ab·ro·ga·tion (æbrəgéiʃən) *n.* the act of abrogating (e.g. a law) [fr. L. *abrogatio* (*abrogationis*)]

ab·rupt (əbrʌpt) *adj.* sudden, unexpected, *an abrupt halt* ‖ steep, precipitous ‖ rough, brusque in manner ‖ disconnected, *an abrupt style* [fr. L. *abrumpere* (*abruptus*), to break away]

→ Guide words showing the alphabetical range of entries on the page

→ Pronunciation respelling See Part 2.

A·bruz·zi e Mo·li·se (ɑbrúːttsiːemɔ́liːze) a region (area 5,954 sq. miles, pop. 1,221,900) in central Italy, formed of the provinces of Aquila, Campobasso, Chieti, Pescara and Teramo, lying in the highest and wildest part of the Apennines (Gran Sasso d'Italia, 9,560 ft), and bounded on the east by the Adriatic: olives, vines, almonds, sheep, hydroelectric power, oil

→ Foreign pronunciation See Part 2.

Ab·sa·lom (æbsələm) the third and best-loved son of David, king of Judah (11 Samuel xiii-xix)

ABSCAM (æbsxǽm) an investigation conducted by the Federal Bureau of Investigation in 1978–80. Seven U.S. Congressmen and various state and local officials were convicted of bribery, conspiracy, and related charges after FBI agents impersonating an Arab sheikh and his associates had videotaped government officials accepting bribes. Critics accused the FBI of entrapment, but the courts ruled that the FBI acted within legal limits

ab·scess (æbses) *n.* a localized collection of pus occurring anywhere in the body **ab·scessed** *adj.* [fr. L. *abscessus*, a going away]

→ Etymology See Part 5.

ab·scis·sa (æbsísə) *n.* (*math.*) the horizontal or x-coordinate in a plane coordinate system [L. = (part) cut off]

→ Field label See Part 4A.

ab·scis·sion (æbsíʒən) *n.* a cutting off [fr. L. *abscissio* (*abscissionis*)]

ab·scond (æbskónd) *v.i.* to flee secretly, esp. to escape the law [fr. L. *abscondere*, to hide]

ab·sence (æbsəns) *n.* a being away ‖ a failure to be present ‖ lack, *absence of proof* [F.]

absence of mind inattention, mental abstraction

ab·sent (æbsənt) *adj.* away, not present ‖ abstracted, *an absent air* [F.]

ab·sent (æbsént) *v. refl.* to keep (oneself) away, *to absent oneself from a meeting* **ab·sen·tee** (æbsəntiː) *n.* a person who is absent **ab·sen·tee·ism** *n.* persistent absence from work, usually without good reason [F. *absenter*]

→ Stress-marked derivative See Part 1D.

absentee landlord a proprietor who does not live on his estate and care for his tenants but merely exploits his property

→ Unsyllabicated main entry See Part 1A.

ab·sent·ly (æbsəntliː) *adv.* in an absent way, inattentively

ab·sent·mind·ed (æbsəntmáindid) *adj.* preoccupied and for that reason not paying attention to what one is doing

ab·sinthe, ab·sinth (æbsinθ) *n.* the plant wormwood ‖ a strongly alcoholic liqueur made from high-proof brandy, wormwood and other aromatics [F.]

→ Spelling variants See Part 1B.

ab·sis·sic acid (æbsísik) (*chem.*) [C₁₅H₂₀O₄] organic inhibitor of plant growth marketed as Dormin. *abbr* ABA

$[C_{15}H_{20}O_4]$

ab·so·lute (æbsəluːt) 1. *adj.* whole, complete ‖ pure, *absolute alcohol* ‖ having unrestricted power, *an absolute ruler* ‖ not conditioned by, or dependent upon, anything else ‖ (*gram.*) of a case not determined by any other word in the sentence (*ABLATIVE*) ‖ (*philos.*) existing independently of any cause outside itself and of our sense perceptions 2. *n.* something that is absolute **the Absolute** the self-existent, the First Cause, God [F. *absolut*]

→ Multiple definitions in several parts of speech See Part 3A.

→ Cross-reference to related term See Part 3C.

absolute address location of stored information in a digital computer

absolute alcohol ethyl alcohol containing not less than 99% pure ethyl alcohol by weight

absolute altimeter radio or similar apparatus designed to indicate the true vertical height of an aircraft above the terrain

absolute code (*computer*) code for an absolute address

absolute dud (*mil.*) a nuclear weapon that fails to explode when launched at, or emplaced on, a target

absolute expansion the true expansion of a liquid irrespective of the expansion of the containing vessel

absolute film *ABSTRACT FILM*

→ Defining cross-reference See Part 3C.

absolute humidity the humidity of the air measured by the number of grams of water vapor present in one cubic meter of the air

absolute music music which does not illustrate or depict (in contrast to program music)

absolute pitch the pitch of a note as determined by a simple frequency, not a combination

---

PRONUNCIATION KEY USED IN THIS DICTIONARY

(Continued)

Symbol	Examples
ʃ	*fi*sh, a*c*tion, fi*ss*ion
t	*t*ime, we*t*, le*tt*er
θ	*th*ick, tru*th*
ð	mo*th*er, *th*ough
ʌ	d*u*ck, t*ou*gh, r*u*dder
ə:	b*ir*d, l*ear*n
u	b*u*ll, c*u*shion, b*oo*k
uə	p*oor*, s*ewer*
u:	f*oo*d, tr*u*e
ju:	*u*nite, conf*u*se
v	*v*erb, o*v*er, wa*v*e
w	*w*ell, *w*aver
x	lo*ch*
j	*y*outh, *y*ellow
z	*z*oom, ro*s*e

Foreign Sounds

Symbol	Examples
y	l*u*ne
ɔ̃	b*on*
ɑ̃	*an*
ɛ̃	*vin*
œ̃	br*un*

Stress

The symbol ´ marks the primary stress in pronouncing the word. The syllable in which the primary stress symbol appears is pronounced with greater emphasis than other syllables.

The symbol ˌ marks the secondary stress of a word. The syllable under which this symbol appears is pronounced with less emphasis than the syllable with primary stress.

THE
NEW LEXICON
WEBSTER'S
DICTIONARY
OF THE ENGLISH LANGUAGE

THE
NEW LEXICON
WEBSTER'S
DICTIONARY
OF THE ENGLISH LANGUAGE

1988 EDITION

LEXICON PUBLICATIONS, INC.
NEW YORK

COPYRIGHT © 1987 BY LEXICON PUBLICATIONS, INC.

Main dictionary section © 1972 Librairie Larousse as *The Larousse Illustrated International Encyclopedia and Dictionary.* Revised and updated 1987.

PRINTED AND MANUFACTURED IN THE UNITED STATES OF AMERICA

ISBN 0-7172-4554-3

Contents

Contents

Preface

This book unites two prominent traditions of reference publishing that have thrived both separately and in combination. These are the encyclopedic and the lexicographical.

Encyclopedias. The encyclopedic tradition is the older, in the European context, being traceable to classical Greek times. Aristotle and the other early writers of encyclopedia-like works shared the impulse to gather a wide range of knowledge into one place, making it easier to expand and increase learning by giving a summary account of its present state.

The Christian Middle Ages, assuming the task of reclaiming classical learning and fitting it for the propagation of an invigorated faith, produced the immediate models of the modern encyclopedia. The pioneering work was the *Etymologiarum,* "the etymologies," of the 7th century Archbishop Isidore of Seville, later canonized. The so-called 12th Century Renaissance produced the most influential medieval encyclopedia, the *Speculum maius,* "the greater looking-glass," of the French Dominican friar Vincent of Beauvais. Vincent used the common medieval metaphor of "mirror" as an instrument for seeing things clearly and undistorted. His work consists of three parts: the *Speculum naturale,* dealing with natural history; the *Speculum doctrinale,* treating theology and the other subjects of the university curriculum; and the *Speculum historiale.* In printed editions of the 15th century, a *Speculum morale* was added by another writer.

The premier encyclopedic work that signaled the Renaissance and bridged medieval and modern times was Sir Francis Bacon's *Instauratio magna,* "the great renewal." It is fair to say that the medieval encyclopedists believed they were writing the whole and mostly permanent truth, whereas Bacon intended both to illustrate and encourage a revolutionary examination of the world in the scientific spirit.

During the full flow of the Enlightenment that succeeded the Renaissance period, leadership in encyclopedia making passed to France, with the publication between 1751 and 1772 of the *Encyclopédie, ou dictionnaire raisonné des sciences, des arts, et des métiers* ("Encyclopedia, or systematic dictionary of arts, sciences, and manual and mechanical trades"), edited by Denis Diderot and Jean Le Rond d'Alembert. Based on a translation of Ephraim Chambers' *Cyclopedia, or an Universal Dictionary of Arts and Sciences* of 1728, the beautifully printed and illustrated 17-volume French work established the principles of the modern encyclopedia. It is noteworthy that the set was not written by one person but was an edited compilation of articles by numerous authorities. Moreover, it was not addressed from experts to experts, in what is called the "monographic method," but to the general literate public.

Before the French Encyclopedia was finished, the first edition of *The Encyclopedia Britannica* appeared in Edinburgh, published by "a society of gentlemen in Scotland," and initiated the longest tradition of encyclopedias in English. The first nine editions, through 1889, were edited in the monographic method, but since the great 11th edition of 1910–1911, the *EB,* as it is called, has been a modern and authoritative monument. With the 14th edition of 1929 the ownership and editorship became American, so that the name is something of a relic.

The Encyclopedia Americana, the first considerable American encyclopedia, appeared in 1829–1833. First edited by Francis Lieber, it was to some extent a translation of Friedrich Brockhaus's *Konversations-Lexikon* of 1796–1808. The *Americana,* published by Grolier Incorporated, has been kept admirably up to date and employs a permanent staff of editors for continuous renewal.

Dictionaries. Single-language dictionaries, as distinct from glossaries and lexicons that give the native equivalents of words in foreign languages, are a newer artifact than encyclopedias and are clearly a consequence of some profound social changes: the spread of literacy, the rise of the middle class, and the increased access of women to the controlling circles of the culture. To take up the last point, the book considered by many to be the pioneer general dictionary in English was Robert Cawdrey's *A Table Alphabeticall,* which defined "hard words" for the "benefit and helpe of Ladies, Gentlewomen, or any other unskillful persons." "Hard words" lexicons like Cawdrey's were the rule for nearly a hundred years, until the appearance in 1702 of *A New English Dictionary,* probably the work of John Kersey. During the fifty-odd years before Samuel Johnson's dictionary, lexicographers such as Nathan Bailey, Thomas Dyche, and Benjamin Martin progressively perfected and modernized the English dictionary.

Dr. Samuel Johnson, known in his time and still reverentially regarded as "the Great Lexicographer," brought out his *Dictionary of the English Language* in 1755, and it is fair to say that all subsequent British and American dictionaries have resulted from imitating, updating, or improving that formidable work.

For example, it was the increasingly poor fit between Johnson's dictionary and the burgeoning and distinct American culture that stimulated Noah Webster to produce the *American Dictionary of the English Language* in 1828, a book in direct line of ancestry to the Merriam-Webster dictionaries of today. The absence of a healthy successor to Johnson caused Dean Richard Chenevix Trench and others, almost exactly a century after Johnson's dictionary appeared, to plan what they called *The New English Dictionary on Historical Principles,* which was published between 1884 and 1928, ultimately as the *Oxford English Dictionary.* The *OED,* as all who know it call it, was extensively updated by a four-volume supplement edited by Dr. Robert Burchfield.

Encyclopedic Dictionaries. The *OED* aimed to trace and define what it called the "common words" of English, and it set these apart from "the peculiar technicalities of trades and processes, of the scientific terminology common to all civilized nations," and from "an infinite number of *Proper* or merely *denotative* names, outside the province of lexicography." So doing it set a distinction between dictionaries and encyclopedias that has been prominent in the subsequent history of such reference books. Lexicographical purists have maintained that "a dictionary defines words, not things," while encyclopedists have pointed out that useful reference books might explain both word-words and thing-words without contamination. At best a rigorous distinction is difficult to maintain in the mind.

Debate between lexicographers and encyclopedists is still going on; this book confidently supports the encyclopedist side. In the history of lexicography it has forbears as respectable as the puristic faction. One need only mention Pierre Larousse's 15-volume *Grand dictionnaire universel du XIX siècle* of 1866–1876, the American William Dwight Whitney's *Century Dictionary and Cyclopedia* of 1889–1899, the Funk and Wagnalls *Standard Dictionary* and *New Standard* of 1913, as well as the Merriam-Webster series through the *New International, 2d Edition* of 1934.

The present book aims to combine the best features of the general dictionary and the short-entry encyclopedia, and hence to be of maximum usefulness to those who seek word-facts and fact-facts. In this effort, the editors have simplified the format by using a single alphabetical listing rather than separate ones for biographies, gazetteer, historical events, and so forth, and have not hesitated to give the encyclopedic entries the space they require.

DICTIONARY STAFF

EDITORIAL

EDITORIAL DIRECTOR   Bernard S. Cayne   MANAGING EDITOR   Doris E. Lechner

EDITORS

Donald O. Bolander
Alyce Bolander
Sara A. Boak
Grace F. Buonocore
Suzanne Stone Burke

James E. Churchill, Jr.
Manuela Izquierdo
Elizabeth J. Jewell
Rebecca Lyon
Jean Munoz
Meghan O'Reilly

Ronald B. Roth
Pauline M. Sholtys
Valerie Law Stodden
Diane Bell Surprenant
Jean A. McCormick Vreeland

PROOFREADERS

David Michael Buskus
Linda Buskus
Merla C. Davies
Nancy Domoff

Carol B. Dudley
Gretchen Korman Ferrante
Jan Jamilkowski
Ruth Lofgren
Laurie M. Romanik

Stephen Romanoff
Judi Sprague
Elise Washington-Davis
Ronald Wertz

ART DIRECTOR   Eric E. Akerman   ARTISTS   Nancy Hamlen   Tone Imset

PHOTO RESEARCH   Ann Eriksen   J.H. Carruth

DESIGN   Richard Glassman   ART ASSISTANT   Elizabeth Farrington

PRODUCTION EDITORS   Diane L. George   Carolyn F. Reil

EDITORIAL ASSISTANTS   Jennifer Pickett Vogt   Monica J. Lechner   Susan Lorimer Reil

MANUFACTURING

DIRECTOR OF MANUFACTURING   Joseph J. Corlett

PRODUCTION MANAGERS   Alan Phelps   Teresa Kluk

PRODUCTION ASSISTANT   Barbara L. Persan

History of the English Language

English is one of the major languages of the world. At the beginning of the 19th century, English was the native speech of barely 15 million people. Today it is used regularly by more than 320 million and is second only to Chinese, whose world primacy in number of speakers is accounted for largely by the vast population of mainland China.

Of the 3,000 or more tongues spoken today, about half a dozen predominate, having among their speakers two thirds of the world's population. English, as one of those influential and growing languages, is spoken in areas widely scattered over the globe. It is the native or official language of one fifth of the earth's land surface, being used throughout most of the North American continent and in the British Isles, Australia, New Zealand, and the Republic of South Africa. Of the languages of colonization it has been the one most important in Africa, Asia, and the islands of the central and southern Pacific.

At present, English is the most widely studied language in areas where it is not native. It is the chief foreign language taught in the schools of Latin American and European countries. In Japan, children begin the study of English in the seventh grade, and in the Philippines all classes are conducted in English from the fourth grade on. In India, English is an official language alternative to Hindi, the chief official language.

In addition, the use of English is widespread in international trade, international scholarship, and scientific research. More than half of the world's scientific and technical journals, as well as newspapers, are printed in English. Three fourths of the world's mail is written in English, and English is the language of three fifths of the world's radio stations. The Soviet Union and China use English to a great extent in their propaganda broadcasts to the developing countries of Africa and Asia. The U.S. Information Agency, with its centers and libraries in various countries, and the British Council and its English-language schools aid greatly in spreading the knowledge of English. As a result a speaker of English can travel around the world and almost never find it necessary in major cities to employ a language other than his own in order to be understood.

INDO-EUROPEAN AND GERMANIC BEGINNINGS

English belongs to the Germanic branch of the Indo-European family of languages. Indo-European is the major linguistic family of the world, in that languages belonging to it have the widest geographic distribution and are spoken by the greatest number of people. Several thousand years ago the "ancestral" language from which the Indo-European languages are all descended was the language of a comparatively small group of primitive people, apparently cattle-raising nomads of a Stone Age culture. The breakup of this Proto-Indo-European into a number of dialects is thought to have occurred around 3000 B.C., or earlier, when the original speakers supposedly began to migrate from east central or southern Europe.

Indo-European Family. The various Indo-European languages usually are divided into two groups—eastern and western. The chief languages in the western group, to which English belongs, are (1) Celtic, including the ancient tongue of the Gauls, whom Caesar conquered; the modern non-English languages of Wales, Ireland, the Highlands of Scotland, and the Isle of Man, and the language of Brittany in northwestern France; (2) Germanic, consisting of English as well as Gothic, German, Dutch, Flemish,

Frisian, Danish, Swedish, Norwegian, and Icelandic, and local dialects spoken in Scandinavia, Germany, Austria, and Switzerland; (3) Greek, including the ancient and modern Greek languages and dialects; and (4) Italic, consisting of Latin with its modern descendants, the Romance languages—the chief of which are French, Spanish, Italian, Portuguese, and Rumanian.

Germanic Branch. Our concern is with the Germanic branch, since it includes English and its nearest relatives. It is divided into three main groups: East Germanic, North Germanic, and West Germanic. The chief dialect of East Germanic was Gothic, now known chiefly from fragments of a 4th century translation of the Bible by Ulfilas, the Arian bishop of the West Goths.

Modern Germanic Languages. North Germanic, derived from Old Norse, now includes the Scandinavian languages—Danish, Swedish, Norwegian, and Icelandic. West Germanic consists of two groups: High German and Low German. High German is so called because it was spoken originally in the southern highlands of Germany. Low German was the dialect spoken in the lowlands along the northern coast. High German is the standard language of present-day Germany. The Low German languages include Dutch, Flemish, Frisian, and English.

The nearest relative of English is Frisian, spoken in the Frisian Islands off the coasts of the Netherlands, Germany, and Denmark. That English is a Germanic language can easily be perceived by comparing it to German, Dutch, and Frisian—all West Germanic languages. The word *water* is common to English and Dutch, and other words are not very different in the two languages. The relation between English *That is good* and German *Das ist gut* is evident.

Characteristics of Germanic Languages. The Germanic group has features in common with the other branches of the Indo-European family, which are all inflectional and have a common word stock. But the Germanic group has its own individual characteristics. These are (1) the development of a weak verb conjugation along with the strong conjugation, (2) the twofold declension of the adjective as strong and weak, (3) a fixed stress accent, and (4) a regular shifting of consonants.

In comparing the Modern English verb, as representative of the Germanic verb, with the Latin verb, as representative of another Indo-European group, one can see the distinguishing characteristics of the Germanic verb. English verbs are of two classes: (1) The weak class, or conjugation, comprises the majority of verbs and is therefore sometimes called "regular"; a verb of this class forms its past tense and past participle by adding -ed, -d, or -t to the present or infinitive stem, as work, worked, worked. (2) The strong class forms its tenses by an internal change of the radical vowel of the verb, as drink, drank, drunk. Latin, however, expresses an idea by changing the form of the root of the verb, as audiō ("I hear"), the present tense, and audīvi ("I have heard"), the perfect tense. Latin verbs fall into conjugations distinguished by the vowel of the present active infinitive. There is no principle of tense formation in Latin so simple as that characterizing the English (Germanic) verb.

Just as the Germanic verb developed a twofold classification, so the Germanic adjective developed a twofold declension. The simple principle of it is that when a demonstrative, a possessive pronoun, or the definite article preceded the adjective or when it was used substantively (as a noun), it was declined in one way, called "weak." Otherwise, it was declined in another way, called "strong." For example, the forms corresponding to *wise* in the Modern English expressions *wise men* and *these wise men* are *wīse menn* and *ðās wīsan menn* in Old English, and *weise Männer* and *diese weisen Männer* in Modern High German. Modern English does not distinguish between the weak and the strong forms, having lost all declension of the adjective. But the earlier presence in English of the two forms shows that English belongs to the Germanic group—because of its history, not because of its present usages.

The third trait characterizing the Germanic languages is the fixed accent. In Germanic, the stress became fixed upon the root syllable, whereas the word stress in Indo-European was free or variable. In Modern English we can generally recognize native words, as distinguished from those that have been borrowed from some non-Germanic tongue, by observing the stressed syllable when affixes are added in forming new words. For example, compare Modern English *friend'*, *friend'ly*, *friend'ship*, *friend'liness*, *unfriend'ly* with *pure'*, *purify'*, *purifica'tion* and to *cin'ema*, *cinemat'ograph*, *cinematog'raphy*, *cinematograph'ic*. The native word *friend* keeps the accent on the root syllable, but *pure* and *cinema*, borrowed from the Latin and Greek, respectively, shift the accent as affixes are added.

The fourth distinctive feature of the Germanic languages is the almost regular shifting, according to a certain pattern, that particular Indo-European consonants underwent in these languages. For example, *p* became *f*, and *t* became *th*, as seen in the Latin *pater* and English *father*. Linguists became aware of this consonant shift as a result of studies in the early 19th century. This knowledge has helped them in grouping the Germanic languages, in discovering the derivation and history of their vocabularies, and in finding out which words are borrowed and which are native.

GENERAL LINES OF DEVELOPMENT

Historically, Modern English is the result of a number of tribal migrations and invasions. Before the first of these, the linguistic ancestors of English-speaking people were wandering along the northern coast of Europe, using Low West Germanic dialects so similar to one another that members of the various tribes could understand one another.

Invasions and Their Results. About the middle of the 5th century A.D., three Germanic tribes—the Angles, the Saxons, and the Jutes—began a successful invasion of what is now England, or a mass migration into it. The gradual fusion of their three dialects resulted in Old English. By the end of the 6th century the former inhabitants of England—the Celts—had been killed, driven into Wales, or enslaved, and the Anglo-Saxons were securely established. English held sway in England. Only some place-names and a few ordinary words of the Celts remained.

The second major invasion was that of the Vikings, which began as a series of raids about the 9th century and also developed into a mass migration. Their language gradually merged with the related Anglo-Saxon dialects, and a great deal of interchange and borrowing of words occurred. Raids by the Danes continued throughout the 10th century, and in the early years of the 11th century Danish kings actually reigned in England. The linguistic consequence of the Viking invasion was a considerable injection of Scandinavian words into English. Examples are the nouns *sky*, *skull*, *egg*, and *leg* and the pronouns *they*, *their*, and *them*.

The third invasion to have a major influence on the language was the Norman Conquest, led by William the Conquerer in 1066. The Normans were descendants of Vikings who had earlier settled in Normandy and had adopted the French dialect of their new home as their own. After the Conquest, the business of the government, or the court, was conducted in Norman French. The French were in control, and French became the language of the nobility, the court, polite society, and literature. English as a written language almost disappeared. But despite the prestige and use of French among the rulers and landlords, French did not replace English as the speech of the common people.

Another, but peaceful, invasion was that of Latin, which began in 597 A.D., when the Roman missionary St. Augustine arrived in England and converted the kingdom of Kent to Christianity. Thus began an influence that has continued to enrich English through Latin borrowings.

Subsequent Trends. English developed and changed with the passing of time, as do all living entities. During the long period after the Norman Conquest when English was neglected in favor of French, English became practically a spoken dialect. At this time it was transformed into a new standard speech, casting off much that was superfluous and borrowing from its rival, Norman French. By the time it emerged again as a literary language, around 1200, it had assumed the form known as Middle English.

Middle English is Old English changed first by French influence and second by the transforming power of popular speech. The consequences were profound. From a rather highly inflected language, English changed to one of few inflections; and as inflectional endings were lost, so was "grammatical" gender, which gave way to "natural" gender. Along with the simplification of the grammatical structure went an increase in vocabulary and idiom, principally under the influence of the French language.

As a product of two merging strains, Germanic and Romance—French is a Romance language, descended from Latin—English became a language capable of expressing a wide range of thought and feeling, as exemplified in the works of Chaucer, the greatest literary figure of medieval England. Chaucer wrote in the East Midland dialect, which had risen to a commanding position among three competing forms—Northern, Midland, and Southern.

East Midland was the dialect of London, the capital and metropolitan center of England, politically, commercially, socially, and intellectually preeminent. It held a middle course between the more conservative Southern dialect and the more advanced Northern, and developed into the speech Chaucer used. It is also the dialect from which standard Modern English is derived.

In the Modern English period the people of England followed a generally peaceful line of development in their thought and language, as they were not subjected to foreign invasion or any extensive external ethnic influences. The language developed along with the political, industrial, and intellectual growth of the country and of the world as a whole.

THE THREE PERIODS OF ENGLISH

Considered in more detail, the periods of English are (1) the Old English (Anglo-Saxon) period, starting with the coming of the Germanic tribes into England—traditionally 449 A.D.—and ending around 1100; (2) the Middle English period, 1100–1500; and (3) the Modern English period—from 1500 to the present, with the Early Modern English period extending to about 1700.

Old English. In Old English there were four main dialects—Northumbrian, Mercian, Kentish, and West Saxon. Two of these were Anglian: Northumbrian, spoken north of the river Humber, and Mercian, spoken in the Midlands between the rivers Humber and Thames. Northumbrian was the language of the first significant literature and the best of Old English literature, including the epic poem *Beowulf*. Kentish was the dialect of the Jutes, who lived in the southeast. West Saxon—the chief Saxon dialect, spoken south of the Thames—is the dialect in which the great bulk of Old English writing has come down to us.

The reason for the preeminence of West Saxon is that in the 9th century the center of culture and influence, formerly in Northumbria and then in Mercia, shifted to Wessex, the home of the West Saxons. Most of the prose was originally West Saxon, inspired by Alfred the Great, who succeeded to the West Saxon throne in 871. The poetry, chiefly Anglian, was copied by West Saxon scribes, whose transcriptions have been preserved. The early West Saxon period centered on King Alfred, who was not only a military leader, successful in opposing the Danish invasions and keeping peace, but also a champion of learning. Late West Saxon centered on the writer and churchman Ælfric, whose works, dated mainly in the late 900's, have made him a major figure in the development of English prose.

Spelling and Sound. The following is the West Saxon version of the Lord's Prayer, from Matthew 6 of the King James Version of the Bible:

. . . Fæder ūre þū þe eart on heofonum, sī þīn nama gehälgod. Tō becume þīn rīce. Gewurþe ðīn willa on eorðan swā swā on heofonum. Ūrne gedæghwāmlīcan hlāf syle ūs tō dæg. And forgyf ūs ūre gyltas, swā swā wē forgyfað ūrum gyltendum. And ne gelæd þū ūs on costnunge, ac ālȳs ūs of yfele . . . . Sōþlīce.

At first glance the passage may seem strange because of the differences between Old English and Modern English spelling. The character æ spells the sound of *a* in *hat,* and the characters þ and ð are used as *th* is used in Modern English. Many differences in sound exist. Modern *our* developed from *ūre,* the first vowel of which sounded like *oo* in *moon.* The word *hlāf* is the ancestor of modern *loaf,* although we have lost the *h* sound and changed the vowel, which sounded approximately like the first vowel in *father.* Old English had some sounds that do not occur in Modern English; for example, the sound represented by Old English *y,* which may be approached by pronouncing *i* in *sit* with the lips rounded. This was a rounded front vowel with approximately the value of German *ü* or French *u.* In later English this sound disappeared, and *y* was used interchangeably with *i.*

Other words that can be recognized in this passage are *eart* (archaic second person singular form of the verb *be; present are*), *heofonum* (*heofon,* with dative plural ending; Modern English *heaven*), *nama* (*name*—nominative singular, weak declension), *eorðan* (*earth,* with dative singular ending, weak declension), *forgyf* (*forgive,* imperative form), *gyltas* (*guilt,* with accusative plural ending), and *forgyfað* (*forgive,* with present indicative plural ending).

Some words in the passage have undergone changes in sound, which are reflected in altered spellings; for example, the combination æg in *dæg* became in Middle English a diphthong, *æy,* illustrated in Modern English *day.* Actually, more than 70% of the words in this passage are still current, though changed somewhat in spelling and pronunciation and occasionally in meaning. The word order is also different from that in Modern English. At the beginning we find "*Fæder ūre*" instead of "Our Father."

Grammar and Vocabulary. From the passage, it is clear that in grammar Old English is more highly inflected than Modern English. There are various case endings for nouns, numerous endings for adjectives, a more complicated system of pronouns, more person and number endings for verbs, and the like. Nouns had four cases—nominative, genitive, dative, and accusative. Adjectives had all these plus an instrumental case. In Modern English, nouns have only two cases—the common case, for both subject and object, and the possessive—and adjectives have no case at all. However, to express relationships, Modern English employs a more rigid word order and more structure words, such as prepositions and auxiliaries, than did Old English.

The vocabulary of Old English is likewise different from that of Modern English. Most of the words were native words, though there were borrowings from other sources. Some words were coming in from Norse, and others had been taken over from Latin. Even while the Anglo-Saxons were still on the Continent, they had adopted from Roman merchants such Latin words as those from which *cheese, kitchen,* and *wine* are derived, and more Latin words came into English after the conversion to Christianity—for example, the original forms of *candle, cloister, creed, dirge,* and *font.* However, only about 400 to 500 words of Latin origin appear in Old English manuscripts.

Middle English. Sometime between the years 1000 and 1200, numerous significant changes took place in the structure of English, and Old English became Middle English. The transition was gradual and did not proceed at a uniform rate in all dialects. In the North, where changes were earlier and more rapid than in the South, the dialect had already definitely assumed the appearance of Middle English by the year 1100, whereas the Southern dialect remained essentially Old English until at least 1150.

The main difference between Old English and Middle English was the great reduction in inflectional endings. This development resulted chiefly from a change in the way words were accented. In the Old English period, a general or distributed stress existed, spread over the word as a whole, thus preserving the full inflectional endings. In the Middle English period the stress shifted to the first syllable, weakening and obscuring the later syllables.

Another factor contributing to change was the complete overthrow of the English social and political system that accompanied the period of Danish rule and, somewhat later, the Norman Conquest. For several generations, confusion reigned and the language developed in an untrammeled and popular way, since the constraints of a rigid social system were removed. The usages of the uneducated were not held in check by conservative forces, and the old standards of correctness were more or less forgotten as the language followed the free impulses of the people. Consequently, when the language achieved a stable literary form in the time of Chaucer and his predecessors, it was very different from that of Alfred and Ælfric.

Changes in the Sound System and in Grammar. Owing to the shift in word accent, the final syllables of words, particularly inflectional syllables, tended to become weak and eventually disappeared. The development of a standard word order compensated for the loss of inflectional endings. In general, the *-um* of the dative plural of nouns and adjectives appeared as *-un, -on, -an,* or *-en,* the last form becoming the predominant one and finally weakening to *-e.* Likewise, all unstressed end vowels leveled under the vowel *-e,* which was later dropped. The present participle in early Middle English ended in *-inde* in the South, *-ende* in the Midlands, and *-ande* in the North. These presumably merged with certain nouns naming actions, which regularly ended in *-ung* (present *-ing*), as in *learnung* ("learning").

As the vowel endings leveled, the classification of nouns disappeared. So did grammatical gender in favor of the natural gender of Modern English. With the loss of grammatical gender in the noun went the loss of agreement in inflection between the noun and its adjective. The same leveling of inflectional endings, therefore, took place in the adjective as in the noun. Only one ending persisted after the loss of those indicative of gender—the vowel *-e,* which marked the plural number and the weak inflection of the adjective.

That Middle English is closer to Modern English than Old English can be seen from lines of Chaucer's Prologue to the *Canterbury Tales:*

> A knyght ther was and that a worthy man,
> That fro the tyme that he first bigan
> To riden out, he loved chivalrie,
> Trouthe and honour, fredom and curteisie.

Changes in Vocabulary. In addition to the changes already mentioned, there were great changes in vocabulary. French words from all walks of life came into English. In some instances we have pairs of words, one from Norman French and one from Parisian French, as in *catch, chase; cattle, chattel;* and *warden, guardian.* The Latin *ca* was preserved in Norman French but was changed to *ch* in Central French. Likewise, many Norman words begin with *w,* whereas the Central form is *gu.*

Many of the borrowed words dealt with things in which the French influence was strong—government, law, religion, and military affairs. Illustrations are *reign, court, revenue, clergy, faith,* and *sergeant.* Architecture, literature, and science, as well as fashion, dress, and social life, added terms like *sculpture, palace, pillar, romance, tragedy, surgeon, anatomy, clock,* and *tournament.* Many words were introduced that had to do with the table and preparation of food, such as *appetite, beef, veal, pork, pastry, broil,* and *boil.* These and thousands of others were added to the English vocabulary between 1100 and 1500. Yet the very core of the vocabulary remained English. The pronouns, prepositions, conjunctions, and auxiliaries and many ordinary nouns, verbs, and adjectives were not supplanted by borrowings.

Latin words, along with French, continued to be added to Middle English. An important source of Latin borrowings was Wycliffe's translation of the Bible into English. The French and Latin borrowings made English a richer language, with many synonyms. For example, one finds *ask* (Old English), *inquire* (French), and *interrogate* (Latin). Flemish, Dutch, and Low German also contributed a number of words, such as *deck, dock,* and *freight,* as a result of the constant communication between England and the Low Countries, principally in connection with trade. The greatest contribution, however, came from French.

The use of French words in Middle English texts gradually increased, reaching its height between 1300 and 1400, the period in which English was reestablishing itself as a national language after some 200 years. English began to be used in the schools, and in 1362 a parliamentary statute required its use in the King's courts. Eventually, the laws of the land were in the language of the people, and a literary standard English, based on the normal spoken English of the London dialect, had been established to a considerable extent, through its use by such writers as Chaucer, Wycliffe, Malory, and Caxton.

Early Modern English. Between the years 1500 and 1700, the language developed many of the features that characterize it today. Some of these came as the result of basic linguistic changes, and some followed in the wake of the Renaissance and other movements—social, political, religious, and scientific.

Linguistic Changes. Between 1400 and 1600, English experienced changes in sound that made Shakespeare's language quite different from that of Chaucer. One modification was the loss of an unstressed vowel sound at the end of some words. For example, *space, grace,* and *large* were pronounced as two syllables by Chaucer but as one by Shakespeare. The *-e* represented a vowel sound for Chaucer. It was not "silent." Likewise, the modern words *looked* and *loved* would have had two syllables for Chaucer. These changes were significant in that they affected thousands of words.

Another alteration was the systematic shifting of some half a dozen tense vowels and diphthongs in stressed syllables. For instance, Middle English *mine* had the vowel of modern *we,* whereas *we* was pronounced like *way. Louse* in Middle English sounded like modern *loose,* and *noon* had the vowel of *known.* This shift, known as the Great Vowel Shift, affected most of the long vowels and all the words containing them.

Changes Brought About by the Printing Press. The invention of printing, which William Caxton introduced into England about 1476, released a force that was to have an almost immeasurable effect on both language and thought. In time, books were available for all, not merely for the favored few. More and more people learned to read and write, and education increased. On the English language itself, the chief effect of the invention of printing was to be in making the language more uniform and in standardizing it, particularly the spelling.

Effects of the Renaissance. The main influence on the development of Modern English was the great humanistic movement of the Renaissance, which exerted its greatest force in England during the period of 1500–1625, enabling Englishmen to partake of the cultural riches of the rest of contemporary Europe as well as of the ancient world. The study of the classics was stressed, and the enthusiastic classicists deliberately attempted to enrich the English language by borrowing from Latin and Greek.

Thousands of words poured in from the classical languages. Such words as *education, external, exist,* and *meditate* came directly from the Latin. Others, like *chaos, climax,* and *crisis,* came in from Greek through the Latin. Some like *catastrophe* and *lexicon,* came directly from the Greek. The English often adapted a Latin term by modifying an ending (*frivolous,* for example, from Latin *frivolus*) or by substituting one final cluster for another (*corporeal,* from Latin *corporeus*). The Latin endings of nouns *-antia* and *-entia* became in English *-ance, -ence,* or *-ancy, -ency,* as in *countenance, concurrence, constancy, frequency.* The borrowing

of Latin words was strengthened by the borrowing of French words, which continued from the Middle English period. In many cases it is difficult to determine whether a word came directly from Latin or came in through French, for many Latin words were entering French, and French was passing them on into English.

Along with the learned words from Greek and Latin in the Renaissance period came loanwords from more than 50 languages, the major sources being the three Romance languages, French, Spanish, and Italian. Words like *detail, genteel,* and *surpass* poured in from French. From Italy came *balcony, piazza,* and *portico.* Spain contributed *alligator* and *armada.* Many words also came from other parts of the world as a result of exploration, trade, and colonization.

The classicists were concerned not only about vocabulary but about style as well, their chief models being such writers as Vergil and Cicero. Many works, therefore, were translated in the great effort to improve the English language. Among the most famous were Sir Thomas North's translation of Plutarch's *Lives* (1579), an important source for Shakespeare's plays; and George Chapman's translations of Homer, which began to appear in 1598. One important classicist, Sir Thomas More, wrote his *Utopia* (1516) in Latin. But the man who no doubt had the greatest influence in spreading the use of Latin was William Lily (or Lilye), the first high master of St. Paul's School in London and the author of a famous Latin grammar that was used by Shakespeare and his contemporaries, as well as by later generations of students. Among the Greek scholars were Thomas Linacre, William Grocyn, and John Colet. The great Dutch humanist Erasmus taught Greek at the University of Cambridge at this time.

Reaction Against Classicism. As strong as the humanistic movement was in Renaissance England, growing patriotism produced a healthy pride in the use of English. Some Englishmen thought that their language should depend upon its own resources. To them, importations from foreign sources meant corruption. Among the linguistic purists holding this theory and praising English were George Pettie, who expounded his position in his *Civile Conversation* (1581; 1586), a translation of a work by Stefano Guazzo; and Richard Mulcaster, the author of the principal treatise on English spelling in the 16th century and the teacher of Edmund Spenser. Spenser supported his master by praising the riches of the English language, by reviving old words, such as *astound, doom, ydrad* (for "dreaded"), and by coining new words, many of which were derivatives of old ones, such as *wrizzled* (probably from "wrinkled" and "frizzled").

Men like Sir John Cheke, first regius professor of Greek at Cambridge, opposed the introduction of inkhorn (pedantic) terms from Latin and Greek. Among the followers of Cheke were Roger Ascham, the tutor of Queen Elizabeth I and the author of *Toxophilus* (1545), a dialogue on archery in English, and of the more famous educational treatise, *The Scholemaster* (1570), and Sir Thomas Elyot, author of what has been called the first book on education written and printed in English, *The Boke Named the Governour* (1531). Others were Thomas Wilson, author of the popular *Arte of Rhetorique* (1553), and Richard Carew, author of *The Excellencie of the English Tongue* (1614). Sir Philip Sidney praised English as a tongue equal to any other. Despite these advocates of English, the Latinists triumphed for a time. Children had to learn Latin at school, to the neglect of English.

Reemergence of English. But once more English emerged and established itself. Its position in the nation had not been questioned, for it had continued as the language of government and of trade. Then came three great English poets, all within a century: Spenser, "the poet's poet" of the English Renaissance and the great advocate of the English language; Shakespeare, the popular, unequaled dramatist and the outstanding literary artist of Early Modern English, credited with using 90% of native words in his working vocabulary of 20,000 to 25,000 words; and Milton, who wrote both in Latin and in English but chose English for *Paradise Lost,* his great blank verse epic. These three literary giants, along with many other poets and prose writers, have proved the versatility and power of the language.

The prose writers of the Renaissance not only borrowed words from Latin but also imitated the Latin style as illustrated by John Lyly in his *Euphues* (1578). In striving for elegance, he employed an excessive use of antithesis, alliteration, and far-fetched similes, cultivating a highly self-conscious and artificial language. The Renaissance writers favored the ornate, although there is one notable exception—the King James Version of the Bible.

Effects of the Reformation. Biblical translation has had a great effect on literary style in Modern English, beginning with the translation by Wycliffe and his friend and collaborator John Purvey in the 14th century. As a result of the Reformation many translations appeared. The first of these was William Tyndale's, which established a standard on which the others were based, including the King James (1611). This literary monument is noted for its native vocabulary and its simplicity and beauty of phrase. The fact that native words make up 94% of its vocabulary has placed it in the forefront of English prose writing and accounts for its powerful and widespread influence on English style.

Summary. With the heritage of the European Renaissance and the Reformation, the influence of the printing press and of increased popular education, and the influx of new ideas from around the globe, Early Modern English, through its experimentations and innovations, gradually became the language of scholarship, replacing Latin. It likewise produced a body of literature unequaled at any other time. The authors of the Elizabethan Age were inspired, highly imaginative, versatile, and experimental, giving to the world writings of all types—long narrative poems, sonnet sequences, lyrics, songs, romances, histories, literary criticism, and, above all, dramas, the greatest since the Golden Age of Greece.

Development Since 1700. After 1700, many movements and countermovements characterized the history of English, one of which was the attempt to regulate and control the language. The freedom of the Renaissance disappeared, and in its place came order and restraint. Formulation of rules began; efforts were made to stabilize the language—to determine what was right and what was wrong. Many demanded an academy, similar to the Académie Française, to decide on correctness of language and, in effect, to legislate on the permanent form of English. Chief among these advocates were Dryden, Swift, and Defoe, who did not wish English to be corrupted. They wanted it to be pure and eloquent.

18th Century. This authoritarian attitude reached its height in the 18th century, the age of reason and logic. The idea of an academy failed, but the desire to stabilize the language resulted in the development of the dictionary and a great interest in grammar.

The first English dictionary, by Robert Cawdrey, had appeared in 1604, briefly explaining 2,500 "hard words." Many others followed, making gradual improvements, until Samuel Johnson's *Dictionary of the English Language* was published in 1755. It dominated the field for about a century and paved the way for the monumental *Oxford English Dictionary*, the standard authority for the history of English words, published during the period 1884–1933. It laid the foundation for the great advance in lexicography that has continued to the present.

The doctrine of "correctness," supported by the authoritarian sense of order and conformity to a standard, was responsible for a succession of English grammars based on Latin rules of grammar and written by grammarians who had no knowledge of the processes of linguistic change. The influence of the most popular of these grammars—one by Robert Lowth, published in 1762, and another by Lindley Murray, in 1795—is still felt.

There were, however, a few thinkers who realized that all linguistic problems could not be solved by logic and that standards must be based on usage. Chief among them were Joseph Priestley, author of *The Rudiments of English Grammar* . . . (1761), and George Campbell, who wrote his *Philosophy of Rhetoric* in 1776.

The principles established in such works as these were the forerunners of the modern doctrine of usage, which is basic in all sound investigations of linguistic questions—that is, that usage and social acceptance determine correctness.

While authoritarian English was being codified lexically and grammatically at home, the British Empire was expanding around the world and extending tremendous influence. Supremacy in trade on the high seas and political supremacy among far-flung colonies brought Britain into contact with strange lands, peoples, cultures, and climates. As a result, thousands of new terms poured into English from around the globe, resulting in a more cosmopolitan vocabulary. From the North American Indians came words like *hickory, persimmon, squash;* from Mexico, *chili, coyote;* from South America, *alpaca, llama, pampas;* from India, *bungalow, cashmere, chintz;* from Africa, *chimpanzee, voodoo, zebra;* and from Australia, *boomerang, kangaroo, wombat.*

19th and 20th Centuries. In both Britain and the English-speaking areas abroad, the romantic period, following the conservative 18th century, was a time of liberalism in literature and language. Obsolete words were revived, and new words were coined. In Britain, great changes were occurring in society, making it more democratic, and the upper and lower classes were brought closer together by industrial reforms. Greater economic and cultural advantages came to the common man, aided by the first cheap newspapers around 1820, by cheap postage about 1840, and by great advances in science.

The large circulation of the newspaper afforded a means of renewing the language, of approving its informal, colloquial usage, and of bringing the spoken standard closer to the written. Means of telecommunication and of travel were likewise increasingly improved and speeded up, thereby bringing the people of the world closer and closer together and enlarging the English vocabulary by word borrowings from many areas. Scientific progress also meant development of the vocabulary, since each new technological advance brought a new stock of words. Thus the vocabulary increased by leaps and bounds as one scientific development followed another in the 19th and 20th centuries.

LEXICAL GROWTH AND CHANGE

The ever-increasing size of the English vocabulary results from a variety of processes, mainly of two kinds: (1) processes of growth, through which words enter the language, and (2) processes of change, whereby words already in use undergo alterations in meaning.

Methods of Forming Words. Although there are many words of unknown origin, there are almost no "originals"—words created without a source of some kind. The following represent the chief sources of the English vocabulary:

Borrowing from Other Languages. The English language has vast debts. In any dictionary some 80% of the entries are borrowed. The majority are likely to come from Latin, and of those more than half will come through French. A considerable number will derive directly or indirectly from Greek. A substantial contribution will come from Scandinavian languages, and a small percentage from Portuguese, Italian, Spanish, and Dutch. Scattered words will be from various sources around the globe. The vocabulary has grown from the 50,000 to 60,000 words in Old English to the tremendous number of entries—650,000 to 750,000—in an unabridged dictionary of today. The bulk of the words spoken and written by English-speaking people, however, are native words, the nine most frequently used being *and, be, have, it, of, the, to, will,* and *you.* Borrowed words are nevertheless immensely useful in enriching the vocabulary and making the language flexible and resourceful.

Compounding. The most evident method of forming new words is joining two or more words to make a new entry. It has been common in all periods of English. Some of the shortest and simplest-appearing words were formed originally in this way—for example, *hussy*, from Old English *hūs* and *wīf* ("housewife").

Almost all parts of speech lend themselves to compounding, though some combinations are far more useful than others.

Examples of nouns formed by compounding are *houseboat* or *motorway* (from two nouns), *blackberry* or *greenhouse* (from adjective and noun), *popcorn* (from verb and noun), *touchdown* (from verb and adverb), and *downpour* or *output* (from adverb and verb). Adjectives so formed include *footsore* (from noun and adjective) and *overdue* (from adverb and adjective). There are also connective and particle compounds, such as *notwithstanding* and *insofar*, and phrase oddities, such as *up-and-coming*.

Formation by Affixes. Another common process of word making is that of adding a prefix or suffix to a single word. Some affixes have existed from the Old English period, such as *un-*, *-ness, -less*, and *-ish*, in words like *undo, frankness, useless*, and *childish*. Examples of living prefixes—those that can be applied freely to new words—are *anti-, ex-, pro-, super-, hyper-, post-*, and many more. A similar morphological wealth is seen in the suffixes. Consider, for example, Latin *-ation* and *-ative;* French *-al, -able, -ous*, and *-ary* (all ultimately Latin); and Greek *-ist, -ize*, and *-itis*. The number of words formed by affixes is constantly growing.

Functional Shift. The free interchange of functions, whereby one part of speech is changed to another, is a significant feature of Modern English. Functional shift between noun and verb is common; for example, one may sew a *button* on a coat and then *button* the coat. But many other changes are possible. A noun may become an adjective, as in "*home* run," or an adverb, in "go *home*." An adjective may become a noun, as in "none but the *brave*," or a verb, in "*brave* the storm." A preposition may become an adjective, as in "a *through* train"; and an adverb may become an adjective, as in "the *then* minister."

Figures of Speech. In the creation of words, imagery plays a great role, as in the original combination *the day's eye*, which finally became *daisy*, now a fossilized image. Metaphors of this type were common in the English vocabulary, as can be seen from names of other flowers, such as *bleeding heart* and *lady's slipper* (or *lady slipper*). Likewise, imagery is evident in *numskull* (also spelled *numbskull*) or *pip-squeak* and in the various uses of the word *head*, originally naming a part of the body. Now, because of the resemblance in shape, we speak of a "*head* of cabbage," or in considering function, of the "*head* of a government." Metaphor also is used in the "*head* of a pin," but in "fifty *head* (of cattle)," synecdoche—the naming of a part to indicate the whole—is employed.

Poetic imagery is evident in slang, where one finds a definite contrast between the literal and the figurative meanings of the word. Slang is generally a bold and metaphoric presentation of an idea, originating from the attempt to be novel and fresh. For example, the literal meaning of *pull* is transformed into the metaphorical meaning "influence." In slang there is no lack of creative and vivid expression. The difficulty is that it is overused, and as a result it often drops out of use after a feverish circulation. Nevertheless, it is an important method of rejuvenating the language, for many slang creations remain.

Clipping and Back-Formation. Two methods of word creation, which result in shortening, may be considered together—clipping and back-formation. Clippings occur frequently in informal situations, especially in spoken language. Student speech is filled with examples like *exam, lab, math*, and *gym*. Such abbreviations may become so well established that they supersede the original. An example is the word *mob*, the use of which was opposed by Jonathan Swift in the 18th century. He preferred the Latin *mobile vulgus* ("vacillating crowd"). Today no one thinks of using the long form. Other common clipped words are *cab* (from *cabriolet*) and *phone* (from *telephone*).

Many back-formations in English come from words ending in *-s* that were singular but were mistaken for plurals or from words having what appear to be (but are not) suffixes, especially the *-er*, *-ar*, or *-or* of agent. Examples of the former are *sherry* (from the

earlier *sherris*, taken as a plural) and *pea* (from *pease*). Instances of the latter include *rove* (from *rover*), *beg* (from *beggar*), and *edit* (from *editor*).

"Initial" Words, or Acronyms. Combining the initial letters of a series of words to form a new word is another method of shortening. *NATO*, for example, is an acronym for "North Atlantic Treaty Organization." Not only may initial letters be used, but initial syllables or parts of words may be combined, as in *EURO-MART* ("European Common Market") and *radar* for "radio detecting and ranging." Acronyms have become increasingly popular. In many cases one uses words like *laser* and *UNESCO* without knowing the words from which they were formed.

Imitation of Sounds. Some words are formed as imitations of natural sounds. These words are onomatopoeic, or echoic. Examples are *bang, crash, fizz, hiss, pop*, and *sizzle*. Some are iterative in form, as *tweet-tweet* and *pitter-patter*. Such imitative words are expressive and vivid.

"Name" Words. A limited but interesting group of words comes from the names of persons or places. The names of scientists, for example, have come to be employed as common nouns—*faraday, joule, ohm*, and *watt*. Words such as *epicurean, platonic, stoic*, and *jeremiad* remind us of classical and biblical times. Other "name" words include *cardigan, macintosh*, and *guillotine*. Words coming from place-names include *meander, canter, mackinaw, canary*, and *tweed*.

Blending. Telescoping two words into one, called "blending," is another process of word creation, as in *slide* (from *slip* and *glide*), *twirl* (*twist* and *whirl*), and *brunch* (*breakfast* and *lunch*). Other examples are *nucleonics, radiotrician, sportscast, astronaut*, and *smog*. Many humorous blends appear, such as *alcoholiday, slanguage*, and *insinuendo*.

Changes in Words. After entering the language, words continue to have a history. They change, even as people do, and many have varied "careers." The changes that occur may be considered under the following headings:

Degeneration and Elevation. Words may rise or fall in status. The word *villain*, which originally meant "farm laborer," is one example of degeneration in meaning. Others are *knave, imp*, and *varlet*, which at one time merely meant "boy"; *lust*, which meant simply "pleasure"; and *wench*, "young girl." Names for lowly positions for rural inhabitants (as opposed to presumably sophisticated city-dwellers), for foreigners, and for death are subject to degeneration and at times to euphemistic substitutions. For example, *cemetery* took the place of *graveyard*, but today in the United States, *memorial park, cloister*, and *burial abbey* are being substituted for *cemetery*, as are *casket* for *coffin* and *funeral car* for *hearse*.

Along with the many pejorative changes, one may observe the opposite tendency in a number of words. Some terms for position or rank have risen in prestige from lowly origins. Originally a *minister* was a servant, and a *marshal* was a stableboy who looked after the horses. In like manner, throughout the centuries a number of organized groups have accepted derisive names and have made them respected. Instances are *Quaker, Shaker*, and *Hoosier*. The word *fond* has risen from its etymological meaning of "foolish" to "affectionate," and *smart* has been elevated from an earlier meaning pertaining to pain to a meaning pertaining to mental alertness and elegance in dress or appearance.

Generalization and Specialization. In the process of change, words also expand or contract. At times a word acquires an extended meaning instead of the narrower one it once had. For example, the words *throw*—from Old English *ðrāwan*, originally meaning "to turn, to twist"—has become so generalized that we are no longer aware of its having any connection with twisting. For centuries the word *free* meant "noble" or "of high birth." Gradually it has gained a wider sense until it now means "unrestricted."

Far more frequent than the foregoing are words that have narrowed their significance. In Old English, the meaning of *wedd* was "pledge." It appeared in the compound *wedlāc,* the second element meaning "an offering." The modern word *wedlock* has narrowed itself to one particular kind of pledge. To Chaucer, *rent* meant "revenue," and *rape* signified any kind of forcible deprival. Many Modern English terms in science, all minutely specialized, represent more generalized predecessors.

Exaggeration and Understatement. Meanings of words are also changed by the use of hyperbole, or exaggeration, and by understatement. Hyperbole—deliberate exaggeration—causes expressions of strength to diminish in effect and grow toward feebleness, as may be seen in the use of intensives. Adverbs like *awfully, enormously, frightfully,* and *tremendously* are now employed for quite trivial matters. Adjectives indicating approval and disapproval, such as *grand, gorgeous, superb, dreadful, horrible,* and *outrageous,* are employed similarly, thereby weakening the distinctive qualitites of each word.

As there is "too much" in exaggeration, so there is "too little" in understatement, the tradition of which reaches back to the Old English period. Understatement is heard in such negative statements as "not bad," when giving approval. Another instance may be found in *rather,* which has been in English from the earliest period, although Old English *hraðe* had the meaning of "quick" and "early," rather than "preferred." The modern *rather* is the comparative of *rathe.* From the meaning "earlier," *rather* changed to include the idea of "prefer," as shown in Shakespeare's line from *Hamlet,* "And makes us rather bear those ills we have . . . ." In addition to signifying preference, *rather* has come to mean "moderately," as in "rather good."

Abbreviation and Extension. Abbreviating may affect the end, the beginning, or the middle, or a combination of these, of the words it shortens. Generally, clipped words lose sounds at the end as *gas* for *gasoline.* Occasionally a word will lose a sound or syllable at the beginning, as *mend* from *amend, tend* from *attend.* In each case here, the vocabulary has been enriched, for there is a useful differentiation in meaning between the original word and the abbreviated form. Phrase shortenings may be observed in *good-bye* from "God be with you" and *farewell* from "fare you (thee) well." The extension of words is not so prevalent as abbreviation. Occasionally a word adds an extra letter and perhaps an extra sound, as *thunder* (from *þunor*) and *sound* (from *soun*).

Metathesis and Folk Etymology. The kinds of changes discussed thus far result mainly in alteration of meaning. The changes caused by metathesis and folk etymology primarily affect the sounds. Metathesis refers to the interchanging of certain phonemes (speech sounds) by the human tongue, principally *l, r,* and *s,* as may be observed in the pronunciation *aks* for *ask.* The modern word *grass* was *gærs* in Old English; *bird* was *brid,* and *fresh* was *fersc.* Other words that show metathesis are *third, thresh,* and *through.*

In folk (popular) etymology, the form of a word is altered to make it reflect a fancied likeness to another word with which it has no connection but which it resembles in sound, as in *belfry* from French *berfrei* ("tower"). *Ber* sounded somewhat like *bell,* and everyone knows that bells belong in towers; therefore, *ber* became *bell* and gave us *belfry.* Similarly, *hangnail* came from *angnail.* The first syllable is from Old English *ang* ("pain"), but it has become *hang,* because *hang* seemed more plausible. Other instances are *mushroom* from Old French *mouscheron* and *cockroach* from Spanish *cucaracha.*

Shifts in Association. Each word is an idea-complex made up of a primary meaning with a number of associated meanings. For example, the basic meaning of *begin* is "to set in motion, to start." But associated with this are other meanings, such as "creation," "youth," and "birth."

The shift of association may be observed in the word *ambition,* from the Latin *ambitio,* signifying "going around." This meaning was applied to the going about of a politician to get votes, and the resulting secondary meaning grew to be the chief one attached to the word. Since politicians eagerly pursue a particular aim, the idea

of going about became generalized, so that it denoted desire for anything that involved a struggle. To Shakespeare and Milton, ambition was not a good quality. But a later shift of emphasis was ameliorative, and today ambition is considered desirable and is even urged on youth. Thus we see four shifts in the development of the meaning of *ambition:* (1) "a going around," (2) "electioneering," (3) "evil pursuit of place or power," and (4) "initiative."

Similarly, *nice* has shifted from its etymological meaning "ignorant," through its early English sense "foolish" and later ones such as "particular" and "discriminating," to its broad meaning of "pleasant" and "desirable," although "discriminating" is still a living meaning.

Radiation of Meaning. It is the nature of a word to have one principal meaning with a periphery of associated meanings. One can see, therefore, why words multiply, either by splitting into two or more separate words or by gaining many key meanings so that they are employed in different contexts to indicate distinct things or ideas. This feature accounts for the doublets in the language—a pair of words from the same origin, differently derived. For example, in English we find *ward* (Norman French) and *guard* (Parisian French), both from the same Germanic source. Pairs from the Greek, the first being the earlier borrowing and the second the later, are *balm, balsam; blame, blaspheme;* and *priest, presbyter.* Other doublets in Modern English from the same root, one from Old English and one from Scandinavian, are *no* and *nay* and *shirt* and *skirt,* the first of each pair being from Old English.

That a word itself need not multiply in order to have radiation in meaning is evident from looking into any large dictionary. A simple word may have dozens of separate meanings, all developed by association from the same source. Each meaning develops a new referent and undergoes a semantic shift, as in the case of the "eye" of a potato or of a needle. A physical similarity causes a transfer of meaning. By this process, meanings of words are always broadening and shifting. We speak of the "legs" of a table, "hands" of a clock, "foot" of a mountain, and "root" of a tooth or even "root" of the matter," the last involving a higher level of abstraction. Many ordinary words such as *brand, break, color, deep,* and *draft* illustrate the radiation of meanings in English words.

PRONUNCIATION AND SPELLING

The English language has some 40 simple sounds plus 8 diphthongs, consonantal and vocalic. For expressing these sounds in writing, there is an alphabet of only 26 letters. It is therefore necessary for some letters to represent more than one sound. In fact, the letters and letter combinations express an average of five sounds apiece.

If the sounds of English are considered and an attempt is made to count the letters and combinations of letters that may represent certain sounds, the situation is indeed complex. For example, one may give a number of possible sounds with the spelling *ai*—as in *ai*sle, m*ai*l, s*ai*d, p*ai*r, and porcel*ai*n. Even more striking is the number of sounds connected with an unphonetic group of letters *ough*—in b*ough,* c*ough,* r*ough,* thr*ough,* d*ough,* and thor*ough.* The numerous spellings of the sound represented by the International Phonetic Alphabet symbol [ʃ] provide yet another instance: *ch*ivalry, o*ce*an, mousta*ch*e, fu*ch*sia, politi*ci*an, *sch*wa, con*sci*ous, nau*se*a, *sh*ell, fa*sh*ion, man*si*on, pre*ss*ure, pa*ss*ion, ini*ti*ate, posi*ti*on, comple*xi*on, an*xi*ous. From these examples it is evident that the present alphabet is inadequate to express the sounds of Modern English. Old English and Middle English were much more phonetic in representing sounds.

Some changes have been made in the alphabet since the Old English period. During the Middle English period the Old English symbols æ, þ, and ð were lost, and the symbols *j, z, q,* and *v* were added, owing to French influence. Finally, in the 17th century *u* and *v* were separated—*u* for vowel use and *v* for consonant use.

Certain changes in spellings of symbols took place in the Middle English period. The symbols þ and ð came to be spelled *th,* and the digraph *æ* became *a*. Also Old English *ū,* reflecting the French orthographical conventions, came to be spelled *ou* or *ow*. As a result, Old English *þū* became Middle English *thou,* and Old English *fæder* became Middle English *fader*.

With the introduction of printing many Middle English spellings became well established as visual representations of words. Thus there gradually emerged a generally accepted system of spelling, which has continued to the present with a few slight modifications. Since a revolution in English pronunciation was taking place at the time the spelling was being standardized, the present orthography does not indicate the phonology very well. Nevertheless, the written word has had a strong unifying effect on the language. Today the principal forms of Modern English (British, American, and Commonwealth) are practically the same on the printed page, thereby providing linguistic and cultural unity despite the almost endless variations in spoken English.

It is therefore not likely that a significant change will occur in the present written English alphabet for the sake of making it phonemic. If a phonemic alphabet were adopted, all literary masterpieces and other writings would have to be translated into the new system, or readers would have to learn the old spellings as well as the new. Then would come the problem of what pronunciation system to use. In addition, the present spelling often indicates the etymology of the word. Thus the quandary of English spelling remains unsolved. There seems to be a tendency toward greater tolerance of misspellings than formerly, but the standardizing effect of the printed page seems certain to prevent absolute individuality in orthography.

THE FUTURE OF ENGLISH

If World Wars I and II and the vigorous participation of English-speaking nations in international commerce carried English to every inhabited quarter of the globe—as they did—the nature of the language itself helped make it virtually a second tongue to millions of users of other languages. Among features of English favoring its widespread use are its sentence structure, based on a simple word order instead of complicated inflections, and its "natural" gender, instead of the "grammatical" gender system of some other leading languages.

English is almost overwhelming in the richness of its vocabulary, estimated to contain more than a million words and to be the world's largest. From this vast storehouse, users of the language can coin words to suit their needs or give new meanings to existing words in ways that seem natural and effortless. Many other features lend force and flexibility to the language. Among them is the fact that an action verb can be linked with a variety of prepositions to convey both literal and figurative meanings, as in combining *put* with *across, away, down, on, over,* and *through*. Another is the ease with which a word can be made to function as more than one part of speech. For example, many nouns may be used as verbs in popular speech, and vice versa, as *table, chair, seat, curtain,* and *shop*. No other Indo-European language can approach English in this freedom of conversion.

Examples of the flexibility of English are not nullified by its unphonetic and often irrational spelling. And even here a defense of sorts can be made. Users of other languages sometimes get a clue to the meaning of a word written in English because in that form it is similar to a word in their own languages, even though the English pronunciation may fall strangely on their ears.

Whatever the future may hold for English, it has proved to be eminently suitable for almost all forms of written expression as well as for everyday use. It is sure to develop and change, for such is the nature of a living language. Probably it will become increasingly informal and utilitarian, under the impact of mass education and the mass media. Thus the written and the spoken forms of the language will be drawn closer together, making for greater flexibility. In the view of some, English might in time become the one generally accepted international language, although national political rivalries and the reluctance of speakers of other major tongues to yield primacy to English are formidable barriers.

MARGARET M. BRYANT
Author of "Modern English and Its Heritage"

Languages of the World

The number of languages spoken in the world may be estimated at about 5,000. No definite figure can be given for two reasons: the incompleteness of our knowledge of human speech varieties and the definitional vagueness of the term "language" itself, as distinguished from dialect. In popular usage a language is superior in dignity to a dialect in that a language has a written orthographic, grammatical, and lexical norm; characteristically serves as a medium of literary expression and educational instruction; and often has official status as a national language or at least embodies the aspirations of its speakers for political recognition. Other forms in nontechnical usage are labeled "dialects" and are often popularly believed to be mere corrupted forms of standard languages.

In technical usage, however, both written standard languages and dialects, which are infrequently or never written, are equally dialects of the same overall language, providing mutual intelligibility exists. Thus standard French and the local patois of, say, Gascony are equally variants of a single French language, assuming mutual intelligibility. Indeed, standard languages arise from the modification of some particular local dialect variant that has acquired priority for a variety of nonlinguistic reasons, usually some combination of cultural, economic, and political factors. Unfortunately, rigorous application of the criterion of mutual intelligibility has not proven to be possible because of variable factors that enter into its determination—relative intelligence, breadth of linguistic experience, and even emotional attitudes.

The great existing variety of languages has arisen through the local differentiation of previously uniform means of communication. As local dialect variants diverge in the course of time, what were formerly dialect variations of the same language develop their differences to the point of mutual unintelligibility and become separate languages. Thus the local variants of Latin spoken in different sections of the Roman Empire moved farther and farther apart, to the point where they became a number of distinct standard languages, including Spanish, Portuguese, French, Italian, and Romanian, and many more distinct local dialects. Such languages are said to be genetically related. Along with this diversification, however, is a countermovement toward language unification, as some forms become extinct and, in particular, as standard forms, with their greater prestige, replace local unwritten dialects.

In a few instances new varieties arise, not from the local differentiation of a previously uniform language but from an auxiliary form of speech known as *pidgin*. A pidgin is based always on some existing language from which its vocabulary is predominantly drawn but usually with a highly simplified grammatical structure. Pidgins are, by definition, auxiliary modes of communication employed among peoples of diverse linguistic backgrounds. They are not native languages of anyone and tend to be restricted in their powers of expression because of their limited use. However, in a few cases, a pidgin has acquired the role of first language of a population and thereafter has been transmitted in the normal fashion. Such languages are called *creoles*. An example is Haitian creole, originally a pidginized form of French used among themselves by African slaves of differing first languages and with their masters. This is now the regular speech of the population of Haiti and has developed along normal linguistic lines.

In modern times a number of artificial languages have been devised as international auxiliary languages. Even the most successful of these, such as Esperanto, have had only limited use. There is no reason to believe that any existing language has originated from such an artificial language.

MODES OF LINGUISTIC CLASSIFICATION

Languages may be classified from a number of viewpoints and for various purposes. One basic kind of classification is typological, and another is genetic.

Typological Classification. Unlike genetic classifications, which reflect the historical fact of the differentiation in the course of time of an original homogeneous speech community, a typological classification has no necessary historical implications. To take one instance of a typological classification, all languages may be divided between those that are tonal and those that are nontonal. In tonal languages, a difference in pitch in an otherwise identical syllable may provide a drastic change of meaning. Such differences, therefore, function as do distinctions among the ordinary phonemes in a nontonal language. Thus in Yoruba, a tonal language of West Africa, *ko* on a high pitch means "to learn"; on a middle pitch, "to write"; and on a low pitch, "to refuse."

Membership in the group of tonal languages has no necessary historical implications. There are tonal languages in Africa, Southeast Asia, aboriginal Mexico, and elsewhere, and all the indications point to the fact that tonalism arose independently in the different areas. Indeed, languages that originally had a tonal system may lose it; those lacking one may develop it.

Typologies are generally either phonological, as the division into tonal and nontonal languages, or grammatical. An example of grammatical typology is a classification of language according to the presence of absence of noun gender. Similar gender systems—for example, the sex gender systems of Latin (masculine, feminine)—recur independently in other areas, as with certain native American languages, such as Chinook (masculine, feminine, neuter).

A popular grammatical typology has been one that divides the languages of the world into isolating, agglutinative, and inflective types. Its basic criteria pertain to internal word structures. At one end are languages in which each word is an unchangeable and unanalyzable unit—that is, not divisible into such characterizing features as root or inflection. Having no internal means of indicating grammatical connections with other words in the sentence, word order becomes the method of indicating relationships. Languages using this method, called *isolating*, form an ideal type to which no known language actually conforms, although some approximate it—for example, Vietnamese in Southeast Asia. The opposite to isolating languages in this typological scheme are languages in which the word is analyzable into a number of highly fused individual elements expressing a variety of syntactic functions. Such languages are called *inflective*. The classical languages (ancient Greek and Latin and Sanskrit) are considered models of this type. Between these extremes is the *agglutinative* type, in which, while the words have internal structures, the individual parts are clearly distinguishable, so that they may be considered agglutinated (literally, glued together) in mechanical fashion.

In the 19th century this typological classification was widely interpreted as a developmental scheme. The isolating type was regarded as the most primitive, the agglutinative as more advanced, and the inflective as the most highly developed. This scheme was clearly ethnocentric in that the most advanced inflectional stage was believed to have been attained only in the Indo-European and Semitic families. A discrepancy in the scheme was immediately obvious because the most frequently cited example of the isolating, supposedly the most primitive type, was

Chinese, hardly the language of a primitive people. Moreover, as reliable knowledge concerning the grammatical structure of American Indian languages began to accumulate, it became apparent that many of these had complex grammatical structures. This fact was explained away by contending that these languages were overelaborated and lacked true inflectional structure. Such languages were called *polysynthetic*.

Implicit in this interpretation was a scale analogous to that of the isolating-agglutinative-inflective typology—namely, a scale based on the complexity of word structure, running from analytic, through synthetic, to polysynthetic. In *Language* (1921), the American anthropologist Edward Sapir sought to put this by-then obsolescent classification on a new, objective basis, freed from any developmental connotations. The new classification was necessarily more complex because notions that merged and were confused in the traditional classification had to be disengaged and separated. Thus, for example, Sapir proposed a distinct scale of synthesis based on the gross complexity of the word. He also distinguished two different senses of inflection. One had to do with the degree of irregularity of the morphological systems. Such irregularity, which led to difficulty in assigning a clear boundary between stem and inflection, he renamed *fusion,* opposing it to agglutination. The other, distinguished from fusion, had to do with inflection proper, in the sense of the existence of affixes expressing grammatical relations. The direct opposite of inflection is the isolating technique by which word order rather than affixes fulfills the function of expressing grammatical relations.

Although it is now generally agreed that historical and developmental conclusions cannot legitimately be derived from typologies, they prove to have uses for other purposes. Such uses of typologies will be considered later.

Genetic Classification. In genetic classification languages are divided into groups of which each contains only languages that are believed on direct or indirect evidence to have originated as diverging forms of what was once the same language. In such a classification there is a direct and obvious reference to real historical events, in that languages that are classified together have developed in the course of time from a single ancestral language. This ancestral language, for which the prefix "proto" frequently is employed, must, of course, once have developed as a dialect of some still earlier language. For example, the various Germanic languages—English, Dutch, German, Swedish, Norwegian, Danish, and Gothic—show similarities of a sort that lead us to posit a single ancestral language, Proto-Germanic. Proto-Germanic itself, however, shows resemblances to a series of reconstructed languages or to languages attested from an older period in written documents. From these resemblances we conclude that Proto-Germanic, Proto-Slavic, Proto-Italic, Proto-Celtic, and others originated from distinct dialects of a still earlier language, Proto-Indo-European.

An overall genetic classification takes a form analogous to a genealogical tree, and, indeed, the subfamilies of a larger family often are called branches. Of course languages, whether related or not, also affect each other by contact, leading to the borrowing of vocabulary and to influences on grammatical structure and sound systems. In principle, however, it is possible to distinguish the borrowed elements of resemblance from those due to common origin. Between English and French, for instance, certain resemblances are the result of remote common descent from Proto-Indo-European—for example, the resemblance between the English word "two" [too] and the French word "deux" [dû]—whereas other resemblances result from much later borrowings—for example, the English word "chance" [chans] borrowed from the French word "chance" [shaNs].

Related forms like those for the English and French words for numeral 2 are called *cognates*. Cognate words are descended, usually with both phonetic and semantic modification, from a hypothetical or directly attested form in the ancestral language. For the example cited, the Proto-Indo-European of the French and English forms is reconstructed as *dwō* on a variety of evidence. (Such reconstructed forms usually are preceded by an asterisk.)

The resemblances relevant for genetic classification involve, then, both sound and meaning in conjunction, occurring in etymologically connected cognates. These may be either in root vocabulary or in grammatical elements. The existence of pairs, such as English "sun" and German "Sonne," English "hand" and German "Hand," and English "foot" and German "Fuss," are relevant vocabulary evidence in relationship. Likewise, the German comparative and superlative adjective endings, -er and -est, identical to the English forms, and the English past-tense ending, -ed, similar to the German -et, constitute important grammatical evidence.

The distinction between genetic classification criteria, involving sound and meaning, and those for typological classification is apparent. Typological criteria deal with sound in isolation from meaning (phonological typologies) or meaning in isolation from sound (grammatical and semantic typologies). Thus in the typological classification into tonal and nontonal languages cited earlier the specific meanings of the forms containing particular sounds are disregarded. In like manner a grammatical typology based on noun gender classes places Arabic, with masculine and feminine genders, in the same type as French, which also has masculine and feminine genders, and treats the specific sounds of the affixes that express the genders as irrelevant.

Uses of Genetic and Typological Classifications. Since a genetic classification has direct historical meaning, its usefulness as a historical source is obvious. For example, for the unity of the Romance languages, which form a genetic group, there is the corresponding historical fact of the Roman Empire. Further, a comparison of related languages leads, under favorable circumstances, to the reconstruction with considerable detail of many features of the ancestral language. Such reconstruction of linguistic history by the methods of comparative linguistics is a highly developed subdiscipline of linguistics. The study of Indo-European is the classic example of using comparative linguistics, but its use is by no means confined to that family or even to those with written evidence of the linguistic past. Examples of reconstructions of other families are those for Proto-Bantu in Africa, Proto-Austronesian in Oceania, and Proto-Central-Algonkian in North America.

The work of reconstruction is greatly facilitated by the fact that sound changes in language are normally regular. A specific sound in a particular phonetic environment almost always undergoes the same change in different words. Thus in true cognates between English and German there is a regular correspondence between English *t* and German *ts* (orthographically *z*)—for example, English "two" and German "zwei," English "tell" and German "zahlen," and English "ten" and German "zehn." This correspondence arises because of the regular German sound change from an earlier *t* in word-initial, while English maintains the original sound in this position. There almost always are a few exceptions, but these are generally attributed to other factors of change.

Genetic classification leads to the reconstruction of linguistic history, and this in turn provides valuable clues to nonlinguistic theory. For example, the present distribution of related languages furnishes probable hypotheses about the past movements of peoples. Thus the presence of an Austronesian language in Madagascar, off the coast of Africa, whose nearest linguistic relative is in Borneo, provides indisputable evidence of a migration from the Indonesian area to Madagascar. Also, the reconstructed vocabulary of the proto-language leads to inferences regarding the natural environment, family organization, basic economy and religious concepts of the original community. Because in most cases it is possible to distinguish inherited from borrowed words, we often derive valuable historical information concerning cultural diffusion between one people and another.

Typological classification, which does not provide specific historical inferences, leads to general conclusions about the psychological nature of human speech behavior. For example, the absence or relative rarity of instances of certain logically possible types enables us to generalize about human behavior in the area of language. In a typology of word order based on the normal arrangement of noun subject (S), verb (V), and noun object (O) in declarative sentences, there are six logically possible orders: VSO, SVO, SOV, VOS, OVS and OSV. Of these, the first three are common, while the last three are rare or nonexistent. The corresponding feature of the occurrent types is the placement of the nominal subject before the nominal object. In such instances, typological classification has led to general conclusions about human speech that must be taken into account in any general theory of human behavior.

GENETIC CLASSIFICATIONS

Languages of Europe, the Middle East, and Related Areas. The largest language family of Europe and the Middle East is Indo-European. The European colonization of the Western Hemisphere and other parts of the world after the 1500's by speakers of Indo-European languages resulted in their dominance in extensive areas outside Europe. The unity of Indo-European first was recognized by the British Orientalist Sir William Jones in 1786, and beginning with the pioneer work of the Germans Franz Bopp and Jacob Grimm and the Dane Rasmus Rask in the early part of the 19th century, the comparative study of Indo-European languages has progressed further than that of any other language family.

The Indo-European family falls into a number of distinct, well-marked branches: Celtic, Germanic, Italic, Balto-Slavic, Albanian, Greek, Armenian, Indo-Iranian, Tocharian, and Anatolian. The westernmost is Celtic, which once was spoken over an extensive area of western Europe. The extinct Celtic language of the ancient Gauls is known to some extent from inscriptions and materials recorded by the Romans. Celtic languages are divided into two groups: Gaelic, including Irish, Manx (the language of the Isle of Man), and Scottish, and Brythonic, including Welsh, Breton, and the extinct Cornish and Pictish. Breton is not a remnant of ancient Gaulish, but was taken to northwestern France from Britain, with Old Breton dating from the 9th to the 11th century.

The Germanic subfamily of Indo-European is divided into the extinct Gothic recorded in the Bible translation of Ulfilas and the existing West Germanic languages. These consist of three groups: Anglo-Frisian (English and Frisian), Scandinavian (Norwegian, Swedish, Danish, and Icelandic), and German-Dutch. The German-Dutch branch contains two dialect areas, High German in the south and Low German in the north. The German literary language for the Flemish inhabitants of Belgium, as well as for the Netherlands, is a form of Low German. Yiddish developed from the High German dialect spoken by German Jews. Dutch as spoken in South Africa changed along distinctive lines, giving rise to a new literary language, Afrikaans.

The Italic branch of the Indo-European is at present represented only by the Romance languages. In ancient times, Latin was but one of a number of languages of the Italic group, spoken chiefly in Italy. Of the others, the best documented are Oscan, the language of southern Italy, and Umbrian.

The modern standard languages of the Romance group include Portuguese, Spanish, Catalan (Spain), Provençal (France), French, Italian, Rhaeto-Romanic or Romansh (Switzerland), and Romanian. Spanish today is the dominant language of Latin America, except Brazil, where Portuguese is the official language. French has bilingual status in Canada, and creolized forms of French are current in Haiti and other West Indian Islands, in French Guiana, and on the island of Mauritius.

Eastern Europe is dominated linguistically by the Slavic branch of Indo-European. The Slavic branch may be divided into three main groups of literary languages: eastern, with Russian, White Russian, and Ukrainian; western, with Polish, Czech, and Slovak; and southern with Slovene, Serbo-Croatian, Bulgarian, and Macedonian. An archaic form of Slavic, still used in the liturgy of the Orthodox churches, is called Old Church Slavonic. It is probably ancestral to present-day Bulgarian and therefore is sometimes called Old Bulgarian. The smaller Baltic branch comprises Lithuanian and Latvian.

In the Balkans, Greek and Albanian form distinct branches of Indo-European. With regard to Greek, except for the local dialect of Sparta, which is a continuation of the ancient Doric of the area, modern Greek developed from the *koinē*, or common language, of the Hellenistic period. The *koinē* was based on the Attic of Athens. In ancient Greece a variety of dialects existed, most commonly divided into three main groups: Ionic, Doric, and Aeolic. It now is known that the language of the Linear B Cretan inscriptions was an early dialect of Greek.

Indo-European languages also are spoken in southwestern Asia. Here are two branches: Armenian, spoken mostly in the Armenian republic of the USSR, and Indo-Iranian. Indo-Iranian in the ancient period was represented by Avestan, the Iranian language of the sacred writings of the Zoroastrians; Old Persian, the language of the inscriptions of the Achaemenid kings; and Sanskrit, the language of the sacred texts of the Hindu religion as well as of a considerable secular literature. A later stage of Old Persian is represented by the Pahlavi (Pehlavi) of the early Middle Ages, which developed into the modern Persian literary language. In addition to Persian, the modern Iranian languages include Pashto, the chief language of the Afghanistan, and Baluchi, Kurdish, and Tajik. The later forms of the Indic branch, as spoken after the period of Sanskrit, are called Prakrits. One of these, Pali, is the language of the extensive Buddhist canon. A number of important literary languages, spoken chiefly in the northern part of India, are the modern representatives of the Indic subbranch of Indo-Iranian. Among these are Hindi, the present official language of India; Gujarati, Sindhi, Panjabi, Kashmiri, Marathi, Bengali, Assamese, Oriya, and Nepali. In Sri Lanka (Ceylon), Sinhalese, an Indic language geographically separated from its northern congeners, is the chief language.

One of the extinct branches of Indo-European is Tocharian, consisting of two closely related languages (A and B) of central Asia, known from Buddhist written documents of the early Middle Ages. A number of extinct languages of Asia Minor form the Anatolian group of languages. These are chiefly known from the cuneiform records excavated at Bogazköy in Turkey. The best known is cuneiform Hittite, with written documents as early as 1600 B.C. Some scholars consider Anatolian a branch of Indo-European, while others believe the relationship to be a more distant one and reckon Indo-Europeans and Hittite as the two branches of a single family, which they call Indo-Hittite.

Among the non–Indo-European languages of Europe are Basque of northern Spain and adjoining southern France and ancient Etruscan of Italy. Basque has most often been connected with the Caucasian family of languages, but this relationship has not been generally accepted.

Afroasiatic, traditionally known as Hamito-Semitic, is the chief language family of the Middle East and the northern part of Africa. It consists of five branches: Semitic, Egyptian, Berber, Cushitic, and Chadic. Of these, Semitic and Egyptian are known from written records of considerable antiquity. Semitic usually is divided into eastern and western branches. The only known member of the eastern branch is the extinct Akkadian language, of which there is a vast literature in the cuneiform system of writing. Akkadian had two chief dialect variants: northern, or Assyrian, and southern, or Babylonian.

The western branch of Semitic has two divisions, Northwest Semitic and Southwest Semitic. The Northwest subfamily includes Aramaic and Canaanite. Aramaic was once the lingua franca of a vast area in the Middle East, from the Persian Achaemenid period on. It was the language of Palestine at the time of Jesus and was employed by the Jews alongside Hebrew in the literature of the talmudic period. In the form of Syriac it still remains the liturgical language of certain Middle Eastern Christian churches. Today, Aramaic survives as a spoken language only in a few scattered areas, having been superseded by Arabic. The Canaanite branch of Northwest Semitic included, in ancient times, Phoenician, Moabite, Hebrew, and other languages. After becoming extinct as a spoken language before the Christian era, Hebrew has been revived and is the official language of Israel. Ugaritic, the language of inscriptions from Ras Shamra in Syria, dating from the 2d millennium B.C., should be considered an early form of Canaanite.

Southwest Semitic is divided into North Arabic and South Arabic-Ethiopic. North Arabic includes the colloquial Arabic dialects that extend from Morocco to Iraq, as well as literary Arabic. South Arabic is represented by the languages of South Arabian inscriptions: Sabean, Minean, Himyaritic, and Qatabanian. South Arabic languages still are spoken by certain populations in South Arabia (Mehr, Hadhramaut) and on the island of Socotra. Among Ethiopian Semitic languages, classical Ethiopic (Geez) still is in use as a liturgical and literary language. It belongs to the northern group, which is represented among contemporary languages by Tigre and Tigrinya. The southern Ethiopic Semitic group has as its chief member Amharic, the official language of Ethiopia. It also includes the Gurage group, Argobba, and Harari.

The second branch of Afroasiatic is the extinct ancient Egyptian. This language is known in its earliest form from hieroglyphic inscriptions. The later form of the language, Coptic, written in an alphabet derived from Greek, was spoken into the 17th century and still is used in the liturgy of the Coptic Church.

The Berber languages are the third group within Afroasiatic. They are spoken alongside Arabic in much of North Africa. The Tuareg of the Sahara also speak a Berber language.

Cushitic, the fourth group of Afroasiatic languages, consists of a large number of languages spoken in Ethiopia, Somalia, and even as far south as mainland Tanzania. The most important are Somali and Gallinya, the latter a major language of Ethiopia.

The fifth group of Afroasiatic languages, Chadic, is represented by a large number of languages in the vicinity of Lake Chad in black Africa. Of these, the most important is Hausa, which had official status in northern Nigeria and is widely employed as a lingua franca.

Some extinct languages of the Middle East and Africa are not affiliated with the major families just described. It is possible, in some cases, that an increase in the available material will assist in their ultimate assignment to some major group. Such languages include Sumerian, Elamite, Hurrian, and Meroitic.

Languages of Subsaharan Africa. The non-Afroasiatic languages of Africa may be classified into three linguistic groups: Niger-Kordofanian, Nilo-Saharan, and Khoisan. The first, Niger-Kordofanian, consists of Niger-Congo, the most extensive linguistic grouping in Subsaharan Africa, and the small Kordofanian stock of Sudan. Niger-Congo occupies almost all of West, Central, and East Africa. It tentatively may be divided into six major subgroups. The first, and most westerly, is the West Atlantic subgroup, including, among others, Wolof of Senegal, Temne of Sierra Leone, and the widespread Fulani spoken in a number of separate regions from Senegal to Lake Chad and beyond. The second subgroup is Mande, including Vai of Liberia, for which an indigenous syllabary was invented; Mende of Liberia; and Malinke and Bambara of Mali. The extensive Voltaic, or Gur, the third subgroup, is spoken largely in the basin of the Volta River system. Its largest single member is Mossi of Upper Volta. The fourth subgroup is Kwa, extending in general along the coastal belt of West Africa from Liberia to Nigeria. Among the major languages of Kwa are Twi of Ghana; Ewe of Ghana, Togo, and Dahomey; Yoruba, the dominant language of the western region of Nigeria; Bini, the language of Benin; Nupe, spoken in central Nigeria; and Ibo, the chief language of eastern Nigeria. The fifth subgroup of Niger-Congo is Benue-Congo, which includes a number of languages in Nigeria, such as Tiv and Jukun. Its most important member, however, is the vast Bantu subgroup that consists of some

300 languages covering most of the Congo basin and eastern and southern Africa. Among the important Bantu languages are Kikongo, Zulu, Chwana, Nyanja, Luganda, and Swahili. Swahili, originally spoken by an Islamicized black populaion of the Tanganyika-Kenya coast and on Zanzibar and Pemba, has become the most widely spoken lingua franca of East Africa and is the official language of Tanzania. It is quite probable that Bantu-Congo and Kwa really form a single subgroup. The sixth subgroup of Niger-Congo is Adamawa-Eastern, which extends north of the Congo basin eastward into Sudan. Among the important languages are Zande and Sango, the latter being the chief language of the Central African Republic.

The other large linguistic stock of black Africa is Nilo-Saharan. It includes, in West Africa, Songhai, the language of the great medieval Songhai Empire, and the Kanuri-Teda group. Kanuri was the chief language of the former Muslim kingdom of Bornu in the Lake Chad area. Teda is spoken in the eastern Sahara. However, most of the languages in the Nilo-Saharan family are found in the eastern portion of the continent. Among these are Nubian, spoken in the Nile Valley, and the large Nilotic group, which includes Shilluk, Nuer, Acholi, Masai, Bari, and Nandi. Some Christian religious documents in Nubian from the medieval period were written in a modified form of the Coptic alphabet.

The third linguistic family of Subsaharan Africa is Khoisan, which is unique in the world because of its use of click sounds. Except for the Negroid Bergdama, Khoisan languages are spoken mostly by the racially distinct Khoikoin (Hottentots) and San (bushmen). Other exceptions are a few neighboring Bantu groups that have borrowed the click sounds. Two languages of the family, Sandawe and Hatsa, are found in mainland Tanzania (Tanganyika), much farther north than the main body of speakers.

Languages of Southeast Asia and Oceania. Five major language stocks occupy practically all of southern and eastern Asia and Oceania: Dravidian, Sino-Tibetan, Austroasiatic, Thai-Austronesian, and Indo-Pacific. The Dravidian languages are a group of quite closely related languages, which, except for the detached Brahui of Baluchistan, are spoken entirely in the southern portion of the Indian subcontinent and on the island of Sri Lanka (Ceylon). The Dravidian group includes four literary languages—Tamil, Malayalam, Kanarese, and Telugu—as well as a number of others, such as Ghond and Kui, that have not undergone such cultivation.

The Sino-Tibetan family is of vast extent and great internal diversity. The Sinitic branch includes literary Chinese as well as the numerous local variants of Chinese, of which Mandarin is the most important. The other large branch is Tibeto-Burman, which includes the Tibetan group, the Naga languages of Assam, the Kuki-Chin of northern Burma, Burmese proper, and the Karen languages.

Austroasiatic is the third major language group of Southeast Asia. It may be divided into the following subfamilies: (1) the aboriginal Munda languages of central and eastern India; (2) Mon-Khmer, with Mon spoken in southern Burma, and Khmer in Kampuchea (Cambodia), of which it is the official language; (3) Palaung-Wa, spoken in Burma; (4) Semang-Sakai, spoken in southern Burma and in Malaysia; (5) Khasi, spoken in the Assam hills of India; (6) Nicobarese, spoken in the Nicobar islands; and (7) Annamite-Muong, a group of languages of which the most important is Vietnamese (Annamite).

Thai-Austronesian has two branches: Thai-Kadai and Austronesian. Thai-Kadai consists of the Thai group, long erroneously included in Sino-Tibetan, and the Kadai languages, spoken in southwestern China and in the interior of the island of Hainan off the southeast coast of Asia. Thai-Kadai is related to the large Austronesian family, sometimes called Malayo-Polynesian. The Austronesian languages extend from Madagascar off the southeast coast of Africa to Easter Island, the farthest east of the Polynesian Islands. Austronesian languages are found in Madagascar, the mainland of Southeast Asia, Taiwan, the Philippines, Indonesia,

Melanesia, Micronesia, and Polynesia. Among the important Austronesian languages are Malay, widely used as a trade language and, in modified form (Bahasa Indonesia), the official language of Indonesia; Tagalog in the Philippines; Batak in Sumatra; Javanese; Samoan; Fijian; and Hawaiian.

The thesis of the German ethnologist Wilhelm Schmidt, linking the Austronesian languages with Austroasiatic in a larger Austric unity, is probably valid. It requires restatement, however, on the basis of the later linkage of Thai-Kadai with Austronesian, to include Thai-Austronesian and Austroasiatic. The Miao-Yao group of southwestern China is also affiliated with Austric.

It has been customary to apply the term Papuan to all non-Austronesian languages of the Pacific area except Australia and Tasmania. Such languages are spoken over most of New Guinea and in various parts of eastern Indonesia and in Melanesia. It appears highly probable that all of these non-Austronesian languages except those of Australia and the hitherto unclassified languages of the Andaman Islands in the Bay of Bengal are to be linked in a single Indo-Pacific family. Indo-Pacific may be divided into the following subgroups (1) Andaman; (2) Northern Halmahera; (3) Timor-Alor; (4) Vogelkop-Kamoro (New Guinea); (5) Ekari-Moni (New Guinea); (6) Hollandia (New Guinea); (7) Merauke (New Guinea); (8) Kiwai (New Guinea); (9) Highland (New Guinea); (10) Astrolabe Bay (New Guinea); (11) Kate (New Guinea); (12) Eastern New Guinea; (13) Northern Solomons (Russell, Rendova, Vella la Vella, and Savo); (14) New Britain; (15) Bougainville; and (16) Tasmania.

The languages of the Australian aborigines form a single linguistic group. One subgroup, Pama-Nyungan, covers most of the continent, but approximately 30 others are concentrated chiefly in the northwest, with some in north central Australia.

Languages of Central and Northern Eurasia. In addition to Basque, other non—Indo-European languages are spoken in Europe. These are branches of the Uralic family, which is composed of the Samoyed languages spoken in Siberia and the more important Finno-Ugric group. The Finnic languages include Finnish, Estonian, Lapp, the Permian languages (Zyryan and Votyak) of northern European Russia, and the more distantly related Mordvin and Cheremiss of the Middle Volga region. The Ugric languages include Hungarian and Ob-Ugric (Vogul and Ostyak) of western Siberia.

A second major linguistic family of northern Eurasia is Altaic, consisting of Turkic, Mongolian, and Tungusic. The Turkic subfamily, which has not yet been properly subclassified, includes Osmanli Turkish, the standard language of Turkey; Azerbaijani, the chief language of Azerbaijan; Nogai in the Caucasus; Chuvash in the Middle Volga; Turkuman, Kirghiz, Kazak, Karakalpak, and Uzbek, all major languages of Russian central Asia; Uigur of Chinese Turkestan; and Yakut, used far to the northeast in Siberia. Mongolian is spoken in several varieties, chiefly Khalkha in Outer Mongolia and Buryat in Inner Mongolia. Languages of the Tungusic branch of Altaic are spoken over a vast but sparsely settled area in eastern Siberia and south of the Amur River. The only form of Tungusic that has received literary cultivation is Manchu. A third major family of languages of this general area is Caucasian, consisting of two distinct groups, South Caucasian or Khartvelian, of which the main language is Georgian, and North Caucasian, consisting of an eastern (Daghestan) group and a western (Circassian and Ubykh) group.

Outside of these larger groupings are the following individual languages or small-scale groups: Burushaski, an isolated language of Kashmir; the Yenisseian group, now extinct; Yukaghir, spoken in eastern Siberia; Gilyak, spoken both in the Amur region on the mainland of Asia and on Sakhalin; the Luorwetlan, or Paleosiberian, group (Chukchee, Koryak, and the various Kamchadal dialects of Kamchatka); Ainu, the language of the aborigines of Hokkaido and southern Sakhalin; Korean; and Japanese (Japanese proper and the language of the Ryukyu Islands). An Asiatic dialect of Eskimo is spoken at the northwestern tip of Siberia.

The Eurasiatic stocks that have been discussed are all conventionally considered to be independent, but various hypotheses have been advanced linking one or more of these. Thus as early as 1730, Count Philip J. von Strahlenberg of Sweden proposed the Ural-Altaic hypothesis of linkage, which was generally accepted in the 19th century, went out of fashion in the early 20th century, but is being revived. Among other later proposals are those linking Yukaghir and Uralic; Korean and Altaic; Korean, Ainu, and Japanese; and Uralic and Eskimo-Aleut. In fact, it seems highly likely that the following groups form a single large family that might be called Eurasiatic: Uralic, Altaic, Yukaghir, Paleosiberian, Gilyak, Ainu, Korean, Japanese and Eskimo-Aleut. It is also probable that they are related to the Indo-European. In fact, the notion of an Indo-European relationship with Uralic has received fairly wide acceptance.

Aboriginal Languages of the Western Hemisphere. Much research remains to be done in the classification of the numerous and diverse languages spoken by the aboriginal inhabitants of the Western Hemisphere. Among the questions involved is that of their ultimate unity and of possible links to languages of the Eastern Hemisphere. The Amerind languanges may, for convenience, be divided into those of North America north of Mexico, those of Mexico and Central America, and those of South America. This division is based, not on linguistic criteria, but on the relatively distinct history of classificational attempts and the fact that specialists have tended to confine themselves to one of these three areas.

The first overall classification of languages north of Mexico was that of Major John W. Powell of the Bureau of American Ethnology, who in 1891 divided these languages into 55 independent stocks. This extremely conservative classification became the basis for more extensive hypotheses in the first decades of the 20th century, notably by the American anthropologists Alfred Kroeber and Roland Dixon. These results were restated and further reductions proposed in an influential article by Edward Sapir, published in the *Encyclopaedia Britannica* in 1929. Sapir's classification of all American Indian languages north of Mexico into six families became the basis of all subsequent work and gave rise to a considerable literature of controversy. It is becoming clear that some of Sapir's families are substantially correct, while others are in serious need of revision, leading to a somewhat different overall view of language classification in the northern part of the Americas.

Sapir's first family is Eskimo-Aleut. The Eskimo branch falls into two well-marked dialect groups, a western in Alaska and Siberia (Yupik) and an eastern covering the remainder of the vast Eskimo domain. The dialects of the Aleutian Islands form the other branch of Eskimo-Aleut. As indicated earlier, the relationships of Eskimo-Aleut are in all probability to be sought in the west in the large Eurasiatic group of languages.

The second family in Sapir's classification is Algonkian-Mosan, consisting of three branches: (1) Algonkian-Ritwan; (2) Mosan; and (3) Kutenai. The large Algonkian group covered most of the central and northeastern United States and eastern Canada and can be divided into four subgroups: (1) Eastern (including Mohican, Delaware, and Abenaki) and Central (including Fox, Sauk, Menomini, Ojibwa, and Cree); (2) Arapaho; (3) Cheyenne; and (4) Blackfoot. The Ritwan Languages are Wiyot and Yurok in northern California. The Mosan family consists of the Salishan, Chemakuan (Chemakum and Quilete), and Wakashan (Kwakiutl and Nootka) subfamilies, all spoken in the northwestern United States and southwestern Canada. The third branch is formed by the Kutenai language of the same general region as the Mosan.

The third family is Na-Dene, consisting of (1) Haida; (2a) Tlingit; and (2b) Eyak-Athapaskan. Athapaskan is an extensive group spoken as far north as Alaska and as far south as the Navajo and Apache of the American southwest.

The fourth Sapir family is Penutian, extending from the Tsimshian of British Columbia to the Maya of Mexico and Guatemala. It includes (1) California Penutian (Yokuts, Maidu, Wintun, and

Miwok); (2) Oregon Penutian (Takelma, Coos, and others); (3) Plateau Penutian (including Sahaptin and Klamath); (4) Chinook; (5) Tsimshian; (6) Mexican Penutian (consisting of Sapir's Mixe-Zoque and Huave, to which should be added Mayan and Totonac).

Sapir's fifth family, Hokan-Siouan, probably has aroused the greatest controversy and is surely not valid in the form he presented. Sapir divided Hokan-Siouan into six groups. The first is Hokan-Coahuiltecan, including Hokan, Subtiaba-Tlappanec, and Coahuiltecan. Individual Hokan languages include, mostly in California, Yana, Pomo, Karok, Chimariko, Shasta-Achomawi, Washo, Esselen, Yuman, Chumash, Seri, and Chontal. To these, Jicaque in Honduras and Subtiaba in Nicaragua should be added. The Coahuiltecan group contains various extinct languages of Texas and Mexico. The other five groups are Yuki, Keres (spoken in certain Pueblos), Tunican (Louisiana and Arkansas), Iroquois-Caddoan, and Eastern (Siouan-Yuchi, Natchez-Muskogean, and possibly the extinct Timucua of Florida). It now appears that, except for Hokan-Coahuiltecan, all of these languages should be assigned either to Penutian (Yuki, Tunican, and Natchez-Muskogean) or to a new group, Keres-Siouan, consisting of Iroquoian, Caddoan, Siouan-Yuchi, and Keres.

The sixth family in Sapir's classification is Azteco-Tanoan. It contains two certain branches (Uto-Aztecan and Tanoan-Kiowan) and a third, doubtful one (Zuni). Uto-Aztecan includes the Shoshonean languages of the southwestern United States (for example, Ute, Comanche, and Hopi), Pima-Papago, and the Aztecan group (including Cora, Huichol, and Nahuatl). Tanoan is the language of certain Pueblos (Taos, Picuris, and others).

It is likely that a third branch should be added to Uto-Aztecan and Kiowa-Tanoan, namely Oto-Mangue, to form a major stock, Central Amerind, and that Zuni is part of Penutian. Oto-Mangue, the single major group spoken exclusively in Middle America, includes Otomi, Zapotec, Mixtec, and others.

The southern part of the area between the Rio Grande and South America is almost entirely occupied by northern outliers of the vast Chibchan family, which is concentrated in northwestern South America but has southward extensions as far as Argentina.

For South America, a large number of independent families were posited by John Alden Mason in 1950 and, largely following him, by Norman McQuowan in 1955. In 1965, Joseph Greenberg proposed an overall reduction to three families: (1) Macro-Chibchan; (2) Andean-Equatorial; and (3) Gê-Pano-Carib. Macro-Chibchan consists of Chibchan proper (including Chibcha, Cuna, Rama, Paya, Xinca, and Lenca) and Paezan (including Paez, Choco, Colorado, and Warrau). Andean-Equatorial has two main branches: Andean, which includes Quechua (the language of the Inca Empire), Aymará, Zaparo, Araucanian, Ona, and Yahgan; and Equatorial, including Tupí-Guaraní and Arawakan, as well as many smaller or extinct languages. Tupí served as the lingua geral (trade language) of the Brazilian interior. Guaraní still is spoken alongside Spanish as one of the two major languages of Paraguay. The third major stock of South America is Gê-Pano-Carib. Its main subdivisions are (1) Macro-Gê, including the Gê language of Brazil, as well as Bororo and Caraja; (2) Macro-Panoan, including the Panoan languages spoken largely in Bolivia, and the Guaycuruan languages of the Chaco; and (3) Macro-Carib, which consists chiefly of the large Carib group. The aboriginal inhabitants of the West Indies spoke Arawakan languages (Andean-Equatorial).

From the foregoing survey it can be seen that, outside of Eskimo-Aleut, the American Indian languages can be divided tentatively into nine families. These are Na-Dene, Algonkian-Mosan, Hokan-Coahuiltecan, Keres-Siouan, Penutian, Central Amerind, Macro-Chibchan, Andean-Equatorial, and Gê-Pano-Carib. A relation among all of these except Na-Dene is highly likely. Thus the indigenous languages of the Americas would consist of (1) a large general Amerindian stock; (2) Na-Dene in the extreme northwest; and (3) Eskimo-Aleut, with affiliations in the Eastern Hemisphere.

Although a small number of isolated languages remain unassigned to larger groupings, the indictions are that further work on the problems of language classification may lead to an overall genealogical classification of the languages of the world into a fairly small number of major branches.

JOSEPH H. GREENBERG
Stanford University

Guide to the Use of the Dictionary

1. ENTRY WORDS AND PHRASES

A. The Main Entry

Main entry words and phrases are set in boldface type and indented from the lefthand margin. Main entry words are syllabicated, with boldface center periods between the syllables: **bal·le·ri·na, Bot·swa·na.** Main entry words are not syllabicated, nor are they pronounced, if the form has already been so treated: **barrow** in the sense of "grave mound" follows **bar·row** "wheeled handcart".

Main entry phrases are not syllabicated if each word in the phrase is syllabicated in its own main entry position: **barrel organ.** If any word of a main entry phrase is not entered in its normal alphabetical place, it is syllabicated at the phrasal main entry: **bar mitz·vah.**

Certain main entry phrases are inverted so that the most logical reference word may be consulted at its alphabetical place. These entries are mainly surnames, geographical names, or the names of historical events or periods. Surnames are syllabicated and pronounced, with given names following in Roman (ordinary text type): **An·der·son** (ændərs'n), Carl David. The key or reference word of a geographical or historical main entry phrase is syllabicated, followed by the beginning of the phrase in main-entry boldface: **A·zov, Sea of; Bau·tzen, Battle of.** Such surnames or reference words are not syllabicated and pronounced, however, if they have already been so treated previously: **Buenos Aires, Lake** occurs after the syllabicated and pronounced entry for the city of Buenos Aires.

B. Variant Forms

Spelling variants are given, separated by commas, in the main entries: **adze, adz; As·wan Dam, As·suan Dam.** The first form is regarded as the more common. If the variation represents a difference between American and British spelling conventions, this is noted, with the American form listed first: **balloon tire,** *Br.* **balloon tyre.**

Spelling variants are treated in the same manner when they occur within the definition block itself as a variant of a subentry: **ac·knowl·edg·ment, ac·knowl·edge·ment.**

For other variants reflecting British usage, see *Usage Labels* below.

C. Inflected Forms

The spellings of plurals (when these are not simply formed by the addition of -s or -es), of participial and past tense forms of verbs, and of comparative and superlative forms of adjectives and adverbs are given in a boldface slightly smaller than the main-entry face and identified by abbreviated italicized labels: **bus·by** . . . *pl.* **bus·bies; brakes·man** . . . *pl.* **brakes·men; ar·tic·u·late** . . . *pres. part.* **ar·tic·u·lat·ing** *past* and *past part.* **ar·tic·u·lat·ed; brave** . . . *comp.* **brav·er** *superl.* **brav·est.**

D. Derivatives and Compounds

When a word is formed by the affixing of a derivational suffix or a compounding word to a base form, the derivative or compound may be entered, and when necessary defined, within the definition block for the base form, rather than treated separately as a main entry: **blame·a·ble, blame·less,** and **blame·wor·thy** appear as derivatives within the definition block of the verb **blame; bounc·er** is entered within the definition block of **bounce; af·fix·a·tion** and **af·fix·ture** are entered in the main entry for the verb **af·fix.**

Such subentries are made when the editor judges that the derivative term within the definition block will be both readily and logically located by the reader. If the derivative is of great currency or is otherwise regarded as sufficiently prominent for separate main entry status, it appears in its own alphabetical place: **bot·a·nist** is a main entry and not a subentry under **bot·a·ny.** Occasionally a less common derivative is entered as a sort of variant in the definition block of a more common form: **brach·y·ceph·a·lous** is entered under main entry **brach·y·ce·phal·ic.**

This dictionary does not attempt to enter all possible derivatives. For instance the regular agent nouns in -er and the very numerous nouns formed with -ment are not entered unless the derivative differs in meaning from what is predictable from the use of the suffix. "Bouncer" above is a case where the sense is not predictable from the meaning of "bounce" plus -er.

Pronunciations are given for derivatives and compounds if these are not readily inferrable from the main entry. Even if the pronunciation is not shown, derivatives and compounds are syllabicated and stresses are marked: under **bu·reauc·ra·cy,** the derivative **bu·reau·crat** is pronounced because two of the vowels have altered sounds, but the additional derivatives **bu·reau·crát·ic** and **bu·reau·crát·i·cal·ly** are marked for primary stress only.

E. Run-in Phrasal Entries

The English language is rich in set phrases, especially in idiomatic phrases whose meaning cannot readily be inferred from the meanings of the separate words, and in phrases consisting of verbs plus adverbs or particles, which are used and understood as if they were linguistic units rather than combinations of units. When a word, especially a verb, enters into many of these phrases, they are "run in" under the main entry for the key word. Under **break,** for instance, the dictionary defines **to break a record, to break away, to break down, to break in,** and ten other such phrases, showing variants where they exist: **to break loose** (or **free**). In a related sort of run-in phrasal entry, **the blind** is entered and defined under the main entry **blind.**

2. PRONUNCIATION

The respelling system of this dictionary is based upon the International Phonetic Alphabet, a scientific notation devised by phoneticians for recording every possible speech sound. It therefore will require, for most persons, a little effort of memory to retain and use the symbols. This system will repay such effort, since it is superior in precision and accuracy over any other system based on "natural" spelling, where in English especially one letter or group of letters may have many pronunciations. The complete respelling system and pronunciation guide will be found inside the front and rear covers and opposite the first page of the dictionary. For the user's convenience, a brief version of the respelling system is printed at the bottom of each page.

This dictionary does not attempt the enormous and probably impossible task of transcribing the pronunciation variants of all the American (and British) dialects, but it does show variant pronunciations that occur within the "General American" (something like educated Northern or North Midwestern) patterns taken here as the standard. For example, **bear** is given only the pronunciation including -r, which does not represent the "-r-less" speech of Southern and Northeastern Americans, whereas words like **a·de·nine** and **a·dieu** show pronunciations that might be heard among educated speakers of the adopted standard. The variant given first is not meant to be "preferred to" or "more correct than" those given second or third.

When the pronunciation of a word changes to indicate a change in part of speech, this is indicated by showing the altered pronunciation at the beginning of the appropriate definition:**ab·stract** (æbstrækt) for the adjective and noun senses, and (æbstrǽkt) for one verb sense and (ǽbstrækt) for another as the situation requires; differing pronunciations are similarly recorded for the verb, adjective, and noun senses of **ag·gre·gate.**

Foreign words, which are especially frequent among the encyclopedic entries, are not always shown as they would be pronounced in the source language, but rather as they would be spoken and recognized by educated American speakers. In practice this means that when a word or name is well "naturalized" in English, it is respelled with a normal English sound (see **Ab·bas**), but when the word still feels foreign, or is new to most American ears, it is given the proper foreign-language pronunciation (see **A·bruz·zi e Mo·li·se**). In the intermediate case, the word or name is often given both an English and a foreign-language pronunciation (see **Ar·a·gon**).

3. DEFINITIONS

The generic-word definitions of this dictionary aim above all to be brief and to be clear. They are designed to be substitutable for the word defined. The encyclopedic "definitions," or descriptions, interspersed with the generic ones aim to give the appropriate information briefly and clearly. The dictionary conforms to the best practices of those dictionaries—more common in American lexicography than in European—that do not puristically rule factual information out of lexicography, but treat word-information and thing-information as equally valid and equally deserving of space in a useful reference work.

The initial words of definitions are not capitalized. If the definition requires more than one sentence, the first word of the subsequent sentence is capitalized in the customary way.

A. The Definition Block

The definitions are organized in three kinds for ready and easy consultation. First, when a word or phrase has one or more senses and only one part of speech, it is written as a single block with the senses introduced by a single italicized part-of-speech label (see the list of abbreviations for these), and the various senses are then separated by double bars (‖). See, for example, the entry at **ba·cil·lus.**

Second, when the term has several definitions in several parts of speech, all senses in one part of speech are introduced by a boldface numeral, and then separated again from one another by double bars. See the entry at **bal·loon.**

Third, when the word or phrase is defined in several parts of speech and many senses, but one part of speech is not dominant over another, or is not clearly the source of another, the definition is divided among two or more main entries and definition blocks. See, for example, the entries at **bal·ance.**

These slightly varying styles of definition block contribute not only to simplicity of use but to a grasp of the particular semantics of the term.

Within the definition block, senses are ordered logically by frequency of use and by apparent semantic derivation. For example, under **busi·ness,** the first sense is the basic occupational one, and

the more specialized or transferred senses follow; under **butch·er,** the noun is defined before the verb, and so on.

B. Examples

The examples in this dictionary are brief and precise, with the aim not merely of showing the term in a possible or random context but also in one where the sense distinction becomes sharper. For instance, the examples under **burn** set the word or phrase in precise contexts where the particular sense is both illustrated and required: *to burn a hole, the pepper burned her throat, the fire is burning brightly, to burn with shame, to burn into one's memory, her burst of energy soon burned out.*

Examples are printed in italics, as here, and their initial words are not capitalized.

C. Cross-references

Cross-references are printed in small capital letters and are preceded by an asterisk or by an abbreviated label in Roman (ordinary text) type.

They are used most commonly to refer the reader to a related word or phrase that supplements or complements the definition at hand: under **ac·count·ant** cross-reference is made to *CERTIFIED PUBLIC ACCOUNTANT and to *CHARTERED ACCOUNTANT; under **ac·ti·nide series** cross-reference is made to *PERIODIC TABLE; under **accrued dividend** the cross-reference is cf. CUMULATED DIVIDEND: under **ac·i·do·sis** it is opp. ALKALOSIS. Such cross-references enrich the semantic field of the term being defined.

Cross-references are also used as a form of quick definition that refers the user from one main entry to another that is synonymous and is judged to be the more current and "normal" term: the main entry **action painting** is defined by the cross-reference *ABSTRACT EXPRESSIONISM.

4. RESTRICTIVE LABELS

Restrictive labels are of several sorts, and all aim to narrow, specify, modify, or otherwise restrict the term and distinguish it from or within current educated standard American English. Labels are printed in italics within parentheses. All labels are simple and self-explanatory, though the user may need to consult the table of abbreviations from time to time.

A. Field Labels

Field labels indicate, often with an abbreviation, the occupational, technical, or other specialized use of the term at hand: one sense under **ac·tion** is labeled *(horol.)*; one sense under **ag·ate** is labeled *(games)*; one sense under **a·pron** is labeled *(theater)*.

B. Usage Labels

Usage labels indicate the relation of the word or phrase to the dictionary's target language, current educated standard American English. Such labels most often either show a regional or geographical peculiarity of the word or phrase, or they indicate how it differs from strict and accurate standard speech: under **a·gree** two verb senses are labeled (Br.), British use; under **al·so-ran** one sense is labeled *(loosely)*; under **an·te** one sense is labeled *(pop.)*; at **belle** the label *(old fash.)* is used, and so on.

5. ETYMOLOGIES

Etymological derivations are shown at the end of the definition block and within square brackets. The names of source languages or language families are usually abbreviated and are printed in Roman type.

When the word or phrase has simply been borrowed from the source language without change of form or meaning, the etymology shows only the language of origin: under **ab·do·men** the etymology is [L.]

When the English word or phrase differs in form but not in meaning from the source term, only the language of origin and the source form are shown: under **ace** the etymology is [O.F. *as*].

When the word or phrase is an English translation or version of the foreign source, the etymology shows the language of origin, and then the English gloss after the equal sign: under **aard·wolf** the etymology is [Du.=earth wolf].

In the most common case, the language of origin and the cognate form are shown, with the form in italics and the meaning of the form is shown in Roman, following a comma: under **ac·count** the etymology is [O.F. *aconter*, to count].

When the source word appears in a form that does not closely resemble the English word, as often happens in the case of derivatives from Greek or Latin, the basic source (usually an infinitive or a noun in the nominative case) will be supplemented with the immediate source (often a noun in the accusative case): under **a·tro·cious** the etymology is [fr. L. *atrox (atrocis)*, cruel].

When the source term itself is derived from another language, this is shown by the abbreviation "fr.": under **ap·sis** the etymology is [L.=arch fr. Gk]; under **bail·iff** the etymology is [M.E. *baillif, custodian* fr. O.F.].

When the actual source of the word or phrase is not entirely certain, a range of related possible source words may be given: under **ba·bel** the etymology is [Heb. *bábel*, Assyrian-Babylonian *Báb-ilu*, Babylon (Gate of God)].

When the elements of a compound word or a phrase, or the base of a derivative, are entered elsewhere in the dictionary, and the etymologies are given at those main entries, the etymology is in effect a cross-reference printed in small capitals directing the user to look in those places for a full etymology: under **ac·et·al·de·hyde** the etymology is [ACETYL + ALDEHYDE].

ROBERT L. CHAPMAN
Professor Emeritus, Drew University

Dictionary Usage Guide

abnegate

Guide words showing the alphabetical range of entries on the page

Syllabicated main entry
See Part 1A.

Usage labels
See Part 4B.

Derivative forms
See Part 1D.

Encyclopedic entry
See Part 3.

Pronounced derivative
See Part 1D.

Plural form
See Part 1C.

Multiple definitions in single part of speech
See Part 3A.

ab·ne·gate (ǽbnigeit) *pres. part.* **ab·ne·gat·ing** *past* and *past part.* **ab·ne·gat·ed** *v.t.* to renounce, give up (a right etc.) [fr. L. *abnegare* (*abnegatus*), to deny]

ab·ne·ga·tion (æbnigéiʃən) *n.* renunciation, denial [fr. L. *abnegatio* (*abnegationis*)]

ab·nor·mal (æbnɔ́rməl) *adj.* different from the norm or average, unusual ‖ pertaining to that which is not normal, *abnormal psychology* **ab·nor·mal·i·ty** (æbnɔrmǽliti:) *pl.* **ab·nor·mal·i·ties** *n.* [fr. F. *anormal* and L. *abnormis*]

ABO a classification of blood groups (A, B, AB or O) with regard to their use in transfusion

a·board (əbɔ́rd, əbóurd) **1.** *adj.* and *adv.* on or into a ship, plane, train etc. **2.** *prep.* on board, *aboard the last ship*

a·bode (əbóud) *n.* (*old-fash., rhet.*) the place someone lives in (*old-fash., rhet.*) residence, *he took up his abode at the east gate of the city* [fr. ABIDE]

abode alt. *past* and *past part.* of ABIDE

ab·ohm (æbóum) *n.* the cgs electromagnetic unit of resistance equal to 10^{-9} ohm

a·bol·ish (əbɔ́liʃ) *v.t.* to do away with completely, put an end to (laws, customs, taxes, privileges etc.) [F. *abolir* (*aboliss-*)]

ab·o·li·tion (æbəliʃən) *n.* the act of abolishing ‖ (esp. *hist.*) the movement against slavery **ab·o·li·tion·ism, ab·o·li·tion·ist** *ns* [F. or fr. L. *abolitio* (*abolitionis*)] —The movement to abolish the international slave trade and the institution of chattel slavery was largely religious. It centered in Great Britain, the U.S.A. and western Europe, between c. 1783 and 1888. Following the pioneer work of Granville Sharp, the struggle was led by the Quakers, who had outlawed slavery in Pennsylvania as early as 1675. Under the leadership of William Wilberforce they obtained, almost single-handedly, the abolition of the slave trade in the British Empire and the U.S.A. by acts of Parliament and Congress in 1808. In England the struggle then became one for emancipation, while in the U.S.A. the act of Congress was blatantly defied. The U.S. movement, led chiefly by William Llyod Garrison, Theodore Dwight Weld, and Frederick Douglass, was obstructed by the U.S. Constitution's toleration of slavery and by the South's economic defense of it. Only after the Civil War could the 13th amendment outlawing slavery be enacted. In 1862 the U.S.A. adhered to an international agreement reached in 1842 affording the reciprocal right of search, which thereafter put an end to the slave trade

ab·o·ma·sum (æbəméisəm) *pl.* **ab·o·ma·sa** (æbəméisə) *n.* the fourth chamber of the stomach of a ruminant [Mod. L. fr. *ab*, from + *omasum*, bullock's tripe]

A-bomb (éibɒm) *n.* atomic bomb

a·bom·i·na·ble (əbɔ́minəb'l) *adj.* causing intense disgust, *an abominable crime* [F.]

abominable snowman a bearlike creature said to inhabit the high Himalayas

a·bom·i·na·bly (əbɔ́minəbli:) *adv.* in an abominable way

a·bom·i·nate (əbɔ́mineit) *pres. part.* **a·bom·i·nat·ing** *past* and *past part.* **a·bom·i·nat·ed** *v.t.* (*rhet.*) to detest [fr. L. *abominari* (*abominatus*)]

a·bom·i·na·tion (əbɒminéiʃən) *n.* disgust ‖ a loathsome act or thing [F.]

ab·o·rig·i·nal (æbəridʒinəl) **1.** *adj.* existing from the earliest times ‖ pertaining to aborigines **2.** *n.* an aborigine **ab·o·rig·i·nal·i·ty** (æbəridʒinǽliti:) *n.* [fr. L. *ab origine*, from the beginning]

ab·o·rig·i·ne (æbəridʒini:) *n.* a native inhabitant of a country, esp. before colonization. *an Australian aborigine* ‖ (*pl.*) the native plants and animals of a region [fr. L. *aborigines* pl. n., inhabitants from the beginning]

a·bort (əbɔ́rt) *v.i.* (*med.*) to give birth to a fetus before it is viable ‖ (*biol.*) to become arrested in development ‖ to come to nothing, *their plans aborted* ‖ (*space*, of a missile) to stop before completion of the scheduled flight ‖ *v.t.* (*space*) to bring (a missile flight) to an end before completion of schedule [fr. L. *aboriri* (*abortus*), to die, to abort]

a·bor·ti·fa·cient (əbɔrtiféiʃənt) **1.** *n.* something which produces an abortion **2.** *adj.* producing an abortion [fr. L. *aboriri* (*abortus*), to abort + *faciens* (*facientis*), causing]

a·bor·tion (əbɔ́rʃən) *n.* the spontaneous or induced expulsion from the womb of a nonviable human fetus ‖ a monstrous person or thing ‖ the failure of a project or attempt **a·bor·tion·ist** *n.* a

ab·ro·ga·tion (æbrəgéiʃən) *n.* the act of abrogating (e.g. a law) [fr. L. *abrogatio (abrogationis)*]

ab·rupt (əbrʌpt) *adj.* sudden, unexpected, *an abrupt halt* ‖ steep, precipitous ‖ rough, brusque in manner ‖ disconnected, *an abrupt style* [fr. L. *abrumpere (abruptus)*, to break away]

A·bruz·zi e Mo·li·se (abrú:ttsi:emɔ́li:ze) a region (area 5,954 sq. miles, pop. 1,221,900) in central Italy, formed of the provinces of Aquila, Campobasso, Chieti, Pescara and Teramo, lying in the highest and wildest part of the Apennines (Gran Sasso d'Italia, 9,560 ft), and bounded on the east by the Adriatic: olives, vines, almonds, sheep, hydroelectric power, oil

Ab·sa·lom (æbsələm) the third and best-loved son of David, king of Judah (11 Samuel xiii–xix)

ABSCAM (æbsxæm) an investigation conducted by the Federal Bureau of Investigation in 1978–80. Seven U.S. Congressmen and various state and local officials were convicted of bribery, conspiracy, and related charges after FBI agents impersonating an Arab sheikh and his associates had videotaped government officials accepting bribes. Critics accused the FBI of entrapment, but the courts ruled that the FBI acted within legal limits

ab·scess (æbses) *n.* a localized collection of pus occurring anywhere in the body **ab·scessed** *adj.* [fr. L. *abscessus*, a going away]

ab·scis·sa (æbsísə) *n.* (*math.*) the horizontal or x-coordinate in a plane coordinate system [L. = (part) cut off]

ab·scis·sion (æbsíʒən) *n.* a cutting off [fr. L. *abscissio (abscissionis)*]

ab·scond (æbskónd) *v.i.* to flee secretly, esp. to escape the law [fr. L. *abscondere*, to hide]

ab·sence (æbsəns) *n.* a being away ‖ a failure to be present ‖ lack, *absence of proof* [F.]

absence of mind inattention, mental abstraction

ab·sent (æbsənt) *adj.* away, not present ‖ abstracted, an *absent air* [F.]

ab·sent (æbsént) *v. refl.* to keep (oneself) away, *to absent oneself from a meeting* **ab·sen·tee** (æbsənti:) *n.* a person who is absent **ab·sen·tee·ism** *n.* persistent absence from work, usually without good reason [F. *absenter*]

absentee landlord a proprietor who does not live on his estate and care for his tenants but merely exploits his property

ab·sent·ly (æbsəntli:) *adv.* in an absent way, inattentively

ab·sent·mind·ed (æbsəntmáindid) *adj.* preoccupied and for that reason not paying attention to what one is doing

ab·sinthe, ab·sinth (æbsinθ) *n.* the plant wormwood ‖ a strongly alcoholic liqueur made from high-proof brandy, wormwood and other aromatics [F.]

ab·sis·sic acid (æbsísik) (*chem.*) [C₁₅H₂₀O₄] organic inhibitor of plant growth marketed as Dormin. *abbr* **ABA**

ab·so·lute (æbsəlu:t) **1.** *adj.* whole, complete ‖ pure, *absolute alcohol* ‖ having unrestricted power, *an absolute ruler* ‖ not conditioned by, or dependent upon, anything else ‖ (*gram.*) of a case not determined by any other word in the sentence (*ABLATIVE) ‖ (*philos.*) existing independently of any cause outside itself and of our sense perceptions **2.** *n.* something that is absolute **the Absolute** the self-existent, the First Cause, God [F. *absolut*]

absolute address location of stored information in a digital computer

absolute alcohol ethyl alcohol containing not less than 99% pure ethyl alcohol by weight

absolute altimeter radio or similar apparatus designed to indicate the true vertical height of an aircraft above the terrain

absolute code (*computer*) code for an absolute address

absolute dud (*mil.*) a nuclear weapon that fails to explode when launched at, or emplaced on, a target

absolute expansion the true expansion of a liquid irrespective of the expansion of the containing vessel

absolute film *ABSTRACT FILM

absolute humidity the humidity of the air measured by the number of grams of water vapor present in one cubic meter of the air

absolute music music which does not illustrate or depict (in contrast to program music)

absolute pitch the pitch of a note as determined by a simple frequency, not a combination

---

Guide words showing the alphabetical range of entries on the page

Pronunciation respelling
See Part 2.

Foreign pronunciation
See Part 2.

Etymology
See Part 5.

Field label
See Part 4A.

Stress-marked derivative
See Part 1D.

Unsyllabicated main entry
See Part 1A.

Spelling variants
See Part 1B.

Multiple definitions in several parts of speech
See Part 3A.

Cross-reference to related term
See Part 3C.

Defining cross-reference
See Part 3C.

PRONUNCIATION KEY USED IN THIS DICTIONARY

(Continued)

ʃ	*fish, action, fission*
t	*time, wet, letter*
θ	*thick, truth*
ð	*mother, though*
ʌ	*duck, tough, rudder*
ə:	*bird, learn*
u	*bull, cushion, book*
uə	*poor, sewer*
u:	*food, true*
ju:	*unite, confuse*
v	*verb, over, wave*
w	*well, waver*
x	*loch*
j	*youth, yellow*
z	*zoom, rose*

Foreign Sounds

y	*lune*
ɔ̃	*bon*
ɑ̃	*an*
ɛ̃	*vin*
œ̃	*brun*

Stress

The symbol ′ marks the primary stress in pronouncing the word. The syllable in which the primary stress symbol appears is pronounced with greater emphasis than other syllables.

The symbol ‚ marks the secondary stress of a word. The syllable under which this symbol appears is pronounced with less emphasis than the syllable with primary stress.

Editorial Abbreviations

Å	Angstrom unit	comp.	comparative	Gk	Greek
abbr.	abbreviation, abbreviated	conj.	conjunction	gm	gram
A.C.	alternating current	contr.	contraction	Gmc	Germanic
A.D.	anno domini	Copt.	Coptic	gram.	grammar
adj.	adjective	Corn.	Cornish	Heb.	Hebrew
adv.	adverb	Corp.	Corporation	Hind.	Hindustani
aeron.	aeronautics	corrup.	corruption	hist.	history
A.F.	Anglo-French	craniol.	craniology	H.M.	Her (His) Majesty('s)
Afrik.	Afrikaans	crystall.	crystallography	hort.	horticulture
agglom.	agglomeration	cu.	cubic	hr, hrs	hour, hours
agric.	agriculture	Czech.	Czechoslovakian	Hung.	Hungarian
alt.	alternative	d.	died	I.	Island
Am.	American	Dan.	Danish	Icel.	Icelandic
anat.	anatomy	Dec.	December	i.e.	id est, that is to say
Anglo-L.	Anglo-Latin	Dept.	Department	imit.	imitative
anthrop.	anthropology	dial.	dialectal	imper.	imperative
Antiq.	Antiquity	dim.	diminutive	impers.	impersonal
approx.	approximately	Du.	Dutch	in., ins	inch, inches
Apr.	April	dynam.	dynamics	incl.	including
Arab.	Arabic	E.	East	indef.	indefinite
Aram.	Aramaic	eccles.	ecclesiastical	infin.	infinitive
archaeol.	archaeology	econ.	economics	infl.	influenced
archit.	architecture	ed.	edition	interj.	interjection
A.S.S.R	Autonomous Soviet Socialist Republic	e.g.	exempli gratia, for example	internat.	international
astron.	astronomy	Egypt.	Egyptian	Ir.	Irish
at.	atomic	elec.	electricity	Is	Islands
attrib.	attributive, attributively	embry.	embryology	Ital.	Italian
Aug.	August	Eng.	English	Jan.	January
Austral.	Australian	engin.	engineering	Jap.	Japanese
b.	born	entom.	entomology	kc.	kilocycle, kilocycles
bacteriol.	bacteriology	Esk.	Eskimo	kg.	kilogram, kilograms
B.C.	Before Christ	esp.	especially	km.	kilometer, kilometers
Belg.	Belgian	etc.	et cetera	kv.	kilovolt, kilovolts
biochem.	biochemistry	ethnol.	ethnology	kw.	kilowatt, kilowatts
biol.	biology	etym.	etymology	L.	Latin
bot.	botany	Eur.	Europe, European	lb., lbs	pound, pounds
Br.	British	eV	electron volt, electron volts	L.G.	Low German
Braz.	Brazilian	excl.	excluding	L. Gk	Late Greek
Bulg.	Bulgarian	F.	French; Fahrenheit	lit.	literally
C.	Centigrade	fam.	family	L.L.	Late Latin
c.	century; circa	Feb.	February	m.	meter, meters
Canad.	Canadian	fem.	feminine	mach.	machinery
Capt.	Captain	ff.	and following	mag.	magnetism
Carib.	Caribbean	fig.	figuratively	Malay.	Malayalam
cc.	centuries	Fin.	Finnish	Mar.	March
c.c.	cubic centimeter	fl.	fluid	math.	mathematics
Celt.	Celtic	Flem.	Flemish	mc.	megacycle, megacycles
cf.	confer	fr.	from	M. Du.	Middle Dutch
c.g.s.	centimeter/gram/second	ft	foot, feet	M.E.	Middle English
chem.	chemistry	G.	German	mech.	mechanics
Chin.	Chinese	Gael.	Gaelic	med.	medicine
cm.	centimeter, centimeters	gen.	genitive	metall.	metallurgy
Co.	Company, County	Gen.	general	meteor.	meteorology
collect.	collective, collectively	geog.	geography	Mex.	Mexican
comb.	combined, combining	geol.	geology	M.F.	Middle French
		geom.	geometry	mil.	military

min., mins	minute, minutes	*part.*	participle	*Sept.*	September
mineral.	mineralogy	*pass.*	passive	*sing.*	singular
mistrans.	mistranslation	*perh.*	perhaps	*Skr.*	Sanskrit
M.L.	Medieval Latin	*Pers.*	Persian	*Span.*	Spanish
M.L.G.	Middle Low German	*Peruv.*	Peruvian	*specif.*	specifically
mm.	millimeter, millimeters	*petrog.*	petrography	*sp. gr.*	specific gravity
Mod.	Modern	*pharm.*	pharmacy	*sq.*	square
M.P.	Member of Parliament	*philos..*	philosophy	*S.S.R.*	Soviet Socialist Republic
m.p.h.	miles per hour	*phon.*	phonology	*st.*	stone, stones
Mt	Mount	*photog.*	photography	*St*	Saint
Mtns	Mountains	*phys.*	physics	*Sta*	Santa
mus.	music	*physiol.*	physiology	*superl.*	superlative
mythol.	mythology	*pl.*	plural	*surg.*	surgery
N.	North	*pop.*	popular; population	*survey.*	surveying
n.	noun	*Port.*	Portuguese	*S.W.*	southwest
naut.	nautical	*pred.*	predicate	*Swed.*	Sweden, Swedish
N.E.	northeast	*prep.*	preposition	*telecomm.*	telecommunications
neg.	negative	*pres.*	present	*theol.*	theology
N.F.	Northern French	*Pres.*	President	*trans.*	translation
no.	number	*prob.*	probably	*Turk.*	Turkish
Norw.	Norwegian	*pron.*	pronoun	*T.V.*	television
Nov.	November	*Prov.*	Provençal	*U.K.*	United Kingdom
N.W.	northwest	*psychoanal.*	psychoanalysis	*ult.*	ultimately
N.Y.	New York	*psychol.*	psychology	*univ.*	university
O. Arab.	Old Arabic	*R.*	river	*U.S.*	American
obs.	obsolete	*rail.*	railroad, railroads	*U.S.A.*	United States of America
Oct.	October	*redupl.*	reduplication	*U.S.S.R.*	Union of Soviet Socialist
O.E.	Old English	*refl.*	reflective		Republics
O.F.	Old French	*rel.*	related	*v.*	volt, volts
O.H.G.	Old High German	*rhet.*	rhetorical	*var.*	variant
O. Ir.	Old Irish	*Rom.*	Roman	*vet.*	veterinary
old-fash.	old-fashioned	*Rum.*	Rumanian	*v.i.*	verb intransitive
O.L.G.	Old Low German	*R.S.F.S.R.*	Russian Soviet Federal	*vol., vols*	volume, volumes (of a book)
O.N.	Old Norse		Socialist Republic	*v.t.*	verb transitive
O.N.F.	Old Northern French	*Russ.*	Russian	*W.*	West
O. Pers.	Old Persian	*S.*	South, *(Ital.)* Santo	*wd*	word
opp.	opposite of, opposed to	*Scand.*	Scandinavian	*wt*	weight
orig.	originally	*Scot.*	Scottish	*yd, yds*	yard, yards
O. Scand.	Old Scandinavian	*S.E.*	southeast	*zool.*	zoology
oz.	ounce, ounces	*sec., secs*	second, seconds		
p.a.	per annum	*Sem.*	Semitic		

Pronunciation Key

ə	adjust, bacillus, colony	l	life, lily, dull	əː	bird, learn
æ	cat, apple, laugh	'l	rabble, trouble	u	bull, cushion, book
ɑ	father, guitar, art	m	moon, lemon, dam	uə	poor, sewer
ɛə	bear, aerial	n	night, train, canal	uː	food, true
ei	snake, alien, parade	'n	redden	juː	unite, confuse
b	banana, rebel, ebb	ŋ	bring, wearing	v	verb, over, wave
tʃ	charm, fetch, ratchet	ɒ	lock, rotten	w	well, waver
d	dog, elder, feed	ɔ	fawn, court	x	loch
e	egg, exit, request	ou	vote, elope, low	j	youth, yellow
iː	even, relief, sneeze	au	cow, round	z	zoom, rose
iə	fear, career, earring	ɔi	void, royal		
f	fee, effort, rough	p	pack, slipper, wrap		
g	goat, hog, bigger	r	rise, errand, paper	**Foreign Sounds**	
h	house, behind	s	silly, whisper, juice		
i	fish, kitten, corrosive	ʃ	fish, action, fission	y	lune
ai	tiger, bright	t	time, wet, letter	ɔ̃	bon
dʒ	general, legend, dodge	θ	thick, truth	ɑ̃	an
ʒ	leisure, corsage	ð	mother, though	ɛ̃	vin
k	kill, luck, vacation	ʌ	duck, tough, rudder	œ̃	brun

Stress ′ over the sign (or first sign of a diphthong) indicates primary stress, under the sign indicates secondary stress.
Derived words in black type show primary stress only, the stress mark being incorporated in the word (though the word is never written in this way) where no change of vowel sound from that shown at the headword is involved.

	EARLY NORTH SEMITIC	PHOENICIAN	EARLY HEBREW (GEZER)	EARLY GREEK	CLASSICAL GREEK	ETRUSCAN Early	ETRUSCAN Classical	EARLY LATIN	CLASSICAL LATIN
A	K	∢	⟨	A	A	A	A	A	A

CURSIVE MAJUSCULE (ROMAN)	CURSIVE MINUSCULE (ROMAN)	ANGLO-IRISH MAJUSCULE	CAROLINE MINUSCULE	VENETIAN MINUSCULE (ITALIC)	N. ITALIAN MINUSCULE (ROMAN)
λ	u	a	a	a	a

A.C. SYLVESTER, CAMBRIDGE, ENGLAND

Development of the letter A, beginning with the early North Semitic letter. Evolution of both the majuscule, or capital, letter A and the minuscule, or lowercase, letter a are shown.

A, a (ei) the first letter in the English alphabet ‖ (*mus.*) a note, and the key of which it is the tonic ‖ a blood group, normally permitting transfusion to people of Group A or AB and from people of O or A

a (ə) historically *prep.* but confused with *indef. art,* (It remains in many words, 'aglow', 'ablaze' etc.) each, every, per, *three times a day* [O.E. *an,* on]

a (ə or, *with emphasis,* ei) *adj.* the singular indefinite article, one ‖ any, each one of a kind, *a man must eat* ‖ denoting an apparent plural, *many a man.* Before vowels and a silent h, 'an' replaces 'a', *an apple, an hour* [O.E. *an,* one]

a- (ə) *prefix* on ‖ in at [O.E. *a-, an, on*]

a- (ei) *prefix* not, without. It changes to 'an-' before vowels and usually before h [L. fr. Gk]

Aa·chen (ákən, áxən) (*F. Aix-la-Chapelle*) a city and spa (pop. 242,000) in N. Rhine-Westphalia, W. Germany, near the Dutch and Belgian frontiers. Manufactures: textiles, needles, machinery. It was the first important German city to be captured in the 2nd world war, falling (1944) to U.S. troops after bitter fighting

Aal·borg, Ål·borg (ólbɔr) an old city (pop. 154,218) on Limfjord, N. Jutland, Denmark, a port and communications center: cement, engineering, shipbuilding

Aalst (alst) (Alost) a town (pop. 44,000) in Belgium, northwest of Brussels: textiles, brewing

Aal·to (áltou), Alvar (1898–1976), Finnish architect. In stressing an organic approach rather than strict adherence to the international style, he produced works beautifully related to environment and human needs. He is also well known for his designs for laminated-wood furniture. He taught (1940–7) at Massachusetts Institute of Technology, where he designed (1947) Baker House. After World War II he supervised urban planning in Finland and designed Helsinki's cultural center (1967–75)

Aar (ar) a river (175 miles) of Switzerland, flowing from glaciers in the Bernese Oberland to the Rhine near Waldshut. It is navigable as far as Lake Thun and provides hydroelectric power

Aar·au (árau) an industrial town (pop. 14,000) in Aargau, Switzerland, on the Aare: engineering, textiles, foundries

aard·vark (árdvark) *n. Orycteropus afer,* an African anteater. It has a strong heavy body, is about 5 ft long, is nocturnal in habit and lives on ants and termites [Du. = earth hog]

aard·wolf (árdwʊlf) *pl.* **aard·wolves** (árdwʊlvz) *n. Proteles cristata,* a carnivorous, burrowing animal of S. Africa, allied to the hyena. It feeds on carrion, small mammals, insects etc. and is nocturnal in habit [Du. = earth wolf]

Aa·re (árə) the Aar River

Aar·gau (árgau) a German-speaking canton (pop. 453,442) in N. Switzerland, relatively flat and heavily industrialized. Capital: Aarau (pop. 14,000)

Aar·hus, År·hus (órhu:s) ancient port (pop. 245,565) in E. Jutland, Denmark's second largest town. University (1928), St. Clements Cathedral (12th c.), town hall (1942)

Aar·on (éərən, ǽrən) Jewish patriarch, who with his brother Moses led Israel out of Egypt and became the first Jewish high priest (Exodus iv ff.)

AAUP American Association of University Professors

AB a blood group, normally permitting transfusion to people of the same AB group and from people of groups O, A, B or AB

A.B. Bachelor of Arts ‖ ablebodied seaman

ab- *prefix* from ‖ away, outside of [O. F. fr. L.]

a·ba·ca (æbəká, æbəkə) *n.* Manila hemp [Span. *abacá*]

a·back (əbǽk) *adv.* (*naut.*) with sails pressed back against the mast by head winds **taken aback** disagreeably astonished

ab·a·cus (ǽbəkəs) *pl.* **ab·a·ci** (ǽbəsai), **ab·a·cus·es** *n.* a calculating instrument consisting of a frame with beads on rods or wires ‖ (*archit.*) the uppermost component of a capital [L. fr. Gk *abax (abakos)*, tablet]

A·ba·dan (æbədán) a town and island (pop. 296,081) in the delta of the Shatt-el-Arab, the principal port of Iran, and a vast oil-refining center

a·baft (əbǽft, əbáft) *adv.* and *prep.* (*naut.*) in or towards the stern of a ship [A (*hist. prep.*) + O.E. *beæftan,* behind]

ab·a·lo·ne (æbəlóuni:) *n.* a haliotis [Span.]

ab·am·pere (æbǽmpiər) *n.* the cgs electromagnetic unit of electric current equal to 10 amperes. The abampere is the basic unit of the cgs electromagnetic system and is defined in terms of the force acting between two parallel conductors when each is carrying a current (*CURRENT BALANCE)

a·ban·don (əbǽndən) *n.* lighthearted yielding to impulse, letting go of restraint [F.]

abandon *v.t.* to give up, *to abandon an attempt* ‖ to forsake ‖ to yield (oneself), *to abandon oneself to the waves* **a·ban·doned** *adj.* forsaken, *an abandoned wife* ‖ dissolute, *an abandoned woman* [O.F. *abandoner,* to put under someone's control]

a·ban·don·ment (əbǽndənmənt) *n.* the act of abandoning ‖ (*law*) the giving up of an interest, particularly of an insurance claim, author's copyright or inventor's patent ‖ lack of restraint [O. F. *abandonnement*]

a·base (əbéis) *pres. part.* **a·bas·ing** *past* and *past part.* **a·based** *v.t.* to degrade, to humiliate **a·based** *adj.* humiliated ‖ (*heraldry,* of a charge) lowered (cf. ENHANCED) **a·báse·ment** *n.* [fr. O.F. *abaissier,* to lower]

a·bash (əbǽʃ) *v.t.* to cause a slight feeling of embarrassment to, disconcert (used mostly in the passive) **a·básh·ment** *n.* [fr. O.F. *esbair,* to astonish]

a·bate (əbéit) *pres. part.* **a·bat·ing** *past* and *past part.* **a·bat·ed** *v.t.* to reduce, do away with, *so abate the anger of the mob* ‖ *v.i.* to grow less, *the storm abated* **a·báte·ment** *n.* [fr. O.F. *abatre,* to beat down]

ab·at·toir (ǽbətwar) *n.* a slaughterhouse [F.]

ab·ba·cy (ǽbəsi:) *pl.* **ab·ba·cies** *n.* the office or jurisdiction of an abbot ‖ his period of office [earlier Eng. *abbatie* fr. L. L. *abbatia*]

Ab·bas (ǽbəs) (566–652) the uncle of Mohammed and ancestor of the Abbasid dynasty

Abbas I 'the Great' (c. 1557–1629), shah of Persia (1587–1629). He crushed the Uzbek rebels (1597), advanced into Afghanistan, and defeated the Turks (1605). Under his rule, Persian territory extended from the Tigris to the Indus

Abbas II (Hilmi Pasha, 1874–1944), khedive of Egypt (1892–1914), son of Tewfik Pasha. He was deposed (1914) by Britain under suspicion of plotting with Turkey against British rule

Ab·bas Ef·fen·di (æbəseféndi:) *ABDUL BAHA

Ab·bas·id (ǽbəsid, əbǽsid) a member of the dynasty which ruled Islam (750–1258) from Baghdad, reaching its height in the reigns of Harun al-Rashid (786–809) and his son Mamun (Caliph 813–33)

Ab·ba·te (æbátei), Niccolò dell' (c. 1512–71), Italian painter known esp. for his frescoes at Fontainebleau

ab·bé (æbei) *n.* a title of respect given in France to secular clergy [F.]

ab·bess (ǽbis) *n.* the woman superior of a nunnery or convent [O.F. *abaësse*]

Abbe·vill·ian (æbvíljən) *adj.* of the earliest Paleolithic period, characterized by the use of bifacial stone axes [after *Abbeville* in N. France]

ab·bey (ǽbi:) *n.* a monastery under an abbot or convent under an abbess ‖ a church that is, or was once, part of such a monastery or convent [O.F. *abaïe*]

ab·bot (ǽbət) *n.* the superior of the community of an abbey **áb·bot·cy, áb·bot·ship** *ns* [O.E. *abbad, abbod* fr. L. fr. Gk fr. Syriac]

Abbott (ǽbət), Berenice (1898–), U.S. photographer. She began as an assistant to surrealist Man Ray and later won acclaim for her documentary photographs of New York City. Her books include 'Changing New York' (1939) and 'Greenwich Village Today and Yesterday' (1949)

ab·bre·vi·ate (əbri:vi:eit) *pres. part.* **ab·bre·vi·at·ing** *past* and *past part.* **ab·bre·vi·at·ed** *v.t.* to shorten (usually, a word) ‖ to reduce in extent (e.g. a story, a film etc.) [fr. L. *abbreviare (abbreviatus)*]

abbreviated dialing telephone service with fewer-than-normal digits, e.g., 911 for calling police

ab·bre·vi·a·tion (əbri̩:vi:éiʃən) *n.* the act or result of abbreviating a word [F. *abréviation*]

ABC (éibi:si:) **1.** *n.* the alphabet ‖ the first principles of a subject ‖ (*abbr.*) for advance booking charter, round-trip airfare that must be booked 30–45 days in advance **2.** *adj.* (*mil. abbr.*) for atomic, biological, and chemical

ABC Coding System computer programming language, used at the Atomic Research Establishment, England

ab·cou·lomb (æbkú:lɒm) *n.* the unit of charge in the cgs electromagnetic system of units equal to the quantity of charge that passes in 1 second through any crosssection of a conductor carrying a steady current of 1 abampere

ABC powers Argentina, Brazil and Chile, the three leading nations of southern South America. The association began informally in 1905 through a friendly exchange of official visits. Its greatest achievement was its successful mediation of a dispute between the U.S. and Mexico in 1914. It also took the lead in expressing the sensitivity of Latin American nations to U.S. intervention in their affairs. The association as such disintegrated in 1936

Abd el-Ka·der (əbdelkádiər) (c. 1807–83), Arab leader who led the resistance to the French conquest of Algeria until his defeat (1847)

Abd el Krim (əbdelkrí:m) (1882–1963), Moroccan chief who led a revolt (1920–6) against Spain and France. Prisoner of the French (1926–47), he escaped to Egypt to lead the movement for N. African independence

ab·di·cate (æbdikeit) *pres. part.* **ab·di·cat·ing** *past* and *past part.* **ab·di·cat·ed** *v.t.* to give up (a throne, position or responsibility) ‖ *v.i.* to resign from power [fr. L. *abdicare (abdicatus)*, to disown]

ab·di·ca·tion (æbdikéiʃən) *n.* the renouncing of power or high office, esp. of kingship [fr. L. *abdicatio (abdicationis)*]

ab·do·men (æbdəmən, æbdóumən) *n.* that part of the human body below the diaphragm containing the major organs of digestion and reproduction as well as the spleen, kidneys, adrenal and lymph glands. The whole cavity is lined inside by the peritoneum ‖ (*zool.*) the hind part of insects, spiders etc. **ab·dom·i·nal** (æbdómin'l) *adj.* [L.]

ab·du·cent (æbdú:sənt, æbdjú:sənt) *adj.* (*med.*) e.g. of the nerve responsible for moving the eyeball outwards) drawing away (opp. ADDUCENT) [fr. L. *abducens (abducentis)* fr. *abducere*, to lead away]

ab·duct (æbdʌkt) *v.t.* to kidnap, take away (esp. a woman or child) by force ‖ (*med.*) to draw (a part of the body) away from the midline [fr. L. *abducere (abductus)*, to lead away]

ab·duc·tion (æbdʌkʃən) *n.* the act of kidnapping, of forcibly taking away ‖ (*med.*) movement of a part of the body away from the midline [fr. L. *abductio (abductionis)*, a carrying away]

ab·duc·tor (æbdʌktər) *n.* a person who kidnaps or takes away forcibly ‖ (*med.*) a muscle that moves a limb or other part of the body away from the midline [Mod. L. fr. *abducere*, to lead away]

Abd·ul Ba·ha (əbdulbahá) (1844–1921) the title of Abbas Effendi, Persian religious leader, son of Baha'ullah and his successor as head of the Bahai faith. He advocated spiritual unity and disarmament as steps to universal peace

Abd·ul Ha·mid II (əbdulhamí:d) (1842–1918), sultan of Turkey (1876–1909) till deposed by the Young Turks. A reactionary despot, he was noted for his unscrupulous and brutal policies (e.g. Armenian massacres, 1894–6). He started a pro-German foreign policy which lasted until 1918

Abdul-Jabbar, Kareem (əbdúldʒʌbár, xʌríəm) (1947–), U.S. basketball player. Born Ferdinand Lewis Alcindor, Abdul-Jabbar led his University of California, Los Angeles team to 3 NCAA titles (1967–9), before joining the Milwaukee Bucks and then the Los Angeles Lakers of the NBA. He held the career record for points scored

Abdullah et Taaisha (əbdúlættaɪ:ʃa) *KHALIFA

Abd·ul·lah ibn Hus·sein (əbdulaib'nhu:sén) (1882–1951), king of the Hashimite Kingdom of Jordan (1946–51) and emir (1921–46) when Transjordan was a British mandate. He attacked Israel (1948) and annexed Arab Palestine to Jordan (1950). He was assassinated in Jerusalem

Abd·ul Rah·man (əbdulrámən), Tunku (1903–), Malaysian statesman, first prime minister of the Federation of Malaysia (1963–70), which he helped to establish. He was the first prime minister of the Federation of Malaya (1957–63), and was influential in negotiations with Great Britain for independence in Aug. 1957

Abd·ur Rah·man (əbduərrámən) (d. 732), Arab governor of Andalusia whose defeat by Charles Martel at Poitiers (732) stopped the Moslem invasion of Europe

Abdur Rahman (1844–1901), emir of Afghanistan. Subsidized by Britain, he centralized the administration and began to create modern Afghan institutions

a·beam (əbi:m) *adv.* (*naut.*) at right angles to the length of a ship

A·bel (éibəl) the second son of Adam and Eve, murdered by his brother, Cain (Genesis iv). Cain was jealous at seeing Abel preferred by God

A·bel (ábəl), Niels Henrik (1802–29), Norwegian mathematician who created the theory of elliptic functions

Ab·e·lard (æbəlɑrd), Peter (1079–1142), French scholastic philosopher and theologian who championed the conceptualist against the universalist position in medieval thought, and was opposed by Bernard of Clairvaux. His most notable follower was Peter Lombard. His works include 'Historia calamitatum'(c. 1136) and'Sic et non' (1121). His love for Heloise (c. 1101–64), niece of a canon of Notre Dame, was perpetuated in their famous correspondence. Some Latin hymns by him survive

Ab·e·o·ku·ta (æbi:oukú:tə) a trading center (pop. 187,000) in Nigeria, 61 miles north of Lagos: palm products, cotton, cocoa

A·ber·dare Mtns (æbərdɛər) a mountain range (up to 13,000 ft) north of Nairobi, the chief region of European settlement in Kenya

Aber·deen (æbərdi:n) formerly a county in N.E. Scotland; its county town (pop. 190,200), a fishing port and from the mid 1970s the supply center for the North Sea petroleum industry. Cathedral (1378). University (1494)

Ab·er·deen (æbərdi:n) *n.* a Scotch terrier of a small, wirehaired breed [after *Aberdeen*, Scotland]

a·ber·rance (əbérəns) *n.* a deviating ‖ an instance of this **a·ber·ran·cy** *n.* the quality of being aberrant

a·ber·rant (əbérənt) *adj.* straying from normal standards ‖ (*biol.*) deviating from the normal type [fr. L. *aberrans (aberrantis)* fr. *aberrare*, to wander away]

ab·er·ra·tion (æbəréiʃən) *n.* a deviation from right or normal standards ‖ (*astron.*) the angular difference between the true and apparent position of an observed heavenly body due to the movement of the observer while light from the body travels to him ‖ (*optics*) the failure of reflected or refracted light to give a point image of a point source, due either to the geometry of spherical surfaces of mirrors or lenses (*SPHERICAL ABERRATION, *COMA, *ASTIGMATISM, *DISTORTION) or to the different speeds at which different wavelengths travel through glass etc. (*CHROMATIC ABERRATION) [fr. L. *aberratio (aberrationis)*]

Ab·er·yst·wyth (æbərístwiθ) a port and resort (pop. 8,666) of Cardiganshire, Wales. University College of Wales (1872), part of the University of Wales

a·bet (əbét) *pres. part.* **a·bet·ting** *past* and *past part.* **a·bet·ted** *v.t.* to encourage, support (someone) in wrongdoing **a·bét·ment, a·bét·ter** (*law*), **a·bét·tor** *ns* [O.F. *abeter*, to bait]

a·bey·ance (əbéiəns) *n.* temporary suspension, usually of a custom, rule or law [A.F. *abeiance*]

ab·far·ad (æbfǽræd) *n.* the cgs electromagnetic unit of capacitance equal to 10^9 farads

ab·hen·ry (æbhénri:) *pl.* **ab·hen·ries** *n.* the cgs electromagnetic unit of inductance equal to 10^{-9} henry

ab·hor (æbhɔ́r) *pres. part.* **ab·hor·ring** *past* and *past part.* **ab·horred** *v.t.* to detest, regard with horror or disgust [fr. L. *abhorrere*, to shrink in horror]

ab·hor·rence (æbhɔ́rəns, æbhɔ́rəns) *n.* detestation, horror, disgust [ABHORRENT]

ab·hor·rent (æbhɔ́rənt, æbhɔ́rənt) *adj.* arousing detestation, horror or disgust [fr. L. *abhorrens (abhorrentis)*]

a·bid·ance (əbáid'ns) *n.* (with 'by') compliance, *strict abidance by the rules*

a·bide (əbáid) *pres. part.* **a·bid·ing** *past* and *past part.* **a·bode** (əbóud), **a·bid·ed** *v.t.* to bear patiently, tolerate (used negatively and interrogatively), *she can't abide him* ‖ *v.i.* to continue in being; remain **to abide by** to accept (rules or a ruling) to stick to (one's decision) **a·bíd·ing** *adj.* constant, enduring [O.E. *abidan*, to remain]

Ab·i·djan (æbidʒán) largest city and former capital, a port and commercial center (pop. 2,000,000) of Ivory Coast, W. Africa: oil refinery. University (1964). Cathedral

a·bil·i·ty (əbíliti:) *pl.* **a·bil·i·ties** *n.* skill or power in sufficient quantity, the *ability to see a job through* ‖ (often *pl.*) cleverness, talent [O.F. *abieté*, skill]

a·bi·o·gen·e·sis (eibaioudʒénisis) *n.* the process, once thought possible, by which life could proceed from nonliving matter (*cf.* BIOGENESIS)

a·bi·ot·ic (eibaiótik) *adj.* of an inorganic resource, e.g., water, sand, gravel

ab·ject (æbdʒekt) *adj.* despicable, *an abject liar* ‖ very humble, *abject apologies* ‖ without any moral resource, *abject despair* ‖ servile, *abject submission* ‖ wretched, *abject poverty* [fr. L. *abjicere (abjectus)*, to throw away]

ab·jec·tion (æbdʒékʃən) *n.* the state of being abject [F.]

ab·ju·ra·tion (æbdʒuréiʃən) *n.* a formal renunciation, esp. of an allegiance or claim [fr. L. *abjuratio (abjurationis)*]

ab·jure (æbdʒúər) *pres. part.* **ab·jur·ing** *past* and *past part.* **ab·jured** *v.t.* to renounce, give up solemnly, repudiate [F. *abjurer*]

Ab·kha·zian A.S.S.R. (æbkéiʒən) an autonomous republic (area 3,358 sq. miles, pop. 400,000) in Georgia, U.S.S.R. Capital: Sukhumi

ab·late (æbléit) *pres. part.* **ab·lat·ing** *past* and *past part.* **ab·lat·ed** *v.t.* (*space*) to remove by ablation ‖ *v.i.* (*space*) to undergo ablation [fr. L. *auferre (ablatus)*, to take away]

ab·la·tion (æbléiʃən) *n.* the removal of part of the body by surgery ‖ (*geol.*) the carrying away of material or ice from the surface of rocks or glaciers ‖ (*space*) the burning away of parts of a nose cone by the heat generated when a missile reenters the earth's atmosphere [fr. L. *ablatio (ablationis)*, a carrying away]

ablation shield *n.* a laminated glass shield

ab·la·tive (æblətiv) **1.** *n.* (in Latin, Sanskrit, Finnish and Hungarian grammar), the case indicating direction from a place, time, agent, instrument or source of an action **2.** *adj.* of or in such a case [F. *ablatif*]

ablative absolute (in Latin grammar) a grammatically independent construction in the ablative case of noun and participle expressing cause, time or circumstance

ab·laut (æblaut) *n.* patterned gradation of the root vowels in related bases of verbs due to a shift of stress in the IndoEuropean parent language [G.]

a·blaze (əbléiz) *pred. adj.* and *adv.* on fire, *the ship was ablaze, to set ablaze* ‖ (fig.) lit up, *ablaze with lights, ablaze with excitement*

a·ble (éib'l) *adj.* clever, competent, skilled ‖ having the means or opportunity to do something, *able to be present* [O. F. *hable*, apt]

a·ble-bod·ied (éib'lbódi:d) *adj.* robust and in good health

able-bodied seaman a trained sailor ‖ (*Br.*, *abbr.* A.B.) a sailor in the Royal Navy of the middle grade (between ordinary seaman and leading seaman)

a·bloom (əblú:m) *pred. adj.* (*rhet.*) in bloom, blooming

ab·lu·tion (əblú:ʃən) *n.* washing for ritual purification, generally with water ‖ (*pl.*) the washing of hands and face **ab·lu·tion·ar·y** *adj.* [fr. L. *ablutio (ablutionis)*]

a·bly (éibli:) *adv.* in an able, competent way

ABM antiballistic missile

Abnaki (æbnáki:), a confederacy of Algonquian-speaking Indian tribes living along the Maine river valleys. Allies of the French from 1607, they were forced to move north or west during the 1670's or make peace with the English

ab·ne·gate (æbnigeit) *pres. part.* **ab·ne·gat·ing** *past* and *past part.* **ab·ne·gat·ed** *v.t.* to renounce, give up (a right etc.) [fr. L. *abnegare* (*abnegatus*), to deny]

ab·ne·ga·tion (æbnigéiʃən) *n.* renunciation, denial [fr. L. *abnegatio* (*abnegationis*)]

ab·nor·mal (æbnɔrməl) *adj.* different from the norm or average, unusual ‖ pertaining to that which is not normal, *abnormal psychology* **ab·nor·mal·i·ty** (æbnɔrmǽliti) *pl.* **ab·nor·mal·i·ties** *n.* [fr. F. *anormal* and L. *abnormis*]

ABO a classification of blood groups (A, B, AB or O) with regard to their use in transfusion

a·board (əbɔ́rd, əbóurd) **1.** *adj.* and *adv.* on or into a ship, plane, train etc. **2.** *prep.* on board, *aboard the last ship*

a·bode (əbóud) *n.* (*old-fash., rhet.*) the place someone lives in ‖ (*old-fash., rhet.*) residence, *he took up his abode at the east gate of the city* [fr. ABIDE]

abode alt. *past* and *past part.* of ABIDE

ab·ohm (æbóum) *n.* the cgs electromagnetic unit of resistance equal to 10^{-9} ohm

a·bol·ish (əbɒliʃ) *v.t.* to do away with completely, put an end to (laws, customs, taxes, privileges etc.) [F. *abolir* (*aboliss-*)]

ab·o·li·tion (æbəliʃən) *n.* the act of abolishing ‖ (esp. *hist.*) the movement against slavery **ab·o·li·tion·ism, ab·o·li·tion·ist** *ns* [F. or fr. L. *abolitio* (*abolitionis*)] —The movement to abolish the international slave trade and the institution of chattel slavery was largely religious. It centered in Great Britain, the U.S.A. and western Europe, between c. 1783 and 1888. Following the pioneer work of Granville Sharp, the struggle was led by the Quakers, who had outlawed slavery in Pennsylvania as early as 1675. Under the leadership of William Wilberforce they obtained, almost singlehandedly, the abolition of the slave trade in the British Empire and the U.S.A. by acts of Parliament and Congress in 1808. In England the struggle then became one for emancipation, while in the U.S.A. the act of Congress was blatantly defied. The U.S. movement, led chiefly by William Llyod Garrison, Theodore Dwight Weld, and Frederick Douglass, was obstructed by the U.S. Constitution's toleration of slavery and by the South's economic defense of it. Only after the Civil War could the 13th amendment outlawing slavery be enacted. In 1862 the U.S.A. adhered to an international agreement reached in 1842 affording the reciprocal right of search, which thereafter put an end to the slave trade

ab·o·ma·sum (æbəméisəm) *pl.* **ab·o·ma·sa** (æbəméisə) *n.* the fourth chamber of the stomach of a ruminant [Mod. L. fr. *ab*, from+*omasum*, bullock's tripe]

A-bomb (éibɒm) *n.* atomic bomb

a·bom·i·na·ble (əbɒminəb'l) *adj.* causing intense disgust, *an abominable crime* [F.]

abominable snowman a bearlike creature said to inhabit the high Himalayas

a·bom·i·na·bly (əbɒminəbli:) *adv.* in an abominable way

a·bom·i·nate (əbɒmineit) *pres. part.* **a·bom·i·nat·ing** *past* and *past part.* **a·bom·i·nat·ed** *v.t.* (*rhet.*) to detest [fr. L. *abominari* (*abominatus*)]

a·bom·i·na·tion (əbɒminéiʃən) *n.* disgust ‖ a loathsome act or thing [F.]

ab·o·rig·i·nal (æbəridʒinəl) **1.** *adj.* existing from the earliest times ‖ pertaining to aborigines **2.** *n.* an aborigine **ab·o·rig·i·nal·i·ty** (æbəridʒinǽliti:) *n.* [fr. L. *ab origine*, from the beginning]

ab·o·rig·i·ne (æbəridʒini:) *n.* a native inhabitant of a country, esp. before colonization. *an Australian aborigine* ‖ (*pl.*) the native plants and animals of a region [fr. L. *aborigines* pl. n., inhabitants from the beginning]

a·bort (əbɔ́rt) *v.i.* (*med.*) to give birth to a fetus before it is viable ‖ (*biol.*) to become arrested in development ‖ to come to nothing, *their plans aborted* ‖ (*space*, of a missile) to stop before completion of the scheduled flight ‖ *v.t.* (*space*) to bring (a missile flight) to an end before completion of schedule [fr. L. *aboriri* (*abortus*), to die, to abort]

a·bor·ti·fa·cient (əbɔrtiféiʃənt) **1.** *n.* something which produces an abortion **2.** *adj.* producing an abortion [fr. L. *aboriri* (*abortus*), to abort+*faciens* (*facientis*), causing]

a·bor·tion (əbɔ́rʃən) *n.* the spontaneous or induced expulsion from the womb of a nonviable human fetus ‖ a monstrous person or thing ‖ the failure of a project or attempt **a·bor·tion·ist** *n.* a

doctor or other person who induces abortions [fr. L. *abortio* (*abortionis*)]

a·bor·tive (əbɔ́rtiv) *adj.* of premature birth ‖ ending in failure [fr. L. *abortivus*]

A·bou·kir Bay, Battle of (ɑbu:kíər) the Battle of the Nile

a·bound (əbáund) *v.i.* to be abundant, *fish abound in that river* ‖ (with 'in' or 'with') to teem, *a river abounding in fish* [O.F. *abunder, abonder*]

a·bout (əbáut) **1.** *adv.* all around, *there's a lot of flu about* ‖ here and there, *papers lying about* ‖ in action again, *to be up and about after an illness* ‖ in the opposite direction, (*mil.*) *about face!, (Br. mil.) about turn!* **about to** (do something) on the point of (doing something) **to come about** to happen **turn and turn about** (esp. *Br.*) alternately, in turn **2.** *prep.* concerning, in connection with, *he worries about his health* ‖ approximately ‖ in the area of, *somewhere about the house* ‖ everywhere in, *the toys were strewn about the garden* [fr. O.E. *onbūtan*, around]

a·bout-face (əbáutféis) **1.** *n.* a military command to face in the opposite direction, or the execution of it ‖ a sharp reversal of policy, opinion etc. **2.** *v.i.* to execute an about-face ‖ *v.t.* to cause to do this

a·bout-ship (əbáutʃip) *v.i.* to place a ship on the opposite tack [obs. v. *about* +SHIP]

a·bove (əbʌ́v) **1.** *adj.* preceding, just mentioned, *the above evidence is conclusive* **2.** *adv.* higher up, overhead, *on the floor above* ‖ earlier (in a book), *see . p. 71 above* **3.** *prep.* higher than, *the chorus was seated above the orchestra* ‖ beyond, *the water is smoother above the dam, above criticism* ‖ more than (in number or quantity), *men above 18 years of age* **above all** more than anything else **over and above** in addition to, *five men over and above the usual crew* [O.E. *abufan, onbufan*, overhead, above]

a·bove-board (əbʌ́vbɔrd, əbʌ́vbourd) *pred. adj.* without deception or trickery

a·bove-ground (əbʌ́vgráund) *adj.* on or above the ground ‖ (*old-fash.*) alive, esp. somewhat surprisingly

ab·ra·ca·dab·ra (æbrəkədǽbrə) *n.* a word used in spells and incantations gibberish [L.]

a·brade (əbréid) *pres. part.* **a·brad·ing** *past* and *past part.* **a·brad·ed** *v.t.* to roughen or wear away the surface of by rubbing or scraping [fr. L. *abradere*]

A·bra·ham (éibrəhæm) (early 2nd millennium B.C.), Hebrew patriarch, the founder of Judaism. He was the progenitor of the Jews, and, through Ishmael, of the Arabs. A native of Ur, he journeyed to Canaan, which God promised to his descendants (Genesis xi–xxv). As a sign of this covenant with God, he instituted the rite of circumcision among the Jews

Abraham, Heights of a plateau near Quebec, the scene of the decisive battle (1759) in the French and Indian War. The British under Wolfe defeated the French under Montcalm

A·brams (éibræmz), Creighton Williams, Jr (1914–74), U.S. general, commander of the U.S. forces in Vietnam (1968–72), army chief of staff (1972–4)

a·bra·sion (əbréiʒən) *n.* the action of wearing by friction, esp. of grazing the skin ‖ the result of rubbing [fr. L. *abrasio* (*abrasionis*)]

a·bra·sive (əbréisiv, əbréiziv) **1.** *adj.* tending to scrape or wear down by friction **2.** *n.* a substance which does this [fr. L. *abradere* (*abrasus*), to wear away]

ab·re·ac·tion (æbri:ǽkʃən) *n.* (*psychoanal.*) the emotional release experienced by a patient when, in the presence of a therapist, he puts into words an idea that he has been repressing [trans. of G. *abreagierung*]

a·breast (əbrést) *adv.* side by side and facing in the same direction **to keep abreast of** to keep oneself informed about

a·bridge (əbrídʒ) *pres. part.* **a·bridg·ing** *past* and *past part.* **a·bridged** *v.t.* to shorten, to abridge a book ‖ to curtail, *an abridged visit* [O.F. *abregier*]

a·bridg·ment, a·bridge·ment (əbridʒmənt) *n.* the act of shortening or curtailing ‖ a shortened version, *an abridgment of Toynbee's book* [O.F. *abregement*]

a·broad (əbrɔ́d) *adv.* in a foreign land ‖ (*rhet.*) in public circulation, *rumors of troop movements are abroad*

ab·ro·gate (æbrəgeit) *pres. part.* **ab·ro·gat·ing** *past* and *past part.* **ab·ro·gat·ed** *v.t.* to cancel, repeal, annul, *to abrogate a law* [fr. L. *abrogare* (*abrogatus*), to repeal]

ab·ro·ga·tion (æbrəgéiʃən) *n.* the act of abrogating (e.g. a law) [fr. L. *abrogatio* (*abrogationis*)]

ab·rupt (əbrʌ́pt) *adj.* sudden, unexpected, *an abrupt halt* ‖ steep, precipitous ‖ rough, brusque in manner ‖ disconnected, *an abrupt style* [fr. L. *abrumpere* (*abruptus*), to break away]

A·bruz·zi e Mo·li·se (əbru:ttsi:emóli:ze) a region (area 5,954 sq. miles, pop. 1,221,900) in central Italy, formed of the provinces of Aquila, Campobasso, Chieti, Pescara and Teramo, lying in the highest and wildest part of the Apennines (Gran Sasso d'Italia, 9,560 ft), and bounded on the east by the Adriatic: olives, vines, almonds, sheep, hydroelectric power, oil

Ab·sa·lom (æbsələm) the third and best-loved son of David, king of Judah (11 Samuel xiii–xix)

ABSCAM (æbsxǽm) an investigation conducted by the Federal Bureau of Investigation in 1978–80. Seven U.S. Congressmen and various state and local officials were convicted of bribery, conspiracy, and related charges after FBI agents impersonating an Arab sheikh and his associates had videotaped government officials accepting bribes. Critics accused the FBI of entrapment, but the courts ruled that the FBI acted within legal limits

ab·scess (æbses) *n.* a localized collection of pus occurring anywhere in the body **áb·scessed** *adj.* [fr. L. *abscessus*, a going away]

ab·scis·sa (æbsísə) *n.* (*math.*) the horizontal or x-coordinate in a plane coordinate system [L. = (part) cut off]

ab·scis·sion (æbsíʒən) *n.* a cutting off [fr. L. *abscissio* (*abscissionis*)]

ab·scond (æbskɒ́nd) *v.i.* to flee secretly, esp. to escape the law [fr. L. *abscondere*, to hide]

ab·sence (æbsəns) *n.* a being away ‖ a failure to be present ‖ lack, *absence of proof* [F.]

absence of mind inattention, mental abstraction

ab·sent (æbsənt) *adj.* away, not present ‖ abstracted, *an absent air* [F.]

ab·sent (æbsént) *v. refl.* to keep (oneself) away, *to absent oneself from a meeting* **ab·sen·tee** (æbsənti:) *n.* a person who is absent **ab·sen·tee·ism** *n.* persistent absence from work, usually without good reason [F. *absenter*]

absentee landlord a proprietor who does not live on his estate and care for his tenants but merely exploits his property

ab·sent·ly (æbsəntli:) *adv.* in an absent way, inattentively

ab·sent-mind·ed (æbsəntmáindid) *adj.* preoccupied and for that reason not paying attention to what one is doing

ab·sinthe, ab·sinth (æbsinθ) *n.* the plant wormwood ‖ a strongly alcoholic liqueur made from high-proof brandy, wormwood and other aromatics [F.]

ab·sis·sic acid (æbsísik) (*chem.*) $[C_{15}H_{20}O_4]$ organic inhibitor of plant growth marketed as Dormin. *abbr* ABA

ab·so·lute (æbsəlu:t) **1.** *adj.* whole, complete ‖ pure, *absolute alcohol* ‖ having unrestricted power, *an absolute ruler* ‖ not conditioned by, or dependent upon, anything else ‖ (*gram.*) of a case not determined by any other word in the sentence (*ABLATIVE) ‖ (*philos.*) existing independently of any cause outside itself and of our sense perceptions **2.** *n.* something that is absolute **the Absolute** the self-existent, the First Cause, God [F. *absolut*]

absolute address location of stored information in a digital computer

absolute alcohol ethyl alcohol containing not less than 99% pure ethyl alcohol by weight

absolute altimeter radio or similar apparatus designed to indicate the true vertical height of an aircraft above the terrain

absolute code (*computer*) code for an absolute address

absolute dud (*mil.*) a nuclear weapon that fails to explode when launched at, or emplaced on, a target

absolute expansion the true expansion of a liquid irrespective of the expansion of the containing vessel

absolute film *ABSTRACT FILM

absolute humidity the humidity of the air measured by the number of grams of water vapor present in one cubic meter of the air

absolute music music which does not illustrate or depict (in contrast to program music)

absolute pitch the pitch of a note as determined by a simple frequency, not a combination

---

of frequencies ‖ the ability to identify a note sounded in isolation

absolute scale the Kelvin scale

absolute temperature temperature measured on the Kelvin scale

absolute zero the lowest temperature theoretically attainable on the Kelvin scale: approximately -273.16° on the Centigrade scale (*LAW OF THERMODYNAMICS)

ab·so·lu·tion (æbzəlú:ʃən) n. the forgiveness of sin, setting free from guilt ‖ the act of a Christian priest in pronouncing the forgiveness of a penitent sinner [F.]

ab·so·lut·ism (æbsəlu:tizəm) n. autocratic government unrestrained by law ‖ (theol.) the doctrine of the absolute sovereignty of God, esp. as manifest in predestination **ab·so·lut·ist 1.** adj. of or relating to absolutism **2.** n. a believer in absolutism

ab·solve (æbzɒlv, æbsɒlv) pres. part. **ab·solv·ing** past and past part **ab·solved** v.t. to set free from obligation, guilt or sin ‖ to remit (a sin) by absolution ‖ to acquit [fr. L. absolvere, to loosen]

ab·sorb (æbsɔ́rb, æbzɔ́rb) v.t. to take up (a substance) into or throughout a system by physical or chemical means (cf. ADSORB) ‖ to take in as if by swallowing or sucking, to absorb water like a sponge ‖ to assimilate, receive without adverse effects, to absorb refugees into the local population ‖ to interest profoundly, occupy completely, absorbed in politics, running the workshop absorbs all his energies ‖ (phys.) to take up (energy) in a particular form in a system and transform it into a different type [F. absorber]

absorbed dose the amount of energy (in rads) imparted by nuclear (or ionizing) radiation to unit mass of absorbing material

ab·sor·be·fa·cient (æbsɔrbəféiʃənt, æbzɔrbəféiʃənt) **1.** adj. causing absorption **2.** n. an agent for this [fr. L. absorbere, to absorb + faciens (facientis), causing]

ab·sorb·en·cy (æbsɔ́rbənsi:, æbzɔ́rbənsi:) n. the state or quality of being absorbent

ab·sorb·ent (æbsɔ́rbənt, æbzɔ́rbənt) **1.** adj. having the ability, capacity or tendency to absorb **2.** n. a substance having this ability, capacity or tendency [fr. L. absorbens (absorbentis)]

absorbent cotton (Am. =Br. cotton wool) raw cotton, esp. as prepared for surgical dressings, packing, lining clothes etc.

ab·sorp·tion (æbsɔ́rpʃən, æbzɔ́rpʃən) n. an absorbing or being absorbed (cf. ADSORPTION, *SORPTION) [fr. L. absorptio (absorptionis)]

absorption spectrum an electromagnetic spectrum in which the intensity distribution of the original radiation has been characteristically modified by its passage through a selectively absorbing substance (*EMISSION SPECTRUM, *SPECTROSCOPY)

ab·sorp·tive (æbsɔ́rptiv, æbzɔ́rptiv) adj. having a tendency to absorb **ab·sorp·tiv·i·ty** n. (phys.) the relative ability of the surface of a substance to absorb energy, that for radiant energy is usually compared with that of a blackbody [fr. L. absorbere (absorptus), to absorb]

ab·stain (æbstéin) v.i. (with 'from') to choose not to participate, to abstain from voting (with 'from') to curb oneself, to abstain from comment ‖ (with 'from') to choose not to indulge oneself, to abstain from meat [F. abstenir]

ab·ste·mi·ous (æbsti:mi:əs) adj. abstaining in regard to food, drink or pleasure [fr. L. abstemius]

ab·sten·tion (æbsténʃən) n. the act or practice of abstaining [F.]

ab·sti·nence (æbstinəns) n. refraining from, or doing without, food, drink or pleasure ‖ a moderate form of fasting [F.]

ab·sti·nent (æbstinənt) adj. practicing abstinence [F.]

ab·stract (æbstrækt) **1.** adj. considered apart from perception or any concrete object, idealized, the abstract world of ideals ‖ theoretical, abstract politics **2.** n. a summary ‖ a short version of a piece of writing, report etc. **the ab·stract** (æbstrækt) the ideal **3.** (æbstrækt) v.t. to take out, remove ‖ to steal ‖ (æbstrækt) to make a written summary of [fr. L. abstrahere (abstractus), to draw from, separate]

abstract art modern art (roughly since 1910) tending to dispense with the treatment of natural objects and using pictorial elements alone to express ideas, feelings or sensations (e.g. abstract expressionism, constructivism) or to create works in which natural objects are transformed in accordance with ideas, feelings or

sensations (e.g. cubism, surrealism, futurism)

ab·stract·ed (æbstræktid) adj. absentminded, lost in thought

abstract expressionism a movement in American painting (since 1940), with parallels in Europe, based on the theory that color, line, form and texture, used freely in informal combination, have greater power of expression and of visual excitement than when they are used in accordance with prescribed formal concepts or to represent objects. It has evolved from ideas inherent in surrealism and expressionism, Kandinsky being a direct precursor. It seeks expression of the artist's whole being: the artist paints spontaneously, and the method is often called 'action painting'. The originators of the movement are Pollock, de Kooning, Tobey, Kline, Gorky, Rothko and Gottlieb. European 'tachisme' or 'art autre', represented by Wols, Fautrier and Hartung, is commensurate with abstract expressionism

abstract film a nonrepresentational film made showing shapes, lines, and color. Syn **absolute film**

ab·strac·tion (æbstrækʃən) n. the act of taking away, abstracting ‖ formation of an idea apart from concrete things, situations etc. ‖ the idea so formulated, e.g. goodness, anger, whiteness ‖ absentmindedness [F.]

abstract noun a noun denoting something intangible, the name of a quality, e.g. 'wickedness', 'wit'

ab·struse (æbstrú:s) adj. not easy to understand [fr. L. abstrudere (abstrusus), to push away]

ab·surd (æbsə́:rd, æbzə́:rd) adj. foolishly contrary to reason, an absurd statement ‖ ridiculous, absurd antics [F. absurde]

ab·surd·ism (æbsə́:rdizəm) n. philosophy that the world is irrational and meaningless and humanity is in conflict with it in searching for order; associated with Albert Camus, Jean-Paul Sartre, Eugène Ionesco, Samuel Beckett —absurd n. —absurdist n. adj. Cf THEATER OF THE ABSURD

ab·surd·i·ty (æbsə́:rditi:, æbzə́:rditi:) pl. **ab·surd·i·ties** n. the state or quality of being absurd ‖ something absurd [F. absurdité]

A·bu Bekr (ábu:békər) (573–634), father-in-law of Mohammed, on whose death he became the first Arab caliph (632)

A·bu Dha·bi (ábu:dábi:) an Arabian town and Gulf state (*TRUCIAL STATES). Oil production has replaced fishing as its primary source of income

A·bu-l'A·la al Ma'ar·ri (ábu:ləláælmáári:) (973–1057), blind Syrian poet whose works include the 'Epistle of Forgiveness', in which the old poets explain their presence in paradise

a·bun·dance (əbʌ́ndəns) n. richness, plenty [O.F. abondance]

a·bun·dant (əbʌ́ndənt) adj. plentiful, copious [O.F.]

a·buse (əbjú:z) pres. part. **a·bus·ing** past and past part. **a·bused** v.t. to use badly or wrongly, to abuse a privilege ‖ to ill-treat, injure ‖ to call (somebody) foul names [F. abuser]

a·buse (əbjú:s) n. misuse ‖ ill-treatment ‖ an instance of injustice or corruption ‖ vituperation [F. abus]

A·bu Sim·bel (ábu:símbəl) the site in the Nile valley of a temple (c. 1250 B.C.) the entrance of which is flanked by colossal statues of Ramses II. The flooding of the area as a result of the building of Aswan High Dam led to the lifting of the temple to a higher place of safety. UNESCO played the leading part in securing finance for this lifting operation

a·bu·sive (əbjú:siv) adj. characterized by abuse ‖ (of language) vituperative [F. abusif]

a·but (əbʌ́t) pres. part. **a·but·ting** past and past part. **a·but·ted** v.i. (with 'on' or 'against') to border, to have a common boundary or frontier, his land abuts on mine ‖ to end or lean for support, the barn abuts against the house **a·but·ment** n. the place where one thing abuts on another ‖ (archit.) the lateral support at the end of an arch or bridge [O.F. abouter, to join two things end to end, and O.F. abuter, to touch with an end]

ab·volt (æbvoult, æbvóult) n. the cgs electromagnetic unit of electrical potential equal to 10^{-8} volt

A·by·dos (əbáidɒs) a sacred burial city of Egyptian kings (3185–2815 B.C.), dedicated to Osiris, in the Nile valley about 200 miles south of Cairo. Temple of Seti I (14th c. B.C.)

a·bysm (əbízəm) n. (rhet.) an abyss **a·bys·mal** (əbízməl) adj. (fig.) bottomless, unfathomable, abysmal ignorance [O.F. abisme]

a·byss (əbís) n. a chasm, deep gorge **a·bys·sal** (əbísəl) adj. of the lower depths of the sea [fr. L. abyssus fr. Gk]

abyssal zone water below 300 fathoms

Ab·ys·sin·i·a (æbisíni:ə) *ETHIOPIA

AC (elec.) alternating current

Ac (chem.) actinium

a·ca·cia (əkéiʃə) n. a member of Acacia, fam. Papilionaceae, a genus of woody plants. There are 500 species, mostly trees. They show typically bipinnate leaves, with stipules, often thornlike. Some yield gum arabic, also tanbark, and some are good timber trees [L.]

a·cad·e·mese (əkædəmí:z) n. overly scholarly style of writing

ac·a·dem·ic (ækədémik) **1.** adj. scholarly ‖ related to a school, college or university, the academic year ‖ of theoretical interest rather than practical value **2.** n. a member of a university [fr. M.L. academicus, of the school of Plato]

ac·a·dem·i·cal (ækədémik'l) adj. of or pertaining to a college or university **ac·a·dem·i·cals** pl. n. academic costume (cap and gown, hood)

academic art art that is formally in some accepted tradition, without originality or passion

academic freedom intellectual freedom in teaching and learning within the academic community, without fear of unwarranted dismissal or other sanction. In the U.S.A., the American Association of University Professors set forth (1915) principles of freedom and tenure, thereafter incorporated into many university bylaws. Under these principles a scholar enjoys freedom to participate in public affairs and is protected outside his institution, not only by his personal rights under the U.S. Constitution, but by his professional rights as well. Academic freedom is accompanied by the obligation to preserve scholarly objectivity, to refrain from using the classroom for extraneous purposes, and to distinguish the individual's personal role from his institutional capacity

a·cad·e·mi·cian (əkædəmíʃən, ækədəmíʃən) n. member of an academy, esp. of certain learned or artistic societies [F. académicien]

ac·a·dem·i·cism (ækədémisizəm) n. (fine arts) uninspired working within some traditional mode

A·ca·dé·mie Fran·çaise (ækædeimi:frɑ́:sez) *FRENCH ACADEMY

a·cad·e·my (əkædəmi:) pl. **a·cad·e·mies** n. a school devoted to specialized training, a military academy, an academy of art ‖ a society of scholars or artists ‖ (in Scotland) a grammar school **Academy** the place near Athens where Plato taught [F. académie fr. L. fr. Gk]

A·ca·di·a (əkéidi:ə) (hist.) the name given by the French to the country comprising Nova Scotia, New Brunswick and Prince Edward Island

A·ca·di·an (əkéidi:ən) adj. (geol.) of a North American mountain-making episode in or about the Devonian period [fr. Acadia]

ac·a·leph (ækəlef) n. a member of Acalepha, a class of marine radiate animals including jellyfish, capable of stinging [fr. Mod. L. acalepha fr. Gk acalēphē, nettle]

A·ca·ma·pich·tli (ɑkɑmɑpí:ʃtli) the first king (1350–1403) of the Aztecs

a·can·thus (əkǽnθəs) pl. **a·can·thus·es, a·can·thi** (əkǽnθai) n. a member of Acanthus, a genus of prickly plants of fam. Acanthaceae. There are about 25 species, mostly xerophytes, with thorny leaves ‖ a leaf design, perhaps inspired by A. spinosus, used by Callimachus (5th c. B.C.) for the sculptured decoration of Corinthian capitals. Its history may be even older [L. fr. Gk akanthos, thorny]

a cap·pel·la (ɑ kəpélə) (of choral music) unaccompanied instrumentally [Ital. = in chapel style]

A·ca·pul·co (ɑ kəpúlkou) Mexico's chief Pacific port (pop. 462,144), in Guerrero state, with a fine harbor and famous as a resort and for fishing

Acarahy *SERRA ACARAHY

Ac·ar·na·ni·a (ækɑrnéini:ə) an ancient region of west central Greece

a·cau·les·cent (ækɔlésənt) adj. (bot.) without a stem [fr. L. acaulis fr. a-, without + caulis, stem]

Accad *AKKAD

Accadian *AKKADIAN

---

ac·cede (æksíːd) *pres. part.* **ac·ced·ing** *past and past part.* **ac·ced·ed** *v.i.* to agree, *to accede to a request* ‖ (with 'to') to come to (the throne), become invested with (an office), attain (some honor) ‖ to come to the throne ‖(with 'to') to become a member of (an organization) [fr. L. *accedere*, to come]

ac·cel·er·an·do (ækselərándou) (*mus.*) gradually speeding up [Ital.]

ac·cel·er·ant (æksélərənt) *n.* (*chem.*) a catalyst [fr. L. *accelerans* (*accelerantis*) fr. *accelerare*, to quicken]

ac·cel·er·ate (ækséləreit) *pres. part.* **ac·cel·er·at·ing** *past and past part.* **ac·cel·er·at·ed** *v.i.* to go faster ‖ *v.t.* to make (something) go faster [fr. L. *accelerare* (*acceleratus*)]

ac·cel·er·a·tion (ækseləréiʃən) *n.* an increase of speed or velocity ‖ (*phys.*) the vector representing the time rate of change, a velocity vector [fr. L. *acceleratio* (*accelerationis*)]

acceleration due to (or **of**) **gravity** (symbol *g*) the acceleration imparted to a body of any mass falling through the gravitational field that exists between the body and the earth. It is equal to the product of the mass of the earth × the gravitational constant divided by the square of the radius of the earth

$$\frac{GM \text{ (earth)}}{R^2 \text{ (earth)}} = g = 9.806 \text{ m/sec}^2$$

in latitude 45° at sea level

ac·cel·er·a·tive (æksélərətiv, ækséləreitiv) *adj.* of or causing acceleration

ac·cel·er·a·tor (ækséləreitər) *n.* a device for increasing speed, e.g. in a car ‖ (*anat., zool.*) a muscle or nerve used to increase motion ‖ (*chem.*) a substance which increases the speed of a reaction ‖ (*phys.*) a device for imparting a high velocity to charged atomic particles

ac·cent (æksent) *n.* the emphasis by stress or pitch on a word or syllable, specifically in poetic rhythms ‖ the mark used to indicate such a stress ‖ a mark used esp. to distinguish different sounds of the same letter, e.g. French acute ´, grave `, circumflex ^ ‖ (*printing*) a mark used with a number or letter to indicate measures of length (2′5″ = 2 ft 5 ins) or time (2′ 5″ = 2 mins 5 secs) or a mathematical variable (á) ‖ tone of the voice ‖ a local or national quality in pronunciation, *a Scottish accent* ‖ (*mus.*) rhythmical stress ‖ (*loosely*) emphasis of any kind, *the accent is on youth* [F.]

ac·cent (æksent, æksént) *v.t.* to pronounce with emphasis ‖ to write the accents on (words etc.) ‖ to emphasize [F. *accenter*]

ac·cen·tu·al (ækséntʃuəl) *adj.* characterized by accent, having rhythm based on stress [fr. L. *accentus*, accent]

ac·cen·tu·ate (ækséntʃueit) *pres. part.* **ac·cen·tu·at·ing** *past and past part.* **ac·cen·tu·at·ed** *v.t.* to emphasize, attribute special importance to [fr. M.L. *accentuare* (*accentuatus*)]

ac·cen·tu·a·tion (æksentʃuéiʃən) *n.* an accentuating or accenting [fr. M.L. *accentuatio* (*accentuationis*)]

ac·cept (æksépt) *v.t.* to take (something offered), *to accept a gift, accept an apology* ‖ to admit the truth or correctness of ‖ to agree to meet (an obligation) ‖ to take on the responsibility of (an office) ‖ to receive into e.g. a community ‖ to allow as being right or proper ‖ to give an affirmative answer to (an invitation) ‖ (of a committee) to receive (a report) [F. *accepter*]

ac·cept·a·bil·i·ty (ækseptəbíliti) *n.* the state or quality of being acceptable

ac·cept·a·ble (ækséptəb'l) *adj.* agreeable, satisfactory ‖ worth accepting ‖ welcome ‖ barely satisfactory **ac·cept·a·bly** *adv.* [F.]

ac·cept·ance (ækséptəns) *n.* a taking or consenting to take something offered ‖ approval, *your acceptance of the conditions is needed* ‖ agreement to meet an obligation ‖ (*commerce*) a signed agreement to pay a draft or bill of exchange when it is due, or the draft or bill itself [O.F.]

acceptance house (*Br.*) a bank specializing in the handling of bills of exchange for foreign trade

acceptance trials *mil.* trials carried out by nominated representatives of the eventual military users of a weapon or equipment to determine if the specified performance and characteristics have been met

ac·cep·ta·tion (ækseptéiʃən) *n.* the accepted sense in which a word is used [F.]

ac·cept·ed (ækséptid) *adj.* generally agreed on or approved

ac·cess (ækses) *n.* way of approach, *access from two roads* ‖ right of approach, *access to the prime minister* ‖ right to consult, *access to the files* ‖ a sudden emotional outburst, *an access of fury* or *sudden onset of illness* ‖ (*broadcasting*) availability of material to the media, e.g., by news sources [fr. L. *accessus*, approach and F. *accès*, fit]

accessary *ACCESSORY

ac·ces·si·bil·i·ty (æksesəbíliti) *n.* the state or quality of being accessible

ac·ces·si·ble (æksésəb'l) *adj.* easy to approach ‖ able to be reached ‖ able to be influenced, open, *accessible to reason* **ac·cés·si·bly** *adv.* [F.]

ac·ces·sion (ækséʃən) *n.* something added, an addition, e.g. to a collection ‖ a coming to an office, or to a special status, e.g. full membership ‖ a coming to the throne ‖ an acquisition, esp. by a non-profit institution [F.]

ac·ces·so·ry, ac·ces·sa·ry (æksésəri) 1. *n. pl.* **ac·ces·so·ries, ac·ces·sa·ries** (usually *pl.*) something added for more convenience or usefulness ‖(*pl.*) accompanying items for a woman's dress, such as handbag, shoes, gloves etc. 2. *adj.* additional ‖ (*law*) concerned in a crime without being the chief protagonist [fr. L.L. *accessorius*, additional]

accessory after the fact (*law*) someone who knows that a crime has been committed and who tries to impede justice by sheltering or aiding the criminal

accessory before the fact (*law*) someone who instigates or forwards a criminal act but is not present when the crime is committed

accessory bud (*bot.*) a bud growing near an axillary bud and in addition to it

accessory fruit (*bot.*) a pseudocarp

access time the time it takes a computer storage unit to provide information, reckoned from the moment of calling for the information ‖ television time provided, e.g., by cable television to members of the public

ac·ci·dence (æksidəns) *n.* the part of grammar which deals with changes in the forms of words, e.g. inflections for gender, number, case etc. [fr. L. *accidentia*, accidentals, nonessentials]

ac·ci·dent (æksidənt) *n.* a mishap ‖ a chance event commonly involving catastrophe, suffering or damage, *railroad accidents* ‖ chance, *we met by accident* ‖ (*geog.*) an irregularity in surface structure ‖ (*philos.*) an attribute, property or quality not belonging to the essence or specific character of a thing ‖ the material qualities remaining in the sacramental bread and wine after transubstantiation [F.]

ac·ci·den·tal (æksidént'l) 1. *adj.* happening by chance, fortuitous ‖ (*mus.*) relating to an accidental 2. *n.* a nonessential ‖ (*mus.*) a sign such as sharp, flat etc. attached to single notes and not in the key signature [F.]

Ac·ción De·mo·crá·ti·ca (aksjóndemɔkráti:ka) a Venezuelan political party, founded (1945) by Rómulo Betancourt. It advocates agrarian reform and industrial development

ac·cip·i·ter (æksípitər) *n.* a member of *Accipiter*, a genus of hawks with a small compact body, short wings and narrow tail. They hunt below the level of the treetops and subsist chiefly on birds. They are widely distributed [Mod. L.]

ac·claim (ækléim) 1. *v.t.* to applaud by shouting, hail enthusiastically 2. *n.* loud applause, vociferous welcome ‖ enthusiastic praise [fr. L. *acclamare*, to shout]

ac·cla·ma·tion (ækləméiʃən) *n.* a shouting of assent [fr. L. *acclamatio* (*acclamationis*)]

ac·cli·mate (ækláimət, ækləmeit) *pres. part.* **ac·cli·mat·ing** *past and past part.* **ac·cli·mat·ed** *v.t.* to acclimatize **ac·cli·ma·tion** (ækləméiʃən) *n.* [F. *acclimater*]

ac·cli·ma·ti·za·tion (ækl̦aimətizéiʃən, ækl̦aimətaizéiʃən) *n.* the process of acclimatizing, esp. (*biol.*) the process by which plants and animals can live and reproduce in an environment different from their native one

ac·cli·ma·tize (ækláimətaiz) *pres. part.* **ac·cli·ma·tiz·ing** *past and past part.* **ac·cli·ma·tized** *v.t.* to accustom to a new climate or to new conditions ‖ *v.i.* to become accustomed to a new climate or to new conditions [fr. F. *acclimater*]

ac·cliv·i·ty (æklíviti) *pl.* **ac·cliv·i·ties** *n.* an upward slope (opp. DECLIVITY) [fr. L. *acclivitas*, sloping]

ac·co·lade (ækəleid) *n.* a ceremonial touch of the sword to mark the conferment of knighthood ‖ any solemn recognition of merit ‖ (*mus.*) a vertical line or brace connecting two or more staves [F. fr. Ital. *accollare*, to embrace about the neck]

ac·com·mo·date (əkúmədeit) *pres. part.* **ac·com·mo·dat·ing** *past and past part.* **ac·com·mo·dat·ed** *v.t.* to provide lodging for ‖ to hold, have space enough for ‖ to oblige, esp. with a loan of money ‖ to adapt, adjust, *to accommodate oneself to circumstances* ‖ to settle (a difference) **ac·cóm·mo·dat·ing** *adj.* obliging, willing to adapt oneself to other people's convenience [fr. L. *accommodare* (*accommodatus*), to fit]

ac·com·mo·da·tion (əkɒmədéiʃən) *n.* (*Am. pl.*, *Br. sing.*) lodgings ‖ space, capacity to receive people, *accommodation for 600* ‖ a loan of money ‖ a settlement or agreement ‖ (*optics*) alteration of the focal length of the crystalline lens of the eye by muscles which attach it to the choroid, in order to bring light from near or distant objects into focus on the retina ‖ something designed for convenience, *sanitary accommodation* [F.]

accommodation ladder a ladder hung from the side of a ship

ac·com·pa·ni·ment (əkʌmpəni:mənt) *n.* a thing which goes naturally or inevitably with something ‖ (*mus.*) an instrumental part which supports a solo instrument or singer [F. *accompagnement*]

ac·com·pa·nist (əkʌmpənist) *n.* (*mus.*) someone who plays an accompaniment for a performer

ac·com·pa·ny (əkʌmpəni:) *pres. part.* **ac·com·pa·ny·ing** *past and past part.* **ac·com·pa·nied** *v.t.* to go with (someone), to escort ‖ to cause something specified to be done, uttered etc. conjointly with (something), *to accompany words with actions* ‖ to occur in association with, *lightning accompanied the storm* ‖ (*mus.*) to play an accompaniment for or to ‖ *v.i.* (*mus.*) to play in accompaniment [F. *accompagner*]

ac·com·plice (əkɒmplis) *n.* an active partner in a misdemeanor or crime [fr. F. *complice*]

ac·com·plish (əkɒmpliʃ) *v.t.* to bring to a successful conclusion, fulfil **ac·cóm·plished** *adj.* proficient ‖ competent in the social graces [O.F. *accomplir* (*accompliss-*)]

ac·com·plish·ment (əkɒmpliʃmənt) *n.* a superficial rather than a thorough skill ‖ a feat ‖ a bringing to completion ‖ a social grace [F. *accomplissement*]

ac·cord (əkɔ́rd) *n.* an agreement ‖ harmony, esp. of tone, color, sounds etc. **of one's own accord** willingly, without constraint [O. F. *acord, acorde*, agreement]

accord *v.t.* to grant (a favor or mark of esteem), *they accorded him a hero's welcome* ‖ *v.i.* to agree, tally, be consistent, *his evidence does not accord with the policeman's* [O.F. *acorder*]

ac·cord·ance (əkɔ́rd'ns) *n.* agreement, conformity [O.F. *accordance*]

ac·cord·ant (əkɔ́rd'nt) *adj.* in harmony, in agreement [O.F. *acordant*]

ac·cord·ing·ly (əkɔ́rdiŋli:) *adv.* therefore, in consequence ‖ in accordance with the circumstances

ac·cord·ing to (əkɔ́rdiŋ) *prep.* in a manner consistent with or depending on, *promotion according to seniority, we will swim or play bridge according to the weather* ‖ on the authority or declaration of, *according to the police he was drunk*

ac·cor·di·on (əkɔ́rdi:ən) *n.* a small wind instrument, with bellows and studs, or more usually both studs and a keyboard, used in popular music **ac·cór·di·on·ist** *n.* [fr. Ital. *accordare*, to attune]

accordion pleats narrow pleats used in dressmaking, lampshade making etc.

ac·cost (əkɔ́st,əkɒ́st) *v.t.* to approach and start a conversation with ‖ (of a prostitute) to solicit [F. *accoster*]

ac·count (əkáunt) *v.t.* to consider, believe to be **to account for** to explain, answer for ‖ to render an explanatory statement for (expenses etc.) ‖ to capture or kill, *they accounted for 20 of the enemy* [O.F. *aconter*, to count]

account *n.* a statement of income and expenditure ‖ a bill for work done or services rendered ‖ a statement, description, explanation, *to give an account of one's behavior* **of no (some, any, little) account** of no (some etc.) value, importance **on account** in part payment of a sum owed or as an advance payment of earnings **on account of** because of **on any account** for any reason **on one's own account** in one's own interest **to give a good account of oneself** to perform well **to square accounts** to settle what is owing ‖ to redress a grievance **to take into account, to take account of** to take into consideration (when coming to a decision) **to**

turn to account to put to advantageous use [O.F. *acont*]

ac·count·a·bil·i·ty (əkáuntəbiliti:) *n.* the quality or state of being accountable

ac·count·a·ble (əkáuntəb'l) *adj.* answerable, bound to give an explanation || able to be explained, explicable **ac·cóun·ta·bly** *adv.*

ac·count·an·cy (əkáuntənsi:) *n.* the profession of an accountant, the recording and interpreting of e.g. a company's finances to allow it to determine its profit or loss, to check and guide policy and to facilitate tax assessment

ac·count·ant (əkáuntənt) *n.* a person skilled in keeping accounts, or someone who examines or inspects the accounts of a business or company (*CERTIFIED PUBLIC ACCOUNTANT, *CHARTERED ACCOUNTANT) [F. *accomptant*]

account sale (*finance*) purchase and sale (P&S) statement, i.e., statement made by a broker to a commodity customer when futures transaction is closed out, showing net profit or loss on the transaction, commission, and other proper charges

ac·cou·ter, esp. *Br.* **ac·cou·tre** (əku:tər) *v.t.* to equip [F. *accoutrer*]

ac·cou·ter·ment, esp. *Br.* **ac·cou·tre·ment** (əku:tərmənt) *n.* equipment [F.]

Ac·cra (əkrá) the capital (pop. 700,000) of Ghana, a seaport and fishing port on the Gulf of Guinea, and a fast-growing administrative and trading center. International airport. The University of Ghana (1961) lies 5 miles north, at Achimota

ac·cred·it (əkrédit) *v.t.* to cause (an ambassador, envoy etc.) to be officially recognized || to recognize (an educational institution) as meeting defined standards **ac·cred·i·tá·tion** *n.* **ac·créd·it·ed** *adj.* officially recognized [F. *accrediter*]

ac·crete (əkrí:t) *pres. part.* **ac·cret·ing** *past and past part.* **ac·cret·ed** *v.i.* to become joined together || to grow together [fr. L. *accrescere* (*accretus*), to grow, increase]

ac·cre·tion (əkrí:ʃən) *n.* growth, esp. organic growth || an adhesion of things usually separate || the act of accreting || the result of this act, e.g. (*geol.*) limestone deposited on some other rock [fr. L. *accretio* (*accretionis*), increase]

ac·cru·al (əkrú:əl) *n.* something which has accrued || the process of accruing

ac·crue (əkrú:) *pres. part.* **ac·cru·ing** *past and past part.* **ac·crued** *v.i.* to come about as a natural consequence, *certain advantages accrue from building cities high* || (of interest on investments) to accumulate [fr. older *accrue n.* fr. F.]

accrued dividend presumed earnings of stocks since the last declaration of dividend (cf. CUMULATED DIVIDEND)

accrued interest interest earned on a bond since the last interest payment but not yet due for payment

ac·cul·tur·ate (əkʌltʃəreit) *pres. part.* **ac·cul·tur·at·ing** *past and past part.* **ac·cul·tur·at·ed** *v.t.* to cause to undergo acculturation || *v.i.* to undergo acculturation [back-formation fr. ACCULTURATION]

ac·cul·tur·a·tion (əkʌltʃəréiʃən) *n.* the process of social adaptation of a group or individual, or the result of this **ac·cul·tur·á·tion·al** *adj.* [AD-+CUL+TURE]

ac·cul·tur·a·tive (əʌltʃəreitiv) *adj.* of or relating to acculturation

ac·cu·mu·late (əkjú:mjəleit) *pres. part.* **ac·cu·mu·lat·ing** *past and past part.* **ac·cu·mu·lat·ed** *v.t.* to gather together in large numbers or quantity, amass || *v.i.* to increase in number or quantity [fr. L. *accumulare* (*accumulatus*), to heap]

ac·cu·mu·la·tion (əkju:mjəléiʃən) *n.* an accumulating or being accumulated || something accumulated || increase of money by the additiun of interest [fr. L. *accumulatio* (*accumulationis*)]

ac·cu·mu·la·tive (əkjú:mjəlativ, əkjú:mjuleitiv) *adj.* produced by accumulation, cumulative [fr. L. *accumulare* (*accumulatus*), to accumulate]

ac·cu·mu·la·tor (əkjú:mjəleitər) *n.* a person who accumulates objects || an apparatus which accumulates, (esp. *Br.*, *elec.*) a storage cell [fr. L.]

ac·cu·ra·cy (ækjərəsi:) *n.* the quality of being accurate, precision

ac·cu·rate (ækjərit) *adj.* precise, exact [fr. L. *accurare* (*accuratus*), to perform with care]

ac·curs·ed (əké:rsid,əké:rst) *adj.* cursed, damned [fr. older *accurse*, to curse]

ac·cus·al (əkjú:zəl) *n.* the act of accusing

ac·cu·sa·tion (ækjuzéiʃən) *n.* a charge of having done wrong || an indictment **to bring an accusation against** to charge with doing wrong

ac·cu·sa·ti·val (əkju:zətáivəl) *adj.* per- taining to the accusative case

ac·cu·sa·tive (əkjú:zətiv) **1.** *adj.* referring to the case in grammar which indicates the object of an action, e.g. (in Latin grammar) the case occurring in the direct object of a verb or after some prepositions, or (in English grammar) the objective case shown in the forms of pronouns, 'him', 'her', 'me', 'us','them', 'whom' **2.** *n.* the accusative case [F.]

ac·cu·sa·to·ri·al (əkju:zətóri:əl, əkju:zətóuri:əl) *adj.* (*law*) of a prosecution made in public before a judge who is not himself the prosecutor (cf. INQUISITORIAL)

ac·cu·sa·to·ry (əkjú:zətɒri:, əkjú:zətouri:) *adj.* implying an accusation, *an accusatory tone of voice* [fr. L. *accusatorius*]

ac·cuse (əkjú:z) *pres. part.* **ac·cus·ing** *past and past part.* **ac·cused** *v.t.* to charge with doing wrong || to blame **the accused** the person or persons charged in a court of law [O.F. *acuser*]

ac·cus·tom (əkʌstəm) *v.t.* (esp. *refl.* ar.d *pass.*) to get used, *he cannot accustom himself to their diet* || to habituate, *she accustomed the child to sleeping alone* **ac·cús·tomed** *adj.* usual, habitual [O.F. *acostumer*]

AC/DC *adj.* (*slang*) both heterosexual and homosexual

ace (eis) *n.* a playing card bearing a single pip || the single spot on dice, dominoes || a person who excels at anything || a fighter pilot who has shot down a large number of enemy aircraft || (*tennis*) an unreturnable service **within an ace of** very close to, *within an ace of being captured* [O.F. *as*]

a·ce·di·a (əsí:di:ə) *n.* spiritual apathy, sloth (one of the seven deadly sins) [L.L. fr. Gk *akēdia*]

a·cel·lu·lar (eiséljələr) *adj.* not made up of cells

a·ceph·a·lan (eiséfələn) *n.* a lamellibranch [fr. Gk *akephala*, headless]

a·ceph·a·lous (eiséfələs) *adj.* having no head [fr. L.L. *acephalus* fr. Gk]

a·cer·bic (əsé:rbik) *adj.* bitter, sour || (of wit etc.) edged with harshness [L. *acerbus*, bitter]

a·cer·bi·ty (əsé:rbiti:) *pl.* **a·cer·bi·ties** *n.* sourness, harshness, esp. of manner or language || an instance of this [F. *acerbité*]

ac·et·al·de·hyde (æsitáldəhaid) *n.* a colorless volatile liquid, CH_3CHO. It can be made by oxidizing ethyl alcohol. lt boils at 21 ° C. It has a pungent, fruity smell. Many organic compounds are prepared from it [ACETYL+ALDE-HYDE]

a·cet·amin·o·phen [$CH_3CONH_6C_6H_4OH$] (əsi:təmínəfən) *n.* (*pharm.*) a pain- and fever-relieving drug

a·cet·a·nil·ide [$C_6H_5NHCOCH_3$] (æsətǽnəlaid) *n.* (*pharm.*) an analgesic and mild antiseptic that causes toxic symptoms with prolonged use

ac·e·tate (ǽsiteit) *n.* a salt or ester of acetic acid || a synthetic fabric or yarn derived from the acetic ester of cellulose [fr. L. *acetum*, vinegar +-ATE]

a·ce·tic (əsí:tik) *adj.* relating to vinegar [fr. L. *acetum*, vinegar]

acetic acid a colorless, pungent, liquid acid, CH_3COOH, that is the chief acid of vinegar. Its salts and esters (acetates) are used in textile, pigment and paint manufacture. lts derivative cellulose acetate is important in the plastics industry

a·ce·to·hex·a·mide [$C_{15}H_{20}N_2O_4S$] (æsetouhéksamaid) *n.* (*pharm.*) drug for oral treatment of mild diabetes

ac·e·tone (ǽsitoun) *n.* a colorless volatile inflammable liquid (CH_3COCH_3) commonly used as a solvent for organic compounds, esp. in the production of rayon (cellulose acetate), and in organic syntheses **ac·e·ton·ic** (æsitónik) *adj.*[G. *azeton* ult. fr. L. *acetum*, vinegar]

a·ce·tyl·cho·line (əsi:t'lkóuli:n) *n.* a compound, ($CH_3)_3N(CH_2OOCCH_3$) OH, (*CHOLINE) formed at the synapses of the autonomic nervous system and thought to play a role in the transmission of impulses across them as well as in the neuron itself. It is formed and destroyed enzymatically

a·cet·y·lene (əsét'li:n) *n.* a colorless inflammable gas. It is a highly unsaturated compound of carbon and hydrogen, C_2H_2. It is industrially important as a starting point in organic syntheses [ult. fr. L. *acetum*, vinegar]

acetylene torch an industrial tool using a mixture of acetylene and oxygen which burns at a

very high temperature (3,300° C). It is used for cutting and welding metal

A·chae·a (əkí:ə) the northernmost region of the Peloponnese, Greece. It was settled by Indo-European tribes who invaded (early 2nd millennium B.C.) and conquered most of Greece. The Achaeans helped to colonize S. Italy (8th c. B.C.)

A·chae·an (əkí:ən) **1.** *n.* a native of Achaea **2.** *adj.* relating to Achaea

Achaean League a confederacy of 10 cities formed (280 B.C.) against Macedon. It became the leading power in Peloponnesus and overcame Sparta (188 B.C.). It was defeated and dissolved by the Romans (146 B.C.)

A·chae·men·id (ækiménid) *n.* a member of a Persian dynasty (c. 550–331 B.C.) which, under Cyrus II, Cambyses II, Darius I, Xerxes I and Artaxerxes I, built up a vast empire, conquered Egypt and attacked Greece. It was overthrown by Alexander the Great at Arbela (331 B.C.)

A·chai·a (əkáiə) Achaea

A·cha·tes (əkéiti:z) companion of Aeneas in Virgil's 'Aeneid'

ache (eik) **1.** *n.* a continuous dull pain as opposed to a sharp, sudden pain **2.** *v.i. pres. part.* **ach·ing** *past and past part.* **ached** to suffer continuous dull pain || to have painful yearnings [O.E. *æce* n. fr. *acan* v.]

Achebe, Chinua (ətʃéibei, chin-wah) (1930–), Nigerian author of 'Things Fall Apart' (1958), 'Arrow of God' (1964), and 'A Man of the People' (1966). His novels are written in English and deal with Ibo society

Acheh *ATJEH

a·chene (əkí:n) *n.* a dry, one-seeded fruit which ripens without bursting [fr. Mod. L. *achænium* fr. Gk]

Ach·er·on (ǽkərɒn) *n.* (*Gk mythol.*) one of the rivers of Hades, over which Charon ferried the dead [Gk]

Ach·e·son (ǽtʃis'n), Dean Gooderham (1893–1971), U.S. lawyer, diplomat and secretary of state (1949–53) under Pres. Harry Truman. He was largely responsible for the Bretton Woods Agreement, the groundwork for the Marshall Plan, the North Atlantic Treaty Organization agreement, the Japanese peace treaty, the diplomacy on the Korean conflict, the non-recognition of Communist China and the aiding of Chiang Kai-shek, and the rearming of West Germany

Acheson, Edward Goodrich (1856–1931), U.S. inventor. He discovered silicon carbide and perfected a method for making graphite

A·cheu·li·an (əʃú:li:ən) *adj.* of the Paleolithic epoch following the Abbevillian, characterized by the use of bifacial and flake tools [after *St Acheul*, N. France]

a·chiev·a·ble (ətʃí:vəb'l) *adj.* able to be achieved

a·chieve (ətʃí:v) *pres. part.* **a·chiev·ing** *past and past part.* **a·chieved** *v.t.* to carry out successfully || to attain || *v.i.* (*Am.*) to reach a required standard of performance [O.F. *achever*, to finish]

a·chieve·ment (ətʃí:vment) *n.* something carried out successfully || the act of achieving || (*heraldry*) an escutcheon granted in memory of something achieved [F. *achévement*]

A·chil·les (əkíli:z) son of the Phthian king Peleus and the sea-goddess Thetis, who plunged him into the Styx so as to make him invulnerable (except for the heel by which she held him). He was the greatest of the Greek heroes in the 'Iliad'. He killed Hector during the siege of Troy but was himself mortally wounded in the heel by an arrow from Paris

Achilles and the Tortoise *ZENO OF ELEA

A·chil·les heel (əkíli:z) a vulnerable spot

Achilles' tendon a tendon joining the calf muscles to the bone in the heel

ach·la·myd·e·ous (ækləmídi:əs) *adj.* (*bot.*) having neither calyx nor corolla [fr. Gk *a-*, without+*chlamus* (*chlamudos*), cloak]

A·cho·li (ətʃóuli:) *n.* a Nilotic-speaking Negro people of N. Uganda || a member of this people || a Nilotic language of this people

ach·ro·mat·ic (ækrəmǽtik) *adj.* (*optics*) free from chromatic aberration || colorless || (*mus.*) free from accidentals or modulation || (*biol.*) not readily stained **ach·ro·mát·i·cal·ly** *adv.* [fr. Gk *achromatos* fr. *a-*, without+*chróma*, color]

a·chro·ma·tin (eikróumətin, əkróumətin) *n.* (*biol.*) that part of the cell nucleus which is not easily colored by basic stains **a·chro·ma·tin·ic** *adj.* [fr. Gk *achrōmatos*, colorless]

CONCISE PRONUNCIATION KEY: **(a)** æ, c*a*t; ɑ, c*a*r; ɔ f*aw*n; ei, sn*a*ke. **(e)** e, h*e*n; i:, sh*ee*p; iə, d*ee*r; ɛə, b*ea*r. **(i)** i, f*i*sh; ai, t*i*ger; ə:, b*i*rd. **(o)** o, *o*x; au, c*ow*; ou, g*oa*t; u, p*oo*r; ɔi, r*oy*al. **(u)** ʌ, d*u*ck; u, b*u*ll; u:, g*oo*se; ə, b*a*cill*u*s; ju:, c*u*be. x, lo*ch*; θ, *th*ink; ð, bo*th*er; z, *Z*en; ʒ, cor*s*age; dʒ, sava*ge*; ŋ, ora*n*guta*n*g; j, *y*ak; ʃ, fi*sh*; tʃ, fe*tch*; 'l, rabb*le*; 'n, redd*en*. Complete pronunciation key appears inside front cover.

a·chro·ma·tism (eikróumətizəm, əkróumətizəm) *n.* the quality or state of being achromatic

ac·id (ǽsid) **1.** *adj.* having a sour, sharp taste, like a lemon ‖ relating to or having the characteristics of an acid ‖ acidproducing ‖ looking or sounding bitter or sour, *an acid remark* **2.** *n.* a compound containing hydrogen which, dissolved in water, provides hydrogen ions (protons) ‖ a molecule or ion which can give up protons to a base ‖ (*slang*) LSD or d-lysergic acid diethylamide, an hallucinogenic drug [F. *acide*]

acid casein casein (insoluble protein used in coating etc.)

acid fallout natural precipitation falling through atmosphere containing sulfur dioxide and nitrogen oxide pollutants, thus creating an acid bias in the atmosphere and soil *syn* **acid rain**

acid fascism eclectic violence resulting from brainwashing under the influence of psychedelic drugs

acid head *n.* a user of LSD

a·cid·ic (əsídik) *adj.* acid-forming ‖ acid

a·cid·i·fi·a·ble (əsídifaiəb'l) *adj.* capable of being acidified

a·cid·i·fi·ca·tion (əsidifikéiʃən) *n.* the act or process of acidifying

a·cid·i·fy (əsídifai) *pres. part.* **a·cid·i·fy·ing** *past and past part.* **a·cid·i·fied** *v.t.* to make sour ‖ (*chem.*) to make acid, i.e. to increase the concentration of hydrogen ions in a solution ‖ *v.i.* to become sour

ac·i·dim·e·ter (æsidímitər) *n.* an instrument or solution for determining the strength of acids **ac·i·di·met·ric** (æsidəmétrik), **ac·i·di·met·ri·cal** *adjs.* **ac·i·dim·e·try** (æsidímitri:) *n.*

a·cid·i·ty (əsíditi:) *pl.* **a·cid·i·ties** *n.* the state or quality of being acid ‖ an acid remark [F. *acidité*]

ac·id·ly (ǽsidli) *adv.* (of a manner of speaking) bitterly

ac·i·do·sis (æsidóusis) *n.* (*med.*) abnormally high acidity of the blood and body fluids (opp. ALKALOSIS)

ac·i·dot·ic (æsidótik) *adj.* having or relating to acidosis

acid rain *ACID FALLOUT

acid rock rock music suggestive of a psychedelic experience

acid rocks (*geol.*) rocks containing over 65% silica, e.g. granite

acid salt (*chem.*) a salt formed by the replacement, usually by a metal, of part of the acidic or replaceable hydrogen of an acid

acid test the test that settles a matter [from testing a metal with an acid to prove its being gold or not]

acid test ratio (*finance*) the degree of liquidity of an organization, i.e., its ability to convert assets into cash

acid trip *n.* an hallucinatory experience resulting from the ingestion of LSD

a·cid·u·late (əsídjəleit, əsídʒəleit) *pres. part.* **a·cid·u·lat·ing** *past and past part.* **a·cid·u·lat·ed** *v.t.* to make slightly acid

a·cid·u·lous (əsídjələs, əsídʒələs) *adj.* slightly acid [fr. L. *acidulus*]

ac·i·nus (ǽsənəs) *pl.* **ac·i·ni** (ǽsənai) *n.* a drupe in a multiple fruit, e.g. the raspberry ‖ a grape seed ‖ (*anat.*) a small sac of a racemose gland [L.=a berry growing in a cluster]

ac·knowl·edge (æknɔ́lidʒ) *pres. part.* **ac·knowl·edg·ing** *past and past part.* **ac·knowl·edged** *v.t.* to recognize as a fact, admit the truth of, *to acknowledge an opponent's superiority* ‖ to recognize as an authority ‖ to report the receipt of, *to acknowledge a letter* ‖ to recognize in a legal form, *he wished to acknowledge the child as his* ‖ to recognize and answer (a greeting, nod etc.) **ac·knówl·edg·ment, ac·knówl·edge·ment** *n.* the act of acknowledging ‖ a receipt for something given **in acknowledgment of** in gratitude for, in recognition of [fr. obs. *acknow* fr. O.E. *on*+*cnawen*, to know]

a·clin·ic (eiklínik) *adj.* without dipping or inclination [fr. Gk *aklinēs*, without inclination]

aclinic line an imaginary line near the equator where the compass needle has no dip

A.C.L.U. American Civil Liberties Union

ac·me (ǽkmi:) *n.* the highest point, peak of perfection [Gk *akmē*]

ac·ne (ǽkni:) *n.* a skin disease caused by chronic inflammation of the sebaceous glands, common in adolescents. It consists of pimples and blackheads, esp. on the face and neck, which if not

properly treated may leave scars [Mod. L., origin unknown]

ac·o·lyte (ǽkəlait) *n.* a person who assists a priest at Mass. (In the Roman Catholic Church he may be ordained to the highest of the four minor orders) ‖ an admiring follower [fr. M.L. *acolitus*, follower fr. Gk]

ACOM (*computer*) acronym for "automatic coding," system used on IBM 701 and 705 by General Motors Corporation

A·con·ca·gua (ækɔŋkágwə) a mountain (23,081 ft) of Argentina, the highest in the Andes

ac·o·nite (ǽkənait) *n.* a member of *Aconitum*, a genus of poisonous plants, esp. *A. napellus* ‖ (*med.*) the dried root of this **a·con·i·tine** (əkɔ́niti:n) *n.* a very poisonous alkaloid obtained from the root and leaves of aconite [F. *aconit* fr. L. fr. Skr.]

a·corn (éikɔrn) *n.* the nut or seed of the oak [O.E. *æcern*, fruit (of the field)] **acorn squash** a North American acorn-shaped winter squash with sweet, tawny-colored flesh

A·cos·ta (akɔ́sta), Joaquín (1800–52), Colombian scientist, historian and statesman. He served as an officer in the patriot army under Simón Bolívar

a·cot·y·le·don (eikɔt'li:d'n, eikɔt'li:d'n) *n.* a plant without cotyledons (ferns, fungi etc.) [fr. Mod. L. fr. Gk *a-*, without+*kotulēdōn*, socket]

a·cous·tic (əkú:stik) *adj.* pertaining to sound ‖ pertaining to acoustics ‖ designed to improve hearing **a·cóus·ti·cal** *adj.* [F. *acoustique* fr. Gk]

acoustical hologram (*electr.*) patterns formed by exposure to high-frequency sound waves that can form threedimensional pictures when viewed by laser light

acoustic burglar alarm a security device activated by the sounds made by an intruder *syn* **acoustic intrusion detector**

acoustic circuit (*mil.*) a mine circuit that responds to the acoustic field of a target

acoustic clarifier arrangement of cones attached to a loudspeaker baffle that absorb excess energy when sounds become suddenly too loud, suppressing the sounds

acoustic data coupler (*electr.*) device for telephone circuit transmission without electrical connection, used to send messages to a computer

acoustic intrusion detector *ACOUSTIC BURGLAR ALARM

acoustic jamming (*mil.*) the deliberate radiation or reradiation of mechanical or electroacoustic signals with the objectives of obliterating or obscuring signals that the enemy is attempting to receive, and of deterring enemy weapon systems

acoustic mine (*mil.*) a mine that can be exploded by the impact of sound waves **acoustic minehunting** *n.* (*mil.*) the use of a sonar to detect mines or minelike objects that may be on or protrude from the seabed or buried in it

acoustic perfume *WHITE NOISE

a·cous·tics (əkú:stiks) *n.* the science of sound waves and their production, transmission, reception and control ‖ the study of hearing ‖ the acoustic properties, e.g. of an auditorium

acoustic warfare (*mil.*) action involving the use of underwater acoustic energy to determine, exploit, reduce, or prevent hostile use of the underwater acoustic spectrum, and actions that retain friendly use of the underwater acoustic spectrum

acoustic wave filter (əkú:stikweiv) (*electr.*) device for separating sound of different frequencies

a·cous·to·e·lec·tric (əkú:stouilɛktrik) *adj.* (*music*) of a sound created by an electronic musical instrument

a·cous·to·e·lec·tron·ics (əku:stouilɛktrɔ́niks) *n.* (*pretersonics*) conversion of electrical signals into acoustic waves that travel on a surface

a·cous·to·op·tic (əku:stouəɔ́ptik) *adj.* of optical devices involving sound

ac·quaint (əkwéint) *v.t.* to familiarize, inform **to be acquainted with** to know (a person or thing) [O.F. *acointer*]

ac·quaint·ance (əkwéintəns) *n.* someone whom one knows only slightly ‖ knowledge of something, *his acquaintance with the language will be useful to him* **ac·quáint·ance·ship** *n.* [O.F. *acointance*]

ac·qui·esce (ækwi:és) *pres. part.* **ac·qui·esc·ing** *past and past part.* **ac·qui·esced** *v.i.* to agree, sometimes reluctantly, to a decision made by

others ‖ to concur in an arrangement, suggestion etc. [F. *acquiescer*]

ac·qui·es·cence (ækwi:és'ns) *n.* the act of acquiescing [F.]

ac·qui·es·cent (ækwi:és'nt) *adj.* acquiescing ‖ submissive, compliant by nature [fr. L. *acquiescens* (*acquiescentis*)]

ac·quire (əkwáiər) *pres. part.* **ac·quir·ing** *past and past part.* **ac·quired** *v.t.* to gain for oneself, to come to have [O.F. *acquerre*]

acquired characteristics somatic modifications in plants and animals effected by environment (*EVOLUTION)

acquired characters acquired characteristics

acquired taste a liking that is gained by degrees (as opposed to a natural liking) or the object of such liking

ac·quire·ment (əkwáiərmənt) *n.* the act of acquiring ‖ a skill acquired or mental attainment

ac·qui·si·tion (ækwiziʃən) *n.* the gaining of something for oneself, act of acquiring ‖ the thing gained or acquired [fr. L. *acquisitio* (*acquisitionis*)]

acquisition laser (*electr.*) wide-angle laser used in an optical guidance system to find and chase a target until a narrow-beam tracking laser can lock into it

acquisition radar (*electr.*) device to detect an approaching target and to convey data to a fire-control radar that can track the target

ac·quis·i·tive (əkwízitiv) *adj.* very anxious to acquire [fr. L. *acquirere* (*acquisitus*), to acquire]

ac·quit (əkwít) *pres. part.* **ac·quit·ting** *past and past part.* **ac·quit·ted** *v.t.* to declare (a person) not guilty of an offense ‖ to settle (a debt) ‖ to discharge from responsibility **to acquit oneself** to conduct oneself, esp. to show one's quality, *the boy acquitted himself well in his first flight* **ac·quít·tal** *n.* [O.F. *aquiter*]

ac·quit·tance (əkwít'ns) *n.* full payment of a debt [O.F. *aquitance*]

ac·quo·ren (əkwóren) *n.* (*biol.*) a protein secreted by the jellyfish *Acquorea aequorea*, which emits a blue light useful for optical examination of cells

A·cre (éikər) a port (pop. 38,700) of Israel, the scene of much fighting in the Crusades (notably between Saladin and Richard I). Held by the Knights of St John (as St Jean d'Acre) as part of the Latin kingdom of Jerusalem (1191), it was reconquered by the Saracens (1291). Captured by the Turks (1517), it successfully resisted a two-month siege by Napoleon (1799). It became part of the British Mandate of Palestine (1918). In 1948 Israel took it from the Arabs

a·cre (éikər) *n.* a measure of land, 4,840 sq. yds. or approx. 4,000 sq. meters [O.E. *æcer*, a field]

a·cre·age (éikəridʒ) *n.* the area of land in acres ‖ acres collectively

ac·rid (ǽkrid) *adj.* bitter to the smell or taste, like the smell of burning rubber or the taste of smoked fish ‖ of sour or sharp temper [fr. L. *acer* (*acris*), sharp]

Ac·rid (*mil.*) Soviet air-to-air missile (AA-6), radar-guided or with infrared homing, on MIG-25s since 1975

ac·ri·dine (ǽkridi:n) *n.* a colorless cystalline compound, $C_{13}H_9N$, occurring in coal tar, used esp. in dye compounds and pharmaceuticals

ac·ri·dine [$C_{13}H_9N$] (ǽkridi:n) *n.* (*pharm.*) a coal-tar derivative used in the process of making dyes and some antiseptics

a·crid·i·ty (əkríditi:) *n.* the state or quality of being acrid

Ac·ri·lan (ǽkrəlæn) *n.* an acrylic fiber used in textiles for its soft, wrinkleresisting qualities [Trademark]

ac·ri·mo·ni·ous (ækrəmóuni:əs) *adj.* harsh, bitter, *an acrimonious quarrel*

ac·ri·mo·ny (ǽkrəmouni:) *pl.* **ac·ri·mo·nies** *n.* harshness or bitterness of temper or manner ‖ an instance of this [fr. L. *acrimonia*]

ac·ro·bat (ǽkrəbæt) *n.* someone who performs gymnastic feats such as turning somersaults, tightrope walking etc. **ac·ro·bát·ic** *adj.* **ac·ro·bát·i·cal·ly** *adv.* **ac·ro·bát·ics** *pl. n.* feats performed by acrobats [F. *acrobate* fr. Gk]

ac·ro·car·pous (ækrəkárpəs) *adj.* (*bot.*) bearing fruit at the top of the main stem [fr. Gk *akros*, highest+ *karpos*, fruit]

ac·ro·lect (ǽkrəlekt) *n.* dialect of the upper classes *Cf* BASILECT

a·cro·le·in (əkróuli:in) *n.* a suffocating volatile liquid, $CH_2=CHCHO$, obtained by the decomposition of glycerol and used in the synthesis of

CONCISE PRONUNCIATION KEY: **(a)** æ, c*a*t; ɑ, c*a*r; ɔ f*aw*n; ei, sn*a*ke. **(e)** e, h*e*n; i:, sh*ee*p; iə, d*ee*r; ɛə, b*ea*r. **(i)** i, f*i*sh; ai, t*i*ger; ə:, b*i*rd. **(o)** o, *o*x; au, c*ow*; ou, g*oa*t; u, p*oo*r; ɔi, r*oy*al. **(u)** ʌ, d*u*ck; u, b*u*ll; u:, g*oo*se; ə, b*a*cillus; ju:, c*u*be. x, lo*ch*; θ, *th*ink; ð, bo*th*er; z, *Z*en; ʒ, cor*s*age; dʒ, sa*v*age; ŋ, oranguta*n*g; j, *y*ak; ʃ, *fi*sh; tʃ, fe*tch*; 'l, rabb*le*; 'n, redd*en*. Complete pronunciation key appears inside front cover.

pharmaceutical products etc. [fr. L. *acer* (*acris*), sharp + *olere*, to smell +-IN]

ac·ro·meg·a·ly (ækrəmégəli) *n.* (*med.*) a disease caused by excessive secretion of growth hormone from the pituitary gland in adult life, and manifested by headache and enlargement of the hands, feet and jaw [fr. Gk *akros*, extremity+*megalē*, large]

ac·ro·nym (ǽkrənim) *n.* a name made up of the initial letters of an official title. e.g. UNESCO [fr. Gk *akros*, upper+*onoma*, name (modeled on 'homonym']

a·crop·e·tal (əkrópit'l) *adj.* (*bot.*) of leaves, flowers or roots developing successively from an axis so that the youngest arise at the apex [fr. Gk *akros*, peak + L. *petere*, to seek]

a·crop·o·lis (əkrópəlis) *n.* a fortified citadel at a high point in a Greek city **Acropolis** the hill citadel of Athens, site of the Parthenon and Erechtheum [fr. Gk *akros*, highest+*polis*, city]

ac·ro·sin (ǽkrəsin) *n.* (*biol.*) enzyme involved in breaking down proteins to penetrate protective layers of an ovum

a·cross (əkrós,əkrós) **1.** *adv.* crosswise, *folded twice across* ‖ from side to side, *they swam across twice* ‖ to or on the other side, *to go across by ferry* **2.** *prep.* on the other side of, *the house across the street* ‖ from one side to the other side of, *the cable goes across the river* **to come across** to meet or find by chance ‖ (*pop.*) to pay out money ‖ (*pop.*) to give out information **to get across** (*someone*) (*Br.*, *pop.*) to irritate (someone)

a·cross-the-board (əkrósðəbórd, əkrósðəbórd, əkrósðəbourd, əkrósðəbóurd) *adj.* (of a wager) covering the chances that the horse bet on will win, place or show ‖ (of an industrial award etc.) having general application

a·cros·tic (əkróstik, əkróstik) *n.* a composition, usually in verse, in which the initial, final or other prearranged letters in each line when taken together spell out a word [fr. L. *acrostichis* fr. Gk]

ac·ro·ter (ǽkrətər) *n.* (*archit.*) a pedestal placed above the lower corners or apex of a pediment to receive a statue or other ornament [F. *acrotère* fr. L. fr. Gk]

a·cryl·ic (əkrilik) **1.** *adj.* of or relating to acrylic acid, acrylic fiber or acrylic resin **2.** *n.* acrylic resin ‖ acrylic fiber [fr. ACROLEIN]

acrylic acid a colorless, corrosive liquid obtained by oxidation from acrolein

acrylic fiber any of various synthetic fibers obtained by polymerization of acrylonitrile

acrylic resin any of various thermoplastic resins obtained by the polymerization of the esters of amides of acrylic acid or methacrylic acid

ac·ry·lo·ni·trile (ækrəlounáitril, ækrəlounáitri:l, ækrəlounáitrail) *n.* a poisonous, colorless, flammable liquid, $CH_2=CHCN$, used in the polymerization of plastics, textile fibers etc.

ac·si·mat·ic (æksimǽtik) (*acronym*) for Chief of Staff for Intelligence, computer language, storage-and-retrieval system used by the office

act (ækt) *n.* a deed ‖ the doing of a deed, *caught in the act* ‖ one of the main divisions of a play ‖ a feature in a variety show, circus etc. ‖ a law passed by a legislative body [F. *acte*]

act *v.t.* to perform (a play or a part in a play) ‖ to play the part of, *stop acting the fool* ‖ *v.i.* to behave in a certain way, *to act wisely* ‖ to fulfil a particular function, *to act as arbitrator* ‖ to intervene effectively, *the police acted quickly to prevent his escape* ‖ to produce an effect, *the acid acts on the metal* **to act for** to represent with full authority [fr. L. *agere* (*actus*), to do]

Ac·tae·on (æktí:ən) (*Gk mythol.*) a hunter who surprised Artemis bathing. He was punished by being changed into a stag, and was killed by his own hounds

ACTH a pituitary hormone which stimulates the cortex of the suprarenal gland [A(DRENO)C(ORTICO)T(ROPIC)H(ORMONE)]

act·ing (ǽktiŋ) **1.** *adj.* doing temporary duty for someone else, *the acting mayor* **2.** *n.* the art of performing in plays or films ‖ this as a profession

acting copy a copy of a play used by the actors showing cuts, producer's directions, cues etc.

ac·tin·i·a (æktíni:ə) *pl.* **ac·tin·i·ae** (æktíni:i:), **ac·tin·i·as** *n.* a sea anemone [Mod. L. fr. Gk *aktis* (*aktinos*), a ray]

ac·tin·ic (æktínik) *adj.* possessing photochemical properties [fr. Gk *aktis* (*aktinos*), a ray]

actinic rays electromagnetic radiations capable of producing photochemical changes and including infrared, ultraviolet and X rays as well as visible light

ac·ti·nide (ǽktinaid) *n.* a radioactive element with an atomic number in the series from 89–103

ac·ti·nide series (ǽktinaid) a series of radioactive elements starting at actinium (at. no. 89) and continuing to uranium (92) and the transuranic elements. There are analogies with the lanthanum or rare-earth series (*PERIODIC TABLE*) [fr. Mod. L. fr. Gk *aktin-*. ray]

ac·tin·i·um (æktíni:əm) *n.* a radioactive element (symbol Ac at no. 89 mass of isotope of longest known half-life 227). It occurs in uranium ores and can be manufactured from radium by transmutation in nuclear reactors [fr. Gk *aktis* (*aktinos*), a ray]

ac·ti·nom·e·ter (æktinómitər) *n.* (*phys.*) instrument for measuring intensity of radiation by measuring the fluorescence produced by it

ac·ti·no·mor·phic (æktinoumórfik) *adj.* radially symmetrical (cf. ZYGOMORPHIC) [fr. Gk *aktis* (*aktinos*), ray+*morphé*, shape]

ac·ti·no·my·cete (æktənoumaisi:t, æktənoumáisi:t) *n.* any of various aerobic or anaerobic bacteria of fam. *Actinomycetaceae*, some of which are pathenogenic for men and animals [ult. fr. Gk *aktis* (*aktinos*), ray+*mukēs*, fungus]

ac·ti·non (ǽktənɒn) *n.* (*chem.*) an inert gaseous radioactive isotope of radon (symbol An, at. no. 86, half-life 3.92 secs) [fr. ACTINIUM]

ac·ti·no·spec·to·cin (æktinouspéktousin) *n.* broad-spectrum antibiotic drug obtained from soil fungus, used in treating penicillin-resistant venereal diseases

ACTION (ǽkʃən) an independent U.S. government agency that administers such voluntary programs as the Peace Corps, VISTA (Volunteers in Service to America), the Senior Companion Program, the Foster Grandparent Program, University Year for Action, and others. The Peace Corps, an autonomous agency within ACTION, was created in 1961 by Pres. Kennedy. Volunteers spend 2 years in a foreign country, working in agriculture, rural development, health, and education. VISTA is the domestic counterpart of the Peace Corps

ac·tion (ǽkʃən) *n.* the process of doing, acting ‖ something done, a deed ‖ effective intervention, *his prompt action prevented an accident* ‖ the working of one thing on another, *the action of an acid on a metal* ‖ enterprise, deeds as compared with words, *a man of action* ‖ the operating mechanism of a piano, typewriter, pump, gun etc. ‖ a bodily movement performed repeatedly, *leg action* ‖ the series of events in a play or novel, *the action takes place in Europe* ‖ (*law*) a proceeding in a court of law where someone seeks to enforce his rights ‖ combat in war, *killed in action* ‖ (*horol.*) the functioning of the escapement in the movement of a timepiece **to take action** to begin to be effective ‖ (*pop.*) goings on, *where the action is* ‖ to initiate practical measures **ác·tion·a·ble** *adj.* giving ground for an action at law **ác·tion·a·bly** *adv.* [F.]

action of trover *TROVER*

action painting *ABSTRACT EXPRESSIONISM*

Ac·ti·um (ǽkti:əm) a promontory in N.W. Greece, near which the fleet of Octavian (*AUGUSTUS*) won a decisive victory over the forces of Antony and Cleopatra in 31 B.C.

ac·ti·vate (ǽktiveit) *pres. part.* **ac·ti·vat·ing** *past* and *past part.* **ac·ti·vat·ed** *v.t.* to make particularly active, esp. by chemical reaction

activated carbon carbon from which hydrocarbons have been removed to increase its powers of adsorption

activated sludge sewage aerated and used to hasten the decomposition of raw sewage by bacterial action

ac·ti·va·tion (æktivéiʃən) *n.* the act or process of activating

activation analysis 1. (*nuclear phys.*) technique for identifying and measuring chemical elements by measuring radiation emitted after exposure to radioactivity *Cf* NEUTRON ACTIVATION ANALYSIS **2.** (*electr.*) treatment of an electron tube to increase emissions. **3.** (*automotives*) addition of water to a battery to make it active

ac·ti·va·tor (ǽktiveitər) *n.* a substance which activates

ac·tive (ǽktiv) *adj.* busy, energetic, *active in local politics* ‖ (of a volcano) erupting from time to time ‖ (*commerce*) productive, bearing interest, *active assets* ‖ (*gram.*) descriptive of a voice or form of the verb which shows the subject as performer of the action of the verb (cf. PASSIVE) ‖ in or of the active voice [F. *actif*]

active duty the full-time service of members of the armed forces who are not reserves and not retired

active homing (*mil.*) homing device in a missile with capability of receiving energy reflected from a target and illuminating the target

active homing guidance (*mil.*) a system of homing guidance in which both the source for illuminating the target and the receiver for detecting the energy reflected from the target as the result of illuminating the target are carried within the missile

active list a roll of service officers available for active service

active mass the concentration (usually expressed in moles per liter) of a reacting substance .

active material (*nuclear phys.*) material capable of supporting a fission chain reaction, e.g., plutonium, and certain isotopes of uranium

active service active duty

active transport (*chem.*) movement of a substance across a membrane in a nonnormal direction, e.g., from a low concentration to a higher concentration

ac·tiv·ism (ǽktivizəm) *n.* a theory that calls for militant propaganda action by individuals or the practice (esp. political) of such action

ac·tiv·ist (ǽktivist) *n.* someone who takes militant action in the service of a party or doctrine

ac·tiv·i·ty (æktíviti:) *pl.* **ac·tiv·i·ties** *n.* the state of being active ‖ capacity for being active ‖ (*chem.*) readiness of a substance to undergo chemical change, depending on the degree of instability of its atomic or molecular structure ‖ the apparent or thermodynamic concentration of a substance ‖ (*pl.*) ways in which people use their energies, *social and cultural activities* [F. *activité*]

activity ratio (*computer*) fraction of stored records that are processed or updated

act of God (*law*) an accident or catastrophe due to natural causes (e.g. an earthquake, hurricane) which could not be controlled

Act of Settlement *SETTLEMENT, ACT OF*

Act of Supremacy *SUPREMACY, ACT OF*

Act of Union *UNION, ACT OF*

Ac·ton (ǽktən), John Emerich Edward Dalberg, 1st Baron Acton (1834–1902), British historian. His posthumously published works include 'Lectures on Modern History' and 'Lectures on the French Revolution'

ac·tor (ǽktər) *n.* a man who performs a part in a play or film [L.=doer]

ac·tress (ǽktris) *n.* a woman actor

Acts of the Apostles the fifth book in the New Testament. It is variously dated from 62 A.D. to the end of the 1st c. Its authorship is ascribed to St Luke. Together with his gospel it tells the story of the Christian movement from its humble origins in Galilee to its establishment in Rome as a universal Church

ac·tu·al (ǽktʃu:əl) *adj.* existing as a fact of experience, real as opposed to potential [F. *actuel*]

actual ground zero the point on the surface of the earth at, or vertically below, or above, the center of an actual nuclear detonation. abbr AGZ

ac·tu·al·i·ty (æktʃu:ǽliti:) *pl.* **ac·tu·al·i·ties** *n.* reality ‖ (*pl.*) realities, things having existence [fr. M.L. *actualitas* (*actualitatis*)]

ac·tu·al·i·za·tion (æktʃu:əlizéiʃən) *n.* the act or process of actualizing

ac·tu·al·ize (ǽktʃu:əlaiz) *pres. part.* **ac·tu·al·iz·ing** *past* and *past part.* **ac·tu·al·ized** *v.t.* to make actual ‖ *v.i.* to become actual

ac·tu·al·ly (ǽktʃu:əli:) *adv.* in fact, really, *he pretended to be deaf but actually he was not* ‖ strange as it may seem, *he actually sells those terrible paintings* ‖ at this moment, *the government actually in office*

ac·tu·ar·i·al (æktʃu:éəri:əl) *adj.* of an actuary or his activity

ac·tu·ar·y (ǽktʃu:əri:) *pl.* **ac·tu·ar·ies** *n.* a statistician who estimates risks and probabilities, particularly in insurance, lotteries etc. [fr. L. *actuarius*, clerk]

ac·tu·ate (ǽktʃu:eit) *pres. part.* **ac·tu·at·ing** *past* and *past part.* **ac·tu·at·ed** *v.t.* to put into action or motion, *this switch actuates the mechanism* ‖ to motivate the actions of (a person). *actuated by envy* **ac·tu·á·tion** *n.* [fr. M.L. *actuare* (*actuatus*)]

a·cu·i·ty (əkjú:iti:) *n.* shrewdness, acuteness of perception [F. *acuité*]

CONCISE PRONUNCIATION KEY: **(a)** æ, c*a*t; ɑ, c*a*r; ɔ f*aw*n; ei, sn*a*ke. **(e)** e, h*e*n; i:, sh*ee*p; iə, d*ee*r; ɛə, b*ea*r. **(i)** i, f*i*sh; ai, t*i*ger; ə:, b*i*rd. **(o)** o, *o*x; au, c*ow*; ou, g*oa*t; u, p*oo*r; ɔi, r*oy*al. **(u)** ʌ, d*u*ck; u, b*u*ll; u:, g*oo*se; ə, b*a*cillus; ju:, c*u*be. x, lo*ch*; θ, *th*ink; ð, bo*th*er; z, *Z*en; ʒ, corsa*g*e; dʒ, sava*g*e; ŋ, orangutan*g*; j, *y*ak; ʃ, *fi*sh; tʃ, fe*tch*; 'l, rab*ble*; 'n, red*den*. Complete pronunciation key appears inside front cover.

a·cu·le·ate (əkjúːliːit,ˌəkjúːliːeit) *adj.* of or characterized by an aculeus or aculei

a·cu·le·us (əkjúːliːəs) *pl.* **a·cu·le·i** (əkjúːliːai) *n.* a prickle growing from bark, e.g. of a rose ‖ (*zool.*) a sting or hairlike projection [L.]

a·cu·men (əkjúːmən, ækjumən) *n.* keen insight or perceptiveness, *financial acumen* [L.]

a·cu·mi·nate (əkjúːmənit) *adj.* (*biol.*) pointed, tapering to a point [fr. L. *acumisnare* (*acuminatus*), to come to a point]

A·cu·ña (akúːnja), Manuel (1849–73), Mexican romantic poet, the author of 'Nocturno'

ac·u·punc·ture (ˈækjupʌŋktʃər) *n.* a therapeutic practice of Chinese origin consisting in the introduction of fine needles at certain points in the skin along vital 'lines of force', sometimes far removed from the point where pain is suffered [fr. L. *acus*, a needle+*punctura*, a pricking]

a·cute (əkjúːt) *adj.* penetrating, perceptive, *an acute observer* ‖ severe, sharp, *acute pain* ‖ crucial, critical, *an acute shortage* ‖ (of the senses) keen, *acute hearing* ‖ marked with an acute accent ‖ (*med.*) beginning suddenly, developing rapidly and not prolonged (cf. CHRONIC) [fr. L. *acuere* (*acutus*), to sharpen]

acute accent a mark (´) used to show vowel quality (as in 'René'), length, stress, or tone or pitch (e.g. in Chinese)

acute angle an angle less than 90°

acute radiation dose total ionizing radiation dose received at one time and over a period so short that biological recovery cannot occur

ACV 1. (*acronym*) for air-cushion vehicle 2. (*acronym*) for actual cash value

a·cy·clic (eisáiklik, eisíklik) *adj.* not cyclic, not in cycles ‖ (*chem.*) having an open-chain structure

a·cy·clo·vir (əsáiklouviːr) *n.* (*pharm.*) experimental drug believed to prevent cold sores and genital herpes infections in transplant patients *Cf* HERPES TYPE II

ad (æd) *n.* (*pop.*) an advertisement

ad- (æd) *prefix* to, towards. It usually changes to 'ac-' before c, k, q, to 'af-' before f, to 'ag-' before g, to 'al-' before l, to 'ap-' before p, to 'as-' before s, to 'at-' before t [ult. fr. L.]

A.D. *ANNO DOMINI

A·da (*computer, mil.*) Department of Defense high-order computer language using recognizable words and phrases in instructions and responses

ad·age (ædidʒ) *n.* an ancient piece of popular wisdom, a saw or saying [F.]

a·da·gio (ədáːdʒou) 1. *adv.* and *adj.* (*mus.*) in slow tempo (as an instruction for the execution of a musical piece) 2. *n.* a slow piece or a slow movement [Ital.]

Ad·am (ædəm), Robert (1728–92), Scottish architect. The details of his work were borrowed from Classical and Italian Renaissance architecture: his gift was in combining them into a graceful whole, often of great extent. He was assisted by his brother James (1730–94). The search for harmony in all the elements of a work led him to design furniture and internal fittings as well. He set out his principles in the 'Ruins of the Palace of the Emperor Diocletian at Spalato' (1764) and The Works in Architecture' (1773)

Ad·am (ædəm) *n.* the first man (*ADAM AND EVE) **not to know someone from Adam** (emphatic expression) not to know a person at all [Heb. *ádám*, man]

Adam and Eve names given to the first pair of human beings in Jewish-Christian tradition (Genesis 1, 1 - ii, 3 and ii,4 - iv,2)

ad·a·mant (ædəmənt) 1. *n.* a substance of utmost hardness ‖ (*mythol.*) unbreakable stone 2. *adj.* (of a person), unyielding **ad·a·man·tine** (ædəmæntain, ædəmænti:n) *adj.* [O.F. *adamaunt*]

A·da·ma·wa (ædəmáwə) a hilly region (average height 2,000 ft) of the Sudan, partly in Nigeria, partly in Cameroun: cattte, palm oil, bananas

Adams (ædəmz), Abigail (1744–1818), wife of John Adams, the second U.S. president, and mother of John Quincy Adams, the sixth president. Born Abigail Smith, she is credited with influencing her husband's distinguished career. Her correspondence demonstrates her lively intelligence and strong opinions, including a proposal to her husband that the new government guarantee women's rights

Adams, Ansel (1902–84), U.S. photographer known for his poetic black and white landscape photographs of the American West. With Imogen Cunningham, Edward Weston, and others, he founded the influential Group F/64. His collections included 'My Camera in Yosemite Valley' (1949), 'Portfolio Two: The National Parks' (1950), and 'The Portfolios of Ansel Adams' (1977)

A·dams (ædəmz), Charles Francis (1807–86), U.S. diplomatist, son of John Quincy Adams and grandson of John Adams. He served as minister to Great Britain in the Lincoln administration

Adams, Sir Grantley Herbert (1898–1971), premier of Barbados (1954–8) and prime minister of the Federation of the West Indies (1958–62)

Adams, Henry Brooks (1838–1918), American historian, author of 'History of the United States from 1801 to 1817' (1889–91), of works on the European Middle Ages, and of 'The Education of Henry Adams' (privately printed 1907, published 1918)

Adams, John (1735–1826), the first vice-president (1789–97) and the second president (1797–1801) of the U.S.A. He was a leader of American opposition to British rule prior to the Revolutionary War and a chief negotiator of the Treaty of Paris (1783). He served (1785–8) as American ambassador to Britain. Although a Federalist he interceded between the Hamiltonians and Jeffersonians and, by conciliation, prevented war with France over the X-Y-Z Affair

Adams, John Couch (1819–92), British astronomer who predicted the existence and position of the planet Neptune by calculations on irregularities in the orbit of Uranus

Adams, John Quincy (1767–1848), sixth president (1825–9) of the U.S.A., a Democratic Republican, son of John Adams. As secretary of state (1817–25) under President Monroe he drew up the Monroe Doctrine. He was unjustly accused by the Jacksonians of corruption in his appointment of Henry Clay, who had lent him key support in the disputed presidential contest, as his secretary of state. As a result his administration failed to implement his broad reform program

Adams, Samuel (1722–1803), American revolutionary, organizer of the Boston Tea Party and a signatory of the Declaration of Independence (1776)

Adam's apple the projection of the thyroid cartilage, prominent esp. in a man

Adam's Bridge the Bridge of Rama, a chain of rocks and sandbanks between Sri Lanka and India. According to legend it is the remains of a causeway built by Rama so that his army could cross to Ceylon and rescue his wife Sita

Adam's Peak a conical mountain (7,365 ft) on the southwest edge of the Kandyan Hills, Sri Lanka, a place of pilgrimage. The excavation on the summit is (to Buddhists) a footprint of the Buddha or (to Moslems) of Adam, who stood there for a thousand years after being driven from Paradise

A·da·na (ædənə) a town (pop. 562,200) in S. Turkey: tobacco, textiles

a·dapt (ədǽpt) *v.t.* to put (oneself) in harmony with changed circumstances, *to adapt oneself to a lower standard of living* ‖ to make more suitable by altering, *to adapt a play for broadcasting* **a·dapt·a·bil·i·ty** *n.* **a·dápt·a·ble** *adj.* [F. *adapter*]

ADAPT (*computer*) a computer compiler language designed by Computer Science Corporation for IBM 1401

ad·ap·ta·tion (ædæptéiʃən) *n.* the act or process of adapting ‖ the condition of being adapted ‖ (*physiol.*) the power of the eye to adjust to variations in light ‖ (*biol.*) an inherited or acquired structure or function serving to fit a plant or animal for its environment ‖ something adapted, *a screen adaptation of a play* [F.]

a·dapt·er (ədæptər) *n.* a device for connecting two pieces of apparatus, esp. in electrical equipment

a·dap·tive (ədǽptiv) *adj.* tending or able to adapt ‖ showing adaptation

adaptive control system device that monitors its own performance and automatically adjusts itself to perform within specified parameters

adaptive filter (*electr.*) a device that automatically responds to specified signals that may be buried in noise, used to extend the capability of radar-sonar, and electromagnetic reconnaissance

ADAR (*mil. acronym*) for advanced design array radar system used to locate and identify enemy intercontinental ballistic missiles

ad·con·duc·tor cath·ode (ædkəndʌktər) (*electr.*) device used in gas lasers that emits electrons from absorbed alkali metal atoms

add (æd) *v.t.* to join, unite or combine (something) with something else so as to increase in size, number or quantity, or so as to contribute a new or further quality, idea, ingredient etc., *add your letters to mine, this book adds nothing to what is already known on the subject* ‖ to say or write (something) further, *as he left he added 'I won't be long'* ‖ to add up, *add 6 and 4* ‖ *v.i.* to do addition **to add in** to include, *add this in with the rest* **to add to** to increase, *losing the rope added to our difficulties* **to add up** to find the sum of (two or more numbers) ‖ (*Br.*) to do addition ‖ to make sense, bear close inspection, *his story doesn't add up* ‖ (with 'to') to reach a specified total [fr. L. *addere*, to add]

Ad·dams (ædəmz), Jane (1860–1935), U.S. social reformer, suffragette and author. She founded (1889) Hull House in Chicago, Ill., a group of social reformers who initiated pioneer welfare laws

ad·dax (ædæks) *n. Oryx nasomaculata*, a large antelope with twisted horns, allied to the gnu, native to Arabia and N. Africa [L.]

ad·ded-val·ue tax (ædədvælju:) *n.* *VALUE-ADDED TAX

ad·dend (ædend, ədénd) *n.* (*math.*) a quantity added to another in forming a sum [shortening of ADDENDUM]

ad·den·dum (adéndəm) *pl.* **ad·den·da** (ədéndə) *n.* something to be added ‖ a supplementary part or appendix of a book [L]

ad·der (ædər) *n. Vipera berus*, a small poisonous snake common in Europe ‖ one of several small harmless snakes, e.g. the hognose snake ‖ one of several poisonous snakes, e.g. the puff adder of Africa or the krait of India ‖ an electronic circuit that combines two or more signals to amplify the output signal; used in color television for combining chrominance and luminance [O.E. *naedre*, a snake (*a nadder* being separated as *an adder*)]

ad·der's-tongue (ædərztʌŋ) *n.* a member of *Ophioglossum*, a genus of small spiked ferns ‖ any of various spiked plants resembling these

ad·der-sub·tract·or (ædərsʌbtræktər) *n.* (*electr.*) an electronic circuit that outputs the sum of, or the difference between, the signal input of two signals in accordance with a control signal

ad·dict (ədíkt) 1. *v.t.* to habituate, esp. **to be** (or **become**) **addicted to** to have given oneself up to (a practice or habit, usually bad) and to become unduly dependent upon (it) 2. (ædikt) *n.* a person addicted to something harmful, usually a drug ‖ (*loosely*) someone inordinately fond of something not harmful, *a jazz addict* [fr. L. *addicere* (*addictus*), to assign, devote]

ad·dic·tion (ədíkʃən) *n.* the state of being addicted [fr. L. *addictio* (*addictionis*)]

ad·dic·tive (ədíktiv) *adj.* causing addiction [ADDICT]

adding machine a keyboard machine which adds numbers rapidly ‖ a calculating machine

Ad·ding·ton (ædiŋtən) *SIDMOUTH

Ad·dis A·ba·ba (ædisæbəbə) the capital (pop. 1,277,159) of Ethiopia, at 8,000 ft, 480 miles from the Gulf of Aden: coffee, tobacco, tanning, flour milling

Ad·di·son (ædisən), Joseph (1672–1719), English essayist, one of the principal figures in Augustan literature. With Richard Steele he founded 'The Spectator' (1711–14) and wrote most of its essays. Together they developed a literary journalism which formed the tastes and ideals of an educated urban upper-middle-class public. His tragedy 'Cato' (1713) was popular in his day

Addison's anemia, esp. *Br.* **Addison's anaemia** (*med.*) pernicious anemia (*ANEMIA, *DIET) [after Thomas *Addison* (1793–1860), British doctor]

Addison's disease (*med.*) a disease of the suprarenal glands (*ADRENAL), causing great weakness and a brown discoloration of the skin [after Dr. Thomas *Addison*]

ad·di·tion (ədíʃən) *n.* the process of adding ‖ an arithmetic sum ‖ an increase, something extra **in addition to** as well as **ad·dí·tion·al** *adj.* extra [F.]

ad·di·tion·al·i·ty (ədiʃənæliti:) *n.* the principle whereby a country granted U.S. aid funds is required to spend all or part of the funds on the purchase of U.S. goods

---

CONCISE PRONUNCIATION KEY: **(a)** æ, c*a*t; a, c*a*r; ɔ f*aw*n; ei, sn*a*ke. **(e)** e, h*e*n; iː, sh*ee*p; iə, d*ee*r; ɛə, b*ea*r. **(i)** i, f*i*sh; ai, t*i*ger; əː, b*i*rd. **(o)** o, *o*x; au, c*ow*; ou, g*oa*t; u, p*oo*r; ɔi, r*oy*al. **(u)** ʌ, d*u*ck; u, b*u*ll; uː, g*oo*se; ə, b*a*cillus; juː, c*u*be. x, lo*ch*; θ, *th*ink; ð, bo*th*er; z, *Z*en; ʒ, corsa*g*e; dʒ, sava*g*e; ŋ, orangutan*g*; j, *y*ak; ʃ, *fi*sh; tʃ, fet*ch*; 'l, rabb*le*; 'n, red*den*. Complete pronunciation key appears inside front cover.

ad·di·tive (ǽditiv) *n.* something added to a food product to give it color, make it keep etc. ‖ something added to a substance (e.g. paint) to give it a desired quality [fr. L. *additivus*]

additive identity (*math.*) unit added to a mathematical combination merely to identify it, e.g., zero in a group

additive inverse (*math.*) number that, added to another number, equals zero, e.g., −9 added to +9

additive printed circuit (*electr.*) input that integrates a circuit by depositing the copper conductor pattern on the board vs. etching out the excess

ad·dle (ǽd'l) 1. *adj.* (of an egg) rotten, or not producing a chicken ‖ (in compounds) confused, muddled 2. *v. pres. part.* **ad·dling** *past* and *past part.* **ad·dled** *v.t.* to muddle, confuse ‖ *v.i.* (of eggs) to go bad [O.E. *adela*, mud]

ad·dress (ədrés) 1. *v.t.* to make a speech or deliver a sermon to ‖ to speak or write formally to ‖ to write the destination on (a letter, parcel etc.) ‖ (with 'to') to apply oneself to (a task), to turn to, *he then addressed himself to the main criticism* 2. (ədrés, ǽdres) *n.* the place where a person lives, *permanent address* or can be reached by letter, *forwarding address* ‖ the written direction on a letter, parcel etc. ‖ a speech or sermon ‖ skill, adroitness ‖ (*old-fash.*) a way of speaking and behaving, *a man of pleasing address* **ad·dress·ee** (ədresí:) *n.* the person to whom a letter, parcel etc. is addressed [F. *adresser*]

ad·dress·able (ədrésibəl) *adj.* (*computer*) data that can be located in the memory storage

'Address of 1848' an address signed (1848) by 48 U.S. Congressmen, condemning northern obstruction in the return of fugitive slaves and censuring the prohibition of slavery in the new territories. It demonstrated the Union's deepening division over the slavery question

Ad·dres·so·graph (ədrésəgræf, ədréssəgrɑf) *n.* a business machine which prints addresses from metal stencils on to envelopes, circulars etc. [a trademark fr. ADDRESS+Gk *graphein*, to write]

ad·duce (ədú:s, ədjú:s) *pres. part.* **ad·duc·ing** *past* and *past part.* **ad·duced** *v.t.* to bring forward (as proof or example) **ad·duc·a·ble** *adj.* [fr. L. *adducere*, to lead toward]

ad·du·cent (ədú:sənt, ədjú:sənt) *adj.* (*physiol.*, of a muscle) leading toward a given point (opp. ABDUCENT) [fr. L. *adducens* (*adducentis*) fr. *adducere*, to lead toward]

ad·du·ci·ble (ədú:səb'l, ədjú:səb'l) *adj.* able to be adduced

ad·duct (ədʌ́kt) *v.t.* (*physiol.*) to draw together (opp. ABDUCT) [fr. L. *adducere* (*adductus*), to lead toward]

ad·duc·tion (ədʌ́kʃən) *n.* (*physiol.*) the action of adducting, a drawing toward a median line or another part [F.]

ad·duc·tive (adʌ́ktiv) *adj.* bringing forward or to

Ad·e·laide (ǽdəleid) the capital (pop. 899,300) of S. Australia, on the Torrens River: woolen, leather, iron and earthenware goods. Port Adelaide, 7 miles away, exports wheat, wool and copper ore. University (1874)

A·dé·lie Land (ǽdəli:lænd) *FRENCH SOUTHERN AND ANTARCTIC TERRITORIES

A·den (éid'n, ɑ́d'n) the capital (pop. 264,000) of the People's Democratic Republic of Yemen, near the entrance to the Red Sea. It is an oil-refining and oil-bunkering port and an important entrepôt ‖ (*hist.*) a British-protected State (formerly colony, pop. 200,000) which was a member of the former Federation of South Arabia. Aden was controlled by Britain (1839–1967) (*YEMEN, PEOPLE'S DEMOCRATIC REPUBLIC OF)

A·de·nau·er (ɑ́dənauər), Konrad (1876–1967), chancellor of West Germany (1949–63). His firm Christian Democrat government allowed the West Germans to recover from Nazism and defeat in war, and ensured the economic prosperity and rearmament of his country

Aden, Gulf of a gulf (550 miles long, 300 miles wide) on the western arm of the Arabian Sea, lying on the Mediterranean–Indian Ocean shipping lane. Chief ports: Aden and Mukalla on the north coast, Djibouti and Berbera on the south coast

ad·e·nine (ǽd'nain, ǽdəni:n) *n.* a purine base ($C_5H_5N_5$) or 6-amino-purine, obtained by the hydrolysis of deoxyribonucleic acid [fr. Gk *adēn*, gland]

ad·e·noid (ǽd'nɔid) *adj.* of or resembling a lymphoid tissue **ad·e·noid·al** *adj.* of or relating to the adenoids ‖ having enlarged adenoids ‖ (of the voice) unpleasantly nasal in quality **ad·e·noids** *pl. n.* a soft mass of lymphoid tissue at the back of the nose and throat which, when enlarged, impedes breathing [fr. Gk *adēn*, a gland+*eidos*, form]

ad·e·no·ma (æd'nóumə) *pl.* **ad·e·no·ma·ta** (æd'nóumətə), **ad·e·no·mas** *n.* (*med.*) a benign tumor composed of glandular tissue [fr. Gk *adēn*, gland]

a·den·o·sine (ədénəsi:n, ədénəsin) *n.* an organic compound, $C_{10}H_{13}N_5O_4$, obtained by partial hydrolysis of ribonucleic acid [irregular blending of ADENINE and RIBOSE]

ad·e·no·vi·rus (ædinouváirəs) *n.* 1. (*cytol.*) one of viruses found in animals containing DNA; causative of respiratory diseases, possibly of malignant tumors 2. (*med.*) group of medium-size DNA viruses that affect mucous membranes of nose, eyes, and lungs **also** APC virus

ad·e·nyl cylase (ǽdənil) (*cytol.*) enzyme located in surface of cell that produces cyclic ampase from adenosine triphosphate (ATP)

ad·ept (ədépt) 1. *adj.* clever, particularly proficient 2. *n.* (ǽdept, ədépt) someone thoroughly clever or skilled in anything, an expert [fr. L. *adipisci* (*adeptus*), to obtain (skill)]

ad·e·qua·cy (ǽdikwəsi:) *n.* the state of being adequate

ad·e·quate (ǽdikwit) *adj.* equal to or sufficient for a special requirement [fr. L. *adaequare* (*adaequatus*), to make equal]

ADES (*computer*) acronym for automatic digital encoding system, language in use by United States Naval Ordnance Laboratory on IBM 704 System —**ADES II** *language* for use in IBM 650

ad·here (ædhíər) *pres. part.* **ad·her·ing** *past* and *past part.* **ad·hered** *v.i.* to cling, cleave, stick fast (to a thing, a person or an idea) [F. *adhérer*]

ad·her·ence (ædhíərəns) *n.* the action of adhering, attachment [F.]

ad·her·ent (ædhíərənt) 1. *adj.* clinging, sticking 2. *n.* a follower, supporter [F.]

ad·he·sion (ædhí:ʒən) *n.* the act or condition of adhering ‖ (*phys.*) intermolecular attraction holding together surfaces in contact (cf. COHESION) ‖ (*med.*) an abnormal union of surfaces, caused by inflammation [F.]

ad·he·sive (ædhí:siv) 1. *adj.* sticky, able to stick fast 2. *n.* a substance used to stick two surfaces together [F. *adhésif*]

adhesive tape tape coated on one side with a sticky substance, used for holding medical dressings in place. It also has many industrial uses

ad hoc (ædhók) exclusively for some understood special purpose, *an ad hoc committee will organize the appeal* [L.=toward this]

ad ho·mi·nem (ædhóminem) (esp. in phrase) **argument ad hominem** an argument directed to the personality, prejudices, previous words and actions etc. of an opponent, rather than an appeal to pure reason [L.=to the man]

ADI (*acronym*) for area of dominant influence, the geographic boundaries of television markets; *e.g.*, the New York City ADI includes 22 counties and 8.9% of all U.S. television households

a·di·a·bat·ic (eidaiəbǽtik, ædi:əbǽtik) 1. *adj.* (*phys.*) of a physical change during which no heat enters or leaves the system 2. *n.* (*phys.*) a curve obtained by plotting pressure against volume, or temperature against entropy, for a change taking place adiabatically **a·di·a·bát·i·cal·ly** *adv.* [fr. Gk *adiabatos*, impassable]

adiabatic expansion (*phys.*) expansion without loss or gain of heat

a·di·a·bet·ic (eidaiəbétik) *adj.* (*phys.*) without change in heat content

a·dieu (ədú:, ədjú:) *pl.* **a·dieus, a·dieux** (ədú:z, ədjú:z) 1. *interj.* good-bye, farewell 2. *n.* a farewell ‖ a leave-taking [F.]

A·di·ge (ɑ́di:dʒe) Italy's second largest river (220 miles). It rises in the Tyrol and runs into the Adriatic immediately north of the Po

ad in·fi·ni·tum (ædinfináitəm) *adv.* forever,or as if forever [L.]

ad·i·pose (ǽdipous) 1. *adj.* fatty, pertaining to animal fat 2. *n.* animal fat **ad·i·pos·i·ty** (ædipósəti) *n.* [fr. Mod. L. *adiposus* fr. *adeps*, lard]

Ad·i·ron·dack Mtns (ædəróndæk) a group of peaks in northeastern New York State (Mt Marcy 5,344 ft) where the Hudson and Mohawk Rivers rise

ADIS (*acronym*) for a data interchange system, communication system designed for Teletype Corporation

A display (*electr.*) the presentation on a radar oscilloscope with targets shown as vertical deflection lines

ad·ja·cen·cies (ədʒéiənsi:s) *n.* (*advertising*) announcements or programs preceding or following each other on a broadcasting station

ad·ja·cen·cy (ədʒéiənsi:) *pl.* **ad·ja·cen·cies** *n.* the condition of being adjacent ‖ an adjacent thing [fr. L.L. *adjacentia*]

ad·ja·cent (ədʒéisənt) *adj.* near, nearby ‖ next, bordering [fr. L. *adjacens* (*adjacentis*) fr. *adjacere*, to lie near]

adjacent angles two angles which have one side in common and the same vertex

ad·jec·ti·val (ædʒiktáivəl) *adj.* of the nature of an adjective ‖ of an adjective

ad·jec·tive (ǽdʒiktiv) *n.* (*gram.*) a part of speech used to qualify, define or limit a substantive [F. *adjectif*]

ad·join (ədʒɔ́in) *v.t.* to lie next to, be adjacent to ‖ *v.i.* to be immediately next to another [O.F. *ojoindre*]

ad·journ (ədʒɔ́:rn) *v.t.* to suspend, defer (a meeting etc.) with a view to later resumption ‖ *v.i.* to suspend or defer a meeting etc. ‖ to move to another place, *let's adjourn to the next room* **ad·journ·ment** *n.* [O.F. *ajorner*]

ad·judge (ədʒʌ́dʒ) *pres. part.* **ad·judg·ing** *past* and *past part.* **ad·judged** *v.t.* to judge or declare after careful consideration, *they adjudged him the winner* ‖ (*law*) to find, *adjudged guilty* ‖ (*law*) to award, *the estate was adjudged to the claimant* [O.F. *ajuger*]

ad·ju·di·cate (ədʒú:dikeit) *pres. part.* **ad·ju·di·cat·ing** *past* and *past part.* **ad·ju·di·cat·ed** *v.t.* to determine (an issue) judicially, *to adjudicate a claim for damages* ‖ *v.i.* to act as judge in a contest [fr. L. *adjudicare* (*adjudicatus*)]

ad·ju·di·ca·tion (ədʒu:dikéiʃən) *n.* the action of adjudicating ‖ (*law*) a judge's decision ‖ (*law*) a decree in bankruptcy that the bankrupt is insolvent [fr. L.L. *adjudicatio* (*adjudicationis*)]

ad·ju·di·ca·tive (ədʒú:dikeitiv) *adj.* pertaining to adjudication

ad·ju·di·ca·tor (ədʒú:dikeitər) *n.* a person who adjudicates

ad·junct (ǽdʒʌŋkt) *n.* something added or extra but subordinate, *knowledge of book production is a useful adjunct to authorship* ‖ (*gram.*) a word or phrase added to another with the purpose of qualifying or defining it ‖ (*logic*) a nonessential quality **ad·junc·tive** (ədʒʌ́ŋktiv) *adj.* [fr. L. *adjungere* (*adjunctus*), to join to]

ad·ju·ra·tion (ædʒuréiʃən) *n.* earnest command, entreaty

ad·jure (ədʒúər) *pres. part.* **ad·jur·ing** *past* and *past part.* **ad·jured** *v.t.* to charge (a person) to do something as though on oath, *he adjured him, on pain of death, to leave at once* ‖ (*rhet.*) to beseech [fr. L. *adjurare*, to swear (an oath)]

ad·just (ədʒʌ́st) *v.t.* to set right, make orderly ‖ to regulate for proper use ‖ to harmonize (differences of opinion) ‖ to adapt (oneself) **ad·jús·ter, ad·jús·tor** *n.* someone who, or something which adjusts (machines or equipment) **ad·júst·ment** *n.* the action of adjusting ‖ a settlement ‖ the means of adjusting an instrument [fr. 16th-c. F. *adjuster*]

ad·ju·tant (ǽdʒətənt) *n.* an army officer who assists a commanding officer in administration, correspondence etc. ‖ an assistant or helper in any capacity ‖ an adjutant bird [fr. L. *adjutans* (*adjutantis*) fr. *adjutare*, to help]

adjutant bird *Leptoptilus dubius*, a large stork found commonly in India

ad·ju·vant (ǽdʒəvənt) *n.* that which reinforces, assists or enhances the action of an ingredient or treatment [F.]

Ad·ler (ǽdlər), Alfred (1870–1937), Austrian psychologist and psychiatrist, and founder of the school of 'individual psychology', which sees the desire for power as the chief human driving force. He is best known for his concept of the 'inferiority complex'. His books include 'The Practice and Theory of Individual Psychology' (1924), 'Understanding Human Nature' (1927), 'The Pattern of Life' (1931)

Adler, Felix (1851–1933), a U.S. educator and founder of the Ethical Culture movement, which taught that an ethical reality existed independently of a personal God. His New York Society for Ethical Culture worked for child welfare, medical care for the poor, slum im-

---

CONCISE PRONUNCIATION KEY: **(a)** æ, c*a*t; ɑ, c*a*r; ɔ f*aw*n; ei, sn*a*ke. **(e)** e, h*e*n; i:, sh*ee*p; iə, d*ee*r; ɛə, b*ea*r. **(i)** i, f*i*sh; ai, t*i*ger; ə:, b*i*rd. **(o)** o, *o*x; au, c*ow*; ou, g*oa*t; u, p*oo*r; ɔi, r*oy*al. **(u)** ʌ, d*u*ck; u, b*u*ll; u:, g*oo*se; ə, b*a*cillus; ju:, c*u*be. x, lo*ch*; θ, *th*ink; δ, bo*th*er; z, *Z*en; ʒ, cor*s*age. dʒ, sava*g*e; ŋ, orangutan*g*; j, *y*ak; ʃ, *fi*sh; tʃ, fet*ch*; 'l, rabb*le*; 'n, redd*en*. Complete pronunciation key appears inside front cover.

provement, and labor relations. Adler also advocated free kindergartens and vocational training

Adler, Mortimer Jerome (1902–), U.S. philosopher and editor, an advocate of adult and general education by study of the great books of the Western world

ad-lib (ædlíb) *pres. part.* **ad-lib-bing** *past and past part.* **ad-libbed** *v.i.* to speak or perform without preparation || *v.t.* to improvise (a speech, performance etc.) **ad lib** *adv.* in unrestricted plenty [AD LIBITUM]

ad lib-i-tum (ædlíbitəm) (*mus., abbr.* ad lib) in whatever manner (esp. as regards tempo) the performer chooses || (*mus.,* of a pact) to be included or excluded as the performer chooses (cf. OBBLIGATO) [L.]

ad-mass (ædmæs) *n.* cultural system dominated by a drive to consume material goods; created by mass advertising media, originally by J. P. Priestly —**admass** *adj.*

ad-min-is-ter (ædmínistər) *v.t.* to manage, direct (business affairs, an estate etc.) || to serve out, dispense, *to administer the sacraments, to administer punishment* || to give, provide, *to administer relief aid* || to tender (the oath) to someone || *v.i.* to act as administrator [O. F. *aministrer*]

ad-min-is-tra-tion (ædministréifən) *n.* the act of administering || the art or practice of carrying out a policy in government, business or public affairs || the act of administering a sacrament, oath, remedy, punishment etc. || (*law*) management of a dead person's property **the Administration** the government of the day [fr. L. *administratio (administrationis)*]

ad-min-is-tra-tive (ædmínistreitiv, ædmínistrətiv) *adj.* concerned with administration [fr. L. *administrativus*]

administrative lie a law designed to satisfy a contingency, but left so toothless or ambiguous as to be unenforceable

ad-min-is-tra-tor (ædmínistreitər) *n.* someone who administers || (*law*) a person appointed by a law court to take charge of an estate etc. [L.]

ad-mi-ra-ble (ædmərəb'l) *adj.* worthy of admiration || excellent **ád-mi-ra-bly** *adv.* [F.]

ad-mi-ral (ædmərəl) *n.* the naval rank above vice-admiral and below (*Am.*) fleet admiral or (*Br.*) admiral of the fleet || the commander of a fleet || the ship in which the admiral sails, the flagship [O.F. *amiral* fr. Arab. *amir-al-*, commander (of) the]

admiral of the fleet the highest rank of officer in the British Royal Navy, ranking immediately above an admiral

ad-mi-ral-ty (ædmərəlti:) *n.* (*old-fash.*) the office of admiral || (*Br.*) that part of a government which controls naval administration **the Ad-mi-ral-ty** the headquarters of the British naval administration [O.F. *admiralté*]

Admiralty Islands a group of 40 volcanic and coral islands (pop. 27,600) in Bismarck Archipelago, north of New Guinea, administered by Australia as part of the trust territory of New Guinea. An important Japanese airbase during the 2nd world war, it was captured (1944) by Allied troops

ad-mi-ra-tion (ædməréifən) *n.* delighted contemplation of something worthy or beautiful || esteem, respect || a person or thing arousing such feelings [F.]

ad-mire (ædmáiər) *pres. part.* **ad-mir-ing** *past and past part.* **ad-mired** *v.t.* to contemplate or consider with pleasure or respect || to express admiration for **ad-mir-er** *n.* someone who admires || (*old-fash.*) a lover [F. *admirer*]

ad-mis-si-bil-i-ty (ædmisəbíliti:) *n.* the state or quality of being admissible

ad-mis-si-ble (ædmísəb'l) *adj.* (of ideas or propositions) that may be allowed or conceded || able to be admitted to a post or office || (*law*) allowable as evidence or judicial proof **ad-mís-si-bly** *adv.*

ad-mis-sion (ædmíʃən) *n.* the action of admitting, of giving access or entrance || the price of admission || entry into an office or status, *admission to the bar* || acknowledgment of the truth of a fact or statement [fr. L. *admissio (admissionis)*]

ad-mis-sive (ædmísiv) *adj.* tending to admit, allowing admission or inclusion [fr. L. *admissivus*]

ad-mit (ædmít) *pres. part.* **ad-mit-ting** *past and past part.* **ad-mit-ted** *v.t.* to allow to enter or have access to a place || to recognize as true, *to admit an assumption* || to acknowledge, *he admits stealing it* || (of an enclosed space) to have

room for, *this hall admits a thousand people* || *v.i.* (with 'to') to make an acknowledgment, *he admits to stealing it* || (*rhet.*) to give entrance, *the gate admits to the tower* **to admit of** to allow as a possibility, *his actions admit of no other interpretation* **ad-mit-tance** *n.* the act of admitting || right of entry || (*elec.*) reciprocal impedance **ad-mit-ted-ly** *adv.* as is generally admitted || as I am willing to admit [O. F. *amettre*]

ad-mix (ædmíks) *v.t.* to mingle, blend (with)

ad-mix-ture (ædmíkstʃər) *n.* addition by mixture || an ingredient which is mixed with another [fr. L. *admixere (admixtus),* to mix in]

ad-mon-ish (ædmóniʃ) *v.t.* to reprove mildly, *he admonished the boy for smoking* || to warn, *he admonished the boys against the dangers of smoking* || to urge, exhort **ad-món-ish-ment** *n.* [O. F. *amonester*]

ad-mo-ni-tion (ædməníʃən) *n.* warning || rebuke [O.F. *amonition*]

ad-mon-i-to-ry (ædmónitəri:, ædmónitouri:) *adj.* giving admonition [fr. L. *admonitorius*]

a-do (ədú:) *n.* fuss and bother, excitement, activity (only in the phrases) **without further ado, without more ado, without much ado** [M.E. fr. *at do,* northern form of the infinitive (=to do)]

a-do-be (ədóubi:) *n.* sun-dried brick, not fired in a kiln || a building made of such bricks [Span.]

ad-o-les-cence (æd'lésəns) *n.* that period of life in which the child changes into the adult [F.]

ad-o-les-cent (æd'lésənt) **1.** *n.* a person who is no longer a child but is not fully adult **2.** *adj.* of, belonging to or characteristic of such a person [F.]

A-do-nis (ədóunis, ədónis) (*Gk mythol.*) a beautiful youth loved by Venus (Aphrodite). He was killed by a wild boar but restored for six months of each year to Venus by the gods in answer to her beseechings

a-don-is (ədónis) *n.* a strikingly handsome young man [Gk fr. Phoenician *adon,* lord]

a-dopt (ədópt) *v.t.* to make one's own (an idea, belief, custom etc. that belongs to or comes from someone else), *some Eastern peoples are adopting Western forms of dress* || to become the legal parent of (a child not one's own) || to accept (recommendations etc.) [F. *adopter*]

a-dop-tion (ədópʃən) *n.* an adopting or being adopted [fr. L. *adoptio (adoptionis)*]

a-dop-tive (ədóptiv) *adj.* of a relationship acquired by adoption, *an adoptive father, an adoptive country*

a-dor-a-ble (ədórəb'l, ədóurəb'l) *adj.* worthy of adoration || lovable (often in trivial contexts), *an adorable puppy* **a-dór-a-bly** *adv.* [F.]

ad-o-ra-tion (ædəréifən) *n.* the act of adoring, worshiping [F.]

a-dore (ədór,ədóur) *pres. part.* **a-dor-ing** *past and past part.* **a-dored** *v.t.* to worship, venerate || to love || (in trivial contexts) to like very much **a-dór-ing** *adj.* [F. *adorer*]

a-dorn (ədórn) *v.t.* to add beauty or splendor to (something) by decoration **a-dórn-ment** *n.* the act of adorning || something which adorns [F. *adorner*]

ADP (*acronym*) for automatic data processing

ad-re-nal (ədrí:n'l) *adj.* situated near the kidney || of or from the adrenal glands [fr. AD-+L. *renes,* kidney]

adrenal gland either of a pair of endocrine glands situated near the kidney and consisting of an inner fatty cortex and an outer vascular portion (the medulla). The cortex produces a group of hormones which assist in maintenance of the salt and water balance in the organism as well as certain steroids related to sex hormones. The medulla produces adrenalin

a-dren-al-in, a-dren-a-line (ədrén'lin) *n.* a pair of hormones produced by the medulla of the adrenal glands that prepares the organism for emotional stress by increasing blood pressure and blood sugar level, and by widening air passages in the lungs etc. It is synthetized by methyl - amino - ethanol - catechol, $C_9H_{13}NO_3$. Its overall stimulant action makes it useful in the treatment of heart failure etc. (*EPINEPHRINE, *NOREPINEPHRINE*)

ad-ren-er-gic (ædrənə:rdʒik) *adj.* (*med.*) stimulated by adrenaline or similar substance

ad-re-no-cor-ti-co-troph-in (ədrí:noukɔrtəkoutróufin) *n.* (*pharm.*) pituitary gland hormone, usu. referred to as ACTH, that maintains growth and stimulates the adrenal gland **also** adrenocorticotrophic hormone —**adrenocorti-costeroid** *n.* a steroid with a similar effect

a-dre-no-cor-ti-co-trop-ic (ədrí:noukɔrtəkoutrópik) *adj.* stimulating the cortex of the adrenal gland (*ACTH) [ADRENAL+CORTICAL+TROPIC]

A-dri-a (ádri:ə) a town (pop. 34,000) in N. Italy on the Po delta near the Adriatic, to which it gave its name

A-dri-an (éidri:ən) (Publius Aelius Hadrianus) *HADRIAN

Adrian I (d. 795), pope (772–95). He extended papal influence in the West by an alliance with Charlemagne

Adrian IV (c. 1100–59) pope (1154–9). Born Nicholas Breakspear, he was the only English pope

Adrian VI (1459–1523), pope (1522–3). He was the tutor to the future Emperor Charles V

A-dri-an-o-ple (eidri:ənóup'l) *EDIRNE

Adrianople, Treaty of the treaty (1829) ending the Russo-Turkish War (1828–9). Russia gained control of the northeast coast of the Black Sea and Moldavia and Walachia, and Turkey recognized Greek independence

A-dri-at-ic Sea (eidri:ætik) an arm of the Mediterranean separating Italy from the Balkan peninsula. It is 500 miles long, and up to 110 miles wide, narrowing to 45 miles at the Strait of Otranto (its southern limit)

a-drift (ədríft) *pred. adj.* and *adv.* afloat without control, at the mercy of wind and sea || at the mercy of circumstances, *adrift in Paris with no money*

a-droit (ədróit) *adj.* dextrous, nimble || lively and resourceful in dealing with difficult situations or people [F.]

ad-sorb (ædsórb, ædzórb) *v.t.* to retain by adsorption (cf. ABSORB) **ad-sórb-ate** *n.* an adsorbed substance **ad-sórb-ent 1.** *adj.* having the tendency or capacity to adsorb **2.** *n.* an agent with this property **ad-sórp-tion** *n.* a process by which molecules are taken up on the surface of a solid by chemical or physical action. Large amounts of gases, for example, may be adsorbed on the surface of a porous material such as charcoal (*ABSORPTION, *SORPTION) **ad-sórp-tive** *adj.* and *n.* [fr. AD-+ L. *sorbere,* to suck]

ad-u-late (ædʒəleit) *pres. part.* **ad-u-lat-ing** *past and past part.* **ad-u-lat-ed** *v.t.* (*rhet.*) to praise fulsomely || to admire to excess [fr. L. *adulari (adulatus),* to flatter]

ad-u-la-tion (ædʒəléifən) *n.* fulsome flattery || excessive admiration [O.F. *adulacion*]

ad-u-la-tor (ædʒəleitər) *n.* a person who adulates

ad-u-la-to-ry (ædʒələtɔri:, ædʒələtouri:) *adj.* fulsomely flattering || excessively admiring [fr. L. *adulatorius*]

a-dult (ædʌlt,ədʌlt) **1.** *n.* a mature, fully grown person, one who has passed adolescence || (*law*) a person who has come of age || a fully grown plant or animal **2.** *adj.* of, for, belonging to or characteristic of an adult [fr. L. *adolescere (adultus),* to grow up]

a-dul-ter-ant (ədʌltərənt) **1.** *adj.* used in adulterating **2.** *n.* an agent with this property [fr. L. *adulterans (adulterantis)* fr. *adulterare,* to corrupt]

a-dul-ter-ate (ədʌltərit, ədʌltəreit) *adj.* (of medicines, mixtures, texts) impure, spurious [fr. L. *adulteratus*]

a-dul-ter-ate (ədʌltəreit) *pres. part.* **a-dul-ter-at-ing** *past and past part.* **a-dul-ter-at-ed** *v.t.* to make impure, debase by the addition of an inferior ingredient **a-dul-ter-á-tion, a-dúl-ter-a-tor** *ns* [fr. L. *adulterare (adulteratus),* to corrupt]

a-dul-ter-er (ədʌltərər) *n.* a man who commits adultery **a-dul-ter-ess** (ədʌltəris) *n.* a woman who commits adultery [M.E. *avouterer, avoutrer* etc. fr. *avouter,* to commit adultery]

a-dul-ter-ine (ədʌltərain,ədʌltəri:n) *adj.* (*rhet.*) spurious, false || (*rhet.*) relating to adultery [fr. L. *adulterinus*]

a-dul-ter-ous (ədʌltərəs) *adj.* of or characterized by adultery [fr. older *adulter,* to commit adultery]

a-dul-ter-y (ədʌltəri:) *n.* voluntary sexual intercourse of a married man with a woman other than his wife or of a married woman with a man other than her husband [M.E. *avoutrie* fr. O.F., altered after L. *adulterium*]

ad-um-brate (ædəmbreit, ædʌmbreit) *pres. part.* **ad-um-brat-ing** *past and past part.* **ad-um-brat-ed** *v.t.* (*rhet.*) to give a vague or shadowy indication or account of || (*rhet.*) to foreshadow in a very general way **ad-um-brá-tion** *n.* [fr. L. *adumbrare (adumbratus),* to shade]

CONCISE PRONUNCIATION KEY: (a) æ, cat; ɑ, car; ɔ fawn; ei, snake. **(e)** e, hen; i:, sheep; iə, deer; ɛə, bear. **(i)** i, fish; ai, tiger; ə:, bird. **(o)** o, ox; au, cow; ou, goat; u, poor; ɔi, royal. **(u)** ʌ, duck; u, bull; u:, goose; ə, bacillus; ju:, cube. x, loch; θ, think; ð, bother; z, Zen; ʒ, corsage; dʒ, savage; ŋ, orangutang; j, yak; ʃ, fish; tʃ, fetch; 'l, rabble; 'n, redden. Complete pronunciation key appears inside front cover.

ad·vance (ædvǽns, ædváns) **1.** *v. pres. part.* **ad·vanc·ing** *past* and *past part.* **ad·vanced** *v.i.* to go forward ‖ to progress, move towards completion, *the book is advancing slowly* ‖ to go up in rank, status etc., *to advance to colonel* ‖ *v.t.* to move forward, *to advance a pawn* ‖ to cause (an event) to happen sooner than planned or expected or to bring forward in time, *they advanced the wedding date* ‖ to suggest, propose, *to advance a theory* ‖ to move up in rank etc., *he advanced three of them to captain* ‖ to pay over (money) before the date when it is due, *his employer advanced him a month's salary* ‖ to raise the price of, *he advanced his charges by 50%* ‖ to further, help to progress, *this will advance our cause* **2.** n. a moving forward, progress ‖ (*mil.*) a planned operation for a move forward ‖ an improvement in knowledge, technique etc. ‖ a payment of money before it is due ‖ a rise in price or value, *an advance in the cotton market* ‖ (*pl.*) attempts to make one's personal relations with someone intimate **in advance** beforehand, *send your luggage in advance* ‖ in front **ad·vánced** *adj.* (of ideas etc.) progressive, in front of most other people's ‖ further developed than is normal for one's age ‖ far developed, *an advanced stage of disease* ‖ (of knowledge) developed beyond the ordinary or elementary level, *advanced mathematics* **of advanced years** old. [O.F. *avancer*]

advanced booking charter round-trip airfare that must be booked 30 to 45 days in advance, *abbr* **ABC**

advanced integrated landing system all-weather instrument landing system, *abbr* **AILS**

Advanced Mars U.S.S.R. spacecraft that failed to achieve a Mars orbit

Advanced Venera U.S.S.R. spacecraft, first to return pictures from Venus

advance guard a detachment of troops sent ahead to make reconnaissance and protect the line.

advance man representative who precedes political, entertainment, or business personality to prepare for an appearance —**advance** *adj., v.*

ad·vance·ment (ædvǽnsmənt, ædvánsmənt) *n.* moving forward, progress, furtherance, *the advancement of science* ‖ promotion in rank or position

ad·van·tage (ædvǽntidʒ, ædvúntidʒ) *n.* a condition or position conferring superiority ‖ a condition or set of circumstances which helps one to reach a desired end ‖ something which gives benefit or profit ‖ (*tennis*) the first point scored after deuce **to advantage** in a favorable way **to take advantage of (someone)** to mislead or trick (someone) by abusing his good nature, trading on his ignorance etc. **to take advantage of (something)** to make the most of, profit by (an opportunity etc.) **ad·van·ta·geous** (ædvæntéidʒəs) *adj.* [F. *avantage*]

ad·vec·tion (ædvékʃən) *n.* (*phys.*) transportation by horizontal movement of air, e.g., moisture —**advect** *v.*

ad·vent (ædvent) *n.* arrival, coming, *the advent of atomic power in industry* **Advent** the coming of Christ ‖ the period of the four Sundays before Christmas ‖ *SECOND ADVENT [O.F. *advent*]

Ad·vent·ism (ædventizəm) *n.* the doctrine of a number of religious bodies which, in the early 19th c., focused their interest on the prophetic portions of the Bible and predicted, as a principal article of faith, the imminent second coming of Christ

Ad·vent·ist (ædventist, ædvéntist) *n.* someone who holds the doctrine of Adventism

ad·ven·ti·tious (ædvəntíʃəs) *adj.* accidental, casual, *an adventitious meeting* ‖ not intrinsic, something added from without, *his resignation was an adventitious factor in the crisis* ‖ (*biol.*, e.g. of buds or shoots) occurring sporadically or elsewhere than is normal [fr. L. *adventicius*, coming from the exterior]

ad·ven·ture (ædvéntʃər) *n.* a dangerous or exciting incident, or a hazardous enterprise ‖ a delightful experience, *childhood adventures* ‖ a commercial or financial speculation [O.F. *aventure*]

adventure *pres. part.* **ad·ven·tur·ing** *past* and *past part.* **ad·ven·tured** *v.t.* (*rhet.*) to risk, expose to danger ‖ *v.i.* (*rhet.*) to venture [O.F. *aventurer*]

ad·ven·tur·er (ædvéntʃərər) *n.* someone who lives by his wits ‖ an unscrupulous speculator ‖ any seeker after adventure (for whatever motive) [F. *aventurier*]

ad·ven·ture·some (ædvéntʃərsəm) *adj.* (*rhet.*) venturesome

ad·ven·tur·ess (ædvéntʃəris) *n.* a woman out to get money or social position by guile and charm

ad·ven·tur·ous (ædvéntʃərəs) *adj.* enterprising, liable to take risks ‖ requiring courage, fraught with danger, *an adventurous journey* [O.F. *aventuros*]

ad·verb (ædvə·rb) *n.* (*gram.*) a part of speech which modifies or limits a verb, an adjective, or another adverb (in the sentence 'He was very old and lived quietly', 'very' and 'quietly' are adverbs). It is generally placed immediately before or after the word which it modifies. Many adverbs in English are formed by addingly to an adjective and such regular formations are not listed in this book **ad·ver·bi·al** (ædvə́ːrbiəl) *adj.* [F. *adverbe*]

ad·ver·sa·ry (ædvərseri) *pl.* **ad·ver·sa·ries** *n.* opponent, enemy [O.F. *aversier*]

ad·ver·sa·tive (ædvə́ːrsətiv) *adj.* expressing opposition or antithesis, *'but' and 'never the less' are adversative conjunctions* [fr. L. *adversativus*]

ad·verse (ædvə·rs, ædvə́·rs) *adj.* contrary, opposing, *adverse winds* ‖ unfavorable, unpropitious, *an adverse weather report* [F. *advers*]

adverse selection (*insurance*) disproportionate risks, e.g., those who are poorer or more prone to suffer loss or make more claims than the average risk. It may result from the tendency for poorer risks or less desirable insureds (sick people) to seek or continue insurance to a greater extent than do better risks (healthy people), or from the tendency for the insured to take advantage of favorable options in insurance contracts *Cf* SKIM

ad·ver·si·ty (ædvə́ːrsiti:) *pl.* **ad·ver·si·ties** *n.* misfortune, trouble, affliction ‖ a misfortune [F. *adversité*]

ad·vert (ædvə·rt) *n.* (*Br.*, *pop.*) an advertisement

ad·ver·tise, ad·ver·tize (ædvərtaiz) *pres. part.* **ad·ver·tis·ing, ad·ver·tiz·ing** *past* and *past part.* **ad·ver·tised, ad·ver·tized** *v.t.* to make known, proclaim publicly, esp. in order to promote sales ‖ to draw attention to, make conspicuous, *to advertise one's presence* ‖ *v.i.* to publish an advertisement **to advertise for** to ask for (someone or something) by public notice **ad·ver·tise·ment, ad·ver·tize·ment** (ædvərtáizmənt, advə́ːrtismənt) *n.* public notice or announcement, usually offering goods or services for sale **ád·ver·tis·ing, ád·ver·tiz·ing** *n.* the business of compiling and placing advertisements ‖ the act of announcing by any of the techniques of advertisement (newspapers, radio, television, films, handbills etc.) [F. *avertir* (*avertiss-*)]

ad·vice (ædváis) *n.* a stated opinion meant to help to determine correct action or conduct ‖ (*commerce*) a notification of a transaction ‖ (*pl.*) information sent by an agent or agency, *advices of the recession came in hourly* **to take advice** to consult the opinion of a specialist ‖ to do what one has been advised to do [O.F. *advis*, opinion]

ad·vis·a·bil·i·ty (ædvąizəbíliti:) *n.* the quality of being advisable

ad·vis·a·ble (ædvąizəb'l) *adj.* prudent, expedient ‖ to be recommended **ad·vis·a·bly** *adv.*

ad·vise (ædváiz) *pres. part.* **ad·vis·ing** *past* and *past part.* **ad·vised** *v.t.* to give advice to, recommend a course of action to ‖ (*commerce*) to notify ‖ *v.i.* to give advice **ad·vis·ed·ly** (ædvąizidli:) *adv.* with due deliberation **ad·vís·er, ad·ví·sor** *n.* someone who gives advice ‖ a teacher who helps students to plan their work **ad·vi·so·ry** (ædváizəri:) *adj.* having the power to advise ‖ consisting of advice [M.E. *avisen* fr. O.F.]

ad·vo·ca·cy (ædvəkəsi:) *pl.* **ad·vo·ca·cies** *n.* advocating, or an instance of it ‖ support (for a cause)or recommendation (of a line of action) ‖ the work of advocates [F. *advocacie*]

advocacy planning urban planning by professionals representing special groups

ad·vo·cate (ædvəkit, ædvəkeit) *n.* a person who pleads on behalf of another, esp. in a court of law ‖ a person who speaks or writes in support of some cause, argument or proposal [O.F. *avocat*]

ad·vo·cate (ædvəkeit) *pres. part.* **ad·vo·cat·ing** *past* and *past part.* **ad·vo·cat·ed** *v.t.* to plead on behalf of, use persuasion in support of [fr. L. *advocare* (*advocatus*)]

advocate approach supportive measure for aiding mental-health patients in dealing with bureaucracy to show that difficulties can be mastered

ad·vo·ca·to·ry (ædvókətɔri:, ædvókətouri:) *adj.* of or relating to an advocate

ad·vow·son (ædváuzən) *n.* (*Br. law*) the right of presentation to a church benefice [O.F. *avoeson*, patronage]

A·dy (ɔ́di:), Endre (1877–1919), Hungarian poet

ad·y·tum (ædítəm) *pl.* **ád·y·ta** (ædítə) *n.* the sanctum, innermost sanctuary in a temple [L. fr. Gk *aduton*, inaccessible (place)]

adze, adz (ædz) **1.** *n.* a tool with a blade set at right angles to the handle for cutting or shaping wood **2.** *v.t. pres. part.* **adz·ing** *past* and *past part.* **adzed** to cut or shape with an adze [O.E. *adesa*, axe]

A·dzhar·i·an A.S.S.R. (ædʒɑri:ən) an autonomous republic (area 1,080 sq. miles, pop. 294,000) in Georgia, U.S.S.R. Capital: Batumi

a·e·des (eií:di:z) *pl.* **a·e·des** (eiín:di:z) *n.* a member of *Aedes*, a genus of mosquitoes, many species of which transmit disease to men and animals. A. *aegypti* is the yellow-fever mosquito (cf. ANOPHELES) [Mod. L. fr. Gk *aēdēs*, unpleasant]

ae·dile, e·dile (i:dail) *n.* (*Rom. hist.*) a magistrate responsible for supervising public buildings, the police, public games and the grain supply **áe·dile·ship, é·dile·ship** *n.* [fr. L. *aedilis*]

Ae·ge·an (idʒí:ən) *adj.* of or pertaining to the Aegean Sea and the islands in it ‖ or pertaining to the Bronze Age civilization (*MINOAN, *MYCENAEAN) of this region [L. *Aegaeus* fr. Gk]

Aegean Sea part of the Mediterranean between Greece and Anatolia, 400 miles long, 200 miles wide

Ae·gi·na (idʒáinə) (*Gk* Aigina) a Greek island (area 32 sq. miles, pop. 9,000) in the Saronic Gulf of the Aegean Sea. Chief town: Aegina (pop. 5,704). Products: almonds, sponges. Aegina was a commercial power from the 7th c. B.C. until conquered by Athens (c. 456 B.C.)

ae·gis, e·gis (í:dʒis) *n.* patronage, sponsorship ‖ direction, control, *under the aegis of the local council* ‖ (in Homer) the shield of Zeus or Athene [L. fr. Gk *aigis*, a shield]

Ae·gos·pot·a·mi (i:gəspótəmai) a river of ancient Thrace, at the mouth of which the final battle of the Peloponnesian War was fought (405 B.C.). The Athenian fleet was destroyed by the Spartans under Lysander

ae·gro·tat (í:groutæt) *n.* (in English universities) an unclassified degree given to a candidate prevented by illness from attending the examination [L.=he is ill]

A-18 (*mil.*) ground-attack version of F-18 (which see)

Ael·fric (ǽlfrik) (c. 955–c. 1020), abbot of Eynsham, English monastic reformer and grammarian. His works include 'Homilies', 'Metrical Lives of Saints', a Latin grammar and translations of Latin religious literature

Ae·ne·id (iní:id) Virgil's epic poem. Aeneas the hero, Trojan leader, son of Anchises and the goddess Aphrodite, is shipwrecked off Africa. Received by Dido, queen of Carthage, he tells her about his wanderings since the fall of Troy. He renounces their mutual love, and sails on to Italy to fulfil his destiny as founder of Latium and so of the Roman state

Ae·o·li·an (i:óuli:ən) **1.** *n.* (*hist.*) a member of a group of ancient Greeks. The Aeolians migrated from Thessaly (c. 1000 B.C.) to Boeotia and western Peloponnesus, to Aegean islands (Lesbos) and to N.W. Asia Minor **2.** *adj.* relating to Aeolis ‖ of Aeolus, Greek god of the wind [fr. L. *Aeolius* fr. Gk]

aeolian accumulations deposits due to the action of the wind, such as sand dunes and loess

aeolian harp a musical instrument which 'plays' automatically when the wind blows through its strings

Aeolian mode (*mus.*) an authentic mode introduced in the 16th c., represented by the white piano keys ascending from A

ae·o·light (í:oulait) *n.* (*optics*) device used to produce a modulated light for motion picture sound recording utilizing a cold cathode and a mixture of inert gases

Ae·o·lis (i:əlis) an ancient district of N.W. Asia Minor settled by the Aeolians (11th–8th cc. B.C.). Twelve city-states formed the Aeolian League until conquered by Croesus of Lydia (6th c. B.C.)

CONCISE PRONUNCIATION KEY: **(a)** æ, c*a*t; ɑ, c*a*r; ɔ f*aw*n; ei, sn*a*ke. **(e)** e, h*e*n; i:, sh*ee*p; iə, d*ee*r; ɛə, b*ea*r. **(i)** i, f*i*sh; ai, t*i*ger; ə:, b*i*rd. **(o)** o, *o*x; au, c*ow*; ou, g*oa*t; u, p*oo*r; ɔi, r*oy*al. **(u)** ʌ, d*u*ck; u, b*u*ll; u:, g*oo*se; ə, b*a*cillus; ju:, c*u*be. x, lo*ch*; θ, *th*ink; ð, bo*th*er; z, *Z*en; ʒ, cor*s*age; dʒ, sava*g*e; ŋ, oranguta*ng*; j, *y*ak; ʃ, *fi*sh; tʃ, fe*tch*; 'l, rabb*le*; 'n, redd*en*. Complete pronunciation key appears inside front cover.

ae·o·lo·trop·ic, e·o·lo·trop·ic (i:əloutrópik) *adj.* anisotropic [fr. Gk *aiolos*, quick-moving + *tropos*, turning]

Ae·o·lus (íːələs) (*Gk mythol.*) the god of the winds

ae·on, e·on (íːən, íːɒn) *n.* an immeasurably long period of time [L. fr. Gk *aeōn*, age]

ae·rate (éəreit, éiəreit) *pres. part.* **aer·at·ing** *past* and *past part.* **aer·at·ed** *v.t.* to impregnate with air, *frequent digging aerates the soil* ‖ to charge (a liquid) with gas or air **aer·á·tion** *n.* [fr. L. *aer*, air]

aer·i·al (éəriəl) **1.** *adj.* of the air or atmosphere ‖ existing or moving in the air ‖ thin as air ‖ ethereal, insubstantial, *aerial fancies* ‖ overhead, in the air, *an aerial railway* **2.** *n.* an antenna (device for converting electrical currents) [fr. L. *aer*, air]

aer·i·al·ist (éəriəlist) *n.* an acrobat who performs feats in the air, e.g. on a trapeze

aerial perspective (*art*) the expression of space in a painting or drawing by gradations of color and tone

aerial port an airfield that has been designated for the sustained air movement of personnel and materiel and to serve as an authorized port for entrance or departure from the country in which it is located

aer·ie, aer·y, eyr·ie (éəri) *pl.* **aer·ies, eyr·ies** *n.* a nest, usually on a high crag or mountainside, of a bird of prey ‖ (*rhet.*) a high and remote human dwelling [O.F. *aire*, a nest]

aer·i·form (éərifɔrm) *adj.* gaseous, of the nature of air ‖ unsubstantial, unreal [fr. L. *aer*, air]

aer·o·al·ler·gen (εərouǽlərdʒən) *n.* (*med.*) an airborne allergy-producing substance

aer·o·bat·ics (εərəbǽtiks) *n.* the performance of acrobatic feats with an aircraft, stunt flying [fr. Gk aēr, air+*batos*, walking (as 'acrobatics')]

aer·obe (éəroub) *n.* (*biol.*) an organism which is able to live only in the presence of oxygen (opp. ANAEROBE) **aer·ó·bic** *adj.* [fr. Mod. L. *aerobia* fr. Gk aēr, air+*bios*, life]

aerobic digestion utilization of bacteria, with oxygen, to reduce the volume of waste, producing carbon dioxide, water, and organic and inorganic compounds **ant** ANAEROBIC DIGESTION

aerobics system of exercise based on increasing oxygen intake to stimulate heart and lung activity

aer·od·esy (εəródəsi:) *n.* (*math.*) the branch of mathematics that determines by observation and measurement the exact positions of points on, and the figures and areas of large portions of the surface of, the planet Mars, or the shape and size of the planet Mars —**aerodetic** *adj.*

aer·o·do·net·ics (εəroudounétiks) *n.* the science and theory of gliding and soaring [fr. Gk aēr, air+*donein* (*donetos*), to drive]

aer·o·drome (éərədroum) *n.* (*Br.*) an airport [fr. Gk aēr, air+*dromos*, racetrack]

aer·o·dy·nam·ic (εəroudainǽmik) *adj.* of or relating to aerodynamics

aer·o·dy·nam·ics (εəroudainǽmiks) *n.* the science of air flow, particularly the study of the motion of solid bodies (e.g. aircraft, bullets) through air, and their control and stability [fr. Gk aēr, air+DYNAMICS]

aer·o·dyne (éərədain) *n.* a heavier than-air flying machine [fr. Gk aēr, air+*dunamis*, power]

aer·o·foil (éərəfɔil) *n.* (*Br.*) an airfoil [fr. Gk aēr, air+FOIL]

aer·o·gram (éərəgræm) *n.* a message conveyed by radio ‖ an air letter [fr. Gk aēr, air+*gramma*, letter]

aer·og·ra·phy (εərógrəfi:) *n.* the measurement of atmospheric data, esp. with an aerograph (self-recording instrument)

aer·o·lite (éərəlait) *n.* a meteorite [fr. Gk aēr, air+*lithos* a stone]

aer·o·lith (éərəliθ) *n.* an aerolite

aer·o·lit·ik (εərəlítik) *adj.* of or relating to an aeronite

aer·o·lo·gy (εərólədʒi:) *n.* the branch of meteorology concerned with the study of the upper air [fr..Gk aēr, air+*logos*, discourse]

aer·o·me·chan·ic (εərouməkǽnik) *n.* a mechanic skilled in aeronautics [fr. Gk aēr, air+MECHANIC]

aer·o·me·chan·i·cal (εərouməkǽnik'l) *adj.* of or relating to aeromechanics

aer·o·me·chan·ics (εərouməkǽniks) *n.* the science of the forces associated with the motion of air and other gases [fr. Gk aēr, air+MECHANICS]

aero metal (éərou) a light, strong alloy of aluminum, zinc and copper

aer·o·naut·ics (εərənɔ́tiks, εərənútiks) *n.* the science and practice of flight by aircraft [fr. Mod. L. *aeronautica* fr. Gk]

aer·on·o·my (εərónəmi:) *n.* study of the upper atmosphere

aer·o·plane (éərəplein) *n.* (*Br.*) an airplane [fr. Gk aēr, air+*planos*, wandering]

aer·o·sol (éərəsɔl, éərəsoul) *n.* a dispersion of solid or liquid particles in a gas or air (e.g. smoke, fog) ‖ a substance (e.g. an insecticide, germicide) in a container with a propellant gas, sprayed out through a valve [fr. Gk aēr, air+SOL]

aer·o·space (éərəspeis) **1.** *n.* the earth's atmosphere together with cosmic space beyond **2.** *adj.* of or pertaining to the technology of flight or ballistics in aerospace [fr. Gk aēr, air+SPACE]

aer·o·stat (éərəstæt) *n.* a lighter-than-air flying machine, such as a balloon or a zeppelin **aer·o·stát·ic** *adj.* pertaining to aerostatics **aer·o·stát·ics** *n.* the physics of the equilibrium of gases [fr. Gk aēr, air+*statos*, placed]

aer·o·ther·mo·dy·nam·ics (εərouθəːrmoudainæmiks) *n.* the science dealing with the thermodynamics of gases, esp. air, esp. in the context of supersonic flight [fr. Gk aēr, air+THERMODYNAMICS]

Aer·o·train (éəroutrein) *n.* a vehicle riding on a cushion of air and guided by a raised central concrete rail, on a special track [Trademark]

aery *AERIE

Aes·chi·nes (éskini:z, esp. *Br.* íːskini:z) (c. 389–c. 314 B.C.), Athenian orator, rival of Demosthenes

Aes·chy·lus (éskiləs, esp. *Br.* íːskiləs) (c. 525–c. 456 B.C.), Greek poetic dramatist, author of about 90 plays, of which seven complete tragedies survive. His plots were simple and mostly concerned with showing the ultimate justice of the gods. His extant plays are the 'Agamemnon', 'Choephoroe', 'Eumenides', 'Seven Against Thebes', 'Suppliants', 'Persians' and 'Prometheus Bound'

Aes·cu·la·pi·us (eskjəléipi:əs, esp. *Br.* iːskjuléipjəs) the Roman god of medicine, identified with the Greek Asclepius

Ae·sop (íːsɒp) (6th c. B.C.), Greek beast-fable writer. He was a freed slave, usually represented as ugly and hunchbacked. The surviving collections include many fables of later date from different sources

aes·thete (ésθi:t, *Br.* iːsθi:t) *n.* a person who professes to put beauty before other considerations [fr. Gk *aisthētēs*, perceiving through the senses]

aes·thet·ic (esθétik, *Br.* iːsθétik) *adj.* concerning appreciation of the beautiful, esp. in the arts, *aesthetic standards* ‖ (of persons) appreciative of the beautiful **aes·thét·i·cal** *adj.* **aes·the·tí·cian** *n.* a person devoted to, or professionally occupied with, aesthetics **aes·thét·i·cism** *n.* inordinate concern with aesthetic matters as against ethical or practical considerations **aes·thét·ics** *n.* the part of philosophy which deals with the perception of the beautiful as distinguished from the moral or the useful ‖ the branch of psychology which deals with the sensations and emotions evoked by beauty [fr. Gk *aisthētikos*, perceptible to the senses]

aes·ti·val (éstəvəl, *Br.* iːstáivəl) *adj.* pertaining to summer [F. *estival*]

aes·ti·vate (éstəveit, *Br.* íːstəveit) *pres. part.* **aes·ti·vat·ing** *past* and *past part.* **aes·ti·vat·ed** *v.i.* (*biol.*) to spend summer in a torpid state (opp. HIBERNATE) **aes·ti·vá·tion** *n.* (*biol.*) the state of torpidity in the heat of summer (opp. HIBERNATION) ‖ (*bot.*) the arrangement of flower petals in the bud before opening [fr. L. *aestivare* (*aestivatus*), to spend the summer]

Aethelbald *ETHELBALD

Aethelbert *ETHELBERT

Aethelred *ETHELRED

Aethelstan *ATHELSTAN

Aethelwulf *ETHELWULF

aether *ETHER

aetiological *ETIOLOGICAL

aetiology *ETIOLOGY

Ae·ti·us Fla·vi·us (éiti:əsfléivi:əs) (c. 396–454), Roman general. Together with the Visigoths, he decisively defeated Attila at Chalons (451)

Aetna *ETNA

Ae·to·li·a (iːtóuli:ə) an ancient region of central Greece

Ae·to·li·an League (iːtóuli:ən) a confederacy of independent tribes of Aetolia, formed late 4th c. B.C. It expanded (3rd c. B.C.) to include many regions and cities of Thrace, Epirus, Peloponne-

sus and Asia Minor, and by 220 B.C. controlled most of central Greece and was the chief rival of Macedonia. The League was attacked by Philip V of Macedon (218 and 211 B.C.) and defeated him (200 B.C.). In alliance with Antiochus of Syria, the League was defeated by the Romans (189 B.C.) and was dissolved (167 B.C.)

AF Air Force

a·far (əfár) *adv.* far off, at a distance **from afar** from a distance

Afars and of the Issas, French Territory of the *DJIBOUTI

af·fa·bil·i·ty (æfəbíliti) *n.* the quality or state of being affable [F. *affabilité*]

af·fa·ble (æfəb'l) *adj.* easy to talk to, good-natured, courteous ‖ mild, not aggressive, *an affable reply* **áf·fa·bly** *adv.* [F.]

af·fair (əféər) *n.* concern, business, *this is no affair of hers* ‖ (*pl.*) daily concerns of a business organization or government, *a man of affairs, affairs of state* ‖ (intentionally vague) an incident, *an unfortunate affair* ‖ a love affair [O.F. *afaire*]

affair of honor, *Br.* affair of honour (*hist.*) a duel

af·fect (æfekt, əfékt) *n.* (*psychol.*) a feeling or mood [fr. L. *affectus*, disposition]

af·fect (əfékt) *v.t.* to make an impression on, move, *her words affected him deeply* ‖ to have an effect on (something), *does this change affect your plans?* ‖ to have a hurtful effect on, *it has affected his mind* ‖ (of a disease etc.) to attack, cause a particular condition in, *the swelling affected the entire leg* [fr. L. *afficere* (*affectus*), to attack]

affect *v.t.* to pretend, feign, *to affect indifference* ‖ to make a whimsical or ostentatious display of, *to affect a cloak* [F. *affecter*, to win at]

af·fec·ta·tion (æfektéiʃən) *n.* a pretense made for effect ‖ studied artificiality in behavior and speaking [fr. L. *affectatio* (*affectationis*), a striving after]

af·fect·ed (əféktid) *adj.* (of behavior etc.) artificial, not natural ‖ (of people) insincere, full of pretensions

af·fec·tion (əfékʃən) *n.* fondness, tender feelings ‖ friendly feelings of attachment ‖ an illness, disease ‖ (*psychol.*) the aspect of consciousness manifested in feelings and emotions [F.]

af·fec·tion·ate (əfékʃənit) *adj.* showing fondness, tenderness, affection [fr. F. *affectionné*]

af·fec·tive (əféktiv) *adj.* (*psychol.*) concerning the affections or the emotions generally [F.]

affective fallacy reaction to a literary work in terms of its effect on the mind of an audience; originally by W. K. Wimsatt and Monroe C. Beardsley

af·fec·tive-neu·tral·i·ty (əféktivnu:træliti:) *n.* (*psych.*) a value or attitude that subordinates expression of feeling and self-gratification to other values

af·fer·ent (æfərənt) *adj.* leading inwards or towards something, e.g. an organ ‖ (*physiol.*, of nerves) bringing impulses towards a nerve center (opp. EFFERENT) [fr. L. *afferens* (*afferentis*) fr. *affere*, to bring to]

af·fi·ance (əfáiəns) *pres. part.* **af·fi·anc·ing** *past* and *past part.* **af·fi·anced** *v.t.* (*rhet.*) to betroth, to promise in marriage [O.F. *afiance*]

af·fi·da·vit (æfidéivit) *n.* a written statement, sworn on oath to be true, esp. one signed in the presence of (*Am.*) a notary, (*Br.*) a lawyer [L.=he has made an oath]

af·fil·i·ate (əfíli:eit) **1.** *v. pres. part.* **af·fil·i·at·ing** *past* and *past part.* **af·fil·i·at·ed** *v.i.* (usually of societies, institutions etc., with 'with' or 'to') to enter into association, *our club has affiliated with a national society* ‖ *v.t.* to add as an associate ‖ (*rare*) to adopt (a son) into a family ‖ to fix the paternity of (an illegitimate child) **2.** (əfíli:it, əfíli:eit) *n.* an associate. a person affiliated to something ‖ a subsidiary organization [fr. L. *affiliare* (*affiliatus*), to adopt]

af·fil·i·a·tion (əfili:éiʃən) *n.* an affiliating or being affiliated [F.]

affiliation order (*Br., law*) a magistrate's order requiring a man to help to maintain his illegitimate child for a period of years

af·fin·i·ty (əfíniti:) *pl.* **af·fin·i·ties** *n.* any close link or connection, *affinities of language and culture* ‖ a strong liking or attraction between one person and another ‖ relationship by marriage ‖ (*biol.*) relationship between species which indicates a common origin ‖ (*chem.*) attraction between elements which causes them to enter into combinations with each other [F. *affinité*]

af·firm (əfə́:rm) v.t. to state positively, with conviction ‖ v.i. (law) to make a declaration of truthfulness (in place of the oath) ‖ to make a statement in the affirmative (as opposed to the negative) [O. F. *afermer*]

af·fir·ma·tion (æfərméiʃən) n. an assertion, a positive statement ‖ (law) a solemn declaration (in place of the oath) [F.]

af·firm·a·tive (əfə́:rmətiv) 1. adj. asserting that a fact is so, affirming by answering 'yes', *an affirmative answer* 2. n. the affirmative mode upholding a proposition, *he answered in the affirmative* ‖ an affirmative word or expression [F.]

affirmative action practices in hiring, promotions, and college admissions that favor a group previously hurt by discrimination against it

af·firm·a·to·ry (əfə́:rmətɔri:, əfə́:rmətouri:) adj. affirmative

af·fix (æfiks) n. something affixed, an appendage ‖ (gram.) a prefix, infix or suffix [F. *affixe*]

af·fix (əfíks) v.t. to fasten ‖ to attach. *to affix a seal to a document* ‖ to append (usually a signature) ‖ to ascribe (censure, a salary etc.) **af·fix·a·tion** (æfikséiʃən) n. the act or process of affixing ‖ the use of an affix **af·fix·ture** (əfíkstʃər) n. the state of being affixed [fr. M.L. *affixare*]

af·fla·tus (əfléitəs) n. inspiration, divine communication of knowledge [L.]

af·flict (əflíkt) v.t. to trouble or distress ‖ to inflict grievous physical or mental suffering on (usually pass.) [older F. *afflict* adj., downcast]

af·flic·tion (əflíkʃən) n. something which causes trouble or distress ‖ physical or mental suffering [F.]

af·flic·tive (əflíktiv) adj. causing affliction

af·flu·ence (æflu:əns) n. wealth ‖ (rhet.) profusion [F.]

af·flu·ent (æflu:ənt) 1. adj. rich 2. n. a tributary stream [F.]

affluent society a milieu in which basic needs have been replaced with sufficient abundance for comfortable living; originally by John K. Galbraith

af·flux (æflʌks) n. a flowing or something which flows to or towards a point [fr. L. *affluxus*, flowing towards]

af·ford (əfɔ́rd, əfóurd) v.t. (with 'can' or 'be able to') to be in a position (to do something), *can we afford to speak out?* ‖ (with 'can') to be able to buy (something), *can we afford a new car?* ‖ (with 'can') to spare, *I can't afford the time to read it* ‖ to give, provide, *the tower affords a fine view* [fr. O.E. *geforthian*, to provide]

af·for·est (æfɔ́rist, əfɔ́rist) v.t. to convert (land) into forest **af·for·est·a·tion** n. [fr. M.L. *afforestare*]

af·fran·chise (əfrǽntʃaiz) pres. part. **af·fran·chis·ing** past and past part. **af·fran·chised** v.t. to set free from servitude **af·frán·chise·ment** n. [F. *affranchir* (*affranchiss-*)]

af·fray (əfréi) n. (law) a fight or brawl constituting a disturbance of the peace [O.F. *effrei*]

af·fri·cate (æfrikit) n. (phon.) a complex consonant unit composed of a stop followed by a fricative, e.g. 'ch' in 'chop' **af·fric·a·tive** (æfríkətiv) adj. [fr. L. *affricare* (*affricatus*), to rub against]

af·front (əfrʌ́nt) 1. v.t. to insult, cause offense to 2. n. an insult, deliberate act of disrespect [O.F. *affronter*]

Af·ghan (æfgæn, æfgən) n. a native of Afghanistan ‖ the language (Pushtu) spoken there **afghan** a crocheted or knitted coverlet

Afghan hound a hunting dog of a breed with long silky hair

af·ghan·i (æfgæni:, æfgúni:) n. the basic monetary unit of Afghanistan, divided into 100 puls ‖ a coin or note of the value of one afghani [Pushtu *afghāni*]

Af·ghan·i·stan (æfgǽnistæn), Democratic Republic of, an independent republic (area c. 245,000 sq. miles, pop. 16,113,000) of W. Asia. Capital: Kabul. Official languages: Persian and Pushtu. Religion: mainly Sunnite Moslems, with a minority of Shi'ite Moslems. Afghanistan is very mountainous in the center and north, dominated by the Hindu Kush (15,000–20,000 ft). There are many fertile valleys, but the south is mainly desert. The climate varies from intense heat (up to 90°F. in Kabul, 120° in the south) to severe cold. Precipitation averages 7 ins a year, much of it snow. Agricultural products: fruit, cereals and nuts. Livestock: sheep, cattle, horses, camels. About 1 million Afghans are nomadic herdsmen. Mineral re-

sources (largely unexploited): copper, coal, oil, topgrade lapis lazuli, iron, silver, mica, gold, asbestos, lead and salt. Half of the country's trade is with the U.S.S.R. Exports: wool, cotton, fruit, nuts, karakul skins, resins, carpets. Imports: cement, gasoline, cloth, sugar, tea, paper. There are few railways. Access to Peshawar in Pakistan is by the Khyber Pass. There is one hydroelectric plant (Sarobi) and an international airport (Kandahar). Monetary unit: afghani (divided into 100 puls). HISTORY. Afghanistan formed a part of the ancient Persian empires and was conquered by Alexander (330 B.C.). It was converted to Islam (9th c.). The Ghaznavid dynasty (c. 977–1155) acquired great wealth from attacks on India. Afghanistan was conquered by Timur (c. 1400) and became part of the Mogul Empire (1504) until it was seized by Nadir Shah (1738). It became independent (1747). Anglo-Russian rivalry in the area led to the wars of 1838–42 and 1878–80 between the Afghans and the British. Afghanistan remained neutral in both world wars. It was recognized as independent (1919) and was a kingdom until 1973, a republic (1973–8), and under Marxist control after a 1978 coup. The U.S.S.R. intervened militarily in 1979 and retained control despite Afghani resistance

Af·ghan·i·stan·ism (æfgǽnistænizəm) n. excessive interest in affairs of distant places at the expense of everyday concerns

a·field (əfi:ld) adv. (rhet.) in or to the field **far afield** at or to a distance, far from home

a·fire (əfáiər) pred. adj. and adv. on fire

a·flame (əfléim) pred. adj. and adv. in flames, burning ‖ glowing as though on fire

af·la·tox·in (æflətɒksən) n. (biol.) mycotoxin produced by molds in animal food. Aflatoxins are believed to affect the liver, to be fatal to livestock, and to be carcinogenic in humans *Cf* MYCOTOXICOSIS

A.F.L.-C.I.O. *AMERICAN FEDERATION OF LABOR AND CONGRESS OF INDUSTRIAL ORGANIZATIONS

a·float (əflóut) pred. adj. and adv. floating ‖ not aground ‖ flooded, nearly submerged in water ‖ (fig.) in circulation, *rumors are afloat that he will resign* ‖ free of debt, solvent

a·foot (əfút) pred. adj. and adv. walking, on foot ‖ beginning to make progress, *plans are afoot for a national theater*

a·fore (əfɔ́r, əfóur) adv. and prep. (naut.) before, *afore the mast* [O.E. *onforan*]

a·fore·said (əfɔ́rsed, əfóursed) 1. pron. (in documents) that which has been said or named before 2. adj. (in documents) said or named before

a·fore·thought (əfɔ́rθɔt, əfóurθɔt) *MALICE AFORETHOUGHT

A-4 *SKYHAWK

AFP (med.) alpha-fetoprotein secretion of the fetus through its urine into the amniotic fluid, an excess of which signals a fetal abnormality

a·fraid (əfréid) adj. frightened, *snakes are afraid of people* ‖ apprehensive, fearful, *afraid of the consequences* ‖ (loosely) regretful, *I am afraid that I must leave* [past part. of older *affray*, to alarm fr. A.F. *afrayer*]

A-frame adj. describing a structure shaped like an A **A-frame** n. a triangular house

a·fresh (əfréʃ) adv. anew, again, *to start afresh*

Af·ri·ca (æfrikə) the second largest continent (area 11,600,000 sq. miles, pop. c. 530,000,000). Political units (see separate entries): Algeria, Angola, Benin, Botswana, Burkina, Burundi, Cameroon, Canary Is, Cape Verde Is, Central African Republic, Chad, Comoro Is, the Republic of the Congo, the Democratic Republic of the Congo, Djibouti, Egypt, Equatorial Guinea, Ethiopia, Gabon, Gambia, Ghana, Guinea, Guinea-Bissau, Ivory Coast, Kenya, Lesotho, Liberia, Libya, Madagascar, Malawi, Mali, Mauritania, Mauritius, Morocco, Mozambique, Namibia (South-West Africa), Niger, Nigeria, Réunion, Rwanda, São Tomé and Principe, Senegal, Sierra Leone, Somalia, Republic of South Africa, Sudan, Swaziland, Tanzania, Togo, Tunisia, Uganda, Zaïre, Zambia, Zimbabwe. HISTORY. The population cultivating the lower Nile valley (late 5th and 4th millennia B.C.) gave rise to the development of Egyptian civilization (late 4th millennium B.C.). By 2000 B.C. Egypt had trade contacts with the coasts of Eritrea, Somaliland, S. Arabia and S. Ethiopia. Nubia was occupied (2nd millennium B.C.), and gave rise to the kingdom of Kush, where Egyptian culture survived while Egypt was conquered by Assyrians, Persians, Greeks and Romans. Kush

expanded south (6th c. B.C.) from the Nile cataracts to the Sudan, founding a new capital at Meroë (mid-3rd c. B.C. to 1st c. A.D.). It was conquered (mid-4th c. A.D.) by the kingdom of Axum in the N. Ethiopian highlands. This dispersion from the Nile valley (1st–6th cc. A.D.) mingled with Arabian influence, spread west and south. The civilizations of the Sudanic peoples included the states of Ghana, Kanem, Songhai and Hausa, most of which are known to have existed by the 8th or 9th cc. A.D., Ghana perhaps by the 4th–5th cc. Meanwhile the north coast of Africa had been colonized by the Phoenicians (8th c. B.C.), who founded Carthage (c. 814 B.C.). The Greeks colonized Cyrenaica and Egypt (4th c. B.C.). The Romans destroyed Carthage (146 B.C.) and spread their influence west as far as Morocco and east to Egypt (1st c. B.C.). Carthage and Alexandria became centers for the spread of Christianity, which extended, in its Coptic form, to Nubia (5th and 6th cc. A.D.). The Roman empire in N. Africa collapsed when the Vandals invaded from Spain (415). The area was reconquered (533–48) by the Byzantine Empire. Trade routes had been established across the Sahara to Ghana, Hausa, Kanem and Songhai by the 8th c., spreading Berber influence southwards. The spread of Islam in Africa began with the conquest of Egypt by the Arabs (c. 640), and had extended by 700 to the whole of the north coast. Under the Almoravides, Islam penetrated (11th c.) across the Sahara to the Sudanic kingdoms. Meanwhile Islam had spread along the east coast (10th–12th cc.), extending into E. Africa (14th c.). European exploration beyond the north coast began when the Portuguese, seeking a new trade route to the Far East and contact with the mythical Prester John, rounded the Cape of Good Hope (1497) and explored Ethiopia (16th c.). England, France and Holland began trading in goods and slaves along the coast of W. Africa (16th c.). The British explored the upper reaches of the Nile (18th c.) and the Niger (early 19th c.) and the Germans the regions of the Niger and Lake Chad. The Dutch settled the Cape Colony (17th c.), which passed to Britain (1814), causing the Great Trek of the Boers inland to the Orange Free State and the Transvaal (1835–6). Napoleon failed to conquer Egypt (1798) but France conquered Algeria (1830–47). Among explorers, Caillié penetrated Central Africa (1827–8), and Nachtigal explored the area around Lake Chad (1869–74). Livingstone crossed the continent from west to east (1851–6) and Stanley from east to west (1874–7). The Suez Canal was cut by de Lesseps (1869). Great trading companies were formed by the colonizing powers and by 1912 the whole continent, except Liberia and Ethiopia, was partitioned among the European powers. The Berlin Conference (1884–5) tried to settle colonial rivalries, but many clashes occurred in the period prior to 1914. France clashed with Belgium over the Congo, with Britain over Egypt, the Sudan and E. Africa, and with Germany over Morocco. Britain came into conflict with Germany over S.W. and S.E. Africa, and with the Boers over S. Africa. Italy conquered Libya (1931) and Ethiopia (1936). Germany lost her colonies in 1918 and Italy lost hers in 1945. The League of Nations and the U.N. held certain former colonies in trusteeship (from 1918 and 1945). Since the 2nd world war, Africa has experienced political struggles against European powers, over Algeria, Suez and Angola, and much internal trouble, in Kenya, the Congo, South Africa, and between Israel and Egypt. There has been rapid economic development, and increasing nationalism has led to political independence for much of the continent. In 1956 Egypt, which had been independent by 1922, was evacuated by the British, and Tunisia, Morocco and the Sudan became independent. Ghana gained independence (1957), then Guinea (1958), Mali (1959), Nigeria, the Congo, Somaliland and 12 former French colonies (1960), Tanganyika (1961), Algeria, Uganda, Rwanda and Burundi (1962). The United Arab Republic of Egypt and Syria was set up (1958) but Syria withdrew (1961). Katanga seceded from the Congo (1960) and was reintegrated (1963). The Republic of South Africa left the Commonwealth (1961). In 1963, the Central African Federation, which had been set up ten years earlier, was dissolved, and Kenya became independent. Zanzibar gained independence (1963) and joined Tanganyika to form Tanzania (1964). Nyasaland became independent as Malawi, and Northern Rhodesia as Zambia (1964). Gambia became independent (1965). Bechuanaland became independent (1966) and changed its name to Botswana. Basutoland took the name Lesotho on gaining independence (1966). Equatorial Guinea and Swaziland became independent (1968). By 1975 former Portuguese colonies Angola, Mozambique, Cape Verde, Guinea-Bissau (formerly Portuguese Guinea) and São Tomé and Principe became independent, as did the French Comoros (1975) and Djibouti (1977) (formerly Afars and Issas) and the British Seychelles (1976). In the face of opposition from most other African countries, Britain, and the Commonwealth, white-ruled Rhodesia made a unilateral declaration of independence (1965) and later became independent Zimbabwe under black rule in 1980. Upper Volta changed its name to Burkina Faso (1984). Western Sahara, relinquished by Spain (1976) and divided between Morocco and Mauritania (who disclaimed it in 1979), was fought over by Morocco and the Polisario, an armed independence movement, through the 1980s. Unrest over the white government's traditional policy of *apartheid* in South Africa drew international attention

Af·ri·can (ǽfrikən) **1.** *adj.* pertaining to Africa **2.** *n.* a native of Africa **Af·ri·can·ist** *n.* a specialist in African cultures or African languages **Af·ri·can·ize** *pres. part.* **Af·ri·can·iz·ing** *past* and *past part.* **Af·ri·can·ized** *v.t.* to make African, esp. to make African appointments to (positions formerly held by Europeans) [fr. L. *Africanus*]

African languages the Hamito-Semitic languages of Africa, together with the native languages belonging mostly to three families: Khoi-San, Sudanese and Bantu. The Khoi-San family is divided into Bushman and Hottentot. The Sudanese group is spoken by over 50 million and includes a great number of different languages. The Bantu family is spoken by over 60 million

African marigold *Tagetes erecta*, an annual plant with large yellowish-orange flower heads, native to Mexico

Af·ri·kaans (æfrikáns) *n.* the form of the Dutch language developed in South Africa [Du. *Afrikaansch*]

Af·ri·kan·der (æfrikǽndər) *n.* an Afrikaner

Af·ri·ka·nen·dom (æfrikánəndəm) *n.* area of the Republic of South Africa settled and dominated by Dutch descendants, now principally South Africa

Af·ri·ka·ner (æfrikánər) *n.* a native of South Africa, of European, esp. Dutch, descent, a Boer [Taal *Afrikaander* fr. Du.]

Af·ro-A·mer·i·can (ǽfrouəmérikən) **1.** *adj.* pertaining to American blacks **2.** *n.* an American black ‖ dialect spoken by some U.S. blacks

Afroism (ǽfrouizəm) *n.* related to African culture

Af·ro-Sax·on (ǽfrousǽksən) *n.* (usu. used disparagingly) black person working as part of the white establishment

aft (æft, aft) *adv.* (*naut.*) at or near the stern of a ship [O.E. *œftan*, behind]

af·ter (ǽftər, áftər) *adj.* next, later, following, *in after years* ‖ (*naut.*) towards the stern of a ship, *the after cabin* ‖ hinder, posterior, towards the rear, *the after parts of a steer* [O.E. *œfter*]

after 1. *prep.* in search of, in pursuit of, *run after the postman* ‖ later than, subsequent to, following in time, *after a week we ought to reconsider* ‖ in spite of, *after all our help he still went the wrong way* ‖ in imitation of, in the manner of, *paintings after the Dutch masters* ‖ copied from, *an engraving after Poussin* **to be** (or **get**, etc.) **after** to be in angry pursuit of, *the farmer will be after you if you trample his hay* **to be named after** someone to be given someone's name, *he was named after his grandfather* **to look after** to take care of **to take after** to be like in looks or character **2.** *adv.* behind in time or place, later, *the dog came following after,* **3.** *conj.* subsequently to the time when, *after he went away we discussed the situation* [O.E. *œfter*]

af·ter·birth (ǽftərbə:rθ, áftərbə:rθ) *n.* the placenta, tissue connected with the fetus in the womb. The expulsion of this (with the membranes and umbilical cord) constitutes the final stage of labor

af·ter·burn·er (ǽftərbə:rnər) *n.* device for destroying (usually by burning) carbon wastes,

e.g., from the engine of a motor vehicle to reduce air pollution —**afterburn** *v.*

af·ter·care (ǽftərkçər, áftərkçər) *n.* further treatment of patients after discharge from the hospital ‖ rehabilitation of offenders leaving prison

af·ter·damp (ǽftərdæmp, áftərdæmp) *n.* toxic gases remaining in a mine after the explosion of firedamp

af·ter·deck (ǽftərdek, áftərdek) *n* (*naut.*) the part of a deck toward the stern, abaft the midships

af·ter·din·ner (ǽftərdínər, áftərdínər) *adj.* following dinner, *an after-dinner speech*

af·ter·ef·fect (ǽftərifekt, áftərifekt) *n.* a delayed effect ‖ (*med.*) an effect occurring after the first result of a drug has disappeared

af·ter·glow (ǽftərglou, áftərglou) *n.* a glow which remains after the source of light has gone, *a glow in the sky after the sun has set* ‖ the sensation that remains after a pleasant experience ‖ the period in phosphorescence or fluorescence after the excitation has been removed

af·ter·heat (ǽftərhi:t) *n.* heat remaining in a nuclear reactor during its operation

af·ter·life (ǽftərlaif, áftərlaif) *n.* life after death **in afterlife** in the later part of a person's lifetime

af·ter·math (ǽftərmæθ, áftərmæθ) *n.* outcome, consequence (usually of a disastrous nature) ‖ (of grass etc.) the crop taken from a second growth [AFTER+O.E. *mœth*, mowing]

af·ter·most (ǽftərmoust, áftərmoust, esp. *Br.* áftəməst) *adj.* (*naut.*) nearest the stern, hindmost, *the aftermost cabin* [O.E. *œoftermest*]

af·ter·noon (ǽftərnú:n, áftərnú:n) *n.* the time of day between midday and evening ‖ (*rhet.*) the later stages or periods, *the afternoon of life*

af·ter·pain (ǽftərpein, áftərpein) *n.* pain not felt until some interval after the time when it was caused ‖ (*pl.*) pains following childbirth associated with the contraction of the uterus

af·ter·part (ǽftərpart, áftərpart) *n.* (*naut.*) the area around the stern of a ship

af·ter·taste (ǽftərteist,áftərteist) *n.* the taste that remains in the mouth after eating or drinking ‖ the feeling remaining after an experience

af·ter·tax (ǽftərtæks) *adj.* of the balance of earnings after payment of income taxes

af·ter·thought (ǽftərθɔt, áftərθɔt) *n.* further thought after action, subsequent reflection

after·ward (ǽftərwərd, áftərwərd) *adv.* at a later time, subsequently [O.E. *œfteweard*, behind]

af·ter·wards (ǽftərwərdz, áftərwərdz) *adv.* afterward [O.E. *œofteweardes*]

A·ga·des (ǽgədés) a town (pop. 5,000) in central Niger, in the Aïr foothills

A·ga·dir (ǽgədíər) a Moroccan seaport (pop. 61,192). It was the scene of a serious incident between France and Germany (1911) in the struggle for control of N.W. Africa. The town was almost destroyed by an earthquake (1960)

a·gain (əgén) *adv.* once more, *try and do it again* ‖ furthermore, in addition, *and again, remember that... * **again and again** very often **as many** (or **much**) **again** the same quantity in addition, *fill my sack and then give me half as much again* **over again** once more [O.E. *ongean*]

a·gainst (əgénst) *prep.* opposite to, contrary to, *against his wishes* ‖ in contrast to, *it stood out against the sky* ‖ in anticipation of, *preparations against a hard winter* ‖ into contact with, *hailstones against the window,* put the ladder *against the wall* ‖ about, *they were warned against the danger* ‖ in exchange for, *will you take my French stamps against your Brazils?* ‖ in the opposite direction to, *against the tide* ‖ to be charged to or deducted from (an account, or something thought of as an account), *set it against expenses* ‖ next to, *put the chair against the wall* **to be** (or **come**) **up against it** (*Br.*, *pop.*) to suffer (or to encounter) hardship or difficulty **to run up against** (*Br.*) to meet by chance, to run across ‖ to encounter, *to run up against difficulties* [fr. O.E. *agenes*]

A·ga Khan (ágəkán) the hereditary spiritual head of the Isma'ili sect of Moslems, claiming descent from Fatima

A·ga·mem·non (ægəmémnən, ægəmémnɒn) a legendary king of Argos and Mycenae and the leader of the Greek expedition against Troy. He sacrificed his daughter Iphigenia to appease Artemis and calm the winds which were holding back his ships. On his return home from

Troy he was murdered by his wife Clytemnestra and her lover Aegisthus. His death was avenged by his son Orestes at the urging of Electra, his daughter

a·gam·ic (eigǽmik) *adj.* (*biol.*) asexual [fr. Gk *agamos*, without marriage]

a·gam·o·gen·e·sis (eigæmoudʒénisis) *n.* (*biol.*) parthenogenesis ‖ asexual reproduction **a·gam·o·ge·net·ic** (eigæmoudʒənétik) *adj.* **a·gam·o·ge·nét·i·cal·ly** *adv.* [fr. Gk *agamos*, without marriage+*genesis*, birth]

ag·a·mous (ǽgəmɒs) *adj.* (*biol.*) asexual [fr. L. fr. Gk *agamos*, wihout marriage]

A·ga·ña (əgánjə) the capital (pop. 2,119) of Guam, on the west coast

a·ga·pe (ǽgəpei,əgápei) *n.* the meal of fellowship among early Christians, commemorating the Last Supper ‖ spiritual love (cf. EROS) [Gk= brotherly love]

a·gape (əgéip) *pred. adj.* openmouthed with surprise

a·gar (ágər, éigər) *n.* agar-agar

a·gar-a·gar (águrágar, éigəréigər) *n* a gelatinous substance, allied chemically with the carbohydrates, obtained from certain seaweeds, esp. in Ceylon, Java, Japan and Malaysia. After being mixed with hot water and cooled, it sets to a firm jelly and is used as the base of media for bacteriological culture and in the industrial preparation of jam, sauces etc. [Malay.]

ag·a·ric (ǽgərik, əgǽrik) **1.** *n.* a fungus of fam. *Agaricaceae* (*MUSHROOM) **2.** *adj.* of or relating to this fungus [L. *agaricum* fr. Gk]

Ag·as·siz (ǽgəsi:), Jean Louis Rodolphe (1807–73), Swiss–U.S. naturalist, geologist and teacher. His studies ranged from fish fossils to glaciers

ag·ate (ǽgit) *n.* a very hard cryptocrystalline form of silica, marked with bands or clouds of color due to the infiltration of other minerals, used for the knife-edges of chemical balances, for mortars in which hard substances are ground, and for ornaments ‖ a burnishing tool used in bookbinding ‖ an instrument used in drawing gold wire ‖ (*printing*) ruby type ‖ (*games*) a marble [F. *agathe* fr. Ital.]

a·ga·ve (əgéivi:,əgávi:) *n.* a member of *Agave*, fam. *Amaryllidaceae*, a genus of tropical plants cultivated for their fiber (*SISAL, *PITA), as the source of a Mexican drink (* PULQUE,* MESCAL, *TEQUILA), and for ornament (*CENTURY PLANT) [mod. L. fr. Gk *agauē*, fem. adj., illustrious]

age (eidʒ) **1.** *n.* the length of time that a person or thing has lived or existed, *ten years of age* ‖ the time of life when one is legally, socially, physically or mentally qualified for a particular purpose, *to come of age* ‖ old age ‖ a generation ‖ an epoch ‖ a great period of time distinguished from others by its special characteristics. *Middle Ages* ‖ (*geol.*) a subdivision of an epoch ‖ (*pop.*, often *pl.*) a very long time, *it's an age since we last met* **2.** *v. pres. part.* **ag·ing, age·ing** *past* and *past part.* **aged** *v.t.* to make older, *his war experiences aged him* ‖ *v.i.* to become perceptibly older, *his hasn't aged a bit* ‖ to mellow, *this whisky hasn't aged enough yet* **a·ged** (éidʒid) *adj.* old, showing visible signs of old age ‖ (éidʒd) of the age of, *a boy aged ten* ‖ (éidʒd, of animals) having reached maturity (e.g.of a horse, seven years old) [O.F. *aage*]

Agee (eidʒi:), James (1909–55), U.S. author of various genres, including poetry, 'Permit Me Voyage' (1934); non-fiction, 'Let Us Now Praise Famous Men' (1941); two volumes of film review, 'Agee on Film' (1958, 1960); an autobiographical novel, 'A Death in the Family' (1957, Pulitzer Prize 1958, film 1963); and screenplay, 'The African Queen' (1951)

age·ism (éidʒizəm) *n.* discrimination against the elderly

age·less (éidʒlis) *adj.* not affected by age or time

age·long (éidʒlɒŋ, éidʒlɒŋ) *adj.* (*rhet.*) lasting for centuries ‖ transmitted down the ages, *age-long wisdom*

a·gen·cy (éidʒənsi:) *pl.* **a·gen·cies** *n.* an organization (or its building) existing to promote the exchange of goods and services, *a travel agency* ‖ instrumentality, *through the doctor's agency he got full compensation* ‖ the profession of being an agent [fr. M. L. *agentia*, the faculty of doing]

Agency for International Development (AID), a U.S. government agency within the State Department, established (1961) to provide nonmilitary aid to underdeveloped countries in the form of loans and grants. It guarantees U.S. private investors against cer-

---

CONCISE PRONUNCIATION KEY: (**a**) æ, c*a*t; ɑ, c*a*r; ɔ f*aw*n; ei, sn*a*ke. (**e**) e, h*e*n; i:, sh*ee*p; iə, d*ee*r; ɛə, b*ea*r. (**i**) i, f*i*sh; ai, t*i*ger; ə:, b*i*rd. (**o**) o, *o*x; au, c*ow*; ou, g*oa*t; u, p*oo*r; ɔi, r*oy*al. (**u**) ʌ, d*u*ck; u, b*u*ll; u:, g*oo*se; ə, b*a*cillus; ju:, c*u*be. x, lo*ch*; θ, *th*ink; ð, bo*th*er; z, *Z*en; ʒ, cor*s*age; dʒ, sa*v*age; ŋ, ora*n*gutang; j, *y*ak; ʃ, *fi*sh; tʃ, fe*tch*; 'l, rabb*le*; 'n, redd*en*. Complete pronunciation key appears inside front cover.

tain specified risks. The U.S. aspect of Alliance for Progress is administered by AID

a·gen·da (ədʒéndə) n. (construed as pl.) things to be done ‖ (construed as sing.) a list of things to be discussed at a business meetings ‖ a memorandum book [L., pl. of agendum]

a·gen·e·sis (eidʒénisis) n. (med.) congenital absence or imperfect development of any part of the human body [fr. Gk a, without+genesis, birth]

a·gent (éidʒənt) n. someone who represents a person or a firm in business ‖ an intermediary ‖ a means, instrument (person or thing) used to secure some effect ‖ (chem.) a substance or element capable of taking part in a reaction [fr. L. agens (agentis). doing]

Agent Orange (chem.) defoliant mixture of 2,4-D and 2,4,5-T and highly toxic dioxin. It was used in Vietnam as a jungle denuder and sometimes in U.S. as a weed killer

a·gent pro·vo·ca·teur (æʒăprɔvɔkæta:r) pl. a·gents pro·vo·ca·teurs (æʒăprɔvɔkæta:r) n. a paid agent who, by pretended sympathy, seeks to induce suspect persons to expose themselves, esp. one who provokes seditious movements in order to justify official reprisals [F.]

Age of Aquarius period in U.S. history dominated by discontent among young adults seeking freedom and brotherhood, esp. in 1960s

age of consent (law) the age of a girl before which sexual intercourse with her is considered rape, whether or not she has consented

age of discretion the earliest age at which the law credits a person with responsibility for certain actions

a·er·a·tum (ædʒəréitəm) n. a member of Ageratum. fam. Compositae, a large genus of tropical American plants with small heads of blue or white flowers [Mod. L. fr. Gk agēraton, not growing old]

Agesilaus II, (ədʒesileíəs) King of Sparta (c. 444–360 B.C.), one of the two Spartan kings from 399. He defeated the Persian satrap Tissaphernes and then the Thebans and their allies at Coronea, but was defeated by Thebes at Leuctra, which signaled the end of Sparta's military strength

ag·gior·na·men·to (əʒɔrnaméntou) n. an updating, esp. with regard to the policy of modernizing Roman Catholic institutions, one of goals of the second Vatican Council, 1962–1965

ag·glom·er·ate (əglóməreit) 1. v. pres. part. ag·glom·er·at·ing past and past part. ag·glom·er·at·ed v.t. to gather into a ball or mass ‖ v.i. to grow into a ball or mass 2. adj. (əglómərit) collected into, forming, growing into a ball or mass 3. n. (əglómərit) a mass, collection ‖ (geol.) an unstratified rock formed from volcanic fragments united by heat (cf. CONGLOMERATE) **ag·glom·er·á·tion** n. a cohesive mass, e.g. a town's suburbs **ag·glom·er·a·tive** (əglómərəitiv, əglómərətiv) adj. [fr. L. agglomerare (agglomeratus), to wind into a ball]

ag·glu·ti·nate (əglú:t'neit) 1. v. pres. part. ag·glu·ti·nat·ing past and past part. ag·glu·ti·nat·ed v.t. to join together as if with glue ‖ v.i. to combine by agglutination ‖ to turn into glue 2. adj. (əglú:t'nit) glued together ‖ (gram.) of forms made up of simple words joined together to form compounds without changed form or loss of meaning [fr. L. agglutinare (agglutinatus), to glue together]

ag·glu·ti·nat·ing (əglú:t'neitiŋ) adj. (linguistics) of a language made up of sequence of roots that have been joined to produce a word with each element having its own meaning

ag·glu·ti·na·tion (əglu:t'néiʃən) n. the action of joining as if with glue ‖ the object composed of the parts thus joined ‖ (chem.) the adhering in a mass of suspended particles ‖ (med., bacteriol.) the massing of particles (e.g. red blood cells, microorganisms etc.) suspended in a liquid ‖ (gram.) the combination of simple words to form compounds without alteration of the form or meaning of the parts [fr. L. agglutinatio (agglutinationis)]

ag·glu·ti·na·tive (əglú:t'neitiv) adj. causing or produced by agglutination ‖ (gram.) characterized by agglutination

ag·gran·dize (əgrǽndaiz, ǽgrandaiz) pres. part. ag·gran·diz·ing past and past part. ag·gran·dized v.t. to make (a person or nation) greater in power, rank, prestige or wealth ‖ to exaggerate, to give the appearance of greatness to ag·gran·dize·ment (əgrǽndizmənt) n. [fr. F. agrandir (agrandiss-)]

ag·gra·vate (ǽgrəveit) pres. part. ag·gra·vat·

ing past and past part. **ag·gra·vat·ed** v.t. to make (an existing trouble) more serious ‖ (pop.) to irritate or exasperate **ag·gra·vá·tion** n. [fr. L. aggravare (aggravatus), to make heavy]

ag·gre·gate (ǽgrigeit) 1. v. pres. part. **ag·gre·gat·ing** past and past part. **ag·gre·gat·ed** v.t. to collect together into a mass ‖ to total ‖ v.i. to come together in a mass 2. (ǽgrigit) adj. formed of parts making a collection, massed together ‖ total, collective ‖ (bot.) having many similar fruits from one flower, e.g. magnolia ‖ (geol.) made up of different mineral crystals, e.g. granite 3. (ǽgrigit) n. a total derived by addition (cf. PRODUCT) ‖ materials mixed with cement to make concrete **in the aggregate** collectively **ag·gre·gá·tion** n. [fr. L. aggregare (aggregatus), to gather into a herd]

ag·gres·sion (əgréʃən) n. a deliberate, unprovoked attack by one country or group on another ‖ (psychol.) energetic activity of the mind or body, whether innate or a product of frustration, and either healthily expressed in proper self-assertion or in the use and perfecting of skills etc., or morbidly expressed in bullying, masochism, destructiveness etc., or sublimated in play [F.]

ag·gres·sive (əgrésiv) adj. wanting to dominate by attacking, domineering ‖ involving attack ‖ enterprising and forceful, an aggressive advertising policy [fr. L. aggredi (aggressus), to approach]

ag·gres·sor (əgrésər) n. a person, nation etc. making a deliberate attack [L.]

ag·grieved (əgrí:vd) adj. having a grievance [past part. of older aggrieve v. fr. O.F.]

a·ghast (əgǽst, əgást) pred. adj. filled with terror or amazement or both [A (hist. prep.)+gast, past part. of O.E. gæstan, to terrify]

ag·ile (ǽdʒil, esp. Br. ǽdʒail) adj. quick moving, nimble, active in body or mind **a·gil·i·ty** (ədʒíliti) n. [F.]

Ag·in·court, Battle of (ǽdʒinkɔrt, ǽdʒinkourt) a battle fought on Oct. 25, 1415 near Agincourt (Pas de Calais). Henry V's English longbowmen defeated the French knights who were made helpless by the weight of their armor. The longbowmen are said to have killed between 5,000 and 10,000 of the French army and to have taken 1,000 prisoners for the loss of 13 men-at-arms and 100 foot soldiers

ag·i·tate (ǽdʒiteit) pres. part. **ag·i·tat·ing** past and past part. **ag·i·tat·ed** v.t. to shake, stir up ‖ to upset (feelings, people) ‖ v.i. (politics) to stir up the public by means of slogans, demonstrations etc. either to produce disorder or to secure reform [fr. L. agitare (agitatus), to move to and fro]

ag·i·ta·tion (ædʒitéiʃən) n. a disturbance, mental or physical, esp. worry ‖ public disturbance on a large scale, or the process of creating it [F.]

ag·i·ta·tor (ǽdʒiteitər) n. a person who provokes social, political or religious disaffection ‖ an apparatus for mixing or shaking

ag·let (ǽglit) n. the metal tag of a lace ‖ a tagged point hanging from cords or braids used on some uniforms, often from shoulder to breast [fr. F. aiguillette dim. of aiguille, needle]

a·glow (əglóu) adv. and pred. adj. in a glow, his face was aglow with pleasure

AGM-84 *HARPOON
AGM-53 *CONDOR
AGM-45 *SHRIKE
AGM-78 *STANDARD ARM
AGM-65 *MAVERICK
AGM-28 *HOUND DOG

ag·nail (ǽgneil) n. a sore at the root of a fingernail or toenail ‖ a hangnail [O.E. ang, tight, painful+naegl, nail]

ag·nate (ǽgneit) 1. n. a relative only on the male side of a family 2. adj. allied, related through a common male ancestor, or by clan or nation ‖ (rare) akin, similar **ag·nat·ic** (ægnǽtik) adj. **ag·na·tion** (ægnéiʃən) n. [F. agnat]

Ag·nes (ǽgnis), St (290–303), of Salerno, a martyr under Diocletian. Feast: Jan. 21

Agnew (ǽgnu:) Spiro Theodore (1918–   ), U.S. Republican vice-president under Richard Nixon and governor of Maryland. He was charged with accepting bribes while governor and resigned from the vice-presidency Oct. 10, 1973. He pleaded no contest to one count of income tax evasion and after a civil suit paid Maryland $270,000 as reimbursement for alleged kickbacks

Ag·ni (ǽgni) pl. **Ag·ni, Ag·nis** n. a member of a W. African people related to the Ashanti

ag·no·men (ægnóumən) pl. **ag·nom·i·na** (ægnómina), **ag·no·mens** n. an additional or fourth name, added as title or epithet to an ancient Roman name, e.g. 'Africanus' in Publius Cornelius Scipio Africanus (cf. NOMEN, cf. COGNOMEN, cf. PRAENOMEN) [L.]

Agnon, (ágnɔn) Shmuel Yosef (1888–1970), Hebrew author and winner of the Nobel Prize for literature in 1966. Born in Galicia (now in Poland), he lived mostly in Jerusalem. Agnon's topics were the decline of Eastern European Jewish life in the 1930's and the struggles of early Jewish settlers in Palestine. Sometimes compared to Franz Kafka, his works include 'The Bridal Canopy' (1930), 'In the Heart of the Seas' (1933), and 'Temol Shilshom' ('The Day Before Yesterday,' 1945)

ag·nos·tic (ægnóstik) 1. n. a person who thinks that nothing can be known about the existence or nature of God ‖ a person who thinks that knowledge of all matters is relative 2. adj. referring to agnosticism **ag·nos·ti·cal·ly** adv. **ag·nos·ti·cism** (ægnóstisizəm) n. the doctrine of an agnostic (cf. ATHEISM, cf. SKEPTICISM) [fr. Gk agnostos, unknown]

Ag·nus De·i (ágnusdéii:) a triple prayer for mercy and peace at the Mass during the breaking of the Host ‖ this part of the Mass ‖ music for it ‖ a disk of wax stamped with the figure of a lamb and blessed by the pope [L.=lamb of God]

a·go (əgóu) 1. adj. (always follows the word it modifies) past, two years ago 2. adv. in the past, long ago [M.E. agone, past part. of obs. ago v. fr. O.E. a-, forth+gan, go]

a·gog (əgóg) pred. adj. eager, excited with anticipation [perh. fr. O.F. engogues fr. en, in + gogue, fun]

a·go·go (əgóugou) n. (Fr.) discotheque; an intimate spot for dancing

a·gon·ic (eigónik, əgónik) adj. not forming an angle [fr. Gk agōnos fr. a-, without+gōnia, angle]

agonic line an imaginary line on the earth's surface joining places at which the magnetic needle points geographically north and south (*DECLINATION)

ag·o·nis·tic (ægənístik) adj. of interactions (fidgeting, cooperating, submitting) between members of the same species

ag·o·nize (ǽgənaiz) pres. part. **ag·o·niz·ing** past and past part. **ag·o·nized** v.t. to cause intense suffering in mind or body to ‖ v.i. to suffer intensely in mind or body, writhe with pain (esp. in the death agony) [fr. M.L. agonizare, to contend in the arena, fr. Gk]

ag·o·ny (ǽgəni:) pl. **ag·o·nies** n. intense mental or physical suffering ‖ an intense feeling. an agony of joy ‖ (pl., loosely) a hard struggle, to go through agonies to get something **last agony** the pangs of death **the Ag·o·ny** the sufferings of Jesus in Gethsemane [fr. L. agonia, struggle, fr. Gk]

agony column (Br. pop.) a column of personal news in a newspaper

a·go·ra (ægorá) pl. **a·go·rot** (ægorɔ́t) n. an Israeli unit of currency equal to one hundredth of a pound

a·go·ra (ǽgərə) n. (hist.) the shoplined open square of ancient Greek cities which was the marketplace and religious and civic center [Gk]

ag·o·ra·pho·bi·a (ægərəfóubi:ə) n. morbid dread of public or open spaces **ag·o·ra·phó·bic** adj. [Mod. L. fr. Gk agora, place of assembly+phobia, fear]

a·gou·ti (əgú:ti:) n. a member of Dasyprocta, a genus of South American rodents, like guinea pigs. They are herbivorous and damage sugarcane [F. fr. S. American Indian]

A·gra (ágrə) a city (pop. 591,917) of Uttar Pradesh, India, on the Jumna River. Built (1566) by Akbar, it was a Mogul capital until 1658, and has many fine examples of Mogul architecture, including the Taj Mahal, Akbar's fort, the Pearl Mosque and the Imperial Palace. It is a commercial and manufacturing center

a·grar·i·an (əgréəri:ən) adj. relating to land or its management or distribution. agrarian laws **a·grár·i·an·ism** n. the theory or practice of distributing the land more equitably or facilitating more productive ways of cultivating it [fr. L. agrarius]

a·gra·ris·mo (agrari:smɔ) n. a native Mexican movement for agrarian reforms, esp. for a more equitable redistribution of the land to the peasants [Span.]

CONCISE PRONUNCIATION KEY: (a) æ, cat; ɑ, car; ɔ fawn; ei, snake. (e) e, hen; i:, sheep; iə, deer; ɛə, bear. (i) i, fish; ai, tiger; ə:, bird. (o) ɔ, ox; au, cow; ou, goat; u, poor; ɔi, royal. (u) ʌ, duck; u, bull; u:, goose; ə, bacillus; ju:, cube. x, loch; θ, think; ð, bother; z, Zen; ʒ, corsage; dʒ, savage; ŋ, orangutang; j, yak; ʃ, fish; tʃ, fetch; 'l, rabble; 'n, redden. Complete pronunciation key appears inside front cover.

a·grav·ic (eigrǽvik) *adj.* of a condition where gravity is zero

a·gree (əgri:) *pres. part.* **a·gree·ing** *past and past part.* **a·greed** *v.i.* to assent, *she'll never agree to that* ‖ to be in harmony, *we don't agree about the dog* ‖ to be suitable (as regards one's tastes, health etc.), *this climate doesn't agree with me* ‖ (of accounts) to balance ‖ (*gram.*) to correspond in number, gender, case or person ‖ *v.t.* to consent, *he agreed never to smoke* ‖ (*Br.*) to check, *please agree my total* ‖ (*Br.*) to confirm, *do you agree the bill?* [O.F.]

a·gree·a·bil·i·ty (əgri:əbiliti:) *n.* the state or quality of being agreeable

a·gree·a·ble (əgri:əb'l) *adj.* pleasant ‖ prepared to consent, *are they agreeable to our plan?* **a·grée·a·bly** *adv.* [F. *agréable*]

a·gree·ment (əgri:mənt) *n.* the act of agreeing ‖ the state of agreeing, *in agreement with the facts* ‖ (*law*) a contract legally binding the contracting parties ‖ (*gram.*) concord in gender, number, case or person [O.F.]

ag·ri·busi·ness (ǽgribiznis) *n.* production, trade, processing, storage, and marketing of farm products

A·gric·o·la (əgríkələ), Gnaeus Julius, Roman general (40–93), and father-in-law of Tacitus, who wrote his biography. He completed the conquest of Britain

ag·ri·cul·tur·al (ægrikʌltʃərəl) *adj.* related to or characteristic of agriculture

ag·ri·cul·tur·al·ist (ægrikʌltʃərəlist) *n.* a person competent in farming theory

agricultural pollution liquid and solid wastes from farming, including runoff from pesticides, fertilizers, and feedlots; erosion and dust from plowing; animal manure and carcasses; crop residues and debris

ag·ri·cul·ture (ǽgrikʌltʃər) *n.* the science or practice of large-scale soil cultivation (cf. HORTICULTURE), farming [F.]

ag·ri·cul·tur·ist (ægrikʌltʃərist) *n.* an agriculturalist

A·gri·gen·to (ɑgri:dʒéntɔ) (formerly Girgenti) a town (pop. 50,000) near the south coast of Sicily exporting sulfur, fruit, olives and wine. Greek temple ruins, cathedral (14th c., restored)

ag·ri·mo·ny (ǽgrəmouni:) *n.* a member of *Agrimonia*, fam. *Rosaceae*, a genus of yellow-flowered plants, with toothed leaves, burr-like fruits and bitter taste ‖ hemp agrimony [fr. L. *agrimonia* fr. Gk *agremōnē*, a kind of poppy]

A·grip·pa (əgrípə), Marcus Vipsanius (63–12 B.C.), Roman general who distinguished himself at Actium, the trusted adviser and minister of Augustus, and his son-in-law. He had the Pantheon built at Rome

A·grip·pi·na (ægripí:nə) (15–59), daughter of Germanicus. She married (as her third husband) her uncle, the Emperor Claudius I, made him adopt her son Nero, and secured Nero's accession by murdering Claudius (54). She was subsequently assassinated on instructions from Nero

ag·ro·in·dus·tri·al (ægrouindʌstri:əl) *adj.* of an activity favoring both agriculture and industry **—agro-industry** *n.*

ag·ro·nom·ic (ægrənómik) *adj.* of or relating to agronomy **ag·ro·nóm·i·cal** *adj.*

a·gron·o·mist (əgrónəmist) *n.* someone who specializes in agronomy

a·gron·o·my (əgrónəmi:) *n.* the theory and practice of crop production and soil science [F. *agronomie* fr. Gk]

a·ground (əgráund) *adv.* and *pred. adj.* (of a ship) touching the bottom in shallow water

A·guas·ca·lien·tes (ɑgwɑskɑljéntes) an inland state (area 2,499 sq. miles, pop. 504,300) of central Mexico, on a plateau about 6,000 ft above sea level: agriculture (wine, fruits), stock raising (bulls, cattle, horses, mules), metallurgy (zinc, copper, gold, silver, lead and antimony). Thermal springs ‖ its capital (pop. 257,179), 364 miles northwest of Mexico City, Mexico

a·gue (éigju:) *n.* fever and paroxysms associated with malaria ‖ a chill or fit of shivering **á·gu·ish** *adj.* [O.F.]

A·gui·nal·do (ɑgi:nɑ́ldɔ), Emilio (1869–1964), Filipino resistance leader, of Chinese and Tagalog parentage. He joined forces with the U.S.A. to rid the Philippines of Spanish rule. He then broke with the U.S. authorities in his desire for complete independence for his country. He led the insurrection which proclaimed (1898) the first Republic of the Philippines. After his capture and the end of the insurrection, he took an oath of allegiance to the U.S.A., which in return granted him a pension. During the 2nd world war he was accused of collaborating with the Japanese invaders, but received a presidential amnesty. Thereafter he devoted himself to the promotion of nationalism and democracy in the Philippines and to the improvement of U.S.-Filipino relations

A·gul·has, Cape (əgʌ́ləs) the southern extremity of Africa

A·hab (éihæb) king of Israel (c. 875–c. 853 B.C.). The husband of Jezebel, he allowed the worship of Baal, and defended his kingdom against the Syrians and Assyrians (I Kings xvi–xxii)

a·head (əhéd) **1.** *adj.* in front, in advance ‖ forward **2.** *adv.* in or to the front ‖ forward **ahead of** in front of ‖ before **to get ahead** to be successful

a·heap (əhí:p) *adv.* in a heap

a·he·mer·al (eihemé:rəl) *adj.* a day of less than 24 hrs

a·him·sa (əhímsɑ) *n.* nonviolence or nonkilling as a creed, affirmed in the belief (taught by Buddhist, Brahman and Jainist philosophies) that all life is sacred [Skr.]

Ahmad Fuad *FUAD I

Ah·ma·di·ya Movement (ɑmədí:jə) the Islamic sect founded (1879) in the Punjab by Mirza Ghūlam Ahmad, who claimed to be the Mahdi

Ah·mad Shah (ɑ́mədʃɑ́) (1724–73), the creator and first king of Afghanistan

Ah·med·a·bad (ɑmədɑbɑ́d) the capital (pop. 1,040,000) of Gujarat, India, on the Sabarmati River: textiles

Ah·med Khan (ɑ́mədkɑ́n), Sir Syed (1817–98), Indian social reformer and educationalist, founder of the Moslem University at Aligarh (1875)

Ah·med·na·gar (ɑmədnʌ́gər) a town (pop. 119,000) in Maharashtra, W. India: textiles

Ah·mose I (ɑ́mous) (or Aahmas I or Amasis I), Egyptian king (c. 1580–c. 1558 B.C.). The founder of the 18th dynasty, he freed Egypt from the Hyksos

AH-1 *SEA COBRA

a·hoy (əhɔ́i) *interj.* (*naut.*) a cry used in hailing. *Ship ahoy!* [A interj. + *hoy*, var. of HEY]

Ah·ri·man (ɑ́rimɑn) *n.* the spirit of evil in the Zoroastrian religion, opposed to Ormazd [Pers.]

Ah·ve·nan·maa (ɑ́xvenɑnmɑ) *ALAND

Ah·waz (ɑwɑ́z) a town (pop. 120,000) of S.W. Iran on the Karun River, a commercial center linked by oil pipeline to Abadan. University

ai (ɑi) *n. Bradypus tridactylus*, the three-toed sloth of South America [Tupi]

AI (*abbr.*) for artificial intelligence, the capability of computers to create new knowledge

AID *AGENCY FOR INTERNATIONAL DEVELOPMENT

AID (*computer*) algebraic computer language for applications in conversational mode

aid (eid) **1.** *n.* help, assistance ‖ someone who helps or something which helps **2.** *v.t.* and *i.* to help [O.F. *aider*]

Ai·dan (éid'n), St (*d.* 651), a monk sent from Iona in 635 to become bishop of Northumbria. Holy Island was the base for his missionary journeys throughout northern England

aide-de-camp (eiddikǽmp) *pl.* **aides-de-camp** (eidzdikǽmp) *n.* an officer attached to a high-ranking officer or governor etc. to assist him personally and confidentially [F.]

aide-mé·moire (eidmemwɑ́r) *pl.* **aides-mé-moire** (eidzmemwɑ́r) *n.* a summary of the main items of a document to be drafted [F.]

AIDS (eidz) or Acquired Immune Deficiency Syndrome, a disease that attacks the body's immune system, rendering it unable to fight cancer, pneumonia, and a wide variety of other diseases. Appearing in the U.S. in 1979, it has reached epidemic proportions, especially among male homosexuals and intravenous-drug abusers. It appears to be transmitted through intimate contacts involving blood or semen and blood donors are now being tested for exposure to AIDS. The fatality rate of 50% is rising

aid station a dressing station

ai·grette (eigret) *n.* an egret ‖ a tuft of feathers or spray of gems worn on the head [F.]

ai·guille (eigwi:l) *n.* a sharp pinnacle of rock ‖ an instrument for boring holes [F. =needle]

ai·guil·lette (eigwilét) *n.* an aglet [F.]

Aiken, (éikin) Conrad (1889–1973), U.S. poet, prose fiction writer, and critic. He sought an 'absolute' poetry in which emotion was employed with detachment, but much of his poetry is concerned with metaphysical and psychological insights. His works include 'The Charnel Rose' (1918), 'Selected Poems' (1929, Pulitzer Prize), and 'Collected Poems' (1953). Aiken also helped establish Emily Dickinson's reputation

Ai·ken solution (éikən) proposal by Senator George Aiken (1966) that U.S. simply declare a victory in Vietnam and withdraw its forces

ai·ki·do (eikaídou) *n.* Japanese method of self-defense depending on high, nonresistance, mental concentration, coordination of body movements, and using the opponent's momentum to create holds, throws, and locks

ail (eil) *v.i.* to be slightly ill ‖ *v.t.* (*rhet.*) to trouble, afflict, *what ails him?* [O.E. *eglan*, to trouble]

ai·lan·thus (eilǽnθəs) *n.* a member of *Ailanthus*, fam. *Simaroubaceae*, a genus of tropical Asiatic trees having pinnate leaves, small greenish flowers and bitter bark. *A. glandulosa* or *A. altissima*, the tree of heaven, is grown in S. Europe for shade and for its leaves, which silkworms feed on [fr. Amboinese *aylanto*, tree of, heaven]

ai·ler·on (éilərɒn) *n.* a hinged flap on the rear edge of an airplane's wing, used mainly for lateral control [F.]

Ailey, (éili:) Alvin (1931–), U.S. choreographer and modern dancer. He dances and choreographs for his own highly successful Alvin Ailey American Dance Theater as well as choreographing such works as 'Feast of Ashes' for the Joffrey Ballet. He combines African ethnic dance, modern dance, ballet, and jazz in his work

ail·ment (éilmənt) *n.* an illness of a trivial nature

aim (eim) **1.** *v.t.* to direct (a missile, blow, gun etc. or a remark, purpose etc.) at an objective ‖ *v.i.* to take aim, direct a weapon or missile, *aim at that stick* ‖ to direct efforts, purposes etc., *aim at quick scoring* **2.** *n.* the action of aiming, *the noise spoiled his aim* ‖ a purpose, intention, *the main aim is to finish quickly* **to take aim** to aim

áim·less *adj.* without purpose [O.F. *esmer*, to estimate]

AIMACO (*computer acronym*) for air material command, a U.S. Air Force computer compiling system for Univac 1105

AIM-54 *PHOENIX

AIM-4 *FALCON

AIM-47 *FALCON

AIM-9 *SIDEWINDER

AIM-7 *SPARROW

AIM-26 *FALCON

Ain (ɛ̃) a department (area 2,248 sq. miles, pop. 376,500) of S.E. France, northeast of Lyon (*LYONNAIS). Chief town: Bourg

ain·hum (ainjú:m) *n.* a disease of dark-skinned races in which a groove grows around a toe, gradually cutting it off [Port. fr. Yoruba]

Ain·tab (aintǽb) *GAZIANTEP

Ai·nu (áinu:) *n.* one of the hairy aboriginal inhabitants of Japan. The race is reduced to about 15,000 people, living on the islands of Sakhaline and Hokkaido ‖ their language, which is unrelated to Japanese

A·ïr (ǽiər) (Azbine) the central highlands of Niger, rising to over 5,000 ft. Chief town: Agadès

air (εər) **1.** *n.* the atmosphere, the mixture of gases surrounding the earth which all people and land animals breathe ‖ the space above us, *to throw a ball up into the air* ‖ a melody ‖ appearance, manner, *a jaunty air* ‖ (*pl.*) affectations of superiority **by air** in an airplane **in the air** unsettled, uncertain, *our plans are in the air* ‖ prevalent, circulating, *rumors are in the air* **on the air** in or by means of a radio broadcast **to give (someone) the air** to send away or dismiss (someone) **to walk on air** to be lightheaded with happiness **up in the air** vague ‖ not yet decided **2.** *v.t.* to expose to fresh air, ventilate ‖ (*Br.*) to dry in a warm place, *to air freshly ironed clothes* ‖ to display in public (e.g. a grievance) [O.F. *air*]

—At sea level, the composition by volume of dry air is 78% nitrogen, 21% oxygen, with small quantities of carbon dioxide, ozone and the inert gases. The water content of air varies up to 4% (in the tropics), and sulfur compounds may be present as industrial pollution

air·bag (éərbæg) *n.* plastic bag for automobile dashboard, designed to inflate upon collision to form a protective cushion

air battery rechargeable battery powered by oxidation of metal

air bearing a bearing or moving part supported by jets of air

air bladder (in fishes) a swim bladder ‖ (in some seaweeds, e.g. bladder wrack) a hollow dilatation of the thallus

air-borne (éərbɔrn, éərbourn) *adj.* carried by air ‖ in the air, *the squadron was airborne in a few minutes*

air brake a brake worked by compressed air ‖ an aileron or flap that can be made to resist the airstream so as to slow down an aircraft or car

air brick a brick perforated to allow ventilation

air bridge a massive connection by aircraft between two places

air-brush (éərbrʌʃ) *n.* an atomizer operated by compressed air which propels paint or ink etc. as a fine spray

Air-bus (éərbʌs) *n.* trademark of wide-bodied (but narrower than jumbo jet), short- and medium-range transport plane by Airbus Industrial (French-German-Spanish-British), with 200–270 seats, 2,500–3,000-mi range; 1979 model is A-300, used by Eastern Airlines *Cf* JUMBO JET

air cavalry (*mil.*) military unit equipped with air transport, for reconnaissance and combat *syn* **air vac**

air chamber in hydraulic machines, a cavity containing air whose elasticity serves to equalize pressure ‖ a cavity filled with air in an organic body

air chief marshal an officer in the British Royal Air Force ranking below a marshal and above an air marshal

air coach coach (class of air travel)

air combat fighter (F-16) a single-engine, supersonic, turbofan, all-weather multi-purpose tactical fighter-bomber, with air refueling capability, capable of employing nuclear and nonnuclear weapons. Air superiority is its primary mission, with air interdiction and close air support as secondary uses

air command (*mil.*) a major subdivision of the U.S. Air Force, for operational purposes, normally consisting of two or more squadrons or wings

air commodore an officer in the British Royal Air Force ranking above a group captain and below an air vice-marshal

air-con-di-tion (éərkəndiʃən) *v.t.* to equip (a building) with air-conditioning apparatus

air conditioner an air-conditioning device

air conditioning a process by which air is purified and its temperature and humidity are regulated before it enters a room or building

air-cool (éərkuːl) *v.t.* to cool (an engine) by a current of air rather than by water

air corridor an internationally agreed (and frequently patrolled) air channel. Aircraft using it may not leave the route

air corridors (*mil.*) restricted routes of air travel specified for use by friendly aircraft and established for the purpose of preventing friendly aircraft from being fired on by friendly forces

air-craft (éərkræft, éərkrɑft) *sing.* and *pl. n.* any flying machine: an airplane, airship, glider or balloon

aircraft arrestment controlled stopping of an aircraft by external means

aircraft carrier a warship with specially constructed decks designed to carry operational aircraft

aircraft flutter (*electr.*) flickering on a television screen caused by reflection of signals from an aircraft flying between sender and receiver

air-craft-man (éərkræftmən, éərkrɑftmən) *pl.* **air-craft-men** (éərkræftmən, éərkrɑftmən) *n.* a man of the lowest rank in the British Royal Air Force

air-crafts-man (éərkræftsmən, éərkrɑftsmən) *pl.* **air-crafts-men** (éərkræftsmən, éərkrɑftsmən) *n.* (*Br.*) an aircraftman

air-crafts-wom-an (éərkræftswumən, éərkrɑftswumən) *pl.* **air-crafts-wom-en** (éərkræftswimin, éərkrɑftswimin) *n.* (*Br.*) an aircraftwoman

air-craft-wom-an (éərkræftwumən, éərkrɑftwumən) *pl.* **air-craft-wom-en** (éərkræftwimin, pərkrɑftwimin) *n.* a woman of the lowest rank in the British Women's Royal Air Force

air-crew (éərkruː) *n.* the complete body of men manning an aircraft

air curtain method of containing oil spills by emitting air bubbles through a perforated pipe, causing an upward water flow that slows the spread of oil and causing a barrier that stops fish from entering polluted water

air cushion an inflatable cushion ‖ a means of keeping a moving vehicle raised just clear of the ground by a blast of low-pressure air under the chassis,or similarly a ship above the water (*HOVERCRAFT, *AEROTRAIN)

air-cush-ion vehicle (éərkuʃən) transit unit that travels on cushion of air created by propellers between vehicle and surface, such as, British Hovercraft *abbr* ACV. *Cf* GROUND EFFECT MACHINE, HOVERCRAFT, SKIM

air defense warning conditions (*mil.*) a degree of air raid probability according to the following code. *Air defense warning yellow:* attack by hostile aircraft and/or missiles is probable, hostile aircraft and/or missiles are en route, or unknown aircraft and/or missiles suspected to be hostile are en route toward, or are within, an air defense division/sector. *Air defense warning red:* attack by hostile aircraft and/or missiles is imminent or is in progress, hostile aircraft and/or missiles are within an air defense division/sector or are in the immediate vicinity of an air defense division/sector, with high probability of entering the division/sector. *Air defense warning white:* attack by hostile aircraft and/or missiles is improbable. This may be called either before or after air defense warning yellow or red

air door device in an entrance consisting of a strong upward current of air usually cooled or heated, e.g., in a store entrance

air-drome (éərdroum) *n.* an airport

air-drop (éərdrɔp) *n.* the unloading of personnel or materiel from aircraft in flight

Aire-dale (éərdeil) *n.* a terrier of a large breed with rough coat, dark tan with a black saddle [after *Airedale* in Yorkshire, England]

air engine an engine using externally heated air as the working medium ‖ an engine driven by compressed air

air equivalent standard for thickness of materials equivalent to that of air, used for stopping nuclear particles, e.g., for walls of ionization chambers

air-field (éərfiːld) *n.* an airdrome ‖ the field of an airdrome

air-foil (éərfɔil) *n.* (*Am.=Br.* aerofoil) a wing, fin or tail plane of an aircraft

air force a country's armed air power, generally possessing fighter, bomber and reconnaissance wings

air-frame (éərfreim) *n.* the body of an aircraft without the engines ‖ the framework, envelope, and cabin of an airship ‖ the assembled principal structural components of a missile, excluding its propulsion system, control and electronic equipment, and payload

air-freight (éərfreit) **1.** *n.* a system of transporting freight by aircraft ‖ freight transported ‖ the cost of this transport **2.** *v.t.* to send by airfreight

air-glow (éərglou) *n.* (*meteor.*) aura in the night sky due to emission from sodium, oxygen, and nitrogen activated by the sun during the day

air-gram (éərgræm) *n.* (*Br.*) an air letter, aerogram

air gun a gun whose propelling force is compressed air

air-head (éərhed) *n.* (*mil.*) **1.** a designated area in a hostile or threatened territory that, when seized and held, enables the continuous air landing of troops and materiel and provides maneuver space necessary for projected operations. Normally, it is the area seized in the assault phase of an airborne operation **2.** a designated location in an area of operations used as a base for supply and evacuation by air. Analogous to beachhead

air hole an air pocket

air hostess a stewardess in an aircraft

air-house (éərhaus) *n.* an inflated plaster structure, usu. temporary, esp. one used in construction operations and over tennis courts, etc.

air-i-ly (éərili) *adv.* in an airy manner, gaily ‖ unconcernedly, jauntily

air-i-ness (éəriːnis) *n.* the state or quality of being airy ‖ lack of concern

air-ing (éəriŋ) *n.* an exposure to fresh air, a ventilation ‖ (*Br.*) the final process of drying clothes etc. in a warm place ‖ a going out into the fresh air ‖ (*fig.*) exposure to consideration by others, *to give one's views an airing*

air-less (éərlis) *adj.* stuffy, oppressive, without movement of air

air letter a single sheet of lightweight writing paper designed to fold and seal up, for airmail

air-lift (éərlift) *n.* a large-scale system of replacing sea or land transport of goods or men by air in an emergency

air-line (éərlain) *n.* a regular air service for the transport of goods and passengers ‖ the route covered by such a service

air-lin-er (éərlainər) *n.* a large passenger aircraft

air lock a stoppage of the flow of liquid through a pipe or pump caused by a bubble of air ‖ a double-doored, sealed chamber to allow safe passage of men and materials from a segregated area

air-mail (éərmeil) *n.* letters and parcels, carried by air ‖ the system for transporting such letters and parcels

air-man (éərmən) *pl.* **air-men** (éərmən) *n.* a member of the crew of an aircraft (usually the flying crew) ‖ an enlisted man or woman in the U.S. Air Force

air marshal an officer of the British Royal Air Force ranking below an air chief marshal and above an air vice-marshal

air mattress a lightweight inflatable rubber or plastic mattress used commonly in camping

air-mind-ed (éərmaindid) *adj.* keenly interested in aviation

air-mo-bile (éərməbiːl) *n.* (*mil.*) military unit equipped with helicopter transportation

air monitor warning device for detecting and measuring airborne radioactivity

air piracy *SKYJACKING.* —**air pirate** *n.*

air-plane (éərplein) *n.* (*Am.=Br.* aeroplane) a heavier-than-air flying machine powered by motors or jets

air pocket a condition in the atmosphere, usually a partial vacuum, which causes an aircraft in flight to drop suddenly

air-port (éərpɔrt, éərpourt) *n.* an expanse of level ground (or water) with control buildings, hangars, workshops etc., equipped to deal with aircraft passengers, refueling and repair of aircraft etc.

air pump a pump for withdrawing air from a container or closed space ‖ a pump for compressing air

air raid an attack by aircraft

AIRS (*computer acronym*) for automatic information retrieval system, a computer program language and storage system for IBM 7090

AIRS (*mil. acronym*) for advanced initial reference sphere guidance system. For the proposed MX missile system, AIRS would permit automatic relocation determination at each movement of individual missiles without further instruction

air-screw (éərskruː) *n.* (*Br.*) the propeller of an aircraft

air-shed (éərʃed) *n.* **1.** (*mil.*) area supplied by a single air defense system **2.** the supply system for an area **3.** (*environ.*) an atmospheric zone unit that could be influenced by air pollution from various sources

air-ship (éərʃip) *n.* a flying machine lighter than air and mechanically driven

air shower cosmic ray particles in the atmosphere

air shuttle air transportation scheduled at regular, short intervals, usu. between major urban centers, often with guaranteed service to all who apply

air-sick (éərsik) *adj.* afflicted with nausea, vomiting etc. when (and as a result of) flying in an aircraft

air-space (éərspeis) *n.* the part of space immediately over some specified territory or area, esp. with regard to jurisdiction

air-speed (éərspiːd) *n.* the speed of an aircraft relative to the air through which it is moving rather than to the earth (*GROUND SPEED)

air-stream (éərstriːm) *n.* the flow of air with respect to the surface of an object immersed in it ‖ a wind, esp. a high wind at high altitude

air-strip (éərstrip) *n.* a strip of ground cleared for aircraft to land and take off

air target mosaic (*mil.*) large-scale mosaic of photographs providing photographic coverage of an area and permitting comprehensive portrayal of pertinent target detail

air taxi aircraft for hire for local flights

air-tel (cərtél) *n.* (*slang*) airport hotel

air-tight (éərtait) *adj.* closed tightly so that air cannot get in or out ‖ watertight, sure, certain, *an airtight alibi*

air-time (éərtaim) *n.* **1.** a broadcast **2.** the period of the broadcast

air trooping (*mil.*) the nontactical air movement of personnel

CONCISE PRONUNCIATION KEY: (**a**) æ, c*a*t; ɑ, c*a*r; ɔ f*aw*n; ei, sn*a*ke. (**e**) e, h*e*n; iː, sh*ee*p; iə, d*ee*r; ɛə, b*ea*r. (**i**) i, f*i*sh; ai, t*i*ger; əː, b*i*rd. (**o**) o, *o*x; au, c*ow*; ou, g*oa*t; u, p*oo*r; ɔi, r*oy*al. (**u**) ʌ, d*u*ck; u, b*u*ll; uː, g*oo*se; ə, b*a*cill*u*s; juː, c*u*be. x, lo*ch*; θ, *th*ink; ð, bo*th*er; z, *Z*en; ʒ, corsa*g*e; dʒ, sava*g*e; ŋ, orangutan*g*; j, *y*ak; ʃ, *fi*sh; tʃ, fe*tch*; 'l, rabb*le*; 'n, red*den*. Complete pronunciation key appears inside front cover.

AIR-2 *GENIE

air vac *AIR CAVALRY

air vice-marshal an officer in the British Royal Air Force ranking below an air marshal and above an air commodore

air-waves (éɔrwẹivz) pl. n. radio and television as mass media

air-way (éɔrwẹi) n. an established route for aircraft, esp. one equipped with navigational aids ‖ a ventilation passage in a mine ‖ (pl.) the radio frequencies allotted to a station for broadcasting

air-wor-thi-ness (éɔrwẹ:rði:nis) n. the condition of being airworthy

air-wor-thy (éɔrwẹ:rði:) adj. (of aircraft) in suitable condition for flying

airy (éɔri:) adj. open to the air, an airy room ‖ light-hearted, cheerful, an airy wave of the hand ‖ lacking proper seriousness, airy unconcern ‖ self-complacent, airy condescension ‖ graceful, delicate, moving freely as the air ‖ immaterial, without reality

A·i·sha, A·ye·sha (ái:ʃə) (c. 614–78), Mohammed's second wife, daughter of Abu Bekr. She survived Mohammed for nearly 50 years, and had great influence in the early history of Islam

aisle (ail) n. (archit.) a side division of a church, flanking the nave ‖ the passage between rows of seats in a church, theater etc. **aisled** (aild) adj. [O.F. ele, wing]

Aisne (en) a department (area 2,866 sq. miles, pop. 526,000) in N. France (*PICARDY, *ÎLE-DE-FRANCE). Chief town: Laon

Aisne a river (175 miles long) in N. France, rising in Meuse department and flowing into the Oise above Compiègne. It formed an important battle line during the 1st world war

aitch (eitʃ) n. the letter h, H

aitch·bone (éitʃboun) n. the bone of the rump of an animal ‖ the cut of beef over this bone [M.E. a nache bone separated as an ache bone fr. O.F. nache. buttock]

Ait·ken (éitkin), Robert Grant (1864–1951), American astronomer, who specialized in the study of double stars

Aix-en-Pro·vence (eksɑ̃prɔvɑ̃s) a town (pop. 114,014) in Provence, France, founded by the Romans (123 B.C.). Cathedral (mainly 12th–15th cc., with a 6th-c. baptistry). University (1409)

Aix-la-Cha·pelle (ekslɑːʃæpel) *AACHEN

Aix-la-Chapelle, Congress of a meeting (1818) of diplomats from Austria, Britain, Prussia and Russia to discuss problems arising from the Congress of Vienna (1815)

Aix-la-Chapelle, Treaty of a treaty (May 2, 1668) ending the War of Devolution. It gave France 11 towns in the Spanish Netherlands ‖ a treaty (Oct. 18, 1748) ending the War of the Austrian Succession

A·jac·cio (æʒæksi:ɔ) a port and the capital (pop. 51,770) of Corsica, on the west coast. It was the birthplace of Napoleon I

A·jan·ta (ədʒʌ́ntə) a village in Maharashtra, S. central India, famous for the frescoes on the walls and ceilings of its caves, which between 200 B.C. and 700 A.D. served as Buddhist assembly halls and monasteries

a·jar (ədʒɑ́r) pred. adj. and adv. (of doors and gates) slightly open [A hist. prep.+O.E. cyrr, a turn]

A·jax (éidʒæks) son of Telamon, the brave leader of the Salaminian contingent in the Trojan War. He went mad and committed suicide because the armor of Achilles, which he coveted, had been given to Ulysses

Ajax son of Oïleus, leader of the Locrians in the Trojan War. He was shipwrecked and drowned by Poseidon for blasphemy

Aj·mer (ʌdʒmíɔr) a town (pop. 257,000) in Rajasthan, India: textiles, food products, railway workshops. Moslem saint's tomb (13th c.), Jain temple ruins, temple to Brahma

Akaba *AQABA

Ak·an (ǽkæn) pl. **Ak·an, Ak·ans** n. a language common to several peoples of Ghana ‖ (pl.) the peoples speaking this language, incl. the Ashanti

Ak·bar (ǽkbɑr) (1542–1605), Mogul emperor of India (1156–1605), the greatest ruler of the Mogul period. He conquered and united the country, reformed its administration, and instituted religious toleration

Akh·na·ton (ɑknátən) IKHNATON

A·ki·ku·yu (ækikú:ju:) Kikuyu

a·kim·bo (əkímbou) adv. with hand on hips and elbows turned outward [etym. doubtful]

a·kin (əkín) adj. related by blood ‖or similar nature or character [OF+KIN]

A·ki·ta (akí:tə) a port (pop. 126,000) on the northwest coast of Honshu, Japan: oil refining, zinc metallurgy, silk

Ak·kad, Ac·cad (ǽkæd) the northern part of ancient Babylonia ‖ a native of this region ‖ any of several dialects spoken by the natives of this region

Ak·ka·di·an, Ac·ca·di·an (əkéidi:ən) adj. of the Semitic dialect spoken by the ancient Akkads ‖ pertaining to Akkad, its inhabitants etc.

A·kla·vik (əklávik) a village (pop. 1,500) and principal trading center for the Arctic region, in the N.W. Mackenzie District near the mouth of the Mackenzie River, Canada

Ak·ron (ǽkrən) a city (pop. 237,177, with agglom. 660,328) in Ohio, in the Great Lakes region: rubber industry. University (1870)

Aksum *AXUM

Al (chem.) aluminum

Ala. Alabama

a·la (éilə) pl. **a·lae** (éili:) n. (bot.) a winglike growth on a flower, fruit, seed etc. ‖ (zool.) any flat, winglike process or part, e.g. the lateral cartilage of the nose [L.=a wing]

Al·a·bam·a (æləbǽmə) (abbr. Ala.) a Southern state (area 51,609 sq. miles, pop. 3,943,000) of the U.S.A. Capital: Montgomery. Chief city: Birmingham. With the exception of the northeastern mountains, it is low-lying plain country. Products: cotton, corn, beef cattle, poultry, peanuts. Resources: timber, coal, iron ore, limestone. Industries: iron and steel, textiles, fertilizers and nitrates, pulp and paper. State university (1831) at Tuscaloosa. Alabama was explored by the Spanish (mid-16th c.), settled by the French (18th c.) and ceded (1763) to Britain. It passed (1783) to the U.S.A., of which it became the 22nd state (1819)

Alabama a navigable river (300 miles long) flowing southwest from central Alabama into Mobile Bay at Mobile, Alabama

'Alabama' arbitration a peaceful settlement of a Civil War dispute between the U.S.A. and Great Britain. The U.S.A. claimed indemnity for damage inflicted by the 'Alabama' and other vessels, which had been launched from British shipyards in the service of the Confederate States and were attacking the U.S. merchant marine. U.S. protest at this alleged violation of international neutrality laws was unsuccessful from 1863 to 1871, when an Anglo-U.S. commission negotiated the Treaty of Washington. The treaty provided for an arbitration commission to convene at Geneva, composed of representatives from Great Britain, the U.S.A., Italy, Switzerland, and Brazil. The commission, which awarded $15.5 million to the U.S.A. for direct loss and damage caused by Confederate vessels of British origin, served as a bellwether in the development of the process of international arbitration

al·a·bam·ine (æləbǽmin, æləbæmi:n) n. (a former name for) astatine [after Alabama]

al·a·bas·ter (ǽləbæstər, æləbɑstər) n. a translucent, fine-grained variety of gypsum, CaSO₄·2H₂O. It is usually white, is very soft, and takes a high polish [O.F. alabastre fr. L. fr. Gk]

al·a·bas·trine (æləbǽstrin, æləbástrin) adj. made of alabaster ‖ like alabaster in whiteness or smoothness [fr. Gk alabastrinos]

a·lack (əlǽk) interj. (rhet.) alas [fr. older a, oh! + LACK, (obs.) fault, failing]

a·lac·ri·ty (əlǽkriti:) n. briskness ‖ eager readiness [F. alacrité]

A·lain-Four·nier (ælɛ̃fuːrnjei) (Henri-Alban Fournier, 1886–1914), French novelist, author of 'le Grand Meaulnes' (1913)

A·la·mein, Battle of (ǽləmein) a decisive British victory (Oct. 23-Nov. 4, 1942) under General Montgomery over the Germans and Italians under Field Marshal Rommel, in the N. African campaign. Alamein is a town in N. Egypt on the Mediterranean coast about 70 miles west of Alexandria. The battle stopped Rommel's advance on Egypt, and marked the beginning of Montgomery's advance to Tripoli

à la mode (ɑləmóud) (cooking, of beef) larded and cooked with carrots and onions ‖ (cooking, of pie or other dessert) served with ice cream ‖ in the style or fashion of the day [F.]

Al·a·mo, the (ǽləmou) a mission fort in San Antonio, Texas, site of a heroic stand (Feb. 23-Mar. 6, 1836) by an outnumbered American garrison against the Mexican army under Santa Anna during the Texas revolution (*CROCKETT)

Al·an·brooke (ǽlənbruk), Field-Marshal Alan Francis Brooke, 1st Viscount (1883–1963), British Chief of the Imperial General Staff (1941–6)

A·land (áland, ɔ́land) (Fin. Ahvenanmaa) a province of Finland, consisting of 6,554 islands at the mouth of the Gulf of Bothnia (total area 581 sq. miles, pop. 22,000, Swedish-speaking). Chief town: Marienhamn. Industries: fishing, shipping and tourism. The islands were surrendered to Russia by Sweden in 1809. The League of Nations awarded them to Finland (1921)

A·lans (éilinz, éilænz) pl. n. a barbarian people (Alani) of Persian origin, living between the Sea of Azov and the Caucasus. Driven by the Huns, they penetrated into the Roman Empire, then invaded Gaul (406), where one group settled in the region of the Loire. A second group entered Spain and was wiped out by the Visigoths

a·lar (éilər) adj. of an ala or wing ‖ having alæ or wings ‖ wing-shaped ‖ (anat.) axillary [fr. L. alaris fr. ala, wing]

A·lar·cón (alarkón), Pedro Antonio de (1833–91), Spanish poet and novelist. 'The Three-cornered Hat' (1874) and 'El niño de la bola' (1880) are his best known novels

Alar·cón y Men·do·za (alarkóni:mendθóa), Juan Ruiz de (c. 1581–1639), Spanish author of many comedies and dramas

Al·a·ric (ǽlərik) (c. 370–410), king of the Visigoths who pillaged the Byzantine Empire (395–9) and then the Western Roman Empire (401–10), sacking Rome (410)

a·larm (əlárm) 1. n. a signal warning of danger ‖ an excited, frightened anticipation of danger, to spring up in alarm ‖ (fencing) a sharp stamp made on the ground with the foot advanced ‖ (hist.) the call to arms 2. v.t. to inspire with fear [O.F. alarme]

alarm clock a clock with a device which rings at a previously set time

a·larm·ist (əlármist) n. a person who spreads alarm ‖ a person who tends to become alarmed

a·la·ry (éiləri:) adj. pertaining to a wing,or winglike part [fr. L. alarius]

Alas. Alaska

a·las (əlǽs) interj. expressing grief, regret, pity, concern [O.F.]

A·las·ka (əlǽskə) (abbr. Alas.) a state (area 586,400 sq. miles, pop. 438,000, 15% Aleuts and Eskimos) of the U.S.A. in the far northwest of North America, 51 miles from the U.S.S.R. Capital: Juneau. Largest town: Anchorage. The mountains of the south, many of them volcanic, rise to over 20,000 ft (Mt McKinley 20,300 ft) and are extended in the Aleutian Is. The interior is a plain, cut into small plateaus by broad river valleys, notably the Yukon. The Brooks Range (highest point 9,239 ft) extends across the north, sloping down to a coastal plain where the largest oil and gas deposits are found. Settlement is concentrated in the basin of the S. Alaska Range. Average temperatures (F.) in Jan. and July: coastal belt 20°–35° and 45°–57°, interior -2°– -16° and 38°–58°. Rainfall: coast 60–150 ins, interior 4–32 ins. Agriculture: dairy products, hay, oats, vegetables, reindeer herding. Resources: timber, furs (esp. seal), fish, coal, oil, natural gas, gold, mercury, chromite, sand and gravel, hydroelectricity. State university (1922) near Fairbanks. HISTORY. Alaska was inhabited by native Indians when Russian fur traders settled there (18th c.). The U.S.A. bought it (1867) from Russia for $7,200,000. The discovery of gold (1896) just over the border at Klondike brought thousands of prospectors to Alaska. During the 2nd world war it was developed strategically and linked to the U.S.A. by the Alaska Highway (1942). It became (1959) the 49th state of the U.S.A. Vast deposits of petroleum and natural gas were discovered in the North Slope region (1968) and commercial oil production began there (1977) after completion of a pipeline to Valdez

Alaska, Gulf of a broad inlet of the Pacific on the south coast of Alaska between the Alaska Peninsula and the Alexander Archipelago, including the Kodiak Is

Alaska Highway the section (1,523 miles) of the Pan-American Highway that runs from Dawson Creek, British Columbia, to Fairbanks, Alaska

Alaska Peninsula a long, narrow extension (500 miles long) of S.W. Alaska, between the Bering Sea and the Pacific Ocean, with the Aleutian Is extending southwest from its tip

---

CONCISE PRONUNCIATION KEY: (a) æ, cat; ɑ, car; ɔ fawn; ei, snake. (e) e, hen; i:, sheep; iə, deer; ɛə, bear. (i) i, fish; ai, tiger; ə:, bird. (o) o, ox; au, cow; ou, goat; u, poor; ɔi, royal. (u) ʌ, duck; u, bull; u:, goose; ə, bacillus; ju:, cube. x, loch; θ, think; ð, bother; z, Zen; ʒ, corsage; dʒ, savage; ŋ, orangutang; j, yak; ʃ, fish; tʃ, fetch; 'l, rabble; 'n, redden. Complete pronunciation key appears inside front cover.

Alaska Range a mountain range curving along the south coast of Alaska (Mt McKinley, 20,300 ft)

a·late (éileit) *adj.* having winglike attachments [fr. L. *alatus* fr. *ala,* wing]

Á·la·va (álava) a province (area 1,175 sq. miles, pop. 260,580) of N. Spain (*BASQUE PROVINCES). Capital: Vitoria (pop. 192,773)

Al-Az·har, University of (alazár) the great university at Cairo, nearly 1,000 years old, and the chief theological university of Islam. It also has modern science and languages faculties

alb (ælb) *n.* a white linen vestment reaching to the feet worn by priests when officiating at Mass, also by certain consecrated kings, symbolizing purity [fr. L.L. *alba (tunica),* white (tunic)]

Al·ba, Al·va (álva), Ferdinand Álvarez de Toledo, duke of (1507–82), Spanish general who crushed the revolt of the Netherlands (1567–73) and conquered Portugal (1580)

Al·ba·ce·te (alvaθéte) a province (area 5,737 sq. miles, pop. 334,468) of S.E. Spain (*MURCIA) ‖ its capital (pop. 117,126)

al·ba·core (ǽlbəkɔr, ǽlbəkour) *n. Thunnus germo,* a small tuna with pectoral fins. It weighs up to 80 lbs, and is good to eat ‖ any of several smaller related fishes, e.g. the bonito [Port. fr. Arab. *al,* the + *bakr,* young camel]

Al·ban (ɔ́lbən), St (*d. c.* 287), the first British martyr. Feast: June 22

Al·ba·ni·a (ælbéini:ə, ælbéinjə) a republic (area 10,631 sq. miles, pop. 2,862,000) of Europe in the W. Balkans. Capital: Tirana. The two dialects of Albanian are Gheg (in the north) and Tosk (in the south). Religion: mainly Moslem, with Orthodox and Roman Catholic minorities, the latter mainly in the north. Ethnic minorities: Greeks, Vlachs, Serbs and Bulgars. The land is mountainous and almost inaccessible in the northeast and southeast. The climate is Mediterranean in the fertile coastal lowlands, but rainfall increases and conditions are harsher inland. Average summer and winter temperatures (F.): 80° and 40°. Rainfall: 40–60 ins. Livestock: sheep, goats, cattle, pigs. Crops: corn, wheat, olives, sugar beet, vines, tobacco, nuts. Resources: forest (40% of the land, largely unexploited), fresh and salt-water fisheries, oil, coal, asphalt, lignite, iron, copper, gold, silver, chromite, salt (all largely unexploited), gypsum and stone. Manufactures: cement, beer, flour. Chief ports: Durrës, Vlona, Sarandë. Exports: oil, chrome ore, tobacco, nuts. Imports: equipment for heavy industry. Monetary unit: lek (divided into 100 quintars). HISTORY. Albania formed part of the Roman and Byzantine Empires. It was conquered by the Goths (4th–5th cc.), by the Serbs in the north (640), and by the Bulgars in the south (861). It came under Greek, Norman, Serbian and Turkish rule, being part of the Ottoman Empire until 1912. Albanian independence was declared (1912), after risings (1908–12). The country was occupied by French, Italian and Serb troops during the 1st world war. Italy proclaimed Albania an independent state under Italian protection (1917), but Italy withdrew and Albania was recognized as a sovereign state (1920). It was a constitutional republic (1925–8), and became a monarchy under Zog (1928). Treaties were signed between Albania and Italy (1926, 1927). Italy invaded the country, and placed it under the king of Italy (1939). The Greek army invaded (1941), but was driven out by the Germans, who retained control until the Allies and the Resistance forces liberated it (Nov. 1944). After the war the Communists gained political power, and Albania was proclaimed a people's republic (1946). It was allied with the U.S.S.R. (1948–61) and with China (1961–78). After China discontinued all aid (1978) Albania moved cautiously to establish trade and diplomatic relations with its European neighbors. Trade with China resumed (1983)

Al·ba·ni·an (ætbéini:ən) **1.** *adj.* of or pertaining to Albania **2.** *n.* a native or inhabitant of Albania ‖ the language of Albania

Al·ba·ny (ɔ́lbəni:) the capital (pop. 101,727, with agglom. 658,000) of New York State, on the Hudson River, an industrial and communications center

Albany a river (610 miles long) flowing east and then northeast from a chain of lakes in W. Ontario, Canada, into the James Bay

Albany Congress an intercolonial conference called by the British Board of Trade and held at Albany, N.Y., in 1754. Its chief purpose was to conciliate the Iroquois, but it also considered the problem of French encirclement and proposed a colonial union based on a plan submitted by Benjamin Franklin. This plan proved unacceptable both to the colonies and to the Crown

Albany Regency a group of politicians, headed by Martin Van Buren and W.L. Marcy, who largely controlled the Democratic Party in the state of New York from c. 1820 to 1854

al·ba·tross (ǽlbətrɔs, ǽlbətrɔs) *pl.* **al·ba·tross·es al·ba·tross** *n.* a bird of the genus *Diomedea,* the largest seabird, with a wingspan of up to 12 ft, found generally in the southern hemisphere [corrup. fr. Port. *alcatraz,* pelican]

al·be·do (ælbí:dou) *n.* (*astron.*) **1.** ratio of light or neutrons reflected from an object, esp. a celestial body **2.** the neutron field above earth produced by primary cosmic rays

albedo neutrons (*geophys.*) electrons, protons, or neutrons that leave the atmosphere. They are produced by nuclear interaction in the atmosphere

Al·bee (ɔ́lbi:), Edward Franklin (1928–), U.S. playwright whose grim but witty plays depict man's sadistic and masochistic tendencies. His 'Who's Afraid of Virginia Woolf!', an analysis of two childless marriages, won every major drama award of the 1962 Broadway season. *A Delicate Balance* (1966) and *Seascape* (1975) won Pulitzer prizes

al·be·it (ɔlbí:it) **1.** *conj.* (*rhet.*) even if, although **2.** *adv.* (*rhet.*) although, *he went, albeit unwillingly* [M.E.=although it be that]

Al·be·marle Sound (ǽlbəmɑrl) an inlet (about 60 miles long) of the Atlantic Ocean in N.E. North Carolina. It is the site of the earliest (1660s) permanent settlements in North Carolina. It was first explored in 1585 and was named after George Monk, Duke of Albemarle, one of the original lords proprietor of Carolina

Al·bé·niz (albéniθ), Isaac (1860–1909), Spanish pianist and composer, known for his pianoforte music, esp. 'Iberia'

Al·ber·di (albérdi:), Juan Bautista (1810–84), Argentine political theorist and diplomat. Exiled by dictator Juan Manuel de Rosas, he took a leading role in Uruguay, Chile and Europe in the liberal opposition to Rosas. His stress on the need to create a central, federalized government and to encourage immigration and foreign investment strongly influenced the constituent assembly which in 1853 wrote Argentina's enduring constitution

Al·be·ro·ni (alberóni:), Giulio (1664–1752), Spanish-Italian cardinal and statesman. As prime minister of Spain (1715–19) he instituted reforms with the aim of getting back the Italian possessions which Spain had lost by the Treaty of Utrecht (1713). He was defeated by the Quadruple Alliance of Britain, France, the Netherlands and Austria, and forced into exile (1719)

Albers, (ɔ́lberz) Josef (1888–1976), German-born U.S. painter, associated with Constructivism and Hard-edge Painting. He taught at the Bauhaus School, Black Mountain College, and Yale. His theoretical writings include 'Interaction of Color' (1963), and his artwork is typified by his 'Homage to the Square' series

Al·bert I (ǽlbərt) (c. 1250–1308), king of Germany (1298–1308), duke of Austria and Styria (1282–1308), son of Rudolf I of Hapsburg

Albert II (1397–1439), Holy Roman Emperor and king of Germany, Hungary and Bohemia (1438–9), duke of Austria (as Albert V of Hapsburg, 1404–39)

Albert the first duke of Prussia (1490–1568). As grand master of the Teutonic Knights (1511–25), he turned Prussia into a secular duchy (1525)

Albert of Saxe-Coburg-Gotha (1819–61), husband (1840–61) of Queen Victoria of England. He was styled Consort in 1842 and Prince Consort after 1857. He affirmed the constitutional role of the Crown. His interest in science and industry fostered the Great Exhibition (1851) and the Imperial Science Museum (1856)

Albert I (1875–1934), king of Belgium (1909–34). He resisted German invasion in 1914, and fought with the Allies (1914–18). He consolidated the monarchy in Belgium by his personal popularity

Al·ber·ta (ælbə́rtə) a prairie province (area 255,285 sq. miles, pop. 2,345,100) in W. Canada, on a high plateau to the east of the Rocky Mountains. Capital: Edmonton. Agriculture: wheat, oats and barley (leading producer), cattle, pigs. Resources: timber, oil and natural gas (leading producer), coal. Industries: food processing, oil refining, iron and steel. Settlers moved into Alberta in the 1880s. The province became a member of the Canadian Confederation (1905)

Al·ber·ti (albérti:), Leon Battista (1404–72), a genius of the Italian Renaissance, distinguished in painting, poetry, philosophy, music and architecture. His 'De re aedificatoria libri X' (printed 1485) has had great influence on architecture. His buildings include the main facade of Sta Maria Novella and the Palazzo Rucellai at Florence, and S. Francesco at Rimini. His treatise on painting (1436) discussed the imitation of nature, perspective, beauty and ancient art. His treatise on sculpture (1464) dealt with human proportions

Albert, Lake a freshwater lake (area 2,000 sq. miles, average depth 30 ft) situated at 2,200 ft in the west Rift Valley, Uganda. It is fed by the Semliki River and the Victoria Nile, and its outlet is the Albert Nile. Sir Samuel Baker was the first European to reach it (1864)

Albert Ny·an·za (naiǽnzə) Lake Albert

Al·ber·tus Mag·nus (ælbə́:rtəsmǽgnəs), St (c. 1193–1280), count of Bollstädt, German philosopher and teacher of Thomas Aquinas. He entered the Dominican order in 1223 and became its provincial in Germany in 1254. He did much to bring about the union of Aristotelianism and theology which is the basis of Scholasticism. His work as an experimental scientist bore on the action of nitric acid on metals, and refining of gold, researches on sulfur and potassium etc. Feast: Nov. 15

Al·bert·ville (ǽlbərtvil) *KALEMIE

Al·bi·gen·ses (ælbidʒénsi:z, ælbigénsi:z) a heretical Christian sect whose influence became widespread in S. France about 1200. Its theology was based on Manichaean dualism (*MANICHEE). It denied the divinity of Christ and the Incarnation. The Dominican Order was founded (1205) in order to combat the heresy. The assassination (1208) of the papal legate provoked a crisis, and Pope Innocent III declared a crusade against the Albigenses (1209). This developed into a political conflict with civil war between the north and south of France. Peace was made in 1229

Al·bi·gen·si·an (ælbidʒénsi:ən, ælbigénsi:ən) **1.** *adj.* of or pertaining to the Albigenses **2.** *n.* a member of the Albigenses

al·bi·nism (ǽlbinjzəm) *n.* the state or quality of being an albino

al·bi·no (ælbáinou, esp. *Br.* ælbi:nou) *n.* a person with a congenital deficiency of pigment in the skin and hair, which are white, and in the eyes, which have a deep red pupil and pink or blue iris and are unable to bear ordinary light ‖ any animal or plant similarly deficient in coloring pigment [Span. or. Port. (orig. of white African Negroes) fr. L. *albus,* white]

Al·bi·no·ni (albi:nóni:), Tomaso (1671–1750), Italian composer and violinist, admirer of Vivaldi. He wrote many operas, but is chiefly known now for his instrumental music

Al·bi·on (ǽlbi:ən) (*rhet.*) Britain (as called by the Greeks and Romans) [fr. L. *albus,* white]

al·bite (ǽlbait) *n.* white or soda feldspar, a sodium aluminum silicate, NaAlSi₃O₈, found in granite, esp. in the Alps [fr. L. *albus,* white]

Al·borg *AALBORG

al·bum (ǽlbəm) *n.* a book for keeping autographs, photographs, stamps etc. in [L.=a blank tablet]

al·bu·men (ǽlbju:mən, ǽlbjumən) *n.* the white of an egg ‖ (*bot.*) a nutritive substance inside many developing seeds ‖ (*biochem.*) albumin

al·bu·men·ize *pres. part.* **al·bu·men·iz·ing** *past* and *past part.* **al·bu·men·ized** *v.t.* (*photog.*) to coat with an albuminous solution [L.]

al·bu·min (ælbjú:mən, ǽlbjumən) *n.* (*biochem.*) one of a group of heat coagulable colloidal proteins, soluble in water, and occurring in egg white, blood plasma or serum, milk and many animal and vegetable tissues. Albumins are used in cookery, wine making, sugar refining, also in photography, printing etc. [F. *albumine*]

al·bu·mi·noid (ælbjú:mənɔid) **1.** *n.* any complex protein, esp. one resembling albumin in origin or properties **2.** *adj.* of or like albumin [fr. L. *albumen (albuminis),* egg white]

CONCISE PRONUNCIATION KEY: **(a)** æ, c*a*t; ɑ, c*a*r; ɔ f*aw*n; ei, sn*a*ke. **(e)** e, h*e*n; i:, sh*ee*p; iə, d*ee*r; ɛə, b*ea*r. **(i)** i, f*i*sh; ai, t*i*ger; ə:, b*i*rd. **(o)** o, *o*x; au, c*ow*; ou, g*oa*t; u, p*oo*r; ɔi, r*oy*al. **(u)** ʌ, d*u*ck; u, b*u*ll; u:, g*oo*se; ə, b*a*cillus; ju:, c*u*be. x, lo*ch*; θ, *th*ink; ð, bo*th*er; z, *Z*en; ʒ, cor*s*age; dʒ, sava*g*e; ŋ, oranguta*ng*; j, *y*ak; ʃ, *fi*sh; tʃ, fe*tch*; 'l, rabb*l*e; 'n, redd*en*. Complete pronunciation key appears inside front cover.

al·bu·min·ous (ælbjúːmənəs) *adj.* having the properties of albumen or albumin

Al·bu·quer·que (ælbəkəːrkiː), Afonso de (1453–1515), Portuguese navigator. He was appointed viceroy of the Portuguese Indies in 1509, and established Portuguese power there by taking Goa in 1510 and Malabar, the coast of Ceylon and Malacca in 1511

Albuquerque a city (pop. 331,767, with agglom. 454,499) in New Mexico, on the Rio Grande, a resort and industrial center. University of New Mexico (1889)

al·bur·num (ælbəːrnəm) *n.* sapwood [L. fr. *albus*, white]

Al·cae·us (ælsíːəs) (7th c. B.C.), Greek lyric poet of Mytilene to whom the creation of the Alcaic stanza is attributed

Al·ca·ic (ælkéiik) 1. *adj.* of a four-lined complex stanza of dominantly iambic pattern, using spondees, trochees and dactyls, first found in Alcaeus and later used by Horace 2. *n.* an Alcaic stanza

al·cal·de (ɑlkáldiː) *n.* the mayor of a Spanish, Portuguese or Spanish-American town, with certain judicial powers [Span. fr. Arab. *al*, the+*quadi*, judge]

Al·ca·traz (ælkətræz) a small island in San Francisco Bay, formerly a federal prison

al·ca·zar (ælkəzár) *n.* a type of Spanish fortress or palace built during the Moorish occupation [Span. fr. Arab.]

Al·ces·tis (ælséstis) (*Gk mythol.*) the wife of Admetus. She gave up her own life to save her husband, and Heracles brought her back from Hades

al·chem·ic (ælkémik) *adj.* pertaining to alchemy [fr. M.L. *alchimicus*]

al·che·mist (ælkəmist) *n.* a person who studied or practiced alchemy [O.F. *alquemiste*]

al·che·my (ælkəmiː) *pl.* **al·che·mies** *n.* a medieval chemical art whose principal objectives were to find the panacea, and to transmute base metals into gold ‖ the power to transform something base into something precious, *the alchemy of words* [O.F. *alquimie* fr. M.L. fr. Arab. *al, the+kimia* perh. fr. Gk *chemia*, transmutation]

Al·ci·bi·a·des (ælsəbáiədiːz) (c. 450–404 B.C.), Athenian general and statesman, pupil of Socrates, brilliant but irresponsible leader of the democrats. He sponsored the Sicilian expedition (415). Exiled, he helped the enemies of Athens. Recalled, he won several naval successes in the Hellespont, but was again exiled after a subordinate's defeat at Notium (406)

ALCM (*mil. acronym*) for air-launched cruise missile

Alc·man (ælkmɑn) (7th c.), Greek lyric poet. Fragments of hymns and chorales survive

Al·cock (ælkɒk), Sir John (1892–1919), English airman who, with A.W. Brown, made the first flight across the Atlantic (June 1919) from Newfoundland to Ireland (16 hours 12 minutes). He was killed in an accident six months later

al·co·hol (ælkəhɒl, ælkəhɒl) *n.* a colorless, volatile, intoxicating, inflammable liquid, C_2H_5OH, ethyl alcohol, obtained commercially by distilling wine or other fermented liquors and by the hydration of ethylene. It is chiefly used as a raw material in the manufacture of organic chemicals, as a solvent and as a fuel ‖ (*chem.*) a class of organic chemicals regarded as arising from the hydrocarbons by replacing one or more hydrogen atoms with hydroxyl (-OH) groups **al·co·hól·ic** 1. *adj.* of alcohol ‖ containing or using alcohol ‖ caused by alcohol 2. *n.* a person who is addicted to alcohol **al·co·hól·i·cal·ly** *adv.* [Mod. L.=liquid produced by distillation fr. M.L.=a finely powdered antimony used to darken women's eyelids fr. O. Span. fr. Arab. *al*, the+*kohl*, powdered antimony]

al·co·hol·ism (ælkəhɒlizəm, ælkəhɒlizəm) *n.* dipsomania ‖ the action of alcohol on the human system [fr. Mod. L. *alcoholismus*]

al·co·hol·i·za·tion (ælkəhɒlizéiʃən, ælkəhɒlizéiʃən) *n.* the act or process of alcoholizing or the condition of being alcoholized

al·co·hol·ize (ælkəhɒlaiz, ælkəhɒlaiz) *pres. part.* **al·co·hol·iz·ing** *past* and *past part.* **al·co·hol·ized** *v.t.* to saturate with alcohol ‖ to change into alcohol

al·co·hol·om·e·ter (ælkəhɒlómitər, ælkəhɒlómitər) *n.* an instrument used to determine alcoholic strength of spirits **al·co·hol·óm·e·try** *n.*

ALCOM (*computer acronym*) for algebraic compiler computer, mathematical program compiled for Bendix G-20

Al·cott (ɔ́lkət), Louisa May (1832–88), American author of 'Little Women' and other well-known books for girls

al·cove (ælkouv) *n.* a recess in the wall of a room, esp. (*hist.*) to contain a bed ‖ any similar recess [F. fr. Span. fr. Arab. *al*, the + *gobbah*, vault, arch]

Al·cuin (ælkwin) (c. 755–804), English theologian and scholar, adviser to Charlemagne. He made the court at Aachen from 782 a center of culture, and was the principal agent in Charlemagne's reform of the Liturgy. He was abbot of Tours 796–804

al·cy·o·nar·i·an (ælsiːənéəriən) 1. *n.* a member of *Alcyonaria*, an order of coelenterates whose polyps have eight tentacles. They live mostly in colonies, and include coral 2. *adj.* of *Alcyonaria* [fr. Mod. L. *Alcyonaria* fr. *Alcyonium*, a genus of soft corals fr. Gk]

ALD (*computer acronym*) for analog line driver, amplifier for an analog computer designed to increase output

Al·dan (ɑldæn) a river (1,400 miles long) in Yakut, U.S.S.R., flowing from the Stanovoi Mtns, round the Aldan Plateau into the Lena north of Yakutsk. It is navigable for 600 miles

al·de·hyde (ældihaid) *n.* one of a series of organic compounds of general formula R.CHO, where R is a monovalent hydrocarbon radical [fr. ALCOHOL+ Mod. L. *dehydrogenatum*, without hydrogen]

Al·den (ɔ́ldən), John (c. 1599–1687), one of the pilgrim founders of the Plymouth Colony, immortalized by Henry W. Longfellow in 'The Courtship of Miles Standish'

al den·te (ɑldéntei) (*It.*) *adj.* of vegetables or macaroni cooked to retain a firm texture

al·der (ɔ́ldər) *n.* a member of *Alnus*, fam. *Betulaceae*, a genus of trees of cool temperate climates, with simple leaves and bearing catkins. Alders flourish on riverbanks, and help to prevent erosion at flood periods. Their wood is water-resistant, and is used for pumps, millwheels, bridges etc. The bark yields a brownish dye [O.E. *alor, aler*]

al·der·man (ɔ́ldərmən) *pl.* **al·der·men** (ɔ́ldərmən) *n.* a member of the governing body of a city ‖ a senior councillor in a city, borough or county in England, holding office for six years, and elected by the council, not by the electorate [O.E. *ealdormann*, a man of high rank]

Al·der·ney (ɔ́ldərniː) the northernmost island (area 3 sq. miles, pop. 1,500) of the Channel Islands. Capital: St Anne

Al·der·shot (ɔ́ldərʃɒt) a municipal borough (pop. 31,000) of Southampton, in N.E. Hampshire, England. It is the largest military training center in Great Britain

Ald·helm (ældhelm), St (c. 640–709), Anglo-Saxon scholar and bishop of Sherborne (705), England. A great builder of churches, he was probably responsible for the one that still stands at Bradford-onAvon. He wrote Latin works in verse and pose. Feast: May 25

al·di·carb (ældicarb) *n.* (*chem.*) a pesticide used in potato farming to combat California potato beetle and golden nematode. It inhibits cholinesterase, transmitter of information from muscles to nerves; marketed as Temik

Al·dine (ældain) *adj.* relating to the press of Aldus Manutius or to the editions of the classics printed by it

Al·drich–Vree·land Act (ɔ́ldritʃvríːlənd) a currency act (1908) introduced by Nelson Wilmarth Aldrich (1841–1915), U.S. senator and financier, which prepared the way for the Federal Reserve Act of 1913

Aldrin, (ɔ́ldrin) Edwin E. 'Buzz' (1930–), U.S. astronaut. During his first flight in 1966 on Gemini 12, he took a 5½-hour space walk. On the Apollo 11 mission to the moon, Aldrin was the second man to walk on the moon. His autobiography is entitled 'Return to Earth' (1973)

Al·dus Ma·nu·ti·us (ɔ́ldəsmənjúːʃiəs, ɔ́ldəsmanúːʃiəs) (Aldo Manuzzio, 1450–1515), humanist scholar and printer of Venice. He printed Greek and Latin texts in convenient format at a price scholars could pay, setting high standards of scholarly editing and accuracy in composition. The first italic alphabet used in books (1501) was one he had cut. He was succeeded by his son Paulus Manutius (1512–74), who was succeeded by his son Aldus Manutius Junior (1547–97)

ale (eil) *n.* alcoholic beverage brewed from an infusion of malt and flavored with hops, sugar etc., often stronger in alcohol and heavier in body than beer [O.E. *alu*]

a·le·a·tor·ic (éiliːətɔrik) *adj.* of a musical performance or painting whose outcome depends on chance —**aleatorism** *n.* —**aleatory** *adj.* Cf ACTION PAINTING

a·le·a·to·ry (éiliːətɔri:, éiliːətɔuri:) *adj.* depending on chance ‖ (*law*) depending on a contract on an uncertain contingency [fr. L. *aleatorius*, of gambling]

A·le·grí·a (ɑlegríːɑ), Ciro (1909–67), Peruvian novelist. His greatest novel, 'El mundo es ancho y ajeno' (1941) (trans. 'Broad and Alien is the World'), depicts the struggle of an Indian tribe to survive against the avarice of land-hungry white men

Aleichem, (aléikem) Sholem (1859–1916), pen name of Yiddish humorist Solomon Rabinowitz. Born in the Ukraine, he served as a rabbi before turning to writing. He left Russia (1905) after a pogrom and lived in New York and Switzerland. He wrote of small Eastern European Jewish towns and resilient, optimistic characters such as Menachem Mendel, the orphan boy Mottel, and the dairyman Tevye, upon whose adventures the musical 'Fiddler on the Roof' (1964, film 1971) is based. Collections of Aleichem's stories include 'Adventures of Mottel, the Cantor's Son' (1953), 'Great Fair, Scenes from My Childhood' (1955), and 'Tevye Stories' (1966)

Aleixandre, (aleiksándrei) Vicente (1898–1984), Spanish poet and 1977 winner of the Nobel Prize for literature. A life-long invalid, his poetry deals with annihilation and darkness initially but progresses to an affirmation of life and love in such works as 'La destrucción del amor' (Destruction of Love, 1933) and 'Diálogos del conocimiento' (Dialogues of Knowledge, 1974). He and poet García Lorca were members of the group Generation of 1927

A·le·mán (alemán), Mateo (1547–c. 1614), Spanish novelist contemporary with Cervantes. He wrote the picaresque novel 'Guzmán de Alfarache' (1599)

Alemán, Miguel (1902–83), president of Mexico (1946–52). He served as Minister of the Interior under president Manuel Ávila Camacho, whom he succeeded as the first non-military president since Madero. He encouraged economic development, esp. in the private sector, and constructed roads

A·le·man·ni (æləmænai) *pl. n.* (*hist.*) a Germanic tribe occupying (5th c.) what is now Alsace and Baden. They were defeated (496) by the Franks under Clovis

A·lem·bert (dælɑ̃bɛr), Jean le Rond d' (1717–83), French mathematician and philosopher. In his 'Traité de la dynamique' (1743) he proved that Newton's third law of motion applies to moving as well as stationary bodies. This is known as d'Alembert's principle. He collaborated with Diderot in founding and editing the Encyclopédie and was responsible for the 'Discours préliminaire de l'Encyclopédie' (1751). An empiricist and a skeptic, he summed up his position in 'Essai sur les eléments de philosophie' (1759)

a·lem·bic (əlémbik) *n.* an apparatus used in distilling ‖ anything which distils or refines, *the alembic of the imagination* [F. *alambic* fr. L. fr. Arab. *al*, the + *anbiq*, a still, fr. Gk *ambix*, cup]

A·len·çon (əlénsən, F. ælɑ̃sɔ̃) a town (pop. 33,000) and commercial center in N.W. France, famous for its lace manufactures (*POINT D'ALENÇON)

A·lep·po (əlépou) an ancient town (pop. 881,458) in Syria, mentioned in Egyptian and Assyrian documents. Under Arab rule it was a bastion against the Byzantine Empire, and under Ottoman rule it was the clearing house for European trade with the Levant. Railways from Egypt, Turkey and Iraq meet there. It is an industrial (esp. textiles) and commercial center

a·lert (əléːrt) 1. *adj.* watchful, vigilant ‖ brisk, nimble 2. *n.* a warning, alarm, esp. of an air raid **on the alert** tensely watchful 3. *v.t.* to warn, put on guard, call to a state of readiness [F.]

ALERT (*computer acronym*) for automated linguistic extraction and retrieval, technique used for indexing and retrieval on RW 400 system

A·les·san·dri (alesándri:), Palma Arturo (1868–1950), Chilean statesman, president (1920–5, 1932–8). Elected president in 1920 as the candidate of a Liberal coalition, he was driven into exile in 1924 by the armed forces, but returned

CONCISE PRONUNCIATION KEY: **(a)** æ, c*a*t; ɑ, c*a*r; ɔ f*aw*n; ei, sn*a*ke. **(e)** e, h*e*n; iː, sh*ee*p; iə, d*ee*r; ɛə, b*ea*r. **(i)** i, f*i*sh; ai, t*i*ger; əː, b*i*rd. **(o)** o, *o*x; au, c*ow*; ou, g*oa*t; u, p*oo*r; ɔi, r*oy*al. **(u)** ʌ, d*u*ck; u, b*u*ll; uː, g*oo*se; ə, b*a*cillus; juː, c*u*be. x, lo*ch*; θ, *th*ink; ð, bo*th*er; z, *Z*en; ʒ, corsa*g*e; dʒ, sava*g*e; ŋ, orangutan*g*; j, *y*ak; ʃ, *fi*sh; tʃ, fe*tch*; 'l, rabb*le*; 'n, redd*en*. Complete pronunciation key appears inside front cover.

with his constitutional powers strengthened. In his second term he leaned politically to the right, which facilitated economic recovery from the Depression, but alienated most of his labor and middle-class supporters

A·les·san·dri Ro·drí·guez (alesándri:rɔðrí:ges), Jorge (1896–   ), Chilean statesman and president (1958–64)

al·eu·ron (ǽljərnn) n. (bot., biochem.) protein, usually in the form of crystalloids, found in seeds ‖ granular protein found in protoplasm and used as reserve food material ‖ the layer containing protein of the endosperm in mon cotyledons [Gk=flour]

al·eu·rone (ǽljəroun) n. aleuron

A·leu·tian Islands (əlú:ʃən) a chain of small volcanic islands (pop. 7,768, of Eskimo origin) belonging to the U.S.A., stretching for 1,100 miles between Alaska and Kamchatka. Industries: whaling and sealing. During the 2nd world war they were heavily bombed (1942) by the Japanese, who occupied Dutch Harbor, Kiska and Attu Is. U.S. forces counter-attacked the Japanese positions from bases established on Adak and Amchitka Is, Kodiak and Cold Bay. U.S. bases were later established on Shemya and Umnak Is. U.S. forces recaptured (1943) the last Japanese bastion on Attu after three weeks of bitter fighting. After the war the bases were retained by the U.S.A. for their strategic importance

ale·wife (éilwaif) pl. **ale·wives** (éilwaivz) n. Pomolobus pseudoharengus, an edible fish of the shad family common on the Atlantic coast of America (etym., doubtful)

Al·ex·an·der I (æligzǽndər, æligzǽndər) (1777–1825), czar of Russia (1801–25), son of Paul I. His early liberal reforms were later abandoned. Defeated by Napoleon at Austerlitz (1805) and Friedland (1807), he made an alliance with him at Tilsit (1807), but opposed his invasion of Russia in 1812. In 1815 he instigated the Holy Alliance

Alexander II (1818–81), czar of Russia (1855–81), son of Nicholas I. A liberal, he emancipated the serfs (1861), and introduced the zemstvo system of local government (1864) and legal and military reforms. He extended Russia's frontiers into Caucasia (1859) and central Asia (1865–8) and defeated the Turks (1877–8) in the last of the Russo-Turkish Wars. He was assassinated by Populist extremists

Alexander III (1845–94), czar of Russia (1881–94), son of Alexander II, a reactionary. He abandoned the Dreikaiserbund in favor of an entente with France (1892)

Alexander III 'the Great' (356–323 B.C.), king of Macedon (336–323 B.C.), son of Philip II and pupil of Aristotle. He defeated the Persians at Issus (333 B.C.), conquered Egypt (332 B.C.) and founded Alexandria (331 B.C.) He decisively defeated the Persians at Arbela (331 B.C.), occupied the easternmost Persian provinces, and then overran the Punjab (327–325 B.C.). His army refused to advance further and he returned to Babylon, where he died of fever (323 B.C.). Alexander tried to unify his empire by a Graeco-Persian partnership. His military achievement did not survive him, and the empire was divided among his generals, but the Hellenistic culture which he spread was to radiate from three centers: Alexandria, Pergamum and Antioch

Alexander I (1888–1934), prince regent of Serbia (1914–21), king of the SerbCroat-Slovene state (1921–34), the name of which he changed to Yugoslavia (1929).His absolutist rule failed to prevent political chaos in Yugoslavia. He was assassinated at Marseilles (1934)

Alexander III (d. 1181), pope (1159–81), a great lawgiver who imposed papal authority on Emperor Frederick I and his antipopes, and on Henry II of England, who quarreled with Becket over Investiture

Alexander VI (Rodrigo de Borgia, 1431–1503), pope (1492–1503), a profligate Spaniard who built up his family estates by fraud and murder. He was attacked by Savonarola. He was a great patron of the arts. He divided the New World between Spain and Portugal in 1493, charging their kings to spread Catholicism

Alexander, Harold Rupert Leofric George, 1st Viscount Alexander of Tunis (1891–1969), British field marshal. In the 2nd world war he commanded the retreats of Dunkirk and Burma, and the victories of N. Africa (1943), Sicily and Italy (1944–5). He was then Supreme Allied Commander in the Mediterranean. He

was governor general of Canada (1946–51) and was minister of defense (1952–4)

Alexander Archipelago about 1,100 islands and islets (area 13,000 sq. miles) along the coast of S. Alaska

Alexander Nev·ski (njévski:), St (c. 1220–63), Russian grand duke and national hero, called Nevski after his defeat of the Swedes (1240) at the R. Neva. Feast: Nov. 23

Alexander of Hales (heilz) (c. 1180–1245), English Scholastic philosopher known as the 'irrefragable doctor'. He held the Franciscan chair of theology in Paris

Alexander Se·ve·rus (siviərəs), Marcus Aurelius (c. 208–35), Roman emperor (222–35). He was murdered in a mutiny on the Rhine

'Alexander v. Holmes' a decision (1969) of the U.S. Supreme Court, which ordered the immediate desegregation of schools throughout the South

Ale·xan·dra Fyo·do·rov·na (æligzándrə fjódə rɔvnə) (1872–1918), last czarina of Russia. Under the influence of Rasputin she encouraged the reactionary policies of her husband Nicholas II. Both were shot by the Bolsheviks in 1918

Al·ex·an·dra, Mt (æligzándrə, æligzándrə) *RU WENZORI

Al·ex·an·dret·ta (æligzændrétə, æligzandrétə) *ISKENDERUN

Alexandretta (Hatay) (hist.) a semiautonomous region (area 2,140 sq. miles) of N.W. Syria from 1920. It became the Republic of Hatay (1938) and was reincorporated into Turkey in 1939. It had a mixed population of 250,000 Turks and Syrian Christians, and included the towns of Alexandretta and Antioch

Al·ex·an·dri·a (æligzándri:ə, æligzándri:ə) a port (pop. 2,317,705) on the Nile Delta, former capital of Egypt. It was founded by Alexander III (331 B.C.), and became an administrative, commercial and cultural center under the Ptolemies and the Romans: its library of 700,000 volumes was the greatest of ancient times. It declined with the discovery of a route around the Cape of Good Hope, but flourished again in the 19th c. under Mohammed Ali. Again the principal Egyptian port, it is an industrial center (food and chemical products, cigarettes, textiles). University (1943)

Al·ex·an·dri·an philosophy (æligzándri:ən, æligzándri:ən) the Neoplatonic system exemplified by Plotinus and Porphyrus which flourished from the beginning of the 3rd c. until 529 (*JUSTINIAN)

Alexandrian school the literature, science and thought of Alexandria under the Greeks and Romans, 300–146 B.C.

al·ex·an·drine (æligzændrin,æligzándrin) 1. n. a line of poetry containing regularly six iambic feet (i.e. 12 syllables), with a caesura after the third 2. adj. of such a line of poetry [F. alexandrin, after its use in early French poems on Alexander the Great]

al·ex·an·drite (æligzændrait, æligzándrait) n. (mineral.) a green chrysoberyl [after Alexander I of Russia]

A·lex·an·drovsk (æligzándrɔvsk) *ZAPOROZHE

a·lex·i·a (əléksi:ə) n. the inability to distinguish words as such, though the individual letters are all grasped (a condition found in some children learning to read, and in some adults with brain injury) [fr. A-(without)+ Gk lexis, word]

a·lex·in (əléksin) n. a defensive substance in the blood plasma which, combining with an antiserum, is essential for destroying bacteria [G. fr. Gk]

Alexis, (əléksis) Tsar of Russia (1629–76), tsar of Russia after his father Tsar Michael, the first Romanov. Alexis suppressed the revolt of the Don Cossacks under Stenka Razin and acquired territory from Poland. He was succeeded in turn by his sons Fyodor III, Ivan V, and Peter I

a·lex·i·thym·i·a (əlexiθaími:ə) n. (psych.) inability to express feelings verbally

A·lex·i·us I Comnenus (əléksi:əs) (1048–1118), Byzantine emperor (1081–1118). He repulsed Norman and Turkish invasions with the aid of the Latin Crusaders

al·fal·fa (ælfǽlfə) n. Medicago sativa, fam. Papilionaceae, a perennial hay crop of the highest quality grown widely in the U.S.A., in temperate regions of South America and Asia, and in the Mediterranean area [Span. fr. Arab. al, the+fachfacha, very good fodder]

Al-Fatah (Arabic: victory) group of Palestine Arab guerillas, the leading group in the Pales-

tinian Liberation Organization (PLO). Formed in 1956 as a paramilitary organization opposing the State of Israel; includes Jihaz al-Rasd, a covert organization, and Black September, a special terrorist group

Al·fie·ri (ɑlfjéri:), Count Vittorio (1749–1803), Italian poet, famous in his day for his classical tragedies, satires and political writings

Al·fold (ɔ́lfɔ:ld) the great central plain of Hungary

Alfonsín, Raúl (ælfonsí:n) (1927–   ), president of Argentina (1983–   ). A civilian elected after 8 years of military rule, he prosecuted those responsible for the disappearance of thousands of people in the 1970's and moved to alleviate Argentina's economic crisis

Alfonso I (ælfonzou, ælfonsou), King of Portugal (c. 1109–85), first king of Portugal. He resisted neighboring Spanish kingdoms and attacked Muslim lands

Alfonso II, King of Portugal (c. 1185–1223), succeeded his father Sancho I as king in 1211. He helped Castile defeat the Moors at Las Navas de Tolosa (1212) and captured Alcácer do Sal (1217). He attempted to curtail the church's power and was excommunicated (1220)

Alfonso III, King of Portugal (1210–79), younger son of Alfonso II who was regent for his deposed brother Sancho II and then king on Sancho's death (1248). He conquered the Algarve (1249). Conflict with the church led to his summoning (1254) representatives of the towns to Cortes for the first time. He was succeeded by his son Dinis

Al·fon·so VI (ælfónzou, ælfónsou) (1030–1109), king of León (1065–1109), of Castile (1072–1109), and of Galicia (1073–1109). Despite defeats by the Moors (1086 and 1108), he began the Christian reconquest of Spain

Alfonso VIII (c. 1156–1214), king of Castile (1158–1214). He led a Christian coalition against the Moors, winning a decisive victory (1212). He married Eleanor, daughter of Henry II of England

Alfonso XIII (1886–1941), the last king of Spain (1886–1931). He went into exile when internal crises and elections showed that the people wanted a republic

Al·fred (ǽlfrid, ǽlfred) 'the Great' (849–99), king of Wessex (871–99), son of Ethelwulf. He drove the Danes from Wessex, confining them to E. England. He made Wessex the Anglo-Saxon center of learning by introducing teachers and scholars, founding new monasteries, and promoting translations into the vernacular from Latin works, and he inspired the compilation of the Anglo-Saxon Chronicle. He began the building of permanent fortifications, created a mobile land army, and attempted to build a fleet

al·fres·co (ælfréskou) 1. outdoor 2. adv. outdoors (e.g. of meals) [Ital.]

al·ga (ǽlgə) pl. **al·gae** (ǽldʒi:), **al·gas** n. a member of a larger group of nonvascular plants belonging to any of seven phyla of thallophytes. They vary widely in size, form (e.g. from single-celled microscopic forms to large, complex, multicellular plant bodies), degree of differentiation, and habitat (aquatic or terrestrial). Almost all algae possess chlorophyll and are autotrophic, and many possess as well one or more other pigments that mask the chlorophyll-producing red, brown, yellow etc. organisms. The colors so produced serve to a great extent to classify the algae. Algae are the most important source of food for aquatic animals (*PLANKTON), and many marine species (*SEAWEED) are important as a source of human food (*DULSE, *CARRAGEEN), or as a source of industrially important substances (*ALGIN, *AGAR-AGAR, *DIATOMACEOUS EARTH) **ál·gal** adj. [L.]

al·gar·ro·ba (ælgəróubə) n. the carob ‖ the mesquite tree or its pods [Span. fr. Arab. al, the+kharrūbah, carob]

al·ge·bra (ǽldʒəbrə) n. a branch of mathematics in which symbols are used to represent numbers, variables or entities, either as a means of expressing general relationships or to indicate quantities satisfying particular conditions **al·ge·bra·ic** (ældʒəbréiik), **al·ge·brá·i·cal** adjs. **al·ge·brá·i·cal·ly** adv. **al·ge·brá·ist** n. [Ital. fr. Arab. al, the+jebr, reunion of broken parts]

Al·ge·ci·ras (ældʒisíərəs, Span. alðeθí:ras) a city, port and resort (pop. 86,042) on the Strait of Gibraltar, S.W. Spain, founded (713) by the Moors

Algeciras Conference a conference (Jan. 16, 1906) held in Spain to discuss the attempt by

France to intervene in Morocco, which in March 1905 had brought the indignant German kaiser to Tangier. At the conference, which was called principally by President Theodore Roosevelt at Germany's behest, Germany received the support only of Austria-Hungary. Italy, Russia, and —significantly for future alliances— Britain and the U.S.A. aligned themselves with France

al·ge·don·ic (ældʒidónik) adj. of the act of regulating an action without any explanation

Al·ger (ældʒər), Horatio (1834–99), U.S. author, perhaps the most popular and influential of his generation. 'Ragged Dick' (1867) introduced his perennial hero-type, the honest lad of cheerful perseverance who, with 'luck and pluck', achieves his just reward

Al·ge·ri·a (ældʒíəri:ə) a republic (area 952,198 sq. miles, pop. 21,351,000) in N. Africa. Capital: Algiers. People: Arab and Berber, with a small minority of Europeans. Languages: Arabic (official), French, Berber dialects. Religion: Moslem, with Roman Catholic and Jewish minorities. The land (excluding the Sahara) is 24% arable and 17% forest. Fertile lowlands along the coast give way to the Maritime Atlas. Semi-arid plateaus (over 3,500 ft) containing swamps and lakes stretch south to the Sahara Atlas, beyond which lies the Sahara (1,500 ft). The sirocco blows in spring, and northeast trade winds prevail in summer. Rainfall: 20 ins along the coast, 10 ins in the highlands, nil in the desert. Average summer and winter temperatures (F.): 50°–75° along the coast, 40°–80° in the highlands, 40°–95° in the Sahara. Livestock: sheep, goats, cattle, camels. Agricultural products: wheat, barley, oats, tobacco, wine, fruit, dates, vegetables, wool, olive oil, cork, esparto. Resources: fish (esp. sardines), iron, phosphates, oil, natural gas, zinc, lead, salt. Manufactures: carpets, leather, pottery. Exports: wine, iron ore, citrus fruits, vegetables, phosphates, esparto. Imports: iron and steel, manufactured goods, textiles, vehicles, petroleum products, sugar. Ports: Algiers, Oran, Annaba. University: Algiers (1909, by amalgamation of older faculties). Monetary unit: dinar. HISTORY. The area was peopled by Berbers when the Phoenicians started to colonize (12th c. B.C.). After the battle of Thapsus (46 B.C.), the area became the Roman province of Numidia, which passed (395 A.D.) to the Byzantine Empire. (The country is rich in Roman antiquities.) Vandals invaded (429), but Byzantine rule was restored (533). The area was controlled by the Arabs (from the 7th c.) and by the Turks (1518–1830). It became the base for Barbary pirates until France conquered the coastal region (1830). After a prolonged struggle (1835–47) with Abd el-Kader, France began to colonize Algeria, which was declared a French territory (1848). The Sahara, explored by the French (1827 onwards), passed into French control (1852) and its administration was separated from that of Algeria (1902). In the 2nd world war, Algeria became (1943–4) the headquarters of the French Committee of National Liberation. Algerian nationalists began guerrilla warfare (1954) to obtain independence, under the National Liberation Front (FLN). After seven years of fighting, a referendum in France and Algeria approved (1961) the principle of self-determination for Algeria. The country, including the two Saharan departments, became independent (July 3, 1962). Ben Bella was elected president (1963). He was deposed (1965) in a coup d'état led by Boumedienne, who became prime minister and president (1965). He nationalized French oil and natural gas concessions (1971) and was succeeded on his death (1979) by Chadli Benjedid, who was reelected (1984). Algeria mediated the Iranian hostage crisis (1980)

Al·ge·ri·an (ældʒíəri:ən) 1. adj. of or relating to Algeria 2. n. a native or inhabitant of Algeria

Al Ghazzali *GHAZZALI

al·gic acid (ældʒik) alginic acid

al·gi·cide (ældʒisaid) n. a chemical applied to kill or control algae growth

al·gid (ældʒid) adj. (esp. of the shivering which accompanies an ague) cold **al·gíd·i·ty** n. [F. *ai-gide*]

Al·giers (ældʒíərz) an ancient Mediterranean port, the capital (pop. 1,721,607) of Algeria. Founded in the 10th c., it became (1518) part of the Ottoman Empire. It was the center of the Barbary pirates until captured by the French (1830). In 1943–4 it was the seat of the French

provisional government. It is the administrative, financial and intellectual center of Algeria. Exports: wines, vegetables, fruit, cork, minerals. University (1909)

al·gin (ældʒin) n. any of various soluble colloidal salts of alginic acid (esp. the sodium salt) extracted commercially from certain seaweeds (e.g. giant kelp) and used as a stabilizing, moisture-holding, emulsifying or thickening agent for foods (e.g. ice cream), cosmetic creams and pastes and pharmaceuticals, and as a sizer and coating agent in the paper and textile industries [ALGA]

al·gi·nate (ældʒineit) n. a salt of alginic acid

al·gin·ic acid (ældʒinik) an insoluble, polymeric, naturally occurring polysaccharide $(C_6H_8O_6)_n$ that is extracted from the cell walls of some marine brown algae. Alginic acid and its salts are nontoxic, hydrophilic colloidal substances that have wide industrial Use (*AL-GIN)

ALGOL (computer acronym) for algorithm-oriented language, arithmetic computer language formalized in the late 1950s. It is particularly suitable to mathematical computations and the descriptions of computer algorithms but with limited IO facilities. There are many dialects, the most prominent of which are ALGOL GO (widely used in Europe) and ALGOL W (developed at Stanford University). A variant, ALGOL 68, is much more elaborate and complex and nothing like the original

al·go·log·i·cal (ælgələdʒik'l) adj. of or relating to algology

al·gol·o·gist (ælgólədʒist) n. a specialist in algology

al·gol·o·gy (ælgólədʒi:) n. the science that deals with algae [fr. L. *alga*, seaweed + Gk *logos*, discourse]

Al·go·man (ælgóumən) adj. (geol.) of a North American mountain-making episode during the mid-Proterozoic period [fr. *Algoma*, a district in Ontario, Canada]

Al·gon·qui·an (ælgónkwi:ən) 1. n. a family of North American Indian languages surviving in eastern and central Canada, New England and the Great Lakes region, and in the west of North America in a few isolated communities || a member of any tribe using these languages 2. adj. of the languages of the Algonquians

Al·gon·quin (ælgónkwin) n. Algonquian || a member of a tribe of Algonquian Indians who lived around the Ottawa River, Canada (now called Ottawa Indians, about 1,000 of whom live in villages in Quebec and Ontario) || the language of this tribe

al·go·rithm (ælgəriðəm) n. (computer) a formula for solving a problem —**algorithmic** adj. —**algorithmically** adv.

Algren, (álgren) Nelson (1909–81), U.S. author of 'The Man with the Golden Arm' (1949, film 1955), which won a 1950 National Book Award. Other works include 'A Walk on the Wild Side' (1956), 'The Neon Wilderness' (1947), and 'The Last Carousel' (1973)

ALGY (computer) a program for algebraic manipulation on the Philco 2000 system

Al Ha·kim (ælhákim) *DRUSE

Al·ham·bra (ælhæmbrə) the alcazar (palace) of the Moorish kings at Granada, built mainly 1250–1350 but frequently restored. It was partly destroyed to allow the building of Charles V's palace. There are magnificent gardens

A·li (áli:) (c. 600–660), cousin and son-in-law of Mohammed. He and his descendants are regarded by the Shi'ites as the only lawful successors of Mohammed. On the Prophet's death he contested the caliphate but submitted to Abu Bekr. He was elected caliph in 656

Ali, (alí:) Muhammad (1942–), U.S. boxer, born Cassius Marcellus Clay, Jr., who won the Olympic light-heavyweight championship (1960) and then the professional heavyweight championship from Sonny Liston (1964). A convert to the Black Muslim religion, Ali lost his title in 1967 for refusing military service in Vietnam, but his appeal of the decision was upheld by the U.S. Supreme Court (1971). He regained the title in 1974 in a match with George Foreman, lost it in 1978 to Leon Spinks, but regained it the same year. He retired in 1981

a·li·as (éili:əs) pl. **a·li·as·es** 1. adv. otherwise called, *Smith alias Strauss* 2. n. an assumed name || (computer) alternate designation of data in the computer [L.=otherwise]

al·i·bi (æləbai) pl. **al·i·bis** n. (law) the plea of having been somewhere else at the time of a crime || (pop.) an excuse [L.=elsewhere]

A·li·can·te (ɑli:kánte) a province (area 2,185 sq. miles, pop. 1,148,597) of Valencia, S.E. Spain || its capital (pop. 226,600), with an excellent harbor. Exports: wine and fruit. It has tobacco and food-preserving factories and oil refineries

Alice acronym for Alaska Integrated Communications, radio station network linking early warning system radar stations **also** White Alice

Al·ice Springs (ælis) the chief settlement (pop. 18,395) in the Northern Territory of Australia, in the middle of the continent, a pastoral and mining center

al·i·cy·clic (ælisáiklik, ælisíklik) adj. (chem.) of organic compounds which are both aliphatic and cyclic || of nonaromatic compounds which contain a ring of carbon atoms [fr. ALIPHATIC+CYCLIC]

al·i·dad (ælidæd) n. an alidade

al·i·dade (ælideid) n. the indicator of a surveying or measuring instrument || such as a quadrant, sextant etc. [F. fr. M.L. fr. Arab. *al*, the+*idādah*, rule]

al·ien (éiljən, éili:ən) 1. adj. belonging to another country, foreign, *an alien land, alien speech* || (with 'from') differing in character, *alien from what was anticipated* || (with 'to') opposed in nature, *a tradition alien to one's natural taste* 2. n. a non-naturalized foreigner, someone living in a country of which he is not a citizen || intelligent extraterrestrial being come to earth [O.F.]

al·ien·a·ble (éiljənəb'l, éili:ənəb'l) adj. capable of being alienated

al·ien·ate (éiljəneit, éili:əneit) pres. part. **al·ien·at·ing** past and past part. **al·ien·at·ed** v.t. to cause (affection) to be withdrawn || to cause (someone) to withdraw affection || (law) to transfer (property, title) from one person to another || to lose or give up (some natural right) **al·ien·á·tion** n. an alienating or being alienated || (psychol.) mental change preventing the person affected from leading a normal existence and taking part in social life [fr. L. *alienare alienatus*)]

al·ien·ism (éiljənizəm, éili:ənizəm) n. the study and treatment of diseases of the mind **ál·ien·ist** n. (law) a physician who specializes in the legal aspects of psychiatry

a·li·form (éilifɔrm) adj. wing-shaped [fr. Mod. L. *aliformis*]

A·li·garh (ʌligar) (Koil) a town (pop. 185,000) in Uttar Pradesh, N. India, 50 miles north of Agra: flour and cotton milling. Moslem University (1920)

a·light (əláit) pres. part. **a·light·ing** past and past part. **a·light·ed**, rarely **a·lit** v.i. to get down from a vehicle || to come to rest after flight [O.E. *alīhtan*]

alight pred. adj. and adv. on fire, in flames || lighted, lit up || bright, sparkling, *eyes alight with mischief* [past. part. of obs. *alight* v., to light, fr. O.E. *alihtan*]

a·lign, a·line (əláin) pres. part. **a·lign·ing, a·lin·ing** past and past part.

a·ligned, a·lined v.t. to line up || to bring into line or into correct relative position, *align the markers on the corner flag* || to join in sympathy, *they aligned themselves with the Republicans* || v.i. to be in proper line, *the letters don't align well in this new typeface* **a·lign·ment, a·line·ment** n. being in line, being in correct relative position to something else, *the front wheel alignment needs adjusting* [F. *aligner*]

a·like (əláik) 1. adv. in the same manner 2. pred. adj. similar, like each other [fr. O.N. *alíkr* and O.E. *gelíc*]

Ali Khan (kán), Liaquat (1895–1951), prime minister of Pakistan (1947–51). He was assassinated during the conflict with Afghanistan

al·i·ment (æləmənt) 1. n. food for body or mind 2. (æləmént) v.t. to provide with the means of support **al·i·mén·tal** adj. [F.]

al·i·men·ta·ry (æləméntəri) adj. of or relating to the function of nutrition [fr. L. *alimentarius*]

alimentary canal the passage in the body through which food travels, comprising the mouth, pharynx, esophagus, stomach and intestines, and which serves digestion, absorption of food and the elimination of solid waste products

al·i·men·ta·tion (æləmentéiʃən) n. an alimenting or being alimented || nourishment [F.]

Ali Mohammed of Shi·raz (ʃiəráz) the Bab

al·i·mo·ny (ǽləmouni:) *pl.* **al·i·mo·nies** *n.* money payable on a judge's order by a man to his wife or former wife, or (sometimes) by a woman to her husband or former husband, for maintenance after separation or divorce [fr. L. *alimonia*, nutriment]

aline *ALIGN

A-line *adj.* of a woman's garment with close fitting top and a flaring skirt, resembling an A

alinement *ALIGNMENT

al·i·ped (éiliped) 1. *adj.* wing-footed (like the bat) 2. *n.* a wing-footed creature [fr. L. *alipes* (*alipedis*)]

al·i·phat·ic (ælifǽtik) *adj.* (*chem.*) of a substance derived from fat, esp. of one of a large class of organic compounds characterized by an open-chain structure of carbon atoms and including both saturated (paraffin) and unsaturated (olefinic, acetylenic) hydrocarbons and their derivatives (cf. ALICYCLIC, cf. AROMATIC. cf. HETERO-CYCLIC) [fr. Gk *aleipha* (*aleiphatos*) fat]

a·live (əláiv) *pred. adj.* and *adv.* living ‖ brisk, lively ‖ (with 'to') alert, *to be alive to a problem* ‖ in existence, *to keep a tradition alive* ‖ (with 'with') swarming, *his coat was alive with fleas* [O.E. *on*, *in*+*life*, life]

a·li·yah (alí:ja) *n.* (*Hebrew*) immigration of Jews to Israel

a·liz·a·rin (əlizarin) 1. *n.* an orange-red dye formerly prepared from madder, now produced synthetically 2. *adj.* of any of a number of dyes similar to alizarin [F. *alizarine*, madder, prob. fr. Arab.]

a·liz·a·rine (əlízəri:n) *n.* and *adj.* lizarin

al·ka·hest (ǽlkəhest) *n.* the universal solvent of the alchemists [pseudo-Arab. coinage, probably by Paracelsus]

al·ka·le·mi·a, *Br.* esp. **al·ka·lae·mi·a** (ælkəlí:mi:-ə) *n.* (*med.*) an abnormal condition of increased alkalinity of the blood due to a decrease of hydrogen ion concentration in the blood [fr. ALKALI+Gk *haima*, blood]

al·ka·les·cence (ælkəlésəns) *n.* the process of becoming alkaline

al·ka·les·cen·cy (ælkəlésənsi:) *n.* alkalescence

al·ka·les·cent (ælkəlésənt) *adj.* slightly alkaline

al·ka·li (ǽlkəlai) *pl.* **al·ka·lis, al·ka·lies** *n.* a usually soluble hydroxide or carbonate of the alkali metals,or less often of the alkaline earth metals (e.g. calcium or barium), having strongly basic properties ‖ (*loosely*) a substance having similar properties to a true alkali **al·ka·li·fi·a·ble** (ælkəlifáiəb'l) *adj.* capable of being converted into an alkali,or of being made alkaline **al·ka·li·fy** (ǽlkəlifai) *pres. part.* **al·ka·li·fy·ing** *past* and *past part.* **al·ka·li·fied** *v.t.* to make alkaline ‖ *v.i.* to become alkaline [F. fr. Arab. *al*, *the*+*qalīy*, calcined ashes of saltwort]

Alkali (*mil.*) U.S.S.R. air-to-air missile (AA-1) with solid propulsion, speed of Mach 2.2, on MIG 17 and SU-9 aircraft

alkali metals the univalent metals of group I of the periodic table: lithium, sodium, potassium, rubidium, cesium and francium

al·ka·lim·e·try (ælkəlímitri:) *n.* the determination by titration of the amount of alkali present in a solution [fr. ALKALI+Gk -*metria*, measuring]

al·ka·line (ǽlkəlain) *adj.* having the properties of an alkali

alkaline earth metals the bivalent metals of group II of the periodic table: beryllium, magnesium, calcium, strontium, barium and radium. Their hydroxides are weaker bases than those of the alkali metals

al·ka·loid (ǽlkəlɔid) *n.* any of a group of organic bases,often of plant origin, containing nitrogen in a cyclic structure and usually oxygen, and that frequently have marked physiological activity and hence are used as drugs

al·ka·lo·sis (ælkəlóusis) *n.* a relatively high bicarbonate content in the blood or body fluids (opp. ACIDOSIS). It can lead to alkalemia

al·kane (ǽlkein) *n.* one of a homologous series of saturated hydrocarbons, C_nH_{2n+1} [ALKYL+-*ane*]

al-Kin·di (ɒlkíndi:), Abu Yusuf (9th c.), Arabian philosopher. He was the author of treatises on Plato and Aristotle, and wrote on various subjects, including medicine and astrology. He expounded the unity and righteousness of God

al·kyl radical (ǽlkil) any of the univalent hydrocarbon radicals, esp. of hydrocarbons of the paraffin series, having the general formula C_nH_{2n+1}, e.g. CH_3, methyl [prob. fr. G., fr. *alkonol*, alcohol]

all (ɔl) 1. *adj.* the whole quantity of, *all the harvest* ‖ the whole sum or number of, *all our friends* ‖ any whatever, *beyond all doubt* ‖ everyone of, *all people* ‖ the greatest possible, *in all sincerity* 2. *pron.* everyone, *all agreed to go* 3. *n.* everything, one's total possessions, *he gave his all to them* **in all** in total 4. *adv.* entirely, completely, *his face was all tear-stained* ‖ each, apiece, *the score is four games all* **all at once** suddenly **all but** very nearly, *he all but choked* **all in** exhausted **all in all** on balance, having considered every aspect of the question **all the better** better still, *it will be all the better if you can stay* **all told** counting everything, *that makes 64 sacks all told* **all very well** used to express discontent, *that's all very well but I won't have anywhere to sleep* **at all** in any way whatever, *you are lucky to be able to take holidays at all* **for good and all** for ever, finally **not at all** used as a polite disclaimer of thanks or praise **not at all bad** used as an understatement for something rather good [O.E. *all*, *eall*]

Al·lah (ǽlə, álə) the divine name used by Moslems

Al·la·ha·bad (æləhəbǽd, æləhəbád) a town (pop. 490,622) in Uttar Pradesh, India, at the confluence of the Ganges and the Jumna. It is a place of pilgrimage for Hindus. University (1887)

al·lan·to·is (əlǽntouis) *pl.* **al·lan·to·i·des** (æləntóuidi:z) *n.* (*embry.*) a vascular fetal membrane in higher vertebrates serving as a respiratory organ, while its cavity stores fetal excretions. In placental mammals, the allantois and the chorion take part in the formation of the placenta [Mod. L. fr. M.F. *allantoide*]

all-a·round (ɔ́lərəund) *adj.* general, *a good all-around education*

al·lay (əléi) *v.t.* to make less, alleviate, *the drug allayed his pain* ‖ to put at rest, make calm, *his promises allayed their fears* [O.E. *ālecgan*]

al·le·ga·tion (æligéiʃən) *n.* an assertion or statement yet to be proved [F.]

al·lege (əléd3) *pres. part.* **al·leg·ing** *past* and *past part.* **al·leged** *v.t.* to affirm without necessarily being able to prove **al·leg·ed·ly** (əlédʒidli:) *adv.* [fr. N.F. *alegier*. O.F. *esligier*]

Al·le·ghe·ny (æligéini:) a river (365 miles long) rising in W. Pennsylvania, looping northwest into New York State, and reentering Pennsylvania to help form the Ohio River at Pittsburgh

Allegheny Mtns *APPALACHIAN MTNS

al·le·giance (əlí:dʒəns) *n.* devotion, loyalty ‖ the duty of a subject to his sovereign, his rulers or his country [fr. O.F. *a*, to + *ligeance*, liege]

al·le·gor·ic (æligórik, æligórik) *adj.* containing, of the nature of, allegory **al·le·gór·i·cal** *adj.*

al·le·go·rist (æligɔrist, æligərist, æligərist) *n.* a maker of allegory

al·le·go·rize (æligəraiz) *pres. part.* **al·le·go·riz·ing** *past* and *past part.* **al·le·go·rized** *v.t.* to make into allegory ‖ *v.i.* to use allegory [F. *allégoriser*]

al·le·go·ry (æligɔri:, æligɔuri:) *pl.* **al·le·go·ries** *n.* a work of art in which a deeper meaning underlies the superficial or literal meaning ‖ the carrying of one meaning by another in this way [fr. L. *allegoria*, speaking of one thing under the guise of another, fr. Gk]

al·le·gret·to (æligrétou) 1. *adv.* and *adj.* (*mus.*) a little slower than allegro but not so slow as andante 2. *n.* (*mus.*) a piece or movement for allegretto performance [Ital.]

al·le·gro (əléigrou) 1. *adv.* and *adj.* (*mus.*) rather fast (as an instruction for the execution of a musical piece) 2. *n.* a lively piece or movement [Ital.]

al·lele (əlí:l) *n.* (*genetics*) one of any pair of alternative hereditary characters, e.g. red or white eyes in the fruit fly ‖ the gene regarded as the carrier of either of a pair of alternative hereditary characters [G. *allel*, shortened from ALLE-LOMORPH]

al·le·lo·morph (əléləmɔrf,əli:ləmɔrf) *n.* an allele **al·le·lo·mór·phic** *adj.* [fr. Gk *allēlōn*, of one another+ *morphē*, shape]

al·le·lu·ia (ælɔlú:jə) *n.* a song of praise to God, hallelujah [L. fr. Gk fr. Heb.]

al·le·mande (æləmǽnd, æləmánd) *n.* a court dance in moderate 4/4 time, popular in the 17th and 18th cc. ‖ a dance movement often at the beginning of the classical suite [F.=German]

Al·len (ǽlin), Ethan (1738–89), American soldier during the Revolutionary War. As leader of the Green Mountain Boys, he promoted the independence of Vermont

Allen, William (1532–94), English cardinal. He lived from 1565 at Douai in France for 20 years, and there founded an English college. (Similar establishments followed at Rome, 1575–8 and Valladolid, 1589.) He also established a printing press, from which issued the Douai Bible

Allen, Woody (1935–   ), U.S. comedian, actor, and film director, born Allen Stewart Konigsberg. His movies 'What's New, Pussycat?' (1965), 'Bananas' (1975), 'Sleeper' (1973), 'Interiors' (1978), and 'Hannah and Her Sisters' (1986) portray current fears and insecurities. 'Annie Hall' (1977) won four Academy Awards, and he wrote 'Play It Again, Sam' (1969) for Broadway

Al·len·by (ǽlinbi:), Edmund Henry Hynman, 1st Viscount (1861–1936), British field marshal. He commanded British forces in Palestine (1917–18) in the 1st world war and was British high commissioner in Egypt (1919–25)

Al·len·de Gos·sens (ɑjéndegɔséns), Salvador (1908–73), Chilean politician, leader of the Marxist Socialists and of the Popular Unity coalition of six leftist parties, incl. the Communists. He became (1970) the world's first freely elected Marxist president. His nationalization of many industries and land reform policies as well as severe economic problems led to widespread unrest. He died during a military coup that overthrew his government

Al·lep·pey, Al·lep·pi (ǽlépi:) a seaport (pop. 202,000) in Kerala, S.W. India, exporting copra, rubber, spices etc.

al·ler·gen, al·ler·gin (ǽlərdʒən) *n.* a substance that acts as an antigen producing an allergy [G. fr. *allergie*, allergy]

al·ler·gic (ələ́:rdʒik) *adj.* caused by, of the nature of, an allergy ‖ (with 'to') having an allergy or allergies

allergin *ALLERGEN

al·ler·gist (ǽlərdʒist) *n.* a doctor specializing in the treatment of allergies

al·ler·gy (ǽlərdʒi:) *pl.* **al·ler·gies** *n.* an exaggerated and specific antigen-antibody reaction marked by sneezing, difficulty in breathing, swelling, itching, rash or other symptoms. Certain individuals show this extreme sensitivity and others remain unaffected. The allergens responsible are diverse and may include pollen, dust, animals, bacteria, drugs, food etc. Disorders such as asthma, hay fever, eczema etc. are recognized as having allergic origin [fr. G. *allergie* fr. Gk]

al·le·vi·ate (əli:vi:eit) *pres. part.* **al·le·vi·at·ing** *past* and *past part.* **al·le·vi·at·ed** *v.t.* to lessen, relieve (esp. pain) ‖ to make lighter, mitigate, moderate, *to alleviate the tax burden* **al·le·vi·a·tion** *n.* **al·lé·vi·a·tive** *adj.* and *n.* **al·lé·vi·a·to·ry** *adj.* [fr. L. *alleviare* (*alleviatus*), to lighten]

al·ley (ǽli:) *n.* a narrow lane between buildings, esp. in a city ‖ a wide path in a garden or park ‖ an enclosure for bowling games **up** (or **down**) **one's alley** just what one likes best or does best or is most interested in [O.F. *alee*]

al·ley (ǽli:) *n.* a choice playing marble, usually with spirals of color inside [short for ALABASTER]

alley cat a homeless, stray cat

Alley Cat fad dance developed in New York City

al·ley·way (ǽli:wei) *n.* a narrow passage for pedestrians between buildings

All Fools' Day April Fool's Day (Apr. 1)

All·hal·lows (ɔ̀lhǽlouz) All Saints' Day, Nov. 1 in the Christian calendar [O.E. *ealra halgena*, of all saints]

al·li·ance (əláiəns) *n.* a treaty between governments ‖ the relationship formed by it between nations ‖ the state of being allied ‖ connection through marriage ‖ a uniting of qualities in a perceived relationship, *an astute alliance of tact and firmness* ‖ (*bot.*) a group of orders [O.F. *aliance*]

Alliance for Progress an agreement between the U.S.A. and the Latin American states to cooperate in the economic development and social betterment of Latin America. It was proposed by John F. Kennedy and created (1961) by the Charter of Punta del Este. Its objective was an economic growth of 2.5 % per year through accelerated industrialization, increased agricultural productivity, a more equitable distribution of national income, and an elimination of illiteracy. The U.S.A. pledged $10 billion in aid over a ten-year period, the sum to be matched by the Latin American

---

CONCISE PRONUNCIATION KEY: **(a)** æ, c*a*t; ɑ, c*a*r; ɔ f*aw*n; ei, sn*a*ke. **(e)** e, h*e*n; i:, sh*ee*p; iə, d*ee*r; ɛə, b*ea*r. **(i)** i, f*i*sh; ai, t*i*ger; ə:, b*i*rd. **(o)** o, *o*x; au, c*ow*; ou, g*oa*t; u, p*oo*r; ɔi, r*oy*al. **(u)** ʌ, d*u*ck; u, b*u*ll; u:, g*oo*se; ə, b*a*cillus; ju:, c*u*be. x, lo*ch*; θ, *th*ink; ð, bo*th*er; z, *Z*en; ʒ, cor*sa*ge; d3, sava*g*e; ŋ, orangutan*g*; j, *y*ak; ʃ, *fi*sh; tʃ, fe*tch*; 'l, rabb*le*; 'n, redd*en*. Complete pronunciation key appears inside front cover.

nations. Extended in 1965, the program ended in 1974

al·lied (əláid, ǽláid) *adj.* joined in alliance ‖ related in subject or kind ‖ (*biol.*) assumed to have an ancestral relationship **Al·lied** of or relating to the Allies

Al·lier (ǽljei) a department (area 2,848 sq. miles, pop. 378,400) of central France at the northern edge of the Massif Central (*BOUR-BONNAIS, *NIVERNAIS, *AUVERGNE). Chief town: Moulins

Allies, the the 23 countries allied against the Central Powers in the 1st world war, notably the British Empire, France, Italy, Russia and the U.S.A. ‖ the 49 countries allied against the Axis in the 2nd world war, notably Belgium, China, Denmark, France, Great Britain and the Commonwealth, Greece, the Netherlands, Norway, the U.S.A., the U.S.S.R. and Yugoslavia

al·li·ga·tor (ǽligeitər) *n.* a member of *Alligator*, a genus of large reptiles of the crocodile family found mostly in the rivers of tropical America ‖ the leather made from its hide [fr. Span. *el lagarto*, the lizard]

alligator pear the avocado

all in (*pop.*) exhausted, utterly fatigued

all-in (5lin) *adj.* (*wrestling*) in which almost no holds are barred ‖ (*Br.*) inclusive, *an all-in charge*

all in all 1. *n.* the person or thing one loves best or sets most store by 2. *adv.* all things being considered, on the whole ‖ altogether, as a whole, *taken all in all*

al·lit·er·ate (əlítəreit) *pres. part.* **al·lit·er·at·ing** *past and past part.* **al·lit·er·at·ed** *v.i.* to write or speak in words beginning with the same letter ‖ to constitute alliteration **al·lit·er·a·tion** *n.* the repetition of the same initial letter (usually a consonant) in a group of words, e.g. 'a deep, dark ditch' **al·lit·er·a·tive** (əlítəreitiv, əlítərətiv) *adj.* of or characterized by alliteration [fr. L. *ad*, to + *littera*, letter]

all-night·er (ɔlnáitər) *n.* an activity lasting through the night, e.g., movie, meeting, party

al·lo·bar·bi·tal [C₁₀H₁₂N₂O₃] (æloubárbitɔl) *n.* a barbiturate used with other drugs

al·lo·cate (ǽləkeit) *pres. part.* **al·lo·cat·ing** *past and past part.* **al·lo·cat·ed** *v.t.* to distribute, share out, to allocate the available seats ‖ to assign, earmark. *to allocate funds* ‖ (*computer*) to assign locations for storage, thus fixing addresses in absolute terms [fr. M.L. *allocare* (*allocatus*)]

al·lo·ca·tion (æləkéiʃən) *n.* the act of allocating ‖ the amount allocated ‖ something allocated [fr. L. *allocatio* (*allocationis*)]

al·lo·ca·tor (ǽləkeitər) *n.* (*computer*) an assembly and compiler program for patching and calling other parts for use on UNIVAC

al·lo·cu·tion (æləkjú:ʃən) *n.* a formal speech of some gravity ‖ (*eccles.*) a solemn speech by the pope in secret consistory (which may later be published) [fr. L. *allocutio* (*allocutionis*)]

allodium *ALODIUM

al·log·a·my (əlɔ́gəmi:) *n.* (*bot.*) cross-fertilization (cf. AUTOGAMY) [fr. Gk *allos*, other + *gamos*, marriage]

al·lo·ge·ne·ic, al·lo·gen·ic (æloudʒí:ni:ək) *adj.* of a transplant not sufficiently alike genetically to be accepted by the body. *Cf* SYNGENEIC

al·lo·graft (ǽləgræft) *n.* (*biol.*) tissue graft from a donor of the same species to a genetically dissimilar body. **syn** homograft. *Cf* XENOGRAFT

al·lo·morph (ǽləmɔrf) *n.* (*linguistics*) one of two or more variants of a morpheme as conditioned by position or by neighboring sounds ‖ (*mineral.*) any of two or more crystalline forms of the same substance [fr. Gk *allos*, other + *morphē*, shape]

al·lo·path (ǽləpæθ) *n.* a practitioner of aliopathy [F. *allopathe*]

al·lo·path·ic (æləpæθik) *adj.* of or pertaining to allopathy **al·lo·path·i·cal·ly** *adv.* [fr. F. *allopathique*]

al·lo·path·ic physician a physician practicing by a philosophy of medicine that views the physician as an interventionist who attempts to counteract the effect of a disease with surgical or medical treatment that produces effects opposite to those of the disease. A *homeopathic* physician generally uses a drug therapy that reinforces the body's natural self-healing process. Most U.S. physicians would be considered allopathic. **—allopathy** *n.*

al·lo·path·y (əlɔ́pəθi:) *n.* the science of treating a disease by inducing effects different from those produced by the disease (cf. HOMEOPATHY)

[fr. *G. allopathie* fr. Gk *allos*, other + *-patheia*, suffering]

al·lo·pat·ric (æləpǽtrik) *adj.* having separate and mutually exclusive distribution areas

al·lo·phone (ǽləfoun) *n.* a phonetic variant of a phoneme [fr. Gk *allos*, other + PHONE (simple speech sound)]

al·lo·pu·ri·nol [C₅H₄N₄O] (æloupjúarinɔl) *n.* (*pharm.*) a diuretic drug used to deter uric-acid formation in blood

al·lo·some (ǽləsoum) *n.* (*genetics*) a nontypical chromosome, e.g., X, Y, W, etc. *Cf* AUTOSOME

al·lo·ste·ric (æloustérik) *adj.* (*biochem.*) of the property of an enzyme to change from active to inactive and vice versa —**allostery** *n* the condition or effect

al·lot (əlɔ́t) *pres. part.* **al·lot·ting** *past and past part.* **al·lot·ted** *v.t.* to assign in portions, *of the various tasks, we were allotted the digging* ‖ to distribute by lot [O. F. *aloter*]

al·lot·ment (əlɔ́tmənt) *n.* the share of something allotted to a person ‖ the act of allotting ‖ an allowance from the pay of a member of the armed forces which is paid on his instructions directly to another person ‖ (*Br.*) a small plot of land which can be rented from the local authority for cultivation [F. *allotement*]

al·lo·trans·plant (æloutrǽnsplænt) *n.* organ transplant between like species of different heredity —**allotransplant** *v.* —**allotransplantation** *n.*

al·lo·tri·o·mor·phic (əlɔtri:əmɔ́rfik) *adj.* (*geol.*, of the minerals in igneous rock) not having the characteristic crystalline form (cf. IDIOMOR-PHIC) [fr. Gk *allotrios*, strange + *morphē*, form]

al·lo·trope (ǽlətroup) *n.* structure containing an element that exists in more than one form; e.g., graphite and diamond, each containing carbon

al·lo·trop·ic (æiətrópik) *adj.* of or showing allotropy [fr. Gk *allotropos*, in another manner]

al·lot·ro·py (əlɔ́trəpi:) *n.* (*chem.*) the occurrence of certain elements in more than one structural form, e.g. of carbon as graphite, charcoal and diamond (*POLYMORPHISM) [fr. Gk *allotropia* fr. *allos*, other + *tropos*, manner]

al·lo·type (ǽlətaip) *n.* (*genetics*) 1. one of the opposite sex of the specimen used as an example in a protein description 2. a genetic variant *Cf* HOLOTYPE

al·lo·ty·py (ǽlətaipi:) *n.* condition in which immunoglobins of different individuals of the same species are made up of different chemical classes

all-ov·er (5louvər) *adj.* covering every part, *an allover pattern*

all over 1. *prep.* on or in every part of, *you have ink all over your face* 2. adv. over every part, *painted yellow all over* ‖ in every part, everywhere, *to search all over* ‖ typically, completely, *that's John all over* ‖ quite finished, *the fighting is all over*

al·low (əláu) *v.t.* to permit, let ‖ to permit to have (something) ‖ to admit as true or acceptable ‖ to grant as a concession, *he was allowed a start of 20 yards* ‖ to give regularly by arrangement, *he allows his son $1000 a year* ‖ to keep in hand as a working margin, *allow one eighth for the trim* ‖ *v.i.* (with 'for') to plan with an adequate margin, *to allow for unexpected expenses* ‖ (with 'of') to admit, *the passage allows of only one interpretation* **al·lów·a·ble** *adj.* **al·lów·a·bly** *adv.* [fr. O.F. *alouer* fr. L. *allaudare*, to praise, and L. *allocare*, to bestow]

allowable charge in health care, a maximum fee that a third party will use in reimbursing a provider for a given service; not necessarily a reasonable, customary, or prevailing charge, as the terms are defined under the Medicare program

allowable costs in health care, items or elements of an institution's costs reimbursable under a payment formula. They may exclude uncovered services, luxury accommodations, unreasonable costs, expenditures unnecessary in the efficient delivery of health services to persons covered under the program in question

al·low·ance (əláuəns) *n.* a regular periodical sum of money paid to a dependant ‖ a price reduction granted e.g. on used goods traded in ‖ money paid to people with certain responsibilities, *family allowances* (money granted to assist in bringing up children) ‖ money granted for the performance of certain tasks, *traveling allowance* ‖ permission **to make allowances for** to take (something) into account and so make a more lenient judgment [O.F. *alouance*]

al·loy (əlɔ́i) *v.t.* to blend (metals) so as to form an alloy ‖ to impair or debase through mingling, *public success alloyed with private failure* [F. *aloyer*]

al·loy (ǽlɔi,əlɔ́i) *n.* a metallic substance composed of two or more metals esp. in solid solution [F. *aloi*]
—An alloy may be a mixture, a compound or a solid solution, its physical properties often differing markedly from those of its constituents. Prehistoric man formed bronze from copper and tin. Brass was later made from copper and zinc. Manganese, chromium, nickel etc. alloyed in small quantities with steel give it properties of special value, i.e. hardness, resistance to corrosion, nonexpansibility etc. (*INVAR). Alloys of aluminum, preserving the lightness of aluminum, can be hard, tough and heat-resistant, and are much used in aircraft construction

Allport, (5lpourt) Gordon W. (1897–1967), U.S. psychologist known for his theory of personality that emphasized individual uniqueness. He was editor of the 'Journal of Abnormal and Social Psychology' (1937–49) and wrote 'Personality' (1937) and 'The Nature of Prejudice' (1954)

all-pow·er·ful (5lpáuərfəl) *adj.* having unlimited authority

all right 1. *adv.* well, well enough, *we can manage all right* ‖ agreed, *all right, you may go* ‖ beyond question, *he's alive all right* 2. *adj.* satisfactory ‖ agreeable ‖ proper ‖ well or recovered in health

all-round (5lráund) *adj.* all-around **áll·róund·er** *n.* someone whose skills or interests are developed in balanced variety, not in a narrowly specialized way

All Saints' Day the feast day (Nov. 1) in the Christian year, instituted by Gregory III, in honor of all saints

all·seed (5lsi:d) *n.* any of several manyseeded plants, e.g. *Polygonum aviculare*, knotgrass

All Souls' Day Nov. 2, a day of remembrance of Christians who died in the faith

all·spice (5lspais) *n. Pimenta officinalis*, fam. *Myrtaceae*, a small evergreen tree, grown chiefly in Jamaica ‖ the spice made from its small berries, which are dried and marketed whole or powdered. Bay rum is produced from the foliage

All·ston (5lstən), Washington (1779–1843), the first important U.S. romantic painter. He experimented in dramatic subject matter and the use of light and atmospheric color

all-time (5ltaim) *adj.* never reached or achieved until now, *an all-time record*

al·lude (əlú:d) *pres. part.* **al·lud·ing** *past and past part.* **al·lud·ed** *v.i.* to refer briefly ‖ to refer indirectly [fr. L. *alludere*, to play with, refer to]

al·lure (əlúər) 1. *v.t. pres. part.* **a·lur·ing** *past and past part.* **al·lured** to attract, entice 2. *n.* attraction, fascination **al·lure·ment** *n.* [O. F. *aleurrer*]

al·lu·sion (əlú:ʒən) *n.* an indirect reference [fr. L. *allusio* (*allusionis*)]

al·lu·sive (əlú:siv) *adj.* containing an allusion or a great number of allusions [fr. L. *alludere* (*allusus*), to play with, refer to]

al·lu·vi·al (əlú:vi:əl) *adj.* relating to a deposit of alluvium (*ALLUVIUM)

al·lu·vi·on (əlú:vi:ən) *n.* the wash of water against a bank or shore ‖ (*law*) the formation of land through the action of water, by the deposit of alluvium [F.]

al·lu·vi·um (əlú:vi:əm) *pl.* **al·lu·vi·ums, al·lu·vi·a** (əlú:vi:ə) *n.* a deposit of earth, sand etc. laid down by rivers chiefly in the lower parts of their courses [L.]

al·ly (ǽli) *pl.* **al·lies** *n.* an alley (playing marble)

al·ly (əlái) 1. *v.t. pres. part.* **al·ly·ing** *past and past part.* **al·lied** to unite in an alliance (esp. of countries by treaty, and families by marriage) ‖ to relate by certain similarities, *jazz is allied to primitive folk music* 2. *n.* (ǽlai,əlái) *pl.* **al·lies** a country or person allied to another [O.F. *alier*]

Al·ma-A·ta (álmaáta) (formerly Vyerny) the capital (pop. 871,000) of Kazakhstan, U.S.S.R.: food processing, leather, textiles, metallurgy, 'champagne'. University

Al·ma, Battle of the (ǽlma) a victory (1854) of the British, French and Turkish over the Russians during the Crimean War

Al-Madina *MEDINA

al·ma·gest (ǽlmədʒest) *n.* a medieval work on astronomy or alchemy the **Al·ma·gest** the great

---

CONCISE PRONUNCIATION KEY: **(a)** æ, c*a*t; ɑ, c*a*r; ɔ f*aw*n; ei, sn*a*ke. **(e)** e, h*e*n; i:, sh*ee*p; iə, d*ee*r; ɛə, b*ea*r. **(i)** i, f*i*sh; ai, t*i*ger; ə:, b*i*rd; **(o)** o, *o*x; au, c*ow*; ou, g*oa*t; u, p*oo*r; ɔi, r*oy*al. **(u)** ʌ, d*u*ck; u, b*u*ll; u:, g*oo*se; ə, b*a*cill*u*s; ju:, c*u*be. x, lo*ch*; θ, *th*ink; ð, bo*th*er; z, *Z*en; ʒ, cor*s*age; dʒ, sava*ge*; ŋ, oranguta*ng*; j, *y*ak; ʃ, *fi*sh; tʃ, fe*tch*; 'l, rabb*le*; 'n, redd*en*. Complete pronunciation key appears inside front cover.

treatise on astronomy by Claudius Ptolemy of Alexandria, written c. 140 A.D. [O.F. *almageste* fr. Arab. fr. Gk]

Al·ma·gro (almágrɔ), Diego de (c. 1475–1538), Spanish conquistador who with Pizarro conquered Peru and discovered Chile (1535–7)

al·ma ma·ter (ælməméitər, ælməmátər, úlməmátər) *n.* (*rhet.*) one's school or university [L.=foster mother]

al·ma·nac (ɔ́lmənæk) *n.* a calendar of the year with information about the sun, moon, stars, tides, public holidays etc. ‖ a regular publication of a generally informative or statistical kind [Span. fr. Arab. *al*, the+*manakh*, calendar]

al·man·dine (ælməndi:n) *n.* a purplish-red variety of garnet stone [corrup. of *alabandine* after *Alabanda*, a city in Caria]

al·man·dite (ælməndait) *n.* the almandine

al·me·mar (ælmí:mar) *n.* the platform in a Jewish synagogue on which the reading desk stands [Heb. fr. Arab. *al*, the + *minbar*, pulpit]

al·me·mor (ælmí:mor) *n.* an almemar

Al·me·rí·a (almerí:a) a province (area 3,360 sq. miles, pop. 405,513) of S Spain (*ANDALUSIA) ‖ its capital (pop. 120,100), with a fine harbor

al·might·y (ɔlmáiti) 1. *adj.* all-powerful 2. *n.* **the Al·might·y God** [O.E. *ælmihtig*]

Al·mo·hades (ælməheidz) a Moslem dynasty. They overthrew the Almoravides in Morocco (1110) and established themselves in Spain and N.W. Africa (by 1147). The dynasty was overthrown in Spain (1212) and in Africa (1269). It destroyed (1591) the Songhai Empire

al·mond (ámənd) *n. Prunus amygdalus*, fam. *Rasaceae*, a small, pink-flowered tree ‖ the high-protein nut obtained from the stone (fruit) of this tree. Bitter almonds come from *P. a. amara* and dessert almonds from *P. a. dulcis* [O.F. *almande* fr. L. fr. Gk]

almond oil the oil of bitter almonds, used medicinally or for flavoring ‖ the oil from either bitter or sweet almonds, used as a lubricant (e.g. for watches) and in cosmetics and pharmaceuticals

al·mon·er (ámənər) *n.* (*Br.*) a specially trained social worker, usually a woman, responsible for the welfare of patients in a hospital [O.F. *aumosnière*]

Al·mo·ra·vides (ælmərávi:dz) a Moslem dynasty of N.W. Africa and Spain (11th c.), founders of Marrakesh and the empire of Morocco. They destroyed (mid-11th c.) the kingdom of Ghana. They were replaced by the Almohades (1110)

al·most (ɔ́lmoust, ɔlmóust) *adv.* nearly, all but [O.E. *ealmǽst*]

Alm·quist (ǽlmkvist), Karl Jonas Love (1793–1866), Swedish writer. He lived mostly in America. His 'Törnrosens Bok' (1832–51) is a 14-vol. miscellany which includes short stories, novels, essays, songs and a dictionary

alms (ámz) *sing.* and *pl. n.* money or goods given to the poor ‖ a charitable gift [O.E. *ælmysse* fr. L. fr. Gk]

alms·house (ámzhɑus) *n.* (*Br.*) a house for old and needy people, founded by charity

Al·ni·co (ælnikɔu) *n.* an alloy of iron, nickel, aluminum and cobalt (and/or copper, titanium) used for permanent magnets [Trademark]

a·lo·di·um, al·lo·di·um (əlóudi:əm) *n.* (*hist.*) land held in absolute possession, free from obligations to an overlord (cf. FEUD) [M.L.]

a·loe (ǽlou) *n.* a member of *Aloe*, fam. *Liliaceae*, a genus of xerophytes having fleshy leaves with a waxy epidermis from which a juice is obtained. It is dried and used as a purgative ‖ (*pl.*) this drug **a·lo·et·ic** (ælouétik) *adj.* (*med.*) containing aloes [O.E. *aluwan* fr. L. fr. Gk]

a·loft (əlɔ́ft, əlɔ́ft) *adv.* and *pred. adj.* high up, in the air ‖ (*naut.*) among the top masts, in the upper rigging [O.N. á *lopt*, *in* air]

a·lo·in (ǽlouin) *n.* a bitter, yellow crystalline substance obtained from the aloe and used as a purgative

a·lone (əlóun) 1. *adj.* (usually follows the word it modifies) by oneself, away from all others, unaccompanied, solitary 2. *adv.* only, solely, exclusively, *he alone knows why* **let alone** not considering, not taking into account, *I haven't the time, let alone the money* **to leave alone** to leave unaccompanied ‖ to ignore, not touch or molest, *leave him alone!* [ALL *adv.* +ONE]

a·long (əlɔ́ŋ,əlɔ́ŋ) 1. *prep.* from one end to the other end of, *a hedge grows along the path* 2. *adv.* with you (or with him, her etc.), *bring your*

bathing things along ‖ onward, forward, *to stroll along* **all along** all the time, *I knew it all along* **to get along with** to be on terms of tolerant understanding with ‖ to proceed with, *get along with your work* **to go along with** to have the same opinion as [O. E. *andlang* fr. *and-*, facing +*lang*, long]

a·long·side (əlɔ́ŋsáid, əlɔ́ŋsáid) 1. *prep.* by the side of, *park alongside the wall* ‖ in company with, *the families grew up alongside each other* 2. *adv.* close to one side (e.g. close to and parallel with a ship or the side of the road), *pull in alongside*

a·loof (əlú:f) 1. *adv.* away, at a physical or spiritual distance 2. *adj.* reserved, cold in manner [fr. A (*hist. prep.*)+Du. *loef*, windward]

a·lo·pe·cia (æləpí:ʃə, æləpí:ʃi:ə) *n.* (*med.*) baldness, loss of hair [L. fr Gk *alōpēkia*, fox mange]

A·lost (ælɔst) *AALST

a·loud (əláud) *adv.* in a normal speaking voice, so as to be heard, *read this story aloud* **to cry aloud for** to demand urgently, *an evil which cries aloud for remedy*

a·low (əlóu) *adv.* (*naut.*) below, in the lower part of a ship

alp (ælp) *n.* a mountain ‖ a pasture high on a mountain [F. *Alpes* (pl.)]

al·pac·a (ælpǽkə) *n.* a species of llama with fine woolly hair ‖ the hair itself, or the cloth made from it [Span. *alpaca* fr. Arab. *al*, the+Peruv. *paco*]

Alp Ars·lan (alparslán) (1029–72), sultan of the Seljuk Turks (1063–72). He conquered Georgia and Armenia (1064) and won a decisive victory over the Byzantine Empire (1071)

al·pen·stock (ǽlpənstɔk) *n.* a long, iron-tipped stick used in mountain climbing [G.=stick of the Alps]

Alpes-de-Haute-Provence (ǽlpdəoutprɔvɑ̃s) a department (area 2,697 sq. miles, pop. 112,200) of S.E. France (*PROVENCE). Chief town: Digne

Alpes, Hautes- *HAUTES-ALPES

Alpes-Ma·ri·times (ælpmæri:ti:m) a department (area 1,443 sq. miles, pop. 816,700) of S.E. France, bordering Italy and the Mediterranean (*PROVENCE). Chief town: Nice

al·pha (ǽlfə) *n.* the first letter (A, *a*=a) of the Greek alphabet ‖ (*astron.*) the brightest star in a constellation ‖ (*math*) probability of error in estimating statistics in scientific studies using sampling; the probability of rejecting a true null hypothesis ‖ (*computer*) (*abbr.*) for alphanumeric; the capacity of representing data in letters rather than numbers [L. fr. Gk fr. Heb. *aleph*, first letter of the Hebrew alphabet, an ox, a leader]

Alpha NATO term for U.S.S.R. submarines with titanium hull, capable of a speed of 40 knots; launched in 1980

al·pha·bet (ǽlfəbet) *n.* the letters or signs representing speech sounds used in writing a language, arranged in a conventional order (cf. SYLLABARY, cf. IDEOGRAM) **al·pha·bét·i·cal** *adj.* of or following the alphabet, *alphabetical order* **ál·pha·bet·ize** *pres. part.* **al·pha·bet·iz·ing** *past* and *past part.* **al·pha·bet·ized** *v.t.* to arrange in alphabetical order [L. *alphabetum* fr. Gk *alpha*+*beta*, the first two letters in the alphabet]

alpha decay (*nuclear phys.*) disintegration of an atomic nucleus due to an emission of a-particles

alpha globulin, a-globulin (*chem.*) a group of serum globulins with high mobility under an electric field in a fluid

alpha helix (*biochem.*) single coil structure characteristic of some proteins discovered by Linus B. Pauling —**alpha-helical** *adj. Cf* DOUBLE HELIX

al·pha·met·ic (ælfəmétik) *adj.* (*math.*) 1. of a numerical computer utilizing letters restored to numbers 2. of a coding system using numbers and letters of the alphabet as characters

alpha particle (*phys.*) an atomic particle composed of two protons and two neutrons having mass 4 and carrying two positive charges, indistinguishable from the nucleus of a helium atom. It is emitted at high speed during certain radioactive transformations (*RADIOACTIVITY)

alpha ray (*phys.*) a stream of alpha particles

al·pha·scope (ǽlfəskoup) *n.* (*computer*) cathode ray tube screen that displays words and symbols

alpha wave brain wave of 8–13 cycles, 9–14 Hz frequency, noted in sleep and in pleasant, relaxed wakefulness. **syn** alpha wave. *Cf* DELTA WAVE, THETA WAVE

Al·phon·sus Li·guo·ri (ælfónsəsligwɔ́ri:), St (Alfonso Maria de' Liguori, 1696–1787), Italian prelate. He founded the Redemptorists (1732). Feast: Aug. 2

al·pine (ǽlpain) *adj.* like or belonging to the Alps **Al·pine** (*geol.*) of a European mountain-making episode during the Tertiary period

alpine hat man's hat with pointed crown and narrow brim, usually green, with a feather or brush ornament; common to Swiss Alps

al·pin·ism (ǽlpinjzəm) *n.* mountain climbing, esp. in the Alps

al·pin·ist (ǽlpinist) *n.* a mountaineer, esp. in the Alps [F. *alpiniste*]

ALPS (*computer acronym*) for advanced linear programming system, a technique utilizing linear programming and equations to optimize conditions; developed by Minneapolis Honeywell

Alps (ælps) the greatest mountain range in Europe, forming an arc 660 miles long around N. Italy, passing through France, Switzerland, Italy, Germany, Austria, Yugoslavia. The Alps cover an area of about 80,000 sq. miles. Three principal groups are distinguished. The Western Alps separate France and Italy and include as subsidiary ranges the Maritime, Ligurian, Cottian, Graian, Dauphiné and Savoy Alps. Highest peak: Mont Blanc (15,781 ft). The Central Alps lie chiefly in Switzerland and include the Pennine, Lepontine, Rhaetian and Bernese Alps. Highest peak: Monte Rosa (15,217 ft). The Eastern or Austrian Alps include the Dolomites, the Hohe Tauern, the Noric, Carnic, Julian, Karawanken and Dinaric Alps. Highest peak: Gross Glockner (12,461 ft). There are many deep valleys and large lakes. Roads and railways cross some of the many narrow passes (St Gotthard, Brenner etc.) and tunnels have also been built (Simplon, St Gotthard, Mont Blanc etc.). The climate is continental in the east and Mediterranean in the southwest. Dairy farming and forestry are important. The upper level of crops is 6,000 ft, though little is cultivated above 4,500, and the tree line lies at 7,000 ft. Tourism is a large source of income. Mineral resources are poor, but hydroelectric schemes are well developed

Al-Qá·hi·rah (ælkáhira) *CAIRO

al·read·y (ɔlrédi:) *adv.* by this time, before a particular moment, *when we arrived they had already begun* [M.E., ALL+READY]

al·right (ɔlráit) *adv.* all right (a commonly written form, still often held to be incorrect)

Al·sace (ælzǽs) a former province of E. France between the Vosges massif and the Rhine, forming the modern departments of Bas-Rhin and Haut-Rhin. The river plain produces corn, tobacco, wheat, barley, hops and sugar beet. The foothills support vineyards (white wines) and dairy herds. Chief towns: Strasbourg Mulhouse, Colmar. Industries: textiles, chemicals, food processing. Resources: potash, petroleum. The region was included in Lotharingia, then (from the 10th c.) in the Holy Roman Empire. Large portions came under Hapsburg control and were transferred (1648) to France. The rest was annexed forcibly (1678–97). The whole was ceded to Germany in 1871 but subsequently restored (*ALSACE-LORRAINE)

Al·sace-Lor·raine (ælzæsləren) a French territory (Alsace and the Moselle region of Lorraine) on the Rhine annexed by Prussia after the Franco-Prussian War, under the Treaty of Frankfurt (1871). It was liberated by French troops (who entered Strasbourg on Nov. 22, 1918, the official date of its reunion with France). It was formally returned to France by the Treaty of Versailles (1919). It was again ceded to Germany by the Armistice of June 1940 but was liberated by the Allies (1944–5) and restored to France (May 1945). It forms the French departments of Haut-Rhin, Bas-Rhin and Moselle

Al·sa·tian (ælséiʃən) 1. *adj.* of Alsace, its inhabitants etc. 2. *n.* an inhabitant of Alsace [fr. older *Alsatia*, Alsace fr. M.L. fr. O.H.G.]

Alsatian *n.* (esp. *Br.*) a German shepherd

al·ser·ox·y·lon (ælsə:rɔ́ksilɔn) *n.* (*pharm.*) purified alkoidal fraction of rauwolfia, antihypertensive and tranquilizer drug; marketed as Rau-Tab and Rauwiloid

al·sike (ǽlsik, ǽlsaik) *n. Trifolium hybridum*, a species of clover [after *Alsike*, a place in Sweden]

al·so (ɔ́lsou) *adv.* as well, in addition, besides [O.E. *all*+*swā*]

CONCISE PRONUNCIATION KEY: **(a)** æ, c*a*t; ɑ, c*a*r; ɔ f*aw*n; ei, sn*a*ke. **(e)** e, h*e*n; i:, sh*ee*p; iə, d*ee*r; ɛə, b*ea*r. **(i)** i, f*i*sh; ai, t*i*ger; ə:, b*i*rd. **(o)** o, *o*x; au, c*ow*; ou, g*oa*t; u, p*oo*r; ɔi, r*oy*al. **(u)** ʌ, d*u*ck; u, b*u*ll; u:, g*oo*se; ju:, c*u*be. x, lo*ch*; θ, *th*ink; ð, bo*th*er; z, *Z*en; ʒ, cor*s*age. dʒ, sa*v*age; ŋ, oranguta*ng*; j, *y*ak; ʃ, *fi*sh; tʃ, fe*tch*; 'l, rabb*le*; 'n, redd*en*. Complete pronunciation key appears inside front cover.

al·so·ran (ɔ́lsourǽn) *n.* a horse which does not come in among the first three in a race ‖ a candidate heavily defeated in elections ‖ (*loosely*) a person who is a nonentity

ALTAC (*computer acronym*) for the transac algebraic translator, computer language for Philco 2000

Al·tai (ǽltái) a mountainous region running northwest-southeast in the south of W. Siberia and the west of the Mongolian People's Republic: coal, iron

Al·ta·ic (ǽltéiik) *adj.* of a postulated family of languages including the Turkic, Mongol and Tungus families (*URALALTAIC)

Al·ta·mí·ra (ɑltɑmírɑ) the site of caves near Santander, N. Spain, with fine Paleolithic animal paintings

Al·ta·mi·ra·no (ɑltɑmi:ránɔ), Ignacio (1834–93), Mexican writer, novelist, poet and politician, of pure Indian blood. His verse works include 'Rimas,' and his novels include 'Clemencia' and 'El zarco'

al·tar (ɔ́ltər) *n.* the structure on which bread and wine are consecrated in a Christian church ‖ any raised structure for offering sacrifices to a deity [O.E. fr. L. *altare*]

altar boy an acolyte (priest's assistant at Mass)

altar cloth a white linen cloth used on Christian altars

al·tar·piece (ɔ́ltɑrpi:s) *n.* a work of art placed above and behind an altar, a reredos

alt·az·i·muth (ǽltǽzimǝθ) *n.* an instrument for determining the altitude and azimuth of celestial bodies [ALTITUDE+ AZIMUTH]

Alt·dor·fer (ɑ́ltdɔrfǝr), Albrecht (c. 1480–c. 1538), German painter and engraver, a very early landscape painter. He made many etchings and drawings of pure landscape, and pictures in which the landscape background has great importance. 'The Victory of Alexander' (1529) at Munich is among his chief works

al·ter (ɔ́ltǝr) *v.t.* to make different, modify, change ‖ to resew (a garment or parts of it) for a new fit or style ‖ *v.i.* to become different, *she has not altered since we last saw her* [F. *altérer*]

al·ter·a·tion (ɔ̀ltǝréiʃǝn) *n.* the act or result of altering [F.]

al·ter·a·tive (ɔ́ltǝrǝtiv, ɔ̀ltǝréitiv) **1.** *n.* (*med.*) something producing healthy alteration, esp. in nutritive processes **2.** *adj.* having this quality or effect

al·ter·cate (ɔ́ltǝrkeit) *pres. part.* **al·ter·cat·ing** *past* and *past part.* **al·ter·cat·ed** *v.i.* to dispute with anger or violence, wrangle [fr. L. *altercari* (*altercatus*)]

al·ter·ca·tion (ɔ̀ltǝrkéiʃǝn) *n.* a quarrel, angry dispute [fr. L. *altercatio* (*altercationis*)]

al·ter e·go (ɔ́ltǝrí:gou) *pl.* **al·ter e·gos** someone so perfectly sharing the views, intentions, tastes etc. of another that he can be regarded as that other's second self ‖ an inseparable friend [L.=other self]

al·ter·nate (ɔ́ltǝrnit, *Br.* ɔ:ltǝ́:nit) **1.** *adj.* (of things which occur in series) every other, *he goes on alternate Mondays* ‖ (*bot.*) of leaves distributed at different heights on either side of a stem in turns **2.** *n.* a substitute **3.** (ɔ́ltǝrneit) *v. pres. part.* **al·ter·nat·ing** *past* and *past part.* **al·ter·nat·ed** *v.t.* to interchange (two things) by turns, *she alternated bullying and cajoling* ‖ *v.i.* to take turns, happen by turns, *day alternates with night* [fr. L. *alternare* (*alternatus*), to alternate]

alternate angles (*math.*) a pair of nonadjacent angles formed on opposite sides of a transversal at its intersections with two lines. They are equal if the two lines are parallel

alternating current (*abbr.* AC) an electrical current which reverses its direction at regular, very short, intervals (cf. DIRECT CURRENT)

al·ter·na·tion (ɔ̀ltǝrnéiʃǝn) *n.* an alternating, an occurrence of things by turns [F.]

alternation of generations a phenomenon characteristic of most plants and found in some invertebrate animals in which the life cycle includes two or more forms differently produced, involving either the regular alternation of a sexual with an asexual generation (e.g. ferns) or an alternation of a dioecious with a parthenogenic generation (e.g. some jellyfish) (*SPOROPHYTE, *GAMETOPHYTE, *MEDUSA, *HYDROID)

al·ter·na·tive (ɔltǝ́:rnǝtiv) **1.** *adj.* offering a choice of two things, or (*loosely*) of several things, *alternative routes for a journey* **2.** *n.* one of two things which must be chosen, or (*loosely*)

one of a number of things [fr. M. L. *alternativus*]

al·ter·na·tor (ɔ́ltǝrneitǝr) *n.* a dynamo or generator which produces alternating current

Alt·geld (ɔ́ltgeld), John Peter (1847–1902), Democratic governor of Illinois (1892–6), famous for his pardon (1893) of three of the men convicted of complicity in the Haymarket riot in Chicago (1886)

Al·thing (ɑ́lθiŋ) the parliament of Iceland, the oldest in Europe, first convened in 930. It was dissolved in 1800, revived in 1843 as an advisory body, and in 1874 became a legislative body

al·though (ɔlðóu) *conj.* in spite of the fact that, though [M.E., ALL+THOUGH]

al·ti·me·ter (ǽltimitǝr, ǽltmí:tǝr) *n.* an instrument for measuring height, e.g. the aneroid barometer fitted in aircraft or a sextant [fr. L. *altus*, high+METER]

Al·ti·pla·no (ɑlti:plánɔ) a high plateau (c. 12,000 ft) between the Western and Eastern Cordilleras of the Andes, mainly in W. Bolivia but extending into S.E. Peru and the northwest corner of Argentina. Lakes Titicaca and Poopó are its principal interior basins. Copper mining

al·ti·tude (ǽltitu:d, ǽltitju:d) *n.* height above sea level ‖ (*astron.*) the angle of elevation of a heavenly body measured from the plane of the observer's horizon ‖ (*geom.*) the length of a perpendicular from the base of a figure to the apex ‖ (*pl.*) regions at a great height above sea level **al·ti·tú·di·nal** *adj.* [fr. L. *altitudo* (*altitudinis*), height]

altitude signal reflection of a radar signal sent from an airborne craft to the earth's surface; used to measure altitude

altitude test *HYPSOMETRIC TINTING

altitude tinting *HYPSOMETRIC TINTING

al·to (ǽltou) **1.** *n.* (esp. choral singing) the lowest female voice, contralto ‖ (esp. choral singing) the highest male voice, countertenor ‖ a singer with such a voice, esp. a contralto ‖ the part sung by such a voice ‖ the second highest in a family of musical instruments, *the viola is the alto of the violin family*, or the one whose relative position in its family is the equivalent of a choral alto's, *alto recorder* **2.** *adj.* playing or singing alto ‖ written for alto [Ital.=highest male voice]

Alto Adige *TRENTINO-ALTO ADIGE

al·to·cu·mu·lus (ǽltoukjú:mjulǝs) *pl.* **al·to·cu·mu·li** (ǽltoukjú:mjulai) *n.* a cloud formation at 10,000–25,000 ft, made up of numerous white patches of small clouds with shaded areas, a mackerel sky [fr. L. *altus*, high+CUMULUS]

al·to·geth·er (ɔ̀ltǝgéðǝr, ɔ́ltǝgeðǝr) *adv.* completely, thoroughly, *altogether in agreement* ‖ on the whole, all things considered

al·to·stra·tus (ǽltoustréitǝs, ǽltoustrǽtǝs) *pl.* **al·to·stra·ti** (ǽltoustréitai, ǽltoustrǽtai) *n.* a cloud formation at 10,000–25,000 ft., made up of wide expanses of gray, flat clouds, somewhat similar to cirrostratus but lower and heavier [fr. L. *altus*, high+STRATUS]

al·tru·ism (ǽltru:izǝm) *n.* consideration for other people without any thought of self as a principle of conduct (cf. EGOISM) ‖ (*loosely*) unselfishness **ál·truist** *n.* **al·tru·ís·tic** *adj.* **al·tru·ís·ti·cal·ly** *adv.* [F. *altruisme*]

ALU (*computer acronym*) for arithmetic logic unit

al·um (ǽlǝm) *n.* any of a group of double salts of formula $M^+_2SO_4M^{3+}_2(SO_4)_3·24H_2O$ or $M^+M^{3+}(SO_4)_2·12H_2O$ where M^+ is a univalent metal ion or radical, usually potassium or ammonium, and M^{3+} is a trivalent metal ion, usually aluminum ‖ a double sulfate of potassium and aluminum, $K_2SO_4·Al_2(SO_4)_3·24H_2O$, used as a mordant in dyeing, in sizing paper and for fireproofing, also called potassium alum or potash alum [O.F.]

a·lu·mi·na (ǝlú:minǝ) *n.* aluminum oxide [Mod. L. fr. *alumen* (*aluminis*), alum]

a·lu·min·i·um (ǽljumíni:ǝm) (*Br.*) aluminum

a·lu·mi·no·sil·i·cate (ǝlu:mousílikit) *n.* any of a class of crystalline compounds that may be regarded as silicates in which a variable number of silicon atoms have been replaced by aluminum atoms in the crystal lattice

a·lu·mi·no·ther·my (ǝlu:minouθǝ́rmi) *n.* a process in which finely divided aluminum is oxidized with the evolution of great heat, the oxygen being taken from a metal oxide which is vigorously reduced to the molten metal. This principle has been used in welding, incendiary bombs and the extraction of certain metals from

their oxides (*THERMITE) [fr. ALUMINUM+Gk *thermē*, heat]

a·lu·mi·nous (ǝlú:minǝs) *adj.* relating to or containing alum or aluminum

a·lu·mi·num (ǝlú:minǝm) *n.* (*Am*= *Br.* aluminium) a light, silvery-white metallic element (symbol Al, at. no. 13, at. mass 26.9815), trivalent, ductile and malleable. It is extracted chiefly from bauxite and is an easily worked metal which resists corrosion. It is extensively used, either pure or alloyed, where lightness is an advantage, e.g. in aircraft, cooking utensils, electrical apparatus and, in paper-thin sheets, for wrappings [fr. L. *alumen* (*aluminis*), alum]

aluminum brass (*Am.*=*Br.* aluminium brass) an alloy of copper and zinc with some aluminum

aluminum bronze (*Am.*=*Br.* aluminium bronze) an alloy of copper with some 5–10 % aluminum

aluminum foil metal in a paper-thin sheet used as a wrapping to keep moisture out, keep juices in etc.

aluminum oxide (*Am.*=*Br.* aluminium oxide) the oxide of aluminum Al_2O_3 found naturally as corundum, in a hydrated form as bauxite, and in impure crystalline forms as ruby, emery etc., and used variously as a refractory, gemstone, abrasive etc.

aluminum screen (*electr.*) a coating of aluminum behind the phosphor layer of a television picture tube, designed to reflect light outward to improve the image

a·lum·na (ǝlʌ́mnǝ) *pl.* **a·lum·nae** (ǝlʌ́mni:) *n.* a woman or girl who is a former student of a school, college or university [L.=foster child]

a·lum·nus (ǝlʌ́mnǝs) *pl.* **a·lum·ni** (ǝlʌ́mnai) *n.* a man or boy who is a former student of a school, college or university [L.=foster child]

a·lu·nite (ǽljunait) *n.* a hydrated aluminum and potassium sulfate. It occurs naturally and is a source of potash alum [F. fr. *alun*, alum]

Alva *ALBA

Al·va·ra·do (ɑlvaráðɔ), Pedro de (c. 1475–1541), Spanish conquistador. After accompanying Cortés in the conquest of Mexico (1519–21), he led an expedition to Guatemala (1523–7), and later became its governor (1530–41)

Al·va·rez (álvareθ), Juan (1790–1867), Mexican revolutionary patriot, of Indian blood. He was provisional president (1854–5). He joined José María Morelos in the abortive campaign of 1811 for independence from Spain, and Antonio López de Santa Anna in the overthrow of Agustín de Iturbide in 1823

Al·ve·ar (ɑlveár), Marcelo Torcuato de (1868–1942), president of Argentina (1922–8) and a member of the Radical (democratic) party from its inception (1889–91)

al·ve·o·lar (ælví:ǝlǝr) **1.** *adj.* of, like or pertaining to an alveolus or alveoli ‖ (*phon.*) articulated by the tongue on or near the upper alveoli, e.g. the English consonants t, d, s, z, n **2.** *n.* a sound articulated in this way

alveolar point (*anat.*) the central point of the upper jaw

al·ve·o·late (ælví:ǝlit, ælví:ǝleit) *adj.* pitted with small holes like a honeycomb **al·ve·o·lá·tion** *n.* [fr. L. *alveolatus*, pitted]

al·ve·o·lus (ælví:ǝlǝs) *pl.* **al·ve·o·li** (ælví:ǝlai) *n.* a small pit or depression ‖ the socket of a tooth ‖ an air cell of a lung ‖ a cavity in a gland ‖ a cell in a honeycomb [L.]

al·ways (ɔ́lweiz, ɔ́lwǝz) *adv.* at all times, on all occasions ‖ invariably, without exception ‖ continually ‖ in any case, *we can always try again* [M.E., gen. of ALL WAY]

Al·za·ga (álsɑgɑ), Martín de (1756–1812), Argentinian politician and mayor of Buenos Aires at the time of the British invasion of 1806–7. He was executed

am (æm) *1st pers. sing. pres. indicative* of BE [O.E. *eom, am*]

AM (*radio*) amplitude modulation

A.M. Master of Arts [L. *artium magister*]

AMA American Medical Association

A·ma·ga·sa·ki (ámɑgɑsáki:) a town (pop. 448,000) of Honshu, Japan, on Osaka Bay: glass and chemical industries

A·ma·ku·sa Islands (ɑmɑkú:sɑ) a Japanese archipelago of 67 islands (area 341 sq. miles, pop. 261,000) in the E. China Sea, off the coast of Kyushu. Chief town: Hondo. Products: rice, fish, camellia oil, porcelain

A·mal·fi (ɑmálfi:) a town (pop. 6,052) on the north shore of the Bay of Salerno, Italy, famous for its beautiful position on the cliffside. It was

---

CONCISE PRONUNCIATION KEY: **(a)** æ, c*a*t; ɑ, c*ar*; ɔ f*aw*n; ei, sn*a*ke. **(e)** e, h*e*n; i:, sh*ee*p; iǝ, d*ee*r; ɛǝ, b*ear*. **(i)** i, f*i*sh; ai, t*i*ger; ǝ:, b*ir*d. **(o)** o, *o*x; au, c*ow*; ou, g*oa*t; u, p*oor*; ɔi, r*oy*al. **(u)** ʌ, d*u*ck; u, b*u*ll; u:, g*oo*se; ǝ, b*a*cillus; ju:, c*u*be. x, lo*ch*; θ, *th*ink; ð, bo*th*er; z, *Z*en; ʒ, cor*s*age. dʒ, sava*g*e; ŋ, orangutan*g*; j, *y*ak; ʃ, *fi*sh; tʃ, fe*tch*; 'l, rabb*le*; 'n, redd*en*. Complete pronunciation key appears inside front cover.

a republic of great commercial importance in the 10th and 11th cc.: its code of maritime law, 'Tabula Amalfitana', was observed throughout the Mediterranean until 1750. Cathedral (9th c.) with bronze doors from Constantinople (1066)

a.m., A.M. (éiém) *ANTE MERIDIEM

am·a·da·vat (ǽmədəvæt) *n.* a small Indian songbird, often kept for fighting [after *Ahmadabad*]

am·a·dou (ǽmədu:) *n.* a dried fungus soaked in saltpeter and used to ignite fireworks [F.]

a·mal·gam (əmǽlgəm) *n.* an alloy of mercury. Silver amalgams and others are used in dentistry for filling cavities ‖ a combination of characteristics, *an amalgam of pride and vanity* [F. *amalgame* fr. M.L. perh. fr. Arab. fr. Gk]

a·mal·ga·mate (əmǽlgəmeit) *pres. part.* **a·mal·ga·mat·ing** *past* and *past part.* **a·mal·ga·mat·ed** *v.t.* (*chem., mining*) to alloy with mercury ‖ to join together, mix, unite (companies, movements, clubs, ideas etc.) ‖ *v.i.* (of companies etc.) to unite, join together (*MERGER) **a·mal·ga·ma·tion** *n.* **a·mál·ga·ma·tor** *n.* someone who amalgamates, or a machine which amalgamates, or the machine minder [fr. L. *amalgamare* (*amalgamatus*)]

a·man·dine (ámandi:n) *adj.* with almonds; garnished with almonds

a·man·ta·dine, amantadine hydrochloride [C₁₀H₁₇N] (əmǽntədi:n) *n.* (*pharm.*) synthetic chemical used to inhibit cell penetration by viruses; used to protect against Parkinson's disease and Asian influenza

a·man·u·en·sis (əmænju:énsis) *pl.* **a·man·u·en·ses** (əmænju:énsi:z) *n.* someone employed to write from dictation or to copy a manuscript [L.]

am·a·ranth (ǽmərænθ) *n.* a plant of fam. *Amaranthaceae*, e.g. love-lies-bleeding ‖ (*rhet.*) an imaginary flower which never fades **am·a·ran·thine** (əmərǽnθain) *adj.* of or relating to amaranth ‖ (*rhet.*) undying, fadeless [F. *amarante* fr. L. fr. Gk]

Am·a·ril·lo (æmərílou) a city and commercial-industrial center (pop. 149,230) of the Texas panhandle, in N.W. Texas: zinc smelters, foundries, grain elevators, oil refineries, meat-packing plants. It is a supply center for oil and helium gas

am·a·ryl·lis (æmərílis) *n.* a plant of fam. *Amaryllidaceae*, e.g. the narcissus ‖ the belladonna [L. fr. Gk girl's name]

a·mass (əmǽs) *v.t.* to gather together, accumulate (esp. wealth) [F. *amasser*]

am·a·teur (ǽmətə:r, ǽmətʃuər, æmətjuər) **1.** *n.* someone who cultivates an activity as a pastime rather than as a means of making money (cf. PROFESSIONAL) ‖ (*derogatory*) a dabbler, dilettante **2.** *adj.* of or done by amateurs ‖ amateurish **am·a·téur·ish** *adj.* lacking proficiency, without professional finish **ám·a·teur·ism** *n.* the state or quality of being an amateur ‖ that which characterizes an amateur ‖ restriction of a sport to amateurs [F.]

A·ma·ti (amáti:) a famous family of Italian violin makers of 16th and 17th-c. Cremona. The name is also given to any instrument made by them

am·a·tive (ǽmətiv) *adj.* disposed towards love or sexual passion [fr. L. *amare* (*amatus*), to love]

am·a·tol (ǽmətɒl, ǽmətɒl) *n.* an explosive made from ammonium nitrate and trinitrotoluene (TNT) [AMMONIA+TOLUENE]

am·a·to·ry (ǽmətɒri:, ǽmətɒuri:) *adj.* dealing with or inducing love or sexual passion (cf. AMOROUS, cf. EROTIC) [fr. L. *amatorius*]

am·au·ro·ais (æmɔróusis) *n.* (*med.*) loss of sight from disease of the optic nerve **am·au·rot·ic** (æmɔrótik) *adj.* [Mod. L. fr. Gk fr. *amauros*, dark]

a·maze (əméiz) *pres. part.* **a·maz·ing** *past* and *past part.* **a·mazed** *v.t.* to astonish, astound, overwhelm with wonder **a·máze·ment** *n.* [O.E. *āmasian*, to perplex]

Am·a·zon (ǽməzən, ǽməzɒn) one of a race of female warriors in Greek and Asiatic legend said to have cut off the right breast so as to draw the bow more easily

Amazon the river with the largest basin and greatest volume of water in the world, draining nearly half of South America. It rises in the Andes as the Alto Marañón, joins the Ucayali in Peru above Iquitos, and flows 3,400 miles to the Atlantic coast of Brazil. Above Rio Negro it is called the Solimoes. Oceangoing vessels can navigate to Iquitos, 2,300 miles from the sea.

With the Ucayali its total length is over 4,000 miles

am·a·zon (ǽməzən, ǽməzɒn) *n.* a strong, manly woman, lacking feminine graces [L. fr. *Amazon* fr. Gk explained as *a*, without+*mazos*, breast]

am·a·zo·ni·an (æməzóuni:ən) *adj.* of or like an amazon **Am·a·zó·ni·an** relating to an Amazon or to R. Amazon

am·ba·ri (æmbári:) *n. Hibiscus cannabinus*, an East Indian plant with tough fiber ‖ the fiber itself, used in rope making [Hind. *ambārā*]

am·bas·sa·dor (æmbǽsədər) *n.* an official of highest rank who represents his government in the capital of another country [F. *ambassadeur*]

ambassador extraordinary an envoy sent to another country on a special mission

am·bas·sa·do·ri·al (æmbæsədóri:əl, æmbæsədóuri:əl) *adj.* of or relating to an ambassador or ambassadors

ambassador plenipotentiary an ambassador with full powers to act on behalf of his government in signing treaties etc.

am·bas·sa·dor·ship (æmbǽsədərʃip) *n.* the position or function of an ambassador

am·bas·sa·dress (æmbǽsədris) *n.* a woman ambassador ‖ the wife of an ambassador

Am·ba·to (ambútə) a manufacturing and commercial city (pop. 90,000) in central Ecuador. It is the 'garden city' (8,435 ft) of Ecuador, with an excellent climate. Manufactures include boots and shoes, and textiles

am·ber (ǽmbər) *n.* a fossilized form of resin, derived from certain extinct coniferous trees. It is yellowish in color and translucent, and is used for making jewelry, fine varnishes, mouthpieces of pipes etc. ‖ the color of amber [F. *ambre* fr. Arab. '*anbar*, ambergris]

am·ber·gris (ǽmbərgri:s) *n.* a waxy substance found floating in tropical seas and formed as a secretion in the intestines of sperm whales. It is used in the manufacture of perfume [F. *ambre gris*, gray amber]

am·bi·dex·ter·i·ty (æmbidekstériti:) *n.* the state of being ambidextrous

am·bi·dex·trous (æmbidékstrəs) *adj.* (of people) able to use both hands with equal ease ‖ two-faced, double-dealing, giving support to both sides in a dispute [fr. M.L. *ambidexter*, having two right hands]

am·bi·ence (ǽmbi:əns) *n.* (*acoustics*) the total acoustic environment of a sound-reproducing system, including reflections from walls, floor, and ceiling, which determines the placement of loudspeakers

am·bi·ent (ǽmbi:ənt) *adj.* on all sides, surrounding [fr. L. *ambiens* (*ambientis*) fr. *ambire*, to go around]

am·bi·gu·i·ty (æmbigjú:iti:) *pl.* **am·bi·gu·i·ties** *n.* the quality of having more than one meaning ‖ an idea, statement or expression capable of being understood in more than one sense [F. *ambiguité*]

am·big·u·ous (æmbígju:əs) *adj.* having more than one meaning or interpretation, equivocal ‖ doubtful, uncertain, *an ambiguous victory* [fr. L. *ambiguus*]

am·bi·plas·ma (æmbiplæzmə) *n.* (*astron.*) hypothetical ionized gas in space consisting of both matter and antimatter

am·bi·sex·trous (æmbisékstrəs) *adj.* (*slang*) attracted to both sexes; bisexual

am·bi·son·ics (æmbisóniks) *n.* acoustical reproduction as it would be heard at a certain point in the original production

am·bit (ǽmbit) *n.* bounds, precincts ‖ extent, limit,, *it is outside my ambit as chairman* [fr. L. *ambire* (*ambitus*), to go around]

am·bi·tion (æmbíʃən) *n.* eagerness to attain success, honor, power, fame etc. ‖ the object of a person's aspirations [F.]

am·bi·tious (æmbíʃəs) *adj.* full of ambition ‖ showing or requiring ambition, *an ambitious project* [fr. F. *ambitieux*]

am·biv·a·lence (æmbívələns) *n.* the state of being ambivalent [fr. L. *ambi-*, on both sides+VALENCE]

am·biv·a·lent (æmbívələnt) *adj.* having conflicting feelings about something (e.g. simultaneously attracted and repelled) or characterized by or expressing such feelings [fr. L. *ambi-*, on both sides+VALENT]

am·ble (ǽmb'l) **1.** *v.i. pres. part.* **am·bling** *past* and *past part.* **am·bled** (of horses) to walk at an easy gait ‖ (of people) to stroll, walk in a leisurely manner **2.** *n.* (of horses) an easy gait [F. *ambler*]

am·bly·o·pi·a (æmbli:óupi:ə) *n.* (*med.*) impaired vision without apparent change in the eye itself **am·bly·op·ic** (æmbli:ópik) *adj.* [Mod. L. fr. Gk *amblus*, dull+*ōps*, eye]

Am·brose (ǽmbrouz), St (c. 339–97), Father of the Latin Church. He was of Christian Roman parentage, though unbaptized when called to the bishopric of Milan in 373. He successfully maintained that the Church should be free in its own sphere from secular interference, but should be protected by secular power. He was a founder of Latin hymnody. Feast: Dec. 7

am·bro·sia (æmbróuʒə) *n.* (*Gk mythol.*) the food of the gods **am·bró·sial** *adj.* [L. fr. Gk]

Am·bro·sian (æmbróuʒən) *adj.* of or relating to St Ambrose

Ambrosian chant the plainsong of the Milanese liturgy, now part of the Gregorian chant

am·bry, aum·bry (ǽmbri:, áimbri:) *pl.* **am·bries, aum·bries** *n.* a recess in the chancel wall of a church for the Communion vessels [fr. L. *armarium*]

am·bu·lance (ǽmbjuləns) *n.* a special vehicle for transporting sick or injured people [F.]

am·bu·la·to·ry (ǽmbjulətɒri:, ǽmbjulətɒuri:) **1.** *adj.* of or concerning walking, adapted to walking, movable ‖ (*med.*) able to walk about, not confined to bed **2.** *n.* (*eccles.*) a place for walking or processing, esp. the apse aisle of a church, or a passage behind the chancel, or the gallery of a cloister [fr. L. *ambulatorius* fr. *ambulator*, a walker]

am·bus·cade (æmbəskéid) *n.* an ambush, esp. by soldiers [F. *embuscade* fr. Ital. *imboscata*]

am·bush (ǽmbuʃ) *n.* a hidden body of soldiers waiting to attack a passing enemy ‖ the place where they are hidden [O. F. *embusche*]

ambush *v.t.* to attack from an ambush [O.F. *embuscher*]

am·cin·o·mide [C₂₈H₅FO₇] (æmsínəmaid) *n.* topical cream (formerly called amcinopol) effective because of antiinflammatory, antipruritic, and vasoconstrictive actions; marketed as Cuclocart

am·cin·o·pol (æmsinəpəl) *n.* *AMCINOMIDE

ameba *AMOEBA

amebic *AMOEBIC

a·mel·io·rate (əmí:ljəreit) *pres. part.* **a·mel·io·rat·ing** *past* and *past part.* **a·mel·io·rat·ed** *v.t.* to improve, make better ‖ *v.i.* to become better **a·mel·io·ra·tion** *n.* **a·mel·io·ra·tive** (əmí:ljərətiv, əmi:ljərətiv) *adj.* [F. *améliorer*]

a·men (ámén, éimén) *interj.* so be it, truly it is so (used after a prayer) [L. fr. Gk fr. Heb. *āmēn*, certainty, truth]

a·me·na·bil·i·ty (əmi:nəbíliti:, əmɛnəbíliti:) *n.* the state or quality of being amenable

a·me·na·ble (əmí:nəb'l, əménəb'l) *adj.* responsive, *amenable to suggestion* ‖ answerable, responsible, *amenable to the law* ‖ able to submit to a test or to particular conditions, *amenable to very high temperatures* **a·mé·na·bly** *adv.* [prob. A.F. *amenable* fr. *amener*, to bring]

a·mend (əménd) *v.t.* to correct, free from faults ‖ *v.i.* to change for the better [O.F. *amender*]

a·mend·ment (əméndmənt) *n.* the act or result of amending ‖ a revision or change made in a law, bill etc. ‖ (in a public meeting or committee) a proposed modification (of a resolution) put forward for adoption ‖ a correction [O.F. *amendement*]

a·mends (əméndz) *sing.* and *pl. n.* (only in) **to make amends** to make compensation, reparation or restitution (for loss or injury) [O.F. *amendes*]

A·men·ho·tep III (əmenóutep) (d. c. 1360 B.C.), Egyptian pharaoh (c. 1397–c. 1360 B.C.) of the 18th dynasty. He built the Colossus of Memnon and most of the Temple of Luxor

Amenhotep IV (d. c. 1353 B.C.), Egyptian pharaoh (c. 1370–c. 1353 B.C.) of the 18th dynasty. He abandoned the cult of Ammon for the monotheistic, universal religion of Aton, took the name Ikhnaton, and founded a new capital at Tell-el-Amarna

a·men·i·ty (əméniti:, əmí:niti:) *pl.* **a·men·i·ties** *n.* the quality of being pleasant ‖ something that tends to make life more comfortable, adds to the convenience of a place, increases the delightfulness of an area etc. **the amenities** courtesies, civilities [F. *aménité*]

am·ent (ǽmənt) *n.* (*bot.*) a catkin **am·en·tá·cious** *adj.* like, consisting of, or bearing catkins [fr. L. *amentum*, a thong]

a·men·tia (eiménʃə) *n.* (*med.*) mental deficiency from birth, imbecility [L. fr. *a-*, away from+ *mens* (*mentis*), mind]

CONCISE PRONUNCIATION KEY: **(a)** æ, c*a*t; ɑ, c*a*r; ɔ f*aw*n; ei, sn*a*ke. **(e)** e, h*e*n; i:, sh*ee*p; iə, d*ee*r; ɛə, b*ea*r. **(i)** i, f*i*sh; ai, t*i*ger; ə:, b*i*rd. **(o)** o, *o*x; au, c*ow*; ou, g*oa*t; u, p*oo*r; ɔi, r*oy*al. **(u)** ʌ, d*u*ck; u, b*u*ll; u:, g*oo*se; ə, b*a*cillus; ju:, c*u*be. x, lo*ch*; θ, *th*ink; ð, bo*th*er; z, *Z*en; ʒ, corsa*g*e; dʒ, sava*g*e; ŋ, oranguta*ng*; j, *y*ak; ʃ, *fi*sh; tʃ, fe*tch*; 'l, rabb*le*; 'n, redd*en*. Complete pronunciation key appears inside front cover.

am·en·tif·er·ous (æməntífərəs) adj. bearing catkins

A·mer·i·ca (əmérikə) the two continents North America and South America, extending from beyond the Arctic Circle to the subantarctic regions and joined by a central isthmus. North America is centered on longitude 100°W. while South America lies further east centered on longitude 60°W. The name is from Americus Vespucius (Amerigo Vespucci). The total land area is over 15,000,000 sq. miles and the estimated total pop. 500,000,000 (*CENTRAL AMERICA, *WEST INDIES). Linguistically and culturally the Americas are known as Anglo-America (the U.S.A. and Canada) and Latin America (Mexico, Central America, most of the West Indies, and South America)

America First Committee a noninterventionist pressure group organized in the U.S.A. in Sept. 1940. It opposed any aid to the victims of Axis aggression which might involve the U.S. in war. After the Japanese attack on Pearl Harbor (Dec. 7, 1941) the Committee freely dissolved

A·mer·i·can (əmérikən) **1.** adj. of or belonging to the American continent ‖ of, characteristic of, or belonging to the U.S.A. or its people etc. **2.** n. a person born in or inhabiting the American continent (usually qualified), Latin Americans, South Americans ‖ a citizen of the U.S.A. ‖ the English language as used in the U.S.A.

American aboriginal languages the languages spoken by the original American Indian inhabitants of the New World and by some of their modern descendants. These languages do not derive from a common historical source. At the time of the coming of the white man, America north of Mexico had about 300 distinct languages spoken by a population of 1 ½ million. Mexico and Central America had 250–300 languages spoken by 5 million inhabitants. South America had over 1,400 languages spoken by 9 million inhabitants. Although many Indian languages disappeared after European colonization, at mid-20th c. a number still flourished, notably Navaho (spoken by 80,000 people in New Mexico and Arizona), Nahuatl (spoken by 700,000 in Mexico), and Quechua (spoken by several million in Ecuador, Peru, Bolivia, and Argentina)

American aloe the century plant (*AGAVE)

American An·ti·slav·er·y Society (ænti·sléivəri:) a U.S. society founded (1833) by William Lloyd Garrison to obtain by moral means alone the immediate and unconditional abolition of slavery

American Association of University Professors (abbr. AAUP) a U.S.–Canadian professional association of teachers and research scholars founded (1915) to promote higher education and research and to advance all aspects of the college and university teaching profession.

American Bible Society one of the oldest interdenominational agencies in the world, founded in 1816 to encourage worldwide circulation of the Bible. It publishes the Bible in more than 275 languages

American Civil Liberties Union (abbr. A.C.L.U.) a U.S. non-partisan organization offering legal aid and other assistance in cases of violation of civil liberties

American Civil War *CIVIL WAR, AMERICAN

American cloth (Br.) oilcloth

American Colonization Society an organization founded in 1816 by Robert Finley, a Presbyterian minister, and encouraged by influential U.S. leaders, notably Henry Clay and President James Madison, to aid freed black slaves to emigrate from the U.S.A. to Africa. The society, supported by antislavery groups, founded (1822) a settlement in Liberia, naming its capital, Monrovia, after President James Monroe. Between 1821 and 1867 it repatriated c. 6000 Blacks and was instrumental in the proclamation (1847) of the Republic of Liberia. Opposition in the U.S.A. and lack of finances caused its dissolution in 1912

American coot Fulica americana, a common American marsh bird

American English the English language, spoken and written, as it has developed in the U.S.A. and as distinguished from British English

American Farm Bureau Federation the largest U.S. farm organization, formed from county and state farm bureaus and founded (1919) in Chicago, Ill. 'to promote, protect and represent

the ... interests of the farmers of the nation, and to develop agriculture'. It has sponsored various bills, including the Agricultural Adjustment acts of 1933 and 1938

American Federation of Labor and Congress of Industrial Organizations (abbr. A.F.L.–C.I.O.) the American labor organization formed (1955) by the merger of two earlier organizations: the A.F.L., a federation of craft unions set up in 1886, and the C.I.O., a federation of mass-production workers, which had been expelled from the A.F.L. in 1937

American football (Br.) *FOOTBALL

American Hustler 1975-designed, twin-engine business/utility STOL aircraft with 1,289-mi range

American Independence, War of (Br.) the Revolutionary War

American Indian *NORTH AMERICAN INDIANS

A·mer·i·can·ism (əmérikənızəm) n. a word or phrase peculiar to American English ‖ devotion to the interests of the U.S.A. ‖ an American custom

A·mer·i·can·ist (əmérikənist) n. a specialist in the study of American Indians ‖ (Br.) a person who studies America, e.g. with respect to its history, geology etc.

American ivy the Virginia creeper

A·mer·i·can·i·za·tion (əmérikənizéiʃən) n. the act or process of Americanizing

A·mer·i·can·ize (əmérikənaiz) pres. part. A·mer·i·can·iz·ing past and past part. A·mer·i·can·ized v.t. to make (somebody or something) American in character ‖ v.i. to adopt the American way of life

American Labor Party a minor U.S. political party in N.Y. State, organized in 1936 by labor union leaders, Liberal Democrats and old-line Socialists, and joined from 1938 by the Communists. The party opposed Tammany Hall but generally endorsed Democrats, including notably Franklin D. Roosevelt in 1936, 1940 and 1944. In 1948 it supported Henry A. Wallace, thereby forfeiting much of its strength. It was dissolved in 1956

American Legion a nonpolitical, nonsectarian organization of U.S. war veterans founded in Paris (1919) on the initiative of Lieutenant-Colonel Theodore Roosevelt, Jr. It received its national charter from Congress in the same year and established its headquarters in Indianapolis, Ind. It has sponsored many programs in support of disabled veterans and their families as well as programs of national defense and of youth training

American Medical Association (abbr. AMA) a physicians' organization founded (1847) in Philadelphia, Pa. Its purpose is the improvement of public health. Although it has no legal power, its reputation exerts a strong moral influence in all matters of medicine

American Missionary Association an interdenominational organization incorporated (1846) by the merger of three antislavery societies. Formed to develop educational opportunities for freed Negroes, it founded more than 500 schools

American National Theatre and Academy (abbr. ANTA) an organization chartered (1935) by Congress to promote professional and non-professional U.S. theater

A·mer·i·can·ol·o·gist (əmérikənólədʒist) n. one who studies the personalities and powers of U.S. leaders Cf KREMLINOLOGIST

American organ a reed organ in which suction bellows draw air in through the reeds

American plan a system of payment in hotels where the price includes room, service and meals [cf. EUROPEAN PLAN]

American Revolution *REVOLUTIONARY WAR

Americans for Democratic Action an independent political organization (abbr. ADA) formed (1947) in Washington, D.C. to propagate liberal ideas, to help elect liberals, and to enact liberal legislation. It was attacked by the extreme left for exposing the Communist domination of the Progressive party and by the extreme right for campaigning against Senator Joseph McCarthy's movement. Many ADA leaders were appointed to key positions in the John Kennedy administration

American Telephone and Telegraph Company the key organization of the Bell Telephone system. It developed from the transfer in 1899 of assets of the American Bell Telephone Company and provides the bulk of telephone service in the U.S.A.

America's Cup, the the foremost prize of international yacht racing. It was named after the 101-ft schooner yacht 'America', which won (1851) the Hundred-Guinea Cup in England in a race against 17 British yachts around the Isle of Wight. The Hundred-Guinea Cup became known (1857) as the America's Cup after it was deeded to the New York Yacht Club as an international challenge trophy. The original ruling required a challenger to cross the Atlantic to qualify for competition, but the requirement was dropped (1958) to permit smaller yachts to enter the contest. All cup winners had been Americans until an Australian yacht won in 1983

am·er·i·ci·um (æmərisíːəm, æməríʃiːəm) n. a chemical element (symbol Am. at. no. 95, mass of isotope of longest known half-life 243) formed by nuclear reaction [Mod. L. fr. AMERICA]

A·mer·i·co·logue (əmérikəlɒg) n. a student of American society

Am·er·ind (æmərind) n. an American Indian or Eskimo **Am·er·in·di·an** adj.

am·e·throp·ter·in [$C_{20}H_{22}N_8O_5$] (æməθróptərin) n. (pharm.) toxic anticancer drug Cf METHOTREXATE

am·e·thyst (æmiθist) n. a precious stone (crystallized quartz), purple or violet in color ‖ oriental amethyst **am·e·thys·tine** (æmiθístain) adj. [M.E. ametist fr. O.F. fr. L. fr. Gk amethustos, not drunken, the stone being regarded as a remedy for, or a prophylactic against, drunkenness]

Am·har·ic (æmhærik, ɑmhárik) n. the southern, Semitic, official language of Ethiopia [fr. Amhara, a province of Ethiopia]

Am·herst (æmərst, æmhəːrst), Jeffrey Amherst, 1st Baron (1717–97), British commander against the French in Canada (1758–60). He captured Louisburg and Montreal

a·mi·a·bil·i·ty (eimiːəbíliti:) n. the quality of being amiable

a·mi·a·ble (éimiːəbˈl) adj. good-natured, friendly **á·mi·a·bly** adv. [O.F.]

am·i·an·thus (æmiːænθəs) n. a fine, greenish, glossy mineral variety of asbestos [L. fr. Gk amiantos (lithos), unstained (stone)]

am·i·ca·bil·i·ty (æmikəbíliti:) n. the quality of being amicable

am·i·ca·ble (æmikəbˈl) adj. friendly, peaceable **ám·i·ca·bly** adv. [fr. L. amicabilis]

am·ice (æmis) n. a white linen vestment worn by the officiating priest at Mass or Holy Communion [M.E. amyse, a wrap, fr. O.F.]

a·mid (əmid) prep. in the midst of, among [O.E. on, in + middan, middle]

am·ide (æmaid) n. (chem.) a compound formed by the replacement of an atom of hydrogen in ammonia by an organic acid radical. Amides have the general formula $R \cdot CONH_2$ where R is an alkyl or aryl radical **a·mid·ic** (əmidik) adj. [AMMONIA]

a·mid·ship (əmídʃip) adv. amidships

a·mid·ships (əmídʃips) adv. (naut.) in the middle of a ship

a·midst (əmídst) prep. amid

A·miel (æmjel), Henri Frédéric (1821–81), Swiss philosopher and diarist. His introspective 'Fragments d'un journal intime' was published in 1883

A·miens (æmjẽ) a trading and industrial city (pop. 131,332) in N.E. France, the chief town of Somme and historic capital of Picardy. Products: textiles, metallurgy, food. Gothic cathedral (13th c.)

Amiens, Peace of a truce (1802) between France and Britain after the French Revolutionary Wars. Dispute over Malta caused the war to be resumed (*NAPOLEONIC WARS)

a·mik·a·cin [$C_{22}H_{43}N_5O_{13}$] (æmíkəsin) n. (pharm.) semisynthetic antibiotic derived from kanamycin; marketed as Amikin

Amin Dada, Idi (íːdi: ɑmíːn dɑ́dɑ) (c. 1925–   ), Ugandan president and dictator (1971–9), often accused of erratic leadership. He overthrew Milton OBOTE in 1971, but was overthrown himself in 1979. He went into exile in Libya and Saudi Arabia

Am·in·di·vi Islands (ʌmindíːviː) *LACCADIVE, MINICOY AND AMINDIVI ISLANDS

a·mine (əmíːn, æmin) n. (chem.) a compound formed by the replacement of one, two or three atoms of hydrogen in ammonia by organic radicals [AMMONIA]

a·mi·no acid (əmíːnou, æminou) one of a class of organic acids having amino (NH₂–) groups in place of hydrogen atoms, in the hydrocarbon groups of fatty acids or other organic acids.

CONCISE PRONUNCIATION KEY: **(a)** æ, cat; ɑ, car; ɔ fawn; ei, snake. **(e)** e, hen; iː, sheep; iə, deer; ɛə, bear. **(i)** i, fish; ai, tiger; əː, bird. **(o)** o, ox; au, cow; ou, goat; u, poor; ɔi, royal. **(u)** ʌ, duck; u, bull; uː, goose; ə, bacillus; juː, cube. x, loch; θ, think; ð, bother; z, Zen; ʒ, corsage; dʒ, savage; ŋ, orangutang; j, yak; ʃ, fish; tʃ, fetch; 'l, rabble; 'n, redden. Complete pronunciation key appears inside front cover.

They occur in all plant and animal tissue and are considered the basic units of proteins, from which they may be obtained by hydrolysis [AMINE]

a·mi·no·ac·id·ur·i·a (əmi:nouæsidjúəri:ə) *n.* (*med.*) condition in which some amino acids are excreted excessively in urine

a·mi·no·trans·fer·ase (əmi:noutrænsfəreis) *TRANSAMINASE

amir *EMIR

Amis (éimis), Kingsley (1922–), English novelist, who was a member of England's 'Angry Young Men.' His novels include 'Lucky Jim' (1954), 'That Uncertain Feeling' (1955), and 'Take a Girl Like You' (1960), all made into films. He also wrote detective novels and science fiction

A·mish (ámiʃ) 1. *adj.* pertaining to the conservative Mennonite branch deriving from Jakob Ammann, a late 17th-c. Swiss Mennonite bishop 2. *n.* the members of this branch of the Mennonites, which settled in North America in 1683 [fr. G. *Amisch* fr. *Ammann*+*-isch*]

a·miss (əmís) 1. *pred. adj.* wrong, not as one would wish it to be, *is there anything amiss?* 2. *adv.* wrongly || away from the mark **to come amiss** to happen at the wrong moment **to take amiss** to take offense at (a remark etc.)

a·mi·to·sis (eimaitóusis, æmitóusis) *n.* cell division in which cleavage of the undifferentiated nucleus precedes cytoplasmic division

am·i·trole, a·mi·no·tri·a·zole [C₂H₄N₄] (æmítroul) *n.* (*chem.*) a toxic systemic herbicide

am·i·ty (æmiti:) *n.* friendship, esp. between nations [F. *amitié*]

AMM *mil.* acronym of antimissile missile

Am·man (æmæn, əmán) the capital (pop. 648,587) of Jordan, 50 miles east of the Jordan River. Products: textiles, handicrafts, cement. Originally the capital of the Ammonites, rebuilt (3rd c. B.C.) by Ptolemy II, it flourished under the Romans. It was conquered by the Arabs (635). It became the capital of Transjordan (1921)

am·me·ter (æmmi:tər) *n.* an instrument for measuring electric current (*GALVANOMETER) [AMPERE+METER]

am·mine (æmi:n) *n.* an inorganic salt (not to be confused with an organic amine) in which there are molecules of ammonia NH₃ attached to a salt molecule in a coordination complex [AMMONIA]

Am·mon, Am·on, Am·un (æmən) Egyptian god of the 16th c. B.C., worshipped at Thebes, in Ethiopia, and Libya, and often represented in the form of a ram. Alexander the Great visited his principal temple in the Libyan desert || an epithet of Jupiter as worshipped in N. Africa

am·mo·nal (æmənæl) *n.* an explosive mixture of ammonium nitrate, trinitrotoluene and aluminum powder [AMMONIUM+ALUMINUM]

am·mo·nia (əmóunjə, emóuni:ə) *n.* a gaseous compound of nitrogen and hydrogen (NH₃), having a pungent smell and very soluble in water to give an alkaline solution. It is manufactured directly from nitrogen and hydrogen by the Haber process or as a by-product in the manufacture of coal gas. It is important chemically and in industry. It is used e.g. in refrigerators, in the manufacture of nitric acid, and in fertilizers (*AMMONIUM SULFATE) [AMMONIAC]

am·mo·nia-beam ma·ser (əmóunjabi:m) *n.* a gas maser utilizing ammonia as a paramagnet

am·mo·ni·ac (əmóuni:æk) *adj.* of the nature of, or having the properties of, ammonia (*GUM AMMONIAC, *SAL AMMONIAC) **am·mo·ni·a·cal** (æmənáiək'l) *adj.* [F. fr. L. fr. Gk *ammōniakon*, a gum taken from plants growing near the temple of Ammon]

Am·mo·nite (æmənait) *n.* a member of a Semitic people of ancient Transjordan, whose chief city was Rabbath Ammon, now Amman. The Ammonite kingdom was established in the 13th c. B.C. and flourished until the 6th c. B.C.

ammonite *n.* (*geol.*) a fossil genus of cephalopods, of spiral form and often very large, abundant in the Triassic era [fr. M.L. *cornu Ammonis*, horn of Ammon]

am·mo·ni·um (əmóuni:əm) *n.* the positive, univalent ion NH₄⁺ known only in solution and as combined with acid radicals in ammonium salts [Mod. L. fr. *ammonia*]

ammonium carbonate the unstable ammonium salt of carbonic acid (NH₄)₂ CO₃, which breaks down to give the bicarbonate and ammonia. It is a constituent of smelling salts

ammonium chloride a volatile white crystalline salt (NH₄Cl) used in dry cells. It is a by-product of the soda industry

ammonium hydroxide NH₄OH, a weak base, formed by the direct combination of water and ammonia, and existing only in solution

ammonium nitrate NH₄NO₃, a white crystalline salt, which decomposes on heating and is used in explosives such as ammonal and in fertilizers

ammonium sulfate (NH₄)₂SO₄, a white crystalline salt obtained as a byproduct of the gas industry by passing the ammonia from the coal distillation into sulfuric acid. It is widely used as a nitrogenous fertilizer

Am·mo·ni·us Sac·cas (əmóuni:əssækəs) (c. 160–242), Greek philosopher and founder of Neoplatonism. Plotinus studied with him in Alexandria

am·mu·ni·tion (æmjuníʃən) *n.* everything (projectiles, charges, fuses etc.) necessary to feed guns or small arms [F. *amunition*]

am·ne·sia (æmní:ʒə) *n.* loss of memory caused by shock, injury etc. **am·ne·sic** (æmní:zik) *adj.* [Mod. L. fr. Gk *amnēsia*, forgetfulness]

am·nes·tic (æmnéstik) *adj.* causing loss of memory [fr. Gk *amnēstos*, forgotten]

am·nes·ty (æmnisti) 1. *n. pl.* **am·nes·ties** an act of pardon by a legislative authority which effaces not merely a punishment inflicted but the cause of it as well, so that no fresh proceedings can be instituted. Amnesties are usually granted to large groups, esp. of political prisoners 2. *v.t. pres. part.* **am·nes·ty·ing** *past* and *past part.* **am·nes·tied** to grant an amnesty to, to pardon [F. *amnestie* fr. L. fr. Gk]

Amnesty Act of 1865 a proclamation issued by U.S. President Andrew Johnson at the end of the Civil War. It granted full pardon to all former Confederates (except certain leaders) who took an unqualified oath of allegiance to the United States. Its provisions were modified in 1867 and 1868

Amnesty Act of 1872 a U.S. Congressional act of the Grant administration which rescinded the act disqualifying Confederate veterans from participating in politics. Only about 500 men were thereafter banned from serving in public office

Amnesty International an apolitical humanitarian organization with its headquarters in London. It requires its various groups (about 700, throughout the world) each to select three victims of political, religious, or racial persecution, one in the capitalist world, one in the Communist, and one in the unaligned, and to work for their release by making the injustice known. It seeks to comfort the victim and help his dependents. It has also sent observers and missions to various countries and, where fundamental rights are found to have been violated, submits reports in detail to the U.N. and the Council of Europe. In 1977 the group was awarded the Nobel peace prize

am·ni·o·cen·te·sis (æmni:ousentí:sis) *n.* (*med.*) process of withdrawing amniotic fluid from the uterus of a pregnant female for analysis to determine sex of the fetus or to diagnose possible fetal defects; e.g., for Down's syndrome

am·ni·og·ra·phy (æmni:ógrəfi:) *n.* (*med.*) X-ray of uterine cavity of a pregnant female after injection of radio-opaque substance

am·ni·on (æmni:ɒn) *pl.* **am·ni·ons, am·ni·a** (æmni:ə) *n.* (*anat.*) a thin, membranous, fluid-filled sac enclosing the embryo of higher vertebrates and formed together with much of the chorion from folds of ectodermal and mesodermal tissue [Gk=caul, dim. of *amnos*, a lamb]

am·ni·os·co·py (æmni:óskəpi:) *n.* (*med.*) visual examination of uterine cavity of a pregnant female through surgically inserted optical instruments —**amnioscope** *n* instrument for examining fetus within the uterus *Cf* FETOLOGY

am·ni·ot·ic fluid (æmni:ótik) the fluid in the amnion

a·moe·ba, a·me·ba (əmí:bə) *pl.* **a·moe·bae** (əmí:bi:), **a·moe·bas, a·me·bae, a·me·bas** *n.* a microscopic, freshwater protozoan, the simplest form of animal, consisting of a naked mass of protoplasm (*CELL). It moves by sending out pseudopodia (false feet), engulfs its particles of solid food, and reproduces by binary fission **a·móe·bic, a·mé·bic** *adj.* [fr. Gk *amoibē*, change]

amoebic dysentery, amebic dysentery *DYSENTERY

a·mok, a·muck (əmók, əmʌk) 1. *n.* an outbreak of violent madness, occurring chiefly in S.E. Asia, in which the victim is liable to kill anyone in sight 2. *adv.* (in the phrase) **to run amok** to be seized with this frenzy [Malay *amok*]

Amon *AMMON

a·mong (əmʌŋ) *prep.* surrounded by, in the midst of, *a house among the trees* || in the company of, *among friends* || in the class of, esp. outstanding in the class of, *a prince among princes* || in or from the number of, *choose one from among the lot* || by the common or collective action of, *decide among yourselves* || in relation to, with (each other), *they fought among themselves* || with a share for each of, *divide it among them* [O.E. *on gemang.* in a grouping]

a·mongst (əmʌŋst) *prep.* among

a·mon·til·la·do (əmɒnt'ládou) *n.* a pale dry sherry [Span. fr. *Montilla*, a town in Andalusia]

a·mor·al (eimɔ́rəl, eimórəl) *adj.* indifferent to morality (cf. IMMORAL) **a·mo·ral·i·ty** (eimæráliti:) *n.*

A·mo·rim (ɑmɔrí:m), Enrique (1900–60), Uruguayan novelist whose works, notably 'La carreta', 'El paisano Aguilar', and 'El caballo y su sombra', depict rural life

am·o·rist (æmərist) *n.* a person having a great many love affairs [fr. L. *amor*, love]

Am·o·rite (æmərait) *n.* a member of a race of Semitic nomads who dominated most of the Middle East (c. 2200–1700 B.C.) until defeated by the Hittites

am·o·rous (æmərəs) *adj.* much given to making love || concerned with love, *amorous verses* || showing or betraying love, *amorous looks* [O.F.]

a·mor·phous (əmɔ́rfəs) *adj.* formless, *an amorphous mass* || (*bot.*) not conforming to the normal structural organization || (*chem.*) having no crystalline form. *amorphous carbon* (charcoal) || (*geol.*) unstratified [Mod. L. fr. Gk *a*, without+*morphē*, form]

a·mor·phous film film deposited on a material without a necessity of having a crystal substrate; used on semi-conductor for magnetic bubble memories

amorphous laser *GLASS LASER

am·or·ti·za·tion (æmərtizéiʃən, əmɔrtizéiʃən) *n.* the act or process of amortizing **am·or·tize** (æmərtaiz, əmɔ́rtaiz) *pres. part.* **am·or·tiz·ing** *past* and *past part.* **am·or·tized** *v.t.* to provide for paying off gradually (a large capital outlay or a debt), usually by means of a sinking fund || (*law*) to sell in mortmain (i.e. under posthumous control) to an ecclesiastical or other corporation [F. *amortir* (*amortiss-*)]

A·mos (éiməs) a Minor Prophet (8th c. B.C.) of the Old Testament. He was the first to assert ethical monotheism || the book of the Old Testament containing his prophecies

a·mount (əmáunt) 1. *n.* the sum total, *the full amount* || a quantity, *a large amount of cement* 2. *v.i.* (with 'to') to add up, *the bill amounts to $10, his arguments do not amount to much* || (with 'to') to be equivalent, *a statement amounting to libel* [O.F. *amonter*, to mount upward]

a·mour (əmúər) *n.* a love affair, esp. an illicit one [F.=love]

a·mour cour·tois (æmu:rku:rtwæ) *n.* courtly love [F.]

a·mour pro·pre (æmu:rprɔpr) self-esteem || self-respect [F.]

Am·oy (æmɔ́i) (Hsia-men) a seaport and trading center (pop. 950,000) on islands of the Kiulung estuary, in Fukien province, S.E. China. University (1921)

amp (æmp) *n.* an ampere [shortening]

amp. ampere || amperage

am·pe·lop·sis (æmpəlópsis) *n.* a member of *Ampelopsis*, fam. *Vitaceae*, a genus of woody creeping plants || *Parthenocissus quinquefolia*, the Virginia creeper or American ivy [Mod. L. fr. Gk *ampelos*, a vine+*opsis*, appearance]

am·per·age (æmpərid3) *n.* the magnitude of an electric current expressed in amperes

am·pere (æmpiər) *n.* the mks unit of electric current, equivalent to a flow of one coulomb per second [after André Marie *Ampère* (1775–1836), French physicist] **am·pere-hour** (æmpiəráuər) *n.* a unit of electric charge, being the quantity of electricity transferred in one hour by a current of one ampere

Ampere's law either of two statements in electromagnetism: the first gives the magnitude and direction of the magnetic field at a point produced by a current-carrying conductor and

---

CONCISE PRONUNCIATION KEY: **(a)** æ, c*a*t; ɑ, c*a*r; ɔ f*aw*n; ei, sn*a*ke. **(e)** e, h*e*n; i:, sh*ee*p; iə, d*ee*r; ɛə, b*ea*r. **(i)** i, f*i*sh; ai, t*i*ger; ə:, b*i*rd. **(o)** o, *o*x; au, c*ow*; ou, g*oa*t; u, p*oor*; ɔi, r*oy*al. **(u)** ʌ, d*u*ck; u, b*u*ll; u:, g*oo*se; ə, b*a*cillus; ju:, c*u*be. x, lo*ch*; θ, *th*ink; ð, bo*th*er; z, *Z*en; 3, corsa*g*e; d3, sava*g*e; ŋ, oranguta*ng*; j, *y*ak; ʃ, *fish*; tʃ, fe*tch*; 'l, rabb*le*; 'n, redd*en*. Complete pronunciation key appears inside front cover.

the second is a relation between the tangential components of magnetic field intensity at points on a closed curve and the net current passing through the area bounded by the curve (*GAUSS'S LAW)

am·pere-turn (ǽmpiərtǝːrn) n. the mks unit defined as that magnetomotive force around one turn of wire carrying a current of 1 amp. One ampere-turn equals 0.4π gilberts

am·per·sand (ǽmpərsænd) n. the sign &, symbol for 'and' [corrup. of & per se=and (i.e. & by itself)]

am·phet·a·mine (æmfétǝmin, æmfétǝmiːn) n. a substance used as a nasal spray or inhalant or in its sulfate or phosphate form as a central nervous system stimulant [alphamethyl-phenethylamine]

am·phib·i·an (æmfíbi:ǝn) 1. n. (biol.) a member of Amphibia, a class of vertebrates intermediate between fish and reptiles. The larvae breathe by gills in water and the adults partly or wholly by lungs on land (frogs, toads, salamanders) ‖ an aircraft which can land on the ground or on water ‖ a military vehicle which can operate on land or water 2. adj. of or pertaining to one of the Amphibia ‖ pertaining to craft operating on land or in water [fr. L. amphibia, amphibious beings fr. Gk]

am·phi·bi·ol·o·gy (æmfɪbiːɔ́lǝdʒi:) n. that part of zoology which deals with amphibians [fr. L. amphibia, amphibious beings+Gk logos, word]

am·phib·i·ous (æmfíbi:ǝs) adj. able to live on land and in the water ‖ (mil.) involving coordinated action by land and naval forces, amphibious warfare [fr. L. amphibia, amphibious beings fr. Gk]

am·phic·ty·on·ic (æmfɪktiːɔ́nik) adj. (Gk hist.) of or relating to an amphictyony or the amphictyons (deputies from ancient Greek States composing a council)

am·phic·ty·o·ny (æmfíktiːǝni:) n. (Gk hist.) a league of neighboring states to protect some common interest [Gk amphiktyonia]

am·phi·mix·is (æmfimíksis) n. (biol.) the union of maternal and paternal characteristics in sexual reproduction [Mod. L. fr. Gk amphi-, both+ mixis, mingling]

am·phi·neur·an (æmfinjúǝrǝn) n. a member of Amphineura, a class of bilaterally symmetrical marine molluscs including the chitons [fr. Mod. L. Amphineura]

am·phi·ox·us (æmfi:ɔ́ksǝs) n. a lancelet of genus Branchiostoma [Mod. L. fr. Gk amphi-, both +oxus, sharp]

am·phi·pod (ǽmfipɒd) n. a member of Amphipoda, a large order of marine crustaceans, including also a few freshwater and parasitic forms **am·phip·o·dan** (æmfípǝdǝn), **am·phip·o·dous** (æmfípǝdǝs) adjs [Mod. L. fr. Gk amphi-, both+pous (podos), foot]

am·phi·pro·style (æmfíprǝstail, æmfǝpróustail) adj. (archit.) of a classical temple; prostyle at front and rear [F.]

am·phi·the·a·ter, Br. **am·phi·the·a·tre** (ǽmfiθiǝtǝr) n. a round or oval arena enclosed by rising tiers of seats, used (esp. by the Romans) for games and other contests ‖ a flat piece of land encircled by hills ‖ the gallery of a modern theater ‖ a large room arranged with tiers of seats for lectures, medical demonstrations etc. **am·phi·the·at·ri·cal** (æmfi:θi:ǽtrik'l) adj. [fr. L. amphitheatrum fr. Gk]

Am·phi·tri·te (æmfitráiti:) (Gk mythol.) goddess of the sea, daughter of Oceanus and wife of Poseidon

Am·phit·ry·on (æmfítri:ɔn) (Gk mythol.) son of Alceus, husband of Alcmena. Zeus disguised himself as Amphitryon and deceived Alcmena, who bore Hercules

am·pho·ra (ǽmfǝrǝ) pl. **am·pho·rae** (ǽmfǝriː), **am·pho·ras** n. a vase of ancient Greece or Rome with a tapering eggshaped body, often a pointed base, concave shoulders, and two slender handles rising on either side of a narrow neck from the shoulders almost to the mouth (cf. AMPULLA) [L. fr. Gk]

am·phor·ter·i·cin B [C₄₆H₇₃NO₂₀] (æmfǝrtérǝsin) n. (pharm.) antibiotic drug used to treat fungal and deep-seated mycotic infections

am·pho·ter·ic (æmfǝtérik) adj. (chem.) of a substance capable of reacting as an acid or a base [fr. Gk amphoteros, both]

Am·pi·cil·lin [C₁₆H₁₉N₃O₄S] (æmpisílin) n. (pharm.) semisynthetic variety of penicillin taken orally; used to combat resistant gram-negative bacteria, esp. in treating urinary and

respiratory infections; trade name for D-aminobenzyl penicillin

am·ple (ǽmp'l) adj. abundant, copious ‖ enough, easily sufficient [F.]

am·pli·dyne (ǽmplidain) n. (electr.) a rotating power amplifier, consisting of a motor and generator with special windings and brush connections used in servosystems and electronic amplifiers

am·pli·fi·ca·tion (æmplifikéiʃǝn) n. an extension or enlargement of something ‖ an amplified statement [fr. L. amplificatio (amplificationis)]

am·pli·fi·er (ǽmplifaiǝr) n. an apparatus used to increase the volume of sound, e.g. from a radio

am·pli·fy (ǽmplifai) pres. part. **am·pli·fy·ing** past and past part. **am·pli·fied** v.t. to expand or enlarge, esp. by adding details to (a statement or story) ‖ (elec., radio) to use (input of power, current, voltage) so as to increase the output ‖ v.i. to explain oneself in greater detail [F. amplifier]

am·pli·tron (ǽmplitron) n. (electr.) a microwave backward-wave amplifier utilizing a space-charge rotor with little mass and high speed

am·pli·tude (ǽmplitu:d, ǽmplitju:d) n. largeness, breadth, extent (esp. of opinions, explanations etc.) ‖ (astron.) the arc of the horizon between the point of true east or west and the foot of the vertical circle passing through any star ‖ the maximum numerical value attained by a periodically varying quantity measured from its mean value taken as zero and giving a measure of the magnitude of the energy of a vibrating or oscillatory disturbance [F.]

amplitude modulation a system of radio broadcasting that modulates the amplitude of a carrier wave (of constant frequency) in accordance with the strength of the audio signal, i.e. the signal produced by a microphone (cʾ. FREQUENCY MODULATION)

am·ply (ǽmpli:) adv. in an ample way

am·poule (ǽmpju:l, ǽmpu:l) n. a small glass vessel containing liquid, esp. for a hypodermic injection [F.]

am·pule (ǽmpju:l) n. an ampoule

am·pul·la (ǽmpúlǝ) pl. **am·pul·lae** (æmpúli:) n. an ancient Roman vase, with a globe-shaped body and two handles at the neck (cf. AMPHORA). It was used for ointments, perfume or wine ‖ (biol.) a sac or vesicle of this shape **am·púl·lar** adj. [origin uncertain]

am·pu·tate (ǽmpjuteit) pres. part. **am·pu·tat·ing** past and past part. **am·pu·tat·ed** v.t. to cut off, esp. in surgery **am·pu·tá·tion**, **ám·pu·ta·tor**, **am·pu·tée** ns [fr. L. amputare (amputatus), to cut]

AMRAMM (mil.) Navy-Air Force advanced medium-range air-to-air missile with 50-lb warhead, operational in 1979; made by Hughes Aircraft Co.

Am·ra·va·ti (Ámrǝvá:ti:) a town (pop. 138,000) in Maharashtra, W. India, 90 miles west of Nagpur. It is a cotton-trading and milling center

Am·rit·sar (æmrítsǝr) a city (pop. 589,229) of the Punjab, India, the main center of Sikh religion and culture. Industries: textiles, carpets, brocades, ivory carving, agriculture. University (1897)

Amritsar, Massacre of the shooting of 380 of Gandhi's followers at Amritsar in 1919 by Gen. Dyer's troops

Am·ster·dam (ǽmstǝrdæm) the capital and largest town (pop. 955,515) of the Netherlands but not the seat of the government (*HAGUE, THE), a great trading center and port at the southwest corner of the IJsselmeer, connected with the North Sea by canal. One of the world's richest towns, with an important money market, it has many industries (food, clothing, small-arms manufacture, marine and aircraft engineering, shipbuilding, diamond cutting), two universities (1877, 1905), and magnificent art collections. It grew up during the 13th c., and was particularly prosperous during the 17th c. It is built on about 100 islands, separated by canals and connected by about 300 bridges

AMTRAK a U.S. 23,700-mi railway system, since 1971 under Federal supervision; officially, National Railroad Passenger Corporation Cf CONRAIL, METROLINER

a·m·u. *ATOMIC MASS UNIT

amuck *AMOK

A·mu-Dar·ya (ǝmú:dárjǝ) (ancient Oxus) a river (1,350 miles long) rising in the Pamirs

and flowing down the Hindu Kush, forming the U.S.S.R.-Afghanistan frontier, and across Uzbekistan to its delta on the Aral Sea

am·u·let (ǽmjulit) n. an ornament or gem worn on the body as a protection against evil spirits [F. amulette]

Amun *AMMON

A·mund·sen (ámundsǝn), Roald (1872–1928), Norwegian explorer and navigator. He made the first crossing of the Northwest Passage (1903–6). He was the first man to reach the South Pole (Dec. 14, 1911). He took part in early Arctic flights (1925), and made the first trans-Arctic journey by airship over the North Pole to Alaska (1926). He was lost while searching for Nobile's airship

Amundsen Gulf a body of water between Victoria Is. and the northwest coast of the Mackenzie District, Northwest Territories, Canada

A·mur (ǝmúǝr) (Chin. Heilung-kiang) a river (2,700 miles) in N.E. Asia formed by the confluence of the Argun and the Shilka. With the Argun and the Ussuri it constitutes almost the entire boundary between Manchuria and Siberia, and flows into the Strait of Sakhalin. Entirely navigable May–Nov., it is the chief means of transport for Siberian grain and timber

a·muse (ǝmjuːz) pres. part. **a·mus·ing** past and past part. **a·mused** v.t. to cause to laugh or smile ‖ to divert pleasantly **a·múse·ment** n. pleasant diversion or entertainment ‖ quiet laughter ‖ (pl.) amusement park devices [O.F. amuser, to cause to stare stupidly]

amusement arcade (Br.) a penny arcade

amusement park a place where mechanical amusement devices are run as a business

AMVER (acronym) for Automated Merchant Vessel Report, computerized vessel and aircraft location sighting service of the U.S. Coast Guard for use in SOS transmission

AMX 13 (mil.) Char de 13X à Canon, French 13-ton light-infantry tank, carrying 75-mm or 105-mm guns, for use by airborne troops

AMX 32 (mil.) French Main Battle Tank with 120-mm gun, 20-mm cannon, 7.65-mm machine gun; planned operational in 1982

a·myg·da·la (ǝmígdǝlǝ) pl. **a·myg·da·lae** (ǝmígdǝli:) n. a tonsil **am·yg·dal·ic** (æmígdǽlik) adj. of or pertaining to almonds **a·myg·da·loid** (ǝmígdǝloid) 1. adj. almond-shaped 2. n. (geol.) any igneous rock containing almond-shaped nodules of minerals [L. fr. Gk amygdale, almond]

a·myg·da·lin [C₂₀H₂₇NO₁₁] (ǝmígdǝlin) n. (chem.) a glycoside found in pits of cherries and peaches and in bitter almonds that yields an hydrolysized glucose, benzaldehyde, and hydrocyanic acid

am·yl (ǽmil) n. (chem.) a hydrocarbon radical (C₅H₁₁) whose compounds are constituents of fusel oil, fruit essences etc. **am·y·la·ceous** (æmiléiʃǝs) adj. starchy, of or pertaining to starch [F. fr. L. amylum, starch+Gk ulē, oil]

amyl acetate an ester with an acrid smell of pears, used as a solvent for lacquers, and for flavoring and in perfumes

am·yl·ase (ǽmileis) n. (biochem.) any enzyme which accelerates the hydrolysis of starch to dextrin, and of dextrin to maltose

am·y·loid (ǽmiloid) 1. adj. like starch, containing starch 2. n. a starchy food

am·y·lop·sin (æmilópsin) n. (biochem.) pancreatic amylase, an enzyme present in the pancreatic juice, converting starch into sugar

A·myot (æmjou), Jacques (1513–93), French humanist and translator of Greek and Latin classics. His translation of Plutarch's 'Lives' was translated into English by Sir Thomas North (1579), and was much used by Shakespeare

an (æn) indef. art. (the form used before a vowel or a silent 'h'), an egg, an hour (*A, indef. art.) [O.E. ān, one]

an- prefix (the form used before a vowel, and usually before 'h') not, without, as in 'anhydrous' (*A- prefix) [fr. Gk]

-an suffix of or pertaining to, as in 'Nigerian'

-ana (ǽnǝ, ánǝ) suffix (used with a proper name) denoting sayings of, writings about, anecdotes concerning [L.]

ANAB (mil.) a U.S.S.R. missile (AA-3) with range of 15 or more km

An·a·bap·tism (ǝnǝbǽptizǝm) n. the doctrine of the Anabaptists ‖ the doctrine that those baptized in infancy must be rebaptized when they are adult [fr. L. *anabaptismus*, rebaptism, fr. Gk]

An·a·bap·tist (ænəbǽptist) 1. *n.* a member of a sect which arose in Germany in 1521 with the object of withholding baptism until it could be accompanied by a confession of faith, opposing Church establishment, and teaching that Christians should renounce private possessions. Anabaptism became a highly spiritualized religion of 'inner light', and also a focus for general peasant discontent. Anabaptists were persecuted by Catholics and Protestants (Luther) alike. They established a theocracy (1534–5) at Münster under John of Leyden, but the movement was stamped out when Münster was recaptured. Offshoots of it persisted in various countries (*MENNONITES, *BAPTISTS) 2. *adj.* of or relating to the sect or a member of it [fr. Mod. L. *anabaptista* fr. *anabaptismus*, rebaptism, fr. Gk]

an·a·bas (ǽnəbæs) *n.* a small freshwater fish, genus *Anabas*, of Africa and S.E. Asia, which can leave water and travel some distance over land. *A. scandens* can climb trees [Mod. L. fr. Gk *anabainein (anabas)*, to ascend]

an·a·bat·ic (ænəbǽtik) *adj.* (of air currents and winds) upward-moving [fr. Gk *anabatikos*, ascension]

an·a·bol·ic ste·roids (ænəbólik) *n.* (*pharm.*) group of muscle-building drugs, banned for use by amateur athletes

a·nab·o·lism (ənǽbəlizəm) *n.* constructive metabolism, in which simpler compounds are converted into more complex ones (opp. KATABOLISM) [fr. Gk *anabolē*, upward thrust]

an·a·branch (ǽnəbrænt∫, ǽnəbrɑnt∫) *n.* a stream that leaves a river and reenters it lower down [Gk *ana*, again+BRANCH]

a·nach·ro·nism (ənǽkrənizəm) *n.* something which does not fit in with its context chronologically (e.g. the smoking of a cigarette by an actor playing Julius Caesar) || an error in calculating time, esp. in historical writing **a·nach·ro·nis·tic** *adj.* [F. *anachronisme* fr. L. fr. Gk]

a·nach·ron·ous (ənǽkrənəs) *adj.* anachronistic

a·na·co·lu·thic (ænəkəlú:θik) *adj.* of or relating to anacoluthon

an·a·co·lu·thon (ænəkəlú:θɒn) *n.* (*gram.*) the abandoning of one grammatical construction for another in the middle of a sentence (e.g. 'which would you rather do, or go fishing?') [L. fr. Gk *anacolouthon*, not following]

an·a·con·da (ænəkɒ́ndə) *n. Eunectes murinus*, a large tree-climbing boa of tropical South America || (*loosely*) any large snake that crushes its prey [prob. fr. native name of a python of Ceylon]

an·a·cous·tic zone (ænəkú:stik) *n.* area in aerospace above 160 km altitude, from which sound waves can no longer be created because distance between molecules is greater than sound wavelength; **syn** zone of silence

A·nac·re·on (ənǽkri:ən) (c. 563–478 B.C.), Greek lyric poet from Ionia. Wine and love were his subjects in the surviving fragments of his poems

a·nac·re·on·tic (ənǽkri:ɒ́ntik) 1. *adj.* in the style or meter of Anacreon's poems || light, elegant, convivial, erotic 2. *n.* a poem in this style [fr. L. *anacreonticus* fr. Gk]

an·a·cru·sis (ænəkrú:sis) *n.* (*prosody*) one or more unstressed syllables at the beginning of a line of poetry not included in the metrical scheme || (*mus.*) an up beat [L. fr. Gk *anakrousis*, a recoil or striking back]

a·na·dam·a bread (ænədǽmə) *n.* bread made of flour, cornmeal, and molasses

a·nad·ro·mous (ənǽdrəməs) *adj.* (*zool.*, of fishes) ascending rivers at certain seasons for breeding (opp. CATADROMOUS) [fr. Gk *anadromos*, running upward]

anaemia *ANEMIA

an·aer·obe (ǽnəroub, ænέəroub) *n.* (*biol.*) a microscopic organism capable of living without free oxygen **an·aer·ó·bic** *adj.* **an·aer·ó·bi·cal·ly** *adv.* [fr. Gk *an*, without+*aēr*, air+*bios*, life]

anaerobic bacteria (*microbiol.*) bacteria capable of surviving with little or no air. They are of two types, facultative and obligate

anaerobic digestion utilization of bacteria without oxygen to reduce the volume of waste ant AEROBIC DIGESTION

anaesthesia *ANESTHESIA
anaesthetic *ANESTHETIC
anaesthetize *ANESTHETIZE

an·a·gen phase (ǽnədʒən) *n.* (*physiol.*) period of hair growth in the follicle

an·a·gen·e·sis (ænədʒénisis) *n.* (*gen.*) the evolution of a group without forming branch groups —**anagenetically** *adv.*

an·a·glyph (ǽnəglif) *n.* an embossed ornament, e.g. a cameo, worked in low relief || (*photog.*) a picture showing two images of the same object, with differently colored plates to give a stereoscopic effect when looked at through color-filter spectacles [fr. Gk *anagluphē*]

an·a·go·ge, an·a·go·gy (ǽnəgoudʒi:) *pl.* **an·a·go·ges, an·a·go·gies** *n.* a mystical or allegorical interpretation of something **an·a·gog·ic** (ænəgódʒik), **an·a·gó·gi·cal** *adjs* [L. fr. Gk *anagōgē*, a leading up]

an·a·gram (ǽnəgræm) *n.* a word or phrase made by changing the order of letters in another word or phrase (in the best anagrams there is a connecting idea between the original word and the anagram, e.g. 'best in prayer' is an anagram of 'presbyterian') **an·a·gram·mat·ic** (ænəgrəmǽtik), **an·a·gram·mát·i·cal** *adjs* [fr. Mod. L. *anagramma* fr. Gk]

an·a·gram·ma·tize (ænəgrǽmətaiz) *pres. part.* **an·a·gram·ma·tiz·ing** *past* and *past part.* **an·a·gram·ma·tized** *v.t.* to make an anagram of (something) [fr. Gk *anagrammatizein*]

An·a·heim (ǽnəhaim) a city and the largest industrial center (pop. 221,847) of Orange county, Calif. It is the site of Disneyland

A·na·huac (ɑnáwɑk) the central plateau of Mexico (average height 7,500 ft)

a·nal (éin'l) *adj.* related to, or situated near, the anus [fr. Mod. L. *analis*]

an·a·lects (ǽn'lekts) *pl. n.* miscellaneous writings, a collection of literary gleanings [fr. L. *analecta*, fr. Gk]

an·a·lep·tic (æn'léptik) 1. *adj.* (*med.*) tonic, restorative, strengthening 2. *n.* a medicine with these properties [fr. Mod. L. *analepticus* fr. Gk]

an·al·ge·sia (æn'ldʒí:ʒə, æn'ldʒí:zi:ə) *n.* insensibility to pain **an·al·ge·sic** (æn'ldʒí:zik) 1. *adj.* producing analgesia 2. *n.* a drug which does this [Mod. L. fr. Gk *an*, without+*algēsia*, pain]

an·a·log (ǽn'lɒg) *adj.* 1. (*electr.*) of a device that represents numerical quantities in terms of physical variables, e.g., in terms of voltages where resistance represents mechanical loss, or space in a slide rule, or rotation in a gear system 2. (*computer*) representing numerical data by physical variables factor, e.g., voltage, presented graphically on a cathode ray tube Cf ANALOGUE, DIGITAL

analog channel information presented between two valve parameters, e.g., a voice channel

analog computer device that provides continuous readings in contrast to a digital device that provides discrete readings, e.g., a water or electric meter, a slide rule

analog device control utilizing variables in continuous measurement units, e.g., voltage

an·a·log·ic (æn'lódʒik) *adj.* pertaining to analogy **an·a·lóg·i·cal** *adj.* founded on, or according to, analogy [fr. L. *analogicus* fr. Gk]

a·nal·o·gist (ənǽlədʒist) *n.* a person who uses analogy

a·nal·o·gize (ənǽlədʒaiz) *pres. part.* **a·nal·o·giz·ing** *past* and *past part.* **a·nal·o·gized** *v.i.* to use analogy || *v.t.* to bring into analogy

a·nal·o·gous (ənǽləgəs) *adj.* similar, corresponding in some respects || (*biol.*) similar in function though differing in structure (cf. HOMOLOGOUS) [fr. L. *analogus* fr. Gk]

analog recording (*acoustics*) reproduction of sounds by recording sound wave vibrations Cf DIGITAL RECORDING

analog signal (*computer*) a signal whose magnitude represents information

an·a·logue, an·a·log (ǽn'lɒg, æn'lɒg) *n.* a thing analogous to some other thing || (*biol.*) an organ of an animal or plant similar in function but different in origin to a corresponding organ in another animal or plant, e.g. the fish's gill is the analogue of the mammalian lung (cf. HOMOLOGUE) [F. fr. Gk *analogon*]

a·nal·o·gy (ənǽlədʒi:) *pl.* **a·nal·o·gies** *n.* the relationship between two things which are similar in many, though not in all, respects || either of these two things in relation to the other || (*biol.*) similarity of function between organs which are different in structure and development (cf. HOMOLOGY) || (*linguistics*) the process depending on correspondence of pairs or sets of words etc. by which certain changes come about in language, e.g. in the creation of new words and in the adjustment of minor structural patterns to the model of major patterns || (*logic*) the

assumption that if two things are similar in one or more respects, they will be similar in other respects || (*math.*) proportion, similarity [fr. L. fr. Gk *analogia*, similarity]

a·nal·y·sand (ənǽlisænd) *n.* a person undergoing psychoanalysis

analyse *ANALYZE

a·nal·y·sis (ənǽlisis) *pl.* **a·nal·y·ses** (ənǽlisi:z) *n.* the process of analyzing (cf. SYNTHESIS) || a document setting out the results of this process || psychoanalysis || *QUALITATIVE ANALYSIS, *QUANTITATIVE ANALYSIS [M.L. fr. Gk *analusis*, a dissolving]

an·a·lyst (ǽn'list) *n.* someone skilled in analysis, esp. in chemical analysis or in psychoanalysis [F. *analyste*]

an·a·lyst (ǽn'list) *n.* (*computer*) one skilled in defining problems and developing algorithms to solve them

an·a·lyt·ic (æn'litik) *adj.* pertaining to analysis || given to the use of analysis || (*gram.*) obtaining differences in meaning by the use of additional words rather than by inflections (*INFLECTION, *AGGLUTINATION) **an·a·lýt·i·cal** *adj.* [fr. M.L. *analyticus* fr. Gk]

analytical geometry geometry in which the analytic method is applied by means of coordinates which determine relative positions in space

analytic inertial navigation technique for obtaining navigational data based on readings of accelerometers that contain inertia-maintained orientation

an·a·lyt·ics (æn'lítiks) *n.* the science of analysis

an·a·lyze, *Br.* esp. **an·a·lyse** (æn'laiz) *pres. part.* **an·a·lyz·ing**, *Br.* esp. **an·a·lys·ing** *past* and *past part.* **an·a·lyzed**, *Br.* esp. **an·a·lysed** *v.t.* to study (a problem) in detail by breaking it down into various parts, *to analyze the cause of failure* || (*chem.*) to submit (a substance) to certain tests in order to identify its constituents || to break up (a substance) into its simplest elements || (*gram.*) to describe (a sentence) in terms of its grammatical components || to psychoanalyze [F. *analyser*]

an·a·lyz·er (æn'laizər) *n.* (*computer*) procedure to analyze another program

am·am·nes·tic (ænæmnéstik) *adj.* (*med.*) of a rapid increase in antibodies following a second immunogenic infusion after response to a first infusion is no longer detectable

A·nan·da-Tir·tha (ʌnándatí:rtə) or Madhva, Indian philosopher and theologian of the 13th c. He wrote Sanskrit commentaries on the Brahmasutras and the main Upanishads, bringing a dualistic interpretation to bear on them

a·nan·drous (ənǽndrəs) *adj.* (*bot.*) without stamens [fr. Gk *anandros*, not male]

an·a·pest, an·a·paest (ǽnəpest) *n.* a metrical foot consisting of two short syllables followed by a long **an·a·pés·tic an·a·paes·tic** *adj.* [fr. L. fr. Gk *anapaistos*, reversed (i.e. opposite to a dactyl)]

an·a·phase (ǽnəfeiz) *n.* the third stage in mitosis and meiosis during which the newly separated chromosomes move toward the poles of the elongating spindle (*PROPHASE, *METAPHASE, *TELOPHASE) [fr. Gk *ana*, up+*phasis*, aspect]

a·naph·o·ra (ənǽfərə) *n.* the repetition of a word or phrase in successive clauses as a literary device, e.g. 'for them he worked, for them he went hungry, for them he was tempted to steal' || the portion of the liturgy in the Greek Orthodox Church in which the Eucharistic elements are offered as an oblation, or the Eucharistic prayer [L. fr. Gk *anaphora*, carrying back]

an·aph·ro·dis·i·ac (ænæfrədízi:æk) 1. *n.* something capable of reducing sexual desire 2. *adj.* capable of reducing sexual desire [fr. Gk *an*, not +*aphrodisiakos*, sexually desiring]

an·a·phy·lac·tic (ænəfilǽktik) *adj.* of, or affected by, anaphylaxis

anaphylactic shock the condition resulting from the second or later introduction of a specific allergen into an anaphylactic organism. It is characterized by contraction of the smooth muscle and increased loss of body heat (*ALLERGY)

an·a·phy·lax·is (ænəfilǽksis) *n.* (*med.*) hypersensitivity to certain substances, characterized by a tendency to acute systemic reaction, and induced by the introduction of one of those substances into the organism (*ALLERGY) [L. fr. Gk *ana*, back again+*phulaxis*, protection]

an·ar·chic (ænárkik) *adj.* of, or characterized by, anarchy **an·ár·chi·cal** *adj.*

CONCISE PRONUNCIATION KEY: **(a)** æ, c*a*t; ɑ, c*a*r; ɔ f*aw*n; ei, sn*a*ke. **(e)** e, h*e*n; i:, sh*ee*p; iə, d*ee*r; εə, b*ea*r. **(i)** i, f*i*sh; ai, t*i*ger; 'ə:, b*i*rd. **(o)** o, *o*x; au, c*ow*; ou, g*oa*t; u, p*oo*r; ɔi, r*oy*al. **(u)** ʌ, d*u*ck; u, b*u*ll; u:, g*oo*se; ə, b*a*cillus; ju:, c*u*be. x, lo*ch*; θ, *th*ink; δ, bo*th*er; z, *Z*en; ʒ, corsa*g*e; dʒ, sava*g*e; ŋ, orangutan*g*; j, *y*ak; ∫, *fi*sh; t∫, fe*tch*; 'l, rabb*le*; 'n, redd*en*. Complete pronunciation key appears inside front cover.

an·ar·chism (ǽnərkizəm) n. the political theory that individual freedom should be absolute and that all government and law is evil. Capitalism and private property would be abolished and be replaced by voluntary cooperation [fr. Gk *anarchos*, without government]

an·ar·chist (ǽnərkist) n. someone who believes in anarchism ‖ (*loosely*) a terrorist [fr. Gk *anarchos*, without government]

an·ar·chy (ǽnərki:) pl. **an·ar·chies** n. the absence of law and order ‖ a general state of disorder and confusion (cf. ANARCHISM) [fr. Gk *anarchia*, absence of government]

an·as·tig·mat·ic (ænəstigmætik)81adj. without astigmatism, used esp. of compound optical lenses in which the astigmatism of one is corrected by an equal and opposite astigmatism of another

a·nas·to·mose (ənǽstəmouz) pres. part. **a·nas·to·mos·ing** past and past part. **a·nas·to·mosed** v.i. to communicate by anastomosis [fr. F. *anastomoser*]

a·nas·to·mo·sis (ənæstəmóusis) pl. **a·nas·to·mo·ses** (ənæstəmóusi:z) n. (*bot.*) the union of ramifications of leaf veins ‖ (*anat.*) the union of an artery and vein or blood vessels arising from a common trunk ‖ (*anat.*) the union of nerves ‖ an intercommunication of rivers, tree branches etc. [Mod. L. fr. Gk *anastomoein*, to supply a mouth]

an·a·tase (ǽnəteis) n. (*mineral.*) crystalline titanium dioxide (TiO₂) found in some rocks [F. fr. Gk *anatasis*, prolongation]

a·nath·e·ma (ənǽθəmə) n. the gravest ecclesiastical censure. 'Let him be anathema' involves total expulsion from the Church and consignment to Satan (cf. EXCOMMUNICATION) ‖ (*loosely*) something intensely disliked, *making speeches is anathema to him* **a·nath·e·ma·tize** pres. part. **a·nath·e·ma·tiz·ing** past and past part. **a·nath·e·ma·tized** v.t. to pronounce anathema against [L. fr. Gk *anathema*, something devoted or set apart]

An·a·to·lia (ænətóuljə, ænətóuli:ə) (*Turk.* Anadolu) Asia Minor ‖ the part of Turkey in Asia

an·a·tom·ic (ænətómik) adj. pertaining to, or dealing with, anatomy **an·a·tóm·i·cal** adj. [fr. L. *anatomicus* fr. Gk *anatomē*, a cutting up]

a·nat·o·mist (ənǽtəmist) n. a specialist in anatomy [F. *anatomiste*]

a·nat·o·mize (ənǽtəmaiz) pres. part. **a·nat·o·miz·ing** past and past part. **a·nat·o·mized** v.t. to dissect, esp. so as to reveal anatomical detail ‖ to analyze minutely [fr. M.L. *anatomizare*]

a·nat·o·my (ənǽtəmi:) pl. **a·nat·o·mies** n. the branch of morphology concerned with the structure of animals or plants ‖ the science of dissection ‖ the structure of an organism [F. *anatomie* fr. L. fr. Gk]

an·au·tog·e·nous (ænotódʒənəs) adj. (*biol.*) requiring a feeding of blood in order to produce eggs, as some types of mosquitoes

An·ax·ag·o·ras (ænəksǽgərəs) a philosopher and scientist of the Ionian school (c. 500–428 B.C.). He was the friend and teacher of Pericles. He regarded the ultimate elements as 'particles' which were set in order by an eternal intelligence

A·nax·i·man·der (ənæksimǽndər) (c. 610–c. 547 B.C.), Ionian scientist and philosopher who believed the Infinite was the origin of all things. He was probably the first to regard the earth as spherical and draw a map of it

An·ax·im·e·nes of Miletus (ænæksíməni:z) (6th c. B.C.), Ionian philosopher who maintained that air is the origin of all things

-ance suffix state of, as in 'permanence' ‖ act of, as in 'attendance'

an·ces·tor (ǽnsestər) n. a forefather, a person from whom one is descended (usually referring further back than a grandparent) ‖ (*biol.*) an earlier type of a species [O.F. *ancestre*]

ancestor worship the ritualistic veneration of the spirits of dead ancestors. It is practiced by most religious men other than Jews, Christians and Moslems, in the belief that after death souls continue to be involved in this world, having influence and being receptive to invocation

an·ces·tral (ænséstrəl) adj. coming from, or belonging to, one's ancestors ‖ (*biol.*) relating to an original or earlier type of a species [O.F. *ancestrel*]

an·ces·tress (ǽnsestris) n. a female ancestor

an·ces·try (ǽnsestri:) pl. **an·ces·tries** n. the line of descent from ancestors [fr. O. F. *anceserie*]

An·chi·ses (æŋkáisi:z) Trojan prince, father of Aeneas by Aphrodite. Aeneas carried him on his shoulders out of burning Troy, down to the ships

an·chor (ǽŋkər) v.t. to secure by an anchor ‖ v.i. to cast anchor by [F. *ancrer*]

anchor n. a heavy iron instrument, consisting of a shank and two arms, which is lowered from a ship to grip the bottom and so hold her fast ‖ any instrument which secures firmly ‖ a person or a thing on which full reliance can be placed **to cast anchor** to lower the anchor **to ride** (or **lie**) **at anchor** (of a ship) to be held securely by the anchor (*DRAG ANCHOR) **to weigh anchor** to take up the anchor, to depart [O.E. *ancor* fr. L.]

An·chor·age (ǽŋkəridʒ) the most populous city (pop. 173,017) of Alaska, at the head of Cook Inlet, a transportation and marketing center. It was nearly destroyed (1964) by an earthquake. Alaska's oil, coal, and natural gas industries are centered here

an·chor·age (ǽŋkəridʒ) n. a place where ships may lie at anchor ‖ the fee for anchoring ‖ something that can be absolutely relied on

an·cho·ress (ǽŋkəris) n. a female anchorite [fr. O. E. *ancra* fr. L. *anachoreta*]

an·cho·rite (ǽŋkərait) n. a hermit, recluse who withdraws from the world for religious reasons without joining an order [fr. L. fr. Gk *anachorētēs*, one who has withdrawn from the world]

anchor man (*sports*) the member of a relay team who performs last ‖ someone on whose utter reliability the steady functioning of a business or enterprise is said to depend

an·chor·man (ǽŋkərmæn) n. (*broadcasting*) in television news, the prime announcer to whom each correspondent refers back

anchor tenant (*real estate*) a well-known business that draws the public to a shopping center

anchor watch a watch (or guard) on board a ship while she lies at anchor

an·cho·vy (ǽntʃouvi:, ǽntʃəvi:) pl. **an·cho·vies** n. *Engraulis encrasicholus*, a small bony fish of the herring family eaten raw or marinated, mainly in hors d'œuvre or in sauces [Span. *anchova*]

anchovy pear *Grias cauliflora*, a West Indian tree ‖ its fruit

an·chu·sa (æŋkjú:sə) n. a member of *Anchusa*, fam. *Boraginaceae*, a genus of plants including bugloss [L.]

anchylose *ANKYLOSE

anchylosis *ANKYLOSIS

anchylostomiasis *ANKYLOSTOMIASIS

an·cien ré·gime (ãsjẽreiʒi:m) n. the political and social organization of France before the French Revolution [F.]

an·cient (éinʃənt) **1.** adj. belonging to times long past, esp. before the fall of the Roman Empire in the West (476 A.D.) ‖ antique, old-fashioned ‖ (*loosely*) old, decrepit **2.** n. someone who lived in the ancient world the ancients the civilized peoples of the ancient world [M.E. *ancien*, fr. O. F.]

ancient history history from prehistory up to the fall of the Roman Empire (476 A.D.) ‖ some commonly known, rather stale piece of news, gossip etc.

an·cil·lar·y (ǽnsələri:, Br. esp. ænsíləri) adj. subordinate, subsidiary [fr. L. *ancillarius* fr. *ancilla*, a handmaiden]

an·con (ǽŋkɒn) pl. **an·co·nes** (æŋkóuni:z) n. (*anat.*) the elbow ‖ (*archit.*) a console, support for a cornice [L. fr. Gk *ankōn*]

An·co·na (aŋkóna) a port (pop. 107,800) on the Adriatic in central Italy, with a good harbor; shipbuilding, textiles. Trajan's mole (200 ft long) and arch (1st c.), cathedral (11th–13th cc.)

an·co·ne·al (æŋkóuni:əl) adj. of or relating to the elbow [ANCON]

ANCP (*computer*) an automatic coding system for use in the Burroughs 205

an·cress (ǽŋkris) n. an anchoress

ancylostomiasis *ANKYLOSTOMIASIS

and (ænd) conj. a joining word, used between two words, two phrases or two clauses, sometimes written & (*AMPERSAND) ‖ in order to, *run along and catch him* **and so forth, and so on** et cetera (etc.), and other more or less similar things, *you will need books, rulers, pencils and so forth* [O.E. *and*, *ond* prep., against, and O.E. *end* conj.]

AND (*computer*) a logical operator that has the property that it is true if two statements are true, expressed by 1, false if either or both of two statements are false, expressed by 0

An·da·lu·sia (ændəlú:ʒə) (*Span.* Andalucía) a region of southernmost Spain between the Sierra Morena and the Mediterranean, forming the provinces of Huelva, Cádiz, Málaga, Granada and Almería on the coast, and Seville, Cordova and Jaén inland. In the south and east are mountain ranges (including the Sierra Nevada), in the center and southwest the fertile Guadalquivir valley. Agricultural products: olive oil (half the Spanish supply), wheat, citrus fruit, esparto, vines, sherry, wool. Livestock: sheep, horses, bulls. Industries: mining (copper, iron pyrites, lead, gold), fishing, iron and steel, textiles. Historic capitals: Cordova, Seville. Colonized by Phoenicians (11th c. B.C.), Greeks and Carthaginians (6th c. B.C.) before the Romans, Andalusia was the center of a brilliant Moorish civilization before being conquered by Castile (13th c.). Granada held out until 1492

An·da·lu·sian (ændəlú:ʒən) **1.** adj. of Andalusia or its people **2.** n. a native of Andalusia ‖ a Mediterranean breed of domestic fowl

An·da·man and Nic·o·bar Islands (ændəmæn, níkəbər) an Indian territory (area 3,135 sq. miles, pop. 115,500) in the Bay of Bengal. Capital: Port Blair. People: Indians, with a small Negrito aborigine minority. There are over 200 islands (Andaman group 2,500 sq. miles, Nicobar 635 sq. miles). N. Andaman rises to 2,400 ft, Great Nicobar to 2,105 ft. Average temperatures (F.): Great Nicobar 64°–92°. Rainfall: 90–135 ins. Livestock: cattle, goats. Products: timber, coconuts, copra, softwood for matches, coffee, rubber, rice. The Nicobar Islands were Danish (1756–1869) until taken over by Britain. The British established a settlement in the Andaman Islands (1789), and a penal colony (1858–1945). The islands were occupied by the Japanese (1942–5)

an·dan·te (ændǽnti:) **1.** adj. and adv. (*mus.*) at a moderate speed **2.** n. a piece or movement for andante performance [Ital.]

An·der·sen (ǽndərs'n), Hans Christian (1805–75), Danish writer of fairy tales and stories. Many have affinities with other European folktales, but he imbued them with a grace and tender melancholy quite his own

An·der·son (ǽndərs'n), Carl David (1905–), American physicist. His discovery of the positron (1932) won a half share in the Nobel prize for physics (1936)

Anderson, Marian (1902–), U.S. opera singer, a contralto and the first black to sing at the Metropolitan Opera House (1955). In 1939 she gave a concert, arranged by Eleanor Roosevelt, at the Lincoln Memorial. An alternate delegate to the U.N. (1958), she was a recipient of the first Kennedy Center Honors (1978)

Anderson, Maxwell (1888–1959), U.S. playwright. He wrote comedy ('What Price Glory?', 1924), historical plays ('Elizabeth the Queen', 1930) and satire ('Both Your Houses', 1933), and two poetic plays with a contemporary setting ('Winterset', 1935, and 'High Tor', 1936)

Anderson, Sherwood (1876–1941), U.S. author. His 'Winesburg, Ohio' (1919) strongly influenced the technique of the American short story. As in his novel 'Poor White' (1920), it depicted the effect of isolation on the people of the small midwest town

An·der·son·ville (ǽndərsɒnvil) a village 60 miles southwest of Macon, Ga., site of a Confederate military prison and hospital (1864–5). The North made propaganda material out of the atrocious conditions there

An·ders·son (ǽndərs'n), Karl Johan (1827–67), Swedish explorer in S. Africa who reached Lake Ngami and the Okavango and Cunene Rivers

An·des (ǽndi:z) a mountain system (average height: 13,000 ft) running the length of W. South America, crossed by few roads or railways. Highest peak (Aconcagua, in Argentina): 23,081 ft. There are many volcanoes, the most active being Cotopaxi and Chimborazo (Ecuador). The Andes are rich in minerals, esp. copper, gold and silver. The Amazon, Orinoco and La Plata Rivers flow from their eastern terraces

an·de·sine (ǽndizi:n) n. (*mineral.*) a plagioclase feldspar between albite and anorthite, and an ingredient of andesite **an·de·sin·ic** (ændizínik) adj. [G. *andesin* after the *Andes*]

an·des·ite (ǽndizait) n. (*mineral.*) a dark gray igneous rock consisting essentially of plagioclase feldspar **an·de·sit·ic** (ændizítik) adj. [G. *andesit* after the *Andes*]

An·dhra Pra·desh (ándraprədéiʃ) a state (area 106,052 sq. miles, pop. 53,592,605) of S.E. India, bordering the Bay of Bengal. Capital: Hyderabad. Crops: rice, millet, sugar, peanuts, tobacco. Industries: shipbuilding, cement, tanning, glass

and·i·ron (ǽndɑiərn) *n.* one of a pair of metal supports for burning wood in a fireplace [O.F. *andier*, influenced by O.E. *yren*, iron]

and/or (ǽndɔ́r) *conj.* indicating that what follows may be taken separately or together, according to context or circumstances, thus 'fish and/or meat' means 'fish and meat' or 'fish or meat'

and or gate (*computer*) gate that outputs for any of several possible computations of inputs

An·dor·ra (ændɔ́rə, ændɔ́rə) a semiautonomous principality (area 190 sq. miles, pop. 38,050), in the E. Pyrenees. Capital: Andorra la Vella (pop. 2,300). Language: Catalan. Religion: Roman Catholic. Lowest pass: 7,792 ft. Lowest valley: 3,000 ft. Highest point: 9,550 ft (Pic de Serrère). Industries: agriculture and tourism. Currency: French and Spanish. Andorra received its independence (9th c.) from Charlemagne, and was ruled jointly from 1278 by the bishop of Urgel and the comte de Foix. Since 1607, the latter's rights have been exercised by the French head of state

An·dra·da e Sil·va (ɑndrádəesí:lvə), José Bonifácio de (c. 1763–1838), Brazilian scholar, statesman, and leader in the struggle for Brazilian independence from Portugal. He was instrumental in the establishment (1822) of the Brazilian Empire, and became prime minister under Dom Pedro. He was exiled (1823–9) for opposing Pedro's counsellors, but returned to support the emperor and became (1831) tutor to Pedro II

an·dra·dite (ændrádait) *n.* a garnet, $Ca_3Fe_2(SiO_4)_3$, ranging from green and yellow to brown and black [after José Bonifácio de *Andrada* e Silva (1763–1838), Braz. scientist and statesman]

An·dras·sy (ændræsi:), Count Gyula (1823–90), Hungarian statesman. He played an important part in the setting up of the dual monarchy of Austria-Hungary (1867). He was the first prime minister of Hungary after the restoration of self-government (1867) and imperial minister for foreign affairs (1871–9)

Andrea del Castagno (ɑndréia del kɑstánjou) (c. 1421–57), Italian painter. known for his frescoes, he worked in Venice and Florence, where his fresco 'Last Supper' (1497) is in the Monastery of Sant'Apollonia

Andrea del Sarto *SARTO

An·drew (ǽndru:), St (*d.* 62 or 70), one of the 12 Apostles, brother of Peter. Tradition holds that he was martyred on an X-shaped cross at Patraea in Achaia. He is the patron saint of Scotland and Russia. Feast: Nov. 30

Andrew, John Albion (1818–67), U.S. political leader and Civil War governor of Massachusetts (1861–6). He anticipated the military conflict, and prepared Massachusetts in advance

An·drewes (ǽndru:z), Lancelot (1555–1626), English theologian. He was one of the translators of the Bible (*AUTHORIZED VERSION). He became bishop of Winchester (1619), after Chichester and Ely. His devotional prayers 'Preces privatae' (1648) are often reprinted

An·drews (ǽndru:z), Thomas (1813–85), Irish chemist and physicist, important for his work on the liquefaction of gases, esp. carbon dioxide, and his discovery of critical temperature

An·dre·yev (ɑndréiəf), Leonid Nikolayevich (1871–1919), Russian author of short stories and plays marked by profound disillusion

an·droe·ci·um (ændrí:ʃiəm) *pl.* **an·droe·ci·a** (ændrí:ʃiə) *n.* (*bot.*) the collective name for all the male organs of a flower [Mod. L. fr. Gk *andro-*, male+*oikion*, little house]

an·dro·gen (ǽndrədʒən) *n.* (*biochem.*) a sex hormone produced in the testicles and adrenal glands and capable of inducing male characteristics **an·dro·gen·ic** (ændrədʒénik) *adj.* [fr. Gk *andro-*, male+-*gen*, producing, fr. *gignesthai*, to be born]

an·drog·y·nous (ændrɔ́dʒinəs) *adj.* combining characteristics of both sexes, hermaphrodite ‖ (*bot.*) having stamens and pistils in the same flower or in the same inflorescence [fr. L. fr. Gk *aner* (*andros*), man+*gune*, woman]

an·droid (ǽndrɔid) *n.* a human-seeming robot

an·dro·lep·sy (ǽndrəlepsi:) *n.* seizure of hostages from one nation by another nation to enforce a political claim

An·drom·a·che (ændrɔ́məki:) wife of Hector. After the fall of Troy she became Pyrrhus's slave, and later married Hector's brother Helenus. In the 'Iliad' she is a symbol of conjugal love

An·drom·e·da (ændrɔ́midə) (*Gk mythol.*) the daughter of Cepheus, legendary king of Ethiopia. When her mother, Cassiopeia, boasted that Andromeda was more beautiful than the Nereids, they persuaded Poseidon to have her chained to a rock for a sea monster to devour, but Perseus rescued her. Her name is given to a constellation of the northern hemisphere

Andropov (ændrɔ́pɒf), Yuri Valdimirovich (1914–84), Soviet leader (1982–84). He served as Soviet ambassador to Hungary (1953–6), on the Central Committee (1961–7), and as KGB (secret police) head before succeeding Leonid Brezhnev as president

An·dros (ǽndrɒs), Sir Edmund (1637–1714), outstanding colonial governor (1674–89, 1692–7). His conservative policies and loyalty to the Crown antagonized the colonists, resulting first in his recall (1681) as governor of New York and the Jerseys and later in his overthrow (1689) as governor of the Dominion of New England. Returning as governor of Virginia, he promoted cotton culture and established William and Mary College

An·dros (ǽndrɒs) the northernmost, very fertile island (area 156 sq. miles, pop. 19,000) of the Cyclades in the Aegean Sea

an·dro·stene·di·one [$C_{19}H_{26}O_2$] (ændroustí:ndri:oun) *n.* (*biochem.*) a steroid hormone highly determinant of male characteristics

an·ec·do·tal (ænikdóut'l) *adj.* relating to or characteristic of anecdotes

an·ec·dote (ǽnikdout) *n.* a short account of an interesting or amusing incident or event, often biographical **an·ec·dot·ic** (ænikdótik), **an·ec·dót·i·cal** *adjs* **án·ec·dot·ism**, **án·ec·dot·ist** *ns* [fr. M.L. fr. Gk *anekdota*, things not published]

an·e·cho·ic room (ænikóuik) *n.* **1.** (*acoustics*) a room constructed so that it absorbs sound waves **2.** room that absorbs radio waves of certain frequencies, esp. microwave frequencies. **syn** dead room, free-field room

a·ne·mi·a, esp. *Br.* **a·nae·mi·a** (əní:mi:ə) *n.* a reduction in the amount of hemoglobin or the number of red cells in the blood ‖ a sudden reduction in the total amount of blood, e.g. in hemorrhage **a·né·mic**, esp. *Br.* **a·næ·mic** *adj.* [Mod. L. fr. Gk fr. *an*, without+ *haima*, blood]

a·nem·o·graph (ənéməgræf, ənéməgrɑf) *n.* an instrument for recording the force and direction of wind **an·e·mo·graph·ic** (ənɛməgræfik) *adj.* [fr. Gk *anemos*, wind + -*graphos*, written]

an·e·mom·e·ter (ænəmɔ́mitər) *n.* an instrument for measuring the force of wind **an·e·mo·met·ric** (ænəmoumétrik) *adj.* **an·e·móm·e·try** *n.* [fr. Gk *anemos*, wind+METER]

a·nem·o·ne (ənéməni:) *n.* a member of *Anemone*, fam. *Ranunculaceae*, a genus of plants bearing colorful flowers. *A. pulsatilla* is the pasqueflower [L. fr. Gk *anemōnē*, daughter of the wind]

an·e·moph·i·lous (ænəmɔ́fələs) *adj.* (*bot.*) pollinated by the wind **an·e·móph·i·ly** *n.* [fr. Gk *anemos*, wind + -*philos*, loving]

an·en·ceph·a·lus (ænənséfələs) *n.* (*med.*) a fetus showing defective skull and brain —**anence· phalic** *adj.*—**anencephaly** *n.* absence of brain in a fetus

an·er·oid (ǽnərɔid) **1.** *adj.* (of an instrument) containing no liquid **2.** *n.* an aneroid barometer [F. *anéroide* fr. Gk]

aneroid barometer a barometer consisting of a shallow, cylindrical metal box, partly exhausted of air. The thin, corrugated upper face is prevented from collapsing by an external clip spring. Changes in air pressure disturb the equilibrium between the spring and the internal pressure, and result in displacements of the upper face. These movements are transmitted by a system of levers to a pointer moving over a calibrated scale

an·es·the·sia, esp. *Br.* **an·aes·the·sia** (ænisθi:ʒə) *n.* (*med.*) loss of the normal perception of pain

an·es·thet·ic, esp. *Br.* **an·aes·thet·ic** (ænisθétik) **1.** *n.* a substance or gas (e.g. ether or chloroform) which produces anesthesia **2.** *adj.* producing anesthesia ‖ relating to anesthesia

an·es·the·tist, esp. *Br.* **an·aes·the·tist** (ənésθitist) *n.* someone who administers anesthetics

an·es·the·ti·za·tion, esp. *Br.* **an·aes·the·ti·za·tion** (ənɛsθitizéiʃən) *n.* **an·es·the·tize**, esp. *Br.* **an·aes·the·tize** (ənésθitaiz) *pres. part.* **an·es·the·tiz·ing**, esp. *Br.* **an·aes·the·tiz·ing** *past* and *past part.* **an·es·the·tized**, esp. *Br.* **an·aes·the·tized** *v.t.* to render insensible by the use of anesthetics [Mod. L. fr. Gk fr. *an*, without+ *aisthēsis*, sensation]

an·es·the·si·o·lo·gist (ænisθi:zi:ɔ́lədʒist) *n.* a specialist in anesthesiology

an·es·the·si·o·lo·gy (ænisθi:zi:ɔ́lədʒi:) *n.* the science of administering anesthetics [fr. ANESTHESIA+ Gk *logos*, discourse]

an·eu·rysm, **an·eu·rism** (ǽnjurizəm) *n.* (*med.*) the dilation of a section of an artery, due to weakness of the artery wall, often resulting eventually in hemorrhage (e.g. in apoplexy) [fr. Gk *aneurusma*, a broadening]

a·new (ənjú:,ənú:) *adv.* again ‖ in a new form or way [O.E. *of*+NEW]

an·frac·tu·os·i·ty (ænfræktʃu:ɔ́siti:) *pl.* **an·frac·tu·os·i·ties** *n.* intricacy ‖ a winding passage or channel [F.]

an·frac·tu·ous (ænfræktʃu:əs) *adj.* winding, sinuous ‖ intricate [fr. L. *anfractuosus*]

An·ga·ra (ɑŋgɑrá) a river of Siberia, U.S.S.R., about 1,100 miles long, flowing northeast from Lake Baikal, a main source of hydroelectric power

an·ga·ry (ǽŋgəri:) *n.* (*internat. law*) the right of a belligerent to use and destroy the property of a neutral, from military necessity (the neutral having the right to compensation) [fr. F. *angarie* fr. L. fr. Gk *angaros*, a courier]

an·gel (éindʒəl) *n.* a messenger of God ‖ a member of the lowest order in the celestial hierarchy, classified by Dionysius the Areopagite as: seraphim, cherubim, thrones, dominions, virtues, powers, principalities, archangels, angels ‖ a person of exceptional goodness or loveliness ‖ (*theater, pop.*) the financial backer of a theatrical production ‖ radar echo from an invisible target ‖ (*hist.*) an English gold coin, stamped with a figure of St Michael and worth varying sums [fr. L. fr. Gk *angelos*, a messenger]

angel dust (*slang*) phencyclidine hydrochloride, a highly dangerous animal tranquilizer sometimes smoked with marijuana to heighten hallucinogenic effects; once used medically by veterinarians. Also called nog crystal, PCP, rocket fuel

an·gel·fish (éindʒəlfiʃ) *pl.* **an·gel·fish**, **an·gel·fish·es** *n. Squatina angelus*, a viviparous fish closely allied to sharks. Its pectoral fins spread like wings

an·gel·ic (ændʒélik) *adj.* belonging to, or characteristic of, angels ‖ of exceptional goodness or loveliness [fr. F. *angelique* fr. L. fr. Gk]

an·gel·i·ca (ændʒélikə) *n. Angelica archangelica*, fam. *Umbelliferae*, an aromatic plant used esp. in cooking. The petioles are often candied [M.L. *herba angelica*, root of the Holy Ghost]

an·gel·i·cal (ændʒélik'l) *adj.* angelic

An·ge·li·co (ɑndʒéli:kɔ), Fra (1387–1455), Italian fresco painter, and Dominican friar. His real name was Guido di Pietro, and his name in religion Fra Giovanni da Fiesole. He decorated the convent of S. Marco at Florence (1437–45), Nicholas V's chapel in the Vatican (1445–7), and part of Orvieto Cathedral. He was important as a Christian iconographer. His colors are pure and fresh, and his compositions are rhythmic, using large forms

an·gel·ol·a·try (eindʒəlɔ́lətri:) *n.* the worship of angels [fr. ANGEL + Gk *latreia*, worship]

an·gel·ol·o·gy (eindʒəlɔ́lədʒi:) *n.* doctrine concerning angels [fr. ANGEL+ Gk *logos*. discourse]

an·gels (éindʒels) *n.* (*mil.*) in air intercept and close air support, a code meaning aircraft altitude (in thousands of feet)

An·ge·lus (ǽndʒələs) *n.* a Roman Catholic prayer commemorating the Incarnation, and imploring the intercession of the Mother of God ‖ the Angelus bell [first words of the prayer (from the Gospel) *Angelus domini*, angel of the Lord]

Angelus bell a signal to say the Angelus, rung at morning, noon and evening

an·ger (ǽŋgər) **1.** *n.* rage, passionate displeasure **2.** *v.t.* to make angry, to enrage [O.N. *angr*, trouble, affliction]

An·gers (ɑ̃ʒéi) the ancient capital (pop. 137,437) of Anjou, N.W. France, on the Maine, an industrial center (textiles, metallurgy, distilleries etc.). It has an early Gothic cathedral, 13th-c. castle, and medieval and Renaissance houses and churches

CONCISE PRONUNCIATION KEY: (**a**) æ, c*a*t; ɑ, c*a*r; ɔ f*aw*n; ei, sn*a*ke. (**e**) e, h*e*n; i:, sh*ee*p; iə, d*ee*r; ɛə, b*ea*r. (**i**) i, f*i*sh; ai, t*i*ger; ə:, b*i*rd. (**o**) o, *o*x; au, c*ow*; ou, g*oa*t; u, p*oo*r; ɔi, r*oy*al. (**u**) ʌ, d*u*ck; u, b*u*ll; u:, g*oo*se; ə, b*a*cillus; ju:, c*u*be. x, lo*ch*; θ, *th*ink; ð, bo*th*er; z, *Z*en; ʒ, corsa*g*e. dʒ, sava*g*e; ŋ, oranguta*ng*; j, *y*ak; ʃ, *fi*sh; tʃ, fe*tch*; 'l, rabb*le*; 'n, redd*en*. Complete pronunciation key appears inside front cover.

An·ge·vin (ǽndʒivin) 1. *adj.* of Anjou ‖ of the house of Plantagenet 2. *n.* a native of Anjou [F.]

an·gi·na (ændʒáinə) *n.* (*med.*) inflammation of the throat, quinsy [L.]

angina pec·to·ris (péktəris) *n.* a disease of the heart causing momentary pain in the chest, sometimes spreading to the arms and neck (*CORONARY THROMBOSIS) [L.=angina of the chest]

an·gi·og·ra·phy (ændʒi:ógrəfi:) *n.* (*med.*) nonsurgical technique and process for determining arrangement of blood or lymph vessels by radiography via injection of radio-opaque material, or by capillaroscopy or fluoroscopy, etc. — **angiogram** *n.* —**angiographic** *adj.*

an·gi·o·sperm (ændʒi:əspə:rm) *n.* a seed plant of the class *Angiospermae* (*PTEROPSID), comprising those which produce seed enclosed in an ovary, i.e. the vast majority of seed plants, divided into dicotyledons and monocotyledons (cf. GYMNOSPERM) **an·gi·o·spér·mous** *adj.* [fr. Gk *angeion*, a vessel + *sperma*, seed]

an·gi·o·ten·sin·ase (ændʒi:outénsineis) *n.* (*biol.*) any enzyme that degrades angiotension

Ang·kor (ǽŋkɔr, ǽŋkour) an area of Cambodia containing the ruins (9th–15th cc.) of the Khmer Empire: Angkor Thom, the capital, and the temple of Angkor Wat

An·gle (ǽŋg'l) *n.* a member of a Germanic tribe which conquered eastern, central and northern England in the 5th c. A.D. and settled there [O.E. fr. L. *Angli*]

an·gle (ǽŋg'l) *n.* the difference in the direction of two intersecting lines or planes, measured in degrees, minutes and seconds (*ACUTE, *OBTUSE, *RIGHT ANGLE) ‖ that part of a solid body which is bounded by planes at an acute angle (its corner) ‖ a point of view, *our readers want the woman's angle on this* [F.]

angle *pres. part.* **an·gling** *past* and *past part.* **an·gled** *v.i.* to fish with line and hook, attracting the fish by bait (usually a worm, grub or artificial fly) ‖ to use wiles or artifice, *to angle for praise* [O.E. *angul* n., hook]

an·gled (ǽŋg'ld) *adj.* having an angle or angles ‖ being at an angle

angle iron an L-shaped metal strip employed for strengthening a corner and in wire fencing etc.

angle of contact (*phys.*) the angle made by the meniscus of a liquid with the solid surface which cuts it. It is measured in the liquid, between the solid surface and the tangent to the meniscus at the point of contact

angle of deviation (*optics*) the angle between the incident and emergent rays when light passes through a prism or any other optical system

angle of elevation the angle made by an ascending line with the horizontal

angle of incidence (*phys.*) the angle between the direction of a moving body or light ray and the normal drawn at the point of incidence on a surface

angle of reflection (*phys.*) the angle between the direction of a moving body or light ray after reflection from a surface and the normal to the surface at the point of incidence

angle of refraction (*phys.*) the angle between a refracted ray and the normal to the interface at the point where refraction occurs

an·gler (ǽŋglər) *n.* a person who fishes with rod and line ‖ *Lophius piscatorius*, a sea fish which preys upon smaller fish, attracting them by filaments on its head

An·gle·sey (ǽŋgəlsi:) a former island county (area 276 sq. miles) of N. Wales across the Menai Strait, a livestock and dairy region. The county included Holyhead Island

angle T (*mil.*) the angle formed at a target by the intersection of the target line and the observer-target line

an·gle·worm (ǽŋg'lwə:rm) *n.* the earthworm

An·gli·an (ǽŋgli:ən) 1. *adj.* of the Angles, their dialect etc. 2. *n.* one of the Angles ‖ the dialect spoken by the Angles, esp. the Old English of Mercia and Northumbria

An·gli·can (ǽŋglikən) 1. *adj.* of the Church of England or the Anglican Communion 2. *n.* a member of the Church of England or the Anglican Communion [M.L. *Anglicanus*, English]

Anglican chant a simple type of harmonized melody used mainly in the Church of England for singing unmetrical texts, e.g. the Psalms and Canticles

Anglican Communion a fellowship of Churches in communion with the see of Canter-

bury (*CHURCH OF ENGLAND). These Churches are not bound together by any centralized authority, but are bound only 'by mutual loyalty sustained through the common counsel of the bishops in conference'. The conference takes place at Lambeth every decade. The Churches share the Catholic, Apostolic faith of the Book of Common Prayer, but as autonomous Churches they each promote a national expression of faith and life. Besides many Churches within the Commonwealth, the Anglican Communion includes the Protestant Episcopal Church in the U.S.A. and many scattered dioceses or chaplaincies throughout the world

An·gli·can·ism (ǽŋglikənizəm) *n.* the Anglican faith or practices

An·gli·ci·za·tion (ædglisizéiʃən) *n.* an Anglicizing or being Anglicized

An·gli·cize (ǽŋglisaiz) *pres. part.* **An·gli·ciz·ing** *past* and *past part.* **An·gli·cized** *v.t.* to make English in form, character or pronunciation (esp. words and names) [fr. L. *Anglicus*, English]

Anglo- (ǽŋglou) *prefix* indicating Great Britain or the English ‖ half English (and half something else), *Anglo-Dutch* [fr. L. *Anglus*, English]

An·glo-A·mer·i·can (ǽŋglouəmérikən) 1. *n.* a native of England, or a descendant, settled in America 2. *adj.* relating to England and the U.S.A., *Anglo-American solidarity*

An·glo-Ca·thol·i·cism (ǽŋgloukəθólisizəm) *n.* the beliefs of those members of the Anglican Communion who hold that the Reformation did not involve a change of doctrine or Church government in the Church of England, that the Anglican episcopate is in direct descent from the apostles, and that its faith is the faith accepted by all Catholics as revealed truth. It derives from the Oxford movement

An·glo-French (ǽŋgloufréntʃ) *n.* the Anglo-Norman language

An·glo-Lat·in (ǽŋgloulǽtin, ǽŋgloulǽt'n) *n.* the medieval Latin used in England

An·glo-Nor·man (ǽŋglounɔ́rmən) 1. *n.* the official language in England for three centuries after the Norman Conquest (1066), a variety of French spoken by Normans (Northmen) who had settled in France, and brought to England by the invaders ‖ a Norman who settled in England after the Norman Conquest 2. *adj.* of the Anglo-Normans or their language

An·glo·phil (ǽŋgləfil) *n.* an Anglophile

An·glo·phile (ǽŋgləfail) *n.* someone who admires the English and their customs [fr. ANGLO-+ Gk *philos*, loving]

An·glo·phobe (ǽŋgləfoub) *n.* someone who dislikes the English and their customs [F.]

An·glo·pho·bi·a (ǽŋgləfóubi:ə) *n.* dislike of the English and their customs [fr. ANGLO-+ Gk -*phobia*, fear]

an·glo·phone (ǽŋgləfoun) *n.* (often cap.) one who speaks English in an area where other languages are usually spoken —**anglophonic** *adj.*

An·glo-Sax·on (ǽŋglousǽksən) 1. *n.* a member of the Germanic tribes which settled in England in the 5th c. A.D. ‖ a member of the mixed race which developed in England between the Anglo-Saxon invasions and the Norman Conquest ‖ a person of English descent in any country ‖ Old English 2. *adj.* concerning the Anglo-Saxons or their language

Anglo-Saxon Chronicle (c. 891–c. 1154), an important series of national as opposed to local histories begun under Alfred, attempting a catalog of events from 1 A.D. In its later part the Chronicle describes the sufferings of the native population under Norman rule

An·go·la (ǽŋgóulə) Peoples Republic of, a country (area 481,226 sq. miles, pop. 7,567,000) in S.W. Africa. Capital: Luanda. It includes the territory of Cabinda north of the Congo. People: mainly Bantu, Bushman minority, 1.8% white. Official language: Portuguese. The coastal plain is unhealthy and infertile, but the central plateau (5,000 ft) is productive. Savanna prevails in the northeast, and dense forest in the center, southeast and river valleys. Annual rainfall (mostly in summer): 55 ins in the highlands, 10–20 ins on the coast. Average temperature at Luanda: 74°F. Livestock: cattle and goats. Minerals: diamonds, iron ore, copper, manganese. Exports: diamonds, coffee, corn, sugar, palm oil and kernels, tobacco, sisal. Imports: textiles, machinery, coal, foodstuffs. Chief ports: Lobito, Luanda, Moçâmedes. Monetary unit: kwanza (100 lwei). HISTORY. Angola, in-

habited by Bantus, was discovered by the Portuguese (1483) and colonized by them (1575 onwards). It was a source of slaves for plantations in Brazil (17th and 18th cc.) In 1961 the Angolese rose against the Portuguese, and a state of guerrilla warfare ensued. Angola became an autonomous province of Portugal (1972), but fighting continued until Portugal withdrew (1975) and Angola became independent. It is a one-party state with the National People's Assembly as the supreme state body

an·go·ra (ǽŋgɔrə, æŋgóurə) *n.* a soft, fluffy fabric made from the hair of the angora goat or angora rabbit [after *Angora*, ancient name of Ankara]

Angora cat a variety of domestic cat with long silky hair

Angora goat a breed of domestic goat yielding mohair

Angora rabbit a variety of domestic rabbit with long silky hair

An·gos·tu·ra (ɑŋgɔstú:rɑ) the former name of Ciudad Bolívar, where in 1819 Simon Bolívar called delegates from the free provinces of Venezuela, Casanare and Nueva Granada. The congress took the lead in the independence movement and established (1819) the republic of Gran Colombia

an·gos·tu·ra (æŋgəstúərə, æŋgəstjúərə) *n.* the bitter, aromatic bark of the tree (*Galipea febrifuga* of tropical America and the West Indies, used as a febrifuge and as a tonic and in various cocktails [after *Angostura*, town in Venezuela, now Ciudad Bolívar]

An·gou·mois (ɑ̃gu:mwɑ) a historic region of W. France, in the N. Aquitaine basin. The north, rich dairy-farming country, with vines grown for cognac, is in modern Charente, the south (sparse woods and sheep pasture) is in Dordogne. Chief towns: Angoulême (the old capital), Cognac. Its existence as a countship, intermittent from the 4th c., ended definitively when it was included in Limousin (16th c.)

an·gries (ǽŋgri:s) *n.* (*slang*) protestors, angry opponents

an·gri·ly (ǽŋgrili:) *adv.* in an angry way

an·gry (ǽŋgri:) *comp.* **an·gri·er** *superl.* **an·gri·est** *adj.* (with 'about', 'at' or 'with') feeling or showing anger (*rhet.*) menacing, stormy, *an angry sky* ‖ (of a wound) sore, inflamed [ANGER]

angry brigade an antiestablishment left-wing British group composed of ex-students, esp. in the 1960s and early 1970s

ang·strom unit (ǽŋstrəm) (*phys.*, symbols Å, A.U.) a unit of length equal to 10^{-8} cm., chiefly used in recording wavelengths of light, X rays etc. [after A. J. *Ångström* (1814–74), Swedish physicist]

An·guil·la (æŋgwílə) an island (area 35 sq. miles, pop. 6,000) of the Leeward Islands. In 1967 it became a part of the St Kitts-Nevis-Anguilla State in association with Britain, but subsequently declared its independence. A small British force invaded (1969), with the promise that Anguilla would not be compelled to reintegrate a federation it had rejected. Anguilla became a separate dependency with internal self-government, a status confirmed by the Anguilla Act (1980)

an·guish (ǽŋgwiʃ) *n.* severe mental suffering, often involving anxiety [M.E. *anguise* fr. O.F.]

an·guished (ǽŋgwiʃt) *adj.* acutely distressed, suffering or expressing anguish [past part. of older *anguish* v.]

an·gu·lar (ǽŋgjulər) *adj.* having angles or sharp corners ‖ (*phys.*) measured in terms of angles ‖ (of people) bony, spare, scraggy ‖ stiff, ungracious in manner [fr. L. *angularis*]

angular acceleration (*phys.*) the time rate of change of angular velocity

angular displacement (*math.*, *phys.*) the angle through which something has rotated about a specified axis

angular distance (*phys.*) the distance between two points in terms of the angle they subtend at a third, which in astronomy is the point of observation

angular frequency (*phys.*) the frequency of a periodic process expressed in radians, and equal to the frequency expressed in cycles multiplied by 2π

angular impulse (*phys.*) the product of the average torque and its duration, being equal to the change in angular momentum during the same interval of time and in the absence of other torques

---

CONCISE PRONUNCIATION KEY: (a) æ, c*a*t; ɑ, c*ar*; ɔ f*aw*n; ei, sn*a*ke. (e) e, h*e*n; i:, sh*ee*p; iə, d*eer*; ɛə, b*ear*. (i) i, f*i*sh; ai, t*i*ger; ə:, b*ir*d. (o) o, *o*x; au, c*ow*; ou, g*oa*t; u, p*oo*r; ɔi, r*oy*al. (u) ʌ, d*u*ck; u, b*u*ll; u:, g*oo*se; ə, b*a*cillus; ju:, c*u*be. x, lo*ch*; θ, *th*ink; ð, bo*th*er; z, *Z*en; ʒ, cor*s*age; dʒ, sava*g*e; ŋ, oranguta*ng*; j, *y*ak; ʃ, fi*sh*; tʃ, fe*tch*; 'l, rabb*le*; 'n, redd*en*. Complete pronunciation key appears inside front cover.

an·gu·lar·i·ty (æŋgjulǽriti:) *n.* the quality of being angular

angular momentum (*phys.*) a vector quantity defined as the product of the angular velocity and the moment of inertia of a rotating body with respect to the same axis

angular parallax *ANGLE OF CONVERGENCE

angular speed the magnitude of angular velocity vector

angular velocity the time rate of change of angular displacement, being a vector whose direction is such that when the motion is viewed in that direction it appears clockwise

an·gu·late (æŋgjulit, æŋgjuleit) **1.** *adj.* (*bot.*) formed with angles or corners **2.** (æŋgjuleit) *v. pres. part.* **an·gu·lat·ing** *past* and *past part.* **an·gu·lat·ed** *v.t.* to make angular || *v.i.* to become angular **an·gu·la·tion** *n.* a making angulate || (*med.*) an abnormal curve in an organ || the measurement of angles [fr. L. *angulare (angulatus)*, to make angular]

An·gus (æŋgəs) (until 1928 Forfar) a former county (area 874 sq. miles, pop. 279,000) in E. Scotland, incorporated into the Tayside Administrative region (1975)

An·hwei (ánhwéi) a province (pop. 49,665,724) of E. China, watered by the Yangtze-kiang. Capital: Hofei

an·hy·dride (ænháidraid) *n.* (*chem.*) a substance derived from a compound by the removal of water or its elements which, when combined with water, again produces the original compound, e.g. sulfur trioxide, the anhydride of sulfuric acid $SO_3 + H_2O{\rightarrow}H_2SO_4$ [fr. Gk *anudros*, without water]

an·hy·drite (ænháidrait) *n.* a naturally occurring anhydrous calcium sulfate ($CaSO_4$), used in the manufacture of ammonium sulfate, sulfuric acid and plaster [fr. Gk *anudros*, without water]

an·hy·drous (ænháidrəs) *adj.* (*chem.*) without water, esp. of crystallization [fr. Gk *anudros*, without water]

an·hys·ter·e·sis (ænhistərí:sis) *n.* (*electr.*) an alternating magnetization field superimposed on a magnetic field in one direction

an·i·lin (æn'lin) *n.* aniline

an·i·line (æn'li:n, æn,lin) *n.* an aromatic organic chemical having one amino group attached to the benzene ring ($C_6H_5NH_2$). It is obtainable from coal tar but is normally synthesized by the reduction of nitrobenzene, and is the basis of many important dyestuffs, plastics, drugs etc. [G. *anilin* fr. *anil*, indigo ult. fr. Arab.]

an·i·ma (ǽnəmə) *n.* (*Jung's psychol.*) a figure symbolizing the feminine aspect of a man's psyche [Mod. L. fr. L.=soul]

an·i·mad·ver·sion (ænəmædvə:rʒən, ænəmædvə́:rʃən) *n.* adverse criticism, censure [fr. L. *animadversio (animadversionis)*, notice, warning]

an·i·mad·vert (ænəmædvə́:rt) *v.i.* (*rhet.*) to express adverse criticism or censure [fr. L. *animadvertere*, to turn the mind to]

an·i·mal (ǽnəmal) **1.** *n.* any of various organisms of the kingdom *Animalia*, distinguished from plants by their voluntary movement, by their nonphotosynthetic methods of nutrition, by their usually requiring complex organic nutriments, by a more or less centralized nervous system, and by their noncellulose cell membrane || such an animal other than man || a man who behaves like a brute **2.** *adj.* like or relating to animals [L. *animal* for *animale*, having breath]

animal charcoal a very porous mixture of carbon with some calcium phosphate. It is usually obtained by charring bones, and is used as a decolorizing filter

an·i·mal·cule (ænəmǽlkju:l) *n.* an animal too small to be seen by the naked eye, e.g. amoeba [fr. L. *animalculum*, dim. of *animal*, animal]

animal heat the heat generated in a living body

animal husbandry the breeding, rearing and marketing of cattle, sheep, pigs etc.

an·i·mal·ism (ǽnəməlizəm) *n.* the functions or qualities characteristic of animals, and their exercise || the doctrine that there is no fundamental distinction between men and animals **án·i·mal·ist** *n.* someone who holds this doctrine

an·i·mal·i·ty (ænəmǽliti) *n.* the nature proper to animals || that part of man's nature which he has in common with the animals [F. *animalité*]

an·i·mal·ize (ǽnəmalaiz) *pres. part.* **an·i·mal·iz·**
ing *past* and *past part.* **an·i·mal·ized** *v.t.* to make into animal matter || to debase (human nature) to a brutish level || to represent in animal form

animal magnetism (*old-fash.*) hypnotism

animal spirits the vigor and gaiety of the young and healthy

an·i·mate (ǽnəmit) **1.** *adj.* living (opp. INANIMATE) || pertaining to animal as opposed to plant life **2.** (ǽnəmeit) *v.t. pres. part.* **an·i·mat·ing** *past* and *past part.* **an·i·mat·ed** to give life to || to have a direct or inspiring influence upon, motivate || to enliven, make cheerful **án·i·mat·ed** *adj.* (of a scene or street etc.) full of the movement of people, esp. those busily engaged in some activity || (of a picture) giving this impression || (of a sculpture or portrait) seeming alive, esp. suggesting movement || (of a person) full of communicative liveliness || (of a lecture, argument etc.) infused with the energy, enthusiasm etc. of the protagonist or protagonists [fr. L. *animare (animatus)*, to give life to]

animated cartoon a film made from very many drawings. Each drawing involves a change of position in characters or objects, and projection converts the successive changes into the illusion of movement

an·i·ma·tion (ænəméiʃən) *n.* the act of animating || the state or quality of being animate or animated || (*cinema*) the preparation of an animated cartoon [fr. L. *animatio (animationis)*]

an·i·ma·tism (ǽnəmətizəm) *n.* the basic religious response to external phenomena, the awed recognition of a force in life, other than the individual self, manifested esp. in the strange and terrible

an·i·ma·tor (ǽnəmeitər) *n.* someone or something that animates || (*movies*) an artist who draws animated cartoons

an·i·mé (ǽnəméi) *n.* a resin used in making copal varnishes [Span. prob. fr. native name]

An·i·mism (ǽnəmizəm) *n.* the belief, widely held esp. in Central Africa, parts of Asia and some Pacific islands, that souls are quasi-physical and can exist outside the body (in dreams and visions), can be transferred from one body to another and persist after the death of the body (ghosts and reincarnation) **An·i·mist** *n.* **An·i·mis·tic** *adj.* [fr. L. *anima*, soul]

an·i·mos·i·ty (ænəmósiti:) *pl.* **an·i·mos·i·ties** *n.* a feeling of hatred or ill will, strong dislike [F. *animosité*]

an·i·mus (ǽnəməs) *n.* (*sing. only*) animosity, hostility || (*Jung's psychol.*) a figure symbolizing the masculine aspect of a woman's psyche [L.=spirit, passion]

an·i·on (ǽnaiən) *n.* a negative ion, which, in electrolysis, travels to the anode and is there discharged (cf. CATION) [Gk = a going up]

an·ise (ǽnis) *n. Pimpinella anisum*, fam. *Umbelliferae*, a plant native to the Mediterranean, cultivated widely [M.E. *anys* fr. F. fr. L. fr. Gk]

an·i·seed (ǽnisi:d) *n.* the seed of the anise plant. It has a strong aromatic flavor. The oil (chiefly anethol), obtained by distilling the seed, is used in medicine and as a fla voring

an·i·sette (ænizét, ænisét) *n.* a colorless liqueur flavored with aniseed [F.]

an·i·so·trop·ic (ænaisətrópik) *adj.* (*phys.*) having different values for one or more properties (e.g. compressibility, refractive index) when these are measured along different axes (cf. HETEROTROPIC) [fr. Gk *anisos*, unequal + *tropikos*, turning]

An·jou (ɑ̃ʒu:) a former province of N.W. France, comprising part of Mayenne in the Armorican Massif, Maine-et-Loire department and parts of Indre-et-Loire and Sarthe in the Paris basin, bordering the Armorican Massif on the west. Products: wine (esp. rosé), fruit, market produce (Loire valley), livestock. Main towns: Angers (the old capital), Saumur. A countship belonging (from the 10th c.) to the Plantagenets, it was attached to the English Crown (1156) after the accession of Henry II, recovered by Philippe II (1205) and secured (1487) as Crown land

An·ka·ra (æŋkərə) (formerly Angora) the capital (pop. 646,000, with agglom. 1,698,500) of Turkey, in the Anatolian highland, at 3,400 ft. It is a market for angora wool and agricultural products, and has textile and engineering industries. The new town is an administrative center, with two universities, including the Middle East Technical University. Ankara was the capital of the Roman province of Galatia (1st c. A.D.), and, after many invasions, was

taken (1360) by the Ottoman Turks. It had declined considerably when it became (1923) the capital of Turkey

ankh (æŋk) *n.* a cross-shaped figure, with a looped handle, symbolizing life and prosperity [Egypt.=life]

An·king (ánkíŋ) (formerly Hwaining) a port (pop. 120,000) in Anhwei province, China, on the north bank of the Yangtze, with a seven-storied pagoda

an·kle (æŋk'l) *n.* the joint between the foot and the leg || the narrowest part of the leg [O.E. *ancleow*]

an·kle·bone (æŋk'lboun) *n.* the astragalus (bone) in man

an·klet (æŋklit) *n.* an ornament worn around the ankle || a short sock || (*Br., mil.*) a canvas or leather gaiter worn around the ankle over a boot

an·ky·lose, an·chy·lose (æŋkəlous), *pres. part.* **an·ky·los·ing, an·chy·los·ing** *past* and *past part.* **an·ky·losed, an·chy·losed** *v.i.* to undergo ankylosis

an·ky·lo·sis, an·chy·lo·sis (æŋkəlóusis) *n.* a partial or total stiffening of joints by the growing together of bones [Gk=crookedness]

an·ky·los·to·mi·a·sis, an·chy·los·to·mi·a·sis, an·cy·los·to·mi·a·sis (æŋkələstəmáiəsis) *n.* (*med.*) a disease due to infestation by hookworms [fr. Mod. L. *ancylostoma*, hookworm fr. Gk *ankulos*, crooked + *stoma*, mouth]

Anna, (ænə) Empress of Russia (1693–1740), born Anna Ivanovna. She succeeded Peter II in 1730 and although initially restricted in authority soon became a strong ruler. During her reign (1730–40) Russian influence was extended to Poland and Turkey, and the aristocracy gained more control over the peasants

an·na (ænə) *n.* a former monetary unit and coin of India and Pakistan, one sixteenth of a rupee [Hind.]

An·na·ba (ænəbə) (formerly Bône) a port (pop. 165,000) in N.E. Algeria, an industrial and commercial center, with metallurgical plant. Exports: iron ore, minerals, phosphates, wheat, wine. The ruins of the Roman city of Hippo (Regius) lie to the south

An·na Com·ne·na (ænəkɒmníːnə) (c. 1083–c. 1148), daughter of the Byzantine emperor Alexius I Comnenus, and author of the 'Alexiad', a valuable description of the Byzantine world

an·nal·ist (æn'list) *n.* a writer of annals **an·nal·is·tic** *adj.*

an·nals (æn'lz) *pl. n.* a year-by-year record of events, a chronicle || (*fig.*) un- written history, *the gravest crisis in the annals of the club* [fr. L. *annales (libri)*, year (books)]

An·nam (ænæm) (*hist.*) the name (until 1945) of Vietnam. Annam originally designated the kingdom (3rd c. B.C.–1428 A.D.) formed by Tonkin and part of southern China. The name was then used for an empire (1428–1884) extending through Vietnam. The French, conquering the region (1859–83), used the name to designate the central provinces of Vietnam, declaring this area a protectorate (1884) and incorporating it (1887) in French Indochina. It became a region of the republic of Vietnam (1945) and was divided (1954) between North Vietnam and South Vietnam, which were ultimately reunited (1975)

An·nam·ese (ænəmíːz, ænəmiːs) **1.** *adj.* (*hist.*) of or pertaining to Annam, its people or their language **2.** *pl.* **An·nam·ese** *n.* (*hist.*) a native or inhabitant of Annam || (*hist.*) the Vietnamese language

An·nam·ite (ænəmait) **1.** *adj.* (*hist.*) Annamese **2.** *n.* (*hist.*) an Annamese || (*hist.*) the Vietnamese language

An·nap·o·lis (ənǽpəlis) the capital (pop. 31,740) of Maryland, a seaport and the site of the U.S. Naval Academy

Annapolis Convention a meeting held (1786) at Annapolis, Md, in order to revise the Articles of Confederation. When only five of the 13 states sent delegates, James Madison and Alexander Hamilton initiated an action resulting eight months later in the drafting of a new federal constitution in Philadelphia

An·na·pur·na (ænəpúərnə) a massif and peak (26,502 ft) in the Himalayas, N. central Nepal. It was first climbed (1950) by a French expedition

Ann Arbor a city (pop. 67,000) in S.E. Michigan. It is a center of trade and agriculture, and the seat of the University of Michigan

an·nat·ta (ənǽtə, ənátə) *n.* annatto

---

an·nat·to, an·na·to (ənǽtou) *n.* an orange-red dye from the pulp of the tropical American tree *Bixa orellana*, used for coloring some cheeses and in textiles and varnishes, and by South American Indians for body paint [origin unknown]

Anne (æn), St (1st c. B.C.), traditionally the mother of the Virgin Mary. Feast: July 26

Anne (1665–1714), queen of Great Britain and Ireland (1702–14), daughter of James II. She was dominated till 1710 by the Whig party through Sarah, duchess of Marlborough, and afterwards by the Tories through Abigail Masham and Robert Harley, earl of Oxford, and Henry St John (Lord Bolingbroke). Her reign was important for the development of party politics, for Marlborough's successes in the War of the Spanish Succession, and for the union with Scotland (1707)

an·neal (əníːl) *v.t.* to improve the properties of by heating and then cooling ‖ to fix (color) applied to glass, by heating [O.E. *ancælan*, to burn on]

Anne Bol·eyn (búlin, bulin) (1507–36), second wife of Henry VIII of England, and mother of Elizabeth I

Anne·cy (ænsi:) a town and tourist resort (pop. 54,954) in Savoy, S.E. France, on Lake Annecy

an·ne·lid (ǽnlid) *n.* one of the invertebrate phylum *Annelida* of round segmented worms, with a soft cuticle (earthworms, leeches etc.) **an·nel·i·dan** (ənélidn) *adj.* [F.]

Anne of Austria (1601–66), queen of France, wife of Louis XIII and daughter of Philip III of Spain. She was regent (1643–61) for her son Louis XIV, with Mazarin as her chief minister

Anne of Brittany (1476–1514), Anne de Bretagne, duchess of Brittany (1488–1514) and queen consort of France. She married successively Maximilian of Austria (1490), Charles VIII of France (1491) and Louis XII (1499), thus uniting Brittany with France

Anne of Cleves (1515–57), fourth wife of Henry VIII. Her marriage, arranged by Thomas Cromwell in 1540 for political reasons, was annulled the same year

an·nex, *Br.* also **an·nexe** (ǽneks) *n.* a building attached to, or depending on, a larger building ‖ an appendix or supplement to a book or document [F.

an·nex (ənéks) *v.t.* to take possession of (a territory etc.) and incorporate it ‖ to add or attach as a condition, penalty etc. ‖ to append [F. *annexer*]

an·nex·a·tion (ænikséiʃən) *n.* an annexing or being annexed ‖ something annexed

annexe *ANNEX

an·ni·hi·late (ənáiəleit) *pres. part.* **an·ni·hi·lat·ing** *past and past part.* **an·ni·hi·lat·ed** *v.t.* to destroy completely, wipe out **an·ni·hi·lá·tion** *n.* [fr. L. *annihilare (annihilatus)*, to reduce to nothing]

an·ni·hi·la·tion (ənaiəléiʃən) *n.* (*phys.*) the result of the meeting of an elementary particle and its antiparticle, which convert into protons **—annihilate** *v.*

annihilation radiation the mutual destruction, with the emission of gamma rays, of an electron and a positron

an·ni·ver·sa·ry (æniváːrsəri) *pl.* **an·ni·ver·sa·ries** *n.* the yearly return of the date of an event, or the particular day on which such a return is celebrated, *wedding anniversary* [fr. L. *anniversarius*, returning yearly]

an·no Dom·i·ni (ænoudómənai) (*abbr.* A.D.) in the year specified of the Christian era, *he was born A.D. 68* [L.=in the year of the Lord]

an·no·tate (ǽnouteit) *pres. part.* **an·no·tat·ing** *past and past part.* **an·no·tat·ed** *v.t.* to write explanatory or critical notes on or for (a book or document) **an·no·tá·tion**, **án·no·ta·tor** *ns* [fr. L. *annotare (annotatus)*, to note]

an·nounce (ənáuns) *pres. part.* **an·nounc·ing** *past and past part.* **an·nounced** *v.t.* to make known publicly or formally ‖ to give the name of (a guest or new arrival) at a formal reception ‖ to say esp. with the intention of startling or shocking, *he announced that he was leaving home* ‖ to introduce (a radio or television item) ‖ *v.i.* to be a radio or television announcer **an·nóunce·ment** *n.* **an·nóunc·er** *n.* someone who announces esp. on the radio or television [O.F. *anoncer*]

an·noy (ənɔ́i) *v.t.* to vex, irritate, trouble ‖ *v.i.* to have an annoying effect or behave in an annoying way [O.F. *anuier*]

an·noy·ance (ənɔ́iəns) *n.* the physical or mental discomfort caused by being annoyed ‖ something that vexes or irritates, a nuisance [O.F. *anuiance*]

an·noy·ing (ənɔ́iŋ) *adj.* irritating, troublesome

an·nu·al (ǽnju:əl) **1.** *adj.* occurring regularly once a year ‖ measured by the year, *annual income* **2.** *n.* a yearly publication ‖ a plant which grows from seed, comes to maturity and dies within one year [O.F. *annuel*]

annual percentage rate (*banking*) percentage cost on an annual basis of interest charged on balances (true interest) adapted from discounted or periodic charges, declining balances, etc.

annual ring one of the concentric rings on the cross section of a tree, marking a year's growth

an·nu·i·tant (ənúːitənt, ənjúːitənt) *n.* a person who receives an annuity

an·nu·i·ty (ənúːiti:, ənjúːiti:) *pl.* **an·nu·i·ties** *n.* a fixed yearly payment or pension, which may end either after an agreed period or at the death of the recipient (*DEFERRED ANNUITY, *PERPETUAL ANNUITY) [F. *annuité*]

annuity certain *pl.* **annuities certain** an annuity under which payment will in any event be made for a certain number of years

an·nul (ənʌ́l) *pres. part.* **an·nul·ling** *past and past part.* **an·nulled** *v.t.* to make null and void (e.g. a rule or law) [O.F. *annuller*]

an·nu·lar (ǽnjulər) *adj.* ring-shaped [fr. L. *annularis*]

annular eclipse an eclipse when the moon, intervening between the earth and the sun, is encircled by a ring of light

annular ligament a ligament around the wrist joint or ankle joint

an·nu·late (ǽnjuleit, ǽnjulit) *adj.* made up of rings, having ringlike markings **an·nu·lat·ed** (ǽnjuleitid) *adj.* **an·nu·lá·tion** *n.* [fr. L. *annulatus*]

an·nu·let (ǽnjulit) *n.* a small ring ‖ (*archit.*) a ring-shaped molding [fr. L. *annulus*, ring]

an·nul·ment (ənʌ́lmənt) *n.* an annulling or being annulled, esp. the invalidation of a marriage

an·nun·ci·ate (ənʌ́nsi:eit, ənʌ́nʃi:eit) *pres. part.* **an·nun·ci·at·ing** *past and past part.* **an·nun·ci·at·ed** *v.t.* (*rhet.*) to announce [fr. L. *annunciare (annunciatus)*]

an·nun·ci·a·tion (ənʌnsi:éiʃən, ənʌnʃi:éiʃən) *n.* (*rhet.*) an announcement **the An·nun·ci·a·tion** the announcement made by the Archangel Gabriel to the Virgin Mary that she was to be the mother of Christ (Luke i, 28–35) ‖ the feast, Mar. 25, on which this is celebrated [F. *annonciation*]

an·nun·ci·a·tor (ənʌ́nsi:eitər, ənʌ́nʃi:eitər) *n.* (*rhet.*) an announcer ‖ the automatic indicator on a telephone switchboard [fr. L. *annunciator*]

An·nun·zio (dɑnnúːntsjɔ), Gabriele d' (1863–1938), Italian poet, novelist and adventurer

an·ode (ǽnoud) *n.* a positive electrode, the point of exit of electrons from a device to the external circuit (cf. CATHODE) **án·o·dize** *pres. part.* **an·o·diz·ing** *past and past part.* **an·o·dized** *v.t.* to produce a durable film on the surface of (a metal) by electrolytic action in which the metal acts as the anode [fr. Gk *anodos*, way up]

an·o·dyne (ǽnədain) **1.** *adj.* painkilling, soothing **2.** *n.* something which kills pain [fr. L. fr. Gk *anodunos*, painless]

a·noint (ənɔ́int) *v.t.* to apply oil or ointment to, either medically or sacramentally (as at the crowning of a sovereign) **a·nóint·ment** *n.* [fr. O. F. past. part. *enoint*, anointed]

a·nom·a·lis·tic (ənɒməlístik) *adj.* characterized by anomaly [fr. Gk *anomalos*, irregular]

anomalistic month the mean time taken by the moon's passage from one perigee to the next, approx. 27.55 days

anomalistic year the time taken by the earth's passage from one perihelion to the next, 365 days 6 hours 13 minutes 53 seconds

a·nom·a·lous (ənɒmələs) *adj.* not in conformity with what is usual or expected, often involving an apparent contradiction or paradox [fr. L. fr. Gk *anomalos*, irregular]

a·nom·a·ly (ənɒməli) *pl.* **a·nom·a·lies** *n.* something contrary to the general rule or to what is expected ‖ (*astron.*) the angular distance between the position of a planet and its last

perihelion, or between that of a satellite and its last perigee [fr. L. *anōmalia*, irregularity fr. Gk]

anomaly finder (*computer*) a device for measuring abnormalities in seismic, gravitational, magnetic, and other factors; used in locating underwater deposits

an·o·mie (ǽnəmi:) *n.* a social condition similar to alienation, caused by the disintegration of accepted codes, esp. in 1950–1970; coined by social theorist Emile Durkheim

a·non (ənɒ́n) *adv.* (*archaic*) soon, presently [O.E. *on ān*, into one, in one moment]

an·o·nym (ǽnənim) *n.* a person who conceals his name or whose name is not known ‖ a pseudonym **an·o·ným·i·ty** *n.* the state of being anonymous [F. *anonyme* fr. Gk]

a·non·y·mous (ənɒ́nəməs) (*abbr.* anon.) *adj.* without a known or disclosed name, *an anonymous donor* ‖ written or given by a person whose name is not known or not disclosed [fr. Gk *anōnumos*, nameless]

a·noph·e·les (ənɒ́fəli:z) *n.* a member of *Anopheles*, a genus of mosquitoes which transmit the parasitic protozoans causing malaria in man [Mod. L. fr. Gk *anōphelēs*, harmful]

an·o·rak (ǽnəræk) *n.* a jacket of cloth or skin, with a hood, orig. as worn in the Arctic [Greenland Eskimo]

an·o·rex·i·a (ænəréxi:ə) *n.* (*med.*) extreme loss of appetite **—anorectic** *adj.* causing loss of appetite **—anorexia nervosa** *n.* aversion-to-food syndrome **—anorexigenic** *adj.* causing a lowering of appetite

an·or·thite (ənɔ́rθait) *n.* (*mineral.*) a white, gray or reddish mineral composed of calcium aluminum silicate, found in igneous rocks [F. fr. Gk *an*, without+ *orthos*, straight]

an·os·mi·a (ænɒ́zmi:ə) *n.* (*med.*) loss of the sense of smell **an·ós·mic** *adj.* [Mod. L. fr. Gk *an*, without + *osmē*, smell]

an·oth·er (ənʌ́ðər) **1.** *adj.* (not preceded by def. art.) additional, *another cup of tea* ‖ different, *find another way to go* ‖ the equal of, *another Shakespeare* **2.** *pron.* an additional one of the same kind, *do take another* ‖ a different one, *he lost his pen and had to buy another* ‖ a similar thing, person etc., *we shall never see another like him* ‖ (*old-fash.*) somebody else, *he loves another* [M.E. orig. *an other* fr. O.E. *ōðer*]

A·nouilh (ænuːj), Jean (1910–), French dramatist. His works include 'le Bal des voleurs' (1938),'Antigone' (1944), 'l'Invitation au château' (1947), 'l'Hurluberlu' (1959), 'Becket' (1959)

an·ou·ran (ənúərən) *n.* and *adj.* anuran, salientian [fr. Gk *an*, without+ *oura*, tail]

an·o·vu·la·tion (ænouvjuléiʃən) *n.* (*med.*) stopping ovulation **—anovulant** *n.* drug causing ovulation to cease **—anovulant** *adj.* **—anovulatory** *adj.*

ans. answer

An·schluss, the (ǽnʃlus) the political union (1938) of Austria with Germany [G. = a joining]

An·selm (ǽnselm), St (1033–1109), archbishop of Canterbury (1093–1109) and one of the originators of Scholasticism. He upheld papal claims (esp. on Investiture) against William II and Henry I. His works include 'Monologion', 'Proslogion', 'Cur Deus Homo?'. Feast: Apr. 21

an·ser·ine (ǽnsərain) *adj.* pertaining to a goose ‖ (*rhet.*) gooselike, silly [fr. L. *anserinus* fr. *anser*, a goose]

Ans·gar (ǽnsgər), St (801–65), Frankish missionary to the Danes (826) and the Swedes (829). Feast: Feb. 3

An·shan (ɑ́nʃɑn) a great iron and steel center (pop. 1,210,000) in Liaoning, N.E. China

ANSI (*acronym*) for American National Standards Institute

An·son (ǽnsən), George Anson, 1st Baron Anson (1697–1762), English admiral. The last of the great corsairs, he circumnavigated the globe when fighting against Spain (1740–4) and defeated the French at Cape Finisterre (1747). He established the Royal Marines in 1755

an·swer (ǽnsər, ɑ́nsər) *v.t.* to reply to, *to answer a letter, answer the telephone* ‖ to defend oneself against, *can you answer the charges?* ‖ to fit, agree with, satisfy, *to answer a purpose* ‖ to correspond to, *he answers the description* ‖ *v.i.* to reply in words, actions etc., *answer to your names, they answered with two quick goals* ‖ to act in response, *the car would not answer to the steering wheel* ‖ to correspond, *to answer to a description* ‖ to be suitable (to a purpose, need),

---

CONCISE PRONUNCIATION KEY: **(a)** æ, cat; ɑ, car; ɔ fawn; ei, snake. **(e)** e, hen; i:, sheep; iə, deer; εə, bear. **(i)** i, fish; ai, tiger; əː, bird. **(o)** o, ox; au, cow; ou, goat; u, poor; ɔi, royal. **(u)** ʌ, duck; u, bull; u:, goose; ə, bacillus; ju:, cube. x, loch; θ, think; ð, bother; z, Zen; ʒ, corsage; dʒ, savage; ŋ, orangutang; j, yak; ʃ, fish; tʃ, fetch; 'l, rabble; 'n, redden. Complete pronunciation key appears inside front cover.

does this answer to your requirements? **to answer back** to give a saucy answer when scolded **to answer for** to vouch or take responsibility for ‖ to be judged for, pay the penalty for, *to answer for one's actions* [O.E. *andswarian*, to reply]

answer *n*. a reply (in speech, writing, or action) ‖ a solution, *the answer to a sum, the answer is to try harder* ‖ (*mus.*) an imitation of a fugue subject in another voice [O.E. *andswaru*, reply]

an·swer·a·ble (ænsərəb'l, ɑ́nsərəb'l) *adj.* responsible, *is he answerable for her debts?*

answering service service that responds to telephone calls for clients, taking and delivering messages

ant (ænt) *n*. a small insect, related to bees and wasps, of the order *Hymenoptera*. There are many species, widely distributed [O.E. *æmete*, *ēmete*]

—Ants show a highly developed social organization and complex behavior patterns. Many exhibit parental care, carrying food to their larvae, cleaning and guarding nests. Each colony has a queen. The only function of the male is to fertilize her. All the workers are sterile females, as in the beehive. Ants eat a variety of foods. Some keep 'cows' in the form of aphids (plant lice) for their sweet excretion, honeydew, some are agriculturists, growing fungus gardens underground, some species depend on the work of 'slave' ants so that the 'master' ants become almost parasitic on them. Many species are belligerent, constantly trying to extend their territory and commandeering the food supply of other colonies. 'Soldier' ants may have such large scimitarlike mandibles that they are no longer able to feed themselves. All have well-developed sense organs

-ant *suffix* denoting an activity, as in 'consultant' ‖ equivalent to '-ing', as in 'expectant'

ANTA (often æntə) *AMERICAN NATIONAL THEATRE AND ACADEMY

ant·ac·id (æntǽsid) **1.** *adj.* preventing or counteracting acidity, esp. in the stomach **2.** *n*. an agent which does this [fr. ANTI-+ACID]

an·tag·o·nism (æntǽgənizəm) *n*. open opposition or resistance, hostility [fr. Gk *antagōnisma*, rivalry]

an·tag·o·nist (æntǽgənist) *n*. an open enemy, rival ‖ (*physiol.*) a muscle which contracts another and is then itself con- tracted by the latter **an·tag·o·nis·tic** *adj.* **an·tag·o·nis·ti·cal·ly** *adv.* [fr. L. fr. Gk *antagōnistēs*, contender, rival]

an·tag·o·nize (æntǽgənaiz) *pres. part.* **an·tag·o·niz·ing** *past* and *past part.* **an·tag·o·nized** *v.t.* to provoke to enmity or hostility [fr. Gk *antagōnizesthai*, to compete with]

An·ta·kya (ɑntɑkjɑ́) *ANTIOCH

An·tal·ci·das (æntǽlsidæs) (4th c. B.C.), Spartan diplomat. He concluded the Peace of Antalcidas (c. 386 B.C.) with Athens, by which Athens recognized Persian sovereignty in Asia Minor

ant·al·ka·li (æntǽlkəlai) *adj.* counteracting or preventing alkalinity **ant·al·ka·line** *adj.* and *n*. [fr. ANTI-+ALKALI]

An·ta·nan·a·ri·vo (æntənænərí:vou) the capital (pop. 270,000) and commercial center of Madagascar on the central plateau. Industries: food and tobacco processing. University (1961)

Ant·arc·tic (æntárktik, æntúrtik) **1.** *adj.* South polar **2.** *n*. **the Antarctic** the South polar regions [M.E. *antartyk* fr. O. F. fr. L. fr. Gk]

Ant·arc·ti·ca (æntárktikə, æntúrtikə) a continent (area 5,000,000 sq. miles) with a coastline of about 14,000 miles, largely within the Antarctic Circle. There are no permanent inhabitants. Political sovereignty is disputed. The continent, surrounded by pack ice and icebergs, is an ice-covered plateau (6,000–10,000 ft) with mountain peaks rising to 15,000 ft, some of them volcanic. Average temperatures all over the continent are below freezing. Precipitation (as snow) is equivalent to 10–20 ins of rainfall on the coast, more in the mountains, and 2 ins at the South Pole. There is little plant life other than mosses and lichens. Seals, penguins and sea birds are found in coastal areas. HISTORY. Ptolemy first postulated the existence of an Antarctic continent. Palmer, an American sealer. sighted it (1821). Ross discovered the Ross Sea and Ross Shelf Ice (1841). Scott crossed Ross Shelf Ice (1902–4) and Shackleton's expedition passed south of it (1908). Amundsen reached the South Pole (Dec. 1911), then Scott (*Jan.* 1912). The continent was mapped from the air by Wilkins (1928–9) and by Byrd (1928–30, 1934–5). Since the Interna-

tional Geophysical Year (1957–8) much geophysical, meteorological and zoological research has been done around the Antarctic coast. Fuchs and Hillary crossed the continent (1957–8). British explorers Fiennes and Burton crossed both poles in a single circumnavigation of the Earth (1982). The Antarctic Treaty (1961) froze all territorial claims until 1991 and specified that the Antarctic will be used for peaceful purposes

Antarctic Circle the parallel of latitude distant 23°27′ from the South Pole, i.e. 66°33′s.

Antarctic Ocean the ocean comprising the southern reaches of the Pacific, Atlantic, and Indian Oceans, surrounding the Antarctic continent. It is measured sometimes from the Antarctic Circle, sometimes from the northern limit of floating ice, a line varying from 47° to 61°S. (area by the latter measure: 5,700,000 sq. miles). Greatest sounded depth: 4,000 fathoms

Antarctic Peninsula the largest peninsula of the Antarctic continent, lying south of Cape Horn. The northern part is now called Graham Land (the former British name for the whole) and the southern part is called Palmer Peninsula. The peninsula is claimed by Argentina, Britain and Chile

Antarctic Pole the South Pole

ante- (ænti:) *prefix* before [L. *ante*]

an·te (ænti:) **1.** *n*. (*poker*) the stake a player must put in the pool before drawing his first cards or the stake he must put in before he can lake part in a jackpot or similar hand ‖ (*pop.*) the share one must pay in something **2.** *v.i. pres. part.* **an·te·ing** *past* and *past part.* **an·ted** (esp. with 'up') to stake the ante [L.=before]

ant·eat·er (ænti:tər) *n*. one of several edentates of Central and South America, southern Africa and Australasia. *Myrmecophagus jubata* is the great anteater of South America. It is a mammal about 4 ft long, with a bushy tail. It feeds on ants (termites) by means of a long sticky tongue, which it protrudes from its long slender snout

an·te·bel·lum (ænti:béləm) *adj.* existing before the war, esp. before the Civil War [L. *ante bellum*, before the war]

an·te·ced·ence (æntisí:d'ns) *n*. priority in time or in a sequence of cause and effect (cf. PRECEDENCE) [fr. L. *antecedentia*]

an·te·ced·ent (æntisí:d'nt) **1.** *adj.* going before, in time or in any other sequence, preceding ‖ (*gram.*) serving as an antecedent **2.** *n*. that which precedes ‖ an earlier type ‖ (*pl.*) a man's past life or origins ‖ (*pl.*) ancestors ‖ (*gram.*) the noun or pronoun to which a following relative pronoun refers ‖ (*logic*) the conditional clause in a hypothetical proposition ‖ (*math.*) the first term of a ratio [F. *antécédent*]

an·te·cham·ber (ænti:tʃeimbər) *n*. a room leading to a main room or apartment [O. F. *antichambre*]

an·te·chap·el (ænti:tʃǽp'l) *n*. a subsidiary chapel, sometimes called a Galilee, in the western entrance to a church ‖ (*Br.*) a screened-off part at the west end of a college chapel

an·te·date (ænti:deit) *pres. part.* **an·te·dat·ing** *past* and *past part.* **an·te·dat·ed** *v.t.* to predate

an·te·di·lu·vi·an (ænti:dilú:vi:ən) **1.** *n*. an antiquated person or thing **2.** *adj.* from before the Flood ‖ very old fashioned or antiquated, *antediluvian ideas* [fr. ANTE-+ L. *diluvium*, flood]

ant egg an ant's white pupa or cocoon. They are dried and sold as food for fish, birds etc.

an·te·lope (ænt'loup) *pl.* **an·te·lope, an·te·lopes** *n*. a deerlike ruminant mammal, esp. of fam. *Bovidae*, with cylindrical, unbranched hollow horns. They are found widely in Africa (e.g. duiker, gazelle, eland, springbok), in Asia (gazelle), in India (blackbuck), and in North America (pronghorn) ‖ their hide used as leather [O.F. *antelop* fr. L. fr. Gk]

an·te·me·rid·i·an (ænti:mərídi:ən) *adj.* before noon [L. *ante meridiem*]

an·te me·rid·i·em (ænti:mərídi:əm) *adj.* (*abbr.* a.m., A.M.) after midnight and before noon [L.]

an·te·na·tal (ænti:néit'l) *adj.* before birth, *antenatal care, antenatal disease*

an·ten·na (ænténə) *pl.* **an·ten·nae** (ænténi:), **an·ten·nas** *n*. the sensitive jointed feeler or horn of an insect or crustacean ‖ either of the two sensitive pollinia in an orchid ‖ a device for converting electrical currents into electromagnetic waves, or vice versa. Size and shape are determined by the wavelength of the radiation and by directional requirements [L. = sailyard]

antenna array (*radio, radar* etc.) an arrangement of receiving or transmitting antennas to cover a particular area

antenna mine (*mil.*) in naval mine warfare, a contact mine fitted with antennae that, when touched by a steel ship, set up galvanic action to fire the mine

an·te·nup·tial (ænti:nʌ́pʃəl) *adj.* (*law*) occurring or relating to the time before the ceremony of marriage

an·te·pen·di·um (ænti:péndi:əm) *pl.* **an·te·pen·di·ums, an·te·pen·di·a** (ænti:péndi:ə) *n*. a veil or screen covering the front of an altar [M.L. fr. *ante-*, before + *pendere*, hang]

an·te·pe·nult (ænti:pinʌ́lt, ænti:pí:nʌlt) *adj.* and *n*. antepenultimate [fr. L. *antepenultima* (*syllaba*), last (syllable) but two]

an·te·pe·nul·ti·mate (ænti:pinʌ́ltəmit) **1.** *adj.* the third in order counting from the end, the third last **2.** *n*. an antepenultimate syllable [fr. L. *antepenultimus* fr. ante-, before+*paenultima*, last but one]

an·te·ri·or (æntíəri:ər) *adj.* nearer the front (cf. POSTERIOR) ‖ (*anat.*) toward or relating to the head, in human anatomy sometimes ventral (opp. POSTERIOR) ‖ (*bot.*) away from the axis ‖ earlier in time **an·te·ri·or·i·ty** (æntiəri:ɔ́riti:, pntjəri:ɔriti:) *n*. [L. = former]

an·te·room (ænti:ru:m, ænti:rum) *n*. a room leading into another, generally larger room ‖ a waiting room ‖ (*Br.*) the common room in an officer's mess

ant·he·li·on (ænthí:li:ən, ænθí:li:ən) *pl.* **ant·he·li·a** (ænthí:li:ə, ænθí:li:ə), **ant·he·li·ons** *n*. a white diffuse image sometimes appearing at the same altitude as the sun, but opposite to it [Mod. L. fr. Gk *anti*-, against + *hēlios*, sun]

ant·hel·min·thic (ænthelmínθik, ænθelmínθik) *n*. and *adj.* anthelmintic

ant·hel·min·tic (ænthelmíntik, ænθelmíntik) **1.** *adj.* getting rid of or destroying intestinal worms **2.** *n*. a product which does this [fr. ANTI-+Gk *helmins* (*helminthos*), worm]

an·them (ænθəm) *n*. a piece of choral music sung in church, often verses of scripture sung antiphonally ‖ a song of praise or joy, *national anthem* [O.E. *antefn* fr. L. fr. Gk]

an·ther (ænθər) *n*. the part of the stamen which produces pollen and to which the filament is usually attached [F. *anthère* fr. L. fr. Gk]

an·ther·id·i·al (ænθərídi:əl) *adj.* of an antheridium

an·ther·i·di·um (ænθərídi:əm) *pl.* **an·ther·i·di·a** (ænθərídi:ə) *n*. the male or sperm-producing structure in the sexual generations of lower plants, e.g. algae, fungi (*OGONIUM) [Mod. L. fr. Gk *anthēros*, blooming+*-idion*, diminutive suffix]

ant·hill (ænthil) *n*. a mound of earth thrown up by ants or termites as they dig their nest ‖ a building or locality crammed with people and full of activity

an·thol·o·gist (ænθɔ́lədʒist) *n*. a person who compiles an anthology

an·thol·o·gize (ænθɔ́lədʒaiz) *pres. part.* **an·thol·o·giz·ing** *past* and *past part.* **an·thol·o·gized** *v.t.* to collect into an anthology

an·thol·o·gy (ænθɔ́lədʒi:) *pl.* **an·thol·o·gies** *n*. a collection of poetry or prose chosen to represent the work of a particular writer, a literary school or a national literature [fr. L. *anthologia* fr. Gk *anthos*, flower + *-logia*, collection]

An·tho·ny (æntəni:, ænθəni:), St (of Egypt) *ANTONY, ST

Anthony, St (of Padua) *ANTONY, ST

An·tho·ny (æntəni:, ænθəni:), Susan Brownell (1820–1906), U.S. reformer. She campaigned esp. for women's rights, helping to pave the way for the 19th Amendment (1920, granting suffrage to women)

an·tho·zo·an (ænθəzóuən) **1.** *n*. a member of *Actinozoa*, a class of marine coelenterates, including sea anemones and coral polyps, without alternation of generations **2.** *adj.* relating to anthozoans [Mod. L. fr. Gk *anthos*, flower + *zōon*, animal]

an·thra·cene (ænθrəsi:n) *n*. a tricyclic crystalline hydrocarbon ($C_{14}H_{10}$) obtained from coal tar. It is white with violet fluorescence and is used for its luminescent properties and as a starting material in the synthesis of dyestuffs [fr. Gk *anthrax*, coal]

an·thra·cite (ænθrəsait) *n*. a form of coal which is hard and very rich in carbon. It burns slowly, and emits very little smoke **an·thra·cit·ic** (ænθrəsítik) *adj.* [fr. L. *anthracites* fr. Gk *anthrax*, coal]

---

an·thrax (ǽnθræks) pl. **an·thra·ces** (ǽnθrəsi:z) n. an infectious, often fatal disease in sheep and cattle, caused by the bacterium *Bacillus anthracis* ‖ a virulent infectious disease in man, contracted by exposure to infected animals or animal products (e.g. bristle shaving brushes), and characterized by malignant pustules [L. fr. Gk *anthrax*, coal, carbuncle]

an·thro·po·cen·tric (ǽnθrəpouséntrik) adj. regarding man as the center or purpose of the universe **an·thro·po·cén·tri·cal·ly** adv. [fr. Gk *anthrōpos*, man + *kentron*, center]

an·thro·po·graph·ic (ǽnθrəpəgrǽfik) adj. relating to anthropography **an·thro·po·gráph·i·cal·ly** adv.

an·thro·pog·ra·phy (ǽnθrəpógrəfi:) n. the branch of anthropology which studies the geographical distribution of men according to physical type, language, culture etc. [fr. Gk *anthrōpos*, man + *graphia*, writing]

an·thro·poid (ǽnθrəpɔid) 1. adj. manlike in appearance ‖ of the anthropoid apes 2. n. an anthropoid ape [fr. Gk *anthrōpos*, man+*eidos*, form]

anthropoid ape a member of fam. *Pongidae*, comprising the chimpanzee, gibbon, gorilla and orangutan. They are tailless, semierect and long-armed, and use their hands and feet in the way a man uses his hands. They live mainly in tropical forests, feeding esp. on fruits and vegetables

an·thro·po·log·i·cal (ǽnθrəpəlódʒikʹl) adj. of or pertaining to anthropology

an·thro·pol·o·gist (ǽnθrəpólədʒist) n. a specialist in anthropology

an·thro·pol·o·gy (ǽnθrəpólədʒi:) n. the science which studies man both as an animal and as living in society, his origins, development, distribution, social habits, culture etc. (*PHYSICAL ANTHROPOLOGY, *SOCIAL ANTHROPOLOGY) [fr. Gk *anthrōpos*, man + *logos*, discourse]

an·thro·po·met·ric (ǽnθrəpoumétrik) adj. of or pertaining to anthropometry **an·thro·po·mét·ri·cal** adj.

an·thro·pom·e·try (ǽnθrəpómitri:) n. the science that deals with human measurements, in particular the bones and skull of the human skeleton and its segments [coined fr. Gk *anthrōpos*, man + *metria*, measure]

an·thro·po·mor·phic (ǽnθrəpəmórfik) adj. of, like or showing anthropomorphism [fr. Gk *anthrōpomorphos*, like man]

an·thro·po·mor·phism (ǽnθrəpəmórfizəm) n. the attribution of human form and character to God, or a god, or of human character to things in nature **an·thro·po·mór·phize** pres. part. **an·thro·po·mor·phiz·ing** past and past part. **an·thro·po·mor·phized** v.t. [fr. Gk *anthropomorphos*, like man]

an·thro·po·mor·phous (ǽnθrəpəmórfəs) adj. having the form of a human being (cf. ANTHROPOMORPHIC) [fr. Gk *anthrōpomorphos*, like man]

an·thro·poph·a·gi (ǽnθrəpófədʒai, ǽnθrəpófəgai) pl. n. eaters of human flesh, cannibals **an·thro·póph·a·gite** n. a cannibal **an·thro·poph·a·gous** (ǽnθrəpófəgəs) adj. [L. fr. Gk *anthrōpos*, man + *phagein*, to eat]

an·thro·poph·a·gy (ǽnθrəpófədʒi:) n. the eating of human flesh, cannibalism [fr. Gk *anthrōpophagia*]

an·thro·pos·o·phy (ǽnθrəpósəfi:) n. a form of theosophy associated with Rudolf Steiner [fr. Gk *anthrōpos*, man + *sophia*, wisdom]

an·throp·o·sphere (ǽnθrópəsfiər) n. the ecology as affected by human activity, total human knowledge syn NOOSPHERE

anti- (ǽnti:, ǽntai) prefix against, opposite, instead [Gk]

an·ti (ǽnti) 1. n. (pop.) a person who opts against some action etc. 2. adj. (pop.) against, opposed [Gk= against]

an·ti·a·bor·tion·ist (ǽnti:əbórʃənist) n. one opposed to abortion **—antiabortion** n.

an·ti·air·craft (ǽnti:éərkræft, ǽnti:éərkrɑft) 1. n. guns, rockets, guided missiles etc. for use against hostile aircraft 2. adj. of such weapons

antiaircraft missile (mil.) a guided surface-to-air missile

an·ti·al·ler·gen·ic, **an·ti·al·ler·gic** (ǽnti:ælərdʒénik) (ǽntiələ́:rdʒik) adj. (med.) providing relief from the symptoms of allergy **—antiallergenic** or **antiallergic** n.

an·ti·anx·i·e·ty (ǽnti:æŋzáiiti:) adj. (med.) providing relief for anxiety, e.g., an antianxiety drug

an·ti·ar (ǽnti:ɑr, ǽntʃər) n. *Antiaris toxicaria*, fam. *Moraceae*, the upas tree of Java and Indochina ‖ the poisonous resin it produces [Javanese *antjar*]

an·ti·ar·rhyth·mic (ǽnti:əríðmik) adj. (med.) providing relief from abnormal cardiac rhythm

an·ti·art (ǽnti:árt) n. an art form rejecting traditional forms, attributed to mechanical and electronic devices, and the mere placement of ordinary objects

an·ti·at·om (ǽnti:ǽtəm) n. (phys.) atoms of an antiparticle

an·ti·au·thor·i·tar·i·an opposed to authoritarianism **—antiauthoritarianism** n.

an·ti·bac·te·ri·al (ǽnti:bæktíəri:əl) 1. adj. useful in curing or preventing the action of harmful bacteria 2. n. such a substance

antiballistic missile (mil.) defensive guided missile that intercepts and destroys a ballistic missile in flight abbr **ABM**

an·ti·bar·y·on (ǽnti:bǽri:ɒn) n. (phys.) one of a group of eight known fundamental particles that are the antiparticles of the baryons, incl. the antiproton and antineutron

an·ti·bi·o·sis (ǽnti:baióusis) n. an antagonism between two microorganisms which makes it impossible for them to live in contact with one another [Mod. L. fr. ANTI-+ Gk *biosis* fr. *bios*, mode of life]

an·ti·bi·ot·ic (ǽnti:baiɒtik) 1. adj. capable of inhibiting or destroying life, esp. of a substance produced by a microorganism that affects other microorganisms 2. n. a substance usually produced by a microorganism (e.g. a fungus or a bacterium) that is used therapeutically to destroy or inhibit the growth of a pathogen (usually another bacterium or a virus) [fr. ANTI-+ Gk *biotikos*, pertaining to life]

an·ti·black (ǽnti:blǽk) adj. hostile to persons of African ancestry **—antiblack** n. **—antiblackism** n.

an·ti·bod·y (ǽntibɒdi:, ǽnti:bɒdi:) pl. **an·ti·bo·dies** n. any of a group of proteins produced by the body of higher organisms in response to the presence of foreign substances called antigens. Antibodies possess the ability to render these foreign substances innocuous (*IMMUNITY)

an·ti·bus·ing (ǽnti:bʌsiŋ) adj. opposed to busing children to schools beyond their residential neighborhoods for the purposes of desegregating schools Cf BUSING

an·tic (ǽntik) n. a caper, extravagant or grotesque gesture ‖ (pl.) foolish, annoying or irresponsible behavior [perh. fr. Ital. *antico*, ancient]

an·ti·cath·ode (ǽnti:kǽθoud) n. the metal target for the stream of electrons in an electronic tube

an·ti·chlor (ǽntiklɔr, ǽntiklour) n. a substance used, after bleaching, to remove any excess of chlorine

An·ti·christ (ǽnti:kraist) the great enemy of Christ. In the New Testament it is said that his coming will precede the second coming of Christ and the end of the world [O.F. *antecrist* fr. L. fr. Gk]

an·tic·i·pate (æntísəpeit) pres. part. **an·tic·i·pat·ing** past and past part. **an·tic·i·pat·ed** v.t. to look forward to, feel in advance, often with either a pleasant or a painful emotion ‖ to assume, use or realize in advance, *to anticipate an inheritance* ‖ to achieve before (another person) or happen before (another event) ‖ to meet in advance, *to anticipate someone's wishes* ‖ to prevent by prior action ‖ (pop.) to expect [fr. L. *anticipare* (*anticipatus*)]

an·tic·i·pa·tion (æntisəpéiʃən) n. an anticipating or being anticipated ‖ (mus.) the sounding of a note belonging to the resolution of a discord, just before the resolving chord itself is sounded [fr. L. *anticipatio* (*anticipationis*)]

an·tic·i·pa·tor (æntísəpeitər) n. one who anticipates **an·tic·i·pa·to·ry** (æntísəpətɔri:, æntísəpətouri:) adj. [L.]

an·ti·clas·tic (ǽnti:klǽstik) adj. of a surface whose curvatures at one or more points are in opposite direction, e.g. a saddle (cf. SYNCLASTIC) [ANTI- + Gk *klastos*, broken fr. *klaein*, to break]

an·ti·cler·i·cal (ǽnti:klérikʹl) 1. adj. opposed to the social or political influence of the clergy or of the Church 2. n. someone who holds this view **an·ti·clér·i·cal·ism** n.

an·ti·cli·mac·tic (ǽnti:klaimǽktik) adj. of the nature of an anticlimax **an·ti·cli·mác·ti·cal·ly** adv.

an·ti·cli·max (ǽnti:kláimæks) n. a disappointing or unimpressive end to what promised well

an·ti·cli·nal (ǽntikláin'l) adj. pertaining to an arched formation of rock in which the strata slope down from a crest (opp. SYNCLINAL) **an·ti·cline** (ǽntiklain) n. such a formation of rock strata (opp. SYNCLINE) [fr. ANTI- + Gk *klinein*, to lie]

an·ti·cline (ǽnti:klain) n. (geol.) a configuration of folded, stratified rocks that dips in two directions from a crest Cf SYNCLINE

an·ti·clock·wise (ǽnti:klókwaiz) adj. and adv. counterclockwise

an·ti·co·ag·u·la·tion (ǽnti:kouægjuléiʃən) n. (med.) hindering clotting, esp. of blood, e.g., by the drug heparin **—anticoagulant** n. **—anticoagulate** v. **—anticoagulative** adj.

an·ti·co·dan (ǽnti:koudən) n. (biol.) three nucleotide bases that define the amino acid in transfer RNA, binding it to a complementary codan in messenger RNA

an·ti·col·li·sion radar (ǽnti:kəlíʒən) n. radar system that warns of collision possibility

an·ti·con·vul·sant (ǽnti:kənvʌ́lsənt) n. (med.) convulsion preventative or mitigator such as used in treating epileptics **—anticonvulsive** adj.

An·ti·cos·ti (ǽntikósti:) n. a large forestcovered island (140 miles long, c. 30 miles wide) in the Gulf of St Lawrence E. Canada

an·ti·crop (ǽnti:krɒp) adj. antagonistic to crops; destroying crops Cf ANTIFOLIANT

an·ti·cy·clone (ǽnti:sáikloun) n. a region in the atmosphere marked by high pressure at the center, the outward radial movement of the air being deviated by the earth's rotation to give a clockwise wind system in the northern hemisphere, counterclockwise in the southern. An anticyclone is generally associated with fine weather **an·ti·cy·clon·ic** (ǽnti:saiklónik) adj.

an·ti·de·pres·sant (ǽnti:diprésənt) 1. n. any of several drugs used for treating mental depression 2. adj. (of a drug) tending to raise a patient's spirits

an·ti·deu·tron (ǽnti:dú:trɒn) n. (phys.) counterpart of the nucleus of deuterium in antimatter

an·ti·di·u·ret·ic (ǽnti:daijurétik) n. (med.) drug that reduces urine flow **—antidiuretic** adj. **—antidiuretic hormone** n pituitary gland secretion that increases blood pressure to cause decrease in urine flow

an·ti·do·ron (ǽnti:dóron, ǽnti:dóurɒn) n. *EULOGIA [L. fr. Gk *antidōron*, a returned gift]

an·ti·dot·al (ǽntidout'l) adj. of or serving as an antidote

an·ti·dote (ǽntidout) n. a remedy counteracting a poison etc. [fr. L. fr. Gk *antidoton*]

an·ti·dump·ing (ǽnti:dʌ́mpiŋ) adj. of measures to discourage importation of manufactures at prices below the market in countries of origin

an·ti·e·lec·tron (ǽnti:əléktrɒn) n. (phys.) positively charged electron, counterpart of an electron Cf POSITRON

an·ti·e·met·ic (ǽnti:imétik) n. (med.) drug to restrain vomiting **—antiemetic** adj. designed to restrain vomiting

an·ti·en·vi·ron·ment, **an·ti·en·vi·ron·men·tal** (ǽnti:inváirənmənt) adj. of a condition or action that contrasts or conflicts with the natural environment

an·ti·es·tab·lish·ment (ǽnti:istǽbliʃmənt) adj. opposed to the ruling group and its principles

An·tie·tam, Battle of (æntí:təm) (Battle of Sharpsburg) a decisive battle (Sept. 17, 1862) of the American Civil War. Lee's first invasion of the North was stopped by Union forces

an·ti·Fed·er·al·ist (ǽnti:fédərəlist, ǽnti:fédrəlist) n. (Am. hist.) a member of the political group which opposed the Federalists in the controversy (1787–8) over the adoption of the constitution. Led by Jefferson, the anti-Federalists were the forerunners of the Democratic party

an·ti·fer·til·i·ty (ǽnti:fərtíliti:) adj. (med.) causing a destruction or reduction of fertility, e.g., a contraceptive drug

an·ti·fluor·i·da·tion·ist (ǽnti:fluərideíʃənist) n. one opposed to fluoridation of the water supply

an·ti·form (ǽnti:fɔrm) adj. rejection of accepted materials in creating works of art, with preference for raw substances

an·ti·foul·ant (ǽnti:fáulənt) n. substance used to reduce fouling, e.g., a paint

an·ti·freeze (ǽnti:fri̱:z) n. a substance which, dissolved in the coolant of an engine, lowers its freezing point sufficiently to keep it from freezing

an·ti·fun·gal (ǽnti:fʌ́ŋgəl) adj. having the capability of deterring fungus growth **syn** fungicidal

an·ti·gal·ax·y (ǽnti:gǽləksi:) n. (astron.) a hypothetical antimatter galaxy

an·ti·gen (ǽntidʒən) n. a substance which provokes the formation of an antibody when it is introduced in another organism. A vaccine acts as an antigen [fr. ANTI-+Gk genos, producing]

an·ti·glob·u·lin (ǽnti:glóbjulin) n. (pharm.) material that precipitates globulin by combining with it

An·tig·o·ne (æntígəni:) (Gk mythol.) daughter of Oedipus and Jocasta. Condemned to death by Creon, king of Thebes, for performing funeral rites over her brother Polynices, she killed herself

An·tig·o·nus Go·na·tas (æntígənəsgənátəs) (c. 319–239 B.C.), king of Macedonia (276–239 B.C.). He repelled the invasion of the Gauls, but was temporarily driven out of his kingdom by Pyrrhus (274 B.C.)

an·ti·grav·i·ty (ænti:grǽviti:) n. (phys.) 1. a force that counteracts gravity 2. the hypothetical effect —**antigravitational** or **antigravity** adj.

An·ti·gua (ʊntí:gwʊ) a commercial and tourist center (pop. 17,000) in the highlands of S. central Guatemala: coffee, sugarcane, grain, fodder crops. It is surrounded by volcanoes and is frequently subject to volcanic eruption and floods. Its many 16th–18th c. ruins make it a museum of Spanish colonial history

Antigua and Barbuda (bɑrbú:də) an island republic in the Caribbean (area 170.5 sq. miles, pop. 80,000), part of the Leeward Islands. It includes the islands of Antigua, Barbuda and Redonda. Capital: St. John's (pop. 25,000). People: African descent. Official language: English. The land is mostly flat with deeply indented coastlines lined with reefs and beaches. The climate is dry. Average temperature: 82° F. Products: tourism, cotton, sugar, fruits and vegetables. Exports: clothing, rum, lobsters. Chief port: St. John's. Monetary unit: East Caribbean dollar (100 cents). HISTORY. Antigua was discovered by Columbus (1493) and first settled by the English in 1632. With Barbuda and Redonda, it formed a British colony until Feb. 27, 1967, when the three islands became a state in association with Britain. In 1981 the islands became an independent state

an·ti·he·mo·phil·ic (ænti:hi:məfíllik) adj. (med.) having the ability to stop hemophilic bleeding

an·ti·he·ro (ǽnti:hi̱ərou) pl. **an·ti·he·roes** n. a main character in a novel or play whose idea of the good life is conspicuously in opposition to that of the conventional hero

an·ti·her·o·ine (ǽnti:hérouin) *ANTIHERO

an·ti·his·ta·mine (ænti:hístəmi:n) n. one of a group of synthetic drugs used in the treatment of such allergic reactions as hay fever

an·ti·hu·man (ænti:hjú:mən) adj. being against humanity; not beneficial to the human species

an·ti·hy·per·ten·sive (ænti:haipərténsiv) n. (med.) drug effective against high blood pressure —**antihypertensive** adj.

an·ti·Jac·o·bin (ænti:dʒǽkəbin) 1. adj. (hist.) opposed to the Jacobins in particular, or to the French Revolution in general 2. n. someone who was thus opposed

an·ti·knock (ǽnti:nɒk) n. a substance added to automobile fuel to prevent knocking

An·ti·Leb·a·non Mtns (ænti:lébənən) (Arab. Jabal-esh-Sharqi) a range (60 miles long) between Syria and Lebanon (Mt Hermon, 9,232 ft)

an·ti·lep·ton (ænti:léptɒn) n. (phys.) a group of four known fundamental particles incl. the positron (antielectron), antimuon and two antineutrinos, constituting the antiparticles of the leptons

An·til·le·an (æntíli:ən, æntəlí:ən) adj. of or relating to the Antilles

An·til·les (æntíli:z) the whole West Indian archipelago excepting the Bahamas. The Greater Antilles consist of Cuba, Hispaniola, Jamaica and Puerto Rico and the adjacent small islands. The Lesser Antilles consist of the remaining islands: Leeward Islands, Windward Islands, Netherlands Antilles, Trinidad and Tobago, the Venezuelan islands and Barbados

an·ti·log·a·rithm (ænti:lógərìðəm, ænti:lógərìðəm) n. (math., abbr. antilog) the number represented by a logarithm

an·til·o·gy (æntílədʒi:) pl. **an·til·o·gies** n. a contradiction in terms [fr. Gk antilogia]

an·ti·ma·cas·sar (ænti:məkǽsər) n. a covering to protect the back of an upholstered chair or sofa from dirty marks

An·ti·Ma·son·ic Party (ænti:məsónik) a U.S. political organization (1827–36) formed in New York State to expose the corruption of the Order of the Masons. It was composed of church groups, temperance and antislavery elements. The Anti-Masonic nominating convention in Baltimore (1831) required a special three-fourths majority to nominate, establishing the precedent for the two-thirds rule which was adopted for more than a century by the major U.S. political parties

an·ti·masque, an·ti·mask (ænti:mǽsk, ænti:mɑsk) n. an interlude in the Tudor or Jacobean masque, often introduced as comic relief

an·ti·mat·ter (ǽnti:mætər) n. matter built up from antiparticles having an existence predicted on the basis of the relativity theory and quantum mechanics. An atom of antihydrogen, for example, would comprise a negative proton (antiproton) as nucleus, with a positive electron (positron) orbiting about it. Antimatter does not exist except fleetingly on earth, but there is a possibility that some regions of the universe are composed of antimatter

an·ti·me·son (ænti:mí:zɒn, ænti:mézɒn) n. (phys.) one of a group of five known fundamental particles that are the antiparticles of the mesons

an·ti·mis·sile (ænti:mísəl) 1. n. a guided missile used for intercepting and destroying guided missiles 2. adj. concerned with or designed for the interception and destruction of guided missiles

an·ti·mo·nar·chi·cal (ænti:mənárkik'l) adj. opposed to the rule of a single sovereign, or to the institution of monarchy, whether absolute or constitutional

an·ti·mo·ny (ǽntimouni:) n. a metallic element (symbol Sb, at. no. 51, at. mass 121.75). It is a constituent of type metal and other alloys. Its oxide is used as a pigment in paints. Some of its compounds are used in medicine [fr. M.L. antimonium, probably fr. Arab.]

an·ti·mu·on (ænti:mjú:ɒn) n. (phys.) an unstable antilepton of the same rest mass as the muon but with opposite charge

an·ti·mu·sic (ænti:mjú:zik) n. 1. dissonance 2. dissonant music

An·ti·Ne·bras·ka Democrats (ænti:nəbrǽskə) a faction within the Democratic party, formed in 1854 and composed of Democrats outraged by the Kansas-Nebraska Act. They helped to create the new Republican party

an·ti·ne·o·plas·tic (ænti:ni:ouplǽstik) adj. inhibiting the growth of malignant cells

an·ti·neu·tri·no (ænti:nu:trí:nou, ænti:nju:trí:nou) n. (phys.) either of two antileptons having the same mass and charge as the neutrino but left-hand orientation of spin

an·ti·neu·tron (ænti:nú:trɒn, ænti:njú:trɒn) n. (phys.) an antibaryon, the antiparticle corresponding to the neutron having the same spin and mass, but differing from the neutron in the nature of its charge distribution

an·ti·node (ǽntinoud) n. (phys.) the point of maximum displacement in a field of wave interference

an·ti·noise (ænti:nɔ́iz) adj. designed to reduce noise, e.g., an antinoise law

an·ti·no·mi·an (æntinóumi:ən) 1. adj. denying that one is bound to obey the moral law 2. n. someone who adhered to the view, esp. put forward during the Reformation, that Christians are justified by faith alone and that salvation does not depend upon obedience to the moral law **an·ti·no·mi·an·ism** n. [fr. M.L. Antinomi fr. Gk anti-. against+nomos, law]

an·tin·o·my (æntínəmi:) pl. **an·tin·o·mies** n. a contradiction between two ideas ‖ self-contradiction or paradox [fr. L. fr. Gk antinomia fr. anti-, against + nomos, law]

an·ti·nov·el (ænti:nɒvəl) n. a work of fiction without a plot or character development customarily found in a novel —**antinovelist** n.

an·ti·nu·cle·ar (ænti:nú:kli:ər) adj. 1. opposed to development of nuclear weapons or power plants 2. (biol.) a tending to react with the nuclei or other components of cells, e.g., in DNA

an·ti·nu·cle·on (ænti:nú:kli:ɒn) n. (phys.) the antiparticle of a nucleon with the same mass but an opposite magnetic movement

an·ti·nu·cle·us (ænti:nú:kli:əs) n. (phys.) hypothetical factor of antimatter

an·ti·ob·scen·i·ty (ænti:əbséniti:) adj. opposing dissemination of obscene material, e.g., antiobscenity laws

An·ti·och (ǽnti:ɒk) (Turk. Antakya) a city (pop. 77,518) in Turkey on the Orontes. The center of ancient trade routes between the Euphrates and the Mediterranean, it was the capital of Seleucid and Roman Syria, famous for its architectural beauty. It was an early Christian missionary center, where Christ's followers were first called Christians (Acts xi, 26). It reached its greatest prosperity in the 4th and 5th cc. declining after Arab capture (638)

Antioch College a nonsectarian, coeducational college founded (1852) in Yellow Springs, Ohio. It was one of the first to adopt the cooperative work-study plan

An·ti·o·chus III (æntáiəkəs) 'the Great' (c. 241–187 B.C.) king of Syria (223–187 B.C.). He strengthened and expanded the Seleucid Empire, but was defeated by the Romans (190 B.C.) and ceded most of Asia Minor

Antiochus IV E·piph·a·nes (ipífəni:z) (c.215–c. 163 B.C.), Seleucid king of Syria (175 –c. 163 B.C.). His attempt to Hellenize the Jews provoked the revolt of the Maccabees (c. 168 B.C.)

Antiochus VII (c. 159–129 B.C.), Seleucid king of Syria (138–129 B.C.). He reconquered Palestine (135–134 B.C.)

an·ti·par·a·sit·ic (ænti:pærəsítik) adj. destructive of parasites

an·ti·par·ti·cle (ænti:pɑrtik'l) n. (phys.) one of a group of fundamental particles that have fleeting existence on the earth. Every electrically charged particle has a counterpart that is identical with it in some respects and opposite to it in others: the masses and spins may be identical but the electric charge opposite (e.g. the electron, constituting ordinary matter, and the positron or antielectron, with identical mass and spin, have charge −e and +e respectively). Neutral particles may have antiparticles or they may be their own antiparticle. When a particle and its antiparticle interact they annihilate each other, producing energy according to the mass-energy equation or in some cases producing lighter particles moving with great speeds

an·ti·pas·to (ænti:pǽstou, ænti:pástou) pl. **an·ti·pas·ti** (ænti:pǽsti:, ænti:pásti:), **an·ti·pas·tos** n. hors d'oeuvre [Ital. = before food]

An·tip·a·ter (æntípətər) (d. 319 B.C.), Macedonian general under Alexander the Great. He was regent in Macedon (334–323 B.C.)

an·ti·pa·thet·ic (ænti:pəθétik) adj. feeling antipathy ‖ arousing antipathy **an·ti·pa·thét·i·cal** adj. [fr. Gk antipathētikos]

an·tip·a·thy (æntípəθi:) pl. **an·tip·a·thies** n. a strong hostility or lack of sympathy [fr. L. antipathia fr. Gk]

an·ti·per·son·nel (ænti:pərsənél) adj. designed to kill or wound enemy troops

an·ti·per·spi·rant (ænti:pərspərənt) n. a preparation applied to the skin to reduce or retard perspiration

an·ti·phlo·gis·tic (ænti:floudʒistik) 1. adj. reducing inflammation 2. n. a medication having this property

An·ti·phon (ǽntifɒn, ǽntifən) (c. 480–411 B.C.), Attic orator and leader of the oligarchic conspiracy (411)

an·ti·phon (ǽntifɒn, ǽntifən) n. a verse or other scriptural passage sung alternately by two parts of a choir liturgically (e.g. the introit, offertory or communion chants of the Mass) ‖ such a passage sung or recited before and after a psalm [fr. M.L. antiphona]

an·tiph·o·nal (æntífən'l) 1. adj. sung as an antiphon 2. n. a book containing a collection of antiphons [O.F.]

an·tiph·o·nar·y (æntífənɛri:) pl. **an·tiph·o·nar·ies** n. a book containing a collection of antiphons ‖ a book containing all the sung parts of the liturgy [fr. M. L. antiphonarius]

an·tiph·o·ny (æntífəni:) pl. **an·tiph·o·nies** n. antiphonal singing [fr. Gk antiphōnos, responsive in sound]

an·ti·po·dal (æntípəd'l) adj. of the antipodes

an·ti·pode (ǽntipoud) n. an exact opposite [back-formation fr. ANTIPODES]

an·tip·o·des (æntípədi:z) pl. n. that part of the earth's surface which is diametrically opposite to one's own position [L. fr. Gk *antipodes*, having feet opposite. standing upside down]

an·ti·pol·lu·tion (æntɪpəlúːʃən) *adj.* designed to reduce or eliminate pollution —**antipollutionist** *n.*

an·ti·pope (ǽntɪpoup) *n.* (*hist.*) a pope elected or claiming papal authority in opposition to the legitimate pope, during the Great Schism 1378–1417

an·ti·pov·er·ty (æntɪpóvərtiː) *adj.* designed to relieve or eliminate poverty

an·ti·pro·ton (æntɪpróutɒn) *n.* (*phys.*) an antibaryon, the antiparticle corresponding to the proton having the same spin and mass but opposite net charge (i.e. −7). The antiproton differs from the proton in that it consists of a shell of negative charge surrounding a negative core

an·ti·psy·chot·ic (æntɪsaɪkótɪk) *adj.* designed to relieve or cure psychosis —**antipsychotic** *n.* a drug that relieves psychotic symptoms

an·ti·quar·i·an (æntɪkwéəriːən) **1.** *adj.* interested in or concerned with the study of ancient times or with ancient objects **2.** *n.* such a person **án·ti·quary** *pl.* **an·ti·quar·ies** *n.* an antiquarian [fr. L. *antiquarius*, ancient]

an·ti·quark (ǽntɪkwɒrk) *n.* a quark in antimatter *Cf* QUARK

an·ti·quat·ed (ǽntɪkweɪtɪd) *adj.* out-of-date, obsolete, ancient [fr. L. *antiquare* (*antiquatus*), to make obsolete]

an·tique (æntíːk) **1.** *adj.* old and precious ‖ belonging to or surviving from distant times, esp. from classical Greece and Rome ‖ antiquated, old-fashioned ‖ (of paper) with a rough surface ‖ (of typefaces) designed so that all lines are uniformly thick **2.** *n.* an object, often beautiful and valuable, surviving from the past **the antique** the classical style of Greek or Roman sculpture and architecture [fr. L. *antiquus*, ancient]

an·tiqu·ing (æntíːkɪŋ) *n.* (*slang or colloq.*) visiting antique shops

an·tiq·ui·ty (æntíkwɪtiː) *pl.* **an·tiq·ui·ties** *n.* the far-distant past ‖ great age ‖ the people who lived in the distant past ‖ (*pl.*) remains of ancient times and culture [F. *antiquité*]

an·ti·ra·cism (æntɪréɪsɪzəm) *n.* being opposed to racial discrimination —**an·ti·ra·cist** *n.*

an·ti·rad·i·cal (æntɪrǽdɪkˈl) *adj.* opposed to political or social radicals or radicalism

an·ti·rheu·mat·ic (æntɪruːmǽtɪk) *adj.* (*med.*) designed to relieve or prevent rheumatism —**antirheumatic** *n.*

an·ti·roll·bar (æntɪróulbɑr) *n.* device in a motor vehicle to aid stability, especially in rounding curves

an·tir·rhi·num (æntɪráɪnəm) *n.* a member of *Antirrhinum*, fam. *Scrophulariaceae*, a genus of flowers of the northern hemisphere [L. fr. Gk *antirrhinon*, resembling a nose]

an·ti·sat·el·lite interceptor (æntɪsǽt'laɪt) *n.* (*mil.*) a satellite interceptor (SAINT); an orbiting weapon system capable of destroying satellites, developed by the U.S.S.R. in 1977 **acronym ASAT**

antisatellite missile (*mil.*) a missile that can destroy a satellite

an·ti·sci·ence (æntɪsáɪəns) *adj.* opposed to scientific methods —**antiscientific** *adj.* —**antiscientism** *v.* —**antiscientist** *n.*

an·ti·scor·bu·tic (æntɪskɔrbjúːtɪk) **1.** *adj.* useful in preventing or curing scurvy **2.** *n.* an agent (e.g. lime juice, fresh vegetables) having this property

an·ti·Sem·ite (æntɪsémaɪt, *Br.* esp. æntɪsíːmaɪt) *n.* someone who is prejudiced against Jews ‖ someone who discriminates against or persecutes Jews **an·ti·se·mit·ic** (æntɪsəmítɪk) *adj.* **an·ti·Sem·i·tism** (æntɪsémɪtɪzəm) *n.*

an·ti·sep·sis (æntɪsépsɪs) *n.* an antiseptic condition ‖ the use of antiseptics [fr. ANTI + Gk *sēpsis*, rot]

an·ti·sep·tic (æntɪséptɪk) **1.** *adj.* counteracting the putrefying effect of bacteria in a wound or cut (cf. ASEPTIC) **2.** *n.* something which does this **an·ti·sep·ti·cize** (æntɪséptɪsaɪz) *pres. part.* **an·ti·sep·ti·ciz·ing** *past* and *past part.* **an·ti·sep·ti·cized** *v.t.* to make antiseptic [fr. ANTI- + Gk *septikos*, rotting]

an·ti·sex, an·ti·sex·u·al (æntɪséks) (æntɪsékʃuːəl) *adj.* opposed to undue emphasis on sexual activity

an·ti·skid (æntɪskíd) *adj.* designed to prevent skidding

an·ti·smog (æntɪsmɒ́g) *adj.* designed to reduce smog, e.g., by reducing causative pollution

an·ti·so·cial (æntɪsóuʃəl) *adj.* contrary to the interests of society ‖ rejecting the laws on which

the security of society depends ‖ disliking or disinclined for social intercourse

an·ti·spas·mod·ic (æntɪspæzmódɪk) *n.* a preventive or remedy for spasms

an·ti·stat·ic (æntɪstǽtɪk) *adj.* designed to reduce or prevent buildup of static electricity —**antistatic** *n.*

An·tis·the·nes (æntísθəniːz) (c. 444–365 B.C.), Greek philosopher, pupil of Socrates, head of the Cynic school, and master of Diogenes. He considered that the supreme good was virtue, which was achieved through contempt of riches, honors, pleasure and the passions

an·tis·tro·phe (æntístrəfiː) *n.* the answer, in a Greek chorus, to the preceding strophe, recited or sung to the same meter and accompanied by a reverse movement of the chorus from left to right **an·ti·stroph·ic** (æntɪstrófɪk) *adj.* [L. fr. Gk]

an·ti·sub·ma·rine rocket (æntɪsʌ́bməriːn) *n.* (*mil.*) homing torpedo launched at sea but traveling principally above water to attack a submerged target directly or by a nuclear depth charge **acronym ASROC**

an·ti·surge mechanism (æntɪsɔ́ːrdʒ) U.S. federal government process that triggers investigation of imports when volume reaches unusual levels

an·ti·tank (æntɪtǽŋk) *adj.* (of a weapon or obstacle) designed for use against tanks

an·ti·the·a·ter or **antitheatre** (æntɪθíːətər) *n.* a radically different form of theater without traditional dramatic conventions

an·tith·e·sis (æntíθɪsɪs) *pl.* **an·tith·e·ses** (æntɪθɪsiːz) *n.* a direct opposite (e.g. 'peace' to 'war', 'beautiful' to 'ugly') ‖ a bringing together, for literary or rhetorical effect, of two contrasting ideas (e.g. 'Peter was a spendthrift, Paul a miser') ‖ the second of two such contrasting ideas ‖ the statement opposed to the thesis of a syllogism [L. fr. Gk]

an·ti·thet·ic (æntɪθétɪk) *adj.* contrasted, containing opposite ideas **an·ti·thét·i·cal** *adj.* [fr. Gk *antithetikos*]

an·ti·throm·bin (æntɪθrómbɪn) *n.* (*med.*) an antienzyme produced in the liver that inhibits thrombin, causing clotting of the blood

an·ti·tox·in (æntɪtóksɪn) *n.* a serum which counteracts the toxin of a particular disease

an·ti·trade (æntɪtréɪd) *adj.* (of winds) blowing in the opposite direction to the trade winds **an·ti·trades** *pl. n.* such winds

an·ti·trust (æntɪtrʌ́st) *adj.* opposed to, or designed to prevent, the concentration of industry and commerce under the control of large combines, e.g. (*Am. hist.*) the Sherman Act of 1890 and later acts

an·ti·type (æntɪtaɪp) *n.* the reality represented by a type or symbol ‖ an opposite type **an·ti·typ·i·cal** (æntɪtípɪk'l) *adj.* [fr. M.L. *antitypus* fr. Gk]

an·ti·u·to·pi·a (æntɪjuːtóupiːə) *n.* dystopia —**antiutopian** *n.*

an·ti·ve·nene (æntɪvəníːn) *n.* an antivenin

an·ti·ven·in (æntɪvénɪn) *n.* an antitoxin, esp. an antidote to snakebite [fr. ANTI + L. *venenum*, poison]

an·ti·vi·ral (æntɪváɪrəl) *adj.* (*med.*) capable of destroying or inhibiting growth of a virus —**antiviral** *n.* a substance destroying a virus

ANTIVOX (*abbr.*) for antivoice-operated transmission, radio communication in which transmission is held back so that messages can be received on another receiver

an·ti·white (æntɪhwáɪt) *adj.* hostile to members of the so-called white race —**antiwhitism** *n.*

an·ti·world (æntɪwɔ́ːrld) *n.* (*particle phys.*) hypothetical world made up of antimatter

ant·ler (ǽntlər) *n.* the branched horn of animals of the deer family **ánt·lered** *adj.* [M.E. *auntol·ier, auntelere* fr. O.F.]

ant lion a member of *Myrmeleon*, a genus of neuropterous insects whose larvae dig traps for ants and other insects

An·to·fa·gas·ta (ɑntɔfagásta) a province (area 47,575 sq. miles, pop. 233,000) of N. Chile ‖ its capital (pop. 149,700), a port exporting nitrate products

An·to·nel·lo da Mes·si·na (ɑntɔnélloˈdamessíːna) (c. 1430–c.1479), Italian painter. Influenced by van Eyck, he introduced Flemish techniques of oil painting into Italy. His San Cassiano altarpiece in Venice (1476) influenced Bellini and the Venetian school

An·to·nes·cu (æntɔnésku), Ion (1882–1946), Rumanian politician and soldier. As prime minister of Rumania (1940–4) he set up a mil-

itary dictatorship (1941) and united with Germany against the U.S.S.R. He was executed as a war criminal (1946)

An·to·ni·nus Pi·us (æntɔnáɪnəspáɪəs) (86–161), Roman emperor (138–161). A patron of the arts and sciences, he instituted legal and social reforms. During his reign the Antonine wall was built in Britain from the Forth to the Clyde

An·to·ny (ǽntɔniː), Mark (Marcus Antonius, c. 82–30 B.C.), Roman general. He was Caesar's lieutenant in Gaul, and a member of the 2nd Triumvirate with Lepidus and Octavian (43 B.C.). He defeated Brutus and Cassius at Philippi (42 B.C.), and received the eastern provinces. Infatuated with Cleopatra, queen of Egypt, he repudiated his wife Octavia and broke with her brother Augustus, who decisively defeated him at Actium (31 B.C.). He committed suicide

an·to·nym (ǽntɔnim) *n.* a word which means the exact contrary of another (cf. SYNONYM) [fr. Gk *antōnumia*]

Antony of Egypt, Anthony of Egypt, St (c. 251–356), Christian hermit in the deserts of Egypt who is regarded as the father of monasticism. Feast: Jan. 17

Antony of Padua, Anthony of Padua, St (c. 1195–1231), Portuguese-born Franciscan theologian. He is invoked by people wanting to get lost property back. Feast: June 13

An·trim (ǽntrim) the northeastern county (area 1,176 sq. miles, pop. 355,716) of Northern Ireland. County town: Belfast

an·trum (ǽntrəm) *pl.* **an·tra** (ǽntrə) *n.* a cavity or sinus in the body, esp. the cavity in the upper jawbone [L. fr. Gk=cave]

Ant·si·ra·ne (ɑntsəránei) *DIEGO SUAREZ

An·tung (úntúŋ) a treaty port (pop. 360,000) on the Korean frontier of Liaotung Province, China, opened to foreign trade in 1907. It has silk, timber and food industries fed by hydroelectric power from the Yalu River

Ant·werp (ǽntwərp) (*Flem.* Antwerpen, *F.* Anvers) one of the world's greatest ports and the main commercial center (pop. 206,800) of Belgium, on the Scheldt estuary, 58 miles from the North Sea (Flushing). Industries: diamond cutting, oil refining, chemicals, glass, engineering, ship repairing. Cathedral (c. 1395–1520), town hall (1561–5). University (1923). The most important commercial and banking center in N. Europe in the 15th and 16th cc., it declined after the closing of the Scheldt by the Treaties of Westphalia (1648). It was revived by Napoleon, as his empire's chief military harbor, and has continued to develop ‖ a Belgian province (area 1,104 sq. miles, pop. 1,519,000)

A·nu·bis (ənjúːbis, ənúːbis) an Egyptian god of the dead, represented as part jackal or dog, part human. In Hellenistic times Anubis was identified with Hermes and appears under the name Hermanubis

A·nu·ra·dha·pu·ra (ʌnuərɑdəpúərə) the ancient ruined capital (5th c. B.C.–8th c. A.D.) of Sri Lanka

an·u·ran (ənjúərən, ənúərən) **1.** *n.* a salientian **2.** *adj.* pertaining to anurans

an·u·rous *adj.* [fr. Gk an, without+oura, tail]

a·nus (éɪnəs) *n.* the lower opening of the rectum [L.]

An·va·ri (ænvári) (Auhad ad-Din, c. 1120–c. 1190), Persian poet famous for his panegyrics and the elegiac 'Tears of Khorasan'

an·vil (ǽnvil) *n.* the iron block on which a smith hammers metal into shape ‖ the incus [O.E. *anfilt*]

anx·i·e·ty (æŋzáiitiː) *pl.* **anx·i·e·ties** *n.* intense dread, apprehension ‖ nagging worry or an instance of this ‖ eagerness, *in his anxiety to win he fell* [fr. L. *anxietas* (*anxietatis*), fear]

anx·ious (ǽŋkʃəs) *adj.* worried and uncertain ‖ causing worry and uncertainty, *running a small workshop can be an anxious business* ‖ eager, *he is anxious to see you* [fr. L. *anxius*, fearful]

an·y (éni) **1.** *adj.* one, one or more, some, *is there any reason for it?*, *we found hardly any mushrooms* ‖ every, whichever you care to choose, *any policeman will tell you* ‖ unlimited, *you can invest any amount* **2.** *sing.* and *pl. pron.* any person or thing, any persons or things, *any who wish to may go* **3.** *adv.* at all, to any degree, *is that any better?*, *his advice did not help me any* [O.E. *ænig*]

an·y·bod·y (éni:bɒdi:, éni:bʌdi:) **1.** *pron.* any person **2.** *n.* a person of importance, *he isn't anybody*

an·y·how (éni:hạu) *adv.* carelessly, in a slap-dash manner ‖ whatever may happen, in any event, *we won't give up, anyhow* ‖ at least, *he is sincere, anyhow, even if he is rather slow*

an·y·one (éni:wʌn) *pron.* any person, anybody

an·y·thing (éni:θiŋ) **1.** *pron.* and *n.* any kind of thing, *she likes anything classical* ‖ something, *is anything amiss?* **2.** *adv.* in any degree or way, *is a frog anything like a toad?*

an·y·way (éni:wẹi) *adv.* anyhow

an·y·where (éni:hwẹər, éni:wẹər) *adv.* in, at or to any place

An·zac (ǽnzæk) **1.** *n.* the Australian and New Zealand Army Corps, in the 1st world war ‖ a member of the corps **2.** *adj.* of this corps

Anzac Day Apr. 25, a public holiday in New Zealand and Australia, commemorating the Anzac landing in Gallipoli on Apr. 25, 1915

An·zus Pact (ǽnzəs) a Pacific defense pact signed in 1951 between Australia, New Zealand and the U.S.A.

A-OK *adj.* or *adv.* without any defect

A·o·mo·ri (ɑɔmɔ́ri:) the chief port (pop. 184,000) of N. Honshu, Japan: fishing, fish canning

A1 (éiwʌn) *adj.* (*naut.*) of a first-class ship (in Lloyd's Register of Ships, for insurance purposes) ‖ (*mil.* and *pop.*) in perfect health ‖ (*pop.*) excellent, being the best of his or its kind, *an A1 cook*

A-110 *THUNDERBOLT

A·o·ran·gi (ɑourángi:) *COOK, MT

a·o·rist (éiərist, éərist) **1.** *n.* (*Gk gram.*) a past tense which does not imply that the action was continued or repeated **2.** *adj.* of or in this tense **a·o·rís·tic** *adj.* fr. Gk *aoristos*, unlimited]

a·or·ta (eiɔ́rtə) *n.* the principal artery through which the blood leaves the heart and passes to the body **a·ór·tal, a·ór·tic** *adjs* [Mod. L. fr. Gk *aortē*, that which is hung]

Aosta *VALLE D'AOSTA

AP Associated Press (U.S. News Agency of world repute)

a·pace (əpéis) *adv.* (*rhet.*) quickly

A·pach·e (əpǽtʃi:) *n.* an Indian (Athapaskan) people of southwestern U.S.A. and New Mexico ‖ a member of this people ‖ a language spoken by Apache Indians

a·pache (əpáʃ,əpǽʃ) *n.* a violent city tough, esp. a Parisian tough [F. fr. APACHE]

Ap·a·lach·ee (æpəlǽtʃi:) *n.* an extinct American Indian people belonging to the Muskogean linguistic stock, formerly living around Apalachee Bay, Florida. They were almost annihilated by the British in the 18th c. and many were sold as slaves ‖ a member of this people ‖ their language [prob. fr. Choctaw *apelachi*, helper]

ap·a·nage, ap·pa·nage (ǽpɔnidʒ) *n.* (*hist.*) the land or income left by a medieval ruler to his younger children ‖ the share that a person receives of any property ‖ a territory that depends upon a more powerful neighbor ‖ a usual adjunct or accompaniment [F.]

APARN (eipárn) (*computer acronym*) for automatic programming and recording, a compiler language developed by Sandia Corporation

a·part (əpárt) **1.** *pred. adj.* separate, *a thing apart* **2.** *adv.* in parts, in pieces, *to tear something apart* ‖ one from the other, *can you tell them apart?* ‖ aside, *he stood apart while talked* **apart from** aside from, *apart from other issues* **to take apart** to separate (something) into its component parts ‖ to be able to be separated in this way [F. *a part*]

a·part·heid (əpártheit,əpárthait) *n.* the racial policy of the government of South Africa, under which white, African, Asiatic and Colored communities live separately, in principle so that each group may develop to the full its own society and culture. It is largely resisted by the segregated non-white communities and by many liberal white South Africans, though not by the Dutch Reformed Church. South Africa left the Commonwealth and is under heavy pressure from other African states on this issue [Afrik, lit. = separateness]

a·part·ment (əpártmənt) *n.* a set of rooms on one floor of a building used as a separate residence ‖ (*esp. Br.*) hired lodgings in a private house ‖ a room in a palace etc. [F. *appartement*]

apartment house a building containing a number of apartments (separate residences)

ap·a·thet·ic (æpəθétik) *adj.* uninterested, unfeeling, showing apathy **ap·a·thét·i·cal·ly** *adv.* [fr. APATHY, infl. by'pathetic']

ap·a·thy (ǽpəθi:) *n.* lack of interest, indifference ‖ lack of emotion [F. *apathie* fr. L. fr. Gk]

ap·a·tite (ǽpətait) *n.* a naturally occurring calcium phosphate containing other radicals, e.g. chloride or fluoride. It is used in fertilizers [fr, Gk *apate*, deceit]

APC (*electr. acronym*) for automatic phase control **1.** a color television receiver circuit used to synchronize with a color-burst signal transmitted **2.** a frequency-control circuit, into which the difference between two frequencies is fed in order to produce the control signal required

APC virus *ADENOVIRUS

ape (eip) **1.** *n.* an anthropoid ape ‖ a person who copies or mimics others in a way which makes him ridiculous **2.** *v.t. pres. part.* **ap·ing** *past* and *past part.* **aped** to copy or mimic in such a way as to make oneself ridiculous **3.** (*adj.*) (*slang*) beyond reason or restraint, *to go ape* [O.E. apa]

a·peak (əpí:k) *adj.* and *adv.* (*naut.*) raised or rising towards the vertical, *oars apeak* [F. *à pic*, to a point]

A·pel·doorn (ápəldɔrn, ápəldourn) a town (pop. 102,000) in the Dutch province of Gelderland: textile and paper industries

ape·like (éiplaik) *adj.* resembling an ape

A·pel·les (əpéli:z) Greek painter (4th c. B.C.). He worked at the court of Macedon. His most famous works were a portrait of Alexander holding a thunderbolt, and an Aphrodite at Cos. No work by him survives, and his fame rests on the witness of Pliny and others. His treatise on painting is also lost

Ap·en·nines (ǽpənainz) a mountain range extending 800 miles along the length of Italy into Sicily, 25 to 85 miles wide and tectonically connected with the Atlas mountains in N. Africa. Highest peak: Monte Corno (9,585 ft). There are 13 important passes and many minor ones. The range contains no valuable minerals and has been largely deforested

a·per·i·ent (əpíəri:ənt) **1.** *adj.* loosening the bowels **2.** *n.* an agent which does this [fr. L. *aperiens* (*aperientis*), opening (i.e. the bowels)]

a·per·i·od·ic (eipiəri:ódik) *adj.* not happening at regular intervals ‖ (*phys.*) of a phenomenon or apparatus which reaches a position of equilibrium without oscillations

a·pé·ri·tif (əperití:f, əpérití:f) *n.* a short alcoholic drink taken before a meal to whet the appetite [F.]

a·per·i·tive (əpéritiv) *adj.* and *n.* aperient [O. F.]

ap·er·ture (ǽpərtʃər, ǽpərtiuər) *n.* an opening, space between two things ‖ an opening in an optical or other kind of instrument that controls the diameter of a beam of emitted or entering radiation or particles, e.g. the opening in a photographic lens (which is usually altered by means of a diaphragm) ‖ the diameter of such an opening, usually measured as it appears from in front of the lens (*RELATIVE APERTURE) [fr. L. *apertura* fr. *aperire*, to open]

aperture card data processing card on which microfilms are mounted

aperture ratio (*photog.*) relative aperture

aperture sight the backsight of a rifle, pierced with a hole, in which the tip of the foresight should appear aligned on the target

ap·er·y (éipəri:) *pl.* **ap·er·ies** *n.* mimicking, foolish aping ‖ a monkey house in a zoo

a·pet·al·ous (eipét'ləs) *adj.* without petals [Mod. L. fr. Gk *a-*, without+*petalon*, leaf]

a·pex (éipeks) *pl.* **a·pex·es, a·pi·ces** (éipisi:z, ǽpisi:z) *n.* the topmost point, climax ‖ the vertex of a triangle or cone [L.]

a·phaer·e·sis, a·pher·e·sis (əférisis) *n.* the dropping of the first letters or syllables from a word, e.g. 'bus' for 'omnibus', 'midships' for 'amidships' [L. fr. Gk *apo-*, away +*hairein*, to take]

a·pha·sia (əféiʒə) *n.* loss of the power to speak, through damage to the brain **a·pha·sic** (əféizik) *n.* and *adj.* [Mod. L. fr. Gk *a-*, without+*-phasia*, speech]

a·phe·lion (əfí:ljən,əfí:li:ən) *pl.* **a·phe·lions, a·phe·lia** (əfí:ljə, əfí:li:ə) *n.* the point furthest from the sun in the orbit of a planet or comet (cf. PERIHELION) [fr. Gk *apo*, from+*helios*, sun

a·phe·li·o·trop·ic (æfi:li:ətrópik) *adj.* (of plants) turning away from the sun

a·phe·li·ot·ro·pism (æfi:li:ótrəpizəm) *n.* [fr. Gk *apo*, from+*hēlios*, sun+*tropikos*, turning]

apheresis *APHAERESIS

aph·e·sis (ǽfisis) *n.* the gradual disappearance of an unaccented vowel at the beginning of a word, e.g. 'special' for 'especial' **a·phet·ic** (əfétik) *adj.* **aph·e·tize** (ǽfitaiz) *pres. part.* **aph-**

e·tiz·ing *past* and *past part.* **aph·e·tized** *v.t.* [Gk=a letting go]

a·phid (éifid, ǽfid) *n.* any of several insects of the superfamily Aphidoidea, order Homoptera, which are destructive to plants and serve as vectors of several viruses [fr. Mod. L. *aphis* (*aphides*)]

Aphid (éifid) U.S.S.R. air-to-air missile (AA-8) for close combat mounted on Flogger aircraft [MiG 23]

a·phis (éifis, ǽfis) *pl.* **a·phi·des** (éifidi:z, ǽfidi:z) *n.* a member of *Aphis*. the type genus of *Aphididae*, order *Homoptera*, a family of small soft-bodied plant lice. They pierce plant tissues and suck the cell sap, causing much damage. Winged and wingless forms occur ‖ an aphid [Mod. L., origin unknown]

a·pho·ni·a (eifóuni:ə) *n.* loss of speech through paralysis of the vocal chords (cf. APHASIA) [Mod. L. fr. Gk *a-*, without+ *phonē*, voice]

aph·o·ny (ǽfəni:) *n.* aphonia

aph·o·rism (ǽfərizəm) *n.* a short, neatly expressed general truth, e.g. 'waste not, want not' **aph·o·ris·mic, aph·o·rís·tic** *adjs.* **aph·o·rís·ti·cal·ly** *adv.* [F. *aphorisme* fr. M.L. fr. Gk]

a·phox·i·dide [$C_6H_{12}N_3OP$] (əfóksidaid) *n.* (*chem.*) compound used against insects, in textile flameproofing, and in cancer therapy

aph·ro·dis·i·ac (æfrədízi:æk) **1.** *adj.* increasing sexual desire **2.** *n.* a drug, food etc. which does this [fr. Gk *aphrodisiakos*]

Aph·ro·di·te (æfrədáiti:) (*Gk mythol.*) the goddess of love, fertility and beauty (corresponding to the Roman Venus) [Gk=foam-born. (She was said to have been born of the sea foam, and was also goddess of seafarers)]

a·phyl·lous (eifíləs) *adj.* not producing leaves, e.g. of a cactus [fr. Mod. L. fr. Gk *a-*, without+*phullon*, leaf]

A·pi·a (ɑpí:ɑ) the capital (pop. 33,800) and chief port of Western Samoa

a·pi·ar·y (éipi:eri:) *pl.* **a·pi·ar·ies** *n.* a place in which a number of beehives are kept, a bee farm [fr. L. *apiarium*]

ap·i·cal (ǽpik'l) *adj.* at or of the peak or apex [fr. L. *apex* (*apicis*), a point]

apices *pl.* of APEX

a·pi·cul·tur·al (eipikʌltʃərəl) *adj.* of or relating to apiculture

a·pi·cul·ture (éipikʌltʃər) *n.* beekeeping **a·pi·cúl·tur·ist** *n.* [fr. L. *apis*, bee +*-cultura*, culture]

a·piece (əpí:s) *adv.* to or for each one of several, as each one's share, *we had two blankets apiece*

A·pis (éipis, ápis) the sacred bull worshipped in the temple of Ptah at Memphis in ancient Egypt [L. fr. Gk fr. Egypt. *Hapi*]

ap·ish (éipiʃ) *adj.* very foolish ‖ copying in a witless, servile way (cf. APELIKE)

APL (*computer*) very concise programming language developed by Kenneth Iverson and useful for complex mathematical computations and array manipulation, widely used for actuarial and economic computations and in various research environments

ap·la·nat·ic (æplənǽtik) *adj.* (*optics*) of a mirror or lens which is free from spherical aberration [fr. Gk *a-*, not+*planatikos*, wandering]

ap·lite (ǽplait) *n.* a close-grained granite [fr. Gk *haploos*, simple]

a·plomb (əplóm) *n.* self-assurance, self-possession [F.]

ap·ne·a, ap·noe·a (æpni:ə, æpní:ə) *n.* (*med.*) cessation of breathing **ap·né·al, ap·nóe·al, ap·né·ic, ap·nóe·ic** *adjs.* [Mod. L. fr. Gk *a-*, without+pnoiē, *pnoia*,pnoē, wind]

a·po·ap·sis (æpouǽpsis) *n.* farthest point in an orbit

a·poc·a·lypse (əpókəlips) *n.* any prophetic writing or utterance, esp. one concerned with the end of the world (*REVELATION) **a·poc·a·lýp·tic, a·poc·a·lýp·ti·cal** *adjs.* [fr. L. fr. Gk *apokalupsis*, an uncovering]

a·po·chro·mat·ic (æpəkroumǽtik) *adj.* of an optic lens, corrected for color distortion, especially along the edges

a·poc·o·pe (əpókəpi:) *n.* dropping the final sound or syllable of a word, e.g. *and* in "thick an' thin" for "thick and thin" [L. fr. Gk *apokopē*, a cutting off]

A·poc·ry·pha (əpókrifə) certain books of the Old Testament not regarded as canonical by Jews or Protestants, as being of uncertain authorship or legendary, but mostly still included in the Roman Catholic canon. Many of them had been included in the Greek Septuagint and were original Greek writings. They are valu-

---

CONCISE PRONUNCIATION KEY: (**a**) æ, cat; ɑ, car; ɔ fawn; ei, snake. (**e**) e, hen; i:, sheep; iə, deer; εə, bear. (**i**) i, fish; ai, tiger; ə:, bird. (**o**) o, ox; au, cow; ou, goat; u, poor; ɔi, royal. (**u**) ʌ, duck; u, bull; u:, goose; ə, bacillus; ju:, cube. x, loch; θ, think; ð, bother; z, Zen; ʒ, corsage; dʒ, savage; ŋ, orangutang; j, yak; ʃ, fish; tʃ, fetch; 'l, rabble; 'n, redden. Complete pronunciation key appears inside front cover.

able to theologians as showing some current Jewish beliefs at the time when Christ was born

A·poc·ry·phal (əpɒ́krifəl) *adj.* concerning the Old Testament Apocrypha ‖ concerning certain writings of New Testament times and later (e.g. the Gospel of Thomas, the Gospel of Nicodemus, the Falling Asleep Of Mary), which the Church at large has never accepted as canonical **a·póc·ry·phal** legendary, untrue, *an amusing but apocryphal story* [fr. L.L. fr. Gk *apokruphos*, hidden]

ap·o·dal (ǽpəd'l) 1. *adj.* relating to an apodan 2. *n.* an apodan

ap·o·dan (ǽpədən) *n.* an animal without feet (e.g. a worm), or a fish without a ventral fin (e.g. an eel) [fr. Gk a-, without+ *pous* (*podos*), foot]

ap·o·deic·tic (æpədáiktik) *adj.* apodictic **ap·o·déic·ti·cal·ly** *adv.*

ap·o·dic·tic (æpədiktik) *adj.* necessarily true, such that its truth can be absolutely proved **ap·o·díc·ti·cal·ly** *adv.* [fr. L. fr. Gk *apodeiktikos.* demonstrating]

a·pod·o·sis (əpɒ́dəsis) *pl.* **a·pod·o·ses** (əpɒ́də·si:z) *n.* the conclusion of a conditional sentence (cf. PROTASIS) [L. fr. Gk *apodōsis*, a giving back]

ap·o·ge·al (æpədʒí:əl) *adj.* apogean

ap·o·ge·an (æpədʒí:ən) *adj.* pertaining to an apogee

ap·o·gee (ǽpədʒi:) *n.* the point in the orbit of the moon, or in that of a planet round the sun, when it is farthest from the earth (opp. PERIGEE) ‖ the farthest or highest point, climax [F. *apogée* fr. L. fr. Gk]

A·pol·li·naire (æpɒli:nɛər), Guillaume (Wilhelm Apollinaris de Kostrowitzki, 1880–1918), French lyric poet stemming from the Romantic tradition of Gérard de Nerval. He was a precursor of the surrealist movement in poetry. 'Alcools' (1913) and 'Calligrammes' (1918) are among his collections of poems, which strongly influenced the development of modern poetry

A·pol·li·nar·i·an (əpɒlinéəri:ən) *adj.* of the heresy originated by Apollinaris

A·pol·li·nar·is (əpɒlinéəris) (c. 313–c. 390), bishop of Laodicea. His heresy, that Christ did not have a human mind, was condemned (375) by Pope Damasus

A·pol·lo (əpɒ́lou) (*Gk mythol.*) Greek god of the arts, prophecy, medicine and light, protector of herds and flocks, son of Zeus and Leto and brother of Artemis. His principal sanctuary and oracle were at Delphi. As god of the sun he is called Phoebus Apollo. He is represented in art as the ideal of young male beauty, e.g. the Apollo Belvedere (4th c. B.C.) in the Vatican Museum

A·pol·lo·dor·us of Damascus (əpɒlədɔ́rəs) Greek architect and town planner of the late 1st c. and early 2nd c. A.D., responsible for Trajan's Forum and the Basilica Ulpia at Rome, and a bridge over the Danube at the Iron Gates

A·pol·lo·ni·us of Rhodes (æpəlóuni:əs) (3rd c. B.C.), Greek epic poet of Alexandria, author of the 'Argonautica'

Apollonius of Ty·a·na (taiéinə) Greek Neo-Pythagorean philosopher of the 1st c. A.D.

Apollo Program a U.S. manned space-flight project sponsored by President John Kennedy in 1961 and designed to land a man on the moon by 1970. This objective was achieved in July 1969 by the crew of Apollo XI, commanded by Neil Armstrong

Apollo-Soyuz test project U.S.-U.S.S.R. docking in orbit to test international docking system, July 17, 1975

A·pol·lyon (əpɒ́ljən) the destroying angel (Revelation 11, 11) ‖ the Devil (particularly in Bunyan's 'Pilgrim's Progress')

a·pol·o·get·ic (əppɒlədʒétik) 1. *adj.* asking pardon, self-excusing ‖ defending by argument, esp. the Christian faith, *an apologetic treatise* 2. *n.* (often *pl.*) a defense, esp. of Christianity **a·pol·o·gét·i·cal** *adj.* [F. *apologétique* fr. L. fr. Gk]

a·pol·o·gia (æpəlóudʒə, æpəlóudʒi:ə) *n.* a writing in defense of actions or beliefs [L. fr. Gk]

a·pol·o·gist (əpɒ́lədʒist) *n.* someone who, by argument, defends a person or point of view, esp. the Christian faith [F. *apologiste* fr. Gk]

a·pol·o·gize (əpɒ́lədʒaiz) *pres. part.* **a·pol·o·giz·ing** *past* and *past part.* **a·pol·o·gized** *v.i.* to say that one is sorry (for something one has done wrong)

ap·o·logue (ǽpəlɒg, ǽpəlɒg) *n.* a little story, generally with a moral [F. fr. L. fr. Gk]

a·pol·o·gy (əpɒ́lədʒi:) *pl.* **a·pol·o·gies** *n.* an expression of regret for wrongdoing ‖ an excuse or defense ‖ (*pop.*) an unworthy substitute, *an apology for a meal* [fr. L. *apologia*, defense against accusation fr. Gk]

ap·o·lune or **ap·o·cyn·thi·on** (ǽpəlu:n) (æpəsínθi:ən) *n.* most distant point in an elliptic orbit around the moon *Cf* APSIS

a·po·mor·phine (æpəmɔ́rfi:n) *n.* (*pharm.*) fast-acting drug used in calming schizophrenics; useful in treating drug overdose

apophthegm *APOTHEGM

a·poph·y·sis (əpɒ́fisis) *pl.* **a·poph·y·ses** (əpɒ́fi·si:z) *n.* a natural excrescence on the surface of a bone [Gk *apophusis*]

ap·o·plec·tic (æpəpléktik) 1. *adj.* suffering or appearing to suffer from apoplexy ‖ liable to apoplexy ‖ causing apoplexy 2. *n.* an apoplectic person **ap·o·pléc·ti·cal** *adj.* [fr. F. *apoplectique* fr. Gk]

ap·o·plex·y (ǽpəpleksi:) *n.* (*med.*) a sudden and total loss of movement and consciousness, commonly called 'a stroke', due to rupture or clotting of one of the blood vessels in the brain (*ANEURYSM) [F. *apoplexie* fr. L. fr. Gk]

ap·o·si·o·pe·sis (æpəsaiəpí:sis) *n.* breaking off in the middle of a sentence, e.g.'And there, lying before me, was— but I can't describe the horror of it' [L. fr. Gk]

a·pos·ta·sy (əpɒ́stəsi:) *pl.* **a·pos·ta·sies** *n.* the public abandoning of a religious faith, esp. Christianity, for another ‖ a similar abandoning of a doctrine or party [fr. L. fr. Gk *apostasia*, renunciation]

a·pos·tate (əpɒ́stit, əpɒ́steit) 1. *n.* someone who abandons his religious faith (or party etc.) for another 2. *adj.* guilty of doing this [F. fr. Gk]

a·pos·ta·tize (əpɒ́stətaiz) *pres. part.* **a·pos·ta·tiz·ing** *past* and *past part.* **a·pos·ta·tized** *v.i.* to become an apostate [L.L. *apostizare*]

a pos·te·ri·o·ri (eipɒsti:əri:ɔ́rai, eipɒsti:əri:óurai) *adj.* and *adv.* referring to principles and judgments based on inductive reasoning ‖ (*logic*) proceeding from effect to cause (opp. A PRIORI) [L. = from what is after]

a·po·stilb (ǽpəstilb) *n.* (*optics*) unit of luminance equal to 1/10,000th lambert. *abbr* **asb** *Cf* CANDELA

A·pos·tle (əpɒ́s'l) *n.* one of the 12 men chosen by Christ to preach the gospel: Peter and his brother Andrew, James and John (sons of Zebedee), Philip, Bartholomew, Thomas, Matthew, James (son of Alphaeus), Thaddaeus (*JUDE), Simon (the Zealot) and Judas Iscariot, replaced by Matthias, together with Barnabas and Paul (the Apostle of the Gentiles), early missionaries **a·pós·tle** the first to introduce Christianity in a pagan land, *Saints Cyril and Methodius were the apostles of the Slavs* ‖ any early or prominent advocate of a belief ‖ a member of the 'council of 12' in the Mormon Church, belonging to the highest order of priesthood, acting chiefly as administrators [O.F. fr. L. fr. Gk *apostolos.* one sent out]

Apostles' Creed a short Christian creed formerly believed to have been drawn up by the Apostles and basically certainly the oldest creed

a·pos·tle·ship (əpɒ́s'lʃip) *n.* the office or work of an apostle

a·pos·to·late (əpɒ́stəlit, əpɒ́stəleit) *n.* the mission of an apostle [fr. L. *apostolare* (*apostolatus*) fr. *apostolus*, apostle]

ap·os·tol·ic (æpəstɒ́lik) *adj.* of, like, or of the time of, the apostles ‖ spreading the Gospel, *the apostolic work of the Church* ‖ papal, *an apostolic letter* **ap·os·tól·i·cal** *adj.* [F. *apostolique* fr. L. fr. Gk]

Apostolic Fathers Christian writers of the 2nd c.: St Clement of Rome, St Ignatius of Antioch, St Barnabas, St Polycarp of Smyrna, the authors of the Didache and The Shepherd of Hermas

Apostolic See the see of Rome, founded by St Peter ‖ a see founded by an Apostle

Apostolic succession the continuous descent, through validly ordained priests and bishops, of the powers and mission entrusted by Christ to the Apostles

a·pos·tro·phe (əpɒ́strəfi:) *n.* a break in writing or speaking in order to address a remark or an exclamation to an imagined person or thing or idea, e.g. 'among their crimes—patriotism, what horrors are done in your name!'—was the burning of the capital' [L. fr. Gk *apostrophē*]

apostrophe *n.* (*printing* or *writing*) a punctuation mark (') marking the omission of a letter or letters, the possessive case, or the plural of let-

ters, e.g. can't (cannot), men's (of men) [F. fr. L. fr. Gk *apostrophos*]

ap·os·troph·ic (æpəstrɒ́fik) *adj.* in the nature of an apostrophe [APOSTROPHE (a break in writing)]

apostrophic *adj.* characterized by use of the apostrophe ‖ being an apostrophe [APOSTROPHE (a sign)]

a·pos·tro·phize (əpɒ́strəfaiz) *pres. part.* **a·pos·tro·phiz·ing** *past* and *past part.* **a·pos·tro·phized** *v.t.* to use an apostrophe in, *to apostrophize a word* ‖ *v.i.* to use an apostrophe [APOSTROPHE (a sign)]

apostrophize *pres. part.* **a·pos·tro·phiz·ing** *past* and *past part.* **a·pos·tro·phized** *v.t.* to address an apostrophe to ‖ *v.i.* to utter an apostrophe [APOSTROPHE (a break in writing)]

apothecaries' measures *MEASURES AND WEIGHTS

apothecaries' weights *MEASURES AND WEIGHTS

a·poth·e·car·y (əpɒ́θikɛri:) *pl.* **a·poth·e·car·ies** *n.* (*old-fash.*) a dispensing chemist, druggist ‖ (*hist.*) someone who prescribed, as well as made up, drugs and medicines [O.F. *apotecaire*]

ap·o·thegm, ap·o·phthegm (ǽpəθem) *n.* a short, instructive maxim, e.g. 'feed a cold, starve a fever' **ap·o·theg·mat·ic, ap·o·phtheg·mat·ic** (æpəθegmǽtik) *adj.* [fr. Gk *apophthegma*]

ap·o·them (ǽpəθem) *n.* a line drawn from the center of a regular polygon perpendicular to any side of it [fr. Gk *apotithemai*, to set down, after *thema*, proposition]

a·poth·e·o·sis (əpɒθi:óusis) *pl.* **a·poth·e·o·ses** (əpɒθi:óusi:z) *n.* deification ‖ glorification **a·poth·e·o·size** (əpɒ́θi:əsaiz, æpəθí:əsaiz) *pres. part.* **a·poth·e·o·siz·ing** *past* and *past part.* **a·poth·e·o·sized** *v.t.* [L. fr. Gk]

ap·pal, ap·pall (əpɔ́l) *pres. part.* **ap·pal·ling, ap·pall·ing** *past* and *past part.* **ap·palled** *v.t.* to shock with terror, horrify ‖ to fill with dismay [O.F. *apalir*, to become or to make pale]

Ap·pa·la·chi·a (æpəléitʃi:ə) *n.* 1. impoverished area in West Virginia, Pennsylvania, etc. 2. (*geol.*) Paleozoic period border of south-eastern North America seaward of the geosyncline — **Appalachian** *adj.*

Ap·pa·la·chian (æpəléitʃən, æpəléitʃi:ən) *adj.* (*geol.*) of a North American mountain-making episode in or about the Pennsylvanian period [fr. APPALACHIAN MTNS]

Appalachian Mtns a mountain system of the eastern U.S.A. extending 1,500 miles from the St Lawrence to Alabama, divided lengthwise by the Great Appalachian Valley, and including a number of ranges of which the chief are (in the north) the White Mtns, the Green Mtns and the Catskills, (in the center) the Alleghenies and the Blue Ridge Mtns, (in the south) the Black and Great Smoky Mtns. The highest peaks are Mt Washington (6,288 ft) in the White Mtns, and Mt Mitchell (6,684 ft) in the Black Mtns. In the north the coal measures of Pennsylvania are among the world's most productive

appal *APPAL

ap·pal·ling (əpɔ́liŋ) *adj.* horrifying ‖ very bad in quality

appanage *APANAGE

ap·pa·ra·tus (æpərǽtəs, æpəréitəs) *pl.* **ap·pa·ra·tus, ap·pa·ra·tus·es** *n.* the equipment (material, tools etc.) needed for a certain task ‖ the equipment used in gymnastics ‖ a group of organs performing a given function in the body ‖ a complex administrative organization, *the apparatus of government* [L.= preparation]

apparatus crit·i·cus (krítikəs) *n.* the notes on a text which give the readings of different manuscripts or editions [L.]

ap·par·el (əpǽrəl) 1. *n.* (*rhet.*) clothes ‖ (*commerce*) clothing ‖ embroidery on certain church vestments 2. *v.t. pres. part.* **ap·par·el·ing,** esp. *Br.* **ap·par·el·ling** *past* and *past part.* **ap·par·eled,** esp. *Br.* **ap·par·elled** (*rhet.*) to clothe, adorn [M.E. *aparail* fr. O.F.]

ap·par·ent (əpǽrənt, əpéərənt) *adj.* seeming, but not real, *his apparent coldness is mere shyness* ‖ real and evident, obvious, *his warm heart was apparent in everything he wrote* ‖ *HEIR APPARENT [O.F. *aparant*, visible]

apparent expansion (*phys.*) the observed expansion of a liquid which is less than its true expansion because of the expansion of the containing vessel

ap·par·ent·ly (əpǽrəntli:, əpéərəntli:) *adv.* seemingly ‖ clearly, obviously

ap·pa·ri·tion (æpəríʃən) *n.* an appearance, in particular of a being from another world ‖ an

CONCISE PRONUNCIATION KEY: **(a)** æ, c*a*t; ɑ, c*ar*; ɔ, f*aw*n; ei, sn*a*ke. **(e)** e, h*e*n; i:, sh*ee*p; iə, d*ee*r; ɛə, b*ea*r. **(i)** i, f*i*sh; ai, t*i*ger; ə:, b*i*rd. **(o)** o, *o*x; au, c*ow*; ou, g*oa*t; u, p*oo*r; ɔi, r*oy*al. **(u)** ʌ, d*u*ck; u, b*u*ll; u:, g*oo*se; ə, b*a*cillus; ju:, c*u*be. x, lo*ch*; θ, *th*ink; ð, bo*th*er; z, *Z*en; ʒ, cor*s*age; dʒ, sava*g*e; ŋ, oranguta*ng*; j, *y*ak; ʃ, *fi*sh; tʃ, fe*tch*; 'l, rabb*le*; 'n, redd*en.* Complete pronunciation key appears inside front cover.

appearing, coming into sight ‖ the being or thing that appears, a ghost ‖ (*astron.*) the first appearance of a star, planet etc. after obscurity or the duration of its visibility [F.]

ap·peal (əpí:l) *v.t.* (*law*) to call upon a higher authority to review (the decision of a lower), *to appeal a case* ‖ *v.i.* to address oneself to a higher authority, *to appeal to a higher court* ‖ to turn for an opinion or judgment, *I appeal to you: was it unreasonable?* ‖ to make an earnest request ‖ to ask for voluntary contributions, *to appeal on behalf of the blind* ‖ to be pleasing, *it appeals to all readers* **to appeal to the country** (*Br.*) to dissolve parliament and hold a general election [M.E. *apelen* fr. O.F.]

appeal *n.* the act of appealing ‖ the right to appeal to a higher authority ‖ the power to arouse or stimulate desire, *consumer appeal, sex appeal* [O.F. *apel*]

ap·peal·a·ble (əpí:ləb'l) *adj.* (*law*, of a case) that can be referred to a higher court

ap·peal·ing (əpí:liŋ) *adj.* moving, endearing ‖ beseeching ‖ pleasing

ap·pear (əpíər) *v.i.* to come in sight ‖ to be in sight ‖ to come on the scene, arrive ‖ to present oneself, e.g. in court or before a committee ‖ to be present for a very short time, *to appear at a party* ‖ to act or perform in public ‖ to be published ‖ to be found, *the motif appears on pots from many sites* ‖ to be first found, *French epic poetry appears in the 11th c.* ‖ to seem or look what a person or thing is or is not, *she appears most charming* (and she is), *he appears generous* (but is mean) ‖ to be evident or probable, *it appears from the evidence that he was drunk* [O.F. *apareir*]

ap·pear·ance (əpíərəns) *n.* the act of appearing ‖ looks ‖ dress and general bearing ‖ (*pl.*) outward or superficial evidence, *appearances are against him* ‖ (*pl.*) outward show hiding the real conditions, *for the sake of appearances* ‖ (in Plato) the transitory or changeable, as opposed to the eternal or essential **to all appearances** so far as one can see or judge **to make an appearance** to put in an appearance ‖ to appear in public **to put in an appearance** to be present for only a short time (e.g. at a meeting) [O. F. *aparance*]

ap·peas·a·ble (əpí:zəb'i) *adj.* capable of being appeased [O.F. *apaisable*]

ap·pease (əpí:z) *pres. part.* **ap·peas·ing** *past and past part.* **ap·peased** *v.t.* to calm or pacify, esp. by making concessions to ‖ to satisfy, *to appease one's hunger* [O. F. *apaisier*]

ap·pease·ment (əpí:zmənt) *n.* the act of appeasing or being appeased [O.F. *apaisement*]

ap·pel·lant (əpélənt) 1. *adj.* (*law*) appealing to a higher court 2. *n.* someone who makes an appeal to a higher court [F.]

ap·pel·late (əpélit) *adj.* (*law*) hearing appeals, *appellate courts* [fr. L. *appellare* (*appellatus*), to call to]

ap·pel·la·tion (æpəléiʃən) *n.* a descriptive addition to or in place of a proper name, e.g. 'Richard Cœur de Lion' [F.]

ap·pel·la·tive (əpélətiv) 1. *n.* (*gram.*) a common as opposed to a proper noun 1. *adj.* relating to a common noun [fr. L. *appellativus*]

ap·pend (əpénd) *v.t.* to attach, add, esp. as an appendix [fr. L. *appendere*, to hang on]

ap·pend·age (əpéndidʒ) *n.* (*biol.*) an external organ, e.g. a tail ‖ an adjunct or accompaniment, *royalty and all its ceremonial appendages* [fr. APPEND]

ap·pend·ant (əpéndənt) *adj.* (*Br., law*) held as a subsidiary right [F.]

ap·pen·dec·to·my (æpəndéktəmi) *n.* the surgical operation of removing the appendix [fr. APPENDIX+Gk *ektome-*, a cutting out]

ap·pen·di·cec·to·my (əpəndiséktəmi) *n.* (*Br.*) an appendectomy

ap·pen·di·ci·tis (əpendisáitis) *n.* an inflammation of the appendix, characterized by severe abdominal pain [Mod. L. fr. *appendix* (*appendicis*), appendage+*-itis*, inflammation]

ap·pen·dix (əpéndiks) *pl.* **ap·pen·dix·es, ap·pen·di·ces** (əpéndisi:z) *n.* an addition to a document or book (generally at the end) which supplements or illustrates the text ‖ the vermiform part of the intestinal canal in the lower right abdomen [L.= appendage]

Ap·pen·zell (ápentsel) a mountainous German-speaking canton in N.E. Switzerland. It has two divisions: to the north, Ausser Rhoden (area 101 sq. miles, pop. 47,600, capital: Herisau), largely Protestant, and to the south, Inner Rhoden (area 61 sq. miles, pop. 12,844, capital: Appenzell), largely Roman Catholic

ap·per·ceive (æpərsí:v) *pres. part.* **ap·per·ceiv·ing** *past* and *past part.* **ap·per·ceived** *v.t.* to take in (new ideas or knowledge) and understand in the light of what is already known [O.F. *aperceveir*]

apperceiving mass the apperceptive mass

ap·per·cep·tion (æpərsépʃən) *n.* conscious perception, consciousness of perception ‖ the act or process of apperceiv*ing* [fr. F. *aperception*]

apperception mass the apperceptive mass

ap·per·cep·tive (æpərséptiv) *adj.* relating to apperception

apperceptive mass (*psychol.*) the body of ideas or experience called on in the grasping of a new idea

ap·per·tain (æpərtéin) *v.i.* to belong by right or custom, *the execution of justice appertains to the state* ‖ to be appropriate, relate, *prudence appertains to moral actions* [O.F. *apartenir*]

ap·pe·tence (æpitəns) *n.* (esp. *psychol.*) strong natural desire, inclination ‖ (*chem.*) an affinity or tendency to combine [F.]

ap·pe·ten·cy (æpitənsi:) *pl.* **ap·pe·ten·cies** *n.* appetence [fr. L. *appetentia*]

ap·pe·tite (æpitait) *n.* a natural desire to satisfy hunger ‖ some other natural desire of the body, *sexual appetite* ‖ a strong desire which demands gratification, *appetite for power* [O.F. *appetit*]

ap·pet·i·tive (æpétitiv, æpitaitiv) *adj.* of, relating to or characterized by appetite [F. *appetitif, appetitive* fr. L.]

ap·pe·tiz·er (æpitaizər) *n.* a short drink or snack that whets the appetite

ap·pe·tiz·ing (æpitáiziŋ) *adj.* arousing appetite [fr. F. *appétissant*]

Ap·pi·an (æpi:ən) (2nd c.), Greek historian, author of a history of Rome

Appian Way (Via Appia) the road from Rome to Brindisi begun (c. 312 B.C.) by Appius Claudius

ap·plaud (əplɔ́d) *v.i.* to show approval by clapping or cheering ‖ *v.t.* to demonstrate approval of by clapping or cheering ‖ (*rhet.*) to declare one's approval of [fr. L. *applaudere*, to clap hands]

ap·plause (əplɔ́z) *n.* approval shown by clapping or cheering ‖ (*rhet.*) praise [fr. L. *applausus* fr. *applaudere*, to clap hands]

ap·ple (æp'l) *n. Pyrus malus*, fam. *Rosaceae*, a tree of the temperate regions bearing roundish, firm, juicy fruit ‖ the fruit (a pome) of this tree, which can be eaten raw or cooked, and can be dried, or made into preserves and drinks etc. [O. E. *oeppel*]

apple brandy spirit distilled from cider (fermented apple juice)

ap·ple·cart (æp'lkɑrt) *n.* (in the phrase) **to upset the** (or **his** etc.) **applecart** to reduce a person's plans or schemes to confusion

apple green a light, clear green

ap·ple·jack (æp'ldʒæk) *n.* apple brandy

apple of discord a cause of dispute [from the golden apple for which the three goddesses Hera, Athene and Aphrodite contended]

apple of one's eye a person or possession greatly cherished [fr. APPLE in older sense of 'pupil' of the eye. (The pupil was thought to be a solid body)]

ap·ple-pie order (æp'lpai) perfectly neat and tidy condition

ap·ple-pol·ish (æp'lpɒliʃ) *v.t.* to try to win the approval of (someone) esp. by a combination of flattery and servility

ap·ple-sauce (æp'lsɔs) *n.* apples stewed to pulp and sweetened ‖ (*Am., old-fash.*) nonsense

Ap·ple·seed (æp'lsi:d), Johnny (John Chapman, 1774–1845), U.S. pioneer. For over 40 years he wandered in the Ohio, Indiana, W. Pennsylvania area cultivating apple orchards

Ap·ple·ton (æp'ltən), Sir Edward Victor (1892–1965), English physicist. Nobel prize in physics (1947) for researches into the upper atmosphere

Appleton layer a layer occurring in the F region of the ionosphere [discovered by Sir Edward *Appleton*]

ap·pli·ance (əpláiəns) *n.* a piece of apparatus for a particular use ‖ a fitting that can be put on a machine or tool to adapt it to a particular use ‖ a mechanical or electrical device using a power supply ‖ the act of applying

ap·pli·ca·bil·i·ty (æplikəbíliti:) *n.* the state or quality of being applicable

ap·pli·ca·ble (æplikəb'l) *adj.* capable of being applied, intended to apply ‖ suitable, appropriate [fr. L. *applicare*, to attach to]

ap·pli·cant (æplikənt) *n.* someone making an application [fr. L. *applicans* (*applicantis*) fr. *applicare*, to attach to]

ap·pli·ca·tion (æplikéiʃən) *n.* the act of applying ‖ a putting on (e.g. of a poultice ointments etc.) to a part of the body ‖ a putting into effect of a general rule or principle ‖ a turning to practical use, *the application of ballistic theory to aircraft design* ‖ a using of a force or a method, *iron is softened by the application of heat* ‖ a using as a name or description, *application of 'rhetorical' to this expression is questionable* ‖ concentrated effort, diligence in work or duty ‖ a request, esp. to be considered as a candidate, made in person or in writing **on application** to anyone making the appropriate request, *available on application* ‖ (*computer*) the system or problem to which a computer is applied. Reference is often made to an application as being either of the computational type, wherein arithmetic computations predominate, or of the data processing type, wherein data handling operations predominate [F.]

ap·plied (əpláid) *adj.* turned or related to practical use (cf. PURE)

applied epistemology (*computer*) the science of utilizing computer programs or models to simulate perception, learning, selection, categorization, etc., in retrieval of data; and of machine design to perform these tasks

applied magnetism *MAGNETIC BUBBLE

ap·pli·qué (æpli:kéi) *n.* a fabric decoration made by cutting out different materials and attaching them on another ‖ a comparable process in metalwork [F. *appliqué*, applied]

ap·ply (əplái) *pres. part.* **ap·ply·ing** *past* and *past part.* **ap·plied** *v.t.* to put (something on another thing), *to apply polish to brasswork* ‖ to bring into use or action, *to apply a tourniquet* ‖ to devote so as to make specified use, *to apply one's experience to a situation* ‖ to use (a word or expression) in order to name or describe ‖ to devote attentively, *apply yourself to your books* ‖ to use for a particular purpose, *the profits are applied to the building fund* ‖ *v.i.* to pertain, *this rule applies only to children* ‖ to make a request, *to apply for a job* [O.F. *aplier*, to attach to]

ap·point (əpɔ́int) *v.t.* to select for an office or position ‖ to set, choose (a date, time, place etc.)

ap·point·ed *adj.* decided or determined beforehand, *the appointed time* ‖ (combined with 'well-', 'ill-' etc.) fitted out, *a well-appointed ship* [O.F. *apointer*, prepare, decide]

ap·point·ment (əpɔ́intmənt) *n.* a prearranged meeting, date ‖ a selecting for an office or position, *the appointment of a secretary* ‖ this office or position ‖ (*pl., commerce*) useful and decorative fittings, equipment to work **to keep an appointment** to be present at the right time and place for a prearranged meeting **to make an appointment** to agree on a time and place to meet [O.F. *apointment*, an appointing]

Ap·po·mat·tox (æpəmǽtɒks) a village in Virginia, U.S.A., where Lee and the Confederate army surrendered (Apr. 9, 1865) to Grant and the Union army, thus ending the American Civil War

Ap·po·nyi (ópponji), Count Albert (1846–1933), Hungarian statesman. He spent most of his career in opposition. He represented Hungary at the League of Nations (1924–5)

ap·por·tion (əpɔ́rʃən, əpóurʃən) *v.t.* to share out, divide into shares **ap·por·tion·ment** *n.* an apportioning or being apportioned ‖ the determination of the number of members of the U.S. House of Representatives on the proportional basis of State population to total U.S. population [O.F. *apportionner*]

ap·po·site (æpəzit) *adj.* neatly appropriate [fr. L. *apponere* (*appositus*), to put near]

ap·po·si·tion (æpəzíʃən) *n.* an application, addition, e.g. of a seal or signature to a document ‖ the addition to a word of another word or words having the same grammatical function, by way of explanation or qualification, e.g. the words between commas in 'his health, never robust, grew worse' **in apposition** in the grammatical relationship of words so used **ap·po·si·tion·al** *adj.* [fr. L. *appositio* (*appositionis*), a putting near]

ap·prais·al (əpréiz'l) *n.* the act of appraising ‖ a judgment formed by appraising

ap·praise (əpréiz) *pres. part.* **ap·prais·ing** *past* and *past part.* **ap·praised** *v.t.* to judge the quality of ‖ (*Am.=Br.* value) to give an expert opinion on the value or cost of [O.F. *apreiser*]

CONCISE PRONUNCIATION KEY: **(a)** æ, c*a*t; ɑ, c*a*r; ɔ f*a*wn; ei, sn*a*ke. **(e)** e, h*e*n; i:, sh*ee*p; iə, d*ee*r; ɛə, b*ea*r. **(i)** i, f*i*sh; ai, t*i*ger; əː, b*i*rd. **(o)** o, *o*x; au, c*ow*; ou, g*oa*t; u, p*oo*r; ɔi, r*oy*al. **(u)** ʌ, d*u*ck; u, b*u*ll; u:, g*oo*se; ə, b*a*cillus; ju:, c*u*be. x, lo*ch*; θ, *th*ink; δ, bo*th*er; z, *Z*en; ʒ, corsa*ge*; dʒ, sava*ge*; ŋ, ora*ng*utan*g*; j, *y*ak; ʃ, *f*ish; tʃ, fe*tch*; 'l, rabb*le*; 'n, redd*en*.   Complete pronunciation key appears inside front cover.

ap·prais·er (əpréizər) n. (Am.=Br. valuer) someone whose profession is to estimate the market value of something

ap·pre·cia·ble (əprí:ʃəb'l, əprí:ʃi:əb'l) adj. large or important enough to be taken into account or noticed **ap·pre·cia·bly** adv. noticeably [fr. L. appreciare, to price]

ap·pre·ci·ate (əprí:ʃi:eit) pres. part. **ap·pre·ci·at·ing** past and past part. **ap·pre·ci·at·ed** v.t. to perceive the nature and quality of, to appreciate someone's point of view ‖ to enjoy intelligently ‖ to be grateful for ‖ to make an estimate of, to appreciate a military situation ‖ to raise in value, to appreciate the reserves of a business ‖ v.i. to rise in value [fr. L. appretiare (appretiatus), to prize]

ap·pre·ci·a·tion (əprí:ʃi:éiʃən) n. understanding of the nature and quality of something ‖ intelligent enjoyment ‖ gratitude ‖ an increase in money value ‖ a critical estimate or judgment [F.]

ap·pre·cia·tive (əprí:ʃətiv, əprí:ʃi:ətiv) adj. showing enjoyment or gratitude

ap·pre·ci·a·to·ry (əprí:ʃətɔri:, əprí:ʃi:ətɔri:, əprí:ʃi:ətɔuri:) adj. appreciative

ap·pre·hend (æprihénd) v.t. to arrest, capture ‖ to become aware of, the mind apprehends the outside world through the senses ‖ to understand ‖ to expect with anxiety [F. appréhender]

ap·pre·hen·si·ble (æprihénsəb'l) adj. capable of being apprehended by the mind or senses [fr. L. apprehensibilis]

ap·pre·hen·sion (æprihénʃən) n. anxious expectation ‖ capture, arrest ‖ mental perception, understanding [fr. L. apprehensio (apprehensionis), seizure]

ap·pre·hen·sive (æprihénsiv) adj. anxious ‖ relating to or capable of apprehending, apprehensive powers [fr. M.L. apprehensivus fr. apprehendere, to seize]

ap·pren·tice (əpréntis) 1. n. someone learning a craft or trade from an employer to whom he is bound by legal agreement for a specified period (*INDENTURE) ‖ a beginner. 2. adj. concerning apprenticeship ‖ made or done by a learner, an apprentice play 3. v.t. pres. part. **ap·pren·tic·ing** past and past part. **ap·pren·ticed** to bind as an apprentice **ap·prén·tice·ship** n. the state or period of being an apprentice [M.E. aprentis fr. O.F.]

ap·prise, ap·prize (əpráiz) pres. part. **ap·pris·ing, ap·priz·ing** past and past part. **ap·prised, ap·prized** v.t. (rhet.) to inform [fr. F. apprendre (appris, apprise), to teach, inform]

ap·proach (əpróutʃ) 1. v.i. to come close or closer or go near or nearer ‖ v.t. to come close to ‖ to seek a way of dealing with, to approach a problem ‖ to resemble somewhat, approximate to, his passion for collecting approaches madness ‖ to address oneself to, to approach the bank for a loan 2. n. the act of coming close or closer, or of going near or nearer ‖ a way by which one approaches ‖ the stretch of railroad track before an area controlled by a signal ‖ the descent of an aircraft towards the landing area ‖ a method of beginning ‖ (pl.) efforts to establish personal or business relations ‖ (pl., mil.) trenches or other means of approaching fortifications **ap·proach·a·bíl·i·ty** n. **ap·próach·a·ble** adj. able to be approached ‖ (of a superior) easy to talk to, friendly [O. F. aprochier]

ap·pro·ba·tion (æprəbéiʃən) n. approval [F.]

ap·pro·ba·tive (æprəbeitiv, əpróubətiv) adj. approving, favorable [F.]

ap·pro·ba·to·ry (æprəbətɔri:, æprəbətɔuri:, əpróubətɔri:, əpróubətɔuri:) adj. expressing approbation

ap·pro·pri·ate (əpróupri:eit) 1. v.t. pres. part. **ap·pro·pri·at·ing** past and past part. **ap·pro·pri·at·ed** to take for one's own property, the régime appropriated foreign industrial undertakings ‖ to steal ‖ to set aside for a special purpose, to appropriate profits to a reserve fund 2. adj. (əpróupri:it) suitable [fr. L. appropriare (appropriatus), to annex]

ap·pro·pri·a·tion (əproupri:éiʃən) n. the act of appropriating ‖ a sum of money devoted to a special purpose [fr. L. appropriatio (appropriationis)]

ap·pro·pri·a·tive (əpróu..ieitiv, əpróupri:ətiv) adj. relating to appropriation

ap·pro·pri·a·tor (əpróupri:eitər) n. someone who appropriates

ap·prov·al (əprú:vəl) n. favorable opinion or judgment ‖ official recognition or sanction **on** approval (of goods ordered) to be sent back if not satisfactory

ap·prove (əprú:v) pres. part. **ap·prov·ing** past and past part. **ap·proved** v.i. to give or have a favorable opinion or judgment ‖ v.t. to give official agreement or sanction to ‖ to be favorably disposed towards, consider to be right, good, advantageous etc. [O.F. aprover]

approved school (Br.) a school for boys or girls who need to be removed from morally dangerous companions or circumstances, or who have been guilty of offenses but should not be dealt with as criminals

approved securities securities described in paragraph 1.25 of the CFTC regulations, authorized for the investment of customers' moneys: "... obligations of the United States, in general obligations of any State or any political subdivision thereof, and in obligations fully guaranteed as to principal and interest by the United States. . . ."

ap·prox·i·mal (əpróksəml) adj. (anat.) touching, in contact with one another [fr. L. approximare, to come close to]

ap·prox·i·mate (əpróksəmeit) 1. v. pres. part. **ap·prox·i·mat·ing** past and past part. **ap·prox·i·mat·ed** v.t. to come close to, be almost the same as, the figure approximates my guess ‖ to give as roughly correct, you can approximate the population figures ‖ v.i. (with 'to') to be almost the same 2. adj. (əpróksəmit) unverified but not far from being correct or exact, approximate weight **ap·prox·i·má·tion** n. the act or process of approximating ‖ the result of this process ‖ (math.) a method of solving problems by a progressive approach to the exact solution ‖ (math. and phys.) a method of calculation which first ascribes to all interrelated measured quantities no less a degree of error than that of the least precisely measured one **ap·prox·i·ma·tive** (əpróksəmeitiv) adj. [fr. L. approximare (approximatus), to come close, be almost the same]

Appuleius *APULEIUS

APRA (Alianza Popular Revolucionaria Americana), a Peruvian political party founded (1924) by V.R. Haya de la Torre

a·près-ski (apreiskí:) (Fr.) 1. n. the social event following skiing 2. adj. après-ski of the clothing worn after skiing

ap·sis (æpsis) n. (astron.) one of the two points in the orbit of a celestial body nearest and furthest from the center of attraction Cf HIGHER APSIS, PERIAPSIS

Ap star (astron.) spectral type-A star whose specter shows peculiarities in chemical composition

APT 1. (computer acronym) for automatic programming tool computer program, used for machine tool operations; developed by Sperry Rand Corporation 2. (acronym) for advanced passenger train, with speeds to 150 mph

Ap·u·le·ius, Ap·pu·le·ius (əpjulí:əs), Lucius (2nd c. A.D.), Latin prose writer, author of the 'Metamorphoses or Golden Ass'

A·pu·lia (əpjú:ljə) (Ital. Puglia) a region (area 7,442 sq. miles, pop. 3,828,300) occupying the southeast promontory (or 'heel') of Italy, formed by the provinces of Bari, Brindisi, Foggia, Lecce and Ionio. It consists of a fertile coastal plain and a dry chalk plateau, with a coastline of 800 miles. It is the driest region in Italy, with hot summers and moderate winters. Products: grain, almonds, figs, cherries, tobacco, cotton, wine and olive oil. Minerals: bauxite, saltpeter

a·pur·te·nance (əpə̀:rt'nəns) n. an accessory, adjunct **ap·púr·te·nant** adj. [A.F. apurtenance, a belonging]

a·pri·cot (éiprikɒt, æprikɒt) n. Prunus armeniaca, fam. Rosaceae, a fruit tree, native to China ‖ its round, yellowishorange fruit (a drupe) ‖ the color of this fruit [fr. Port. albricoque and F. abricot]

A·pril (éiprəl) n. (abbr. Apr.) the fourth month of the year, having 30 days [O.F. avrill]

April fool the victim of a practical joke played on April Fools' Day ‖ the joke itself

April Fools' Day Apr. 1, when, traditionally, people play practical jokes

a pri·o·ri (eipraiɔ́rai, eipraióurai) adj. and adv. referring to principles and judgments valid without reference to sense impressions ‖ (logic) proceeding from cause to effect, deductive (opp. A POSTERIORI) ‖ (loosely) at first reaction, offhand, an a priori verdict [L.=from what is before]

a·pron (éiprən) n. a protection for the clothes, generally made of cloth, leather or canvas, worn in front, and tied around the waist ‖ the symbolic or conventional apron worn as part of the official dress of a bishop or freemason ‖ anything like an apron either in shape or in purpose, e.g. a guard over the moving or vulnerable parts of a machine ‖ (theater) the part of the stage in front of the curtain ‖ the open space in front of the hangars on an airfield **tied to his mother's (wife's) apron strings** completely dependent on or dominated by his mother (wife) [O.F. naperon, a cloth ('a napron' was separated as 'an apron')]

apron stage a stage which projects into the auditorium

ap·ro·pos (æprəpou, æprəpóu) 1. adj. to the point 2. adv. by the way ‖ fitly, suitably as regards time or circumstances 3. prep. with reference to **apropos of** with reference to [F. à, to + propos, purpose]

apse (æps) n. (in early Christian churches) the semicircular altar end of the church ‖ (in later, esp. Gothic, churches) the semicircular or many-sided end to the chancel, aisles or transepts [fr. L. apsis (apsidis), arch fr. Gk]

ap·si·dal (æpsid'l) adj. of or shaped like an apse ‖ (astron.) relating to the apsides (*APSIS)

ap·sis (æpsis) pl. **ap·si·des** (æpsidi:z, æpsáidi:z) n. the point on an orbit furthest from the center of attraction, higher apsis, or nearest to it, lower apsis. Thus for a planet the apsides are the aphelion and the perihelion, and for the moon the apogee and the perigee. The line of apsides joins these two points, constituting the principal axis of the orbit [L.=arch fr. Gk]

apt (æpt) adj. to the point, cleverly suited or timed, an apt retort ‖ liable or likely, the engine is apt to stall ‖ quick to understand or learn, an apt pupil [fr. L. aptus, fitted]

ap·ter·ous (æptərəs) adj. (zool.) wingless, esp. of insects of the suborder Aptera, e.g. lice and springtails ‖ (bot.) having no membranous expansions on stems, petioles. fruits or seeds [fr. Gk apteros fr. a, without + pteron, wing]

ap·ter·yx (æptəriks) n. a New Zealand flightless bird, order Apterygiformes, about the size of a goose [fr. Gk a, without + pterux, wing]

ap·ti·tude (æptitu:d, æptitju:d) n. a natural talent, bent, musical aptitude ‖ ability to learn easily and quickly, an aptitude for languages ‖ (psychol.) a set of factors which can be assessed and which show what occupation a person is probably best suited to [F.]

'A·qa·ba, A·ka·ba (ǽkəbə, á:kəbə) the only seaport (pop. 10,000) of Jordan, at the head of the Gulf of 'Aqaba, the northeastern arm of the Red Sea

aq·ua·cul·ture or **aq·ui·cul·ture** (ǽkwəkʌltʃər) n. mass production of sea foods, e.g., lobster, shrimp, carp, clams Cf MARICULTURE

aq·ua·farm (ǽkwəfarm) n. small artificially made body of water for breeding aquatic forms of life

aq·ua for·tis (ǽkwəfɔrtis, á:kwəfɔrtis) n. concentrated nitric acid [L.=strong water]

aq·ua·lung (ǽkwəlʌŋ, á:kwəlʌŋ) n. a device, consisting essentially of a face mask and a cylinder of compressed air, which enables the user to breathe under water for some time and dive to considerable depths [fr. L. aqua, water + LUNG]

aq·ua·ma·rine (ǽkwəmərí:n, a:kwəmərí:n) 1. n. a semiprecious blue-green stone, a variety of beryl ‖ this color 2. adj. of this color [fr. L. aqua marina, water of the sea]

aq·ua·naut (ǽkwənɔt) n. 1. one who lives underwater, usually in an underwater shelter 2. an underwater researcher

aq·ua·plane (ǽkwəplein, á:kwəplein) 1. n. a board towed behind a speedboat to carry a rider who stands up on it as it skims the surface 2. v.i. pres. part. **aq·ua·plan·ing** past and past part. **aq·ua·planed** to ride on such a board [fr. L. aqua, water + PLANE]

aq·ua re·gi·a (ǽkwərí:dʒi:ə, á:kwərí:dʒi:ə) n. a corrosive mixture of concentrated hydrochloric and nitric acids in the ratio of 3 or 4 to 1. It attacks such metals as gold and platinum (the noble metals), forming soluble chlorides [L.=royal water]

aq·ua·relle (ækwərél, a:kwərél) n. a painting in watercolors [F.]

A·quar·i·an (əkwéəri:ən) *AGE OF AQUARIUS

a·quar·i·um (əkwéəri:əm) pl. **a·quar·i·ums**, **a·quar·i·a** (əkwéəri:ə) n. a tank (often of glass) or pond in which fishes, aquatic plants and animals are kept alive ‖ a place where these aquatic collections are kept for study and exhibition [L.=reservoir]

A·quar·i·us (əkwέəri:əs) a central constellation ‖ the 11th sign of the zodiac, represented as a water carrier

A·quas·ca·lien·tes (ɑkwɑskɑljéntes) a spa (pop. 127,000) of N. central Mexico in the Western Sierra Madre, at 6,200 ft, with hot springs. Baroque cathedral

aq·ua·tel (ǽkwətel) n. marina where houseboats and other live-on craft are moored

a·quat·ic (əkwǽtik,əkwɔ́tik) **1.** adj. living or growing in or near water ‖ taking place on or in water, aquatic sports **2.** n. an aquatic plant or animal ‖ (pl.) water sports [F. aquatique]

aq·ua·tint (ǽkwətint, úkwɔtint) n. a method of etching esp. a copper plate, which is grained by covering it with powdered resin or a resinous suspension. The plate is immersed in nitric acid (aqua fortis), those parts of the design which are to appear as white being protected from the acid by coating of varnish. Varying tones are produced by etching and varnishing by turns. The process is particularly suitable for reproducing watercolors ‖ a print from a plate so produced [F. aquatinte]

aq·ua vi·tae (ǽkwəváiti:, úkwəváiti:) n. a liqueur fortified with alcohol, often colorless, made from wine, cider etc. [L.=water of life]

aq·ue·duct (ǽkwidʌkt) n. a channel constructed to carry a supply of water by gravity from one place to another, esp. one carried on arches across a valley or river ‖ (anat.) a small canal or passage [fr. L. aquaeductus]

a·que·ous (éikwi:əs, ǽkwi:əs) adj. watery, like water, an aqueous fluid ‖ made with or from water, an aqueous solution ‖ (geol.) made by the action of water, an aqueous deposit [fr. L. aqua, water]

aqueous humor, Br. **aqueous humour** the liquid in the space between the cornea and the crystalline lens of the eye

aq·ui·fer (ǽkwəfər) n. (geol.) **1.** an underground layer of earth or stone that contains water **2.** a permeable rock holding water **3.** any subsurface area capable of yielding economically significant amounts of water

Aq·ui·la (ǽkwilə) (early 2nd c.), the author of a Greek version of the Old Testament surviving only in fragments

aq·ui·le·gia (ækwilí:dʒə, ækwilí:dʒi:ə) n. a member of Aquilegia, fam. Ranunculaceae, a genus of elegant plants with spurred flowers [Mod. L., etym. doubtful]

A·qui·le·ia (ɑkwi:léjə) a former city of the Roman Empire at the head of the Adriatic. Founded in 181 B.C., it was an important trade and art center, but was destroyed by Attila (452 A.D.)

aq·ui·line (ǽkwilain) adj. of or like an eagle ‖ (esp. of a nose) hooked like the beak of an eagle [fr. L. aquilinus]

Aquinas *THOMAS AQUINAS

A·qui·nist (əkwáinist) n. a specialist in the study of St Thomas Aquinas, a Thomist

Aquino (əkí:nou), Corazon (1933–), Philippines president (1986–) who succeeded Ferdinand Marcos when he fled the country under accusations of election fraud. She is the widow of Benigno Aquino, a Marcos opponent assassinated upon his return to the Philippines in 1983. She worked at economic and political reform

Aq·ui·taine (ǽkwitein) a former duchy in S.W. France, known as Guyenne after the 13th c. The Roman Aquitania comprised that part of Gaul lying between the Pyrenees and the Garonne. It became an English possession (1152) upon the marriage of Eleanor of Aquitaine to Henry II. It was regained by France at the end of the Hundred Years' War (1337–1453)

Ar·ab (ǽrəb) **1.** n. one of the Semitic people inhabiting the Arabian peninsula (*ARABIA) ‖ a member of the Beduin tribes in the north of this area and east of Palestine ‖ a member of any Arab-speaking people ‖ a horse of a breed from Arabia famous for speed, elegance and spirit **2.** adj. of, relating to or characteristic of the Arabs ‖ of or relating to an Arab horse [F. Arabe]

Ar·ab Boy·cott (ǽrəb) agreement among members of the Arab League to boycott foreign enterprises that do business with Israel, 1973

ar·a·besque (ærəbésk) **1.** n. a complex intertwining design of geometric patterns, used decoratively in early Islamic architecture ‖ an elaborate or fantastic interlaced design, which may introduce natural objects and human figures ‖ (ballet) a position in which the dancer

leans forward on one leg, the arm on the same side held forward horizontally, the other leg and arm held backward horizontally ‖ (mus.) a title sometimes given to a short ornate composition **2.** adj. showing an arabesque design [F. arabesque fr. Ital.]

A·ra·bi·a (əréibi:ə) a great peninsula (area 1,200,000 sq. miles) of W. Asia in the Middle East, bounded on the west by the Gulf of 'Aqaba and the Red Sea, on the east by the Persian Gulf, on the south by the Gulf of Aden and the Indian Ocean, and on the north by the frontiers of Iraq and Jordan. Politically Arabia consists of Saudi Arabia, Yemen, the People's Democratic Republic of Yemen, Oman, Kuwait, Bahrain, Qatar and the United Arab Emirates. HISTORY. The early history of Arabia was dominated by three kingdoms, the Minaean (c. 1200–650 B.C.), the Sabaean (c. 930–115 B.C.), and the Himyarite (115 B.C.–525 A.D.). The Romans attempted unsuccessfully (24 B.C.) to conquer Arabia in order to control the spice trade. The Abyssinians invaded S. Arabia and established a kingdom (340–378 A.D. and 525–575 A.D.). The south then came under Persian rule (c. 579), while the north was influenced by Christian culture from Byzantium and Syria. The rise of Islam changed the history of Arabia. Mecca and Medina became the spiritual centers of the Arab world. Mohammed's successors, the Orthodox caliphs, unified Arabia into a single Islamic state (632–661), and conquered Syria, Lebanon, Palestine, Iraq, Egypt and Persia. But the Omayyad caliphate (661–750) moved its capital to Damascus, and the Abbasids (750–1258) moved it to Baghdad, causing Arabia to diminish in importance. The Mamelukes (1250–1516) and the Ottoman Turks (1516–24) claimed or held parts of Arabia. The Portuguese seized Oman (1508) but were expelled (c. 1650). Britain secured Aden (1839). Revolt against Turkish rule was begun (18th c.) by the Wahhabis and brought to success by ibn Saud with the creation (1932) of Saudi Arabia. The Federation of S. Arabia was absorbed in the Peoples' Republic of South Yemen (later the People's Democratic Republic of Yemen). Oil production on the Persian Gulf coast, begun in the 1940s, has greatly increased Arabia's economic importance and made public welfare improvements possible

A·ra·bi·an (əréibi:ən) **1.** adj. native to, or belonging to, Arabia **2.** n. an Arab (native of Arabia)

Arabian Desert the desert of E. Egypt, between the Nile and the Red Sea, merging with the Nubian Desert in the south. Parts are rocky mountain areas (rising to 7,000 ft). There are oil and phosphate deposits (*SAHARA)

Arabian Nights the popular title of the 'Thousand and One Nights', Arabian stories of adventure, humor and love, of the 14th and 15th cc.

Arabian Sea part of the Indian Ocean, between Arabia and India

Ar·a·bic (ǽrəbik) **1.** adj. of the Arabs or their language **2.** n. the Arabic language [O.F.]

Arabic language a member of the western branch of the Semitic family of languages. It is spoken by about 60 million people and is the language of Iraq, Syria, Lebanon, Jordan, Saudi Arabia, Yemen, the United Arab Republic, Kuwait, Libya, Tunisia, Algeria, Morocco and the Sudan. It is also spoken in Israel and Zanzibar. It is the religious and literary language of Islam

Arabic numerals the figures 1, 2, 3 etc., in common use, as opposed to the Roman numerals I, II, III etc. The system was invented in India, passed through Persia to the Arabs, and was introduced in Europe in the 10th c.

Ar·a·bin or **ar·a·bic acid** (ǽrəbin) n. (chem.) magnesium and potassium salts derived from acacia gum

A·ra·bi Pa·sha (ærúbi:pǽʃə) (c. 1841–1911), Egyptian revolutionary. As Egyptian undersecretary for war he attempted to rebel against Anglo-French financial control (1882) and was banished to Ceylon

Ar·ab·ist (ǽrəbist) n. a specialist in the Arabic language or Arabic literature

ar·a·ble (ǽrəb'l) **1.** adj. (of land) plowed or suited to plowing ‖ produced from plowland, arable crops **2.** n. arable land, plowland [fr. L. arabilis]

Arab League the League of Arab States, a confederation organized in 1945. The founder-members were Iraq, Jordan, Lebanon, Saudi Arabia, Egypt, Syria and Yemen. They were

joined by Libya (1953), the Sudan (1956), Morocco and Tunisia (1958), Kuwait (1961) and Algeria (1962). The Palestine Liberation Organization was admitted in 1976. The league has maintained an economic boycott of Israel since the Arab-Israeli war (1948–9). Its members voted (1979) to suspend Egypt's membership indefinitely

Arab States, League of *ARAB LEAGUE

a·rach·nid (ərǽknid) **1.** n. a member of Arachnida, a class of arthropods, including scorpions, spiders, ticks and mites. They are distinguished from insects by having four pairs of walking legs and by having the head and thorax in a single prosoma **2.** adj. pertaining to arachnids **a·rách·ni·dan** n. and adj. [Mod. L. fr. Gk arachnē, spider]

a·rach·noid (ərǽknɔid) **1.** adj. like a cobweb (applied to a thin membrane between two other membranes surrounding the brain and spinal cord (*MENINGES) and to plants covered with long fibers or hairs which give the appearance of a cobweb) ‖ belonging to, or of, the arachnid class of animals **2.** n. an arachnid ‖ the arachnoid membrane **a·rach·noid·al** (ærəknɔid'l) adj. [fr. Mod. L. fr. Gk arachnoeidēs, like a spider or cobweb]

A·rad (ɑrúd) a town (pop. 112,000) in Rumania, on the Mures River, a communications, industrial and trading center

A·ra·fat (úrəfɑt), Yasser (1929–), Palestinian statesman, leader of the anti-Zionist al-Fatah from 1968 and president of the Palestine Liberation Organization from 1969

A·ra·fu·ra Sea (ærəfúərɑ) a sea (800 miles long, 350 miles wide) between N. Australia and the East Indies. With the Timor Sea it connects the Coral Sea with the Indian Ocean

A·ra·go (ærægou), Dominique François Jean (1786–1853), French scientist and politician whose main contributions were to astronomy, magnetism and optics

Ar·a·gon (ǽrəgon, ǽrəgɒn) a region of N.E. Spain in the fertile Ebro valley and the central plateau, forming the modern provinces of Huesca, Teruel and Saragossa. Agricultural products: cereals, root vegetables, olives, wine. Livestock: sheep, cattle. Industries: textiles, some mining (copper, sulfur). A Christian kingdom from the 11th c., it expanded (12th–15th cc.) to possess Roussillon, Provence, Sardinia, Sicily, and Naples. Its union with Castile (1479) led to the formation of the Spanish state

A·ra·gon (ærægɔ̃), Louis (1897–1982) French poet, novelist and essayist, one of the founders of the surrealist movement. He was one of the principal poets of the French Resistance (1940–4)

a·rag·o·nite (ərǽgənait) n. a mineral consisting of orthorhombic crystals of calcium carbonate (cf. CALCITE) [after Aragon, in Spain]

A·ra·kan (ɑrɑkán) the northern coastal region of Burma, on the Bay of Bengal: fishing

Arakan Yo·ma (jóumɑ) a mountain range in Burma rising to 10,000 ft, stretching north-south from Manipur to Cape Negrais

A·raks (ɑrǽks) (Pers. and Turk. Aras, ancient Araxes) a river (635 miles long) flowing east from Turkish Armenia to the Caspian Sea. It forms the border of the U.S.S.R. with E. Turkey and Iran

Ar·al Sea (ǽrəl, úrəl) a lake (300 miles long and up to 170 miles wide, area nearly 25,000 sq. miles) partly in Uzbekistan and partly in Kazakhstan, U.S.S.R., fed by the Rivers Amu-Darya and Sir-Darya. It is shallow and has a high salt content

Ar·am (έərəm, ǽrəm) ancient Syria

Ar·a·mae·an, Ar·a·me·an (ærəmí:ən) **1.** n. an inhabitant of ancient Syria and Mesopotamia ‖ the Aramaic language **2.** adj. of the ancient Syrians or their language

Ar·a·ma·ic (ærəméiik) n. a group of northwest Semitic languages spoken in Biblical times. It included the language of Palestine spoken by Christ

A·ram·bu·ru (ɑrɑmbú:ru:), Pedro Eugenio (1903–70), Argentinian general and president (1955–8). He was murdered

A·ran·da (ɑrúndɑ), Pedro Pablo Abarca y Bolea, count (1718–98), Spanish diplomat and minister of Charles III

ar·a·ne·id·an (ærəní:idən) **1.** n. a spider of the class Araneida **2.** adj. pertaining to the araneidans [fr. Mod. L. fr. L. aranea, spider]

A·rany (órɒnj), János (1817–82) Hungarian scholar, ballad writer and epic poet

A·rap·a·ho, A·rap·a·hoe (ərǽpəhou) *pl.* **A·rap·a·ho, A·rap·a·hos, A·rap·a·hoe, A·rap·a·hoes** *n.* an Indian tribe belonging to the Algonquian family. The northern Arapaho were given a reservation in Wyoming in 1876 and the southern Arapaho one in Oklahoma in 1867 ‖ a member of this tribe ‖ their language

ar·a·pai·ma (ærəpáimə) *n.* a very large South American edible river fish, up to 15 ft in length [Port. fr. Tupi]

Ar·a·rat (ǽrəræt) a volcanic mass (height 16,873 ft) in E. Turkey (Armenia) and Iran, the legendary resting place of Noah's Ark

A·rau·can (ərɔ́kən,əráukən) *n.* the language of the Araucanians ‖ an Araucanian

Ar·au·ca·ni·an (ærɔkéiniːən, əraukúniːən) **1.** *n.* one of a South American Indian people who formerly lived in central Chile ‖ the language spoken by the Araucanians, Araucan **2.** *adj.* of or pertaining to the Araucanians or their language

ar·au·car·i·a (ærɔkéəriːə) *n.* a member of *Araucaria*, a genus of tall coniferous trees of the southern hemisphere, e.g. the monkey puzzle [Mod. L. fr. Span. *Araucano*, Araucanian]

A·rav·al·li Hills (ərávəliː) an arid range (average height 1,500 ft) in Rajasthan, N.W. India, reaching 5,650 ft (Mount Abu): limestone, marble

Ar·a·wak (ǽrəwɑk) **1.** *n.* an Indian people of northeastern South America ‖ a member of this people **2.** *adj.* of or pertaining to the Arawaks **Ar·a·wák·an** *adj.* belonging to the linguistic family of the Arawaks

ar·ba·lest (árbəlist) *n.* a medieval crossbow, which shot a heavy, often metal, bolt with great force ‖ an early nautical instrument for measuring the altitude of the sun or of a star [O.F. *arbaleste*]

ar·ba·list (árbəlist) *n.* an arbalest

Ar·be·la, Battle of (ɑrbíːlə) the decisive victory (331 B.C.) of Alexander the Great over Darius III. The battle overthrew the Persian Empire and opened the way for Alexander's eastward expansion

Ar·benz Guz·mán (árbensguːsmán), Jacobo (1913–71), president of Guatemala (Mar. 1951–June 1954). His agrarian reform program led to an army coup d'etat in 1954. Arbenz resigned and was exiled

ar·bi·ter (árbitər) *n.* someone who decides what will or should be accepted ‖ someone who controls, *man is not the arbiter of his destiny* (*computer*) unit that sets the sequence of inputs from various terminals [L.=witness, judge]

ar·bi·trage (arbitráːʒ) *n.* (*commerce*) the buying of goods in one place in order to sell them immediately in another at a higher price ‖ (*commerce*) the buying of bills of exchange or stocks and shares for the same purpose [F.]

ar·bi·tral (árbitrəl) *adj.* belonging or appropriate to an arbiter [F.]

ar·bi·tra·ment, ar·bit·re·ment (arbítrəmənt) *n.* the decision of an arbiter [O. F. *arbitrement*]

ar·bi·trar·i·ly (árbitreriliː, arbitréəriliː) *adv.* in an arbitrary manner

ar·bi·trar·i·ness (árbitreriːnis) *n.* the quality or state of being arbitrary

ar·bi·trar·y (árbitreriː) *adj.* arrived at without allowing argument or objection ‖ resulting from personal inclination entirely ‖ decided by chance or whim ‖ prejudiced, not based on reasoned examination ‖ absolute, despotic [fr. L. *arbitrarius* fr. *arbiter*, judge]

ar·bi·trate (árbitreit) *pres. part.* **ar·bi·trat·ing** *past* and *past part.* **ar·bi·trat·ed** *v.i.* to decide a dispute by arbitration ‖ to act as an arbitrator ‖ *v.t.* to settle (a dispute) by arbitration ‖ to judge (a dispute) as an arbitrator [fr. L. *arbitrari (arbitratus)*, to judge]

ar·bi·tra·tion (arbitréiʃən) *n.* the settling of a dispute by an arbitrator or arbitrators [O.F.]

arbitration of exchange the fixing of the rate of exchange between two countries or agencies

ar·bi·tra·tive (árbitreitiv) *adj.* of or relating to arbitration

ar·bi·tra·tor (árbitreitər) *n.* an impartial judge, or one of a number, whose decision both parties to a dispute agree to accept [O.F. *arbitrateur*]

arbitrement *ARBITRAMENT

ar·bo (árbou) *adj.* (*med.*) pertaining to diseases spread by anthropods, e.g., by mosquitoes

ar·bor, Br. ar·bour (árbər) *n.* a pleasant shady spot in a garden or wood, either natural or made by training foliage over a framework [O.F. *herbier*, a grassy lawn]

arbor *n.* the main shaft of a machine ‖ a device that holds cutting tools on a lathe [L. = tree]

Arbor Day (in most states of the U.S.A. and in some other countries) a day in spring fixed each year for planting trees

ar·bo·re·al (orbóriːəl, orbóuriːəl) *adj.* living in trees ‖ of or relating to trees [fr. L. *arboreus*, of a tree]

ar·bo·res·cence (orbərésəns) *n.* a branching, treelike formation (e.g. in some minerals)

ar·bo·res·cent (orbərésənt) *adj.* somewhat like a tree in appearance ‖ (*archit.*) branched [fr. L. *arborescens (arborescentis)*, growing like a tree]

ar·bo·re·tum (orbəríːtəm) *pl.* **ar·bo·re·tums, ar·bo·re·ta** (orbəríːtə) *n.* a collection of trees, usually of rare species, for display [L.]

ar·bo·ri·cul·ture (árbərikʌltʃər) *n.* the cultivation of trees and shrubs [fr. L. *arbor, tree+cultura*, cultivation]

ar·bo·ri·za·tion (orbəraizéiʃən, *Br.* esp. orbəraizéiʃən) *n.* the formation of a natural pattern or design which resembles the branches of a tree, e.g. by frost on a windowpane or in crystallization ‖ (*anat.*) the branchlike arrangement of dendrites around adjacent nerve cells [fr. L. *arbor*, tree]

ar·bo·vi·rus (orbərváirəs) *n.* (*med.*) one of some 200 RNA viruses transmitted by bloodsucking anthropods, e.g., mosquitoes, causing encephalitis, yellow fever, dengue

ar·bor·vi·tae (árbərváitiː) *n.* a tree or shrub of the genus *Thuja. T. plicata*, the giant arborvitae, is native to the forests of western U.S.A. It is frequent from coastal California to coastal British Columbia. *T. occidentans*, an American tree, yields soft and brittle wood which is unusually durable and is used for shingles. Its cedar-leaf oil, obtained by distillation, is used in perfumery and as a fixative. *T. orientals* is the Chinese or oriental arbovitae **arbor vitae** (*anat.*) an arborization, e.g. the white matter of the brain in cross section [L.=tree of life]

arbour *ARBOR

ar·bu·tus (arbjúːtəs) *n.* a member of *Arbutus*, fam. *Ericaceae*, a genus of evergreen shrubs or trees with red peeling bark. *A. unedo*, the strawberry tree, is cultivated for ornament, having white flowers and red strawberrylike fruits. *A. Menziesii*, the tall madrona laurel, yields a brown dye from the bark [L.]

arc (ɑrk) *n.* part of the circumference of a circle or part of any other curve ‖ (*astron.*) part of the circle above the horizon (diurnal arc), or below the horizon (nocturnal arc), through which the sun or any other heavenly body appears to pass ‖ (*phys.*) an electric arc, a sustained luminous electrical discharge between separated electrodes. The current is carried across the gap by the vapor of the electrode or by ionized gas (*CARBON ARC, *MERCURY ARC) [O.F.]

ar·cade (arkéid) *n.* a roofed-in passage, often with arches on one or both sides, and sometimes with shops or stalls ‖ (*archit.*) a row of arches, either let into a wall, *blind arcade* or supporting an upper structure **ar·cad·ed** *adj.* [F.]

Ar·ca·di·a (arkéidiːə) a mountainous part of the central Peloponnesus, Greece. After Theocritus, Arcadia symbolized the happy life and loves of shepherds. **Ar·cá·di·an** *adj.*

Ar·ca·di·us (arkéidiːəs) (c 377–408) first emperor of the Byzantine Empire (395–408), son of Theodosius I. Under his weak rule, Greece was attacked by the Visigoths. St John Chrysostom was banished (404)

Ar·ca·dy (árkədiː) Arcadia as symbolizing the happy life of shepherds

ar·ca·na (arkéinə) *pl. n.* secret things, esp. the objects of alchemical research [pl. of L. *arcanum*]

ar·cane (arkéin) *adj.* mysterious, secret [fr. L. *arcanus*]

Ar·ces·i·la·us (arsesiléiəs) (c. 316–241 B.C.), Greek philosopher, founder of the New Academy

arch (artʃ) *n.* a curved construction built to bridge a gap and support weight above it, or used ornamentally ‖ a curve or curved shape [O.F. *arche*]

arch *v.t.* to span with, or as though with, an arch ‖ to shape with or like an arch ‖ *v.i.* to serve or appear as an arch **to arch one's eyebrows** to show surprise or disapproval by raising one's eyebrows [O. F. *archer*]

arch *adj.* supreme of its kind (usually pejorative when not compounded), *an arch villain, archpriest* ‖ consciously roguish or playful, *an arch smile* [O.E. *arce-* fr. L. fr. Gk *archos*, ruler]

Archaean *ARCHEAN

ar·chae·o·log·i·cal, ar·che·o·log·i·cal (arkiːəlódʒikˡ) *adj.* of or pertaining to archaeology [fr. Gk *archaiologikos*, pertaining to antiquity]

ar·chae·ol·o·gist, ar·che·ol·o·gist (arkiːólədʒist) *n.* a specialist in archaeology

ar·chae·ol·o·gy, ar·che·ol·o·gy (arkiːólədʒiː) *n.* the study of prehistory and of ancient periods of history, based on the examination of their physical remains ‖ the body of knowledge obtained from this [fr. Gk *archaiologia* fr. *archaios*, ancient + *logos*, discourse]

ar·chae·op·ter·yx (arkiːóptəriks) *n.* the oldest known fossil bird, having a lizardlike tail, teeth, and well-developed wings [fr. Gk *archaios, ancient+pterux*, wing]

Archaeozoic *ARCHEOZOIC

ar·cha·ic (arkéiik) *adj.* belonging to ancient times ‖ fallen into disuse **ar·chá·i·cal·ly** *adv.* [fr. Gk *archaikos*, primitive]

ar·cha·ism (árkiːizəm, árkeiizəm) *n.* a word or phrase that has long passed out of the language ‖ (in the arts generally) imitation of the ancient **ar·cha·is·tic** *adj.* [fr. Gk *archaismos*, a copy of the ancient]

ar·cha·ize (árkiːaiz, árkeiaiz) *pres. part.* **ar·cha·iz·ing** *past* and *past part.* **ar·cha·ized** *v.t.* to make archaistic ‖ *v.i.* to imitate language or style that has long passed out of use [fr. Gk *archaizein*, to copy the ancient]

Arch·an·gel (árkeindʒəl) (Arkhangelsk) the chief White Sea trading and fishing port (pop. 398,000) of the U.S.S.R. on the Dvina estuary, R.S.F.S.R. It is the terminal of the Northern Sea Route to the Pacific, and is ice-free May–Oct.

arch·an·gel (árkeindʒəl) *n.* a member of an order of angels (*ANGEL) **arch·an·gel·ic** (arkændʒélik) *adj.* [fr. L. fr. Gk *archangelos*]

arch·bish·op (artʃbíʃəp) *n.* a bishop who has a certain limited authority and precedence in dignity over other bishops in an ecclesiastical province, a metropolitan ‖ (in the Eastern Churches) a bishop who is directly beneath a patriarch but who has no suffragans

arch·bish·op·ric (artʃbíʃəprik) *n.* the diocese, or office, of an archbishop

arch·dea·con (artʃdíːkən) *n.* (*Anglican Churches*) a dignitary charged with matters of discipline on behalf of the bishop of a diocese ‖ (*Roman Catholic Church*) an honorary official ‖ (*Eastern Churches*, where the archdeacon is often still a deacon and not a priest) a church officer with administrative duties **arch·déa·con·ate** *n.* the jurisdiction of an archdeacon **arch·déa·con·ry** *pl.* **arch·déa·con·ries** *n.* the office of an archdeacon, or his residence [O.E. *archediacon*, chief deacon fr. L. fr. Gk]

arch·di·oc·e·san (artʃdaiósis'n) *adj.* of or relating to an archdiocese

arch·di·o·cese (artʃdáiəsis, artʃdáiəsiːs) *n.* the diocese or see of an archbishop

arch·du·cal (artʃdúːkˡl, artʃdjúːkˡl) *adj.* of an archduke or an archduchy

arch·duch·ess (artʃdʌtʃis) *n.* the wife of an archduke ‖ (*hist.*) the daughter of the Austrian emperor [fr. F. *archiduchesse*]

arch·duch·y (artʃdʌtʃiː) *pl.* **arch·duch·ies** *n.* the territory of an archduke or an archduchess [fr. F. *archiduché*]

arch·duke (artʃdúːk, artʃdjúːk) *n.* (*hist.*) a son of the Austrian emperor [O. F. *archeduc*]

Ar·che·an, Ar·chae·an (arkíːən) *adj.* (*geol.*) of the oldest known rocks in the earth's crust [fr. Gk *archaios*, ancient]

ar·che·go·ni·al (arkigóuniːəl) an archegonium

ar·che·go·ni·ate (arkigóuniːit) **1.** *adj.* having archegonia **2.** *n.* a plant having archegonia

ar·che·go·ni·um (arkigóuniːəm) *pl.* **ar·che·go·ni·a** (arkigóuniːə) *n.* (*bot.*) the female or egg-producing structure in the gametophyte generation of lower plants, e.g algae, liverworts, mosses [Mod L. fr. Gk *archegonos*, the first of a race]

arch·en·e·my (artʃénəmiː) *n.* **arch·en·e·mies** *n.* the direst enemy ‖ (*rhet.*) Satan, the devil

ar·chen·ter·on (arkéntərɔn) *n.* the cavity formed in the gastrula stage of many embryos [Mod. L. fr. *archi-*, primitive, primary + Gk *enteron*, intestine]

archeological *ARCHAEOLOGICAL
archeologist *ARCHAEOLOGIST
archeology *ARCHAEOLOGY

Ar·che·o·zo·ic, Ar·chae·o·zo·ic (arkiːəzóuik) *adj.* of the earliest era in geological history, characterized by the Archean rocks (*GEOLOGICAL TIME) the Archeozoic this era

arch·er (ártʃər) *n.* someone who shoots with a bow and arrow **the Archer** the constellation Sagittarius (*ZODIAC) [O. F. *archier*]

archer fish *Toxotes jaculator,* a fish found in East Indian fresh waters. It catches insects by aiming a jet of water at them as they rest on plants above the water, so that they fall in

ar·cher·y (ártʃəri) *n.* the sport of shooting arrows from varying distances up to 100 yds at a target 48 ins in diameter, marked with rings of different values. Long-distance shooting, up to 220 yds, at a small target, is called clout shooting ‖ the equipment necessary for the sport. Bows are made of supple wood (usually yew) and a linen or hemp string, arrows of deal or pine, or both may be metal [O. F. *archerie*]

ar·che·typ·al (ɑrkitáip'l) *adj.* pertaining to an archetype

ar·che·type (árkitaip) *n.* the model from which later examples are developed, or to which they conform, a prototype ‖ the assumed exemplar or perfect model which inferior examples may resemble but never equal ‖ (*psychol.*) one of the inherited unconscious patterns which Jung held to constitute the fundamental structure of the mind. Archetypes can be observed only through their effects, e.g. images recurring in dreams, behavior patterns etc. [fr. L. *archetypum* fr. Gk]

arch·fiend (ɑrtʃfíːnd) *n.* Satan, the devil ‖ a person of devilish wickedness

ar·chi·di·ac·o·nal (ɑrki:daiǽkən'l) *adj.* pertaining to an archdeacon [fr. L. *archidiaconus*]

ar·chi·e·pis·co·pal (ɑrki:ipískəp'l) *adj.* of or pertaining to an archbishop [fr. L. L. *archiepiscopus*]

ar·chi·e·pis·co·pate (ɑrki:ipískəpit, ɑrki:ipískəpeit) *n.* the office, function, or term of office of an archbishop [fr. L.L. *archiepiscopus*]

ar·chil (ártʃil) *n.* a deep purple dye obtained from lichens, sometimes used in dyeing wool and silk ‖ a member of *Roccella* or *Lecanora,* genera of lichens yielding this dye [M.E. *orchell* fr. O.F. *orchel* fr. Ital.]

Ar·chil·o·cus (ɑrkíləkəs) (7th c. B.C.), Greek lyric and satirical poet of Paros

ar·chi·man·drite (ɑrkimǽndrait) *n.* (*Eastern Churches*) the head of a large monastery ‖ (*Eastern Churches*) an honorary title applied, sometimes irregularly, to both monks and secular clergy [fr. M.L. *archimandrita* fr. Gk]

Ar·chi·me·des (ɑrkimí:di:z) (287–212 B.C.), mathematician of Syracuse. He discovered the ratio of the radius of a circle to its circumference and the formulas for the surface and volume of a cylinder and of a sphere, and demonstrated the hydrostatic law known as Archimedes' Principle. He invented machines which greatly helped in the defense of Syracuse against the Romans

Archimedes' principle a law stating that when a body is immersed in a fluid its loss of weight is equal to the weight of the fluid displaced

Archimedes' screw a pump consisting of a spiral screw revolving inside a closefitting cylinder. It is canted at an angle, with the lower end immersed in water. Rotating the screw causes water to be raised to the level of the higher end

ar·chi·pe·lag·ic (ɑrkəpəlǽdʒik, ɑrtʃəpəlǽdʒik) *adj.* of or constituting an archipelago

ar·chi·pel·a·go (ɑrkəpéləgou, ɑrtʃəpéləgou) *pl.* **ar·chi·pel·a·goes, ar·chi·pel·a·gos** *n.* a group of islands ‖ a sea with many islands **the Archipelago** the Aegean Sea, studded with islands, to which the name was first given [fr. Ital. *arcipelago* fr. Gk *archos,* original + *pelagos,* sea]

Ar·chi·pen·ko (ɑrkəpénkou), Alexander (1887–1964), Russian sculptor, painter and designer. He lived in the U.S.A. after 1923. He was one of the chief representatives of cubism

ar·chi·tect (árkitekt) *n.* someone whose profession is to design buildings etc., and to see that his plans are correctly followed by the builders [F. *architecte* fr. L. fr. Gk]

ar·chi·tec·ton·ic (ɑrkitektónik) *adj.* relating to architecture as a technique, architectural ‖ constructive and orderly ‖ (*philos.*) relating to the systematic arrangement of knowledge **ar·chi·tec·tón·ics** *n.* the art or science of architecture ‖ structural order achieved in building and design, *the architectonics of the new civic center* ‖ (*philos.*) the arrangement of knowledge in a systematic manner [fr. L. *architectonicus* fr. Gk]

ar·chi·tec·tur·al (ɑrkitéktʃərəl) *adj.* of or pertaining to architecture ‖ used in architecture

ar·chi·tec·ture (árkitektʃər) *n.* the art, science or profession of designing buildings ‖ buildings with reference to their style, *Romanesque architecture, the architecture of Frank Lloyd Wright* [F.]

ar·chi·trave (árkitreiv) *n.* (*archit.*) the lowest part of the entablature, resting on supporting columns [F. fr. Ital.]

ar·chives (árkaivz) *pl. n.* a place in which are kept records of interest to a government, or to an institution, a firm, a family etc. ‖ the records themselves, which may be written or printed papers, pictures, photographs, films etc., and include muniments **ar·chi·vist** (árkivist) *n.* [F. fr. L. fr. Gk *archeion,* public office]

ar·chi·volt (árkivoult) *n.* a molding, sometimes with decorative carving, which follows the curve of an arch [fr. Ital. *archivolto*]

ar·chon (árkən, árkɒn) *n.* (*Gk hist.*) one of the nine chief officers of the ancient city-state of Athens, elected annually after 683 B.C. [Gk *archōn*]

arch·priest (ɑrtʃprí:st) *n.* (*Eastern Churches*) the highest honorary title of the secular clergy [F. *archeprestre*]

arch·way (ártʃwei) *n.* an arch under which people pass ‖ a passage roofed by a vault held up by arches

arc·jet or **arc-jet engine** (árkdʒet) *n.* gas-propelled rocket engine ignited by an electric arc

Arc, Joan of *JOAN OF ARC

arc lamp a lamp producing an intense white light by the passing of an electric arc between heavy, incandescent carbon rods or other electrodes

arc light an arc lamp ‖ the light of the arc lamp

ar·col·o·gy (ɑrkólədʒi:) *n.* a structure or larger unit (such as a city) providing a total, planned environment for human habitants

ARC system (*computer*) datapoint trade name for a wired integrated electronic office in which a single computer terminal is linked to telephone, typewriters, copiers, microfiche, and other filing systems

Arc·tic (árktik, ártik) *adj.* near or relating to the North Pole **arc·tic** (*pop.*) intensely cold **the Arctic** the Arctic Regions [O.F. *artique* fr. L. fr. Gk *arktikos,* northern]

Arctic Circle the parallel of latitude 66°33′ N., the limit of the northern region in which there is at least one day in the year on which the sun never sets and one day on which it never rises

Arctic Ocean the ocean (area 5,541,000 sq. miles), largely covered with floating ice, lying north of the Arctic Circle. It is generally considered part of the Atlantic. Greatest depth: 2,975 fathoms, north of the Bering Strait, its link with the Pacific

Arctic Regions the Arctic Ocean and the land areas surrounding it, north of the limit of tree growth. This includes parts of N. Alaska, Canada, Greenland, Svalbard, Novaya Zemlya, and N. Siberia. Climate: long, dark, cold winters, short summers with temperatures often above freezing. Native peoples include Eskimos, Lapps and Samoyeds. Resources: reindeer, whales and seals, oil, minerals

arc·tics (árktiks, ártiks) *pl. n.* rubber overshoes with a cloth lining. They reach to the ankle or above and may be zipped or buckled

Arc·tu·rus (ɑrktúərəs, ɑrktjúərəs) the brightest star in Boötes

ar·cu·ate (árkjuit, árkjueit) *adj.* bow-shaped **ar·cu·at·ed** (árkjueitid) *adj.* [fr. L. *arcuare* (*arcuatus*), to bend in an arc]

arc welding a method of welding in which metal parts are joined by fusion using the heat of an electric arc struck between two electrodes or an electrode and the metal

Ar·dèche (ærdeʃ) a department (area 2,144 sq. miles, pop. 257,100) of S.E. France between the Cévennes and the Rhône Valley (*VIVARAIS). Chief town: Privas

ar·den·cy (árdnsi:) *n.* ardor

Ar·dennes (ærden) a department (area 2,027 sq. miles, pop. 309,300) of N.E. France comprising parts of Lorraine and Champagne. Chief town: Mézières

Ardennes a wooded hill region in S.E. Belgium, Luxembourg and N.E. France, the westernmost part of the Rhenish schistose mountains. It was the scene of heavy fighting in both world wars (Aug. 1914 and Dec. 1944), the latter engagement being known as the Battle of the Bulge (*BULGE, BATTLE OF THE)

ar·dent (árd'nt) *adj.* passionate ‖ eager [M.E. *ardaunt,* burning fr. O.F.]

Ar·dha·ma·ga·dhi (ʌrdəmʌgádi:) *n.* one of the Prakrit languages of India. A great part of Jain literature is written in it

ar·dor, esp. *Br.,* **ar·dour** (árdər) *n.* passion ‖ eagerness, enthusiasm [O.F. *ardour*]

ar·du·ous (árdʒuəs, esp. *Br.* árdjuəs) *adj.* steep, hard to climb ‖ difficult, trying ‖ strenuous [fr. L. *arduus,* steep]

are (ɑr) *pres. indicative* of BE with 'we,' 'you' (*sing.* and *pl.*) and 'they'

are (ɑr, ɛər) *n.* a metric unit of area, equal to 100 square meters (119.6 sq. yds) [F.]

ar·e·a (ɛəri:ə) *n.* the extent of a surface as measured by the number of squares it contains each with side 1 unit long or by another standard measure (e.g. for a circle or triangle) when it cannot be so measured ‖ a district or region, vicinity ‖ a sphere of operation. *the sterling area* ‖ a field of academic activity ‖ (*Br.*) an areaway [L. =piece of vacant ground]

area bombing (*mil.*) bombing of a target that is in effect a general area rather than a small or pinpoint target

area code a code number prefixed to the local telephone number and used in automatic systems to dial from one telephone area to another

area composition terminal (*computer*) video screen that allows a compositor to see exactly how the message will appear in a printed product

area formulas

triangle	$A = \dfrac{bh}{2}$
rectangle	$A = cd$
parallelogram	$A = bh$
trapezoid (*Br.* trapezium)	$A = \dfrac{h(p+q)}{2}$
regular polygon	$A = \dfrac{bhn}{2}$
circle	$A = \pi r^2$
sector	$A = \dfrac{\pi r^2 a}{360} = \dfrac{r^2 \beta}{2}$
ellipse	$A = \dfrac{\pi xy}{4}$
cone	$A = \pi r_b s + \pi r^2 b$
sphere	$A = 4\pi r^2$

A = surface area, b = base length, c and d = adjacent sides, h = perpendicular height, n = number of sides, p and q = parallel sides, r = radius, r_b = base radius, s = slant height, x and y = major and minor axes, a = sector angle (degrees), β = sector angle (radians), π = 3.1416 or $^{22}/_7$ approx. (*VOLUME FORMULAS)

area navigation a computer-controlled aircraft navigation system using ground radio signals to determine flight position

area rug a small rug

ar·e·a·way (ɛəri:əwei) *n.* (*Am.* = *Br.* area) a sunken yard or enclosure outside the basement of a house, often with an entry to it

ar·e·ca (ǽrikə, ərí:kə) *n.* a member of *Areca,* a genus of palms of tropical Asia and the Malay archipelago. *A. catechu* yields the areca nut or betel nut [Port. fr. Tamil]

A·ref (æréf),'Abd al-Salām (1921–66), Iraqi soldier and statesman, president of the republic (1963–6). He was succeeded by his brother, 'Abd al-Rahmān (1916–), deposed in 1968 by a military coup d'état

a·re·na (ərí:nə) *n.* the open central area of the Roman amphitheater, in which games and fights between gladiators or wild animals took place ‖ any large area, indoors or outdoors, used for sport, exhibitions, concerts etc. ‖ a sphere of action, influence or contest [L. *arena,* sand, a sandy place (the Roman arena was strewn with *sand*)]

ar·e·na·ceous (ærənéiʃəs) *adj.* (of rocks) sandy or made principally of sand ‖ like sand in texture ‖ growing in sand or sandy soil [fr. L. *arenaceus*]

ar·e·nic·o·lid (ærəníkəlid) **1.** *n.* a member of *Arenicola,* a genus of sandworms or lugworms, used for fishing bait **2.** *adj.* relating to this genus [Mod. L. fr. *arena,* sand+*colere,* to dwell]

ar·e·nic·o·lous (ærəníkələs) *adj.* (*zool.*) living in sand [fr. L. *arena,* sand+*colere,* to dwell]

CONCISE PRONUNCIATION KEY: **(a)** æ, c*a*t; ɑ, c*ar*; ɔ f*aw*n; ei, sn*a*ke. **(e)** e, h*e*n; i:, sh*ee*p; iə, d*ee*r; ɛə, b*ear*. **(i)** i, f*i*sh; ai, t*i*ger; ə:, b*i*rd. **(o)** o, *o*x; au, c*ow*; ou, g*oa*t; u, p*oor*; ɔi, r*oy*al. **(u)** ʌ, d*u*ck; u, b*u*ll; u:, g*oo*se; ə, b*a*cill*u*s; ju:, c*u*be. x, lo*ch*; θ, *th*ink; ð, bo*th*er; z, *Z*en; ʒ, cor*s*age; ʒ, sava*g*e; ŋ, oranguta*ng*; j, *y*ak; ʃ, fi*sh*; tʃ, fe*tch*; 'l, rabb*le*; 'n, redd*en*. Complete pronunciation key appears inside front cover.

ar·e·nose (ǽrənəus) *adj.* arenaceous [fr. L. *arenosus,* sandy]

aren't (ɑrnt,ɑ́rənt) contr. of ARE NOT

a·re·o·cen·tric (æri:ousɛ́ntrik) *adj.* (*astron.*) having Mars as its center

ar·e·od·e·sy (æri:ɔ́dəsi) *n.* (*math.*) the branch of mathematics that determines by observation and measurement the exact positions of points and the figures and areas of large portions of the surface of the planet Mars, or the shape and size of the planet Mars —**aerodetic** *adj.* pertaining to, or determined by, areodesy

a·re·o·la (ərí:ələ) *pl.* **a·re·o·lae** (ərí:əli:), **a·re·o·las** *n.* (*biol.*) a small area, e.g. between the veins of a leaf ‖ (*anat.*) a circular area, e.g. around the nipple of the breast ‖ (*med.*) the inflamed area around a spot or pimple **a·ré·o·lar** *adj.* [L., dim. of *area,* an open space]

areolar tissue a layer of loose connective tissue, often containing fat cells, between the skin and deeper tissues

a·re·o·late (ərí:əlit, ərí:əleit) *adj.* divided into or marked by areolae **a·re·o·lat·ed** (ərí:əleitid) *adj.*

ar·e·ole (ǽri:oul) *n.* an areola

Ar·e·op·a·gite (æri:ɔ́pəgait, æri:ɔ́pədʒait) *n.* (*hist.*) a member of the court of the Areopagus ‖ *DIONYSIUS THE AREOPAGITE [fr. L. *areopagites* fr. Gk]

Ar·e·op·a·gus (æri:ɔ́pəgəs) originally the highest council of the Athenian state, later a court for the trial of cases of homicide. It was famous for its wisdom and impartiality [L. fr. Gk *Areios,* of Ares+*pagos,* hill]

A·re·qui·pa (æriki:pə) a city (pop. 386,000, altitude 7,600 ft) of Peru, founded by Pizarro (1540) on the site of an Inca city. It is a commercial and intellectual center. University (1821)

Ar·es (έ:ri:z) (*Gk mythol.*) the god of war, son of Zeus and Hera, and lover of Aphrodite, identified with the Roman Mars

a·rête (æréit) *n.* a sharp ridge running up the side of a mountain or crossing a valley between two peaks [F.=fish skeleton, ridge]

ar·e·thu·sa (ærəθú:zə) *n.* a member of *Arethusa,* a genus of North American orchids found in bogs and swamps [Mod. L. after *Arethusa,* a nymph who, trying to escape from Alpheus, the river god, was changed into a spring

A·re·ti·no (ɑretí:nɔ), Pietro (1492–1556), Italian author of plays, satire and licentious verse

A·ré·va·lo (ɑrévalɔ), Juan José (1904–), Guatemalan president (1944–51) after elections held (1944) by a revolutionary triumvirate

A·rez·zo (ɑréttsɔ) an old market town (pop. 67,000) in Tuscany, Italy, with silk and clothing industries. It has a Gothic cathedral. The church of San Francesco contains frescos by Piero della Francesca

ar·ga·li (ɑ́rgəli:) *pl.* **ar·ga·li, ar·ga·lis** *n. Ovis ammon,* the largest, big-horned, Asiatic sheep ‖ *Ovis canadensis,* the American bighorn [Mongolian]

ar·gent (ɑ́rdʒənt) **1.** *n.* (*heraldry*) silver **2.** *adj.* (*heraldry*) silver ‖ (*rhet.*) silvery white, shining [F.]

ar·gen·tif·er·ous (ɑrdʒəntífərəs) *adj.* containing silver [fr. L. *argentum,* silver+*ferre,* to bear]

Ar·gen·ti·na (ɑrdʒəntí:nə) a federal republic (area 1,072,744 sq. miles, pop. 30,708,000) in S.E. South America. Capital: Buenos Aires. People: European (mainly of Italian and Spanish origin), with some Asians and a dwindling Indian minority. Language: Spanish. Religion: mainly Roman Catholic, with small Protestant and Jewish minorities. The land is 41% pasture, 32% forest and 11 % cultivated. The crest of the Andes (rising to Aconcagua, 23,081 ft) forms most of the Chilean frontier. The eastern two-thirds of the country is plain: the Gran Chaco in the north (sugar, rice) between the Paraná and Uruguay Rivers, the Pampas (the east rich farmland, the west grain fields and cattle ranges) in the center, and the arid plain of Patagonia in the south. Average winter and summer temperatures (F.): in the north 56° and 83°, in Buenos Aires 49° and 74°, and in the south 35° and 59°. Rainfall: 68 ins in the northeast and in Tucumán, 38 ins at Buenos Aires, 7–15 ins in Patagonia and the Andes. Livestock: cattle on the Pampas, sheep in Patagonia, pigs, horses and goats. Products: meat, wheat, corn, linseed, sugar, cotton, butter, cheese, sunflower seeds, rice, fruit, vines, wool, tobacco, edible oils. Mineral resources: oil, tungsten, beryllium, iron ore, mica, lead, copper, gold, silver, uranium. Industries: meat packing, flour milling, textiles, leather, brewing, tanning, furniture, glass, cement, pig iron, rubber, chemicals. Exports: raw meat (1st in the world), cereals (4th in the world), oils, linseed, dairy produce, wool, hides and skins. Imports: machinery, vehicles, iron, fuels. Ports: Buenos Aires, La Plata, Bahia Blanca, Rosario, Santa Fé (the last two being river ports). There are six universities, the oldest being Córdoba (1613) and Buenos Aires (1821). Monetary unit: gold peso (peso oro, divided into 100 centavos). HISTORY. The Río de la plata was discovered by Solis (1516) and explored by Sebastian Cabot (1526–30). Buenos Aires was colonized by the Spanish under Mendoza (1536) but was destroyed by Indians and rebuilt (1580). The area formed part of the Spanish viceroyalty of Peru (1617) and became the Spanish viceroyalty of Río de La Plata (1776). It won its independence from Spain after a revolutionary struggle (1810–16) and under San Martín, and the United Provinces of the Plate River were set up (1816). Warfare between Federalists and Unitarians followed, checked by the dictatorship (1829–52) of Juan Manuel Rosas. A federal constitution was drawn up in 1853. Argentina, with Brazil and Uruguay, fought Paraguay (1865–70). British capital developed the railways, ports, and the meat export industry (from 1860). Argentina was governed under military dictatorships (1930–45). In the 2nd world war it declared war on Germany in March 1945. Perón became president in 1946 but he was overthrown by a military revolt in 1955, leaving grave economic problems. Gen. Pedro E. Aramburu, provisional president (1955–8) restored the constitution of 1853 and called (1958) elections. The new president, Arturo Frondizi, failed to improve the economy and was deposed (1962) by a military coup. The elections of 1963 were won by Arturo Illia. His strong nationalistic line in foreign affairs failed to satisfy the military, who feared the return to Peronismo and he too was deposed (1966). A military junta presided over by Gen. Juan Carlos Onganía proceeded to dissolve Congress, suppress political parties, and deprive the universities of their autonomy. In 1968 he rid himself of a significant liberal opposition to his idea of a tightly controlled corporate state by dismissing his army, navy and air force chiefs, but in 1970 he fell to a coup led by Gen. Roberto M. Levingston, who then assumed the presidency. Levingston was in turn ousted (1971) by the junta he had led, and was replaced by Lieut. Gen. Alejandro Lanusse. Perón became president again in 1973 but died the following year and was succeeded by his third wife, Isabel, who was overthrown by the military (1976). Following an unsuccessful war with Great Britain (1982) over possession of the Falkland Islands, Argentina elected Raúl Alfonsín, a civilian, as president. He faced an economic crisis with uncontrolled inflation and a huge foreign debt

Ar·gen·tine (ɑ́rdʒəntí:n, ɑ́rdʒəntain) **1.** *adj.* of or pertaining to Argentina, the inhabitants, or their culture **2.** *n.* a native or inhabitant of Argentina **the Argentine** Argentina

ar·gen·tine (ɑ́rdʒəntí:n, ɑ́rdʒəntin) **1.** *adj.* like silver, silvery **2.** *n.* any of various metals resembling silver ‖ a small silvery fish of fam. *Salmonidae* ‖ a silvery variety of calcite [F. *argentin*]

Ar·gen·tin·e·an (ɑrdʒəntíni:ən) *n.* an Argentine

Argentine Milanga dance from which the tango derived

Ar·gen·ti·no, Lake (ɑrhentí:nɔ) a lake (c. 570 sq. miles) in S. Argentina

ar·gen·tite (ɑ́rdʒəntait) *n.* natural silver sulfide, Ag₂S, a valuable silver ore found esp. in America and Europe [fr. L. *argentum,* silver]

ar·gil·la·ceous (ɑrdʒiléiʃəs) *adj.* containing clay ‖ claylike in composition or texture [fr. L. *argillaceus*]

ar·gi·nae·mi·a (ɑrdʒiní:mi:ə) *n.* (*med.*) an inherited blood condition characterized by a low level of arginase and resulting metabolic deficiency

Ar·give (ɑ́rdʒaiv,ɑ́rgaiv) **1.** *adj.* of, belonging to or native to the ancient Greek city of Argos **2.** *n.* (in Homer) any ancient Greek [fr. L. *Argivus*]

ar·gol (ɑ́rgɑl,ɑ́rgɔl) *n.* crude cream of tartar, potassium hydrogen tartrate, which is deposited as a brownish red crust on the vats used in wine making, and from which purified cream of tartar is manufactured [etym. doubtful]

Ar·go·lis (ɑ́rgəlis) a region of the E. Peloponnesus, Greece

ar·gon (ɑ́rgɑn) *n.* an odorless, colorless, chemically inert gaseous element (symbol Ar, at. no. 18, at. mass 39.948) which makes up just under 1% of atmospheric air. It is used in electric bulbs and for fluorescent lighting [Gk, neut. of *argos,* idle, inert]

Ar·go·naut (ɑ́rgənɔt) (*Gk mythol.*) any one of the heroes who sailed with Jason in the ship 'Argo'

ar·go·naut (ɑ́rgənɔt) *n.* a paper nautilus

Ar·gonne (ɑ́rgɔn) a wooded hilly region of France in the east of the Paris basin. It was the site of bitter fighting (the Meuse-Argonne offensive) during the 1st world war, notably at Verdun (1916) and Saint-Mihiel (1918), the latter engagement joined by U.S. troops. In the 2nd world war it was the site of engagements (1940) at Dinant, Monthermé and Sedan

Ar·gos (ɑ́rgɔs) a Greek city-state which fought Sparta in the Peloponnesian War (431–404 B.C.) and in the Corinthian War (395–387 B.C.). It became a member of the Achaean League 229 B.C.) and was conquered by Rome 146 B.C.)

ar·go·sy (ɑ́rgəsi:) *pl.* **ar·go·sies** *n.* (*hist.*) a large merchant ship of the 16th and 17th cc. ‖ (*hist.*) a fleet of such treasure-laden ships [earlier *ragusy* perh. fr. Ital. *Ragusea,* a ship of Ragusa (Dubrovnik). (The spelling was influenced by 'Argo', Jason's ship)]

ar·got (ɑ́rgou,ɑ́rgət) *n.* the slang of a social group, e.g. thieves, students [F.]

ar·gu·a·ble (ɑ́rgju:əb'l) *adj.* for which good, if not necessarily convincing, reasons may be found ‖ open to doubt **ár·gu·a·bly** *adv.* not certainly, but reasonably held to be

argue (ɑ́rgju:) *pres. part.* **ar·gu·ing** past and past part. **ar·gued** *v.t.* to apply reason to (a problem), *to argue a point* ‖ to maintain (an opinion) ‖ to persuade by talk, *she argued him into going* ‖ to be a sign of, to prove, *his behavior argues lack of willpower* ‖ *v.i.* to dispute ‖ to wrangle [O.F. *arguer*]

Ar·güe·das (ɑrgwéðɑs), Alcides (1879–1946), Bolivian author and diplomat whose novels, notably 'Raza de bronce' (1919) and 'Los caudillos bárbaros' (1929), expose the sufferings of the oppressed Aymara Indians

ar·gu·ment (ɑ́rgjumənt) *n.* a reason put forward (for or against something) ‖ a chain of reasoning. ‖ a discussion, debate ‖ a dispute ‖ a wrangling ‖ a summary of the contents of a book [F.]

ar·gu·men·ta·tion (ɑrgjumentéiʃən) *n.* the mental process of constructing a chain of reasoning ‖ its expression in words or writing ‖ discussion [F.]

ar·gu·men·ta·tive (ɑrgjuméntətiv) *adj..* excessively fond of arguing or raising objections [F. *argumentatif*]

Ar·gus (ɑ́rgəs) (*Gk mythol.*) the many-eyed monster set by Hera to guard Io. Hermes killed it. Hera decked the peacock's tail with its eyes

ARGUS (ɑ́rgus) (*computer*) acronym for automatic routine generating and updating system, a computer compiler system for Honeywell 800

argus shell *Cypraea argus,* a tropical marine gastropod shell marked with an eyelike pattern

Ar·gyle (ɑ́rgail) **1.** *adj.* (of socks, sweaters etc.) knitted in a diamond pattern of two or more colors **2.** *n.* such a pattern ‖ a sock in this pattern [var. of ARGYLL, after the Argyll tartan]

Ar·gyll (ɑrgáil) a former county in W. Scotland. Its county town was Inverary. Administrative center: Lochgilphead

Arhus *AARHUS

Ar·i·a (έ:ri:ə) *HERAT

a·ri·a (ɑ́ri:ə) *n.* an air, melody, esp. in opera [Ital.]

Ar·i·ad·ne (æri:ǽdni:) *THESEUS

Ar·i·an (έ:ri:ən, æri:ən) **1.** *adj.* of the heresiarch Arius **2.** *n.* one of his followers **Ar·i·an·ism** *n.* the first widespread Christian heresy, originating in the N. African Church, preached by Arius and Eusebius of Nicomedia in the early 4th c. A logical development from Origen, Arianism denied the divinity of Christ. Arius was excommunicated (323). The heresy spread in the Near East, and Constantine called the Council of Nicaea (325) to establish an orthodox doctrine of the Trinity. The quarrel became political, led to the persecution of the Orthodox Christians (337–61), and rent the Christian East up to the Council of Constantinople (381).

CONCISE PRONUNCIATION KEY: (**a**) æ, c*a*t; ɑ, c*ar*; ɔ f*aw*n; ei, sn*a*ke. (**e**) e, h*e*n; i:, sh*ee*p; iə, d*eer*; ɛə, b*ear*. (**i**) i, f*i*sh; ai, t*i*ger; ə:, b*ir*d. (**o**) o, *o*x; au, c*ow*; ou, g*oa*t; u, p*oor*; ɔi, r*oy*al. (**u**) ʌ, d*u*ck; u, b*u*ll; u:, g*oo*se; ə, *a*bacillus; ju:, c*u*be. x, lo*ch*; θ, *th*ink; ð, bo*th*er; z, *Z*en; ʒ, cor*s*age; dʒ, sava*g*e; ŋ, orangutan*g*; j, *y*ak; ʃ, *f*ish; tʃ, fe*tch*; 'l, rabb*le*; 'n, redd*en*. Complete pronunciation key appears inside front cover.

The Christianity of the Germanic tribes was Arian until the 7th c. [fr. L. *Arianus*]

A·rias (árjas), Arnulfo (1901–   ), Panamanian politician and president (1940–1, 1949–51, 1968)

Arias Dávila *PEDRARIAS

ar·id (ǽrid) *adj.* dry, barren ‖ dull, uninteresting [fr. L. *aridus*]

a·rid·i·ty (əríditi:) *n.* the state or quality of being arid [fr. L. *ariditas*]

A·riège (ærjeʒ) a department (area 1,892 sq. miles, pop. 137,900) of S. France in the Pyrenees (*GASCOGNE, *LANGUEDOC, *FOIX). Chief town: Foix

Ar·ies (ɛ́əri:z, ǽri:z) a northern constellation ‖ the first sign of the zodiac, represented as a ram [L.=ram]

a·right (əráit) *adv.* (*rhet.*) rightly, *have I understood you aright?*

ar·il (ǽril) *n.* an outer coating to some seeds, often bright in color, e.g. the fruit of *Taxus* (yew) **ar·il·late** (ǽrileit, ǽrilit), **ár·il·lat·ed** *adjs.* [fr. Mod. L. *arillus*, dried grape]

ar·il·lode (ǽriloud) *n.* a false aril, not arising from the placenta but from the region of the micropyle

A·ri·os·to (ɑri:ɔ́stɔ), Ludovico (1474–1533), Italian poet, author of the epic 'Orlando Furioso' (1516)

a·rise (əráiz) *pres. part.* **a·ris·ing** *past* **a·rose** (əróuz) *past part.* **a·ris·en** (əriz'n) *v.i.* to come into being, begin ‖ to originate from a particular source or as a natural consequence ‖ to come up for notice or into consideration ‖ (*rhet.*) to get up, stand up [O.E. *ārīsan*]

A·ris·ta (arí:sta), Mariano (1802–55) Mexican general and president of the Republic (1851–3)

a·ris·ta (ərísta) *pl.* **a·ris·tae** (ərísti:) *n.* an awn or bristle, e.g. in the beard of barley ‖ a slender bristle as on the terminal joint of the antennae of some insects [L.]

Ar·is·tar·chus of Samos (æristárkəs) (3rd c. B.C.), Greek astronomer who put forward the theory that the earth revolves round the sun

Ar·is·ti·des (æristáidi:z) 'the Just' (c. 530–c. 468 B.C.), Athenian statesman and general. He fought at Marathon (490 B.C.), and was ostracized (483–480 B.C.) through the influence of Themistocles. He played a leading part in the victories at Salamis (480 B.C.) and Plataea (479 B.C.)

ar·is·toc·ra·cy (æristɔ́krɔsi:) *pl.* **ar·is·toc·ra·cies** *n.* government by a small, privileged, hereditary class, drawn from the leading families in the state (cf. DEMOCRACY) ‖ a state so governed ‖ the members of such a governing class, in particular those who bear titles of nobility (even when they no longer control government) ‖ (in Plato and Aristotle) government by those whose character best fits them for the task ‖ the best or most prominent of any class, *aristocracy of intellect* [fr. L. *aristocratia* fr. Gk *aristos*, best + *kratia*, rule]

ar·is·to·crat (ərístəkræt, ǽristəkræt) *n.* a member of the ruling class in an aristocracy ‖ a noble [F. *aristocrate*]

ar·is·to·crat·ic (ərìstəkrǽtik, æristəkrǽtik) *adj.* of or pertaining to an aristocracy ‖ patrician (in origin, manners, taste etc.) [F. *aristocratique*]

Ar·is·toph·a·nes (æristɔ́fəni:z) (c. 450–c. 385 B.C.), Athenian comic playwright, 11 of whose comedies survive entire. He had a shrewd insight into the hidden causes of many evils of his day, and wrote boldly and sarcastically, with coarse jokes. He attacked Cleon in 'The Knights', Socrates in 'The Clouds' and Euripides in 'The Frogs'. He satirized Athenian litigation in 'The Wasps', the constitutional theorists in 'The Ecclesiazusae' and the high hopes placed in the Sicilian expedition in 'The Birds'. He pleaded for peace with Sparta in 'The Acharnians', 'The Peace' and the 'Lysistrata'

Ar·is·to·te·lian (ærìstətí:ljən, ərìstəti:ljən) **1.** *adj.* of or pertaining to Aristotle **2.** *n.* a follower of Aristotle, one who shares his philosophy **Ar·is·to·té·lian·ism** *n.*

Aristotelian logic traditional formal logic, based on the syllogism, developed from the foundation laid by Aristotle

Ar·is·tot·le (ǽristɔt'l) (384–322 B.C.), Greek philosopher, pupil of Plato, tutor of Alexander the Great, and founder of the Peripatetic School at Athens (335 B.C.). His philosophy grew away from the idealism of Plato and became increasingly concerned with science and the phenomena of the world. His analyses were original and profound and his methods exercised an

enormous influence on all subsequent thought. His works include 'Organon' (logic), 'Ethics', 'Politics', 'Poetics', 'On the Soul' (a biological treatise). 'Metaphysics', 'Historia animalium'

Arithmatic (*computer*) trade name for a compiler and coding system for Univac II, manufactured by Sperry-Rand Corp.

a·rith·me·tic (əriθmətik) **1.** *n.* the manipulation of numbers by addition, subtraction, multiplication, division **2.** (ærɪθmétik) *adj.* arithmetical [O.F. *arismetique*, L. *arithmetica* fr. Gk]

ar·ith·met·i·cal (ærɪθmétik'l) *adj.* concerned with, in accordance with the rules of, arithmetic [fr. L. fr. Gk *arithmētikos*]

a·rith·me·ti·cian (ərɪθmətiʃən) *n.* someone skilled in the science or practice of arithmetic [F.]

arithmetic mean an average found by adding a group of values and dividing by the number of values in the group

arithmetic progression a series of numbers which increase or decrease by the same amount at each step, e.g. 3, 6, 9, 12, 15 (cf. GEOMETRIC PROGRESSION)

Ar·i·us of Alexandria (ɛ́əri:əs) (c. 280–336), Libyan churchman and heresiarch (*ARIANISM)

Ariz. Arizona

Ar·i·zo·na (ærizóunə) (*abbr.* Ariz.) a state (area 113,909 sq. miles, pop. 2,860,000) in the southwestern U.S.A. Capital: Phoenix. It is divided by mountains with a high plateau in the northeast and desert in the southwest. Agriculture: cattle and sheep ranching, cotton, fodder crops, some fruit and vegetables (under irrigation). Resources: copper (12% of world supply), some gold and silver, zinc, lead. Industries: metal refining, electronics, aircraft parts. University (1885) at Tucson. The U.S.A. acquired most of the state from Mexico (1848) and the rest as part of the Gadsden Purchase (1854). It became (1912) the 48th state of the U.S.A.

Ark. Arkansas

ark (ɑrk) *n.* (*Bible*) the vessel Noah built at God's command [O.E. fr. L. *arca*, a chest]

Ar·kan·sas (árkansɔ) (*abbr.* Ark.) a state (area 53,104 sq. miles, pop. 2,291,000) of the S. central U.S.A. Capital: Little Rock. The Mississippi alluvial plain lies in the east, while the north and west are mountainous. Agriculture (the principal industry): cotton, rice, poultry, soybeans. Resources: timber, oil and natural gas, bauxite (90% of American supply), some coal. Industries: timber, wood products, food processing. State university (1871) at Fayetteville. Arkansas was explored by the Spanish (mid 16th c.) and the French (late 17th c.), and passed as part of the Louisiana Purchase (1803) to the U.S.A., of which it became (1836) the 25th state

Arkansas River a river 1,450 miles long which rises in the mountains of central Colorado, flows through S. Kansas and Oklahoma, across Arkansas, and into the Mississippi

Ar·khan·gelsk (arhángelsk) *ARCHANGEL

Ark of Testimony the Ark of the Covenant

Ark of the Covenant the sacred chest containing the tablets of the Ten Commandments, carried by the Israelites during their wandering in the wilderness (Exodus XXV, 10–22 and XXXVII, 1–5). It symbolized God's presence among his chosen people, and was heavily guarded and so holy that to touch it was punishable by death. It was captured in battle by the Philistines but was recovered after many years and placed in the Holy of Holies in the Temple of Solomon. It disappeared after the burning of the Temple by the Babylonians (c. 587 B.C.)

Ark·wright (árkrait), Sir Richard (1732–92), English cotton manufacturer. He invented the water frame (1769) and other mechanical spinning processes, thus helping to start the factory system of the Industrial Revolution

ARL (*acronym*) for acceptable reliability level

Arles (arl) a market town (pop. 50,345) of Bouches-du-Rhône, S. France, on the Rhône delta, famous for its Roman ruins (esp. the arena, theater and necropolis). It was the capital of the kingdom of Burgundy (c. 933–1246). Romanesque church (11th–15th cc.)

Arles, Synod of a council (314) of the Western Church, convened by the emperor Constantine, at which the Donatist schism was condemned

Ar·ling·ton National Cemetery (árliŋtən) a burial ground occupying more than 400 acres on the Potomac River in Virginia, opposite

Washington, D.C. It is the resting place of many soldiers and leaders of the U.S. military and other professions

ARM (*acronym*) for automated route management, IBM program for control of distribution systems, e.g. sales routes

arm (ɑrm) *n.* the upper limb of the human body, from the shoulder to the hand (called 'upper arm' above the elbow, and 'forearm' below the elbow) ‖ a similar limb of an animal, e.g. of a bear or monkey, or a limb roughly resembling an arm, e.g. of an octopus ‖ a part attached to or projecting from something, *an arm of the sea, the arm of a chair* ‖ a sleeve of a garment **the long arm of the law** the power of the police to arrest wrongdoers **with open arms** joyfully, *to welcome someone with open arms* [O.E. *arm, earm*]

arm *n.* (often *pl.*) a weapon ‖ a branch of the fighting services, *the air arm* ‖ (*pl.*) the heraldic devices on the shield of a family, diocese, institution, state etc. (*COAT OF ARMS) **in arms** (*rhet.*) armed and ready for war **to bear arms** (*rhet.*) to serve actively as a soldier **to stand to arms** to come to a state of readiness to meet attack **to take up arms** (*rhet.*) to prepare for war or wage war **under arms** mobilized for war **up in arms** vexed and prepared to offer resistance [F. *armes*]

arm *v.t.* to provide with weapons, or other means of fighting or attacking ‖ to protect or defend. *to arm oneself against the cold* ‖ to provide with what is needed, *to arm oneself with letters of introduction* ‖ to fit with some device, tool, or equipment, *the lead is armed with wax to sample the sea bottom* ‖ *v.i.* to build up armaments [F. *armer*]

ar·ma·da (ɑrmádə) *n.* a fleet of warships ‖ any large fleet of ships or aircraft **the Ar·ma·da** the Spanish fleet sent (1588) by Philip II in an attempt to invade England. An English fleet under Howard and Drake prevented it from joining up with the Spanish army in the Netherlands, and it was finally scattered by storms [Span.]

ar·ma·dil·lo (ɑrmədílou) *n.* a member of *Dasypodidae*, a family of edentate mammals, allied to anteaters, but having some teeth. They inhabit Central and South America, and are characterized by an armor of horny scales covering the body. Some species roll into a ball if attacked. They are nocturnal in habit and eat insects, worms, fruit etc. The giant armadillo is about 3 ft in length, the fairy armadillo about 5 ins [Span., dim. of *armado*, armed]

Ar·ma·ged·don (ɑrməgéd'n) the scene of the final battle between the forces of good and evil, foretold in the New Testament 'Revelation of St John the Divine' (xvi, 16) ‖ the battle itself

Ar·magh (armá) a county (area 512 sq. miles, pop. 133,969) in the south of Northern Ireland ‖ its county town (pop. 9,000), seat of the Roman Catholic archbishop, primate of Ireland, and the Anglican archbishop of the Church of Ireland

Ar·ma·gnac (ærmɑnjæk) a subregion of Aquitaine in S.W. France, a former province (roughly equivalent to modern Gers). It is famous for its brandy

ar·ma·ment (ɑrməmənt) *n.* the weapons, guns, rockets etc. with which a ship, aircraft, army, fighting vehicle etc. is equipped ‖ (*pl.*) the weapons and munitions of war [fr. L. *armamentum*, an equipment]

ar·ma·ture (ɑrmətʃər) **1.** *n.* a piece of soft iron or steel which connects the poles of a magnet or of two magnets placed side by side ‖ (*elec.*) an iron framework wound with copper wire, fixed between the poles of a magnet. When such an armature is made to revolve in the magnetic field, an electric current is induced in the windings (e.g. in a dynamo). When current is passed through the windings of the armature (e.g. in an electric motor), electromagnetic induction causes it to revolve in the magnetic field ‖ the metal frame on which a modeler in clay builds up his work ‖ any metal skeleton which supports a structure ‖ in an electric instrument, e.g. a bell, the arm which moves to and fro as the magnetic field varies **2.** *v.t. pres. part.* **ar·ma·tur·ing** *past* and *past part.* **ar·ma·tured** to fit an armature to [fr. L. *armatura*, arms]

arm·band (ármbænd) *n.* an armlet (sleeve band)

arm·chair (ármtʃear) **1.** *n.* a chair, wooden or upholstered, with arms **2.** *adj.* theoretical and lacking practical experience, *armchair strategy*

armed sweep (*mil.*) sweep vehicle fitted with cutters or other devices to increase its ability to cut mine moorings

Ar·me·nia (ɑrmíːnjə, ɑrmíːniːə) a former country of W. Asia, a region of high plateaus and mountain ranges, southeast of the Black Sea, and west of the Caspian Sea. It is now divided between the U.S.S.R., Turkey and Iran. The kingdom of Urartu flourished between the 9th and 7th cc. B.C. and was ruled successively by the Medes, Persians, Romans, Arabs and Ottoman Turks (from 1514). It was the first country to adopt Christianity as a national religion (303). Parts were ceded to Russia (1828, 1829, 1878, 1918) and in 1921 these were set up as a Soviet Republic. In 1936 it became a constituent republic (area 11,490 sq. miles, pop. 3,222,000) of the U.S.S.R. Capital: Erevan. Agriculture: cattle raising in the mountains, cotton, fruit, wheat, root crops in the irrigated valleys. Resources: copper, zinc, aluminum, molybdenum, building materials. Industries and products: mining, chemical fertilizers, synthetic rubber, textiles, food processing

Ar·me·nian (ɑrmíːnjən, ɑrmíːniːən) **1.** *n.* a native of Armenia ‖ the Armenian language ‖ a member of the Armenian Church (also known as the Gregorian, from its founder, St Gregory the Illuminator), a monophysite Church in communion with no other Christian body. It has about four million members **2.** *adj.* pertaining to Armenia or its inhabitants ‖ pertaining to the Indo-European language of the Armenians ‖ pertaining to or belonging to the Armenian Church

arm·ful (ɑ́rmful) *pl.* **arm·fuls, arms·ful** *n.* the amount that can be held in both arms

arm·hole (ɑ́rmhoul) *n.* the hole through which the arm is put into a garment

ar·mil·lar·y (ɑ́rməleri:, ɑrmíləri:) *adj.* made up of rings ‖ like a ring [fr. L. *armilla*, bracelet]

armillary sphere an early astronomical instrument made up of rings representing the circles (horizon, meridian, ecliptic etc.) of the celestial sphere

arm in arm (of two or more persons) with arms linked

arm·ing (ɑ́rmiŋ) *n.* the equipment with which something is made complete or fit for action, e.g. the tallow on a sounding lead

Ar·min·i·an (ɑrmíniːən) **1.** *adj.* pertaining to the teaching of Jacobus Arminius **2.** *n.* one of his followers **Ar·min·i·an·ism** *n.*

Ar·min·i·us (ɑrmíniːəs), Jacobus (Jacob Harmensen, 1560–1609), Dutch Protestant theologian who rejected the Calvinist doctrines of predestination, election and grace. His teaching influenced Wesleyan and Methodist theology

ar·mi·stice (ɑ́rmistis) *n.* an agreement by which fighting is suspended while peace terms are negotiated [fr. Mod. L. *armistitium*]

Armistice Day *VETERANS DAY

arm·let (ɑ́rmlit) *n.* a sleeve band worn around the upper arm for identification, as a sign of mourning etc. ‖ a little arm of the sea, of a lake etc.

ar·mor, *Br.* **ar·mour** (ɑ́rmər) *n.* (*hist.*) protection for the body worn in battle, e.g. mail, plate armor, leather etc. ‖ the steel protective skin of a battleship, tank etc. ‖ tanks, armored cars and other armored forces ‖ the protective covering of an animal (e.g. the shell of a turtle) [O.F. *armeüre*]

ar·mor·clad, *Br.* **ar·mour·clad** (ɑ́rmərklæd) *adj.* covered with armor

ar·mored, *Br.* **ar·moured** (ɑ́rmərd) *adj.* equipped with steel armor ‖ making use of armored forces, *an armored attack*

ar·mor·er, *Br.* **ar·mour·er** (ɑ́rmərər) *n.* a maker of arms or (*hist.*) armor ‖ someone who looks after and repairs the arms of a fighting unit, incl. the guns of aircraft [A. F. *armurer*]

ar·mo·ri·al (ɑrmóːriːəl, ɑrmóuriːəl) **1.** *adj.* of, pertaining to or bearing heraldic devices **2.** *n.* a book of heraldic arms

Ar·mor·i·can (ɑrmóːrikən, ɑrmóurikən) *adj.* Hercynian

ar·mor·ist (ɑ́rmərist) *n.* someone interested or skilled in heraldry

armor plate, *Br.* **armour plate** a protective covering of steel plates on a warship, tank etc. **ár·mor·plat·ed,** *Br.* **ár·mourplat·ed** *adj.*

ar·mo·ry (ɑ́rməri:) *pl.* **ar·mo·ries** *n.* the branch of heraldry concerned with coat armor ‖ a book of coats of arms listed in the order of the names of the bearers [O.F. *armoirie*, arms]

ar·mor·y, *Br.* **ar·mour·y** (ɑ́rməri:) *n.* a place in which arms and ammunition are kept, a large building with offices, drill hall etc. ‖ a factory, generally owned by the government, for the manufacture of arms and ammunition, an arsenal [prob. O.F. *armoierie*]

armour *ARMOR

armour·clad *ARMOR-CLAD

armoured *ARMORED

armourer *ARMORER

armour plate *ARMOR PLATE

armoury *ARMORY (place for arms and ammunition)

arm·pit (ɑ́rmpit) *n.* the hollow (axilla) under the joint of the shoulder and arm

Arm·strong (ɑ́rmstrɒŋ, ɑ́rmstrɔːŋ), John (1758–1843), U.S. soldier, diplomat and political leader. He served as U.S. minister to France (1804–10), as brigadier general in the War of 1812, and as Secretary of War (1813–14) under President James Madison

Armstrong, Louis 'Satchmo' (1900–71), U.S. trumpeter and composer and 'king' of the New Orleans jazz style

Armstrong, Neil Alden (1930–), U.S. pioneer astronaut who commanded the Apollo XI mission, becoming (July 1969) the first man to stand on the surface of the moon

arm·strong (ɑ́rmstrɒŋ) *v.* (*mil.*) a term, peculiar to the U.S. Army Air Support Radar Team, indicating both the command and response for arming and fusing-circuit activation

arm·twist·ing (ɑ́rmtwisti) *n.* exertion of extreme pressure upon someone — **arm-twisting** *adj.*

arm-wres·tling (ɑ́rmres'liŋ) *n.* Indian wrestling contest to force an opponent's erect forearm (with elbow on the surface) to the surface

ar·my (ɑ́rmi:) *pl.* **ar·mies** *n.* a body of men (or women, or both) organized for war on land ‖ the whole of a nation's military force ‖ some part of it fighting a campaign on its own or with a similar unit, *field army* [F. *armée*]

army ant a foraging ant

army corps a military unit typically of two divisions and auxiliary troops, with headquarters

army of occupation troops assuring the military government of a defeated enemy and the respect of peace terms

Army War College a U.S. military school founded (1901) in Washington, D.C. to provide a progressive scheme of instruction for Army officers. Its emphasis was changed (1916) by the National Defense Act to give more attention to theory, abstract problem solving, and the development of doctrines. It was reestablished (1950) at Carlisle, Pa., to prepare selected Army officers for the highest positions in the U.S. Army

Ar·nauld (ærnou), Antoine (1612–94), French theologian, chief defender of the Jansenists. He wrote the treatise 'De la fréquente communion' (1643). His sister, Mère Angélique (1591–1661), was abbess of Port-Royal from 1602

Arne (ɑrn), Thomas Augustine (1710–78), English composer. He wrote mainly operas and masques, e.g. 'Comus' (1738), 'Artaxerxes' (1762). 'Rule Britannia' is from his 'Alfred' (1740)

Arn·hem (ɑ́rnhem) the capital (pop. 125,500) of the Dutch province of Gelderland, on the Lower Rhine, with a good harbor and chemical and metallurgical industries. There was an unsuccessful British airborne attack on the German positions here in Sept. 1944

Arnhem Land the extreme northern part of Australia's Northern Territory, mainly an aborigine reserve

ar·ni·ca (ɑ́rnikə) *n.* a member of *Arnica*, fam. *Compositae*, a genus of small, perennial plants found in temperate regions ‖ a tincture prepared particularly from *A. montana* and used as an embrocation for treating bruises and sprains [Mod. L., origin unknown]

Ar·no (ɑ́rnou) the chief river in Tuscany, Italy, 140 miles long. It rises in the Apennines and flows through Florence and Pisa into the Ligurian Sea

Ar·nold (ɑ́rnəld), Benedict (1741–1801), American general in the Revolutionary War. After fighting gallantly, he plotted unsuccessfully (1780) to betray West Point to the British and deserted to them (1780)

Arnold, Henry Harley (1886–1950), U.S. general, commanding U.S. army air forces in the 2nd world war

Arnold, Matthew (1822–88), English poet, critic and educationalist, son of Thomas Arnold. His main theme is the condition of modern man without religious faith. As a critic he encouraged the study in England of continental literature. In his essays he attacked the philistinism of prosperous industrialism. He wrote the classic political treatise 'Culture and Anarchy' (1869)

Arnold, Thomas (1795–1842), headmaster of Rugby School (1828–42). He reformed English public school education, which was almost entirely devoted to classical studies, by introducing the study of modern languages and modern history. He made sports an integral part of education and reformed boarding methods

Arnold of Brescia (c. 1100–55), Italian religious and political reformer, pupil of Abélard, and abbot of an Augustinian house at Brescia. He challenged the temporal power of the papacy and was condemned to death

a·ro·ma (əróumə) *n.* the characteristic, usually pleasant, odor given off by certain plants, spices etc. [O.F. *aromat* fr. L. fr. Gk]

ar·o·mat·ic (ærəmǽtik) **1.** *adj.* with a sharp, pleasant smell, like that of spices **2.** *n.* an aromatic plant or drug [F. *aromatique* fr. L. fr. Gk]

aromatic compound (*chem.*) an organic compound containing at least one benzene ring

arose *past* of ARISE

A·ro·se·me·na (ɑroseména), Carlos Julio (1920–), Ecuadorian politician and president (1961–3)

Arosemena, Justo (1817–86), Colombian jurist, writer and politician, the author of 'El Estado Federal'. He championed the federalist cause against the centralist

A·rou·et (æruːei), François Marie *VOLTAIRE

a·round (əráund) **1.** *adv.* more or less in a circle, on all sides, *we stood around and watched* ‖ near, more or less in the vicinity, *you will find some food around somewhere* **to have been around** to be worldly wise ‖ to have traveled widely **2.** *prep.* round about, encircling, *wrap your coat around you* ‖ approximately, *around midnight* ‖ within, in the area of, *somewhere around the house*

a·rous·al (əráuz'l) *n.* an arousing or being aroused

a·rouse (əráuz) *pres. part.* **a·rous·ing** *past* and *past part.* **a·roused** *v.t.* to excite, stir up ‖ (*old-fash., rhet.*) to wake up

Arp (ærp), Jean (Hans Arp, 1887–1966), French sculptor, an originator of dada and surrealism. He produced abstract forms of smooth, curved contours, usually in white stone, most of which suggest derivation from the human figure or natural forms

ar·peg·gi·o (ɑrpédʒiːou) *n.* (*mus.*) the playing of the notes in a chord successively instead of simultaneously [Ital.]

ar·que·bus (ɑ́rkwəbəs) *n.* (*hist.*) an early type of portable firearm (mid 15th-late 16th cc.), fired either slung from a tripod or placed on a forked rest [F. *arquebuse* fr. M.H.G.]

ar·rack (ǽrək) *n.* a spirit distilled in many Eastern countries from fermented coconut-palm juice or fermented rice etc. [fr. Arab. *araq*, juice]

ar·raign (əréin) *v.t.* to call before a court to answer a charge ‖ (*rhet.*) to denounce, censure **ar·ráign·ment** *n.* [A. F. *arraigner*, to accuse in court]

Ar·ran (ǽrən) an island (area 166 sq. miles, pop. 4,500) of Buteshire, Scotland, in the firth of Clyde

ar·range (əréindʒ) *pres. part.* **ar·rang·ing** *past* and *past part.* **ar·ranged** *v.t.* to put in order ‖ to dispose with taste, *to arrange flowers* ‖ to settle (a dispute etc.) ‖ to plan, *to arrange a meeting* ‖ (*mus.*) to adapt (a composition) for voices or instruments for which it was not originally written ‖ *v.i.* to make arrangements, *to arrange about a work permit* [O. F. *arangier*]

ar·range·ment (əréindʒmənt) *n.* the act of arranging ‖ the way in which arranging is done, *change the arrangement of the kitchen* ‖ a settlement (of a dispute etc.) ‖ something decided in advance, *the arrangement was to meet at 6* ‖ something made up from different things, or parts of things, *a plaster-and-string arrangement* ‖ (*pl.*) plans, preparations, *wedding arrangements* ‖ the arranging of a musical composition ‖ the composition so arranged [F.]

ar·rant (ǽrənt) *adj.* out-and-out, notorious [var. of ERRANT, wandering (first in *arrant thief* etc.)]

Ar·ras (ǽrɑs) the capital (pop. 46,446) of Pas-de-Calais, and ancient capital of Artois, N.E. France, an agricultural market with engineering and textile industries

ar·ras (ǽrəs) n. a wall hanging or screen made of tapestry [after *Arras*, France, noted in the 14th c. for tapestry]

ar·ray (əréi) n. military order, *battle array* ‖ (*hist.*) a fighting force in battle order ‖ a grand or impressive series or collection ‖ ceremonial dress or outward adornment, *chiefs in splendid array* ‖ (*law*) the composition of a jury, the persons making up a jury ‖ (*computer*) memory elements arranged in a meaningful pattern [O.F. *arei*]

array v.t. to arrange (troops etc.) in order ‖ to dress (oneself) magnificently ‖ (*law*) to impanel (a jury) [O.F. *areer* or *aroier*]

array processor (*computer*) specialized computer designed to perform repetitive arithmetic calculations on large groups of data, effective because of speed

array sonar sonar system incorporating state-of-the-art computer capacity for penetration of sea water and for detection and mapping

ar·rears (əríərz) pl. n. things outstanding or overdue for appropriate action (e.g. a backlog of work) **in arrears** behind time, waiting to be dealt with or paid up [O.F. *arere*, behind]

ar·rest (ərést) v.t. to seize and hold by legal authority or superior force ‖ to bring to a stop, check, *measures to arrest inflation* ‖ to attract and hold (one's sight or attention) [O.F. *arester*, to stop]

arrest n. seizure and imprisonment by legal authority or superior force ‖ a check, a stopping of forward movement or progress ‖ (*metall.*) discontinuity in heating or cooling, *arrest point* **under arrest** held in confinement or prison **under house arrest** not allowed to leave one's house **under open arrest** (esp. *mil.*) not allowed to leave one's quarters [O.F. *areste*, stoppage and *arrest*, act of arresting]

arrested development failure to maintain normal progress towards emotional (and sometimes physical) maturity

ar·rest·er gear (əréstər) *ARRESTING GEAR

arrester hook the retractable hook with which a carrier-based aircraft engages the arresting gear on landing

ar·rest·ing (əréstiŋ) adj. striking, attracting attention

arresting gear (*Am.*=*Br.* arrester gear) wires running across the flight deck of an aircraft carrier, with which the arrester hook of the aircraft engages as it lands, so as to halt in a short distance

Ar·rhe·ni·us (æréini:əs), Svante August (1859–1927), Swedish chemist and physicist. His work includes studies in physical and biological chemistry, and cosmology. He was awarded the Nobel prize in chemistry (1903) for his theory of ionic dissociation of electrolytes

Ar·ri·an (æri:ən), Flavius Arrianus (2nd c. A.D.), governor of Cappadocia and Greek historian, best known for his history ('Anabasis') of the campaigns of Alexander the Great

ar·ris (ǽris) n. (*archit.*) the edge formed by the meeting of two straight or curved surfaces, e.g. in a molding [O. F. *areste*, spine]

ar·ri·val (əráivəl) n. the act of arriving ‖ a person or thing that has arrived, *early arrivals at a flower market* [A.F. *arrivaille*]

ar·rive (əráiv) pres. part. **ar·riv·ing** past and past part. **ar·rived** v.i. to come to a place, reach a destination, end a journey ‖ to appear, come on the scene ‖ to win success, be recognized as successful **to arrive at** to gain (an object), reach (an end or state) [O.F. *ariver*, to come to shore]

ar·ri·viste, ar·ri·vist (æri:ví:st) n. a calculating self-centered person, determined to succeed at all costs [F.]

ARRL (*acronym*) for American Radio Relay League, a group made up of licensed amateur radio operators

ar·ro·gance (ǽrəgəns) n. haughtiness, an overbearing manner [F.]

ar·ro·gan·cy (ǽrəgənsi:) n. arrogance [fr. L. *arrogantia*]

ar·ro·gant (ǽrəgənt) adj. haughty, having or showing too high an opinion of one's own position or rights, contemptuous of others [F.]

ar·ro·gate (ǽrəgeit) pres. part. **ar·ro·gat·ing** past and past part. **ar·ro·gat·ed** v.t. to claim for oneself improperly **ar·ro·ga·tion** n. [fr. L. *arrogare* (*arrogatus*), to claim for oneself]

ar·row (ǽrou) n. the weapon shot from a bow (*ARCHERY) with a pointed (often barbed) head, and slender shaft, to the end of which feathers are attached ‖ a directing sign (→) ‖ a shoot on sugarcane [O.E. *earh*, *arwe*]

ar·row·head (ǽrouhed) n. the tip of an arrow, formerly of flint or stone, now usually metal

ar·row·root (ǽrouru:t, ǽrourʊt) n. a starchy flour made from the roots of a number of plants, but chiefly from *Maranta arundinacea*, West Indian arrowroot, used to make foods for invalids and arrowroot cookies ‖ the plant itself [formerly used by American Indians to absorb the poison from wounds made by poisoned arrows]

ar·row·y (ǽroui:) adj. having the shape or speed of an arrow

ar·roy·o (əróiou) pl. **ar·roy·os** n. a driedup water course, dry gully [Span.= stream]

Ar·sac·id (ɑrsǽsid) a member of a royal dynasty of Parthia (c. 250 B.C.–226 A.D.). They extended their kingdom from Bactria and the Caspian Sea to the Euphrates and India. The dynasty was overthrown (c. 226) by the Sassanids

arse (ɑrs) *ASS (buttocks)

ar·se·nal (ɑrsən'l) n. a place for the making and storing of weapons and munitions [Ital. *arsenale*, dock fr. Arab. *dar-al-sinah*, workshop]

ar·se·nic (ɑrsnik, ɑrsənik) **1.** n. a semimetallic element (symbol As, at. no. 33, at. mass 74.922). Its compounds are highly poisonous and are used in pest control and in medicine **2.** (ɑrsénik) adj. (*chem.*) of a compound in which arsenic is pentavalent **ar·sen·i·cal** (ɑrsénik'l) adj. of or containing arsenic **ar·se·ni·ous** (ɑrsí:ni:əs) adj. of a compound in which arsenic is trivalent **ár·se·nous** adj. arsenious [O.F. fr. L. fr. Gk fr. Arab. fr. Pers.]

ar·se·no·py·rite (ɑrsənoupáirait) n. a hard whitish or grayish mineral, FeAsS, the principal ore of arsenic [G.]

ar·sis (ɑrsis) pl. **ar·ses** (ɑrsi:z) n. the stressed syllable in a metrical foot (opp. THESIS) [L. fr. Gk=lifting (in poetry and music)]

ar·son (ɑrs'n) n. the crime of maliciously burning somebody else's buildings or property, or of burning one's own to get insurance money [O.F.]

ARSR (*mil. acronym*) for air route surveillance radar

art (ɑrt) n. the use of the imagination to make things of aesthetic significance ‖ the technique involved ‖ the theory involved ‖ one of the fine arts ‖ objects made by creative artists ‖ a sphere in which creative skill is used, *the art of shipbuilding* or other skill, *the art of lying* ‖ one of the humanities (as distinct from a science) ‖ (*pl., old-fash.*) artifice, wiles ‖ one of the liberal arts [O.F.]

ART an assembly system that responds to English language to produce routines, assignments, error control, etc., designed by Sperry-Rand Corp.

Ar·ta·xerx·es I (ɑrtəgzá:rksi:z) (d. 424 B.C.), king of Persia (c. 465–424 B.C.), son of Xerxes. He reconquered Egypt (c. 455 B.C.), which had revolted with Athenian help

Artaxerxes II (d. 358 B.C.), king of Persia (404–358 B.C.), son of Darius II. He crushed Cyrus the Younger's rebellion and the satraps' revolt and repelled Spartan intervention, but under his rule the empire progressively declined

Artaxerxes III (d. 338 B.C.), king of Persia (358–338), son of Artaxerxes II. After a reign of terror, he was assassinated (338 B.C.), and, after his son had been deposed (336 B.C.), was succeeded by Darius III

artefact *ARTIFACT

Ar·te·mis (ɑrtəmis) (*Gk mythol.*) goddess of chastity and of hunting, daughter of Zeus and twin sister of Apollo, helper of women in childbirth. She was later identified with the Roman Diana

Ar·te·mis (ɑrtəmis) n. (*mil.*) U.S. underwater warning system with listening posts beyond the continental shelf

ar·te·ri·al (ɑrtíəri:əl) adj. (*anat.*) of, from or like an artery ‖ of or pertaining to an artery in a system of communication or transport [F. *artériel*]

ar·te·ri·og·ra·phy (ɑrtiəri:ógrəfi:) n. (*med.*) **1.** process for X-raying arteries injected with radio-opaque dyes **2.** graphic record of the pulse —**arteriogram** n. diagnostic technique (and the instrument) to record the pulse; the record of arteriography

ar·te·ri·o·scle·ro·sis (ɑrtiəri:ouskləróusis) n. a chronic disease of the arteries characterized by the progressive hardening and thickening of the walls, leading to complete blockage and rupture [Mod. L. fr. *arterio-*, arterial+SCLEROSIS]

ar·ter·y (ɑrtəri:) pl. **ar·ter·ies** n. (*anat.*) one of the tubular, thick-walled, elastic vessels through which blood is pumped by the heart throughout the body (to return through the veins) ‖ an important channel (road, railway, river) in a system of communication and transport [fr. L. *arteria*, windpipe, artery fr. Gk]

ar·te·sian well (ɑrtí:ʒən) a well bored into the earth (often to a great depth) until water is forced to the surface by the pressure below [fr. F. *artésien*, of the old province of Artois, where such a well was first bored in the 12th c.]

art for art's sake the theory that the fine arts are free to seek beauty without regard for moral purpose or social effect

art·ful (ɑrtfəl) adj. tricky, crafty

ar·thrit·ic (ɑrθrítik) adj. of or having arthritis

ar·thri·tis (ɑrθráitis) n. inflammation of a joint or joints [fr. Gk *arthron*, ajoint]

ar·thro·pod (ɑrθrəpɒd) n. (*zool.*) a member of *Arthropoda*, an animal phylum characterized by a segmented body, a chitinous exoskeleton, and jointed appendages, which are modified for feeling, feeding, walking etc. The three main classes are arachnids, crustaceans and in sects **ar·throp·o·dal** (ɑrθrópəd'l) **ar·throp·o·dous** (ɑrθrópədəs) adjs [Mod. L. fr. Gk *arthron*, joint+*pous* (*podos*), foot]

Ar·thur (ɑrθər) *ARTHURIAN LEGEND

Arthur, Chester Alan (1830–86), 21st president (1881–5) of the U.S.A., following the assassination of President Garfield. A Republican handicapped by his complicity in New York machine politics, he nevertheless introduced (1883) a civil service reform act, vetoed (1882) a Chinese exclusion bill which violated a treaty with China, and prosecuted the Star-Route trials

Ar·thu·ri·an legend (ɑrθúəri:ən) stories of King Arthur, who was, probably, a Romano-British leader in the wars against the Saxon invaders. Although he held a 'court' he was not a king. A great body of legend grew around him, his knights, their quest for the Holy Grail, and his famous Round Table. This was elaborated (12th c.) by Geoffrey of Monmouth. Arthur holds chief place in English literature of heroic imagination, which includes 'Sir Gawayn and the Grene Knight' (c. 1346) and Sir Thomas Malory's 'Morte Darthur' (1485)

ar·ti·choke (ɑrtitʃouk) n. *Helianthus tuberosus*, the Jerusalem artichoke, closely related to the sunflower. It is tall, with a yellow flower, and has edible tubers somewhat like potatoes in appearance ‖ *Cynara scolymus*, the globe artichoke, related to the thistle. It produces flower heads enclosed in an involucre of edible fleshy bracts. It grows in Mediterranean countries and in parts of the U.S.A. ‖ *Stachys tuberifera*, the Chinese artichoke, which produces small, edible, jointed roots [fr. Ital. *articiocco*, fr. O. Span. fr. Arab. *al-karshuf*]

ar·ti·cle (ɑrtik'l) **1.** n. a particular thing of a distinct class, *skirts and other articles of clothing* ‖ a particular piece of writing in a larger work (book, encyclopedia, newspaper, periodical) ‖ a clause in a document ‖ a statement, regulation etc., *articles of apprenticeship* or a tenet, *articles of belief* ‖ (*zool.*) a segment of a jointed part ‖ (*gram.*) the words 'the', 'a', 'an' or analogous words in other languages, used as adjectives (*DEFINITE ARTICLE, *INDEFINITE ARTICLE) **2.** v. pres. part. **ar·ti·cling** past and past part. **ar·ti·cled** v.t. to bind by articles of apprenticeship ‖ to state (someone's offenses) in articles ‖ v.i. (with 'against') to bring charges [F.]

Articles of Confederation *CONFEDERATION, ARTICLES OF

ar·tic·u·lar (ɑrtíkjulər) adj. of or affecting the joints [fr. L. *articularis*]

ar·tic·u·late (ɑrtíkjulit) **1.** adj. divided by joints ‖ (of speech) divided into distinct words and syllables ‖ intelligible, able to speak intelligibly ‖ able to speak with fluency ‖ clearly and distinctly arranged or expressed **2.** v. (ɑrtíkjuleit) pres. part. **ar·tic·u·lat·ing** past and past part. **ar·tic·u·lat·ed** v.t. to pronounce (words and syllables) clearly and distinctly ‖ (generally in passive) to join together in sections, to joint ‖ v.i. to pronounce sounds distinctly [fr. L. *articulare* (*articulatus*), to utter distinctly]

ar·tic·u·la·tion (ɑrtíkjuléiʃən) n. the pronouncing of distinct sounds of speech ‖ (of man, animals, plants) the way in which different parts are joined together ‖ a joint [F.]

CONCISE PRONUNCIATION KEY: **(a)** æ, c*a*t; ɑ, c*a*r; ɔ f*aw*n; ei, sn*a*ke. **(e)** e, h*e*n; i:, sh*ee*p; iə, d*ee*r; ɛə, b*ea*r. **(i)** i, f*i*sh; ai, t*i*ger; ə:, b*i*rd. **(o)** o, *o*x; au, c*ow*; ou, g*oa*t; u, p*oo*r; ɔi, r*oy*al. **(u)** ʌ, d*u*ck; u, b*u*ll; u:, g*oo*se; ə, b*a*cillus; ju:, c*u*be. x, lo*ch*; θ, *th*ink; ð, bo*th*er; z, *Z*en; ʒ, cor*s*age. dʒ, sa*v*age; ŋ, orangutan*g*; j, *y*ak; ʃ, *f*ish; tʃ, fe*tch*; 'l, rabb*le*; 'n, redd*en*. Complete pronunciation key appears inside front cover.

ar·tic·u·la·tor (ɑrtíkjuléitər) n. someone who or something which articulates ‖ (pron.) an organ which gives speech sounds their acoustic character, e.g. lips, tongue, glottis **ar·tic·u·la·to·ry** (ɑrtíkjulətɔːri:,ɑrtíkjulətouri:) adj.

ar·ti·fact, ar·te·fact (ɑ́rtifækt) n. (archaeol.) a simple man-made object, such as a knapped flint, that provides evidence of an ancient culture ‖ a work of art (stressing its character as a product of making) ‖ (histology) a structure or changed appearance produced artificially or by death [fr. L. ars (artis), skill+acere (factus), to make]

ar·ti·fice (ɑ́rtifis) n. cunning, ingenuity in scheming ‖ (rhet.) skill in contriving, ingenuity (without guile) **ar·tif·i·cer** n. a skilled craftsman, esp. one whose work calls for great precision ‖ (mil.) a technician such as an armorer, mechanic etc. ‖ a maker, someone who devises [F.]

ar·ti·fi·cial (ɑrtifíʃəl) adj. man-made (as opposed to natural), an artificial lake ‖ made to imitate a natural product, an artificial leg ‖ synthetic, artificial leather ‖ insincere, artificial gaiety ‖ affected, an artificial way of writing [F. artificiel]

artificial horizon a small trough of mercury, the surface of which is always horizontal and in which the reflected image of the sun or a star is observed through a sextant ‖ an instrument giving the orientation of an aircraft to the horizontal

artificial insemination the introduction of semen into the uterus by artificial means, without coition

ar·ti·fi·ci·al·i·ty (ɑrtifíʃi:ǽliti:) pl. **ar·ti·fi·ci·al·i·ties** n. the state or quality of being artificial ‖ something artificial

artificial language a synthetic language based on a given set of specifications as to its use, e.g., for a computer

artificial respiration the artificial inducement of breathing, esp. by manual means, in a person suffering from asphyxia

artificial turf plastic ground cover resembling grass

Ar·ti·gas (ɑrtígas), José Gervasio (1764–1850), champion of Uruguayan independence against Spain, Buenos Aires and Brazil

ar·til·ler·y (ɑrtíləri:) n. guns, cannon etc., as opposed to portable firearms (used only of land forces, such as in a ship or aircraft being its armament) ‖ the branch of the army equipped with such weapons [O.F. artillerie]

ar·til·ler·y·man (ɑrtíləri:mən) pl. **ar·til·ler·y·men** (ɑrtíləri:mən) n. a soldier who serves with the artillery, a gunner

ar·ti·san (ɑrtíz'n) n. a trained craftsman, e.g. a printer, cabinetmaker, fitter [F. fr. Ital.]

art·ist (ɑ́rtist) n. a person who uses deliberate skill in making things of beauty, esp. (pop.) a painter ‖ a person who uses skill and taste in any activity ‖ an artiste [F. artiste]

ar·tiste (ɑrtí:st) n. a person who appears in public as a singer, dancer, pianist, actor etc. [F.]

ar·tis·tic (ɑrtístik) adj. relating to the fine arts, artistic theory ‖ of or connected with artists ‖ made or done with taste and skill, with an eye to beauty ‖ proficient in, fond of, or appreciative of the fine arts **ar·tis·ti·cal·ly** adv. [fr. F. artistique]

ar·tist·ry (ɑ́rtistri:) n. the exercise of an artist's gifts‖ artistic quality

artist's proof one of the first copies pulled from an engraved plate, for the engraver's approval

art·less (ɑ́rtlis) adj. simple and natural ‖ open, guileless

art·mo·bile (ɑ́rtməbi:l) n. traveling art exhibition housed in a trailer

art music unconventional compositions defined by the intention and method of the composer

art nou·veau (ærnu:vou) n. a style of design in architecture and crafts, also known as modern style or Jugendstil, which flourished 1890–1910. Formed in reaction to industrialization, it is characterized by sinuous, undulating lines often involving plant forms, mannered asymmetry and exotic coloring. Inspired by Morris, it was developed architecturally by Horta and Mackintosh [F.]

Ar·tois (ærtwa) a former province in extreme N.E. France, forming most of modern Pas-de-Calais, a hilly plateau producing wheat, sugar beet and vegetables. Historic capital: Arras. A countship cut (1180) out of Flanders, it passed to Burgundy and to the Hapsburgs before it was finally united to France (1659)

Arts and Crafts Movement the 19th-c. attempt (led chiefly by William Morris) to restore the skill and responsibility of the individual craftsman to the making of things in common use, in the face of machine standardization

art·sy (ɑ́rtsi:) adj. (slang or colloq.) simulating art; overly decorative

art·sy-craft·sy (ɑrtsi:kræftsi:, ɑrtsi:krɑ́ftsi:) adj. arty

art trouvé (Fr.) shapes or patterns perceived in ordinary objects and comparable in evocative force to work produced by artists; literally, "found art"

art·y (ɑ́rti:) adj. (of persons) posing as artistic, bohemian ‖ (of things) designed to be artistic, but pretentious in conception and feeble in impact

art·y-craft·y (ɑrti:kræfti:, ɑrti:krɑ́fti:) adj. arty

A·ru·ba (ərú:bə) *NETHERLANDS ANTILLES

ar·um (éərəm) n. a member of Arum, fam. Araceae, a genus of mainly tropical, herbaceous plants, sometimes climbing. They have a complicated inflorescence on a spadix, with female flowers at the base, male flowers above and sterile hairs above the male flowers. All are enveloped in a spathe. Their fetid smell attracts flies, which pollinate them. The fruit is a poisonous berry. Examples are the cuckoopint and the white-flowered Zantedeschia aethiopica, generally called calla lily (Am.=Br. arum lily), or lily of the Nile [L. fr. Gk aron]

ARVN (acronym) for Army of the Republic of South Vietnam

Ar·yan (éərjən, éəri:ən) 1. adj. (formerly) of the Caucasian race from which sprang the Indo-European peoples ‖ (formerly) of the Indo-Iranian branch of the Indo-European languages ‖ (formerly) of the Indo-European languages ‖ (in the teaching of the Nazis) belonging to a supposed master race (also called Nordic) of the original Caucasian stock with no mixture of Semitic 2. n. a member of the so-called Nordic race ‖ (formerly) the hypothetical parent language of the Indo-European family of languages (now called Indo-European) [fr. Skr. ārya, noble]

Ar·ya Sa·maj (ɑ́rjəsʌmɑ́ʒ) a 20th-c. reform movement within Hinduism. It rejects all polytheistic and idolatrous worship in favor of the Vedas alone

as (æz,əz) 1. conj. because, as he is late, we must wait ‖ at the time when, tell me your story as we walk on ‖ in the way in which, do as I tell you ‖ in accordance with that which, as he predicted, the wind changed ‖ though, sick as he was, he came to work ‖ (often with a correlative 'so' or 'as') to the same amount or degree that, as many as you wish ‖ (with a preceding 'so' or 'such') in such a way or to such an extent that, he so exaggerated as never to be believed **as it were** so to speak **as you were** (mil.) oral cancellation of a statement or order to troops, four of you— as you were—four of you will leave at once 2. prep. in the aspect, role, function, capacity of, he came as an observer ‖ like, he wandered as one in a dream **as a rule** usually 3. adv. to the same amount or degree, he drives as well as you ‖ for example, many words, as in English, are imitative in formation **as for** with reference to **as from** dating from ‖ written or sent as though from **as if** as it would if, he looked as if he had not slept **as long as** provided that **as of** at or on (a specified time or date), the law is effective as of midnight tonight **as regards** with reference to, our tastes differ as regards music **as though** in a way that resembles, like, she looks as though she had seen a ghost **as to** with reference to, he has no complaint as to salary **as well** also, in addition, bring a raincoat as well [O.E. allswā, all so]

As (chem.) arsenic

ASA (acronym) for American Standards Association

as·a·fet·i·da, as·sa·fet·i·da, as·a·foet·i·da, as·sa·foet·i·da (æsəfétidə, æsəfi:tidə) n. a gum resin from the roots of some W. Asian plants of genus Ferula, smelling of garlic, used in medicine as an antispasmodic [M.L. asa, fr. Pers. aza, mastic+foetida, stinking]

A·sa·hi·ga·wa (əsɑhí:gɑwɑ) (Asahikawa) a city (pop. 183,000) of central Hokkaido, Japan, an agricultural market: engineering, textile and chemical industries

ASALM (mil. acronym) for advanced strategic air-launched USAF air-to-air and air-to-surface defensive missile in development by McDonnell Douglas and Martin Marietta; operational in late 1980s

A·san·sol (əsɑnsóul) an industrial center (pop. 104,000) of W. Bengal, India, on the Calcutta-Varanasi railroad: coal mines, metallurgy (iron and steel, aluminum, tin)

ASAT (mil.) U.S.S.R.'s anti-satellite interception system Cf SAINT

as·bes·tos (æsbéstəs, æzbéstəs) 1. n. fibrous silicate materials, chiefly calcium magnesium silicate, used in the manufacture of flameproof fabrics and building materials, and for heat insulation 2. adj. made of or containing asbestos [Gk = unquenchable]

As·bur·y (ǽzbəri:), Francis (1745–1816), the first Methodist bishop consecrated in America (1784), an original leader of Methodism

A-scale sound level (acoustics) a measurement of sound approximating the sensitivity of the human ear, used to note the intensity or annoyance of sounds

As·ca·lon (ǽskələn) an ancient Philistine city in Israel north of Gaza, a center of the cult of Astarte from 1200 B.C.

as·cend (əsénd) v.i. to go or come up ‖ to rise ‖ to slope upwards ‖ (of sounds) to rise in pitch ‖ to rise from a lower degree or level ‖ v.t. to climb ‖ (rhet.) to mount, to ascend the throne ‖ to go up towards the source of, to ascend a river [fr. L. ascendere, to climb]

as·cend·ance, as·cend·ence (əséndəns) n. ascendancy

as·cend·an·cy, as·cend·en·cy (əséndənsi:) pl. **as·cend·an·cies, as·cend·en·cies** n. dominating influence or control

as·cend·ant, as·cend·ent (əséndənt) 1. adj. (astron., of a heavenly body) climbing towards the zenith, before beginning to set ‖ (astrol.) rising over the eastern horizon 2. n. (astrol.) the point of the ecliptic that is rising above the eastern horizon at any given instant (believed to have a dominating influence) ‖ (pl.) ancestors [O.F.=ascending]

as·cend·er (əséndər) n. (printing) the tall stroke of b, d, f, h, k, l, t

as·cend·ing (əséndiŋ) adj. rising, mounting ‖ (bot.) curving upwards

as·cen·sion (əsénʃən) n. (rhet.) the act of ascending or rising **the As·cen·sion** Christ's bodily ascent into heaven 40 days after his Resurrection [fr. L. ascensio (ascensionis)]

Ascension Day the feast celebrating Christ's Ascension, the 40th day after Easter

Ascension Island a solitary volcanic island (area 35 sq. miles, pop. 1,372) in the S. Atlantic, British since 1815 and inhabited only since then. In 1922 it became part of the colony of St Helena

as·cent (əsént) n. the act of ascending ‖ a climbing ‖ a rising from a lower degree or level ‖ a way up ‖ an amount of upward slope ‖ a going back in time, e.g. in a genealogy [fr. ASCEND by analogy with DESCENT]

as·cer·tain (æsərtéin) v.t. to find out **as·cer·tain·a·ble** adj. **as·cer·tain·a·bly** adv. **as·cer·tain·ment** n. [O.F. accrtener (acertain-)]

as·cet·ic (əsétik) 1. adj. practicing self-discipline with a view to spiritual improvement, esp. by learning to do without things good in themselves (e.g. warmth, comfort) ‖ frugal, austere ‖ (of personal appearance) giving the impression of self-denial, gaunt, spare 2. n. a person who practices asceticism ‖ a person who lives an austere life **as·cet·i·cal** adj. ascetic ‖ of or relating to asceticism ‖ like an ascetic **as·cét·i·cal·ly** adv. **as·cét·i·cism** n. the theory or practice of an ascetic [fr. Gk askētikos, industrious or like a hermit]

ascetic theology theology dealing with the operation of God's grace on all human effort to win perfection

Asch, (æʃ) Sholem (1880–1957), Yiddish novelist and dramatist, born in Poland. He spent time in France and England, became a naturalized citizen of the U.S., and, after 1954, lived in Israel. His many novels and plays include 'The Little Town' (1904), 'Uncle Moses' (1918), 'The Witch of Castle' (1926), 'Three Cities' (1929–32), 'The Nazarene' (1939), 'The Apostle' (1943), 'Mary' (1949), 'Moses' (1951), and 'The Prophet' (1957)

As·cham (ǽskəm), Roger (c. 1515–68), English classical scholar and humanist. He was tutor to Elizabeth I and author of 'The Schole-Master' (published 1570) and 'Toxophilus' (1565)

as·cid·i·an (əsídi:ən) n. (biol.) a tunicate, esp. a tunicate of the order Ascidiaceae [fr. Gk askidion, dim. of askos, wineskin, bladder]

as·cid·i·um (əsídi:əm) pl. **as·cid·i·a** (əsídi:ə) n. the trap of a pitcher plant, e.g. Nepenthes, which produces a fluid in which trapped insects are drowned [Mod. L. fr. Gk askidion, dim. of askos, wineskin, bladder]

ASC II (computer abbr.) of American Standard Code for Information Exchange, an alphanumeric information code for data processing

As·cle·pi·us (æsklí:pi:əs) (Gk mythol.) hero and god of healing, killed by Zeus for daring to restore Hippolytus to life. He corresponds to the Roman Aesculapius

as·co·carp (æskəkɑrp) n. the fully developed body (including the asci, spores and paraphyses) of an ascomycetous fungus **as·co·cárp·ous** adj. [fr. Gk askos, bladder + karpos, fruit]

as·co·go·ni·um (æskəgóuni:əm) pl. **as·co·go·ni·a** (æskəgóuni:ə) the oogonium of an ascomycete (*ANTHERIDIUM) [Mod. L.]

as·co·my·cete (æskoumáisi:t) n. a member of Ascomycetes, the largest class of fungi, both saprophytic and parasitic, showing great variation in morphology and reproduction, but all possessing an ascus. The class includes yeasts, truffles, the fungi that produce penicillin, many common mildews and molds, as well as the fungi responsible for elm and chestnut tree blights **as·co·my·cé·tous** adj. [fr. Mod. L. Ascomycetes]

a·scor·bic acid (əskórbik) vitamin C, used against colds and scurvy. It is present in citrus fruits, green leafy vegetables etc., and is also manufactured synthetically [fr. A-(without) + Mod. L. scorbutus, scurvy]

as·co·spore (æskəspɔr, æskəspour) n. a spore carried in an ascus [prob. F.]

as·cot (æskət) n. a dressy scarf worn by men [after Ascot Heath, a racetrack in Berkshire, England]

a·scrib·a·ble (əskráibəb'l) adj. capable of being ascribed

as·cribe (əskráib) pres. part. **as·crib·ing** past and past part. **as·cribed** v.t. to assign to a cause or source, he ascribes his success to prudence || to assign (to an author) as a conjecture, or from the available evidence || to regard as belonging, you can hardly ascribe such courage to him [O.F. ascrire]

as·crip·tion (əskrípʃən) n. a document or statement which ascribes || an ascribing [fr. L. ascriptio (ascriptionis)]

As·cu·lum (æskjuləm) an ancient town in S.E. Italy near which Pyrrhus defeated the Romans with heavy losses to his own army (279 B.C.)

as·cus (æskəs) pl. **as·ci** (æsai, æski) n. the spore sac in ascomycetes typically bearing after fusion eight ascospores [Mod. L. fr. Gk askos, bladder]

ASDIC 1. (Br.) (acronym) for Anti-Submarine Detection Investigation Committee, echo-ranging equipment, underwater detection devices **2.** (lower case) a forerunner of U.S. sonar

ASEAN group (acronym) for Association of Southeast Asian Nations, five non-Communist countries of Southeast Asia: Thailand, Malaysia, Singapore, Indonesia, and the Philippines

a·sep·sis (eisépsis,əsépsis) n. freedom from bacteria || the method or process of excluding bacteria, esp. in surgery (cf. ANTISEPSIS, *LISTER, *PASTEUR) [fr. A-(without) + Gk sepsis, decay]

a·sep·tic (eiséptik,əséptik) **1.** adj. free from bacterial infection || (of surgical instruments or materials) sterilized || designed to exclude bacteria (cf. ANTISEPTIC) **2.** n. a self-sterilizing substance **a·sép·ti·cal·ly** adv. [fr. A-(not) + Gk séptikos, decaying]

A-7 (mil.) U.S. Army attack aircraft

a·sex·u·al (eisékʃu:əl) adj. without sex, sexless || (biol., of reproduction) by other than sexual action, without the union of male and female germ cells (e.g. by sporangia in fungi, gemmae in bryophytes, spores in ferns, bilateral fission in protozoans) **a·sex·u·ál·i·ty** n. **a·séx·u·al·ly** adv.

ash (æʃ) n. the powder left when something has been burned, wood ash (cf. ASHES) [O.E. asce]

ash n. a member of Fraxinus, fam. Oleaceae, a genus of trees of temperate regions with pinnate leaves and roughish gray-green bark. They show black or dark gray buds in winter || the smooth-grained, springy wood of the ash, used for tool handles [O.E. æsc]

a·shamed (əʃéimd) adj. feeling shame, dishonor or disgust, at one's own bad or unworthy behavior or because or on behalf of another || refusing, or reluctant, to do something through pride or fear of ridicule, I am ashamed to go in these clothes [past part. of obs. v. ashame, to shame]

A·shan·ti (əʃænti:) an administrative region (area 24,379 sq. miles, pop. 1,109,000) of Ghana. Capital: Kumasi. Language: Akan. It was an independent kingdom from the late 17th c. until its annexation by the British in 1901. Its civilization flourished in the 18th c. The Ashanti resisted British rule and four wars were fought (1824–7, 1873–4, 1893–4, 1895–6)

Ashbery, (æʃberi:) John (1927–), U.S. poet noted for his imagery and inventive verse. His works include 'Turandot' (1953), 'Some Trees' (1956), 'Rivers and Mountains' (1966), 'Self Portrait in a Convex Mirror' (1975; Pulitzer Prize), 'Shadow Train' (1981), and 'The Wave' (1984)

Ash·bur·ton (æʃbə:rt'n), Alexander Baring, Baron (1774–1848), British financier and diplomat. He negotiated (1842) with Daniel Webster the Webster-Ashburton Treaty

ash can (Am.=Br. dustbin) a receptacle for ashes and household refuse

Ash·can school (æʃkæn) a school of American realist painters of the early 20th c., who painted scenes of city life. John Sloan and George Bellows are best known

Ash·dod (æʃdɒd) the chief port of Israel, 20 miles south of Jaffa, inaugurated Oct. 1965

Ashe, (æʃ) Arthur (1943–), U.S. tennis player and coach, who was the first black to win a major tennis title. He won the U.S. Open (1968), the Australian Open (1970), and Wimbledon (1975). Due to ill health, he retired in 1980 and then coached the U.S. Davis Cup team

ash·en (æʃən) adj. of an ash tree || made of the wood of an ash || (of persons) deathly pale

Ash·er (æʃər) Hebrew patriarch, son of Jacob || the Israelite tribe of which he was the ancestor

ash·es (æʃiz) pl. n. what is left when a fire has burned itself out || powdery matter ejected by volcanoes || the remains of a human body (whether or not cremated) **the Ashes** a symbol of victory in a series of cricket matches (test matches) between England and Australia, or the series itself **to lay in ashes, reduce to ashes** to burn to the ground, destroy **to turn to ashes in one's mouth** to become a bitter disappointment, to become repugnant after being pleasant

Ash·ke·lon (æʃkələn) Ascalon

Ash·ke·naz·ic (aʃkənázik) adj. of the Ashkenazim or their culture and language (Yiddish)

Ash·ke·naz·im (aʃkənázim) pl. n. the Jews of E. and N. Europe (cf. SEPHARDIM) [Heb.]

Ash·kha·bad (æʃkəbæd, æʃkəbad) the capital (pop. 332,000) of Turkmenistan U.S.S.R., near the Iranian border. Industries: glass, food, textiles, leather, printing, film making, carpets. An earthquake almost destroyed it in 1948. University

ash·lar, ash·ler (æʃlər) n. a building stone cut and squared by a mason || stone work or stone facing made of such stones **ash·lar·ing, ash·ler·ing** n. a boarding which runs from the floor of an attic to meet the rafters of the sloping roof || stone work built with ashlars [O.F. aiseler, a little board]

a·shore (əʃór, əʃáur) pred. adj. and adv. to or on the shore, on land

ash·ram (æʃrəm) n. a Hindu religious retreat

ash·tray (æʃtrei) n. a receptacle for cigarette ends, ashes, used matches etc.

A·shur·ba·ni·pal (aʃuərbáni:pal) (d. c. 633 B.C.), the last great king of Assyria (668–c. 663 B.C.), son of Esarhaddon. He built the palace and library at Nineveh

Ash Wednesday the first day of Lent, so called from the ceremony of putting ashes on the forehead as a sign of penitence. The ash is from palms blessed on Palm Sunday of the previous year

ash·y (æʃi:) comp. **ash·i·er** superl. **ash·i·est** adj. of or made of ashes || (of persons) ashen in color

A·si (æsi:) *ORONTES

A·sia (éiʒə, éiʃə) the largest continent (area 17,600,000 sq. miles, pop. 2,693,255,000). Political units: Afghanistan, Bahrain, Bangladesh, Bhutan, Bonin Is, Brunei, Burma, China, Cyprus, part of Egypt, Gaza Strip, Hong Kong, India, Indonesia, Iran, Iraq, Israel, Japan, Jordan, Kampuchea, the Democratic People's Republic of Korea, the Republic of Korea, Kuwait, Laos, Lebanon, Macao, Malaysia, Maldive Is, Mongolian People's Republic, Oman, Nepal, Pakistan, Papua New Guinea, the Philippines, Qatar, Ryukyu Is, Saudi Arabia, Sikkim, Singapore, Sri Lanka, Syria, Taiwan, Thailand, part of Turkey, United Arab Emirates, part of the U.S.S.R., Vietnam, the Republic of Yemen, the Peoples' Democratic Republic of Yemen. HISTORY (see also separate entries). The earliest Asian civilizations were those of Sumer and Akkad in Mesopotamia and of the Indus valley in India (3rd millennium B.C.). In the 2nd millennium B.C. first the Amorites and then the Kassites invaded Mesopotamia, while Asia Minor was invaded by the Hittites, and the Indus valley by the Aryans. Chinese civilization developed under the Chou dynasty (1122–221 B.C.). The Assyrians conquered Babylonia (13th c. B.C.) and created an empire which reached its peak in the 7th c. B.C., to be captured by the Medes and Babylonians (605 B.C.) and then by the Persians (539 B.C.). The 5th c. B.C. saw the spread of the teachings of Confucius, Zoroaster and Buddha. The Persian Empire was destroyed (331 B.C.) by Alexander the Great, who extended Greek power from the Mediterranean to the Indus. Central Asia came under the domination of China during the Han dynasty (206 B.C.–220 A.D.). The Roman Empire spread as far as the Euphrates, but Constantinople and its Eastern Empire separated from Rome (395 A.D.), and Roman power in Asia was opposed by Persia under the Sassanids. In the 7th c. the Arabs extended the power of Islam to Persia, Syria and Israel, ruling their empire from Baghdad (750–1258). The Turks conquered most of Asia Minor, and their capture of Jerusalem (1072) led to the Crusades (1095–1291). The Mongols, under Genghis Khan and his descendants, conquered China, Manchuria, Korea, N. India and E. Russia (13th–14th cc.). Persia regained independence under the shahs, and China under the Ming dynasty (1368–1644). Constantinople was taken by the Ottoman Turks (1453), and the Mogul Empire was established in India (16th–17th cc.).

European conquest in Asia dates from the voyage of Vasco da Gama round the Cape to India (1498). The Portuguese monopoly of Asian trade was destroyed by Holland, England and France. Trade with the coasts and islands was developed by the English East India Company (1600) and the Dutch East India Company (1602), and colonization followed. Britain defeated France (1763) in the struggle for control of India, and established the British Raj. The East Indies were colonized by Holland (17th–20th cc.) and Indo-China by France (1862–83).

In Russia, Ivan the Great threw off the domination of the Tatars (1480) and the Cossacks began settling Siberia (16th c.). By the 17th c., Russia had spread to the Pacific and collided with Japanese expansion (1904–5). Japan, which had already defeated China (1895), emerged victorious, annexed Korea (1910), and occupied Manchuria (1932–45). China, which had been a republic since 1912, was invaded by Japan (1937), which then overran S.E. Asia until defeated by the Allies (1945).

European influence has given place politically since 1945 to national independence and self-government. India, Pakistan, Sri Lanka, Cyprus, Burma, Malaya and Singapore were granted independence by Britain, Indochina won independence from France, and Indonesia from Holland. The state of Israel was created, Arab nationalism began to assert itself, China came under a communist government (1949) and anti-communist alliances (SEATO, 1954, and the Baghdad Pact, 1955) were formed. Malaya, Singapore, Sarawak and North Borneo united to form the Federation of Malaysia (1963), but Singapore seceded (1965). Vietnam became a communist country following a long civil war (1975). Laos and Cambodia (Kampuchea) also fell to the communists that same year. The U.S.S.R. invaded Afghanistan (1979) but resistance to their control continued. In many parts of Asia ethnic and religious differences have led to conflicts: Iran-Iraq, India-Pakistan, Arabs-Israelis, and Muslims-Christians in Lebanon among others, making much of Asia the scene of hostilities

Asia dollar (economics) money market term for U.S. currency based in Singapore, controlled by Monetary Authority of Singapore Cf EURODOLLAR

Asia Minor the historic name for that peninsula (area about 200,000 sq. miles) of W. Asia which now forms the greater part of Turkey. It is bordered by the Black Sea, the Sea of Marmara, the Aegean and the Mediterranean, and by the Armenian plateau on the east. It is separated from Europe by the Bosporus and Dardanelles on the northwest. It forms an elevated plateau sloping northwards and westwards, with mountain ranges in the east. After the decline of the Hittite kingdom (1900–1200 B.C.) and the conquest of Troy and the Trojan allies, the coast was colonized by the Greeks (1000 B.C.) while Phrygia and Lydia developed in the interior. It was conquered by Cyrus II of Persia (546 B.C.) and by Alexander (333 B.C.) and was divided into several small Hellenic states. It became part of the Roman and Byzantine Empires and was raided by Arabs (from the 7th c.) and by the Seljuk Turks (11th c.). The Crusaders set up the empire of Trebizond (1204–1461), overrun successively by the Seljuk Turks, the Mongols and the Ottoman Turks. Asia Minor gradually became part of the Ottoman Empire (14th and 15th cc.)

A·sian (éiʒən, éiʃən) 1. *adj.* of or relating to the continent or people of Asia 2. *n.* a native of Asia

A·si·at·ic (eiʒiːǽtik, eifiːǽtik) 1. *n.* a member of one of the peoples of Asia 2. *adj.* of or pertaining to Asia or its peoples [fr. L. *Asiaticus* fr. Gk]

Asiatic beetle *Anomala orientalis*, a beetle whose larva destroys sugarcane and grass. It is native to Japan and is established in the U.S.A.

a·side (əsáid) 1. *adv.* to or on one side, *to step aside* ‖ out of the way, *to lay aside* ‖ apart, *joking aside* 2. *n.* words spoken in a play which by convention are heard by the audience but not by the actors ‖ words spoken low to a person or group which by-standers are not meant to hear ‖ a digression

aside from besides in addition to ‖ with the exception of

a·sien·to (asjéntɔ) *n.* a contract under which the Spanish government farmed out the slave trade to a private contractor (power, company or an individual), who would sell licenses and direct the shipment to the Spanish colonies. It was won (1685) by Louis XIV and (1713, Treaty of Utrecht) by Britain [Span.]

as·i·nine (ǽsinain) *adj.* stupid **as·i·nin·i·ty** (æsiníniti:) *pl.* **as·i·nin·i·ties** *n.* crass stupidity or an instance of this [fr. L. *asininus*, asslike]

A·sir (æsíər) a plateau region of S. Saudi Arabia, bordering Yemen and the Red Sea. Chief town: Abha (pop. 10,000). It gained independence (1915) from the Ottoman Empire, but was largely occupied by Saudi Arabia (1920–33) and annexed

A-6 *INTRUDER

ask (æsk, ɑsk) *v.t.* to request (something) of someone, *may I ask a favor of you?* ‖ to inquire about, *ask the way home* ‖ to inquire of (someone), *ask him about mealtimes* ‖ to demand (a price) ‖ to invite ‖ *v.i.* to make a request ‖ to inquire ‖ (with 'for') to necessitate, *this asks for great prudence* **for the asking** simply by asking, without charge **to ask after someone** to ask for news of someone, esp. to inquire about his health **to ask for it** (or **trouble**) to behave in a way that will get one into trouble [O.E. *ascian*]

a·skance (əskǽns) *adv.* (in the phrase) **to look askance at** to view with suspicion or disapproval [etym. doubtful]

a·skew (əskjúː) *adv. and pred. adj.* crooked, out of line [etym. doubtful, perh. rel. to SKEW V.]

ask out *v.* to withdraw

a·slant (əslǽnt, əslánt) 1. *adv.* slantwise, across at an angle 2. *prep.* obliquely across

a·sleep (əslíːp) 1. *pred. adj.* sleeping ‖ numb, esp. through cramp 2. *adv.* into a state of sleep **to fall asleep** to pass from waking to sleeping ‖ (*euphemistic*) to die

a·slope (əslóup) *adv. and pred. adj.* sloping, aslant

As·ma·ra (ɑzmɑ́rə) the capital (pop. 474,241) of Eritrea, Ethiopia, on Hamasen plain, at 7,765 ft

ASMD (*mil. acronym*) for air-ship missile defense system

a·so·cial (eisóuʃəl) *adj.* tending to avoid social intercourse ‖ self-centered and indifferent to the social needs of others

A·so·ka (əsóukə) (d. c. 232 B.C.), Indian emperor (c. 273–c. 232 B.C.), whose empire extended from Afghanistan over all the present area of

India except for South Deccan. Remorse at his wars converted him to Buddhism, which he raised from being a minor sect to the official religion of his empire

AS-1 *KENNEL

asp (æsp) *n. Vipera aspis*, a viper, a small poisonous European snake ‖ *Cerastes cornutus*, the horned viper of N. Africa [fr. L. *aspis* fr. Gk]

ASP (*acronym*) for Anglo-Saxon Protestant

A·spa·ra·gin·ase (əspǽrədʒineis) *n.* (*pharm.*) drug containing the enzyme L-asparinase created by *E coli* used in treating leukemia; marketed as Elspar *Cf* INTERFERON

as·par·a·gus (əspǽrəgəs) *n.* a member of *Asparagus*, fam. *Liliaceae*, a perennial plant native to the E. Mediterranean region. Each spring the plant (or 'crown') produces edible, leafless, thick green shoots, which are cut by hand when a few inches tall [L. fr. Gk *asparagos*]

as·par·tine (æspɑrtiːn) *n.* artificial sugar substitute introduced by G. D. Searle & Co, Skokie, Ill., in 1981, marketed as Nutra-Sweet

as·par·to·kin·ase (aspɑrtoukíneis) *n.* (*biochem.*) enzyme that catalyzes the reaction of aspartic acid with adenosine triphosphate to create aspartyl phosphate

As·pa·sia (æspéiʒə) (5th c. B.C.), a courtesan from Miletus of great beauty and intelligence who became the mistress of Pericles

as·pect (ǽspekt) *n.* look, outward appearance ‖ the direction in which a thing faces ‖ the angle from which a thing may be regarded, *from a selfish aspect* ‖ (*aeron.*) the way in which a wing enters the air, the relation between span and mean chord ‖ (*astron.*) the relative position of one planet to another, as seen from the earth, which astrologers held to influence human fortunes ‖ (*gram.*) a form of the verb expressing inception, duration or completion of the action [fr. L. *aspicere* (*aspectus*), to look at]

aspect ratio ratio between height and width of a view in a television screen or projected on a film screen

as·pen (ǽspən) *Populus tremula*, *P. tremuloides*, *P. grandidentata*, or any of various other small poplar trees whose leaves quiver in the slightest breeze [O.E. *œsp*, *œps*]

as·per·a·tion (æspəréiʃən) *n.* (*med.*) mechanical removal of dead skin cells

as·per·ges (æspé:rdʒi:z) *n.* (*eccles.*) the ceremony of sprinkling holy water on the altar, clergy and congregation before High Mass ‖ the antiphon sung during the sprinkling [L. (opening words, *Asperges me, Domine*, Thou shalt sprinkle me, Lord)]

as·per·gil·lo·sis (æspərdʒiloúsis) *n.* rare infection usually in the lungs, caused by a genus of fungi *Aspergillus funigatus*

as·per·gil·lum (æspərdʒíləm) *pl.* **as·per·gil·la** (æspərdʒílə) *n.* the brush or metal ball with perforated holes used for sprinkling in the asperges [M.L. fr. *aspergere*, to sprinkle]

as·per·i·ty (əspériti:) *pl.* **as·per·i·ties** *n.* (of the temper or the tongue) sharpness ‖ (of a surface) roughness, unevenness ‖ (of weather) severity [O.F. *asprete*]

as·perse (əspé:rs) *pres. part.* **as·pers·ing** *past and past part.* **as·persed** *v.t.* to malign, try to hurt the reputation of [fr. L. *aspergere* (*aspersus*), to sprinkle, spatter]

as·per·sion (əspé:rʒən, əspé:rʃən) *n.* an oblique assault on a person's reputation ‖ a sprinkling with holy water [fr. L. *aspersio* (*aspersionis*), sprinkling]

as·per·so·ri·um (æspərsóri:əm, æspərsóuri:əm) *pl.* **as·per·so·ri·a** (æspərsóri:ə, æspərsóuri:ə), **as·per·so·ri·ums** *n.* a holy-water vessel ‖ an aspergillum [M.L.]

as·phalt (ǽsfolt, ǽsfælt) 1. *n.* a bituminous derivative of petroleum occurring as an industrial residue or naturally, and containing varying proportions of other organic and mineral materials, used principally for surfacing roads and flat roofs 2. *adj.* with a surface of asphalt 3. *v.t.* to apply a surface of asphalt to [fr. L.L. *asphaltum* fr. Gk prob. fr. Semitic]

asphalt cloud (*mil.*) an antimissile technique dispersing asphalt particles to disable heat shields of offensive missiles, causing the missiles to burn up or deflect

asphalt jungle (*colloq.*) violence-prone urban area *Cf* BLACKBOARD JUNGLE

as·pho·del (ǽsfədel) *n.* a member of *Asphodelus*, fam. *Liliaceae*, a genus of Old World perennial plants with long racemes of white flowers ‖ (*Gk mythol.*) the flower that adorned the Elysian Fields [fr. L. *asphodelus* fr. Gk]

as·phyx·i·a (æsfíksi:ə) *n.* the condition in which a person is not able to get air into his lungs. The commonest causes are drowning, poisoning by coal gas or other vapors, and obstruction of the respiratory passages by external pressure, i.e. suffocation or strangulation, or by internal blockage, e.g. in diseases of the throat or windpipe **as·phyx·i·al** 1. *adj.* causing asphyxia or suffocation 2. *n.* an agent with this property **as·phyx·i·ate** (æsfíksi:eit) *pres. part.* **as·phyx·i·at·ing** *past and past part.* **as·phyx·i·at·ed** *v.t.* to cause asphyxia in ‖ *v.i.* to be a victim of asphyxia **as·phyx·i·a·tion, as·phýx·i·á·tor** *ns* [Mod. L. fr. Gk. Gk=stopping of the pulse]

as·pic (ǽspik) *n.* a clear jelly made from meat (or fish) stock and often used as a mold for meats [F.]

as·pi·dis·tra (æspidístrə) *n.* a plant of genus *Aspidistra*, fam. *Liliaceae*, with large dark-green parallel-veined leaves, native to Asia [Mod. L. fr. Gk *aspis* (*aspidos*), shield + *astron*, star]

as·pir·ant (əspáiərənt, ǽspərənt) *n.* a person anxious to win a desirable thing or position, *an aspirant to the priesthood* [F.]

as·pi·rate (ǽspəreit) 1. *v.t. pres. part.* **as·pi·rat·ing** *past and past part.* **as·pi·rat·ed** *v.t.* to pronounce with an h sound, *do not aspirate the h of 'honesty'* ‖ (*phon.*) to pronounce as an aspirate ‖ (*med.*) to remove (fluid or gas) with an aspirator 2. (ǽspərit) *n.* the sound represented by the letter h ‖ an aspirate consonant 3. *adj.* pronounced as an aspirate, *the h of 'how' is aspirate, the h of 'honor' is not* ‖ (*phon.*, of a consonant) followed by a slight puff of breath [fr. L. *aspirare* (*aspiratus*), to breathe upon]

as·pi·ra·tion (æspəréiʃən) *n.* ambition or an ambition ‖ the pronunciation of an aspirate or the sign that marks one (e.g. the rough breathing in Greek) ‖ (*med.*) the action or use of an aspirator [fr. L. *aspiratio* (*aspirationis*), a breathing]

as·pi·ra·tor (ǽspəreitər) *n.* a suction pump or similar device ‖ (*med.*) an instrument used to suck fluid or poison from the body **as·pir·a·to·ry** (əspáiərətɔːri, əspáiərəlouri:) *adj.* relating to suction [fr. L. *aspirare* (*aspiratus*), to breathe upon]

as·pire (əspáiər) *pres. part.* **as·pir·ing** *past and past part.* **as·pired** *v.i.* to be eager (to *win* something), to have an ambition (to achieve something desirable or lofty) [fr. L. *aspirare*, to breathe upon]

as·pi·rin (ǽspərin, ǽsprin) *n.* acetylsalicylic acid. It is widely used in powder or tablet form to relieve pain or reduce fever, and has a beneficial effect on certain forms of rheumatism [fr. G.]

a·squint (əskwínt) *adv. and pred. adj.* with a squint

As·quith (ǽskwiθ), Herbert Henry, 1st earl of Oxford and Asquith (1852–1928), British statesman, leader of the Liberal party (1908–26) and prime minister (1908–16)

Asraam (æsrám) *n.* (*mil.*) U.S. Navy project for advanced short-range air-to-air missile

ASROC (*mil. acronym*) for antisubmarine rocket

ass (æs) *n.* any of several mammals of the genus *Equus*, esp. *E. asinus*, the donkey. It can live on a smaller quantity and coarser quality of food than the horse, can carry heavy burdens over uneven ground, and has been domesticated since ancient times. By mating the horse with the she-ass, the hybrid hinny is produced. The jackass and mare produce the mule, which is larger and more useful than the hinny ‖ a stupid person **to make an ass of oneself** to do something foolish [O.E. *assa*]

ass *n.* (Am.=Br. arse, not in polite usage) the buttocks [O.E. *œors*]

-ass (æs) *suf.* (*colloq.*) derogatory intensive combining suffix, e.g., fancy-ass, smart-ass

Assad, Hafez al- (hɑfez ʌl ɑsɑ́d) (c. 1928–), Syrian president (1971–). He served as Syria's defense minister (1966–70) before being elected president

assafetida, assafoetida *ASAFETIDA

assagai *ASSEGAI

as·sa·i (ʌsɑi:) *n. Euterpe edulis*, a palm tree of Brazil with purple edible fruit ‖ a drink or flavor made from the fruit [Port. *assahy*, fr. Tupi]

as·sail (əséil) *v.t.* to attack vigorously [O.F. *assalir*, to leap at]

as·sail·ant (əséilənt) *n.* an attacker [F.]

As·sam (ǽsæm) a state (area 84,899 sq. miles, pop. 19,902,826) in N.E. India including the valley of the Brahmaputra River. Capital: Shil-

CONCISE PRONUNCIATION KEY: **(a)** æ, c*a*t; ɑ, c*a*r; ɔ f*aw*n; ei, sn*a*ke. **(e)** e, h*e*n; i:, sh*ee*p; iə, d*ee*r; ɛə, b*ea*r. **(i)** i, f*i*sh; ai, t*i*ger; əː, b*i*rd. **(o)** o, *o*x; au, c*ow*; ou, g*oa*t; u, p*oo*r; ɔi, r*oy*al. **(u)** ʌ, d*u*ck; u, b*u*ll; uː, g*oo*se; ə, b*a*cillus; juː, c*u*be. x, lo*ch*; θ, *th*ink; ð, bo*th*er; z, *Z*en; ʒ, cor*s*age; dʒ, sava*g*e; ŋ, orangutan*g*; j, *y*ak; ʃ, *fi*sh; tʃ, fe*tch*; 'l, rabb*le*; 'n, red*den*. Complete pronunciation key appears inside front cover.

long. It has a tropical climate and is forested. Agricultural products: tea, rice and jute. Coal and crude oil are exploited

As·sas·sin (əsǽsin) a member of a fanatical secret order of the Ismaʻilis which flourished in the 11th and 12th cc. in Persia and Syria. It became notorious for its terrorist murders, which its members considered to be a religious duty

as·sas·sin (əsǽsin) *n.* a person who kills, or tries to kill, another by violent means, generally for political or religious motives and often by treachery [after ASSASSIN, the Ismaʻili sect, fr. Arab. *hashshāshīm*, hashish-eaters]

as·sas·si·nate (əsǽsineit) *pres. part.* **as·sas·si·nat·ing** *past* and *past part.* **as·sas·si·nat·ed** *v.t.* to kill as an assassin ‖ death at the hands of an assassin [fr. M. L. *assassinare (assassinatus)*]

as·sault (əsɔ́lt) *n.* a vigorous armed attack, esp. a head-on charge ‖ a violent critical attack ‖ (*law*) an unlawful threat to use force against another person [O.F. *asaut*]

assault *v.t.* to make an assault on ‖ (*law*) to use violence against [O.F. *asauter*]

assault and battery (*law*) an attack on a person accompanied by blows and use of force

as·say (əséi) *v.t.* to test (an ore) for the amount of metal it contains ‖ to determine the purity of (a metal) ‖ *v.i.* to make an assay **as·say·a·ble** *adj.* [O. F. *assayer*]

as·say (ǽsei,əséi) *n.* the determination of the proportion of a metal in an ore or alloy, esp. determination of the purity of precious metals ‖ a sample of metal for such trial ‖ the result of the trial [O. F. *assai, assay*]

as·se·gai, as·sa·gai (ǽsigai) *n.* the throwing-spear, with a flat iron head, of S. African tribes ‖ *Curtisia faginea*, the S. African tree whose hard wood is used for the shaft [F. or Port. fr. Arab. *al*, the+*zaghāyah*, spear fr. Berber]

as·sem·blage (əsémblidʒ) *n.* a number of persons or things gathered together ‖ an assembling ‖ art form or composition of scraps of various materials, e.g., cloth, hardware, paper [F.]

as·sem·ble (əsémb'l) *pres. part.* **as·sem·bling** *past* and *past part.* **as·sem·bled** *v.t.* to bring together, *assemble your men* ‖ to fit together, *to assemble the parts of a radio* ‖ *v.i.* to come together, *a crowd assembled* [O. F. *asembler*]

as·sem·bler (əsémblər) *n.* (*computer*) program that produces a machine language program on which the processor can operate

assembler language symbolic representation of the internal language of a machine. Symbols are used as memories to make programs easier to read and write —**assembler** *n* device that translates these symbols into machine language

as·sem·bly (əsémbli:) *pl.* **as·sem·blies** *n.* a gathering of people ‖ (of machines etc.) assemblage ‖ (*mil.*) a signal sounded for troops to fall in on parade ‖ (*computer*) conversion of a source program to a machine language [O.F. *assemblee*]

assembly language (*computer*) memoric programming language approximating a machine language, e.g., Argus, Easy

assembly line (in mass-production factories) an arrangement by which components can be progressively put together as they travel through the factory on a conveyor belt or moving platform

as·sem·bly·man (əsémbli:mən) *pl.* **as·sem·bly·men** (əsémbli:mən) *n.* a member of the assembly (lower house) of the legislature in some states of the U.S.A.

as·sent (əsént) *n.* an acceptance (of a doctrine, statement, logical proposition etc.) as true [O.F.]

assent *v.i.* to give expressed or unexpressed mental acceptance to the truth or rightness of a doctrine, conclusion etc. ‖ to say yes [O.F. *assenter*]

as·sert (əsə́:rt) *v.t.* to state as true, *to assert one's innocence* ‖ to maintain, insist on, *to assert a claim* ‖ to make effective, use with effect, *can you assert your influence on him?* **to assert itself** to become active, make its effect felt **to assert oneself** to impose one's proper authority ‖ to be domineering [fr. L. *asserere (assertus)*, to claim or set free a slave by laying one's hand on his head]

as·ser·tion (əsə́:rʃən) *n.* a positive statement ‖ the act of asserting [fr. L. *assertio (assertionis)*, a setting free]

as·ser·tive (əsə́:rtiv) *adj.* dominating, *an assertive manner* ‖ positive, allowing no denial or opposition, *an assertive statement*

as·ser·tor (əsə́:rtər) *n.* a person who asserts

as·sess (əsés) *v.t.* to fix the value or amount of, esp. for the purpose of taxation ‖ to impose a charge for, *damages were assessed at $5,000* ‖ to judge the value or worth of (other than in money), to estimate, *to assess character* **as·sess·a·ble** *adj.* **as·sess·ment** *n.* the amount assessed ‖ the act of assessing ‖ an estimate [O.F. *assesser*]

as·ses·sor (əsésər) *n.* a person who assesses value for taxation, or apportions taxes, fines etc. ‖ (*insurance*) a person who estimates the value of property for which a claim is made and investigates the legality of the claim ‖ (esp. *hist.*) an expert assistant who listens to a case and advises the judge **as·ses·so·ri·al** (æsisɔ́ri:el psisɔ́uri:əl) *adj.* [O. F. *assessor*]

as·set (ǽset) *n.* anything one owns or any quality one has that is of value or use ‖ (*pl.*) the total property of a person, firm or institution, esp. that part which can be used to pay debts ‖ (*pl.*) the positive items on a balance sheet [A.F. *assets*, orig. sing. but now treated as pl., with sing. *asset*]

as·sev·er·ate (əsévəreit) *pres. part.* **as·sev·er·at·ing** *past* and *past part.* **as·sev·er·at·ed** *v.t.* to affirm solemnly **as·sev·er·á·tion** *n.* the act of asseverating ‖ the statement made [fr. L. *asseverare (asseveratus)*, to speak in earnest]

as·si·du·i·ty (æsidú:iti:, əsidjú:iti:) *n.* untiring diligence or attention [fr. L. *assiduitas (assiduitatis)*]

as·sid·u·ous (əsídʒu:əs) *adj.* constant in working or giving attention [fr. L. *assiduus*]

as·sign (əsáin) *n.* (*law*) a person to whom property or a right is legally assigned, (esp.) *heirs and assigns* [F. *assigne*]

assign *v.t.* to give as a share, allot, to *assign positions to people* ‖ to nominate, appoint, *to assign a person to a position* ‖ to give or make over (property or a right) ‖ to fix or determine (a day, time etc.) ‖ to ascribe to a given time, authorship, origin, class ‖ to give as a task [O.F. *assigner*]

as·sig·nat (ǽsignæt) *n.* (*F. hist.*) a piece of paper currency issued (1789-96) during the French Revolution. The assignats were originally secured on the sale of confiscated estates, but rapidly became worthless as a result of overissue and inflation [F.]

as·sig·na·tion (æsignéiʃən) *n.* a secret arrangement to meet, usually between lovers or conspirators ‖ an attribution of origin and esp. of date ‖ the act of assigning [O.F. *assignacion*]

assigned risk (*insurance*) a risk that underwriters do not care to insure (such as person with hypertension seeking health insurance), but which, because of state law or otherwise, must be insured. Assigned risks are usually handled through a group of insurers, in proportion their share of the business

as·sign·ee (æsini:, əsaini:) *n.* (*law*) a person who has been given the right or duty of acting in place of another ‖ a person to whom property or a right has been legally assigned [F. *assigné*]

as·sign·ment (əsáinmənt) *n.* the act of assigning ‖ the thing (task) assigned ‖ an attribution, assignation ‖ (*law*) transference of property or a right ‖ (*law*) the document by which this is done [O.F. *assignement*]

as·sim·i·la·ble (əsímələb'l) *adj.* capable of being assimilated [fr. L.L. *assimilabilis*]

as·sim·i·late (əsíməleit) *pres. part.* **as·sim·i·lat·ing** *past* and *past part.* **as·sim·i·lat·ed** *v.t.* to absorb (food etc.) into the body's system ‖ to absorb, make one's own, *to assimilate knowledge* ‖ to adapt, *to assimilate oneself to new surroundings* ‖ (*phon.*) to make like by assimilation ‖ *v.i.* (*phon.*) to become like by assimilation ‖ (of people) to become absorbed into a society [fr. L. *assimilare (assimilatus)*, to make like]

as·sim·i·la·tion (əsiməléiʃən) *n.* an assimilating or being assimilated ‖ the incorporation of food by plants and animals ‖ (*phon.*) the process by which one speech sound is altered to a pronunciation more like that of another sound following or preceding it [fr. L. *assimilatio (assimilationis)*]

as·sim·i·la·tive (əsímələtiv, əsíməleitiv) *adj.* causing, or concerning, assimilation

as·sim·i·la·to·ry (əsímələtɔri:, əsímələtɔuri:) *adj.* assimilative

As·si·si (əsí:zi:) a town (pop. 24,500) in Perugia, Italy, birthplace of St Francis, who founded the Franciscan order there (1208). Church of S. Francesco (1228–53): frescos by Giotto and Cimabue

as·sist (əsíst) **1.** *v.t.* to help (someone) ‖ *v.i.* to be of service ‖ (*games*) to make an assist **2.** *n.* (games) help given to another player, e.g. in a putout in baseball ‖ (*acronym*) for advanced scientific instruments symbolic translator, a computer assembly program designed by Advanced Scientific Instruments, Inc. [F. *assister*]

as·sis·tance (əsístəns) *n.* usefulness, service ‖ financial or other practical help [F.]

as·sis·tant (əsístənt) **1.** *n.* a helper ‖ a person holding a subordinate position **2.** *adj.* helping ‖ subordinate [F.]

Assiut *ASYÛT

as·size (əsáiz) *n.* a law-court session ‖ (*Br.*, usually *pl.*) the judicial sessions, held regularly in every English county, when civil and criminal cases are tried before a judge of the High Court and a jury ‖ (in Scotland) the jury in a case tried by jury [O.F. *assise*]

as·so·ci·a·bil·i·ty (əsouʃəbíliti:, əsouʃi:əbíliti:) *n.* the quality of being associable

as·so·ci·a·ble (əsóuʃəb'l, əsóuʃi:əb'l) *adj.* that can be associated or connected (in thought) [F.]

as·so·ci·ate (əsóuʃi:it) **1.** *adj.* acting on equal terms, *associate editors* ‖ subordinate, *an associate member* ‖ accompanying, allied, *war and its associate horrors* **2.** *n.* a fellow worker or partner ‖ a subordinate ‖ a person whom one is friendly with or much in company with ‖ a member (of a society) with less than full rights **3.** *v.* (əsóuʃi:eit) *pres. part.* **as·so·ci·at·ing** *past* and *past part.* **as·so·ci·at·ed** *v.t.* to connect in one's mind, *we associate war with misery* ‖ to cause to participate in some cooperative capacity ‖ *v.i.* to join as companion etc., *he likes associating with such people* **to associate oneself with** to manifest publicly one's solidarity with (a corporate act of protest etc.) **as·só·ci·ate·ship** *n.* less than full membership [fr. L. *associare (associatus)*]

as·so·ci·a·tion (əsousi:éiʃən) *n.* the act of associating or being associated ‖ an organized body of people with a common interest or object ‖ an idea identified in one's mind with some object and recalled by it, *Paris has happy associations for her* ‖ companionship, social or business relationship ‖ (*statistics*) a statistical relationship between two or more variables such that change in one variable results in a change in one or more other variables [fr. L. *associatio (associationis)*]

association copy a book connected with some famous person, e.g. by annotations, presentation, inscription etc.

association football (*Br.*) soccer

as·so·ci·a·tion·ism (əsousi:éiʃənizəm) *n.* (*philos.*) a philosophical system or theory of psychology based on the concept that mental and moral phenomena derive from an association of ideas, known chiefly by introspection. Hartley's system of philosophical psychology was repeatedly examined and modified in the 19th c. It influenced James Mill ('Analysis of the Phenomena of the Human Mind', 1829) and J. S. Mill (whose 'mental chemistry' laid the foundations for a science of psychology), Bentham's utilitarian ethics, Spencer's evolutionary treatment of mental life and, through Alexander Bain, William James's 'Principles of Psychology' (1890)

association of ideas (*philos.*) a thought process by which one mental state, frequently met in connection with another mental state, becomes in itself evocative of this other state (e.g. some taste or sound vividly recalls a childhood experience). The notion has been assimilated into literature as the basis of an artistic method, notably in the works of Proust, Joyce and Virginia Woolf (cf. ASSOCIATIONISM)

as·so·ci·a·tive (əsóuʃətiv, əsóuʃi:ətiv) *adj.* concerning association ‖ tending to associate ‖ (*math.*) of an operation whose result is unchanged when a partial operation affecting consecutive elements is carried out

as·so·ci·a·tive processor (əsóuʃətiv) (*computer*) ultraspeed digital computer for searching memory, used in air traffic control systems, etc

as·so·ci·a·to·ry (əsóuʃi:ətɔri:, əsóuʃi:ətɔuri:) *adj.* associative

as·so·nance (ǽsənəns) *n.* a similarity of sound between words or syllables ‖ the controlled repetition in verse of an accentuated vowel, but not

CONCISE PRONUNCIATION KEY: **(a)** æ, c*a*t; ɑ, c*a*r; ɔ f*aw*n; ei, sn*a*ke. **(e)** e, h*e*n; i:, sh*ee*p; iə, d*ee*r; ɛə, b*ea*r. **(i)** i, f*i*sh; ai, t*i*ger; ə:, b*i*rd. **(o)** o, *o*x; au, c*ow*; ou, g*oa*t; u, p*oo*r; ɔi, r*oy*al. **(u)** ʌ, d*u*ck; u, b*u*ll; u:, g*oo*se; ə, b*a*cillus; ju:, c*u*be. x, lo*ch*; θ, *th*ink; ð, bo*th*er; z, *Z*en; ʒ, corsa*g*e; dʒ, sava*g*e; ŋ, oranguta*ng*; j, *y*ak; ʃ, *f*ish; tʃ, *f*etch; 'l, rabb*le*; 'n, redde*n*. Complete pronunciation key appears inside front cover.

of the consonants following, esp. in the last words of consecutive lines, e.g. pale/brave **ás·so·nant** adj. [F.]

as·sort (əsórt) v.t. (old-fash.) to sort, classify ‖ v.i. to harmonize, go together **as·sórt·ed** adj. classified ‖ of various kinds, miscellaneous ‖ (in combined words) matched, an ill-assorted couple [O.F. assorter]

as·sort·ment (əsórtmənt) n. a mixture or collection made up of different things, or different kinds of the same thing

as·suage (əswéidʒ) pres. part. **as·suag·ing** past and past part. **as·suaged** v.t. to soothe, lessen (a pain or an emotion) ‖ to satisfy (hunger, thirst, or other desire) **as·suáge·ment** n. [O.F. assouagier]

Assuan Dam *ASWAN DAM

as·sume (əsú:m) pres. part. **as·sum·ing** past and past part. **as·sumed** v.t. to suppose, accept or believe (something) to be true, we assume his guilt ‖ to suppose, believe or accept (someone) to be something, we assume him guilty ‖ to put on as a pretense, to assume a disguise, assume a foreign accent ‖ to adopt (e.g. an attitude or role) ‖ to manifest itself under, the disease assumes many forms ‖ to begin effectively in (office) ‖ to begin to exercise (control) **as·súmed** adj. accepted as, or believed to be true, supposed, assumed innocence (until guilt is proved) ‖ pretended, false, assumed friendliness, an assumed title ‖ taken as one's right, assumed powers **as·súm·ing** adj. proud, arrogant [fr. L. assumere, to take to oneself]

as·sump·tion (əsʌmpʃən) n. the act of assuming ‖ something taken for granted **the Assumption** (Roman Catholicism) the bodily taking up of the Virgin Mary into heaven ‖ the feast commemorating this (Aug. 15) [fr. L. assumptio (assumptionis)]

As·sur (æsər) the early capital of Assyria, destroyed by the Medes in 606 B.C. Its ruins at Sharqat in N. Iraq, on the Tigris, have been extensively excavated in the 20th c. ‖ the supreme god of the Assyrian pantheon

as·sur·ance (əʃúərəns) n. something, e.g. a promise, pledge, convincing reason etc. on which one can rely as a guarantee of truth ‖ certainty ‖ self-confidence ‖ (esp. Br.) insurance [O. F. asseürance]

as·sure (əʃúər) pres. part. **as·sur·ing** past and past part. **as·sured** v.t. to make certain, to assure success ‖ to tell as a certain fact, I assure you that there is no danger ‖ to insure (*INSURANCE) **as·súred** adj. certain, safe ‖ self-confident **as·sur·ed·ly** (əʃúəridli:) adv. certainly, emphatically yes **as·sur·ed·ness** (əʃúəridnis) n. certainty ‖ self-confidence **as·súr·er** n. someone who assures **as·súr·or** n. (law.) an underwriter ‖ someone who insures his life [O.F. asseürer, to make safe]

As·syr·i·a (əsíri:ə) an ancient kingdom in N. Mesopotamia lying mainly between the Tigris and Euphrates Rivers, with its capital first at Assur and later at Nineveh. Linked culturally with Babylonia, Assyria expanded to form an empire (c. 1950–c. 1750 B.C.), but then declined until c. 1500 B.C. A new period of conquest, esp. during the reign (c. 1116–1078 B.C.) of Tiglath-pileser I, created a state typified by bureaucracy and harsh laws. The reigns of Shalmaneser III (858–c. 824 B.C.) and Tiglath-pileser III (746–728 B.C.) saw renewed conquests over neighboring peoples. Assyria attained its greatest extent, reaching Armenia, Arabia and Egypt, in the reigns of Sargon II (721–705 B.C.), Sennacherib (705–681 B.C.), Esarhaddon (680–669 B.C.) and Ashurbanipal (668–633 B.C.). Under these kings Assyrian art and architecture were at their height, notable particularly for the bas-reliefs on temples and palaces. A vast library of cuneiform tablets was assembled at Nineveh. After Ashurbanipal's death, the empire fell to the Medes and Babylonians (c. 616–606 B.C.)

As·syr·i·an (əsíri:ən) 1. adj. of or relating to Assyria, the Assyrians or their language 2. n. a member of the Semitic race which peopled Assyria ‖ their language, a dialect of Akkadian

As·syr·i·ol·o·gy (əsiri:ólədʒi:) n. the study of the history, remains, language and culture of ancient Assyria [fr. ASSYRIA+Gk logos, discourse]

As·tar·te (æstúrti:) Phoenician goddess of love, identified with the Greek Aphrodite

a·stat·ic (eistǽtik) adj. (phys.) without fixed position or direction or movement **a·stát·i·cal·ly** adv. [fr. Gk astatos, not stable]

astatic coils two coils so arranged as to produce zero external magnetic field when a current passes through them. Variations in the external magnetic field do not induce any electromotive force

astatic galvanometer a moving magnet galvanometer in which the effect of the earth's magnetic field is reduced

a·stat·i·cism (eistǽtisizəm) n. the state or quality of being astatic

as·ta·tine (æstəti:n) n. a radioactive element in the halogen group (symbol At, at. no. 85, mass of isotope of longest known half-life 210) made artificially and formerly known as alabamine [fr. Gk astatos, not stable]

as·ter (æstər) n. a member of Aster, fam. Compositae, a genus of perennial plants native to temperate regions whose 500 species include the Michaelmas daisies [L. fr. Gk astēr, star]

as·ter·isk (æstərisk) 1. n. (in printing or writing) a mark like a star [*] which calls attention to a note, or distinguishes a word or words 2. v.t. to mark with an asterisk [fr. L. fr. Gk asteriskos, a little star]

as·ter·ism (æstərizəm) n. (astron.) a group of stars or constellation, a star cluster ‖ (printing) three asterisks [*** or **] marking an omission, a pause, or a further (or changed) line of thought, or calling special attention to a passage ‖ (crystall.) a star-shaped reflection of light, e.g. as seen in the star sapphire [fr. Gk asterismos fr. astēr, star]

a·stern (əstə́:rn) adv. (naut.) in, at, or towards the rear of a vessel) ‖ (naut.) backwards

as·ter·oid (æstəroid) 1. n. (astron.) one of the small planets occupying orbits mainly between those of Mars and Jupiter. The orbits of over 1,500 asteroids have been plotted and their total weight is estimated to be 1/3000 that of the earth. Ceres is the largest (diameter about 480 miles). Their origin is not known ‖ (zool.) a starfish 2. adj. like the conventional shape of a star **as·ter·oi·dal** adj. **as·ter·oi·de·an** adj. and n. [fr. Gk asteroeidēs, star-shaped]

as·the·ni·a (æsθí:ni:ə) n. (med.) weakness, muscular underdevelopment [Mod. L. fr. Gk astheneia fr. a, without+sthenos, strength]

as·then·ic (æsθénik) adj. (med.) like or pertaining to asthenia, weak ‖ (anthrop.) slight in build and muscular strength [fr. Gk asthenikos]

as·then·o·sphere (æsθénəsfiər) n. (geol.) a weak plastic zone in the interior of the earth in the upper part of the mantle below the crust, 2,900 km below the surface, extending 100 to 400 km

asth·ma (æzmə, æsmə) n. a disease which causes wheezing and difficulty in breathing, due to swelling and congestion of the air passages in the lungs. This is the result of an allergic reaction to various substances [Gk=breathlessness]

asth·mat·ic (æzmætik, æsmætik) 1. adj. caused by asthma or affected with asthma 2. n. someone who suffers from asthma **asth·mát·i·cal** adj. [fr. L. asthmaticus fr. Gk]

AS-3 *KANGAROO

as·tig·mat·ic (æstigmætik) adj. affected by astigmatism ‖ (of a lens) correcting, or corrected for, this defect [fr. Gk a, without+stigma (stigmatos), point, focus]

a·stig·ma·tism (əstígmətizəm) n. (phys.) a defect of the eye, of a lens or of an image formed by either, the curvature of the refracting surface or surfaces being different in different planes. This results in the focal lengths also being different in different planes (the curvature of the cornea in the case of the eye) [fr. Gk a, without+stigma (stigmatos) point, focus]

a·stir (əstə́:r) pred. adj. and adv. out of bed, up ‖ (rhet.) in movement, stirring

As·ti·spu·man·te (ásti:spu:mánti:) n. trade name of a white Italian sparkling wine from Piedmont region

as·told-to (æstóuldtu:) adj. euphemism for a book, usu. an autobiography, written for a well-known person. The "as-told-to" author is the person presumed to be the authority about the facts presented

As·ton (æstən), Francis William (1877–1945), English physicist. His studies of electrical discharge in gases led to his discovery of isotopes. He constructed the first mass spectrograph, and used it to investigate isotopes. Nobel prize for chemistry (1922)

as·ton·ish (əstóniʃ) v.t. to strike with amazement or wonder ‖ to shock **as·tón·ish·ing** adj. amazing, wonderful ‖ shocking **as·tón·ish·ment**

n. the state of being astonished ‖ a cause for astonishment [M.E. astonien fr. O.F.]

As·tor (æstər) an Anglo-American family founded by John Jacob Astor (1763–1848). The family's wealth derived mainly from a virtual monopoly of the U.S. fur trade and from real estate in New York City. William Vincent Astor (1891–1959) bequeathed his fortune to the Astor Foundation, a philanthropic organization which he had created

Astor (mil. acronym) for antisubmarine torpedo

as·tound (əstáund) v.t. to shock with fear, wonder or amazement ‖ to surprise greatly **as·tóund·ing** adj. [past part. of obs. M.E. astonen, to astonish]

astrachan *ASTRAKHAN

a·strad·dle (əstrǽd'l) adv., pred. adj. and prep. astride

as·tra·gal (æstrəg'l) n. (archit.) a narrow band of ornamental molding around a column ‖ a ring around the mouth of an old-fashioned cannon [fr. L. astragalus fr. Gk]

a·strag·a·lus (æstrǽgələs) pl. **a·strag·a·li** (æstrǽgəlai) n. a bone of the ankle joint, on which the tibia rests, a tarsal bone ‖ a member of Astragalus, a genus of leguminous shrubs, from which tragacanth is made. The gum, produced chiefly in Iran, is used as an adhesive and in medicine [L. fr. Gk astragalos, anklebone]

As·tra·khan (æstrəkǽn) a port (pop. 465,000) on the Caspian Sea in the Volga delta, R.S.F.S.R., U.S.S.R., a transit center for bulk oil traffic from Baku, with fishing and fish-preserving industries. University (1919)

as·tra·khan, as·tra·chan (æstrəkən) n. the skin of newborn lambs of the Karakul or Astrakhan sheep. With its close-curled wool it makes a valuable fur (*PERSIAN LAMB)

as·tral (æstrəl) adj. pertaining to or consisting of stars, starry ‖ star-shaped ‖ (spiritualism) of an alleged substance neither wholly spiritual nor wholly material [fr. L. astrolis, starlike]

a·stray (əstréi) adv. on the wrong road ‖ wandering, lost ‖ mistaken, wrong [etym. doubtful, perh. O.F. past part. estraié]

a·stride (əstráid) 1. pred. adj. and adv. with one leg on each side ‖ in the position of striding 2. prep. with one leg on each side of

a·strin·gen·cy (əstríndʒənsi:) n. the quality of being astringent

a·strin·gent (əstríndʒənt) 1. adj. (of something acting on the tissues of the body etc.) tightening ‖ (of flavor) causing the mouth to feel dry and puckered ‖ (of medicine) styptic ‖ (of style or criticism) dry and sharply to the point 2. n. an astringent agent [F.]

as·tri·on·ics (æstri:óniks) n. acrospace electronics

as·tro- (æstrou) adj. combining form meaning pertaining to outer space, e.g., astrodog, astronaut, astrophysics, astromouse, astrochronologist

astro altitude the arc of a vertical circle measured from the celestial horizon to the body

as·tro·bi·ol·o·gy (æstroubaiólədʒi:) n. space biology **syn** exobiology —**astrobiologist** n. —**astrobiological** adj.

as·tro·bleme (æstroubléim) n. (geol.) a depression on earth's surface created by an object from space, e.g., a meteor

as·tro·chem·is·try (æstrəkémistri:) n. chemistry of space objects —**astrochemist** n.

as·tro·com·pass (æstrəkʌmpəs) n. an instrument for finding direction by celestial observations, not subject to the errors of magnetic compasses or gyrocompasses [fr. Gk astron, star+COMPASS]

as·tro·cyte (æstrəsait) n. (zool.) a many-branched, star-shaped cell that attaches itself to brain or spinal-cord blood vessels

as·tro·dy·nam·ics (æstroudainæmiks) n. study of mechanics involving the motion of objects in space —**astrodynamicist** n. —**astrodynamic** adj.

as·tro·ge·ol·o·gy (æstroudʒi:ólədʒi:) n. geology of celestial bodies —**astrogeologist** n. —**astrogeologic** adj.

as·tro·labe (æstrəleib) n. a circular ring or metal disk on which the heavenly sphere was projected, fitted with a sight and marked on the edge with degrees, known to the ancient Greeks and used from early times to measure the altitudes of stars, but now replaced by the sextant [O.F. astrelabe fr. L. fr. Gk]

as·trol·o·ger (əstrólədʒər) n. a person who practices astrology

as·tro·log·i·cal (æstrəlódʒik'l) adj. pertaining to astrology or astrologers [fr. Gk astrologikos]

as·trol·o·gy (əstrólədʒi:) n. the art of predicting or determining the influence of the planets and stars on human affairs [F. astrologie fr. Gk astron, star+logos, discourse]

as·tron (æstrɒn) n. (nuclear phys.) technique of producing controlled nuclear reactions, using rotating electrons to produce a plasma beam that is shot into a chamber containing deuterium

as·tro·naut (æstrənɔt, æstrənɒt) n. a space traveler [fr. Gk astron, star+nautēs, sailor]

as·tro·nau·tics (æstrənɔtiks, æstrənɒtiks) n. the science of travel in outer space [fr. Gk astron, star+nautikos fr. nautēs, sailor]

as·tro·nav·i·ga·tion (æstrounævigéiʃən) n. navigation by observation of heavenly bodies [fr. Gk astron, star+NAVIGATION]

as·tron·o·mer (əstrónəmər) n. a person skilled or learned in astronomy

astronomer royal a British government post dating from the foundation of the Royal Observatory at Greenwich by Charles II (1675).

as·tro·nom·ic (æstrənómik) adj. pertaining to astronomy ‖ (fig., of figures, quantity, distance) enormous **as·tro·nóm·i·cal** adj. **as·tro·nóm·i·cal·ly** adv.

astronomical clock a very accurate clock used in observations of the movements of celestial bodies, and which may be used as a standard timepiece

astronomical telescope a telescope with no image erector, used for the observation of celestial bodies

astronomic unit a unit of distance equal to the mean radius of the earth's orbit about the sun, 93,003,000 miles, used for the measurement of distance within the solar system

as·tron·o·my (əstrónəmi) n. the science of the heavenly bodies [O.F. astronomie fr. L. fr. Gk fr. astron, star+nomos, law, arrangement]

as·tro·phys·ics (æstroufíziks) n. the study of the physical and chemical nature of the heavenly bodies, and their origin and evolution [fr. Gk astron, star+PHYSICS]

As·tu·rias (əstú:rjəs), Miguel Angel (1899–1974), Guatemalan novelist, poet, and winner of the 1967 Nobel prize for literature. His works include studies of folklore ('Leyendas de Guatemala') and sociological novels ('El señor presidente', 'Hombres de maiz', 'El papa verde', and 'Weekend en Guatemala')

As·tu·ri·as (æstúəri:əs) a region in N. Spain, forming the modern province of Oviedo. It rises from a narrow coastal plain to the Cantabrian Mtns, rich in minerals (coal, copper, iron, zinc, lead) which make it one of Spain's most industrialized areas (specializing in metallurgy, esp. steel). Other products: livestock, grain, potatoes, olives, figs, citrus fruits, fish, timber. Historic capital: Oviedo. Asturias was the first center of the Christian reconquest of Spain from the Moors. It was united to León in the 10th c., and to Castile in 1037

as·tute (əstjú:t,əstú:t) adj. shrewd ‖ ready-witted, clever, an astute answer [fr. L. astutus, cunning]

AS-2 *KIPPER

A·sun·ción (asu:nsjɔ́n) the capital (pop. 455,517) of Paraguay, a port 935 miles up the Paraguay River from Buenos Aires

a·sun·der (əsʌ́ndər) adv. (rhet.) into two or more parts, into pieces, torn asunder [O.E. on sundran, apart]

A supply (electr.) power source for heating the electrotube cathode

As·wan Dam, As·suan Dam (æswɑn) a dam built in 1902 on the first cataract of the Nile. It is 1¼ miles long with a road along the top, and 176 feet high. A new dam (Aswan High Dam) has been built (the financing of it produced an international crisis in 1956) for hydroelectric power, flood control and irrigation (*ABU SIMBEL). It was built with Soviet financial and technological assistance, and was inaugurated Jan. 1971

as yet until now ‖ until that moment

a·sy·lum (əsáiləm) n. a mental home, hospital for the mentally ill ‖ (rhet.) a place affording safety from attack, or shelter ‖ refuge, to seek political asylum [L. fr. Gk asulon fr. a, without+sulē, right of seizure]

a·sym·met·ric (eisimétrik, æsimétrik) adj. showing asymmetry **a·sym·mét·ri·cal** adj.

a·sym·met·ric bars (gymnastics) apparatus consisting of parallel bars, with one bar higher than the other

asymmetric carbon atom a carbon atom with each of its four valencies satisfied by a different atom or group. Two different arrangements in space are possible, giving rise to optical isomerism and stereoisomerism

a·sym·me·try (eisímitri:, æsímitri:) n. lack of symmetry, uneven disposition on each side of an (imaginary) central line or point

as·ymp·tote (æsimtout) n. (math.) a line which approaches but never meets a plane curve within any finite distance. It would be tangential to the curve at infinity **as·ymp·tot·ic** (æsimtótik), **as·ymp·tót·i·cal** adjs **as·ymp·tót·i·cal·ly** adv. [fr. Gk asumptótos, not meeting]

a·syn·chro·nous computer (eisí:ŋkrənəs) device that starts automatically when a previous operation has been completed

as·yn·det·ic (æsindétik) adj. using asyndeton

a·syn·de·ton (æsínditən, əsínditɒn) pl. **a·syn·de·tons, a·syn·de·ta** (əsíndítə) n. the omission of conjunctions between coordinate parts of a sentence, e.g.'men, dogs, birds, all these are animals' [L. fr. Gk a, not+sundetos, united]

A·syût, As·siut (æsjú:t) a town (pop. 213,983) of Upper Egypt. Crafts: weaving, carpetmaking, pottery. From the Asyût barrage (1902) runs the Ibrahimiya Canal, irrigating central Egypt and the Faiyum. As ancient Egyptian Siut and Greek Lycopolis, Asyût was the terminus of the caravan route to Dar-fur. There are many rock tombs nearby

at (æt) prep. expressing position, at home, at a great distance, at Melbourne, at 66 Main Street ‖ expressing place in time, at 6 o'clock, at Easter ‖ expressing the direction or end of movement, or the end towards which action or will is directed, we arrived at the house, he came at me with a knife, aim at the center ‖ expressing manner of action or employment, at work, good at arithmetic, sitting at dinner, he's at his tricks again ‖ expressing situation or condition, at war, do it at leisure, still at liberty ‖ expressing cause or occasion of an action or state, sad at leaving, he suffered at your hands ‖ expressing position in a scale that measures degree, amount, price etc., at 50 m.p.h., at a trot, at three dollars each, at boiling point **at all** (in a question, or after a negative or a word implying a negative), to any degree, are you at all frightened? [O.E. œt]

A·ta·ca·ma Desert (ætəkáma) a desert of N. Chile extending into Argentina and Bolivia. It contains the world's chief deposits of nitrates

A·ta·hual·pa (ætəwálpə) (c. 1500–33), last king of the Incas (1525–33). He was executed by order of Pizarro

At·a·lan·ta (ætəlǽntə) (Gk mythol.) the daughter of Iasos. She would marry no one who could not beat her in a race, and killed any suitors who failed. As they were running, her suitor Hippomenes threw down the three golden apples of Hesperides, which she stopped to pick up. By this stratagem he won her

A·ta·türk (ætətə:rk), Kemal (Mustafa Kemal, c. 1880–1938), Turkish statesman. An army officer, he led a successful movement against the dismemberment of Turkey after the 1st world war. After the Treaty of Lausanne (1923) had recognized Turkey's independence, he became the republic's first president (1923–38). He abolished (1924) the Ottoman caliphate and introduced many western reforms during his dictatorship

at·a·vism (ætəvizəm) n. (biol.) the reappearance of certain forms, derived from an ancestor, which had not manifested themselves in the intermediate generations ‖ (of man) a reversion to primitive instincts **át·a·vist** n. **at·a·vis·tic** adj. [F. atavisme]

a·tax·i·a (ətǽksi:ə) n. (med.) loss of the power to control movement or muscular action **a·táx·ic** adj. **a·tax·y** (ətǽksi:) pl. **a·tax·ies** n. ataxia [Mod. L. fr. Gk ataxia, disorder]

At·ba·ra (ǽtbərə, átbərə) a town (pop. 36,000) in the Sudan at the confluence of the Nile and the Atbara. It is a junction on the Port Sudan-Khartoum railway and has railway workshops

Atbara the last tributary of the Nile, 800 miles long. It rises (as Takazze River) in the Ethiopian mountains and flows through the Sudan

ate past of EAT

-ate suffix used to form verbs indicating that a process or change or development is involved, as in 'chlorinate' ‖ used to form adjectives from nouns, indicating what is characteristic, as in 'lanceolate' [fr. L. -atus, past part. termination of 1st conjugation verbs ending in -are]

-ate suffix indicating office or authority, as in 'protectorate' or a group of officials, as in 'episcopate' [fr. L. noun ending -atus]

at·el·ier (ætəljei) n. an artist's studio ‖ a workroom used for crafts, dressmaking etc. [F.]

Ath·a·bas·can, Ath·a·bas·kan (æθəbǽskən) adj. and n. Athapaskan

Ath·a·bas·ka (æθəbǽskə) a river rising in the Rocky Mtns, Canada, and flowing for 765 miles through N. Alberta ‖ a lake (area 2,842 sq. miles) in Alberta and Saskatchewan into which the River Athabaska flows. The lake drains into the Mackenzie River

Ath·a·na·sian Creed (æθənéiʒən, æθənéiʃən) the third principal creed (Quicunque Vult) of the Christian Church, stating in particular the doctrine of the Trinity and of the Incarnation

Ath·a·na·sius (æθənéiʃəs), St (c. 296–373), patriarch of Alexandria. He championed the definition of the Christian faith accepted at Nicaea in the Arian controversy (*ARIANISM). His best-known treatise is 'De Incarnatione' (c. 319). Feast: May 2

Ath·a·pas·kan, Ath·a·pas·can (æθəpǽskən) 1. adj. of one of the chief N. American linguistic families which covered most of N.W. Canada, and much of the southwestern U.S.A., together with many isolated groups in California, and including Navaho and Apache 2. n. one of the languages of the family ‖ an Athapaskan Indian

a·the·ism (éiθi:izəm) n. the denial of the existence of God, particularly with regard to theistic formulations (cf. AGNOSTICISM, cf. SKEPTICISM) ‖ godlessness in belief or as a guide in conduct **á·the·ist** n. and adj. **a·the·is·tic** adj. **a·the·ís·ti·cal·ly** adv. [F. athéisme fr. Gk a, without+theos, God]

Ath·el·stan, Aeth·el·stan (æθəlstən) (c. 895–940), king of the English (924–40), son of Edward the Elder. He extended his father's kingdom by conquering Northumbria (925) and by defeating a coalition of Welsh, Scots and Danes at Brunanburh (937). He issued a body of law, and his court established continental connections

A·the·na (əθí:nə) Athene

Ath·e·nag·o·ras (æθənǽgərəs) (2nd c.), Greek Christian apologist who defended Christians against charges of atheism, addressing himself to Marcus Aurelius in his 'Embassy on behalf of the Christians' (c. 177)

Athenagoras I (1886–1972), archbishop of Constantinople and patriarch of the Orthodox Eastern Church (1948–72)

A·the·ne (əθí:ni:) (Gk mythol.) the presiding deity of Athens, the Greek goddess of wisdom and the arts and handicrafts, daughter of Zeus. She was identified with the Roman Minerva

A·the·ni·an (əθí:ni:ən) 1. adj. of or relating to Athens 2. n. a native or inhabitant of Athens [fr. L. atheniensis]

Ath·ens (æθinz) the capital (pop. 565,000, with agglom. 3,300,000) of modern Greece. It lies four miles from the port of Piraeus, and is enclosed by hills on three sides. It is a modern city, developed since 1834 on the site of the ancient city (*ACROPOLIS). It is a commercial and manufacturing center for textiles, chemicals, tobacco, engineering and printing. Athens has a university (1837), museums, and archaeological schools. Ancient Athens had developed into a strong city-state, which (by the 7th c. B.C.) included Attica. It was destroyed by Xerxes (480 B.C.) but was rebuilt on a magnificent scale under Pericles and became the prosperous leader of a large confederacy of Greek states (460–31 B.C.). This was the era of Aeschylus, Sophocles, Euripides, Aristophanes and Socrates. Athens was defeated in the second Peloponesian war (431–404 B.C.) and by Philip of Macedon (338 B.C.). It became subject to Rome (146 B.C.) and formed part of the Roman province of Achaea after 27 B.C. It was conquered by the Goths (c. 267 A.D.) and by the Ottoman Turks (1456). It had declined to a village of a few thousand people when it was chosen as the capital of the new independent Greece (1834). It was occupied by the Germans (1941) but liberated by the British (1944)

a·ther·man·cy (æθə́:rmənsi:) n. the quality of being athermanous

a·ther·ma·nous (æθə́:rmənəs) adj. not transmitting infrared radiation [A (without)+Gk thermē, heat]

ath·er·o·gen·ic (æθəroudʒénik) adj. (med.) causing degeneration of arterial walls —**athero-**

genesis *n* the process, —**atheron**- combining form meaning fatty degeneration —**atherona** *n* plaque in the artery

ath·er·o·scle·ro·sis (æθərouskləróusis) *n.* a stage of arteriosclerosis in which the inmost wall of the artery undergoes fatty degeneration [Mod. L. fr. L. *atheroma*, tumor containing matter like groats +SCLEROSIS]

a·thirst (əθɔ́:rst) *adj.* (*rhet.*) eager, *athirst for knowledge* [O.E. *ofthyrstan v.*, to be very thirsty]

A-37B (*mil.*) U.S. military aircraft for light strikes, carrying 7.62-mm guns; manufactured by Cessna

ath·lete (æθli:t) *n.* a person with the skill and training to be good at sports, esp. (*Br.*) as an individual competitor (in running, jumping, throwing etc.) rather than as one of a team [fr. L. *athleta*, contestant, fr. Gk]

athlete's foot a contagious skin disease, most common between the toes, a form of ringworm

ath·let·ic (æθlétik) *adj.* of or pertaining to athletes ‖ strong, fit and agile **ath·lét·ics** *n.* the sports practiced by athletes. In American usage athletics include gymnastics, baseball, football and many other sports. In British usage only track and field events are included [fr. L. *athleticus* fr. Gk]

ath·o·dyd (æθədid) *n.* a ramjet [AEROTHERMODYNAMIC DUCT]

at home a reception for guests in one's own home

Ath·os (æθɒs, éiθɒs) a Greek peninsula (area 111 sq. miles, pop. 3,000) in Chalcidice (Macedonia). The only inhabitants are Greek Orthodox monks, whose churches (10th–14th cc.) and libraries are magnificent. Athos is an autonomous republic under Greek sovereignty ‖ the mountain at its tip (6,349 ft)

a·thwart (əθwɔ́rt) **1.** *adv.* across the length of a ship or across her course **2.** *prep.* across the length of (a ship) or across (her course) **a·thwart·ships** (əθwɔ́rtʃips) *adv.* from side to side across a ship

-ation *suffix* indicating a process or the result of a process, as in 'asphyxiation'

At·jeh, A·cheh (útʃe) a province (area 21,381 sq. miles, pop. 1,500,000) of Indonesia in N.W. Sumatra. Capital: Kotaradja. The people are Moslems of Indonesian-Dravidian stock. Crafts: wood and gold work, silk weaving. Exports: rubber, pepper, copra

At·kin·son (ætkinsən), Sir Harry Albert (1831–92), prime minister of New Zealand noted for financial and social reforms, and the introduction of protective duties

At·kins, Tommy (ætkinz), *TOMMY

At·lan·ta (ætlǽntə) a city (pop. 425,022, with agglom. 2,029,618) of Georgia, commercial and financial capital of the Southeast. University (1865). Atlanta was the Confederate center in Georgia around which several engagements of the Civil War were fought. The Atlanta conflict (July 20–Sept. 2, 1864) ended with Gen. William T. Sherman forcing the Confederate forces to evacuate the city. The victory assured Abraham Lincoln's success in the presidential elections of 1864

atlantes *pl.* of ATLAS (a pillar)

At·lan·tic (ətlǽntik) **1.** *adj.* of or close to the Atlantic Ocean **2.** *n.* the Atlantic Ocean [fr. L. fr. Gk *Atlantikos* fr. *Atlas* (*ATLAS)]

Atlantic Charter a joint declaration by F. D. Roosevelt and Winston Churchill (who met at sea, Aug. 14, 1941) of eight principles to guide a postwar settlement

Atlantic City a noted resort and amusement center in S.E. New Jersey (pop. 40,119). A longtime attraction was a 4-mile boardwalk of steel and concrete (1896). After gambling was legalized (1976), casinos were built along the boardwalk. Gambling revenues revitalized the city

At·lan·ti·cism (ətlǽntisizəm) *n.* policy of greater cooperation between United States and Western Europe —**Atlanticist** *n.*

Atlantic Ocean the ocean (area incl. the Arctic Ocean, Antarctic waters, seas and gulfs, 41,000,000 sq. miles) separating America from Europe and Africa. Length (Bering Strait–Antarctica): 12,800 miles. Width from Florida, U.S.A. to Portugal: 4,000 miles. The Atlantic Ridge (300–500 miles wide), of which the Azores, Ascension, St Helena and Tristan da Cunha are summits, divides it into eastern and western valleys (mainly 2,000–3,000 fathoms). Deeps reach 4,800 fathoms (Puerto Rico trench)

Atlantic Pact *NORTH ATLANTIC TREATY ORGANIZATION

Atlantic Standard Time Atlantic Time

Atlantic Time (in Nova Scotia, New Brunswick, Prince Edward Island, E. Quebec) time as reckoned from the sun's crossing the 60th meridian west of Greenwich (four hours behind Greenwich Mean Time)

At·lan·tis (ətlǽntis) a mythical continent of the Atlantic Ocean

At·las (ǽtləs) (*Gk mythol.*) a giant who held up the heavens on his shoulders, identified later with Mt Atlas in N. Africa

at·las (ǽtləs) *n.* (*physiol.*) the first vertebra in the neck, which supports the head ‖ a book containing a collection of maps, after the famous one of Mercator (1594) ‖ *pl.* **at·lan·tes** (ætlǽnti:z) a pillar in the form of a man, supporting a weight (cf. CARYATID) [L. fr. Gk *Atlas*]

At·las (ǽtləs) *n.* (*mil.*) surface-to-surface intercontinental ballistic missile used in launching spacecraft

Atlas Mtns a mountain system running for 1,500 miles parallel to the N. African coast from Cape Ghir to the Gulf of Gabes. The main range is High Atlas (over 6,500 ft) in Morocco, flanked on the northwest by Middle Atlas and on the southwest by Anti-Atlas (a tableland). The Maritime Atlas stretches from Ceuta to E. Algeria, the Sahara Atlas of Algeria from Figuig to Biskra. Minerals, esp. phosphates, are exploited

at·mol·y·sis (ætmɔ́lisis) *n.* a method of separation of a mixture of gases by means of the differential diffusion of the constituent molecules through a porous partition [Mod. L. fr. Gk *atmos*, vapor + *lusis*, a loosening]

at·mos·phere (ǽtməsfiər) *n.* the gases that surround the earth, divided into layers according to such criteria as rate of temperature change with increasing altitude, composition and electrical nature (*TROPOSPHERE, *TROPOPAUSE, *STRATOSPHERE, *STRATOPAUSE, *MESOSPHERE, *MESOPAUSE, *IONOSPHERE) ‖ the air in any enclosed space with respect to its effects on people or things subjected to it, *a stuffy atmosphere* ‖ a set of prevailing moral or mental influences on an institution, locality, group etc., *an atmosphere of suspicion* ‖ a unit of pressure equal to that exerted by a column of mercury 76 cm high at 0°C and under standard gravity

at·mos·pher·ic (ætməsférik) *adj.* **at·mos·pher·i·cal** *adj.* [fr. M od. L. *atmosphera* fr. Gk]

atmospheric pressure the pressure exerted by the earth's atmosphere: 14.72 lb. per sq. in. at sea level, decreasing with height above sea level and varying with the weather. The unit of pressure is the atmosphere

at·mos·pher·ics (ætməsfériks) *n.* natural electromagnetic radiations of radio frequency, or the resulting disturbances in radio equipment

at·mo·sphe·ri·um (ætməsfíəri:əm) *n.* area or device created in which to simulate atmospheric or meteorological phenomena, e.g., a planetarium

a·toll (ǽtɒl) *n.* a coral reef in the shape of a ring or horseshoe enclosing a lagoon [Maldive]

at·om (ǽtəm) *n.* the smallest portion of matter displaying the characteristic properties of a particular chemical element ‖ (*hist.*) the ultimate, indestructible particle taken by some early Greek and Indian thinkers, and by the Roman Lucretius, to be the basis of all matter ‖ a very small quantity, *not an atom of truth in it* [F. fr. L. fr. Gk *atomos*, indivisible]
—The atom consists of a heavy nucleus composed of neutrons and protons held together by extremely strong nuclear forces surrounded by a cloud of electrons. The number of protons is given by the atomic number (cf. ATOMIC MASS. The number of neutrons varies from isotope to isotope (*NUCLIDE) for a given element. In the neutral atom the number of electrons equals the number of protons, thus balancing the nuclear charge. The electrons are grouped in shells (energy levels, *QUANTUM THEORY) and, within the shells, in orbitals and suborbitals in such a manner that the Pauli exclusion principle is obeyed (*PERIODIC TABLE). According to Heisenberg's uncertainty principle it is not possible to determine exactly both the position and the momentum of an electron, and hence no particular electron can be assigned a definite orbit, but rather definite values representing the probability of finding the electron in that region at a given time are assigned to regions in the neighborhood of the nucleus (*QUANTUM

MECHANICS). The number of electrons which can be added to or withdrawn from the atom, esp. the valence shell and the energy required for this, determine the chemical reactivity of the element. The atom has a very open structure. The diameter of a nucleus is of the order of 10^{-14}. The nucleus is separated from the even smaller electrons by a distance of the order of 10^{-8} cm.

at·om·ar·i·um (ætəméiri:əm) *n.* room or structure created to provide illustration of phenomena of atomic and nuclear physics for study

atom bomb an atomic bomb

a·tom·ic (ətɔ́mik) *adj.* of, related to, or characterized by atoms **a·tóm·i·cal·ly** *adv.*

atomic bomb a very powerful bomb whose energy is derived from an extremely rapid nuclear chain reaction in which heavy nuclei of uranium or plutonium are broken down (*NUCLEAR FISSION, cf. NUCLEAR FUSION)

atomic clock a very accurate timepiece consisting of a quartz crystal or other electrical oscillator regulated by natural vibration frequencies from an atomic system

atomic energy *NUCLEAR ENERGY

Atomic Energy Commission formerly an independent U.S. agency (*abbr.* AEC) of the executive branch of government created (1946) to administer the national atomic energy program which stemmed from the development of the atomic bomb in the 2nd world war. *NUCLEAR REGULATORY COMMISSION

atomic heat specific heat (expressed in calories/gram) multiplied by the atomic mass of an element (*DULONG AND PETIT'S LAW)

at·o·mic·i·ty (ætəmísiti:) *n.* the state of being made up of atoms ‖ (*chem. and phys.*) the number of atoms in a molecule of an element

atomic lamp light source in which radio activity provides the energy, e.g., zinc sulfide phosphor activated by radioisotope of krypton gas

atomic mass (*abbr.* at. mass) the mass of an atom of an element on the atomic mass scale

atomic mass scale the scale, adopted in 1962, used for comparing the masses of atoms, molecules and nuclear particles. The mass unit is defined as one twelfth of the mass of the carbon isotope C^{12}, which was adopted as the standard substance. Before 1962 two scales existed, one based on the chemical a.m.u. defined as one sixteenth of the mass of naturally occurring oxygen, and the other on the physical a.m.u. defined as one sixteenth of the oxygen isotope O^{16}

atomic mass unit (*abbr.* a.m.u.) the unit of mass on the atomic mass scale (1 a.m.u.= 1.66x 10^{-24} gm)

atomic number (*symbol* Z, *abbr.* at. no.) the number characteristic of an element, including all its isotopes and equal to the number of protons in the nucleus of any atom of that element, also equal to the number of electrons in a neutral atom. It determines the position of the element in the periodic table

atomic physics (*phys.*) science concerned with structure of the atom and the particles which compose it *Cf* PARTICLE PHYSICS

atomic pile a nuclear reactor

atomic spectrum the emission or absorption spectrum of an atom or monatomic ion. Spectra of atoms are particularly simple because atoms do not interact with infrared or microwave radiation (i.e. they do not have quantized vibrational or rotational states). In an effort to explain the noncontinuous nature of atomic spectra Bohr invoked the quantum hypothesis, arguing that radiation of energy by circulating electrons could only occur between discrete values of energy (*QUANTUM THEORY), and that there were minimum energy levels for electrons in atoms

atomic theory the theory that all matter is composed of a limited number of discrete particles, separate or in combination with each other ‖ any of a number of theories of the structure of such atoms, modern ones being in terms of a small heavy nucleus surrounded by electrons (*QUANTUM THEORY)

atomic time time based on the frequency of atomic emissions of certain substances *Cf* ATOMIC CLOCK

atomic weight atomic mass

at·om·ism (ǽtəmizəm) *n.* (*philos.*) the doctrine, esp. as taught by the Greek philosophers Leucippus and Democritus, that all matter consists of different arrangements of a limited number of indivisible particles or atoms **át·om·ist** *adj.* and *n.* **at·om·ist·ic** *adj.*

---

at·om·ize (ǽtəmaiz) *pres. part.* **at·om·iz·ing** *past and past part.* **at·om·ized** *v.t.* to convert (a liquid, e.g. a perfume, insecticide or medicine) into very fine particles, generally as a spray forced through a nozzle **at·om·iz·er** *n.* a device for atomizing a liquid

at·om·om·e·ter (ǽtəmómətər) *n.* (*meteor.*) device for measuring capacity of air to absorb moisture

atom probe a spectrometer of single-atom sensitivity consisting of a field-ion microscrope with a hole in its fluorescent screen, a flight table, and a detection device for single-particle sensitivity; invented by Dr. Erwin Muller in 1967

atom smashers atomic-particle accelerators *Cf* BETATRON

a·ton·al (eitóun'l) *adj.* (*mus.*) written without key, i.e. using all 12 semitones of the chromatic scale equally (*SCHONBERG) **a·ton·al·ism** *n.* the theory or principle of such composition **a·ton·al·is·tic** *adj.* **a·to·nal·i·ty** (eitounǽliti:) *n.* the musical quality of atonal composition

a·tone (ətóun) *pres. part.* **a·ton·ing** *past and past part.* **a·toned** 1. *v.i.* to make amends (for some sin, wrong or omission) 2. *v.t.* (used only passively and with 'for') to make amends for, *these crimes will have to be atoned for someday* [back-formation from ATONEMENT]

a·tone·ment (ətóunmənt) *n.* the act of atoning || that which is done in order to atone **the A-tone·ment** in Christian theology, Christ's incarnation and death on the cross, which made up for the original sin of Adam and Eve, and enabled mankind to be at one with God again [fr. AT+obs. *onement*, union]

a·ton·ic (eitónik) *adj.* (*phon.*) without stress, *the first syllable of 'atone' is atonic* || (*mus.*, sometimes preferred to 'atonal') describing a composition not in a key but based on several tonic centers [fr. M.L. *atonicus* fr. Gk *atonos* fr. *a*, without + *tonos*, tone]

at·o·ny (ǽt'ni:) *n.* (*med.*) lack of vitality, weakness of a muscle or of an organ || (*phon.*) lack of stress or accent [F. *atonie* fr. L. fr. Gk]

AT Pase adenosine triphosphatase, an enzyme common to all body cells, that helps pump sodium and potassium across cell membranes; responsible for 10% to 50% of body heat energy production

at·ra·bil·iar (ǽtrəbíljər) *adj.* atrabilious

at·ra·bil·ious (ǽtrəbíljəs) *adj.* gloomy and sour-tempered || overanxious and fussy about one's health [fr. L. *atra bilis*, black bile]

ATRAN ((ǽtræn) (*mil. acronym*) for automatic terrain recognition and navigation, system for missile navigation based on superimposing radar data over prior map

at·ra·zin or **at·rar·zine** [C₈H₁₄N₅C] (ǽtrəzi:n) *n.* a weed killer used esp. in raising corn and sorghum

A·tre·us (éitri:əs) (*Gk mythol.*) a son of Pelops and king of Mycenae. After his brother, Thyestes, seduced Atreus's wife, Atreus murdered three sons of Thyestes, and had them served to their father at a banquet. Thyestes laid a curse on the house of Atreus which manifested itself bloodily in the next generation. It was lifted when Athena pardoned Orestes's murder of Clytemnestra and her lover Aegisthus, another son of Thyestes, who had murdered Agamennon. Atreus himself had been killed by Aegisthus

a·trip (ətríp) *adj.* (*naut.*, of an anchor) just tripped, i.e. just raised clear of the bottom

a·tri·um (éitri:əm) *pl.* **a·tri·a** (éitri:ə) *n.* the central hall of a Roman house, where the household gods were. It was used for receiving visitors || an open court with a covered passage on three or four sides leading e.g. to a basilica || (*anat.*) a cavity in the body, esp. the main chamber of the auricle of the heart [L.]

a·tro·cious (ətróuʃəs) *adj.* shockingly cruel or wicked || of very bad quality || extremely painful || very unpleasant [fr. L. *atrox* (*atrocis*), cruel]

a·troc·i·ty (ətrósiti:) *pl.* **a·troc·i·ties** *n.* shocking cruelty or wickedness || extreme painfulness || an atrocious deed || something ridiculous or very bad of its kind, *are you going to wear that atrocity?* [fr. L. *atrocitas* (*atrocitatis*)]

at·ro·phy (ǽtrəfi:) 1. *n.* a wasting or withering away or failure to develop normally, from lack of food or use || (*fig.*) loss of power or vigor 2. *v. pres. part.* **at·ro·phy·ing** *past and past part.* **at·ro·phied** *v.t.* to cause atrophy in || *v.i.* to suffer atrophy [F. *atrophie* fr. L. fr. Gk]

at·ro·pine (ǽtrəpi:n) *n.* a white crystalline alkaloid occurring naturally in belladonna.

It is used medically to dilate the pupil of the eye, and to relieve spasms etc. [fr. Mod. L. *Átropa*, deadly nightshade fr. Gk *Atropos*]

At·ro·pos (ǽtrəpɒs) *FATES

ATS (*abbr.*) for administrative terminal system, an IBM word-processing system permitting a typist to recall previously recorded texts for insertion in material being typed

at·tach (ətǽtʃ) *v.t.* to fasten, connect (one thing to another), *attach a hook to the line, two conditions are attached to his offer* || to bind by love or esteem || to appoint or assign in some added role, *he is attached to the commission as an observer* || (*mil.*) to place temporarily under the orders of some other unit for specified purposes || (*law*) to seize (a person or property) by legal authority || to attribute, *to attach blame* || *v.i.* to be fastened in some specified way || (*fig.*) to adhere, *no blame attaches to him* [O.F. *atachier*]

at·ta·ché (ǽtæʃéi, *Br.* esp. ətǽʃei) *n.* a person attached to an embassy for some specific activity, *press attaché* [F.]

attaché case a small rectangular case (often of leather) for carrying papers or personal effects

at·tach·ment (ətǽtʃmənt) *n.* the act of attaching one thing to another || the device or method by which one object is attached to another || the object attached || a bond of affection or friendship || (*law*) the legal seizure of persons or property [F. *attachement*]

at·tack (ətǽk) *n.* the act of attacking || a bout of illness, *an attack of flu* || (*mus.*) the action or manner of beginning a piece or phrase || (*sport*) offensive rather than defensive play [F. *attaque* or ATTACK V.]

attack to set upon, try to get the better of or destroy or win || to assail in words or writing || to start upon (a difficulty, task or occupation) || to have a harmful or destructive effect on || (*chess*) to threaten with a view to capturing || *v.i.* to make an attack [F. *attaquer*]

attack man (*sports*) team player assigned to offensive position

at·tain (ətéin) *v.t.* to arrive at, obtain, win **to attain to** to arrive at, *to attain to full maturity* **at·tain·a·bíl·i·ty** *n.* **at·táin·a·ble** *adj.* [M.E. *ateyne, ateine* fr. O.F.]

at·tain·der (ətéindər) *n.* the loss of all rights as a citizen, part of the punishment of a person condemned to death or outlawry for treason or felony (now abolished) [O.F. *ataindre, ateindre*, to accuse]

at·tain·ment (ətéinmənt) *n.* the act of attaining || an acquired personal skill

at·taint (ətéint) *v.t.* (*hist.*) to pass sentence of attainder upon [O.F. *ataint, ateint*, convicted]

at·tar of roses (ǽtər) a sweetsmelling essential oil distilled from the petals of *Rosa damascena* [fr. Pers. *itr*, perfume fr. Arab.]

at·tempt (ətémpt) 1. *v.t.* to try (to do something), to try or make trial of, *I am attempting to answer you, don't attempt more than three questions* || to try to achieve, *to attempt a rescue* **to attempt the life of** (*rhet.*) to try to kill 2. *n.* the act of attempting, often unsuccessful || a failed attack by a killer [O.F. *attempter*]

at·tend (əténd) *v.t.* to be present at, *a huge crowd attended the game* || to go regularly to, *he attends evening classes* || to visit and treat (as doctor, nurse etc.) || to accompany as attendant || to accompany (often as a result), *success attended his final effort* || *v.i.* (*Br.*) to pay attention **to attend to** to apply oneself to || to care for, look after || to wait upon, serve **to attend upon** to accompany (esp. royal personages) for the purpose of giving service [M.E. *atende* fr. O.F.]

at·tend·ance (əténdəns) *n.* the act or habitual practice of attending, being present, *attendance at school* || those who are present or attend, *the attendance at his lectures is increasing* **to dance attendance on** to run about after (somebody) to do their least bidding [O.F. *atendance*]

at·tend·ant (əténdənt) 1. *n.* a servant, an employee in charge, *a cloakroom attendant* || a companion, usually of lower rank, *the prince's attendants* || (*rhet.*) an accompaniment, *ignorance and its attendants: fear and prejudice* 2. *adj.* accompanyng *war and its attendant horrors* [O.F. *atendant*]

at·ten·tion (əténʃən) *n.* the giving of one's mind to something, mental concentration || notice, *wave to attract attention* || nursing, care, looking after, *he needs attention* || a mending or overhauling, *the brakes need attention* || service by a

waiter etc. || (*mil.*) the formal position of readiness on parade: upright and still, hands held stiffly at the seam of the trousers or skirt, fingers pointing downward, feet together || (*mil.*) the order to come to this position || (*interj.*) used as a warning word before an important announcement to impress the need to listen || (*pl.*) attentiveness, acts of politeness, *his constant attentions annoyed her* **to call attention to** to point out [fr. L. *attentio* (*attentionis*)]

at·ten·tive (əténtiv) *adj.* paying attention, giving one's mind to what is going on || thoughtful for others, esp. so as to meet their immediate needs or wishes [F. *attentif*]

at·ten·u·ant (əténju:ənt) 1. *adj.* (*med.*) making thin, diluting, e.g. by adding water 2. *n.* a substance used for this purpose [F.]

at·ten·u·ate (əténju:eit) 1. *v. pres. part.* **at·ten·u·at·ing** *past and past part.* **at·ten·u·ated** *v.t.* to make thin or slender || to dilute (a liquid) || to weaken, *inbreeding can attenuate the vigor of a breed* || *v.i.* to become thin, weak etc. 2. (əténju:it) *adj.* attenuated **at·ten·u·a·tion** (əténju:éiʃən) *n.* [fr. L. *attenuare* (*attenuatus*), to make thin]

at·ten·u·a·tion (əténju:éiʃən) *n.* 1. a reduction in an observed correlation or because of measurement error 2. (*electr.*) decrease in intensity of a signal, beam, or wave as a result of absorption of energy and of scattering out of the path of a detector, but not including the reduction due to geometric spreading, i.e., the inverse square of distance effect 3. (*mil.*) in mine warfare, the reduction in intensity of an influence as distance from the source increases

attenuation factor the ratio of the incident radiation dose or dose rate to the radiation dose or dose rate transmitted through a shielding material; the reciprocal of the transmission factor

at·test (ətést) *v.t.* to bear witness to, esp. by signing (a statement) || to confirm as authentic, *his secretary attests the truth of his statement* || to administer an oath to || (*Br.*) to certify the freedom of (livestock) from a specific disease || *v.i.* to testify [F. *attester*]

at·test·ant (ətéstənt) 1. *adj.* attesting 2. *n.* someone who attests [fr. L. *attestans* (*attestantis*) fr. *attestari*, to bear witness]

at·tes·ta·tion (ǽtestéiʃən) *n.* the act of bearing witness || the evidence given by a witness || confirmation of truth or authenticity, *the company's seal is sufficient attestation* || the administering of an oath [F.]

at·tes·tor (ətéstər) *n.* someone who attests

At·tic (ǽtik) 1. *adj.* (esp. of classical times) of Attica or Athens || of the dialect of Attica || (of literature and the arts) elegant in style, classical 2. *n.* the Attic dialect of ancient Greek [fr. L. fr. Gk *Attikos*]

at·tic (ǽtik) *n.* a room just under the roof of a house [F. *attique*, Attic fr. the Attic order]

At·ti·ca (ǽtikə) a region of east central Greece, incl. Athens

At·ti·ca (ǽtikə) *n.* (*eponym*) for prison riot; derived from an incident in which lives were lost unnecessarily from the 1968 riot at Attica, NY

At·ti·cism (ǽtisizəm) *n.* (in Greek style) an expression, a way of writing, peculiar to Attic Greek

Attic order an architectural order using pilasters, employed in Renaissance architecture for a low story set over the much higher order of the main facade of a building

Attic salt neat, elegant wit

Attic wit Attic salt

At·ti·la (ǽt'lə, ətílə) (c. 406–53), king of the Huns, who overran much of the Byzantine and Western Roman Empires. In 451 he advanced as far as Orléans in Gaul and in 452 to the River Mincio in Italy. His empire collapsed after his death. He later came to be called 'Scourge of God'

at·tire (ətáiər) 1. *v.t. pres. part.* **at·tir·ing** *past and past part.* **at·tired** (usually very formal) to dress grandly, *the bridesmaids attired her for her wedding* 2. *n.* fine clothing || (*venery and heraldry*) a stag's antlers [O.F. *atirier*]

at·ti·tude (ǽtitju:d, ǽtitu:d) *n.* posture, *what attitude was the body in?, a threatening attitude* || a mental position, *a favorable attitude* || **to strike an attitude** to assume a histrionic pose **at·ti·tú·di·nize** *pres. part.* **at·ti·tu·di·niz·ing** *past and past part.* **at·ti·tu·di·nized** *v.i.* to strike an attitude [F.]

Att·lee (ǽtli:), Clement Richard, 1st Earl Attlee (1883–1967), British statesman, leader of the

CONCISE PRONUNCIATION KEY: **(a)** æ, c*a*t; ɑ, c*a*r; ɔ f*aw*n; ei, sn*a*ke. **(e)** e, h*e*n; i:, sh*ee*p; iə, d*ee*r; ɛə, b*ea*r. **(i)** i, f*i*sh; ai, t*i*ger; əː, b*i*rd. **(o)** o, *o*x; au, c*ow*; ou, g*oa*t; u, p*oo*r; ɔi, r*oy*al. **(u)** ʌ, d*u*ck; u, b*u*ll; uː, g*oo*se; ə, b*a*cillus; juː, c*u*be. x, lo*ch*; θ, *th*ink; ð, bo*th*er; z, *Z*en; ʒ, corsa*g*e; dʒ, sava*g*e; ŋ, orangutan*g*; j, *y*ak; ʃ, *f*ish; tʃ, fe*t*ch; 'l, rabb*le*; 'n, redd*en*.   Complete pronunciation key appears inside front cover.

Labour party (1935–55), deputy prime minister (1943–5), and prime minister of the first majority Labour government (1945–51). His government nationalized the basic industries, greatly expanded the welfare state, ended the Palestine mandate and control of India, rearmed Britain against Communism and strengthened ties with the U.S.A.

at·to- (ǽtou) combining form meaning one quintillionth of a standard unit or 10^{-18} (0.0000000000000000001)

at·tor·ney (ətə́:rni:) *n.* a person who has legal authority to act on behalf of another, *power of attorney* ‖ a legal agent qualified to act for someone engaged in legal proceedings ‖ *DISTRICT ATTORNEY* [O.F. *atorné*, one appointed]

at·tor·ney-at-law (ətə́:rni:ətlɔ́:) *pl.* **at·tor·neys-at-law** *n.* a lawyer

attorney general *pl.* **attorneys general, attorney generals** the principal law officer of a nation, who represents the nation in all cases which involve public rights, and is the government's chief legal adviser, elected by every successive government. In the U.S.A. he heads the department of justice

at·tract (ətrǽkt) *v.t.* to draw towards itself or oneself, cause to move towards itself, *magnets attract nails, jam attracts wasps* ‖ to appear lovely or pleasing to the mind and senses ‖ to cause to center on itself, direct towards itself or oneself, *the play attracted a lot of notice* [fr. L. *attrahere (attractus)*, to draw in]

at·trac·tion (ətrǽkʃən) *n.* the power or act of attracting ‖ a desirable or pleasant quality or thing ‖ *(phys.)* the force, due to gravitational, electric, magnetic or other effects, causing or tending to cause two bodies to approach one another [fr. L. *attractio (attractionis)*]

at·trac·tive (ətrǽktiv) *adj.* charming, good-looking ‖ pleasant, enticing, *an attractive idea* [F. *attractif*]

at·tra·zine [$C_8H_{14}CIN_5$] (ǽtrəzi:n) *n.* persistent herbicide (weed killer)

at·tri·bute (ǽtribju:t) **1.** *n.* a quality proper to or characteristic of a person or thing, *hardness is an attribute of steel, reason is an attribute of man* ‖ a symbol often associated with a person or thing, *the sword and scales are attributes of Justice* ‖ *(logic)* an essential quality ‖ *(gram.)* a word or phrase used adjectivally **2.** *v.t.* (ətríbju:t) *pres. part.* **at·trib·ut·ing** *past* and *past part.* **at·trib·ut·ed** to consider (something) as being proper to or belonging to a person or thing ‖ to consider (a thing) as being ascribable to a cause, *he attributes his poverty to her extravagance* ‖ to consider (a thing) as having its origin in a certain time or place, or as being the work of a certain person or persons [fr. L. *attribuere (attributus)*, to assign]

at·tri·bu·tion (ætribjú:ʃən) *n.* the act of attributing ‖ the thing or quality attributed [F.]

at·trib·u·tive (ətríbju:tiv) **1.** *adj.* *(gram.,* of an adjective or other modifier) preceding the word it modifies, e.g. in 'a wrong answer', 'wrong' is attributive, but in 'your answer is wrong', 'wrong' is predicative **2.** *n.* an attributive word [F.]

at·tri·tion (ətríʃən) *n.* a wearing away by rubbing or friction ‖ a constant loss of strength or of resistance ‖ *(theol.)* a valid but imperfect form of contrition, sorrow for sin based not on hatred of the offense to God but on fear of punishment or disgrace ‖ normal reduction, e.g., by death, retirement, graduation ‖ the reduction of the effectiveness of a force caused by loss of personnel and material [fr. L. *attritio (attritionis)*]

attrition minefield *(mil.)* in naval mine warfare, a field intended primarily to cause damage to enemy ships

attrition rate a factor, normally expressed as percentage, reflecting the degree of losses of personnel or materiel due to various causes within a specified period of time

at·tune (ətjú:n,ətú:n) *v.t. pres. part.* **at·tun·ing** *past* and *past part.* **at·tuned** to bring (a musical instrument) into harmony, to tune ‖ to make (one thing) suit or agree with another, *attune your speech to the mood of your audience*

ATV (acronym) for all-terrain vehicle

A₂ (med.) Asian flu virus

Atwood, (ǽtwud) Margaret (1939–), Canadian novelist and poet. Her works include the poetry volumes 'The Circle Game' (1964) and 'Selected Poems' (1976) and novels 'Surfacing' (1972), 'Life Before Man' (1980), 'Bodily Harm' (1982), 'Second Words' (1984), and 'The Handmaid's Tale' (1986)

At·wood's machine (ǽtwudz) an apparatus used to study laws of dynamics and gravitation, consisting of a light frictionless wheel over which is passed a light string supporting at its ends two masses whose small difference provides an accelerating force for the system [after George *Atwood* (1746–1807), English physicist]

a·typ·i·cal (eitípik'l) *adj.* not like the regular type

Au *(chem.)* gold [fr. L. *aurium*]

au·bade (oubǽd, oubád) *n.* a morning serenade [F.]

Aube (oub) a department (area 2,326 sq. miles, pop. 285,000) of N.E. France, in the southeastern Paris basin (*CHAMPAGNE, *BURGUNDY). Chief town: Troyes

Au·ber (ouber), Daniel François Esprit (1782–1871) French composer of opera, e.g. 'Fra Diavolo' (1830)

au·ber·gine (óubərʒi:n, oubeərʒí:n) *n.* *(Br.)* the fruit of the eggplant [F.]

au·bre·ti·a (ɔbrí:ʃi:ə) *n.* a member of *Au brietia,* fam. *Cruciferae,* a genus of cushionlike perennial plants, with flowers whose colors range through pinks, reds and mauves, commonly grown in rock gardens and borders [after Claude *Aubriet* (c. 1665–1742), French painter]

Au·brey (ɔ́bri:), John (1626–97), English author and antiquarian. His 'Brief Lives' (edited 1898) contains vivid character sketches and anecdotes, chiefly of his contemporaries

au·burn (ɔ́bərn) **1.** *adj.* reddish-brown (esp. of hair) **2.** *n.* the color auburn [O.F.]

Au·bus·son (oubysɔ́) a French tapestry-weaving and carpet-making center (pop. 7,000) on the Creuse, in the department of the Creuse

Au·cas·sin and Ni·co·lette (oukæsǽn, nįkəlét) one of the chief works of medieval French literature, a love story told in alternate song and recitative in a light, humorous style

Auck·land (ɔ́klənd) a region (area 25,420 sq. miles, pop. 915,768) of North Island, New Zealand. Products: butter, wool, mutton, citrus fruit, newsprint, forest products, coal ‖ its capital (pop. 150,708), the largest city and chief port of New Zealand. Industries: dairy processing, timber, clothing, chemicals, engineering, steel and aluminum processing, shipbuilding. Founded in 1840, it was the national capital until 1865. University (autonomous since 1962)

auc·tion (ɔ́kʃən) **1.** *n.* a public sale at which the goods are sold to the highest bidder ‖ an offer to give something to whoever will pay the most ‖ *(cards,* esp. auction bridge) the bids which the players make to establish trumps ‖ *DUTCH AUCTION* **2.** *v.t.* to sell by auction [fr. L. *auctio (auctionis)*]

auction bridge *(cards)* an early variety of bridge in which tricks over contract count towards game (cf. *CONTRACT BRIDGE*)

auc·tion·eer (ɔkʃəníər) *n.* a person who sells by auction, esp. one licensed to do so

au·da·cious (ɔdéiʃəs) *adj.* daring, ready to take calculated risks ‖ too daring by conventional moral standards, *audacious language* [fr. L. *audax (audacis)*]

au·dac·i·ty (ɔdǽsiti:) *pl.* **au·dac·i·ties** *n.* boldness or an instance of it ‖ impudence, shamelessness, or an instance of it [fr. L. *audax (audacis),* bold]

Aude (ɔd) a department (area 2,448 sq. miles, pop. 272,000) of S. France between Toulouse and the Mediterranean (*LANGUEDOC). Chief town: Carcassonne

Au·den (ɔ́d'n), Wystan Hugh (1907–73), English lyric and dramatic poet, critic, librettist and translator, British by birth, naturalized American. He combined intellectual force with lyricism and a dazzling technique

au·di·bil·i·ty (ɔdəbíliti:) *n.* the ability to be heard

au·di·ble (ɔ́dəb'l) **1.** *n.* *(football)* a surprise substitute play or formation called at the scrimmage line **2.** *adj.* able to be heard **áu·di·bly** *adv.* [fr. M.L. *audibilis*]

au·di·ence (ɔ́di:əns) *n.* a group of persons assembled to listen to or watch something, esp. a public performance or speech ‖ those who read a publication or listen to a broadcast ‖ an official or formal interview, *a papal audience* [F.]

au·dien·cia (audjénsjə) *n.* *(hist.)* the highest court throughout colonial Latin America, often exercising administrative functions. It is the origin of the local government bodies set up after independence in Latin American countries [Span. = hearing]

au·dile (ɔ́dail) **1.** *adj.* (of spiritualistic, psychic or ghostly happenings) heard, as opposed to seen or felt **2.** *n.* *(psychol.)* a person in whose mind things appear as noises rather than pictures or movement [fr. L. *audire,* to hear]

au·di·o (ɔ́di:ou) **1.** *adj.* of electronic apparatus using audio frequencies ‖ of or relating to sound broadcasting, or to sound transmission or reception in television **2.** *n.* the part of television, or of television equipment, concerned with sound (cf. *VIDEO*) ‖ sound transmission or reception in broadcasting [fr. *audio-* combining form, fr. L. *audire,* to hear]

audio frequency the frequency of an oscillation which produces an audible sound ‖ a frequency lying between 20 and 20,000 cycles per second [fr. L. *audire,* to hear]

au·di·o·lin·gual (ɔdi:oulíŋgwəl) *adj.* of speech and sounds

au·di·om·e·ter (ɔdi:ɔ́mitər) *n.* an electrical instrument which produces a range of notes of adjustable frequency and intensity, by which hearing can be tested [fr. L. *audire,* to hear + *METER*]

au·di·o·phile (ɔ́di:oufail) *n.* high-fidelity hobbyist

audio tape sound recording on magnetic tape

au·di·o·typ·ing (ɔdi:outáipiŋ) *n.* typewriting performed from tape recordings — **audiotypist** *n.*

au·di·o·vis·u·al (ɔdi:ouvíʒu:əl) *adj.* *(television, education* etc.) relating to both sound and sight

au·dit (ɔ́dit) **1.** *n.* a full check and examination of account books ‖ the final account after the examination **2.** *v.t.* to make such an examination of (accounts) ‖ *v.i.* to examine account books in such a way [fr. L. *auditus,* hearing]

au·di·tion (ɔdíʃən) **1.** *n.* a trial of talent in which a prospective employer assesses an actor, singer etc. ‖ the sense or act of hearing **2.** *v.t.* to submit (candidates) to an audition ‖ *v.i.* to compete in an audition [fr. L. *auditio (auditionis),* hearing]

au·di·tive (ɔ́ditiv) *adj.* auditory [F. *auditif*]

au·di·tor (ɔ́ditər) *n.* a person who makes an audit, either professionally or in an amateur, honorary capacity ‖ a listener, e.g. to a broadcast ‖ a person who attends a high school or college course without aiming to obtain the attached credit **au·di·to·ri·al** (ɔditɔ́ri:əl, ɔditóuri:əl) *adj.* [A.F. *auditour*]

au·di·to·ri·um (ɔditɔ́ri:əm, ɔditóuri:əm) *n.* the part of a theater or movie theater etc. in which the audience sits ‖ a lecture hall or assembly room [L.]

au·di·to·ry (ɔ́ditɔri:, ɔ́ditɔuri:) *adj.* relating to the sense of hearing [fr. L. *auditorius*]

auditory meatus the channel leading from the outer ear to the eardrum

audit trail *(computer)* error-finding technique that traces dataflow from input to output

Au·du·bon (ɔ́dəbɒn), John James (1785–1851), American naturalist and bird painter. 'The Birds of America' was originally published 1827–33 and 'Ornithological Biography' 1831–9

Au·er (áuər), Karl, Baron von Welsback (1858–1929), Austrian chemist. He studied the rare earths and the alloy ferrocerium, used for flints for lighters, and invented the gas mantle

Auf·klä·rung (áufklɛəruŋ) the Enlightenment (*ENLIGHTEN *v.t.*)

Au·ge·an stables (ɔdʒí:ən) *(Gk mythol.)* the stalls in which King Augeas of Elis kept 3,000 oxen. They had not been cleaned out for years, and Hercules had to do it as one of his labors. He did the job in one day, by diverting the River Alpheus to sluice out the stalls (*HERCULES)

aug·end (ɔ́dʒend) *n.* *(math.)* the quantity to which an addend is added to form a sum [fr. L. *augendum* fr. gerundive *augendus* of *augere,* to increase]

au·ger (ɔ́gər) *n.* a tool, larger than a gimlet, for boring holes in wood ‖ any tool similar in shape and principle for boring holes or drilling (e.g. into the ground) [O.E. *nafugār,* a tool for boring the nave of a wheel (*a nauger* being separated as *an auger*)]

aught, ought (ɔt) *n.* *(archaic)* anything [O.E. *āwiht* fr. *ā,* ever + *wiht,* whit, thing]

Au·gier (ouʒjei), Guillaume Victor Émile (1820–89), French dramatist, part author of the comedies 'le Gendre de M. Poirier' (with Sandeau), and 'le Prix Martin' (with Labiche). He also wrote many dramas on social themes

---

CONCISE PRONUNCIATION KEY: **(a)** æ, c*a*t; ɑ, c*a*r; ɔ f*aw*n; ei, sn*a*ke. **(e)** e, h*e*n; i:, sh*ee*p; iə, d*ee*r; ɛə, b*ea*r. **(i)** i, f*i*sh; ai, t*i*ger; ə:, b*i*rd. **(o)** o, *o*x; au, c*ow*; ou, g*oa*t; u, p*oo*r; ɔi, r*oy*al. **(u)** ʌ, d*u*ck; u, b*u*ll; u:, g*oo*se; ə, b*a*cillus; ju:, c*u*be. x, lo*ch*; θ, *th*ink; ð, bo*th*er; z, *Z*en; ʒ, cor*s*age. dʒ, sava*g*e; ŋ, oranguta*ng*; j, *y*ak; ʃ, *f*ish; tʃ, *f*etch; 'l, rabb*le*; 'n, redd*en*. Complete pronunciation key appears inside front cover.

au·gite (ɔ́dʒait) n. (mineral.) a complex aluminous silicate, a variety of pyroxene, found in many igneous rocks [fr. L. augites, precious stone fr. Gk]

aug·ment (ɔgmént) v.t. to add to, his wife works to augment their income || (mus.) to increase (certain intervals) by sharpening the higher note || v.i. to increase [f. augmenter]

aug·men·ta·tion (ɔgmentéiʃən) n. an increasing or being increased || something which is an increase or addition || (mus., in counterpoint) the repeating of a phrase in notes longer than those first used [O. F. augmentacion]

aug·men·ta·tive (ɔgméntətiv) 1. adj. (of words) having the effect of strengthening or enlarging the force or meaning, 'almighty' is an augmentative form of 'mighty' 2. n. an augmentative word [F. augmentatif]

aug·men·tor (ɔgméntər) n. robot for performing difficult or dangerous work

au grat·in (ougrát'n, ougræt'n) (cooking) covered with breadcrumbs or grated cheese or both, and cooked in the oven [F.]

Augs·burg (áuksbu:rk) a town (pop. 248,000) on the Lech in Bavaria, Germany, with chemical and machine industries. It was the seat of great merchant houses in the 15th and 16th cc. (*FUGGER)

Augsburg Confession the 28 articles of faith, doctrine and rule which constitute the main confessional declaration (1530) of the Lutheran Church. The Confession was drawn up by Melanchthon and approved by Luther. It follows Luther's emphasis on justification by faith alone (the sacraments being valid only as aids to faith), and his teaching that the Scriptures constitute the one necessary guide to truth

Augsburg, League of the alliance formed by the Austrian emperor, some German princes, Sweden and Spain in 1686 and joined (1689) by the Netherlands, Savoy and England to form the Grand Alliance against Louis XIV of France

Augsburg, Peace of a temporary settlement of Reformation conflicts in the German empire between Catholics and Lutherans (1555). It allowed 'cuius regio, eius religio', i.e. that each state could determine whether Catholicism or Lutheranism should prevail within its territory

au·gur (ɔ́gər) 1. n. (Rom. hist.) one of a college of officials who divined whether or not an action would be approved by the gods (by watching how hens pecked at their grain, observing the flight or cries of birds etc.) || a person who interprets omens 2. v.t. to presage, point to, his early successes augured a brilliant career **to augur well (ill) for** to suggest a good (bad) future for [L.]

au·gu·ry (ɔ́gjuri) pl. **au·gu·ries** n. the art of an augur || an omen || (rhet.) a promising sign of the future [O.F. augurie]

Au·gust (ɔ́gəst) n. (abbr. Aug.) the 8th month of the year, having 31 days [after the first Roman emperor, Augustus Caesar]

au·gust (ɔgʌ́st) adj. majestic, noble and impressive [fr. L. augustus]

Au·gus·ta (ɔgʌ́stə) a city, commercial center and winter resort (pop. 42,532) of E. Georgia at the head of navigation on the Savannah River

Augusta the capital city (pop. 21,819) of Maine

Au·gus·tan (ɔgʌ́stən) 1. adj. of the Roman emperor Augustus Caesar or his reign (27 B.C.–14 A.D.) || of the literature of that period || belonging to the classical period of a country's literature (in England, the first half of the 18th c.) 2. n. a writer belonging to such a period [fr. L. Augustanus fr. Augustus Caesar]

Au·gus·tine of Canterbury (ɔgʌ́stin, ɔ́gəsti:n) St (d. c. 604). He was appointed missionary of England by Pope Gregory I. He landed in 597 and became the first archbishop of Canterbury (601), but his missionary success was limited. Feast: May 28

Augustine of Hippo, St (354–430), African Latin Church Father. His 'Confessions' tell of his spiritual pilgrimage and dramatic conversion to Christianity, influenced by his mother, St Monica. The profundity of his thought was such that both Catholics and Protestants look to him (esp. to his treatise on grace) for doctrinal authority. His speculations on freedom, history, time and the nature of man give him a prominent place in the history of philosophy. His 'De civitate Dei' (413–26) has been the basis of much political theory. He sought to reconcile Platonic thought and Christian dogma, reason and faith. His 'Letters' embody his rule of life. His tomb is at Hippo (which was his bishopric), an ancient city of Numidia near modern Annaba. Feast: Aug. 28

Au·gus·tin·i·an (ɔgəstíni:ən) 1. adj. of, or relating to, St Augustine (of Hippo) or to his teaching 2. n. a follower of St Augustine's teaching || a member of a religious order following the rule of St Augustine **Au·gus·tin·i·an·ism, Au·gus·tin·ism** (ɔgʌ́stinizəm) ns. the theological and philosophical system of St Augustine

Au·gus·tus (ɔgʌ́stəs) (Gaius Julius Octavianus, 63 B.C.–14 A.D.), first Roman emperor (27 B.C.–14 A.D.), great-nephew and adopted son of Julius Caesar. He became a member of the 2nd Triumvirate with Antony and Lepidus (43 B.C.). After his victory over Antony at Actium (31 B.C.), he was sole master of the Roman world. Previously known as Octavian, he was granted the name 'Augustus' as a title of honor. He received wide powers previously divided among several magistrates, and his firm government brought peace and prosperity to a world long torn by civil wars. His greatness showed itself in administrative reform, social and financial measures (public works, grants for improved agriculture), reorganization of the army, and encouragement of the arts. He was succeeded by his stepson Tiberius

au jus (ouʒú:s, oudʒú:s) (cooking, of meat) served in the natural juices extracted during cooking [F.]

auk (ɔk) n. a member of Alcidae, a family of web-footed, short-winged birds, often flightless, which live in large colonies on the edges of the seas of the northern hemisphere. They include the little auk, razorbill, guillemot and puffin || *GREAT AUK [O.N. ālka]

auld lang syne (ɔ́ldlæŋzáin,ɔ́ldlæŋsáin) (rhet.) the good old days || (rhet.) long friendship [Scot.=old long ago]

aumbry *AMBRY

Au·nis (ouni:s) a former province of W. France, now parts of Charente-Maritime and Deux-Sèvres, a treeless, partly sandy plain, with mixed farming. The coast lives on fishing and tourism. Old capital: La Rochelle. It was detached from Poitou in the 10th c. and attached to the Crown in 1373. In the 16th and 17th cc. it was a stronghold of Protestantism

aunt (ænt,ɑnt) n. a sister of one's mother or father || (by courtesy) the wife of one's uncle [O.F. aunte]

Aunt Sal·ly (sǽli:) (Br.) a game played at fairs, in which balls or sticks are thrown at a painted wooden head || (Br.) a target for questions or reproaches, a butt or scapegoat

au pair (oupéər) adj. of an arrangement for reciprocal services between two parties which often avoids money payment or a wages relationship It is used esp. of the arrangement whereby a girl wishing to learn a foreign language goes abroad and gives domestic help in return for food, lodging, (sometimes) pocket money, and the opportunity to learn [F.]

au·ra (ɔ́rə) n. the atmosphere of a thing, an aura of romance || (spiritualism) a vague, luminous glow surrounding a figure or object || (med.) a warning of an impending epileptic fit. It may take the form of a sound, sight, smell or feeling not perceptible to others **áu·ral** adj. [L. fr. Gk aura, breeze]

au·ral (ɔ́rəl) adj. relating to the ear or to hearing [fr. L. auris, ear]

Au·ran·ga·bad (áurʌŋgəbæd) a market town (pop. 61,000) in Maharashtra, India, 175 miles northeast of Bombay. It contains the beautiful mausoleum built by Aurangzeb for his favorite wife

Au·rang·zeb (ɔ́rʌŋzeb) (1618–1707), Mogul emperor (1658–1707), son of Shah Jahan. Under his reign the Mogul Empire reached the height of its prosperity, but his bigoted policies and the rise of Maratha power weakened the Moguls

au·re·lia (ɔri:ljə,ɔrɪ́:li:ə) n. a member of Aurelia, a genus of jellyfish common in N. Atlantic waters [Ital.=silkworm]

Au·re·lian (ɔrɪ́:ljən, ɔrɪ́:li:ən) (Lucius Domitius Aurelianus, c. 214–275), Roman emperor (270–5). He reasserted Roman authority by the capture of Palmyra (273)

Aurelius *MARCUS AURELIUS

au·re·o·la (ɔrɪ́:ələ) n. an aureole

au·re·ole (ɔ́ri:oul) n. the heavenly crown which is the symbolic reward of sanctity, often represented in art by a halo || this halo || the halo of light seen around a heavenly body or bright light in misty weather || the clear space between the sun or moon and a surrounding halo or corona [fr. L. aureola (corona), golden (crown)]

au·re·o·my·cin (ɔri:oumáisin) n. the yellow crystalline 'broad-spectrum' antibiotic chlortetracycline, active against many organisms resistant to penicillin and streptomycin, and used to stimulate animal growth [trade name fr. L. aureus, olden + mukēs fungus]

Au·ric (ouri:k), Georges (1899–1983), French composer, one of 'les Six'. His ballet music includes 'les Fâcheux' (of Molière) and 'les Matelots' for Diaghilev, and he composed for many films

au·ric (ɔ́rik) adj. of or containing gold || (chem) in which gold is trivalent [fr. L. aurum, gold]

au·ri·cle (ɔ́rik'l) n. (anat.) the external part of the ear || the chamber or either of the two chambers in the heart connecting the veins with the ventricles || (bot.) an earlike growth [fr. L. auricula, dim. of auris, ear]

au·ric·u·la (ɔrɪ́kjulə) pl. **au·ric·u·las, au·ric·u·lae** (ɔrɪ́kjuli:) n. Primula auricula, a species of primula || an auricle [L.]

au·ric·u·lar (ɔrɪ́kjulər) 1. adj. of or concerned with the ear or hearing || spoken in the ear, in private, auricular confession || known by hearing || of or concerned with an auricle of the heart || like an ear in shape 2. n. (usually pl.) one of the feathers covering a bird's ear [fr M.L. auricularis]

au·ric·u·late (ɔrɪ́kjulit) adj. with ears or with appendages resembling ears or lobes [fr. L. auricula, dim. of auris, ear]

au·rif·er·ous (ɔrɪ́fərəs) adj. containing or producing gold [fr. L. aurifer]

au·ri·form (ɔ́rifɔrm) adj. shaped like an ear [fr. L. auris, ear]

Au·ri·gna·cian (ɔrinjéiʃən) adj. of a late Paleolithic cultural period, associated with Cro-Magnon man and marked by the use of finely finished flint pointed tools, and by the appearance of bone implements and of cave art [after Aurignac, in the French Pyrenees]

Au·ri·ol (ouri:ɔl), Vincent (1884–1966), French statesman, president of the Fourth Republic (1947–54)

au·rochs (ɔ́rɔks, áurɔks) n. the urus || the wisent [etym. doubtful]

Au·ro·ra (ɔrɔ́rə, ɔróurə) (Rom. mythol.) the goddess of the dawn, identified with the Greek Eos

au·ro·ra (ɔrɔ́rə, ɔróurə) n. the redness of the sky just before sunrise || the aurora australis or the aurora borealis [AURORA, Rom. goddess]

aurora aus·tra·lis (ɔstréilis) n. a phenomenon in the southern hemisphere analogous to the aurora borealis [Mod. L.]

aurora bo·re·al·is (bɔri:ǽlis, bɔurɪ:ǽlis) n. a colored glow visible at night in high latitudes. It has the appearance of a fan of ascending luminous streamers near the northern horizon, and is supposed to be of electrical origin [Mod. L.]

aur·ous (ɔ́rəs) adj. containing gold || (chem.) in which gold is monovalent [fr. L. aurum, gold]

Ausch·witz (áuʃvits) (Polish Oświęcim) a town near Katowice in Upper Silesia, Poland, site of the most notorious Nazi extermination camp (1940–5). Estimates of the number of Jews who were gassed there vary between 2 and 4 million

aus·cul·tate (ɔ́skəlteit) pres. part. **aus·cul·tat·ing** past and past part. **aus·cul·tat·ed** v.t. (med.) to examine (the heart, lungs etc.) by auscultation [fr. L. auscultare (auscultatus), to listen to]

aus·cul·ta·tion (ɔskəltéiʃən) n. (med.) examination by listening to the heart, lungs etc. with a stethoscope **aus·cul·ta·tive** (ɔ́skəlteitiv), **aus·cul·ta·to·ry** (ɔskʌ́ltətɔri:, ɔskʌ́ltətɔuri:) adjs [fr. L. auscultatio (auscultationis), a listening]

aus·forg·ing (ɔ́sfɔrdʒiŋ) n. (metallurgy) process of shaping austentite steel of gamma iron and carbon aftercooling, by hammering or pressing, designed to increase resistance to metal fatigue

Au·so·ni·us (ɔsóuni:əs), Decimus Magnus (c. 310–c. 395), Latin poet born at Bordeaux, tutor to the emperor Gratian. He celebrated the Moselle country and S. Gaul in his Idylls

aus·pice (ɔ́spis) n. (Rom. hist.) the observation of the flight and behavior of birds, and observation of other animals, so as to learn whether the gods would be pleased or displeased by a proposed action || a sign so observed **under the**

auspices of under the patronage of, by care and favor of [F. *auspice*]

aus·pi·cious (ɔspíʃəs) *adj.* giving promise of good fortune ‖ (*rhet.*) fortunate [fr. L. *auspicium*, omen]

Aus·ten (ɔ́stin), Jane (1775–1817), English novelist. Her six finished novels are 'Sense and Sensibility' (1811), 'Pride and Prejudice' (1813), 'Mansfield Park' (1814), 'Emma' (1816), 'Northanger Abbey' (1818) and 'Persuasion' (1818). Her material is the contemporary life of the English upper middle class in the country, and in London and Bath. Her wit is pervasive and vigorous. Her implicit themes are positive: right judgment, right behavior, the formation of character

aus·tere (ɔstíər) *adj.* stern and strict ‖ stern in appearance, grim ‖ simple and without decoration ‖ marked by the absence of comfort or luxury [O.F. fr. L. fr. Gk *austēros*, dry, rough]

aus·ter·i·ty (ɔstériti) *pl.* **aus·ter·i·ties** *n.* the quality of being austere ‖ (*esp. pl.*) an austere habit or practice [O.F. *austerité*]

Aus·ter·litz (ɔ́stərlits) Napoleon's most brilliant victory (1805), against Austria and Russia, sometimes called the 'battle of the three emperors'

Aus·tin (ɔ́stin), Herbert Austin, 1st Baron (1866–1941), British industrialist, founder of the Austin Motor Company (in 1905). His 'Austin seven' was the first successful small family car

Austin, Stephen Fuller (1793–1836), a U.S. frontier colonizer and founder of the chief English-speaking settlements in Texas in the 1820s. He took a leading part in the Texan struggle for independence from Mexico, and served as secretary of state (1836) under Sam Houston in the Republic of Texas

Austin the capital (pop. 345,496) of Texas, on the Colorado River, center of a rich farming district, with varied industries. University of Texas (1883)

Austin Friar an Augustinian Friar

aus·tral (ɔ́strəl) *adj.* (*rare*) southern, *austral signs of the zodiac* (those south of the ecliptic) [fr. L. *australis*]

Aus·tral·a·sia (ɔstrəléiʒə, ɔstrəléiʃə) *n.* Australia, Tasmania, New Zealand, Malaysia, Melanesia, Micronesia and Polynesia as a biogeographical unit ‖ (*loosely*) Australia, Tasmania, New Zealand and their island territories as a biogeographical unit **Aus·tral·á·sian** *adj.*

Aus·tral·ia (ɔstréiljə) a continent in the southern hemisphere, and (Commonwealth of Australia) federal dominion (area 2,271,081 sq. miles, pop. 15,862,000, incl. Tasmania) within the British Commonwealth. Federal capital: Canberra. Largest towns: Sydney, Melbourne, Brisbane, Adelaide. Outlying territories administered by Australia include: Australian Antarctic Territory, Christmas Is., Cocos (Keeling) Is, Norfolk, and Papua and New Guinea. People: mainly of British stock, with small minorities from other European countries, 40,000 full aborigines, and 39,000 part aborigines. Language: English. Religion: 82% Protestant, 9% Roman Catholic, small Orthodox minority. Three quarters of Australia lies between the 600 ft and the 1,500 ft contours, in the form of a huge dry plateau (incl. the Great Sandy Desert, the Great Victoria Desert and the Nullarbor Plain). The arable land is mainly on the coastal plains of the eastern coast and in the southwest corner of Australia, but hitherto arid parts are being brought under cultivation by irrigation. The longest rivers include the Murray, the Darling and the Murrumbidgee. The mountains of Australia are relatively low, Mt Kosciusko on the Victoria-New South Wales border in the Great Dividing Range being only 7,316 ft. The biggest lakes are the shallow salt lakes in the center: Lake Eyre, Lake Torrens. The Great Barrier Reef runs for 1,200 miles 10–100 miles off the eastern coast. 39% of Australia lies within the Tropics. Most of the northerly areas have a monsoon climate (wet season Jan.–Apr.). Rainfall along the coast is 30–60 ins, but most of Australia receives less than 30 ins. Livestock: sheep, cattle. Agricultural products: wool (29% of world output), meat, cereals, sugarcane, dairy products. Mineral resources: coal, copper, gold, lead, uranium, silver, zinc, iron. Manufactures: steel, food processing, ships, machinery, plastics, textiles, chemicals, vehicles, airplanes. Exports: wool, wheat, meat, cane sugar, fruit, ores and concentrates, hides and skins, butter, flour, barley, lead. Imports: machinery, vehicles, fertilizers, textiles, petroleum products, chemicals, paper. Main ports: Sydney, Newcastle, Adelaide, Melbourne. There are 14 universities, the oldest being Sydney (1850) and Melbourne (1853). Monetary unit: Australian dollar (100 cents). HISTORY. Australia, sparsely inhabited by aboriginal tribes, was discovered by the Portuguese in the 16th c. The north and west coasts were explored by the Dutch early in the 17th c., and were named New Holland. Tasman discovered Tasmania (1642–3). Dampier navigated the west coast (1688). Cook discovered Botany Bay and claimed the east coast region for Britain, naming it New South Wales (1770). The English began to transport convicts to Australia (Jan. 26, 1788) after the loss of the American colonies, and continued transportation until c. 1840. Flinders circumnavigated the continent (1801–3), and introduced the name Australia for the whole continent. Settlements developed early in the 19th c., esp. after the crossing of the Blue Mtns in 1813 and the introduction of merino sheep. Self-government was adopted in the separate colonies in the 1850s. The aborigines lost their food-gathering grounds and dwindled. There were rapid developments after the gold rush (1851) and the opening up of the Murray-Darling basin. Six colonies were founded: New South Wales (1788), Tasmania (1803), Western Australia (1829), Victoria (1835), South Australia (1836), Queensland (1859). These became states forming the Commonwealth of Australia (1901), to which were added the Northern Territory and the Australian Capital Territory (1911). Australia fought in both world wars as an ally of Britain and joined the ANZUS pact (1951) and the Colombo Plan (1950). It granted independence to Papua New Guinea (1975). Active in Asian and Pacific affairs, Australia has taken a stand in favor of a nuclear-free zone in the South Pacific

Aus·tral·ian (ɔstréiljən) **1.** *n.* a native or an inhabitant of Australia **2.** *adj.* pertaining or belonging to Australia, its inhabitants etc.

Australian Alps *GREAT DIVIDING RANGE

Australian Antarctic Territory the sector of the Antarctic continent and adjacent islands between 45°E and 160°E south of 60°S. (except Adélie Land)

Australian antigen (*med.*) substance associated with, and the carrier of, serum hepatitus

Australian Capital Territory a territory (area 939 sq. miles, pop. 236,600) ceded by New South Wales to contain Canberra, capital of Australia. It consists of two enclaves, one (area 911 sq. miles, ceded 1911) inland and the other (area 28 sq. miles, ceded 1915) providing a port area at Jervis Bay

Aus·tral Islands (ɔ́strəl) (Tubuaï Is) a chain (about 850 miles long) of 7 small volcanic islands and atolls (total land area 67 sq. miles, pop. 4,000) in the S. Pacific, part of French Polynesia. Religion: Protestant. Capital: Moerai

Aus·tra·sia (ɔstréiʒə, ɔstréiʃə) the eastern dominion of the Merovingian Franks, centered on Metz. It existed from the death of Clovis (511) to the reign of Charlemagne (768–814)

Aus·tri·a (ɔ́stri·ə) a republic (area 32,373 sq. miles, pop. 7,559,440) in central Europe. Capital: Vienna. Language: German, apart from small Croat and Magyar minorities in Burgenland, and small Slovene groups along the Yugoslav border. Religion: nine-tenths Roman Catholic, with a small Protestant minority. Jews formed 4% of the population in 1938, but were almost exterminated under Nazi rule. The land is about 28 % arable, 30% pasture and 37% forest. The eastern Alps, rising to 12,000 ft in the Hohe Tauern, cover the west and part of the center and east. The fertile Alpine foreland forms a narrow plateau (1,000–2,000 ft) between the Alps and the Danube. North of the Danube stretch the hills of the Bohemian Forest. The extreme east is lowland, joining the Hungarian plain. Average winter and summer temperatures (F.): 27° and 65°. Average annual rainfall: 28 ins. Livestock: cattle, pigs, poultry. Crops: rye, oats, barley, wheat, potatoes, sugar beet, vines. Mineral resources: lignite, iron ore, magnesite, top-grade graphite, oil, salt. Manufactures: pig iron, steel, cotton, wool, chemicals, machinery, electrical goods, paper, pulp, timber, glass, aluminum, synthetic fibers, beer. Tourism is important. Exports: timber, electric power, steel, pulp, pig iron, graphite, magnesite, textiles, chemicals, machinery. Imports: vegetables, coal. Large sections of the Austrian economy were nationalized in 1946–7. The Danube is an important waterway. Nearest seaport: Trieste (in Italy). There are three universities (Vienna, Graz and Innsbruck). Monetary unit: schilling (divided into 100 groschen). HISTORY. The area was inhabited by Celts when Rome conquered it (c. 15 B.C.). It was invaded by Vandals, Visigoths and Huns (5th c. A.D.) and settled by Alemanni, Avars and Slavs (5th and 6th cc.). Charlemagne defeated the Avars (795) and set up (803) the East Mark (later Österreich). Otto I finally repelled the Magyars (955). Austria was ruled by the Hapsburgs (1278–1918), who took the title of Holy Roman Emperor (1438–1806) (*HOLY ROMAN EMPIRE, *GERMANY). The empire was weakened and reduced by wars: the Thirty Years' War (1618–48), the War of the Spanish Succession (1701–14), the War of the Austrian Succession (1740–8), the Seven Years' War (1756–63) and the Napoleonic Wars. Francis II united the territories under the new title of Emperor of Austria (1804). Austria took the dominant part in the German Confederation under the direction of Metternich (1815–48), but was forced by Prussia to withdraw from German affairs (1866). The dual monarchy of Austria-Hungary lasted from 1867 to 1918. Austria then became a federal republic (1919–38). It was annexed by Germany (1938–45) and occupied by the Four Powers (1945–55). A state treaty (1955) reestablished the 1938 frontiers and ended the occupation. Austria joined the U.N. later that year. Its series of coalition governments was broken from 1966–70 on a People's party administration and from 1970–83 by a Socialist government, after which another coalition took power

Aus·tri·a-Hun·ga·ry (ɔ́stri·əhʌ́ŋɡəri:) the dual monarchy of the Hapsburg Empire (1867–1918). It included Austria, Hungary, and parts of modern Czechoslovakia, Italy, Poland, Rumania, Russia and Yugoslavia. Austria and Hungary formed two separate kingdoms under one crown, united for foreign affairs, defense and finance. (The total area in 1910 was 261,239 sq. miles, pop. 51,000,000). It was a member of the Triple Alliance with Germany and Italy (1882–1914). It annexed the Turkish provinces of Bosnia and Herzegovina (1908). The assassination of the heir to the throne, Archduke Franz Ferdinand, by Bosnian Serbs (1914) precipitated the 1st world war. The monarchy ceased to exist with the proclamation of the Austrian republic (1918). There emerged the independent states of Austria, Hungary, Czechoslovakia and Poland. Parts of the old monarchy passed to Italy, Rumania and Yugoslavia (1919)

Aus·tri·an (ɔ́stri·ən) **1.** *n.* a native or inhabitant of Austria ‖ the German dialect spoken in Austria **2.** *adj.* of Austria, its people, dialect etc.

Austrian Succession, War of the (1740–8), a series of European conflicts following the death of Emperor Charles VI (Oct. 20, 1740), despite his attempt to settle his succession by the Pragmatic Sanction. France had decided to support Spain in the War of Jenkins' Ear against Britain. Frederick II of Prussia invaded Silesia (1741), which was ceded to him by the Treaty of Berlin (1742) and by the Treaty of Dresden (1745). France formed a coalition of Spain, Bavaria and Saxony against Austria. An alliance of Britain, Holland and Austria was defeated by France at Fontenoy (1745). The Prussians won notable victories over Austria at Mollwitz (1741), Hohenfriedberg and Kesselsdorf (1745). By the Treaty of Aix-la-Chapelle (1748), France and Britain restored their conquests, while Prussia kept Silesia

Aus·tro·ne·sia (ɔstroní:ʒə, ɔstroní:ʃə) the islands of the central and S. Pacific

Aus·tro·ne·sian (ɔstroní:ʒən, ɔstroní:ʃən) *adj.* of Austronesia, its peoples etc. ‖ of a family of languages, also called Malayo-Polynesian, extending from Madagascar through the Malay Peninsula to Easter Island and from Formosa to New Zealand. There are about 90 million speakers of these languages. They are grouped into four families: Indonesian, Melanesian, Micronesian and Polynesian

Aus·tro-Prus·sian War (ɔ́strouprʌ́ʃən) *SEVEN WEEKS' WAR

au·tar·chic (ɔtárkik) *adj.* of or characteristic of an autarchy **au·tar·chi·cal** *adj.*

au·tar·chy (ɔ́tɑrki:) *pl.* **au·tar·chies** *n.* despotism, the rule of an autocrat ‖ a country under

CONCISE PRONUNCIATION KEY: **(a)** æ, c*a*t; ɑ, c*ar*; ɔ f*aw*n; ei, sn*a*ke. **(e)** e, h*e*n; i:, sh*ee*p; iə, d*ee*r; ɛə, b*ear*. **(i)** i, f*i*sh; ai, t*i*ger; ə:, b*ir*d. **(o)** o, *o*x; au, c*ow*; ou, g*oa*t; u, p*oo*r; ɔi, r*oy*al. **(u)** ʌ, d*u*ck; u, b*u*ll; u:, g*oo*se; ə, b*a*cill*u*s; ju:, c*u*be. x, lo*ch*; θ, *th*ink; ð, bo*th*er; z, *Z*en; ʒ, cor*s*age; dʒ, sava*g*e; ŋ, orangutan*g*; j, *y*ak; ʃ, *f*ish; tʃ, fe*tch*; 'l, rabb*le*; 'n, redd*en*. Complete pronunciation key appears inside front cover.

such rule [fr. Gk *autarchia* fr. *autos*, self+*archos*, ruler]

au·tar·kic (ɔtárkik) *adj.* of or relating to autarky **au·tár·ki·cal** *adj.*

au·tar·ky (ɔ́tarki:) *n.* national self-sufficiency in the production of all a country's needs [fr. Gk *autarkeia* fr. *autos*, self+ *arkeein*, to suffice]

au·teur (ɔtə:r) *n.* film director who exerts substantial personal influence on his or her productions —**auterism** *n.*

auteur theory critical hypothesis that the director of a film is the chief creator of the product —*auteur n.* film director —**auteurist** *n.* the critic who subscribes to this view

au·then·tic (ɔθéntik) *adj.* genuine ‖ true, reliable **au·thén·ti·cal·ly** *adv.* [O.F. *autentique* fr. L. fr. Gk]

au·then·ti·cate (ɔθéntikeit) *pres. part.* **au·then·ti·cat·ing** *past* and *past part.* **au·then·ti·cat·ed** *v.t.* to prove the genuineness or truth of, *to authenticate a claim* **au·then·ti·cá·tion**, **au·thén·ti·ca·tor** *ns* [fr. M.L. *authenticare (authenticatus)*]

au·then·tic·i·ty (ɔθentísiti:) *n.* the quality of being authentic

authentic mode (*mus.*) a mode of which the keynote is also the lowest note of its range, e.g. the Dorian (cf. PLAGAL)

au·thor (ɔ́θər) *n.* the writer of a book, article etc. ‖ a person whose profession is writing ‖ a writer's books, *this author is often asked for in the library* ‖ a maker, originator, *the author of the universe* **au·tho·ri·al** (ɔθɔ́ri:əl) *adj.* [A.F. *autour*, inventor fr. L.]

au·thor·i·tar·i·an (əθɔritéəri:ən, əθɔritéəri:ən) **1.** *adj.* favoring, or relating to, the theory that respect for authority is of greater importance than individual liberty ‖ domineering **2.** *n.* a person supporting this theory ‖ economist who espouses government actions to direct economic trends **au·thor·i·tári·an·ism** *n.*

authoritarian personality (*psych.*) a complex of personality traits including rigid adherence to conventional values, uncritical submission to moral authorities, aggressive attitudes toward social deviants, preoccupation with power and toughness, and a generalized hostility

au·thor·i·ta·tive (əθɔ́riteitiv, əθɔriteitiv) *adj.* coming from an official source or from an appropriate authority ‖ fully expert, *an authoritative work on the subject* ‖ with an air of command, *an authoritative tone of voice*

au·thor·i·ty (əθɔ́riti:, əθɔriti:) *pl.* **au·thor·i·ties** *n.* the right and power to command and be obeyed, or to do something ‖ such power, or proof of such power, entrusted to another, *this letter is my authority to inspect the accounts* ‖ an official body which controls a particular department or activity, *the Port of London Authority* ‖ (esp. *pl.*) the government, those in charge ‖ someone whose knowledge and opinions command respect and belief ‖ the power of such knowledge, *the authority of long experience* ‖ a book or other writing which is trusted or quoted as evidence, or its author ‖ evidence, reasons for a statement, *on the authority of an eyewitness* [F. *autorité*]

au·thor·i·za·tion (ɔθərizéiʃən) *n.* an authorizing or being authorized

au·thor·ize (ɔ́θəraiz) *pres. part.* **au·thor·iz·ing** *past* and *past part.* **au·thor·ized** *v.t.* to give legal power or right to ‖ to give permission for ‖ to delegate power to **áu·thor·ized** *adj.* officially approved or appointed, holding or done with the necessary rights or powers [F. *autoriser*]

Authorized Version (*Br., abbr.* A.V.) the King James Bible (*BIBLE)

au·thor·ship (ɔ́θərʃip) *n.* writing as an activity or profession ‖ the identity of the author of a literary work, *to deduce the authorship of a poem* ‖ the source of an event or deed, *the authorship of the discovery is disputed*

au·tism (ɔ́tizəm) *n.* (*psychol.*) psychiatric disturbance in which the subject is withdrawn into himself. It includes indifference to external realities, the impulse to find oneself in some constant situation, absence of contact with individuals (but strong affective contact with objects). In children it is often accompanied by language troubles **áu·tist** *n.* **au·tís·tic** *adj.* [fr. Gk *autos*, self]

auto- (ɔtou) *prefix* self ‖ same ‖ self-induced [Gk fr. *autos*]

au·to (ɔ́tou) *n.* (*pop.*) an automobile

au·to·an·a·lyz·er (ɔtouǽnəlaizər) *n.* device that performs chemical analysis

Au·to·bahn (ɔ́təban) *n.* a German superhighway [G.= road for cars]

au·to·bi·og·ra·pher (ɔtoubaiógrəfər) *n.* a person who writes the story of his life

au·to·bi·o·graph·ic (ɔtoubaiəgrǽfik) *adj.* relating to, consisting of or characterized by autobiography **au·to·bi·o·gráph·i·cal** *adj.*

au·to·bi·og·ra·phy (ɔtoubaiógrəfi) *pl.* **au·to·bi·og·ra·phies** *n.* a written account of one's own life ‖ autobiographical writing as a literary genre

au·to·bus (ɔ́toubʌs) *n.* (*Fr.*) a bus

au·to·ca·tal·y·sis (ɔtoukətǽlisis) *n.* the catalysis of a reaction by one of the reaction products

au·to·ceph·a·lous (ɔtouséfələs) *adj.* (*Orthodox Eastern Church*) self-governing, appointing its own chief bishop but remaining in communion with the patriarch of Constantinople

au·to·change·r (ɔ́tətʃeindʒər) *n.* automatic record changer

au·to·chrome (ɔtəkroum) *n.* a plate or film used in the Lumiére process of color photography ‖ the process, patented in 1906 by A. and L. Lumiére [fr. Gk *autos*, same + *chrōma*, color]

au·toch·thon (ɔtókθən) *pl.* **au·toch·thons, au·toch·tho·nes** (ɔtókθəni:z) *n.* one of the original or earliest known inhabitants of a place, an aborigine ‖ an animal or plant which is native to a place **au·toch·thon·ic** (ɔtɔkθónik), **au·tóch·tho·nous** *adjs* [fr. Gk *autochthōn* fr. *autos*, self+*chthōn*, land]

au·toch·tho·ry (ətókθəri:) *n.* original and independent quality of a constitution of a nation, esp. newly independent of the British Commonwealth; originally coined by K. C. Wheare

au·to·cide (ɔ́tousaid) *n.* **1.** self-destruction **2.** suicide by motor vehicle

au·to·clave (ɔ́təkleiv) *n.* an apparatus for sterilizing or cooking etc. by steam under pressure ‖ a vessel in which chemical reactions are carried out at elevated temperatures and pressures [F. fr. Gk *autos*, self+ L. *clavis*, key]

au·to·code (ɔ́təkoud) *n.* (*computer*) a computer system utilizing memoric machine code to simplify programming

au·toc·ra·cy (ɔtókrəsi:) *pl.* **au·toc·ra·cies** *n.* government by a single absolute ruler ‖ a state so governed [fr. Gk *autokrateia* fr. *autos*, self+*krateia*, rule]

au·to·crat (ɔ́təkræt) *n.* an absolute ruler, a despot ‖ someone who insists on his own way and will not defer to others **au·to·crát·ic**, **au·to·crát·i·cal** *adjs* [F. *autocrate* fr. Gk]

au·toc·ra·trix (ɔtókrətriks) *n.* a female absolute ruler (the title assumed by Catherine II of Russia) [L., fem. or *autocrator*, autocrat]

au·to·cross (ɔ́toukrɔs) *n.* place for auto-racing competitions

au·to·cue (ɔ́toukju:) *n.* device that prompts speakers or singers by exposing text line by line; e.g., Tele Prompter

au·to·da·fé (àutoudəféi), *pl.* **au·tos·da·fé** *n.* (*hist.*) the ceremony which concluded a session of the Spanish or Portuguese Inquisition. Unrepentant or relapsed heretics were handed over to the secular authorities to be burned, and penances were imposed on those who recanted ‖ the public burning of a heretic [Port.=act of faith]

au·to de fé (àutoudəféi) *pl.* **au·tos de fé** *n.* auto-da-fé [Span.]

au·to·de·struc·tive art (ɔtoudistrʌ́ktiv) art objects that obliterate or destroy themselves

au·to·drome (ɔ́tədroum) *n.* automobile race track

au·toe·cious (ɔtí:ʃəs) *adj.* (*biol.*), of some parasites) passing the entire life cycle on one host **au·tóe·cism** *n.* [fr. Gk *autos*, same+*oikos*, house]

au·to·en·code (ɔ́touinkoud) *n.* (*computer*) to choose words from input material that will create a pattern for location and retrieval of information

au·to·e·rot·ic (ɔtouirótik) *adj.* of or relating to autoerotism **au·to·e·rot·i·cism** (ɔtouirótisizəm) *n.*

au·to·er·o·tism (ɔtouérətizəm) *n.* sexual gratification not involving the participation of another person

au·tog·a·mous (ɔtógəməs) *adj.* of or characterized by autogamy

au·tog·a·my (ɔtógəmi:) *n.* (*biol.*) conjugation of nuclei within a single cell ‖ conjugation of two protozoans originating from the division of the same individual ‖ (in plants) self-fertilization [fr. Gk *autos*, self+*gamos*, marriage]

au·to·gen·e·sis (ɔtoudʒénisis) *n.* spontaneous generation

au·to·ge·net·ic (ɔtoudʒənétik) *adj.* of or resulting from autogenesis

au·tog·e·nous (ɔtódʒənəs) *adj.* produced by an organism without outside influence, endogenous ‖ (*med.*, e.g. of a vaccine) produced within the body of the patient (opp. HETEROGENOUS) [fr. Gk *autogenēs* fr. *autos*, self+*genesis*, origin]

au·tog·e·ny (ɔtódʒəni:) *n.* autogenesis [fr. Gk *autos*, self+-*geneia*, origin]

au·to·ges·tion (ɔtədʒéstʃən) *n.* management by a committee of workers

au·to·gi·ro, **au·to·gy·ro** (ɔtoudʒáirou) *n.* aircraft driven by a conventional propeller but with the wings wholly or partly replaced by a freely revolving horizontal rotor (cf. HELICOPTER) allowing vertical take-off and slow flight [*Autogiro*, a trademark fr. Gk *autos*, self+*guros*, circle]

au·to·graph (ɔ́təgræf, ɔ́təgrɑf) **1.** *n.* something written in a person's own handwriting, esp. his signature ‖ a manuscript in the author's handwriting, not necessarily exclusively (cf. HOLOGRAPH) **2.** *v.t.* to sign with one's name **au·to·gráph·ic** (ɔtəgrǽfik), **au·to·gráph·i·cal** *adjs* [fr. L. *autographum* fr. Gk]

autogyro *AUTOGIRO

au·to·im·mune (ɔtouimjú:n) *adj.* (*med.*) of reactions to one's own tissues or antigens —**auto·immunizations** *n.* —**autoimmunization** *v.*

autoimmune disease (*med.*) ailment resulting from breakdown of the body's immune system so that the immune response is directed against the body's own organisms **syn** autoaggressive diseases

au·to·in·fec·tion (ɔtouinfékʃən) *n.* an infection which originates within the body itself, e.g. from bacteria already present

au·to·in·oc·u·la·tion (ɔtouinɔkjuléiʃən) *n.* inoculation with a substance produced within the body of the patient ‖ the spread of a disease from an infected part of the body to other parts

au·to·in·tox·i·ca·tion (ɔtouintɔksikéiʃən) *n.* poisoning by a substance produced within the body itself

au·tol·y·sis (ɔtólisis) *n.* (*biochem.*) cell or tissue disintegration by the action of autogenous enzymes, self-digestion **au·to·lyt·ic** (ɔt'lítik) *adj.* [fr. Gk *autos*, self+ *lusis*, dissolution]

au·to·ma·nip·u·la·tion (ɔtoumənipju:léiʃən) *n.* self-stimulation of genital organs. **syn** masturbation —**automanipulative** *adj.*

au·to·mat (ɔ́təmæt) *n.* a restaurant where prepared food is served in locked glass compartments. Customers put a coin or token in the slot which opens the chosen compartment ‖ an automatic device, e.g. one used in controlling machinery [*Automat*, a trademark fr. Gk *automatos*, self-moving]

automata alt. *pl.* of AUTOMATON

au·to·mate (ɔ́təmeit) *pres. part.* **au·to·mat·ing** *past* and *past part.* **au·to·mat·ed** *v.t.* to convert (a factory) to automation

automated blood analysis process of blood analysis by mechanical equipment

automated teller machine (*banking*) machine that can process simple money transactions, e.g., deposits, small withdrawals; it is activated by a plastic card. *abbr* ATM

au·to·math (ɔ́təmæθ) *n.* (*computer*) computer language for Honeywell processing systems

au·to·mat·ic (ɔtəmǽtik) **1.** *adj.* mechanically self-acting ‖ (*firearms*) of a gun in which the spent cartridge is ejected, and the gun reloaded and fired, by the action of the gas generated in firing or by the force of the recoil ‖ not controlled by the will, *physical growth is automatic* ‖ done or said without consideration or hesitation, *an automatic refusal* ‖ (of artistic creation) done unconsciously or subconsciously ‖ happening without the need for, or in spite of, some further action, *automatic promotion* **2.** *n.* an automatic rifle, pistol etc. **au·to·mát·i·cal·ly** *adv.* [fr. G k *automatos*, self-moving]

automatic check (*computer*) checking system encoded into a computer that provides an automatic alert when an error is made

automatic control *AUTOMATION

automatic dialer device that dials a preset telephone number when a single button is pushed or by insertion of magnetically coded plastic card

automatic drive *AUTOMATIC TRANSMISSION

automatic exchange a telephone exchange in which connections between subscribers are made by impulse-operated switches, not by operators

---

automatic focusing (*television*) adjustment to picture tube, through the connection of the focusing anode to the cathode tube through a resistor, avoiding the need for external voltage control

automatic pilot (in aircraft) a device for maintaining a set course and level flight without human control. It consists essentially of two gyroscopes, one horizontal and one vertical

automatic shutoff device that switches off a record player or tape recorder when the record or tape ends

automatic tint control (*television*) in a television receiver, a device that automatically adjusts color by correcting phase errors

automatic transfer service *banking* procedure permitting commercial banks to pay interest on checking accounts

automatic transmission a system in a motor vehicle whereby engine power is transmitted to the wheels etc. by means of gears engaged automatically according to vehicle speed, or using a torque converter

automatic typewriter device that records material typed on correctible magnetic tape, on a cassette, or on punched tape so that some or all of the material may be reproduced without manually retyping

automatic writing writing by a person who (as in surrealism) intentionally blots out the rational structure of his thinking, or who is in a state of trance

au·to·ma·tion (ɔtəméiʃən) *n.* a technique by which mechanical processes are subject to some degree of automatic control, without human intervention [coined fr. Gk *automatos*, self-moving]
—Automation ranges from the operation of a simple device, such as the governor used to control engine speeds, to the fully automatic factory. All automatic control systems depend on the feedback principle. The servomechanism is a common device for achieving such control. In automatically controlled production lines automatic transfer machines feed each machine tool in turn, testing the work and rejecting defective pieces, under the control of a digital computer

au·tom·a·tism (ɔtómətizəm) *n.* the philosophical theory that what one thinks or feels or wills is determined by physical changes in one's body ‖ an action or event in the mind or body over which one has no control (e.g. a dream, a sneeze) ‖ (*med.*) behavior of a person who is apparently fully conscious but is in fact not so (as sometimes after epileptic attacks) ‖ a method of writing or painting used esp. by surrealists and depending on the re-emergence of subconscious images **au·tóm·a·tist** *n.* someone who holds a theory of automatism

au·tom·a·ton (ɔtómətən) *pl.* **au·tom·a·tons**, **au·tom·a·ta** (ɔtómətə) *n.* a person or animal whose actions are not controlled by his own will or intelligence ‖ a robot (mechanical device) [Gk, neut. of *automatos*, self-moving]

au·to·mo·bile (ɔtəməbi:l, ɔtəməbi:l, ɔtəmóubi:l) *n.* a (usually) four-wheeled vehicle which may seat from two to eight people, driven by an engine (gasoline, diesel, electric etc.) [F.]

au·to·mo·tive (ɔtəmóutiv) *adj.* of or to do with automobiles or other self-propelling machines [fr. Gk *autos*, self + M.L. *motivus*, moving]

au·to·net·ics (ɔtənétiks) *n.* science of automatic guidance systems

au·to·nom·ic (ɔtənómik) *adj.* (*physiol.*) of the autonomic nervous system ‖ (*bot.*) originating within the plant without any external cause **au·to·nóm·i·cal** *adj.* [fr. Gk *autonomia*, self-government]

autonomic nervous system the part of the vertebrate nervous system innervating the smooth muscles and glands, comprising sympathetic and parasympathetic nervous systems

au·ton·o·mous (ɔtónəməs) *adj.* self-governing (generally used not of a sovereign state or completely independent body but of one which, under the general control of a larger body, enjoys self-government in its internal affairs) ‖ (*bot.*) autonomic [fr. Gk *autos*, self + *nomos*, law]

autonomous operation (*mil.*) in air defense, the mode of operation assumed by a unit after it has lost all communication with higher echelons. The unit commander assumes full responsibility for control of weapons and engagement of hostile targets

autonomous spending (*economics*) statistical nomenclature for total voluntary expenditures by government, business, and consumers

au·ton·o·my (ɔtónəmi:) *pl.* **au·ton·o·mies** *n.* self-government ‖ a self-governing political community ‖ (in the philosophy of Kant) the subjection of human will to its own laws, independently of God (opp. HETERONOMY) [fr. Gk *autonomia*]

au·to·pes·ta (ɔtoupəstə) *n.* (*Sp.*) auto expressway

au·to·pha·gy (ɔtoufeidʒi:) *n.* (*biol.*) digestion of cells by enzymes in the cell —**autophagic** *adj.*

au·to·phyte (ɔtəfait) *n.* a plant which can synthesize its food from simple inorganic substances (cf. SAPROPHYTE, cf. HETEROPHYTE, cf. AUTOTROPH) **au·to·phyt·ic** (ɔtəfítik) *adj.* [fr. Gk *autos*, self + *phuton*, plant]

au·to·pi·a (ɔtoúpi:ə) *n.* an area completely dominated by motor vehicles

AUTOPIC (ɔtópik) (*computer acronym*) for Automatic Personal Identification Code, a computer program code designed by IBM

au·top·sy (ɔtópsi:) *pi.* **au·top·sies** *n.* the examination of a dead body to determine the cause of death [fr. Gk *autopsia*, a seeing for oneself]

AUTOPSY (*computer acronym*) for operating system, computer compiler, and assembly language designed for IBM 704

au·to·reg·u·la·tion (ɔtəregjuléiʃən) *n.* the capability of adusting to varying conditions to maintain physiological processes —**autoregulative** or **autoregulatory** *adj.*

au·to·route (ɔtouru:t) *n.* (*Fr.*) auto expressway

au·to·some (ɔtəsoum) *n.* a chromosome other than a sex chromosome ‖ a typical chromosome [fr. Gk *autos*, self + *sōma*, body]

au·to·stra·da (ɔtoustrádə) *n.* (*It.*) multilane auto expressway

au·to·sug·ges·tion (ɔtousədʒéstʃən, ɔtousəg-dʒéstʃən) *n.* the process of influencing one's conduct, or state of mind or body, by an idea which one keeps constantly in mind, e.g. to help oneself to get to sleep by telling oneself that one is sleepy

au·to·tel·ic writing (ɔtoutélik) literary art as only art, with no place in life

au·to·tim·er (ɔtoutaimər) *n.* device that turns electric lights or devices on or off at preset times

au·tot·o·my (ɔtótəmi:) *n.* (*zool.*) the reflex breaking off or sacrificing of part of the body (as a starfish will break if grasped by one of its arms) or the division of the body into two or more pieces (as in worms) [fr. Gk *autos*, self + *tomé*, a cutting]

au·to·tox·in (ɔtoutóksin) *n.* a poison produced within the body itself

au·to·trans·duc·tor (ɔtoutrænsdʌktər) *n.* (*Br.*) magnetic amplifier with windings that serve for both control and power

au·to·troph (ɔtətrof, ɔtətrɔf) *n.* (*biol.*) an autotrophic organism [G.]

au·to·troph·ic (ɔtətrófik) *adj.* (*biol.*) relating to organisms, e.g. green plants, that do not depend on others for their nutritive processes but can use inorganic sources of carbon and nitrogen (opp. HETEROTROPHIC, cf. AUTOPHYTIC) [fr. Gk *autos*, self + *trophē*, food]

au·tumn (ɔtəm) *n.* the third season of the year in temperate zones, between summer and winter. In the northern hemisphere it is roughly Sept.–Nov., and in the southern hemisphere roughly Feb.–Apr. a fully mature period approaching the decline, *the autumn of life* [O. F. *autompne*]

au·tum·nal (ɔtʌmn'l) *adj.* of autumn, appearing in, or suggesting, autumn [fr. L. *autumnalis*]

autumnal equinox *EQUINOX

autumn crocus the colchicum

Au·tun (outœ̃) a town (pop. 23,000) in Saône-et-Loire, France. The 12th-c. cathedral is famous esp. for its Last Judgment portico and the carved pillars of the nave (*GISLEBERTUS). The town is also rich in Roman antiquities

au·tun·ite (óut'nait) *n.* a natural phosphate of uranium and calcium [after *Autun*]

Au·vergne (ouvernj) a former province of France in the Massif Central, forming the modern department of Cantal and parts of Puy-de-Dôme, Haute-Loire, Allier and Aveyron. Historic capital: Clermont (now Clermont-Ferrand, an industrial center). The region consists largely of volcanic peaks with their surrounding plateaus (forests and pasture), and fertile central valleys (fruit, vines, wheat, root crops). The climate is severe. After resisting Roman rule (2nd–1st cc. B.C.), Auvergne long defended itself against the Visigoths (5th c.), and continued as a center of learning and art through the

medieval period. The original countship (8th and 9th cc.), a fief of Aquitaine, was divided up (10th c.). The Crown acquired most of it in the 16th c.

aux·il·ia·ry (ɔgzíljəri:, ɔgzíliəri:) **1.** *adj.* helping, providing additional help when needed, *auxiliary engine* ‖ supplementary, *auxiliary troops* **2.** *n. pl.* **aux·il·ia·ries** a supplementary group or organization ‖ an auxiliary verb ‖ (*pl., hist.*) troops recruited from subject or allied nations to supplement regular forces [fr. L. *auxiliarius*]

auxiliary verb (*gram.*) a verb used in conjunction with other verbs to form their tense, mood or voice, e.g. 'be', 'do', 'have', 'may', 'can', 'must' etc.

aux·in (ɔksin) *n.* a growth-stimulating plant hormone [fr. Gk *auxein*, to increase]

aux·o·troph·ic (ɔksətrófik) *adj.* (*biol.*) requiring special substances for normal growth and reproduction —**auxotroph** *n.* —**auxotrophy** *n.* the study of auxotrophic organisms

A·va (ávə) a village and ruined city on the Irrawaddy River, Upper Burma, six miles south of Mandalay. It was the capital (1364–1783 and 1823–37)

av·a·da·vat (ævədəvæt) *n.* the amadavat

a·vail (əvéil) **1.** *v.t.* (*rhet.*) to help, be useful to ‖ *v.i.* to be effective to **avail oneself of** to put to good use, enjoy the benefit of **2.** *n.* use, benefit, advantage, *of no avail, to no avail, without avail* **a·vail·a·bíl·i·ty** *n.* **a·vail·a·ble** *adj.* ready or free for use, capable of being used, *every available man* ‖ obtainable [perh. fr. O.F. *a*, to + *vaille* fr. *valoir*, to be worth]

av·a·lanche (ævəlæntʃ, ævəlɑntʃ) *n.* a great mass of snow, ice, earth, rocks etc. which breaks away on a mountainside and pours down the slope ‖ any sudden flood or massive descent, *an avalanche of reproaches* [F.]

avalanche cone the area of debris piled up by an avalanche

avalanche effect *CASCADE

av·a·lanch·ol·o·gist (ævəlæntʃólədʒist) *n.* expert on avalanches

Av·a·lon, Av·al·lon (ævəlɒn) the blessed island of medieval romance to which King Arthur was carried wounded after his last battle, and from which it was believed he would one day return to rule again (*ARTHURIAN LEGEND)

a·val·u·a·tive (əvæljuːətiv) *adj.* not capable of being evaluated

a·vant-garde (ævãgærd, ɑvɑŋgárd) *n.* those who experiment boldly in the arts and are in advance of their time ‖ those who experiment in the arts without discipline and make a virtue of novelty [F.=vanguard]

A·var (ávar) *n.* a member of a tribe of Tatar nomads who established a kingdom in central Asia (407–653). The Avars crossed the Urals in 558, and settled in Dacia. Their supremacy in E. Europe threatened Constantinople (619–26), Italy (8th c.) and Bavaria (788). Subdued by Charlemagne (791–9), they were absorbed by the Slavs, Bulgarians and Germans (9th c.)

av·a·rice (ævəris) *n.* greed for money and abnormal hatred of parting with it [O.F.]

av·a·ri·cious (ævəriʃəs) *adj.* characterized by avarice [F. *avaricieux*]

a·vast (əvǽst, əvást) *interj.* (*naut.*, used with pres. part.) stop, cease from, *avast heaving!* [perh. fr. Du. *houd vast, holdfast*]

av·a·tar (ævətár) *n.* (*Hinduism*) the appearance on earth, in bodily form, of a god (e.g. of Vishnu as Rāma and Krishna) [fr. Skr. *avatāra*, descent]

a·ve (ávi:,ávei) *n.* an Ave Maria

AV-8 (*mil.*) *HARRIER

AV-8A (*mil.*) *HARRIER

A·vel·la·ne·da (ɑveʃanéðɑ) a city (pop. 330,000) in E. Argentina, a suburb of Buenos Aires

A·ve Ma·ri·a (ávi:mɑrí:ə) (*Roman Catholicism*) the 'Hail Mary', a prayer to the Virgin Mary taken from the greetings addressed to her as the future Mother of God by the Archangel Gabriel and by her cousin Elizabeth (Luke I, 28 and 42) [L.= Hail Mary]

a·venge (əvéndʒ) *pres. part.* **a·veng·ing** *past and past part.* **a·venged** *v.t.* to inflict just punishment in return for, to take vengeance for (something) or on behalf of (someone) (cf. REVENGE) to avenge oneself to obtain satisfaction for an injury or wrong [O.F. *avengier*]

av·ens (ævinz) *n.* a member of *Geum*, fam. *Rosaceae*, a genus of perennial plants with flowers of various colors. *G. rivale* is the water avens, *G. urbanum* the wood avens or herb bennet [O.F. *avence*]

CONCISE PRONUNCIATION KEY: **(a)** æ, c*a*t; ɑ, c*a*r; ɔ f*aw*n; ei, sn*a*ke. **(e)** e, h*e*n; i:, sh*ee*p; iə, d*ee*r; ɛə, b*ea*r. **(i)** i, f*i*sh; ai, t*i*ger; ə:, b*i*rd. **(o)** o, *o*x; au, c*ow*; ou, g*oa*t; u, p*oo*r; ɔi, r*oy*al. **(u)** ʌ, d*u*ck; u, b*u*ll; u:, g*oo*se; ə, b*a*cillus; ju:, c*u*be. x, lo*ch*; θ, *th*ink; ð, bo*th*er; z, *Z*en; ʒ, corsa*g*e; dʒ, sava*ge*; ŋ, orangutan*g*; j, *y*ak; ʃ, *f*ish; tʃ, fe*tch*; 'l, rabb*le*; 'n, red*den*. Complete pronunciation key appears inside front cover.

Av·en·tine (ǽvəntain) one of the seven hills of Rome

a·ven·tu·rine (əvéntʃuəri:n, əvéntʃuərin) *n.* an ornamental glass, used for tableware, which contains opaque sparkling traces of copper, *gold aventurine* or chromic oxide, *green or chrome aventurine* ‖ a quartz in which flakes of mica or iron oxide produce a glittering effect ‖ a feldspar, flashing fiery red because of minute particles of red iron oxide [F. fr. Ital.]

av·e·nue (ǽvinju:, ǽvinu:) *n.* a formally designed or planted approach or road, *an avenue of elms* ‖ a wide street ‖ a road or path which leads to or through a place [F.]

a·ver (əvə́:r) *pres. part.* **a·ver·ring** *past* and *past part.* **a·verred** *v.t.* to assert, declare firmly [F. *avérer*]

av·er·age (ǽvəridʒ) **1.** *n.* the arithmetic mean, the value arrived at by adding the quantities in a series and dividing the total by their number, *the average of 20+18+4 is 14* ‖ a common or usual standard, *his height is above average* ‖ the estimate of the loss involved in shipping damage and its division between those responsible ‖ (*insurance*) a less than total loss incurred by a ship or cargo ‖ expenses for damage at sea, generally shared by all concerned (*GENERAL AVERAGE) **2.** *adj.* worked out as a mathematical average, *the average age of women employed in industry* ‖ undistinguished, ordinary **3.** *v. pres. part.* **av·er·ag·ing** *past* and *past part.* **av·er·aged** *v.t.* to work out the average of ‖ to divide as an average, *average the loss among all the departments* ‖ *v.i.* to be on average [perh. fr. O.E. *aveir*, goods]

average adjuster, average adjustor an investigator of claims for damaged property etc.

a·ver·ment (əvə́:rmənt) *n.* the act of asserting or stating firmly ‖ the statement so made [F. *averement*]

A·ver·nus (əvə́:rnəs) (*Rom. mythol.*) a lake in the crater of a volcano in Campania, Italy, regarded by the ancients as the entrance to the underworld or the underworld itself

A·ver·ro·es (əvérouiːz) (*Arab.* ibn Rushd, 1126–98), Arab philosopher and writer on medicine, commentator on Aristotle. He profoundly influenced Scholasticism. His doctrines tended towards materialism and pantheism and were condemned by the pope

a·verse (əvə́:rs) *adj.* opposed, *averse to the use of slang, not averse to a glass of beer* ‖ (*bot.*) turned away from the stem or axis [fr. L. *avertere* (*aversus*), to turn away]

a·ver·sion (əvə́:rʒən,əvə́:rʃən) *n.* an active or pronounced dislike ‖ the object of such dislike [fr. L. *aversio* (*aversionis*), a turning away]

aversion therapy (*psych.*) psychological program designed to induce aversion to an undesirable habit or addiction —**aversive** *adj* tending to avoid certain stimuli *Cf* BEHAVIOR MODIFICATION

a·vert (əvə́:rt) *v.t.* to turn away or aside, *to avert one's mind from* (not think about), *to avert one's eyes from* (not look at) ‖ to prevent, ward off, *to avert a danger* [F. *avertir*]

A·ves·ta (əvéstə) the collection of Zoroastrian sacred writings in Old Iranian (Zend). There are seven main parts, one of which (the Yasna) is ascribed to Zoroaster. Others are believed to have been composed in the 4th c. A.D.

A·ves·tan (əvéstən) **1.** *adj.* concerning the Avesta or the Old Iranian language (Zend) of the Avesta **2.** *n.* the language of the Avesta

A·vey·ron (æveirṍ) a department (area 3,385 sq. miles, pop. 278,000) of S. France in the S. Massif Central (*ROUERGUE, *QUERCY). Chief town: Rodez

av·go·lem·o·no (ɑvɡoulémənou) *n.* (*Gr.*) dish of chicken soup with egg yolks, rice, lemon juice

a·vi·an (éivi:ən) *adj.* relating to birds [fr. L. *avis*, bird]

a·vi·a·ry (éivi:əri) *pl.* **a·vi·a·ries** *n.* an enclosure or cage for breeding and rearing birds [fr. L. *aviarium* fr. *avis*, bird]

a·vi·a·tion (eivi:éiʃən) *n.* the science of flying aircraft ‖ aircraft manufacture, *the aviation industry* [F.]

a·vi·a·tor (éivi:eitər) *n.* a pilot or member of an aircraft crew, in the early days of flying [fr. L. *avis*, bird]

aviator glasses lightweight tinted eyeglasses with protective metal frames

Av·i·cen·na (æviséna) (*Arab.* ibn Sina, 980–1037), Persian philosopher and physician, called the 'prince of physicians'. His summary of medical literature in his 'Qanun' was authoritative until after the Renaissance. He also wrote on philosophy, astronomy, mathematics, physics, alchemy, geology and music

a·vi·cul·ture (éivikʌltʃər) *n.* the rearing of birds [fr. L. *avis*, BIRD+CULTURE]

av·id (ǽvid) *adj.* intensely eager, *avid for fame* ‖ very keen, *an avid reader* [fr. F. *avide*]

a·vid·i·ty (əvíditi:) *n.* the quality or state of being avid [fr. F. *avidité*]

a·vi·fau·na (eivifɔ́nə) *n.* the bird population of a district **a·vi·fáu·nal** *adj.* [fr. L. *avis*, bird + FAUNA]

A·vi·gnon (ævi:njṍ) a town (pop. 90,900) on the lower Rhône, S. France, an agricultural and trading center. Industries: metallurgy, textiles, food processing, shoes. The popes lived there during their exile from Rome (1309–76). So did two antipopes (1378–1417). The massive fortified papal palace was built c. 1333–c. 1362

A·vi·la (ávi:la) a province (area 3,042 sq. miles, pop. 178,997) of Old Castile, W. Spain ‖ its capital, a medieval, walled, pilgrimage city (pop. 86,584), birthplace of St Teresa

A·vi·la Ca·ma·cho (ávi:lɑkɑmátʃo), Manuel (1897–1955), President of Mexico (1940–6) whose administration closely cooperated with the U.S.A. in the 2nd world war and greatly promoted the modernization and industrialization of Mexico

a·vi·on·ics (eivi:óniks) *n.* the application of electronics to aviation and astronautics

a·vi·ta·min·o·sis (eivaitəminóusis) *pl.* **a·vi·ta·min·o·ses** (eivaitəminóusi:z) *n.* (*med.*) any of the diseases resulting from vitamin deficiency

av·o·ca·do (ævəkádou, ɑvəkádou) *pl.* **av·o·ca·dos, av·o·ca·does** *n.* the fruit (a drupe) of trees of the genus *Persea*, fam. *Lauraceae*, the alligator pear, native to tropical America. It is roughly pearshaped, greenish or purple, and provides a rich source of digestible fats (up to 30 %) and proteins (2%) ‖ a tree bearing this fruit. There are about 400 species [Mex. Span. *avogato* fr. Nahuatl]

av·o·ca·tion (ævəkéiʃən) *n.* an occupation, esp. one followed for pleasure, or one of minor importance [fr. L. *avocatio* (*avocationis*)]

av·o·cet (ǽvəset) *n.* a member of *Recurvirostra*, a genus of birds with webbed feet, a long, upwardly curved bill, and long legs for wading in marshes [F. *avocette* fr. Ital.]

A·vo·ga·dro number (ævəɡádrou) the number (6.023 x 10^{23}) of molecules or atoms in a mole of any element or compound [after Count Amadeo *Avogadro* di Quaregna (1776–1856), Italian physicist]

Avogadro's law the law that equal volumes of all gases, measured at the same pressure and temperature, contain equal numbers of molecules

a·void (əvɔ́id) *v.t.* to keep out of the way. of ‖ to refrain from ‖ (*law*) to invalidate **a·vóid·a·ble** *adj.* **a·vóid·ance** *n.* [A.F. *avoider*, to empty out]

a·void·ance (əvɔ́idəns) *n.* (*psych.*) measures taken in advance to avoid an unpleasantness, e.g., tax avoidance, conditioned avoidances — **avoidant** *adj* of the avoidance behavior

av·oir·du·pois (ævərdəpɔ́iz) (*abbr.* avoir.) *n.* a system of reckoning weight in English-speaking countries based on the pound equal to 16 ounces ‖ (*pop.*) portliness [corrup. of O.F. *avoir de pois*, property of weight]

A·von (éivən), Robert Anthony Eden, 1st earl of (1897–1977), British statesman. As foreign secretary (1935–8), he opposed Chamberlain's policy of appeasement towards Hitler and Mussolini. Under Churchill he was secretary of state for war (1940) and for foreign affairs (1940–45). He became Conservative prime minister in 1955 but resigned (1957) after the controversy caused by the Anglo-French armed occupation of the Suez Canal zone (1956)

a·vouch (əváutʃ) *v.t.* to state as a positive fact, esp. in the face of contradiction ‖ (*rhet.*) to vouch for, guarantee [O.F. *avochier*, to appeal to authority]

a·vow (əváu) *v.t.* to admit to be true, openly acknowledge **a·vów·al** *n.* open admission **a·vówed** *adj.* openly admitted, *an avowed agnostic* ‖ declared, *an avowed enemy* **a·vow·ed·ly** (əváuidli:) *adv.* [O.F. *avouer*, to bind by a vow]

a·vun·cu·lar (əvʌ́ŋkjulər) *adj.* of, like, or in the relationship of, an uncle [fr. L. *avunculus*, uncle]

AWAC (*mil. acronym*) for airborne warning and control system, U.S. Air Force system designed to detect low-flying and high-altitude bombers and to provide commands to intercept them

a·wait (əwéit) *v.t.* to wait for, look out for ‖ to be in store for, *a disappointment awaits you* ‖ *v.i.* to wait ‖ to be in store as a future experience [O.F. *awaitier*]

a·wake (əwéik) *pres. part.* **a·wak·ing** *past* **a·woke** (əwóuk) *past part.* **a·wak·en** (əwóukən), **a·waked, a·wak·ened** (əwéikənd) *v.i.* to stop sleeping, *she awoke at noon* ‖ (with 'to') to realize, *she awoke to the unpleasant facts* ‖ *v.t.* to rouse from sleep, wake up ‖ (*fig.*) to stir up, *he awoke the fury of the mob* [confusion of O.E. *awæcnan*, to awake and *awacian*, to be awake]

awake *pred. adj.* not asleep ‖ with a full realization of, *to be awake to a risk* ‖ alert [orig. *awaken*, past part. of AWAKE V.]

a·wak·en (əwéikən) *v.t.* to wake up (someone) ‖ *v.i.* to awake **a·wák·en·ing** *n.* the act of ceasing to sleep or rousing from sleep ‖ a realization of circumstances ‖ an arousal of interest or activity [O.E. *a wæcnan*]

a·ward (əwɔ́rd) *n.* a judicial decision, esp. after arbitration ‖ a prize, grant etc. won or given [A.F. *award*, observation]

award *v.t.* to give as a prize, reward, or judgment [A.F. *awarder*, to observe]

a·ware (əwéər) *pred. adj.* conscious, informed, *are you aware that you are late?, he is aware of being late* [O.E. *gewær*, wary]

a·wash (əwɔ́ʃ, əwɒ́ʃ) *pred. adj.* and *adv.* just covered by water (e.g. of a ship's deck in a storm) ‖ (e.g. of flotsam) washing about in the sea ‖ (*coloq.*) inebriated

a·way (əwéi) **1.** *adv.* to, or at, a distance, *run away, throw it away, keep away from danger* ‖ far, *away beyond the hills* ‖ in a different direction, *turn your face away* ‖ at an end or to a weakened or lessened condition or degree, *the fire burned away, his courage faded away* ‖ continuously, steadily, *he is working away at his book* **far and away** beyond all doubt, *he is far and away the cleverest* **to do away with** to get rid of, murder or cause to be murdered **to fall away** to give up, fail or desert, *six set out but three fell away before the finish* ‖ to work less well, *he has fallen away after a good start* **to get away with** to succeed in stealing, *they got away with a fine haul* ‖ to escape with only, *he got away with torn ligaments* ‖ to do or say with impunity, *you can't get away with that story* **to take away** to detract, *the discomfort of the journey takes away the pleasure* ‖ to subtract **2.** *adj.* (*sports*) played on the ground of one's opponents, *away matches* ‖ absent, *she's away at present* ‖ at a distance, *the leaders are well away* (i.e. far ahead) **3.** *n.* (*Br.*, esp. in football pools) a match not played on the home ground [O.E. *on weg*, on way]

awe (ɔ) **1.** *n.* a feeling of deep wonder and respect for overpowering grandeur ‖ fear and respect, *she goes in awe of the manager* **2.** *v.t. pres. part.* **aw·ing** *past* and *past part.* **awed** to fill with awe ‖ to subdue or overcome by so doing [O.E. *ege*]

a·weigh (əwéi) *pred. adj.* (*naut.*, of an anchor) free of the bottom so that the ship may move

awe·some (ɔ́səm) *adj.* inspiring awe

awe·strick·en (ɔ́strikən) *adj.* awestruck

awe·struck (ɔ́strʌk) *adj.* struck with awe, astounded

aw·ful (ɔ́fəl) *adj.* very bad, *an awful mess* ‖ shocking, appalling, *an awful disaster* ‖ inspiring awe, *awful grandeur* ‖ (*pop.*) very great or large, extreme, *an awful lot to do, an awful fool* **áw·ful·ly** *adv.* very, *awfully sorry, awfully kind*

a·while (əhwáil, əwáil) *adv.* for a while, for a short time [O.E. *āne hwīle*]

awk·ward (ɔ́kwərd) *adj.* not quite right, *an awkward fit* ‖ inconvenient ‖ difficult to deal with, *an awkward problem* ‖ obstinate, unhelpful, unaccommodating ‖ clumsy, uncouth ‖ causing inconvenience or embarrassment [fr. obs. adj. *awk* fr. O.N. *afug*, the wrong way round+-*ward* (indicating direction)]

awl (ɔl) *n.* a short pointed tool used for making holes, esp. in leather by a shoemaker [O.E. *oel*]

awn (ɔn) *n.* (*bot.*) the bristle or threadlike projection from the fruit of some plants and from the ear of some cereals (e.g. barley) **awned** *adj.* [perh. O.N. *ǫgn*]

awn·ing (ɔ́niŋ) *n.* a sheet of canvas, used chiefly to protect against strong sunlight or rain, e.g. over a shop window or ship's deck [etym. doubtful]

awoke past of AWAKE

awoken past part. of AWAKE

A.W.O.L. (mil.) absent without leave (but not intending to desert)

a·wry (ərái) adv. and adj. crooked, not straight **to go awry** to go wrong, turn out badly

ax, axe (æks) 1. n. a tool consisting of a wooden handle fitted with a steel cutting head (sometimes a double head), used for cutting down trees, or chopping, splitting or roughly shaping wood ‖ (hist.) such an ax used as a battle weapon, or by an executioner in beheadings ‖ drastic cutting of expenditure **to have an ax to grind** to have a personal interest at stake in something 2. v.t. pres. part. **ax·ing** to shape with an ax ‖ to put an end to, they axed his pet scheme ‖ to reduce drastically [O.E. oex]

Ax·el·rod (æksəlrod), Julius (1912–), U.S. pharmacologist and co-winner (with Sir Bernard Katz and Ulf von Euler) of the 1970 Nobel prize in medicine for their individual discoveries concerning the humoral transmitters in the nerve terminals and the mechanisms for their storage, release and inactivation

ax·i·al (æksi:əl) adj. of, relating to, or like an axis, or relating to the central structure of an organism

ax·i·al·flow (æksi:əlfloú) adj. of a device in which a fluid flows parallel to the axis

axial route (mil.) a route for supplies, etc., running through the rear area and into the forward military area

ax·il (æksil) n. (bot.) the upper angle between a leaf and the stem on which it is borne, where a bud (axillary) usually develops [L. = armpit]

ax·ile (æksail) adj. (bot.) of the placentation of seeds in the ovary situated in or belonging to the axis [fr. L. axis, axis]

ax·il·la (æksílə) pl. **ax·il·lae** (æksíli:) n. (anat.) the armpit **ax·il·lar** 1. adj. relating to the axilla 2. n. an axillary part [L.]

ax·il·lar·y (æksəlɛri) 1. adj. (anat.) of or relating to the armpit ‖ (bot.) relating to an axil, growing in the axil (of buds) 2. n. pl. **ax·il·lar·ies** an axillar ‖ (zool.) an articular sclerite of an insect's wing [F. axillaire]

ax·i·ol·o·gy (æksi:óləd͡ʒi:) n. philosophy advocating value judgments embracing ethics and aesthetics

ax·i·om (æksi:əm) n. (logic and math.) a self-evident truth or proposition, e.g. that there can be no effect without a cause ‖ an accepted principle ‖ a maxim or proverbial truth [F. axiome fr. L. fr. Gk]

ax·i·o·mat·ic (æksi:əmǽtik) adj. self-evident, obvious ‖ making use of axioms **ax·i·o·mát·i·cal·ly** adv. [fr. Gk axiōmatikos]

ax·is (æksis) pl. **ax·es** (æksi:z) n. the line, real or imaginary, around which a thing rotates, the earth's axis runs through the poles ‖ the central line around which a structure, pattern or figure is built or formed, the Mediterranean was once the axis of European trade ‖ one of the reference lines in a coordinate system ‖ (bot.) a main stem or central cylinder ‖ (zool.) the central skeleton or nervous chord of an organism ‖ a structure at the base of an insect's wing ‖ (anat.) the vertebra in the neck on which the head turns ‖ an alliance between countries to ensure solidarity of foreign policy **the Ax·is** (hist.) the alliance of Bulgaria, Finland, Germany, Hungary, Italy, Japan and Rumania during the 2nd world war [L.]

axis deer Cervus axis, a deer native to India and S. Asia. The horn of its antlers is much used for the handles of pocketknives etc. [L. axis, such an animal (Pliny)]

ax·le (æksəl) n. the bar or pin on which the hub of a wheel turns or which turns with the wheel ‖ the arm or axletree joining two wheels of a vehicle [fr. O.N. öxull, axletree]

ax·le·tree (æksəltri:) n. the bar connecting the axles of two wheels

Ax·min·ster (æksminstər) n. any of several kinds of machine-woven carpet imitating handtufted Eastern carpets [made at Axminster, Devon, England]

ax·o·lotl (æksəlót'l) n. a Mexican amphibian, the larval form of members of Amblystoma, resembling the salamander. They bear three pairs of feathery gills, and are plump and shortlegged. They may fail to metamorphose if water conditions are unfavorable, keeping gills throughout life, but can reproduce. The full growth is about 9 ins [Aztec=servant of water]

ax·on (ækson) n. (anat., physiol.) a typically long and single process of a nerve cell which ends in short branches. Impulses are generally conducted away from the cell body [fr. Gk axón, axis]

ax·one (æksoun) n. an axon

ax·seed (æksi:d) n. Coronilla varia, fam. Papilionaceae, a plant native to Europe, cultivated in the U.S.A. The flowers resemble lotus flowers

Ax·um, Ak·sum (æksu:m) an ancient kingdom (1st–6th cc. A.D.) including much of modern Ethiopia and the Sudan ‖ its capital, a trading center between India, Arabia, Greece and Rome

ay *AYE

A·ya·cu·cho (ɑjɑku:tʃo) the battle (1824) in Peru in which the Spanish forces on the mainland of America were finally defeated. The victory of the revolutionary forces under Antonio José de Sucre resulted in the independence of Peru. All Spanish troops were withdrawn by 1826

A·ya·la, Plan of (ɑjálɑ) a plan formulated (1911) by the Mexican revolutionary leader Emiliano Zapata. It called for the redistribution of land to the Indians

a·ya·tol·lah (ɑiətóulə) n. a Shiite Moslem spiritual leader in Iran

aye (ei) adv. (archaic) always, ever **for aye** for ever [O.N. ei]

aye, ay (ai) adv. (in restricted naval, dialectal or parliamentary usage) yes **ayes** pl. n. affirmative votes or voters [origin unknown]

aye-aye (áiai) n. Daubentonia madagascariensis, a nocturnal, tree-climbing animal found in Madagascar. It is as big as a large cat and is black, with a long bushy tail and finger-like claws. It has very sharp hearing. It is classed with lemurs, and is allied to monkeys [F. fr. Malagasy]

Ayesha *AISHA

Ay·ma·ra (aimɑrá) n. a South American Indian of one of the chief linguistic groups. They flourished before the Incas. A few still remain in Peru and they make up the majority of the rural population of Bolivia ‖ their language **Ay·ma·rán** adj.

'Ayn-Sālih *IN SALAH

Ayr (ɛər) a former county (area 1,132 sq. miles) of S.W. Scotland ‖ its county town (pop. 45,000), a port near the mouth of River Ayr, an ancient strategic and trade center. Industries: carpets, shipbuilding, drop forging

A·yub Khan (áiju:bkɑn), Mohammed (1907–74), Pakistani soldier and statesman. As president of Pakistan (1958–69), he introduced land reforms and promulgated (1962) a new constitution. He led his country to war with India (1965) over the Kashmir dispute. He resigned (Mar. 1969) in favor of Gen. Yahya Khan

A·yudh·ya (ɑju:·dja) a city (pop. 25,000) in Thailand on the Chao Phraya, 40 miles north of Bangkok, founded in 1350 and formerly the Siamese capital. It contains ruins (temples, pagodas, royal palace) of early Thai civilization

Ay·yu·bid (ɑju:·bid) a member of the Moslem dynasty founded by Saladin (1171). The Ayyubids supplanted the Fatimids and ruled Egypt, Syria, Jordan and southern Arabia until destroyed by the Mamelukes in the 13th c.

a·zal·ea (əzéiljə) n. a member of Azalea, fam. Ericaceae, often classified as a subgenus of Rhododendron, a flowering deciduous shrub, cultivated for the beauty and variety of its flowers [Mod. L. fr. Gk azalea, dry]

a·zan (æzɑn, ɑzán) n. the muezzin's call from the minaret of the mosque, which summons Moslems to prayer five times a day [fr. Arab. adhan, invitation]

A·zan·de (əzǽndi:) n. a federation of tribes in the Sudan, central Africa. Each has a distinct territory and paramount chief belonging to a special ruling class of 'Avongara', who are said to have a common ancestor. They are patrilineal and patrilocal. They number about 3,000,000. Their territory is 48,000 sq. miles ‖ a member of one of these tribes

a·za·ser·ine [C₅H₇N₃O₄] (æzǽsəri:n) n. (pharm.) an antibiotic amino acid used in tumor therapy

a·za·tad·ine [C₂₀H₂₂N₂] (æzǽtadi:n) n. (pharm.) an antihistamine used in treating perennial and seasonal allergies and chronic urticaria; marketed as Optimine

a·za·thio·prine [C₉H₇N₇O₂S] (æzəθáiəpri:n) n. (pharm.) a drug used in treatment of leukemia to suppress production of antibodies

A·ze·glio (æzéljo), Massimo Taparelli, Marchese d' (1798–1866), Italian author and statesman. A leader of the Risorgimento, he took part in the 1848 revolution and was prime minister of Sardinia (1849–52)

a·ze·o·trop·ic (eizi:ətrópik) adj. (phys.) of a mixture of two or more liquids which boils at a constant temperature higher or lower than that of any one of the constituent liquids and which distils without their separating [fr. Gk a, not + zein, to seethe + tropos, turning, change]

A·zer·bai·jan (ɑzərbaid͡ʒán) a constituent republic (area 33,430 sq. miles, pop. 6,028,000) of the U.S.S.R. in S.E. Caucasia, on the Caspian Sea. Capital: Baku. A broad, rather arid central plain lies between the Caucasus Mtns to the north and the Armenian Mtns to the south. Agriculture: cotton, tea, wheat, corn, grapes, fruit, sheep raising in the mountains. Resources: vast oil reserves around Baku, iron, aluminum, copper, lead, zinc, sulfur pyrites, limestone. Industries: oil refining, iron and steel, aluminum and copper, chemical engineering, cement. It joined the U.S.S.R. in 1922

Azerbaijan a region of N.W. Iran, in the mountainous area west of the Caspian Sea, divided from Soviet Azerbaijan by the Araks River. It is very fertile, producing wheat, cotton and tobacco. Sheep are raised. Chief towns: Tabriz, Rezayeh

az·ide (æzaid) n. a derivative of hydrazoic acid HN₃, containing the univalent group N₃- [fr. Azo + -ide]

A·zik·i·we (əzíkiwei), Nnamdi (1904–), Nigerian statesman, president of Nigeria (1963–6). He was prime minister of the Eastern Region (1954–9) and governor-general of Nigeria (1960–3), and was influential in the nationalist movement. His books include 'The African in Ancient and Medieval History' (1938) and 'Political Blueprint of Nigeria' (1943)

A·zil·ian (əzí:ljən) adj. of a mesolithic culture centered in N. Spain and S. France. Bone and horn implements were used, and curiously painted pebbles have been found [Mas d'Azil in France]

az·i·muth (æzimɵ) n. (astron., navigation, surveying) the horizontal arc expressed as the clockwise angle between a fixed point (such as true north) and the vertical plane through the object, the azimuth of a star ‖ a bearing, course or direction **az·i·muth·al** (æzimú͡ɵəl) adj. [F. azimut fr. Arab. al, the + sumūt, way]

azimuth circle a great circle in the heavens which runs through both the zenith and the nadir

azimuth compass a magnetic compass with sights for measuring the azimuth angle or bearing

a·zine (éizi:n, æzi:n) n. a six-membered heterocyclic compound that contains two or more cyclic atoms, other than carbon, of which at least one is nitrogen ‖ a hydrazine derivative of the general formula R₂C = NN = CR₂ [fr. AZOTE +-ine]

a·zin·phos·meth·yl [C₁₀H₁₂N₃O₃PS₂] (æzinfóz-meɵəl) n. pesticide, used esp. against mites

az·o (æzou) adj. relating to compounds, often dyes, containing the bivalent radical —N = N — [AZOTE]

a·zo·ic (eizóuik,əzóuik) adj. lifeless, esp. (geol.) of a period leaving no trace of living organisms [fr. Gk azöos, lifeless]

a·zole (éizoul, æzoul) n. a five-membered heterocyclic compound that contains two or more cyclic atoms, other than carbon, of which at least one is nitrogen [fr. AZOTE + L. oleum, oil]

A·zores (əzɔ́rz, əzóurz) a group of volcanic islands (total land area 888 sq. miles, pop. 280,000) in the Atlantic, 800 miles west of Portugal. Capital: Ponta Delgada on São Miguel. Language: Portuguese. There is an airfield at Santa Maria (built by the U.S.A.) in the 2nd world war). Crops: tea, tobacco, wheat, sugar, fruit (esp. pineapples) and grape vines. Livestock-breeding and fishing are important. The islands were annexed by Portugal (1432) and are administered as a province of Portugal

A·zo·rín (ɑzorí:n), pseudonym of José Martínez Ruiz (1873–1967), Spanish novelist and critic

a·zote (æzóut, æzout) n. nitrogen [coined by Lavoisier fr. Gk a-, without+ zöe, life (because nitrogen does not support life)]

Azov, Sea of (æzov) a shallow sea (area 14,520 sq. miles) northeast of the Crimea, U.S.S.R. Almost landlocked, it is connected with the

---

Aztec

Black Sea by the Kerch Strait. It supports fishing industries

Az·tec (ǽztek) n. (hist.) a member of a Nahuatl Indian people who settled in Mexico (late 12th c.) and established an empire which was overthrown (1521) by Cortés. The Aztec civilization was marked by fine public architecture and by the advancement of learning and the arts. It was based on a caste system and a polytheistic religion involving human sacrifice. The Aztecs created a pictorial alphabet and an elaborate calendar

Az·tlán (ɑztlán) (land of the heron), the mythical region in N.W. Mexico or California from which the Aztecs came

A·zue·la (ɑswéla), Mariano (1873–1952), Mexican novelist. His novels deal mostly with the social aspects of the Mexican Revolution, through which he lived. 'Los de abajo' (trans. 'The Underdogs'), set a literary style for realism in Mexico

a·zu·le·jo (ɑzu:léihou) n. (Sp.) colored tile (usu. blue) from Spain or Portugal

az·ure (ǽʒər, éiʒər) 1. adj. of a light, bright blue, sky-blue ‖ (heraldry) blue 2. n. azure color [O.F. azur fr. Pers.]

azure stone lapis lazuli

az·ur·ite (ǽʒərait) n. a naturally occurring, blue basic copper carbonate, $CU_2(CO_3)_2(OH)_2$ ‖ a semiprecious stone derived from it

Azusa (əzú:zə) n. (Br. mil.) a continuous-wave single station missile tracking station operating on C-band waveguide (s.48 × 1.58 cm) to provide two directions that place position and velocity

az·y·gous (ǽzigəs) 1. adj. (biol.) not paired 2. n. an azygous part [fr. Gk azugos, unyoked]

az·yme (ǽzaim, ǽzim) n. unleavened bread, eaten by Jews at the Passover, and consecrated at Mass in the Western Church [fr. L. fr. Gk azumos, unleavened]

CONCISE PRONUNCIATION KEY: (a) æ, cat; ɑ, car; ɔ fawn; ei, snake. (e) e, hen; i:, sheep; iə, deer; ɛə, bear. (i) i, fish; ai, tiger; ə:, bird. (o) o, ox; au, cow; ou, goat; u, poor; ɔi, royal. (u) ʌ, duck; u, bull; u:, goose; ə, bacillus; ju:, cube. x, loch; θ, think; ð, bother; z, Zen; ʒ, corsage; dʒ, savage; ŋ, orangutang; j, yak; ʃ, fish; tʃ, fetch; 'l, rabble; 'n, redden. Complete pronunciation key appears inside front cover.

Development of the letter B, beginning with the early North Semitic letter. Evolution of both the majuscule, or capital, letter B and the minuscule, or lowercase, letter b are shown.

A.C. SYLVESTER, CAMBRIDGE, ENGLAND

B, b (bi:) the second letter of the English alphabet ‖ (*mus.*) a note, and the key of which it is the tonic ‖ a blood group normally permitting transfusion to people of the same B group or group AB, and from people of group O or B ‖ (*chem.*) boron

b *abbr* for 1. (*computer*) bit, a unit of data measurement 2. (*nuclear phys*) barn, a unit of nuclear cross section

B *electr* in transistor circuit diagrams, symbol for base

B.A. Bachelor of Arts

Baa·der-Mein·hof gang (bádər máinhouf) former guerrilla terrorist group in West Germany; supplanted by Red Army Faction

Ba·al (béiəl, bɑl) *pl.* **Ba·al·im** (béiəlim, bálim) *n.* a Phoenician god. The name was given by ancient Canaanitish peoples to local male deities considered responsible for the fertility of land and flocks [Heb. *ba'al*, lord]

Ba·al·bek (béiəlbek, búlbek) a town (pop. 14,000) in Lebanon. It was a Phoenician city, and a Roman colony (1st c. A.D.). Ruins, esp. Roman temples of Helios and Bacchus (1st–3rd cc.)

Ba'·ath (bɑ́ɑθ) *n.* dominant political party in Syria and Iraq

Bab (bɑb) the title assumed by the Persian founder of Babism, Mirza Ali Mohammed (1821–50). He was executed and about 20,000 of his followers were killed (1844–50) [fr. Pers. *Bab-ad-Din*, Gate of the Faith]

ba·ba·coo·te (bɑbəkú:ti:) *n. Lichanotus brevicaudatus*, a species of short-tailed lemur, native to Madagascar [fr. Malagasy *babakoto*]

bab·bing (bǽbiŋ) *n.* (*angling*) technique for catching eels at night using worms threaded on coarse wool that catches onto eel's teeth

Bab·bitt (bǽbit), Irving (1865–1933), American critic, author of 'The New Laokoön' (1910), 'The Masters of Modern French Criticism' (1912), 'Rousseau and Romanticism' (1919) etc.

Babbitt metal an alloy of tin with antimony and copper, and often lead, used for low-friction bearings [after the inventor, Isaac *Babbitt* (1799–1862)]

bab·ble (bǽb'l) 1. *v. pres. part.* **bab·bling** *past* and *past part.* **bab·bled** *v.i.* to chatter idly or continuously ‖ (of a brook etc.) to murmur ‖ *v.t.* to utter confusedly or incoherently 2. *n.* indistinct or confused speech ‖ idle talk ‖ a continuous murmur (of water) **bab·bler** (bǽblər) *n.* someone who chatters ‖ a bird of fam. *Timaliidae* [M.E. *babelen*, prob. imit.]

babe (beib) *n.* (*rhet.*) an infant ‖ an innocent or inexperienced person [M.E.]

ba·bel (béib'l, bǽb'l) *n.* a confused noise, an uproar of indistinguishable voices (*TOWER OF BABEL) [Heb. *bāb̩el*, Assyrian-Babylonian *Bābilu*, Babylon (Gate of God)]

Bab El Man·deb (bǽbelmǽndeb, bábelmándeb) a strait (about 20 miles wide) between S.W. Arabia and Africa, linking the Red Sea and the Gulf of Aden.

bab·e·si·o·sis (bæbəzáiəsis) *n.* 1. malarialike tick-borne parasite, native to islands Northeast U.S., affecting principally animals 2. (*med*) the disease caused by these ticks

Ba·beuf (bæbə:f), François Noël (1760–97), French revolutionist, one of the first to propound a form of socialism ('Babouvism') as a practical policy.

Ba·bi (bábi:) *n.* a sect following Babism ‖ a follower of Babism

Bab·ing·ton (bǽbiŋtən), Anthony (1561–86), English conspirator, executed for plotting (1586) to murder Queen Elizabeth I and to restore Roman Catholicism in England. The complicity of Mary Queen of Scots in the plot led to her execution (1587)

Bab·in·ski reflex (bəbínski:) a reflex movement in which the big toe turns upward when the sole is tickled, indicating an organic lesion of the nervous system [after J. F. F. *Babinski* (1857–1932), French neurologist]

bab·i·ru·sa, bab·i·rous·sa (bɑbirú:sə, bæbirú:sə) *n.* a wild hog of the East Indies with upcurved tusks [fr. Malay *bābi*, hog + *rūsa*, deer]

Bab·ism (bábizəm) *n.* the doctrines of a Persian religious sect founded in 1844, which sought to reconcile certain teachings of Islam, Judaism and Christianity (*BAB, *BAHAISM)

ba·boon (bæbú:n, *esp. Br.* bəbú:n) *n.* a member of *Papio* and other genera of large, ferocious, terrestrial, dog-faced monkeys of Africa and Arabia. They have cheek pouches and naked callosities on the buttocks. They are found in groups ranging from a single family to a troop of 200 or more (*MANDRILL) [F. *babouin*, origin unknown]

Ba·bou·vism (bəbú:vizəm) *BABEUF

BABS (*acronym*) for blind approach beacon system, used to aid approach of aircraft at airports

Ba·bur (bɑbú:r, bábər) 'the Tiger' (Zahir Ud-Din Mohammed, 1483–1530), first Mogul emperor (1526–30) of India. From Turkestan he invaded and conquered the Afghan Empire (1504). Entering Delhi (1526), he became the master of an empire stretching from the Oxus to Patna

ba·bush·ka (bəbú:ʃkə) *n.* a scarf worn by a woman over her hair and tied under the chin [Russ.= grand-mother]

ba·by (béibi:) 1. *pl.* **ba·bies** *n.* an infant ‖ a young child ‖ the youngest member of a family ‖ a timorous person **to be left to hold** (or hold-ing) **the baby** (*Br.*=*Am.* to be left holding the bag) to be left to take the blame or assume unwanted responsibility 2. *adj.* of or belonging to a baby, *baby clothes, baby talk* ‖ of a thing small of its kind, *a baby car* 3. *pres. part.* **ba·by·ing** *past* and *past part.* **ba·bied** *v.t.* to treat with inordinate care or indulgence [dim. of BABE]

baby bond a bond whose face value does not exceed $100

baby bonus payment to families for having children

baby carriage (*Am.*= *Br.* perambulator, pram) a four-wheeled carriage for a baby, moved by pushing

baby grand a smaller version (5–6 ft long) of the grand piano

ba·by·hood (béibi:hud) *n.* the state or age of being a baby

ba·by·ish (béibi:iʃ) *adj.* like a baby

Bab·y·lon (bǽbilən, bǽbilɒn) the ancient capital of Babylonia, now ruins, on the Euphrates 55 miles south of Baghdad, probably founded c. 4000 B.C. It was known for its luxury, and its hanging gardens were one of the Seven Wonders of the World. The Jews were held captive here by Nebuchadnezzar II (II Kings, xxv) [L. fr. Gk *Babulon* fr. Heb. *Bābel*]

Bab·y·lo·ni·a (bæbilóuni:ə) an ancient kingdom on the Tigris and Euphrates in S. Mesopotamia (now Iraq). Sumerian city-states (*UR) developed in the valleys (from about 3500 B.C.) and from 2200 B.C. were united by the Amorite dynasty of Akkad. Hammurabi created a great empire (1750–c. 1600 B.C.) based on a code of laws of widespread and lasting influence. Hittites, Cassites and Assyrians ruled until 626 B.C., when a new and greater neo-Babylonian empire arose which stretched to the borders of Egypt, and included Palestine (the Jews being taken into the 'Babylonian Captivity' 586–538 B.C.). Nebuchadnezzar II, its king (605–562 B.C.), rebuilt Babylon as a great city, but the empire fell to Cyrus II of Persia (539 B.C.) and later to Alexander the Great, the Seleucids and Parthians. The Babylonians were traders, notable for their law and administration, the temples built to their many gods, and achievements in astronomy, mathematics, medicine and music

Bab·y·lo·ni·an (bæbilóuni:ən) 1. *adj.* of or pertaining to ancient Babylonia ‖ of or pertaining to an inhabitant of Babylonia 2. *n.* an inhabitant of Babylonia ‖ the Semitic language of Babylonia

Babylonian Captivity *CAPTIVITY, THE BABYLONIAN

ba·by·sit (béibi:sit) *pres. part.* **ba·by·sit·ting** *past* and *past part.* **ba·by·sat** (béibi:sæt) *v.i.* to act as a paid or unpaid baby-sitter **bá·by·sít·ter**

n. a person who looks after children for short periods of time in the absence of the parents

baby tooth a milk tooth

bac·ca·lau·re·ate (bækəlɔ́ri:it) *n.* the bachelor's degree ‖ a religious service for a graduating class, or the sermon preached at it [fr. M.L. *baccalaureatus*, of a bachelor]

bac·ca·rat, bac·ca·ra (bǽkərɑ, bɑ́kərɑ) *n.* a gambling game with playing cards. There are two forms, 'chemin de fer' and 'banque' [F.]

bac·cate (bǽkeit) *adj.* bearing berries, bacciferous ‖ berrylike [fr. L. *baccatus*]

bac·cha·nal (bǽkən'l) **1.** *n.* (*hist.*) a dance or festival in honor of Bacchus ‖ a drunken orgy ‖ a person taking part in such festivities **2.** *adj.* bacchanalian ‖ riotous [fr. L. *bacchanalis* fr. *Bacchus*]

bac·cha·nal·ia (bækənéiljə) *pl. n.* (*hist.*) the festival of Bacchus ‖ drunken revels **bac·cha·nál·ian** *adj.* [L.]

bac·chant (bǽkənt) *n.* a priest, priestess or votary of Bacchus ‖ a bacchanal **bac·chan·te** (bəkǽnti:) *n.* a priestess of Bacchus, a woman taking part in a bacchanal **bac·chán·tic** *adj.* [fr. L. *bacchans* fr. *bacchari*, to celebrate the feast of Bacchus]

bac·chic (bǽkik) *adj.* of Bacchus and his rites ‖ orgiastic [fr. L. *Bacchicus* fr. Gk]

Bac·chus (bǽkəs) (*Gk and Rom. mythol.*) the son of Zeus and Semele, the god of wine and fertility, better known to the Greeks as Dionysus

Bac·chyl·i·des (bækílidi:z) Greek lyric poet of Ceos (5th c. B.C.)

bac·cif·er·ous (bæksífərəs) *adj.* (of plants) bearing berries [fr. L. *baccifer* fr. *bacca*, berry + *ferre*, to bear]

Bach (bɑx), baron Alexander von (1813–93), Austrian statesman. As head of the Austrian government (1852–9), he tried to subject the Hapsburg lands to a strong, centralized bureaucracy

Bach, Carl Philipp Emanuel (1714–88), German musician and composer, third son of J. S. Bach. His most influential work was with the sonata (for clavier), but he also wrote much church music

Bach, Johann Christian (1735–82), German musician and composer, the 11th son of J. S. Bach. He lived in London from 1762, where his operas were very popular. He was one of the first to write for the piano

Bach, Johann Sebastian (1685–1750), German musician and composer, the most famous member of the Bach family of musicians. His enormous output included over 190 cantatas and oratorios, concertos for various instruments, chamber music, and a vast body of organ and keyboard music. Since the early 19th c. he has been recognized as one of the greatest of European composers, although in his own time he was not fashionable. He continued the traditions of northern European polyphonic music of the 17th c., much of his work being church music at a time when the secular and the gallant were becoming popular. The formality of his polyphony was no constriction: the elaborate prescribed forms were, in his hands, the vehicle of extraordinary musical vigor in thematic development, rhythmic vitality and melodic invention, e.g. in the great organ and keyboard works such as the 'Toccata and Fugue in D minor', the 'Fantasia and Fugue in G minor' (1720), 'The Well-Tempered Clavier' (1722, 1744), and the Leipzig Preludes and Fugues (1727–39), and in such orchestral works as the six 'Brandenburg Concertos' (1721). His strong Christian faith is manifested in the 'Passion according to St John' (1723), the 'Passion according to St Matthew' (1729), the 'Mass in B minor' (1733–8), and the cantatas and chorale preludes. As a brilliant practitioner, theorist and teacher of music he also left works of instruction (esp. for his own family) and recreation ('Art of Fugue', 'Goldberg Variations' etc.). All show the same genius in the penetration and transformation of musical form

Bach, Wilhelm Friedemann (1710–84), German musician and composer, the eldest son of J. S. Bach. He wrote nine symphonies, music for the organ and harpsichord, church cantatas etc.

bach·e·lor (bǽtʃələr, bǽtʃlər) *n.* an unmarried man ‖ a man or woman who has taken the first university (or college or professional school) degree ‖ a knight bachelor [O.F. *bacheler*, a young knight]

bachelor girl an unmarried woman living independently

bach·e·lor·hood (bǽtʃələrhud, bǽtʃlərhud) *n.* the state of being a bachelor ‖ the time when one is or was a bachelor

Bachelor of Arts the first university or college degree awarded in the liberal arts ‖ a person who has been awarded this degree

bac·il·la·ry (bǽsələri) *adj.* connected with bacilli ‖ rod-shaped, made up of little rods (e.g. of the retina) [fr. Mod. L. *bacillarius* fr. *bacillus*, little rod]

bacillary dysentery *DYSENTERY

ba·cil·li·form (bəsíliform) *adj.* rodshaped [BACILLUS]

ba·cil·lus (bəsíləs) *pl.* **ba·cil·li** (bəsílai) *n.* a member of *Bacillus*, fam. *Bacillaceae*, a large genus of aerobic, rod-shaped bacteria which reproduce by endospores. It includes saprophytes of importance in the decay of natural wastes in soil and water, and the anthrax pathogen (among other parasitic members) ‖ a rod-shaped bacterium, as distinguished from spirillum and coccus [L.L. dim. of *baculus*, a stick]

back (bæk) **1.** *n.* the hinder part of the body, or, in most animals, the upper part from the neck to the end of the spine ‖ the less important side or surface of a thing, opposite the front, *the back of a knife* ‖ the remoter part, *the back of a house* ‖ (*football*) a mainly offensive player whose position is behind the line of scrimmage ‖ a defensive position in certain games (e.g. field hockey) ‖ the player occupying that position ‖ a support for the back, *a chair back* **at the back of** (*fig.*) behind, in support of, *he has his wife's fortune at the back of his venture* **behind one's back** without one's knowledge, deceitfully or treacherously **in back of** behind **to be on one's back** to be ill in bed **to be on someone's back** to harass someone with constant urgings and scoldings **to break one's back** to overwork **to break the back of a task** to achieve the greater or more difficult part of a task **to have one's back to the wall** to be hard pressed and fighting for survival ‖ to be thrown on one's defenses **to put one's back into** to work very hard at **to put someone's back up** to irritate, offend, antagonize someone **to turn one's back on** to turn one's back on (someone) in order to snub him ‖ to go away from ‖ to relegate (something) to the past, put (something) behind one **2.** *v.t.* to give moral or material support to, *to back a colleague, back a venture* ‖ to support or line, *to back a curtain with heavy material* ‖ to cause to move backwards ‖ to furnish with a background or serve as a background to ‖ to bet on the success of ‖ *v.i.* to move backwards ‖ to retreat ‖ (of the wind, when it changes in a direction opposite to the course of the sun, or of a driver) to reverse direction **to back down** to stop asserting something **to back out** to withdraw from an undertaking, contest etc. **to back up** to give moral support to **3.** *adj.* to the rear, *the back door* ‖ remote, *the back country* ‖ in arrears, *back rent* ‖ (of a magazine or journal) of an earlier date than the current issue **to take a back seat** to take a minor part in some activity, esp. after being prominent in it **4.** *adv.* to the rear, backward, at a distance, *they stood back from the fire* **to get back** to return, *he got back home late last night* ‖ to recover, *to get one's money back* **to get back at someone** to get even with someone **to give back** to restore (something borrowed or taken) **to go back** to return ‖ to extend back in time, *this coat of arms goes back to the 13th century* **to go back on** to fail to keep (a promise, one's word etc.) **to keep back** to withhold ‖ to conceal (a fact etc.) **to pay back** to discharge (a debt), return in kind (something borrowed) **to pay someone back** to return a loan to someone ‖ to avenge oneself on somebody **to play back** to listen to (what one has recorded on tape or disk) **to take back** to return (something sold) to stock and refund the purchase money ‖ to retract, unsay [O.E. *bæc*]

back and forth to and fro

back answer (*Br.*) a cheeky retort

back·beat (bǽkbi:t) *n.* a strong, steady, underlying rhythm, e.g., in rock and disco music

back bench (*Br.*) any of the rows of seats in the House of Commons occupied by members who are not of ministerial or shadow cabinet rank (cf. FRONT BENCH) **back·bench·er** (bǽkbéntʃər) *n.* someone who occupies such a seat

back·bite (bǽkbait) *pres. part.* **back·bit·ing** *past* **back·bit** (bǽkbit) *past part.* **back·bit·ten**

back·bit'n *v.t.* to slander with petty malice ‖ *v.i.* to talk malicious gossip

back·blocks (bǽkblɒks) *n.* land in the remote interior of Australia

back·board (bǽkbɔrd, bǽkbourd) *n.* (*med.*) a board which supports the back of a person ‖ a board which forms the back of a thing (e.g. of a framed picture) ‖ (*basketball*) the board or surface behind the basket

back·bone (bǽkboun) *n.* the spinal column ‖ courage, determination ‖ chief support, *farmers are the backbone of the nation* ‖ the spine of a book

back burner (*colloq.*) a position of less priority

back·chat (bǽktʃæt) *n.* (*Br.*) back talk

back-cloth (bǽkklɔθ, bǽkklɒθ) *pl.* **back-cloths** (bǽkklɔðs, bǽkklɒθs, bǽkklɔðz, bǽkklɒðz) *n.* (*Br.*) a backdrop

back-comb (bǽkkoum) *v.* (*cosmetology*) to tease hair

back door a door of a building other than the front door ‖ a way of avoiding controls which usually apply, *there is no back door into the civil service* **back-door** (bǽkdɔr, bǽkdour) *adj.* relating to an entrance (to a house etc.) other than the principal one ‖ surreptitious, kept hidden, *back-door methods* ‖ (*golf*) the back or side of a hole through which a ball falls

back·drop (bǽkdrɒp) *n.* a painted cloth or drop curtain at the back of the stage

back·er (bǽkər) *n.* someone who gives financial support ‖ a person placing a bet

back·field (bǽkfi:ld) *n.* (*football*) the players in positions behind the line of scrimmage ‖ (*football*) their area

back·fill (bǽkfil) *n.* material used to refill an excavation — **backfill** *v.* — **backfilling** *n.*

back·fire (bǽkfaiər) **1.** *n.* a premature explosion in the cylinder of an internal combustion engine, or in the breach of a gun ‖ an explosive ignition of gases in the exhaust after a cylinder has misfired **2.** *v.i. pres. part.* **back·fir·ing** *past* and *past part.* **back·fired** to explode in this way ‖ (*fig.*) to go wrong, esp. in such a way as to have the reverse effect of what was intended, *his plans backfired*

Back·fire (bǽkfaiər) *n.* (*mil.*) U.S.S.R. intercontinental missile-carrying plane

back·flip (bǽkflip) *n.* (*gymnastics*) a recovery from a headstand to the normal standing position, the feet going over the head and no part of the body touching the floor

back-for·ma·tion (bǽkfɔrmeiʃən) *n.* a word (e.g. to broke) supplied from an existing word (broker) itself mistakenly supposed to be derived from the newly made word: other examples include 'to laze' (lazy), 'to grovel' (groveling) ‖ the supplying of such parts of speech in this way

back-gam·mon (bǽkgæmən, bǽkgæmən) **1.** *n.* a table game of chance for two players, played with dice and pieces ‖ the complete form of win in the game **2.** *v.t.* to win by getting a gammon from [BACK + M.E. *gamen*, game]

back-ground (bǽkgraund) **1.** *n.* the part of a picture against which the principal figures are shown, or a surface on which there are patterns, *red triangles on a green background* ‖ the part of a picture or photograph reproducing distance and distant objects ‖ an inconspicuous position, *keep in the background* ‖ a person's past history, family circumstances and social class etc. ‖ the accumulation of knowledge and experience that a person can draw on ‖ music or sound effects to accompany e.g. a radio broadcast ‖ the events, circumstances and conditions leading up to or underlying some event, *the background to the revolution* ‖ any accompanying noise **2.** *adj.* of an off-the-record, official, informal news conference designed to provide nonquotable information

back·hand (bǽkhænd) **1.** *adj.* (*racket games,* of a stroke) made with the back of the hand turned in the direction of the stroke **2.** *adv.* with a backhand stroke **3.** *n.* a backhand stroke, or the capacity to play backhand strokes ‖ handwriting whose strokes slope to the left **back·hand·ed** *adj.* made with the back of the hand ‖ (of an apparent compliment) double-edged, e.g. 'she's beautiful for her age' **back·hand·er** *n.* a backhand blow ‖ an indirect verbal attack

back·ing (bǽkiŋ) *n.* support or aid ‖ a body of supporters ‖ something which forms a thing's back or support or protective covering

back judge (*football*) timekeeper and the official designated to identify team members eligible to receive passes

CONCISE PRONUNCIATION KEY: (**a**) æ, c*a*t; ɑ, c*a*r; ɔ f*aw*n; ei, sn*a*ke. (**e**) e, h*e*n; i:, sh*ee*p; iə, d*ee*r; ɛə, b*ea*r. (**i**) i, f*i*sh; ai, t*i*ger; ə:, b*i*rd. (**o**) o, *o*x; au, c*ow*; ou, g*oa*t; u, p*oo*r; ɔi, r*oy*al. (**u**) ʌ, d*u*ck; u, b*u*ll; u:, g*oo*se; ə, b*a*cillus; ju:, c*u*be. x, lo*ch*; θ, *th*ink; ð, bo*th*er; z, *Z*en; ʒ, corsa*g*e; dʒ, sava*g*e; ŋ, oranguta*ng*; j, *y*ak; ʃ, *f*ish; tʃ, fe*tch*; 'l, rabb*le*; 'n, redd*en*. Complete pronunciation key appears inside front cover.

back·lash (bǽklæʃ) *n.* a jarring reaction or striking back caused in badly fitting machinery by a change in velocity or reverse of motion ‖ (*sociology*) an angry group response to what is seen as a threat or provocation ‖ play, looseness, esp. in a steering mechanism ‖ a snarl or tangle in the part of a fishing line that is wound on the reel

back·light·ed transparency (bǽklaited) color film lighted from behind the screen, esp. in advertising displays *Cf* BACK PROJECTION

back·list (bǽklist) *n.* books in a publisher's catalogue which have appeared before the current season and are still in demand

back·log (bǽklɔg, bǽklog) *n.* a reserve of unfilled orders for goods, or an accumulation of uncompleted work

back marker (*auto racing*) one who falls far behind in a race

back·most (bǽkmoust, *esp. Br.* bǽkməst) *adj.* (*Br.*) furthest back

back number an out-of-date issue of a publication ‖ a person who has outlived his fame or popularity

back of beyond, the (*Br.*) somewhere thought of as inaccessible, esp. the remote countryside

back order quantity of an item ordered or requested that is not immediately available for issue but is recorded as a stock commitment for future issue **back order** *v.* to place on requisition list

back·out (bǽkaut) *n.*(*mil.*) in a missile launching countdown, reversal of the numbering sequence, e.g., 10, 9, 8, 7, etc.

back·plane (bǽkplein) *n.* (*computer*) in mini- and micro-computers, a printed circuit board that provides wiring between input/output, memory, and logic operations

back·plate (bǽkpleit) *n.* a metal plate forming the back of a suit of armor

back pressure the resistance offered by external pressure to the motion of a piston in a cylinder

back projection screen presentation projected from the rear of a translucent screen —**back project** *v.* —**back-projected** *adj.*

back scattering (*electr.*) radio-wave propagation in which the direction of the incident and scattered waves, resolved along a reference direction (usually horizontal), are oppositely directed —**back-scatter** *v.* the signal

back·scat·ter radar (bǽkskætər) system to detect elements beyond the horizon from energy reflected from ionized disturbances

back score (*curling*) the rear borderline of play

back·side (bǽksaid) *n.* the buttocks

back·sight (bǽksait) *n.* the lining-up device on a rifle etc. nearest the butt ‖ (*survey.*) a reading to a previously occupied survey station ‖ (*survey.*) a reading on a leveling rod at a known elevation

back·slide (bǽkslaid) *pres. part.* **back·slid·ing** *past* **back·slid** (bǽkslid) *past part.* **back·slid**, **back·slid·den** (bǽkslid'n) *v.i.* to fall away or lapse from former virtuous beliefs or conduct

back·spin (bǽkspin) *n.* a backward rotary motion, such as can be given to a ball in billiards etc.

back·stage (bǽkstéidʒ) **1.** *adv.* (*theater*) at or to a backstage area or position **2.** (bǽksteidʒ) *adj.* (*theater*) of or relating to a backstage **3.** (bǽksteidʒ) *n.* (*theater*) the stage area behind the proscenium, esp. the dressing rooms

back stairs stairs other than the main staircase (generally those used by servants) **back stairs** (bǽkstɛərz) *adj.* (*fig.*, esp. of intrigue or gossip) secret and rather despicable

back·stay (bǽkstei) *n.* (*naut.*) a rope or cable extending aft in support of a mast ‖ a support at the back of a machine ‖ a piece of leather at the back and sides of a shoe above the heel to give added support

back·stitch (bǽkstitʃ) **1.** *n.* an overlapping stitch in sewing **2.** *v.t.* to sew (something) with this stitch ‖ *v.i.* to sew with this stitch

back·stop (bǽkstop) *n.* a screen or fence (e.g. behind the home plate in baseball) to stop balls from going too far out of the area of play ‖ something that serves as a safeguard or support

back street a place where illegal or socially unacceptable acts are performed —**back-street** *adj.* not legitimate

back·stroke (bǽkstrouk) *n.* a return or backhand stroke with a racket ‖ a swimming stroke rather like the crawl, but performed on the back

back talk (*Am.*=*Br.* backchat) retorts, answering back

back tell the transfer of information from a higher to a lower echelon of command *Cf* TRACK TELLING

back·up (bǽkʌp) *n.* someone or something that reinforces ‖ a reserve supply ‖ an accumulation built up as the result of stoppage in flow (e.g. of traffic) ‖ (*cartography*) image printed on the reverse side of a map sheet already printed on one side

backup ball (*bowling*) a ball spin that curves in the direction of the throwing hand

back·ward (bǽkwərd) **1.** *adj.* turned or directed to the back, *a backward glance* ‖ not progressing normally, behind in growth or mentality ‖ shy **2.** *adv.* backwards

back·ward·a·tion (bækwərdéiʃən) *n.* (*commodities*) market situation in which future prices are progressively lower in the distant delivery months, e.g., if the quotation for Feb. is $160 per oz and that for June is $155 per oz, the backwardation for four months against Jan. is $5 per oz

back·wards (bǽkwərdz) *adv.* toward the back, *to lean backwards* ‖ back first, *if you run backwards you'll fall* ‖ in the reverse way or order, *to count backwards* ‖ into the past, *to look backwards in time* ‖ from a better to a worse state

back·ward-wave oscillator (bǽkwərdweiv) *CARCINOTRON

back·wash (bǽkwɔʃ, bǽkwoʃ) *n.* water thrown back by the passage of a ship ‖ the drag of a receding wave ‖ the unwelcome repercussions of some social action

back·wa·ter (bǽkwɔtər, bǽkwotər) *n.* water dammed back, cut off from the main stream ‖ an isolated place out of touch with new ideas

back·woods (bǽkwúdz) *pl. n.* the remote, sparsely settled areas of a country

back·woods·man (bǽkwúdzmən) *pl.* **back·woods·men** (bǽkwúdzmən) *n.* a person who lives in the remote countryside and has none of the townsman's urbanity

bac·lo·fen [C₁₀H₁₂ClNO₂] (bǽkləfən) *n.* (*pharm.*) muscle-relaxant drug used to alleviate spasticity from multiple sclerosis; marketed as Lioresal

Ba·con (béikən), Francis, Baron Verulam of Verulam, Viscount St Albans (1561–1626), English statesman, philosopher and essayist. In natural philosophy he completed the break from the medieval scholastic method, laid down for the first time a classification of the natural sciences, and founded a new inductive method of reasoning which challenged traditional authority (and revelation) and prepared the way for modern experimental science. His incomplete 'Instauratio magna', a project for the entire reorganization of human knowledge, includes 'The Advancement of Learning' (1605), 'Novum organum' (1620) and 'De argumentis scientiarum' (1623). The 'Essays' (1st edition 1597) are his chief literary work. After a distinguished parliamentary career under Elizabeth I, he won promotion under James I, and became lord chancellor (1618). He lost this office and retired in disgrace when the House of Lords found him guilty of accepting bribes (1621)

Bacon, Francis (1910–   ), Irish painter of grotesquely deformed human figures and images expressive of tormented states of mind. His richly colored compositions tend to be abstract, though they are clearly derived from natural appearances

Bacon, Nathaniel (1647–76), aristocratic Virginia planter and leader of 'Bacon's rebellion' (1676) against colonial governor William Berkeley, who opposed his expedition to wipe out the Indians in Virginia. For a time Bacon's forces controlled the colony, but they collapsed at his death

Bacon, Roger (c. 1220–92), English Franciscan philosopher called the 'doctor mirabilis' because of his great learning. His interest lay in mathematics and in experimental science generally, esp. optics. He understood the need for experimental checking of deduced principles. His main work was the 'Opus maius', an encyclopedia of the sciences of his time

ba·con (béikən) *n.* the flesh from a pig's back and sides, cured dry or in pickle and smoked [O.F. *bacon*]

BACON (*computer*) self-programming (thinking) computer, named for Sir Francis Bacon

BAC I-II British short-to-medium range, 89-passenger transport with twin turbofan engines and a 1,650-mi range

Ba·co·ni·an (beikóuni:ən) **1.** *adj.* relating to Francis Bacon or his works or doctrines ‖ of or relating to the theory that Bacon wrote Shakespeare's plays **2.** *n.* someone who accepts Bacon's doctrines ‖ someone who believes that Bacon wrote Shakespeare's plays

BACT (*computer acronym*) for best available control technology

bac·te·re·mi·a (bæktərí:mi:ə) *n.* the presence, usually transitory, of bacteria or other microorganisms in the blood [fr. BACTERIA+Gk -*emia* fr. *haima*, blood]

bac·te·ri·a (bæktíəri:ə) *BACTERIUM

bac·te·ri·al (bæktíəri:əl) *adj.* of or resulting from bacteria

bac·te·ri·cide (bæktíərisaid) *n.* a substance which kills bacteria [fr. BACTERIUM+L. -*cida*, killing]

bac·te·ri·o·cin (bæktíəri:əsən) *n.* (*chem.*) bacteria-produced antibacteriacide, e.g., colicin

bac·te·ri·o·log·i·cal (bæktíəri:ələdʒikˈl) *adj.* of or relating to bacteriology

bacteriological warfare biological warfare

bac·te·ri·ol·o·gist (bæktíəri:ɒlədʒist) *n.* someone who studies bacteriology

bac·te·ri·ol·o·gy (bæktíəri:ɒlədʒi:) *n.* the scientific study of bacteria [fr. BACTERIUM +Gk *logos*, discourse]

bac·te·ri·o·ly·sin (bæktíəri:əláis'n) *n.* an antibody which destroys a specific microorganism (e.g. a bacterium)

bac·te·ri·ol·y·sis (bæktíəri:ɒlisis) *n.* destruction of bacteria by antibodies **bac·te·ri·o·lyt·ic** (bæktíəri:əlítik) *adj.* [fr. BACTERIUM+Gk *lusis*, dissolution]

bac·te·ri·o·phage (bæktíəri:əfeidʒ) *n.* a bacteriolytic virus normally found in blood, pus or sewage, or in the intestines of animals recovering from bacterial infection [fr. BACTERIUM+Gk -*phagos*, eating]

bac·te·ri·o·stat·ic (bæktíəri:əstǽtik) *adj.* preventing or inhibiting the growth or multiplication of bacteria without destroying them [BACTERIUM+STATIC]

bac·te·ri·um (bæktíəri:əm) *pl.* **bac·te·ri·a** (bæktíəri:ə) *n.* a member of *Schizomycophyta*, a large class of microscopic unicellular plants lacking chlorophyll and fully defined nuclei. They are often motile, by means of flagella, and occur in three main forms: spherical (coccus), rod-shaped (bacillus), and spiral (spirilla). They reproduce mostly by fission and by asexual spore formation. They occur in water, soil, organic matter or living bodies of plants and animals, being saprophytic, parasitic and autotrophic in nutrition. They are of significance because of their chemical effects (nitrogen fixation, fermentation etc.) and as pathogens [Mod. L. fr. Gk *baktērion*, a small rod or stick]

Bac·tri·a (bǽktri:ə) an ancient kingdom, once a part of the Persian and Seleucid empires, between the Hindu Kush (N.W. India) and the Oxus. It was the home of Zoroastrianism

Bac·tri·an (bǽktri:ən) *adj.* of Bactria

Bactrian camel the two-humped camel

ba·cu·li·form (bækjəlifɔrm, bəkjú:lifɔrm) *adj.* rod-shaped [fr. L. *baculus*, rod]

bac·u·lite (bǽkjəlait) *n.* a fossil cephalopod with a straight, elongated shell [fr. L. *baculum*, a stick]

bad (bæd) **1.** *adj. comp.* **worse** (wə:rs) *superl.* **worst** (wə:rst) wicked, evil ‖ defective, inadequate, *a bad light for reading* ‖ not prosperous, *his business is in a bad way* ‖ decayed, rotten ‖ severe, *a bad cold* ‖ serious, *a bad mistake* ‖ faulty, *bad grammar* ‖ unwelcome, distressing, *bad news* ‖ disagreeable, *a bad taste* ‖ (*pop.*) distressed, upset, *to feel bad about something* ‖ harmful, *spices are bad for him* ‖ unskilled, not clever, *bad at arithmetic* **to go bad** to decay **to go from bad to worse** to become more and more deplorable **2.** *n.* that which is bad, *the bad in him comes from his background* ‖ misfortune, *take the good with the bad* ‖ the debit side of an account, *$1,000 to the bad* **to go to the bad** to become criminal, corrupt etc. **3.** *adv.* (*substandard*) badly, *how bad do you need it?* [M.E. *badde* perh. from O.E. *bæddel*, hermaphrodite]

Ba·da·joz (badaxóθ) a province (area 8,451 sq. miles, pop. 635,375) of Estremadura, W. Spain ‖ its capital (pop. 114,361) a fortress town on the Guadiana River. Cathedral (13th c.)

bade *BID

bad egg (*pop.*) a bad lot (man who has a bad character)

Ba·den (bád'n) a former state of Germany. It became a margravate (1112), but was divided

CONCISE PRONUNCIATION KEY: **(a)** æ, c*a*t; ɑ, c*a*r; ɔ f*aw*n; ei, sn*a*ke. **(e)** e, h*e*n; i:, sh*ee*p; iə, d*ee*r; ɛə, b*ea*r. **(i)** i, f*i*sh; ai, t*i*ger; ə:, b*i*rd. **(o)** o, *o*x; au, c*ow*; ou, g*oa*t; u, p*oo*r; ɔi, r*oy*al. **(u)** ʌ, d*u*ck; u, b*u*ll; u:, g*oo*se; ə, b*a*cillus; ju:, c*u*be. x, lo*ch*; θ, *th*ink; ð, bo*th*er; z, *Z*en; ʒ, corsa*g*e. dʒ, sava*g*e; ŋ, orangutan*g*; j, *y*ak; ʃ, *f*ish; tʃ, *f*etch; 'l, rabb*le*; 'n, redd*en*. Complete pronunciation key appears inside front cover.

many times until united (1771) under Charles Frederick. It prospered and joined the German Confederation (1815). Prussian intervention suppressed the revolutions of 1848–9. Baden allied with Austria against Prussia (1866), but made a separate treaty with Prussia, and became a state (1871) of the new German Empire, a constitutional republic (1918), a unit of the Reich (1934), and part of the Land of Baden-Württemberg (1949) in W. Germany (*GERMANY)

Ba·den-Ba·den (bád'nbád'n) a spa (pop. 49,400) in Baden-Württemberg, W. Germany, in the Black Forest

Ba·den-Pow·ell (béid'npóuəl), Robert Stephenson Smyth (1857–1941), founder of the Boy Scouts (1908) and (with his sister Agnes) of the Girl Guides (1909)

Ba·den-Würt·tem·berg (bɑd'nvýrtəmberk) a state (area 13,800 sq. miles, pop. 9,235,600) of West Germany in the southern highland bordering France and Switzerland, including (in Baden, the western part) the Rhine Valley and the Black Forest, and (in Württemberg) the Upper Danube and the Neckar Valleys. Lake Constance is at the southeast end. Agricultural products: cereals, root vegetables, wine, tobacco. Industries: forestry, mechanical engineering, textiles, tourism. Main towns: Stuttgart (the capital), Karlsruhe, Heidelberg, Freiburg. Württemberg emerged from the old duchy of Swabia as a countship (12th c.), then a duchy (1495). Baden was unified by Napoleon, who made it a grand duchy (1803–6) and Württemberg a kingdom (1806). Baden was the center of the radical revolutionary movement (1848–9). Both sided with Austria against Prussia (1866) but joined the German Empire (1871). They were merged in 1951

badge (bædʒ) n. a distinctive device worn as a sign of office, employment or membership ‖ an award for attainment, *a lifesaving badge* [M.E. *bag, bagge,* origin unknown]

badg·er (bædʒər) 1. n. a burrowing, carnivorous, nocturnal mammal of fam. *Mustelidae,* inhabiting the northern hemisphere. Badgers are related to weasels and skunks. They have thick bodies and short legs and stiff, bristly hair. The coat is gray or brown, with white patches as facial markings ‖ badger's hair, used in shaving brushes and artists' brushes ‖ (in Australia) the wombat or bandicoot 2. v.t. to nag with requests [prob. fr. BADGE, a mark]

bad hat (*Br., pop.*) a bad lot (man who has a bad character)

bad·i·nage (bædinázʒ) n. playful teasing ‖ joking and repartee [F.]

Bad·i·us A·scen·si·us (bádi:usɑskénsi:us), Jodocus (1462–1535), Flemish scholar and one of the first great humanist printers

bad·lands (bædlændz) pl. n. stretches of rugged land dissected into narrow, steep-sided gullies. They mostly lack animal life and flora, but often abound in fossils. They are typified by the badlands district of S.W. South Dakota, and by S. Algeria and S. Morocco

bad lot (*pop.*) a man who has a bad character

bad·ly (bædli) *comp.* **worse** (wə:rs) *superl.* **worst** (wə:rst) *adv.* not well (made, done etc.) ‖ wickedly or in poor taste, *to behave badly* ‖ by much, *badly beaten in the match* ‖ very much, *to need money badly*

badly off poor, impoverished ‖ (with 'for') ill-supplied (with), in need (of)

bad·min·ton (bædmint'n) n. a game similar to tennis, but with shuttlecocks instead of balls and lighter rackets, usually played indoors. The court is 44 ft by 20 ft and the net 5 ft high. Play consists entirely of volleying

bad-mouth (bædmauθ) v. (*slang*) to denigrate *Cf* DUMP ON

bad news n. (*colloq.*) an unwelcome person or situation

Ba·do·glio (bɑdɔ́ljɔ), Pietro (1871–1956), Italian marshal, viceroy of Ethiopia (1936). He became head of the Italian government after Mussolini's fall, and capitulated to the Allies in 1943

Bae Hawk British turbojet training plane (Hawk T Mk 1) with speed of 621 mph launched in 1974

Bá·ez (báes), Buenaventura (1810–84), president of the Dominican Republic, except for periods of exile, between 1844 and 1878. He attempted to secure Dominican freedom from Haiti by seeking the support and protection of a foreign power. He persuaded President Ulysses

Grant to annex the country, but the U.S. Senate refused ratification

Baez (baiéz), Joan (1941–), U.S. folk-singer, composer, and guitarist, who became known for her roles in the antiwar and civil rights movements. She wrote 'Daybreak' (1968), an autobiography

Baf·fin Bay (bæfin) an arm of the Arctic Ocean between Baffin Is. and Greenland. The eastern section is ice-free in summer

Baffin Island the largest island (area 201,600 sq. miles, pop. 2,000) of the Canadian Arctic, first visited by Frobisher and first explored (1615–16) by the English navigator William Baffin (c. 1584–1622)

baf·fle (bæfəl) 1. v.t. pres. part. **baf·fling** past and past part. **baf·fled** to puzzle, perplex 2. n. a device to direct or control the flow of a fluid or the propagation of light and sound waves [etym. doubtful]

baffle plate a plate used to change the direction of gases of combustion ‖ a grating placed in a channel to promote uniform flow of a fluid through it, or a plate similarly placed to deflect the flow of the fluid

bag (bæg) 1. n. a receptacle of leather, cloth, paper etc. often shaped like a sack and easily opened and closed ‖ game shot by a sportsman or party of sportsmen in one shoot ‖ loose, pouchy skin, *bags under the eyes* ‖ (pl., Br.) trousers **a bag of bones** a thin, scrawny creature **bag and baggage** (with) all one's belongings **in the bag** as good as secured **in the bottom of the bag** to be used as a last resource **to be left holding the bag** (Am.=Br. to be left holding the baby) to be left to take the blame for something or to assume an unwanted responsibility ‖ (slang) something one likes; one's way of life; a packet of drugs 2. v. pres. part. **bag·ging** past and past part. **bagged** v.t. to put into a bag or bags ‖ to kill or capture (game) ‖ v.i. to fill out like a bag (e.g. of a skirt gone shapeless) ‖ to hang loosely (e.g. of a sail) [M.E. bagge perh. fr. O.N. baggi]

Ba·gan·da (bəgándə) n. a member of a Bantu people inhabiting Buganda. Their economy is based on cotton and coffee

ba·gasse (bəgǽs) n. waste products in sugar making used for fuel and in the manufacture of paper [F. fr. Span.]

bag·a·telle (bægətél) n. something of no importance ‖ (mus.) a short, light composition, esp. for the piano ‖ a game played on a board with cue and ball [F. fr. Ital.]

Bage·hot (bædʒət), Walter (1826–77), English social scientist and literary critic. He was editor of 'The Economist' (1861–77). His 'The English Constitution' (1867) long remained the standard work. His work on the English banking system, 'Lombard Street' (1873), was followed by 'Literary Studies' (1879 and 1895), and 'Economic Studies' (1880). In 'Physics and Politics' (1872) he analyzed the interrelations of natural and social sciences

bag·gage (bægidʒ) n. personal luggage ‖ (old-fash.) a saucy girl ‖ (mil. and hist.) an army's belongings other than equipment taken into battle [O.F. bagage]

bag·gi·ly (bægili) adv. in a baggy manner

bag·gi·ness (bægi:nis) n. the quality of being baggy

bag·gy (bægi:) comp. **bag·gi·er** superl. **bag·gi·est** adj. stretched out of shape and hanging loosely, *a baggy sweater*

bag·gys (bægi:s) n. loose-fitting shorts worn by athletes

Bagh·dad (bægdæd) the capital (pop. 2,800,000) of Iraq, on the Tigris, one of the most important communication and trade centers in the Middle East. Products: leather, silk, cotton and woolen goods. University (1958). It was a leading cultural center (8th and 9th cc.) under the Abbasid caliphate

Baghdad Pact *CENTRAL TREATY ORGANIZATION

Baghdad Railway a railroad started (1903) by a German company to connect Berlin via Constantinople with Baghdad as part of Kaiser Wilhelm II's policy of 'Drang nach Osten' (drive toward the East). It was regarded with suspicion by France and Great Britain and was a contributory cause of the 1st world war. It was not completed until 1940

bag·house (bæghaus) n. air-pollution abatement device used to trap particulates by filtering gas streams through large fabric bags, usually made of glass fibers

bag man one who receives illicit payments — **bag woman**

Bag·ot (bægət), Charles (1781–1843), British minister to Washington who negotiated with Richard Rush the Rush-Bagot Treaty

bag·pipe (bægpaip) n. (usually pl.) a musical wind instrument, very popular in Scotland, consisting of a leather bag which acts as bellows, and pipes **bag·pip·er** n.

ba·guette (bægét) n. (archit.) a small rounded molding ‖ a gem cut in the shape of a long rectangle [F. baguette and Ital. bacchetta]

bag·wig (bægwig) n. (hist.) an 18th-c. wig with the back hair caught in a bag

Ba·ha·i (bəhái:) n. an adherent of Bahaism **Ba·ha·ism** n. a religion originating in Persia in 1863, developing from Babism. Its founder was Baha'ullah who, after periods of violent persecution, settled near Mt Carmel in Palestine. On his death (1892) the leadership passed to his son, Sir Abdul Baha, and then to his great-grandson. After the death of the latter (1957) administration was transferred to an international council. Bahaism has adherents in most Moslem countries (even though it is classed there as heretical), but its strongest support comes from the U.S.A. and certain European countries. It stresses the unity of mankind and of all divine revelation, which is progressive and relative. Thus Baha'ullah is God's prophet for this present age, just as Mohammed was for his contemporaries, and Jesus, Moses etc., were for theirs

Ba·ha·mas (bəháməz) an independent member of the Commonwealth of Nations consisting of about 700 islands (area 4,404 sq. miles, pop. 209,505, 75% of African descent) in the West Indies. Their subtropical climate makes them a favorite resort. 20 are inhabited. Main islands: New Providence, Andros, Eleuthera, Grand Bahama. Capital: Nassau, on New Providence. Products: sugar, fruit, sisal, salt, lumber. Monetary unit: Bahamas dollar (100 cents). One of the islands, probably San Salvador, was where Columbus first made landfall (1492). Most of the original inhabitants, the Arawaks, were taken away in Spanish slave raids (16th c.). England occupied the islands (1629) and they became a Crown Colony (1729), receiving internal self-government (1964) and achieved full independence in 1973. Governed by prime minister and 42-member House of Assembly

Ba·ha·'ul·lah (baháulá) (1817–92), the Persian religious leader Mirza Hosain Ali, founder of the Bahai faith. He proclaimed (1863) that he was the universal prophet whose coming the Bab had foretold, and that he was to unify mankind

Ba·ha·wal·pur (bəháwʌlpuər) a town (pop. 133,956) in Pakistan on the Sutlej River, an agricultural center for wheat, rice, dates and cotton. Industries: textiles, chemicals and machinery

Ba·hi·a (bəhí:ə) *SALVADOR

Ba·hí·a Blan·ca (bɑí:ɑblánkɑ) a port (pop. 233,126) of Argentina at the mouth of the Napostá River. Exports: cattle, wool, wheat

Bah·rain, Bah·rein (bɑréin) an archipelago and fully independent sovereign state (area 231 sq. miles, pop. 350,798) in the Persian Gulf. Capital: Manama. Race: Arab, with Persian, Indian and Pakistani minorities. Language: Arabic. Religion: Moslem. Chief islands: Bahrain and Muharraq (connected by causeway). The land is low, flat and sandy, with oases, supporting donkeys and cattle, and date and vegetable cultivation. Main industry: the production, refining and export of oil (discovered 1932). Bahrain has well-equipped deep-water anchorages and harbors, and an entrepôt trade. Monetary unit: dinar (1000 fils). Famous in ancient times for their pearls, the islands were ruled by the Portuguese (16th c.) and the Persians (17th c.). They signed (1820) a treaty of friendship with Britain, becoming a protected sheikdom (1862). Bahrain became (1971) a sovereign state. Iran received old claim to Bahrain in 1979

Bahr-el-A·biad (bárəlábjad) *WHITE NILE

Bahr-el-Az·raq (bárəlʌzræk) *BLUE NILE

Bahr-el-Je·bel (bárəldʒébel) *WHITE NILE

baht (bɑt) n. the basic monetary unit of Thailand ‖ a coin or note of the value of one baht [Thai bāt]

Bai·ae (báii:) a ruined city 11 miles west of Naples, popular with ancient Romans as a resort because of its hot springs

Ba·if (baí:f), Jean-Antoine de (1532–89), learned French poet, member of the Pléiade

CONCISE PRONUNCIATION KEY: (a) æ, cat; ɑ, car; ɔ fawn; ei, snake. (e) e, hen; i:, sheep; iə, deer; εə, bear. (i) i, fish; ai, tiger; ə:, bird. (o) o, ox; au, cow; ou, goat; u, poor; ɔi, royal. (u) ʌ, duck; u, bull; u:, goose; ə, bacillus; ju:, cube. x, loch; θ, think; ð, bother; z, Zen; ʒ, corsage; dʒ, savage; ŋ, orangutang; j, yak; ʃ, fish; tʃ, fetch; 'l, rabble; 'n, redden. Complete pronunciation key appears inside front cover.

Bai·kal (baikál) the world's deepest freshwater lake (area 13,197 sq. miles, greatest depth 5,170 ft, frozen in winter) in E. Siberia, U.S.S.R., emptying into the lower Angara: fisheries; summer resort

bail (beil) *n.* a money or property security deposited to obtain a prisoner's freedom of movement, pledging that he will appear before the court when called **out on bail** having one's freedom on these conditions **to go bail** to put up the bail money for someone **to jump** (or **forfeit**) **one's bail** to fail to appear as pledged [O.F. *bail*, custody]

bail *n.* a hoop, or half hoop for supporting wagon covers etc. ‖ the curved handle of a pail or kettle ‖ a frame used for holding a cow's head during milking [M.E. *beyl* prob. fr. O.N. *beygla*, hoop]

bail, bale 1. *n.* a vessel used to scoop water out of a boat, a bailer **2.** *v.t.* to scoop out (water) from inside a boat ‖ to empty (a boat) of water by scooping ‖ *v.i.* to scoop the water out of a boat **to bail out** to bail ‖ to make a parachute jump, esp. in an emergency [F. *baille*, bucket]

bail *n.* (*Br.*) a bar separating horses in a stable ‖ (*cricket*) one of the two crosspieces resting on the stumps [perh. O.F. *bail*, enclosure]

bail *v.t.* to grant bail to, release on security ‖ to secure someone's temporary freedom of movement by putting up security for (him) **to bail out** to get (someone) out of prison on these terms [O.F. *baillier*, to be guardian]

bail·ee (beilí:) *n.* (*law*) someone to whom goods are entrusted in bailment

bail·er (béilər) *n.* a bat for scooping out water

Bai·ley (béili:), Gamaliel (1807–59), U.S. abolitionist. He was editor of the first U.S. abolitionist journal, 'The National Era' (1847–60), which first published Harriet Beecher Stowe's 'Uncle Tom's Cabin' as a serial, in 1851–2

bai·ley (béili:) *n.* (*hist.*) the outer wall of a castle ‖ the space or courts enclosed by it [M.E. *baili*, var. of BAIL, enclosure]

Bailey bridge a bridge made of easily transported latticed metal parts which can be quickly assembled [after the English inventor Sir Donald *Bailey* (1901–)]

bail·ie (béili:) *n.* a Scottish municipal magistrate elected by town councils from their own members. In royal boroughs the office corresponds to that of the English alderman [O.F. *bailli*, bailiff]

bail·iff (béilif) *n.* the agent or steward of an estate ‖ a court officer who keeps order in court ‖ the title of the chief magistrates of various British towns and of the keepers of some royal castles ‖ (*Br.*) a bumbailiff ‖ (*hist.*) the title given in England to the local deputy of the king, or a lord, charged with rent collection, the administration of justice etc. [M.E. *baillif*, custodian fr. O.F.]

bail·i·wick (béiliwik) *n.* the district or jurisdiction of a bailie or bailiff ‖ one's special field of interest

bail·ment (béilmənt) *n.* the act of bailing an accused person ‖ (*law*) delivery of personal property by a bailor to a bailee

bail·off (béilɒf) *n.* vaporization

bail·or (béilər) *n.* (*law*) someone who delivers personal property to a bailee in trust

bail·out (béilaut) *n.* **1.** parachuting from a plane in distress **2.** rescue of an enterprise through the injection of funds to pay creditors **3.** assumption by an outside agency (usually governmental) of a business in financial difficulty

bails·man (béilzmən) *pl.* **bails·men** (béilzmən) *n.* (*law*) someone who gives bail for another

bain-ma·rie (bɛ̃mæri:) *pl.* **bains-ma·ries** (bɛ̃mæri:) *n.* a vessel of hot water in which certain food dishes are ɔet to stand in their own container for slow cooking ‖ a double boiler [F.]

Bai·on (baióun) *n.* slow, sensual dance related to Samba, native to Brazil

Bai·ram (bairám) *n.* either of two annual Moslem festivals (Lesser and Greater) after Ramadan [Turk. and Pers.]

bairn (bɛərn) *n.* (mainly in Scotland and N. England) a child [O.E. *bearn*]

bait (beit) *v.t.* to put food on (a hook) or in (a trap) to lure a fish or animal ‖ to tease, provoke ‖ (*hist.*) to torment (bulls, bears etc.) by setting dogs on them, for sport [O.N. *beita*, to cause to bite]

bait *n.* food used to lure prey ‖ an enticement or temptation [O.N. *beita*, food]

bait-and-switch (béitændswɪtʃ) *n.* trade policy designed to attract customers to an advertised bargain to induce sale of something else

Ba·ius, Ba·jus (bájus), Michael (Michel de Bay, 1513–89), Flemish Roman Catholic theologian, chancellor of Louvain University and forerunner of Jansenism. Influenced by Protestant views on original sin, predestination and grace, his interpretation of Augustine in the form of 76 propositions was condemned as heretical by papal bull (1567)

bai·za (báizə) *n.* unit of currency in Oman, equal to 1/1000 rial

baize (beiz) *n.* a thick woolen cloth used for coverings (on billiard tables etc.) [fr. F. *baies* fem. pl. of *bai*, bay-colored]

Ba·ja California (báhə) *LOWER CALIFORNIA

Baja California Sur *LOWER CALIFORNIA

Ba·ja·zet I (bædʒəzét) (1347–1403), sultan of the Ottoman Empire (1389–1402). He rapidly overran Bulgaria, part of Serbia, Macedonia and Thessaly, and defeated Sigismund of Hungary at Nicopolis (1396). He was defeated by Timur (1402)

Bajus, Michael *BAIUS

bake (beik) *pres. part.* **bak·ing** *past* and *past part.* **baked** *v.t.* to cook (food) in dry heat, esp. in an oven ‖ to make hard by heating ‖ to expose to the heat of the sun ‖ *v.i.* to bake bread etc. ‖ to become baked ‖ to become hard and dry in the sun [O.E. *bacan*, to roast]

bake·house (béikhaus) *pl.* **bake·hous·es** (béikhauziz) *n.* a bakery

ba·ke·lite (béikəlait) *n.* the trademark for a synthetic thermosetting plastic resin [fr. G. *bakelit* after L. H. *Baekeland* (1863–1944)]

Bak·er (béikər), Sir Benjamin (1840–1907), British consulting engineer who, in partnership with Sir John Fowler, designed and constructed the Forth Bridge (Scotland), the Aswan Dam (Egypt), and much of the London underground railway system

Baker, Howard Henry (1925–), U.S. Republican senator from Tennessee (1967–85). He served on the Watergate Investigation Committee (1973), was Senate minority leader (1977–81), and Senate majority leader (1981–5)

Baker, James Addison 3d (1930–), U.S. lawyer and politician, who served as Secretary of the Treasury (1985–) under Ronald Reagan. He was also Reagan's chief of staff (1981–85) and was known for his ability to achieve consensus

Baker, Ray Stannard (pen name: David Grayson, 1870–1946), U.S. author. He wrote the authorized biography of Woodrow Wilson (1927–39), in eight volumes

Baker, Sir Samuel White (1821–93), British explorer. He began to explore the Nile in 1861, and discovered Lake Albert and Murchison Falls in 1864. In Egyptian service (1869–73), he completed the annexation of the equatorial regions of the Upper Nile and made efforts to suppress the slave trade

bak·er (béikər) *n.* a professional breadmaker ‖ someone who sells bread and pastries

baker's dozen thirteen

bak·er·y (béikəri:) *pl.* **bak·er·ies** *n.* a place where bread is baked ‖ a baker's shop

Bake·well (béikwel), Robert (1725–95), British agriculturist who pioneered experiments in the breeding and raising of livestock

Ba·ki (báki:), Mahmut Abdül (1526–1600), Turkish classical poet

bak·ing (béikiŋ) *n.* (*cosmetology*) technique for drying large, fantasy-styled hairpieces

baking powder a substitute for yeast in cooking, essentially a carbonate and an acidic agent which on moistening react to give carbon dioxide

baking soda sodium bicarbonate

Bakke Case U.S. Supreme Court decision (1978) ruling that a medical school had violated a white male applicant's rights by an affirmative action policy but could consider race in choosing among applicants

Ba·kony Forest (bɔ́kounj) a mountain range (rising to 2,333 ft) of W. Hungary, northwest of Lake Balaton

Bakst (bakst), Léon (1866–1924), Russian painter and stage designer. His best work was done (1909–21) for the Russian Ballet under Diaghilev

Ba·ku (bakú:) the capital (pop. 1,435,000) of Azerbaijan, U.S.S.R., a port on the Caspian Sea, with the largest oil fields in the U.S.S.R. Other industries: metallurgy, textiles, food processing. University

Ba·ku·nin (bakú:njin), Mikhail (1814–76), Russian anarchist and militant atheist, an exile prominent in the Communist International, from which he was expelled in 1872

BAL (*computer acronym*) for basic assembly language, general programming language with minimal memory

Ba·laam (béiləm) the prophet sent by the king of Moab to curse Israel. After being reproved by his ass, he blessed Israel instead (Numbers xxii–xxiv)

Bal·a·cla·va, Battle of (bæləklávə) an inconclusive battle fought (Oct. 25, 1854) by the British and French against the Russians during the Crimean War. It was the scene of the heroic charge of the Light Brigade

bal·a·cla·va helmet (bæləklávə) a close-fitting woolen covering for the head and neck

Ba·la·guer (bɑlɑgér), Joaquín (1907–78), Dominican politician and president (1960, 1966–78). He developed a large tourist trade but 1978 elections brought defeat because of corruption and economic troubles

Ba·la·ki·rev (balákirəf), Mily Alexeyevich (1837–1910), Russian composer. His works include folksong arrangements, much piano music ('Islamey' 1868), two symphonies and two symphonic poems. He was a leader of the 'nationalist' movement in music and influenced many Russian composers, e.g. Mussorgsky and Borodin

bal·a·lai·ka (bæləláikə) *n.* a triangular, guitar-like musical instrument popular esp. in Russia [Russ.]

bal·ance (bǽləns) *pres. part.* **bal·anc·ing** *past* and *past part.* **bal·anced** *v.t.* to weigh in a balance ‖ to weigh by comparing (two arguments, advantages, choices etc.) ‖ to match, offset, *his prudence balances her ardor* ‖ to keep in equilibrium ‖ to compare both sides of (an account) and make the entry needed to equalize them ‖ (*dancing*) to move away from and then toward (a partner) ‖ *v.i.* to remain in equilibrium ‖ (of account entries) to be equal on the credit and debit sides [F. *balancer*]

balance *n.* an instrument for measuring the weight of a body, either by comparison with other calibrated weights or by the force it exerts on a calibrated spring ‖ the weighing of actions or opinions, *his fate is in the balance* ‖ equilibrium ‖ mental or emotional stability ‖ (*art*) harmony in design ‖ a regulating mechanism in a clock or watch ‖ (*accounts*) the difference between the debit and credit sides ‖ the remainder ‖ the greater amount, *the balance of advantage lies on his side* **to hold the balance** to have the power to decide [F.]

balance of nature normal capacity of natural forces in the biosphere to renew themselves without human intervention

balance of payments the export-import tabling of a country's financial transactions with other countries. It covers both goods ('visible') and services ('invisible')

balance of power parity between rival nations or groups of nations, preserved by systems of military or economic alliances, or both

balance of terror concept that the U.S. and U.S.S.R. have capability of exterminating each other, giving them military equality

balance of trade the difference in total value over a period between imports and exports

bal·anc·er (bǽlənsər) *n.* (*radio*) an appliance used in conjunction with a direction finder to enable direction to be determined more easily

balance reef a reef band across a fore-and-aft sail ‖ the last reef on a fore-and-aft sail

balancer meal a composite poultry food containing essential foodstuffs

balance sheet a written statement of assets and liabilities

balance spring a hairspring

balance wheel the vibrating wheel of a watch or clock, which, with the hairspring, regulates its timing

Bal·an·chine (bǽləntʃi:n), George (1904–83), Russian–U.S. dancer and choreographer. Following his association with the Diaghilev Ballet Russe (1924–33), he organized the American Ballet Company (1934), later the New York City Ballet (1948–83). His works include 'Prodigal Son' and 'Apollo'

Ba·lante (bəlɒ́nt) *n.* a member of a Sudanese Negro people of W. Africa, esp. Senegal and Portuguese Guinea ‖ this people ‖ their language [F.]

bal·as (bǽləs) *n.* a semiprecious stone, a variety of spinel ruby, rose-red or inclining to orange, an aluminate of magnesium [O.F. *balais* fr. Arab. fr. Pers. *Badakhshan* near Samarcand]

CONCISE PRONUNCIATION KEY: **(a)** æ, c*a*t; ɑ, c*a*r; ɔ f*aw*n; ei, sn*a*ke. **(e)** e, h*e*n; i:, sh*ee*p; iə, d*ee*r; ɛə, b*ea*r. **(i)** i, f*i*sh; ai, t*i*ger; ə:, b*i*rd. **(o)** o, *o*x; au, c*ow*; ou, g*oa*t; u, p*oo*r; ɔi, r*oy*al. **(u)** ʌ, d*u*ck; u, b*u*ll; u:, g*oo*se; ə, b*a*cillus; ju:, c*u*be. x, lo*ch*; θ, *th*ink; ð, bo*th*er; z, *Z*en; ʒ, corsa*ge*. dʒ, sava*g*e; ŋ, orangutan*g*; j, *y*ak; ʃ, *f*ish; tʃ, fe*tch*; 'l, rabb*le*; 'n, red*den*. Complete pronunciation key appears inside front cover.

bal·a·ta (bəlátə) *n.* the tree *Mimusops globosa* ‖ the rubberlike exudate from this tree, used in golf balls, insulation etc. [Span.]

Ba·la·ton (bǽlətɒn) S. Europe's largest lake (area 266 sq. miles), in W. Hungary: fishing, tourism

Bal·bo (búlbɔ), Cesare (1789–1853), Italian statesman. His book, 'The Hopes of Italy' (1844), was important for the Risorgimento

Bal·bo·a (bælbóuə), Vasco Núñez de (c. 1475–1517), Spanish explorer, the first European to see the Pacific Ocean, after crossing the Panama isthmus (1513)

balboa *n.* the basic monetary unit of Panama ‖ a coin of the value of one balboa [Span. after Vasco Núñez de *Balboa*]

Bal·bue·na (balbwéna), Bernardo de (1568–1627), Spanish epic poet and bishop of Puerto Rico. His 'Bernardo o victoria de Roncesvalles' established him as the patriarch of American poetry

Balch (bɔltʃ), Emily Greene (1867–1961), U.S. economist, political scientist, and Nobel Peace prizewinner (with John Mott) in 1946

bal·co·ny (bǽlkəni:) *pl.* **bal·co·nies** *n.* an accessible platform, usually with a safety rail or parapet, projecting outwards from the window or wall of a building ‖ (*theater*) a tier of seats usually between the dress circle and the gallery ‖ (*movies*) a similar tier above the orchestra [Ital. *balcone* fr. O.H.G. *balcho*, a beam]

bald (bɔld) *adj.* without (or partly without) hair or fur, feathers etc., where these normally grow ‖ (*fig.*) unadorned, *bald narrative* ‖ featureless, *a bald landscape* [M.E. *balled*, origin unknown]

bal·da·chin, bal·da·quin (bɔ́ldəkin, bǽldəkin) *n.* a canopy of rich material carried in religious processions or placed over an altar ‖ a similar drapery e.g. over a bed ‖ (*archit.*) a structure (usually over an altar) like such a drapery [F. fr. *Baldacco* Ital. form of Baghdad, the place of origin of a rich gold and silk fabric used for vestments etc.]

bald eagle *Haliaeetus leucocephalus,* the common eagle of North America

bal·der·dash (bɔ́ldərdæʃ) *n.* nonsense, foolish talk [origin unknown]

bald·ing (bɔ́ldiŋ) *adj.* beginning to be bald

bal·dric (bɔ́ldrik) *n.* (*hist.*) a belt, passing from one shoulder to the opposite hip, to carry a sword, bugle etc. [M.E. *bauderik* fr. O.F. *baudrei*]

Bald·win I (bɔ́ldwin) (1058–1118), ruler of Edessa (1098–1100) and king of Jerusalem (1100–18). He extended the Latin Kingdom of Jerusalem by capturing Acre (1104), Beirut and Sidon (1110)

Baldwin II (*d.* 1131), count of Edessa (1100–31) and king of Jerusalem (1118–31). In a reign of almost incessant fighting, he extended the Latin Kingdom of Jerusalem to its widest limits

Baldwin I (c. 1171–c. 1205), leader of the 4th Crusade (1202–4). He captured Constantinople and became the first ruler of the Latin Empire of Constantinople (1204–5)

Baldwin, James (1924–   ), U.S. black novelist, essayist, and civil rights spokesman in the 1960s. His works, notably 'Go Tell It on the Mountain' (1953), 'Nobody Knows My Name' (1962), and 'The Fire Next Time' (1963), depict the Black as victimized by the 'guilty imagination of the white people who invest him with their hates and longings.' Other works include 'Another Country' (1962) and 'Tell Me How Long the Train's Been Gone' (1968)

Baldwin, Robert (1804–58), Canadian statesman prominent in the struggle for responsible government (1841–6)

Baldwin, Stanley, 1st Earl Baldwin of Bewdley (1867–1947), British statesman, three times Conservative prime minister between the two world wars. His popularity and cleverness helped to keep the country together in the crisis of the general strike (1926), in the subsequent depression, and in the abdication of Edward VIII (1936). He failed to rearm Britain in the face of growing German militarism

Bâle *BASLE

bale (beil) 1. *n.* a quantity of cotton, wheat, straw etc., tightly bound for ease of handling ‖ a large package of goods wrapped in canvas and corded 2. *v.t. pres. part.* **bal·ing** *past* and *past part.* **baled** to make up (wheat etc., or merchandise) into such bundles [perh. O.F. *bale*, bundle]

bale *BAIL (vessel used to scoop water)

Ba·le·a·res (bəleárɛs) *BALEARIC ISLANDS

Bal·e·ar·ic Islands (bæli:ǽrik) a Spanish province (Baleares, area 1,935 sq. miles, pop. 585,000) in the W. Mediterranean. The largest islands are Majorca (*Span.* Mallorca, area 1,352 sq. miles, pop. 270,000, with the capital Palma), Minorca (*Span.* Menorca, area 264 sq. miles, pop. 60,000) and Ibiza (area 230 sq. miles, pop. 12,000). They are mountainous, with a mild, sunny climate. Occupations: farming (fruit and vines), fishing, quarrying and mining, tourism. The islands were conquered in turn by the Phoenicians, Romans, Vandals and Moors. Aragon took them (1229) and made them a separate kingdom, which became part of Spain (1349). They were ceded to Britain (1713) and restored to Spain (1802)

bale cubic capacity the space available in a hold or container for cargo, measured in cu ft

ba·leen (bəlí:n) *n.* whalebone [O.F. *baleine*, whale]

bale·ful (béilfəl) *adj.* willing evil, *a baleful look* ‖ causing evil, *a baleful influence* [O.E. *bealuful*]

bal·er (béilər) *n.* a bail for scooping out water ‖ a machine for putting up straw, cotton etc., in bales

Ba·le·wa (bəléiwæ), Alhaji Sir Abubakar Tafawa (1912–66), Nigerian statesman. He was the first prime minister of Nigeria (1957–66). He was killed (Jan. 1966) in a military coup d'état

Bal·four (bǽlfər), Arthur James, 1st earl of Balfour (1848–1930), British Conservative statesman and philosopher. He succeeded his uncle, Lord Salisbury, as prime minister (1902–5), and was foreign secretary (1916–19). He was responsible for the Balfour Declaration (1917) and represented Britain at the first meeting of the League of Nations (1920). His philosophical works include 'A Defense of Philosophic Doubt' (1879) and 'Theism and Humanism' (1914–15)

Balfour Declaration a declaration made by Lord Balfour in 1917 that the British government favored a national home for the Jews in Palestine, without prejudice to the civil and religious rights of the non-Jewish people already living there

Ba·li (báli:) a mountainous, fertile volcanic island (area 2,243 sq. miles, pop. 2,469,930) between Java and Lombok in the Indonesian archipelago. Capital: Singaradja. Products: rice (grown in irrigated terraces), cotton, tobacco, sugar, coffee. Java was converted to Hinduism in the 7th c. and an elaborate Hindu culture developed by the 10th c. Bali was under Javanese rule from the 10th c. to the late 15th c. It was reached by the Dutch (1597), periodically invaded, subdued (1845–1906) and became part of the Netherlands E. Indies (1906). After Japanese occupation (1942–5), it became part of the United States of Indonesia (1945), then a province of the Republic of Indonesia (1950)

Ba·lik·pa·pan (bálikpápan) the chief port (pop. 137,340) of Kalimantan, center of the petroleum industry

Bal·iol (béiljəl), John de (1249–1315), king of Scotland (1292–6). His claim to the throne was disputed by Robert the Bruce, but supported by Edward I of England, who later defeated and imprisoned him (1296)

ba·li·sage (bæləsaʒ) *n.* the marking of a route by a system of dim beacon lights, enabling vehicles to be driven at near daytime speed under blackout conditions

balk, baulk (bɔk) 1. *n.* a hindrance or stumbling block ‖ the sanctuary area on a billiard table behind the balkline ‖ (*baseball*) a foul by a pitcher who, having begun the action of pitching to home plate, fails to complete the delivery or turns to throw to a base instead: each runner takes an extra base ‖ a ridge of land left unplowed ‖ a roughly squared length of lumber ‖ the tie beam, or main horizontal beam, of a roof ‖ the headline of a fishing net 2. *v.t.* to hinder, thwart ‖ *v.i.* to pull up, refuse to proceed, *the pony balked at the fence* ‖ (*baseball*) to commit a balk [O.E. *balca*, ridge and O.E. *bolca*, gangway]

Bal·kan (bɔ́lkən) *adj.* of the peninsula bounded by the Adriatic, Aegean and Black Seas ‖ of its peoples or countries

Balkan Entente a loose defensive alliance formed (1934) by Yugoslavia, Rumania, Greece and Turkey, dissolved in the 2nd world war

Balkan frame a framework with weights and pulleys for suspension, traction and extension

of a limb in the treatment of fractures [first used in the *Balkan* countries]

Balkan Mtns (*Bulg.* Stara Planina) a range (370 miles long) crossing Bulgaria parallel to the Danube from the Yugoslav border to the Black Sea, rising to 7,850 ft

Balkan Pact a military treaty of alliance (1954) between Greece, Turkey and Yugoslavia

Balkan Wars two wars fought (1912–13) in the Balkans. The 1st Balkan War began Oct. 8, 1912, between the Balkan League (Bulgaria, Serbia, Greece and Montenegro) and Turkey. It resulted in the recognition (1913) of Albanian independence. In the 2nd Balkan War (June 29–July 30, 1913) Greece, Serbia, Montenegro, Rumania and Turkey fought Bulgaria. A provisional agreement was reached at the Treaty of Bucharest (Aug. 10, 1913)

Balkans, the the peninsula of S.E. Europe bounded by the Rivers Danube and Sava in the north and by the Adriatic, the Aegean, the Mediterranean, the Sea of Marmara and the Black Sea, and including Albania, Bulgaria, Greece, Rumania, Yugoslavia and European Turkey

Bal·khash (balxáʃ) a shallow freshwater lake (area 7,200 sq. miles) below the Tien Shan in Kazakhstan, U.S.S.R.

balk·line (bɔ́klain) *n.* the line across a billiard table from behind which the opening shots are made and any ball in hand is played

balk·y (bɔ́ki:) *comp.* **balk·i·er** *superl.* **balk·i·est** *adj.* given to balking

Ball (bɔl), John (14th c.), English heretical priest and social reformer, executed for his part in the Peasants' Revolt of 1381

ball (bɔl) 1. *n.* a spherical object of any size ‖ the object (hard or soft, hollow or solid, round or oval, according to the game it is used in) which is kicked, hit, thrown etc., in various sports ‖ (*sport*) such an object with reference to its delivery, *a slow ball* ‖ (*baseball*) a ball pitched outside home plate at which the batter does not swing ‖ (*hist.*) shot fired from a cannon etc. ‖ the rounded part of the foot near the base of the big toe ‖ the mound at the base of the thumb, set in the palm **on the ball** alert **to have the ball at one's feet** (*Br.*) to have a clear path to success **to keep the ball rolling** to do one's share in conversation, or any activity **to play ball** to play a game in which a ball is thrown, kicked or hit ‖ to cooperate **to set** (or **start**) **the ball rolling** to start some cumulative action, *to set the ball rolling with a donation* 2. *v.t.* to wind up into a ball ‖ *v.i.* to form a ball **balled up** (*pop.*) confused, muddled [M.E. *bal* fr. O.N. *böllr*]

ball *n.* a formal assembly for social dancing **to give a ball** to invite people to such an assembly **to open the ball** to lead off the first dance [F. *bal*]

bal·lad (bǽləd) *n.* a narrative poem, usually in short stanzas, generally about heroic or tragic deeds, or love, often in vivid, unliterary language ‖ any simple song, esp. a romantic or sentimental one, having the same melody for each stanza [O.F. *balade*]

bal·lade (bæláːd) *n.* a verse form consisting of three symmetrical stanzas and a short concluding verse called an envoy (addressed to some imagined hearer), all four stanzas sharing a refrain ‖ (*mus.*) an instrumental piece suggesting a story (e.g. Chopin's 'Ballades') [F.]

ballad meter, (*Br.*) ballad metre the meter usual in English ballads, the quatrain stanza, with a rhyme at the end of the 2nd and 4th lines, based on the Latin septenarius of two long lines of 7 accents

bal·lad·mon·ger (bǽlədmʌ́ŋgər) *n.* (*hist.*) a person who sold ballad sheets

ballad opera an opera using popular tunes of the day and spoken dialogue, e.g. Gay's 'The Beggar's Opera' (1728)

bal·lad·ry (bǽlədri:) *n.* ballads ‖ the art or activity of composing ballads

ball and socket joint a joint which allows a rotary movement in every direction within limited arcs

Bal·la·rat (bǽləræt) a city (pop. 57,000) in Victoria, Australia, the center of a mining area: textiles, machinery, dairy products

bal·last (bǽləst) 1. *n.* any heavy substance placed in a ship's hold, or balloon basket, to improve stability ‖ broken stone or slag used to form a bed for railroad track, or the lower layer of a road ‖ (of a ship) to carry ballast but no goods 2. *v.t.* to steady with bal-

CONCISE PRONUNCIATION KEY: **(a)** æ, c*a*t; ɑ, c*a*r; ɔ f*aw*n; ei, sn*a*ke. **(e)** e, h*e*n; i:, sh*ee*p; iə, d*ee*r; ɛə, b*ea*r. **(i)** i, f*i*sh; ai, t*i*ger; ə:, b*i*rd. **(o)** o, *o*x; au, c*ow*; ou, g*oa*t; u, p*oo*r; ɔi, r*oy*al. **(u)** ʌ, d*u*ck; u, b*u*ll; u:, g*oo*se; ə, b*a*cillus; ju:, c*u*be. x, lo*ch*; θ, *th*ink; ð, bo*th*er; z, *Z*en; ʒ, cor*s*age; dʒ, sava*g*e; ŋ, oranguta*ng*; j, *y*ak; ʃ, *f*ish; tʃ, fe*tch*; 'l, rabb*le*; 'n, redd*en*. Complete pronunciation key appears inside front cover.

last, stabilize ‖ to fill in with ballast [perh. Low G. *ballast*, bad lading]

ball bearing a bearing consisting of hardened steel balls rolling between a race on a shaft and a race held in a housing ‖ one of these balls

ball control (*basketball*) strategy involving holding possession of the ball to maintain a leading score

bal·le·ri·na (bæləríːnə) *n.* a female ballet dancer

bal·let (bǽlei, bǽléi) *n.* a performance, usually by two or more dancers, in which music, movement and mime are combined [F.]

bal·let·o·mane (bǽlitoumein, bəlétəmein) *n.* a person passionately fond of ballet [coined fr. Ital. *balleto*, ballet+Gk *mania*, mania]

bal·lis·ta (bəlístə) *n.* (*hist.*) a weapon for hurling missiles [L. fr. Gk]

bal·lis·tic (bəlístik) *adj.* of or connected with projectiles [fr. L. *ballista*, catapult, fr. Gk *ballein*, to throw]

ballistic galvanometer an instrument for measuring the amount of electricity flowing during the momentary closing of a circuit

ballistic missile (*rocketry*) a missile which follows an unpowered trajectory (after being initially self-powered and guided), controlled only by gravity

ballistic pendulum an instrument for measuring the speed of a projectile ‖ an instrument for measuring the coefficient of restitution when bodies collide

bal·lis·tics (bəlístiks) *n.* the scientific study of projectiles (shells, bombs, rockets), their ejection, flight through the air, and impact with the target

ballistic separator a machine that sorts organic from inorganic matter for composting

ballistic wave the compressed air in front of a projectile in flight

Ba·lli·vián (bɑji:vján), José (1804–52), Bolivian general and president (1841–7). He routed (1841) the Peruvian force under Gen. Augustín Gamarra (1785–1841) at Ingaví, and this assured the independence of Bolivia

ball mill a mill containing the material to be pulverized in a drum together with a number of heavy balls. The mill is rotated and the material is crushed by the rolling balls

bal·loon (bəlúːn) **1.** *n.* an envelope of gasproof fabric distended by the pressure of a gas less dense than air at ground level. Helium is usual, formerly hot air or hydrogen were used. In accordance with Archimedes' principle the balloon rises because it is filled with gas lighter than an equal volume of air. The density of the surrounding air decreases as the balloon rises until an equilibrium is reached ‖ a toy inflatable sphere of thin rubber ‖ (*chem.*) a hollow glass sphere used in distillations ‖ (*archit.*) a large ball surmounting a pillar, pinnacle or spire ‖ something balloon-shaped, esp. a brandy glass ‖ a balloon sail ‖ (in a comic strip) the frame enclosing the words or written-out thoughts of the characters **2.** *v.i.* to go up in a balloon ‖ to swell out like a balloon [fr. Ital. *ballone*, a large ball]

balloon cloth a strong cotton material with special finishes used esp. for balloons

bal·loon·fish (bəlúːnfiʃ) *pl.* **bal·loon·fish, bal·loon·fish·es** *n.* a globefish

balloon foresail a light foresail between the foretopmasthead and the jib-boom end

balloon glass (*Br.*) a snifter (brandy glass)

bal·loon·ing (bəlúːniŋ) *n.* the practice of sending a bouquet of balloons instead of flowers

bal·loon·ist (bəlúːnist) *n.* someone who goes up in a balloon

balloon tire, (*Br.*) **balloon tyre** a pneumatic tire with a large cross section which lessens shock because of low inflation

bal·lot (bǽlət) **1.** *n.* a paper used in secret voting ‖ a vote cast by this method ‖ a drawing of lots ‖ the total votes cast at an election **2.** *v.i.* to vote by ballot papers ‖ to draw lots [fr. Ital. *ballotta*, dim. of *balla*, ball]

bal·lotte·ment (bəlótmənt) *n.* (*med.*) a manual method of determining the presence or absence of a floating object, esp. of diagnosing pregnancy or of diagnosing floating kidney [F.]

Bal·lou (bəlúː), Hosea (1771–1852), U.S. theologian, and the most influential leader of the Universalist Church of his age. In 'A Treatise on Atonement' (1805) he rejected the doctrines of original sin and vicarious atonement and advocated a unitarian and not a trinitarian base. Later he argued that punishment for sin is limited to this life

ball park an enclosed tract of grassland where ball games are played, with stands for spectators

ball·park (bɔ́ːlpɑːrk) *adj.* (*colloq.*) approximate, e.g., a ballpark figure

ball-point (bɔ́ːlpɔint) *n.* a ball-point pen

ball-point pen a pen with a tiny steel ball as a writing point, revolving at the end of a tube of semifluid ink

ball race one of the races in a ball bearing

ball·room (bɔ́ːlruːm, bɔ́ːlrum) *n.* a large room for dancing

bal·lute (bəlúːt) *n.* a small supplementary parachute or balloon used to stabilize a jumper until a principal parachute opens

ball valve a ball resting on a cylindrical inlet and allowing fluid to pass one way through the valve according to the pressure exerted by the fluid

bal·ly·hoo (bǽlihuː) **1.** *n.* sensational or noisy publicity ‖ factitious and exaggerated claims **2.** *v.t.* to promote by ballyhoo [fr. *Ballyhooly*, a village in County Cork, Eire]

balm (bɑm) *n.* a member of *Melissa,* fam. *Labiatae,* a genus of perennial fragrant herbs widely cultivated in temperate regions for the oil in the leaves, which is used for flavoring ‖ an aromatic and medicinal resin obtained from certain trees ‖ balsam ‖ (*loosely*) an ointment used for soothing and healing ‖ any calming or consoling influence [O.F. *basme*]

Bal·ma·ce·da (bɑlmaséðə), José Manuel (1840–91), Chilean liberal reformer and president (1886–91). As president he strove to prevent the legislature from eroding the powers of the executive. This led to civil war, ending in his defeat and suicide

balm·i·ly (bɑ́mili) *adv.* in a balmy manner

balm·i·ness (bɑ́miːnis) *n.* the state or quality of being balmy

balm of Gil·e·ad (gíliːəd) a liquid resinous balsam used for centuries medicinally and for its fragrance, derived from *Commiphora meccanesis,* a small Abyssinian and Arabian tree ‖ this tree

balm·y (bɑ́mi) *comp.* **balm·i·er** *superl.* **balm·i·est** *adj.* of or like balm ‖ fragrant, gentle, refreshing, *a balmy breeze* ‖ (*pop.*) crazy, weak in the head

bal·ne·al (bǽlniːəl) *adj.* of or pertaining to baths and bathing **bal·ne·ar·y** (bǽlniːəri) *adj.* [fr. L. *balneum,* bath]

bal·ne·o·ther·a·py (bǽlniːouθérəpi) *n.* (*med.*) treatment by baths [fr. L. *balneum,* bath+THERAPY]

ba·lo·ney, bo·lo·ney (bəlóuni) *n.* (*pop.*) bologna (sausage) ‖ (*slang*) nonsense, humbug [alteration of BOLOGNA (sausage)]

bal·op or **bap·li·con** (bǽləp) *n.* **1.** projection device that creates images by reflection, used as background for a TV or motion picture setting **2.** the artwork for it

bal·sa (bɔ́lsə) *n.* *Ochroma lagopus,* fam. *Bombaceae,* an American tree ‖ the wood of this tree, which is lighter than cork and used for rafts, floats etc. ‖ a raft or float, esp. a raft made of two wooden or metal cylinders joined by a framework, used for landing through surf [Span.]

bal·sam (bɔ́lsəm) *n.* a mixture of resins in volatile oils often used in medicines and perfumes ‖ any plant or tree yielding balsam (*CANADA BALSAM, *FRIAR'S BALSAM) ‖ balm of Gilead [fr. L. *balsamum*]

balsam apple a vine of genus *Momordica,* fam. *Cucurbitaceae,* with brightly colored fruit, grown in the West Indies

balsam fir *Abies balsamea,* a fir of North America used for pulp and Christmas trees

balsam of Peru an oleoresin from *Myroxylon Pereirae,* a tropical American tree, used in medicine and in perfume

balsam of Tolu a medicinal, resinous product from *Myroxylon balsamum,* a South American tree

balsam poplar *Populus balsamifera,* a shade tree of North America

Bal·sas, Rí·o de las (ríːəðelas búlsas) (or Mexcala) a river (426 miles long) rising in Tlaxcala state, Mexico, and flowing through Guerrero state into a bay on the Pacific. Its lower course forms the Michoacán-Guerrero boundary. Rapids

Bal·tic (bɔ́ltik) **1.** *adj.* of or pertaining to the Baltic Sea or to a Baltic state or language **2.** *n.* a branch of the Indo-European languages including Latvian and Lithuanian

Baltic Provinces the name given before 1918 to the Russian governments of Kurland, Livo-

nia, Estonia, Petrograd and Finland (*BALTIC STATES). Kurland and Livonia formed the independent republic of Latvia (1918), and Estonia and Finland also became independent (1918)

Baltic Sea a sea (area 157,000 sq. miles, average depth 180 ft) separating lower Scandinavia from the rest of N. Europe, bordered by Sweden, Denmark, Germany, Poland, Finland and the U.S.S.R. It is connected with the North Sea by a channel between Sweden and Denmark and by the Kiel Canal, and with the White Sea by canals (1933) via Lakes Ladoga and Onega

Baltic States the independent Baltic republics of Estonia and Latvia set up (1918) in place of the former Baltic Provinces, together with Lithuania, which also became independent in 1918. They were all annexed (1940) by the U.S.S.R. and became constituent republics

Bal·ti·more (bɔ́ːltəmər), George Calvert, 1st Baron (c. 1580–1632), English statesman who procured (1623) a charter for a colony in America and founded (1629) what became the state of Maryland. He attempted to impose strict Roman Catholic practices on the colonists

Baltimore (bɔ́ːltəmər, bɔ́ːltəmour) a port (pop. 786,775, with agglom. 1,879,000) and import-export center of Maryland, on the estuary of the Patapsco River, which flows into the Chesapeake Bay. Industries: iron and steel. Johns Hopkins University. Recent urban renewal concentrated on the waterfront and the downtown office district

Baltimore Canyon off-shore New Jersey area explored for oil

Baltimore chop (*baseball*) a ball hit to bounce too high for the infielder to make a put-out at first base while other players move

Baltimore oriole *Icterus galbula,* a songbird of America, orange and black in the male [after Lord *Baltimore*]

Bal·ti·stan (bʌltistán) a region (pop. 50,000), cut by the Indus valley, of N.E. Azad Kashmir, Pakistan, rising to the Karakorams. Capital: Skardu

Ba·lu·chi (bəlúːtʃi) *pl.* **Ba·lu·chi, Ba·lu·chis** *n.* a member of a Sunni Moslem people living in southern West Pakistan and in Iran ‖ the Iranian language spoken by this people

Ba·lu·chi·stan (bəlúːtʃistan) a special province of Iran, included in the 'ustan' of Kerman. Capital: Zahedan

Baluchistan a mountainous, sparsely inhabited desert region in S.W. Pakistan and S.E. Iran. The inhabitants (*BALUCHI, *PATHAN) are mainly nomadic herdsmen (sheep, goats, camels), oasis farmers (dates, cereals, cotton) or coastal fishermen. Handicrafts: carpets, textiles, pottery, metalwork ‖ (*hist.*) a state of British India and former province of Pakistan, consisting of the portion of Baluchistan lying within Pakistan. Capital: Quetta

bal·us·ter (bǽləstər) *n.* one of the small pillars which support the railing of a staircase or balcony etc., a banister [fr. Ital. *balausta* (*balaustra),* wild-pomegranate blossom]

bal·us·trade (bǽləstreid) *n.* a row of balusters surmounted by a rail or coping to form the parapet of a balcony, terrace etc. ‖ a banister [F.]

Bal·zac (bǽlzæk), Honoré de (1799–1850), French novelist, born at Tours. His great work was nearly all done in his last 20 years. It included nearly 100 novels, with well over 2,000 characters, under the general title 'la Comédie humaine'. His theory that character is largely conditioned by environment and tends to crystallize into a single dominating obsession led to minute cataloging of detail in setting and to a procession of grotesque protagonists, but Balzac's imagination and dramatic gift burst the limitations of the theory. He presents a rich, detailed picture of life in early 19th c. France, creating characters of formidable individuality and willpower. 'Eugénie Grandet' (1833) and 'le Père Goriot' (1834) are among his best-known works

Ba·ma·ko (bæmækóu) a port (pop. 215,700) on the Niger, capital of the Republic of Mali, terminus of the railroad from Dakar, and a road, air and river junction with oil and soap industries. It is the seat of an archbishop

BAMARC (*mil.*) long-range interceptor missile

Bam·ba·ra (bombɑ́ra) *n.* a member of a people of Senegal and Mali notable for their antelope and human masks ‖ this people ‖ their Mande language

bam·boo (bæmbúː) *n.* an arborescent grass of the tribe *Bambuseae,* fam. *Gramineae,* grown in the tropics and subtropics. The hollow stems are so hard and durable that they are used in buildings, furniture and some agricultural tools, and split bamboo is also used for mats and paper. The young shoots and grain are edible [Hindi *bambu*]

bamboo curtain border barrier between Communist states of Asia and the West-oriented states

bam·boo·zle (bæmbú:z'l) *pres. part.* **bam·boo·zling** *past* and *past part.* **bam·boo·zled** *v.t.* to hoax, mystify or trick, in jest or malevolently [etym. doubtful]

Bam·bu·co (bambú:kou) *n.* dance native to Colombia, fusing Indian and Spanish influences; described as a samba in waltz rhythm in 3/4 time with 6/8 accompaniment

ban (bæn) *pres. part.* **ban·ning** *past* and *past part.* **banned** *v.t.* to prohibit, forbid [O.N. *banna*, to curse]

ban *n.* a formal prohibition || (*eccles.*) a formal interdict [O.F. *ban*, proclamation and BAN v.]

ban (bɑn) *pl.* **ba·ni** (bâni:) *n.* one-hundredth of a leu || a coin of this value [Rumanian]

ba·nal (béin'l, bənǽl, bənǽl) *adj.* commonplace, flat [F.]

ba·nal·i·ty (bənǽliti:) *pl.* **ba·nal·i·ties** *n.* triteness || something commonplace [fr. F. *banalité*]

ba·nal·ize (bǽnəlaiz) *v.* to make ordinary

ba·nan·a (bənǽnə) *n.* the edible fruit of *Musa*, fam. *Musaceae*, a genus of plants cultivated widely in tropical and subtropical areas. Bananas are internationally important as a foodstuff, esp. in S.E. Asia || the tall, coarse plant itself (up to 30 ft), having large clusters of fruit [Port. or Span.]

banana oil a colorless liquid with a fruity smell derived from a commercial amyl alcohol and used in the manufacture of artificial fruit essences || a lacquer containing amyl acetate used in cosmetics, dentistry, etc.

ba·nan·a·seat (bənǽnəsi:t) *n.* (*bicycling*) saddle with upward-curved back

Ban·at (bɑ́nat) a region of the middle Danube with a largely fertile plain with mountains in the southeast. Formerly a Hungarian province, it is now divided between Rumania and Yugoslavia

Ban·croft (bǽnkroft, bǽnkroft), George (1800–91), American historian and statesman. His great work is the 'History of the United States' (10 vols., 1834–74). He was secretary of the Navy (1845–6), minister to Great Britain (1846–9), to Prussia (1867–8), to the N. German Confederation (1868–71) and the German Empire (1871–4)

band (bænd) *v.t.* to put a band on || to tie with a band || to mark with stripes || *v.i.* to form into a group or company, to *band together in protest* [F. *bander* and BAND n.]

band *n.* a flat strip of material, e.g. a narrow strip for strengthening a garment || a flat strip or stripe differing from the rest of the material or decoration of an object || a broad group of closely spaced lines found in molecular spectra || a range of sound frequencies or wavelengths between two stated limits || an item of music, on a record including several pieces || (*pl.*) two strips of white cloth sometimes worn at the neck as an item of academic, clerical or legal dress [late M.E. *bande* fr. F.]

band *n.* a group of musicians playing together (usually percussion and brass or wind, never a symphonic or chamber group) || an organized group of persons, a *band of robbers* or animals, a *band of performing dogs* [late 15th-c. *bande* fr. F.]

Ban·da (bǽndə), Hastings Kamuzu (1905–   ), Malawi statesman. He became (1963) the first prime minister of Nyasaland, which he led to independence (1964) as Malawi. He became (1966) the first president of Malawi

band·age (bǽndidʒ) **1.** *n.* a strip of cloth used to protect or bind an injured part of the body, so as to immobilize or apply pressure **2.** *v.t. pres. part.* **band·ag·ing** *past* and *past part.* **band·aged** to tie up with a bandage [F.]

Band-Aid (bǽndeid) *n.* (*trademark*) **1.** combination gauze and adhesive tape used to cover small cuts and bruises **2.** metaphorically, emergency temporary 'patch' applied to a basic problem

Banda Islands a group of volcanic islands (area 16 sq. miles, pop. 13,000) in the Banda Sea between Ceram and Timor, Indonesia: spices, esp. nutmeg

ban·dan·na, ban·dan·a (bændǽnə) *n.* a large decorative handkerchief [fr. Hindi *bāndhnū*, a method of dyeing]

Bandaranaike, Sirimavo (si:ri:mávou bandranáiki:) (1916–   ), prime minister of Sri Lanka (1960–5; 1970–7). She entered politics after the assassination of her husband, Prime Minister Solomon W.R.D. Bandaranaike. During her terms industry was nationalized, a new constitution was adopted, and Sinhalese became the national language

band·box (bǽndbɒks) *n.* a cardboard hatbox, orig. for clerical bands

ban·deau (bǽndou) *pl.* **ban·deaux** (bǽndouz) *n.* a narrow band of ribbon, esp. one for binding a woman's hair || the fitting band inside a hat [F.]

bandeau hairpiece headband with small wiglet attached covering the hairline *also* bandwig

Ban·dei·ra, Pi·co da (pí:kudəbandéirə) *BRAZIL*

Ban·de·lier (bǽndəliər), Adolph Francis Alphonse (1840–1914), U.S. archaeologist and anthropologist. He conducted extensive investigations into Indian cultures of the southwest U.S.A., Mexico, and Peru-Bolivia

ban·de·ri·lla (bænderí:lja, bænderí:ja) *n.* (*bullfighting*) a barb decorated with ribbons, which the banderillero plants in the bull's shoulder muscles [Span.]

ban·de·ri·lle·ro (bænderi:ljérɔ, bænderi:jérɔ) *n.* (*bullfighting*) the bullfighter who plants the banderillas [Span.]

ban·de·role, ban·de·rol (bǽndərɔl) *n.* a long, narrow flag or pennant flown from a masthead, lance etc. || a surveyor's flag || (*archit.*) a sculptured band like a ribbon or scroll, often inscribed [F.]

ban·di·coot (bǽndiku:t) *n.* a member of *Peramelidae*, a family of small marsupials native to Australia, Tasmania and New Guinea || *Nesokia bandicota*, a large rat which damages rice fields in India and Ceylon [fr. Telegu *pandikokku*, pig rat]

ban·dit (bǽndit) *n.* a robber, esp. one of a group roving in uninhabited districts [Ital. *bandito*, someone outlawed]

Band·jar·mas·in (bándʒarmásin) a seaport and trading center (pop. 281,673) of S. Kalimantan, Indonesia, on the Martapura River

band·mall (bǽndmɔl) *n.* a groupie who attaches to a rock group

Bandoeng *BANDUNG*

ban·do·lier, ban·do·leer (bændəlíər) *n.* a shoulder belt with pockets or loops for cartridges [F. *bandoulière*]

band·pass (bǽndpæs) *n.* (*electr.*) in an amplifier, the number of cycles per sec expressing the difference between the limiting frequencies at which the desired fraction (usu. half power) of the maximum output is obtained

band·ra·zor (bǽndreizər) *n.* shaving razor that contains roll of edged steel that is advanced for use as required

band saw a saw consisting of an endless steel belt running over wheels

band spectrum a molecular spectrum

Ban·dung, Ban·doeng (bándún) the capital (pop. 1,202,730) of W. Java, Indonesia: textiles, chemical industry. University (1958)

Bandung Conference the first Afro-Asian Conference (1955): it set out to promote concerted economic and cultural cooperation and opposed colonialism, and affirmed the right to independence and to neutral coexistence in the cold war between East and West

band·wag·on (bǽndwægən) *n.* a decorated wagon carrying a band of musicians, e.g. in a parade || a movement, party, or faction with a very strong popular appeal **to climb aboard** (or **jump on**) **the bandwagon** to shift one's vote or support to the winning side

ban·dy (bǽndi:) *pres. part.* **ban·dy·ing** *past* and *past part.* **ban·died** *v.t.* (with 'about') to chuck back and forth, often carelessly || to exchange (words, compliments, insults etc.) || to discuss or mention superficially or too freely [etym. doubtful, perh. fr. M.F. *bander*, to strike a ball to and fro in tennis]

ban·dy-legged (bǽndi:legd) *adj.* bowlegged

bane (bein) *n.* a cause of misery, worry, or anxiety || a person who constantly gets on one's nerves || (only in compounds, e.g. ratbane) poison **báne·ful** *adj.* harmful [O.E. *bana*, destroyer]

Banff (bæmf, bænf) former county in N.E. Scotland, now part of Grampian administrative region

bang (bæŋ) *n.* (*Am.*, often *pl.*,=*Br.* fringe) hair cut straight across the forehead

bang 1. *v.t.* to strike suddenly and violently || to cause to make a loud, sudden noise, *don't bang the door* || *v.i.* to make the sound of a blow or explosion **2.** *n.* a hard knock || a loud, sudden noise || (*pop.*) a thrill of pleasure **3.** *adv.* abruptly || explosively **4.** *interj.* the conventional imitation of a gun going off [imit.]

bang *BHANG*

Ban·ga·lore (bæŋgəlór) a town (pop. 2,482,507) in Karnataka (formerly Mysore) India, on the Deccan plateau. Industries: textiles, leather, aircraft engineering

Bangka *BANKA*

Bang·kok (bæŋkók) the capital (pop. 5,396,997) of Thailand, a seaport at the mouth of the Chao Phraya. It is the center of a great rice-producing district and the country's chief entrepôt

Bangladesh (bæŋlədéʃ) (formerly East Pakistan), independent nation in S. Asia on Bay of Bengal (area 55,126 sq. mi.; pop. 93,849,000). Capital: Dacca. It is an agricultural country, producing rice and jute. It has a tropical monsoon climate. Before 1947 most of the country was part of British-ruled East Bengal. In 1947 it joined with Assam to become East Pakistan in a new state of Pakistan, and declared itself independent in 1971. More than 95% of population is Bengali. Since 1975 when the first president, Shiekh Mujibur Rahman, was assassinated Bangladesh has alternately been ruled by military and elected governments. A 1985 referendum approved the policies of Lt. Gen. H. M. Ershad, self-proclaimed president since 1983

ban·gle (bæŋg'l) *n.* a narrow bracelet [Hind. *bangrī*]

Ban·gor (bǽŋgər) a port (pop. 14,000) on the Menai Strait in Caernarvonshire, Wales. Cathedral (16th c.). University College of N. Wales (1884), part of the University of Wales

bang time the period between the sighting of an explosion and the hearing of it

Ban·gui (bɑ́gi:) the capital (pop. 350,000) of Central African Republic, on the Ubangi River: archbishopric, international airport

Bang·we·u·lu (bæŋwi:ú:1u:) a lake (area 1,670 sq. miles, elevation 3,700 ft) in Zambia, fed by the Chambezi, and emptying into the Luapula, the headstream of the Congo

bang·zone (bǽŋzoun) *n.* the range of sonic boom

ban·ish (bǽniʃ) *v.t.* to compel (someone) to leave a country || to drive away from home or an accustomed place || to dismiss from one's presence or thoughts **bán·ish·ment** *n.* [fr. O.F. *banir* (*baniss-*)]

ban·is·ter (bǽnistər) *n.* the upright support of a stair rail or handrail || the row of supports and the rail together [corrup. of BALUSTER]

ban·jo (bǽndʒou) *pl.* **ban·jos, ban·joes** *n.* a stringed musical instrument, strummed or plucked with the fingers, having a neck like a guitar and a round sound box covered with parchment, traditionally in the days of slavery a favorite instrument of American blacks **bán·jo·ist** *n.* [corrup. of *bandore* fr. Span. fr. Gk]

Banjul (bándʒu:l), formerly Bathurst, the capital city (41,000) of Gambia, a port. Exports: peanuts, hides, ivory, gold

bank (bæŋk) **1.** *n.* a place where money is kept and paid out, lent, borrowed, issued or exchanged || (*gambling*) the fund of the keeper of the table || a reserve supply of a thing, *blood bank* **to break the bank** (*gambling*) to win all the dealer's money **2.** *v.t.* to deposit (money or valuables) at a bank || *v.i.* to use the services of a bank || to carry on bank business || (*gambling*) to be in charge of the table fund **to bank on** to rely upon **bánk·a·ble** *adj.* [F. *banque* fr. Ital. *banca*, (money) bench]

bank 1. *n.* (*hist.*) a galley rower's bench || (*hist.*) a tier of oars in a galley || a row of organ keys || (*elec.*) a grouping of transformers, cells etc. **2.** *v.t.* to arrange (cells etc.) in a bank [M.E. *baunk* fr. O.F. *banc*]

bank 1. *n.* the rising ground bordering a lake, river etc. || earth raised above the ground, esp. to mark a dividing line || an elevation of mud or sand etc., in a sea or river bed || a mound or pile, esp. of earth, but also of sand, clouds etc. || the ground at the top of a mining shaft || the cushion in billiards || the tilting of an aircraft rounding a curve **2.** *v.t.* to raise or form in a bank, *to bank* earth *around a building* ‖ to build a slope into (a road) to enable a car to maintain speed on bends ‖ to cause (a ball) to hit the cushion of a billiard table ‖ (sometimes with 'up') to cover (a fire) with fuel and reduce the draft (for slow burning) ‖ *v.i.* to tilt sideways when rounding a curve in flight ‖ (with 'up') to pile up into a bank, *clouds are banking up* [M.E. *banke*, prob. fr. O.N.]

Ban·ka, Bang·ka (báŋka), an island (area 4,610 sq. miles, pop. 205,000) of Indonesia, off E. Sumatra, one of the world's main tin-mining centers since its discovery in 1710. The inhabitants are mainly Malay emigrants. Capital: Pangkalpinang

bank account money which a depositor entrusts to a bank and on which he can draw

bank bill a bank note ‖ (*Br.*) a bill of exchange

bank club a group of creditors set up to administer orderly liquidation or rehabilitation of endangered companies, esp. in Argentina

bank credit an arrangement by which a customer may overdraw on security given

bank·er (báŋkər) *n.* a person conducting the business of a bank ‖ (*gambling*) the person who keeps the bank

banker *n.* a man or vessel employed in cod fishing on the Newfoundland banks [BANK, the ground bordering a sea, etc.]

banker *n.* a stonemason's or sculptor's workbench [BANK, bench]

bank holiday a period when banks are closed by government order to effect monetary or banking reforms ‖ (*Br.*) a day on which banks are legally closed and which is kept as a public holiday

bank·ing (báŋkiŋ) *n.* the business of a banker [BANK, to keep money]

banking *n.* fishing on a sea bank, esp. the Newfoundland banks [BANK, the ground bordering a sea, etc.,]

bank note a piece of paper money with the value printed on it

Bank of England the central bank of England and Wales, founded (1694) to finance loans to the government. Its note-issuing functions were separated from its other banking activities (1842) and it was nationalized (1945)

Bank of the United States, a private corporation designed by Alexander Hamilton and governed by a federal charter (1791). Meant to keep public funds safe, serve as fiscal agent for the federal government, and provide credit, it also served as a check on state banks. The charter was not renewed in 1811. By 1816 a second Bank of the United States had been chartered and existed until 1836

BANKPAC (*computer acronym*) for Bank Pack, a software packed for the banking industry designed by General Electric Co

bank rate the discount rate fixed by a central bank

bank·rupt (báŋkrəpt) **1.** *n.* a person who cannot pay his debts ‖ (*law*) a person declared by a court unable to pay his debts and whose property will be administered by the court for the benefit of the creditors **2.** *adj.* insolvent, unable to pay one's debts ‖ lacking something one used to have or ought to have, *spiritually bankrupt* **3.** *v.t.* to reduce to bankruptcy **bank·rupt·cy** (báŋkrəptsi:) *n.* the state of being actually or legally bankrupt, insolvency ‖ complete failure, *bankruptcy of the imagination* [fr. Ital. *banca rotta*, broken bank]

Banks (báŋks), Nathaniel Prentiss (1816–94), U.S. political leader and Civil War general. He was elected speaker of the House of Representatives (1855) and governor of Massachusetts (1858) before serving in the army as major general of volunteers (1861–4)

bank·si·a (báŋksi:ə) *n.* a member of *Banksia*, fam. *Proteaceae*, a genus of Australian evergreen shrubs (Australian honeysuckle) with leathery leaves and yellowish flowers [after Sir Joseph *Banks* (d. 1820), English naturalist]

Bank·side (báŋksaid) the Thames bank at Southwark, the site of Elizabethan theaters in London

bank statement a record of his account issued to a customer by a bank

bank swallow *Riparia riparia*, a small swallow of the northern hemisphere which often nests in holes in sandy cliffs and feeds chiefly over water

ban·ner (bánər) *n.* a cloth flag on a pole used as a military standard ‖ the flag of a country ‖ a piece of cloth, cardboard etc., bearing a slogan

and carried in religious or political demonstrations [O.F. *banere*]

banner headline (often *pl.*) a bold headline running entirely across the page of a newspaper

Ban·nock·burn, Battle of (bánəkbərn) a battle (1314) in which Robert I of Scotland inflicted a crushing defeat on Edward II of England

banns (bænz) *pl. n.* a public announcement of an intended marriage given out on the same three Sundays in the parish churches of the engaged pair, to give an opportunity for objection if there is some impediment **to call** (or **publish** or **ask**) **the banns** to make this announcement [fr. BAN in older sense of proclamation]

ban·quet (báŋkwit) **1.** *n.* a feast ‖ an official celebration dinner with speeches **2.** *v.t.* to honor with a banquet ‖ *v.i.* to be a guest at a banquet [F.]

banquet lamp tall kerosene lamp used as table centerpiece

ban·shee (bænʃí:, bǽnʃi:) *n.* (*Ir. mythol.*) a female spirit whose wailing foretells death in a house [Ir. *bean sidhe*, woman of the fairies]

ban·tam (bántəm) *n.* a small variety of domestic fowl of which the cock is very aggressive ‖ a small but spirited person [after *Bantam* in Java]

ban·tam·weight (bántəmweit) *n.* a professional boxer whose weight does not exceed 118 lbs ‖ an amateur boxer whose weight does not exceed (*Am.*) 119 lbs or (*Br.*) 118 lbs

ban·ter (bántər) **1.** *n.* playful teasing **2.** *v.t.* to make good-humored fun of ‖ *v.i.* to talk jokingly [origin unknown]

Ban·ting (bántiŋ), Sir Frederick (1891–1941), Canadian scientist who with J. J. Macleod isolated insulin and thus made possible the successful treatment of diabetes. They shared a Nobel prize for medicine (1923)

Ban·tu (bántu:) *pl.* **Ban·tu, Ban·tus** *n.*a member of any of several peoples of equatorial and southern Africa speaking a Bantu language

Bantu languages a family of African languages with some 50 million speakers, distributed south of a line between the Gulf of the Cameroons and the mouth of the Tana River

Ban·tu·stan (bántustæn) *n.* a district enclave in the Republic of South Africa where nonwhites dominate and govern. A feature of South Africa's policy of apartheid, Bantustans are designed as a 'homeland' for black people

Ban·ville (bávi:l), Théodore de (1823–91), French poet of the Parnassian school

ban·yan (bánjən) *n. Ficus bengalensis*, fam. *Moraceae*, an East Indian tree characterized by aerial roots forming supporting pillars [Hindi *baniyā* fr. Skr. *vārija*, merchant, from the setting up of markets under its shade]

Ban·zer Suá·rez (bánsərswáres), Hugo (1926–), Bolivian colonel and president (1971–78) after the overthrow of Juan José Torres. He himself was overthrown by military

ba·o·bab (béiəbæb, báubæb) *n. Adansonia digitata*, fam. *Bombacaceae*, a softwood tree grown esp. in Africa, Asia and Australia, one of the world's largest trees (40-60 ft high, trunk diameter up to 30 ft, branch spread up to 30 ft). Products derived from it include the edible pulp of the fruit, medicine, rubber, fertilizer, soap etc., and its wood is used in canoes, musical instruments etc. [perh. central African]

Ba·o Dai (báudái) (1913–), emperor of Annam (1925–45). In 1945 he proclaimed (Mar. 11) the independence of Vietnam and abdicated (Aug. 25). He was again head of state 1949–55. In 1954, by the Geneva Conference, the independence of Vietnam was recognized. The North came under Communist control. In 1955 Ngo Dinh Diem deposed Bao Dai and took control of the South

bap·tism (báptizəm) *n.* the religious practice, one of the sacraments commanded by Christ (Matthew xxviii, 19), of sprinkling a person with water, or immersing him in it, in the name of the Trinity, to symbolize the washing away of sin and (with most Christian sects) to mark admission to the Church, generally accompanied by christening ‖ the naming of church bells or ships ‖ an experience that initiates a new way of life **bap·tis·mal** (bæptízməl) *adj.* [F. fr. L. fr. Gk]

Baptist (báptist) *n.* a member of a worldwide Christian Protestant denomination dating from the 17th c. Baptists practice baptism by immersion, and hold that this rite should be performed only when the person is old enough to

appreciate its meaning. They are congregationalist in polity ‖ someone who baptizes (cf. JOHN THE BAPTIST) [O.F. fr. L. fr. Gk]

bap·tis·te·ry (báptistəri:, bæptistri:) *pl.* **bap·tis·ter·ies** *n.* a baptistry

bap·tis·try (báptistri:) *pl.* **bap·tis·tries** *n.* the part of a church (or formerly a separate building) used for baptism ‖ in a Baptist chapel, the tank used for immersion [O.F. fr. L. fr. Gk]

bap·tize (bæptáiz, bǽptaiz) *pres. part.* **bap·tiz·ing** *past* and *past part.* **bap·tized** *v.t.* to administer baptism to as a sign of purification or initiation, esp. into the Christian Church ‖ to give a name to ‖ to nickname ‖ to administer baptism [F. *baptizer* fr. L. fr. Gk]

bar (bɑr) *n.* a long piece of wood, metal etc. used as a support, an obstruction or a lever ‖ a barrier of any kind, *deafness is a bar to many careers* ‖ a rectangular slab of rigid material (metal, soap, chocolate etc.) ‖ a metal strip on the ribbon of a medal as an additional award ‖ the solid mouthpiece of a horse's bit ‖ a strip (of light or color) ‖ a straight line considerably longer than it is broad, e.g. the horizontal stroke of the letter t ‖ (*heraldry*) two horizontal stripes across a shield ‖ (*mus.*) a vertical line across a staff dividing it into equal measures of time ‖ (*law*) a plea arresting an action or claim ‖ a barrier in a law court where the prisoner stands ‖ any tribunal, *the bar of public opinion* ‖ the legal profession ‖ a counter over which liquor and food may be served ‖ the space behind this counter ‖ the room containing it ‖ (*Br.*) the rail near the door of parliament cutting off the space to which nonmembers may be admitted to the chamber on business **to be called to the bar** (*Br.*, with reference to the bar in the Inns of Court before which students when qualified were called to debate) to be admitted a barrister **to be called within the bar** (*Br.*, with reference to the bar in the courts where K.C.s plead) to be appointed a King's (Queen's) Counsel [M.E. *barre* fr. O.F.]

bar *n.* a unit of pressure equal to 10^6 dynes per square centimeter or 0.99 atmospheres ‖ a unit of pressure in the cgs system equal to 1 dyne per square centimeter [G. fr. Gk *baros*, weight]

bar 1. *v.t. pres. part.* **bar·ring** *past* and *past part.* **barred** to fasten, secure ‖ to obstruct, *to bar a passage* ‖ to prohibit ‖ to exclude, *to bar a topic from discussion* ‖ to mark with stripes **2.** *prep.* except, excluding [O.F. *barrer*]

Bar·ab·bas (bərábəs) the thief released instead of Jesus (Matthew xxvii, 15–26)

Ba·ra·bu·dur (bá:rabudúər) a great Buddhist temple of central Java (c. 850), each story of which is carved in low relief

Baraka, Imamu Amiri (i:mámu:amí:ri:baráka) (1934–), U.S. poet and playwright, formerly LeRoi Jones. An advocate of black power, he wrote the plays 'Dutchman' (1964), 'The Slave' (1965), and 'The Toilet' (1965). His poetry is collected in 'Preface to a Twenty-Volume Suicide Note' (1961). Jones changed his name in 1968 and founded a Muslim group, the Black Community Development and Defense Organization

ba·ra·ni or **ba·ro·ni** (bəráni:) *n.* (*gymnastics*) front somersault with a half twist

bar·a·the·a (bærəθí:ə) *n.* a fine woolen cloth, sometimes interwoven with silk or cotton [origin unknown]

barb (bɑrb) *n.* a pigeon of a breed native to Barbary and related to the carriers **Barb** a horse of a breed related to the Arab and originally from Barbary. It is noted for its speed and stamina [F. *barbe* (*Barbarie*)]

barb 1. *n.* the part of an arrow, fishhook, bee's sting etc., that points backwards and prevents or hinders removal ‖ the beardlike feelers of a barbed fish ‖ the chinpiece of a nun's headdress ‖ one of the lateral processes branching from the shaft of a feather ‖ an awn, e.g. in certain grasses **2.** *v.t.* to supply (an arrow etc.) with barbs [F. *barbe*, beard]

Bar·ba·dos (bɑrbéidouz) an independent state (area 166 sq. miles, pop. 246,082, 80% of African descent) in the Lesser Antilles, West Indies, about 100 miles east of St Vincent in the Windward Is. Capital: Bridgetown (pop. 7,517). Tourism has become an important industry. Chief exports: sugar, molasses, rum. Imports: machinery, foodstuffs. Barbados College (University of the West Indies College of Arts and Sciences, at Cave Hill near Bridgetown). It was settled as a British colony (1627) and attained full internal self-government (1691). It became an independent state (Nov. 30, 1966) within the

---

Commonwealth and became (1967) a member of the Organization of American States

Bar·ba·ra (bárbərə), St (d. c. 235), virgin martyr, patroness of artillerymen and naval gunners, miners, firemen and quarrymen

bar·bar·i·an (bɑrbéəriːən) **1.** *n.* a savage, uncivilized person ‖ an uncultured person ‖ (for the ancient Greeks) a non-Greek ‖ (for the ancient Romans) a person from outside the Roman empire **2.** *adj.* of or like a barbarian [F. *barbarien*]

bar·bar·ic (bɑrbǽrik) *adj.* savage, *barbaric cruelty* ‖ utterly lacking in taste, breeding, etc. ‖ (of a work of art) having a rough or primitive quality, forceful and without finish **bar·bár·i·cal·ly** *adv.* [O.F. *barbarique* fr. L. fr. Gk]

bar·bar·ism (bárbərizəm) *n.* a barbaric condition ‖ the use of unapproved expressions in speech or writing ‖ such an expression [F. *barbarisme* fr. L. fr. Gk *barbarizein*, to speak like a foreigner]

bar·bar·i·ty (bɑrbǽriti) *pl.* **bar·bar·i·ties** *n.* savage cruelty ‖ barbaric taste or an object showing this [fr. L. *barbarus*]

bar·bar·ize (bárbəraiz) *pres. part.* **bar·bar·izing** *past* and *past part.* **bar·bar·ized** *v.t.* to make barbarous ‖ to corrupt (language) ‖ *v.i.* to become barbarous

Bar·ba·ros·sa (bɑrbərósə), Frederick *FREDERICK I

bar·bar·ous (bárbərəs) *adj.* uncivilized ‖ cruel ‖ uncouth ‖ characterized by or consisting of barbarisms in speech or writing [fr. L. *barbarus* fr. Gk]

Bar·ba·ry (bárbəri) (*hist.*) N. Africa from Egypt to the Atlantic and from the Sahara to the Mediterranean. It was a center of piracy (16th–early 19th cc.)

Barbary ape *MACAQUE

bar·bate (bárbeit) *adj.* (*biol.*) bearded, having hairy tufts, or long stiff hairs [fr. L. *barbatus*]

bar·be·cue (bárbikjuː) **1.** *n.* an ox, hog etc. roasted whole (or split) over a wood fire in a pit for a feast ‖ a feast at which a barbecue is served ‖ (*loosely*) any party where food is grilled on a metal frame over charcoal ‖ the grill itself ‖ the food cooked on the grill with a highly seasoned sauce **2.** *v.t. pres. part.* **bar·be·cu·ing** *past* and *past part.* **bar·be·cued** to roast over a barbecue pit or grill on a metal frame over charcoal, and serve with a highly seasoned sauce [fr. Span. *barbacoa*, a raised frame, fr. Haitian]

barbed wire a steel wire to which pointed steel barbs are attached at close intervals, for fences or defense works

bar·bel (bárbəl) *n. Barbus fluviatilis*, a large European freshwater fish having four tactile processes on its upper jaw ‖ one of these filaments ‖ any species of the genus *Barbus* [O.F.]

bar·bell (bárbəl) *n.* a bar with adjustable weights used in weight lifting

Bar·ber (bárbər), Samuel (1910–81), American composer. His works include 'Adagio for Strings', an overture to 'The School for Scandal', the opera 'Vanessa' etc.

bar·ber (bárbər) *n.* a person whose business is cutting and dressing men's hair, shaving, etc. [O.F. *barbeor*]

bar·ber·ry (bárbəriː, bárbəri) *pl.* **bar·ber·ries** *n.* any shrub of genus *Berberis* [fr. M.L. *barbaris, berberis*]

bar·ber·shop (bárbərʃɒp) **1.** *n.* a barber's premises **2.** *adj.* of or relating to an amateur male quartet singing sentimental popular songs unaccompanied, in homemade arrangements, or relating to the harmony characteristic of such groups

barber's pole a pole painted with red and white spiraling stripes and displayed as a sign of the barber's trade

barber's rash a skin disease spread by barbers' unsterilized shaving brushes

bar·bette (bɑrbét) *n.* an armored protection of a warship's revolving turret ‖ a mound or platform from which guns are fired over a parapet [F. dim. of *barbe*, beard]

Bar·bey d'Aure·vil·ly (bærbeidɔrviːjiː), Jules (1808–89), French Catholic romantic novelist, critic and writer of long short stories, e.g. 'les Diaboliques' (1874)

bar·bi·can (bárbikən) *n.* an outer defense work of a city or castle, esp. towers over a gate or bridge [F. *barbacane*, perh. fr. Arab. or Pers.]

bar·bi·cel (bárbisel) *n.* one of the small hooked processes on the lower margin of the barbule of a feather [fr. Mod. L. *barbicella*, dim. of *barba*, beard]

bar·bi·tal (bárbitɔl) *n.* diethylbarbituric acid, $C_8H_{12}N_2O_3$, a habit-forming sedative [fr. BARBITURIC]

bar·bi·tu·rate (bɑrbítʃurit, bɑrbítʃureit) *n.* one of a group of drugs derived from barbituric acid. They are mainly used as sedatives and anesthetics

bar·bi·tu·ric acid (bɑrbitjúərik, bɑrbitúərik) the compound $C_4H_4N_2O_3$, from which the barbiturates are derived [etym. doubtful]

Bar·bi·zon school (bárbizɒn) a group of French naturalist painters incl. Théodore Rousseau, Millet, Corot and Daumier, associated with the village of Barbizon near Fontainebleau, France

Bar·bu·da (bɑrbúːdə) an island (area 62 sq. miles, pop. 1,000) of the Leeward Islands. *ANTIGUA AND BARBUDA became an independent nation in 1981

bar·bule (bárbjuːl) *n.* one of the processes along the side of the barb of a feather. The ones on the upper face mesh with the hooks of the adjacent barbicels [fr. L. *barbula*, dim. of *barba*, beard]

barb·wire (bárbwáiər) *n.* barbed wire

bar·ca·role, bar·ca·rolle (bárkəroul) *n.* the song of a gondolier or an imitation of it [F. *barcarolle*, fr. Ital.]

Bar·ce·lo·na (bɑrsəlóunə) Spain's second city (pop. 1,754,900) and largest port, on the Mediterranean, the chief town of Catalonia and capital of the modern province of Barcelona (area 2,968 sq. miles, pop. 4,618,734). It is Spain's greatest industrial center: textiles, machinery, shipbuilding, chemical industries etc. Said to have been founded by Hamilcar Barca in 230 B.C., it was a Roman colony. Under the counts of Barcelona, it became (12th c.) one of the greatest ports of the Mediterranean, and one of the strongest banking centers in Europe. In modern times it has been the center of Catalan separatism and Spanish republicanism. Cathedral and cloister (14th c.). University (1450)

Barcelona chair armless chair with stainless-steel frame and leather-covered cushions

Barc·lay de Tol·ly (bɑrkláidetɔ́ljiː), Michael, Prince (1761–1818), Russian soldier. His scorched-earth policy of retreat before Napoleon's invasion of Russia (1812) led to his replacement as commander in chief of the army in the west by Kutuzov, but he was reinstated (1813)

bar·code reader (bárkoud) device that reads combinations of bars and numbers, e.g., on food packages

bard (bɑrd) *n.* a national poet, perhaps originally a minstrel, a narrator or singer of folk poetry, esp. ballads. Among the Celts, the bards became a highly organized society. In modern Wales a bard is a poet recognized at an eisteddfod **bárd·ic** *adj.* relating to bards and to lyric poetry [Ir.]

Bar·deen (bɑrdíːn), John (1908–   ), U.S. theoretical physicist and co-winner of the Nobel prize for physics (1956) for his research on the transistor and (1972) for his development of the theory of superconductivity

bare (béər) **1.** *adj.* uncovered, naked, *barefeet* ‖ without trees or any tall growth, *a bare hillside* ‖ empty, *a bare cupboard* ‖ without decoration, *a bare room* ‖ scant, meager, *a bare living* ‖ plain, unconcealed, *the bare truth* ‖ very slight, *a bare chance* **2.** *v.t. pres. part.* **baring** *past* and *past part.* **bared** to uncover, *to bare one's head* ‖ to reveal (feelings) [O.E. *bær*]

bare·back (béərbæk) *adj.* and *adv.* (of riders or riding) without a saddle

Bare·bone's Parliament (béərbounz) the nickname for Cromwell's assembly which in 1653 had Praise God Barbon (or Barebone or Barebones) as a member. He was a rich London leather merchant (and Fifth Monarchy man) who was an ardent preacher, mocked at for his prophetic ecstasies

bare·faced (béərfeist) *adj.* insolent, blatant, shameless, *a barefaced lie*

bare·foot (béərfut) *adj.* and *adv.* without shoes and stockings

bare·hand·ed (béərhændid) *adj.* and *adv.* without any covering on the hands ‖ with just the hands (*i.e.* without a tool or weapon)

bare·head·ed (béərhédid) *adj.* and *adv.* without a hat or cap

Ba·reil·ly (bəréiliː) a town (pop. 296,248) in Uttar Pradesh, India: textiles, lumber, sugar

bare·ly (béərliː) *adv.* only just, merely, *barely four years old* ‖ scantily, *a barely furnished room*

Bar·ents (bǽrents), William (c. 1550–97), Dutch navigator. While searching for the Northeast Passage he explored Novaya Zemlya (1594–5) and discovered Barents Island and Spitsbergen (1596)

Barents Sea the eastern part of the northernmost Arctic Ocean between Spitsbergen, Novaya Zemlya and N. Scandinavia: fisheries

bar·gain (bárgin) *v.i.* to haggle over terms ‖ *v.t.* to offer as terms of a bargain, *he bargained his own life in return for his son's safety* **to bargain for** to estimate, expect, *more guests arrived than she had bargained for* [fr. O.F. *bargainer*]

bargain *n.* an agreement on terms of give and take ‖ something acquired or offered cheaply, or advantageously **into the bargain** in addition to the terms agreed, as well **to conclude** (or **drive** or **make** or **settle** or **strike**) **a bargain** to come to terms [O.F. *bargaine*]

bargain basement the section of a department store where cheap goods are sold

barge (bɑrdʒ) **1.** *n.* a flat-bottomed freight boat without sails, chiefly used on rivers and canals ‖ a lighter, a similar boat with one dandy-rigged mast ‖ the second boat of a man-of-war, used by chief officers ‖ a large, ornamental, oared boat for state occasions **2.** *v.i. pres. part.* **barging** *past* and *past part.* **barged** to move about clumsily ‖ (with 'in', 'into') to intrude ‖ (with 'into') to collide (with someone) [O.F.]

barge·board (bárdʒbɔrd, bárdʒbɔurd) *n.* a board, sometimes ornamental, running along the edge of a house gable, to prevent rain from driving in

bar·gee (bɑrdʒíː) *n.* (*Br.*) a bargeman **to swear like a bargee** (*Br.*) to swear fluently and often

bar·gel·lo (bɑrdʒélou) *n.* a hand stitch in zig-zag pattern

barge·man (bárdʒmən) *pl.* **barge·men** (bárdʒmən) *n.* (*Am.* = *Br.* bargee) a man in charge of a barge, or who works on one

barge pole a pole used for propelling a barge, and for fending **not to touch with a barge pole** (*Br.* = *Am.* not to touch with a 10-ft pole) to have nothing at all to do with

bar·girl (bárgərl) *n.* a prostitute headquartered at a bar

Bar·ham (bǽrəm), the Rev. Richard Harris (1788–1845), English author of the 'Ingoldsby Legends' (1837–46), comic tales in verse written under the pseudonym Thomas Ingoldsby

Ba·ri (bári:) S.E. Italy's largest town (pop. 376,500) on the Adriatic, in Apulia, a trade center since Roman times. Exports: olive oil, almonds, wine, grain. University (1936). Cathedral, church of San Nicola (both 11th c.)

Bari *pl.* **Ba·ris** *n.* a Nilotic people of S. Sudan ‖ a member of this people ‖ their Nilotic language

ba·ri·at·rics (bəariːǽtriks) *n.* medical science of weight reduction and nutrition —**bariatrician** *n.*

Ba·ri·san Mtns (bɑrisán) two largely volcanic ranges (1,000 miles long) along the western side of Sumatra, Indonesia (Kerintji: 12,467 ft)

bar·ite (bǽrait, béərait) *n.* barytes

bar·i·tone, bar·y·tone (bǽritoun) **1.** *n.* a male voice between tenor and bass ‖ a man having such a voice **2.** *adj.* having the range and quality of a baritone voice [F. *barytone* fr. Gk]

bar·i·um (bǽriːəm, béəriːəm) *n.* a silver-white, toxic, divalent, metallic element in the alkaline earth group (symbol Ba, at. no. 56, at. mass 137.34). It occurs in combination with other elements. It is used in insecticides, paints, steel etc. [fr. Gk *barus*, heavy]

barium hydroxide the base $Ba(OH)_2$

barium meal a solution of barium sulfate swallowed by a patient before X-ray examination. It helps diagnosis because it is opaque to X rays and so reveals an obstruction

bark (bɑrk) **1.** *n.* (not used technically) the tissue in woody stems and roots external to the cambium. It usually includes phloem, pericycle, cortex and epidermis ‖ cinchona bark ‖ tanbark **2.** *v.t.* to strip or peel bark from (a tree) ‖ to tan ‖ to scrape the skin from, *to bark one's shins* [M.E. *barke* fr. O.N.]

bark 1. *v.i.* to make the sharp, explosive, vocal noise characteristic of dogs ‖ *v.t.* to snap out sharply and abruptly, *to bark an order* **to bark up the wrong tree** to misdirect one's attack, be on the wrong track **2.** *n.* the brief, explosive cry of esp. dogs and foxes ‖ any similar sound, a very bad cough *his bark is worse than his*

bite he speaks angrily but is really harmless [O.E. *beorcan*]

bark, barque (bɑrk) *n.* a three-masted vessel with fore and main masts square-rigged, and mizzenmast fore-and-aft-rigged [F. *barque* fr. Ital.]

bark beetle any of several beetles of fam. *Scolytidae* which damage the bark of pine, ash, elm and other trees

bark cloth tapa (cloth)

bar·keep (bárki:p) *n.* a barkeeper

bar·keep·er (bárki:pər) *n.* a person who keeps or tends a bar for the sale of alcoholic drinks

bark·en·tine, bar·quen·tine (bárkənti:n) *n.* a three-masted vessel with the foremast square-rigged and the others fore-and-aft-rigged [fr. BARK, like *brigantine*]

bark·er (bárkər) *n.* a person who drums up trade by shouting, e.g. for a sideshow

Bark·ley (bárkli:), Alben William (1877–1956), 35th U.S. vice-president. He served as senate majority leader (1937–47) prior to his election (1948) as vice-president under Harry S. Truman

Bark·ly Tableland (bárkli:) a belt of rich pasture country (area 500,000 sq. miles) in N.E. Northern Territory, Australia, between the desert and the Gulf of Carpentaria

bark pit a pit of bark and water for tanning

bark tree cinchona

bar·ley (bárli:) *n.* a cereal grass of genus *Hordeum*. Barley is adapted to higher altitudes, colder weather and a shorter growing season than most other cereals. The grain is used for animal feed, breakfast foods, malt syrup, brewing etc. [O.E. *bœrlic*]

bar·ley·corn (bárli:kɔrn) *n.* a grain of barley

Bar·low (bárlou), Joel (1754–1812), U.S. poet and diplomat. His poems include his paean to America, 'Vision of Columbus' (1787) and his pastoral 'Hasty Pudding' (1796). He served as U.S. plenipotentiary to France (1811–12)

barm (bɑrm) *n.* the yeast formed during the fermenting of liquor [O.E. *beorma*]

bar·maid (bármeid) *n.* a female bartender

bar·man (bármən) *pl.* **bar·men** (bármən) *n.* a bartender

Bar·me·cides (bármisaidz) a Persian family, many of whom were viziers in the caliphate of Baghdad in the 8th c.

bar mitz·vah (bɑrmítsvə) *n.* the Jewish ceremony admitting a boy to adult membership of the Jewish community ‖ the boy himself **bas mitzvah** similar ceremony for a Jewish girl [Heb. *bar miswâh*, son of the divine law]

barm·y (bármi:) *adj.* full of barm, frothy ‖ (*pop.*) daft, balmy

barn (bɑrn) *n.* the unit of cross section in scattering experiments equal to 1 x 10^{-24} cm^2

barn *n.* a farm building for storing grain, hay, farm implements etc. or for housing animals ‖ a large, sparsely furnished building, esp. a house too big to run conveniently [O.E. *bere-ern*, barley-place]

Bar·na·bas (bárnəbəs), St (1st c.), Apostle and martyr, companion of St Paul. Feast: June 11

Bar·na·bite (bárnəbait) *n.* a member of the order of Clerics Regular of St Paul, founded in Milan in 1530

bar·na·cle (bárnək'l) *n.* (usually *pl.*) pincers for a horse's nose to restrain it, esp. during shoeing [O.F. *bernac*, muzzle]

barnacle *n. Branta leucopsis*, a goose of N. Europe ‖ a crustacean of the sub-class *Cirripedia*. It has a motile larval stage, but in the adult stage attaches itself permanently to a rock or ship's bottom etc. [M.E. *bernekke, bernake*, O.F. *bernaque*, M.L. *bernaca*, the goose]

Bar·nard (bárnárd), Christian (1922–), South African surgeon. He performed (1967) the first successful heart transplant. In 1974 he was first to implant a second heart, linking it with original to provide blood and circulation

Barnard, Edward Emerson (1857–1923), U.S. astronomer, at Lick Observatory (1887–95) and Yerkes Observatory (1895–1923). His contributions to observational astronomy and celestial photography included the discovery of 16 comets, Jupiter's fifth satellite, and Barnard star (1916)

Barnard, Frederick Augustus Porter (1809–89), U.S. educator, academic reformer, and president of Columbia College (1864–89). He transformed the small undergraduate institution into a world-famous university, open to women. Barnard College for women was named (1889) after him

Bar·nard College (bárnərd) a women's undergraduate college of Columbia University established (1889) shortly after the death of Frederick A.P. Barnard, after whom it was named

Bar·nar·do (bɑrnárdou), Thomas John (1845–1905), British philanthropist, founder and director of homes for destitute children

Bar·na·ul (bərnaú:l) a city (pop. 549,000) of the R.S.F.S.R., U.S.S.R., in Siberia on the Ob River: engineering and food industries. Cotton from central Asia and Siberia is processed

Bar·nave (bɑrnáv), Antoine Pierre Joseph (1761–93), French politician and revolutionary orator in the Constituent Assembly. After escorting the French royal family from Varennes to Paris (1791), he negotiated with Marie Antoinette to establish a constitutional monarchy. He was guillotined

barn dance a social dance in a barn, usually featuring square dances

Barnes (bɑrnz), Thomas (1785–1841), English journalist, editor (1817–41) of the (London)'Times'. He gave it its particular weight and authority as a responsible paper independent of government or party

Barnes, the Rev. William (c. 1801–86), English (Dorset) dialect poet, author of 'Poems of Rural Life' (1844–62)

Bar·ne·veldt (bárnəvelt), Jan van Olden (1547–1619), Dutch statesman. Having supported the union of Holland (1579) and the appointment of Maurice of Nassau as stadtholder (1584), Barneveldt became political ruler of Holland (1586). He was involved in the quarrels between Remonstrants and orthodox Calvinists and was executed on the orders of Maurice

barn owl *Tyto alba*, a common species of whitebreasted, grayish-brown owl useful to man because it destroys rodents

barn·storm (bárnstɔrm) *v.i.* to perform plays or make political speeches etc. in rural districts ‖ to give sightseeing air trips for a living, or to perform exhibition stunts in an airplane

Bar·num (bárnəm), Phineas Taylor (1810–91), American showman, who created 'The Greatest Show on Earth', a combination of museum, menagerie and circus, with which he traveled around the world

barn·yard (bárnjɑrd) *n.* a farmyard

ba·ro·co·co (bærəkóukou) *adj.* of grotesquely elaborate (baroque plus rococo) style

Ba·ro·da (bəróudə) a former Maratha state now included in Gujarat, India ‖ a city (pop. 467,442) of Gujarat, a textile center. University (1949)

bar·o·gram (bǽrəgræm) *n.* a curve drawn on scaled paper, giving a continuous record of changes in air pressure as measured by an aneroid barometer [fr. Gk *baros, weight+gramma*, a letter]

bar·o·graph (bǽrəgræf, bǽrəgrɑf) *n.* a recording barometer

Ba·ro·ja (baróxa), Pío (1872–1956), Spanish novelist, a realist, anticlerical, last-ditch defender of the freedom of the individual. His works include 'Aurora Roja' (1904) and 'Zalacaín el Aventurero' (1909)

Ba·ro·lo (baróulou) *n.* an Italian dry, red wine

ba·rol·o·gy (bərólədʒi:) *n.* the science of weight [fr. Gk *baros*, weight+*logos*, discourse]

ba·rom·e·ter (bərómitər) *n.* an instrument for measuring atmospheric pressures, used in forecasting weather and in estimating heights above sea level (*MERCURY BAROMETER, *ANEROID BAROMETER) **bar·o·met·ric** (bærəmétrik), **bar·o·mét·ri·cal** *adjs* **ba·róm·e·try** *n.* the science of making barometric measurements [fr. Gk *baros*, weight+METER]

ba·ron (bǽrən) *n.* (*Br.*) a member of the lowest order of nobility (called Lord —, not Baron —) ‖ (in other countries) a nobleman (called Baron —) ‖ a great merchant in some particular commodity, *a beef baron* [O.F. *barun*]

ba·ron·age (bǽrənidʒ) *n.* the whole body of barons ‖ (*Br.*) a book listing peers [O.F. *barnage*]

ba·ron·ess (bǽrənis) *n.* a baron's wife ‖ a lady holding a baronial title in her own right [O.F. *barnesse*]

bar·on·et (bǽrənit, bǽrənet) *n.* (*Br., abbr.* bart) a member of the lowest hereditary titled order, a commoner with precedence over all knights except knights of the Garter

bar·on·et·age (bǽrənitidʒ, bǽrənetidʒ) *n.* baronets collectively ‖ a book listing them

bar·on·et·cy (bǽrənitsi:, bǽrənetsi:) *n.* a baronet's rank or patent

ba·ro·ni·al (bəróuni:əl) *adj.* of, belonging to, or befitting a baron or the baronage

baron of beef a joint of beef consisting of the undivided loins

Bar·ons' War (bǽrənz) a civil war (1264–6) in England between Henry III and a baronial faction led by Simon de Montfort, caused by the barons' attempt to bind Henry to the Provisions of Oxford (1258). The king was captured at Lewes (1264), and Montfort set up one of the earliest parliaments (1265). He was defeated at Evesham (1265) and the king restored

bar·o·ny (bǽrəni:) *pl.* **bar·o·nies** *n.* (*Br.*) a baron's rank or domain ‖ (*Ir.*) a division of a county ‖ (*Scot.*) a large manor [O.F. *baronie*]

ba·roque (bəróuk) *adj.* of painting and sculpture, architecture, literature and music of the late 16th and 17th cc., giving way to rococo art in the 18th c., and having these general characteristics: devices which make the beholder feel he is involved (esp. Bernini's architecture and sculpture), sinuosity of line and form, the portrayal of spiritual ecstasy in terms of physical passion (and vice versa), theatricality (not necessarily in a bad sense). The forms in the visual arts are developed from the classical modes of the Renaissance, but agitated, as it were, and characterized by distortion. Baroque art flourished chiefly in Italy, Spain, Portugal, France, Austria and S. Germany, countries of the Counter-Reformation. Here learning and education were influenced or controlled by the Jesuits, who can be said to have found in baroque art an expression of a reinvigorated Catholicism. Baroque has been adopted in literary criticism to denote esp. the use of the conceit in poetry (by Marino in Italy, Scéve and Sponde in France, and the Metaphysical poets in England) [F. fr. Port. *barroco*, rough pearl, origin unknown]

baroque pearls irregularly shaped pearls, usually obtained from mussels

ba·roq·ue·rie (bəróukæri:) *n.* baroque elements

bar·o·re·cep·tor (bærouriséptər) *n.* (*physiol.*) **1.** nerve cells sensitive to stretching induced by blood pressure changes **2.** any peripheral nerve responsive to mechanical deformation

bar·o·trau·ma (bǽrətrɔumə) *n.* (*med.*) injury to the auditory tube or middle ear resulting from change of pressure

Ba·rot·se·land (bərótsəlænd) a protectorate (area 44,920 sq. miles, pop. 366,000) in Zambia, inhabited by the Barotse tribe. Capital: Mongu Lealui. Very many of its young men go to work in Zimbabwean and South African mines

ba·rouche (bərú:ʃ) *n.* (*hist.*) a fourwheeled carriage with a driver's seat in front, and two double seats inside facing each other, and a collapsible top over the back seat [fr. G. *barutsche* fr. Ital.]

barque *BARK

barquentine *BARKENTINE

Bar·qui·si·me·to (barkí:si:mèto) the capital (pop. 430,000) of Lara state, W. Venezuela, on the Barquisimeto River: sugar, coffee, cacao, rum

bar·rack (bǽrək) **1.** *n.* (esp. *pl.*) a large building for lodging soldiers ‖ (esp. *pl.*) any large, drab building **2.** *v.t.* to place in barracks ‖ (*Br.*) to hoot, jeer (players in a match etc.) [F. *baraque* fr. Ital.]

barracks bag a soldier's duffel bag

bar·ra·cou·ta (bærəkú:tə) *pl.* **bar·ra·cou·ta, bar·ra·cou·tas** *n. Thyrsites atun*, a large food fish (snoek) found off New Zealand, Australia and S. Africa

bar·ra·cu·da (bærəkú:də) *pl.* **bar·ra·cu·da, bar·ra·cu·das** *n.* a member of fam. *Sphyraenidae*, predatory fishes found in warm seas. They have pikelike bodies, long snouts and sharp teeth [fr. Sp.]

bar·rage (barɑ́ʒ, esp. *Br.* bǽraʒ) *n.* the barring of a watercourse to increase its depth ‖ a barrier, esp. of artillery shellfire, to impede enemy action ‖ a formidable number (of questions, protests etc.) poured out in a rush [F.]

barrage balloon a large captive balloon used to support wires to prevent the approach of lowflying aircraft

Bar·ran·qui·lla (bɑrɑŋkí:jɑ) the chief port (pop. 855,195) of Colombia on the delta of the Magdalena River, an industrial city and air terminal. University

Bar·ras (bǽræs), Paul François, Vicomte de (1755–1829), French revolutionist, president of the Convention (1795). As a member of the Directory (1795–9), he was virtual dictator of France

bar·ra·tor, bar·ra·ter (bǽrətər) *n.* someone guilty of barratry [fr. O.F. *barateor*, trickster]

CONCISE PRONUNCIATION KEY: **(a)** æ, c*a*t; ɑ, c*a*r; ɔ f*aw*n; ei, sn*a*ke. **(e)** e, h*e*n; i:, sh*ee*p; iə, d*ee*r; ɛə, b*ea*r. **(i)** i, f*i*sh; ai, t*i*ger; ə:, b*i*rd. **(o)** o, *o*x; au, c*ow*; ou, g*oa*t; u, p*oo*r; ɔi, r*oy*al. **(u)** ʌ, d*u*ck; u, b*u*ll; u:, g*oo*se; ə, b*a*cill*u*s; ju:, c*u*be. x, lo*ch*; θ, *th*ink; ð, bo*th*er; z, *Z*en; ʒ, corsa*g*e. dʒ, sava*g*e; ŋ, orangutan*g*; j, *y*ak; ʃ, *fish*; tʃ, fe*tch*; 'l, rabb*le*; 'n, redd*en*. Complete pronunciation key appears inside front cover.

bar·ra·trous (bǽrətrəs) *adj.* involving or constituting barratry

bar·ra·try (bǽrətri:) *pl.* **bar·ra·tries** *n.* (*marine law*) fraud or negligence on the part of the master to the prejudice of the shipowner ‖ the purchase or sale of Church or State office or preferment ‖ the offense of stirring up lawsuits, quarrels etc. [O.F. *baraterie*, trickery]

barred (bard) *adj.* obstructed by bars ‖ fastened with bars ‖ marked with bars

bar·rel (bǽrəl) 1. *n.* a flat-ended, curved cylindrical container, usually made of wood hooped by metal bands, a cask ‖ the amount that a barrel holds ‖ the metal tube of a gun ‖ the cylindrical body or trunk of an animal ‖ the part of a fountain pen containing the ink ‖ the case containing the mainspring of a clock or a watch ‖ the body of a capstan 2. *v. pres. part.* **bar·rel·ing, bar·rel·ling** *past* and *past part.* **bar·reled, bar·relled** *v.t.* to put in barrels ‖ to cause to travel very fast ‖ *v.i.* to travel very fast [fr. F. *baril*]

barrel chair an easy chair with a high rounded back and sides

barrel distortion in a television receiver, the bulging-out distortion of the picture received

barrel organ an instrument from which music is ground out by turning a handle and causing a cylinder to act mechanically on keys

barrel roll (bǽrəlroul) an aerial maneuver in which the plane turns in a complete sideways revolution

bar·ren (bǽrən) 1. *adj.* sterile, incapable of bearing (children, fruit etc.) ‖ unprofitable, without result, *barren talk* ‖ unable to produce new ideas, dull 2. *n.* (esp. *pl.*) a tract of poor sandy country with little vegetation [O.F. *brahain*, original form uncertain]

bar·re·ra (bərérə) *n.* bullfighting terrain between the matador and the fence, enclosing the bull ring

Bar·rès (bǽres), Maurice (1862–1923), French writer, author of 'les Déracinés' (1897), 'la Colline inspirée' (1913), etc.

bar·rette (bərét) *n.* (*Am.=Br.* hair slide) a hinged clip shaped in the form of a short, slightly curved bar, for keeping a girl's hair in place [F.]

bar·ri·cade (bǽrikeid, bærikéid) 1. *n.* a defense or obstruction, esp. one hastily made across a road or street 2. *v.t. pres. part.* **bar·ri·cad·ing** *past* and *past part.* **bar·ri·cad·ed** to block with a barricade [F.]

Bar·rie (bǽri:), Sir James Matthew (1860–1937), Scottish playwright and novelist, author of 'The Admirable Crichton' (1902), 'Peter Pan' (1904) etc.

Bar·ri·en·tos Or·tu·ño (barrjéntɔsɔrtú:njo), René (1920–69), Bolivian air force general who became president (1964) after a coup d'état. As leader of the new Bolivian Revolutionary Front, he was reelected (1966) constitutionally

bar·ri·er (bǽri:ər) *n.* an obstacle barring advance or access ‖ (*horse racing*) the movable gate at the starting line ‖ something that hinders progress ‖ a mental or emotional obstacle [O.F. *barrière*]

barrier reef a coral reef lying parallel to the shore and separated from it by a lagoon **Barrier Reef** *GREAT BARRIER REEF

bar·ring (bárin) *prep.* excluding, bar

bar·ri·o (bǽri:ou, bárrjo) *n.* the Spanish-speaking quarter of a U.S. town or city ‖ a district of a town or city in Spain or in a Spanish-speaking country

Bar·rios (bárrjɔs), Eduardo (1884–1963), Chilean novelist. His works, notably 'El hermano asno' (1922), show the influence of French skepticism on Spanish social and religious tradition

Barrios, Justo Rufino (1835–85), president of Guatemala (1873–85) and a champion of Central American unity. When his diplomatic efforts failed to restore the five-nation Central American confederation, he led an invasion of El Salvador (1885)

bar·ris·ter (bǽristər) *n.* (*Br.*) a lawyer having the right to speak and argue in the superior courts [etym. doubtful]

bar·ris·ter-at-law (bǽristərətlɔ́) *pl.* **bar·ris·ters-at-law** *n.* (*Br.*) a barrister

bar·row (bǽrou) *n.* a small wheeled handcart ‖ a wheelbarrow [M.E. *barewe*]

barrow *n.* (*archaeol.*) a grave mound, tumulus ‖ (*Br.*, in place names) a hill [O.E. *beorg*, hill]

Bar·row, Point (bǽrou) the northernmost point of Alaska, on the Arctic Ocean

Bar·ry (bǽri:), Sir Charles (1795–1860), British architect. He promoted the neo-Gothic style. His best-known building is the Palace of Westminster

Bar·ry (bǽri:), Jeanne Bécu, comtesse du (1743–93), mistress of Louis XV of France. She was guillotined on her return to France (1793) from England, where she had fled

Bar·ry (bǽri:), John (1745–1803), the first U.S. commodore. He won important naval engagements during the Revolutionary War, including the last sea battle of the war in the Gulf of Florida (1783), in which he repulsed three British frigates. His successful training of naval officers, including Stephen Decatur, earned him the title 'Father of our Navy'

Barrymore (bǽrimɔr), Anglo-American family of stage and film. Maurice Barrymore (1847–1905), father, and Georgianna Drew (1856–93), mother, acted in England and the U.S. and appeared together in 'Diplomacy' (1886). Their son Lionel (1878–1954), especially known for his role of Dr. Gillespie, appeared in other movies such as 'A Free Soul' (1931; Academy Award), 'Grand Hotel' (1932), and 'Dinner at Eight' (1933). His sister Ethel (1879–1959) appeared on the stage in 'Captain Jinks of the Horse Marines' (1901) and 'The Corn is Green' (1940), and in the film 'None But the Lonely Heart' (1944; Academy Award). Their brother John (1882–1942) became a matinee idol who acted in films such as 'A Bill of Divorcement' (1932) and 'Twentieth Century' (1934). They appeared together in 'Rasputin and the Empress' (1932)

Bar·sac (barsǽk) *n.* a semisweet white Bordeaux wine from near the Garonne [after *Barsac* in the Gironde]

bar sinister an oblique reference to a person's bastardy, from the heraldic term 'bend sinister'

bar·tend·er (bártendər) *n.* an attendant at a bar serving alcoholic drinks

bar·ter (bártər) 1. *v.t.* to exchange (goods or services against something else) without using money ‖ *v.i.* to engage in such trade 2. *n.* trade by exchange ‖ the thing exchanged [perh. fr. O.F. *barat*, fraud]

Barth, Heinrich (1821–65), German explorer. His travels in the Sahara, Sudan and Central Africa (1850–55) began a new era in the exploration of Africa

Barth, John (1930–), U.S. writer, noted for his experimental fiction. His novels include 'The Floating Opera' (1956), 'The End of the Road' (1958), 'The Sot-Weed Factor' (1960), 'Giles Goat-Boy' (1966), 'Letters' (1979), and 'Sabbatical' (1982). Short stories are collected in 'Lost in the Funhouse' (1968)

Barth, Karl (1886–1968), Swiss Protestant theologian who rejected what he held to be the errors of post-Renaissance humanism in the name of revealed religion and a doctrine of total grace. His teaching is called 'crisis' (Gk.=judgment) theology, emphasizing the gulf between the Creator and his creatures, which can be bridged only by God

Bar·thé·le·my (bærteilmi:), François, marquis de (1747–1830), French statesman. He negotiated the Treaties of Basle (1795), and became a member of the Directory (1797)

Bar·thol·di (bærtɔldi:), Frédéric Auguste (1834–1904), French sculptor. He made the Statue of Liberty presented by the French people to the U.S.A. in 1886, and the Lion of Belfort (1880) carved in the living rock, commemorating the defenders of Belfort against the Germans in 1870

Bar·thol·o·mew (barθɔ́ləmju:), St (1st c.). one of the 12 Apostles. Feast: Aug. 24

Bartholomew, Massacre of St the murder of Huguenots by Catholics in Paris, Orléans, and other French towns which began on St. Bartholomew's Day, Aug. 24, 1572. Catherine de' Medici and the Guises persuaded Charles IX to consent to it

bar·ti·zan (bártiz'n, bartizǽn) *n.* a small turret projecting from a wall or tower [form of *bratticing*, *BRATTICE]

Bar·tók (bártɔk), Béla (1881–1945), Hungarian composer, editor, folksong scholar and pianist, one of the outstanding European composers of the 20th c. His music often draws on Magyar folk melodies and their strong dance rhythms. He was also a master of classical theory. His work includes six string quartets, concertos for piano, violin, and viola, concerto for orchestra, etc.

Bar·to·lom·me·o (bartɔləméiou), Fra (1472–1517), Florentine painter, and member of the Dominican order. His secular name was Baccio della Porta. Most of his work was devotional

Bar·ton (bárt'n), Clara (1821–1912), founder of the American Red Cross (1881–2)

Barton, Sir Edmund (1849–1920), first federal prime minister of Australia (1901)

Bar·uch (báruk) disciple and scribe of Jeremiah and presumed author of the book of Baruch in the Old Testament Apocrypha

Bar·uch (bərú:k), Bernard Mannes (1870–1965) U.S. financier and statesman, unofficial adviser to Presidents Wilson, Roosevelt and Truman, and also to Winston Churchill, and U.S. representative (1946–51) to the U.N. Atomic Energy Commission

bar·ye (bǽri:) *n.* a bar (in the cgs system) [F. fr. Gk *barys*, heavy]

bar·y·on (bǽri:ɒn) *n.* one of a group of eight known fundamental particles having spin quantum number ½, large rest mass and variable electric charge. Baryons include the nucleons in addition to other known particles [fr. Gk *barys*, heavy + *-on*, fundamental particle]

Ba·rysh·ni·kov (baríʃnɒkʌf), Mikhail (meekhyl') (1948–), Russian ballet dancer and choreographer who defected to the West in 1974. With the Kirov Ballet at the time of defection, he joined the American Ballet Theatre (1974–8). He is noted for dancing the classics as well as modern dances. 'Push Comes to Shove' (1976) was created for him. He joined the New York City Ballet in 1978 and became its director in 1980. He has also appeared in the films 'The Turning Point' (1978) and 'White Nights' (1985)

ba·ry·ta (bəráitə) *n.* any of several compounds of barium [fr. Gk *barus*, heavy]

baryta water a suspension of barium hydroxide in water

ba·ry·tes (bəráiti:z) *n.* native barium sulfate, heavy spar [fr. Gk *barus*, heavy]

barytone *BARITONE

ba·sal (béis'l, béiz'l) *adj.* of, or forming, the base ‖ at or near the base

Ba·sal·gan·li·a (beis'lgǽnli:ə) *n.* (*physiol.*) nerve cells connecting cerebrum with other nerves

basal metabolic rate the rate at which heat is given off by an organism at complete rest. Measurement of it indicates an individual's general metabolism or state of health

basal metabolism the metabolism of an organism in the dormant state, when it uses just enough energy to maintain vital activities, as measured by the basal metabolic rate

ba·salt (bəsɔ́lt, bǽsɔlt) *n.* black or dark gray rock, chiefly sodium or potassium alumino-silicates, with some iron, basic in character, supposed to constitute the bulk of the earth beneath its solid crust, and found as intrusions at the surface in some places ‖ black stoneware invented by Wedgwood [fr. L. *basaltes*, perh. fr. African]

bas·cule (bǽskju:l) *n.* a counterbalancing apparatus [F.=seesaw]

bascule bridge a counterpoised lift bridge or drawbridge

base (beis) *adj.* morally low, contemptible ‖ menial, degrading ‖ (of metals) low in value, not precious ‖ (of coins) debased, spurious ‖ (*mus.*) bass [F. *bas*]

base 1. *n.* the bottom, the lowest part, *the base of the skull* ‖ that on which something is mounted or to which it is fixed and on which it stands ‖ groundwork ‖ foundation ‖ the stem or root of a word, to which suffixes are added ‖ (*archit.*) the lower part of a column or wall when treated as a separate feature ‖ the place from which an army or military force starts and where its supplies are ‖ a starting place in certain games, or a place to which players try to get ‖ the essential ingredient of a mixture ‖ (*chem.*) a substance which, dissolved in water, provides hydroxyl ions from its own molecules ‖ (*chem.*) a molecule or ion which can accept protons ‖ (*geom.*) the line or area on which a figure stands ‖ (*securities*) level at which the pressure of lower prices meets strong resistance in creating demand ‖ (*math.*) a number of reference upon which mathematical tables are built, e.g. in logarithmic tables ‖ (*biol.*) that end of a part which is attached to the main portion ‖ (*survey.*) the precisely measured distance from which triangulation starts **off base** (*baseball*) not on one's base ‖ (*pop.*) wrong, mistaken 2. *v.t. pres. part.* **basing** *past* and *past part.* **based** to found (deductions etc.), *what do you base your suspicions on?* [F. fr. L. fr. Gk]

base address (*computer*) a number that modifies related addresses, noting a reference point for each program. When added to the relative addresses, this provides an absolute address necessary for machine transfer of data

base·ball (béisbɔl) *n.* the national game of the U.S.A. The field is divided into infield, or diamond, and outfield. The bases are at the corners of the diamond. There are two teams of 9 players, a game having 9 innings. The ball, which is semisoft and covered in leather, is thrown, or pitched, by the pitcher from about the center of the diamond to the batter on the home plate or base. The bat is about 3 ft long. The catcher stands behind the batter, one fielder guards each of the three bases and the rest (other than shortstop) are placed strategically in the outfield. The object of the game is to score 'runs' by hitting the ball and running round the diamond. There are two main professional baseball leagues and about 40 minor ones in the U.S.A., and the game has spread to many countries ‖ the ball used

base·board (béisbɔrd, béisbourd) *n.* (*Am.=Br.* skirting board) a board, often with a decorative molding, running along the bottom of an interior wall and covering the join of wall and floor

Ba·se·dow's disease (bázədouz) exopthalmus [after Karl von *Basedow* (1799-1854), G. physician]

base exchange commissary at an armed forces base

base hit (*baseball*) a hit which enables a batter to reach first base before the ball is thrown there

Ba·sel (báz'l) *BASLE

base·less (béislis) *adj.* groundless, without foundation

Ba·sel-Land (báz'llɒnt) *BASLE

Ba·sel-Stadt (báz'lʃtɒt) *BASLE

base·ment (béismənt) *n.* the story of a building below the ground floor ‖ (*archit.*) a supporting structure on which the main order, e.g. of a Renaissance château, rests

base·ness (béisnis) *n.* the state or quality of being base ‖ a base act

ba·sen·ji (bəséndʒi:) *n.* a small dog of an ancient African breed. It is chestnut brown in color, and rarely barks [Afrik.=bush thing]

base pair (*gen.*) two nucleotides in a nucleic acid-cytosine and guanine or adenine and thymine or uracil, all of which constitute DNA

ba·ses (béisi:z) *pl.* of BASIS ‖ (béisiz) *pl.* of BASE

bash (bæʃ) **1.** *v.t.* (*pop.*) to strike violently ‖ (*pop.*) to smash or buckle ‖ *v.i.* to crash, collide **2.** *n.* (*pop.*) a violent blow ‖ (*pop.*) the damage caused by such a blow [imit.]

bash·ful (bæʃfəl) *adj.* shy, self-conscious [fr. obs. v. *bash*, abash]

bash·i·ba·zouk (bæʃi:bəzú:k) *n.* (*hist.*) a soldier belonging to the irregular Turkish troops, notorious for plundering and cruelty [Turk. *bashi*, head+*bazuq*, disorderly]

Bash·kir·i·an A.S.S.R. (bʌʃkíəri:ən) an autonomous republic (area 54,233 sq. miles, pop. 3,860,000) of the R.S.F.S.R., U.S.S.R. in S.E. Europe: oil, coal, steel, copper, agriculture (esp. grain), horse breeding

Bash·kirt·seff (bʌʃkjíərtsef), Marie (1860–84), Russian painter who lived in Paris, famous for her 'Journal' (1887)

Ba·shō (báʃou), Matsuo (1643–94), Japanese poet and teacher of haiku prosody, author of 'Oku no Hosomichi' (1689)

ba·sic (béisik) *adj.* fundamental ‖ forming a basis ‖ (*chem.*) relating to or having the characteristics of a base ‖ (*geol.*) an igneous rock containing between 45% and 55% silica ‖ (*metall.*) steel made by a nonsilica process

BASIC (*computer acronym*) for Beginners All-purpose Symbolic Instruction Code, computer language using many terms in English in its programs

basic encyclopedia (*mil.*) compilation of identified military installations and physical areas of potential significance as objectives for attack

Basic English a selection of 850 English words intended as a possible international language and for use in learning English, invented b C. K. Ogden. 'Basic' is formed from the initial letters of British, American, Scientific, International, Commercial

basic health services minimum supply of health services that should be generally and

uniformly available in order to assure a population's adequate health and protection from disease, or to meet some other criteria or standards

ba·sic·i·ty (beisísiti:) *n.* the degree to which a compound is basic ‖ the number of ionizible hydrogen atoms in an acid, being equal to the number of equivalents of a base that will react with 1 mole of the compound

basic slag a by-product of steel manufacture, used as a fertilizer because of its high content of phosphorus

basic training training in the basic elements of military service etc.

ba·sid·i·o·my·cete (bəsidi:oumaisí:t) *n.* a member of *Basidiomycetes*, a large class of the most highly developed fungi, predominantly sexual in their mode of reproduction and possessing a basidium. The class includes both parasitic forms (e.g. rusts and smuts) and saprophytic forms (e.g. mushrooms) **ba·sid·i·o·my·cé·tous** *adj.* [fr. N.L. *Basidiomycetes*]

ba·sid·i·o·spore (bəsidi:ouspɔr, bəsidi:ouspour) *n.* a spore produced by a basidium

ba·sid·i·um (bəsidi:əm) *pl.* **ba·sid·i·a** (bəsidi:ə) *n.* (*bot.*) a conidiophore characteristic of basidiomycetes, bearing usually a fixed number (four) of basidiospores [fr. L. fr. Gk dim. of *basis*, base]

Bas·il (bæz'l), St (c. 329–79), Greek patriarch. He preserved his Church from Arianism and secured the triumph of the Nicene definitions at the Council of Constantinople (381). He is one of the founders of monasticism. Feast: June 14

bas·il (bæz'l) *n.* a member of *Ocimum*, fam. *Labiatae*, a genus of aromatic plants, esp. *O. basilicum*, sweet basil, and *O. minimum*, bush basil, used as culinary herbs [O.F. *basile* fr. L. *basilisca*]

bas·i·lar membrane (bæsələr) the membrane partitioning part of the cochlea which translates mechanical vibrations into nerve impulses

ba·si·lect (béisilekt) *n.* dialect of the lower classes *Cf* ACROLECT

Basil I 'the Macedonian' (c. 812–86), Byzantine emperor (867–86). He gained the throne by murdering two rivals. He introduced legal and financial reforms and tried unsuccessfully to heal the religious schism between East and West

Basil II 'Bulgaroctonus' (c. 957–1025), Byzantine emperor (963–1025). In a reign of almost continuous warfare and expansion, he inflicted great atrocities on the Bulgarians (986–1018)

ba·sil·ic (bəsílik) *adj.* (*anat.*) of a large vein of the upper arm [fr. F. fr. L. *basilicus*, kingly fr. Gk]

ba·sil·i·ca (bəsílikə, bəzílikə) *n.* a large Catholic church ranking next to a cathedral, and having certain privileges. There are four major basilicas, all in Rome, and several minor ones. A basilica is built to an oblong ground plan, with an apse. The nave roof is generally higher than that of the flanking aisles [L. fr. Gk *basilikē*, royal (edifice)]

Ba·si·li·ca·ta (bɑzi:li:kátə) (formerly Lucania) a mountainous region (area 3,856 sq. miles, pop. 617,300) on the Gulf of Taranto, S. Italy

bas·i·lisk (bæsəlisk, bæzəlisk) *n.* a member of *Basiliscus*, fam. *Iguanidae*, a genus of small Central American lizards. They have a crest on the head which can be inflated at will ‖ a mythical African reptile allegedly hatched by a serpent from a cock's egg, its breath or look being said to be fatal [fr. L. fr. Gk *basiliskos*, little king]

ba·sin (béis'n) *n.* a hollow vessel for holding a liquid ‖ a dock, or group of docks ‖ a tract of land drained by a river and its tributaries ‖ (*geol.*) a depression in older strata in which more recent strata may have been deposited [O.F. *bacin*]

bas·i·net (bæsinet) *n.* (*hist.*) a light steel helmet with a visor [O.F. *bacinet*, dim. of *bacin*, basin]

ba·si·on (béisi:ɒn) *n.* the midpoint of the front rim of the foramen magnum [Mod. L.]

ba·sis (béisis) *pl.* **ba·ses** (béisi:z) *n.* a foundation, base ‖ an underlying principle ‖ the main ingredient in a mixture ‖ (*commodities*) the difference between the spot or cash price of a commodity and the futures price of the same or a related commodity, usu. computed to the near future. This difference may represent different time periods, product forms, qualities and locations ‖ (*math*) a set of linearly independent vectors in a vector space, in which each vector

in the space is a linear combination of vectors from the set [fr. L. fr. Gk]

bask (bæsk, bɑsk) *v.i.* to luxuriate in warmth and light, or in something compared with these, *to bask in reflected glory* [O.N. *bathask*, to bathe oneself]

Bas·ker·ville (bæskərvil), John (1706–75), English printer. His editions of Milton, the Bible and the Latin classics were set in type designed by himself. This has been revived for machine composition

bas·ket (bæskit, báskit) *n.* a vessel (often of wicker or other flexible material), for containing shopping, laundry, wastepaper etc. ‖ the quantity contained in a basket ‖ the passenger part of a balloon ‖ a goal in basketball [origin unknown]

bas·ket·ball (bæskitbɔl, báskitbɔl) *n.* a fast indoor or outdoor ball game played by two teams of five men or six women. A circular open-bottomed basket is fixed 10 ft above the ground at each end of the court, and a goal is scored by throwing the ball into the opponent's basket. Basketball originated at Springfield College, Mass., in 1891 ‖ the ball used

basket chair a deep wicker armchair

Basket Maker a member of an early Indian culture supposed by archaeologists to have inhabited the southwest region of North America between 100 and 700 A.D.

bas·ket·ry (bæskitri:, báskitri:) *n.* the art of making baskets ‖ things worked in cane, osiers etc.

Basket Three accord negotiated at Helsinki, Finland, espousing belief in the free movement of people and ideas and national self-determination; signed by 33 nations at Helsinki as part of 1975 Conference on Security and Cooperation in Europe *Cf* HELSINKI AGREEMENT

basket weave a style of weaving in which the pattern imitates the interlacing of a plaited basket

bas·ket·work (bæskitwəːrk, báskitwəːrk) *n.* basketry

basking shark *Cetorhinus maximus*, the largest species of shark

Basle (bɑːl) (F. Bâle, G. Basel) a former canton of Switzerland at the junction of the Swiss, German and French frontiers, divided since 1833 into Basel-Land (area 164 sq. miles, pop. 219,822, capital Liestal) and Basel-Stadt (area 14 sq. miles, pop. 203,915) ‖ the capital (pop. 182,143) of the latter, a commercial center with chemical, pharmaceutical and silk ribbon industries. University (1460), Romanesque cathedral

Basle, Council of an ecclesiastical council (1431–49) for Church reform, the settlement of the Hussite wars, and the reunion of Christendom. It became a struggle for supremacy between pope and council

Basle, Treaties of treaties signed Apr. 5 and July 22, 1795 by Prussia, Spain and France. France retained the left bank of the Rhine, and gave up all her conquests beyond the Pyrenees. Spain surrendered Santo Domingo to France, which gave the latter all Hispaniola, but Spain recovered Santo Domingo in the Treaty of Paris (1814). Prussia and Spain left the coalition against France (*FRENCH REVOLUTIONARY WARS)

ba·so·phil (béisəfil) *n.* a basophile

ba·so·phile (béisəfail) *n.* (*biol.*) a cell or tissue readily stained with basic dyes, e.g. a leucocyte possessing this property **ba·so·phil·ic** (beisəfílik) *adj.* readily stained with basic dyes

Basque (bæsk) **1.** *n.* a native of the Pyrenees region on the Bay of Biscay in France and Spain. The Basques, thought to be one of the oldest races in Europe, resisted conquest by the Romans, Visigoths, Moors and Franks, and defeated Charlemagne at Roncesvalles (778). They established (824) the kingdom of Navarre ‖ the Basque language **2.** *adj.* of the Basques or their language [F.]

basque (bæsk) *n.* a continuation of the bodice of a dress below the waist, separate from the skirt and over it [F.]

Basque country (F. Pays basque) a region of France in the Western Pyrenees, now included in Pyrénées Atlantiques department. It consists of the French share of old Navarre, with smaller former Basque states north of it. The mountains produce cattle, lumber, cereals, vines, and hydroelectricity. The coast, on the Bay of Biscay, has many resorts (Biarritz, Hendaye, Saint-Jean-de-Luz)

CONCISE PRONUNCIATION KEY: **(a)** æ, c*a*t; ɑ, c*a*r; ɔ f*aw*n; ei, sn*a*ke. **(e)** e, h*e*n; i:, sh*ee*p; iə, d*ee*r; ɛə, b*ea*r. **(i)** i, f*i*sh; ai, t*i*ger; əː, b*i*rd. **(o)** o, *o*x; au, c*ow*; ou, g*oa*t; u, p*oo*r; ɔi, r*oy*al. **(u)** ʌ, d*u*ck; u, b*u*ll; uː, g*oo*se; ə, b*a*cillus; juː, c*u*be. x, lo*ch*; θ, *th*ink; ð, bo*th*er; z, *Z*en; ʒ, corsa*g*e; dʒ, sava*g*e; ŋ, orangutan*g*; j, *y*ak; ʃ, *f*ish; tʃ, *f*etch; 'l, rabb*le*; 'n, redd*en*. Complete pronunciation key appears inside front cover.

Basque language a language spoken in the W. Pyrenees by about half a million people. Basque is unrelated to any other present-day European language. It constitutes an isolated remnant of an Iberian language which may have been spoken in France and Spain. It can be traced back only as far as the 16th c.

Basque provinces (*Span.* Vascongadas) a group of Spanish provinces at the west end of the Pyrenees: Guipúzcoa and Vizcaya, bordering the Bay of Biscay, and Alava, in the dry inland mountains. Crops: vegetables, cereals, olives, vines. Livestock: cattle, sheep. Fishing is important. Mines (iron, lead, copper) make this a great industrial region. Chief town: Bilbao. Previously included in Navarre, the provinces were taken by Castile (13th–14th cc.). Movement for Basque separation developed 19th–20th centuries. A militant separatist organization, ETA, has led movement since 1959. Home rule was granted in 1980 but ETA continued fight. The Spanish government and ruling Basque Nationalist party formed peace alliance in 1985

Bas·ra (bæzrə) a town and port (pop. 720,000) of Iraq on the Shatt-el-Arab, exporting petroleum and dates

bas-re·lief (bɑrilí:f, bæsrilí:f) *n.* carving or sculpture in which the figures or designs project less than halfway from the background (cf. HIGH RELIEF) [F. fr. Ital. *basso-rilievo*, low relief]

Bas-Rhin (bɑrɛ̃) a department (area 1,848 sq. miles, pop. 882,100) in N.E. France. (*ALSACE) Chief town: Strasbourg

bass (bæs) *pl.* **bass, bass·es** *n. Perca fluviatilis,* a European freshwater fish ‖ any of numerous fish of fam. *Serranidae* or fam. *Centrarchidae.* They are spiny-rayed food and game fishes of both saltwater and freshwater [O.E. *bœrs,* name of a fish]

bass (beis) 1. *n.* the lowest part in harmonized music ‖ the lowest male singing voice, extending 1½ octaves or more below middle C ‖ a singer with such a voice 2. *adj.* deep in tone or pitch [F. *bas,* respelled after Ital. *basso,* low]

bass (bæs) *n.* bast

bass clef (beis) (*mus.*) the symbol indicating F below middle C as the next to top line of the staff

bass drum (beis) the largest and deepest-toned of the drums used in a symphony orchestra or military or dance band. It is shallow and has two heads

Bas·sein (bəséin) a port (pop. 126,045) on the Irrawaddy delta, S. Burma, 80 miles from the sea: rice milling

Basses-Py·ré·nées (bɑspi:reinei) *PYRÉNÉES-ATLANTIQUES

bas·set (bæsit) 1. *n.* (*geol.*) the exposure of a stratum at the surface of the ground 2. *v.i.* to crop out at the surface [etym. doubtful]

Basse-Terre Is. *GUADELOUPE

Basse-Terre, La (bɑstɛər) the capital (pop. 14,700) of Guadeloupe, a seaport on the southwest coast of Basse-Terre Is.

basset horn a musical instrument like a clarinet, but lower in pitch, now rarely used [trans. of Ital. *corno di bassetto*]

basset hound a short-legged hunting dog of a breed used for digging out foxes and badgers [F.]

Bas·sett (bæsit), Richard (1745–1815), U.S. political leader. He served his state, Delaware, as a representative to the Constitutional Convention (1787), as U.S. senator (1789–93), as chief justice of the court of common pleas (1793–9), and as governor (1799–1801). He was appointed judge of the U.S. circuit court (1801) by President John Adams

bass horn (beis) a tuba

bas·so (bæsou) *n.* a bass voice ‖ a bass singer [Ital.]

bas·soon (bəsú:n) *n.* a wooden musical instrument of the double reed type, the lowest of all the woodwind instruments in pitch except the double bassoon **bas·sóon·ist** *n.* a bassoon player [fr. F. *bassoon*]

bass staff (beis) *pl.* **bass staves** (*mus.*) the staff carrying the bass clef

Bass Strait (bæs) a channel 80 to 150 miles wide and 180 miles long, separating Australia and Tasmania

bass viol (beis) the viola da gamba ‖ the double bass, contrabass

basswood (bæswʊd) *n. Tilia americana,* fam. *Tiliaceae,* the American lime or linden ‖ its wood

bast (bæst) *n.* the phloem ‖ any flexible fibrous bark, esp. that of the lime used in ropemaking etc., or the fiber commonly used for tying up plants [O.E. *bœst,* inner bark of a lime tree]

bas·tard (bæstərd) 1. *n.* an illegitimate child (used also as a term of abuse) ‖ something false or of questionable origin or departing from standard ‖ a hybrid 2. *adj.* illegitimate ‖ not genuine, counterfeit ‖ of an unusual shape or size, *a bastard type* ‖ hybrid [O.F.]

bas·tard·ize (bæstərdaiz) *pres. part.* **bas·tard·iz·ing** *past* and *past part.* **bas·tard·ized** *v.t.* to declare to be illegitimate

bastard wing a process on the first digit of a bird's wing, usually consisting of three quill feathers

bas·tar·dy (bæstərdi) *n.* illegitimacy

baste (beist) *pres. part.* **bast·ing** *past* and *past part.* **bast·ed** *v.t.* to pour hot liquids over (esp. meat) during roasting to prevent its drying out ‖ to pour melted wax on (wicks) in candle making ‖ (*pop.*) to thrash or batter (someone) [etym. doubtful]

baste *pres. part.* **bast·ing** *past* and *pastpart.* **bast·ed** *v.t.* to stitch temporarily with large loose stitches [O.F. *bastir*]

Bas·ti·a (bɑstí:ɑ) an old port (pop. 50,100) in N.E. Corsica, the island's chief trading center. Products: cheese, olive oil, tobacco. Citadel (14th c.)

Bas·ti·das (bɑstí:ðɑs), Rodrigo de (1460–1526), Spanish explorer and conquistador. He led an expedition to the Venezuelan and Colombian coasts and reached Panama (1501), founding Santa Marta

Bas·tille (bæsti:l, bæsti:j) a former state prison in Paris, built 1369–83 and now completely demolished. The storming of the Bastille (July 14, 1789) by the citizens of Paris was a symbol of the destruction of absolute royal power and is still celebrated as a national holiday (*FRENCH REVOLUTION)

bas·ti·na·do (bæstinéidou) 1. *pl.* **bas·ti·na·does** *n.* the punishment of beating someone on the soles of his feet 2. *v.t.* to administer a bastinado to [Span. *bastonada* fr. *baston,* stick]

bast·ing (béistin) *n.* a temporary stitching with large, loose stitches ‖ the thread used in basting

bas·tion (bæstʃən, bæsti:ən) *n.* part of a fortification, with two flanks, which juts out from the main defense work ‖ any strong defense [F. fr. Ital.]

Ba·su·to·land (bəsú:toulænd) *LESOTHO

bat (bæt) *n.* a member of *Chiroptera,* an order of nocturnal, mouselike, flying mammals **to have bats in the belfry** to be crazy or eccentric [perh. fr. Scand.]—Bats inhabit temperate and tropical areas. While most genera are insectivorous, some are fruit eaters and a few (vampires) suck mammalian blood. They are the only flying mammals, having forelimbs and hands modified to form wings

bat *pres. part.* **bat·ting** *past* and *past part.* **bat·ted** *v.t.* to wink (an eyelid), blink (one's eyes), as a sign of surprise or emotion [var. of obs. V. *bate,* to flutter]

bat 1. *n.* the special club or implement used for hitting the ball in baseball, cricket etc. ‖ a turn at batting (in cricket, baseball) ‖ a blow with or as if with a bat ‖ the rounded signaling instrument used for guiding aircraft on to aircraft carriers ‖ a moist lump of potter's clay **off one's own bat** (*Br.=Am.* on one's own hook) unaided, on one's own initiative **off the bat** immediately 2. *v. pres. part.* **bat·ting** *past* and *past part.* **bat·ted** *v.t.* to strike with or as if with a bat ‖ *v.i.* to take a turn at batting [etym. doubtful]

Ba·taan Peninsula, Battle of (bətǽn, bətɑ́n) a battle of the 2nd world war in the Philippines in which U.S. and Filipino troops were defeated (1942) by Japanese forces. Bataan is a province of W. Luzon

Ba·ta·vi·a (bətéivi:ə) the former name for Djakarta ‖ (*hist.*) an island at the mouth of the Rhine inhabited (c. 1st–3rd cc.) by the Batavi **Ba·tá·vi·an** 1. *n.* an inhabitant of Batavia in Java or of ancient Batavia 2. *adj.* of or concerning Batavia (Java) or ancient Batavia

Batavian Republic (*hist.*) the name given to the Seven United Provinces of the Netherlands (1795–1806)

batch (bætʃ) *n.* a quantity (of loaves or cakes) produced at one baking ‖ a number or quantity of things produced at one time or to be taken together as a set, *a batch of recruits* ‖ (*computer*) several items capable of being processed with the same program at one time [M.E. *bache* fr. O.E. *bacan,* to bake]

batch process an industrial process which is not continuous, one cycle of operations being completed and the product removed or utilized before the cycle is repeated

bate (beit) 1. *n.* an alkaline lye for making hides supple 2. *v.t. pres. part.* **bat·ing** *past* and *past part.* **bat·ed** to soak in this [etym. doubtful]

bated breath breath held in fear, apprehension, anticipation etc. [older *bate* v. fr. ABATE]

Bates (beits), Katharine Lee (1859–1929), U.S. author and educator. Her works include the hymn, 'America the Beautiful' (1911), written while she was a professor at Wellesley College

Bath (bæθ, bɑθ) a county borough (pop. 84,300) in Somerset, England, noted since Roman times for its medicinal springs and esp. fashionable during the 18th c., the date of much of its architecture

bath (bæθ, bɑθ) 1. *n.* the immersion of the body or part of it in water to clean it, or as a minor pleasure ‖ (*pl.*) an indoor swimming pool, or public building where a person can go to wash himself ‖ water for a bath ‖ exposure of the body to the sun, steam etc. ‖ (*chem.*) a medium (water, air, sand, soil etc.) for regulating the temperature of anything placed in it ‖ the vessel containing such a medium ‖ a medium (e.g. oil) in a container, used for some special purpose (e.g. lubrication), or the container itself 2. *adj.* accessory to a bath, used for a bath 3. *v.t.* (*Br.*) to wash (someone) in a bathtub ‖ *v.i.* (*Br.*) to bathe (in a bathtub) [O.E. *bœth*]

Bath chair a three-wheeled chair for taking out an invalid

bathe (beið) *pres. part.* **bath·ing** *past* and *past part.* **bathed** *v.t.* to wash by immersion ‖ to apply water or other liquid to, *to bathe one's eyes* ‖ to surround or envelop, *bathed in sunshine* ‖ *v.i.* to go swimming ‖ to wash oneself in a bathtub [O.E. *bathian*]

ba·thet·ic (bəθétik) *adj.* marked by bathos

bath·house (bǽθhaus, bɑ́θhaus) *pl.* **bath·houses** (bǽθhauziz, bɑ́θhauziz) *n.* a building for bathers to undress in on a beach ‖ a building containing public baths

bathing costume (*Br.*) a bathing suit

bathing suit a garment worn for swimming

bath·o·lith (bǽθəliθ) *n.* (*geol.*) a deep-sited intrusion of igneous rock [fr. Gk *bathos,* depth + *lithos,* rock]

ba·thom·e·ter (bəθómitər) *n.* an instrument for measuring the depth of water [fr. Gk *bathos,* depth + *-meter*]

ba·thos (béiθos) *n.* a sudden drop from the sublime or elevated to the ludicrous ‖ an anticlimax [Gk = depth]

bath·robe (bǽθroub, bɑ́θroub) *n.* a wrap put on before or after bathing or used as a dressing gown

bath·room (bǽθru:m, bɑ́θru:m, bǽθrum, bɑ́θrum) *n.* a room containing a bathtub and shower and often a washbasin and toilet ‖ (a euphemism for) a toilet

Bath·she·ba (bæθʃí:bə, bæθʃəbə) the mother of Solomon. She married David after he had secured the death of her first husband, Uriah the Hittite

bath·tub (bǽθtʌb, bɑ́θtʌb) *n.* the receptacle in which one washes one's body

Bath·urst (bǽθərst) *BANJUL

ba·thym·e·try (bəθímitri:) *n.* 1. the measurement of water 2. underwater topography

bath·y·scaphe (bǽθiskæf) *n.* a spherical bell for diving to great depths in the ocean for purposes of exploration [F. fr. Gk fr. *bathys,* deep + *skaphē,* light boat]

bath·y·sphere (bǽθisfjer) *n.* a large spherical steel chamber able to withstand great pressure, used for deep-sea observation [fr. Gk *bathys,* deep + SPHERE]

ba·tik (bətí:k, bǽtik) *n.* a method of working designs in dyes on fabric by coating with wax any parts to be left undyed, the wax being boiled off after the dyeing process. The technique is repeated for each color used in a pattern ‖ a fabric so printed [Malay]

Ba·tis·ta (bətí:stɑ), General Fulgencio (1901–73), Cuban soldier and dictator. After a coup d'état (1933) Batista was president (1940–4, 1952–4). He was reelected (1954) but deposed by the Castro revolution (1959)

ba·tiste (bətí:st, bætí:st) *n.* a fine fabric of linen or cotton [F., after Jean *Baptiste* of Cambrai, who first made it]

CONCISE PRONUNCIATION KEY: **(a)** æ, c*a*t; ɑ, c*a*r; ɔ f*aw*n; ei, sn*a*ke. **(e)** e, h*e*n; i:, sh*ee*p; iə, d*ee*r; ɛə, b*ea*r. **(i)** i, f*i*sh; ai, t*i*ger; ə:, b*i*rd. **(o)** o, *o*x; au, c*ow*; ou, g*oa*t; u, p*oo*r; ɔi, r*oy*al. **(u)** ʌ, d*u*ck; u, b*u*ll; u:, g*oo*se; ə, b*a*cillus; ju:, c*u*be. x, lo*ch*; θ, *th*ink; ð, bo*th*er; z, *Z*en; ʒ, cor*s*age; dʒ, sava*g*e; ŋ, orangutan*g*; j, *y*ak; ʃ, *f*ish; tʃ, fe*tch*; 'l, rabb*le*; 'n, redd*en*. Complete pronunciation key appears inside front cover.

Bat·lle Ber·res (bátjebéres), Luis (1897–1964), Uruguayan politician, leader of the Colorado party, and president (1947–51). He initiated the law (1952) abolishing the four-year presidency in favor of a nine-man National Council of Government, over which he presided (1955–9)

Bat·lle y Or·dó·ñez (bátjeiɔrɔ́ɔ́njes), José (1856–1929), president of Uruguay (1903–7, 1911–15). As a journalist he founded 'El Día', which became Uruguay's leading newspaper. He then joined the Colorado party. During his two presidential terms, he fought to improve the lot of the lower-income groups, to eliminate the influence of the Church in government, and to create a plural bipartisan executive, which he achieved by dividing the executive powers between the president and a new independent national council of administration (1917). He was an early advocate of a world political organization

bat·man (bátmən) pl. **bat·men** (bátmən) n. (Br., mil.) an officer's servant [fr. F. bat, pack saddle+MAN]

ba·ton (bətón, bæt'n) n. a short stick used by policemen as a weapon, or in some countries for directing traffic ‖ (mus.) the stick with which the conductor beats time ‖ a staff which is a symbol of office ‖ the stick carried in a relay race ‖ the stick twirled by a drum majorette in a parade ‖ round rubber bullet fired from a baton gun [F.]

baton gun riot control device that fires large hard rubber bullets Cf STUN GUN

Bat·on Rouge (bæt'nrú:ʒ) the capital (pop. 219,486) of Louisiana, on the Mississippi. Industries: sugar, oil refining. University (1860)

baton sinister (heraldry) a truncheon in a shield, a sign of bastardy [F.]

ba·tra·chi·an (bətréiki:ən) 1. adj. of or relating to the Batrachia, the salientians 2. n. a salientian ‖ an amphibian [fr. Mod. L. Batrachia fr. Gk batrachos, a frog]

ba·tra·chi·tox·in [C₃₁H₄₂N₂O₆] (bətréikətpksin) n. (pharm.) steroid venom derived from a frog's skin

bats·man (bætsmən) pl. **bats·men** (bætsmən) n. (cricket) the player whose turn it is to bat ‖ a person who signals with bats in his hands to guide aircraft landing on carriers

bat·tal·ion (bətæljən) n. (mil.) a unit of infantry consisting of a headquarters and two or more companies ‖ (pl.) a large fighting or warlike force, battalions of ants [F. battalion fr. Ital. battaglione (battaglia, battle)]

bat·ten (bæt'n) 1. n. a long board used for flooring etc. ‖ a strip of wood for nailing or clamping across others ‖ (theater) a strip of wood from which stage lights are suspended ‖ (naut.) a strip of wood nailed on to a spar to prevent rubbing, or for fastening down the edges of tarpaulins covering the hatches ‖ (naut.) a wooden bar from which hammocks are slung 2. v.t. to strengthen with battens to **batten down the hatches** to fasten the hatches of a ship [var. of BATON]

batten n. the bar used in silk weaving to strike the weft [fr. F. battant]

batten v.i. (with 'on') to seize on (someone) and profit at his expense ‖ (with 'on') to seize on (an excuse, argument etc.) [perh. fr. O.N. batna, get better]

bat·ter (bætər) n. (baseball and cricket) the player whose turn it is to bat

batter 1. v.t. to strike (something or someone) violently and often ‖ to beat out of shape ‖ to impair by hard usage ‖ v.i. to strike, heavily and often, waves battered on the cliff 2. n. a semiliquid mixture, esp. of eggs, flour and milk beaten before cooking ‖ a damaged surface in printing type or stereotype plate [fr. bat-, beat, as in O.F. batre]

batter 1. v.i. (of a wall) to slope slightly out of the vertical 2. n. the slope of a wall from the ground as it narrows towards the top [etym. doubtful]

battered child syndrome condition or group of symptoms, esp. bodily injuries, indicating physical abuse of a young child

battering ram (hist.) a long, heavy beam with an iron head, used as an engine of war to break into a fortification against which it was rammed (either carried forward by a number of men or swung by ropes from a framework)

bat·ter·y (bætəri) pl. **bat·ter·ies** n. a battering ‖ a verbal attack ‖ (mil.) a unit of artillery ‖ the emplacement of a unit's guns and the men who use them ‖ a double row of cannon on a warship ‖

(elec.) a grouping of cells, condensers etc., for making electricity, esp. for a car, radio etc. ‖ (mus.) an orchestra's percussion section ‖ (optics) a combined series of lenses or prisms ‖ (law) a blow or a menacing touching of a person or his clothes or anything he is carrying or holding, assault and battery ‖ (baseball) the pitcher and catcher together [F. batterie]

bat·ting (bætiŋ) n. the act of using a bat ‖ a cotton fiber prepared in sheets for quilting etc.

batting average (baseball) the average obtained by dividing the number of a player's safe hits by the number of times at bat ‖ (cricket) the ratio of runs scored to innings completed

bat·tle (bæt'l) n. a fight between armies or forces ‖ a combat between two individuals **to do battle** (rhet.) to fight [O.F. bataille]

battle pres. part. **bat·tling** past and past part. **bat·tled** v.t. to fight, to battle one's way ‖ v.i. to struggle

bat·tle-ax, bat·tle-axe (bæt'læks) n. a medieval long-handled ax used as a weapon ‖ (pop.) a sour, formidable woman

battle cruiser a heavily armed warship, faster but more vulnerable than a battleship

battle cry (hist.) a rallying cry or cry to inspire courage ‖ a slogan

bat·tle·dore (bæt'ldɔr, bæt'ldour) n. a light racket used to bat a shuttlecock in the game of battledore and shuttlecock [perh. fr. Port. batedor, beater]

battledore and shuttlecock a children's game, a primitive form of badminton

battle dress a soldier's uniform of belted blouse and trousers

bat·tle·field (bæt'lfi:ld) n. a place where a battle is or was fought

battle group (mil.) a standing naval force consisting of an aircraft carrier, surface combatants, and submarines as assigned in direct support, operating in mutual support with the task of destroying hostile forces on land or sea within the group's assigned area of responsibility

bat·tle·ment (bæt'lmənt) n. (usually pl.) a crenelated parapet formerly used for defense [M.E. bateillment fr. O.F.]

bat·tle·ship (bæt'lʃip) n. the most heavily armored warship, largely replaced by aircraft carriers, themselves being superseded by missile-carrying submarines

bat·tue (bætú:, bætjú:) n. the act of beating undergrowth etc. to drive game on to the guns ‖ a shooting party conducted in this manner, a beat [F.]

bat·ty (bæti:) comp. **bat·ti·er** superl. **bat·ti·est** adj. (pop.) crazy

Ba·tu·mi (bátu:mi:) (Batum) the capital (pop. 126,000) of the Adzharian A.S.S.R., U.S.S.R., on the east coast of the Black Sea, terminus of the oil pipeline from Baku

Ba·twa (bátwa) pl. **Ba·twa, Ba·twas** n. a pygmy people inhabiting the Republic of the Congo and Rwanda ‖ a member of this people

bau·ble (bɔb'l) n. a bright, showy trinket of no value ‖ (hist.) a stick carried by a jester or court fool [fr. O.F. babel, child's toy]

Baucis *PHILEMON AND BAUCIS

baud (bɔd) n. (computer) unit of signaling data transmission equal to the number of code elements per sec

Bau·de·laire (boud'lɛar), Charles (1821–67), French poet, critic and moralist. His chief work is the collection of poems 'les Fleurs du mal' (1857). He deals with the most sordid aspects of life in Paris, and of life in general, in exact and beautiful language. 'Les Fleurs du mal' was the object of public prosecution on its publication, yet in these poems voluptuous pleasures are set against an ideal order, and judged inferior. He influenced the Symbolists both through his own approach to writing and technique, and by his theory (formulated in the sonnet 'Correspondances') that all the arts are one and are a manifestation of the universal essence.

Bau·doin I (boudwɛ̃) (1930–), king of the Belgians (1951–)

Bau·dot code (bɔdóu) a binary code based on five or six binary digits to represent each character; also known as Standard Teletypewriter Code

Bau·haus (báuhaus) a German art school, the first to stress collaboration in pure art, architecture and crafts and to insist that problems of design must be solved in accordance with the spirit of an industrial, mechanized age. Founded at Weimar by Gropius in 1919, the school's faculty included Klee, Kandinsky,

Breuer and Mies van der Rohe. The Bauhaus was at Dessau (1925–32). When the Nazis came to power the chief teachers went to the U.S.A. Many of their ideas, e.g. functionalism and the refusal to conceal structure or the nature of material, have become standard practice

Ba·u·lé (bau:léi) pl. **Ba·u·lé, Ba·u·lés** n. a people living in the savanna of the Ivory Coast, famous for their goldsmiths' work (cire perdue) and sculpted masks in wood ‖ a member of this people

baulk *BALK

Bau·tzen, Battle of (báuts'n) a decisive victory (1813) of Napoleon over the allied armies of Prussia and Russia

baux·ite (bɔ́ksait, bóuksait) n. a naturally occurring aluminum oxide, Al₂O₃·nH₂O, the commercial source of aluminum, consisting of various proportions of the trihydrated and the monohydrated forms. The most important deposits occur in the Guianas, U.S.A., Ghana, Jamaica, Brazil and Hungary [fr. Baux, in France]

Ba·var·i·a (bəvéari:ə) (G. Bayern) the southeastern state (area 27,239 sq. miles, pop. 10,849,200) of West Germany, a wooded highland between the northern Alps and the Bohemian Forest (Austrian and Czech frontiers), largely arable. Agriculture: cereals, potatoes, fruit, hops, vines, pig and cattle breeding. Industries: brewing, textiles, precision instruments, tourism. Main towns: Munich (the capital), Nuremberg, Augsburg. The area was controlled by the Magyars (10th c.) and Guelphs (1070–1180). Otto I of Wittelsbach founded a line which ruled Bavaria as a duchy (1180–1806), then as a kingdom until 1918. It became an electorate (1623). It suffered in the struggles between Prussia and Austria, but gained strength during the Napoleonic Wars. After leading the smaller states in the struggle against Prussia, it joined the German Empire (1871)

bawd (bɔd) n. a woman who keeps a brothel [etym. doubtful]

bawd·i·ly (bɔ́dili:) adv. in a bawdy way

bawd·i·ness (bɔ́di:nis) n. the quality or state of being bawdy

baw·dry (bɔ́dri:) n. bawdiness

bawd·y (bɔ́di:) comp. **bawd·i·er** superl. **bawd·i·est** adj. obscene, lewd

bawdy house a brothel

bawl (bɔl) v.t. to shout, to bawl curses ‖ v.i. to cry loudly and without restraint [perh. fr. M.L. baulare, to bark]

Bax (bæks), Sir Arnold (1883–1953), English composer. His best-known works are the tone poem 'Tintagel' (1917) and his violin concerto (1937)

bay (bei) n. a wide inlet of the sea ‖ a recess in a mountain range [F. baie]

bay 1. adj. (of a horse) reddish brown 2. n. a reddish-brown horse [F. bai]

bay n. Laurus nobilis, the European laurel ‖ (hist., pl.) a wreath of laurel leaves given to conquerors, poets etc. [O.F. baie, berry]

bay n. one of the divisions into which an architectural whole may be divided, e.g. by columns, arches etc. ‖ a recess or part of a structure set aside for a particular purpose, a bomb bay ‖ a railroad platform with a blind end used as the terminus of a side line ‖ the cul-de-sac of such a platform [F. baie fr. bayer, to gape]

bay 1. n. the cry of hounds on the scent ‖ a dog's wail **at bay** (of an animal) forced to face its pursuers and defend itself **to bring to bay** to force (a quarry or victim) to turn and defend itself **to keep** (or **hold**) **at bay** to prevent from coming in to attack ‖ to ward off 2. v.i. to bark (esp. during pursuit of a quarry) ‖ v.t. to bark at, to bay the moon [O.F. bay, suspense and abai, barking]

Bay·ard (bæjær), Pierre du Terrail, Seigneur de (c. 1474–1524), French soldier, 'le chevalier sans peur et sans reproche'. He was killed in battle after covering himself with glory in the wars of Charles VIII, Louis XII and Francis I

Ba·yard (báiard), Thomas Francis (1828–98), U.S. lawyer, statesman, and diplomat. As U.S. Senator from Delaware (1869–85), he became a leader of the Democrats in the Senate. Under President Grover Cleveland, he served as secretary of state (1885–9), and as ambassador to Great Britain (1893–7), the first U.S. envoy to London to hold that rank. His views were considered too sympathetic to Britain, and the House of Representatives passed a vote of censure against him

---

CONCISE PRONUNCIATION KEY: **(a)** æ, cat; ɑ, car; ɔ fawn; ei, snake. **(e)** e, hen; i:, sheep; iə, deer; ɛə, bear. **(i)** i, fish; ai, tiger; ə:, bird. **(o)** o, ox; au, cow; ou, goat; u, poor; ɔi, royal. **(u)** ʌ, duck; u, bull; u:, goose; ə, bacillus; ju:, cube. x, loch; θ, think; ð, bother; z, Zen; ʒ, corsage; dʒ, savage; ŋ, orangutang; j, yak; ʃ, fish; tʃ, fetch; 'l, rabble; 'n, redden. Complete pronunciation key appears inside front cover.

Ba·ya·zid I (bajazí:d) *BAJAZET I

bay·ber·ry (béiberi:) *pl.* **bay·ber·ries** (béiberi:z) *n. Myrica pennsylvanica,* fam. *Myricaceae,* a wax myrtle ‖ *Pimenta racemosa* or *P. acris,* fam. *Myrtaceae,* a species of pimento yielding all-spice, native to the West Indies (*BAY RUM)

Bay·er (bájɛər), Johann (1572–1625), German astronomer whose 'Uranometria' (1603) included a catalog of the stars and an improved method of naming them which has been universally adopted

Ba·yeux Tapestry (bæjœ:, beijú:) a panorama, embroidered on a band of linen 231 ft long by 20 ins wide, in wools of eight colors, representing in 72 scenes the conquest of England by William the Conqueror in 1066. It was probably designed by an artist of the Canterbury school, and worked by English craftsmen c. 1088–92. It is now preserved in the Bayeux Museum, France

Bay Islands a group of islands in the Caribbean Sea off the coast of N. Honduras

Bayle (bel), Pierre (1647–1706), French philosophical writer whose 'Dictionnaire historique et critique' (1696–7) breathed the spirit of skepticism later found esp. in Voltaire

Bay of Pigs (*Span.* Bahía de Cochinos) a bay in S. Cuba and site of an unsuccessful invasion (Apr. 1961) by anti-Castro exiles secretly supported by the U.S.A. Some 1,100 of the invaders were taken prisoner. They were ransomed (1962) by the U.S. government

Bay of Plenty a large bay on the northeast coast of Auckland, New Zealand, bordered by a narrow alluvial plain: a noted dairy area

bay·o·net (béiənit, béiənet) 1. *n.* a dagger which can be attached to a rifle 2. *v.t. pres. part.* **bay·o·net·ing, bay·o·net·ting** *past* and *past part.* **bay·o·net·ed, bay·o·net·ted** to stab with a bayonet ‖ to compel or coerce with or as if with a bayonet [F. *baïonette* perh. fr. *Bayonne*]

bayonet joint a joint in which two mechanical parts are so interlocked that they cannot be separated by longitudinal movement

Ba·yonne (bæjɔn) a fortified port (pop. 44,706) and trade and industrial center in the Basque region of S.W. France. Gothic cathedral

bay·ou (báju:, báijou) *n.* (*Am.*) a marshy creek or tributary to another river (used of offshoots of the lower Mississippi basin and rivers in the Gulf coast region) [Choctaw *bayoue*]

Bay·reuth (bairɔ́it) a town (pop. 66,900) on the upper Main, Bavaria, Germany, famous as the home of Richard Wagner and (since 1876) for the performance of his operas at yearly festivals in the opera house which he himself designed. Manufactures: textiles, porcelain, machine tools

bay rum a fragrant medicinal and cosmetic liquid, orig. made by distilling rum with leaves of the West Indian bayberry

bay window a window projecting out, usually in a curve, from the outside wall of a building

bay·wood (béiwud) *n.* mahogany from the Bay of Campeche, Mexico, or Honduras

ba·zaar (bəzár) *n.* an Oriental marketplace or permanent market, where goods of all kinds are bought and sold ‖ a sale of goods donated by people in order to raise money for some charity etc. [fr. Pers. *bāzār,* market]

ba·zoo·ka (bəzú:kə) *n.* (*mil.*) a portable antitank rocket launcher used in the 2nd world war [origin unknown]

BB (bí:bi:) *n.* a shot pellet of 0.18 in. diameter for use in cartridges ‖ a shot pellet of 0.175 in. diameter for use in a BB gun

B.B.C. British Broadcasting Corporation

BB gun a smooth-bore air gun firing BB ammunition

B.C. (following the date) before Christ ‖ British Columbia

BCAS (*mil. acronym*) for beacon collision avoidance system

BCD (*computer*) abbr for binary coded decimal, a typewriter code method of transmitting each figure in a decimal number by a 4-figure binary number

B cell or **B lymphocyte** derived from the bone marrow, a cell that carries antigens on its surface that, when stimulated, produce circulating antibodies *Cf* T CELL

bdel·li·um (déli:əm, déljəm) *n.* a member of *Commiphora,* a genus of trees yielding a gum resin like myrrh ‖ this gum resin [L. fr. Gk *bdellion* for Heb. *b'dolakh* (of uncertain meaning)]

be (bi:) (*pres.* **I am, you are, he, she, it is, we, you, they are** *past* **I was, you were, he, she, it was, we, you, they were**) *pres. part.* **be·ing**

past part. **been** (bin) *v.i.* used as a copulative or connective verb, *tomorrow is Monday, the shirt is green* ‖ to equal, *let x be* 3 ‖ to add up to, *three threes are nine* ‖ to cost, *the fare is 60 cents* ‖ to become, *he intends to be rich* ‖ to exist, *they maintain that God is* ‖ to live ‖ to continue, *will it always be like this?* ‖ to remain, *will you be here long?* ‖ (followed by the infinitive) used to express obligation, *you are to go at once* or intention, *she is to stay two weeks* or possibility, *it was not to be denied* ‖ used as an auxiliary verb with the past participle of transitive verbs to form the passive voice, *the damage was repaired* ‖ used with the present participle to form the continuous tenses (active and passive), *they are working, plans were being made* **to be for** to be in favor of, *he is for abolishing exams* ‖ **to wish or intend to partake of,** *who's for a drink?* ‖ **to be the way to,** *this is the road for Manchester* ‖ (*Br.*) to be on the way to, *is anyone here for Brighton?* **to be oneself** to be behaving in a normal or usual fashion ‖ to be in good health [irregular defective verb made up of the surviving inflections of three originally independent verbs (themselves irregular) i.e. the orig. Aryan substantive verb, stem *es-* (whence *is*), the verb *wes,* O.E. *wesan,* to remain, stay, continue to be (whence *was*) and the stem *ben,* O.E. *bēon,* to become (whence *be*)]

Be (*chem.*) beryllium

be- *prefix* around, about ‖ (in verbs, with 'with') to surround or cover, *bedewed with sweat* ‖ (with 'with') to affect in any way, *befuddled with wine* [O.E. weak form of *bi,* prep. and adv., by]

beach (bi:tʃ) 1. *n.* the shore of the sea or a lake washed by the water and covered by sand, shingle or larger rocks 2. *v.t.* to draw (a boat) up on to the shore [origin unknown]

beach capacity an estimate, expressed in terms of measurement tons or weight tons, of cargo that may be unloaded over a designated strip of shore per day

beach·comb·er (bí:tʃkoumər) *n.* a person who loafs about beaches and wharves to gather flotsam and jetsam for sale, esp. a white person who does this in the Pacific Islands ‖ a long wave rolling upon the beach

beach·head (bí:tʃhed) *n.* a fortified position established on an enemy shore by landing troops ‖ the physical objective of an amphibious operation ‖ by extension, *business* a foothold in a new market for a product or service

beach·mas·ter (bí:tʃmæstər, bí:tʃmɑstər) *n.* an officer in charge of disembarking troops

beach·wear (bí:tʃwɛər) *n.* clothing designed especially to be worn on the beach

bea·con (bí:kən) *n.* a fire or light used as a signal, e.g. to guide sailors to shore or warn them of a shoal, reef, etc. ‖ a lighthouse ‖ (*Br.,* in place names) a conspicuous hill [O.E. *bēacn*]

Bea·cons·field (bí:kənzfi:ld), earl of *DISRAELI

bead (bi:d) 1. *n.* a small ball pierced for threading and used with others for ornament, e.g. in a necklace or fabric trimming, or for a rosary, an abacus etc. ‖ a small round drop, *a bead ofsweat* ‖ a small metal knob used for a front sight on a gun ‖ (*archit.*) a molding like a row of beads, beading ‖ that part of a tire which grips the rim of a wheel ‖ (*pl.*) a necklace ‖ (*pl.*) the rosary **to draw a bead on** to aim at **to tell one's beads** to say the rosary 2. *v.t.* to supply or cover with beads or as if with beads, *beaded with dew* ‖ to adorn with beading ‖ *v.i.* to form or grow into beads [O.E. *gebed,* prayer]

bead·ing (bí:diŋ) *n.* a beaded molding ‖ beadwork ‖ a narrow lacework through which a ribbon may be run

Bea·dle (bí:d'l), George Wells (1903–), U.S. geneticist and co-winner of the Nobel prize for physiology and medicine (1958), for his experiments at Stanford University on the red bread mold *Neurospora crassa,* bringing to light new information on genes and biochemical processes. He was appointed president of the University of Chicago in 1961

bea·dle (bí:d'l) *n.* (*Br.*) an attendant who walks before dignitaries in procession, a mace-bearer ‖ (*Br.,* in some universities) an officer who precedes processions of staff and students ‖ (*Br., hist.*) a parish officer whose duties include keeping order in church [O.E. *bydel* fr. *bēodan,* to announce]

bea·dle·dom (bí:d'ldəm) *n.* (*Br.*) tiresome officiousness

beads·man, bedes·man (bí:dzmən) *pl.* **beads·men, bedes·men** (bí:dzmən) *n.* (*hist.*) a pensioner bound to pray for his benefactor

bead·work (bí:dwə:rk) *n.* ornamental work in beads

bead·y (bí:di:) *comp.* **bead·i·er** *superl.* **bead·i·est** *adj.* beadlike ‖ (of eyes) small, round and glittering

bea·gle (bí:g'l) *n.* a small, short-legged hound for hunting hares **béa·gling** *n.* hunting hares with beagles, the huntsmen following on foot [perh. fr. F. *bégueule,* open-mouthed]

'Bea·gle', H.M.S. *DARWIN, Charles

beak (bi:k) *n.* the projecting jaws of a bird, made of hard material and differently adapted for ripping, striking etc. ‖ the similar curving mandible of certain other animals, e.g. the turtle ‖ a hooked nose ‖ any beaklike projection, e.g. the prow of an ancient warship ‖ a spout [F. *bec*]

beak·er (bí:kər) *n.* an antique drinking vessel ‖ a tumbler-shaped drinking mug in pottery, plastic etc. ‖ a deep, widemouthed, thin-walled, cylindrical vessel with a pouring lip for scientific experiments [M.E. *biker* fr. O.N. *bikarr,* goblet]

beaker folk a Stone Age people who spread from Spain to central Europe and Britain in the 2nd millennium B.C. They are identified by the characteristically decorated beakers and bowls generally found in graves

beam (bi:m) 1. *n.* a long, heavy piece of wood used with others in building for supporting a roof, ceiling etc. ‖ a ray of light ‖ a gleam ‖ a bright smile ‖ a cylinder of wood in a loom, on which the warp is wound ‖ the bar of a balance from which the scales hang ‖ the lever in an engine connecting the piston rod and crank ‖ one of the horizontal timbers which join the two sides of a ship and support the deck ‖ the widest part of a ship ‖ (*phys.*) a group of parallel light rays as used in geometrical optics ‖ a directional radio or other electromagnetic-radiation signal used to maintain aircraft on course ‖ a stream of electrons or other particles, e.g. in a vacuum tube or particle accelerator **on the beam** on course ‖ functioning well **on the starboard (port) beam** on the right (left) side of a ship **to fly (or ride) the beam** to fly an aircraft on the course given by a radio beam 2. *v.i.* to send forth rays of heat or light ‖ to smile broadly ‖ *v.t.* (*radio*) to aim (a broadcast) in a particular direction [O.E. *bēam,* tree]

beam compass a compass with sliding sockets used for drawing large circles

beam-ends (bí:mendz) *pl. n.* the ends of beams, usually on a ship **on her beam-ends** (of a ship) on her side, almost capsizing **to be on one's beam-ends** to have no money, be broke

beam·ing (bí:miŋ) *adj.* sending forth rays ‖ smiling broadly

beam rider (*mil.*) a missile guided by radar, radio beam, or electronic beam

beam·width (bí:mwidθ) *n.* (*electr.*) the angle of radio beam reception

bean (bi:n) *n.* one of the seeds from any of several climbing or erect leguminous plants, esp. of genus *Phaseolus* ‖ a plant producing these seeds ‖ the edible pod of certain of these plants and the seeds in it, *runner beans* ‖ any of several fruits or seeds that resemble beans, *coffee bean* [O.E. *bēan*]

bear (bɛər) *n.* a member of *Ursidae,* a family of heavily built, thick-furred, plantigrade, carnivorous mammals found throughout all the northern hemisphere and some parts of the tropics ‖ a rough, ill-mannered person ‖ (*stock exchange*) someone who sells stock in the hope of buying it at a lower price later, esp. one who speculates for a decline by selling short [O.E. *bera*]

bear *pres. part.* **bear·ing** *past* **bore** (bɔr, bour) *past part.* **born, borne** (bɔrn, bourn) *v.t.* to support, *to bear weight* ‖ to sustain, *to bear expense* ‖ to carry, *to bear arms* ‖ to be marked with, *to bear an inscription* ‖ to have and be known by, *to bear a well-known name* ‖ to conduct, *crowds bore her to her car* ‖ to tolerate, *to bear pain* ‖ to admit of, *to bear several meanings* ‖ to be suitable for, *the joke does not bear repetition* ‖ to give birth to ‖ to produce, *to bear fruit* ‖ to carry or conduct (oneself) ‖ to give, offer, *to bear witness* ‖ *v.i.* to change direction by something less than a turn, *to bear to the right* **to bear down** to press downwards ‖ (*naut.*) to sail to leeward **to bear down on (or upon)** to sail or move rapidly towards, esp. in a menacing way ‖ to be a burden on **to bear on (or upon)** to relate to the **bear out** to confirm **to bear up** to uphold ‖ (*naut.*) to bring a boat's head into the wind ‖ to remain courageous **to bear up for** (*naut.*) to change a ship's direction so as to sail towards (some point

CONCISE PRONUNCIATION KEY: **(a)** æ, c*a*t; ɑ, c*a*r; ɔ f*aw*n; ei, sn*a*ke. **(e)** e, h*e*n; i:, sh*ee*p; iə, d*ee*r; ɛə, b*ear*. **(i)** i, f*i*sh; ai, t*i*ger; ə, b*i*rd. **(o)** o, *o*x; au, c*ow*; ou, g*oa*t; u, p*oo*r; ɔi, r*oy*al. **(u)** ʌ, d*u*ck; u, b*u*ll; u:, g*oo*se; ə, b*a*cillus; ju:, c*u*be. x, lo*ch*; θ, *th*ink; ð, bo*th*er; z, *Z*en; ʒ, cor*s*age; dʒ, sava*g*e; ŋ, ora*ng*utang; j, *y*ak; ʃ, *fi*sh; tʃ, fe*tch*; 'l, rabb*le*; 'n, red*den*. Complete pronunciation key appears inside front cover.

or mark) **to bear with** to be patient with [O.E. *beran*]

bear animalcule a tardigrade

bear·bait·ing (béərbeitiŋ) *n.* (*hist.*) the sport of setting dogs on a chained bear

beard (bíərd) **1.** *n.* the hair that grows on the lower part of men's faces ‖ the chin hair of a goat, or similar appendage of other animals ‖ the gills of an oyster ‖ the awns of grasses, e.g. barley ‖ (*printing*) the part of the type metal which accommodates ascenders and descenders **2.** *v.t.* to face up to (someone) boldly, to defy [O.E.]

Beards·ley (bíərdzli:), Aubrey Vincent (1872–98), English artist in black and white. His work, chiefly illustrations to Malory's 'Le Morte Darthur', Pope's 'Rape of the Lock', Wilde's 'Salome' etc., is distinguished by refined and mannered craftsmanship, sometimes applied to the grotesque and the obscene

bear·er (béərər) *n.* a load-bearing beam etc. ‖ someone who helps to carry a coffin ‖ (in India), a servant or messenger ‖ someone holding a check etc. for payment, *payable to bearer* or someone carrying a communication to or from someone ‖ a tree etc. in respect to its yield, *a poor bearer*

Bear Flag Republic a republic proclaimed (1846) by American settlers in California led by John Charles Frémont. During the Mexican War (1846–8) it was supported by U.S. army and naval forces

bear garden a scene of rowdiness (formerly a place for bearbaiting and other rough sports)

bear grass any of various plants of fam. *Liliaceae*, esp. *Yucca glauca* of Oklahoma and New Mexico

bear·ing (béəriŋ) *n.* the action of carrying ‖ carriage, deportment ‖ (*heraldry*) a single charge ‖ relevancy, *that has no bearing on the matter* ‖ endurance, the capacity to tolerate, *behavior past all bearing* ‖ (*pl.*) position in relation to some reference point ‖ (*pl.*) grasp of one's situation, *to find one's bearings* ‖ a part of a machine that bears the friction set up by a moving part. Sliding friction is reduced by making the bearing of Babbitt metal, and by separating it and its moving part by a thin film of lubricant. By the introduction of ball bearings (or roller bearings) sliding friction is replaced by rolling friction, which is much less in effect ‖ an angle measured from true north, magnetic north, or from some given survey line **to lose one's bearings** to be lost ‖ to be puzzled

bearing rein a rein fixed from bit to saddle to keep a horse's head up and its neck arched

bear·ish (béəriʃ) *adj.* surly, bad-tempered ‖ (*stock exchange*) tending to show a price decline ‖ (*stock exchange*) acting on the assumption that prices will decline

Bé·arn (beiærn) a former province of France in the S.W. Aquitaine basin, bordering the Pyrenees, a plateau growing vines and cereals (esp. corn). It is now included in Pyrénées Atlantiques department. Historic capitals: Orthez (until 1620), Pau. A viscountship from the 10th c., it passed to Foix (13th c.), Navarre (15th c.) and the French crown (1620)

bear·skin (béərskin) *n.* a rug etc. made of a bear's fur ‖ (*Br.*) a guardsman's tall fur hat

Be·as (bí:as) a tributary (400 miles long) of the Sutlej, flowing from the W. Himalayas through Himachal Pradesh and the N. Punjab, India

beast (bi:st) *n.* any four-legged animal, esp. a wild one ‖ a farm animal ‖ a person with savage, brutal ways **béast·ly** *comp.* **beast·li·er** *superl.* **beast·li·est** *adj.* revolting to any of the senses ‖ (of a man) behaving like a beast ‖ (of human conduct) befitting a beast rather than a man [O.F. *beste*]

beastings *BEESTINGS

beast of burden a pack animal

beast of prey an animal that kills other animals for its food

beat (bi:t) **1.** *v. pres. part.* **beat·ing** *past* **beat** *past part.* **beat·en** (bí:t'n) *v.t.* to strike deliberately and often, *to beat a carpet* ‖ to flap vigorously, *the cock beat its wings* ‖ to strike repeatedly so as to whip or mix, *to beat eggs* ‖ to strike with a cane etc. in punishment ‖ to work (metal) by hammering ‖ to clear (a path) by striking etc., *to beat a way through the undergrowth* ‖ to give the measure for (musical time) ‖ to baffle, *it beats me how you solve this problem* ‖ to surpass, *to beat a record* ‖ to strike the bushes etc. in (specified woods etc.) in order to make game leave cover ‖ *v.i.* to dash, *waves beat against the shore* ‖ to throb, *fear makes the heart*

beat faster ‖ to produce a noise by dealing blows, *to beat on a door* ‖ to strike bushes etc. in order to make game leave cover **beat it!** (*pop.*) go away! **to beat about** (*naut.*) to tack against the wind **to beat about** (or **around**) **the bush** to approach a subject indirectly ‖ to avoid the main issue **to beat a retreat** to run away, withdraw to safety **to beat back** to repulse, fight off **to beat down** (of the sun) to be intensely hot without respite ‖ (of rain) to fall heavily and steadily or in a storm **to beat** (**someone**) **down** to force (a seller) to lower his price in bargaining **to beat the air** to fail to come to grips with a problem **to beat the bounds** (*Br.*) to mark the parish boundaries by going around them in procession and striking certain points with rods **to beat up** to knock (someone) about with great physical violence ‖ to drive (the weft) into its right position in weaving ‖ (*pop.*) to raise, muster ‖ (*naut.*) to tack against the wind **2.** *n.* a stroke (on a drum etc.) or the noise made ‖ a throb or pulsation ‖ (*acoustics*) a maximum in the combined amplitudes of two or more waves (e.g. sound waves, radio waves, electric currents) that recurs periodically and is due to the union of waves of slightly different frequency. The frequency of the beats is the sum or difference of the frequencies of the waves or currents (*INTERFERENCE) ‖ the movement of a conductor's baton or hand ‖ a rhythmic pulse in music ‖ the stroke of a bird's wing ‖ a policeman's or watchman's round ‖ (*naut.*) a tack **3.** *adj.* characteristic of or relating to the beat generation ‖ exhausted [O.E. *beatan*]

beat·en (bí:t'n) *adj.* defeated ‖ made smooth by constant treading, *a beaten path* ‖ shaped or made thin by hammering **off the beaten track** little-frequented ‖ aside from what is well known or familiar

beat·er (bí:tər) *n.* an implement for beating ‖ a machine in which beating is done, e.g. (*papermaking*) a machine for reducing pulp to the required state ‖ someone who beats to make game leave cover

beat generation disillusioned members (esp. writers) of the generation following the 2nd world war, professing philosophical detachment and affirming social and sexual freedom

be·a·tif·ic (bi:ətífik) *adj.* of or belonging to a state of bliss ‖ making blessed [fr. L. *beatificus*]

be·at·i·fi·ca·tion (bi:ætifikéiʃən) *n.* a beatifying or being beatified ‖ the act by which the pope permits the establishment of a limited public cult of a deceased person and bestows the title of 'blessed' upon him [F.]

beatific vision the sight of heavenly glory promised to faithful Christians

be·at·i·fy (bi:ætifai) *pres. part.* **be·at·i·fy·ing** *past* and *past part.* **be·at·i·fied** *v.t.* to declare the beatification of [F. *béatifier*]

beat·ing (bí:tiŋ) *n.* punishment by repeated striking ‖ a severe defeat

be·at·i·tude (bi:ætitju:d, bi:ætitu:d) *n.* blessedness ‖ bliss **the Be·at·i·tudes** (*Bible*) a passage from the Sermon on the Mount declaring what makes a man blessed (Matthew V, 3–12) [F.]

Bea·tle·ma·ni·a (bi:t'lméini:ə) *n.* great enthusiasm for the Beatles, group of four Englishmen who adapted a complex variety of rock-and-roll songs to reflect the mood of youth culture of the 1960s

Beatles, (bi:t'lz) **The,** English rock music group consisting of John Lennon (1940–80), Paul McCartney (1942–   ), George Harrison (1943–   ), and Ringo Starr (1940–   ) that set the tone for music from the 1960's on. Their hits include 'Love Me Do' (1962) and 'I Want to Hold Your Hand' (1964) and the albums 'Sergeant Pepper's Lonely Hearts Club Band' (1967) and 'Let It Be' (1970). They also made films, among them 'A Hard Day's Night' (1964) and 'Help' (1965). The members of the group went their separate ways in 1970. In 1980, John Lennon was shot and killed by former mental patient Mark Chapman

beat·nik (bí:tnik) *n.* a member of the beat generation

Be·a·trice (bíətris) (1938–   ), queen of the Netherlands (1980–   ), daughter of Queen Juliana, who abdicated the throne in favor of Beatrice. She is married to Germany's Prince Claus von Amsberg; they have 3 sons

Beatrice the woman immortalized by Dante in 'Vita Nuova' and the 'Divine Comedy'

beau (bou) *pl.* **beaus, beaux** (bouz) *n.* (*old-fash.*) a man with respect to the girl he is paying

amorous attentions to ‖ (*hist.*) a dandy [F. adj.=beautiful]

Beau Brummell *BRUMMELL

Beauce (bous) the very fertile, grain-producing plain in the northern Orléanais, France

Beau·fort scale (bóufərt) a scale for indicating the force of the wind (measured at 33 ft above the ground) by conventional numbers, invented (1806) by Admiral Sir Francis Beaufort (1774–1857) and used internationally since 1874

Beau·har·nais (bouarnei), Eugène de (1781–1824), French general, son of the Empress Josephine. He served with distinction in the Napoleonic Wars (1803–15) and was viceroy of Italy (1805–14)

Beauharnais, Josephine de *JOSEPHINE

Beau·jo·lais (bouʒəlei) *n.* a red wine from the northern Lyonnais, France. The center of the Beaujolais trade is at Villefranche-sur-Saône

Beau·mar·chais (boumærʃei), Pierre-Augustin Caron de (1732–99), French playwright. His most famous plays are 'le Barbier de Séville' (1775) and 'le Mariage de Figaro' (1784)

Beau·mont (bóumənt), Francis (1584–1616), English dramatist. He wrote, with John Fletcher, about 50 comedies and tragedies, including 'The Knight of the Burning Pestle' (c. 1607) and 'Philaster' (c. 1609)

Beau Nash *NASH

Beaune (boun) *n.* a variety of red Burgundy [after the region of *Beaune*, Côte d'Or, France]

Beau·re·gard (bóuregard), Pierre Gustave Toutant de (1818–83), Confederate general. One of the eight full generals of the Confederacy, he participated in most of the major American Civil War engagements as an effective combat officer but revealed serious deficiencies as a general officer

beau·ti·cian (bju:tíʃən) *n.* a person who gives beauty treatments

beau·ti·ful (bjú:tifəl) **1.** *adj.* having beauty ‖ physically lovely ‖ morally or intellectually pleasing, *a beautiful solution to a problem* **2.** *n.* (with 'the') beauty in the abstract, the ideal to which all beautiful things are referred

beautiful people persons whose names appear frequently in newspaper society pages

beau·ti·fy (bjú:tifai) *pres. part.* **beau·ti·fy·ing** *past* and *past part.* **beau·ti·fied** *v.t.* to make beautiful, adorn

beau·ty (bjú:ti:) *pl.* **beau·ties** *n.* that which delights the senses or exalts the mind ‖ physical loveliness ‖ qualities pleasing to the moral sense ‖ (*pop.*) a particularly good example or specimen of a thing [O.F. *beauté*]

beauty parlor, *Br.* **beauty parlour** a place where women go for professional beauty treatment of the hair, skin etc.

beauty sleep (*pop.*) sleep before midnight

beauty spot (*hist.*) a small patch worn on the face as a foil to a flawless complexion ‖ a little mole ‖ a place noted for its fine scenery

Beau·vais (bouvei) a French town (pop. 56,725) 41 miles north of Paris, famous for tapestry and carpet making. Gothic cathedral (unfinished)

Beau·voir (bouvwár), Simone de (see-muhn' duh) (1908–86), French writer, feminist, and existentialist. A companion of Jean Paul SARTRE, she wrote about existentialism through her novels 'She Came to Stay' (1943), 'The Blood of Others' (1945), and 'The Mandarins' (1954). 'The Second Sex' (1949) portrayed woman's secondary role in society, and 'Memoirs of a Dutiful Daughter' (1958) and 'All Said and Done' (1972) were among her autobiographical works

beaux arts (bouzær) *pl. n.* the fine arts [F.]

bea·ver (bí:vər) *pl.* **bea·ver, bea·vers** *n. Castor fiber* or *C. canadensis,* a semiaquatic rodent having webbed hind feet and a very broad scaly tail ‖ its fur [O.E. *beofor*]

—Beavers are chiefly North American. They fell trees by gnawing and construct complex lodges of them, built with great skill and ingenuity into river banks. They often dam rivers to maintain the water level

beaver *n.* (*armor*) the piece of a helmet protecting the lower part of the face [O.F. *bavière,* bib]

Bea·ver·brook (bí:vərbruk), William Maxwell Aitken, 1st Baron (1879–1964), Canadian-born British newspaper proprietor and Conservative politician. His chain of newspapers, led by the 'Daily Express', campaigned for free trade within the British Empire. He was minister of information (1918) and served (1940–5) in Churchill's coalition government, notably as minister of aircraft production (1940–1)

---

be·bee·ru (bibíǝru:) n. *Nectandra rodioei*, fam. *Lauraceae*, a tropical tree native to Guiana ‖ its hard, heavy, durable wood, used for fishing rods and formerly in shipbuilding. The bark yields bebeerine, an alkaloid used in medicine [Span. and Port. *bibirú*, of Cariban origin]

be·calm (bikám) v.t. (usually passive) to make calm (the sea etc.) ‖ to deprive (a sailing ship) of wind

became past of BECOME

be·cause (bikɔ́z, bikʌ́z, bikʌ́z) conj. for the reason that **because of** on account of

bêche-de-mer (beʃdǝmér) pl. **bêche-de-mer**, **bêches-de-mer** (beʃdǝmér) n. a trepang

Bech·u·a·na (betʃu:ánǝ) n. a member of one of the peoples living between the Orange and Zambesi Rivers in Central Africa ‖ the Bantu language spoken by these peoples

Bech·u·a·na·land (betʃu:ánǝlænd) *BOTSWANA

Beck (bek), Ludwig (1880–1944), German general, leader of a bomb plot against Hitler, which failed (July 20, 1944). Beck was killed that same night

beck (bek) n. (in the phrase) **at someone's beck and call** ready to do instant service for someone [fr. obs. v. *beck*, shortening of BECKON]

beck n. (Br.) a stream, esp. a pebbly mountain brook [O.N. *bekk*]

Beck·et (békit), St Thomas (c. 1118–70), English prelate and royal minister. He was of a merchant family. He gained the favor of Theobald, archbishop of Canterbury, and became (1155) high chancellor to Henry II. Henry appointed him (1162) archbishop of Canterbury, in the belief that he would support royal claims to control the Church. He showed increasing hostility to Henry's policy and refused to sign the Constitutions of Clarendon (1164). Becket was murdered (1170) in Canterbury Cathedral by barons acting on Henry's orders. His shrine rapidly became a popular place of pilgrimage. He was canonized in 1173

beck·et (békit) n. (naut.) a contrivance for holding ropes, tackle etc. in place [origin unknown]

becket bend a sheet bend

Beck·ett (békit), Samuel (1906–), Irish writer of novels and plays (many in French) celebrating the absurdity of the human condition. His works include 'En attendant Godot' ('Waiting for Godot', 1952, first performed 1953) and (in English) 'All that Fall' (1957) and 'Krapp's Last Tape' (1959), 'Happy Days' (1961), 'That Time' (1976) and 'Footfalls' (1976). Novels include 'Malone meurt' ('Malone Dies', 1951)

Beck·mann (békmǝn), Max (1884–1950), German expressionist painter known for his use of symbolic imagery and portrayal of brutality. His works include 'The Night' (1918–9), the destruction of a tenement building by thugs, and 'Departure' (1932–3), the first of his triptychs that symbolizes flight from Nazism. He later emigrated to the U.S. and taught in St. Louis (1947–9) and the Brooklyn Museum School in New York (1949–50)

Beckmann thermometer (békmǝn) a mercury-in-glass thermometer with a very large bulb so that a small temperature rise results in expansion up a long section of the stem. This permits subdivision of a degree on the scale into 100 parts. The instrument can be set for a desired initial temperature by varying the amount of mercury in the bulb, using a reservoir at the top for this purpose. The scale extends over only 6-7 degrees

beck·on (békǝn) v.t. to summon e.g. by a nod or motion of the finger or hand ‖ (fig.) to invite, *the prospect of wealth beckoned him on* ‖ v.i. to wave, nod or make some other gesture recognized as an invitation, summons or signal [O.E. *bīecnan*]

bec·lo·meth·a·sone [$C_{22}H_{29}ClO_5$] (bɛkloumeθǝsoun) n. (pharm.) antiasthmatic steroid drug marketed as Vanceril

be·cloud (bikláud) v.t. (rhet.) to cover with clouds ‖ (rhet.) to obscure

be·come (bikʌ́m) 1. v. pres. part. **be·com·ing** past **be·came** (bikéim) past part. **be·come** v.i. to come to be, *to become a grandmother* ‖ to be in process of change or development ‖ v.t. to suit, enhance the attractiveness of ‖ to be fitting or proper in **to become of** to happen to, *what will become of me if you go?* **be·cóm·ing** 1. adj. suitable, attractive 2. n. (philos.) the state of undergoing development ‖ (philos.) a coming into being [O.E. *becuman*, to arrive]

Becque·rel (bekrel), Antoine Henri (1852–1908), French physicist who studied a, β and γ rays emitted by radioactive substances. Nobel prize (1903)

bed (bed) n. a piece of furniture for sleeping in or resting on, usually comprising a bedstead, mattress, pillows, bedclothes and a bedspread ‖ a resting place for animals, *a bed of straw* ‖ the firm base on which something is supported ‖ the ground at the bottom of the sea or a river etc. ‖ a piece of ground prepared for plants etc. ‖ the ballast or foundation of a road or railroad ‖ the central part of a gun carriage ‖ the level surface of a printing press on which the type rests ‖ a layer or stratum of rock etc. **to get out of bed on the wrong side, get out of the wrong side of bed** to be in a bad temper for the day **to go to bed** to retire to one's bed ‖ (of a newspaper etc.) to go to press **to lie on the bed one has made** to accept the consequences of one's actions **to make a bed** to arrange the bedclothes on a bed **to put to bed** to prepare for sleep and place in bed ‖ to work on (an edition of a newspaper) until it is ready to go to press **to take to one's bed** to go to bed and stay there because one is ill [O.E. *bedd*]

bed pres. part. **bed·ding** past and past part. **bed·ded** v.t. to provide with a place to sleep ‖ to fix in a foundation, *posts bedded in concrete* ‖ to arrange or form·in a bed or layer **to bed out** to put (plants) in a bed [O.E. *beddian*]

be·daub (bidɔ́b) v.t. to smear with paint or anything sticky or garish

be·daz·zle (bidǽz'l) pres. part. **be·daz·zling** past and past part. **be·daz·zled** v.t. to dazzle completely ‖ to impress (someone) in such a way that he is blinded to the truth

bed·bug (bédbʌg) n. a member of fam. *Cimicidae*, order *Hemiptera*, esp. *Cimex lectularius* or *C. rotundus*, a small, oval, reddish brown, wingless, parasitic insect which sucks blood with its piercing and sucking mouthparts. It inhabits most of the world

bed·cham·ber (bédtʃeimbǝr) n. a bedroom (now only in titles of court officials)

bed·clothes (bédklouðz, bédklouz) pl. n. the sheets, blankets etc., used on a bed

bed·cov·er (bédkʌvǝr) n. a bedspread ‖ (pl.) bedclothes

bed·ding (bédiŋ) n. bedclothes ‖ hay, straw etc. used as litter for animals ‖ a foundation, *a bedding of concrete* ‖ (geol.) stratification ‖ the growing of many plants of the same species in outdoor flowerbeds to achieve effects of massed color etc.

bed·do (bédou) n. beds of Japanese design that can be raised, rotated, or rocked electronically

Bede (bi:d), the Venerable (c. 672–735), English monk, scholar and historian, author of 'Historia ecclesiastica gentis Anglorum' (731). He also wrote many works of exegesis, scientific works largely concerning chronology and the calendar, lives of St Cuthbert in verse and prose, and other historical treatises. His influence was carried by Alcuin to the Continent, where it became a major factor in the revival of learning under Charlemagne

be·deck (bidék) v.t. to adorn

bed·e·guar (bédigɑr) n. a gall on rosebushes, caused by the gall wasp *Rhodites rosae*, whose females lay eggs in young leaf buds in spring [F. fr. Pers. *bādāwar*, wind-brought]

bedesman *BEADSMAN

be·dev·il (bidévǝl) pres. part. **be·dev·il·ing**, esp. Br. **be·dev·il·ling** past and past part. **be·dev·iled**, esp. Br. **be·dev·illed** v.t. to interfere with and throw into confusion ‖ to pester ‖ (rhet.) to beset with devils **be·dév·il·ment** n. exasperating interference and trouble ‖ a pestering ‖ (rhet.) a besetting with devils

be·dew (bidjú:, bidú:) v.t. (rhet.) to cover with dew or dewlike drops

bed·fast (bédfæst, bédfɑst) adj. bedridden

bed·fel·low (bédfelou) n. someone with respect to the person one shares a bed with

Bed·ford (bédfǝrd), John of Lancaster, duke of *JOHN OF LANCASTER

Bedford cord a cloth with thick ribbing

Bed·ford·shire (bédfǝrdʃǝr) (abbr. Beds.) a Midland county (area 473 sq. miles, pop. 491,000) of England. County town: Bedford

be·dim (bidím) pres. part. **be·dim·ming** past and past part. **be·dimmed** v.t. (rhet.) to make dim (esp. the eyes or the mind)

Bed·i·vere, Sir (bédiviǝr) King Arthur's steward, in the Arthurian legend

be·di·zen (bidáiz'n, bidíʒ'n) v.t. (rhet.) to dress flamboyantly ‖ to overload with ornament [BE-+16th-c. *disen*, to dress a distaff with flax]

bed·lam (bédlǝm) n. a scene of uproar [after *Bedlam*, the hospital of St Mary of Bethlehem, Bishopsgate, London, founded as a priory and converted into a lunatic asylum in 1547]

bed linen sheets and pillowcases, of whatever material

Bed·ling·ton terrier (bédliŋtǝn) a terrier of a gray, short-haired, rough-coated, lightly built, swift breed [after *Bedlington* in Northumberland, England]

bed of roses a comfortable, easy situation

bedouin *BEDUIN

bed·pan (bédpæn) n. a shallow chamber pot used by invalids in bed

bed·plate (bédpleit) n. a metal plate forming the base of a machine

bed·post (bédpoust) n. one of the upright supports of a bed

be·drag·gled (bidrǽg'ld) adj. with clothing, hair, fur etc. wet or hanging limply and unbecomingly

bed·rid·den (bédrid'n) adj. compelled to stay in bed because of illness or infirmity [O.E. *bedreda*, bed-rider]

bed·rock (bédrɒk) n. the solid rock underlying superficial deposits ‖ basic issues, *to get down to bedrock*

bed·room (bédru:m, bédrum) n. a room for sleeping in

bed·side (bédsaid) 1. n. a position by a sickbed 2. adj. relating to a sickbed ‖ for placing beside a bed, *bedside table* ‖ for light reading in bed, *a bedside book*

bedside manner the solicitous or reassuring manner of a doctor

bed·sit·ter (bédsitǝr) n. (Br.) a bedsitting-room

bed·sit·ting·room (bédsitiŋru:m, bédsitiŋrum) n. (Br.) a rented furnished living room containing a divan on which the occupant sleeps at night

Bed·son·i·a (bédsouniǝ) n. (miol.) any of the microorganism genus *Chlamydia* that causes psittacosis, trachoma, and lymphogranuloma venereum; named for Samuel P. Bedson, British bacteriologist

bed·sore (bédsɔr, bédsour) n. a body sore caused by lack of nourishment in tissues under prolonged pressure, esp. affecting bedridden invalids

bed·space (bédspeis) n. number of beds available, e.g., in a hostel or hospital

bed·spread (bédspred) n. a cover, usually ornamental, for the bedding on a bed

bed·stead (bédsted) n. the framework of a bed supporting the springs and mattress

bed·time (bédtaim) n. time to go to bed or the time when one habitually goes to bed

Bed·u·in, Bed·ou·in (bédu:in) pl. **Bed·u·in, Bed·u·ins, Bed·ou·in, Bed·ou·ins** n. a nomadic Arab of the Arabian peninsula and N. Africa, traditionally claiming descent from Ishmael. The Beduin are known for their pride and their courage in the face of privation. Camel breeding is their main livelihood [F. fr. Arab. *badáwi*, dweller in the desert]

bed warmer (hist.) a long-handled pan holding charcoal for warming a bed

bee (bi:) n. any of numerous insects belonging to the suborder *Apoidea*, order *Hymenoptera*, esp. *Apis mellifera*, a fourwinged insect producing wax and honey, *hive bee* ‖ a gathering of people for work or amusement, *sewing bee, spelling bee* **to have a bee in one's bonnet** to be obsessed about some matter, esp. a matter to which one is opposed [O.E. *bēo*]
—Bees are allied to wasps and ants. Their mouthparts are adapted for chewing and sucking. Food consists of nectar and pollen from which the honeybees make and store honey. The social honeybees have a queen, workers and drones. The queen copulates once and this enables her to lay fertile eggs during her lifetime. She lays up to 2,000 or more eggs in a day, each in a cell of the hive. Fertilized eggs produce workers (sterile females), unfertilized eggs produce drones (males). The larvae are fed by workers for three days on royal jelly, then on pollen and honey. After 9 days the cell is sealed, metamorphosis occurs, and the adult emerges in 21 days. Eggs laid in large cells and fed only on royal jelly produce young queens in 16 days. Bees are invaluable to man in the pollination of food crops

bee *n.* a strip of iron or wood on the bowsprit of a vessel through which are reeved the fore-top-mast stays [O.E. *béag,* ring]

beech (bi:tʃ) *n.* a member of *Fagus,* fam. *Fagaceae,* a genus of temperate, deciduous, smooth, gray-barked trees ‖ their hardwood timber **béech·en** *adj.* [O.E. *béce*]

Bee·cher (bí:tʃər), Henry Ward (1813–87), U.S. clerical leader and spokesman for the Protestantism of his time. His sermons in the 1850s at Plymouth Church, Brooklyn, N.Y., won him the largest congregation in the U.S.A. He was a fervent advocate of the emancipation of slaves and of woman suffrage

beech mast beechnuts collectively

beech·nut (bí:tʃnʌt) *n.* the fruit of the beech tree, usually consisting of two edible, three-cornered nuts

bee-eat·er (bí:i:tər) *n.* a member of fam. *Meropidae* of mainly tropical birds with vivid plumage, which feed on bees

beef (bi:f) **1.** *n.* the flesh of a bull, cow or ox ‖ (*pl.* **beeves** (bi:vz), **beefs,** or collectively **beef**) a bull, cow or ox fully or nearly grown, esp. when fattened for food **2.** *v.i.* (*pop.*) to complain [O.F. *boef*]

beef Bourguignon dish of beef chunks cooked in Burgundy wine or sometimes cognac

beef·eat·er (bí:i:tər) *n.* a yeoman of the guard ‖ a warder of the Tower of London

beef·steak (bí:fsteik) *n.* a cut of beef, esp. from the rump, for grilling or frying

beef tea an extract made by cooking lean beef in water and serving it strained

beef Wellington dish of beef fillet and pâté surrounded by pastry

beef·wood (bí:fwud) *n.* red timber from various esp. tropical trees

beef·y (bí:fi:) *comp.* **beef·i·er** *superl.* **beef·i·est** *adj.* (of people) brawny

bee glue propolis

bee·hive (bí:haiv) *n.* a hive ‖ (*cosmetology*) high, circular hairstyle shaped like a beehive

bee·keep·ing (bí:ki:piŋ) *n.* the art of keeping bees in hives

bee·line (bí:lain) *n.* (in the phrase) **to make a beeline for** to go straight and quickly towards

Be·el·ze·bub (bi:élzəbʌb) *n.* the Devil ‖ one of the chief devils [L. fr. Gk *beelzeboub,* fr. Heb. *ba'alz'būb,* lord of the flies]

been (bin, *Br.* bi:n) *past part.* of BE **to have been** (*Br.*) to have called, *has anyone been while I was out?* **to have been to** to have visited

beer (biər) *n.* an alcoholic drink brewed from fermented malt flavored with hops ‖ any of some other slightly fermented drinks, *ginger beer* [O.E. *béor*]

beer *n.* one of the divisions (e.g. of 40 threads) of the end of a warp [=BIER, a framework]

beer and skittles (*Br.*) carefree pleasure

Beer·bohm (bíərboum), Sir Max (1872–1956), English wit, critic, satirical writer ('Zuleika Dobson', 1911), parodist ('A Christmas Garland', 1912) and caricaturist ('Poet's Corner', 1904)

Beer·she·ba (biərʃí:bə, bíərʃəbə) the largest town (pop. 96,500) of the Negev, Israel, 48 miles southwest of Jerusalem

beer·y (bíəri:) *comp.* **beer·i·er** *superl.* **beer·i·est** *adj.* affected by drinking a lot of beer, *beery voices* ‖ smelling of beer

beest·ings, beast·ings (bí:stiŋz) *pl. n.* the colostrum of a cow [O.E. *bēost*]

bees·wax (bí:zwæks) *n.* wax secreted by bees to make a honeycomb ‖ a product from this used in polishes, and for modeling

bees·wing (bí:zwiŋ) *n.* a film of shining scales formed in some wines after long keeping, so called from its appearance

beet (bi:t) *n.* a member of *Beta,* fam. *Chenopodiaceae,* a genus of fleshy roots, used as a source of sugar (white or sugar beet) or (esp. *Am.=Br.* beetroot) in salads and cookery (red beet) [O.E. *bete* fr. L. *beta*]

Bee·tho·ven (béitouvən), Ludwig van (1770–1827), German composer who lived in Vienna after 1792. Beethoven vastly expanded the expressive possibilities of sonata form in his sonatas, chamber music and symphonies, through his genius for developing and unifying thematic material. He was recognized as a great composer even in his own day, but became increasingly cut off from the world by deafness. This began when he was 31 and became total by c. 1824, before he wrote his last three string quartets. His works include nine symphonies (no. 3 'Eroica', no. 9 the 'Choral'), 32 piano sona-

tas, 16 string quartets, five piano concertos, a violin concerto, the opera 'Fidelio', several overtures and incidental music, choral music, many chamber works etc.

bee·tle (bí:t'l) **1.** *n.* an insect of the order *Coleoptera* ‖ any of various insects resembling the beetle, e.g. the cockroach **2.** *v.i. pres. part.* **bee·tling** *past* and *past part.* **bee·tled** to project, jut out as though menacing, *beetling cliffs* [O.E. *bitula,* a biter]

beetle 1. *n.* a heavy-headed tool for crushing ‖ a heavy wooden mallet ‖ a machine in which hammers a revolving roll of cloth to give it a soft finish **2.** *v.t. pres. part.* **bee·tling** *past* and *past part.* **bee·tled** to beat or crush with a beetle [O.E. *bietel*]

beet leafhopper *Circulifer tenellus,* a homopterous insect which transmits a virus disease to sugar beet and similar plants in the western U.S.A.

Bee·ton (bí:t'n), Isabella Mary (1836–65), English writer on cookery. Her 'Book of Household Management' (1859) is the classic work in English on how to prepare good food and run a household

beet·root (bí:tru:t, bí:trut) *n.* (esp. *Br.=Am.* beet) the crimson root of the beet plant, used as a vegetable

beet sugar sugar made from the sugar beet

beeves *alt. pl.* of BEEF

be·fall (bifɔ́l) *pres. part.* **be·fall·ing** *past* **be·fell** (biféll) *past part.* **be·fall·en** (bifɔ́lən) *v.t.* (*rhet.*) to happen to ‖ *v.i.* (*rhet.*) to come to pass [O.E. *befallan*]

be·fit (bifít) *pres. part.* **be·fit·ting** *past* and *past part.* **be·fit·ted** *v.t.* to be suitable or proper for **be·fit·ting** *adj.*

be·flag (biflæg) *pres. part.* **be·flag·ging** *past* and *past part.* **be·flagged** *v.t.* to adorn or cover with flags

be·fog (bifɔ́g, bifóg) *pres. part.* **be·fog·ging** *past* and *past part.* **be·fogged** *v.t.* to envelop in fog ‖ to obscure

be·fool (bifú:l) *v.t.* (*rhet.*) to delude

be·fore (bifɔ́r, bifóur) **1.** *adv.* previously, already ‖ (*old-fash.*) in front **2.** *prep.* in front of ‖ ahead of ‖ under the impulse of, *to recoil before a shock* ‖ in or into the presence of, *brought before the judge* ‖ which concerns and awaits, *the task before us* ‖ earlier than, *finish this before supper* ‖ higher in rank, nobility or worth, *generals come before colonels* ‖ rather than, *choose virtue before everything else* **3.** *conj.* sooner in time than, *think before you answer* [O.E. *beforan*]

be·fore·hand (bifɔ́rhænd, bifóurhænd) *adv.* and *adj.* in advance, *to make preparations beforehand*

be·fore-tax (bifɔrtǽks) *adj.* of sums earned before deduction for U.S. federal income taxes *syn* pretax

be·foul (bifául) *v.t.* to make filthy ‖ to traduce

be·friend (bifrénd) *v.t.* to be helpful to with friendly sympathy

be·fud·dled (bifʌ́d'ld) *adj.* thoroughly confused (with liquor) [*past part.* of *befuddle*]

beg (beg) *pres. part.* **beg·ging** *past* and *past part.* **begged** *v.i.* to solicit money, clothing, food etc. for a living ‖ (of a holy person) to ask alms ‖ (of an animal) to express demands by making noises or assuming beseeching postures ‖ to ask earnestly ‖ *v.t.* to solicit as charity, *he begged a hot meal* ‖ to ask for as a favor, *to beg a cigarette* ‖ to ask earnestly, *she begged him not to go* **to beg off** to back out of an undertaking and ask to be excused **to beg someone off** to get someone excused from a penalty etc. **to beg the question** to avoid the issue *to go begging* to be unwanted [perh. fr. O.F. *begart*]

began *past* of BEGIN

be·get (bigét) *pres. part.* **be·get·ting** *past* **be·got** (bigót) *past part.* **be·got·ten** (bigót'n) *v.t.* (*rhet.*) to procreate, usually said of the father, sometimes of both parents ‖ to cause, *grumbling begets deeper dissatisfaction* **be·gét·ter** *n.* [O.E. *begitan*]

beg·gar (bégər) **1.** *n.* someone who begs food, clothes, money etc. for a livelihood ‖ a pauper ‖ (esp. *Br.*) a fellow, *he's a silly beggar* **2.** *v.t.* to ruin, reduce to poverty **to beggar description** to be so magnificent as to be impossible to describe [O.F. *begard*]

beg·gar·ly (bégərli:) *adj.* like or befitting a beggar ‖ mean, contemptible, *a beggarly reward*

beg·gar-my-neigh·bor, *Br.* **beg·gar-my-neigh·bour** (bégərmíneibər) *n.* a card game for children

beg·gar·y (bégəri:) *n.* the state of being a beggar ‖ extreme poverty

Be·gin (béigin), Menachem (1913–), Israeli prime minister (1977–83). Born in Russia, he emigrated to Palestine in 1942 and fought the British for the establishment of a Jewish homeland. Chairman of Herut, the right-wing party, from 1948, he became prime minister when Herut won the 1977 elections. He received the 1978 Nobel Peace Prize (with Anwar SADAT) for Middle East peace efforts and took a hard line against compromise with the Arabs. He resigned in 1983

be·gin (bigín) *pres. part.* **be·gin·ning** *past* **began** (bigǽn) *past part.* **be·gun** (bigʌ́n) *v.i.* to start, *begin when you're ready* ‖ to come into existence, *when the world began* ‖ *v.t.* to cause to start, *what began the revolution?* ‖ to commence, *she begins school this week* **not to begin to** to be in no position to, *he can't begin to compete with you* ‖ not to manage in the least degree to, *it doesn't begin to do what it's supposed to* **be·gin·ner** (bigínər) *n.* someone beginning, a novice **be·gin·ning** (bigíniŋ) *n.* a start ‖ the early part, *the beginning of the book* ‖ the time when life started ‖ origin, *the beginning of his downfall* ‖ (*pl.*) early stages [O.E. *beginnan*]

be·gird (bigə́:rd) *pres. part.* **be·gird·ing** *past* and *past part.* **be·girt** (bigə́:rt) *v.t.* (*rhet.*, used esp. in *past part.*) to surround [O.E. *begyrdan*]

be·gone (bigɔ́n, bigón) *v.i.* (*rhet.*, only *imper.* and *infin.*) to go away [O.E. *bēgan*]

be·gon·ia (bigóunjə, bigóuni:ə) *n.* a member of *Begonia,* fam. *Begoniaceae,* a genus of tropical and subtropical plants cultivated for their handsome flowers and foliage. They are perennials, usually with rhizomes or tubers [after Michel *Bégon* (1638–1710), French governor of Santo Domingo]

begotten *past* of BEGET

be·grime (bigráim) *pres. part.* **be·grim·ing** *past* and *past part.* **be·grimed** *v.t.* to soil with grime

be·grudge (bigrʌ́dʒ) *pres. part.* **be·grudg·ing** *past* and *past part.* **be·grudged** *v.t.* to envy (someone something) ‖ to feel unwillingness or dissatisfaction at, *to begrudge spending money on repairs*

be·guile (bigáil) *pres. part.* **be·guil·ing** *past* and *past part.* **be·guiled** *v.t.* (esp. with 'into', 'out of') to fool, deceive ‖ to charm ‖ to relieve the tedium of, *the book beguiled his journey*

Bé·guine (bégi:n, béigi:n) *n.* a member of certain lay sisterhoods of the Netherlands which are not bound by vows [F. *béguine* fr. Lambert le *Bègue,* founder (c. 1170)]

be·guine (bigí:n) *n.* an energetic popular dance of the islands of Saint Lucia and Martinique, resembling the rumba [F. dialect *béguine,* fr. F. *béguin,* flirtation]

be·gum (bí:gəm) *n.* a title given to an Indian Moslem princess or woman of high rank

begun *past part.* of BEGIN

Bé·hague, Pointe (pwɛ̃tbeiæg) a cape on the east coast of French Guiana, just north of the Oyapock River

Be·haim (béihaim), Martin (c. 1459–1507), German cosmographer. His terrestrial globe (1492) summed up geographical knowledge on the eve of the discovery of the New World

be·half (bihǽf, biháf) *n.* (only in phrases) **in** (or **on**) **behalf of** in the interest of [M.E. a mixture of *on his halve* and *bihalve him,* on his side]

be·have (bihéiv) *pres. part.* **be·hav·ing** *past* and *past part.* **be·haved** *v.i.* to conduct oneself, *to behave badly* ‖ to conduct oneself well, *you must behave* ‖ *v. refl.* to conduct (oneself) well, *behave yourself* [BE-+HAVE]

be·hav·ior, *Br.* **be·hav·iour** (bihéivjər) *n.* manners, deportment ‖ moral conduct ‖ the way in which a machine, organ or organism works, with respect to its efficiency ‖ the way in which something reacts to environment, *the behavior of a kite in the wind* **be·hav·ior·al,** *Br.* **be·háv·iour·al** *adj.*

be·hav·ior·ism, *Br.* **be·hav·iour·ism** (bihéivjərizəm) *n.* (*psychol.*) the doctrine that psychological theories should be based on the outwardly observable data of human actions without reference to the products of introspection **be·háv·ior·ist,** *Br.* **be·háv·iour·ist** *n.* and *adj.*

behavior modification (*psych.*) system of changing personal relations based on motivation, e.g., determining real needs, providing sense of belonging and accomplishment, teamwork, developed by B.F. Skinner *Cf* SKINNERIAN

behavior therapy (*psych.*) program designed to replace undesirable behavior patterns with new ones —**behavioral scientist** *n.*

CONCISE PRONUNCIATION KEY: **(a)** æ, c*a*t; ɑ, c*a*r; ɔ: f*aw*n; ei, sn*a*ke. **(e)** e, h*e*n; i:, sh*ee*p; iə, d*ee*r; ɛə, b*ea*r. **(i)** i, f*i*sh; ai, t*i*ger; ə:, b*i*rd. **(o)** o, *o*x; au, c*ow*; ou, g*oa*t; u, p*oo*r; ɔi, r*oy*al. **(u)** ʌ, d*u*ck; u, b*u*ll; u:, g*oo*se; ə, b*a*cillus; ju:, c*u*be. x, lo*ch*; θ, *th*ink; ð, bo*th*er; z, *Z*en; ʒ, cor*s*age; dʒ, sava*g*e; ŋ, orangutan*g*; j, *y*ak; ʃ, *fi*sh; tʃ, fe*tch*; 'l, rabb*le*; 'n, redd*en.* Complete pronunciation key appears inside front cover.

be·head (bihéd) v.t. to cut off the head of [O.E. *behéadian*]

beheld past and past part. OF BEHOLD

Be·he·moth (bihí:məθ, bí:əməθ) (*Bible*) a mythical beast of gigantic proportions, mentioned with Leviathan in Job xi

be·hest (bihést) n. (*rhet.*) a command or authoritative request [O.E. *behæs*]

be·hind (biháind) **1.** adv. in the rear ‖ in the past, *his troubles lie behind* ‖ in a place where one is no longer, *he left his pajamas behind* ‖ in arrears, *behind with one's work* **2.** prep. in back of, *behind the house* ‖ in the past for, *our youth is behind us* ‖ remaining after when one has gone on, *to leave a good reputation behind one* ‖ in an inferior position to, *behind him in rank* ‖ motivating but not disclosed or made evident by, *what is behind his refusal?* ‖ in support of, *whose money is behind him?*, *all your colleagues are behind you* ‖ running later than, progressing more slowly than, *behind schedule* **to put something behind one** to get over some past incident and concentrate on the future **3.** n. the buttocks [O.E. *behindan*]

be·hind·hand (biháindhænd) adv. and pred. adj. behind (in progress, payments etc.) ‖ backward

Be·his·tun (beihistú:n) *RAWLINSON

be·hold (bihóuld) pres. part. **be·hold·ing** past and past part. **be·held** (bihéld) v.t. (*rhet.*) to look at and consider ‖ (*Bible*) to see in a vision [O.E. *bihaldan*]

be·hold·en (bihóuldən) pred. adj. under an obligation, bound in gratitude

be·hoove (bihú:v) pres. part. **be·hoov·ing** past and past part. **be·hooved** v.t. impers. (*rhet.*) to be morally necessary to ‖ (esp. *Br.*) to be suitable to, *it ill behooves you to criticize* [O.E. *bihófian*]

be·hove (bihóuv) pres. part. **be·hov·ing** past and past part. **be·hoved** v.t. impers. (esp. *Br.*) to **be·hoove**

Beh·rens (béərəns), Peter (1868–1940), German architect, among the first to develop a style corresponding to the demands of industrialized society, and to instigate effective design in the production of consumer goods. His massive, powerful buildings are characterized by functional efficiency and logical use of modern materials, e.g. the AEG Turbine Factory, Berlin (1909). He influenced Le Corbusier, Gropius and Mies van der Rohe

beige (beiʒ) n. the color of natural wool [F.]

Bei·jing Peking, China, as spelled under the new spelling system

be·in (bí:ín) n. a gathering for the purpose of being together, esp. of like-minded

be·ing (bí:iŋ) **1.** n. existence, *to bring into being* ‖ the substance or essence of an existing person or thing ‖ one who exists, *a human being* **2.** adj. (in the phrase) **for the time being** for the present

Be·i·ra (báiərə, béiirə) *SOFALA

Bei·rut, Bey·routh (beirú:t) the capital (pop. 1,100,000) of Lebanon, at the foot of the Lebanon Mtns, a seaport and an old trading and a banking center. Four universities

Be·ja (bí:dʒə) n. a member of an African Moslem people of Hamitic origin living between the Nile and Red Sea. They are mainly nomadic herdsmen, but are cultivating cotton in increasing numbers

Beke (bi:k), Charles Tilstone (1800–74), English geographer and biblical critic. He traveled principally in Ethiopia and was the first to determine the course of the Blue Nile

be·ke (bi:ki:) n. among French Creoles, a white settler

bel (bel) n. ten decibels [after A. G. *Bell*]

be·la·bor, *Br.* **be·la·bour** (biléibər) v.t. (*rhet.*) to thrash ‖ to abuse with words ‖ to wear to exhaustion, *to belabor a subject*

Bel and the Dragon (bel) (*Bible*) a book of the Apocrypha. Bel (an idol) and the dragon were worshiped by the Babylonians until Daniel proved that they were not living gods by destroying them

be·la·ted (biléitid) adj. late ‖ retarded [past part. of obs. v. *belate*, to delay]

be·laud (bilɔ́d) v.t. (*rhet.*) to lavish praises on

Be·la·ún·de Ter·ry (beluú:ndetérri:), Fernando (1913–), Peruvian architect, politician, and president (1963–8). He introduced various programs of social reform but was replaced by a junta under Gen. Juan Velasco Alvarado. Coming out of exile, he again served as president (1980–85)

be·lay (biléi) **1.** v.t. (*naut.*) to make fast, secure (a running rope) round a cleat or belaying pin ‖ (mountaineering) to take a strong position and act as a belay to (another climber) ‖ v.i. (of ropes and cables) to be made fast **2.** interj. (*naut.*) stop! **3.** n. a projection round which a mountaineer's running rope may be passed to secure it [O.E. *belecgan*, to enclose]

belaying pin (*naut.*) a pin of wood or metal around which a rope can be made fast

bel can·to (belkántou) n. the art of singing operatic arias calling for agility in technique and for a pure, lyrical style and finely cultivated voice. It characterized the castrati and sopranos of Italian opera from the 17th c. up to Verdi, then gave place (with Wagner) to the melodic recitative [Ital.]

belch (beltʃ) **1.** v.i. to expel gas or wind from the stomach through the mouth ‖ v.t. (of a gun, volcano etc.) to throw forth (its contents) **2.** n. an instance of belching ‖ a sudden, violent emission, *a belch of steam* [O.E. *bealcian*]

be·lea·guer (bilí:gər) v.t. (*rhet.*) to besiege [Du. *belegeren*, to camp round]

Be·lém (belém) the capital (pop. 758,117) of Pará state, Brazil, a port on the lower Amazon exporting rubber, rice, sugar and forest products

bel·em·nite (béləmnait) n. (*geol.*) the internal skeletal fossil of an extinct cephalopod of fam. *Belemnitidae* related to the squid, belonging to the Mesozoic era [fr. Mod. L. fr. Gk *belemnon*, dart]

Bel·fast (bélfæst, bélfast, belfǽst, belfúst) a seaport (pop. 322,600) in county Antrim, the capital of Northern Ireland. Industries: shipbuilding, linen. Queen's University

Bel·fort (belfór) a territory (area 235 sq. miles, pop. 57,317) of E. France between the Vosges and Switzerland, administered as a department (*BURGUNDY). Chief town: Belfort (pop. 56,000)

bel·fry (bélfri:) pl. **bel·fries** n. a bell tower ‖ the room in a tower (esp. of a church) where the bells hang [M.E. *berfrey* fr. O.F. *berfrei* fr. Gmc]

Bel·gae (béldʒi:, bélgai) pl. n. an ancient Germanic and Celtic people who inhabited N. Gaul. Some migrated (1st c. B.C.) to S. Britain. They were conquered (57 B.C.) by Caesar

Bel·gian (béldʒən) **1.** n. a native or inhabitant of Belgium ‖ a draft horse of a heavy breed originating in Belgium **2.** adj. of or pertaining to Belgium

Bel·gic (béldʒik) adj. of or concerning the Belgae

Bel·gium (béldʒəm) a constitutional monarchy (area 11,775 sq. miles, pop. 9,854,589) in N.W. Europe. Capital: Brussels. People and language: Flemish in the north (55%), Walloons (French-speaking) in the south, 11% bilingual, with a small German minority in the east. All three languages are official in their respective regions. Brussels is officially bilingual. Religion: Roman Catholic, with small Protestant and Jewish minorities. The land is 60% arable and 20% forest. It slopes gently from the Ardennes to the North Sea. North of the Ardennes (rising to 2,200 ft) is the Sambre-Meuse valley, a rich coal belt and industrial region. Central Belgium is a fertile, undulating plain (300–600 ft). The Campine, in the north and east, is a region of sand, woods and heath. The rivers are linked by canals to form an excellent system of inland waterways. Average winter and summer temperatures (F.): 38° and 64°. Average annual rainfall: 35 ins. Livestock: cattle, pigs. Agricultural products: wheat, barley, oats, rye, potatoes, sugar beet, dairy produce. Mineral resources: coal and iron (also lead, manganese and zinc). Manufactures: iron and steel, textiles, machinery, chemicals, glassware, beer, matches, sugar. Exports: metals, textiles, chemicals and pharmaceutical products, precious stones, glassware. Imports: textiles, machinery, vehicles. Chief ports: Antwerp, Ghent, Ostend. Belgium has the densest road and railroad network in the world. There are four universities, the oldest being Louvain. Monetary unit: Belgian franc. HISTORY. The Celtic Belgae were conquered by the Romans (58–50 B.C.), by the Franks (3rd and 4th cc. A.D.), and were raided by the Vikings (9th c.). Semi-independent federal states developed. The Netherlands passed to the House of Burgundy (1384) and to the Hapsburgs (1477), being united to Spain (1555). The southern states remained under Spanish rule (Union of Utrecht, 1579) after

the Netherlands revolt (1568). They became part of the Hapsburg Austrian Empire (Treaty of Utrecht, 1713) after the War of the Spanish Succession. They were occupied by France in the War of the Austrian Succession, but were returned to Austria (1748). France overran them (1792) and incorporated them (1801). Belgium and Holland united to form the Kingdom of the Netherlands (1815–30), but Belgium revolted (1830) and was recognized as an independent kingdom (1831) whose neutrality was guaranteed by the Great Powers (1839). Prince Leopold of Saxe-Coburg was elected King Leopold I (1831–65). He was succeeded by Leopold II (1865–1909), who acquired the Congo (1878), which became a Belgian colony (1908). Belgium was overrun by Germany (1914–18). It suffered financial crises (1926, 1935). It was invaded and occupied by the Germans during the 2nd world war (1940–4). Leopold III abdicated (1951) after a national crisis, and was succeeded by his son Baudouin. With the Netherlands and Luxembourg Belgium formed a customs union, Benelux (1948), which became an economic union (1960). It joined NATO (1949) and the European Common Market (E.E.C.) (1958). It lost the Congo (Zaïre) when that country became independent (June 30, 1960) and in 1962 granted independence to Ruanda-Urundi (now Rwanda and Kingdom of Burundi). In 1980 parliament established regional assemblies in Flanders and Wallonia, but postponed action on autonomy of Brussels

Bel·grade (belgréid, bélgreid) (*Serbian* Beograd) the capital (pop. 976,000) of Yugoslavia, and of the federated republic of Serbia, at the confluence of the Sava and the Danube. Its position on the waterways and on the Orient railroad makes it the gateway to the Balkans, and it is a great commercial city. Industries: textiles, engineering, chemicals. University (1863). Belgrade, a Roman fort, was destroyed (372) by the Huns, settled by the Avars (627) and Bulgars (9th c.), disputed (12th and 13th cc.) between the Magyars and Byzantium and taken (1521) by the Turks. It was captured (1688, 1717 and 1789) by the Austrians, but remained Turkish until 1867, when it became the capital of Serbia and (1929) of Yugoslavia

Bel·gra·no (belgránɔ), Manuel (1770–1820), Argentine patriot and general. As commander of the army (1811–14) early in the Argentine war for independence, he fought Spanish forces in Banda Oriental, Upper Peru, and Chile, losing his command to José de San Martín

Be·li·al (bí:li:əl, bí:ljəl) n. (*Old Testament*) the power of evil ‖ the Devil [Heb. *b'li-yaal*, worthlessness, destruction]

be·lie, be·ly (biléi) pres. part. **be·ly·ing** past and past part. **be·lied** v.t. to give a false impression of, esp. by hiding, *his smile belied his true feelings* ‖ to fail to fulfil (expectations or a promise) [O.E. *beléogan*, to deceive by lying]

be·lief (bilí:f) n. the conviction that something is true, esp. the teachings of a religion ‖ the conviction that something exists, *belief in fairies* ‖ the conviction that something is right, *belief in a cause* ‖ something accepted as true ‖ a religion or creed ‖ an opinion **to the best of one's belief** as far as one knows [M.E. *beleave* fr. O.E. (ge)leafa]

be·liev·a·ble (bilí:vəb'l) adj. able to be believed

be·lieve (bilí:v) pres. part. **be·liev·ing** past and past part. **be·lieved** v.t. to accept as true, *to believe a story* ‖ to give credence to (a person) ‖ to hold as one's opinion, *I believe it is going to rain* ‖ v.i. to have religious faith **to believe in** to have confidence in the existence, truth or efficacy of, *to believe in ghosts, to believe in planning* **be·liev·er** n. a person who has beliefs, esp. one who has religious faith [M.E. *bileven* fr. O.E. *geliefan*]

Bel·i·sar·i·us (bəlisǽri:əs) (c. 494–565), Byzantine general. Under Justinian I, he drove the Vandals out of most of N. Africa (533–4) and the Ostrogoths out of Italy (535–40), and repulsed the attacks of the Persians (541–2)

Be·li·sha beacon (bəlí:ʃə) (*Br.*) an orange globe on a pole to mark a pedestrian crossing on a street [after Sir Leslie Hore-*Belisha* (d. 1957), Br. minister of transport (1934–7)]

be·lit·tle (bilít'l) pres. part. **be·lit·tling** past and past part. **be·lit·tled** v.t. to make (an achievement, effort etc.) seem of less than its true worth, to disparage

Be·li·tung (bəlí:tuŋ) (Billiton) an island (area 1,866 sq. miles, pop. 74,000, Chinese and Malay) between Borneo and Sumatra, Indonesia, a major tin source

Be·lize (beli:z) (formerly British Honduras) nation (area 8,866 sq. miles, pop. 118,000) in Central America. Capital: Belmopan, replacing coastal Belize (largely destroyed by a hurricane in 1961). People: 38% African, 31% Mulatto, 17% Maya Indians, together with East Indian, Syrian and Chinese minorities. Official language: English. Spanish is widely spoken. Religion: 60% Roman Catholic, 35% Protestant, with Mennonite, Hindu and Moslem minorities. The land is 90% forest and 5% arable. The north is low and swampy. Inland and south are the Cockscomb Mtns, which rise to 3,681 ft. Annual rainfall: 80 ins in the north, 100 ins in the south (the wet season is May–Feb.). Average temperature (F.) at Belize: 73° (Dec.), 83° (July). The forests produce mahogany, cedar, Santa Maria trees, pine, rosewood and gums (chicle etc.). Agricultural products: citrus fruit, sugar. Fisheries (esp. lobsters and shrimps) are important. Exports: lumber, sugar, oranges, grapefruit. Imports: machinery, vehicles, fuels, oil, foodstuffs. Monetary unit: Belizean dollar (100 cents). HISTORY. The country is the site of an ancient Maya civilization. By the 1530s the Spanish had conquered the peninsula, failing, however, to extend their influence to the Belize area. The British first settled there in 1638. It was completely self-governing until 1786, when a British superintendent was sent to administer its affairs. In 1862 it was officially proclaimed a British Crown Colony, responsible to Jamaica, but it became an independent unit in 1884. Guatemalan claims to the territory, derived from old Spanish treaties, caused tension in the 1930s and 1946–8. Internal self-government was granted in 1964 and independence in 1981

Bel·knap (bélnæp), William Worth (1829–90), U.S. Civil War general. He gained distinction in the Atlanta campaign and received (1865) the rank of major general. Later he became U.S. secretary of war (1869) but was forced to resign when impeached (1876) on charges of corruption. He was acquitted by the Senate

Bell (bel), Alexander Graham (1847–1922), a Scot who emigrated to America, where he invented the telephone (1876) and obtained a U.S. monopoly for the Bell system of telephone communication

bell (bel) 1. *n.* the bellow of a stag at rutting time 2. *v.i.* to make this sound [O.E. *bellan*, to bellow]

bell 1. *n.* a hollow, usually cup-shaped instrument, widening at the lip, which makes a ringing sound when struck. It may be very small, or weigh many tons ∥ an electric device sounding a note when made to do so ∥ its sound ∥ (*naut.*) a halfhourly division of the watch (4, 8 and 12 are marked by 8 bells, then 4:30, 8:30 and 12:30 are each marked by one bell, and progressively one more marks each further half hour up to 8 bells) ∥ something shaped like a bell, such as the corolla of certain flowers **sound as a bell** morally or physically in perfect condition ∥ (of schemes, investments etc.) stable 2. *v.i.* to take the form of a bell ∥ *v.t.* to provide with a bell **to bell the cat** to undertake a risky venture, esp. on behalf of others (from the mice in the fable who wanted to tie a warning bell around the cat's neck) [O.E. *belle*]

bel·la·don·na (belədónə) *n. Atropa belladonna*, fam. Solanaceae, the roots and leaves of which are used in the preparation of atropine ∥ *Amaryllis belladonna*, fam. Amaryllidaceae, the belladonna lily, which grows in S. Africa [Ital.=beautiful lady]

Bel·lar·mine (bélɑrmi:n), St Robert (1542–1621), Italian Jesuit cardinal who was theological adviser to Clement VIII at a time of great religious controversy. He was canonized in 1930. Feast: May 13

bellarmine (bélɑrmi:n, bélɑrmí:n) *n.* a salt-glaze jug stamped with a bearded human image [perh. after Cardinal *Bellarmine*]

Bel·lay (belei), Joachim du (1522–60), French poet, friend and collaborator of Ronsard. He drew up the manifesto of the Pléiade, 'Deffence et Illustration de la langue française' (1549)

bell·boy (bélbɔi) *n.* a hotel or club page boy ∥ trade name for one-way personal signaling service enabling subscribers to get in touch with people in the field; operated by the Bell System

bell buoy a buoy fitted with a warning bell rung by the action of the water

belle (bel) *n.* (*old-fash.*) a beautiful woman, esp. the most beautiful of a group or a place [F.]

Bel·leau Wood, Battle of (bélou) the second engagement between U.S. and German troops in the 1st world war. It took place in Aisne, France, in June 1918, and was won by a U.S. Marine brigade

Belle Isle, Strait of (bɛláil) a channel (10–15 miles wide) between the northern tip of Newfoundland and S.E. Labrador, connecting the Gulf of St Lawrence with the Atlantic

Bel·ler·o·phon (bəlérəfən, bəlérəfɒn) (*Gk mythol.*) the hero who destroyed the fire-breathing monster Chimera with the help of his winged horse Pegasus

belles let·tres (belletr) *pl. n.* the lighter forms of literary writing, esp. elegant essays in criticism [F.]

bell founder a person who casts bells

bell·hang·er (bélhæŋər) *n.* a person who puts bells into position for service

bell·hop (bélhɒp) *n.* a bellboy

bel·li·cism (bélisizəm) *n.* belligerence

bel·li·cose (bélikous) *adj.* warlike ∥ aggressive ∥ fond of fighting **bel·li·cos·i·ty** (belikɒsiti:) *n.* [fr. L. *bellicosus*]

bel·lig·er·ence (bəlídʒərəns) *n.* aggressiveness

bel·lig·er·en·cy (bəlídʒərənsi:) *n.* the state of being at war ∥ belligerence

bel·lig·er·ent (bəlídʒərənt) 1. *adj.* (*internat. law*) waging a war ∥ (of international or personal relations) aggressive, hostile 2. *n.* a nation at war [fr. L. *belligerans* (*belligerantis*) fr. *belligerare* fr. *bellum, war* + *gerere*, to wage]

Bel·li·ni (belí:ni:), Giovanni (c. 1429– 1516), Venetian painter. A great initiator, he was a master of color, with a new understanding of light and a growing feeling for landscape. All this served a profoundly spiritual imagination. His pupils included Titian and Giorgione. He was of a family of painters: Jacopo (c. 1400–70) was his father, Gentile (c. 1429–1507) his brother. Mantegna was his brother-in-law

bell jar a bell-shaped vessel, esp. of glass, used in a laboratory, esp. to contain gases

bell metal an alloy of copper and tin, a bronze for casting large bells

Bel·lo (béjɔ), Andrés (1781–1865), South American poet and statesman. Born in Venezuela, he founded the University of Chile (1842), which he served as Rector until his death. He was a major contributor to the drafting (1855) of the Chilean civil code, of great influence throughout South America. His varied writings include 'Gramática de la lengua castellana' (1847) and his pastoral poems 'Silvas americanas' (1826–7)

Bel·loc (bélɒk), Hilaire (1870–1953), British essayist, historian, novelist and poet, of mixed French and English origin. He wrote 'The Path to Rome' (1902) and other travel books, various biographies, and comic verse ('Cautionary Tales', 1907)

Bel·lo·na (bəlóunə) (*Rom. mythol.*) the goddess of war and sister or wife of Mars. In her temple at Rome the senators gave audience to foreign ambassadors and returning generals

Bel·low (bélou), Saul (1915–), U.S. novelist. His works include 'The Adventures of Augie March' (1953), 'Mr. Sammler's Planet' (1970), 'Humboldt's Gift' (1975), 'The Dean's December' (1982), and 'Him With His Foot in His Mouth' (1984)

bel·low (bélou) 1. *v.i.* (of a bull) to roar ∥ (of guns, men in pain or anger, children in a temper etc.) to make a similar noise ∥ to shout very loudly ∥ *v.t.* to shout out, *to bellow abuse* 2. *n.* the noise of a bull ∥ any comparable noise [M.E. *belwen*, etym. doubtful]

Bel·lows (bélouz), George Wesley (1882–1925), American painter and lithographer. He is known for his paintings of simple realism and for his lithographs, of which 'Billy Sunday' and 'Dempsey and Firpo' are classics

bel·lows (bélouz) *pl.* and *sing. n.* an instrument which, by expanding and collapsing, draws air in through a valve and forces it out, to give draft to a fire, cause organ pipes to sound etc. ∥ the expanding part of a folding camera [M.E. *belowes*]

bell·pull (bélpul) *n.* a rope or handle attached to a wire which operates a bell

bell ringer a campanologist

bell ringing campanology

bell-shaped curve (bélʃeipʼd) the curve of a normal distribution of a general characteristic in a population, named for its shape

Bell's palsy a paralysis of the face, caused by a lesion of a cranial nerve [after Sir Charles *Bell* (1774–1842), Scottish anatomist]

bell·weth·er (bélweðər) *n.* the sheep around whose neck a bell is hung and which leads the flock ∥ someone or something taking the lead

bel·ly (béli:) 1. *n. pl.* **bel·lies** the abdomen ∥ the front part of the human body between the diaphragm and the thighs ∥ the corresponding part of an animal, esp. in relation to food or appetite ∥ anything resembling the rounded exterior of the belly, e.g. the rounded part of a flask ∥ the lower or undersurface of anything, e.g. of a large piece of machinery standing off the ground ∥ the upper plate of the sounding box of a violin etc. 2. *v.t. pres. part.* **bel·ly·ing** *past* and *past part.* **bel·lied** to cause to swell out ∥ *v.i.* to become swollen out [O.E. *bœlig*, bag]

bel·ly·ache (béli:eik) 1. *n.* (*pop.*) an abdominal pain 2. *v.i. pres. part.* **bel·ly·ach·ing** *past* and *past part.* **bel·ly·ached** (*pop.*) to grumble, complain peevishly

bel·ly·band (béli:bænd) *n.* a band passing under a horse's belly to keep a pack or saddle etc. in place

belly board short surfboard designed for riding by lying horizontally upon it

bel·ly·flop (béli:flɒp) 1. *n.* a bad dive, when the body smacks flat on the water, often painfully, instead of entering it obliquely ∥ (of an aircraft) a crash landing made on the underside of the fuselage 2. *v.i. pres. part.* **bel·ly·flop·ping** *past* and *past part.* **bel·ly·flopped** to dive, or land an aircraft, in a bellyflop

bel·ly·ful (béli:ful) *pl.* **bel·ly·fuls** *n.* (*pop.*) as much as, or more than, one wants of anything

bel·ly·hold (béli:hould) *n.* cargo hatch of a passenger aircraft

Be·lo Ho·ri·zon·te (bélɔri:zóntə) a city (pop. 1,442,483) of Brazil: cotton, mining, agriculture

be·long (bilɔ́ŋ, bilóŋ) *v.i.* to have a rightful place, *does the chair belong here?* **to belong to** to be a possession of, *this dog belongs to him* ∥ to be a member of, *do you belong to the choir?* ∥ to be classified with, *do buttercups and kingcups belong to the same family?* **be·long·ings** *pl. n.* possessions, property [M.E. *belongen*]

Belorussia *BYELORUSSIA

be·loved (bilʌvd, bilʌ́vid) 1. *adj.* much loved, favored 2. (bilʌ́vid, bilʌ́vd) *n.* someone who is dearly loved [fr. M.E. *biluven*, to love]

be·low (bilóu) 1. *adv.* under, in a lower place ∥ (*rhet.*) on earth, *mortals here below* ∥ downstream ∥ further down a page or further on in a book **to go below** (*naut.*) to go belowdecks 2. *prep.* lower than, under, *below the surface* ∥ lower in quality than, *below standard* ∥ lower in rank than ∥ downstream from ∥ unworthy of, not befitting the dignity of, *she felt it was below her to do housework* [LOW]

be·low·decks (bilóudɛks) *adv.* in or into a ship's cabin or hold

Bel·sen (bélzʼn) (Bergen-Belsen) the site of a Nazi concentration camp (1943–5) near Lüneburg, N.W. Germany

Bel·shaz·zar (belʃǽzər) (6th c. B.C.), son of the last Babylonian emperor. At a great feast he saw the 'writing on the wall' (Daniel v) which told his fate and the fate of Babylon. That same night Cyrus took the city (539 B.C.)

belt (belt) 1. *n.* a strip of fabric, leather etc., worn around the waist to support clothes or to draw them in ∥ a strip of canvas, leather etc., worn over one shoulder and across to the opposite hip for carrying grenades, a sword etc. ∥ a district characterized by certain physical or climatic conditions, or by the prevalence of a mineral, species, crop etc., *cotton belt* ∥ (*mech.*) an endless band connecting wheels or pulleys ∥ (*shipbuilding*) a row of armor plates below the waterline ∥ a girdle conferred as an honor on a knight or earl **to tighten one's belt** to take austerity measures 2. *v.t.* to fasten with a belt ∥ to encircle, *belted with trees* ∥ to be marked with a band, *belted pigs* ∥ (*pop.*, with 'out') to sing in a loud, coarse voice ∥ (*pop.*) to thrash, esp. with a belt ∥ *v.i.* (*pop.*) to run, rush, *he belted down the street* [O.E. *belt*]

bel·tane (béltein) *n.* (*hist.*) the Celtic fire festival, when all fires were extinguished and the home fires then rekindled from one public sacrificial bonfire. Some modern May Day festivals and various surviving customs are a link [fr. Gael. *bealltainn*, the first day of May]

bel·ted-bi·as tire (béltədbáiəs) motor vehicle tire with ply cords laid at an angle, surrounded

CONCISE PRONUNCIATION KEY: **(a)** æ, c*a*t; ɑ, c*a*r; ɔ f*aw*n; ei, sn*a*ke. **(e)** e, h*e*n; i:, sh*ee*p; iə, d*ee*r; ɛə, b*ea*r. **(i)** i, f*i*sh; ai, t*i*ger; ə:, b*i*rd. **(o)** o, *o*x; au, c*ow*; ou, g*oa*t; u, p*oo*r; ɔi, r*oy*al. **(u)** ʌ, d*u*ck; u, b*u*ll; u:, g*oo*se; ə, b*a*cillus; ju:, c*u*be. x, lo*ch*; θ, *th*ink; ð, bo*th*er; z, *Z*en; ʒ, corsa*g*e; dʒ, sava*g*e; ŋ, oranguta*ng*; j, *y*ak; ʃ, *fi*sh; tʃ, fet*ch*; ʼl, rabb*le*; ʼn, redd*en*. Complete pronunciation key appears inside front cover.

by metal or cord fabric on which the tread is laid; introduced in 1966

belt highway (*Am.=Br.* ring road) a road enabling traffic to bypass a town

belt·ing (béltiŋ) *n.* material for belts

Bel·trán (beltrán), Washington (1914–), Uruguayan editor, politician, Blanco Party leader and 1965–6 president

belt·way (béltwẹi) *n.* a belt highway

be·lu·ga (bəlú:gə) *n.* Acipenser huso, the great sturgeon of the Caspian and Black Seas ‖ *Delphinapterus leucas,* fam. *Delphinidae,* a white whale found in herds in northern seas [Russ. *beluga* and *belucha* fr. *belo-,* white]

bel·ve·dere (bélvidiər, belvidíər) *n.* a tower built to command a fine view [Ital. fr. *bel,* beautiful+*vedere,* see]

bely *BELIE

belying *pres. part.* of BELIE

be·ma (bí:mə) *pl.* **be·ma·ta** (bí:mətə) *n.* the enclosure about the altar of an Orthodox Eastern church [Gk *bēma,* a step]

Bem·bo (bémbou), Pietro (1470–1547), Italian cardinal, poet and humanist, a Latinist of Ciceronian purity, author of a 'History of Venice 1487–1513', secretary to Pope Leo X (1513–20)

be·mean (bimí:n) *v. refl.* to degrade, demean

bem·e·gride [C₈H₁₃NO₂] (bémigri:d) *n.* (*pharm.*) drug to assist recovery from overdose of barbiturates; marketed as Megimide

be·mire (bimáiər) *pres. part.* **be·mir·ing** *past* and *past part.* **be·mired** *v.t.* (*rhet.*) to cover with mud

be·moan (bimóun) *v.t.* to moan over ‖ to express deep sorrow or regret for [O.E. *bemœnan*]

be·mused (bimjú:zd) *adj.* deep in thought ‖ dazed

Be·nal·cá·zar (benɑlkɑ́θɑr, benɑlkɑ́sɑr), Sebastián de (1480–1551), Spanish conquistador and explorer of the Isthmus of Panama. He led an expedition to Ecuador, where he founded Quito (1534) and Guayaquil (1535)

Be·nar·es (bənɑ́ri:s, bənɑ́ri:z) *VARANASI

Be·na·ven·te (benavénte), Jacinto (1866–1954), Spanish dramatist. His works include 'Los intereses creados'

Ben Bel·la (benbélə), Mohammed (1916–), Algerian statesman. He was imprisoned by the French (1949–52, 1956–61) for directing the Algerian movement for independence. He was the first prime minister of independent Algeria (1962), was elected president (1963) and was deposed in a coup d'état (1965)

bench (bentʃ) 1. *n.* a long wooden or stone seat (often with no back) for two or more people ‖ a work table ‖ a judge's seat or the office of judge or magistrate, *appointed to the bench* ‖ judges or magistrates, *the opinion of the bench* ‖ (*Br. parl.*) seats occupied by certain officials or groups or the officials or groups themselves, *treasury bench* ‖ a narrow shelf of ground, esp. a former shoreline of a river or lake ‖ a raised shelf in a mine ‖ a platform on which a dog is exhibited at a show **Bench** (in titles) a law court, *King's Bench* 2. *v.t.* to exhibit (a dog) in a show ‖ to send (a player in a game) to the bench, i.e. remove him from the game [O.E. *benc*]

bench·er (béntʃər) *n.* (*Br.*) a senior member of one of the four Inns of Court

bench mark (*survey.*) a datum point used when leveling ‖ a reference point for making measurements

bench·work (béntʃwə:rk) *n.* handwork at the bench (as distinguished from machine work)

bend (bend) *n.* (*naut.*) a knot ‖ (*heraldry*) a band running from top right to bottom left of the shield ‖ (*leather trade*) a half butt shape, of thickest leather [O.E.]

bend 1. *v. pres. part.* **bend·ing** *past* and *past part.* **bent** (bent) *v.t.* to make curved or crooked ‖ to render (something curved or crooked) straight ‖ to fold, *don't bend these photos* ‖ to focus, to apply, *to bend one's energies to a task* ‖ to force to submit, *to bend someone to one's will* ‖ *v.i.* to become curved or crooked ‖ to change direction, *the road bends to the right* ‖ to submit, *to bend to someone's will* ‖ to stoop 2. *n.* a curve or turn ‖ a part that is not straight, *a bend in a road* **bénd·er** *n.* (*pop.*) a spree [O.E. *bendan,* to bend (a bow), to confine]

Ben·dec·tin (bendéktin) *n.* (*pharm.*) drug used for treating morning sickness, suspected of causing birth defects

bend sinister (*heraldry*) a band denoting bastardy, running from top left to bottom right of the shield

bends, the caisson disease

be·neath (biní:θ) 1. *adv.* under, in a lower place 2. *prep.* under, at, in or to a position lower than ‖ lower in amount, quality or rank than ‖ unworthy of, not befitting **to marry beneath one** to marry a social inferior [O.E. *binithan, beneothan*]

ben·e·dic·i·te (benidáisiti:, benidísiti:) *n.* a grace said at table ‖ the canticle 'Benedicite, omnia opera Domini' [L.=2nd pers. pl. imper. of *benedicere,* to bless]

Ben·e·dict XIV (bénidikt) (1675–1758), pope (1740–58). A great scholar, he is remembered for his writings on beatification and canonization

Benedict XV (1854–1922), pope (1914–22). He denounced inhumanities in the 1st world war, and offered (Aug. 1, 1917) to act as mediator

Benedict Bisc·op (bíʃəp) (c. 628–90), Anglo-Saxon ecclesiastic. He brought masons and glassmakers from Gaul to build the monasteries which he founded at Wearmouth (674) and Harrow (682) and which he equipped with manuscripts and art treasures from the Continent. He had Bede as his pupil

Ben·e·dic·tine (benidíktin, benidíktain) 1. *adj.* of or relating to St Benedict of Nursia, or the religious order founded by him 2. *n.* a member of this order —Founded (c. 529) at Monte Cassino, the order grew rapidly, esp. through the efforts of St Gregory the Great. Notable among later reforms of the order were the Cluniac and the Cistercian. The order is widely distributed throughout W. Europe and the U.S.A. Benedictines are noted for scholarship and for their chanting of Gregorian plainsong. There is an order of nuns

ben·e·dic·tine (benidíkti:n) *n.* a liqueur [after the *Benedictine* monastery where it was orig. made]

ben·e·dic·tion (benidíkʃən) *n.* a blessing, esp. a formal prayer of blessing ‖ a Catholic service of blessing in which the priest makes the sign of the cross over the congregation with the Host [fr. L. *benedictio* (*benedictionis*)]

Benedict of Nur·si·a (né:rsi:ə), St (c. 480– c. 547), Italian monk. He founded (c. 529) the Benedictine order at Monte Cassino, and was the author of the rule followed by Benedictines and Cistercians. Feast: Mar. 21

ben·e·dic·to·ry (benidíktəri:) *adj.* of or expressing benediction [fr. M.L. *benedictorius*]

Ben·e·dic·tus (benidíktəs) *n.* the prayer in the Mass beginning with the word 'Benedictus', following the Sanctus ‖ a canticle in the Book of Common Prayer [L. = blessed]

ben·e·fac·tion (benifǽkʃən) *n.* a financial gift to a charity ‖ a handsome donation or gift to an organization, club etc. [fr. L. *benefactio* (*benefactionis*), doing good]

ben·e·fac·tor (bénifæktər, benifǽktər) *n.* someone who helps, esp. financially **ben·e·fac·tress** (bénifæktris, benifǽktris) *n.* a woman benefactor [L.=one who does good]

ben·e·fice (bénifis) *n.* a church living, the material livelihood of a priest in charge of a parish **bén·e·ficed** *adj.* [O.F. *bénéfice,* a kindness]

ben·ef·i·cence (bənéfisəns) *n.* kindness on a large scale ‖ a particular instance of it **be·néf·i·cent** *adj.* actively good, producing good results [fr. L. *beneficentia*]

ben·e·fi·cial (benifíʃəl) *adj.* helpful, causing improvement ‖ (*law*) receiving (property etc.) for one's own benefit or enjoyment [F.]

ben·e·fi·ci·ar·y (benifíʃi:ẹri:, benifíʃəri:) 1. *n. pl.* **ben·e·fi·ci·ar·ies** someone receiving a benefit, esp. the income of a trust estate or the benefits of an insurance policy etc. ‖ someone who holds a benefice 2. *adj.* pertaining to a benefice ‖ pertaining to charity [fr. L. *beneficiarius*]

ben·e·fit (bénifit) 1. *n.* help, profit, *to derive benefit from* ‖ advantage ‖ an allowance, pension, etc., to which a person may be entitled under private or state welfare arrangements, *maternity benefit* ‖ a performance whose proceeds are given to a particular charity or person 2. *v.t. pres. part.* **ben·e·fit·ing, ben·e·fit·ing** *past* and *past part.* **ben·e·fit·ted, ben·e·fit·ed** to do good to, *exercise will benefit her* ‖ *v.i.* to receive help or benefit, *to benefit by good advice* [M.E. *benfet*=O.F. *bienfait*]

ben·e·fit-cost ratio (bénifitkɒst) indicator of economic efficiency, equal to cost divided by benefits

benefit of clergy (*Br., hist.*) the privilege which entitled a member of the clergy to be tried before an ecclesiastical court although accused in a temporal court

benefit of the doubt the assumption of innocence rather than guilt for lack of proof

benefit society (*Am.=Br.* friendly society) a voluntary association of members paying regular contributions in order to secure certain benefits for sickness, old age etc.

Ben·e·lux (bén'lʌks) an economic union between Belgium, the Netherlands and Luxembourg. The customs union came into operation on Jan. 1, 1948 and the full economic union on Nov. 1, 1960. Benelux holds fourth place in volume of world trade, and joined the European Economic Community in 1959 [*Belgium, Netherlands* and *Lux*embourg]

Be·neš (bénej), Eduard (1884–1948), Czech statesman, president of Czechoslovakia (1935–8 and 1946–8). He left Czechoslovakia after the Munich Agreement, headed its government-in-exile, and returned (1945). He resigned after the Communist coup d'état (1948)

Be·nét (benéi), Stephen Vincent (1898–1943), American poet, author of 'John Brown's Body' (1928), a ballad-style narrative of the American Civil War

Benét, William Rose (1886–1950), American poet, author and editor, brother of Stephen Vincent Benét

Be·ne·ven·to (benevéntɔ) (ancient Maleventum) a town (pop. 59,016) in Campania, S. Italy, rich in monuments, having known Samnite, Roman, Gothic, Lombard, Saracen, Norman and Napoleonic occupations. It belonged to the papacy (1077–1860). Trajan's arch (114 A.D.)

Be·ne·ven·tum (benivéntəm) an ancient city of S.W. Italy, site of Pyrrhus's defeat (275 B.C.) by the Romans

be·nev·o·lence (bənévələns) *n.* kindheartedness ‖ generous giving [O.F.]

be·nev·o·lent (bənévələnt) *adj.* wellwishing, friendly ‖ charitable, *benevolent fund* [O.F.]

Ben·gal (beŋgɔ́l) the area of the Ganges and Brahmaputra deltas, partitioned in 1947 between India (West Bengal, capital Calcutta, area 29,664 sq. miles) and Pakistan (East Bengal, capital Dacca, area 52,550 sq. miles). Its rich alluvial plains produce rice and jute. It is a heavily overpopulated industrial area. E. Bengal claimed (1971) its independence as *BANGLADESH

Bengal, Bay of part of the Indian Ocean, between India and Burma, fed by the Ganges and Brahmaputra (in the north), by the Irrawaddy (in the east), and by the Mahanadi (in the west). It contains many islands, including Andaman and Nicobar

Ben·ga·li (beŋɔ́li:) 1. *n.* an inhabitant or the language of Bengal 2. *adj.* of Bengal, its people or its language

Bengali language a member of the eastern branch of the Indo-Iranian family of languages. It is spoken by about 50 million in Bengal and has literary importance

Bengal light a firework with a blue flame used in signaling

Ben·gha·zi (beŋgázi:) a port (pop. 530,000) of Libya, on the Mediterranean. It was the center of much fighting during the 2nd world war. National University of Libya (1955)

Ben·gue·la (beŋgélə) a port (pop. 40,996) of W. Angola

Benguela current a cold ocean current flowing northwards from the southern Atlantic and carrying low temperatures to the region of Benguela, S.W. Africa

Ben Gu·rion (bengúrjɔn, bengúari:ən), David (1886–1973), Israeli socialist statesman. As the first prime minister of Israel (1948–53, 1955–63) he carried out large economic and social reforms

Be·ni (béni:) a river (c. 1,000 miles long) rising in the Andes of W. Bolivia and flowing to unite with the Mamoré River near the Brazilian border

be·night·ed (bináitid) *adj.* (*rhet.*) lost in moral darkness or ignorance

be·nign (bináin) *adj.* kind, well-disposed ‖ (of climate etc.) mild, favorable ‖ (of diseases) not dangerous (cf. MALIGNANT) [O.F. *benigne*]

be·nig·nan·cy (binígnənsi:) *n.* the state or quality of being benignant

be·nig·nant (binígnənt) *adj.* kind, gracious

be·nig·ni·ty (binígniti:) *n.* kindliness [O. F. *benignité*]

benign neglect policy of watchful inactivity, advocated as a U.S. policy toward the extension of black civil rights by Daniel Patrick Moynihan in 1970; originally phrased by the Earl of Durham in 1839

Be·nin (benín, benírn) (formerly Dahomey) a republic (area 43,484 sq. miles, pop. 3,636,000) in W. Africa. Capital: Porto Novo. Chief commercial center and port: Cotonou. Official language: French. The land is made up of lagoons, palm forests and swamps in the south, rising through plateaus to the Atakora Mtns (1,600 ft) in the north. Mean temperature (F.) 80° in the south, lower in the north. Rainfall: 20–40 ins. The cold, dry harmattan wind blows from the north in winter. Livestock: sheep and cattle. Agricultural products: corn, manioc, yams, cotton (in the north), coffee (in the south). Freshwater fishing is important in the south. Exports: palm kernels and oil, peanuts. Imports: textiles, wine, cement. Monetary unit: C.F.A. franc. HISTORY. The four kingdoms of Ouidah, Allada, Dahomey and Porto Novo flourished in the south in the 17th c. Dahomey defeated Allada (1724) and Ouidah (1729) and took over their slave trade, which continued with Central and South America until the mid-19th c. A commercial treaty was negotiated by France (1851), which annexed the region (1893). The colony became a territory of French West Africa (1899), a member state of the French Community, and an independent republic (Aug. 1, 1960). The army mounted a series of coups d'état (1963, 1965, 1967, 1969, 1972). In 1975 the name was changed to Benin. A military council rules and the national ideology has become Marxism-Leninism

Benin, Bight of part of the northern Gulf of Guinea, W. Africa. Several rivers, including the Niger delta, cut its marshy, sandy shore

ben·i·son (bénizˈn, bénisˈn) n. (archaic) a blessing [O.F. beneiçun]

Ben·ja·min (béndʒamin) Hebrew patriarch, son of Jacob ‖ the Israelite tribe of which he was the ancestor

Benjamin, Judah Philip (1811–84), Anglo-U.S. lawyer. He served as secretary of state for the Confederacy (1862–5) during the Civil War. Escaping to England after Appomattox, he became (1872) a Queen's Counsel. His 'Law of Sale of Personal Property' (1868) long remained the leading authority on the subject in England and the U.S.A.

ben·ja·min (béndʒəmən) n. Styrax benzoin, a tree yielding benzoin ‖ the North American aromatic shrub, spicebush [corrup. of benjoin fr. BENZOIN]

Ben·ja·mite (béndʒəmait) n. a member of the Israelite tribe of Benjamin

Ben·nett (bénit), Arnold (1867–1931), English novelist, best known for his 'The Old Wives' Tale' (1908) and other works set in his native country, the industrial midlands of England

Bennett, James Gordon (1795–1872), U.S. journalist, founder and editor of the 'New York Herald'. His editorial policy of seeking 'not to instruct but to startle' greatly influenced U.S. journalism

Bennett, Richard Bedford Bennett, 1st Viscount (1870–1947), Canadian statesman. As Conservative prime minister of Canada (1930–5) he initiated the Ottawa Conference and championed the protective tariff system

Ben Nev·is (bennévis) the highest mountain (4,406 ft) in Great Britain, in Inverness, Scotland

Be·no·ni (benóunai) a town (pop. 206,810) in the Transvaal, a gold mining center: foundries, electrical manufactures

Ben·son (bénsən), William Shepherd (1885–1932), U.S. admiral. He served as the U.S. naval representative in the drafting of the naval terms of the 1918 Armistice

bent (bent) past and past part. OF BEND ‖ **1.** adj. altered from a previous straight or even state by bending or being bent, a bent pole ‖ (with 'on' or 'upon') determined, resolved, bent on succeeding **2.** n. a mental inclination, a bent for languages ‖ a leaning, tendency **at the top of one's bent** in one's best form

bent n. any of several species of coarse grass ‖ a member of Agrostis, a genus of grasses, some species of which are used for forage and turf [O.E. beonet]

Ben·tham (bénθəm, béntəm), Jeremy (1748–1832), English radical jurist and philosopher. His utilitarian doctrine rests on the arithmetical calculability of the pleasure principle ('men seek pleasure and avoid pain'): the test of an institution's utility lies in how far it tends to promote 'the greatest happiness of the greatest

number', which can be measured. Benthamism produced many reforms in English law. His works include 'Introduction to the Principles of Morals and Legislation' (1789). He founded University College, London

Ben·tham·ism (bénθəmizəm, béntəmizəm) n. the utilitarian doctrine of Jeremy Bentham

ben·thic (bénθik) adj. of or found on the bottom of the deep sea

ben·thos (bénθɒs) n. the bottom of the deep sea ‖ (biol.) the flora and fauna living there [Gk=depth of the sea]

Ben·tinck (béntiŋk), Lord William Cavendish (1774–1839), British governor-general of India (1828–35) who prohibited suttee and put down thuggee. He made English the medium for higher education, with important consequences for the modernizing of India

Ben·ton (béntən), Thomas Hart (1889–1975), U.S. painter. His murals set out to show the wide variety of American life. He wrote an informative autobiography, 'An Artist in America' (1937)

ben·ton·ite (béntənait) n. (geol.) any of a number of valuable claylike materials, similar to fuller's earth [after Fort Benton, Montana]

Be·nue (béinwei) the largest eastern tributary of the Niger, which it joins at Lokoja. It rises in the hills above the Adamawa plateau and is navigable for 700 miles. It was explored in the second half of the 19th c. by Barth, Flegel and others

be·numb (binʌm) v.t. to deprive of the sense of feeling, benumbed by cold ‖ to paralyze (the mind etc.) [O.E. benumen, past part. of beniman, to deprive]

Benz (bents), Carl Friedrich (1844–1929), German engineer. He constructed (1885) one of the first efficient gasoline-driven motor vehicles

benz·al·de·hyde (benzældihaid) n. C₆H₅·CHO, a colorless liquid smelling of essence of almonds, used in perfume and dye manufacture [fr. BENZOIN+ALDEHYDE]

Ben·ze·drine (bénzidri:n, bénzidrin) n. a trademark for amphetamine

ben·zene (bénzi:n, benzí:n) n. (chem.) a distillation product from coal and petroleum. It is a colorless, inflammable, toxic, liquid hydrocarbon boiling at 80.1°C and is used as a solvent and as a fuel. The simplest ring compound, it has six carbon atoms arranged in a ring, with a hydrogen atom attached to each. Its compounds, aromatics, are formed by substituting other elements or groups of elements for one or more of the hydrogen atoms [BENZOIN]

ben·zine (bénzi:n, benzí:n) n. a mixture of the paraffin series of hydrocarbons obtained during the fractional distillation of crude petroleum. It is used as a solvent for fats and in dry cleaning. It boils between 120°C and 150°C [BENZOIN]

ben·zo·in (bénzouin, bénzɔin, benzóuin) n. a resinous substance obtained from Styrax benzoin (*BENJAMIN). It is used in medicines, perfumes etc. ‖ a member of Lindera, a genus of aromatic plants ‖ a member of Benzoin, a genus of aromatic shrubs, esp. the spicebush ‖ a crystalline hydroxy ketone, C₆H₅COCHOHC₆H₅, a condensation product of benzaldehyde reacting both as a ketone and a secondary alcohol [F. benjoin fr. Arab.]

ben·zol (bénzɔl, bénzoul, bénzɒl) n. unrefined benzene [BENZOIN]

Ben-Zvi (benzví:), Izhak (1884–1963) Israeli statesman. One of the founders of Israel, he was president 1952–63

Be·o·wulf (béiəwulf) an Anglo-Saxon epic (c. 700 A.D.), in alliterative verse and heroic style, of unknown authorship. The story is set in Denmark or S. Sweden and tells how the hero, Beowulf, defeats the monster Grendel and his mother but is eventually himself killed in killing a dragon

be·queath (bikwí:ð, bikwí:θ) v.t. to will (money, possessions etc.) at one's death ‖ to hand down (intangibles) to posterity [O.E. becwethan, to say]

be·quest (bikwést) n. something that is left under a will [M.E. biqueste, prob. fr. bi-, BE-+cwiss, a saying]

Be·rar (beirár) a cotton-growing region of Madhya Pradesh, India, in the Deccan. It was a 16th-c. Moslem kingdom

be·rate (biréit) pres. part. **be·rat·ing** past and past part. **be·rat·ed** v.t. to scold, chide

Ber·ber (bé:rbər) n. a member of one of various branches of an indigenous people inhabiting the area between the Mediterranean and the Sahara from Egypt to the Atlantic. They have

fair complexions, usually with dark hair and brown eyes, and have largely remained unmixed with Arab and other invaders. Their language is Hamitic

Ber·ber·a (bé:rbərə) a seaport (pop. 65,000) of N. Somalia on the Gulf of Aden

Berber languages a branch of the Semitic-Hamitic family of languages spoken in N. Africa, represented by various languages, including Tuareg and Kabyle, spoken by 6-7 millions (*AFRICAN LANGUAGES)

Ber·bice (bə:rbí:s) a river (c. 300 miles long) of E. Guyana, flowing north into the Atlantic: navigable for 125 miles

Berch·told (bérxtɔlt), count Leopold von (1863–1942), Austro-Hungarian foreign minister (1912–15). His reckless policy after the assassination of Franz Ferdinand (1914) precipitated the 1st world war

be·reave (birí:v) pres. part. **be·reav·ing** v.t. (past and past part. **be·reaved**) to leave desolate, esp. by death ‖ (past and past part. **be·reft** (biréft)) to deprive (usually of immaterial things, such as reason, comfort etc.) **be·reave·ment** n. [O.E. berēafian]

Be·re·si·na, Battle of the (berəsí:nə) (or Berezina) a battle (Nov. 26–9, 1812) in which Napoleon lost more than 20,000 men while crossing the River Beresina in Byelorussia during the retreat from Moscow

be·ret (bəréi, bérei) n. a soft, round, flat woolen cap of Basque origin [F.]

Berg (berk), Alban (1885–1935), Austrian composer of chamber music and of the operas 'Wozzeck' (1917–21) and 'Lulu' (1928–35). A pupil of Schönberg, he was a master of the twelve-tone technique. His works also include songs, with piano and with orchestra, a 'Lyric Suite' (1925–6) for string quartet, and a violin concerto 'In memory of an angel'

Ber·ga·mo (bérgamɔ) a town (pop. 121,846) in N. Italy, 30 miles northeast of Milan: textile and metal industries

ber·ga·mot (bé:rgəmɒt) n. Citrus bergamia, fam. Rutaceae. The rind of its fruit yields an oil used in perfumery ‖ this oil or perfume ‖ any of several varieties of mint, esp. Mentha citrata [after Bergamo in Italy]

bergamot n. any of several varieties of pear [F. bergamotte fr. Ital. fr. Turk. beg armudi, prince's pear]

Ber·gen (bé:rgən) Norway's second largest town, a great port and fishing center (pop. 207,419) on the west coast: shipbuilding, metal and clothing industries, food processing. Old merchant houses and the cathedral (13th c.). University (1946)

Bergen-Belsen *BELSEN

Berg·man (bé:rgmən, bǽrjmæn), Ingmar (1918–), Swedish play producer and film director. His films include 'The Seventh Seal' (1956), 'Wild Strawberries' (1958), 'Scenes from a Marriage' (1978), 'Autumn Sonata' (1978), 'Fanny and Alexander' (1983)

Bergman, Ingrid (1915–82), Swedish actress who received Academy Awards for her roles in 'Gaslight' (1944), 'Anastasia' (1956), and 'Murder on the Orient Express' (1974). She came to Hollywood in the late 1930's to make 'Intermezzo' (1939). Other films include 'Casablanca' (1942), 'For Whom the Bell Tolls' (1943), 'The Bells of St. Mary's' (1945), 'Spellbound' (1945), 'Notorious' (1946), and 'Autumn Sonata' (1978). She made 'A Woman Called Golda' (1981) for television

Berg·slag·en (bérkzlɑgən) an iron-mining and industrial region in central Sweden

Berg·son (berks5), Henri (1859–1941), French philosopher, the most influential of modern temporalistic, antimechanistic thinkers, whose leading ideas (esp. through their influence on Proust) reached a very wide public. His system rests on the liberation of mental intuitions from the idea of space and the scientific notion of time, and on the affirmation of an 'élan vital', a creative life-force. His main works were 'Essai sur les données immédiates de la conscience' (1889), 'Matière et Mémoire, (1896), 'l'Évolution créatrice' (1907) and 'les Deux Sources de la morale et de la religion' (1932)

Ber·i·a (béəri:ə), Lavrenti (1899–1953), Soviet politician. He was minister of the interior (1942–6). He was created (1945) Marshal of the Soviet Union. He was executed for treason after Stalin's death

beri·ber·i (béri:béri:) n. a disease due to deficiency of vitamin B₁, common esp. among people who live mainly on polished rice. Its principal effect is nerve degeneration, but edema and heart failure can be symptoms [Singhalese *beri*, weakness]

Ber·ing (bérin, bíərin), Vitus (1680–1741), Danish navigator. He explored the coasts of N.E. Asia, discovering the Bering Strait (1728) and Bering Is. (1741)

Bering Sea an arm (area 875,000 sq. miles) of the Pacific between the Aleutian Islands and Bering Strait

Bering Strait a passage 56 miles wide, dividing America from Asia and linking the Arctic and Pacific Oceans

Berke·ley (bá:rkli:, *Br.* bákli), George (1685–1753), Irish bishop and philosopher who held that all reality reduces itself to human thought, but that the existence of the human mind argues the existence of a universal mind, a God. Major works: 'Essay towards a New Theory of Vision' (1709), 'Treatise concerning the principles of Human Knowledge' (1710) and 'Dialogues between Hylas and Philonous' (1713)

Berke·ley (bá:rkli:), Sir William (1606–77), colonial governor of Virginia (1641–52, 1660–77). His failure to provide his colonists with security against Indian attacks resulted in Bacon's rebellion (1676)

Berkeley a city (pop. 112,000) in California, near San Francisco, seat of the University of California

berke·li·um (bé:rkli:əm, bə:rkí:li:əm) *n.* a radioactive element artificially produced in a cyclotron (symbol Bk, at. no. 97, mass of isotope of longest known half-life 247) [after the University of California at *Berkeley*]

Berk·shire (bá:rkʃər, *Br.* bákʃə) (*abbr.* Berks.) a county (area 725 sq. miles, pop. 659,000) in the south Midlands of England. County town: Reading

Ber·lich·ing·en (bérlixinən), Götz von (1480–1562), German knight, known as 'Götz of the Iron Hand'. Goethe based his Sturm und Drang drama 'Götz von Berlichingen' (1773) on his life

Ber·lin (bə:rlín) a city of Brandenburg, Germany, connected by river and canal with the North Sea, the Baltic, and industrial regions inland. It owed its rise to the Hohenzollern dynasty. It was in turn capital of Brandenburg, Prussia, and finally (1871) all Germany, and became a great industrial and cultural center. In the 2nd world war about 4/5ths of its dwellings were destroyed. The Russians withdrew from the quadripartite Allied government of the city in 1948, set up a separate municipal government in their eastern sector, and for over a year stopped all supplies by land to West Berlin, which was supplied by an American and British airlift. West Berlin (pop. 1,890,300) is a 'Land' (state) of the Federal Republic. It contains the Free University (1948) and Berlin Museum (esp. for Renaissance painting). There are electrical and mechanical engineering, clothing, printing and steel industries. East Berlin (pop. 1,152,500) is the capital of East Germany. Industries: electrical and mechanical engineering (esp. machine tools), iron and steel, paper and printing. University (1810), Berliner Ensemble theater and the Brandenburg Gate (1788). A wall built (Aug. 13, 1961) by the East Germans separates the two sectors

ber·lin (bə:rlín) *n.* (*hist.*) a fourwheeled carriage with a hood, having a platform behind for footmen ('tigers') [after *Berlin* in Germany]

Berlin, Congress of a meeting of European statesmen held (1878) under the presidency of Bismarck to discuss problems arising from the Russo-Turkish War (1877–8). The Treaty of San Stefano (1878) was undone. Bosnia and Herzegovina became Austro-Hungarian protectorates, Bulgaria was split in two, and the independence of Rumania, Serbia and Montenegro was guaranteed

Berlin Decree *CONTINENTAL SYSTEM

ber·line (bə:rlí:n) *n.* (*hist.*) a berlin

Berlin, Treaty of a treaty signed July 28, 1742 during the war of the Austrian Succession. Austria ceded Silesia to Prussia

Ber·lioz (berljɔz), Hector (1803–69), French composer, a master of orchestration and pioneer of 'program music', a key figure in the French Romantic movement. His works include 'la Damnation de Faust' (cantata), 'Symphonie fantastique' and 'Harold in Italie' (orchestral), 'l'Enfance du Christ' (oratorio), 'les Troyens' (opera) and the great funeral pieces:

the 'Grande messe des morts' and the 'Symphonie funèbre et triomphale'

berm (bə:rm) *n.* a narrow path in a fortification between the ditch and the base of the parapet ‖ a narrow path along a road [F. *berme* fr. G.]

Ber·me·jo (berméhɔ) a river (c. 1,000 miles long) in N. Argentina, rising on the Bolivian border and flowing into the Paraguay River (Paraguay-Argentina boundary). Its middle course is called the Teuco

Ber·mu·da (bərmjú:də) a British colony (area 20½ sq. miles, pop. 60,000) including over 300 coral islands (20 inhabited) in the N. Atlantic, 600 miles east of the southern U.S.A. Capital: Hamilton (pop. 2,800). Main island: Bermuda (or Great Bermuda). Crops: fruit, flowers, vegetables. Industries: tourism, fishing, pharmaceutics. Bermuda was visited (c. 1515) by the Spaniard Bermudez, but the islands were first settled (1609) by shipwrecked English Puritans. The Bermuda Company developed the islands rapidly (17th c.). They became a Crown Colony (1684). Naval and air bases were leased (1941) to the U.S.A. for 99 years. Bermuda has been self-governing since 1968

Bermuda grass *Cynodon dactylon*, a trailing grass used for making lawns and pastures, esp. in the U.S.A. and India

Bermuda petrel an almost-extinct nocturnal bird with brown and white coloring, noted for burrowing into earth; formerly native to Bermuda

Bermuda triangle triangular area between Bermuda, Cape Hatteras, and Puerto Rico (440,000 sq mi) where ships and planes have disappeared without a trace

Bern, Berne (bə:rn, bɛərn) a canton (area 2,658 sq. miles, pop. 912,022) of N.W. Switzerland (since 1353), mainly German-speaking and Protestant ‖ its capital (pop. 145,254), capital of Switzerland (since 1848), on the Aar, a rail center, with weaving and metal industries. University (1834)

Ber·na·dette (bə:rnədét), St (Bernadette Soubirous, 1844–79), a Lourdes girl whose visions of the Virgin Mary have made Lourdes a great center of pilgrimage. Feast: Apr. 10

Ber·na·dotte (bɛərnædɔ́t), Folke, Count (1895–1948), Swedish humanitarian, prominent in Red Cross work in the 2nd world war. He was assassinated by a Jewish extremist while acting as United Nations mediator in Palestine

Ber·na·dotte (bernædɔt), Jean (1763–1844), French marshal and king of Sweden (Charles XIV, 1818–44). After a distinguished military career in the French Revolutionary Wars he was created a marshal of the French Empire (1804). He became (1810) heir apparent to the Swedish throne, and allied (1812) with Russia against Napoleon. He obtained the union of Norway and Sweden (1814) and acceded to the throne (1818). He was the founder of the present Swedish royal family

Ber·na·nos (bernænous), Georges (1888–1948), French novelist and Catholic apologist. His novels include 'Sous le soleil de Satan' (1926) and 'Journal d'un curé de campagne' (1936)

Ber·nard (bernɑr), Claude (1813–78), French physiologist. He made important discoveries relating to the action of secretions of the alimentary tract, the glycogenic action of the liver, and the sympathetic nerves

Bernard, Samuel (1651–1739), French banker, who supplied Louis XIV with the millions he needed for his wars and his glory, and whose influence continued under Louis XV

Ber·nar·din de Saint-Pierre (bernærdɛ̃dəsɛ̃pjer), Jacques-Henri (1737–1814), French writer. His works, esp. the sentimental romance 'Paul et Virginie' (1788), helped to bring in a romantic taste for nature, the picturesque and the exotic

Ber·nard·ine (bé:rnərdi:n) *adj.* of St Bernard of Clairvaux or of his branch of the Cistercian order

Bernard of Clair·vaux (bé:rnərdəvklɛərvóu), St (c. 1090–1153), French theologian and ecclesiastical reformer. Trained as a Cistercian, he founded (1115) a monastery at Clairvaux, in N.E. France, of which he remained the abbot for the rest of his life. He did much to spread the Cistercian order throughout W. Europe and exercised a controlling influence on the affairs of the Church. He was responsible for the recognition of Innocent II as pope (1130), and Eugenius III was his disciple. He secured the condemnation of Abelard's rationalist teaching, and preached the 2nd Crusade. His writings include

hundreds of treatises, sermons and letters. Feast: Aug. 20

Ber·ners (bá:rnərz), John Bourchier, 2nd Baron (1467–1533), English statesman and translator of 'The Chronicles of Froissart' (1523–5) etc.

Bern·hardt (bá:rnhɑrt), Sarah (Henriette Rosine Bernard, 1844–1923), French actress. Her personality, voice and command of emotion made her probably one of the greatest tragediennes of all time. She also played in comedy

Ber·ni·ni (berní:ni:), Gian Lorenzo (1598–1680), Italian painter, sculptor and architect. His great colonnade at St Peter's, Rome, is his most famous work (*BAROQUE)

Ber·noul·li, Ber·nouil·li (bərnú:li:) Swiss family of Dutch extraction, several members of which made distinguished contributions to physics and mathematics. Jacques (1654–1705) worked on analytical geometry, his brother Jean (1667–1748) discovered the exponential calculus and a method of integrating rational functions, and Jean's son Daniel (1700–82) developed the kinetic theory of gases

Bernoulli effect the phenomenon observed in hydrodynamics that the pressure in a stream of fluid falls as the rate of flow increases [after Daniel *Bernoulli*]

Bernoulli's theorem a fundamental principle of statistics, sometimes called the law of averages, that as the number of trials of an event of given theoretical probability is increased indefinitely the ratio of the observed events to total trials approaches the theoretical probability [after Jacques *Bernoulli*]

Bern·stein (bá:rnstain, bá:rnsti:n), Leonard (1918–), U.S. conductor and composer. He served (1958–69) the New York Philharmonic as permanent conductor and occasional pianoforte soloist. His compositions range from jazz and musical comedy to symphonies and ballet music. His major works include the symphonies 'Jeremiah' (1944), 'The Age of Anxiety' (1949), and 'Kaddish' (1963); ballets 'Fancy Free' (1944), 'Facsimile' (1946), and 'Dybbuk' (1974); musical scores 'On the Town' (1944), 'Wonderful Town' (1952), 'Candide' (1956), and 'West Side Story' (1957); and operas 'Trouble in Tahiti' (1952) and 'A Quiet Place' (1983)

Ber·ry (beri:) a former province of central France in the S. Paris basin, forming most of modern Cher and Indre, and parts of Loiret, Indre-et-Loire and Creuse. The west is swampy, the south sandy, but the center, round the Cher (cereals, fruit, sheep pasture) and the Sancerre hills by the Loire (vineyards) are productive. Historic capital: Bourges. Acquired gradually by the Crown (11th–12th cc.), it was a duchy given in apanage to princes of the blood (1360–1601)

ber·ry (béri:) **1.** *n. pl.* **ber·ries** any small, juicy fruit with seeds ‖ (*bot.*) a many-seeded fleshy fruit, e.g. tomato, grape, gooseberry, banana etc. (cf. DRUPE) ‖ one of the eggs of a fish, crab or lobster **2.** *v.i. pres. part.* **ber·ry·ing** past and past part. **ber·ried** to bear berries ‖ to gather or look for berries, *to go berrying* [O.E. *berie*]

Ber·ry·man (béri:mən) John (1914–72), U.S. poet who dealt with innovative forms and techniques and probed the psychological in most of his works. His poems include 'Homage to Mistress Broadstreet' (1956), '77 Dream Songs' (1964; Pulitzer Prize), 'Berryman's Sonnets' (1967), and 'The Dream Songs' (1970). Poems collected in 'Delusions' (1972) and a novel 'Recovery' (1973) were published after his suicide

ber·serk (bə:rsé:rk, bə:rzé:rk) *adj.* frenzied **to go berserk** to have a sudden fit of frenzy [Icel. *berserkr*, (prob.) bear shirt]

berth (bə:rθ) **1.** *n.* a bunk in a ship or train ‖ a place at a wharf where a ship can lie at anchor ‖ an appointment, job **to give a wide berth to** to give (a ship) plenty of room to maneuver ‖ to take care to avoid **2.** *v.t.* to moor (a ship) at a suitable place ‖ to assign a berth to ‖ *v.i.* to take up moorings [origin unknown]

Ber·tha (bá:rθə) (d. 783), queen of the Franks, known as 'Berthe au grand pied', mother of Charlemagne

Ber·trand (bertrɑ̃), Jean-Jacques (1916–), Canadian politician, leader of the Quebec National Union party, and premier of Quebec (1968–70)

Ber·tran de Born (bɛərtrɑ̃dəbɔrn) (1140 – c. 1215), a famous troubadour, mentioned by Dante

Ber·wick (bérik) a former border county (area 457 sq. miles) of S. E. Scotland.

beryl

93

better

ber·yl (béril) *n.* a semiprecious or precious stone, a beryllium aluminum silicate, varying in color from white through yellow (heliodor), greenish-blue (aquamarine), green (emerald) to pink (morganite) [O.F. fr. L. fr. Gk]

be·ryl·li·um (bəríli:əm) *n.* a divalent element (symbol Be, at. no. 4, at. mass 9.0122), the lightest alkaline earth, more stable in moist air than magnesium. It is used in light alloys as a resistant to corrosion, and to slow down neutrons emitted during nuclear fission

Ber·ze·li·us (bə:rzí:li:əs), Baron Jöns Jacob, (1779–1848), Swedish chemist who, by an extensive use of the newly invented chemical balance, amassed data used by Dalton to formulate the atomic theory. He also formalized the symbols for chemical elements

Be·san·çon (bəzãsɔ̃) a fortress town (pop. 126,187) on the Doubs, E. France, ancient capital of Franche-Comté, a rail and industrial center (watches, paper, silk), with Renaissance buildings, university (1485), and a citadel built by Vauban

be·seech (bisí:tʃ) *pres. part.* **be·seech·ing** *past and past part.* **be·sought** (bisɔ́t) *v.t.* to implore **be·seech·ing** *adj.* [BE-+M.E. *secen* fr. O.E. *sēcan*, to seek]

be·seem (bisí:m) *v.t. impers.* (*old-fash.*) to be fitting in, become

be·set (bisét) *pres. part.* **be·set·ting** *past and past part.* **be·set** *v.t.* to surround, hem in, *beset with difficulties* ‖ to set upon, waylay **be·set·ting** *adj.* continually harassing or assailing, *besetting sin* [O.E. *besettan*]

be·side (bisáid) *prep.* by the side of, close to ‖ compared with, *his efforts look feeble beside yours* **beside the point** irrelevant **to be beside oneself** to be so overcome with worry, rage, joy etc. as to be almost out of one's mind [O.E. *besīdan*]

be·sides (bisáidz) **1.** *adv.* moreover ‖ also, in addition **2.** *prep.* in addition to

be·siege (bisí:dʒ) *pres. part.* **be·sieg·ing** *past and past part.* **be·sieged** *v.t.* to surround with armed forces, lay siege to ‖ to throng around ‖ to assail (with requests etc.) [M.E. *besegen*]

Bes·kids (beskí:dz) (*Polish* Beskidy) a range of the Carpathians between Poland and Czechoslovakia (Babia Gora, 5,658 ft)

be·smear (bismíər) *v.t.* to smear with dirt, or with something sticky or greasy [O.E. *besmierwan*]

be·smirch (bismé:rtʃ) *v.t.* to cast a slur on, sully

be·som (bí:zəm) *n.* a stiff sweeping broom made of twigs [O.E. *besma*, broom]

be·sot (bisɔ́t) *pres. part.* **be·sot·ting** *past and past part.* **be·sot·ted** *v.t.* to make besotted **be·sot·ted** *adj.* drunken ‖ infatuated ‖ mentally confused

besought *past and past part.* of BESEECH

be·span·gle (bispǽŋg'l) *pres. part.* **be·spangling** *past and past part.* **be·span·gled** *v.t.* to cover with spangles

be·spat·ter (bispǽtər) *v.t.* to spatter all over (with mud, blood etc.)

be·speak (bispí:k) *pres. part.* **be·speak·ing** *past* **be·spoke** (bispóuk) *past part.* **be·spoke**, **bespoken** (bispóukən) *v.t.* to order in advance ‖ to indicate, show evidence of, *his arrogance bespeaks his youth* [O.E. *besprecan*]

be·sprin·kle (bispríŋk'l) *pres. part.* **be·sprin·kling** *past and past part.* **be·sprin·kled** *v.t.* to sprinkle over [M.E. *besprengil*]

Bes·sa·ra·bi·a (besəréibi:ə) a region of steppe land (area 17,147 sq. miles) in S.E. Europe between the Dniester and Prut Rivers, the Danube delta and the Black Sea. Part of Moldavia, it became subject to the Ottoman Empire (16th c.), and was annexed by Russia (1812). It was again part of Moldavia (1856) and of Russia (1878). It was occupied by Rumania (1918–44) and formally ceded to Russia (1947). It is incorporated in Moldavia, Rumania, and the Ukraine, U.S.S.R.

Bes·sel (bés'l), Friedrich Wilhelm (1784–1846), German astronomer who gave his name to a series of mathematical functions of great practical importance in mathematical physics

Bes·se·mer (bésəmər), Sir Henry (1813–98), English metallurgist, inventor of a process (1856) for converting cast iron into steel by forcing air through the molten metal (*BLAST FURNACE). The impurities escape as gases or form a slag of their oxides, and the percentage of combined carbon is greatly reduced

best (best) **1.** *adj.* (*superl.* of GOOD) finest in quality ‖ most advantageous ‖ largest, *the best part of an hour* **2.** *n.* anything which is best ‖ greatest effort, utmost, *to try one's best* ‖ best clothes, *Sunday best* ‖ (*pl.*) persons superior in any category, *the best of the recruits* **it's all for the best** it will work out advantageously in the long run **to be at one's best** to be in one's best form or state **to get** (or **have**) **the best of** to dominate, have the advantage over or be the winner of, *he had the best of the argument* **to make the best of** to do as well as one can in (a difficult, situation) **to the best of one's ability** as well as one can **to the best of one's belief** (or **knowledge**) as far as one knows **with the best** as well as anyone else, *he can dance with the best* **3.** *adv.* (*superl.* of WELL) most, *bears like honey best* ‖ in the most excellent way, *the engine runs best at night* **at best** in the most hopeful circumstances, *at best we can only hope to finish third* **had best** would find it wisest to, *he had best hurry up* **4.** *v.t.* to do better than, *she can best him at swimming* ‖ to get the better of [O.E. *betst*]

best bower *BOWER

best-ef·forts (bésteferts) *adj.* of a commitment to use one's best effort in a project with no guarantee of the outcome

best·er (béstər) *n.* variety of sturgeon that does not migrate, developed in the U.S.S.R.

bes·tial (béstʃəl, bésti:əl) *adj.* of or like a beast ‖ vile ‖ obscene, lustful **bes·ti·al·i·ty** *n.* [O.F.]

bes·ti·ar·y (béstʃi:eri:, bésti:eri:) *pl.* **bes·ti·ar·ies** *n.* a type of didactic illustrated book popular esp. in the 12th and 13th cc., in which pseudo-scientific descriptions of known animals were mixed with legends, fables and accounts of mythological creatures [fr. L. *bestiarium*]

best man the bridegroom's attendant at a wedding

be·stow (bistóu) *v.t.* to confer, to *bestow a medal* ‖ to devote (thought, time) [M.E. *bistowen*]

be·strad·dle (bistrǽd'l) *pres. part.* **be·straddling** *past and past part.* **be·strad·dled** *v.t.* to bestride

be·strew (bistrú:) *pres. part.* **be·strew·ing**, **be·strewed** *past part.* **be·strewed**, **be·strewn** (bistrú:n) *v.t.* to scatter over, *bestrewn with leaves* [O.E. *bestrēowian*]

be·stride (bistráid) *pres. part.* **be·strid·ing** *past* **be·strode** (bistróud) *past part.* **be·strode**, **be·strid·den** (bistríd'n) *v.t.* to have a leg on either side of ‖ to mount (a bicycle etc.) [O.E. *bestrīdan*]

best seller an article of merchandise, most frequently a book or record, the sales of which are conspicuously large ‖ the author or performer of a best-selling work

bet (bet) **1.** *n.* a wager of money etc. against someone else's on the outcome of a doubtful event ‖ the money etc. that is staked ‖ the thing that is wagered upon **one's best bet** one's safest course of action **2.** *v.* *pres. part.* **bet·ting** *past and past part.* **bet**, **bet·ted** *v.t.* to wager (a sum etc.) ‖ *v.i.* to lay a bet ‖ to be in the practice of laying bets [etym. doubtful]

be·ta (béitə, *Br.* bí:tə) *n.* the second letter (B, β=b) of the Greek alphabet ‖ the second brightest star in a constellation ‖ (*securities*) unit in the measurement of risk in stock trading based on sensitivity to performance of the stock market as a whole

beta adrenergic *adj.* (*biol.*) causing stimulation of the sympathetic nervous system that releases adrenalinelike substance

beta decay or **beta disintegration** (*particle phys.*) radioactive disintegration of a nuclide with emission of a beta particle or a neutrino or an antinutrino and an increase or decrease of the atomic number by one

beta emitter (*particle phys.*) a radionuclide that changes to another element by emitting beta particles

be·ta·en·dor·phin (beitəendɔ́rfin) *n.* (*biol.*) natural substance in the pituitary gland that acts as a painkiller more potent than morphine

be·take (bitéik) *pres. part.* **be·tak·ing** *past* **betook** (bitúk) *past part.* **be·tak·en** (bitéik'n) *v. refl.* (*rhet.*) to take oneself off, go, *he betook himself to bed* [M.E. *bitaken*]

Be·tan·court (bétəkour:), Rómulo (1908–81), Venezuelan statesman, and founder of the Acción Democrática, the spearhead of Latin American parties of social reform. He served (1945–8, 1959–64) as a democratically elected president

beta particle an electron or positron emitted by radioactive substances

beta ray a stream of beta particles

be·ta·tron (béitətron, *Br.* bí:tətron) *n.* (*phys.*) a device in which electrons are accelerated in circular orbits, and restricted to them, by the inductive effect of a powerful and varying field applied perpendicularly to the plane of motion. Electrons having energies of 10^8 eV are produced by the larger betatrons [BETA+ ELECTRON]

be·tel (bí:t'l) *n. Piper betle,* a climbing pepper (*BETEL NUT) [prob. Port. *betel* fr. Tamil]

Be·tel·geuse (bí:t'ldʒu:z, bét'ldʒə:z) *n.* a giant red star near one shoulder of the constellation Orion [F. fr. Arab.]

betel nut the kernel of the betel palm. Enclosed in betel leaves, and mixed with an aromatic paste, it is chewed extensively in Africa and the East

betel palm *Areca catechu,* an Asian palm whose fruit, a drupe, contains the betel nut

bête·noire (betnwær) *pl.* **bêtes noires** (betnwær) *n.* a pet aversion, a person or thing causing feelings of irritation [F.=black beast]

beth·el (béθəl) *n.* a house of worship, esp. (*Br.*) a Nonconformist chapel [fr. *Bethel,* a city of ancient Palestine where, according to the Bible (Genesis xxviii, 18-19), God appeared to Abraham and Jacob]

be·thes·da (bəθézdə) *n.* a Nonconformist chapel [Heb. = house of mercy]

be·think (biθíŋk) *pres. part.* **be·think·ing** *past and past part.* **be·thought** (biθɔ́t) *v. refl.* (*rhet.*) to remember, call to mind [O.E. *bithencan*]

Beth·le·hem (béθlihem, béθli:əm) a town (pop. 15,000) in Israeli-occupied Jordan five miles south of Jerusalem, birthplace of Jesus Christ (the 4th-c. Church of the Nativity is on the assumed site) and the early home of King David

Bethlehem an industrial city and music center (pop. 70,419) in E. Pennsylvania. It is one of the most important steel production areas in the U.S.A., and also supplies large quantities of cement. It is the chief site of the Moravian sect in the U.S.A.

Beth·len (bétlən), Gabor (1580–1629), prince of Transylvania (1613–29) and elected king of Hungary (1620–1). A champion of Protestantism, he fought the Emperor Ferdinand III in the Thirty Years' War

Beth·mann Holl·weg (béitmanhɔ́lveik), Theobald von (1856–1921), chancellor of Germany (1909–17)

Beth·sa·i·da (beθséiidə) a site on the northern side of Lake Tiberias, Israel, traditionally the birthplace of the Apostles Peter, Andrew and Philip

be·tide (bitáid) *pres. part.* **be·tid·ing**, *past and past part.* **be·tid·ed** *v.t.* (only in) **woe betide (you** etc.) may ill befall (you etc.) [M.E. *bitiden*]

be·times (bitáimz) *adv.* (*old-fash.*) early, in good time

be·to·ken (bitóukən) *v.t.* to give evidence of, be a sign of [M.E. *bitacnien*]

betook *past* of BETAKE

be·tray (bitréi) *v.t.* to act treacherously towards, *to betray one's country* ‖ to reveal treacherously, *to betray information* ‖ to reveal accidentally, *to betray a secret* ‖ to fail to justify, *to betray the trust put in one* ‖ to give evidence of, *the gleam in his eye betrayed his interest* **be·tráy·al** *n.* [M.E. *betraien* fr. BE-+O.F. *traïr*]

be·troth (bitróuð, bitrɔ́θ) *v.t.* (*rhet.*) to affiance, promise in marriage **be·tróth·al** *n.* an engagement to marry **be·tróthed 1.** *n.* the person to whom one is engaged **the betrothed** an engaged couple **2.** *adj.* engaged to be married [M.E. *bitreuðien* fr. BE-+M.E. *treowthe,* truth]

bet·ter (bétər) **1.** *adj.* (*comp.* of GOOD) having good qualities in a greater degree ‖ preferable ‖ improved ‖ improved in health ‖ larger, *the better part of a day* **better off** richer ‖ in a more satisfactory situation **no better than** just as bad as, virtually the same as, *he's no better than a thief* **to be better than one's word** to do what one promised and more besides **2.** *adv.* (*comp.* of WELL) in a more excellent manner, *he swims better than most* ‖ in a higher degree, *your efforts are better appreciated now* ‖ (of preference) more, *to like beer better than wine* **had better** would find it wiser, *you had better come early* **to know better** to be wiser (than to think or do a thing), *you should know better than to tease him* **to think better of it** to change one's mind **3.** *n.* someone superior in age, rank, knowledge etc. ‖ advantage, *to get the better of someone* [O.E. *betera*]

CONCISE PRONUNCIATION KEY: **(a)** æ, c*a*t; ɑ, c*a*r; ɔ f*aw*n; ei, sn*a*ke. **(e)** e, h*e*n; i:, sh*ee*p; iə, d*ee*r; ɛə, b*ea*r. **(i)** i, f*i*sh; ai, t*i*ger; ə:, b*i*rd. **(o)** o, *o*x; au, c*ow*; ou, g*oa*t; u, p*oo*r; ɔi, r*oy*al. **(u)** ʌ, d*u*ck; u, b*u*ll; u:, g*oo*se; ə, b*a*cillus; ju:, c*u*be. x, lo*ch*; θ, *th*ink; ð, bo*th*er; z, *Z*en; ʒ, corsa*g*e; dʒ, sava*g*e; ŋ, oranguta*ng*; j, *y*ak; ʃ, *fi*sh; tʃ, fe*tch*; 'l, rabb*le*; 'n, redd*en*. Complete pronunciation key appears inside front cover.

better v.t. to improve ‖ to surpass, *they raised $500 and we must better that sum* [M.E. *beteren* fr. O.E.]

better *BETTOR

Better Business Bureau a bureau administered by businessmen for the purpose of safeguarding standards of honesty in business transactions

bet·ter·ment (bétərmənt) n. improvement ‖ (*law*) the increased value of an estate or property because of improvements beyond mere repairs

betting shop (*Br.*) licensed public betting premises

bet·tor, bet·ter (bétər) n. a person who bets

be·tween (bitwí:n) 1. prep. in the intervening space of, *the house is between two oaks* ‖ within two limits (of distance, time or amount), *between 60 and 70, between 7 and 7:30* ‖ intermediate to in quality, degree etc., *between fair and excellent* ‖ to and from, *between Le Havre and Southampton* ‖ common to, *there is an understanding between them* ‖ distinguishing, *the difference between a crow and a rook* ‖ linking, *the ramp between the boat and the jetty* ‖ with respect to either the one or the other of (two people or things), *he must choose between them* ‖ jointly among (two or more persons etc.), *we shared the work between us* ‖ what with the combined several effects of, *between the whiskey, the atmosphere and the crowd, she felt ready to faint* **between ourselves** in confidence 2. adv. in an intermediate space ‖ in an interval of time [O.E. *betwēonum, betwēon*]

be·tween·times (bitwí:ntạimz) adv. in the interval or intervals

be·tween·whiles (bitwí:nhwạilz, bitwí:nwạilz) adv. betweentimes

be·twixt and between (bitwíkst) in a midway position

Beust (bɔist), Friedrich Ferdinand, Count von (1809–86), Saxon and Austrian statesman. As prime minister of Austria (1867–71), he negotiated the establishment (1867) of the dual monarchy of Austria-Hungary

Beu·then (bɔít'n) *BYTOM

BeV (abbr.) for 1 billion electrovolts

Bev·an (bévən), Aneurin ('Nye') (1897–1960), British statesman, Welsh Labour M.P. (1927–60). As minister of health (under Attlee) he created the National Health Service. He resigned as minister of works (1951) over rearmament

bev·el (bévəl) 1. n. the angle formed at the junction of two nonperpendicular lines or surfaces ‖ the surface at such an angle ‖ (*printing*) the angled part of the body of a piece of type between the face and the shoulder ‖ an instrument for measuring angles 2. v.t. pres. part. **bev·el·ing**, esp. *Br.* **bev·el·ling** past and past part. **bev·eled**, esp. *Br.* **bev·elled** to reduce (a square edge) to a sloping edge [etym. doubtful]

bevel gear a gear whose teeth lie across a bevel

bev·er·age (bévəridʒ, bévridʒ) n. (*catering trade, administration*) a drink [fr. O.F. *bevrage*]

Bev·er·idge (bévəridʒ, bévridʒ), William Henry, 1st Baron Beveridge (1879–1963), British economist, author of 'Report on Social Insurance and Allied Services' (1942), on which subsequent social security legislation in Britain was based, and of 'Full Employment in a Free Society' (1944)

Bev·in (bévin), Ernest (1881–1951), British statesman. He created the Transport and General Workers' Union (1922) by amalgamation, and was elected chairman of the Trades Union Congress General Council (1937). He was minister of labor in Churchill's coalition government (1940–5). As foreign secretary in the Labour government (1945–51) he played an important part in the granting of independence to India, and the creation of O.E.E.C. and NATO. He was a strong supporter of the U.N.

bev·y (bévi) n. pl. **bev·ies** n. a group or company (correctly of women, quails, larks or roes) [origin unknown]

be·wail (biwéil) v.t. to wail over ‖ to lament

be·ware (biwéər) v.i. (only infin. and imper.) to be careful, be on one's guard [fr. BE+O.E. *wœr*, cautious]

Bew·ick (bjú:ik), Thomas (1753–1828), English artist who revived and advanced the art of wood engraving. He is famous esp. for his 'History of Quadrupeds' (1790) and 'History of British Birds' (1797–1804)

be·wil·der (biwíldər) v.t. to throw into mental confusion ‖ v.i. to be a cause of mental confusion

be·wil·der·ment n. [BE-+obs. *wilder*, to cause to lose one's way]

be·witch (biwítʃ) v.t. to fascinate or charm ‖ to affect by witchcraft **be·witch·ing** adj. [fr. BE-+O.E. *wiccian*, enchant]

bey (bei) n. (*hist.*) an Islamic title of rank used by higher army officers and dignitaries of state ‖ (*hist.*) the title of rulers who were vassals of the Turkish sultan [Turk. = prince, governor]

Beyle (beil), Marie Henri *STENDHAL

be·yond (bijónd, bi:ónd) 1. adv. further, *come to the gateway but not a step beyond* 2. prep. on the further side of ‖ later than, *it is beyond your bedtime* ‖ past the comprehension of ‖ ahead of ‖ past, *beyond redemption* 3. n. **the beyond** what lies after death [O.E. *begeondan*]

Beyrouth *BEIRUT

Be·za (béizə) (Latinized name of) Théodore de Bèze

Bèze (bez), Théodore de (1519–1605), French nobleman and Renaissance scholar, author of a Latin translation of the New Testament. He was Calvin's successor at Geneva, a playwright ('The Sacrifice of Abraham', 1550), a diplomat, and a protector of persecuted French Protestants

bez·el (béz'l) n. the oblique face of a cut gem, esp. the part projecting from the setting ‖ the groove and flange of a watchcase to hold the watch glass ‖ a sloping edge, e.g. on a chisel [etym. doubtful]

be·zique (bəzí:k) n. a complicated card game for two players, usually played with two packs from which all cards below 7 have been discarded [fr. F. *besique*]

Bez·wa·da (beizwǣdə) *VIJAYAWADA

B-52 *See* STRATOFORTRESS

Bha·gal·pur (bágəlpuər) a town (pop. 172,202) in Bihar, N.E. India, on the Ganges: silk industry

Bha·ga·vad-gi·ta (bágəvədgí:tə) one of the sacred books of Hinduism, variously dated between the 5th c. B.C. and the 3rd c. A.D. It is generally thought to have been originally independent of the Mahabharata, into which it is now placed. It is a philosophical treatise in the form of a dialogue between one of the chief characters of the Mahabharata, Arjuna, and his charioteer, Krishna (an incarnation of Vishnu)

bhang, bang (bæŋ) n. hemp (*Cannabis sativa*) ‖ any intoxicant and narcotic made from it, usually eaten as a sweet, drunk in water, or smoked [fr. Skr. *bhangā*, hemp]

Bha·ra·vi (bárəvi:) Indian poet of the 6th c., author of the Sanskrit epic 'Kiratarjuniya'

Bhar·tri·har·i (bʌrtri:hári:) (d. c. 650 A.D.), Indian poet, author of three 'Satakas' or 'Centuries' of poems in Sanskrit

Bha·sa (bázə) the assumed author of about 13 dramas in Sanskrit which were discovered in MS in 1909. They are the oldest extant in Sanskrit (c. 375 A.D.)

Bhát·gá·on (bádgaun) a town (pop. 84,000) in E. Nepal. Founded in 865, it was the capital of Nepal for two centuries

Bha·va·bhu·ti (bɑvəbú:ti:) (probably 7th to 8th c. A.D.), author of Sanskrit dramas

Bhav·na·gar (baunágər) a port (pop. 225,358) of Gujarat, W. India, a rail terminus and airport: cotton trade

Bhil (bi:l) n. a member of an aboriginal pre-Aryan people of central India, driven by invading Aryans into the hills. They are nomads, living in jungles of the states of Maharashtra, Rajasthan and Madhya Pradesh. They number about 2,500,000

Bho·ja (bóudʒə) (11th c. A.D.), king of Dhar, assumed author of Sanskrit writings on theology, poetics, philosophy, government and the care of horses

Bho·pal (boupál) the capital (pop. 900,000) of Madhya Pradesh and of the former state of Bhopal on the headwaters of the Betwa River, an agricultural market and center for traditional crafts. Scene of worst industrial accident in history (Dec. 3, 1984) when toxic gas leaked from a chemical plant, killing at least 2,500 and injuring 200,000

Bhu·ba·nes·war (bubanéiʃwər) the capital of Orissa, India, 30 miles from the coast, between Cuttack and Puri: Hindu temples (8th–12th cc.)

Bhu·mi·bol A·dul·ya·dej (bú:mi:bɔlædú:ljædɛ) (1927–), king of Thailand since 1950

Bhu·tán (bu:tán) an autonomous kingdom (area 18,000 sq. miles, pop. 1,364,000) on the south slopes of the E. Himalayas, between Tibet, China and Assam, with forests and some fertile valleys. Products: rice, corn, millet, cloth, lac, wax, metalwork. Winter capital: Punakha. Summer capital: Tashi-Cho-Dzong. Bhután is ruled by a hereditary maharaja and receives a subsidy from India, which looks after its external affairs

Bhut·to (bú:tou), Zulfikar Ali (1928–79), Pakistani statesman, president (1971–3) and prime minister (1973–7). He was minister of foreign affairs (1963–6). He formed (1967) the People's Party. A military coup after the 1977 elections led to his trial and hanging

Bi (chem.) bismuth

bi- (bai), prefix twice ‖ having two ‖ doubly ‖ occurring every two [fr. L.]

Bi·a·fra (bi:æfrə, bi:úfrə) the name under which the former Eastern Region of Nigeria seceded (May 1967–Jan. 1970) from Nigeria as an independent republic (*NIGERIA)

Bia·lik (bjálik), Chaim Nahman (1873–1934), Hebrew poet from Russia who settled in Israel (1924). He was largely responsible for the revival of Hebrew as a modern literary tongue

bi·al·y (bi:æli:) n. an onion roll made of bagel dough; named for Polish city of Bialystok

Bia·ly·stok (bjalístɔk) a department (area 11,000 sq. miles, pop. 1,102,000) of N.E. Poland, a poor farming area with light industries ‖ its capital (pop. 218,000), a railway junction, trade and industrial center: textiles, food processing

bi·an·nu·al (baiænju:əl) adj. happening twice a year

Biar·ritz (bjæri:ts) a famous resort (pop. 27,595) on the Bay of Biscay, S.W. France

bi·as (báiəs) 1. n. a temperamental or emotional leaning to one side, *a bias in favor of the French* ‖ the weight on one side of the wood used in the game of lawn bowling (so that the bowl rolls in a curved path) ‖ an unchanging component of the potential difference between an electrode and the cathode in a thermionic valve ‖ (*dressmaking*) an oblique direction to the run of the threads in the material 2. v.t. pres. part. **bi·as·ing**, esp. *Br.* **bi·as·sing** past and past part. **bi·ased**, esp. *Br.* **bi·assed** to cause to incline to one side ‖ to cause to be prejudiced in opinion, judgment etc. [F. *biais*, oblique]

bi·as-belt·ed tire (báiəsbɛltəd) *See* BELTED-BIAS TIRE

bi·as-ply tire (báiəsplai) pneumatic tire with inner ply cord laid diagonally

bi·as·tro·naut·ics (bɑiæstrɔnɔtiks) n. branch of astronautics that deals with the effects of space flight factors on living creatures

bi·ath·lon (baiæθlɔn) n. (*sports*) combination cross-country skiing and rifle shooting at targets as a competitive sport —**biathlete** n. a participant in a biathlon

bi·ax·i·al (baiæksi:əl) adj. (*crystall.*, of optical properties) with two axes

bib (bib) n. a small piece of cloth placed under a child's chin at mealtimes to protect his clothes ‖ the top of an apron or overalls coming above the waist in front [perh. fr. obs. v. *bib*, to drink]

bibb (bib) n. (*naut.*) a bracket for supporting the trestletrees [var. of BIB]

Bibb lettuce (bib) small-headed, dark green variety of lettuce

bib·cock (bíbkɔk) n. a faucet with a downbent nozzle

bi·be·lot (bí:blou, bíblou) n. a small decorative curio [F.]

bi·bi·ru (bibíru:) n. the bebeeru

Bi·ble (báib'l) n. the sacred writings of the Christian faith **bi·ble** the authoritative book on a subject [F. fr. L. fr. Gk *ta biblia*, the books (the sacred books)]

—The Bible is a collection of religious books comprising the Old Testament, sacred to both the Jewish and Christian faiths and the New Testament, acknowledged only by Christians. The Old Testament consists of 39 books, most of which were written originally in Hebrew, some in Aramaic. Its books were written, revised, edited and reedited between approximately 1000 B.C. and 100 A.D. It is divided into the Pentateuch, the five books of the Law, the Prophetical books (including the main historical books as well as the works of the Prophets), and the Hagiographa, or sacred writings, containing the poetical and sapiential books and the remainder of the historical books. Some of the Old Testament books, the Apocrypha, were not placed within the sacred canon by the Jews of

Palestine, and are regarded by Protestants as sources of edification rather than doctrine: they are included in the canon of the Vulgate and are therefore regarded as authoritative by the Roman Catholic Church. The Old Testament treats of the creation and fall of man, of God's covenant with his chosen people, the Jews, the law and ritual of the Jewish faith, the vicissitudes of the Jews, the utterances of the prophets and apocalyptists, and the wisdom and poetry attributed to David and Solomon. (Modern scholarship doubts the authorship of many of the books, e.g. of the first five, ascribed to Moses: most books should be regarded as traditional material, collected and edited later.)

The New Testament, written originally in Greek, comprises 27 books. The four Gospels record the life and teaching of Jesus Christ, regarded by Christians as the savior foretold in the Old Testament. They affirm his reconciling mission from God to man, and describe his crucifixion. Acts records the spreading of the gospel by his Apostles. The Epistles are letters by the Apostles to the young Christian Churches of the Mediterranean world. It is thought that the Gospels are based on collections of the sayings and acts of Christ, current in the 50 years or so after his death.

The Jewish community, in which Christianity developed, was mainly Greek-speaking, and was spread throughout the Roman Empire. The Old Testament was early translated (3rd and 2nd cc. B.C.) into Greek (*SEPTUAGINT). This version, and an old Latin one, were used by Jerome in the 4th c. A.D. as the basis for a new version, the Vulgate, still the official version of the Roman Catholic Church.

During the Latin Middle Ages, the Vulgate was the source of all biblical teaching. Theology took the form largely of expositions of the Scripture, more allegorical than literal. But textual scholarship was not unknown. Alcuin circulated a purified Latin text, and later scholars debated with learned Jews. There were attempts to render the Bible into the vernaculars, and versions circulated in France, Germany, Italy, Holland and England. But they were associated, sometimes rightly, with heresy. In England in the 14th c. (*WYCLIF), and in Bohemia in the 15th c. (*Hus), the Church actively suppressed vernacular versions.

Philological scholarship was a main concern of the Renaissance. Lorenzo Valla in the early 15th c., and later Erasmus, pioneered a new critical attitude to the text. Erasmus produced a new edition of the Greek text of the New Testament (1516) derived from the comparison of manuscripts. It was realized that incessant copying had introduced corruptions, and that it was necessary to find reliable witnesses to the originals. The Protestant reformers thought it important to make the Bible available to the laity in the vernacular. Luther's German version (from 1521) was the stimulus to others, in every European language. The opening of the Bible to the laity became a main source of conflict. In Protestant territories, aided by the new technique of printing, the Bible became the source and guarantee of doctrine. In Catholic countries interpretation of the Scriptures remained the province of the clergy, and was held less important than the tradition of the Church. But even so, versions with approved annotations were eventually allowed some currency.

During the 17th, 18th and 19th cc. the techniques of scholarship improved, refining the critical attitude to the text. The discovery of old and more reliable manuscripts in the original tongues culminated in some sensational finds in the 19th c., and, most sensational of all, the discovery of the Dead Sea Scrolls in the 20th c. They are the oldest witnesses to the Hebrew text. No complete manuscript even approaching contemporaneity with the time of writing has been found, but the text of both Testaments has been established with reasonable certainty for most purposes.

The other great activity of the 19th c., coinciding with mass-production methods, the spread of literacy in Europe, the colonization of overseas territories, and the concomitant missionary activity, was the production of Bibles in very large numbers and at very cheap prices by the Bible societies. Since then the Bible has been translated into more than 1,100 languages.

Bible societies nonsectarian Protestant societies formed to translate, print and distribute Bibles. An early German example is the Canstein Bible Society formed at Halle (1710). The British and Foreign Bible Society was formed in 1804 in London. The American Bible Society dates from 1816. Gideon's International, which places the Bible in hotel rooms, was formed at the turn of the century. A supranational body, United Bible Societies, was formed in 1946

bib·li·cal (bíblik'l) *adj.* of or relating to the Bible [fr. Med. L. *biblicus*]

bib·li·og·ra·pher (bibli:ógrəfər) *n.* someone who writes or compiles bibliographies ‖ someone who has a knowledge of bibliography

bib·li·o·graph·i·cal (bíbli:əgrǽfik'l) *adj.* of or relating to bibliography

bib·li·og·ra·phy (bibli:ógrəfi:) *pl.* **bib·li·og·ra·phies** *n.* a complete list of a writer's work ‖ a list of books on a particular subject ‖ a list of references at the end of a book ‖ the history of books, authorship, editions etc. ‖ a book containing such information [Gk *bibliographia*, bookwriting]

bib·li·o·la·ter (bibli:ólətər) *n.* (*rhet.*) someone whose devotion to the Bible is marked by an irrational lack of criticism **bib·li·ol·a·trous** *adj.*

bib·li·ol·a·try *n.* excessive and uncritical passion for the Bible [fr. BIBLE+Gk *-lateria*, worship]

bib·li·o·ma·ni·a (bibli:ouméini:ə) *n.* excessive love of books ‖ a passion or craze for collecting books **bib·li·o·ma·ni·ac** (bibli:ouméini:æk) *n.* [fr. Gk *biblion*, book+MANIA]

bib·li·o·phile (bíbli:əfail, bíbli:əfil) *n.* a booklover [F. *bibliophile* fr. Gk *biblion*, book+philos, loving]

bib·li·o·ther·a·py (bibli:ouθérəpi:) *n.* (*psych.*) form of psychotherapy utilizing printed material to structure, explain, and universalize problems, e.g., tracts on masturbation, pregnancy, sexual response, depression, etc.

bib·u·lous (bíbjuləs) *adj.* (*rhet.*) addicted to alcoholic drink [fr. L. *bibulus*]

bi·cam·er·al (baikǽmərəl) *adj.* (of a system of government) having two legislative chambers [fr. BI-+L. *camera*, chamber]

bi·car·bo·nate of soda (baikárbənit, baikárbəneit) sodium bicarbonate

bice (bais) *n.* any of certain blue and green pigments usually prepared from carbonates of copper [F. *bis*, etym. doubtful]

bi·cen·te·nar·y (baisenténəri:, baiséntənəri:) 1. *n. pl.* **bi·cen·te·nar·ies** a 200th anniversary or its celebration 2. *adj.* relating to a 200th anniversary ‖ occurring every 200 years

bi·cen·ten·ni·al (baisenténi:əl) 1. *n.* a 200th anniversary or its celebration 2. *adj.* occurring every 200 years ‖ lasting 200 years

bi·ceph·a·lous (baiséfələs) *adj.* two-headed [fr. BI-+Gk *kephalē*, head]

bi·ceps (báiseps) *pl.* **bi·ceps, bi·ceps·es** (báisepsiz) *n.* a muscle with two heads or origins, two attachments to the bone, esp. the large flexor muscle in the upper arm **bi·cip·i·tal** (baisípit'l) *adj.* having two heads, esp. relating to a biceps muscle [L.=*two-headed*, fr. *bi-*, two+*caput*, head]

bi·chlo·ride (baiklóraid, baiklóuraid) *n.* dichloride

bichloride of mercury mercuric chloride

bick·er (bíkər) 1. *v.i.* to squabble ‖ to quarrel about trifles 2. *n.* snappish quarrel of a not very serious kind [M.E. *bikeren*, etym. doubtful]

Bick·er·dyke (bíkərdaik), Mary Ann (known as 'Mother Bickerdyke', 'General Bickerdyke', and 'the General in Calico' 1817–1901), U.S. organizer and chief of nursing, hospital and welfare services for the troops commanded by General U.S. Grant during the Civil War. Her campaign against filth, malnutrition and disease resulted in the introduction of effective medical facilities for the military

bi·col·or, *Br.* **bi·col·our** (báikʌlər) *adj.* of two colors **bi·col·ored,** *Br.* **bi·col·oured** *adj.*

bi·con·cave (baikɒnkeiv, baikɒnkéiv) *adj.* concave on both sides

bi·con·vex (baikɒnveks, baikɒnvéks) *adj.* convex on both sides

bi·cul·tur·al (baikʌltʃərəl) *adj.* of two cultural heritages co-existing in a single social group or person —**biculturism** *n.*

bi·cus·pid (baikʌspid) 1. *adj.* having two cusps or points 2. *n.* a doublepointed tooth in man ‖ the mitral valve **bi·cus·pi·dal, bi·cus·pi·date** *adjs.* [fr. BI-+ L. *cuspis* (*cuspidis*), point]

bi·cy·cle (báisik'l) 1. *n.* a vehicle esp. for one person, consisting of two large, spoked, tandem wheels, a steering handle and a saddle on which the rider sits to work two pedals which, by making a chain engage in a series of cogs, drive the back wheel. A bicycle may also be fitted with a small motor 2. *v.i. pres. part.* **bi·cy·cling** *past* and *past part.* **bi·cy·cled** to cycle **bi·cy·clist** *n.* a cyclist [F. fr. L. *bi-*, two+Gk *kuklos*, wheel]

bid (bid) 1. *v. pres. part.* **bid·ding** *past* and *past part.* **bid** *v.t.* to offer (a price), esp. at an auction sale ‖ (*card games*) to make (a bid) ‖ (*past* also **bade** (beid) *past part.* also **bid·den** (bíd'n) to command ‖ *v.i.* to make a bid in an auction, card games etc. **to bid fair** (*rhet.*) to promise favorably 2. *n.* an offer of a price, esp. at a sale ‖ an offer to do a job etc. for a certain price ‖ (*card games*) a statement of the number of tricks a player hopes to win **to make a bid for** to try to gain (e.g. freedom) **bid·da·ble** (bídəb'l) *adj.* (of a hand of playing cards) capable of being bid **bid·der** *n.* someone who bids **bid·ding** *n.* a command or commands ‖ the offers made at an auction **to do someone's bidding** (*rhet.*) to obey someone [O.E. *biddan*, to beg, and *bēodan*, to command]

Bid·dle (bíd'l), James (1783–1848), U.S. naval commander of the 'Hornet' (1813) during the War of 1812. He negotiated the first treaty between the U.S.A. and China (1846). During the Mexican War he assumed command on the Pacific coast

Biddle, Nicholas (1786–1844), U.S. diplomat, financier, and president of the Second Bank of the U.S.A. (1822–36 and 1839–41), where he helped to develop the theory and practice of central banking. The bank's restrictive policies and Biddle's political ineptitude, however, resulted in the dissolution of the bank (1841)

bid·dy (bídi:) *pl.* **bid·dies** *n.* a grown chicken, domestic fowl ‖ a young chick ‖ a fussy old woman [etym. unknown]

bide (baid) *pres. part.* **bid·ing** *past* **bid·ed, bode** (boud) *past part.* **bid·ed** *v.t.* (only in the phrase) **to bide one's time** to wait for the right opportunity [O.E. *bīdan*]

bi·det (bi:déi) *n.* a low, oval bathroom appliance used esp. for washing the genitals [F.]

bi·di·a·lec·ti·cal (baidaiəléktikəl) *adj.* using two dialects of a language —**bidialectalism** *n.* —**bidialectical** *adj.* —**bidialectical** *n.*

bi·don·ville (bí:dənvil) *n.* shantytown; from the French word *bidon*, meaning tin can

Bie·der·mei·er (bí:dərmaijər) a bourgeois style of furniture and interior decoration in Germany 1815–48, roughly a heavy version of French Empire. The term is applied generally to philistinism in art and excessive middle-class social conventionalism [fr. Gottlieb *Biedermeier*, a fictional character in the humorous poetry of Ludwig Eichrodt, 1827–92]

Biel (bi:l) (F. Bienne) a town (pop. 53,793) on Lake Biel, N.W. Switzerland: watchmaking, metallurgy

Bie·le·feld (bí:ləfelt) a town (pop. 312,600) in North Rhine-Westphalia, W. Germany, a metalwork and textile center

bi·en·ni·al (baiéni:əl) 1. *adj.* lasting for two years ‖ occurring once every two years 2. *n.* an event occurring once every two years ‖ (*bot.*) a plant which vegetates one year and flowers, fruits and dies in the second [fr. L. *biennis* fr. *bi-*, two+ *annus*, year]

Bien·ville (bjévi:l), Jean Baptiste Le Moyne, sieur de (1680–1768), French Canadian colonial governor. He continued the work of his brother Iberville in Louisiana, of which he was governor (1713–26 and 1733–43)

bien vu (bi:en vu:) *adj.* (*Fr.*) well regarded

bier (biər) *n.* the frame on which a coffin or corpse is taken to its burial [O.E. *bær*]

Bierce (biərs), Ambrose Gwinett (1842–c. 1914), U.S. journalist and author of sardonic short stories, notably 'In the Midst of Life' (1891) and 'Can Such Things Be?' (1893), which treat of death and horror

Bier·stadt (bíərstat), Albert (1830–1902), U.S. painter of scenes from the West, esp. the Rocky Mtns and the Yosemite Valley

bi·fa·cial (baiféiʃəl) *adj.* (e.g. of some chipped flint tools) having two faces

bi·fid (báifid) *adj.* evenly divided in two lobes by a cleft [fr. L. *bifidus*]

bi·fo·cal (baifóuk'l) *adj.* having two points of focus (esp. of spectacles with lenses having upper and lower segments ground for long and near vision) **bi·fó·cals** *pl. n.* bifocal spectacles

bi·fo·li·ate (baifóuli:it, baifóuli:eit) *adj.* (*bot.*) two-leaved [fr. BI-+L. *folium*, leaf

bi·fur·cate (báifə:rkeit, baifə́:rkeit) 1. *v. pres. part.* **bi·fur·cat·ing** *past* and *past part.* **bi·fur·cat·ed** *v.i.* to divide into two branches or forks ∥ *v.t.* to cause to bifurcate 2. (baifə́:rkit, báifə:rkeit) *adj.* (esp. *bot.*) forked **bi·fur·ca·tion** *n.* a division into two branches ∥ one or both of the branches [fr. M.L. *bifurcatus* fr. L. *bi-*, two+*furca*, fork]

big (big) 1. *adj. comp.* **big·ger** *superl.* **big·gest** large, *a big book* ∥ grown-up, *when you are a big girl* ∥ important, *big, news* ∥ boastful, *big words* ∥ (*pop.*) magnanimous 2. *adv.* boastfully, *to talk big* [M.E. *big* perh. fr. Norse]

big·a·mist (bígəmist) *n.* a person who makes a second marriage illegally while the first marriage remains valid

big·a·mous (bígəməs) *adj.* guilty of bigamy ∥ involving bigamy [fr. M.L. *bigamus*]

big·a·my (bígəmi:) *n.* illegally having two wives or husbands at the same time [F. *bigamie* fr. L. fr. *bi-*, two+Gk *-gamos*, married]

Big Bang theory hypothetical account for the formation of the universe by an explosion 10–15 billion yrs ago *Cf* STEADY STATE THEORY

big-beat or **Big Beat** (bigbí:t) *n.* rock music

Big Ben a bell which strikes the hours in the clock tower of the houses of parliament in London. It weighs 13½ tons, is 9 ft across, and was named for Sir Benjamin Hall, First Commissioner of Works at the time it was hung

Big Bird (*mil.*) U.S. 12-ton surveillance satellite

big business large-scale commerce (sometimes with a suggestion of the political pressure exerted by it)

big dipper (*Br., pop.*) a roller coaster (in an amusement park) **Big Dipper** *URSA MAJOR

big end the crank end of an engine connecting rod

Big Foot hypothetical human precursor reported to exist in northwestern U.S. and southwestern Canada. Analogous to Sasquatch

big game the larger wild animals (lions, tigers etc.) hunted for sport

big-heart·ed (bíghártid) *adj.* generous, full of charitable spirit

big·horn (bíghɔrn) *pl.* **big·horn, big·horns** *n.* the wild sheep of the mountains of western North America

bight (bait) 1. *n.* a bend in a coast or river line ∥ a small bay ∥ the loop or coil of a rope 2. *v.t.* to fasten with a bight [O.E. *byht*, bend]

big-mouth·ing (bígmauðiŋ) *n.* self-promotion

big·no·ni·a (bignóuni:ə) *n.* a member of *Bignonia*, fam. *Bignoniaceae*, a genus of woody vines with tendrils thickened with discs, and trumpet-shaped flowers [after J. P. Bignon (1662–1743), librarian to Louis XIV]

big·ot (bígət) *n.* someone obstinately and intolerantly devoted to his own beliefs, creed or party **big·ot·ed** *adj.* narrow-minded, prejudiced **big·ot·ry** *n.* the mental attitude and behavior of a bigot, obstinate narrow-mindedness [F., origin unknown]

bi·gou·di (bigú:di:) *n.* (*Fr.*) wooden curler used to make curls for wigs

big top the main tent in a circus ∥ (*rhet.*) the circus

big tree *Sequoiadendron giganteum*, a conifer of California growing up to 300 ft high

big·wig (bígwig) *n.* (*pop.*) someone who is treated with ceremonious deference because of his authority or influence

Bi·har (bi:hár) a state (area 62,198 sq. miles, pop. 66,210,000) of India, west of Bengal, in the heavily overpopulated Ganges valley. Capital: Patna. Rice, oilseed and sugarcane are intensively cultivated. There are coal and nonferrous metal mines and steel works

Bi·isk (bjí:isk) a town (pop. 146,000) of the R.S.F.S.R., U.S.S.R., in the Altai Mtns, center of an agricultural region with engineering, food and textile industries. It is the starting point of a highway to Mongolia

bi·jou (bí:ʒu:, bi:ʒú:) 1. *n. pl.* **bi·joux** (bí:ʒu:z, bi:ʒú:z) a jewel 2. *adj.* miniature and charming or finely ornamented etc., *a bijou theater* [F.]

Bi·ka·ner (bíkənɛər) a city (pop. 188,518) of Rajasthan, India: carpets, camel-hair fabrics

bike (baik) 1. *n.* (*pop.*) a bicycle 2. *v.i. pres. part.* **bik·ing** *past* and *past part.* **biked** (*pop.*) to bicycle, cycle

bik·er (báikər) *n.* member of a motorcycle gang

bike·way (báikwei) *n.* road or lane in a road reserved for bicycling

Bi·ki·ni (bikí:ni:) an atoll in the Marshall Islands where the U.S.A. conducted atom-bomb tests (1946–58). The islands are expected to contain dangerous levels of radiation for another 30–50 years

bi·ki·ni (bikí:ni:) *n.* a woman's minimal two-piece bathing suit

bi·la·bi·al (bailéibi:əl) 1. *adj.* (*phon.*, of consonants, e.g. b, m, p) articulated with both lips 2. *n.* a consonant articulated with both lips

bi·la·bi·ate (bailéibi:eit, bailéibi:it) *adj.* (*bot.*, of some corollas) having two lips

bi·lat·er·al (bailǽtərəl) *adj.* affecting each of two sides or parties, *a bilateral agreement* ∥ having two sides ∥ ranged upon two sides ∥ (*sociology*) indicating or tracing descent through both maternal and paternal lines

bilateral symmetry the quality in a structure of being symmetrical with respect to a single plane only, hence divided into right and left halves (cf. RADIAL SYMMETRY)

Bil·ba·o (bilbáou) N. Spain's largest commercial center and port (pop. 452,921), capital of Vizcaya province, near the Bay of Biscay, exporting local iron ores: iron works, shipyards, cotton spinneries, paper works

bil·ber·ry (bílberi:, bílbəri:) *pl.* **bil·ber·ries** *n.* the blue-black fruit of a dwarf moorland shrub, *Vaccinium myrtillus*, fam. *Ericaceae* ∥ the shrub itself [etym. doubtful]

bile (bail) *n.* a bitter, greenish-yellow alkaline fluid secreted by the liver of many vertebrates. It is stored between meals and upon eating is discharged into the duodenum where it aids the digestion esp. of fats ∥ ill humor [F. fr. L. *bilis*]

bile duct a duct which conveys bile between the liver and the duodenum

bile stone a gallstone

bi·lev·el (bailévəl) *adj.* of a two-story dwelling, one partially below ground —**bilevel** *n. Cf* RANCH HOUSE

bilge (bildʒ) 1. *n.* the bottom of a ship from the keel to where the sides begin to rise ∥ the swelling part of a barrel ∥ bilge water ∥ (*pop.*) foolishly mistaken ideas or remarks 2. *v. pres. part.* **bilg·ing** *past* and *past part.* **bilged** *v.t.* to cause to fracture in the bilge ∥ *v.i.* to have a fracture in the bilge [corrup. of BULGE, fr. O.F. *boulge*]

bilge keel a keel on either side of a ship's bottom to prevent rolling

bilge water the foul water collecting in a ship's bilge

bil·har·zi·a (bilhárzi:ə) *n.* a disease common in many parts of the Far East, Africa and South America, caused by a parasite which invades and destroys many body organs. The disease is contracted by washing or swimming in contaminated water containing certain snails and mollusks which act as hosts to the parasites [after Theodor *Bilharz* (1825–62), G. zoologist]

bil·i·ar·y (bíli:eri:) *adj.* of or connected with the bile [fr. F. *biliaire*]

bi·lin·e·ar (bailíni:ər) *adj.* of or relating to two lines

bi·lin·gual (bailíŋgwəl) 1. *adj.* speaking two languages with equal fluency ∥ (of a text) written in two languages 2. *n.* a person with complete mastery of two languages **bi·lin·gual·ism** *n.* the habitual use of two languages by an individual or group of individuals [fr. L. *bilinguis*]

bil·ious (bíljəs) *adj.* of or connected with the bile ∥ having or resulting from a liver or bile disorder ∥ ill-tempered ∥ sickly looking [fr. F. *bilieux*]

bilk (bilk) *v.t.* to defraud (a creditor) by avoiding payment of one's debts ∥ to evade, give (someone) the slip [origin unknown]

bill (bil) 1. *n.* an account for goods sold or services rendered ∥ the draft of a law ∥ a poster ∥ a handbill or leaflet ∥ a concert or theater program ∥ a piece of paper money 2. *v.t.* to charge (an account) for goods or services ∥ to announce by means of playbills [fr. L. *billa, bulla*, seal]

bill 1. *n.* a beak ∥ a narrow promontory ∥ the end of an anchor fluke 2. *v.i.* (of doves) to stroke each other with their bills

bil·la·bong (bíləbɔŋ) *n.* (*Austral.*) a channel from a river, coming to a dead end ∥ a stagnant backwater [Austral. native word]

bill·board (bílbɔrd, bílbɔrd) *n.* (*Am.=Br.* hoarding) a wall of planks etc. for the display of advertisement posters

billboard *n.* (*naut.*) a ledge fixed to a ship's bow for the anchor to rest on

bill broker (*Br.*) a person dealing in bills of exchange

bil·let (bílit) *n.* a section of a log split lengthwise (for firewood) ∥ (*archit.*) an ornamental device in molding resembling a billet of wood ∥ a small bar of iron or steel ∥ a strap buckled on a harness ∥ the loop holding the end of the strap after the buckle [F. *billette* and *billot*]

billet 1. *n.* the quarters to which a soldier etc. is officially assigned ∥ an official note directing a householder to provide the bearer with board and lodging 2. *v.t.* to find or provide quarters for (soldiers, refugees etc.) [A.F. *billette*, a short document]

bill·fold (bílfould) *n.* a wallet for paper money

bill·hook (bílhuk) *n.* a pole or a short handle with a curved blade at one end for lopping or pruning [fr. obs. *bill*, a sword +HOOK]

bil·liards (bíljərdz) *n.* any of several games played on a large, rectangular, cushioned, clothcovered table, ivory balls being driven by a tapering wooden cue. Certain games, e.g. pool, are played on a table with pockets [F. *billiard*]

bil·li·bi (bíli:bi:) *n.* hot or cold soup of mussels, white wine, and cream, named for William B. Leeds (1972)

Bil·lings (bílinz), Josh (Henry Wheeler Shaw, 1818–85), U.S. antebellum cracker-barrel philosopher-humorist, known for his rustic aphorisms

bil·lion (bíljən) *n.* *NUMBER TABLE [F.]

bil·lion·aire (bíljənɛ́ər) *n.* someone whose possessions are worth a billion dollars (or pounds etc.)

bil·lionth (bíljənθ) 1. *adj.* being number 1,000,000,000 in a series (*NUMBER TABLE) ∥ being one of the 1,000,000,000 equal parts of anything 2. *n.* the person or thing next after the 999,999,999th ∥ one of 1,000,000,000 equal parts of anything (1/ 1,000,000,000)

Bil·li·ton (bili:tɔn) *BELITUNG

bill of attainder (*Eng. hist.*) a bill (the earliest was passed by the English parliament in 1459) under which the penalties of attainder were inflicted on persons without any trial in a judicial court

bill of exchange (abbr. B/Ex., B/E, b.e.) a written order by a drawer to a drawee for the drawee to pay a specified sum to the drawer or to a payee on a specified date

bill of fare a menu

bill of health a certificate given to a ship's master regarding infectious diseases on a ship or in port at sailing time

bill of lading (abbr. B/L, b.l.) the receipt given by a ship's master to a consigner of goods

bill of quantities a statement of work, material, labor etc. involved in a building job

Bill of Rights (*Am. hist.*) the first ten amendments to the constitution of the U.S.A.

Bill of Rights (*Eng. hist.*) an act passed by Parliament (1689) settling the succession on William III and Mary II, and stating the terms under which they were to rule. It included clauses making it illegal to suspend laws or levy taxes without parliamentary consent, or to raise a standing army in time of peace. It demanded freedom of speech in parliament and the right to petition the Crown. It attempted to secure the independence of juries and frequent meetings of parliament

bill of sale (abbr. B/S, b.s.) a document transferring property, or agreeing to its seizure if payment is not made

bil·lon (bílən) *n.* silver largely alloyed with copper, used for coinage [F.=mass]

bil·low (bílou) 1. *n.* a large wave ∥ anything that sweeps along like a wave, *a billow of laughter* 2. *v.i.* to roll along or rise and fall like a wave ∥ to bulge or swell **bil·low·y** *adj.* [perh. fr. O.N. *bylgja*]

bill·post·er (bílpoustər) *n.* a person who sticks up posters

bill·stick·er (bílstikər) *n.* a billposter

bil·ly (bíli:) *pl.* **bil·lies** *n.* a policeman's nightstick

billy *n.* (*Austral.*) a container for water that can be put on a camp fire [fr. BILLYCAN]

billy board (*surfing*) a surfboard of less than 3 ft.

bil·ly·can (bíli:kæn) *n.* a tin can with a lid ∥ (*Austral.*) a billy

billy goat a male goat

Billy Jo fad dance in medium tempo rock'n'roll, introduced in 1966

Billy the Kid (William H. Bonney, 1859–81), U.S. outlaw. As leader (from 1878) of a gang of

CONCISE PRONUNCIATION KEY: (a) æ, c*a*t; ɑ, c*a*r; ɔ f*aw*n; ei, sn*a*ke. **(e)** e, h*e*n; i:, sh*ee*p; iə, d*ee*r; ɛə, b*ea*r. **(i)** i, f*i*sh; ai, t*i*ger; ə:, b*i*rd. **(o)** o, *o*x; au, c*ow*; ou, g*oa*t; u, p*oo*r; ɔi, r*oy*al. **(u)** ʌ, d*u*ck; u, b*u*ll; u:, g*oo*se; ə, b*a*cillus; ju:, c*u*be. x, lo*ch*; θ, *th*ink; ð, bo*th*er; z, *Z*en; ʒ, corsa*g*e; dʒ, sava*g*e; ŋ, ora*ng*utang; j, *y*ak; ʃ, *fi*sh; tʃ, fe*tch*; 'l, rabb*le*; 'n, red*den*. Complete pronunciation key appears inside front cover.

killers and cattle thieves in New Mexico, he was finally gunned down by Sheriff Pat F. Garrett

bi·lo·bate (bailóubeit) *adj.* (*biol.*) having two lobes

Bi·lox·i (bilóksi:, bilʌ́ksi:) *pl.* **Bi·lox·i, Bi·lox·is** *n.* a Siouan Indian people living in lower Louisiana and Mississippi until the 20th c., when very few remained ‖ a member of this people ‖ their language

bil·tong (bíltɒŋ) *n.* sun-dried strips of esp. ox, antelope or buffalo meat [*Afrik.* fr. *bil,* buttock + *tong,* tongue]

bi·man·u·al (baimǽnju:əl) *adj.* done with, or requiring the use of, two hands

bi·mar·gin for·mat (bɑimárdʒin) (*cartology*) the format of a map or chart on which the cartographic detail is extended to two edges of the sheet, normally on North and East, thus leaving only two margins

bi·mes·tri·al (baiméstri:əl) *adj.* lasting two months ‖ bimonthly [fr. L. *bimestris,* of two months]

bi·me·tal·lic (bɑimətǽlik) *adj.* composed of two metals ‖ relating to a system of double currency, based on two metals (gold and silver) with a value ratio fixed by law **bi·met·al·lism** (baimét'lizəm) *n.* **bi·mét·al·list** *n.* and *adj.* [fr. F. *bimétallique*]

bi·month·ly (baimʌ́nθli) 1. *adj.* happening every two months ‖ happening twice a month 2. *n. pl.* **bi·month·lies** a bimonthly publication 3. *adv.* once in two months ‖ twice a month

bin (bin) *n.* a receptacle for storing e.g. bread, coal or flour [O.E. *binn,* manger]

bi·na·ry (báinəri) *adj.* consisting of two [fr. L. *binarius*]

binary *pl.* **bi·na·ries** *n.* (*astron.*) two stars revolving around one another, a double star

binary code (*computer*) a computer number system based on two characters, one of which is formed of binary (on or off, yes-no) digits

binary compound (*chem.*) a substance which is a compound of two elements

binary fission (*biol.*) the splitting of a nucleus into two daughter nuclei, followed by similar division of the whole cell body (a form of asexual reproduction among certain simple plants and animals)

binary form (*mus.*) a form in which a movement is in two sections: the first modulates to a new key, and the second comes back to the key with which the first movement opened

binary nerve gas (*mil.*) a nerve gas made of two parts for storage safety. For the gas to become effective, the two parts must be combined

binary scale (*math.*) a number scale based on two digits 0 and 1, other numbers being powers of 1. It was invented by Leibniz, but is thought to have been used formerly in China

Decimal scale	Binary equivalent
1	1
2	10
3	11
4	100
5	101
6	110
7	111
8	1000
9	1001
10	1010

binary star a double star (two stars rotating about a common center of mass)

bi·nate (báineit) *adj.* (*bot.*) growing in pairs ‖ double [fr. Mod. L. *binatus*]

bin·aural (bainɔ́rəl) *adj.* of or relating to both ears ‖ of a system of radio broadcasting using two microphones and two receivers to create a stereophonic effect [*bin-,* bi- + AURAL]

bind (baind) *pres. part.* **bind·ing** *past* and *past part.* **bound** (baund) *v.t.* to tie up ‖ to fasten together ‖ to bandage ‖ to provide a decorative or strengthening border for ‖ to fasten (pages or fascicles) together and put them into a cover ‖ to place (someone) under an agreement or obligation ‖ to constipate ‖ to cause to cohere or adhere, *to bind paint with oil* ‖ *v.i.* to stick together in a hard lump or cohesive mass ‖ to become jammed ‖ to be obligatory **to bind off** (*knitting*) to finish a piece of work with interlocking loops **to bind over** to impose a legal

obligation on, *the court bound him over to appear at the assizes* [O.E. *bindan*]

bind·er (báindər) *n.* someone who binds, esp. a bookbinder ‖ the part of a reaping machine for binding sheaves, or the part of a harvester which binds the straw into bales ‖ a binding substance, e.g. tar ‖ a tie beam ‖ a cover for fastening loose papers together ‖ a strip of material sometimes fastened around the abdomen of a newly born baby

bind·er·y (báindəri, báindri) *pl.* **bind·er·ies** *n.* a factory or workshop where books are bound

bind·ing (báindiŋ) 1. *n.* the action of someone who binds ‖ a bookcover ‖ material used to strengthen or decorate the edges e.g. of a blanket, mat or garment 2. *adj.* involving moral obligation, *the promise is binding* ‖ (*bookselling*) of a book not immediately available because the publisher has no bound stock

binding energy the energy required to break a molecule or atom into its simplest constituent parts

bind·weed (báindwi:d) *n. Convolvulus arvensis,* a perennial twining weed ‖ any of several other species of *Convolvulus*

bine (bain) *n.* a flexible shoot ‖ a climbing stem, esp. of the hop [dial. form of BIND n.]

binge (bindʒ) *n.* (*pop.*) a drinking spree [origin unknown]

Bing·ham (bíŋəm), George Caleb (1811–79), U.S. genre painter. His subjects range from Midwestern river life (e.g.'Raftsmen Playing Cards') to the political scene (e.g. 'Stump Speaking')

Bingham, Hiram (1875–1956), U.S. archaeologist and Senator (1925–33) from Connecticut. He discovered (1911) the lost Inca city and traditional refuge of the Quechua kings, and named it Machu Picchu (Old Peak). He wrote its best known history

bin·go (bíŋgou) *n.* a gambling game in which each of several players has a numbered card on which he covers the numbers as they are called or indicated on a wheel. The first player to complete his card (or, in some cases, one complete row of numbers on his card) wins the 'jackpot', part of the money staked by players for their cards ‖ code word when originated by pilot meaning "I have reached minimum fuel for safe return to base or to designated alternate" ‖ when originated by controlling activity, it means "proceed to alternate aircraft or carrier as specified"

bin·na·cle (bínək'l) *n.* a case containing the ship's compass, with a lamp for night use [earlier *bittacle* perh. fr. Span. *bitacula*]

bin·oc·u·lar (binókjulər, bainókjulər) *adj.* having or requiring the use of two eyes **bin·óc·u·lars** *pl. n.* an optical instrument composed of two terrestrial telescopes mounted on a frame and equipped with a screw that focuses both objectives simultaneously, while the focus of the eyepieces is independent (*PRISM BINOCULARS) [fr. L. *bini,* both + *oculi,* eyes]

bi·no·mi·al (bainóumi:əl) 1. *n.* (*math.*) an expression consisting of the sum or difference of two terms. 2. *adj.* of such an expression ‖ (*biol.*) of the system of double names (generic and specific) given to plants and animals [fr. L.L. *binomius*]

binomial theorem (*math.*) the nth power of a binomial worked out in detail, attributed to Newton

bi·nom·i·nal (bainómin'l) *adj.* consisting of two names, binomial [fr. L.L. *binominis* fr. *bi-,* two + *nomen,* name]

bin·tu·rong (bintú:rɒŋ) *n. Arctictis binturong,* a mammal allied to civets, having a prehensile tail, inhabiting S.E. Asia [Malay]

bi·nu·cle·ar (bainjú:kli:ər, bainú:kli:ər) *adj.* having two nuclei **bi·nu·cle·ate** (bainjú:kli:eit, bainú:kli:eit) *adj.*

bio- *prefix* life, organic life [Gk fr. *bios,* way of living, course of life]

bi·o·as·say (báiouəséi, báiouæsei) 1. *n.* determination of the strength of a drug or biological product by testing its effects on living organisms under standardized conditions, or an instance of such determination 2. *v.t.* to test by bioassay

bi·o·as·tro·nau·tics (báiouæstrənɔ́tiks) *n.* biological science applied to space travel —**bioastronautical** *adj.*

bi·o·au·tog·ra·phy (báiouɔtɒ́grəfi:) *n.* classification of organic material by using solid absorbents that have affinities for specific elements —**bioautograph** *n.* —**bioautographic** *adj.*

bi·o·a·vail·a·bil·i·ty (báiouəveiləbíliti:) *n.* (*med.*) the extent and rate of absorption of a dose of a given drug, measured by the time-concentration curve for appearance of the administered drug in the blood. Bioavailability is used to determine whether different brand-name drugs, a generic name as opposed to a brand-name drug, or, in some cases, different batches of the same brand name drug, will produce the same therapeutic effect *Cf.* BIOEQUIVALENCE

Bí·o-Bí·o (bí:ɔbí:ɔ) a river (238 miles long) in S. Chile, rising in the Andes and flowing into the Pacific at Concepción

bi·o·cat·a·lyst (báioukǽt'list) *n.* a substance (a vitamin, enzyme etc.) which activates or accelerates a biological process, e.g. metabolism

bi·o·ce·no·sis or **bi·o·coe·no·sis** (báiousənóusis) *n.* (*envir.*) 1. science of animals and plants living together 2. an ecological unit comprising both plant and animal populations of a habitat 3. a biological or biotic community 4. the organisms comprising a biological community —**biocenotic** or **biocoenotic** *adj.*

bi·o·chem·i·cal (báioukémik'l) *adj.* of or relating to biochemistry

bi·o·chem·ist (báioukémist) *n.* someone trained or engaged in biochemistry

bi·o·chem·is·try (báioukémistri:) *n.* the study of the chemical processes and substances of living matter

bi·o·cide (báiousaid) *n.* 1. destruction of life 2. an agent that destroys life —**biocidal** *adj.*

bi·o·clean (báioukli:n) *adj.* free of living organisms

bi·o·crat (báiəkræt) *n.* bureaucrat representing the interests of the biological sciences or environment protection

bi·o·cy·ber·net·ics (báiousaibərnétiks) *n.* science applying computer mathematics to emotions

bi·o·de·grad·a·ble (báioudigréidəb'l) *n.* a substance capable of natural decomposition into harmless elements in a short period —**biodegradability** *n.* —**biodegradable** *adj.* —**biodegrade** *v.* —**biodegradation** *n.*

bi·o·de·struct·i·ble (báioudistrʌ́ktəb'l) *adj.* capable of being decomposed into harmless elements without danger to the environment —**biodeterioration** *n.*

bi·o·e·lec·tro·gen·e·sis (báiouilektrədʒénisis) *n.* electrical production by living organisms —**bioelectricity** *n.*

bi·o·e·lec·tron·ics (báiouilektróniks) *n.* science of electronic effect and control of living organisms

bi·o·en·gi·neer·ing (báiouendʒiniɛ́riŋ) *n.* application of engineering techniques to biological processes, e.g., creation of drugs utilizing bacteria, molds, yeasts, etc. —**bioengineer** *n.*

bi·o·en·vi·ron·ment (báiouinváirənmənt) *n.* environment as it affects and is affected by living organisms —**bioenvironmental** *adj.*

bi·o·e·quiv·a·lence (báiouikwívələns) *n.* chemically and therapeutically equivalent drugs that have the same bioavailability (indistinguishable by chemical means). Bioequivalence is a function of bioavailability, and the terms are often used synonymously. Therapeutically equivalent preparations need not be either chemically equivalent or bioequivalent

bi·o·eth·ics (báiouéθiks) *n.* study of ethical problems involved in biological research, e.g., in genetics, organ transplants, artificial insemination

bi·o·feed·back (báioufí:dbæk) *n.* conditioning technique designed to observe, control, and modify emotional, nervous, and muscular responses including blood pressure and heartbeat

bi·o·gen (báiədʒən) *n.* a hypothetical protein molecular unit of which it is assumed that cells are built [fr. BIO- + Gk *genos,* producing]

bi·o·gen·e·sis (báioudʒénisis) *n.* the hypothesis that living organisms can arise only from preceding living organisms (cf. ABIOGENESIS) [fr. BIO- + Gk *genesis,* origin]

bi·og·ra·pher (baiógrəfər, bi:ógrəfər) *n.* an author of a biography or biographies

bi·o·graph·ic (báiəgrǽfik) *adj.* of or relating to biography **bi·o·gráph·i·cal** *adj.*

bi·og·ra·phy (baiógrəfi:, bi:ógrəfi:) *pl.* **bi·og·ra·phies** *n.* a written account of a person's life ‖ biographical writing as a literary genre [fr. Mod. L. *biographia* fr. Gk *bios,* life + *graphein,* to write]

bi·o·haz·ard (báiouhæzərd) *n.* danger from natural life

bi·o·in·stru·men·ta·tion (baiouinstrəməntéiʃən) *n.* devices for recording and transmitting physiological data —**bioinstrumentation** *n.* the development, the installation of these devices

bi·o·log·ic (baiəlódʒik) *n.* (*med.*) any virus, therapeutic serum, toxin, antitoxin, or analogous product of plant or animal origin used in the prevention, diagnosis, or treatment of disease, e.g., vaccines, blood plasma products ‖ *adj.* of or relating to biology **bi·o·lóg·i·cal** *adj.*

biological clock body-function rhythms

biological engineering creation of life forms toward an objective such as creating greater crop yield in a type of plant *Cf* GENETIC ENGINEERING

biological father natural father

biological mother natural mother

biological warfare warfare waged with organisms (e.g. pathogens and their toxins) against men, animals or plants

bi·ol·o·gist (baiólədʒist) *n.* a specialist in biology

bi·ol·o·gy (baiólədʒi:) *n.* the science of life and all its manifestations: an area of study concerned with living organisms, their form and structure, their behavior, their function, their origin, development and growth and their relationship to their environment and to like and unlike organisms, both living and extinct ‖ the plant and animal life of a given region [fr. BIO-+Gk *logos*, discourse]

bi·o·lu·mi·nes·cence (baioulu:minésəns) *n.* the giving off of light by living organisms, e.g. plankton, fireflies etc. **bi·o·lu·mi·nés·cent** *adj.*

bi·o·mass (báioumæs) *n.* (*ecology,* esp. of plankton) the living matter of a given habitat, expressed as weight of living matter per unit area of habitat or as weight or volume of living matter per unit volume of habitat

bi·o·ma·te·ri·al (baioumətíari:əl) *n.* material suitable for use as a substitute for living material, e.g., prosthetics

bi·ome (báioum) *n.* a large community of organisms having a peculiar form of vegetation and characteristic animals

bi·o·med·i·cine (baioumédisin) *n.* branch of medicine dealing with functioning and survival of man in abnormal environments, esp. in space —**biomedical** *adj.*

bi·o·met·ric (baioumétrik) *adj.* of or relating to biometry **bi·o·mét·ri·cal** *adj.*

bi·o·me·tri·cian (baioumətríʃən) *n.* a specialist in biometry

bi·o·met·rics (baioumétriks) *n.* biometry

bi·om·e·try (baiómitri:) *n.* estimation of the probable length of human life ‖ the science of applying statistical techniques to biological knowledge [fr. BIO-+Gk *metron*, measure]

bi·o·mon·i·tor·ing (baioumónitəriŋ) *n.* (*envir.*) method of testing water quality at a site by using living organisms *Cf* BIOASSAY

bi·on·ics (baióniks) *n.* study of electronic systems that act like living systems and application to engineering of biological structure, e.g., birds' wings to flying, brain workings to computers —**bionic** *adj.* —**bionics** *n.*

bi·o·nom·ics (baiənómiks) *n.* ecology [fr. BIO-+ *nomics* (after 'economics')]

bi·o·par·ent (báioupɛərənt) *n.* natural parent

bi·o·pho·tol·y·sis (baioufoutóləsis) *n.* hypothetical process of splitting water by solar energy to produce hydrogen

bi·o·phys·i·cist (baioufízisist) *n.* a specialist in biophysics

bi·o·phys·ics (baioufíziks) *n.* the study of biological material and processes by physical methods, and the study of physical phenomena in living organisms. Biophysics is thus concerned with the states and properties of matter and the effects, transformation and production of various forms of energy in the biological state

bi·op·sy (báiopsi:) *pl.* **bi·op·sies** *n.* (*med.*) the examination of tissue taken from the living body [fr. BIO-+Gk *opsis*, sight]

bi·o·re·search (baiourí:sə:rtʃ) *n.* research in the biological sciences

bi·o·rhythm (báiouriðəm) *n.* natural rhythms and cycles in bodily functions

bi·o·sa·line (baiouséili:n) *adj.* of systems suitable for making deserts economically useful

bi·o·sat·el·lite (baiousæt'lait) *n.* artificial satellite containing living organisms

bi·o·sci·ence (baiəsáiəns) *n.* the study of biology beyond the earth, including exobiology and biomedicine —**bioscientific** *adj.* —**bioscientist** *n.*

bi·o·sen·sor (báiousensər) *n.* device to monitor and transmit information about biological processes, e.g., effect of motion on an animal in space

bi·o·spe·le·ol·o·gy (baiouspi:li:ólədʒi:) *n.* study of organisms that live in caves —**biospeleologist** *n.*

bi·o·sphere (báiəsfiər) *n.* the part of the world where organisms can live

bi·o·ster·e·o·met·rics (baiousteri:əmétriks) *n.* three-dimensional measurement of the body utilizing two stereo cameras to make bodygrams, used in medical diagnosis and anthropological research

bi·o·syn·the·sis (baiousínθisis) *n.* chemical synthesis produced by and within a living organism, e.g. the manufacture of hormones

bi·o·ta (baióutə) *n.* the plants and animals in an area

biotelemetry (baioutəlémətri:) *n.* transmission of measurements of body activity —**biotelemetric** *adj. Cf* TELEMETRY

bi·ot·ic (baiótik) *adj.* relating to life [fr. L. fr. Gk *biotikos*]

biotic potential the highest possible rate of population increase, resulting from maximum natality and minimum mortality

bi·o·tin (báiətin) *n.* a member of the vitamin B complex [fr. Gk *bios,* life]

bi·o·tite (báiətait) *n.* a form of mica found as black crystals in igneous rocks, esp. in granites. It is a silicate of iron, magnesium, potassium and aluminum [after J. B. Biot (1774-1862), French physicist]

biotransformation (baioutrænsfərméiʃən) *n.* change of one chemical into another while within a living organism

biotron (báiətron) *n.* chamber with controlled climate; used in experiments of the effect of environment on organisms

bi·o·type (báiətaip) *n.* (*biol.*) a group of plants or animals having the same genotype ‖ the genotype itself

bip·a·rous (bípərəs) *adj.* bringing forth two at a birth [fr. BI-+L. -*parus,* bearing]

bi·par·ti·san (baipártizən) *adj.* of the two-party system in politics ‖ marked by the cooperation of both parties **bi·pár·ti·san·ship** *n.*

bi·par·tite (baipártait) *adj.* having two parts ‖ drawn up in two parts, one for each of two sides, *bipartite agreement* ‖ (*bot.*) divided into two parts, e.g. of a leaf divided nearly to its base **bi·par·ti·tion** (baipartíʃən) *n.*

bi·ped (báiped) **1.** *adj.* having two feet **2.** *n.* a two-footed animal, e.g. man [fr. BI-+L. *pes* (*pedis*), foot]

bi·pin·nate (baipíneit) *adj.* (*bot.*) having leaflets growing in pairs on paired petioles

bi·plane (báiplein) *n.* an airplane with two sets of wings, one above the other

bi·pod (báipod) *n.* a two-legged support for a gun etc. [fr. BI-+Gk *pous* (*podos*), foot]

bi·po·lar (baipóulər) *adj.* having, or at, two poles **bi·po·lar·i·ty** (baipoulæriti:) *n.*

bi·prism (báiprizəm) *n.* two prisms of glass, base to base, of very small refracting angles, employed by Fresnel to obtain interference between the light deviated by the two prisms

bi·quar·tic filter (baikwórtik) (*electr.*) energy or sound filter made up of amplifiers, resistors, and capacitors used to provide infinite values of electrical charge adjustments

bi·ra·di·al (bairéidi:əl) *adj.* arranged bilaterally and radially

bi·ra·mous (bairéiməs) *adj.* having, or consisting of, two branches

Biran *MAINE DE BIRAN

birch (bə:rtʃ) **1.** *n.* a member of *Betula,* fam. *Betulaceae,* a deciduous forest tree of the temperate areas of the northern hemisphere, with light, smooth bark ‖ the wood of this tree, valuable for furniture, veneers etc. ‖ a bundle of its twigs used for flogging **2.** *v.t.* to flog with a birch [O.E. *berc*]

birch·bark (bə́:rtʃbɑrk) *n.* a canoe of birch bark

birch·en (bə́:rtʃ'n) *adj.*

Birch·er (bə́:rtʃər) *n.* member of the right wing extremist John Birch society, formed in 1958 — **Bircher, Birchite,** or **Birchist** *n.*

bird (bə:rd) *n.* a warm-blooded vertebrate of the class *Aves,* covered with feathers except for the legs and feet, which are scaly, and having the forelimbs converted into wings ‖ a game bird ‖ the shuttlecock in badminton **birds of a feather** people of similar character **to kill two birds with one stone** to achieve two aims simultaneously [O.E. *brid*]

bird·bath (bə́:rdbæθ, bə́:rdbɑθ) *n.* a garden ornament filled with water for birds to drink and bath in

bird·call (bə́:rdkɔl) *n.* the characteristic call of a bird ‖ an instrument imitating this, for decoying birds

bird dog a gundog

bird·house (bə́:rdhaus) *pl.* **bird·hous·es** (bə́:rdhauziz) *n.* a box for a bird to nest in ‖ an aviary

bird·ie (bə́:rdi:) *n.* (*golf*) a score of one stroke under bogey in playing a hole

bird·lime (bə́:rdlaim) *n.* a sticky substance spread on trees in order to catch birds

bird of paradise a bird of fam. *Paradisaeidae,* native to New Guinea and neighboring islands. They are characterized by the splendor and brilliance of their plumage

bird of passage a migratory bird ‖ a person who never stays long in one place

bird of prey a carnivorous bird which hunts for its food (as distinct from eating carrion)

bird·seed (bə́:rdsi:d) *n.* small seed, esp. of the grass *Phalaris canariensis,* fed to cage birds

bird's-eye (bə́:rdzai) *adj.* marked with little spots, *bird's-eye piqué* (fabric), *bird's-eye maple* (a spotted wood) ‖ seen from above, *a bird's-eye view of a target area* ‖ wide-ranging, general, *a bird's-eye view of a situation*

bird's-foot trefoil (bə́:rdzfut) a member of *Lotus,* fam. *Papilionaceae,* esp. *L. corniculatus,* having yellow flowers

bird's-nest (bə́:rdznest) *v.i.* to look for birds' nests or their contents

bird's nest soup a soup made from swifts' nests because of the choice flavor of the bird's saliva used in their fabrication. It is regarded as a delicacy, esp. in S.E. Asia and China

bird·song (bə́:rdsoŋ, bə́:rdsoŋ) *n.* the singing of birds

bird watcher someone who makes a practice of observing wild birds

bird·y·back or **bird·ie back** (bə́:rdi:bæk) *n.* transport of truck-loaded containers by air *Cf* PIGGYBACK

bi·re·frin·gence (baiirifríndʒəns) *n.* the refraction of a beam of incident light as two polarized beams along slightly diverging paths, as in most crystals (*POLARIZATION)

bi·re·frin·gent (baiirifríndʒənt) *adj.* having the property of birefringence

bi·reme (báiri:m) *n.* an ancient galley with two banks of oars [fr. L. *biremis* fr. *bi-,* two+*remus,* oar]

bi·ret·ta (birétə) *n.* the square cap worn by Catholic and some Anglican clergy [Ital. *berretta* and Span. *birreta*]

Bir·ken·head (bə́:rkənhed), Frederick Edwin Smith, 1st earl of (1872–1930), English statesman, lawyer, journalist and orator

Birkenhead a seaport and county borough (pop. 123,907) in Cheshire, N.W. England, on the Mersey, with shipyards and flour mills. It is linked with Liverpool by a tunnel (two and a half miles long) under the Mersey

Birk·hoff (bə́:rkɔf), George David (1884–1944), U.S. mathematician. His research contributed greatly to the fields of mathematical analysis and analysis applied to dynamics

Bir·ming·ham (bə́:rmiŋəm) an industrial and manufacturing city (pop. 1,041,000, with agglom. 2,292,000) and county borough in Warwickshire, the second largest city in England, and the market center of the Black Country. It is famous for metal goods, hardware, cars, electrical equipment, machine tools, jewelry, small arms and plastics. University (1899)

Bir·ming·ham (bə́:rmiŋhæm) a city (pop. 284,413, with agglom. 847,360) in Alabama, the leading industrial center of the South. It has iron, steel and cotton industries, and is a market for softwoods

Bir·ney (bə́:rni:), James Gillespie (1792–1857), U.S. politician and abolitionist. As founding editor (1836) of the 'Philanthropist', and as executive secretary (1837–9) of the American Anti-Slavery Society, he was instrumental in the creation of the Liberty party and was its candidate for U.S. president in 1840 and 1844

Bi·ro·bi·jan (birəbidʒán) a Jewish autonomous region (pop. 193,400) of the R.S.F.S.R., U.S.S.R., in E. Siberia. It was colonized by Jews in 1928, and was made an autonomous region in 1934. Industries: mining, forestry, agriculture ‖ its capital (pop. 41,000)

birr (bə:r) *n.* unit of currency in Ethiopia, equal to 100 cents

CONCISE PRONUNCIATION KEY: **(a)** æ, c*a*t; ɑ, c*ar*; ɔ, f*aw*n; ei, sn*a*ke. **(e)** e, h*e*n; i:, sh*ee*p; iə, d*ee*r; ɛə, b*ea*r. **(i)** i, f*i*sh; ai, t*i*ger; ə:, b*i*rd. **(o)** o, *o*x; au, c*ow*; ou, g*oa*t; u, p*oo*r; ɔi, r*oy*al. **(u)** ʌ, d*u*ck; u, b*u*ll; u:, g*oo*se; ə, bacill*u*s; ju:, c*u*be. x, lo*ch*; θ, *th*ink; ð, bo*th*er; z, *Z*en; ʒ, cor*s*age; dʒ, sava*g*e; ŋ, oranguta*n*g; j, *y*ak; ʃ, *f*ish; tʃ, fe*tch*; 'l, rabb*le*; 'n, redd*en*. Complete pronunciation key appears inside front cover.

birth (bə:rθ) *n.* the event of being born ‖ the act of bringing forth young ‖ a coming into existence, *the birth of dadaism* ‖ lineage, descent ‖ noble lineage **to give birth to** to bring forth (young) [M.E. *byrthe* fr. O.E. *beran*, to bear]

birth certificate a certificate showing the place and date of a person's birth, the names of the parents etc.

birth control the avoidance of unwanted pregnancies, esp. by preventing fertilization by the use of contraceptives or by continence (*RHYTHM METHOD)

birth·day (bə́:rθdei) *n.* the day of one's birth or the anniversary of this day

birthday honours (*Br.*) titles etc. bestowed on people on the official birthday of the sovereign

birth·mark (bə́:rθmɑrk) *n.* a mark on the skin at birth

birth·place (bə́:rθpleis) *n.* the place of one's birth

birth·rate (bə́:rθreit) *n.* the ratio of births to population within a given time

birth·right (bə́:rθrait) *n.* the rights or privileges to which one is entitled by birth

birth·stone (bə́:rθstoun) *n.* a precious stone considered astrologically proper to the month of one's birth

bis (bis) *dv.* twice ‖ (*mus.*) a direction to repeat ‖ (*in references*) a mark of repetition [L.]

Bis·cay, Bay of (bískei, bíski:) a bay of the Atlantic Ocean formed by the north coast of Spain and the west coast of France, notorious for its storms

bis·cuit (bískit) 1. *n.* a soft unsweetened roll or bun, usually eaten hot with butter (*Br.*) a cracker ‖ (*Br.*) a cookie ‖ pottery fired once before glazing and refiring ‖ (*Br.*) part of a soldier's mattress ‖ a very light brown color 2. *v.t.* to fire (raw pottery) without glaze [O.F. *bescuit* fr. *bis*, twice+*cuit*, cooked]

bi·sect (baisékt) *v.t.* to cut or divide into two equal parts ‖ to cut or divide into two parts (not necessarily equal) **bi·séc·tion** *n.* **bi·séc·tion·al** *adj.* **bi·séc·tor** *n.* a bisecting line [fr. BI-+L. *secare* (*sectus*), to cut]

bi·sex·u·al (baisékʃuəl) *adj.* of or relating to both sexes ‖ having both sexes, e.g. the earthworm

bish·op (bíʃəp) *n.* a member of the highest order in the Christian Church ‖ (*chess*) one of the two pieces which move only diagonally [O.E. *bisceop* fr. L. fr. Gk]
—A bishop administers a diocese, and for some Christian sects the office is merely a convenient unit of administration. For most Christians, however, the office represents the essential nature of Church order, and the reality of the Church's authority delivered by Christ to his Apostles and transmitted by them

bish·op·ric (bíʃəprik) *n.* the office of a bishop ‖ a diocese [O.E. *bisceoprīce* fr. *bisceop*, bishop+*rīce*, realm]

Bishops' Bible the English translation of the Bible produced in 1568, under the authority of Archbishop Parker, as a challenge to the Calvinistic Geneva Bible

Bishops' Wars two short wars (1639 and 1640) between Charles I of England and the Scots, caused by Charles's attempt to force the English liturgy on the Presbyterian Scots. Charles's defeat caused him to call the Long Parliament

bisk *BISQUE (soup)

Bis·marck (bízmɑrk), Otto Eduard Leopold, Prince von (1815–98), German statesman and Prussian junker, known as 'The Iron Chancellor'. He was appointed prime minister of Prussia (1862) by Wilhelm I, in order to push von Roon's army reform through parliament. He invaded Schleswig-Holstein (1864) and defeated Austria in the Seven Weeks' War (1866). He formed the North German Confederation (1867), excluding Austria. His editing of the Ems Telegram precipitated the Franco-Prussian War (1870–1). He became the first chancellor of the German Reich (1871). At home, he faced a Catholic opposition (*KULTURKAMPF) and tried to forestall the rise of socialism by social reform (1883–7). Abroad, he maintained peace by the Dreikaiserbund (1872) and alliances with Austria (1879) and Italy (1882). His protective tariff (1879) and colonial policy (1883) fostered trade and industry. Friction with Wilhelm II led to Bismarck's dismissal (1890)

Bismarck the capital (pop. 44,485) of North Dakota. It is the center for navigation on the upper Missouri, a rail junction, and the wholesale market for a large agricultural area

Bismarck Archipelago a group of about 200 mountainous, wooded, volcanic islands (area 22,920 sq. miles, pop. 250,000) in the Pacific (Melanesia) northeast of New Guinea. It includes New Britain, New Ireland and the Admiralty Is. It was a German possession (1884–1919) and was administered under mandate by Australia until it became independent as *PAPUA NEW GUINEA. Chief products: copra, cocoa, shellfish

Bismarck Sea a part of the S.W. Pacific stretching 500 miles between the Bismarck Archipelago and New Guinea

bis·muth (bízməθ) *n.* a trivalent metallic element (symbol Bi, at. no. 83, at. mass 208.980). Alloys with tin, lead and cadmium (Rose's metal, type metal, Wood's metal) have low melting points and give good castings by expanding when they solidify ‖ (*pop.*) bismuth subnitrate [G., origin unknown]

bismuth subnitrate a basic salt obtained from bismuth nitrate and used to treat some gastrointestinal disorders ‖ a mixture of such salts

bi·son (báis'n, báiz'n) *pl.* **bi·son, bi·sons** *n.* a member of *Bison*, fam. *Bovidae*, a genus of large, shaggy, bovine mammals, often called buffalo, having a large hump on the withers and back. Two species are extant, *B. bison* of America and the European wisent ‖ the gaur [L.]

Bi·son (báis'n) *n.* (*mil.*) U.S.S.R. 4-engine jet bomber (M-4) similar to U.S. B-52 Stratofortress; with 45,000-ft ceiling, launched in 1954

bisque (bisk) *n.* (in certain games) the right of taking one extra point or turn when desired [F., origin unknown]

bisque *n.* biscuit (pottery fired once) ‖ vitreous, hardfired porcelain not meant to be glazed [BISCUIT]

bisque, bisk *n.* a rich soup made from shellfish etc. [F. *bisque*, crayfish soup]

bis·sex·tile (baisékstil, bisékstail) 1. *adj.* (of a year) containing 366 days 2. *n.* a leap year [fr. L. *bissextilis*]

Bis·sière (bi:sjer), Roger (1888–1964), French painter. Influenced by cubism, he has painted abstract compositions of ordered, regular forms and subtle, harmonious colors

bi·sta·ble (baistéib'l) *adj.* (*computer*) capable of accepting either one or the other of two conditions at the same time, e.g., computer switches **bistability** *n.*

bi·stat·ic (baistǽtik) *adj.* utilizing a receiver and transmitter at different locations

bis·ter, esp. *Br.* **bis·tre**(bístər) 1. *n.* a dark brown pigment made from wood soot and used in watercolor painting 2. *adj.* of this color [F., origin unknown]

bis·tort (bístɔrt) *n.* a member of *Polygonum*, fam. *Polygonaceae*, a genus of herbaceous plants with a stout and contorted rhizome, used as an astringent, and a spike of pale flowers, esp. *P. bistorta* [fr. L. *bistorta* fr. *bis*, twice+*torta*, fem. past part. of *torquere*, to twist]

bistre *BISTER

bit (bit) *n.* a small piece or amount ‖ a short time, *wait a bit* ‖ a piece, part ‖ a small coin or its value, two bits (=25 cents) **a bit** rather, a *bit cross* **a bit of** rather a, *a bit of a dandy* **every bit as** quite as, *you're every bit as good as he is* **not a bit** not at all **to do one's bit** to do one's share of work or duty [O.E. *bita*, a piece broken off]

bit *n.* the metal bar of a bridle, which is put into the horse's mouth ‖ the part of a key which enters the lock and grips the lever ‖ the cutting edge of a tool, esp. the cutting iron of a plane ‖ the boring piece of a drill used in a brace ‖ the gripping part of pincers **to take the bit between the teeth** (of a horse) to run away, bolt ‖ (of a person) to reject control [O.E. *bite*, a biting]

bit *n.* (*computer technology*) a basic unit of information [B(INARY DIG)IT]

bit *past* and alt. *past part.* of BITE

bit by bit gradually, piecemeal

bitch (bitʃ) *n.* the female of the dog or other canine ‖ a spiteful, malicious woman ‖ a sexually promiscuous woman **bitch·y** *comp.* **bitch·i·er** *superl.* **bitch·i·est** *adj.* [O.E. *bicce*]

bite (bait) 1. *v. pres. part.* **bit·ing** *past* **bit** (bit) *past part.* **bit·ten** (bít'n), **bit** *v.t.* to seize and grip with the teeth ‖ to cut with the teeth ‖ to cut or pierce, the *handcuff bit his flesh* ‖ (of insects, snakes etc.) to sting ‖ to cause sharp pain to, *the wind bit his face* ‖ to damage, *the dahlias were bitten by frost* ‖ to corrode ‖ to grip, *the anchor bit the coral* ‖ *v.i.* to seize and grip something with the teeth ‖ to have a tendency to make attacks in this way ‖ to cause a biting sensation ‖ (of a fish) to take the bait ‖ to yield to a lure ‖ to have a corrosive action **to bite off more than one can chew** to attempt more than one can manage **to bite the dust** (*rhet.*) to fall to the ground, esp. mortally wounded 2. *n.* a biting ‖ the wound made by biting ‖ something bitten off, *a bite of apple* ‖ a snack ‖ the nibbling or swallowing of bait by a fish ‖ sharp pain ‖ sharpness, pungency, *his criticism lacks bite* ‖ a grip or hold [O.E. *bītan*]

bite plate plastic and wire device used by orthodontists to restrain or pressure movement of teeth

bite the bullet *v.* accept an unpleasant duty

Bi·thyn·i·a (biθíni:ə) an ancient district in N.W. Asia Minor. It became a Roman province (74 B.C.)

bit·ing (báitiŋ) *adj.* stinging, painful, *biting cold* ‖ caustic, sarcastic, *biting words*

bit rate (*computer*) number of bits per specified period passing a point

bitt (bit) *n.* (*pl.*) a single or double post on a ship's deck for fastening cables etc. [etym. doubtful]

bit·ten (bít'n) *past part.* of BITE ‖ *adj.* (with 'with') filled with enthusiasm for

bit·ter (bítər) 1. *adj.* acrid-tasting, tart ‖ hard to bear, *a bitter disappointment* ‖ caused by or expressing deep grief, *bitter tears* ‖ harsh, biting, *a bitter wind* ‖ acrimonious, showing deep resentment, *bitter remarks* ‖ (of ale, beer) very dry and strongly flavored with hops **to the bitter end** to the very last, come what may 2. *adv.* bitingly, *the night was bitter cold* 3. *n.* (*Br.*) bitter beer ‖ (*pl.*) angostura [O.E. *biter*]

bit·ter·ling (bítərliŋ) *n. Rhodeus amarus*, fam. *Cyprinidae*, a small carplike fish of Central Europe [G. fr. *bitter*, bitter]

bit·tern (bítərn) *n.* a member of *Botaurus*, fam. *Ardeidae*, a genus of long-legged marsh birds allied to herons. There are European and American species [perh. M.E. *botor* fr. O.F. *butor*]

bittern *n.* the liquid remaining after crystallization in the manufacture of salt [perh. fr. *bittering*, making bitter]

bitter orange the Seville orange

bit·ter·root (bítərru:t, bítərrut) *n. Lewisia tediviva*, fam. *Portulaceae*, a plant of the Rocky Mtns having fleshy roots and pink flowers

Bit·ter·root Range (bítərru:t, bítərrut) a range (about 400 miles long) of the Rocky Mtns, extending along the Idaho-Montana boundary. Highest peak: Garfield Mt (10,961 ft)

bit·ter·sweet (bítərswi:t) 1. *adj.* mingling bitter and sweet qualities ‖ mingling pain and pleasure 2. *n. Celastrus scandens*, a North American woody vine having orange or yellowish fruits ‖ *Solanum dulcamara*, a nightshade of Eurasia having purple flowers and poisonous scarlet berries

bi·tu·men (bitjú:mən, bitú:mən) *n.* any of several viscous or solid mixtures of hydrocarbons and their nitrogen and sulfur derivatives ‖ asphalt, found in great quantity native in Trinidad ‖ tar residue from the distillation of coal [L.=mineral pitch]

bi·tu·mi·nous (bitjú:minəs, bitú:minəs) *adj.* of the nature of bitumen ‖ containing or made with bitumen [F. *bitumineux*]

bituminous coal soft coal rich in volatile hydrocarbons

bituminous paint paint including bitumen, used for rustproofing and waterproofing iron pipes, gutters etc.

bi·u·nique (baiju:ní:k) *adj.* of an exclusive exchange on a one-to-one basis —**biuniqueness** *n.*

bi·va·lent (baivéilənt, bívələnt) *adj.* (*chem.*) having two valencies (cf. DIVALENT) ‖ (*biol.*, of paired homologous chromosomes associated in synapsis) double [fr. L. *bi-*, two+*valens* (*valentis*) fr. *valere*, to be strong]

bi·valve (báivælv) 1. *n.* an animal that has a hinged double shell, e.g. a member of the class *Lamellibranchia* 2. *adj.* having a shell consisting of two hinged valves, allowing the shell to open and close

biv·ou·ac (bívuːæk, bívwæk) 1. *n.* a temporary camp without tents or with pup tents only ‖ a makeshift shelter 2. *v.i.* pres. part. **biv·ou·ack·ing** *past* and *past part.* **biv·ou·acked** to spend the night in a bivouac [F. fr. G. *beiwacht*, an additional night watch]

CONCISE PRONUNCIATION KEY: (**a**) æ, cat; ɑ, car; ɔ fawn; ei, snake. (**e**) e, hen; i:, sheep; iə, deer; ɛə, bear. (**i**) i, fish; ai, tiger; ə:, bird. (**o**) o, ox; au, cow; ou, goat; u, poor; ɔi, royal. (**u**) ʌ, duck; u, bull; u:, goose; ə, bacillus; ju:, cube. x, loch; θ, think; δ, bother; z, Zen; ʒ, corsage; dʒ, savage; ŋ, orangutang; j, yak; ʃ, fish; tʃ, fetch; 'l, rabble; 'n, redden. Complete pronunciation key appears inside front cover.

bi·week·ly (baiwí:kli:) **1.** adj. happening or appearing once every two weeks ‖ happening or appearing twice a week **2.** adv. once every two weeks ‖ twice a week **3.** n. pl. **bi·week·lies** a biweekly publication

bi·year·ly (baijɪ́ərli:) **1.** adj. biennial ‖ (substandard) happening twice a year **2.** adv. every two years ‖ (substandard) twice a year

bi·zarre (bizár) adj. fantastic, strange (often with a suggestion of the ridiculous or the uncanny) [F.]

Bi·zer·ta (bizá:rtə) (Bizerte) a port (pop. 62,856) in Tunisia, on the Mediterranean at the mouth of Lake Bizerta

Bi·zet (bi:zei), Georges (1838–75), French composer. The opera 'Carmen' (1875) and the incidental music to 'l'Arlésienne' (1872) are his most popular works

Björn·son (bjǿ:rnsɒn), Björnstjerne (1832–1910), Norway's greatest dramatist after Ibsen, and her chief novelist and poet. The plays include 'Beyond our Power' (1895), and the novels 'The Fisher Girl' (1868) and 'In God's Way' (1889)

blab (blæb) **1.** v. pres. part. **blab·bing** past and past part. **blabbed** v.i. to give away secrets thoughtlessly, talk indiscreetly ‖ to chatter wearisomely ‖ v.t. to reveal (a secret etc.) thoughtlessly or indiscreetly **2.** n. vague, windy talk ‖ chatter [etym. doubtful]

blab·ber (blǽbər) pres. part. **blab·ber·ing** past and past part. **blab·bered** v.i. to talk drivel, chatter tiresomely or without proper restraint ‖ v.t. (often with 'out') to say (something) in an uncontrolled spate of remarks [M.E. blaberen]

Black (blæk), Hugo Lafayette (1886–1971), Associate Justice (from 1937) of the U.S. Supreme Court. He opposed isolations by Congress or the States of free speech and due process

Black, Jeremiah Sullivan (1810–83), U.S. lawyer. As attorney general (1857–60) under President James Buchanan, he successfully challenged Mexican land grants in California. As secretary of state (1860), he solicited foreign support for the Union on the eve of the Civil War. His arguments before the Supreme Court in the Reconstruction Slaughterhouse cases encouraged a narrow interpretation of the rights of citizens conferred by the 14th amendment

Black, Joseph (1728–99), Scottish chemist who discovered that a change of physical state is accompanied by the evolution or absorption of heat (*LATENT HEAT, *SPECIFIC HEAT)

black (blæk) **1.** adj. without light, or not able to reflect it ‖ colorless, or so dark as to appear colorless ‖ the opposite of white ‖ lowering, black clouds ‖ not hopeful, the prospects look black ‖ (rhet.) sad, a black day for our team ‖ angry, sullen or disapproving, a black look ‖ very dirty ‖ (rhet.) wicked, black villainy ‖ evil, black magic ‖ darkskinned, belonging to a race with dark pigmentation ‖ reflecting discredit, a black mark ‖ illegal, black market ‖ inveterate, a black Republican, a black liar ‖ (Br.) not to be handled or worked in by trade unionists while other trade unionists are on strike ‖ of the members of a religious order wearing a black habit ‖ of or concerning a black or blacks **2.** n. a black pigment, fabric etc. ‖ dirt, soot ‖ (board games) the dark-colored men or pieces or the player having these ‖ a person whose natural skin color is black **3.** v.t. to make black ‖ to polish with blacking ‖ v.i. to become black, blacken **to black out** to darken, cause to give out or receive no light ‖ (esp. of pilots of planes pulling out of a dive or very sharp turn) to lose consciousness or memory, usually temporarily (*BLACKOUT) [O.E. blæc]

black-and-blue (blǽkənblú:) adj. discolored because of broken blood vessels beneath the skin due to a bruise

Black and Tans auxiliary police used by the British to crush Irish republicans (1920–1)

black and white writing or print, a statement in black and white ‖ a drawing (pencil, pen and ink, wash etc.) not using color ‖ a photographic print, reproduction, television image etc. not using color

black art (esp. pl.) magic in the service of evil

black bag job an illegal entry by a law enforcement agent

black·ball (blǽkbɒl) **1.** n. a small black ball (or some equivalent) used in a secret ballot to vote against (or exclude in some cases) a candidate for some privilege or office **2.** v.t. to exclude (e.g. from a club etc.) by the use of a blackball ‖ to ostracize

black bear Ursus americanus, a North American bear ‖ Selenarctos thibetanus, an Asian bear

black·bee·tle (blǽkbi:t'l) n. (Br., pop.) a cockroach

black belt 1. in judo or karate, certification of highest proficiency; one who has earned the degree **2.** (agriculture) region with extremely fertile soil **3.** (usu. cap.) area inhabited by black people, e.g., south of the Sahara Desert

black·ber·ry (blǽkbəri:; blǽkbəri) pl. **black·ber·ries** n. a member of Rubus, fam. Rosaceae, a genus of trailing or erect, usually prickly, bushes bearing edible berries which consist of numerous small drupes on a receptacle ‖ one of the berries

black·bird (blǽkbə:rd) n. Turdus merula, a thrush common throughout Europe and found in N. Africa. The male is characterized by black plumage and a bright orange-yellow beak ‖ any bird of fam. Icteridae, esp. Agelaius phoeniceus, the red-winged blackbird

black·board (blǽkbɔrd, blǽkbourd) n. a large piece of slate or painted wood with a dark smooth surface which can be written or drawn on with chalk. The marks easily rub off and the board can be used repeatedly

blackboard jungle 1. an urban school where discipline is enforced with great difficulty if at all, against student violence **2.** the condition in a school with a high potential for student violence Cf ASPHALT JUNGLE

black·bod·y (blǽkbɒdi:) pl. **black·bod·ies** n. (phys.) a hypothetical perfect absorber and emitter of radiant energy

black book a book containing a blacklist **to be in someone's black books** to be out of favor with someone

black box 1. in an aircraft, any removable unit of electronic equipment, e.g., receiver, amplifier **2.** portable electronic device of unknown workings controlling an operation or making a recording

black bread coarse bread, of a dark color, made of rye flour

black buck Antilope cervicapra, the common medium-sized antelope of India. The male has long, spiraling horns

Black·burn (blǽkbərn) a county borough (pop. 88,236) in Lancashire, N.W. England: textiles, mainly cotton

black·cap (blǽkkæp) n. any of several species of black-headed birds, esp. Sylvia atricapilla, the black warbler of Europe ‖ Rubus occidentalis, the black raspberry

black capitalism principle of greater participation by blacks in entrepreneurship

Black Caucus *CONGRESSIONAL BLACK CAUCUS

black·cock (blǽkkɒk) n. the male black grouse ‖ the black grouse

'Black Codes' codes of racial law passed (1865–6) in southern states of the U.S.A. which appeared to confer second-class status on blacks. Congress responded with an act, over President Andrew Johnson's veto, which strengthened the Freedmen's Bureau

black comedy black humor, humor derived from morbid, grotesque, unpleasant or absurd situations. syn black humor —**black humorist** n.

Black Country a prosperous industrial area of about 50 sq. miles in S. Staffordshire and N. Worcestershire, England, incl. Birmingham, Walsall, Wolverhampton, Dudley, Stourbridge and West Bromwich

black currant Ribes nigrum, a European shrub or bush cultivated for its small, black, succulent berries ‖ one of these fruits

black·damp (blǽkdæmp) n. air in which carbon dioxide replaces oxygen because of explosion or combustion, causing suffocation

Black Death the deadly plague, most probably bubonic, which was widespread in Asia and Europe in the 14th c. It struck Europe (1347–50) and returned intermittently until 1383

black earth the rich dark soil of the grain-producing grasslands of central European Russia and central North America

black·en (blǽkən) v.t. to make black or dark ‖ to speak ill of, defame ‖ v.i. to grow black or dark [M.E. blaknen fr. O.E. blæc, black]

Black English dialect common among Afro-Americans

Black·ett (blǽkit), Patrick Maynard Stuart (1897–1974), British physicist. His perfecting of the Wilson cloud chamber led to the discov-

ery of the positive electron, and to important work on cosmic rays. Nobel prize (1948)

black eye an eye surrounded by a dark bruise ‖ an eye with a dark iris **black-eyed** (blǽkaid) adj. having black eyes ‖ with a dark center or spot, blackeyed peas

black-eyed Su·san (súːz'n) Rudbeckia hirta, a flower of central and eastern North America having flower heads with yellow to orange ray florets and dark conical disks ‖ R. serotina, the similar flower of the southeastern U.S.A.

black·face (blǽkfeis) n. a darkfaced sheep ‖ (printing) boldface ‖ a minstrel comedian ‖ makeup for a black role

black·fel·low (blǽkfelou) n. an Australian aboriginal

black·fish (blǽkfiʃ) pl. **black·fish, black·fish·es** n. any of several varieties of English and American dark-hued fishes, e.g. Centrolophus niger, fam. Stromateidae, and the tautog ‖ the salmon after spawning ‖ Dallia pectoralis, fam. Umbrididae, a small edible fish of the Arctic seas which can survive being frozen ‖ a member of Globicephala, fam. Delphinieae, a genus of small toothed whales

black flag (hist.) a black flag with a white skull and crossbones on it, used as an emblem of piracy ‖ (Br.) a black flag flown to show that an execution has been carried out

black-fly (blǽkflai) pl. **black-flies** n. any small, chunky, blackish fly of fam. Simuliidae, order Diptera ‖ Aphis fabae, the bean aphid, a garden pest which attacks broad beans particularly

Black·foot (blǽkfut) pl. **Black·feet** (blǽkfi:t) n. a North American Indian of the Blackfoot tribes of the Algonquin group

Black Forest an area in southern W. Germany of forest highland (Feldberg, 4,905 ft), stretching for 100 miles along the east bank of the upper Rhine. Resources: timber, hydroelectric power. There are many lakes and mineral springs and many resorts (*BADEN-WÜRTTEMBERG)

Black Friar a Dominican friar

black frost a hard frost without rime or snow

black·guard (blǽgard, blǽgərd) **1.** n. a scoundrel ‖ an utterly unscrupulous person **2.** v.t. to destroy the character of (someone) with false accusations **black·guard·ly** adj. typical of a scoundrel [etym. doubtful]

Black Hand (Am. Hist.) a secret organization of Italian criminals and blackmailers which operated in the U.S.A. It was formed c. 1868 ‖ an organization of Spanish anarchists repressed in 1883

Black Hawk War a conflict (1832) between the U.S. government and the Sac and Fox Indians, resulting from a U.S. demand (1804) that the Indians withdraw west of the Mississippi River. Ignoring the white flag of surrender, a U.S. volunteer force ended the war by massacring almost the entire tribe of Sac chieftain Black Hawk

black·head (blǽkhed) n. any of several black-headed birds, esp. gulls ‖ a plug of grease and dirt blocking a sebaceous gland duct ‖ a usually fatal infectious disease of turkeys etc. attacking the liver and intestines

Black Hills mountains in South Dakota and Wyoming, many over 5,000 ft: minerals (gold, silver), forest reserve

black hole (astron.) hypothetical area in space postulated to be a collapsed star into which matter has contracted so that it vanishes except for an intense gravitational effect. A black hole can even "swallow" light. syn collapsor. Cf ERGOSPHERE, SCHWARZSCHILD RADIUS

Black Hole of Calcutta *CALCUTTA, BLACK HOLE OF

black humor *BLACK COMEDY

black·ing (blǽkiŋ) n. a polish for making shoes, stoves etc. shiny black

black·jack (blǽkdʒæk) **1.** n. a pirate flag ‖ a card game in which each player tries to assemble a hand whose value adds up to, but does not exceed, 21. Players bet against a banker, who is himself a player ‖ a small rubber club with lead in it and a flexible handle **2.** v.t. to strike or menace with this weapon

black knot a destructive fungus disease causing dark, knotlike growths in plum and cherry trees, gooseberries, filberts and hazels

black lead graphite

black·leg (blǽkleg) **1.** n. a swindler, esp. a cheat at gambling ‖ a disease affecting cattle ‖ a plant disease (e.g. of cabbages) ‖ (Br.) a strikebreaker **2.** v. pres. part. **black·leg·ging** past and past part. **black·legged** v.t. (Br.) to break (a strike)

CONCISE PRONUNCIATION KEY: **(a)** æ, cat; ɑ, car; ɔ fawn; ei, snake. **(e)** e, hen; i:, sheep; iə, deer; ɛə, bear. **(i)** i, fish; ai, tiger; ə:, bird. **(o)** o, ox; au, cow; ou, goat; u, poor; ɔi, royal. **(u)** ʌ, duck; u, bull; u:, goose; ə, bacillus; ju:, cube. x, loch; θ, think; ð, bother; z, Zen; ʒ, corsage; dʒ, savage; ŋ, orangutang; j, yak; ʃ, fish; tʃ, fetch; 'l, rabble; 'n, redden. Complete pronunciation key appears inside front cover.

by being a blackleg ‖ *v.i.* (*Br.*) to act as a black-leg in a strike

black letter (*printing*) Gothic type

black·list (blǽklist) **1.** *n.* a list of names of guilty or suspect persons, firms etc. **2.** *v.t.* to put on a blacklist

black lung (*med.*) form of pneumoniosis (lung disease) caused by long-term inhalation of coal dust; prevalent among miners. *Cf* BROWN LUNG

black·mail (blǽkmeil) **1.** *n.* an attempt to extort money by threats, esp. of exposure ‖ the money extorted in this way **2.** *v.t.* to extort money from (someone) by intimidation, esp. by threats of exposure [BLACK adj.+obs. *mail*, tribute]

black magic magic used in the service of evil

Black Ma·ri·a (məráiə) the patrol wagon in which prisoners are taken to and from prison

black mark something less than a grave fault that causes a person to be viewed critically

black market an illegal setup for changing money or buying and selling goods in violation of officially controlled quotas or rates **black·mar·ke·teer** (blǽkmɑrkitíər) *n.* someone who buys or sells on the black market

black mass a travesty, in Devil worship, of the Christian Mass

black money unreported (and untaxed) income

Black Monk a Benedictine monk

Black·more (blǽkmɔr, blǽkmour), Richard Doddridge (1825–1900), English author of 'Lorna Doone' (1869) and other novels

Black Mountains the highest range in the Appalachian Mtns. It is a spur of the Blue Ridge, in W. North Carolina. Highest peak: Mt Mitchell

Black·mun, (blaékmən) Harry (1908–   ), U.S. Supreme Court associate justice. After graduation from Harvard Law School in 1932, he practiced and taught law in Minnesota. Appointed to the Supreme Court by Pres. Nixon in 1970, he was considered a moderate conservative

Black Muslims (Nation of Islam), an exclusively nonwhite socio-politico-religious movement in the U.S.A., founded in 1930 by Wali Farad, a Meccan orthodox Muslim. Under Farad's successor, Elijah Muhammad, the movement became imbued after the 2nd world war with the spirit of black nationalism and protest. The Black Muslims believe in the superiority of the black man and his eventual domination of all extant white civilizations

black nationalism philosophy advocating formation of Afro-American self-governing communities —**black nationalist** *n.*

black·ness (blǽknis) *n.* **1.** negritude **2.** black humor

black night shade *Solanum nigrum,* a weed with white flowers and black edible berries. The foliage is poisonous

black·out (blǽkaut) *n.* a preventing of lights inside a building from being seen outside, or the condition of having lights screened in this way, or a period of time in which lights are thus screened ‖ a temporary loss of consciousness or memory

Black Panthers a U.S. black militant organization advocating 'Black Power'. It was originally associated with SNCC (the Student Non-violent Coordinating Committee), first presented candidates for public office in local Mississippi elections in 1966, and eventually became an independent force. It was long in open conflict with the police and many of its leaders were killed or imprisoned

black pepper a powdered condiment obtained by grinding the entire peppercorn

black·ploi·ta·tion (blǽkplɔitéiʃən) *n.* exploitation of blacks or black movements, esp. in films

Black·pool (blǽkpu:l) a town and seaside resort (pop. 147,000) in Lancashire, England, on the Irish Sea, catering particularly for the industrial Midlands

Black Power the ideology of the black militant movement in the U.S.A., which seeks to achieve social, economic, and political power for U.S. blacks. It aims at restoring black pride and independence in a white-dominated society

Black Prince Edward of Woodstock, Prince of Wales (1330–76), son of Edward III of England. He distinguished himself in battle at Crécy (1346) and Poitiers (1356). His son became Richard II

black project (*mil.*) U.S. Defense Department term for extremely secret program

black propaganda propaganda that purports to emanate from a source other than the true one

black pudding blood sausage

black radio propaganda broadcasts made under false sponsorship, esp. psychological warfare

Black Rod (*Br.*) an official of the House of Lords responsible for the maintenance of order (the office was instituted in 1350) and usher of the Order of the Garter

black salsify *Scorzonera hispanica,* a European plant with a black edible taproot

Black Sea an inland sea (area 168,500 sq. miles) between S.E. Europe and Asia Minor, bordered by the U.S.S.R., Turkey, Bulgaria and Rumania, with an outlet to the Mediterranean through the Bosporus

Black September extremist element in Al-Fatah group of Palestine Liberation Organization; dedicated to the use of terrorism against Israel

black sheep a member of a family (or other group) of whom the other members are ashamed

black signal in facsimile transmission, the reproduction of a maximum-density portion of the original copy

black·smith (blǽksmiθ) *n.* a man who works iron in a forge, shoes horses etc.

black snake any of several black or dark-colored snakes, esp. *Coluber constrictor,* fam. *Colubridae,* found in North America

black spot removal in South Africa, the apartheid policy of relocating black people to areas exclusively for blacks under 1948 Group Areas Act

Black·stone (blǽkstoun, blǽkstən), Sir William (1723–80), English jurist. His 'Commentaries on the Laws of England' (1765–9) had a great influence on jurisprudence, esp. in the U.S.A.

black studies school courses at high-school or college level, dealing with history and culture of black people in the U.S. and Africa

black tea *TEA

black·thorn (blǽkθɔrn) *n.* the sloe ‖ a walking stick cut from a sloe

blackthorn winter (*Br.*) frosty weather at the spring planting time, when the blackthorn is in flower

black·top (blǽktɒp) *n.* a bituminous surfacing material used for roads, runways etc. ‖ a road etc. finished with this material

black·wa·ter fever (blǽkwɒtər, blǽkwɒtər) a malaria characterized by dark urine

black widow the female of *Latrodectus mactans,* fam. *Therididiae,* an American spider with a venomous bite. It is black, with a red hourglass-shaped mark on its underside

blad·der (blǽdər) *n.* (*anat.*) a membranous sac filled with fluid or air, esp. the musculo-membranous receptacle for urine ‖ any hollow bag that can be inflated ‖ (*bot.*) an inflated pericarp ‖ a hollow vesicle, e.g. in various seaweeds **blad·der·y** *adj.* [O.E. *blǽdre*]

blad·der·nose (blǽdərnouz) *n.* the hooded seal

bladder worm a saclike tapeworm larva, e.g. the cysticercus, the hydatid

blad·der·wort (blǽdərwɔ:rt) *n.* a member of *Utricularia,* fam. *Lentibulariaceae,* a genus of aquatic insectivorous plants. The leaves bear small bladders which trap insects

bladder wrack *Fucus vesiculosus,* a seaweed used for manure and in kelp

blade (bleid) *n.* the cutting part of a knife, sword, razor, scissors etc. ‖ a long slender leaf, esp. of grass ‖ (*bot.*) the outspread part of a leaf, excluding the stalk ‖ a thin flattened edge, e.g. of an oar or propeller ‖ the flat upper part of the tongue ‖ a flattened bone, esp. the scapula or shoulder blade **in the blade** (of cereal crops) not yet having produced ears [O.E. *blæd, leaf*]

blahs (blaz) *n.* (*colloq.*) (often with "the") feeling of malaise

blain (blein) *n.* (*rare,* esp. of animals) a blister or sore on the skin [O.E. *blegen*]

Blaine (blein), James Gillespie (1830–93), U.S. statesman. He served (1869–75) as Speaker of the House. Although known to his followers as the 'Plumed Knight', he was defeated by Rutherford Hayes in the 1876 Republican presidential nomination, partly because of a charge of corruption that had been brought against him. As secretary of state (1880–4) under President James Garfield, he sought an agreement for a U.S.-dominated Panama canal and envisioned

a system of inter-American arbitration. This agreement, later realized in the Hay-Pauncefote treaty, marked the first step in the Pan-American movement. After losing to Grover Cleveland by a small margin in the 1884 presidential race, he served (1889–92) as secretary of state under President Benjamin Harrison. Assuming the chairmanship of the first Pan-American conference (1889), he fought to include a reciprocity clause in the high-tariff McKinley bill of 1890 in order to improve trade relations with Latin America

Blair (blɛər), Francis Preston (1791–1876), U.S. journalist and politician. He founded (1830) and owned (until 1845) the Washington 'Globe', a mouthpiece for the Jacksonian Democrats, and also published the 'Congressional Globe'. He served in Andrew Jackson's 'kitchen cabinet' and helped to found the Republican party. He gave influential advice to Abraham Lincoln and support to Andrew Johnson in his Reconstruction plan

Blake (bleik), Eugene Carson (1906–85), American church leader. He was general secretary of the World Council of Churches (1966–72)

Blake, Robert (1599–1657), English admiral who commanded Cromwell's navies against the Royalists (1649–51) and against the Dutch and Spanish

Blake, William (1757–1827), English poet, painter, engraver and mystic. His early works, e.g. 'Songs of Innocence' (1789) and 'Songs of Experience' (1794), were never free from symbolism, but the lyrical element predominated. His later works, e.g. 'Milton' (1804–8) and 'Jerusalem' (1804–20), were almost entirely symbolic. 'The Four Zoas' (1796–1804) was not published in its entirety until 1925. A professional engraver all his life, he also painted in watercolors. Most of his books were self-manufactured by his original process of 'illuminated printing': text and pictures done in reverse on metal with acid-proof ink, then treated with acid, printed by hand and hand-colored. He also engraved a series of illustrations to his own Prophetic Books, to 'The Book of Job' (1825), and to Dante and other poets

blam·a·ble, blame·a·ble (bléiməb'l) *adj.* deserving blame

blame (bleim) **1.** *v.t. pres. part.* **blam·ing** *past and past part.* **blamed** to hold responsible, *he blamed the weather for his poor crops* ‖ to attribute the cause of, lay the fault for, *he blamed his poor crops on the weather* **to be to blame** to be held responsible **2.** *n.* censure, expression of disapproval ‖ responsibility for something wrong or unsatisfactory **to lay the blame on** to hold responsible **blame·a·ble** *adj.* *BLAMABLE **blame·less** *adj.* free from fault or blame ‖ innocent **blame·wor·thy** *adj.* deserving blame, at fault [O.F. *blâmer* fr. L. fr. Gk]

Blanc (blɑ̃), Louis (1811–82), French socialist politician and historian. In his 'Organisation du travail' (1839) he put forward the principle: 'From each according to his abilities, to each according to his needs.' His attempt to achieve this by a system of social workshops (a form of cooperative trade union) failed in 1848, but the idea of the right to work played an important part in the development of socialist thought

blanc fixe (blãfí:ks) *n.* artificial barium sulfate precipitated by sulfuric acid from a solution of a barium salt and used as a white pigment and extender [F.]

blanch (blæntʃ, blɑntʃ) *v.t.* to make white or pale ‖ to make white by peeling away the skin of (almonds), by depriving (e.g. celery) of light, by scalding (meat) etc. ‖ to give a white luster to (silver coins, before stamping) ‖ to coat (sheet iron or steel) with tin ‖ *v.i.* to grow pale [F. *blanchir*]

Blanche of Cas·tile (blæntʃəvkæstí:l) (1188–1252), queen of France, regent during her son Louis IX's minority (1226–36), and again when he was at the Crusades (1248–52). She used great firmness in pacifying the kingdom and defeating baronial reaction

blanc·mange (bləmã́nʒ) *n.* a pudding made mainly of milk solidified by gelatin or starch and variously flavored [fr. O.F. *blancmanger,* white food]

Blanc, Mont *MONT BLANC

Blan·co Fom·bo·na (blánkɔfombóna), Rufino (1876–1944), Venezuelan novelist, poet and polemicist. His novels, notably 'El hombre de hierro' (1907) and 'El hombre de oro' (1920), denounce the dictatorship of Gómez and the political corruption in Caracas

CONCISE PRONUNCIATION KEY: **(a)** æ, c*a*t; a, c*a*r; ɔ f*a*wn; ei, sn*a*ke. **(e)** e, h*e*n; i:, sh*ee*p; iə, d*ee*r; ɛə, b*ea*r. **(i)** i, f*i*sh; ai, t*i*ger; ə:, b*i*rd. **(o)** o, *o*x; au, c*ow*; ou, g*oa*t; u, p*oo*r; ɔi, r*oy*al. **(u)** ʌ, d*u*ck; u, b*u*ll; u:, g*oo*se; ə, b*a*cillus; ju:, c*u*be. x, lo*ch*; θ, *th*ink; ð, bo*th*er; z, *Z*en; ʒ, cor*s*age; dʒ, sava*g*e; ŋ, orangutan*g*; j, *y*ak; ʃ, *fish*; tʃ, fe*tch*; 'l, rabb*le*; 'n, red*den*. Complete pronunciation key appears inside front cover.

Blan·co party (bláŋkɔ) the conservative party of Uruguay (now called the Nationalists), rival of the Colorado or liberal party

bland (blænd) n. mild, *a bland climate* ‖ suave, *a bland manner* ‖ soothing and nonirritating, *a bland diet* [fr. L. *blandus*]

blan·del (blǽndel) *APOSTILB

blan·dish (blǽndiʃ) v.t. to coax or flatter ‖ to tempt with flattering words **blán·dish·ment** n. (often *pl.*) [F. *blandir* (*blandiss-*)]

blank (blæŋk) 1. *adj.* not written on, *a blank paper* ‖ expressionless, *blank faces* ‖ empty, without incident, *a blank future* ‖ unrelieved, without variety, *a blank wall* (one without doors or windows) 2. *n.* an empty space left in printed matter ‖ a void, *her mind became a blank* ‖ a dash written instead of a letter or word (often a swearword) or instead of a name, *tell that —to clear off* ‖ a blank cartridge ‖ a coin before stamping ‖ a key before the notches have been cut ‖ a raffle ticket which does not win a prize for its holder **to draw a blank** to be unsuccessful, e.g. in an inquiry or search 3. *v.t.* (with 'out') to blot out [F. *blanc*, white]

blank cartridge an explosive charge without any projectile

blank check, *Br.* **blank cheque** a check which the payer signs, leaving the amount to be filled in by the payee ‖ a free choice of action accorded to someone

blan·ket (blǽŋkit) 1. *n.* a warm woolen (or nylon etc.) covering used esp. on a bed ‖ any extended covering, *a blanket of mist* 2. *v.t.* to cover as if with a blanket, *snow blanketed the fields* ‖ to stifle (noise, rumors, questions etc.) ‖ to take the wind from the sails of (another boat) by passing to windward 3. *adj.* applicable to all persons or in all circumstances, *a blanket ban* [O.F. *blanquette* dim. of *blanc*, white]

blanket stitch a buttonhole stitch worked round the border of heavy material instead of hemming

blank verse unrhymed verse, esp. the five-foot iambic

Blan·qui (blɑ̄ki:), Louis Auguste (1805–81), French socialist who took a leading part in the revolutions of 1830, 1848 and 1871. He formulated the economic doctrine of French radical socialists or 'Blanquistes's

Blan·tyre (blæntáiər) the main commercial and industrial center (pop. 219,011) of Malawi, in the Shire Highlands. It joined with Limbe in 1959

blare (blɛər) 1. *v. pres. part.* **blar·ing** *past* and *past part.* **blared** *v.i.* to make a loud, harsh sound ‖ *v.t.* to proclaim loudly, *loudspeakers blared the news* 2. *n.* any continuous, loud, harsh noise or trumpeting [etym. doubtful]

blar·ney (blɑ́rni:) 1. *n.* persuasive cajolery, wheedling talk 2. *v.t.* to try to influence or persuade by blarney ‖ *v.i.* to talk blarney [after *Blarney*, an Irish castle near Cork, with a stone supposed to make those who kiss it proficient in blarney]

Blas·co I·bá·ñez (blúskɔi:bánjeθ), Vicente (1867–1928), Spanish novelist, notable for his vivid portrayals of the life of action. His many novels include 'The Cabin' (1898), 'Blood and Sand' (1908) and 'The Four Horsemen of the Apocalypse' (1916)

bla·sé (blɑzéi,blázei) *adj.* satiated with pleasure and left without enthusiasm ‖ affectedly sophisticated in a world-weary way [F.]

blas·pheme (blæsfí:m) *pres. part.* **blas·phem·ing** *past* and *past part.* **blas·phemed** *v.t.* to speak impiously of (God and things regarded as sacred) ‖ *v.i.* to utter blasphemy **blas·phe·mous** (blǽsfəməs) *adj.* [O.F. fr. L. fr. Gk]

blas·phe·my (blǽsfəmi:) *pl.* **blas·phe·mies** *n.* contemptuous or irreverent speech about God or things regarded as sacred [O.F. fr. L. fr. Gk]

blast (blɑːst, blast) 1. *n.* a strong gust of wind ‖ a draft of air used to increase the heat of a furnace ‖ a wave of highly compressed air created by an explosion ‖ a ringing sound from a trumpet etc. **(at) full blast** at top capacity ‖ (*biol.*) an undeveloped cell ‖ (*slang*) an exciting event 2. *v.t.* to make by the use of explosives, *to blast a tunnel* ‖ to shatter ‖ to attack violently, *to blast the opposition* ‖ *v.i.* (with 'off', of a rocket or guided missile) to take off under selfpropulsion 3. *interj.* an expletive expressing annoyance **blást·ed** *adj.* damnable, annoying [O.E. *blœst*, a blowing]

blas·te·ma (blæstí:mə) *pl.* **blas·te·mas, blas·te·ma·ta** (blæstí:mətə) *n.* undifferentiated embry-

onic tissue capable of growth and differentiation [Gk *blastēma*, bud]

blast furnace a large vertical furnace for the production of iron from its ores, generally the oxides. Hot air is blasted through a charge consisting of ore, limestone and coke. Carbon monoxide from the ignited coke reduces the oxides to iron and the limestone acts as a flux allowing the molten iron to flow to the bottom of the furnace, where it is tapped off and cast into blocks ('pigs'). Cast iron (or pig iron) contains approx. 4% of combined carbon, as well as traces of silicon, manganese, phosphorus, and sulfur. The carbon content is reduced, and the impurities removed, by the Bessemer process

blast·ing (blǽstiŋ, blústiŋ) *n.* the disintegration of solid masses (e.g. stone) by the use of explosives ‖ an abrasive action caused by small particles rubbing against a larger body

blasting gelatin a powerful explosive formed chiefly of nitroglycerin and cellulose nitrate

blas·to·coel, blas·to·coele, blas·to·cele (blǽstəsi:l) *n.* (*biol.*) the fluid-filled cavity of a blastula [fr. Gk *blastos*, bud + *koilos*, hollow]

blas·to·cyst (blǽstəsist) *n.* (*embryology*) early stage of development before formation of human embryo in which cells are formed into a sac

blas·to·derm (blǽstədə:rm) *n.* a sheet of cells formed from the blastodisc after the completion of cleavage [fr. Gk *blastos*, bud + *derma*, skin]

blas·to·disc, blas·to·disk (blǽstədisk) *n.* the region of a meroblastic ovum (i.e. usually one containing large amounts of yolk) in which cleavage first appears [fr. Gk *blastos*, bud + DISC]

blast·off (blǽstɔf, blǽstɒf, blústɔf, blústɒf) *n.* (of a rocket or guided missile) the action of taking off under self-propulsion

blas·to·gen·e·sis (blæstoudʒénisis) *n.* gemmation, reproduction by budding ‖ transmission of inherited characters by means of germ plasm only **blas·to·gen·ic** (blæstoudʒénik) *adj.* [fr. Gk *blastos*, bud + *genesis*, birth]

blas·to·mere (blǽstəmiər) *n.* a blastula cell [fr. Gk *blastos*, bud + *meros*, part]

blas·to·pore (blǽstəpɔr, blǽstəpour) *n.* (*embry.*) the opening of the archenteron of a gastrula [fr. Gk *blastos*, bud + *póros*, passage]

blas·tu·la (blǽstʃulə) *pl.* **blas·tu·las, blas·tu·lae** (blǽstʃuli:) *n.* an early metazoan embryo consisting of a single layer of cells forming a hollow ball (cf. MORULA, cf. GASTRULA) **blas·tu·lá·tion** *n.* the formation of a blastula [dim. fr. Gk *blastos*, bud]

blat (blæt) *n.* (Russian; italics) nonofficial exchange of supplies and services, a common practice in U.S.S.R. industry

bla·tan·cy (bléit'nsi:) *n.* the state or quality of being blatant

bla·tant (bléit'nt) *adj.* very obvious, *a blatant lie* ‖ (of voices, colors, clothes etc.) strident, harsh [etym. doubtful]

bla·ther (blǽðər) 1. *v.i.* to talk foolishly ‖ *v.t.* to utter foolishly 2. *n.* foolish talk [fr. O.N. *blathr*, nonsense]

Blau·e Rei·ter, der (derbláuəráitər) (the Blue Rider) a German expressionist art movement (1911–14) founded by Kandinsky and Marc and joined by Klee. It furthered the abstract tendencies of expressionism and introduced foreign abstract art (e.g. cubism, futurism) into Germany

Bla·vat·sky (bləvǽtski:), Helena Petrovna (1831–91), Russian-born theosophist. Her works include 'Isis Unveiled' (1887) and 'The Secret Doctrine' (1888)

blaze (bleiz) 1. *n.* a bright fire ‖ an unintended fire ‖ a bright display (of color, light) ‖ an outburst, *a blaze of fury* ‖ full, direct light, *the blaze of noon, the blaze of publicity* 2. *v.i. pres. part.* **blaz·ing** *past* and *past part.* **blazed** to burn brightly ‖ to be bright with light or color ‖ to shine or glow fiercely ‖ to burst forth (with anger etc.) **to blaze away** to shoot or fire continuously or very frequently [O.E. *blase*, blœse, torch]

blaze 1. *n.* a patch of white fur or hair on an animal's face, esp. a longitudinal stripe down the center ‖ a mark made on a tree by cutting a chip of bark from it, either to mark it for felling or to show a track through a wood 2. *v.t. pres. part.* **blaz·ing** *past* and *past part.* **blazed** to mark with a blaze **to blaze a trail** to mark out a route by blazing trees ‖ to be a pioneer in some activity [etym. doubtful]

blaze *pres. part.* **blaz·ing** *past* and *past part.* **blazed** *v.t.* ‖ to proclaim ‖ to spread (news) far and wide [etym. doubtful]

blaz·er (bléizər) *n.* a lightweight flannel jacket, brightly colored for sports wear, or commonly navy blue or some other solid color [BLAZE (to burn brightly)]

bla·zon (bléiz'n) 1. *n.* a coat of arms ‖ a heraldic shield ‖ a technical description of armorial bearings 2. *v.t.* to describe or paint armorial bearings ‖ (*old-fash.*) to proclaim boastfully **bla·zon·ry** *pl.* **bla·zon·ries** *n.* a coat of arms ‖ the art of describing or representing armorial bearings [F. *blason*, shield]

bleach (bli:tʃ) 1. *v.t.* to remove the color or stains from (something) by converting colored chemical compounds into colorless ones ‖ to lighten the color of (hair) by hydrogen peroxide or other chemicals ‖ to lighten the color of, as if by chemical bleaching, *hair bleached by the sun* 2. *n.* a chemical used in bleaching **bléach·er** *n.* someone who bleaches (clothes etc.) ‖ a machine or chemical used for bleaching ‖ (*pl.*) a section in a stadium etc. containing uncovered seats for spectators of outdoor sports [O.E. *blœcean*]

bleaching powder a mixture containing calcium hydroxide saturated with chlorine, used as a bleaching agent and disinfectant

bleak (bli:k) *adj.* exposed, desolate, *a bleak hillside* ‖ cheerless, *a bleak reception* ‖ cold, bitter, *bleak winds* [rel. to O.E. *blāc*, pale]

bleak *n.* *Alburnus lucidus*, fam. *Cyprinidae*, a small European river fish [perh. fr. O.N. *bleikja*]

blear (bliər) 1. *adj.* (of the eyes) bleary 2. *v.t.* to blur, *rain bleared the outline of the hills* **bléar·i·ness** *n.* **bléar·y** *comp.* **blear·i·er** *superl.* **blear·i·est** *adj.* dim, misted, filmy [origin unknown]

bleat (bli:t) 1. *v.i.* (of a sheep or goat) to make its characteristic cry ‖ to speak plaintively ‖ *v.t.* to say in a bleating manner 2. *n.* the cry of a sheep or goat [O.E. *blœtan*]

bleb (bleb) *n.* a small blister on the skin ‖ a small bubble in glass or water [imit.]

bleed (bli:d) *pres. part.* **bleed·ing** *past* and *past part.* **bled** (bled) *v.i.* to lose or emit blood ‖ (of plants) to lose sap ‖ (*printing*, of illustrations) to extend right to the edge of a page so that there is no white margin ‖ *v.t.* to draw blood from (surgically) ‖ to take sap from ‖ to extort money from ‖ (*printing*) to cause (an illustration) to extend to the edge of a page without a margin **bléed·er** *n.* a hemophiliac [O.E. *blédan*]

bleeding heart the popular name for *Dicentra spectabilis*, fam. *Fumariaceae*, a garden plant with racemes of drooping, pink, heart-shaped flowers ‖ someone who gushes with anguish over the misfortunes of others

bleep (bli:p) *n.* sound from an electronic device used to send a signal, e.g., in a pocket instrument receiving an alert to call one's office — **bleeper** *n.* instrument used for a remote communication

blem·ish (blémiʃ) 1. *v.t.* to spoil or impair 2. *n.* a physical or moral defect or flaw [fr. O.F. *blemir* (*blemiss-*) perh. fr. O.N.]

blench (blentʃ) *v.i.* to flinch, recoil (in fear or disgust) [perh. fr. O.E. *blencan*, to deceive]

blend (blend) 1. *n.* a harmonious mixture 2. *v. pres. part.* **blend·ing** *past* and *past part.* **blend·ed, blent** (blent) *v.t.* to mix together ‖ *v.i.* to merge harmoniously [M.E. *blenden* prob. fr. O.N. *blanda*]

blende (blend) *n.* naturally occurring zinc sulfide, often looking like metallic lead [fr. G. *blenden*, to deceive (because it yields no lead)]

Blen·heim, Battle of (blénəm) a battle (1704) in which an Anglo-Austrian army under Marlborough and Eugène decisively defeated the French and Bavarian armies in the War of the Spanish Succession

Blenheim orange a golden-colored variety of eating apple

Blenheim spaniel a red and white variety of English spaniel

blen·ny (bléni:) *pl.* **blen·nies** *n.* any of several small fishes of fam. *Blenniidae* and related families with spiny-rayed fins, frequenting rocky coasts [fr. L. fr. Gk *blennos*, slime]

Blé·riot (bleirjou), Louis (1872–1936), French aviator who made the first flight across the English Channel (1909). He was an early advocate of the monoplane

bless (bles) *v.t. pres. part.* **bless·ing** *past* and *past part.* **blessed** (less frequently) **blest** (blest) to call down God's favor upon ‖ to consecrate, *to bless a new church* ‖ to enrich, *the marriage was*

blessed *with ten children* ‖ to praise, to *bless God* ‖ (in expressions of surprise) may God bless, *bless my soul!* **to bless oneself** to make the sign of the cross over oneself [O.E. *bletsian*, to mark with blood]
bless·ed (blésid) **1.** *adj.* holy, revered, *the blessed martyrs* ‖ (*Roman Catholicism*) beatified, accorded the second of three degrees of sanctity ‖ (*blest*) lucky, favored, *blessed with an easy-going nature* ‖ (*ironic*) cursed **2.** *n.* **the bless·ed** (blésid) the souls in Heaven **bless·ed·ness** (blésidnis) *n.* a state of happiness, esp. through the enjoyment of God's favor
Bles·sed Sacrament (blésid) the consecrated Host
Bless·ed Virgin Mary (blésid) *MARY, THE VIRGIN
bless·ing (blésiŋ) *n.* divine favor or the invocation of it ‖ a source of consolation ‖ a piece of good fortune **a blessing in disguise** something unwelcome at first, which turns out to be fortunate
Bles·sing·ton (blésiŋtən), Marguerite, countess of (1789–1849), an Irishwoman who was a brilliant society hostess, a friend of Byron, and the mistress of Count d'Orsay from 1822. She wrote many novels to make money
blest (blest) *adj.* blessed
blew *past* of BLOW
Bligh (blai), William (1754–1817), British rear admiral. He took part in Cook's last voyage (1776). He was commander of the 'Bounty' in 1789 when the crew mutinied in the South Seas and set him adrift in an open boat. On a later voyage (1791) he made discoveries in Tasmania, Fiji and the Torres Straits. He was governor of New South Wales (1805–8) and served with distinction in the Napoleonic Wars
blight (blait) **1.** *n.* any plant disease or injury characterized by or resulting in withering, growth cessation, and a more or less general death of parts without rotting. Blight is caused by microorganisms, fungi, insect attack or unfavorable environmental conditions ‖ an organism which causes this ‖ something which spoils hope, plans, festivity etc. **2.** *v.t.* to wither ‖ to spoil, destroy ‖ to frustrate **blight·er** *n.* (*Br.*) a person who makes one temporarily cross (often used mildly or affectionately) [origin unknown]
blimp (blimp) *n.* a small, nonrigid dirigible used esp. for observation [type B+LIMP]
blimp *n.* (esp. *Br.*) an extreme, rather stupid, chauvinistic conservative [after Col. *Blimp*, a cartoon figure invented by David Low (1891–1963)]
blind (blaind) **1.** *adj.* without sight ‖ undiscerning or unwilling to judge, *blind to faults* ‖ without foresight or thought, *a blind decision* ‖ without seeing objects or facts, *blind flying, blind guessing* ‖ drunken, *a blind stupor* ‖ having no outlet, *a blind passage* ‖ having no opening, *a blind wall* ‖ (*hort.*) producing leaves rather than flowers **2.** *n.* something which prevents strong light from coming through a window ‖ a cover-up to conceal the truth ‖ (*Am.=Br.* hide) a concealed place for a hunter or observer of wildlife ‖ (*Br., pop.*) a bout of hard drinking **the blind** blind people collectively **3.** *v.t.* to deprive of the faculty of sight ‖ to dazzle [O.E.]
blind alley any path, lane or road that is closed at one end ‖ an occupation, without prospects of advancement ‖ a line of inquiry, or way of search leading nowhere
blind date an engagement to go out with a person whom one has not met
blind·er (bláindər) *n.* one of two pieces of leather sometimes fixed on each side of a bridle so that the horse can see only directly ahead, not sideways (to discourage it from shying or bolting)
blind·fold (bláindfould) **1.** *v.t.* to cover the eyes of (someone) with a cloth **2.** *adj.* having the eyes covered to restrict vision **3.** *n.* a cloth tied around the eyes to prevent vision [M.E. *blindfellen*, to strike blind]
blind·ing (bláindiŋ) *n.* the filling in of the cracks in a newly made road with fine material ‖ the material itself
blind·ly (bláindli:) *adv.* not being able to distinguish objects, facts etc., to *stumble blindly forward* ‖ without resisting or questioning, to *obey blindly*
blind·man's buff (bláindmænzbʌf) a children's game in which one blindfold player tries to catch one of the others, who are not blindfold

blind·ness (bláindnis) *n.* lack of sight ‖ lack of perception or understanding
blind spot the part of the retina in the eye insensitive to light ‖ a part of one's understanding where one's judgment does not act fairly or competently
blind stamp (*bookbinding*) a tooled cover impression not brought out with gold leaf or colored foil etc. **blind-stamp** (bláindstæmp) *v.t.* to make such impressions in (a binding cover)
blind·sto·ry (bláindstɔri:, bláindstɔuri:) *pl.* **blind-sto·ries** *n.* the triforium below the clerestory in a church, admitting no light
blind trust trust arrangement for management of assets in which the owner has no voice, used esp. to avoid conflict of interests
blind·worm (bláindwəːrm) *n.* a limbless lizard with small eyes, esp. *Anguis fragilis,* fam. *Anguidae*
blink (bliŋk) **1.** *n.* a quick shutting and opening of the eyes ‖ a momentary glimmer **2.** *v.i.* (of the eyes) to shut and open quickly ‖ to shut and open one's eyes quickly ‖ to shine with an unsteady light *v.t.* to shut and open (the eyes) quickly ‖ to make (eyes, light etc.) blink [origin unknown]
blink·er (blíŋkər) *n.* a blinder for a horse ‖ a warning light that flashes at intervals
blink·ing (blíŋkiŋ) *adj.* (*Br.*) a substitute for 'bloody' in curses
blip (blip) **1.** *n.* the light image on a radar screen that indicates the presence of an object ‖ a short, sharp, repeated sound ‖ the display of a received pulse on a cathode ray tube **2.** *v.* to excise a portion of a tape recording, leaving a space, e.g., eliminating obscene language [prob. imit.]
bliss (blis) *n.* great but quiet enjoyment ‖ perfect happiness, heavenly joy **bliss·ful** *adj.* [O.E. *bliths*]
blis·ter (blístər) **1.** *n.* a portion of skin raised by the pressure of fluid beneath it ‖ a portion of a surface similarly raised, e.g. by water vapor in a film of paint **2.** *v.t.* to cause blisters to form in or on ‖ to criticize (a person) harshly ‖ *v.i.* to become covered with blisters [M.E. *blester,* etym. doubtful]
blister agent a chemical agent that injures the eyes and lungs and burns or blisters the skin
blister beetle a beetle of fam. *Meloidae* still able, when dried and powdered, to blister the skin, e.g. cantharides
blister copper (*metall.*) impure copper with a blistered appearance due to the escape of gases during its manufacture
blister rust (*bot.*) any of several diseases of pine trees caused by rust fungi which produce blisters on the bark
blister steel (*metall.*) steel with a blistered surface formed by heating wrought iron with carbon to increase the percentage of combined carbon
blithe (blaið, blaiθ) *adj.* lightheartedly cheerful, happy [O.E. *blithe,* kindly]
blith·er·ing (blíðəriŋ) *adj.* talking nonsense, babbling, *a blithering idiot* [var. of BLATHER]
blithe·some (bláiðsəm, bláiθsəm) *adj.* blithe
blitz (blits) **1.** *n.* an air attack ‖ any sudden concerted attack ‖ (*football*) to rush by lineman or safety man to disconcert a passer **blitzer** *n.* one who does **2.** *v.t.* to attack, to bomb [short for G. *blitzkrieg,* lightning war]
bliz·zard (blízərd) *n.* a blinding snowstorm accompanied by a strong wind [etym. doubtful]
bloat (blout) **1.** *n.* (*vet.*) a windy swelling of the abdomen, esp. in cattle and horses, caused by eating too quickly **2.** *v.t.* to inflate with air or water ‖ to cause to swell with excessive pride, make vain ‖ *v.i.* to swell up [etym. doubtful]
bloat·er (blóutər) *n.* a herring cured by light smoking and salting [fr. obs. v. *bloat,* to cure]
blob (blob) *n.* a drop of liquid ‖ a small lump or globule ‖ a spot of color **to score a blob** (*Br.*) to make no score [imit.]
bloc (blok) *n.* a group of parties, governments etc. associating together to achieve (or prevent) something [F.=block]
Bloch (blok), Ernest (1880–1959), American composer born in Switzerland. His work includes string quartets, an opera ('Macbeth', 1909), a symphony ('Israel') and much orchestral writing. Jewish folklore and liturgy were a strong source of inspiration for him
Bloch, Felix (1905–), U.S. physicist, known for his theoretical work in solid state, magnetism, and the stopping of charged particles in matter. At Stanford University he developed the principle of nuclear induction which earned him (and

E.M. Purcell of Harvard University) the Nobel prize in physics (1952)
block (blok) *n.* a large solid piece of stone, wood etc. ‖ (*hist.*) a large piece of wood upon which condemned people were beheaded ‖ a wooden mold for shaping hats ‖ a pulley ‖ a piece of wood or metal engraved for use in printing ‖ a prepared piece of stone for building ‖ a large building consisting of offices, shops etc. ‖ an area in a city enclosed by four intersecting streets, often rectangular, or the length of one side of this area ‖ an obstruction ‖ something which results from obstruction, a *traffic block* ‖ (*psychol.*) a mental mechanism preventing a topic with unpleasant associations from being thought about ‖ a number of seats all together, e.g. in a theater (*Austral.*) an area of land offered by the government to a settler ‖ a piece of wood or other material used in sets by children playing at building ‖ a large number of shares [F. *bloc*]
block *v.t.* to cause obstruction in, prevent the passage of ‖ to make difficult or impossible, put obstacles in the way of ‖ (*finance*) to forbid the conversion of (money held abroad) into foreign exchange ‖ (*finance*) to restrict the use of (money held abroad) to the country concerned ‖ (*med.*) to prevent sensation in (a nerve) by the use of a local anesthetic ‖ (*theater*) to place characters in position and define movement ‖ to shape (a knitted garment) or mold (a hat) on a block ‖ to stamp (a book cover) ‖ (*sports*) to stop (a cricket ball) without attempting to drive it ‖ (*sports*) to obstruct (a player) ‖ to be blocked ‖ to cause a block **to block in** (or out) to mark out the general lines of (a drawing etc.) **to block in** (or **up**) to close off, seal [F. *bloquer*]
block·ade (blokéid) **1.** *n.* an attempted starving into surrender of an enemy by preventing goods from reaching or leaving him **to raise a blockade** to stop blockading **to run a blockade** to succeed in breaking through blockading forces, or attempt to do so **2.** *v.t. pres. part.* **block·ad·ing** *past* and *past part.* **block·ad·ed** to subject to blockade by surrounding with troops or warships etc.
block·ade-run·ner (blokéidrʌnər) *n.* a person or ship trying to get through a blockade
block and tackle a system consisting of a pulley with ropes or chains for lifting great weights
block book (*hist.*) a popular devotional book printed from blocks, text and picture being cut at the same time. They date from c. 1460: the printing method survived after the invention of movable type (*GUTENBERG)
block·bust·er (blókbʌstər) *n.* a bomb weighing several tons dropped from an aircraft to do some large piece of demolition, e.g. breech a dam ‖ someone or something that has the immediate effect of startling or impressing in a big way
block busting technique for inducing white property owners to sell their properties on the advice that black people are moving into the neighborhood —**blockbust** *v.* —**blockbuster** *n.*
block chain a chain, such as is fitted to a bicycle, the solid sections of which (engaging with the teeth of the driving wheel) are joined by side links and pins, so that the whole has flexibility
block·ette (blokét) *n.* (*computer*) **1.** small group of consecutive information units transferred. **2.** the subdivision of a block of units
block·head (blókhed) *n.* a very dullwitted person
block·house (blókhaus) *pl.* **block·hous·es** (blókhauziz) *n.* a small fortification or roofed gun emplacement [etym. doubtful]
block ice a fine mist of fog that forms a cumulative coating of ice when in contact with certain materials
Block island (blok) an island (7 miles long, 3½ miles wide) 9 miles southwest of Rhode Island. It is a popular summer resort
block letters capitals without serifs
block printing a method of printing designs on material from wooden blocks
block system (*rail.*) an arrangement by which no train is allowed to enter a section of line until the section is free of traffic
block tin refined tin cast into blocks (cf. TINPLATE)
block·y *comp.* **block·i·er** *superl.* **block·i·est** *adj.* stockily built ‖ squarish and massive in shape
bloc voting policy of voting on issues based on a

CONCISE PRONUNCIATION KEY: **(a)** æ, c*a*t; ɑ, c*a*r; ɔ f*aw*n; ei, sn*a*ke. **(e)** e, h*e*n; i:, sh*ee*p; iə, d*ee*r; ɛə, b*ea*r. **(i)** i, f*i*sh; ai, t*i*ger; əː, b*i*rd. **(o)** o, *o*x; au, c*ow*; ou, g*oa*t; u, p*oo*r; ɔi, r*oy*al. **(u)** ʌ, d*u*ck; u, b*u*ll; u:, g*oo*se; ə, b*a*cillus; ju:, c*u*be. x, lo*ch*; θ, *th*ink; ð, bo*th*er; z, *Z*en; ʒ, cor*s*age. dʒ, sava*ge*; ŋ, orangu*tang*; j, *y*ak; ʃ, *f*ish; tʃ, fe*tch*; 'l, rabb*le*; 'n, redd*en*. Complete pronunciation key appears inside front cover.

group decision, often involving group allegiances rather than the merits of an issue — **block vote** n.

Bloem·fon·tein (blú:mfɒntein) the capital (pop. 230,688) of the Orange Free State, and judicial capital of the South African Republic, with important livestock markets. Its altitude (4,518 ft) and dry climate make it a health resort. University College of the Orange Free State

Blois (blwæ) the chief town (pop. 51,950) of Loir et Cher, France, on the Loire. The countship of Blois was united to the French crown (1498). Château (13th–17th cc.)

Blok (blɒk), Alexander Alexandrovich (1880–1921), Russian poet. After early symbolist poems (1904, 1906) he became more and more messianic, giving a mystical interpretation to the revolution ('The Scythians' and 'The Twelve', 1918)

bloke (blouk) n. (Br., pop.) a guy (man, fellow) [origin unknown]

blond, blonde (blɒnd) **1.** adj. (of hair) yellowish in color ‖ (of the complexion) pale **2.** n. (**blond** only) a boy or man with yellowish hair and fair skin ‖ (**blonde** only) a girl or woman with such hair and skin [F., origin unknown]

Blon·din (blɔ̃dɛ̃), Charles (Jean François Gravelet, 1824–97), French ropewalker. He crossed Niagara Falls on a tightrope four times (1859–60)

blood (blʌd) **1.** n. a fluid circulating throughout the vertebrate body, carrying nutrients and oxygen to the tissues and removing wastes and carbon dioxide ‖ (hist.) one of the four humors **in cold blood** deliberately, not in an access of passion **in one's blood** as an inborn passion or natural capacity, esp. through the influence of parents and grandparents etc., acting is in his blood **of the blood royal** of royal family by birth **to have blood on one's hands** to be guilty of having caused someone's death **to have one's blood up** to be in a fighting mood **to make one's blood boil** to make one passionately angry **2.** v.t. to give the first taste of blood to (a hound) ‖ (Br., ceremonially in fox hunting) to give (a person) a dab with the severed brush of the dead fox [O.E. blōd]

—Blood has four main constituents: plasma, erythrocytes, leucocytes, and platelets. Plasma, the fluid part of the blood, is composed of numerous chemicals, including sugars, minerals and proteins (*ALBUMIN, *GLOBULIN, *FIBRINOGEN). Erythrocytes, containing hemoglobin, carry oxygen, supplying it to all the tissues and organs. Leucocytes, of which there are several types, serve principally to combat infections (*PHAGOCYTOSIS). Platelets are important in the mechanism of blood clotting

blood agent (physiol.) a chemical compound, including the cyanide group, that affects bodily functions by preventing the normal transfer of oxygen from the body to body tissues

blood bank a stock of whole blood or plasma for blood transfusions ‖ a place where whole blood or plasma is stored

blood·bath (blʌdbæθ, blʌdbɑːθ) n. brutal killing on a large scale, a pogrom

blood count the determination of the number of blood cells in a given volume of blood, usually as a diagnostic aid

blood·cur·dling (blʌdkə:rdliŋ) adj. horrific

blood·ed (blʌdid) adj. bred from pedigree stock ‖ (in compounds) having blood of a specified kind, warm-blooded

blood feud a vendetta involving bloodshed between two families or clans, murder exacting retaliatory murder

blood group a group of individuals classified according to whether their blood contains certain antigens or not, the compatibility of the groups determining whether or not blood transfusion can be carried out between donor and patient. There are four main groups (O, A, B and AB) and various subgroups (cf. RHESUS FACTOR). The groups are determined by laws of heredity

blood horse a thoroughbred horse

blood·hound (blʌdhaund) n. a powerful dog with a keen sense of smell, sometimes used for tracking escaped prisoners

blood·i·ly (blʌdli) adv. in a bloody manner

blood·i·ness (blʌdinis) n. the state or quality of being bloody

blood·less (blʌdlis) adj. lacking blood, unaccompanied by bloodshed ‖ without verve or energy ‖ lacking in emotion

Bloodless Revolution (Eng. hist.) *GLORIOUS REVOLUTION

blood·let·ting (blʌdletiŋ) n. the process of removing blood from a vein for therapeutic reasons

blood money money paid to a person for murdering somebody, or for giving information leading to someone's death ‖ compensation paid to the next of kin of a murdered person by the murderer, his family or tribe

blood plasma the fluid portion of whole blood (i.e. whole blood lacking erythrocytes, leucocytes and platelets)

blood poisoning disease resulting from the introduction of infection into the blood, often through an open wound

blood pressure the pressure exerted by the blood on the walls of the blood vessels, measured usually by a sphygmomanometer and expressed usually as a fraction, the numerator being the maximum pressure in mm. of mercury immediately following the systole of the left ventricle of the heart, and the denominator being the minimum pressure in the same units of the diastole of the heart's action

blood·red (blʌdréd) adj. of a red suggesting the color of blood

blood relation a person related by kinship, not by marriage

blood·root (blʌdru:t, blʌdrʊt) n. Sanguinaria canadensis, fam. Papaveraceae, a North American woodland plant with a red root, red sap, and single white flower

blood sausage a dark-colored sausage containing a large amount of pig's blood and pig's fat

blood serum blood plasma which has had fibrin removed

blood·shed (blʌdʃed) n. violent death or injury as a phenomenon, a revolution without bloodshed

blood·shot (blʌdʃɒt) adj. (of the eyes) suffused with blood

blood·stain (blʌdstein) n. a mark made by blood **blóod·stained** adj. stained with blood ‖ (rhet.) guilty of taking human life

blood·stock (blʌdstɒk) n. blood horses collectively

blood·stone (blʌdstoun) n. a semiprecious stone consisting of quartz in which red grains of jasper are embedded

blood·stream (blʌdstri:m) n. the circulating stream of blood in a body (*HEART)

blood·suck·er (blʌdsʌkər) n. a leech ‖ a person who repeatedly extorts money, e.g. a blackmailer

blood test a sampling of the blood, e.g. to determine blood group, kind of infection etc. (e.g. Wassermann test)

blood·thirst·i·ness (blʌdθə:rsti:nis) n. the state or quality of being bloodthirsty

blood·thirst·y (blʌdθə:rsti) adj. eager for blood, for slaughter ‖ delighting in tales of horror

blood type blood group

blood vessel a tube or canal in an animal through which blood circulates, e.g. an artery, vein, capillary

blood·worm (blʌdwə:rm) n. one of several vivid red (or sometimes pale red) worms esp. used as bait in fishing

blood·y (blʌdi) **1.** adj. comp. **blood·i·er** superl. **blood·i·est** of the nature or appearance of blood ‖ stained with blood ‖ in which blood is shed, a bloody battle ‖ concerned with bloodshed ‖ vicious, murderous ‖ (Br., not in polite usage) expletive used for emphasis, a bloody swindle **2.** adv. (Br., not in polite usage) expletive used for emphasis, not bloody likely **3.** v.t. pres. part. **blood·y·ing** past and past part. **blood·ied** to stain or cover with blood [O.E. blōdig]

Bloody Mary (blʌdi:méəri:) *MARY I

blood·y-mind·ed (blʌdi:máindid) adj. (Br., pop.) awkward, contrary, obstinate ‖ (Br., pop.) bad-tempered **blóod·y·mínd·ed·ness** n.

bloom (blu:m) n. a mass of iron wrought in a forge or puddled and shaped into an oblong block ‖ a mass of steel formed by hot rolling into a square block ‖ a mass of iron or steel formed by hammering or rolling scrap consolidated at high temperature [O.E. blōma]

bloom 1. n. the state of flowering, roses in full bloom ‖ a flower, blossom ‖ (of people) the time of physical perfection ‖ a flush or glow on the cheek ‖ the fine, powdery covering on freshly picked fruit such as grapes, plums or peaches ‖ a pleasing, glowing surface, the bloom on new coins ‖ a kind of raisin ‖ a cloudy defect on a varnished surface ‖ (ecol.) colored area in water caused by heavy reproduction of plankton or algae **2.** v.i. to blossom, to be or come into flower ‖ to be in, or come into, fullness of beauty ‖ (of

people) to look radiant ‖ v.t. (Br., phys.) to coat (an optical surface) with a thin layer of material so as to improve transmission [O.N. blóm, flower and blómi, prosperity]

bloom·er (blú:mər) n. (hist.) a woman's short skirt and loose trousers gathered at the ankles, designed by Mrs. Amelia Bloomer (c. 1849), U.S. social reformer ‖ (pl.) loose trousers or knickers tied at the knee, and formerly worn by women for cycling or athletics

bloomer n. (Br., pop.) a blunder, blooper, boner

bloom·er·y (blú:məri:) pl. **bloom·er·ies** n. a forge for making wrought-iron blooms

bloom·ing (blú:miŋ) adj. blossoming ‖ radiant with health ‖ (Br., pop.) used as an expression of emphasis, a blooming shame

Blooms·bur·y (blú:mzbəri:) a district in Holborn, central London, England, containing the British Museum, University College, London University Senate House etc. In the late 19th c. it became the main intellectual and cultural center of London, and in the 20th c. between the world wars it was the center for a number of writers and other intellectuals known as the 'Bloomsbury Group', whose principal figures included Virginia Woolf and Lytton Strachey

bloop·er (blú:pər) n. (pop.) a blunder

blos·som (blɒsəm) n. a flower, usually of a fruit-producing tree or bush ‖ the mass of bloom on a fruit tree or bush ‖ a youthful, fresh stage of growth **blós·som·y** adj. full of blossoms ‖ resembling a blossom [O.E. blōstm]

blossom v.i. to open into flower ‖ to develop, Mozart's genius blossomed early **to blossom out** to lose reserve, develop an attractive personality [O.E. blōstmian]

blot (blɒt) **1.** n. a spot of ink ‖ something which spoils appearance, an eyesore ‖ something causing disgrace, a blot on one's reputation **2.** v. pres. part. **blot·ting** past and past part. **blot·ted** v.t. to spoil by dropping a blob of ink on, or as though by doing so ‖ to dry (writing or other ink marks) with specially absorbent paper ‖ (with 'out') to cover with ink so as to obscure ‖ (with 'out') to hide from view, fog blotted out the landscape ‖ v.i. to make a blot or blots ‖ to become blotted ‖ to have an absorbent quality, as in poor quality paper **to blot one's copybook** to mar one's hitherto good reputation [etym. doubtful]

blot n. (backgammon) an exposed piece liable to be taken or the action of exposing a piece [perh. Dan. blot, uncovered]

blotch (blɒtʃ) **1.** n. a patch of ink or color ‖ a disfiguring spot on the skin **2.** v.t. to make a blotch on (something) ‖ v.i. to make a blotch **blotched** adj. **blótch·y** comp. **blotch·i·er** superl. **blotch· i·est** adj. [etym. doubtful]

blot·ter (blɒtər) n. a piece or pad of blotting paper ‖ a book in which transactions, happenings etc. are noted before being permanently recorded elsewhere, police blotter

blotting pad a pad of blotting paper

blotting paper absorbent paper for drying the ink just used in writing

blouse (blaus, blauz) **1.** n. a woman's shirt, worn e.g. with a skirt and usually tucked inside it, made of cotton, silk etc. ‖ (in some countries) the top part of a naval or army uniform ‖ a loose working garment **2.** v. pres. part. **blous·ing** past and past part. **bloused** v.t. to make (the bodice of a garment) fit loosely like a blouse ‖ v.i. to fit loosely like a blouse [F.]

blou·son (blúːsɒn) n. woman's belted garment with material hanging loosely over the waist to cover the belt

blow (blou) **1.** v. pres. part. **blow·ing** past **blew** (blu:) past part. **blown** (bloun) v.i. (of the wind) to move ‖ to direct air from the mouth, to blow on one's fingers to warm them ‖ to sound when blown into, the whistle blew ‖ to make a noise as of blowing ‖ (of whales) to eject air forcibly from the lungs through blowholes ‖ (of a fuse) to melt when overloaded with electric current ‖ (colloq.) to smoke, esp. marijuana ‖ to leave ‖ v.t. to cause (air, steam etc.) to move ‖ to direct (air) from the mouth at something ‖ to sound by blowing, to blow a horn ‖ (of the wind) to buffet ‖ to clear (the nose) of mucus by forcing air through it ‖ to shape (molten glass) by forcing one's breath into it ‖ to work the bellows of (an organ) ‖ (of flies) to lay eggs in **to be blown** (Br.) to be out of breath **to blow away** (of the wind) to carry away ‖ (of a thing) to be carried away by the wind **to blow hot and cold** to look on something favorably one moment and unfavorably the next **to blow one's top (off)** to lose one's temper **to blow out** to extinguish by blowing ‖ to become extinguished, *the candles blew out* **to blow over** (of a storm) to be blown away by the wind ‖ to die down, pass off, *the fuss will blow over soon* **to blow up** to inflate (e.g. a balloon) ‖ to destroy by exploding ‖ (*Br.*) to rebuke severely ‖ to enlarge greatly (a picture or detail of a picture) ‖ to explode ‖ to lose one's temper **2.** *n.* a blowing of wind, esp. a gale ‖ a blast of air from the mouth or nose, or from an instrument or machine ‖ a violent rush of gas from or into a coal seam [O.E. *blāwan*]

blow *n.* a sudden vigorous stroke with the hand or an instrument ‖ a sudden shock ‖ a stroke of bad luck **at one blow** by a single action, in one go **to come to blows** to begin fighting [etym. doubtful]

blow·back (blóubæk) *n.* **1.** escape, to the rear and under pressure, of gases formed during the firing of a defective weapon. **2.** type of weapon operation in which the force of expanding gases acting to the rear against the face of the bolt furnishes all the energy required to initiate the complete cycle of operation. A weapon employing this method of operation is characterized by the absence of any breech-lock or bolt-lock mechanism

blow·down (blóudɑun) *n.* (*envir.*) water from an industrial system drawn to eliminate some solid waste, esp. salts, usu. previously treated for pH adjustment and slime control

blow drying (*cosmetology*) drying and styling hair in a single process using a hand-held hair dryer

blow·er (blóuər) *n.* that which blows, e.g. something which increases the draft of air to a fire or supplies air to the bellows of an organ ‖ an escape of gas, or the opening giving vent to it, in a coal mine

blow·fly (blóuflɑi) *pl.* **blow·flies** *n.* any of numerous two-winged flies of fam. *Calli-phoridae* that lay eggs on carcasses and meat or in wounds of living animals

blow·gun (blóuɡʌn) *n.* a tube by which a missile such as an arrow or dart may be projected by blowing

blow·hole (blóuhɒul) *n.* a hole in an enclosed space, such as a tunnel, by which air, smoke or gas may escape ‖ a flaw in a metal casting due to a bubble of air caught during solidification ‖ a hole in the ice by which seals, whales etc. can breathe, an air hole ‖ the nostril of a whale

blow·lamp (blóulæmp) *n.* a blowtorch

blown (bloun) *adj.* (of flowers) fully open

blow·off (blóuɒf, blóuɔf) *n.* an expelling of air, water etc. ‖ an apparatus for blowing off steam, water from a boiler etc. ‖ an outburst of furious talk to relieve one's feelings

blow·out (blóuɑut) *n.* the bursting of a tire or a burst in a tire ‖ the melting of an electric fuse ‖ a sudden and violent escape of gas or steam ‖ (*cosmetology*) hairstyling accomplished with brush and hand-held hair dryer

blow·pipe (blóupɑip) *n.* a short pipe through which air is blown to deflect a portion of a flame and enrich it with air, in order to direct intense heat on to a small area ‖ a blowgun ‖ a blowtube ‖ (*anat., zool.*) a tube used for cleaning out a cavity

blow·torch (blóutɔrtʃ) *n.* a device for obtaining a high-temperature flame by burning a mixture of kerosene vapor (forced out of a nozzle by pressure) and air

blow·tube (blóutjuːb, blóutuːb) *n.* a long tube used by a glassworker to blow into molten glass and so shape it ‖ a blowgun

blow·up (blóuʌp) *n.* an explosion ‖ a violent quarrel or fit of temper ‖ a big photographic enlargement

blow·y (blóui) *comp.* **blow·i·er** *superl.* **blow·i·est** *adj.* windy

blowz·y (blávzi) *comp.* **blowz·i·er** *superl.* **blowz·i·est** *adj.* (of a woman) slovenly, untidy, and bulging out of her clothes [origin unknown]

Bloy (blwæ), Léon (1846–1917), French writer. His works include the autobiographical novel 'le Désespéré' (1886), his masterpiece 'la Femme pauvre' (1897), and his journal in 8 volumes

blub (blʌb) *pres. part.* **blub·bing** *past* and *past part.* **blubbed** *v.i.* (*Br., pop.*) to cry, blubber

blub·ber (blʌbər) **1.** *n.* fat from the whale or other marine mammal, from which oil is extracted ‖ noisy weeping and complaining **2.** *v.t.* to utter with gasping sobs ‖ *v.i.* to weep noisily and with choking sobs **blub·ber·y** *adj.* having

lots of blubber or (of people) loose fat [M.E. *blu-ber*, prob. imit.]

Blü·cher (blýʃər), Gebhard Leberecht von, prince of Wahlstadt (1742–1819), Prussian field marshal. After a distinguished career in the Napoleonic Wars, he commanded the Prussian army at Waterloo (1815), where his opportune arrival helped to ensure Napoleon's final defeat

bludg·eon (blʌdʒən) **1.** *n.* a heavy stick or stick-like weapon, with one end weighted **2.** *v.t.* to hit repeatedly with such a weapon ‖ to force (someone into a course of action) by violent argument etc. [origin unknown]

blue (bluː) **1.** *adj.* of the color sensation stimulated by the wavelengths of light in that portion of the spectrum between green and violet, being the color of e.g. a cloudless sky ‖ having pallid skin due to cold or fear ‖ depressing in outlook, *things look blue* ‖ unhappy, melancholy ‖ belonging to the Conservative party in Britain **2.** *n.* a blue color, pigment, fabric etc. ‖ (*Br.*) bluing ‖ (*Br.*) a member of Oxford or Cambridge University selected to represent his university in a match (rugby, cricket etc.) against the other **out of the blue** without any warning **3.** *pres. part.* **blue·ing, blu·ing** *past* and *past part.* **blued** *v.t.* to use bluing on ‖ to cause to become blue [O.F. *bleu*]

blue baby a child born with a blue tinge to the skin because of insufficient oxygenation of the blood. The condition indicates a congenital heart or lung defect

blue·back salmon (blúːbæk) the sockeye

blue·beard (blúːbiərd) *n.* a man who has a succession of wives, murdering each in turn [after a character in a folktale]

blue·bell (blúːbel) *n.* a plant of the genus *Campanula*, fam. *Campanulaceae*, esp. the harebell ‖ either of two European flowers having racemes of nodding blue flowers: the wood hyacinth and the grape hyacinth

blue·ber·ry (blúːberi:, blúːbəri:) *pl.* **blue·ber·ries** *n.* a member of *Vaccinium*, fam. *Ericaceae*, a genus of shrubs which produce blue or blackish, sweet, edible fruit. Many American species are cultivated for food. The British species (bilberry) usually bears single berries, whereas the American species have clusters of many berries ‖ the fruit itself

blue·bird (blúːbəːrd) *n.* a member of *Sialia*, a genus of American songbirds related to the robin

blue bird a member of the Blue Birds, the junior (ages 7–9) Camp Fire Girls

blue blood aristocratic lineage

blue·bon·net (blúːbɒnit) *n.* a broad, flat, Scottish cap, made of blue wool ‖ (*pop.*) a Scot ‖ the cornflower

blue book a directory of prominent persons, esp. government officials ‖ a notebook in which college examination answers are written ‖ the examination itself ‖ (*Br.*) a report published by the privy council or parliament

blue·bot·tle (blúːbɒtˈl) *n.* any of several blow-flies ‖ the cornflower ‖ the grape hyacinth

blue box illegal device capable of connecting long distance calls, avoiding telephone company charges

blue cheese any of various kinds of strong cheese with artificially matured blue mold

blue chip a chip of high value used in playing poker ‖ a stock highly priced and valued for its security

blue-collar (bluːkólər) *adj.* of the factory working class; (British) cloth cap. *Cf* WHITE COLLAR

Blue Collar Caucus group of members of Congress, esp. those who have previously worked in factories, concerned with the political viewpoint of blue-collar workers

blue-eyed boy (blúːɑid) (*Br.*) fairhaired boy

blue·fish (blúːfiʃ) *pl.* **blue·fish, blue·fish·es** *n. Pomatomus saltatrix*, fam. *Pomatomidae*, a widely distributed, bright blue, edible fish

blue forces (*mil.*) those forces used in a friendly role during military exercises

blue funk (esp. *Br., pop.*) a state of utter self-distrust and fright

blue·grass (blúːɡræs, blúːɡrʌs) *n.* any of several grasses of the genus *Poa* with bluish-green culms, esp. the Kentucky bluegrass, good for pasture ‖ southern U.S. country music, esp. improvised and produced by unaccompanied string instruments

blueing *BLUING

blueish *BLUISH

blue·jack·et (blúːdʒækit) *n.* a seaman of the American or British navy

blue jay *Cyanocitta cristata*, a crested jay of Eastern North America with bright blue feathers on its back

blue jeans blue work trousers of jean or denim

blue key configuration of blue lines, etc., any art medium that is dropped out when the superimposed work is photographically reproduced. These lines are used as a guide for scribing or drawing, or to show locations to a printer

blue law (*Am. hist.*) a severe law of a puritanical nature enforced in the early days of the New England colonies ‖ any severe, restrictive law regulating the observance of Sunday

Blue Light highly trained U.S. Army Commando Force. *Cf* GREEN BERET

blue mold a fungus of genus *Penicillium*, esp. one forming a blue mold, e.g. on bread

Blue Mountains a spur of the Great Dividing Range in New South Wales, Australia

Blue Mountains a range in Pennsylvania, part of the Appalachian system

Blue Mountains a range in E. Jamaica, West Indies. Highest peak: Blue Mtn Peak (7,520 ft)

blue movie pornographic cinema production

Blue Nile (*Arab.* Bahr-el-Azraq) the second headstream (850 miles long) of the Nile (cf. WHITE NILE). It flows from two springs in the highlands of Ethiopia as the Abbai, through Lake Tana, then over a long series of cataracts into the Sudan to join the White Nile at Khartoum. Its immense volume in the rainy season (four times that of the White Nile) causes the annual Nile floods

Blue·nose (blúːnọuz) *n.* a native of Nova Scotia **blue·nose** a rigidly puritanical person

blue note (*mus.*) a flatted third or seventh, occurring characteristically in the blues

blue pages government-agency listings in the telephone directory

blue pencil a pencil used for corrections or for editing **blue-pen·cil** (blúːpénsˈl) *pres. part.* **blue-pen·cil·ing,** esp. *Br.* **blue-pen·cil·ling** *past* and *past part.* **blue-pen·ciled,** esp. *Br.* **blue-pen·cilled** *v.t.* to obliterate from a writing

blue peter a blue flag with a white square in the middle, hoisted before setting sail

blue·point (blúːpɔint) *n.* an oyster from a bed near Blue Point, Long Island

blue point a strain of Siamese cat with a faintly bluish cream body and gray points (cf. SEAL POINT)

blue·print (blúːprint) **1.** *n.* (*engin., archit.*) a copy of an original diagram or plan, used as a working drawing. Sensitized paper, coated with potassium ferricyanide and an organic ferric salt, is placed beneath the original and exposed to light. The organic ferric salt is reduced by the light to a ferrous salt which forms Prussian blue with the ferricyanide. The exposed paper, after being washed with water, is blue except where the dark lines of the diagram shielded it from light. The diagram appears in white lines on a blue background ‖ a detailed plan for achieving some large undertaking **2.** *v.t.* to make a blueprint of

blue ribbon the badge of the Order of the Garter ‖ a badge indicating the first prize in a competition

Blue Ridge Mtns a range of the Appalachians extending from N.W. Maryland through Virginia and North Carolina into Georgia. It rises in the south to 5,000 ft and is famous for the grandeur of its scenery. Highest peak: Mt Mitchell

blues (bluːz) *pl. n.* (with 'the') a mood of profound melancholy, depression ‖ a type of jazz, originally a form of Afro-American song, consisting essentially of a 12-bar chorus made up of three four-measure sequences, in AAB form, the harmonic basis consisting essentially of chords on the tonic, dominant and subdominant, and characterized by the use of flatted thirds and sevenths. Departures are often made from the basic form, which is generally improvised upon in performance. An emotional charge indicating desolation of spirit is characteristic, but not invariably present

blue slip historic veto privilege of a U.S. senator to block appointment of a federal judge from his or her own state

blue·stock·ing (blúːstɒkiŋ) *n.* a female intellectual, esp. a pedant [fr. the name 'Bluestocking society' applied to certain 18th-c. literary coteries of London where informal dress was allowed]

CONCISE PRONUNCIATION KEY: **(a)** æ, c*a*t; ɑ, c*a*r; ɔ f*aw*n; ei, sn*a*ke. **(e)** e, h*e*n; iː, sh*ee*p; iə, d*ee*r; ɛə, b*ea*r. **(i)** i, f*i*sh; ai, t*i*ger; əː, b*i*rd. **(o)** o, *o*x; au, c*ow*; ou, g*oa*t; u, p*oo*r; ɔi, r*oy*al. **(u)** ʌ, d*u*ck; u, b*u*ll; uː, g*oo*se; ə, b*a*cill*u*s; juː, c*u*be. x, lo*ch*; θ, *th*ink; ð, bo*th*er; z, *Z*en; ʒ, corsa*ge*; dʒ, sava*ge*; ŋ, oranguta*ng*; j, *y*ak; ʃ, *fish*; tʃ, fe*tch*; 'l, rabb*le*; 'n, red*den*. Complete pronunciation key appears inside front cover.

blu·et (blú:it) n. *Vaccinium arboreum*, a small tree or shrub having dry black berries with stony seeds ‖ a member of *Houstonia*, fam. *Rubiaceae*, a plant with bluish flowers [F. *bleuet* dim. of *bleu*, blue]

blue tit *Parus caeruleus*, a European titmouse having bright blue wings, tail and head crown

blue vitriol hydrated copper sulfate

blue·weed (blú:wɪ:d) n. viper's bugloss

blue whale *Sibbaldus musculus*, a rorqual whale of the Arctic seas. It can grow to over 80 ft in length and is the largest of all mammals

bluff (blʌf) 1. v.t. to mislead deliberately by pretending to be in a more favorable or advantageous position than one really is ‖ to intimidate by threats one cannot fulfill ‖ (in poker) to make (an opponent) think one is holding better cards than one really is ‖ v.i. to use deception in these ways 2. n. a bluffer, a person who bluffs ‖ the act of bluffing ‖ a taking in by bluffing **to call someone's bluff** to make someone expose his real weakness [etym. doubtful]

bluff 1. adj. hearty, blunt and direct but good-natured ‖ (of a ship's bows or a coastline) rising abruptly, but with a broad, rounded front 2. n. a steep cliff or headland with a broad, rounded front [origin unknown]

blu·ing, blue·ing (blú:iŋ) n. (*Am.*=*Br.* blue) a product used in laundering to make clothes white by counteracting with blue coloring the tendency of cloth to become yellow

blu·ish, blue·ish (blú:iʃ) adj. rather blue in color ‖ tinged with blue

Blum (blu:m), Léon (1872–1950), French statesman, writer, socialist leader and creator of the Popular Front government of 1936–7. He was interned first by the Vichy government, then by the Nazis (1940–5). He became France's caretake prime minister (1946–7) after the defeat of Blume

Blume, (blu:m) Judy (1938–), U.S. writer, whose novels for young readers deal with early adolescent problems. Her works include 'Are You There God? It's Me, Margaret' (1970), 'Then Again, Maybe I Won't' (1971), 'Deenie' (1973), 'Forever' (1976), and 'Superfudge' (1980). She wrote the adult novels 'Wifey' (1978) and 'Smart Women' (1984)

blun·der (blʌndər) 1. n. a crass, stupid mistake 2. v.i. (often with 'along', 'into', 'through') to move heavily and clumsily ‖ to make a crass mistake ‖ (with 'upon') to find by chance ‖ v.t. to make a clumsy failure of ‖ (with 'out') to blurt out stupidly or clumsily [M.E. *blondren*, to mix, etym. doubtful]

blun·der·buss (blʌndərbʌs) n. an old-fashioned, inaccurate, large-bored, short-barreled, flintlock handgun [fr. Du. *donderbus*, thunder gun]

blunge (blʌndʒ) pres. part. **blung·ing** past and past part. **blunged** v.t. (pottery) to mix (clay) with water by beating, usually by a machine **blúng·er** n. an apparatus for blunging [origin unknown]

Blunt (blʌnt), Wilfrid Scawen (1840–1922), English poet. He championed Egyptian and Arab nationalist interests at a time of English jingoism. His verse includes 'Love Sonnets of Proteus' (1880)

blunt (blʌnt) 1. adj. having an edge or point that is not sharp ‖ (of wits) insensitive, unperceptive, slow in understanding ‖ (of manner or character) lacking in finesse, scorning tact 2. v.i. to become less sharp ‖ v.t. to make less sharp [origin unknown]

blur (blə:r) 1. n. a confused visual impression ‖ a blemish or smudge ‖ indistinct appearance ‖ indistinct sound, *a blur of voices* 2. v. pres. part. **blur·ring** past and past part. **blurred** v.t. to make indistinct ‖ v.i. to become spoiled by smudging etc. ‖ to become indistinct [etym. doubtful]

blurb (blə:rb) n. a publisher's commendation of one of its books, usually printed on the wrapper or in advertising notices ‖ any similar sales copy or fulsome piece of publicizing [orig. U.S. slang]

blur·ry (blə́:ri:) comp. **blur·ri·er** superl. **blur·ri·est** adj. marked by blurs ‖ indistinct

blurt (blə:rt) v.t. (with 'out') to say impulsively, or under pressure, *to blurt out the truth* [etym. doubtful]

blush (blʌʃ) 1. n. a suffusion of the cheeks with red, from pleasure, shame, modesty etc. ‖ a rosy color, e.g. of a peach or an apple **at first blush** at first glance 2. v.i. (esp. of the cheeks) to become red, esp. from pleasure, shame, mod-

esty, etc. ‖ (with 'for') to feel shame (because of or on behalf of) [M.E. *bluschen*, etym. doubtful]

blush·er (blʌʃər) n. face rouge that creates a natural-seeming shining quality

blus·ter (blʌstər) 1. n. a loud, gusty wind ‖ noisy, ineffectual anger 2. v.i. (of wind) to blow violently and gustily ‖ (of weather) to be violently windy ‖ to talk with histrionic anger, usually so as to assert one's own importance ‖ v.t. to force by overbearing talk, *to bluster one's way into a leading role* **blús·ter·ous, blús·ter·y** adjs [origin uncertain]

B lymphocyte *B CELL

BMEWS (mil. acronym) for ballistic missile early warning system

BMP-1 (mil.) U.S.S.R. mobile, amphibious infantry combat vehicle, with 73-mm smooth-base gun, speed of 55 km/hr.

bo·a (bóuə) n. a member of *Boa*, fam. *Boidae*, a genus of tropical American nonpoisonous snakes ‖ any large snake which crushes its prey, e.g. the boa constrictor ‖ (*old-fash.*) a long, light scarf of fur or feathers worn by a lady [L. *boa*, a water serpent]

Bo·ab·dil (bouəbðí:l) (d. c. 1538), as Mohammed XI the last Moorish king of Granada (1482–3, 1486–92). He was expelled by Ferdinand and Isabella, and fled to Morocco

boa constrictor *Constrictor constrictor*, fam. *Boidae*, a boa measuring 10 ft or more which goes on land or in water, and is capable of climbing trees. It crushes small animals to death and then swallows them whole

Bo·ad·i·ce·a (bouædisí:ə) (Boudicca, 1st c.), queen of the British tribe of the Iceni. She revolted against Roman rule in Britain, and when defeated took poison (c. 62 A.D.)

boar (bɔr, bour) n. the uncastrated male pig ‖ its flesh ‖ *Sus scrofa*, fam. *Suidae*, the male or female wild hog of continental Europe, S.W. Asia and N. Africa. It is the origin of the domestic hog [O.E. *bār*]

board (bɔrd, bourd) 1. n. a piece of sawn lumber longer than it is broad ‖ a square or oblong piece of thin wood or other similar material used for a special purpose, *diving board*, *cheese board*, *sounding board* ‖ the stiff panel over which the paper, cloth, leather etc., is stretched to form the side of a bound book ‖ (*naut.*) the distance sailed by a ship on one tack ‖ (*basketball*) the backboard behind the basket ‖ (*hockey*) the wall surrounding the ice ‖ (*surfing*) the buoyant surfboard ‖ a council or authoritative body, *board of managers* ‖ daily meals served in exchange for payment or services **above board** openly, without deceit **on board** aboard a ship, train etc. **to go by the board** (of nautical equipment) to be lost in a heavy sea ‖ to fall into disuse, be made or allowed to lapse **to sweep the board** (in gambling) to win all the stakes **boards** (*rhet.*) the theater stage 2. v.t. (often with 'up') to cover with boards or planks, close up (an opening) with boards ‖ to provide with meals, and often with lodging ‖ to make one's way onto (a ship, train or aircraft) as a passenger ‖ (*hist.*) to come alongside, attack and take possession of (a ship) ‖ v.i. (usually with 'at' or 'with') to be given meals at a fixed rate over a certain period of time **to board out** to have meals in a house other than the one where one sleeps ‖ to place (children) in families for meals **bóard·er** n. a person who is given food and lodging by someone in exchange for a fee, esp. a pupil at boarding school [O.E. *bord*, plank, table]

board foot a unit of measure for measuring lumber, equal to the volume of a piece of wood 1 ft long, 1 ft wide and 1 in. thick

board·ing (bórdiŋ, bóurdiŋ) n. boards collectively ‖ a covering made of boards

board·ing·house (bórdiŋhaus, bóurdiŋhaus) pl. **board·ing·hous·es** (bórdiŋ hauziz, bóurdiŋhauziz) n. a house where people pay to reside and have their meals

boarding school a school where pupils are lodged and fed as well as taught

board of health a government department dealing with matters of public health

board of trade a grouping of businessmen, bankers etc. to promote trade

board of trade unit (*Br.*, *abbr.* B.T.U.) a legal and commercial unit of electrical energy, defined as the amount consumed when 10^{10} ergs of work are performed per second for 1 hour (= 1 kilowatt-hour)

board·sail·ing (bórdseiliŋ) n. (sports) combination of surfing and sailing on a floating board equipped with a sail 12–15 ft. high

board·walk (bórdwɔk, bóurdwɔk) n. a walk made of planking ‖ (*Am.*) a promenade esp. of planking, alongside a beach, esp. the one in Atlantic City, N.J.

boar·hound (bórhaund, bóurhaund) n. a big dog, esp. the Great Dane, used for hunting wild boar

boast (boust) 1. n. a claim about oneself, or something connected with oneself, whether made with proper pride or with inordinate pride ‖ (boasting) one is proud of 2. v.i. to brag, make an exaggerated claim ‖ v.t. to be justly proud of (a possession), *Germany can boast excellent roads* **bóast·ful** adj. [etym. doubtful]

boast·er (bóustər) n. a broad chisel used in paring stone [origin unknown]

boat (bout) 1. n. any small open vessel propelled by oars, sail, an engine, or paddles ‖ any ship from a liner to a dinghy ‖ a boat-shaped vessel for the table, *gravy boat* **in the same boat** running the same risks or sharing the same misfortunes 2. v.i. to go out rowing in a small boat for amusement [O.E. *bāt*]

boat·build·er (bóutbildər) n. a person who constructs boats

boat·er (bóutər) n. (*Br.*) a hard straw hat with a flat top and wide ribbon band

boat·hook (bóuthuk) n. a pole with a hook at one end for catching hold of boats

boat·house (bóuthaus) pl. **boat·hous·es** (bóuthauziz) n. a shed by the water in which a boat is kept

boat·ing (bóutiŋ) n. the activity of rowing a boat for relaxation

boat·load (bóutloud) n. a full cargo

boat·man (bóutmən) pl. **boat·men** (bóutmən) n. a man who works a boat or raft

boat people refugee emigrants, esp. Vietnamese, who escape their country by boat with no authorized destination

boat·swain (bóus'n, bóutswein) n. a ship's officer who calls men on duty. On sailing ships he was in charge of sails and rigging [BOAT+SWAIN fr. O.N. *sveinn*, a servant]

boatswain's chair a cradle suspended by ropes and pulleys, used esp. by seamen as a seat for working at heights

boat·tail (bóuteil) n. the conical section of a ballistic body that progressively decreases in diameter toward the tail to reduce overall aerodynamic drag

boat·tel (bóutél) n. hotel at a marina, for use of boat owners. *Cf* AQUATEL

boat train a train timed to catch or meet a boat

bob (bɒb) 1. v. pres. part. **bob·bing** past and past part. **bobbed** v.t. to lower and quickly raise again, *to bob one's head* ‖ to perform with a quick jerky movement, *to bob a curtsy* ‖ v.i. to move up and down in quick jerky movements ‖ to curtsy **to bob for** to try to seize (floating or suspended fruit) in the mouth without using one's hands as a party game 2. n. a short, bouncing or jerky movement ‖ a curtsy [origin unknown]

bob pl. **bob** n. (*Br.*, *pop.*) a shilling [origin unknown]

bob 1. n. a short, straight hair style for women ‖ the docked tail of a horse 2. v. pres. part. **bob·bing** past and past part. **bobbed** to style (hair) short and straight ‖ to dock (a horse's tail) [origin unknown]

bob n. (campanology) a modification of the order in which bells course in long peals ‖ a method of change ringing using such modifications [origin unknown]

bob n. a weight on the end of a pendulum, plumb line etc. [origin unknown]

Bo·ba·di·lla (bɒbaðí:lja, bɒbaðí:ja), Francisco de (d. 1502), Spanish governor of Hispaniola. He ordered the arrest of Christopher Columbus and his family and sent them to Spain in chains

bob·ber (bóbər) n. a cork float used in fishing

bob·bin (bóbin) n. a roller or spool for holding thread or yarn, used on sewing machines, and in spinning and weaving ‖ a small cylinder or pin used in making lace ‖ a device consisting of a small bar and string for lifting a wooden door latch [F. *bobine*]

bobbin lace pillow lace

bob·ble (bób'l) n. (waterskiing) a misstep quickly recovered. —**bobble** v.

bob·by (bóbi:) pl. **bob·bies** n. (*Br.*, *pop.*) a policeman [after Sir *Robert* Peel who established (1829) the London police]

bobby pin (*Am.*=*Br.* hair clip) a small metal clasp for fastening the hair by the pressure of one prong against the other

bobby socks, bobby sox (spks) socks reaching above the ankle, worn by girls. They were popular esp. in the 1940s

bob·cat (bóbkæt) *pl.* **bob·cats, bob·cat** *n. Lynx rufus*, fam. *Felidae*, a North American lynx having long legs and a stubby tail [BOB, short tail+CAT]

bob·o·link (bóbəlink) *n. Dolichonyx oryzivorus*, a North American migratory songbird [imit.]

bob·sled (bóbsled) **1.** *n.* a long sled with independent runners at front and back. Racing bobsleds have a steering mechanism on the front runners and a braking mechanism on the back ones and are used by 2-man or 4-man teams in the sport of coasting down specially built courses of snow-covered ice at speeds in the region of 70 m.p.h. ‖ either of the two sets of runners of such a sled **2.** *v.i. pres. part.* **bob·sled·ding** *past* and *past part.* **bob·sled·ded** to ride on a bobsled.

bob·sleigh (bóbslei) **1.** *n.* a bobsled **2.** *v.i.* to bobsled

bob·stay (bóbstei) *n.* (*naut.*) the rope or wire running from the end of the bowsprit to a point on the hull, holding the bowsprit in position [origin unknown]

bob·tail (bóbteil) **1.** *adj.* with a short tail or the tail cut short **2.** *n.* a cat, dog or horse with such a tail

bob·white (bóbhwáit, bóbwáit) *n.* a North American game bird of the genus *Colinus*, fam. *Phasianidae*, esp. *C. virginianus*, having buff and black mottled plumage and a distinctive call (*QUAIL, *PARTRIDGE)

boc·age (bókidʒ) *n.* background material supporting a ceramic figure

Boc·cac·ci·o (boukátʃiou), Giovanni (1313–75), Italian author. He wrote romances, epic poems and idylls before he began his great story collection, the 'Decameron', about the time when the Black Death reached Florence (1348). He also wrote a life of Dante and various encyclopedic works, and had some influence on the development of calligraphy

Boc·che·ri·ni (bɔkkerí:ni:), Luigi (1743–1805), Italian composer and cellist. He wrote many works for the cello, 120 string quintets, over 100 string quartets and 20 symphonies

Boc·cio·ni (bɔtʃóni:), Umberto (1882–1916), Italian painter and sculptor, an originator of futurism

Bo·chum (bóuxum) a town (pop. 413,400) in the Ruhr district, West Germany: iron and steel works, coal mines

bode *past* of BIDE

bode (boud) *pres. part.* **bod·ing** *past* and *past part.* **bod·ed** *v.t.* to portend, indicate by signs (something to come) ‖ *v.i.* (with 'well' or 'ill') to be a (good or bad) omen **bóde·ful** *adj.* (*rhet.*) warning of evil to come [O.E. *bodian*, to announce fr. *boda*, messenger]

Bo·den·see (bóud'nzei) *CONSTANCE

Bo·dhi·dhar·ma (bóudidá:rmə) (early 6th c.), Indian monk and traditional founder of Zen. A Mahayana Buddhist, he went to China (c. 525) and developed a Chinese Buddhist school

bo·dhi·satt·va (boudisætvæ) *n.* (*Mahayana Buddhism*) a being who has attained Buddhahood but forgoes entering Nirvana to help others [Skr.]

bod·ice (bódis) *n.* the top part of a woman's dress [orig. a pair of *bodies*=a pair of stays, a corset]

bod·i·less (bódilis) *adj.* without a body, incorporeal

bod·i·ly (bód'li:) **1.** *adj.* pertaining to the body, *bodily harm* **2.** *adv.* in person, *he was removed bodily from the meeting* ‖ altogether, in its entirety, *the castle was transported bodily to America*

Bo·din (bodɛ̃), Jean (1530–96), French political thinker and economist whose treatise 'De la république' sets out a theory of limited monarchy, while condemning rebellion

bod·kin (bódkin) *n.* a large-eyed, thick, blunt needle for drawing elastic, tape etc. through a hem ‖ (*hist.*) a dagger, stiletto [origin unknown]

Bod·lei·an Library (bpdlí:ən, bódli:ən) Oxford University Library, containing over a million and a half books and valuable manuscripts. It receives a free copy of every book published in Great Britain under British copyright regulations [after Sir Thomas *Bodley*]

Bod·ley (bódli:), Sir Thomas (1545–1613), British statesman and founder of the Bodleian Library at Oxford (1602)

Bo·do·ni (bədóuni:) *n.* a very black and condensed printing type [invented by the Italian printer Giambattista *Bodoni* (1740–1813)]

bod·y (bódi:) *pl.* **bod·ies** *n.* the physical substance of a man or animal ‖ a corpse ‖ (*boxing*) the trunk ‖ the main portion of an army, plant, building etc. ‖ the main part of a document or printed article ‖ (*old-fash.*) a person ‖ a collective unit of people, *a body of soldiers, the legislative body* ‖ a mass (of facts, ideas etc.) ‖ a mass of matter, *heavenly bodies* ‖ a rich, full flavor in wine ‖ the quality in cloth which makes it firm and durable ‖ (*printing*) the block of metal supporting the typeface ‖ (*pottery*) the clay of which a work is made as distinct from the glaze on it **in a body** (of people) as a single group **to keep body and soul together** to manage to stay alive (on very little food or money) [O.E. *bodig*]

body bag plastic or rubber bag used to transport corpses

body burden undesirable radioactive or toxic materials ingested and carried by the body, e.g., radioactive particles, lead

body clock natural mechanism that regulates diurnal activities in the body. *syn* biological clock, biorhythm

body corporate (*law*) a corporation

body count 1. number killed. **2.** number present

body drop (*judo*) throw made by grasping competitor, and tripping him or her over an outstretched leg

bod·y·guard (bódi:gard) *n.* a man or group of men guarding the safety of another

body heat animal heat

bod·y·jewel (bódi:dʒu:əl) *n.* a precious stone worn on the body, e.g., in the navel or nose

body language conscious or unconscious positions, movements, or gestures that communicate one's attitudes and emotional responses to others

body microphone a microphone worn on the person, usu. concealed

body paint cosmetic for decorating or coloring body

body politic the State

body shaper woman's long-legged girdle

body shirt 1. close-fitting blouse or shirt. **2.** a woman's top that fastens at the crotch

body slam (*wrestling*) illegal maneuver in which competitor is lifted and thrown to the mat

body snatcher (*hist.*) a person who dug up corpses and sold them to hospitals for dissection

body stocking tight-fitting, one-piece undergarment covering the torso

bod·y·suit (bódi:su:t) *n.* woman's tight-fitting one-piece informal outerwear garment, usu. worn with skirt or slacks

bod·y·surf (bódi:sə:rf) *v.* to ride the waves horizontally without a surfboard

Boe·ing 707 (bóuing) 1954-designed four-engine jet transport for 219 passengers (U.S. Airforce VG 137), capable of a 146,200-lb load, with 627 mph speed, and a 5,000-mi range. — **737** a four-engine short-range transport for 115 passengers, capable of a 117,000-lb load with 1,900-mi range. —**747** 1969-produced wide-body commercial jet transport of 452 passengers; 200,000-lb cargo weight with 5,700-mi range. —**757** 1979-produced two-engine, 200-passenger wide-body fuel-economy jet transport with 2,500-mi range; planned for 1982. —**777** proposed long-range jet plane

Boe·o·tia (bi:óuʃə) a region of central Greece, northeast of the Gulf of Corinth. Ten of the city-states of Beotia formed (c. 575 B.C.) the Boeotian League, led by Thebes. Under Epaminondas, Boeotia dominated Greece (371–62 B.C.), but then declined, becoming part of the Aetolian League (245 B.C.) and a Roman protectorate (194 B.C.)

Boer (bor, bour) **1.** *n.* an early Dutch or Huguenot settler in S. Africa. The Boers established themselves mainly in Cape Colony, the Orange Free State and the Transvaal. They fought two wars (1880–1 and 1899–1902) with the British before the formation of the Union of South Africa (1910) ‖ a South African descendant from these settlers **2.** *adj.* relating to the original Dutch settlers or to a modern descendant [Du.=farmer]

Boer War a war (1899–1902) between the British Empire and the two Dutch Boer republics, the Orange Free State and the Transvaal. The presence of Uitlanders in the Witwatersrand goldfields, and the question of their civic rights under Boer rule, worsened Anglo-Boer relations and led to an unsuccessful rising (*JAMESON RAID, 1895). In 1899, the Boers under Kruger, the Transvaal president, declared war on Britain, and besieged Mafeking, Kimberley and Ladysmith. These towns were relieved (1900) by Kitchener and Roberts, who rapidly captured Bloemfontein, Johannesburg and Pretoria, and declared the annexation of the Boer states. The Boers, under Botha, De Wet and Smuts, continued guerrilla warfare for two years, but surrendered (May 31, 1902) at Vereeniging. The republics became the British Transvaal and Orange River colonies, and were embodied (1910) in the Union of South Africa. Britain was criticized for her use of internment camps, and the war led to a demand for army reform and to a reaction against imperialism

Bo·e·thi·us (bouí:θi:əs), Anicius Manlius Severinus (c. 480–524), Roman statesman and philosopher, author of 'De consolatione philosophiae'. He sought to interpret Greek philosophy (esp. Aristotle and Plato) to the Romans, and to expound orthodox Christian doctrine. He was put to death by Theodoric on a false charge of treason

bof·fo (bófou) *adj.* sensational

bog (bɔg, bog) **1.** *n.* an area of ground saturated with water and decayed vegetation **2.** *v. pres. part.* **bog·ging** *past* and *past part.* **bogged** *v.t.* (often with 'down') to submerge into or as if into a bog ‖ *v.i* (usually with 'down') to become sucked into or as if into a bog [fr. Ir. *bogach* fr. *bog*, soft]

Bo·gart (bóugart) Humphrey (1899–1957), U.S. actor known for his portrayals of tough, cynical, but moral characters. Among his more noted films are 'The Petrified Forest' (1936), 'The Maltese Falcon' (1941), 'Casablanca' (1942), 'The Big Sleep' (1946), 'The Treasure of Sierra Madre' (1948), and 'The African Queen' (1951) for which he won an Academy Award. He was married to actress Lauren Bacall

Bo·gaz·koy (bougazkó:i:) a village of central Turkey. As Hattusas it was the ancient capital of the Hittite Empire (14th and 13th cc. B.C.)

bo·gey (bóugi:) *pl.* **bo·geys, bo·gies** *n.* (*golf*) one over par ‖ (*Br.*) the ideal number of strokes in which a hole or the course should be played

bo·gey, bo·gy (bóugi:) *pl.* **bo·geys, bo·gies** *n.* an imaginary source of fear, a bugbear ‖ (*mil.*) an air or contact or radar screen image that is unidentified but assumed to be hostile ‖ an evil goblin [etym. doubtful]

bogey *BOGIE (swiveling truck)

bo·gey·man (bóugi:mæn) *pl.* **bogey·men** (bóugi:men), *n.* an imaginary man who makes children afraid, esp. in the dark

bog·gi·ness (bógi:nis, bógi:nis) *n.* the state or quality of being boggy

bog·gle (bóg'l) *pres. part.* **bog·gling** *past* and *past part.* **bog·gled** *v.i.* to hesitate or hold back because one is startled or fearful [origin unknown]

bog·gy (bógi:, bógi:) *comp.* **bog·gi·er** *superl.* **bog·gi·est** *adj.* of or resembling a bog ‖ containing a bog

bo·gie, bo·gey, bo·gy (bóugi:) *pl.* **bo·gies** *n.* a swiveling truck forming part of a road or rail vehicle ‖ a weight-carrying wheel on the inner side of the tread of a tank ‖ (*Br.*) the wheels and short undercarriage at the end of a locomotive giving it a pivoted support [origin unknown]

bog myrtle sweet gale ‖ buckbean

Bo·gor (bóugor) (formerly Buitenzorg) a town (pop. 195,882) in Indonesia near Djakarta, with a famous botanic garden and agricultural research station

Bo·go·tá (bəgotá) the capital (pop. 2,855,065) and industrial and intellectual center of Colombia. It is on a high plateau (8,563 ft) of the eastern Andes, 200 miles from the coast, and is the center of a fertile agricultural region. Founded (1538) by Gonzalo Jiménez de Quesada under the name Santa Fe de Bogotá, it became the capital of the viceroy of Nueva Granada

bo·gus (bóugəs) *adj.* sham [etym. doubtful]

bogy *BOGIE (swiveling truck)

bogy *BOGIE (imaginary source of fear)

bo·hea (bouhí:) *n.* a black tea of inferior quality, often the last crop of a season [fr. Chin. *Wu-i*, the hill district where this tea is cultivated]

CONCISE PRONUNCIATION KEY: **(a)** æ, cat; ɑ, car; ɔ, fawn; ei, snake. **(e)** e, hen; i:, sheep; iə, deer; ɛə, bear. **(i)** i, fish; ai, tiger; ə:, bird. **(o)** o, ox; au, cow; ou, goat; u, poor; ɔi, royal. **(u)** ʌ, duck; u, bull; u:, goose; ə, bacillus; ju:, cube. x, loch; θ, think; ð, bother; z, Zen; ʒ, corsage; dʒ, savage; ŋ, orangutang; j, yak; ʃ, fish; tʃ, fetch; 'l, rabble; 'n, redden. Complete pronunciation key appears inside front cover.

Bo·he·mi·a (bouhíː·miː·ə, bouhíːmjə) a former province of W. Czechoslovakia; the historic kingdom of Bohemia, enclosed by mountains: the Bohemian Forest on the southwest, the Erzgebirge on the northwest, the Sudetens on the northeast, and the Bohemian-Moravian highlands on the southeast. Settled by Slavs (5th–6th cc.), Bohemia emerged as an independent principality under the Premyslides (9th–13th cc.). It became a tributary kingdom of the Holy Roman Empire and its crown passed to the Luxembourg dynasty (1310–1437) and to the Hapsburgs (1526–1918). It suffered heavily and lost its independence in the Thirty Years' War (1618–48). With the Austrian defeat in the 1st world war, it became (1918) part of the new republic of Czechoslovakia. The province was replaced by administrative regions in 1949

bo·he·mi·an (bouhíː·miː·ən, bouhíːmjən) **1.** *n.* a person, esp. with literary or artistic interests, who lives in an easygoing way untroubled by middle-class social standards **2.** *adj.* descriptive of this way of life **bo·hé·mi·an·ism** *n.* [F. *bohémien*, gipsy]

Bohemian Forest (G. Böhmerwald) a wooded mountain range (summit: Arber, 4,780 ft) extending the length of the frontier between Bavaria (S. Germany) and Bohemia (Czechoslovakia)

Bohemian language Czech

Bo·he·mund I (bóuəmənd) (c. 1052–1111), prince of Antioch, son of Robert Guiscard. He was a leader of the 1st Crusade, and of wars against the Byzantine Empire

Böh·me (bə́ːmə), Jakob (1575–1624), German theosophist and mystic, a precursor of Spinoza, Schelling and Hegel

Bo·hol (bohóːl) an island (area 1,492 sq. miles, pop. 553,000) of the central Philippine Is (Visayas), producing esp. rice and textiles

Bohr (bɔr, bour), Niels Henrik David (1885–1962), Danish physicist awarded a Nobel prize (1922) for his theory of the structure of the atom

Bohr mag·ne·ton (mǽgnitɒn) the quantized component of magnetic moment of an electron oriented in a magnetic field. It is equal to 0.927 x 10^{-20} erg/gauss

Bo·iar·do (bɔjárdɔ), Matteo Maria (c. 1441–94), Italian poet. His 'Orlando Innamorato' was continued by Ariosto in the 'Orlando Furioso'

boil (bɔil) *n.* a localized, inflamed swelling of the skin caused by a bacterium [O.E. *byl*]

boil 1. *v.i.* (of a liquid) to bubble at a high temperature and give off vapor ‖ to be cooked in boiling liquid ‖ to seethe like a boiling liquid ‖ to be very agitated, *to boil with rage* ‖ *v.t.* to cook in boiling liquid ‖ to heat to the boiling point ‖ to make or clean by boiling **to boil away** to evaporate as a result of long boiling **to boil down** to reduce by boiling ‖ to condense ‖ to simplify **to boil down to** to signify basically **to boil over** to overflow while boiling ‖ **to keep the pot boiling** to make sure one has enough of a thing (usually money) **2.** *n.* the boiling point ‖ the state of boiling **to bring to a boil** to heat until the boiling point is reached [O.F. *boillir*]

Boi·leau (bwǽlou), Nicolas (Nicolas Boileau-Despréaux, 1636–1711), French poet and critic. His satires and his 'l'Art poétique' (1674) influenced French and English literature. The apostle of 'bon sens', he expressed in elegant, pithy alexandrines many of the theories of French classicism

boiled sweet (*Br.*) a hard candy

boil·er (bɔ́ilər) *n.* (*engin.*) a container in which water can be heated under pressure and converted into steam ‖ a stove which heats water for conveyance to a hot-water system ‖ (*pop.*) a fowl too old to roast but suitable for boiling

boiling point the temperature at which a liquid boils, i.e. at which its vapor pressure equals atmospheric pressure (for water, 212°F. or 100°C. at sea level)

boil·off (bɔ́ilɔf) *n.* evaporation of a liquid, esp. of a rocket fuel

Boi·se (bɔ́isiː, bɔ́iziː) the capital (pop. 102,451) of Idaho, center of a large irrigated region producing mainly wool, hides and fruit

bois·ter·ous (bɔ́istərəs, bɔ́istrəs) *adj.* gusty, *boisterous winds* ‖ agreeably rough, a *boisterous sea* ‖ cheerfully loud, *boisterous shouts* [origin unknown]

Bokhara *BUKHARA

Bok·mal (bákməl) *n.* literary Norwegian language evolved from Danish

Bo·lan Pass (boulán) a narrow 30-mile mountain pass (summit: 5,900 ft) in Pakistan

between Quetta and the Indus basin, crossed by rail

bo·las (bóulas) *pl.* **bo·las** (bóuləz), **bo·las·es** *n.* a South American Indian weapon made of two or more stone balls attached to long, thin ropes and used primarily in hunting (rhea, guanaco, puma). It is twirled and thrown to entangle the legs of the creature being hunted, and so immobilize it

bold (bould) *adj.* brave, *a bold action* ‖ daring, *a bold idea* ‖ confidently original, *a bold piece of architecture* ‖ well defined, *a bold headland* ‖ strongly assertive, *a bold outline* ‖ impudent, *a bold look* ‖ (*printing*) of boldface type [O.E. *bald*]

bold·face (bóuldfeis) *n.* heavy black printing type

bold·faced (bóuldfeist) *adj.* showing an impudent lack of shame

bole (boul) *n.* the trunk of a tree, esp. the lower part [O.N. *bolr*]

bo·lec·tion (boulékʃən) *n.* (*archit.*) a molding projecting beyond the face of the panel it decorates [origin unknown]

bo·le·ro (bəléərou) *pl.* **bo·le·ros** *n.* a Spanish national dance in ¾ time with characteristic rhythm, or its music ‖ a waist-length jacket worn open in the front [Span.]

bo·le·tus (boulíːtəs) *pl.* **bo·le·tus·es**, **bo·le·ti** (boulíːtiː) *n.* a member of *Boletus*, fam. *Boletaceae*, a genus of spore fungi. Some are edible, others poisonous [F. fr. Gk *bōlítēs*, mushroom]

Boleyn *ANNE BOLEYN

bo·lide (bóulaid) *n.* a large meteor, usually one that explodes [F. fr. L. fr. Gk *bolis*, missile]

Bol·ing·broke (bɔ́liŋbruk), Henry St John, 1st Viscount (1678–1751), English Tory statesman who negotiated the Treaty of Utrecht (1713). His writings include 'The Idea of a Patriot King', setting the monarch above party politics as representative of the whole nation

Bolingbroke *HENRY IV of England, *PLANTAGENET

Bol·í·var (bɔlíːvɑr), Simón (1783–1830), Venezuelan soldier and statesman. During nine years of fighting (1813–22) he liberated Venezuela, New Granada (*COLOMBIA) and Ecuador from Spanish rule, uniting the first two as Greater Colombia (1819) under his presidency, and adding Ecuador (1822). With San Martín and Sucre, he liberated Peru and Upper Peru in 1824 (*BOLIVIA), but failed to achieve a union of these countries in one confederation

bol·i·var (bɔlíːvɑr, bóləvər) *pl.* **bol·i·va·res** (bɔli:vɑ́res), **bol·i·vars** (bóləvərz) *n.* the basic monetary unit of Venezuela [after Simón *Bolívar*]

Bo·liv·i·a (bəlíːviə, bɔlíːvjə) a republic (area 424,000 sq. miles, pop. 5,914,844) of central South America. Official capital (and seat of the judiciary): Sucre. Actual seat of government: La Paz. People: 54% Indian, 31% Mestizos, 15% of European origin. Official language: Spanish. Indian languages: Aymará and Quechua in the west, Guaraní in the east. State religion: Roman Catholic. The land is 2% cultivated. Two chains of the Andes, the Cordillera Occidental and the Cordillera Real or Oriental (averaging 15,000 ft, highest peak: Illampu, 22,000 ft), cross W. Bolivia, enclosing a plateau, the Altiplano (averaging 13,000 ft), which contains most of the mines and two thirds of the population (mainly subsistence farmers). The eastern seven tenths is an alluvial plain covered with rain forest in the north, grassland and savanna in the south. The eastern foothill valleys (the yungas) are the most productive agricultural region. Average temperatures (F.): 45° in the Altiplano, 50°–70° in the yungas, 73°–80° in the plains. Rainfall: 23 ins. at La Paz, 25–35 ins. in the yungas, 70 ins. (heaviest Nov.–Mar.) in the northeast, 20 ins. in the southeast. Livestock: sheep, cattle, goats, llamas, alpacas. Crops: sugar cane, corn, quinoa, coffee, tobacco, root vegetables, cacao, rubber. Mineral resources: tin (15% of world output), lead, salt, oil, silver (mined at Potosí since 1545), copper, antimony, wolfram, tungsten, zinc. Exports: minerals (95% of exports, tin comprising 64%). Imports: agricultural products (30% of imports), iron and steel products, textiles. Bolivia has free access to the Chilean port of Arica and the Brazilian port of Santos. Other ports used: Antofagasta (Chile), Mollendo (Peru), and river ports on tributaries of the Amazon. Chief navigable rivers: Paraguay, Mamore, Beni. There are seven universities, the oldest being Sucre (1624). Monetary unit: Bolivian peso. HISTORY. The In-

cas overcame the Aymará Indians (14th c.) but were conquered by the Spaniards (1538), who made the country part of the viceroyalty of Peru, and joined it to the viceroyalty of Río de la Plata (1776). It was liberated by Bolívar and Sucre and proclaimed an independent republic (1825), but suffered from political instability (revolution and military dictatorships) and unsuccessful wars. It lost its coastal possessions to Chile in the War of the Pacific (1879–83), it ceded the rich rubber-growing region of the Acre River after disputes with Brazil (1903), and lost the Gran Chaco to Paraguay after a war (1932–5) which exhausted Bolivia. Economic depression and political upheavals continued, culminating in civil war (1949–52). The National Revolutionary Movement, which came to power in 1952, nationalized the big tin industries and estates, and with U.S. aid began to stabilize the economy. But the social revolution began to lose direction and enthusiasm. Although its leader, Víctor Paz Estenssoro, was twice reelected (1960, 1964), he was replaced (1964) by a military junta headed by Gen. René Barrientos Ortuño. As leader of the new Bolivian Revolutionary Front, Barrientos was elected (1966) constitutional president. Following his death in a plane crash (1969), vice president Luis Adolfo Siles Salinas assumed the presidency, introducing to Bolivia the leftist nationalism already established in Peru. In the 186th change of government in less than a century and a half of national existence, Ovando was deposed (1970) by the conservative army chief Gen. Rogelio Miranda. As the country drifted toward armed conflict between the conservative and liberal factions of the army, a compromise was found in the appointment of leftist Gen. Juan José Torres. Torres was overthrown (1971) and replaced by Col. Hugo Banzer Suárez, whose Frente Popular Nacionalista was a coalition of left-wing and right-wing parties. The military took over in 1978 following an election dispute until an interim civilian government was chosen by Congress in 1979. Former pres. Siles Zuazo was reelected in 1980 but prevented from taking office until 1982. Following an election in which no candidate won the necessary majority, in 1985 Congress elected Paz Estenssoro president

Böll, (bəl), Heinrich (1917–85), German writer whose satirical works explored post-war German society; winner of the Nobel Prize for literature (1972). 'Adam, Where Art Thou?' (1955), 'Tomorrow and Yesterday' (1957), and 'Billiards at Half-past Nine' (1962) are among his early novels. In 'The Clown' (1965), 'Group Portrait with Lady' (1971), 'The Lost Honor of Katharina Blum' (1974), and 'Safety Net' (1979), Böll looks at dehumanization by institutions and political terrorism

boll (boul) *n.* a capsule, esp. of cotton or flax [O.E. *bolla*, bowl]

Bol·land (bɔ́lɑ), Jean (1596–1665), Belgian Jesuit who published the first eight volumes of the lives of the saints, 'Acta sanctorum'. This work has been continued by his successors, known as Bollandists

bol·lard (bólərd) *n.* a short, strong wooden or metal post on a ship's deck or a quayside, to which mooring ropes can be tied ‖ (*Br.*) an obstacle like this in appearance, used for closing roads to traffic [etym. doubtful]

boll weevil *Anthonomus grandis*, fam. *Curculionidae*, a small gray weevil which lays its eggs in the bolls and squares of the cotton plant, doing very great damage

Boll Weevil conservative Southern Democratic member of Congress who votes with Republicans

boll·worm (bóulwərm) *n. Heliothis armigera*, a moth, larva or grub which feeds on bolls and unripe pods of cotton, and on the ears of corn, beans, peas etc.

Bo·lo·gna (bolónjə), Giovanni (1524–1608), French-born sculptor, who did his best work in Italy for the Medici family

Bologna a walled city (pop. 454,703) of N. Italy, on the Emilian plain at the foot of the Apennines. It is a communications center and agricultural market, with food-processing, mechanical engineering and chemical industries. Originally Etruscan, it passed after the fall of Rome under Byzantine, Frankish (8th c.) and nominal papal control, but flourished as a free commune from the 12th c., reaching its greatest prosperity in the 15th c. Papal rule was effective, except for the Napoleonic period, from the

16th c. until 1860, when Bologna joined the kingdom of Sardinia. Its university (11th c.), with Paris the oldest in Europe, was the European center of medieval legal studies. A number of medieval and Renaissance buildings remain

bo·lo·gna (bəlóuni) n. a seasoned, boiled and smoked sausage of ground beef, pork and veal [after BOLOGNA, Italy]

bo·lom·e·ter (boulómitər) n. (phys.) a resistance thermometer for measuring very small amounts of radiant energy [fr. Gk bolē, ray of light+METER]

boloney *BALONEY

Bolos *VOLOS

bo·lo·tie or **bo·la·tie** (bóuloutai) n. necktie made of a cord and ornament

Bol·she·vik (bólʃivik, bóulʃivik) n. (hist.) a member of the Russian Communist party, constituted in 1903 by the majority faction of the congress of the Russian Social Democratic party (cf. MENSHEVIK) **Ból·she·vism, Ból·she·vist** ns

bol·ster (bóulstər) 1. n. a long cylindrical pillow stretching from one side of a bed to the other or an often wedge-shaped pillow along the back of a sofa etc. ‖ a support, bolsterlike in shape, in some machines or instruments ‖ (archit.) a support, e.g. the crosspiece capping a pillar under a beam 2. v.t. (fig., usually with 'up') to support, prop, to bolster up a person's confidence [O.E.]

bolt (boult) 1. n. a sliding bar for keeping a door closed ‖ the sliding piece moved in a lock by the key ‖ a metal pin, headed at one end and often with a screw thread to take a nut at the other ‖ a thick tight roll of cloth ‖ a bundle of osiers or straw ‖ a roll of wallpaper of a certain length ‖ (hist.) a short, heavy arrow shot from a crossbow ‖ a thunderbolt ‖ a quick dash, esp. one made so as to flee a **bolt from the blue** an utter surprise, often disagreeable **to have shot one's bolt** to have taken a decisive action and be left with no possibility of turning back etc. **to make a bolt for it** to try to escape by running away 2. v.t. to secure (a door or window) with a bolt ‖ to fasten together with bolts ‖ to eat very quickly ‖ to break with, withdraw support from (a political party) ‖ v.i. to make off at a run ‖ to run away out of control ‖ to withdraw support from a political party [O.E. bolt, a crossbow bolt]

bolt v.t. to sift (flour) [O.F. bulter fr. bure, coarse woolen cloth]

Bol·ton (bóultən) a county borough (pop. 261,000) in Greater Manchester County, England, on River Croal, center of the fine-cotton spinning industry: also textiles, tanning, metalwork, engineering

bolt·rope (bóultroup) n. a cord round the edge of a sail to prevent its tearing

bolt upright adj. and adv. rigidly straight

Boltz·mann (bóltsmɑn), Ludwig (1844–1906), Austrian physicist who formulated mathematical laws for the distribution of energy, of particular importance in constructing the kinetic theory of gases

Bol·za·no (boltsánɔ) (G. Bozen) a communications center (pop. 107,300) and capital (alternating with Trento) of Trentino-Alto Adige, Italy, in Alto Adige

bomb (bɔm) 1. n. an explosive missile dropped from an aircraft, fired from a mortar or thrown by hand, which explodes on contact or by means of a time mechanism (*ATOMIC BOMB, *HYDROGEN BOMB) ‖ (basketball) a long shot ‖ (football) a long pass ‖ (theater) a flop 2. v.t. to drop bombs upon ‖ v.i. to drop bombs **to bomb out** to deprive (someone) of home, business premises etc. by bombing **to bomb up** to put bombs into (an aircraft) ‖ to take on a load of bombs ‖ (colloq.) to fail 3. adj. **bombed** drunk [F. bombe fr. Ital.]

Bomb (bɔm) n. (preceded by 'the') annihilating nuclear weaponry

bom·bard (bɔmbárd) v.t. to attack with big guns, hurl shells and bombs repeatedly at ‖ to pester (with questions, complaints etc.) ‖ (phys.) to subject (a substance) to rays or the impact of small particles [fr. F. bombarder, to fire a cannon]

bom·bar·dier (bɔmbərdíər) n. that member of a bomber crew who aims the bombs at the target ‖ (Br.) a noncommissioned officer below the rank of sergeant in the artillery [F.]

bom·bard·ment (bɔmbárdmənt) n. a bombarding or being bombarded ‖ a bombarding attack

bom·bar·don (bɔmbárd'n, bómbərdən) n. (hist.) a deep-toned double-reed wind instrument,

from which the bassoon was developed ‖ an organ stop imitating this [Ital. bombardone]

bom·ba·sine, bom·ba·zine (bómbəziːn, bɔmbəzíːn) n. a twilled dress material made of worsted, often with cotton or silk [F. bombasin]

bom·bast (bómbæst) n. swollen rhetoric, pretentious language, hollow ranting **bom·bás·tic** adj. **bom·bás·ti·cal·ly** adv. [O.F. bombace, cotton padding]

Bom·bay (bombéi) a former state of W. India, divided (1960) into two new states, Gujarat and Maharashtra ‖ the capital (pop. 5,970,575) of the state of Maharashtra, and the second city of India, a port and railway terminus. The cotton industry, established in the 19th c., remains important but, with hydroelectric power, engineering, chemical and other industries have been developed. Bombay was given to England by the Portuguese in 1534, and in 1671 became the center of British influence in W. India. The Parsees have led in commercial and professional activities

Bombay duck Harpodon nehereus, a small fish found off S. Asiatic coasts and eaten dried with curry

bombazine *BOMBASINE

bomb bay the compartment in an aircraft for carrying bombs

bomb disposal the rendering harmless and removing of unexploded bombs

bomb·er (bómər) n. an aircraft designed for bombing

bomb·load (bómloud) n. the full quota of bombs carried in an aircraft

bomb·proof (bómpruːf) adj. strong and thick enough to be protection against a bomb

bomb·shell (bómʃel) n. a sudden, amazing or appalling shock

bomb·sight (bómsait) n. the mechanism in an aircraft by which a bomb is aimed

Bon (boun) the Japanese festival called 'Feast of Lanterns', held July 13–15, when ancestral spirits are believed to come back to the household altars

bo·na fide (bóunəfaid, bónəfaid, bóunəfaidi:) adj. made, said, done, offered etc. without any intention to deceive or defraud, a bona fide bargain ‖ genuine, bona fide antiques [L.=with good faith]

Bon·aire (bonéər) *NETHERLANDS ANTILLES

Bon·am·pak (bonɑmpák) a ruined city in Chiapas, near Tuxtla, in the forests of S. Mexico, formerly a center of Mayan civilization. It is noted for its frescoes (discovered in 1946)

bo·nan·za (bənǽnzə) n. a very rich deposit of ore in veins of gold or silver ‖ something bringing profit or prosperity [Span.=fair weather, prosperity]

Bo·na·parte (bóunəpɑrt) the Corsican family which produced Napoleon I of France, his brothers Joseph, Lucien, Louis and Jérôme, and his sisters Elisa, Marie-Pauline and Caroline

Bonaparte, Jérôme (1784–1860), youngest brother of Napoleon I, who appointed him king of Westphalia (1807–13)

Bonaparte, Joseph (1768–1844), eldest brother of Napoleon I. His brother made him king of Naples (1806–8) and of Spain (1808–13)

Bonaparte, Louis (1778–1864), younger brother of Napoleon I, who made him king of Holland (1806–10). His youngest son became Napoleon III

Bonaparte, Louis Napoleon *NAPOLEON III

Bonaparte, Lucien (1775–1840), younger brother of Napoleon I. He was elected a member of the Council of Five Hundred (1796). Pius VII made him prince of Canino

Bonaparte, Napoleon *NAPOLEON I

Bo·na·part·ism (bóunəpɑrtizəm) n. (hist.) the ideas and policies of Napoleon I ‖ advocacy of strong government by a leader given a popular mandate

Bo·na·part·ist (bóunəpɑrtist) n. (hist.) a follower of Napoleon I or of his ideas and policy, or of the Napoleonic dynasty

Bon·a·ven·tu·ra (bonəventúːrə), St (1221–74), Italian Franciscan and theologian. He became general of the Franciscans (1257). He wrote a 'Life of St Francis' (1262) and an exposition of the rule (1266–8) which helped to remold the order. He also wrote classic works of devotion. Famous as a mystical theologian, he was known as 'the seraphic doctor'. Feast: July 14

bon·bon (bónbɔn, bɔ̃bɔ̃) pl. **bon·bons** (bónbɔnz, bɔ̃bɔ̃) n. a sweet candy [F. fr. bon, good]

Bond (bond), William Cranch (1789–1859), U.S. astronomer. He discovered a new ring system and a new satellite (Hyperion) of Saturn, and constructed an improved type of recording chronograph. He directed the Harvard Observatory (1847–59), and greatly advanced the application of photography to astronomy

bond (bond) 1. n. that which unites, the bond of friendship ‖ a written legal agreement by someone to pay money to another person ‖ a document issued by a government or a company recording money borrowed and the promise to pay back with interest to the holder ‖ bond paper ‖ an insurance policy covering losses suffered by an employer as the result of some contingency out of his control or of the actions of a specified employee ‖ (chem.) any of several mechanisms by which atoms, groups of atoms, or ions are held together in a molecular or crystal structure (*COVALENT BOND, *IONIC BOND, *HYDROGEN BOND, *COORDINATE BOND) ‖ a method of laying bricks or stone to give strength and pleasing appearance, English bond ‖ (rhet.) a shackle **in bond** kept in charge of customs officers in a warehouse until the appropriate duty is paid **to take out of bond** to remove (goods) from the customs warehouse after paying the duty 2. v.t. to place bricks in building (a structure) in such a way as to hold them firmly together ‖ to place (imported goods) in bond ‖ to mortgage [M.E. var. of band]

bond·age (bóndidʒ) n. (hist.) slavery ‖ (rhet.) subjection to the constraint of duty or of some strong desire etc.

bond·ed (bóndid) adj. (of goods) placed in bond ‖ (of a warehouse) under bond to pay duty on goods stored ‖ attached by adhesive to make a single product of two components

bond·ing (bóndiŋ) n. (dentistry) use of a synthetic tooth material fused onto teeth or between teeth in the shape desired; used as a substitute for dental crowns

bond paper strong paper made originally for government bonds etc., now used for letterheads etc.

bonds·man (bóndzmən) pl. **bonds·men** (bóndzmən) n. (hist.) a man standing surety for another under legal bond

bond·stone (bóndstoun) n. a stone or brick going right through the thickness of a wall

B-1 (mil.) proposed U.S. intercontinental bomber with four engines, subsonic wing, and four- to five-man crew

Bône (boun) *ANNABA

bone (boun) 1. n. one of the hard parts of the skeleton of a vertebrate animal ‖ the hard substance which composes it ‖ something made of bone or of similar material, e.g. one of a pair of dice or clappers ‖ the stiffening material in a corset etc. ‖ (pl.) an end man in a minstrel show (who plays bone clappers) ‖ (pl.) the living body, my old bones ache ‖ (pl.) the dead body, his bones were laid to rest **to feel in one's bones** to know intuitively **to have a bone to pick with someone** to have a reproach or complaint to make to someone **to make no bones about (something)** to be blunt about (a matter) 2. v.t. pres. part. **bon·ing** past and past part. **boned** to remove the bones from (fish, poultry) ‖ to stiffen with bone (a bodice or corset) 3. adv. extremely, bone idle [O.E. bán, bone]

—Bone is a hard living tissue which forms the framework of the body. It also serves to protect such organs as the brain, heart, and lungs. The center of most bones contains bone marrow, where many of the blood cells are produced (*BLOOD). Bone can develop directly from soft tissue or from intermediate cartilage. It has the property of repairing itself when broken (*FRACTURE)

bone ash the white ash (largely calcium phosphate) obtained when bones are heated in air. It is used in industrial chemistry, the manufacture of porcelain etc.

bone black finely ground animal charcoal, used as a pigment

bone china semiporcelain made of a combination of bone ash, china stone and china clay, and used for fine tableware

bone·less (bóunlis) adj. without a bone or bones ‖ (of people) lacking spirit or verve, without determination or strength of character ‖ (of prose etc.) feeble, without vigor

bone meal meal made of crushed or ground bone and fed to animals or used as fertilizer

bone oil a black, foul-smelling oil obtained from carbonized bones and used for sheep dipping ‖ the liquid part of bone fat, used in making leather and as a lubricant

bon·er (bóunər) n. (pop.) a painful or embarrassing mistake **to pull** (or **make**) **a boner** to make such a mistake

bone·set·ter (bóunsetər) n. a person who sets broken or dislocated bones, often without being a qualified physician

bone spavin a new bone growth on a horse's hock

bon·fire (bónfaiər) n. a fire built outdoors, for burning rubbish, for festivity or celebration, or sometimes as a signal [orig. bonefire, a fire for burning bodies]

bon·go (bóŋgou, bóŋgou) pl. **bon·gos, bon·goes** n. one of a pair of small, tuned drums, played with the hands [Span. bongó]

bongo drum the bongo

Bon·i·face (bónifeis), St (c. 675–754), English monk and missionary, 'the apostle of Germany', who gave the German Church its organization and its earliest bishops. He was martyred, with 50 companions

Boniface VIII (c. 1235–1303), pope (1294–1303). His attempts to maintain the rights of the papacy led to clashes with Edward I of England and Philippe IV of France over the taxation of the clergy

bon·i·ness (bóuni:nis) n. the state or quality of being bony

Bon·ing·ton (bóniŋtən), Richard Parkes (1802–28), English painter, trained in France, notable for his landscapes. His watercolors show great freedom of technique

Bo·nin Islands (bóunin) a group of small volcanic islands (area 40 sq. miles, pop. 800) in the Pacific, southeast of Japan. They were returned (June 1968) by the U.S.A. to Japan. Their Japanese name is Ogasawara

bo·ni·to (bəní:tou) pl. **bo·ni·tos, bo·ni·to** n. any of several Atlantic and Pacific fish of fam. Scombridae having dark stripes running from head to tail with a silver underside [Span.]

bon·kers (bón·kers) adj. (colloq.) insane

bon mot (bɔmou) pl. **bons mots** (bɔmou) n. a witty remark [F. bon, good+mot, word]

Bonn (bɔn) the capital (pop. 289,400) of West Germany, in North Rhine-Westphalia, on the Rhine. Manufactures: pottery, chemicals, leather, textiles. University (1786)

Bon·nard (bɔnar), Pierre (1867–1947), French painter. After painting early lowtoned pictures using pure flat color (he was influenced by Gauguin, ToulouseLautrec and Japanese engravings), he developed into a rapturous colorist, with a free and intensely lyrical handling of esp. domestic subjects

bon·net (bónit) n. a kind of hat worn mainly by babies, fastened under the chin with ribbons or strings ‖ (hist.) a woman's headdress fitting closely round the head ‖ a cap worn by Scotsmen ‖ (Br.) a hood for an open fireplace ‖ (Br.) a car hood (cover over the engine) ‖ a protective cover over parts of some machines ‖ (naut.) a piece of canvas laced to the foot of a sail to give extra sail area in moderate winds [O.F. bonet]

bon·ny (bóni:) comp. **bon·ni·er** superl. **bon·ni·est** adj. (esp. Scot., of babies) healthy-looking ‖ (esp. Scot., of girls) fresh and attractive [etym. doubtful]

bon·sai (bónsai) pl. **bon·sai** (bónsai) n. a potted tree or shrub dwarfed (e.g. by pruning the roots) for ornamental effect ‖ the art of cultivating such trees or shrubs [Jap.]

bon·spiel (bónspi:l) n. (curling) a grand tournament

bo·nus (bóunəs) pl. **bo·nus·es** n. a grant of money as a gratuity to workers, discharged soldiers etc. ‖ a special earned payment based e.g. on production ‖ an extra dividend or gift of stock or shares from a company to its shareholders ‖ a distribution of profits to certain insurance policy holders ‖ anything welcome that one receives over and above what is expected or usual [L.=good]

bon vi·vant (bõvi:vã) pl. **bon vi·vants, bons vi·vants** (bõvi:vã) n. a person who appreciates good wine and good food and is of a cheerful and easy good nature [F.]

bon vo·yage (bɔnvɔiáʒ) a conventional wish to someone setting off on a journey, that it may be safe and pleasant [F.]

bon·y (bóuni:) comp. **bon·i·er** superl. **bon·i·est** adj. (of persons) with large, prominent bones ‖ (of persons and animals) very thin ‖ full of bones ‖ like or consisting of bone or bones

bonze (bɔnz) n. a Far Eastern Buddhist monk [prob. F. fr. Port. fr. Jap. fr. Chin. fan seng, a religious person]

boo (bu:) **1.** n. a cry of contemptuous disapproval, e.g. after bad acting ‖ an interjection made suddenly and loudly to cause fright ‖ (slang) marijuana **2.** v. pres. part. **boo·ing** past and past part. **booed** v.t. to shout contemptuous boos at ‖ v.i. to shout contemptuous boos [imit.]

boob tube (bu:b) (slang) television set

boo·by (bú:bi:) pl. **boo·bies** n. a stupid fool, a clumsy lout [prob. fr. Span. bobo]

booby prize a prize awarded to the person with the least score in a game, or who comes last in a race

booby trap a trap laid for the unwary as a practical joke, often humiliating ‖ (mil.) a harmless-looking object containing an explosive charge liable to go off when disturbed

boo·ga·loo (bu:gəlú:) n. a slow-motion dance in two-beat rhythm with the body swiveling from side to side, shoulders and hips rotating. — **boogalou** v. to dance the boogalou

boog·ie-woog·ie (búgi:wúgi:, bú:gi:wú:gi:) n. a fast style of playing jazz on the piano, having a persistent bass rhythm, and intricate figurations of a simple melody, often moving contrary to the bass

book (buk) n. a number of printed pages fastened together and enclosed in a cover ‖ a literary composition ‖ a treatise ‖ a major unit of a literary composition, Book I of Milton's 'Paradise Lost' ‖ one of the works which make up the Bible ‖ a libretto ‖ a number of blank or lined sheets strung or bound together, on which notes, accounts, exercises etc. may be written ‖ (pl.) business accounts ‖ a number of stamps, tickets, checks etc. fastened together as in a book ‖ (betting) a record of bets made by a bookmaker at a race, esp. a horserace, **to make book** **in someone's bad** (or **black**) **books** out of favor with someone **in someone's good books** in favor with someone **on the books** included in a list of members **to read someone like a book** to know by intuition what someone is thinking **to speak by the book** to speak authoritatively, with appropriate information **to suit someone's book** to be acceptable to, or convenient for, somebody **to take a leaf out of someone's book** to learn a lesson from someone and imitate him [O.E. bōc, writing tablet]

book v.t. to reserve in advance (seats in a theater, hotel accommodation, travel tickets etc.) ‖ to put down someone's name for or issue (such advance tickets) ‖ to enter (someone's name) on a reservation list ‖ to engage in advance (a speaker or performer) ‖ to record (an order) ‖ to issue a ticket to [O.E. bōcian, to assign (land) by charter]

book·bind·er (búkbaindər) n. someone who binds books

book·bind·ing (búkbaindiŋ) n. the craft of binding books by hand or machine. Technically, a bound book is one in which the cover is attached in the sewing press, before the adhesion of an outer skin of leather or cloth. Books to which prefabricated covers are applied are said to be cased

book·case (búkkeis) n. a number of shelves in one unit for containing books

book·end (búkend) n. an end support for a row of books

book·ie (búki:) n. (pop.) a bookmaker

booking office (Br.) the ticket office in a railroad station etc.

book·ish (búkiʃ) adj. of or relating to books ‖ fond of reading and studying ‖ reflecting vicarious experience gathered from books, rather than practical experience

book·keep·er (búkki:pər) n. someone keeping the accounts of a business etc.

book·keep·ing (búkki:piŋ) n. the regular recording of the essential facts about the transactions of a business or enterprise. It is traditionally distinguished from accounting, which deals with the analysis and presentation of the recorded data

book learning knowledge gained from books (as distinct from that gained by experience)

book·let (búklit) n. a book of not very many pages, usually in paper covers

book·mak·er (búkmeikər) n. a man whose business is taking bets and paying out on winners

book·mark (búkmark) n. anything used for inserting between the pages of a book to mark one's place

book·mo·bile (búkməbi:l) n. a truck fitted out as a traveling library for rural areas etc. [BOOK+(AUTO)MOBILE]

Book of Common Prayer the service book of the Anglican Communion. Based on the missal and the breviary, but influenced also by continental reforms, it was produced under the direction of Cranmer, and first published in 1549. A revised version (1552), also by Cranmer, showed more Protestant influence, but was abolished in the Catholic reaction (1553–8) under Mary. It reappeared (1559) under Elizabeth in a version which restored certain details of the 1549 book. It was abolished during the Commonwealth (1649–60), but restored (1662) with some liturgical improvements. A modern revi- sion was submitted to parliament (1927 and 1928) but was rejected by the Commons. The 1928 book is nevertheless in partial use in many churches. In the U.S.A. the Episcopal Church adopted a revised version of the Book of Common Prayer (1789), and other revisions took place in 1892 and 1928

Book of Hours a book of prayers or offices for the canonical hours

book·plate (búkpleit) n. a label with the owner's name, crest or other distinguishing mark, for sticking inside the cover of a book

book·rest (búkrest) n. a support for an open book, at a convenient slant for reading or consultation

book review a critic's remarks on a book, esp. on a new publication

book·sel·ler (búkselər) n. someone whose business is selling books

book·shelf (búkʃelf) pl. **book·shelves** (búkʃelvz) n. a shelf for holding books

book·shop (búkʃɔp) n. a bookstore

book·stall (búkstɔl) n. an open-air stand for displaying books on sale ‖ (Br.) a kiosk selling chiefly magazines and newspapers

book·stand (búkstænd) n. a bookstall selling books

book·store (búkstɔr, búkstour) n. a bookseller's store

book token (Br.) a voucher having a certain money value and exchangeable for books in a bookshop

book value the monetary worth of an article as noted in a firm's books

book·work (búkwə:rk) n. the study of theory or texts as opposed to practical work ‖ paper work

book·worm (búkwə:rm) n. a person who reads voraciously ‖ the larva of any of various moths and beetles which eat holes in the covers and pages of books

Boole (bu:l), George (1815–64), English mathematician and logician. He showed the relationship of mathematics and logic in 'Mathematical Analysis of Logic' (1847) and 'Investigation of the Laws of Thought' (1854)

bool·ean algebra (bú:li:ən) (computer) algebraic system with two bases, used in computer processing

boom (bu:m) **1.** n. a hollow-sounding roar, as of a distant explosion ‖ a sudden increase in a particular business or commodity etc., or in general prosperity ‖ a surge in popularity **2.** v.i. to make a hollow roar ‖ to be notably successful or prosperous or in demand, steel is booming again ‖ v.t. to cause to boom [imit.]

boom n. a long spar, usually of wood, with one end attached to the mast, used to stretch the sail foot ‖ a long spar jutting out from the mast of a derrick, used to support or guide the object being lifted ‖ a floating barrier, usually of wood or chain, across a harbor or river mouth, used to prevent the access of enemy ships, or to keep sawmill logs from floating away ‖ a mass of floating logs thus contained [Du.=tree, beam]

boom·er·ang (bú:məræŋ) n. a curved or smoothly angular wooden missile used by Australian aborigines. When thrown it returns to its thrower if it hits nothing ‖ an argument or idea which rebounds and harms the originator [native Australian]

boom·town (bú:mtaun) n. a town which has sprung up or grown very quickly as the result of a boom

boon (bu:n) n. a blessing, something that comes as a help or comfort [O.N. bón, prayer]

boon adj. convivial, (only in) boon companion [O.F. bon, good]

boon·docks (bú:ndɔks) n. rural areas

Boone (bu:n), Daniel (1734–1820), American frontiersman and fighter against the Indians in Kentucky and Missouri

boor (búər) n. an uncouth, insensitive, ill-bred person **boor·ish** adj. [Du. boer, peasant]

boost (bu:st) **1.** *n.* a lifting up, *to give someone a boost over a wall* ‖ something that gives an impetus or encouragement **2.** *v.t.* to push from below, hoist ‖ to increase the power, value etc., of (an industrial scheme, person etc.) ‖ to help, assist, *to boost a candidate's chances* ‖ (*elec.*) to raise the voltage in (a battery, circuit etc.)
bóost·er *n.* a substance which increases the efficiency of an immunizing agent, or a dose renewing it ‖ (*engin.*) a machine which increases pressure, voltage etc. (*rocketry*) the first stage of a multistage rocket, used to supply the main thrust for takeoff [origin unknown]
booster shot a booster (substance which increases the efficiency of an immunizing agent, or a dose renewing it)
boost·glide vehicle (bú:stglaid) spacecraft based on an airplane that is carried to the upper atmosphere, whence it is rocket-boosted into space, returning to earth by aerodynamic control. *Cf* SPACE SHUTTLE
boot (bu:t) **1.** *n.* an article of footwear coming to the ankle or higher, made of leather, rubber or canvas, often for particular uses (riding, skiing, etc.) ‖ the part of a reed pipe encasing the reed ‖ (*baseball*) a fielding error ‖ the box containing the lower pulley of a grain elevator ‖ a naval or marine recruit in the first stage of training ‖ (*Br.*) the trunk of a car ‖ (*pop.*) dismissal, *to get the boot* ‖ (*hist.*) a torture device which encased and crushed the foot and leg **the boot** (or **shoe**) **is on the other foot** the precise opposite is the case **to have one's heart in one's boots** to feel sudden despairing apprehension **to lick someone's boots** to flatter someone in a servile way **2.** *v.t.* to kick [O.F. *bote*, etym. doubtful]
boot·black (bú:tblæk) *n.* someone who cleans and polishes the shoes of passers-by for a small fee
boot camp a military training camp for new recruits
boot·ee (bú:ti:) *n.* a knitted or crocheted baby's boot
Bo·ö·tes (bouóuti:z) a northern constellation at the tail of Ursa Major (*ARCTURUS)
Booth (bu:θ), John Wilkes (1839–65), American actor, the assassin of Abraham Lincoln
Booth, William (1829–1912), the founder and first general of the Salvation Army
booth (bu:θ, *Br.* bu:ð) *pl.* **booths** (bu:θs, bu:ðz) *n.* a temporary structure of canvas and boards, esp. a covered stall in a fair or market ‖ a small permanent structure affording privacy, *telephone booth* [M.E. *bôthe* prob. fr. Scand.]
Boo·thi·a, Gulf of (bú:θi:ə) a gulf in the Northwest Territories, Canada, between the Boothia Peninsula to the west, Baffin Is. and the Melville Peninsula to the east
Boothia Peninsula the northernmost point on the North American mainland, between Baffin Is. and Prince of Wales Is. in the Northwest Territories, Canada. It is up to 130 miles wide
boot·jack (bú:tdʒæk) *n.* a device for pulling off boots
boot·lace (bú:tleis) *n.* a lace for a boot
boot·leg (bú:tleg) **1.** *v.t. pres. part.* **boot·legging** *past* and *past part.* **boot·legged** (*pop.*) to smuggle (alcoholic liquor) ‖ (*pop.*) to sell or make (alcoholic liquor) illegally **2.** *adj.* (*pop.*, esp. of alcoholic liquor) illicit, *bootleg gin* **bóot·leg·ger** *n.* a smuggler of liquor, esp. during Prohibition in America [fr. hiding goods in the leg of a boot]
boot·less (bú:tlis) *adj.* (*rhet.*) yielding no success, *bootless efforts* [O.E. *bótléas*, not expiable by payment]
boots (bu:ts) *pl. n.* construed as *sing.* (*Br.*) a hotel servant who cleans shoes, carries bags, etc.
boot·strap (bú:tstræp) *n.* (*computer*) instructions that provide for other instructions. — **bootstrap** *v.*
bootstrap loader (*computer*) short program used to facilitate the input of more complex programs into the memory of a processor
boot strapping 1. (*electr.*) technique for lifting a generator by the power it generates. **2.** any self-generating or self-sustaining process
boot tree a device inserted into boots for keeping them in shape when not worn
boo·ty (bú:ti:) *pl.* **boo·ties** *n.* spoils taken in war, or by thieves ‖ any rich prize [fr. O.N. *bÿti*, exchange]
booze (bu:z) **1.** *v.i. pres. part.* **booz·ing** *past* and *past part.* **boozed** (*pop.*) to drink alcoholic liquor to excess **2.** *n.* (*pop.*) alcoholic drink **booz·y**

comp. **booz·i·er** *superl.* **booz·i·est** *adj.* [Du. *buizen*]
Bo·phu·tha·tswa·na (boupu:tatswúnə) *n.* quasi-self-governing unit within the Republic of South Africa for the Bantu nation, established according to the South African apartheid policy of separate development
bo·rac·ic (bəræsik, borǽsik, bouræsik) *adj.* boric
bor·age (bá:ridʒ, bóridʒ, bóridʒ) *n. Borrago officinalis,* fam. *Borraginaceae,* an annual plant with hairy leaves, cymose inflorescence, and bright blue petals, used in salads [fr. M.L. *borrago*]
bo·rane or **bo·ron·hy·dride** [H₃BO₃ or B₂O₃] (bóurein) (bouranháidraid) *n.* (*chem.*) explosive, toxic, and unstable compound of boron and hydrogen used as fuel
bo·rate (bóreit, bóureit) *n.* a salt of boric acid [BORON]
bo·rax (bóræks, bóuræks) *n.* sodium tetraborate, $Na_2B_4O_7$, used as a flux, as a detergent, and as a mild antiseptic [O.F. *boras* perh. fr. Pers.]
bor·bo·ryg·mus (bɔrbərígməs) *n.* rumbling, gurgling noise in the intestines
Bor·deaux (bordou) the chief town (pop. 200,000, with agglom. 472,000) of the Gironde, S.W. France, on the Garonne, 60 miles from the sea: one of France's largest ports and a great center of the wine trade. Industries: shipbuilding, petroleum, oil and soap making, metallurgy, engineering, sugar-refining. Cathedral (12th–14th cc.). University (1441)
Bordeaux *n.* a red (*CLARET) or white wine from the Bordeaux region of France
Bor·den (bórd'n), Gail (1801–74), U.S. inventor. He developed the first commercial method of condensing milk (patented by the U.S.A. and Great Britain in 1856). He was also a pioneer in Texan affairs
Borden, Sir Robert Laird (1854–1937), Canadian prime minister. Heading a Conservative government (1911–17) and a Union government (1917–20), he defined the new status of the self-governing dominions in the British Empire
Bor·den·ize (bórdənaiz) *v.* to dip in phosphate to prevent rusting
bor·der (bórdər) **1.** *n.* an edge, an outer side ‖ a frontier, a boundary between two countries ‖ the state between one condition and another, *the borders of sleep* ‖ a strip (often ornamental) around the edge of a handkerchief, dress etc. **2.** *v.t.* to put or be a border around ‖ *v.i.* (with 'on') to be in an adjoining position ‖ (with 'on' or 'upon') to come near to something specified, *his remarks bordered upon rudeness* [M.E. *bordure* fr. O.F.]
bordered pit a plant cell pit in which the secondary wall forms an overarching rim esp. characteristic of gymnosperm tracheids
bor·der·er (bórdərər) *n.* someone who lives on or near a frontier, e.g. between England and Scotland
bor·der·land (bórdərlænd) *n.* a frontier district ‖ an area without clear bounds, *the borderland between physics and chemistry*
border line the line, real or imagined, marking a frontier or boundary **bor·der·line** (bórdərlain) *adj.* being on a frontier ‖ indeterminate, not falling into one clear category
bor·dure (bórdʒər) *n.* (*heraldry*) a bearing running around and parallel to the outline of the shield, always a fifth of the shield in width [fr. BORDER]
bore (bɔr, bour) **1.** *n.* a deep hole made by drilling in the ground to find oil etc. ‖ the internal cylinder of a gun barrel ‖ the gauge of a shotgun barrel ‖ the caliber of other gun barrels **2.** *v. pres. part.* **bor·ing** *past* and *past part.* **bored** *v.t.* to drill (a hole) ‖ to create by boring, *to bore a tunnel* ‖ to force (a way) as if by drilling ‖ (*racing*) to push off course ‖ *v.i.* to make a hole by drilling or as if by drilling ‖ (of a horse) to thrust the head forward and down [O.E. *borian,* to pierce]
bore 1. *n.* an uninteresting person inflicted on others in talk ‖ a nuisance ‖ anything protractedly dull **2.** *v.t.* *pres. part.* **bor·ing** *past* and *past part.* **bored** to weary or irritate by dullness **bored to death** (or **tears**) very bored [etym. doubtful]
bore *n.* a high tidal wave rushing up an estuary into the narrowing channel of a river. The Canadian Bay of Fundy and the English Severn are examples [O.N. *bára,* wave]
bore *past* of BEAR

bo·re·al (bóri:əl) *adj.* of the north or north wind [fr. L. *borealis*]
Bo·re·as (bóri:əs, bóuri:əs) *n.* (Gk *mythol.*) the god of the north wind ‖ the north wind personified [Gk]
bore·dom (bórdəm, bóurdəm) *n.* the state or quality of being bored, the condition of having one's interest either unaroused or extinguished
bor·er (bórər, bóurər) *n.* a person, tool or machine which bores holes ‖ a horse which bores ‖ a boring insect or its larva, *corn borer*
bore·safe fuse (bórseif) type of fuse having an interrupter in the explosive train that prevents a projectile from exploding until after it has cleared the muzzle of a weapon
Bor·ges (bórhes), Jorge Luis (1899–1986), Argentine poet and novelist. His sense of the metaphor and his creative imagination, evident in his verse ('Fervor de Buenos Aires', 'Luna de enfrente', 'Cuaderno San Martín', short stories 'A Universal History of Infamy,' 'The Aleph,' 'Ficciones,' 'Dreamtigers,' 'The Book of Imaginary Beings,' 'Doctor Brodie's Report,' and 'The Book of Sand', and essays ('Inquisiciones', 'Otras inquisiciones'), placed him in the front rank of contemporary writers in Spanish
Bor·gia (bórdʒə) Italian family of Spanish origin, powerful in the second half of the 15th c. Pope Alexander VI was a Borgia. His illegitimate children included Cesare (1475–1507), duke of Valentinois, a consummate and criminal politician (the model of Machiavelli's 'The Prince') and Lucrezia (1480–1519), famous for her beauty and for her patronage of science and the arts. The cruelty, crimes, profligacy, bad faith and ambition of many of the Borgias made them hated by Italians
Bor·glum (bórgləm), (John) Gutzon (de la Mothe) (1867–1941), U.S. sculptor. He carved in the Mount Rushmore National Memorial (South Dakota) the colossal portraits of Washington, Jefferson, Lincoln and Theodore Roosevelt. He also sculpted the huge head of Lincoln in the Capitol Rotunda in Washington, D.C.
Bor·gu (bórgu:) a region west of the Niger in Benin and Nigeria
bo·ric (bórik, bóurik) *adj.* of, relating to or derived from boron
boric acid H_3BO_3, a white crystalline weak acid which occurs naturally [BORON]
bor·ing (bóriŋ, bóuriŋ) *n.* a hole made by boring ‖ the process of boring holes
Bo·ris III (bóris, bóuris) (1894–1943), king of Bulgaria (1918–43), ally of Hitler
Bor·laug (bórlang), Norman Ernest (1914–), U.S. agriculturalist. He was awarded the 1970 Nobel peace prize for his 'green revolution': the campaign to ease world hunger by the development and application, largely in the underdeveloped countries, of new high-yield cereals, esp. wheat, rice and corn
Born (bɔrn), Max (1882–1970), German atomic physicist who settled in Great Britain in 1933. He provided the mathematical link between classical physics and quantum mechanics
born (bɔrn) *past part.* of BEAR (to give birth) ‖ *adj.* having a certain natural characteristic, *a born poet* or one so marked as to seem natural, *a born fool* **born of** (*rhet.*) arising from
Bor·na disease (bórnə) encephalomyelitis in horses
born-a·gain (bórnəgen) *adj.* of one taking a new, different, and more religious course, e.g., a born-again Christian
Born approximation (bɔrn) (*quantum mechanics*) system of solving a scattering problem by successive approximations based on the premise that the effect of the scattering process is not large; named for Max Born
borne *past part.* of BEAR (except in the sense 'to give birth')
Bor·ne·o (bórni:ou) an island (area 290,000 sq. miles, pop. 8,272,000) in the Malay Archipelago, S.E. Asia. It is divided into Kalimantan (Indonesia), Sabah and Sarawak (Malaysia) and Brunei. The forested mountainous interior (highest point: Gunong Kinabulu 13,455 ft, in Sabah), encircled by a swampy coastal belt, is cut by river valleys (largest rivers: Kapuas, Rajang, Barito, Mahakam). The island is extremely well watered. Average temperature (F.): 72°–93°. Average rainfall: 160 ins. Chief products: rubber, metals, petroleum, lumber. Livestock: hogs, water buffalo, goats, cattle. HISTORY. The Chinese had settlements here by the 12th c., and later the island came under the power of the Javanese. The Spanish and Portu-

---

CONCISE PRONUNCIATION KEY: **(a)** æ, c*a*t; ɑ, c*a*r; ɔ f*aw*n; ei, sn*a*ke. **(e)** e, h*e*n; i:, sh*ee*p; iə, d*ee*r; ɛə, b*ea*r. **(i)** i, f*i*sh; ai, t*i*ger; ə:, b*i*rd. **(o)** o, *o*x; au, c*ow*; ou, g*oa*t; u, p*oo*r; ɔi, r*oy*al. **(u)** ʌ, d*u*ck; u, b*u*ll; u:, g*oo*se; ə, b*a*cillus; ju:, c*u*be. x, lo*ch*; θ, *th*ink; ð, bo*th*er; z, *Z*en; ʒ, corsa*g*e; dʒ, sava*g*e; ŋ, oranguta*ng*; j, *y*ak; ʃ, *f*ish; tʃ, fe*tch*; 'l, rabb*le*; 'n, redd*en*. Complete pronunciation key appears inside front cover.

guese visited Brunei (16th c.) but were expelled. The Dutch and British then struggled for control (17th c.). Increased piracy along the north coast (18th c.) caused British reprisals. The Dutch expanded their influence in the south, and the boundaries of Sarawak, Brunei, North Borneo and Dutch Borneo were defined (1891). Sarawak and North Borneo (now Sabah) joined (1963) the Federation of Malaysia. Brunei gained its independence in 1984

Born·holm (bórnhǫlm) a Danish island (area 228 sq. miles, pop. 47,357) in the Baltic, south of Sweden

born·ite (bórnait) n. Cu₅FeS₄, a compound of copper sulfide with iron sulfide and one of the chief ores of copper, copper pyrites [after I. von Born (1742–91), Austrian mineralogist]

Bor·nu (bornú:) a vast agricultural plain of Nigeria southwest of Lake Chad || (hist.) an influential Sudanic kingdom (10th–19th cc.) in this region

Bo·ro·bu·dur, Bo·ro·boe·doer (bouroubu:dúər) a site near Magelang (Java) of the ruins of a great Buddhist temple (8th c.). It is a pyramid covered with carved blocks of stone illustrating episodes in the Buddha's life

Bo·ro·din (bórədi:n, bʌrʌdjí:n), Alexander Porfyrievich (1834–87), Russian composer. The Polovtsian dances from his unfinished opera 'Prince Igor' were made famous by Diaghilev's Russian Ballet

Bo·ro·di·no, Battle of (bǫrədí:nou, bʌrʌdjinó) a battle (Sept. 7, 1812) in which the Russians under Kutuzov failed to stop Napoleon's march to Moscow. There were 80,000 casualties

bo·ron (bórɒn, bóurɒn) n. a chemical element (symbol B, at. no. 5, at. mass 10.81 1). It has a very high melting point and is non-metallic. It hardens steel when alloyed with it. With carbon it forms a solid solution which is extremely hard and is used as an abrasive [fr. BORAX+CARBON]

Bo·ro·ro (bourouróu) pl. **Bo·ro·ro, Bo·ro·ros** n. an Indian people of Brazil of matrilineal descent, now occupying a large area near the headwaters of the Paraguay River. Their main occupations are hunting, fishing and agriculture. They perform elaborate ceremonial dances, usually connected with funerals || a member of this people || their language [Port. Bororó]

bor·ough (bә́rou, bʌ́rou) n. a municipal corporation resembling an incorporated town || one of five political divisions of Greater New York || a county in Alaska || (Br.) a town or urban district with corporation and privileges granted by royal charter || (Br.) a town or urban constituency which sends a member or members to parliament [O.E. burg, burh, fortified place or town]

Borromeo, St Charles *CHARLES BORROMEO

Bor·ro·mi·ni (bǫrǫmí:ni:), Francesco (1599–1667), one of the chief Italian baroque architects (churches of S. Carlo alle Quattro Fontane and S. Agnese Piazza Navona in Rome)

Bor·row (bórou, bórou), George Henry (1803–81), English writer and linguist. His travels on behalf of the British and Foreign Bible Society led to 'The Bible in Spain' (1843). His knowledge of gipsy life provided the material for 'Lavengro' (1851) and 'The Romany Rye'(1857)

bor·row (bórou, bórou) v.t. to take (something) on the understanding that it will be returned later || to appropriate, to take and use (an idea etc.) not thought of by oneself || when subtracting, to take 1 from a figure in the minuend in order to add 10 to the next lower denomination, when the latter is less than the corresponding figure in the subtrahend [O.E. borgian]

borrowed light light let in by an internal window or opening

borsch (bɔrʃ) n. a cold soup made of grated beets and beet juice, beaten eggs and sour cream || a hot soup of Russian origin, mainly of beets and cabbage [Russ. borshch]

borscht (bɔrʃt) n. borsch

bort (bɔrt) n. fragments made in cutting diamonds || imperfectly crystallized or poor quality diamonds, useless as gems but industrially valuable, or one such diamond [perh. O.F. bort, bastard]

bor·zoi (bórzɔi) n. the Russian wolfhound [Russ. borzoy, swift]

Bo·san·quet (bóuzænkit), Bernard (1848–1923), British philosopher. His idealism derives from Hegel. His works include 'Logic or the Morphology of Knowledge' (1888) and, in metaphysics,

his Gifford Lectures, 'The Principle of Individuality and Value' (1912) and 'The Value and Destiny of the Individual' (1913)

Bosch (bɔs, bɒs), Hieronymus (Jerome) (c. 1460–1516), Dutch painter who greatly influenced Cranach and Bruegel. He was a satirist, with a keen interest in the grotesque and the symbolic

Bosch (bɒʃ), Juan (1909–), Dominican writer and politician. Elected president (1963), he was overthrown in the same year

Bose (bous), Sir Jagadis Chandra (1858–1937), Indian physicist who founded the Bose Research Institute, Calcutta

Bose-Ein·stein statistics (bóusáinstain) a quantum mechanical statistical system which demonstrates that particles having integral spin quantum number interact with one another in such a way as to permit two or more particles to be in exactly the same quantum state (cf. FERMI-DIRAC STATISTICS)

bosh (bɒʃ) n. meaningless talk, nonsense [Turk.=empty]

bosh n. the lower sloping part of a blast-furnace shaft [etym. doubtful]

bosk·y (bóski) adj. (rhet.) having lots of trees || (rhet.) provided by trees, bosky shade [fr. archaic bosk, bush fr. M.E.]

bo's'n (bóus'n) n. a boatswain

Bos·ni·a-Her·ze·go·vi·na (bózni:əhȩ̌ərtsəgouví:nə) a constituent republic (area 19,904 sq. miles, pop. 4,029,000) of Yugoslavia, between the Sava and the Adriatic. Capital: Sarajevo. It is barren, mountainous country, cut by deep river valleys, and forested in the east. Industries: agriculture (corn, sugar beet, tobacco, fruit, wine and liqueurs), cattle breeding, lumber, iron and coal mining. Textile, chemical and metallurgical industries are being developed. It was a Turkish province (from 1463), and was occupied (1878) and annexed (1908) by Austria-Hungary. It became a province of the kingdom later called Yugoslavia (1918) and a federated republic of Yugoslavia (1945)

Bos·ni·an (bózni:ən) 1. n. an inhabitant of Bosnia 2. adj. of or pertaining to Bosnia or to its inhabitants

bos·om (búzəm, bú:zəm) 1. n. a human being's breast || a woman's breasts || strong, protective affection, the bosom of the family || something suggesting the human breast, the bosom of the earth || that part of a dress etc. covering the breast || the space between this part of the dress and the body 2. adj. intimate, beloved, a bosom friend [O.E. bōsm]

bos·on (bóusɒn) n. any fundamental particle having integral spin quantum number (e.g. 0, 1, 2 etc.) and that obeys Bose-Einstein statistics [after S. N. Bose (b. 1894), Indian physicist]

Bos·po·rus (bóspərəs) a strait 17 miles across, joining the Black Sea to the Sea of Marmara, and separating Europe from Asia Minor. Of great strategic importance in history, the Bosporus played an important part in the Eastern Question

boss (bɔs, bɒs) 1. n. an employer || a foreman || a person in charge || the professional manager of a political organization 2. v.t. to direct or manage (a business, a show etc.) **to boss about** (or **around**) to order about in a domineering way [fr. Du. baas, master]

boss 1. n. a rounded protuberance || the round ornamental knob on the center of a shield || (archit.) a projecting part at the point of intersection of vault ribs || (mech.) the enlarged part of a shaft 2. v.t. to ornament with bosses [O.F. boce]

bos·sa no·va (bósə nóuvə) n. 1. sophisticated Brazilian version of the samba, sometimes with strong jazz influence. 2. the music

boss-eyed (bósaid, bɒ́said) adj. (Br., pop.) crosseyed

boss-shot (bósʃɒt, bɒ́sʃɒt) n. (Br., pop.) a bad shot or guess

Bos·suet (bɒswei), Jacques-Bénigne (1627–1704), French divine. He was an impassioned preacher, a prolific author, a historian, a political thinker, and the defender of orthodoxy against Protestantism and against the quietism of Fénelon. He was tutor to the dauphin (1670–80) and was made bishop of Meaux (1681). His works include 'Discours sur l'histoire universelle' (1681), 'Histoire des variations des églises protestantes' (1688) and 'Politique tirée de l'Ecriture Sainte' (1709). His sermons and funeral orations are masterpieces of eloquence

bos·sy (bósi:, bɒ́si:) comp. **bos·si·er** superl. **bos·si·est** adj. domineering, fond of giving orders

Bos·ton (bóstən, bɒ́stən) the capital (pop. 562,944, with agglom. 2,589,000) of Massachusetts, a port, important industrially and commercially and a center of learning. First settled in 1630, Boston was one of the centers of resistance to British rule during the Revolutionary War (1775–83). City has grown more than 35 times its colonial size. It was site of 1st American public school and public library. Urban renewal in 1960s added several prominent skyscrapers to the city's skyline

Boston arm electronically operated prosthetic limb that responds to will; developed in four Boston hospitals

Boston ivy Japanese ivy

Boston Massacre (Am. hist.) a riot (Mar. 5, 1770) in Boston, Massachusetts, in which several townspeople were killed by British troops. It was one of the incidents leading up to the Revolutionary War (1775–83)

Boston Tea Party (Am. hist.) an incident (Dec. 16, 1773) in which three shiploads of tea were dumped into Boston harbor by citizens demonstrating against British taxation of tea. The struggle against 'taxation without representation' led up to the Revolutionary War (1775–83)

bo·sun (bóus'n) n. a boatswain

Bos·well (bózwəl, bɒ́zwel), James (1740–95), Scottish author and lawyer. His friendship with Dr. Johnson began during the period in which he attempted, and failed, to obtain by court influence a livelihood in London, and ended only with Johnson's death. Of his works the most famous are the 'Life of Samuel Johnson, LL.D.' (1791), a classic of English biography, and the 'Journal of a Tour to the Hebrides with Samuel Johnson, LL.D.' (1785). He chronicled his own racy private life voluminously

Bos·worth Field, Battle of (bózwərθ) the final battle (Aug. 22, 1485) of the Wars of the Roses, in which Richard III was defeated and killed by Henry Tudor, who then became Henry VII

Bot·a·ny Bay (bót'ni:) a bay on the east coast of Australia, discovered by Cook (1770). The first Australian penal settlement was established nearby (1788)

bot, bott (bɒt) n. the parasitic larva of the botfly, esp. that attacking the horse [origin unknown]

bo·tan·ic (bətǽnik) adj. botanical **bo·tán·i·cal** adj. of or pertaining to botany [fr. M.L. botanicas fr. Gk]

botanical garden a place in which plant collections are grown for display and scientific study. It usually comprises herbarium, laboratories and museum, and frequently offers teaching and training facilities

botanical pesticide plant-produced chemical used to control pests, e.g., nicotine or strychnine

bot·a·nist (bót'nist) n. a specialist in botany [F. botaniste]

bot·a·nize (bót'naiz) pres. part. **bot·a·niz·ing** past and past part. **bot·a·nized** v.i. to study plants where they grow || to collect plants for study [fr. Mod. L. botanizare fr. Gk]

bot·a·ny (bót'ni:) n. the branch of biology concerned with plant life and all its manifestations (cf. ZOOLOGY) || the plant life of a given region

botany wool a fine grade of wool from Merino sheep, mainly supplied by Australia [after Botany Bay, Australia]

botch (bɒtʃ) 1. n. a badly done piece of work 2. v.t. to bungle (a piece of work) **botched** adj. [M.E. bocchen]

bot·fly (bótflai) pl. **bot·flies** n. any of several two-winged, large or medium-sized flies whose larvae are parasitic in sheep, horses, man etc.

both (bouθ) 1. adj. the two, each of two, both girls are pretty 2. pron. the one and the other, both are pretty, they are both pretty, both of them are pretty 3. adv. (with 'and') at the same time, she is both pretty and rich, both Europe and Asia are involved [M.E. bāthe prob. fr. O.N. bāthar]

Bo·tha (bóuta), Louis (1862–1919), South African statesman and general. He fought Britain in the Boer War, then became the first prime minister (1910–19) of the Union of South Africa. He advocated cooperation with the British and took South Africa into the 1st world war against Germany

Bo·tha, (bóuta) Pieter Willem (1916–), South African prime minister (1978–). After serving in various government posts, he began his prime ministership amid a bribery scandal. His attempts to soften South Africa's *apartheid* policies, such as relaxation (1986) of the hated pass laws for blacks, were opposed by many whites and criticized as inadequate by blacks

both·er (bóðər) 1. *n.* inconvenience ‖ a nuisance ‖ disturbance ‖ a fuss 2. *v.t.* to worry persistently ‖ *v.i.* (with 'about' or 'with') to take trouble, *they never bother with repairs* ‖ (with the infinitive) to take the trouble, *don't bother to get supper for me* 3. *interj.* an expression of impatience [origin unknown]

both·er·a·tion (bɒðəréiʃən) 1. *n.* (*pop.*) something that bothers, a nuisance 2. *interj.* an exclamation of impatience

both·er·some (bóðərsəm) *adj.* causing bother

Both·ni·a, Gulf of (bóθni:ə) a northern arm of the Baltic Sea, between Sweden and Finland, generally frozen in winter

Both·well (bóθwəl, bóθwel), James Hepburn, earl of (1535–78), Scottish nobleman, third husband of Mary queen of Scots, generally regarded as the leader of Darnley's murderers

bo tree (bou) *Ficus religiosa*, fam. *Moraceae*, the pipal tree of India, esp. the sacred tree at Buddh Gaya, under which Gautama received heavenly enlightenment and became the Buddha [fr. Singhalese *bo* fr. Pali *bodhi*, perfect knowledge tree]

Bot·swa·na (bɒtswánə) (formerly Bechuanaland) a republic (area 222,000 sq. miles, pop. 1,038,000) in central S. Africa. Capital: Gaberones. Chief tribes: Bamangwato (capital: Serowe), Bakwena, Bangwaketse, Batawana. Languages: Bantu (chief language: Tswana). The land (only 5% arable) is arid and undulating (3,000 ft), rocky in the southeast, marshy in the north (Okavango basin) and semi-desert in the west. The Kalahari desert covers the center and south. The climate is subtropical with summer rain (25 ins. in the north, 10 ins. in the southwest). Occupations: cattle raising, dairy farming. Mineral resources: gold, kyanite, asbestos, manganese. Exports: livestock, meat, hides, skins. Imports: textiles, corn, manufactured goods. Monetary unit: South African rand. HISTORY. The country was torn by intertribal warfare when British missionaries arrived (early 19th c.). A long struggle with the Boers of the Transvaal led to the establishment of the British protectorate of Bechuanaland (1885). The southern part was incorporated in Cape Colony (1895). Bechuanaland was a High Commission Territory (1891–1964). Seretse Khama was elected its first prime minister (1965–80). It became an independent republic within the Commonwealth (Sept. 30, 1966) and changed its name to Botswana. It joined the U.N. (1966)

bott *BOT

Bot·ti·cel·li (bɒtitʃéli:), Sandro (Alessandro di Mariano dei Filipepi, 1444–1510), Florentine painter, illustrator and engraver. He was patronized by the Medicis. 'Primavera' and the 'Birth of Venus' are his most famous works. Their grave, elaborate and delicate beauty is seen also in his religious paintings (e.g. frescos in the Sistine Chapel, Rome) and in other mythological and allegorical works. Their impact depends much on outline, and his illustrations to Dante (drawings) further reveal his genius for contour

bot·tle (bót'l) 1. *n.* a narrow-necked vessel without a handle, usually of glass, for containing liquid ‖ the contents of a bottle ‖ the amount contained by a bottle **the bot·tle** alcoholic liquor 2. *v.t.* *pres. part.* **bot·tling** *past* and *past part.* **bot·tled** to put into bottles ‖ to preserve in glass jars **to bottle up** to restrain (feelings etc.) [O.F. *bouteille*]

bot·tle-fed (bót'lfed) *adj.* (of a child or animal) not fed with mother's milk

bot·tle·feed (bót'lfi:d) *v.* to feed with a bottle, e.g., as an infant is fed; often used metaphorically meaning "to coddle"

bottle glass coarse, dark green glass

bot·tle·neck (bót'lnek) *n.* a narrowing in a road, where traffic may become congested ‖ any similar obstruction to flow

bottleneck guitar glissando style created by pressing a bar or neck of a bottle on guitar strings

bottle party a party to which each guest is expected to bring a bottle of alcoholic drink

bot·tom (bótəm) 1. *adj.* lowest, last, *bottom price* ‖ frequenting the bottom, *bottom fish* ‖ **bet one's bottom dollar** to stake everything one has 2. *n.* the lowest interior or exterior part

of anything ‖ the seat (of a chair) ‖ the buttocks ‖ the bed of the sea, a lake, river, or pond ‖ the low land in a river basin ‖ any low-lying land ‖ the less exalted or distinguished end of a table, class etc. ‖ the innermost, remotest part, e.g. of a bay ‖ (*naut.*) that part of a hull under water when a ship is floating ‖ the basic facts, foundation, reality, *to get to the bottom of a mystery* ‖ the source, *who is at the bottom of the scheme?* **at bottom** essentially **from the bottom of my heart** with deep feeling **to go to the bottom** (of a ship) to sink **to send to the bottom** to sink (a ship) 3. *v.i.* to touch the bottom (of the sea etc.) ‖ *v.t.* to put a bottom on ‖ to bring (a submarine etc.) to the bottom [O.E. *botm*]

bottom dollar lowest possible price. *ant* top dollar

bottom drawer (*Br.*) a hope chest

bottom gear (*Br.*) low gear, first gear, the lowest gear in a car etc.

bottom lands (*envir.*) area adjacent to, and only slightly higher than, a stream channel

bot·tom·less (bótəmlis) *adj.* very deep, too deep to fathom

bottom line the ultimate result. **—bottomline** *adj.* **—bottomline** *v.* to consider only the ultimate result

bot·tom·most (bótəmmoust, *esp. Br.* bótəmməst) *adj.* that is at the very bottom

bottom out (*securities*) the point in graph of security prices at which strong resistance to sales at a lower price is met, indicating a potential rise in price. **—bottom out** *v* to reach a low point

bot·tom·ry (bótəmri:) 1. *n.* (*marine law*) a system of lending money to a shipowner on the security of his ship 2. *v.t.* *pres. part.* **bot·tom·ry·ing** *past* and *past part.* **bot·tom·ried** to pledge (a ship) in such a way

bot·u·lism (bótʃəlizəm) *n.* (*med.* and *vet.*) food poisoning caused by eating the toxin of the bacillus *Clostridium botulinum*, sometimes found in sausages or in preserved food [fr. L. *botulus*, sausage]

Boua·ké (bwækéi) a market and communications center (pop. 805,356) in central Ivory Coast, on the northern edge of the tropical forest

bou·bou (bú:bu:) *n.* traditional long, shapeless dress of men and women in Mali, Senegal, and other areas in West Africa

Bou·cher (bu:ʃéi), François (1703–70), French painter. His delicately voluptuous handling of pastoral and mythological subjects makes him one of the most admired painters of the 18th c.

Bouches-du-Rhône (bu:ʃdyroun) a department (area 2,025 sq. miles, pop. 1,633,000) of S.E. France on the east side of the Rhône delta. Chief town: Marseille (*PROVENCE)

Bou·dic·ca (bu:díkə) *BOADICEA

Bou·din (bu:dẽ), Louis Eugène (1824–98), French marine painter, and a forerunner of the Impressionists, to whose first exhibition in 1874 he contributed

Boud·i·not (búd'nou), Elias (1740–1821), U.S. lawyer and public official. He served as president (Nov. 1782–Oct. 1783) of the Continental Congress. He was later director (1795–1805) of the U.S. Mint in Philadelphia. He was president of the American Bible Society, and he published 'The Age of Revelation' (1790)

bou·doir (bú:dwɑr, bú:dwɔr) *n.* a lady's small private room [F. fr. *bouder*, to sulk (= a place to sulk in)]

bouf·fant (bu:fánt) *adj.* (of skirts) giving a puffed-out appearance ‖ (of hairdos) given a puffed-out appearance [F. = swelling]

Bou·gain·ville (bú:gənvil) the largest island (area 3,500 sq. miles, pop. 120,000) of the Solomon Is. in the Pacific. Named after the French navigator Louis Antoine de Bougainville (1729–1811), it is part of Papua New Guinea

bou·gain·vil·le·a (bu:gənvíli:ə) *n.* a member of *Bougainvillaea*, fam. *Nyctaginaceae*, a genus of plants of tropical America with lilac or red persistent bracts. They are luxuriant flowering creepers, cultivated in the tropics and subtropics [after L.A. de *Bougainville*]

bough (bau) *n.* a branch of a tree, esp. a main branch [O.E. *bóg, bóh*, bough]

bought *past* and *past part.* of BUY

bou·gie (bú:ʒi:, bú:dʒi:) *n.* (*med.*) a tapering instrument for dilating narrowed body passages, esp. the urethra [F.]

Bou·guer (bu:gei), Pierre (1698–1758), French hydrographer and mathematician. He was one of the founders of photometry

bouil·la·baisse (bu:jæbés, bu:ljəbéis) *n.* a Provençal dish containing various Mediterranean fish and shellfish cooked in water or white wine, with olive oil, garlic, tomato, saffron, and herbs [F. fr. Prov. *bouiabaissi*]

bouil·lon (búljɒn, búljən) *n.* a clear soup made esp. from beef [F. fr. *bouillir*, to boil]

Bou·lan·ger (bu:lɑ̃ʒéi), Georges (1837–91), French general and minister of war (1886–7), who attempted a coup d'état (1889) against the Third Republic, failed, and fled to Belgium

boul·der (bóuldər) *n.* a large stone, or mass of rock, rounded and smoothed by water, ice or wind [etym. doubtful]

boulder clay tough, stony clay, with embedded boulders, transported by glaciers and deposited when the ice melted

boule (bu:l) *n.* a synthetic crystallized form of aluminum oxide, of great hardness, used for the pivot cups of instruments such as watches [F. = ball]

boul·e·vard (búləvɑrd, bú:ləvɑrd) *n.* a broad street, usually with trees on either side or down the middle [F. fr. G. *bollwerk*, bulwark, the flat promenade on a rampart]

Boulle (bu:l), André Charles (1642–1732), French cabinetmaker, whose method of inlaying, esp. of chased brass devices into ebony, ivory etc. came to be, called buhl work

Bou·logne-sur-Mer (bu:lɒnjsyrmer) a Channel port (pop. 49,284) of N.E. France: fishing, fish canning, boatbuilding, cross-Channel tourist traffic

boul·ter (bóultər) *n.* a long fishing line with many hooks, used for bottom fishing [origin unknown]

Boul·ton (bóult'n), Matthew (1728–1809), English engineer. In partnership with James Watt, he was responsible for the manufacture and development of steam engines (1775–1800). He produced a new copper coinage for Great Britain (1797)

Boul·war·ism (bu:lwɔrizəm) *n.* method of collective bargaining based on making a "fair" offer and not deviating from it; conceived by Lemuel Boulware for General Electric Co. in the 1950s

Bou·me·dienne (bu:mədjen), Houari (1927–78), Algerian soldier and statesman. He seized power in Algeria (1965) after deposing Ben Bella and became prime minister (1965–78)

bounce (bauns) 1. *n.* a sudden rebound, e.g. of a rubber ball ‖ vitality ‖ (*Br.*) self-importance 2. *v. pres. part.* **bouncing** *past* and *past part.* **bounced** *v.t.* to cause to rebound, *to bounce a ball* ‖ (*pop.*) to throw out of a bar etc. ‖ *v.i.* to rebound ‖ to jump up ‖ (*pop.*, of a check) to be refused by a bank because there is not enough money in the account to cover it **bóunc·er** *n.* (*Am.=Br.* chucker-out) an attendant employed to eject people who make themselves a nuisance in dance halls, nightclubs etc. **bóunc·ing** *adj.* full of health and vitality [M.E. *bunsen*, to thump fr. Du. or L.G.]

bound (baund) *adj.* (often with 'for') making the trip to, on the way to, *a ship bound for Rio* ‖ going, *homeward bound* [M.E. *boun* fr. O.N. *búinn*, repaired]

bound 1. *n.* a springy jump, a leap up or forward ‖ a rebound, a bounce e.g. of a ball 2. *v.i.* to leap ‖ to run leaping, *the dog went bounding after the ball* [F. *bondir*, to leap]

bound 1. *n.* a limit of an estate etc. ‖ (usually *pl.*) restraining rules, laws or standards, *beyond the bounds of decency* **out of bounds** not to be entered 2. *v.t.* to set limits to ‖ (*computer*) to set maximum output where input voltage is greater than planned ‖ to set upper or lower permitted limits ‖ (esp. in passive, with 'by') to delimit by boundaries, *a garden bounded by a stream* [O.F. *bonde, bodne*]

bound *past* and *past part.* of BIND ‖ *adj.* sure, *he's bound to see you there* ‖ obliged, *he was bound to admit he was wrong* ‖ (*fig.*) morally attached, *bound by ties of friendship* ‖ (*pop.*) determined, *she's bound to get up whatever the doctor says* ‖ provided with a binding ‖ constipated ‖ tied by binding **bound up** (with 'with') involved in ‖ (with 'in') devoted to

bound·a·ry (báundəri:, báundri:) *pl.* **bound·a·ries** *n.* the real or understood line marking a limit ‖ (*cricket*) a hit which sends the ball over the line limiting the field: it scores 4 runs, or 6 if it does not bounce inside the line

bound·er (báundər) *n.* (*Br.*, *old-fash.*) a pushing, loud, ill-mannered fellow ‖ (*Br.*) a man who behaves in an unprincipled manner, esp. in his relations with women

---

CONCISE PRONUNCIATION KEY: **(a)** æ, cat; ɑ, car; ɔ fawn; ei, snake. **(e)** e, hen; i:, sheep; iə, deer; ɛə, bear. **(i)** i, fish; ai, tiger; ə:, bird. **(o)** o, ox; au, cow; ou, goat; u, poor; ɔi, royal. **(u)** ʌ, duck; u, bull; u:, goose; ə, bacillus; ju:, cube. x, loch; θ, think; δ, bother; z, Zen; ʒ, corsage; dʒ, savage; ŋ, orangutang; j, yak; ʃ, fish; tʃ, fetch; 'l, rabble; 'n, redden. Complete pronunciation key appears inside front cover.

bound·less (báundlis) *adj.* without limits ‖ vast

boun·te·ous (báuntiəs) *adj.* (*old-fash.*) generously giving ‖ freely and generously given, *a bounteous gift* ‖ plentiful, *a bounteous crop* [M.E. *bontyous* fr. O.F.]

boun·ti·ful (báuntifəl) *adj.* bounteous, freely giving ‖ (*old-fash.*) abundant

boun·ty (báunti:) *pl.* **boun·ties** *n.* liberality in giving, generosity ‖ a sum of money given as a subsidy or reward, esp. by a government [O.F. *bontet*, goodness]

'Boun·ty', Mutiny of the (báunti:) a famous mutiny (Apr. 1789) on a British merchant ship near the Friendly Is. in the South Seas. The commander, William Bligh, and several crew members sailed 4,000 miles in a small open boat, reaching Timor in June. The mutineers settled on Pitcairn Is.

bou·quet (bu:kéi, boukéi) *n.* a bunch of flowers ‖ the distinctive perfume of a wine [O.F.]

bouquet mine (*mil.*) in naval mine warfare, a mine in which a number of buoyant mine cases are attached to the same sinker, so that when the mooring of one mine case is cut, another mine rises from the sinker to its set depth

Bour·bon (buəːrbõ) a European royal dynasty. The first house of Bourbon was founded in France (late 13th c.), when a Capetian prince married the Bourbonnais heiress. Descendants held the title from 1327 to 1527, until dispossessed by François I. The title passed to a younger branch, who ruled France 1589–1792 and 1814–30 (Henri IV, Louis XIII, Louis XIV, Louis XV, Louis XVI, Louis XVII and Charles X). Another younger branch, the Orléans family, returned to power (1830–48) under Louis Philippe. Other branches of the Bourbons ruled in Spain (1700–1931), the Two Sicilies (1734–1860) and Parma (1748–1860)

bour·bon (bə́:rbən) *n.* a whiskey distilled from mainly corn mash ‖ (búərbən) *Rosa borboniana*, a rose probably resulting from a cross between *R. chinensis* and *R. gallica*

Bour·bon·nais (buərbɔnei) a former province of France in the N. Massif Central, forming modern Allier and part of Puy-de-Dôme. In the west are wooded hills, in the east the alluvial plain of the Loire. Products: lumber, cattle. Main towns: Moulins (historic capital), Montluçon, Vichy. The domain of the first house of Bourbon, it passed to the crown (1527) by confiscation

Bour·da·loue (bu:rdælu:), Louis (1632–1704), French preacher. He was penetrating in psychology, fearless in attack, and popular with the court and with the people. He abandoned preaching for work in prisons and hospitals

Bour·delle (bu:rdel), Antoine (1861–1929), French monumental sculptor, painter and teacher, much influenced by Rodin

bour·don (búərd'n, bɔ́rd'n, bóurd'n) *n.* an organ stop of low (16-ft) pitch ‖ a similar stop in a harmonium ‖ the lowest bell in a peal of bells ‖ the drone pipe of bagpipes [F.=drone]

Bour·don gauge (búərd'n) a partly flattened, curved tube which, tending to straighten under internal pressure, indicates the fluid pressure applied to it. It is used e.g. with steam boilers [after Eugène *Bourdon* (1804-84), F. engineer, its inventor]

bour·geois (búərȝwɑ, burȝwá) 1. *adj.* belonging to or typical of the middle classes ‖ having self-centered, materialistic and conformist ideas 2. *n.* someone having such limited ideas ‖ a member of the middle classes ‖ (bərdȝóis) an old size of type (about 9 point) [F.]

bour·geoi·sie (buərȝwɑzí:) *n.* the middle classes ‖ (in Marxist ideology) the capitalist class [F.]

bour·geoi·si·fi·ca·tion (buərȝwɑzifikéifən) *n.* becoming, or making into, a middle-class person, or instilling or applying middle-class ideas. **—bourgeoisified** *adj.* *syn* (French) embourgeoisement

bourgeon *BURGEON

Bourges (bu:rȝ) the chief town (pop. 80,379) of the Cher, central France, in the Berry. Industries: aeronautical and metallurgical engineering, metalwork, woolen goods. Cathedral (13th c.) with splendid stained glass. Jacques Cœur's palace (c. 1443)

Bour·ges (bə́:rdȝes) *n.* transport sheets overlaid to provide color in artwork for reproduction

Bour·get (bu:rȝei), a lake (11 miles long, area 17 sq. miles) in the Savoy Alps, France

Bour·gogne (bu:rgɔnj) *BURGUNDY

Bour·gui·ba (burgí:bə), Habib ibn Ali (1903–

), Tunisian statesman, principal architect of Tunisian independence, and first president of Tunisia from 1957. In 1975 he was proclaimed president for life

Bourne·mouth (bɔ́rnməθ, bóurnməθ, búərnməθ) a resort and county borough (pop. 144,803) in Hampshire, England, on the English Channel

Bourse (bu:rs) *n.* the Paris stock exchange [F.]

bou·stro·phe·don (baustrəfíːd'n, bustrəfíːd'n) *n.* (*hist.*) the early Greek method of writing from right to left, then left to right, etc. ‖ layer of microforms with rows alternating successively from left to right and right to left to facilitate the location of successive frames; used in reference to microfiche and microfilm [Gk fr. *bous*, ox + *strophos*, a turning]

bout (baut) *n.* a period (of work or other activity), *a bout of exercise, a drinking bout* ‖ a fit or period (of illness) ‖ a fight, trial of strength, *a wrestling bout* [origin doubtful]

bou·tique (bu:tí:k) *n.* a chic little store selling smart or fashionable clothes and accessories [F.]

bou·tiqui·er (bu:tí:ki:éər) *n.* one who operates a boutique

bou·ton·niere (bu:t'njéər, bu:t'ní:r) *n.* (*Am.*=*Br.* buttonhole) a flower worn on the lapel [F. *boutonnière*]

Bou·troux (bu:tru:), Etienne Emile Marie (1845–1921), French philosopher. His works include 'De la contingence des lois de la nature' (1874). He taught Bergson

Bouts (bauts), Dirk (or Dierick, c. 1415–75), Netherlands painter who worked at Louvain and Brussels. Only two paintings certainly by him survive, the 'Five Mystic Meals' at Louvain, and two panels of the unfinished 'Justice of the Emperor Otto', at Brussels. A deep calm and a strange blend of intimacy and majesty mark his style

Bou·vines, Battle of (bu:vi:n) the victory (1214) of Philippe II of France over the combined forces of King John of England, Otto IV of Germany, and the count of Flanders

bou·zou·ki or bou·sou·ki (buzú:ki:) *n.* Greek stringed musical instrument

Bo·ves (bóves), José Tomás (1783–1814), Spanish guerrilla fighter. At the head of his irregulars, he harassed and defeated the Venezuelan patriots under Simón Bolívar

bo·vine (bóuvain, bóuvin, bóuvi:n) *adj.* of or pertaining to an ox or a cow ‖ (of humans) cowlike [fr. L. *bovinus*]

bow (bau) *n.* (*naut.*, often *pl.*) the forepart of a ship ‖ the bow oar **on the port** (or **starboard**) **bow** within 45° left (or right) of the point straight ahead [perh. Dan. *boug* or Du. *boeg*, ship's bow]

bow (bou) 1. *n.* a weapon made of a long strip of wood, tensely arched by means of a cord stretched between the ends, used for shooting arrows (*CROSSBOW, *LONGBOW) ‖ a strip of wood with horsehairs stretched between the ends, used in playing the violin and some other string instruments ‖ a stroke of such a bow ‖ a slipknot, often ornamental, formed by doubling a shoelace, ribbon, etc., into one or two loops **to draw the long bow** (*Br.*) to exaggerate **to have more than one string to one's bow** to have more than one plan or idea 2. *v.t.* to use a bow on (a violin etc.) ‖ *v.i.* to use the bow on a violin etc. ‖ to curve in an arch [O.E. *boga*]

bow (bau) 1. *n.* a bending of the head or body, in respect, greeting, assent etc. 2. *v.t.* to cause to bend, *to bow one's head* ‖ to express by bowing, *to bow one's appreciation* ‖ (with 'in' or 'out') to show (a person) in or out with a bow ‖ *v.i.* to submit or give in, *to bow to the inevitable* ‖ to bend the head or body in respect, greeting, politeness etc. **to bow one's knee** to genuflect [O.E. *būgan*]

Bow bells (bou) the bells of St. Mary-le-Bow, a Wren church in the City of London **within the sound of Bow bells** in the City of London, the birthplace of a true Cockney

bow compass (bou) a pair of compasses whose legs are joined by spring steel, with a screw-thread adjustment

bowd·ler·ism (báudlərizəm, bóudlərizəm) *n.* bowdlerization

bowd·ler·i·za·tion (baudlərizéifən, boudlərizéifən) *n.* the act or result of bowdlerizing

bowd·ler·ize (báudləraiz, bóudləraiz) *pres. part.* **bowd·ler·iz·ing** *past* and *past part.* **bowd·ler·ized** *v.t.* to expurgate (a book etc.) by removing or modifying parts considered improper or in-

delicate [after Thomas *Bowdler*, who published an expurgated edition of Shakespeare in 1818]

bowed (baud) *adj.* (often with 'down') having the head inclined, through grief, age, cares etc.

bow·el (báuəl, baul) *n.* (usually *pl.*) the intestine, the lower end of the alimentary canal ‖ entrails ‖ (*rhet.*) the innermost part, *deep in the bowels of the earth* [O.F. *boel*]

bow·er (báuər) *n.* (*naut.*) either of two anchors, the best bower and small bower, carried at a ship's bow [BOW, fore-end of a ship]

bower *n.* a leafy shelter, an arbor [O.E. *bur*, dwelling]

bower anchor a bower

bow·er·bird (báuərbə:rd) *n.* a bird of fam. *Paradiseaidae* found in Australia (esp. in New South Wales) and New Guinea. They make bowerlike structures adorned with feathers, shells and brightly colored objects. These are not nests, but resorts used esp. during the breeding season

bow·er·y (báuəri:, báuri:) *pl.* **bow·er·ies** *n.* a Dutch colonial farm or plantation and its buildings **the Bow·er·y** a section and street in lower Manhattan, New York City, known as a place where homeless derelicts live [Du. *bouwerij*, farm]

bow·head (bóuhed) *n.* a Greenland whale

Bo·wie (bouí:) James (1796–1836), U.S. Western frontier hero who was killed at the ALAMO during the Texas Revolution. He is credited with the invention of the Bowie knife

bow·ie knife (bóui:, bú:i:) a long hunting knife, straight, single-edged, but double-edged at the point [after James *Bowie* (1799-1836), U.S. soldier, or his brother Rezin]

bow·ing acquaintance (báuiŋ) (with 'a') a slight friendship, limited to conversational politeness ‖ (with 'a') a person with whom one is on these terms

bowl (boul) 1. *n.* a heavy wooden ball for rolling in the game of lawn bowling, esp. one shaped and weighted on one side to make it run a curved course ‖ a flattened or spherical wooden ball for English ninepins ‖ a heavy cylindrical roller used in a calender 2. *v.t.* to make (something, esp. a hoop) roll along the ground ‖ (*cricket*) to deliver (a ball) to the batsman ‖ to get (a batsman) out by hitting the wicket in bowling ‖ to score at bowling ‖ *v.i.* to play lawn bowling ‖ to go bowling ‖ to have a turn at bowling or lawn bowling ‖ to move smoothly and rapidly, esp. in a vehicle, *to bowl along* **to bowl over** to knock down ‖ to overwhelm [M.E. *boule* fr. F.]

bowl *n.* a deep, round basin or dish for holding liquids, food etc. ‖ the contents of such a dish ‖ the bowl-shaped part of anything [O.E. *bolla*]

bow·leg·ged (bóulegid, bóulegd) *adj.* with legs curved outwards

bow·ler (bóulər) *n.* (*Br.*) a derby [after *Bowler*, 19th-c. English hatter]

bow·line (bóulain) *n.* (*naut.*) a rope from the weather side of a sail to the bow, used for keeping that edge of the sail stretched tight ‖ a simple but very secure knot [etym. doubtful]

bowl·ing (bóuliŋ) *n.* any of several games in which pins are bowled at, e.g. ninepins, tenpins ‖ the action of delivering the ball in cricket ‖ the activity of playing lawn bowling

bowling alley (*Br.*) a long enclosed piece of ground for the playing of English ninepins ‖ a long wooden lane for bowling ‖ the building containing the alleys

bowling crease (*cricket*) the line marking the end of the bowler's run before he delivers the ball

bowling green a very smooth lawn for playing lawn bowling

bowls (boulz) *n.* lawn bowling

Bow·man (bóumən), Isaiah (1878–1950), U.S. geographer and educator. He published the first comprehensive work on the physiographic divisions of the U.S.A. ('Forest Physiography', 1911). As director of the American Geographical Society (1915–35), he made it into a world-famous institution. He was president (1935–48) of Johns Hopkins University

bow·man (bóumən) *pl.* **bow·men** (bóumən) *n.* an archer

bow oar (bau) the oarsman nearest the bow

bow·shot (bóufɔt) *n.* the range within which an arrow is effective

bow·sprit (bóusprit, báusprit) *n.* (*naut.*) a spar jutting forwards from the bow of a boat, to which forestays are fastened [etym. doubtful]

CONCISE PRONUNCIATION KEY: (a) æ, c*a*t; ɑ, c*a*r; ɔ f*aw*n; ei, sn*a*ke. **(e)** e, h*e*n; i:, sh*ee*p; iə, d*ee*r; ɛə, b*ea*r. **(i)** i, f*i*sh; ai, t*i*ger; ə:, b*i*rd. **(o)** o, *o*x; au, c*ow*; ou, g*oa*t; u, p*oo*r; ɔi, r*oy*al. **(u)** ʌ, d*u*ck; u, b*u*ll; u:, g*oo*se; ə, b*a*cillus; ju:, c*u*be. x, lo*ch*; θ, *th*ink; δ, bo*th*er; z, *Z*en; ȝ, corsa*g*e; dȝ, sava*g*e; ŋ, orangutan*g*; j, *y*ak; ʃ, *fi*sh; tʃ, fe*tch*; 'l, rabb*le*; 'n, redd*en*. Complete pronunciation key appears inside front cover.

bow·string (bóustriŋ) *n.* the string of a bow
bow thruster forward propeller in ship's bow that forces water through underwater tubes to turn the ship and to facilitate docking
bow tie a man's necktie tied in a bow
bow window (bou) a curved bay window
box (bɒks) **1.** *n.* a container, usually lidded, made of a stiff material such as pasteboard, wood, metal etc. ‖ the contents of a box ‖ the quantity a box will hold ‖ a small separate compartment in a theater (usually at the side) with a few chairs in it ‖ a special compartment in a court of law, *jury box, witness box* ‖ a small hut or wooden shelter for a sentry or a signalman ‖ a compartment in a stable for a horse ‖ (*baseball*) the space where the batter stands ‖ a wide gash cut in a tree to collect sap or resin **2.** *v.t.* to enclose in a box, or a small space ‖ to divide off from other compartments **to box the compass** (*naut.*) to name the 32 points of the compass in their right order ‖ (*naut.*) to make a complete turn, ending where one began ‖ to turn in a circle in argument, etc. **to box up** to confine [O.E. fr. L.]
box 1. *n.* a cuff or slap (esp. on the ear) **2.** *v.i.* to fight with the fists covered in thickly padded gloves, in sport (*BOXING) *v.t.* to cuff (a person's ears)
box *n.* a member of *Buxus*, fam. *Buxaceae*, a genus of evergreen shrubs with small, dark, stiff leaves, used for hedging [O.E. fr. L. fr. Gk]
Box and Cox (bóksənkóks) (*Br.*) alternating or in alternation [from J. M. Morton's farce turned into the musical play 'Cox and Box' (1867) by F. C. Burnand and Arthur Sullivan, about two people never at home at the same time]
box barrage a barrier of shellfire laid down on three sides to isolate an area
box calf calfskin tanned with chrome salts, with square markings on the grain [after Joseph *Box*, London bootmaker]
box·car (bókskɑr) *n.* (*rail.*) a closed, roofed freight car
box drain a drain of rectangular section, usually of brickwork or concrete, used in sanitary engineering
box elder *Acer negundo*, a maple of E. and central U.S.A.
Box·er (bóksər) a member of a Chinese antiforeign secret society which organized the Boxer Rebellion (1900) in N. China and besieged the legations in Peking. Foreign forces restored order (1901) and obtained increased privileges. Russia extended its tutelage to Manchuria (*RUSSO-JAPANESE WAR)
box·er (bóksər) *n.* a medium-sized, short-haired, fawn or brindle dog, of a strong, playful breed originating in Germany [etym. doubtful]
box·haul (bókshɔl) *v.t.* (*naut.*) to bring (a square-rigged ship) on to the other tack by luffing and then veering around shortly on her heel, when space for turning is limited
box·ing (bóksiŋ) *n.* the sport of fighting with the fists, in accordance with the rules laid down. Boxing is governed by the Queensberry rules, set up by the marquis of Queensberry in 1865, revised 1890. The ring is 14-20 ft square, with ropes around it. Gloves, not less than 6 oz. in weight, must be worn. A contest is divided into not more than 15 three-minute rounds. Each boxer tries to knock his opponent out or score points for well-placed blows, skill or style. Hitting below the belt, hitting with unclenched fist or with the elbow, butting with the head or shoulders, or holding on to an opponent are fouls
boxing *n.* material for making boxes
Box·ing Day the first weekday after Christmas, a legal holiday in England, Wales, N. Ireland, New Zealand, Australia and South Africa. Christmas boxes (tips) are traditionally given to garbage collectors and a few other public servants
boxing gloves heavily padded, laced leather mittens worn in boxing
box kite a kite of paper or canvas stretched over a light frame in two boxlike sections
box office the ticket office in a theater ‖ receipts from a play ‖ appeal to a large popular audience, *the play was good box office*
box pleat a double pleat, with the cloth folded under at both sides, usually in a skirt
box spanner (*Br.*) a socket wrench
box spring mattress a mattress consisting of a honeycomb arrangement of spiral springs which are prevented from buckling by being

isolated from each other, in cloth compartments
box stall (*Am.=Br.* loose-box) a wide stall in which a horse is free to move about
box·wood (bókswʊd) *n.* the closegrained wood of the box shrub, used in turning and wood engraving
boy (bɔi) *n.* a male child, till puberty or young manhood ‖ a son of any age ‖ a familiar name for any man, old or young [M.E. *boi*, etym. doubtful]
Bo·ya·cá (bɔjɑká) a river in Colombia, and village on it that was the site of a battle (1819) in which Simón Bolívar routed the monarchists, ending Spanish rule in Nueva Granada
bo·yar (boujár, bɔiər) *n.* a member of the old Russian aristocracy before the time of Peter the Great [fr. Russ. *boyarin*, grandee]
boy·cott (bóikɒt) **1.** *v.t.* to join with others in refusing to have any dealings with (some other individual or group) ‖ (*commerce*) to exclude (a product) from a market by united action **2.** *n.* the act of boycotting [after Charles *Boycott*, ostracized in Ireland, 1880]
Boyd Orr, John, 1st Baron (1880–1971), British scientist. He founded and directed the Imperial Bureau of Animal Nutrition (1929). He became director-general of the Food and Agriculture Organization of the United Nations (1945–7), and received the Nobel peace prize (1949)
Boy·er (bwæjei), Jean Pierre (c. 1773–1850), president of Haiti (1818–43). He led the struggle that resulted in Haiti's independence. As president, he initiated the basic law codes of Haiti. Unpopular later, on account of his autocratic policy, he was ousted by a revolution
boy·friend (bóifrend) *n.* a male sweetheart or lover
boy·hood (bóihud) *n.* the period of being a boy
boy·ish (bóiiʃ) *adj.* characteristic of a boy
Boyle (bɔil), the Hon. Robert (1627–91), Anglo-Irish scientist who developed the air pump invented by von Guericke and used it to investigate what he termed 'the Spring and Weight of Air'. This led him to formulate Boyle's law. A founder member of the Royal Society, he also did pioneer work in chemistry
Boyle's law (*phys.*) the statement that at constant temperature the volume of a given mass of gas is inversely proportional to its pressure. It was formulated by Robert Boyle in 1662
Boyne (bɔin) a river in Eire rising in Kildare and flowing into the Irish Sea, famous as the scene of the defeat of James II by William III (1690) when James's hopes of regaining the English throne were destroyed
Boys (bɔiz), Charles Vernon (1855–1944), English physicist. He devised and used a greatly refined version of Cavendish's torsion balance for determining the mass of the earth and the gravitational constant. He invented the radio-micrometer. He discovered the properties of quartz fibers
boy scout a member of the movement founded (1908) in England by Lord Robert Baden-Powell to help boys to develop qualities, e.g. leadership, responsibility, usefulness to others, and comradeship, by training them in enjoyable open-air activities such as camping, tracking etc. There are groups all over the world. 'Scout' is now the preferred term
boy·sen·ber·ry (bóiznberi) *pl.* **boy·sen·ber·ries** *n.* the fruit of a large reddish-black bramble, with the taste of a raspberry ‖ the plant which bears this, developed in California by crossing blackberries and raspberries [after Rudolf *Boysen*, the breeder]
Bozen (bótsən) *BOLZANO
BP *n.* (*acronym*) for **1.** beautiful people. **2.** acronym for Black Panther
bpi acronym for bits or bytes per in
BQM-34 *FIREBEE
bra (brɑ) *n.* a brassiere
Bra·bant (brəbænt, bræbɑ̃) a province (area 1,267 sq. miles, pop. 2,221,782) of central Belgium, in which Brussels lies. It was part of the powerful medieval duchy of Brabant which passed to the house of Burgundy in 1406, and to the Hapsburgs in 1477 (*BELGIUM)
brace (breis) *n.* (*carpentry*) the tool into which a bit is inserted for boring holes ‖ (*engin.*) a rod, girder etc., used to strengthen a structure by its power to hold under tension ‖ a cord or rod for tightening (a drum) and keeping it tense ‖ (often *pl.*) a dental appliance worn to straighten crooked teeth ‖ (*pl., Br.*) suspenders for trousers ‖ a linking mark } in printing ‖ (*pl.* **brace**) a

pair, couple, esp. of pistols and of certain game birds or hunted animals, 10 *brace of pheasants*, *a brace of hares* ‖ (*naut.*) a rope attached to the end of a yard for trimming the sail (by pulling in or letting out) [O.F. *brace*, pair of arms]
brace *pres. part.* **brac·ing** *past* and *past part.* **braced** *v.t.* to fasten tightly ‖ to stretch into a state of tension ‖ to strengthen so as to resist pressure or weight, or to support ‖ to prepare to take a strain or a shock, *to brace one's back* ‖ to stimulate, *bracing air* ‖ (*naut.*) to move (a sail) by braces [fr. O.F. *bracier*, to embrace]
brace·let (bréislit) *n.* an ornamental band or chain worn on the arm [O.F.]
brac·er (bréisər) *n.* something which strengthens morale, e.g. an alcoholic drink or a piece of welcome news
bracer *n.* an archer's wrist guard [O.F. *brasseüre*]
bra·chi·al (bréiki:əl, bræki:əl) *adj.* (*physiol.*) pertaining to the arm ‖ like an arm [fr. L. *brachialis*]
bra·chi·ate (bréiki:it, bréiki:eit, bræki:it, bræki:eit) *adj.* (*bot.*) branched ‖ having opposite paired branches on alternate sides [fr. L. *brachiatus*, having arms]
bra·chi·o·pod (bréki:əpod) *n.* a member of *Brachiopoda*, a small phylum of marine invertebrates. A pair of 'arms' with tentacles, which cause a current of water to bring microscopic food to the mouth, protrude through the bivalve shell. This gives brachiopods a superficial resemblance to mussels and oysters [fr. Mod. L. *brachiopoda* fr. Gk *brachión*, arm+*pous* (*podos*), foot]
bra·chi·o·saur (bræki:əsɔr) *n.* a member of *Brachiosaurus*, a genus of very big dinosaurs of the Upper Jurassic [fr. Gk *brachión*,arm+*sauros*, lizard]
bra·chi·um (bréiki:əm, bræki:əm) *pl.* **bra·chi·a** (bréiki:ə, bræki:ə) *n.* (*anat.* and *zool.*) an arm or branching structure ‖ an upper limb between the shoulder and the elbow or forelimb of a vertebrate [L.= arm]
brach·y·ce·phal·ic (bræki:səfælik) *adj.* short-headed or broad-headed (of a skull whose breadth is at least four fifths its length) ‖ of a person or race characterized by such a skull (opp. DOLICHOCEPHALIC, *CEPHALIC INDEX)
brach·y·ceph·a·lous (bræki:séfələs) *adj.* [fr. Gk *brachus*, short+*kephalē*, head]
brach·y·ur·an (bræki:júərən) **1.** *adj.* of or relating to *Brachyura*, a suborder of decapod crustaceans consisting of the common crabs **2.** *n.* a brachyuran crustacean **brach·y·úr·ous** *adj.* [fr. Gk *brachus*, short+*oura*, tail]
brack·en (brækən) *n.* a member of *Pteridium*, a large genus of ferns distributed from the Arctic to the Tropics [fr. Scand.]
brack·et (brækit) **1.** *n.* a right-angled piece of metal, wood, stone etc. of which one surface bears on the upright and so allows the other surface to form a support ‖ one of a pair of punctuation marks [ ] to isolate the words enclosed in them from the surrounding text ‖ (*loosely*) one of a pair of parentheses ( ) or (*math.*) braces { } ‖ (*mil.*) in ranging, the distance between two shots on either side of a target ‖ a social classification, involving an upper and a lower limit, *income bracket, age bracket* **2.** *v.t.* to enclose within brackets, esp. (*math.*) to enclose (certain figures) in brackets to establish a relationship with other figures ‖ to couple together to show some kind of equality ‖ (*mil.*) to drop one shot short of, and one beyond (the target) in firing ranging rounds [older *bragget* fr. Span. *bragueta*, dim. of *braga*, breeches]
bracket creep (*economics*) the tendency of income tax rates to increase with inflation as taxpayers fall into higher brackets without an increase in real income
brack·ish (brækiʃ) *adj.* (of water) impure, slightly salt ‖ of unpleasant taste [perh. fr. Du. *brak*]
bract (brækt) *n.* a leaf in whose axil a flower grows ‖ a leaf on the floral axis, esp. one subtending the flower or flower cluster **brac·te·al** (brækti:əl), **brac·te·ate** (brækti:it) *adjs* [fr. L. *bractea*, thin leaf of metal]
brad (bræd) *n.* a thin, flat, slight-headed, short nail of uniform thickness, tapering in width [fr. O.N. *broddr*, spike]
brad·awl (brædɔl) *n.* a small non-spiral chiseledged tool for boring holes for screws etc.
Brad·dock (brædək), Edward (1695–1755), British general. He commanded (1755) all British forces in North America during the

French and Indian War. His force cut the first road across the Allegheny Mtns

Brad·ford (brǽdfərd), William (c. 1590–1657), one of the Pilgrims, elected governor of Plymouth Colony (1621–57)

Bradford an industrial city (pop. 457,677) in West Yorkshire, England, center of the English woolen industry since medieval times. Textile machinery is also manufactured

Brad·ley (brǽdli:), Andrew Cecil (1851–1935), English critic, best known for his 'Shakespearean Tragedy' (1904) and 'Oxford Lectures on Poetry' (1909). One of the first 'psychological' critics, he made detailed analyses of the characters of Shakespeare's tragedies

Bradley, Francis Herbert (1846–1924), English metaphysical thinker, author of 'Appearance and Reality' (1893)

Bradley, James (1693–1762), British astronomer who discovered the aberration of light (*ABERRATION) and the oscillation of the earth's axis. He became astronomer royal in 1742

Bradley, Omar Nelson (1893–1981), U.S. Army general. In Europe during the 2nd world war, he commanded the 12th Army Group under General Eisenhower. He served as Army Chief of Staff (1948–9) and as the first chairman of the Joint Chiefs of Staff (1949–53)

Bra·dy (bréidi:), Mathew B. (c. 1823–96), U.S. photographer, known for his battlefield pictures of every phase of the Civil War. He was the prototype of the 20th-c. war photographer. He also photographed all but one of the presidents of his age

brad·y·ki·nin (breidikaínin) n. (biochem.) protein that stimulates blood-vessel dilation, believed to produce swelling and pain. Cf NEUROKININ

brae (brei) n. (Scot.) a hillside [M.E. fr. O.N. brá]

Brae·mar (breimár) a district in Aberdeenshire, Scotland, in the Grampians, containing Balmoral and other royal residences, but no towns. It is famous for its annual Highland Games

brag (bræg) 1. n. a boast ‖ boasting talk ‖ that which is boasted about ‖ a card game like poker 2. v.i. pres. part. **brag·ging** past and past part. **bragged** (often with 'of' or 'about') to boast [origin unknown]

Bra·ga (brága) a town (pop. 48,730) in N.W. Portugal. Its archbishop is primate of Portugal

Bra·gan·ça, Bra·gan·za (brəgánsə) the reigning house of Portugal (1640–1910)

Bragg (bræg), Braxton (1817–76), Confederate general in the Civil War. An ineffective commander whose greatest failing lay in not following up his successes, he was nevertheless retained through the personal favor of President Jefferson Davis

Bragg, Sir William Henry (1862–1942), and Sir William Lawrence (1890–1971), English physicists, father and son, who used X rays to elucidate atomic and crystal structures. They shared a Nobel prize (1915)

brag·ga·do·ci·o (brægədóuʃi:ou) n. (rhet.) a boaster ‖ (rhet.) windy boasting [after Braggadocchio, a boastful character in Spenser's 'Faerie Queene', prob. fr. BRAG]

brag·gart (brǽgərt) n. someone who brags, a habitual boaster

Brahe (bra), Tycho (1546–1601), Danish astronomer whose observations of the sun and planets enabled his pupil Kepler to deduce his three laws of planetary motion. Brahe considered the earth to be fixed in space and that the other planets orbited the sun which, together with the moon and stars, revolved around the earth

Brah·ma (bráma) n. the Hindu creator of the universe, first god of the Hindu trinity (*VISHNU, *SIVA) [Hind.]

Brah·man (brámən) pl. Brah·mans n. a Brahmin ‖ an animal of a breed of cattle raised in the southern U.S.A., by crossbreeding from Indian stock, to increase the hardiness of U.S. breeds of beef cattle Brah·man·ic (brəmǽnik), Brah·mán·i·cal adjs

Brah·ma·nas (brámənəz) a collection of sacred Sanskrit texts (10th–7th cc. B.C.) representing explanatory commentaries on the relation of sacrificial and other ceremonial rites to the Vedas

Brah·man·ism (brámənizəm) n. the religious and social discipline of the Brahmins originating c. 550 B.C. and regarded as the orthodox Hindu religion because of its continuity with

the Vedic tradition of the Brahmanas and the Upanishads (*HINDUISM)

Brah·ma·pu·tra (brəməpú:trə) a river (1,800 miles long, navigable for 800 miles) of central Asia whose unity was unrecognized until the late 19th c. It rises in Tibet as the Tsangpo and flows east, then flows south and west through the Himalayas (as the Dihang), through the plains of Assam and East Pakistan to join the Ganges at its delta

Brah·ma·su·tras (brəməsú:trəz) a Vedanta philosophical treatise (prob. second half of the 4th c. A.D.)

Brah·min (brámin) pl. **Brah·min, Brah·mins** n. a Hindu of the first and highest of the four chief castes, comprising the priests (*KSHATRIYA, *SUDRA, *VAISYA) **Brah·min·ic, Brah·min·i·cal** adjs **Bráh·min·ism** n. [fr. Skr. brahmana fr. brahman, worship]

brah·mi·nee (brámini:) 1. adj. of the Brahmin caste 2. n. a female Brahmin

brahminee bull a white male zebu. These bulls are never slaughtered by Hindus

Brahms (brəmz), Johannes (1833–97), German composer. His music, esp. his early work and some of his piano and chamber music, shows a rhapsodic element, vigorous and strongly rhythmical. He is well known for his four symphonies, large compositions full of personal feeling, two piano concertos (1854–9 and 1882), a violin concerto (1879) and the 'German Requiem' (1868). His songs have an important place in the lieder tradition (*LIED)

braid (breid) n. a plait of hair made by weaving several strands together ‖ anything plaited ‖ silk etc. woven into an ornamental binding and used esp. on uniforms [O.E. brægd]

braid v.t. to plait (esp. hair) ‖ to ornament or trim by binding with ribbon ‖ to edge with braid [O.E. bregdan, to brandish, weave]

braided (bréidəd) adj. (geol.) of streams having diverging and converging channels separated by bars and islands

brail (breil) 1. n. (naut.) a thin rope attached to the edge of a sail for pulling the sail up or in for furling 2. v.t. (with 'up') to pull up by the brails [O.F. braiel, a band around the top of breeches]

Braille (breil) n. a system of representing letters and figures by raised dots, for use by the blind [after Louis Braille (1809-52), F. inventor]

Braille trail a nature trail designed for the blind

brain (brein) 1. n. that part of the central nervous system within the cranium that is the organ of thought, memory and emotion. It contains all the higher centers for various sensory impulses, and it initiates, controls and coordinates muscular movements ‖ in invertebrates, the corresponding regulating ganglion ‖ (loosely) the intellect **to have** (or **get**) **something on the brain** to be (or become) obsessed by something, e.g. a song or a fixed idea **to pick someone's brain** (or **brains**) to find out and use another's ideas **to rack one's brain** (or **brains**) to think very hard **to turn someone's brain** to cause someone to become insane 2. v.t. to dash out the brains of [O.E. brægn, brægen] —The brain is generally divided into three areas: the cerebrum, cerebellum and brainstem. The cerebrum, which is divided into two hemispheres, is the largest area of the brain. It is the origin of all voluntary actions. The cerebellum is the area that controls muscle coordination. The brainstem is continuous with the spinal cord through the foramen magnum. It is differentiated into four areas: medulla oblongata, pons Varolii, midbrain, and diencephalon. The motor and sensory tracts and the nuclei of the cranial nerves all originate in the brainstem

brain·child (bréintʃaild) pl. **brain·chil·dren** (bréintʃildrən) n. a person's invention (often of a practical order)

brain death (med.) cessation of brain activity as recorded for 5 hours on an electroencephalogram and constituting legal death in some jurisdictions. syn cerebral death

brain drain emigration of highly educated persons to areas with more opportunity, e.g., from England, India to U.S. —**brain-drain** v. — **brain-drainer** n one who emigrates

brain fever inflammation of the brain or its coverings

brain hor·mone (entomology) insect brain secretion that stimulates creation of moulting hormone ecdysone. Cf MOULTING HORMONE

brain·less (bréinlis) adj. witless, silly

brain·rins·ing (bréinrinsin) n. technique of creating a mental climate by immobility and constant verbal pressure. —**brainrinse** v.

brain·stem (bréinstem) n. the vertebrate brain excluding the cerebellum and cerebrum

brain·storm (bréinstɔrm) n. a sudden attack of uncontrolled emotion or confusion ‖ a brain wave (sudden good idea)

brain·storm·ing (bréinstɔrmin) n. technique for eliciting ideas, decisions, or solutions to problems by concentrated, uninhibited discussion among a small group of knowledgeable persons

brains trust a brain trust

brain trust a group of experts used for consultation, planning etc. ‖ a panel of experts giving unprepared answers to questions asked by an audience, esp. as a form of entertainment

brain·wash (bréinwɔʃ, bréinwɒʃ) v.t. to perform the act of brainwashing on (someone)

brain·wash·ing (bréinwɔʃin, bréinwɒʃin) n. the changing of a person's political or religious ideas by relentless indoctrination often to the point of mental torture

brain wave a sudden good idea, esp. one which resolves some problem ‖ the periodic changes in potential difference between different parts of the brain resulting in a detectable current ‖ the current produced (*ELECTROENCEPHALOGRAPH)

brain·y (bréini:) comp. **brain·i·er** superl. **brain·i·est** adj. (pop.) intelligent, clever above average

braise (breiz) pres. part. **brais·ing** past and past part. **braised** v.t. to cook slowly in fat and very little liquid in a tightly covered pan [F. braiser fr. braise, hot charcoal]

brake (breik) n. (Br.) a station wagon [etym. doubtful]

brake 1. n. a device for diminishing or preventing the motion of a body, usually by opposing a frictional force 2. v. pres. part. **brak·ing** past and past part. **braked** v.t. to slow down (a moving body) ‖ v.i. to operate or apply a brake [perh. fr. O.F. brac, lever or O. Du. braike, bridle]

brake n. a thicket ‖ bracken [rel. to M.L.G. brake]

brake 1. n. a toothed instrument for beating hemp or flax to separate the fiber ‖ an instrument for stripping off bark, esp. of willow ‖ a heavy harrow 2. v.t. pres. part. **brak·ing** past and past part. **braked** to crush (flax or hemp) by beating [M.L.G. brake or O. Du. braeke]

brake horsepower the maximum rate at which an engine can do work as measured by the resistance of an applied brake, expressed in horsepower

brake lining the part of a braking mechanism, usually made of asbestos and other materials, that produces friction and so arrests rotation

brake·man (bréikmən) pl. **brake·men** (bréikmən) n. the employee on a railroad train who operates the hand brakes etc. and assists the conductor

brake shoe a brake lining

brakes·man (bréiksmən) pl. **brakes·men** (bréiksmən) n. (Br.) a man responsible for the braking mechanism on a train

Bram·ah (bráma), Joseph (1748–1814), English inventor of the beer pump. He also improved the toilet mechanism and developed the hydraulic press

Bra·man·te (bramánte), Donato (c. 1444–1514), Italian architect of the Renaissance, who first used the forms of classical Roman architecture as an expression of the Renaissance spirit. He worked in Milan (e.g. the churches of S. Satiro with its octagonal sacristy and S. Maria delle Grazie) and Rome (e.g. the Tempietto di S. Pietro in Montorio), established the Greek-cross form of St. Peter's, and began the building of it in 1506. (Eventually responsibility passed to Michelangelo, who changed Bramante's designs)

bram·ble (brǽmb'l) n. a brier, any prickly bush or vine ‖ (esp. Br.) a blackberry [O.E. brǽmiel, brǽmbel]

bram·bling (brǽmblin) n. Fringilla montifringilla, the mountain finch or bramble finch, often bred as a cage bird

bram·bly (brǽmbli:) comp. **bram·bli·er** superl. **bram·bli·est** adj. resembling or having brambles

bran (bræn) n. the broken husks of grain separated from the ears by threshing [O.F. bren]

branch (bræntʃ, brʊntʃ) 1. n. a stem growing out from the trunk or from a bough of a tree ‖ a similar division, a river branch ‖ a subunit, the Canadian branch of the family 2. (computer) leaving the normal sequence of instructions ‖ an instruction to leave the normal procedure ‖ instructions completed as a result of a decision instruction ‖ selection of one of several paths based on a standard branch instruction 3. *v.i.* to put forth branches ‖ to subdivide ‖ (with 'out' or 'off') to spring as though in branches, *many minor roads branch off the main road* to **branch away** to diverge **to branch out** to expand in scope, enlarge one's activities [F. *branche*]

bran·chi·a (brǽŋki:ə) *pl.* **bran·chi·ae** (brǽŋki:i:) *n.* (*zool.*) a gill **brán·chi·al, bran·chi·ate** (brǽŋki:it, brǽŋki:eit) *adjs* [L. fr. Gk *branchia*, gills]

bran·chi·o·pod (brǽŋki:əpɔd) *n.* a member of *Branchiopoda*, a subclass of *Crustacea*. They are aquatic, with elongated bodies and many pairs of flattened limbs [fr. Gk *branchia*, gills+*pous* (*podos*), foot]

Bran·cu·si (brɑŋkúːzi:), Constantin (1876–1957), Rumanian sculptor, of the Ecole de Paris. His works are almost completely abstract, reducing the subjects (heads, birds, animals) to their quintessential form

Brand (brænt), Jan Hendrik (1826–88), president of the Orange Free State (1864–88)

brand (brænd) 1. *n.* a mark made by a hot iron, e.g. on cattle to identify ownership ‖ (*hist.*) an identification mark put on prisoners ‖ a trademark ‖ a proprietary make, blend etc., *a brand of tea* ‖ a piece of burning or charred wood ‖ an iron stamp for burning a mark ‖ a blight on leaves etc., characterized by a burnt look 2. *v.t.* to mark (cattle etc.) with a hot iron ‖ to stigmatize morally, *to brand a man a liar* [O.E. *brand, brond,* burning wood]

Bran·deis (brǽndais), Louis Dembitz (1856–1941), U.S. jurist, who served as unpaid counsel on behalf of consumers, labor unions, and investors. He influenced the enactment of the Clayton Antitrust Act (1914) and the creation of the Federal Trade Commission (1914). He served as associate justice of the U.S. Supreme Court (1916–39)

Bran·den·burg (brǽndənbə:rg) a former state of East Germany on the northern plain east of the Elbe, a region of sandy soil, heath, lakes and forest, now comprising Cottbus, Frankfurt an der Oder and Potsdam districts. Crops: rye, oats, root vegetables. Industries: mechanical engineering, textiles, precision instruments. Communications center: Berlin. Historic capital: Potsdam. Brandenburg was conquered (12th c.) from the Wends by the house of Ascania, who ruled as margraves until 1320. It became an electorate (1361) and developed under the Hohenzollerns (from 1415), becoming the nucleus of the Prussian state. In 1945 the part east of the Oder was placed under Polish rule

Brandenburg a town (pop. 94,091) on the Havel, East Germany: textile industries, mechanical engineering. Cathedral (12th c.)

bran·died (brǽndi:d) *adj.* preserved in brandy **branding iron** an implement of iron used to brand cattle etc.

bran·dish (brǽndiʃ) *v.t.* to wave about or flourish (a weapon etc.), often menacingly [O.F. *brandir* (*brandiss-*)]

brand·ling (brǽndliŋ) *n. Eisenia foetida,* a red or yellowish earthworm marked by purplish-brown rings, found in dunghills, and used as bait by anglers

brand-new (brǽndnjúː, brǽndnúː) *adj.* obviously entirely new

Bran·do, (brǽndou) Marlon (1924–), U.S. stage and film actor, a product of the method school of acting. He played Stanley Kowalski in 'A Streetcar Named Desire' on stage (1947) and in the movies (1951) and won an Academy Award for 'On the Waterfront' (1954) and 'The Godfather' (1972). Other films include 'The Men' (1950), 'The Young Lions' (1958), 'Last Tango in Paris' (1972), and 'Apocalypse Now' (1978)

brand rating measure of consumer awareness of a brand name

brand-stand·ing (brǽndstændiŋ) *n.* (*advertising*) short-term brand promotion

Brandt (brɑnt), Willy (1914–), German statesman. A Social Democrat leader, he became foreign minister of the Federal Republic in 1966, after being mayor of West Berlin from 1957, and was elected chancellor (1969–74). He was awarded (1971) the Nobel peace prize

bran·dy (brǽndi:) *pl.* **bran·dies** *n.* a spirit distilled from wine. The finest brandy is made from the white wine of Cognac in France. Other producer countries are Spain, Portugal, Australia, and South Africa ‖ a liquor distilled from fermented fruit juices, *cherry brandy* [fr. Du. *brandewijn,* 'burnt' (distilled) wine]

bran·dy·ball (brǽndi:bɔl) *n.* (*Br.*) a hard candy flavored with brandy

brandy butter a sauce of creamed butter and sugar saturated with brandy and eaten with plum pudding

brandy snap a crisp, very thin rolled wafer flavored with ginger

Bran·dy·wine, Battle of (brǽndi:wain) an engagement during the American Revolution, fought at Brandywine Creek in S.E. Pennsylvania on Sept. 11 1777. Washington's forces were defeated by the British force under William Howe

Brant (brænt), Joseph (1742–1807), Mohawk chief (Thayendanegea), a Christian convert. He commanded his people, who remained loyal to the British, throughout the Revolutionary War and settled them on Canadian land

brant (brænt) *pl.* **brant, brants** *n.* a member of *Branta,* a genus of small, wild arctic geese which migrate south in winter

bran tub (*Br.*) a tub filled with bran in which presents are hidden to make a grab bag at charity bazaars etc.

Braque (bræk), Georges (1882–1963), French painter. In 1905 he joined, briefly, the Fauves in Paris. He and Picasso, working together from 1908 to 1914, developed cubism. The still-life paintings which make up the great body of Braque's work are marked by intense refinement of form and color and by an exquisite harmony between the two, combining lyricism with intellectual force and a complex organization of the subject matter. Many later works are dominated by the invention of majestic signs (birds, suns). Braque also designed for Diaghilev ('les Fâcheux', 1924), sculpted, made lithographs, illustrated books with wood engravings, etched etc. and wrote

brash (bræʃ) *n.* useless bits of hedge clippings, floating ice, chipped rock etc. [etym. doubtful]

brash *adj.* tiresomely self-satisfied and bragging, cocky ‖ reckless, foolhardy [etym. doubtful]

Bra·si·das (brǽsidæs) (d. 424 B.C.), Spartan general in the Peloponnesian War. He decisively defeated Cleon (424), but was killed in the battle

Bra·sil·ia (brɑsíːljə) the capital (1960) and a federal district (pop. 411,305, growing rapidly) of Brazil on the central plateau (3,500 ft). Its plan, based on an equilateral triangle, is by Lucio Costa (1902–). Its chief public buildings are by Niemeyer, with sculpture and decoration by Brazilian artists. It came into being from wilderness in less than four years (1956–60)

Bra·sov (braʃɔv) (formerly Orasul Stalin) (G. Kronstadt, *Hung.* Brasso) a town (pop. 320,168) in central Rumania on the foothills of the Transylvanian Alps, founded (13th c.) by the Teutonic Knights. Industries: textiles, chemicals, steel, lumber, leather and metalwork

brass (bræs, brɑs) *n.* a yellow alloy of copper and zinc. Brass takes a high polish, is malleable, resists corrosion, and has high electrical conductivity ‖ the color of this alloy ‖ impudence ‖ (*pl.*) the brass ‖ (*pop.*) brass hats collectively **the brass** the brass wind instruments of an orchestra **bold as brass** pushing oneself forward without any modesty **to get down to brass tacks** to get to the (often financial) heart of a matter, and stop talking peripherally [O.E. *bræs*]

brass·age (brǽsidʒ, brɑsidʒ) *n.* a charge made by a mint for coining money [F.]

bras·sard (brǽsɑrd) *n.* a badge worn on the arm [F. fr. *bras,* arm]

brass band a band comprising mainly brass instruments and drums

brass hat (*pop.*) a high-ranking officer

brass·ie, brass·y (brǽsi:, brɑsi:) *n.* (*golf*) a wood with a brass-plated sole, for long shots from the fairway

bras·siere, bras·sière (brəzír, *Br.* brǽsjə) *n.* a light garment which supports a woman's breasts [F.]

bras·sin (brǽsin) *n.* group of plant hormones that stimulate enlargement and division of plant cells

brass knuckles an iron or brass cover for the knuckles, used in vicious fighting

brass·y (brǽsi:, brɑsi:) *comp.* **brass·i·er** *superl.* **brass·i·est** *adj.* of or like brass, esp. in color or sound ‖ (of a voice) harsh and suggesting self-satisfaction (of manner) cocksure

brassy *BRASSIE

brat (bræt) *n.* (usually contemptuous or impatient) a child, esp. a bad-mannered or troublesome one [etym. doubtful]

Bra·ti·sla·va (brǽtislɑ́və) (G. Pressburg) a town (pop. 394,644) in Czechoslovakia on the Danube near the Austrian frontier, with engineering, chemical and textile industries. It was the capital of Hungary (1541–1784). University (1919)

Brat·tain (brǽt'n), Walter Houser (1902–), U.S. physicist who shared with John Bardeen and William Shockley the 1956 Nobel prize in physics for investigations in semiconductors and the invention of the point-contact transistor

brat·tice (brǽtis) *n.* (*mining*) a wooden wall for controlling ventilation in a shaft or gallery ‖ (*hist.*) a wooden parapet on a fortress [O.F. *bretesche,* wooden tower]

Brau·chitsch (bráuxitʃ), Walther von (1881–1948), German field marshal who directed the 2nd world war campaigns in Poland, France, the Balkans and (at first) Russia. Hitler relieved him of his post in 1941, when he failed to take Moscow

Braun (braun), Wernher von (1912–77) U.S. engineer, born German. He worked on rockets after 1930. In 1944 his V2 missiles wrought havoc in London. In 1945 he went to the U.S.A., perfected the 'Jupiter-C' 3-stage rocket which made possible the launching of the first American artificial satellite, and became civil director of the research station at Redstone Arsenal, Huntsville (Alabama). His work on the giant rocket 'Saturn', and the successful landing of men on the moon, mark a decisive stage in U.S. interstellar travel research. He was then (1970–72) assistant director of NASA

Braun·schweig (bráunʃvaig) *BRUNSWICK

bra·va·do (brəvádou) *n.* a bold front, a pretense of indifference to risk or misfortune [fr. Span. *bravada* and F. *bravade*]

brave (breiv) 1. *comp.* **brav·er** *superl.* **brav·est** *adj.* bold, courageous, mastering fear, *a brave man* ‖ testifying to this quality, *a brave act* ‖ displaying well, *a brave show of poppies* 2. *n.* a North American Indian warrior 3. *v.t. pres. part.* **brav·ing** *past* and *past part.* **braved** to face the risk of, *to brave death* **to brave it out** to see a thing through to the end with courage [F. fr. Ital. *bravo,* fine]

brav·er·y (bréivəri:, bréivri:) *n.* courage [prob. F. *braverie*]

bra·vo (brávou, bravóu) 1. *interj.* Well done! 2. *n.* (*pl.*) enthusiastic cries of approval [Ital.]

bra·vu·ra (brəvúərə, brəvjúərə) *n.* swagger ‖ (*mus.*) technical daring and display ‖ (*painting*) spirited brushwork [Ital.=bravery]

brawl (brɔl) 1. *n.* a noisy, undignified fight 2. *v.i.* to quarrel or fight noisily [origin unknown]

brawn (brɔn) *n.* muscular strength ‖ the pickled and potted flesh of a pig **brawn·y** *comp.* **brawn·i·er** *superl.* **brawn·i·est** *adj.* muscular [O.F. *braon,* fleshy part]

brawn drain emigration of unskilled laborers and/or athletes to nations of greater opportunity. *Cf* BRAIN DRAIN

brax·y (brǽksi:) 1. *n.* an infectious bacterial disease of the intestines of sheep 2. *adj.* (of mutton) infected with braxy ‖ suffering from braxy [etym. doubtful]

bray (brei) 1. *n.* the cry of an ass ‖ a similar loud, rasping noise 2. *v.i.* to make the cry or noise of an ass ‖ *v.t.* (with 'out') to utter harshly and loudly ‖ to sound harshly and loudly, *the trumpets brayed out a fanfare* [F. *braire,* to cry, perh. fr. Celt.]

bray·er (bréiər) *n.* (*printing*) an ink roller for a handpress [fr. obs. v. *bray,* to crush fr. O.F.]

braze (breiz) *pres. part.* **braz·ing** *past* and *past part.* **brazed** *v.t.* to solder with certain hard solders, esp. an alloy of copper and zinc, or one of copper, zinc and silver, or with nickel-silver alloys [perh. F. *braser,* to solder]

braze (breiz) *pres. part.* **braz·ing** *past* and *past part.* **brazed** *v.t.* to give the color of brass to ‖ to make, cover or decorate with brass [O.E. *brasian*]

bra·zen (bréiz'n) 1. *adj.* (*rhet.*) made of brass ‖ of a harsh yellow color like brass ‖ harsh and loud ‖ bold and shameless 2. *v.t.* **to brazen it out, brazen one's way out** to extricate oneself from a difficult situation by putting on a bold act [O.E. *brœsen*]

bra·zier (bréizər) *n.* a metal holder for burning coal or coke in the open, used esp. by night watchmen, roadmen etc. [F.]
brazier *n.* someone who works in brass **brá·ziery** *n.* the work of a brazier
Bra·zil (brəzíl) a federal republic (area 3,288,000 sq. miles, pop. 137,502,000) in South America. Capital: Brasília. Chief cities: Rio de Janeiro, São Paulo. People: 62% European, 11% African, 26% mixed race, with some Asians and a dwindling Indian minority. Language: Portuguese. Religion: 93% Roman Catholic, with Protestant, Spiritist and other minorities. The land is 56% forest, 40% pasture and 4% cultivated. The Amazon basin covers the northern half of the country. Rain forest (selva) along the river gives way to grassland (campos) and savanna as the land rises, north and south, to the Guiana and Brazilian highlands. The latter (mainly 1,500–3,000 ft) culminate in a mountain system running along the Atlantic from Porto Alegre to Salvador (highest point: Pico de Bandeira, 9,462 ft). The eastern part contains the great plantations, the west (Mato Grosso) is arid savanna, as also is the northeastern bulge (the Sertao). The coastal plain is tropical and subtropical. Rainfall: 70–90 ins in the Amazon basin, 43 ins in Rio de Janeiro, 40–70 ins in the Brazilian highland, 10–30 ins in the northeast. Average winter and summer temperatures (F.): Manaus 80° and 83°, Rio de Janeiro 70° and 79°, Goiaz 72° and 78°, Recife 77° and 82°, Belo Horizonte 62° and 72°, Porto Alegre 56° and 76°. Livestock (Brazil is the world's biggest producer, ahead of Argentina): cattle, hogs, sheep, goats, horses. Crops: coffee (southeast), castor beans (world's chief producer of both), oranges and cocoa (northeast), sugar and tobacco (northeast). Other produce: bananas, cotton lint and seed, vegetable oils, rice, manioc, corn (south), rubber (Amazon basin), vines. The fishing industry is nationalized. Mineral resources: high-grade quartz crystal, iron (in Minas Gerais, E. central Brazil, rich deposits largely unexploited), chrome ore, mica, zirconium, beryllium, graphite, titanium ore, magnesite, thorium, manganese ore, tungsten, coal, gold, silver, oil, salt. Manufactures: cotton (employing 25% of all industrial workers), food processing, paper. Exports: coffee (60% of exports), cotton, hides, wool, meat, cocoa, lumber, tobacco, carnauba wax, foodstuffs. Imports: machinery, petroleum, vehicles, wheat. Chief ports: Rio de Janeiro and Santos. There are 22 state universities and three Roman Catholic ones. Monetary unit: cruzeiro (100 centavos). HISTORY. Brazil, inhabited by seminomadic Indian tribes, was allocated to Portugal by the Treaty of Tordesillas (1494), although it was actually discovered (1500) by Cabral. The Spanish, Dutch and French disputed various territories (16th and 17th cc.). By the 18th c. Brazil supplied most of Europe's sugar, and imported African slaves in great numbers to work in the plantations. The Portuguese court fled to Brazil (1808) when Napoleon invaded Portugal, and the united kingdom of Portugal and Brazil was ruled from Brazil (1815–21). The independent empire of Brazil was proclaimed (1822). Brazil fought Argentina (1825–8), and Paraguay (1865–70). After a bloodless military coup, it became a federal republic (1889) with separation of Church and State, and the constitution of the United States of Brazil was adopted (1891). It declared war on Germany (1917). Brazil suffered from the interwar world depression (losing its markets for coffee and rubber). Getulio Vargas, after a revolt (1930), established a dictatorship (1930–45). Brazil declared war on Germany and Italy (1942). After a new constitution (1946), Vargas resumed power (1951–4). Under the presidency (1956–61) of Juscelino Kubitschek, attempts were made to develop the economy, and the capital was transferred (1960) to the new city of Brasília. João Goulart became president (1961) under a parliamentary constitution, which was amended to give more power to the president (1963). Goulart was overthrown (1964) and replaced by Castelo Branco, who was succeeded by Costa e Silva (1967) and Gen. Medici (1969). The military rulers suspended constitutional liberties and imposed censorship of the press. Opposition parties made some gains in 1982 elections, and in 1985 civilian government was reinstated under José Sarney

bra·zil (brəzíl) *n.* a red dye extracted from brazilwood ‖ brazilwood
Bra·zil·ian (brəzíljən) **1.** *adj.* of or pertaining to Brazil or an inhabitant of Brazil **2.** *n.* an inhabitant of Brazil
Brazil nut the edible, oily seed of the tropical South American tree *Bertholletia excelsa*, fam. *Lecythidaceae*
bra·zil·wood (brəzílwʊd) *n.* the heavy wood of several tropical American trees of genus *Caesalpinia*, from, which red dyes are extracted [Span. and Port. *brasil*, etym. doubtful]
Braz·os (brǽzas) a river (800 miles long) of central Texas, flowing southeast into the Gulf of Mexico
Braz·za (brǽzæ), Pierre Savorgnan de (1852–1905), French colonizer. He explored parts of equatorial Africa (1873–7), founded Brazzaville and Franceville (1880), and governed the Congo (1887–97), which he acquired by peaceful means for France
Braz·za·ville (brǽzævi:l) the capital and a commercial and industrial center (pop. 184,000) of the Republic of the Congo, on the Congo River at Stanley Pool, opposite Kinshasa. It is connected by rail to the port of Pointe Noire on the Atlantic
breach (bri:tʃ) **1.** *n.* the breaking of a legal or moral obligation, *breach of contract* or of a convention, *breach of manners* ‖ an estrangement ‖ a gap made by guns in a wall or fortifications ‖ a gap in a hedge, wall etc. ‖ a whale's leap out of the water **to stand in the breach** to be ready to beat off an attack ‖ to be ready to take responsibility in a crisis **to throw oneself into the breach** to hurl oneself wholeheartedly into some emergency task **2.** *v.t.* to break through ‖ to make a gap in ‖ *v.i.* (of a whale) to leap right out of the water [O.E. *bryce* and O.F. *brèche*, a fracture]
bread (bred) **1.** *n.* a food made by moistening and kneading flour (usually leavened by yeast) or meal and baking it **to know which side one's bread is buttered on** to know what is to one's advantage or when one should count oneself lucky **2.** *v.t.* (*cookery*) to coat with breadcrumbs [O.E. *brēad*, fragment, bread]
bread and butter a buttered slice or slices of bread ‖ a livelihood **bread-and-but·ter** (bréd'nbʌtər) *adj.* concerned with earning a livelihood ‖ (of a letter) written to thank someone for a present or hospitality
bread·board (brédbɔrd) *v.* (*electr.*) to create an experimental circuit on a surface without regard to its placement, e.g., to prove feasibility or facilitate change. —**breadboarding** *n.*
bread·fruit (brédfru:t) *n. Artocarpus altilis*, fam. *Moraceae*, a tree probably native to the E. Indies, but spread throughout all tropical lowlands. It produces a large, round, starchy, edible fruit, which when baked has the consistency of bread ‖ this fruit
bread·line (brédlain) *n.* a line of people waiting for food given out by relief workers
Bread·ner (brédnər), Lloyd Samuel (1894–1952), Canadian air force officer, commanding the Royal Canadian Air Force overseas during the 2nd world war. He was the first R.C.A.F. offficer to be promoted to the rank of Air Chief Marshal (1945)
bread·stuff (brédstʌf) *n.* (esp. *pl.*) flour, grain etc. used in making bread
breadth (bredθ, bretθ) *n.* the linear dimension measured from side to side of a surface or volume and at right angles to its length ‖ a piece of cloth etc. considered in respect to its width ‖ spaciousness ‖ largeness, generosity (of mind, sympathies etc.) [M.E. *brede*, breadth+-*th* (like *length*)]
breadth·ways (brédθweiz, brétθweiz) *adj.* and *adv.* in the sense of the breadth
breadth·wise (brédθwaiz, brétθwaiz) *adj.* and *adv.* breadthways
bread·win·ner (brédwinər) *n.* the person who earns money to support a family
break (breik) **1.** *v. pres. part.* **break·ing** *past* **broke** (brouk) *past part.* **bro·ken** (bróukən) *v.t.* to cause to fall into pieces, by force or by accident, *to break a chair* ‖ to cause to snap in two, *to break a bone* ‖ to interrupt the continuity of, *to break a silence* ‖ to reduce the damaging power of, *the hedge broke the force of the wind, to break a fall* ‖ to shatter, destroy ‖ to suppress, bring to an end, *to break a strike* ‖ to demote, *to break an officer* ‖ to disobey, *to break the law* ‖ to disre-

gard, violate, *to break a contract* ‖ to announce (startling or bad news) ‖ to discover or work out the secret of (a code) ‖ to open the surface of, *to break the skin* ‖ to split into smaller units, *to break a dollar* ‖ *v.i.* to fall suddenly to pieces ‖ (of waves) to curl over and crash down in foam ‖ (e.g. of a seedpod or abscess) to burst ‖ to happen explosively or suddenly, *the storm broke, dawn broke* ‖ to disintegrate under pressure, *his health broke under the strain* ‖ (of the voice) to change from one register to another ‖ to show a dramatic fall in prices or values ‖ to come to an end, *the drought broke at last* ‖ to come out of a clinch, huddle etc. ‖ to come into general knowledge, *the scandal broke* ‖ (*phon.*, of vowels) to change into a diphthong ‖ (of a pitched baseball) to curve near the plate ‖ (of a cricket ball) to swing in or out after hitting the ground **to break a record** to do better than the best competitive performance officially recorded **to break away** to leave suddenly ‖ to abandon, forget purposefully, *to break away from the past* ‖ (in a race) to start too soon **to break down** to destroy, *the mob broke down the barriers* ‖ to analyze, *to break down population figures* ‖ to go out of working condition ‖ to have an emotional, physical or nervous collapse **to break in** to force an entry ‖ to make (a young horse) tractable ‖ to train (a person) to a new job ‖ to wear off the newness of, *to break in a pair of shoes* **to break in on** to interrupt (e.g. a conversation) **to break into** to enter forcibly ‖ to enter in order to rob ‖ to begin, *to break into a run* **to break loose** (or **free**) to escape (from clutches, handcuffs etc.) **to break (someone) of** to make give up, *she broke him of smoking* **to break off** to separate (a part) from the whole ‖ to put an abrupt end to **to break open** to force open **to break out** to start suddenly, *fighting broke out, measles broke out* ‖ to become covered with pimples ‖ (with 'of' or 'from') to escape from **to break the bank** to spend so much that there is nothing left in the bank ‖ (*gambling*) to win all the dealer's money **to break up** to come to an end ‖ to put a stop to, *to break up a fight* **to break with** to sever relations with ‖ to stop conforming to, *to break with tradition* **2.** *n.* a gap, the result of breaking, a rupture ‖ (*rhet.*, of day) the beginning ‖ an interruption, *a break in a wiring circuit* ‖ a short pause, e.g. between periods of work, *coffee break* ‖ (good or bad) fortune, *a lucky break, a bad break* ‖ (*mus.*) the point where one register of the voice, or of certain wind instruments, changes to the next ‖ (*prosody*) a caesura ‖ a sudden drop in prices on the exchange ‖ (*billiards*) a sequence of caroms ‖ (*pool*) the shot that scatters the balls ‖ (*bowling*) the playing of a frame without a strike or a spare ‖ (*baseball, cricket*) an induced deflection of the ball from the straight when thrown or bowled ‖ an attempt to run away, *to make a break for it* **bréak·a·ble** *adj.* **bréak·a·bles** *pl. n.* articles easily broken **bréak·age** *n.* a breaking ‖ a thing broken ‖ a fee or allowance for what has been broken [O.E. *brecan*]
break-bulk (bréikbʌlk) *adj.* of creating smaller packages for carload shipments for distribution to different destinations
break·down (bréikdaun) *n.* a collapse of mental or bodily health ‖ a stoppage of machinery etc. ‖ chemical decomposition ‖ a division into categories, classes or component parts ‖ a division of a complete job into several separate processes
breakdown lorry (*Br.*) a tow truck
break·er (bréikər) *n.* a wave breaking into foam on the shore ‖ a huge wave with a foaming white crest ‖ a structure for breaking, sorting and cleaning large masses of anthracite coal ‖ a strip of fabric put on a tire before the tread in order to distribute the pressure of the tire in contact with the ground
break·fast (brékfəst) **1.** *n.* the first meal of the day **2.** *v.i.* to eat breakfast
breakfast food (*commerce*) a cereal eaten for breakfast
breaking out (*show business*) achieving wide public recognition for the first time
break·neck (bréiknɛk) *adj.* very dangerous, risking life, *breakneck speed*
break·out (bréikaut) *n.* (*electr.*) point at which conductors are brought out of a multiconductor cable
break·point (bréikpɔint) *n.* (*computer*) point in an operation when the processing can be stopped for checking or other reasons
break·through (bréikθru:) *n.* the forcing of a way through an obstruction ‖ the result of this action ‖ (*mil.*) a successful attack on some lim-

ited sector of defenses ‖ the opening up of some new way of achievement in scientific or artistic technique, with large consequences

break·up (bréikʌp) *n.* a disintegration

break·wa·ter (bréikwɔtər, bréikwptər) *n.* a protective seawall built to break the force of the waves, in order to stop cliff erosion, damage to a harbor, sweeping away of shingle etc.

bream (bri:m) *pl.* **bream, breams** *n. Abramis brama,* a N. European freshwater fish of the carp family ‖ a fish of fam. *Sparidae,* the sea bream ‖ (brim) a member of *Leponis,* a genus of freshwater sunfishes [F. *brême*]

bream *v.t.* (*naut.*) to clean (a ship's bottom) by heating and scraping [etym. doubtful]

breast (brest) 1. *n.* the upper front part of the human body between the neck and the abdomen ‖ the corresponding part of an animal ‖ a mammary gland ‖ that part of a coat or dress covering the breast ‖ the center of the emotions ‖ anything analogous to a human or animal breast, *the breast of a hill, a chimney breast* **to make a clean breast of** to confess 2. *v.t.* to struggle up and over, *to breast a hill, breast a crisis* [O.E. *brēost*]

breast·bone (bréstboun) *n.* the sternum

breast-high (brésthái) *adj.* up to the breast in height or depth ‖ (of a scent) so strong that the hounds run with their heads up

breast·pin (bréstpin) *n.* a jeweled or otherwise ornamented pin worn in the tie

breast·plate (bréstpleit) *n.* (*hist.*) a piece of armor protecting the breast

breast·stroke (bréststrouk) *n.* a swimming stroke in which the arms are extended forward and then swept back palms outwards, while the feet are drawn up towards the hips and then thrust sideways and backwards so as to close together in the horizontal plane, the body being flat in the water. The main forward movement occurs when the arms and legs relax after the effort of the stroke

breast·sum·mer (brésəmər, bréssʌmər) *n.* a beam, lintel etc. placed over an opening (of a window etc.) to support the superstructure

breast wall a breast-high bank of earth forming a parapet

breast·work (bréstwə:rk) *n.* (*mil. hist.*) a temporary, hastily built parapet

breath (breθ) *n.* air drawn into or expelled from the lungs ‖ a slight movement of air ‖ air carrying fragrance, *a breath of spring* ‖ respiration ‖ (*rhet.*) the capacity to breathe ‖ a whisper, suggestion, *a breath of scandal* ‖ a slight pause, a moment ‖ (*phon.*) a hiss or puff, produced e.g. in pronouncing 's' or 'p' **a breath of fresh air** an invigorating influence **in the same breath** at the same moment, *he denied and admitted the mistake in the same breath* **out of breath** unable to draw breath quickly enough after violent exercise **to catch one's breath** to gasp in a little air as the result of an emotional reflex ‖ to stop to rest so as to breathe normally again **to draw breath** (*rhet.*) to breathe, live **to save one's breath** to keep quiet, stop talking, because argument is useless **to take one's breath away** to shock or astonish one **to waste one's breath** to talk to no avail **under** (or **below**) **one's breath** in a whisper [O.E. *brœth,* breath, smell]

breath·a·lyse (bréθəlɑiz) *v.* (Br.) to receive an intoxication test of the breath. —**breathalyser** *n.* a breath-testing device to measure sobriety

breath·a·lys·er *Br.* **breath·a·lys·er** (bréθəlɑizər) *n.* a portable device, used esp. by police in investigating traffic accidents or misdemeanors, for measuring instantly, but with limited accuracy, the alcoholic content of the breath which the person being tested breathes out [BREATH+ANALYZE]

breathe (bri:ð) *pres. part.* **breath·ing** *past* and *past part.* **breathed** *v.i.* to draw in air and send it out from the lungs ‖ (*rhet.*) to live ‖ (of wind) to blow gently ‖ *v.t.* to take in (air etc.) into the lungs ‖ to exhale (esp. fragrance) ‖ to make naturally evident, *her bearing breathed simplicity* **not to breathe a word** to say nothing of, not tell anyone about **to breathe again** (or **freely**) to recover from fear or anxiety **to breathe new life into** to revive, encourage or invigorate **to breathe one's last** (or **last breath**) (*rhet.*) to die [M.E. *brethen* fr. *breth,* breath]

breath·er (bríːðər) *n.* (*pop.*) a short rest

breath·i·ness (bréθi:nis) *n.* the state or quality of being breathy

breath·ing (bríːðiŋ) *n.* respiration ‖ (*Gk gram.*) a mark to indicate that a vowel is or is not aspi-

rated. Rough breathing is shown by ' (aspirated), smooth breathing by ' (unaspirated)

breathing space a pause for rest

breathing spell a breathing space

breath·less (bréθlis) *adj.* out of breath, exhausted ‖ lifeless ‖ utterly absorbed, *breathless interest* ‖ utterly windless

breath·tak·ing (bréθteikiŋ) *adj.* thrilling ‖ such as to take one's breath away

breath·y (bréθi:) *comp.* **breath·i·er** *superl.* **breath·i·est** *adj.* (of the speaking or singing voice) characterized by the sound of more breathing than is used vocally

brec·ci·a (brétʃi:ə) *n.* (*geol.*) a rock consisting of angular fragments usually bound together in a matrix (cf. AGGLOMERATE, cf. CONGLOMERATE) [Ital.=gravel]

Brecht (brext), Bertolt (1898–1956), German expressionist dramatist. His 'Dreigroschenoper' (1928) was an adaptation of Gay's 'The Beggar's Opera.' Brecht sought to obtain 'Entfremdungseffekt', literally 'alienation' or 'distancing': neither the actors nor the audience were wholly to identify themselves with any character, nor to forget that they were acting or watching a theatrical representation. This was meant to lead to a cooler response and a more secure judgment. In practice it increased the sense of the mystery of human character and action. His plays include: 'Galileo Galilei' (1942) and 'Mother Courage' (1941)

Brecht·ian (brékti:ən) *adj.* following the theatrical concepts of Bertolt Brecht. German playwright and poet

Breck·in·ridge (brékənridʒ), John Cabell (1821–75), U.S. lawyer, soldier, and political leader. He was elected (1856) vice-president of the U.S.A. under James Buchanan and nominated (1860) for the presidency by the southern proslavery Democrats. He resigned (1861) his seat on the U.S. Senate to join the Confederate army as brigadier general. He served (1865) as Confederate secretary of war

Breck·nock·shire (bréknəkʃər) an inland county (area 733 sq. miles, pop. 56,000) of S. Wales. County town: Brecon

Bre·con·shire (brékənʃər) Brecknockshire

bred *past* and *past part.* of BREED

Bre·da (breidá) a town (pop. 117,259) in N. Brabant, Netherlands, with machinery, leather, food and textile industries, formerly a key fortress town. Charles II of England lived there during his exile

Breda, Declaration of a proclamation (Apr. 4, 1660) by Charles II of England, in which he promised religious toleration, liberty of conscience and a general amnesty. Charles was proclaimed king (May 8, 1660)

breech (bri:tʃ) *n.* (*mil.*) the part of a cannon behind the barrel, where the shell is inserted ‖ the back part of a rifle, where the round is inserted [O.E. *brēc* (pl.), trousers]

breech·block (bri:tʃblɒk) *n.* the loading mechanism closing the breech of a gun

breech-cloth (bri:tʃklɔθ, bri:tʃklɒθ) *pl.* **breech-cloths** (bri:tʃklɔθs, bri:tʃklɒθs, bri:tʃklɔðz, bri:tʃklɒðz) *n.* a loincloth [fr. *breech,* the buttocks+CLOTH]

breech delivery the birth of a baby with the buttocks appearing first

breech·es (brítʃiz) *pl. n.* pants fitted below the knee

Breech·es Bible (brítʃiz) *GENEVA BIBLE

breeches buoy (*naut.*) a lifesaving apparatus consisting essentially of a lifebuoy with an attached breeches-like support in which someone can be hauled from ship to ship or from ship to shore along a suspended rope

breech·ing (brítʃiŋ, bri:tʃiŋ) *n.* the part of the leather harness going around a shaft-horse's hindquarters ‖ (*naut.*) a rope fastening a gun to a ship's side or deck

breech-load·ing (bri:tʃloudiŋ) *adj.* (of a gun) loaded at the breech, not at the muzzle

breed (bri:d) 1. *n.* a particular group of domestic animals related by descent from common ancestors, visibly similar in most characteristics and usually incapable of maintaining its distinctive qualities in nature ‖ a similar group of plants 2. *v. pres. part.* **breed·ing** *past* and *past part.* **bred** (bred) *v.t.* to produce (young) ‖ to give rise to, *to breed discontent* ‖ to raise (a breed of animals or plants) ‖ to mate (animals) ‖ to train, educate, *bred to the law* ‖ *v.i.* to reproduce [O.E. *brēdan,* to nourish]

breed·er (bri:dər) *n.* a breeder reactor

breeder document false proof of birth used to obtain other identification

breeder reactor a reactor in which a non-fissionable element is transmuted to a fissionable one by neutron bombardment from a radioactive source, more fissionable material being produced than is used up. In this way plutonium 239 can be produced from uranium 238

breed·ing (brí:diŋ) *n.* the propagation of plants or animals, esp. so as to improve their useful properties ‖ the manifestation in domestic animals and plants of the select use of forbears for the improving of the breed ‖ distinction of manners

Breed's Hill (bri:dz) a hill about 700 yards from Bunker Hill, in Boston, Mass., the actual site of the Revolutionary War engagement (June 17, 1775) known as the Battle of Bunker Hill

breeze (bri:z) 1. *n.* a gentle wind ‖ (*pop.*) something easy 2. *v.i. pres. part.* **breez·ing** *past* and *past part.* **breezed** (*pop.,* with 'in') to pay a casual call ‖ to move at a pleasantly easy speed [earlier *brize* fr. Span. and Port. *briza,* northeast wind]

breeze *n.* (Br.) bits of cinder, coke or coke dust used with cement to make cinder blocks [perh. F. *braise,* cinders]

breeze block (Br.) a cinder block

breeze·way (brí:zwei) *n.* an open, roofed passage linking two separate buildings ‖ (*electr.*) the time interval preceding the appearance of the color on television reception

breez·i·ly (brí:zili) *adv.* in a breezy manner

breez·i·ness (brí:zi:nis) *n.* the state or quality of being breezy

breez·y (brí:zi:) *comp.* **breez·i·er** *superl.* **breez·i·est** *adj.* played over by pleasant light winds ‖ pleasantly windy ‖ cheerful and casual

Brei·ten·feld, Battle of (bráit'nfelt) a battle (Sept. 17, 1631) in which Gustavus Adolphus of Sweden defeated the Imperial forces under Tilly ‖ a battle (Nov. 2, 1642), in which the Swedes under Torstensson defeated the Imperial army (*THIRTY YEARS WAR) ‖ a battle (Oct. 16, 1813) forming part of the Battle of the Nations at Leipzig

Brem·en (bréimən) a town (pop. 553,500) on the Weser, West Germany, 35 miles from the sea, a great port and industrial city: shipbuilding, oil refining, machine and automobile manufacturing ‖ the state (area 154 sq. miles, pop. 545,100) in which it lies

Brem·er·ha·ven (bréimərháfən) a town (pop. 140,505) at the mouth of the Weser, West Germany. Founded in 1827 as a port for Bremen, it is a passenger traffic, shipbuilding and fisheries center

Bre·mond (brem5), Henri, Abbé (1865–1933), French historian and critic, author of the 11-volume 'Histoire littéraire du sentiment religieux en France' (1916–36), and of critical works on poetry

Bren (bren) *n.* a Bren gun

Bren carrier a small bulletproof tracked vehicle for the transport of a Bren and the gunners who man it

Bren gun a fast, light machine gun firing .303 ammunition, gas-operated and air-cooled [fr. *Br*no, in Czechoslovakia where originally made, and *En*field, in England]

Bren·nan (brénən), William Joseph, Jr. (1906–), U.S. Supreme Court associate justice (1956–). After graduation from Harvard Law School he specialized in labor law in New Jersey and served on that state's superior (1949–52) and supreme courts (1952–6) before being appointed to the U.S. Supreme Court by Pres. Eisenhower. A liberal concerning civil rights, he wrote the majority opinion for 'Baker v. Carr' (1962) and 'New York Times v. Sullivan' (1964)

Bren·ner Pass (brénər) the lowest pass over the Alps. Its summit (4,494 ft) marks the Austrian-Italian frontier

Bren·ta·no (brentánou), Franz (1838–1917), German philosopher and psychologist. His doctrine of self-evident truths and his psychology of acts and intentions were particularly influential, esp. on Husserl. His works include 'Psychologie vom empirischen Standpunkt' (1874)

brent goose (brent) the brant

brer (brɛər, brə:r) *n.* (in fable personifications) brother, *Brer Rabbit* [Am. dial. contraction]

Bre·scia (bréiʃə) a town (pop. 213,939) of Lombardy, Italy, a rail junction with engineering and textile industries. Medieval walls and moats, Duomo Vecchio (12th c.), cathedral (1604)

Bres·lau (bréslau, brézlau) *WROCLAW

Brest (brest) a naval station and town (pop. 167,500) in Finistère, France: shipbuilding, textiles, fisheries

Brest-Li·tovsk, Treaty of (bréstlitɔ́fsk) a separate peace treaty signed (1918) by Russia and the Central Powers during the 1st world war. Russia was forced to recognize the independence of Poland, the Baltic states, Georgia and the Ukraine, and to pay a large indemnity. The general armistice (1918) declared the treaty void

brethren (esp. *hist.* and *Bible*) *alt. pl.* of BROTHER

Bré·ti·gny, Treaty of (breiti:nji:) a treaty (1360) between Edward III of England and Jean II of France, at the end of the first part of the Hundred Years' War. Edward renounced his claim to the French throne, but gained Aquitaine and all its dependencies

Bre·ton (brɔtɔ́) André (1896–1966), French poet, creator and leader of surrealism. His collected poems were published in 1948

Bret·on (brét'n) **1.** *adj.* of Brittany, or the Bretons **2.** *n.* a native of Brittany ‖ the Celtic language of Brittany

Bret·ton Woods Conference (brét'n) the United Nations Monetary and Financial Conference (1944) at Bretton Woods, New Hampshire, as a result of which the International Monetary Fund and the International Bank for Reconstruction and Development (*WORLD BANK) were created

bre·tyl·ium tosylate ($C_{11}H_{17}BrNC_7H_7SO_3$) (brɔtíli:əm) (*pharm.*) drug used to control high blood pressure; marketed as Daronthin

Breu·er (brɔ́iər) Joseph (1842–1925), Austrian physician who developed the method of treating the mentally ill by getting them to express repressed desires, esp. under hypnosis (*FREUD, *PSYCHOANALYSIS)

Breuer, Marcel Lajos (1902–81), Hungarian-born American architect and furniture designer. He taught at the Bauhaus (1925–8) and at Harvard University (1937–46), and has worked in partnership with Gropius. He worked with Nervi and Bernard Zehrfuss on the Unesco building in Paris (1953–8)

Breuil (brə:j) Abbé Henri (1877–1961), French archaeologist, famous for his work on prehistoric cave paintings in Spain, France and South Africa

breve (bri:v, brev) *n.* (*mus.*) a note equal to two whole notes ‖ a curved mark used to indicate a short vowel (e.g. ĕ as distinct from ē) or syllable [older *bref, brefe,* brief n.]

bre·vet (brɔvét, *Br.* brévit) **1.** *n.* (*mil.*) a commission promoting an officer to a higher nominal rank than that for which he is paid **2.** *adj.* of a rank or of rank obtained or bestowed by brevet **3.** *v.t. pres. part.* **bre·vet·ting, bre·vet·ing** *past and past part.* **bre·vet·ted, bre·vet·ed** to confer such a rank upon [F., dim. of *bref,* short]

bre·vi·ar·y (bri:vi:ɛri:, brévi:ɛri:) *pl.* **bre·via·ries** *n.* a book containing the offices to be said daily by Catholic priests [fr. L. *breviarium,* summary]

bre·vier (brɔvíər) *n.* an old size of type (about 8 point) [O.F., used in printing breviaries]

brev·i·ty (bréviti:) *n.* shortness, esp. of time ‖ conciseness of speech or writing [prob. A.F. *brevete*]

brevity code any code that provides no security but that has as its sole purpose the shortening of messages rather than the concealment of their content

brew (bru:) **1.** *n.* a drink made by brewing ‖ the process of brewing ‖ the amount or quality of something brewed **2.** *v.t.* to make (beer or ale) (*BREWING) ‖ to make (tea) by infusion ‖ to foment (trouble, mischief, a rebellion etc.) ‖ *v.i.* to brew ale or beer ‖ (of beer, tea etc.) to be being prepared ‖ to gather force, *mischief is brewing, a storm is brewing* [O.E. brēowan]

brew·er·y (brú:əri:, brú:ri:) *pl.* **brew·er·ies** *n.* a building housing machinery for brewing beer or ale

brew·ing (brú:iŋ) *n.* the making of beer or ale. Barley, allowed to germinate, then heated and dried to form malt, is ground and mixed with water. The enzyme diastase converts the starch into the sugar maltose, resulting in the sweetish liquid wort. Hops are added and the liquid is boiled. It is cooled, cleared of solids, and yeast is added. The enzyme zymase converts the sugar into alcohol, with the evolution of carbon dioxide

Brew·ster (brú:stər) Sir David (1781–1868), Scottish physicist who did pioneer work on the

polarization of light and on the effect of light on the electrical resistance of certain conductors

Brewster's Law the law stating that the tangent of the angle of incidence which gives maximum polarization by reflection at the surface of a transparent medium is numerically equal to the index of refraction of the medium

Brezh·nev (bréʒnəf) Leonid Ilyich (1906–82), Russian statesman, first secretary of the Soviet Union Communist party (1964–82). After working on various regional committees (1939–56) he became party leader. In 1968 he proclaimed the 'Brezhnev Doctrine' that the U.S.S.R. would not remain passive when those countries within the Soviet sphere of influence demonstrated 'anti-socialist degeneration,' as shown in the Soviet invasion of Afghanistan (1979) and the suppression of Poland's Solidarity labor union movement (1981)

Brezh·nev Doctrine (bréʒnef) Soviet principle of international law asserting right of the Communist community to intervene where internal and external forces hostile to Communism try to turn the development of a socialist nation toward capitalism, a situation seen as threatening to all Communist nations

Bri·an Bo·ru (bráiənbərú:) (c. 926–1014), king of Ireland (1002–14). He decisively defeated the Norse invaders (1014) but was killed in the battle

Bri·and (bri:ɑ̄) Aristide (1862–1932), French socialist statesman, 10 times prime minister between 1909 and 1929. He took a leading part in bringing about the separation of Church and State (1905), the formation of the League of Nations, and the signing of the Locarno Pact (1925) and the Kellogg-Briand Pact (1928), and he advocated a federal European union

briar *BRIER

bribe (braib) **1.** *n.* a secret gift (usually of money) offered to a person in a position of trust, e.g. a public servant, to persuade him to turn his power to the advantage of the person offering the gift ‖ any enticement meant to condition behavior **2.** *v.t. pres. part.* **brib·ing** *past and past part.* **bribed** to give a bribe to ‖ to secure by bribes, *to bribe one's way* **brib·er·y** *n.* [perh. O.F. *bribe,* scrap of bread fr. *briber,* to beg]

bric-a-brac (bríkəbræk) *n.* small articles of little value ‖ antique or decorative miscellaneous objects such as small pieces of furniture, vases etc., valued often because they are old or curious rather than beautiful [F.]

brick (brik) **1.** *n.* a block of fired clay and sand used in building ‖ a child's building block of wood, plastic etc. ‖ anything brick-shaped, *a brick of ice cream* ‖ the red color of brick ‖ (*pop.*) someone brave or good-hearted **to drop a brick** (*Br.*) to say something indiscreet **2.** *v.t.* (with 'up', 'in') to fill in (a space) with bricks [prob. F. *brique*]

brick·bat (bríkbæt) *n.* a bit of brick, esp. used as a missile ‖ a wounding remark

brick·lay·er (bríkleiər) *n.* a builder's workman who lays bricks

brick·work (bríkwə:rk) *n.* construction of bricks set with mortar or cement and bonded together in a regular interlocking pattern

brick·yard (bríkjɑrd) *n.* a place where bricks are made

brid·al (bráid'l) *adj.* relating to a bride or a wedding [O.E. brýd-ealo, wedding-ale]

bride (braid) *n.* a delicate loop or other link connecting lace patterns [F.=bridle]

bride *n.* a woman on her wedding day ‖ a newly married woman [O.E. brýd]

bride·groom (bráidgru:m, bráidgrum) *n.* a man on his wedding day [O.E. brýdguma, bride man]

brides·maid (bráidzmeid) *n.* a girl or a young woman, usually unmarried, who attends the bride on her wedding day

bridge (bridʒ) **1.** *n.* a structure carrying a road, railroad or path over a road, railroad, river or ravine ‖ the movable wooden part of a violin or related instrument, over which the strings are stretched ‖ the part of a pair of glasses fitting over the nose ‖ (*naut.*) a platform amidships for the officers on watch, from which the vessel is commanded ‖ (*dentistry*) a device for anchoring artificial to natural teeth ‖ (*mus.*) a passage joining two more important passages, sometimes by a change of key ‖ (*billiards, pool*) a support for the cue in play made by thumb and forefinger of the left hand, or a special notched gadget at the end of a rod ‖ (*phys.*) an arrangement for measuring or comparing various electrical quantities by balancing opposed voltages

so that no current flows in the circuit, indicating the equality of a known to an unknown ratio ‖ (*engin.*) a gantry ‖ the upper bony part of the nose **2.** *v.t. pres. part.* **bridg·ing** *past and past part.* **bridged** to make a bridge over ‖ to cross over, *to bridge a gap in conversation* [O.E. brycg, bricg]

bridge *n.* a skilled card game of E. European origin, derived from whist, for four people, one of whom (dummy) looks on while his exposed cards are played by his partner [origin unknown]

bridge-build·er (brídʒbildər) *n.* one who strives to bring opposing persons or groups together

bridge·head (brídʒhed) *n.* (*mil.*) an advanced position occupied in enemy territory

Bridge of Sighs a covered 16th-c. bridge in Venice leading from the Doges' palace to the prisons. Prisoners crossed it on the way to execution

Bridge·port (brídʒpɔrt, brídʒpourt) an industrial city (pop. 142,546, with agglom. 335,000) of Connecticut, on Long Island Sound

Bridger (brídʒər) James (1804–81), U.S. frontiersman, fur trader, explorer, and guide. He trapped along the upper Missouri River (1822) and is credited with the discovery of the Great Salt Lake in 1825. A founder of the Rocky Mountain Fur Company (1830), he built Fort Bridger (1838–43), which later became a military post and pony express station

Bridges (brídʒiz) Robert Seymour (1844–1930), English poet, critic and poet laureate (1913–30). He is known for his 'Testament of Beauty' (1929), a long philosophical poem, and for his lyrical poems. He was a friend of Gerard Manley Hopkins, whose poems he first edited for publication

Bridge·town (brídʒtaun) the capital and port (pop. 8,789, with agglom. 73,000) of Barbados, on Carlisle Bay

bridge train (*mil.*) engineers with material for building bridges

bridge·work (brídʒwə:rk) *n.* bridge-building as a technique or occupation ‖ (*dentistry*) dental bridges collectively or a dental bridge

bri·dle (bráid'l) **1.** *n.* the headgear, made up of headstall, bit and reins, by which a horse is guided and controlled ‖ a check, a restraining influence ‖ (*mach.*) a strip of metal joining two parts of a machine and controlling or restraining their motion ‖ (*naut.*) a mooring cable **2.** *v. pres. part.* **bri·dling** *past and past part.* **bri·dled** *v.t.* to put a bridle on (a horse) ‖ to restrain (emotions, ambitions etc.) ‖ *v.i.* to show that one has taken offense or that one's vanity is wounded by a movement of the head as though suddenly jerked back by a curb [O.E. brídel]

bridle path a path for riders, not for vehicles

Brie (bri:) *n.* a soft fermented French cheese made from cow's milk [after *Brie,* a region of the Paris basin]

brief (bri:f) **1.** *adj.* lasting a short time ‖ concise ‖ short in length ‖ curt **2.** *n.* an official letter from the pope, less formal than a bull, on matters of discipline ‖ (*law*) a concise presentation of the facts of a client's case for counsel ‖ (*Br.*) a case for a barrister ‖ (*mil., aviation*) instructions for an operation ‖ any concise summary prepared for someone else to act on ‖ (*pl.*) shorts, underpants **in brief** in short **to hold no brief for** not to advocate **3.** *v.t.* to instruct by brief ‖ to employ as counsel ‖ to summarize (facts) in a brief ‖ (*mil., aviation*) to instruct as preparation for action ‖ to inform [O.F. bref]

brief·case (bri:fkeis) *n.* a flat, flexible case of leather, etc., for carrying papers

brief of title (*law*) an abstract of all the legal documents affecting a title to a property

brief psychotherapy (*psych.*) various techniques for mental-health therapy based on solution, correction, or amelioration of a selected central problem or symptom

bri·er, bri·ar (bráiər) *n.* any prickly bush or wooded plant e.g. of the genera *Rosa, Rubus* or *Smilax,* or a single branch of one of these [O.E. brēr, brœr]

brier, briar *n. Erica arborea,* a heath of S. Europe whose root is used in making tobacco pipes ‖ a pipe made from this wood [F. *bruyere,* heath]

brier rose the dog rose

bri·ar·wood, bri·ar·wood (bráiərwud) *n.* the root wood of the brier

brig (brig) *n.* a brigantine

brig *n.* (*Am. Navy*) a ship's prison

bri·gade (brigéid) **1.** *n.* (*mil.*) one of the subdivisions of an army ‖ (outside an army) a disciplined group, *fire brigade* **2.** *v.t. pres. part.* **bri·gad·ing** *past* and *past part.* **bri·gad·ed** to form into a brigade [F. fr. Ital.]

brig·a·dier (brigədíər) *n.* a brigadier general ‖ (*Br.*) an army officer ranking above a colonel and below a major general [F.]

brigadier general an officer in the U.S. army, air force or marine corps, ranking above a colonel and below a major general

brig·and (brígənd) *n.* a member of a band of men who rob and plunder, a bandit **bríg·and·age** *n.* [O.F. prob. fr. Ital.]

brig·an·tine (brígəntain, brígənti:n) *n.* a two-masted vessel with square sails on the foremast and fore-and-aft sails on the mainmast [F. fr. Ital. *brigantino*, a pirate boat]

Bright (brait), John (1811–89), British Liberal statesman. With Richard Cobden, he campaigned against the Corn Laws. He entered parliament (1843) and was noted for his oratory against the Crimean War and against slavery in America

bright (brait) **1.** *adj.* reflecting or giving out light ‖ cheerful, *a bright smile* ‖ (of color) brilliant, vivid ‖ hopeful, promising success, *a bright future* ‖ clever, *a bright remark* **2.** *adv.* brightly [O.E. *beorht*]

bright·en (bráit'n) *v.t.* to make light or cheerful ‖ *v.i.* to light up ‖ to become cheerful, lively etc. [M.E. *brightnen*]

bright·ness (bráitnis) *n.* the quality of a source by which the light emitted varies from dim to bright (*COLOR)

brightness control (*electr.*) in a television radar and other cathode ray receivers, a device that varies tube brightness by changing the tube's grid bias. *syn* brilliance control

Bright·on (bráit'n) a seaside resort and county borough (pop. 146,134) in E. Sussex, England, with fine Regency terraces and squares and a mock-oriental pavilion (1782). University of Sussex (1959)

Bright's disease any of several diseases of the kidneys [after Richard *Bright* (1789-1858), English doctor]

brill (bril) *pl.* **brill, brills** *n. Bothus rhombus* or *Rhombus laevis*, a European flatfish related to the turbot [origin unknown]

bril·liance (bríljəns) *n.* the quality of being brilliant ‖ extreme clarity in musical performance or richness in overtones etc. of a sound recording **bríl·lian·cy** *n.*

bril·liant (bríljənt) **1.** *adj.* sparkling, very bright ‖ outstanding in intelligence or imagination ‖ very distinguished, *a brilliant career* **2.** *n.* a cut diamond with very many facets ‖ an old small size of type (about 3½ point) [F. *brillant*]

bril·lian·tine (bríljənti:n) *n.* a cosmetic hair dressing used mainly by men [F.]

brim (brim) **1.** *n.* the edge or lip of a cup, bowl or other hollow dish ‖ the projecting rim or edge of a hat **2.** *v.i. pres. part.* **brim·ming** *past* and *past part.* **brimmed** (with 'over') to be so full as to overflow, *to brim over with excitement* **brim·ful** *adj.* full to the brim, *brimful of ideas* **brim·mer** *n.* (*old-fash.*) a very full glass, cup etc. [M.E. *brimme*, origin unknown]

brim·stone (brímstoun) *n.* sulfur ‖ hellfire [M.E. fr. *brinnen*, to burn+STONE]

Brin·di·si (bríndizi:) a port (pop. 79,784) on the Adriatic (mainly passenger traffic). Apart from Ancona it is the only good natural harbor on Italy's east coast. There are food processing and chemical industries. It marks the end of the Via Appia, and has many Roman remains

brin·dle (bríndl) **1.** *adj.* gray or tawny with darker streaks **2.** *n.* an animal marked in this way **brín·dled** *adj.* [etym. doubtful]

Brind·ley (bríndli:), James (1716–72), British canal engineer. The canal which he built (1760–1) from Worsley to Manchester launched the 18th-c. boom in canal construction

brine (brain) *n.* very salt water (seawater, or salted water used e.g. for pickling) ‖ sodium or calcium chloride solution used as a refrigerant ‖ (*rhet.*) the sea [O.E. *brȳne, brine*]

brine pan a shallow iron vessel, or pit, for extracting salt from water by evaporation

bring (briŋ) *pres. part.* **bring·ing** *past* and *past part.* **brought** (brɔt) *v.t.* to carry, lead, convey, or otherwise cause to come along with oneself, *bring your report to the office, bring him home to dinner* ‖ to persuade, *I can't bring myself to ask, try to bring him to accept* ‖ to cause to come, *it brought a smile to her face* ‖ (*law*) to institute (proceedings), *to bring an action* ‖ (*law*) to pre-

fer, *to bring a charge* ‖ to adduce, advance (an argument) ‖ to fetch (a price) **to bring about** to cause to happen ‖ to turn (a ship) around **to bring around,** *esp. Br.* **bring round** to win over to a new point of view ‖ to restore to consciousness **to bring back** to recall **to bring down** to cause to fall wounded or dead ‖ to lower (a price) ‖ to cause to fall, *to bring down a curse on someone* **to bring forth** (*rhet.*) to give birth to ‖ to produce **to bring forward** to introduce (a topic or proposal) for discussion ‖ to put at the top of a page or new column of an accounts book (the sum of the figures of the previous page or column) **to bring in** to cause to appear, *bring in the meat course* ‖ to yield (income etc.), *night work brings in extra money* ‖ to pronounce (a verdict in court) ‖ to introduce (e.g. a topic, a quotation) **to bring into play** to cause to be effective, begin using **to bring off** to achieve (something difficult or risky) **to bring on** to cause, *to bring on a fainting attack* **to bring out** to publish or have published on one's behalf ‖ to clarify and stress (an argument, a distinction etc.) ‖ to call forth, cause to be seen or realized, *to bring out the best in someone* ‖ to introduce (a girl) formally into society **to bring (someone) to** to restore (someone) to consciousness **to bring to bear** to concentrate, *to bring one's mind to bear on a problem* ‖ to cause to have effect, *to bring pressure to bear on a person* **to bring to one's senses** to restore to reasonableness or sanity **to bring under** (*Br.*) to subdue **to bring up** to rear, train (a child) ‖ to vomit [O.E. *bringan*]

bring·ing-up (bríŋiŋʌp) *n.* upbringing

brink (briŋk) *n.* the top or edge of a steep place ‖ the verge, *on the brink of collapse* ‖ the bank of a river or other stretch of water [M.E. *brink* perh. fr. Scand.]

brink·man·ship (bríŋkmənʃip) *n.* tactic of international relations involving the deliberate creation of a recognizable state of war, not completely controlled, and applying intolerable pressure to the other party; based on a 1956 remark by U.S. Secretary of State John Foster Dulles

brin·y (bráini:) *comp.* **brin·i·er** *superl.* **brin·i·est** *adj.* of or like brine

bri·quette, bri·quet (brikét) *n.* a brick-shaped block, esp. of compressed coal dust [F. dim. of *brique*]

Bris·bane (brízbən, brízbein) the chief port, capital and commercial center (pop. 942,836) of Queensland, E. Australia, on Brisbane River near Moreton Bay, first settled as a penal station (1824). Queensland University (1909)

brisk (brisk) *adj.* lively and quick, *a brisk trade, a brisk walk* ‖ sharply refreshing and keen, *a brisk breeze* ‖ (of a person or manner) lively, alert ‖ (of a drink) sparkling [etym. doubtful]

bris·ket (brískit) *n.* the breast or lower part of the chest of an animal, as meat for the table [etym. doubtful]

bris·ling, bris·tling (brísliŋ) *n. Clupea sprattus,* a small fish resembling the sardine [origin unknown]

Bris·sot de War·ville (bri:soudəvarvi:1), Jacques Pierre (1754–93), French politician, a leader of the Girondists. Elected to the Legislative Assembly (1791), he was largely responsible for the French declaration of war against Austria (1792)

bris·tle (bris'l) **1.** *n.* a short, stiff hair on the back of an animal, esp. on swine ‖ anything resembling this **2.** *v.i. pres. part.* **bris·tling** *past* and *past part.* **bris·tled** (of an animal's hair) to stand on end, usually through fear, anger etc. ‖ (of people) to take offense ‖ to abound in, *to bristle with difficulties* **brís·tly** *comp.* **bris·tli·er** *superl.* **bris·tli·est** *adj.* [M.E. *brustel*]

bristling *BRISLING

Bris·tol (bríst'l) a port (pop. 390,697) on River Avon, in S.W. England, important in the port and sherry trade: chocolate, tobacco and soap factories, engineering industries (locomotives, bicycles, automobiles, aircraft). University (1909)

Bristol board a fine, smooth-surfaced cardboard for drawing on, made of many sheets of paper pasted together

Bristol Channel an inlet of the Atlantic in S.W. England dividing Wales from Devon and Somerset, ending in the Severn estuary. About 80 miles long, and 5 to 43 miles wide, it serves Bristol (by the Avon), Cardiff, Swansea and other industrial towns. Tides rise to 53 ft at Chepstow, causing a bore with tides 9 ft high

Brit·ain (brít'n) *GREAT BRITAIN

Britain, Battle of the struggle (Aug. 1940–May 1941) over S. England in which the Germans failed to win mastery of the air and so were prevented from carrying out their planned seaborne invasion of Britain

Bri·tan·ni·a (britæni:ə, britænjə) *n.* a personification of Britain [L.]

Britannia metal an alloy of tin with about 10% of antimony and smaller amounts of copper, zinc or lead. It takes a dull silvery polish and was formerly used for domestic utensils

Bri·tan·nic (britǽnik) *adj.* of Britain, (chiefly in) *His* (*Her*) *Britannic Majesty* [fr. L. *Britannicus*]

Bri·tan·ni·cus (britǽnikəs), Tiberius Claudius (c. 41–56), Roman prince, son and heir of Claudius I, poisoned by his stepmother Agrippina

britch·es (brítʃiz) *pl. n.* (*pop.*) breeches

Brit·i·cism (brítisizəm) *n.* an English word or phrase or idiom used only by British people and differing esp. from American usage [BRITISH, after 'Gallicism']

Brit·ish (brítiʃ) **1.** *adj.* of Great Britain and its inhabitants ‖ (*hist.*) of the ancient Britons **2.** *n.* (with 'the') the people or inhabitants of Great Britain ‖ (*hist.*) the language spoken by the ancient Britons [O.E. *Brettisc, Brittisc*]

British Aerospace *BAC 1–11

British Antarctic Territory a sector of Antarctica between 20°W. and 80°W., south of 60°S., claimed by Great Britain. It includes Graham Land, the South Shetland Is and the South Orkney Is. It was formerly part of the Falkland Is Dependencies

British Broadcasting Corporation (*abbr.* B.B.C.) a public corporation set up by royal charter in 1927, with a monopoly in sound radio in Britain. It succeeded the British Broadcasting Company, a private monopoly controlled by radio manufacturers, set up in 1922. The corporation is financed out of license fees which are paid by the public to the Treasury, then voted annually to the corporation by parliament. Since 1947 it has received grants-in-aid from parliament for its external services. Its television service competes with those provided by the commercial companies of the Independent Television Authority

British Columbia a province (area 366,255 sq. miles, pop. 2,851,700) on the Pacific coast of Canada. Capital: Victoria. Chief city: Vancouver. It is almost entirely mountainous and densely forested. Settlement is concentrated in the southwest and on Vancouver Is. Agriculture: dairy and beef cattle, fruit, vegetables. Fur production. Fisheries (leading province). Resources: zinc, lead, copper, silver, tungsten, timber (over half Canada's production), hydroelectric power. Industries: forestry products, pulp, paper, metal and oil refining, food processing. Vancouver Is. became a British colony (1849) and the mainland developed as New Caledonia. The two colonies united (1866) as British Columbia and joined the Canadian Confederation (1871)

British Commonwealth of Nations *COMMONWEALTH

British Council an official body established 1934 and incorporated by royal charter (1940) to promote knowledge abroad of Britain and the English language, and to establish reciprocal cultural relations with other countries. It works in many parts of the Commonwealth and in over 40 foreign countries. It organizes courses and exhibitions, provides literature and visual aids etc., trains teachers in English, and establishes cultural centers (e.g. British Institutes). Its publications include 'British Book News' and 'British Language Teaching'

British East India Company *EAST INDIA COMPANY, BRITISH

British Empire *COMMONWEALTH

Brit·ish·er (brítiʃər) *n.* a British subject of British descent

British Guiana the former name of Guyana

British Honduras the former name of *BELIZE

British Indian Ocean Territory a British colony in the Indian Ocean, comprised of the Chagos Archipelago (area 29 sq. mi.); a former dependency of Mauritius. The Territory was created in 1965 and originally included the islands of Aldabra, Farquhar, and Desroches, which were returned to the Seychelles, after that country became independent in 1976. Diego Garcia is the largest island, and in early 1980s it was returned to Mauritius' sovereignty. The Territory was leased until 2025 for a U.S. military base

British Isles a group of islands off N.W. Europe, comprising Great Britain, Ireland, the Hebrides, Orkney, the Shetland Is. and adjacent islands

British Museum a museum in Bloomsbury, London, founded by act of parliament in 1753. It houses one of the richest and most varied collections of antiquities in existence. Its treasures were acquired by private donations, archaeological expeditions undertaken at public expense, and state grants. They include the 'Elgin marbles' from the Parthenon at Athens (438 B.C.). The museum library contains 6 million volumes and receives a free copy of every book published in the U.K. under the British copyright regulations

British North America Act *CANADA

British North West Company *NORTH WEST COMPANY

British Solomon Islands Protectorate *SOLOMON ISLANDS

British Somaliland *SOMALIA

British thermal unit (*abbr.* B.T.U., Btu) unit quantity of heat needed to raise the temperature of 1 lb. avoir. of water by 1° F., usually from 39.2° F. to 40.2° F.

British Togoland *TOGOLAND, *GHANA

British Virgin Islands *VIRGIN ISLANDS, BRITISH

British West Indies dollar (*abbr.* B.W.I. dollar) the monetary unit of the Commonwealth countries of the Eastern Caribbean ‖ a note of the value of one B.W.I. dollar

Brit·on (brít'n) n. (*hist.*) a member of one of the tribes found by the Romans in Britain ‖ a native of Great Britain [M.E. *breton* fr. F.]

Brit·ta·ny (brít'ni:) (*F.* Bretagne) a former province occupying the northwestern peninsula of France (Armorican Massif), now forming the departments of Ille-et-Vilaine, Loire-Atlantique, Côtes-du-Nord, Morbihan and Finistère. It is a plateau, broken by hills in the west, with a deeply indented coast. Chief industries: farming (cereals, market produce, fruit and cattle), fishing, shipbuilding, tourism. Except for Rennes (historical capital) the main towns are ports: Nantes (on the Loire), Brest, St Nazaire, St Malo. Armorica was renamed Britannia Minor by the Romans, but the Celtic Breton language, still spoken in the west, was brought (5th and 6th cc.) by immigrants from Wales and Cornwall. A duchy from the 10th c., it was disputed by Britain and France until 1365, united to the French crown (1491) by the marriage of Anne of Brittany to Charles VIII, and finally annexed in 1532. A separatist tradition continues

Brit·ta·ny Spaniel (brítəni:) breed of medium-size, compact spaniel with a short tail or no tail, a dense, flat coat of orange, white, or tan color; native to Brittany and Wales

Brit·ten (brít'n), Benjamin (1913–76), English composer, known for his operas, esp. 'Peter Grimes' (1945). Other works include 'A War Requiem', the musical 'mystery play' 'Noye's Fludde', and vocal works, some in combination with orchestra, e.g. 'Serenade for Tenor, Horn and String Orchestra' and 'Spring Symphony', and song-settings of Rimbaud and Donne

brit·tle (brít'l) *adj.* of a solid (e.g. cast iron) in which the cohesion between the molecules is fairly easily destroyed by a sudden stress, causing either fragmentation or cleavage along one or more planes [M.E. *britil*, rel. to O.E. *brēotan*, to break]

brittle fracture (*metall.*) the failure of a metal in one or more planes, at the crystal interfaces. This cleavage takes place without any signs of plastic deformation

Br·no (bə́:rnou) (*G.* Brünn) Czechoslovakia's second largest town (pop. 363,179), capital of Jihomoravsky region, Moravia. Manufactures: textiles, machinery, porcelain and glass. University (1919)

broach (brout∫) 1. n. a roasting spit ‖ any of various other pointed tools, e.g. a boring bit 2. *v.t.* to tap, pierce (a cask) so as to let out the liquor ‖ to open and start using (e.g. a bale, stores, cargo etc.) ‖ to introduce (a subject) into conversation [F. *broache*]

broach *v.t.* (*naut.*) to cause (a ship) to veer so that she is broadside on to the waves ‖ *v.i.* (*naut.*, esp. with 'to') to veer so as to be broadside on to the waves and risk capsizing [etym. doubtful]

Broad (brɔd), Charlie Dunbar (1887–1971), English philosopher. His works include 'The Mind and its Place in Nature' (1925), 'Five Types of Ethical Theory' (1930), 'Examination of McTaggart's Philosophy' (1933, 1938)

broad (brɔd) 1. *adj.* of great width, *a broad expanse of sea* ‖ clear and explicit, easily understandable, *a broad hint* ‖ full and clear, *broad daylight* ‖ (of ideas or the mind) liberal, free from prejudice ‖ extensive, *broad acres* ‖ racy, unrestrained, *broad farce* ‖ free in treatment (e.g. of brushwork in painting) ‖ general, not detailed ‖ strongly marked, *a broad Scottish accent* ‖ (of a vowel) pronounced with a wide gap between tongue and palate, open **as broad as it is long** amounting to the same thing, with no advantage one way or the other 2. n. the broad part of something, *the broad of one's back* [O.E. *brad*]

broad arrow an arrow with a broad head ‖ (*hist.*) this mark on British ordnance and government property

broad·ax, broad·axe (brɔ́dæks) *pl.* **broad·axes** n. a large, broad-bladed ax for hewing timber

broad·band (brɔ́dbænd) *adj.* (*electr.*) efficient over a wide band of frequencies

broad·band·ing (brɔ́dbændiŋ) n. system of combining employee categories under a single title to provide a wider channel of selection and promotion. —**broadband** v.

broad bean an annual of fam. *Papilionaceae*, grown since prehistoric times throughout S. Europe for its large, flattened, edible seed ‖ this seed ‖ *Vicia faba*, a vetch used chiefly for fodder

broad·brush (brɔ́dbrʌʃ) *adj.* being rough, outlined, and/or without detail

broad·cast (brɔ́dkæst, brɔ́dkɑst) 1. *adj.* transmitted by radio or television, *a broadcast speech* ‖ (of seed or fertilizer) scattered by handfuls, not in rows and drills 2. n. a speech or other item sent out by radio or television 3. *v. pres. part.* **broad·cast·ing** *past* and *past part.* **broad·cast** *v.t.* to transmit by radio or television ‖ to scatter (seed or fertilizer) freely by hand ‖ to spread (news, rumors etc.) about ‖ *v.i.* to speak or perform on the radio

broad·cloth (brɔ́dklɔθ, brɔ́dklɒθ) n. a fine woolen or worsted cloth, chiefly used for men's garments ‖ a fine silk or cotton cloth used for shirts etc.

broad·en (brɔ́d'n) *v.t.* to make broader, wider ‖ *v.i.* to become wider

broad gauge, broad gage (*rail.*) a gauge of more than 4 ft 8½ ins

broad jump (*athletics*) a jump for length, not height

broad·loom (brɔ́dlu:m) *adj.* (of a carpet) woven on a wide loom (at least 4 ft 6 ins, seamless)

broad·mind·ed (brɔ́dmáindid) *adj.* tolerant in thought and views, not bigoted or petty

broad pendant (*Royal Navy*) a short pennant flown by the commodore of a squadron

broad·sheet (brɔ́dʃi:t) n. a large sheet of paper printed on one side only, e.g. with advertising or electioneering matter

broad·side (brɔ́dsɑid) 1. n. (*naut.*) the side of a ship from bow to quarter above the waterline ‖ all the guns on one side of a ship ‖ their simultaneous firing ‖ a spate of vigorous abuse ‖ a broadsheet 2. *adv.* with the broadside fully turned (towards an object)

Broads, the (brɔdz) a region in Norfolk and Suffolk, England, consisting of shallow lakes connected by narrow channels to rivers. The Broads are noted for their bird sanctuaries and for yachting

broad·sword (brɔ́dsɔrd, brɔ́dsɔərd) n. (*hist.*) a sword with a broad, flat blade for cutting rather than thrusting, esp. a claymore

broad·tail (brɔ́dteil) n. the skin or fur of a prematurely born Karakul lamb, flat and wavy in appearance, yielding valuable fur

broad·tape (brɔ́dteip) *adj.* of newswires carrying price and background information on securities and commodities markets, in contrast to the exchanges' own price-transmission wires, which use narrow ticker tape

Broad·way (brɔ́dwei) a street in New York City, famous for its theaters

broad·ways (brɔ́dweiz) *adv.* broadwise

broad·wise (brɔ́dwaiz) *adv.* with the broadest part foremost

bro·cade (broukéid) 1. n. a rich fabric with raised patterns woven in gold or silver thread ‖ any woven fabric with a raised design woven into it by additional weft threads, usually an allover floral pattern 2. *v.t. pres. part.* **bro·cad·ing** *past* and *past part.* **bro·cad·ed** to work (a cloth) with a raised design [earlier *brocado* fr. Span.]

broc·co·li, bro·co·li (brɔ́kəli:) n. a hardy variety of cauliflower ‖ sprouting broccoli [Ital.=little stalks]

bro·chette (brouʃét) n. a skewer for use in cooking [F.]

bro·chure (brouʃúər) n. a pamphlet, esp. a small stitched booklet [F. fr. *brocher*, to stitch]

Brock·en specter, *Br.* **Brock·en spectre** (brɔ́k'n) an atmospheric phenomenon seen by an observer between the sun and a cloudbank, in which his vastly enlarged shadow and that of surrounding objects is projected on to the cloud and is often circled by rings of colored lights [after *Brocken*, peak in the Harz Mtns, Germany]

brock·et (brɔ́kit) n. a second-year stag with its first horns [fr. F. *brocart*]

brocoli *BROCCOLI

Bro·glie (brɔi, *Eng.* brɔgli:), Louis, prince (later duc) de (1892–   ), French theoretical physicist who has made many contributions to quantum mechanics. In 1924, he laid the foundations of wave mechanics, which describes certain properties of atomic particles in terms of waves. He predicted the diffraction of an electron beam, which has since been experimentally confirmed. Nobel prize (1929)

Broglie, Maurice, duc de (1875–1960). French physicist, elder brother of prince Louis de Broglie. He was a pioneer in obtaining X-ray spectra of crystals

brogue (broug) n. a strong shoe for golf, walking etc., usually with perforations decorating the uppers [Gael. and Ir. *brōg*]

brogue n. a soft local pronunciation, esp. of Irish English [perh. fr. Ir. *barrog*, defective pronunciation]

broil (brɔil) *v.t.* to cook by direct exposure to a fire or other radiant heat ‖ to expose to great heat ‖ *v.i.* to be cooked in this way ‖ to be exposed to great heat **broil·er** n. a grill or part of a stove used for broiling ‖ a young chicken suitable for broiling ‖ a very hot day [O.F. *bruiller*, to burn]

broke (brouk) *pres. part.* **brok·ing** *past* and *past part.* **broked** *v.i.* to act as broker [BROKER]

broke *past* and archaic *past part.* of BREAK ‖ *adj.* (*pop.*) having no money ‖ (*pop.*) bankrupt **to go for broke** to use all one's strength, assets etc. in an undertaking

bro·ken (bróukən) *past part.* of BREAK ‖ *adj.* fractured ‖ interrupted, *broken sleep* ‖ uneven, *broken ground* ‖ emotionally crushed ‖ ruined and despairing, *a broken man* ‖ violated, betrayed, *a broken vow* ‖ imperfectly spoken, esp. by a foreigner, *broken English* or as a result of strong emotion ‖ consisting of remains or siftings, *broken orange pekoe tea* ‖ (of weather) uncertain ‖ (of cloud) covering much of the sky but not all of it

bro·ken-down (bróukəndáun) *adj.* reduced physically or morally to very poor condition

bro·ken·heart·ed (bróukənhártid) *adj.* grieving inconsolably

Broken Hill *KABWE

Broken Hill a mining town (pop. 27,700) in New South Wales, Australia: silver, lead and zinc ‖ a small ridge of the Barrier Range where a silver lode was discovered in 1883

broken home family in which the parents are separated or divorced

broken wind (wind) the heaves **bro·ken-wind·ed** (bróukənwíndid) *adj.*

bro·ker (bróukər) n. a stockbroker ‖ a professional middleman in some special market, *a tea broker* **bró·ker·age** n. the commission earned by a broker ‖ his business **brók·ing** n. the profession of being a broker [O.F. *brocheor*, a wine retailer]

bro·ma·crip·tine [$C_{32}H_{40}BrN_5O_5$] (broumǝkríptï:n) n. (*pharm.*) dopamine reception agonist used to inhibit secretions of prolactin that stimulate mammary secretions; marketed as Parlodel

Brom·field (brɔ́mfi:ld), Louis (1896–1956), U.S. novelist, known for his 'The Green Tree' (1924) and 'Early Autumn' (1926)

bro·mide (bróumaid) n. any compound of a metal with bromine (*BINARY COMPOUND) ‖ potassium bromide used medicinally as a sedative ‖ (*loosely*) a trite remark, or anything that tends to slow down mental excitement

bro·mi·dro·sis (bróumədrousis) n. (*med.*) foul-smelling perspiration

bro·mine (bróumi:n) n. a chemical element (symbol Br, at. no. 35, at. mass 79.909), a dark red liquid at room temperature, boiling at 58.8°

C. It is obtained from the magnesium bromide in the Stassfurt deposits and occurs in sea water as bromides [fr. F. *brome* fr. Gk *bromos*, stink]

bro·mo·u·ra·cil [$C_4H_3N_2O_2Br$] (brɒumoujú:rə-sil) *n.* (*biochem.*) in the genetic process, a derivative of RNA uracil that replaces thymine and pairs with adenine during bacterial synthesis

bronchi *pl.* of BRONCHUS

bron·chi·a (brɒ́ŋkiːə) *pl. n.* the branches of the bronchi within the lungs **brón·chi·al** *adj.* pertaining to the bronchia or the bronchi [L. fr. Gk]

bron·chi·ole (brɒ́ŋkiːoul) *n.* one of the last, minute ramifications of the bronchi, inside the lungs

bron·chi·o·pneu·mo·nia (brɒŋkiːounuːmóunjə, brɒŋkiːounjuːmóunjə) *n.* bronchopneumonia

bron·chit·ic (brɒŋkítik) *adj.* of, relating to or having bronchitis

bron·chi·tis (brɒŋkáitis) *n.* an inflammation of the mucous membrane in the bronchial tubes

broncho *BRONCO

bron·cho·pneu·mo·nia (brɒŋkounuːmóunjə, brɒŋkounjuːmóunjə) *n.* an inflammation of the lungs

bron·cho·scope (brɒ́ŋkəskoup) *n.* a narrow tubular instrument for inspecting the large bronchi, to remove foreign bodies from them, or to treat disease **bron·chos·co·py** (brɒŋkɒ́skəpi:) *n.* [fr. BRONCHIA+Gk *skopein*, to look at]

bron·chus (brɒ́ŋkəs) *pl.* **bron·chi** (brɒ́ŋkai:, brɒ́ŋki:) *n.* either of the two main divisions of the trachea leading directly into the lungs, where they ramify [Mod. L. fr. Gk]

Bron·co (brɒ́ŋkou) *n.* a light, twin turboprop, twin-seat observation and support aircraft (OV 10), sometimes equipped with machine guns and light ordnance for close air-support missions

bron·co, bron·cho (brɒ́ŋkou) *pl.* **bron·cos, bron·chos** *n.* a wild or halftrained horse or pony of the western U.S.A. [Span. =rough]

bron·co·bust·er (brɒ́ŋkoubˌʌstər) *n.* a man who breaks in wild horses

Bron·të (brɒ́nti:), Anne (1820–49), English novelist, author of 'The Tenant of Wildfell Hall' (1847). Her work gained some recognition, but she was overshadowed by her sisters, Charlotte and Emily. She wrote under the name of Acton Bell

Bron·të, Charlotte (1816–55), English novelist, author of 'The Professor' (published 1857), 'Jane Eyre' (1847), 'Shirley' (1849) and 'Villette' (1853). The second and fourth of these drew largely on her own experiences as a child at school, as a governess, and as a student teacher in a Belgian School. The third is a portrait of her sister Emily, set in a Yorkshire mill town. She wrote at first under the name of Currer Bell

Bron·të, Emily (1818–48), English novelist and poet. 'Wuthering Heights' (1847), her only novel, which vividly evokes the wild, bleak Yorkshire moors, violates almost every convention of Victorian fiction: it is direct and uncompromising in its treatment of love and hatred. The excellence of her poetry was long unrecognized. She wrote at first under the name of Ellis Bell

bron·to·saur (brɒ́ntəsɔr) *n.* a member of *Brontosaurus*, a genus of dinosaurian reptiles of the Jurassic and Cretaceous periods, often over 65 ft long and 12 ft high [Mod. L. fr. Gk *bronte*, thunder+*sauros*, lizard]

Bronx cheer (brɒŋks) (*pop.*) a rude sound made by vibrating the tongue between the lips, to show contempt or derision [fr. the *Bronx*, New York City]

Bronx, the a chiefly residential borough (pop. 1,168,972) of New York City, on the mainland

bronze (brɒnz) **1.** *n.* an alloy of copper and tin, special types also containing other elements. It expands when it solidifies and so makes good castings when poured into molds. It is very hard, and resistant to moisture or weathering. It was used for weapons, tools and ornaments (*BRONZE AGE) before iron was smelted, and is used in statuary and coinage ‖ an object made of bronze ‖ the color of bronze, golden or reddish-brown **2.** *v.t. pres. part.* **bronz·ing** *past and past part.* **bronzed** to make the color of bronze [F. fr. Ital.]

Bronze Age (brɒnz) the era between the Stone and Iron Ages, when bronze was used for tools and weapons. Starting in the East in the 5th

millennium it spread to all Europe, India and China by 1500 B.C. Writing and arithmetic date from this age, and other inventions which profoundly altered society: the plow, wheeled vehicles, and the use of animals for pulling and riding. Life became more settled, townships were formed, men became specialized in their work, and trading and shipping began their civilizing effects

bronze cancer corrosion process that frequently destroys statuary

bronz·ing (brɒ́nziŋ) *n.* (*cosmetology*) creation of gold-red shading to hair by successive applications of lightener

Bron·zi·no (brɒndzí:nɔ), Il (Agnolo di Cosimo di Mariano, 1503–72), Florentine painter, esp. of portraits

brooch (broutʃ, bru:tʃ) *n.* an ornamental, sometimes jeweled clasp worn esp. as a neck fastening or on a lapel [M.E. *broche*, var. of BROACH]

brood (bru:d) **1.** *n.* the young birds from one clutch of eggs ‖ (*rhet.*) a large family of children **2.** *v.i.* (of a bird) to sit on eggs and hatch them ‖ *v.t.* (of a bird) to sit on (eggs) so as to hatch them **to brood on** (or **over**) to think about and weigh in one's mind ‖ to think about sullenly, esp. after an injury or insult, *to brood over one's grievances* **bróod·er** *n.* a heated device for rearing chicks artificially ‖ someone who broods [O.E. *bröd*]

brood·mare (brú:dmɛər) *n.* a mare kept for breeding purposes

brood·y (brú:di:) *comp.* **brood·i·er** *superl.* **brood·i·est** *adj.* (of a hen) wanting to sit on eggs ‖ (of people) moody

brook (bruk) *n.* a small stream [O.E. *brōc*]

brook *v.t.* (only in negative constructions and *rhet.*) to put up with, endure, tolerate [O.E. *brūcan*, to use, enjoy]

Brooke (bruk), Sir James (1803–68), 1st raja of Sarawak (1841–63), appointed by the sultan of Brunei after settling a revolt. The Brooke family ruled until 1946, when Sarawak was handed over to the British government

Brooke, Rupert Chawner (1887–1915), English lyric poet who died on active service in the 1st world war

brook·let (brúklit) *n.* a very small stream

Brook·lyn (brúklin) an industrial and residential borough (pop. 2,230,936) of New York City, at the southwest end of Long Island

Brooks (bruks), Van Wyck (1886–1963), American critic of New England life and literature, author of a literary history of the U.S.A. (1936–52)

broom (bru:m, brum) *n.* a longhandled brush for sweeping floors etc., originally made with twigs of broom, heather etc. ‖ any shrub of the genera *Cytisus*, *Genista* and *Spartium*, fam. *Papilionaceae*, generally having yellow flowers [O.E. *brom*, a shrub]

broom·corn (brú:mkɔrn, brúmkɔrn) *n.* *Sorghum vulgare*, common millet, a sorghum with a jointed stem bearing a long, stiff-branched panicle and used for making brooms

broom·rape (brú:mreip, brúmreip) *n.* a member of *Orobranche*, a genus of leafless parasitic plants growing on the roots of broom and other plants

broom·stick (brú:mstik, brúmstik) *n.* a broom handle serving as a witch's mount for riding through the air

bros. brothers

broth (brɔθ, brɒθ) *n.* a thin soup made from meat stock and vegetables, esp. with rice or barley ‖ meat stock [O.E. *broth*]

broth·el (brɒ́θəl) *n.* a house of prostitutes [M.E. *brothel*, a base person fr. O.E. *breothen* (*brothen*), to go to ruin]

broth·er (brʌ́ðər) *pl.* **broth·ers**, *alt. pl.* **breth·ren** (brέðrin) *n.* a son in his relationship to another child of the same parents ‖ a man sharing with others the same citizenship, profession, religion etc., *our African brothers* ‖ a title in certain religious orders, sects, guilds, corporations etc. [O.E. *brōthor*]

broth·er-ger·man (brʌ́ðərʒə́rmən) *pl.* **broth·ers-ger·man** *n.* one's full brother, i.e. born of the same two parents [BROTHER+*german*, akin fr. O.F. *germain*]

broth·er·hood (brʌ́ðərhud) *n.* the condition of being a brother ‖ a group of men living a communal life ‖ men of the same profession, business or other occupational tie, a fraternity [prob. fr. O.E. *brotherred*]

broth·er-in-law (brʌ́ðərinlɔ) *pl.* **broth·ers-in-**

law *n.* the brother of one's husband or wife ‖ the husband of one's sister

broth·er·ly (brʌ́ðərli:) *adj.* of or like a brother ‖ displaying characteristics of a brother, such as loyalty or steady affection

Brothers of the Christian Schools *JEAN BAPTISTE DE LA SALLE

Brough·am (bru:m), Henry Peter, Baron Brougham and Vaux (1778–1868), British statesman. Having helped to found the 'Edinburgh Review' (1802), he entered parliament (1810) and attacked the slave trade. As lord chancellor (1830–4), he devoted himself to legal and educational reform

brought *past and past part.* of BRING

Brou·wer (bráuwər), Adriaen (c. 1606–38), Flemish painter of tavern scenes

brow (brau) **1.** *n.* the forehead ‖ (usually *pl.*) the eyebrow ‖ the rounded top of a hill or projecting edge of a cliff [O.E. *brū*]

brow·beat (bráubi:t) *pres. part.* **brow·beat·ing** *past* **brow·beat** *past part.* **brow·beat·en** (bráubi:t'n) *v.t.* to bully mentally and spiritually

Brow·der (bráudər), Earl (Russell) (1891–1973), U.S. Communist Party leader. He served as its general secretary (1930–45) and as its candidate (1936, 1940) for the U.S. presidency. He was expelled (1946) from the party for advocating coexistence

Brown (braun), Sir Arthur Whitten *ALCOCK

Brown, Ford Madox (1821–93), English painter. He was associated with the Pre-Raphaelites and, by his close attention to detail, his passionate sincerity and his use of vivid colors, he led the breakaway from Victorian traditions

Brown, George (1818–80), Canadian journalist and statesman. As a member of the Canadian parliament (1851–65) he opposed the political power of the Roman Catholic Church. This led (1854) to the secularization of the clergy's reserves, and his fight for proportional representation of the two Canadas in parliament led (1867) to the British North America act. He strongly influenced the unification of Canada and the acquisition of the Northwest Territories by the new dominion

Brown, John (1800–59), American abolitionist. In the cause of freedom for black slaves he incited (Oct. 16, 1859) an insurrection at Harper's Ferry, Virginia (now W. Virginia). The attempt failed, and he was hanged for treason. His hanging increased the dissension over slavery

Brown, Lancelot (1716–83), known as 'Capability' Brown, English landscape gardener of vision who laid out the gardens of many great English country houses. He was a product of (and an influence on) the 18th-c. taste for the picturesque

brown (braun) **1.** *n.* any color of an orange-black mixture ‖ such a pigment, fabric etc. **2.** *adj.* of the color brown **3.** *v.t.* to make brown, esp. by exposure to sun or heat ‖ *v.i.* to become brown [O.E. *brūn*]

brown bagging 1. carrying one's lunch to work. **2.** carrying liquor to places where its sale is illegal. —**brown bag** *v.* —**brown bagger** *n.*

brown bear *Ursus arctos*, a very large European bear having a brown coat

brown belt 1. in judo or karate a degree of proficiency below that of black belt. **2.** one who holds such a certification

Brown Berets Mexican-American organization seeking to create better conditions for Mexican Americans in U.S.

brown bread dark bread of unbolted flour ‖ steamed bread, usually made of rye and cornmeal, graham or white flour, molasses, soda and milk or water

brown coal lignite

Browne (braun), Sir Thomas (1605–82), English doctor and author of prose works: curious, personal, and informative observations and meditations, notably 'Religio Medici' (1642) and 'Hydriotaphia, or Urneburiall' (1658). His prose is splendidly rhythmic and decorative

Brown·i·an movement (bráuni:ən) erratic movement of extremely small particles in suspension, due to the impacts of the molecules of the fluid in which they are suspended. They were first observed in 1827 under the microscope by Robert Brown (1773-1858, Scottish botanist), who realized that it was striking evidence in support of the molecular kinetic theory

CONCISE PRONUNCIATION KEY: **(a)** æ, c*a*t; ɑ, c*a*r; ɔ f*aw*n; ei, sn*a*ke. **(e)** e, h*e*n; i:, sh*ee*p; iə, d*ee*r; εə, b*ea*r. **(i)** i, f*i*sh; ai, t*i*ger; əː, b*i*rd. **(o)** o, *o*x; au, c*ow*; ou, g*oa*t; u, p*oo*r; ɔi, r*oy*al. **(u)** ʌ, d*u*ck; u, b*u*ll; u:, g*oo*se; ə, b*a*cillus; ju:, c*u*be. x, lo*ch*; θ, *th*ink; ð, bo*th*er; z, *Z*en; ʒ, corsa*g*e; dʒ, sava*g*e; ŋ, orangutan*g*; j, *y*ak; ʃ, *fi*sh; tʃ, fet*ch*; 'l, rabb*le*; 'n, redd*en*. Complete pronunciation key appears inside front cover.

brown·ie (bráuni:) *n.* a good-natured goblin supposed to do helpful chores at night ‖ a junior girl scout, (*Br.*) junior girl guide ‖ a square of rich chocolate cake with walnuts

brownie point (used pejoratively) credit earned by doing a favor, esp. for a boss

Brown·ing (bráunin), Elizabeth Barrett (1806–61), English poet and critic, wife of Robert Browning and author of 'Sonnets from the Portuguese' (1850)

Browning, John Moses (1855–1926), U.S. inventor. He designed small arms and automatic weapons, many of which were adopted for use by the U.S. army

Browning, Robert (1812–89), English poet. His dramatic monologues (a genre in which he was unrivaled) are penetrating studies of personality as well as vigorous poetry. In his lyrics and occasionally elsewhere (e.g. 'Andrea del Sarto') he reveals great tenderness and compassion. 'The Ring and the Book' (1868–9) explores the human mind by telling the same story 12 times, each time from the point of view of a different character

Brown·ist (bráunist) (*Eng. hist.*) a member of a Puritan sect of Congregationalist views founded by Robert Browne (c. 1550–c. 1633), English clergyman (*PILGRIM)

brown lung (*med.*) popular name for byssinosis, a chronic, disabling lung disease caused by long-term inhalation of cotton dust; prevalent among textile workers. *Cf* BLACK LUNG

brown·out (bráunqut) *n.* loss of electric power that causes dimming of an area's lighting

brown paper coarse paper used for parcels

Brown Power policy designed to provide greater influence for Mexican-Americans and other hispanics in U.S.

brown rice hulled, unpolished rice that largely retains the bran layers and germs

brown·stone (bráunstoun) *n.* a reddish-brown sandstone used in building, esp. for front elevations, and formerly esp. associated with smart residential districts of New York City ‖ a house with a facade of this stone

brown study a reverie in which one is unaware of surrounding persons and things

brown sugar unrefined or half-refined sugar, with a film of dark syrup covering its crystals

Brown University a university which was originally Rhode Island College (1764) at Warren, R.I. It was moved (1770) to Providence, R.I., and renamed (1804)

'Brown v. Board of Education of Topeka, Kansas' a decision (1954) of the U.S. Supreme Court, which held that officially segregated schools were inherently unequal (contrary to an older Supreme Court decision upholding the separate but equal doctrine) and therefore unconstitutional

brown·ware (bráunwɛər) *n.* **1.** primitive brown or reddish pottery. **2.** kitchen pottery with a brown glaze

browse (brauz) **1.** *n.* the act of browsing **2.** *v. pres. part.* **brows·ing** *past* and *past part.* **browsed** *v.t.* to nibble or feed on (leaves, bushes etc.) ‖ *v.i.* to nibble, feed, on leaves, bushes etc. ‖ to graze ‖ to dip into a book, read without concentration ‖ to explore a library or bookshop unsystematically, or in a leisurely, desultory fashion [perh. early F. *broust,* sprout]

brows·er (bráuzər) *n.* (*biol.*) an animal that feeds on leaves, twigs, etc.; e.g., a deer

Bruce (bru:s), James (1730–94), Scottish explorer. He reached the source of the Blue Nile in Abyssinia (1770), and traced it to its confluence with the White Nile (1771)

Bruce, Robert the *ROBERT I

bru·cel·lo·sis (bru:səlóusis) *n.* undulant fever [after Sir David *Bruce* (1855–1931), Scottish physician]

Bruce of Melbourne, Stanley Melbourne Bruce, 1st Viscount (1883–1967), Australian statesman. He became prime minister of Australia (1923–9). He was president of the council of the League of Nations (1936), Australian high commissioner in London (1933–45), and chairman of the World Food Council (1947–51)

Brü·cke, die (brýkə) (the Bridge) a German expressionist art movement active 1905–13, originated by Kirchner, Schmidt-Rottluff and Heckel, and joined by Nolde. Its participants introduced the influence of primitive art into works which have affinities with those of the Fauve group

Bruck·ner (brúknər), Anton (1824–96), Austrian composer. His symphonies are of great length and elaboration. An organist and a devout Catholic, he also wrote church music, e.g. four Masses, and 'Te Deum' in C major for soprano, chorus, orchestra and organ

Brue·gel (brɔ́:gəl), Jan (1568–1625), Flemish painter, second son of Bruegel the Elder. He painted still lifes and allegorical landscapes remarkable for their detail and color. He was known as ' Velvet' Bruegel

Bruegel, Pieter, the Elder (c. 1525–69), Flemish painter of landscape and scenes of low life. The landscapes are ideal and yet have an intense feeling of reality, and of space and majesty. The peasant scenes are sometimes cruelly satirical. He also painted biblical scenes in terms of contemporary life, e.g. 'Massacre of the Innocents'

Bruegel, Pieter, the Younger (c. 1564- c. 1638), Flemish painter, elder son of Bruegel the Elder. His diabolical scenes of the lower regions earned him the nickname 'Hell' Bruegel

Bruges (bru:ʒ, bry:ʒ) (*Flem.* Brugge) a town (pop. 119,400) in Flanders, Belgium. Products: lace and textiles. A leading medieval port, important for its woolen manufactures, it was ruined in the 16th c. by the silting up of the Zwin, the arm of the North Sea on which it lay. Its prosperity was revived by the building of a canal to the sea at Zeebrugge. Its museum contains works esp. of its 15th-c. school of painting (the van Eycks, Memling, Van der Goes)

bruise (bru:z) **1.** *n.* a surface injury to the body, caused by a fall or a blow. Small broken blood vessels discolor the skin, which is not broken ‖ a similar injury to fruit or plants **2.** *v. pres. part.* **bruis·ing** *past* and *past part.* **bruised** *v.t.* to inflict a bruise on, *a bruised arm, bruised feelings* ‖ to pound and crush into small particles, as in a mortar ‖ to make a dent in (e.g. wood or metal) ‖ *v.i.* to be susceptible to, show the effect of, bruises, *ripe fruit bruises easily* **brúis·er** *n.* (*pop., old-fash.*) a professional boxer ‖ (*pop.*) a heavy aggressive man [O.E. *brȳsan,* to crush]

bruit (bru:t) *v.t.* (*rhet.*) (with 'about') to cause (something) to spread among the public as hearsay or rumor, *it was being bruited about that he had been fired* [F.=noise]

Bru·maire (brymer) (F. *hist.*) the 2nd month of the French Revolutionary calendar ‖ the coup d'etat of 18 Brumaire (Nov. 9, 1799) in which the Directory was replaced by the Consulate under Napoleon

Brum·mell (brʌ́məl), George Bryan (1778–1840), English dandy known as 'Beau Brummell', a friend of George IV and a leader of fashion, who had a lasting influence on the taste of polite society in England

Bru·nan·burh, Battle of (brú:nænbərg) the battle (937) in which Athelstan, king of the West Saxons and Mercians, defeated an army of Scots, Danes, and Welsh, and became king of most of what is now England. The poem 'Brunanburh', contained in the Anglo–Saxon Chronicle, recounts the battle

brunch (brʌntʃ) *n.* a light meal that does duty as both a late breakfast and an early lunch [BR(EAKFAST)+(L)UNCH]

Bru·nei (brú:nai) Islamic sultanate (area 2,226 sq. miles, pop. 252,000) on the northwest coast of the island of Borneo. It is in two parts, both surrounded by Sarawak, and has a coastline of about 100 miles. Capital: Bandar Seri Begawan (pop. 49,902) on Brunei River, 9 miles from its mouth. Religions: Moslem, Buddhist, Christian, Animist. Languages: Malay (official), Chinese, English, Iban and other local languages. The land rises to the south from a narrow coastal plain and is heavily forested. Crops include rice, sugarcane and fruit. Rubber, lumber, natural gas, cutch and sago are exported. There is a large oil field and refinery and offshore oil production is developing. The sultan of Brunei ceded Sarawak to James Brooke (1841). Brunei was placed under British protection (1888). It was occupied by the Japanese (1941–5). It decided (1963) not to join Malaysia as had been proposed. It is ruled by the sultan, a privy council, and executive and legislative councils. Brunei became a fully independent nation on Jan. 1, 1984

Bru·nel (bru:nél), Isambard Kingdom (1806–59), English engineer who constructed suspension bridges at Clifton (1834), Hungerford (1845) and Saltash (1859). He pioneered the design of giant steamships, notably the 'Great Western' (1838), the 'Great Britain' (1845) and

the 'Great Eastern' (1858). His work invariably combined utility with beauty

Bru·nel·les·chi (bru:n'léski:), Filippo (1377–1446), outstanding Italian architect of the early Renaissance, painter and sculptor. His masterpieces are the dome of S. Maria del Fiore (the Cathedral), the small domed Pazzi chapel of S. Croce, and the Pitti Palace, in Florence

bru·net, bru·nette (bru:nét) **1.** *adj.* having dark hair and complexion (cf. BLOND) **2.** *n.* someone with such hair and complexion [F., dim. of *brun,* brown]

Brun·hild (brú:nhild) the legendary heroine of several myths, esp. in the Old Norse 'Edda', in the 'Völsunga Saga', and in the 'Nibelungenlied'

Brun·hil·da (bru:nhíldə) (c. 534–613), Visigoth queen and regent of Austrasia, noted for her beauty, wisdom and cruelty. Dynastic feuds and war with the Franks made her reign bloody. She was captured by Fredegund's son, tortured, and dragged to death at the heels of a wild horse

Bru·no (brú:nɔ), Giordano (1548–1600), Italian Renaissance philosopher. He taught at Paris and at Oxford, attacking Scholasticism and Aristotelianism. He was greatly influenced by Nicholas of Cusa. Under the influence of the new Copernican astronomy he evolved a naturalistic and mystical pantheism. He was burnt at Rome as a heretic

Bruno, St. (c. 1030–1101), German monk. He founded the Carthusians

Bruns·wick (bránzwik) (G. Braunschweig) a town (pop. 261,500) in Lower Saxony, West Germany, founded c. 860, a publishing and printing center: cars, pianos, optical instruments, calculating machines. It was capital of the former Duchy of Brunswick, which joined the German Empire (1781), became a republic (1918) and joined the Reich (1934)

brunt (brʌnt) *n.* the main force or shock of a blow, attack, etc. [etym. doubtful]

brush (brʌʃ) *n.* an implement made of bristles, wire, hair, or nylon etc. set in wood, etc., different kinds being used for sweeping floors, scrubbing, painting, grooming the hair etc. ‖ the act of brushing ‖ a bushy tail, esp. of a fox or squirrel ‖ (*elec.*) a bundle of conducting wires or strips used to convey electricity to or from a surface with which it makes contact ‖ (*phys.*) brush-shaped dark regions, often in the form of a Maltese cross, seen when biaxial crystals are viewed through a mineralogical microscope. They are caused by interference between beams of polarized light ‖ a short, quick fight, a skirmish ‖ a controversy ‖ small trees and shrubs, land covered with thicket ‖ brushwood (undergrowth) [O.F. *brosse,* brush, brushwood]

brush *v.t.* to apply a brush to ‖ to apply with a brush ‖ to force (one's way) ‖ to touch lightly in passing ‖ *v.i.* to make a brushing action ‖ to force one's way, esp. through a crowd **to brush aside** to dismiss summarily **to brush away** to remove with a brush or with a brushing action of one's fingers **to brush off** to dismiss curtly ‖ to remove with a brush or a brushing action of one's fingers **to brush over** to paint lightly ‖ to touch lightly in passing, esp. to treat lightly or superficially, *to brush over a problem* **to brush up** to refresh by starting to study again, *to brush up one's French* [perh. fr. F. *brosser*]

brush·back (brʌ́ʃbæk) *n.* (*baseball*) pitch closely missing batter's head, designed to force him to move back from the plate

brush discharge a stream of electrically charged air molecules repelled by sharp points on a charged conductor

brushed wool a woolen fabric on which a nap has been raised by brushes

brush·fire war (brʌ́ʃfqiər) *n.* (*mil.*) relatively small military or police action, usu. for harassment of one side by another

brush-off (brʌ́ʃɔf, brʌ́ʃɑf) *n.* a curt dismissal

brush·stroke (brʌ́ʃstrouk) *n.* the single movement of a paint-filled brush against a surface ‖ the contour or pattern made by this movement

brush·up (brʌ́ʃʌp) *n.* a brushing up of something imperfectly retained in the mind

brush wheel a wheel with brushes or some buffing material on it, so that it polishes as it revolves

brush·wood (brʌ́ʃwud) *n.* undergrowth, thicket ‖ wood from small branches that have broken off

CONCISE PRONUNCIATION KEY: **(a)** æ, c*a*t; ɑ, c*ar*; ɔ f*aw*n; ei, sn*a*ke. **(e)** e, h*e*n; i:, sh*ee*p; iə, d*eer*; ɛə, b*ear*. **(i)** i, f*i*sh; ai, t*i*ger; ə:, b*ir*d. **(o)** o, *o*x; au, c*ow*; ou, g*oa*t; u, p*oo*r; ɔi, r*oy*al. **(u)** ʌ, d*u*ck; u, b*u*ll; u:, g*oo*se; ə, b*a*cillus; ju:, c*u*be. x, lo*ch*; θ, *th*ink; ð, bo*th*er; z, *Z*en; ʒ, cor*s*age; dʒ, sa*v*age; ŋ, oranguta*ng*; j, *y*ak; ʃ, *f*ish; tʃ, fe*tch*; 'l, rabb*le*; 'n, redd*en.* Complete pronunciation key appears inside front cover.

brush·work (brʌ́ʃwəːrk) n. (art) the style or technique of applying paint with brushes

brusque (brʌsk) adj. abrupt, short ‖ curt, slightly hostile in manner or speech [F. fr. Ital.]

brus·que·rie (brʌ́skəri:) n. the quality or state of being brusque, brusqueness [F.]

Brus·sels (brʌ́səlz) (F. Bruxelles, Flem. Brussel) the capital (pop. 169,000, with agglom. 1,000,221) of Belgium. It is officially bilingual (French and Flemish). It is a road, rail and canal junction. Industries: food processing, tobacco, clothing, chemicals, textiles, engineering, printing. In the 16th and 17th cc. Brussels was the capital of the Spanish Netherlands. It has been the Belgian capital since 1830. There are many medieval, Renaissance and baroque buildings, including the Gothic church of St Gudule (1220–73) and the town hall (1402–54). University (1834)

Brussels carpet a wool carpet fixed in a strong linen foundation

Brussels lace needlepoint or bobbin lace worked in floral designs, originally made at Brussels

Brussels sprout a small edible green sprout or bud on the plant Brassica oleracea gemmifera ‖ the plant

brut (bryt) adj. (of champagne) very dry [F.]

bru·tal (brú:t'l) adj. harsh to the point of cruelty, brutal punishment ‖ savagely violent, a brutal attack ‖ plain and direct with no regard for feeling, the brutal truth **bru·tal·i·ty** (bru:tǽliti:) pl. **bru·tal·i·ties** n. harshness to the point of cruelty, or an instance of this ‖ savage violence, or an instance of this [fr. L. brutus, irrational]

bru·tal·ism (brú:t'lizəm) n. 1. art style involving distortion and exaggeration used to create effect of massiveness. 2. in architecture, use of large exposed concrete areas without windows to suggest massiveness and strength. —**brutalist** n, adj.

bru·tal·i·za·tion (bru:t'lizéiʃən) n. a brutalizing or being brutalized

bru·tal·ize (brú:t'laiz) pres. part. **bru·tal·iz·ing** past and past part. **bru·tal·ized** v.t. to render brutal, inhuman, savage ‖ to treat brutally

brute (bru:t) 1. n. an animal ‖ a brutal person 2. adj. not endowed with reason, a brute beast ‖ (of actions, motives, ideas etc.) like a beast's in strength or savagery, brute force **brút·ish** adj. [F. brut]

Bru·tus (brú:təs), Lucius Junius (6th c. B.C.), Roman statesman, principally responsible for the expulsion of Tarquinius Superbus and the establishment of the Roman republic (510 B.C.). He became one of its first praetors

Brutus, Marcus Junius (c. 85–42 B.C.), Roman statesman. A supporter of Pompey in the civil war, he was pardoned by Caesar after the Battle of Pharsalus. Despite Caesar's favors he supported the senatorial party and was a leader of the conspiracy against the dictator. He committed suicide after his defeat by Antony and Augustus at Philippi

Bry·an (bráiən), William Jennings (1860–1925), U.S. political leader and orator. As champion of the Democratic free-silver movement to relieve the depressed conditions of agriculture and industry, he unsuccessfully ran twice (1896, 1900) against William McKinley and (1908) against Howard Taft for the U.S. presidency. Appointed (1913) secretary of state by President Woodrow Wilson, he resigned (1915) when Wilson protested to Germany over the sinking of the 'Lusitania'. He proposed progressive measures including the popular election of senators, a tax on income, and women's suffrage which were eventually adopted. As a fundamentalist and opponent of Darwinism, he assisted (1925) the prosecution in the Scopes Trial

Bryan-Chamorro Treaty a treaty (1916) signed between William Jennings Bryan and Nicaraguan president Emiliano Chamorro, giving the U.S. the right to construct a canal through Nicaragua

Bry·ansk (bri:ánsk) a city (pop. 407,000) of the W. European R.S.F.S.R., U.S.S.R.: rolling stock, cement, clothing, meat processing

Bry·ant (bráiənt), William Cullen (1794–1878), U.S. nature poet and editor (1829–78) of the New York Evening Post, through which he promoted liberal causes

Bryce (brais), James Bryce, 1st Viscount (1839–1922), British statesman, ambassador to the U.S.A. (1907–12), and writer. His works

include 'The Holy Roman Empire' (1864), 'The American Commonwealth' (1888), 'Studies in History and Jurisprudence' (1901)

bry·o·log·i·cal (braiəlɑ́dʒik'l) adj. of or relating to bryology

bry·ol·o·gist (braiɑ́lədʒist) n. someone who studies bryology

bry·ol·o·gy (braiɑ́lədʒi:) n. the branch of botany relating to the bryophytes [fr. Gk bruon, moss+logos, word]

bry·on·y (bráiəni:) pl. **bry·o·nies** n. a member of Bryonia, fam. Cucurbitaceae, a genus of climbing plants, with coiled tendrils, large leaves and red fruit, esp. B. dioica, white bryony ‖ Tamus communis, fam. Dioscoreaceae, black bryony, a plant which resembles this but is unrelated and has no tendrils [fr. L. bryonia fr. Gk]

bry·o·phyte (bráiəfait) n. a member of Bryophyta, a phylum of Embryophyta, comprising primitive land plants (i.e. liverworts and mosses) characterized by a rhizoid foot with a nonvascular moisture-transport system and marked alternation of generations in which the gametophyte possessing chlorophyll supports the sporophyte with food and moisture [Mod. L. fr. Gk bruon, moss+phuton, plant]

bry·o·zo·an, **bry·o·zo·on** (braiəzóuən) pl. **bry·o·zo·ans**, **bry·o·zo·a** (braiəzóuə) n. a member of the phylum Bryozoa of aquatic animals, superficially resembling coelenterates. They have a tubular body with a crown of ciliated tentacles, and are usually found in colonies, in fresh water, like a coat of moss [fr. Gk bruon, moss+zōe, life]

Bryth·on (bríθɒn) n. a Celt of Britain **Bry·thón·ic** 1. adj. of or pertaining to the Brythons or their language 2. n. a division of the Celtic family of languages [Welsh]

Bryu·sov (brjú:sʌf), Valery Yakovlevich (1873–1924), Russian symbolist poet, novelist, critic and translator

b/s (abbr.) for bit per sec.

B-school (abbr.) colleges of business administration, esp. on the graduate level

Bu·bas·tis (bju:bǽstis) *ZAGAZIG

bub·ble (bʌ́b'l) 1. n. a small volume of air or gas surrounded by a liquid, a solid or an elastic membrane such as a soap solution film. The internal pressure exceeds the external pressure of liquid or the atmosphere by an amount which, for equilibrium, balances the surface tension of the surface or surfaces ‖ dome or semicylindrically shaped structure, e.g., of rubber or plastic ‖ a tightly fitting plastic package covering objects on display or for sale ‖ something transient without substance and liable to burst, a bubble of excitement 2. v.i. pres. part. **bub·bling** past and past part. **bub·bled** to form bubbles ‖ to make gurgling sounds **to bubble over** to be exuberant [imit.]

bubble car automobile with a transparent plastic top so that passengers may see and be seen from without

bubble chamber a device used to detect and study the properties of fundamental particles. It consists of a chamber containing a liquid at a temperature slightly above its boiling point. The ions formed by high-energy charged particles traversing the liquid serve as centers of formation of small vapor bubbles, which define the tracks of the particles

bubble gum 1. chewing gum that can be expanded to form a bubble. 2. simplistic rock music for young listeners

bubble memory (computer) solid-state magnetic device that stores data in bubbles that move in films of magnetic material with no friction points. It is capable of retaining data when power is shut off, used esp. in automatic numeric control of machine tools

bub·ble·top (bʌ́b'ltɒp) n. transparent dome shape used in umbrellas, automobiles, trains, and buses to permit greater visibility. Cf BUBBLE CAR

bub·bly (bʌ́bli:) comp. **bub·bli·er** superl. **bub·bli·est** adj. full of bubbles

Bub·er (bú:bər), Martin (1878–1965), Austrian-born Israeli writer, philosopher, sociologist and Jewish theologian. His best known works are 'I and Thou' (1923),'Between Man and Man' (1946), and 'Tales of Hasidism' (1947, 1948)

bu·bo (bjú:bou) pl. **bu·boes** n. (med.) an inflamed swelling of a lymph gland, esp. in the groin or armpit **bu·bon·ic** (bjubɒ́nik) adj. [L.L. fr. Gk boubōn, groin]

bubonic plague an epidemic disease symptomized by fever, chills, prostration, and buboes. It

is spread by rats and transmitted to man by fleas

bubu (bú:bu:) n. *BOU-BOU

Bu·ca·ra·man·ga (bu:kɑrɑmáŋgɑ) a city (pop. 209,000) of N. central Colombia, a tobacco and coffee center

buc·cal (bʌ́k'l) adj. (anat.) of the cheeks or mouth cavity [fr. L. bucca, cheek]

buc·ca·neer (bʌkəníər) n. a pirate **Buc·ca·neer** a member of an Anglo-French pirate confederacy which fought Spain in the Caribbean (16th and 17th cc.). The most famous of the Buccaneers was Sir Henry Morgan. The confederacy began to dissolve when Britain went to war with France (1689) [F. boucanier, a hunter of wild oxen (used of the French settlers in Haiti)]

Bu·cer (bú:sər, bú:tsər), Martin (1491–1551), German Protestant reformer, midway in his views between Luther and Zwingli. He led the Reformed Church in Strasbourg (1523–48). In 1549 Cranmer invited him to Cambridge to teach theology and to assist the English Reformation

Buch·an (bʌ́kən), John, 1st Baron Tweedsmuir (1875–1940), Scottish statesman and author of adventure stories, e.g. 'The Thirty-Nine Steps' (1915). He was governor-general of Canada (1935–40)

Bu·chan·an (bju:kǽnən), George (1506–82), Scottish scholar and Latin poet

Buchanan, James (1791–1868), 15th president (1857–61) of the U.S.A., a Democrat. As minister to Great Britain (1853–6), he helped to draw up the Ostend Manifesto. Despite his vigorous attempts to placate the pro-slavery and anti-slavery factions, the U.S.A. drifted during his administration toward civil war

Bu·cha·rest (bú:kərest, bjú:kərest) the capital (pop. 2,165,997) of Rumania, on the Walachian plain, a rail junction and trading center (petroleum, lumber, agricultural produce), with food processing, textile, chemical and engineering industries. University (1864)

Bucharest, Treaty of a treaty signed (1913) by Rumania, Greece, Montenegro, Serbia and Bulgaria, ending the 2nd Balkan War, and defining the boundaries of Bulgaria

Bu·chen·wald (bú:xənvɑlt) n. the site of a Nazi concentration camp (1937–45) near Weimar in Germany

Buch·man (bú:kmən), Frank Nathan Daniel (1878–1961), American-born evangelist who used modern propaganda techniques to further his campaign for individual and national moral regeneration (*MORAL RE-ARMAMENT)

Buch·man·ism (bú:kmənizəm) n. *MORAL RE-ARMAMENT

Buch·ner (bú:xnər), Eduard (1860–1917), German chemist, awarded a Nobel prize in 1907 for his work on fermentation. He isolated the enzymes invertase, zymase and lactase

Büch·ner (bý́xnər), Georg (1813–37), German poet and playwright. His works include 'Dantons Tod' (1835) and 'Wozzeck' (or 'Woyzeck', 1836), which inspired Berg's opera

Büchner funnel (chem.) a cylindrical porcelain funnel, with a flat circular perforated base, used for filtration under reduced pressure [after Ernst Büchner, 19th-c. G. chemist]

Buck (bʌk), Pearl (1892–1973), U.S. author and Nobel prizewinner (1938) in literature. Her novel 'The Good Earth' (1931), describing the hardship of Chinese peasant life, won the Pulitzer prize (1932)

buck (bʌk) 1. n. the male of hares, goats, rabbits, deer, antelope, rats ‖ (hist.) a dandy ‖ (poker) a counter or other object given to the winner of each jackpot, who then deals ‖ the act of bucking ‖ (football) a charge into the opposing rush line ‖ (pop.) a dollar ‖ (Br.) an eel-trap basket **to pass the buck** to dodge responsibility by passing it on to someone else 2. v.t. to throw (a rider) by bucking ‖ (football) to charge (the opponent's rush line) ‖ to resist, oppose ‖ v.i. (of a horse or mule) to spring up vertically clear off the ground with the back arched ‖ (with 'up') to become more cheerful or energetic **buck up!** pull yourself together! ‖ cheer up! ‖ (Br.) hurry up! **to feel bucked** (Br.) to feel confident and happy (usually because one has done something well or received a compliment) [O.E. buc, male deer and bucca, he-goat]

buck n. a sawhorse, sawbuck ‖ a padded, leather-covered, thick, short, adjustable vaulting block [Du. (zaag-) boc]

buck·board (bʌ́kbɔrd, bʌ́kbouərd) *n.* (*hist.*) a light, four-wheeled, horse-drawn carriage with a board in place of body and springs

buck·et (bʌ́kit) 1. *n.* a container for holding water, milk etc., a pail ‖ the amount contained in this ‖ a similar container, e.g. the scoop of a grain elevator 2. *v.t.* to lift in buckets ‖ (*Br., pop.*) to ride (a horse) fast ‖ *v.i.* to drive fast, rush along ‖ (*Br., rowing*) to row hurriedly, hurry the forward swing of a stroke [perh. O. F. buket, washing-tub]

bucket seat a low, round-backed, separate seat, often arranged to tip or fold forward, mostly used in automobiles

bucket shop an office for speculating on current stock exchange prices, but without any actual buying or selling of stock

buck·eye (bʌ́kai) *pl.* **buck·eyes** *n. Aesculus glabra,* the American horse chestnut

Buckholdt, John *JOHN OF LEYDEN

Buck·ing·ham (bʌ́kiŋəm), George Villiers, 1st Duke of (1592–1628), English nobleman and favorite of James I and Charles I. Hated by parliament for his profitable monopolies, his Roman Catholic sympathies and his disastrous attempts to intervene in the Thirty Years' War, he was impeached (1626) but saved by a rapid dissolution of parliament. His expedition to aid the Huguenots of La Rochelle failed (1627) and he was assassinated (1628)

Buckingham, George Villiers, 2nd Duke of (1627–87), English courtier. After the fall of Clarendon (1667), he became chief minister of Charles II, and a member of the Cabal (1667–73). He wrote a number of plays, including the satirical 'The Rehearsal' (1671)

Buckingham Palace the London home of the British sovereign, constructed by Nash (1821–36) and partly redesigned early in the 20th c.

Buck·ing·ham·shire (bʌ́kiŋəmʃər) (*abbr.* Bucks.) a county (area 749 sq. miles, pop. 512,000), in the south Midlands of England. County town: Aylesbury

buck·le (bʌ́kl) 1. *n.* a stiff fastening attached to one end of a belt, ribbon, strap etc., the other end being threaded through it and secured by a hole over its spiked tongue as and when required ‖ a similar device in the form of an ornament, e.g. on some shoes 2. *v. pres. part.* **buck·ling** *past and past part.* **buck·led** *v.t.* (often with 'on', 'up') to fasten with a buckle ‖ to bend sharply, kink, crumple ‖ *v.i.* to give way ‖ to bend out of shape, twist, crumple **to buckle down** to to force oneself to concentrate and work hard at [F. *boucle*]

buck·ler (bʌ́klər) *n.* (*hist.*) a small round shield held on the arm to protect the body ‖ (*naut.*) a wooden shutter preventing water from coming in at a hawsehole ‖ (*anat. and zool.*) a hard, protective covering, e.g. of armadillos or some crustaceans [O.F. *boucler*]

buck private (*pop.*) a private soldier, esp. a recruit

buck·ram (bʌ́krəm) 1. *n.* a coarse linen or hemp cloth stiffened with sizing (gum or paste), and used for binding books, stiffening belts etc. 2. *adj.* made of buckram [origin unknown]

buck·saw (bʌ́ksɔ) *n.* a saw used for sawing on a sawbuck

buck·shot (bʌ́kʃɒt) *n.* coarse lead shot between .24 and .36 in. across, for big-game hunting

buck·skin (bʌ́kskin) *n.* the skin of a buck ‖ a strong, yellowish, soft leather ‖ a cream-colored, closely-woven wool cloth

buck·thorn (bʌ́kθɔrn) *n. Rhamnus catharticus,* fam. *Rhamnaceae,* a thorny deciduous bush, with dark bud scales. Its bark and berries yield the purgative cascara sagrada, and its berries a greenish dye

buck·toothed (bʌktú:θt) *adj.* having a projecting upper front tooth or teeth

buck·wheat (bʌ́khwi:t, bʌ́kwi:t) *n.* a member of *Fagopyrum,* fam. *Polygonaceae,* esp. *F. esculentum* and *F. tataricum* grown as a cereal crop, tolerating a short growing season and notably free from disease. Buckwheat is fed to livestock, and in North America is made into flour. It is also a source of rutin. The U.S.S.R. and the U.S.A. are the biggest producers [etym. doubtful]

bu·col·ic (bju:kɒ́lik) 1. *adj.* rustic ‖ pastoral 2. *n.* (esp. *pl.*) a pastoral poem [fr. L. fr. Gk fr. *boukolos,* herdsman]

Bucovina *BUKOVINA

bud (bʌd) 1. *n.* (*bot.*) a much condensed, undeveloped shoot end of the axis, composed of closely crowded young leaves, with very short internodes, e.g., cabbage, lettuce, Brussels sprout ‖

(*zool.*) a protruding part of a simple animal organism which grows into a new organism, e.g. in the hydra ‖ a gemma ‖ a half-opened flower **in bud** putting forth buds ‖ *NIP 2. v. pres. part.* **bud·ding** *past and past part.* **budded** *v.t.* (*hort.*) to engraft by inserting a bud of one variety of tree or shrub under the bark of another stock, usually a wild or less desirable type ‖ to develop, *to bud horns* ‖ *v.i.* to put forth buds **búd·ding** *adj.* promising, *a budding writer* [M.E. *budde, bodde,* origin unknown]

Bu·da·pest (bjú:dəpest, bú:dəpest) the capital (pop. 2,063,745) of Hungary, formed by the union (1872) of Buda on the right bank of the Danube and Pest on the left bank. Industries (concentrated in Pest): textiles, machinery, chemicals, flour, tobacco, brewing, leather, glass. Buda, the old Magyar capital, became the capital of the Hungarian kingdom (1867). The city suffered heavily in the Russian advance (1945), but rapidly recovered. It was the center of an unsuccessful revolt against the Communist regime (1956)

Bud·da·hood (búdəhud, bú:dəhud) *n.* (*Mahayana Buddhism*) a state of enlightenment

Bud·dha (búdə, bú:də), Gautama (563–483 B.C.), the Indian founder of Buddhism. The son of a nobleman and member of the Kshatriya caste, Siddhārtha Gautama was born on the present borders of India and Nepal. It is told that at 29 he first saw a senile old man, a sick man, a corpse and a wandering ascetic. With eyes opened to aspects of life newly revealed to him, he broke with his past and became an ascetic, but after six years he abandoned rigorous asceticism for the deep meditation that brought enlightenment. He soon collected many disciples, and spent his remaining 45 years of life teaching, organizing and serving the order of mendicants which he founded. He is also known by the titles Sakyamuni ('the sage of the Sakya family') and Tathagata ('the follower of truth') [Skr. = the enlightened one]

Bud·dha·gho·sa (budəgóusə, bu:dəgóusə) (5th c. A.D.), orthodox and encyclopedic commentator on Buddhist doctrine, probably of Ceylon

Bud·dhism (búdizəm, bú:dizəm) *n.* a religious and philosophical system springing from the life and teaching of Gautama Buddha, who in the 6th c. B.C. rejected certain features of his native Hinduism, particularly the caste system, animal sacrifice and undue asceticism. He founded an order of mendicant preachers, including both sexes, and his first sermon to his disciples at Benares is the root of all later developments. In this sermon he preached the Four Noble Truths: (1) that sorrow is the universal experience of mankind (2) that the cause of sorrow is desire, and the cycle of rebirths is perpetuated by desire for existence (3) that the removal of sorrow can only come from the removal of desire (4) that desire can be systematically abandoned by following the Noble Eightfold Path. With the cessation of desire man passes from the world of individual existence into the world of pure Being (Nirvana). Because his concern was primarily practical, Gautama refused to speculate on the nature of Being, or on the nature of the individual self. He did, however, show the fallacies of some of the current theories, and has been regarded as a naturalistic atheist by many among both critics and disciples. He taught that man's release from sorrow was not obtainable by any act of sacrifice or pilgrimage which might be interpreted as trying to gain the favor of a deity. He also taught that this release came from the all-absorbing knowledge that man's selfish desires were rooted in dualistic delusions about the self.

Gautama's original teachings have been developed along two distinct and often conflicting lines: Theravada, disparagingly called Hinayana (found mainly in Ceylon, Burma, Thailand, and parts of Malaysia), and Mahayana (which developed in China, Tibet, Korea, and Japan). Theravada has laid stress on monastic disciplines, and has resisted any attempts to compromise with theism in any form. Within Mahayana, however, the idea of Gautama as an incarnation of 'the Buddha-spirit' has grown up. Closely linked with this is the concept of the bodhisattva. In Theravada the ideal, the 'saint', is the arhat, the man who has gained personal enlightenment; in Mahayana it is the bodhisattva, the man who has attained enlightenment (Buddhahood) but who has set aside his enjoyment of Nirvana in order to help others

make the journey that he has already completed. The furthest development of Mahayana in this soteriological direction is to be found in the Pure Land (Jodo) school, particularly in its Japanese form. Here, salvation comes solely from faith in the loving grace of the bodhisattva Amida. The Jodo doctrine is classified as tariki ('by another's effort'), in contrast with the more orthodox forms of Buddhism which are jiriki ('by self-effort'). Another well-known form of Mahayana is the Zen school. According to some, Zen is a fusion of Buddhism with Taoism. It shares with the latter a profound distrust of the human intellect, and points its adherents to an enlightenment (satori) which comes only when the subconscious is set free to resolve the false dualities of existence which cannot be resolved by rational means. Buddhism has some 500,000,000 adherents, largely in Asia

Bud·dhist (búdist, bú:dist) 1. *n.* a follower of Buddhism 2. *adj.* of or pertaining to Buddhism **Bud·dhís·tic** *adj.*

bud·dle (bʌ́dl) 1. *n.* (*mining*) a trough or plane at an angle, on which crushed ore is washed 2. *v.t. pres. part.* **bud·dling** *past and past part.* **bud·dled** to wash (ore) using such an apparatus [origin unknown]

bud·dle·ia (bʌ́dli:ə, bʌdlí:ə) *n.* a member of *Buddleia,* fam. *Loganiaceae,* a genus of shrubs or trees, many of which are cultivated, e.g. *B. Davidii,* which flowers in dense cymes with lilac or violet petals, and *B. globosa* from Chile, which has orange flowers in globose heads [Mod. L. after Adam *Buddle* (d. 1715), English botanist]

bud·dy (bʌ́di) *pl.* **bud·dies** *n.* a pal, friend ‖ a fellow soldier

Bu·dé (bydei), Guillaume (1467–1540), French philologist, humanist and Hellenist, who persuaded François I to create the Collège de France (1529)

budge (bʌdʒ) *pres. part.* **budg·ing** *past and past part.* **budged** *v.t.* to cause (something heavy or resisting) to move slightly ‖ to cause (a person) to modify his opinion ‖ *v.i.* to move ‖ to yield ‖ to modify an opinion [F. *bouger,* to stir]

budg·er·i·gar (bʌ́dʒərigar) *n.* the Australian lovebird or grass parakeet, much kept as a cage bird [native name=good cockatoo]

budg·et (bʌ́dʒit) 1. *n.* a written statement of money: where it is drawn from, its amount, how it is to be spent ‖ the annual estimate of revenue and expenditure for governing a country, fixing the level of taxation until the next budget ‖ (*pop.*) personal or household expenses 2. *v.t.* to allow for in a budget ‖ *v.i.* to plan expenditure with a given amount of money **búdg·et·ar·y** *adj.* [fr. F. *bougette,* bag, wallet]

bud scale one of the external, sometimes sticky, scalelike leaves covering a bud in winter

Bue·nos Ai·res (bwénəséəri:z) the capital (pop. 2,908,001) and federal district (area 72 sq. miles), of Argentina, a rail center and port on the Rio de la Plata estuary, the largest city in the southern hemisphere. Export industries: meat packing, dairy food processing, flour milling, tanning, chemicals, textiles ‖ a province (area 118,752 sq. miles, pop. 8,774,529) of Argentina, from which the federal district was separated in 1880. Capital: La Plata. Chief port: Bahía Blanca

Buenos Aires, Lake a lake (75 miles long) in S.E. Chile, on the Chile-Argentina boundary

buff (bʌf) 1. *adj.* like buff in color, yellowish ‖ made of buff 2. *n.* a thick, good-quality soft leather made from buffalo or oxhide ‖ the pale brownish yellow color of this ‖ a stick or wheel covered with leather etc., and used for polishing ‖ (*pop.*) an enthusiast 3. *v.t.* to polish with a buff ‖ to dye or stain buff ‖ to give (leather) a velvety surface [perh. fr. F. *buffle,* buffalo]

Buf·fa·lo (bʌ́fəlou) a port (pop. 357,870, with agglom. 1,242,573), of New York State, on Lake Erie, a market for grain, flour, timber and fish. Industries, served by hydroelectricity from Niagara: iron and steel, car and aircraft manufacture, meat packing

buf·fa·lo (bʌ́fəlou) 1. *n. pl.* **buf·fa·lo, buf·fa·loes, buf·fa·los** any of several wild oxen, e.g. the water buffalo, the cape buffalo or bison ‖ buffalo fish 2. *v.t.* (*pop.*) to trick, bamboozle ‖ (*pop.*) to overawe [Ital. fr. Gk *boubalos,* African antelope]

buffalo berry the scarlet, edible berry of *Shepherdia argenta* and *S. canadensis,* fam. *Elaeagnaceae,* of North America ‖ either of these shrubs

CONCISE PRONUNCIATION KEY: **(a)** æ, c*a*t; ɑ, c*a*r; ɔ, f*aw*n; ei, sn*a*ke. **(e)** e, h*e*n; i:, sh*ee*p; iə, d*ee*r; ɛə, b*ea*r. **(i)** i, f*i*sh; ai, t*i*ger; ə:, b*i*rd. **(o)** o, *o*x; au, c*ow*; ou, g*oa*t; u, p*oo*r; ɔi, r*oy*al. **(u)** ʌ, d*u*ck; u, b*u*ll; u:, g*oo*se; ə, b*a*cillus; ju:, c*u*be. x, lo*ch*; θ, *th*ink; ð, bo*th*er; z, *Z*en; ʒ, cor*s*age; dʒ, sava*g*e; ŋ, orangutan*g*; j, *y*ak; ʃ, *fi*sh; tʃ, fe*tch*; 'l, rabb*le*; 'n, red*den*. Complete pronunciation key appears inside front cover.

Buffalo Bill the nickname of W. F. Cody (1846–1917), American plainsman and showman. He toured the U.S.A. and Europe (1883–1916) with his 'Wild West' shows

buffalo bush either of the buffalo berry shrubs

buffalo robe a shaggy rug of bison skin with the hair left on the hide

buf·fer (bʌfər) n. (Br.) a man with out-of-date ideas [origin unknown]

buffer n. something which deadens or softens the force or shock of a collision, esp. the apparatus for this on a locomotive or rail truck ‖ (computer) device that stores data to compensate for differences in the rates of input in the process of transferring data from one system to another ‖ (chem.) a solution whose hydrogen ion concentration changes very little on dilution or on the addition of small amounts of acids or alkalis. It can thus be used to stabilize the pH of a system [origin unknown]

buffer n. something used for shining or polishing, esp. a leather-covered wheel

buffer species (envir.) a species subject to prey when another preferred species is in short supply

buffer state a small independent state between two potentially hostile larger ones, thought (historically) to lessen the chances of war between the two

Buf·fet (byfei), Bernard (1928–), French painter and engraver, ascetically spare in style and highly mannered

buf·fet (bʌfit) 1. n. a blow given by a storm, or strong waves, or (old-fash.) with the hand ‖ (rhet.) a stroke of bad luck 2. v.t. (old-fash.) to strike, hit ‖ to knock about ‖ to force by striking out about one, to buffet one's way through a crowd [perh. O.F., dim. of buffe, blow]

buf·fet (buféi) n. a sideboard ‖ a recessed cupboard or set of shelves for displaying china etc. ‖ in informal entertaining, a table laid with food and drink to which guests help themselves ‖ (búfei) a refreshment bar, as in a railroad station [F.]

Buf·fon (byfɔ̃), Georges Louis Leclerc, comte de (1707–88), French naturalist and writer, famous for his 'Histoire naturelle' (36 vols., 1749–88) written with collaborators and translated into many languages. His theories and speculations are important in the study of the theory of evolution

buf·foon (bʌfúːn) 1. n. someone noted for playing the fool ‖ a clownish fellow 2. v.i. to act like a clown **buf·foon·er·y** (bʌfúːnəri) pl. **buf·foon·er·ies** n. [F. fr. Ital.]

Bug *SOUTHERN BUG, *WESTERN BUG

bug (bʌg) 1. n. any small insect ‖ a bedbug or other hemipteran ‖ (pop.) a disease-producing organism, bacterium ‖ (pop.) a fault in an apparatus or in its working ‖ (pop.) a concealed microphone 2. v.t. pres. part. **bug·ging** past and past part. **bugged** (pop.) to conceal a microphone in ‖ (pop.) to listen to by means of a concealed microphone ‖ (pop.) to pester, annoy [origin unknown]

bug·a·boo (bʌgəbuː) n. a bugbear

Bu·gan·da (buːgǽndə) a kingdom and federated state (area 17,311 sq. miles, pop. 1,900,000, largely of the Baganda tribe) in S. Uganda. Capital: Kampala. Buganda was an important power in central Africa from the mid-17th c. It became a British protectorate in 1894, and gained limited internal self-government in 1900

bug·bear (bʌgbɛər) n. a belief, idea, obsession etc. causing fear or strong dislike ‖ a tiresome source of difficulties [etym. doubtful]

bug·ger (bʌgər) 1. n. a sodomite ‖ (Br., term of abuse) a harsh or unjust person in authority ‖ (used affectionately) a scamp, rascal 2. v.t. to commit buggery with **bug·ger·y** n. sodomy [F. bougre fr. M.L. Bulgarus, 11th-c. Bulgarian heretic of a sect thought capable of any crime or vice]

bug·gy (bʌgi) pl. **bug·gies** n. a light, usually one-horse carriage (Am. fourwheeled, Br. two-wheeled) for one or two persons ‖ a baby carriage [origin unknown]

bu·gle (bjuːgl) 1. n. a brass wind instrument like a trumpet, but with a shorter, more conical tube and no valves 2. v. pres. part. **bu·gling** past and past part. **bu·gled** v.i. to sound a bugle ‖ v.t. to sound (a call) on a bugle [orig. short for bugle horn, a hunting horn made from the horn of a wild ox or bugle, fr. O.F. bugle]

bugle n. a long tube-shaped glass bead, often black, sewn on a dress as an ornament [origin unknown]

bugle n. Ajuga reptans, fam. Labiatae, a perennial with rooting stolons and blue corolla [F.]

bu·gloss (bjuːglɔs, bjuːglɒs) n. Lycopsis arvensis, fam. Borraginaceae, a hairy annual or biennial, widely distributed [F. bugloss, fr. L. fr. Gk bous, ox+glōssa, tongue]

bug off v. (slang) go away

buhl work *BOULLE

Buh·ra·ky (bǽraːkiː) n. Japanese puppet theater featuring a visible puppeteer and chanter on stage

buhrstone *BURRSTONE

build (bild) 1. n. shape, proportions of body, of heavy build 2. v. pres. part. **build·ing** past and past part. **built** (bilt) v.t. to construct (e.g. a house) by putting together materials and parts ‖ v.i. to construct a house etc. ‖ to cause a house etc. to be constructed ‖ to earn one's living by constructing houses etc. **to build into** to incorporate into **to build on** to rely hopefully upon **to build up** to establish by means of hard work, to build up a practice ‖ to endow with imaginary qualities, they built him up to be a hero **build·er** n. someone who builds ‖ a building contractor [M.E. bulden fr. O.E. bold, dwelling]

build·ing (bildiŋ) n. a permanent construction (house, factory etc.) ‖ the work of constructing houses etc.

building lease a contract requiring the lessee of ground to build on it

building society (Br.) a finance society which lends a percentage of the purchase price of a house at a certain rate of interest over a number of years (usually 10, 15, or 20). Money for such loans comes from investments made by members of the society, who receive a small percentage of interest every year and can deposit or withdraw money from their share account as in a savings bank (cf. SAVINGS AND LOAN ASSOCIATION)

build-up (bildʌp) n. an increase in tension or expectation before the climax is reached (as in a drama) ‖ an extremely favorable account of a person (esp. of a candidate for a job) who has yet to prove himself, or of a thing not yet seen

built past and past part. of BUILD

built-in (biltin) adj. made a permanent part of the structure of something, a built-in bookcase

Bu·jum·bu·ra (buːdʒumbúːræ) (or Usumbura) the capital (pop. 141,000), port and airport of Burundi, at the northeast corner of Lake Tanganyika. University college

Bu·ka·vu (buːkávuː) (formerly Costermansville) a town (pop. 209,051) of Zaïre, at the southern end of Lake Kivu: a commercial and communications center

Bu·kha·ra, Bo·kha·ra (bukára) a commercial center (pop. 192,000) of W. Uzbekistan, U.S.S.R., on a fertile oasis, with many fine mosques. Products: cotton and leather goods, silk, carpets

Bu·ko·vi·na (buːkəviːna) a region consisting of the wooded eastern slopes of the Carpathians and, to the east, a fertile plain. It was conquered by Austria (1775) and ceded to Rumania (1919). The U.S.S.R. annexed N. Bukovina (which contains gypsum, oil, alabaster and coal deposits) to the Ukraine in 1940. Main town: Tchernovtsy, in Soviet territory

Bu·la·wa·yo (buːləwájou) a town (pop. 363,000) in Matabeleland, Zimbabwe, a commercial and distributing center, connected by rail with various ports. It has metallurgical plants, food and textile industries. It was built over the kraal of the last Matabele king, Lobengula. Cecil Rhodes is buried nearby. Bushman paintings (Matopo Hills)

bulb (bʌlb) n. the erect underground stem of a plant, reduced to a mere plate, surrounded by fleshy overlapping leaf bases, which are covered with brown scale leaves. The roots grow adventitiously. Buds and flowers are terminal or axillary ‖ any plant or flower growing from a bulb, e.g. onion, tulip, lily ‖ (anat.) a rounded part or end of a cylindrical organ, as of a hair root, urethra etc. ‖ the medulla oblongata ‖ any bulb-shaped part, esp. of a glass tube ‖ that part of an electric lamp which encloses the filament [fr. L. bulbus fr. Gk]

bul·bil (bʌlbil) n. (bot.) an aerial deciduous fleshy leaf bud capable of becoming a new individual when detached from the parent plant [fr. Mod. L. bulbillus, little bulb]

bulb·ous (bʌlbəs) adj. growing from, having or like a bulb

bul·bul (búlbul) n. the Persian name for the nightingale ‖ an Asian and African bird of genus Pycnonotus, related to the thrush, with brilliant plumage [Pers. fr. Arab.]

Bul·ga·kov (bulgákəf), Sergei Nikolayevich (1871–1944), Russian philosopher and theologian. He founded the Institute of Orthodox Theology in Paris (1925) after his exile from Russia (1923). His writings include 'The Wisdom of God'(1937)

Bul·ga·nin (bulgánin), Nikolai Alexandrovitch (1895–1975), Russian leader. He became first deputy chairman of the council of ministers after Stalin's death (1953) and chairman (1955). He was replaced (1958) by Khrushchev

Bul·gar (bálgar, búlgar) n. a member of a people, probably of Finnic language, who set up a state (8th-13th cc.) at the confluence of the Volga and the Kama

Bul·gar·i·a (bʌlgɛ́əriːə) a republic (area 42,818 sq. miles, pop. 8,940,000) of S.E. Europe. Capital: Sofia. National minorities (150,000 Gipsies, Macedonians, Turks, Armenians and Rumanians) form 14% of the population. Languages: Bulgarian (88%) and Turkish (10%). Religion: Orthodox (89%), Moslem (10%), Roman Catholic, Protestant and Jewish minorities. The land is 40% arable, 33% forest and 27% pasture. The Balkan Mtns (3,500–7,800 ft) cross the country from west to east. To the north the Danube plateau slopes down to the Rumanian border. To the south and center the fertile Maritsa valley separates the Balkan Mtns from the Rhodope Mtns (highest point 9,595 ft). Average summer and winter temperatures (F.): Pleven 90° and −15°, Plovdiv 90° and 40°. The climate is mainly continental, with intensely cold winters in the north, but is more temperate along the Black Sea coast, and Mediterranean in the south. Average annual rainfall: 25 ins. Livestock: sheep, cattle, hogs, poultry. Agricultural products: wheat, corn, tobacco, sugar beet, vegetables, fruit, cotton, roses. Mineral resources: iron, manganese, coal, copper, lignite, lead, zinc, salt, oil. Hydroelectric power and irrigation have been greatly developed. Manufactures: cement, fertilizers, cotton, wool, silk, rose oil, sugar. Exports: tobacco, eggs, ships, rose oil. Imports: machinery, vehicles, petroleum. Chief ports: Varna and Burgas. Communist nationalization of the economy began in 1944. There are 20 institutions of higher learning, including the University of Sofia. Monetary unit: lev. HISTORY. The Bulgars of Asiatic origin crossed the Danube (7th c.) and established the first Bulgarian kingdom, which became part of the Byzantine Empire (1018–1185). The second Bulgarian Empire (1185–1396) was founded by the Asens. It was conquered and ruled by the Turks (1396–1908). Numerous uprisings, esp. the 'Bulgarian atrocities' (1876), were crushed by the Turks. Bulgaria was made an autonomous principality after the Russo-Turkish War (1877–8), but was made dependent on Turkey, and the province of Eastern Rumelia was separated by the Congress of Berlin (1878). Alexander of Battenberg was elected prince of Bulgaria (1879–86). Bulgaria annexed Eastern Rumelia and was attacked by Serbia (1885). Ferdinand of Saxe-Coburg was elected prince (1887), and took the title of czar when Bulgaria was declared a kingdom, independent of Turkey (1908). Bulgaria joined Serbia and Greece against Turkey in the 1st Balkan War (1912) but attacked Serbia and Greece (1913), losing Macedonia and Thrace. It was an ally of the Central Powers and invaded Serbia (1915), but lost its Aegean coast (1919). It signed the Axis pact and declared war on Britain and the U.S.A. (1941). Russia declared war and occupied Bulgaria (1944), and a pro-Soviet government was formed which declared war on Germany. The Communists gained control and a people's republic was proclaimed (1946). The peace treaty was signed in 1947. Bulgaria joined (1955) the Warsaw Pact and the U.N. The Bulgarian secret service was implicated in several acts of terrorism in the 1970s and 1980s, notably in the assassination attempt on Pope John Paul II in 1981

Bul·gar·i·an (bʌlgɛ́əriːən) 1. n. a native or citizen of Bulgaria ‖ the Slavic language spoken there 2. adj. pertaining to Bulgarians or their language

bulge (bʌldʒ) *n.* a curving outwards, esp. when this is ugly or involves asymmetry ‖ a rounded part ‖ an abnormal increase In numbers, *a bulge in the birthrate* 2. *v. pres. part.* **bulg·ing** *past* and *past part.* **bulged** *v.t.* to cause to curve or swell outwards ‖ *v.i.* to curve or swell out **búlg·i·ness** *n.* **búlg·y** *comp.* **bulg·i·er** *superl.* **bulg·i·est** *adj.* [O.F. *boulge*, bag]

Bulge, Battle of the a German counter-attack (1944–5) in the Ardennes during the 2nd world war. Concentrating all his remaining reserves, Marshal von Rundstedt took advantage of foggy weather and a thinly held American front to break through and penetrate deep into Belgium, creating a bulge in the Allied lines. Antwerp, the main Allied supply base, was simultaneously bombed. A greatly outnumbered U.S. force held out heroically at Bastogne, until relieved by Allied forces which attacked the salient from the north and south, regained the initiative and resumed the offensive. The German advance was checked (Jan. 1945) after it had penetrated fifty miles

bu·lim·i·a (bju:lími:ə) *n.* (*med.*) a disease symptomized by a never-satisfied hunger [fr. Gk *boulimia* fr. *bous*, ox + *limos*, hunger]

bulk (bʌlk) 1. *n.* mass ‖ thickness ‖ a very large or fat human body ‖ the largest part, *the bulk of the nation* ‖ food taken in to help digestion rather than for nutritional value **in bulk** as one mass, not packaged or bottled ‖ in large amounts, *to buy in bulk* **to break bulk** to begin unloading a ship 2. *v.t.* (with 'out') to increase the size of (usually by adding something of little intrinsic worth), *to bulk out a journal with advertisements* ‖ to pile in a heap (e.g. fish or tobacco) ‖ *v.i.* to occupy space **to bulk large** to be or seem very important [etym. doubtful]

bulk eraser device utilizing a strong magnetic field to erase a reel of magnetic tape. *syn* tape eraser

bulk·head (bʌlkhɛd) *n.* a partition dividing a ship into separate watertight compartments so that if one compartment is holed the ship is still kept afloat by the others ‖ a partition dividing a ship's hold to prevent cargo from piling up on one side as the ship rolls or pitches ‖ a sloping door in a jutting framework, shutting off a mine shaft etc. [etym. doubtful]

bulk·i·ness (bʌlki:nis) *n.* the state or quality of being bulky

bulk modulus (*phys.*) the constant ratio, for an elastic body, between an applied stress and the resulting change in volume of unit volume

bulk·y (bʌlki:) *comp.* **bulk·i·er** *superl.* **bulk·i·est** *adj.* having bulk ‖ taking up a lot of room, and often of a shape difficult to handle

Bull (bul), John (c. 1562–1628), English composer and organist. He wrote mainly for voices and for the keyboard. The attribution to him of the British national anthem is disputed

bull (bul) 1. *adj.* male, esp. of large animals, *a bull elephant* ‖ very strong-looking or massive, *a bull neck* ‖ (*stock exchange*) marked by rising prices, marked by the activity of bulls, *a bull market* 2. *n.* an uncastrated male of the bovine or ox family ‖ the male of certain other large animals, e.g. whale, elephant, elk, or moose ‖ (*stock exchange*) a person buying as a speculation in the hope that prices will rise (cf. BEAR) ‖ **bull in a china shop** a person who is destructively clumsy in a situation requiring delicacy or tact **to take the bull by the horns** to deal boldly and directly with a difficult situation 3. *v.t.* (*stock exchange*) to try to raise the price of (stocks) by speculative buying ‖ *v.i.* (of stocks) to rise in price because of speculative buying [M.E. *bole, bule*]

bull *n.* an official letter or edict from the pope [fr. L. *bulla*, a seal]

bul·lace (búlis) *n. Prunus domestica insititia,* a plum no longer much cultivated. Damson is usually regarded as a cultivated form of it [etym. doubtful]

bul·late (búleit) *adj.* (*bot.* and *physiol.*) blistered-looking ‖ puckered, like a savoy cabbage leaf [fr. L. *bullatus* fr. *bulla*, bubble]

bull·dag·ger (búldægər) *n.* (*slang*) a masculine-looking lesbian. *syn* butch

bull·dog (búldɔg, búldɒg) 1. *n.* a very powerful, short-haired dog of a breed noted for courage and determination ‖ 2. *v.t. pres. part.* **bull·dog·ging** *past* and *past part.* **bull·dogged** *v.t.* to throw (a steer) by catching its horns and twisting its neck

bull·doze (búldouz) *pres. part.* **bull·doz·ing** *past* and *past part.* **bull·dozed** *v.t.* to move (earth) with a bulldozer ‖ to force, *to bulldoze one's way in* ‖ to bully **búll·doz·er** *n.* a powerful caterpillar tractor with a broad steel blade or ram in front for clearing land and leveling uneven earth surfaces, esp. in preparation for building roads, airfields etc. ‖ a bully [etym. doubtful]

bul·let (búlit) *n.* a small, round or conical piece of lead, fired from a rifle or pistol [F. *boulette,* dim. of *boule,* ball]

bul·let-head·ed (búlithɛdid) *adj.* with a round head

bul·le·tin (búlitin) *n.* a short official statement of news ‖ a periodical publication, e.g. of a club or society [fr. Ital. *bullettino,* a short note]

bulletin board a board on which written announcements are displayed

bul·let·proof (búlitpru:f) *adj.* hard enough to resist bullets

bulletproof vest fabric vest of nylon plastic, sometimes with overlapping fiberglass, capable of stopping a bullet. *Cf* FLAK JACKET

bullet train Japanese high-speed (130 mph) rail line between Tokyo and Nagoya

bull·fight (búlfait) *n.* a Spanish sporting event (found also in South America, Portugal, S. France, and Mexico) in which, observing ritual conventions, men fight specially bred bulls, usually to a kill but under some laws in order to pluck a rosette from between the horns **búll·figh·ter** *n.* **búll·fight·ing** *n.*

bull·finch (búlfintʃ) *n.* a quickset hedge, too high and strong to put a horse over, with a ditch on one side [perh.= bull fence]

bullfinch *n. Pyrrhula pyrrhula,* a strong-beaked European songbird, with red breast, throat and cheeks, allied to the grosbeaks

bull·frog (búlfrɔg, búlfrɒg) *n. Rana pipiens,* a large American frog

bull·head (búlhɛd) *n.* any of several small, big-headed fish, esp. *Ameiurus nebulosus,* American catfish

bull·head·ed (búlhɛdid) *adj.* obstinate ‖ thoughtlessly impetuous

bull·horn (búlhɔrn) *n.* (*Am.=Br.* loud-hailer) a megaphone with a built-in amplifier

bul·lion (búljən) *n.* a fringe of gold or silver lace or thread [perh. F. *bouillon*]

bullion *n.* gold or silver in bars or ingots, i.e. before coining or manufacturing processes [etym. doubtful]

bull·ish (búliʃ) *adj.* (*stock-exchange*) characterized by rising prices ‖ optimistic ‖ like a bull, esp. obstinate

Bull, John *JOHN BULL

bull·ock (búlək) *n.* a castrated bull ‖ an ox, steer [O.E. *bulluc,* young bull]

bull·pen (búlpɛn) *n.* an enclosure for bulls or a bull ‖ a barracks in a lumber camp ‖ (*baseball*) a place where relief pitchers limber up and practice during a game

Bullpup U.S. air-to-surface missile (AGM-12) weighing 100 to 250 lbs.

bull·ring (búlriŋ) *n.* a circular, roofless building containing many rows of tiered seats enclosing a sanded arena in which bullfighting takes place

bull·roar·er (búlrɔrər, búlrɔurər) *n.* a thonged slat of wood which makes a roaring noise when whirled, used to scare novices in certain tribal ceremonies

Bull Run, Battles of two battles (July 21, 1861, Aug. 30, 1862) of the American Civil War. The Confederates won both: the first under Beauregard and Jackson, the second under Lee and Jackson

bull session an informal group discussion on some large topic

bull's-eye (búlzai) *pl.* **bull's-eyes** *n.* the center ring of a target ‖ a shot which hits it ‖ a guess, remark etc. which exactly hits on the truth ‖ a hard, round candy with a strong peppermint flavor ‖ a boss of glass at the center of a sheet of blown glass ‖ a thick disk of glass, e.g. in a ship's side, to let in light or air ‖ a hemispherical lens of short focal distance, or a lantern with such a lens ‖ (*naut.*) a small, round, wooden block without sheaves, having a groove around it and a hole through it to take a rope

bull·ter·ri·er (búltéri:ər) *n.* a very strong, short-haired dog of a breed said to have been created by crossing the bulldog with now extinct breeds of terrier. They are swift and full of courage, with long, powerful jaws and no stop

bul·ly (búli:) *n.* (*Br.*) bully beef [prob. fr. F. *bouilli,* boiled (beef)]

bully 1. *pl.* **bul·lies** *n.* someone who enjoys oppressing others weaker than himself ‖ (*Am.=Br.* bully-off) the putting into play of the ball at the start of a game of hockey and after

each goal 2. *v. pres. part.* **bul·ly·ing** *past* and *past part.* **bul·lied** *v.t.* to persecute physically or spiritually ‖ to oppress (a weaker person or subordinate) ‖ to intimidate or force, *she bullied him into accepting the invitation* ‖ *v.i.* to be a bully or act like one [etym. doubtful]

bully beef (*Br.*) canned, pressed beef, corned beef

bul·ly-off (búli:ɔf, búli:ɒf) *n.* (*Br.,* hockey) the bully

Bul·nes (bú:lnes), Manuel (1799–1866), Chilean general and president (1841–51). He defeated (1839) the Peru-Bolivian Confederation at Yungay, founded (1841) the University of Chile, and established (1843) Chilean sovereignty in the Magellan strait

Bü·low (býlou), Prince Bernhard von (1849–1929), German chancellor (1900–9). His threatening foreign policy toward France and Russia increased German isolation before the 1st world war

bul·rush (búlrʌʃ) *n.* a sedge of genus *Scirpus* ‖ (*Br.*) the cattail

Bult·man (búltmən), Rudolf (1884–1976), German Lutheran theologian advocating a demythologizing of the New Testament and an existentialist interpretation of the gospel. His works include the 'Theologie des Neuen Testaments' (1948), 'Glaube und Verstehen' (1952)

bul·wark (búlwərk) *n.* a defensive wall, ramparts ‖ (usually *pl.*) a ship's side above the upper deck ‖ any defensive or safeguarding structure, e.g. a breakwater ‖ a person, institution, moral principle etc. thought of as being a defense or protection [etym. doubtful, cf. Du. *bolwerk* or G. *bollwerk,* logwork]

Bul·wer (búlwər), Sir Henry (1801–72), British author and diplomat. As minister to Washington (1849–52), he negotiated the Clayton-Bulwer Treaty of 1850

Bul·wer-Lyt·ton (búlwərlít'n), Edward George Earle Lytton, 1st Baron Lytton of Knebworth (1803–73). He was the author of highly colored historical novels, e.g. 'The Last Days of Pompeii' (1834) and 'The Last of the Barons' (1843)

bum (bʌm) 1. *adj.* (*pop.*) of poor quality 2. *n.* (*pop.*) a loafer ‖ (*pop.*) a vagrant **on the bum** (*pop.,* of people and machines) not working 3. *v. pres. part.* **bum·ming** *past* and *past part.* **bummed** *v.t.* (*pop.*) to get (something) by sponging ‖ *v.i.* (*pop.*) to sponge ‖ (*pop.*) to idle [etym. doubtful]

bum *n.* (*Br.,* not in polite usage) the buttocks, backside ‖ (*Br.*) a bumbailiff [M.E. *bom*]

bum·bail·iff (bʌmbéilif) *n.* (*Br.*) an official sent to seize the property of someone unable to pay his debts

bum·ble·bee (bʌmb'lbi:) *n.* a member of *Bombus,* a genus of big, hairy, social bees which make a loud humming noise in flight [obs. *bumble,* to hum + BEE]

bum·boat (bʌmbout) *n.* a trader's boat peddling provisions or goods among ships in port [perh. L.G. *bumboot,* beamed boat]

bum·ma·lo (bʌmələu) *n.* the Bombay duck [fr. Mahratti *bombil*]

bum·mer (bʌmər) *n.* (*colloq.*) a bad experience, esp. when due to the effect of drugs

bump (bʌmp) 1. *n.* a heavy jolt, blow or collision ‖ the swelling caused by a bump ‖ (*phrenology*) a protuberance on the skull supposed to indicate character and mental capacity etc. ‖ the faculty indicated by it, *a bump of locality* ‖ (*Br., boat racing*) a touching of one boat by a following boat in a bumping race, in which boats start at fixed intervals ‖ the win constituted by this ‖ (*pl.*) the races of this kind ‖ (*aviation*) a jolt felt by an aircraft in flight ‖ the variation in wind or air pressure which causes this 2. *v.t.* to knock or strike ‖ (*Br.,* of schoolboys) to grasp (someone) by the arms and legs and lower him so that his bottom bumps the floor, e.g. to celebrate a victory, birthday etc. ‖ to preempt a place, particularly on a public carrier or for an event ‖ (*Br., boat racing*) to overtake and touch (another boat) in a bumping race ‖ to shape (metal) into curves ‖ *v.i.* (often with 'into' or 'against') to knock or collide suddenly **to bump into** to meet accidentally **to bump off** (*pop.*) to kill [imit.]

bump·er (bʌmpər) 1. *n.* (*old-fash.*) a glass filled to the brim, *a bumper of ale* 2. *adj.* unusually good or abundant, *a bumper harvest* [etym. doubtful]

bumper *n.* a device for reducing (by absorbing) the shock of a collision, esp. the metal guards at the front and back of a car ‖ (*Br.*) a fender (shock absorber on a locomotive)

bumper sticker narrow adhesive label carrying a message, designed to be attached to an automobile bumper. *syn* bumper strip

bump·i·ly (bʌ́mpili:) *adv.* in a bumpy manner

bump·i·ness (bʌ́mpi:nis) *n.* the state or quality of being bumpy

bump·kin (bʌ́mpkin) *n.* (a citydweller's term) an awkward ignorant country person [perh. Du. *boomken*, little tree]

bump·tious (bʌ́mpʃəs) *adj.* self-assertive, full of noisy conceit

bump·y (bʌ́mpi:) *comp.* **bump·i·er** *superl.* **bump·i·est** *adj.* having or causing jolts or bumps

bun (bʌn) *n.* a small, soft, slightly sweetened roll, often with raisins ‖ a soft bread roll ‖ a woman's long hair done in a tight coil at the back of the head [M.E. *bunne* perh. fr. O.F. *bunge*, bump]

Bu·na (bú:nə, bjú:nə) *n.* any of a number of synthetic rubbers derived from butadiene [Trademark]

Bu·nau-Va·ril·la (bynouværi:jæ), Philippe Jean (1859–1940), French engineer. As director of the French undertaking to construct a canal in Panama, he persuaded the U.S.A. to buy the company's rights and organized with U.S. aid the insurrection in Panama which led to its independence from Colombia. He was appointed (1903) minister plenipotentiary to Washington, where he negotiated the Hay-Bunau-Varilla Treaty

bunch (bʌntʃ) **1.** *n.* a cluster of things growing or tied together ‖ a number of things of the same kind ‖ (*pop.*) a group of people, *a bunch of students* **2.** *v.t.* to tie or gather together in bunches ‖ to work (material) in folds or gathers ‖ *v.i.* to gather into a close group ‖ (*mil.*, of convoys, troops in file etc.) to fail to keep regular intervals [etym. doubtful]

Bunche (bʌntʃ), Ralph Johnson (1904–71), American sociologist and United Nations official who received the Nobel peace prize in 1950 for his work as U.N. mediator in Palestine (1948–9). He was the U.N. secretary-general's personal representative in the Congo for a period until Sept. 1960

bunch·y (bʌ́ntʃi:) *comp.* **bunch·i·er** *superl.* **bunch·i·est** *adj.* (of material) unevenly or too thickly gathered

bun·dle (bʌ́nd'l) **1.** *n.* a number of things wrapped, rolled or tied together ‖ a set of parallel fibers, e.g. of nerves or muscles (*VASCULAR BUNDLE) **2.** *v.t. pres. part.* **bun·dling** *past* and *past part.* **bun·dled** to tie up in a bundle ‖ to stow (things) untidily ‖ (with 'off') to hustle [etym. doubtful]

bundle sheath the layer of large parenchymatous cells surrounding the vascular tissue of a leaf vein

bung (bʌŋ) **1.** *n.* the stopper of the bunghole in a cask or barrel **2.** *v.t.* to stop with or as if with a bung ‖ (*Br., pop.*) to toss, *bung that knife over to* **bung up** (*Br.*) to clog, choke ‖ to bruise, batter, damage [etym. doubtful]

bun·ga·loid (bʌ́ŋgəloid) *adj.* (esp. *pejorative*) like or consisting of a bungalow or bungalows

bun·ga·low (bʌ́ŋgəlou) *n.* a one-storied house [fr. Hindi *banglā*, belonging to Bengal]

bung·hole (bʌ́ŋhoul) *n.* the opening for filling a cask or barrel

bun·gle (bʌ́ŋg'l) **1.** *n.* a clumsy, unsuccessful piece of work **2.** *v. pres. part.* **bun·gling** *past* and *past part.* **bun·gled** *v.i.* to work clumsily and unsuccessfully ‖ *v.t.* to botch, spoil [imit.]

bun·ion (bʌ́njən) *n.* an enlargement from chronic inflammation of the small sac on the first joint of the big toe [etym. doubtful].

bunk (bʌŋk) **1.** *n.* a narrow sleeping berth, e.g. in a ship **2.** *v.i.* (often with 'down') to occupy a bed [etym. doubtful]

bunk *n.* (*pop.*) humbug, nonsense [shortened from BUNKUM]

bunk·er (bʌ́ŋkər) **1.** *n.* a large bin ‖ a compartment on a ship for storing fuel ‖ (*golf*) a sandpit or other rough hazard on the course ‖ (*mil.*) a bombproof underground shelter or dugout **2.** *v.t.* (*golf*) to hit (a ball) into a bunker ‖ to put (oneself) in the position of having to play from a bunker ‖ to put (fuel) into a bunker ‖ *v.i.* to take on coal or oil [origin unknown]

Bunker Hill, Battle of a battle (June 17, 1775) in which American troops were defeated by the British. The battle galvanized American resistance in the Revolutionary War (1775–83)

bunk·er·ing (bʌ́ŋkəriŋ) *n.* the fueling of ships or vehicles

bunk·house (bʌ́ŋkhaus) *pl.* **bunk·hous·es** (bʌ́ŋkhauziz) *n.* a cabin with bunks, e.g. for workers on a building site, ranch hand etc.

bun·kum (bʌ́ŋkəm) *n.* humbug, nonsense [fr. *Buncombe*, N. Carolina, whose member spoke needlessly in Congress to impress his constituents]

bun·ny (bʌ́ni:) *pl.* **bun·nies** *n.* (child's name for) a rabbit [origin uncertain]

bun·ny (bʌ́ni:) *n.* (often cap.) minimally dressed female, esp. a waitress wearing the Playboy trademark costume with rabbit tail and ears

buns (bʌnz) *n. pl.* (*colloq.*) buttocks

Bun·sen (bʌ́ns'n, bú:ns'n), Robert Wilhelm (1811–99), German chemist. He developed spectrum analysis (with Kirchhoff), and they discovered and isolated the elements cesium and rubidium. He invented the filter pump, the vapor calorimeter, and the ice calorimeter, and developed the Bunsen burner

Bunsen burner a burner used esp. in laboratories. It mixes air with combustible gas, the air being drawn in by the draft of the gas, giving a hot flame free from carbon particles

bunt (bʌnt) *n.* the baggy part of a fishing net or of a sail [origin unknown]

bunt 1. *n.* (*baseball*) a push or short hit infield ‖ (*aviation*) half an outside loop followed by a half roll **2.** *v.i.* (*aviation*) to perform a bunt ‖ *v.t.* (*baseball*) to bat (the ball) lightly to the infield [etym. doubtful]

bunt *n.* a smut affecting wheat grains, with bad-smelling spores [origin unknown]

bunt·ing (bʌ́ntiŋ) *n.* a member of *Emberiza*, fam. *Fringillidae*, a genus of small birds found in the northern hemisphere. They live in flocks in winter and pair off in summer [origin unknown]

bunting *n.* thin wool or cotton stuff used for flags and similar decorations ‖ flags [etym. doubtful]

bunting *n.* a hooded sleeping bag to put a baby in outdoors

bunt·line (bʌ́ntlain, bʌ́ntlin) *n.* (*naut.*) the cord attached to the foot of a square sail, used for hauling the sail up to the yard for furling

Bu·ñu·el (bu:nwél), Luis (1900–83), Spanish film director. His films include 'Un Chien Andalou' (with Salvador Dali, 1928), 'L'Age d'Or' (1930), 'Los Olvidados' (1950), 'Viridiana' (1962), 'Discreet Charm of the Bourgeoisie' (1972), 'That Obscure Object of Desire' (1977), and 'My Last Sigh' (1983)

Bun·yan (bʌ́njən), John (1628–88), English religious writer and preacher. He worked with his father as a tinker at Elstow, near Bedford, until he was conscripted into the parliamentary army (1644–7). He became High Anglican, but joined the Puritan congregation at Bedford (1653) and began to preach (1655). He was imprisoned in Bedford county jail (1660–72) for preaching without a license, and while there wrote 'Grace Abounding' (1666) and other works. Rearrested (1675), he was imprisoned for nearly two more years in Bedford town jail, where he wrote the first part of 'The Pilgrim's Progress' (1678), the second part being published in 1685. It is an allegory written in a majestic yet simple style, derived from deep love of mankind and profound knowledge of the English Bible. Other works include 'The Life and Death of Mr Badman' (1680), and 'The Holy War' (1682)

Bunyan, Paul, a mythical folk hero of the American lumber camps. The first Bunyan tales, depicting a gigantic lumberman who overcame fantastic hazards, were published (1910) in the 'Detroit News-Tribune'. The stories were restyled by lumber publicists to attract a national audience

bu·oy (bú:i:, bɔi) **1.** *n.* an anchored float marking a navigable channel, dangerous shallows etc. **2.** *v.t.* (usually with 'up') to keep afloat ‖ (usually with 'up') to raise to the surface ‖ (usually with 'up') to encourage, raise (hopes etc.) ‖ to mark with buoys [perh. fr. O.F. *boye*]

buoy·an·cy (bɔ́iənsi:, bú:jənsi:) *n.* the ability to float or (of a fluid) to keep something afloat ‖ (*hydrostatics*) loss of weight by immersion in a fluid ‖ resilience of spirits, prices etc.

buoy·ant (bɔ́iənt, bú:jənt) *adj.* able to float or rise to the surface ‖ able to keep things floating ‖ resilient in spirit, lighthearted [perh. fr. O.F. *buoyant*]

bu·pren·or·phine (bjuprenɔ́rfi:n) *n.* (*pharm.*) antidrug addiction drug, said to have 40 times the pain-relieving effect of morphine

bur (bə:r) *n.* (*dentistry*) a small drill

bur, burr *n.* a prickly or sticky seed vessel or flower head of a plant, e.g. burdock ‖ a rough or prickly covering of a fruit, e.g. chestnut ‖ a person or thing that clings like a bur [etym. doubtful]

Bur·bage (bə́:rbidʒ), Richard (c. 1567–1619), English actor, leader of the theatrical company which first presented Shakespeare's plays, and builder of the Globe Theater

bur·ble (bə́:rb'l) **1.** *n.* (*aeron.*) the breaking up of the flow of air about a traveling body, e.g. over a wing of an aircraft climbing too steeply **2.** *v.i. pres. part.* **bur·bling** *past* and *past part.* **bur·bled** to make inarticulate sounds of laughter or rage ‖ (of running brooks) to chuckle over the stones ‖ (of babies) to gurgle [imit.]

bur·bot (bə́:rbət) *n. Lota lota,* fam. *Gadidae,* a flatheaded, bearded freshwater fish related to the cod. The North American subspecies is *Lota lota maculosa* [F. *bourbotte*]

Burck·hardt (bə́:rkhɑrt), Jacob (1818–97), Swiss historian. Major works: 'The Cicerone' (1860), a critique of Italian art, and 'The Civilization of the Renaissance in Italy' (1860)

Burck·hardt, Johann Ludwig (1784–1817), Swiss traveler and Orientalist. He traveled widely in the East disguised as a Moslem, visiting Mecca, Medina and Cairo. He wrote vivid journals

bur·den (bə́:rd'n) *n.* the refrain or chorus of a song or ballad ‖ the gist or main idea of a poem, speech etc. [M.E. *burdoun,* musical bass, fr. O.F.]

burden 1. *n.* a heavy load ‖ a heavy moral obligation ‖ the capacity or tonnage of a ship's cargo **2.** *v.t.* to put a weight on ‖ to take on (oneself) or put on (others) a mental or moral burden [O.E. *byrthen*]

burden of proof the obligation to prove a statement or accusation

bur·den·some (bə́:rd'nsəm) *adj.* heavy ‖ troublesome

bur·dock (bə́:rdɔk) *n.* a member of *Arctium,* fam. *Compositae,* a genus of annual or biennial herbs with a prickly involucre of bracts on the flower head and fruit

bu·reau (bjúərou) *pl.* **bu·reaus, bu·reaux** (bjúərouz) *n.* a chest of drawers (esp. with a mirror) for a bedroom ‖ (*Br.*) a writing desk with drawers ‖ a government department or its subdivision ‖ an organization or agency, *employment bureau* [F.=office, desk]

bu·reauc·ra·cy (bjuərɔ́krəsi:) *pl.* **bu·reauc·ra·cies** *n.* government by officials ‖ officialdom, the routine world of regulations ‖ government officials **bu·reau·crat** (bjúərəkræt) *n.* **bu·reau·crat·ic** *adj.* **bu·reau·crat·i·cal·ly** *adv.* [F. *bureaucratie*]

bu·reau·crat·ese (bjuərəkrætí:z) *n.* legalistic, wordy style of communication often characteristic of government announcements. *syn* gobbledegook

bu·rette, bu·ret (bjuərét) *n.* a graduated glass tube with stopcock and narrow outlet, used for delivering a measured volume of a liquid or measuring the quantity of a gas or liquid collected or discharged [F., dim. of *buire,* a vase]

burg (bə:rg) *n.* (*pop.*) a town or small city [fr. L.L. *burgus*]

Bur·gas (buərgás) a Bulgarian port (pop. 148,200) on the Black Sea, linked by rail with Sofia

bur·gee (bə́:rdʒi:, bə:rdʒí:) *n.* (*naut.*) a swallow-tailed or three-cornered flag or pennant flown by yachts, esp. in races [etym. doubtful]

Bur·gen·land (búərgənlɑnt) a province (area 1,529 sq. miles, pop. 272,568) in E. Austria, formerly a part of Hungary. Capital: Eisenstadt (pop. 5,000)

bur·geon, bourgeon (bə́:rdʒən) **1.** *n.* a bud ‖ a shoot **2.** *v.i.* to send forth shoots or other new growth ‖ to begin to grow [O.F. *burjon*]

Bur·ger, Warren Earl (1907–) U.S. lawyer and Supreme Court chief justice (1969–86). After studying law in Minnesota he was in private practice until serving as an assistant U.S. attorney general (1953–6). He served on the U.S. Court of Appeals for the District of Columbia (1956–69) before being appointed chief justice (1969) by Pres. Richard M. Nixon in an attempt to swing the Court to the conservative side. Known as a 'strict constructionist' he favored the death penalty (*Furman v. Georgia*, 1972), the limitation of defendants' rights (*Ashe v. Swenson*, 1970; *Coleman v. Alabama*, 1970; *Harris v. New York*, 1971) and the right of government intelligence agencies to keep secret their activities (*Central Intelligence Agency v.*

Sims, 1985). His tenure as chief justice was noted for administrative changes in the U.S. court system

bur·gess (bə́ːdʒis) *n.* (*Br.*, *hist.*) a freeman of a borough, a citizen with full municipal rights ‖ (*Am. hist.*) a member of the lower house of the colonial legislature of Virginia or Maryland ‖ (*Br. hist.*) the representative of a borough, corporate town or university in parliament [M.E. *burgeis* fr. O.F.]

burgh (bə́ːrə) *n.* a Scottish borough or chartered town [var. of BOROUGH]

burgh·er (bə́ːrgər) *n.* (*hist.*) a citizen, esp. of Dutch or German towns ‖ (esp. *ironic*) a conventional middle-class citizen [G. or Du. *burger*]

Burgh·ley (bə́ːrli:), William Cecil, 1st Baron (1520–98), English statesman. As secretary of state (1558–72) and lord high treasurer (1572–98), he was Elizabeth I's principal adviser for 40 years

bur·glar (bə́ːrglər) *n.* someone who commits burglary [fr. Anglo-Latin *burglator*]

burglar alarm a device, usually electric, which sets off an alarm when a house, safe etc. is forced

bur·gla·ry (bə́ːrgləri) *pl.* **bur·gla·ries** *n.* the act of breaking into houses, shops etc. to steal, esp. at night

bur·gle (bə́ːrg'l) *pres. part.* **bur·gling** *past* and *past part.* **bur·gled** *v.t.* to rob by burglary ‖ *v.i.* to be a burglar

bur·go·mas·ter (bə́ːrgəmæstər, bə́ːrgəmɑstər) *n.* the chief magistrate in a Dutch, Flemish, German, or Austrian town [fr. Du. *burgemeester*]

Bur·gos (búːrgɔs) a province (area 5,480 sq. miles, pop. 363,474) of Castile, N. Spain ‖ its capital (pop. 136,400), the capital of Old Castile (1037–1492). It was the seat of the Falangist government during the Spanish Civil War. Gothic cathedral (13th c.)

Bur·goyne (bə́ːrgɔin), John (c. 1722–92), British general. He led the British expeditionary force from Canada during the Revolutionary War, and surrendered (1777) at Saratoga

Bur·gun·di·an (bəːrgʌ́ndiːən) **1.** *n.* an inhabitant of Burgundy **2.** *adj.* of Burgundy or of a Burgundian

Bur·gun·dy (bə́ːrgəndi:) (*F.* Bourgogne) a former province of S.E. France, between the Massif Central and the Lower Rhône, composing modern Saône-et-Loire department and parts of Nièvre, Côte d'Or and Yonne. It includes the Saône valley and the hills of Côte d'Or, whose slopes produce the Burgundy wines. Main towns: Dijon (historic capital), Beaune, Auxerre. Historic Burgundy at times included a much larger area. KINGDOM OF BURGUNDY. The first kingdom was established in the Saône-Rhône valley by the Germanic Burgundians (5th c. A.D.), who were conquered by the Franks (534) and absorbed into the Frankish Empire. The second kingdom, founded after the partition of the Carolingian middle kingdom (843), extended from the Mediterranean to N. Switzerland, and from the Rhône to the Alps. It became known as the kingdom of Arles. It was absorbed by the Holy Roman Empire (1032) and the western parts were gradually acquired by France. COUNTY OF BURGUNDY. A countship in the north of the kingdom which became known as Franche-Comté. DUCHY OF BURGUNDY. A duchy founded to the northwest of the kingdom (9th c.), ruled by the Capetian dukes (1031–1361) and by the house of Valois (1363–1477), who also acquired Franche-Comté, Artois, N. Picardy, Lorraine and the Low Countries. It was annexed (1477) by Louis XI (*CHARLES THE BOLD) and formally united to the French crown (1482), but most of its northern possessions went by marriage to the Hapsburgs. The province of Burgundy was constituted from the duchy (1477)

Bur·gun·dy *pl.* **Bur·gun·dies** *n.* a red or white wine from Burgundy in France ‖ a dark purplish red

bur·i·al (béri:əl) *n.* a burying or being buried [M.E. *buryel* fr. O.E. *byrgels*, tomb]

burial ground a cemetery ‖ disposal site for unwanted radioactive materials using earth or water for a shield

Bur·iat A.S.S.R. (burját) an autonomous republic (area 127,020 sq. miles, pop. 673,000) in the R.S.F.S.R., U.S.S.R., in S. central Siberia. Capital: Ulan Udé

Bur·i·dan's Ass (bjúːridənz) a parable attributed to Jean Buridan (c. 1300–58), French Scholastic philosopher: an ass, moved equally by hunger and thirst, was put equidistant between a bundle of hay and a bucket of water. Unable to choose between them, it died of hunger and thirst. By contrast man has effective freedom of will

buried *past* and *past part.* of BURY

bu·rin (bjúːrin) *n.* a pointed steel tool for engraving, or for carving stone [F.]

Burke (bə́ːrk), Edmund (1729–97), British statesman and conservative political theorist. An Irishman, and a Rockingham Whig, he opposed George III's personal rule, defending parliamentary government. He supported the American colonies in their fight (1775–83) for independence. He put forward the trusteeship of backward peoples as an imperial idea, in the course of his unjust impeaching of Warren Hastings. He attacked legal abuses and the slave trade. Later he joined the Tories under Pitt, to oppose the French Revolution ('Reflections on the Revolution in France', 1790), which he attacked as wanton destruction of the immemorial organic partnership which formed a State. He was a brilliant pamphleteer

Burkina Faso, formerly Upper Volta, a republic (area 105,839 sq. miles, pop. 6,733,000) in W. Africa. Capital: Ouagadougou (pop. 51,000). People: mainly Mossi (36%). There are Fulani and Tuareg minorities in the north. Language: French (official), local African languages. Religion: traditional African religions, with Moslem and Christian minorities. The land is a savanna plateau, highest (2,350 ft) in the Banfora escarpment in the southwest, crossed by the Black, White and Red Voltas. Average temperatures (F.): Jan. 68°, July 90°. Rainfall: south 40 ins, north 10 ins. Livestock: cattle, sheep, goats. Crops: millet, sorghum, corn, rice, yams, karite, cotton, peanuts. Mineral resources: manganese, copper, gold, diamonds. Exports: labor, livestock, dried fish, peanuts, cottonseed. Monetary unit: franc CFA. HISTORY. The area was dominated (c. 10th–16th cc.) by a feudal empire ruled by the Mossi. The French established a protectorate (1896) and made the Upper Volta a separate colony (1919). It was divided among Niger, the French Sudan and the Ivory Coast (1932) but was restored (1947) and became self-governing (1958). It became an independent republic (Aug. 5, 1960) outside the French Community, and joined the U.N. (1960). A military government was set up (1966) and frequent military coups followed. The country's name was changed in 1984

Burk·itt's lymphoma (bə́ːrkəts) cancer of lymphatic system afflicting African children, identified in 1957 by British surgeon Dennis Burkitt

burl (bə́ːrl) **1.** *n.* a knot or lump in wool, thread or cloth ‖ a growth, often round and flat, on tree trunks ‖ a veneer made from such growths **2.** *v.t.* to free (cloth) from burls [O.F. *bourle*, tuft of wool]

bur·lap (bə́ːrlæp) *n.* a coarse fabric of hemp, jute or flax [etym. doubtful]

bur·lesque (bəːrlésk) **1.** *adj.* intentionally comic through light-hearted, exaggerated imitation ‖ unintentionally ludicrous, through inadequacy **2.** *n.* a literary or dramatic imitation mocking its model by going to comic extremes, for fun (not with the serious purposes of satire) ‖ (*hist.*) a popular musical entertainment in Victorian England, which travestied plots from popular novels or the classics ‖ a parody ‖ an unintentionally ludicrous entertainment ‖ a theatrical entertainment of low comedy, esp. incorporating striptease **3.** *v.t. pres. part.* **bur·les·quing** *past* and *past part.* **bur·lesqued** to represent grotesquely, in fun [F. fr. Ital. *burlesco*]

bur·li·ness (bə́ːrli:nis) *n.* the state or quality of being burly

Bur·lin·game (bə́ːrliŋgeim), Anson (1820–70), U.S. Congressman and diplomat. He served (1861–7) as U.S. minister to China, so successfully that he was named (1867–70) imperial envoy empowered to conduct China's international relations. His 'Burlingame treaty' (1868) proclaimed U.S. respect for China's territorial integrity

bur·ly (bə́ːrli:) *comp.* **bur·li·er** *superl.* **bur·li·est** *adj.* big and strong, heavily built [M.E. *borlich*, stately]

Bur·man (bə́ːrmən) **1.** *pl.* **Bur·mans** *n.* an inhabitant of Burma **2.** *adj.* of or pertaining to the Burmans

Bur·ma Road (bə́ːrmə) a military highway from the Burmese railhead at Lashio to Kunming in Yunnan (700 miles), completed in 1938. The road was extended (1942–4) westward to Ledo in India

Burma, Union of a republic (area, 261,610 sq. miles, pop. 36,196,000) in S.E. Asia. Capital: Rangoon. It includes Burma proper, four semiautonomous states (Shan, Karen, Kachin and Kayah) and one special division (Chin). Ethnic and linguistic groups: Burmese (66%), Karens (7.5%), Shans (6.5%), and smaller groups of Kachins, Indians, Chins, Mons, Chinese, Palaung-Was. Official language: Burmese. Religion: 84% Hinayana Buddhist (the state religion), with Animist, Moslem, Hindu and Christian minorities. The land is 57% forest. Lower Burma is the coastal region, Upper Burma is inland. Four great rivers, the Irrawaddy and Chindwin, which form a central plain, and in the east the Sittang and Salween, run north-south between mountain ranges (3,000–8,000 ft). In the north are the mountains of Tibet (passes at 12,000 ft, the highest point in Burma being Hkakabo Razi, 19,296 ft). In the south lies the Irrawaddy delta. The west coasts are swampy. The climate is hot and humid, dominated by the wet summer monsoon: May–Sept., wettest in July. Rainfall: Rangoon 100 ins, Mandalay 35 ins, Arakan and Tenasserim 200 ins. Average temperature (F.): Rangoon 77° (Jan.), 88° (Apr.), Mandalay 70° (Jan.), 90° (Apr.). Livestock: oxen, water buffalo. Crops: rice, sesame, pulses, peanuts, millet, cotton, sugarcane. Minerals: tin, jade, ruby, gold, silver, lead, wolfram, zinc, sapphire, amber, tungsten, petroleum. Industries: rice milling, tanning, rubber processing. Exports: rice, rubber, cotton, teak, vegetables, gums. Imports: machinery, textiles. Chief port: Rangoon. The Irrawaddy is navigable up to Bhamo (900 miles) and its tributary the Chindwin for 390 miles. University (1920), at Rangoon. Monetary unit: kyat (divided into 100 pyas). HISTORY. Burma was settled (7th c.) by the Pyus, the Shans and the Mons. The Burmese came from Yunnan (9th c.) and founded a kingdom (11th c.) at Pagan. After the Mongol invasion (1287), most of the country was ruled by the Shans (1287–1531) and the Mons (1740–52). Under the reign (1752–60) of the Burmese Alaungpaya and his descendants, Siam was defeated (1767) and Arakan, Manipur and Assam were annexed (1785–1819). After three AngloBurmese wars (1824–6, 1852–3, and 1885–6), Burma became a province of British India (1886–1937) and a Crown Colony (1937). Following the Japanese invasion (1942–5) Burma became independent (Jan. 4, 1948). Rebellions, discontent among minorities, and economic instability culminated in civil war in the late 1950s. In 1958, Premier U Nu asked Gen. U Ne Win to take over the government; order was restored and in 1960 a civilian government under Nu was returned to power. However, in 1962 Ne Win led a military coup and resumed control of the government. He resigned as president in 1981 in favor of U San Yu, former army chief. A 1981 legislative act restricts politico/economic rights to descendants of Burmese nationals

Bur·mese (bəːrmíːz, bəːrmíːs) **1.** *adj.* of Burma **2.** *n.* a native of Burma ‖ the Burmese language of the Tibeto-Burman group

burn (bə́ːrn) *n.* (*Br.*) a brook [O.E. *burn*, a spring]

burn 1. *n.* damage or injury caused by fire, heat or acid **2.** *v. pres. part.* **burn·ing** *past* and *past part.* **burned, burnt** (bə́ːrnt) *v.t.* to consume or destroy by flames or heat ‖ to injure by fire or heat or acid ‖ to make by fire or heat or acid, *to burn a hole* ‖ (*cooking*) to scorch, to cause to stick to the pan ‖ (*med.*) to cauterize (a wound etc.) ‖ (*chem.*) to cause to undergo combustion ‖ to cause (candles, electricity, gas, oil etc.) to give light or heat ‖ to cause a sensation of heat in, *the pepper burned her throat* ‖ (of sun, radiation etc.) to cause injury or discomfort to ‖ *v.i.* to flame, blaze, *the fire is burning brightly* ‖ to be destroyed by fire or heat ‖ (of fires, electric lamps, gas stoves etc.) to give out light or heat ‖ (*cooking*) to stick to a pan and char ‖ to suffer injury or discomfort by exposure to the sun, radiation etc. ‖ to be passionately excited or heated with anger etc. ‖ to feel hot, *to burn with shame* ‖ (*chem.*) to undergo combustion **to burn a hole in one's pocket** (of money) to give one an urge to spend **to burn away** to diminish by burning, to burn to nothing ‖ to continue to burn **to burn down** to destroy or be destroyed by fire **to burn into** (esp. of acid) to eat into ‖ to

CONCISE PRONUNCIATION KEY: (a) æ, c*a*t; ɑ, c*a*r; ɔ f*aw*n; ei, sn*a*ke. **(e)** e, h*e*n; i:, sh*ee*p; iə, d*ee*r; ɛə, b*ea*r. **(i)** i, f*i*sh; ai, t*i*ger; əː, b*i*rd. **(o)** o, *o*x; au, c*ow*; ou, g*oa*t; u, p*oo*r; ɔi, r*oy*al. **(u)** ʌ, d*u*ck; u, b*u*ll; u:, g*oo*se; ə, b*a*cillus; juː, c*u*be. x, lo*ch*; θ, *th*ink; δ, bo*th*er; z, *Z*en; ʒ, corsa*g*e. dʒ, sava*g*e; ŋ, oranguta*n*g; j, *y*ak; ʃ, *fi*sh; tʃ, fe*tch*; 'l, rabb*le*; 'n, redd*en*. Complete pronunciation key appears inside front cover.

make an indelible impression on, *to burn into one's memory* **to burn one's bridges** (*Am.=Br.* **to burn one's boats**) to take some irrevocable step **to burn oneself out** to use up one's energy by overwork or dissipation **to burn one's fingers** to suffer the result of rash behavior **to burn out** to stop burning because of lack of fuel ‖ to come to nothing, *her burst of energy soon burned out* ‖ to force to emerge by setting fire to a dwelling etc. **to burn up** to consume or be consumed by fire [O.E. *bœrnan v.t.* and *brinnan v.i.*]

burn bag container ready for burning for classified material

burn center section of a hospital especially equipped to treat massive burns

burned (bə:rnd) *adj.* used to indicate a clandestine operator whose cover has been exposed (esp. in a surveillance) or whose reliability as a source of information has been compromised

Burne-Jones (bə́:rndʒóunz), Sir Edward (1833–98), English painter and designer. He worked with William Morris as a designer of stained glass windows, and as an illustrator for the Kelmscott Press

burn·er (bə́:rnər) *n.* the part of an oil lamp, gas stove, gas bracket, oil kiln etc. which gives out the flame ‖ a person or thing that burns

bur·net (bə́:rnit) *n.* a member of *Sanguisorba*, fam. *Rosaceae*, a genus of brown-flowered plants, esp. the widely distributed *S. officinalis* and *S. canadensis* of eastern North America

Bur·ney (bə́:rni:), Frances ('Fanny') (1752–1840), English novelist and diarist. 'Evelina' (1778) was highly praised by Dr. Johnson. Her most valuable work was her 'Diary and Letters of Madame D'Arblay' (published 1842–6)

Burn·ham (bə́:rnəm), Lindon Forbes Sampson (1923–85), Guyanan lawyer and statesman. He was prime minister (1964–6) of British Guiana, which he led to independence (1966) as Guyana. He became Guyana's first president (1980–5) under a new constitution

burn·ing (bə́:rniŋ) *adj.* on fire ‖ intense ‖ exciting passion, *a burning question*

burning bush the wahoo

burning glass a convex lens or concave mirror that concentrates the sun's rays, making the object focused upon burst into flame

bur·nish (bə́:rniʃ) 1. *n.* a gloss, luster produced by burnishing 2. *v.t.* to polish by rubbing with a hard and smooth instrument ‖ *v.i.* to take a polish in this way [fr. O.F. *burnir* (*burniss-*), to make brown]

burn notice an official statement by one intelligence agency to other agencies, domestic or foreign, that an individual or group is unreliable for any of a variety of reasons

bur·nous, bur·noose (bə:rnú:s) *n.* a hooded cloak worn by Arabs [F. fr. Arab. *burnus*]

burn-out (bə́:rnout) *n.* point in time or in the missile trajectory when combustion of fuels in the rocket engine is terminated by other than programmed cutoff

Burns (bə:rnz), Robert (1759–96), Scottish poet. The son of a poor farmer, and himself a farm laborer until he was 27, he became famous on the publication of his first book of poems (1786), mostly songs and narrative poems written in the vernacular. In an age of overliterary gentility they were direct, passionate, frank, bawdy, downright funny, shrewdly satirical, or passionately tender. His own musical gift made him a supreme songwriter

burnt alt. *past* and *past part.* of BURN

burnt ocher, esp. *Br.* **burnt ochre** a brick-red pigment obtained by heating ocher

burnt offering (*hist.*) a sacrifice made by burning an offering at an altar

burnt sienna raw sienna calcined and ground, giving a reddish-brown pigment

burnt umber umber calcined to give it a much more reddish hue ‖ the dark reddish-brown color of this (cf. RAW UMBER)

burp (bə:rp) 1. *n.* a belch 2. *v.i.* to belch ‖ *v.t.* to pat or rub (a baby) on the back, to help it to bring up wind [imit.]

Burr (bə:r), Aaron (1756–1836), U.S. political leader, and vice-president (1800–4) under Thomas Jefferson. He killed his political enemy, Alexander Hamilton, in a duel (1804). With James Wilkinson he conspired to launch an invasion of Mexico. Betrayed by Wilkinson, Burr was tried for treason. He was acquitted

burr (bə:r) 1. *n.* (*bot.*) a bur ‖ a trilling pronunciation of *r* ‖ a rough, country pronunciation ‖ a whirring, humming sound ‖ (*dentistry*) a bur ‖ a roughness left on cut or punched metal or paper

‖ any rough edge or ridge ‖ a disk seen around the moon or a star ‖ a small washer placed on the end of a rivet before it is made fast ‖ a coarse rock with quartz crystals used in millstones ‖ any of various limestones ‖ a whetstone 2. *v.i.* to speak with a burr ‖ to make a burring sound (e.g. of a drill) ‖ *v.t.* to pronounce with a burr [perh. imit.]

Bur·ritt (bə́:rit, bʌ́rit), Elihu (1810–79), U.S. philanthropist. As a leader (from 1837) of the American Peace Society and editor of its organ 'The Advocate of Peace', he organized (1848) the Brussels Congress of 'Friends of Peace' and urged the adoption of an international law code

bur·ro (bə́:rou, búərou, bʌ́rou) *n.* a small donkey used as a pack animal [Span.]

Bur·roughs (bə́:rouz, bʌ́rouz), Edgar Rice (1875–1950), U.S. novelist who created Tarzan. His works include 'Tarzan of the Apes' (1914) and many jungle and science fiction thrillers

bur·row (bə́:rou, bʌ́rou) 1. *n.* a hole dug underground by some animals (e.g. foxes, rabbits) as a shelter and home 2. *v.t.* (of animals) to dig (such a hole) ‖ *v.t.* (of animals) to dig a burrow or move forward by doing this ‖ (of people) to make a way underground or as though underground ‖ to delve, *to burrow into a mystery* [etym. doubtful]

burr·stone, buhr·stone (bə́:rstoun) *n.* a coarse rock with quartz crystals used in millstones ‖ such a millstone

Bur·sa (bu:rsá) a town (pop. 445,113) of N.W. Anatolia, Turkey, famous for fruit and vegetables, and center of the silk, cutlery and wool industries. It is sacred to Moslems

bur·sa (bə́:rsə) *pl.* **bur·sae** (bə́:rsi:), **bursas** *n.* a pouch or sac of connective tissue containing a thick fluid to lessen friction between the joints of the body **búr·sai** *adj.* [M.L. fr. Gk *bursa*, hide]

bur·sar (bə́:rsər, bə́:rsɑr) *n.* a treasurer, esp. of a college ‖ (*Br.*) the holder of a scholarship in some universities **bur·sar·i·al** (bə:rséəri:əl) *adj.* [fr. M.L. *bursarius* fr. *bursa*, bag fr. Gk]

bur·sa·ry (bə́:rsəri:) *pl.* **bur·sa·ries** *n.* the accounts office, esp. of a college ‖ (*Br.*) a scholarship in some universities and schools

burse (bə:rs) *n.* (*eccles.*) a silk or brocade case enclosing the folded corporal, and carried to and from the altar [F. *bourse* fr. L. fr. Gk]

bur·si·tis (bərsáitis) *n.* inflammation of a bursa [Mod. L. *bursa*, bursa+*itis*, inflammation]

burst (bə:rst) *n.* an explosion, a sudden disintegration ‖ a sudden outbreak ‖ a spouting forth, a spurt ‖ a sudden short intensive period, *a burst of energy* [O.E. *byrst*, damage]

burst *pres. part.* **burst·ing** *past* and *past part.* **burst** *v.i.* to explode, disintegrate suddenly and forcefully from inner pressure ‖ to come open suddenly, *to burst into flower* ‖ to collapse, *to burst into tears* ‖ to be full to overflowing, *to burst with pride* ‖ to rush suddenly and violently, *to burst into a room* ‖ *v.t.* to cause to burst, *to burst a balloon* ‖ to make by bursting, *to burst a hole in a canoe* ‖ to break, *the river will burst its banks* ‖ (with 'open') to open forcibly **to burst into view** to appear with startling suddenness **to burst out** (with *pres. part.*) suddenly to begin, *to burst out laughing* ‖ (with 'into') to launch oneself, *to burst out into a tirade* [O.E. *berstan*]

bur·then (bə́:rðən) *n.* a ship's carrying capacity ‖ (*rhet.*) a burden

Bur·ton (bə́:rt'n), Sir Richard Francis (1821–90), British explorer, linguist and Orientalist. He visited Mecca (1853) and was the first European to reach Harar, the capital of Somaliland (1854). With Speke, he discovered Lake Tanganyika (1858). He translated 'The Thousand Nights and a Night' ('The Arabian Nights') into English (1885–8)

Burton, Robert (1577–1640), English divine, author of 'The Anatomy of Melancholy' (1621), a compendium of medical knowledge, classical and Renaissance learning, history and fantasy

bur·ton (bə́:rt'n) *n.* a light hoisting tackle with a double and a single block [origin unknown]

Bu·run·di (burú:ndi:) (formerly Urundi) a republic (area 10,747 sq. miles, pop. 4,438,000) in central Africa. Capital: Bujumbura. People: Bahutu (85%), with Watutsi (the traditional rulers) and Batwa minorities. Language: Kirundi (Bantu) and French (both official), Swahili for trading. Religion: mainly Animist and Roman Catholic. The Nile-Congo dividing range (6,000–7,000 ft) crosses the country in the west,

dropping to the Great Rift Valley (Congo border). The east (averaging 5,000 ft) is part of the E. African plateau. Little woodland remains. Average temperature (F.): valley 81°, plateau 68°. Rainfall: Bujumbura (Lake Tanganyika) 31 ins, mountains 57 ins. Main industries: subsistence agriculture (beans, cassava, peanuts, cereals, bananas, palm products), cattle raising, fishing (Lake Tanganyika). Exports: coffee, cotton. Monetary unit (1965): Rwanda-Burundi franc. Formerly part of Ruanda-Urundi, it became an independent kingdom July 1, 1962. The king was deposed (Nov. 1966) and a republic was declared. In a 1972 unsuccessful attempt to restore the monarchy King Ntare was killed and many Hutu were slaughtered. In 1976, Lt. Col. Jean Baptiste Bagaza led a successful military coup; he was elected president in 1979 and 1984

bur·y (béri:) *pres. part.* **bur·y·ing** *past* and *past part.* **bur·ied** (béri:d) *v.t.* to put in the ground so as to be hidden from view ‖ to place in a grave or tomb ‖ to perform funeral rites over, *to be buried at sea* ‖ to dismiss from the mind ‖ to cover over ‖ to hide, *to bury one's face in one's hands* ‖ to preoccupy (oneself), *to bury oneself in one's books* ‖ to isolate (oneself), *to bury oneself in the country* **to bury one's head in the sand** to refuse to face a difficulty [O.E. *byrgan*]

bus (bʌs) 1. *pl.* **bus·es**, **bus·ses** *n.* a large public passenger vehicle serving fixed routes ‖ a similar vehicle used privately, e.g. by firms for transporting employees **to miss the bus** (*Br.*) to miss an opportunity ‖ to fail ‖ (*computer*) conductor used to transmit data from one or several sources to one or several destinations. A bus can be a coaxial cable, a fiber optic link, or any other wide-band (high-throughput) physical structure for transmitting data and control information ‖ (*mil.*) low-thrust final state of MIRV rocket 2. *v.i. pres. part.* **bus·sing** *past* and *past part.* **bussed** to go by bus [shortened from L. *omnibus*, for all]

bus·bar or **bus** (bʌ́sbɑr) *n.* (*electr.*) heavy conductor used to carry or make a mutual connection between several circuits

bus·boy (bʌ́sbɔi) *n.* a restaurant or cafeteria employee whose job is to clear the tables of dirty dishes

bus·by (bʌ́zbi:) *pl.* **bus·bies** *n.* (*Br.*) a tall fur headdress worn ceremonially by certain regiments [origin unknown]

bush (buʃ) 1. *n.* a cylindrical metal lining forming the bearing for a shaft or pin 2. *v.t.* to line with a bush [perh. fr. M. Du. *busse*, box]

bush 1. *n.* a shrub ‖ a clump of shrubs ‖ rough, shrubby, uncultivated country ‖ (*pop.*, with 'the') undeveloped, remote, thinly populated country occupying a large area ‖ (*hist.*) a bunch of ivy hung at a vintner's door 2. *v.i.* to branch out or cluster thickly [M.E. *busk* fr. O.N.]

bush baby a galago

bush basil *BASIL

bush bean any of various bushy varieties of bean plant, having no tendency to form vines

bushed (buʃt) *adj.* (*pop.*) exhausted

bush·el (búʃəl) *n.* any of various measures of capacity, esp. (*Am.*) a dry unit equal to 2150.42 cu. ins. and (*Br.*) a dry and liquid unit equal to 2219.36 cu. ins. or 8 gallons **to hide one's light under a bushel** to keep some ability etc. secret [M.E. *boyschel* fr. O.F.]

bush·ham·mer (búʃhæmər) *n.* a mason's hammer with a sharply grooved striking surface, used for dressing stone [prob. fr. G. *bosshammer*]

bush hat Australian military-style, wide-brim hat with one side pinned up

bu·shi·do (bu:ʃi:dó) *n.* the code of honor of the samurai [Jap. *bushidō* fr. *bushi*, warrior+*dō*, doctrine]

bush·i·ness (búʃi:nis) *n.* the state or quality of being bushy

bush·ing (búʃiŋ) *n.* (*elec.*) an insulator allowing the passage of a live conductor through an earthed wall ‖ a metal (usually bronze) lining in a piece of machinery that serves as a bearing and can be replaced ‖ a hardened steel tube in a machine tool etc. that serves as a guide and can be replaced [BUSH, a bearing]

Bush·man (búʃmən) 1. *pl.* **Bush·men** (búʃmən) *n.* a member of a nomadic people, an aboriginal race in S. Africa, inhabiting the Kalahari desert and similar areas in the southwest ‖ their language, characterized by clicking sounds 2. *adj.* pertaining to the Bushmen or their language

---

CONCISE PRONUNCIATION KEY: **(a)** æ, c*a*t; ɑ, c*a*r; ɔ f*aw*n; ei, sn*a*ke. **(e)** e, h*e*n; i:, sh*ee*p; iə, d*ee*r; ɛə, b*ea*r. **(i)** i, f*i*sh; ai, t*i*ger; ə:, b*i*rd. **(o)** o, *o*x; au, c*ow*; ou, g*oa*t; u, p*oo*r; ɔi, r*oy*al. **(u)** ʌ, d*u*ck; u, b*u*ll; u:, g*oo*se; ə, b*a*cillus; ju:, c*u*be. x, lo*ch*; θ, *th*ink; ð, bo*th*er; z, *Z*en; ʒ, corsa*g*e; dʒ, sava*g*e; ŋ, ora*ng*utang; j, *y*ak; ʃ, *fi*sh; tʃ, fe*tch*; 'l, rabb*le*; 'n, redd*en*. Complete pronunciation key appears inside front cover.

bush·man (búʃmən), pl. **bush·men** (búʃmən) n. a woodsman, esp. a farmer, traveler etc. in the Australian bush

bush·mas·ter (búʃmæstər, búʃmɑstər) n. Lachesis mutus, the largest poisonous snake in the Americas, found in tropical America

Bush Negro one of a tribal people descended from escaped African slaves, inhabiting the interior forests of Guyana, French Guiana and Surinam, having a common language based on English

Bush·on·go (bu:ʃɔŋgou) pl. **Bush·on·go, Bush·on·gos** n. a Bantu-speaking people of the central Congo noted esp. for their wood carving ‖ a member of this people

bush pilot an airplane pilot who flies over largely uninhabited country, off the regular routes

bush·rang·ers (búʃreindʒərz) pl. n. (Austral. hist.) armed robbers, usually escaped convicts, who terrorized outlying districts of Australia in the 19th c.

bush·rid·er (búʃraidər) n. (Austral.) a ranger in the bush regions

bush·rope (búʃroup) n. a liana

bush·veld (búʃvelt, búʃfelt) n. the low country of Transvaal ‖ any veld consisting mainly of bush [fr. Du. boschveld]

bush·whack·er (búʃhwækər, búʃwækər) n. someone used to traveling through rough country, esp. applied (hist.) to Civil War Confederate guerrillas **bush·whack·ing** n.

bush·y (búʃi) comp. **bush·i·er** superl. **bush·i·est** adj. covered with bushes ‖ growing thickly, a bushy beard

Bu·si·a (bú:si:ə), Kofi (1913–), Ghanaian statesman. He became (1969) prime minister in the first civilian administration in Ghana after Nkrumah's fall. He was overthrown (1972) by a coup d'état

bus·i·ly (bízili:) adv. in a busy manner

busi·ness (bíznis) n. one's regular employment, profession, occupation ‖ one's personal affair, concern, duty ‖ something requiring attention, the business before a committee ‖ a situation, matter, happening ‖ the activity of buying and selling, trade ‖ active selling, transactions, doing brisk business ‖ a commercial firm or enterprise ‖ (theater) silent acting, interpretation by gesture, movement etc. **to go about one's business** to do what concerns oneself **to have no business to** to have no right to **to make it one's business to** to choose to be personally responsible for **to mean business** to be in earnest **to mind one's own business** to refrain from interfering **to send someone about his business** to dismiss someone, esp. without giving him satisfaction [O.E. bisignis, the state of being busy]

business cycle (Am.=Br. trade cycle) the recurring succession of trade conditions alternating between boom and slump

busi·ness·like (bíznislaik) adj. practical-minded, a businesslike attitude ‖ methodical, a businesslike arrangement

business machine a computing or other machine used for office work

busi·ness·man (bíznismæn) pl. **busi·ness·men** (bíznismen) n. a person concerned with commerce or trading

busi·ness·man's risk moderate investment risk in which other factors, e.g., return and/or growth potential, are involved. It is less than a speculative risk. Cf PRUDENT INVESTMENT

bus·ing (básiŋ) n. transporting students from one school area to another to promote racial integration

bus·kin (báskin) n. a cothurnus [etym. doubtful]

bus·man's holiday (básmənz) a holiday spent in an activity the same as (or similar to) one's regular occupation

Bu·so·ni (bu:zɔ́ni:), Ferruccio Benvenuto (1866–1924), Italian pianist, conductor and composer. He transcribed many of Bach's organ works for the piano

bus principle (computer) group of parallel lines used as a pathway of communication throughout the computer

buss (bás) 1. v.t. pres. part. **buss·ing** past and past part. **bussed** to kiss 2. n. a kiss [origin unknown]

bust (bást) n. a piece of sculpture showing head, neck and something of shoulders and chest ‖ the upper front part of a woman's body ‖ the measurement around a woman's body at the breasts [F. buste fr. Ital.]

bust 1. n. (pop.) a burst ‖ (Am., pop., of a person) a complete failure ‖ a spree **2.** v.t. pres. part. **bust·ing** past **bust** past part. **bust, bust·ed** (pop.) to burst, break ‖ to make bankrupt ‖ (pop.) to demote (a soldier) ‖ (slang) to arrest ‖ to raid **3.** adj. bankrupt [var. of BURST]

Bus·ta·man·te (bʌstəmǽnti:), Sir William Alexander (1884–1977), Jamaican statesman and trade unionist. He was chief minister (1953–5) and became (1962–7) the first prime minister of independent Jamaica

bus·tard (bástərd) n. a member of Otis, fam. Otididae, a genus of large European and Australian game birds related to cranes and plovers. They are largely terrestrial, feeding on plants and insects [etym. doubtful]

bus·tle (bás'l) n. (hist.) a pad or framework worn under a woman's skirt to make it puff out behind [fr. G. buschel, a pad]

bustle 1. n. a stir ‖ brisk movement **2.** v. pres. part. **bus·tling** past and past part. **bus·tled** v.i. to move with busy or fussy purpose ‖ v.t. to cause to bustle [perh. imit.]

bu·sul·fan [$C_6H_{14}O_6S_2$] (bju:sʌ́lfən) n. (pharm.) drug used to treat myelogenous leukemia

bus·y (bízi:) comp. **bus·i·er** superl. **bus·i·est** adj. engaged in work or other occupation, to be busy sewing ‖ having plenty to do ‖ full of activity, a busy day ‖ always moving or working, busy fingers ‖ (of a telephone line) in use [O.E. bisig]

busy pres. part. **bus·y·ing** past and past part. **bus·ied** v.t. to occupy (someone, one's hands etc.) [O.E. bisgian]

bus·y·bod·y (bízi:bɒdi:) pl. **bus·y·bod·ies** n. a meddlesome person who pries into other people's affairs

but (bát) **1.** adv. (rhet.) only, merely, she is but a child ‖ just, I saw her but a moment ago **2.** conj. yet, and on the other hand, the work is hard, but you are well paid ‖ except (that), they would hear of nothing but that we should stay to dinner ‖ (after a negative) without the result that, he never speaks but she contradicts him **3.** prep. except, he grew nothing but rice **all but** almost, he was all but dead with fatigue **but for** except for, without, you couldn't have done it but for him **4.** n. (pl.) objections, ifs and buts [O.E. bútan, adv. and prep.]

bu·ta·di·ene (bju:tədáii:n, bju:tədaif:n) n. $CH_2=CH—CH=CH_2$, a gas used in making synthetic rubber by copolymerization [BUTANE]

bu·tane (bjú:tein) n. a hydrocarbon, C_4H_{10}, of the paraffin family, a gas obtained in large quantities in the refining of petroleum, and distributed, liquefied by pressure, as a fuel (gas, cigarette lighter fuel) [fr. L. butyrum, butter]

butch (butʃ) adj. **1.** a masculine appearance. **2.** a homosexual woman playing a male role in a lesbian relationship. **3.** a tough. **4.** a very short men's haircut. **5.** (slang) female homosexual who acts like a man in public

butch·er (bútʃər) **1.** n. someone who sells meat that he has prepared for sale ‖ someone who slaughters animals for market ‖ (of bad surgeons, generals etc.) a man who causes needless killing or suffering through brutality or incompetence **2.** v.t. to slaughter (animals) for food ‖ to kill cruelly or in great numbers ‖ to ruin the impact of (a work) by bad reading, performing or editing **butch·er·ly** adj. [O.F. bochier]

butcher's broom Ruscus aculeatus, a European low, leafless, evergreen plant, with stiff-pointed, spiny, leaflike branches (cladophylls), bearing greenish flowers on the surface, followed by red berries

butch·er·y (bútʃəri:) pl. **butch·er·ies** n. cruel slaughter on a large scale ‖ the butcher's trade [F. boucherie, slaughterhouse]

Bute (bju:t), John Stuart, 3rd earl of (1713–92), British statesman, the power behind the throne on George III's accession, secretary of state (1761), first lord of the treasury (1762), and prime minister for one year. He ended the Seven Years' War by the Treaty of Paris (1763), and retired completely from politics

Bute a former county (area 218 sq. miles) of S.W. Scotland, consisting of several islands (Bute, Arran and the Cumbraes are the largest) in the Firth of Clyde

bu·te·o (bjú:ti:ou) pl. **bu·te·os** n. a member of Buteo, a genus of medium-sized hawks, with heavy bodies and broad wings and tail. They soar high up for long periods searching for food (mice, frogs, snakes etc.). They are widely distributed [Mod. L.]

But·ler (bátlər), Benjamin Franklin (1818–93), U.S. lawyer, Civil War general, and politician

who championed the rights of workers, women, and blacks. During the Civil War he was governor (1862) of captured New Orleans. He confiscated property of Confederate sympathizers and executed a citizen for tearing down the U.S. flag

Butler, Nicholas Murray (1862–1947), U.S. educator. While president (1901–45) of Columbia University, he shared (with Jane Addams) the 1931 Nobel peace prize

Butler, Samuel (1612–80), English poet. Almost his only published work was 'Hudibras' (1663–78), a long, entertaining satire on contemporary religious factions, written in a deliberately low style

Butler, Samuel (1835–1902), English author and satirist. His works include 'Erewhon' (1872), a satirical story of an imaginary country, the novel 'The Way of all Flesh' (published posthumously, 1903), and his notebooks

but·ler (bátlər) n. the chief manservant of a house, usually in charge of the wine cellar, plate etc. [O.F. bouteillier, bottle bearer]

butt (bát) n. the thicker or handle end, esp. of a tool or weapon, rifle butt ‖ the base of a petiole or end of a plant nearest the roots ‖ the unburned part of a smoked cigarette etc. or used candle ‖ any of various flatfish, e.g. sole, turbot, plaice ‖ the thickest leather, from an animal's back or sides, trimmed rectangularly (*BEND) [etym. doubtful]

butt n. an object of ridicule, teasing or criticism ‖ the mound for catching bullets, arrows etc. behind a shooting or archery target ‖ (pl.) a shooting range ‖ a mark or target ‖ a grouse shooter's stand protected by a low stone wall ‖ (esp. of a goat) a sudden thrust with the head [F. but, goal]

butt n. a large cask for wine or beer (capacity 108-140 gals) [L.L. butta, cask]

butt v.t. to strike with the head or horns ‖ to join by making a butt joint, without overlapping ‖ to place (a plank etc.) end to end with another ‖ v.i. to bump ‖ to project, a building butting out over a river **to butt in** to interrupt suddenly **to butt in on** to intrude in [O.F. boter, buter, to thrust]

butte (bju:t) n. an isolated hill, with steep, even sides, and a flat top [F.=knoll]

but·ter (bátər) **1.** n. the fatty substance made by churning cream, used at the table and in cooking **2.** v.t. to spread with butter **to butter up** to flatter [O.E. butere fr. L. fr. Gk]

butter bean a lima bean, esp. a large, dried lima bean ‖ (Br.) a large, dried haricot bean

but·ter·bur (bátərbə:r) n. a member of Petasites, fam. Compositae, a genus of plants with large soft leaves once used for wrapping butter in

but·ter·cup (bátərkʌp) n. a member of Ranunculus, fam. Ranunculaceae, a genus of plants of Europe, Asia and North America, visited by many different insects for the nectar found in pockets at the base of the shining, bright yellow petals

but·ter·fat (bátərfæt) n. a fatty material obtained from milk

But·ter·field (bátərfi:ld), William (1814–1900), English architect. He built many fine churches in a neo-Gothic style. His best-known is All Saints, Margaret Street, London (1849–59)

but·ter·fin·gers (bátərfiŋgərz) n. a person who fails to catch or hold things

but·ter·fly (bátərflai) pl. **but·ter·flies** n. an insect of the division Rhopalocera of the order Lepidoptera. They are lively by day and have large, broad wings, erect when at rest and often brightly colored ‖ a frivolous person, a social butterfly ‖ a fast swimming stroke in which the extended arms make a circular movement simultaneously and are out of the water during recovery. The feet make two up-and-down kicks to each full circling of the arms **to have butterflies in one's stomach** to be in a state of acute nervous anticipation [O.E. buttorflēoge]

butterfly clamp (cosmetology) device for holding hair for sectioning during coloring processes

butterfly fish any of several species of vividly colored, spiny-finned tropical fish of fam. Chaetodontidae, or any of various other fish so named because of their coloring or broad fins

butterfly nut (mach.) a nut with wings to be turned by thumb and finger

butterfly valve a damper or throttle valve in a pipe, consisting of a disk turning on a diametrical axis or of two hinged semicircular plates

but·ter·is (bΛtəris) *n.* a farrier's tool for paring a hoof [origin unknown]

butter knife a blunt knife for cutting and serving butter at the table

but·ter·milk (bΛtərmilk) *n.* the liquid left after churning butter

butter muslin (*Br.*) cheesecloth

but·ter·nut (bΛtərnΛt) *n.* the souari nut of South America ‖ *Juglans cinerea,* a North American tree of the walnut family

butter print a wooden stamp for marking butter for market

but·ter·scotch (bΛtərskɒtʃ) *n.* a candy made chiefly of butter and brown sugar

but·ter·wort (bΛtərwəːrt) *n.* a member of *Pinguicula,* fam. *Lentibulariaceae,* a genus of insectivorous plants found in boggy land in the northern hemisphere. Their leaves are covered with glands which secrete a fluid, to which small insects adhere. The leaf rolls over when stimulated, secretes a ferment, digests the prey, absorbs the products, and then unrolls

but·ter·y (bΛtəri) *adj.* having the appearance or consistency of butter ‖ containing or covered with butter

buttery *pl.* **but·ter·ies** *n.* a storeroom for liquors or provisions ‖ (*Br.*) the room in colleges etc. where wines, ales and some provisions are kept for sale to students ‖ (*Br.*) a restaurant department (often separate) serving grilled foods etc. [perh. O.F. *boterie=bouteillerie,* a place where bottles are kept]

butt hinge a hinge with two leaves used on a door and jamb etc.

butt joint (*carpentry*) a joint between two pieces whose ends are squared and jointed but do not overlap ‖ (*engin.*) a joint between two plates held together by a butt strap

butt·leg·ging (bΛtlegin) illegal transportation and sale of cigarettes on which local taxes have not been paid

but·tock (bΛtək) **1.** *n.* one of the two rounded, muscled parts of the body on which a person sits ‖ (*esp. Br., wrestling*) a throw over the head from across the back **2.** *v.t.* (*esp. Br., wrestling*) to throw (an opponent) by using a buttock [M.E. *buttok* prob. fr. *butt,* stump]

but·ton (bΛtn) **1.** *n.* a small disk or knob sewn on material and passed through a hole or loop to provide a loose fastening, or this used ornamentally ‖ a disk worn during political campaigns to identify one's party, candidate etc. ‖ a flower bud ‖ an unopened mushroom ‖ a knob, a small device to be pressed, e.g. to start machinery working, or on an electric bell ‖ (*fencing*) the knob on the tip of a foil to render it harmless **2.** *v.t.* (often with 'up') to fasten the buttons of or enclose within a buttoned garment ‖ *v.i.* to have buttons for fastening ‖ to admit of being buttoned [O.F. *boton,* bud]

but·ton-down (bΛtndaun) *adj.* **1.** of one who is conservative, urbane. **2.** of one not easily changed from conventional attitudes

but·ton·hole (bΛtnhoul) **1.** *n.* the hole or loop through which a button is passed ‖ (*Br.*) a boutonniere **2.** *v.t. pres. part.* **but·ton·hol·ing** *past* and *past part.* **but·ton·holed** to make buttonholes in ‖ to detain (an unwilling listener)

buttonhole stitch a close loop stitch worked around the edges of buttonholes to prevent fraying

but·ton·hook (bΛt'nhuk) *n.* (*football*) a pass on which the receiver hooks back to the passer

but·ton·man (bΛt'nmæn) *n.* in underworld organizations, the lowest ranking member, usu. assigned to undesirable, dangerous, or unpleasant tasks

but·tons (bΛt'nz) *n.* (*Br.*) a bellboy

button stick a soldier's appliance for keeping polish off his uniform and equipment when he polishes his buttons etc.

but·ton·wood (bΛt'nwud) *n. Platanus occidentalis,* the sycamore of eastern North America

but·tress (bΛtris) **1.** *n.* a support built against a wall ‖ a prop, a supporting factor **2.** *v.t.* to prop or support with buttresses ‖ (often with 'up') to support, *to buttress a statement with statistics* [perh. fr. O.F. *bouterez,* flying buttress]

butt strap a strap welded or riveted to two plates and covering the butt joint between them

but·tut (butúːt) *n.* monetary unit in Gambia, equal to 1/100th dalasi

butt weld a butt joint made by welding

bu·tyl (bjúːt'l) *n.* any of four isomeric univalent organic radicals, C_4H_9- [fr. L. *butyrum,* butter fr. Gk]

butyl rubber a synthetic rubber made by copolymerization of isobutylene with a small quantity of butadiene or isoprene

bu·tyr·ic acid (bjuːtírik) C_3H_7COOH, a colorless liquid acid of unpleasant odor found in rancid butter. Synthetic butyric acid is used in the manufacture of plastics

bux·om (bΛksəm) *adj.* (of a woman) well rounded and attractive, esp. full-bosomed [M.E. *buhsum,* tractable, fr. O.E. *bugan,* to bend]

Bux·te·hu·de (bukstəhúːde), Diderik (c. 1637–1707), Danish composer (generally called Dietrich from his being organist at Lübeck). He wrote for the organ and harpsichord, also church cantatas and chamber music, and influenced Bach and Handel

Bux·ton (bΛkstən), Sir Thomas Fowell (1786–1845), English social reformer who, as a member of Parliament (1818–37) and leader of the emancipation movement, introduced the bill (1833) which ended slavery in the British Empire

buy (bai) **1.** *v.t. pres. part.* **buy·ing** *past* and *past part.* **bought** (bɔt) to acquire by paying money, purchase ‖ to obtain at some cost or sacrifice ‖ to win over by bribery or promises ‖ to be the price of, *$4000 will buy the machine* **to buy in** to buy a stock of ‖ to buy for oneself (possessions) which one has put up for auction or sale, by going beyond the highest rival bid **to buy into** to buy stocks or shares in (esp. a company) **to buy off** to get rid of (a blackmailer, claimant etc.) by payment **to buy out** to pay (a person) to give up certain privileges or rights **to buy up** to purchase (a firm etc., or a big part of it) **2.** *n.* something bought, esp. a bargain **búy·er** *n.* someone who selects and buys stock for a big store [O.E. *bycgan*]

buyers' market a market in which prices are low because of the plentiful supply of the goods concerned and weak demand

buy-in (báiín) **1.** *v.* to join a group, esp. in a business transaction. **2.** *v.* to cover a short position in the securities or commodities market. **3.** *n.* stock-exchange procedure in which a broker who does not receive delivery of a security by the time specified buys elsewhere and charges the resulting loss to the nondelivering broker

buy-out (báiáut) *n.* purchase of an entire inventory

buzz (bΛz) **1.** *n.* a humming noise, esp. of bees ‖ a muted sound of many people talking ‖ a general stir **2.** *v.t.* to fly an airplane low and fast over (something) ‖ to cause to buzz ‖ *v.i.* to make a humming sound ‖ to murmur ‖ to be filled with a hum, *the hall buzzed with excitement* ‖ to circulate, *the rumor buzzed around the village* ‖ to use a buzzer **to buzz off** (*Br., pop.*) to go away [imit.]

buz·zard (bΛzərd) *n.* the turkey buzzard ‖ (*Br.*) a buteo [O.F. *basart*]

Buz·zards Bay (bΛzərdz) an inlet (30 miles long, 5–10 miles wide) in S.E. Massachusetts. Cape Cod Canal connects it with Cape Cod Bay

buz·zer (bΛzər) *n.* a signaling apparatus making a buzzing noise, e.g. in a factory or office

buzz off *v.* (*slang*) (usu. an imperative) to go away

buzz saw a circular saw

buzz session informal discussion in small groups

buzz word 1. a term from a business or technical area applied to a different situation, e.g., yardstick, catalyst. **2.** expression designed to impress the uninitiated, usually consisting of technical or esoteric terms. **3.** expression that triggers a strong emotional reaction

BWO *CARCINOTRON

by (bai) **1.** *adv.* past (in space), *a man walked by* ‖ past (in time), *in years gone by* ‖ near, *to stand by* ‖ aside, *to put some savings by* **2.** *prep.* beside, *a day by the sea* ‖ close to, *sit by the fire* ‖ in the direction of, *west by south* ‖ along, over, *come by the quickest road* ‖ through, via ‖ past, *she walked by him without speaking* ‖ during, *by night* ‖ not later than, *be here by noon* ‖ to the extent of, *to win by a meter* ‖ concerning, with respect to, *to do one's duty by a friend* ‖ through the means of, *to travel by car,* *to lead someone by the hand* ‖ with, born of, *two children by a previous wife* ‖ (indicating progression or quantity), *little by little,* *to go forward by degrees,* *to emigrate by the thousand* ‖ (in oaths) in the name of, *to swear by God* [O.E. *bi*]

by-and-by (baiənbái) *n.* the remote future ‖ the hereafter [M.E. adv.=one by one]

by and by soon, before long

by and large on the whole

Byb·los (bíblɔs) a city of ancient Phoenicia (modern Jubail in Lebanon) important for the cult of Adonis, Isis and Osiris. The tomb of Ahiram (13th c. B.C., contemporary of Ramses II) has been excavated, yielding a sculptured sarcophagus and Phoenician inscriptions

Byd·goszcz (bídgɔʃtʃ) (G. *Bromberg*) a town (pop. 352,400) in N. Poland, a rail and waterways center. Its canal links the Vistula and Oder river systems. Industries: lumber, leather, metal etc.

bye (bai) *n.* (*cricket*) a run scored on a ball which passes both batsman and wicketkeeper ‖ (in certain sports matches) a player left after pairs are drawn, who proceeds to the next round without playing ‖ (*golf*) the hole or holes left unplayed in a match, and played as a new game [var. of BY]

byelaw *BYLAW

by-e·lec·tion, bye-e·lec·tion (báiilekʃən) *n.* (*Br.*) a local election held when a vacancy has been caused by a death or resignation

Bye·lo·rus·sia (bjelourΛʃə) (White Russia) a constituent republic (area 80,314 miles, pop. 9,744,000) of the U.S.S.R. in E. Europe, bordering Poland. Capital: Minsk. It is largely wooded hill country with extensive marshland in the southwest. Agriculture: dairy and beef cattle, pigs, flax, root crops. Resources: peat (the main source of power), rock salt. Industry: mechanical engineering. It became a Soviet Republic (1919) and joined the U.S.S.R. in 1922

by·gone (báigɔn, báigɒn) **1.** *adj.* (*rhet.*) past, of the past **2.** *n.* (*pl.*) past offenses etc. (esp. in phrase) **to let bygones be bygones** to forgive and forget

by·law, bye·law (báilɔ) *n.* a regulation or law made by a corporation, company, club, or (*Br.*) local authority, for controlling its affairs ‖ a secondary law or regulation

by·line (báilain) **1.** *n.* the line naming the writer at the head of a newspaper or magazine article **2.** *pres. part.* **by·lin·ing** *past* and *past part.* **by·lined** *v.t.* to write under a by-line

Byng (bin), George *TORRINGTON

Byng, John (1704–57), English admiral shot 'pour encourager les autres' as Voltaire said, after his failure to relieve Minorca

Byng, Julian Hedworth George Byng, 1st Viscount (1862–1932), British general in the 1st world war who commanded the Canadian Corps at Vimy Ridge. He was governor-general of Canada (1921–6)

by·o·bu (biːóubuə) *n.* (*s* or *pl*) Japanese painted screen with six panels

by·pass (báipæs, báipɑs) **1.** *n.* an alternative road around a town or through its outskirts designed to make through traffic avoid the town ‖ (*engin.*) a device to direct flow around a fixture or pipe, etc., instead of through it ‖ (*elec.*) a shunt **2.** *v.t.* to make a detour round

by·path (báipæθ, báipɑθ) *pl.* **by·paths** (báipæðz, báipɑðz, báipæθs, baipɑθs) *n.* a side path ‖ a little known or not very important episode, *bypaths of history*

by·play (báiplei) *n.* action aside or apart from main events, esp. that of minor characters during a scene on the stage

by·prod·uct (báiprɒdəkt) *n.* something produced during the manufacture of something else

Byrd (bəːrd), Richard Evelyn (1888–1957), American rear admiral and polar explorer. He was a pioneer in transatlantic and transpolar flights and led four scientific expeditions to the Antarctic (1928–30, 1933–5, 1939–41 and 1946–7)

Byrd, William (1543–1623), English composer of Masses, madrigals and music for the virginals. Perhaps his greatest works are the Masses, which reveal his attachment to the old (and then proscribed) Catholic religion. He also contributed greatly to the new Anglican liturgy, writing responses, services and anthems

byre (báir) *n.* (*Br.*) a cow shed [O.E. *býre*]

by·road (báiroud) *n.* an unimportant, little-used road

By·ron (báirən), George Gordon Noel, 6th Baron (1788–1824), English poet. A journey in the Near East (1809–11) inspired several of his poems, esp. 'Childe Harold's Pilgrimage', the appearance of the first part of which (1812) made him immediately and wildly popular. In 1823 he joined the insurgent Greeks, for several

CONCISE PRONUNCIATION KEY: **(a)** æ, c*a*t; ɑ, c*a*r; ɔ f*aw*n; ei, sn*a*ke. **(e)** e, h*e*n; iː, sh*ee*p; iə, d*ee*r; ɛə, b*ea*r. **(i)** i, f*i*sh; ai, t*i*ger; əː, b*i*rd. **(o)** o, *o*x; au, c*ow*; ou, g*oa*t; u, p*oo*r; ɔi, r*oy*al. **(u)** Λ, d*u*ck; u, b*u*ll; uː, g*oo*se; ə, b*a*cillus; juː, c*u*be. x, lo*ch*; θ, *th*ink; ð, bo*th*er; z, *Z*en; ʒ, corsa*g*e; dʒ, sava*ge*; ŋ, orangutan*g*; j, *y*ak; ʃ, *fi*sh; tʃ, fe*tch*; 'l, rabb*le*; 'n, redd*en*. Complete pronunciation key appears inside front cover.

months helping their fight for liberty against the Turks. He died of fever at Missolonghi. As a poet he was uneven, capable of dramatic, romantic and sometimes deeply moving lyricism, and with a gift for satire, swift narration and vivid description. At other times his verse was puerile and sentimental. The romanticism both of his life and of his work won him a vast popularity in England and the Continent. He is now most admired for his satirical verse, 'Don Juan' (1819–24), 'Beppo' (1818), 'The Vision of Judgement' (1822), which is close to the poetry of the 18th–c. Augustans, esp. Pope, whom he admired. He had little sympathy for contemporary English poets

By·ron·ic (bairónik) *adj.* of or pertaining to Lord Byron ‖ of or resembling Byron's work, romantic appearance or temperament etc., *a Byronic hero*

bys·si·no·sis (bịsənóusəs) *n.* (*med.*) brown lung (which see)

bys·sus (bísəs) *n.* (*zool.*) a tuft of strong filaments secreted by a gland of certain bivalve mollusks, which cling to rocks by means of them ‖ (*bot.*) the stipe of some fungi ‖ (*hist.*) a precious ancient linen fabric [L. fr. Gk *bussos*, linen]

by·stand·er (báistændər) *n.* a person present when some action takes place but not involved in it, a casual spectator

by·street (báistrị:t) *n.* a side street

byte (bait) *n.* (*computer*) unit of binary digits, usually in eight bits representing two numerals or one character

byte per second (*computer*) unit of measuring speed of digital transmission. (*abbr.* byte/s)

by the by incidentally

By·tom (bítɔm) (former Beuthen) a town (pop. 236,000) in Upper Silesia, Poland: coal, zinc and iron mines, ironworks

by·way (báiwẹi) *n.* a quiet track ‖ a shortcut ‖ a little-known line of research or department of a subject

by·word (báiwə:rd) *n.* proverbial status accorded to some person, place etc., usually held in contempt, *his drunken habits were a byword in the village* ‖ a word or phrase often used [O.E. *biword*, proverb]

Byz·an·tine (bízənti:n, bizǽntain) **1.** *adj.* of Byzantium or the Byzantine Empire ‖ (*archit.*) describing the style of architecture of the Byzantine Empire, esp. of the 5th and 6th cc., characterized by a central dome over a square space sometimes surrounded by groups of smaller domes, round arches, mosaics on walls and floors, marble veneering etc. ‖ involving intrigue **2.** *n.* an inhabitant of Byzantium [fr. L. *Byzantinus*]

Byzantine Empire the Eastern Roman Empire from 395 A.D. to 1453. Constantine I rebuilt Byzantium (330 A.D.), renamed it Constantinople, and made it the new capital of the Roman Empire. The Empire was divided (395), and the western part was overrun by the barbarians (5th c.). The Eastern Empire, ruled from Constantinople, chiefly comprised Asia Minor, the Balkan peninsula and Egypt. The dominant language was Greek, though Latin was in official use. Constantine I made Christianity the official religion (313), and the Orthodox Church refuted the heresies of Arianism (381) and Nestorianism (431). Under the reign (527–65) of Justinian I, the Empire was extended to Italy and N. Africa. Roman law was codified, and there was a revival of art, architecture, literature and music. N. Italy was lost to the Lombards (by 580). The Avars threatened Constantinople (610), but were driven back by the Heraclian dynasty (610–711). The Arabs captured Egypt, N. Africa and Syria, and attacked Constantinople (673–8). Under the Syrian dynasty (717–802) the Arabs were finally crushed (717–8), and Asia Minor was recovered. With the outbreak of iconoclasm, and the crowning of Charlemagne as Emperor of the West (800), the Byzantine Empire lost its claim to universality. The Macedonian dynasty (876–1057) consolidated the Empire. Economic prosperity brought progress in science, philosophy and architecture. After 1025, most of Asia Minor was lost to the Turks, S. Italy was conquered by the Normans, and the Bulgars and Serbs revolted, but parts of Asia Minor were recovered under the Comnenus dynasty (1081–1185). The Greek and Roman Churches split definitively (1054). Constantinople was sacked (1204) by the 4th Crusade, and the Latin Empire of Constantinople was set up. The rest of the Byzantine Empire was broken up into independent states, but was partially restored under the Palaeologus dynasty (1261–1453). The Empire finally collapsed with the capture (1453) of Constantinople by the Ottoman Turks. The Byzantine Empire protected western Europe against barbarian attacks, and preserved the classical traditions, esp. of Roman political theory and of Greek culture, from which the Renaissance developed

By·zan·ti·um (bizǽnti:əm, bizǽnʃi:əm) (now Istanbul) a Greek colony founded c. 660 B.C. It was generally a free city in Hellenic and Roman times, though subject to frequent attack. Constantine I rebuilt the city as a new (and Christian) capital of the Roman Empire, naming it Constantinople after himself (330 A.D.)

BZ (*mil.*) Army code name for nerve gas that incapacitates both mentally and physically, causing drowsiness, disorientation, hallucinations

---

CONCISE PRONUNCIATION KEY: **(a)** æ, c*a*t; ɑ, c*a*r; ɔ f*a*wn; ei, sn*a*ke. **(e)** e, h*e*n; i:, sh*ee*p; iə, d*ee*r; ɛə, b*ea*r. **(i)** i, f*i*sh; ai, t*i*ger; ə:, b*i*rd. **(o)** o, *o*x; au, c*o*w; ou, g*oa*t; u, p*oo*r; ɔi, r*oy*al. **(u)** ʌ, d*u*ck; u, b*u*ll; u:, g*oo*se; ə, bacill*u*s; ju:, c*u*be. x, lo*ch*; θ, *th*ink; ð, bo*th*er; z, *Z*en; ʒ, corsa*g*e; dʒ, sava*ge*; ŋ, orangutan*g*; j, *y*ak; ʃ, *fi*sh; tʃ, fe*tch*; 'l, rabb*le*; 'n, redd*en*. Complete pronunciation key appears inside front cover.

	EARLY NORTH SEMITIC	PHOENICIAN	EARLY HEBREW	EARLY GREEK	CLASSICAL GREEK	ETRUSCAN		EARLY LATIN	CLASSICAL LATIN
						Early	Classical		
C	⌐	∧	⌐	⊓	Γ	⌐	>	<	C

	CURSIVE MAJUSCULE (ROMAN)	CURSIVE MINUSCULE (ROMAN)	ANGLO-IRISH MAJUSCULE	CAROLINE MINUSCULE	VENETIAN MINUSCULE (ITALIC)	N. ITALIAN MINISCULE (ROMAN)
	⌐	C	C	c	C	C

A. C. SYLVESTER, CAMBRIDGE, ENGLAND

Development of the letter C, beginning with the early North Semitic letter. Evolution of both the majuscule, or capital, letter C and the minuscule, or lowercase, letter c are shown.

C, c (si:) the third letter in the English alphabet ‖ (*mus.*) a note, and the key of which it is the tonic ‖ C Roman numeral = 100

C. Centigrade

CA (*pharm. acronym*) for chloradinone acetate [$C_{21}H_{27}ClO_3$], a progestogen in the form of a minipill to inhibit pregnancy

Caaba *KAABA

cab (kæb) *n.* a taxi, car for hire ‖ the closed part of a truck or locomotive where the driver sits ‖ a closed horse-drawn carriage for hire [shortened fr. CABRIOLET]

ca·bal (kəbǽl) **1.** *n.* a plot, intrigue ‖ an association of persons secretly united to further their interests by plotting ‖ (*hist.*) a secret cabinet of ministers which governed England under Charles II (1667–73). The members were Clifford, Ashley, Buckingham, Arlington, and Lauderdale **2.** *v.i. pres. part.* **ca·bal·ling** *past* and *past part.* **ca·balled** to plot, form a cabal [F. *cabale*]

cabala *CABBALA

ca·bal·le·ro (kæbəljéɑrou, *Span.* kɑvɑljérɔ) *n.* (*Span. and south west U.S.A.*) a horseman ‖ (*Span.*) a knight, gentleman [Span.]

ca·ba·na (kəbǽnə, kəbǽnjə) *n.* a light, tentlike structure for changing in at a beach or swimming pool [Span. *cabaña*, cabin]

cabana set men's beachwear of loose shirt and shorts

cab·a·ret (kæbəréi) *n.* a place serving alcoholic drinks and providing entertainment ‖ (*Br.*) the entertainment given in a nightclub [F., etym. doubtful]

cab·bage (kǽbidʒ) *n. Brassica oleracea,* fam. *Cruciferae,* a plant whose tightly packed, unopened leaves are eaten as a vegetable ‖ any of various other hearting or nonhearting varieties of *Brassica* [M.E. *caboche* fr. F. fr. L.]

cabbage palmetto *Sabal palmetto,* a fan palm of the southeastern U.S.A. having an edible terminal bud

cabbage rose *Rosa centifolia,* fam. *Rosaceae,* a sweet-smelling rose with large pink or white flowers

cabbage tree *Oreodoxa oleracea,* fam. *Palmaceae,* a palm whose terminal bud is eaten as a vegetable. The fruit yields an oil, and a form of sago is obtained from the stem ‖ a member of *Sabal,* fam. *Palmaceae,* a genus of palms used for thatching

cabbage white *Pieris brassica,* a butterfly whose larvae destroy esp. the leaves of cabbages. The adult has white wings with black markings

cab·ba·la, ca·ba·la (kǽbələ, kəbálə) *n.* a method of interpreting scripture by explaining the occult meaning of letters and words, used esp. by rabbis ‖ any occult science [M.E. fr. Heb. *qabbálāh,* tradition]

cab·by, cab·bie (kǽbi:) *pl.* **cab·bies** *n.* a cabdriver

cab·driv·er (kǽbdrɑivər) *n.* the driver of a taxi or horse-drawn carriage for hire

ca·ber (kéibər) *n.* the trunk of a young tree tossed in the Scottish sport of tossing the caber [Gael. *cabar,* pole]

ca·bes·tro (kəbéstrou) *n.* (*bullfighting*) tamed steer used to direct fighting bulls

Ca·be·za de Va·ca (kɑbéθɑðeváka), Alvar Núñez (c. 1490–c. 1557), Spanish conquistador. He explored the Mississippi and New Mexico and, as adelantado (governor) of the province of Rio de la Plata, the Chaco. He is the author of 'Naufragios y comentarios'

ca·bil·do (kɑbí:ldɔ) *n.* (in colonial Spanish America) a town council. When the citizens participated in the council, it was known as a 'cabildo abierto' [Span.]

cab·in (kǽbin) *n.* a small wooden house ‖ a room on board ship where passengers sleep ‖ a room belowdecks for crew or passengers ‖ an aircraft's closed compartment for passengers, cargo etc. [M.E. *cabane* fr. F.]

cabin boy a young sailor who waits on the ship's officers and passengers

cabin class a class of accommodation on a passenger ship ranking between first class and tourist class

Ca·bin·da, Ka·bin·da (kəbíndə) an exclave, or outlying territory, of Angola (area 3,000 sq. miles, pop. 81,300) north of River Congo. Bounded on the S. by Zaire and on the N. by the Congo, its principal product is oil ‖ its capital

cab·i·net (kǽbinit) *n.* a piece of furniture with display shelves ‖ a metal or wood container with drawers or shelves for storing things ‖ the committee of chief ministers under a president or prime minister [dim. of CABIN]

—In the U.S.A. there is no provision for a cabinet in the constitution, but it early became a recognized part of executive policy to work with a cabinet. It is the president's advisory body, composed of secretaries in charge of departments, who are not allowed to be members of either house of Congress. There is no theory of collective responsibility and no responsibility to Congress. The cabinet is responsible to the president alone, and he is free to accept or reject its advice.

The British cabinet is composed of the chief members of the government appointed by, and under the chairmanship of, the prime minister. Historically, it evolved from the 'cabinet council', a committee of the privy council, under Charles I. The king attended its meetings until the reign of George I, and royal control of the cabinet was further weakened under George III. Today it is technically an informal body with no executive authority, but its decisions become those of the sovereign and of the government. Its deliberations are secret and the principles of collective responsibility and unanimity in public are maintained. It is responsible to parliament and has the sole right of advising the sovereign. Its functions are the final determination of the policy of government, the order, manner, and form of proposals to be submitted to parliament, and the settlement of interdepartmental matters. Cabinet government has been adopted by most of the self-governing Commonwealth countries

cab·i·net·mak·er (kǽbinitmeikər) *n.* a person skilled in working wood for furniture

cab·i·net·mak·ing (kǽbinitmeikiŋ) *n.* the trade of the cabinetmaker

cabinet minister a member of the committee of chief ministers under a president or prime minister

cab·i·net·work (kǽbinitwəːrk) *n.* furniture or wooden fittings made by a cabinetmaker

ca·ble (kéib'l) **1.** *n.* a strong length of rope, wire or chain ‖ a rope of wire used to transmit electricity or messages, a telegraph line ‖ a message sent by this means ‖ a rope or chain holding a ship at anchor **2.** *v. pres. part.* **ca·bling** *past* and *past part.* **ca·bled** *v.t.* to send by cable or telegraph ‖ *v.i.* to send a cable or telegraph [M.E. *cable, cabel* fr. O.F.]

cable car a passenger car on a cable railway

cable cast *v.* to broadcast on cable television. —**cablecaster** *n.* the program. —**cablecaster** *n.*

ca·ble·gram (kéib'lgræm) *n.* a message sent by an underwater telegraph cable

ca·ble-laid (kéib'lleid) *adj.* (of a rope) having three three-stranded, plain-laid ropes twisted counterclockwise

cable length one tenth of a nautical mile, 608 feet ‖ 100 fathoms ‖ 120 fathoms

cable railway a railway used esp. for short, steep climbs, the passenger cars gripping and being hauled by an endless belt driven by a stationary engine

cable stitch a knitting stitch producing a pattern resembling intertwining strands

ca·blet (kéiblit) *n.* a cable-laid rope of under 10 ins. in circumference

cable television system delivered by direct wire for providing more varied television shows to paid subscribers by utilizing better and wider reception, amplification, and sometimes special programs. *abbr* CATV.

cab·man (kǽbmən) *pl.* **cab·men** (kǽbmən) *n.* a taxi driver

cab·o·chon (kǽbəʃɒn) **1.** *n.* a gem cut in a convex curve and polished but not given facets **2.**

CONCISE PRONUNCIATION KEY: **(a)** æ, c*a*t; ɑ, c*a*r; ɔ f*aw*n; ei, sn*a*ke. **(e)** e, h*e*n; i:, sh*ee*p; iə, d*ee*r; ɛə, b*ea*r. **(i)** i, f*i*sh; ai, t*i*ger; əː, b*i*rd. **(o)** o, *o*x; au, c*ow*; ou, g*oa*t; u, p*oo*r; ɔi, r*oy*al. **(u)** ʌ, d*u*ck; u, b*u*ll; uː, g*oo*se; ə, bacill*u*s; juː, c*u*be. x, lo*ch*; θ, *th*ink; ð, bo*th*er; z, *Z*en; ʒ, cor*s*age; dʒ, sava*g*e; ŋ, oranguta*n*g; j, *y*ak; ʃ, *fi*sh; tʃ, fe*tch*; 'l, rabb*le*; 'n, redd*en*. Complete pronunciation key appears inside front cover.

adv. (of a gem) cut in this style [F. fr. *caboche*, a head]

ca·boo·dle (kəbú:d'l) *n.* (*pop.*, in the phrase) **the whole caboodle** the whole lot (of things or people) [fr. *kit, kith,* relatives + boodle, possessions fr. Du. *boedel*]

ca·boose (kəbú:s) *n.* a ship's galley ‖ the rear car of a freight train used by trainmen [perh. of L.G. origin]

Ca·bot (kǽbət), John (1450–98), Venetian navigator. Under letters patent from Henry VII of England, he sailed west (1497) in search of the Northwest Passage, and reached the coast of America, probably at Cape Breton Is. In 1498 he explored the coast of Greenland and visited Baffin Land, Labrador and Newfoundland

Cabot, Sebastian (c. 1476–1557), Venetian (or possibly English) navigator and cartographer, John's son. He explored the La Plata region of Brazil (1526–30) and was internationally famous as cartographer to Emperor Charles V

cab·o·tage (kǽbətidʒ) *n.* the navigation and movement of ships in coastal waters ‖ restriction of the use of coastal waters and air space by a country to its own domestic traffic [F. fr. *caboter,* to coast]

Cabot Strait a channel (c. 60 miles wide) between Cape Breton Is. and S.W. Newfoundland, connecting the Gulf of St. Lawrence with the Atlantic

Ca·bral (kəbról), Pedro Álvarez (c. 1460– c. 1526), Portuguese navigator who took possession of Brazil (1500) for the Portuguese crown

cab rank (*Br.*) a taxi stand

Cab·ri·ni (kəbrí:ni:), Saint Frances Xavier (1850–1917), Roman Catholic saint. As founder (1880) of the Missionary Sisters of the Sacred Heart of Jesus, she established schools, hospitals and orphanages throughout the Americas and Europe. She became (1946) the first U.S. citizen to be canonized

cab·ri·ole (kǽbri:oul) *n.* a curved leg on furniture of the Queen Anne and Chippendale styles [F. *cabriole*, a goat's leap, from the similarity with a goat's foreleg]

cab·ri·o·let (kæbri:əléi) *n.* a motorcar with a folding top and glass windows ‖ (*hist.*) a light, hooded, one-horse carriage [F. dim. of *cabriole,* a goat's leap]

ca·ca·o (kəkéiou, kəkáuou) *n.* the seed of *Theobroma cacao,* from which cocoa and chocolate are made ‖ the tree itself (*COCOA) [Span. fr. Nahuatl]

cacao bean the seed of the cacao tree

cacao butter a substance extracted from cacao seeds, used in soaps, cosmetics etc.

cac·cia·to·re (kɑtʃətóri:) *n.* meat dish served with tomatoes, green peppers, onions, and olive oil

Cá·ce·res (kúsəreis, kúθəreis) a province (area 7,667 sq. miles, pop. 414,744) of W. Spain ‖ its capital (pop. 71,852) (*ESTREMADURA)

cach·a·lot (kǽʃəlɒt, kǽʃəlou) *n.* the sperm whale [F.]

cache (kæʃ) **1.** *n.* a hiding place for treasure or stores ‖ the goods in such a hiding place, a hoard or store **2.** *v.t. pres. part.* **cach·ing** *past* and *past part.* **cached** to hide away (valuables or stores) [F.]

ca·chec·tic (kəkéktik) *adj.* of or relating to cachexia **ca·chéc·ti·cal** *adj.*

cache memory (*computer*) a supplementary memory bank

ca·chet (kæʃéi, kǽʃei) *n.* a mark of distinction or quality ‖ a capsule containing a dose of a drug [F.]

ca·chex·i·a (kəkéksi:ə) *n.* physical ill health, with loss of weight and emaciation [Mod. L. fr. Gk *kakos*, bad + *hexis*, condition]

cach·in·nate (kǽkineit) *pres. part.* **cach·in·nat·ing** *past* and *past part.* **cach·in·nat·ed** *v.i.* (*rhet.*) to laugh so loudly as to give offense **cach·in·na·tion** *n.* **cach·in·na·to·ry** (kǽkineitəri:) *adj.* [fr. L. *cachinnare* (*cachinnatus*)]

cach·o·long (kǽʃəlɒŋ) *n.* a white or yellow opaque variety of opal [perh. fr. *Cach,* a river in Bokhara + Kalmuck *cholong,* stone]

ca·chou (kəʃú:, kæʃú:) *n.* a pastille sucked to sweeten the breath ‖ a catechu [F.]

ca·cique (kəsí:k) *n.* a member of *Cacicus* and other genera of American orioles, having the base of the beak enlarged for protection ‖ a title borne by the chiefs of Indian tribes in Central and S. America, Haiti and Cuba [Span. or F. fr. Haitian]

cack·le (kæk'l) **1.** *n.* the harsh, clucking noise of a hen ‖ a raucous laugh ‖ (*pop.*) idle talk **2.** *v. pres. part.* **cack·ling** *past* and *past part.* **cack·-**

led *v.i.* to make such a noise ‖ to chatter or laugh shrilly ‖ *v.t.* to utter in a harsh, shrill tone [M.E. *cakelen,* imit.]

cac·o·de·mon, cac·o·dae·mon (kækədí:mən) *n.* an evil spirit, a demon [Gk *kakodaimōn*]

cac·o·mis·tle (kǽkəmis'l) *n. Bassariscus astutus,* a carnivorous animal of Mexico and southwest U.S.A., related to the raccoon [Span. fr. Mex. *tlacomiztli*]

ca·coon (kəkú:n) *n.* one of the large polished pods (1 yd long) of the tropical climbing shrub *Entada scandens,* fam. *Papilionaceae* ‖ this shrub [etym. doubtful]

ca·coph·o·nous (kəkɒfənəs) *adj.* characterized by cacophony

ca·coph·o·ny (kəkɒfəni:) *pl.* **ca·coph·o·nies** *n.* a harsh discord ‖ dissonance [F. *cacophonie* fr. Gk]

cac·ta·ceous (kæktéiʃəs) *adj.* of or related to the cactus [fr. Mod. L. *Cactaceae,* cactus family]

cac·tus (kǽktəs) *pl.* **cac·ti** (kǽktai), **cac·tus·es** *n.* a member of *Cactus,* a genus of spiny plants of fam. *Cactaceae.* There are 1,500 species, chiefly found in dry regions of the Tropics. Cacti are xerophytes, exhibiting reduction of the transpiring surface and able to store up water. They often have flowers of great size and beauty. There are a few edible forms, and certain species are important as the food plant of the cochineal insect [L. fr. Gk]

cad (kæd) *n.* a man offending against the accepted code of gentlemanly behavior, esp. in his relations with women [perh. shortened fr. CADDIE, CADET]

CAD (*computer acronym*) for computer-aided design, system for testing proposed alternative designs by computer

ca·das·tral (kədǽstrəl) *adj.* pertaining to landed property [F.]

cadastral survey a large-scale map for the purpose of making a cadastre

ca·das·tre (kədǽstər) *n.* (*law*) an official register of the extent and value of real estate for purposes of taxation [F.]

ca·dav·er (kədǽvər, kədéivər) *n.* a human corpse **ca·dav·er·ous** (kədǽvərəs) *adj.* corpselike ‖ gaunt ‖ deathly pale [L.]

cad·die, cad·dy (kǽdi:) **1.** *n.* an attendant paid to carry a golfer's clubs around the course **2.** *v.i. pres. part.* **cad·dy·ing** *past* and *past part.* **cad·died** to serve as a caddie [fr. F. *cadet,* a younger son or brother]

cad·dis fly (kǽdisflai) a mothlike insect of order *Trichoptera,* having a hairy body covering and four iridescent wings. It lays its eggs in water [perh. fr. O.F. *cadas,* floss silk]

cad·dish (kǽdiʃ) *adj.* of or relating to a cad

cad·dis·worm (kǽdiswə:rm) *n.* the larva of the caddis fly. It lives under water and forms a case of silk and stones, shells or grasses etc. It is used as bait for fishing

Cad·do (kǽdou) *pl.* **Cad·do, Cad·dos** *n.* a North American Indian linguistic group which occupied most of the eastern Great Plains area. Epidemics reduced the population from many thousands to about 1,000, who settled on a reservation in east central Oklahoma ‖ a member of this group

caddy *CADDIE

cad·dy (kǽdi:) *pl.* **cad·dies** *n.* a small container for tea [fr. Malay *kati,* a weight of 1⅓ lb.]

Cade (keid), John (commonly known as Jack Cade, d. 1450), English rebel. He led the Kentish rebellion (1450) against Henry VI, but was captured and killed

cade (keid) *adj.* (of animals) reared by hand instead of by the mother [origin unknown]

ca·dence (kéid'ns) *n.* the fall or modulation of the voice ‖ the rhythmic flow of sound, esp. of words in verse or prose ‖ a beat, measure ‖ the closing of a musical phrase [F. fr. Ital. *cadenza*]

ca·den·cy (kéid'nsi:) *pl.* **ca·den·cies** *n.* cadence ‖ the status of being a younger son or brother, or a younger branch of a family or member of such a branch

ca·den·za (kədénzə) *n.* (*mus.*) a passage for solo voice or instrument, interrupting the flow of a work and allowing the performer to display virtuosity and achieve effects of brilliance. Cadenzas occur most often in concertos. They were generally improvised up to the end of the 18th c., but are now written out [Ital.]

ca·det (kədét) *n.* a student at a military or naval college ‖ a member of the army being trained to be an officer ‖ a younger son or a junior branch of a family ‖ a youth being given premilitary training [F. = a younger son]

cadge (kædʒ) *pres. part.* **cadg·ing** *past* and *past part.* **cadged** *v.t.* to obtain by subtle begging or sponging ‖ *v.i.* to scrounge, sponge [etym. doubtful]

ca·di, ka·di (kúdi:, kéidi:) *n.* a judge in a Moslem society whose judgments rest on Moslem religious law [Arab. *qādi*]

Cá·diz (kéidiz, kúdi:θ) a province (area 2,834 sq. miles, pop. 1,001,716) of Andalusia, Spain ‖ (*ancient* Gades) its capital (pop. 157,766), a fortified port of Phoenician origin, on a narrow peninsula forming the Bay of Cádiz, at the east end of the Gulf of Cádiz, a shallow, wide depression in the southwestern coast. Cádiz was long a center for trade with America

cad·mic (kǽdmik) *adj.* of or related to cadmium

cad·mi·um (kǽdmi:əm) *n.* a white, malleable, ductile, divalent, toxic, metallic element (symbol Cd, at. no. 48, at. mass 112.40). It is used in alloys and for electroplating. Certain of its compounds are used as pigments [Mod. L. fr. *cadmia,* calamine]

cadmium arsenide [CaAs] (*electr.*) semi-conductor used to produce colored light when applied with phosphor coatings to light-emitting divides

ca·dre (kǽdri:, kúdrə) *n.* the permanent nucleus of an organization (esp. *mil.*), to be expanded when the need arises [F. fr. Ital. fr. L.]

ca·du·ce·us (kədú:si:əs, kədjú:si:əs) *pl.* **ca·du·ce·i** (kədú:si:ai, kədjú:si:ai) *n.* (*mythol.*) the staff carried by Hermes or Mercury ‖ the symbol of the art of medicine [L. fr. Gk]

ca·du·ci·ty (kədú:siti:, kədjú:siti:) *n.* the tendency to decay and grow feeble ‖ (*biol.*) the dropping or early disappearance of parts or organs (e.g. the calyx of poppies, stipules) [fr. F. *caducité*]

ca·du·cous (kədú:kəs, kədjú:kəs) *adj.* (*biol.*, of parts or organs) falling off easily when they have fulfilled their function (cf. FUGACIOUS) [L. *caducus*]

caecal *CECAL

cae·cil·i·an (si:síli:ən) *n.* a tropical wormlike, limbless amphibian of fam. *Caeciliidae* with small, skin-covered eyes, which burrows into the earth [fr. L. *caecilia,* a kind of lizard]

caecum *CECUM

Caed·mon (kǽdmən) late 7th-c. Anglo-Saxon poet and monk of Whitby, who composed an inspirational 'Hymn' and devotional poems

Caen (kɑ̃) a town (pop. 119,500) in Normandy, France. It was rich in historic buildings and art treasures, but much was destroyed in the Allied liberation of Europe (1944). University (1432)

Caenozoic *CENOZOIC

Cae·re (síri:) (*Ital.* Cerveteri) an ancient city of Etruria about 20 miles northwest of Rome. The Roman civilization probably derives in part from Caere

Caer·nar·von·shire (karnárvənʃər) a county (area 569 sq. miles, pop. 121,000) of N. Wales. County town: Caernarvon

Caer·phil·ly (kɑrfíli:) *n.* mild white whole-milk cheese named for city in Wales

Cae·sar (sí:zər), Gaius Julius (101–44 B.C.), Roman statesman, general and historian. A supporter of the popular party, suspected of complicity in the Catiline conspiracy, he joined Pompey and Crassus in the 1st Triumvirate (60 B.C.). He conquered Gaul (58–51), defied the senate's order to lay down his military command, overran Italy (49), and defeated Pompey's army at Pharsalus, pursuing Pompey to Alexandria, and later defeating the Pompeian force in Africa at Thapsus (46). He extended Roman citizenship to Cisalpine Gaul. He became dictator in 48, and was made dictator for life in 44. Caesar's measures were liberal and moderate: but his excessive powers and almost regal honors led to the conspiracy of Brutus and Cassius, who assassinated him in the senate (44 B.C.). His commentaries on the Gallic Wars and on the civil war are models of succinct Latin

Cae·sar (sí:zər) *n.* the title (in honor of Julius Caesar) of Roman emperors up to Domitian's death (96) and, from 96, of the heir to the throne

Cae·sar (sí:zər) *n.* (*mil.*) code for underwater sonar warning system at edge of continental shelf

Caes·a·re·a (sesərí:ə, sezəri:ə) *KAYSERI

Caesarea Ma·za·ca (mǽzəkə) *KAYSERI

Cae·sar·e·an, Cae·sar·i·an (sizéəri:ən) *adj.* of Julius Caesar or of other Roman emperors styled Caesar [fr. L. *Caesarianus*]

Caesarean section, *CESAREAN SECTION

CONCISE PRONUNCIATION KEY: **(a)** æ, c*a*t; ɑ, c*a*r; ɔ f*aw*n; ei, sn*a*ke. **(e)** e, h*e*n; i:, sh*ee*p; iə, d*ee*r; ɛə, b*ea*r. **(i)** i, f*i*sh; ai, t*i*ger; ə:, b*i*rd. **(o)** o, *o*x; au, c*ow*; ou, g*oa*t; u, p*oo*r; ɔi, r*oy*al. **(u)** ʌ, d*u*ck; u, b*u*ll; u:, g*oo*se; ə, b*a*cillus; ju:, c*u*be. x, lo*ch*; θ, *th*ink; ð, bo*th*er; z, *Z*en; ʒ, cor*s*age; dʒ, sa*v*age; ŋ, ora*n*gutan*g*; j, *y*ak; ʃ, *f*ish; tʃ, fe*tch*; 'l, rabb*le*; 'n, redd*en.* Complete pronunciation key appears inside front cover.

Caesarea Phi·lip·pi (fílipai, fəlípai) a city founded (3rd–2nd cc. B.C.) by Philip, tetrarch of Galilee, near the source of the Jordan

Caesarian *CAESAREAN

cae·sar·ism (síːzərizəm) n. absolute dictatorship

Caesar salad tossed salad of romaine lettuce, anchovies, coddled egg, croutons with garlic, lemon juice, and grated cheese

caesium *CESIUM

cae·su·ra, ce·su·ra (siȝúərə, sizúərə, sizjúərə) n. a pause in a metrical line. It can serve to introduce a rhythmic pattern related to ordinary speech rhythm into the strict metrical flow, and so enrich it **cae·su·ral** adj. [L. caesura, a cutting]

ca·fé, ca·fe (kæféi) n. a place providing light meals or snacks, usually cheaper than a restaurant and not licensed to serve alcohol ‖ a place where coffee, other drinks and occasionally food are served ‖ a cheap restaurant [F.=coffee, coffeehouse]

café filtre (French, usu. italics) coffee prepared by filtering hot water through finely ground beans or a filter cup; originated in France. also filter coffee.

caf·e·te·ri·a (kæfitíəri:ə) n. a self-service restaurant [Span. cafeteria, coffeeshop]

caff (kæf) n. (Br.) coffee shop

caf·feine (kæfíːn, kæfiːn) n. an organic compound (alkaloid) of the purine group, occurring in esp. the coffee bean and tea leaf. It is the stimulant in tea, coffee and cocoa, and is used in medicine as a heart stimulant [fr. F. caféine]

caf·tan, kaf·tan (kæftən, kɑftán) n. a long sashed gown worn by men and women in the Middle East [Turk. and Pers.]

cage (keidȝ) 1. n. an airy container made with bars for keeping birds etc. in ‖ an open protective framework enclosing a platform, esp. used as a hoist or lift ‖ any skeleton framework ‖ sheer dress with no waistline ‖ dress worn over a slip, usually gathered at the neck ‖ (baseball) an enclosed space for practice 2. v.t. pres. part. **cag·ing** past and past part. **caged** to place or keep in a cage [F.]

cage·y, cag·y (kéidȝi:) comp. **cag·i·er** superl. **cag·i·est** adj. (pop.) secretive, reluctant to give oneself away ‖ wary **cá·gi·ly** adv. **cá·gi·ness** n. [etym. doubtful]

Ca·glia·ri (kæljúri:) (ancient Caralis) a port (pop. 240,300) of Phoenician origin in S. Sardinia. Industries: salt, shipbuilding. Cathedral (14th and 17th cc.), university (1626)

Ca·glios·tro (kæljóustrɔ, kaljóstrɔ), Count Alessandro (Giuseppe Balsamo, 1743–95), Italian adventurer notorious throughout Europe as necromancer and alchemist. He was condemned to death by the Inquisition (1791) for his association with freemasonry, but his sentence was commuted to life imprisonment

cagy *CAGEY

Ca·hi·ta (kɑhíːtɑ) pl. **Ca·hi·ta, Ca·hi·tas** n. a North American Indian people, in the 16th c. the most numerous of any language group in northern Mexico. They farmed their land, were effective warriors, and developed a religion combining Christianity with Indian belief. In the early 20th c. they were dispersed throughout Mexico and the U.S.A. ‖ a member of this people ‖ their language [Span.]

Ca·ho·ki·a Mounds (kəhóuki:ə) the largest prehistoric artificial earth mounds in America north of Mexico, in Illinois. The largest is in the form of a rectangular, flat-topped, terraced pyramid (100 ft high by 1,000 x 720 ft at the base). They are named after the Cahokia Indians

ca·hoots (kəhúːts) pl. n. (pop., only in the phrase) **in cahoots** in partnership, esp. one which involves shady dealings [prob. fr. F. cahute, cabin]

CAI (acronym) for computer-assisted instruction

Cai·a·phas (káiəfəs, kéiəfəs) Jewish high priest (c. A.D. 18–c. A.D. 36) who presided at the council which put Jesus to death (Matthew XXVI, 57–68)

Cai·cos Islands (káikous, kéikəs) *TURKS AND CAICOS ISLANDS

Cail·lié (kæjei), René (1799–1838), French explorer in Africa. He was the first European to reach Tombouctou (Timbuctoo) and survive (1828)

cai·man, cay·man (kéimən) n. an alligator of genus Caiman of tropical America [Span. caiman fr. Carib.]

Cain (kein) the first son of Adam and Eve. He killed his brother Abel (Genesis iv)

cain (kein) n. (only in the phrase) **to raise cain** to create an angry fuss [after Cain, in the Bible]

ca·ique (kɑíːk) n. a light rowing boat or skiff used on the Bosporus ‖ a Levantine sailing ship [F. fr. Turk. kaik]

cairn (kɛɔrn) n. a heap of stones placed as a landmark or memorial ‖ a terrier of a small, short-legged, shaggy breed [Scot. fr. Gael. carn, a heap of stones]

cairn·gorm (kɛɔrngɔrm) n. a semiprecious stone of yellow or brownish quartz [after the Cairngorm Mtns]

Cairngorm Mtns part of the Grampian Range on the borders of Banff, Inverness and Aberdeen, Scotland, intensely glaciated and popular for climbing and winter sports (Ben Macdhui, 4,296 ft)

Cai·ro (káirou) (Arab. Al-Qāhirah) the capital (pop. 5,074,016) of the Arab Republic of Egypt on the Nile, at a strategic point on the convergence of routes from the delta toward Upper Egypt, founded in 969. It is the country's administrative, commercial and cultural center, the site of Al-Azhar University (972, the focus of Moslem intellectual life) and two state universities (1925, 1950). It has 400 mosques. Industries: iron and steel, textiles, chemicals, engineering, food, tobacco and leather processing, gold, silver and ivory work. It was occupied by the Turks (1517–1798), the French (1798–1801) and the British (1882–1922)

cais·son (kéisən, kéisɒn) n. a watertight chamber used in constructional work under water ‖ a hollow vessel used as a gate of a dock or basin ‖ a pontoon, watertight box or cylinder used to lift submerged vessels ‖ a chest or wagon containing ammunition for artillery [F.]

caisson disease the bends, a serious and sometimes fatal condition, characterized by cramping pain and paralysis, induced by a too rapid return to normal atmospheric pressure after a period in a compressed atmosphere. It is caused by bubbles of gas forming in the blood on decompression

Caith·ness (kéiθnes, keiθnés) a former county of extreme N.E. Scotland

Caius (káiəs, kéiəs) *Gaius

Ca·ja·mar·ca (kɑhɑmárkɑ) a river, and the town (pop. 23,000) in N. Peru where Pizarro and Atahualpa met and where Atahualpa was imprisoned

Ca·je·tan (kǽjətæn) (Tommaso de Vio, 1469–1534), Italian cardinal. He failed to obtain Luther's recantation at Augsburg (1518)

ca·jole (kədȝóul) pres. part. **ca·jol·ing** past and past part. **ca·joled** v.t. to persuade or coax by flattery, try to win over by playing on the sympathies of **ca·jóle·ment, ca·jól·er·y** ns [F. cajoler, origin doubtful]

cake (keik) 1. n. a baked mixture of flour, leaven, eggs, fats, sugar and other sweet or fruity ingredients ‖ an edible, round, flattened mixture, fried or baked, fish cake ‖ a small quantity of a substance molded into a bar, a cake of soap **a piece of cake** (Br.) something very easily done, an easy victory **to have one's cake and eat it** to enjoy simultaneously two conflicting pleasures or advantages **to take the cake** to be so extreme or excessive as to astonish 2. v. pres. part. **cak·ing** past and past part. **caked** v.t. to cover (a surface) or fill (a space) with a hardened mass ‖ v.i. to become a hardened mass [prob. fr. O.N. kaka]

cake urchin an echinoderm of a discoid shape, a much flattened sea urchin

cake·walk (kéikwɔk) 1. n. (hist.) an Afro-American promenade: cakes were given to the couple performing the most intricate steps ‖ (hist.) a stage dance based on this ‖ a moving platform in a fun fair ‖ a raised horizontal plank for crawling along in a playground 2. v.i. to walk or dance in the manner of the cakewalk

cal. calorie

Cal·a·bar (kæləbár, kæləbɑr) the capital (pop. 103,000) of the South Eastern State, Nigeria, and commercial center (lumber, palm products, rubber)

calabar *CALABER

calabar bean the poisonous seed of Physostigma venenosum, fam. Papilionaceae, an African climbing plant, used medicinally

cal·a·bash (kæləbæʃ) n. a member of Crescentia, fam. Bignoniaceae, a genus of tropical American trees ‖ the hard shell of the fruit, used throughout the Tropics as a container for liquids, and for other domestic utensils and tobacco pipes ‖ any of various gourds, esp. La-

genaria sicraria, the bottle gourd [F. calebasse fr. Span. perh. fr. Pers.]

cal·a·ber, cal·a·bar (kæləbər) n. the fur of the gray Siberian squirrel [F. Calabre, Calabria]

cal·a·boose (kæləbuːs, kæləbúːs) n. (pop.) jail [Span. calabozo]

Ca·la·bri·a (kəléibri:ə) a region (area 5,824 sq. miles, pop. 2,048,900) forming the 'toe' of Italy. Chief town: Reggio di Calabria. It is almost entirely filled by part of the Apennines, and is an earthquake area. It was settled (8th c. B.C.) by the Greeks and conquered (268 B.C.) by the Romans, came under Byzantine rule (9th c. A.D.) and was conquered (11th c.) by the Normans. It was united to Italy (1860). Products: olives, fruit, nuts, lumber, salt, sulfur

Ca·lais (kælei) a port (pop. 78,000) in N.E. France, esp. for passenger traffic to and from Dover. Industries: fishing, lace and tulle manufacture, paper pulp and metal. Calais was held by the English 1347–1558

cal·a·man·der (kæləmændər) n. Diospyros quaesita, fam. Ebenaceae, a tree yielding ebony wood. It grows in India and Ceylon. The sapwood is white and soft, the heartwood hard and black [perh. fr. Coromandel, Bay of Bengal]

cal·a·mar·y (kæləmeri:, kæləməri:) pl. **cal·a·mar·ies** n. a squid, esp. the giant squid [fr. L. calamarius fr. calamus, a pen]

cal·a·mine (kæləmain, kæləmin) n. a pink powder consisting of zinc oxide and some ferric oxide used in lotions, ointments etc. ‖ a former name for basic zinc silicate ‖ (Br.) a former name for zinc carbonate (*HEMIMORPHITE, *SMITHSONITE) [F. fr. L.L. calamina, prob. corrup. of cadmia]

ca·lam·i·tous (kəlæmitəs) adj. causing great pain and distress, disastrous

ca·lam·i·ty (kəlæmiti:) pl. **ca·lam·i·ties** n. a disastrous event causing great misery ‖ a state of great distress or adversity [F. calamité]

Calamity Jane (kəlæmiti:dȝein) (1852–1903), U.S. frontierswoman. Born Martha Jane Canary, she became Wild Bill Hickok's companion. She dressed in men's clothing, frequented bars, and toured in Wild West shows

cal·a·mus (kæləməs) n. a member of Calamus, fam. Palmae, a genus of tropical leaf climbers, up to 600 ft. long, whose stripped stems form rattan canes used for chairs, baskets etc. ‖ Acorus calamus, fam. Araceae, a marsh plant yielding a perfume oil like patchouli from distillation of its rhizomes ‖ (zool.) the horny part or quill of a feather [L.=reed]

Ca·las (kæləs), Jean (1698–1762), French Calvinist falsely accused of murdering his son to prevent him from abjuring Protestantism. He was tortured and executed in 1762. He was declared innocent in 1765 after an intensive campaign by Voltaire

cal·car·e·ous, cal·car·i·ous (kælkéari:əs) adj. (esp. of soils) consisting of or containing calcium carbonate or limestone ‖ of the nature of chalk and limestone [fr. L. calcarius, of limestone]

cal·ce·o·lar·i·a (kælsi:əléəri:ə) n. a member of Calceolaria, fam. Scrophulariaceae, a genus of cultivated herbaceous plants from America and New Zealand [fr. L. calceolus, slipper]

cal·ce·o·late (kælsi:əleit) adj. (bot.) shaped like a slipper [fr. L. calceolus, slipper]

calces pl. of CALX

Cal·chas (kælkəs) (Gk mythol.) a priest who accompanied Agamemnon to the siege of Troy. He ordered Iphigenia's sacrifice and advised the building of the Trojan horse (*TROJAN WAR)

cal·cic (kælsik) adj. of or containing calcium or lime [fr. L. calx (calcis), lime]

cal·cif·er·ol (kælsífəroul, kælsífərɔl, kælsífərɒl) n. vitamin D₂ [CALCIFEROUS+ ERGOSTEROL]

cal·cif·er·ous (kælsífərəs) adj. producing or containing calcium, calcium carbonate or other calcium compounds [fr. L. calx (calcis), lime+ -fer, bearing]

cal·ci·fi·ca·tion (kælsifikéiʃən) n. conversion to calcium carbonate ‖ the deposition of insoluble calcium salts in a tissue ‖ a calcified formation or structure ‖ a process in which surface soil is supplied with calcium

cal·ci·fy (kælsifai) pres. part. **cal·ci·fy·ing** past and past part. **cal·ci·fied** v.t. to change into calcium carbonate or into a calciferous state by the reaction of calcium salts ‖ v.i. to be changed in this way ‖ to harden and become calcareous [fr. L. calx (calcis), lime]

cal·ci·mine (kælsəmain, kælsəmin) 1. n. a white or colored wash for walls and ceilings 2. v.t. pres. part. **cal·ci·min·ing** past and past part.

cal·ci·mined to wash or cover with calcimine [fr. L. *calx* (*calcis*), lime]

cal·ci·na·tion (kælsinéiʃən) *n.* the action or process of calcining

cal·cine (kælsain) *v.t. pres. part.* **cal·cin·ing** *past* and *past part.* **cal·cined** to effect a physical or chemical change in (usually inorganic materials), by heating to high temperature without fusing. Calcining is used to drive off volatile constituents or products, to convert to powder form, or to oxidize (esp. metals) ‖ *v.i.* to undergo calcination [fr. M.L. *calcinare*, an alchemist's term]

cal·ci·phy·lax·is (kælsifiláksis) *n. pl* **-es 1.** *med* inflammation and sclerosis caused by excess of calcium or vitamin D. **2.** an experimentally induced calcification. —**calciphylactic** *adj.* — **calciphylactically** *adv.*

cal·cite (kælsait) *n.* a mineral consisting of hexagonal crystals of calcium carbonate and including chalk, limestone, marble, Iceland spar, stalactites, stalagmites etc. (*ARAGONITE) [fr. L. *calx* (*calcis*), lime]

cal·ci·to·nin (kælsətóunən) *n.* (*biochem.*) one of two polypeptide hormones from the thyroid that regulate calcium content in blood. *syn* chryrocacitonin, thyrocalcitonin.

cal·ci·trol (kælsitról) *biochem* a natural hormone that increases vitamin D activity, used in management of calcium deficiency; marketed as Rocaltrol

cal·ci·um (kælsi:əm) *n.* a white divalent element of the alkaline earth group (symbol Ca, at. no. 20, at. mass 40.08), found chiefly as a carbonate (chalk, limestone, marble, coral). It is used chiefly in alloys [fr. L. *calx* (*calcis*), lime]

calcium bicarbonate a soluble salt formed when carbon dioxide from the air forms a solution of carbonic acid with water and this solution comes into contact with calcium carbonate in one of its forms. It is useful to vertebrates as a bone-builder. It is responsible for the temporary hardness of water

calcium carbide a colorless compound, CaC_2, commonly dark gray or brown in color due to impurities, usually formed by heating together lime and carbon in an electric furnace. It reacts with water to give acetylene

calcium carbonate an insoluble salt, $CaCO_3$. Its common natural form is calcite. It is used to make quicklime and cement

calcium chloride a white deliquescent salt, $CaCl_2$, with many industrial and scientific applications

calcium cy·an·a·mide (saiǽnəmaid, saiǽnəmid) a compound, $CaCN_2$, used as a fertilizer and produced artificially by heating calcium carbide in the presence of nitrogen. It releases ammonia slowly in the presence of water

calcium hydroxide the alkali $Ca(OH)_2$, a white solid (slaked lime)

calcium oxide a white solid, CaO, the chief constituent of lime

calcium phosphate any of several phosphates of calcium used in medicine and industry and as a fertilizer

calcium silicate a silicate which, when mixed with those of the alkali metals, and fused, forms ordinary glass

calcium sulfate a white salt, $CaSO_4$, occurring naturally as anhydrite, and in hydrated form as gypsum

calc·spar (kælkspar) *n.* calcite

cal·cu·la·ble (kælkjuləb'l) *adj.* able to be ascertained or measured by mathematical or logical reasoning [fr. L. *calculare*, to calculate]

cal·cu·late (kælkjuleit) *pres. part.* **cal·cu·lat·ing** *past* and *past part.* **cal·cu·lat·ed** *v.t.* to find out or ascertain by means of mathematics, *to calculate the size of the moon* ‖ to figure out in one's head ‖ (usually *pass.*) to intend, plan, arrange for a particular purpose, *a promise calculated to win votes, calculated rudeness* ‖ *v.i.* to make a calculation ‖ (with 'on') to rely, *he calculated on darkness making escape easy* **cal·cu·lat·ing** *adj.* working out mathematical processes ‖ planning and scheming for one's own ends [fr. L. *calculare*]

calculating machine a machine which performs arithmetical operations rapidly (*COMPUTER)

cal·cu·la·tion (kælkjuléiʃən) *n.* the act, process or result of using mathematical processes ‖ careful thinking ‖ self-seeking deliberation [F.]

cal·cu·la·tor (kælkjuleitər) *n.* someone who calculates ‖ a set of tables used in mathematics ‖ a calculating machine

cal·cu·lous (kælkjuləs) *adj.* (*med.*) pertaining to, or suffering from, a deposit of small stones or gravel in the kidneys etc. [fr. L. *calculosus*, stony]

cal·cu·lus (kælkjuləs) *pl.* **cal·cu·li** (kælkjulai), **cal·cu·lus·es** *n.* a hard concretion formed in parts of the body such as the gall bladder or kidneys ‖ (*math.*) any branch of mathematics that employs symbolic computations, esp. integral calculus and differential calculus [L. dim. of *calx*, stone]

Cal·cut·ta (kælkʌtə) a town and port (pop. 3,291,655, with agglom. 9,165,650) in N.E. India, the capital of W. Bengal, on the Hooghly River 80 miles from the Bay of Bengal. It controls about a third of India's export and import trade. University (1867). Industries: shipping, textiles, sugar refining, iron smelting. The town was founded (1690) by the British East India Company and was the capital of India (1833–1912)

Calcutta, Black Hole of an incident (1756) during the Anglo-French struggle for India, when the nawab of Bengal attacked Calcutta and imprisoned 146 British residents in a dungeon, causing 123 deaths by suffocation

Cal·das (káldas), Francisco José de (c. 1770–1816), Colombian botanist, cartographer of the vice-royalty of Peru, and patriot. He was executed by the Spaniards

Cal·der (kóldər), Alexander (1898–1976), American sculptor, specializing in abstract designs in metal, wire etc. named by him 'mobiles' (articulated forms moving in currents of warm air or in a breeze) and 'stabiles' (static abstract sculptures)

Cal·de·ra (kaldéra), Rafael (1916–), Venezuelan politician, founder and leader of the Christian Democratic Party (COPEI), and the first opposition leader in Venezuela to serve as a democratically elected president (1969–74)

Cal·de·rón de la Bar·ca (kaldəróndelabárka), Pedro (1600–81), Spanish dramatist. In addition to about 120 plays ('La Vida es Sueño' being the most famous) Calderón wrote many 'autos sacramentales', plays comparable with the English and French mystery plays

cal·dron, caul·dron (kóldrən) *n.* a large deep cooking pot of iron used over an open fire [O.N.F. *caudron*]

Cald·well (kóldwel, kóldwəl), Erskine Preston (1903–), American Southern novelist. 'Tobacco Road' (1932) is his best-known work

Caldwell, Sarah (1924–), U.S. conductor. She founded (1957) the Boston Opera Group (now Opera Company of Boston) and also conducted the New York City Opera (1973), the Metropolitan Opera (1975–6)), and a television production of 'The Barber of Seville'

Cal·e·do·ni·a (kælidóuni:ə) the Roman name for northern Britain ‖ (*rhet.*) Scotland

Cal·e·do·ni·an (kælidóuni:ən) **1.** *adj.* pertaining to Scotland ‖ of a European mountain-making episode during the Paleozoic era **2.** *n.* a native of Scotland, Scotsman

Caledonian Canal a waterway (60 miles long) in N. Scotland linking the Atlantic with the North Sea, built (1804–47) by connecting a natural series of lakes, incl. Loch Ness. The locks are too small for modern heavy shipping

cal·e·fa·cient (kæliféiʃənt) **1.** *adj.* producing warmth **2.** *n.* a substance used in medicine to increase bodily heat [fr. L. *calefaciens* (*calefacientis*) fr. *calere*, to be warm and *facere*, to make]

cal·e·fac·tion (kælifékʃən) *n.* a warming or being warmed ‖ thermal pollution through release of waste heat into the environment *THERMAL POLLUTION [fr. L. *calefactio* (*calefactionis*)]

cal·e·fac·to·ry (kæliféktəri:) **1.** *adj.* producing warmth **2.** *pl.* **cal·e·fac·to·ries** *n.* a room in a monastery in which monks warm themselves [fr. L. *calefactorius*]

cal·en·dar (kæləndər) **1.** *n.* a table of the days, weeks and months of the year noting public holidays etc. ‖ a system of fixing the length and divisions of a year for the purposes of a community, *a school calendar* ‖ a register or schedule of persons, events etc., usually arranged in chronological order, *a calendar of cases for trial* **2.** *v.t.* to enter or write in a register ‖ to arrange and index (documents) [A.F. *calender*]

—The natural units of our calendar are the day (one rotation of the earth on its axis) and the year (one revolution of the earth around the sun), whereas the month and week are conventional subdivisions of the solar year. In ancient times, however, the month was equated with a natural division of time, i.e. the lunar cycle (the revolution of the moon around the earth). As 12 lunations comprise only 354 of the solar year's 365 days, peoples using lunar calendars were forced to intercalate a 13th month from time to time to keep a fixed relationship between months and seasons, or else accept that each month goes the round of the seasons within a certain period. Julius Caesar introduced the solar, Julian calendar in 45 B.C. It contained an error of intercalation amounting to eight days in a thousand years and was therefore revised in the 16th c. by Pope Gregorius XIII. The shift that had occurred between months and seasons since Caesar's day was put right by the abolition of ten days and by a revision of the Julian method of calculating leap years. Protestant Europe did not immediately adopt the Gregorian calendar: in England it was not introduced until 1752. In Russia the transition was not accomplished until after the Bolshevik Revolution

cal·en·der (kæləndər) **1.** *v.t.* to press (cloth, paper etc.) so as to produce a smooth, glossy or other special finish, or to adjust thickness **2.** *n.* a machine containing rollers to carry out this process [F. *calandre* fr. L. fr. Gk]

cal·ends, kal·ends (kæləndz) *pl. n.* the first day of the month in the Roman calendar [fr. L. *kalendae*]

ca·len·du·la (kəléndʒələ) *n.* a member of *Calendula*, fam. *Compositae*, a genus of herbaceous plants including *C. officinalis*, the marigold [fr. Mod. L. *calendae*, the first day of the month in the Roman calendar]

cal·en·ture (kæləntʃər, kæləntʃuər) *n.* a tropical fever with delirium, caused by exposure to excessive heat [F. fr. Span. *calentura*, fever]

calf (kæf, kaf) *pl.* **calves** (kævz, kavz) *n.* the fleshy part of the back of the leg below the knee [perh. fr. O.N. *kálfi*]

calf *pl.* **calves** *n.* the young of a cow, elephant, whale etc. ‖ leather made from the skin of a young cow, esp. light-brown leather used in bookbinding ‖ (*naut.*) a floating piece of ice separated from a larger mass **in calf** (of a cow) pregnant [O.E. *cealf*]

calf love a strong, usually short-lived emotional attachment of an adolescent for one of the opposite sex

calf-skin (kæfskin) *n.* leather from the skin of a calf

Cal·ga·ry (kælgəri:) a city (pop. 592,743) of Alberta, Canada, center of a wheat-growing and stock-raising prairie region and a railroad junction. Industries: metallurgy, petroleum refining

Cal·houn (kælhú:n), John Caldwell (1782–1850), U.S. vice-president (1825–32) and political philosopher. In such works as 'A Disquisition on Government' and 'A Discourse on the Constitution and Government of the United States' he strove to protect minority rights, especially Southern economic interests, against unrestricted majority rule embodied in a centralized government

Ca·li (kúli:) a city (pop. 923,400) of S.W. Colombia, commercial and industrial center of the rich Cauca valley: sugar, tobacco and coffee. Coal mines

cal·i·ber, cal·i·bre (kælibər) *n.* the diameter of the bore of a gun or rifle or of a bullet or a shell ‖ (Br.) also kælí:bə) the quality of a person's mind or character [F. *calibre*]

cal·i·brate (kælibreit) *pres. part.* **cal·i·brat·ing** *past* and *past part.* **cal·i·brat·ed** *v.t.* to indicate a scale on (a measuring instrument) ‖ to measure the internal diameter of (a tube) ‖ to test the accuracy of (a measuring instrument) by comparison with an independent standard ‖ to find out by firing what range and elevation corrections must be applied to (a field gun) to make it conform to a standard **cal·i·bra·tion** *n.*

calibre *CALIBER

ca·li·che (kalí:tʃi:) *n.* a crude form of sodium nitrate, $NaNO_3$, found naturally in Chile ‖ a natural form of calcium carbonate, $CaCO_3$, found encrusting dry, stony soil [Span.]

cal·i·co (kælikou) *pl.* **cal·i·coes, cal·i·cos** *n.* inexpensive printed cotton cloth ‖ (Br.) plain white cotton cloth [after *Calicut*, a town in India from which cloth was originally imported]

Cal·i·cut (kælikət) *KOZHIKODE

Calif. California

calif *CALIPH

califate *CALIPH

Cal·i·for·nia (kælifôrnjə) (*abbr.* Calif.) a state (area 158,693 sq. miles, pop. 24,724,000) on the Pacific coast of the U.S.A. Capital: Sacramento. Chief cities: Los Angeles, San Francisco. It is formed by a great valley bounded on the east by the Sierra Nevada Mountains and Cascade Range and on the west by the Coast Ranges, giving way in the south to desert. There is a narrow, fertile coastal plain. Agriculture: cotton, poultry, dairy produce, beef cattle, sheep, fruit (esp. citrus), vegetables, cereals, vines, sugar beet. Much is under irrigation. Fishing (first state producer). Resources: hydroelectric power, lumber, oil and natural gas, mercury (60% national supply), gold, salt, tungsten. Industries: shipyards, aircraft and missile engineering, electronics, food processing, metal products, chemicals, films. Universities: University of California (1868) mainly at Berkeley and Los Angeles, California Institute of Technology (1891) at Pasadena, and Stanford (1891) at Palo Alto. California was explored (16th–18th cc.) by the Spanish and was first colonized in 1769. It was under Mexican rule (1822–48). After a revolt, it was ceded (1848) to the U.S.A., of which it became (1850) the 31st state. The gold rush (1849) brought many immigrants

California, Gulf of an arm of the Pacific (about 750 miles long) separating the peninsula of Lower California from the Mexican mainland

California, Lower *LOWER CALIFORNIA

California poppy the eschscholtzia

California, University of an institution of higher education founded in 1868, with campuses at Berkeley, Davis, Irvine, Los Angeles, Riverside, San Diego at La Jolla, San Francisco, Santa Barbara, and Santa Cruz

cal·i·for·ni·um (kælifôrni:əm) *n.* an element (symbol Cf, at. no. 98, isotope of longest known half-life 249) obtained by bombarding curium 242 with alpha particles [after *California*]

Ca·lig·u·la (kəlígjulə) (Gaius Caesar Germanicus, 12–41), Roman emperor (37–41), son of Germanicus. His cruelty and tyranny are said to have resulted from madness. After plotting against the senate, he was assassinated (41)

cal·i·pash (kǽlipæʃ) *n.* the greenish, edible, gelatinous part of a turtle under its upper shell, considered a delicacy [origin unknown]

cal·i·pee (kǽlipi:) *n.* the yellowish, edible, gelatinous part of a turtle above its lower shell, considered a delicacy [origin unknown]

cal·i·per, cal·li·per (kǽlipər) *n.* (often *pl.* construed as *sing.*) an instrument for measuring a distance where a straight rule cannot be used. It consists of two hinged legs, with the terminal points turned inwards or outwards. Contact is made with these points, the hinge is fixed, and the instrument can then be transferred to a straight scale [perh. same as CALIBER]

ca·liph, ca·lif (kéilif, kǽlif) *n.* a successor to Mohammed as head of Islam, originally having full political as well as religious power **cal·i·phate, cal·i·fate** (kǽlifeit) *n.* (*hist.*) the office of caliph, established (632) on the death of Mohammed, and abolished (1924) by Turkish revolutionaries. Among several rival caliphates, the major ones were the Medinese (632–61), the Umayyad (661–750), the Abbasid (750–1258), the Fatimid (909–1171), the Abbasid in Egypt (1259–1517, under the patronage of the Mamelukes) and the Ottoman (1517–1924) (*ISLAM) [F. *caliphe* fr. Arab. *khalīfa*]

cal·i·sa·ya bark (kæliséiə) the yellow bark of *Cinchona calisaya*, from which quinine is extracted [Span. prob. fr. Peruvian native name]

cal·is·then·ic, *Br.* esp. **cal·lis·then·ic** (kælisθénik) *adj.* producing health and beauty in the body **cal·is·thén·ics**, *Br.* **cal·lis·thén·ics** *n.* the exercise of the body and limbs to promote strength and beauty, e.g. in certain gymnastics [fr. *Gk* kalli-, beauty + *sthenos*, strength]

Ca·lix·tus II (kəlíkstəs) (*d.* 1124), pope (1119–24). He reached agreement with Emperor Henry V in the Concordat of Worms (1122) after the Investiture Controversy

calk (kɔk) 1. *n.* a piece of iron with a sharp point fitted to a horseshoe or a boot to prevent slipping 2. *v.t.* to provide with calks [perh. fr. L. *calx* (*calcis*), heel]

calk *CAULK

cal·kin (kɔ́kin, kǽlkin) *n.* the ridged edge on the heel and front of a horseshoe ‖ an iron guard on boots to prevent slipping [older *kakun* fr. L. *calx* (*caicis*), heel]

call (kɔl) 1. *v.t.* to say loudly in order to get attention ‖ to summon ‖ to speak to by telephone or send a message to by radio etc. ‖ (usually *pass.*) to summon or invite to carry out some special mission in life, *called to the priesthood* ‖ to wake and tell to get up ‖ to convoke, *to call a meeting* ‖ to bring under consideration or discussion, *call the next case* ‖ to name descriptively ‖ to give a personal name to ‖ to consider, regard as, *I call that dishonest* ‖ to estimate roughly, *I call that a good 20 miles* ‖ to attract (animals, birds) by an imitative cry or signal ‖ (*finance*) to demand payment of, or give notice of payment on (a loan or a bond) ‖ (*bridge*) to bid ‖ (*poker*) to demand to see the cards held by (an opponent) ‖ (*baseball*) to indicate (a pitched ball) as a strike ‖ (*baseball*) to end (a game) because of bad weather ‖ *v.i.* to shout or exclaim in order to gain attention ‖ to telephone ‖ (of a bird) to make its characteristic sound ‖ to pay a visit ‖ to stop (at a port) **to be called to the bar** to qualify as a lawyer ‖ (*Br.*) to be allowed to practice as a barrister **to call away** to summon to another place **to call back** to summon back, recall ‖ to retract **to call down** to invoke ‖ to reprimand **to call for** to request, *to call for help* ‖ to require, *skating calls for good balance* **to call forth** to draw out, *the job called forth unsuspected talents* **to call in** to withdraw from circulation, *to call in an old coinage* ‖ to summon for assistance ‖ to demand payment of, *to call in debts* ‖ to invite **to call into question** to challenge the truth of **to call (someone) names** to use insulting epithets to or about (someone) **to call off** to order to desist ‖ to postpone or cancel **to call on** to pay a visit to (someone) **to call out** to summon for emergency service ‖ to shout **to call to account** to demand an explanation from **to call to order** to request (someone) to be quiet or orderly **to call the roll** to check a list of names so as to find absentees **to call up** to telephone or contact by radio etc. ‖ to summon for military service **to call upon** (or **on**) to appeal to 2. *n.* a cry or shout to attract attention ‖ a message, esp. by telephone ‖ a short visit ‖ a doctor's consultation at the patient's home ‖ the notes of a bird ‖ an instrument imitating the cry of an animal, used as a lure ‖ a vocation, *a call to the priesthood* ‖ an inner urging ‖ a summons or invitation, *the call of the sea* ‖ an invitation to become a minister of a church or a professor in a university ‖ a claim on time, money etc. ‖ (*finance*) a demand for payment of money ‖ (*poker*) a demand for a show of hands ‖ an instalment of the nominal share capital which a shareholder is asked to pay ‖ grounds, necessity, *there's no call for you to be upset* **on call** (of a doctor, ambulance etc.) available for duty [O.E. *ceallian* fr. O.N.]

cal·la (kǽlə) *n.* a member of *Calla*, fam. *Araceae*, a bog plant with a white spathe surrounding a yellow spike ‖ a calla lily [etym. doubtful]

call·a·ble (kɔ́ləb'l) *adj.* capable of being called, esp. (*finance*) subject to payment on demand or subject to redemption upon notice

Callaghan, (kǽləhæn) James (1912–), British politician, Labour party leader, and prime minister (1976–9). Elected to the House of Commons (1945), he served in cabinet positions under Harold Wilson (1964–9, 1974–6). Against Britain joining the EEC (European Economic Community), he was plagued by economic woes as prime minister. He was followed by the Conservative party's Margaret Thatcher

calla lily *Zantedeschia aethiopica*, a plant native to Africa, with a large white spathe surrounding a yellow spike, much grown as a house plant and in greenhouses

Ca·lla·o (kɑjáo) the chief port (pop. 296,920) of Peru, on the Pacific: minerals, sugar, hides and wool

call-back (kɔ́lbæk) *n.* recall by a manufacturer of a defective product, usu. for correction of the defect, sometimes for rebate

call-board (kɔ́lbɔrd, kɔ́lbourd) *n.* a theater notice board giving rehearsal times

call box a street phone for calling the police or fire department ‖ (*Br.*) a public telephone booth

call-boy (kɔ́lbɔi) *n.* a person who summons actors to the stage

callenia *STROMATOLITE

call·er (kɔ́lər) *n.* a person paying a visit ‖ a person making a telephone call

Ca·lles (kájes), Plutarco Elías (1877–1945), Mexican politician and president (1924–8), and defender of constitutionalism in Mexico's revolutionary movement. As president he initiated enlarged reform programs in agriculture, irrigation and road construction. His application of the anticlerical religious and educational provisions of the constitution precipitated (1926) the Catholic cristeros rebellion. Following the assassination (1928) of president-elect Obregón, he remained the power behind interim president Emilio Portes Gil until he was forced into exile (1936) by President Lázaro Cárdenas

call forwarding system for relaying incoming telephone calls to another number for any period of time

call girl a prostitute with whom engagements can be made by phone

Ca·llia·ri (kúljari:) an ancient town (pop. 169,000) on the south coast of Sardinia, with a good harbor, shipbuilding and salt industries. Cathedral. University (1626)

Cal·lic·ra·tes (kəlíkrəti:z) (5th c. B.C.), Athenian architect responsible, with Ictinus, for the Parthenon

cal·li·gram or **cal·li·gramme** (kǽligræm) *n.* poem whose lines are set in type to form a picture appropriate to its subject. *Cf* CONCRETE POEM

cal·lig·ra·pher (kəlígrəfər) *n.* someone who practices calligraphy

cal·li·graph·ic (kæligrǽfik) *adj.* of or relating to calligraphy

calligraphic display (*computer*) computer output arranged to form a picture on a cathode tube. *Cf* RASTER DISPLAY

cal·lig·ra·phist (kəlígrəfist) *n.* a calligrapher

cal·lig·ra·phy (kəlígrəfi) *n.* the art of beautiful handwriting ‖ handwriting in general [fr. Gk *kalligraphia*]

Cal·lim·a·chus (kəlíməkəs) (c. 310–c. 235 B.C.), Alexandrian poet, author of hymns and epigrams

call-in (kɔ́lin) *n.* radio or television program that invites listeners to call a station so that questions or conversations may be broadcast. *syn* phone-in

call·ing (kɔ́liŋ) *n.* a profession or occupation ‖ a spiritual summons, a deep impulse to carry out some mission

calling card (*Am.*=*Br.* visiting card) a small card of introduction bearing the name, and usually the address, of the visitor

Cal·li·o·pe (kəláiəpi:) the Muse of epic poetry

cal·li·o·pe (kəláiəpi:) *n.* a musical instrument consisting of a set of steam whistles played from a keyboard [after the Muse CALLIOPE]

calliper *CALIPER

callisthenic *CALISTHENIC

Cal·lis·to (kəlístou) (*Gk mythol.*) a nymph loved by Zeus. Changed into a bear, she became the constellation Ursa Major

Cal·lis·tus (kəlístəs) *CALIXTUS II

call loan (*stockbroking*) a loan payable on demand of either party

call market (*finance*) a market on which call money is raised

call money (*finance*) money borrowed subject to repayment at a moment's notice

call number (*Am.*=*Br.* pressmark) a symbol with which a librarian marks a book to show location and classification

cal·los·i·ty (kəlósiti:) *pl.* **cal·los·i·ties** *n.* a hardening or thickening of the skin, usually caused by continual pressure or rubbing [F. *callosité*]

Cal·lot (kǽlou), Jacques (1592–1635), French engraver. Among his best-known works are 'Miseries of War' and 'Temptations of St Anthony'

cal·lous (kǽləs) 1. *adj.* indifferent to the pain or distress of others ‖ (of the skin) hardened 2. *n.* a callus [fr. L. *callosus*, hardened]

call-o·ver (kɔ́louvər) *n.* (*Br., betting*) the reading of the latest odds

cal·low (kǽlou) *adj.* lacking experience of life, immature ‖ (of young birds) featherless, unfledged [O.E. *calu*, bald, without feathers]

call rate the rate of interest on call money

call the shots *v.* (*colloq.*) to make the decisions

cal·lus, cal·lous (kǽləs) *pl.* **cal·lus·es, cal·lous·es** *n.* a thickened area of skin or plant tissue ‖ a bony substance formed around a fractured bone [L.]

calm (kɑm) 1. *adj.* (of the sea) still, without rough motion ‖ (of a person) unruffled, unexcited, unperturbed, esp. when it would be natural not to be so ‖ (of a person) placid ‖ (*pop.*) impudent, brazen 2. *n.* a period of serenity ‖ a windless period ‖ a motionless, undisturbed state ‖ an ominous and uneasy peace, *the calm* *before the storm* **3.** *v.t.* to soothe, pacify ‖ *v.i.* to become calm **to calm down** to regain emotional self-control after anger etc. [F. *calme* fr. Ital. fr. L. fr. Gk]

cal·ma·tive (kǽlmətiv, kúmətiv) **1.** *n.* a sedative **2.** *adj.* having a quietening effect

cal·o·mel (kǽləmel) *n.* mercurous chloride [F. fr. Gk.]

Ca·lonne (kælɔn), Charles-Alexandre de (1734–1802), French statesman. As controller-general of finances (1783–7), he failed to break the fiscal privileges of the nobility and upper clergy in prerevolutionary France

cal·o·res·cence (kælərésəns) *n.* the absorption of visible light and its conversion into infrared radiation. Thus, the glass of a greenhouse admits the wavelengths of visible light, but is opaque to the longer, infrared wavelengths subsequently emitted by objects inside the greenhouse (cf. INCANDESCENCE) [fr. L. *calor*, heat]

ca·lor·ic (kəlórik, kəlórik) *adj.* of or pertaining to heat ‖ of or pertaining to calories [F. *calorique*]

cal·o·rie, cal·o·ry (kǽləri:) *n.* (*phys.*, *abbr.* cal.) a unit of heat energy in the cgs system, defined as the quantity of heat required at 1 atmosphere to raise the temperature of 1 gram of water through 1°C, usually from 14.5°C to 15.5°C (*MEAN CALORIE) ‖ (*physiol.*) a unit of heat energy derived by the body from food, equal to 1 kilogram calorie [F. fr. L. *calor*, heat]

cal·o·rif·ic (kælərífik) *adj.* producing or relating to heat [F. *calorifique*]

calorific value the heat produced by the complete combustion of a unit weight of a fuel

cal·o·rim·e·ter (kælərímətər) *n.* an instrument used to measure quantities of heat or determine specific heats **cal·o·ri·met·ric** (kælərimétrik), **cal·o·ri·mét·ri·cal** *adjs.* **cal·o·rim·e·try** (kælərímətri:) *n.* [fr. L. *calor* (*caloris*), heat+METER]

calory *CALORIE

ca·lotte (kəlɔt) *n.* a skullcap, esp. as worn by priests [F.]

cal·o·yer (kǽləjər, kəlóiər) *n.* a monk of the Greek Orthodox Church [F. fr. Ital. fr. Gk *kalos*, good+*geros*, old man]

CALR (*computer acronym*) for computer-assisted legal-research service provided to attorneys for retrieval of decided cases appropriate to a legal problem

Cal·ta·nis·set·ta (kæltənisétə) a town (pop. 60,072) in central Sicily, center of the Sicilian sulfur industry. Baroque cathedral

cal·trap (kǽltrəp) *n.* a military caltrop esp. as represented in heraldry

cal·trop (kǽltrəp) *n.* (*hist.*) an instrument with four iron spikes used on the ground to hinder the approach of cavalry ‖ a member of *Tribulus*, a genus of spiky herbaceous plants [M.E. *calketrappe* fr. O.E. *coltetræppe*, *calcatrippe*, a trap for the feet, prob. fr. L.]

cal·u·met (kǽljumet) *n.* a long-stemmed tobacco pipe used ceremonially by North American Indians, a peace pipe [F.]

ca·lum·ni·ate (kəlʌ́mni:eit) *pres. part.* **ca·lum·ni·at·ing** *past and past part.* **ca·lum·ni·at·ed** *v.t.* to slander ‖ to accuse falsely and maliciously by making untrue statements **ca·lum·ni·á·tion** *n.* the act of slandering ‖ a slander **ca·lúm·ni·a·tor** *n.* someone who slanders **ca·lúm·ni·a·to·ry** *adj.* marked by, or given to, calumny ‖ slanderous **ca·lúm·ni·ous** *adj.* [fr. L. *calumniari* (*calumniatus*)]

cal·um·ny (kǽləmni) *pl.* **cal·um·nies** *n.* a slanderous accusation, made with the intention of harming another [fr. L. *calumnia*]

Cal·va·dos (kǽlvædɔs) a department (area 2,197 sq. miles, pop. 561,000) of N.W. France, west of the Seine estuary. Chief town: Caen (*NORMANDY)

Cal·va·ry (kǽlvəri:) the place near Jerusalem where Jesus was crucified **cal·va·ry** *pl.* **cal·va·ries** *n.* a representation, esp. a carving, of the Crucifixion ‖ intense suffering [fr. L. *Calvaria*, skull, trans. of Aram. *Golgotha*, the place of a skull (Mark xv, 22)]

calve (kæv, kɑv) *pres. part.* **calv·ing** *past and past part.* **calved** *v.i.* to give birth to a calf ‖ (of an iceberg or glacier) to split so that a piece of ice is thrown off ‖ *v.t.* to give birth to (a calf) [O.E. *cealfian*]

Cal·vert (kǽlvərt), George, lst Baron Baltimore (c. 1580–1632), English statesman. His attempt to found (1629) a new American settlement was the origin of the colony of Maryland

calves *pl.* of CALF

Cal·vin (kǽlvin), John (Jean Cauvin, 1509–64), French theologian who spread the Protestant Reformation in France (*HUGUENOT) and Switzerland, where he established a strict Presbyterian government in Geneva. Calvin taught that it was the right and duty of the State to aid the Church, that biblical authority was to be set above Church tradition, that the sacraments were of value but not essential, and he taught predestination. His teachings, contained in his 'Institutes of the Christian Religion' (1536), spread to the Netherlands and Scotland (*KNOX), and influenced the Puritans in England and in New England

Cal·vin·ism (kǽlvinjzəm) *n.* the doctrine of John Calvin (*REFORMED CHURCH)

Cal·vin·ist (kǽlvinist) **1.** *n.* someone who adheres to Calvinism **2.** *adj.* of or relating to Calvinism or Calvinists **Cal·vin·is·tic** *adj.*

calx (kælks) *pl.* **cal·ces** (kǽlsi:z) *n.* the powder or brittle substance remaining after a metal or mineral has been calcined [L.=lime, small stone]

calyces *alt. pl.* of CALYX

ca·lyc·u·lus (kəlíkjuləs) *pl.* **ca·lyc·u·li** (kəlíkjulai) *n.* (*biol.*) a small, cuplike structure, e.g. a taste bud [L., dim. of *calyx*, husk fr. Gk]

Ca·lyp·so (kəlípsou) (*mythol.*) a nymph who received the shipwrecked Odysseus and entertained him for seven years

ca·lyp·so (kəlípsou) **1.** *n.* a W. Indian lilting song, usually improvised and topical like a ballad with a refrain **2.** *adj.* of this style [perh. after *Calypso* the nymph]

Ca·lyp·so (kəlípsou) *n.* modern swing dance of the Caribbean characterized by foot slipping and hip and knees rolling, derived from slave-sung songs of Trinidad

ca·lyp·tra (kəlíptrə) *n.* (*bot.*) the hood covering the lid of the capsule in mosses ‖ the hoodlike covering of a flower or fruit ‖ a root cap [Mod. L. fr. Gk. *kaluptra*, covering]

ca·lyp·tro·gen (kəlíptrədʒən) *n.* (*bot.*) the histogen layer which develops into the root cap [fr. CALYPTRA+Gk -*genēs*, producing]

ca·lyx (kéiliks, kǽliks) *pl.* **ca·lyx·es, cal·y·ces** (kéilisi:z, kǽlisi:z) *n.* an outer whorl of floral leaves forming the protective covering of a flower bud ‖ the cuplike portion of the pelvis of the kidney ‖ the cuplike body of a crinoid [L. fr. Gk *kalux*, case of bud, or husk]

cam (kæm) *n.* an eccentric projection on a shaft which communicates the revolution of the shaft into the linear movement of another part of a machine [prob. Du. *kam*, cog]

CAM (*computer*) **1.** (*acronym*) for content-addressable memory. **2.** computer-sided manufacturing

Ca·ma·güey (kæməgwei, kɑmɑgwéi) the capital (pop. 251,293) of Camagüey province, Cuba: distilleries, sugar refineries

ca·ma·ra·de·rie (kɑmərɑ́dəri:) *n.* the familiar, buoyant spirit proper to good comrades, characterized esp. by mutual trust and loyalty [F. fr. *camarade*, comrade]

Ca·margue (kæmɑrg) a marshy alluvial plain (area 290 sq. miles) in the Rhône delta, S.E. France, lying south of Arles between the Grand Rhône and the Petit Rhône. Bulls and horses are raised. Rice, vines and fodder are grown. The southern part is a zoological and botanical reserve. Chief town: Saintes-Maries-de-la-Mer

cam·a·ron (kæmərɔ́n) *n.* a large freshwater prawn, resembling a crayfish [Span.=shrimp]

cam·as (kǽməs) *n.* a member of *Camassia*, fam. *Liliaceae*, a genus of scapose plants of western North America, esp. *C. quamash*, with edible bulbs [Chinook *quamash*, bulb]

cam·ber (kǽmbər) **1.** *n.* a shallow convex curve on the surface of a road, a roof or the deck of a ship, etc. ‖ (*engin.*) a recess in the side of the entrance to a dock etc., for the sliding caisson **2.** *v.t.* to make (an object) cambered ‖ *v.i.* to be cambered [F. *cambre*]

camber beam a curved roof beam

cam·bi·al (kǽmbi:əl) *adj.* of or relating to cambium

cam·bi·um (kǽmbi:əm) *pl.* **cam·bi·ums, cam·bi·a** (kǽmbi:ə) *n.* (*bot.*) a lateral meristem between the xylem and phloem in woody plants, from which these tissues develop [L.L.=exchange]

Cam·bo·di·a (kæmbóudi:ə) also known as Kampuchea, a Communist republic (area 69,898 sq. miles, pop. c. 6,890,000), in S.E. Asia. Capital: Phnom Penh. Ethnic and linguistic divisions: 85% Khmers (Cambodians), and minorities of Chinese, Vietnamese. Languages: Khmer (official) and French. Religion: chiefly Hinayana Buddhism. The land is 75% forest and 17% arable. The fertile underdeveloped central depression, surrounded by mountains, is traversed by the R. Mekong, which floods during the monsoons. The climate is tropical, with a wet summer monsoon June–Nov. Average temperature (F.): minimum 68°, maximum 97°. Rainfall: 30–80 ins. Agricultural products: rice, corn, cotton, pepper, palm sugar, kapok, castor beans, coffee, tea, silk. Livestock: oxen, water buffalo. Iron ore resources are unexploited. Cambodian fisheries (esp. in the fresh water of Tonle-Sap Lake) are the most productive in S.E. Asia, and the production of salted and smoked fish is an important industry. Exports: rice, rubber, corn, lumber. Imports: textiles, foodstuffs, metal products, machinery and vehicles. Ports: Phnom Penh, on the Mekong, and Kompong Som. Inland waterways provide an extensive transportation network for goods and passengers. Buddhist University at Phnom Penh. Monetary unit: riel. HISTORY. Indian emigrants established the Funan kingdom and introduced their culture and religion in the 1st c. By the 6th c. the Khmer Empire had arisen, reaching its zenith in the 9th c., when it developed a remarkable architecture (*ANGKOR). Invasions by the Thais and Annamese during the subsequent centuries forced the king to ask for French protection in 1863. Cambodia became part of French Indochina (1887). A series of treaties (1904, 1907, 1946) with Laos and Thailand returned several former provinces to Cambodia. In 1947 a constitutional monarchy was created. Cambodia became (1949) an associated state in the French Union and declared (1953) its independence. Following an invasion (1954) of Communist Vietnamese forces, the Geneva Conference (1954) provided for the withdrawal of foreign forces from Cambodian territory. Upon the death of king Norodom Suramarit (1896–1960), his son, Prince Norodom Sihanouk, prime minister since 1955 and previously king (1941–55), became chief of state again. His rule was marked by a policy of neutrality toward the Vietnam War. Following a right-wing coup d'état (Mar. 1970), Cheng Heng became head of the Phnom Penh government, advocating a policy of 'pro-American neutrality.' On Apr. 30, 1970 U.S. President Richard Nixon announced the invasion of Cambodia by U.S. and South Vietnamese forces in search of North Vietnamese headquarters, arms stockpiles, and Vietnamese refugees. U.S. ground combat forces were withdrawn by July 1, 1970, but South Vietnamese forces remained, supported by U.S. air power Cambodia became (1970) a republic. The Communist Khmer Rouge took Phnom Penh (1975) and drove the entire urban population into the countryside. Hundreds of thousands of people died of malnutrition, exhaustion, and through executions and purges within the Khmer Rouge movement. The country was almost totally isolated from the outside world. The Vietnamese army overran Phnom Penh (1979) and Khmer Rouge defectors headed by Heng Samrin established a Vietnamese-style people's republic. Khmer Rouge forces fled to the border with Thailand and began guerrilla resistance. A coalition government was formed (1982) with Sihanouk, Son Sann and the Khmer Rouge. The Association of Southeast Asian Nations (ASEAN) helped arm this group and insisted on Vietnam's leaving the country, and the UN refused to admit the Vietnam-backed government. The Vietnamese, backed by the U.S.S.R., continued assaults along the Thai border

Cam·bo·di·an (kæmbóudi:ən) **1.** *adj.* of or pertaining to Cambodia **2.** *n.* a native or inhabitant of Cambodia ‖ the Khmer language

Cam·brai, League of (kɑ̀brei) an alliance (1508–10) formed by the Emperor Maximilian I, Louis XII of France, Pope Julius II and Ferdinand V of Aragon against the republic of Venice

Cam·brai, Treaty of a treaty (1529) signed by François I of France and Emperor Charles V. France permitted Italy to revert to the Emperor and relinquished her claims over Artois and Flanders

cam·brel (kǽmbrəl) *n.* (*Br.*) a gambrel [origin unknown]

Cam·bri·an (kǽmbri:ən) **1.** *adj.* relating to Wales ‖ (*geol.*) of the earliest period or system of the Paleozoic era, characterized by rocks

CONCISE PRONUNCIATION KEY: **(a)** æ, c*a*t; ɑ, c*a*r; ɔ *faw*n; ei, sn*a*ke. **(e)** e, h*e*n; i:, sh*ee*p; iə, d*ee*r; ɛə, b*ea*r. **(i)** i, f*i*sh; ai, t*i*ger; ə:, b*i*rd. **(o)** o, *o*x; au, c*ow*; ou, g*oa*t; u, p*oo*r; ɔi, r*oy*al. **(u)** ʌ, d*u*ck; u, b*u*ll; u:, g*oo*se; ə, b*a*cillus; ju:, c*u*be. x, lo*ch*; θ, *th*ink; ð, bo*th*er; z, *Z*en; ʒ, cor*s*age; dʒ, sava*g*e; ŋ, orangutan*g*; j, *y*ak; ʃ, *f*ish; tʃ, fe*tch*; 'l, rabb*le*; 'n, redd*en*. Complete pronunciation key appears inside front cover.

formed under shallow sea conditions, e.g. limestones, sandstones, shales, and by invertebrates, e.g. trilobites (*GEOLOGICAL TIME) **2.** *n.* a Welshman **the Cambrian** the Cambrian period or system of rocks [fr. L. *Cambria* fr. Celt.]

cam·bric (kéimbrik) *n.* a fine cloth of linen or cotton [fr. *Kameryk,* Flem. name of Cambray, France, where it was orig. made]

Cam·bridge (kéimbridʒ) the county town (pop. 90,440) of Cambridgeshire, England, on River Cam, the seat of Cambridge University. It is a market town, with light industries

Cambridge a city (pop. 95,322) of Massachusetts, on the Charles River opposite Boston, seat of Harvard University

Cambridge Agreement an agreement reached by the leading stockholders of the Massachusetts Bay Company, unhappy with 'Romish' tendencies in the English Church, to organize a migration to America and a settlement around Massachusetts Bay as a religious refuge for Puritans. The first migrants (1629) were followed by 20,000 persons within twelve years

Cambridge Platonists a group of English Neoplatonist philosophers associated with Cambridge in the second half of the 17th c., including Ralph Cudworth and Henry More

Cam·bridge·shire (kéimbridʒʃər) (abbr. Cambs.), a former county (area 492 sq. miles, pop. 575,177 excluding the Isle of Ely) of E. England

Cambridge University a British university consisting of 31 residential colleges (including three women's colleges). The oldest is Peterhouse (1284) and the newest is Wolfson College (1977). Each college is self-governing, but a senate regulates the university's administrative affairs

Cam·by·ses II (kæmbáisi:z) (d. c. 521 B.C.) king of Persia (529–c. 521 B.C.), son of Cyrus II. He conquered Egypt (525 B.C.), but further expeditions in Africa failed

Cam·den (kæmdən), William (1551–1623), English scholar, chief of the Elizabethan historians. He wrote 'Britannia' (1586), an antiquarian's survey of the British Isles

Camden a port of entry (pop. 84,910) in S.W. New Jersey, an industrial, marketing and transportation center. Manufactures: radios, phonographs, soap, chemicals, oilcloth and linoleum. Railroads and shipyards

came (keim) *n.* one of the narrow, grooved strips of lead for holding the small panes of glass in latticed or stained-glass windows [etym. doubtful]

came *past of* COME

cam·el (kæmǝl) *n.* either of two members of *Camelus,* fam. *Camelidae,* quadruped ruminants used in desert countries for riding or as beasts of burden: *C. dromedarius* of Arabia, having a single hump, and *C. bactrianus* of Turkestan, having two humps. Camels eat rough herbage and their capacity for storing fat in their humps and converting it to water enables them to travel long distances in the desert. Their broad elastic feet prevent them from sinking into the sand. They can travel about 25 miles carrying heavy burdens, but when used for speed only they may reach 90 miles a day ‖ (*engin.*) a machine for lifting vessels or sunken objects out of water, a caisson ‖ a pontoon **cam·el·eer** (kæmǝlíǝr) *n.* a camel driver ‖ (*Br.,* *mil.*) a member of a camel-mounted force [Late O.E. fr. L. fr. Gk fr. Semitic]

camel hair camel's hair

ca·mel·lia, ca·mel·ia (kǝmí:ljǝ) *n.* a member of *Camellia,* fam. *Theaceae,* a genus of widely cultivated evergreen shrubs, with red or white flowers and glossy leaves [after Georg Josef *Kamel,* who discovered the plant (1639) in the Philippines]

ca·mel·o·pard (kǝméloupǝrd) *n.* (*oldfash.*) a giraffe [fr. L. fr. Gk fr. *kamēlos,* camel+*pardalis,* leopard]

Cam·e·lot (kæmǝlot) the seat of King Arthur's court, in the Arthurian legend

Cam·e·lot (kæmǝlot) *n.* an idyllic time and place, esp. descriptive of Washington, D.C., during the John F. Kennedy administration; from the mythical court of King Arthur

cam·el·ry (kæmǝlri:) *pl.* **cam·el·ries** *n.* a force of men mounted on camels

camel's hair the hair of the camel, from the haunch and underpart ‖ cloth made of camel's hair, generally fawn-colored

camel spin (*ice skating*) spin from an arabesque position

Cam·em·bert (kæmǝmbɛǝr, kæmüber) *n.* a very soft, rich, fermented cheese of a kind originally made near Camembert, in Normandy, France

cam·e·o (kæmi:ou) *n.* an engraved design or portrait cut in relief on hard stone or a gem so engraved (cf. INTAGLIO). Often the stone chosen has differently colored layers, the lower serving as a background for the relief carving ‖ an appearance role (usu. in one scene) by a well-known person in a larger theatrical or cinematic production **2.** *adj.* miniature-scale [Ital.]

cam·er·a (kæmǝrǝ, kæmrǝ) *n.* an apparatus for taking photographs, consisting of a light-proof box containing a light-sensitive plate or film which records the image of an external object when light enters the camera through a lens ‖ an apparatus, as used in television, for changing images into electrical impulses, so that they can be transmitted over considerable distances **in camera** in a judge's private chamber ‖ with the public excluded [L.=vault]

camera lu·ci·da (lú:sidǝ) *pl.* **camera lu·ci·das** *n.* an apparatus which, by the use of mirrors or a prism, casts the outline of an object on to paper etc. for tracing [L. =light chamber]

cam·er·a·man (kæmǝrǝmǝn, kæmrǝmæn) *pl.* **cam·er·a·men** (kæmǝrǝmǝn, kæmrǝmǝn) *n.* a man who operates a camera for films or television

camera ob·scu·ra (ɒbskjúǝrǝ) *pl.* **camera obscuras** *n.* a darkened chamber or boxlike apparatus in which light, admitted through a convex lens, casts a detailed image (not an outline only) on ground glass or an opaque surface. It is used for making precise drawings or photographs

Cam·er·on (kæmǝrǝn), Verney Lovett (1844–94), British explorer. Sent (1873) to relieve Dr Livingstone in E. Africa, he found him already dead. He explored Lake Tanganyika and continued to the Atlantic coast. He was the first European to cross equatorial Africa east to west

Cam·e·roons (kæmǝrú:nz) a former German protectorate in W. Africa administered as a League of Nations mandate (1922), then as a U.N. Trust Territory (after the 2nd world war) by France and Britain. The French Cameroons became the Republic of Cameroun (Jan. 1, 1960), which was joined by the southern half of the British Cameroons (Oct. 1, 1961) to form the Federal Republic of Cameroun. The northern half of the British Cameroons joined Nigeria (June 1, 1961)

Cam·e·roun (kæmrú:n) a federal republic (area 183,570 sq. miles, pop. 8,853,000) in W. Africa. Capital: Yaoundé. Chief towns: Douala and Buea. Behind the coastal swamps lies a thick tropical rain forest. Farther north are high grassland plateaus, and in the Chad basin semidesert savanna. Highest point: Mt Cameroun (13,352 ft), near the coast. Rainfall is very heavy in the south (400 ins on Mt Cameroun), light in the north. Livestock: cattle, goats. Agricultural products: cassava, bananas, taro, millet, sorghum, yams, corn, cacao, coffee, tobacco, cotton. Mineral resources: aluminum (smelter at Edéa). Exports: cacao, palm kernels, coffee, bananas, lumber. Imports: beer, wine, chemicals, foodstuffs. Ports: Douala, Victoria. Monetary unit: franc C.F.A. HISTORY. The coast was explored by the Portuguese (15th c.) and French, Dutch and British traders (16th c.). The British settled (19th c.) but the country was declared a German protectorate (1884). This was divided (1919) into the Cameroons, administered by Britain, and Cameroun, administered by France. Cameroun attained independence (Jan. 1, 1960) and united with the southern part of the Cameroons as the Federal Republic of Cameroun (Oct. 1, 1961). The N. Cameroons joined Nigeria (June 1961). Alhaji Ahmadou Ahidjo served as president (1960–82) until he resigned and was succeeded by Paul Biya. There is only one political party, the Union Nationale Camerounaise

Cam·o·ens (kæmouens), Luis Vaz de (1524–80), Portuguese poet, author of 'The Lusiads'

camomile *CHAMOMILE

camomile tea a drink made from an infusion of chamomile flowers

cam·ou·flage (kæmǝflɑʒ) **1.** *n.* the hiding from observation of ships or buildings (e.g. by painting them to blend with the surroundings and break up hard outlines) or guns and other mobile military equipment (e.g. by nets, tree branches etc.) ‖ the disguise used ‖ any concealment by disguise **2.** *v.t. pres. part.* **cam·ou·flag·ing** *past* and *past part.* **cam·ou·flaged** to hide by camouflage [F.]

cam·ou·flet (kæmǝflɛt) *n.* the resulting cavity in a deep underground explosion when there is no rupture of the earth's surface

camp (kæmp) **1.** *n.* (*mil.*) a place where forces are temporarily lodged, in tents, barracks or huts ‖ a temporary resting-place for gypsies etc. ‖ tents collectively, an encampment ‖ the persons sheltered ‖ a holiday recreational center, esp. for children, *riding camp, music camp* ‖ an ideological position ‖ (*pop.*) behavior involving the adoption of false attitudes or false values for purposes of ridicule or to amuse **to break camp** to pack up equipment and leave a campsite **to pitch camp** to set up a camp **2.** *v.i.* to make a camp, pitch tents, etc. ‖ to live in a camp ‖ *v.t.* to station (soldiers) in a camp **to camp out** to live outdoors in a camp **3.** *adj.* of something so outmoded, exaggerated, banal, unnatural, or unsophisticated that it is accepted as clever or amusing ‖ of exaggeratedly effeminate mannerisms by a male homosexual ‖ to live elsewhere than one's home, temporarily, and in conditions involving discomfort or inconvenience ‖ to act in a camp way, e.g., to camp it up [F. *camp*]

Cam·pa·gna di Ro·ma (kɑmpɑnjǝdi:róumǝ) the plain (area c. 800 sq. miles) surrounding Rome, rich in ancient monuments. It was marshy and malarial, but was drained and made more fertile by irrigation (20th c.)

cam·paign (kæmpéin) **1.** *n.* a series of military actions in one area, usually with limited objectives, or a part of some larger warfare ‖ any organized attempt to gain public support **2.** *v.i.* to direct, or take part in, a campaign [F. *campagne* fr. Ital.]

campaign dirty tricks *DIRTY TRICKS.

Cam·pa·nel·la (kɑmpanéllǝ), Tommaso (1568–1639), Italian philosopher, whose 'Civitas Solis' (1623) advocated an egalitarian theocracy, and whose 'Metaphysics' (1638) anticipated the idealistic reactions to Scholasticism

Cam·pa·nia (kɑmpánjǝ) a region (area 5,213 sq. miles, pop. 5,491,658) of S.W. Italy. Chief city: Naples. Along the Tyrrhenian Sea lie the fertile, populous plains (vegetables, wine, fruit) of Naples and Salerno, broken near Sorrento by mountains (notably Vesuvius), and bordered on the north, east and south by the Apennines. Colonized by Greeks, Oscans, Etruscans and Samnites, Campania was conquered by Rome (4th c. B.C.) and contains famous archaeological sites (*HERCULANEUM, *POMPEII, *PAESTUM)

cam·pa·ni·le (kæmpǝní:li:) *n.* a belfry, or bell tower, sometimes detached from the main building to which it belongs [Ital.]

cam·pa·no·log·i·cal (kæmpǝn'lɒdʒik'l) *adj.* of or related to campanology

cam·pa·nol·o·gist (kæmpǝnólǝdʒist) *n.* someone who practices campanology

cam·pa·nol·o·gy (kæmpǝnólǝdʒi:) *n.* the study of bells, of bell making, and esp. of the ringing of bells [fr. Mod. L. *campanologia* fr. *campana,* bell+Gk *logos,* discourse]

cam·pan·u·la (kæmpænjulǝ) *n.* a member of *Campanula,* fam. *Campanulaceae,* a genus of plants of which there are 300 known species. Many are alpine plants, and all have bell-shaped flowers, usually blue or white ‖ a member of *Campanularia,* a genus of hydroid zoophytes, having bell-shaped polyp cells supported on long footstalks [Mod. L., dim. of *campana,* bell]

cam·pan·u·late (kæmpænjulit) *adj.* (*biol.*) bell-shaped [fr. L. *campanula,* little bell]

camp bed a light folding bed

Camp·bell (kæmb'l), Alexander (1788–1866), U.S. religious leader, a founder of the Disciples of Christ (1830). As founding-editor of the 'Christian Baptist' (1823) he opposed revivalism and pressed for a scriptural simplicity in organization and doctrine

Campbell, Sir Colin, Baron Clyde (1792–1863), British general who led the relief of Lucknow and put down the Indian Mutiny (1858)

Campbell, William Wallace (1862–1938), U.S. astronomer. With a 36-inch reflecting telescope at the Lick Observatory, Mt Hamilton, Calif., he calculated the sun's motion in our galaxy and the average random velocities of stars of

CONCISE PRONUNCIATION KEY: **(a)** æ, c**a**t; ɑ, c**a**r; ɔ, f**aw**n; ei, sn**a**ke. **(e)** e, h**e**n; i:, sh**ee**p; iǝ, d**ee**r; ɛǝ, b**ea**r. **(i)** i, f**i**sh; ai, t**i**ger; ǝ:, b**i**rd. **(o)** o, **o**x; au, c**ow**; ou, g**oa**t; u, p**oo**r; ɔi, r**oy**al. **(u)** ʌ, d**u**ck; u, b**u**ll; u:, g**oo**se; ǝ, b**a**cillus; ju:, c**u**be. x, lo**ch**; θ, **th**ink; δ, **bo**ther; z, **Z**en; ʒ, cor**s**age; dʒ, sava**g**e; ŋ, ora**ng**uta**ng**; j, **y**ak; ʃ, fi**sh**; tʃ, fe**tch**; 'l, rabb**le**; 'n, redd**en**. Complete pronunciation key appears inside front cover.

various spectral types. He served as president of the University of California (1923–30) and as president of the National Academy of Sciences (1931–5)

Camp·bell-Ban·ner·man (kæmb'lbænərmən), Sir Henry (1836–1908), British Liberal prime minister (1905–8). He denounced the Boer War and gave the Transvaal and Orange Free State self-government (1907)

Campbell v. Ball a landmark of British jurisprudence (1774) in which Lord Chief Justice Mansfield ruled for the plaintiff in Grenada, denying the right of the British Government to tax his sugar business since an island government had been established

camp chair a light folding chair

camp·craft (kæmpkræft, kæmpkrɑft) n. the art of camping

Cam·pe·che (kæmpétʃe) a southeastern state of Mexico (area 19,672 sq. miles, pop. 337,000) on the peninsula of Yucatán. Capital: Campeche (pop. 69,506). The land ranges from arid or semiarid in the north (some farming, stock raising) to uninhabitable tropical rain forest (hardwoods, chicle) in the south

Campeche, Bay of a wide, shallow bay in the southwest section of the Gulf of Mexico, extending into S.E. Mexico

camp·er (kæmpər) n. a person at a camp or living in a tent etc. on holiday ‖ a pickup truck or any vehicle fitted out with temporary living arrangements

Camp·er·down, Battle of (kæmpərdaun) a British naval victory (1797) over a Dutch fleet which had threatened British naval supremacy

camp·fire (kæmpfaiər) n. an open-air fire, round which people in a camp gather for warmth, cooking and fellowship

camp fire girl a member of the Camp Fire Girls, Inc. organization for girls, promoting character training, good citizenship and good health

camp follower a prostitute, laundress or other nonmilitary person who becomes attached to a soldiers' camp or (hist.) followed the campaign along with the baggage wagons

camp·ground (kæmpgraund) n. an area where a camp may be set up or a camp meeting be held

cam·phire (kæmfaiər) n. henna [M.E. camphire, caumfre, camphor]

cam·phor (kæmfər) n. a white, crystalline, volatile solid of the terpene group, with a characteristic smell. It occurs in the wood of certain trees and is used in the production of celluloid, as an insect repellent and in some pharmaceuticals [F. camfre fr. Arab.]

cam·pho·rate (kæmfəreit) pres. part. **cam·pho·rat·ing** past and past part. **cam·pho·rat·ed** v.t. to treat with camphor [fr. M.L. camphoratus]

camphorated oil cottonseed oil impregnated with camphor, used to soothe irritation, esp. in nose and throat infections

Cam·pi·gli (kampí:lji:), Massimo (1895–1971), Italian painter and lithographer

Cam·pi·on (kæmpi:ən), Edmund (1540–81), English Jesuit priest trained at Douai, Rome and Prague, and sent (1580) to England as a Catholic missionary. He was tortured and hanged as a traitor

Campion, Thomas (1567–1620), English poet and composer noted esp. for his lute songs

cam·pi·on (kæmpi:ən) n. a lychnis ‖ a member of Silene, fam. Caryophillaceae, a genus of widely distributed plants, having flowers of various colors, e.g. S. acaulis, the moss campion, a small mountain plant having purple flowers [etym. doubtful]

camp meeting a religious meeting held in a tent or open air and usually lasting several days

cam·po (kæmpou, kámpou) n. a tropical grassland on the interior plateau of Brazil resembling savanna in climate and vegetation [Port.]

Cam·po-For·mio, Treaty of (kæmpoufɔ́rmjou) a settlement (1797) between France and Austria during the French Revolutionary Wars. France gained the Austrian Netherlands and the Ionian Is, and Austria received Istria, Dalmatia and part of Venetia

camp·o·ree (kæmpərí:) n. a boy scout camp gathering at local or regional level [CAMP+(JAMB)OREE]

camp·site (kæmpsait) n. a place chosen for camping or occupied by campers

cam·pus (kæmpəs) pl. **cam·pus·es** n. the grounds and main buildings of a school or college [L.= field]

cam·shaft (kæmʃæft, kæmʃɑft) n. a shaft having a cam or cams, e.g. to operate the valves of an internal-combustion engine

Ca·mus (kæmy), Albert (1913–60), French writer born in Algeria. Two novels, 'l'Etranger' (1942) and 'la Peste' (1947), and his play 'Caligula' (1945) are among his best-known works. He wrote of man's lonely and absurd condition in an irrational universe. He won a Nobel Prize (1957), chiefly for such philosophical tracts as 'The Rebel' (1951)

cam·wood (kæmwud) n. the wood of the African tree Baphia nitida, fam. Caesalpiniaceae, yielding a red or blue dye [etym. doubtful]

Can. Canada ‖ Canadian

can (kæn) infin. and parts lacking, neg. **can·not** (kænɒt), **can not, can't** (kænt, kɑnt) 3rd pers. sing. **can** past **could** (kud) (or, by suppletion, 'was, were able to') auxiliary v. to be able to, can you come to dinner? ‖ to know how to, can you sew? ‖ to be permitted to, can we park here? **can but** can only **cannot but** must [O.E. cunnan, to know]

can 1. n. a receptacle, often of metal, for liquids, etc. ‖ (Am.=Br. tin) a tinplated container in which foodstuffs are preserved 2. v.t. pres. part. **can·ning** past and past part. **canned** (Am.=Br. tin) to preserve by packing in an airtight can [O.E. canne]

Ca·na (kéinə) the ancient town of Galilee where Jesus worked his first two miracles (John ii, 1–11 and iv, 46–54)

Ca·naan (kéinən) the ancient region corresponding roughly to Palestine, the land promised by God to Abraham [fr. Heb. kena'n]

Ca·naan·ite (kéinənait) n. an inhabitant of ancient Canaan

Can·a·da (kænədə) an independent state (area 3,851,809 sq. miles, pop. 24,343,181) in North America, and a federal dominion within the British Commonwealth. Capital: Ottawa. Largest towns: Montreal, Toronto. The population is 48% of British origin, 31% of French origin, 1% Indian and Eskimo, with German, Ukrainian, Scandinavian, Dutch, Polish and other minorities. French Canada is centered in the province of Quebec. Languages: 67% English only, 20% French only, 13% bilingual. Religion: 46% Roman Catholic, 45% Protestant, with Jewish, Orthodox and Mennonite minorities. The land is 5% arable and 46% forest. The Canadian Shield stretches from the Mackenzie River to the St Lawrence estuary. The maritime provinces of the east comprise a northern continuation of the Appalachians, stretching from the Green Mtns to Gaspé peninsula (rising to 4,160 ft) and to Newfoundland. Half the population lives in the St Lawrence lowlands, between Quebec and Lake Huron. North of the Canadian Shield stretches the largely unexplored Arctic Archipelago with heights over 7,000 ft e.g. in Baffin and Ellesmere Is. North of the vast interior prairies (Manitoba lowland, Alberta upland rising to 4,000 ft and foothills belt) are the sparsely inhabited Northwest Territories. In the west are three belts of mountains (main ranges: Rocky Mtns and Coast Mtns). Highest peak: Mt Logan (19,850 ft) in the W. Yukon. The interior is covered with snow for 3 months of the year, and frost-free for only 2–3 months. Annual rainfall: St John's, Newfoundland 54 ins, Montreal 41, Toronto 32, Winnipeg 21, Dawson 13, Victoria 30. Average temperatures (F., Jan. and July): St John's 23°, 60°, Montreal 14°, 70°, Toronto 23°, 69°. Winnipeg −3°, 67°, Dawson −21°, 60°, Victoria 39°, 60°. Livestock: cattle, horses, sheep, pigs, poultry. Agricultural products: cereals (esp. wheat in Saskatchewan), dairy products (Ontario and Quebec), fruit (Ontario and British Columbia), fur, tobacco, eggs and poultry, maple products, vegetables. There are large irrigation projects in Alberta and British Columbia. Resources: lumber, fish (esp. salmon, lobster and cod), nickel, uranium, copper, gold, zinc, oil (in Alberta), coal, natural gas, asbestos, salt, silver, cobalt, gypsum. Manufactures: foodstuffs, iron and steel, paper goods, transport equipment, machinery, metal products, oil and coal products, wood pulp and products, electricity, textiles. Exports: newsprint, paper, wheat, wood, minerals, fish. Imports: vehicles, machinery, fuel oil. Ports: Montreal, St John's, Halifax on the Atlantic (the last two ice-free all year), Vancouver and Victoria on the Pacific, Fort William and Port Arthur on Lake Superior. Chief universities: McGill (Montreal, 1821), Toronto (1827), Laval (Quebec, French language, 1852), Montreal (French language, 1876). Monetary unit: Canadian dollar (100 cents). HISTORY. John Cabot discovered Canada (1497), Jacques Cartier explored the St Lawrence (1534–42), Samuel de Champlain founded Quebec (1608) and penetrated the interior (1603–16). The French colonized along the St Lawrence and part of this New France was granted by Richelieu to the Company of 100 Associates (1627), and subsequently returned to the French crown in 1663. Montreal was founded by Maisonneuve (1642). Acadia was ceded to the English by the Treaty of Utrecht (1713) and renamed Nova Scotia. Anglo-French rivalry culminated in the Seven Years' War (1756–63) and nearly all the rest of French Canada was ceded to England by the Treaty of Paris (1763), French liberties being guaranteed by the Quebec Act (1774). Upper Canada (British) and Lower Canada (French) were created by an Act of 1791, but were united into one province by the Act of Union (1840) and given internal self-government (1848) (*DURHAM REPORT). The maritime provinces became self-governing (1848–51). The Dominion of Canada was established under the first prime minister, Sir John Macdonald, by the British North America Act (1867), and formed the Confederation of the provinces of New Brunswick, Nova Scotia, Quebec and Ontario, to which were added the provinces of Manitoba (1870), British Columbia (1871), Prince Edward Island (1873), Alberta and Saskatchewan (1905), and Newfoundland (1949). The Hudson's Bay Company, chartered by Charles II (1670), was purchased by the Confederation (1869). Canada settled its boundary disputes with the U.S.A. over Oregon (1846) and Alaska (1903) and now shares a 5,000-mile undefended frontier. The Canadian Pacific Railway (1885) led to the opening up of the prairies and the Northwest. Canada fought on the side of the Allies (1914–18). Independence was formally recognized by the Statute of Westminster (1931). Canada fought as an ally of Britain (1939–45), and greatly developed its industries and agriculture. Except for Diefenbaker's conservative government (1957–63) Canada had liberal governments from 1935 to 1979: Mackenzie King (1935–48), L. Saint-Laurent (1948–57), Lester B. Pearson (1963–8) and P. E. Trudeau (1968–79). Trudeau responded to the terrorist provocation of the separatist Front de Libération du Québec by invoking (1970) emergency police powers under Canada's 1914 War Measures Act, which had never before been used in time of peace. The Parti Québécois, committed to making Quebec an independent republic, came to power (1976), causing a crisis that, together with economic problems, led to the Liberal defeat (1979). Joseph Clark's minority government lasted less than a year and Trudeau and the Liberals took over again (1980). A referendum in Quebec (May 1980) rejected the proposal for political independence. Trudeau resigned (1984) and was succeeded by John Turner, but later that year Brian Mulroney and the Conservatives won an overwhelming victory—211 of the 282 parliamentary seats. Canada has close economic ties with the U.S.A., while maintaining trading connections by preferential tariff with Britain and other Commonwealth countries. It joined the U.N. (1945) and NATO (1949)

Canada balsam the resin of the fir Abies balsamea, used as a transparent cement for mounting objects on microscope slides and in optical systems. Its refractive index is about the same as that of glass

Canada bill *CANADIAN CONSTITUTIONAL ACT

Canada goose pl. **Canada geese** Branta canadensis, a North American wild goose 30-35 ins. long, brownish above and light below. Its head, bill, neck and feet are black and it has a white patch on the throat and sides of the head

Canadian a river (906 miles long) flowing from N. New Mexico southward and eastward across N.W. Texas and through central Oklahoma to the Arkansas River in E. Oklahoma. It is sometimes called the South Canadian River

Ca·na·di·an (kənéidi:ən) 1. n. an inhabitant of Canada 2. adj. of Canada or its people

Canadian Constitutional Act (Canada bill), an act passed by the British legislature which introduced (1791) representative government on the British model into the provinces of Canada. It eventually led to responsible government, but for a time it bolstered authority against the popular will

Canadian Shield (formerly called the Laurentian Plateau) a complex of ancient rocks with its center in Hudson Bay, covering about half of Canada (2,000,000 sq. miles). It is characterized by low relief (rising above 1,500 ft only in W. Quebec, Labrador and Baffin Is), with areas of exposed rock and many lakes, due to glaciation. Resources: copper, gold, nickel, uranium, iron ore, hydroelectricity, lumber

ca·nal (kənǽl) n. an artificial waterway for irrigation or navigation || (zool.) a tube through which lymph and other fluids are conveyed || a sucking groovelike organ in cephalopods, gastropods etc. || (archit.) a groove [F.]

Ca·na·let·to (kæn'létou) (Giovanni Antonio Canal, 1697–1768), Venetian painter, best known for his paintings of Venice, London, Vienna and Warsaw. They are highly detailed, but also suffused with a light which raises the actual scene to an impression of ideal, nostalgic beauty

ca·nal·ize (kənǽlaiz, kǽnəlaiz) pres. part. **ca·nal·iz·ing** past and past part. **ca·nal·ized** v.t. to convert a river into a canal by straightening its course, making it wider or narrower, and if necessary constructing locks, to facilitate navigation || to make a canal through || to direct (feelings or activity) into one channel [F. canaliser]

canal ray (phys.) a positive ray, esp. one which has passed through a perforated cathode

Canal Zone *PANAMA CANAL

can·a·pé (kǽnəpei, kǽnəpi:) n. a piece of bread or toast with savory topping [F. = couch]

ca·nard (kənárd) n. a piece of false information put out as a hoax [F.]

ca·nar·y (kənɛ́əri) pl. **ca·nar·ies** n. any of several varieties of singing cage birds of the finch family. They breed 3 or 4 times a year, lay 4-6 eggs each time, and live 15-16 years || a bright yellow || a sweet wine like Madeira from the Canary Is

Canary creeper Tropaeolum peregrinum, a creeping plant with yellow flowers

Canary Islands (Span. Islas Canarias) a group of islands (area 2,807 sq. miles, pop. 1,444,626) in the Atlantic, about 70 miles off the N.W. African coast, forming two Spanish provinces: Santa Cruz de Tenerife and Las Palmas. Seven are inhabited: Tenerife, Fuerteventura, Gran Canaria, Lanzarote, Palma, Gomera and Hierro. Products: grain, fruit, wine

canary seed the seed of Phalaris canariensis, a grass of the Canary Is, used as food for cage birds

canary yellow canary (a bright yellow)

ca·nas·ta (kənǽstə) n. a card game, somewhat similar to rummy [Span. = basket]

Can·ber·ra (kǽnbɛrə, kǽnbərə) the federal capital (pop. 246,100) of Australia since 1927 and seat of the Australian National University, in the Capital Territory

can·can (kǽnkæn) n. a very gay dance (cabaret or revue), which originated in 19th-c. Paris. It features high kicks and splits [F., origin unknown]

can·cel (kǽnsəl) 1. v.t. pres. part. **can·cel·ing**, esp. Br. **can·cel·ling** past and past part. **can·celed**, esp. Br. **can·celled** to abolish, nullify || to countermand || to cross out, delete || to mark (postage stamps) so that they cannot be used again || to neutralize || (printing) to replace (a leaf or leaves) by corrected matter || to remove (equivalents on opposite sides) from equations or accounts 2. n. the act of canceling || (printing) the replacement for a previously printed part which required canceling [fr. L. cancellare, to cancel, fr. cancelli, lattice]

can·cel·late (kǽnsəleit) adj. (biol.) consisting of slender fibers and lamellae, joining to form a reticular structure || cancellous **cán·cel·lat·ed** adj. [fr. L. cancellare (cancellatus), to crosshatch]

can·cel·la·tion, can·cel·a·tion (kænsəléifən) n. the act of canceling, nullifying or invalidating || something canceled || a standardized marking on mail to indicate invalidation of the postage stamp || the termination of insurance by one or both contracting parties according to the terms of the policy

can·cel·lous (kǽnsələs) adj. of the inner, more spongy portion of bony tissue, e.g. the anterior portion of cuttlebone [fr. L. cancelli (pl. dim. of cancer), little grating]

Can·cer (kǽnsər) n. a northern constellation || the fourth sign of the zodiac, represented as a crab || *TROPIC OF CANCER **can·cer** a malignant tumor || the disease caused by such a tumor **cán·cer·ous** adj. [L.=crab, gangrene]

can·croid (kǽŋkroid) 1. n. a mildly malignant skin cancer 2. adj. resembling a crab || resembling a cancer [fr. L. cancer, crab]

can·de·la (kændí:lə) n. a new candle, a unit of intensity of light defined as one sixtieth of the light emitted by 1 sq. cm. of a black body at the temperature (1773.5°C.) at which molten platinum solidifies (*CANDLEPOWER) [L. candela, candle]

can·de·la·brum (kænd'lúbrəm) pl. **can·de·la·bra** (kænd'lúbrə) (pl. often used as sing., with pl. **can·de·la·bras**) n. a large, branching support for a number of candles [L. fr. candela, candle]

can·des·cence (kændésəns) n. the state or quality of being candescent

can·des·cent (kændésənt) adj. glowing with a brilliant white light [fr. L. candescens (candescentis) fr. candescere, to glow]

Can·di·a (kǽndi:ə) *HERAKLION

can·did (kǽndid) adj. frankly truthful even if the truth is unpleasant || honest, open [fr. L. candidus, white or F. candide]

can·di·da·cy (kǽndidəsi:) pl. **can·di·da·cies** n. the position or status of being a candidate [CANDIDATE]

can·di·date (kǽndideit, kǽndidit) n. a person who offers himself, or is nominated, for some post or office (esp. in elections) || a person taking an examination [fr. L. candidatus, white-robed (the candidates in Roman consular elections wore white)]

can·di·da·ture (kǽndidətʃər) n. (Br.) candidacy [F.]

can·died (kǽndi:d) adj. preserved in or covered with sugar

can·dle (kǽnd'l) n. a cylinder of tallow or wax around a core of wick, burned to give light **the game is not worth the candle** success would not be worth the cost or effort **to burn the candle at both ends** to live too hectic a life (literally to be up late for pleasure and up early for work) [O.E. candel fr. L.]

can·dle·ber·ry (kǽnd'lbɛri:) pl. **can·dle·ber·ries** n. Myrica cerifera, fam. Myrtaceae, the wax myrtle of North America, a source of wax || Aleurites triloba, fam. Euphorbiaceae, a tree of the E. Indies and Polynesia

candle curls (cosmetology) hairstyle with spirally wound, elongated curls. also caline curls

can·dle·light (kǽnd'l lait) n. the light of candles

Can·dle·mas (kǽnd'lməs) n. the Purification || one of the four Scottish quarter days, Feb. 2 [O.E. candelmæsse]

can·dle·nut (kǽnd'lnʌt) n. the fruit of Aleurites moluccana, a tropical tree whose seeds are rich in oil and are used in making candles

can·dle·pow·er (kǽnd'lpauər) n. the illuminating power of a source of light, originally expressed in a unit based on a candle made to precise specification (standard candle), later in terms of comparison with a Harcourt pentane lamp (international candle), now measured in the candela unit (new candle)

can·dle·stick (kǽnd'lstik) n. a holder for a candle

can·dle·wick (kǽnd'lwik) n. a cotton material with raised patterns of tufted soft cotton thread used esp. for bedspreads

can-do (kǽndu:) adj. of one who is enthusiastically effective

Can·dolle (kādɔl), Augustin Pyrame de (1778–1841), Swiss botanist famous for his work on systematic botany

can·dor, Br. **can·dour** (kǽndər) n. frankness, even to the point of telling unwelcome truths || openness of speech or expression, without dissembling [L. candor, radiance, whiteness]

C & W or **C-and-W** (abbr.) for American country and western music, esp. as recorded in Nashville, TN.

can·dy (kǽndi:) 1. n. pl. **can·dies** crystallized sugar || (Am.=Br. sweet) a piece of sugared confectionery 2. v. pres. part. **can·dy·ing** past and past part. **can·died** v.t. to preserve by coating with sugar || to turn into candy || v.i. to become candied [F. candi fr. Arab. fr. Pers.]

candy floss (Br.) cotton candy

candy striper a volunteer nurse's aid; from the red-and-white striped uniform

can·dy·tuft (kǽndi:tʌft) n. a member of Iberis, fam. Cruciferae, a genus of annual and perennial cultivated plants having unequal petals on a dense corymb inflorescence [after Candia, in Crete+TUFT]

cane (kein) 1. n. the long, hollow stem of plants such as bamboo, osier or sugarcane || the stem of certain small soft fruit bushes, raspberry cane || a stem, usually osier, used for furniture, chair seats, baskets, etc. || a thin walking stick || (Br.) a slender rod used (esp. formerly) as an instrument of punishment for schoolboys || a rod for supporting a climbing plant etc. 2. v.t. pres. part. **can·ing** past and past part. **caned** to make (a chair seat or back etc.) with canes || to punish by striking with a cane [O.F. fr. L. fr. Gk perh. fr. Sem.]

cane·brake (kéinbreik) n. a dense growth of sugarcane

ca·nel·la (kənélə) n. a member of Canella, a genus of trees growing in Florida and the West Indies. C. alba yields an orange, aromatic bark, used as a flavoring and as a stimulant [M.E. canele fr. O.F.]

cane sugar sugar obtained from sugarcane

Canetti, (kənéti:) Elias (1905–), a Bulgarian-born Jewish novelist and playwright who writes in German. Awarded the Nobel Prize for literature (1981), his works include 'Crowds and Power' (1960, Eng. trans. 1962), 'Die Blendung' (1935, trans. as 'Auto da Fé' 1946), and memoirs (2 vols., 1979, 1982)

Can Grande del·la sca·la (kuŋgrún-deidélluskúla) (1291–1329), lord of Verona, rich patron and protector of Dante

ca·nic·o·la fever (kəníkələ) an acute gastroenteritis, caused by a spirochete which affects dogs. Humans in contact with dogs so affected occasionally catch the disease [Mod. L. fr. canis, dog]

ca·nine (kéinain) 1. adj. of or pertaining to the family Canidae (dogs, wolves, foxes and jackals) 2. n. a canine tooth [fr. L. caninus]

canine tooth pl. **canine teeth** the pointed tooth between the incisors and the molars. Humans have two in each jaw

canine typhus canicola fever

Canisius *PETER CANISIUS

can·is·ter, can·nis·ter (kǽnistər) n. a small metal box for tea, coffee etc. or tobacco || (mil.) a case containing shot [fr. L. canistrum fr. Gk]

can·ker (kǽŋkər) n. an ulceration on the inside of the mouth or lips || a disease of horses' hooves || a sore in an animal's ear (esp. of a cat or dog) || a disease of fruit trees **cán·ker·ous** adj. [O.N.F. cancre, gangrene]

can·ker·worm (kǽŋkərwərm) n. a caterpillar which attacks fruit trees, destroying leaves and buds

can·na (kǽnə) n. a member of Canna, fam. Cannaceae, a genus of plants growing in warm climates, with long swordlike leaves and a tall flower stem which bears several red, yellow or orange flowers [L. fr. Gk canna, reed]

can·na·bis (kǽnəbis) n. hemp [fr. Gk kannabis]

Can·nae (kǽni:) (Canosa) an ancient village near Barletta, S.E. Italy, the scene of Hannibal's defeat of the Romans (216 B.C.)

canned (kænd) adj. preserved in a can or jar || (pop.) recorded or taped, canned music

can·nel coal (kǽn'l) a bituminous coal, hard and dull in appearance, having 77-80% carbon. It is rich in volatile content and is used in making gas

can·ner (kǽnər) n. someone who cans fruit etc.

can·ner·y (kǽnəri:) pl. **can·ner·ies** n. a place where food is canned

Cannes (kæn) a fashionable resort (pop. 72,259) on the Mediterranean (Côte d'Azur), S. France: metal and textile industries

can·ni·bal (kǽnəb'l) 1. n. a human who eats human flesh || any animal which feeds on its own kind 2. adj. having the habits of a cannibal **cán·ni·bal·ism** n. **can·ni·bal·is·tic** adj. [Span. canibales, Caribs]

can·ni·bal·ize (kǽnəbəlaiz) pres. part. **can·ni·bal·iz·ing** past and past part. **can·ni·bal·ized** v.t. to repair (vehicles or aircraft) by using parts from other vehicles, instead of using spare parts || to repair vehicles or aircraft in this way

can·ni·ly (kǽnili:) adv. in a canny way

can·ni·ness (kǽni:nis) n. the state or quality of being canny

Can·ning (kǽniŋ), Charles John Canning, 1st Earl (1812–62), governor-general of India (1855–7) and viceroy (1858–62)

Canning, George (1770–1827), British Tory statesman. As foreign secretary (1822–7) he maintained the cause of independence in Portugal, Greece and Latin America, claiming the Monroe Doctrine (1823) as a personal triumph

Canning, Stratford, 1st Viscount Stratford de Redcliffe (1786–1880), British diplomat. As ambassador at Constantinople (1842–58), he advised the sultan to resist Russian demands and so was accused, probably unjustly, of helping to cause the Crimean War

can·ning (kǽniŋ) n. the process or industry of sterilizing and preserving foods in cans or jars

cannister *CANISTER

Can·non (kǽnən), Joseph Gurney (1836–1926), U.S. Republican politician and Congressman for 46 years. As Speaker (1903–11) of the House of Representatives he became the eponym of partisanship in that office

can·non (kǽnən) 1. n. (pl. **can·non**) a piece of artillery fired from a mounting ‖ (pl. **cannon**) an automatic gun in an aircraft ‖ the barrel of a watch key ‖ a round bit (on a horse's harness) ‖ (mech.) a hollow cylinder ‖ (Br., billiards) a carom 2. v.i. (with 'with', 'into', or 'against') to collide ‖ (Br., billiards) to carom [F. canon]

can·non·ade (kænənéid) 1. n. continuous fire from cannon ‖ a bombardment 2. v. pres. part. **can·non·ad·ing** past and past part. **can·non·ad·ed** v.t. to bombard (a target) ‖ v.i. to fire continuously at an object [F. canon, tube]

can·non·ball (kǽnənbɔl) n. (hist.) a round, iron missile, fired from a cannon

cannon bone (zool., in hoofed quadrupeds) the metacarpal bone between the knee and fetlock of the foreleg, and the metatarsal bone between the hock and fetlock of the hind leg

can·non·eer (kænəníer) n. an artilleryman [F. canonnier]

cannon fodder men regarded as expendable material of warfare

cannon net a net used for capturing birds or animals by firing it from several positions over an area where the birds or animals are feeding

can·not (kǽnɔt) alt. pres. indicative neg. of CAN

can·ny (kǽni:) comp. **can·ni·er** superl. **can·ni·est** adj. cautious ‖ shrewd ‖ careful [Scot. fr. obs. can, to know how]

Ca·no (kánou), Juan Sebastián del (c. 1460–1526), Spanish navigator, the first to circumnavigate the globe. He sailed on Magellan's expedition (1519), took command after Magellan's death, and reached Spain (1522)

ca·noe (kənú:) 1. n. a light, long, narrow boat, propelled by paddles 2. v.i. to go in a canoe **ca·noe·ist** n. [fr. Span. canoa fr. Haitian]

canoe slalom sport in which a canoeist navigates through a slalom course in white water

can of worms (colloq.) unpleasant packet of problems

can·on (kǽnən) n. a church law ‖ any general principle or body of principles ‖ a list of people venerated as saints ‖ a member of the chapter, or administrative body, of a cathedral ‖ books of the Bible regarded by Christians as holy writ ‖ the list of books by any author regarded as authentically his work ‖ part of the Mass, beginning 'Te igitur' and including the words of consecration ‖ a metal loop on a bell, by which it is suspended ‖ (mus.) a contrapuntal work in which various instruments or voices take up the same melody successively, before the previous one has finished [O.E. fr. L. fr. Gk]

cañon *CANYON

can·on·ess (kǽnənis) n. a member of a religious community of women living under a rule, but not under vows

ca·non·i·cal (kənónik'l) adj. conforming with, or ordered by, canon law ‖ of or belonging to the canon of scriptures or of an author's works [fr. M.L. canonicalis]

canonical dress vestments prescribed by canon law for wear by a priest

canonical Epistles the epistles in the Bible of James, Peter, John and Jude

canonical hours certain hours of the day appointed for prayer, the offices of which are called matins, lauds, prime, tierce, sext, none, vespers and compline ‖ the time (between 8 a.m. and 3 p.m.) when marriage may be legally celebrated in a British church

ca·non·i·cals (kənónik'lz) pl. n. canonical dress

can·on·ic·i·ty (kænənísiti:) n. accepted authenticity ‖ the condition of being admitted to the canon [fr. L. canonicus, canonical]

can·on·ist (kǽnənist) n. a lawyer who specializes in canon law ‖ any person skilled in canon law [F. canoniste]

can·on·i·za·tion (kænənizéiʃən) n. a canonizing or being canonized

can·on·ize (kǽnənaiz) pres. part. **can·on·iz·ing** past and past part. **can·on·ized** v.t. to declare by authority in the Roman and Orthodox churches that a person is to be venerated as a saint ‖ to approve or sanction something by ecclesiastical authority ‖ to include in a canon, esp. the biblical canon [fr. L. canonizare]

canon law ecclesiastical law

canon regular pl. **canons regular** a priest living in a monastic community under a rule and who is either on the staff of a cathedral or doing parish or educational work etc.

can·on·ry (kǽnənri:) pl. **can·on·ries** n. the office or benefice of a canon ‖ canons collectively

Ca·no·pic vase (kənóupik) an ancient Egyptian funerary vase in which the entrails of an embalmed body were placed

can·o·py (kǽnəpi:) 1. pl. **can·o·pies** n. an ornate covering of cloth, wood etc. suspended or held over a bed, throne, shrine or person ‖ a rooflike covering, usually of wood, over a pulpit or lecturer's desk, to reflect sound ‖ (archit.) a rooflike covering over a niche or tomb ‖ (rhet.) anything that covers or overhangs, such as the sky, trees etc. 2. v.t. pres. part. **can·o·py·ing** past and past part. **can·o·pied** to cover with a canopy ‖ to serve as a canopy to [older canape fr. F. fr. L. fr. Gk]

Ca·nos·sa (kənósə) a hamlet near Reggio in N. Italy, the scene of Emperor Henry IV's penance (1077) to Pope Gregory VII

Ca·no·va (kənóuvə), Antonio (1757–1822), Italian neoclassical sculptor. He mingled classical forms and conventions with a cult of the sublime, heroic and demonic

can't alt. neg. of CAN

cant (kænt) 1. n. an external angle of slope ‖ an inclination ‖ the bevel of a sloping surface, e.g. of a buttress ‖ a thrust or movement that tips or deflects an object 2. v.t. to tilt ‖ to deflect ‖ to set at an angle ‖ v.i. to assume a tilted position ‖ (naut.) to swing around [perh. O.F. cant, corner, edge]

cant 1. n. insincere or trite statements, esp. those expressing hypocritical piety ‖ jargon used by members of a particular class or profession, racing cant ‖ the secret jargon of thieves, tramps or gypsies ‖ temporarily fashionable phrases 2. adj. trite ‖ insincere ‖ (of words and phrases) used only by members of a particular group [O.N.F.=singing]

Can·tab. (kǽntæb) adj. of Cambridge University, M.A. (Cantab.) ‖ n. Cantabrigiensis]

can·ta·bi·le (kɑntábilei) adj. (mus.) song-like, flowing smoothly and melodiously [Ital.]

Can·ta·bri·an Mtns (kæntéibriən) (Span. Cordillera Cantabrica) a range (370 miles long) rising to over 8,000 ft in N. Spain, stretching from the Pyrenees to Cape Finisterre. It is rich in coal and iron

Can·ta·brig·i·an (kæntəbrídʒiːən) 1. adj. of the university or city of Cambridge, England 2. n. a student or graduate of Cambridge University ‖ a native or resident of Cambridge, England [fr. Cantabrigia, latinized name of Cambridge]

Can·tal (kɑtǽl) a department (area 2,229 sq. miles, pop. 169,000) of S. central France in the Massif Central. Chief town: Aurillac (*AUVERGNE)

can·ta·loupe, can·ta·loup (kǽnt'loup) n. Cucumis melo cantaloupensis, a variety of chiefly European muskmelon having a warty rind and orange flesh [after Cantalupo in Italy]

can·tan·ker·ous (kæntǽŋkərəs) adj. bad-tempered ‖ quarrelsome [etym. doubtful]

can·ta·ta (kəntátə) n. (mus.) an extended composition for chorus and solo voices, or chorus only, generally with an orchestral accompaniment. Some cantatas (esp. by Bach) are for solo voice or voices [Ital.]

cant dog (kænt) (Br.) a cant hook [Ital. canto, corner, edge]

can·teen (kæntí:n) n. the restaurant of a large institution, e.g. a factory or college ‖ a shop in a military camp or barracks, selling food, liquor, etc. ‖ a box of cooking utensils for army use ‖ a water bottle ‖ (Br.) a case containing cutlery, for household use [F. cantine fr. Ital. cantina, cellar, etym. doubtful]

can·ter (kǽntər) 1. n. the gait of a horse between a trot and a gallop **to win at a canter** to win easily 2. v.i. to move at a canter ‖ v.t. to

make (a horse) move at a canter [short for Canterbury pace, the easy pace at which Canterbury pilgrims rode]

Can·ter·bur·y (kǽntərberi:, kǽntərbari:) a city and county borough (pop. 34,510) in Kent, England, on River Stour, the seat of the archbishop and primate of England. An important Roman town, it became the capital of the Saxon kingdom of Kent and was chosen (597) by St Augustine as the center from which to convert the English. The cathedral (11th–12th cc.) was the scene of the martyrdom of St Thomas Becket (1170). University of Kent (1964)

Canterbury a region (area 16,769 sq. miles, pop. 380,000) of South Island, New Zealand. Chief city: Christchurch. The fertile Canterbury Plain occupies a wide coastal belt, and extends into the interior. Products: wheat, wool, frozen meat, skins and hides, butter, cheese

Canterbury bell the cultivated campanula with pink, mauve or white, large, bell-shaped flowers [fr. the bells on the harness of Canterbury pilgrims' horses]

can·thar·i·des (kænθǽridi:z) pl. n. a pharmaceutical preparation made from dried beetles, esp. the blister beetle or Spanish fly, used externally as a counter-irritant and internally as a diuretic, and formerly used as an aphrodisiac [Gk, pl. of kantharis, blister fly]

can·thar·i·din ($C_{10}H_{12}O_4$) (kænθǽridin) n. active chemical in cantharides and other insect-derived preparations; used medically as a counter-irritant

can·thar·is (kǽnθæris) pl. **cantharides** n. a member of Cantharis, fam. Trochelidae, a genus of coleopterous insects [Mod. L. fr. Gk]

cant hook (Am.=Br. cant dog) an iron hook with a long wooden handle, used for rolling logs

can·thus (kǽnθəs) pl. **can·thi** (kǽnθai) n. the corner of each side of the eye [L. fr. Gk]

can·ti·cle (kǽntik'l) n. a short hymn or chant, esp. one from the Bible and included in the Roman Catholic and Anglican liturgies, e.g. Te Deum, Magnificat, and Nunc Dimittis **Can·ti·cles** (Bible) the Song of Solomon [fr. L. canticulum, little song]

Can·ti·gny (kɑti:nji:) a village in Somme, France, site of the first offensive (May 28, 1918) by U.S. troops in the 1st world war, which forced the Germans to retreat

can·ti·lev·er (kǽntilevər, kǽntiljːvər) n. (mach.) a horizontal part projecting beyond a pier etc., which supports it at one end only ‖ a girder or beam projecting from a wall and supporting a balcony or projecting piece of roof etc.

cantilever bridge a bridge, the span of which is supported by cantilevers which project from the piers on which it rests and which meet in the center of the span, where they are joined together

cantilever spring a laminated spring, supported at one end and bearing a load at its center and at the other end

can·tle (kǽnt'l) n. the high part at the back of a saddle (cf. POMMEL) [O.F. cantel, dim. of cant, corner]

can·to (kǽntou) n. a chief division of a long poem [Ital.=song]

Can·ton (kæntón) *KWANGCHOW

can·ton (kǽntən) 1. n. a division of a country, esp. a Swiss state ‖ (heraldry, kǽnten) a division of the upper part of a shield, less than a quarter of the shield in area 2. v.t. to divide into cantons ‖ (kæntón, kæntóun, Br. kæntú:n) to quarter (soldiers) [O.F. canton, corner]

Canton and En·der·bur·y Islands (éndərberi:) *PHOENIX ISLANDS

Can·ton·ese (kæntəní:z) 1. n. the Chinese dialect spoken in Kwangtung and Kwangsi provinces and in Hong Kong ‖ a native or inhabitant of Kwangtung province 2. adj. of or relating to Cantonese or a Cantonese [fr. CANTON, former name of Kwangchow, capital of Kwangtung]

can·ton·ment (kæntónmənt, kæntóunmənt, Br. kæntú:nmənt) n. quarters occupied by troops on a more than temporary but less than permanent basis [F. cantonnement]

Can·tor (kǽntər, kántɔr) Georg (1845–1918), German mathematician who investigated the properties of irrational and infinite numbers

can·tor (kǽntər) n. the leader of a church choir, a precentor ‖ the singer of the liturgy and leader of chanting in a synagogue **can·to·ri·al** (kæntóːriəl, kæntóuriːəl) adj. pertaining to the north side of the choir in a church (cf. DECANAL) [L.=a singer]

can·tus fir·mus (kǽntəsfə́:rməs) n. (mus.) a melody used (14th-17th cc.) as the basis of a composition, against which new melodies were set in counterpoint ‖ a set melody against which a student must write a counterpoint [L.=fixed song]

Ca·nute (kənú:t, kənjú:t) *CNUT

can·vas, can·vass (kǽnvəs) n. a strong, coarse cloth of unbleached hemp or flax, used for sails, tents, and as a surface for painting on in oils ‖ a light, openweave material used for embroidery ‖ an oil painting on canvas ‖ tents or sails collectively **under canvas** in tents ‖ (of a ship) with sails spread [M.E. *canevas* fr. O.N.F.]

canvas v.t. *CANVASS

can·vas·back (kǽnvəsbæk) n. *Aythya valisineria,* a North American duck (about 20 ins. in length) with black, white, chestnut and slate-colored plumage

canvass n. *CANVAS

can·vass, can·vas (kǽnvəs) **1.** v.t. to seek votes, business orders, subscriptions, etc., from (potential supporters, clients, etc.) ‖ to ascertain (public opinion) by interrogating people in a certain area, etc. ‖ to discuss (a subject) thoroughly ‖ to examine (election returns) for accuracy ‖ (*Br.*) to put forward (an idea) for consideration ‖ v.i. to seek votes, subscriptions etc. **2.** n. a seeking of support, votes etc. ‖ a survey of public opinion regarding a future election etc. **cán·vass·er** n. someone who canvasses ‖ (*Am.=Br.* scrutineer) a person who checks the validity of ballot papers in an election [CANVAS, (obs.) to toss in a sheet]

can·yon, ca·ñon (kǽnjən) n. a deep gorge or natural cleft, with very steep sides, often containing a stream [Span. *cañon,* tube]

can·zo·net (kænzənét) n. (*hist.*) a light song, resembling (but simpler than) a madrigal [fr. Ital. *canzonetta,* short song]

Cão (kaun), Diogo (Diogo Cam), Portuguese navigator. He explored much of the west coast of Africa, and was the first European known to have visited the mouth of the Congo (1482)

Cao·da·ism (kaudáiizəm) n. an Indochinese religion fusing teachings of Buddhism, Confucianism, Christianity, Spiritualism and Taoism. It dates from 1926 **Cao·dá·ist** n. [fr. Vietnamese *Cao Dai,* great palace]

CAORF (*computer acronym*) for computer aides operation research facility, which is used to simulate aerospace conditions

caou·tchouc (káutʃuk) n. pure rubber [F. fr. Tupi]

cap (kæp) **1.** n. a usually brimless head covering ‖ any caplike cover, e.g. on a bottle or fountain pen ‖ a charge (for igniting explosive in a cartridge) ‖ a piece of paper containing a very little explosive used to make toy pistols go bang ‖ (*fox hunting*) a payment for a day's hunting by nonmembers of the hunt association ‖ (*hist.*) a woman's headdress of lace, silk or muslin ‖ (*sports*) a headdress of special form and color denoting membership of a team **if the cap fits** (*Br.=Am.* if the shoe fits) an expression used to invite an individual to apply particularly to himself the uncomfortable truth of some general statement ('wear it' being understood) ‖ (*Br. med.*) diaphragm-like contraceptive *syn.* cervical cap **2.** v.t. pres. part. **cap·ping** past and past part. **capped** to put a cap on (something) ‖ to cover the top or end of (an object) with metal etc. ‖ to cover as if with a cap, *mountains capped with snow* ‖ to put the finishing touch to or come as a climax to ‖ (*Br.*) to give (a player) his cap as a sign that he is included in a cricket team etc. ‖ (*Scot.*) to give a university degree to **to cap a quotation** (or **joke** or **story**) to follow a speaker with another quotation (or joke or story) on the same theme as his [O.E. *cæppe* fr. L.L.]

cap. capital letter ‖ capital city

ca·pa·bil·i·ty (keipəbíliti) pl. **ca·pa·bil·i·ties** n. the quality of being capable, ability ‖ ability to be developed, exploited etc. ‖ (*pl.*) potentially excellent performance

ca·pa·ble (kéipəb'l) adj. able, having many capacities **capable of** with the ability for ‖ sufficiently wicked or foolish for, *he is quite capable of lying under oath* [F.]

ca·pa·cious (kəpéiʃəs) adj. able to hold a large amount [fr. L. *capax,* able]

ca·pac·i·tance (kəpǽsitəns) n. (*elec.*) the property of a nonconductor by which it stores electrical energy when separated surfaces of the nonconductor are maintained at a difference of potential. Capacitance is measured by the ratio of the charge induced to the potential difference and is proportional to the area of the conducting plates and the dielectric constant of the nonconducting material, and inversely proportional to the separation of the plates (mks unit: farad) ‖ part of a circuit possessing capacitance

ca·pac·i·tate (kəpǽsiteit) pres. part. **ca·pac·i·ta·ting** past and past part. **ca·pac·i·tat·ed** v.t. (*law*) to empower

capacitation (kəpæsitéiʃən) n. (*biol.*) process by which a sperm is enabled to penetrate and fertilize an egg—**capacitate** v.

ca·pac·i·tor (kəpǽsitər) n. (*elec.*) a device which gives capacitance, usually consisting of conducting plates or foil separated by layers of a dielectric. A potential difference applied across the plates induces a separation of charge centers in the dielectric, thus storing electrical energy

ca·pac·i·ty (kəpǽsiti:) pl. **ca·pac·i·ties** n. the ability to contain or accommodate ‖ the amount which can be contained or accommodated ‖ the ability of a factory etc. to manufacture or process its product, esp. this as a maximum, *working to capacity* ‖ mental ability ‖ faculty, *no capacity for concentration* ‖ an office or position with respect to a particular function, competence etc., *in his capacity as chairman* ‖ (*elec.*) capacitance **to be filled to capacity** to be completely full [older *capacyte* fr. F.]

cap and bells (*hist.*) a pointed cap with small bells worn by jesters

cap-à-pie (kæpəpí:) adv. (*hist.*) from head to foot, *armed cap-à-pie* [O.F.]

ca·par·i·son (kəpǽrisən) n. ceremonial equipment or dress ‖ an ornamental covering for a horse [F. *caparaisson* fr. Span.]

caparison v.t. to put trappings on (a horse) ‖ to dress or adorn richly [F. *caparassonner*]

cap coif (*cosmetology*) hairstyle cut for a natural neckline

CAPCOM (*acronym*) for capsule communicator, the space flight center liaison with astronauts during flight

cape (keip) n. a sleeveless outer garment hanging from the shoulders, worn fastened at the neck ‖ a very short version of this made up as an integral part of a coat or cloak [F. fr. Span. or Ital.]

cape n. a piece of land jutting out into the sea [fr. F. *cap,* fr. Ital.]

Cape Bret·on Island (brét'n, brít'n) an island (area 3,975 sq. miles) off the east coast of Canada, forming the northern part of Nova Scotia province

Cape buffalo *Syncerus caffer,* fam. *Bovidae,* a S. African buffalo, often savage

Cape Ca·nav·er·al (kənǽvərəl) *CAPE KENNEDY

Cape Coast a town and educational center (pop. 71,594) in Ghana, former capital of the Gold Coast. It was a center of the slave trade in the 16th and 17th cc. and was successively occupied by the Portuguese, Dutch and British

Cape Cod a sandy peninsula (65 miles long) in S.E. Massachusetts; popular resort area. The Pilgrims landed at its tip (Provincetown) in 1620

Cape Cod Bay a bay (c. 25 miles wide) at the southern extremity of Massachusetts Bay in E. Massachusetts, formed within the northwestern curve of Cape Cod peninsula

Cape Colony the name until 1910 of Cape Province

Cape Colored, *Br.* **Cape Coloured** a member of a small group of mixed white and nonwhite racial descent, without political status, dwelling in Cape Province, South Africa

Cape Dutch Afrikaans

Cape Farewell the southernmost point of Greenland

Cape gooseberry *Physalis peruviana,* fam. *Solanaceae,* a ground-cherry with an edible orange berry

Cape Horn a steep headland at the south of Horn Is., Tierra del Fuego, Chile, generally considered the southernmost point of South America

Cape jasmine *GARDENIA

Cape jumping hare *Pedetes cafer,* a S. African rodent about 2 ft long

Ča·pek (tʃápek), Karel (1890–1938), Czech dramatist, author of 'R.U.R.' and (in collaboration with his brother Joseph) of 'The Insect Play'

Cape Kennedy (formerly Cape Canaveral) a cape on the east coast of Canaveral Peninsula,

Florida, the site of a long-range rocket and earth satellite testing center

Cape of Good Hope a southerly promontory of Cape Peninsula, South Africa, discovered (1487) by Dias and rounded for the first time by Vasco da Gama (1497)

Cape Province (Cape of Good Hope Province) a province (area 278,380 sq. miles, pop. 5,091,000) in the Republic of South Africa, at the southern extremity of the continent. Capital: Cape Town. A series of plateaus lies between the mountain ranges of the Karroo. Agriculture: wheat and other cereals, fruit, grapes, tobacco, sheep. Resources: diamonds (major world source), copper, asbestos, manganese, fish. Industries: textiles, food processing, motor-vehicle assembly, chemicals, engineering. The first European settlement was established by the Dutch East India Company (1652) and ceded to Britain (1814). The province joined the Union of South Africa (1910)

ca·per (kéipər) **1.** v.i. to leap or jump about playfully **2.** n. a frisky leap or jump ‖ a fantastic antic [perh. shortened fr. CAPRIOLE]

caper n. *Capparis spinosa,* fam. *Capparidaceae,* a low trailing shrub with small dark-green leaves, and three-petaled white flowers with mauve stamens, growing in the Mediterranean region ‖ (*pl.*) its unopened flower buds pickled for use in sauces, relishes etc. [M.E. *caperis* fr. L. fr. Gk. It was taken as a plural and a new singular *caper* was formed]

cap·er·cail·lie (kæpərkéilji:) n. *Tetrao urogallus,* a European grouse almost as large as a turkey, with handsome black and brown plumage [fr. Gael. *capull coille,* great cock of the wood]

cap·er·cail·zie (kæpərkéilzi:) n. the capercaillie

Ca·per·na·um (kəpə́:rneiəm, kəpə́:rni:əm) an ancient town of Palestine on the northwest shore of the Sea of Galilee, the center of much of the ministry of Jesus

Capet, Hugh *HUGH CAPET

Ca·pe·tian (kəpí:ʃən) **1.** adj. pertaining to the kings of France (987–1328), succeeded by the related house of Valois **2.** n. one of the Capetian kings [after Hugh *Capet*]

Cape Town, Cape·town (kéiptaun) (Kaapstaad) the legislative capital (pop. 1,490,935) of South Africa and port of Cape Province, a commercial, industrial and tourist center. It was founded (1652) by the Dutch East India Co. as a revictualing station on the route to India. University

Cape Verde Islands (və:rd) officially the Republic of Cape Verde, a country (area 1,557 sq. miles, pop. 330,000) in the N. Atlantic, about 350 miles west of Cape Verde, Africa. Capital: Praia (pop. 37,500), on Santiago. There are 10 islands and 5 islets, the largest being Santo Antão (area 301 sq. miles) in the north (Barlavento group), and São Tiago (area 383 sq. miles) in the south (Sotavento group). Language: Creole and Portuguese. Religion: Roman Catholic and Animist. Highest point: Pico da Cano (9,281 ft), a volcano on Fogo. Droughts are frequent, but the mountain valleys are fertile. Average temperatures (F.): Praia 62° (Jan.), 92° (July). Rainfall: 10–20 ins. Exports: coffee, fish, salt. Other products: fruit, vegetables, nuts, tobacco, sugarcane, castor oil. Port and fueling station: Mindelo. The islands were sighted (1456) by a Venetian navigator, and were under Portuguese rule from 1495 until 1975, when it became independent

Cape York Peninsula an area of tropical jungle in N. Queensland, Australia, between the Gulf of Carpentaria and the Coral Sea

Cap Ha·i·tien (kæpæi:sjɛ̃) a port (pop. 54,691) on the north coast of Haiti. It was formerly the capital (to 1770) of Saint-Domingue and was (from 1811) Henri Christophe's capital

cap·il·la·ceous (kæpiléiʃəs) adj. hairlike ‖ capillary [fr. L. *capillaceus*]

cap·il·lar·i·ty (kæpilǽriti) n. (*physiol.*) the quality of being a capillary ‖ (*phys.*) a phenomenon in which the surface of a liquid where it is in contact with a solid is elevated or depressed, depending on differences between intermolecular attraction in the liquid and between the liquid and the solid. An example would be the rise and fall of a liquid in a capillary tube relative to its level outside. The tendency of a liquid to rise up or be depressed at the side of a floating body causes capillary attraction or repulsion between two floating bodies near one another (*SURFACE TENSION) [fr. F. *capillarité*]

cap·il·lar·y (kǽpileri:, *Br.* kəpíləri) **1.** *adj.* hairlike ‖ having a small bore or diameter **2.** *pl.* **cap·il·lar·ies** *n.* one of a system of minute thinwalled blood vessels separating arterial from venous circulation, serving to distribute blood to all the tissues of the body and as the locus of oxygen nutriment and waste-product exchange (*HEART) [fr. L. *capillaris*, of hair]

capillary action capillary

capillary attraction *CAPILLARITY

capillary repulsion *CAPILLARITY

cap·i·tal (kǽpit'l) *n.* the top or head of a pillar, pier or column [fr. L. *capitellum*, little head]

capital 1. *adj.* involving forfeiture of life, *capital punishment, a capital offense* ‖ chief, *capital city* ‖ very great, *capital importance* ‖ very good, *capital entertainment* ‖ having to do with capital (wealth), *capital goods* ‖ (of a letter of the alphabet) in its relatively large form, as used initially in proper nouns etc., e.g. A, B, C **2.** *n.* principal (cf. INCOME) ‖ the value of this in a given instance ‖ the chief city of a country, state etc., esp. the seat of government (or of a branch of it) or of the central administration ‖ the owners of wealth (only vis-à-vis 'labor') ‖ (*econ.*) the stock of goods and commodities in a country at any one time ‖ a capital letter [F.]

capital account an account of the owner's interest in the assets of a business ‖ (*pl., accounting*) net accounts of a business when liabilities have been deducted from assets

capital expenditure money spent on improvements or additions (including debts incurred for this purpose)

capital gain profit from the sale of assets

capital gains distribution dividend from a corporation that represents a sale of assets and is thus taxable as capital gains income

capital-intensive (kǽpit'linténsiv) *adj.* (*economics*) of production by a high ratio of equipment or other investment to the role of labor. *ant.* labor-intensive

cap·i·tal·ism (kǽpitəlizəm, *Br. also* kəpítəlizəm) *n.* an economic system in which the means of production, distribution and exchange are privately owned and operated for private profit

cap·i·tal·ist (kǽpitəlist, *Br. also* kəpítəlist) **1.** *n.* someone who owns capital stock used in business, or who has accumulated wealth from business **2.** *adj.* possessing capital ‖ defending or engaging in capitalism ‖ characterized by capitalism **cap·i·tal·is·tic** *adj.*

cap·i·tal·i·za·tion (kæpitəlizéifən, *Br. also* kəpitəlaizéifən) *n.* the permanent liabilities of a business, including outstanding stock

cap·i·tal·ize (kǽpitəlaiz, *Br.* kəpítəlaiz) *pres. part.* **cap·i·tal·iz·ing** *past* and *past part.* **cap·i·tal·ized** *v.t.* to use as capital ‖ to convert into capital ‖ to provide (a business) with capital ‖ to turn (something) to account ‖ to write with an initial capital letter ‖ to write in capitals

capital levy an exceptional, nonpermanent tax on property and assets, usually involving payment out of capital to deal with an emergency such as war. Levies may also be imposed in order to secure some redistribution of income and wealth

cap·i·tal·ly (kǽpitəli:) *adv.* in a capital manner, very well

capital ship a large warship: a battleship, battle cruiser or aircraft carrier

capital stock the total shares of a joint stock company, or their value

cap·i·tate (kǽpiteit) *adj.* (*anat.,* e.g. of certain bones) enlarged or swollen at the tip ‖ (*bot.,* e.g. in a compound stigma and some inflorescences) gathered into a mass at the apex **cáp·i·tat·ed** *adj.* [fr. L. *capitatus* fr. *caput*, head]

cap·i·ta·tion (kæpitéifən) *n.* a tax levied per head ‖ a uniform fee for each of several people ‖ method of payment for health services in which an individual or institution is paid a fixed per capita amount for each person served, without regard to the actual number or nature of services provided to each person [fr. L. *capitatio* (*capitationis*), poll tax]

capitation grant a grant of money, at so much per head

cap·i·tol (kǽpit'l) *n.* the building in which a state legislature meets **the Capitol** (*hist.*) temple of Jupiter in Rome ‖ the Congressional building in Washington, D.C. [M.E. *capitolie, capitoile* fr. O.N.F. fr. L. *capitolium,* citadel on a hill, the Capitol]

Cap·i·to·line Hill (kǽpit'lain, *Br.* kəpítəlain) one of the seven hills of ancient Rome, esp. the summit of it, on which the Capitol stood

ca·pit·u·lar (kəpítfulər) **1.** *adj.* of the chapter of a cathedral ‖ (*physiol.*) of a capitulum **2.** *n.* (*pl.*) the statutes of an ecclesiastical chapter or council [fr. L. *capitularis* fr. *capitulum,* chapter]

ca·pit·u·lar·y (kəpítfuleri:) **1.** *pl.* **ca·pit·u·lar·ies** *n.* (*hist.*) a collection of ordinances, esp. of the Frankish kings ‖ a member of an ecclesiastical chapter **2.** *adj.* of an ecclesiastical chapter [fr. M.L. *capitularius,* of a chapter]

ca·pit·u·late (kəpítfuleit) *pres. part.* **ca·pit·u·lat·ing** *past* and *past part.* **ca·pit·u·lat·ed** *v.i.* to surrender, often on terms agreed by both sides [fr. M.L. *capitulare* (*capitulatus*), to draw up under headings]

ca·pit·u·la·tion (kəpitfuléifən) *n.* a surrender upon terms [fr. M.L. *capitulatio* (*capitulationis*), a statement under headings]

ca·pit·u·lum (kəpítfuləm) *pl.* **ca·pit·u·la** (kəpítfulə) *n.* (*bot.*) a rounded or flattened head of sessile flowers, a flower head ‖ (*anat.*) the knoblike head of a bone [L.=little head]

capo (kápou) *n.* (*slang*) chief of a crime family

Cap·o·dis·tri·as (kæpoudístri:əs), Count Joannis Antonios (1776–1831), Greek statesman. He was Russian foreign minister (1820–2). He became president of Greece (1827–31). He was assassinated

ca·pon (kéipɒn, kéipən) *n.* a castrated cock [O.E. *capun* fr. L.]

Ca·po·te (kəpóuti:), Truman (1924–84), American author. Most of his work has a Southern background. Among his novels and stories are 'Other Voices, Other Rooms' (1948), 'The Grass Harp' (1951), 'Breakfast at Tiffany's' (1958), 'Music for Chameleons' (1980). 'In Cold Blood' (1966) is a piece of reporting treated as if it were fiction and given a heightened effect

ca·pote (kəpóut) *n.* a long cloak with a hood [F. dim of *cape,* cape]

Cap·pa·do·cia (kæpədóufə) a high plateau region in E. Turkey. First a Persian satrapy, then an independent kingdom, it became a Roman province (17 A.D.)

Cap·pel·le (kæpéle), Jan van der (1624/5–79), Dutch marine painter

cappuccino (kʌpjətfí:no:) *n.* espresso coffee mixed with frothed hot milk, often topped with cinnamon or whipped cream

cap·re·o·late (kǽpri:əleit) (*bot.*) having a tendril ‖ tendril-shaped [fr. L. *capreolus,* tendril]

Ca·pri (kúpri:, kɑprí:) an Italian island (area 5 sq. miles, pop. 8,000) on the south side of the Gulf of Naples: tourism

ca·pric·ci·o (kəprí:tfi:ou) *n.* (*mus.*) a caprice [Ital.]

ca·price (kəprí:s) *n.* a sudden and illogical fancy, a whim ‖ an arbitrary action ‖ (*mus.*) a light, gay piece, esp. used of certain 17th-c. keyboard works [F. fr. Ital.]

ca·pri·cious (kəprífəs) *adj.* unreliable, ruled by whims ‖ changeable, *capricious winds* [fr. F. *capricieux*]

Cap·ri·corn (kǽprikɔrn) *n.* a southern constellation ‖ the tenth sign of the zodiac, represented as a goat ‖ *TROPIC OF CAPRICORN [fr. L. *capricornus* fr. *caper,* goat+ *cornu,* horn]

cap·ri·fi·ca·tion (kæprifikéifən) *n.* pollination of the flowers of the cultivated fig tree by chalcid insects from the wild fig tree [fr. L. *caprificatio* (*caprificationis*) fr. *caprificus,* wild fig]

cap·ri·fig (kǽprifig) *n. Ficus carica sylvestris,* the wild and semicultivated fig which grows in S. Europe and Asia Minor and from which the fig wasp pollinates the edible fig [F. *caprifique*]

cap·ri·ole (kǽpri:oul) **1.** *n.* a leap or caper ‖ a horse's jump completely off the ground without moving forward **2.** *v.i. pres. part.* **cap·ri·ol·ing** *past* and *past part.* **cap·ri·oled** to leap or caper ‖ (of a horse) to make a capriole [F.]

Capri pants (kæprí:) women's closefitting pants for informal wear, with tapered legs slit to the ankle at the bottoms *syn* Capriso

Ca·pri·vi (kɑprí:vi:), Leo, Count von (1831–99), German soldier and statesman. He was a chief of staff in the Franco-Prussian War (1870–1), chief of the admiralty (1883–8), and chancellor of the German Empire (1890–4)

cap·sa·i·cin (kæpséiisin) *n.* a colorless crystalline phenolic amide, $C_9H_{17}CO$ $NHCH_2C_6H_3$-$(OCH_3)OH$, a strong irritant found e.g. in cayenne pepper

cap·si·cum (kǽpsikəm) *n.* a member of *Capsicum,* fam. Solanaceae, a genus of tropical plants or shrubs bearing pungent fruit called peppers ‖

the dried fruit of *Capsicum frutescens,* used as a gastric stimulant [Mod. L. prob. fr. *capsa,* a box]

capsid (kǽpsid) *n.* protein shell of a virus. — **capsidal** *adj. syn* capsomere

cap·size (kǽpsaiz, kæpsáiz) *pres. part.* **cap·sizing** *past* and *past part.* **cap·sized** *v.t.* to upset or cause to founder (esp. a boat or ship) ‖ *v.i.* to turn over or become overturned on water [etym. doubtful]

cap·stan (kǽpstən) *n.* (*naut.*) a revolving barrel or drum for raising weights. A cable (e.g. of an anchor) or the halyard of a heavy sail is wound around it [F. *cabestan*]

capstan lathe (*Br.*) a turret lathe

cap·stone (kǽpstoun) *n.* a coping stone ‖ something that crowns the rest, culmination

cap·su·lar (kǽpsələr) *adj.* of or like a capsule

cap·sule (kǽpsəl, *Br.* kǽpsju:l) *n.* (*anat.*) a saclike membrane enclosing an organ ‖ (*biol.*) a thickened slime layer around certain bacteria ‖ (*bot.*) any closed boxlike vessel containing seeds, spores or fruits, e.g. the sporogonium in bryophytes ‖ a dry, dehiscent fruit composed of two or more carpels ‖ (*zool.*) a membrane surrounding nerve cells of sympathetic ganglia ‖ (*anat.*) either of two layers of white matter in the cerebrum ‖ (*med.*) a small case of gelatin etc., enclosing a medicinal dose ‖ a sealed, pressurized cabin for extremely high-altitude or space flight that provides an acceptable environment for humans, animals, or equipment ‖ an ejectable sealed space-vehicle cabin having automatic devices for safe return of the occupants to the earth's surface ‖ a metal bottle top [F.]

Capt. Captain

cap·tain (kǽptən) **1.** *n.* (*navy*) an officer above a commander and below a rear admiral in rank ‖ (by courtesy) the commander or master of a vessel ‖ (*army*) an officer above a lieutenant and below a major in rank ‖ an officer of the same rank in the U.S. air force or marine corps ‖ a leader, chief ‖ the leader of a team in sports **2.** *v.t.* to be captain of **cáp·tain·cy** *n.* [M.E. *capitain* fr. O.F.]

cap·tion (kǽpfən) *n.* the heading of a chapter ‖ the headline of a newspaper article ‖ a legend to an illustration, or, in silent films, to an image ‖ (*law*) part of a document (cf. INDICTMENT) showing 'where, when and by what authority it is taken, found or executed' [fr. L. *captio* (*captionis*), seizure]

cap·tious (kǽpfəs) *adj.* faultfinding, critical ‖ meant to entangle, *captious questioning* [fr. L. *captiosus,* liable to catch one]

cap·ti·vate (kǽptiveit) *pres. part.* **cap·ti·vat·ing** *past* and *past part.* **cap·ti·vat·ed** *v.t.* to charm, enchant **cap·ti·vá·tion** *n.* [fr. L.L. *captivare* (*captivatus*), to take captive]

cap·tive (kǽptiv) **1.** *n.* a prisoner, esp. a prisoner of war **2.** *adj.* imprisoned, kept in confinement (used both of people and animals) **to hold captive** to keep in prison or in confinement ‖ to fascinate (a listener etc.) **to make** (or **take**) **captive** to capture [F. *captif, captive*]

cap·tiv·i·ty (kæptíviti:) *pl.* **cap·tiv·i·ties** *n.* the period of being a captive ‖ confinement [fr. L. *captivitas* (*captivitatus*)]

Captivity, the Babylonian the deportation (586 B.C.) of the Jewish people to Babylonia by Nebuchadnezzar II. They were allowed to return (538 B.C.) by Cyrus II ‖ the exile of the papacy in Avignon (1309–77)

cap·tor (kǽptər) *n.* someone who takes someone or something captive [L.]

cap·tress (kǽptris) *n.* a female captor

cap·ture (kǽptfər) **1.** *v.t.* to get (someone) into one's power as a prisoner ‖ to subdue, dominate or overcome and get possession of, *it captured our imagination* ‖ to gain control of despite obstacles, *to capture a market* ‖ (*chess, cards*) to put out of play (a card or piece of inferior value) ‖ *v.i.* (*chess*) to take an opponent's chessman **2.** *n.* a capturing or being captured ‖ a thing or person captured [F. fr. L. *captura*]

Cap·u·chin (kǽpju:tfin, kǽpju:fin) *n.* a Franciscan friar of the strict, reformed order of 1528

cap·u·chin a woman's hooded cloak [F. fr. Ital. *capuccino,* hood]

capuchin monkey a member of *Cebus,* a genus of South American monkeys with short-haired heads and hairless foreheads, esp. *C. capucinus*

cap·y·ba·ra (kæpəbárə) *n. Hydrochaerus capybara,* the waterhog of South America, the largest rodent (3–4 ft.). It is allied to the guinea

CONCISE PRONUNCIATION KEY: **(a)** æ, c*a*t; ɑ, c*ar*; ɔ, f*aw*n; ei, sn*a*ke. **(e)** e, h*e*n; i:, sh*ee*p; iə, d*eer*; εə, b*ear*. **(i)** i, f*i*sh; ai, t*i*ger; ə:, b*ir*d. **(o)** o, *o*x; au, c*ow*; ou, g*oa*t; u, p*oor*; ɔi, r*oy*al. **(u)** ʌ, d*u*ck; u, b*u*ll; u:, g*oo*se; ə, *a*bacillus; ju:, c*u*be. x, lo*ch*; θ, *th*ink; δ, *b*o*th*er; z, *Z*en; ʒ, cor*s*age; dʒ, sa*v*age; ŋ, ora*ng*utang; j, *y*ak; ʃ, *fi*sh; tʃ, fe*tch*; 'l, rabb*le*; 'n, redd*en.* Complete pronunciation key appears inside front cover.

pig, aquatic, and mainly vegetarian. It damages sugarcane plantations [native Brazilian] **Ca·que·tá** (kαketá) *JAPURÁ

car (kαr) *n.* a wheeled vehicle, esp. an automobile ‖ a passenger conveyance in an elevator ‖ any railroad carriage or wagon ‖ (*Br.*) any of certain railroad carriages, *buffet car* [M.E. *carre* fr. O.N.F., perh. of Celt. origin]

ca·ra·ba·o (kαrəbáou) *n.* the water buffalo of the Philippine Islands [Span. fr. Malay *rbau*]

Car·a·bo·bo (kαrαbóbɔ) a village in Venezuela, southeast of Valencia, site of Bolívar's victory (1821) which secured the independence of Venezuela

car·a·cal (kærəkæl) *n. Felis caracal,* a lynx found in warm parts of Africa and Asia [F. fr. Turk. *garah-gulak,* black ear]

Car·a·cal·la (kærəkǽlə) (Marcus Aurelius Severus Antoninus, 188–217), Roman emperor (211–17), whose edict of 212 greatly extended Roman citizenship. He was assassinated by Macrinus

ca·ra·ca·ra (kαrəkárə) *n.* any of several South American falconlike hawks, esp. of genera *Polyborus* and *Ibycter* [Span. and Port. fr. Tupian]

Ca·ra·cas (kαrǽkəs) the capital (pop. 1,658,500) of Venezuela, 8 miles from La Guaira, its port on the Caribbean, and an industrial center: paper, cement, food products, textiles, leather. Founded (1567) by Diego de Caracas, it became (1777) the seat of the Captaincy General of Venezuela and (1786) the seat of the Audiencia of Caracas, under the loose control of the viceroy of Nueva Granada. The University of Caracas was founded in 1725. It was the site of the proclamation (July 5, 1811) of the first independent South American republic. An earthquake in 1812 destroyed half the city, killing 12,000 people

car·a·cole (kærəkoul) **1.** *n.* a rider's half-turn to left or right, or a succession of alternate half-left and half-right turns **2.** *v.i. pres. part.* **car·a·col·ing** *past* and *past part.* **car·a·coled** to perform a caracole [F. fr. Ital. fr. Span. *caracol,* spiral snail shell]

car·a·cul (kærək'l) *n.* the skin of a Karakul lamb when the curl begins to be less tight ‖ a cloth imitation of astrakhan [Russ.]

ca·rafe (kəræf, kəráf) *n.* a glass bottle for table water or wine [F. fr. Ital. fr. Arab.]

car·a·mel (kærəməl, kærəmel) *n.* (*cooking*) sugar melted and slightly burned over a low flame ‖ a semi-hard candy that needs chewing ‖ a shade of light brown [F. fr. Span.]

car·a·pace (kærəpeis) *n.* the chitinous or bony shield covering the whole or part of the back of turtles, crabs, lobsters etc. [F. fr. Span., origin unknown]

car·at, kar·at (kærət) *n.* an international measure of weight used for gems, equivalent to 200 milligrams ‖ (*Br.*) karat (measure of the purity of gold) [F. fr. Ital.]

Ca·ra·vag·gio (kærəvádʒou), Michelangelo Merisi (1573–1610), Italian painter. He introduced the strictly 'lifelike' in his paintings, which are almost overwhelmingly tense and dramatic. His great influence on others was chiefly through his use of dramatic chiaroscuro

car·a·van (kærəvæn) *n.* a company of people, e.g. merchants or pilgrims, traveling together for safety, esp. in desert areas of Asia and Africa ‖ a covered wagon, esp. as still used by some gypsies ‖ (*Br.*) a trailer (containing sleeping quarters) [earlier *carouan* fr. Pers.]

caravaner (kærəvænər) *n.* **1.** one who travels with a group of trailers. **2.** (*Br.*) one who travels in a trailer

caravan park (*Br.*) trailer park

car·a·van·sa·ry (kærəvænsəri:) *pl.* **car·a·van·sa·ries** *n.* a caravanserai

car·a·van·se·rai (kærəvænsərai) *n.* an Eastern inn, built around a large court, where caravans can stop for the night [ult. fr. Pers. *kārwān,* caravan + *sarāi,* palace]

car·a·vel (kærəvel) *n.* a small, fast sailing ship of the 15th and 16th cc. [F. *caravelle* fr. Ital. perh. fr. Span.]

Car·a·velle (kærəvel) *n.* twin-engine transport plane (SE 210) for 64–80 passengers produced in France by SudAviation since 1955

car·a·way (kærəwei) *n. Carum carvi,* fam. *Umbelliferae,* a plant with flat yellow flower heads, and seeds used as flavoring. They contain the aromatic oil carvone [perh. fr. M.L. *caᵛui*]

car·bam·ide (kαrbǽmaid, kαrbəmaid) *n.* urea

car·bar·yl [$C_{12}H_{11}O_2N$] (kárbəril) *n.* a biodegradable insecticide used in agriculture

car·baz·o·chrome [$C_{10}H_{12}N_4O_3$] (kαrbéizəkroum) *n. pharm.* systemic hemostatic agent used to control capillary bleeding; marketed as Andrestat, Andrenosem, and Anaroxyl

car·ba·zole (kάrbəzoul) *n.* a weakly basic crystalline compound ($C_6H_4)_2$NH found with anthracene in coal tar. It is used for a number of dyes

carbecue (kárbəkju:) *n.* device for turning an abandoned automobile into compact metal by applying heat and pressure

carbed (kάrbed) *n.* portable bed adapted for auto travel

car·ben·i·cil·lin [$C_{17}H_{18}N_2O_6S$] (kαrbenəsílin) *n.* (*pharm.*) form of semisynthetic penicillin with a broad-spectrum effect against gram-negative and gram-positive organisms; marketed as Geopen and Pyopen

car·bide (kárbaid) *n.* (*chem.*) a binary compound of carbon usually with a metal ‖ calcium carbide

car·bine (kárbain) *n.* (*hist.*) a short, light, cavalry rifle [older *carabine* fr. F.]

car·bi·nol (kárbinoul, kárbinɔl) *n.* methyl alcohol [fr. *carbin,* name used by Kolbe for the methyl radical]

Car·bo·caine [$C_{15}H_{22}N_2O$] (kάrbəkein) *n.* (*pharm.*) trade name for mepivacaine, painkiller used by athletes to enable them to continue to play while injured

car·bo·cy·clic (kαrbousáiklik) *adj.* (*chem.*) of organic compounds which contain a ring of carbon atoms, esp. alicyclic and aromatic compounds

car·bo·hy·drate (kαrbouháidreit) *n.* one of a biologically important group of neutral organic chemicals composed of carbon, hydrogen and oxygen and including sugars, starches and celluloses. Naturally occurring carbohydrates are produced by green plants photosynthetically from carbon dioxide and water, and are used for providing the energy necessary for growth and other functions. The carbohydrates are a major class of animal foods, the others being proteins and fats

car·bol·ic acid (kαrbólik) phenol

car·bon, (kárbən) *n.* a tetravalent element (symbol C, at. no. 6, at. mass 12.01115). It occurs in crystalline forms as diamonds and graphite. Combined with other elements, it occurs in all living things, and in carbonates in the earth's crust. It can be obtained in an amorphous condition as lampblack and charcoal. The study of carbon compounds constitutes organic chemistry. The radioactive isotope, carbon 14, is used as a tracer and in dating archaeological and geological specimens [fr. F. *carbone*]

car·bo·na·ceous (kαrbənéiʃəs) *adj.* like coal or charcoal ‖ (*chem.*) containing carbon ‖ (*geol.*) containing coal [fr. L. *carbo* (*carbonis*), coal]

car·bo·na·do (kαrbənéidou) *n.* a hard black aggregate of diamond particles in a diamond matrix, with valuable industrial uses [Span. *carbonada* fr. *carbón,* charcoal]

carbon arc a continuous discharge of intense light and heat produced when an electric current crosses the gap between two carbon rods close together. It is carried by the vapor of the electrode. The carbon arc is the principle of the arc lamp (*ARC)

Car·bo·na·ri (kαrbənári:) the members of a secret society, dedicated to liberal ideas, which originated (1807) in S. Italy and appeared (1820) in France and Spain. Its part in the fight for Italian unity was taken over by the Risorgimento

car·bon·a·ta·tion (kαrbənətéiʃən) *n.* carbonation

car·bon·ate (kárbəneit, kárbənit) **1.** *n.* a salt of carbonic acid, the acid radical being $(CO_3)^{2-}$ **2.** (kárbəneit) *v.t. pres. part.* **car·bon·at·ing** *past* and *past part.* **car·bon·at·ed** to impregnate (a liquid) with carbon dioxide under pressure (e.g. aerated water) or with carbonic acid ‖ (*chem.*) to form into a carbonate [F. fr. Mod. L.]

car·bon·a·tion (kαrbənéiʃən) *n.* a saturation or reaction with carbon dioxide

carbon black colloidal carbon, usually obtained by combustion and used as a pigment

carbon copy the duplicate of a letter etc. made by using carbon paper

carbon cycle (*astron.*) the process, involving a cycle of thermonuclear reactions by which hydrogen is converted to helium, held to be the source of energy for the sun and for many stars.

Carbon isotopes and nitrogen isotopes play a catalytic role ‖ the cycle followed by carbon in living beings. It consists of photosynthesis by plants and oxidation of photosynthetic products by plants and animals which obtain their food directly or indirectly from them, back to carbon dioxide

carbon dating technique for determining age of an ancient artifact by measuring the proportion to residual carbon of radioactive carbon 14 (14_c), which has a half-life of 5568 yrs). *syn* carbon 14 dating, radiocarbon dating. —**carbon·date** *v.*

carbon dioxide a colorless, heavy gas, CO_2, that does not support combustion, that dissolves in water to form carbonic acid and that is formed by the oxidation of carbon-containing compounds (e.g. in animal respiration) and by the action of acid on carbonates. It is absorbed from air by green plants in the first step of photosynthesis, and it has many scientific, technical and industrial uses

carbon dioxide laser laser utilizing carbon dioxide, helium, and nitrogen. It is used for communication, welding, heating, cutting, drilling, evaporating, and optical radar

carbon disulfide an inflammable liquid, CS_2, used as an insecticide and as a solvent in the vulcanization of rubber and in the manufacture of viscose rayon

carbon fiber carbonized acrylic fiber with great strength and light weight

car·bon·ic (kαrbónik) *adj.* pertaining to or obtained from carbon

carbonic acid a weak dibasic acid, H_2CO_3, known only in aqueous solution and by its salts, the carbonates

carbonic acid gas carbon dioxide

car·bon·if·er·ous (kαrbənífərəs) *adj.* producing coal **Carboniferous** of the period or system of the Paleozoic era characterized by coal-bearing rocks (*GEOLOGICAL TIME) **the Carboniferous** the Carboniferous period or system of rocks [fr. L. *carbo* (*carbonis*), coal + *ferre,* to bear]

car·bon·i·za·tion (kαrbənizéiʃən) *n.* the process of carbonizing

car·bon·ize (kárbənaiz) *pres. part.* **car·bon·iz·ing** *past* and *past part.* **car·bon·ized** *v.t.* to convert into carbon ‖ to turn (coal or wood) by slow combustion into coke or charcoal ‖ to char ‖ to cover (paper) with carbon

carbon microphone (*acoustics*) microphone in which the diaphragm responds to varying pressures, changing the resistance of a container of carbon granules

carbon monoxide a colorless, odorless, highly toxic gas, CO, that may be produced by the incomplete combustion of carbon, e.g. when coal is converted to coke. It burns with a blue flame to give carbon dioxide

carbon monoxide laser (*optics*) gas laser utilizing carbon monoxide

carbon paper a paper coated on one side with loosely adhering dye (originally a carbon composition) used for transferring impressions of writing, typewriting, drawing etc.

carbon spot black spot on a coin, esp. noted in numismatics

carbon star (*astron.*) star with a reddish appearance

carbon tet·ra·chlo·ride (tetrəklóraid, tetrəklóuraid) a colorless, toxic, noninflammable liquid, CCl_4, used as a solvent (e.g. for greases) and as a fire extinguisher

car·bon·yl (kárbənil) *n.* the divalent radical CO in a compound, e.g. in $COCl_2$ (phosgene) ‖ a compound of a metal with the CO group, e.g. nickel carbonyl $Ni(CO)_4$

car·borne (kárbɔrn) *n.* carbon-bonarhydrogen compound with exceptional thermal qualities; used in producing polymers

Car·bo·run·dum (kαrbərándəm) *n.* any of a range of abrasives, esp. silicon carbide [Trademark]

car·box·yl (kαrbóksəl) *n.* the monovalent COOH group or radical characteristic of a large class of organic acids, e.g. acetic acid ‖ the monovalent ion RCOO- formed by the ionization of a carboxylic acid (where R is any organic group) **car·box·yl·ic** (kαrbɔksílik) *adj.* of or containing one or more carboxyl groups [CARBON + OXYGEN]

car·boy (kárbɔi) *n.* a large globular bottle (protected, e.g. by wickerwork) used for containing and transporting acids and other corrosive liquids, or distilled water [fr. Pers. *qarābah,* large flagon]

CONCISE PRONUNCIATION KEY: **(a)** æ, c*a*t; α, c*a*r; ɔ f*a*wn; ei, sn*a*ke. **(e)** e, h*e*n; i:, sh*ee*p; iə, d*ee*r; εə, b*ea*r. **(i)** i, f*i*sh; ai, t*i*ger; ə:, b*i*rd. **(o)** o, *o*x; au, c*ow*; ou, g*oa*t; u, p*oo*r; ɔi, r*oy*al. **(u)** ʌ, d*u*ck; u, b*u*ll; u:, g*oo*se; ə, b*a*cillus; ju:, c*u*be. x, lo*ch*; θ, *th*ink; ð, bo*th*er; z, *Z*en; ʒ, cor*s*age. dʒ, sava*g*e; ŋ, oranguta*ng*; j, *y*ak; ʃ, *f*ish; tʃ, fe*tch*; 'l, rabb*le*; 'n, redd*en*. Complete pronunciation key appears inside front cover.

car·bun·cle (kárbʌŋkʼl) *n.* a garnet cut in a boss, or cabochon ‖ a painful infection of the skin, deeper and severer than a boil **car·bún·cu·lar** *adj.* like a carbuncle [M.E. *charbucle* fr. O.F.]

car·bu·rant (kárbərənt, kárbjərənt) *n.* the fuel used in carburation [F.]

car·bu·ra·tion (karboréiʃən, kɒrbjəréʃən) *n.* carburetion [F.]

car·bu·ret (kárbəreit, kárbjəret) *pres. part.* **car·bu·ret·ing, car·bu·ret·ting** *past* and *past part.* **car·bu·ret·ed, car·bu·ret·ted** *v.t.* to combine (a chemical element) with carbon ‖ to mix a volatile fuel with a gas

car·bu·re·tion (karbəréiʃən, karbjəréʃən) *n.* the process of supplying air and fuel in the proper proportions in an internal combustion engine

car·bu·re·tor, car·bu·re·ter, (*Br.*) **car·bu·ret·ter, car·bu·ret·tor** (kárbəreitər, kárbjəretər) *n.* an apparatus which vaporizes a liquid fuel and controls its mixing with air for combustion in an engine

carburetter, carburettor *CARBURETOR

car·cass (kárkəs) *n.* a dead animal body ‖ an animal's body (without head, entrails etc.) as it reaches the butcher ‖ the human body, alive or dead ‖ the remains of something, e.g. a wrecked ship ‖ the foundation structure of a pneumatic tire [origin unknown]

Car·cas·sonne (karkæsɔn) a town (pop. 42,200) on the Aude in Languedoc, S. France. Restored medieval fortifications. Church of St-Nazaire (12th–13th cc.)

Car·chem·ish (kárkəmiʃ), the ancient seat of Hittite culture on the Euphrates

car·cin·o·gen (karsínədʒən) *n.* an agent or substance producing cancer [fr. CARCINOMA+Gk -*genēs,* producing]

car·ci·no·ma (karsinóumə) *pl.* **car·ci·no·mas, car·ci·no·ma·ta** (karsinóumətə) *n.* (*med.*) an epithelial cancer [L. fr. Gk]

car·ci·no·ma·to·sis (karsinoumətóusis) *n.* (*med.*) a condition in which many carcinomata are produced in the body

car·cin·o·tron (karsínətrɒn) *n. electr.* a backward-wave oscillator tube (BWO) that sends amplified signals in direction opposite that of the electron beam, in a UHF range up to 100 GHz

car coat short overcoat comfortable for driving

card (kard) *n.* a usually rectangular piece of paper or pasteboard suitable for writing or printing on, used for written messages, invitations, announcements, names and addresses, greetings, scores etc. ‖ a playing card ‖ an eccentric or comic person ‖ (*pl.*) the activity of playing with cards **to have a card up one's sleeve** to keep back some fact etc., for use when other arguments or plans fail **to play one's best card** to put forward one's strongest argument **to play one's cards well** to go about obtaining a desired end astutely **to put one's cards on the table** to make one's plans or sentiments known frankly [fr. F. *carte* fr. Ital. fr. L. fr. Gk]

card 1. *v.t.* to clean (wool or flax before it is spun) with a comb or similar instrument ‖ to raise the nap on (woolen fabric) 2. *n.* any instrument used for carding raw wool, flax or hemp, or for raising the nap on woven material [F. *carde,* teasel, originally used for carding cloth]

car·da·mom (kárdəməm) *n.* one of several perennial plants of fam. *Zingiberaceae,* native to Asia, Africa and the Pacific islands, esp. *Amomum cardamon* of Indonesia and *Elettaria cardamomun* of India ‖ the seed of these, used in food spices and in pharmacy [fr. L. fr. Gk]

Cardamom Hills a mountain range (2,000–4,000 ft) in E. Kerala, S.W. India

car·dan (kárdæn) *adj.* (*mech.*) enabling a rotary movement to be transmitted in a different direction of movement [after Jerome *Cardan* (*CARDANO)]

cardan joint a universal joint

Car·da·no (kardánou), Gerolamo or Geronimo (Jerome Cardan, 1501–76), Italian mathematician, physician and astrologer. His 'Ars Magna' (1545) contains the first published solution of cubic equations. He invented the universal joint

cardan shaft a shaft with a universal joint at one or both ends

card·board (kárdbɔrd, kárdbourd) *n.* stiff pasteboard, used for shoe boxes etc.

card cage (*computer*) rack containing slots that hold circuit boards plugged into the back panel

card-car·ry·ing (kárdkæri:iŋ) *adj.* of one who is a member of an organization or group, esp. of the Communist Party; e.g., a card-carrying Communist

Cár·de·nas (kárðenas), Lázaro (1895–1970), Mexican statesman. As president (1934–40) he carried out agrarian reform, and nationalized the oil industry (1938)

car·di·ac (kárdi:æk) 1. *adj.* (*anat.*) pertaining to the heart ‖ pertaining to the cardia, or upper orifice of the stomach connecting it with the esophagus 2. *n.* a medicine or cordial which stimulates the heart ‖ a cardiac patient [fr. Gk *kardiakos*]

cardiac monitor (*med.*) warning device that gauges changes in an electrocardiograph and provides visual or aural alarm if certain parameters are exceeded

cardiac muscle the contractile tissue of the heart wall of vertebrates. Its fibers are faintly striated, frequently branching and in cytoplasmic continuity with each other (cf. SMOOTH MUSCLE, cf. STRIATED MUSCLE, cf. SKELETAL MUSCLE)

cardiac pacemaker *PACEMAKER

Car·diff (kárdif) a port (pop. 278,900) and county borough in S. Wales, on River Taff. Industries: shipping (Bristol Channel), iron and steel. University College of South Wales and Monmouthshire (1863), part of the University of Wales

car·di·gan (kárdigən) *n.* a knitted jacket which buttons down the front [after the 7th Earl of *Cardigan*]

Car·di·gan·shire (kárdigənʃi:ər, kárdigənʃər) a county (area 692 sq. miles, pop. 54,000) in W. Wales. County town: Cardigan. Administrative center: Aberystwyth

car·di·nal (kárdnʼl) 1. *adj.* of fundamental importance ‖ deep red ‖ (*zool.*) pertaining to the hinge of a bivalve shell of mollusks 2. *n.* one of the princes of the Catholic Church who are members of the papal council or Sacred College, and electors of the pope ‖ a member of *Richmondena,* a family of small red birds in the U.S.A. ‖ a deep red color [fr. L. *cardinalis* fr. *cardo,* hinge]

cardinal flower *Lobelia cardinalis,* a North American plant with scarlet flowers

cardinal number a simple number answering the question 'how many?', e.g. one, two, three etc. ‖ (*math.*) the number of elements in a set (cf. ORDINAL)

cardinal point one of the four main points of the compass: north, south, east and west

car·di·nal·ship (kárdnʼlʃip) *n.* the office of a cardinal

cardinal virtues the four virtues: justice, prudence, temperance and fortitude

carding machine a machine for carding wool, etc.

car·di·o·ac·cel·er·a·tor (kardi:ouækséləreitər) *n.* (*med.*) blood thinner that speeds heart action. —**cardioacceleration** *v.* —**cardioacceleratory** *adj.*

car·di·o·ac·tive (kardi:ouæktiv) *adj.* (*med.*) heart-stimulating

car·di·o·gen·ic (kardi:ədʒénik) *adj.* (*med.*) caused by the heart

car·di·o·gram (kárdi:əgræm) *n.* a tracing made by a cardiograph [fr. Gk *kardia,* heart+*gramma,* writing]

car·di·o·graph (kárdi:əgræf, kárdi:əgraf) *n.* an instrument which records the movements of the heart muscle in terms of a graph **car·di·o·graph·ic** (kardi:əgræfik) *adj.* **car·di·og·ra·phy** (kardi:ógrəfi:) *n.* [fr. Gk *kardia,* heart+*graphē,* writing]

car·di·ol·o·gy (kardi:ólədʒi:) *n.* the study of the functions and diseases of the heart [fr. Gk *kardia,* heart+*logos,* discourse]

car·di·o·meg·a·ly (kardi:ómégəli:) *n.* (*med.*) enlargement of the heart

car·di·om·e·ter (kardi:ómətər) *n.* (*med.*) electronic instrument used to measure the force of heart action

car·di·o·my·op·a·thy (kardi:oumaiópəθi:) *n.* (*med.*) 1. progressive enlargement or other disease of the heart. 2. a disease of the heart's muscular tissue

car·di·o·pul·mo·na·ry resuscitation (kardi:oupálməneiri:) emergency method combining clearing a breathing passage with chest massage and sometimes drugs. It is used to start breathing and blood circulation in a cardiac-arrest victim. abbr CPR

car·di·ot·o·co·gram (kardi:ótəkəgræm) *n.* (*med.*) electronic record of the instantaneous fetal heart rate, before, during, and after birth

car·di·o·ver·sion (kárdi:əvə:rʒən) *n.* (*med.*) restoration of normal heart action by electric shock

car·di·tis (kardáitis) *n.* an inflammation of the muscular tissue of the heart [Mod. L. fr. Gk. *kardia,* heart]

card·sharp (kárdʃɑrp) *n.* a cardsharper

card·sharp·er (kárdʃɑrpər) *n.* a professional gambler who lives by cheating at cards

Car·duc·ci (kardú:ttʃi:), Giosuè (1835–1907), Italian poet. His republican views, and his use of classical meters and of modern Italian historical themes, made his reputation as a national poet

care (kɛər) *n.* serious attention, watchfulness, caution ‖ protection ‖ charge ‖ anxiety, concern, worry ‖ an object of anxiety, worry **to take care** to exercise caution or prudence **to take care of** to look after [O.E. *caru, cearu*]

care *pres. part.* **car·ing** *past* and *past part.* **cared** *v.t.* to feel interest in, bother about, *who cares what happens now?* ‖ to be concerned as much as, *he doesn't care a damn what happens* ‖ *v.i.* to be willing, have the wish, *would you care to try it on?* **to care for** to take care of ‖ to like, enjoy [O.E. *carian*]

ca·reen (kərí:n) 1. *n.* (*naut.*) a tilted position of a ship, *on the careen* 2. *v.t.* to turn (a ship) on her side for scraping etc. ‖ to make (a ship) heel or tip over ‖ *v.i.* (of a ship or car) to go forward tilting to one side **ca·réen·age** *n.* the expense of careening ‖ a place for careening [F. *carène,* keel]

ca·reer (kərí:r) 1. *n.* a swift movement, impetus, *the horse's headlong career* ‖ progress through life with respect to one's work ‖ a means of earning a living, a profession (also used attributively, *a career diplomat*) **in full career** at top speed 2. *v.i.* to move swiftly and erratically [F. *carrière,* race-course]

ca·reer·ist (kərí:ərist] *n.* an ambitious person set on success in his career even at others' cost

care·free (kéərfri:) *adj.* free from care

care·ful (kéərfəl) *adj.* cautious ‖ painstaking ‖ done with accuracy or with caution ‖ (with 'of' or 'for') having thoughtful concern, *careful of the rights of others* [O.E. *carful, cearful*]

care·less (kéərlis) *adj.* lighthearted, carefree ‖ relaxed, casual, *dressed with careless ease* ‖ indifferent, thoughtless ‖ negligent ‖ showing negligence [O.E. *carlēas*]

ca·ress (kərés) *n.* a gentle, affectionate touch or embrace [F. *caresse*]

caress *v.t.* to touch gently and lovingly, fondle [F. *caresser*]

car·et (kærit) *n.* a mark (ʌ) made below a line of writing to show that a word or letter is to be inserted [L.=it is lacking]

care·tak·er (kéərteikər) *n.* a person employed to take charge of property etc., and see to routine matters, esp. in the owner's absence

caretaker government a temporary government acting until there is a new permanent government

care·worn (kéərwɔrn, kéərwourn) *adj.* worried and tired by anxiety or responsibility

Ca·rey (kéəri:), Henry Charles (1793–1879), U.S. economist. A leader in the theoretic development of American economic nationalism and an advocate of initial protection for the industrial growth of developing nations, he nevertheless believed that diverse economic interests could progress in harmony. His works, translated into at least eight languages, include 'Principles of Political Economy' (1837–40) and 'The Unity of Law' (1872)

car·fare (kárfɛər) *n.* the charge for a passenger on a streetcar or bus etc.

car·go (kárgou) *pl.* **car·goes, car·gos** *n.* the freight of goods or luggage carried by a ship, aircraft etc. [Span. *cargo* or *carga*]

cargo boat a trading vessel, as distinct from a passenger boat

car·hop (kárhɒp) *n.* a waiter or waitress in a restaurant where people are served in their parked cars

Car·i·a (kéəri:ə) an ancient region of S.W. Asia Minor

car·i·am·a (kæri:æmə) *n.* a seriema

Ca·rí·as An·din·o (karí:asandí:nɔ), Tiburcio (1876– presumed dead), Honduran general and dictator (1932–48)

Car·ib (kǽrib) *n.* one of the Carib Indians inhabiting the S. West Indian islands, Guiana, Venezuela, some of the Lesser Antilles, and the Caribbean coast of Central America ‖ a linguistic group of the West Indies and Central America

Car·i·ban (kǽribən) *n.* a linguistic group of South American Indians including the Caribs, inhabiting Brazil, Colombia, Guiana, Venezuela, parts of Central America and the Lesser Antilles ‖ the Cariban-speaking group of peoples, or a member of the group

Car·ib·be·an (kǽribíːən, kəríbiːən) *adj.* pertaining to the Caribs ‖ of or pertaining to the Caribbean Sea or the islands in it

Caribbean Sea an arm (750,000 sq. miles) of the Atlantic between Central and South America and the West Indies, linked with the Pacific by the Panama Canal

Caribbean, the the West Indies

ca·ri·be (kərí:biː) *n.* a piranha [Am. Span. fr. Span. *caribe,* cannibal]

car·i·bou (kǽribuː) *n.* a member of *Rangifer,* a genus of deer indigenous to Canada, Alaska and Greenland and related to the reindeer, esp. *R. caribou* [Canad. F.]

car·i·ca·ture (kǽrikətʃuər) **1.** *n.* ridicule (by exaggeration and distortion) of a thing or person, e.g. in mime, a picture, or a literary portrait, often with a mocking or offensive intention, and esp. used in political attack ‖ such a picture, literary portrait etc. ‖ a ludicrously poor copy or imitation **2.** *v.t. pres. part.* **car·i·ca·tur·ing** *past* and *past part.* **car·i·ca·tured** to make a caricature of **cár·i·ca·tur·ist** *n.* someone who makes caricatures, esp. pictorial ones [F. fr. Ital.]

car·ies (kέaːriːz, kέariːːz) *n.* the decay of animal tissues, esp. of teeth [L.]

car·il·lon (kǽrələn, *Br.* kəríljən) **1.** *n.* a set of bells sounded either directly by hand or from a keyboard, and playing either a tune or a series of notes repeated without any change ‖ the tune played by a carillon ‖ a musical instrument or organ stop imitating a carillon **2.** *v.i.* to play a carillon (cf. CHANGE RINGING) [F.]

ca·ri·na (kərái nə, kərí:nə) *pl.* **ca·ri·nas, ca·ri·nae** (kərí:ni:) *n.* (*biol.*) a ridge on certain bones like a keel, e.g. the breastbone of birds ‖ the median dorsal plate of a barnacle ‖ the two coherent anterior petals of a papilionaceous flower ‖ the ridge on bracts of some grasses **ca·rí·nal, car·i·nate** (kǽrineit), **cár·i·nat·ed** *adjs* [L.=keel]

Ca·rin·thi·a (kərinθi:ə) (G. Kärnten) a province (area 4,583 sq. miles, pop. 537,212) of S. Austria. Capital: Klagenfurt. It became an independent duchy (976) and then a possession of the Hapsburgs (1276–1918)

cariole *CARRIOLE

car·i·ous (kέaːriːəs) *adj.* (esp. of teeth) decayed [fr. F. *carieux*]

car·i·so·pro·dal [C₁₂H₂₄N₂O₄] (kərisóuproudɔl) *n.* (*pharm.*) muscle-relaxing drug used to relieve muscle pain; marketed as Rela and Soma

cark·ing (kárkiŋ) *adj.* (*rhet.,* of cares or troubles) burdensome [fr. obs. v. *cark,* to burden, fr. O.N.F.]

Car·lism (kárlizəm) *n.* adherence to Don Carlos, second son of Charles IV, as rightful monarch of Spain, or to his descendants **Cár·list 1.** *n.* someone who supports Don Carlos or his descendants **2.** *adj.* pertaining to the support of Don Carlos or his descendants [F. *carlisme* fr. *Carlos*]

Carlist Wars three civil wars (1833–9, 1860, 1872–6) in Spain fought unsuccessfully against Isabella II and her successors by those supporting the Carlist claims to the throne

car·load (kárloud) *n.* a capacity load, esp. of a freight car ‖ the minimum weight that will be accepted for transport at reduced rate

carload lot a carload shipment of freight above the minimum carload amount

Car·lo·man (kárləmən) (751–71), king of the Franks (768–71). He shared the kingdom with his brother Charlemagne

Car·lo·vin·gi·an (kàrləvíndʒi:ən) *n.* and *adj.* Carolingian [fr. F. *Carlovingien*]

Car·low (kárlou) a southeastern county (area 346 sq. miles, pop. 39,814) of Leinster, Irish Republic ‖ its county seat, on River Barrow

Carlowitz, Treaty of *KARLOWITZ, TREATY OF

Carls·bad (kárlzbæd) *KARLOVY VARY

Carlsbad Caverns a series of limestone caves in S.E. New Mexico. The largest is Big Room (c. 4,000 ft long, 625 ft wide, 285 ft high)

Carl·son (kárlsən) Chester Floyd (1906–68), U.S. inventor of xerography (1938), an electro-static dry copying process. Commercial development of his invention was undertaken by the Haloid Company (1947), later known as Xerox Corporation

Car·lyle (karláil), Thomas (1795–1881), Scottish essayist, historian and philosopher. He was greatly influenced by German literature and philosophy. He translated Goethe's 'Wilhelm Meister' (1824), and wrote 'The Life of Schiller' (1825). His first major work, 'Sartor Resartus' (1833–4), was a spiritual autobiography, expounding a passionate antirationalist philosophy. He won fame with 'The French Revolution' (1837), a prose epic rather than a history. His lectures 'On Heroes, Hero-Worship and the Heroic in History' (1841) expounded the principle that human progress is brought about chiefly by great individuals. Other works are 'Frederick the Great' (1857–65) and 'The Letters and Speeches of Oliver Cromwell' (1845)

Car·mar·then·shire (karmárðənʃiər, karmárðənʃər) a county (area 919 sq. miles, pop. 168,000) of S. Wales. County town: Carmarthen

Car·mel·ite (kárməlait) *n.* a mendicant friar of the order of our Lady of Mount Carmel founded (c. 1150) at Mount Carmel ‖ a nun of its second order founded in the mid-15th c.

Car·mel, Mount (kárməl) a mountain ridge in Israel, associated esp. with Elijah (*CARMELITE)

car·min·a·tive (karmínətiv, kárməneitiv) **1.** *adj.* relieving flatulence **2.** *n.* a drug or other agent having this property [fr. L. *carminare* (*carminatus*), to card (wool)]

car·mine (kármin, kármain) **1.** *n.* a bright crimson color made from cochineal **2.** *adj.* of this color [F. or Span. ult. fr. Arab.]

car·mus·tine [C₅H₉Cl₂N₃O₂] (karmésti:n) *n.* (*pharm.*) anticancer drug used with other drugs in treating brain tumors, multiple myeloma, and lymphomas; marketed as Bicnu

Car·nac (karnæk) a village in Brittany famous for its Stone Age monuments: menhirs (standing stones), barrows and burial-chambers

car·nage (kárnidʒ) *n.* slaughter, esp. in battle [F. fr. Ital.]

car·nal (kárn'l) *adj.* pertaining to the flesh, as opposed to the spirit ‖ sexual, *carnal appetite* [fr. L. *canalis*]

car·nall·ite (kárn'lait) *n.* (*mineral.*) a white or reddish double salt, potassiummagnesium chloride KCl·MgCl₂·6H₂O mined from deposits at Stassfurt, Germany and in Iran. It is an important source of potassium and magnesium salts [after R. von *Carnall* (1804–74), G. mining engineer]

Car·nap (kárnæp), Rudolf (1891–1970), U.S. philosopher of German origin. He was the leader of the school of logical positivism, and the American school of constructive language philosophy was very largely influenced by him. His publications include 'Der logische Aufbau der Welt' (1928), 'Logische Syntax der Sprache' (1934, trans. 'Logical Syntax of Language'), 'Introduction to Semantics' (1942), 'Meaning and Necessity' (1948), 'Logical Foundations of Probability' (1951), 'Introduction to Symbolic Logic and its Applications' (1958)

car·nap·per or **car·nap·er** (kárnæpər) *n.* car thief

Car·nat·ic (karnǽtik) the European name for a region lying between the E. Ghats and the Coromandel Coast in Madras state, S. India

car·na·tion (karnéiʃən) *n. Dianthus caryophyllus,* fam. *Caryophyllaceae,* a species of pink, having many usually double-flowering varieties [fr. L. *carnatio* (*carnationis*), flesh-colored]

car·nau·ba (karnáubə) *n.* the Brazilian palm *Copernicia cerifera,* the leaves of which yield wax used for candles, fibers etc. [Port. fr. Tupian]

Car·ne·a·des (karní:ədi:z), Greek philosopher (c. 215–c. 129 B.C.), founder of the New Academy at Athens, noted for his skepticism and his theory of probability

Car·ne·gie (karnéigi: kárnəgi:), Andrew (1835–1919), U.S. steel manufacturer and philanthropist. In his lifetime he built and equipped over 2,500 public libraries in the U.S.A., Canada and Britain, and he devoted millions of dollars to the endowment of educational and research trusts

car·nel·ian (karní:ljən) *n.* a reddish, semitransparent variety of chalcedony [alteration of CORNELIAN]

car·ni·val (kárnivəl) *n.* the festivities in Catholic countries just before Lent (Mardi Gras) and

at mid-Lent (mi-Carême) ‖ any public festivity, usually with processions, dancing and sideshows ‖ a traveling amusement show [Ital. *carnevale*]

car·ni·vore (kárnivɔr, kárnivour) *n.* a member of *Carnivora,* an order of mammals of which most are flesh-eating but some (e.g. bears) omnivorous. They have well-developed canines, small incisors, and shearing molars. The order includes lions, cats, dogs, seals, walruses etc. [F.]

car·niv·o·rous (karnívərəs) *adj.* flesh-eating [fr. L. *carnivorus*]

Car·not (kárnou), Lazare Nicolas Marguerite (1753–1823), French military engineer and statesman. He successfully directed the war effort of the revolutionary armies (1793–5), and was a member of the Directory

Carnot, Nicolas Léonard Sadi (1796–1832), French physicist, son of Lazare Carnot. His 'Réflexions sur la puissance motrice du feu' (1824) deals with the relation between heat and mechanical energy. He formulated the second law of thermodynamics and conceived the mathematical idea of an ideal heat engine (*CARNOT CYCLE, *CARNOT'S PRINCIPLE)

Carnot cycle an ideal reversible heat transfer cycle involving a fluid (usually) as a working substance and consisting of an isothermal expansion, an adiabatic expansion, an isothermal compression and an adiabatic compression back to the original state, where each step is carried out reversibly. The Carnot cycle accomplishes the conversion of heat to work with the theoretical maximum efficiency and was historically important in the development of thermodynamics, particularly for the concept of entropy

Carnot heat engine an idealized arrangement for converting heat energy into mechanical work and vice versa, by means of one or more linked Carnot cycles

car·no·tite (kárnətait) *n.* (*mineral.*) uranium potassium vanadate, a source of uranium and radium [after M. A. *Carnot* (d. 1920), F. inspector general of mines]

Carnot's principle the principle that the efficiency of a reversible heat engine depends not on the working substance used but only upon the temperatures between which the engine works

car·ob (kǽrəb) *n. Ceratonia siliqua,* a tree widely grown in the Mediterranean region. Carob gum is obtained from the pods. These are rich in sugar and protein, and are also used for fodder, and fermented for beverages [F. *carobe* fr. Arab.]

car·ol (kǽrəl) **1.** *n.* a Christmas hymn ‖ (*rhet.*) a joyful song **2.** *v. pres. part.* **car·ol·ing,** esp. *Br.* **car·ol·ling** *past* and *past part.* **car·ol·ed,** esp. *Br.* **car·olled** *v.i.* (*rhet.*) to sing joyfully ‖ to sing Christmas hymns ‖ *v.t.* (*rhet.* esp. of birds) to sing joyfully [O.F.]

Car·o·le·an (kǽrəli:ən) *adj.* characteristic of the time of Charles I and II of England [fr. L. *Caroleus*]

Carol I (kǽrəl) (1839–1914), first king of Rumania (1881–1914). As prince of Moldavia and Walachia (1866–81), he helped Russia in the Russo-Turkish War (1877–8), and obtained Rumanian independence at the Congress of Berlin (1878)

Carol II (1893–1953), king of Rumania (1930–40). He supplanted his son Michael as king (1930), formed a royal dictatorship, and was deposed (1940)

Car·o·li·na (kǽrəláinə) the English colony (1653) that was divided (1729) into what is now North Carolina and South Carolina

Carolinas, the *NORTH CAROLINA, *SOUTH CAROLINA

Car·o·line (kǽrəlain, kǽrəlin) *adj.* pertaining to Charles I and II of Great Britain and their period [fr. L. *Carolus,* Charles]

Caroline Islands a scattered archipelago (area 550 sq. miles, pop. 85,932) of about 500 islets in the Pacific Ocean north of New Guinea, included in Micronesia. Interesting stone remains of ancient cultures survive. The islands were discovered by the Spaniards (1526), were sold to Germany (1899), were a Japanese mandate between the world wars, and are now a U.S. trust territory. Exports: dried bonito, copra, tapioca

Car·o·lin·gi·an (kǽrəlíndʒi:ən) **1.** *n.* one of the second dynasty of Frankish kings (751–987) **2.** *adj.* pertaining to these kings [F. *Carolingien*] —Charles Martel governed the Frankish lands under the nominal rule of the Merovingians,

CONCISE PRONUNCIATION KEY: **(a)** æ, c*a*t; ɑ, c*ar*; ɔ f*aw*n; ei, sn*a*ke. **(e)** e, h*e*n; i:, sh*ee*p; iə, d*ee*r; εə, b*ear*. **(i)** i, f*i*sh; ai, t*i*ger; ə:, b*ir*d. **(o)** o, *o*x; au, c*ow*; ou, g*oa*t; u, p*oo*r; ɔi, r*oy*al. **(u)** ʌ, d*u*ck; u, b*u*ll; u:, g*oo*se; ə, b*a*cill*u*s; ju:, c*u*be. x, lo*ch*; θ, *th*ink; ð, bo*th*er; z, *Z*en; ʒ, cor*s*a*g*e. dʒ, sava*g*e; ŋ, ora*ng*uta*ng*; j, *y*ak; ʃ, *f*i*sh*; tʃ, fe*tch*; 'l, rabb*le*; 'n, redd*en*. Complete pronunciation key appears inside front cover.

who were deposed (751) by Pepin III. His son, Charlemagne, became (800) the first Holy Roman Emperor. After the death of his son Louis I, the Treaty of Verdun (843) divided the Carolingian empire into three parts. Lothaire I inherited the middle kingdom and Louis the German took the eastern part. Charles II founded the French Carolingians, who ruled until supplanted (987) by the Capetians

Car·o·lin·i·an (kærəlíni:ən) **1.** adj. of or relating to North Carolina or South Carolina **2.** n. a native or inhabitant of North Carolina or South Carolina

Carolinian 1. adj. Carolingian **2.** n. a Carolingian

car·om (kǽrəm) **1.** n. (billiards, Am.= Br. cannon) a stroke which causes the player's ball to hit two others in succession **2.** v.i. to make a carom [shortened fr. older carambole fr. Span. carambola, origin unknown]

car·o·tene, car·ro·tene (kǽrəti:n) n. one of a number of yellow or red unsaturated crystalline hydrocarbon pigments, a constituent of e.g. carrots and butter, and a source of vitamin A for animals and man

ca·rot·e·noid, ca·rot·i·noid (kərót'nɔid) n. any of a group of unsaturated pigments occurring in many plants and animals

ca·rot·id (kərótid) **1.** n. either of the two large arteries which carry blood to the head **2.** adj. pertaining to, or near these [fr. Gk karōtides fr. karoun, to stupefy (pressure on these arteries causes unconsciousness)]

car·o·tin, car·ro·tin (kǽrətin) n. carotene

carotinoid *CAROTENOID

ca·rous·al (kəráuzəl) n. (rhet.) a drinking bout

ca·rouse (kəráuz) **1.** v.i. pres. part. **ca·rous·ing** past and past part. **ca·roused** to take part in a drinking bout **2.** n. a drinking bout [fr. G. gar aus (trinken), (to drink) all up]

carousel *CARROUSEL

carp (karp) Cyprinus caprio, fam. Cyprinidae, a long-lived bony, edible, freshwater fish [O.F. carpe]

carp v.i. to complain **to carp at** to nag, find fault with [perh. fr. L. carpere, to slander]

Car·pac·cio (karpáttʃo), Vittore (c. 1465–c. 1522), Italian painter, precursor of the Venetian school

car·pal (kárpəl) adj. pertaining to the carpus, or wrist [fr. Mod. L. carpalis fr. carpus, wrist]

car park (Br.) a parking lot

Car·pa·thi·an Mtns (kɑrpéiθi:ən) the chief range of E. central Europe, an 800-mile arc extending east from the Vienna depression through the edges of Czechoslovakia and Poland, curving southeast into Rumania, then west to run parallel with the lower Danube. It forms a number of chains which are all far lower than the Alps (highest point 8,737 ft, in the Tatra), have no glaciers, and are cut by many low passes. They are forest-covered with wide, level highlands providing cattle pasture. There are large mineral deposits

car·pel (kárpəl) n. part of the structure of a seed plant. The pistil or gynoecium consists of one or more carpels or megasporophylls, which may be joined or free **cár·pel·lar·y** adj. [fr. Gk karpos, fruit]

Car·pen·tar·i·a, Gulf of (kɑrpəntéəri:ə) a gulf on the north coast of Australia, between Cape York and Cape Arnhem. It has a low swampy coast, largely uninhabited

car·pen·ter (kárpəntər) **1.** n. a workman in wood ‖ a person who makes the wooden frames of a house, ship etc. (*CABINETMAKER, *JOINER) **2.** v.i. to work as a carpenter ‖ v.t. to make by carpentry [A.F. carpenter]

carpenter ant an ant which bores holes into wood, esp. dead or decaying wood

carpenter bee one of several large bees which bore holes into sound wood

carpenter moth Prionoxystus robiniae, the American goat moth

car·pen·try (kárpəntri:) n. woodwork ‖ the carpenter's trade

car·pet (kárpit) **1.** n. a heavy fabric, often patterned, of tufts or strands of wool, hemp or silk, often woven into open canvas, used esp. as a covering for floors and stairs ‖ a smooth expanse (of turf, flowers etc.) **on the carpet** (of a topic) under discussion ‖ (of a person) being, or about to be, reprimanded ‖ (electr.) device used to jam radar reception **2.** v.t. to cover with or as if with a carpet [M.E. carpete fr. Ital. carpetta, table cover]

car·pet·bag (kárpitbæg) n. (hist.) a traveling bag originally made of carpet fabric

car·pet·bag·ger (kárpitbægər) n. (Am. hist.) a person from the Northern states who went to the Southern states after the Civil War, esp. to take advantage of the depressed conditions ‖ (Am. hist.) an itinerant wildcat banker in the West

carpet beetle Anthrenus scrophulariae, a beetle whose larvae feed on wool and damage carpets and clothes

car·pet·ing (kárpitiŋ) n. material used for laying as a carpet

carpet rod a rod of metal or wood etc. for holding a stair carpet in place

car·po·log·i·cal (kɑrpəlódʒikəl) adj. of or related to carpology

car·pol·o·gist (kɑrpólədʒist) n. a specialist in carpology

car·pol·o·gy (kɑrpólədʒi:) n. the study of the structure of fruits and seeds [fr. Gk karpos, fruit + logos, discourse]

car·po·phore (kárpəfɔr, kárpəfour) n. (bot.) a slender prolongation of the flora axis which supports the carpels, e.g. in the geranium ‖ the spore body of the higher fungi [fr. Gk karpos, fruit + phoros, bearing]

car·port (kárpɔrt) n. a roofed open shelter for an automobile

car·pus (kárpəs) pl. **car·pi** (kárpai) n. (anat.) the wrist, the bones which join the hand to the forearm [Mod. L. fr. Gk karpos, wrist]

Car·rac·ci (kərátʃi:) the name of three Italian painters born at Bologna: Ludovico (1555–1619) and his two cousins, the brothers Agostino (1557–1602) and Annibale (1560–1609). Annibale was the greatest of the three. Their academy at Bologna influenced a whole movement in Italian art in the 17th c.

car·ra·geen, car·ra·gheen (kǽrəgi:n) n. Chondrus crispus, a dark purple seaweed of N. Europe. When dried and bleached it is used for feeding cattle. A colloidal extract of it and of certain other red algae is used in the preparation of size and for various culinary and medical uses [after Carragheen in Ireland]

Car·ran·za (kɑrránsə), Venustiano (1859–1920), president of Mexico (1917–20). After he had led the Constitutional forces against President Huerta, his restrictive foreign policy and his failure to pursue agrarian reform led to his overthrow and assassination

Car·ra·ra (kərɑ́rə) a town (pop. 67,758) in N.W. Tuscany, Italy, famous for its fine marble

Car·re·ra (kɑrrérə), José Miguel (1785–1821), Chilean revolutionary leader and first president and dictator of Chile (1811–4). He reorganized public finances and the military, created the National Institute and founded the first Chilean newspaper. Internal strife, however, caused by his lust for power, allowed Spain to restore (1814) monarchic rule

Carrera, Rafael (1814–65), Guatemalan dictator. He engineered (1839) the secession of Guatemala from the United States of Central America, established Guatemala as an independent republic, and proclaimed himself (1854) president for life. With the support of the military, the Church, and the Indian peasantry, he brought domestic peace, economic progress, and racial equality, but at the cost of freedom and Central American unity

Carrera An·dra·de, Jorge (karréraandráðe) (1903–), Ecuadorian poet and revolutionary. His poems, notably 'Boletines de mar y tierra' (1930), are noted for their pure aestheticism

car·riage (kǽridʒ) n. a horse-drawn vehicle for people to ride in ‖ the manner of holding oneself in walking and standing ‖ the act of carrying or conveying, esp. the transport of goods from one place to another, or the charge for this ‖ the passing of a bill, proposal before a committee etc. ‖ a framework on which a gun is mounted ‖ a part of a machine in or on which another moving part rides ‖ (Br.) a railroad vehicle for passengers [O.N.F. cariage fr. carier, to carry (in a cart)]

carriage clock a clock with glass sides, back and top (usually in a protective leather case) originally designed as a traveling clock

carriage forward (Br.) with the cost of conveyance to be paid by the receiver of the goods

carriage free with the cost of conveyance paid by the sender of the goods

carriage paid (Br.) carriage free

car·rick bend (kǽrik) (naut.) a knot used for joining the ends of hawsers etc. [etym. doubtful]

carrick bitts (naut.) the bitts or stays which support a windlass or winch

car·ri·er (kǽri:ər) n. a person, company or corporation undertaking transport ‖ a luggage rack on a bicycle ‖ a person or animal carrying the germs of a disease without contracting it himself but able to infect others ‖ an aircraft carrier

carrier bag (Br.) a strong paper bag with handles for carrying groceries etc.

carrier current higher-than-normal frequency current superimposed on telephone or other electric-powered lines. It is used to carry messages or for control purposes

carrier nation a nation which manages overseas trade for other nations

carrier pigeon a pigeon of Eastern origin able to be trained to find its way home over long distances and sometimes used for carrying messages

carrier wave an electric wave or current whose modulations carry signals in telephonic and wireless transmission, television etc.

car·ri·ole, car·i·ole (kǽri:oul) n. a small, one-horse, two-wheeled carriage for one person ‖ a light covered cart [F.]

car·ri·on (kǽri:ən) n. dead, putrefying flesh of man or beast [M.E. caronye fr. O.N.F.]

carrion crow Corvus corone, the common European crow, which feeds on carrion

Car·roll (kǽrəl), Lewis (Charles Lutwidge Dodgson, 1832–98), English author famous esp. for 'Alice's Adventures in Wonderland' (1865) and 'Alice through the Looking-glass' (1871)

car·rot (kǽrət) n. Daucus carota, fam. Umbelliferae, a biennial plant whose yellowish red root is widely used as a vegetable ‖ the root of this plant **cár·rot·y** adj. yellowish red [F. carotte]

car·ro·ten *CAROTENE

car·ro·tin (kárətin) n. carotene

car·rou·sel, car·ou·sel (kærəsél, Br. kæru:zél) n. a cavalry tournament ‖ a merry-go-round [F. fr. Ital.]

car·ry (kǽri:) **1.** v. pres. part. **car·ry·ing** past and past part. **car·ried** v.t. to convey from one place to another by hand or in a vehicle ‖ to convey or transmit in any manner ‖ to conduct, those pipes carry water ‖ to prolong, extend, the wall is carried to the end of the street ‖ to be necessarily accompanied by, the job carries great responsibility ‖ to support, bear (the weight of a stationary object), the bridge is carried by three piers ‖ to win, capture (a position held by an enemy) ‖ to secure or hold the sympathy of (an audience) ‖ to win the votes of, will he carry Minnesota? ‖ to sing (a tune) in tune ‖ to play (an instrument) or sing (a part) ‖ to hold or bear (the body or head or oneself) in a certain way ‖ to secure the election of (a candidate) or the adoption of (a motion) ‖ v.i. to have range, this rifle carries half a mile ‖ (of sound) so strong as to be heard at a distance **to carry all before one** to go from success to success **to carry away** to cause (someone) to be so absorbed or thrilled as to cease to be aware of himself and his immediate concerns ‖ (naut.) to smash and sweep (a mast etc.) away **to carry forward** (accounting) to transfer (a total) from one column of figures to the next ‖ to progress with **to carry off** to remove by force, to carry off a prisoner ‖ to win by prowess, he carried off three medals ‖ to act intelligently and boldly in, to carry off a difficult situation ‖ to cause the death of, fever carried off half the force **to carry on** to continue ‖ to make a scene, be a nuisance ‖ to flirt **to carry out** to fulfil, put (orders etc.) into effect **to carry over** (accounting) to carry forward ‖ (Br., stock exchange) to carry (a customer) until the following settlement, or extend (a settlement date) to the end of the next account ‖ to continue as a survival after a particular period etc. has ended **to carry through** to complete, succeed in doing (something) ‖ to help (someone) to surmount and survive (a hard test etc.) **2.** n. portage between rivers ‖ the range of a gun [O.N.F. carier, to cart]

car·ry·all (kǽri:ɔl) n. a large soft canvas bag for carrying clothes etc. ‖ a light, covered, one-horse family carriage

carrying charge (commodities) trading situation in which each successive contract maturity is set at a higher price

car·ry·ings-on (kǽri:iŋzón, kǽ'ri:iŋzón) pl. n. frivolous or immoral behavior of which one disapproves

car·ry-on (kǽri:ɒn) adj. of luggage permitted to be taken aboard a plane by a passenger

car·ry-o·ver (kǽri:ouvər) n. the act or process of carrying over ‖ an amount brought forward from one page to the next ‖ a practice etc. that is continued out of tradition or habit

carry the can (*Br.*) *v.* (*slang*) to bear responsibility

car·sick (kársįk) *adj.* nauseated by the motion of traveling in a car

Car·son (kárs'n), Christopher ('Kit') (1809–68), U.S. frontiersman. His career as frontier scout, Indian agent, and brigadier general in the southwest during the Civil War was a major contribution to the settlement of the American West

Carson City the capital (pop. 32,022) of Nevada: silver mines

cart (kurt) **1.** *n.* a two-wheeled or four-wheeled horse-drawn or tractor-drawn vehicle, used for carrying loads ‖ a small, shafted vehicle for moving loads by hand **in the cart** (*Br.*) in trouble **to put the cart before the horse** to consider facts in the wrong order or attach wrong relative values to two things **2.** *v.t.* to transport in a cart etc. ‖ to drag, cause to go under compulsion, *to cart a child off to bed* ‖ *v.i.* to move loads by cart **cárt·age** *n.* the act of conveying goods in a cart ‖ the charge for doing this [fr. O.N. *kartr*, cart]

CART (*acronym*) for computerized automatic rating system, a computer program to select and monitor traffic routes with consideration of rates and other factors; designed by Honeywell Electronic Data Processing Division

Car·ta·ge·na (kqrtahéina) a port (pop. 129,200) in Murcia, S.E. Spain, one of the best harbors on the east coast, founded (c. 226 B.C.) by Hasdrubal. It is a naval station, with shipyards

Cartagena a port (pop. 435,361) of Colombia on the Caribbean, exporting petroleum and coffee

Cartagena Manifesto a proposal (1812) by Simón Bolívar calling for a confederation of all peoples of America in an Amphictyonic League of good neighbors. It was backed by San Martín and O'Higgins

carte *QUARTE

carte blanche (kártblá:nʃ) *n.* a blank paper already signed by one party to an agreement and given to another, so that he may state his own terms unconditionally ‖ complete discretionary powers, a free hand [F.=white paper]

car·tel (kartél, kárt'l) *n.* an industrial combination in which several different firms agree on some form of joint action. A cartel differs from a trust in that members retain control of their own affairs instead of being directed by a central management [G. *kartell* fr. F.]
—Cartel agreements have commonly been made for the restriction of production and competition, joint purchase of raw materials, joint distribution of products, allocation of markets and quotas, and price fixing. The most common form is retail price maintenance. Cartels have been most successful in controlling production and distribution of articles for which there are no substitutes, esp. in industries producing raw materials or processing early stages of manufactured goods. They have come to be associated with international trade organizations

Car·ter, Jimmy (kártər) (1924–), 39th U.S. president (1977–81). Born James Earl Carter in Plains, Ga., he was state senator (1962–6) and governor (1971–5) before narrowly defeating incumbent Gerald Ford to become president. He achieved an arms control treaty, transfer of control of the Panama Canal to Panama, and was instrumental in obtaining a peace treaty between Egypt and Israel. The Shah of Iran's downfall, the taking of U.S. citizens as hostages by Iranian militants, and Afghanistan's invasion by the Soviets caught the U.S. by surprise and eroded confidence in Carter's leadership. He ran for a second term against Republican challenger Ronald Reagan, who easily defeated him

cart·er (kártər) *n.* a person who drives a cart ‖ a person who transports goods for others

Car·ter·et (kártəret) *GRANVILLE

Car·te·sian (kartí:ʒən) **1.** *n.* a follower of Descartes **2.** *adj.* pertaining to Descartes, his philosophy, or his mathematical methods **Car·té·sian·ism** *n.* [fr. *Cartesius, Cartisianus*, L. for Descartes]

cartesian control (*mil.*) system for controlling guided missiles utilizing control surfaces, one horizontal and one vertical

Cartesian coordinates (*math.*) system of coordinates in which the position of any point of the plane is determined by distance from two lines or three planes

Car·thage (kárθidʒ) a Phoenician trading station in Tunis (founded c. 814 B.C.) which formed a great agricultural-commercial empire in N. Africa, Sicily, Sardinia and Spain against Greek and Roman opposition (*PUNIC WARS). Carthage was sacked by Scipio Africanus in 202 B.C. and again in 146 B.C. by Scipio Aemilianus. But from 29 B.C. Rome recolonized her as a great city, capital of Roman Africa. Carthage was then a Christian center till destroyed by the Vandals (439) and again by the Arabs (692–8)

Car·tha·gin·i·an (kɑrθədʒíni:ən) **1.** *adj.* of or relating to Carthage **2.** *n.* a native or inhabitant of Carthage

Carthaginian Wars *PUNIC WARS

cart horse a strong, heavily built horse used for dragging loads

Car·thu·sian (kɑrθú:ʒən) **1.** *adj.* of a strict monastic order, founded (1084) by St Bruno at Chartreuse near Grenoble, France (*CHARTERHOUSE) **2.** *n.* a member of this order [fr. L. *Cartusianus* from the *Cartusiani* (*montes*)]

Car·tier (kærtjei), Sir George Etienne (1814–73), Canadian statesman. As premier in the Cartier-MacDonald ministry (1857–62), he took a leading part in the building of the Liberal-Conservative party. He strongly influenced the decision to build the Canadian Pacific railroad and to bring French Canada into federation (1864–7)

Cartier, Jacques (1491–1557), French navigator who made three voyages to Canada (1534, 1535–6, 1541–2), and took possession of the country in the name of François I (1534). He named the St Lawrence River and explored it a little beyond present-day Montreal

car·ti·lage (kárt'lidʒ) *n.* (*anat.*) a very tough, translucent, bluish-white elastic tissue, found in connection with bones in vertebrates **car·ti·lag·i·noid** (kqrt'lǽdʒinɔid) *adj.* resembling cartilage [F.]

car·ti·lag·i·nous (kqrt'lǽdʒinəs) *adj.* formed of cartilage ‖ resembling cartilage [fr. F. *cartilagineux*]

cart·load (kártloud) *n.* as much as a cart holds or is capable of holding

car·to·gram (kártəgræm) *n.* a simple map incorporating diagrammatic statistics [fr. L. *carta*, map+Gk *gramma*, something written]

car·tog·ra·pher (kartógrəfər) *n.* a person who prepares and makes maps

car·to·graph·ic (kqrtəgrǽfik) *adj.* of or relating to cartography **car·to·gráph·i·cal** *adj.*

car·tog·ra·phy (kartógrəfi:) *n.* mapmaking [fr. F. *carte*, map+Gk *graphein*, to write]

car·ton (kárt'n) *n.* a light box made of cardboard or fiber ‖ a white disk in the center of the bull's-eye of a target [F.]

car·toon (kartú:n) *n.* a drawing which puts a comic construction (from mildly humorous to savagely satirical) on current events or on people ‖ a drawing for a tapestry or a painting ‖ an animated cartoon ‖ comic strip **car·tóon·ist** *n.* a person who draws cartoons [Ital. *cartone*, large paper]

car·top·per (kártɒpər) *n.* portable boat transportable atop a car

car·touche (kartú:ʃ) *n.* (*archit.*) a scroll-like ornament ‖ a drawing of a partly open scroll in the corner of a map, with an inscription on it ‖ an oval or oblong design, esp. on an Egyptian monument, bearing the title of a king [F.]

car·tridge (kártridʒ) *n.* a cased explosive charge, also containing the missile when made for rifles or shotguns ‖ a holder for a roll of film or ink refill for a fountain pen [corrup. of CARTOUCHE]

cartridge belt a belt made for carrying a supply of cartridges or bullets around the waist ‖ a long ammunition strip fed into the guns of fighter planes

cartridge clip a metal holder for cartridges

cartridge paper thick, strong paper used esp. for drawings

car·tu·lar·y (kártʃuleri:) *pl.* **car·tu·lar·ies** *n.* a collection of charters or records ‖ the place or book containing them [fr. M.L. *cartularium*, fr. *cartula*, a small card]

cart·wheel (kárthwi:l, kártwi:l) *n.* a feat of agility in which the legs are made to pass over the head in a lateral movement with the limbs kept straight but splayed like the spokes of a wheel

Cart·wright (kártrait), Edmund (1743– 1823), English inventor of the power loom, which he patented (1785)

cart·wright (kártrait) *n.* a man who builds carts

car·un·cle (kǽrəŋk'l, kərʌ́ŋk'l) *n.* a naked fleshy excrescence on the heads of certain birds and on certain caterpillars ‖ (*bot.*) an outgrowth from various regions of the testa of a seed **car·un·cu·lar** (kərʌ́ŋkjulər) **car·ún·cu·late, car·ún·cu·lous** *adjs* [F. *caruncule*]

Ca·ru·so (kɑrú:sɔ), Enrico (1873–1921), Italian operatic tenor of tremendous fame. He made his U.S. debut in New York in 1903

car·va·crol (kárvəkrɔl) *n.* an oil (C₁₀H₁₃OH) extracted from certain plants of the mint family, used as an antiseptic [fr. F. *carvi*, caraway+L. *acer* (*acris*), sharp]

carve (karv) *pres. part.* **carv·ing**, *past and past part.* **carved** *v.t.* to cut (stone, wood etc.) ‖ to form (an image, inscription etc.) by such cutting ‖ to cut (a roast, chicken etc.) into slices or pieces ‖ *v.i.* to make a statue, inscription etc. by cutting ‖ to cut up a roast, chicken etc. **to carve out** to cause to emerge by a process of cutting away surroundings ‖ to obtain by effort, *to carve out a career* **to carve up** to divide into pieces [O.E. *ceorfan*]

car·vel (kárvəl) *n.* a caravel [F. *carvelle*]

car·vel-built (kárvəlbįlt) *adj.* (of a ship) having planks with their edges flush instead of overlapping (cf. CLINKERBUILT)

Car·ver (kárvər), George Washington (c. 1864–1943), U.S. black agricultural chemist. He directed his research in agronomy to the improvement of the South, coaxing southern farmers to diversify their crops by planting soil-enriching peanuts and sweet potatoes

Carver, John (c. 1576–1621), leader of the Pilgrim Fathers

carv·er (kárvər) *n.* a person who carves ‖ a carving knife ‖ (*pl.*) a carving knife and fork ‖ (*Br.*) a dining chair with armrests

carv·ing (kárviŋ) *n.* the act of carving ‖ a carved work or design

car·vone (kárvoun) *n.* an oily liquid ketone of the terpene series, C₁₀H₁₄O, found in essential oils (e.g. caraway, spearmint) and used as a flavoring and perfume [perh. fr. G. *karvon* fr. M.L. *carui*, caraway]

Car·y (kéari:, kǽri:), Joyce (1888–1957), English novelist and writer. His works include 'Mister Johnson' (1939), 'Herself Surprised' (1941), 'The Horse's Mouth' (1944), 'A Fearful Joy' (1949)

car·y·at·id (kǽri:ǽtid) *n.* a support, esp. a pillar of a Greek or neoclassical temple etc., carved in the form of a woman (cf. TELAMON, cf. ATLAS) [fr. Gk *Karyatides*, priestesses of Diana's temple at Karyai]

car·y·op·sis (kæri:ópsis) *pl.* **car·y·op·ses** (kæri:ɒpsi:z), **car·y·op·si·des** (kæri:ópsidi:z) *n.* a small, dry, single-celled, single-seeded indehiscent fruit in which the testa and pericarp are fused, as in cereals, grain etc. [Mod. L. fr. Gk *karuon*, nut+*opsis*, appearance]

CAS (*acronym*) for collision avoidance system

ca·sa·ba, cas·sa·ba (kəsába) *n.* any of several muskmelons with a yellow rind, esp. a subvariety of *Cucumis melo inodorus* [after *Kasaba*, in Asia Minor]

Ca·sa·blan·ca (kɑsɑblánkɑ) the chief port and economic center (pop. 1,952,200) of Morocco. Industries: chemical products, building materials, mechanical engineering, textiles, food processing, fishing. The medieval city is surrounded by modern and industrial quarters

Casablanca Conference the meeting (Jan. 14–26, 1943) between F. D. Roosevelt and Winston Churchill, at which it was agreed to insist on the unconditional surrender of the Axis powers

Ca·sa·no·va de Sein·galt (kɑsɑnóvɑdəsɛ̃gǽl), Giovanni Giacomo (1725–98), Italian amorist and adventurer whose 'Memoirs' give a lively picture of European life and morals of his day

Ca·sa Ros·a·da (kásɑrɔsáðɑ) the presidential palace in Buenos Aires [Span.= pink house]

Ca·sals, Pablo (kəsálz) (1876–1973), Spanish cellist, conductor, and composer. He toured widely with the cello and formed a trio with French violinist Jacques Thibaud and French pianist Alfred Cortot. In 1919 he founded the Orquestra Pau Casals in Barcelona, but left Spain to protest Francisco Franco's regime. He was associated with the Marlboro music festival in Vermont, and composed 'El Pessebre' ('The Manger'), a sacred oratorio (1960)

Casas, Las *LAS CASAS

cas·bah (kǽzbɑ) *n.* the quarter of a N. African town around the citadel or ruler's palace, or the

CONCISE PRONUNCIATION KEY: **(a)** æ, c*a*t; ɑ, c*ar*; ɔ fa*w*n; ei, sn*a*ke. **(e)** e, h*e*n; i:, sh*ee*p; iə, d*ee*r; ɛə, b*ea*r. **(i)** i, f*i*sh; ai, t*i*ger; ə:, b*i*rd. **(o)** o, *o*x; au, c*ow*; ou, g*oa*t; u, p*oo*r; ɔi, r*oy*al. **(u)** ʌ, d*u*ck; u, b*u*ll; u:, g*oo*se; ə, b*a*cillus; ju:, c*u*be. x, lo*ch*; θ, *th*ink; ð, bo*th*er; z, *Z*en; ʒ, cor*s*age; dʒ, sava*g*e; ŋ, orangutan*g*; j, *y*ak; ʃ, *f*ish; tʃ, fe*tch*; 'l, rabb*le*; 'n, redd*en*. Complete pronunciation key appears inside front cover.

citadel or palace itself [F. fr. Arab. *qasbah, quasabah*]

cas·cade (kæskéid) **1.** *n.* a waterfall ‖ a section of a large waterfall ‖ any rush of water falling from a height ‖ anything thought of as like a rush of water, *cascades of laughter* ‖ a series of stages in an apparatus or process in which each stage derives from the preceding one and acts upon its output, *cascade amplifier, cascade liquefaction* ‖ (*electr.*) process in which charged particles, accelerated by an electric field, cause a breakdown in a diode, resulting in an electric field crossing a barrier region so that current carriers collide with valence electrons ‖ the resulting ionization and cumulative multiplication of carriers due to the breakdown **2.** *v.i. pres. part.* **cas·cad·ing** *past* and *past part.* **cas·cad·ed** to fall as or like a waterfall [F. fr. Ital.]

cascade (*electr.*) **1.** process in which charged particles, accelerated by an electric field, cause a breakdown in a diode, resulting in an electric field crossing a barrier region so that current carriers collide with valence electrons. **2.** the resulting ionization and cumulative multiplication of carriers due to the breakdown. *syn* avalanche, avalanche diode, Townsend avalanche

cascade amplifier (*electr.*) device that amplifies in two successive stages

cascade particle *XI PARTICLE

Cascade Range a chain of volcanic peaks, with their foothills running from N. California through W. central Oregon and Washington and, as the Coast Mtns, into British Columbia, Canada: Mt Rainier, 14,410 ft

Cas·ca·di·an (kæskéidiːən) *adj.* (*geol.*) of a North American mountain-making episode during the Cenozoic period [fr. CASCADE RANGE]

cas·car·a (kæskéərə, *Br.* kæskúrə) *n.* the cascara buckthorn ‖ cascara sagrada

cascara buckthorn *Rhamnus purshiana*, a tree growing on the Pacific coast of the U.S.A. It yields cascara sagrada

cascara sa·gra·da (səgrádə) *n.* the dried bark of cascara buckthorn from which a laxative drug is obtained [Span.=sacred bark]

cas·ca·ril·la (kæskərílə) *n. Croton eluteria*, fam. *Euphorbiaceae*, a shrub growing in the Bahamas ‖ its bark, from which a tonic drug is obtained [Span.=thin bark]

case (keis) **1.** *n.* a box or crate ‖ a special box for some article, *an instrument case* ‖ any protective outer covering, *a watch case* ‖ a glass-sided box for exhibiting specimens, e.g. in a museum ‖ the frame in which a window or a door is set, a casing ‖ (*bookbinding*) a completed book cover ready to be fitted to the sheets ‖ (*Br.*) a suitcase **2.** *v.t. pres. part.* **cas·ing** *past* and *past part.* **cased** to enclose in a case or box, encase [O.N.F. *casse*]

case *n.* a set of circumstances or conditions, a state of affairs, *in that case you should sue* ‖ an instance, *four cases of fire* ‖ (*med.*) an instance of an illness ‖ the patient suffering from an illness, *a hopeless case* ‖ someone needing or receiving help other than medical, *a welfare case* ‖ a difficulty, problem, *a case of conscience* ‖ (*law*) a matter for trial ‖ the arguments for either side in a lawsuit, *the case for the defense* ‖ (*gram.*) in inflected languages (e.g. Latin) the form of a noun, pronoun or adjective which indicates its relationship to other words in a sentence (whether subject or object etc.). In English there are only two cases in nouns, the uninflected form (e.g. 'dog') and the genitive form, usually represented by *'s* following a word (e.g. 'dog's') **in any case** in any circumstances **in case** lest, *take a map in case you get lost* ‖ against possible need, *take some money just in case* **in case of** in the event of [O.F. *cas*]

case harden *v.t.* to harden the surface of (iron or steel) **case·hard·ened** (kéishɑrd'nd) *adj.* of a person grown callous through seeing too much misery

case history (*med.*) the facts of a patient's immediate and more remote ancestry, his childhood, education; environment, experiences etc., which could bear on the choice of treatment for his illness

ca·sein (kéisiːn, kéisiːin) *n.* the colloidal protein in milk, caseinogen ‖ the insoluble protein which is the basis and chief protein in cheese and is used in making certain plastics. It is precipitated from milk and curdled by rennet ‖ the insoluble protein (acid casein), precipitated from milk by acid (e.g. in souring) and used in

coating, synthetic fibers etc. [fr. L. *caseus*, cheese]

ca·sein·o·gen (keisíːnədʒən, kеisiːínədʒən) *n.* casein [fr. CASEIN+Gk *-genēs*, producing]

case knife a knife worn in a sheath

case law law established by precedent or judicial decision (cf. STATUTE LAW)

case·mate (kéismeit) *n.* (*hist.*) a chamber in the thickness of the wall of a fortress with small openings through which weapons could be fired ‖ an armored chamber in a warship in which the guns are enclosed **cáse·mat·ed** *adj.* [F. fr. Ital. *casamatta*, etym. doubtful]

Case·ment (kéismənt), Sir Roger David (1864–1916), Irish rebel. He was hanged for treason because of his attempts to induce Germany to support the cause of Irish independence

case·ment (kéismənt) *n.* a frame with a window hinged at the side so as to move in a horizontal plane [O.F. *encassement*]

case-mix (kéismiks) *n.* diagnosis-specific makeup of an institution's or a health program's workload

ca·se·ous (kéisiːəs) *adj.* like or of cheese [fr. L. *caseus*, cheese]

case program (*linguistics*) approach to sentence structure as a verb plus one or more noun phrases, where meaning relations are called cases; e.g., in *Tom saw the car through binoculars, Tom* is agentive case, *car* is objective, *through binoculars* is instrumental. It was conceived by Charles Fillmore in 1968

case shot a collection of small projectiles in a case, fired from a cannon

casette *CASSETTE

case·work (kéiswəːrk) *n.* the study of the history and environment of an individual or family in connection with psychological treatment or social assistance **cáse·work·er** *n.*

case·worm (kéiswəːrm) *n.* an insect larva which makes a case to protect itself (*CADDIS)

cash (kæʃ) **1.** *n.* money in the form of coins or paper, ready money **to pay cash (down)** to pay at the time of purchase **2.** *v.t.* to give or obtain cash in exchange for (a check, money order etc.) **to cash in on** (*pop.*) to turn to account, take advantage of [fr. F. *casse*, or Ital. *cassa*]

cash account an account into which only cash is paid, and from which recorded payments are made

cash-and-car·ry (kǽʃænd kǽriː) *adj.* of a store that sells merchandise at a discount for cash only, without services such as tailoring

cash bar liquor bar at which drinks are sold, esp. in distinction to social event where an open bar might be expected

cash book a book recording cash received and paid out

cash crop a crop grown to be sold (cf. SUBSISTENCE FARMING)

cash discount a percentage deduction from the amount charged if paid within a specified period

cash·ew (kǽʃuː, kəʃúː) *n. Anacardium occidentale*, fam. *Anacardiaceae*, a tropical tree native to Brazil and grown in the West and East Indies. It yields edible fruit, a nut with a high oil content, and resin

cashew nut the seed of the cashew, made edible by roasting. The shells yield a resin

cash flow (*business*) short-term changes in cash and working capital. *Cf* FUNDS FLOW

cash·ier (kæʃíər) *n.* an employee in a bank, who receives and pays out money ‖ an employee in a shop, restaurant etc. who takes and records customers' payments [fr. F. *caissier*]

cashier (kəʃíər) *v.t.* (*armed forces*) to dismiss (an officer) from the service in disgrace [Flem. or Du. *casseren*]

cash·mere (kǽʒmiər, kǽʃmiər) *n.* a very soft, fine wool, or woolen material, made from the fleece of the Kashmir goat

cash on delivery (*abbr.* C.O.D.) payment made for goods at the time of receipt, not of ordering

ca·shoo (kəʃúː) *n.* catechu

cash price the price of goods paid for in cash, lower than the installment plan price

cash register a mechanical till used in shops and restaurants, which records sums of money received

Cas·i·mir III (kǽzimiər) 'the Great' (1310–70), king of Poland (1333–70), known as 'the Peasants' King' for improving their lot

cas·ing (kéisiŋ) *n.* a thing which encases ‖ a material for encasing something else ‖ an enclosing framework, e.g. of a window ‖ the outer part of a tire

ca·si·no (kəsíːnou) *n.* a public room for gambling and dancing ‖ a building containing gambling rooms [Ital.=small house]

cask (kæsk, kɑsk) *n.* a wooden barrel for liquids ‖ a barrel and its contents ‖ the amount a cask holds [etym. doubtful]

cas·ket (kǽskit, kɑ́skit) *n.* a small box, usually of some valuable material and fine workmanship, esp. for holding letters or jewels ‖ a receptacle for the ashes of a cremated person ‖ a coffin [etym. doubtful]

Ca·so (kɑ́sɔ), Antonio (1883–1946), Mexican writer and essayist, author of 'Filosofía de la intuición' and 'Doctrina e ideas'

Cas·pi·an Sea (kǽspiːən) a shallow inland sea, the world's largest (area 275,000 sq. miles) between the European and Asian U.S.S.R., with Iran as its south border. It is 86 ft below sea level. Most of its waters come from the Volga. Fish: sturgeon and herring. Chief ports: Astrakhan and Baku

casque (kæsk) *n.* (*hist.*) a metal helmet, usually covering the face and having a visor [F. fr. Span. *casco*]

Cass (kæs), Lewis (1782–1866), U.S. general, diplomat and politician. He served as minister to France (1836–42) and won the Democratic presidential nomination (1848). He was appointed secretary of state (1857) under Buchanan but resigned (1860) when the president refused to take a firm stand against secession

cassaba *CASABA

Cas·san·dra (kəsǽndrə) (*Gk mythol.*) the daughter of Priam and Hecuba. She was a prophetess, doomed by Apollo never to be believed. Her warning to the Trojans against the Greeks' wooden horse was disregarded

cas·sa·reep (kǽsəriːp) *n.* the concentrated juice of cassava roots, deprived of its poisonous properties by boiling, and flavored with aromatics. It is used as the basis of the West Indian pepper pot, as an antiseptic, and for keeping meat fresh in the Tropics [Carib.]

cas·sa·tion (kæséiʃən) *n.* the annulment or quashing of a legal judgment [fr. L.L. *cassatio* (*cassationis*)]

Cas·satt (kəsǽt), Mary (1845–1926), American painter. Her work (esp. studies of mothers with children) shows the influence of Degas and the Impressionists

cas·sa·va (kəsáva) *n.* a member of *Manihot*, fam. *Euphorbiaceae*, a genus of plants grown in the Tropics to provide a staple food. The swollen roots (mainly starch) are boiled, powdered or dried [fr. Haitian]

Cassegrain antenna (*electr.*) microwave antenna arranged so that a feed radiator located near the main reflector is focused on a mirror, spreading its energy to illuminate the main reflector

Cas·se·grain·i·an telescope (kæsəgréiniːən) a reflecting telescope utilizing a paraboloidal mirror objective with a secondary convex hyperboloidal mirror. They are widely used as astronomical telescopes producing magnified images of very distant objects [after N. *Cassegrain*, F. 17th-c. physicist]

Cas·sel (kǽsəl) (*G.* Kassel) a city (pop. 206,000) in N. Hesse, West Germany, a communications junction. Industries: heavy machinery, textiles

cas·se·role (kǽsəroul) *n.* a covered dish of earthenware or toughened glass etc. in which food needing long, slow cooking is prepared ‖ food cooked in such a dish [F.]

cas·sette (kəsét) *n.* a holder for a photographic film or plate, esp. in X-ray work or for a tape-recorder tape ‖ cartridge containing magnetic tape that can be inserted into a player for listening or viewing, e.g., an audio cassette or video cassette [F., dim. of *casse*, case]

cassette television television equipment that can reproduce programs from cassette recordings.

cas·sia (kǽʃə, kǽsiːə) *n.* a member of *Cassia*, fam. *Papilionaceae*, a genus of trees cultivated in India. Their sun-dried leaves produce senna, and the fruits (pods) produce pectin ‖ Chinese cinnamon [L. fr. Gk fr. Heb.]

Cas·sian (kǽʃən), John (c. 360–c. 432), a monk in the Egyptian desert. He was among the first to pursue the monastic ideal in the West. His 'Institutes' and 'Conferences' influenced St Benedict in composing his rule

Cas·si·ni (kəsíːni) a French family of astronomers and geographers. Jean Dominique (1625–1712), Jacques (1677–1756), César François (Cassini de Thury, 1714–84) and Jean Domi-

CONCISE PRONUNCIATION KEY: **(a)** æ, c*a*t; ɑ, c*ar*; ɔ, f*aw*n; ei, sn*a*ke. **(e)** e, h*e*n; i:, sh*ee*p; iə, d*ee*r; ɛə, b*ea*r. **(i)** i, f*i*sh; ai, t*i*ger; ə, b*i*rd. **(o)** o, *o*x; au, c*ow*; ou, g*oa*t; u, p*oo*r; ɔi, r*oy*al. **(u)** ʌ, d*u*ck; u, b*u*ll; u:, g*oo*se; ə, b*a*cillus; ju:, c*u*be. x, lo*ch*; θ, *th*ink; ð, bo*th*er; z, *Z*en; ʒ, cor*s*age; dʒ, sava*g*e; ŋ, oranguta*ng*; j, *y*ak; ʃ, *fi*sh; tʃ, fe*tch*; 'l, rabb*le*; 'n, redd*en*. Complete pronunciation key appears inside front cover.

nique (comte de Cassini, 1748–1845) successively (father to son) directed the Paris observatory and contributed to the construction of a largescale map of France

Cas·si·no (kəsí:nou) a town in central Italy, 52 miles north-northwest of Naples. The Benedictine monastery on the mountain above the town was almost entirely destroyed in 1944 and has been rebuilt

Cas·si·o·do·rus (kæsi:ədórəs, kæsi:ədóurəs) Magnus Aurelius (c. 480–575), statesman, Christian scholar and Latin writer. He held high office under Theodoric the Great and the Ostrogoths, whose life he portrayed in his 'Variae', a collection of official documents

Cas·si·o·pe·ia (kæsi:əpí:ə) (Gk mythol.) the wife of Cepheus, king of Ethiopia, and mother of Andromeda ‖ a constellation of the northern hemisphere, very close to the North Star

Cas·si·rer (kəsí:rər), Ernst (1874–1945), German philosopher. He immigrated to Sweden in 1933 and to the U.S.A. in 1941. A neo-Kantian, he extended the Kantian critique to modern science. In his most celebrated work, 'The Philosophy of Symbolic Forms' (3 vols, 1923–9) he investigated the symbolic functions of thought as manifested in language, myth and science

Cass·Ir·is·ar·ri Treaty (kæsi:ri:sári:) a treaty (1858) signed by Lewis Cass and Antonio José de Irisarri (1786–1868), Guatemalan writer and politician. It gave the U.S.A. the right of free passage on Nicaraguan soil and the right to intervene in its affairs for whatever purpose the U.S.A. saw fit

cas·sit·er·ite (kəsítərait) n. stannic oxide, SnO₂, the most important ore of tin [fr. Gk kassiteros, tin]

Cas·sius (kæʃəs), Gaius Longinus (d. 42 B.C.), Roman general, a leader of the conspiracy against Julius Caesar (44 B.C.)

Cas·si·ve·lau·nus (kæsivilónəs) British chief who led the resistance to Caesar's invasion of Britain (54 B.C.)

cas·sock (kæsək) n. a long, close-fitting tunic, usually black, worn by priests and choristers [F. casaque, etym. doubtful]

cas·so·war·y (kæsəwęri) pl. **cas·so·war·ies** n. a member of Casuarius, a genus of running birds allied to the ostrich, emu and American rhea [fr. Malay]

cast (kæst, kɑst) 1. v. pres. part. **cast·ing**, past and past part. **cast** v.t. to throw, to cast dice, to cast a shadow ‖ to let drop, throw off, a snake casts its skin ‖ to discard (a card) ‖ to add up ‖ to shape (molten metal, liquid clay, plaster etc) by pouring it into a mold ‖ (an object) by this process ‖ (angling) to throw (a line) into the water ‖ (theater) to distribute (the parts) in a play to the actors ‖ (theater) to assign (an actor) to a role ‖ (naut.) to bring (a boat) around ‖ to register (a vote) ‖ to drop out (an anchor) attached to a rope ‖ (Br.) of a cow) to give birth to (a calf) prematurely ‖ to assemble the data for (a horoscope) ‖ to direct, usually quickly, to cast a glance ‖ (fig.) to cause to be directed on or against, to cast light on a problem, to cast suspicion on a person ‖ v.i. to turn, tack ‖ (angling) to throw the line into the water **to cast about for** to look for **to cast aside** to put away from one **to cast down** to turn (the eyes) downwards **to cast loose** to detach oneself **to cast off** (naut.) to loosen the ropes securing a boat to a pier or jetty ‖ (knitting) to bind off ‖ (printing) to estimate the printed space required for (a manuscript) **to cast on** (knitting) to begin or widen a piece by making loops on a knitting needle 2. n. the act of casting ‖ a throw of a fishing net or line, a sounding lead, or dice ‖ the light piece of gut or nylon on the end of a fishing line, to which the weights, hook and bait are attached ‖ undigested matter (bone, fur etc.) regurgitated by birds of prey ‖ (Br.=Am. roll) the number thrown in a game of dice ‖ the actors in a play ‖ a model made by running molten metal, plaster etc., into a mold ‖ the mold into which metal is poured ‖ a characteristic quality, cast of mind ‖ the distance which something may be thrown ‖ an addition (of figures) ‖ a tinge of some color ‖ a slight squint ‖ (med.) a rigid surgical dressing often of gauze and plaster of paris ‖ (zool.) a coil of sand passed by the lugworm [O.N. kasta]

cas·ta·net (kæstənét) n. (mus.) one of a pair of wooden or ivory attached, shell-like pieces which the player loops over his fingers and holds in the palm and which produce a sharp, clicking sound when struck together [fr. Span. castañeta dim. of castaña, chestnut]

cast·a·way (kæstəwęi, kástəwęi) 1. n. a shipwrecked person 2. adj. shipwrecked

caste (kæst, kɑst) n. an inherited socioreligious rank. Hinduism has traditionally divided its adherents into four basic castes: Brahmin (priest), Ksatriya (noble warrior), Vaisya (merchant or farmer) and Sudra (worker). There are strict rules of behavior, and no orthodox Hindu will seek to break caste. One can rise from one caste to another only in the course of reincarnation. There have been many modern movements within India to ease the hardships brought about by the caste system [fr. Span. and Port. casta, race]

Cas·tel Gan·dol·fo (kəstélgandólfə) the pope's summer residence, 17 miles southeast of Rome

cas·tel·lat·ed (kæst'lęitid) adj. (of a building) like a castle, having battlements [fr. M.L. castellatus]

Cas·te·llón (kəsteljón) a province (area 2,495 sq. miles, pop. 431,755) of E. Spain ‖ its capital (pop. 126,464) (*VALENCIA)

Cas·te·lo Bran·co (kəstélu:bránku:), Humberto de Alançar (1900–67), Brazilian army officer and statesman, president of Brazil (1964–6)

cast·er, cas·tor (kæstər, kástər) n. a small container for sugar, salt or pepper, with holes in the top, used at the table ‖ a small metal wheel fixed to the leg of a piece of furniture to allow it to be moved easily

cas·ti·gate (kæstigeit) pres. part. **cas·ti·gat·ing** past and past part. **cas·ti·gat·ed** v.t. to rebuke or criticize vehemently **cas·ti·gá·tion** n. very severe criticism **cás·ti·ga·tor** n. **cas·ti·ga·to·ry** (kæstigətɔri:, kæstigətóuri:) adj. [fr. L. castigare (castigatus), to punish]

Cas·ti·glio·ne (kəstiljóne), Count Baldassare (1478–1529), Italian diplomat and author of 'Il Libro del Cortegiano' (1528) translated (1561) as 'The Courtyer' by Thomas Hoby

Cas·tile (kæstí:l) (Span. Castilla) a region of Spain occupying most of the central plateau, divided by the Sierra de Guadarrama into Old Castile (north) and New Castile (south). It is largely arid, with a harsh climate. Originally part of León, Castile became an independent kingdom (10th c.) and achieved a dominant position by the 13th c. Its union with Aragon (1479) led to the formation of the Spanish state

Castile soap a hard white soap made from olive oil and sodium hydroxide

Cas·til·ian (kæstíljən) 1. n. the accepted standard spoken Spanish, originally the dialect of Castile ‖ an inhabitant of Castile 2. adj. of Castile, its inhabitants, or their language ‖ of standard Spanish

Cas·ti·lla (kəstí:jə), Ramón (1797–1867), Peruvian general, patriot in the struggle for independence, and president (1845–51, 1854–62). He abolished slavery, modernized Lima, introduced telegraphy and railroads, and organized the guano industry

Cas·ti·llo Ar·mas (kəstí:jɔármɑs), Carlos (1914–57), Guatemalan colonel who became president (1954) after overthrowing the government of Jacobo Arbenz. He was assassinated

cast·ing (kæstiŋ, kástiŋ) n. an object made by casting liquid metal etc. into a mold and allowing it to solidify ‖ the process of making such an object

casting vote a final vote cast (e.g. by the chairman) to decide a question over which voting is equally divided

cast iron an iron-carbon alloy produced in a blast furnace. It contains up to 4% carbon, and is more brittle, but more easily fused, than steel (cf. WROUGHT IRON) **cást-iron** adj. made of cast iron ‖ (fig.) unbreakable, a cast-iron will

cas·tle (kæs'l, kás'l) n. **cas·tling** past and past part. **cas·tled** v.i. (chess) to move the king two squares to either side and then put the corresponding rook on the square skipped by the king ‖ v.t. (chess) to move (the king) in castling

castle n. a fortified building or group of buildings within a defensive wall, a fortress ‖ (chess) a rook [O.E. castel fr. O.N.F.]

Cas·tle·reagh (kæs'lręi, kás'lręi), Robert Stewart, Viscount, afterwards 2nd marquess of Londonderry (1769–1822), British statesman. As Tory foreign secretary (1812–22), he held together the coalition against Napoleon and played a leading role in the reorganization of Europe at the Congress of Vienna (1815) and in subsequent European congresses

castles in Spain daydreams, plans that will never be put into effect

castles in the air castles in Spain

cast-off (kæstɔf, kástɔf, kæstɒf, kástɒf) adj. (of clothes, lovers etc.) not wanted any more **cást-off** n. a person who has been rejected ‖ (pl.) clothes which the owner won't wear again ‖ (printing) an estimate of the number of lines or pages, in type of a given style, required for a given quantity of copy

castor *CASTER

cas·tor (kæstər, kástər) n. a substance obtained from glands of the beaver, used in medicine and perfumery [F. and L. fr. Gk kastor, beaver]

Cas·tor and Pol·lux (kæstər, kástər, póləks) *DIOSCURI

castor bean the seed of the castor-oil plant ‖ the castor-oil plant

castor oil a pale yellow, thick oil, with an unpleasant taste, obtained from the seeds of the castor-oil plant. The oil is used medically as a purgative, and also as a lubricant [origin unknown]

castor-oil plant Ricinus communis, fam. Euphorbiaceae, a plant grown throughout the Tropics. Its seeds yield castor oil

castor sugar (Br.) a white, finely granulated sugar

cas·trate (kæstreit) pres. part. **cas·trat·ing** past and past part. **cas·trat·ed** v.t. to remove the testicles of (a man or male animal) **cas·trá·tion** n. [fr. L. castrare (castratus)]

cas·tra·to (kæstrátou) pl. **cas·tra·ti** (kæstrúti:) n. (hist., esp. 17th and 18th cc.) a male singer castrated as a boy to allow development of the voice in the soprano or contralto ranges [Ital.]

Castriota *SCANDERBEG

Cas·tro (kústrɔ), Cipriano (1858–1924), Venezuelan general and dictator (1899–1908). The corruption of his administration provoked several revolts, the last of which resulted in his overthrow by Gen. Juan Vicente Gómez

Cas·tro (kæstrou, kástro), Fidel (1927–   ), Cuban statesman. He was exiled from Cuba (1953), but returned (1956) to fight a guerrilla war against the regime until President Batista was forced to flee. Castro became prime minister of Cuba (1959). Following the unsuccessful U.S.-backed Bay of Pigs invasion (1961), he consolidated his power and declared himself a Marxist-Leninist. He became Chairman of the Nonaligned Nations Movement (1979) and considered it his obligation to fight imperialism in the Third World to which end he sent troops to Angola and Ethiopia to assist Marxist regimes. His economic policies were less successful, however, and Cuba had to depend on considerable economic aid from the U.S.S.R.

Castro Al·ves (kástrɔálves), Antonio de (1847–71), Brazilian poet and champion of emancipation and republicanism

Cas·tro·ism (kæstrouizəm) n. principles and policies of Fidel Castro in Cuba. syn Fidelism. —**Castroist** n. —**Castroite** n.

cas·u·al (kæʒu:əl) adj. irregular, happening by chance, a casual encounter ‖ without formality, casual manners ‖ free and easy, he is too casual with her ‖ unimportant, not significant, a casual remark [F. casuel]

casual labor temporary employment paid for by the hour

cas·u·al·ty (kæʒu:əlti:) pl. **cas·u·al·ties** n. an accident, esp. one involving injury or loss of life ‖ an injured person ‖ a soldier who is missing or has been captured, wounded or killed in action ‖ (pl.) soldiers or civilians killed or injured in war ‖ someone injured or killed in an accident [F. casualité fr. M.L. casualitas, chance]

cas·u·a·ri·na (kæʒərí:nə) n. a member of Casuarina, a genus of graceful trees with jointed branches and scalelike leaves, somewhat like the larch [fr. Mod. L. casuarius, cassowary bird, because of the feathery look of the branches]

cas·u·ist (kæʒu:ist) n. a person, esp. a theologian, expert in dealing with moral problems and in resolving cases of conscience by applying ethical rules ‖ (pop.) a person who reasons speciously **cas·u·is·tic, cas·u·ís·ti·cal** adjs [F. casuiste]

cas·u·ist·ry (kæʒu:istri:) n. the act or system of dealing with cases of conscience ‖ (pop.) specious argument

cat (kæt) n. Felis catus or F. domesticus, fam. Felidae, a carnivorous furry mammal, long domesticated and useful for keeping down mice. There are about 30 breeds of long-haired and short-haired cats, widely distributed. The average length of the male is 28 ins and of the female 21 ins. The gestation period averages 63 days ‖ the fur or pelt of the domestic cat ‖ any other member of fam. *Felidae*, e.g. a lion, tiger, leopard, wildcat etc. ‖ a malicious or spiteful woman ‖ (*hist.*) the cat-o'-nine-tails **to let the cat out of the bag** to reveal a secret, esp. by a slip of the tongue [O.E.]

cat 1. *v.t. pres. part.* **cat·ting** *past* and *past part.* **cat·ted** (*naut.*) to raise (an anchor) from the surface of the water to the cathead 2. *n.* the cathead

CAT 1. (*acronym*) for clear air turbulence. 2. (*acronym*) for coaxial tomography

catabolic *KATABOLIC

catabolism *KATABOLISM

cat·a·chre·sis (kætəkríːsis) *pl.* **cat·a·chre·ses** (kætəkríːsiːz) *n.* the incorrect use of a word or term **cat·a·chres·tic** (kætəkréstik) *adj.* [L. fr. Gk *katachrēsis*, misuse]

cat·a·clysm (kætəklizəm) *n.* any violent physical upheaval such as a flood or an earthquake ‖ a political upheaval or catastrophe **cat·a·clys·mal, cat·a·clys·mic** *adjs* [F. fr. Gk]

cat·a·comb (kætəkoum) *n.* a series of underground galleries and chambers with recesses for burying the dead [F. *catacombe*]

ca·tad·ro·mous (kətædrəməs) *adj.* tending downwards ‖ (*zool.*) of fish which migrate from fresh to saltwater to breed (cf. ANADROMOUS) [fr. Gk *kata*, down + *-dromos*, running]

cat·a·falque (kætəfælk, kætəfɔk) *n.* a draped platform, supporting the coffin at a funeral or lying-in-state [F. fr. Ital.]

Ca·ta·lan (kætlǽn) 1. *n.* a person from Catalonia ‖ the Romance language spoken in Catalonia 2. *adj.* of such a person ‖ of this language

cat·a·lan·guage (kætələŋgwidʒ) *n.* (*computer*) target language used to translate data for processing by an assembler, compiler, or translator

cat·a·lep·sy (kætlepsiː) *n.* (*med.*) a condition in which the patient maintains his limbs in any position in which they are placed [fr. M.L. *catalepsia* fr. Gk *katalepsis*, a grasping]

cat·a·lep·tic (kætléptik) 1. *adj.* pertaining to catalepsy 2. *n.* a person subject to catalepsy [fr. L.L. *catalepticus*]

cat·a·log, cat·a·logue (kætlɔg, kætlog) 1. *n.* a complete list of articles, e.g. library books, pictures, museum exhibits, or goods for sale, usually in alphabetical order, or under special headings, and often with descriptions of the articles 2. *v.t. pres. part.* **cat·a·log·ing, cat·a·logu·ing** *past* and *past part.* **cat·a·loged, cat·a·logued** to list ‖ to include in a catalog ‖ to describe the bibliographical and technical features of (a publication) **cát·a·log·er, cát·a·logu·er** *n.* [F. fr. Gk *katalogos*, enrollment]

ca·ta·logue rai·son·né (kætlɔgrezonéi, kætlogrezonéi) *pl.* **ca·ta·logues rai·son·nés** *n.* a catalog arranged according to subjects and with descriptions [F.]

Cat·a·lo·ni·a (kætlóuniə, kætlóunjə) (*Span.* Cataluña) a region of Spain bordering France (in the Pyrenees) and the Mediterranean (Costa Brava), comprising Gerona, Barcelona, Lérida and Tarragona provinces. It is one of Spain's most prosperous areas. Main industries: mining (coal, lead, salt), metallurgy, textiles, tourism, fishing. Agricultural products: cereals, olives, wine. Historic capital: Barcelona. Taken from the Moors by Charlemagne, it became independent (9th c.) and united with Aragon (1137). It has maintained a strong separatist tradition and was the center of Republican resistance in the Civil War (1936–9). Catalan is widely spoken

Cat·a·lo·ni·an (kætəlóuniːən) 1. *adj.* of or pertaining to Catalonia or its people 2. *n.* a native or inhabitant of Catalonia

ca·tal·pa (kətælpə) *n.* a member of *Catalpa*, fam. *Bignoniaceae*, a genus of trees with heart-shaped leaves and long racemes of flowers and long pods [fr. Creek Indian *kutuhlpa*]

ca·tal·y·sis (kətælisis) *pl.* **ca·tal·y·ses** (kətælisiːz) *n.* the change in the rate of chemical reaction brought about by a catalyst, usually present in small quantities and unaffected chemically at the completion of the reaction **cat·a·lyst** (kætlist) *n.* a substance that alters the rate of a chemical reaction and is itself unchanged by the process. Catalysts usually increase the rate of chemical reaction, so enabling them, for example, to take place under milder conditions (e.g. at lower temperatures) than would otherwise be possible **cat·a·lyt·ic** (kætlítik) *adj.* causing or relating to catalysis

cat·a·lyt·i·cal·ly *adv.* [Gk *katalusis*, a breaking down]

catalytic attack (*mil.*) attack designed to bring about a war between major powers through the disguised machinations of a third power

catalytic converter device used in automobiles that chemically changes noxious gases (carbon monoxide, nitrogen oxides, and hydrocarbons) to harmless, nonpolluting products (carbon di oxide, nitrogen, and water vapor). It is used in most motor vehicles manufactured after 1974

cat·a·lyze (kætlaiz) *pres. part.* **cat·a·lyz·ing** *past* and *past part.* **cat·a·lyzed** *v.t.* to bring about the catalysis of (a reaction) ‖ to produce (a substance) by catalysis **cát·a·lyz·er** *n.* a catalyst [prob. fr. F. *catalyser*]

cat·a·ma·ran (kætəmərǽn) *n.* a boat with twin hulls connected by a frame, esp. a very fast sailing boat ‖ a raft of two boats lashed together [fr. Tamil *katamaram*, tied tree]

Cat·a·mount (kætəmaunt) *n.* a wild animal of fam. *Felidae* [shortened fr. CATAMOUNTAIN]

cat·a·moun·tain (kætəmáuntən) *n.* the European wildcat ‖ (*hist.*) the leopard [=Cat of the Mountain]

cat-and-dog (kætəndɔg, kætəndóg) *adj.* (of the life lived together by a couple) embittered by perpetual quarreling

Ca·ta·nia (kətánjə) a town (pop. 399,800) at the foot of Etna on the east coast of Sicily, an industrial center (linen, silk, canning) and the island's largest export port (agricultural products, sulfur) founded (729 B.C.) by Greeks. Cathedral (1091). University (1444)

cat·a·pho·re·sis (kætəfərí:sis) *pl.* **cat·a·pho·re·ses** (kætəfərí:siːz) *n.* electrophoresis

cat·a·plec·tic (kætəpléktik) *adj.* of, relating to or affected with cataplexy

cat·a·plex·y (kætəpleksiː) *n.* a condition of transient immobility without loss of consciousness as a result of shock etc. [fr. Gk *kataplēxis*, stupor]

cat·a·pult (kætəpult, kætəpʌlt) 1. *n.* (*hist.*) a machine for hurling stones etc., worked by a lever. It was used by the Romans, and continued in use until the invention of cannon ‖ (*Br.*) a slingshot ‖ a machine for launching aircraft 2. *v.t.* to launch (aircraft) with a catapult ‖ *v.i.* to rise into the air as though shot from a catapult [L. *catapulta* fr. Gk]

cat·a·ract (kætərækt) *n.* a waterfall ‖ any rush of water ‖ (*med.*) a disease of the eye in which the normally transparent lens becomes opaque [F. *cataracte* fr. L. fr. Gk]

ca·tarrh (kətáːr) *n.* an inflammation of any mucous membrane, esp. that of the nasal passages, usually accompanied by discharge from the membrane **ca·tárrh·al** *adj.* [F. *catarrhe* fr. L. fr. Gk]

ca·tas·ta·sis (kətǽstəsis) *pl.* **ca·tas·ta·ses** (kətǽstəsiːz) *n.* the part of a tragedy when the action is heightened to its climax, following the epitasis and just before the catastrophe [Gk *katastasis*, settlement]

ca·tas·tro·phe (kətǽstrəfi) *n.* a sudden and terrible event, e.g. an earthquake, flood or tornado, any disaster affecting one or more persons ‖ (*drama*) the point in a tragedy to which the action has been leading **cat·a·stroph·ic** (kætəstrófik) *adj.* [Gk *katastrophē*, a turning down]

catastrophe insurance (*insurance*) insurance protection against large losses. Such policies generally cover all, or a specified percentage, of expenses above a substantial amount that remains the responsibility of the insured or of another insurance policy of limited liability

cat·a·to·ni·a (kætətóuniːə) *n.* a set of symptoms involving muscular rigidity and mental stupor, with alternating excitement and confusion, most often found in schizophrenia **cat·a·ton·ic** (kætətónik) *adj.* [fr. Gk *kata*, down, through + *tonos*, tension]

ca·taw·ba (kətɔbə) *n. Vitis labrusca*, a light red American grape ‖ the light white wine made from this grape [after the *Catawba* River in North America]

cat·a·zine (kætəziːn) *n.* a catalog that contains some editorial matter designed to extend the period of reader retention; from catalog-magazine

cat·bird (kætbəːrd) *n. Dumetella carolinensis*, a dark gray American songbird with a black head, whose call is like a cat's meow ‖ any of several similar Australian birds

cat·boat (kætbout) *n.* a sailing boat with one mast stepped close to the bows, and a single sail [perh. fr. *catt*, an obsolete type of boat]

cat burglar a thief who breaks into a building after nimble and often dangerous climbing

cat·call (kætkɔl) 1. *n.* a piercing whistle used esp. to show displeasure in theaters etc. 2. *v.i.* to sound catcalls ‖ *v.t.* to express disapproval of by catcalls

catch (kætʃ) 1. *v. pres. part.* **catch·ing**, *past* and *past part.* **caught** (kɔt) *v.t.* to capture, ensnare ‖ to seize in flight ‖ to be in time for, *to catch a train* ‖ to hit or strike, *the stone caught him on the shin* ‖ to surprise or detect (esp. in a crime or misdemeanor), *caught in the act* ‖ to burst into, *to catch fire* ‖ to make brief contact with, *try to catch him for a minute after the meeting* ‖ to contract (an illness) ‖ to be infected with, *to catch someone's enthusiasm* ‖ to hear, *did you catch his name?* ‖ to suspend (breathing) momentarily from surprise or other emotion, *to catch one's breath* ‖ to obtain briefly, *to catch a glimpse* ‖ to attract (attention) or the attention of ‖ *v.i.* to become entangled, *her coat caught on the wire* ‖ (of the voice) to break with emotion ‖ (of breath) to stop momentarily as a result of surprise etc. ‖ (*baseball*) to play as catcher ‖ to take fire **to catch at** to try to seize **to catch it** (*pop.*) to be punished **to catch on** (*pop.*) to understand, grasp an idea **to catch out** (*Br.*) to detect in a mistake ‖ (*cricket* or *baseball*) to dismiss (a batter) by catching a ball immediately after it leaves his bat without bouncing **to catch up** to lift suddenly ‖ to interrupt in order to disagree ‖ to make up arrears **to catch up with** to come level with 2. *n.* the act of catching, esp. of catching a ball in baseball or cricket ‖ the number of fish caught in a fishing expedition ‖ something worth securing (*pop.*, esp. a husband or wife) ‖ a temporary stoppage or interruption, *a catch in the voice* ‖ a fastening on a door, window or gate ‖ (*mus.*) an English popular round of the 17th and 18th cc. for three or more voices ‖ a fragment (of music), *a catch of song* ‖ a game consisting of throwing and catching a ball [O.N.F. *cachier*]

catch-as-catch-can (kætʃəzkætʃkǽn) 1. *n.* a style of wrestling in which no holds are barred 2. *adj.* of anything makeshift and hurried

catch·er (kætʃər) *n.* (*baseball*) the player who stands behind the batter to catch the pitched ball

catch·ing (kætʃiŋ) *adj.* (of disease, enthusiasm etc.) contagious

catch·ment (kætʃmənt) *n.* the whole area from which water drains into a river, lake or reservoir

catchment area geographic area defined and served by a health program, hospital, or other institution, usu. delineated on the basis of such factors as population distribution, natural geographic boundaries, and transportation accessibility

catch·pen·ny (kætʃpeniː) *adj.* of glib, empty sales talk, *catchpenny slogans* ‖ of any facile showmanship, *catchpenny jokes* ‖ made for quick sale at a low price

catch·phrase (kætʃfreiz) *n.* a striking phrase intended to arrest attention, usually often repeated (e.g. in publicity or political propaganda)

catch-22 double-bind situation in which one factor invalidates or makes impossible other factors, usu. used satirically; from the novel *Catch-22* by Joseph Heller

catch·up (kætʃəp) *n.* ketchup

catch·weight (kætʃweit) *n.* (*sports*) the weight that a contestant, e.g. a boxer or a jockey, happens or prefers to be, as distinct from the approved weight in the rules of his particular sport

catch·word (kætʃwəːrd) *n.* a word constantly repeated and taken up, so that it becomes associated with a policy, outlook etc., esp. in politics ‖ a printed word placed so that it catches the attention, e.g. the first word in a dictionary entry ‖ the first word of a new page printed at the foot of the preceding page, to help the reader to pass from one to the other ‖ the last word of an actor's speech, which gives the next speaker his cue

catch·y (kætʃiː) *comp.* **catch·i·er** *superl.* **catch·i·est** *adj.* attractive and easy to remember ‖ tricky, full of snags

Ca·teau-Cam·bré·sis, Treaty of (kætoukăbreizi:), a treaty (1559) between France, Spain and England, concluding the Italian Wars (1494–1559). France recognized Spanish claims in Italy, but received the bishoprics of Metz, Toul and Verdun. England finally lost Calais

---

CONCISE PRONUNCIATION KEY: **(a)** æ, c*a*t; ɑ, c*a*r; ɔ f*aw*n; ei, sn*a*ke. **(e)** e, h*e*n; iː, sh*ee*p; iə, d*ee*r; εə, b*ea*r. **(i)** i, f*i*sh; ai, t*i*ger; əː, b*i*rd. **(o)** o, *o*x; au, c*ow*; ou, g*oa*t; u, p*oo*r; ɔi, r*oy*al. **(u)** ʌ, d*u*ck; u, b*u*ll; uː, g*oo*se; ə, b*a*cillus; juː, c*u*be. x, lo*ch*; θ, *th*ink; ð, bo*th*er; z, *Z*en; ʒ, corsa*g*e; dʒ, sava*g*e; ŋ, oranguta*ng*; j, *y*ak; ʃ, *fi*sh; tʃ, fe*tch*; 'l, rabb*le*; 'n, redd*en*. Complete pronunciation key appears inside front cover.

cat·e·che·sis (kætəki:sis) *pl.* **cat·e·che·ses** (kætəki:si:z) *n.* oral teaching, esp. in the basic principles of any religion, catechizing [L. fr. Gk *katēchēsis*]

cat·e·chet·ic (kætəkétik) *adj.* pertaining to oral teaching, or to getting information, by question and answer ‖ pertaining to the Church catechism **cat·e·chét·i·cal** *adj.* [fr. L. fr. Gk *katēchētēs*, an oral teacher]

cat·e·chism (kætəkizəm) *n.* a set of questions and answers on religious doctrine ‖ (*pop.*) persistent questioning on any matter, esp. if resented [fr. L. *catechismus* fr. Gk *kata*, completely+*ēchein*, to sound]

cat·e·chist (kætəkist) *n.* a catechizer ‖ a teacher of catechumens [fr. L. *catechista* fr. Gk]

cat·e·chize (kætəkaiz) *pres. part.* **cat·e·chiz·ing**, *past* and *past part.* **cat·e·chized** *v.i.* to drill the catechism ‖ *v.t.* to put searching questions to (someone) [fr. L. *catechizare* fr. Gk]

cat·e·cho·la·mine (kætekóuləmi:n) *n.* (*pharm.*) **1.** any of various neurotransmitter drugs or hormones, e.g., epinephrene, dopamine. **2.** *adj.* (*biochem.*) of a class of hormones that act upon the nerve cells, e.g., adrenaline, epinephrine

cat·e·chu (kætətʃu:) *n.* any of several dry, astringent substances, containing 40–55% tannin, obtained from certain Asiatic plants, and used in dyes and for tanning [perh. fr. Malay. *kachu*]

cat·e·chu·men (kætəkjú:mən) *n.* a person receiving instruction in the religion into which he is to be baptized [fr. F. *catéchumène* fr. L. fr. Gk]

cat·e·gor·i·cal (kætəgórik'l, kætəgórik'l) *adj.* unqualified, absolute ‖ explicit, *a categorical denial* ‖ (*logic*) analyzable into a subject and an attribute ‖ of, pertaining to, or in a category [fr. Gk *katēgorikos*, assertive]

categorical imperative (*Kantian ethics*) the obligation to find for every case of conscience a solution which will hold for all men at all times

categorically needy (*sociology*) persons who are economically needy and members of certain categories of groups eligible to receive public assistance

categorically related *adj.* **1.** in the Medicaid program, satisfying requirements (other than income and resources) that one must meet in order to be eligible for benefits. **2.** individuals who meet these requirements

categorical program 1. a health program concerned with research, education, control, and/or treatment of only one disease or a few specific diseases. **2.** a program concerned with only a part of the population or health system. **3.** a program that the federal government should cease to support

cat·e·go·ry (kætəgɔri:, kætəgouri:) *pl.* **cat·e·go·ries** *n.* one of the divisions in a system of classification, e.g. genus and species in biological classification ‖ any general division serving to classify ‖ (*pl.*, *Aristotelian logic*) the fundamental classes among which all things can be distributed: relation, place, time, substance, quality, quantity, posture, possession, action and passion ‖ (*pl.*) similar classes employed by other philosophers [fr. L. fr. Gk *kategoria*, statement]

ca·te·na (kətí:nə) *pl.* **ca·te·nae** (kətí:ni:) *n.* a connected series [L.=chain]

ca·te·nac·cio system (kætənátʃi:ou) (*football*) defensive alignment of four backs and one sweeper

cat·e·nar·y (kæt'neri:, *Br.* kətí:nəri) **1.** *pl.* **cat·e·nar·ies** *n.* the curve made by a flexible cord or chain hanging freely between two points of suspension not necessarily of the same height **2.** *adj.* resembling such a curve [fr. L. *catenarius* fr. *catena*, a chain]

catenary bridge a suspension bridge hung on catenary chains

cat·e·nate (kæt'neit) *pres. part.* **cat·e·nat·ing** *past* and *past part.* **cat·e·nat·ed** *v.t.* to connect in a series, like links in a chain **cat·e·na·tion** *n.* [fr. L. *catenare* (*catenatus*)]

ca·ter (kéitər) *v.i.* to provide meals, refreshments etc. ‖ to provide something other than food, e.g. amusement, *to cater to all tastes* ‖ (*Br.*) to arrange for (but not cook) the meals in an institution or place of public entertainment **cá·ter·er** *n.* a person or company supplying food for public or private entertainment ‖ (*Br.*) a person who arranges the meals in an institution, e.g. a school [M.E. *catour* fr. O.F.]

cat·er·cor·ner (kætəkɔrnər, kætərkɔrnər) *adj.* and *adv.* catercornered

cat·er·cor·nered (kætəkɔrnərd, kæti:kɔrnərd, kætərkɔrnərd) **1.** *adj.* diagonal **2.** *adv.* diagonally [fr. F. *quatre*, four+CORNERED]

cat·er·pil·lar (kætərpilər, kætəpilər) *n.* the larva of a moth or butterfly. It has powerful biting jaws, and has no distinct thorax or abdomen. It crawls slowly on stubby legs. After hatching from the egg, it eats leaves voraciously until fully grown, then forms a hard case around its soft body, becoming a chrysalis **Cat·er·pil·lar** (trademark) a tractor fitted with flexible steel bands around the wheels to enable it to travel over very rough or soft ground [etym. doubtful]

cat·er·waul (kætərwɔl) **1.** *n.* a cat's scream **2.** *v.i.* to make a noise like a cat's scream ‖ to quarrel like cats [CAT+*waul*, to cry]

cat·fall (kætfɔl) *n.* (*naut.*) a rope or tackle used in hoisting the anchor to the cathead

cat·fish (kætfiʃ) *pl.* **cat·fish·es**, **cat·fish** *n.* any of over 1,200 varieties of fish of the suborder *Siluroidea*, order *Ostariophysi*, voracious eaters, having barbels, a scaleless or bony-plated body and a fleshy fin near the tail. Most are freshwater fish and edible. *Malapterurus electricus* is the electric catfish of N. African and tropical African waters (*ELECTRIC ORGANS)

cat·gut (kætgʌt) *n.* a translucent cord with a high tensile strength, made from the twisted intestines of a sheep or a horse (not of a cat). It is used for the strings of violins etc., tennis rackets, and for stitching wounds [etym. doubtful]

Cath·ar (kæθar) *pl.* **Cath·a·ri** (kæθəri:), **Cath·ars** *n.* a member of several heretical medieval Christian sects of Manichaean origin, e.g. the Albigenses

ca·thar·sis, **ca·thar·sis** (kəθársis) *pl.* **ca·thar·ses, ka·thar·ses** (kəθársi:z) *n.* (*med.*) purgation ‖ the (Aristotelian) purification or relief of the emotions through art, esp. tragedy [Mod. L. fr. Gk]

ca·thar·tic (kəθártik) **1.** *n.* a purgative medicine **2.** *adj.* pertaining to catharsis [fr. L. fr. Gk]

Ca·thay (kæθéi) (*hist.*) China

cat·head (kæthed) *n.* (*naut.*) a horizontal beam on each side of a ship's bow, on which the anchor is slung

ca·the·dral (kəθí:drəl) **1.** *n.* the principal church of a diocese, from which the bishop of the diocese takes his title, and where he often officiates and has his throne ‖ any of various large non-episcopalian churches **2.** *adj.* pertaining to or ranking as a cathedral [fr. M.L. *cathedralis* fr. Gk *kathedra*, chair]

ca·thep·sin (kəθépsin) *n.* (*biochem.*) enzyme that breaks down proteins into simpler substances, reducing heavy proteins to proteoses and peptones

Cath·er (kæðər), Willa Sibert (1873–1947), U.S. novelist. Her works, which include 'My Antonia' (1918) and 'A Lost Lady' (1923), often depict pioneer life on the U.S. frontier

Cath·er·ine I (kæθərin, kæθrin) (c. 1684–1727), second wife of Peter the Great, whom she succeeded as empress of Russia (1725–7)

Catherine II 'the Great' (1729–96), empress of Russia (1762–96) after the overthrow of her inept husband, Peter III. A benevolent despot, she reformed local administration (1775) and gave a new charter to the nobility (1785) confirming their privileges. She increased Russian territory in the partitions of Poland (1772, 1793 and 1795) and by the Russo-Turkish Wars (1768–74, 1787–92). She wrote memoirs and plays, and was a patron of writers and artists

Catherine de' Medici (1519–89), queen of France and regent for her son Charles IX. After seeking peace between Catholics and Protestants she later encouraged the Massacre of St Bartholomew

Catherine How·ard (háuərd) (c. 1521–42), fifth wife of Henry VIII of England, beheaded for political reasons, though on a charge of infidelity

Catherine of Alexandria, St (d. 307), patron saint of wheelwrights. Feast: Nov. 25

Catherine of Aragon (1485–1536), first wife of Henry VIII of England, mother of Mary I. The pope's opposition to Henry's divorce from her (1533) was the occasion of the separation of the Church of England from papal authority

Catherine of Bra·gan·za (brəgænzə) (1638–1705), daughter of John IV of Portugal. She married (1662) Charles II of England, bringing Bombay and Tangier as part of her dowry

Catherine of Siena, St (1347–80), patron saint of the Dominican Order, author of the mystical 'Book of Divine Doctrine' and Doctor of the Church. Feast: Apr. 30

Catherine of Valois (1401–37), daughter of Charles VI of France and wife of Henry V of England. The Tudor dynasty was descended from her later marriage to Owen Tudor

Catherine Parr (par) (1512–48), sixth wife of Henry VIII of England, whom she survived

Catherine wheel (*Br.*) a pinwheel (firework) ‖ a circular window with spokes radiating from the center [after St *Catherine* of Alexandria]

cath·e·ter (kæθitər) *n.* a tube of metal, glass or rubber passed along a mucous canal to permit the passage of fluid (esp. from the bladder) or to facilitate breathing [L. fr. Gk *katheter* fr. *ka·thienai*, to send down]

cath·e·tom·e·ter (kæθitómitər) *n.* a small horizontal telescope mounted on a graduated vertical rod used for measuring small differences in height at a distance of a few meters [fr. Gk *kathetos* fr. *kathienai*, to let down+*-meter*]

ca·thex·is (kəθéksis) *pl.* **ca·thex·es** (kəθéksi:z) *n.* (*psychoanal.*) the investment of emotional significance in an object, activity or idea ‖ the charge of psychic energy invested in this way [fr. Gk *kathexis*, a holding, trans. of G. *besetzung*, used by Freud]

cath·ode (kæθoud) *n.* (*elec.*) a negative electrode, the point of entry of electrons into a device from the external circuit (*ANODE) [fr. Gk *kathodos*, descent]

cathode ray a high-speed electron or a stream of them emitted from a cathode into a vacuum tube under the influence of a powerful electric field

cathode ray oscilloscope (*abbr.* C.R.O.) an oscilloscope

cathode-ray tube a vacuum tube in which cathode rays produce a luminous spot or line as they are projected on a fluorescent screen at one end of the tube

Cath·o·lic (kæθəlik, kæθlik) **1.** *adj.* of the original Christian Church before the schism between East and West (*ORTHODOXY) ‖ of the Roman or Western Church after this schism and before the Reformation ‖ pertaining to the whole Christian Church ‖ pertaining or adhering to Catholicism **cath·o·lic** universal, all embracing, *catholic tastes in music* **2.** *n.* someone who subscribes to the beliefs of the universal Christian Church ‖ a member of the Roman Catholic Church [F. *catholique* fr. L. fr. Gk *kath'holou*, as a whole]
—The term is used by the Church of Rome exclusively of itself. The Anglican Church uses the term with reference to the whole body of the Christian Church which claims to have retained the apostolic succession of bishops

Catholic Church of Rome *ROMAN CATHOLIC CHURCH

Catholic Emancipation Act (*Br. hist.*) the law passed (1829) by a ministry led by Wellington and Peel, allowing Roman Catholics to sit in parliament. It was the result of a vigorous campaign led by Daniel O'Connell

Ca·thol·i·cism (kəθólisizəm) *n.* the faith, practice or system of the Catholic Church ‖ the faith, practice or system of the Roman Catholic Church ‖ catholicity

cath·o·lic·i·ty (kæθəlísiti:) *n.* universality ‖ Catholic beliefs ‖ adherence to the Roman Catholic Church

Ca·thol·i·cize (kəθólisaiz) *pres. part.* **Ca·thol·i·ciz·ing** *past* and *past part.* **Ca·thol·i·cized** *v.t.* to make Catholic

Catholic League a union of Catholic German princes formed (1609) in answer to the Protestant Union (1608). The league was headed by Maximilian I of Bavaria, whose army, under Tilly, played an important part in the Thirty Years' War

Catholic University of America a national pontifical institution in Washington, D.C., founded (1884) and opened (1889)

Cat·i·line (kæt'lain) (Lucius Sergius Catilina, 109–62 B.C.) Roman politician, who organized a conspiracy (63 B.C.) against the senate. The plot was denounced by Cicero in his 'Catilinarian Orations' and described in Sallust's 'Bellum Catilinae'

cat·i·on (kætaiən, kætaiɒn) *n.* a positive ion, which, in electrolysis, travels to the cathode and is discharged there (*ANION) [Gk *kation*, a going down]

cat·i·on·ic (kætaiónik) *adj.* of a type of fiber variant that takes deep and brilliant colors. When cationic fibers are mixed or blended with conventional fibers, various multicolor and

---

cross-dye effects are possible in a fabric from one dye bath or treatment

cat·kin (kǽtkin) n. a spike with unisexual flowers and pendulous rachis, e.g. of willow and birch and esp. the male flowers of the hazel [fr. Du. *katteken*, dim. of cat]

Cat·lin, (kǽtlən) George (1796–1872), U.S. painter and author. He painted more than 500 pictures of Indians from over 40 different tribes, and authored 'Letters and Notes on the Manners, Customs, and Condition of the North American Indians' (1841)

cat·mint (kǽtmint) n. catnip

cat·nap (kǽtnæp) n. a short doze by a human being who is not in bed

cat·nip (kǽtnip) n. *Nepeta cataria*, fam. *Labiatae*, an aromatic plant with blue flowers and grayish foliage

Ca·to (kéitou), Marcus Porcius (234–149 B.C.), 'the Elder' or 'the Censor', Roman statesman and writer

Cato, Marcus Porcius (95–46 B.C.), 'the Younger', surnamed Uticensis, great-grandson of Cato the Elder, Roman statesman, soldier and Stoic philosopher

cat-o'-nine-tails (kǽtənáinteilz) *pl.* **cat-o'-nine-tails** n. a whip of nine knotted lashes used (*hist.*) for punishment esp. in the British navy

CAT scanner (*med.*) term for computed axial tomography, a diagnostic X-ray device providing a detailed three-dimensional view of a slice of the body by rotating the X-ray machine completely around the patient, taking pictures at various angles

cat's cradle a game of making geometrical string figures, looped over the fingers, the figures progressing as the string is passed from one person to another

cat's eyes small glass reflectors, esp. those set in rubber and placed at intervals along the central axis of a road to make driving in the dark or in fog safer and easier. The reflectors are caught in the beams of the headlights

Cats·kill Mtns (kǽtskil) a range in New York State, west of the Hudson, part of the Appalachian system. Highest peak: Slide Mt (4,204 ft). Forests, resorts

cat's-paw (kǽtspɔ) n. (*naut.*) a hitch in a rope on to which tackle is hooked ‖ a ruffle on water, caused by a light breeze ‖ a person used by another, a dupe

cat·suit (kǽtsu:t) n. women's form-fitting one-piece garment with flared legs

catsup *KETCHUP

cat's whisker a very fine contact wire in some crystal detectors

Catt (kæt), Carrie Chapman (née Lane) (1859–1947), U.S. leader in the movement for woman suffrage. She also campaigned for world disarmament and for prohibition

Cat·tail (kǽtteil) n. a plant of the genus *Typha*, esp. *T. latifolia*, a reedlike plant growing in marshes, with a dense cylindrical spike of flowers. The long flat leaves are used for making chair seats, rush mats etc.

cat·ti·ly (kǽtəli:) adv. in a catty way

cat·ti·ness (kǽti:nis) n. the quality of being catty

cat·tish (kǽtiʃ) adj. catty

cat·tle (kǽt'l) n. bovine animals collectively. The two domesticated species are *Bos taurus* (European cattle) and *Bos indicus* (Zebu cattle). Cattle are bred for milk or butterfat production, or for meat or as work animals (esp. in Asia), or as dual-purpose animals [O.N.F. *catel*, property or wealth]

cattle lifter (*Br.*) a cattle rustler

cat·tle·man (kǽt'lmən, kǽt'lmæn) *pl.* **cat·tle·men** (kǽt'lmən, kǽt'lmen) n. the owner of a cattle ranch ‖ a man who tends cattle

cattle plague rinderpest

cattle rustler (*Am.*=*Br.* cattle lifter) a cattle thief

cat·ty (kǽti:) comp. **cat·ti·er** superl. **cat·ti·est** adj. spiteful in a petty way

Ca·tul·lus (kətʌləs), Valerius (c. 87–c. 54 B.C.), Latin lyric poet who adopted Greek meters with originality, author of the 'Marriage of Peleus and Thetis' and other shorter poems full of wit, passion and irony

CATV (*acronym*) for community antenna television, an early coaxial cable television system, term now applied to all cable television

cat·walk (kǽtwɔk) n. a narrow footway, usually with a safety rail, e.g. around a large machine ‖ (*movies, theater*) a high bridge in a studio or in the scene loft above a theater stage for handling scenery, ropes etc.

cat whisker a cat's whisker (wire)

catydid *KATYDID

Cau·ca (káuka) a river (c. 600 miles long) in W. Colombia, rising in the Andes and flowing into the Magdalena River

Cau·ca·sia (kɔkéiʒə, kɔkéiʃə) (or Caucasus) the region of the southwest U.S.S.R. between the Black Sea and the Caspian, crossed by the Caucasus. It was formerly divided into Ciscaucasia (now in the R.S.F.S.R.), north of the mountains, considered as being in Europe, and Transcaucasia, south of them, considered as part of Asia (now Georgia, Armenia and Azerbaijan). Because of ethnological diversity there are several autonomous republics (Dagestan, Checheno-Ingush, North Ossetian, Kabardino-Balkarian, Abkhazian, Adzharian and Nakhichevan) and regions. Climate: Mediterranean. The region produces half of Soviet petroleum (*BAKU) and a large part of Soviet cotton. The inhabitants, largely Moslem, long resisted Russian rule (18th–19th cc.) and had to be reconquered after the Russian revolution (1917)

Cau·ca·sian (kɔkéiʒən, kɔkéiʃən) 1. n. a person of the Caucasus ‖ the family of languages spoken there ‖ a member of the predominantly white-skinned race (after a skull found in the Caucasus), one of the three main divisions of mankind, living generally in Europe, western Asia and North Africa (cf. MONGOLIAN, cf. NEGRO) 2. adj. pertaining to the region of Caucasia, its inhabitants, or the languages native to it ‖ of or pertaining to the white race of mankind

Caucasian languages a group of languages (about 40 have so far been distinguished) spoken by about 4 million people in the Caucasus. Georgian has most speakers — about 2 million — and a few others (Mingrelian, Kabardian, Chechen, Avar, Lakk, Hurkili and Kuri) each have over 100,000 speakers. Some languages are spoken only in a few villages. The Caucasian languages are characterized by a very simple vowel system and a wide range of consonants (up to 80 in Aghul) and a complex morphology (there are 50 noun cases in Tabassaran). Only Georgian has the status of a literary language, with a tradition going back to the 5th c.

Cau·ca·soid (kɔ́kəsɔid) 1. adj. of or pertaining to the Caucasian race 2. n. a member of the Caucasian race

Cau·ca·sus (kɔ́kəsəs) a mountain system of the U.S.S.R. whose chief range (about 750 miles long, 30–130 miles wide) runs diagonally across the land bridge between the Black Sea and the Caspian as a solid wall, seldom under 9,000 ft high, with a smaller range along the Iranian border. Summit: Elbruz, 18,470 ft. Chief pass: the Daryal, above Tiflis. No railroads cross it. Above 10,000 ft there are many glaciers. The lower slopes, wooded and rich in game, are inhabited by semi-tribal villagers ‖ Caucasia

cau·cus (kɔ́kəs) 1. n. a preliminary meeting of the leaders of a political party to make policy and decide on candidates ‖ (*Br.*) the system of party organization by committees 2. v.i. to hold a meeting of party leaders ‖ to make use of the caucus system to organize a political party [prob. fr. Algonquian *caucau-asu*, elder]

cau·dal (kɔ́d'l) adj. resembling a tail ‖ pertaining to a tail, *caudal fin* ‖ near the tail or base of the spinal column, *caudal anesthesia* [fr. L. *caudalis*]

cau·date (kɔ́deit) adj. (*zool.*) having a tail or tail-like appendage **cáu·dat·ed** adj. [fr. L. *caudatus* fr. *cauda*, tail]

Cau·di·llo (kauɖí:ljo) *FRANCO

cau·di·llo (kauɖí:jo) n. a Latin American term for a war lord [Span.=chieftain fr. L.L. *capitellum*, little head]

Cau·dine Forks (kɔ́dain) a narrow defile near Capua near Naples where a Roman army was trapped by the Samnites and forced to surrender (321 B.C.)

caught past and past part. of CATCH **to be caught up in** to be involved in, esp. by force of circumstances

caul (kɔl) n. the membrane (amnion) which encloses the fetus ‖ the part of this which sometimes remains on a baby's head at birth (*OMENTUM) [O.F. *cale*, a small cap]

cauldron *CALDRON

cau·les·cent (kɔlésənt) adj. (*bot.*) having a leaf-bearing stem above ground [fr. L. *caulis*, stem]

cau·li·flow·er (kɔ́ləflauər, kɔ́li:flauər, kɔ́ləflauər, kɔ́li:flauər) n. *Brassica oleracea capitata*, fam. *Cruciferae*, a variety of cabbage with a fleshy hypertrophied inflorescence [fr. F. *chou-flori*]

cau·line (kɔ́lin, kɔ́lain) adj. pertaining to a plant stem ‖ applied to leaves growing on the upper portion of a stem [fr. Mod. L. *caulinus* fr. *caulis*, tail]

caulk, calk (kɔk) v.t. to stop up and make watertight the seams of (a wooden ship) with pitch and oakum, or by striking the edges of metal plates of (an iron ship) with a chisel ‖ to stop up the crevices of (windows etc.) [O.F. *cauquer*, squeeze]

Cau·po·li·cán (kɔupoli:kán) (d. 1558), chief of the Araucano Indians. He was defeated and executed by García Hurtado de Mendoza (1535–1609). His exploits are commemorated in Ercilla's 'La Araucana'

cau·ris (káuri:s) n. unit of currency in Guinea, equal to 1/100th syli.

caus·al (kɔ́zəl) adj. being the cause of a state of affairs or an event ‖ pertaining to the cause of an event ‖ having to do with cause and effect ‖ (*gram.*) expressing cause [fr. L. *causalis*]

cau·sal·i·ty (kɔzǽliti:) *pl.* **cau·sal·i·ties** n. the state of being a cause ‖ the relation of cause and effect ‖ the doctrine that all things have a cause [fr. L. *causalis*, causal]

cau·sa·tion (kɔzéiʃən) n. the act of causing ‖ the relation of cause and effect ‖ the doctrine that all things have a cause [fr. L. *causatio* (*causationis*), pretext, but with the meaning from M.L. *causare*, to cause]

cau·sa·tive (kɔ́zətiv) 1. adj. causing, acting as a cause ‖ (*gram.*) expressing or denoting causation, causal 2. n. (*gram.*) a causative word [F. *causatif*]

cause (kɔz) n. that which brings about a result ‖ basis, grounds, *no cause for alarm* ‖ a person whose actions or words lead to some result ‖ a matter of widespread interest and concern, *the cause of world peace* ‖ the side taken in a contest between individuals or between political or religious movements **to plead a cause** to plead a case before a court [F.]

cause pres. part. **caus·ing** past and past part. **caused** v.t. to bring about (a result), be the cause of [fr. M.L. *causare*]

cause cé·lè·bre (kouzseilébr) *pl.* **causes cé·lè·bres** (kouzseilébr) n. a famous lawsuit [F.]

cause·less (kɔ́zlis) adj. having no cause ‖ groundless

cau·se·rie (kouzəri:) n. an informal talk or chat ‖ a short, conversational article or talk, esp. on literary subjects [F.]

cause·way (kɔ́zwei) n. a raised roadway across wet or low-lying ground [fr. older *causey* fr. O.N.F. *caucie* fr. L.L. *calciata*, trodden+WAY]

Causses (kous) limestone plateaus, 3–4,000 ft high, in the Massif Central, France, sloping west from the Cévennes: they are an arid region with spectacular canyons. The chief industry is raising sheep, yielding the milk for Roquefort cheese. Tourism

caus·tic (kɔ́stik) 1. adj. burning, corrosive, e.g. of some chemicals, esp. strong alkalis ‖ (*fig.*) sharply biting, esp. with a sarcastic intention, *a caustic tongue* 2. n. (*phys.*) a surface of maximum concentration of light after reflection from, or refraction through, a spherical or cylindrical mirror or lens face **cáus·ti·cal·ly** adv. [fr. L. *causticus*, burning fr. Gk]

caustic curve the curve of intersection of a caustic by a plane surface

caustic potash potassium hydroxide

caustic soda sodium hydroxide

cau·ter·i·za·tion (kɔtərizéiʃən) n. the act or effect of cauterizing

cau·ter·ize (kɔ́təraiz) pres. part. **cau·ter·iz·ing** past and past part. **cau·ter·ized** v.t. to destroy (living tissue) by means of heat or a caustic agent, esp. in the treatment of wounds [fr. L.L. *cauterizare*, to sear fr. Gk]

cau·ter·y (kɔ́təri:) *pl.* **cau·ter·ies** n. cauterization ‖ an instrument for cauterizing tissue [fr. L. *cauterium*, a hot iron fr. Gk]

Cau·tin (kautín) a province (area 6,707 sq. miles, pop. 460,000) of S. central Chile. Capital: Temuco

cau·tion (kɔ́ʃən) 1. n. carefulness, concern for safety ‖ a warning, esp. one that carries a reprimand ‖ (*pop.*) a person who clowns, or a child who says or does things which are found funny ‖ a money deposit or pledge towards the performance of an obligation ‖ a person who gives such a pledge or deposit **2.** *v.t.* to warn ‖ to warn with a reprimand [F.]

cau·tion·ar·y (kóʃənɛri:) *adj.* containing, or of the nature of, a caution ‖ warning, *cautionary tales*

caution money (*Br.*) money deposited as a security for the good behavior of students esp. at universities and Inns of Court

cau·tious (kóʃəs) *adj.* prudent, attentive to safety

Cau·ver·y (kóvəri:) (Kaveri) a river in S. India, sacred to Hindus. It flows from the W. Ghats across the Mysore plain into a large delta on the Coromandel Coast of the Bay of Bengal. Unnavigable, it has irrigation dams and hydroelectric power stations

cava *KAVA

cav·al·cade (kævəlkéid, kǽvəlkeid) *n.* horsemen in procession ‖ a procession or parade not necessarily of horsemen, *circus cavalcade, cavalcade of history* [F. fr. Prov. *cavalcada* fr. *cavalcar,* to ride]

cav·a·lier (kævəlíər, kǽvəliər) **1.** *n.* (*hist.*) a horseman, esp. a mounted soldier ‖ (*hist.*) a knight **Ca·va·lier** (*Eng. hist.*) a member of the loyalist country gentry (17th c.), who fought for the king in the English Civil War (1642-52), and who later supported the Tory party (cf. ROUNDHEAD) **2.** *adj.* high-handed **Cavalier** of poets of the period of Charles I of England or of their poetry, esp. of the gallant courtier poets or their poetry celebrating wine, women and song [F. fr. Ital.]

Ca·va·llón (kɑvɑljón), Juan de (*d.* 1565), Spanish conquistador. His expedition of 1560, notable for its relative humanity, marks the first colonization of Costa Rica

cav·al·ry (kǽvəlri:) *pl.* **cav·al·ries** *n.* (*hist.*) mounted soldiers ‖ (*mil.*) a motorized unit formerly mounted [F. *cavalerie*]

cav·al·ry·man (kǽvəlri:mən) *pl.* **cav·al·ry·men** (kǽvəlri:mən) *n.* a member of the cavalry

Cav·an (kǽvən) an inland county (area 730 sq. miles, pop. 52,618) of Ulster province, Irish Republic ‖ its county seat

cav·a·ti·na (kævətí:nə) *n.* (*mus.*) an operatic song in one section, of regular form ‖ a short, slow, songlike instrumental movement [Ital.]

cave (keiv) **1.** *n.* a natural hollow in rock, or an underground chamber, with an opening at surface level. Caves are caused by the action of water on the rock, or by marine or volcanic action ‖ an area shielded to protect against radioactivity in which processing is usually done by remote control **2.** *v.t. pres. part.* **cav·ing** *past* and *past part.* **caved** to make a hollow in, *to cave out a hillside* ‖ to scoop or excavate (earth) **to cave in** to smash in ‖ to cause to collapse ‖ (of a wall etc.) to bulge inwards ‖ (of a roof) to sink in ‖ (*pop.*) to collapse, cease resisting [F.]

ca·ve·at (kéivi:æt) *n.* a legal notice to stop some proceeding such as the proving of a will or making over of a property ‖ a warning, a caution, *the chairman entered a caveat* [L.=let him beware]

ca·ve·at emp·tor (kéivi:ætémptɔr) a phrase used to express the trading principle that it is the buyer's responsibility to satisfy himself about the quality of the goods he receives [L., lit.=let the buyer beware]

cave-in (kéivin) *n.* a yielding to pressure and collapsing inwards

Cav·ell (kǽv'l), Edith Louisa (1865–1915), English nurse and national heroine, shot by the Germans as a spy. She helped many Allied prisoners to escape

cave·man (kéivmæn) *pl.* **cave·men** (kéivmen) *n.* a Stone Age cave dweller ‖ a man fatuously pleased with his own strength and behaving with ostentatious aggressiveness

Cav·en·dish (kǽvəndiʃ), Henry (1731–1810), English physicist and chemist. He discovered hydrogen and the inert gases, made a determination of the mass of the earth, established the composition of water, and made important advances in electricity

cav·ern (kǽvərn) *n.* a cave, esp. a large one ‖ an underground chamber [L. *caverna* fr. *cavus,* hollow]

cav·ern·ous (kǽvərnəs) *adj.* full of caverns ‖ suggestive of caverns, *cavernous eye sockets* [fr. L. *cavernosus*]

ca·vet·to (kəvétou) *pl.* **ca·vet·ti** (kəvéti:), **ca·vet·tos** *n.* (*archit.*) a concave molding which is a quarter circle in section [Ital.]

Ca·vi·a·na (kəvjánə) a fertile island (47 miles long, 20 miles wide) in the northern delta of the Amazon River in N.E. Brazil

cav·i·ar, cav·i·are (kǽvi:ɑr, kævi:ɑ́r) *n.* the roes of the sturgeon and sterlet caught in lakes and rivers of the U.S.S.R., salted and eaten as an appetizer [etym. doubtful]

cav·il (kǽv'l) **1.** *v.i. pres. part.* **cav·il·ing,** esp. *Br.* **cav·il·ling** *past* and *past part.* **cav·iled,** esp. *Br.* **cav·illed** (with 'at' or 'about') to raise petty objections ‖ to find fault without reason **2.** *n.* a trivial, frivolous objection, a quibble ‖ the raising of such objections [O.F. *caviller*]

cav·i·ta·tion (kævitéiʃən) *n.* the formation and subsequent collapse of bubbles in a liquid in the path of a fast moving body, e.g. a propeller blade [fr. L. *cavitas* (*cavitatis*), a hollow]

Ca·vi·te (kaví:te) a port in the Philippine Is (S.W. Luzón), in Manila Bay, site of a naval battle (1898) in the Spanish-American War in which the U.S. fleet under Admiral George Dewey destroyed the Spanish squadron

cav·i·ty (kǽviti:) *pl.* **cav·i·ties** *n.* an empty space inside a solid object, e.g. in a decayed tooth [F. *cavité*]

ca·vort (kəvɔ́rt) *v.i.* to prance about [etym. doubtful]

Ca·vour (kævú:r), Count Camillo Benso di (1810–61), Piedmontese statesman. As premier of Sardinia (1852–9, 1860–1), he gained prestige for his country by intervening in the Crimean War. After his pact with Napoleon III at Plombières (1858), he provoked war with Austria (1859), and obtained annexation of southern Italian states in the new kingdom of Italy (1861)

cavu (*acronym*) for ceiling and visibility unlimited

ca·vy (kéivi:) *pl.* **ca·vies** *n.* a tropical American rodent of fam. *Caviidae.* The domesticated species, *Cavia cobaya,* is the common guinea pig [fr. F. *cabiai*]

caw (kɔ) **1.** *n.* the harsh, raucous cry of rooks, crows and ravens **2.** *v.i.* to make such a cry [imit.]

Cawn·pore (kónpɔr, kónpour) *KANPUR

Cax·ton (kǽkstən), William (1422–91), the first English printer (1477). He put out about 80 books from his Westminster press (1477–91). A book printed by him is called a Caxton, and a black letter type like his is named after him

cay (kei, ki:) *n.* a bank or reef of sand [fr. Span. *cayo,* shoal]

Ca·ya·pa (kajápa) *pl.* **Ca·ya·pa, Ca·ya·pas** *n.* a South American Indian people of N. Ecuador ‖ a member of this people ‖ their language [Span.]

Cay·enne (kaién, keién) the capital (pop. 36,215) of French Guiana, a port on the Atlantic

cay·enne pepper (kaién, keién) a very hot powder obtained from the dried pulverized fruit of several pepper varieties, esp. *Capsicum frutescens longum,* and used as a condiment [fr. native Braz.]

cayman *CAIMAN

Cay·man Islands (kaimán) a British colony (area 100 sq. miles, pop. 16,677 mainly of African descent and Mulatto) in the Caribbean, formed of three islands: Grand Cayman, Cayman Brac and Little Cayman. Capital: Georgetown, on Grand Cayman. Occupations: turtle and shark fishing, boatbuilding, rope making. The islands were discovered by Columbus (1503), ceded by Spain to England (1670) and became dependencies of Jamaica (1863–1962)

Ca·yu·ga (keijú:gə, kaijú:gə) *n.* an Indian of a tribe of the Iroquois family formerly inhabiting the western part of New York State and now living in Ontario

Cay·use (kaijú:s, káius) *n.* a North American Indian of a tribe now living on a reservation in Oregon

cay·use (kaijú:s, káius) *n.* an Indian-bred pony [after the Cayuse tribe]

ca·zique (kæsí:k) *n.* a cacique

CB 1. (*abbr.*) for citizen's band radio, a noncommercial, 40-channel, 27 MHz receiver-transmitter. **2.** (*abbr.*) for chemical and biological warfare

CBW (*mil. acronym*) for chemical and biological warfare

C clef (*mus.*) a movable clef (symbol 𝄢) indicating the location of middle C on the staff

CCTV (*acronym*) for closed circuit television

CD (*acronym*) for certificate of deposit

C-day (*mil.*) the unnamed day on which a deployment operation commences or is to commence

cease (si:s) *pres. part.* **ceas·ing** *past* and *past part.* **ceased** *v.t.* to stop, bring to an end ‖ *v.i.* to come to an end, stop [M.E. *cessen* fr. F.]

cease *n.* (only in phrase) **without cease** incessantly [O.F. *ces*]

cease-fire (sí:sfáiər) *n.* (*mil.*) an order to stop shooting ‖ an order for the cessation of hostilities as a preliminary to making peace terms ‖ the period during which the order holds

cease·less (sí:slis) *adj.* without pause or interruption

Ce·au·șes·cu (tʃéiau:sɛsku:) Nicolae (1918–), Rumanian statesman. Secretary general of the Communist party (1965), he became head of state (1967) and president of the republic (1974)

Ce·bu (sebú:) an island (area 1,702 sq. miles, pop. 1,634,200) in the central Philippine Is (Visayas), producing esp. corn, copper, coal ‖ its capital (pop. 418,500), a port on the east coast, the oldest Spanish city (founded 1565) in the islands. Cathedral (18th c.)

ce·cal, cae·cal (sí:k'l) *adj.* of or like a cecum

Cec·chet·ti (tʃekkétti:), Enrico (1850–1927), Italian dancer and ballet master. He taught in St Petersburg (1892–1902 and for Diaghilev, 1905–19), Warsaw, London and Milan. His pupils included Pavlova and Nijinsky

Ce·cil (sés'l), William, 1st Baron Burghley *BURGHLEY

Ce·cil·ia (sisí:ljə), St, virgin martyr of the early Church, decapitated c. 230. She is the patron saint of music, associated esp. with the organ. Feast: Nov. 22

ce·cro·pi·a moth (sikróupi:ə) *Samia cecropia* or *Hyalophora cecropia,* a large silkworm moth of North America, with red, white and black markings [N.L. ult. fr. *Cecropius,* pertaining to CECROPS]

Ce·crops (sí:krɒps) legendary founder of Athens

ce·cum, cae·cum (sí:kəm) *pl.* **ce·ca, cae·ca** (sí:kə) *n.* (*anat.* and *zool.*) a tube or duct closed at one end ‖ the blind pouch in which the large intestine begins and into which the ileum opens from one side [L. (*intestinum*) *caecum,* blind (intestine)]

ce·dar (sí:dər) *n.* a member of *Cedrus,* fam. *Coniferae,* a genus of evergreen trees, producing durable wood used for building ‖ a member of *Cedrela,* fam. *Meliaceae,* a genus of trees native to American tropical forests, yielding cedarwood and gum ‖ a tree of the genus *Juniperus* (*JUNIPER) [O.E. *ceder* fr. L. fr. Gk]

cedar bird the cedar waxwing

cedar waxwing *Bombycilla cedorum,* a yellowish-brown North American waxwing

cede (si:d) *pres. part.* **ced·ing** *past* and *past part.* **ced·ed** *v.t.* to grant ‖ to surrender (esp. territory or legal rights) [fr. L. *cedere,* to yield]

ce·di (sí:di:) *n.* the monetary unit of Ghana divided into 100 pesawas [native word]

ce·dil·la (sidílə) *n.* a mark (¸) under the letter C to show a sibilant pronunciation before a, o, u [Span.]

cef·a·clor (séfəklor) *n.* (*pharm.*) anti-infective antibiotic used in treatment of staphylococcic pneumonia; marketed as Ceclor

cef·a·man·dole [$C_{18}H_{18}N_6O_5S_2$] (séfəmɑmdoul) *n.* (*pharm.*) antibiotic injected intramuscularly to combat serious infections; marketed as Mandol

cef·tox·in (seftóksin) *n.* (*pharm.*) anti-infective injected intravenously to retard growth of susceptible microorganisms; marketed as Mefoxin

cei·ba (séibə) *n. Ceiba pentandra,* the silkcotton tree, which yields kapok ‖ kapok [Span. fr. native name in South America]

ceil (si:l) *v.t.* to line the roof of (a room) with plaster etc. [perh. fr. F. *ciel,* heaven, ceiling]

ceil·ing (sí:liŋ) *n.* the upper, inner surface of a room ‖ the maximum height which can be reached ‖ an imposed upper limit, *a price ceiling* ‖ an upper limit of capacity or ability ‖ the cloud cover above clear air, esp. with respect to altitude

ceiling *CEILOMETER

ceiling price the maximum price for a commodity permitted by law, or judged acceptable by customers

ceil·om·e·ter (si:lómitər) *n.* (*meteorol.*) a device for measuring the altitude of a cloud base, using a narrow beam of light and measuring its angle of reflection

cel·a·don (sélədɒn) *n.* a pale, soft, gray-green color, esp. in porcelain [F.]

CONCISE PRONUNCIATION KEY: **(a)** æ, c*a*t; ɑ, c*a*r; ɔ f*aw*n; ei, sn*a*ke. **(e)** e, h*e*n; i:, sh*ee*p; iə, d*ee*r; ɛə, b*ea*r. **(i)** i, f*i*sh; ai, t*i*ger; ə:, b*i*rd. **(o)** o, *o*x; au, c*ow*; ou, g*oa*t; u, p*oo*r; ɔi, r*oy*al. **(u)** ʌ, d*u*ck; u, b*u*ll; u:, g*oo*se; ə, b*a*cillus; ju:, c*u*be. x, lo*ch*; θ, *th*ink; ð, bo*th*er; z, *Z*en; ʒ, cor*s*age; dʒ, sava*g*e; ŋ, oranguta*ng*; j, *y*ak; ʃ, *f*ish; tʃ, fe*tch*; 'l, rabb*le*; 'n, redd*en*. Complete pronunciation key appears inside front cover.

cel·an·dine (séləndain) *n. Ranunculus ficaria,* fam. *Ranunculaceae,* the lesser celandine or pilewort, a plant with tuberous roots forming at the base of each axillary bud, each capable of producing a new plant ‖ *Chelidonium,* fam. *Papaveraceae,* the greater celandine, a plant sometimes used medicinally as a diuretic [M.F. *celydoine* fr. O.F. fr. Gk]

Cel·e·bes (séləbi:z) *SULAWESI

Celebes Sea an arm of the Pacific between Sulawesi, Borneo and the Philippines

cel·e·brant (séləbrənt) *n.* a priest officiating at the Mass (Eucharist) or other public religious rite [fr. L. *celebrans (celebrantis)* fr. *celebrare,* to celebrate]

cel·e·brate (séləbreit) *pres. part.* **cel·e·brat·ing** *past and past part.* **cel·e·brat·ed** *v.t.* to perform (a religious ceremony) publicly, *to celebrate a wedding* ‖ to honor or observe (some special occasion or event) ‖ to praise, sing the glories of, *her book celebrates a forgotten hero* ‖ *v.i.* to seize an occasion for being festive **cél·e·brat·ed** *adj.* famous [fr. L. *celebrare (celebratus),* to frequent, honor]

cel·e·bra·tion (seləbréiʃən) *n.* the act or process of celebrating [fr. L. *celebratio (celebrationis)*]

ce·leb·ri·ty (səlébriti:) *pl.* **ce·leb·ri·ties** *n.* fame ‖ a famous person [fr. L. *celebritas (celebritatis)*]

cel·er·i·ac (səléri:æk, səli:ri:æk) *n.* a variety of celery with large swollen roots

ce·ler·i·ty (səlériti:) *n.* rapidity, swiftness [F. *célérité*]

cel·er·y (séləri:) *n. Apium graveolens,* fam. *Umbelliferae,* a culinary plant cultivated in fertile, moist, temperate areas. The leafstalks are blanched and eaten raw or cooked [F. *céleri*]

ce·les·ta (səléstə) *n.* a keyboard instrument resembling a small piano, but having steel plates, instead of strings, struck by hammers [F.]

ce·leste (səlést) *n.* a sky-blue color [F.=heavenly]

ce·les·tial (səléstʃəl) *adj.* pertaining to the sky or heavens, *celestial bodies* (the stars, planets etc.) ‖ pertaining to a spiritual heaven, heavenly, divine [O.F. *celestial*]

celestial equator (*astron.*) the circle in which the celestial sphere is intersected by the plane of the earth's equator

celestial map a map showing the positions of the stars etc.

celestial pole (*astron.*) either of the imaginary points at which the extended axis of the earth intersects the celestial sphere

celestial radio tracking air navigation system utilizing emission of microwaves from stars and sun for positioning a vehicle or missile in flight

celestial sphere (*astron.*) an imaginary spherical surface of infinite radius on which a star may be projected, the terrestrial observer being at the center of the sphere

Cel·es·tine V (sélistain, səléstain) (St Peter Celestine, 1215–96), pope (1294). The founder of the Celestine monastic order, he was elected pope against his will, and abdicated soon after. Feast: May 19

cel·es·tite (sélistait) *n.* (*mineral.*) naturally occurring orthorhombic strontium sulfate, SrSO₄, frequently pale blue due to the presence of impurities [prob. fr. Ital. *celestino,* sky-blue]

celiac *COELIAC

ce·li·ac disease, coe·li·ac disease (séli:æk) a disease affecting young children and involving distension of the intestines and inability to absorb fats

cel·i·ba·cy (sélibəsi:) *n.* the unmarried state

cel·i·bate (sélibit, sélibeit) **1.** *n.* a person who has vowed to remain unmarried, or who is bound to do so **2.** *adj.* unmarried [fr. L. *caelebs (caelibis),* unmarried]

Céline (seili:n), (Louis Ferdinand Destouches, 1894–1962), French writer, author of 'Voyage au bout de la nuit' (1932), a ferocious satire on society and the times. Other works include 'Mort à Crédit' (1936)

cell (sel) *n.* a small enclosed space, small chamber, e.g. in a prison, monastery or honeycomb ‖ a small group of militant political members within a community ‖ (*computer*) unit of computer memory with one-word capacity ‖ (*biol.*) the smallest structural unit of living tissue capable of functioning as an independent entity. It consists of a small mass of protoplasm often bounded by a semipermeable membrane, containing usually one or more nuclei and the various nonliving products of its activities, and able to carry on independently all the basic life functions (i.e. reproduction, growth etc.) ‖

(*chem.*) a device for producing an electric current chemically or photoelectrically or for use in electrolysis ‖ (*chem.*) a fuel cell ‖ (*hist.*) a small convent dependent on a large one [O.F. *celle*]

cell (*computer*) unit of computer memory with one-word capacity

cel·lar (sélər) *n.* a room, usually under a building, used as a cool storage place for wine etc. ‖ a collection of wines **cél·lar·age** *n.* storage space in a cellar ‖ a charge made for storing goods in a cellar **cél·lar·er** *n.* the keeper of wine and food in a monastery **cel·la·ret** (selərét) *n.* a cupboard in a sideboard or a cabinet, in which wine bottles are kept [M.E. *celer* fr. A.F.]

cellar (*sports*) bottom position in a league competition

cell division *AMITOSIS, *MITOSIS, *MEIOSIS

cel·li·form (sélifɔrm) *adj.* formed of or resembling cells

Cel·li·ni (tʃelí:ni:), Benvenuto (1500–71), Italian sculptor, engraver and goldsmith, famous also for his 'Autobiography'

cel·list (tʃélist) *n.* a person who plays the cello

cel·lo, 'cel·lo (tʃélou) *n.* a four-stringed, bowed musical instrument developed from the bass viol, tuned an octave below the viola. It has a compass of more than three octaves above C two octaves below middle C [abbr. Ital. *violoncello*]

cel·lo·phane (séləfein) **1.** *n.* a thin, transparent material made from viscose and used esp. for wrapping food and other articles **2.** *adj.* made from cellophane [former trade mark fr. CELLULOSE]

cell·scan (sélskæn) *n.* computer scanning system for counting white blood cells and analyzing their patterns; designed by Perker-Elmer Corp.

cell system *NET SYSTEM

cell therapy program for rejuvenation or physical restoration using injection of suspensions of cells from foetal sheep. *abbr.* CT. *syn* cellular therapy

cel·lu·lar (séljulər) *adj.* formed of cells, *cellular tissue* ‖ having cells or compartments [perh. fr. F. *cellulaire*]

cellular plant a plant without distinct stems, leaves etc., e.g. cactus

cellular radio (*electr.*) communication transmission system used for mobile telephone service and requiring no wires.

cellular therapy *CELL THERAPY

cel·lule (sélju:l) *n.* a cell or interstice in a living organism [fr. L. *cellula,* a small compartment]

cel·lu·lite (séljulait) *n.* hypothetical excess flesh, esp around women's thighs

Cel·lu·loid (séljulɔid) *n.* a highly inflammable, colorless solid made from cellulose nitrate and camphor. It is used in the manufacture of film, packaging materials etc. [trademark, fr. CELLULOSE]

cel·lu·lose (séljulous) *n.* a fibrous carbohydrate having the formula $(C_6H_{10}O_5)_n$. It is the principal structural material of the cell walls of plants and is chiefly obtained from wood pulp and cotton. It is used in making paper, rayon, many plastics and some explosives [fr. Mod. L. *cellulosus* fr. *cellula,* little cell]

cellulose acetate an acetic ester of cellulose used to make artificial fibers and various plastics

cellulose nitrate a nitric ester of cellulose used to make lacquers, explosives (*GUN-COTTON), Celluloid etc. (*COLLODION, *PYROXYLIN)

Cel·si·us scale (sélsi:əs) the international name for the centigrade scale [after Anders *Celsius* (1701–44), the Swedish astronomer who proposed it in 1742]

Cel·sus (sélsəs), Aulus Cornelius (1st or 2nd c.), Latin writer on medicine and surgery

Celt (selt, kelt) *n.* one of one of the ancient peoples speaking Celtic. They originated (c. 1500 B.C.) in S.W. Germany and spread (7th c. B.C.) through France to N. Spain and the British Isles. Successive Celtic invasions reached upper Italy, Bohemia, Hungary, Illyria (4th c. B.C.), and Asia Minor (3rd c. B.C.). They were conquered and absorbed by the Romans and the barbarians, until only Brittany and the west of the British Isles remained Celtic [F. *Celte* fr. L.]

celt (selt) *n.* (*archaeol.*) a prehistoric tool of stone or metal, resembling a chisel [fr. L. *celtes,* chisel (a misreading)]

Celt·i·ber·i·an (seltibíəri:ən, keltibíəri:ən) **1.** *n.* a member of a people of ancient Spain of mixed Celtic and Iberian stock. They served both the

Carthaginians and the Romans as mercenaries. They were put down by Scipio Aemilianus **2.** *adj.* of, relating to, or characteristic of a Celtiberian, or of the mountainous region of N.E. Spain in which they lived

Celt·ic (séltik, kéltik) **1.** *n.* a branch of Indo-European languages spoken by the Celts: Cornish, Breton and Welsh (Cymric or Brythonic) and Irish, Scottish Gaelic and Manx (Goidelic) and ancient Gaulish **2.** *adj.* pertaining to the Celts [fr. L. *celticus*]

celt·i·um (sélti:əm) *n.* hafnium [mod. L. fr. *Celtae,* Celts]

ce·ment (simént) **1.** *n.* a grayish powder made by heating together limestone or chalk and clay or shale, and then grinding. It consists chiefly of aluminates and silicates of calcium. When mixed with water complex chemical changes and crystallizations occur, and a hard solid soon results. When sand or gravel etc. is included in the mixture, the product is concrete ‖ any substance used to make materials cohere ‖ a substance for filling teeth **2.** *v.t.* to join together with, or as if with, cement, *to cement a friendship* ‖ *v.i.* to become cemented **ce·men·ta·tion** (si:məntéiʃən, seməntéiʃən) *n.* the act of cementing ‖ (*metall.*) the heating of a solid body in contact with a powdered substance in order to convey some special property to the solid body by chemical combination. Thus the cementation of steel by carbon makes it possible to harden the surface of the steel [O.F. *ciment*]

ce·ment·ite (siméntait) *n.* a hard and brittle carbide of iron, Fe_3C

cem·e·ter·y (sémiteri:, *Br.* sémitri) *pl.* **cem·e·ter·ies** *n.* a place (*Br.* other than a churchyard) where the dead are buried [fr. L. fr. Gk *koimētērion,* sleeping place]

Cen·drars (sɑ́drɑr), Blaise (Frédéric Sauser, 1887–1961), French writer of Swiss origin. His verse includes 'Pâques à New York' (1912), and his prose 'l'Homme foudroyé' (1945), 'la Main coupée' (1946), 'Bourlinguer' (1948)

Cenis, Mont *MONT CENIS

ce·no·bite, coe·no·bite (sí:nəbait) *n.* a member of a monastic community (cf. ANCHORITE) **cen·o·bit·i·cal, coe·no·bit·i·cal** (si:nəbítikəl) *adj.* **cen·o·bit·ism, coe·no·bit·ism** (sí:nəbaitizəm) *n.* [fr. L.L. *coenobita* fr. *coenobium,* convent fr. Gk]

ce·nog·a·my (senógəmi:) *n.* form of marriage involving two or more parties of each sex

ce·no·spe·cies, coe·no·spe·cies (si:nəspí:ʃi:z) *n.* (*biol.*) a group of closely related biological types distinguished by being able to exchange genetic characteristics within the group (and not outside it) by reason of closely related genotypes. It is usually coextensive with a taxonomic classification below genus [fr. Gk *koinos,* common+SPECIES]

cen·o·taph (sénətæf, sénətaf) *n.* a monument in honour of a person (or persons) buried elsewhere [F. *cenotaphe* fr. Gk *kenos,* empty+*taphos,* tomb]

Ce·no·zo·ic, Cae·no·zo·ic (si:nəzóuik, senəzóuik) *adj.* of the most recent era in geological history, characterized notably by rapid evolution of the mammals (*GEOLOGICAL TIME) **the Cenozoic** this era [fr. Gk *kainos,* new+*zōon,* animal]

cense (sens) *pres. part.* **cens·ing** *past and past part.* **censed** *v.t.* to perfume with burning incense or other spices as part of a religious rite, *to cense an altar* [fr. INCENSE]

cen·ser (sénsər) *n.* a vessel in which incense is burned, usually suspended on a chain so that it can be swung to disperse the smoke [O.F. *censier*]

cen·sor (sénsər) **1.** *n.* a person empowered to suppress publications or excise any matter in them thought to be immoral, seditious or otherwise undesirable ‖ (*mil.*) an official who examines letters, papers etc. to make sure they contain nothing that could interest the enemy ‖ any of various officials in British universities ‖ any person who supervises the morals and conduct of others ‖ (in Freud's system) the psychological mechanism which prevents distasteful unconscious ideas and memories from coming into the consciousness ‖ (*Rom. hist.*) one of two magistrates charged with taking the census of citizens, regulating taxation and controlling public behavior **2.** *v.t.* to examine (letters, literature etc.) in the capacity of a censor ‖ to delete (offensive material) from these, or ban (a work)

cen·so·ri·al (sensɔ́ri:əl, sensóuri:əl) *adj.* [L.=magistrate of ancient Rome]

---

cen·so·ri·ous (sensóri:əs, sensóuri:əs) *adj.* critical, faultfinding [fr. L. *censorius,* fr. *censor*]

cen·sor·ship (sénsərʃip) *n.* the institution or practice of censoring

cen·sur·a·ble (sénʃərəb'l) *adj.* deserving or subject to censure, blamable **cén·sur·a·bly** *adv.*

cen·sure (sénʃər) *n.* adverse criticism, blame, *vote of censure* [F.]

censure *pres. part.* **cen·sur·ing** *past* and *past part.* **cen·sured** *v.t.* to reprove, criticize severely [F. *censurer*]

cen·sus (sénsəs) *n.* an official counting of a country's population, usually with vital statistics etc. ‖ a similar count of items in some other field (e.g. production, distribution) [L.=a registration for taxation]

cent (sent) *n.* (*symbol* [¢]) one hundredth of a dollar ‖ a small coin of this value in the U.S.A., Canada etc. ‖ one hundredth of a gulden, Ceylonese rupee etc. or coin of this value [fr. L. *centum,* a hundred]

cen·tal (sént'l) *n.* a weight of 100 lbs used in measuring grain ‖ (*Am.*) a hundredweight of 100 lbs (the British hundredweight=112 lbs) [fr. L. *centum,* a hundred]

cen·taur (séntɔr) *n.* (*Gk mythol.*) a creature with the legs and body of a horse and the head, shoulders and arms of a man [fr. L. fr. Gk]

cen·tau·ry (séntɔri) *pl.* **cen·tau·ries** *n.* a member of *Centaurium,* fam. *Gentianaceae,* a genus of plants incl. *C. umbellatum,* formerly used in medicine as a tonic [fr. M.L. *centaurea* fr. Gk *kentauros,* because its discovery was attributed to the centaur]

cen·ta·vo (sentávou) *n.* a unit of currency in certain Latin American countries and the Philippines, the hundredth part of a boliviano, a colon, a cordoba, a lempira, a peso, a quetzal, a sol, or a sucre ‖ a coin of the value of one centavo [Span.]

centavo *n.* a unit of currency worth one hundredth of a Portuguese escudo or the Brazilian cruzeiro ‖ a coin of the value of one centavo [Port. fr. Span.]

cen·te·nar·ian (sentənéari:ən) **1.** *n.* a person who is 100 years old or more **2.** *adj.* of or pertaining to a centenary or a centenarian [fr. L. *centenarius*]

cen·te·nar·y (sénteneri:, senténəri:, *Br.* sentí:nəri) **1.** *pl.* **cen·te·nar·ies** *n.* a hundredth anniversary ‖ a period of one hundred years **2.** *adj.* pertaining to a century [L. *centenarius* fr. *centum,* a hundred]

cen·ten·ni·al (senténi:əl) **1.** *n.* a hundredth anniversary **2.** *adj.* lasting one hundred years ‖ happening once in a hundred years [fr. L. *centum,* a hundred+*annus,* year]

cen·ter, *Br.* **cen·tre** (séntər) **1.** *n.* a point equidistant from the extremities of a straight line, circle, sphere or any other object ‖ an axis, pivot or point around which an object moves ‖ the approximate middle part or point of something ‖ a place where activity is concentrated, *shopping center* ‖ a person or group occupying a middle position, esp. the main body of troops ‖ (*politics*) the group of those who hold moderate opinions ‖ (*sports*) the middle player in the attacking line of a hockey or soccer team ‖ the part of a target, e.g. for archery, which encircles the bull's-eye **2.** *v. pres. part.* **cen·ter·ing,** *Br.* *also* **cen·tring** *past* and *past part.* **cen·tered,** *Br. also* **cen·tred** *v.t.* to concentrate at one point ‖ to place in or bring into the middle ‖ to find the center of (an object) ‖ (*soccer, hockey*) to kick or hit (a ball) towards the central axis of the field ‖ *v.i.* (with 'in', 'at', 'on', 'upon') to have a center ‖ to have a chief element, *the conversation centered on tennis* [F. *centre*]

center bit, *Br.* **centre bit** a tool for boring holes in wood with a centered point for guidance, and a lip for cutting away inside a scored circumference

cen·ter·board, *Br.* **cen·tre·board** (séntərbɔrd, séntərbourd) *n.* a wooden plank or iron plate, moving on a pivot, which can be lowered through the keel of a sailing ship to increase its draft, prevent leeway, and counteract a tendency to heel when moving at speed

center field (*baseball*) the part of the outfield between left field and right field

cen·ter·fold (séntərfould) *n.* center pages of a magazine, esp. containing a special photograph or feature, sometimes removable or with an additional foldout, esp. of a nude woman or man

center of gravity, *Br.* **centre of gravity** center of mass ‖ the single point in a body towards which any other body is gravitationally attracted

center of mass, *Br.* **centre of mass** the point in a system such that the sum of the products of the masses (*m*) and distance to that point (x) = 0 i.e. $\sum_i^n m_i x_i = 0$. The system interacts with external forces as if all its mass were concentrated at that point

cen·ter·piece, *Br.* **cen·tre·piece** (séntərpi:s) *n.* a centrally placed unit of a decorative composition or ornament

cen·tes·i·mal (sentésiməl) *adj.* reckoned by hundredths ‖ divided into hundredths [fr. L. *centesimus,* a hundredth]

cen·te·si·mo (tʃentézi:mɔ) *pl.* **cen·te·si·mi** (tʃentézi:mi:) *n.* an Italian unit of currency worth one hundredth of a lira ‖ a coin of this value [Ital.]

cen·té·si·mo (sentési:mɔ) *n.* a unit of currency of Uruguay worth one hundredth of a peso ‖ a coin of this value [Span.]

cen·ti·grade scale (séntigreid) (*abbr.* C.) a temperature scale for which 0° is taken as the freezing point of pure water and 100° is taken as the boiling point of pure water under standard atmospheric pressure, thus establishing the centigrade degree as one hundredth of the temperature difference between these fixed points. A temperature of x°C. corresponds to ⅚x + 32°F. [F. fr. L. *centum,* hundred+*gradus,* step, degree]

cen·ti·gram (séntigræm) *n.* one hundredth of a gram [F. *centigramme*]

cen·ti·li·ter, *Br.* **cen·ti·li·tre** (sént'li:tər) *n.* one hundredth of a liter [F.]

cen·til·lion (sentiljən) *NUMBER TABLE [fr. L. *centum,* hundred+MILLION]

cen·time (sɑːti:m) *n.* a unit of currency worth one hundredth of a franc ‖ a coin of this value [F.]

cen·ti·me·ter, *Br.* **cen·ti·me·tre** (séntimi:tər) *n.* a hundredth part of a meter [F.]

centimeter-gram-second system, *Br.* **centimetre-gram-second system** (*abbr.* cgs) a metric system of units based on the centimeter as the unit of length, the gram as the unit of mass and the second as the unit of time

cén·ti·mo (séntimou, θénti:mou) *n.* one hundredth of a peseta, bolivar, colón (Costa Rica) or guarani, or a coin of the value of any of these [Span.]

cen·ti·pede (séntipi:d) *n.* an arthropod about 1 in. long of class *Chilopoda.* They have a serpentine body of many similar flattened segments, each with a pair of legs, and are voracious and predatory ‖ a member of *Scolopendra,* a tropical genus of centipedes, incl. some very large ones (up to 1 ft) [fr. L. *centum,* hundred+*pes* (*pedis*), foot]

cen·ti·sec·ond (séntisẹkənd) *n.* 1/100th of a second

cent·ner (séntnər) *n.* a commercial measurement of weight used in some European countries, equal to 50 kg. or 1 10.23 lbs avoir. [G. fr. L. *centenarius*]

cen·tral (séntrəl) **1.** *adj.* situated at or near the center or middle point ‖ principal, chief ‖ between extremes, *to take a central position on a problem* ‖ (*phon.*) pronounced with the tongue in a neutral position **2.** *n.* a telephone exchange, esp. in a rural district [fr. L. *centralis*]

Central African Federation a former federation (1953–63) of the then British protectorates of Northern Rhodesia (now Zambia) and Nyasaland (now Malawi) and the self-governing territory of Southern Rhodesia

Central African Republic (République Centrafricaine, former Ubangi-Shari) an independent state (area 238,000 sq. miles, pop. 2,512,000) on the central African plateau. Capital: Bangui. The land (mainly 1,000–3,000 ft) is mostly savanna, with a semidesert region in the east and dense forests in the south. Annual rainfall 40–60 ins in the south, less in the north. Average temperature (F.): 84°. Agricultural products: cotton, corn, rice, peanuts, coffee, rubber. Mineral resources: diamonds, gold. Chief export: cotton. Monetary unit: franc C.F.A. HISTORY. European explorers, following the rivers that for centuries had been used by migrating tribes crossing Central Africa, made contact with the region in the late 18th c. The English and French fixed its boundaries (1899). It became a French colony (1910) within French Equatorial Africa under the name of Ubangi-Shari-Chad. It became a member of the French Community (1958) and achieved complete independence (Aug. 13, 1960). David Dacko, its first president, was ousted by the military (1965). His successor, Jean Bedel Bokassa, crowned himself emperor (1977) and ruled by decree. He was overthrown (1979) and Dacko reestablished the republic and became president until he was ousted in a military coup (1981) led by Gen. André Kolingba

Central America the narrow southern extremity (area 230,000 sq. miles) of North America connecting it with South America. Political units: Belize, Costa Rica, El Salvador, Guatemala, Honduras, Nicaragua, and Panama. HISTORY (see also separate entries). In the northern part of the region (Guatemala, Belize, western Honduras and El Salvador), as well as in southern Mexico, there originated the Maya civilization (prob. c. 1000 B.C.). This flourished (300–900 A.D.), but was in decline when the Spaniards, under Pedro de Alvarado, conquered the area (1524). The southern part of the region (Nicaragua, Costa Rica and Panama) was inhabited by Indian tribes when Columbus explored the Caribbean coast (1502). The whole region except Belize (British Honduras), was ruled by Spain as the captaincy general of Guatemala until 1821, when the colonies declared their independence. They were incorporated into the Mexican Empire (1822–3), and were loosely united as the Central American Federation (1823–39), after which they separated into independent republics. The U.S.A. developed large economic interests in Central America, notably the United Fruit Company and the Standard Fruit and Steamship Company. The Panama Canal was cut (1902–14), and the Canal Zone leased to the U.S.A. The U.S.A. intervened to protect its interests on many occasions until the 'Good Neighbor' policy was followed in the 1930s. The Central American states jointly declared war (Dec. 1941) against the Axis powers. Economic cooperation has been developed through the Organization of American States (1948) and the Organization of Central American States (1951)

Central American 1. *adj.* of or belonging to Central America **2.** *n.* a native or inhabitant of Central America

Central American Federation a loose political federation (1823–38) of the republics of Guatemala, Honduras, Nicaragua, El Salvador and Costa Rica

central bank the main banking institution in a country, usually acting as banker to the government and to the other banks, and exercising a degree of control over national financial policy. Central banks often issue paper currency and hold the country's gold reserves

central casting casting department of a large U.S. film studio. —**from central casting** metaphorically, mediocre, stereotyped, or commonplace

central city center of an urban area, usu. with the greatest concentration of commercial enterprises. *syn* core city

central dogma (*biochem.*) thesis that, in general, genetic information is carried in self-replicating DNA and is transferred in one direction only to messenger RNAs, which specifies the sequence of amino acids in the corresponding proteins; formulated in 1958 by Francis H. C. Crick

central heating a heating system serving many rooms or a whole office block or other unit from one central source

Central India Agency the former official British name for a group of states in Hindustan, formed 1854. They became affiliated to the Indian Union (1947)

Central Intelligence Agency (*abbr.* CIA) a U.S. government independent bureau created by the National Security Act of 1947. It collects and reports information regarding foreign powers. The Central Intelligence Act (1949) exempted its director from accounting for its funds or for the size and selection of his staff. The CIA is not allowed to assume police powers within the United States (*FBI). It has involved itself in the internal affairs of foreign countries to impede the growth of communism. It was criticized for its part in the U-2 plane incident (1960) and the Bay of Pigs invasion (1961). A supervisory committee was reinstated by President Kennedy to ensure that the CIA executed policies and did not formulate them. President Carter ordered tighter restrictions oh clandestine operations (1977), and in 1978 the CIA was

---

CONCISE PRONUNCIATION KEY: **(a)** æ, c*a*t; ɑ, c*a*r; ɔ f*aw*n; ei, sn*a*ke. **(e)** e, h*e*n; i:, sh*ee*p; iə, d*ee*r; ɛə, b*ea*r. **(i)** i, f*i*sh; ai, t*i*ger; ə:, b*i*rd. **(o)** o, *o*x; au, c*ow*; ou, g*oa*t; u, p*oo*r; ɔi, r*oy*al. **(u)** ʌ, d*u*ck; u, b*u*ll; u:, g*oo*se; ə, *ba*cillus; ju:, c*u*be. x, lo*ch*; θ, *th*ink; ð, bo*th*er; z, *Z*en; ʒ, cor*s*age; dʒ, sava*g*e; ŋ, oranguta*ng*; j, *y*ak; ʃ, *fish*; tʃ, fe*tch*; 'l, rabb*le*; 'n, redd*en*. Complete pronunciation key appears inside front cover.

prohibited from making secret contracts with nongovernment institutions. Restraints were also instituted on such intrusive surveillance methods as wiretapping and opening mail. Fears arose, however, that restrictions had reduced the CIA's effectiveness and Pres. Reagan pledged to bolster its ability to ensure U.S. security (1981)

cen·tral·i·ty (sentrǽliti:) *pl.* **cen·tral·i·ties** *n.* the quality or state of being central ‖ a central position or tendency

cen·tral·i·za·tion (sentrəlizéifən) *n.* a centralizing or being centralized

cen·tral·ize (séntrəlaiz) *pres. part.* **cen·tral·iz·ing** *past* and *past part.* **cen·tral·ized** *v.i.* to concentrate at one central point ‖ *v.t.* to bring (the administration of a country, institution etc.) under central control

central limit theorem (*math.*) any of several theorems of probability based on the premise that distribution of n random finite variables tends to normal distribution as N tends to infinity. This is applied as justification for population sampling, with accuracy increasing as the sampling increases

Central Massif (séntrəlmæsif) *MASSIF CENTRAL

central nervous system the portion of the vertebrate nervous system consisting of the brain and spinal cord, which transmits motor impulses and receives sensory impulses (cf. NERVOUS SYSTEM, cf. AUTONOMIC NERVOUS SYSTEM)

Central Powers (*hist.*, 1st world war) Germany, Austria-Hungary, Bulgaria and Turkey

central processing unit (*computer*) the device in a computer that contains logic, arithmetic, and control circuits, and sometimes input and memory units. *abbr* CPU. *syn* mainframe computer

Central Provinces and Be·rar (beirár) *MADHYA PRADESH

Central standard time (*abbr.* C.S.T.) Central time

Central time (*abbr.* C.T.) one of the four standard time divisions of the U.S.A., six hours behind Greenwich time, one hour behind Eastern standard time

Central Treaty Organization (*abbr.* CENTO, known until 1959 as the Baghdad Pact) a mutual defense pact signed (1955) by Turkey, Iraq, the U.K., Pakistan and Iran. Iraq withdrew (1959). The organization was dissolved in 1979

centre *CENTER

centre bit *CENTER BIT

centreboard *CENTERBOARD

centre of gravity *CENTER OF GRAVITY

centre of mass *CENTER OF MASS

centrepiece *CENTERPIECE

cen·tric (séntrik) *adj.* placed in or at the center, central ‖ (*physiol.*) originating at a nerve center **cén·tri·cal** *adj.* **cen·tric·i·ty** (sentrísiti:) *n.* [fr. Gk *kentrikos* fr. *kentron*, center]

cen·trif·u·gal (sentrífjuːˈl, *Br.* also séntrifjuːˈgl) *adj.* acting, moving or tending to move away from a center (opp. CENTRIPETAL) ‖ (*anat.*) of nerves transmitting impulses away from a nerve center (cf. EFFERENT) ‖ (*bot.*) of flowering beginning at the summit and gradually extending downwards along a stem [fr. Mod. L. *centrifugus* fr. *centrum*, center+*fugere*, to fly from]

centrifugal force (*phys.*) a force generally considered to act on a body moving along a curved path and to be equal in magnitude but opposite in direction to the centripetal force. It is often invoked to show that an object moving under the influence of a constant centripetal force must be acted upon by a centrifugal force to keep it in its orbit

cen·tri·fuge (séntrifjuːdʒ) *n.* a machine that, by rotating a liquid containing a finely divided or a dispersed liquid at high speeds, increases the rate of sedimentation of the suspended material. This effect is due to the variation of the force acting on a suspended particle as it moves out from the center of rotation [F.]

cen·trip·e·tal (sentrípitˈl) *adj.* (*phys.*) acting, moving or tending to move towards a center (opp. CENTRIFUGAL) ‖ (*anat.*) of nerves transmitting impulses to a nerve center (cf. AFFERENT) [fr. Mod. L. *centripetus* fr. *centrum*, center+*petere*, to seek]

centripetal acceleration (*phys.*) the acceleration of a body moving under the influence of a centripetal force

centripetal force (*phys.*) the net force acting on a body that moves along a curved path. It is directed toward the center of curvature of the path and remains perpendicular to the velocity vector of the body. In the case of a constant centripetal force the path is a circle

cen·trism (séntrizəm) *n.* judicious or noncommittal stance in politics

cen·tro·some (séntrəsəum) *n.* a structure found in the cytoplasm or nucleus in cells undergoing mitosis [fr. Gk *kentron*, center+*sōma*, body]

cen·tro·sphere (séntrəsfiər) *n.* the core of the earth ‖ (*biol.*) the part of a cell in organic matter which includes the aster and the centrosome [fr. L. *centrum*, center+SPHERE]

cen·tu·ple (séntjuːˈl) 1. *adj.* one hundred times as much or as many 2. *v.t. pres. part.* **cen·tu·pling** *past* and *past part.* **cen·tu·pled** to multiply by a hundred [F.]

cen·tu·pli·cate (sentúːplikeit, sentjúːplikeit) *pres. part.* **cen·tu·pli·cat·ing** *past* and *past part.* **cen·tu·pli·cat·ed** *v.t.* to centuple [fr. L. *centuplicare* (*centuplicatus*)] **cen·tu·ri·on** (sentúːriən, sentjúːriən) *n.* (*hist.*) an officer commanding a century in the Roman army [fr. L. *centurio* (*centurionis*)]

Centurion Main Battle Tank (*mil.*) British tank with a 105-mm gun

cen·tu·ry (séntfuri:) *pl.* **cen·tu·ries** *n.* a period of a hundred years ‖ a period of a hundred years counting from a particular point of time, e.g. the assumed birth of Christ, *the 1st century B.C.* (=100–1 B.C.), *the 1st century A.D.* (=1–100 A.D.), *the 17th century* (=1601–1700) ‖ a hundred of anything, esp. a hundred runs scored by one batsman in one inning at cricket ‖ (*hist.*) a company in the Roman army, forming the smallest unit of a legion, orig. a hundred men [fr. L. *centuria* fr. *centum*, a hundred]

century plant a member of genus *Agave*, esp. *A. americana*, fam. *Amaryllidaceae*, the American aloe, pita or maguey, a showy plant native to Mexico which flowers once after many years and then dies

CEO (*acronym*) for chief executive officer

ce·phal·ic (səfǽlik, *Br.* also kefǽlik) *adj.* pertaining to the head ‖ in or near the head [F. *cephalique*]

cephalic index a number indicating whether the cranium is brachycephalic or dolichocephalic. It is found by dividing the head breadth by the length and multiplying by 100

ceph·a·lom·e·ter (sefəlómətər) *n.* instrument for measuring the head, esp. used in facial reconstruction. —**cephalometry** *n.*

Ceph·a·lo·ni·a (sefəlóuni:ə, sefəlóunjə) (*Gk* Kephallinia) the largest island (area 277 sq. miles, pop. 36,742) of the Ionian Is

ceph·a·lo·pod (séfələpɒd) *n.* a member of *Cephalopoda*, the most highly organized class of mollusks, containing the octopus, squid and cuttlefish. They are among the largest invertebrates and are strictly marine. They have a group of elongated muscular tentacles equipped with grasping hooks or suckers, a beaked mouth, and complex, well developed eyes. The higher forms propel themselves by ejecting a jet of water [Mod. L. fr. Gk *kephalē*, head+*pous* (*podos*), foot]

ceph·a·lor·i·dine [$C_{19}H_{17}N_3O_4S_2$] (sefəlóridiːn) *n.* (*pharm.*) broad-spectrum semisynthetic antibiotic, used in treatment of gonorrhea; marketed as Loridine

ceph·a·lo·spor·in (sefəlouspórin) *n.* (*pharm.*) any of various antibiotics produced by the fungus *Cephalosporium*, similar to penicillin in structure, with moderate effectiveness against bacteria. —**cephalosporiosis** *n.* (*med.*) infection caused by the fungus

ceph·a·lo·thin [$C_{16}H_{15}N_2NaO_6S_2$] (séfələθin) *n.* (*pharm.*) broad-spectrum antibiotic similar to cephalosporin used to combat penicillin-resistant staphylococci

ceph·a·lo·tho·rax (sefəlouθóræks, sefəlouθóuræks) *n.* the united head and thorax found in arachnids and crustaceans [fr. Gk *kephalē*, head+THORAX]

ce·pheid (síːfi:id) *n.* a variable giant star having a short-period variation of luminosity over about two magnitudes. The variation is thought to be due to a cyclical expansion and contraction of the stellar material [fr. *Cepheus*, a northern constellation, fr. *Cepheus*, mythical king of Ethiopia]

CEQ (*acronym*) for Council on Economic Quality

ce·ra·ceous (səréifəs) *adj.* waxy [fr. L. *cera*, wax]

Ce·ram (si:ræm, seirám) an island (area 6,621 sq. miles, pop. 100,000) in the Moluccas, Indonesia

ce·ram·ic (sərǽmik) *adj.* of or having to do with pottery **ce·rám·ics** *pl. n.* the art of pottery **cer·a·mist** (séramist) *n.* a potter ‖ someone with expert knowledge of pottery [fr. Gk *keramos*, potter's clay]

ce·ram·o·plas·tic (serǽməplæstik) *n.* a bond of glass and mica used for insulation under high temperatures

ce·ras·tes (sərǽsti:z) *pl.* **ce·ras·tes** *n.* the horned viper [L. fr. Gk *kerastēs* fr. *keras*, horn]

ce·rate (síəreit) *n.* an ointment made basically from wax and oil ‖ a compound having an anion containing tetravalent cerium [fr. L. *cerare* (*ceratus*), to wax]

cer·a·tin (sérətin) *n.* keratin

ce·rat·o·dus (sərǽtədəs) *pl.* **ce·rat·o·des** (sərǽtədiːz) *n.* a member of *Ceratodus*, a genus of Queensland mudfishes of subclass *Dipnoi* (double breathers), related to *Lepidosiren* and *Protopterus* [fr. L. *cera*, wax+Gk *odous*, tooth]

ce·ra·tose (sérətous) *n.* keratose

Cer·ber·us (sə́ːrbərəs) (*Gk mythol.*) a three-headed, monstrous dog that guarded Hades (*HERACLES)

cer·car·i·a (sərkéəri:ə) *pl.* **cer·car·i·ae** (sərkéəri:i:) *n.* the tailed larva of the liver fluke **cer·cár·i·al** *adj.* [Mod. L. fr. Gk *kerkos*, tail]

cer·co·pith·e·cus (sə́ːrkoupíθikəs) *n.* a member of *Cercopithecus*, a genus of longtailed African monkeys, including the baboon, mandrill, macaque, rhesus etc., having cheek pouches and callosities on the buttocks [L. fr. Gk *kerkos*, tail+*pithēkos*, ape]

cere (siər) *n.* a swollen fleshy patch at the proximal end of a bird's bill [F. *cire*, wax]

ce·re·al (síəri:əl) 1. *n.* any of several plants of fam. *Gramineae* (wheat, barley, oats, corn, millet, rice etc.), whose seed (grain) is cultivated for human food and for feeding livestock ‖ (*loosely*) any of various other plant orders incl. beans, peas, buckwheat etc. ‖ breakfast food made from grain 2. *adj.* pertaining to grain used for food [fr. L. *cerealis*, pertaining to Ceres, the goddess of grain]

cereal leaf beetle small chrysomelid beetle from Europe with brown-black head. It feeds on cereal grasses

cer·e·bel·lum (serəbéləm) *pl.* **cer·e·bel·lums**, **cer·e·bel·la** (serəbélə) *n.* a dorsal three-lobed outgrowth of the anterior end of the vertebrate brain (*BRAIN) [L., dim. of *cerebrum*, brain]

cer·e·bral (sérəbrəl, səríːbrəl) *adj.* pertaining to the brain ‖ relating to the cerebrum, *the cerebral hemispheres* ‖ marked by intellectual rather than passionate qualities, *cerebral music* [F. *cérébral*]

cerebral death *BRAIN DEATH

cerebral palsy a malfunction of the motor centers of the brain due to damage to the tissue (usually before or during birth) that results in a lack of muscular coordination e.g. in movement, speech etc.

cer·e·bra·tion (serəbréifən) *n.* the working of the brain, the process of thought [fr. L. *cerebrum*, brain]

cer·e·bro·spi·nal (serəbrouspáinˈl, səríːbrouspáinˈl) *adj.* pertaining to that part of the nervous system including the brain, spinal cord and the cranial and spinal nerves, which transmits impulses from a sense organ to voluntary muscles (cf. AUTONOMIC NERVOUS SYSTEM) [fr. L. *cerebrum*, brain+SPINAL]

cerebrospinal fluid a colorless liquid supplied by the blood, circulating between the meninges and throughout the neurocoele of the body. It primarily maintains uniform pressure within the brain and spinal cord

cerebrospinal meningitis a bacterial infection of the meninges which produces a high fever and is often fatal (*MENINGOCOCCUS)

cer·e·brum (sérəbrəm, səríːbrəm) *pl.* **cer·e·brums**, **cer·e·bra** (sérəbrə, səríːbrə) *n.* the enlarged dorsal part of the brain [L.]

cere·cloth (síərklɔθ, síərklɒθ) *pl.* **cere·cloths** (síərklɔ̄ðz, síərklɒðz, síərklɔθs, síərklɒθs) *n.* a waxed cloth used esp. for wrapping corpses [fr. older *cered cloth* fr. L. *cera*, wax]

cere·ment (síərmənt, sérəmənt) *n.* (usually *pl.*) a shroud or winding-sheet, usually treated with wax for the dead [F. *cirement* fr. *cirer*, to wax]

cer·e·mo·ni·al (serəmóuni:əl) 1. *n.* ritual ‖ formalities observed on certain occasions, esp. public ceremonies, often symbolic and picturesque ‖ (*eccles.*) a book of ritual 2. *adj.* pertaining to ceremonies, *a ceremonial banquet* [fr. L. *ceremonialis* fr. *caeremonia*, *ceremony*]

cer·e·mo·ni·ous (serəmóuni:əs) *adj.* observing ceremony ‖ fussily polite [fr. F. *cérémonieux*]

cer·e·mo·ny (sérəmouni:) *pl.* **cer·e·mo·nies** *n.* rites or ritual ‖ an occasion observed with ritual ‖ any formalities observed on a special occasion ‖ punctilious, formal behavior **to stand on ceremony** to insist on formal politeness or rigid regard for convention **without ceremony** casually ‖ brusquely [prob. fr. O.F. *cerymonie*]

Cer·en·kov radiation (tʃérenkəf) (*phys.*) a visible light created when a transparent medium is traversed by charged particle at a greater speed than that of light; named for Paul A. Cerenkov

Ce·res (síəri:z) (*Rom. mythol.*) the goddess of grain and agriculture, identified with the Greek Demeter

ce·re·us (síəri:əs) *n.* a member of *Cereus*, a genus of American cacti incl. *C. giganteus*, the largest cactus, growing to 70 ft high and 2 ft thick, with candelabra-like branching, and *C. grandiflora*, a night-blooming variety [L. fr. *cera*, wax]

ce·ric (síərik, sérik) *adj.* of or pertaining to cerium or containing cerium in the tetravalent state

Ce·ri·go (tʃéri:gou) *CYTHERA

ce·rise (serí:s, serí:z) **1.** *n.* cherry red, a bright red color **2.** *adj.* of this color [F.=*cherry*]

ce·rite (síərait) *n.* a brownish mineral, a hydrous silicate of cerium [CERIUM]

ce·ri·um (síəri:əm) *n.* a metallic element (symbol Ce, at. no. 58, at. mass 140.12) in the rare-earth group. It is used in making alloys which spark when struck or scraped, e.g. flints for cigarette lighters [after the planet *Ceres*]

cer·met (sə́:rmet) *n.* an alloy made of a heat-resistant material (e.g. titanium carbide) and a metal (e.g. nickel) and used for turbine blades [CERAMIC+METAL]

ce·ro·plas·tic (siərəplǽstik, serəplǽstik) *adj.* modeled in wax ‖ pertaining to modeling in wax [fr. Gk *kēroplastikos*]

ce·rous (síərəs) *adj.* of or pertaining to cerium or containing cerium in the trivalent state

Cer·ro Bolívar (sérrɔ) a mountain in Venezuela of almost pure iron ore, 25 miles south of Ciudad Bolívar

Cer·ro de Pas·co (sérrɔðepáskɔ) a mining town (pop. 26,000) in central Peru, at 13,973 ft, long a great source of silver (1630–late 19th c.), and now of copper and other minerals

Cer·ro Gor·do (sérrɔɡórdɔ) a mountain pass between Veracruz and Jalapa, Mexico, site of a battle (1847) in the Mexican War. The victory of the U.S. force, under Gen. Winfield Scott, over Santa Anna cleared the path to the Mexican capital

cer·tain (sə́:rt'n) *adj.* sure ‖ convinced ‖ predictably reliable, *a certain winner* ‖ of a thing or person not specified although the identity is known, *on a certain day* ‖ some, though not very much, *a certain hesitance* **for certain** without a doubt, surely **to make certain** to assure oneself

cer·tain·ly *adv.* definitely ‖ admittedly, *there is certainly some cause for anxiety* ‖ (as an answer) yes ‖ yes, willingly [O.F. *certain*]

cer·tain·ty (sə́:rt'nti:) *pl.* **cer·tain·ties** *n.* something which is certain ‖ conviction, sure knowledge **for a certainty** without any doubt **with certainty** with the conviction of being right [O.F. *certeinté*]

cer·ti·fi·a·ble (sə́:rtifaiəb'l) *adj.* capable of being certified ‖ fit to be certified insane

cer·tif·i·cate l. (sərtífikit) *n.* a written statement attesting some fact, esp. the status and qualifications of the person holding it **2.** (sərtífikeit) *v.t. pres. part.* **cer·tif·i·cat·ing** *past* and *past part.* **cer·tif·i·cat·ed** to grant a certificate to ‖ to license **cer·tif·i·ca·tion** *n.* a certifying or certificating or a being certified or certificated ‖ a certified statement [fr. M.L. *certificare (certificatus)*, to certify]

certified public accountant a state-certified professional accountant (cf. CHARTERED ACCOUNTANT)

cer·ti·fy (sə́:rtifai) *pres. part.* **cer·ti·fy·ing** *past* and *past part.* **cer·ti·fied** *v.t.* to attest formally ‖ to state in a certificate ‖ (of a medical practitioner) to state formally the insanity of (a person) [F. *certifier*]

certiorari *WRIT OF CERTIORARI

cer·ti·tude (sə́:rtitu:d, sə́:rtitju:d) *n.* conviction, the feeling of certainty [F.]

ce·ru·le·an (sərú:li:ən) **1.** *n.* azure blue **2.** *adj.* of this color [fr. L. *caeruleus*]

ce·ru·men (serú:mən) *n.* the waxlike secretion exuded by glands in the outer part of the ear ‖ a wax secreted by scale insects [fr. L. *cera*, wax]

ce·rus·site (síərəsait, sirʌ́sait) *n.* native lead carbonate [fr. L. *cerussa*]

Cer·van·tes (sərvǽnti:z), Miguel de (1547–1616), Spanish author and dramatist, whose best-known work is 'Don Quixote' (1605), a novel episodic in structure with many inserted tales. The hero is a parody of the knight errant and, at the same time, a perfect exponent of chivalric nobility

cer·vi·cal (sə́:rvik'l) *adj.* pertaining to the neck, esp. pertaining to the region of the spinal column between the skull and the thoracic vertebrae [fr. L. *cervex (cervicis)*, neck]

cer·vine (sə́:rvain, sə́:rvin) *adj.* like a deer ‖ pertaining to deer [fr. L. *cervinus*]

Cer·vin, le (servẽ) *MATTERHORN

Cer·vi·no, il (tʃerví:nɔ) *MATTERHORN

cer·vix (sə́:rviks) *pl.* **cer·vi·ces** (sə́:rvisi:z), **cer·vix·es** *n.* (*anat.* and *zool.*) the neck, esp. the back part ‖ the neck of the uterus ‖ a necklike part [L.]

Cé·saire (seizer), Aimé (1913–), French West Indian (Martinique) writer and political leader who turned away from Communism. In his poetry he returns to the sources of the black cultural heritage and frees himself from traditional Western forms. He is also the author of essays ('Discours sur le colonialisme', 1951 and 'Toussaint Louverture', 1956) and his plays include 'la Tragédie du roi Christophe' (1963) and 'Une saison au Congo' (1966)

Ce·sar·e·an section, Ce·sar·i·an section, Cae·sar·e·an section, Cae·sar·i·an section (sizéəri:ən) a surgical operation through the walls of the abdomen and womb for the delivery of a baby [fr. L. *Caesarianus* (after Julius Caesar*, said to have been born in this way)]

ce·si·um, cae·si·um (sí:zi:əm) *n.* a white, ductile element of the alkali metal group (symbol Cs, at. no. 55, at. mass 132.905). It is the most electropositive element and has photoelectric properties [neut. of L. *caesius*, bluish-gray]

cesium clock (*phys.*) device that accurately measures time by the frequency of vibrations of atoms of a cesium atom-beam resonator

cesium 137 (*nuclear phys.*) radioactive isotope component of nuclear fallout with half-life of 12 months

Cés·pe·des (séspeðes), Carlos Manuel de (1819–74), Cuban patriot who freed his slaves and cried out (1868) at Yara 'Viva Cuba Libre' (Long Live Free Cuba). He proclaimed the Republic in Arms, thus provoking the Ten Years War (1868–78). He served (1869–73) as president

ces·sa·tion (seséiʃən) *n.* a ceasing [fr. L. *cessatio (cessationis)*]

ces·sion (séʃən) *n.* the act of ceding or giving up (land, property, rights etc.) [F.]

ces·sion·ar·y (séʃəneri:) *pl.* **ces·sion·ar·ies** *n.* an assignee [fr. M.L. *cessionarius*]

cess·pit (séspit) *n.* a pit holding solid matter from house drains [etym. doubtful]

cess·pool (séspu:l) *n.* a deep hole into which sewage drains [etym. doubtful]

ces·tode (séstoud) *n.* a member of *Cestoda*, a subclass of *Platyhelminthes*, flatworms, all of which are highly adapted internal parasites (*TAPEWORM) [fr. Gk *kestos*, girdle]

cesura, cesural *CAESURA, *CAESURAL

CETA (*acronym*) for Comprehensive Employment and Training Act, which provided subsidized employment for disadvantaged plus training at federal expense

ce·ta·cean (sitéiʃən) **1.** *n.* a member of *Cetacea*, a mammalian order including whales, dolphins and porpoises **2.** *adj.* pertaining to this order

ce·ta·ceous *adj.* [fr. L. *cetus*, a whale fr. Gk]

ce·tane number (sí:tein) *n.* a measurement of the ignition value of diesel oil [fr. *cetane*, a constituent of petroleum fr. L. *cetus*, whale fr. Gk]

cetane rating cetane number

Ceu·ta (sjú:tə, θi:ú:ta) a Spanish town and seaport (pop. 70,864) forming an enclave in Morocco, a trading center since Roman times. Captured by the Portuguese (1415), it was acquired by Spain (1580). Cathedral (15th c.)

Cé·vennes (seiven) a mountain range forming the southeast rim of the Massif Central

ce·viche (səví:ʃ) *n.* raw, spiced marinated white fish

Cey·lon *SRI LANKA

Cey·lo·nese (si:ləní:z) **1.** *adj.* of or pertaining to Ceylon or its people **2.** *pl.* **Cey·lo·nese** *n.* a native or inhabitant of Ceylon

Cé·zanne (seizæn), Paul (1839–1906), French painter. As a young man he was influenced by the Impressionists, but he came to believe that Impressionism was destroying itself in atmosphere and incoherence. He began to create a new world of forms out of natural objects, even distorting appearances and reducing objects to geometrical patterns in order to make a coherent whole in his pictures. His final landscapes are the forerunners of the cubist experiments of Picasso and Braque a few years later

cf. compare [fr. L. *confer*]

C-5A *GALAXY

CGN *GUIDED MISSILE CRUISER

cgs *CENTIMETER-GRAM-SECOND SYSTEM

CGS units system of scientific centimeter-gram-second measurement superseded by SI units. *Cf* SI UNITS

ch. chapter

Cha·blis (ʃæbli:) *n.* a dry white wine made at Chablis on the Serein near Auxerre, N. Burgundy, France

Cha·bri·er (ʃæbri:ei), Alexis Emmanuel (1841–94), French composer of operas and piano music, and of the popular rhapsody for orchestra 'España'

Cha·ca·bu·co (tʃɑkɑbú:kɔ) a branch of the Chilean Andes, and a village north of Santiago which was the site of a battle (1817) in which San Martín routed the Spaniards under Rafael Maroto (1783–1847). The independence of Chile was proclaimed in the following year

chac·ma (tʃǽkmə) *n. Papio comatus*, a S. African baboon [Hottentot]

Chaco *GRAN CHACO

cha·conne (ʃækɔ́n) *n.* (*mus.*) a vocal or instrumental piece in slow 3-beat time, with a repeated theme in the bass, originally for dancing [F. fr. Span. fr. Basque *chucun*, pretty]

Chaco War a conflict (1932–5) between Bolivia and Paraguay over disputed areas of the Chaco Boreal, a region (area 100,000 sq. miles) north of the Pilcomayo River and west of the Paraguay River. The Treaty of Buenos Aires (1938) granted Paraguay c. 90,000 sq. miles of the area in dispute

Chad (tʃæd), St (*d.* 672), bishop of York, later of Mercia. He fixed his see at Lichfield

Chad (F. Tchad) a republic (area 461,200 sq. miles, pop. 4,752,000) on the central African plateau. Capital: Fort Lamy. About half the people are Moslems. The land is mountainous desert (1,000–4,600 ft) in the north (Tibesti Mtns, highest point 11,209 ft) and east (Ennedi and Ouadai Mtns). The Lake Chad depression is in the west. North of Lake Chad a dry Sahara climate prevails. South of Lake Chad summer rainfall (20–48 ins) allows grazing and cultivation. Average temperature (F.) 90°. Livestock: cattle, sheep, goats. Agricultural products: cotton, peanuts, millet, rice, fishing. Exports: cotton, cattle, meat. Monetary unit: franc C.F.A. HISTORY. Because ancient trade routes passed through the region of Lake Chad (*AFRICA), the European powers attempted to establish their influence in the late 18th c. By a series of treaties in the 1890s, the French gained control of the area north and east of Lake Chad. After the 1st world war the German territory of the southeast was incorporated, to form a French overseas territory in French Equatorial Africa. It became a member state of the French Community (1958) and in 1959 formed an economic, technical and customs union with the three other members of the former French Equatorial Africa. Independence was granted (Aug. 11, 1960). Armed uprisings developed (from 1968) in various regions and French troops were called in. Both France and Libya intervened repeatedly in Chad as the government remained unstable and fighting continued into the 1980s. Drought exacerbated the country's problems in the mid-1980s

Chad (F. Tchad) a lake of central Africa, whose area varies seasonally from 7,000 to 20,000 sq. miles, but which is only 10 ft deep

chad tape (tʃæd) (*computer*) paper tape on which codes are prepunched

Chad·wick (tʃǽdwik), Sir James (1891–1974), English physicist. He discovered the neutron (1932) and made many other contributions to atomic physics. Nobel prize (1935)

chae·tog·nath (kí:tɔgnæθ, kí:təgnæθ) *n.* a member of *Chaetognatha*, a phylum of about 30 species of marine swimming animals (arrow-worms), carnivorous, torpedo-shaped, laterally compressed, with paired fins and two groups of bristles (chaetae) at the front end. They are

---

CONCISE PRONUNCIATION KEY: **(a)** æ, c**a**t; ɑ, c**a**r; ɔ f**aw**n; ei, sn**a**ke. **(e)** e, h**e**n; i:, sh**ee**p; iə, d**ee**r; ɛə, b**ea**r. **(i)** i, f**i**sh; ai, t**i**ger; ə:, b**ir**d. **(o)** o, **o**x; au, c**ow**; ou, g**oa**t; u, p**oo**r; ɔi, r**oy**al. **(u)** ʌ, d**u**ck; u, b**u**ll; u:, g**oo**se; ə, b**a**cill**u**s; ju:, c**u**be. x, lo**ch**; θ, **th**ink; ð, bo**th**er; z, **Z**en; ʒ, cor**s**age; dʒ, sava**g**e; ŋ, oranguta**n**g; j, **y**ak; ʃ, **fi**sh; tʃ, **fe**tch; 'l, rabb**le**; 'n, redd**en**. Complete pronunciation key appears inside front cover.

transparent, showing distinct head, trunk and tail [fr. Gk *chaité*, hair + *gnathos*, jaw]

chafe (tʃeif) **1.** *v. pres. part.* **chaf·ing** *past* and *past part.* **chafed** *v.t.* to irritate or make sore by rubbing ‖ to wear by rubbing ‖ to rub so as to warm ‖ to irritate, annoy ‖ *v.i.* to rub, *the boats chafed against each other* ‖ to become worn by rubbing ‖ to be in a state of irritation through frustration, *to chafe at restrictions* **2.** *n.* a sore or irritation ‖ wear caused by rubbing [M.E. *chaufen* fr. O.F. *chaufer*, to warm]

chaf·er (tʃeifər) *n.* a large flying beetle of fam. *Scarabaeidae*, esp. the cockchafer [O.E. *cefer*]

chaff (tʃæf, tʃɑf) **1.** *n.* banter, good-humored teasing **2.** *v.t.* to tease good-humoredly [etym. doubtful]

chaff 1. *n.* the outer husk of grain separated by threshing or winnowing ‖ straw or hay chopped for animal fodder ‖ the bracts of the flower of grasses, esp. the inner pair ‖ useless or worthless writing, talk etc. ‖ (*mil.*) radar reflectors consisting of thin, narrow metallic strips of various lengths and frequency responses, used to reflect echoes to confuse an enemy **2.** *v.t.* to chop (hay or straw) [O.E. *ceaf*]

chaff·cut·ter (tʃæfkʌtər, tʃɑfkʌtər) *n.* a machine for chopping hay etc. for animal fodder

chaf·finch (tʃæfintʃ) *n. Fringilla coelebs*, a small European finch. The male has a pinkish breast and a slate-blue crest on the head

chaf·ing dish (tʃeifiŋ) a heated dish (or stand for a dish) for keeping food warm, or for cooking certain dishes at the dining table

Cha·gall (ʃægæl), Marc (1887–1985), French painter of Russian Jewish origin, a rich colorist with great poetic imagination, often taking subjects from Russian village life or Jewish folklore and religion. He was also an engraver. His work includes illustrations for 'Arabian Nights' and for the Old Testament, 12 stained-glass windows (the tribes of Judah) for Israel, and the ceiling of the Paris opera house. In 1977 he became the first living artist to have an exhibition at the Louvre

cha·grin (ʃəgrín, *Br.* ʃægrin) **1.** *n.* disappointment, mortification **2.** *v.t.* to vex acutely because of disappointment [F.]

Cha·har (tʃáhár) a region (area 107,677 sq. miles, pop. 2,035,000) of Inner Mongolia, N.E. China: iron and coal deposits

chain (tʃein) **1.** *n.* a series of rings or links of metal joined one to another and used for fastening, dragging, suspending, tethering etc. ‖ an ornamental set of links worn as a necklace, as insignia etc. ‖ a series or sequence, *chain of mountains, chain of events* ‖ (*pl.*) a prisoner's fetters ‖ (*pl., fig.*) bonds, bondage ‖ (*chem.*) a linkage of atoms of one or more elements ‖ (*surveying*) a measuring instrument consisting of 100 joined links (*ENGINEERS' CHAIN, *GUNTER'S CHAIN) ‖ a unit of length equal to 66 ft ‖ a number of business concerns all of one kind and owned by one person or group, *a chain of hotels* **2.** *v.t.* to confine with or as if with chains or a chain [M.E. *chayne* fr. O.F.]

chain armor chain mail

chain·belt (tʃéinbelt) *n.* waistband composed of interlocking metal links

chain bridge a suspension bridge suspended by chains

chain coupling a chain linking rail cars as a safeguard, in case the screw coupling breaks

chained list (*computer*) list arranged so that each item identifies the next following item

chain gang a number of convicts chained together, esp. while working outdoors

chain letter a letter sent to a certain number of people, each of whom is asked to send copies to an equal number of people

chain lightning lightning that flashes across the sky in a zigzag course

chain mail armor of small metal links

chain of being the notion of a hierarchy of perfection embracing all entities in unbroken order

chain printer line-printing device contained in a continuous chain, used on some typewriter and office printout machines

chain pump a pump formed by an endless chain in a tube with a series of buckets or disks attached to it, passing over a turning wheel, so that each vessel in turn dips and is filled

chain reaction a process of change in which a product of the change initiates further change, e.g. in atomic fission

chain reactor *REACTOR

chain saw a power saw with the teeth set on an endless chain

chain shot (*hist.*) a missile fired from cannon. It consisted of two balls or halfballs joined by a chain, and was used esp. in naval warfare to damage the enemy's rigging

chain-smoke (tʃéinsmouk) *pres. part.* **chain-smok·ing** *past* and *past part.* **chain-smoked** *v.i.* to smoke one cigarette after another, lighting the fresh one from the stub of the previous one ‖ *v.t.* to smoke (cigarettes) in this way **chain-smok·er** *n.*

chain stitch an embroidery or crochet stitch resembling the links of a chain ‖ the stitch made with two interlocking threads by a sewing machine

chain store one of a number of shops owned by the same person or company, each selling the same range of goods

chain system *NET SYSTEM

chain wheel a toothed wheel with an endless chain so that power can be transmitted or received, e.g. in a bicycle

chair (tʃeər) **1.** *n.* a seat with four legs and a backrest, for one person ‖ the position of a professor in a university ‖ the seat and the office of a person appointed to preside over a meeting ‖ the chairman, *to appeal to the chair* ‖ the electric chair ‖ a rail chair **to take the chair** to act as chairman **2.** *v.t.* to preside over (a meeting) as chairman ‖ to install in office ‖ (*Br.*) to carry (a person who has done something particularly notable) on the shoulders of several people [M.E. *chaere* fr. O.F. fr. L. fr. Gk]

chair car a rail car having single armchairs with adjustable backs, a saloon car

chair·man (tʃéərmən) *pl.* **chair·men** (tʃéərmən) *n.* a person appointed to preside over a meeting ‖ the president of a committee, board or (*Br.*) magistrates' bench **chair·man·ship** *n.*

chair·per·son (tʃéərpə:rsən) *n.* individual who supervises at a committee or formal meeting

chair·side (tʃéərsaid) *adj.* dental equivalent of 'bedside'

chaise (ʃeiz) *n.* (*hist.*) a light, open pleasure carriage, usually with a hood [F. = chair]

chaise longue (ʃéizlɔ̃g) *n.* a couch with a backrest at one end only [F. = long chair]

cha·la·za (kəléizə) *pl.* **cha·la·zae** (kəléizi:), **cha·la·zas** *n.* (*zool.*) a twisted cord of albumen which connects the yolk to either end of the shell membrane in a bird's egg ‖ (*bot.*) the basal portion of the nucellus of an ovule [Mod. L. fr. Gk *chalaza*, hail]

Chal·ce·don, Council of (kælsidɒn, kælsí:d'n) the fourth and last (451) of the Councils of the undivided Church to pronounce on the person of Christ (*CHRISTOLOGY). It condemned monophysitism (*EUTYCHES)

chal·ced·o·ny (kælséd'ni:, kælsədóuni:) *n.* a semi-precious blue-gray variety of quartz, composed of very small crystals packed together with a fibrous, waxy appearance [fr. L. *chalcedonius* fr. Gk]

chal·cid (kælsid) *n.* a member of *Chalcidae*, a family of hymenopterous insects resembling wasps. The larvae are parasitic on other insects [fr. Gk *chalkos*, copper]

Chal·cid·i·ce (kælsídisi:) a three-tongued peninsula projecting into the Aegean from Macedonia, N. Greece

Chal·cis (kælsis) the chief city of Euboea, Greece, famous in antiquity for its metalwork and pottery

chal·co·py·rite (kælkəpáirait, kælkəpíərait) *n.* a yellow mineral, copper pyrites, copper-iron sulfide, CuFeS₂, an important copper ore [fr. Gk *chalkos*, copper + PYRITE]

Chal·de·a, Chal·dae·a (kældí:ə) an ancient region on the Euphrates and the Persian Gulf, originally the southern part of Babylonia

Chal·de·an (kældí:ən) **1.** *adj.* pertaining to Chaldea or the Chaldeans **2.** *n.* an inhabitant of Chaldea, a member of the tribe which lived in Babylon ‖ the Semitic language of the Chaldeans [fr. Gk *chaldaios*]

cha·let (ʃæléi, ʃælei) *n.* a small wooden house in the Alps ‖ a house built in this style [F.]

Cha·lia·pin (ʃəljápin), Fyodor Ivanovich (1873–1938), Russian bass singer

chal·ice (tʃælis) *n.* the cup used at the celebration of the Mass (Eucharist) **chál·iced** *adj.* (of flowers) cup-shaped [O.F.]

chalk (tʃɔk) **1.** *n.* (*geol.*) a soft, friable, earthy, whitish variety of limestone, composed mainly of calcium carbonate. It is of marine origin, consisting principally of deposited shells of foraminifers ‖ a short rod, formerly of chalk but now of calcium sulfate, used for writing and drawing on dark and slightly rough surfaces (esp. a

blackboard) **as different as chalk from cheese** (*Br.*) totally different **not by a long chalk** (*Br.*) not at all **2.** *v.t.* to write or mark with chalk **to chalk out** to make a rough sketch of (a plan or purpose) **to chalk up** to write up on a board ‖ to give credit for, place on record, *to chalk up a good deed* **chálk·i·ness** *n.* [O.E. *cealc* fr. L.]

chalk·board (tʃɔkbɔrd, tʃɔkbourd) *n.* a blackboard, esp. a small one

chalk number (*mil.*) number given to a comboete load and to the transporting carrier. — **chalk commander** *n.* —**chalk troops** *n.*

chalk·stone (tʃɔkstoun) *n.* a deposit of calcium carbonate in the joints of bones, e.g. in persons having gout

chalk·y (tʃɔki:) *comp.* **chalk·i·er** *superl.* **chalk·i·est** *adj.* of or like chalk

challah *HALLAH

chal·lenge (tʃælindʒ) *n.* a question called out by a sentry to halt someone approaching and check his right to be there ‖ a calling in question (of the truth of statements, rights, authority etc.) ‖ something which tests a person's qualities ‖ a calling out to a duel ‖ an invitation to play a game or accept a match ‖ an objection made against someone in respect of his qualification to vote, serve on a jury etc. [O.F. *chalenge*]

challenge *pres. part.* **challeng·ing** *past* and *past part.* **chal·lenged** *v.t.* (of a sentry) to demand a statement of identity of (a person) ‖ to invite or summon to a match or game or to a duel or (*fig.*) to comparison ‖ to dispute the truth of (a statement) ‖ to assert a claim to, *this matter challenges attention* ‖ to take objection to the authority or opinions of ‖ to call forth and test (someone's qualities) ‖ (*law*) to object to (a person) as voter, juryman etc. **chál·leng·er** *n.* someone or something that challenges ‖ (*boxing*) a boxer fighting a champion for his title [O.F. *chalenger*]

chal·lis, chal·lie (ʃæli:) *n.* a light clothing fabric woven from wool, cotton or rayon, printed with a small pattern or dyed a solid color [prob. fr. the surname *Challis*]

Châ·lons, Battle of (ʃuló) a battle (451) in which Attila's attempt to invade Gaul was defeated by a Roman army under Aetius and a Visigoth army under Theodoric

cha·lyb·e·ate (kəlíbi:it, kəlíbi:eit) *adj.* impregnated with iron salts, *chalybeate water* [perh. fr. Mod. L. *chalybeatus* fr. Gk *chalups* (*chalubos*), steel]

chal·y·bite (kælibait) *n.* siderite

Cham (tʃæm, tʃɑm) a Moslem people of Indochina who controlled (3rd–17th cc.) a large region of southern Annam

cham·ber (tʃéimbər) *n.* a legislative or judicial body, esp. either of the divisions in a bicameral legislative body ‖ a large room or hall used for the meetings of a legislative or judicial body ‖ (*hist.*) a private room, esp. a bedroom ‖ (*pl.*) a room where a judge deals with matters not requiring action in court ‖ (*pl., Br.*) lawyers' rooms, esp. in one of the Inns of Court ‖ a compartment or cavity, *burial chambers cut in the rock* ‖ the part of a gun which holds the charge ‖ the part of a firearm which receives the cartridge ‖ any of the ammunition compartments in the cylinder of a revolver [F. *chambre*]

Cham·ber·lain (tʃéimbərlin), Arthur Neville (1869–1940), prime minister of Great Britain (1937–40), son of Joseph Chamberlain. He followed a policy of appeasement toward the Fascist and Nazi dictators, culminating in the Munich Conference (Sept. 1938), when he agreed to German annexation of Sudetenland. Germany's invasion of Poland forced him to declare war (Sept. 3, 1939). He resigned after the invasion of Norway (May 10, 1940), giving place to Winston Churchill

Chamberlain, Joseph (1836–1914), British statesman. As Liberal-Unionist colonial secretary (1895–1903) he was accused of precipitating the Boer War (1899–1902). He resigned the office in order to campaign for his policy of Imperial Preference, finally accepted after his death

Chamberlain, Sir Joseph Austen (1863–1937), British statesman, son of Joseph Chamberlain. As Conservative chancellor of the exchequer (1903–6, 1919–21) he secured parliamentary consent to Imperial Preference, and as foreign secretary (1924–9) he successfully negotiated the signing of the Locarno Pact (1925)

Chamberlain, Owen (1920–), U.S. nuclear physicist and educator who shared (with Emilio

Segrè) the 1959 Nobel prize in physics for the discovery of the antiproton

cham·ber·lain (tʃéimbərlin) n. the official in charge of the household and court of a monarch or nobleman [O.F.]

cham·ber·maid (tʃéimbərmeid) n. a maid who looks after the bedrooms in a house or hotel

chamber music music written for a small number of performers (generally more than two). Originally it signified music meant to be performed in a room, not in a theater, church etc.

chamber of commerce an association of businessmen of a city etc. to further the interests of trade

Chamber of Deputies the lower house of the French legislature

chamber orchestra a small orchestra for playing chamber music

chamber pot a vessel for urine used in a bedroom or child's nursery

Cham·bers (tʃéimbərz), Ephraim (1680–1740), English encyclopedist. His two-volume 'Cyclopædia' or 'Universal Dictionary of Arts and Sciences' (1728) influenced Diderot's 'Encyclopédie'

Cham·bé·ry (ʃábeiri:) the chief town (pop. 56,788) of Savoie, France and former capital of Savoy: castle (15th and 19th cc.), cathedral (16th c.)

cham·bray (ʃámbrei) n. a lightweight cloth woven from silk, cotton or linen, with a white weft and a colored warp [prob. fr. *Cambrai*, France]

cha·me·le·on (kəmí:liːən, kəmí:ljən) n. an insectivorous lizard distinguished by its prehensile tail, long extensible tongue, independently moving eyeballs and esp. its ability to change its skin color to match its surroundings ‖ an inconstant person **cha·me·le·on·ic** (kəmi:liːónik) adj. [L. *chamaeleon* fr. Gk *chamai*, dwarf+*leōn*, lion]

cham·fer (tʃæmfər) 1. v.t. to bevel off the right-angled edge or corner of 2. n. the surface produced by beveling away the right angle between two surfaces [fr. O.F. *chanfraindre*]

Cham·fort (ʃáför), Nicholas Sébastien Roch (1741–95), French man of letters, conversationalist, and maker of epigrams, author of 'Pensées, Maximes et Anecdotes' (published 1803). Although a Republican, he was revolted by the revolutionary Terror and committed suicide

cham·ois (ʃǽmi:, ʃǽmwɑ) n. *Antelope rupicapra*, a horned, goatlike antelope of the high Alps and European mountains. Its skin makes a very soft, warm leather used for making gloves, polishing glass, etc. ‖ (ʃǽmi:) this leather or a sheepskin substitute for it [F.]

cham·o·mile, cam·o·mile (kǽməmail) n. a member of *Anthemis*, fam. *Compositae*, a genus of perennial, strong-scented plants, esp. *A. nobilis*, which yields an antispasmodic and diaphoretic [F. *camomille* fr. L. fr. Gk]

Cha·mo·nix (ʃǽmɔni:) a famous winter sports and mountaineering center (pop. 5,907) in Savoy, France, at the foot of Mont Blanc

Cha·mor·ro (tʃamɔ́rrɔ), Emiliano (1871–1965), Nicaraguan general and president (1917–21, 1926). He signed the Bryan-Chamorro treaty

champ (tʃæmp) v.t. to munch or chew noisily ‖ to bite on ‖ v.i. to make chewing noises or movements ‖ to show impatience, *he's champing to be off* [origin unknown]

champ n. (pop.) a champion [by shortening]

Cham·pa (tʃǽmpə) the kingdom of the Chams (2nd c.–17th c.) which at its zenith occupied the middle and south of Annam

cham·pac, cham·pak (tʃǽmpæk, tʃʌ́mpʌk) n. *Michelia champaca*, fam. *Magnoliaceae*, an E. Asiatic tree cultivated for its sweet-scented yellowish-orange flowers, used in making perfume [Hind. *campak* fr. Skr.]

Cham·pagne (ʃápænj) a former province of France in the E. Paris basin, forming Ardennes, Aube, Marne, and Haute-Marne departments. It is a dry, chalky tableland, largely reafforested, with cereals and sugar beet, pasture and vineyards (around Reims). Historic capital: Troyes. A medieval countship acquired by the house of Blois (11th c.), it was united to the crown in 1361. Its fairs (born of its location in the textile zone and near the Low Countries) drew merchants from all of W. Europe (12th and 13th cc.)

cham·pagne (ʃæmpéin) n. a sparkling white wine made in Champagne

Cham·paigne (ʃápeinj), Philippe de (1602–74), Flemish painter. He lived and worked in Paris. His portraits (Richelieu, the religious of Port Royal etc.) show the classical qualities of rational severity, lucidity and restraint

champak *CHAMPAC

cham·pi·on (tʃǽmpiːən) 1. n. a winner of a competition in a particular field, *tennis champion*, (often used attributively) *champion baseball team* ‖ a flower or vegetable or animal which has won first prize in competition ‖ someone who defends another person or a cause, *a champion of liberty* 2. v.t. to fight or argue on behalf of 3. adj. first among all competitors ‖ (pop.) first-rate **chám·pi·on·ship** n. the state or honor of being a champion ‖ a competition in which the title of champion is contested ‖ advocacy [O.F.]

Cham·plain (ʃæmpléin, ʃáplɛ̄), Samuel de (c. 1567–1635), French explorer and colonizer. He explored the lower St Lawrence River (1603), the coast of Nova Scotia (1604), and Lakes Huron and Ontario (1615–16). He founded the settlements of Quebec (1608) and Place Royale, later Montreal (1611), and governed New France (1612–29, 1633–5)

Cham·plain (ʃæmpléin) a lake (area 600 sq. miles) on the U.S.A.-Canadian frontier. A canal joins it to the Hudson, providing an inland waterway between New York and the St Lawrence. It was the site of a naval engagement (1814) during the War of 1812, in which a U.S. naval force commanded by Thomas McDonough (1783–1825) defeated a British naval force, thereby preventing a British invasion from Canada

champ·le·vé enamel (ʃɑ̄ləvéi) enamel work in which the colored powdered glass is placed into depressions in the surface of the metal before the article is fired (cf. CLOISONNÉ) [F. *champlevé* a raised field]

Cham·pol·lion (ʃápɔljɔ̄), Jean-François (1790–1832), French Orientalist who deciphered (1823) Egyptian hieroglyphics from the Rosetta stone, independently of Thomas Young

chance (tʃæns, tʃɑns) 1. n. an occurrence that cannot be accounted for by any pattern of cause and effect, nor by the working of providence ‖ a supposed power (cf. FATE) behind such occurrences, *chance made me go there* ‖ an opportunity ‖ (baseball) an opportunity in fielding for a put-out or an assist ‖ (cricket) an occasion when a batsman should be out but isn't (a dropped catch etc.) **by chance** fortuitously **to leave it to chance** to trust to luck **to take a chance** to run a risk and trust to luck 2. adj. unintentional, fortuitous 3. v.i. pres. part. **chanc·ing** past and past part. **chanced** to happen fatefully (often impers.), *it so chanced that we met again* ‖ to happen by accident ‖ v.t. to leave to luck, *we may be too late, but let's chance it* ‖ to risk, *to chance one's neck* **to chance upon** to find, meet by accident [O.F. *cheance*]

chan·cel (tʃǽnsəl, tʃánsəl) n. the choir and sanctuary of a church [O.F.]

chan·cel·ler·y, chan·cel·lor·y (tʃánsələri:, tʃánsələri:) pl. **chan·cel·ler·ies, chan·cel·lor·ies** n. the offices and administration of a chancellor [O.F.]

Chan·cel·lor (tʃǽnsələr, tʃánsələr), Richard (d. 1556), English navigator whose journey (1553) to the White Sea and to Moscow led to the opening of English trade with Moscow

chan·cel·lor (tʃǽnsələr, tʃánsələr) n. the chief minister of state in Germany and Austria ‖ the chief administrative officer of some U.S. universities, or the titular head of some British universities ‖ the presiding judge in a court of equity ‖ (Br.) a bishop's law officer ‖ (Br.) a title of various high officials, *chancellor of the exchequer* (=finance minister) ‖ (Br.) the chief secretary of an embassy **chán·cel·lor·ship** n. [O.F. *chancelier*]

Chan·cel·lors·ville, Battle of (tʃǽnsələrzvil, tʃánsələrzvil) the last great victory (May 2–4, 1863) of Lee and the Confederate forces in the American Civil War. It led to the Confederate invasion of the North in the campaign of Gettysburg

chancellory *CHANCELLERY

chan·cer·y (tʃǽnsəri:, tʃánsəri:) pl. **chan·cer·ies** n. the office or department of a chancellor ‖ an office of public records **in chancery** in litigation in a court of chancery **Chan·cer·y** a court of equity ‖ (Br.) a division since 1875 of the Supreme Court of Judicature. Presided over by the lord chancellor, it is the highest court of judicature next to the House of Lords

Chan Chan (tʃántʃán) ruins on the north coast of Peru, near Trujillo, formerly the capital of the Chimú Empire, a pre-Inca civilization (c. 500–15th c.)

chan·cre (ʃǽŋkər) n. a syphilitic ulcer **chan·croid** (ʃǽŋkrɔid) n. a venereal ulcer resembling a chancre, but caused by a different microorganism [F.]

chanc·y (tʃǽnsi:, tʃánsi:) comp. **chanc·i·er** superl. **chanc·i·est** adj. uncertain, hazardous

chan·de·lier (ʃændəlíər) n. a branched holder for several candles or electric lights, suspended from a ceiling [F.]

Chan·der·na·gore (tʃʌ̀ndərnəgór, tʃʌ̀ndərnəgóur) a town (pop. 75,960) in West Bengal, India, on the Hooghly River, a former French settlement (1686–1950), transferred to India after a plebiscite

Chan·di·garh (tʃʌ́ndigár) a union territory in N.W. India (pop. 218,700). The modern city, intended eventually for 500,000 inhabitants, was planned in the 1950s by Le Corbusier. He was also the architect of several of its main buildings

chan·dler (tʃǽndlər, tʃándlər) n. (Br., old-fash.) a merchant who sells candles, oil, paint and groceries **chán·dler·y** n. the goods sold by a chandler [O.F. *chandeler*, candlestick]

Chan·dler's wobble (tʃǽndlərz) 14-month cyclical, elliptical variation in the earth's rotation

Chan·dra·gup·ta I (tʃʌ̀ndrəgúptə) (d. c. 330), Indian ruler (c. 320–c. 330), founder of the Gupta dynasty

Chandragupta Maurya (d. c. 286 B.C.), Indian ruler, founder of the Maurya dynasty

Chang·an (tʃʌ́ŋán) *SIAN

Chang·chow (tʃʌ́ŋtʃáu)*LUNGKI

Changchow *WUTSIN

Chang·chun (tʃʌ́ŋtʃún) (former Sinking) a town (pop. 1,604,000) in N.E. China (Manchuria), on the Shenyang-Harbin railroad at the junction with the line to Kirin, developed by the Japanese as capital (Hsinking) of their protectorate Manchukuo (1932–45)

change (tʃeindʒ) n. alteration ‖ the exchange of one thing for another ‖ a new occupation or fresh outlook ‖ the passing from one form, phase, place or state to another ‖ a balance of money remaining out of what is tendered in payment of a smaller sum ‖ coins of small denomination ‖ (pl., campanology) the different orders in which a peal can be rung ‖ (Br.) the place where merchants meet for business, an exchange **to get no change out of (someone)** (Br.) to get no satisfaction from (someone) **to ring the changes** to practice change ringing ‖ to use variety

change pres. part. **chang·ing** past and past part. **changed** v.i. to become altered ‖ to put on different clothes ‖ to get out of a bus, train etc. and into another so as to continue a journey ‖ to make a change or exchange ‖ v.t. to alter ‖ to take off (clothes) and put on different ones ‖ to exchange (money) for the same amount in another denomination ‖ to abandon (one thing or person) for another, *to change one's address, change one's hairdresser* ‖ to exchange, *to change places* ‖ to put a clean diaper on (a baby) ‖ to put fresh sheets on (a bed) **to change color** to flush or grow pale, usually from sudden emotion **to change hands** to pass from one owner to another **to change key** (mus.) to modulate from one key to another, or from minor to major, major to minor **to change one's mind** to go back on a decision and make a different one **to change one's tune** to be humbled, be made to be less self-assertive **to change step** in walking or marching) to miss a pace deliberately [F. *changer*]

change·a·bil·i·ty (tʃeindʒəbíliti:) n. the capacity of being changeable ‖ a tendency to change

change·a·ble (tʃéindʒəb'l) adj. able to be changed ‖ variable, inconstant **change·a·bly** adv.

change·ful (tʃéindʒfəl) adj. changing ‖ inconstant

change·less (tʃéindʒlis) adj. unchanging

change·ling (tʃéindʒliŋ) n. a child secretly substituted for another ‖ (mythol.) an elf substituted by the fairies for a mortal baby

change of heart a complete change of attitude

change of life the menopause

change ringing the ringing of a chime of bells to a set series of different combinations, so that no one sequence is rung twice (cf. CARILLON)

changing room locker room

Chang·kia·kow (tʃǽŋkjǽkóu) (formerly Wanchuan, *Mongolian* Kalgan) the capital (pop. 229,000) of Chandar province, N. China, 95 miles northwest of Peking, a trade center

Chang·sha (tʃǽŋʃá) the capital (pop. 703,000) of Hunan province, central China, on the Siangkiang, and on the Canton-Wuhan railroad. It is an industrial center, with a university

chan·nel (tʃǽn'l) 1. *n.* a natural or artificial course for running water ‖ a part of a river or harbor where the water is deeper than the water on either side of it ‖ (*geog.*) a narrow stretch of water linking two larger stretches ‖ any closed passage or conduit for liquid ‖ (*radio*) a narrow band of frequencies wide enough for one-way communication ‖ the course or agency through which something passes, *legislation must go through the usual channels* **Chan·nel** the English Channel 2. *v.t. pres. part.* **chan·nel·ing**, esp. *Br.* **chan·nelling** *past* and *past part.* **chan·neled**, esp. *Br.* **chan·nelled** to make a channel or groove in ‖ to canalize, *to channel one's energies* [M.E. *chanel* fr. O.F.]

channel *n.* a broad wooden or metal ledge projecting from a ship's deck abreast the masts to broaden the spread of the shrouds [fr. older *chain-wale*]

channel black gas black

Channel Islands British islands (total area 75 sq. miles, pop. 130,000) in the English Channel: Jersey, Guernsey, Alderney and Sark and a few islets. Part of the duchy of Normandy under William the Conqueror, they remained British thereafter. They govern themselves under Norman law, with lieutenant-governors appointed by the Crown. Germany occupied them 1940–5. Industries: market gardening, cattle, tourism. Languages: English, Norman patois, French (in Jersey)

Chan·ning (tʃǽniŋ), William Ellery (1780–1842), U.S. author, Unitarian minister, and leader of apostates from Calvinism. Advocating religious humanitarianism and tolerance rather than a new creed, he organized (1820) what became (1825) the American Unitarian Association. His works on slavery greatly aided the abolition movement

chan·son (ʃãsó) *n.* (*mus.*) a secular composition for several voices, with or without instruments, esp. as composed in the 14th–16th cc. in France [F.]

Chan·son de Geste (ʃãsõdəʒest) one of the early French epic poems (11th–14th cc.) based on heroic deeds (*gestes*), historical or legendary. The best are written in unrhymed 10-syllable verse, with a regular pattern of stanzas (*ROLAND, CHANSON DE)

chant (tʃænt, tʃɑnt) *n.* a simple melody to which a psalm may be sung ‖ a singing, esp. in choir ‖ a repetitive singsong utterance [F.=song]

chant *v.t.* to sing (a chant) ‖ to utter in a singsong voice ‖ *v.i.* to sing a chant **chánt·er** *n.* a person who chants ‖ the melody pipe of a bagpipe, on which the tune is played, as distinct from the drones [F. *chanter*, to sing]

chan·te·relle (ʃæntərél, tʃæntərél) *n. Cantharellus cibarius*, an edible, yellow fungus [F.]

chant·ey (ʃǽnti:, tʃǽnti:) *pl.* **chant·eys** *n.* a sailors' song from the days of sailing ships. The songs have swinging rhythms which helped men e.g. to haul together [perh. fr. F. *chantez* imper. of *chanter*, to sing]

Chan·til·ly lace (ʃæntíli:) a delicate silk or linen bobbin lace, often black [after *Chantilly*, a town north of Paris, France]

chan·try (tʃǽntri:, tʃántri:) *pl.* **chan·tries** *n.* an endowment made to a church, for Masses and prayers to be said, usually for the repose of the donor's soul [O.F. *chanterie*, a chanting]

chantry chapel a chapel endowed by a chantry, often in a larger church or cathedral

chant·y (ʃǽnti:) *pl.* **chant·ies** *n.* a chanty

Cha·nu·kah (xánuka) *n.* the Jewish feast Hanukkah [Heb.]

Chao·an (tʃáuán) (Chaochow) a town (pop. 170,000) in E. Kwangtung, China, at the head of the Han delta: textiles, machinery, porcelain

Chao Phra·ya (tʃáuprajá) the chief river of Thailand. Its two headstreams, the Ping and the Nan, join about 160 miles above the Gulf of Siam. The whole system is navigable by small craft for most of its length. It floods annually, irrigating rice fields. Chief port: Bangkok

cha·os (kéiɒs) *n.* complete confusion ‖ the formless void before the creation of the universe **Cha·os** (Gk *mythol.*) the oldest of the gods, the

mother of Erebus and Night **cha·ót·ic** *adj.* **cha·ót·i·cal·ly** *adv.* [L. fr. Gk. *chaos*]

chap (tʃæp) *n.* (*pop.*) a man or boy [shortened fr. *chapman*, a peddler]

chap 1. *v. pres. part.* **chap·ping** *past* and *past part.* **chapped** (*usually of skin*) to crack or split ‖ to become rough and sore ‖ *v.t.* to make rough and sore **2.** *n.* a crack or split in the skin [M.E. *chappen*]

Cha·pa·la (tʃɑpɑ́lɑ) the largest lake in Mexico, 50 miles long and 8 miles wide

chap·ar·ral (tʃæpərǽl, ʃæpərǽl) *n.* xerophytic scrub of the Californian hills including dwarf oaks, buckeye etc. ‖ any dense tangled brushwood, e.g. in Mexico and Texas [Span. *chaparra*, evergreen oak]

Chaparral (*mil.*) short-range, lowaltitude, surface-to-air, solid-fuel Army air defense artillery system (MIM-72) with infrared homing. *Cf* SIDEWINDER

chaparral cock *Geococcyx californianus*, a species of North American cuckoo [Span.]

chaparral pea *Pickeringia montana*, a thorny Californian shrub which grows in chaparral thickets

chap·book (tʃǽpbuk) *n.* (*hist.*) a small book of stories, ballads or tracts sold by peddlers [fr. *chapman*, a peddler]

chape (tʃeip) *n.* the metal tip of a scabbard ‖ the part of a buckle by which it is attached to a strap etc. ‖ a sliding loop on a belt etc. [F. fr. L.L. *capa*, cape]

chap·el (tʃǽp'l) *n.* a place of Christian worship other than a parish or cathedral church, e.g. one attached to a school, college, private house etc. ‖ a part of a cathedral or large church, divided off from the rest, and having a separate altar and dedication ‖ (*Br.*) a nonconformists' place of worship ‖ a service held in a chapel, or attendance at chapel, esp. in a college ‖ (*printing*) an association of workers in a printing house [O.F. *chapele* fr. L.L. *cappella*, a short cloak, after the sanctuary where St Martin's cloak was kept]

chapel of ease a chapel dependent upon a parish church, for parishioners who live far from the church

chap·er·on, chap·er·one (ʃæpəroun) 1. *n.* (*esp. hist.*) someone responsible for the moral protection of a girl or the good behavior of young people at social gatherings or for providing a show of propriety 2. *v.t. pres. part.* **chap·er·on·ing** *past* and *past part.* **chap·er·oned** to act as chaperon to [F. dim. of *chape*, a cape]

chap·fall·en (tʃɒ́pfɔlən, tʃǽpfɔlən) *adj.* dejected, dispirited

chap·lain (tʃǽplin) *n.* a priest or minister who officiates in a private chapel ‖ a priest, minister or rabbi who serves a school, college, prison or hospital ‖ a priest, minister or rabbi attached to the armed forces **cháp·lain·cy** *n.* the office of being chaplain [O.F. *chapelain*]

chap·let (tʃǽplit) *n.* a circlet of flowers, jewels etc., worn on the head ‖ a string of beads ‖ (*eccles.*) one third of a rosary ‖ (*archit.*) a narrow line of bead molding [O.F. *chapelet*, dim. of *chape*, cape]

Chap·lin (tʃǽplin), Sir Charles Spencer ('Charlie Chaplin', 1889–1977), film actor, scriptwriter and director, born in London. His films include 'Shoulder Arms' (1918), 'The Kid' (1921), 'The Gold Rush' (1925) etc. as well as later, longer ones (incl. 'City Lights', 1931, 'Modern Times', 1936) in which he satirized contemporary industrial society from the point of view of the 'little man' always threatened by its large organizations and inhuman institutions, but triumphing over them. He received an Academy Award (1973) and was knighted (1975)

Chap·man (tʃǽpmən), George (1559–1634), English poet and dramatist, 'philosophical' exponent of the Elizabethan tragedy of revenge. His plays exemplify stoic determination. He translated Homer

chaps (tʃæps) *pl. n.* a covering of leather or sheepskin for the front of the legs, worn over trousers, esp. by cowboys as a protection against brush [fr. Mex. *chaparejos*]

chaps *pl. n.* the jaws of an animal or the folds of flesh over them [etym. doubtful]

chap·ter (tʃǽptər) *n.* a division of a book (*abbr.* chap., ch., and c.) ‖ a phase of existence, *that chapter of his life is closed* ‖ the administrative body of canons of a cathedral or abbey ‖ a meeting of such a body ‖ a meeting of members of a religious community or order ‖ a local section of a national club, lodge etc. ‖ (*Br.*) an act of par-

liament as numbered in the statute book **to quote chapter and verse** to give an exact reference in support of a statement of fact [fr. O.F. *chapitre*]

chapter house the building or room where a chapter meets

chapter of accidents a series of accidents or misfortunes

Chapter 77 manifesto signed in Jan. 1977 by citizens of Czechoslovakia demanding that the government abide by guarantees of freedom of expression in constitution and honor the human rights provisions of 1975 Helsinki agreement

Cha·pul·te·pec (tʃapultepék) (lit. 'grasshopper hill'), a castle and park in Mexico City, site of Montezuma's hunting lodge, later a presidential palace and military academy, and now the National Museum of History and Anthropology. The resistance of the U.S. invasion of 1847 by its cadets has made it a national shrine

char (tʃɑr) *pres. part.* **char·ring** *past* and *past part.* **charred** *v.t.* to reduce to carbon by slow, intense heating, or by burning ‖ to scorch ‖ *v.i.* to be burned to charcoal [origin unknown]

char (*Br., pop.*) 1. *n.* a charwoman 2. *v.i. pres. part.* **char·ring** *past* and *past part.* **charred** to work as a charwoman

char·a·banc (ʃǽrəbæŋ) *n.* (*Br.*) a motor coach with seats facing forward, for holiday excursions [F. *char à bancs*, carriage with benches]

char·ac·ter (kǽriktər) 1. *n.* the total quality of a person's behavior, as revealed in his habits of thought and expression, his attitudes and interests, his actions, and his personal philosophy of life ‖ (*genetics*) a detectable quality of an organism that is the result of the presence of a gene or group of genes, a unit of character ‖ the qualities that distinguish one people from another, *national character* ‖ a set of qualities or attributes distinguishing one place or country from another ‖ an imaginary person in a book or play etc. ‖ any symbol representing information ‖ a well-known person, *a public character* ‖ a person of a bizarre or eccentric nature ‖ nature, kind, *what is its exact character?* ‖ reputation, *a bad character* ‖ a figure or sign used in writing **in (out of) character** in accordance (not in accordance) with a person's nature 2. *adj.* of or relating to character ‖ (of actors and parts in plays) portraying types, not individuals (*cf.* STRAIGHT) [F. *caractère* fr. L. fr. Gk]

character disorder the inability of an individual to come to terms with society. Some who suffer from this, psychopaths, are frequently in trouble with the law through criminal behavior. Others, the 'inadequate psychopaths', have great difficulty in being self-reliant and may be permanently dependent on other people or on institutions

char·ac·ter·is·tic (kæriktərístik) 1. *n.* a quality typical of a person, place or object ‖ (*genetics*) a unit character ‖ (*math.*) the whole-number part of a logarithm 2. *adj.* typical **char·ac·ter·is·ti·cal·ly** *adv.* [fr. Gk *charaktēristikos*]

char·ac·ter·i·za·tion (kæriktərizéiʃən) *n.* the act, process or result of characterizing

char·ac·ter·ize (kǽriktəraiz) *pres. part.* **char·ac·ter·iz·ing** *past* and *past part.* **char·ac·ter·ized** *v.t.* to be the distinguishing feature of ‖ to describe the character of (a person, landscape, etc.) [fr. M.L. fr. Gk *charaktērizein*, to engrave]

char·ac·ter·less (kǽriktərlis) *adj.* undistinguished, featureless, *a characterless landscape* ‖ lacking in personality

character recognition system of reading written or typewritten letters or symbols and translating to a machine code. —**character reader** *n.* —**character set** *n.* the original sound represented by a character. *Cf* OPTICAL SCANNING

character reference a testimonial given to an employee by his employer when he leaves his service

cha·rade (ʃəréid, *Br.* ʃərád) *n.* (*esp. pl.*) a party game in which each syllable of a word to be guessed is acted out or mimed [F., origin unknown]

Char·bin (tʃárbin) *HARBIN

char·broil (tʃárbrɔil) *v.* to cook by direct heat using charcoal

Char·cas (tʃárkəs) the former name of Sucre, Bolivia. During the colonial period it was the seat of the Real Audiencia, governing Bolivia, Argentina, Paraguay and part of Brazil, until it passed (1776) into the jurisdiction of the viceroy of the River Plate. It was also the seat of a university of repute

CONCISE PRONUNCIATION KEY: **(a)** æ, c*a*t; ɑ, c*a*r; ɔ f*aw*n; ei, sn*a*ke. **(e)** e, h*e*n; i:, sh*ee*p; iə, d*ee*r; ɛə, b*ea*r. **(i)** i, f*i*sh; ai, t*i*ger; ə:, b*i*rd. **(o)** o, *o*x; au, c*ow*; ou, g*oa*t; u, p*oo*r; ɔi, r*oy*al. **(u)** ʌ, d*u*ck; u, b*u*ll; u:, g*oo*se; ə, b*a*cillus; ju:, c*u*be. x, lo*ch*; θ, *th*ink; ð, bo*th*er; z, *Z*en; ʒ, cor*s*age; dʒ, sava*g*e; ŋ, orangutan*g*; j, *y*ak; ʃ, *fi*sh; tʃ, *f*etch; 'l, ra*bb*le; 'n, re*dd*en. Complete pronunciation key appears inside front cover.

char·coal (tʃárkoul) n. the amorphous form of carbon obtained by the destructive distillation of animal or vegetable matter in a limited supply of air. It is used as a fuel, for drawing and sketching with, and in many scientific and industrial processes

Char·cot (ʃærkou), Jean-Martin (1825–93), French doctor noted for work on nervous disorders, esp. hysteria, which was to influence Freud

chard (tʃɑrd) n. Swiss chard

Char·din (ʃærdɛ̃), Jean-Baptiste Siméon (1699–1779), French painter of still lifes and quiet domestic scenes

Char·don·net (ʃærdɔne), comte Hilaire Bernigaud de (1839–1924), French chemist, physiologist and industrialist. He developed and manufactured rayon, the first synthetic fiber

Cha·rente (ʃærãt) a department (area 2,305 sq. miles, pop. 337,100) of W. France. (*ANGOUMOIS, *SAINTONGE, *POITOU) Chief town: Angoulême

Cha·rente-Ma·ri·time (ʃærãtmæri:ti:m) a department (area 2,791 sq. miles, pop. 497,900) of W. France, north of the Gironde. (*AUNIS, *SAINTONGE, *POITOU) Chief town: La Rochelle

charge (tʃɑrdʒ) n. the price to be paid for goods or services ‖ an entry in an account of something due ‖ a duty, responsibility ‖ safekeeping ‖ a judge's or bishop's directive ‖ a legal accusation ‖ a record of accusation kept at a police station ‖ (mil.) a swift concerted attack on a limited objective ‖ an explosive for a gun, or for blasting ‖ an electric charge ‖ the electricity stored in a battery ‖ a financial responsibility ‖ (heraldry) a blazon **in charge** in command, having supervision ‖ (Br.) under arrest by the police **in charge of** having supervision of, the teacher in charge of the class ‖ under the supervision of, he left it in charge of the doorman **to lay something to a person's charge** to accuse him of something **to take charge** to assume control or responsibilty [F. charge, a burden]

charge pres. part. **charg·ing** past and past part. **charged** v.t. to accuse, they charged him with murder ‖ (old-fash.) to give a solemn order to, he charged her to be careful ‖ (old-fash.) to entrust or burden with, they charged him with presents for the family ‖ to ask as a price, he charged me $10 ‖ to record (a debt), charge it to my account ‖ to fill (a magazine) with bullets ‖ to give electrical energy or charge to (a battery) ‖ to saturate ‖ to load ‖ (esp. of a bishop or judge) to instruct authoritatively ‖ (heraldry) to place a bearing on (a shield) ‖ to rush at, the bull charged the campers ‖ v.i. to rush forward in assault, the men charged with bayonets ‖ to ask payment, he charges for his services ‖ to accumulate electrical energy or charge ‖ (pop.) to hurry, he charged off down the road **chárge·a·ble** adj. liable to be accused ‖ liable or proper to be charged as debts, alterations chargeable to the customer [O.F. charger, chargier, to load]

charge account a customer's account at a store etc. Items are grouped for payment periodically, individual purchases being taken on credit

char·gé d'af·faires (ʃarʒéidəfɛər) pl. **char·gés d'af·faires** (ʃarʒéizdəfɛ́ər) n. a temporary substitute for an ambassador or minister during his absence ‖ an envoy in a country where diplomatic representation is at a level lower than ambassadorial or ministerial [F.]

charge nurse nurse assigned to the management of a ward

charg·er (tʃárdʒər) n. (elec.) a device for charging batteries ‖ (rhet.) a cavalry officer's mount

Charger See TU-144

Chari *SHARI

char·i·ly (tʃéərili) adv. in a chary manner

char·i·ness (tʃéəri:nis) n. the state or quality of being chary

char·i·ot (tʃæri:ət) n. (hist.) a two-wheeled, horse-drawn vehicle used in warfare and for racing, esp. in classical times **char·i·ot·eer** (tʃæri:ətíər) n. the driver of a chariot [O.F. fr. char, cart]

char·ism (kǽrizəm) n. charisma

cha·ris·ma (kərízmə) pl. **cha·ris·ma·ta** (kərízmətə) n. (theol.) a special spiritual gift bestowed temporarily by the Holy Spirit on a group or an individual for the general good of the Church ‖ an extraordinary power in a person, group, cause etc. which takes hold of popular imagination, wins popular support etc. **cha·ris·mat·ic** (kærizmǽtik) adj. [Gk=favor, gift]

char·i·ta·ble (tʃǽritəb'l) adj. using Christian charity in human dealings ‖ generous in giving

to the needy ‖ tolerant in judging other people ‖ of or relating to charity **chár·i·ta·bly** adv. [O.F.]

char·i·ty (tʃæriti:) pl. **char·i·ties** n. spiritual love for others ‖ the virtue by which we love God above all other things, and our neighbor as ourself, for the love of God ‖ tolerance in judging other people ‖ generosity to the needy ‖ alms given to the poor ‖ an organization dispensing relief to the poor [O.F. charité]

charity school (Br., hist.) one of the day schools for poor children organized (18th and 19th cc.) largely by the Church of England. Some developed into fee-paying boarding schools, others became national elementary schools in the 19th c., others gave place to Sunday schools

Charity, Sister of a member of any of several Roman Catholic orders of women, the oldest of which was founded (1633) by St. Vincent de Paul to nurse the sick

cha·riv·a·ri (ʃərívəri:, ʃivəri:, ʃərivári:) n. (rare) a confused medley of sounds, babel [F., origin unknown]

char·la·dy (tʃárleidi:) pl. **char·la·dies** n. (Br.) a charwoman

char·la·tan (ʃárlətən) n. a person who pretends to have knowledge or skill that he does not possess, esp. medical knowledge **chár·la·tan·ism** n. [F. fr. Ital. ciarlatano fr. ciarlare, to speak glibly]

Char·le·magne (ʃárləmein) (c. 742–814), Charles I, emperor of the West (800–14) and king of the Franks (768–814), son of Pépin the Short. After defeating the Lombards (774), he conquered Saxony (772–804), thus ruling a vast empire bounded by the North Sea, the Elbe, Bavaria, Carinthia, Lombardy, the Mediterranean, the Pyrenees and the Atlantic. He intervened (799) to save Pope Leo III from deposition, and was rewarded with the title of Holy Roman Emperor (800). At the end of his reign he had to defend his frontiers from attacks by Vikings and Saracens. His reign was notable for administrative, judicial and ecclesiastical reforms, and for the development of foreign trade. Charlemagne's palace was the center of a great intellectual revival under the leadership of Alcuin

Char·le·roi (ʃærlərwæ) a Belgian coal-mining town (pop. 221,911), on the Sambre, center of S.W. Belgium's chief industrial region (iron and engineering industries)

Charles (ʃærl), Jacques Alexandre César (1746–1823), French physicist. He was the first to use hydrogen in balloons (1783), and he formulated Charles's law

Charles I (tʃɑrlz) Holy Roman Emperor *CHARLEMAGNE

Charles II 'the Bald' (823–77), Holy Roman Emperor (875–7) and as Charles I, king of France (843–77), son of Louis I. With his brothers Louis the German and Lothair I, he divided Charlemagne's empire by the Treaty of Verdun (843), receiving most of what is now France

Charles III 'the Fat' (839–88), Holy Roman Emperor (881–7), king of Italy (879–87) and as Charles II, king of France (884–7), son of Louis the German. He failed to relieve Paris from a Norman siege (885), and was deposed (887)

Charles IV (1316–78), Holy Roman Emperor (1355–78), king of Germany and Bohemia (1346–78). After fighting the deposed Louis IV for the German throne, he issued (1356) the Golden Bull, which laid down rules for the election of the German king

Charles V (1500–58), Holy Roman Emperor (1519–58), king of Franche-Comté and the Netherlands (1506–55), and of Spain (as Charles I, 1516–56), son of Philip I of Castile. The growing power of his vast Hapsburg empire brought him into conflict with the Italian states (1526) and with France (from 1521) and England (PEACE OF *CAMBRAI, 1529). He presided at the diet of Worms which outlawed Luther (1521). He tried to adopt a moderate attitude to Protestants, though a decree against them provoked the formation of the Schmalkaldic League (1531), which he crushed in the Schmalkaldic War (1546–7). He failed to unite Protestants and Catholics, and was attacked (1552) by Maurice, elector of Saxony, and Henri II of France. The Peace of Augsburg resulted (1555). Disillusioned, he transferred his Austrian lands to his brother Ferdinand I, and abdicated as king of Spain in favor of his son Philip (1556). He retired (1557) to a monastery. Dur-

ing his reign, Spain had conquered large areas of Mexico, Peru and the Antilles

Charles VI (1685–1740), Holy Roman Emperor and, as Charles III, king of Hungary (1711–40), son of Leopold I. His claim to the Spanish throne involved the Empire in the War of the Spanish Succession (1701–14). To ensure the succession of his daughter Maria Theresa to his dominions he induced the great powers to guarantee the Pragmatic Sanction (1713). He again fought with France and Spain in the War of the Polish Succession (1733–5), and with the Turks (1737–9)

Charles VII (Karl Albrecht, 1697–1745), Holy Roman Emperor (1742–5) and elector of Bavaria (1726–45). Having married a daughter of Joseph I, and refusing to recognize the Pragmatic Sanction, he allied with Frederick II of Prussia in the War of the Austrian Succession (1740–8). He was accordingly elected emperor (1742)

Charles I (1600–49), king of England, Scotland and Ireland (1625–49), son of James I. His conflict with parliament began with his marriage (1625) to Henrietta Maria of France, and grew as he confided in such favorites as Buckingham and pursued the High Church policy of Laud. His early parliaments tried to control royal policy by withholding supplies, and Charles attempted to levy taxes without parliamentary consent. Financial difficulties forced him to sign (1628) the Petition of Right. Buckingham was assassinated (1628). Charles ruled (1629–40) without parliament, through his minister Strafford, but conflict continued in the courts, notably in the case (1638) of John Hampden. A Scottish invasion (1640) forced Charles to summon (1640) the Long Parliament, which executed Strafford and Laud, and drew up (1641) the Grand Remonstrance. The king attempted to arrest the five members responsible for this (1642) but was forced to flee to York. With the battle of Edgehill (1642) began the Civil War (1642–52). Charles took refuge (1646) with the Scottish army, and was betrayed (1647) to the English army under Cromwell. After Pride's Purge (1648), Charles was tried and executed (1649)

Charles II (1630–85), king of England, Scotland and Ireland (1660–85), son of Charles I. In exile after the battle of Naseby (1645), he returned (1650) to Scotland, was defeated (1651) at Worcester by Cromwell, and fled to France. He was restored (1660) to the throne, and was at war (1665–7) with the Netherlands, in the course of which a Dutch fleet ravaged the Thames (1667). London had been hit by plague (1665) and fire (1666). Charles dismissed his minister Clarendon (1667) and gave power to the even less popular cabal of five ministers. The king signed (1670) the secret Treaty of Dover, promising to join France in war against the Netherlands and to declare himself a Roman Catholic. The Dutch War (1672–4) was unpopular and unsuccessful, and parliament forced Charles to revoke the Declaration of Indulgence (1672) and to consent to the Test Act (1673). Fears of a Popish plot grew with the affair (1678) of Titus Oates, and a Whig opposition arose (*RYE HOUSE PLOT, 1683). The king's pleasure-loving character set the tone of a dissolute court, reflected in the Restoration comedies. Nevertheless, his reign saw great colonial, maritime and commercial expansion, the foundation of the Royal Society (1660), and great advances in science

Charles I king of France *CHARLES II, Holy Roman Emperor

Charles II 'the Fat', king of France *CHARLES III, Holy Roman Emperor

Charles III 'the Simple' (879–929), French king (898–923), son of Louis II. He ended the Norse raids on his territory by ceding (911) Normandy to Rollo. He was deposed and imprisoned (923)

Charles IV 'the Fair' (1294–1328) king of France and, as Charles I, king of Navarre (1322–8), son of Philippe IV and last of the direct Capetian line

Charles V 'the Wise' (1338–80), king of France (1364–80). As regent (1356–60, 1364) during the captivity of his father Jean II in England, he dealt with the Jacquerie. He reformed the royal administration and finances, and the army. With the aid of his general, du Guesclin, he had almost driven the English from France by 1380

Charles VI (1368–1422), king of France (1380–1422), son of Charles V. During his troubled reign, civil war between the Burgundians and the Armagnacs was almost continuous. France was invaded (1415) by Henry V of England, and heavily defeated at Agincourt (1415). Charles was forced by the Treaty of Troyes (1420) to recognize the English king as his successor

Charles VII (1403–61), king of France (1422–61), son of Charles VI. Crowned at Poitiers (1422), he tried to win back the French crown from Henry VI of England. His efforts were unsuccessful until Joan of Arc led the French to victory at Orléans and Charles was again crowned at Reims (1429). By 1453, the French had expelled the English from all of France except Calais. French economic recovery was aided by Jacques Cœur

Charles VIII (1470–98), king of France (1483–98), son of Louis XI. He acquired Brittany by marriage (1491) with Anne of Brittany. He invaded Italy (1494), thus beginning the Italian Wars

Charles IX (1550–74), king of France (1560–74), son of Henri II. The religious conflict between Huguenots and Catholics broke into open war (1562) and continued intermittently during the reign. Charles's mother, Catherine de' Medici, persuaded him to consent (despite his Huguenot adviser Coligny) to the Massacre of St Bartholomew (1572)

Charles X (1757–1836), king of France (1824–30), brother of Louis XVI and Louis XVIII. His reactionary rule ended when his attempt at a coup d'état provoked a revolution in Paris, forcing him into exile

Charles I king of Spain *CHARLES V, Holy Roman Emperor

Charles II (1661–1700), last Hapsburg king of Spain, Naples and Sicily (1665–1700). With the outbreak of the War of Devolution (1667–8) and the War of the Grand Alliance (1689–97), Spanish power was greatly weakened

Charles III (1716–88), king of Spain (1759–88) and (as Charles IV) king of Naples and Sicily (1734–59). An enlightened despot, he inaugurated reforms in finance, trade and agriculture. He expelled the Jesuits (1767) from all Spanish territories

Charles IV (1748–1819), king of Spain (1788–1808) till replaced by Joseph Bonaparte

Charles XII (1682–1718), king of Sweden (1697–1718). A military genius, he won initial successes in the Northern War (1700–21), defeating Denmark (1700), Poland (1704) and Saxony (1706). His later defeats, notably by Russia (1709), and his long absence from Sweden, including captivity in Turkey (1713–14), marked the end of Sweden as a great power

Charles XIII (1748–1818), king of Sweden (1809–18) and of Norway (1814–18). He ceded Finland to Russia (1809), but gained Norway (1814) as a reward for his prudence in the Napoleonic Wars

Charles XIV of Sweden *BERNADOTTE

Charles I (Charles of Anjou) (1226–85), king of Naples and Sicily (1266–85), son of Louis VIII of France. His rule in Sicily was ended by the Sicilian Vespers (1282)

Charles IV king of Naples and Sicily *CHARLES III of Spain

Charles I king of Navarre *CHARLES IV, king of France

Charles II 'the Bad' (1332–87), king of Navarre (1349–87). He spent much of his reign disputing his claim to the French throne with Jean II

Charles I (Charles Robert of Anjou) (1288–1342), king of Hungary (1308–42). His reign established the Angevin dynasty in Hungary on a feudal basis. Increased prosperity made Hungary a great power

Charles III king of Hungary *CHARLES VI, Holy Roman Emperor

Charles IV king of Hungary *CHARLES I, emperor of Austria

Charles I (G. Karl Franz Josef, 1887–1922), emperor of Austria and, as Charles IV, king of Hungary (1916–18), nephew of Archduke Franz Ferdinand. The last ruler of Austria-Hungary, he abdicated (Nov. 12, 1918) and, after unsuccessful attempts to regain the Hungarian throne (1921), was exiled to Madeira

Charles 'the Bold' (1433–77), duke of Burgundy (1467–77), son of Philippe the Good. He attempted to conquer the lands between his possessions of Luxembourg, Burgundy, the Low Countries and Franche-Comté, but was killed

in battle. Burgundy then passed (1482) to the French crown, and the rest of his lands to the Hapsburgs

Charles, Prince of Wales (1948–), eldest son of Queen Elizabeth II of Britain and Prince Philip; heir to the throne. He married Lady Diana Spencer (1981); they have two sons, Prince William (*b*. 1982) and Prince Henry (*b*. 1984)

Charles Albert (1798–1849), king of Sardinia (1831–49). At first liberal, but later more reactionary, he sought to free northern Italy from Austrian control. After heavy defeats at Custozza (1848) and Novara (1849), he abdicated in favor of his son Victor Emmanuel II

Charles Bor·ro·me·o (bɔrəméiou), St (1538–84), Italian churchman. As papal secretary he was largely responsible for the success of the Council of Trent, and continued his zeal for reform (esp. in strengthening the discipline of the clergy) as cardinal archbishop of Milan. Feast: Nov. 4

Charles Edward Stuart *STUART, CHARLES EDWARD

Charles Mar·tel (martél) (c. 688–741), Frankish ruler of Austrasia (715–41). He subdued the tribes of western Germany, Burgundy, Aquitaine and Provence, and stopped the Moslem invasion of Europe, by defeating the Moors at Poitiers (732)

Charles of Anjou *CHARLES I of Naples and Sicily

Charles Robert of Anjou *CHARLES I, king of Hungary

Charles's law (*phys.*) the statement that at constant pressure the volume of a given mass of gas is directly proportional to its temperature measured on the Kelvin scale. It was formulated by J. A. C. Charles in 1787 and independently by J. L. Gay-Lussac

Charles's Wain *WAIN

Charles·ton (tʃárlstən) an Atlantic port, the oldest city (pop. 69,510) of South Carolina: naval base

Charleston the capital (pop. 63,968) of West Virginia: coal, oil, lumber

charles·ton (tʃárlstən) 1. *n.* a ballroom dance of the 1920s, in which the dancers kick sideways with one foot while pivoting on the other 2. *v.i.* to dance the charleston [after *Charleston*, South Carolina]

Charleston, Battle of a siege (July 1864– Feb. 1865) ending in the capture of the Confederate-held city by Union forces during the Civil War

Charles·town (tʃárlztaun) a part of Boston, Mass., between the Mystic and Charles Rivers, site of the battle of Bunker Hill

char·ley horse (tʃárli:) (*pop.*) painful stiffness in the leg caused by strain, or an attack of such stiffness

char·lock (tʃárlək) *n. Sinapis arvensis*, a wild mustard plant, with bright yellow flowers [O.E. *cerlic*]

Char·lotte (ʃárlət) a city (pop. 314,447) of North Carolina, heart of the hydroelectric development and the textile industry of the southern Appalachians

Char·lotte·town (ʃárləttaun) the capital (pop. 15,282) of Prince Edward Is., Canada, on the estuary of the Hillsborough River, a fishing port

charm (tʃárm) *n.* a softly or gently pleasing quality ‖ an incantation, esp. as a protection against evil or danger ‖ a formula or action supposed to have a supernatural power against evil ‖ an object worn to avert danger by magic ‖ (*particle phys.*) hypothetical quark (the fourth) discovered in 1974, created to account for j or psi particle ‖ a small trinket worn esp. on a bracelet **like a charm** perfectly, without the least hitch etc. [F. *charme*]

charm *v.t.* to please and attract, esp. in a relaxed or gentle way ‖ to allay as if by magic, *to charm away all difficulties* **to bear** (or **lead**) **a charmed life** to be so lucky as to suggest supernatural protection **chármed** *adj.* pleased, *he will be charmed to see you home* **chárm·ing** *adj.* delightful [F. *charmer*]

char·nel house (tʃárn'l) (*hist.*) a vault for the bones of the dead [O.F. *charnel*, burying-place]

Char·on (kéərən, kærən) (*Gk mythol.*) the ferryman who took the souls of the dead across the River Styx to Hades [Gk]

char·rette (tʃáret) *n.* group assembled to examine a problem or disputed matters, aided by specialists

Char·ron (ʃærɔ), Pierre (1541–1603), French moralist, friend of Montaigne and author of the skeptical treatise 'de la Sagesse'

Char·rua (tʃárrwa) *pl.* **Char·rua, Char·ruas** *n.* a South American Indian people, now extinct, formerly inhabiting the north coast of the River Plate ‖ a member of this people ‖ their language

chart (tʃart) 1. *n.* a map used by navigators, showing coastlines, deeps, rocks, currents etc. ‖ an outline map giving information on a particular subject, e.g. climatic conditions ‖ a graph showing fluctuations, e.g. in temperature or prices 2. *v.t.* to make a map of ‖ to record on a chart or graph [O.F.]

char·ter (tʃártər) 1. *n.* an official document granting rights, esp. to a new borough, company, university etc. ‖ the articles of incorporation of an organization or company, usually including a statement of principles or objectives ‖ the lease of an airplane, yacht, ship or bus etc. to a hirer for his exclusive use 2. *v.t.* to grant a charter to ‖ to hire (an airplane, yacht etc.) for the exclusive use of the hirer [O.F. *chartre*, a leaf of paper]

chartered accountant (*Br.*) an accountant qualified in accordance with the standards laid down by the Institute of Accountants, a body which was given a royal charter in 1880

char·ter·house (tʃártərhaus) *pl.* **char·ter·hous·es** (tʃártərhauziz) *n.* a Carthusian monastery [var. of A.F. *chartrouse*]

charter member (*Am.*=*Br.* foundation member) an original member of a corporation or society

Chart·ism (tʃártizəm) *n.* (*Br. hist.*) a working-class movement (19th c.) to achieve the political reforms contained in the 'People's Charter' (1838). It demanded manhood suffrage, vote by ballot, payment of M.P.s, equal electoral districts, the abolition of the property qualification for M.P.s, and annual parliaments. The movement led to riots (1839–42) and organized petitions to parliament (1840, 1842 and 1848). It collapsed (1848), but all its aims, except the last, have been wholly or partly achieved

Char·tres (ʃærtr) a French town (pop. 38,928) 55 miles southwest of Paris. Its cathedral (1194–1240) is a great work of Gothic architecture, with magnificent stained glass and stone carving

char·treuse (ʃartrú:z) *n.* a Carthusian monastery ‖ a liqueur first made by Carthusian monks ‖ a yellow-green color [after the monastic house of La Grande *Chartreuse*]

char·wom·an (tʃárwumən) *pl.* **char·wom·en** (tʃárwimin) *n.* a woman employed to clean homes or offices [fr. O.E. *cerre*, a turn (of work)+WOMAN]

char·y (tʃéəri:) *comp.* **char·i·er** *superl.* **char·i·est** *adj.* cautious, wary ‖ sparing, *he's chary of his praise* [O.E. *cearig*]

Cha·ryb·dis (kəríbdis) *SCYLLA AND CHARYBDIS

Chase (tʃeis), Salmon Portland (1808–73), U.S. statesman and abolitionist. As secretary of the treasury (1861–4) under President Abraham Lincoln, he established a national banking system. Despite his opposition to Lincoln, he was appointed (1864) Chief Justice of the Supreme Court. In 'Texas v. White' (1869), he declared secession a nullity and the federal union indissoluble. He presided over the impeachment trial of President Andrew Johnson

chase (tʃeis) *n.* a running after, a pursuit **the chase** (*rhet.*) the sport of hunting **to give chase** to set off in pursuit [M.E. *chace* fr. O.F.]

chase *n.* (*printing*) a frame holding type set ready for printing [F. *châsse*, case]

chase *pres. part.* **chas·ing** *past* and *past part.* **chased** *v.t.* to follow at speed in order to catch ‖ to drive (someone, something) away ‖ to pursue amorously ‖ *v.i.* to rush, hurry [O.F. *chacier*]

chase *pres. part.* **chas·ing** *past* and *past part.* **chased** *v.t.* to engrave or emboss (metal) [older *enchase* fr. F. *enchasser*, to encase]

chase 1. *n.* the part of a gun which encloses the bore ‖ a groove for a tenon ‖ a trench (e.g. in a wall) for a pipe or for wiring 2. *v.t. pres. part.* **chas·ing** *past* and *past part.* **chased** to groove for a joint etc. ‖ to cut (a screw thread) ‖ to ornament (silver etc.) with a noncutting tool by hammering ‖ to impress (a design) by this method **chás·er** *n.* a tool used in cutting internal or external screw threads [F. *chas*, enclosure]

chaser *n.* a short drink usually of beer or water taken after drinking neat liquor

CONCISE PRONUNCIATION KEY: **(a)** æ, c*a*t; ɑ, c*a*r; ɔ f*aw*n; ei, sn*a*ke. **(e)** e, h*e*n; i:, sh*ee*p; iə, d*ee*r; ɛə, b*ea*r. **(i)** i, f*i*sh; ai, t*i*ger; ə:, b*i*rd. **(o)** o, *o*x; au, c*ow*; ou, g*oa*t; u, p*oo*r; ɔi, r*oy*al. **(u)** ʌ, d*u*ck; u, b*u*ll; u:, g*oo*se; ə, b*a*cillus; ju:, c*u*be. x, lo*ch*; θ, *th*ink; ð, bo*th*er; z, *Z*en; ʒ, corsa*g*e; dʒ, sava*g*e; ŋ, orangutan*g*; j, *y*ak; ʃ, *fi*sh; tʃ, fe*tch*; 'l, rabb*le*; 'n, redd*en*. Complete pronunciation key appears inside front cover.

chasm (kǽzəm) n. a deep cleft in the earth ‖ a deep division of opinion or interests [fr. L. fr. Gk *chasma*]

chas·seur (ʃasə́:r) n. sauce of mushrooms, shallots, tomato puree, butter, seasoned with tarragon, esp. for veal

chas·sis (ʃǽsi, tʃǽsi:) n. the frame, wheels and engine of an automobile, without the bodywork [F. *chassis*, frame]

chaste (tʃeist) adj. innocent of immoral sexual intercourse ‖ deliberately abstaining from sexual intercourse ‖ (of manner, speech, dress etc.) modest, restrained ‖ (of literary or artistic style) pure, unadorned [O.F.]

chas·ten (tʃéis'n) v.t. to cause to think less well of oneself ‖ to subject to moral or spiritual discipline [older *chaste* fr. O.F. *chastier*]

chas·tise (tʃæstáiz) pres. part. **chas·tis·ing** past and past part. **chas·tised** v.t. to punish by whipping or beating ‖ to denounce or criticize vehemently **chas·tise·ment** (tʃǽstizmənt, tʃæstáizmənt) n. [fr. earlier *chaste*, to chasten fr. O.F.]

chas·ti·ty (tʃǽstiti:) n. the state or virtue of being chaste ‖ total sexual abstention, continence [O.F. *chasteté*]

chas·u·ble (tʃǽzjub'l) n. the outer, sleeveless robe worn by a priest celebrating Mass (the Eucharist) [F.]

chat (tʃæt) 1. n. light, gossipy conversation ‖ the stonechat or whinchat ‖ a member of *Icteria*, a genus of North American songbirds 2. v.i. pres. part. **chat·ting** past and past part. **chat·ted** to talk light gossip [shortened fr. CHATTER]

châ·teau (ʃætóu) pl. **châ·teaus**, **châ·teaux** (ʃætóuz) n. a French feudal castle or country mansion [F.]

Cha·teau·bri·and (ʃætoubri:ā) François-René, Vicomte de (1768–1848), French author and statesman. His most famous works were 'le Génie du christianisme' (1802), in which he emphasized the aesthetic and moral appeal of Christianity, and 'Mémoires d'outretombe', a passionate autobiography

Châ·teau-Thier·ry, Battle of (ʃatoutjeri:), a 1st world war battle fought (1918) on the Marne in north-central France. U.S. troops halted a German offensive

Chat·ham (tʃǽtəm), 1st earl of *PITT

Chatham a port (pop. 61,909) in Kent, S.E. England on River Medway, a shipbuilding center and naval dockyard from the 17th c.

Chatham House *ROYAL INSTITUTE OF INTERNATIONAL AFFAIRS

Chatham Islands two islands in the S. Pacific, 536 miles east of New Zealand: Chatham (area 347 sq. miles) and Pitt (25 sq. miles), constituting a county (pop. 716) of South Island, New Zealand

Chat·ta·hoo·chee (tʃætəhú:tʃi:) a navigable river (c. 400 miles long) rising in N.E. Georgia and flowing southwest to the Alabama border at W. central Georgia, continuing south as part of the Alabama-Georgia and Georgia-Florida boundaries

Chat·ta·noo·ga (tʃætənú:gə) a manufacturing city (pop. 169,565) of Tennessee, on the Tennessee River, center of the Tennessee Valley Authority's development area

Chattanooga, Battle of a decisive Civil War engagement fought (1863) at Chattanooga, Tenn. The besieged Union forces under Gen. George H. Thomas seized the offensive and routed the Confederate troops under General Braxton Bragg

chat·tel (tʃǽt'l) n. (law) a piece of property other than real estate or a freehold [O.F. *chatel*, property, cattle]

chattel mortgage a mortgage on personal property

chat·ter (tʃǽtər) 1. n. light, inconsequential talk ‖ (of birds) quick, short notes suggesting human speech ‖ any light persistent sound, *the chatter of a stream* ‖ (surfing) the bending of the board in a rough sea ‖ the rattling together of teeth from cold, fear etc. 2. v.i. to talk lightly and inconsequentially, chat ‖ (of birds) to utter quick short notes suggesting human speech ‖ (of teeth) to rattle together ‖ (of a machine or tool) to skid or vibrate on a surface instead of cutting it cleanly, leaving a line of irregular notches or a spiral pattern ‖ v.t. to say by way of gossip, to *chatter a lot of nonsense* [imit.]

chat·ter·box (tʃǽtərbɑks) pl. **chat·ter·box·es** n. a person who talks too much and too fast, often foolishly

Chat·ter·ton (tʃǽtərtən), Thomas (1752–70), English poet, of Bristol. He wrote 'medieval'

prose and verse which he claimed to have 'discovered', and the vogue for medievalism gave them wide currency. He failed to make his way in London and at 17 took his own life

chat·ti·ly (tʃǽtli:) adv. in a chatty manner

chat·ti·ness (tʃǽti:nis) n. the state or quality of being chatty

chat·ty (tʃǽti:) comp. **chat·ti·er** superl. **chat·ti·est** adj. liking to chat ‖ like chat

Chau·cer (tʃɔ́sər), Geoffrey (c. 1340–1400), English poet. 'The Canterbury Tales' are his most popular work, for their comedy, realism, insight and warm humanity. His greatest innovation was the introduction of the French and Italian styles in prosody, which rapidly ousted the native tradition of alliterative verse. Chaucer did not greatly reform the English language, but by the sheer weight and popularity of his writings he set it firmly on its way toward modern English

chauf·feur (ʃóufər, ʃoufə́:r) 1. n. a person employed to drive a car for a private person or for a firm 2. v.t. to be or act as chauffeur to ‖ v.i. to be or act as chauffeur [F.]

Chaus·son (ʃousɔ̄), Ernest (1855–99), French composer. A pupil of César Franck, he wrote orchestral and choral works

chau·vin·ism (ʃóuvinizəm) n. exaggerated and aggressive patriotism **chau·vin·ist** n. **chau·vin·is·tic** adj. **chau·vin·is·ti·cal·ly** adv. [F. *chauvinisme* after Nicolas *Chauvin*, a devoted adherent of Napoleon Bonaparte]

Chá·vez (tʃáves), Carlos (1899–1978), Mexican composer and conductor. He was director (1928–34) of the National Conservatory of Mexico. A strongly national musical idiom is dominant in his works

Chávez, César Estrada (1927–), U.S. labor leader of Mexican-American farm workers

chay (tʃei, tʃai) n. the root of *Oldenlandia umbellata*, fam. *Rubiaceae*, an East Indian plant from which a red dye is obtained [fr. Tamil *saya*]

cheap (tʃi:p) 1. adj. inexpensive ‖ easily obtained, *a cheap victory* ‖ (of goods) worth more than the price paid ‖ poor in quality, tawdry ‖ facile, *a cheap joke* ‖ held in little esteem, *to make oneself cheap* ‖ (by the sheer weight and popularity) low, mean 2. adv. inexpensively 3. n. (only in) **on the cheap** (Br.) cheaply, *to travel on the cheap* [O.E. *ceap*, bargain]

cheap and nasty (Br.) of low cost and poor quality

cheap·en (tʃí:pən) v.t. to lower in price ‖ to lower in cost, *to cheapen production* ‖ to lower or degrade, cause to be less esteemed ‖ v.i. to become cheap or cheaper

cheap-jack (tʃí:pdʒæk) n. a hawker

cheap money money obtainable at a low rate of interest

cheap·skate (tʃí:pskeit) n. (pop.) someone who is stingy [CHEAP+*skate*, a contemptible person]

cheap sterling sterling held in the U.K. by nonresidents, sold below the official rate of exchange

cheat (tʃi:t) 1. v.t. to trick or deceive ‖ v.i. to play a game not according to the rules ‖ to use unfair methods ‖ to practice fraud **to cheat (someone) out of (something)** to swindle, *he cheated his brother out of his inheritance* 2. n. a person who cheats ‖ a fraud [fr. older *escheat*, to confiscate (property)]

Che·bo·ksa·ry (tʃibʌksári) the capital (pop. 340,000) of Chuvash A.S.S.R., U.S.S.R. on the Volga: textile and lumber industries

Che·chen-o-In·gush A.S.S.R. (tʃitʃénouiŋgúʃ) an autonomous republic (area 6,060 sq. miles, pop. 1,170,000, mainly Moslems) of the R.S.F.S.R., U.S.S.R. in N. Caucasia.

check (tʃek) 1. n. a sudden interruption of movement ‖ a control to verify information etc., *keep a check on his movements* ‖ a controlled test ‖ a means of preventing error, fraud ‖ a small crack ‖ a mark to show that something has been verified or checked ‖ a person employed to check or control ‖ a bill for a meal in a restaurant ‖ a receipt for deposit (of luggage etc.) ‖ a counter used in a gambling game ‖ a reverse in military strategy ‖ (hunting) the loss of the scent by the hounds ‖ (falconry) pursuit of poorer game rather than the real quarry ‖ (chess) the position of the king when exposed to attack **to keep in check** to hold under restraint 2. adj. serving to control, verify, *a check list* 3. interj. (chess) a call to warn one's opponent that his king is exposed to direct

attack [M.E. fr. Pers. *shāh*, king, the king in chess]

check n. a pattern of crossing lines or alternating squares of colors ‖ a fabric woven or printed with such a pattern [prob. fr. CHECKER]

check v.t. to arrest or restrain the progress or motion of, *the rope checked his fall* ‖ to restrain, *to check a tendency* ‖ to curb (a horse) ‖ to verify the correctness of (e.g. accounts) ‖ to verify the state or condition of (something) to see if it is all right ‖ (mil.) to rebuke ‖ (chess) to expose (the opponent's king) to attack ‖ to deposit or accept for safekeeping, receiving a check as a receipt ‖ to send or accept for conveyance, using a passage ticket ‖ v.i. to crack or split (e.g. of paint) ‖ (of hounds) to lose the scent or cast about to make certain of it ‖ (falconry) to cease the pursuit of poorer game and fly after poorer game **to check in** to register (e.g. at a hotel) **to check off** to tick off, mark as verified correct or attended to **to check out** to withdraw (money) by check ‖ to leave and pay for hotel accommodation **to check up on** (pop.) to investigate, find out about [M.E. *cheken* fr. O.F. *eschequier*, to play chess]

check, Br. **cheque** n. an order (on a specially printed form) to a bank to pay a stated sum to a named person

check·book, Br. **cheque·book** (tʃékbuk) n. a number of checks bound in paper covers and issued by a bank to an account holder

checked (tʃekt) adj. having a pattern of checks ‖ checkered

check·er (tʃékər) n. (Am.=Br. draughtsman) a piece used in a game of checkers [back-formation fr. CHECKERS]

check·er, Br. esp. **chequ·er** 1. n. (often pl.) a pattern of squares of alternating dark and light colors 2. v.t. to mark with squares **check·ered**, Br. esp. **chéq·uered** adj. (fig.) varied, dramatically uneven, *a checkered career* [M.E. *cheker* fr. O.F. *eschekier*, chessboard]

check·er·ber·ry (tʃékərberi:) pl. **check·er·ber·ries** n. *Gaultheria procumbens*, fam. *Ericaceae*, a wintergreen plant whose foliage yields wintergreen oil ‖ the spicy red berry of this plant

check·er·board (tʃékərbɔrd, tʃékərbourd) n. (Am.=Br. draughtboard) the squared board on which the game of checkers is played

check·ered (tʃékərd) adj. checked

check·ers (tʃékərz) n. (Am.=Br. draughts) a game for two played on a checkered board with opposing sets each of 12 pieces

check·er·wise, Br. esp. **chequ·er·wise** (tʃékərwaiz) adv. in alternating squares

checking account (Am.=Br. current account) a bank account operated by checks, drawn on it without notice. The bank pays no interest (cf. SAVING ACCOUNT)

check·list (tʃéklist) n. a list of items for convenient reference

check·mate (tʃékmeit) 1. n. (chess) a move or position which places the opponent's king inescapably in check 2. v.t. pres. part. **check·mat·ing** past and past part. **check·mat·ed** to place (the opponent's king) in this position ‖ to defeat or frustrate (a plan) 3. interj. the announcement of such a move in chess [M.E. *chek mate* ult. fr. Arab. *shāh māta*, the king is dead]

check-off (tʃékɔf, tʃékɒf) n. a collection of union dues by the employer, deducted from wages

check off v. (football) to change a play plan in the huddle at the line of scrimmage

check-out (tʃékaut) n. process of verifying before proceeding

check·point (tʃékpɔint) n. a place on a route where vehicles are stopped for inspection

check point (mil.) 1. predetermined point on the earth's surface used as a means of controlling movement, a registration target for fire adjustment, or a reference for location. 2. center of impact; abürst center. 3. geographical location on land or water above which the position of an aircraft in flight may be determined by observation or by electronic means. 4. place where military police check vehicular or pedestrian traffic in order to enforce circulation control measures and other laws, orders, and regulations. 5. (computer) point in routine when processing can be stopped for a printout and for making any necessary corrections

check·rein (tʃékrein) n. a bearing rein ‖ a rein connecting the snaffle rein of one of a pair of horses to the bit of the other

check·room (tʃékru:m, tʃékrʊm) n. a cloakroom, usually with an attendant in control ‖ (Am.=Br. left-luggage office) a storeroom at a railroad station etc. where luggage can be checked temporarily for a fee

check trading (*banking*) form of loan in which a customer purchases a check from the bank for a specified amount and repays the amount to the bank with interest

check-up (tʃékʌp) *n.* a physical examination ‖ a scrutiny for verification

Ched-dar (tʃédər) *n.* a yellow cheese originating in Cheddar, a village in Somerset, England

cheek (tʃi:k) **1.** *n.* the soft fleshy part of the face between the eye, mouth and edge of the jaw ‖ the side wall of the mouth ‖ impudence ‖ (*pl.*) machine parts arranged in pairs, e.g. the gripping parts of a vise **to turn the other cheek** to react with submissiveness rather than retaliate in the face of injury or provocation **2.** *v.t.* to speak or behave impudently to [O.E. *cēce*, jaw]

cheek-bone (tʃí:kboun) *n.* the projecting bone below the eye

cheek by jowl very close together

cheek-i-ly (tʃí:kili:) *adv.* in a cheeky manner

cheek-i-ness (tʃí:ki:nis) *n.* the state or quality of being cheeky

cheek pouch a bag for carrying food in the cheek of certain animals, e.g. squirrels

cheek-y (tʃí:ki:) *comp.* **cheek-i-er** *superl.* **cheek-i-est** *adj.* impudent

cheep (tʃi:p) **1.** *n.* the feeble sound of a very young bird **2.** *v.i.* to make such a sound [imit.]

cheer (tʃiər) **1.** *n.* a shout of joy, esp. from a crowd ‖ (*pl.*) applause ‖ (*rhet.*) heart-warming comfort **to give three cheers** to shout 'hip hip hooray' three times as a form of congratulation **2.** *v.i.* to shout for joy ‖ *v.t.* to applaud by shouts ‖ to fill with gladness, hope or comfort **to cheer up** to help (someone) to get over depression ‖ to get over depression [M.E. *chere*, face or facial expression, fr. O.F.]

cheer-ful (tʃíərfəl) *adj.* happy, goodhumored ‖ bright and attractive

cheer-i-ly (tʃíərili:) *adv.* in a cheery manner

cheer-i-ness (tʃíəri:nis) *n.* the state or quality of being cheery

cheer-i-o (tʃíəri:ou, tʃiəri:óu) *interj.* (*Br., pop.*) good-bye

cheer-lead-er (tʃíərli:dər) *n.* a person who leads organized cheering esp. at a football game

cheer-less (tʃíərlis) *adj.* gloomy

cheer-y (tʃíəri:) *comp.* **cheer-i-er** *superl.* **cheer-i-est** *adj.* showing cheerfulness, *a cheery greeting* ‖ promoting lightheartedness, *cheery music*

cheese (tʃi:z) *n.* a solid food of high protein content made from the pressed curds of milk ‖ a mass of this food set into characteristic shape [O.E. *cēse* fr. L.]

cheese-burg-er (tʃí:zbərgər) *n.* a hamburger with cooked cheese on top

cheese-cake (tʃí:zkeik) *n.* a cake made of cottage cheese or cream cheese, eggs and sugar baked in a pastry shell ‖ (*bowling*) a lane where high scores are made easily ‖ (*pop.*) photographs of sexually attractive women posed with hardly any clothing on

cheese-cloth (tʃí:zklɔθ, tʃí:zklɒθ) *n.* a soft, thin, loosely woven cotton fabric, used for wrapping food, for surgical dressings etc.

cheese cutter a curved scoop of steel or silver for cutting cheese ‖ a very strong wire attached to a flat board, used by grocers for cutting cheeses

cheese-par-ing (tʃí:zpɛ́?riŋ) **1.** *adj.* mean, stingy **2.** *n.* miserliness, mean economy ‖ rigorous attention to detail in saving

cheese straw an appetizer consisting of a thin strip of short pastry flavored with cheese

chees-y (tʃí:zi:) *comp.* **chees-i-er** *superl.* **chees-i-est** *adj.* tasting of cheese ‖ resembling cheese in consistency or smell

chee-tah (tʃí:tə) *n. Felis jubata*, a small leopard formerly used for hunting deer and antelope in India, where it is now virtually extinct. Other species inhabit Africa. It has a catlike head backed by a short mane [Hind. *chītā*]

Chee-ver, (tʃí:vər) John (1912–82), U.S. writer of satirical short stories and socially critical novels about the mostly Protestant, upper middle class. His short story collections include 'The Way Some People Live' (1943), 'The Enormous Radio' (1953), 'The Brigadier and the Golf Widow' (1964), and 'The Stories of John Cheever' (1978, Pulitzer Prize 1979). His novels include 'The Wapshot Chronicle' (1957), 'The Wapshot Scandal' (1964), and 'Oh What a Paradise It Seems' (1982)

cheewink *CHEWINK

chef (ʃef) *n.* the head cook, esp. in a hotel or restaurant [F.]

chef-d'oeu-vre (ʃeidə:vr) *pl.* **chefs-d'oeu-vre** (ʃeidə:vr) *n.* a masterpiece, esp. in art, music or literature ‖ the best piece of work of an artist, composer or writer [F.]

Che-foo (tʃí:fú:) (Yentai) a town (pop. 250,000) and port in N. Shantung, China

chef's salad dish including lettuce and small chunks of chicken, ham, hard-boiled eggs, cheese, and tomatoes

cheiropteran *CHIROPTER

Che-ju (tʃə́:dʒú:) *KOREA, REPUBLIC OF

Che-khov (tʃékɔf, tʃékɒf), Anton Pavlovich (1860–1904), Russian dramatist and short-story writer. His plays and stories are penetratingly observant of Russian upper-middle-class life in the late 19th c., and dominated by an irony so exquisitely balanced that the spectator is both amused at the wit and exactness of the observation and full of pity at the characters' helplessness. The most famous plays are 'The Seagull' (1895), 'Uncle Vanya' (1900), 'The Three Sisters' (1901) and 'The Cherry Orchard' (1903)

Che-kiang (tʃékjáŋ) the easternmost province (area 39,750 sq. miles, pop. 31,000,000) of S.E. China, on the East China Sea. Capital: Hang-chow

che-la (kí:lə) *pl.* **che-lae** (kí:li:) *n.* the pincerlike claw of a crab or lobster, and of some arachnids [fr. Gk *chēlē*, claw]

che-la (tʃéílə) *n.* a pupil, disciple (esp. of an Eastern spiritual teacher) [Hindi=disciple, pupil]

che-late (kí:leit) *adj.* like or having chelae

chelate 1. *n.* a coordination complex, with a cyclic structure usually of five or six members, in which the coordinated groups have at least two bonds to the central ion **2.** *v. pres. part.* **che-lat-ing** *past* and *past part.* **che-lat-ed** *v.i.* to react so as to form a chelate ‖ *v.t.* to combine with so as to form a chelate **che-la-tion** (ki:léiʃən) *n.* a chelating or being chelated [Gk *chēlē*, hoof, claw]

chelate laser liquid laser that utilizes chelate compounds. *syn* rare-earth chelate laser

che-la-tion (ki:léiʃən) *n.* (*organic chem.*) chemical process in which a heterocyclic compound is formed with a metal containing positive-charge ion or hydrogen ion

chel-i-cer (kélisər) *n.* a chelicera [F. *chélicère* fr. Gk]

che-lic-er-a (kəlísərə) *pl.* **che-lic-er-ae** (kəlísəri:) *n.* one of the anterior pair of appendages of an arachnid **che-lic-er-al** *adj.* [L.]

Che-lif (ʃelí:f) the largest river (430 miles long) in Algeria, flowing into the Mediterranean near Mostaganem

che-li-form (kí:ləfɔrm) *adj.* having the form of a chela

Chel-le-an (ʃéli:ən) *adj.* Abbevillian

che-loid, ke-loid (kí:lɔid) *n.* (*med.*) an overgrowth of scar tissue [F. *kéloïde* fr. Gk. *chēlē*, crab's claw]

che-lo-ni-an (kilóuni:ən) **1.** *adj.* testudinate **2.** *n.* a testudinate [fr. Mod. L. *Chelonia*]

Chel-ya-binsk (tʃiljábinsk) a town (pop. 1,019,000) in the R.S.F.S.R., U.S.S.R., east of the Urals, center of a grain-producing region: agricultural machinery

chem-i-cal (kémík'l) **1.** *adj.* relating to the science of chemistry, *chemical symbol* ‖ relating to the applications of chemistry, *chemical analysis* **2.** *n.* a substance used in or obtained by a chemical process [fr. older *chemic* fr. ALCHEMIC]

chemical agent chemical substance intended for use in military operations to kill or incapacitate humans through its physiological effects, not including riot-control agents, herbicides, smoke and flame

chemical engineer a specialist in chemical engineering **chemical engineering** the branch of engineering which deals with the manufacture of chemicals on a large scale, esp. with the design and operation of the plant and equipment involved

chemical horn (*mil.*) mine horn containing an electric battery, for which the electrolyte is in a glass tube protected by a thin metal sheet. *also* Hertz horn

chemical laser gas laser that depends on a chemical reaction between gases, e.g., deuterium and fluorine, hydrogen and chlorine, either internally or with the aid of external energy

chemical warfare the use of chemical substances other than explosives in warfare, esp. poison gases

chem-i-lu-mi-nes-cence (kémilu:minésəns) *n.* (*chem.*) light without heat produced by chemical action

che-min de fer (ʃəmɛ̃dəfɛ́r) *n.* a form of baccarat [F.]

chem-i-o-tax-is (kémi:ətǽksis, ki:mi:ətǽksis) *n.* chemotaxis

chem-ist (kémist) *n.* a person trained or engaged in chemistry ‖ (*Br.*) a pharmaceutical chemist [F. *chimiste*]

chem-is-try (kémistri:) *n.* the study of the composition, properties and structure of substances, and of the changes they undergo (*INORGANIC CHEMISTRY, *ORGANIC CHEMISTRY, *PHYSICAL CHEMISTRY)

Chem-nitz (kémnits) *KARL-MARXSTADT

che-mo-nu-clear (ki:mənú:kliər) *adj.* (*nuclear phys.*) of a chemical reaction resulting from nuclear radiation

che-mo-sen-so-ry (ki:məsénsəri:) *adj.* (*biochem.*) of the sensory perception of a chemical stimulus

che-mo-sphere (kí:məsfiər) *n.* (*meteorology*) zone of the atmosphere 20–50-mi. above the earth's surface in which photochemical activity takes place and radio signals are reflected by ionized clouds formed by nitric oxide

che-mo-ster-i-lant (ki:məstérilənt) *n.* (*biochem.*) chemical that controls pests by preventing reproduction. —**chemosterilization** *v.*

che-mo-sur-ger-y (ki:mousə́rdʒəri:) *n.* (*med.*) removal of tissue by use of chemicals. —**che-mosurgical** *adj.*

chem-o-syn-the-sis (kɛməsínθisis, ki:məsínθisis) *n.* (*bot.*) a synthesis of organic substances with energy derived from other chemical reactions (*PHOTOSYNTHESIS) [fr. older *chemic* adj.+SYNTHESIS]

chem-o-tax-is (kɛmətǽksis, ki:mətǽksis) *pl.* **chem-o-tax-es** (kɛmətǽksi:z, ki:mətǽksi:z) *n.* movement or orientation of cells or freely mobile organisms in response to chemical stimuli (*TAXIS) [fr. older *chemic* adj.+TAXIS]

che-mo-tax-on-o-my (ki:moutæksónəmi:) *n.* (*biochem.*) classification of flora and fauna in accordance with biochemical composition. —**chemotaxonomist** *n.* —**chemotaxonic** *adj.* —**chemotaxonomically** *adv.*

chem-o-ther-a-py (kɛməθérəpi:, ki:məθérəpi:) *n.* the use of chemical agents to prevent or treat disease

che-mot-ro-pism (kimótrəpizəm) *n.* the orientation of an organism (e.g. a plant) in response to a chemical stimulus

Che-mul-pho (tʃémulpó) *INCHON

chem-ur-gic (kemə́rdʒik) *adj.* relating to or produced by chemurgy **chem-ur-gi-cal** *adj.*

chem-ur-gy (kémərdʒi:) *n.* the study of the use of organic raw materials in industry, esp. farm products, such as soybean oil used for paints and varnishes [fr. older *chemic* adj.+Gk *-ergos*, working]

Che-nab (tʃináb) a tributary (675 miles long) of the Indus rising in the Himalayas in the N. Punjab, India. It flows through Himachal Pradesh and Kashmir, and joins the Sutlej in Pakistan (forming the Panjnad) before joining the Indus

Cheng-chow (tʃə́ŋdʒóu) (Chenghsien) the capital (pop. 766,000) of Honan, N. China, near the Hwang-ho, at the intersection of the Sian-Nanking and Peking-Canton railroads

Chenghsien *CHENGCHOW

Cheng-teh (tʃʌ́ndʌ́) (formerly Jehol) a town (pop. 60,000) in Hopei, China, northeast of Peking in the Lwan valley, a trade center (wool, hides, furs, silk). Imperial palace (c. 1700)

Cheng-tu (tʃʌ́ndú:) the capital (pop. 1,107,000) of Szechwan province, northwest of Chungking, one of China's oldest towns, now a great industrial center

Ché-nier (ʃeinjei), André (1762–94), French poet. At first inspired by the classics, he later showed strong romantic feeling, esp. in 'la Jeune Captive'. He was guillotined and most of his work was published posthumously

che-nille (ʃəni:l) *n.* a fabric with a pile slightly deeper and rougher than velvet, used esp. for furnishings ‖ a cotton fabric with a candlewick pattern used for bedspreads ‖ a tufted cord of silk, cotton or worsted used e.g. in fringes [F.=hairy caterpillar fr. L.]

Chenkiang *CHINKIANG

Chen-nault (ʃənɔ́lt), Claire Lee (1890–1958), U.S. army general, commander of U.S. air

CONCISE PRONUNCIATION KEY: (a) æ, c*a*t; ɑ, c*a*r; ɔ f*aw*n; ei, sn*a*ke. (e) e, h*e*n; i:, sh*ee*p; iə, d*ee*r; ɛə, b*ea*r. (i) i, f*i*sh; ai, t*i*ger; ə:, b*i*rd. (o) o, *o*x; au, c*ow*; ou, g*oa*t; u, p*oo*r; ɔi, r*oy*al. (u) ʌ, d*u*ck; u, b*u*ll; u:, g*oo*se; ə, b*a*cill*u*s; ju:, c*u*be. x, lo*ch*; θ, *th*ink; ð, bo*th*er; z, *Z*en; ʒ, corsa*g*e. dʒ, sava*g*e; ŋ, orangutan*g*; j, *y*ak; ʃ, *fi*sh; tʃ, fe*tch*; 'l, rabb*le*; 'n, redd*en*. Complete pronunciation key appears inside front cover.

forces in China during the 2nd world war. He organized and trained (1941) the 'Flying Tigers', U.S. pilots recruited to fight for the Chinese

cheong·sam (tʃɔ́ŋsam) *n.* traditional Oriental women's garment consisting of a long gown, split skirt, and high mandarin collar

Che·ops (kíːɒps) *KHUFU

cheque *CHECK (order to a bank)

chequebook *CHECKBOOK

chequer *CHECKER

chequerwise *CHECKERWISE

Cher (ʃɛər) a department (area 2,819 sq. miles, pop. 316,400) of central France south of the Loire. (*BARRY, *NIVERNAIS, *BOURBONNAIS, *ORLÉANAIS) Chief town: Bourges

Cher·bourg (ʃɛərbuːr) a naval station and passenger port (pop. 30,112) of Manche department on the Cotentin peninsula, N. France

Che·rem·kho·vo (tʃirjémkəvə) a city (pop. 104,000) of the R.S.F.S.R., U.S.S.R., in S.E. Siberia, on the Trans-Siberian railroad, center of the Cheremkhovo coal basin

Cher·en·kov (tʃirénkɔf), Pavel Alekseyevich (1904–), Soviet physicist known for his discovery of the radiation produced by certain high-energy particles traveling faster than light in a transparent medium, known as Cherenkov radiation. He shared the 1958 Nobel Prize for physics with I.M. Frank and I.Y. Tamm

cher·ish (tʃériʃ) *v.t.* to treasure, *a cherished possession* ‖ (esp. in the marriage vow) to take loving care of ‖ to keep alive (an emotion, illusion, etc.) [F. *chérir (chériss-)* fr. *cher,* dear]

Cher·nen·ko (tʃɛərnjénkou), Konstantin (1911–85), general secretary of the Soviet Union's Communist party and effective head of state from the death of Yuri V. Andropov (1984) until his own death 13 months later, when he was succeeded by Mikhail Gorbachev. Long a member of the party, Chernenko served as head of the propaganda department of the party's Central Committee in Moscow and became a member of the Politburo. His poor health while head of state precluded his being a forceful leader

Cher·no·byl (tʃɛənoúbəl) nuclear power plant located in Pripyat, a town about 60 miles north of Kiev in the Soviet Ukraine, site of a serious nuclear accident in April, 1986

Cher·o·kee (tʃérəkiː, tʃérəkiː) *pl.* **Cher·o·kee, Cher·o·kees** *n.* a member of a North American Indian tribe of the Iroquoian family, formerly exclusively of the S. Alleghenies, now in North Carolina and Oklahoma ‖ an Iroquoian language

che·root (ʃərúːt) *n.* a thin cigar cut, instead of tapered, at both ends [fr. F. *cheroute* fr. Tamil]

cher·ry (tʃériː) 1. *pl.* **cher·ries** *n.* a member of *Prunus,* fam. *Rosaceae,* a genus of flowering trees bearing small fruit on long stems, each having a small smooth stone, and a skin varying in color from pink to dark red. *P. avium* (sweet cherry) is diploid. *P. cerasus* (sour cherry) is tetraploid. Native to Asia Minor, both are widely cultivated ‖ the fruit (drupe) of these species ‖ the wood of these species ‖ a bright red color **to make two bites at a cherry** (*Br.*) to do a job by unnecessary stages, instead of completing it at once 2. *adj.* bright red [prob. fr. O.N.F. *cherise*]

cherry bean the cowpea

cherry brandy a sweetened brandy in which cherries have been steeped

cher·ry·stone (tʃériːstoun) *n.* the clam *Venus mercenaria* when larger than a littleneck

chert (tʃəːrt) *n.* a dark-colored flintlike quartz ‖ (*biol.*) microscopic primitive life form found in a cryptocrystalline black rock in Swaziland ‖ (*geol.*) the rock [origin unknown]

cher·ub (tʃérəb) *pl.* **cher·ubs,** (*Bible*) **cher·u·bim** (tʃérəbim) *n.* an order of angels (*ANGEL) ‖ a representation of such a creature, e.g. in art as a winged child's head, or a rosy baby boy **che·ru·bic** (tʃərúːbik) *adj.* (esp. of a child) having a round rosy face [O.E. *cherubin* fr. Heb.]

Che·ru·bi·ni (kerubíːniː), Maria Luigi Carlo Zenobio Salvatore (1760–1842), Italian composer, later a French citizen. He wrote about 30 operas and many church cantatas, Masses etc.

cher·vil (tʃəːrvil) *n. Anthriscus cerefolium,* fam. *Umbelliferae,* an aromatic herb. Its leaves are used in soups and salads [O.E. *cerfille* fr. L. fr. Gk]

Ches·a·peake Bay, the (tʃésəpiːk) the largest inlet on the Atlantic coast of the U.S.A., receiving the Susquehanna, Potomac, Rappahan-

nock, York and James Rivers, all navigable, and others

'Chesapeake', U.S.S. a frigate captured (June 22, 1807) by the British flagship 'Leopard' after it refused to allow the right of search for deserters. The U.S. public, including the pro-British Federalists, were outraged by the indignity. In the War of 1812 it was captured (1813) outside Boston by the British vessel 'Shannon'

Chesh·ire (tʃéʃər) (*abbr.* Ches.) a county (area 900 sq. miles, pop. 913,900) of the western Midlands of England. County town: Chester

chess (tʃes) *n.* an ancient, conventional, elaborate game of skill for two players, played on a chessboard. Each player has 16 chessmen with which he tries to checkmate the other player's king [M.E. *ches* fr. O.F.]

chess·board (tʃésbɔːrd, tʃésbourd) *n.* a board divided into 64 equal squares, used in the game of chess

ches·sel (tʃésəl) *n.* a mold for making cheese [prob. CHEESE+WELL]

chess·man (tʃésmæn, tʃésmən) *pl.* **chess·men** (tʃésmən, tʃésmən) *n.* one of the 16 pieces (king, queen, 2 bishops, 2 knights, 2 rooks or castles, 8 pawns), each kind moving in its proper way, which each player of a game of chess has on the board at the start

chest (tʃest) *n.* the thorax, that part of the body between the neck and abdomen which contains the lungs and heart, parts of the esophagus, windpipe, greater blood vessels and some nerves. They are enclosed in a bony protective cage formed by the spine, ribs and breastbone ‖ a large, strong box with a hinged lid ‖ the funds of an institution ‖ a chest of drawers **to get something off one's chest** to unburden oneself by speaking about what is weighing on one's mind or conscience [O.E. *cest, cist,* perh. fr. L. fr. Gk]

Ches·ter·field (tʃéstərfiːld), Philip Dormer Stanhope, 4th earl of (1694–1773), English statesman and author. His fame rests on his 'Letters to his Son' (1774). He is also remembered because of Dr. Johnson's rebuke for his failure as a patron during the writing of Johnson's dictionary. He stood for aristocratic worldliness, redeemed by intelligence, elegance and wit

ches·ter·field (tʃéstərfiːld) *n.* (*Br.*) a large sofa with back and arms ‖ a style of overcoat [after an Earl of *Chesterfield*]

Ches·ter·ton (tʃéstərtən), Gilbert Keith (1874–1936), English poet, novelist and essayist. He was a prolific writer, stimulating, epigrammatic and provocative. He is associated with Belloc as a Catholic propagandist

chest note a note produced in the lowest part of the singing register

chest·nut (tʃésnʌt) 1. *n.* a tree of genus *Castanea,* fam. *Fagaceae* ‖ its sweet, edible nut ‖ its wood ‖ the horse chestnut ‖ a warm brown color ‖ an old or outworn joke 2. *adj.* reddish-brown [fr. older *chesten* fr. F. *chastaine* fr. L. fr. Gk+NUT]

chest of drawers a set of drawers in a frame, for keeping clothes in

chest-on-chest (tʃéstɒntʃést, tʃéstɔːnttʃést) *n.* a highboy

che·val glass (ʃəvǽl) a long, narrow mirror, pivoting on an upright stand [F. *cheval,* horse=frame or stand]

chev·a·lier (ʃəvəlíər) *n.* a member of certain orders of knighthood or merit [A.F. fr. L.L. *caballus,* horse]

che·val·ine (ʃəvælíːn) *n.* (*Fr.*) horsemeat sold for human consumption in Europe

che·vaux-de-frise (ʃəvóudəfríːz) *pl. n.* (*hist.*) a plank or barrel covered with sharp iron spikes projecting at all angles, as a defense against cavalry in warfare ‖ projecting spikes on a wall or on railings ‖ a line of protective hair in plants etc. [F.= Frisian horses, the defense being invented in Friesland, which had no cavalry force]

Chev·i·ot (tʃévi:ət, tʃíːviːət) *n.* a breed of meat-type, medium-wooled sheep originating in the Cheviot hills ‖ cloth made from the fleece of these sheep

Cheviot Hills a range on the borders of England and Scotland, mainly in Northumberland, rising to 2,676 ft (Mt Cheviot): moorland and grass country, noted for sheep

chev·ron (ʃévrən) *n.* the symbol ∧ as a heraldic device, or as an indication of rank, or (in some forces) length of service worn on service uniform [F.]

chev·ro·tain (ʃévrətein, ʃévrətin) *n.* a member of *Tragulus,* a genus of musk deer of S.E. Asia [F. dim. of O.F. *chevrot,* little goat]

chew (tʃuː) 1. *v.t.* to reduce (food) to a pulp in the mouth by grinding it between the teeth with the help of the tongue etc. ‖ to bite repeatedly, *to chew one's nails* ‖ (with 'on' or 'over') to think carefully and at length about the various aspects of (a matter) *v.i.* to chew something ‖ to chew tobacco 2. *n.* the act of chewing [O.E. *cēowan*]

chew·i·ness (tʃúːiːnis) *n.* the quality of being chewy

chewing gum a preparation of sweetened, flavored gum, esp. chicle, for chewing

che·wink, chee·wink (tʃiwíŋk) *n. Pipilo erythrophthalmus,* a bird of eastern North America, the common towhee [perh. imit.]

chew·y (tʃúːiː) *comp.* **chew·i·er** *superl.* **chew·i·est** *adj.* for chewing, that needs to be chewed, *chewy candies*

Cheyenne the capital (pop. 47,283) of Wyoming

Chey·enne (ʃaién, ʃaiǽn) *n.* a subdivision of the large Algonquian tribe of Indians of North America, formerly inhabiting the area between the Arkansas and Missouri Rivers ‖ a member of this people ‖ their Algonquian language

CH-53 *SEA STALLION

chi (kai) *n.* the twenty-second letter (Χ, χ=ch) of the Greek alphabet

Chiang Kai-shek (dʒiǽŋkáiʃék) (1887–1975), Chinese general and head of the Nationalist government. He assumed control of the Kuomintang (1926) and alternately campaigned against the warlords, the Japanese, and the Chinese Communists until he withdrew to Taiwan (1949), ruling until his death

Chi·an·ti (kiːánti, kiːǽnti) *n.* a dry (esp. red) wine from Chianti, a hill region in Tuscany, Italy, southeast of Florence

Chi·an turpentine (káiən) the oleoresin yielded by the terebinth

chiao (ʒau) *n.* unit of China currency, equal to 1/10 yuan

Chi·a·pas (tʃiːápəs) a Pacific coast state (area 28,732 sq. miles, pop. 2,097,500) of southern Mexico, on the Guatemalan frontier. Capital: Tuxtla Gutiérrez (pop. 42,000). Main occupations: agriculture, stock raising, forestry, fruit farming. The northeast jungle contains early Maya ruins

Chia·ri (tʃjáriː), Roberto Francisco (1905–), Panamanian president (1960–4) who demanded (1964) of the U.S.A. a revision of the agreements relative to the Canal

chi·a·ro·scu·ro (kiːɑrouskjúərou) *n.* the disposition of highlight and shadow in a painting [Ital. fr. *chiaro,* bright +*oscuro,* dark]

chi·as·ma (kaiǽzmə) *pl.* **chi·as·ma·ta** (kaiǽzmətə), **chi·as·mas** *n.* (*anat.*) a structure of the central nervous system, formed by the crossing over of fibers from either side to the other [Gk fr. *chiazein,* to mark with a chi (χ)]

Chi·ba (tʃíːbá) a city (pop. 746,000) on Tokyo Bay, Honshu, Japan

Chib·cha (tʃíbtʃə) *pl.* **Chib·cha, Chib·chas** *n.* a member of a group of Indian tribes of the Eastern Cordillera of the Colombian Andes ‖ their extinct Chibchan language **Chib·chan** (tʃíbtʃən) *adj.* of a group of Indian languages spoken in Colombia and S. Central America [Span.]

chic (ʃiːk) 1. *n.* stylishness 2. *adj.* elegant, stylish [F.]

chicadee *CHICKADEE

Chi·ca·go (ʃikáːgou, ʃikɔ́gou) the second largest city (pop. 3,005,072), with agglom. 7,102,328) in the U.S.A., at the south end of Lake Michigan in Illinois: chief railroad center for the U.S.A., with a harbor opened to ocean traffic by the St Lawrence Seaway. Exports: grain, livestock, lumber and meat. It is a major financial, commercial and industrial center

Chicago Seven Trial a trial in which five members of what was originally the Chicago Eight were convicted (1970) of crossing State lines with intent to incite disorders at the 1968 Democratic National Convention in Chicago. The defense filed (1971) an appeal that the Federal anti-riot statute 'violates on its face' the provisions of the First Amendment and its cardinal purpose: 'to keep American government out of the business of thought control.' The defense also argued that the judge and jury were not impartial

Chicago, University of a private, coeducational university, founded in 1890, in Chicago,

---

Illinois. Its reputation has been made esp. in the social sciences, education and nuclear physics

chi·ca·lo·te (tʃiːkɑlóte) n. *Argemone platyceras*, a prickly poppy with white flowers, found in Mexico and the western U.S.A. [Span. fr. Nahuatl]

chi·cane (ʃikéin) n. chicanery ‖ (*bridge*) a hand with no trumps ‖ (*racing*) an artificially contrived difficulty (e.g. a hairpin bend around barriers in a straight stretch) [F. *chicane*]

chicane v. *pres. part.* **chi·can·ing** *past* and *past part.* **chi·caned** v.t. to trick by quibbling ‖ to quibble over ‖ v.i. to use chicanery [F. *chicaner*, origin unknown]

chi·can·er·y (ʃikéinəːɪ) pl. **chi·can·er·ies** n. trickery, esp. legal trickery [F. *chicanerie*]

Chi·ca·no (masc.) **Chi·ca·na** (fem.) (tʃikɑ́nou) n. U.S. resident of Mexican descent

Chi·ca·no movement (tʃikɑ́nou) a movement in California led by César Chávez whose main purpose was to win better conditions for Mexican-American agricultural workers, by protracted strikes

Chi·chén It·zá (tʃiːtʃéiniːtsɑ́) the site, in N. central Yucatán, Mexico, of the capital of the Maya Empire. Temple pyramids, astronomical observatory

chi·chi (ʃiːʃiː) adj. pretentiously elegant

Chi·chi·cas·te·nan·go (tʃiːtʃiːkɑsteːnɑ́ŋɡɔ) a town (pop. 2,000) in the highlands of W. central Guatemala. It is a market center of the Quiché Indians and much visited by tourists: cotton and wool weaving, agriculture (corn, beans)

Chi·chi·me·ca (tʃiːtʃəméikə) pl. **Chi·chi·me·ca, Chi·chi·me·cas** n. an Indian people of the Nahuatl race which migrated southward, defeating (12th c.) the Toltecs and settling in Tenayuca and later Texcoco. They were overcome (13th c.) by the Aztecs

chick (tʃik) n. a newly hatched chicken ‖ any very young bird

chick·a·dee, chic·a·dee (tʃíkədiː) n. a member of *Penthestes* or *Parus*, comprising several species of crestless titmice, esp. *P. atricapillus*, the blackcapped chickadee, one of the tamest North American birds [imit.]

Chick·a·mau·ga, Battle of (tʃikəmɔ́ɡə) a Civil War victory (1863) for the Confederate forces under Gen. Braxton Bragg over Union troops commanded by Gen. William S. Rosecrans, at Chickamauga, Tenn. Bragg's failure to follow up the victory led to his defeat at Chattanooga

chick·a·ree (tʃíkəɪi) n. *Sciurus hudsonius*, the larger American red squirrel [imit.]

Chick·a·saw (tʃíkəsɔ) pl. **Chick·a·saws, Chick·a·saw** n. an Indian of a Muskogean tribe, now living in Oklahoma ‖ this tribe ‖ the Choctaw dialect of the tribe

chick·en (tʃíkən) 1. n. the domestic fowl, *Gallus gallus*, or its flesh as food 2. adj. (pop.) cowardly [O.E. *cicen*]

chicken breast pigeon breast

chicken feed food for hens ‖ a trifling sum of money

chick·en·heart·ed (tʃíkənhɑːtid) adj. cowardly

chicken Kiev dish of boned breast of chicken, stuffed with seasoned butter; named for the Ukranian city

chicken pox an infectious disease, commonest in children and rarely dangerous. It is manifested by small blisters on the skin which eventually become scabs and fall off. It is infectious until the last scab has fallen

chicken Tetrazzini dish of chicken, mushrooms, noodles, and almonds in velouté sauce; named for Luisa Tetrazzini, opera singer

chick·ling (tʃíklin) n. *Lathyrus sativus*, the common European purple vetch cultivated as a forage plant [etym. doubtful]

chick·pea (tʃíkpiː) n. *Cicer arietinum*, fam. *Papilionaceae*, a plant cultivated esp. in S. Europe, India and the Middle East for its edible seeds ‖ a seed of this plant [after F. *pois chiche*]

chicks (mil.) friendly fighter aircraft

chick·weed (tʃíkwiːd) n. a member of *Stellaria*, fam. *Caryophyllaceae*, a genus of small wild annual or perennial plants, comprising about 85 species ‖ a plant of the genera *Alsine, Arenaria* or *Cerastium*

Chi·cla·yo (tʃiklɑ́jo) a coastal city (pop. 187,809) of N.W. Peru, in a rice, cotton and sugar district

chic·le (tʃík'l) n. the gum obtained from the latex of the sapodilla, used in making chewing gum [Span. fr. Nahuatl]

Chicom or **ChiCom** Chinese Communist

chic·o·ry (tʃíkəɪi) n. *Cichorium intybus*, fam. *Compositae*, a perennial plant whose root is roasted, pulverized and used as a coffee adulterant or substitute. The leaves are eaten in salad [F. *cichorée, chicorée*]

chide (tʃaid) *pres. part.* **chid·ing** *past* **chid** (tʃid), **chid·ed** *past part.* **chid, chid·den** (tʃid'n), **chid·ed** v.t. to reprove, rebuke ‖ to compel by chiding, *he chid him into going* [O.E. *cīdan*]

chief (tʃiːf) 1. n. a leader or ruler, esp. of a tribe or clan ‖ the head of a department in an institution ‖ (*heraldry*) the upper part of a shield **in chief** (*Br.*) especially 2. adj. most important, *the chief export is oil* ‖ highest in rank, *Chief Scout* [M.E. *chef, chief* fr. F.]

Chief Executive the president of the U.S.A.

chief justice the presiding judge of a court having several judges **Chief Justice** the presiding judge of the U.S. Supreme Court

chief·ly (tʃíːfli) adv. mainly, but not altogether ‖ pertaining to a chief

chief of staff the senior officer on a military commander's staff

chief·tain (tʃíːftən) n. the leader of a group, esp. a clan or tribe **chief·tain·cy** n. [M.E. *chieftayne* fr. O.F.]

Chieftain (mil.) British Main Battle Tank (Mk 5) with 120-mm gun, laser range finder; operational since 1963

Chieng Mai (tʃéŋmái) a teak-trading town (pop. 40,000) in N. Thailand, terminus of the northern railroad

chiff·chaff (tʃíftʃæf, tʃíftʃɑf) n. *Phylloscopus collybita*, a small European warbler, with an olive-green back and yellow-white breast and rump [imit.]

chif·fon (ʃifɒn, ʃifɒn) 1. n. a very soft, fine transparent material, usually of silk, used in dressmaking etc. 2. adj. made of chiffon ‖ (*cooking*) light and fluffy in consistency [F.=rag]

chif·fo·nier (ʃifəníər) n. a small chest of drawers [F. fr. *chiffon*, a rag]

Chif·ley (tʃífli), Joseph Benedict (1885–1951), Australian statesman, leader of the Australian Labor movement, and prime minister (1945–9)

chig·ger (tʃíɡər) n. a chigoe ‖ a harvest bug ‖ any of various larval mites that suck the blood of many vertebrates, incl. man

chi·gnon (ʃíːnjɒn, ʃiːnjɑ́n) n. a bun, a knot or twist of hair worn esp. on the nape of the neck, and sometimes dressed over false hair [F.]

chig·oe (tʃíɡou) n. *Tunga penetrans*, a tropical flea. The female burrows beneath the skin of human feet and hands, causing irritation and sores ‖ a harvest bug, chigger [West Indian, perh. corrup. of Span. *chico*, small]

Chih·li (dʒɑʌlí:) *HOPEI

Chihli, Gulf of *PO HAI

Chi·hua·hua (tʃiːwɑ́wɑ) the largest state (area 95,400 sq. miles, pop. 2,005,477) of Mexico, bounded north and northeast by the U.S.A. The land is mostly elevated plain, while in the western mountains there are fertile valleys. Capital: Chihuahua. Important city: Ciudad Juárez. Principal industry: mining (iron, antimony, gold, silver, copper). Its silver mines are among Mexico's richest. Cotton farming and meat packing have developed ‖ its capital (pop. 406,830), c. 1,000 miles northwest of Mexico City. It contains the church of San Francisco, one of the finest specimens of 18th-c. architecture in Mexico

Chihuahua (tʃiːwɑ́wɑ) n. a dog of a very small breed originally from Mexico [Mex.]

Chi·ka·mat·su (tʃíːkɑmɑ́tsu:), Monzaemon (1653–1724), Japanese dramatist, author of over 100 plays

Chi·lám Ba·lám (tʃiːlɑ́mbɑlɑ́m) chronicles containing the traditional history of the northern Mayas of Yucatán, written by an unknown author at the time of the Conquest, in Mayan language but in Spanish script. They include a prophetic vision of the Conquest, and of Christianity, with an injunction to the Mayan people: 'Let us receive our guests heartily. Our elder brothers, the white men, come!'

chil·blain (tʃílblein) n. an inflamed, itching swelling or sore, esp. on the hands or feet, caused by exposure to the cold

child (tʃaild) pl. **chil·dren** (tʃíldrən) n. a boy or girl at any age between infancy and adolescence ‖ a newborn infant ‖ a person of any age in relation to his parents ‖ (*rhet.*) a follower or disciple, *a child of the devil* ‖ (*fig.*) a product, *a child of the imagination* **with child** pregnant [O.E. *cild*]

Child abuse includes physical abuse, sexual abuse, and neglect and may result in bruises, broken bones, permanent physical or developmental impairment, emotional trauma, or death. Estimates of the extent of child abuse vary greatly, as do theories about the cause. Recent evidence suggests that abusive parents are likely to have been abused children and that poverty, unemployment, and other stresses contribute to child abuse. In 1974 the U.S. government established the National Center on Child Abuse and Neglect (NCCAN), now part of the Dept. of Health and Human Services. Child abuse is also dealt with by law enforcement, medical, mental-health, and social agencies

child abuse psychological or physical abuse of a child under one's care

child·bear·ing (tʃáildbɛəriŋ) n. a giving birth to a child, parturition

child·birth (tʃáildbəːθ) n. the expulsion of an infant from its mother's womb into the outside world, labor (*OBSTETRICS)

Chil·dé·ric I (tʃíldərik) (c. 436–81), Merovingian king of the Salian Franks (c. 457–81), father of Clovis

Chil·der·mas (tʃíldərmɑs) n. the former name for Holy Innocents' Day (*INNOCENTS, MASSACRE OF THE) [O.E. *cildra*, of children+MASS]

child·hood (tʃáildhud) n. the state of being a child ‖ the years between infancy and adolescence [O.E. *cildhād*]

child·ish (tʃáildiʃ) adj. like or proper to a child ‖ pertaining to childhood ‖ immature ‖ (of remarks or behavior) puerile, not befitting an adult [O.E. *cildisc*]

child labor, *Br.* **child labour** the employment of children. This is regulated in most countries by conventions of the International Labor Organization covering minimum age, length of working day, overtime etc.

child·like (tʃáildlaik) adj. possessing what are commonly thought of as the good qualities of a child's character, such as trust, wonder, candor and innocence

child·proof (tʃáildpruːf) adj. designed to avoid danger to or from children

children pl. of CHILD

chil·dren·ese (tʃíldrəniːz) n. vocabulary for an exchange of information with one's children

Children's Crusade an incident (1212) during the Crusades, in which thousands of children embarked at Marseille, but were sold into slavery before they reached the Holy Land

child·snatch·ing (tʃáildsnætʃiŋ) n. kidnapping of a child by his or her parent

child's play something very easy to do

Chil·e (tʃíli:) a republic (area incl. Easter Is. 286,451 sq. miles, pop. 11,882,000) of South America. Capital: Santiago. Outlying possessions include Easter Is. and the Juan Fernandez Is. Language: Spanish. The land is 5% arable, 13% pasture, and 22% forest. The northern two thirds consists of a coast range (1,000–7,000 ft) and the Andes (15,000—over 23,000 ft), and the valley between them. The highest peaks (Ojos del Salado, 23,293 ft), many of them volcanic, are on the Argentine border. The valley is desert (*ATACAMA) in the north, fertile in the center and south. S. Chile consists of the forested S. Andes (3,000–9,000 ft), with grassy tableland (Chilean Patagonia) in the far southeast, fiords and many islands (the extension of the coast range) in the west. Climate: subtropical to subantarctic. Earthquakes are frequent. Annual rainfall: practically nil in the north. 14 ins at Santiago, 100 ins at Valdivia, 100 ins in the S.W. Andes, 19 ins at Punta Arenas. Average temperatures (F.): 66° in the north (without seasonal variation), 46° (winter) and 69° (summer) in Santiago, below freezing in the south. Livestock: sheep (in the south), cattle (south central). Crops:. wheat, oats, barley, corn, sugar beet, vegetables, rice, cotton, vines, fruit. Fisheries (whales, oysters) are important. Forestry products: lumber, paper, cellulose. Mineral resources: 40% of the world's copper reserves, nitrates and the by-product iodine (75% of world production), iron, coal, oil (output increased by ten times between 1950 and 1960), silver, manganese. Manufactures: food processing, textiles, steel, iodine, cement, pig iron. Hydroelectric power is being developed. Exports: copper (60% of exports), nitrates, lumber, iron ore, wine. Imports: foodstuffs, machinery, sugar, chemicals. Chief port: Valparaíso. Universities: three in Santiago, two in Valparaíso and one each in Concepción, Valdivia and Antofagasta. Monetary unit: escudo (100 centesimos). HISTORY. The Atacama Indians had developed settlements by the l0th c. Chile was conquered in the north by the Incas (l5th c.), and was penetrated and settled (16th c.) by Spain, but the Araucanian Indians kept control of the south until the mid-19th c. In 1818, thanks to the liberating army which San Martín brought over the Andes from Argentina the previous year, Chile won independence from Spain after a revolutionary war (1810–18) led by Bernardo O'Higgins. The first constitution was introduced in 1833. Conservative and liberal governments were followed after 1891 by a succession of dictator-presidents. Chile fought wars against Peru and Bolivia (1836–9 and 1879–84), and against Spain (1866). She settled her boundary disputes with Argentina (1899–1902) and with Peru (1929). A popular front government was in power (1938–58), after which Jorge Alessandri followed (1958–64) a pro-U.S. policy which kept the economy tied to copper. In the 1964 elections, remarkable for the absence of any rightist party, Eduardo Frei, leader of the moderate leftist Christian Democrats, defeated Salvador Allende, leader of the far left Popular Action Front (FRAP). Impressive gains (1969) by the conservative National Party, though partly the result of recent natural disasters, led Frei to decide (1969) on the widely popular move to nationalize, with compensation, the Anaconda Co., the world's biggest producer of copper. Constitutionally barred from a second consecutive term in office, Frei was replaced as leader of the Christian Democrats by Radomiro Tomic, whose platform in the 1970 elections was, if anything, to the left of Allende's. In the elections Allende narrowly led the conservative Alessandri, but his lack of a majority required Congress to decide the winner. Since Tomic, and ultimately even Alessandri, gave their support to Allende, he was duly endorsed, to become the first Marxist ever to win a free federal election. He nationalized all other U.S. copper firms and all private banks. He died during a military coup financed by the U.S. CIA and was replaced by a junta headed by Gen. Augusto Pinochet Ugarto (1974). A 1980 plebiscite confirmed Pinochet in office until 1989 and a new constitution provided for a bicameral legislature to be installed in 1989. The Pinochet government restored many banks and industries to private ownership. An economic recession (1982–3) led to increased political opposition, which continued despite slight improvement in the economy (1984)

Chile niter, *Br.* **Chile nitre** Chile saltpeter

Chile saltpeter, *Br.* **Chile saltpetre** sodium nitrate, esp. in its natural form as caliche

chil·i, *Br.* **chil·li** (tʃíli:) *pl.* **chil·ies,** *Br.* esp. **chil·lies** *n. Capsicum frutescens,* fam. *Solanaceae,* a garden pepper grown from Chile to the middle of North America [Span. *Chile,* Mex. *chilli*]

Chil·i con car·ne (tʃíli:kɒnkárni:) *n.* a Mexican dish of chopped meat stewed with minced red chilies and kidney beans [Span.=chili with meat]

chili sauce, *Br,* esp. **chilli sauce** a sauce made with chilis and tomatoes

chill (tʃil) **1.** *adj.* cold to the touch ‖ unpleasantly cold, *a chill wind* ‖ unemotional, undemonstrative ‖ unfriendly, *a chill reception* **2.** *n.* an unpleasant sensation of coldness, *a chill in the air* ‖ a depressing influence, *to cast a chill over one's spirits* ‖ (esp. *Br.*) an illness characterized by shivering and fever ‖ a metal mold for making chilled castings **to take the chill off** to warm slightly **3.** *v.t.* to make cold ‖ to refrigerate but not freeze (food) ‖ to bring (champagne etc.) down to the right temperature for drinking ‖ to depress or dishearten ‖ to surface harden (iron) by making it cold quickly ‖ *v.i.* to become cold ‖ (*metall.*) to become surface hardened by rapid cooling [O.E. *cele,* cold]

chill factor increased feeling of a cold temperature caused by wind

chilli *CHILI

chil·li·ly (tʃílili:) *adv.* in a chilly manner

chil·li·ness (tʃíli:nis) *n.* the state or quality of being chilly

chil·ly (tʃíli:) *comp.* **chil·li·er** *superl.* **chil·li·est** *adj.* rather cold ‖ unfriendly, undemonstrative ‖ sensitive to cold ‖ producing a sensation of cold

Chi·lo·é (tʃi:lɔé) an island (area 3,241sq. miles) off the southwest coast of Chile, forming (with

other islands) a province of Chile: coal deposits

chi·lo·pod (káiləpɒd) *n.* a member of *Chilopoda,* an order of predacious and mostly nocturnal arthropods, having a body of numerous segments each with a pair of legs, and two anterior pairs of legs converted into foot jaws, e.g. the centipede [fr. Mod. L. fr. Gk *cheilos,* lip+*pous* (*podos*), foot]

Chil·pan·cin·go de los Bra·vos (tʃi:lpan-sí:ŋgɔðelɔzbrávɔs) a town in Mexico, capital of the state of Guerrero.It was the site (1813) of the First Constituent Congress, called by Morelos

Chil·tern Hundreds (tʃíltərn) (*Br., Parliament*) a manor in Buckinghamshire belonging to the Crown **to apply for the Chiltern Hundreds** to relinquish a seat in the House of Commons. A British M.P. cannot resign his seat, but a person who holds a place of honor or profit under the Crown cannot be an M.P. Since 1750 it has been the practice for an M.P. who wishes to resign to apply for the stewardship of the Chiltern Hundreds, a nominal Crown appointment. Once obtained, it is immediately resigned. The stewardship of the Manor of Northstead in Yorkshire has been used in the same way since 1841

Chi·lung (tʃí:lúŋ) *KILUNG

chi·mae·ra (kimíərə, kaimíərə) *n.* a member of *Chimaera,* deep-sea cartilaginous fish with large eyes in a leathery case [L.]

chimaera *CHIMERA

chimb *CHIME

Chim·bo·ra·zo (tʃimbərázou) an extinct volcano (20,702 ft) of Ecuador, one of the highest peaks of the Andes

chime (tʃaim) **1.** *n.* a set of bells ‖ the sound made by a bell or bells, esp. (*pl.*) the bells in a striking clock ‖ a musical instrument consisting of a set of vertical metal tubes, struck with a hammer **2.** *v. pres. part.* **chim·ing** *past* and *past part.* **chimed** *v.i.* (of a chime of bells) to ring ‖ *v.t.* to ring (a bell or bells) ‖ to tell (the time) by ringing **to chime in** to break into a conversation, usually agreeably **to chime in with** to agree fully with ‖ to fit in well with [M.E. *chimbe, chymbe* fr. O.F.]

chime, chimb (tʃaim) *n.* the projecting edge or rim of a cask or barrel [M.E. *chimbe*]

chi·me·ra, chi·mae·ra (kimíərə, kaimíərə) *n.* (*Gk mythol.*) a fire-breathing monster, having a lion's head, goat's body and dragon's tail ‖ any imaginary monster ‖ a wild or foolish idea ‖ (*biol.*) a graft hybrid, an organism having tissues of two or more kinds differing genetically [M.E. *chimere* fr. F. fr. L. fr. Gk]

chi·mere (tʃimíər, ʃimíər) *n.* a bishop's sleeveless robe, worn for public worship etc. when a cope is not used [O.F. *chamaire,* a loose gown]

chi·mer·i·cal (kimérik'l, kimíərik'l, kaimérik'l, kaimíərik'l) *adj.* unreal, imaginary

chim·ney (tʃímni:) *pl.* **chim·neys** *n.* an enclosed vertical channel or flue in the wall of a house for carrying away the smoke from a fire ‖ the part of a flue projecting above the roof of a house ‖ the high brick or metal stack of a factory furnace ‖ anything resembling a chimney in purpose, e.g. the glass tube above the flame in an oil lamp, the opening of a volcano etc. ‖ (*mountaineering*) a narrow, climbable crack in a cliff face ‖ (*Br.*) the smokestack of a steamship or locomotive [M.E. *chimenee* fr. O.F.]

chimney corner a seat by the fire in a wide open fireplace

chim·ney·piece (tʃímni:pi:s) *n.* the overmantel, usually of wood or stone, above a fireplace

chimney pot a short, narrow earthenware or metal tube fixed to the top of a chimney to increase the draft

chimney stack several chimney flues built adjacently and projecting above a roof as a single mass

chimney sweep a man who cleans soot from chimneys

chimney swift *Chaetura pelagica,* an American Swift that likes nesting inside a chimney

chimp (tʃimp) *n.* (*pop.*) a chimpanzee [by shortening]

chim·pan·zee (tʃimpænzí:, tʃímpænzi:) *n. Pan troglodytes* or *Anthropopithecus troglodytes,* an African ape allied to the gorilla and resembling man more closely than do most apes. It stands 5 ft, weighs up to 175 lbs and walks fairly erect [native W. African]

Chin (tʃin) *n.* a member of a tribal people speaking a language related to Burmese, occupying a special division (area 10,377 sq. miles, pop.

250,000) in W. Burma, the former Chin Hills district. Capital: Falam

chin (tʃin) **1.** *n.* the part of the face below the lower lip, esp. the front part of the lower jaw **2.** *pres. part.* **chin·ning** *past* and *past part.* **chinned** *v.t.* (*gymnastics*) to bring one's chin up to the level of (the horizontal bar etc.) by bending the elbows while the body hangs straight from it by the hands ‖ (*gymnastics*) to bring (oneself) to this position in this way [O.E. *cin*]

Chi·na (tʃáina) (since 1949 People's Republic of China) a country (area 3,745,000 sq. miles, pop. estimated at 1,031,882,511 excluding Taiwan) of central and E. Asia. Capital: Peking. There are 21 provinces and five ethnic autonomous regions, divided among six administrative regions. Minorities: aborigines (Chuan, Yi, Miao, Manchu, Puyi) and Koreans in the east, Mongols, Turks (Uighurs) and Tibetans in the west. Language: several dialects (80% speak Mandarin) of the Chinese language, plus minority languages. Religion: chiefly Confucian, 25% Buddhist, 5% Taoist, 5% Moslem, with 3,000,000 Roman Catholics. Except for vast desert basins (*TAKLA MAKAN, *DZUNGARIA, *GOBI) stretching east to Manchuria in the north, the western half of China (Tibet, Sinkiang-Uighor, Tsinghai, Ningsia-Hui) is a plateau (partly desert, partly steppe) mainly above 14,000 ft, with great mountain ranges running east-west (*HIMALAYAS, *KUNLUN, *TIFN SHAN, *NAN SHAN). Highest peak: Ulagh Muztagh, 25,340 ft. The plateau is wooded along the India-Burma border and in W. Szechwan. In central China it drops (along a line running through Kansu, W. Szechwan and Yunnan) to 1,500–6,000 ft, except in the Chinling Shan Mtns. This region is partly cultivated (esp. central Szechwan and the loess-covered Hwang-ho basin in Shensi and Shansi), but parts (esp. in Kweichow and Kwangsi-Chuang) are rugged and uninhabited. The far north (Inner Mongolia and adjoining regions) is steppe. The plateau continues (except for the low Si-kiang delta region, Kwangtung) across the southeast (Hunan, Kiangsi, Fukien, Chekiang), most of which is intensely cultivated (rice, tea), with forests near the coast. Central E. China (E. Hupei, Honan, Hopei, Shantung, Kiangsi, Anhwei) is a great cultivated plain around the Yangtse-kiang and Hwang-ho deltas (cereals, cotton). The northeast (Manchuria) is a cultivated plain watered by the Amur, Shungari and Yalu, and enclosed by forested mountains (*KHINGAN) on the northwest, north, and east. N.E. China has cold, dry, windy winters. S.E. China is warm and humid all the year and muggy in summer. Rainfall is heaviest in the southeast, where there are regularly four or five typhoons a year. Annual rainfall: N. Manchuria 9 ins, Harbin 21 ins, Peking 25 ins, Shanghai 44 ins, Chungking 43 ins, Canton 65 ins. Average winter and summer temperatures (F.): N. Manchuria −15° and 70°, Peking 24° and 79°, Shanghai 38° and 81°, Chungking 46° and 70°, Canton 56° and 84°. 80% of the population is rural. In 1958, 500,000,000 peasants were grouped in 26,578 'Peoples' Communes'. Livestock: sheep and goats, cattle, horses, pigs. The water buffalo is the principal farm animal. Main crops (N. and central E. China): wheat, cotton, sorghum, millet, tobacco, barley, oats, flax, peas, soya beans (esp. in Manchuria), hemp, cotton (S.E. China), rice, tea, silk, beans, tung seeds, bamboo, sugarcane, (far south) citrus fruits, litchis, bananas, ginger, cassia (65% of world total). Fisheries are important. Chief forest products: tung oil (90% of the world's production) and teak, the country's most important wood. Bamboo grows in the south. Mineral resources: (in the west and north) coal, gold, iron, copper, lead, zinc, silver, tungsten (principal world producer), mercury, antimony, tin, manganese, oil, salt. Manufactures: textiles, esp. cotton, flour milling, rice milling, steel (in Anshan, Wuhan and Paotow), pig iron, lumber, tobacco, electricity, leather, chemicals, cement, matches, paper, porcelain, lacquer, parasols, fans. Exports: raw materials. Imports: oil, food and manufactured goods. Ports: Talien, Tientsin, Shanghai, Canton. The Grand Canal (1,000 miles) links Hangchow and Peking. New roads link Szechwan and Chinghai with Tibet. New railroads link Peking with Ulan Bator, and N.W. Kansu with Sikiang and the Trans-Siberian. There are 227 institutes for higher learning, including 15 universities. Monetary unit: jen min piao (yuan), divided into 10 chiao

and 100 fen. HISTORY. Early Chinese history consists of legends and myths concerning the emperor, Son of Heaven, and the origin and development of Chinese society along the Yellow River. The historic period began with the Chou dynasty (1122–221 B.C.), the third of 22 dynasties. It was the age of great Chinese philosophy, of Confucianism, Taoism, Mohism, Legalism. The Ch'ins (221–209 B.C.) created an empire based on Legalist principles. The Hans (206 B.C.–220 A.D.) ended Chinese isolation, created stability, and attempted to control their barbarian neighbors. Buddhism was introduced (1st c. A.D.) and dominated the period of the Three Kingdoms (220–589). The empire was reunited and considerably expanded under the Suis (590–618) and consolidated by the T'angs (618–906). After another period of fragmentation (907–960), peace was restored under the Sungs (960–1279) and the arts flourished. The Mongol invasion (1210) under Genghis Khan established the Yuan dynasty (1279–1368). By 1360 revolt was widespread. Mongol oppression provoked a new isolation policy under the Mings (1368–1644), whose power was weakened by corruption and foreign infiltration. The early Manchu rulers reestablished the Chinese Empire under the Ch'ing dynasty (1644–1912) (*TZU HSI). Government ineptitude in the 18th c. and the increasing efforts of foreign powers to exploit trade relations led to six major clashes, notably the Taiping rebellion (1850–65), the Opium War (1839–42), the Arrow War (1856–60), and the 1st Sino-Japanese War (1894–95), and the development of secret antiforeign societies (e.g. Triad, Boxer). By 1900 China was divided into spheres of influence, the European powers claiming special rights. After many attempts at reform, the dynasty was overthrown (1911) and Sun Yat-sen was installed as provisional president of the republic. Yüan Shih-kai, an imperial general, was appointed president (1912), but his monarchist policies led to anarchy and an increase in the power of the warlords after his death (1916). The Kuomintang and the Nationalist government formed under Chiang Kai-shek (1926) restored order and the Chinese Communists went to Yenan. Japan invaded Manchuria (1931). The 2nd Sino-Japanese war (1931–45) temporarily stopped the conflict between the Nationalists and the Communists under Mao Tse-tung. At the end of the 2nd world war civil war was resumed until Chiang Kai-shek was expelled to Taiwan (1949). A people's republic was formed (Sept. 21, 1949) and economic rehabilitation progressed rapidly under the five-year plan of 1953–7 and 1959–62. In 1966 Mao Tse-tung launched the Cultural Revolution. Border disputes arose with India (1964-6) and with the U.S.S.R. (1969). The first Chinese earth satellite was launched (Apr. 1970). The People's Republic replaced (Oct. 1971) Taiwan in the United Nations. Soon after Mao's death (1976) the moderate leader Teng Hsaio-p'ing took control and ties with the U.S. were strengthened; diplomatic relations were restored (1979). The excesses of the Cultural Revolution were officially condemned and a campaign of party reform began (1984). An agreement was reached with Britain on the future of Hong Kong (1984) and tensions eased with the U.S.S.R. in the early 1980s
chi·na (tʃáinə) 1. *n.* a twice-fired, finegrained ceramic ware used esp. for eating and drinking utensils and ornaments ‖ porcelain ‖ any crockery 2. *adj.* made of china [after *China*=ware from China]
chi·na·ber·ry (tʃáinəbẹri:) *pl.* **chi·na·ber·ries** *n. Sapindus saponaria,* a shrub found in the U.S.A. and Mexico. Its stem and roots contain saponin, which forms a lather with water
china clay kaolin
chi·na·graph pencil (tʃáinəgræf, tʃáinəgrʊf) a pencil for marking a hard glazed surface, e.g. the talc of a map case
china grass ramie
China, Great Wall of *GREAT WALL OF CHINA
China Sea part of the Pacific Ocean, lying between China, Indochina, Borneo, the Philippines and Japan. North of Formosa it is called the East China Sea, south of Formosa the South China Sea
china stone partly decomposed granite, used as a flux in making glass and glaze
Chi·na·town (tʃáinətạun) *n.* the part of any non-Chinese town where the Chinese colony

mainly lives (e.g. in San Francisco, Liverpool etc.)
chi·na·ware (tʃáinəwçɐr) *n.* china
China watcher one specially knowledgeable of China and its government
China White 1. a pure, rare strain of heroin from Southeast Asia (which see). **2.** (lowercase) a white paint often used as a correction fluid
chincapin *CHINQUAPIN
chinch (tʃintʃ) *n.* a chinch bug ‖ a bedbug [Span. *chinche*]
chinch bug *Blissus leucopterus,* a small black and white insect destructive to grasses and cereal crops, esp. in dry weather ‖ a bedbug [Span. *chinche*]
chin·chil·la (tʃintʃílə) *n.* a member of *Chinchilla,* a genus of South American rodents, closely allied to rabbits, with long hind legs and a bushy tail. The soft, pearl-gray fur, used for coats, is very valuable ‖ a breed of rabbit with a fur resembling that of the chinchilla ‖ a woolen fabric with a long soft nap [Span. perh. dim. of *chinche,* a bug]
Chin-chow (dʒíndʒóu) *CHINHSIEN
Chin·dit (tʃíndit) *n.* a Burmese who fought in Wingate's task force in the 2nd world war
Chin·dwin (tʃíndwin) a river in W. Upper Burma about 550 miles long, chief tributary of the Irrawaddy
chine (tʃain) 1. *n.* a cut of meat or fish including part of the backbone ‖ (*geol.*) a ridge or arête 2. *v.t. pres. part.* **chin·ing** *past* and *past part.* **chined** to cut through or remove the backbone of [fr. O.F. *eschine,* spine]
Chin·ese (tʃainí:z, tʃainí:s) 1. *n.* a native of China ‖ the Chinese language 2. *adj.* belonging to China ‖ coming from China ‖ in Chinese style
Chinese artichoke *ARTICHOKE
Chinese cinnamon an essence produced by distillation of the bark of *Cinnamonium cassia*
Chinese fire drill (*used disparagingly*) highly disorganized event
Chinese language the most important member of the Indo-Chinese group, spoken by over 600 million people in China, Mongolia and S.E. Asia. Dialects: Northern (official), Southern and Southwestern Mandarin (together spoken by 80% of the mainland population), Cantonese, Kan-Hakka (Kiangsi), Amoy-Swatow, Foochow, Wu (Kiangsu-Chekiang), Hsiang (Hunan). It has had a great influence on other Eastern languages, comparable to that of Greek and Latin in the West. It is a tone language and is monosyllabic, with no grammatical inflection. The standard dialect is that of Peking. The written language has remained largely unchanged for over 1,000 years and is common to all the dialects. It consists of characters representing a combination of sounds and ideas, and is written vertically. A roman script was introduced by government order (1958) for the transcription of Chinese characters in books and newspapers. A Chinese script, simplified in its form and with fewer characters, and written horizontally from left to right, has also been introduced. Both systems are in use, alongside the older form
Chinese lantern a collapsible paper lantern used esp. for decoration at outdoor parties
Chinese puzzle any intricate puzzle such as those made by the Chinese ‖ a highly complicated situation, set of instructions, genealogical table etc.
Chinese restaurant syndrome temporary symptoms affecting some who have ingested monosodium glutamate, esp. in Chinese cuisine
Chinese white zinc white
Ch'ing (tʃiŋ) *MANCHU
Chingan *KHINGAN
Chin Hills (tʃin) a mountain range, largely jungle-covered, of N.W. Burma in the special division of the Chins
Chin·hsien (dʒinʃjén) a town (pop. 352,000) in Liaoning province, N.E. China, on the Tientsin-Shenyang railroad, at the head of the Gulf of Liaotung
chink (tʃiŋk) 1. *n.* a narrow crack or opening, e.g. in a wall or door **a chink in someone's armor** (*Br.* **armour**) a factor in a person's character which makes them susceptible to persuasion, or vulnerable in some way 2. *v.t.* to fill up the chinks in [origin unknown]
chink 1. *n.* a light, ringing sound, e.g. of coins or glasses knocking together 2. *v.i.* to make this sound ‖ *v.t.* to cause (something) to make this sound [imit.]

chinkapin *CHINQUAPIN
Chin·kiang (tʃínkjáŋ), a port (pop. 201,000) on the Yangtze-kiang, the Grand Canal, and the Nanking-Shanghai railroad in Kiangsu province, E. China: textiles
Chin-ling Shan, Tsin-ling Shan (tʃínlínʃán) a mountain range (rising to 12,000 ft), rich in coal, forming a barrier between N. and S.E. central China
chi·no (tʃí:nou) *n.* Mexican term for a Spanish-American
chi·noi·se·rie (ʃi:nwazərí:, ʃi:nwózəri:) *n.* a style in costume, furniture, decoration, architecture etc., much in vogue in Europe in the 18th c., that was Chinese in inspiration or was intended to look so [F.]
Chi·nook (tʃinúk, ʃinúk) *n.* an Indian belonging to the linguistic group of Chinookan Indians of North America, formerly from the region of the Columbia River in Oregon ‖ this people ‖ either of their languages (Lower Chinook, Upper Chinook)
chi·nook (tʃinúk, ʃinúk) *n.* a warm dry wind blowing down the eastern slopes of the Rocky Mountains at intervals ‖ a warm, moist southwest wind of the coastal regions of Oregon and Washington
chin·qua·pin, chin·ca·pin, chin·ka·pin (tʃíŋkəpin) *n. Castanea pumila,* fam. *Fagaceae,* a sweet chestnut tree of North America ‖ the nut of this tree ‖ *Castanopsis chrysophylla,* a tree of California and Oregon ‖ its edible nut [N. Am. Indian]
chin turret (*mil.*) in a bomber or gunship, a gun turret located below the nose of the plane
chintz (tʃints) 1. *n.* a strong, sometimes glazed, cotton fabric with a printed design, used for upholstery etc. 2. *adj.* made of chintz **chintz·y** *comp.* **chintz·i·er** *superl.* **chintz·i·est** *adj.* (*pop.*) cheap, of poor quality [fr. Hindi *chint* fr. Skr.]
Chin·wang·tao (tʃínhwáŋdáu) an ice-free port (pop. 186,000) in N.E. Hopei, China
Chiog·gia (kjódʒa) Italy's largest fishing port (pop. 50,000), on the lagoon of Venice
Chi·os (káios, káious, kí:ɒs, kí:ous) (Khios) a Greek island (area 320 sq. miles, pop. 67,000) of the Cyclades in the Aegean. First colonized by the Ionians, it was held by the Turks (1566–1912). Products: wine, fruit, marble, antimony ‖ its capital (pop. 24,000)
chip (tʃip) 1. *n.* a small fragment broken or cut from wood, china, glass, stone etc. ‖ (*electr.*) miniaturized wafer disc of silicon on which an integrated circuit is printed ‖ a mark made by chipping ‖ the place in an object where a chip has broken away ‖ a counter in a gambling game ‖ (*Br.*) a chip basket or one of its thin strips of split wood ‖ (*Br.*) a French fry ‖ *PO-TATO CHIP* **to be a chip off the old block** to be just like one's father in appearance or character **to have a chip on one's shoulder** to be aggressively touchy 2. *v. pres. part.* **chip·ping** *past* and *past part.* **chipped** *v.t.* to cut or break a fragment off (wood, stone etc.) (*Br.*) to cook (potatoes) as French fries ‖ *v.i.* to become chipped ‖ to be liable to become chipped, *this china chips easily* ‖ (*golf*) to play a chip shot **to chip in** to place a chip or chips (counters) as a share of the stake in a gambling game ‖ to share expenses ‖ (*Br.*) to interrupt conversation in order to assert something [prob. O.E. *cippian*]
chip basket (*Br.*) a very light basket of strips of split wood with air spaces between the slats, used esp. for marketing soft fruit
chip·munk (tʃípmʌŋk) *n.* any of several species of small, squirrel-like animals of the genera *Tamias* and *Eutamias,* found in North America [N. Am. Indian]
chipped beef smoked beef cut in very thin slices
Chip·pen·dale (tʃípəndeil), Thomas (c. 1718–79), English cabinetmaker whose graceful, fundamentally strong furniture is much reproduced. At various periods he worked in Louis XV, Chinese and Gothic styles
chip·per (tʃípər) *adj.* (*pop.*) lively, cheerful [perh. rel. to CHIRRUP]
Chip·pe·wa (tʃípəwɑ, tʃípəwei, tʃípəwə) *pl.* **Chip·pe·was, Chip·pe·wa** *n.* one of the Ojibwa Indians of North America ‖ their language
Chip·pe·way (tʃípəwei) *pl.* **Chip·pe·ways, Chip·pe·way** *n.* a Chippewa ‖ the Chippewa language
chipping sparrow *Spizella passerina,* a common North American sparrow that likes to nest where there are houses
chip shot (*golf*) a short, steeply rising shot

Chi·qui·to·an (tʃikíːtouən) *n.* an independent linguistic family of South American Indians of E. Bolivia [Span.]

chi·ral (tʃírəl) (*particle phys.*) characteristic of the spin of a particle, positive if always parallel to its momentum, negative if antiparallel. — **chirality** *n.*

chi-rho (kíːróu, káirou) a symbol for Christ, formed of Greek X (chi) and P (rho) from 'Christos'(*LABARUM)

Chi·ri·co (kíːriːkɔ), Giorgio de (1888–1978), Italian painter, born in Greece, whose work had a profound influence on surrealism. He painted hallucinatory landscapes in which realistic images create an emotional effect by being placed in vast, dreamlike space. Stark architectural forms and sharp contrast of light and shade intensify the sense of strangeness

Chi·ri·quí (tʃiːriːkíː) a volcanic peak (11,070 ft) in W. Panama, near the Costa Rican border

chi·ro·man·cer (káirəmænsər) *n.* a person skilled in chiromancy

chi·ro·man·cy (káirəmænsiː) *n.* palmistry, the art of divining a person's character and future by studying the palm of his hand [fr. Gk *cheir*, hand + *manteia*, divination]

Chi·ron (káirɒn) (*Gk mythol.*) one of the centaurs, son of Kronos, and teacher of Achilles

chi·rop·o·dist (kairópədist, kirópədist) *n.* a person professionally qualified to treat minor disorders of the feet **chi·rop·o·dy** (kairópədiː, kirópədiː) *n.* the care of the feet and treatment of ailments of the feet [fr. Gk *cheir*, hand + *pous* (*podos*), foot]

chi·ro·prac·tic (kairəpræktik) *n.* the manipulation of the spinal vertebrae in an attempt to cure various ailments **chi·ro·prac·tor** *n.* [fr. Gk *cheir*, hand + *praktikos*, effective]

chi·rop·ter (kairóptər) *n.* a member of *Chiroptera* (*Cheiroptera*), the order of mammals comprising the bats **chi·róp·ter·an, chei·róp·ter·an** *n.* and *adj.* [Mod. L. fr. Gk *cheir*, hand + *pteron*, wing]

chirp (tʃəːrp) 1. *n.* a short, sharp sound made by a small bird, a cricket or grasshopper ‖ sound or other wave variation due to a variation of frequency 2. *v.i.* to make such a sound ‖ to talk brightly ‖ *v.t.* to say with a chirping sound [imit.]

chirp·i·ness (tʃéːrpiːnis) *n.* the state or quality of being chirpy

chirp·y (tʃéːrpiː) *comp.* **chirp·i·er** *superl.* **chirp·i·est** *adj.* bright, lively, in good spirits

chirr (tʃəːr) 1. *n.* a long, dry, trilling sound, e.g., of a cricket or grasshopper 2. *v.i.* to make such a sound [imit.]

Chir·ri·pó Gran·de (tʃirriːpóːgránde) a mountain (12,589 ft) in central Costa Rica, the highest point in the country

chir·rup (tʃírəp, tʃéːrəp) 1. *n.* a series of short sharp sounds or chirps 2. *v.i. pres. part.* **chir·rup·ing** *past* and *past part.* **chir·ruped** to make this noise [imit.]

chis·el (tʃíz'l) 1. *n.* any of various steel hand tools with a beveled cutting edge for cutting or shaping wood, stone or metal (*COLD CHISEL) 2. *v.t. pres. part.* **chis·el·ing,** *Br.* also **chis·el·ling** *past* and *past part.* **chis·eled,** *Br.* also **chis·elled** to cut or shape (wood, stone or metal) with a chisel ‖ to cheat or defraud **chis·eled,** *Br.* also **chis·elled** *adj.* worked with a chisel ‖ fine, clear-cut, *chiseled features* [O.N.F.]

chisel bond wire attached to a contact pad of a semiconductor with a chisel-shape tool

Chis·holm Trail (kízəm) (*Am. hist.*) a cattle trail, famous in frontier lore, by which drovers brought Texas herds to the Kansas rail heads for 20 years after the Civil War. It ran from San Antonio, Texas, to Abilene, Kansas [after Jesse *Chisholm* (1806–68), a Cherokee Indian trader]

chi-square test (tʃáiskwéər) (*statistics*) test of statistical significance for nominal variables. *Cf* FISHER EXACT PROBABILITY TEST

chit (tʃit) *n.* a pert girl or young woman [var. of *kit* (kitten)]

chit *n.* a short note, esp. a requisition ‖ a note of a sum owed, esp. for food or drink [shortened fr. Hindi *citthi*]

Chi·ta (tʃitá) a town (pop. 315,000) in E. Siberia, U.S.S.R., center of a mining and lumber district: iron foundries, leather and fur industries

chit-chat (tʃíttʃæt) *n.* gossip [CHAT]

Chit·i·ma·cha (tʃiːtəmáʃə) *pl.* **Chit·i·ma·cha, Chit·i·ma·chas** *n.* an Indian people of Louisiana. The murder (1706) of the French missionary St Cosme involved them in war with

France, which they ended by presenting the French with the head of his murderer ‖ a member of this people ‖ their language [perh. Choctaw *Chutimasha*=they have pots for cooking]

chi·tin (káitin) *n.* a nitrogenous polysaccharide forming the horny exoskeletal substance in arthropods [F. *chitine* fr. Gk *chitōn*, tunic]

chi·ton (káitɒn, káitɒn) *n.* a member of fam. *Chitonidae,* esp. genus *Chiton,* of eyeless, gill-breathing amphineurans. Chitons have a shell consisting of eight overlapping plates, are oval and flattened, and adhere to rocks ‖ a garment hanging from the shoulders, worn in ancient Greece [Gk *chitōn,* tunic]

Chit·ta·gong (tʃíttəgɒŋ) the chief port (pop. 1,388,476) of Bangladesh on the Karnaphuli River. Exports: tea, mineral oil, jute, cotton, rice, hides

chit·ter·ling (tʃítərliŋ, tʃílin) *n.* (usually *pl.*) the smaller intestines of animals, esp. fried or boiled for food [origin unknown]

chit·ty (tʃíti) *pl.* **chit·ties** *n.* a chit (short note) [Hindi]

chiv·al·ric (ʃívəlrik, ʃivælrik) *adj.* chivalrous of chivalry

chiv·al·rous (ʃívəlrəs) *adj.* (of men) respectful of women ‖ having the characteristics of the ideal medieval knight: courteous, honorable, ready to help those in need ‖ pertaining to the age of chivalry [O.F. *chevalerous* fr. *chevalier,* knight]

chiv·al·ry (ʃívəlri) *n.* honorable behavior, esp. to women ‖ the social and moral conventions of the medieval knights ‖ the qualities (courtesy, honor, defense of the weak etc.) of an ideal knight ‖ (*hist.*) knights and fighting noblemen collectively, *England's chivalry* [F. *chevalerie,* horsemen]

—Orders of chivalry are of three kinds: (a) religious orders of lay nobles, founded during the Crusades to protect pilgrims, e.g. the Knights Hospitalers (b) princely orders, founded by various rulers, e.g. the Order of the Garter (c) orders of merit, founded in the 18th and 19th cc. as a means of honoring subjects, e.g. the Legion of Honor

chive (tʃaiv) *n. Allium schoenoprasum,* fam. *Liliaceae,* an Old World hardy perennial plant allied to the onion. The leaf is used for seasoning [fr. F. *cive*]

chiv·y, chiv·vy (tʃívi) *pres. part.* **chiv·y·ing, chiv·vy·ing** *past* and *past part.* **chiv·ied, chiv·vied** *v.t.* to urge persistently, nag, worry to make **chivy someone up** (*Br.*) to make someone hurry [orig. *chevy,* perh. fr. the Battle of Chevy Chase, a skirmish near the Cheviot Hills]

Chka·lov (tʃkáləf) *ORENBURG

Chlam·y·dom·o·nas (klæmidómənəs) *n.* a genus of flagellates or algae found in vast numbers in fresh water and damp soil [Mod. L. fr. Gk *chlamus,* a mantle+ Mod. L. *monas* fr. Gk *monos,* single]

chla·myd·o·spore (kləmídəspɔr, klæmídəspour) *n.* a single-celled, thick-walled resting spore in certain fungi and bacteria [fr. Gk *chlamyd-* fr. *chlamys,* a mantle+SPORE]

chlo·ral (klɔ́rəl, klóurəl) *n.* a colorless, oily liquid, CCl₃CHO, used in the manufacture of DDT ‖ (*loosely*) chloral hydrate [fr. CHLORINE+ALCOHOL]

chloral hydrate [CCl₃CH(OH)₂] a compound having anesthetic and narcotic properties

chlor·am·bu·cic [C₁₄H₁₉Cl₂NO₂] (klɔræmbjúːsik) *n.* (*pharm.*) drug product of nitrogen mustard used in treatment of leukemia and Hodgkins disease; marketed as Leukeran

chlo·ra·mine (klɔ́rəmiːn, klóurəmiːn, klɔræmiːn, klouræmiːn) *n.* any of three products formed from the reaction of dilute hypochlorous acid with ammonia, esp. NH₂Cl, a pungent, colorless, bactericidal liquid [CHLORINE+AMINE]

chlo·ram·phen·i·col (klɔræmféniːkɔl, klouræmféniːkɔl) *n.* (*med.*) an antibiotic obtained from a soil microorganism and also manufactured synthetically, used in the treatment of certain diseases caused by bacteria, viruses or rickettsia, esp. typhoid fever. Chloromycetin is its trade name [CHLORINE+AMIDE+PHENOL+NITRATE+GLYCOL]

chlo·rate (klɔ́reit, klóureit, klɔ́rit, klóurit) *n.* a salt of chloric acid [CHLORINE]

chlor·di·a·ze·pox·ide [C₁₆H₁₄ClN₃O] (klɔrdaiəzepɒ́ksaid) *n.* (*pharm.*) tranquilizer used in treatment of alcoholism and other mental diseases; marketed as Librium

chlo·ric (klɔ́rik, klóurik) *adj.* pertaining to or obtained from chlorine

chloric acid a strong unstable acid, HClO₃

chlo·ride (klɔ́raid, klóuraid, klɔ́rid, klóurid) *n.* a compound of chlorine with some other substance

chloride of lime bleaching powder

chlo·rin·ate (klɔ́rineit, klóurineit) *pres. part.* **chlo·rin·at·ing** *past* and *past part.* **chlo·rin·at·ed** *v.t.* to treat or cause to combine with chlorine or a chlorine compound **chlo·rin·a·tion** *n.* treatment with chlorine, esp. the disinfecting of swimming pools

chlorinated hydrocarbon (*chem.*) class of persistent broad-spectrum nondegradable, synthetic pesticides, e.g., DDT, dieldrin, aldrin, endrin, lindare, chlordane, etc.

chlo·rine (klɔ́riːn, klóuriːn, klɔ́rin, klóurin) *n.* a gaseous greenish-yellow element (symbol Cl, at. no. 17, at. mass 35.453). It occurs widely in nature in combination with metals, e.g. as sodium chloride in seawater. It is extremely reactive, and is used as a bleaching, disinfecting and oxidizing agent [fr. Gk *chlōros,* green]

chlor·ma·di·none acetate [C₂₁H₂₇ClO₃] (klɔrmádinoun) *n.* (*pharm.*) pregnancy-preventive drug; *abbr.* CA.

chlor·mer·o·dren [C₅H₁₁ClHgN₂O₂] (klɔrméroudrin) *n.* (*pharm.*) oral diuretic used in treatment of edema and kidney diseases; marketed as Neohydrin

chlor·o·a·ce·to·phe·nome [C₈H₇ClO] (klɔroupsetóufenoum) *n.* (*chem.*) an intermediate product in organic synthesis, with an apple-blossom odor. It is used as a tear gas

chlo·ro·fluo·ro·car·bon (klɔroufluəroukárbən) *FLUOROCARBON

chlo·ro·form (klɔ́rəfɔrm, klóurəfɔrm) 1. *n.* a colorless, volatile heavy liquid, CHCl₃, used as an anesthetic and as a solvent 2. *v.t.* to anesthetize with chloroform ‖ to treat with chloroform [F. *chloroforme* fr. CHLORINE+FORMYL]

chlo·ro·my·ce·tin (klɔroumaisíːt'n, klourou maisíːt'n) *n.* *CHLORAMPHENICOL

chlo·ro·phyll, chlo·ro·phyl (klɔ́rəfil, klóurəfil) *n.* a green pigment found in chloroplasts in plant cells, that is essential to photosynthesis and is formed only in the presence of light [F. *chlorophylle* fr. Gk]

chlo·ro·plast (klɔ́rəplæst, klóurəplæst) *n.* a plastid containing chlorophyll found in plant cells. It is the site of photosynthesis and starch formation [fr. Gk *chlōros,* green+*plastos,* formed]

chlo·ro·sis (klɔróusis, klouróusis) *n.* an anemic disease in young women, a symptom of which is a greenish color in the skin ‖ (*bot.*) an abnormal condition in plants characterized by absence of green pigments, due to magnesium or iron deficiency **chlo·rot·ic** (klɔrótik, klourótik) *adj.* [fr. Gk *chlōros,* green]

chlor·pro·ma·zine [C₁₇H₁₉ClN₂S] (klɔrpróməziːn) *n.* (*pharm.*) antipsychotic, depressant drug, developed as an antiemetic and useful in treatment of radiation sickness and some symptoms of carcinoma; marketed as Thorazine

chlor·prom·pa·mide [C₁₀H₁₃ClN₂O₃S] (klɔrprópamaid) *n.* (*pharm.*) drug used in treatment of hypoglycemia; marketed as Diabinese

Choate (tʃout), Joseph Hodges (1832–1917), U.S. trial lawyer and diplomat. He obtained the repeal (1895) of the income tax law of 1895. He served (1899–1905) as ambassador to Great Britain and (1907) as leader of the U.S. delegation to the second Hague Conference

Cho·ca·no (tʃokáno), José Santos (1875–1934), Peruvian lyric poet, protector of the Indians, and exponent of socialist and revolutionary ideas

chock (tʃɒk) 1. *n.* a block or wedge used to fix something in position temporarily, or prevent its rolling ‖ (*naut.*) a metal or wooden fitting with two restraining arms between which ropes may pass in mooring etc. 2. *adv.* as close or tight as possible, *chock against the wall* 3. *v.t.* to make fast, prevent from rolling with chocks ‖ to place a boat on chocks ‖ (with 'up') to fill too full, *a cupboard chocked up with odds and ends* [perh. fr. O.N.F. *choque,* log]

chock-a-block (tʃɒ́kəblɒk) *adv.* crammed, filled to capacity

chock-full (tʃɒ́kfúl) *adj.* chockablock

choc·o·late (tʃɒ́kəlit, tʃɒ́kəlit, tʃɒ́klit, tʃɒ́klit) 1. *n.* a food product made from the seeds of cacao, roasted and ground, often sweetened ‖ a small candy made e.g. of fondant, caramel or nuts, coated with chocolate ‖ a hot drink made from chocolate and milk 2. *adj.* flavored with chocolate ‖ of a brown color resembling that of chocolate [F. *chocolat* fr. Mex.]

Choc·taw (tʃɔ́ktɔ) *pl.* **Choc·taws, Choc·taw** *n.* a North American Indian of Muskogean people now living in Oklahoma ‖ this people ‖ their language

choice (tʃɔis) *adj.* (esp. commercial contexts) of high quality, carefully selected [perh. M.E. *chīs*, nice + CHOICE n.]

choice *n.* the act of choosing or selecting, *to make a choice* ‖ the right or possibility of choosing, *to have no choice* ‖ something chosen ‖ a variety from which to choose, *a wide choice* ‖ an alternative **for choice** (*Br.*) preferably [M.E. *chois* fr. O.F.]

choir (kwáiər) **1.** *n.* a group of singers giving public performances, a choral society ‖ a group of singers leading the singing in a church ‖ the part of a cathedral, abbey or church between the nave and the sanctuary **2.** *v.t.* (*rhet.*) to sing (a hymn etc.) in chorus ‖ *v.i.* (*rhet.*) to sing in chorus [M.E. *quere* fr. O.F. *cuer* fr. L. fr. Gk]

choir·boy (kwáiərbɔi) *n.* a boy member of a choir in a church, cathedral etc.

choir loft a gallery in a church, where the choir can be near the organ

choir·mas·ter (kwáiərmæstər, kwáiərmɑstər) *n.* the musical director and conductor of a church choir or of a choral society

Choi·seul (ʃwæzə:l), Etienne François, duc de (1719–85), French statesman. As foreign minister (1758–70) he negotiated the Family Compact (1761) and the Treaty of Paris (1763). He acquired Lorraine (1766) and Corsica (1768) for France

choke (tʃouk) **1.** *v. pres. part.* **chok·ing** *past* and *past part.* **choked** *v.t.* to stop or almost stop from breathing, by applying pressure on the windpipe or by blocking it ‖ to asphyxiate ‖ to block up, *weeds choked the river* ‖ to restrict the air intake of (an internal-combustion engine) so as to produce a richer fuel mixture ‖ (with 'back', 'down') to repress (emotion) with difficulty ‖ (with 'down') to force oneself to eat (something) ‖ (with 'off') to silence or discourage (someone) ‖ *v.i.* to be unable to breathe ‖ to be inarticulate (with emotion) ‖ to suffer strangling or suffocation **2.** *n.* the act of choking ‖ the sound of choking ‖ the valve controlling the air intake in an internal-combustion engine ‖ (*elec.*) a reactor [M.E. *cheken, choken,* fr. O.E. *acēocian*]

choke·ber·ry (tʃóukbɛri:) *pl.* **choke·ber·ries** *n.* the small berrylike fruit of any shrub of the genus *Aronia* ‖ any shrub of this genus ‖ the astringent cherrylike fruit of *Pyrus arbutifolia*

choke·bore (tʃóukbɔr, tʃóukbouʀ) *n.* the slightly narrowed part of a sporting gun barrel at the muzzle end

choke·cher·ry (tʃóuktʃeri:) *pl.* **choke·cher·ries** *n.* the bitter cherry borne by *Prunus virginiana* and *P. demissa* ‖ either of these North American cherry trees

choke·damp (tʃóukdæmp) *n.* blackdamp ‖ white damp

chok·er (tʃóukər) *n.* a necklace fitting closely around the neck ‖ a narrow neckpiece of fur ‖ (*hist.*) a man's high stiff collar

chok·y, chok·ey (tʃóuki:) *comp.* **chok·i·er** *superl.* **chok·i·est** *adj.* tending to choke, esp. with emotion, *a choky voice* ‖ causing choking, *a choky atmosphere*

chol·er (kɔ́lər) *n.* (*hist.*) one of the four humors ‖ (*rhet.*) anger, bad temper [M.E. *coler* fr. O.F. fr. L. fr. Gk]

chol·er·a (kɔ́lərə) *n.* a highly dangerous and infectious disease, outbreaks of which occur esp. in India and central China. The cholera bacterium is transmitted through infected food and water. It causes a profuse, painless, watery diarrhea with consequent extreme dehydration, weakness and often death [L. fr. Gk = name of a disease]

chol·er·ic (kɔ́lərik, kəlérik) *adj.* inclined to be irritable [F. *cholérique* fr. L. fr. Gk]

cho·le·sta·sis, *pl* **-ses** (kɔləstéisis) *n.* (*med.*) obstruction of gall bladder and flow of bile. — **cholestatic** *adj.*

cho·les·ter·ol (kəléstəroul, kəléstərɔl, kəléstərɔl) *n.* (*biochem.*) a fat-soluble crystalline steroid alcohol, found in all animal tissues and fluids, esp. in nervous tissue [fr. Gk *cholē,* bile + *stereos,* stiff]

cho·line (kóuli:n, kóli:n, kóulin, kólin) *n.* a nitrogenous base, $C_5H_{15}NO_2$, found in lecithin. It is essential in fat metabolism in many plants and animals and is a vitamin of the B complex [fr. Gk *cholē,* bile]

cho·lin·o·lyt·ic (kɒlinɒlítik) *adj.* of interference with the sympathetic and parasympathetic system. —**cholinolytic** *n.*

Cho·lon (ʃɔlõ) a town (pop. 230,000) of Vietnam outside Ho Chi Minh City, a rice market and industrial center (*SAIGON)

Chom·ski·an or **Chomskyani** (tʃɔ́mski:ən) *adj.,* (*linguistics*) of generative conception of linguistic principles established by Avram Noam Chomsky of MIT. *Cf* DEEP STRUCTURE; GENERATIVE GRAMMAR

chon·ta (tʃɔ́ntə) sharpened dowel used as a defensive weapon in India

choose (tʃu:z) *pres. part.* **choos·ing** *past* **chose** (tʃouz) *past part.* **cho·sen** (tʃóuz'n) *v.t.* to select from a number, or between alternatives ‖ (*theol.* esp. *past part.*) to select for salvation ‖ *v.i.* to make a choice ‖ to decide **cannot choose but** have no alternative but **chóos·y, chóos·ey** *comp.* **choos·i·er** *superl.* **choos·i·est** *adj.* (*pop.*) fastidious, hard to please [O.E. *cēosan*]

chop (tʃɒp) **1.** *v. pres. part.* **chop·ping** *past* and *past part.* **chopped** *v.t.* to cut by striking or dividing with a sharp instrument, *to chop wood* ‖ to hit (a ball) with a short cutting stroke, usually so that it spins ‖ *v.i.* to use a chopper ‖ to hit a ball with a short cutting stroke **2.** *n.* a cutting stroke with a sharp instrument ‖ a cut of pork, mutton or veal including a rib or part of a rib ‖ (*boxing*) a short, downward blow ‖ the short, irregular, broken motion of waves [var. of CHAP]

chop *pres. part.* **chop·ping** *past* and *past part.* **chopped** *v.i.* (in phrases) **to chop and change** (*Br.*) to decide first one thing then another, be always changing one's mind, plans etc. **to chop about** (or **around**) (*naut.,* of the wind) to veer, change direction suddenly ‖ *v.t.* (in the phrase) **to chop logic** (*Br.*) to be argumentative [etym. doubtful]

chop·fall·en (tʃɒpfɔlən) *adj.* chapfallen

Cho·pin (ʃɔpẽ), Frédéric François (1810–49), Polish composer and pianist. His father was French. His work is almost entirely for the piano (mazurkas, waltzes, nocturnes, polonaises etc.). It is characterized by its romantic, penetrating, utterly personal character, often melancholy or elegiac. Chopin's exploration of technique, extension of the piano's scope, and his harmonic imagination are all prodigious

chop·per (tʃɒpər) *n.* a short-handled ax for cutting wood etc. ‖ a butcher's chopping tool ‖ a kitchen utensil for chopping vegetables ‖ (*pop.*) a helicopter ‖ (*electr.*) device that interrupts an electrical current, light, or other radiation at regulated intervals to create an alternating signal that can be more easily amplified ‖ (*pop.*) custom-made motorcycle

chop·py (tʃɒpi:) *comp.* **chop·pi·er** *superl.* **chop·pi·est** *adj.* (of the sea) agitated, with small tossing waves ‖ (of the wind) changing suddenly or irregularly

chops (tʃɒps) *pl. n.* the chaps of an animal

chop·stick (tʃɒpstik) *n.* a slender stick of wood or ivory used in pairs by the Chinese and other Eastern peoples for eating with [pidgin English = nimble stick]

chop su·ey (tʃɒpsú:i:) *n.* a Chinese dish of chopped meat fried or stewed with rice, onions, pea shoots, soy sauce etc. [Chin. = mixed bits]

cho·ral (kɔ́rəl, kóurəl) *adj.* sung or intended for singing by a choir ‖ pertaining to a choir [F.]

cho·rale, cho·ral (kərǽl, kɔ́rəl, kóurəl) *n.* a hymn tune of simple rhythm, adapted from plainsong, and sung originally in the German Protestant Church ‖ (in some titles) a choir [G. *choral*]

chorale prelude an instrumental work (esp. for organ) based on a chorale

choral speaking the speaking of poetry or prose by a group in unison (esp. in classical drama as a commentary on the action of the play)

chord (kɔrd) *n.* an emotional response, *to touch the right chord* ‖ (*physiol.*) a part of the body resembling a string ‖ (*math.*) a straight line joining two points on a curve ‖ (*engin.*) a principal member of a truss framework, usually horizontal along the top or bottom edge ‖ (*aeron.*) a straight line joining the trailing and leading edges of an airfoil section [respelling of CORD like L. *chorda*]

chord *n.* (*mus.*) a simultaneous combination of notes, either concord or discord **chórd·al** *adj.* [orig. *cord* fr. *accord*]

chor·date (kɔ́rdeit) **1.** *n.* a member of *Chordata,* the highest phylum of animals, including vertebrates having at some stage in their develop-ment a dorsal notochord, a tubular dorsal nervous system, and pharyngeal gills or gill clefts **2.** *adj.* of or relating to a chordate [fr. L. *chorda,* cord]

chord organ simplified organ producing chords when buttons are pressed

chore (tʃɔr, tʃour) *n.* an odd job ‖ a boring or tiresome job ‖ a recurrent farm or household task [var. of CHAR]

cho·re·a (kərí:ə, kɔrí:ə, kourí:ə) *n.* any of various nervous diseases, of either infectious or organic origin, causing uncontrollable spasmodic twitching of the body (commonly called St. Vitus's dance) [L. *chorea (Sancti Viti),* dance (of St Vitus), fr. Gk]

cho·re·o·graph (kɔ́ri:əgræf, kɔ́ri:əgrɑf, kóuri:əgræf, kóuri:əgrɑf) *v.t.* to create the choreography for ‖ *v.i.* to be a choreographer [back formation fr. CHOREOGRAPHY]

cho·re·og·ra·pher (kɔri:ógrəfər, kouri:ógrəfər) *n.* someone who composes choreography

cho·re·o·graph·ic (kɔ̀ri:əgrǽfik, kòuri:əgrǽfik) *adj.* of or relating to choreography

cho·re·og·ra·phy (kɔ̀ri:ógrəfi:, kòuri:ógrəfi:) *n.* the art of arranging a dance performance and the notation of the steps of the dances in detail [fr. Gk *choreia,* dancing + *graphē,* writing]

cho·re·ol·o·gist (kɔ̀ri:ɒ́ləʒist) *n.* one who records dance steps, esp. for ballet

cho·ri·amb (kɔ́ri:æmb, kóuri:æmb) *n.* a metrical foot (– ‿ ‿ –) made up of a trochee and an iamb [fr. L. fr. Gk *choriambos* fr. *choreios,* dancing + *iambos,* iamb]

cho·ric (kɔ́rik, kóurik) *adj.* in the style of a chorus in a Greek play ‖ pertaining to such a chorus [fr. L. *choricus* fr. Gk]

cho·ri·on (kɔ́ri:ɒn, kóuri:ɒn) *n.* a vascular embryonic membrane enclosing the amnion, a specialized portion of which acts as the site of nutriment absorption from the parent. The chorion and the allantois take part in placenta formation in higher mammals **cho·ri·ón·ic** *adj.* [Gk = skin]

cho·ri·pet·al·ous (kɔ̀ripét'ləs, kòuripét'ləs) *adj.* having separate petals [fr. Gk *chori-,* apart + PETAL]

chor·is·ter (kɔ́ristər, kóristər) *n.* a member of a church or cathedral choir, esp. a choirboy [fr. M.L. *chorista*]

cho·roid (kɔ́rɔid, kóurɔid) **1.** *adj.* of delicate and highly vascular membranes **2.** *n.* a layer ('coat') of heavily pigmented tissue in an eye, between the retina and the sclerotic covering [fr. Gk *chorioeidēs*]

cho·rol·o·gy (kɔróləʒie) *n.* (*biol.*) the study of geographic distributions of organisms

cho·ro·pleth map (klɔ́rɔpleθ) shaded map in which degrees of shading indicate relative frequencies of certain phenomena, or, for some commodities, etc., the number per unit in the area

Cho·ro·te·ga (tʃɔrɔtéga) *pl.* **Cho·ro·te·ga, Cho·ro·te·gas** *n.* an Indian people of Honduras, Nicaragua and Costa Rica. Their language and customs disappeared during the colonial period ‖ a member of this people ‖ their language [Span.]

Cho·ro·tí (tʃəroutí:) *pl.* **Cho·ro·tí, Cho·ro·tís** *n.* a South American Indian people, numbering about 3,000, inhabiting the Bolivia-Paraguay-Argentina boundary region and subsisting on agriculture, fishing and simple pottery making ‖ a member of this people ‖ their language [Span., of Amerind origin]

chor·tle (tʃɔ́rt'l) **1.** *n.* a gleeful chuckle **2.** *v.i. pres. part.* **chor·tling** *past* and *past part.* **chor·tled** to utter such a chuckle [coined by Lewis Carroll]

cho·rus (kɔ́rəs, kóurəs) **1.** *n.* a group of singers or dancers in musical comedy etc. ‖ a secular choir ‖ the refrain of a song in which a number of singers join the solo voice ‖ the group of singers and dancers in early Greek plays, esp. those who commented chorally on the action ‖ one of the speeches of such a chorus ‖ the person speaking the prologue and commenting on the action in 16th-c. English plays ‖ any remark made by several people simultaneously, *a chorus of 'hellos'* **in chorus** (speaking) simultaneously **2.** *v.t.* to sing (music) or utter (greetings etc.) in chorus ‖ *v.i.* to sing or speak in chorus [L. fr. Gk *choros*]

chorus girl a girl in the chorus of a musical show, cabaret etc.

Cho·rzów (xɔ́ʒu:f) (former Königshütte) a Polish town (pop. 150,000), center of the Upper Silesian industrial region: iron and steel works,

CONCISE PRONUNCIATION KEY: **(a)** æ, c*a*t; ɑ, c*a*r; ɔ f*a*wn; ei, sn*a*ke. **(e)** e, h*e*n; i:, sh*ee*p; iə, d*ee*r; ɛə, b*ea*r. **(i)** i, f*i*sh; ai, t*i*ger; ə:, b*i*rd. **(o)** o, *o*x; au, c*ow*; ou, g*oa*t; u, p*oo*r; ɔi, r*oy*al. **(u)** ʌ, d*u*ck; u, b*u*ll; u:, g*oo*se; ə, b*a*cill*u*s; ju:, c*u*be. x, lo*ch*; θ, *th*ink; ð, bo*th*er; z, *Z*en; ʒ, cor*s*age; dʒ, sa*v*age; ŋ, oranguta*ng*; j, *y*ak; ʃ, fi*sh*; tʃ, fe*tch*; 'l, rabb*le*; 'n, redd*en*. Complete pronunciation key appears inside front cover.

chose 175 **christy**

coal, zinc and iron mining, glass, brick and chemical works

chose past of CHOOSE

Cho·sen (tʃóusen) *KOREA

chosen (tʃóuz'n) past part. of CHOOSE

Chosen People (Bible) the Jews

chos·ism (kouʒəm) n. (Fr.) characteristic detailed description of trivia in the New Novel, esp. by Alain Robbe-Grillet of France

Chos·ro·es (kósroui:z) *KHOSRU

Cho·ta Nag·pur (tʃóutənágpuər) a lac-producing plateau region (area 27,112 sq. miles, pop. 7,516,000) in S.E. Bihar, India. Chief town: Ranchi

Chou (dʒou) a Chinese dynasty (1122–221 B.C.) under which feudalism was introduced into China and the Chinese borders were extended. The great schools of philosophy, Confucianism, Taoism, Mohism and Legalism, arose in this classical period of China's history

Chou En-lai (dʒóuénlái) (1898–1976), Chinese Communist statesman. He was foreign minister and premier from 1949 until his death and served continuously on the Politburo (1927–76)

chough (tʃʌf) n. a member of Pyrrhocorax, a genus of birds of the crow family, generally black with red beak, legs and toes [M.E. choge]

chou pastry (ʃuː) a light soufflé pastry used for éclairs etc.

Chow (tʃau) n. a dog of a breed believed to have come from N. China, with a very thick, soft coat, prick ears, and purplish tongue, resembling a husky in build [origin unknown]

chow·chow (tʃáutʃau) n. a Chinese preserve of pickled orange peel and ginger [pidgin English]

Chow Chow a Chow

chow·der (tʃáudər) n. a New England dish of fish or clams or other foods stewed in milk with bacon, onion etc. [fr. F. chaudière, saucepan fr. chaud, hot]

chow mein (tʃaumein) n. a Chinese dish of noodles fried with meat (chicken, pork, beef etc.) or fish, and vegetables. Chinese restaurants in the West usually serve shredded chicken with mushrooms, celery, onions etc. and fried noodles [Chin. ch'ao, to fry + mien, flour]

chres·tom·a·thy (krestóməθiː) pl. **chres·tom·a·thies** n. a collection of literary passages, esp. intended for those learning a language [fr. Gk chrēstomatheia, fr. chrēstos, useful + mathein, learn]

Chré·tien de Troyes (kreitjɛ̃dətrwæ) 12th-c. French poet, author of poems based on the Arthurian legends, notably 'Erec et Enide' (c. 1170), 'Yvain' (c. 1177), 'Lancelot' and the unfinished 'Perceval', works which established the tradition of courtly love in French literature

chrism, chris·om (krízəm) n. the consecrated oil used for anointing in baptism, confirmation and ordination in the Catholic and Orthodox Churches [O.E. crisma fr. L. fr. Gk]

Christ (kraist) the anointed king or Messiah of Jewish prophecy, sometimes conceived of as a military leader who would conquer the Jews' oppressors, sometimes held to be a supernatural being sent by God to destroy and recreate the earth, purging it of evil ‖ the title given to Jesus by his followers, who believed that his coming fulfilled the Messianic prophecies [O.E. crist fr. L. fr. Gk christos, anointed]

Chris·ta·del·phi·an (krjstədélfiːən) n. a member of a sect originating (1844) with John Thomas (1805–71), an English doctor who immigrated to Brooklyn, New York. It accepts the whole Bible as a divine guide, rejects much of orthodox Christian doctrine, and seeks the establishment of a universal theocracy

Christ·church (kráisttʃəːrtʃ) the largest city (pop. 172,400, with agglom. 325,700) of South Island, New Zealand, on the east coast. It is the capital of Canterbury province, with its port at Lyttelton, 7 miles away. Industries: meat-packing, tanning. University of Canterbury (autonomous since 1962)

chris·ten (krís'n) v.t. to receive (a person usually an infant) into the Christian Church by baptism ‖ to name (a child) formally, at baptism ‖ to name (a ship) at its launching [O.E. cristnian, to make Christian]

Chris·ten·dom (krís'ndəm) n. the whole body of members of the Christian Church ‖ all countries professing Christianity as opposed to those professing other religions [O.E. cristendōm]

chris·ten·ing (krís'niŋ, krísniŋ) n. the religious ceremony of baptizing and naming a child, and the social festivities which normally follow

Chris·tian (krístʃən, Br. esp. krístjən) 1. n. a person who believes in the doctrines of Jesus and acknowledges his divinity ‖ (loosely) a person having the qualities expected of one who professes Christianity 2. adj. pertaining to the doctrines of Jesus ‖ believing in the doctrines and divinity of Jesus ‖ (loosely) having the qualities expected of a Christian [fr. L. Christianus]

Christian I (1426–81), king of Denmark (1448–81), Norway (1450–81) and Sweden (1457–64), founder of the Oldenburg dynasty. He failed (1471) to subdue Sweden, but brought Schleswig and Holstein under the Danish crown (1460)

chris·ti·a·ni·a (kristjúːni:ə, kristʃi:æni:ə, kristi:æni:ə) n. a swinging movement of the body used in skiing, in order to make a turn during descent [after Christiania, former name of Oslo]

Christian II (1481–1559), king of Denmark and Norway (1513–23) and Sweden (1520–3). His massacre (1520) of Swedish nobles and his legal reforms in Denmark provoked a rebellion by the nobles (1522). He was deposed (1523) and imprisoned (1532) until his death

Chris·ti·an·i·ty (kristʃi:æniti:) n. the religion of those who accept Jesus Christ as God incarnate, are guided by the Holy Spirit, and participate in the fellowship of the Christian Church ‖ the state of being a Christian [fr. L. Christianitas]

—Christianity came into being (c. 30 A.D.) when the Apostles received the power of the Holy Spirit to preach the resurrection and gospel of Christ. Jesus had placed the Jewish idea of the Kingdom of God at the center of his teaching, but gave the idea a new spiritual, universal meaning. He taught that God is present wherever individuals enter into the relationship of love which God is seeking to establish with them. This relationship was established by Jesus at the cost of his crucifixion by men who rejected his claims. The relationship of love transcends time and space: the disciples of Jesus felt a continuing relationship with him which, though broken by his crucifixion, was restored by his resurrection. The most influential of the Apostles was Paul, the founder of Christian theology, whose missionary journeys ensured that Christianity would not be simply another Jewish sect. Between two periods of persecution in the latter half of the 1st and 3rd cc., Christianity established itself throughout the Roman Empire as a highly organized hierarchy separate from the State and predominantly Gentile. By the 2nd c. bishops, presbyters and deacons had emerged. In the 3rd c. diocesan bishops replaced congregational bishops, and the jurisdiction of the bishops of Rome, Constantinople, Antioch, Alexandria and Jerusalem (the patriarchs) extended beyond the diocese. In 313 Constantine accorded to Christianity the rights and toleration previously enjoyed by paganism, and in 380 Theodosius established it as the one and only State religion. From the outset Christianity nourished controversy and heresy. In the 2nd c. the early Church safeguarded its institutional orthodoxy against the perils of Arianism, Montanism and Gnosticism (in its early form of Marcionism) by convoking synods and ecumenical councils, formulating creeds, establishing the canon of the Bible, and setting up the Apostolic succession. Following the Council of Nicaea (325), the Origen controversy and the Apollinarian, Nestorian and Monophysite heresies provoked further conciliar definition of the nature of the Trinity at Chalcedon (451) and Constantinople (680).

Monasticism, based on ascetic discipline, was already a feature by the 4th c. In the West Christianity stopped the advance of Islam in 732 (by arms) and of Saxon paganism in the 9th c. (by conversion). The issue of papal authority led to a schism between Rome and Constantinople, apparent in the 9th c. and made permanent in 1054 (*ORTHODOX EASTERN CHURCH). In the 13th and 14th cc. further schismatic tendencies appeared in the West with the Waldensian, Albigensian, Hussite and Lollard movements. In the early 16th c. the Reformation led to the division of Western Christianity into Protestants and Roman Catholics, a schism rendered permanent by the Council of Trent (1545–63).

In the 20th c. Protestants, Orthodox and Catholics began to come together in the ecumenical movement.

Christianity has molded the shape of Western civilization, and has been carried by missionaries to nearly all the countries of the world. It has almost 890,000,000 adherents

Christian IV (1577–1648), king of Denmark and Norway (1588–1648). He was at war with Sweden (1611–13 and 1643–5). He invaded Germany (1625) in support of the Protestants in the Thirty Years' War, but was defeated (1626). His court was an intellectual center, and commerce prospered during his reign

Christian IX (1818–1906), king of Denmark (1863–1906). He annexed Schleswig (1863), precipitating war (1864) with Prussia and Austria, which resulted in the loss of both Schleswig and Holstein

Chris·tian·ize (krístʃənaiz, Br. esp. krístjənaiz) pres. part. **Chris·tian·iz·ing** past and past part. **Chris·tian·ized** v.t. to convert to Christianity ‖ to give a Christian character to

Christian name the name or names given at baptism, as distinct from the family name (*SURNAME)

Christian X (1870–1947), king of Denmark (1912–47) and of Iceland (1918–44)

Christian Brothers the Brothers of the Christian schools (*JEAN BAPTISTE DE LA SALLE)

Christian era the years since Christ's birth (Roman year 753)

Christian Schools, Order of the Brothers of the *JEAN BAPTISTE DE LA SALLE

Christian Science a Protestant sect founded (1866) in the U.S.A. by Mrs Mary Baker Eddy (1821–1910), who claimed that health depends only on right mental attitudes, illness being an illusion of nonexistent matter. Her 'Science and Health with Key to the Scriptures' (1875) is the sect's textbook

Christians of St Thomas indigenous Christians of the Malabar coast of India, who claim to have been evangelized by St Thomas (Didymus)

Chris·ti·na (kristí:nə) (1626–89), queen of Sweden (1632–54), whose court was a center of learning, attracting such men as Descartes and Grotius. A convert to Roman Catholicism, she abdicated (1654), and retired (1667) to Rome

Christ·mas (krísməs) n. the annual festival observed by Christians on Dec. 25, commemorating the birth of Christ ‖ the Christmas season [O.E. Cristes mæsse, Christ's Mass]

Christmas box (Br.) money given at Christmas to the garbage collectors and others who provide a service throughout the year (*BOXING DAY)

Christmas card a greeting card sent at Christmas

Christmas Island an island (area 55 sq. miles, pop. 3,018, mainly Chinese and Malayan) southwest of Java. Sole industry: exporting phosphate of lime from guano deposits. The island, visited by the Dutch (17th c.), was annexed (1888) by the British, and transferred (1958) to Australian jurisdiction

Christmas Island *LINE ISLANDS

Christmas pudding a rich steamed pudding containing dried fruit and candied peel with sugar, spices etc., eaten traditionally at Christmas

Christmas rose Helleborus niger, fam. Ranunculaceae, a dark-leaved evergreen plant whose white or purplish flowers blossom during winter months

Christ·mas·tide (krísməstaid) n. the days around the festival of Christmas

Christmas tree a conifer decorated at Christmas time with candles, colored lights, tinsel etc.

Christ of the Andes a statue on the border between Argentina and Chile, on the Buenos Aires–Santiago highway, symbolizing eternal peace between the two republics

Chris·tol·o·gy (kristólədʒi:) n. the aspect of theology concerned with definitions of the limits of the human and divine nature of Jesus Christ [fr. CHRIST + Gk logos, discourse]

Chris·tophe (kri:stóf), Henri (1767–1820), Haitian black emancipated slave, president (1806) and king (from 1811) of northern Haiti. He built his capital at Cap Haïtien

Chris·to·pher (krístəfər), St (3rd c.), the patron saint of travelers, martyred c. 250. Feast: July 25

chris·ty (krísti:) pl. **chris·ties** n. a christiania

CONCISE PRONUNCIATION KEY: (a) æ, cat; ɑ, car; ɔ fawn; ei, snake. (e) e, hen; iː, sheep; iə, deer; ɛə, bear. (i) i, fish; ai, tiger; ə:, bird. (o) o, ox; au, cow; ou, goat; u, poor; ɔi, royal. (u) ʌ, duck; u, bull; uː, goose; ə, bacillus; juː, cube. x, loch; θ, think; ð, bother; z, Zen; ʒ, corsage; dʒ, savage; ŋ, orangutang; j, yak; ʃ, fish; tʃ, fetch; 'l, rabble; 'n, redden. Complete pronunciation key appears inside front cover.

chro·ma (króumə) n. (of a color) saturation [fr. Gk chróma, color]

chro·mate (króumeit) n. (chem.) a salt or ester of chromic acid [CHROMIUM]

chro·mat·ic (kroumǽtik, krəmǽtik) adj. colored or relating to color, esp. with respect to hue or saturation ‖ (mus.) having notes other than those in the diatonic scale ‖ (biol.) relating to the staining properties of cell material ‖ (biol.) of or like chromatin [fr. Gk chrómatikos fr. chróma, color]

chromatic aberration distortion of an optical image produced by the dispersion of light passing through a lens and generally characterized by blurred multicolored edges

chro·mat·i·cal·ly (kroumǽtikli:, krəmǽtikli:) adv. in a chromatic manner

chro·mat·ics (kroumǽtiks, krəmǽtiks) n. the science of color

chromatic scale (mus.) a scale composed of semitones

chromatic semitone (mus.) the interval between a note and its sharp or flat

chro·ma·tid (króumətid) n. (biol.) one of the chromosomal strands resulting from chromosomal duplication (*MITOSIS, *MEIOSIS) [fr. Gk chróma (chrómatos), color]

chro·ma·tin (króumətin) n. (biol.) a substance in cells consisting of deoxyribonucleic acid and basic proteins, distinguished by its staining properties at different stages in cell development, and considered to be the bearer of genes [fr. Gk chróma (chrómatos), color]

chro·ma·tism (króumətizəm) n. natural coloring ‖ (optics) chromatic aberration [fr. Gk chróma (chrómatos), color]

chro·ma·to·graph·ic (kroumətəgrǽfik, kroumætəgrǽfik) adj. of or pertaining to chromatography **chro·ma·to·graph·i·cal·ly** adv.

chro·ma·tog·ra·phy (kroumətógrəfi:) n. a modern method of continuous or batch chemical analysis and separation based on the preferential adsorption of different components of a gas, liquid or solid mixture or solution as it contacts an adsorbent medium (e.g. paper, certain liquids, chalk). Each component appears at a different zone or at a different time in a flow process and may then be identified. Widely used chromatographic techniques are gas-liquid, liquid-solid and liquid-liquid chromatography (where the first term is the state of the mixture to be separated and the second the state of the separating medium) [fr. Gk chróma (chrómatos), color+graphé, writing]

chro·ma·tol·o·gy (kroumətóladʒi:) n. chromatics ‖ a treatise on color [fr. Gk chróma, color+logos, discourse]

chro·ma·to·phore (króumətəfɔr, kroumǽtəfɔr, kroumǽtəfour) n. a cell containing pigment, whose contractile processes enable the skin of some animals (e.g. chameleon, frog, cephalopods) to change color **chro·ma·to·phor·ic** (kroumətəfɔ́rik, kroumǽtəfɔ́rik) adj. [fr. Gk chróma, color+-phoros, bearing]

chro·ma·tron (króumətron) n. television color picture tube with one gun that deposits phosphorous on the screen in sequential strips (vs. dots), with the beam deflected by horizontal grid wires. also Lawrence tube

chrome (kroum) n. chromium ‖ chrome yellow [F. fr. Gk chróma, color]

chrome green chromic oxide (Cr_2O_3), anhydrous or hydrated, used in green pigments

chrome red basic lead chromate, Pb_2OCrO_4, used as a pigment

chrome steel a steel and chromium alloy whose characteristics include hardness and resistance to oxidation and corrosion, depending on the percentage of chromium present (*STAINLESS STEEL)

chrome yellow lead chromate, $PbCrO_4$, used as a pigment

chro·mic (króumik) adj. of, derived from or containing chromium, esp. when chromium is tervalent

chro·mite (króumait) n. an ore containing chromium, in the compound $FeCr_2O_4$, from which chromium is obtained

chro·mi·um (króumiəm) n. a metallic element (symbol Cr, at. no. 24, at. mass 51.996), not occurring freely in nature, but produced from chromite. Its special properties, e.g. hardness, resistance to corrosion and wear, are used in alloys with steel (*CHROME STEEL) and nickel, and in electroplating

chro·mo·lith·o·graph (kroumɔlíθəgræf, kroumɔlíθəgrɑf) n. a colored picture printed by lithography **chro·mo·li·thog·ra·pher** (krou-mouliθógrəfər) n. **chro·mo·lith·o·graph·ic** (kroumouliθəgrǽfik) adj. **chro·mo·li·thog·ra·phy** (kroumouliθógrəfi:) n. [fr. Gk chróma, color+LITHOGRAPH]

chro·mo·ne·ma (kroumouní:mə) pl. **chro·mo·ne·ma·ta** (kroumouní:mətə) n. the coiled core of a chromatid, thought to contain the genes [Mod. L. fr. Gk chróma, color+nema, thread]

chro·mo·plast (króuməplæst) n. a colored plastid or pigment body ‖ (bot.) a colored plastid other than a chloroplast, containing pigments [fr. Gk chróma, color+plastos, formed]

chro·mo·ra·di·om·e·ter (kroúmoureidi:ómitər) n. gauge to measure X-ray radiation, indicated by color changes

chro·mo·some (króuməsoum) n. a microscopic, thread-like bundle of deoxyribonucleic acid molecules which collectively carry the hereditary material in subunits called genes. They may be observed during meiosis and mitosis [fr. G. chromosom fr. Gk]

chromosome number the number of chromosomes in the nucleus characterizing a species of plant or animal

chro·mo·sphere (króuməsfiər) n. (astron.) a colored, irregular incandescent layer of ionized and neutral gases (mostly hydrogen) surrounding the photosphere to a distance of about 3,000 miles. There are many small, transient, high-speed jets of gas ejected to heights reaching 10,000 miles from the low chromosphere. The temperature of the chromosphere increases with distance outward, reaching 20,000°C. from a minimum of 4,500°C. in the upper photosphere (*CORONA, cf. SOLAR PROMINENCE, cf. SOLAR FLARE) ‖ a similar gaseous layer around a star **chro·mo·spher·ic** (krouməsférik) adj. [fr. Gk chróma, color+SPHERE]

chro·mous (króuməs) adj. of, derived from or containing chromium, esp. when chromium is bivalent

chron·ic (krónik) adj. (of disease) longlasting, deep-seated (cf. ACUTE) ‖ constant, inveterate, a chronic smoker ‖ (Br. pop.) very bad, a chronic performance **chrón·i·cal·ly** adv. **chro·nic·i·ty** (krɔnís-iti:) n. (of disease) the state or quality of being chronic [F. chronique fr. L. fr. Gk]

chronic dose radiation dose absorbed in circumstances such that biological recovery may be, or have been, possible, e.g., absorption occurring after 24 hours following a nuclear explosion

chron·i·cle (krónik'l) 1. n. a list of events in the order in which they happened ‖ a narrative of events, esp. a medieval history 2. v.t. pres. part. **chron·i·cling** past and past part. **chron·i·cled** to record (events) in a chronicle **chrón·i·cler** n. a writer of chronicles, esp. a medieval historian [M.E. cronikle fr. A.F.]

Chron·i·cles (krónik'lz) two books of the Old Testament, which reinterpret the history of Judah given in Kings

chron·is·tor (krónistər) n. (electr.) miniaturized timing device to compute the use of equipment

chron·o·gram (krónəgræm) n. a phrase or motto, the Roman numeral letters of which can be added up to make a date, e.g. 'haLLoweD be thy naMe'= 50+ 50+500+1000=1600. Cabalists find significance in such things **chron·o·gram·mat·ic** (krɔnougrəmǽtik) adj. [fr. Gk chronos, time+gramma, letter]

chron·o·graph (krónəgræf, krónəgrɑf) n. an instrument for recording and measuring time [fr. Gk chronographos fr. chronos, time+graphé, writing]

chron·ol·o·ger (krɔnólədʒər) n. someone practicing or skilled in chronology

chron·o·log·i·cal (krɔn'lódʒik'l) adj. of or relating to chronology

chro·nol·o·gist (krɔnólədʒist) n. a chronologer

chro·nol·o·gy (krɔnólədʒi:) pl. **chro·nol·o·gies** n. the science of measuring time and fixing dates ‖ order of occurrence, the chronology of Shakespeare's plays is still uncertain ‖ an arrangement (list, table, treatise etc.) in order of occurrence [fr. Gk chronos, time]

chro·nom·e·ter (krɔnómitər) n. an instrument measuring the passage of time with great accuracy, esp. one used in navigation for determining position [fr. Gk chronos, time+METER]

chron·o·met·ric (krɔnəmétrik) adj. relating to or done by chronometry **chron·o·mét·ri·cal** adj.

chro·nom·e·try (krɔnómitri:) n. the science of measuring time [fr. Gk chronos, time+metria, process of measurement]

chron·o·scope (krónəskoup, króunəskoup) n. an instrument for measuring very small intervals of time [fr. Gk chronos, time+skopos, watcher]

chrys·a·lid (krísəlid) 1. n. a chrysalis 2. adj. of or relating to a chrysalis

chrys·a·lis (krísəlis) pl. **chrys·a·li·des** (krisǽlidi:z), **chrys·a·lis·es** n. the pupa of certain insects, esp. butterflies and moths at the state between caterpillar or larva and fully developed imago [L. fr. Gk chrusallis fr. chrusos, golden]

chry·san·the·mum (krisǽnθəməm) n. a member of Chrysanthemum, fam. Compositae, a genus of widely cultivated, autumn-flowering, perennial plants from China and Japan. There are many varieties [L. fr. Gk chrysanthemon, golden flower]

chrys·el·e·phan·tine (kriseləfǽntin, kriseləfǽn-tain) adj. overlaid or decorated with gold and ivory, as in classical sculpture [fr. Gk chrusos, gold+elephantinos, ivory]

Chrys·ler Corporation (kráislər) a U.S. automobile manufacturing company founded (1924) by Walter Percy Chrysler (1875–1940). Chrysler and Dodge merged in 1928, to form one of the largest companies in the U.S. automotive industry

chrys·o·ber·yl (krísəberəl) n. yellowish-green beryllium aluminate. The best varieties are used as gems [fr. L. chrysoberyllus fr. Gk]

chrys·o·lite (krísəlait) n. any of various magnesium iron silicates of an olive-green or yellow color, the most common of which is olivine. Some forms are used as gems [M.E. crisolite fr. O.F. fr. L. fr. Gk]

chrys·o·prase (krísəpreiz) n. an applegreen variety of chalcedony, used as a gem [fr. Gk chrusos, gold+prason, leek]

Chrysostom *JOHN CHRYSOSTOM

chub (tʃʌb) n. Leuciscus cephalus, a European fish of the carp family. It frequents deep holes in rivers shaded by trees. It rarely weighs over 5 lbs, and makes poor food [origin unknown]

chub·bi·ness (tʃʌ́bi:nis) n. the state or quality of being chubby

chub·by (tʃʌ́bi:) comp. **chub·bi·er** superl. **chub·bi·est** adj. (of people, esp. children) nicely plump [CHUB]

Chu·but (tʃu:bú:t) a river (c. 500 miles long) in S. Argentina, rising in the Andes Mtns and flowing east into the Atlantic

chuck (tʃʌk) n. the cut of beef or lamb between the neck and shoulder blade ‖ a block used as a chock ‖ a mechanical screw device for holding a tool in a machine (e.g. a bit in a drill) [perh. var. of CHOCK]

chuck 1. v.i. (of chickens) to cluck ‖ (of persons calling chickens) to imitate a hen's clucking 2. n. a cluck [imit.]

chuck 1. v.t. (pop.) to throw lightly, toss ‖ to tap playfully (under the chin) **chuck it!** (Br., pop.) stop that! to chuck away (pop.) to throw away, to chuck away a chance **to chuck out** (pop.) to eject **to chuck up** (pop.) to give up (something), esp. as the result of a sudden decision or whim, to chuck up one's job 2. n. a playful tap under the chin ‖ (pop.) a short throw [perh. imit.]

Chuck·chee (tʃúktʃi:) n. a Mongolic people inhabiting N.E. Siberia, U.S.S.R., on the shores of the Arctic Ocean and the Bering Sea ‖ a member of this people

chuck·er·out (tʃʌ́kəráut) pl. **chuck·ers-out** n. (Br.) a bouncer

chuck·full (tʃʌ́kful) adj. chock-full

chuck·le (tʃʌ́k'l) 1. v. pres. part. **chuck·ling** past and past part. **chuck·led** v.i. to laugh quietly with amusement, satisfaction, glee or triumph ‖ to make a sound suggesting quiet laughter, e.g. of water flowing over stones 2. n. such a laugh or sound suggesting laughter [imit.]

chuck wagon a wagon carrying provisions etc. for cowboys

chuf·fing (tʃʌ́fiŋ) n. characteristic of some rockets to burn intermittently and with an irregular noise

Chü·foo (tʃyfú:) the birthplace and burial place of Confucius in Shantung province, China

chug (tʃʌg) 1. n. the short explosive sound of an engine going steadily and rather slowly 2. v.i. pres. part. **chug·ging** past and past part. **chugged** to make such a sound **to chug along** to drive or go slowly but steadily [imit.]

chug-a-lug v. (colloq.) to drink a draft of beer without stopping

---

chuk·ker, chuk·kar (tʃʌkər) n. a period of play in the game of polo [Hindi *chakar* fr. Skr. *cakra*, wheel]

Chu·kot·ski Peninsula (tʃukótski:) (Chukchi) the northeastern extremity of Asia. It forms part of the Chukot National Area (Okrug) of the U.S.S.R.

chum (tʃʌm) n. (esp. of young people) a close friend **chúm·my** comp. **chum·mi·er** superl. **chum·mi·est** adj. intimately friendly **to be chummy with** to have as a friend [origin unknown]

chump (tʃʌmp) n. (pop.) a person who has said or done something silly ‖ (Br.) the thick end of a loin of mutton, *a chump chop* ‖ a thick lump of wood [etym. doubtful]

chun (tʃʌn) n. currency unit of South Korea, equal to 1/100 won

Chung·king (tʃúŋkíŋ, Chin. dʒúŋgíŋ) (Pahsien) an ancient town (pop. 6,000,000) on the Yangtze-kiang in Szechwan, central China, mentioned as early as 1100 B.C. It is a trade and industrial center. It was opened (1891) as a treaty port. It was the Chinese capital during the Sino-Japanese war (1937–45)

chunk (tʃʌŋk) n. a short, thick piece (of wood, bread etc.) ‖ a large amount **chúnk·y** comp. **chunk·i·er** superl. **chunk·i·est** adj. (of people) short and thickset ‖ (of objects) rather thick or heavy [perh. fr. CHUCK]

chun·nel (tʃʌnəl) n. railroad tunnel under a water channel, esp. the English Channel

Church (tʃə:rtʃ), Frederick Edwin (1826–1900), U.S. landscape painter and member of the Hudson River School. The only pupil of Thomas Cole, the school's founder, Church painted enormous landscapes, flooded with light and using multiple perspectives and meticulous detail, as in 'Niagara' (1857), 'Heart of the Andes' (1859), and 'Twilight in the Wilderness' (1860)

Church, George Earl (1835–1910), U.S. explorer. After his Amazonian explorations (1868–79), he became the leading authority on the Amazon

church (tʃə:rtʃ) 1. n. a building for Christian worship ‖ a service held in it ‖ baptized Christian men and women ‖ **Church** a particular body of Christians, *the Church of Scotland* ‖ ecclesiastical government, *Church and State* **the Church** (pop.) the clerical profession 2. v.t. to take (a woman) through the service of thanksgiving for the birth of a child [O.E. *cirice* fr. Gk]

Church Army a Church of England mission organizing canteens and hostels for servicemen and the poor, founded (1882) by Prebendary Wilson Carlile (1847–1942)

Church Father *FATHER OF THE CHRISTIAN CHURCH

church·go·er (tʃə́:rtʃgouər) n. a regular worshipper at church **church·go·ing** n. and adj.

Church·ill (tʃə́:rtʃil), Charles (1731–64), English poet and satirist, author of 'The Rosciad' (1761) etc.

Churchill, John *MARLBOROUGH, 1ST DUKE OF

Churchill, Sir Winston Leonard Spencer (1874–1965), British statesman, operator and writer, son of Lord Randolph Churchill. He was a soldier and journalist in Cuba, India, Egypt and South Africa before being elected to parliament as a Conservative member (1900). He held office in Liberal and Conservative governments (1908–29) and, out of office, he advocated military preparations after the rise of Nazi Germany and was an opponent of appeasement. He was a great war leader as prime minister, first lord of the treasury and minister of defense (1940–5). He became leader of the Opposition in parliament (1945), and was prime minister (1951–3). His writings include 'Lord Randolph Churchill' (1906) 'The World Crisis, 1916–18' (1923–9), 'Marlborough' (1933–8), 'The Second World War' (1948–53), 'A History of the English-speaking Peoples' (1956–8)

Churchill a river (1,000 miles long) of Saskatchewan and Keewatin district, Canada ‖ the town in N.E. Manitoba at its mouth, the best harbor on the south of Hudson's Bay

Church in Wales an Anglican Church disestablished from the Church of England in 1920. It has almost 200,000 members

church key (slang or colloq.) pointed instrument used for piercing the tops of cans containing liquids

church·man (tʃə́:rtʃmən) pl. **church·men** (tʃə́:rtʃmən) n. an adult male member of a

Church (old-fash.) a minister ‖ clergyman, priest **chúrch·man·ship** n.

Church Militant Christians regarded as being in constant warfare with the powers of evil

Church of Christ, Scientist *CHRISTIAN SCIENCE

Church of England the established Church in England. It was created as a national institution by the Act of Supremacy (1534), which replaced the pope's authority by that of the king as 'the only supreme head on earth of the Church of England'. The change was occasioned by Henry VIII's need to divorce Catherine of Aragon, and by his financial difficulties, which were relieved by Thomas Cromwell's suppression of the monasteries (1535–6). Few doctrinal changes were made until the reign (1547–53) of Edward VI, when the Books of Common Prayer of 1549 and 1552 showed increasingly the influence of the Reformation. After the brief return to Roman Catholicism in the reign (1553–8) of Mary, the Church of England was restored under Elizabeth I. Its doctrine, set out in the 39 Articles (1571), met growing opposition from the Puritans, whose views were rejected at the Hampton Court Conference (1604). The Authorized Version of the Bible appeared (1611). The attempts of Laud to increase the Church's ceremonial further alienated the Puritans. The Civil War ensued (1642–52), and the Long Parliament established Presbyterianism (1646). At the Restoration (1660), the episcopacy was restored. The Clarendon Code (1661–5) and a Test Act (1673) against both Nonconformists and Roman Catholics were passed. James II's attempts to evade this ended with the revolution of 1688, after which Protestantism was secured by the Bill of Rights (1689) and the Act of Succession (1701). In the 18th c. the Church of England waned, until the spiritual revival led by John Wesley, whose followers eventually separated from the Church (*METHODISM). An Evangelical party grew up within the Church. Civil disabilities were removed from non-Anglicans by the repeal (1828) of the Test and Corporation Acts and by the emancipation (1829) of Roman Catholics. In the early 19th c., High Church traditions were revived by Keble and Newman in the Oxford Movement. Parliament rejected (1928) a proposal to revise the Prayer Book. The Church is organized in 43 dioceses in the two provinces of Canterbury and York. The archbishop of Canterbury is the primate of all England. The Church Assembly (set up in 1919) submits to parliament matters relating to the Church. The convocations of York and Canterbury are the ancient assemblies of bishops and clergy. The Lambeth Conference (set up in 1867) brings together the bishops of the 327 dioceses of the worldwide Anglican Communion every 10 years

Church of Jesus Christ of Latterday Saints *MORMON

Church of Rome *ROMAN CATHOLIC CHURCH

Church of Scotland the established Church in Scotland, which is Presbyterian in polity and Calvinist in doctrine. Under the leadership of John Knox, Presbyterianism was adopted (1560) as the established religion by the Scottish parliament. The Stuarts attempted to restore episcopacy but the National Covenant (1638) reaffirmed Presbyterianism. The Scottish Presbyterians joined the parliamentary forces in the English Civil War. The Westminster Confessions were adopted (1648). The Presbyterian Church was reestablished (1690) and reconfirmed in the Act of Union (1707)

Church of South India an ecumenical Church formed in India in 1947 by the union of several Protestant Churches. Membership: about 1 million

Church slavic *OLD SLAVIC

church·ward·en (tʃə́:rtʃwɔrd'n) n. (Anglican Communion) one of two lay parish officers with limited responsibilities in parish administration (e.g. upkeep of the church fabric) ‖ (Br., hist.) a long clay tobacco pipe

church·wom·an (tʃə́:rtʃwumən) pl. **church·wom·en** (tʃə́:rtʃwimin) n. an adult female member of a Church

church·y (tʃə́:rtʃi:) comp. **church·i·er** superl. **church·i·est** adj. (pop.) absorbed in Church matters, but not necessarily spiritually minded

church·yard (tʃə́:rtʃjɑrd) n. the ground around a church, often used for burial

churl·ish (tʃə́:rliʃ) adj. ill-mannered ‖ surly [O.E. *ceorl*, a man of low rank]

churn (tʃə:rn) 1. n. a vessel in which milk or cream is shaken or stirred to produce butter ‖ (Br.) a large metal container for transporting milk 2. v.t. to make butter by beating (milk or cream) in a churn ‖ to make (butter) by working a churn ‖ to agitate violently, *the propeller churned the water* ‖ (securities) to buy and sell securities in an investment account for the purpose of generating excessive broker's commissions ‖ (with 'up') to stir with force and make soft, *its wheels churned up the path* ‖ v.i. to work a churn **chúrn·ing** n. the amount of butter made at one time [O.E. *cyrin*]

churn out to produce without thought or regard to quality

chur·ri·gue·resque (tʃuəri:gərésk) adj. of or relating to the exuberant style of baroque architecture associated with José Churriguera (1665–1723), Spanish architect

Chu·ru·bus·co (tʃu:ru:bú:skɔ) a suburb (pop. 8,000) of Mexico City. It was the site of a battle (1847) in which Gen. A. López de Santa Anna's forces were defeated by U.S. forces under Gen. Winfield Scott

Chu·shan (dʒóuʃán) an archipelago of 100 islands (pop. 400,000) off Chekiang, E. China ‖ its largest island (22 miles long, 10 miles wide)

chute (ʃu:t) n. a steep slide or trough down which things (e.g. parcels, coal) are made to pass to a lower level ‖ a quick descent of water over a slope ‖ (Br.) a swimming-pool slide wet with running water [fr. F. *chute* and Eng. SHOOT]

chut·ney (tʃʌtni:) n. a spicy condiment originating in India and made chiefly from mangoes. In other climates, tomatoes etc. are substituted [Hindi *chatni*]

chutz·pah or **chutz·pa** (xútspə) n. (Yiddish) brass, boldness, impertinence, insolence, effrontery

Chu·vash A.S.S.R. (tʃú:vaʃ) an autonomous republic (area 6,909 sq. miles, pop. 1,311,000) of the R.S.F.S.R., U.S.S.R., south of the Volga. Capital: Cheboksary

chyle (kail) n. a milky fluid in the lymphatic vessels of the abdomen. It contains emulsified fats etc. absorbed from the partly digested food in the intestines **chý·lous** adj. [F. fr. L. fr. Gk]

chyme (kaim) n. the semifluid mass of partly digested food after passing from the stomach into the small intestine, where it is digested **chý·mous** adj. [fr. L. *chymus*, stomach juice fr. Gk]

CIA Central Intelligence Agency

Cia·no (tʃánou), Count Galeazzo (1903–44), Mussolini's son-in-law and Italian foreign minister (1936–43). One of the Fascist Grand Council which ousted Mussolini (1943), he was captured and shot by the Nazis

ciao (tʃau) interj. (colloquial Italian) 1. goodbye. 2. hello

Cí·bo·la (sí:bɔla) a legendary region in N. Mexico (now New Mexico) that was believed to comprise seven cities of gold. The Spanish conquistadores went for it but found only miserable adobe huts

ci·bo·ri·um (sibóri:əm, sibóuri:əm) pl. **ci·bo·ri·a** (sibóri:ə, sibóuri:ə) **ci·bo·ri·ums** n. (eccles.) a vessel for the consecrated Host ‖ (archit.) a canopy, often over an altar or shrine [M.L. fr. Gk *kibórion*, cup]

ci·ca·da (sikéida, sikádə) n. a member of *Cicada*, a genus of homopteran insects, known for the whirring noise made by the males [L.]

cic·a·trice (síkətris) n. a scar left when a wound heals ‖ a scar left where an organ was previously attached [F.]

cic·a·tri·cle (síkətrik'l) n. a cicatrice ‖ the blastoderm in bird and reptile eggs [fr. L. *cicatricula*, little scar]

cic·a·trix (síkətris, sikéitriks) pl. **cic·a·tri·ces** (sikətráisi:z) **cic·a·trix·es** n. a cicatrice [L.]

cic·a·trize (síkətraiz) pres. part. **cic·a·triz·ing** past and past part. **cic·a·trized** v.t. to induce healing in a scar ‖ v.i. to heal by the formation of a scar [fr. F. *cicatriser*]

cic·e·ly (sísəli:) pl. **cic·e·lies** n. any of several plants of fam. *Umbelliferae*, esp. sweet cicely [perh. fr. L. *seselis*, Gk *seselis, seseli*]

Cic·e·ro (sísərou), Marcus Tullius (106–43 B.C.), Roman orator and statesman. He came from an equestrian family and supported the senatorial party. As consul, he crushed Catiline's conspiracy (63 B.C.). He sided with Pompey during the civil war (49–48 B.C.) but was subsequently allowed by Caesar to return to Rome. After Caesar's murder (44 B.C.), he violently attacked

Antony, was proscribed by the 2nd Triumvirate, and murdered by Antony's agents. Cicero was a moderate, loyal to the constitution, but his political career was often marred by timidity and irresolution. His legal and political speeches are models of Latin diction, and his clear, elegant style enormously influenced the subsequent development of Latin prose. His letters are an important source for his own life and character, and for contemporary events

cic·e·ro·ne (sɪsəróuni:, tʃɪtʃəróuni:) *n.* (*rhet.*) a guide who conducts sightseers [Ital. after *Cicero* (*Ciceronis*), the Roman orator]

Cic·e·ro·ni·an (sɪsəróuni:ən) *adj.* eloquent, oratorical in style, resembling the writings or speeches of Cicero [fr. L. *Ciceronianus*]

Cid (**Cam·pe·a·dor, the** (sid kæmpeiadɔ́r, kæmpeiadóur), (Rodrigo Diaz de Vivar, c. 1043–99), Castilian noble whose exploits in the Christian-Moorish wars (on both sides) are described in the 12th-c. Spanish 'Poem of the Cid' and in innumerable ballads. They inspired Corneille's tragicomedy 'le Cid'

ci·der (sáidər) *n.* a nonalcoholic drink made from apple juice, sweet cider ‖ (*Br.*) hard cider [M.E. *sidre* fr. O.F. fr. L. fr. Gk fr. Heb.]

Cien·fue·gos (jenfwégɔs) a town (pop. 85,200) of W. central Cuba: sugar exportation

Cie·za de Le·ón (θjéθaðeleɔ́n) Pedro (1518–60), Spanish historian. His 'Crónica del Perú' (1553) describes the exploits of Francisco Pizarro

C.I.F., c.i.f. cost, insurance and freight included in the price quoted

ci·fox (sífɒx) *n.* (*computer*) facsimile communication device that scrambles input and reassembles output

ci·ga·la (sigéilə, sigálə) *n.* a cicada [Prov. fr. L. *cicada*]

ci·gar (sigár) *n.* a roll of tobacco leaves for smoking [fr. Span. *cigarro*]

cig·a·rette, cig·a·ret (sigərét, sígərɛt) *n.* a short cylinder of finely cut tobacco rolled in very thin paper, for smoking [F.]

cigarette hull (*boat racing*) open-cockpit boat with inboard engine, used in offshore races

ci·lan·tro (silǽntrou) *n.* garnish of coriander leaves

cil·i·a (síli:ə) *sing.* **cil·i·um** (síli:əm) *pl. n.* short, hairlike cytoplasmic processes projecting from the free surface of certain cells. They are constantly in a state of active movement **cil·i·ar·y** *adj.* [L. pl. of *cilium*, eyelid]

ciliary body *pl.* **ciliary bodies** (*anat.*) the thick rim of choroid, surrounding the vertebrate eye, to which the lens is attached

cil·i·ate (síli:it, síli:eit) **1.** *n.* a member of *Ciliata*, a class of protozoans having cilia. Very varied in form and habit, they are found in waters throughout the world. Some are solitary, some colonial, and most are highly active **2.** *adj.* provided with cilia **cil·i·a·tion** (sili:éiʃən) *n.* the state or extent of being ciliate [fr. Mod. L. *ciliatus* fr. *cilia*, eyelids]

Ci·li·cia (silíʃə) an ancient region of S.E. Asia Minor which occupied the region around modern Adana, Turkey

Ci·li·cian Gates (silíʃən) *TAURUS MTNS

cilium *n.* sing. of CILIA

Ci·ma·bue (tʃi:mabú:e) (Cenni di Pepi, 1240-c. 1302), Florentine painter, pioneer of the naturalism which, in his successors, was to displace the Byzantine style. The only work certainly his is a mosaic in the cathedral at Pisa, but paintings attributed to him include frescoes at Assisi

Ci·ma·ro·sa (tʃi:maróuzə), Domenico (1749–1801), Italian composer. His many operas include 'Il Matrimonio Segreto'

ci·met·i·dine [$C_{10}H_{16}N_6S$] (saimétidi:n) *n.* (*pharm.*) histamine preceptor antagonist used in treating duodinal ulcers; marketed as Tagamet

ci·mex (sáimeks) *pl.* **cim·i·ces** (sími·si:z) *n.* the bedbug [L.=bug]

cim·me·ri·an (simíəri:ən) *adj.* shrouded in darkness, gloomy [fr. L. fr. Gk *kimmerios*, of the mythical people dwelling in perpetual gloom, as related by Homer]

Ci·mon (sáimən) (c. 502–449 B.C.), Athenian statesman and general. He defeated the Persians at Eurymedon (c. 469 B.C.) and became the chief statesman of Athens until c. 461 B.C.

cinangiograph (sinǽndʒi:əgræf) *n.* motion picture camera to record movement of isotopes, opaque dyes, etc., in the body; projected on a fluoroscope screen. —**cinangiocardiograph** *n.* —**cinangiographic** *adj.* —**cinangiography** *v.*

cin·an·gi·o·di·og·ra·phy (sinændʒi:odi:ɒgrəfi) *n.* making a motion picture of an angiograph. —**cinangiograph** *n.* —**cinangiographic** *adj.* —**cinangiodicardiography** *n.* making a film of an angiography specifically of the heart and large blood vessels. —**cinangiodicardiographic** *adj.*

cinch (sintʃ) **1.** *n.* a strong girth for a saddle ‖ (*pop.*) something done very easily ‖ (*pop.*) someone or something sure to be successful ‖ (*pop.*) a tight grip **2.** *v.t.* to put a cinch on ‖ (*pop.*) to make sure of [fr. Span. *cincha*]

cin·cho·na (sɪnkóunə) *n.* a member of *Cinchona*, fam. *Rubiaceae*, a genus of trees and shrubs native to the Andean Highlands, now widely cultivated in South America and Indonesia, yielding alkaloids from their bark (e.g. cinchonine, quinine) used medically in the treatment of malaria and coronary diseases [after the Countess of *Chinchón*, vicereine of Peru, who brought the drug to Spain]

cin·cho·nine (sɪ́nkənin, sɪ́nkənin) *n.* an alkaloid, $C_{19}H_{22}N_2O$, obtained from the cinchona and used medicinally as a quinine substitute [F.]

Cin·cin·nat·i (sinsinǽti:) an industrial city (pop. 385,457, with agglom. 1,401,403) in Ohio, on the Ohio River: machine tools, meat packing. University of Cincinnati (1873)

Cincinnati, Society of the a hereditary military organization, founded (1783) by officers of the American Revolutionary army to promote comradeship and patriotism and named after Lucius Quinctius Cincinnatus. Its headquarters are in Washington, D.C. Its branches are restricted to the 13 original states and France

Cin·cin·na·tus (sinsinéitəs), Lucius Quinctius (519–438 B.C.), Roman dictator in 458 and 439 B.C.

cinc·ture (síɲktʃər) *n.* (*old-fash.*) a girdle ‖ (*archit.*) a ring at the top and bottom of a column shaft, marking off capital and base [fr. L. *cinctura*, a girding]

cin·der (síndər) *n.* a piece of partly burned coal or other combustible material no longer flaming ‖ slag from a furnace ‖ (*pl.*) the residue of burned coal ‖ (*pl.*) lava from a volcano [O.E. *sinder*, slag]

cinder block (*Am.=Br.* breeze block) a slab made of cement and coke or coke dust or bits of cinder, used as a construction unit

Cin·der·el·la (sindərélə) *n.* (*rhet.*) a woman who is imposed on by being given all the menial jobs to do ‖ a woman who has a sudden stroke of good fortune after an unhappy period of obscurity [after the heroine of Perrault's 'Cinderella' fairy tale]

cinder track a running track made of cinders

cin·der·y (síndəri:) *adj.* of, resembling or relating to cinders

cin·e (sínə) *adj.* relating to the motion picture industry

cin·e·cam·er·a (sínəkæmərə) *n.* (*Br.*) a movie camera

cin·e·ho·log·ra·phy (sinəhoulágrəfi:) *n.* three-dimensional motion pictures utilizing laser light split into two beams

cin·e·ma (sínəmə) *n.* the art or technique of making movies ‖ (esp. *Br.*) a building where movies are shown in public [fr. F. *cinéma* fr. Gk *kinêma*, motion]

cin·e·ma·go·er (sínəməgouər) *n.* (*Br.*) a moviegoer

cin·e·ma·theque (sinəmætí:k) *n.* movie house noted for screening avant-garde, historic, unconventional, or underground films

cin·e·mat·ic (sinəmǽtik) *adj.* of, for or like the cinema **cin·e·mát·ics** *n.* the art of the cinema

cin·e·mat·o·graph (sinəmǽtəgræf, sinəmǽtəgrɑf) *n.* (*Br., old-fash.*) a film projector **cin·e·mat·o·graph·ic** (sinəmǽtəgrǽfik) *adj.* of or relating to cinematography **cin·e·ma·tog·ra·phy** (sinəmətógrəfi:) *n.* the art of motion-picture photography [F. *cinematograph* fr. Gk]

cin·e·ma vé·ri·té (sínəmə véritei) *n.* **1.** candidly realistic documentary motion pictures, esp. using on-the-scene interviews. **2.** commercial films that simulate newsreels

cin·e·phile (sínəfi:l) *n.* lover of motion pictures

cin·e·rar·i·a (sinəréəri:ə) *n.* any of the bright flowering pot plants originating from *Senecio cruentus*, fam. *Compositae*, of the Canary Islands, having ashy down on the leaves [fr. L. *cinerarius*, of ashes]

cin·e·rar·i·um (sinəréəri:əm) *pl.* **cin·e·rar·i·a** (sinəréəri:ə) *n.* a place where the ashes of the cremated dead are kept in urns [L. fr. *cinerarius*, of ashes]

cin·e·rar·y (sínərɛri:) *adj.* relating to ashes [fr. L. *cinerarius*]

cinerary urn an urn holding the ashes of the dead after cremation

cin·e·ra·tor (sínəreitər) *n.* a furnace for cremating corpses [fr. L. *cinis* (*cineris*), ashes]

cine record (sínə) *n.* a motion picture record. —**cine-record** *v.*

ci·ne·re·ous (siníəri:əs) *adj.* (esp. *biol.*) ashen gray in color [fr. L. *cinereus*, ashy]

cine-strip (sínəstrip) *n.* a sequence of motion pictures

Cin·ga·lese, Cin·ghe·lese, Sin·gha·lese (siŋgəli:z, siŋgəli:s) *n.* and *adj.* Sinhalese

cin·gu·lum (síŋgjuləm) *pl.* **cin·gu·la** (síŋgjulə) *n.* the part of a plant between the root and stem ‖ the ridge around the base of the crown of a tooth ‖ the clitellum of worms [L.=belt]

Cin·na (sína), Lucius Cornelius (d. 84 B.C.), patrician leader of the democrats at Rome and opponent of Sulla

cin·na·bar (sínəbər) *n.* the bright red mineral mercuric sulfide ‖ the artificial red form of mercuric sulfide used as a pigment [fr. L. *cinnabaris* fr. Gk perh. fr. Pers.]

cin·nam·ic (sinǽmik, sínəmik) *adj.* (*chem.*) relating to or obtained from cinnamon

cin·na·mon (sínəmən) *n.* a spice made from the bark of certain trees of the genus *Cinnamomum* ‖ a tree yielding this ‖ the yellowish-brown color of this spice ‖ its flavor [F. *cinamome* fr. L. fr. Gk]

cinq·a·sept (sáŋkəset) *n.* a 5 to 7 p.m. visit to one's lover

cinqfoil *CINQUEFOIL

cinque, cinq (siŋk) *n.* the number five, esp. at dice and cards [O.F. *cink*, five]

cin·que·cen·to (tʃiŋkwitʃéntou) *n.* the Renaissance in 16th-c. Italy, esp. with respect to its art and literature [Ital.=five hundred, short for 1500]

cinque·foil, cinq·foil (síŋkfɔil) *n.* a member of *Potentilla*, fam. *Rosaceae*, a genus of plants of temperate regions ‖ (*archit.*) an ornamental design having five cusps [M.E. *sink foil* fr. M.F. fr. L. *quinquefolium* trans. of Gk]

Cinque Ports (siŋk) the English towns Hastings, Romney, Hythe, Dover and Sandwich, together with Winchelsea and Rye. They were important for the medieval naval defense of England. The office of Lord Warden is given for distinguished service to the Crown

CIO *AMERICAN FEDERATION OF LABOR AND CONGRESS OF INDUSTRIAL ORGANIZATIONS

ci·pher, *Br.* also **cy·pher** (sáifər) **1.** *n.* a 0, zero, naught (*NUMBER TABLE) ‖ a person or thing of no importance ‖ a method of transforming a text to conceal its meaning by systematic substitution or transformation of its letters (cf. CODE) ‖ the key to such a text ‖ interwoven letters, e.g. in a monogram ‖ the continued sounding of an organ note because of a defective valve **2.** *v.i.* (of an organ) to sound one note continually ‖ *v.t.* to put (a message) into cipher [O.F. *cyfre* fr. M.L. fr. Arab. *cifr*, empty, zero (from the empty row of an abacus)]

ci·phon·y (sáifəni:) *n.* process of scrambling and unscrambling voice messages in telephone or radio communication by converting speech into on-off pulses

cir·ca (sə́:rkə) *prep.* (*abbr.* **c., ca.,** used with numerals) about, *built circa 1640* [L.]

cir·ca·di·an (sə:rkéidi:en) *adj.* repeating or performing in a 24-hr cycle, esp. in an organism. —**circadianly** *adv.* —**circadian rhythm** *n.*

cir·can·nu·al (sə:rkǽnu:əl) *adj.* of annual cycles. *syn* circannean

Cir·cas·sia (sərkǽʃə, sərkǽʃi:ə, *Br.* sə:kæsjə) a European region in the southern U.S.S.R. on the northeast coast of the Black Sea, northwest of the Caucasus Mtns. It was part of the Ottoman Empire until 1829, when it was ceded to Russia. It forms part of the R.S.F.S.R.

Cir·cas·sian (sərkǽʃən, sərkǽʃi:ən, *Br.* sə:kæsjən) **1.** *n.* a member of a group of tribes from the Caucasus in the U.S.S.R. ‖ the language of this people **2.** *adj.* of or relating to these tribes or their language [fr. *Circassia* fr. *Tcherkess*]

Cir·ce (sə́:rsi:) the enchantress in Homer's 'Odyssey' who charmed her victims and then turned them into swine

cir·ci·nate (sə́:rsineit) *adj.* (*bot.*) rolled up so that the apex is in the center (e.g. the young leaves of many ferns) [fr. L. *circinare* (*circinatus*), to make round]

cir·cle (sə́:rk'l) **1.** *n.* (*geom.*) a plane figure with a bounding edge (circumference), all points on which are equidistant from a fixed point (*RA-

DIUS ‖ (*pop.*) the circumference ‖ the area of intersection of a sphere by a plane ‖ a group of objects on the circumference of a circle ‖ a group of persons with a common interest or an exclusive group within society, *court circles* **to argue in a circle** to base a conclusion upon a premise which is itself derived from the conclusion **to come full circle** (esp. of ideas) to return to the point of departure by a circuitous path **to run around in circles** to achieve nothing because one is in a dither **2.** *v. pres. part.* **cir·cling** *past* and *past part.* **cir·cled** *v.t.* to put a circle around ‖ *v.i.* to move around, or around in, the circumference of a circle [O.E. *circul* fr. L.]

circ·le-dot mode (sá:rk'ldɒt) (*computer*) storage of binary units using a code of circles and circles with dots

cir·clet (sá:rklit) *n.* a small band or ring, e.g. of flowers, worn esp. as an ornament [F. *cerclet*, little circle]

cir·cuit (sá:rkit) **1.** *n.* a movement around an object, *they made a circuit of the city* ‖ a roughly circular boundary or route ‖ (*law*) a geographical group of towns having courts of law, visited in turn by a judge ‖ a chain of movie houses or theaters under the same ownership ‖ (*Methodism*) a group of churches associated together for organizational purposes ‖ the complete path traversed by an electric current ‖ the diagram of the connections of an electrical apparatus **2.** *v.t.* to make the circuit of ‖ *v.i.* to go or move in a circuit [F.]

circuit breaker a device for interrupting an electric circuit

circuit court a court held in different towns of a judicial district (cf. COURT OF ASSIZE)

circuit court of appeals the federal intermediate court which reviews judgments of the federal district courts

cir·cu·i·tous (sərkjú:itəs) *adj.* roundabout, indirect [fr. L. L. *circuitosus*]

circuit rider a preacher who regularly visits a number of towns and villages

cir·cu·i·ty (sərkjú:iti) *pl.* **cir·cu·i·ties** *n.* a being circuitous ‖ roundabout character, *circuity of language* [O.F. *circuité*]

cir·cu·lar (sá:rkjulər) **1.** *adj.* having the shape of a circle ‖ moving in a circle **2.** *n.* a printed advertising leaflet, notice etc., sent out in large numbers **cir·cu·lar·i·ty** (sə:rkjulǽriti) *n.* **cir·cu·lar·i·za·tion** *n.* the act of circularizing **cir·cu·lar·ize** (sá:rkjuləraiz) *v.t. pres. part.* **cir·cu·lar·iz·ing** *past* and *past part.* **cir·cu·lar·ized** *v.t.* to send circulars to ‖ to make into a circular letter [M.E. *circuler* fr. A.F.]

Circular Letter (1767) a statement issued by the Massachusetts legislature, rebutting the Townshend Acts and declaring that the colonists could be taxed only by their own assemblies. It received support from other resolutions issued by George Washington and Thomas Jefferson, but led to the dissolution of the Massachusetts Assembly the following year

circular letter a letter sent (each in manuscript or top-copy typescript) without change of wording to several people

circular measure (*math.*) the expression of an angle in radians

circular mil (*mech.*) unit of area equal to that of a circle 1 mm diameter, used in computing the cross section of round conductors, *abbr* **cir. mil.**

circular plane a compass plane

circular polarization an observable fact in which magnetically influenced polarization of light revolves clockwise or counter clockwise

circular saw a serrated disk, revolved by machinery, for sawing

circular tour a trip ending where it begins without taking the traveler over the same ground twice

cir·cu·late (sá:rkjuleit) *pres. part.* **cir·cu·lat·ing** *past* and *past part.* **cir·cu·lat·ed** *v.i.* to move around and return to a starting point ‖ to pass from place to place or from person to person, *the news quickly circulated* ‖ *v.t.* to send or pass around, *to circulate rumors* [fr. L. *circulare* (*circulatus*)]

circulating capital capital transformed in production or exchanged, e.g. raw materials, commodities, fuel

circulating library a lending library

cir·cu·la·tion (sə:rkjuléiʃən) *n.* movement in a circuit, e.g. of water or air, usually with a return to the starting point ‖ the movement of blood in the blood vessels of the body induced by the pumping of the heart, serving to distribute nutrients and oxygen and remove wastes and

carbon dioxide ‖ distribution, *circulation of a leaflet* ‖ (*fig.*) flow, *traffic circulation* ‖ the number of copies of a newspaper or magazine regularly sold [F.]

cir·cu·la·tive (sá:rkjuleitiv, sá:rkjulativ) *adj.* promoting circulation

cir·cu·la·to·ry (sá:rkjulətɔri:, sá:rkjulətouri:) *adj.* concerned with the circulation of the blood or sap [fr. L. *circulatorius*]

circulatory system the system of blood, lymph, veins, arteries, arterioles, capillaries, lymphatics and heart that is found in vertebrates

circum- (sá:rkəm) *prefix* around, surrounding [fr. L. *circum*, round about]

cir·cum·am·bi·ence (sə:rkəmǽmbiːəns) *n.* a being circumambient

cir·cum·am·bi·ent (sə:rkəmǽmbiːənt) *adj.* surrounding, esp. of air and fluids ‖ enclosing

cir·cum·am·bu·late (sə:rkəmǽmbjuleit) *pres. part.* **cir·cum·am·bu·lat·ed** *past* and *past part.* **cir·cum·am·bu·lat·ed** *v.i.* to wander about ‖ *v.t.* to walk around (an object) **cir·cum·am·bu·la·tion** *n.* **cir·cum·am·bu·la·to·ry** (sə:rkəmǽmbjulətɔri:, sə:rkəmǽmbjulətouri:) *adj.* [fr. L. *circumambulare* (*circumambulatus*)]

cir·cum·cise (sá:rkəmsaiz) *pres. part.* **cir·cum·cis·ing** *past* and *past part.* **cir·cum·cised** *v.t.* to cut off the foreskin of (males) or the clitoris of (females) as a religious rite or on medical grounds **the circumcised** (*Bible*) the Jewish race [O.F. *circonciser*]

cir·cum·ci·sion (sə:rkəmsíʒən) *n.* the act of circumcising ‖ the religious rite of purification and initiation by circumcising as practiced by Jews, Moslems etc. **Circumcision** *n.* the festival (Jan. 1) commemorating the circumcision of Christ [O.F. *circumcisiun*]

cir·cum·fer·ence (sərkʌ́mfərəns) *n.* the line bounding a circle, or its length [fr. L. *circumferentia*]

cir·cum·flex (sá:rkəmflɛks) **1.** *n.* a mark, or marks, used in ancient Greek to denote rise and fall of the voice ‖ a mark (ˆ) used in French and other languages to indicate an omitted consonant which was once part of the word ‖ a vowel so marked or pronounced **2.** *adj.* of such an accent [fr. L.] (*anat.*) curved, bending around, esp. of the nerve which winds around the shoulder bone to supply the shoulder muscles, and of certain arteries **3.** *v.t.* to mark with a circumflex accent [fr. L. *circumflectere* (*circumflexus*), to bend around]

cir·cum·flu·ent (sərkʌ́mfluːənt) *adj.* flowing around, surrounding in the manner of a fluid [fr. L. *circumfluens* (*circumfluentis*) fr. *circumfluere*, to flow around]

cir·cum·fuse (sə:rkəmfjúːz) *pres. part.* **cir·cum·fus·ing** *past* and *past part.* **cir·cum·fused** *v.t.* (*rhet.*) to pour, spread about or around ‖ to surround (with) **cir·cum·fu·sion** (sə:rkəmfjúːʒən) *n.* [fr. L. *circumfundere* (*circumfusus*)]

cir·cum·gy·rate (sə:rkəmdʒáireit) *pres. part.* **cir·cum·gy·rat·ing** *past* and *past part.* **cir·cum·gy·rat·ed** *v.i.* to turn, move around in a circling or whirling manner **cir·cum·gy·ra·tion** *n.* [fr. CIRCUM·+L. *gyrare* (*gyratus*), to turn]

cir·cum·ja·cent (sə:rkəmdʒéisənt) *adj.* situated around, bordering on every side [fr. L. *circumjacens* (*circumjacentis*) fr. *circumjacere*, to lie around]

cir·cum·lo·cu·tion (sə:rkəmloukjúːʃən) *n.* the use of many words when a few would do ‖ an indirect or roundabout expression **cir·cum·loc·u·to·ry** (sə:rkəmlɒ́kjutɔri:, sə:rkəmlɒ́kjutouri:) *adj.* [fr. L. *circumlocutio* (*circumlocutionis*)]

cir·cum·me·rid·i·an (sə:rkəmmərídiːən) *adj.* (*astron.*) about or near the meridian

cir·cum·nav·i·ga·ble (sə:rkəmnǽvigəb'l) *adj.* capable of being circumnavigated

cir·cum·nav·i·gate (sə:rkəmnǽvigeit) *pres. part.* **cir·cum·nav·i·gat·ing** *past* and *past part.* **cir·cum·nav·i·gat·ed** *v.t.* to sail around (the earth, Australia etc.) **cir·cum·nav·i·ga·tion** *n.* **cir·cum·nav·i·ga·tor** *n.* [fr. L. *circumnavigare*]

cir·cum·nu·ta·tion (sə:rkəmnu:téiʃən, sə:rkəmnju:téiʃən) *n.* (*bot.*) a movement of the growing part of a plant forming ellipses, spirals or irregular curves

cir·cum·plan·e·tar·y (sə:rkəmplǽnetery) *adj.* closely around a planet

cir·cum·po·lar (sə:rkəmpóulər) *adj.* (*astron.*) above the horizon throughout its diurnal course ‖ (*geog.*) about or near one of the earth's poles [fr. CIRCUM·+L. *polus*, pole]

cir·cum·scis·sile (sə:rkəmsísil) *adj.* (*bot.*, applied to the dehiscence exhibited by a pyxidium) splitting along a circular line [fr. L. *circumscindere* (*circumscissus*), to cut around]

cir·cum·scribe (sə:rkəmskráib, sá:rkəmskraib) *pres. part.* **cir·cum·scrib·ing** *past* and *past part.* **cir·cum·scribed** *v.t.* to draw a line around ‖ to mark the boundary of ‖ to set limits to, restrict ‖ (*geom.*) to draw a plane figure) so as to enclose another [fr. L. *circumscribere*]

cir·cum·scrip·tion (sə:rkəmskrípʃən) *n.* the act of limiting ‖ the state of being limited or confined ‖ the inscription written around anything, esp. a coin ‖ a boundary or thing which confines ‖ a circumscribed space or district **cir·cum·scrip·tive** *adj.* [fr. L. *circumscriptio* (*circumscriptionis*)]

cir·cum·so·lar (sə:rkəmsóulər) *adj.* closely around the sun

cir·cum·spect (sá:rkəmspekt) *adj.* attentive to the consequences of one's actions, cautious, discreet, prudent **cir·cum·spéc·tion** *n.* [fr. L. *circumspicere* (*circumspectus*), to look around]

cir·cum·stance (sá:rkəmstæns) *n.* an essential fact or detail ‖ (of storytelling) detail ‖ stiff ceremonial ‖ chance, fate, *the web of circumstance* ‖ (*pl.*) the elements of a total situation ‖ (*pl.*) the particular elements directly affecting a matter ‖ (*pl.*) the financial state of a person, *in easy circumstances* **cir·cum·stanced** *adj.* placed in a set of conditions, esp. with regard to financial state [O.F.]

cir·cum·stan·tial (sə:rkəmstǽnʃəl) *adj.* giving full and precise details, *a circumstantial report* ‖ incidental, related but not essential **cir·cum·stan·ti·al·i·ty** (sə:rkəmstænʃi:ǽliti:) *n.* [fr. L. *circumstantia*, conditions]

circumstantial evidence evidence made up of details tending to prove a fact by inference, but giving no direct proof

cir·cum·stan·ti·ate (sə:rkəmstǽnʃi:eit) *pres. part.* **cir·cum·stan·ti·at·ing** *past* and *past part.* **cir·cum·stan·ti·at·ed** *v.t.* to confirm or support by a statement of relevant details **cir·cum·stan·ti·a·tion** *n.* [fr. L. *circumstantia*, circumstance]

cir·cum·stel·lar (sə:rkəmstélər) *adj.* rotating around or encompassing a star

cir·cum·ter·res·tri·al (sə:rkəmteréstri:əl) *adj.* closely around the earth

cir·cum·val·late (sə:rkəmvǽleit) *adj.* (*anat.*) surrounded by a ridge ‖ (*hist.*) surrounded by a rampart **cir·cum·val·la·tion** *n.* [fr. L. *circumvallare* (*circumvallatus*), to put a rampart around]

cir·cum·vent (sə:rkəmvént, sá:rkəmvent) *v.t.* to prevent by counterstrategy, outwit, get around **cir·cum·vén·tion** *n.* [fr. L. *circumvenire* (*circumventus*), to surround, cheat]

cir·cum·vo·lu·tion (sə:rkəmvəlú:ʃən) *n.* a turning, or a turn, around an axis, a rotation ‖ a rolling or folding of one thing around another [fr. L. *circumvolvere* (*circumvolutus*), to roll around]

cir·cus (sá:rkəs) *n.* the entertainment made up of acts including performing animals, horseback riders, acrobats, clowns etc., usually held in a big tent ‖ the arena with seats around it in which the show is performed ‖ the persons and animals making up the show ‖ (*Br.*) a circular space where streets intersect ‖ (*Rom. hist.*) an arena, with tiers of seats on three sides, used for chariot races etc. ‖ (*aeron.*) a team of stunt flyers [L.]

ci·ré (siréi) *n.* lustrous patent-leather effect produced on fabric surfaces, derived from the French verb *cirer*, meaning to wax and polish

cirque (sə:rk) *n.* (*geol.*) a circular recess confined by steep mountain walls, a corrie [F. fr. L. *circus*, ring]

cir·rate (síreit) *adj.* (*biol.*) bearing a cirrus ‖ shaped like a cirrus

cir·rho·sis (siróusis) *n.* a chronic, noninfectious disease of the liver characterized by excessive formation of scar tissue, hardening and contraction. It is due to unknown causes but is associated with chronic poisoning (e.g. from excessive alcohol consumption), malnutrition or parasites [Mod. L. fr. Gk *kirros*, orange-colored]

cir·ri·ped (síriped) *n.* a member of *Cirripedia*, a subclass of sessile crustaceans including barnacles and a few parasitic forms. All are freeswimming in the larval stage [fr. L. *cirrus*, curl+*pes* (*pedis*), foot]

cir·ro·cu·mu·lus (siroukjú:mjuləs) *pl.* **cir·ro·cu·mu·li** (siroukjú:mjulai) *n.* (*meteor.*) a cloud formation of small, white, rounded masses at high altitudes, usually regularly grouped to form a mackerel sky [fr. L. *cirrus*, curl+*cumulus*, heap]

cir·rose (síərous, siróus) *adj.* (*biol.*) cirrate

CONCISE PRONUNCIATION KEY: (**a**) æ, c*a*t; ɑ, c*ar*; ɔ f*aw*n; ei, sn*a*ke. (**e**) e, h*e*n; i:, sh*ee*p; iə, d*ee*r; ɛə, b*ea*r. (**i**) i, f*i*sh; ai, t*i*ger; əː, b*i*rd. (**o**) o, *o*x; au, c*ow*; ou, g*oa*t; u, p*oor*; ɔi, r*oy*al. (**u**) ʌ, d*u*ck; u, b*u*ll; uː, g*oo*se; ə, b*a*cillus; ju:, c*u*be. x, lo*ch*; θ, *th*ink; ð, bo*th*er; z, *Z*en; ʒ, cor*s*age; dʒ, sava*ge*; ŋ, orangutan*g*; j, *y*ak; ʃ, *f*ish; tʃ, fe*tch*; 'l, rabb*le*; 'n, redd*en*. Complete pronunciation key appears inside front cover.

cir·ro·stra·tus (sịroustréitəs, sịroustrǽtəs) *pl.* **cir·ro·stra·ti** (sịroustréitai, sịroustrǽtai) *n.* (*meteor.*) a thin, wispy sheet of cloud or haze at high altitudes, darker than the cirrus and either horizontal or very slightly inclined [fr. L. *cirrus*, curl + *stratum*, strewn]

cir·rous (síras) *adj.* resembling cirrus clouds ‖ cirrate

cir·rus (síras) *pl.* **cir·ri** (sírai) *n.* (*meteor.*) a lofty, white, fleecy cloud formation usually made up of ice crystals at heights between 20,000 and 40,000 ft ‖ (*bot.*) a tendril ‖ (*zool.*) a slender, tactile appendage e.g. on mollusks [L. = curl]

cir·vis (sə́:rvis) (*acronym*) for communications instructions for reporting vital intelligence sightings

cis·al·pine (sisǽlpain, sisǽlpin) *adj.* on the south side of the Alps (cf. TRANSALPINE) [fr. L. *cisalpinus*, on this side of the Alps (i.e. closest to Italy)]

Cisalpine Gaul *GAUL

Cisalpine Republic a state created (1797) in N. Italy by Napoleon. Capital: Milan. It was known successively as the Italian Republic (1802–4) and the Kingdom of Italy (1804–15)

ci·sel·é (siázəlẹi) *n.* form of velvet with a distinctive pattern formed by contrasting cut and uncut loops of yarn

cis·lu·nar (sislú:nər) *adj.* of or relating to the area separating the earth and moon

Cis·ne·ros (θi:snérəs), Francisco de Jiménez (1436–1517), Spanish cardinal and statesman. Appointed (1492) confessor to Isabella I, he was regent of Castile (1506–7) and of Spain (1516–17) and chief inquisitor for Castile and León (1507). He supervised the editing of the Polyglot Bible (1502–17)

cissie *SISSY

cis·soid (sísɔid) **1.** *n.* (*math.*) a curve converging into an apex **2.** *adj.* included between the concave sides of two intersecting curves [fr. Gk *kissoeidēs*, ivylike]

cissy *SISSY

cist (sist) *n.* a Neolithic type of grave or burial chamber [Welsh = chest]

Cis·ter·cian (sistə́:rʃən) **1.** *adj.* of the religious order founded (1098) at Cîteaux in Burgundy **2.** *n.* a member of this order [fr. M.L. *Cistercium*, Cîteaux]

—The Cistercian order was founded to restore the Benedictine rule to its former austerity. It expanded rapidly (12th c.) under the rule of St Stephen Harding and St Bernard. As Cistercian monasteries were supported by the labor of their own monks, the order played an important part in the development of medieval agriculture, and in the growth of the English wool trade. The Cistercians declined in the 14th c. The most notable among later attempts at reform was that of the Trappists. The order underwent a revival (19th c.) and is now divided into the Cistercians of the Common Observance and the Cistercians of the Strict Observance (Trappists). There is an order of nuns

cis·tern (sístərn) *n.* a tank for storing water, usually at the top of a house ‖ a reservoir for storing rainwater, often underground, esp. in the U.S.A. ‖ (*anat.*) a closed space containing fluid, e.g. in arachnids [O.F. *cisterne*]

cis·ter·na (sistə́:rnə) *pl.* **cis·ter·nae** (sistə́:rni:) *n.* (*anat.*) a cistern [L.]

cis·tron (sístrɒn) *n.* (*cyt. biochem.*) chromosome in the DNA chain that controls a functional protein or enzyme unit. —**cistronic** *adj.*

cis·tus (sístəs) *n.* a member of *Cistus*, fam. *Cistaceae*, a genus of mainly Mediterranean (some South American) shrubs and plants, often yielding the resin ladanum. Many are cultivated ornamental shrubs [Mod. L. fr. Gk]

cit·a·del (sítəd'l, sítədel) *n.* a fortress protecting or dominating a town ‖ (*hist.*) a place of refuge ‖ something thought of as a defensive stronghold, *a citadel of freedom* [F. *citadelle* fr. Ital.]

ci·ta·tion (saitéiʃən) *n.* the act of citing ‖ a quotation ‖ (*mil.*) a mention in dispatches in praise of an act of courage or other soldierly virtue ‖ a summons to appear in court [F.]

cite (sait) *pres. part.* **cit·ing** *past* and *past part.* **cit·ed** *v.t.* to give (an example), or quote (an authority) e.g. in support of an argument ‖ (*mil.*) to mention in official dispatches ‖ to summon to court to answer an accusation [F. *citer*]

Ci·teaux (si:tou) *CISTERCIAN

cit·i·fy (sítifai) *pres. part.* **cit·i·fy·ing** *past* and *past part.* **cit·i·fied** *v.t.* to cause to have city ways

cit·i·zen (sítiz'n, sítis'n) *n.* an inhabitant of a city or town ‖ a member of a country, native or naturalized, having rights and owing allegiance **cit·i·zen·ry** *n.* (*old-fash.*) citizens as a body **cit·i·zen·ship** *n.* the state of being a citizen ‖ the rights and duties of this state [M.E. *citesein* fr. A.F.]

citizens band or **citizens wave band** frequencies allocated for citizen radio communications (460–470 or 26.965–27.405 MHz) widely used by drivers of motor vehicles. *abbr* **CB.**

Ci·tlal·te·petl (si:tlaltéipet'l) (Orizaba) a volcano in S. Mexico, the highest peak in the country (18,701 ft)

cit·ral (sítrəl) *n.* a liquid aldehyde, present in oil of lemon and orange etc., used in making perfumes [CITRON + ALDEHYDE]

cit·rate (sítreit) *n.* a salt or ester of citric acid

cit·ric (sítrik) *adj.* of or pertaining to the citron [fr. L. *citrus*, orange tree]

citric acid a soluble tribasic acid, $C_6H_8O_7$, in the juice of citrus fruits, esp. lemons, used as a flavoring agent

cit·rin (sítrin) *n.* vitamin P (*DIET) [fr. L. *citrus*, orange tree]

cit·ron (sítrən) *n. Citrus medica*, fam. *Rutaceae*, a small citrus tree bearing a fruit similar to a lemon, but larger and without a terminal nipple. It is the parent species of many varieties, e.g. lemon, lime, sweet lime ‖ the fruit of this tree ‖ its rind, candied or used in cakes, puddings etc. [F. fr. L. fr. Gk]

cit·ron·el·la (sịtrənélə) *n. Cymbopogon nardus*, fam. *Gramineae*, a sweet-smelling grass of S. Asia [Mod. L.]

cit·ron·el·lal (sịtrənélæl) *n.* (*chem.*) a colorless, liquid aldehyde, used in perfumes and as a flavoring agent

citronella oil a fragrant essential oil used in perfumes and insect repellents

cit·rous (sítrəs) *adj.* of or pertaining to trees of the genus *Citrus* or their fruit

cit·rus (sítrəs) *n.* a member of *Citrus*, fam. *Rutaceae*, a genus of trees and shrubs yielding fruits which include the orange, lemon, lime, grapefruit, shaddock, tangerine and citron [M.L.]

citrus red spider or **citrus red mite** *Panonychus citri*, a destructive citrus foliage pest

cit·y (síti:) *pl.* **cit·ies** *n.* an important town ‖ a municipal corporation whose powers are confined to a fixed area and subject to the authority of the state ‖ (*Canada*) a municipality of highest rank ‖ (*Br.*) a town given special rights by charter from a monarch, often one which is an episcopal see ‖ the collective body of people living in a city, its citizens **the City** (*Br.*) the commercial center of London governed by the lord mayor and corporation ‖ the worldwide financial interests centered there, *he has the City behind him* [M.E. *cite* fr. O.F.]

cit·y·bil·ly (síti:bíli:) *n.* country music singer from the city

city block a city division bounded by four streets ‖ one side of the block so formed

City company (*Br.*) a London charitable corporation of businessmen developed from the ancient trade guilds of the City of London

City editor the news editor of a newspaper ‖ (*Br.*) the editor of the financial section of a journal or newspaper

city father a prominent citizen, esp. a civic official, e.g. an alderman

city hall the building from which a city government administers a city ‖ the city government as a body

city manager a person appointed by a city council to manage the affairs of the city

cit·y·scape (síti:skẹip) *n.* the visual effect created by architecture, street furniture (lighting, trash cans, etc.), use of space and urban activities; analogous to landscape

cit·y·state (síti:stẹit) *n.* a city which is an independent sovereign state, often extending its authority over outlying regions, e.g. ancient Athens or Sparta

Ciu·dad Juá·rez (sju:ðáðhwáres) a frontier town (pop. 567,365) in Chihuahua State, Mexico, on the right bank of the Rio Grande, opposite El Paso, Texas: a marketing center (mainly cotton) and rail terminus. The city was Benito Juárez's headquarters (1865) during his struggle with the French

Ciu·dad Re·al (θju:ðáðreiál) a province (area 7,620 sq. miles, pop. 468,327) in S. central Spain ‖ its capital (pop. 41,708) (*NEW CASTLE*)

Ciu·dad Tru·jil·lo (sju:ðáðtru:xíːjɔ) *SANTO DOMINGO

civ·et (sívit) *n.* any of several fierce carnivorous mammals of fam. *Viverridae* of N. Africa and Asia ‖ a fatty substance produced in the perineal glands of these animals, and used in perfume [F. *civette* fr. Arab.]

civet cat *Civettictis civetta*, fam. *Viverridae*, a mammal 2–3 ft long of central Africa, yielding the bulk of commercial civet

civ·ic (sívik) *adj.* relating to a city, its citizens or citizenship [fr. L. *civicus*]

civic center, *Br.* civic centre a group of municipal buildings and services, comprising e.g. a theater, dance hall, movie house, swimming pool

civ·ics (síviks) *n.* the study of the rights and duties of citizens

civ·il (sív'l) *adj.* relating to a community or to citizens, *civil rights* ‖ relating to civilian as opposed to military matters ‖ conforming to normal standards of politeness ‖ (*law*) relating to the private rights of individuals and disputes between them (cf. CRIMINAL) ‖ legally determined, *civil disabilities* ‖ of a system of time legally recognized for use by the public, *civil year* (cf. SIDEREAL) [F.]

civil death a legal change of status with consequences in law tantamount to those resulting from natural death

civil defense, *Br.* civil defence the organization responsible for protecting civilians from enemy attack, esp. air attack

civil disobedience refusal to obey civil laws, as a way of securing reforms

civil engineer a person trained or engaged in civil engineering

civil engineering *ENGINEERING

ci·vil·ian (sivíljən) **1.** *adj.* not belonging to the armed forces **2.** *n.* a person not a member of the armed forces [O.F. *civilien*, civil]

Civilian Conservation Corps (*abbr.* CCC), a U.S. government organization created (1933) as Emergency Conservation Work and renamed (1937). Established to provide training and work for the unemployed and a national program of conservation, the entire program employed about 3 million persons and expended about $2.9 billion. It ceased activities in 1942

ci·vil·i·ty (sivíliti:) *pl.* **ci·vil·i·ties** *n.* conformity with normal conventions of politeness ‖ an act or expression conforming to these conventions [O.F. *civilité*]

civ·i·li·za·tion, **civ·i·li·sa·tion** (sịvilizéiʃən, also *Br.* sịvilaizéiʃən) *n.* a making or becoming civilized ‖ the state of being civilized ‖ the sum of qualities of a particular civilized society, *Greek civilization*

civ·i·lize (sívəlaiz) *pres. part.* **civ·i·liz·ing** *past* and *past part.* **civ·i·lized** *v.t.* to endow with law, order and the conditions favorable to the arts and sciences ‖ to refine the manners and tastes of [fr. F. *civilizer*]

civil liberty the traditional rights of individuals with respect to state control: freedom to assemble, freedom of speech etc.

civil list the annual income granted by parliament to the British sovereign for personal and royal household expenses. It is fixed by Act of Parliament at the beginning of the reign

civil list pension a pension awarded by the sovereign in Great Britain, on the advice of the prime minister, to persons (or their dependents) distinguished for public service or in literature, arts or science. The awards originated with Queen Victoria

civil marriage marriage involving a civil contract but no religious rite or vow

civil rights the rights to personal liberty established by the 1st, 2nd, 3rd, 4th, 5th, 6th, 7th, 8th, 13th, 14th and 15th amendments to the Constitution (*CONSTITUTION OF THE UNITED STATES)

Civil Rights Act of l866 a U.S. Congressional act following the Civil War which extended U.S. citizenship to all except Indians. Found unconstitutional by the Supreme Court as a federal encroachment on states rights, it led to the adoption of the 14th amendment

Civil Rights Act of l875 a U.S. Congressional act, giving citizens of whatever race equal rights to public facilities and to serve on juries. It was passed to thwart the activities of secret terrorist societies, notably the Ku Klux Klan

Civil Rights Act of l964 a U.S. Congressional act, passed after a 75-day filibuster. It prohibited racial discrimination in voting, employment, public accommodation, and vocational training. The constitutionality of the accommodation clause, denounced by business proprietors as a violation of property rights, was upheld (1964) by the Supreme Court as falling within the power of Congress to regulate commerce

Civil Rights Cases a decision (1883) of the U.S. Supreme Court written by Morrison R. Waite. By ruling that the federal guarantee against racial discrimination, contained in postbellum amendments to the Constitution, applied only to state and not to private actions, it served to emasculate the 14th and 15th amendments

civil servant a member of a civil service

civil service the secretariat of a government. It can be limited to central government administration, or include all state employees (except the military). In the U.S.A. all government officers are appointed by the president, by and with the advice and consent of the Senate. Entrance by competitive examination has been introduced to counter the effect of the spoils system whereby state offices were subject to partisan appointment and removal. The British civil service is largely recruited by open competitive examination. The treasury supervises it, the permanent head of the treasury being 'head of the civil service'

civil war war between the citizens of one country

Civil War, American the struggle (1861–5) between the Union of 23 Northern states (together with Dakota, Colorado, Nebraska, Nevada, New Mexico, Utah and Washington) and the Confederate States of the South. Its causes were political and economic, aggravated by the issue of slavery and expansion to the west. Despite the Missouri Compromise (1820) and the Compromise of 1850, America was split between an agricultural, slave-owning South and an industrialized North favoring free soil and protectionism. Hostility was increased by the Kansas-Nebraska Act (1854) and the Dred Scott Decision (1857) and brought to a head by the election (1860) of Lincoln as president. This provoked seven Southern states to secede from the Union (1860–1), setting themselves up as the Confederate States under Jefferson Davis (Feb. 8, 1861). Lincoln declared that secession was illegal and that he would hold federal forts in the South. The attack on one of these, Fort Sumter, by Confederate forces (Apr. 12, 1861) started the war. The Union forces were led by Grant, Sherman, Sheridan and Meade, and those of the South by Lee and Jackson. After bitter fighting, including the battles of Bull Run, Shiloh, Antietam, Fredericksburg, Chancellorsville, Gettysburg and Cold Harbor, the Southern states surrendered (Apr. 9, 1865) at Appomattox. The war, which cost over 600,000 lives, had been fiercely contested from Pennsylvania to Georgia and west to Missouri. It increased the political and economic dominance of the North over the South. Many issues were left unsettled, but the Union had been preserved, and slavery had been abolished (1863) in the Emancipation Proclamation

Civil War, English the struggle (1642–52) between Charles I and his son and parliament, also known as the Great Rebellion. The war was the culmination of middle-class Puritan opposition to the Stuarts' claims to rule by divine right. It was caused by the Long Parliament's attempts to control royal policy by withholding supplies. The royalists, or 'Cavaliers', faced the parliamentarians, or 'Roundheads', at Edgehill (1642). Parliament gained the support of the Scots (1643) and Cromwell's army reversed earlier royal successes, gaining decisive victories at Marston Moor (1644) and Naseby (1645). Charles fled from Oxford (1646), surrendered to the Scots, and was handed over to parliament (1647). Cromwell's army defeated a royalist invasion by the Scots, and removed the Presbyterian majority from parliament by Pride's Purge (1648). Charles was tried and executed (1649). The Commons set up the Commonwealth, abolishing the monarchy and the House of Lords. Cromwell invaded Ireland (1649), and defeated the Presbyterian Scots at Dunbar (1650). Charles II made terms with the Scots and advanced into England, but was defeated by Cromwell at Worcester (1651) and forced into exile

Civil War, Spanish the struggle (1936–9) between Fascist and republican forces in Spain. After the replacement of the monarchy by a republic (1931), Spain was governed (1931–3

and 1936) by an anticlerical popular front of republicans, socialists, communists and syndicalists. A Falangist military revolt in Spanish Morocco (July 17, 1936) led by Franco spread quickly to Spain and was supported by monarchists, the Catholic right, landowners and industrialists. The main republican centers were Madrid, Barcelona, Valencia and Oviedo. The Falangists received massive military aid from Germany and Italy, while the International Brigade was formed (Nov. 1936) to defend the republican cause. By Oct. 1937, Franco held the Portuguese frontier and the north, and bisected (Apr. 1938) the remaining republican territory. The war ended with the fall of Barcelona, the republican capital (Jan. 25, 1939), and of Madrid (Mar. 28, 1939) after a siege of 29 months. The war was fought at the cost of a million lives and economic devastation. Franco's victory led to the establishment of a dictatorship and the restoration of Church property and privileges

clab·ber (klǽbər) **1.** *n.* sour clotted milk **2.** *v.i.* to become sour and clotted [shortened fr. *bonny clabber* fr. Ir. *bainne clabair,* lit. milk of the clapper]

clack (klæk) **1.** *n.* a sharp sound, e.g. of clappers being struck together ‖ loud, continual, rapid chatter **2.** *v.i.* to make sharp, staccato sounds ‖ to cackle ‖ to chatter rapidly and continually ‖ *v.t.* to cause to make a sharp noise [imit.]

clack valve a valve allowing flow of a liquid in only one direction. It is usually hinged on one side, and shuts with a clack

clad (klæd) esp. *archaic* and *rhet.* past and past part. of CLOTHE ‖ *adj.* clothed (in a specified way), *warmly clad, clad in armor*

clad·ding (klǽdiŋ) *n.* **1.** structural technique utilizing lightweight materials, e.g., steel frame to perform a load-bearing function as in greenhouses, railroad stations, exhibition halls **2.** process of covering a base with metals, e.g., silver over copper-base coins. —**clad** *adj.*

cla·dis·tic (klədístik) *adj.* (*genetics*) of systems of classification of organisms based on similar lines of descent or hereditary factors. —**cladistics** *n.* —**cladistically** *adv. Cf* PHENETIC

clad·o·gen·e·sis (klædədʒénisis) *n.* (*genetics*) genetic changes due to changes in environment, esp. in isolated areas. —**cladogenetic** *adj.* —**cladogenetically** *adv.*

clad·o·phyll (klǽdəfil) *n.* a leaflike branch borne in the axil of a true leaf, often bearing leaves or flowers around its edges [Mod. L. *cladophyllum*]

claim (kleim) *v.t.* to demand as a right ‖ to assert as true ‖ to profess, *to claim peaceful intentions* ‖ (of things) to need, require, *it claims all his spare time* [fr. O.F. *claimer,* to call out for]

claim *n.* the demanding of something as a right, *to make a claim* ‖ (*insurance*) a request for payment of compensation ‖ a right to demand assistance, *to have a claim on someone* ‖ an assertion of right to possession of a thing, *a claim to a title* ‖ an assertion (esp. of superiority) ‖ the thing claimed, esp. land claimed by a settler or prospector **to lay claim to** to demand ownership of **to stake out a claim to** to mark boundaries of (land) to prove ownership **claim·ant** *n.* a person making a claim [O.F. *claime*]

Clairvaux *BERNARD OF CLAIRVAUX

clair·voy·ance (klɛərvɔ́iəns) *n.* second sight **clair·voy·ant 1.** *adj.* having second sight **2.** *n.* someone who is clairvoyant [F.]

clam (klæm) **1.** *n.* one of various bivalve marine or freshwater mollusks of the class *Lamellibranchia,* esp. those that are edible and equivalved and that live partly or completely buried in sand or mud **to shut up like a clam** to become suddenly uncommunicative **2.** *v.i. pres. part.* **clam·ming** past and past part. **clammed** to gather clams **to clam up** to shut up like a clam [older *clamshell* for *clamp shell*]

cla·mant (kléimənt) *adj.* noisy ‖ demanding attention [fr. L. *clamans* (*clamantis*), clamorous]

clam·bake (klǽmbeik) *n.* a social gathering where clams are baked or other food is prepared and eaten outdoors

clam·ber (klǽmbər) **1.** *v.i.* to get over something, esp. with difficulty, using hands and feet **2.** *n.* physical progress between a climb and a scramble [prob. fr. CLIMB v.]

clam·mi·ly (klǽmili:) *adv.* in a clammy manner

clam·mi·ness (klǽmi:nis) *n.* the state or quality of being clammy

clam·my (klǽmi:) *comp.* **clam·mi·er** *superl.* **clam·mi·est** *adj.* damp, cold and sticky to the touch [fr. older *clam* fr. *clæman,* to smear]

clam·or, *Br.* **clam·our** (klǽmər) **1.** *n.* a loud confused noise, a hubbub ‖ a noisy outcry, a loud demanding **2.** *v.i.* to make demands or complain loudly ‖ to make a loud noise **clám·or·ous** *adj.* [O.F. *clamor,* outcry]

clamp (klæmp) **1.** *n.* a device for holding things together tightly ‖ any of various appliances with parts brought together by screws for holding or compressing **2.** *v.t.* to fasten with, or place in, a clamp ‖ *v.i.* to close with a clamp **to clamp down on** to become more strict about, esp. in order to prohibit [etym. doubtful]

clamp 1. *n.* a pile, esp. of raw bricks for burning, of potatoes under straw and earth for storage, of turf, peat etc. **2.** *v.t.* to pile up (bricks, potatoes etc.) in a clamp [perh. fr. Du. *klamp,* a heap]

clamp *v.i.* to tread noisily (of people or their boots) [imit.]

clamp·down (klǽmpdaun) *n.* a suddenly stricter enforcement of rules or administrative controls

clan (klæn) *n.* a social group, esp. Scots, with a common ancestor, usually under patriarchal control ‖ a tribe ‖ (*pop.*) a large united family ‖ (*pop.*) a clique, a coterie [Gael. *clann*]

clan·des·tine (klændéstin) *adj.* existing or done in forced secrecy ‖ surreptitious [fr. L. *clandestinus*]

clang (klæŋ) **1.** *n.* a loud ringing sound, esp. of metal striking metal **2.** *v.i.* to make such a sound ‖ *v.t.* to cause to make such a sound [imit.]

clan·ger (klǽŋər) *n.* (*Br. slang*) a gross blunder

clang·or, *Br.* also **clang·our** (klǽŋər) *n.* a clang ‖ a series of clangs making a confused din **cláng·or·ous** *adj.* [fr. L. *clangor*]

clank (klæŋk) **1.** *n.* a sharp, ringing sound, e.g. of chains rattling **2.** *v.i.* to make such a sound ‖ *v.t.* to cause to make such a sound [imit.]

clan·nish (klǽniʃ) *adj.* banding together in small, closed groups

clans·man (klǽnzmən) *pl.* **clans·men** (klǽnzmən) *n.* a member of a clan

clap (klæp) *n.* a sharp, loud noise, *a clap of thunder* ‖ the sound of hands struck together [M.E. *clappe,* imit.]

clap *pres. part.* **clap·ping** past and past part. **clapped** *v.i.* to strike the palms of the hands together, esp. so as to applaud, summon or scare off ‖ *v.t.* to strike (the palms of the hands) together ‖ to slap lightly in friendly gesture, *to clap someone on the back* ‖ (*pop.*) to put, impose etc. with force **to clap eyes on** to see ‖ to see suddenly [M.E. *clappen*]

clap·board (klǽbərd, klǽpbɔrd, klǽpbourd) **1.** *n.* a narrow board for weatherboarding houses **2.** *v.t.* to cover with clapboards [partial trans. of Du. *klaphout,* stave wood]

clap·net (klǽpnet) *n.* a net shut by pulling a string, used by entomologists, fowlers etc.

clapped-out *n.* (*Br. slang*) worn-out, fatigued

clap·per (klǽpər) *n.* the striker of a bell ‖ a device making a clapping sound, e.g. a bird scarer ‖ a flat stick used by minstrels

clap·ping (klǽpiŋ) *n.* massage technique of striking the flesh with cupped palms

clap·trap (klǽptræp) *n.* pretentious language ‖ empty, insincere talk, humbug

claque (klæk) *n.* a group of paid applauders in a theater, or any group of hangers-on [F.]

clar·a·bel·la (klærəbélə) *n.* a fluty organ stop [fr. L. *clarus,* clear + *bellus,* beautiful]

Clare (klɛər), John (1793–1864), English poet, called 'the peasant poet' and admired for his simple, direct presentation of rural subjects

Clare, Richard de *PEMBROKE, 2nd earl of

Clare, St (1193–1253), foundress of the order of Poor Clares, the second order of Franciscans. Feast: Aug. 12

Clare the northwestern county (area 1,231 sq. miles, pop. 75,008) of Munster province, Irish Republic. County seat: Ennis

clar·ence (klǽrəns) *n.* a closed fourwheeled carriage with seats for four inside and for two outside on a box [after the duke of *Clarence,* later William IV of England]

Clar·en·don (klǽrəndən), Edward Hyde, 1st earl of (c. 1609–74), English statesman and historian. Having drawn up the Declaration of Breda (1660), he became chief minister (1660–7) to Charles II. A moderate, he opposed the Clarendon Code. He wrote the 'History of the Rebellion'

CONCISE PRONUNCIATION KEY: (a) æ, c*a*t; ɑ, c*a*r; ɔ f*aw*n; ei, sn*a*ke. **(e)** e, h*e*n; iː, sh*ee*p; iə, d*ee*r; ɛə, b*ea*r. **(i)** i, f*i*sh; ai, t*i*ger; əː, b*i*rd. **(o)** o, *o*x; au, c*ow*; ou, g*oa*t; u, p*oo*r; ɔi, r*oy*al. **(u)** ʌ, d*u*ck; u, b*u*ll; uː, g*oo*se; ə, b*a*cillus; juː, c*u*be. x, lo*ch*; θ, *th*ink; ð, bo*th*er; z, *Z*en; ʒ, corsa*g*e; dʒ, sava*g*e; ŋ, oranguta*ng*; j, *y*ak; ʃ, *f*ish; tʃ, fe*tch*; 'l, rabb*le*; 'n, redd*en*. Complete pronunciation key appears inside front cover.

clar·en·don (klǽrəndən) n. a boldfaced printing type

Clarendon Code (Eng. hist.) a series of statutes to enforce adherence to the Church of England. They comprised the Corporation Act (1661), the Act of Uniformity (1662), the Conventicle Act (1664) and the Five-Mile Act (1665)

Clarendon, Constitutions of (Eng. hist.) a code of laws drawn up (1164) by the great council of Henry II to increase the jurisdiction of the civil courts at the expense of the Church courts. The refusal of Becket to agree to the constitutions precipitated his breach with the king

clar·et (klǽrit) 1. n. red Bordeaux wine 2. adj. the reddish-purple color of this wine [O.F. dim. of clair, clear]

clar·i·fi·ca·tion (klærifikéiʃən) n. the act or process of clarifying

clar·i·fy (klǽrifai) pres. part. **clar·i·fy·ing** past and past part. **clar·i·fied** v.t. to make understandable, explain, the minister clarified his proposals ‖ to make (a liquid) pure and transparent ‖ v.i. to become easier to understand ‖ (of a liquid) to become pure and transparent [O.F. clarifier]

clar·i·net (klærinét) n. a woodwind instrument with a single reed and keys **clar·i·nét·ist, clar·i·nét·tist** n. someone who plays the clarinet [F. clarinette]

clar·i·on (klǽri:ən) 1. n. an organ stop imitating a trumpet ‖ (hist.) a shrill war trumpet 2. adj. loud and very clear [O.F. claron, clairon]

clar·i·ty (klǽriti) n. clearness (of liquids, sounds, meaning etc.) [M.E. clarté fr. O.F.]

Clark (klɑrk), George Rogers (1752–1818), American pioneer and soldier. He fought the British and Indians in Kentucky and Illinois during the Revolutionary War. His victories enabled the 13 colonies to secure extensive northwest territories when the peace was signed (1783)

Clark, John Bates (1847–1938), U.S. economist. His chief work, 'The Distribution of Wealth' (1899), defended the fairness of the competitive system and strongly influenced the economic thinking of his time

Clark, Joseph (1939–   ), youngest prime minister in Canada's history (1979–80). His Progressive Conservative party (PCP) narrowly defeated Pierre Elliott Trudeau and the Liberal party. Trudeau regained leadership in 1980; when Brian Mulroney became prime minister in 1984, Clark was appointed foreign secretary

Clark, Mark Wayne (1896–1984), U.S. army general. During the 2nd world war he commanded (1943–5) Allied forces in Italy. He later commanded (1952–3) all United Nations troops in Korea

Clark, William *LEWIS, MERIWETHER

Clark Memorandum a statement issued (1928) by J. Reuben Clark, spokesman for the U.S. State Department, repudiating the Roosevelt Corollary

Clarke (klɑrk), Arthur C. (1917–   ), English author of science fiction, including 'Childhood's End' (1953), '2001: A Space Odyssey' (book and screenplay, 1968), and its sequel '2010' (1984). He also wrote scientific/technical nonfiction, such as 'Ascent to Orbit' (1984)

Clarke-Bump·us sampler (klɑrkbʌ́mpəs) instrument towed behind a boat to collect samples from a horizontal stratum of a body of water, e.g., of plankton

Clark·son (klɑ́rks'n), Thomas (1760–1846), Englishman who devoted most of his life to working for the abolition of slavery and slave trading. He was chiefly responsible with Wilberforce for the abolition of the British slave trade (1807)

clash (klæʃ) 1. v.i. to make the loud, resonant noise of metal striking metal ‖ to skirmish ‖ to conflict by disagreeing, military duties can clash with moral principles ‖ to conflict by occurring at the same time, the first night of the play clashes with his concert ‖ (of colors) not to harmonize ‖ v.t. to strike together violently, usually noisily 2. n. a loud strident noise as of metal being struck ‖ a skirmish ‖ a conflict [imit]

clasp (klɑsp) 1. v.t. to hold tightly in one's arms, embrace ‖ to seize in a firm hold, or with the hand, to clasp a dagger ‖ to fasten together with a clasp ‖ to interlace the fingers of (one's hands) ‖ v.i. (of hands) to close tensely 2. n. a fastening device ‖ a clip on a brooch etc. ‖ a firm hold, a grasp ‖ (mil.) a bar on a medal ribbon inscribed with the name of the action or campaign at which the wearer was present [origin unknown]

clasp knife a knife with a blade folding into the handle

class (klæs, klɑs) 1. n. a group of people of the same rank or status in a community, the working class ‖ the concept or system of social divisions ‖ a division by cost, first class on a train ‖ a division by quality, grapes of the first class ‖ a group of students taught together ‖ the period when they meet ‖ a course of instruction ‖ the year of graduation from school or college, class of '59 ‖ an age group for conscription, the 1940 class ‖ (Br. universities) the grading of candidates after examination ‖ (biol.) a comprehensive group of animals or plants ranking above an order and below a phylum **in a class apart, in a class by itself** different from, esp. better than, all others 2. v.t. to place in a class ‖ to classify ‖ v.i. to be classed [F. classe]

class action jurisprudential proceeding enacted on behalf of all to whom the litigation has a bearing

class-con·scious (klæskɒ́nʃəs, klɑskɒ́nʃəs) adj. characterized or motivated by class consciousness **class consciousness** awareness of differences between social groups, esp. between one's own and another, as manifested in attitudes and behavior

class day a day in the commencement season in colleges and schools when members of the senior class present a show celebrating the finish of their studies

clas·sic (klǽsik) 1. adj. received into the accepted canons of excellence, the classic works of the 19th century ‖ conforming to Greco-Roman canons of taste, classic beauty ‖ authoritative, a classic reference ‖ having familiar historical or literary association, classic ground ‖ (of dress) having simple tailored lines which never go out of fashion 2. n. a great work of ancient Greek or Roman literature ‖ a later work commonly received as having permanent greatness ‖ a writer or artist of recognized excellence, other than a contemporary ‖ (Br.) a student of the Greek and Latin classics ‖ (Br.) one of the classic horse races: the Two Thousand Guineas, One Thousand Guineas, Derby, Oaks and St Leger [fr. L. classicus]

clas·si·cal (klǽsik'l) adj. of the ancient civilization of Greece and Rome ‖ (of literature and art) having the formal beauty and emotional control typical of the works of that civilization ‖ (of education) humane as distinct from scientific ‖ traditional, as distinct from modern or experimental ‖ (mus.) compact in form and emotionally controlled (cf. ROMANTIC) ‖ (pop.) of all music other than jazz or popular music ‖ (loosely) orthodox, within a received tradition, academic [fr. L. classicus]

classical architecture architecture, esp. of the Renaissance and of the classical revival in W. Europe c. 1770—c. 1840, based on that of ancient Greece and Rome

classical economics the body of thought developed in the late 18th and early 19th cc. by British economists (including Adam Smith, Malthus and Ricardo), who proposed that wealth is promoted by free competition and division of labor

Classical Latin the Latin characteristic of Rome's greatest literary period (c. 100 B.C.—c. 175 A.D.) as found in the works of Cicero, Caesar, Virgil, Horace, Ovid etc.

clas·si·cism (klǽsisizəm) n. the spirit informing the works of Greco-Roman civilization: order, clarity, harmony, grace, humanity, etc. ‖ any later art imitating the ancient masters or pursuing an abstract ideal of rational beauty ‖ scholarship in the ancient Greek and Roman writers

—Classicism as commonly opposed to Romanticism, and in particular as the ideal of 17th-c. France, implies a social ideal: man is viewed as a social being consciously and willingly subject to certain disciplines. Corneille depicts man as a rational analytical being capable of heroically mastering his passions. Moliére postulates a reasonable form of behavior and satirizes departures from it. Racine, with a shift of emphasis, shows man as a highly analytical being, well aware of good and evil but often powerless to stop himself from choosing evil: none the less the ideal is still in view. Romanticism, on the other hand, cultivates the individual ego, esp. in the rare gifted person, and brings that ego into opposition with a formalistic, unimagina-

tive, or sordidly materialist society. T. E. Hulme makes the non-Romantic view of man's nature rest on the Christian doctrine of original sin and the limited possibilities of human nature, requiring discipline.

Classicism tends naturally to be expressed in classical forms: the alexandrine, the heroic couplet, the ode, the Palladian building, the ideal landscape of Claude and Poussin. It tends also to foster a certain type of analysis: that which leads to self-discipline or irony, as in the great French moralists

clas·si·cist (klǽsisist) n. someone who follows a classical ideal ‖ a classical scholar

clas·sics (klǽsiks) pl. n. the study of the languages and literatures of ancient Greece and Rome ‖ authors or books of traditional excellence

clas·si·fi·a·ble (klǽsifaiəb'l) adj. capable of being classified

clas·si·fi·ca·tion (klæsifikéiʃən) n. the act or result of classifying ‖ a system of classifying

clas·si·fi·ca·to·ry (kləsifikətɔ́ri:, klǽsifikətɔ̀uri:, klæsifikətɔ́ri:, klæsifikətɔ̀uri:) adj. relating to or involving classification

clas·si·fied (klǽsifaid) adj. (of information) forbidden to be disclosed for reasons of national or military security ‖ put into a certain category or categories

classified advertisement a small advertisement in a newspaper etc. under a heading ('wanted', 'for sale' etc.)

clas·si·fi·er (klǽsifaiər) n. a machine which separates the constituents of a substance (ore, coal etc.) according to relative size and density by settling

clas·si·fy (klǽsifai) pres. part. **clas·si·fy·ing** past and past part. **clas·si·fied** v.t. to arrange in classes ‖ to put into groups systematically because of common characteristics or properties [fr. L. classis, class]

class·less (klǽslis, klɑ́slis) adj. (of a society) without distinctions of class ‖ (of a person) not assignable to a social class

class·mate (klǽsmeit, klɑ́smeit) n. a member of the same class at school or college

class·room (klǽsru:m, klǽsrum, klɑ́sru:m, klɑ́srum) n. a room in a school in which students are taught

class warfare (in Marxist theory) the inevitable opposition between the workers who put the means of production into action and the capitalists who own the means of production: inevitable because the capitalist appropriates to his own benefit part of the value of the workers' labor

clas·tic (klǽstik) adj. (geol.) composed of fragments of older rocks [fr. Gk klastos, broken]

clath·rate (klǽθreit) n. 1. (botany) like latticework. 2. (chem.) a compound formation in which one kind of molecule is enclosed in the structure of another, e.g., 1,4, dihydroxybenzene. — **clathration** n. formation of a clathrate

clat·ter (klǽtər) 1. v.i. to make, or move with, the noises of impact of many hard objects, the train clattered over the switch ‖ v.t. to cause to make such a confused sound 2. n. a confused sharp banging, rattling or clashing ‖ noisy, confused chatter [O.E. clatrian]

Clau·del (kloudel), Paul Louis Charles Marie (1868–1955), French poet, playwright and diplomat. His plays include 'l'Otage' (1911),'l'Annonce faite à Marie' (1912), 'le Soulier de satin' (1930), and 'Partage de midi' (1905). The main theme of much of his work is man's resistance, and final surrender, to the love of God. His published correspondence with Gide is important for the history of 20th-c. thought and letters

Claude Lor·rain (kloudlɔrɛ̃) (Claude Gelée or Gellée, 1600–82), French painter. With Poussin he was the creator of the late 17th-c. and early 18th-c. ideal of landscape. In creating a taste for the natural sublime Claude prepared the way for the Romantic poets, and for Turner, who was heavily indebted to him

Clau·di·us (klɔ́di:əs), Appius (4th–3rd cc. B.C.), Roman statesman, censor (312–308 B.C.) who built the Appian Way and the first aqueduct at Rome

Claudius I, Tiberius (10 B.C.–54 A.D.), Roman emperor (41–54). His rule became increasingly corrupt under the influence of his wives and freedmen. He was poisoned by his fourth wife, Agrippina

Claudius II, 'Gothicus' (c. 214–270), Roman emperor (268–270). An energetic soldier, he decisively defeated (269) the Gothic invaders in the Balkans

claus·al (klɔ́z'l) *adj.* relating to or of the nature of a clause

clause (klɔz) *n.* a distinct article or proviso in a legal document, agreement or treaty ‖ a part of a sentence having a subject and predicate of its own [O.F.]

Clau·se·witz (kláuzəvits), Karl von (1780–1831), Prussian general and military theorist. His 'On War', advocating total war, greatly influenced German (and Russian) military strategy

Clau·si·us (kláuzi:əs), Rudolf Julius Emmanuel (1822–88), German physicist and mathematician who made important contributions to thermodynamics and the kinetic theory of gases

claus·tral (klɔ́strəl) *adj.* of or like a cloister [fr. L.L. *claustralis*]

claustral prior a prior acting as an abbot's assistant in an abbey

claus·tro·pho·bi·a (klɔstrəfóubi:ə) *n.* a morbid dread of being in confined spaces **claus·tro·pho·bic** (klɔstrəfóubik, klɔstrəfóbik) *adj.* [Mod. L. fr. *claustrum*, a confined place + *phobia*, fear]

cla·vate (kléiveit) *adj.* (*biol.*) club-shaped [fr. L. *clava*, a club]

clav·i·chord (klǽvikɔrd) *n.* a soft-toned keyboard instrument, a precursor of the piano, with strings struck by tangents (hammers) which remain in contact so long as the key of the keyboard is depressed (cf. HARPSICHORD) [fr. L. *clavis*, a key + *chorda*, a string]

clav·i·cle (klǽvik'l) *n.* the vertebrate bone forming part of the pectoral arch, joined to the breastbone and the shoulder blade, in man called the collarbone **cla·vic·u·lar** (kləvíkjulər) *adj.* [fr. L. *clavicula*, dim. of *clavis*, key]

clav·ier (kləvíər, klǽvi:ər, kléivi:ər) *n.* the keyboard of a musical instrument (used attributively of works for keyboard instruments, not specifying piano, harpsichord etc.) [F.]

claw (klɔ) **1.** *n.* the sharp, hooked nail on an animal's foot ‖ the whole foot or leg so armed ‖ a pincer of a crustacean ‖ anything shaped like an animal's claw, esp. a device for grappling, holding and extracting **2.** *v.t.* to scratch or tear with claws or fingernails ‖ *v.i.* to make scratching or tearing attacks with or as if with claws ‖ to make febrile grasping motions ‖ (*naut.*, esp. with 'off') to beat to windward **clawed** *adj.* having claws ‖ scratched and torn by claws [O.E. *clawu*]

claw·back (klɔ́bæk) *n.* (*Br.*) retrieval by government, via taxes, of special benefits received. *Cf* WINDFALL

claw hammer a hammer with one end of the metal head double-pronged for taking out nails etc.

Clay (klei), Cassius Marcellus, *ALI, MUHAMMAD

Clay, Henry (1777–1852), U.S. nationalist statesman who advocated expansion westward and an 'American system' stressing tariff protection. As leader of the 'War Hawks', he pressed President Madison into the War of 1812. He influenced the enactment of the Compromise of 1850 which helped postpone the Civil War for a decade

Clay, Lucius Dubignon (1897–1978), U.S. army general and diplomat. He was appointed (1947) commander in chief of U.S. forces in Europe and military governor of the U.S. zone of Germany, where he was responsible for the success of the Allied air lift into Berlin

clay (klei) *n.* a firm earthy substance essentially composed of aluminum silicate. It is plastic when wet, but loses its plasticity when heated to high temperature. Clays include fireclays, brick and tile clays, and pottery clays. China clay is the purest form **clay·ey** *adj.* [O.E. *clæg*]

clay·more (kléimɔr, kléimour) *n.* (*hist.*) the two-edged sword of Scottish Highlanders [fr. Gael. *claidheamh mor*, great sword]

clay pigeon a saucer-shaped piece of baked clay etc. catapulted from a trap, and used for shooting practice or shooting matches

Clay·ton (kléit'n), John Middleton (1796–1856), U.S. politician. As secretary of state (1849–50) under President Zachary Taylor, he negotiated with British representative Sir Henry Lytton Bulwer the Clayton-Bulwer Treaty

Clayton Antitrust Act a Congressional act (1914) introduced by Henry De Lamar Clayton, designed as an amendment to the Sherman Antitrust Act. It prohibited price discrimination and the acquisition by any company of

stock in another, limited the use of the injunction in labor disputes, and legalized strikes, picketing, and boycotts

Clay·ton-Bul·wer Treaty (kléit'nbúlwər) an Anglo-American treaty (Apr. 19, 1850) composed by John Middleton Clayton and Sir Henry Lytton Bulwer to safeguard the construction and operation of an isthmian canal in Central America. Power rivalry led to its abrogation by the second Hay-Pauncefote Treaty (1901)

clean (kli:n) **1.** *adj.* not dirty ‖ free from imperfections, *clean land* (land free from weeds), *clean proof* (printer's proof with no or few corrections) ‖ fresh, not soiled, *a clean shirt* ‖ pure, without moral defilement ‖ free from ceremonial defilement ‖ (of animals and food) considered on hygienic or religious grounds fit to be eaten ‖ (*Br.*, of pets) housebroken ‖ trim and definite, *a ship with clean lines* ‖ even, without obstructions or rough edges, *a clean cut* ‖ dexterous and free from imprecision, *clean brushwork* **to come clean** to own up **to make a clean sweep of** to leave nothing on, remove every piece from ‖ (*colloq.*) not possessing drugs ‖ not addicted to drugs ‖ not possessing any stolen merchandise **2.** *adv.* completely, *it cut clean through the bone* **3.** *v.t.* to make clean ‖ *v.i.* to remove dirt **to clean down** to remove dirt from by brushing or wiping **to clean out** to remove rubbish etc. from ‖ to take all the money from, *the game cleaned him out* **to clean up** to make tidy ‖ to put the finishing touches to ‖ (*pop.*) to gain as profit, *to clean up a fortune* ‖ (*mil.*) to mop up (the enemy) **4.** *n.* the act or process of cleaning [O.E. *clæne*]

clean aircraft 1. an aircraft in flight configuration, i.e., with landing gear retracted, etc. **2.** an aircraft that does not have external storage for weaponry, etc.

clean bill of health a certificate or assurance of freedom from sickness

clean breach (*naut.*) the sweeping away by breaking waves of everything on deck

clean-cut (klí:nkʌt) *adj.* as though chiseled, *clean-cut features*

clean·er, (klí:nər) *n.* a person who cleans ‖ a device or product used to clean ‖ (esp. *pl.*) a person or a firm cleaning clothes etc. by a chemical process

clean float (*economics*) money exchange rates allowed to adjust to market conditions with no government intervention

clean·hand·ed (klí:nhǽndid) *adj.* guiltless

clean·li·ness (klénli:nis) *n.* the habit or condition of being clean

clean·ly (klí:nli:) *adv.* in a clean manner

clean·ly (klénli:) *comp.* **clean·li·er** *superl.* **clean·li·est** *adj.* (of a person or animal) habitually clean ‖ habitually kept clean [O.E. *clænlic*]

clean·ness (kli:nnis) *n.* the quality or condition of being clean

clean room an area that has been completely disinfected and/or has had dust removed and temperature and humidity controlled for use as a laboratory or work room, esp. for assembly of delicate instruments

cleanse (klenz) *pres. part.* **cleans·ing** *past* and *past part.* **cleansed** *v.t.* to make thoroughly clean, *to cleanse a wound* ‖ to purify (from sin) ‖ (*Bible*) to cure, esp. of leprosy **cleans·er** *n.* an agent which cleanses [O.E. *clænsian*]

clean-shav·en (klí:nʃéivən) *adj.* having the beard and moustache shaved off

clean weapon (*mil.*) a nuclear weapon that leaves no radioactive residue

clear (kliər) **1.** *adj.* transparent, unclouded, *clear water* ‖ bright, luminous, *a clear flame* ‖ distinct to the vision, *a clear print* ‖ free from blemishes or defects, *clear skin* ‖ untroubled, *a clear conscience* ‖ (of sounds) easily audible, distinct, pure ‖ perceiving distinctly, *clear sight* ‖ easy to understand, plain, *a clear statement* ‖ convinced, certain, *he was clear that it shouldn't have happened* ‖ free from difficulty, obstruction or danger ‖ at a safe distance, *keep clear of the machinery* ‖ complete, entire, *a clear profit of $50* **all clear** perfectly safe to proceed ‖ the signal that raiding aircraft have gone away **2.** *n.* (in phrases) **in clear** not in code or cipher **in the clear** innocent, having an alibi **3.** *adv.* completely, *the dog followed him clear into town* **4.** *v.t.* to free from obstructions, *to clear a street of snow* ‖ to remove (an obstruction), *to clear snow from the streets* ‖ to free from suspicion, *the evidence cleared him* ‖ to get over or past ‖ to make as a net profit ‖ to settle (a debt) ‖ to free (a ship,

cargo or luggage) from port restrictions by payment of customs dues etc. ‖ to get rid of by selling ‖ to get (a check) approved for payment ‖ to rid (land) of bushes, weeds etc. ‖ to remove (dirty dishes etc.) from a table ‖ to rid (the throat) of phlegm by coughing slightly ‖ *v.i.* to become clear **to clear away** to remove so as to leave a place clear **to clear out** (*pop.*) to go away ‖ to clear by emptying **to clear the air** to dissipate misunderstandings etc. **to clear the decks for action** to put things away so as to be untrammeled **to clear up** to tidy up ‖ to explain ‖ to become clear ‖ to become sunny after cloudy or rainy weather [M.E. *cler* fr. O.F.]

clear air turbulence (*meteor.*) sudden, substantial air movement encountered by an aircraft in a cloudless area, usu. due to radical temperature changes. *acronym* CAT

clear·ance (klíərəns) *n.* the act or process of clearing, *slum clearance* ‖ an unobstructed space allowing passage, *the bridge has a clearance of 10 ft* ‖ the amount of space between two objects, *1 ft clearance between cars* ‖ the act of clearing a ship, goods etc. at a customhouse ‖ the certificate showing that this has been done ‖ the passing of a check through a clearinghouse

clearance sale a sale held to clear out old goods so as to make room for new stock

Clear and Present Danger Doctrine a doctrine created by U.S. Supreme Court Justice Oliver Wendell Holmes in 'Schenck v. U.S.' (1919), to the effect that speech could incur penalties only when it created a clear and present danger of abetting evil. It was frequently invoked in the 1940s

clear breach (*naut.*) a wave rolling over without breaking

clear-cut (klíərkʌt) **1.** *adj.* sharply defined, *clear-cut issues* ‖ having distinct forms or masses, *clear-cut features* ‖ free of vagueness or uncertainty **2.** *v.* to remove trees to clear an area

clear·head·ed (klíərhédid) *adj.* mentally precise and sound in judgment

clear·ing (klíəriŋ) *n.* a making or becoming clear ‖ a piece of land in a wood free from trees ‖ the bank process of honoring checks ‖ (*pl.*) the total of claims settled at a clearinghouse

clear·ing·house (klíəriŋhaus) *pl.* **clear·ing·hous·es** (klíəriŋhauziz) *n.* a central office at which checks of different banks are exchanged and balances paid ‖ any agency used for sorting and distribution, *a clearinghouse for news*

clear·ly (klíərli:) *adv.* in a clear manner, distinctly, *to speak clearly* ‖ lucidly, *to explain clearly* ‖ undoubtedly, manifestly

clear·ness (klíərnis) *n.* the quality of being clear or distinct ‖ transparency ‖ freedom from ambiguity or confusion ‖ freedom from obstruction

clear-sight·ed (klíərsáitid) *adj.* discerning

clearstory *CLERESTORY

clear·way (klíərwei) *n.* (*Br.*) a section of a high-speed road on which no parking is allowed and where there are no crossroads ‖ (*air traffic control*) defined rectangular area at the end of a strip or channel in the direction of take-off selected or prepared as a suitable area over which an aircraft may make its initial climb to a specified height

cleat (kli:t) **1.** *n.* a device used to secure a rope by belaying it around two projecting arms ‖ a wedge-shaped piece bolted on to a spar etc. to prevent a rope from slipping ‖ one of the studs on the sole of a shoe to prevent sliding (e.g. on golf shoes) ‖ (*pl.*) the main cleavage planes in a coal seam **2.** *v.t.* to fasten to, or by, a cleat [O.E. *clēat*, lump, wedge]

cleav·age (klí:vidʒ) *n.* a cleaving or being cleft ‖ (*biol.*) cell division, esp. the series of mitotic divisions of a zygote in which it becomes a multicellular embryo ‖ (*chem.*) the splitting of a crystal along certain directions parallel to certain actual or possible crystal faces, when subjected to tension ‖ (*chem.*) the breaking down of complex molecules into simpler molecules ‖ any sharp division (e.g. of ideas)

cleave (kli:v) *pres. part.* **cleav·ing** *past* **clove** (klouv), **cleaved**, **cleft** (kleft) *past part.* **clo·ven** (klóuv'n), **cleaved**, **cleft** *v.t.* to split with an ax or chopper ‖ to make a way through as if by cutting, *to cleave the waves* ‖ *v.i.* to become split in two [O.E. *clēofan*]

cleave (kli:v) *pres. part.* **cleav·ing** *past* **cleaved**, **clave** (kleiv) *past part.* **cleaved** *v.i.* (archaic) to be steadfast, adhere, hold fast, *to cleave to one's wife* [O.E. *clīfan* and *clifian*, to stick]

CONCISE PRONUNCIATION KEY: **(a)** æ, c*a*t; ɑ, c*ar*; ɔ f*aw*n; ei, sn*a*ke. **(e)** e, h*e*n; i:, sh*ee*p; iə, d*eer*; ɛə, b*ear*. **(i)** i, f*i*sh; ai, t*i*ger; ə:, b*ir*d. **(o)** o, *o*x; au, c*ow*; ou, g*oa*t; u, p*oo*r; ɔi, r*oy*al. **(u)** ʌ, d*u*ck; u, b*u*ll; u:, g*oo*se; ə, b*a*cillus; ju:, c*u*be. x, lo*ch*; θ, *th*ink; ð, bo*th*er; z, *Z*en; ʒ, corsa*g*e; dʒ, sava*g*e; ŋ, orangutan*g*; j, *y*ak; ʃ, *f*ish; tʃ, fe*tch*; 'l, rabb*le*; 'n, red*den*. Complete pronunciation key appears inside front cover.

cleav·er (klí:vər) *n.* a splitting instrument esp. a wide heavy knife with a short handle used by butchers to split up carcasses

clef (klef) *n.* (*mus.*) a sign at the beginning of the staff to show pitch by locating a particular note on the staff. Extant clefs: G (treble), F (bass), C (tenor or alto) [F.]

cleft (kleft) *n.* an opening made by splitting, a crack, a fissure ‖ a hollow in the chin [M.E. *clift* perh. fr. O.E.]

cleft alt. *past* and *past part.* of CLEAVE ‖ *adj.* divided ‖ split ‖ (of a leaf) divided halfway to the midrib, with narrow sinuses **a cleft stick** a dilemma

cleft palate a split or opening in the roof of the mouth, with or without a harelip

Cleis·the·nes (kláisθəni:z), Athenian statesman who established the democratic constitution (508 B.C.) after the expulsion of the tyrant Hippias

cleis·to·gam·ic (klạistəgǽmik) *adj.* cleistogamous

cleis·tog·a·mous (klaistógəməs) *adj.* of or relating to cleistogamy

cleis·tog·a·my (klaistógəmi:) *n.* self-pollination in closed flowers (e.g. violets) [fr. Gk *kleistos*, closed+*gamos*, marriage]

clem·as·tine fumarate [C₂₁H₂₆ClNO] (kléməs-ti:n fú:məreit) *n.* (*pharm.*) an antihistamine, anticholinergic, and sedative; marketed as Tavist

clem·a·tis (klémətis) *n.* a member of *Clematis*, fam. *Ranunculaceae*, a genus of mostly climbing plants [L. fr. Gk *klēmatis*]

Cle·men·ceau (klemãsou), Georges (1841–1929), French statesman. A radical, he became known as 'the Tiger', and was prime minister 1906–9 and 1917–19. He led France to victory in the first world war, and negotiated the Treaty of Versailles, although he thought it too lenient to Germany

clem·en·cy (klémənsi:) *pl.* **clem·en·cies** *n.* the disposition to be merciful ‖ mercy ‖ mildness (of weather) [fr. L. *clementia*]

Clem·ens (klémənz), Samuel Langhorne *TWAIN, MARK

clem·ent (klémənt) *adj.* inclined to be merciful ‖ (of climate or weather) mild [fr. L. *clemens* (*clementis*)]

Clem·ent I (klémənt), St, pope (c. 88–c. 97), the first of the Apostolic Fathers. Feast: Nov. 23

Clement IV (*d.* 1268), pope (1265–8). A Frenchman who had been adviser to Louis IX, he used his influence to establish Charles of Anjou on the throne of Naples

Clement V (1264–1314), pope (1305–14). He was the first pope to reside at Avignon, and in policy was generally subservient to Philippe IV. He compiled the medieval collection of ecclesiastical laws, the 'Corpus Juris Canonici'

Clement VII (Giulio de' Medici, 1478–1534), pope (1523–34). He quarreled with Charles V, and was imprisoned (1527) by imperial troops for some months. He refused (1527) to grant Henry VIII of England a divorce from Catherine of Aragon

Clement VIII (1536–1605), pope (1592–1605). He ended Rome's dependence on Spain, and established friendly relations with France on Henri IV's abjuration of Protestantism

Clement XI (1649–1721), pope (1700–21). He issued (1713) the bull 'Unigenitus' against Jansenism

Clement XIV (1705–74), pope (1769–74). He suppressed (1773) the Jesuits at the instigation of the courts of France and Spain

Cle·men·ti (kləménti:), Muzio (1752–1832), Italian composer of piano sonatas and of the 'Gradus ad Parnassum' piano studies

Clement of Alexandria (c. 150–215), pagan philosopher turned Christian theologian, who taught Origen at the Alexandrian catechetical school. He was one of the Greek Church Fathers

clench (klentʃ) 1. *v.t.* to press closely together, *to clench one's teeth* ‖ to grasp firmly 2. *n.* the act of clenching ‖ a grip [M.E. *clenchen* fr. O.E. *clencan*]

Cle·on (klí:ɒn) (*d.* 422 B.C.), Athenian politician and general. He defeated the Spartans on the island of Sphacteria in the Ionian Sea (425 B.C.). He was satirized as a demagogue by Aristophanes

Cle·o·pa·tra (kli:əpǽtrə, kli:əpátrə) the name of seven queens of Egypt. The most famous was Cleopatra VII (69–30 B.C.), queen (51–30 B.C.), mistress of Julius Caesar and later of Antony. After the Battle of Actium she killed herself

with an asp to avoid becoming the prisoner of Octavian

clere·sto·ry, clear·sto·ry (klíərstɔri:; klíərstɒu-ri:) *pl.* **clere·sto·ries, clear·sto·ries** *n.* a series of church windows above the roofs of the aisles and below the nave roof [older *clere*, *clear*+STORY (floor)]

cler·gy (klɔ́:rdʒi:) *n.* ordained Christian ministers collectively (cf. LAITY) **cler·gy·man** (klɔ́:rdʒi:mən) *pl.* **cler·gy·men** (klɔ́:rdʒi:mən) *n.* a member of the clergy [O.F. *clergie*]

cler·ic (klérik) *n.* (*old-fash.*) a clergyman [fr. L.L. *clericus* fr. Gk]

cler·i·cal (klérik'l) *adj.* relating to the work of a clerk in an office ‖ connected with the clergy

cler·i·cal·ism (klérikəlizəm) *n.* a policy favoring the political influence of the clergy ‖ adherence to this policy **cler·i·cal·ist** *n.* [fr. L. *clericalis*]

cler·i·hew (klérihju:) *n.* a mildly witty, pseudo-biographical verse of four lines of varying length rhyming aabb, e.g.,

> Jonathan Swift
> Never went up in a lift;
> Nor did the author of 'Robinson Crusoe'
> Do so

[after E. *Clerihew* Bentley (1875–1956), its English originator]

cler·i·sy (klérisi:) *n.* the intelligentsia [perh. fr. G. *clerisei*]

clerk (klɔ:rk, *Br.* klɑk) 1. *n.* an officeworker in a position of minor responsibility ‖ an official who acts as secretary to a council ‖ (*archaic* and *legal*) a clergyman, *a clerk in holy orders* ‖ a layman who performs minor ecclesiastical duties, *parish clerk* ‖ a shop assistant, salesman or saleswoman 2. *v.i.* to work as a clerk **clérk·ly** *adj.* [O.E. *clerc* fr. L.]

clerk of the works (*Br.*) an overseer of construction work

clerk·ship (klɔ́:rkʃip, *Br.* klɑ́kʃip) *n.* the job of a clerk ‖ a situation as clerk

Cler·mont-Fer·rand (klɛɔrmɔ̃ferã) a French town (pop. 253,244), former capital of Auvergne, with rubber industries. The Peace of God and the 1st Crusade were proclaimed here (1095). Gothic cathedral

cleve·ite (klí:vait, kléivəait) *n.* a crystallized variety of uranimite, highly radioactive, found in Norway [after P. T. *Cleve* (1840–1905), Swedish chemist]

Cleve·land (klí:vlənd), (Stephen) Grover (1837–1908), 22nd (1885–9) and 24th (1893–7) president of the U.S.A., a Democrat. He was elected to his first term by the support of the Mugwumps and to his second term by the opposition to the McKinley Tariff (1890). He sent (1894) federal troops into Chicago to quell the Pullman Strike. He refused to recognize the revolutionary government in Hawaii established by Americans, and opposed sending aid to the Cuban revolutionists. By his support of the gold standard, he antagonized the silver Democrats

Cleveland a port (pop. 573,822) in Ohio, on Lake Erie. It is a great ore market, lying between the iron regions of Lake Superior and the coal and oil regions of Pennsylvania and Ohio

clev·er (klévər) *adj.* quick to learn and understand, *a clever pupil* ‖ skillful, good at a job ‖ artful ‖ revealing skill, *a clever trick* ‖ (*Br.*) conceited [etym. doubtful]

Cleves (kli:vz) a former German duchy on the lower Rhine. It was divided (1614) between Brandenburg and Wittelsbach

clev·is (klévis) *n.* a U-shaped iron device for fixing tackle to a beam etc. [etym. doubtful]

clew (klu:) 1. *n.* (*naut.*) the lower corner of a square sail, or the after lower corner of a fore-and-aft sail, or the loop and thimbles at the sail's corner ‖ (*pl.*) the small cords suspending a hammock 2. *v.t.* **to clew up** to haul (a sail) by means of clew lines to the mast, ready for furling [O.E. *cleowen, cliwen*]

clew *CLUE

clew line one of the ropes by which a sail is hauled up to its yard for furling

cli·ché (kli:ʃéi, kliʃéi) *n.* a trite or hackneyed expression or idea [F.]

click (klik) 1. *n.* a slight, sharp momentary sound, as when a switch is put on or off ‖ a momentary electrical disturbance ‖ a catch or detent in machinery acting with this sound ‖ (*phon.*) a speech sound in some African languages made by drawing the breath into the mouth and pressing the tongue against the teeth or palate and pulling it away suddenly 2.

v.i. to make a clicking sound ‖ to fit, *the clues clicked into place* ‖ (*pop.*) to succeed or be lucky ‖ (*pop.*, of two persons) to get along well, be attracted to one another ‖ *v.t.* to cause to click [imit.]

click beetle *ELATER

click·er (klíkər) *n.* (*Br.*, *printing*) a foreman compositor ‖ a foreman shoemaker who cuts out leather and gives out work

cli·ent (kláiənt) *n.* a person who hires the services of a professional man (doctor, lawyer etc.) ‖ a customer [fr. L. *cliens* (*clientis*), someone under the protection of a patron]

cli·en·tele (kląiəntél) *n.* a body of clients of a professional man, shopkeeper, theater etc. [F. *clientèle*]

client state or **client** people or dominion that relies on another government for military and/or economic support

cliff (klif) *n.* a high steep face of rock [O.E. *clif*]

Cliff Dweller a member of the American Indian tribes, ancestors of the Pueblo Indians, who built high rock dwellings in northern Mexico and the southwest U.S.A.

cliff·hang·er (klífhæŋər) *n.* situation fraught with great uncertainty and suspense. —**cliff hang** *v.*

Clif·ford trust (klífɔ:rd) type of family trust in which income is directed to others (usu. in a lower tax bracket) and the principal reverts after a minimum of 20 years, e.g., to provide for college tuition for children

clift sentence (klift) (*grammar*) sentence structure beginning with *what* and ending with a verb, e.g., *What I said is 'go'*

cli·mac·ter·ic (klaimǽktərik, klạimæktérik) 1. *adj.* relating to or constituting a crisis, critical 2. *n.* a period or point in human life in which some crucial change in state, health or fortune tends to take place ‖ the menopause ‖ a similar reduction in reproductive activity and ability in the male [fr. L. *climactericus* fr. Gk]

cli·mac·tic (klaimǽktik) *adj.* of or relating to a climax

cli·mate (kláimit) *n.* the sum of the prevailing weather conditions of a place over a period of time ‖ an area or region with certain weather conditions ‖ the trend of opinions and attitudes pervading a community, nation or period **cli·mat·ic** (klaimǽtik) *adj.* **cli·mát·i·cal·ly** *adv.* [F. *climat* fr. L. fr. Gk]

cli·ma·to·log·i·cal (klạimət'lódʒik'l) *adj.* of or relating to climatology

cli·ma·tol·o·gist (klạimətólədʒist) *n.* someone skilled in climatology

cli·ma·tol·o·gy (klạimətólədʒi:) *n.* the science of climates and their phenomena [fr. Gk *klima*, a slope+*logos*, discourse]

cli·max (kláimæks) 1. *n.* the last of a series of ideas, events, points of interest or situations (esp. dramatic or musical) to which what has gone before seems in retrospect to have been building up ‖ the movement towards such a culmination, *a mounting climax* 2. *v.i.* to come to a climax ‖ *v.t.* to bring to a climax [L. fr. Gk *klimax*, ladder]

climb (klaim) 1. *v.t.* to go up, ascend, esp. using hands and footholds, *to climb a ladder* ‖ *v.i.* to rise to a higher point, *mercury climbs in a thermometer* ‖ to slope upward ‖ (of plants) to grow upward by turning around a support or by tendrils ‖ to gain height in the air, *the plane climbed to 40,000 ft* ‖ to rise in social rank or in reputation, by effort **to climb down** to descend (a hill etc.) on foot ‖ to withdraw from a previously held position by admitting one was wrong or too assertive 2. *n.* a climbing ‖ a place to be climbed **clímb·er** *n.* a person who climbs mountains for sport ‖ a plant which grows vigorously up a support ‖ *SOCIAL CLIMBER [O.E. *climban*]

climb corridor *CLEARWAY

climbing irons steel spikes which may be attached to boots for climbing poles, trees etc., crampons

climbing perch *Anabas scandens*, a fish found in India which can live out of water as long as 5–6 days because of modified gills which retain moisture and form chambers containing air for respiration. It moves by means of spiny fins, erected scales, and gill covers

climb-out (kláimaut) *n.* steep ascent by an aircraft, usu. at take-off

clime (klaim) *n.* (*rhet.*) an area or region ‖ (*rhet.*) climate [fr. L. *clima* fr. Gk]

clinch (klintʃ) 1. *v.t.* to settle, make conclusive, *to clinch a deal* ‖ to bend back the point of (a nail) after it has gone through the wood, and drive it into the wood to secure it ‖ to clench (teeth) ‖ to fasten (a rope) by a clinch ‖ *v.i.* (*boxing*) to grapple as a method of making strong punches impossible, each boxer holding his opponent in at close quarters ‖ (*wrestling*) to struggle at close quarters 2. *n.* the position or practice of clinching by boxers or wrestlers ‖ (*naut.*) a hitch, the end of which is lashed back by seizing **clinch·er** *n.* a thing that clinches ‖ the remark or argument which settles a dispute [var. of CLENCH]

clinch·ing (klíntʃiŋ) *n.* (*computer*) wrinkling in magnetic tape that may be a source of processing errors

cling (kliŋ) *pres. part.* **cling·ing** *past* and *past part.* **clung** (klʌŋ) *v.i.* to hold fast, *the boy clung to his mother* ‖ to keep close, *the boat clung to the coast* ‖ to keep a sentimental feeling for something, *to cling to one's memories* [O.E. *clingen*]

Cling·mans Dome (klíŋmənz) the highest point (6,642 ft) in the Great Smoky Mtns, on the Tennessee-North Carolina border

cling·stone (klíŋstoun) *n.* a variety of peach, nectarine, plum etc., whose flesh adheres to the stone (cf. FREESTONE)

clin·ic (klínik) *n.* a place where hospital outpatients receive medical examination, treatment or advice ‖ a similar institution where people get medical help (often free) ‖ practical instruction of medical students by letting them watch treatment of patients ‖ a class so taught **clin·i·cal** *adj.* of or concerning a clinic ‖ concerning medical teaching by demonstration, *clinical lectures* ‖ concerning the study of disease by observation, *clinical medicine* [F. *clinique* fr. Gk]

clinical thermometer a thermometer for taking body temperature

clink (kliŋk) *n.* (*pop.*) prison [orig. the name of a prison in Southwark]

clink 1. *n.* a sharp high-pitched sound produced by glass, metal etc. knocking lightly against similar material 2. *v.i.* to make this sound ‖ *v.t.* to cause to make this sound [imit.]

clink·er (klíŋkər) *n.* hard, incombustible slag formed in a furnace or boiler ‖ a very hard Dutch brick ‖ a brick with a vitrified surface ‖ a mass of bricks fused together by great heat [fr. older Du. *klinckaerd* fr. *klinken*, to clink]

clink·er-built (klíŋkərbilt) *adj.* (of a ship) having the outer planks overlapping downwards and fastened with clinched nails (cf. CARVEL-BUILT) [fr. obs. *clink*, to clinch]

clink·stone (klíŋkstoun) *n.* phonolite

cli·nom·e·ter (klainómitər, klinómitər) *n.* an instrument for measuring slopes and other angles of elevation or depression, e.g. on a gun [fr. Gk *klinein*, to slope+METER]

Clin·ton (klíntən), De Witt (1769–1828), U.S. political leader. He was the Republican presidential nominee (1812) against President James Madison and chief sponsor of the Erie Canal Project

Clinton, George (1739–1812), U.S. vice-president (1805–9) under Thomas Jefferson and (1809–12) under James Madison. He opposed a strong centralized government in the belief that it threatened finance and banking

Cli·o (kláiou) the Muse of history

Cli·o (klíːou) *n.* statuette presented annually for outstanding professional work in TV commercials

cli·o·quin·ol [C₉H₅ClINO] (kliːoukwínɔl) *n.* (*pharm.*) drug formerly known as iodochlorhydroxyquin; formerly used in treatment of dysentery and vaginitis, now used for dermatitis; sometimes producing neurological symptoms; marketed as Entero-Vioform and Vioform

clip (klip) 1. *v. pres. part.* **clip·ping** *past* and *past part.* **clipped** *v.t.* to fasten together with a clip ‖ *v.i.* (*football*) to hurl oneself from behind across the shins of a player who is not holding the ball, thus committing a foul 2. *n.* a device for fastening things together, *paper clip* ‖ a brooch ‖ (*Br.*) a bobby pin ‖ a device for holding cartridges for a magazine rifle [O.E. *clyppan*, to embrace]

clip 1. *v. pres. part.* **clip·ping** *past* and *past part.* **clipped** *v.t.* to cut, trim, shear, *to clip a poodle* ‖ to cut the edge of (a coin) ‖ to omit final sounds or syllables of in pronouncing, *clipped speech* ‖ (*pop.*) to cuff with the hand, *to clip someone's ear* ‖ *v.i.* (*pop.*) to move swiftly, *to clip along* 2. *n.* the act of clipping, esp. of sheepshearing ‖ the quantity of wool clipped from a sheep ‖ the season's yield of wool ‖ a cutting, esp. a sample piece of cloth ‖ a cuff with the hand ‖ (*pop.*) a rapid pace,

to go at a good clip [M.E. *clippen* prob. fr. O.N.]

CLIP (*acronym*) for compiler language for information processing, a computer program language designed by System Development Corporation

clip·board (klípbɔrd, klípbourd) *n.* a small portable board incorporating a clip to hold papers, convenient for when there is no table to write at

clip·per (klípər) *n.* someone who clips ‖ (often *pl.*) a clipping instrument, *hedge clippers* ‖ (*hist.*) a fast sailing vessel used in the China tea trade

clip·per-built (klípərbilt) *adj.* (*naut.*) built on rakish lines for fast sailing

clipper diode (*electr.*) diode device that holds back voltage peaks beyond preset parameters. —**clipping level** *n.* point at which a circuit is cut back

clip·ping (klípiŋ) *n.* the act of clipping ‖ something clipped off, *nail clippings* ‖ (*Am.=Br.* cutting) a paragraph, article etc. cut from a newspaper or magazine

clique (kliːk, klik) 1. *n.* (*pejorative*) a small, exclusive set of people 2. *v.i.* to form a clique **cli·quey** (klíːkiː, klíːkiː), **cli·quish** (klíːkiʃ, klíkiʃ), **cli·quy** *adjs* [F. fr. *cliquer*, to click]

cli·tel·lum (klaitéləm) *n.* a glandular thickening of the outer body wall of certain annelid worms, which secretes the cocoon and the albuminoid material on which the embryo feeds [Mod. L. fr. *clitellae*, packsaddle]

clit·o·ris (klítəris, kláitəris) *pl.* **clit·o·res** (klítəriːz, kláitəri:z) *n.* (*anat.*) a small erectile organ at the upper part of the vulva [L. fr. Gk *kleitoris* perh. fr. *kleiein*, to shut]

Clive (klaiv), Robert, Baron Clive of Plassey (1725–74), British soldier and statesman. After a distinguished military career (1744–57) in the service of the East India Company, he finally defeated the nawab of Bengal at Plassey (1757), and drove the French from India. As governor of Bengal (1765–6), he reformed British administration in India

clo (klou) *n.* measurement unit for comfort level clothing devised by Cy Chaikin Research Group

clo·a·ca (kloueíkə) *pl.* **clo·a·cae** (kloueísi:) *n.* (*zool.*) the common cavity into which the intestinal, urinary and generative canals discharge in birds, reptiles, amphibians, many fish and monotremate animals ‖ a similar cavity in invertebrates **clo·a·cal** *adj.* [L.=drain, sewer]

cloak (klouk) 1. *n.* a loose, sleeveless outer garment sometimes worn instead of a coat, or as part of uniform (*Br.*, nurses) or habit (priests) ‖ something which hides, *the cloak of darkness* 2. *v.t.* to conceal, disguise, *to cloak one's disapproval with a smile* ‖ to cover as if with a cloak, *mist cloaked the hills* [O.E. *cloke*]

cloak-and-dag·ger (klóukəndǽgər) *adj.* of plays, films etc. of a melodramatic kind with a historical setting and involving adventures and escapes, or of the actors who play in them ‖ of spies or espionage

cloak·room (klóukruːm, klóukrum) *n.* a room, esp. in a hotel, theater etc., where one can leave one's coat, luggage etc. ‖ (esp. *Br.*) a lavatory

cloche (klouʃ, klɔʃ) *n.* a glass frame or bell jar used to protect or force plants ‖ a woman's close-fitting, bell-shaped hat [F. =bell]

clock (klɔk) 1. *n.* a device, other than a watch, for measuring and indicating time, based on some strictly periodic process (e.g. the swing of a pendulum, the vibration of a crystal, the diurnal rotation of the earth about its axis) whose period is regarded as constant ‖ a mechanism with a dial for indicating or recording the working state or output of the machine to which it is attached ‖ a time clock ‖ a speedometer ‖ (*pop.*) the fruiting head of a dandelion 2. *v.t.* to time (a race, competitors) with a stopwatch ‖ *v.i.* (of employees, with 'in', 'out', 'on') to record one's entry or exit on a control mechanism (*TIME CLOCK) [M.E. *clocke* perh. fr. O.N.F.]

clock *n.* a pattern on the side of a sock or stocking [origin unknown]

clock-face (klókfeis) *n.* the dial of a clock

clock-mak·er (klókmeikər) *n.* a maker or repairer of clocks

clock radio combination of a radio and a clock with devices to connect or disconnect radio at set times

clock·wise (klókwaiz) 1. *adv.* in the same direction as the hands of a clock move 2. *adj.* turning or directed thus

clock·work (klókwəːrk) 1. *n.* the mechanism of a clock ‖ a device not unlike that of a clock, containing a spring and cogged wheels, used for timing or as a driving mechanism etc. 2. *adj.* having such a mechanism, *a clockwork train* **like clockwork** smoothly, regularly, in an efficient routine

clod (klɔd) *n.* a lump of earth or mud ‖ a part of the shoulder of beef ‖ a stupid person **clod·dish** *adj.* oafish [var. of CLOT]

clod-hop·per (klódhɔpər) *n.* a country lout ‖ a clumsy fellow ‖ (*pl.*) big heavy shoes **clód·hop·ping** *adj.*

clo·fi·brate [C₁₂H₁₅ClO₃] (klɒfíbreit) *n.* (*pharm.*) drug used to reduce cholesterol and lipid levels in the blood; marketed as Atromio-S

clog (klɔg) 1. *n.* a wooden shoe, or one with a wooden sole, used esp. for walking over wet or muddy ground ‖ a movable weight to which an animal is tied to prevent its straying 2. *v. pres. part.* **clog·ging** *past* and *past part.* **clogged** *v.t.* to choke up, *a clogged drain* ‖ to encumber, make heavy, *clay clogged their boots* ‖ to hamper the movement of (an animal) with a clog ‖ *v.i.* to become choked up [etym. doubtful]

clog dance a dance performed by dancers wearing clogs

cloi·son·né (klɔizənéi, klwæzənéi) 1. *adj.* (of enamel) decorated with colors separated from each other by fine wire or thin metal partitions 2. *n.* cloisonné enamel [F.]

clois·ter (klɔ́istər) 1. *n.* a place of religious seclusion, e.g. a convent, monastery ‖ a covered walk, usually walled on one side and open on to a court or quadrangle on the other, esp. of a religious building **the cloister** (*rhet.*) monastic life 2. *v.t.* to shut up in, or confine to, a convent or monastery ‖ to isolate, *he cloistered himself in the library to write* **clóis·tered** *adj.* monastic ‖ isolated from the outside world **clóis·tral** *adj.* [M.E. *cloistre* fr. O.F.]

cloister garth an open court bounded by a cloister

clo·mi·phene [C₂₆H₂₈ClNO] (klóomifi:n) *n.* (*pharm.*) synthetic drug used to stimulate ovulation, e.g., a fertility aid marketed as Clomid

clone (kloun) *n.* (*biol.*) the descendants produced asexually from a single animal or plant. The clone is of the same genetic constitution and results naturally or otherwise, e.g. by plant grafting, cutting etc. [fr. Gk *klon*, twig]

clon·ic (klónik, klóunik) *adj.* relating to or involving clonus

clo·ni·dine [C₉H₉Cl₂N₃] (klónidi:n) *n.* (*pharm.*) drug used to reduce high blood pressure; marketed as Catapres

clo·nus (klóunəs) *n.* (*med.*) a series of muscular contractions [Mod. L. fr. Gk *klonos*, turmoil]

close (klous) 1. *adj.* near, *a close relative* ‖ intimate, *close friends* ‖ nearly alike, *a close resemblance* ‖ nearly equal, *a close finish* ‖ dense, tightly packed, compact, *a close weave* ‖ careful, thorough, *close examination* ‖ as nearly word-for-word as correct style will allow, *a close translation* ‖ secretive ‖ strictly kept or guarded, *a close secret, a close prisoner* ‖ mean, tight-fisted, *close with money* ‖ stifling, *close weather* ‖ (*phon.*, of vowels) articulated with the tongue near the palate ‖ (*finance*) scarce, hard to obtain, *money is still close* 2. *adv.* in a close manner ‖ nearby, near, *come close* ‖ tightly ‖ nearly ‖ compactly ‖ secretly **to run someone close** to rival someone closely [F. *clos*]

close (klouz) 1. *v. pres. part.* **clos·ing** *past* and *past part.* **closed** *v.t.* to shut ‖ to bring together, *the troops closed their ranks* ‖ to end, finish, *to close a speech* ‖ to settle (an account) finally ‖ to come to an agreement about (a bargain) ‖ *v.i.* to become shut, *when do the bars close?* ‖ to come together, *the waters closed over her head* ‖ to come to an end, *the meeting closed with prayer* **to close about** to encircle, surround **to close down** to cease activity permanently, *to close down through lack of business* or temporarily, *the radio station closes down at midnight* **to close in** to surround and draw near for attack **to close out** to sell at reduced price **to close the door** to make no longer possible **to close up** to stand or sit closer together, fill up gaps, *can you close up a bit?* ‖ to make more compact **to close with** to accept in settlement, *to close with an offer* ‖ to come within striking distance of, or grapple in a clinch with, *to close with an opponent* 2. *n.* an end, conclusion ‖ (*mus.*) a cadence **to come** (or **draw**) **to a close** to finish gradually [M.E. *closen* fr. F.]

close (klous) *n.* an enclosed place, esp. a cathedral precinct ‖ (*Br.*) a narrow alley or court [F. *clos*]

close call (klous) a narrow escape

closed chain (*chem.*) an arrangement of atoms in a ring

closed circuit an electric circuit without any break in continuity ‖ a television channel in which the image and sound are not broadcast but are transmitted only to a restricted number of interconnected receivers

closed-loop (klóuzdlú:p) *adj.* of a device, usu. computer-controlled, that adjusts itself to varying conditions. *Cf* FEEDBACK, OPEN LOOP CONTROL SYSTEM

closed primary a primary in which only registered party members may vote for party candidates

closed season a period in the year when by law certain animals may not be hunted nor certain fish fished

closed shop a trade or establishment which employs union members only

closed shop (*computer*) facility where programmers are not permitted to process or oversee the processing of the programs they prepared

closed society country where people are not permitted to emigrate, write, or speak freely

close-fist·ed (klóusfístid) *adj.* miserly, mean

close-grained (klóusgréind) *adj.* of close texture ‖ having the structural elements close or fine in texture

close harmony (klous) (*mus.*) harmony with the notes of the chord as close together as possible

close-hauled (klóushóld) *adj.* with the sails trimmed for sailing as near to the wind as possible

close-mouthed (klóusmạuŏd, klóusmạuθt) not communicative, esp. not inclined to give information away

close quarters (klous) near range, immediate contact

close season (klous) the closed season

close shave (klous) a narrow escape

clos·et (klózit) 1. *n.* a recess built into a room and shut off with a door, or a small room for storing things, *clothes closet, china closet* ‖ a toilet (room) ‖ a water closet 2. *v.t.* (usually *refl.*) to shut in a room, esp. for private conference 3. *adj.* secret, undisclosed, e.g., *closet homosexual* [O.F.]

closet homosexual a homosexual who conceals his or her sexual preference

close-up (klóusʌp) *n.* a photograph or film shot taken at close range or with a telescopic lens ‖ an intimate account of (some personality or event)

clos·trid·i·um (klɒstrídi:əm) *n.* a bacterium of the anaerobic genus *Clostridium*, e.g. *C. tetani* (tetanus) [Mod. L.]

clo·sure (klóuʒər) *n.* a closing, *the holiday closure is in August* ‖ a conclusion, a bringing to an end, *the closure of a speech* ‖ (*parliament*) a decision taken by vote to put the question without further debate [O.F.]

clot (klɒt) 1. *n.* a lump of coagulated or thickened liquid ‖ (*pop.*) a stupid person 2. *v. pres. part.* **clot·ting** *past and past part.* **clot·ted** *v.i.* to undergo a series of chemical and physical reactions such that a fluid is converted into a coagulum (e.g. blood) (*FIBRINOGEN) ‖ *v.t.* to cause to form into a clot or clots [O.E. *clott*]

Clo·taire I (klɒtéər) (497–561), Frankish king (558–61), son of Clovis

Clotaire II (584–629), Frankish king (613–29), slayer of Brunhilda, the queen of Austrasia

cloth (klɔθ, klɒθ) 1. *pl.* **cloths** (klɔðs, klɒðs, klɔðz, klɒðz) *n.* woven material or fabric ‖ a piece of this material ‖ (*rhet.*) the clerical profession ‖ a drop curtain in a theater 2. *adj.* made of cloth [O.E. *clāth*]

cloth·back (klóθbæk) *n.* book covered with a hard cover and cloth binding

cloth cap (*Br.*) of the factory working class (*Am.*=blue collar). —**cloth-cap** *adj.*

clothe (klouð) *pres. part.* **cloth·ing** *past and past part.* **clothed** esp. *archaic* and *rhet.* **clad** (klæd) *v.t.* and *refl.* to provide with clothes ‖ to cover, *he clothed his meaning in fanciful language* [O.E. *clāthian*]

cloth ears one with defective hearing. —**cloth-eared** *adj.*

clothes (klouðz, klouz) *pl. n.* garments, wearing apparel ‖ bedclothes ‖ laundry [O.E. *clāthas*, pl. of CLOTH]

clothes bag (*Br.*) a bag for clothes waiting to be washed, laundry bag

clothes basket a covered basket, for clothes waiting to be washed ‖ an open basket for clean laundry waiting to be ironed

clothes hanger a coat hanger

clothes·horse (klóuðzhɔrs, klóuzhɔrs) *n.* a frame for drying or airing clothes ‖ someone who pays inordinate attention to dressing conspicuously well

clothes·line (klóuðzlạin, klóuzlạin) *n.* a length of rope, nylon etc. on which laundry is hung to dry

clothes moth a moth whose larvae eat cloth, fur, feathers etc.

clothes·peg (klóuðzpeg, klóuzpeg) (*Br.*) a clothespin

clothes·pin (klóuðzpin, klóuzpin) *n.* (*Am.*=*Br.* clothes-peg) a fastener for hanging out the wash on a clothesline

cloth·ier (klóuðjər) *n.* someone who makes or sells cloth or clothing [older *clother*]

cloth·ing (klóuðiŋ) *n.* clothes in general

Clo·tho (klóuθou) *FATES

cloth of gold a fabric woven with gold threads (*FIELD OF THE CLOTH OF GOLD)

clo·ture (klóutʃər) *n.* the closure of a Congressional debate [F.=closure]

cloud (klaud) 1. *n.* a visible expanse of suspended droplets of water or ice particles in the air, *rain clouds* ‖ any suspension of particles in the air or any gas ‖ (*astron.*) a suspension in outer space of dispersed matter ‖ (*nuclear phys.*) nucleons of an atom nucleus not in closed shells ‖ a multitude forming a cloudlike mass, *a cloud of locusts* ‖ something which casts a gloom or causes depression, *a cloud of suspicion* **to have one's head in the clouds** to be unrealistic, a dreamer 2. *v.t.* to overspread with clouds ‖ to darken, *anger clouded his face* ‖ to make opaque, misty or patchy, *mud clouded the water* ‖ to be suffused with, *a green glaze clouded with rust* ‖ *v.i.* to become cloudy or overcast, *the sky is clouding over* [O.E. *clūd*, a mass]

cloud·burst (kláudbə:rst) *n.* a sudden heavy downpour of rain

cloud-capped (kláudkæpt) *adj.* (of mountains) having the summit covered in clouds

cloud chamber a device for observing the tracks of fundamental particles used in conjunction with particle accelerators and in cosmic ray studies. The cloud chamber contains a gas saturated with water vapor: by sudden expansion the gas is cooled and thus becomes supersaturated, so that droplets of water form. These tend to form around the ions that are produced as high-energy electrically charged particles which traverse the gas, and thus the droplets define the paths of the particles ‖ (*meteorology*) a container of air saturated with water vapor ‖ air that holds moving ionized particles visible as streaks of droplets (*BUBBLE CHAMBER)

cloud form any of the ten forms of cloud classified by the International Cloud Atlas as: high clouds (above 6,000 m. or c. 20,000 ft, cirrus, cirrocumulus, cirrostratus), medium clouds (between 2,000 m., or c. 6,500 ft, and 6,000 m., altocumulus, altostratus, stratocumulus), low clouds (below 2,000 m., nimbostratus, stratus), and ascending clouds (starting from as low as 500 m. or c. 1,600 ft, cumulus and cumulonimbus)

cloud formation the process by which clouds are formed when air containing water vapor is cooled below its saturation point and vapor condenses into droplets on dust particles or ionized molecules of the air itself. Cooling may be caused by the air rising and expanding, by mixing with cold air, or by the radiation of heat into space (*CLOUD FORM)

cloud·i·ly (kláudili:) *adv.* in a cloudy way

cloud·i·ness (kláudi:nis) *n.* the state or quality of being cloudy

cloud·land (kláudlænd) *n.* a utopia, a land of dreams

cloud·let (kláudlit) *n.* a small cloud

cloud nine (*colloq.*) place of extreme bliss; from the highest heaven in Dante's *Paradise*

cloud·y (kláudi:) *comp.* **cloud·i·er** *superl.* **cloud·i·est** of or resembling clouds ‖ overcast with clouds ‖ difficult to understand ‖ vague, inexact, *cloudy ideas* ‖ lacking brightness, *a cloudy mirror*

Clou·et (klu:ei), Jean (or Janet) and François (16th c.), French miniaturists and portrait painters, father and son

Clough (klʌf), Arthur Hugh (1819–61), English poet. Much of his verse expressed the religious doubts of mid-19th-c. England. He was the subject of Matthew Arnold's elegy 'Thyrsis'

clout (klaut) 1. *n.* (*pop.*) a hard blow ‖ a protective plate, e.g. an iron plate on a boot ‖ (*archery*) a white target ‖ (*archery*) a hit ‖ (*colloq.*) leverage, mastery, or authority in a situation, esp. relating to a hold in politics 2. *v.t.* (*pop.*) to hit hard [O.E. *clūt*, a lump]

clout nail a broad-headed nail for attaching clouts, studding boots etc.

clove (klouv) *Eugenia caryophyllata*, fam. *Myrtaceae*, a tropical tree grown esp. in Zanzibar and Madagascar ‖ the spice yielded by its dried flower buds [O.F. *clou* (*de girofle*), a nail (of clove)]

clove *n.* a division of a composite bulb, *a clove of garlic* [O.E. *clufu*]

clove *alt. past of* CLEAVE

clove hitch a knot for fastening a rope about a spar, pole or another rope

cloven *past part. of* CLEAVE

clo·ven-foot·ed (klóuv'nfútid) *adj.* cloven-hoofed

cloven hoof the divided hoof of cows and other ruminant quadrupeds, and traditionally of the devil **clo·ven-hoofed** (klóuv'nhúft, klóuv'nhú:ft) *adj.*

clove oil an essential oil extracted from the flowers of the clove tree and used in perfumery and medicine

clo·ver (klóuvər) *n.* a member of *Trifolium*, fam. *Papilionaceae*, a genus of perennial plants, having trifoliate leaves, cultivated widely in temperate and subtropical regions as forage crops and for soil improvement **in clover** enjoying good fortune or success [O.E. *clafre*]

clo·ver·leaf (klóuvərli:f) *pl.* **clo·ver·leaves** (klóuvərli:vz) *n.* a road construction, resembling a four-leaf clover, where one arterial road passes over another, instead of intersecting

Clo·vis (klóuvis) (c. 466–511), king of the Franks (481–511) and founder of the Frankish monarchy. After routing the Romans (486), the Alemanni (496) and the Visigoths (507), he chose Paris as the capital of his new kingdom, which included most of Gaul and S.W. Germany. He was baptized (c. 496) and championed orthodox Catholicism against Arianism, convening a Church council at Orléans (511). On his death his lands were divided among his four sons

clown (klaun) *n.* a buffoon in a circus ‖ someone who is clumsy, or who behaves stupidly 2. *v.i.* to be a clown ‖ to make people laugh by one's antics **clówn·er·y** *n.* **clówn·ish** *adj.* [etym. doubtful]

clox·a·cil·lin [$C_{19}H_{18}ClN_3NaO_5S$] (klɒksəsílin) *n.* (*pharm.*) semisynthetic penicillin used against staphylococci resistant to other penicillin; marketed as Tegopen

cloy (klɔi) *v.t.* to glut, satiate, esp. with sweetness [fr. obs. *acloy.* to choke, put a nail into, fr. O.F.]

cloze (klouz) *adj.* of a reading-comprehension test requiring the supply of deleted words missing from the text

club (klʌb) 1. *n.* a stout stick with a thickened end, a cudgel ‖ a golf stick ‖ a playing card of the suit marked with black trefoils (♣) ‖ an association of people with some common interest who meet periodically, *a boat club* ‖ (esp. *Br.*) an association of people enjoying premises which provide them with reading and recreation rooms, meals, occasional residence, etc. 2. *v.t. pres. part.* **club·bing** *past and past part.* **clubbed** to beat with a club or similar weapon ‖ to share, *to club expenses* **to club together** to put money in a common fund, *to club together to buy a present* [M.E. *clubbe* prob. fr. O.N.]

club (preceded by "the") organization of the world's uranium producers (formed in Paris in 1972) for control of production

club cut (*cosmetology*) straight haircut leaving hair flat on head without a taper

club·foot (klʌbfut) *pl.* **club·feet** (klʌbfi:t) *n.* a congenital deformity of the forepart of the foot ‖ a foot having such a deformity **clúb·fóot·ed** *adj.*

club·haul (klʌbhɔl) *v.t.* (*naut.*) to drop the lee anchor of (a ship) when the wind is out of the sails, and then, when the head swings around, cut the cable to get off on a new tack (used only as a last resort)

club moss a member of *Lycopsida*, a subphylum of low, spreading, vascular, evergreen plants, the sporophytes of which have stems covered

187 **coast guard**

with many small leaves sometimes bearing sporangia. These latter may resemble normal leaves or may be modified and aggregated into a cluster (strobili). The gametophyte exhibits wide variation in structure and sometimes depends upon the sporophyte for nutriment. Club mosses are widely distributed, but tropical forms predominate

Club of Rome an informal organization of 100 business and government leaders formed in Rome (1968) that advocates a no-growth or negative-growth policy for world population to avert disaster from population explosion and famine

club steak a small cut of beef from the end of the loin

cluck (klʌk) 1. *n.* the sound of a hen calling her chicks 2. *v.i.* (of a hen) to utter this sound ‖ (of a person) to make a similar kindly or fussy sound [imit.]

clue (kluː) *n.* anything serving as a guide in the solution of a mystery [CLEW]

Cluj (kluʒ) (*G.* Klausenburg, *Hung.* Kolozsvar) the chief town (pop. 256,900) of Transylvania, Rumania. Industries: mechanical engineering, metallurgy, food processing. Rumanian university (1872). Hungarian university (1945)

Clum·ber spaniel (klʌmbər) a short-legged spaniel of a breed with a long, heavy body and thick silky coat [after *Clumber*, the estate of the duke of Newcastle]

clump (klʌmp) 1. *n.* a group (of trees, flowers etc.) growing together ‖ a lump or mass ‖ a heavy tramping sound 2. *v.i.* to tramp heavily or clumsily ‖ to form clumps ‖ *v.t.* to put together in a clump ‖ (*bacteriol.*) to cause to form clumps [etym. doubtful]

clum·si·ly (klʌmzili:) *adv.* in a clumsy manner

clum·si·ness (klʌmzi:nis) *n.* the state or quality of being clumsy

clum·sy (klʌmzi:) *comp.* **clum·si·er** *superl.* **clum·si·est** *adj.* awkward, ungainly ‖ poorly made, without refinement or elegance ‖ tactless, *a clumsy remark* [fr. obs. *clumse*, to be stiff with cold]

clunch (klʌntʃ) *n.* (*geol.*) the lower and harder strata of the Upper Chalk, used in building [etym. doubtful]

clung (klʌŋ) *past* and *past part.* of CLING

Clu·ni·ac (kluːniːæk) 1. *adj.* of the reformed Benedictine order founded (910) at Cluny in E. France 2. *n.* a monk of this order [after *Cluny*]
—The Cluniac reform affected worship, learning and liturgy, and was an important force in Western Christendom until the 12th c. It was suppressed during the French Revolution. The 11th-c. abbey at Cluny, a Romanesque masterpiece, was largely destroyed at the end of the 18th c.

Clu·ny (klyni:) *CLUNIAC

clu·pe·id (kluːpiːid) 1. *n.* a member of *Clupeidae*, a family of marine, teleostean fishes, including herrings and sardines 2. *adj.* of or relating to the *Clupeidae* [fr. Mod. L. *Clupeidae* fr. *clupea*, a small freshwater fish]

clu·pe·oid (kluːpiːɔid) 1. *n.* a member of *Clupeoidea*, a suborder of *Isospondyli*, an order of fishes including the clupeids, salmon, smelts etc. 2. *adj.* of or relating to the *Clupeoidea* [fr. Mod. L. *Clupeoidea* fr. *clupea*, a small freshwater fish]

clus·ter (klʌstər) 1. *n.* a number of similar things growing or gathered together, *a cluster of grapes* 2. *v.i.* to gather close together 3. *adj.* of houses built close together to utilize larger spaces for common recreation [O.E. *clyster*]

cluster college small, independent liberal arts college within the framework of a multicollege university

cluster sampling sampling procedure in which the initial sampling from the population consists of clusters or groups of elements rather than the elements themselves

clutch (klʌtʃ) *n.* a tight grip ‖ the act of clutching ‖ (esp. *pl.*) power, control, the *moneylender's clutches* ‖ (*mech.*) a device for connecting and disconnecting driving and driven parts smoothly, used esp. in motor vehicles between the engine and the transmission ‖ the lever or pedal controlling this device ‖ the grab of a crane [M.E. *cloke*, claw and *cluchen*, to clench]

clutch *n.* a nestful of eggs ‖ a brood of chickens [earlier *cletch* fr. O.N.]

clutch *v.t.* to seize, catch hold of ‖ to hold firmly ‖ *v.i.* (with 'at') to make a snatching movement [prob. O.E. *clyccean*]

clut·ter (klʌtər) 1. *n.* an untidy mess, state of disorder ‖ litter, things left around untidily 2. *v.t.* to disorder, make untidy [var. of obs. *clotter*]

Clyde (klaid) a river in Lanark, Scotland, a great commercial waterway. It rises in Dumfries, flows 106 miles, passing through Glasgow, and reaches the North Channel at Dumbarton as the Firth of Clyde

Clyde·bank (kláidbæŋk) an industrial port (pop. 51,656) in Dumbartonshire, Scotland on the outskirts of Glasgow, on the Clyde: shipbuilding, engineering

clyp·e·ate (klípi:eit) *adj.* (*biol.*) shaped like a round shield ‖ (*biol.*) furnished with a shield [fr. L. *clypeare* (*clypeatus*), to arm with a shield]

Cly·tem·nes·tra (klaitəmnéstrə) (*Gk mythol.*) the daughter of Tyndareus and Leda, sister of Castor, Pollux and Helen. She married Agamemnon and was the mother of Iphigenia, Electra and Orestes. Helped by her lover Aegisthus she murdered Agamemnon on his return from Troy, and was herself killed by Orestes

cm. centimeter, centimeters

CN abbr for chloracetophenone, a lacrimatory agent. *Cf* MACE

cni·do·blast (náidəblæst) *n.* a cell containing a nematocyst, typical of coelenterates [fr. Gk *knidē*, nettle + *blastos*, cell]

Cnossus *KNOSSOS

Cnut (kənúːt, kənjúːt) (Canute, c. 995–1035), king of England (1016–35), Denmark (1019–35) and Norway (1028–35). He invaded England (1013) with his father Swein Forkbeard of Denmark, and divided the country (1016) with Edmund II. On Edmund's death (1016) he became king of all England, codifying the laws and aiding the Church. He invaded Scotland (1027) and ruled Schleswig, but his kingdom broke up on his death

c/o care of

c.o. care of ‖ (*accountancy*) carried over

co- (kou) *prefix* jointly, together, mutually, joint, mutual ‖ (*math.*) of the complement of an angle [L. *com-*, *con-*, *co-*]

coach (koutʃ) 1. *n.* a state carriage ‖ (*hist.*) a large four-wheeled carriage usually drawn by four horses, carrying passengers, parcels and mail ‖ a bus for long-distance journeys ‖ a railroad car for passengers ‖ a class of air travel less luxurious than first class ‖ a private tutor ‖ a trainer in athletics ‖ (*baseball*) a team member stationed near 1st or 3rd base who advises the runners 2. *v.t.* to teach (someone) privately ‖ to train (someone, e.g. in athletics) ‖ *v.i.* to give private tuition [older *coche* fr. F. fr. Magyar]

coach box the driver's seat on a coach

coach·built (kóutʃbilt) *adj.* (*Br.*, of car bodies) made by a craftsman, not mass-produced

coach·man (kóutʃmən) *pl.* **coach·men** (kóutʃmən) *n.* the driver of a carriage

co·ad·ju·tor (kouædʒutər, kouədʒúːtər) *n.* an assistant, esp. a bishop assisting a bishop [O.F. *coadjuteur*]

co·ag·u·la·ble (kouægjuləb'l) *adj.* capable of being congealed

co·ag·u·lant (kouægjulənt) *n.* something which causes coagulation

co·ag·u·late (kouægjuleit) *pres. part.* **co·ag·u·lat·ing** *past* and *past part.* **co·ag·u·lat·ed** *v.i.* to turn from a liquid to a curdlike or jellylike consistency, congeal ‖ *v.t.* to precipitate (a suspension) ‖ to cause to congeal **co·ag·u·lá·tion, co·ág·u·la·tor** ns [fr. obs. *coagulate* adj. fr. L. *coagulare* (*coagulatus*), to cause to curdle]

co·ag·u·la·tor (kouægjuleitər) *n.* (*med.*) electronic device used by surgeons to stop bleeding

co·ag·u·lum (kouægjuləm) *pl.* **co·ag·u·la** (kouægjulə) *n.* a coagulated mass [L.]

Co·a·hui·la (kɔawíːla) a northern state (area 58,067 sq. miles, pop. 1,334,000 of Mexico, bounded by Texas in the north and northeast. The land ranges from barren desert to broken plateau, traversed by several mountain ranges. Capital: Saltillo (pop. 118,000). Industries: stock raising, agriculture (cotton, corn, wheat, beans, sugar, grapes), mining (silver, lead, coal, copper, iron)

coal (koul) 1. *n.* (*geol.*) a combustible deposit of vegetable matter (mosses, ferns etc.) which grew in the Carboniferous era, rendered compact and hard by pressure and heat (*ANTHRACITE, *BITUMINOUS COAL, *CANNEL COAL, *LIGNITE, *PEAT) ‖ a burning ember **to carry coals to Newcastle** to perform a superfluous action **to heap coals of fire on (someone)** to make (someone) feel guilty by returning good for evil **to rake** (or **call** or **haul**) **over the coals** to criticize severely 2. *v.t.* to load (a ship) with coal ‖ *v.i.* to take in a supply of coal [O.E. *col*]

coal-black (koulblæk) *adj.* very black

co·a·lesce (kouəlés) *pres. part.* **co·a·lesc·ing** *past* and *past part.* **co·a·lesced** *v.i.* to grow or come together, fuse ‖ to combine in a political coalition **co·a·lés·cence** *n.* **co·a·lés·cent** *adj.* [fr. L. *coalescere*]

coal face an exposed vertical working section in a coal mine reached by tunneling

coal-field (kóulfiːld) *n.* a coal mine ‖ a district where coal is found

coal gas a distillation product produced when suitable coal is strongly heated in the absence of air. It is used as a fuel. Its approximate composition by volume is 50% hydrogen, 30% methane, 8% carbon monoxide, 8% carbon dioxide, oxygen and nitrogen, 4% gaseous hydrocarbons other than methane

coal-heav·er (kóulhiːvər) *n.* (*Br.*) a strong man who works for a coal merchant and esp. one who delivers to customers

coaling station a port at which steamships can refuel with coal

co·a·li·tion (kouəlíʃən) *n.* a coalescing, union ‖ a temporary union of political parties for some common aim **co·a·li·tion·ist** *n.* [fr. L. *coalitio* (*coalitionis*)]

coal measures (*geol.*) the upper division of the Carboniferous rocks, in which seams of coal occur

coal-mouse, cole-mouse (kóulmaus) *pl.* **coal-mice, cole-mice** (kóulmais) *n.* the coal tit [M.E. *colmose* fr. O.E. *colmāse*]

coal oil petroleum or a refined petroleum oil, esp. kerosene

coal-pit (kóulpit) *n.* a coal mine

coal scuttle a utensil for carrying (and sometimes for pouring) small quantities of coal

coal tar a thick, black liquid obtained by the destructive distillation of bituminous coal in a coke oven or retort, to give such important products as benzene, phenol, naphthalene, creosote etc.

coal tit, cole·tit (kóultit) *n. Parus ater*, a small European tit with a black cap and white neck marking

coal-whip·per (kóulhwipər, kóulwipər) *n.* (*Br.*) a man or machine unloading coal from a ship's hold

coam·ing (kóumiŋ) *n.* a raised border around a ship's hatches, cockpit or skylights, to keep water out [origin unknown]

Coanda effect (kouándə) *phys.* property of a fluid to follow a curved surface that it contacts; named for Henri Coanda, in 1932

co·arc·tate (kouárkteit, kouárktit) *adj.* (*biol.*) pressed together, constricted ‖ of insect pupae retaining the last larval skin as a covering [fr. L. *coarctatus*, pressed close together]

coarse (kɔrs, kours) *comp.* **coars·er** *superl.* **coars·est** *adj.* rough, large-grained, not fine, *coarse sugar* ‖ inferior, of poor quality, *coarse stockings* ‖ unrefined, rude, *coarse manners* ‖ vulgar, indecent, *coarse language* [older *course*, ordinary fr. COURSE n.]

coarse aggregate the small gravel or crushed stone used in mixing concrete

coarse-grained (kɔrsgreind, koursgreind) *adj.* having coarse texture

coars·en (kɔrs'n, kours'n) *v.t.* to make coarse ‖ *v.i.* to become coarse

coast (koust) 1. *n.* the seashore, the land bordering the sea ‖ a slope for tobogganing ‖ a ride downhill on a sled etc. ‖ a ride downhill on a bicycle without pedaling or in a motor vehicle with the engine switched off **the coast is clear** the danger has passed ‖ there is no one around ‖ the obstructions holding up advance have been removed 2. *v.i.* to sail along the coast ‖ to trade between ports along the same coast ‖ to toboggan downhill ‖ to cycle downhill without pedaling or drive a car downhill with the engine switched off ‖ *v.t.* to sail near, *we crossed Gibraltar* **cóast·al** *adj.* [M.E. *coste* fr. O.F.]

coast·er (kóustər) *n.* a coasting vessel ‖ a small, low, round stand placed under a decanter ‖ a small tray or mat placed under a bottle or glass to protect a table ‖ a roller coaster ‖ (*Br.*) a wooden stand for a cheese

coast-guard (kóustgard) *n.* (*Br.*) an official keeping lookout from the coast for ships in danger, smuggling of contraband goods, illegal landing of passengers etc.

coast guard the body which organizes lifesaving stations along the coast and enforces customs and immigration laws ‖ a member of this body

Coast Guard Academy, U.S. a military institution in New London, Connecticut, founded (1876) by an act of Congress to train cadet candidates for a commission in the coast guard

coast·line (kóustlaɪn) n. the continuous limit of the land at the sea's edge ‖ the shape this makes on the ground or on the map, *a broken coastline*

Coast Ranges a mountain belt in W. North America, extending along the Pacific coast from Alaska southward into Lower California, Mexico. It contains Mt Logan

coast·wards (kóustwərdz) adv. toward the coast

coast·wise (kóustwaɪz) 1. adj. following the coast 2. adv. along the coast

coat (kout) 1. n. an overcoat ‖ a person's jacket ‖ an animal's protective covering ‖ any outer covering, *a coat of paint* 2. v.t. to cover with a coat, *to coat apples with toffee* [M.E. *cote* fr. O.F.]

coat armor, *Br.* **coat armour** coats of arms

coated lens (*optics*) lens for cameras or instruments designed to reduce light loss by reflection. It is created by applying a film coating made up of magnesium, fluoride, silicon oxide, sodium fluoride, and titanium oxide

coat·ee (koutí) n. a short coat

Coates (kouts), Joseph Gordon (1878–1943), New Zealand statesman and prime minister (1925–8). He introduced wide-ranging economic reforms during the 1930s

coat hanger a shaped support with a central hook, used for hanging up garments to preserve their shape

co·a·ti (kouátiː) pl. **co·a·tis** n. a member of *Nasua*, a genus of mammals related to the raccoon. Two known species, with a long snout, live in tropical America, eating chiefly eggs, insects etc. They are easily domesticated [Tupi fr. *cua*, cincture + *tim*, nose]

coat·ing (kóutɪŋ) n. a covering (e.g. of paint etc.) ‖ cloth used for coats

coat of arms a number of distinctive heraldic devices used on a shield ‖ (*hist.*) a herald's tabard [fr. F. *cotte d'armes*, a tabard]

coat of mail (*armor*) an outer garment covered with overlapping metal plates or with chain mail

coat·room (kóutruːm, kóutrʊm) n. a room where one can leave one's coat etc., cloakroom

coat·tail (kóuteɪl) n. capacity of a more powerful candidate to sustain the weaker one through an election and lead them both to victory

co·au·thor (kouɔ́θər, kóuɔθər) 1. n. a joint author 2. v.t. to be joint author of

coax (kouks) v.t. to persuade by soft words or gentle handling, *to coax a kitten down a tree* ‖ to cause a desired effect in (something) by persistent little efforts, *to coax smoldering twigs into flame* ‖ to get (something) out of someone by cajoling, encouragement etc. ‖ v.i. to wheedle, cajole [fr. obs. *cokes*, a fool]

co·ax·al (kouǽksəl) adj. coaxial

co·ax·i·al (kouǽksiːəl) adj. having a common axis, *coaxial lenses*

coaxial cable a cable consisting essentially of a central conductor surrounded by an insulated conducting tube, used for transmitting esp. television signals

cob (kɒb) n. a male swan ‖ a stocky, short-legged horse for riding and light draft work ‖ a cobnut ‖ (*Br.*) a round crisp loaf ‖ a roundish piece of coal [origin unknown]

cob n. the spike or ear of corn on which the kernels grow, a corncob [origin unknown]

co·balt (kóubɔlt) n. a bivalent, hard, magnetic, silver-white, metallic element (symbol Co, at. no. 27, at. mass 58.933). It is used in the production of magnetic and hard alloys which are resistant to high temperatures, abrasion and corrosion. Its radioisotope Co^{60} is used as a source of gamma rays in radiology and as a trace element in nutrition studies [G. *kobalt* prob. same as *kobold*, mine demon]

co·balt-beam therapy (kóubɔltbiːm) (*med.*) treatment for cancer utilizing gamma radiation from cobalt 60 to destroy malignant cells. —

cobalt bomb n. source of the cobalt beam

cobalt bloom erythrite

cobalt blue a permanent greenish-blue pigment composed of cobalt oxide and alumina ‖ a strong greenish-blue color

co·bal·tic (koubɔ́ltik) adj. of, relating to or containing (esp. trivalent) cobalt

co·bal·tif·er·ous (koubɔltífərəs) adj. containing cobalt

co·bal·tite (koubɔ́ltaɪt, kóubɔltaɪt) n. a sulfarsenide of cobalt (CoAsS) used in making smalt

co·bal·tous (koubɔ́ltəs) adj. of, relating to or containing (esp. divalent) cobalt

Cob·bett (kɒ́bit), William (1763–1835), English writer and radical reformer, author of 'Rural Rides', a discursive account of conditions in the English countryside after the Napoleonic Wars

cob·ble (kɒ́bl) 1. n. a cobblestone ‖ (*Br.*) a piece of coal the size of a small cobblestone 2. v.t. pres. part. **cob·bling** past and past part. **cob·bled** to pave with cobbles [etym. doubtful]

cobble pres. part. **cob·bling** past and past part. **cob·bled** v.t. to mend (shoes) ‖ (*Br.*) to make or mend roughly or clumsily **cób·bler** n. a shoe repairer ‖ a fruit pie made in a deep dish and covered with a thick crust ‖ an iced drink typically of wine, sugar and citrus fruit [origin unknown]

cobblers (*Br.*) bunk

cobbler's wax a resin used for waxing thread

cob·ble·stone (kɒ́blstoun) n. a round, smooth stone used for paving, a cobble

cob·ble-up (kɒ́blʌp) v. (*Br.*) to put together, e.g., like a cobbler

Cob·den (kɒ́bdən), Richard (1804–65), British statesman and economist. With John Bright, he led the campaign (1838–46) of the Anti-Corn-Law League which finally persuaded Peel to repeal (1846) the Corn Laws. He vainly advocated nonintervention in the Crimean War (1854–6), and negotiated (1860) a free-trade treaty with France

Co·blenz (kóublents) (*G.* Koblenz) a West German town (pop. 113,900) at the confluence of the Rhine and the Moselle, a communications center: winemaking

cob·nut (kɒ́bnʌt) n. *Corylus avellana grandis*, a variety of hazel ‖ the nut of this tree [older *cobill* var. of COBBLE + NUT]

COBOL (*computer acronym*) for common business-oriented language used in computer programming, utilizing English statements given through a compiler language that produces the desired program. It was designed by Codaysl, a Department of Defense committee. *Cf* ALGOL, BASIC, FORTRAN

co·bra (kóubrə) n. a member of *Naja*, a genus of very poisonous African and Asian snakes that, when on the defensive, flatten the skin behind the neck by distending and elevating the ribs to form a hood [Port. *cobra de capello* = snake with hood]

cobs (kɒbz) n. aberrations on oscilloscope created by continuous wave jamming

cob·web (kɒ́bweb) n. the fine network of threads spun by a spider to trap its prey ‖ a single thread spun by a spider ‖ something as flimsy as a spider's threads or thought of as entangling **cób·web·by** adj. [M.E. *coppeweb* fr. *coppe*, spider]

co·ca (kóukə) n. a member of *Erythroxylon*, any of several South American and West Indian shrubs whose dried leaves are the source of cocaine and other alkaloids [Span. fr. Peruv. *cuca*]

co·caine (koukéin, kóukein) n. an alkaloid ($C_{17}H_{21}O_4N$) derived from coca leaves or which can be synthesized. If taken internally or sniffed it acts as a stimulant, then as a narcotic. It can cause addiction. It is used medically as a local anesthetic [COCA]

Coc·a·na·da (kɒkənáːdə) *KAKINADA

coc·cid (kɒ́ksid) n. a scale insect or mealybug, a member of the superfamily *Coccoidea* [L. fr. Gk *kokkis*, grain]

Coc·cid·i·um, pl. **-ia** (kɒksídiːəm) n. (*biol.*) group of parasitic soil fungi of the class *Sporozoa* that are pathogenic for many animals but not for humans

coc·coid (kɒ́kɔid) adj. of or resembling a coccus

coc·cus (kɒ́kəs) pl. **coc·ci** (kɒ́ksai) n. (*bot.*) a one-seeded carpel into which a compound fruit splits when ripe ‖ a spherical bacterium (*STREPTOCOCCUS, *STAPHYLOCOCCUS, *DIPLOCOCCUS, *MICROCOCCUS) [Mod. L. fr. Gk *kokkos*, kernel]

coc·cyg·e·al (kɒksídʒiːəl) adj. of or relating to the coccyx

coc·cyx (kɒ́ksiks) pl. **coc·cy·ges** (kɒksáidʒiːz, kɒksídʒiːz), **coc·cyx·es** n. the fused vertebrae at the base of the spinal column in man and certain primates [L. fr. Gk *kokkux*, cuckoo]

Co·cha·bam·ba (kɒtʃəbámbə) a city (pop. 281,962) of Bolivia, 8,448 ft above sea level, a trading center southeast of La Paz

Co·chin (kóutʃin) a former princely state in S.W. India, now part of Kerala ‖ its former capital (pop. 513,081), a port and naval base. It was visited by Vasco da Gama in 1502, and was the site of the first European settlement in India

Co·chin-Chi·na (kóutʃintʃáinə, kɒ́tʃintʃáinə) a former province of S. Vietnam. Part of the Funan and Khmer empires, it was settled (17th and 18th cc.) by the Vietnamese. It became a French colony (1867), the southern division of French Indochina (1887), an independent republic (1946) and part of Vietnam (1949)

coch·i·neal (kɒtʃəniːl, kɒ́tʃəniːl) n. a dye prepared from the dried bodies of the female cochineal insect, used in the preparation of carmine and scarlet pigments [F. *cochenille* fr. Span. or Ital.]

cochineal insect *Dactylopius coccus*, an insect which feeds on plants of the cactus family, esp. *Opuntia*, common in Mexico (*COCHINEAL)

coch·le·a (kɒ́kliːə) pl. **coch·le·ae** (kɒkliːiː) n. the usually spiraled part of the inner ear in mammals and birds which receives sound vibrations and converts them to nerve impulses **cóch·le·ar** adj. [L. fr. Gk *kochlias*, snail]

coch·le·ate (kɒ́kliːit, kɒkliːeit) adj. (*biol.*) spiral, shaped like a snail shell **cóch·le·at·ed** adj. [fr. L. *cochleatus*, spiral-shaped]

Coch·rane (kɒ́krən), Thomas *DUNDONALD

cock (kɒk) 1. n. the male bird of the common domestic fowl ‖ (often in combination) the male of other birds, *cock pheasant* ‖ a weathercock ‖ a tap ‖ the hammer in a gun ‖ the raised position of this hammer ‖ an upward tilt, of a nose, hat etc. **to go off at half cock** to fail because not fully ready or prepared (e.g. of a coup d'état) 2. v.t. to erect or cause to stand on end, *the dog cocked its ears* ‖ to set aslant, tilt upwards, *to cock one's hat* ‖ to raise the cock of (a gun) ready to fire ‖ v.i. to stick up, stand on end **to cock a snook** (*Br.*) to thumb one's nose [O.E. *cocc*]

cock 1. n. a small conical pile of hay set up in a field for drying, a haycock 2. v.t. to set up (hay etc.) in cocks [perh. fr. Scand.]

cock·ade (kɒkéid) n. a rosette, knot of ribbons etc., worn in a hat to show support of a person or party, or as a badge of office **cock·ád·ed** adj. [fr. F. *cocarde* (fem.), pert]

cock-a-doo·dle-doo (kɒ́kədu:d'ldú:) n. an imitation of a cock's crow

cock-a-hoop (kɒ́kəhú:p, kɒ́kəhúp) 1. adj. elated, exultant 2. adv. elatedly, exultantly [origin unknown]

Cock·aigne (kɒkéin) an imaginary land of luxury and leisure [M.E. *cokaygne* fr. O.F.]

cock-a-leek·ie (kɒkəli:kí:) n. a Scotch soup made from chicken and leeks

cock-a-ma·mie or **cock-a-ma·my** (kɒkəméimi:) adj. (*colloq.*) silly, preposterous, illogical

cock-and-bull story (kɒ́kənbúl) an incredible story ‖ a blatantly false excuse

cock·a·too (kɒ́kətu:, kɒkətú:) n. a crested parrot of fam. *Kakatoidae* found in Australia and the East Indies [fr. Malay *kakatúa*]

cock·a·trice (kɒ́kətris) n. a fabulous monster (*BASILISK) [O.F. *cocatris*]

Cock·ayne's syndrome (kɒkéins) (*med.*) rare ailment (50 reported cases) in which physical time is telescoped and the aging process runs out of control; first described by Dr. E. A. Cockayne in 1936

cock·boat (kɒ́kbout) n. a small ship's boat [fr. obs. *cock*, a small boat]

cock·chaf·er (kɒ́ktʃeifər) n. a member of *Melolontha*, a genus of large European beetles whose larvae live 2–3 years. The adult and the larva destroy vegetation

Cock·croft (kɒ́kkrɔft, kɒ́kkroft), Sir John Douglas (1897–1967), English atomic physicist. In 1932 Cockcroft and Walton caused the first artificial transmutation of one element into another. Nobel prize (1951)

cock·crow (kɒ́kkrou) n. dawn

cocked hat a hat with the brim turned up on three sides, worn as part of certain uniforms ‖ a hat with the brim turned up on two sides and worn front to back or crossways, as part of certain uniforms **to knock into a cocked hat** to beat completely, in fight or competition

cock·er (kɒ́kər) n. a breed of spaniel [COCK (from its use as a game dog, starting woodcock etc.)]

cock·er·el (kɒ́kərəl, kɒ́kərl) n. a young cock

Cocker spaniel a cocker

cock·eyed (kɒ́kaid) adj. squinting ‖ (*pop.*) lopsided, awry, *a cockeyed angle* ‖ nonsensical, ridiculous, *a cockeyed scheme* ‖ drunk

CONCISE PRONUNCIATION KEY: **(a)** æ, c*a*t; ɑ, c*a*r; ɔ f*aw*n; ei, sn*a*ke. **(e)** e, h*e*n; i:, sh*ee*p; iə, d*ee*r; ɛə, b*ea*r. **(i)** i, f*i*sh; ai, t*i*ger; əː, b*i*rd. **(o)** ɒ, *o*x; au, c*ow*; ou, g*oa*t; u, p*oo*r; ɔi, r*oy*al. **(u)** ʌ, d*u*ck; u, b*u*ll; u:, g*oo*se; ə, b*a*cillus; ju:, c*u*be. x, lo*ch*; θ, *th*ink; ð, bo*th*er; z, *Z*en; ʒ, corsa*g*e; dʒ, sava*g*e; ŋ, oranguta*ng*; j, *y*ak; ʃ, *f*ish; tʃ, fe*tch*; 'l, rabb*le*; 'n, redd*en*. Complete pronunciation key appears inside front cover.

cock·fight·ing (kókfaitiŋ) n. the sport of setting cocks to fight each other, usually armed with metal spurs. Spectators bet on the outcome

cock·horse (kókhɔrs) n. a hobbyhorse, adult's knee etc. on which a child can pretend to ride astride

cock·i·ly (kókili:) adv. in a cocky manner

cock·i·ness (kóki:nis) n. the state or quality of being cocky

cocking circuit (mil.) in mine warfare, a subsidiary circuit that requires actuation before the main circuits become alive

cock·le (kók'l) 1. v. pres. part. **cock·ling** past and past part. **cock·led** v.i. (of paper etc.) to pucker, curl up because of varying tensions ‖ v.t. to cause to pucker or curl up 2. n. a pucker, wrinkle ‖ a bivalve mollusk of genus Cardium, esp. C. edule, the common edible European species ‖ a cockleshell ‖ (rhet.) a small, frail boat **to warm the cockles of one's heart** to cause one to feel a glow of wellbeing [M.E. cokille fr. O.F. coquille, shell]

cock·le·bur (kók'lbə:r) n. a coarse weed of genus Xanthium, fam. Compositae, with prickly burs ‖ a bur of this weed [fr. cockle, any of certain weeds+BUR]

cock·le·shell (kók'lʃel) n. the shell of a cockle ‖ a small, frail boat

cock·loft (kóklɔft, kóklɒft) n. a small loft or garret under the roof [origin unknown]

cock·ney (kókni:) 1. pl. **cock·neys** n. a dialect spoken in London ‖ a Londoner who speaks this dialect ‖ (strictly) a Londoner born within the sound of Bow Bells 2. adj. of or relating to a cockney [M.E. coken-ey, cock's egg, orig. prob. meaning a small or misshapen egg]

cock of the walk (Br.) the leader of a set, esp. someone who asserts himself domineeringly

cock·pit (kókpit) n. an opening in the fuselage or hull of an airplane without a pilot's cabin, for the pilot (and observer or navigator) ‖ the well at the stern of small yachts and some other small decked boats where the wheel is usually situated ‖ (hist.) the afterpart of the orlop deck in a man-of-war ‖ a small arena for cockfights ‖ a battleground, Belgium has been called the cockpit of Europe

cock·roach (kókroutʃ) n. a member of Blattaria, an order of usually vegetarian insects. Of the more than 2,400 species, some are serious household pests [fr. Span. cucaracha]

cock·shy (kókʃai) pl. **cock·shies** n. (Br., old-fash.) a target for pelting in a fairground booth, or a throw at it ‖ something or someone taken as a target for ridicule or criticism

cock sparrow a cocky little man (usually one who is so to compensate for his smallness of stature or social insignificance)

cock·sure (kókʃúər) adj. self-confident to an irritating degree **cóck·súre·ness** n.

cock·tail (kókteil) n. a drink of liquor mixed with others or with various flavorings ‖ an appetizer served as a first course, shrimp cocktail ‖ a horse with a docked tail

cocktail belt stretch of suburban community considered to be occupied by cocktail imbibers

cock·up (kókʌp) n. (printing) an initial letter taller than the rest

cock·y (kóki:) comp. **cock·i·er** superl. **cock·i·est** adj. cocksure ‖ pert

cock·y·leek·y (kóki:lí:ki:) n. cock-a-leekie

co·co (kóukou) n. a coconut (palm) ‖ a coconut (drupe) [Span. and Port.]

co·coa (kóukou) n. a brown powder obtained after extracting the fats from the cacao bean ‖ a drink prepared from this powder ‖ dull reddish brown [fr. Span. cacao fr. Mex.]

co·coa n. a coco

cocoa butter cacao butter

COCOM (mil.) a coordinating committee of representatives from all NATO countries (except Iceland), 'responsible for compiling lists of strategic goods that the Western powers want to deny the Communists'

co·co·nut, co·coa·nut (kóukənʌt, kóukənət) n. Cocos nucifera, fam. Palmaceae, the coconut palm, which grows on the shores of tropical islands ‖ the edible fruit (a drupe) of this palm. The milk (liquid endosperm) is good to drink and the outer husk yields coir [Span. coco, bogeyman, grinning face+NUT]

coconut oil the fatty oil obtained from coconuts and used for soaps, cosmetics etc. and in cooking

coconut palm *COCONUT

co·coon (kəkú:n) n. the silky covering which the larvae of many insects, e.g. the silkworm, spin about themselves for protection during the

pupa stage ‖ the similar protective coverings produced by some animals, e.g. some annelids [F. cocon]

cocooning the spraying or coating of an aircraft or equipment with a substance, e.g., a plastic, to form a cocoonlike seal against the effects of the atmosphere

coco palm the coconut (palm)

Co·cos Islands (kóukous) (Keeling Islands) an Australian territory (area 5 sq. miles, pop. 546 Malays and Europeans) in the Indian Ocean southwest of Java, producing copra. There are 27 coral islands (3 inhabited). They were discovered in 1609, first settled in 1826, became a British protectorate (1857), and were transferred to Australia (1955)

Coc·teau (kɔktou), Jean (1889–1963), French poet, novelist ('les Enfants terribles'), playwright ('Antigone', 'les Parents terribles', 'l'Aigle à deux têtes' etc.), and maker of films ('le Sang d'un poète', 'la Belle et la Bête', 'Orphée', 'le Testament d'Orphée'). He also illustrated books, decorated churches, designed ballet settings etc.

cod (kɒd) n. a member of Gadus, fam. Gadidae, a genus of bony fishes (2–4 ft long) inhabiting cold and temperate seas of the northern hemisphere, particularly abundant off Newfoundland. They yield food and oil [origin unknown]

c.o.d., C.O.D. cash on delivery, collect on delivery

co·da (kóudə) n. (mus.) a section added at the end of a movement to round it off [Ital.]

CODAP (computer acronym) for control data assembly program, computer assembly program designed by Control Data Corporation for 1604A computers

CODAR (mil. acronym) for correlation, detection and ranging underwater, a sonic detection device utilizing sonobuoys dropped by planes in a special pattern

Cod, Cape *CAPE COD

cod·dle (kɒd'l) pres. part. **cod·dling** past and past part. **cod·dled** v.t. to treat carefully and tenderly, to pamper ‖ to cook slowly in water just below boiling point, coddled eggs [origin unknown]

code (koud) 1. n. a collection of statutes, rules etc. methodically arranged ‖ an accepted way of behavior, esp. the mores of a society ‖ a system of signals, Morse code ‖ a system in which arbitrary values are given to letters, words, numbers or symbols to ensure secrecy or brevity (cf. CIPHER) 2. v.t. pres. part. **cod·ing** past and past part. **cod·ed** to put (a message) into code ‖ (genetics) to particularize the genetic code used in synthesizing [F.]

co·dec·li·na·tion (kóudeklinéiʃən) n. (astron.) the complement of the declination

co·deine (kóudi:n) n. an alkaloid extracted from morphine and used primarily for relieving pain [fr. Gk kōdeia, poppyhead]

Code Noir (kɔdnwær) a French colonial code for the treatment of slaves, introduced (1685) by Colbert and Louis XIV, out of fear of mutiny. It gave slaves the right to a formal trial and prohibited the division of families. The code was ignored

code of honor, Br. **code of honour** the unwritten rules and moral principles of an individual or social group

co·dex (kóudeks) pl. **co·di·ces** (kóudisi:z, kɒdisi:z) n. a manuscript book, esp. of early Bible or classical texts [L.=book]

cod·fish (kódfiʃ) pl. **cod·fish, cod·fish·es** n. the cod

cod·ger (kódʒər) n. (pop.) an old fellow, esp. one slightly eccentric [perh. var. of CADGER]

codices pl. of CODEX

cod·i·cil (kódis'l) n. a supplementary clause added to a will, revoking or modifying it ‖ an additional provision **cod·i·cíl·la·ry** adj. [fr. L. codicillus, dim. of codex, book]

co·di·fi·ca·tion (kɒdifikéiʃən, kɒudifikéiʃən) n. the act, process or result of codifying

cod·i·fi·er (kódifaiər, kóudifaiər) n. someone who codifies

cod·i·fy (kódifai, kóudifai) pres. part. **cod·i·fy·ing** past and past part. **cod·i·fied** v.t. to draw up a code of (laws etc.)

cod·ling (kódliŋ) n. a young cod ‖ a fish of genus Phycis

codling moth Carpocapsa pomonella, a lepidopteran insect which in the larval stages bores into and destroys apples, pears, quinces etc. It pupates on the ground during winter

cod-liv·er oil (kódlivər) oil extracted from the liver of cod and allied fish, rich in vitamins and used in medicine

co·don (kóudon) n. (genetics) a collection of three nucleotide chemicals in DNA in a specific order, creating a genetic code for developing a particular amino acid. 2. (acronym) for Carrier-operated device, an anti-noise device to receive modulated carrier signals without interference

cod·piece (kódpi:s) n. (hist.) a flap or pouch in the front of men's breeches to cover the opening [fr. obs. cod, bag+ PIECE]

cods wallop (Br.) foolish nonsense

Cod War enforcement by Iceland of 200-mi. territorial limit on English fishing vessels resulting in several incidents, including gunfire. The issue was settled by NATO intervention in 1975

Co·dy (kóudi), William F. *BUFFALO BILL

co·ed (kóuéd, kóued) n. (pop.) a female student at a coeducational college

co·ed·u·ca·tion (kóuedʒukéiʃən) n. the education together in a single institution of children or students of both sexes **co·ed·u·cá·tion·al** adj.

co·ef·fi·cient (kouifíʃənt) n. (math.) the non-varying factor of a variable product e.g. the 4 in $4x$ ‖ (phys.) a number expressing the degree to which a substance or process possesses a given characteristic, e.g. the coefficient of expansion of a metal or a gas

coefficient of alienation (math.) measure of the absence of relationship between two variables

coefficient of expansion (phys.) the ratio of the change in length, area or volume of a body per degree rise in temperature to the length, area or volume respectively at some fixed temperature

coefficient of haze 1. (meteorology) measure of visibility interference in the atmosphere. 2. unit of measure of soiling particles. abbr CoH. Cf SMOKE SHADE, SOILING INDEX

coefficient of reliability (statistics) measure of the reliability of consistency of some measuring instrument, e.g., intelligence tests

coe·la·canth (sí:ləkænθ) n. a fish of fam. Coelacanthidae, often considered coextensive with order Actinistia. Its ancestry is believed to go back 300 million years and it was thought extinct until living specimens were found (1938) off the African coasts. Specimens continue to be found (*LATIMERIA) [fr. Mod. L. Coelacanthus fr. Gk koilos, hollow+akantha, thorn]

coe·len·ter·ate (siléntəreit, siléntərit) n. a member of Coelenterata, a phylum of invertebrate, mostly marine animals including hydra, corals, jellyfish and sea anemones, whose basic structure is a sac with two layers of cells, and a central mouth surrounded by tentacles [Mod. L. fr. Gk koilos, hollow+enteron, intestine]

coe·li·ac, ce·li·ac (sí:li:æk) adj. (of arteries, veins, nerves, plexus) pertaining to the abdominal cavity [fr. L. coeliacus fr. Gk]

coeliac disease *CELIAC DISEASE

coeliac plexus the solar plexus

coe·lom (sí:ləm) pl. **coe·loms, coe·lo·ma·ta** (silóumətə) n. (zool.) the body cavity of metazoans above the lower worms. It forms a large space between the alimentary viscera and the body when well developed **coe·lo·mate** (sí:ləmeit, sí:loumit), **coe·lo·mic** (silómik, silóumik) adjs [fr. Gk koilōma fr. koilos, hollow]

coenobite *CENOBITE

coe·no·cyte (sí:nəsait, sénəsait) n. (biol.) a mass of protoplasm with many nuclei resulting from division of the nucleus without division of the cell [fr. Gk koinos, common+kutos, vessel, hollow]

coenospecies *CENOSPECIES

coe·nu·rus (sinúərəs, sinjúərəs) pl. **coe·nu·ri** (sinúərai, sinjúərai) n. the larva of Multiceps multiceps, a tapeworm of dogs, which causes gid in sheep [Mod. L. fr. Gk koinos, common+oura, tail]

co·en·zyme (kouénzaim) n. (biochem.) a nonprotein organic substance that can unite with a protein to form an enzyme or holoenzyme

co·en·zy·mom·e·ter (kouenzimómətər) n. photoelectric device to measure enzyme activity through the amount of light absorbed

co·e·qual (kouí:kwəl) 1. adj. equal in rank or dignity 2. n. a person or thing equal to another in rank or dignity **co·e·quál·i·ty** (kouikwóliti:) n.

co·erce (kouə́:rs) *pres. part.* **co·erc·ing** *past* and *past part.* **co·erced** *v.t.* to compel ‖ to enforce, *to coerce obedience* **co·er·ci·ble** *adj.* [fr. L. *coercere*, to constrain]

co·er·cion (kouə́:rʃən) *n.* compulsion (moral or physical) ‖ government by force [fr. O.F. *cohercion*]

co·er·cive (kouə́:rsiv) *adj.* compelling, intended to coerce

coercive force the strength of the magnetic field needed to demagnetize a given substance

co·er·civ·i·ty (kouə:rsíviti:) *n.* the value of the coercive force of a substance which has been magnetized to saturation

coe·site (kouśait) *n.* crystalline silica material found in meteorite craters created from quartz under great pressure; named for Loring Coes, Jr., American chemist

co·es·sen·tial (kouisénʃəl) *adj.* sharing the same essence

co·e·ter·nal (kouitə́:rn'l) *adj.* jointly or equally eternal

Cœur (kə:r) Jacques (c. 1395–1456), French merchant prince and treasurer (1439–51) to Charles VII. He developed trade with the Levant and restored the stability of French currency. His vast wealth mainly financed the war which drove (1450) the English from Normandy

Cœur d'A·lene (kə:rd'léin) *n.* a U.S. Indian people living in Idaho and Washington and numbering (before 1873) about 2,000 and latterly about 650 ‖ a member of this people

co·e·val (kouí:vəl) **1.** *adj.* contemporary, of the same age ‖ of equal duration **2.** *n.* a contemporary person or thing [fr. L. *coaevus*]

co·ex·ist (kouigzíst) *v.i.* to exist together ‖ (of countries) to live at peace with one another from policy despite conflicting ideologies **co·ex·íst·ence** *n.* **co·ex·íst·ent** *adj.*

co·ex·ten·sive (kouiksténsiv) *adj.* extending over the same space or time

cof·fee (kɔ́fi:, kɔ́fi:) *n.* a member of *Coffea*, fam. *Rubiaceae*, a genus of plants of which two or three species are cultivated commercially ‖ its seeds, raw, roasted or ground ‖ a drink, made (by infusion or decoction) from the roasted and ground seeds ‖ dark brown [Ital. fr. Turk. fr. Arab. *qahwah*, wine, coffee]
—Grown during the Middle Ages by Arabs near the Red Sea, coffee was brought to Europe in the 17th c. through pilgrimages and caravan trade. Mocha was the center of trade for two centuries, but Arabian monopoly declined when coffee growing extended to India, the East Indies, the West Indies and South America. Introduced (1727) into Brazil, coffee found the most favorable soil and climate, and Brazil now produces the major part of world supply

coffee bean the seed of the coffee plant

coffee break a short pause from work for drinking coffee etc. and relaxing

coffee grinder (*gymnastics*) maneuver from squatting position with both hands on floor in which a leg circle is made

coffee grounds the sediment left after the preparation of the coffee drink

cof·fee·house (kɔ́fi:haus, kɔ́fi:haus) *pl.* **cof·fee·hous·es** (kɔ́fi:hauziz, kɔ́fi:hauziz) *n.* a shop selling coffee and other refreshments, esp. (*hist.*) one frequented in the 17th and 18th cc. in England for political and literary discussion and social entertainment

coffee lightener or **coffee whitener** powder substitute for cream in coffee, made of vegetable oils (corn, soybean), sugar, and other substances

coffee mill a small mill for grinding coffee beans

cof·fee·pot (kɔ́fi:pɔt, kɔ́fi:pɔt) *n.* a pot in which coffee is prepared or served

coffee shop a small restaurant, which may be attached to a hotel, serving meals and snacks

cof·fee-ta·ble book (kɔ́fi:teib'l) elaborate, outsize book on a specific subject, with lush illustrations, usually placed in view

cof·fer (kɔ́fər, kɔ́fər) *n.* a large strongbox for storing money or valuables ‖ a place for storing money ‖ (often *pl.*) a store of funds ‖ (*archit.*) a panel sunk in a ceiling, vault or dome for decoration **2.** *v.t.* (*archit.*) to adorn with coffers [M.E. *cofre* fr. O.F. fr. L. fr. Gk]

cof·fer·dam (kɔ́fərdæm, kɔ́fərdæm) *n.* a watertight temporary structure enclosing part of a body of water to enable it to be pumped dry for construction purposes etc. ‖ a watertight structure from which repairs are made below the waterline of a ship

cof·fin (kɔ́fin, kɔ́fin) *n.* a box in which a corpse is placed for burial ‖ the hoof of a horse below the coronet ‖ (*printing*) the carriage of a printing machine ‖ container with radiation-resistant walls used to transport radioactive materials [O.F. *cofin*]

coffin bone the terminal foot bone enclosed in the hoof of horses and allied animals

coffin joint the joint above the coffin bone

co·fig·u·ra·tive (koufígjərətiv) *adj.* of a society in which age-peer influence is dominant, as defined by American anthropologist Margaret Mead Cf POSTFIGURATIVE

cog (kɔg, kɔg) *n.* a projection or tooth on the rim of a wheel which, by fitting between the cogs of another wheel or between the links of a chain, transmits motion and power ‖ a cogwheel ‖ (*carpentry*) a tenon ‖ a person whose efforts must combine with those of others to be effective [M.E. *kogge* fr. Scand.]

cog *pres. part.* **cog·ging** *past* and *past part.* **cogged** *v.i.* to cheat, esp. when throwing dice ‖ *v.t.* to handle (dice) in such a way as to cheat [etym. doubtful]

co·gen·cy (kóudʒənsi:) *n.* the state or quality of being cogent

co·gent (kóudʒənt) *adj.* compelling, convincing, *cogent arguments* [F.]

cog·i·ta·ble (kɔ́dʒitəb'l) *adj.* thinkable, capable of being conceived as an idea [fr. L. *cogitabilis*]

cog·i·tate (kɔ́dʒiteit) *pres. part.* **cog·i·tat·ing** *past* and *past part.* **cog·i·tat·ed** *v.i.* to think ‖ *v.t.* to plan, devise **cog·i·ta·tion** *n.* **cog·i·ta·tive** (kɔ́dʒiteitiv) *adj.* [fr. L. *cogitare* (*cogitatus*)]

Co·gnac (kɔ́njæk) a town (pop. 22,612) in Charente, W. France, famous for its brandy

co·gnac (kɔ́njæk) *n.* brandy distilled in Cognac and the surrounding region

cog·nate (kɔ́gneit) **1.** *adj.* having a common ancestor or origin ‖ (of languages or words) having a common source or root ‖ (of subjects etc.) related, naturally grouped together **2.** *n.* a person or thing cognate with another [fr. L. *cognatus*]

cognate object an object following an intransitive verb and from the same root, e.g. 'life' in 'to live a good life'

cog·na·tion (kɔgnéiʃən) *n.* cognate relationship [fr. L. *cognatio* (*cognationis*)]

cog·ni·tion (kɔgníʃən) *n.* the act or faculty of knowing ‖ the product of this act, a perception or insight **cog·ni·tive** (kɔ́gnitiv) *adj.* [fr. L. *cognitio* (*cognitionis*)]

cognitive consonance (*psych.*) characteristic of a belief system in which knowledge, ideas, and beliefs are without internal contradictions, e.g., when attitude is harmonious with behavior; coined by L. Festinger, *A Theory of Cognitive Dissonance*, 1962. *ant.* cognitive dissonance. —**cognitive system** *n.* the collection of interrelated beliefs about a subject which affects responses

cognitive dissonance (*psych.*) the holding of inconsistent or incompatible ideas, which produces tension and causes the individual to modify the ideas; coined by L. Festinger, *A Theory of Cognitive Dissonance*, 1962. *ant.* cognitive consonance

cognitive psychology (*psych.*) branch of psychology presupposing that responses are affected by the point of view of the receiver of the stimulus as well as by his or her environment; developed by U. Neisser in *Cognitive Psychology*, 1967

cog·ni·za·ble (kɔ́gnizəb'l, kɔ́nizəb'l, kɔgnáizəb'l) *adj.* capable of being perceived or known ‖ capable of being dealt with in a given court of law **cóg·ni·za·bly** *adv.*

cog·ni·zance (kɔ́gnizəns, kɔ́nizəns) *n.* the range of mental observation or awareness ‖ the fact of being aware, knowledge ‖ (*law*) the power given to a court to deal with a given matter, jurisdiction ‖ (*heraldry*) a distinguishing device **beyond one's cognizance** not one's concern, outside one's terms of reference **to have cognizance of** to be fully aware of **to take cognizance of** to take into one's reckoning **cóg·ni·zant** *adj.* **cog·nize** (kɔ́gnaiz) *pres. part.* **cog·niz·ing** *past* and *past part.* **cog·nized** *v.t.* to make (something) an object of cognition [O.F. *connoissance*, knowledge]

cog·no·men (kɔgnóumən) *pl.* **cog·no·mens**, **cog·nom·i·na** (kɔgnóminə) *n.* the third and family name used by the ancient Romans, e.g. 'Caesar' in Gaius Julius Caesar (cf. AGNOMEN,

cf. NOMEN, cf. PRAENOMEN) ‖ a nickname or epithet [L.]

COGO (*computer*) coordinate geometry computer program designed at the Massachusetts Institute of Technology. —**COGO 10** a special code for civil engineering problems

cog·nos·ci·ble (kɔgnɔ́səb'l) *adj.* cognizable [fr. L. *cognoscere*, to know]

cog·wheel (kɔ́ghwi:l, kɔ́gwi:l) *n.* a gear wheel

co·hab·it (kouhǽbit) *v.i.* to live together, esp. as husband and wife when not married **co·hab·i·tá·tion** *n.* [F. *cohabiter*]

cohabitation law legal aspects of property accumulated during a period of cohabitation without marriage

co·heir (kouéər) *n.* a joint heir **co·heir·ess** (kouéəris) *n.* a joint heiress

'Co·hens v. Virginia' (kóuənz) a decision (1821) of the U.S. Supreme Court headed by John Marshall in which the Court affirmed its authority to inquire into the constitutionality of state court decisions

co·here (kouhíər) *pres. part.* **co·her·ing** *past* and *past part.* **co·hered** *v.i.* to stick together, e.g. of the particles of a mass ‖ to stay united ‖ (of style, design, planning etc.) to be consistent throughout [fr. L. *cohaerere*, to stick]

co·her·ence (kouhíərəns) *n.* the state or quality of being coherent

co·her·en·cy (kouhíərənsi:) *n.* coherence

co·her·ent (kouhíərənt) *adj.* cohering ‖ forming a unity ‖ consistent in sequence of thought or design [F. *cohérent*]

co·he·sion (kouhí:ʒən) *n.* a cohering ‖ (*phys.*) intermolecular attraction holding together particles in the mass (cf. ADHESION) ‖ a remaining or becoming united **co·he·sive** (kouhí:siv) *adj.* [F. *cohésion*]

co·hort (kóuhɔrt) *n.* (*Rom. hist.*) the tenth part of a legion ‖ a companion [F. *cohorte*]

Coi·ba (kɔ́ibɑ) an island (20 miles long) off the southwest coast of Panama

coif (kɔif) *n.* a close-fitting cap, esp. as worn by nuns under a veil ‖ (*hist.*) a cap worn by a medieval soldier under a hood of mail to protect the skull ‖ a cap formerly worn by English lawyers, esp. serjeants at law ‖ a coiffure [M.E. *coyfe* fr. O. F.]

coif·fure (kwɑfjúər) **1.** *n.* a way of wearing the hair, *an elaborate coiffure* **2.** *v.t. pres. part.* **coif·fur·ing** *past* and *past part.* **coif·fured** to provide (someone) with a coiffure ‖ to arrange (someone's hair) in a coiffure [F.]

coign of vantage (kɔin) a position good for observing or taking action from

coil (kɔil) **1.** *v.t.* to arrange in rings which lie side by side, *to coil a rope* ‖ *v.i.* to wind itself, *the snake coiled around the tree* **2.** *n.* something coiled, *a coil of hair* ‖ a single turn of something coiled, *a coil of rope* ‖ (*elec.*) a spiral or helix of wire used as a resistance for electromagnetic purposes [etym. doubtful]

Co·im·ba·tore (kouimbətɔ́r, kouim-batóur) a town (pop. 356,368) in W. Madras, India, between the Nilgiri and Anaimalai hills: textiles, leather, light industries

Coim·bra (kwímbrə) a city (pop. 56,000) in central Portugal, the capital until the 13th c. Cathedral (12th c.) university (1306)

coin (kɔin) **1.** *n.* a piece of metal money **to pay someone in his own coin** to avenge an injury by committing a similar one against the offender **2.** *v.t.* to turn (metal) into coins ‖ to mint (coins of a specified sort) ‖ to invent (a new word or expression) ‖ to amass (a fortune, money) quickly [F. *coin*, corner, wedge, die]

coin·age (kɔ́inidʒ) *n.* the making of coins ‖ money ‖ a system of money, *the decimal coinage* ‖ the inventing of a word, phrase or idea ‖ a word, phrase or idea so invented [O.F. *coignaige*]

co·in·cide (kouinsáid) *pres. part.* **co·in·cid·ing** *past* and *past part.* **co·in·cid·ed** *v.i.* to occur at the same time, *their holidays coincide this year, his holiday coincides with hers* ‖ to occupy the same space, esp. in geometry ‖ to be equal, or the same, in some other (non-spatial) respect, *your statement does not coincide with his* [F. *coincider*]

co·in·ci·dence (kouínsidəns) *n.* the state of coinciding ‖ an event or circumstance fortuitously relating in some way to other events or circumstances [F.]

co·in·ci·dent (kouínsidənt) *adj.* coinciding ‖ (*geom.*) occupying the same space ‖ happening at the same time **co·in·ci·den·tal** (kouinsidént'l) *adj.* coincident ‖ happening by chance, not by contrivance [F. *coincident*]

CONCISE PRONUNCIATION KEY: **(a)** æ, cat; ɑ, car; ɔ fawn; ei, snake; i:, sheep; iə, deer; ɛə, bear. **(i)** i, fish; ai, tiger; ə:, bird. **(o)** o, ox; au, cow; ou, goat; u, poor; ɔi, royal. **(u)** ʌ, duck; u, bull; u:, goose; ə, bacillus; ju:, cube. x, loch; θ, think; ð, bother; z, Zen; ʒ, corsage; dʒ, savage; ŋ, orangutang; j, yak; ʃ, fish; tʃ, fetch; 'l, rabble; 'n, redden. Complete pronunciation key appears inside front cover.

coincident indicator (*economics*) statistical index that correlates highly with the current state of the economy, e.g., employment, industrial production, sales. *Cf* LAGGING INDICATORS, LEADING INDICATORS

coin·er (kɔ́inər) *n.* a person who makes coins ‖ (*Br.*) a person who makes false coins

co·in·stan·ta·ne·ous (kɔuinstəntéini:əs) *adj.* happening at the same moment

co·in·sti·tu·tion·al (kɔuinstitú:ʃənəl) *adj.* in a school, having separate activities for boys and girls

Cointelpro (*acronym*) for counterintelligence program, a branch within the FBI during the years 1956–1971

coir (kɔ́iər) *n.* a fiber from the husk of the fruit (drupe) of the coconut, used for rope, cables, mats and coarse brushes [fr. Malay. *kāyar*, cord]

co·i·tion (kouíʃən) *n.* sexual intercourse [fr. L. *coitio* (*coitionis*), coming together]

co·i·tus (kóuitəs) *n.* coition [L.]

Coke (kuk), Sir Edward (1552–1634), English jurist. A brilliant lawyer, he became (1593) Speaker of the House of Commons. As chief justice of the Common Pleas (1606–13) and of the King's Bench (1613–17), he led the defense of the common law against encroachment by James I. He continued to oppose the royal prerogative under Charles I, and took a leading part in drafting the Petition of Right (1628). His 'Law Reports' (1600–15) helped to formulate the common law

coke (kouk) **1.** *n.* the hard, gray, porous residue, mostly carbon, obtained by destructive distillation of coal which is heated in a retort or oven, driving off coal gas and other volatile matter. It is used as a fuel and burns with great heat and little smoke **2.** *v.t. pres. part.* **cok·ing** *past* and *past part.* **coked** to transform into coke [etym. doubtful]

Coke of Norfolk (kuk), (Thomas William Coke, earl of Leicester of Holkham, 1754–1842), British agriculturalist who pioneered far-reaching improvements in farming method on his estate in Norfolk

co·ker·nut (kóukərnʌt) *n.* (*commerce*) a coconut

col (kɒl) *n.* a pass between peaks in a mountain range ‖ (*meteor.*) a region of low pressure between two anticyclones [F.=neck]

col. collected, collector ‖ college, collegiate ‖ colony, colonial ‖ color ‖ column

Col. Colonel ‖ Columbia ‖ Colossians

COLA (*economics acronym*) for cost-of-living adjustment

col·an·der (kʌ́ləndər, kɒ́ləndər) *n.* a bowl perforated with holes, used as a strainer in cooking [L. *colare*, to strain]

cola nut *KOLA NUT

co·lat·i·tude (koulǽtitu:d, koulǽtitju:d) *n.* the complement of the latitude

cola tree *KOLA TREE

Col·bert (kɔlbɛər), Jean-Baptiste (1619–83), French statesman. Chief minister to Louis XIV, he reorganized French finances, reformed the tax system, introduced a protective trade tariff (1664), created a new navy and merchant fleet (1669), and built roads and canals. He promulgated legal codes (1667–85) and was a patron of the arts and sciences

Col·ches·ter (kóultʃestər, *Br.* kóultʃistə) a town (pop. 129,200) in Essex, England, on River Colne: agriculture, oyster fishing. University of Essex (1964)

col·chi·cine (kɔ́ltʃisi:n, kɔ́ltʃisin, kɔ́lkəsi:n, kɒ́lkəsin) *n.* a poisonous alkaloid obtained from the dried seeds and dried corm of the colchicum. It is used as a hormone in plant breeding, and in medicine for treating gout

col·chi·cum (kɔ́ltʃəkəm, kɔ́lkəkəm) *n.* a plant of genus *Colchicum*, fam. *Liliaceae*, esp. *C. autumnale*, autumn crocus or meadow saffron. It yields colchicine [L. fr. Gk *kolchikon*, meadow saffron]

col·co·thar (kɔ́lkəθər) *n.* reddish-brown ferric oxide used as a pigment and by jewelers etc. for polishing [fr. Arab. *qolqotār*]

cold (kould) *n.* absence of heat ‖ low temperature, in comparison with that of the body ‖ (*med.*) coryza, acute infectious catarrh of the nasal mucous membrane, with a running nose and sore throat ‖ cold weather **to be left out in the cold** to be ignored, receive no attention [O.E. *cald*]

cold *adj.* without heat, unheated, *cold water* ‖ without warmth as felt by the human body, *a cold day* ‖ feeling the cold ‖ having cooled,

grown cold, *cold meat* ‖ without warm human feelings, unfriendly ‖ lacking enthusiasm ‖ (of scent in hunting) faint ‖ unconscious, *to knock someone cold* ‖ chilling in effect, *cold white furniture* ‖ (*pop.*, of a searcher) far from the object sought **in cold blood** in complete self-possession, not driven by passion, *to kill in cold blood* **to have** (or **get**) **cold feet** to lose one's courage or confidence about seeing a plan through **to make someone's blood run cold** to cause intense fear in a person [O.E. *cald*]

cold-blood·ed (kóuldblʌ́did) *adj.* unfeeling, not emotional ‖ callous ‖ (of fishes and reptiles) having a body temperature which depends on environment

cold chisel a chisel used with a hammer for cutting away metal or stone

cold comfort little or no consolation

cold cream a soothing and cleansing cosmetic for the skin

Cold Duck trade name of a mixture of sparkling burgundy and domestic champagne

cold frame a shallow, glass-covered structure with a bed of earth, in which young plants are protected from cold and produced early for transplanting

cold front (*meteor.*) the edge of a cold air mass advancing against and under a warmer air mass, usually accompanied by squalls and showers

Cold Harbor, Battle of one of the hardest-fought engagements (June 3, 1864) of the American Civil War, in Virginia. The Confederate army under Lee fought off the Union attacks led by Grant

cold·heart·ed (kóuldhártid) *adj.* feeling no love, sympathy, friendliness etc.

cold shoulder (only in phrases) **to give** (**someone**) **the cold shoulder, to turn a cold shoulder on** (**someone**) to cold-shoulder (someone)

cold-shoul·der (kóuldʃóuldər) *v.t.* to treat (someone) with hostility or marked lack of consideration or (a proposal etc.) with studied indifference

cold sore a mild form of herpes

cold storage the keeping of food, furs etc. in a cold, esp. a refrigerated, room

cold sweat perspiration with a sensation of chill, often accompanying fear or shock

cold war a state of diplomatic tension between nations, esp. between East and West, and in particular between the U.S.S.R. and the U.S.A., deliberately maintained for the winning of political and economic advantages without fighting, and to influence nations not committed to either side

cold warrior one who takes an aggressive role in the cold war

cold·wave (kóuldweiv) *n.* (*cosmetology*) permanent wave created chemically without heat

cold weld *v.* to cause metals to adhere without the use of heat or pressure, e.g., in a vacuum. — **cold weld** *n.*

Cole, (kóul) Thomas (1801–48), U.S. landscape artist and founder of the Hudson River School. He immigrated to the U.S. from England, became a wandering portraitist, and studied at the Philadelphia Academy of Fine Arts before becoming attracted to the scenery of the Hudson River Valley and upstate New York, which he recorded in such works as 'View Near Ticonderoga' (1826), 'Kaaterskill Falls' (1827), 'The Course of Empire' (1835–6), and 'The Voyage of Life' (1840)

cole (koul) *n.* a plant of the genus *Brassica*, esp. rape ‖ sea kale [M.E. *col, cole*, O.E. *cāwel*, fr. L. *caulis*]

colemouse *COALMOUSE

co·le·op·ter·on (kɒli:óptərɒn, kɒli:óptərɒn) *pl.* **co·le·op·ter·a** (kɒli:óptərə, kɒli:óptərə) *n.* a member of *Coleoptera*, an order of insects (beetles) having front wings modified as hard sheaths (elytra) to protect the hind, functional wings **co·le·óp·ter·ous** *adj.* [Mod. L. fr. Gk *koleos*, sheath+*pteron*, wing]

co·le·op·tile (kɒli:óptil, kɒli:óptil) *n.* (*bot.*) the first leaf of grass to appear above ground, forming a sheaf around the other leaves [fr. Gk *koleos*, sheath+*ptilon*, soft feather]

co·le·o·rhi·za (kɒli:əráizə, kɒli:əráizə) *pl.* **co·le·o·rhi·zae** (kɒli:əráizi:, kɒli:əráizi:) *n.* a sheath in some (mostly monocotyledonous) plants through which the radicle grows during germination [fr. Gk *koleos*, sheath+*rhiza*, root]

Cole·ridge (kóulridʒ), Samuel Taylor (1772–1834), English Romantic poet and critic, and friend of Wordsworth. He is famous as a poet for

a relatively small amount of poetry, and later in his career he concentrated rather on philosophy, politics, theology and criticism. His theory of the imagination (expounded at length in 'Biographia Literaria', 1817, but discussed and developed throughout his works) is of primary importance, both as a document of Romantic critical theory, and as an influence upon subsequent critical thought. He often provided new insight into specific authors (esp. Shakespeare and Wordsworth). His political writings had a profound influence: he is the source of (or an influence upon) most 19th-c. antiutilitarianism

cole·seed (kóulsi:d) *n.* the seed of the rape plant [trans. Du. *koolzaad*]

cole·slaw (kóulslɔ) *n.* cabbage salad [Du. *koolsla*]

co·les·ti·pol (koulésti pɔl) (*pharm.*) drug used to decrease serum cholesterol and the lipid level by removing bile acids from the intestines; marketed as Colestid

Co·let (kɔ́lit), John (c. 1467–1519), English humanist and theologian, dean of St Paul's, founder (1512) of St Paul's School in London

co·le·ta (kouléitə) *n.* (*bullfighting*) short, braided pigtail worn by a bullfighter

coletit * COAL TIT

Co·lette (kɔlet), Sidonie-Gabrielle (1873–1954), French writer. Her many stories include 'Chéri', 'Gigi', the 'Claudine' series, 'Sept Dialogues de bêtes' etc. The apparent ease of her writing (she was a tremendous corrector) conceals skillful, subtle analysis of emotion and sensual pleasure

co·le·us (kóuli:əs) *pl.* **co·le·us·es** *n.* a member of *Coleus*, a large genus of plants of fam. *Labiatae*, many forms and hybrids of which are cultivated for their variegated and colored leaves. *C. rotundifolius*, an African species, is cultivated for its edible tubers [Mod. L. fr. Gk *koleos*, sheath]

co·lic (kɒlik) *n.* severe pains in the bowels or abdomen **col·ick·y** (kɒliki:) *adj.* [F. *colique* fr. L. fr. Gk]

Colidar (*acronym*) for coherent light detection and ranging. *Cf* LADAR

co·li·form (kóulifɔrm) *n.* (*biol.*) **1.** a measure of bacterial content of water. **2.** the group of aerobic and anaerobic gram-negative bacteria that ferment lactose in 48 hours at 35°F, e.g., *Escherichia*

coliform index a rating of the purity of water based on a count of fecal bacteria

Co·li·gny (kɔli:nji:), Gaspard II de (1519–72), French statesman and Huguenot leader in the Wars of Religion (1562–3, 1567–8 and 1568–70). He became (1571) chief adviser to Charles IX, but was killed in the Massacre of St Bartholomew

Co·li·ma (kɔlí:ma) a state (area 2,010 sq. miles, pop. 317,000) on the Pacific coast of Mexico. Capital: Colima (pop. 55,450). Principal occupations: agriculture (sugar, rice, corn, palm oil and coffee) and mining (iron, copper, lead)

col·i·se·um (kɒlisí:əm) *n.* a large building, theater, stadium etc. for sports or public entertainment [L. *colosseum* fr. *colosseus*, gigantic]

co·li·tis (kəláitis, kouláitis) *n.* inflammation of the colon [Mod. L. fr. COLON]

col·lab·o·rate (kəlǽbəreit) *pres. part.* **col·lab·o·rat·ing** *past* and *past part.* **col·lab·o·rat·ed** *v.i.* to work together, esp. on work of an intellectual nature ‖ to help an enemy country or an occupying power **col·lab·o·rá·tion, col·lab·o·rá·tion·ist** (only of quislings), **col·láb·o·ra·tor** *ns* [fr. L. *collaborare*]

col·lage (kəláʒ, kouláʒ) *n.* a picture made by gluing fragments of various materials in a composition ‖ the art of creating such compositions [F.=pasting]

col·la·gen (kɒlədʒən) *n.* a gluey protein found in vertebrates. It forms the principal substance in connecting fibers and tissues and in bones, hydrolizing to gelatin when boiled with water (*OSSEIN) [fr. F. *collagène* fr. Gk *kolla*, glue+-*gen*, producing]

col·laps·a·ble (kəlǽpsəb'l) *adj.* collapsible

collapsar *BLACK HOLE

col·lapse (kəlǽps) **1.** *v. pres. part.* **col·laps·ing** *past* and *past part.* **col·lapsed** *v.i.* to fall down or apart when the component parts cease to support one another, *that table will collapse if you sit on it* ‖ to fail, *his plans collapsed* ‖ to suffer a breakdown of body, mind or nerves ‖ (of a table etc. designed to do so) to fold ‖ (of a lung) to come into an airless state ‖ *v.t.* to cause to collapse **2.** *n.* a falling down ‖ a breaking to pieces ‖ a failure (of plans etc.) ‖ a mental or physical breakdown **col·láps·i·ble** adj. made so as to fold up when not in use [fr. L. collabi (collapsus), to fall together]

col·lar (kólər) 1. n. the usually folded part of a coat, shirt, dress etc. around the neck ‖ (zool.) any of various markings or structures suggesting such a collar ‖ (engin.) a ring used to limit motion or hold something in place ‖ any structure comparable to a collar ‖ a leather band or chain put around an animal's neck ‖ part of the harness around a draft horse's neck ‖ an ornamental necklace with insignia of an order 2. v.t. to snatch possession of ‖ to seize ‖ (pop.) to appropriate ‖ to put a collar on ‖ to roll up and bind (meat, fish), for cooking [M.E. coler fr. A.F.]

collar beam a horizontal beam joining the opposite sides of a pointed roof

col·lar·bone (kólərboun) n. the clavicle

col·lared (kólərd) adj. wearing or having a collar ‖ marked as though having a collar

col·lat·ing (kɒléit, kəléit, kóleit) pres. part. **col·lat·ed** past and past part. **col·lat·ed** v.t. to examine (a text) closely against another in order to discover variations (and correct or emend) ‖ to put (pages, illustrations) in correct order ‖ to verify the number and order of the sheets of (a book) [fr. L. conferre (collatus), to bring together]

col·lat·er·al (kəlátərəl) 1. adj. parallel, collateral arguments ‖ (law) subordinate, collateral evidence ‖ (commerce, of money) lent or secured to guarantee another loan as supplement to some more important security ‖ (biol.) descended from a common ancestor but in a different line 2. n. a person so descended ‖ a secondary security for a loan [fr. M.L. collateralis, side by side]

collateral damage (mil.) civilian casualties and destruction as the result of a military action

col·la·tion (kɒléiʃən, kəléiʃən, kouléiʃən) n. the act or result of collating texts ‖ a description of the technical features of a book ‖ (old-fash.) a light meal, snack [O.F.]

col·league (kóli:g) n. a fellow worker, e.g. in a professional organization [F. collègue]

Col·lect (kólekt) n. a prayer appointed for the day, said before the Epistle in the Mass (Eucharist) [F. collecte]

col·lect (kəlékt) 1. v.t. to gather in or together, to collect taxes ‖ to accumulate (things of a similar kind) for pleasure, self-education or profit, to collect stamps ‖ to gain or recover control of (oneself or one's mental faculties) ‖ v.i. to come together, flies collect on food ‖ to take up a collection 2. adj. and adv. to be paid for by the recipient, a collect telegram [O.F. collecter]

col·lect·ed (kəléktid) adj. calm ‖ self-possessed

col·lec·tion (kəlékʃən) n. the act of collecting ‖ things brought together by choice, a collection of pictures ‖ money taken up from members of an audience or congregation for some intention ‖ the season's models designed by a dress designer ‖ (pl., Oxford University) a college terminal examination ‖ an assembly of people, a queer collection of individuals [O.F.]

col·lec·tive (kəléktiv) 1. adj. formed by collection ‖ of, relating to, or done by a number of people, a collective letter, collective ownership 2. n. a collective farm [fr. L. collectivus]

collective agreement a contract between an employer and a trade union ‖ an agreement on wages and working conditions within an industry

collective bargaining direct negotiating between trade unions and employers. The term is generally used for the settlement of wage claims and improvement in working conditions for all workers of one union (or of several), by a collective agreement. The organization into trade unions of workers within the same industry or pursuing the same trade gives the unions power to meet the employers with unified demands and excludes local individual bargaining

collective farm a farm under state supervision, uniting many small farms and operated collectively (esp. in communist countries)

collective fruit (bot.) a fruit formed from the fused cluster of the ovaries of several flowers (e.g. mulberry)

col·lec·tive·ly (kəléktivli) adv. in a collective manner ‖ in a collective sense ‖ in the mass

collective noun a noun designating a number of individuals considered as a group, e.g. 'flock' in 'a flock of sheep'

collective security agreements between any number of countries for mutual defense and for joint measures to discourage aggression. Such agreements have produced the North Atlantic Treaty Organization and the South East Asia Treaty Organization

collective unconscious (psychol.) the underlying region of the mind in which Jung postulated that memories of universal human experience are stored. These arrange themselves into archetypes, which erupt in certain critical situations, provoking neuroses but also providing artistic and other drives

col·lec·tiv·ism (kəléktivizəm) n. a vague term applied to socialism and sometimes to communism, referring to the belief that state action is desirable in matters often left in the hands of private individuals, or to the more definite proposition that the state should own all land and all means of production, distribution and exchange **col·léc·tiv·ist** 1. n. someone having or practicing the principles of collectivism 2. adj. related to or having the characteristics of collectivism ‖ favoring collectivism

col·lec·tiv·i·ty (kɒlektíviti) pl. **col·lec·tiv·i·ties** n. the state or quality of being collective ‖ a collective whole ‖ a group of people acting as a single unit

col·lec·tiv·ize (kəléktivaiz) pres. part. **col·lec·tiv·iz·ing** past and past part. **col·lec·tiv·ized** v.t. to transfer from private to state ownership ‖ to establish collectivism in

col·lec·tor (kəléktər) n. someone who collects, either professionally, a tax collector or for pleasure, a stamp collector ‖ a device for collecting (in various machines), charge collector (in an electrostatic generator) [M.E. fr. O.F.]

col·ledge (kóledʒ) n. (ice skating) jump from forward outer edge of skate to backward inner edge of a skate with 1½ turns intervening

col·leen (kóli:n, kɒlí:n) n. an Irish girl [Ir. cailín, girl]

col·lege (kóledʒ) n. an organized body of people united for the sake of their functions, purposes or rights, the College of Cardinals ‖ an educational institution within a university and part of it for some purposes but organizing its own affairs ‖ an institution for higher education which may grant a bachelor's degree and sometimes higher degrees or which (Br.) is affiliated with a university ‖ the building occupied by an institution for higher education ‖ a school offering specialized professional instruction ‖ (Br.) a secondary school, esp. if independent of the state, Eton College [O.F. collège]

College of Cardinals the body, formed of all the cardinals of the Roman Catholic Church, which elects the pope

col·le·gi·al·i·ty (kəli:dʒi:æliti:) n. the doctrine of the Roman Catholic church's hierarchy (bishops), who collectively determines church policy with the Pope

col·le·gian (kəlí:dʒən, kəlí:dʒi:ən) adj. a member of a college [perh. fr. M.L. collegianus]

col·le·giate (kəlí:dʒit, kəlí:dʒi:it) adj. having the nature of a college ‖ of or pertaining to a college or to college members, collegiate basketball ‖ characteristic of colleges, collegiate dress [fr. L. collegiatus, member of a college]

collegiate church a church which is not a cathedral, but which has a college or chapter of clergy, called canons, and, in the Church of England, a dean ‖ a church or churches whose source of income is administered by several clergy or ministers jointly ‖ (Scotland) a church with two or more ministers equal in rank

col·len·chy·ma (kəléŋkəmə) pl. **col·len·chy·ma·ta** (kɒliŋkímətə) n. (bot.) the temporary supporting tissue in the stems and leaves of young plants, with elongated and variously thickened cells (*PARENCHYMA, *SCLERENCHYMA) [fr. Gk kolla, glue+enchyma, infusion]

col·let (kólit) 1. n. (mach.) a small collar or ring, esp. that which holds the inner end of the balance spring in clocks ‖ a culet ‖ a circle holding a precious stone, e.g. in a ring 2. v.t. pres. part. **col·let·ing** past and past part. **col·let·ed** to provide with a collet [F., dim. of col, neck]

col·lide (kəláid) pres. part. **col·lid·ing** past and past part. **col·lid·ed** v.i. to come into collision ‖ to come into conflict, your ideas collide with his [fr. L. collidere]

col·lie, Br. also **col·ly** (kóli:) n. a sheep dog of a long-haired Scottish breed [etym. doubtful]

col·lier (kóljər) n. a coal miner ‖ a ship used for carrying coal **cól·lier·y** pl. **col·lier·ies** n. a coal

mine and its complete installation [M.E. colier fr. col, coal]

col·li·mate (kólimeit) pres. part. **col·li·mat·ing** past and past part. **col·li·mat·ed** v.t. (phys.) to cause (light) to form a parallel beam ‖ to arrange (lenses) so that they are coaxial ‖ to adjust the line of sight in (a telescope) **col·li·má·tion** n. **cól·li·ma·tor** n. (phys.) a device to produce a beam of parallel rays of light or other radiation, usually by passing the radiation through an adjustable slit placed in the focal plane of an objective lens ‖ a device to produce a parallel beam of nuclear or other particles, molecules etc. [fr. L. collimare, misreading of collineare, to align]

collimating marks index marks fixed on the camera body, which form images on the negative. These images are used to determine the position of the optical center or principal point of the imagery. syn fiducial marks

collimation the aligning of radar antenna with the aid of optical observation of elevation and azimuth. **—collimate** v. (nuclear phys.) to change the path of electrons to make them more parallel as they approach the storage tube for cathode-ray scanning. **—collimating lens** n. **—collimator** n.

col·lin·e·ar (kəlíni:ər) adj. in the same straight line

Col·lins (kólinz), Michael (1890–1922), Irish nationalist, leader of Sinn Féin and the I.R.A. (1916–21). He negotiated the treaty with the British (1921) which created the Irish Free State. He was assassinated by a group of extremist republicans

Collins, Wilkie (1824–89), English novelist. His most famous books, 'The Moonstone' and 'The Woman in White', are sometimes regarded as precursors of the crime novel

Collins, William (1721–59), English poet, generally accounted a precursor of Romanticism (*GRAY). His poetry was influenced by Milton's minor verse. It reflects the 18th-c. taste for the 'pleasing horror' of 'wild' nature, the nocturnal, the medieval ('Gothic'), and the elegiac pastoral. His poems include the odes 'To Evening', 'To the Passions' and 'To Simplicity'

col·li·sion (kəlíʒən) n. the violent coming together of a moving body with another, either moving or stationary ‖ a conflict, esp. of ideas or interests [fr. L. collisio (collisionis)]

col·lo·cate (kóləkeit) pres. part. **col·lo·cat·ing** past and past part. **col·lo·cat·ed** v.t. to arrange together so as to form words into a phrase, shapes into a pattern etc. **col·lo·cá·tion** n. [fr. L. collocare (collocatus), to place together]

collocation (linguistics) a term in Firthian grammar describing regular occurrence of certain descriptive words in relation to other words in various languages, e.g., bar for pub, harbor, steel, soap, etc.

col·lo·di·on (kəlóudi:ən) n. a viscous solution of cellulose nitrate in a mixture of alcohol and ether, for excluding air from a wound and formerly used in photography [fr. Gk kollōdēs, gluelike]

col·loid (kóloid) n. a substance, whether gas, liquid or solid, dispersed in a continuous gas, liquid or solid medium. The particles, consisting of very large molecules or large aggregates of molecules, do not settle (or do so very slowly). The system is neither a solution nor a suspension ‖ the system of the dispersed and continuous phases **col·lói·dal** adj. [fr. Gk kolla, glue]

col·lop (kóləp) n. a small slice of meat [M.E. colhoppe, coloppe, cooked dish, derivation obscure]

col·lo·qui·al (kəlóukwi:əl) adj. (of words, idioms, etc.) thoroughly part of living language, a good knowledge of correct, colloquial English ‖ not part of conventional formal modes of expression (esp. written), though usable in speech without being classified as slang **col·ló·qui·al·ism** n. [fr. L. colloquium, conversation]

col·lo·quy (kóləkwi:) pl. **col·lo·quies** n. a conference of scholars or specialists [fr. L. colloquium, a talking together]

col·lo·type (kólətaip) n. (printing) a fine reproduction process, similar in principle to lithography, in which prints are taken from a hardened gelatin film ‖ a print made by this method [fr. Gk kolla, glue+TYPE]

col·lude (kəlú:d) pres. part. **col·lud·ing** past and past part. **col·lud·ed** v.i. to have a secret agreement with someone (usually unlawfully, e.g. between pretended opponents in a lawsuit [fr. L. colludere, to play with]

CONCISE PRONUNCIATION KEY: **(a)** æ, cat; ɑ, car; ɔ fawn; ei, snake. **(e)** e, hen; i:, sheep; iə, deer; ɛə, bear. **(i)** i, fish; ai, tiger; ə:, bird. **(o)** o, ox; au, cow; ou, goat; u, poor; ɔi, royal. **(u)** ʌ, duck; u, bull; u:, goose; ə, bacillus; ju:, cube. x, loch; θ, think; ð, bother; z, Zen; ʒ, corsage; dʒ, savage; ŋ, orangutang; j, yak; ʃ, fish; tʃ, fetch; 'l, rabble; 'n, redden. Complete pronunciation key appears inside front cover.

col·lu·sion (kəlú:ʒən) *n.* a dishonest, secret agreement ‖ (*law*) a fraudulent secret agreement between litigating parties, esp. one between man and wife to commit an offense to obtain divorce **col·lu·sive** (kəlú:siv) *adj.* [F.]

colly *COLLIE

col·lyr·i·um (kəlíəri:əm) *n.* a lotion for the eyes [L. fr. Gk *kollurion*, poultice]

col·o·cynth (kɔ́ləsinθ) *n. Citrullus colocynthis*, a vine of Asia, Africa and the Mediterranean region ‖ the purgative drug obtained from the dried pulp and seeds of its fruit [fr. L. fr. Gk *kolokunthis*]

Co·logne (kəlóun) (*G.* Köln), an industrial city, Rhine port and commercial center (pop. 1,010,400) in North Rhine-Westphalia, West Germany. Industries: textiles, leather, steel, heavy machinery, perfumes. It was a prosperous city of the Hanseatic League (13th–15th cc.). University (1388). Gothic cathedral (begun 1248)

co·logne (kəlóun) *n.* a scented toilet water composed of alcohol and citrus or other oils [short for Cologne water]

Co·lom·bi·a (kəlámbi:ə) a republic (area 439,825 sq. miles, pop. 24,248,000) in N.W. South America. Capital: Bogotá. People: 71% Mestizo, 20% of European origin, 6% of African origin, 2% Indian. Language: Spanish. Religion: Roman Catholic, with a Protestant minority. The land is 2% arable, 35% pasture and 50% forest. The population is concentrated in the valleys of the Andes (4,000–9,000 ft). The Caribbean plain comprises the dry sandy pampas of Guajira and the hot, often-flooded Urabá region. The Pacific coast is humid, sultry and swampy. The Eastern Plains (llanos) are covered with grasslike plants in the Orinoco basin and thick equatorial forest in the Amazon basin. The Andes are separated into the Eastern, Central and Western Cordilleras, dissected by the Cauca and Magdalena Rivers. Climate: tropical at sea level to polar at 10,000 ft and including a warm, humid zone (3,000–6,500 ft) and a cool, moist zone (6,500–10,000 ft). Rainfall: 42 ins at Bogotá. Average minimum and maximum temperatures (F.): 57° and 59° in Bogotá, 75° and 85° in the lowlands. Livestock: cattle, horses, pigs, mules. Agricultural products: coffee (world's 2nd largest producer), cotton, rice, sugar, rubber, corn, bananas, plantain, yucca, tobacco, cacao. Forestry products: quinine, balsa, lumber. Mineral resources: gold (biggest producer in South America), silver, copper, lead, mercury, manganese, emeralds, platinum (discovered in 1735, the largest deposit in the world), oil, uranium, coal, iron, salt. Manufactures: leather, cement, electricity. Exports: coffee, fuel oil, bananas, gold, precious metals and stones. Imports: machinery, vehicles, textiles, wheat, chemicals. Ports: Cartagena, Barranquilla and Buenaventura. The Magdalena River, navigable for 900 miles, is the main traffic route from the Caribbean to the interior and is served by lateral railroads. There are 25 universities, the oldest in Bogotá (1572). Monetary unit: peso (100 centavos). HISTORY. The Chibchas and other Indian tribes had established settlements when Colombia was colonized by Spain in the 16th c. It formed the Spanish viceroyalty of New Granada (1718). It won independence after the revolution of 1810 with the help of Bolívar (1819). It formed (1819) the state of Greater Colombia with Panama and Venezuela (joined in 1822 by Ecuador) under the leadership of Santander and became the Republic of New Granada when Venezuela and Ecuador seceded (1830). New constitutions renamed it the Granadina Confederation (1858), the United States of New Granada (1861), the United States of Colombia (1863) and the Republic of Colombia (1886). In 1903, Panama seceded. The liberals dominated in the 1930s and opposed U.S. economic control. The liberal leader Jorge Eliécer Gaitán was assassinated (1948) and an estimated 260,000 people were killed in the ensuing political war. The dictatorship (1950–3) of the conservative Laureano Gómez was followed by the military dictatorship of Gustavo Rojas (1954–7). The liberals and conservatives formed a National Front, Rojas was overthrown, and constitutional government was restored with alternating liberal and conservative governments. Alberto Lleras Camargo (1958–62) was succeeded by Guillermo León Valencia (1962–6) and by Carlos Lleras Restrepo (1966–71). Restrepo inherited a stagnant economy and a financial crisis. He curbed

inflation, restored a respectable growth rate and balance of trade, and (1969) negotiated an agreement in Bogotá, signed by Colombia, Bolivia, Chile, Ecuador and Peru, to establish an Andean Common Market. He was succeeded (1971) by the Conservative leader Misael Pastrana. In 1974 the National Front ended and elections were held. The Liberal government of Dr. Tubay Ayala (1978–82) was followed by that of Conservative Belisario Betancur Cuartus. A volcanic eruption in 1985 caused mudslides and floods that killed over 20,000

Co·lom·bo (kəlámbou) the capital and chief port (pop. 602,000) of S.W. Sri Lanka, near the mouth of the Kelani, founded (1517) as a trading station by the Portuguese. It was occupied (1656–1796) by the Dutch and taken (1796) by the British. University (1942)

Colombo Plan a plan for cooperative economic development in S. and S.E. Asia, designed to raise the standard of living of a quarter of the world's population occupying a sixteenth of the world's land surface. It was conceived by the Commonwealth foreign ministers (Jan. 1950) and became operational in July 1951. It embraces Afghanistan, Bhutan, Burma, Cambodia, India, Indonesia, Iran, Laos, Malaysia, the Maldive Is., Nepal, Pakistan, the Philippines, Singapore, South Korea, Sri Lanka, and Thailand, and it includes Australia, Canada, Japan, New Zealand, Great Britain and the U.S.A. It aims at diversifying and increasing production and trade, developing irrigation and hydroelectric power, improving communications and increasing technical knowledge

Co·lón (kɔlón), Bartolomé (c. 1445-c. 1515), cartographer and explorer, brother of Cristóbal (Christopher Columbus). He was appointed governor of Hispaniola, where he founded (1496) Santo Domingo

Co·lón (kɔlón) a city (pop. 59,832) of Panama, the northern gateway to the Panama Canal. The U.S.-built docks and installations at nearby Cristóbal make it the chief Caribbean port

co·lón (kɔlón) *pl.* **co·lo·nes** (kɔlónes), **co·lóns** *n.* the basic monetary unit of Costa Rica and El Salvador ‖ a coin of the value of one colón [after Cristóbal *Colón* (Columbus)]

co·lon (kóulən) *n.* a punctuation mark (:) used chiefly to introduce examples, a list, a statement which illustrates or explains the previous one, or one which expresses a contrast to the previous one [L. fr. Gk *kolon*, limb, clause of a sentence]

colon (kóulən, kóulɒn) *n.* the major portion of the large intestine of vertebrates between the cecum and the rectum ‖ the second portion of the intestine of insects [L. fr. Gk *kōlon*]

Colón archipelago *GALÁPAGOS ISLANDS

colo·nel (kɔ́:rn'l) *n.* an officer in the U.S. army, air force or marine corps ranking below a brigadier and above a lieutenant colonel ‖ (*Br.*) an army officer ranking below a brigadier and above a lieutenant colonel **colo·nel·cy** (kɔ́:rn'lsi:) *n.* [earlier *coronel* fr. F. *coronnel*, Ital. *colonnello*]

Co·lo·nia (kɔlɔ́nja) a town (pop. 13,000) in Uruguay on the River Plate facing Buenos Aires, founded (1680) by the Portuguese

co·lo·ni·al (kəlóuni:əl) **1.** *n.* an inhabitant of a colony **2.** *adj.* of or belonging to a colony ‖ of or pertaining to the 13 colonies which originated the United States of America **Colonial** of or pertaining to works of art or architecture, or artifacts, typical of or dating from the period of the British colonies in America in the 17th and 18th cc. [fr. L. *colonia*, colony]

co·lo·ni·al·ism (kəlóuni:əlɪzəm) *n.* the economic, political and social policies by which colonies are governed ‖ a belief in the merits of the colonial system as promoting the welfare of the nation colonized (cf. IMPERIALISM)

co·lon·ic (koulónik, kəlónik) *adj.* of or relating to the colon

Colonies, the (*Am. hist.*) *THIRTEEN COLONIES

col·o·nist (kɔ́lənist) *n.* someone who helps to establish a colony ‖ an inhabitant of a colony

col·o·ni·za·tion (kɒlənizéiʃən) *n.* the act or policy of colonizing

col·o·nize (kɔ́lənaiz) *pres. part.* **col·o·niz·ing** *past* and *past part.* **col·o·nized** *v.t.* to bring settlers into (a country) ‖ to make (a country) into a colony ‖ *v.i.* to establish a colony or colonies [fr. L. *colonus*, farmer]

col·on·nade (kɒlənéid) *n.* (*archit.*) an evenly spaced line of columns supporting an entabla-

ture ‖ a line of trees making a similar effect [F.]

col·o·ny (kɔ́ləni:) *pl.* **col·o·nies** *n.* a land or place settled by people from another country, to whose government it is in some degree subject ‖ the people who do this, their descendants, and those who join them ‖ people of the same foreign nationality, or of a special occupation, living in an unorganized community, *an artists' colony* ‖ a segregated group, *a leper colony* ‖ a number of animals of the same kind living in one place, *a colony of rats* ‖ (*bot.*) a group of individuals of a species migrant in a new habitat ‖ (*bacteriol.*) a mass of organisms growing in or on a substance ‖ (*biol.*) a group of colonial animals ‖ (*Am. hist.*) *THIRTEEN COLONIES [fr. L. *colonia*]

col·o·phon (kɔ́lafon, kɔ́ləfən) *n.* a note, often treated ornamentally and placed at the end of a book, about the details of manufacture ‖ an emblem, often the publisher's, in the preliminary pages of a book [L.L. fr. Gk *kolophōn*, summit]

col·o·pho·ny (kɔ́ləfouni:, kəlófəni:) *n.* rosin [fr. L. *Colophonia* (*resina*), (resin) of Colophon, in Lydia]

col·o·quin·ti·da (kɒləkwíntidə) *n.* colocynth [M.E. from Med. L.]

co·lor, *Br.* **col·our** (kʌ́lər) **1.** *n.* a sensation experienced usually as a result of light of varying wavelengths reaching the eye ‖ a pigment, *an artist's color* ‖ the complexion of the face, *a healthy color* ‖ the racial complexion of people not of white race, esp. of Africans ‖ (*pl.*) a ribbon used as a symbol of a party, the flag of a ship or a regiment, *to rally to the colors* ‖ (*pl.*) a distinction won by athletic prowess, and the cap, blazer etc. of particular colors, design etc. that go with the distinction ‖ tone of conversation or behavior, *I don't like the color of those remarks* ‖ (in literature) specially heightened effects to give the feeling of truth to life, or of the reality of a particular setting, *local color* ‖ (*mus.*) the quality of tone in a note inseparable from the voice or instrument which sounds it, and that makes the same note sound differently when produced by another voice or instrument ‖ (*art*) the general effect of color in a painting ‖ (*printing*) the quality of the inking ‖ (*pl.*, *navy*) the morning ceremony of hoisting the flag and the evening one of lowering it **to bring the color to** to bring a blush to **to come through** (**or off**) **with flying colors** to achieve great success in a test or enterprise **to give** (**or lend**) **color to** to give an appearance of probability to, *his absence gave color to the rumors of his disgrace* **to join the colors** to enlist in the army **to lose color** to go pale, from fear or ill health **to nail one's colors to the mast** to commit oneself to the consequences of one's opinions **to serve with the colors** to serve in the army **to show one's true colors** to reveal one's true character or opinion **to stick to one's colors** to be loyal to one's opinion or party **under color of** under the pretension of, *he stole money under color of making investments for clients* **2.** *v.t.* to impart color to ‖ (*fig.*) to make (something) seem better or worse, by selection of facts and studied emphasis, than is really the case, *to color a report* ‖ *v.i.* to assume a color, or a deeper color, to blush, *to color with embarrassment* [M.E. *color* fr. O.F.]

—The normal human eye conveys stimuli to the brain which vary according to the wavelength of visible light, and which are interpreted by the brain to give the sensations we know as colors. It is thought that all color sensations are compounds of three or less primary sensations. The color of light depends on its range of wavelengths, the color of an object being the color of the light it reflects or emits or transmits. Thus a red object appears red in white light because it reflects or transmits red light principally. The same object illuminated by light containing no red (e.g. green light) would appear black, since it absorbs all the light falling on it.

A particular color has the qualities of hue, saturation and lightness or brightness. Hue is the attribute by which a color is red, green etc. and such a color is chromatic. A color without hue (black, white, gray, silver etc.) is achromatic. Saturation is the quality of a color that depends on the amount of achromatic color mixed with it. Achromatic colors have zero saturation. The lightness of an object depends on its ability to reflect or transmit more or less light. The lightness of opaque objects varies from black to white, and of transparent objects

CONCISE PRONUNCIATION KEY: **(a)** æ, c*a*t; ɑ, c*a*r; ɔ f*aw*n; ei, sn*a*ke. **(e)** e, h*e*n; i:, sh*ee*p; iə, d*ee*r; ɛə, b*ea*r. **(i)** i, f*i*sh; ai, t*i*ger; ə:, b*i*rd. **(o)** o, *o*x; au, c*ow*; ou, g*oa*t; u, p*oo*r; ɔi, r*oy*al. **(u)** ʌ, d*u*ck; u, b*u*ll; u:, g*oo*se; ə, b*a*cillus; ju:, c*u*be. x, lo*ch*; θ, *th*ink; ð, bo*th*er; z, *Z*en; ʒ, cor*s*age; dʒ, sava*g*e; ŋ, ora*ng*utan*g*; j, *y*ak; ʃ, fi*sh*; tʃ, fe*tch*; 'l, rabb*le*; 'n, redd*en*. Complete pronunciation key appears inside front cover.

from black to colorless. The brightness of a colored source depends on the quality of light emitted, varying from invisible or dim to very bright. A shade is a color containing some black, and a tint is a color containing some white. The primary pigment colors are red, yellow and blue. The primary light colors are red, green and violet. Mixing colored light has a different result from that of mixing pigments. White light was formerly thought to consist of the whole range of wavelengths contained in the visible spectrum, but it has been shown that white is obtained by combining certain pairs of wavelengths

col·or·a·ble, *Br.* **col·our·a·ble** (kʌ́lərəb'l) *adj.* plausible, seeming true || pretending to be true but really false **cól·or·a·bly**, *Br.* **cól·our·a·bly** *adv.* [O.F. *colorable*]

Col·o·rad·an (kɒlərǽd'n, kɒlərɑ́d'n) **1.** *adj.* of or relating to Colorado **2.** *n.* a native or inhabitant of Colorado

Col·o·rad·o (kɒlərǽdou, kɒlərɑ́dou) (*abbr.* Colo., Col.) a state (area 104,247 sq. miles, pop. 3,045,000) of the central U.S.A. Capital: Denver. The east forms part of the Great Plains, while the west includes part of the Rocky Mtns. Agriculture: cattle and sheep, wheat and other cereals, sugar beet, potatoes. Resources: coal, molybdenum, uranium, oil and natural gas, gold and silver. Industries: food processing, iron and steel, machinery. Chief universities: University of Colorado (1876) at Boulder and Colorado School of Mines (1874) at Golden. Part of Colorado was included in the Louisiana Purchase (1803) and the remainder was ceded (1848) by Mexico to the U.S.A., of which it became (1876) the 38th state

Colorado a river (530 miles long) in central Argentina, formed near the Chilean border and flowing southeast into the Atlantic near Bahía Blanca

Colorado a river of southwestern North America rising in the Rocky Mtns, flowing 1,450 miles through Colorado, Utah and Arizona, and northern Mexico, into the Gulf of California. It forms part of the western border of Arizona with Nevada and California. It is famous for the 1,000 miles of canyons along its course (*GRAND CANYON). Its system of dams and canals provides power and water for a vast area of the southwestern U.S.A., esp. S. California and Arizona

Colorado a river of central Texas, flowing 840 miles into the Gulf of Mexico, a source of hydroelectric power

Co·lo·ra·do (kɒlɔrɑ́ðɔ) *n.* an Ecuadorian Indian people, named for their red-painted bodies || a member of this people || their language [Span.=colored]

Colorado beetle *Leptinotarsa decemlineata,* a striped beetle native to North America which has spread to most potato-growing regions of the world. It feeds on the leaves of potato plants, often doing great damage

Colorado Desert an arid region (2,000 sq. miles) in S.E. California, west of the Colorado River

Colorados a Uruguayan liberal political party opposed to the Blancos

Colorado Springs a resort (pop. 215,150) in central Colorado: U.S. Air Force Academy

col·o·ra·tion, *Br.* also **col·our·a·tion** (kʌləréi-ʃən) *n.* the quality or pattern of color || the method of putting on or arranging color [F.]

col·o·ra·tu·ra (kʌlərətúərə, kʌlərətjúərə, kɒlərətúərə, kɒlərətjúərə) **1.** *n.* a much ornamented style of vocal music || a voice suited to this style **2.** *adj.* of this style of music or voice [Ital.]

color bar, *Br.* **colour bar** the segregation of colored from white persons, or the according to different rights or privileges to the two

col·or·blind, *Br.* **col·our·blind** (kʌ́lərblaind) *adj.* afflicted with color blindness || one who is unbiased with regard to a person's skin color or racial identity

color blindness, *Br.* **colour blindness** difficulty in distinguishing chromatic color or inability to do so

color box, *Br.* **colour box** a box holding artists' pigments, brushes etc.

col·or·cast (kʌ́lərkæst, kʌ́lərkɑst) *n.* a TV broadcast in color

col·or-code or color key (kʌ́lərkoud) *v.* to identify by using different colors, e.g., in wiring, pipes, card files

col·ored, *Br.* **col·oured** (kʌ́lərd) *adj.* having

color || belonging to some race other than white || given deliberate bias, *colored remarks* **Col·ored** (South Africa) of or pertaining to the Cape Colored

col·or·field (kʌ́lərfi:ld) *adj.* of abstract art style in which color is the predominant factor. — **color painter** *n.* —**color painting** *v.*

col·or·ful, *Br.* **col·our·ful** (kʌ́lərfəl) *adj.* full of color || vivid, lively, *a colorful account*

col·or·if·ic (kʌlərifik *adj.* giving color || of color [fr. F. *colorifique*]

col·or·im·e·ter (kʌlərímitər) *n.* an instrument for measuring the characteristics of a color || an instrument for chemical analysis of liquids by comparison of their colors with standards **col·or·i·met·ri·cal** (kʌlərimétrik'l) *adj.* of or relating to colorimetry **col·or·im·e·try** *n.* the study and measurement of colors and their characteristics || quantitative chemical analysis by comparison of colors (*SPECTROSCOPY) [fr. L. *color,* color+METER]

col·or·ing, *Br.* **col·our·ing** (kʌ́ləriŋ) *n.* color scheme || the color of the face and hair || appearance, show (esp. false), *the string of names gave a coloring of truth to his story* || (*art*) the way in which an artist uses color || a children's pastime of putting color on outline pictures || a substance used to give color to something (esp. food)

col·or·ist, *Br.* **col·our·ist** (kʌ́lərist) *n.* a painter with regard to his use of color

col·or·less, *Br.* **col·our·less** (kʌ́lərlis) *adj.* without color || dull, characterless || unbiased

color phase, *Br.* **colour phase** (*zool.*) a genetically caused change in the usual skin or pelage color of an animal group || an individual exhibiting such a variation || a seasonally variant skin or pelage color

col·or·plex·er (kʌ́lərplɛksər) *n.* television transmission device that mixes primary colors to create a compatible single picture

color printing, *Br.* **colour printing** reproduction of a subject in two or more colors. Successive printings of each of the different colors into which the subject has been separated are built up by exact register into an image of the original

color scheme, *Br.* **colour scheme** a systematic combination of colors, *the color scheme of a room*

co·los·sal (kəlósəl) *adj.* huge [COLOSSUS]

Col·os·se·um (kɒləsí:əm) an amphitheater in Rome, begun (72 A.D.) under Vespasian, and inaugurated (80 A.D.) by Titus. It could hold more than 80,000 spectators. Public sport included the killing of early Christians there by lions and gladiators. It is now in ruins [L.]

Co·los·sians, Epistle to the (kəlóʃənz) the 12th book of the New Testament, written (c. 60) by St. Paul, probably during his imprisonment in Rome, to the Church at Colossae and Laodicea. It condemns the heretical worship of angels, and stresses the doctrine of the mystical body of Christ

co·los·sus (kəlósəs) *pl.* **co·los·sus·es, co·los·si** (kəlósai) *n.* a person of immense influence or thing of great size, esp. a huge statue || (*mil.*) navy code name for underwater sonic warning system [L. fr. Gk]

Colossus of Rhodes the huge statue of Helios which stood (c. 280–224 B.C.) at the entrance to the harbor at Rhodes (*SEVEN WONDERS OF THE WORLD)

co·los·trum (kəlóstrəm) *n.* the first milk of a mammal after giving birth, which supplies essential immune bodies to its young and aids in the establishment of digestion [L.]

colour *COLOR

col·por·teur (kólpɔrtər, kólpourtər) *n.* a traveling bookseller, esp. a seller of Bibles and religious books [F. fr. *col,* neck +*porteur,* porter]

Colt (koult), Samuel (1814–62), U.S. inventor of the Colt revolver, patented in Europe (1835) and in the U.S.A. (1836). He established (1855) in Hartford, Connecticut, the largest private armory in the world

colt (koult) *n.* the young of the horse and similar animals (ass, zebra etc.), esp. the male young of the horse (cf. FILLY) || an inexperienced person, esp. (*Br.*) a young cricketer [O.E. *colt,* young ass, young camel]

col·ter, *Br.* **coul·ter** (kóultər) *n.* a vertical iron cutter in front of a plowshare [O.E. *culter* fr. L.]

colt·ish (kóultiʃ) *adj.* of or like a colt

col·u·ber (kɒləbər, kóljubər) *n.* a member of *Coluber,* a genus of non-venomous snakes of worldwide distribution, familiar as a symbol of medicine [L.= snake]

col·u·brine (kɒləbrain, kɒləbrin, kóljubrain, kóljubrin) *adj.* like a snake || of or pertaining to the *Colubrinae,* a subfamily of *Colubridae,* a family of non-poisonous snakes [fr. L. *colubrinus*]

Co·lum·ba (kəlʌ́mbə), St (521–97), Irish missionary who founded (563) the monastic community of Iona and preached Christianity to the Picts of Caledonia. Feast: June 9

col·um·bar·i·um (kɒləmbéəri:əm) *pl.* **col·um·bar·i·a** (kɒləmbéəri:ə) *n.* (*Rom. Antiq.*) a building with recesses for urns containing the ashes of cremated people [L.=dovecote]

Co·lum·bi·a (kəlʌ́mbi:ə) the capital (pop. 101,208) of South Carolina, center of a rich farming and lumber region, with cotton mills. University of South Carolina (1801)

Columbia (*rhet.*) a female personification of the U.S.A.

Columbia the largest river of N.W. North America (1,270 miles long), flowing from the Rocky Mtns through British Columbia, Canada, and Washington and Oregon, U.S.A., into the Pacific. It is a great source of electric power and irrigation and an important waterway

Columbia first U.S. space shuttle, launched in April 1981

Columbia, Cape the northernmost point in Canada, on the north coast of Ellesmere Is., N.E. Arctic Archipelago

Columbia, District of *DISTRICT OF COLUMBIA

Columbia University a private university in New York City, founded as King's College (1754), comprising Columbia College for men, Barnard College for women, and important graduate schools

Col·um·bine (kɒ́ləmbain) *HARLEQUIN

col·um·bine (kɒ́ləmbain) *n.* an aquilegia [F. *columbine*]

co·lum·bite (kəlʌ́mbait) *n.* a black mineral compound of iron and niobium [fr. COLUMBIUM]

co·lum·bi·um (kəlʌ́mbi:əm) *n.* niobium [fr. *Columbia,* U.S.A.]

Co·lum·bus (kəlʌ́mbəs), Christopher (*Ital.* Cristoforo Colombo, *Span.* Cristóbal Colón, c. 1451–1506), Genoese born navigator and discoverer (or rediscoverer) of the New World. After much difficulty, he obtained the patronage of Ferdinand V and Isabella of Spain for his project of sailing west to reach the Orient. He left Palos (Aug. 3, 1492) with three ships, the 'Pinta', the 'Nina' and the 'Santa Maria', and reached the Bahamas (Oct. 12, 1492). He sailed to Cuba and Haiti before returning (1493) to Spain. A second voyage (1493–6) took him to the Lesser Antilles, Puerto Rico and Jamaica, and a third (1498–1500) to Trinidad and the coast of Venezuela. On his fourth voyage (1502–4), he explored the coast of Central America

Columbus the capital (pop. 564,871) of Ohio, a trade center (coal, wool, livestock). Industries: iron and steel

Columbus a city (pop. 169,441) in W. Georgia: cotton gins, cotton mills, iron works, meat-packing houses

Columbus a village (pop. 300) in New Mexico on the Mexican frontier, site of a raid (1916) by Pancho Villa. It resulted in the dispatch of Gen. Pershing and his army in a vain attempt to capture Villa

Columbus Day a legal holiday (Oct. 12) in many states of the U.S.A. and many countries of South America, commemorating Columbus' discovery of America in 1492

col·u·mel·la (kɒljuméllə) *pl.* **col·u·mel·lae** (kɒljuméli:) *n.* a prolongation of the stalk into the sporangium of a fungus || the central pillar in gastropod shells || the rod, partly bony, partly cartilaginous, connecting the tympanum with the inner ear in amphibians, reptiles and birds || the lower part of the nasal septum [L.=small column]

col·umn (kɒ́ləm) *n.* a pillar, usually with capital and base, used to support an entablature or an arch, or used decoratively in a building, or alone monumentally || something analogous to such a column, *a column of mercury* || a division of a manuscript or printed page into vertical blocks, or the matter set out in such a block || a journalist's regular feature in a newspaper, or other regular feature, *the gossip column* || (*mil.*) a formation extending in depth behind a narrow front || a similar formation of ships **co·lum·nar** (kəlʌ́mnər) *adj.* **co·lum·ni·form** *adj.* **col·umn·ist** *n.* a journalist who writes a regular newspaper feature [O.F. *colompne*]

co·lure (kəlúər, koulúər, kóuluər) *n.* either of two great circles crossing at right angles at the

CONCISE PRONUNCIATION KEY: (a) æ, c*a*t; ɑ, c*a*r; ɔ f*aw*n; ei, sn*a*ke. **(e)** e, h*e*n; i:, sh*ee*p; i:, d*ee*r; ɛə, b*ea*r. **(i)** i, f*i*sh; ai, t*i*ger; ə:, b*i*rd. **(o)** o, *o*x; au, c*ow*; ou, g*oa*t; u, p*oo*r; ɔi, r*oy*al. **(u)** ʌ, d*u*ck; u, b*u*ll; u:, g*oo*se; ə, b*a*cillus; ju:, c*u*be. x, lo*ch*; θ, *th*ink; ð, bo*th*er; z, *Z*en; ʒ, cor*s*age; dʒ, sava*g*e; ŋ, ora*ng*utang; j, *y*ak; ʃ, *fi*sh; tʃ, fe*tch*; 'l, rabb*le*; 'n, redd*en*. Complete pronunciation key appears inside front cover.

poles, one passing through the equinoctial points and the other through the solstitial points [fr. L. *colurus* fr. Gk *kolouros*, docked tail (because the lower parts are cut off from view)]

col·za (kólzə) *n.* any of several coles, esp. rape ‖ the oil-bearing seed of rape [F.]

colza oil rape oil esp. when refined

com- (kɒm) *prefix* with. It is used before b, p, m. It becomes 'col-' before l and 'cor-' before r [= L. *cum*, with]

COM *abbr* computer-output microfilm or for microfilm used as a substitute for paper printouts

co·ma (kóumə) *n.* the state of deep unconsciousness caused by disease, injury or poison [Gk *kōma*, a deep sleep]

coma *pl.* **co·mae** (kóumi:) *n.* (*bot.*) a tuft or bunch, e.g. of leaves or hairs ‖ (*astron.*) the head of a comet ‖ an imperfection in a lens or mirror which produces a comet-shaped image of a point source of light **có·mal** *adj.* [L.=hair, fr. Gk *komē*]

Co·man·che (koumæntʃi:, kəmæntʃi:) *n.* an Indian of a Shoshonean tribe formerly inhabiting the southwest U.S.A. ‖ the language of this tribe

co·mate (kóumeit) *adj.* (*bot.*) hairy [fr. L. *comatus*]

com·a·tose (kómətous, kóumətous) *adj.* relating to, resembling or affected with coma ‖ drowsy

co·mat·u·lid (kəmætʃulid) *n.* a feather star [L.L. fr. *Comatulidae*, the family containing these]

comb (koum) 1. *n.* a toothed instrument of hard rubber, plastic etc. for arranging the hair ‖ a similar but ornamental instrument of ivory, tortoiseshell, wood etc., used to keep a woman's hair in place ‖ a currycomb for removing dust, loose hairs etc. from a horse's or dog's coat ‖ a toothed instrument for cleaning wool, flax etc. ‖ the fleshy crest on a cock's head or a similar crest on other birds ‖ the crest of a wave ‖ a honeycomb 2. *v.t.* to arrange or clean with a comb ‖ to search through with great care, *to comb the woods* ‖ to card (wool) ‖ *v.i.* (of a wave) to break, curl over **to comb out** to remove by combing, *to comb burrs out of a dog's coat, comb out the weaker applicants* ‖ to comb thoroughly [O.E. *camb*]

com·bat 1. (kómbæt, kʌ́mbæt) *n.* a fight, struggle 2. *v.* (kəmbǽt, kómbæt, kʌ́mbæt) *pres. part.* **com·bat·ing, com·bat·ting** *past* and *past part.* **com·bat·ed, com·bat·ted** *v.t.* to fight or struggle against ‖ to oppose ‖ *v.i.* to fight, struggle [fr. F. *combattre*]

com·bat·ant (kəmbǽt'nt, kómbət'nt, kʌ́mbət'nt) 1. *adj.* fighting ‖ disposed to fight 2. *n.* a fighter [O.F.]

combat fatigue severe nervous disorders caused by strain experienced under the conditions of battle

com·bat·ive (kəmbǽtiv, kómbətiv, kʌ́mbətiv) *adj.* ready and willing to fight

combat team (*mil.* and *navy*) a mixed tactical unit organized for independent fighting, e.g. as a task force

combe *COOMB

combed yarn cotton or woolen yarn made from mechanically straightened fibers

comb·er (kóumər) *n.* a man or machine combing wool or cotton ‖ a beachcomber (wave)

com·bi·na·tion (kɒmbinéiʃən) *n.* a combining or being combined ‖ the single thing formed by two or more other things joining together, e.g. business concerns acting as one unit ‖ (*Br.*) a motorcycle and sidecar ‖ (*chem.*) the act or process of two or more substances joining to form a different substance ‖ the compound so formed ‖ (*math.*) any of the different sets into which a number of objects may be grouped, irrespective of the order within each set (*PERMUTATION) ‖ a set of numbers or other symbols which controls the action of a combination lock ‖ the mechanism operated by this [O.F.]

combination laws (*Br. hist.*) Acts of Parliament (1799 and 1800) which made associations of workers against employers illegal. They were repealed (1824)

combination lock a lock whose action is controlled by the right arrangement of a series of rings etc. inscribed with symbols

combination room (*Cambridge University, England*) a college common room for students, *junior combination room* or fellows, *senior combination room*

com·bi·na·tive (kómbinɛitiv, kəmbáinətiv) *adj.*

tending to combine ‖ of combination [fr. L. *combinare* (*combinatus*), to combine]

com·bi·na·to·ri·al mathematics (kɒmbinətɔ́ri:əl) (*math.*) branch of mathematics dealing with the number of ways in which certain combinations may be formed, i.e., 7 in a pair of dice. *syn* combinatorial topology

combinatorial topology *COMBINATION MATHEMATICS

com·bine 1. (kəmbáin) *v. pres. part.* **com·bin·ing** *past* and *past part.* **com·bined** *v.i.* (of two or more things) to join to form a single unit, *the two businesses have combined* ‖ (*chem.*, of substances) to join to form a different substance ‖ to join with other people in order to achieve a joint purpose, *they all combined to welcome him* ‖ *v.t.* to cause to join together, *he has combined his business with his brother's* ‖ to contain in a fused state, *the trip combined business with pleasure* 2. (kómbain) *n.* a combination of people or organizations, usually for keeping trade prices high or for political ends ‖ art form utilizing various elements, e.g., collage, painting, etc. ‖ a machine which reaps and threshes as a single process [fr. L.L. *combinare*]

combined operation a military operation involving the strategic use of units of air, sea and land forces as a single entity

combine harvester a combine (machine which reaps)

comb·ings (kóuminz) *pl. n.* loose hairs removed with a comb

combining form a word or word element used with another to form a compound, e.g. 'Anglo-' in 'Anglophobia'

comb jelly a ctenophore

comb-out (kóumaut) *n.* process of combing and styling the hair to a desired set. —**comb out** *v.*

com·bus·ti·ble (kəmbʌ́stib'l) 1. *adj.* able to undergo combustion 2. *n.* a substance having this property [F.]

com·bus·tion (kəmbʌ́stʃən) *n.* any chemical process accompanied by the emission of heat and light, typically by combination with oxygen [O.F.]

combustion chamber a compartment in which combustion takes place, e.g. the cylinder of an internal-combustion engine

com·bus·tor (kəmbʌ́stər) *n.* the combustion chamber and its ancillary equipment in a jet engine or gas turbine [fr. O. F. *combust*, burned]

come (kʌm) 1. *v. pres. part.* **com·ing** *past* **came** (keim) *past part.* **come** *v.i.* to approach, *come this way* ‖ to arrive, appear, *to come unexpectedly* ‖ to become, *the boat came adrift* ‖ to happen, *take life as it comes* ‖ to occur, *the explanation comes at the end* ‖ to reach, *the water comes up to my chin* ‖ to occur in sequence, *Tuesday comes after Monday* ‖ to occur to the mind, *the answer came to him in the bathtub* ‖ to fall as inheritance, *the title came to the younger son* ‖ to issue, be born, *he comes of mixed blood* ‖ to result, *you know what comes of drinking too much* ‖ to be available, *this coat comes in all sizes* ‖ *v.t.* (*Br.*) to pretend to be, *don't come the young innocent* **come along!** hurry up! **come off it!** (*pop.*) stop pretending! **to come about** to happen ‖ (*naut.*) to change tack **to come across** to meet with **to come and go** to move about, *come and go as you please* ‖ to pass to and fro ‖ to be transitory **to come around** (or **round**) to visit casually, *come around some time* ‖ to recover consciousness ‖ to recover one's good humor etc. ‖ to change an opinion, *he came around to my view* **to come at** (*old-fash.*) to get access to, to reach ‖ to attack, *the thieves came at him from the shadows* **to come away** to become unfastened, detached **to come back** to return ‖ to regain one's former position ‖ to retort, *he came back with a stinging reply* ‖ to recur to memory, *the name has just come back to me* **to come by** to obtain, *how did you come by that painting?* **to come down** to be handed down, *the folksongs that have come down to us* ‖ to lose status, *he has come down in the world* **to come down on** to rebuke, punish **to come forward** to present oneself (in answer to an appeal etc.), *no one came forward to give evidence* **to come in** to enter ‖ to arrive at the winning post ‖ (*Br.*) to become useful, *that suit will come in for the schoolplay* ‖ to become fashionable, *wigs are coming in again* ‖ to have a place or purpose, *and that's where you come in* **to come in for** to receive as one's share **to come of age** to become adult (as defined by law) **to come off** to become detached ‖ to emerge (from a situation, exam

etc.), *you came off lightly in the accident* ‖ to succeed, *the plan was a gamble but it came off* ‖ to take place, *the concert comes off next week* ‖ (*theater*) to end, *that play comes off tomorrow* **to come on** to meet unexpectedly ‖ to make progress ‖ to appear on the stage ‖ to make a first impression, *to come on strong* **to come out** (*Br.*) to go on strike, *the miners came out in sympathy* ‖ to become covered (with a rash or sweat etc.), *he came out in spots* ‖ to be seen to have specified photographic quality when developed and printed, *the photographs came out badly* ‖ to appear, *her foul temper came out again in her child* ‖ to be published, *it comes out annually* ‖ to be presented in society etc., *she came out when she was 17* ‖ to emerge, *to come out of hiding* **to come out with** to utter, *he came out with some vile oaths* **to come over** to cause to act strangely, *what has come over her?* **to come round** to come around **to come to** (with infinitive) to happen to, *how did you come to do that?* ‖ (with infinitive) to find oneself compelled or persuaded to, *she had come to accept his view* ‖ to amount to, *the bill comes to $10* ‖ (with stress on 'to') to recover consciousness ‖ (*naut.*, with stress on 'to') to take the way off a ship, to anchor etc. **to come true** to turn out to be as wished, *her dreams came true* **to come up** to spring up, *the seeds are coming up at last* ‖ to arise, *the matter came up at the last meeting* **to come upon** to find, meet by chance ‖ to make a surprise attack upon **to come up to** to equal, *he hasn't come up to expectations* ‖ to be as tall as, *she comes up to his shoulder* 2. *interj.* used to call attention or express remonstrance, *come! that's enough* [O.E. *cuman*]

come-back (kʌ́mbæk) *n.* a return to a desirable rank or position, *the old actress made an astonishing comeback* ‖ a retort (reply)

come-back·er (kʌ́mbækər) *n.* (*baseball*) ball hit along the ground directly toward the pitcher

COMECON (Council for Mutual Economic Assistance), an economic association set up (1949) in Moscow. It includes East Germany, Bulgaria, Hungary, Poland, Mongolia, Rumania, Czechoslovakia, Cuba, Vietnam and the U.S.S.R. Albania was expelled (1961). Yugoslavia became an associate member (1964)

co·me·di·an (kəmí:di:ən) *n.* a person who tells jokes in variety shows, nightclubs etc. ‖ an actor in comedy parts [fr. F. *comédien* fr. L. fr. Gk]

com·é·die de moeurs (kɒmædi: də mɜːrs) *n.* (*Fr.*) comedy of manners, usu. satirical

Co·mé·die-Fran·çaise (kɔmeidi:fræsez) the original national theater of France, founded in 1680 by the amalgamation of several theaters (among them Molière's). It was officially renamed 'Théâtre-Français' in 1791 and its constitution was laid down by Napoleon in 1812. Until recent times its performances were restricted to the classical French drama. Its actors are permanent and pensionable

comédie larmoyante (*Fr.*) sentimental comedy, usu. evoking tears

co·me·di·enne (kəmi:di:én, kəmeidi:én) *n.* a woman who tells jokes in variety shows, nightclubs etc. ‖ a comedy actress [F.]

comédie noire (*Fr.*) black comedy, esp. morbid or grotesque. *Cf* BLACK HUMOR

come·down (kʌ́mdaun) *n.* a humiliation

com·e·dy (kómidi:) *pl.* **com·e·dies** *n.* drama which seeks to please by amusing and deals with 'some defect... that is not painful or destructive' (Aristotle) ‖ an example of such drama ‖ a real-life situation that suggests such drama ‖ the laughter-provoking element in a situation, real or imagined [F. *comédie* fr. L. fr. Gk]

—A comedy is generally an amusing play, or a play with a happy ending. Comedy can, however, be serious, almost painful to the spectator (e.g. Shakespeare's 'Troilus and Cressida' and 'Measure for Measure', Molière's 'le Misanthrope', 'l'Ecole des femmes' and 'Don Juan'). Here the basic distinction between comedy and tragedy lies principally in the degree of sympathy extended by author and spectators to the characters. The comic spirit is essentially more critical, usually from the point of view of a society conscious of certain positive values which are endangered or flouted by the characters of the play

comedy of humors psychological drama of the 17th c., esp. Ben Jonson's. The 'humors' are psychological traits: the comedy consists in the portraiture of characters in whom one 'humor' is overdeveloped, making them ridiculous when judged by some norm of behavior

comedy of manners comedy in which current fashions of behavior are ridiculed

com·e·dy·wright (kómidi:rait) n. one who writes comedies

come-hith·er (kʌmhíðər) adj. enticing

come·li·ness (kʌ́mli:nis) n. the state or quality of being comely

come·ly (kʌ́mli:) comp. **come·li·er** superl. **come·li·est** adj. (old-fash.) of handsome appearance [O.E. cȳmlīc]

Co·me·ni·us (kəmí:ni:əs) (Jan Amos Komensky, 1592–1670), Czech educational reformer. He introduced new methods of teaching by object lessons and illustrations. He wrote the first Latin textbook illustrated for children, and many books on practical education

come on v. to make an over-zealous impression; to have a diligent approach

come out v. to reveal oneself, esp. as a homosexual; e.g., to come out of the closet

com·er (kʌ́mər) n. someone who comes, all comers welcome || (pop.) someone likely to make a name for himself

com·es·ti·ble (kəméstib'l) 1. adj. edible 2. n. (pl.) food, eatables [F.]

com·et (kómit) n. a heavenly body subject to the sun's force of attraction, moving in an elliptical or parabolic orbit, which sometimes degenerates into a hyperbola leading to the escape of the comet from the solar system. A comet consists of a hazy gaseous cloud with a bright nucleus. As it approaches the sun, radiation pressure causes it to form a tail which always points away from the sun **com·et·ar·y** (kómitəri:) adj. [O.E. cometa fr. L. fr. Gk]

come·up·pance (kʌ́mʌpəns) n. a punishment due and well deserved

com·fit (kʌ́mfit, kómfit) n. a fruit, nut or seed or other sweetmeat preserved in sugar [M.E. comfyt, fr. O.F.]

com·fort (kʌ́mfərt) n. consolation (for loss etc.) || someone or something that brings consolation || well-being, contentment, to look after the comfort of one's guests || someone or something that contributes to one's well-being [O.F. confort] **comfort** v.t. to console [O.F. conforter]

comfort index (meteorology) numerical value ranging from 70 to 80 reflecting outdoor temperature and humidity; comprised of 15 plus 0.4 times sum of dry-bulb and wet-bulb temperatures Fahrenheit. abbr. **CI**, also **THI**

com·fort·a·ble (kʌ́mftəb'l, kʌ́mfərtəb'l) adj. providing comfort, is your bed comfortable? || enjoying comfort, are you comfortable? || serene, restful, a comfortable atmosphere || quite large, a comfortable income [A.F. confortable]

Comfortable Words the four passages from the Scriptures following the Absolution in the Mass (Eucharist)

com·fort·a·bly (kʌ́mftəbli:, kʌ́mfərtəbli:) adv. in a comfortable way

com·fort·er (kʌ́mfərtər) n. someone who comforts || (Br.) a pacifier (rubber nipple for babies to suck) || a big woolen scarf || a feather quilt the **Comforter** the Holy Ghost

com·fort·less (kʌ́mfərtlis) adj. with grief unassuaged, she went away comfortless || cheerless, austere, a comfortless room || (rhet.) offering no comfort, comfortless messages

com·frey (kʌ́mfri:) n. a plant of genus Symphytum, fam. Boraginaceae, formerly used as a vulnerary [O.F. confirie]

com·fy (kʌ́mfi:) comp. **com·fi·er** superl. **com·fi·est** adj. (pop.) comfortable

com·ic (kómik) 1. adj. funny, amusing, a comic situation || relating to comedy, a comic part 2. n. a comedian || an amusing person || (pl.) comic strips || (Br.) a magazine consisting of such drawings **the comic** the humorous element in life or art **cóm·i·cal** adj. **com·i·cal·i·ty** (kɒmikǽliti:) n. [fr. L. fr. Gk komikos, belonging to comedy]

comic book a magazine consisting of narrative cartoon drawings

comic opera a light or amusing opera in which dialogue may be spoken as well as sung

comic strip a sequence of drawings, not necessarily intended to be funny, recording a story or set of situations usually about some central character. Comic strips may have no printed words, may have dialogue issuing from characters' mouths in balloons, or may have short captions

Com·in·form (kómic) the Communist information bureau set up (1947) by the U.S.S.R. to coordinate the Communist parties of Bulgaria, Czechoslovakia, France, Hungary, Italy,

Poland, Rumania, the U.S.S.R. and Yugoslavia. It was dissolved (1956)

com·ing (kʌ́miŋ) 1. adj. approaching, the coming year || lying in the near future || of increasing importance or soon to become important, a coming actress 2. n. approach || visit, arrival, his coming was quite unexpected

com·int (kómint) n. (mil.) code word for communications intelligence

Com·in·tern (kómintərn, kɒmintə́:rn) the Communist International set up in Russia by the Bolsheviks (1919) to promote revolutionary activity against capitalist governments, dissolved in 1943

COMIT (computer) programming language developed by Massachusetts Institute of Technology for the IBM 704, IBM 709, and IBM 7090

com·i·ty (kómiti:) n. courtesy [fr. L. comitas (comitatis) fr. comis, polite]

comity of nations the reasonable respect paid by one country to the laws and customs of another

COMLOGNET (mil. acronym) for combat logistic network, a computerized long-distance military network for transmitting logistic information on a priority basis

com·ma (kómə) n. a punctuation mark (,) separating words, phrases or clauses in a sentence, items in a list etc. || (mus.) a minute interval or difference in pitch of the same note, caused by different tuning systems [L. fr. Gk komma, clause]

comma bacillus Vibrio comma or Spirillum cholerae asiaticae, the comma-shaped bacterium which causes cholera

com·mand (kəmǽnd, kəmá:nd) 1. v.t. to control, be in authority over, to command a division || to dominate, restrain, to command one's temper || to order, he commanded them to withdraw || to deserve and win, integrity commands respect || to have at one's disposal, to command unlimited capital || to have a view of, overlook, the house commands the whole bay || to be in a position to demand, to command a high salary || v.i. to be in authority 2. n. an order || (mil.) a drilling order, the command to stand at ease || authority, control || (computer) a signal that sets a process in motion || mastery, command of a language || troops or ships under one's authority || view or effective range, the guns had command over both beaches **in command of** in charge of **under the command of** commanded by [M.E. comaunden fr. O.F.]

com·man·dant (kómandænt, kɒmandánt) n. (mil.) a commanding officer [F.]

com·mand·de·struct (kəmǽnddistrʌkt) n. in a rocket system, a signal that brings about destruction of the rocket

com·man·deer (kɒmandíər) v.t. to take possession of for military purposes || (loosely) to take arbitrary possession of [fr. Afrik. kommanderen fr. F.]

com·mand·er (kəmǽndər, kəmá:ndər) n. a leader, someone in command || (navy) an officer ranking below a captain and above a lieutenant commander || a member of a higher class in certain orders of knighthood [O.F. comandere]

commander in chief pl. **commanders in chief** the head of an armed force, esp. at national level || the naval officer in command of all ships on a station

Commander of the Faithful the title of the caliph

com·mand·ing (kəmǽndiŋ, kəmá:ndiŋ) adj. having command || having an impressive manner or appearance, demanding respect || having a fine view, a commanding position

com·mand·ment (kəmǽndmənt, kəmá:ndmənt) n. an order, esp. a divine command (*DECALOGUE) [fr. O.F. comandement]

command module 1. aerospace vehicle containing the operational crew, esp. directing other space craft. 2. directing unit of a group of space ships. abbr **CM**

com·man·do (kəmǽndou, kəmá:ndou) pl. **com·man·dos, com·man·does** n. a band of shock troops, esp. when engaged on raids into enemy territory || a member of such a group [Port.=party commanded]

com·meas·ur·a·ble (kəméʒərəb'l) adj. commensurate

com·me·dia dell'ar·te (kɒmmédjadellá:rte) n. a type of Italian drama created in the mid-16th c. in which the actors improvised the words and actions of a set plot. This was almost invariably an amorous intrigue involving disguises, the outwitting of guardians etc., and was usually

derived from Plautus and Terence [Ital. = comedy of art]

com·mem·o·rate (kəmémareit) pres. part. **com·mem·o·rat·ing** past and past part. **com·mem·o·rat·ed** v.t. to recall to memory, on Good Friday the crucifixion of Christ is commemorated || to serve as a memorial to, a monument to commemorate the dead [fr. L. com- + memorare, to recall to memory]

com·mem·o·ra·tion (kəmeməréiʃən) n. a solemn act of remembrance || a religious service of remembrance || (Oxford University) the annual Trinity term celebration in memory of founders and benefactors [fr. L. commemoratio (commemorationis)]

com·mem·o·ra·tive (kəméməreitiv, kəmémərativ) adj. of or relating to a commemoration

com·mence (kəméns) pres. part. **com·menc·ing** past and past part. **com·menced** v.t. to begin || v.i. to have a beginning [M.E. commence fr. O.F.]

com·mence·ment (kəménsmənt) n. the act of beginning || the time of beginning || the fact of beginning || a ceremony in some universities etc. at which diplomas and degrees are conferred [O. F. commencement, comencement]

com·mend (kəménd) v.t. to recommend, to commend a book to someone || to praise || to entrust, to commend one's soul to God [fr. L. commendare, to commit]

com·mend·a·ble (kəméndəb'l) adj. praiseworthy **com·mend·a·bly** adv. [O.F.]

com·men·da·tion (kɒmendéiʃən) n. praise || the act of commending || something which commends [O.F.]

com·mend·a·to·ry (kəméndətɔri:, kəméndətouri:) adj. commending, praising [fr. L.L. commendatorius]

com·men·sal (kəménsəl) 1. adj. (biol.) of an organism living in a state of commensalism 2. n. an organism **com·men·sal·ism** n. (biol.) a relation between organisms in which one derives benefits (e.g. food or protection) without harming or benefiting the other [F.]

com·men·su·ra·bil·i·ty (kəmensərəbíliti:, kəmenʃərəbíliti:) n. the quality or state of being commensurable

com·men·su·ra·ble (kəménsərəb'l, kəménʃərəb'l) adj. capable of being measured by the same standard || in due proportion **com·mén·su·ra·bly** adv. [fr. L. commensurabilis]

com·men·su·rate (kəménsərit, kəménʃərit) adj. equal in measure || in proper proportion, his abilities are commensurate with the task [fr. L. commensuratus]

com·ment (kóment) 1. n. a remark || a criticism || an explanatory note, esp. to a text 2. v.i. to make comments or remarks || to write explanatory notes [O.F.]

com·men·tar·y (kómənteri:) pl. **com·men·tar·ies** n. an explanatory book || a set of notes or critical remarks || a continuous flow of remarks on an event or performance [fr. L. commentarium, notebook]

com·men·tate (kómənteit) v.i. (esp. radio) to act as commentator [backformation fr. COMMENTATOR]

com·men·ta·tor (kómənteitər) n. the writer of a commentary || (radio) someone who is present at an event and broadcasts a description of it as it takes place || in a religious ceremony, a layman who explains the rituals [L.]

Commerce, U.S. Dept. of, an arm of the U.S. government that provides businesses with information on markets abroad, makes loans to businesses in depressed areas, subsidizes the merchant marine, and oversees the Bureau of the Census, the Patent and Trademark Office, the National Bureau of Standards, the Minority Business Development Agency, and the Maritime Administration

com·merce (kómərs) n. the exchange of goods, esp. on a large scale || (old-fash.) intercourse, esp. illicit sexual intercourse [F.]

com·mer·cial (kəmə́:rʃəl) 1. adj. concerned with commerce, commercial art || (of a radio program) paid for by an advertiser || (of certain films etc.) made with an eye to emphasis on sales appeal rather than artistic worth 2. n. (radio and television) a broadcast advertisement or a program put on by an advertiser [fr. L. commercium, trade]

commercial agency a firm which investigates the business background of individuals and companies for its clients

commercial bank a bank which accepts checking accounts and which makes short term investments

commercial college (*Br.*) a school specializing in commercial subjects to prepare people for business careers

com·mer·cial·ism (kəmə́:rʃəlizəm) *n.* commercial spirit or practice

com·mer·cial·ize (kəmə́:rʃəlaiz) *pres. part.* **com·mer·cial·iz·ing** *past* and *past part.* **com·mer·cial·ized** *v.t.* to make commercial ‖ to lower in quality in order to make more profitable

commercial traveller (*Br.*) a traveling salesman

commercial treaty a bilateral or multilateral agreement between countries, covering special trade and payment arrangements, tariffs, quotas, credits and preferential trade

com·mi·na·tion (kɔminéiʃən) *n.* a cursing, esp. a recital of divine threats against sinners rehearsed on Ash Wednesday in the Anglican Church [F.]

com·min·a·to·ry (kəmínətɔri:, kəmínətɔuri:, kɔ́minətɔri:, kɔ́minətɔuri:) *adj.* threatening [fr. L. *comminatorius*]

Commines, Philippe de *COMMYNES

com·min·gle (kəmíŋg'l) *pres. part.* **com·min·gling** *past* and *past part.* **com·min·gled** *v.t.* and *i.* to mix thoroughly together

com·mi·nute (kɔ́minu:t, kɔ́minju:t) *pres. part.* **com·mi·nut·ing** *past* and *past part.* **com·mi·nut·ed** *v.t.* (*med.*) to reduce to minute fragments, *a comminuted fracture* ‖ (*engin.*) to crush, grind **com·mi·nu·tion** *n.* [fr. L. *comminuere* (*comminutus*)]

com·mis·er·ate (kəmízəreit) *pres. part.* **com·mis·er·at·ing** *past* and *past part.* **com·mis·er·at·ed** *v.i.* (with 'with') to feel or express pity **com·mis·er·a·tion** *n.* **com·mis·er·a·tive** (kəmízəreitiv) *adj.* [fr. L. *commiserari* (*commiseratus*)]

com·mis·sar (kɔ́misɑr, kɔmisɑ́r) *n.* a head of a government department in the U.S.S.R. [Russ.]

com·mis·sar·i·al (kɔmiséɑri:əl) *adj.* relating to a commissary [fr. M.L. *commissarius*]

com·mis·sar·i·at (kɔmiséɑri:ət) *n.* a department in charge of food supplies, esp. in the army ‖ a government department in Russia [F.]

com·mis·sar·y (kɔ́miseri:) *pl.* **com·mis·sar·ies** *n.* an officer in charge of military supplies ‖ a government store supplying food and equipment to army or other governmental personnel ‖ a deputy, esp. (*eccles.*) someone who deputizes for a bishop in outlying parts of his diocese, or in his absence ‖ (in the U.S.S.R.) a commissar ‖ (in France) a senior police officer [fr. M.L. *commissarius*, person in charge]

com·mis·sion (kəmíʃən) **1.** *n.* a paper or warrant conferring authority, esp. one conferring rank and command upon an officer of the army, navy or air force ‖ the entrusting of authority to a person ‖ the business entrusted to a person ‖ a committing or being committed, *the commission of this crime appalled him* ‖ a percentage paid to an agent or employee on the business which he transacts ‖ a group of people appointed to investigate a matter **in commission** ready for active service ‖ in active service **out of commission** not in a state for use **2.** *v.t.* to give a commission to ‖ to order as a commission, *to commission a portrait* ‖ to put (a ship) in commission [F.]

commission agent (*Br.*) a bookmaker

com·mis·sion·aire (kəmiʃənéɑr) *n.* (*Br.*) a uniformed messenger or doorkeeper at a hotel, movie house, theater or department store [F.]

commissioned officer a military officer holding rank by commission (second lieutenant, ensign and above)

com·mis·sion·er (kəmíʃənər) *n.* a member of a commission, esp. of a government board ‖ an official with prime responsibility, esp. of a government department ‖ an official in charge of a branch of the public service

commission merchant a person who buys or sells goods on a commission basis

commission plan a system of municipal administration by a small elective commission

com·mis·su·ral (kəmíʃərəl, kɔmiʃúərəl, kɔmisúərəl) *adj.* of, relating to or having the properties of a commissure

com·mis·sure (kɔ́miʃuər) *n.* a seam, the place where two bodies or two parts of a body (lips, eyelids) join together ‖ a band of connecting nerve tissue linking symmetrical parts, e.g. the right and left side of the brain [fr. L. *commissura*, a joining together fr. *committere* (*commissus*)]

com·mit (kəmít) *pres. part.* **com·mit·ting** *past* and *past part.* **com·mit·ted** *v.t.* to give in keeping, entrust ‖ to be guilty of, *to commit larceny* ‖ to consign officially to custody, *to commit someone to prison* ‖ to consign for preservation, *to commit a thing to memory* ‖ to put in its last place, *to commit a body to the waves* ‖ to bind, pledge, *to commit oneself to an undertaking* ‖ to compromise, *don't commit yourself by saying anything rash* **com·mit·ment** *n.* something which engages one to do something ‖ a continuing obligation, esp. financial ‖ the act of committing, *commitment to prison* ‖ the state of being committed ‖ (*law*) a warrant for imprisonment ‖ the state of intellectual and emotional adherence to some political, social or religious theory or action or practice, esp. the conscious linking of works of literature and art with such theory or action ‖ a promise, pledge ‖ (*stock exchange*) the purchase or sale of a security **com·mit·tal** (kəmít'l) *n.* the point in the burial service at which the body is placed in the grave ‖ the sending to prison of a person ‖ a commitment of oneself [M.E. *committe* fr. L.]

com·mit·tee (kəmíti:) *n.* a body of people appointed or elected to examine or deal with particular matters ‖ (*law*) someone to whom a trust or charge is committed, *committees for minors* [A.F. fr. *committere*, to commit]

Committee for Industrial Organization a committee established (1935) by John L. Lewis within the American Federation of Labor to extend membership in the AFL to the unskilled or low-skilled worker. It separated from the AFL to form (1938) the Congress of Industrial Organizations

Committee of Fifteen a U.S. Congressional committee, dominated by 'radical' reconstructionists led by Charles Sumner, formed (1866) to inquire into the southern franchise after the Civil War. It denied the existence of any southern state government and declared that Congress was the sole agency of reconstruction

committee of the whole (house) a meeting of all members of a legislative body when it resolves itself into committee, in order to discuss some matter with a procedure less formal and more flexible than the usual procedure

Committee on Public Information a U.S. committee established (1917) by President Woodrow Wilson, headed by George Creel, to influence public opinion in favor of the administration's policy during the lst world war

com·mix (kəmíks) *v.t.* and *i.* to mix together ‖ to blend [fr. older *commixt*, adj. fr. L. *commixtus*, mixed together]

com·mix·ture (kəmíkstʃər) *n.* a mixing together ‖ the mixture resulting [fr. L. *commiscere* (*commixtus*), to mix together]

com·mode (kəmóud) *n.* a chest of drawers ‖ a washstand with a cupboard underneath ‖ a box or chair containing a chamber pot [F. (adj.) = convenient]

com·mo·di·ous (kəmóudi:əs) *adj.* roomy [fr. F. *commodieux*, useful]

com·mod·i·ty (kəmɔ́diti:) *pl.* **com·mod·i·ties** *n.* an article of trade ‖ (*econ.*) any concrete thing desired by purchasers, possessing utility, and available in limited supply [fr. F. *commodité*, a useful thing]

commodity agreement an international agreement for the marketing of foodstuffs and industrial raw materials

com·mo·dore (kɔ́mədɔr, kɔ́mədour) *n.* a naval officer ranking below a rear admiral and above a captain ‖ the senior captain of a line of merchant ships ‖ the president of a yacht club [earlier *commandore*, perh. fr. Du.]

Com·mo·dus (kɔ́mədəs), Lucius Aelius Aurelius (161–192), Roman emperor (180–192), son of Marcus Aurelius. A mad tyrant, he was murdered

com·mon (kɔ́mən) *adj.* belonging or relating to more than one ‖ belonging or relating to the public, *common knowledge* ‖ ordinary, usual, of frequent occurrence, *a common weed* ‖ vulgar, *common behavior* ‖ second-rate, inferior ‖ (*math.*) belonging to two or more quantities, *a common factor* [M.E. *comun* fr. O.F.]

common *n.* (often *pl.*) an area of grassland, usually in or near a village, used mainly for recreation. Historically it was common pasture ‖ (*law*) a specific right (e.g. fishing) which one man may have on another's land ‖ (*eccles.*) an office used for certain classes of feast, *common of Martyrs* **in common** owned or shared by all the members of a group, or by two people, *they have little in common* **out of the common** spe-

cially remarkable [COMMON adj. and F. *commune*]

com·mon·age (kɔ́mənidʒ) *n.* (*hist.*) a state of being held in common ‖ something held thus, esp. pasture land ‖ the use or right of use of something held thus

com·mon·al·ty (kɔ́mən'lti:) *pl.* **com·mon·al·ties** *n.* (esp. *hist.*) common people (distinguished from clergy and nobility) as one of the three classes of society [O.F. *comunalté*]

common carrier a person or company whose business is the transporting of goods or passengers for a fee

common chord a chord consisting of any note with its third and fifth above, any of the three notes being the bass note

common cold an acute, contagious disease of the upper respiratory tract caused by a virus. It is characterized by inflammation of the membranes of the nose, throat, eyes and Eustachian tubes, associated with a watery discharge

common denominator a quantity which is divisible without remainder by all the denominators of a number of fractions

common divisor a common factor

com·mon·er (kɔ́mənər) *n.* (*Br.*) one of the common people, not a member of the peerage ‖ (*Oxford University*) an undergraduate other than a scholar or exhibitioner

common factor a quantity by which a number of other quantities may be divided without remainder

common fraction a fraction expressed in terms of both a numerator and a denominator (cf. DECIMAL FRACTION)

common gender either masculine or feminine gender (e.g. of 'person') or a collective gender including both (e.g. of 'audience')

common ground a basis accepted by both sides in an argument

common informer someone who trades incriminating secrets to the police etc. in return for pay or advantage

common language (*computer*) computer language that is compatible with many computers

common law the unwritten law of custom, esp. of England, based on the decisions of judges over a period of years (cf. STATUTE LAW, cf. EQUITY)

common-law marriage a marriage entered into without a civil or religious ceremony, recognized as valid under certain legal systems where documentary evidence etc. can be produced

com·mon·ly (kɔ́mənli:) *adv.* very frequently, generally ‖ in a vulgar manner

Common Market the European Economic Community

common market (*economic*) unit in which border-crossing barriers have been removed, esp. tariffs; e.g., the European Common Market. — **common marketeer** *n.* one who favors membership in a common market

common multiple a quantity divisible, without remainder, by two or more other quantities

common node (*electr.*) having identical amplitude and phase signals at both inputs, e.g., in a differential operational amplifier

common noun a noun designating a thing or being (e.g. cat, mayor) which is one of a class (cf. PROPER NOUN)

common of pis·ca·ry (pískəri:) the right to fish in another's waters [fr. M.L. *piscaria*, neut. pl. of *piscarius* adj., of fish, of fishing]

common or garden ordinary, undistinguished

com·mon·place (kɔ́mənpleis) **1.** *adj.* ordinary ‖ undistinguished ‖ trite **2.** *n.* a trite saying [trans. L. *locus communis*]

commonplace book a book into which a person copies other men's writings or sayings which strike him as worth collecting

Common Pleas (in several states) a civil court ‖ (*Br. hist.*) the chief common-law court for the trial of civil cases, abolished 1875

Common Prayer *BOOK OF COMMON PRAYER

common room (esp. *Br.*) a sitting room shared by all members of a hostel etc. ‖ a room in a college set apart for the social use of students, or one for the teaching staff

Com·mons (kɔ́mənz), John Rogers (1862–1945), U.S. labor economist known for his contribution to industrial research. He published 'Legal Foundations of Capitalism' (1924) and 'Institutional Economics' (1934), and sponsored reform legislation in Wisconsin

CONCISE PRONUNCIATION KEY: **(a)** æ, c*a*t; ɑ, c*a*r; ɔ f*aw*n; ei, sn*a*ke. **(e)** e, h*e*n; i:, sh*ee*p; iə, d*ee*r; ɛə, b*ea*r. **(i)** i, f*i*sh; ai, t*i*ger; ə:, b*i*rd. **(o)** o, *o*x; au, c*ow*; ou, g*oa*t; u, p*oo*r; ɔi, r*oy*al. **(u)** ʌ, d*u*ck; u, b*u*ll; u:, g*oo*se; ə, b*a*cillus; ju:, c*u*be. x, lo*ch*; θ, *th*ink; ð, bo*th*er; z, *Z*en; ʒ, cor*s*age; dʒ, sava*ge*; ŋ, orangutan*g*; j, *y*ak; ʃ, *fish*; tʃ, fe*tch*; 'l, rabb*le*; 'n, redd*en*. Complete pronunciation key appears inside front cover.

com·mons (kómənz) pl. n. the ordinary people of a nation ‖ their parliamentary representatives ‖ provisions, esp. those shared by a monastery or college ‖ **the Commons** the House of Commons (*PARLIAMENT)

common sense the ability to form opinions which reflect practical experience **cóm·mon·sénse** adj.

common stock (Am.=Br. ordinary shares) corporation shares which have rights to assets and dividends, contingent upon the claims of preferred stock

common time (mus.) four quarter notes to the bar

common trust fund an accumulation of investment assets held in trust for many owners in which each investor owns a proportional part

com·mon·weal (kómənwi:l) n. (rhet.) the general good of all ‖ (archaic.) the body politic

com·mon·wealth (kómənwelθ) n. a free association of self-governing units in a federation, with certain common tasks performed by the federal government (e.g. Australia) ‖ (hist.) the body politic ‖ (hist.) government for the common good **the Commonwealth** (Eng. hist.) the republican government established (1649) after the execution of Charles I. Oliver Cromwell became (1653) lord protector of the Commonwealth, and was succeeded (1658) by his son Richard, who resigned (1659). The Commonwealth ended (1660) with the restoration of Charles II

Commonwealth of Nations a free association of Britain and certain sovereign independent states, formerly the colonies of the British Empire, and their dependencies. The British Crown is acknowledged by all members as the symbol of their association. Many members accept the British monarch, represented by a governor-general, as their head of state, but others are republics under a president, while Malaysia, Lesotho and Swaziland have their own monarchs. The Commonwealth has no central government, and unites a fifth of the world's land and population. Its members, with dates of entry, are: Great Britain (1931), Canada (1931), Australia (1931), New Zealand (1931), India (1947), Sri Lanka (1948), Ghana (1957), Nigeria (1960), Cyprus (1961), Sierra Leone (1961), Jamaica (1962), Trinidad and Tobago (1962), Uganda (1962), Malaysia (1963), Kenya (1963), Tanzania (1964), Malawi (1964), Malta (1964), Zambia (1964), The Gambia (1965), Singapore (1965), Guyana (1966), Botswana (1966), Lesotho (1966), Barbados (1966), Mauritius (1968), Swaziland (1968), Tonga (1970), Fiji (1970), Western Samoa (1970), Bangladesh (1972), Bahamas (1973), Grenada (1974), Papua New Guinea (1975), Seychelles (1976), Dominica (1978), Solomon Is. (1978), Tuvalu (1978), Kiribati (1979), St. Lucia (1979), St. Vincent and the Grenadines (1979), Vanuatu (1980), Zimbabwe (1980), Antigua and Barbuda (1981), Belize (1981), Maldives (1982), St. Kitts-Nevis (1983), and Brunei (1984). The main cohesive forces are historical ties, trade, finance and defense interests, and the bond of the English language. The British Empire, out of which the Commonwealth developed, began with the colonization of Newfoundland (1583). In the early 18th c., settlements were made in North America, while commercial companies were chartered to trade with other lands, notably the British East India Company in India. The empire developed on mercantilist lines, the colonies being regarded as sources of raw materials and markets. Canada and India were in effect won from the French during the Seven Years' War (1756–63), but the Thirteen Colonies of North America were lost in the Revolutionary War (1775–83). Many strategic colonies were won during the Napoleonic Wars, the slave trade was abolished (1833), and free trade replaced protectionism (1840s). The report (1839) of Lord Durham changed the emphasis of the empire from exploitation to development. Systematic emigration to Australia and New Zealand began. The Crown took control (1858) of India, of which Victoria was proclaimed empress (1877). Canada became (1867) the first dominion, followed by Australia (1907), New Zealand (1907), Newfoundland (1907) and South Africa (1910). Meanwhile Britain was gaining new territory in the scramble for colonies in Africa and the Pacific, but jingoism was halted by the Boer War (1899–1902). Imperial conferences began (1887). The dominions joined Britain in the 1st world war, after which Britain received mandates over Tanganyika, Palestine and Iraq. The Statute of Westminster (1931) proclaimed the equality of Britain and the dominions, and recognized their complete independence. After the 2nd world war, dominion status was ended and a Commonwealth Relations Office set up (1947). India and Pakistan became independent in 1947, and Ceylon (now Sri Lanka) in 1948. The Irish Republic withdrew (1949), as did South Africa (1961) and Pakistan (1972). Younger colonies, notably in Africa, rapidly advanced to independent Commonwealth status (1960s). Preferential tariff treatment for goods sold in Britain by Commonwealth members was abandoned when Britain joined the European Economic Community (1973)

com·mo·tion (kəmóuʃən) n. a noisy disturbance caused by a number of people ‖ mental turmoil, confused excitement [O.F.]

com·mu·nal (kəmjú:n'l, kómjun'l) adj. belonging to a community, communal fields ‖ (India) of religious or racial communities, communal riots **com·mú·nal·ism** n. a system of decentralized government by which large powers are delegated to small communities in a country **com·mú·nal·ist** n. **com·mu·nal·ís·tic** adj. [F.]

com·mune (kómju:n) n. the smallest administrative division of the country in France, Belgium, Italy, Spain and some other countries ‖ the government or citizens of a commune ‖ a group protesting modern technological civilization and seeking a simpler way of living through a communal effort, usually based on craft or agriculture **the Commune** (F. hist.) a revolutionary government set up in Paris (1789–94) during the French Revolution ‖ a collective organization for living or working in which products and property are shared, i.e., the ultimate of communism and anarchism ‖ a revolutionary government proclaimed (Mar. 18, 1871) in opposition to the National Assembly at Versailles, whose troops crushed the Commune with the loss of thousands of lives (May 21–8, 1871) [F.]

com·mune (kəmjú:n) pres. part. **com·mun·ing** past and past part. **com·muned** v.i. to be in communion (in respect of ideas, feelings) ‖ to communicate, receive Communion [O.F. communer]

com·mu·ni·ca·bil·i·ty (kəmju:nikəbíliti:) n. the quality of being communicable

com·mu·ni·ca·ble (kəmjú:nikəb'l) adj. capable of being communicated [F.]

com·mu·ni·cant (kəmjú:nikənt) n. ‖ (eccles.) someone who receives Communion ‖ someone who communicates information [fr. L. communicans (communicantis) fr. communicare, to communicate]

com·mu·ni·cate (kəmjú:nikeit) pres. part. **com·mu·ni·cat·ing** past and past part. **com·mu·ni·cat·ed** v.t. to give or pass on (information, feelings, disease etc.) ‖ v.i. (eccles.) to receive Communion ‖ to make others understand one's ideas ‖ to be in touch by words or signals ‖ to be joined by a common door, gate etc. [fr. L. communicare (communicatus)]

communicating copier a reproduction device connected with distant word processing machines, computers and other devices

com·mu·ni·ca·tion (kəmju:nikéiʃən) n. a sending, giving or exchanging (of information, ideas, etc.) ‖ a method of such exchange ‖ the state of such exchange, poor communication ‖ an item of such exchange ‖ a scientific paper read to a learned group ‖ (often pl.) travel and transport links between places ‖ (pl., mil.) a system of radio and telegraph liaison from advance troops back to base [O.F. communicacion]

communication gap (colloq.) a failure to convey and/or understand the information, intent, or meaning of another, especially between individuals of different perception

com·mu·ni·ca·tive (kəmjú:nikeitiv, kəmjú:nikətiv) adj. informative, willing to talk informatively [fr. L. communicare (communicatus), to communicate]

com·mun·ion (kəmjú:njən) n. an intimate or sublime exchange or communication of thoughts and feelings ‖ a body of people with common faith ‖ fellowship bridging divisions of the Church, they are in communion with the Greek Orthodox Church **Com·mun·ion** (eccles.) the partaking of the consecrated bread or wine ‖ the sacrament of Holy Communion (*EUCHARIST) [F.]

com·mu·ni·qué (kəmjú:nikéi, kəmjú:nikei) n. an official communication [F.]

com·mun·ism (kómjunizəm) n. the ownership of property, or means of production, distribution and supply, by the whole of a classless society, with wealth shared on the principle of 'to each according to his need', each yielding fully 'according to his ability' ‖ the body of political and economic doctrines which sets forth the establishing of this as a revolutionary aim through the dictatorship of the proletariat **Communism** a social and political movement which is based on Marx's interpretation of history and which seeks to achieve communism by revolutionary means **cóm·mun·ist** 1. n. a person who advocates communism 2. adj. of, pertaining to, favoring communism **Communist** 1. n. a member of a Communist party 2. adj. advocating Communism ‖ relating to a Communist party **com·mu·nís·tic** adj. communist [fr. L. communis, common]
—The history of Communism goes back to Karl Marx's 'Communist Manifesto' published (1848) in England, in which he put forward historical materialism. Lenin developed the Communist party after the Russian Revolution (1917), when the U.S.S.R. was established. Stalin opposed Trotsky's insistence on universal revolution and developed a strong dictatorship, which after his death was denounced by Khrushchev as 'the cult of personality'. Since Stalin, there has been a return in Russia to Marxist-Leninism. There are profound differences in the development of Communism in Russia, China, Poland, Yugoslavia and other countries

Communism, Mt (formerly Stalin Peak, Garmo Peak) a peak (24,590 ft) in the Pamirs, the highest in the U.S.S.R.

Communist Control Act a U.S. Congressional act (1954) which in effect 'outlawed' the U.S. Communist party

Communist Manifesto a statement of the principles of Communism, written (1848) by Karl Marx and Friedrich Engels

com·mu·ni·ty (kəmjú:niti:) pl. **com·mu·ni·ties** n. a body of people living near one another and in social relationship, a village community ‖ a body of people with a faith, profession or way of life in common, the Jewish community in London ‖ a collection of animals and or plants sharing the same environment ‖ common ownership, community of goods ‖ a sharing, a community of interest [O.F. communeté]

Community (preceded by **The**) short form for U.S. foreign policy community made up of those who hold top foreign policy and national security posts

community antenna television system of television in which each subscriber is connected by cable to a base antenna that has access to clearer and more varied programs than are broadcast commercially. abbr CATV

community center, Br. **community centre** a building in which local residents meet for social purposes

community chest (U.S.A. and Canada) a fund built by individual contribution and used for social welfare

community health network a community health system for delivering medical care to the poor. acronym CHN

community medicine 1. community health care 2. public health 3. preventive medicine 4. primary health care

community singing singing in which everyone present joins

com·mu·nize (kómjunaiz) pres. part. **com·mu·niz·ing** past and past part. **com·mu·nized** v.t. to make (esp. land or factories) into common property ‖ to bring (esp. people, countries) under the doctrines of communism [fr. L. communis, common]

com·mut·a·bil·i·ty (kəmju:təbíliti:) n. the state or quality of being commutable

com·mut·a·ble (kəmjú:təb'l) adj. capable of being commuted [fr. L. commutabilis]

com·mu·tate (kómjuteit) pres. part. **com·mu·tat·ing** past and past part. **com·mu·tat·ed** v.t. (elec.) to reverse the direction of (a current) ‖ to convert (alternating current) into direct current [COMMUTATION]

com·mu·ta·tion (kɒmjutéiʃən) n. (law) commuting, reduction of sentence ‖ the substitution of one form of payment for another ‖ reversing, by means of a commutator, of the direction of an electric current ‖ commuting, regular (daily) travel over the same ground, esp. at reduced rail fare ‖ (electr.) reversal of direct-current in armature windings of a direct current rotating machine so as to provide direct current at the brushes ‖ (*math.*) an element that, when multiplied by the product of two other elements, equals the product of the elements in reverse order ‖ in telemetering, sampling transmission of quantities repeatedly over a channel [F. *commutacion*]

com·mu·ta·tive (kəmjúːtətiv, kómjutɐitiv) *adj.* requiring or using substitution of one thing for another ‖ (*math.*) of an operation in which the order in which the elements are placed is irrelevant, e.g., 6 × 3 × 4 [fr. M.L. *commutativus*]

com·mu·ta·tor (kómjutɐitər) *n.* (*elec.*) a device for reversing the direction of an electric current ‖ a rotating device that transmits current to the brushes in a dynamo and collects it from them in an electric motor

com·mute (kəmjúːt) *pres. part.* **com·mut·ing** *past* and *past part.* **com·mut·ed** *v.t.* to change (a mode of payment) to another, *to commute an annuity into a capital sum* ‖ to change (a punishment) into another less severe, *to commute a death sentence to life imprisonment* ‖ (*elec.*) to commutate *v.i.* to travel regularly to and from a city, usually for work [fr. L. *commutare*]

com·mut·er belt (kəmjúːtər) suburbs of a city
commuter tax income tax levied on a nonresident worker

Com·mynes, Com·mines (kɔmiːn), Philippe de, sire d'Argenton (c. 1447–c. 1511), French statesman and historian. His 'Mémoires' (1489–98) are the chief source for the history of the reign of Louis XI, whom he served as adviser

Com·ne·nus (kɔmníːnəs) a dynasty which ruled the Byzantine Empire (1057–9 and 1081–1185)

Co·mo (kóumou) a cathedral town (pop. 76,000) at the south end of Lake Como, N. Italy: silk industry

Como a lake (area 56 sq. miles) in the Alps of N. Italy, 650 ft above sea level. Its beauty draws many tourists

Com·o·ro Islands (kómərou) (F. Comores) an Islamic republic (area 838 sq. miles, pop. 385,000 Malay, Arab, Malagasy, African and European) in the Indian Ocean between N. Madagascar and Mozambique. The main islands are Grande-Comore, Anjouan, Mayotte (containing the capital, Dzaoudzi) and Mohéli. Products: vanilla, perfumes, copra, sugar, lumber, sisal, cloves, rum. The islands were visited by the Portuguese (16th c.), became a French protectorate (1886), and an autonomous overseas territory (Jan. 1, 1947). All the islands except Mayotte voted to become independent (1974) and unilaterally declared independence (1975). Mayotte remained under French administration. Comoros became a federal Islamic republic (1978) and a one-party state (1982). The future of Mayotte remained unsettled

co·mose (kóumous) *adj.* (*bot.*, of seeds) tufted, having a coma [fr. L. *comosus*]

com·pact (kómpækt) *n.* an agreement between individuals or groups [fr. L. *compacisci* (*compactus*), joined]

com·pact 1. (kəmpækt) *adj.* densely packed, *a compact mass* ‖ closely arranged or put together so as to use space economically, *a compact house* ‖ (of an automobile) smaller than average so as to be cheap to run, easy to park etc. ‖ without waste of words, *a compact little book* 2. (kómpækt) *n.* a small container for face powder, and sometimes rouge, with a mirror [fr. L. *compingere* (*compactus*), to fasten together]

com·pact·i·ble (kəmpæktibəl) *adj.* capable of being packed tightly together

com·pan·dor (kəmpændər) *n.* (*electr.*) system to improve signal-to-noise ratio by compressing the signal's volume range at the transmitter or recorder, using a compressor and providing normal receiving with an expander

com·pan·ion (kəmpænjən) 1. *n.* a person who goes with or accompanies another, *a traveling companion* ‖ someone who shares another's experiences, *companions in good fortune* ‖ a person or animal whose company one enjoys ‖ a thing made to match or harmonize with another, *this chair is a companion to that* ‖ a woman paid to live with and help another ‖ a manual (in titles of handbooks), *the Carpenter's Companion* ‖ (*Br.*) a member of the lowest grade of an order of knighthood 2. *v.t.* (*rhet.*) to accompany, go with [O.F. *compaignon*]

companion *n.* (*naut.*) a raised frame on a ship's deck for lighting cabins [ult. fr. Ital. *compagna*]

com·pan·ion·a·ble (kəmpænjənəb'l) *adj.*

friendly, making a good companion **com·pán·ion·a·bly** *adv.*

com·pan·ion·ate marriage (kəmpænjənit) a proposed form of marriage with legalized birth control, and divorce by consent of childless couples, neither partner having financial claims on the other

companion cell one of the elongated parenchyma cells lying next to the sieve tube in many seed plants (*PHLOEM)

companion hatch (*naut.*) a wooden or metal covering over the companion hatchway

companion hatchway (*naut.*) an opening in the deck leading to the cabins

companion ladder (*naut.*) a companionway

com·pan·ion·ship (kəmpænjənʃip) *n.* the fellowship shared by companions ‖ (*Br., printing*) a company of compositors working together

com·pan·ion·way (kəmpænjənwei) *n.* (*naut.*) a staircase from deck to cabin

com·pa·ny (kámpəni:) *pl.* **com·pa·nies** *n.* the state of being with another or others ‖ people with whom one associates, *do not judge a man by the company he keeps* ‖ (*pop.*) a guest or guests ‖ a number of people united in an industrial or commercial enterprise, e.g. a firm of partners ‖ (in the title of a firm) those partners not named, *Brown, Sidebottom and Company* ‖ the officers and men of a ship, *the ship's company* ‖ an infantry unit between a platoon and a battalion in size ‖ companionship ‖ someone or something providing companionship **to keep a person company** to accompany a person ‖ to stay with someone for companionship **to part company** to go each his own way ‖ (of a couple) to separate [O.F. *compaignie*]

company union an association of employees in a single firm for their common advantage, having no connection with another union ‖ such a union dominated by the employer

com·par·a·bil·i·ty provision (kɒmpərəbíliti:) provision in Medicare specifying that the reasonable charge for a service may not be higher than charges payable for comparable services insured under comparable circumstances by an organization for its non-Medicare beneficiaries

com·pa·ra·ble (kómpərəb'l) *adj.* capable or worthy of being compared ‖ similar, *all great cities are comparable* **cóm·pa·ra·bly** *adv.* [F.]

comparable worth doctrine that jobs traditionally held by women automatically receive lower pay than jobs with comparable worth usually held by men; held to be discriminatory by U.S. Supreme Court (1981)

com·pa·ra·tist (kəmpærətist) *n.* (*linguistics*) one who utilizes the technique of comparing words, structure, habit, literature, and other art forms to the study of philology, esp. of parent Indo-European languages

com·par·a·tive (kəmpærətiv) 1. *adj.* using or introducing comparison, *comparative methods of study* ‖ not absolute but existing in some degree, *he is wise despite his comparative youth* 2. *n.* (*gram.*) the comparative degree [fr. L. *comparativus*]

comparative degree (*gram.*) the form of an adjective or adverb expressing a greater degree of the attribute denoted by it than the simple form, e.g. 'fast' has as its comparative degree 'faster' and 'slowly' has as its comparative degree 'more slowly'

com·pa·ra·tor (kómpəreitər) *n.* an instrument for comparing one thing with another like it or with a standard measure, e.g. as used in colorimetry [fr. L. *comparare*, to compare]

com·pare (kəmpéər) 1. *v. pres. part.* **com·par·ing** *past* and *past part.* **com·pared** *v.t.* to examine (two or more things) in order to discover their likenesses or differences ‖ to state a likeness of (one thing to another), *he compared life to a game of skill* ‖ to affirm the excellence of (one thing) by setting it beside another of known excellence, *this wine can be compared with the best claret* ‖ (*gram.*) to form the comparative and superlative degrees of (adjectives and adverbs) ‖ *v.i.* (*usually neg.*) to sustain comparison, *it can't compare with last year's* 2. *n.* (in phrases) **beyond compare, past compare** of such excellence that nothing comparable can be found [O.F. *comparer*]

com·par·i·son (kəmpæris'n) *n.* a comparing, an attempt to discover what is like and unlike, *a comparison of two countries* ‖ a resemblance shown for the sake of explanation, *the comparison of the earth to a ball* ‖ (*gram.*) the change in form of adjectives and adverbs to show differ-

ence of degree, e.g. 'great, greater, greatest' [O. F. *comparaison*]

com·part·ment (kəmpáartmənt) *n.* one part of a space which has been divided, e.g., in an egg carton, or watertight division of a ship ‖ (*Br.*) a separate part of business which may be discussed by parliament within a time limit **com·part·men·tal** (kəmpartmént'l, kɒmpartmént'l) *adj.* [F.]

com·part·men·tal·ize (kəmpartmént'laiz, kɒmpartmént'laiz) *pres. part.* **com·part·men·tal·iz·ing** *past* and *past part.* **com·part·men·tal·ized** *v.t.* to divide into separate compartments, organize by largely self-contained divisions [fr. COMPARTMENTAL]

com·pass (kámpəs) *v.t.* to move around ‖ to surround, *a wall compassed the garden* ‖ to accomplish, attain, *to compass one's ends* ‖ to grasp mentally, *his mind could not compass such a vast problem* **cóm·pass·a·ble** *adj.* [F. *compasser*, to compass]

compass *n.* an instrument for determining direction on the earth's surface, either a magnetic compass, which points to the magnetic north, or any nonmagnetic device (e.g. a gyrocompass) which gives true north ‖ (also *pl.*) an instrument consisting of two legs connected by a metal joint, used for making circles ‖ range, extent, *the compass of a mezzosoprano* ‖ limited extent, *within the compass of a small book* [F. *compas*]

Compass (*computer*) computer program, assembler, and compiler language designed for the SAGE system by U.S. Air Force

compass card (*naut.*) the disk carrying the magnetic needle of a mariner's compass, and marked with points of the compass (North, South etc.)

com·pas·sion (kəmpæʃən) *n.* pity aroused by the distress of others, with the desire to help them [F.]

com·pas·sion·ate (kəmpæʃənit) *adj.* feeling compassion [fr. F. *compassionné*]

compassionate allowance (*Br., mil.*) money granted to a person in special need who is not otherwise entitled to it

compassionate leave (*Br., mil.*) a period of absence from duty granted a person in cases of hardship or suffering

compass plane a woodworking plane for use on convex or concave surfaces

compass, points of the the 32 marked, equidistant spots on the circumference of a compass card indicating direction to the horizon

compass rose a graduated circle printed on a chart, usually showing magnetic and true directions

compass window a bay window in the form of a half circle

com·pat·i·bil·i·ty (kəmpætəbíliti:) *n.* the state or quality of being compatible

com·pat·i·ble (kəmpætəb'l) *adj.* able to exist together without mutual contradiction ‖ capable of living together harmoniously [F.]

com·pat·i·bly (kəmpætəbli:) *adv.* in a compatible manner

com·pa·tri·ot (kəmpéitri:ət, *Br.* kəmpætri:ət) *n.* someone having the same native country as another [F. *compatriote*]

com·peer (kəmpíər, kómpiər) *n.* (*rhet.*) an equal in capacity or rank, peer ‖ a companion [M.E. *comper* O.F.]

com·pel (kəmpél) *pres. part.* **com·pel·ling** *past* and *past part.* **com·pelled** *v.t.* to oblige (someone to do something) ‖ to call forth and secure (something) in others, *his honesty compels respect* **com·pél·la·ble** *adj.* [O. F. *compeller*]

com·pen·di·ous (kəmpéndi:əs) *adj.* short but containing much of what is needed, *a compendious guidebook* [A.F.]

com·pen·di·um (kəmpéndi:əm) *pl.* **com·pen·di·ums, com·pen·di·a** (kəmpéndi:ə) *n.* a concise treatise containing what is needed [L. fr. *compendere*, to weigh together]

com·pen·sate (kómpənseit) *pres. part.* **com·pen·sat·ing** *past* and *past part.* **com·pen·sat·ed** *v.t.* to repay (someone) for a loss ‖ (*phys.*) to provide with a means of counteracting or neutralizing variation ‖ to make up for (something) ‖ *v.i.* to make up for something, *later success compensated for his early struggles* [fr. L. *compensare* (*compensatus*), to counterbalance]

compensating gear differential gear

compensating pendulum a clock pendulum so designed as to remain the same length despite changes caused by temperature variation

com·pen·sa·tion (kɒmpənséiʃən) *n.* an act of compensating or thing which compensates ‖

CONCISE PRONUNCIATION KEY: **(a)** æ, c*a*t; ɑ, c*ar*; ɔ f*aw*n; ei, sn*a*ke. **(e)** e, h*e*n; i:, sh*ee*p; iə, d*ee*r; ɛə, b*ear*. **(i)** i, f*i*sh; ai, t*i*ger; əː, b*i*rd. **(o)** o, *o*x; au, c*ow*; ou, g*oa*t; u, p*oo*r; ɔi, r*oy*al. **(u)** ʌ, d*u*ck; u, b*u*ll; uː, g*oo*se; ə, b*a*cillus; juː, c*u*be. x, lo*ch*; θ, *th*ink; ð, bo*th*er; z, *Z*en; ʒ, cor*s*age; dʒ, sa*v*age; ŋ, orangutan*g*; j, *y*ak; ʃ, *f*ish; tʃ, fe*tch*; 'l, rab*ble*; 'n, red*den*. Complete pronunciation key appears inside front cover.

(psychol.) a behavior mechanism which seeks a substitute for something lacking or unacceptable [fr. L. *compensatio (compensationis)*]

com·pen·sa·tion balance a balance wheel in a clock counteracting variations in its time measurements due to changes in temperature

com·pen·sa·tive (kómpənsẹitiv, kəmpénsətiv) *adj.* compensatory

com·pen·sa·tor (kómpənsẹitər) *n.* something that compensates **com·pen·sa·to·ry** (kəmpénsətori:, kəmpénsətouri:) *adj.*

compensatory lengthening *(phon.)* a lengthening of a vowel sound on the loss of a following consonant

com·pére (kómpɛər) **1.** *n.* *(Br.)* a master of ceremonies who introduces comic acts in cabarets, in broadcasts etc. **2.** *v. pres. part.* **com·pér·ing** *past and past part.* **com·péred** *v.t.* *(Br.)* to act as compère to (a show) || *v.i.* *(Br.)* to act as a compère [F.]

com·pete (kəmpí:t) *pres. part.* **com·pet·ing** *past and past part.* **com·pet·ed** *v.i.* to try to win a contest, *to compete in a tournament* || to try to get what others also seek and which all cannot have, *to compete for export markets* [fr. L. *com+petere*, to seek]

com·pe·tence (kómpitəns) *n.* sufficient ability || a modest income, enough to live on || legal capacity or qualification [F. *compétence*]

com·pe·ten·cy (kómpitənsi:) *pl.* **com·pe·ten·cies** *n.* competence [fr. L. *competentia*]

com·pe·tent (kómpitənt) *adj.* having the necessary qualities or skills || showing adequate skill || *(law)* having legal capacity or qualification, *a competent witness* [F. *compétent*]

com·pe·ti·tion (kɒmpitíʃən) *n.* a contest in which people compete, *an athletic competition* || a competing, *trade competition* [fr. L. *competitio (competitionis)*]

com·pet·i·tive (kəmpétitiv) *adj.* based on competition [fr. L. *competere*]

com·pet·i·tor (kəmpétitər) *n.* someone who takes part in a competition || a rival

Com·piègne (kɔ̃pjenj) a French town (pop. 40,720) northeast of Paris, where Joan of Arc was captured by the Burgundians (1430), and the armistices of both 1918 (the Allies-Germany) and 1940 (Germany-France) were signed. Royal château (18th c.)

com·pi·la·tion (kɒmpiléiʃən) *n.* the act of compiling || something compiled [F.]

com·pile (kəmpáil) *pres. part.* **com·pil·ing** *past and past part.* **com·piled** *v.t.* to collect (materials, facts) for a book etc. || to put together (a history, an account etc.) from facts [F. *compiler*]

com·pil·er (kəmpáilər) *n.* *(computer)* program that translates source program from a high-level language (FORTRAN, COBOL) into a machine-language module or object program. — **compiler language** *n.* the compiler coding system. *Cf* ASSEMBLER LANGUAGE, MACHINE LANGUAGE

com·pla·cence (kəmpléisəns) *n.* complacency [fr. M.L. *complacentia*]

com·pla·cen·cy (kəmpléisənsi:) *n.* self-satisfaction, lack of self-criticism || mild contentment [fr. M.L. *complacentia*]

com·pla·cent (kəmpléisənt) *adj.* self-satisfied, smug [fr. L. *complacere*, to please]

com·plain (kəmpléin) *v.i.* to express dissatisfaction || to express pain or distress || to make a formal, complaint **com·pláin·ant** *n.* *(law)* someone accusing another of an injury [M.E. *compleigne* fr. F.]

com·plaint (kəmpléint) *n.* an expression of dissatisfaction || an accusation || a cause of dissatisfaction, *its poor light was their only complaint against the office* || a minor or recalcitrant illness || *(Am., law)* a formal allegation in a civil action [M. E. fr. F. *complainte*]

com·plai·sance (kəmpléisəns, kəmpléizəns, kómpləzæns) *n.* obligingness, willingness to please or do what is wanted [F.]

com·plai·sant (kəmpléisənt, kəmpléizənt) *adj.* obliging, ready to do what will please or be of service [F.]

complection *COMPLEXION

com·ple·ment 1. (kómpləmənt) *n.* that which serves to complete, *wine is the complement to a good dinner* || the full number required, esp. of men to man a ship, soldiers in an army unit etc. || *(genetics)* chromosomes from a single nucleus consisting of one or more sets, capable of pairing purine and pyrimidine bases between strands of DNA and RNA, with the structure of one determining the other || any of the many factors in normal serum involved in immuno-

logical activity || *(gram.)* that which completes the predicate of a sentence, e.g. the object of a transitive verb or a predicate adjective || *(math.)* the number of degrees by which an angle is less than 90° **2.** (kómpləmənt) *v.t.* to complete, supply (what is lacking) **com·ple·men·tal** (kɒmpləmént'l) *adj.* of or relating to a complement **com·ple·mén·ta·ry** *adj.* serving to complete [fr. L. *complementum* fr. *complere*, to fill up]

complementary angles *(math.)* two angles whose sum is 90°

complementary colors, *Br.* **complementary colours** pairs of colors (not pigments) which, when mixed, give the effect of white

complement fixation *(immunology)* the action of a specific antibody on an antigen (complement), rendering the antigen ineffective

com·plete (kəmplí:t) *adj.* with nothing missing or lacking, *the complete works of Tolstoy* || finished, *his work is now complete* || absolute, entire, *a complete surprise, a complete stranger* [fr. L. *completus*]

complete *pres. part.* **com·plet·ing** *past and past part.* **com·plet·ed** *v.t.* to finish, *to complete a book* || to perfect, round off, *travel completes an education* || to make up a desired amount, *he wants two more volumes to complete his set* **com·plé·tion** *n.* [fr. L. *complere (completus)*, to fill up]

complete round an assemblage of explosive and nonexplosive components necessary to perform a specific function at the time, and under the conditions desired, e.g., separate loading—consisting of a primer, propelling charge and (except for blank ammunition), a projectile and a fuse

com·plet·ist (kəmplí:tist) *n.* one obsessed with completing each piece of work

com·plex (kómpleks) *n.* a whole made up of dissimilar parts or parts in intricate relationship, *a town is a complex of streets, buildings and people* || *(pop.)* a fixed idea or obsession || *(psychol.)* a persistent set of attitudes, having a decisive influence on the personality, and partly determined by unconscious motives || *(chem.)* a complex substance, a substance formed by the union of simpler substances as distinguished from mixtures or compounds, *an enzyme complex* [fr. L. *complexus*]

complex (kəmpléks, kómpleks) *adj.* not simple || consisting of many parts, *complex machinery* || of a distinct chemical species consisting of some combination of ions, radicals, elements or compounds in which the chemical bonds are weaker than those found in compounds [fr. L. *complectere (complexus)*, to embrace]

complex fraction a fraction containing a fraction in the numerator or denominator, or in both

com·plex·ion, com·plec·tion (kəmplékʃən) *n.* the natural color and appearance of the skin, esp. of the face, *a fair complexion* || (of behavior, events, affairs) general appearance, *matters suddenly took on a new complexion* **com·pléx·ioned** *adj.* (chiefly in combinations) having a (specified) complexion, *dark-complexioned* [F.]

com·plex·i·ty (kəmpléksiti:) *pl.* **com·plex·i·ties** *n.* the state or quality of being complex || something complex

complex number *(math.)* a number or expression comprising both real and imaginary parts, of general form $a + ib$ when a and b are both real numbers and $i = \sqrt{-1}$

complex sentence *(gram.)* a sentence which has one main sentence or clause and one clause or more subordinate to it: 'he is a man' is a simple sentence, but 'he is a man who has written books' is a complex one

com·pli·ance (kəmpláiəns) *n.* willingness to follow or consent to another's wishes, *compliance with the regulations* || an instance of this quality

com·pli·ant (kəmpláiənt) *adj.* yielding or willing to comply

com·pli·ca·cy (kómplikəsi:) *pl.* **com·pli·ca·cies** *n.* the state of being complicated || a complex or complicated matter [fr. L. *complicatus*, interwoven]

com·pli·cate (kómplikeit) **1.** *v.t. pres. part.* **com·pli·cat·ing** *past and past part.* **com·pli·cat·ed** to make difficult or confused || to make complex || *(med.)* to cause to be more severe or more difficult to treat **2.** *adj.* *(zool.)* folded lengthwise **cóm·pli·cat·ed** *adj.* complex, with many components || difficult to understand because of its many aspects, *a complicated rela-*

tionship || *(med.*, of a fracture) in which nerves or blood vessels are damaged [fr. L. *complicare (complicatus)*, to fold together]

com·pli·ca·tion (kɒmplikéiʃən) *n.* the state of being complicated || an additional difficulty or accumulation of difficulties which makes something hard to understand or which makes a situation hard to act in || *(med.)* the condition resulting from the coincidence of two diseases or conditions arising in sequence, where the second disease may or may not be attributable to the first [fr. L. *complicatio (complicationis)*, a folding together]

com·plic·i·ty (kəmplísiti:) *pl.* **com·plic·i·ties** *n.* participation in wrongdoing [fr. L. *complex (complicis)*, entwined]

com·pli·ment (kómplimənt) *n.* a verbal expression of courteous praise || an action showing praise and respect || *(pl.)* a formula of greeting, *give my compliments to your wife* [F.]

com·pli·ment (kómpliment) *v.t.* to praise courteously || to congratulate **com·pli·mén·ta·ry** *adj.* of or relating to a compliment [F. *complimenter*]

com·pline, com·plin (kómplin) *n.* the last service of the day, at the seventh of the canonical hours [M.E. *cumplie* fr. O.F.]

com·ply (kəmplái) *pres. part.* **com·ply·ing** *past and past part.* **com·plied** *v.i.* to act in accordance with another's wishes, or with rules and regulations [ult. fr. L. *complere*, to fulfill]

com·po·nent (kəmpóunənt) **1.** *adj.* forming part of a whole, *a component part* **2.** *n.* an essential part of something, *the machine has 28 components* || *(mech.)* one of the parts into which a vector or tensor quality (force, velocity etc.) may be resolved || a substance of fixed composition in a chemical system [fr. L. *componere*, to put together]

com·port (kəmpórt, kəmpóurt) *v. refl.* *(rhet.)* to behave (oneself), *to comport oneself well* || *v.i.* *(rhet.*, with 'with') to be in agreement, harmony, *his behavior did not comport with that of a priest* **com·pórt·ment** *n.* *(rhet.)* one's way of behaving [fr. L. *comportare* and F. *comporter*]

com·pose (kəmpóuz) *pres. part.* **com·pos·ing** *past and past part.* **com·posed** *v.t.* to create in music or literature, *to compose a symphony* || to arrange shapes and colors into (a painting etc.) || to arrange (words or objects) into good order, *to compose a sentence* || to make calm, quiet, bring under control, *to compose one's face* || *(printing)* to set up (copy) in printing types || (of elements, parts etc.) to constitute when put together || *v.i.* to compose music || to lend itself for artistic purposes, *this landscape composes well* **com·pósed** *adj.* calm, in full self-possession **com·pós·er** *n.* a person who composes music [F. *composer*]

composing machine *(printing)* a machine for setting up type

composing stick *(printing)* a small, handy tray in which the typesetter arranges type into words and lines when handsetting

com·pos·ite (kəmpózit) **1.** *adj.* made up of parts, each of which is itself a whole or taken from another whole, *a composite photograph* || *(bot.)* of fam. *Compositae,* in which the flowers are closely packed in a capitulum or head || *(math.)* of a number divisible by some number other than 1 without a remainder (cf. PRIME NUMBER) **Composite** of, relating to, or resembling one of the classical orders of architecture combining the Corinthian and Ionic styles **2.** *n.* a plant of fam. *Compositae* || *(dentistry)* cavity-filling material of plastic and quartz or glass [fr. L. *componere (compositus)*, to compound]

composite circuit *(electr.)* electrical circuit that can be used for both telegraphy and voice at the same time

com·po·si·tion (kɒmpəzíʃən) *n.* the act of creating in music or literature || a work so created || the act of arranging or putting into order || *(printing)* the setting up of type || the building up of a compound from two single words || the arrangement of shapes, color and line in a picture || an essay || content with respect to constituent elements, *the composition of the soil* || material made up of various substances, *composition billiard balls* || *(math.)* the substitution for a number of vector quantities of a single vector that is equivalent to them (cf. RESOLUTION) || the settling of a dispute || the payment of a sum of money to take the place of a larger sum or of some other obligation, *composition of one's debts* [F.]

com·pos·i·tor (kəmpózitər) *n.* a person who sets up type for printing [A.F. *compositour*]

com·pos men·tis (kómpəsméntis) *adj.* (*law*) sane, in one's right mind [L.]

com·post (kómpoust) *v.t.* to treat with compost ‖ to make into compost [O.F. *composter*]

compost *n.* a mixture of vegetable matter, lime etc., used for fertilizing land [O.F. *composte*, compound]

Compostela *SANTIAGO DE COMPOSTELA

com·po·sure (kəmpóuʒər) *n.* a settled state of mind, calm self-possession

com·pote (kómpout) *n.* fruit stewed with sugar [F.]

com·pound 1. (kómpaund, kɑmpáund) *adj.* made up of separate substances or parts ‖ (*bot.*) composed of a number of similar parts forming a common whole **2.** (kómpaund) *n.* something made up from things combined together ‖ (*chem.*) a substance formed of two or more ingredients of constant proportion by weight ‖ (*gram.*) a word composed of two or more other words or elements **3.** (kəmpáund) *v.t.* to make (a new whole) by combining elements ‖ to combine (elements) to make a new whole ‖ to settle (a debt) by agreed partial payment ‖ to compute (interest) on the total of the principal and the interest which has accrued regularly at intervals ‖ *v.i.* to settle a debt by compromise, *they compounded for $100* **to compound a felony** to avoid prosecuting a criminal for private motives [O.F. *compondre*, to put together]

com·pound (kómpaund) *n.* (in many countries) enclosed land around a house, factory etc. [prob. Malay *kampong*, enclosure]

compound eye an eye made up of many simple eyes, arranged in a convex base of tissue and covered by a chitinous cornea, e.g. in insects and crustaceans

compound fraction a complex fraction

compound fracture a broken bone which has lacerated surrounding tissue and usually has pierced the skin

compound interest (*finance*) interest calculated on the sum of principal plus accrued interest

compound leaf a leaf whose blade is divided by one or more commissures into a number of distinct leaflets

compound lens a lens made of two or more pieces joined together or mounted on a common axis and designed to eliminate an aberration or aberrations

compound number a number composed of more than one denomination or unit, e.g. 3 yds 2 ft 6 ins

compound sentence (*gram.*) a sentence made of two or more simple sentences, neither subordinate to the other (e.g. 'he came and I went')

com·pre·hend (kɒmprihénd) *v.t.* to understand, grasp the meaning or significance of, esp. by an effort of sympathy ‖ to include, *education comprehends the training of many kinds of ability* [fr. L. *comprehendere*]

com·pre·hen·si·bil·i·ty (kɒmprihensəbíliti:) *n.* the state or quality of being comprehensible

com·pre·hen·si·ble (kɒmprihénsəb'l) *adj.* capable of being understood **com·pre·hén·si·bly** *adv.* [fr. L. *comprehensibilis*]

com·pre·hen·sion (kɒmprihénʃən) *n.* the act of understanding ‖ the faculty of understanding ‖ the capacity to include ‖ sympathetic understanding of differing opinions [fr. L. *comprehensio (comprehensionis)*]

com·pre·hen·sive (kɒmprihénsiv) *adj.* including much, *politics is a comprehensive term* ‖ all-inclusive, *a comprehensive charge* ‖ able to understand much, *a comprehensive mind.* [fr. L. *comprehensivus*]

com·press (kómpres) *n.* a soft pad of cloth, pressing on to some part of the body to relieve pain etc. ‖ a wet cloth held by a waterproof bandage to relieve inflammation ‖ a device for pressing cotton into bales [F. *compresse*]

com·press (kəmprés) *v.t.* to reduce the volume, duration etc. of, by or as if by pressure ‖ to condense, express concisely **com·préssed** *adj.* pressed together ‖ condensed ‖ flattened ‖ (*bot.*) flattened laterally ‖ (*zool.*, e.g. of flatfish) flattened from side to side [O.F. *compresser*]

compressed air air under a pressure greater than atmospheric pressure, used esp. as a source of power

compressed speech tape-recorded speech with some sounds eliminated and the reproduction speeded up

com·press·i·bil·i·ty (kəmprɛsəbíliti:) *n.* the capacity to be compressed

com·press·i·ble (kəmprésəb'l) *adj.* capable of being compressed

com·pres·sion (kəmpréʃən) *n.* a compressing or being compressed **com·prés·sive** *adj.* having the tendency to compress [F.]

com·pres·sor (kəmprésər) *n.* (*anat.*) a muscle which compresses a part of the body ‖ (*engin.*) a machine, such as a pump, that compresses air, gases, fuel mixtures etc. [L. that which compresses]

com·prise, com·prize (kəmpráiz) *pres. part.* **com·pris·ing, com·priz·ing** *past and past part.* **com·prised, com·prized** *v.t.* to be made up of, consist of, *the course comprises 10 lessons* ‖ to include, contain, *this month's figures are comprised in the total* [fr. F. *comprendre (compris)*]

com·pro·mise (kómprəmaiz) **1.** *n.* a method of reaching agreement in a dispute, by which each side surrenders something that it wants ‖ an agreement so reached ‖ a course of action intermediate between extremes, *he sent flowers as a compromise between calling and writing* ‖ a placing in jeopardy, *a compromise of one's integrity* **2.** *v. pres. part.* **com·pro·mis·ing** *past and past part.* **com·pro·mised** *v.i.* to settle a dispute by a compromise ‖ *v.t.* to bring into danger or under suspicion, or expose to loss of reputation [F. *compromis*]

Compromise of 1850 a series of acts passed (1850) by Congress providing that each newly acquired territory should decide on its own slave or free status. The terms of the compromise aroused great bitterness, and the issue was fought out in the Civil War

Compromise of 1877 an arrangement which settled the disputed U.S. presidential contest of 1876 between Rutherford Hayes and Samuel Tilden. It created an Electoral Commission composed of five representatives each from the House, the Senate, and the Supreme Court, selecting eight Republicans and seven Democrats who voted along party lines. Southern Democrats accepted Hayes' election in return for the demilitarization of the South, the appointment of a southerner in the cabinet, and financial aid in the construction of a southwest railroad. It ended the period of black participation in politics

comp·tom·e·ter (kɒmptómitər) *n.* a calculating machine [fr. F. *compter*, to count fr. L. *computare*, to compute+METER]

Comp·ton (kómptən), Arthur Holly (1892–1962), American physicist distinguished for his work on gamma rays, X rays and other radiations. For his discovery of the Compton effect he was awarded a Nobel prize (1927)

Comp·ton-Bur·nett (kómptənbə́:rnet), Ivy (1892–1969), English novelist, author of 'Men and Wives' (1931), 'Elders and Betters' (1944), 'Mother and Son' (1955) etc., witty novels presenting mainly in dialogue a grotesque world of hypocrisy and wickedness, but arousing compassion

Compton effect the effect whereby X rays are scattered on impact with electrons in matter, accompanied by energy transfer to the electrons and a change in wavelength [after A. H. Compton]

Compton scattering the Compton effect

comp·trol·ler (kəntróulər) *n.* (only in official titles) a controller

com·pul·sion (kəmpʌ́lʃən) *n.* a compelling ‖ (*psychol.*) a feeling of being compelled to some irrational action which is always unnecessary and often repetitive (*OBSESSIVE-COMPULSIVE NEUROSIS) [F.]

com·pul·sive (kəmpʌ́lsiv) **1.** *adj.* compelling ‖ (*psychol.*) irrationally compelling **2.** *n.* (*psychol.*) a person subject to compulsive drives [fr. L. *compellere (compulsus)*, to compel]

com·pul·so·ri·ly (kəmpʌ́lsərili:) *adv.* in a compulsory manner

com·pul·so·ry (kəmpʌ́lsəri:) *adj.* that must be done or suffered, having the force of compulsion [fr. L. *compellere (compulsus)*, to compel]

com·punc·tion (kəmpʌ́ŋkʃən) *n.* the pricking of conscience [O.F.]

com·put·a·ble (kəmpjú:təb'l) *adj.* able to be computed

com·pu·ta·tion (kɒmpjutéiʃən) *n.* the act of computing

computational linguistics study of languages utilizing the computer

com·pute (kəmpjú:t) *pres. part.* **com·put·ing** *past and past part.* **com·put·ed** *v.t.* to calculate **com·pút·er, com·pú·tor** *n.* someone who computes ‖ a computing machine [F. *computer*] —Computers may be designed to carry out complex and lengthy mathematical analytical oper-

ations very rapidly, to control industrial operations, or to undertake routine clerical work. The analogue computer is a specialized calculating machine which operates with numbers represented by measurable quantities of given magnitudes, e.g. mechanical movement, voltages, resistance etc. A digital computer is more versatile and operates electronically with numbers expressed as digits in a given (usually binary) number scale

computer dating system for selecting social or romantic companions by matching compatible personalities through a computer program

computer graphics art derived by programming computer output to create a design or picture

com·put·er·ese (kəmpju:tərí:z) *n.* computer workers' jargon

com·put·er·ize (kəmpjú:təraiz) *v.* **1.** to adapt records and procedures for filing and processing by a computer. **2.** to equip with computers. — **computerizable** *adj.* —**computerization** *v.*

computerized tomography *CAT SCANNER

computer language material organized in a system so as to be comprehensible to a computer, e.g., ALGOL, COBOL, FORTRAN

computer music synthesized music created and produced by computer programming, sometimes including utilization of sounds not produced by musical instruments. *Cf* ELECTRONIC MUSIC

computer science the study of computer hardware and software technology and operations —**computer scientist** *n.*

computer terminal input/output device for a computer system

com·put·er·y (kəmpjú:təri:) *n.* the use of computers

com·rade (kómræd, *Br.* kómrid) *n.* an intimate companion who shares one's work or pleasures **cóm·rade·ship** *n.* [older *camerade* fr. F.]

COMSAT (*acronym*) for Communications Satellite Corporation, a privately owned satellite-launching corporation providing international maritime and domestic satellite services under 1962 Communications Satellite Act

Com·stock (kʌ́mstɒk, kómstɒk), Anthony (1844–1915), U.S. antivice crusader. He sponsored the Act of Congress (1873) which barred from the U.S. mails all matter deemed 'obscene, lewd, lascivious, indecent, filthy or vile'

com·symp (kómsimp) *n.* (used disparagingly) a Communist sympathizer

Com·tat-Ve·nais·sin (kɔ̃tævənessɛ̃) a former papal possession (1274–1791) in France, in the Rhône valley and the Maritime Alps. With Orange and Avignon, it forms Vaucluse department (*PROVENCE). Historic capital: Carpentras

Comte (kɔ̃t), Auguste (1798–1857), French mathematician and philosopher, founder of positivism, and preacher of a religion of humanity. His 'Cours de philosophie positive' (1830–42) was one of the seminal works of the 19th c.

con (kɒn) *pres. part.* **con·ning** *past and past part.* **conned** *v.t.* (*old-fash.*) to learn by heart ‖ to study carefully, *to con a lesson* [fr. O.E. *cunnian*, to test and O.E. *cunnan*, to know]

con *pres. part.* **con·ning** *past and past part.* **conned** *v.t.* (*Am.*) to deceive by a confidence trick or tricks

con *PRO AND CON [shortened fr. L. *contra*, against]

con *CONN

con- *prefix* (used before sounds other than b, p, m, l, r) with [fr. L., form of *com-*]

Co·na·kry (kɒnækri:) the capital and chief port (pop. 527,700) of Guinea, on the island of Tumbo. Exports: ores, bananas. Industries: food processing, engineering

Co·nant (kóunənt), James Bryant (1893–1978), U.S. educator and chemist. He was appointed (1933) president of Harvard University and (1953) U.S. high commissioner for West Germany, becoming ambassador (1955–7)

co·na·tion (kouéiʃən) *n.* (*philos.*) the power or act of willing, striving **con·a·tive** (kónətiv, kóunətiv) *adj.* (*philos.*) pertaining to conation ‖ (*gram.*, of verbal aspect) expressing endeavor [fr. L. *conatio (conationis)* fr. *conari*, to try]

con·cat·e·nate (kɒnkǽt'neit) **1.** *v.t. pres. part.* **con·cat·e·nat·ing** *past and past part.* **con·cat·e·nat·ed** (*rhet.*) to link together **2.** *adj.* (*rhet.*) linked together, forming a chain or series **con·cat·e·ná·tion** *n.* (*rhet.*) linkage, *a concatenation of events* [fr. L. *concatenare (concatenatus)* fr. *catena*, chain]

con·cave (kɒnkéiv, kónkeiv) **1.** adj. curving inwards like the inside of a sphere (opp. CONVEX) **2.** n. a concave surface, line etc. **con·cav·i·ty** (kɒnkæviti:) n. [O.F.]

con·ca·vo-con·cave (kɒnkéivoukɒnkéiv) adj. (esp. of a lens) biconcave

con·ca·vo-con·vex (kɒnkéivoukɒnvéks) adj. concave on one side and convex on the other || (optics) of a lens whose concave side has a greater curvature than the convex side (cf. CONVEXO-CONCAVE)

con·ceal (kənsí:l) v.t. to hide || to keep secret **con·céal·ment** n. [O.F. conceler]

con·cede (kənsí:d) pres. part. **con·ced·ing** past and past part. **con·ced·ed** v.t. to grant to be true in an argument || to grant (a right or privilege) || to admit having lost (a game, election etc.) at some stage before the end [fr. L. concedere, to yield]

con·ceit (kənsí:t) n. excessive satisfaction with one's character or achievements || a complex witty figure of speech, typical e.g. of the English Metaphysical poets **con·céit·ed** adj. having too high an opinion of oneself [M.E. conceite fr. conceiven, to conceive]

con·ceiv·a·ble (kənsí:vəb'l) adj. capable of being thought, imagined or understood **con·céiv·a·bly** adv.

con·ceive (kənsí:v) pres. part. **con·ceiv·ing** past and past part. **con·ceived** v.t. to become pregnant with (a child) || to form (an idea) || v.i. to become pregnant || (with 'of') to form a conception [O.F. conceveir]

con·cel·e·brant (kənséləbrənt) n. priest who celebrates Mass together with another clergyman

con·cen·ter, Br. **con·cen·tre** (kɒnséntər) pres. part. **con·cen·ter·ing**, Br. **con·cen·tring** past and past part. **con·cen·tered**, Br. **con·cen·tred** v.t. to bring to a common center || v.i. to come to a common center [F. concentrer]

con·cen·trate (kónsəntreit) **1.** v. pres. part. **con·cen·trat·ing** past and past part. **con·cen·trat·ed** v.t. to bring together into a mass, concentrate the troops near the station || to render less dilute || to focus, cause to converge on an objective, to concentrate one's energies || (mining) to separate (ore) from sand etc. || v.i. to direct or focus one's powers or actions on some limited object || to come together in a mass, the troops concentrated near the station **2.** n. a concentrated form of something **con·cen·tra·tion** n. a concentrating or being concentrated || (mil.) a body of troops massed in an area || (mil.) the specified duration and intensity of artillery fire on a target || (chem.) an amount present in a given volume. It may be measured by the number of grams in 100 cc but is now more usually measured by the number of moles (molecular weight in grams) present in 1 liter. A square bracket denotes 'concentration of' in a chemical formula, e.g. [H+] means 'concentration of hydrogen ions in moles per liter' [fr. L. con, with+centrum, center]

concentration camp a place of arbitrary internment, not subject to courts and processes of law

con·cen·tra·tive (kónsəntreitiv, kənséntrətiv) adj. characterized by concentration || serving or tending to concentrate

con·cen·tra·tor (kónsəntreitər) n. device permitting numerous users to communicate over the same transmission lines by storing messages

concentre *CONCENTER

con·cen·tric (kənséntrik) adj. having the same center, e.g. of circles or spheres enclosing one another **con·cén·tri·cal** adj. **con·cen·tric·i·ty** (kɒnsəntrísiti:) n. [fr. M.L. concentricus]

Con·cep·ción (kɒnsepsjón) a city (pop. 202,396) of S. central Chile on the Bío-Bío River, a commercial center (wheat, wine, wool, cattle, coal, lumber)

Concepción Bay an inlet of the Pacific in S. central Chile, near the city of Concepción

con·cept (kónsept) n. a thought or opinion, general notion or idea, esp. one formed by generalization from particular examples [fr. L. concipere (conceptus), to conceive]

con·cep·tion (kənsépʃən) n. the act of becoming pregnant || the state of being conceived in the womb || the faculty of conceiving in the mind, he has little conception of the work involved || a thing conceived, designed, or thought out, the city center was a splendid conception **con·cép·tion·al** adj. [F.]

con·cep·tive (kənséptiv) adj. of or relating to conception, esp. mental conception [fr. L. conceptivus]

con·cep·tu·al (kənséptʃu:əl) adj. pertaining to mental conception or concepts **con·cép·tu·al·ism** n. (philos.) the doctrine that universals exist, but only in the mind (cf. NOMINALISM, cf. REALISM) **con·cép·tu·al·ist** n. [fr. M.L. conceptualis]

conceptual art or **concept art 1.** art style designed to reflect the idea of the creator of the work. **2.** art form accenting content and neglecting form, utilizing eccentric and disposable materials, e.g., earth, cloth, human bodies, neon lights, newspapers, photographs, even junk in a collage, creating an awareness of an event or idea; evolved from minimal art and happenings. —**conceptual artist** n. —**conceptualist** n. Cf PROCESS ART

con·cern (kənsə́:rn) **1.** v.t. to have as subject, his new book concerns the betting laws || (refl.) to interest (oneself) in, take part in, don't concern yourself with such matters || to implicate or involve, it concerns him only indirectly **2.** n. a matter of direct interest or importance to one, it's no concern of his || (pl.) private affairs, interfering with my concerns || a share or interest, he has a concern in the industry || a business, firm or organization || anxiety, worry || (pop.) a contrivance or thing of which one thinks little, you should drop the whole concern **a going concern** a business or organization that is active and has gotten beyond the planning stage **con·cérned** adj. worried, disturbed **con·cérn·ing** prep. about, regarding, pertaining to **con·cérn·ment** n. concern, anxiety || relation or bearing, a question of general concernment [fr. F. concerner]

con·cert 1. (kənsə́:rt) v.t. to devise, plan, or frame together **2.** (kónsə:rt) n. agreement or union in an undertaking, to work in concert || a musical performance, usually by several singers or instrumentalists **con·cért·ed** adj. arranged by mutual agreement, a concerted effort || (mus.) arranged in parts for several instruments or voices [fr. F. concerter fr. Ital.]

con·cer·ti·na (kɒnsərtí:nə) n. a small hexagonal musical instrument with bellows, held in the hands. It is played by pressing studs at each end while the bellows are worked

con·cert·mas·ter (kónsərtmæstər, kónsərtmɑstər) n. (Am.=Br. leader) the principal violinist of an orchestra [G. konzertmeister]

con·cer·to (kəntʃéərtou) pl. **con·cer·ti** (kəntʃéərti:), **con·cer·tos** n. a musical composition, usually in three movements, for solo instrument or instruments with orchestra [Ital.]

Concert of Europe an agreement of Austria, Prussia and Russia to defend their common interests after the Congress of Vienna (1815)

con·cer·to gros·so (kəntʃéərtougróusou) pl. **con·cer·ti gros·si** (kəntʃéərti:gróusi:), **con·cer·to gros·sos** n. an orchestral composition, esp. of the 17th and 18th cc., featuring interplay between a smaller and a larger group of players [Ital. = big concerto]

concert overture an orchestral work in a single movement, usually with some literary or pictorial point of departure, meant for concert performance but otherwise resembling an operatic overture

concert pitch the pitch to which concert instruments are normally tuned || a state of complete preparedness

con·ces·sion (kənséʃən) n. a conceding or yielding, a concession to public opinion || the thing yielded or conceded || a grant, esp. of land or property, by a government for a specified purpose, an oil concession || a tract of land granted to a foreign power with extraterritorial rights || a lease of a part of premises for some specific use, an ice cream concession at a sports stadium **con·ces·sion·aire, con·ces·sion·naire** (kənseʃənéər) n. a person or company benefiting from a concession, esp. the beneficiary of a monopoly granted by a government to a foreign company || a person or firm benefiting from the grant of a lease, e.g. to sell retail goods in a special place **con·ces·sion·ar·y** (kənséʃəneri:) **1.** adj. relating to a concession **2.** pl. **con·ces·sion·ar·ies** n. a concessionaire [fr. L. concessio (concessionis)]

con·ces·sive (kənsésiv) adj. of the nature of, or tending to, concession || (gram.) expressing concession, concessive conjunction (e.g. 'although'), concessive clause (e.g. 'though we tried hard') [fr. L. concessivus]

conch (kɒŋk, kɒntʃ) pl. **conchs** (kɒŋks), **conches** (kɒntʃiz) n. any of a group of large spiral-shelled marine mollusks, or the shell or animal individually || (art and mythol.) the shell used by a Triton as a trumpet || (archit.) the domed roof of a church apse || (anat.) the largest concavity of the external ear, or the whole external ear [fr. Gk koncha, shell fr. Gk]

con·cha (kóŋkə) pl. **con·chae** (kóŋki:) n. (anat.) the conch [L.=shell]

con·choi·dal (kɒŋkóid'l) adj. having the shape of a shell [fr. Gk konchoeidēs, like a mussel]

con·chol·o·gist (kɒŋkólədʒist) n. someone specializing in conchology

con·chol·o·gy (kɒŋkólədʒi:) n. the branch of zoology that deals with shells (cf. MALACOLOGY) [fr. Gk konchē, mussel + logos, discourse]

con·cil·i·ar (kənsíli:ər) adj. of, pertaining to or issued by a council [fr. L. consilium, council]

con·cil·i·ate (kənsíli:eit) pres. part. **con·cil·i·at·ing** past and past part. **con·cil·i·at·ed** v.t. to win over from hostility || to win (goodwill) by genial or soothing approaches || to make compatible, reconcile (conflicting views etc.) [fr. L. conciliare (conciliatus), to bring together]

con·cil·i·a·tion (kənsili:éiʃən) n. a bringing of opponents into harmony || reconcilement || a voluntary (and not legally binding) attempt by parties to an industrial dispute to reach agreement without strike action (cf. ARBITRATION) [fr. L. conciliatio (conciliationis), a bringing together]

con·cil·i·a·tive (kənsíli:eitiv, kənsíli:ətiv, kənsíljətiv) adj. conciliatory

con·cil·i·a·tor (kənsíli:eitər) n. someone who conciliates

con·cil·i·a·to·ry (kənsíli:ətɔ:ri:, kənsíli:ətouri:) adj. having the effect of propitiating, or of bringing about harmony

con·cin·ni·ty (kənsíniti:) pl. **con·cin·ni·ties** n. (in literary criticism) neatness and formal elegance of style [fr. L. concinnitas fr. concinnus, well put together]

con·cise (kənsáis) adj. brief, condensed, expressing much in few words [fr. L. concidere (concisus), to cut off]

con·ci·sion (kənsíʒən) n. conciseness [F.]

con·clave (kónkleiv, kóŋkleiv) n. the room in which cardinals meet to elect a pope || the body of cardinals || a private or secret meeting **cón·clav·ist** n. a priest attending cardinals in a conclave [F.]

con·clude (kənklú:d) pres. part. **con·clud·ing** past and past part. **con·clud·ed** v.t. to bring to an end, to conclude a speech || to effect or bring about, to conclude a peace treaty || to decide (something) on the basis of reasoning || v.i. to come to an end [fr. L. concludere (conclusus), to shut up]

con·clu·sion (kənklú:ʒən) n. the end or last part || a reasoned judgment or inference || a settlement or arrangement of an agreement etc., the conclusion of a peace treaty || the summary or upshot of an argument, essay etc., a sound argument but a false conclusion **in conclusion** lastly [F.]

con·clu·sive (kənklú:siv) adj. final, decisive, a conclusive argument || putting an end to further discussion, conclusive evidence || belonging to an end or termination, concluding [fr. L.L. conclusivus]

con·coct (kɒnkókt, kənkókt) v.t. to prepare by mixing ingredients || to make up, invent, devise [fr. L. concoquere (concoctus), to cook up]

con·coc·tion (kɒnkókʃən, kənkókʃən) n. a concocting || something concocted || a lie [fr. L. concoctio (concoctionis)]

Concom coordinating committee set up by Western allies to screen sales of advanced technology to Communist countries

con·com·i·tance (kənkómitəns) n. a coexistence, a state of accompanying, esp. (theol.) the coexistence of the body and blood of Christ in each of the two consecrated elements **con·cóm·i·tan·cy** n. [fr. L.L. concomitantia fr. concomitari, to accompany]

con·com·i·tant (kɒnkómitənt, kənkómitənt) **1.** adj. of that which goes with or accompanies something, concomitant circumstances **2.** n. an accompanying thing, state or quality [fr. L. concomitans (concomitantis) fr. concomitari, to accompany]

Con·cord (kóŋkərd) the capital (pop. 30,400) of New Hampshire

Concord a town (pop. 16,293) in Massachusetts, and site of the first active resistance (Apr. 19, 1775) in the American Revolution when the Minutemen checked the British force

---

con·cord (kónkɔrd, kóŋkɔrd) *n.* a state of agreement or harmony ‖ a treaty or agreement ‖ (*mus.*) a chord harmonious in itself, not needing others to resolve it ‖ (*gram.*) agreement between the forms of words, e.g. (for number) 'this house, these houses' [F. *concorde*]

con·cord·ance (kɒnkɔ́rd'ns, kənkɔ́rd'ns) *n.* an agreement ‖ an alphabetical index of principal words e.g. in the Bible or in a writer such as Dante or Shakespeare, giving references to passages in which these words occur [F.]

con·cord·ant (kɒnkɔ́rd'nt, kənkɔ́rd'nt) *adj.* agreeing, harmonious, consistent ‖ in musical concord [F.]

con·cor·dat (kɒnkɔ́rdæt) *n.* an agreement or compact, esp. an agreement between the pope and a secular government, notably the Concordat of Worms (1122) and that concluded (1801) between Pius VII and Napoleon [F.]

Concord, Battle of *LEXINGTON AND CONCORD, BATTLES OF

Concord, Book of *LUTHERANISM

Concorde Anglo-French supersonic (Mach 2.04) airliner for 128–144 passengers, with 3,870-mi. range; made by Aerospacial/British Aerospace Aircraft and launched in 1973

con·course (kónkɔrs, kónkours, kóŋkɔrs, kóŋkours) *n.* a flocking together of people ‖ a coming together (of things, e.g. streams) ‖ an open space where crowds may gather, e.g. in a railroad station [O.F.]

con·cres·cence (kɒnkrésəns) *n.* (*biol.*) a growing together of parts, esp. of parts originally separate [fr. L. *concrescentia* fr. *concrescere*, to grow together]

con·crete (kónkri:t, kɒnkri:t) **1.** *n.* a hard strong substance made by mixing sand and gravel or crushed stone with cement and water, used as a building and construction material while still moist, and allowed to set in position **2.** *adj.* (of a noun) naming an object as opposed to a quality or attribute, *'gold' is a concrete noun, 'wealth' is an abstract noun* ‖ real, specific, not abstract or ideal, *concrete proposals* ‖ united, compounded, in a condensed or solid state ‖ made of concrete **3.** *v. pres. part.* **con·cret·ing** *past* and *past part.* **con·cret·ed** *v.i.* (kɒnkri:t) to solidify, harden ‖ *v.t.* (kónkri:t) to make from, set in or cover with concrete [fr. L. *concrescere* (*concretus*), to grow together]

concrete poem poem plus drawing in which words, letters, and fragments are arranged to form a pattern. —**concretism** *n.* —**concretist** *n. Cf* CALLIGRAM

con·cre·tion (kɒnkríːʃən) *n.* a mass of coalesced particles ‖ a concreting or being concreted ‖ a hard formation growing in some part of the body, e.g. a stone in the kidney ‖ (*geol.*) a mass (usually round in shape) of mineral matter formed by deposition from water in the rock **con·cre·tion·ar·y** *adj.* [fr. L. *concretio* (*concretionis*)]

con·cu·bi·nage (kɒnkjú:binidʒ) *n.* the living together of two people not legally married ‖ the state of being a concubine ‖ (in primitive law) an inferior system of marriage [F.]

con·cu·bi·nar·y (kɒnkjú:bineri) *adj.* living in, or sprung from, concubinage [fr. M. L. *concubinarius*]

con·cu·bine (kóŋkjubain, kóŋkjubain) *n.* a woman who lives with a man not her husband ('mistress' is the commoner word but does not necessarily imply cohabitation) ‖ (among some peoples) a wife of inferior status [F.]

con·cu·pis·cence (kɒnkjú:pisəns) *n.* sexual desire, lust ‖ (*theol.*) desire for earthly things **con·cú·pis·cent** *adj.* [fr. L. *concupiscentia*]

con·cur (kənkə́:r) *pres. part.* **con·cur·ring** *past* and *past part.* **con·curred** *v.i.* to agree or accord in opinion ‖ to happen together, coincide ‖ (esp. of three or more lines) to meet in one point **con·cur·rence** (kənkə́:rəns, kɒnkʌ́rəns), **con·cur·ren·cy** *ns.* **con·cúr·rent** *adj.* running alongside, existing or happening together ‖ acting together, cooperating ‖ directed to, or intersecting in, the same point, *three concurrent lines* ‖ (*law*) having joint, equal authority [fr. L. *concurrere*, to run together]

concurrent lease a lease made before the previous lease expires

concurrent processing *PARALLEL PROCESSING

con·cuss (kənkʌ́s) *v.t.* (of a heavy blow, fall etc.) to knock out (a person) [fr. L. *concutere* (*concussus*), to shake violently]

con·cus·sion (kənkʌ́ʃən) *n.* violent shaking, e.g. from an impact ‖ (*med.*) a condition of impaired activity of the brain, through a blow or violent shaking [fr. L. *concussio* (*concussionis*)]

concussion bellows a device to regulate the wind supply for an organ

con·cus·sive (kənkʌ́siv) *adj.* of an agitating or shaking nature

con·cy·clic (kɒnsáiklik, kɒnsíklik) *adj.* (*math.*) lying on the circumference of the same circle

Con·dé (kɔ̃dei), Louis I de Bourbon, prince de (1530–69), French Huguenot leader

Condé, Louis II, prince de (1621–86), French soldier ('le grand Condé'). He led Louis XIV's armies against the Fronde (1649), but was himself the leader of a new rising (1650–2) and he commanded the Spanish armies (1653–8)

con·demn (kəndém) *v.t.* to censure, blame ‖ to prescribe punishment for, *they condemned him to death* ‖ to pronounce (esp. a tenement) unfit for use ‖ to pronounce (e.g. smuggled goods) taken over for public use ‖ (*pop.*) to declare incurable **con·dem·na·ble** (kəndémnəb'l) *adj.* [O.F. *condemner*]

con·dem·na·tion (kɒndemnéiʃən) *n.* a condemning or being condemned ‖ grounds for condemning, *his own actions are his condemnation* [fr. L. *condemnatio* (*condemnationis*)]

con·dem·na·to·ry (kəndémnətɔri:, kəndémnətouri:) expressing or implying condemnation [fr. L. *condemnare*, to condemn]

condemned cell the cell in which a prisoner awaiting execution is kept

con·den·sa·bil·i·ty (kəndensəbíliti:) *n.* the ability to be condensed

con·den·sa·ble (kəndénsəb'l) *adj.* able to be condensed

con·den·sa·tion (kɒndenséiʃən) *n.* a condensing or being condensed ‖ a making more concise and brief of written material etc. ‖ the product of such treatment ‖ (*chem.*) the transition of a substance from the vapor to the liquid state ‖ (*chem.*) a class of chemical reactions involving the union of two or more atoms or molecules, often accompanied by the elimination of a simple molecule, e.g. water, ammonia etc., to form a usually more complex molecule [fr. L. *condensatio* (*condensationis*), a making more dense]

condensation pump a diffusion pump

condensation trail a contrail

con·dense (kəndéns) *pres. part.* **con·dens·ing** *past* and *past part.* **con·densed** *v.t.* to make more dense or compact ‖ to express in fewer words ‖ to concentrate, increase the strength of ‖ to reduce (gas or vapor) to a liquid form ‖ to reduce by evaporation ‖ *v.i.* to become more dense or compact ‖ (of gas or vapor) to become liquid or solid [fr. F. *condenser*]

condensed milk milk thickened by evaporation and sweetened

condensed type a typeface narrower than the normal type of its series

con·dens·er (kəndénsər) *n.* (*phys.*) an arrangement for converting a gas or vapor into a liquid or solid, e.g. a Liebig condenser (in which the vapor passes through a tube surrounded by cold water) ‖ (*phys.*) the recipient of the exhaust heat from a heat engine ‖ (*phys.*) a system of lenses which makes light converge on an object, in a projector or a microscope ‖ a capacitor

con·de·scend (kɒndisénd) *v.i.* to behave patronizingly ‖ to agree to do something which one considers beneath one's dignity ‖ to be gracious to people of lower rank **con·de·scénd·ing** *adj.* [fr. F. *condescendre*]

con·de·scen·sion (kɒndisénʃən) *n.* a condescending [fr. L.L. *condescensio* (*condescensionis*)]

con·dign (kəndáin) *adj.* merited (by bad behavior), *condign punishment* [F. *condigne*]

Con·dil·lac (kɔdi:jæk), Etienne Bonnot de (1715–80), French sensualist philosopher influenced by Locke. In revolt against the deductive rationalism of Descartes, he held that all knowledge comes from sensations. His philosophy is set out in his 'Traité des sensations' and his 'Logique'

con·di·ment (kóndəmənt) *n.* a seasoning, e.g. pepper, used to flavor food [F.]

con·di·tion (kəndíʃən) *v.t.* (*pass.*) to be a condition of, *supply is conditioned by demand* ‖ to subject to conditions ‖ to stipulate ‖ to put into the required state, make fit, *to condition a horse for a race* ‖ to subject (a substance) to a technological treatment in order to sterilize or preserve it etc. ‖ to impose a condition on (a student) ‖ (*psychol.*) to affect the reflexes or behavior of (a person or animal) by conditioning [O.F. *condicioner*]

condition *n.* mode or state of existence, *a bicycle in good condition, butter in a liquid condition* ‖ state of health ‖ state of training ‖ a stipulation, provision ‖ a prerequisite ‖ (*pl.*) circumstances, *under existing conditions* ‖ (*pl.*) terms ‖ social rank, *people of every condition* ‖ (*gram.*) a conditional clause, protasis ‖ (*logic*) an antecedent ‖ a stipulation that a student who has failed to reach the required standard in a subject should pass a further examination in it before he may proceed ‖ (*law*) a clause in a contract etc. that modifies, revokes or suspends a stipulation or a given contingency **on condition that** provided that [M.E. *condicion* fr. O.F.]

con·di·tion·al (kəndíʃən'l) **1.** *adj.* dependent, made or granted on certain conditions, not absolute, *a conditional undertaking* ‖ (*gram.*) expressing or containing a condition, *conditional clause* (e.g. 'if you work any harder you will be ill') **2.** *n.* (*gram.*) a conditional word, clause, mood etc. **con·di·tion·al·i·ty** *n.* [M.E. *condicionel* fr. O.F.]

conditional probability chance that something will happen if something else has happened or will happen

con·di·tion·er (kəndíʃənər) *n.* something or someone that conditions ‖ an additive meant to make something better suited for some specified function

con·di·tion·ing (kəndíʃəniŋ) *n.* the process of changing behavior in such a way that an action formerly associated with a particular stimulus becomes associated with a new and unrelated stimulus ‖ the process of influencing thought and behavior patterns in others, so as to bring them into conformity with a set of ideas, esp. this as a technique used for political ends

con·do (kóndou) *n.* shortened form of condominium

con·dole (kəndóul) *pres. part.* **con·dol·ing** *past* and *past part.* **con·doled** *v.i.* to express sympathetic grief, commiserate **con·dó·lence** *n.* [fr. L. *condolere*]

con·dom (kóndəm) *n.* a contraceptive sheath worn over the penis [after Dr *Condom*, 18th-c. Eng. doctor]

con·do·min·i·um (kɒndəmíni:əm) *n.* a region administered jointly by two or more powers ‖ joint sovereignty ‖ part of a building owned usually for use by the purchaser, e.g. a single apartment in a multiple housing structure or office in a commercial structure

con·do·na·tion (kɒndounéiʃən) *n.* the act of condoning

con·done (kəndóun) *pres. part.* **con·don·ing** *past* and *past part.* **con·doned** *v.t.* to overlook (an offense or shortcoming) ‖ to allow to continue (what ought to be stopped) [fr. L. *condonare*]

con·dor (kóndər) *n. Vultur gryphus*, a very large vulture of the High Andes [Span. fr. Peruv. *cuntur*]

Condor (*mil.*) Navy air-to-surface missile with 50-mi range, capable of sighting a target and fixing on it

Con·dor·can·qui (kɒndorkáŋki:), José Gabriel *TUPAC AMARU

Con·dor·cet (kɔ̃dorse), Antoine de Caritat, Marquis de (1743–94), French mathematician, economist and philosopher. As a member of the Legislative Assembly and of the Convention during the French Revolution, he drew up a scheme for universal education and a plan for a constitution. He was proscribed (1793) by the Jacobins, hid for nine months, was captured and took his own life by poison. His 'Esquisse d'un tableau historique des progrès de l'esprit humain' emphasizes reason and brotherly love, and holds to the infinite perfectibility of human nature

con·duce (kəndú:s, kəndjú:s) *pres. part.* **con·duc·ing** *past* and *past part.* **con·duced** *v.i.* (with 'to' or 'toward') to lead or tend towards (a generally desirable result) **con·dú·cive** *adj.* having power to promote, *moderate exercise is conducive to health* [fr. L. *conducere*, to lead]

con·duct 1. (kəndʌ́kt) *v.t.* to lead, guide, escort ‖ to direct, command or manage, *to conduct a business* ‖ to direct (an orchestra, choir or musical work) ‖ to behave (oneself) ‖ to transmit or be capable of transmitting (heat, light, sound or electricity) ‖ *v.i.* to act as a musical conductor **2.** (kóndʌkt) *n.* moral behavior ‖ management, mode of conducting, *the conduct of the war* [fr. L. *conducere* (*conductus*)]

con·duct·ance (kəndʌ́ktəns) *n.* (*elec.*) the ability of a conductor to conduct electricity. It is the reciprocal of resistance (mks unit: mho)

con·duc·tion (kəndʌ́kʃən) *n.* the transfer of heat energy through matter, without translation or flow of the matter, by the transfer of kinetic energy from particle to particle (cf. CONVECTION, cf. RADIATION) ‖ the establishment of an electric current that takes place through metallic conductors by the movement of loosely bound electrons, through gases by the passage of ionized particles, and through electrolytes by the movement of ions [fr. L. *conductio* (*conductionis*), a conducting]

con·duc·tive (kəndʌ́ktiv) *adj.* having conductivity **con·duc·tiv·i·ty** (kɒndʌktíviti:) *n.* the ability of a substance to conduct (e.g. heat or electricity) ‖ electrical conductivity ‖ thermal conductivity

con·duc·tor (kəndʌ́ktər) *n.* the guide or leader of a party ‖ someone who conducts musical performers ‖ the official in charge of passengers on a bus or streetcar ‖ (*Am.=Br.* ticket inspector) a railroad official who examines passengers' tickets during the journey ‖ a material which can conduct heat, electricity etc. (cf. INSULATOR) [L.]

con·duc·tress (kəndʌ́ktris) *n.* a woman conductor, esp. (*Br.*) a woman bus conductor

con·duit (kɒ́ndwit, kɒ́ndu:it, kɒ́ndju:it, kɒ́ndit) *n.* a channel or pipe for carrying fluids, e.g. a pipe, canal, aqueduct ‖ a tube or trough for protecting electric wires [O.F.]

conduit system a system of electric wires carried underground or in lead piping

con·du·pli·cate (kɒndú:plikit, kɒndjú:plikit) *adj.* (*bot.*, of a cotyledon) folded to embrace the radicle ‖ (*bot.*, of a leaf) having one half folded upon the other [fr. L. *conduplicare* (*conduplicatus*), to fold together]

con·dyle (kɒ́ndail, kɒ́ndʼl) *n.* a rounded process on a bone associated with a joint **con·dy·loid** (kɒ́ndʼlɔid) *adj.* [F. fr. L. fr. Gk *kondylos*, knuckle]

con·dy·lo·ma (kɒndʼlóumə) *pl.* **con·dy·lo·mas**, **con·dy·lo·ma·ta** (kɒndəlóumətə) *n.* (*med.*) a wartlike growth on the skin or a mucous membrane, esp. in the genital region **con·dy·lom·a·tous** (kɒndʼlómətəs, kɒndʼlóumətəs) *adj.* [L. fr. Gk]

cone (koun) *n.* (*bot.*) a mass of spirally arranged, woody carpels, bearing pollen or ovules and found in most conifers and cycads ‖ the terminal spike in horsetails and mosses ‖ (*geom.*) a solid figure with circular (or elliptical) base, tapering to a point. One form is the right circular cone, generated by the revolution of a right-angled triangle about one of its sides ‖ a marine shell of the genus *Conus* ‖ something conical in shape, e.g. the formation built up around the crater of a volcano ‖ a cone-shaped meteorological signal used as a wind signal or gale warning ‖ a cone-shaped wafer for ice cream ‖ an indicator used in pyrometry ‖ one of the light-sensitive cone cells in the retina of the eye 2. *v. pres. part.* **con·ing** *past* and *past part.* **coned** *v.t.* to shape like a cone ‖ *v.i.* to bear cones [fr. L. *conus* fr. Gk]

C-123K *PROVIDER

C-130 *HERCULES

C-140 *JET STAR

C-141 *STARLIFTER

cone·nose (kóunouz) *n.* (*entomology*) a blood-sucking insect (order Hemiptera, esp. genus *Triatoma*) with two pairs of wings in the male, none in the female *also* assassin bug, kissing bug

Con·es·to·ga wagon (kɒnistóugə) a heavy, broad-wheeled covered wagon that American pioneers traveled west in [after *Conestoga*, Pa., where the wagons were originally made]

co·ney, co·ny (kóuni:, kʌ́ni:) *pl.* **co·neys, co·nies** *n.* a trade name for rabbit skin or rabbit fur dressed to resemble other fur ‖ a hyrax [M.E. *cunin* fr. O.F.]

con·fab (kɒ́nfæb) **1.** *n.* (*pop.*) a confabulation **2.** *v.i. pres. part.* **con·fab·bing** *past* and *past part.* **con·fabbed** (*pop.*) to confabulate

con·fab·u·late (kənfǽbjuleit) *pres. part.* **con·fab·u·lat·ing** *past* and *past part.* **con·fab·u·lat·ed** *v.i.* to converse or chat **con·fab·u·la·tion** *n.* [fr. L. *confabulari*, (*confabulatus*)]

con·fect (kənfékt) *v.t.* to prepare or make from ingredients ‖ to make up, contrive, put together (a story, excuse etc.) [fr. L. *conficere* (*confectus*), to prepare]

con·fec·tion (kənfékʃən) **1.** *n.* a prepared dish, esp. jam, preserves or dessert ‖ a mixture or

compounding **2.** *v.t.* to prepare or make (confections) **con·féc·tion·er** *n.* a manufacturer of, or shopkeeper selling, candies, cakes etc. [F.]

confectioners' sugar (*Am.=Br.* icing sugar) finely powdered sugar used in icing cakes etc. and in making various confections

con·fec·tion·er·y (kənfékʃəneri:) *n.* candy ‖ the work of a confectioner ‖ a confectioner's shop

con·fed·er·a·cy (kənfédərəsi:, kənfédrəsi:) *pl.* **con·fed·er·a·cies** *n.* a league or alliance ‖ a union of states or peoples for a particular purpose **the Confederacy** *CONFEDERATE STATES OF AMERICA [ult. fr. L. L. *confoederatio*]
—A confederacy (or confederation) in politics is formed mainly for defense, foreign affairs and trade. The stress is on the sovereign independence of each state (cf. German 'Staatenbund'). Matters not regulated in common are fully controlled by member states, and those confided to the confederation are finally controlled by members in some form. In a federation, by contrast, the stress is on the supremacy of the common government (cf. German 'Bundesstaat'), which has full powers over the matters entrusted to it.
— In trade-union usage, a confederation is an association to which member unions have surrendered most of their powers. A federation, by contrast, is an alliance of autonomous unions

con·fed·er·ate (kənfédərit, kənfédrit) **1.** *adj.* allied, leagued together **Confederate** of or pertaining to the Confederate States of America **2.** *n.* an ally (esp. in a pejorative sense), an accomplice **Confederate** an adherent of the Confederate States of America **3.** (kənfédəreit) *v. pres. part.* **con·fed·er·at·ing** *past* and *past part.* **con·fed·er·at·ed** *v.i.* to unite in a league or conspiracy ‖ *v.t.* to bring (a person or state) into an alliance [fr. L. *confoederare* (*confoederatus*)]

Confederate States of America the Confederacy, the government established (1861–5) by the Southern states of the U.S.A. after they had seceded from the Union. They were: South Carolina, Mississippi, Florida, Alabama, Georgia, Louisiana, Texas, Virginia, Arkansas, North Carolina and Tennessee (*CIVIL WAR, AMERICAN, *DAVIS, JEFFERSON)

con·fed·er·a·tion (kənfédəréiʃən) *n.* a confederating or being confederated ‖ an alliance of powers for some mutual benefit (*CONFEDERACY) [F.]

Confederation, Articles of (*Am. hist.*) the agreement under which the Thirteen Colonies became (1781) the U.S.A. and adopted a federal form of association. It gave too little power to the central government and was superseded by thc U.S. Constitution (1789)

Confederation of the Rhine *RHINE, CONFEDERATION OF THE

con·fer (kənfí:r) *pres. part.* **con·fer·ring** *past* and *past part.* **con·ferred** *v.i.* to seek advice, *to confer with a solicitor* ‖ to discuss views, hold a conference ‖ *v.t.* to give or grant, *to confer a knighthood* **con·fer·ee** (kɒnfərí:) *n.* someone on whom something is conferred ‖ someone who takes part in a conference [fr. L. *conferre*, to bring together]

con·fer·ence (kɒ́nfərəns, kɒ́nfrəns) *n.* consultation, *in conference* ‖ a formal meeting at which people confer ‖ the annual meeting which constitutes the governing body of the Methodist Church ‖ an association or league of athletic teams **con·fer·en·tial** (kɒnfərénʃəl) *adj.* [F. *conference*]

conference call telephone or radio conversation connected to more than two persons at different locations

con·fer·ment (kənfá:rmənt) *n.* a conferring

con·fer·ra·ble (kənfá:rəbʼl) *adj.* able to be conferred

con·fess (kənfés) *v.t.* to own up to, admit, *to confess a mistake* ‖ to acknowledge (one's sins) in penitence ‖ to hear the confession of (a penitent) ‖ (*eccles.*) to acknowledge belief in ‖ *v.i.* to acknowledge one's sins, esp. to make them known to a priest and ask for absolution **con·féssed** *adj.* admitted, avowed [O.F. *confesser*]

con·fes·sion (kənféʃən) *n.* an acknowledgment of a crime or fault ‖ a statement of something confessed ‖ a profession of belief, *a confession of faith* ‖ the acknowledging of one's sins, esp. the act of disclosing them to a priest to obtain absolution ‖ the tomb of a martyr or confessor, an altar built over it, or the crypt, chapel etc. in which it is **con·fés·sion·al** *adj.* pertaining to a confession or creed [F.]

con·fes·sion·al (kənféʃənəl) *n.* the enclosure in which a priest hears confession ‖ the practice of confessing sin to a priest [F. *confessionale*]

Confession of Augsburg *AUGSBURG CONFESSION

con·fes·sor (kənfésər) *n.* a person confessing, esp. one who avows his religious faith despite danger but is not martyred ‖ a priest who hears confession and grants absolution [L.]

con·fet·ti (kənféti:) *pl. n.* small pieces of colored paper thrown for fun on festive occasions [Ital.=candies]

con·fi·dant (kɒnfidǽnt, kɒnfidʌ́nt, kɒ́nfidænt, kɒ́nfidɑnt) *n.* someone to whom secrets, esp. love affairs, are confided ‖ a bosom friend **con·fi·dánte** *n.* a female confidant [F. *confident*]

con·fide (kənfáid) *pres. part.* **con·fid·ing** *past* and *past part.* **con·fid·ed** *v.i.* to entrust a secret ‖ to trust, have entire faith, *is there nobody he confides in?* ‖ *v.t.* to tell (something) confidentially ‖ (*old-fash.*) to entrust, *to confide one's child to a neighbor's care* [fr. L. *confidere*]

con·fi·dence (kɒ́nfidəns) *n.* a state of trust ‖ reliance, a feeling of hope on which one relies, *we have every confidence in his future* ‖ self-reliance ‖ something told in confidence, a secret **in confidence** as a secret **to take someone into one's confidence** to tell someone something private [fr. L. *confidentia*]

confidence game (*Am.=Br.* confidence trick) a swindling by winning someone's trust and then defrauding him

confidence man (*Am.=Br.* confidence trickster) a swindler who operates a confidence game

confidence trick *CONFIDENCE GAME **confidence trickster** *CONFIDENCE MAN

con·fi·dent (kɒ́nfidənt) *adj.* self-assured ‖ convinced, *she is confident that he can do it* ‖ bold, sometimes presumptuously, *confident assertions* [fr. L. *confidere*, to trust]

con·fi·den·tial (kɒnfidénʃəl) *adj.* spoken or written in confidence ‖ entrusted with secrets, *a confidential secretary* ‖ indicating close intimacy or confidence, *a confidential tone* ‖ in the secret service, *a confidential agent* [fr. L. *conjidentia*, trust]

con·fid·ing (kənfáidiŋ) *adj.* trustful

con·fig·u·ra·tion (kənfigjuréiʃən) *n.* the assemblage of relative positions of the parts of a material system, which may be represented in models, plans or diagrams ‖ (*psychol.*) a gestalt ‖ (*chem.*) the spacial arrangement of atoms in a molecule ‖ (*astron.*) the relative position of stars **con·fig·u·rá·tion·al** *adj.* relating to or based on a configuration **con·fig·u·rá·tion·ism** *n.* Gestalt psychology **con·fig·u·ra·tive** (kənfígjurətiv, kənfígjureitiv) *adj.* configurational [fr. L. *configuratio* (*configurationis*)]

con·fine (kənfáin) *pres. part.* **con·fin·ing** *past* and *past part.* **con·fined** *v.t.* to limit, keep (something, oneself) within limits, *confine your remarks to the main issue* ‖ to shut in, imprison ‖ (with 'to') to prevent from going out, *confined to bed with a cold* **con·fíned** *adj.* (*old-fash.*) about to have a child [F. *confiner* fr. Ital.]

con·fine·ment (kənfáinmənt) *n.* the state of being confined ‖ imprisonment ‖ inability to go out because of illness ‖ a lying-in, time of giving birth to a child [F.]

confinement farming *FACTORY FARMING

con·fines (kɒ́nfainz) *pl. n.* borders ‖ limits [F. *confins*]

con·firm (kənfá:rm) *v.t.* to make stronger or more persistent, *to confirm a belief* ‖ to corroborate, establish the truth of, *to confirm a report* ‖ to ratify, endorse by writing, *to confirm a treaty* ‖ to make (something provisional) definite, *to confirm an appointment* ‖ to administer the rite of confirmation to **con·fir·mand** (kɒnfərmǽnd, kɒ́nfərmænd) *n.* a candidate for confirmation [M.E. *confermen* fr. O.F.]

con·fir·ma·tion (kɒnfərméiʃən) *n.* a confirming or being confirmed ‖ corroboration ‖ something that confirms, a proof ‖ the Christian rite by which baptized persons, at the age of discretion, are admitted to full communion ‖ the solemn initiation of boys and girls into the Jewish faith [O.F.]

con·firm·a·tive (kənfá:rmətiv) *adj.* confirmatory

con·firm·a·to·ry (kənfá:rmətɔri:, kənfá:rmətɔuri:) *adj.* serving to confirm

con·firmed (kənfá:rmd) *adj.* firmly set in behavior or condition and so stamped as of a specified kind, *a confirmed drunkard, a confirmed bachelor*

CONCISE PRONUNCIATION KEY: **(a)** æ, c*a*t; ɑ, c*ar*; ɔ f*aw*n; ei, sn*a*ke. **(e)** e, h*e*n; i:, sh*ee*p; iə, d*ee*r; ɛə, b*ear*. **(i)** i, f*i*sh; ai, t*i*ger; ə:, b*ir*d. **(o)** o, *o*x; au, c*ow*; ou, g*oa*t; u, p*oor*; ɔi, r*oy*al. **(u)** ʌ, d*u*ck; u, b*u*ll; u:, g*oo*se; ə, b*a*cillus; ju:, c*u*be. x, lo*ch*; θ, *th*ink; ð, bo*th*er; z, *Z*en; ʒ, cor*s*age; dʒ, sava*g*e; ŋ, orangutan*g*; j, *y*ak; ʃ, *f*ish; tʃ, fe*tch*; ʼl, rabb*l*e; ʼn, redd*en*. Complete pronunciation key appears inside front cover.

con·fis·cate (kónfiskeit, kənfískeit) *pres. part.* **con·fis·cat·ing** *past* and *past part.* **con·fis·cat·ed** *v.t.* to seize for the public treasury as a penalty ‖ to take away (something) from somebody under discipline [fr. L. *confiscare* (*confiscatus*)]

con·fis·ca·tion (kɒnfiskéiʃən) *n.* a confiscating or being confiscated [fr. L. *confiscatio* (*confiscationis*)]

con·fis·ca·tor (kónfiskeitər) *n.* someone who confiscates

con·fis·ca·to·ry (kənfískətɔri, kənfískətɔuri:) *adj.* of the nature of or characterized by confiscation, *confiscatory taxation*

con·fla·gra·tion (kɒnfləgréiʃən) *n.* a calamitous fire [fr. L. *conflagratio* (*conflagrationis*)]

con·fla·tion (kənfléiʃən) *n.* a combining or fusing together, esp. of two variant readings of a text [fr. L. *conflatio* (*conflationis*)]

con·flict 1. (kónflikt) *n.* armed fighting, a war ‖ a struggle between opposing principles or aims ‖ a clash of feelings or interests ‖ such a clash as a source of dramatic action **2.** (kənflíkt) *v.i.* to be at variance, clash ‖ to struggle, contend **con·flic·tion** *n.* [fr. L. *confligere* (*conflictus*)]

con·flu·ence (kónflu:əns) *n.* a flowing together of streams, roads etc. ‖ a stream or body formed by such a junction [fr. L. L. *confluentia*]

con·flu·ent (kónflu:ənt) **1.** *adj.* flowing together, uniting ‖ running together (e.g. of smallpox pustules) **2.** *n.* a stream uniting with another [fr. L. *confluens* (*confluentis*)]

con·flux (kónflʌks) *n.* a confluence or flowing together [fr. L. *confluere* (*confluxus*), to flow together]

con·form (kənfɔrm) *v.i.* to comply, *the design conforms with the regulations* ‖ to do as others do, *under discipline you must conform* ‖ *v.t.* to adapt, cause to comply [F. *conformer*]

con·form·a·bil·i·ty (kənfɔrməbíliti:) *n.* the state or quality of being conformable

con·form·a·ble (kənfɔrməb'l) *adj.* that conforms, is in proper harmony or agreement ‖ (*geol.*, of strata formed under the same conditions) following in unbroken sequence **con·form·a·bly** *adv.*

con·form·ance (kənfɔrməns) *n.* the act of conforming, conformity

con·for·ma·tion (kɒnfɔrméiʃən) *n.* a particular form, structure ‖ adaptation ‖ the act of conforming [fr. L. *conformatio* (*conformationis*)]

conformational *adj.* (*phys.*) of various three-dimensional forms of molecules

con·form·ist (kənfɔrmist) **1.** *adj.* tending to conform **2.** *n.* someone who conforms

con·form·i·ty (kənfɔrmiti:) *pl.* **con·form·i·ties** *n.* a conforming to authority or to an accepted or implied standard ‖ compliance, *in conformity with your instructions* ‖ likeness in form, shape or manner [F. *conformité*]

con·found (kɒnfáund, kənfáund) *v.t.* to fail to distinguish between, mix up, confuse ‖ (*rhet.*) to defeat, *his plans were confounded by events* ‖ to perplex deeply, utterly astonish ‖ (kónfáund, as a mild oath) to damn, *confound it!* **con·found·ed** *adj.* utterly confused, astonished ‖ (*pop.*) damned, damnable [O.F. *confondre*]

con·fra·ter·ni·ty (kɒnfrətɔ:rniti:) *pl.* **con·fra·ter·ni·ties** *n.* a brotherhood or society esp. for religious or charitable purposes [fr. M.L. *confraternitas*]

con·front (kənfrʌnt) *v.t.* to face, esp. boldly or in a hostile way ‖ (with 'with') to bring face to face, force to consider something, *to confront one's accusers with the evidence* ‖ to stand in front of, lie before, *the difficulties confronting them* ‖ to put together for comparison **con·fron·ta·tion** (kɒnfrəntéiʃən) *n.* [F. *confronter*]

Confrontation States the Arab states vis à vis Israel; originally used to refer militarily to Arab countries that border on Israel

confrontation therapy (*psych.*) method of treating delinquent or problem adolescents through discipline, punishment (including physical punishment), in which each is allowed to express hostile feelings within a community of peers

Con·fu·cian (kənfjú:ʃən) **1.** *adj.* of, concerning or derived from the philosophy of Confucius **2.** *n.* a follower of the philosophy of Confucius **Con·fú·cian·ism** *n.* the moral and religious system of China founded by Confucius at the end of the 6th c. B.C. His original sayings (Analects) were edited with commentaries by Mencius in the 4th c. B.C., and his philosophy was further developed by Chu Hsi in the 12th c. and by Wang Yang-ming in the 16th c. Basically it is a system of ethical precepts—benevolent love,

righteousness, decorum, wise leadership, sincerity—designed to inspire and preserve the good management of family and society. A theological dimension was introduced in the 2nd c. B.C. when Tung Chung-shu related the five virtues to a cosmic order governed by Shang-Ti (ruler of heaven) to whom the emperor was immediately responsible. It became the official doctrine of Imperial China under the Han dynasty (2nd c. B.C. - 2nd c. A.D.). Ritual sacrifice in appointed shrines characterized Confucianism from the 1st c. A.D. until the People's Republic of 1949. Eclipsed by Taoism and Buddhism from the 3rd to the 7th cc., Confucianism was revived and made the state religion under the Tang dynasty (618–906). Neo-Confucianism, strong between the 10th and 13th cc., opposed the supernatural quietistic tendencies of Buddhism and Taoism, advocating a humanist search for truth. From the 2nd c. B.C. until the 20th c. Confucianism was the distinctive philosophy of China, and the basis of social organization, education and administration **Con·fú·cian·ist** *n.* and *adj.*

Con·fu·cius (kənfjú:ʃəs) (c. 551 B.C.–c. 479 B.C.), Chinese philosopher, born and buried at Chufoo. After 15 years as a public administrator (c. 532 B.C. –c. 517 B.C.) he spent the rest of his life studying and teaching the classics and spreading his philosophy (CONFUCIANISM). His sayings, the Analects of Confucius, were recorded after his death and, together with the classics which he edited, formed the body of traditional Chinese education

con·fuse (kənfjú:z) *pres. part.* **con·fus·ing** *past* and *past part.* **con·fused** *v.t.* to throw into disorder, jumble together, *to confuse issues* ‖ to fail to distinguish between, *to confuse a butterfly with a moth* ‖ to perplex or muddle ‖ to abash, disconcert **con·fus·ed·ly** (kənfjú:zidli, kənfjú:zdli:) *adv.* in a confused manner [fr. F. *confus* or L. *confusus*]

con·fu·sion (kənfjú:ʒən) *n.* the state of being confused, esp. a state of great disorder ‖ the act of confusing, mistaking one thing for another ‖ lack of clarity ‖ bewilderment, perplexity ‖ embarrassment [O. F.]

con·fu·ta·tion (kɒnfjutéiʃən) *n.* a confuting ‖ something which confutes

con·fute (kənfjú:t) *pres. part.* **con·fut·ing** *past* and *past part.* **con·fut·ed** *v.t.* to refute (an argument) ‖ to prove (a person) mistaken [fr. L. *confutare*]

Cong (kɒŋ) *n.* (*slang*) (used disparagingly) during the Vietnam war, a Vietcong person, and by extension all potentially hostile Vietnamese

con·ga (kóŋgə) *n.* a Cuban dance performed in file following a leader, orig. with a bass drum [Span.]

con game confidence game

con·geal (kəndʒí:l) *v.i.* to change from fluid to solid through coldness, freeze ‖ to coagulate, become thick as if frozen ‖ *v.t.* to cause to freeze ‖ to cause to coagulate **con·géal·ment** *n.* a congealing ‖ a congealed mass [M.E. *congelen* fr. O.F.]

con·ge·la·tion (kɒndʒəléiʃən) *n.* a congealing or being congealed ‖ something congealed [F.]

con·ge·ner (kóndʒənər) *n.* a thing or person of the same kind, homologue **con·ge·ner·ic** (kɒndʒənérik) *adj.* of the same race or kind ‖ of the same nature or origin ‖ of the same genus **con·gen·er·ous** (kəndʒénərəs) *adj.* of the same kind, akin [L. fr. *con-*, *con-*+*genus* (*generis*), kind]

con·gen·er·a·tion (kəndʒənəréiʃən) *n.* system for capturing waste heat, e.g., from smoke stacks

congeneric *adj.* of a group of diversified business companies commonly controlled and fitting into a cohesive whole

con·gen·ial (kəndʒí:njəl) *adj.* of the same nature, tastes or interests, *congenial neighbors* ‖ suited to one's nature or tastes, agreeable, *congenial occupations* ‖ suitable, *acid soil is congenial to heather* **con·ge·ni·al·i·ty** (kəndʒí:ni:æliti) *n.* [fr. L. *con-*, *con-*+*genialis* fr. *genius*, tutelary deity or genius of a person]

con·gen·i·tal (kəndʒénit'l) *adj.* present at birth ‖ acquired during fetal development and not hereditary [fr. L. *congenitus*, born with]

con·ger eel (kóŋgər) *Conger conger*, the large sea eel, attaining a length of 6–10 ft [O.F. *congre* fr. L. fr. Gk]

con·ge·ries (kɒndʒíəri:z) *pl.* **con·ge·ries** *n.* an aggregation, collection (of parts or bodies) [L.]

con·gest (kəndʒést) *v.t.* to pack closely, cause clogging in by overcrowding, *holiday traffic congested the roads* ‖ to cause excessive accumulation of blood in the vessels of (an organ or part) ‖ *v.i.* to become crowded together **con·gést·ed** *adj.* closely packed, crowded ‖ overpopulated ‖ overcharged with blood, *congested lungs* ‖ (*bot.*) packed into a tight mass [fr. L. *congerere* (*congestus*), to bring together]

con·ges·tion (kəndʒéstʃən) *n.* the state of being congested, *traffic congestion* ‖ overcrowding ‖ the accumulation of excessive amounts of blood in part of the body [F.]

con·glo·bate (kɒnglóubeit, kóngloubeit) *adj.* formed into a rounded mass, ball-shaped **con·glo·bá·tion** *n.* [fr. L. *conglobare* (*conglobatus*), to form into a globe]

con·glob·u·late (kənglóbjəleit) *v.* to form into a ball

con·glom·er·ate (kənglómərit) **1.** *adj.* gathered or clustered into a ball or mass **2.** *n.* sedimentary rock consisting of rounded rock fragments (cf. AGGLOMERATE, cf. BRECCIA) held together in a mass by hardened clay etc. ‖ an accumulated mass of different materials ‖ corporate entity composed of several companies in a variety of industries **3.** *v.* (kənglóməreit) *pres. part.* **con·glom·er·at·ing** *past* and *past part.* **con·glom·er·at·ed** *v.t.* to gather into a compact mass ‖ *v.i.* to form a compact mass **con·glom·er·á·tion** *n.* the state of being conglomerated ‖ a collection of things of various kinds [fr. L. *conglomerare* (*conglomeratus*), to form into a ball]

con·glom·er·at·or *n.* one who organizes the acquisition or merger of companies into a single entity

con·glu·ti·nate (kənglú:t'neit) **1.** *v.* *pres. part.* **con·glu·ti·nat·ing** *past* and *past part.* **con·glu·ti·nat·ed** *v.t.* to cause to stick together as if with glue ‖ *v.i.* to grow together **2.** *adj.* stuck together **con·glu·ti·ná·tion** *n.* [fr. L. *conglutinare* (*conglutinatus*)]

Con·go (kóŋgou) a river (the Zaïre, about 3,000 miles, navigable for long stretches between rapids) draining the central African basin. It rises as the Lualaba on the plateau of Katanga, flows north to Stanley Falls, then west and south to the Atlantic, forming the border between the Congo and Zaïre. The chief towns of both countries are on the river. Its mouth was discovered (1482) by the Portuguese explorer Diego Cão. It was explored (1867–73) by Livingstone and more thoroughly (1874–7) by Stanley

Congo Free State *ZAÏRE

Con·go·nhas do Cam·po (kɒŋgɔ́njusdɔkúmpɔ) a town (pop. 3,000) in the State of Minas Gerais, Brazil, famous for its baroque art and as a pilgrimage center

Congo, the Democratic Republic of the *ZAÏRE

Congo, the Republic of the (formerly French Congo) a republic (area 135,000 sq. miles, pop. 1,619,000) in W. central Africa. Capital: Brazzaville. Official language: French. The land is half equatorial forest and half savanna and swamps. A mountainous region rising to 4,920 ft separates the coastal plain from the central plateau. There are two seasons of heavy rain and two dry seasons. Agricultural products: copal, rubber, palm oil, peanuts, tobacco. Mineral resources: oil, aluminum, lead, gold. Exports: lumber (ebony, mahogany), palm kernels, palm oil. Port: Pointe Noire. The Congo River network is a main means of transportation over about 1,250 miles. The Congo-Ocean Railway (318 miles) connects Brazzaville and Pointe Noire. Monetary unit: franc C.F.A. HISTORY. Bantu kingdoms were flourishing along the coast north of the Congo estuary when the Portuguese arrived (1482). The explorer de Brazza established (1880) a French protectorate by treaty with Makoko, the Bateke king, and (1882) with the king of Loango. The country was known as French Congo until 1910, when it was renamed Middle Congo and became part of French Equatorial Africa. It was made an overseas territory of the French Union (1946), a member state of the French Community (1958) and an independent republic (Aug. 15, 1960). It was admitted to the U.N. (1960). An army coup d'état (Aug. 1968) was mounted successfully. The republic became (Jan. 1970) a people's republic. Labor uprisings and military coups during the 1960s led to overthrows of the government in 1963 and 1968. By 1969, a Communist state was declared and in 1979 a new constitution was adopted. The Congo has maintained close ties with the U.S.S.R.

con·grat·u·late (kəngrǽtʃuleit) *pres. part.* **con·grat·u·lat·ing** *past and past part.* **con·grat·u·lat·ed** *v.t.* to express pleasure in the success or happiness of (another) ‖ (refl.) to deem (oneself) fortunate or clever in some matter [fr. L. *congratulari (congratulatus)*]

con·grat·u·la·tion (kəngrætʃuléiʃən) *n.* a congratulating ‖ (*pl.*) expressions of congratulation [fr. L. *congratulatio (congratulationis)*]

con·grat·u·la·to·ry (kəngrǽtʃulətɔːri; kəngrǽtʃulətouri) *adj.* expressing congratulations

con·gre·gate 1. (kɔ́ŋgrəgeit) *v. pres. part.* **con·gre·gat·ing** *past and past part.* **con·gre·gat·ed** *v.i.* to collect into a crowd or mass ‖ *v.t.* to cause to collect into a crowd **2.** (kɔ́ŋgrəgit, kɔ́ŋgrəgeit) *adj.* collected, assembled [fr. L. *congregare (congregatus)*]

con·gre·ga·tion (kɔŋgrəgéiʃən) *n.* an assemblage of persons or things, esp. of persons gathered for a religious service ‖ the body of regular attenders at a particular place of worship ‖ a permanent committee of the College of Cardinals ‖ an order or community of religious with a common rule (with or without solemn vows) ‖ (*Br.*) the general assembly of qualified members of a university **con·gre·ga·tion·al** *adj.* pertaining to a congregation **Con·gre·ga·tion·al** of or belonging to Congregationalism **con·gre·ga·tion·al·ism** *n.* a form of Church government which makes the local congregation autonomous **Con·gre·ga·tion·al·ism** the doctrine of a Protestant evangelical and trinitarian Church based on this form of government which began in England (1567) and gained strength esp. in New England (early 17th c.) **con·gre·ga·tion·al·ist, Con·gre·ga·tion·al·ist** *n. and adj.* [F. *congrégation*]

con·gress (kɔ́ŋgris) *n.* a formal meeting, e.g. of delegates, *a biochemical congress* **Con·gress** the federal legislature of the U.S.A. (Senate and House of Representatives) and of some other American republics ‖ the Indian National Congress [fr. L. *congredi (congressus)*, to go together]

—The U.S. Congress consists of a Senate and a House of Representatives. All the legislative powers of the federal government are vested in it by the Constitution. The House of Representatives is composed of 435 representatives, elected for two years. Constitutionally it is the legislative equal of the Senate, but it alone has the right to initiate revenue-raising bills. The Senate is composed of 100 senators elected for six years, one third being elected every two years. There are two senators for each state. Treaties negotiated by the president require ratification by the Senate only, and the president's appointments to major offices in the executive and judiciary require endorsement by the Senate only. Congressional measures are liable to presidential veto, but bills repassed by a two-thirds majority in each house become law without the president's signature. By the constitutional separation of powers, members of Congress may not hold executive office. Contact between the executive and legislature is limited to the formal, nonbinding exchange of presidential messages and congressional resolutions

con·gres·sion·al (kəngréʃən'l) *adj.* of or pertaining to a congress **Con·gres·sion·al** pertaining to the U.S. Congress ‖ pertaining to the Indian National Congress [fr. L. *congressio (congressionis)*]

Congressional Black Caucus group of members of the House of Representatives concerned with the Afro-American viewpoint on domestic and international affairs

Congressional caucus group of members of the House of Representatives representing a special constituency organized to coordinate policies and votes, e.g., Congressional Black Caucus, Congresswomen's Caucus

Congressional Clearinghouse group of members of Congress especially concerned with state and local government legislation

Congressional Medal of Honor the highest U.S. military decoration, authorized (1861) and awarded by Congress, for supreme gallantry in action

con·gress·man (kɔ́ŋgrismən) *pl.* **con·gress·men** (kɔ́ŋgrismən) *n.* a member of the House of Representatives

Congress of Industrial Organizations *AMERICAN FEDERATION OF LABOR AND CONGRESS OF INDUSTRIAL ORGANIZATIONS

Congress of Racial Equality (*abbr.* CORE), a U.S. civil rights organization founded (1942) by

James Farmer. It originally advocated nonviolent forms of protest to fight racial discrimination, but from the mid-1960s became more radical

Congress of the United States, lawmaking body comprising the House of Representatives and the Senate. There are 100 senators (two from each state) elected for 6-year terms; the number of representatives, elected for 2 years, is limited to 435, and the representatives are distributed among the states, based on population

Congress of Vienna *VIENNA, CONGRESS OF

Con·greve (kɔ́ŋgriːv, kɔ́ŋgriːv), William (1670–1729), English Restoration playwright. His witty comedies of manners include 'Love for Love' (1695) and 'The Way of the World' (1700)

con·gru·ence (kɔ́ŋgruːəns) *n.* an accord, a harmonious relation ‖ (*geom.*) an exact coinciding **cón·gru·en·cy** *n.* [fr. L. *congruentia*]

con·gru·ent (kɔ́ŋgruːənt) *adj.* possessing congruity ‖ (*geom.*) equal in all respects, able to be superimposed so as to coincide throughout, *congruent triangles* [fr. L. *congruens (congruentis)*]

con·gru·i·ty (kəngrúːiti:, kɔŋgrúːiti:) *pl.* **con·gru·i·ties** *n.* a state of agreement, harmony, correspondence ‖ (*geom.*) exact coincidence of figures [fr. L. *congruitas (congruitatis)*]

con·gru·ous (kɔ́ŋgruːəs) *adj.* suitable, consistent with, fitting ‖ congruent [fr. L. *congruus*]

con·ic (kɔ́nik) *adj.* having the form of a cone **cón·i·cal** *adj.* **cón·ics** *n.* that part of geometry dealing with the cone and its sections [fr. Gk *kōnikos* fr. *kónos*, cone]

conic section one of a group of mathematical curves which may be formed at the intersection of a plane with a cone. They include the ellipse, hyperbola, parabola, and circle

co·nid·i·al (kounídiːəl, kənídiːəl) *adj.* relating to, resembling or producing conidia

co·nid·i·o·phore (kounídiːəfɔr, kounídiːəfɔr, kənídiːəfɔr, kənídiːəfour) *n.* a structure that bears conidia, esp. specialized fungal hypha bearing conidia

co·nid·i·um (kounídiːəm, kənídiːəm) *pl.* **co·nid·i·a** (kounídiːə, kənídiːə) *n.* (*biol.*) an asexual spore often produced by obstruction of a sterigma and in general not borne within an enclosing structure [ult. fr. Gk *konis*, dust]

co·ni·fer (kóunifər, kɔ́nifər) *n.* a member of *Coniferales*, a large order of gymnospermous trees and shrubs. They are generally evergreen, with slender, prickly leaves or leaves with rounded points, and reproduce by means of cones **co·nif·er·ous** (kounífərəs, kɔnífərəs) *adj.* [fr. L. *conus*, cone + *-ferus*, bearing]

co·ni·form (kóunifɔrm) *adj.* cone-shaped [fr. L. *conus*]

co·ni·ine (kóuniːiːn, kóuniːin, kóuniːn) *n.* a poisonous alkaloid ($C_8H_{17}N$) found in hemlock. It is used medicinally as a sedative [fr. L. *conium*, hemlock fr. Gk]

conj. conjunction

con·jec·tur·al (kəndʒéktʃərəl) *adj.* doubtful, of the nature of conjecture, *conjectural emendations* ‖ given to, prone to conjecture [fr. L. *conjecturalis*]

con·jec·ture (kəndʒéktʃər) *n.* guesswork, opinion or theory based on presumption or insufficient evidence ‖ such an opinion esp. in textual criticism, a proposed reading [fr. L. *conjectura* fr. *conjicere*, to throw together] **conjecture** *pres. part.* **con·jec·tur·ing** *past and past part.* **con·jec·tured** *v.t.* to guess, infer on slight evidence ‖ *v.i.* to make conjectures [fr. F. *conjecturer*]

Con·jee·ve·ram (kəndʒíːvərəm) *KANCHIPURAM

con·join (kəndʒɔ́in) *v.t. and i.* to join together, unite [fr. F. *conjoindre*]

con·joint (kəndʒɔ́int) *adj.* united, conjoined ‖ carried on by two or more in association, *conjoint efforts* [F.]

con·ju·gal (kɔ́ndʒugʼl) *adj.* pertaining to marriage or to married persons **con·ju·gal·i·ty** (kɔndʒugǽliti:) *n.* [fr. L. *conjugalis*]

con·ju·gate 1. (kɔ́ndʒugeit) *v. pres. part.* **con·ju·gat·ing** *past and past part.* **con·ju·gat·ed** *v.t.* to state or set out (a verb) with its various inflectional endings in order, i.e. in its voices, moods, tenses, numbers and persons ‖ *v.i.* to join together ‖ to become fused or united **2.** (kɔ́ndʒugit, kɔ́ndʒugeit) *adj.* yoked or united, joined, connected, esp. in pairs ‖ related by having some properties in common but by being opposite or inverse in some particular feature or in

more than one, *conjugate complex numbers* ‖ (*gram.*) derived from the same root **3.** (kɔ́ndʒugit, kɔ́ndʒugeit) *n.* a conjugate word or conjugate axis, diameter etc. ‖ (*math.*) one of two complex numbers that have identical real parts and imaginary parts differing only in sign [fr. L. *conjugare (conjugatus)*, to yoke together]

con·ju·ga·tion (kɔndʒugéiʃən) *n.* a conjugating or being conjugated ‖ (*gram.*) a statement of the various forms of a verb ‖ a class of verbs having similar inflections, *weak conjugations* ‖ (*biol.*) the fusion of two gametes or unicellular organisms, e.g. in lower plants by a process like fertilization ‖ (*genetics*) contact for the transfer of DNA to another cell ‖ (*chem.*) structure providing single and double bonds with successive carbon atoms ‖ (*biol.*) the pairing of chromosomes ‖ (*zool.*) a temporary union with exchange of nuclear material, e.g. among certain protozoans **con·ju·ga·tion·al, con·ju·ga·tive** (kɔ́ndʒugeitiv) *adjs.* [fr. L. *conjugatio (conjugationis)*]

con·junc·tion (kəndʒʌ́ŋkʃən) *n.* a conjoining or being conjoined ‖ the apparent meeting of two or more heavenly bodies in the same part of the sky ‖ (*gram.*) a word used to connect sentences, clauses, phrases or words, e.g. a coordinating word ('and', 'but', 'or') or a subordinating word ('if', 'as', 'though') ‖ a combination of events or circumstances **in conjunction with** together with [O.F.]

con·junc·ti·va (kɔndʒʌŋktáivə) *pl.* **con·junc·ti·vas, con·junc·ti·vae** (kɔndʒʌŋktáivi:) *n.* (*anat.*) the mucous membrane lining the front of the eyeball and inner surface of the eyelid ‖ the membrane between adjoining parts of an insect's body [Mod. L. (*membrana*) *conjunctiva*]

con·junc·tive (kəndʒʌ́ŋktiv) **1.** *adj.* serving to unite or join, *conjunctive tissue* ‖ (*gram.*) serving as a conjunction, describing a word which links words, phrases etc., e.g. 'hence', 'consequently', 'therefore' **2.** *n.* a conjunctive word or phrase [fr. L. *conjunctivus*]

con·junc·ti·vi·tis (kəndʒʌŋktiváitis) *n.* (*med.*) inflammation of the conjunctiva

con·junc·ture (kəndʒʌ́ŋktʃər) *n.* a combination of events or circumstances that precipitates a critical state of affairs [F. *conjoncture*]

con·ju·ra·tion (kɔndʒuréiʃən) *n.* a summoning by a sacred name ‖ the incantation used ‖ the practice of legerdemain [O.F.]

con·jure (kʌ́ndʒər) *pres. part.* **con·jur·ing** *past and past part.* **con·jured** *v.t.* to summon up (a spirit) by invocation ‖ to produce by sleight of hand, *to conjure a rabbit out of a hat* ‖ (*rhet.* kəndʒúər) to urge with pleading, *he conjured them to keep it secret* ‖ *v.i.* to practice sleight of hand **to conjure up** to bring vividly before the imagination as though by magic **cón·jur·er, cón·ju·ror** *n.* a magician who practices legerdemain [O.F. *conjurer*]

conk (kɔŋk, kɔ́ŋk) **1.** *v.i.* (*pop.*, of a machine, often with 'out') to break down, fail **2.** *n.* congolene, a preparation produced from copal for straightening kinky hair ‖ the hairstyle created [origin unknown]

conk·er (kɔ́nkər, kɔ́ŋkər) *n.* (*Br., pl.*) a game in which a horse chestnut threaded with string is struck against another, also threaded, to try and break it (and risk being broken in the attempt) ‖ (*Br.*) a horse chestnut [dial. *conker*, snailshell, with which the game was originally played]

Con·kling (kɔ́ŋkliŋ), Roscoe (1829–88), U.S. political leader. As senator (1867–81) he strongly influenced the Grant administration in its Reconstruction policy and dominated the Republican party in New York State

con man confidence man

con·man·ship (kɔ́nmənʃip) *n.* the abilities of a confidence man

conn, con (kɔn) **1.** *v.t. pres. part.* **con·ning** *past and past part.* **conned** to direct the steering of (a ship) **2.** *n.* the control exercised by someone who conns [etym. doubtful, perh. rel. to F. *conduire*]

Conn. Connecticut

Con·nacht (kɔ́nəxt, kɔ́nət) (formerly Connaught) the western province (area 6,611 sq. miles, pop. 423,915) of the Irish Republic. It includes counties Galway, Leitrim, Mayo, Roscommon and Sligo ‖ (*hist.*) an ancient kingdom of W. Ireland

Con·naught (kɔ́nɔt) *CONNACHT

connate (kɔ́neit) *adj.* inborn, congenital ‖ (of two or more innate qualities) born or originated together ‖ allied, agreeing in nature ‖ (*biol.*)

firmly joined together from birth [fr. L. *connasci* (*connatus*), to be born together]

con·nat·u·ral (kənǽtʃərəl) *adj.* inborn, innate ‖ of the same nature, cognate [fr. L. *connaturalis*]

con·nect (kənékt) *v.t.* to join, *to connect a circuit* ‖ to establish a connection between in the mind, *to connect crime with emotional insecurity* ‖ *v.i.* to join on, make a connection, *this pipe connects with the sewer* **con·néct·ed** *adj.* joined together ‖ linked ‖ related by birth or marriage ‖ coherent ‖ employed in some capacity or otherwise associated, *connected with a shipping firm* [fr. L. *connectere* (*connexus*), to bind]

connecter *CONNECTOR

Con·nect·i·cut (kənétikət) (*abbr.* Conn.) a predominantly industrial state (area 5,009 sq. miles, pop. 3,153,000) of New England, on the northeastern coast of the U.S.A. Capital: Hartford. It is upland country, divided by the Connecticut River lowlands. Agriculture: poultry and dairy products, tobacco, nursery and greenhouse plants. Resources: building materials. Industries: aircraft engineering, metal products, machinery, electrical machinery, chemicals, textiles. Chief universities: Yale, University of Connecticut (1881) at Storrs, Wesleyan (1831) at Middletown. Connecticut was a Puritan settlement (17th c.) and one of the Thirteen Colonies. It became (1788) the fifth state of the U.S.A.

Connecticut a river (400 miles long) rising near the Canadian border in N. New Hampshire. It flows south to form the New Hampshire-Vermont boundary, passes through Massachusetts and Connecticut, and empties into Long Island Sound: hydroelectric power

connecting rod a rod or bar joined to and connecting two or more moving parts, e.g. in a steam engine

con·nec·tion, *Br.* also **con·nex·ion** (kənékʃən) *n.* a connecting or being connected ‖ a linking mechanism, *a screw connection* ‖ a link or joint ‖ relationship of thought, plot etc., *what connection has it with the previous incident?* ‖ something, esp. a train, timed so as to be convenient for something else, esp. another train ‖ blood relationship or personal relationship, *family connections, embassy connections* ‖ economic and business relations ‖ a body of persons linked by common beliefs, *the Methodist connection* **in connection with** with reference to **in this connection** while speaking of such things [fr. L. *connexio* (*connexionis*)]

con·nec·tive (kənéktiv) **1.** *adj.* connecting or tending to connect **2.** *n.* a word that connects words, clauses or sentences, e.g. a conjunction or relative pronoun

connective tissue (*anat.*) tissue that supports and connects organs of the body, e.g. cartilage, ligaments

con·nec·tor, con·nect·er (kənéktər) *n.* someone who or something which connects

connexion *CONNECTION

conning tower an armored tower on a warship or submarine from which steering or firing is directed

con·nip·tion (kəníp ʃən) *n.* (*pop.*) a fit of anger or hysteria [origin unknown]

con·niv·ance, con·niv·ence (kənáivəns) *n.* complicity, silent agreement ‖ guilty acquiescence in wrongdoing [fr. L. *conniventia*, shutting the eyes]

con·nive (kənáiv) *pres. part.* **con·niv·ing** *past* and *past part.* **con·nived** *v.i.* to pretend ignorance of something one should condemn ‖ (with 'at') to wink, be sympathetically tolerant ‖ (with 'at') to be culpably cooperative [fr. L. *connivere*, to shut the eyes]

connivence *CONNIVANCE

con·niv·ent (kənáivənt) *adj.* (*biol.*) convergent but not joined at the apex [fr. L. *connivens* (*conniventis*) fr. *connivere*, to incline together]

con·nois·seur (kɒnəsɔ́:r, kɒnəsúər) *n.* an expert critic (of the arts) ‖ a judge in matters of taste, *a connoisseur of wine* **con·nois·séur·ship** *n.* [F.]

con·no·ta·tion (kɒnətéiʃən) *n.* the implication of a word, apart from its primary meaning ‖ (*logic*) implication by a general name [fr. M.L. *connotatio* (*connotationis*)]

con·no·ta·tive (kɒ́nəteitiv, kənóutətiv) *adj.* relating to connotation [fr. L. *connotativus*]

con·note (kənóut) *pres. part.* **con·not·ing** *past* and *past part.* **con·not·ed** *v.t.* (of a word) to suggest, imply apart from its primary meaning ‖ to involve by implication, *poverty connotes malnutrition* ‖ (*logic*) to imply by a general name (the

sum of its attributes) [fr. M.L. *connotare*, to mark together]

con·nu·bi·al (kənú:bi:əl, kənjú:bi:əl) *adj.* pertaining to marriage, conjugal **con·nu·bi·ál·i·ty** *n.* [fr. L. *connubialis*]

co·noid (kóunɔid) **1.** *adj.* cone-shaped **2.** *n.* a solid described by the rotation of a conic section about its axis **co·nói·dal** *adj.* like a conoid [fr. Gk *kōnoeidēs*]

con·quer (kɒ́ŋkər) *v.t.* to defeat in war ‖ to take possession of by force, *Spain conquered Mexico* ‖ to overcome by moral power, *to conquer a habit* ‖ *v.i.* to be victorious [O.F. *conquerre*]

con·quer·or (kɒ́ŋkərər) *n.* a victor, a person who conquers [A.F. *conquerour*]

con·quest (kɒ́ŋkwest, kɒ́ŋkwest) *n.* the act of conquering a country or people ‖ something won or acquired by physical or moral victory ‖ someone amorously won [O.F. *conquest*, thing acquired by conquering and *conqueste*, action of conquering]

con·quis·ta·dor (kɒnkwístədɔr, kɒnkwístədour) *pl.* **con·quis·ta·do·res** (kɒnkwístədóri:z, kɒnkwístədóuri:z), **con·quis·ta·dors** *n.* (*hist.*) any of the 16th-c. Spanish conquerors of Mexico, Central America and Peru. The most famous were Cortés and Pizarro [Span.=conqueror]

Con·rad (kɒ́nræd), Joseph (Konrad Korzeniowski, 1857–1924), English novelist of Polish birth. His service in the British merchant navy in the East provided the material for his stories and novels with sea settings (e.g. 'The Nigger of the Narcissus' 1898, 'Lord Jim' 1900, 'Typhoon' 1903). His main theme is the moral nature of man: in particular the kind of integrity which is judged by others, honor. His settings vary from political intrigues in Czarist Russia ('Under Western Eyes') and espionage, blackmail and murder in London ('The Secret Agent') to politics and revolt in a South American republic ('Nostromo'), in addition to the exotic Eastern settings or the more specifically sea-stories

Conrad II (c. 990–1039), Holy Roman Emperor (1027–39), German king (1024–39). The first of the Franconian dynasty, he greatly increased the power of the German monarchy

Conrad III (c. 1093–1152), German king (1138–52), the first of the Hohenstaufen dynasty

Conrad IV (1228–54), German king (1237–54), king of Sicily (1250–4), son of Emperor Frederick II. Germany was plunged into anarchy in his reign, when Pope Innocent IV set up a rival king

Conrail (*acronym*) for Consolidated Rail Corporation, created by Congress in 1978 combining former privately owned rail lines in northeast U.S.; operated under U.S. government auspices

con·san·guin·e·ous (kɒnsæŋgwíni:əs) *adj.* related by blood, descended from the same ancestor [fr. L. *consanguineus*]

con·san·guin·i·ty (kɒnsæŋgwíniti:) *n.* kinship, blood relationship [F. *consanguinité*]

con·science (kɒ́nʃəns) *n.* knowledge of one's own acts as right or wrong **in all conscience** surely, reasonably **to have on one's conscience** to feel guilty about [F.]

conscience clause a proviso in an act ensuring respect for religious or moral scruples

conscience money money paid to relieve the conscience, esp. anonymously, e.g. in payment of evaded debt etc.

con·science-strick·en (kɒ́nʃənsstrìkən) *adj.* suffering pangs of conscience

Conscience Whigs a faction of the U.S. Whig party which, opposed to the Kansas-Nebraska act, helped to form (1854) the Republican party

con·sci·en·tious (kɒnʃi:énʃəs) *adj.* governed by conscience, scrupulous, *a conscientious worker* ‖ characterized by or done with careful attention, *a conscientious piece of research* [fr. F. *conscientieux*]

conscientious objector someone who refuses to be conscripted into a fighting unit because he is convinced that killing (in whatever cause) is wrong

con·scious (kɒ́nʃəs) *adj.* recognizing the existence, truth or fact of something, *he was conscious that his reception was cool* ‖ in the state of knowing what goes on around one, *is the patient conscious yet?* ‖ registered subjectively, *conscious duplicity* ‖ marked by the use of one's rational powers, *a conscious gesture* ‖ self-conscious ‖ intended, *a conscious snub* [fr. L. *conscius*, knowing with others or in oneself]

con·scious·ness (kɒ́nʃəsnis) *n.* the state of being conscious, esp. being in one's senses and aware of one's surroundings ‖ mental activity, including emotion and thought ‖ the upper level of mental life, as opposed to subconscious mental processes

con·scious·ness-ex·pand·ing (kɒ́nʃəsnəsexpǽndiŋ) *adj.* psychic condition in which mind appears to have greater-than-normal sensitivity or potential, e.g., under the influence of LSD

consciousness raising 1. providing a greater awareness. **2.** small-group technique whereby members, esp. feminists, discuss the political implications of their lives to enhance their political awareness —**consciousness-raising group** *n.*

con·script 1. (kənskrípt) *v.t.* to enlist by compulsion ‖ to commandeer for national use **2.** (kɒ́nskript) *n.* a recruit enrolled in the armed forces) by compulsion (cf. VOLUNTEER) **3.** (kɒ́nskript) *adj.* enlisted thus (usually conscripted) [fr. L. *conscribere* (*conscriptus*), to enroll]

conscript fathers (kɒ́nskript) (*hist.*) the senators of ancient Rome

con·scrip·tion (kənskrípʃən) *n.* compulsory enlistment for military or state service [fr. L. *conscriptio* (*conscriptionis*), enrollment]

conscription of wealth taxation or confiscation imposed by government in wartime

con·se·crate (kɒ́nsikreit) *pres. part.* **con·se·crat·ing** *past* and *past part.* **con·se·crat·ed** *v.t.* to make (someone) a king or a bishop by religious rite ‖ to make or declare holy, *the priest consecrated the offerings* ‖ to devote to a purpose, dedicate, *a life consecrated to poetry* [fr. L. *consecrare* (*consecratus*)]

con·se·cra·tion (kɒnsikréiʃən) *n.* the act of consecrating, esp. of the bread and wine in the Mass or Eucharist ‖ the ritual making of a bishop or king ‖ the state of being consecrated [fr. L. *consecratio* (*consecrationis*)]

con·se·cra·to·ry (kɒ́nsikrətɔri:, kɒ́nsikrətouri:) *adj.* serving to consecrate

con·se·cu·tion (kɒnsəkjú:ʃən) *n.* a train or sequence of deductions ‖ a sequence of events or things (words, tenses etc.) [fr. L. *consecutio* (*consecutionis*), sequence]

con·sec·u·tive (kənsékjutiv) *adj.* following in regular or unbroken order, *five consecutive victories* ‖ marked by logical sequence, *consecutive ideas* ‖ (*gram.*) expressing result, *a consecutive clause* ‖ (*mus.*) of intervals of the same kind moving in parallel sequence, e.g. C and G followed by D and A, *consecutive fifths* [F.]

con·sen·su·al (kənsénʃu:əl) *adj.* involving consent or mere consent, esp. (*law*) having validity by mutual consent without a written contract ‖ of actions which are involuntary, but accompanied by awareness of their performance [fr. L. *consensus*, agreement]

con·sen·sus (kənsénsəs) *pl.* **con·sen·sus·es** (kənsénsəs) *n.* concord (of opinion, evidence, authority, testimony etc.) [L.=agreement]

con·sent (kənsént) *n.* permission, acquiescence, approval, *the committee's consent is merely formal* ‖ agreement, *by common consent* **with one consent** unanimously, with no opposition [M.E. *consente* fr. O.F.]

consent *v.i.* to give assent [O.F. *consentir*]

con·sen·tient (kənsénʃənt) *adj.* agreeing in opinion, unanimous ‖ consenting (to something) [fr. L. *consentire*, to consent]

con·se·quence (kɒ́nsikwens, kɒ́nsikwəns) *n.* that which follows something and arises from it ‖ a logical inference, *it follows as a consequence that...* ‖ importance, *a matter of consequence* **in consequence of** as a result of **to take the consequences** to put up with a penalty, punishment or suffering brought about by one's own action [F. *conséquence*]

con·se·quent (kɒ́nsikwent, kɒ́nsikwənt) **1.** *n.* a thing that follows another in time or order ‖ (*math.*) the second term in a ratio, e.g. *y* in the ratio x: *y* **2.** *adj.* following as an effect or outcome, *his interview and consequent appointment, political decisions consequent on an event* ‖ following as a deduction, logically consistent [F. *conséquent*]

con·se·quen·tial (kɒnsikwénʃəl) *adj.* following as a consequence or corollary ‖ self-important, *a consequential manner* [fr. L. *consequentia*, a consequence]

consequential damages (*law*) damages arising indirectly

con·se·quent·ly (kónsikwəntli:, kónsikwəntli:) **1.** *adv.* accordingly, therefore **2.** *conj.* therefore, and so

con·serv·an·cy (kənsə́:rvənsi:) *pl.* **con·serv·an·cies** *n.* (*Br.*) a committee with authority to control a port or river, esp. the fishing rights ‖ conservation of natural resources [fr. L. *conservare*, to conserve]

con·ser·va·tion (kɒnsərvéifən) *n.* the act of keeping free from depletion, decay or injury, esp. works of art ‖ wise management and maintaining, *conservation of natural resources* ‖ official supervision of rivers and forests ‖ a district under such supervision **con·ser·vá·tion·al** *adj.* **con·ser·vá·tion·ist** *n.* someone who is active in the conserving of natural resources [fr. L. *conservatio (conservationis)*]

conservation of baryons (*phys.*) principle that the number of baryons in an isolated system remains constant regardless of decay or transformation

conservation of charge a principle in physics which states that charge is neither created nor destroyed and that when charges combine the resulting charge is the algebraic sum of the single charges

conservation of electricity conservation of charge

conservation of energy a principle in classical physics which states that the total energy of an isolated system remains constant although it may be converted from one form to another

conservation of leptons (*particle phys.*) principle that the number of leptons in an isolated system of elementary particles remains constant regardless of decay or transformation

conservation of mass a principle in classical physics which states that the mass of an isolated system remains constant

conservation of mass-energy a principle in modern physics which states that in an isolated system the sum of the total mass and total energy is constant where the interconversion of mass and energy is given by the mass-energy equation

conservation of momentum a principle in physics which states that the total linear momentum of an isolated system under the influence of no external force remains constant in magnitude and direction

con·serv·a·tism (kənsə́:rvətizəm) *n.* the state or quality of being conservative ‖ a political philosophy based on the maintenance of existing institutions, and preferring gradual development to abrupt change **Con·serv·a·tism** the policies and tenets of the Conservative party

con·serv·a·tive (kənsə́:rvətiv) **1.** *adj.* desiring to preserve existing institutions, and thus opposed to radical changes ‖ tending or desiring to conserve ‖ (*loosely*) moderate, cautious, *a conservative estimate* ‖ (*pop.*, of ideas, views etc.) old-fashioned ‖ considered to involve little risk, *a conservative investment* ‖ tending to preserve, keep from deteriorating **Conservative** of or relating to the Conservative party, its members etc. **2.** *n.* a person of conservative disposition ‖ something that tends to preserve **Conservative** a member of the Conservative party [F.]

Conservative party a British political party which developed (1830s) out of the Tory party, with the maintenance of existing institutions as its policy. It was split by Peel on the question of the repeal of the Corn Laws (1846), and reorganized by Disraeli, who brought in the Reform Act (1867) and much social legislation (1874–80). The Conservatives allied (1886) with the Liberal Unionists, led by Joseph Chamberlain, and had control of the government, except in 1886 and 1892–5, until the party split (1905) on the question of tariff reform. The Conservatives formed the government from 1922 to 1940, except in 1924 and 1929–31, and was generally more successful than its main rival, the Labour party, after the 2nd world war

con·ser·va·toire (kənsə́:rvətwár, kənsé:rvətwər) *n.* a music or art conservatory [F.]

con·ser·va·tor (kónsərveitər, kənsə́:rvətər) *n.* a custodian, someone who preserves from harm, esp. a member of a conservancy or a museum official [A.F. *conservatour*]

con·serv·a·to·ry (kənsə́:rvətɔri:, kənsə́:rvətouri:) *pl.* **con·serv·a·to·ries** *n.* a greenhouse (esp. one forming a room on an outside wall of a house) where exotic plants are kept ‖ a school of music or art [fr. L. *conservatorius*, conserving]

con·serve (kónsə:rv, kənsə́:rv) *n.* fruit etc. preserved in sugar [F.]

con·serve (kənsə́:rv) *pres. part.* **con·serv·ing** *past* and *past part.* **con·served** *v.t.* to preserve in a sound state ‖ to make a preserve of (fruit etc.) by cooking with sugar [F. *conserver*]

con·sid·er (kənsídər) *v.t.* to ponder, think out, weigh the advantages and disadvantages of ‖ to assess before reaching a decision, *the company is considering his claim* ‖ to take into one's reckoning ‖ to make allowances for, *you must consider his youth* ‖ to be sensitively thoughtful about, *consider his feelings* ‖ to believe, *they consider him innocent* ‖ *v.i.* to reflect or deliberate [F. *considérer*]

con·sid·er·a·ble (kənsídərəb'l) *adj.* quite large in amount, extent or degree ‖ important, *a considerable figure in local politics* **con·sid·er·a·bly** *adv.* [fr. M.L. *considerabilis*]

con·sid·er·ate (kənsídərit) *adj.* careful not to hurt the feelings of others or cause inconvenience to them [fr. L. *considerare (consideratus)*, to reflect]

con·sid·er·a·tion (kənsidəréifən) *n.* a considering, deliberation ‖ a point of importance, a thing worth considering as a reason ‖ a financial reward, payment ‖ considerateness, thoughtfulness for others ‖ importance, *of no consideration* **in consideration of** on account of, in return for, *a pension in consideration of long service* **on no consideration** in no circumstances **to leave out of consideration** not to include in one's reckoning **to take into consideration** to include in one's reckoning ‖ to make allowance for **under consideration** being considered, not yet decided [F. *considération*]

con·sid·ered (kənsídərd) *adj.* resulting from careful thought, *his considered opinion*

con·sid·er·ing (kənsídəriŋ) **1.** *prep.* in view of, *he plays well considering his age* **2.** *adv.* (*pop.*) taking all circumstances into account, *he did quite well, considering* **3.** *conj.* seeing that, *he behaves very well considering he was brought up badly*

con·sign (kənsáin) *v.t.* to send, *to consign goods by rail* ‖ to entrust, give over to another's charge ‖ to make over formally **con·sign·ee** (kɒnsaini:, kɒnsiní:, kɒnsainí:) *n.* a person to whom goods etc. are consigned or sent **consigner** *n.* *CONSIGNOR* [fr. L. *consignare*, to mark with a seal]

con·sign·ment (kənsáinmənt) *n.* a consigning ‖ a thing consigned ‖ a set of things sent together, *a large consignment arrived recently* **on consignment** (of goods) delivered to a merchant for sale but remaining the property of the sender until sold

con·sign·or, con·sign·er (kənsáinər) *n.* a person by whom goods are consigned

con·sist (kənsíst) *v.i.* (with 'of') to be made up or composed, *the program consists of three plays* ‖ (with 'in') to reside or lie essentially, *the advantage consists in its simplicity* [fr. L. *consistere*, to stand together]

con·sist·ence (kənsístəns) *n.* consistency **con·sist·en·cy** (kənsístənsi:) *pl.* **con·sist·en·cies** *n.* degree of solidity, or (of liquids) of density ‖ firm coherence in applying principles or a policy ‖ agreement, correspondence, *consistency between versions* [M. F. *consistance*]

con·sist·ent (kənsístənt) *adj.* in accordance, *his conduct is not consistent with his promises* ‖ true to principles or a policy, *a consistent advocate of peace* **con·síst·ent·ly** *adv.* in a consistent way ‖ regularly, *consistently late* [fr. L. *consistens (consistentis)* fr. *consistere*, to stand together]

con·sis·to·ri·al (kɒnsistóri:əl, kɒnsistóuri:əl) *adj.* of or relating to a consistory

con·sis·to·ry (kənsístəri:) *pl.* **con·sis·to·ries** *n.* an ecclesiastical council, esp. of the pope and cardinals ‖ a court or tribunal of any of various Churches [O.N. F. *consistorie*]

con·sol (kónsɒl) *n.* a long-range radio aid to navigation, the emissions of which, by means of their radio-frequency-modulation characteristics, enable bearings to be determined

con·sol·a·ble (kənsóuləb'l) *adj.* able to be consoled

Consolar an aircraft navigation system utilizing only a radio with signals transmitted in a rotating pattern to obtain an approximation of position (within 20 mi. at 2,500 mi.)

con·so·la·tion (kɒnsəléifən) *n.* the alleviation of suffering, grief, disappointment etc. by comforting ‖ an instance of this, or some circumstance which consoles [F.]

consolation prize a prize awarded as solace for failure

consolation race a race open only to those who failed in previous contests

con·sol·a·to·ry (kənsólətɔri:, kənsólətɒuri:) *adj.* offering or providing consolation [fr. L. *consolatorius*]

con·sole (kənsóul) *pres. part.* **con·sol·ing** *past* and *past part.* **con·soled** *v.t.* to bring consolation to, comfort in distress ‖ *v.i.* to be a consolation [F. *consoler*]

con·sole (kónsoul) *n.* a bracket supporting a shelf or cornice ‖ a table supported by brackets against a wall ‖ the part of an organ containing the keyboard or keyboards and stops ‖ a keyboard apparatus for remote control of stage lighting ‖ a grouping of controls, indicators, and similar electronic or mechanical equipment used to monitor readiness of and/or control specific functions of a system, such as a computer, missile checkout, or countdown ‖ a cabinet for a radio or television set standing on the floor [F.]

console table a table supported by brackets against a wall

con·sol·i·date (kənsólideit) *pres. part.* **con·sol·i·dat·ing** *past* and *past part.* **con·sol·i·dat·ed** *v.t.* to strengthen, make firm, *the reforms consolidated his position* ‖ (*mil.*) to strengthen (a recently captured position) ‖ to make or compress into a compact mass ‖ *v.i.* to become solid or firm ‖ to combine, merge, *the companies consolidated for greater efficiency* **con·sol·i·dá·tion** *n.* [fr. L. *consolidare (consolidatus)*, to make firm]

consolidation (*securities*) process of firming the market price following a substantial change in prices. Consolidation is considered customary preceding another price movement

con·sols (kónsɒlz, kənsɒ́lz) *pl. n.* (*Br.*) government securities which the government redeems at its own discretion, paying the fixed amount of interest each year until it decides to repay the capital [CONSOLIDATED ANNUITIES]

con·som·mé (kɒnsəméi) *n.* a clear soup made from poultry or meat [F.]

con·so·nance (kónsənəns) *n.* mutual fitness, agreement, *consonance between words and actions* ‖ harmony of sounds (opp. DISSONANCE) ‖ a sounding of two notes in harmony ‖ a repetition of consonant sounds at the ends of lines of verses after different vowel sounds (cf. ASSONANCE) ‖ (*phys.*) resonance [F.]

con·so·nant (kónsənənt) *adj.* having consonance, consistent, *behavior consonant with principles* ‖ harmonious (opp. DISSONANT) ‖ corresponding in sound, *consonant syllables* ‖ resonant [F.]

consonant *n.* a unit of speech sound (p, t etc.) which differs from a vowel in that there is some obstruction of the breath in its production ‖ the letter representing such a unit **con·so·nan·tal** (kɒnsənǽnt'l) *adj.* [F.]

con·sort 1. (kónsort) *n.* the non-reigning wife or husband of a reigning king or queen ‖ a ship accompanying another, esp. for protection in wartime ‖ a combination of musical instruments or singers, *a consort of viols* **in consort** in harmony ‖ in company (with) **2.** (kənsórt) *v.i.* to associate or keep company, *to consort with criminals* ‖ to harmonize, be in accord, *such behavior hardly consorts with his profession* [F. *consort* and *concert*]

con·sor·ti·um (kənsórfi:əm) *pl.* **con·sor·ti·a** (kənsórfi:ə), **con·sor·ti·ums** *n.* an international (esp. banking or financial) combination, to carry out some common purpose ‖ (*bot.*) the compound thallus of a lichen [L.=partnership]

con·spec·tus (kənspéktəs) *pl.* **con·spec·tus·es** *n.* a comprehensive survey of a subject ‖ a synopsis [L.]

con·spic·u·ous (kənspíkju:əs) *adj.* very readily perceived, *a conspicuous landmark* ‖ attracting attention, *a conspicuous display of wealth* [fr. L. *conspicuus*]

con·spir·a·cy (kənspírəsi:) *pl.* **con·spir·a·cies** *n.* a conspiring, esp. a joining secretly with others for an evil purpose ‖ a plot [fr. L. *conspiratio*]

conspiracy of silence a tacit agreement not to discuss something

con·spir·a·tor (kənspírətər) *n.* a person taking part in a conspiracy **con·spir·a·to·ri·al** (kənspirətóri:əl, kənspirətóuri:əl) *adj.* of or relating to conspiracy [M.E. *conspiratour* fr. L.]

con·spire (kənspáiər) *pres. part.* **con·spir·ing** *past* and *past part.* **con·spired** *v.i.* to combine secretly esp. for unlawful purposes ‖ (*rhet.*) to

CONCISE PRONUNCIATION KEY: **(a)** æ, c*a*t; ɑ, c*a*r; ɔ f*aw*n; ei, sn*a*ke. **(e)** e, h*e*n; i:, sh*ee*p; iə, d*ee*r; ɛə, b*ea*r. **(i)** i, f*i*sh; ai, t*i*ger; ʼ, b*ir*d. **(o)** o, *o*x; au, c*ow*; ou, g*oa*t; u, p*oo*r; ɔi, r*oy*al. **(u)** ʌ, d*u*ck; u, b*u*ll; u:, g*oo*se; ə, b*a*cillus; ju:, c*u*be. x, lo*ch*; θ, *th*ink; ð, bo*th*er; z, *Z*en; ʒ, cor*s*age; dʒ, sava*g*e; ŋ, oranguta*ng*; j, *y*ak; ʃ, *fi*sh; tʃ, fe*tch*; ʼl, rabb*le*; ʼn, redd*en*. Complete pronunciation key appears inside front cover.

cooperate towards an end, *the crowds and the sunshine conspired to make it a success* ‖ *v.t.* (*rhet.*) to devise, *to conspire someone's ruin* [F. *conspirer*]

Con·sta·ble (kʌ́nstəb'l, kɒ́nstəb'l), John (1776–1837), greatest of the English landscape painters. He is remarkable for the boldness of his handling, the 'dewy freshness' of his atmospheric effects, and for using actual recognizable parts of the English landscape, not idealized reminiscences of Italy. He was the last great painter in the tradition received from the Dutch 17th-c. landscape painters, and a forerunner of the Impressionists

con·sta·ble (kɒ́nstəb'l, *Br.* also kʌ́nstəb'l) *n.* a police constable ‖ (*hist.*) a high officer of a royal court ‖ (*Br.*) a warden of a royal castle [M.E. fr. O.F. *conestable*]

con·stab·u·lar·y (kənstǽbjuləri:) 1. *adj.* (*Br.*) pertaining to the police 2. *n. pl.* **con·stab·u·lar·ies** (*Br.*) the body of police in any area or country [fr. M.L. *constabularia*]

Con·stance (kɒ́nstəns) (*G.* Konstanz), an ancient German town (pop. 64,600) on Lake Constance: tourism, textile and other industries

Constance (*G.* Bodensee) a lake (area 207 sq. miles) through which the Rhine flows, at the junction of Switzerland, Germany and Austria, 1,309 ft above sea level

Constance, Council of a great council held (1414–18) to reform the Church. It ended the Great Schism (1378–1417), condemned (1415) the teachings of Wyclif, and executed (1415) Hus

con·stan·cy (kɒ́nstənsi:) *n.* steadfastness, fidelity, esp. in love, friendship etc. ‖ firm adherence to principles ‖ fortitude, endurance ‖ stability, *constancy of temperature* [fr. L. *constantia*]

Con·stant (kɔ̃stɑ̃), Benjamin (Benjamin Henri Constant de Rebecque, 1767–1830), French politician and author. His 'Adolphe' (1806, published 1816) is one of the great psychological novels: Romantic in that it deals with a young introspective sensitive hero and a tragic love affair, classical in the justness with which Adolphe analyzes and judges his behavior

con·stant (kɒ́nstənt) 1. *adj.* continual, unceasing, *constant nagging* ‖ unremitting, *constant attention* ‖ faithful, unwavering, *a constant friend* ‖ not subject to variation, uniform 2. *n.* (*math., phys.*) a quantity or factor that does not change, that may be universal (e.g. the circular ratio [π]), that may apply only to a particular operation or circumstance, or that may be characteristic of a substance or instrument (cf. VARIABLE) [F.]

Con·stan·ta (kɒnstɑ́ntsɑ) Rumania's chief port (pop. 256,900) on the Black Sea, founded by Constantine the Great. It is connected by pipeline to the Ploesti oil fields

con·stant·an (kɒ́nstəntæn) *n.* an alloy of copper and nickel. The variation of its electrical resistance with temperature is almost negligible

constant composition, law of *PROUST, J. L.

constant dollar estimate (*economics*) estimates made removing the effects of price changes from statistical data reported in current dollars

Con·stan·tine I (kɒ́nstəntiːn, kɒ́nstəntain) 'the Great' (c. 280–337), first Christian Roman emperor (306–37), converted (312) on the eve of a battle. He established toleration of Christianity throughout the empire (Edict of Milan, 313), and dealt with the Donatist schism and the Arian heresy (Council of Nicaea, 325). He defeated the Eastern emperor (324) and moved his capital to Constantinople (330) to face the Goths

Constantine V Cop·ron·y·mus (kɒprónimǝs) (718–75), Byzantine emperor (740–75). His suppression of the monasteries led the papacy to look to Pépin, king of the Franks, for support, instead of to Constantinople

Constantine VII Por·phy·ro·gen·i·tus (pɔrfirədʒénitəs) (905–59), Byzantine emperor (913–59). A patron of art and literature, he inspired an exhaustive compilation of all contemporary knowledge

Constantine IX Mo·nom·a·chus (mənómǝkəs) (1000–55), Byzantine emperor (1042–55). His neglect of military matters led to the loss of most of the Italian possessions (1053) and contributed to the weakening of the empire

Constantine XI (or XII) (1405–53), Byzantine emperor (1449–53). He was the last emperor before Constantinople fell to the Turks (1453)

Constantine I (1868–1923), king of Greece (1913–17, 1920–22). He was pro-German, and

was exiled in 1917. He was recalled by plebiscite in 1920, but had to abdicate after defeat by the Turks

Constantine II (1940–), king of Greece (1964–67), son of King Paul. He supported (Apr. 26, 1967) the government set up after an army coup d'état (Apr. 21, 1967), but attempted (Dec. 1967) a counter coup, failed, and went into exile. He was deposed in 1978 by the military government, and a republic was established by a national referendum

Constantine a town (pop. 350,200) of Algeria, on isolated chalk rock and almost surrounded by the gorges of the Rummel. It is a market and industrial center for E. and S. Algeria. University

Con·stan·ti·no·ple (kɒnstæntinóup'l) an ancient city, now part of Istanbul (*BYZANTIUM). It dominates the Golden Horn on the European side of the Bosporus. It remained, after the empire in the west collapsed, the capital of the Byzantine Empire until taken by the Turks (1453), except for an interval as capital of the Latin Empire of Constantinople (1204–61). It was the Turkish capital until 1923

Constantinople, Council of the second ecumenical council, convened (381) by Theodosius I. It confirmed the decisions of the Council of Nicaea (325) and elaborated the Nicene Creed

con·stant-level balloon (kɒ́nstəntlevəl) lighter-than-air vehicle designed to remain at a constant altitude for weeks or months *syn.* constant-pressure balloon

con·stant·ly (kɒ́nstəntli:) *adv.* without stopping, continuously ‖ frequently

con·sta·tive (kɒ́nstətiv) *adj.* (*linguistics*) 1. of a statement of condition, *I am gone* Cf PERFORMATIVE 2. implying a wish, hopes, or plan, but not necessarily a promise

con·stel·late (kɒ́nstəleit) *pres. part.* **con·stel·lat·ing** *past* and *past part.* **con·stel·lat·ed** *v.t.* to stud, adorn in myriads ‖ to unite in a radiant cluster ‖ *v.i.* to cluster like stars in a constellation [fr. L. *constellatus*, starred]

con·stel·la·tion (kɒnstəléiʃən) *n.* a group of fixed stars, arbitrarily considered together, usually named with reference to an imaginary outline enclosing them ‖ a group of brilliant people ‖ (*psychoanal.*) a group of conditions affecting behavior [F.]

con·ster·nate (kɒ́nstərneit) *pres. part.* **con·ster·nat·ing** *past* and *past part.* **con·ster·nat·ed** *v.t.* to fill with dismay or panic [fr. L. *consternare* (*consternatus*)]

con·ster·na·tion (kɒnstərnéiʃən) *n.* surprise and alarm, astonishment, dismay [F.]

con·sti·pate (kɒ́nstəpeit) *pres. part.* **con·sti·pat·ing** *past* and *past part.* **con·sti·pat·ed** *v.i.* to cause constipation ‖ *v.t.* to cause constipation in (someone) [fr. L. *constipare* (*constipatus*), to press together]

con·sti·pa·tion (kɒnstəpéiʃən) *n.* infrequent passage of dry hardened feces due to poor functioning of the bowels [F.]

con·stit·u·en·cy (kənstítʃuːənsi:) *pl.* **con·stit·u·en·cies** *n.* a body of voters represented by an officeholder ‖ an area or community represented thus

con·stit·u·ent (kənstítʃuːənt) 1. *adj.* forming a basic part of a whole, *flour is a constituent element of bread* ‖ having power to elect, *a constituent body* ‖ charged with making or modifying a political constitution, *a constituent assembly* 2. *n.* an essential part, component ‖ a member of a constituency [fr. L. *constituens* (*constituentis*) fr. *constituere*, to constitute]

constituent analysis (*linguistics*) analysis of verbal material into identifiable elements seen as layers of other immediate constituents (IC) and unanalyzable residual material which are termed ultimate constituents (UC)

con·sti·tute (kɒ́nstituːt, kɒ́nstitjuːt) *pres. part.* **con·sti·tut·ing** *past* and *past part.* **con·sti·tut·ed** *v.t.* to appoint to an office or function, *the meeting constituted him chairman* ‖ to set up, establish, *that constitutes a precedent* ‖ to give legal form to (a court, tribunal etc.) ‖ to be the constituent element of, make up, *the best of three games constitutes a win* ‖ (*pass.*) to have certain qualities, *he is so constituted that he needs very little sleep* [fr. L. *constituere* (*constitutus*)]

'Constitution' (kɒnstitúːʃən, kɒnstitjúːʃən) U.S. frigate, one of the first three built for the U.S. Navy, and launched in 1797. She defeated (Aug. 19, 1812) the British frigate 'Guerrière', earning the title 'Old Ironsides' when the

British shot failed to pierce her sides. She was restored (1927–31) and permanently docked in Boston

con·sti·tu·tion (kɒnstitúːʃən, kɒnstitjúːʃən) *n.* the act of constituting, a setting up, *the constitution of a committee* ‖ the total physical condition of the body, *a healthy constitution* ‖ total moral or mental makeup, or way in which something is made up ‖ molecular structure, physical and chemical ‖ the set of principles adopted by a state or society for its government ‖ a decree or ordinance, *the Constitutions of Clarendon* **con·sti·tu·tion·al** 1. *adj.* of, due to, or inherent in one's constitution ‖ of or pertaining to a political constitution ‖ authorized by the constitution, *constitutional changes in the law* ‖ loyal to the constitution, *a constitutional opposition* ‖ limited by the constitution, *constitutional monarchy* 2. *n.* a regular walk taken for one's health [F.]
—A political constitution lays down the manner and means by which power shall be exercised by the executive, legislature and judicature. Some countries, e.g. the U.S.A., have a written constitution Others have unwritten constitutions, although, as in Great Britain, there may be many written rules of law: e.g. Bill of Rights, Parliament Act, Representation of the Peoples Act, Judicature Act, Act of Settlement. Constitutions are defined as flexible or rigid according to the ease with which they may be amended: e.g. the U.S. constitution provides for a long and difficult process for amendment, whereas in Britain the constitution may be modified simply by parliamentary majority

Constitutional Convention (*Am. hist.*) the assembly which drew up (1787) the constitution of the U.S.A.

con·sti·tu·tion·al·ism (kɒnstitúːʃən'lizəm, kɒnstitjúːʃən'lizəm) *n.* a constitutional system of government ‖ adherence to the principles of such government

con·sti·tu·tion·al·ist (kɒnstitúːʃən'list, kɒnstitjúːʃən'list) *n.* a supporter of constitutional government ‖ a writer on or student of constitutionalism

con·sti·tu·tion·al·i·ty (kɒnstitu:ʃənǽliti:, kɒnstitju:ʃənǽliti:) *n.* the state or quality of being constitutional

constitutional law the collection of rules which defines the powers, organization and responsibilities of central and local government. In the U.S.A. the term is restricted to the law that is handed down by the courts in interpreting the written constitution. (The Supreme Court has at times had to resort, however, to common law for defining terms used in the constitution which imply previous common law.) In England the term covers statutes (e.g. Magna Carta, Bill of Rights, Parliament Act), principles evolved from court decisions and common law, and conventions based on precedent and usage which, although not strictly law, if violated might involve a breach of law. In other countries of Europe there has also evolved a large body of administrative law. Administrative courts deal with the relations between state officials and citizens, which in England and the U.S.A. are dealt with by the ordinary courts

con·sti·tu·tion·al·ly (kɒnstitúːʃən'liː, kɒnstitjúːʃən'liː) *adv.* in accordance with a political constitution or the constitution, *to govern constitutionally*

con·sti·tu·tive (kɒ́nstitutiv, kɒ́nstitjutiv) *adj.* of that which essentially constitutes something ‖ of that which enters into the constitution of something [fr. L. *constituere* (*constitutus*), to constitute]

con·strain (kənstréin) *v.t.* to persuade by strong pressure or force, compel **con·strained** *adj.* ill at ease and embarrassed through repression of natural feelings **con·strain·ed·ly** (kənstréinidliː) *adv.* [fr. O. F. *constreindre*]

con·straint (kənstréint) *n.* use of force to influence or prevent an action ‖ the state or quality of being compelled to do or not do something ‖ restricted liberty ‖ the sense of being ill at ease [O.F. *constreinte*]

con·strict (kənstríkt) *v.t.* to compress, make narrower ‖ to cause to contract, *to constrict a vein* **con·strict·ed** *adj.* narrow, limited, *a constricted outlook* **con·stric·tion** *n.* tightness ‖ a constricted part ‖ something that constricts **con·stric·tive** *adj.* tending to constrict [fr. L. *constringere* (*constrictus*)]

con·stric·tor (kənstríktər) *n.* (*anat.*) a muscle which narrows an orifice or constricts an organ ‖ (*biol.*) a snake which kills its prey by squeez-

CONCISE PRONUNCIATION KEY: **(a)** æ, c*a*t; ɑ, c*a*r; ɔ f*aw*n; ei, sn*a*ke. **(e)** e, h*e*n; iː, sh*ee*p; iə, d*ee*r; ɛə, b*ea*r. **(i)** i, f*i*sh; ai, t*i*ger; əː, b*i*rd. **(o)** o, *o*x; au, c*ow*; ou, g*oa*t; u, p*oo*r; ɔi, r*oy*al. **(u)** ʌ, d*u*ck; u, b*u*ll; uː, g*oo*se; ə, b*a*cillus; juː, c*u*be. x, lo*ch*; θ, *th*ink; ð, *b*o*th*er; z, *Z*en; ʒ, cor*s*age; dʒ, sa*v*age; ŋ, oranguta*ng*; j, *y*ak; ʃ, *f*ish; tʃ, fe*tch*; 'l, rabb*le*; 'n, redd*en*. Complete pronunciation key appears inside front cover.

ing or constriction, e.g. a python, boa constrictor etc. ‖ a surgical instrument for constricting [L. =that which constricts]

con·strin·gent (kənstríndʒənt) *adj.* causing constriction [fr. L. *constringens* (*constringentis*) fr. *constringere*, to constrict]

con·stru·a·ble (kənstruː'əb'l) *adj.* able or liable to be construed

con·struct 1. (kənstrʌ́kt) *v.t.* to put together, build ‖ to arrange mentally, *to construct a theory* ‖ (*geom.*) to draw, *construct a triangle on base AB* ‖ to combine (words) meaningfully, *to construct a sentence* **2.** (kónstrʌkt) *n.* (*psychol.*) a mental construction **con·strúc·ter, con·strúc·tor** *n.* [fr. L. *construere* (*constructus*), to pile up]

con·struc·tion (kənstrʌ́kʃən) *n.* a thing constructed ‖ the process of constructing ‖ the manner of building with regard to materials, *the construction is lath and plaster* ‖ the arrangement and interrelation of words in a sentence ‖ meaning, interpretation, *to put a wrong construction on a statement* ‖ a nonrepresentational work of sculpture made from various components **under construction** in process of being constructed **con·strúc·tion·al** *adj.* pertaining to construction ‖ structural **con·strúc·tion·ist** *n.* someone who interprets a law or document in a specified way, *a liberal constructionist* [fr. L. *constructio* (*constructionis*)]

con·struc·tive (kənstrʌ́ktiv) *adj.* tending to or helping to construct (opp. DESTRUCTIVE), *constructive criticism* ‖ of construction, esp. the construction of a building, or comparable activity, *constructive toys* ‖ (*law*) not direct or expressed, inferred, *constructive permission* **con·strúc·tiv·ism** *n.* one of the first movements whose aim was to create completely nonobjective sculpture. Antoine Pevsner and his brother Naum Gabo were its originators. They thought of sculpture essentially in terms of contemporary architecture. Their works give a strong impression of planes turning, moving toward or away from each other in calculated relationships. Thin metal rods, wires or pieces of plastic placed closely together form the planes and emphasize the sense of movement [fr. M.L. *constructivus*]

constructor *CONSTRUCT

Constructs trade name of a computer system designed by Control Data Corporation to produce construction drawings

con·strue (kənstrúː) *pres. part.* **con·stru·ing** *past* and *past part.* **con·strued** *v.t.* to analyze (a sentence or clause) grammatically ‖ to interpret the meaning of (a statement) ‖ to combine (words) grammatically, 'aware' is construed with 'of' or 'that' ‖ *v.i.* to admit of grammatical analysis, *this sentence does not construe* (i.e. is ungrammatical) [M.E. *construen* fr. L.]

con·sub·stan·tial (kɒnsəbstǽnʃəl) *adj.* (esp. *theol.*) of the same kind, essence or nature [fr. L. *consubstantialis*]

con·sub·stan·ti·al·i·ty (kɒnsəbstænʃiːǽliti:) *n.* (esp. *theol.*) the state or quality of being consubstantial [fr. L. *consubstantialitas*]

con·sub·stan·ti·ate (kɒnsəbstǽnʃieit) *pres. part.* **con·sub·stan·ti·at·ing** *past* and *past part.* **con·sub·stan·ti·at·ed** *v.t.* to unite in one common substance [fr. M.L. *consubstantiare* (*consubstantiatus*)]

con·sub·stan·ti·a·tion (kɒnsəbstænʃiːéiʃən) *n.* (*theol.*) the Lutheran doctrine of the mode of Christ's presence in the Eucharist, the divine substance coexisting with the substance of the bread and wine (cf. IMPANATION, cf. TRANSUBSTANTIATION) [fr. L.L. *consubstantiatio* (*consubstantiationis*)]

con·sue·tude (kónswituːd, kónswitjuːd) *n.* (*rhet.*) custom, habit, social usage [O.F.]

con·sue·tu·di·nar·y (kɒnswituː'd'nɛri:, kɒnswitjuː'd'nɛri:) **1.** *adj.* customary, consuetudinary *law* **2.** *n. pl.* **con·sue·tu·di·nar·ies** a manual of ritual devotions or ceremonial usage [fr. L. *consuetudinarius*]

con·sul (kónsəl) *n.* an agent appointed by a country to look after the interests of its citizens and its commerce in a foreign town ‖ (*hist.*) either of two joint chief magistrates of ancient Rome ‖ (*hist.*) one of the rulers of France under the Consulate [fr. L. *consularis*]

con·su·lar (kónsələr) *adj.* pertaining to a consul [fr. L. *consularis*]

con·su·late (kónsəlit) *n.* the premises or establishment of a consul ‖ the term of office of a consul ‖ (*hist.*) the office of a Roman consul **Consulate** the French government Nov. 10, 1799–May 18, 1804. Originally a three-man

government, it was rapidly dominated by Napoleon, who became first consul for life (1802) and emperor (1804) [fr. L. *consulatus*]

con·sult (kənsʌ́lt) *v.t.* to seek advice from, *to consult a lawyer* ‖ to seek information from, *to consult a dictionary* ‖ to test, find out, *to consult someone's feelings* ‖ *v.i.* to reflect (with others), sit in council, *to consult with one's colleagues* [fr. L. *consultare*]

con·sult·ant (kənsʌ́ltənt) *n.* a person (engineer, doctor etc.) giving expert or professional advice [fr. L. *consultans* (*consultantis*) fr. *consultare*, to consult]

Consultants Club exclusive group of industrial nations that consult annually on major economic policy developments

con·sul·ta·tion (kɒnsəltéiʃən) *n.* the act of consulting, *consultation with a lawyer* ‖ a conference to discuss a problem, esp. among lawyers or doctors [F.]

con·sul·ta·tive (kənsʌ́ltətiv) *adj.* of or having to do with consultation

con·sul·ta·to·ry (kənsʌ́ltətɒri, kənsʌ́ltətɒuri:) *adj.* consultative [fr. L. *consultatorius*]

con·sult·ing (kənsʌ́ltiŋ) *adj.* specializing in giving professional advice within a profession or to the public

con·sum·a·ble (kənsúːməb'l) **1.** *adj.* that may be eaten ‖ that may be exhausted, used up (e.g. of nonproductive goods as distinguished from capital goods) **2.** *n.* a consumable commodity

con·sume (kənsúːm) *pres. part.* **con·sum·ing** *past* and *past part.* **con·sumed** *v.t.* to eat or drink up ‖ to destroy by burning, *fire consumed the whole house* or by wastefulness, *to consume an inheritance* ‖ to waste or absorb, *a time-consuming activity* **con·súmed** *adj.* eaten up or as if eaten up, *consumed with envy* [fr. L. *consumere*]

con·sum·er (kənsúːmər) *n.* someone who uses articles made by another (opp. PRODUCER)

consumer durables consumer goods not consumed in a single use, with a minimum useful life of three yrs.; e.g., appliances, homes, and esp. those that perform multiple services, such as automobiles

consumer goods those goods which satisfy individual needs directly, e.g. food, clothing, refrigerators (as opposed to producer goods)

con·sum·er·ism (kənsúːmərizəm) **1.** program to promote consumer interests including protection of the environment, restraints on abuse by business, etc. —**consumerist** *n. Cf* NADERISM **2.** promotion of growth of increased use of goods

consumer price index (*economics*) a monthly index based on the composite cost of selected goods and services used by working-class households based on 1967 costs *Cf* PRICE INDEX

con·sum·mate 1. (kənsʌ́mit, kónsəmit) *adj.* complete, perfect, supreme, *consummate skill, a consummate liar* **2.** (kónsəmeit) *v.t. pres. part.* **con·sum·mat·ing** *past* and *past part.* **con·sum·mat·ed** to bring to completion or perfection, esp. to complete (a marriage) by sexual intercourse [fr. L. *consummare* (*consummatus*), to sum up]

con·sum·ma·tion (kɒnsəméiʃən) *n.* the act of completing (esp. a marriage by sexual intercourse) ‖ perfection, *consummation of bliss* ‖ fulfillment, *the consummation of a life's work* [O.F. *consommation*]

con·sump·tion (kənsʌ́mpʃən) *n.* a consuming ‖ an amount consumed ‖ (*econ.*) the use and enjoyment of goods and services by consumers or producers ‖ (*pop.*) tuberculosis of the lungs [fr. L. *consumptio* (*consumptionis*)]

con·sump·tive (kənsʌ́mptiv) **1.** *adj.* of or for consumption ‖ (*pop.*) suffering from or prone to pulmonary tuberculosis **2.** *n.* (*pop.*) a person suffering from tuberculosis of the lungs [fr. L. *consumere* (*consumptus*)]

con·tact (kóntækt) **1.** *n.* the state of touching or meeting ‖ a coming into association or establishing of communication, *to make contact with one's neighbors* ‖ a person who may be helpful to one, *social contacts* ‖ (*med.*) a person who has been exposed to infection and may carry and transmit a disease ‖ a junction of two conductors enabling an electric current to flow from one to the other ‖ a device for effecting such a junction **to be in contact with** to meet, esp. at intervals **2.** *v.t.* to get in touch with [fr. L. *contingere* (*contactus*), to touch together]

contact angle *ANGLE OF CONTACT

contact electricity electricity arising from the contact of two dissimilar bodies

contact flying the navigating of an aircraft by observing landmarks (cf. INSTRUMENT FLYING)

contact inhibition (*biol.*) the phenomenon of cessation of cell division, when cells in a tissue culture establish contact with other cells

contact lens a thin glass or plastic lens designed to fit over the cornea of the eye to correct certain sight defects

contact lens (*optics*) optically adjusted lens worn over the cornea to correct vision

contact maker (*elec.*) a device for making, or for making and breaking, a contact

con·tac·tor (kóntæktər, kəntǽktər) *n.* a device for repeatedly making and breaking an electric circuit

contact print a photographic print made from exposure through a negative directly in contact with the sensitized paper

con·ta·gion (kəntéidʒən) *n.* the direct or indirect transmission of disease from one person to another ‖ a contagious disease ‖ the spreading of an influence (e.g. enthusiasm, panic) from person to person

con·ta·gious (kəntéidʒəs) *adj.* (of diseases) catching, communicable by direct or indirect contact (cf. INFECTIOUS) ‖ (of persons) liable to pass on such a disease ‖ easily spreading, *contagious laughter* [O.F. *contagieus*]

con·tain (kəntéin) *v.t.* to enclose, *the cupboard contains books* ‖ to have capacity for, hold, *the bottle contains two pints* ‖ to include, *this book contains illustrations* ‖ to comprise, *that block contains 8 garages* ‖ (*math.*) to be a multiple of without remainder, *10 contains 2 and 5* ‖ to enclose, bound, *lines XY, XZ contain the angle YXZ* ‖ to restrain (an enemy force) from moving ‖ to control (oneself or one's feelings) **con·táin·er** *n.* a carton, crate, jar, bottle etc. for receiving and holding something [O.F. *contenir*]

con·tain·er·i·za·tion (kənteinərizéiʃən) *n.* system of packing less-than-carload or less-than-shipload packages destined for a single destination into single standard containers for more efficient handling *syn.* container shipping — **containerize** *v.* to utilize this system —**container ship** *n.* ship adapted for containers

container ship a cargo ship in which all the cargo is packed in uniform containers, to speed up off-loading and turnabout

con·tain·ment (kəntéinmənt) *n.* a containing or being contained

containment U.S. policy of firm and long-term inhibition of U.S.S.R. expansion

con·tam·i·nate (kəntǽmineit) *pres. part.* **con·tam·i·nat·ing** *past* and *past part.* **con·tam·i·nat·ed** *v.t.* to infect with a contagious disease ‖ to pollute ‖ to harm morally **con·tam·i·ná·tion** *n.* [fr. L. *contaminare* (*contaminatus*), to defile]

con·tan·go (kəntǽŋgou) *pl.* **con·tan·gos, con·tan·goes** *n.* (*Br., stock exchange*) a premium paid by a buyer to the seller of stock for postponing delivery till next settling day [perh. fr. Span. *contengo*, check]

contango day (*Br., stock exchange*) continuation day, the second day before settling day

cont. continued

con·temn (kəntém) *v.t.* (*rhet.*) to treat with contempt, despise [O.F. *contemner*]

con·tem·plate (kóntəmpleit, kəntémpleit) *pres. part.* **con·tem·plat·ing** *past* and *past part.* **con·tem·plat·ed** *v.t.* to look steadily at ‖ to consider attentively ‖ to intend, but not as part of an immediate plan, *to contemplate retiring* ‖ *v.i.* to meditate or ponder **con·tem·plá·tion** *n.* meditation, concentration of the mind on an intellectual or religious subject ‖ the act of looking attentively at something ‖ the process of considering with a view to a decision, *no changes are in contemplation* [fr. L. *contemplari* (*contemplatus*)]

con·tem·pla·tive 1. (kəntémplətiv, kóntəmpleitiv) *adj.* concerned with or given to contemplation, thoughtful ‖ (kóntəmplətiv, of religious orders) devoted to prayer and meditation (as distinct from active orders) **2.** *n.* (kəntémplətiv) a contemplative monk or nun [O.F. *contemplatif*]

con·tem·pla·tor (kóntəmpleitər) *n.* someone who contemplates

con·tem·po·ra·ne·i·ty (kəntempərəníːiti:) *n.* the quality or state of being contemporaneous

con·tem·po·ra·ne·ous (kəntempəréiniːəs) *adj.* living, happening at the same time, *early industrialism was contemporaneous with enclosures* ‖ covering the same period of time [fr. L. *contemporaneus*]

CONCISE PRONUNCIATION KEY: (**a**) æ, c*a*t; ɑ, c*a*r; ɔ f*aw*n; ei, sn*a*ke. (**e**) e, h*e*n; iː, sh*ee*p; iə, d*ee*r; ɛə, b*ea*r. (**i**) i, f*i*sh; ai, t*i*ger; əː, b*i*rd. (**o**) o, *o*x; au, c*ow*; ou, g*oa*t; u, p*oo*r; ɔi, r*oy*al. (**u**) ʌ, d*u*ck; u, b*u*ll; uː, g*oo*se; ə, b*a*cill*u*s; juː, c*u*be. x, lo*ch*; θ, *th*ink; ð, bo*th*er; z, *Z*en; ʒ, cor*s*age; dʒ, sava*g*e; ŋ, orangutan*g*; j, *y*ak; ʃ, *fi*sh; tʃ, fe*tch*; 'l, rabb*le*; 'n, redd*en*. Complete pronunciation key appears inside front cover.

con·tem·po·rar·y (kəntémpərɛri:) **1.** *adj.* belonging to the same time, contemporaneous ‖ (*pop.*) modern, *contemporary furniture* **2.** *n. pl.* **con·tem·po·rar·ies** a person living at the same time as another, *he is my contemporary at college* ‖ a person of the same or nearly the same age as another, *he has little in common with his contemporaries* ‖ a newspaper's name for another currently published paper [fr. L. *con-*, with + *temporarius*, of time]

con·tem·po·rize (kəntémpəraiz) *pres. part.* **con·tem·po·riz·ing** *past* and *past part.* **con·tem·po·rized** *v.t.* to make contemporary ‖ *v.i.* to be contemporary [fr. L.L. *contemporare*]

con·tempt (kəntémpt) *n.* an attitude to something which one despises as worthless, insignificant or vile ‖ total disregard, *contempt for danger* ‖ (*law*) disobedience of lawful orders **to bring into contempt** to produce contempt for **to hold in contempt** to feel contempt for [fr. L. *contemnere* (*contemptus*), to despise]

con·tempt·i·bil·i·ty (kəntəmptəbíliti:) *n.* the state or quality of being contemptible

con·tempt·i·ble (kəntémptəb'l) *adj.* worthy of contempt or scorn **con·tempt·i·bly** *adv.* [fr. L. *contemptibilis*]

contempt of court disobedience to the order of a court, or disregard for its dignity

con·temp·tu·ous (kəntémptʃu:əs) *adj.* feeling or showing contempt [fr. L. *contemnere* (*contemptus*), to despise]

con·tend (kənténd) *v.i.* to struggle in rivalry ‖ to conflict, *contending passions* ‖ to argue ‖ (with 'with') to struggle (e.g. with hardship or difficulty) ‖ *v.t.* to assert, esp. against opposition [fr. L. *contendere*, to strive after]

con·tent (kəntént) *v.t.* to make content or satisfied **to content oneself with** to make do with, resign oneself to having only, *to content oneself with a frugal meal* [F. *contenter*]

con·tent (kəntént) **1.** *adj.* satisfied, not displeased **to rest content** to be at peace with oneself, *he won't rest content until she buys it* ‖ to decide to refrain from further effort or research etc., *let us rest content with that* **2.** *n.* the state of being contented or satisfied **to one's heart's content** as much as one could wish [F.]

con·tent (kóntent) *n.* (usually *pl.*) that which is contained, *the contents of a bottle* ‖ (usually *pl.*) a summary of subjects treated in a book, *table of contents* ‖ capacity (of a vessel), *a content of 40 gallons* ‖ the amount of a certain substance contained, *the vitamin content of a food* ‖ the volume of a solid ‖ the gist of a speech or argument ‖ the substance, matter (of a book) ‖ significance (of a work of art), *it is clever but lacks content* [fr. L. *continere* (*contentus*), to contain]

con·tent·ed (kənténtid) *adj.* enjoying or showing contentment

con·ten·tion (kənténʃən) *n.* the act of contending ‖ a struggle, debate, controversy ‖ an opinion maintained in discussion [F.]

con·ten·tious (kənténʃəs) *adj.* given to contention, quarrelsome ‖ likely to cause argument [fr. F. *contentieux*]

con·tent·ment (kənténtmənt) *n.* the state or quality of being content

con·ter·mi·nal (kəntə́:rmin'l) *adj.* having a boundary in common [fr. M.L. *conterminalis*]

con·ter·mi·nous (kəntə́:rminəs) *adj.* conterminal, having common limits ‖ meeting at the ends ‖ occupying the same space or time, coextensive [fr. L. *conterminus*]

con·test 1. (kəntést) *v.t.* to call in question, dispute, *to contest a statement* ‖ to refuse to recognize as lawful, *to contest a will* ‖ to strive to win or hold, *to contest every inch of ground* ‖ (*Br.*) to compete for (esp. a seat in parliament) ‖ (*Br.*) to be a candidate in, *to contest an election* ‖ *v.i.* to strive, struggle **2.** (kóntest) *n.* a trial of skill ‖ a competition ‖ a struggle for domination [F. *contester*]

con·test·ant (kəntéstənt) *n.* someone who contests, in a fight, match, (*Br.*) election, or court of law [F.]

con·tes·ta·tion (kɒntestéiʃən) *n.* a controversy ‖ a contesting ‖ an assertion [fr. L. *contestatio* (*contestationis*)]

con·text (kóntekst) *n.* the parts of a book, speech etc. which precede or follow a word or passage and affect its significance ‖ the conditions or circumstances which affect something, *crime has to be studied in its social context* **con-**

tex·tu·al (kəntékstʃu:əl) *adj.* [fr. L. *contexere* (*contextus*), to weave]

context of situation (*linguistics*) term in Firthian grammar for the nonlinguistic environment of utterances, e.g., number of listeners, the position of speaker

con·ti·gu·i·ty (kɒntigjú:iti:) *n.* the state of being contiguous [fr. F. *contiguité*]

con·tig·u·ous (kəntígju:əs) *adj.* in contact, touching, *contiguous territories* ‖ neighboring ‖ next in order or in time, *contiguous events* [fr. L. *contiguus*]

con·ti·nence (kóntinəns) *n.* the state or quality of being continent

con·ti·nent (kóntinənt) *adj.* abstaining from sexual intercourse ‖ able to retain (feces, urine) voluntarily [O.F.]

continent *n.* one of the seven great land masses of the world (Europe, Asia, Africa, North America, South America, Australia, Antarctica) **the Continent** the mainland of Europe **con·ti·nen·tal** (kɒntinént'l) **1.** *adj.* belonging to or characteristic of a continent ‖ belonging to or characteristic of the mainland of Europe, *continental food* **Continental** (*Am. hist.*) of the colonies collectively at the time of the Revolutionary War **2.** *n.* an inhabitant of the European continent **Continental** (*Am. hist.*) a soldier in the Continental Army in the Revolutionary War [fr. L. *continens* (*continentis*), continuous mass of land]

Continental Army the small regular army of state regiments, raised by the patriots, which provided the hard core of resistance in the American Revolutionary War

continental climate the climate of the center of continents in the temperate latitudes, characterized by large differences between summer and winter temperatures

Continental Congress (*Am. hist.*) one of several legislative congresses (1774–89) held at the time of the Revolutionary War and responsible for the Declaration of Independence (1776) and the Articles of Confederation (1777)

Continental Divide the watershed of North America, separating the rivers flowing west to the Pacific from those flowing north and east to the Arctic and Atlantic. It coincides with the Rocky Mtns, the central plateau of Mexico, and the Central American cordilleras

continental drift the theory that the continents once formed a solid land mass and have very slowly drifted to their present positions

con·ti·nent·al-seat·ing (kɒntinəntlsí:tiŋ) *adj.* of public assemblies that provide no central aisle but allow greater distance between seating rows to facilitate passage

continental shelf the underwater plain on the borders of most continents, descending in a slope to deep water

continental slope the steep slope from the continental shelf to the ocean depths

Continental System (*hist.*) an attempted economic blockade of Britain by Napoleon. It was begun by his Berlin Decree (1806), barring trade between Britain and the ports of continental Europe, but it proved impossible to enforce, and had collapsed by 1812

con·tin·gen·cy (kəntíndʒənsi:) *pl.* **con·tin·gen·cies** *n.* the quality or state of being contingent ‖ something likely but not certain to happen ‖ something dependent on a probable but not certain event ‖ an unforeseeable event or circumstance, such as is prudently allowed for in budgeting ‖ an incidental quality, expense etc. [fr. L. *contingere*, to touch]

contingency account a reserve set aside against unforeseen expense

con·tin·gent (kəntíndʒənt) **1.** *adj.* liable but not certain to happen ‖ dependent on something that may not occur ‖ incidental, *risks contingent to mining* ‖ conditional, dependent, *the agreement is contingent on getting these concessions* ‖ accidental, *shortage of forestry workers was a contingent result of the war* ‖ (*logic*) established by sensory observation, not true ‖ a priori **2.** *n.* a quota, esp. of troops ‖ a representative group of people, e.g. a delegation ‖ a contingent thing [F.]

con·tin·u·al (kəntínju:əl) *adj.* occurring frequently, often repeated, *the continual screeching of brakes* ‖ continuous, unbroken, *the continual thunder of Niagara* [O.F. *continuel*]

con·tin·u·ance (kəntínju:əns) *n.* a continuing in a given state, or the going on of an action or process ‖ the duration of such a continuing, time of lasting ‖ (*law*) postponement of legal proceedings [O.F.]

con·tin·u·ant (kəntínju:ənt) **1.** *n.* that which continues ‖ a consonant sound which can be prolonged during a breath, e.g. f, s, m, n **2.** *adj.* of a consonant which can be continued [F.]

con·tin·u·a·tion (kəntínju:éiʃən) *n.* a prolonging ‖ the action of resuming after an interruption, *continuation of work after lunch* ‖ the next additional part to be published in serial publication [F.]

continuation school a school that enables young workers to continue their education part-time

con·tin·u·a·tive (kəntínju:ɛitiv, kəntínju:ətiv) *adj.* serving as a continuation, tending to continue [fr. L. *continuativus*]

con·tin·u·a·tor (kəntínju:ɛitər) *n.* someone who continues, esp. a writer who continues another's work, e.g. after his death [fr. L. *continuare*, to continue]

con·tin·ue (kəntínju:) *pres. part.* **con·tin·u·ing** *past* and *past part.* **con·tin·ued** *v.t.* to go on with (an action), *to continue working* ‖ to prolong, *continue the hedge beyond the gateway* ‖ to resume, take up again ‖ to prolong the employment or tenure of office of (someone) ‖ *v.i.* to extend, *the forest continues for miles* ‖ to remain in a given place or condition, *he continues to be in poor health* ‖ to be retained in an official position, *to continue to be chairman* ‖ (of a story, speech, speaker etc.) to go on **to be continued** a phrase printed at the end of part of an article, serial story etc. to indicate that a sequel follows in a later issue of the periodical etc. [F. *continuer*]

continued stay review (*med.*) review during a patient's hospitalization to determine the medical necessity and appropriateness of continuation of the patient's stay at a hospital level of care

continuing education formal education for adults after completion of ordinary training

con·ti·nu·i·ty (kɒntinú:iti:, kɒntinjú:iti:) *pl.* **con·ti·nu·i·ties** *n.* the state or condition of being smoothly continuous ‖ (*movies*) a complete scenario ‖ (*radio*) the written material on which the spoken part of a program is based ‖ (*math.*) the property characteristic of a continuous function [F. *continuité*]

continuity girl a person responsible for insuring, after an interruption in the filming of a scene, that when filming starts again all details are the same as before

con·tin·u·o (kəntínju:ou) *n.* (*mus.*) the bass line of 17th-c. and 18th-c. keyboard music requiring the player to find the right harmonies from each given note. Often figures were provided to indicate the harmonies (*FIGURED BASS) [Ital.]

con·tin·u·ous (kəntínju:əs) *adj.* connected throughout, uninterrupted in space, time or sequence ‖ (*math.*, of a function defined at a point) such that the difference between its value at that point and the value at a neighboring point can be made arbitrarily small by taking the neighboring point sufficiently close to that at which the function is defined [fr. L. *continuus*]

continuous creation theory *STEADY STATE THEORY

continuously variable transmission experimental device for automatic shifting of gears according to need without limitation, e.g., first, second, etc., esp. for trucks. It substitutes metal belt drives for gears and adjustable pulleys *acronym* CTV

Continuous Voyage an international law doctrine maintaining that a voyage interrupted at an intermediate port is continuous. It was conceived by the British during the Napoleonic Wars to halt U.S. shipment of goods to France and upheld by the U.S.A. during the Civil War

con·tin·u·um (kəntínju:əm) *pl.* **con·tin·u·a** (kəntínju:ə) *n.* something capable of being divided infinitely, as is assumed of space and time (cf. DICHOTOMY) ‖ a continuous series of identical components [L.]

con·toid (kóntɔid) *n.* (*linguistics*) class of sound made by air escaping over the center of the tongue, including consonants except *y*, *w*, *v*, and *h*

con·tort (kəntɔ́rt) *v.t.* to twist, force out of normal shape, distort [fr. L. *contorquere* (*contortus*)]

con·tor·tion (kəntɔ́rʃən) *n.* a twisting or contorting, *a contortion of the truth* **con·tór·tion·ist** *n.* an acrobat who can contort his body or limbs [fr. L. *contortio* (*contortionis*)]

con·tour (kɔ́ntuər) 1. *n.* the outline of a figure or shape ‖ a contour line 2. *adj.* following contour lines, *contour plowing* 3. *v.t.* to mark with contour lines ‖ to construct (a road etc.) in relation to contour lines [F.]

con·tour-chas·ing (kɔ́ntuərtʃeisiŋ) *n.* system of low-altitude flying to follow surface contours, designed to lessen turbulence

contour line a line drawn on a map passing through all points at the same height above sea level

contour map a map showing contour lines

contra- (kɔ́ntrə) *prefix* against, opposite, contrary [L. *contra*, against]

con·tra·band (kɔ́ntrəbænd) 1. *n.* illegal traffic in goods, smuggling ‖ smuggled goods ‖ goods which may not be imported or exported ‖ (*Am. hist.*) a Negro slave who managed to get within the Union lines during the Civil War 2. *adj.* forbidden by law, prohibited, *contraband goods* ‖ concerned with illegal goods or smuggling, *contraband trade* [fr. Span. *contrabando*, smuggling fr. Ital.]

contraband of war goods on their way to the enemy, which under international law belligerents may seize

con·tra·bass (kɔ́ntrəbeis) 1. *n.* the double bass 2. *adj.* having a range of voice or tone below the usual bass limits [fr. Ital. *contrabasso*, F. *contrebasse*]

con·tra·bas·soon (kɔ́ntrəbəsú:n, kɔ́ntrəbəsú:n) *n.* the double bassoon

con·tra·cep·tion (kɔntrəsépʃən) *n.* birth control

con·tra·cep·tive 1. *adj.* preventing conception, *contraceptive methods* 2. *n.* a contraceptive device [CONTRA-+CONCEPTION]

con·tract (kəntrǽkt) *v.t.* to catch (cold, a disease etc.) ‖ to enter into (a marriage) ‖ to acquire (debts, habits etc.) ‖ to draw together (brows, muscles etc.) ‖ to shorten, *contract 'do not' to 'don't'* ‖ *v.i.* to shrink, become narrower or shorter, *metals contract in cold weather* ‖ (sometimes kɔ́ntrækt) to enter into a contract, *they contracted to build the new bridge* **to contract out** (*Br.*) to free oneself of the terms of an agreement [fr. L. *contrahere* (*contractus*), to draw together]

con·tract (kɔ́ntrækt) *n.* an agreement, a covenant ‖ a document formulating such agreement ‖ an agreement to undertake work or supply goods at a certain price ‖ an order to assault or kill a predetermined victim for a price ‖ the work done or goods supplied under such a contract ‖ an agreement endorsed by law ‖ a promise made and accepted but only morally binding ‖ a marriage agreement ‖ contract bridge ‖ (*bridge*) the number and suit of tricks called by the highest bidder **out to contract** (of work) out on offer to various firms for tendering **under contract** (of a person or group) legally bound to work on given terms [O.F.]

con·tract bridge (kɔ́ntrækt) a form of bridge in which partners bid and try to achieve a contract, using one of many sets of conventions in the calling of the contract

con·trac·tile (kəntrǽktil) *adj.* (*biol.*) prone or able to draw together or contract, *contractile wings, contractile muscles* [F.]

contractile cell any cell in a sporangium or an anther wall which by hygroscopic contraction helps to open the organ

contractile vacuole a vacuole in the cytoplasm of many aquatic protozoans which gradually enlarges and suddenly collapses, dispersing its fluid into the surrounding water. Immediately another begins to form. The process regulates water content in the cell

con·trac·til·i·ty (kɔntræktíliti) *n.* the quality of contracting or capacity to contract

contracting out *v.* substituting contracts with service agencies for work previously done in-house

con·trac·tion (kəntrǽkʃən) *n.* a contracting (of disease, bad habits, debts etc.) ‖ a shrinking, *contraction of a muscle* ‖ a shortened form of a word made by omitting or combining some elements or by reducing vowels or syllables, *'isn't' is a contraction of 'is not'* (cf. ABBREVIATION) [F.]

con·trac·tor (kɔ́ntræktər, kəntrǽktər) *n.* a person or firm undertaking to do work or to supply goods, esp. on a large scale, by signing a contract ‖ a muscle which contracts

con·trac·tu·al (kəntrǽktʃuəl) *adj.* of, or having the nature of, a contract [fr. L. *contractus*, contract]

con·tra·dict (kɔntrədíkt) *v.t.* to deny the truth of (a statement) ‖ to assert the contrary to, *your report contradicts his* ‖ to be inconsistent with, *his account contradicted itself* ‖ *v.i.* to deny the truth or assert the contrary of something [fr. L. *contradicere* (*contradictus*)]

con·tra·dic·tion (kɔntrədíkʃən) *n.* a contradicting ‖ a contradicting statement ‖ opposition, inconsistency, *a contradiction between two versions* [F.]

con·tra·dic·tive (kɔntrədíktiv) *adj.* involving contradiction ‖ tending to contradict [fr. L. *contradictus*, to contradict]

con·tra·dic·to·ri·ly (kɔntrədíktərili:) *adv.* in a contradictory manner

con·tra·dic·to·ri·ness (kɔntrədíktəri:nis) *n.* the state or quality of being contradictory

con·tra·dic·to·ry (kɔntrədíktəri:) 1. *adj.* affirming the contrary, denying the truth of a statement etc., tending to contradict, *a contradictory reply* ‖ inconsistent, *a contradictory attitude* 2. *n.* (*logic*) a contradictory principle or proposition [fr. L. *contradictorius*]

con·tra·dis·tinc·tion (kɔntrədistíŋkʃən) *n.* distinction by means of contrast

con·tra·dis·tinc·tive (kɔntrədistíŋktiv) *adj.* serving to distinguish by contrast

con·tra·dis·tin·guish (kɔntrədistíŋgwiʃ) *v.t.* to distinguish by demonstrating contrasting or opposite qualities

con·trail (kɔ́ntreil) *n.* a visible track of condensed water vapor formed behind an aircraft flying at high altitudes [CONDENSATION+TRAIL]

con·tra·in·di·cate (kɔntrəíndikeit) *pres. part.* **con·tra·in·di·cat·ing** *past* and *past part.* **con·tra·in·di·cat·ed** *v.t.* to render (the treatment or procedure adopted) inadvisable

con·tra·in·di·ca·tion (kɔntrəindikéiʃən) *n.* a symptom etc. which renders it inadvisable to continue the treatment or procedure adopted

con·tral·to (kəntrǽltou) *pl.* **con·tral·tos** *n.* the lowest female singing voice ‖ a singer with such a voice ‖ the part sung by such a singer [Ital.]

CONTRAN (*acronym*) for control translator, compiler language derived from FORTRAN IV and ALGOL 60; designed by Honeywell Data Processing Division

con·trap·tion (kəntrǽpʃən) *n.* an odd gadget, device or contrivance [etym. doubtful]

con·tra·pun·tal (kɔntrəpʌ́nt'l) *adj.* of, or following the rules of, counterpoint **con·tra·pún·tist** *n.* [fr. Ital. *contrapunto* fr. *contra*, counter+*punto*, point]

con·tra·ri·e·ty (kɔntrəráiiti:) *pl.* **con·tra·ri·e·ties** *n.* the state or quality of being contrary or opposite ‖ an inconsistency [O.F. *contrarieté*]

con·tra·ri·ly (kɔ́ntrerili:) *adv.* in a contrary way

con·tra·ri·ness (kɔ́ntreri:nis) *n.* the quality of being contrary

con·tra·ri·wise (kɔ́ntreri:waiz) *adv.* on the contrary ‖ in the opposite way

con·tra·ry (kɔ́ntreri:) 1. *adj.* opposed, *a contrary opinion* ‖ opposite in nature, direction etc., *contrary motion* ‖ (of wind etc.) unfavorable ‖ (esp. kəntréəri) vexatious, perverse, doing the opposite of what is expected or wanted 2. *n. pl.* **con·tra·ries** the opposite, something which is the opposite of something else **on the contrary** (supporting a negative answer to a question etc.) the reverse is the case, *is he sober? On the contrary, he is very drunk* **to the contrary** to the opposite effect, *evidence to the contrary* 3. *adv.* counter, contrarily [O.F. *contrarie*]

con·trast (kəntrǽst) *v.t.* to display the differences between, *contrast his record with his promises* ‖ *v.i.* to show marked differences when compared, *his elegant clothes contrasted with his rough speech* [O.F. *contraster*]

con·trast (kɔ́ntræst) *n.* a divergence between related things, ideas etc. ‖ a relationship of difference demonstrated by juxtaposition, *color contrast* ‖ a person or thing showing this difference relationship when compared with someone or something else, *she is a contrast to her shy husband* ‖ (*optics*) the degree to which a photographic or optical image displays sharp differences in brightness between adjacent areas **con·trast·y** (kɔntrǽsti:, kɔ́ntræsti:) *comp.* **con·trast·i·er** *superl.* **con·trast·i·est** *adj.* (*optics*) displaying marked contrast [F. *contraste* fr. Ital.]

con·tra test (kɔ́ntrə) the control element in an experiment

con·tra·val·la·tion (kɔntrəvəléiʃən) *n.* (*hist.*) a series of earthworks built by the besiegers of a town to discourage sorties by the besieged [fr. F. *contrevallation*]

con·tra·vene (kɔntrəví:n) *pres. part.* **con·tra·ven·ing** *past* and *past part.* **con·tra·vened** *v.t.* to infringe (a rule or law) ‖ to deny, contradict, *these facts cannot be contravened* ‖ to conflict with, go counter to, *to contravene someone's wishes* [fr. F. *contrevenir*]

con·tra·ven·tion (kɔntrəvénʃən) *n.* a contravening ‖ an infringement **in contravention of** in violation of (regulations) [F.]

con·tre·temps (kɔ́ntrətɑ̃) *n.* an untimely, embarrassing or annoying happening, though not one with serious consequences [F.]

con·tri·bute (kəntríbju:t) *pres. part.* **con·tri·but·ing** *past* and *past part.* **con·tri·but·ed** *v.t.* to give, together with others, for a common purpose, *to contribute money to charity* ‖ to supply (an article etc.) to a newspaper or periodical ‖ *v.i.* to give a share, *to contribute to a fund* ‖ to help to bring something about, *the champagne contributed to the success of the party* ‖ to have writings accepted by a publication, esp. frequently [fr. L. *contribuere* (*contributus*), to bestow]

con·tri·bu·tion (kɔntribjú:ʃən) *n.* the act of contributing ‖ something contributed **to lay under contribution** to oblige (someone) to contribute [F.]

con·tri·bu·tive (kəntríbjutiv) *adj.* contributing or tending to contribute

con·tri·bu·tor (kəntríbjutər) *n.* a person who contributes, e.g. money to a cause or articles to a periodical [A.F. *contributour*]

con·trib·u·to·ry (kəntríbjutɔ:ri:, kɔntríbjutɔuri:) 1. *adj.* contributing, giving a share ‖ helping to bring about, serving towards an end, *drought was a contributory cause of the fire* 2. *n. pl.* **con·trib·u·to·ries** (*Br.*) a person liable to contribute towards meeting the debts of a bankrupt company ‖ someone or something which contributes [fr. L. *contribuere* (*contributus*), to contribute]

contributory negligence (*law*) the partial responsibility of an injured person for his injury

contributory pension a retirement pension towards which an employee contributes while he is employed, the employer also making a contribution

con·trite (kəntráit, kɔ́ntrait) *adj.* penitent, thoroughly sorry, esp. for sin [F. *contrit*]

con·tri·tion (kəntríʃən) *n.* remorse, penitence, esp. for sin [O.F. *contriciun*]

con·triv·a·ble (kəntráivəb'l) *adj.* able to be contrived

con·triv·ance (kəntráivəns) *n.* the act of contriving ‖ a mechanical appliance ‖ resource, *it required considerable contrivance to get us there in time* ‖ a dishonest device, *his excuse was a mere contrivance*

con·trive (kəntráiv) *pres. part.* **con·triv·ing** *past* and *past part.* **con·trived** *v.t.* to devise, *to contrive a means of meeting* ‖ to invent, *to contrive a new kind of tool* ‖ to manage by resourcefulness, *she contrived to bring up her family on very little money* [O.F. *controver*, to find fr. Ital.]

con·trol (kəntróul) 1. *v.t. pres. part.* **con·trol·ling** *past* and *past part.* **con·trolled** to govern, exercise control over, *dampers control the intake of air into the kiln* ‖ to restrain, *to control one's temper* ‖ to regulate ‖ to test or verify (an experiment) by setting up a control in which all factors except the variant being tested are kept identical 2. *n.* power, authority ‖ restraint ‖ self-restraint ‖ the right of administering or supervising, *control of finances* ‖ a means of safeguarding the constitution etc. or regulating the economic life of a nation, *wage controls* ‖ dominance over the difficulties of a technique, e.g. in the arts ‖ (*pl.*) the mechanisms operated by the driver's hands and feet in driving a vehicle, or those by which a pilot flies an aircraft ‖ a station where a competitor may stop for repairs, refueling etc., during a motor race etc. or a part of a course not reckoned in timing ‖ a person who acts as a check ‖ a standard of comparison or check in an experiment, *this unfertilized plot acts as control for the experimental ones* ‖ (*spiritualism*) a spirit said to actuate the utterances of the medium [F. *contrôler*]

control column the device in an aircraft that operates the ailerons and elevators

control group in an experiment, a group of subjects matched with an experimental group, but not subject to the treatment under investigation. The control group of an experiment involving human beings is usually unaware of its status

con·trol·ler (kəntróulər) *n.* a person who or device which governs or controls, esp. an officer

CONCISE PRONUNCIATION KEY: (**a**) æ, c*a*t; ɑ, c*a*r; ɔ f*aw*n; ei, sn*a*ke. (**e**) e, h*e*n; i:, sh*ee*p; iə, d*ee*r; ɛə, b*ea*r. (**i**) i, f*i*sh; ai, t*i*ger; ə:, b*i*rd. (**o**) o, *o*x; au, c*ow*; ou, g*oa*t; u, p*oo*r; ɔi, r*oy*al. (**u**) ʌ, d*u*ck; u, b*u*ll; u:, g*oo*se; ə, b*a*cillus; ju:, c*u*be. x, lo*ch*; θ, *th*ink; ð, bo*th*er; z, *Z*en; ʒ, cor*s*age; dʒ, sava*g*e; ŋ, oranguta*ng*; j, *y*ak; ʃ, fi*sh*; tʃ, fe*tch*; 'l, rabb*le*; 'n, redd*en*. Complete pronunciation key appears inside front cover.

controlling expenditure or a device for controlling power, pressure, speed etc. **con·tról·ler·ship** n. [A.F. *contrerollour*]

control tower the building on an airfield from which permanent visual observation of the landing area is maintained and its use by air and ground traffic controlled, normally by radio

con·tro·ver·sial (kɒntrəvə́:rʃəl) *adj.* disputable, *a controversial statement* ‖ prone to controversy, *a controversial manner* ‖ relating to controversy **con·tro·vér·sial·ist** n. [fr. L. *controversialis*]

con·tro·ver·sy (kɒ́ntrəvə:rsi) *pl.* **con·tro·ver·sies** n. a disputing ‖ an argument, esp. a prolonged one, e.g. in newspaper correspondence ‖ a quarrel or wrangle [fr. L. *controversia*]

con·tro·vert (kɒ́ntrəvə:rt, kɒntrəvə́:rt) *v.t.* to deny the truth of ‖ to call in question, dispute [fr. L. *controversus*, opposed]

con·tu·ma·cious (kɒntuméiʃəs, kɒntjuméiʃəs) *adj.* obstinately disobedient, rebellious, esp. against lawful authority, e.g. an order of court **cón·tu·ma·cy** n. [fr. L. *contumax* (*contumacis*), stubborn]

con·tu·me·li·ous (kɒntumí:li:əs, kɒntjumí:li:əs) *adj* contemptuous, arrogant, insolent in language or behavior [O.F. *contumélieus*]

con·tu·me·ly (kɒ́ntuməli:, kɒ́ntjuməli:, kəntu:məli:, kəntjú:məli:, kɒ́ntəmli:) n. insolent or insulting language or treatment [O.F. *contumelie*]

con·tuse (kəntú:z, kəntjú:z) *pres. part.* **con·tus·ing** *past* and *past part.* **con·tuse** *v.t.* to bruise, damage the subcutaneous tissue of, without breaking the skin [fr. L. *contundere* (*contusus*), to thump]

con·tu·sion (kəntú:ʒən, kəntjú:ʒən) n. a bruise, damage to subcutaneous tissue [F.]

co·nun·drum (kənʌ́ndrəm) n. a riddle turning on a play of words ‖ (*fig.*) a problem [origin unknown]

con·ur·ba·tion (kɒnərbéiʃən) n. a large network of urban communities [fr. L. *cum*, with + *urbs*, city]

con·va·lesce (kɒnvəlés) *pres. part.* **con·va·lesc·ing** *past* and *past part.* **con·va·lesced** *v.i.* to recover health, esp. gradually, after prolonged illness **con·va·lés·cence** n. a gradual recovering from illness **con·va·lés·cent 1.** *adj.* gradually recovering from illness ‖ of or suitable for convalescence, *convalescent home* **2.** n. a person recovering from illness [fr. L. *convalescere*]

con·vec·tion (kənvékʃən) n. (*phys.*) transference of heat energy from place to place by the circulatory movement of a mass of fluid (due to variations in temperature and hence density) and the action of gravity, the energy being conveyed by the fluid ‖ (*meteor.*) a mechanically or thermally produced process involving upward or downward transfer of part of the atmosphere **con·véc·tion·al** *adj.* [fr. L. *convectio* (*convectionis*), conveyance]

convection current a stream of fluid produced by convection, e.g. in the atmosphere or in the ocean

convection oven stove in which a fan circulates heated air through the oven for fast, even cooking

con·vec·tor (kənvéktər) n. a heating stove or other device using the principle of convection

con·vene (kənvi:n) *pres. part.* **con·ven·ing** *past* and *past part.* **con·vened** *v.t.* to call together (a committee, assembly etc.) ‖ to summon to appear before a tribunal etc. ‖ *v.i.* to assemble, *the meeting convened yesterday* [F. *convenir*]

con·ven·ience (kənví:njəns) n. advantage, *living near one's work is a convenience* ‖ a convenient time or arrangement, *deal with it at your convenience* ‖ something which makes for one's comfort or for saving work, or any useful appliance ‖ (esp. *Br.*) a public lavatory **to make a convenience of someone** to use someone's services for one's own ends without regard for his interests [fr. L. *convenientia*]

convenience clinic private medical service approximating a hospital emergency room in providing patient care

convenience foods prepared or semiprepared packaged foods sold at retail and substantially ready for eating, e.g., frozen dinners, canned or dehydrated vegetables

con·ven·ient (kənví:njənt) *adj.* favorable to one's comfort, occasioning little trouble or extra work ‖ suitable as an arrangement, *come tomorrow if it is convenient* ‖ easy of access, *a convenient bookshelf* ‖ fitting in with one's require-

ments, *a convenient bus service* [fr. L. *convenire*, to come together, to suit]

con·vent (kɒ́nvent) n. a community of religious, esp. of nuns ‖ the establishment in which they live [M.E. *covent* fr. A.F.]

con·ven·tion (kənvénʃən) n. the act of convening ‖ a conference, a body of delegates assembled for a common purpose ‖ (*Eng. hist.*) parliament assembled without royal summons (1660, 1688) ‖ an agreement or covenant between parties or nations ‖ an arbitrary but consistently observed usage, *italics for examples are a convention in this book* ‖ a polite practice observed by the majority ‖ such a practice that has become a deadening influence, or such practices collectively, *a slave to convention* ‖ any of various accepted and generally understood methods of bidding, leading etc. in various card games ‖ a rule or practice traditionally observed in the arts etc., *the conventions of the novel* [F.]

con·ven·tion·al (kənvénʃən'l) *adj.* depending on or deriving from convention ‖ customary, sanctioned by usage, *conventional clothing* ‖ not original or spontaneous, *a conventional letter of sympathy* ‖ conformist ‖ (*arts*) lacking originality, merely traditional ‖ (of signs, symbols etc., e.g. in mathematics and the sciences) habitually used with a single arbitrary, well understood significance ‖ of or relating to a convention or meeting **con·vén·tion·al·ism, con·vén·tion·al·ist, con·ven·tion·al·i·ty** (kənvenʃənǽliti:) ns **con·ven·tion·al·ize** (kənvénʃən'laiz) *pres. part.* **con·ven·tion·al·iz·ing** *past* and *past part.* **con·ven·tion·al·ized** *v.t.* to make conventional ‖ (*arts*) to treat or represent conventionally [fr. L. *conventionalis*]

Convention of 1818 an Anglo-U.S. convention which determined the U.S.-Canadian boundary along the forty-ninth parallel, from Lake of the Woods to the Rocky Mtns. It provided for a joint ten-year occupation of the disputed Oregon area, comprising the present states of Washington and Oregon and the province of British Columbia

Convention, the National the revolutionary assembly which governed France (Sept. 1792–Oct. 1795) during the French Revolution and founded the First Republic

con·ven·tu·al (kənvéntʃu:əl) **1.** *adj.* of or relating to a convent **2.** n. a member of a convent **Con·ven·tu·al** a member of a branch of the Franciscan order following a less strict regimen than the Observants [fr. L. *conventualis*]

con·verge (kənvə́:rdʒ) *pres. part.* **con·verg·ing** *past* and *past part.* **con·verged** *v.i.* (of two or more directions) to be towards the same point in space ‖ (of two or more things having direction) to be directed towards the same point in space ‖ (with 'upon' or 'towards', of two or more things in motion) to move towards the same specified point in space ‖ (of two or more actions) to be directed towards the same end ‖ (*math.*, of a sequence, series or integral) to tend to a limit ‖ *v.t.* to cause (things) to converge [fr. L.L. *convergere*, to tend towards]

con·ver·gence (kənvə́:rdʒəns) n. the act or state of converging ‖ the buildup of a high-pressure layer due to several air currents meeting in a region ‖ (*math.*) of a sequence, series or integral possessing the property of converging ‖ (*biol.*) the evolutionary development of similarities in different species living in the same environment

con·ver·gen·cy (kənvə́:rdʒənsi:) n. the act or state of converging, convergence

con·ver·gent (kənvə́:rdʒənt) *adj.* of things in motion or of directions or actions which converge, or of that which causes things to converge ‖ of agencies (mirrors, lenses, lens systems etc.) which focus light or other electromagnetic radiation ‖ (*math.*, of an infinite sequence, an infinite series or an improper integral) that tends to a finite limit as the number of terms or domains of integration tends to infinity

con·verg·er (kənvə́:rdʒər) n. one who has special ability in answering rational, unimaginative questions *Cf* DIVERGER, LATERAL THINKING, VERTICAL THINKING

con·vers·a·ble (kənvə́:rsəb'l) *adj.* easy to talk to, sociable ‖ fond of conversation ‖ suitable for conversation **con·vérs·a·bly** *adv.* [F.]

con·ver·sance (kənvə́:rsəns, kɒ́nvə:rsəns) n. acquaintance through study **con·vér·san·cy** n.

con·ver·sant (kənvə́:rsənt, kɒ́nvə:rsənt) *adj.* well acquainted, familiar, *conversant with poli-*

tics ‖ informed about, *he is quite conversant with the matter* [O.F.]

con·ver·sa·tion (kɒnvərséiʃən) n. talk, esp. informal and friendly ‖ good talk practiced as an art ‖ (*pl.*) exploratory discussion of an issue by diplomats of different countries or by officials of institutions **con·ver·sá·tion·al** *adj.* pertaining to or characteristic of conversation, *a conversational tone* ‖ fond of conversation **con·ver·sá·tion·al·ist** n. a practiced or gifted talker [O.F.]

conversation piece a painting etc. of a group of people in free and easy attitudes of conversation ‖ something which sets off conversation

conversation pit dropped living area with seating arranged to promote conversation

con·ver·sa·zi·o·ne (kɒnvərsɑtsi:óuni:) n. a reception given for conversation, esp. an evening gathering given by a learned society [Ital.]

con·verse 1. (kɒ́nvə:rs) n. a statement which transposes the terms of another statement, e.g., 'he has strength but no skill' is the converse of 'he has skill but no strength' ‖ (*logic*) a proposition obtained by conversion ‖ something which is the opposite of something else **2.** (kənvə́:rs, kɒ́nvə:rs) *adj.* of one statement which is the converse of another [fr. L. *conversus*, turned around]

con·verse 1. (kənvə́:rs) *v.i. pres. part.* **con·vers·ing** *past* and *past part.* **con·versed** to have a conversation **2.** (kɒ́nvə:rs) n. spiritual communion, *to hold converse with nature* [F. *converser*]

con·ver·sion (kənvə́:rʒən, kənvə́:rʃən) n. a converting or being converted, esp. to new beliefs or to a new allegiance, e.g. from one Christian denomination to another ‖ a change of role, purpose etc., *the conversion of a house into offices* ‖ a voluntary change of stocks and shares into others of a different kind ‖ (*economics*) a change in a rate of interest to a lower rate ‖ (*real estate*) changeover of a rental apartment building to condominium or cooperative ownership ‖ (*logic*) the act of interchanging the terms of a proposition, *if no two-legged animals are horses, then by conversion no horses are two-legged* ‖ (*math.*) a change or reduction of the form of an expression, e.g. from a fractional to an integral form ‖ (*phys.*) the change from one physical state into another, *the conversion of water into steam* ‖ (*chem.*) the change of one substance into another, *the conversion of quicklime into slaked lime* ‖ (*football*) a score made on a try for point after touchdown [F.]

con·vert 1. (kənvə́:rt) *v.t.* to change, *to convert a wilderness into a garden* ‖ to change the chemical or physical character of, *to convert sugar into starch* ‖ to bring over to a new position, faith etc., *to convert someone to one's own opinion* ‖ to make a spiritual change in ‖ to turn to another use, *to convert stables into a cottage* ‖ (*rugby*) to complete (a try) by kicking the ball between the uprights of the goal above the crossbar from a position 25 yds back from the goal line and level with where the try was scored ‖ (*logic*) to change (a statement etc.) by conversion ‖ to change (stocks, shares etc.) into others by conversion ‖ *v.i.* to undergo a conversion ‖ to be able to be converted ‖ (*football*) to make a conversion ‖ (*rugby*) to convert a try **2.** (kɒ́nvə:rt) n. a person whose religious, philosophical or political beliefs etc. have been changed **con·vért·er** n. an apparatus for converting, esp. a retort used in the Bessemer steel process ‖ a device for transforming electrical voltage [F.]

con·vert·i·bil·i·ty (kənvə:rtəbíliti:) n. the quality of being convertible

con·vert·i·ble (kənvə́:rtəb'l) **1.** *adj.* liable to conversion ‖ able to be converted ‖ interchangeable, *these terms are convertible* **2.** n. a car with a folding top [F.]

convertible currency paper money able to be exchanged at a fixed price for gold, usually restricted to currency held by foreigners. The term is commonly used to mean convertible into U.S. dollars

con·vex 1. (kɒnvéks, kɒ́nveks) *adj.* curving outwards like the outside of a sphere (opp. CONCAVE) **2.** (kɒ́nveks) n. a convex surface, line etc. **con·véx·i·ty** n. [fr. L. *convexus*]

con·vex·o·con·cave (kɒnvéksoukɒnkéiv) *adj.* convex on one side and concave on the other ‖ (*optics*) of a lens whose convex face has a greater curvature than the concave face (cf. CONCAVO-CONVEX)

con·vex·o·con·vex (kɒnvéksoukɒnvéks) *adj.* (esp. of a lens) biconvex

con·vey (kənvéi) *v.t.* to carry, transport, *to convey goods and passengers* || to act as a medium transmitting sound etc., *air is the medium by which sound waves are conveyed* || to impart (information etc.) || to suggest, present as meaning, *what did his speech convey to you?* || to transfer by legal process, *to convey an estate* **con·véy·a·ble** *adj.* [O.F. *conveier*]

con·vey·ance (kənvéiəns) *n.* the act of conveying || a means of conveying, esp. a hired vehicle || (*law*) the transfer of property from one person to another || (*law*) the deed conveying this transfer **con·véy·anc·er** *n.* a lawyer responsible for effecting conveyance of property **con·véy·anc·ing** *n.* the work of drawing up deeds etc. done by a conveyancer

con·vey·or (kənvéiər) *n.* a conveyor belt or other device for moving articles or raw materials in a factory

conveyor belt an endless moving flexible belt, or sequence of rollers, used for conveying finished products or work in progress, esp. in a factory

con·vict (kənvíkt) *v.t.* to prove or find guilty after trial || to show to be in error or to have done wrong, *their embarrassment convicted them* || (*theol.*) to impress with a sense of guilt, *to convict someone of sin* [fr. L. *convincere* (*convictus*), to vanquish by proof]

con·vict (kónvikt) *n.* a person convicted of crime, esp. one serving a long sentence [fr. obs. *convict* adj.]

con·vic·tion (kənvíkʃən) *n.* a convicting or being convicted || firm belief || a convincing or being convinced **to carry conviction** to bear the clear mark of convincing truth [fr. L. *convictio* (*convictionis*)]

con·vince (kənvíns) *pres. part.* **con·vinc·ing** *past* and *past part.* **con·vinced** *v.t.* to persuade by argument or proof [fr. L. *convincere* (*convictus*)]

con·vin·ci·ble (kənvínsəb'l) *adj.* open to persuasion or conviction [fr. L. *convincibilis*]

con·viv·i·al (kənvívi:əl) *adj.* festive, gay, sociable || appropriate to feasting and drinking, *convivial talk* **con·viv·i·ál·i·ty** *n.* [fr. L. *convivialis* fr. *convivium*, feast]

con·vo·ca·tion (kɒnvəkéiʃən) *n.* a calling together or convoking || an assembly of representatives || an ecclesiastical or academic assembly, esp. (*Br.*) a provincial synod of the Church of England || (*Br.*) the legislative assembly of some universities, e.g. Oxford, Durham **con·vo·cá·tion·al** *adj.* [fr. L. *convocatio* (*convocationis*)]

con·voke (kənvóuk) *pres. part.* **con·vok·ing** *past* and *past part.* **con·voked** *v.t.* to call together to an assembly [fr. F. *convoquer*]

con·vo·lute (kónvəlu:t) **1.** *adj.* (*bot.*) rolled, coiled on itself, *a convolute leaf* || (*zool.*) having one part twisted over or rolled over another part **2.** *n.* a coil **3.** *v. pres. part.* **con·vo·lut·ing** *past* and *past part.* **con·vo·lut·ed** *v.t.* to twist or coil about (something) || *v.i.* to twist, coil **cón·vo·lut·ed** *adj.* coiled, twisted, spiral in shape || complex, involved **con·vo·lu·tion** (kɒnvəlú:ʃən) *n.* a coiled or twisted state || a single whorl, twist or fold, one turn of a coil or spiral || (*anat.*) a sinuous fold of the surface of the brain **con·volve** (kənvólv) *pres. part.* **con·volv·ing** *past* and *past part.* **con·volved** *v.t.* to roll together, roll (one part) on another || *v.i.* to roll together [fr. L. *convolvere* (*convolutus*), to roll together]

con·volv·er (kənvólvər) *n.* (*acoustics*) device for processing surface acoustic waves by nonlinear interaction between waves from opposite directions

con·vol·vu·lus (kənvólvjuləs) *pl.* **con·vol·vu·lus·es, con·vol·vu·li** (kənvólvjulai) *n.* a member of *Convolvulus*, fam. *Convolvulaceae*, a genus of annual or perennial plants, often with twining stems which are woody at the base. It includes bindweed and some of the morning glories [L. fr. *convolvere*, to enfold]

con·voy (kónvɔi) *n.* a convoying or being convoyed or escorted || a group of merchant ships under aerial or naval protection || a column of military supplies or motorized troops etc. **under** (or **in**) **convoy** taking part in a convoy [F. *convoi*]

con·voy (kónvɔi, kənvɔi) *v.t.* to provide military or naval escort for [F. *convoyer*]

con·vulse (kənváls) *pres. part.* **con·vuls·ing** *past* and *past part.* **con·vulsed** *v.t.* to throw into spasms or convulsions || to affect with strong emotion, *convulsed with laughter* [fr. L. *convellere* (*convulsus*), to tear up]

con·vul·sion (kənválʃən) *n.* (usually pl.) a violent involuntary spasm of muscles, or irregular movement of limbs etc., resulting from this || any violent disturbance, e.g. an earthquake, tidal wave || (esp. *pl.*) violent political or social upheaval || (esp. *pl.*) uncontrollable laughter [fr. L. *convulsio* (*convulsionis*)]

con·vul·sive (kənválsiv) *adj.* of the nature of a convulsion, *convulsive spasms* || attended with or producing convulsions, *a convulsive seizure* || emotionally violent, *convulsive rage* [fr. L. *convellere* (*convulsus*), to tear up]

Con·way (kónwei), Moncure Daniel (1832–1907), U.S. liberal clergyman, known for his 'Life of Thomas Paine' (1892) and 'Collected Works of Thomas Paine' (1894–96). He contributed to the antislavery and reform press

Con·well (kónwel), Russell Herman (1843–1925), U.S. clergyman and lecturer. He built up Grace Baptist Church, Philadelphia, into a large and flourishing congregation, and founded Temple University from it

cony *CONEY

coo (ku:) **1.** *pres. part.* **coo·ing** *past* and *past part.* **cooed** *v.i.* to make the murmuring sound characteristic of doves, pigeons etc. || (of lovers) to talk tenderly || (of babies) to gurgle contentedly **2.** *n.* the sound produced by doves etc. || (*Br.*) a sound used to express mild surprise [imit.]

Cooch Be·har (ku:tʃbəhár) *BENGAL

Cook (kuk), James (1728–79), British naval captain, navigator and explorer. He led three scientific expeditions to the southern hemisphere (1768–71, 1772–5, 1776–9), making many discoveries in the regions of Australia, New Zealand and the Pacific Is. He was the first to penetrate the Antarctic Circle (1773), and on this voyage demonstrated the efficacy of methods of preventing scurvy. He visited (1778) the Bering Strait in search of the Northwest Passage. He was murdered by natives in Hawaii

cook (kuk) **1.** *n.* a person who cooks food, esp. professionally **2.** *v.t.* to prepare (food) by the action of heat || (*Br., pop.*) to falsify, *to cook the accounts* || (with 'up') to invent, *to cook up an excuse* || *v.i.* to do the work of a cook || to undergo the process of cooking [O.E. *cōc* fr. L.]

cook·book (kúkbʊk) *n.* (*Am.*=*Br.* cookery-book) a book of cooking recipes

Cooke (kuk), Jay (1821–1905), U.S. financier. His sale (1862) of government bonds and his establishment (1863) of two national banks greatly aided the U.S. government during the Civil War

cook·er (kúkər) *n.* a vessel for cooking food, *a pressure cooker* || a fruit better cooked than eaten raw || (*Br.*) a stove for cooking food

cook·er·y (kúkəri:) *n.* the art or process of cooking

cook·er·y-book (kúkəri:bʊk) *n.* (*Br.*) a cookbook

cook·house (kúkhaʊs) *pl.* **cook·hous·es** (kúkhaʊziz) *n.* an outdoor or camp kitchen || a ship's galley

cook·ie, cook·y (kúki:) *pl.* **cook·ies** *n.* a small, sweet cake, usually thin [prob. Du. *koekje*, dim. of *koek*, cake]

cookie jar (*colloq.*) good thing available for a relatively small effort, esp. an unethical or illegal one

Cook Islands a New Zealand territory (area 93 sq. miles, pop. 17,000) 1,500 miles northeast of New Zealand in the S. Pacific. There are (excluding Niue) 15 islands. Race: Polynesian. Religion: Christianity. Chief island and capital: Rarotonga (pop. 8,700). Exports: fruit, mother of pearl, clothing, copra. The islands were discovered (1773–7) by James Cook, became a British protectorate (1888), and were annexed to New Zealand (1901). Full internal self-government was granted (1965)

Cook, Mt (Aorangi) the highest peak (12,350 ft) in New Zealand, in the Southern Alps, South Island

cook·out (kúkaʊt) *n.* a party planned around the cooking and eating of a meal outdoors

Cook Strait the channel (16 to 90 miles wide) between North Island and South Island, New Zealand, discovered by James Cook (1770)

cook·top (kúktɒp) *n.* the top area of a cooking range

cooky *COOKIE

cooky pusher diplomat who spends excessive time at parties

cool (ku:l) **1.** *adj.* rather colder than one would wish || pleasantly cold || not retaining heat, *a cool dress* || self-possessed, calm || unenthusias-

tic, verging on hostility, *a cool reception* || calmly impudent, *a cool stare* || untemperamental, *a cool head in a crisis* || (of money) impressive in amount, *it cost a cool thousand* || (of colors) near green or blue (removed from orange or red) || (*jazz*) showing technical control and virtuosity || (*pop.*) excellent **2.** *n.* cool air, *the cool of the mountains* || a cool time, *the cool of the evening* || a cool place, *it's better in the cool* || coolness [O.E. *cōl*]

cool *v.i.* to become cool || (of temper or enthusiasm) to calm down, moderate || *v.t.* to make cool **to cool down** to become cool || to recover from a fit of temper **to cool off** to become less affectionate, enthusiastic etc. || to become calm after temper **to cool one's heels** to be kept waiting [O.E. *cōlian*]

cool·ant (kú:lənt) *n.* a liquid used to lessen friction in cutting tools, or (in industrial processes) to cool down metals, liquids etc., or (in engines) to cool them

cool·er (kú:lər) *n.* a vessel for cooling liquids, *wine cooler* or solids, *butter cooler*

Coo·ley (kú:li:), Charles Horton (1864–1929), U.S. pioneer sociologist. His 'Human Nature and the Social Order', 'Social Organization', and 'Social Progress' stress that the individual's social development depends on the extent to which he participates with others

Cooley's anemia, (kú:li:z) or beta-thalassemia major, an inherited deficiency in which red blood cells are low in hemoglobin. Death occurs in the teens or early 20's from anemia or heart failure

cool-head·ed (kú:lhédid) *adj.* calm, unexcited

Cool·idge (kú:lidʒ), (John) Calvin (1872–1933), 30th president (1923–9) of the U.S.A., upon the death of President Harding. A Republican, he advocated economy in government, low taxation, and a laissez-faire policy toward business, twice vetoing (1927, 1928) the McNary-Haugen agricultural bill for its price-fixing features. The period of his administration was marked by general prosperity

Coo·lidge tube (kú:lidʒ) (*electr.*) an X-ray tube that utilizes a hot cathode to produce necessary electrons

coo·lie, coo·ly (kú:li:) *pl.* **coo·lies** *n.* an unskilled Oriental laborer [var. of *kulī, kolī*, a Gujarati tribe]

cool·ness (kú:lnis) *n.* the state or quality of being cool || lack of enthusiasm || calm self-assurance

coomb, combe (ku:m, koum) *n.* (*Br.*) a narrow valley running up from the coast || (*Br.*) a grassy hollow in a hillside [O.E. *cumb*]

coon (ku:n) *n.* a raccoon

coop (ku:p) **1.** *n.* a box, cage, pen or enclosure for poultry, small animals etc. || a place of confinement **to fly the coop** to escape from confinement **2.** *v.t.* to put in a coop **to coop up** to confine, *she feels cooped up at home* [M.E. *cupe*, basket, etym. doubtful]

co-op, co·op (kóuɒp, kouóp) *n.* (short for) a cooperative

Coo·per (kú:pər, kúpər), James Fenimore (1789–1851), American author, remembered for his 'Leatherstocking Tales' of Indians, notably 'The Last of the Mohicans'

Cooper, John Montgomery (1881–1949), U.S. anthropologist. He was an authority on South American ethnology. His works include 'An Analytical and Critical Bibliography of Tierra del Fuego' (1917)

Cooper, Peter (1791–1883), U.S. industrialist and inventor. He designed and built (1830) the first U.S. steam locomotive, constructed (1854) the first structural beams, introduced the Bessemer process to the U.S.A., and constructed the largest U.S. blast furnace. He founded the Cooper Union, and was nominated the Greenback Party's presidential candidate (1876)

coop·er (kú:pər, kúpər) **1.** *n.* a maker or repairer of casks, barrels etc. || (*Br.*) a person who bottles, samples or sells wine **2.** *v.i.* to work as a cooper || *v.t.* to make or repair (casks) || to put (wine etc.) into casks **cóop·er·age** *n.* the work done by a cooper || his workshop || a charge made by a cooper [M. Du. *cuper* fr. L.]

co·op·er·ate (kouópəreit) *pres. part.* **co·op·er·at·ing** *past* and *past part.* **co·op·er·at·ed** *v.i.* to work jointly with others to some end || to be helpful as distinct from hostile, *an appeal to the population to cooperate* || to contribute to a joint effect, *everything cooperated to make the day a success* [fr. L. *cooperari* (*cooperatus*)]

co·op·er·a·tion (kouɒpəréiʃən) *n.* a cooperating, working together to a common end || (*econ.*) a group of producers, distributors etc. cooperating and sharing profits [fr. L. *cooperatio (cooperationis)*]

co·op·er·a·tive (kouópəreⁱtiv, kouópərǝtiv) **1.** *adj.* of or pertaining to cooperation ‖ describing an association for producing goods, marketing etc. in which members share profits, and middlemen are eliminated **2.** *n.* a cooperative business or association. Cooperative societies are retail organizations in which the consumers are members who provide the capital and share the trading profits in the form of a dividend on purchases made by each member. In producers' cooperative societies the producers join together to market their products, and share the trading profits. In Europe they operate esp. in agriculture and viticulture ‖ an apartment house in which the apartments are each individually owned ‖ an apartment in such a building [fr. L. *cooperari (cooperatus)*, to work together]

Coo·per pairs (kúːpər) (*particle phys.*) pairs of bound electrons in a metal with twice the charge and mass of an electron; formed in a superconductor through interaction of positive ions. Their existence is proposed by the Bardeen-Cooper-Schreiffer theory

Cooper Union a tuition-free educational institution founded (1859) by Peter Cooper in New York City for the advancement of the arts and sciences. It conducts day and evening classes and has an art museum and public library

coop·er·y (kúːpəriː, kúpəriː) *pl.* **coop·er·ies** *n.* the work done by a cooper ‖ a cooper's workshop

coop·ing (kúːpiŋ) *n.* practice by police in patrol cars of pulling aside for rest or sleep while on duty

co·opt (kouópt) *v.t.* to elect into a body, committee etc. by the votes of existing members **co·op·ta·tion** *n.* the election of members by this procedure **co·óp·ta·tive** *adj.* **co·op·tion** (kouópʃən) *n.* co-optation [fr. L. *cooptare*, to choose]

coopt *v.* to absorb or take over

cooptation technique for maintaining organizational stability by absorbing new ideas and/ or persons into the policymaking structure

co·or·di·nate (kouóːrd'nit, kouóːrd'neⁱt) **1.** *adj.* equal in rank or order, not subordinate ‖ pertaining to or made up of coordinate things **2.** *n.* something that is coordinate ‖ (*math.*) any one of a set of numbers specifying the position of a point on a line, a surface or in space (thus latitude and longitude are the coordinates of a point on the surface of the earth) ‖ (*phys.*) any one of a set of variables used to specify the state of a substance (e.g. its temperature or pressure) or the motion of a particle (e.g. position, velocity or momentum) [fr. L. *co-*, with + *ordinatus* fr. *ordinare*, to arrange]

co·or·di·nate (kouóːrd'neⁱt) *pres. part.* **co·or·di·nat·ing** *past* and *past part.* **co·or·di·nat·ed** *v.t.* to make coordinate ‖ to bring the parts or agents of a plan, process etc. into a common whole, to harmonize, *to coordinate the work of departments* [prob. fr. CO + L. *ordinare*, to arrange]

coordinate bond a covalent bond formed by a pair of electrons originating from one only of the two atoms it joins and characteristic of coordination complexes

coordinate covalence a coordinate bond

coordinate geometry analytical geometry

co·or·di·nates (kouóːrd'nəts) *n.* **1.** portions of a costume that go together in color, texture, and design **2.** crossing lines used to determine a point

co·or·di·na·tion (kouóːrd'neⁱʃən) *n.* a making or being coordinate

coordination complex an ion or compound formed from a central, usually metallic ion attached to a fixed number of ions, atoms or molecules by means of coordinate bonds, and that may exist as a discrete species in solution, e.g. a chelate

coordination of benefits (*insurance*) provisions and procedures used by insurers to avoid duplicate payment for losses insured when more than one insurance policy covers the loss *acronym* COB

co·or·di·na·tive (kouóːrd'neⁱtiv, kouóːrd'nətiv) *adj.* that coordinates ‖ relating to coordination

co·or·di·na·tor (kouóːrd'neⁱtər) *n.* someone who coordinates

Coorg, Kurg (kuərg) a mountainous province (area 1,593 sq. miles, pop. 229,000) in S.W. India. Capital: Mercara

coot (kuːt) *n.* a member of *Fulica*, fam. *Rallidae*, a genus of swimming and diving birds. F. *atra* is distinguished by a conspicuous white frontal shield and bill ‖ (*pop.*) an eccentric or slightly mad person [M.E. *cote*, etym. doubtful]

coot·ie (kúːtiː) *n.* (*pop.*) a body louse [Malay. *kutu*, a louse]

cop (kop) *pres. part.* **cop·ping** *past* and *past part.* **copped** *v.t.* (*pop.*) to catch (something that causes death, suffering, imprisonment etc.) [etym. doubtful]

cop *n.* (*pop.*) a policeman [COPPER (policeman)]

cop *n.* a conical ball of yarn wound on a spindle during spinning [O.E. *cop*, top]

co·pai·ba (koupeⁱbə, koupáⁱbə) *n.* an oleoresin obtained from South American trees of genus *Copaifera* and used as a stimulant, diuretic and antiseptic [Span. fr. Braz. *cupauba*]

co·pal (kóupəl, kóupæl) *n.* a resin from various tropical plants, used in varnishes [Span. fr. Mex. *copalli*, incense]

co·par·ce·nar·y (koupáːrsəneriː) *pl.* **co·par·ce·nar·ies** *n.* (*law*) a joint share in an inheritance ‖ joint ownership

co·par·ce·ner (koupáːrsənər) *n.* (*law*) a joint heir

co·part·ner (koupáːrtnər, kóupɑːrtnər) *n.* one of two or more equal partners or associates **co·part·ner·ship** *n.*

co·pay·ment (koupeⁱmənt) *n.* (*insurance*) type of cost-sharing in which the insured pays a specified flat amount per unit of service (e.g., $2 per visit, $10 per inpatient hospital day), with the insurer paying the rest of the cost

cope (koup) **1.** *n.* a long semicircular ecclesiastical vestment worn by a priest in processions ‖ the outer part of a mold used in founding ‖ a coping **2.** *pres. part.* **cop·ing** *past* and *past part.* **coped** *v.t.* to supply with a cope ‖ to cover with a coping ‖ *v.i.* to project like a coping [M.E. fr. O.F.]

cope *pres. part.* **cop·ing** *past* and *past part.* **coped** *v.i.* (with 'with') to contend (with a situation, problem), esp. successfully [F. *couper*, to strike]

co·peck, ko·peck (kóupek) *n.* one-hundredth of a rouble [fr. Russ. *kopeika*, dim. of *kopyé*, lance]

COPEI the Christian Democratic party in Venezuela, which won its first election in 1968 under Rafael Caldera

Co·pen·ha·gen (koupənhéⁱgən, koupənhágən, kóupənheⁱgən, koupənhɑgən) (*Dan.* Køenhavn) Denmark's capital (pop. 645,200, with agglom. 1,377,000: over a quarter of the country's total) since 1416. It lies on the Sound facing Sweden, on Zealand and Amager islands. Industries: shipbuilding, engineering, brewing, food, clothing, porcelain etc. It is a port and rail center, has Scandinavia's biggest airport, and is its largest commercial center. University (1478)

Copenhagen, Battle of the naval engagement (Apr. 2, 1801) between the British and Danish fleets in the course of which Nelson put the telescope to his blind eye and so 'did not see' Parker's signal to break off the fight. The Danish fleet was destroyed

co·pe·pod (kóupəpod) *n.* a member of *Copepoda*, a subclass of *Crustacea*, including both freshwater and saltwater forms. The group includes minute forms, some parasitic on fish, others free-living and important as fish food **co·pep·o·dan** (koupépəd'n) *n.* and *adj.* **co·pép·o·dous** *adj.* [L. fr. Gk *kōpē*, oar + *pous* (*podos*), foot]

cop·er (kóupər) *n.* (*Br.*) a horse dealer [fr. obs. v. *cope*, to buy fr. L.G.]

Co·per·ni·can (koupéːrnikən, kəpéːrnikən) *adj.* relating to Copernicus

Co·per·ni·cus (koupéːrnikəs, kəpéːrnikəs), Nicolaus (1473–1543), Polish astronomer and administrator. He put forward the ideas, revolutionary at that time, that the earth and other planets orbit about the sun and that the earth is not at the center of the universe (*PTOLEMAIC SYSTEM)

cope·stone (kóupstoun) *n.* the headstone of a wall or building

cop·i·er (kópiːər) *n.* an imitator ‖ a machine for making copies

co·pi·lot (kóupaⁱlət) *n.* an assistant pilot in an aircraft

cop·ing (kóupiŋ) *n.* the top course of a masonry wall etc., often sloping to throw off rain ‖ a protective ledge surrounding a wall on which fruit is grown [fr. COPE v., to supply with a cope]

coping saw a saw for cutting patterns in wood. It consists of a narrow blade in a U-shaped frame with a handle

coping stone a stone shaped for coping

co·pi·ous (kóupiːəs) *adj.* plentiful, overflowing, *a copious supply of drink* ‖ not concise, *a copious style* [fr. L. *copiosus* fr. *copia*, plenty]

Cop·land (kóuplənd), Aaron (1900–), American composer of orchestral, chamber, choral and film music

Cop·ley (kóupli:), John Singleton (1738–1815), American portrait painter, known for his 'Paul Revere' and 'Samuel Adams' and for his huge historical canvases, notably 'The Death of Lord Chatham'

co·pol·y·mer (koupólimər) *n.* a polymer formed by the bonding of unlike molecules usually to form a sequence which may be regarded as the monomer of a polymeric molecule containing an approximately constant proportion of the original reagents

cop-out (kópaut) *v.* to avoid work, embarrassment, responsibility, etc., by resigning, e.g., from school, work, etc.

Cop·pée (kɔpei), François (1842–1908), French poet and dramatist

cop·per (kópər) **1.** *n.* a metallic element (symbol Cu, at. no. 29, at. mass 63.54) easily smelted from its ores ‖ a penny ‖ a large boiler **2.** *v.t.* to sheathe (e.g. a saucepan) with copper **3.** *adj.* made of copper ‖ coppercolored [O.E. *coper* fr. L.L. *cuprum* fr. L. *Cyprium* (*aes*), Cyprian (metal)]

—The metal and its alloy with tin (*BRONZE) were known in prehistoric times (*BRONZE AGE). Malleable and ductile and unaffected by water or steam, it has many domestic uses. A very good conductor of electricity and heat, it is widely used to convey electric current. It is a constituent of many useful alloys in addition to bronze. Several of its salts are used as fungicides

copper *n.* (*pop.*) a policeman [COP v.]

cop·per·as (kópərəs) *n.* hydrated ferrous sulfate, $FeSO_4 \cdot 7H_2O$ [fr. older *coperose* fr. O.F. fr. L. *cuprosa* fr. *cuprum*, copper]

copper beech *Fagus sylvatica*, a variety of beech tree with red sap in the cells of the epidermis, giving the leaves a purplish or coppery color

copper bit a soldering iron

cop·per·bot·tom (kópərbótəm) *v.t.* to sheathe (the bottom of a ship or cooking pan) with copper

cop·per·head (kópərhed) *n. Agkistrodon mokasen* or *A. contortrix*, a poisonous American snake found in the eastern U.S.A. and related to the rattlesnake ‖ (*Am. hist.*) a Northern secret supporter of the Southern Confederates in the Civil War

cop·per·plate (kópərpleⁱt) *n.* a plate of copper prepared for engraving ‖ an impression taken from such a plate ‖ a distinctive style of decorative handwriting (imitated from copperplate engraving)

copper pyrites chalcopyrite

cop·per·smith (kópərsmiθ) *n.* someone who works copper

copper sulfate, *Br.* **copper sulphate** the sulfate of copper, $CuSO_4$, that is white when anhydrous but best known in the blue hydrated form $CuSO_4 \cdot 5H_2O$

cop·per·y (kópəri:) *adj.* mixed with or containing copper ‖ like copper

cop·pice (kópis) *n.* a wood of small trees, grown for periodical cutting [O.F. *copeiz*]

cop·ra (kóprə) *n.* the dried and broken kernel of the coconut, the source of coconut oil [Port. perh. fr. Malay.]

cop·ro·lite (kóprəlait) *n.* fossilized animal dung **cop·ro·lit·ic** (kɔprəlítik) *adj.* [fr. Gk *kopros*, dung + *lithos*, a stone]

cop·rol·o·gy (kɔprólədʒi:) *n.* the treatment of unclean subjects in literature etc. [fr. Gk *kopros*, dung + *logos*, discourse]

cop·roph·a·gous (kɔprófəgəs) *adj.* (of certain beetles, fam. *Lamellicornia*) dung-eating [fr. Gk *kopros*, dung + *phagein*, to eat]

cop·ro·phil·i·a (kɔprəfíliːə) *n.* a tendency to be interested in feces [fr. Gk *kopros*, dung + *philia*, a liking]

cop·ro·pho·bi·a (kɔprəfóubiːə) *n.* irrational dread of feces [fr. Gk *kopros*, dung + PHOBIA]

copse (kops) *n.* a coppice

copse·wood (kópswud) *n.* a coppice

Copt (kopt) *n.* a member of the Coptic Church, an ancient Egyptian Monophysite branch of Christianity dating from the 5th c. A.D., which gave birth to the monastic system and ideal. Persecuted at intervals from the Arab conquest (640) untit 1811, when the Christian minority gained a measure of security, the Copts number about 3,000,000. Only a few monasteries remain. Worship follows the ancient Greek liturgy but is in the Coptic language. The head of the Coptic Church is the patriarch of Alexandria in Cairo **Cóp·tic** 1. *adj.* of, pertaining to Copts or their Church 2. *n.* a Hamitic language derived from ancient Egyptian, since the l5th c. surviving only in the liturgy of the Coptic Church

cop·ter (kóptər) *n.* (*pop.*) a helicopter, chopper

cop·u·la (kópjulə) *pl.* **cop·u·las, cop·u·lae** (kópjuli:) *n.* a bond, tie, or link ‖ (*gram.*) a linking verb, esp. the verb 'to be' ‖ (*logic*) the connecting link between subject and predicate of a proposition (e.g. 'are' in 'all men are mortal') ‖ (*anat.*) any bridging or connecting structure, ligament, bone etc. **cóp·u·lar** *adj.* [L.=a band]

cop·u·late (kópjuleit) *pres. part.* **cop·u·lat·ing** *past* and *past part.* **cop·u·lat·ed** *v.i.* to unite in sexual intercourse [fr. L. *copulare* (*copulatus*), to fasten together]

cop·u·la·tion (kɒpjuléiʃən) *n.* coition, sexual intercourse ‖ (*logic*) the act of joining by a copula [F.]

cop·u·la·tive (kópjuleitiv, kópjulətiv) 1. *adj.* uniting, connecting ‖ (*gram.*) serving as a copula, connecting words or clauses and uniting their senses ‖ relating to sexual union 2. *n.* a word acting as a copula [F.]

copulative verb a linking verb

cop·u·la·to·ry (kópjulətɔri:, kópjulətɔuri:) *adj.* relating to or used in copulation

cop·y (kópi:) *pl.* **cop·ies** *n.* a reproduction, not an original ‖ a duplicate ‖ a work written out from a model or pattern ‖ one of the printed works which as a set comprise an edition ‖ material intended for printing ‖ material for newspaper publication, *the case made good copy* ‖ (*Eng. hist.*) the transcript of the manorial court roll [F. *copie*]

copy *pres. part.* **cop·y·ing** *past* and *past part.* **cop·ied** *v.t.* to make a copy of ‖ to imitate ‖ *v.i.* to cheat, e.g. in examination, by passing off a copy of someone else's work as one's own [F. *copier*]

cop·y·book (kópi:bʊk) *n.* (*hist.*) a book containing samples of penmanship or drawings for imitation

copybook maxims commonplace moralizings typical of copybooks

cop·y·cat (kópi:kæt) *n.* (*pop.*) someone who imitates another slavishly

cop·y·desk (kópi:desk) *n.* the desk in a newspaper editorial room at which articles are revised and headlines added

cop·y·hold (kópi:hould) *n.* (*Eng. hist.*) a tenure of land by copy of the court roll **cóp·y·hold·er** *n.* (*Eng. hist.*) someone holding land thus ‖ a proofreader's assistant where proofing involves reading aloud

copying ink indelible ink suitable for use with some of the older duplicating processes

cop·y·ist (kópi:ist) *n.* a person who makes copies, esp. of old documents etc.

cop·y·right (kópi:rait) 1. *n.* the exclusive right to reproduce literary, dramatic, artistic or musical work, given by law for a certain period to an author etc. or his agent (indicated now through international agreement by the letter 'C' in a circle on the title page of a book or on the page immediately following it, or at the end). It is a property which can be assigned or bequeathed 2. *v.t.* to secure a copyright on (a book, film etc.) 3. *adj.* protected by copyright

cop·y·writ·er (kópi:raitər) *n.* a writer of advertising material

coq au vin (koukouvǽn) *n.* dish of chicken cooked in red wine

co·quet, co·quette (koukét) *pres. part.* **co·quet·ting** *past* and *past part.* **co·quet·ted** *v.i.* to flirt ‖ to show interest but be indecisive, *he has coquetted for weeks with the suggestion* [F. *coqueter*]

co·quet·ry (kóukitri:, koukétri:) *pl.* **co·quet·ries** *n.* behavior (esp. in women) intended to attract mainly for the satisfaction of vanity [F. *coquetterie*]

co·quette (koukét) 1. *n.* a flirtatious woman 2. *v.* *COQUET* **co·quét·tish** *adj.* [F.]

Co·quil·hat·ville (kɒkíːʒævi:l) *MBANDAKA*

co·quil·la nut (kɒkíːljə, kɒkíːjə) *n.* the fruit of *Attalea funifera*, the Brazilian piassava palm ‖

its shell, which can be worked on a lathe [Span. or Port. *coquilla* dim. of *coca*, a shell]

co·qui·na (koukí:nə) *n.* a variety of limestone made up of adhering shells and corals, used for building in the southern U.S.A. [Span. fr. *coca*, Shell]

co·qui·to (koukí:tou) *pl.* **co·qui·tos** *n. Jubaea spectabilis*, a Chilean variety of palm tree, from the sap of which a sweet table-syrup is obtained [Span., dim. of *coco*, coconut]

cor·a·cle (kórək'l, kórək'l) *n.* a small, light, basketlike boat covered with hide, cloth etc., used by ancient Britons, and still sometimes used for fishing in Wales and Ireland [Welsh *cwrwgl*]

cor·a·coid (kórəkoid, kórəkoid) 1. *adj.* (*anat.*) of a bone in the shoulder girdle of many vertebrates 2. *n.* the coracoid bone [fr. Mod. L. fr. Gk *korakoeidēs*, crowlike]

cor·al (kórəl, kórəl) 1. *n.* a coelenterate of class *Anthozoa* or a colony of them. They occur as polyps only and usually are colonial, living in shallow ocean waters ‖ the hard red or white substance secreted by these animals to protect and support the polyps. Coral reefs and atolls are formed from broken coral 'skeletons'. Some corals are prized for necklaces etc. ‖ the bright red ovary of a lobster, or its cooked roe 2. *adj.* of coral, or the color of red coral **coral·lif·er·ous** (kɒrəlífərəs, kɒrəlífərəs) *adj.* [O. F.]

cor·a·lene (kórəli:n) *n.* 1. decoration of beading on glassware 2. the glassware —**coralene** *adj.*

cor·al·line (kórəlin, kórəlain, kórəlin, kórəlain) 1. *n.* a seaweed with calcareous incrustation like coral, e.g. *Corallina officinalis* 2. *adj.* (applied esp. to hydrozoa and polyzoa) resembling a coral ‖ of or made of coral ‖ coral red [fr. Ital. *corallina*, dim. of *corallo*, coral]

coralline zone the sea depths in which growth of coral is frequent

cor·al·lite (kórəlait, kórəlait) *n.* the coral skeleton of a marine polyp ‖ fossil coral ‖ coral-like marble [fr. L. *corallum*, coral]

cor·al·loid (kórəloid, kórəloid) 1. *adj.* like coral, branching like a coral 2. *n.* an organism like coral [fr. L. *corallum*, coral]

coral rag (*geol.*) limestone formed from coral, occurring in the Middle Oolite strata

Coral Sea the southwest arm of the Pacific lying between Australia, New Guinea and New Hebrides. It contains the Great Barrier Reef. The decisive Battle of the Coral Sea (2nd world war) was fought in May 1942. It consisted of air action, U.S. aircraft carriers defeating units of the Japanese navy

coral snake any of several venomous snakes having red in their markings, esp. of genus *Micrurus* found in South and Central America. *M. fulvius* is also found in the southern U.S.A.

cor an·glais (kɔrɒŋgléi, kɔrɑŋgléi) *n.* the English horn ‖ an organ stop of similar tone [F.=English horn]

cor·bel (kórb'l) 1. *n.* (*archit.*) a projection of stone or wood from the face of a wall, supporting the weight above (e.g. of a roof) at the spring of the arch ‖ a short piece of timber placed lengthwise to provide a bearing for a beam 2. *v.* *pres. part.* **cor·bel·ing**, esp. *Br.* **cor·bel·ling** *past* and *past part.* **cor·beled**, esp. *Br.* **cor·belled** *v.t.* to provide with corbels ‖ *v.i.* to project outward like a corbel **cór·bel·ing**, esp. *Br.* **cór·bel·ling** *n.* projecting courses forming a load-bearing ledge [O.F.]

corbel table a projecting course, e.g. of brickwork, resting on corbels

Cor·bett (kórbit), Harvey Wiley (1873–1954), U.S. architect. He helped to design (1932–40) the skyscrapers composing Rockefeller Center in New York City

cor·bie gable (kórbi:) (*archit.*) a gable with corbiesteps

cor·bie·step (kórbi:step) *n.* (*archit.*) one of a set of steps (in place of the more usual slope) along a gable [O.F. *corb*, a raven]

Cor·co·va·do Gulf (kɔrkɔvάðɔ) an inlet of the Pacific between Chiloé Is. and the coast of S.W. Chile

Cor·cy·ra (kɔrsáiərə) *CORFU*

cord (kɔrd) 1. *n.* a rope of small diameter or a fairly thick string ‖ a piece of such rope or string ‖ (*anat.*) a structure of the body resembling a cord, *umbilical cord* ‖ a cordlike rib on textiles ‖ a ribbed fabric ‖ (*pl., Br.*) corduroy trousers ‖ a cubic measure, esp. for cut wood (128 cu. ft) ‖ a quantity of wood so measured ‖ (*elec.*) insulated wire for conveying current 2. *v.t.* to bind with cord ‖ to pile (wood) into

cords **cord·age** (kórdidʒ) *n.* (collective term for) ropes, esp. those used for ship's rigging ‖ (of wood) quantity in cords [F. *corde* fr. L. fr. Gk]

cor·date (kórdeit) *adj.* heart-shaped, *a cordate leaf* [fr. Mod. L. *cordatus* fr. *cor* (*cordis*), heart]

Cor·day (kɔrdei), Charlotte (Charlotte Corday d'Armont, 1768–93), French revolutionist who stabbed Marat to death in his bath to avenge the Girondists. She was guillotined

cord·ed (kórdid) *adj.* bound or supplied with cords ‖ ribbed, *a corded cloth*

cor·de·lier (kɔrd'líər) *n.* a Franciscan friar of the strict rule, so called from his knotted cord worn as a girdle [F.]

Cor·de·liers, Club des (klybdeikɔrdəljei) a democratic club (1790–5) formed by Danton, Desmoulins and Marat during the French Revolution

cor·dial (kórdʒəl, *Br.* esp. kódjəl) 1. *adj.* hearty, sincere, friendly, *a cordial welcome* ‖ deeply felt, *cordial dislike* 2. *n.* a fortifying drink of flavored spirits or a comforting non-alcoholic drink **cor·dial·i·ty** (kɔrdʒælíti:, kɔrdʒi:ǽliti:, *Br.* esp. kɔdiǽliti:) *n.* friendliness, sincerity, cheerfulness [fr. M.L. *cordialis* fr. *cor* (*cordis*), heart]

cor·di·er·ite (kórdi:ərait) *n.* (*mineral.*) a blue silicate of aluminum, iron and magnesium, occurring in metamorphic rocks [after P. L. A. Cordier (1777–1861), F. geologist]

cor·di·form (kórdiform) *adj.* heart-shaped, *cordiform tendon* [fr. L. *cor* (*cordis*), heart]

cor·dil·le·ra (kɔrdiljέərə, kɔrdílərə) *n.* a chain of mountains, esp. one forming the axis of a large land mass [Span.]

Cor·dil·le·ras (kɔrdiljέərəz, kɔrdílərəz) the Spanish term for the range of mountains running the length of the west coast of North and South America. In North America it includes the Rocky Mtns and the Sierra Nevada. In South America it includes the Andes and is the particular name of the ranges of Colombia

cor·dite (kórdait) *n.* a smokeless explosive made from nitroglycerin and guncotton, pressed into cordlike lengths

cord·less (kórdləs) *adj.* with no electrical cord, e.g., battery-operated shavers

Cór·do·ba (kórðɔba) a town (pop. 990,007) in central Argentina, on the Primero River. University (1613), observatory

Córdoba (Spain) *CORDOVA*

cór·do·ba (kórðɔba) *n.* the basic monetary unit of Nicaragua ‖ a coin or note of the value of one córdoba [Span.]

cordoba unit of currency in Nicaragua, equal to 100 centavos

cor·don (kórd'n) 1. *n.* a line or circle of police sentries etc. preventing access to a person or place ‖ a line of guards isolating an infected area ‖ a stringcourse ‖ an ornamental cord on a costume ‖ a cord or braid worn as a badge ‖ a ribbon of an order of knighthood ‖ a fruit tree grown as a single stem or so as to form a single horizontal line 2. *v.t.* (with 'off') to enclose with a cordon, *to cordon an area off* [F.]

cor·don bleu (kɔrdɔblə:) *n.* a first-class cook ‖ dish of meat stuffed with ham and cheese [F.=blue ribbon]

Cor·do·va (kórdəvə) (*Span.* Córdoba) a province (area 5,299 sq. miles, pop. 717,213) in Andalusia, S. Spain ‖ its capital (pop. 284,737) on the River Guadalquivir. Industries: leather, fine metalwork, food processing, distilling, agricultural trading. A chief town in Roman times, it developed a splendid culture as capital of the Umayyad caliphate (756–1031). It was reconquered by the Christians (1263) and a cathedral was built into its 8th-c. Great Mosque

Cor·do·van (kórdəvən) 1. *adj.* of or pertaining to Cordova in Spain ‖ made of leather from Cordova 2. *n.* soft leather, orig. from Cordova [Span. *cordován*]

cor·du·roy (kórdərɔi, kɔrdərói) 1. *n.* a thick cotton material with a velvetlike pile on raised ribs ‖ (*pl.*) trousers made of this 2. *adj.* made of corduroy [etym. doubtful]

corduroy road a road of logs laid side by side across swampy ground

cord·wood (kó dwʊd) *n.* wood for burning tied in bundles with cord ‖ lumber suitable only for firewood and usually cut to 4-ft lengths

CORE (kor, kour) *CONGRESS OF RACIAL EQUALITY*

core (kor, kour) 1. *n.* the inner part of certain fruits containing the seeds ‖ the innermost part of anything ‖ the essence or gist, *the core of a message* ‖ the hard center of a boil or a corn ‖ the

CONCISE PRONUNCIATION KEY: (a) æ, c*a*t; **α,** c*a*r; **ɔ** f*aw*n; **ei,** sn*a*ke. **(e)** e, h*e*n; **i:,** sh*ee*p; **iə,** d*ee*r; **ɛə,** b*ea*r. **(i)** i, f*i*sh; **ai,** t*i*ger; **ə:,** b*i*rd. **(o)** o, *o*x; **au,** c*ow*; **ou,** g*oa*t; **u,** p*oo*r; **ɔi,** r*oy*al. **(u)** ʌ, d*u*ck; **u,** b*u*ll; **u:,** g*oo*se; **ə,** b*a*cillus; **ju:,** c*u*be. **x,** lo*ch*; **θ,** *th*ink; **ð,** bo*th*er; **z,** *Z*en; **ʒ,** cor*s*age; **dʒ,** sava*g*e; **ŋ,** orangutan*g*; **j,** *y*ak; **ʃ,** *fi*sh; **tʃ,** fe*tch*; **'l,** rabb*le*; **'n,** redd*en*. Complete pronunciation key appears inside front cover.

central part of a rock mass removed by boring ‖ (*computer*) magnetic doughnut-shape ring for storing computer information ‖ (*phys.*) the uranium-containing heater of a nuclear reactor where energy is released ‖ the heart of timber ‖ a wood base on which veneers are fastened ‖ an iron bar, bundle of wires etc. forming the center of an induction coil, transformer etc. ‖ the part of a mold forming the inside shape in a hollow casting ‖ the central strand of a rope ‖ the insulated conducting wire of a cable **2.** *v.t. pres. part.* **cor·ing** *past* and *past part.* **cored** to take out the core of (an apple etc.) [etym. doubtful]

core city older, inner part of an urban area *syn.* central city, inner city

co·re·li·gion·ist (kǒurilídʒənist) *n.* a person of the same religion

Co·rel·li (kǒréli:), Arcangelo (1653–1713), Italian violinist and composer of chamber music. A major influence on the development of violin technique, he also helped to establish the form of the concerto grosso

Co·rel·li (kǒréli:, kǒuréli:), Marie (Mary Mills, 1855–1924), English novelist. Her melodramatic novels were immensely popular, esp. 'Thelma' (1887) and 'The Sorrow of Satan' (1895)

core memory (*computer*) data-storage device based on the direction of magnetization

co·re·op·sis (kǒri:ópsis, kǒuri:ópsis) *n.* a member of *Coreopsis*, fam. *Compositae*, a genus of perennial plants, many of which are cultivated. Annual varieties are called *Calliopsis*, tickseed [Mod. L. fr. Gk *koris*, bug+*opsis*, appearance, from the shape of the seeds]

cor·er (kǒrər, kǒurər) *n.* a device for removing cores from fruit

co·re·spond·ent (kǒurispóndənt) *n.* the person accused of adultery with the petitioner's wife or husband in a divorce suit

corf (kǒrf) *pl.* **corves** (kǒrvz) *n.* a small wagon (*hist.*, a basket) for carrying coal in a mine [etym. doubtful]

Cor·fu (kǒrfú:, kǒrfú:) (*Gk* Kerkyra) the northernmost island (area 229 sq. miles, pop. 99,477) of the Ionian group ‖ its chief city (pop. 27,000)

cor·gi (kǒrgi:) *WELSH CORGI

co·ri·a·ceous (kǒri:éiʃəs, kǒuri:éiʃəs, kǒri:éiʃəs) *adj.* (*biol.*) of or like leather, leathery [fr. L. *coriaceus*]

co·ri·an·der (kǒri:ǽndər, kǒuri:ǽndər, kǒri:ǽndər) *n. Coriandrum sativum*, fam. *Umbelliferae*, a plant whose fruits are aromatic seeds used as a carminative and for flavoring [F. *coriandre* fr. L. fr. Gk]

Co·rinth (kǒrínt), Lovis (1858–1925), German Impressionist painter whose works reflect elements of expressionism

Cor·inth (kǒrinθ, kǒrinθ) (*Gk* Kórinthos) a Greek port (pop. 22,495) on the Gulf of Corinth, on the Isthmus of Corinth joining the Peloponnesus to Central Greece. A canal was cut across the Isthmus near the city (1881–93). Settled (8th c. B.C.) by Dorians. Corinth was the largest and richest city-state after Athens, and founded many colonies. It prospered under the Romans (after 44 B.C.), but declined under the Turks (1458–1687 and 1715–1822) and Venetians (1687–1715)

Co·rin·thi·an (kərínθi:ən) **1.** *adj.* of, relating to, or resembling one of the Greek classical orders of architecture, characterized by bell-shaped capitals ornamented with acanthus leaves and pillars 10 times their diameter in height ‖ of or pertaining to Corinth **2.** *n.* an inhabitant of Corinth [fr. L. *Corinthius*]

Corinthians, Epistles to the the seventh and eighth books of the New Testament, written (55–6) by St. Paul to the Church at Corinth. They correct moral abuses, enunciate the doctrine of the mystical body of Christ, and describe the nature of Christian love

Corinthian War a war (394–387 B.C.) in which Corinth, Athens, Thebes and Argos joined together against Sparta. The Persians enforced a peace

Co·ri·o·la·nus (kǒri:əléinəs, kǒri:əléinəs), Gaius Marcius (5th c. B.C.), legendary Roman patrician and soldier. Exiled for his oppression of the plebeians, he led a Volscian army to the gates of Rome, but was dissuaded from further action by his mother, Veturia, and his wife, Volumnia

Co·ri·o·lis force (kǒri:óulis) (*phys.*) distortion of trajectory of a projectile due to the effects of earth's rotation

co·ri·um (kǒri:əm, kǒuri:əm) *pl.* **co·ri·a** (kǒri:ə, kǒuri:ə) *n.* the middle division of an elytron ‖ the dermis [L.=leather]

Cork (kǒrk) a southern county (area 2,880 sq. miles, pop. 402,288) of Munster province, Irish Republic ‖ its county seat and port (pop. 149,792): food processing, distilling, brewing, textiles. University College, National University of Ireland

cork (kǒrk) **1.** *n.* the bark of the cork oak, stripped off by hand every 8–11 years when the cork layer of cells is 1–2 ins thick ‖ a bottle stopper made of cork (or a substitute) ‖ (*bot.*) the protective tissue of dead impermeable cells formed by cork cambium (phellogen) in certain plants, replacing the epidermis as the diameter of stems and roots increases **2.** *v.t.* to furnish with cork ‖ to stop with a cork ‖ to blacken with burned cork [etym. doubtful]

cork·age (kǒrkidʒ) *n.* a charge made by a hotelkeeper etc. for uncorking and serving a bottle of wine not supplied by the hotel

corked (kǒrkt) *adj.* (of wine) gone bad from faulty corking

cork·er (kǒrkər) *n.* something or someone that inserts corks ‖ (*pop.*) something of more than ordinary size or quality, or someone referred to with a gasp of admiration

cork oak *Quercus suber*, an oak of S. Europe and N. Africa yielding cork

cork·screw (kǒrkskru:) **1.** *n.* an implement, usually with a pointed spiral, for removing corks from bottles **2.** *adj.* spiral, twisted, a *corkscrew stairway* **3.** *v.i.* to move spirally or windingly ‖ *v.t.* to cause to move spirally or windingly

corkscrew curl (*cosmetology*) hairstyle involving spiral strands

cork·wood (kǒrkwud) *n.* any of several varieties of tree with light or corky wood, esp. *ochroma lagopus* (*BALSA), *Anona palustris* and *Leitneria floridana*

cork·y (kǒrki:) *comp.* **cork·i·er** *superl.* **cork·i·est** *adj.* like cork

corm (kǒrm) *n.* (*bot.*) an enlarged, round subterranean stem, composed of two or more internodes and covered externally by a few thin, membranous scale leaves. Reproduction occurs when axillary buds develop into new corms (in the crocus, gladiolus etc.) [fr. Gk *kormos*, trunk with boughs lopped off]

cor·mo·rant (kǒrmərənt) *n.* a member of *Phalacrocorax*, a genus of large, black, voracious sea birds, widely distributed over the northern hemisphere [fr. F. *cormoran*]

corn (kǒrn) **1.** *n. Zea mays*, maize, a tall annual American cereal grass having a terminal staminate tassel and lateral pistillate inflorescences covered with protecting leaves. The edible kernels are a source of oil and of cornstarch ‖ small hard seeds of cereals, grain in general esp. (*Br.*) wheat, (*Scot.*) oats ‖ a small hard seed of pepper and a few other plants ‖ a plant producing such seeds ‖ such plants growing or cut ‖ (*pop.*) corny music, dialogue, jokes etc. ‖ (*pop.*) corn whiskey **2.** *v.t.* to preserve with salt, *corned beef* [M.E. fr. O.E.]

corn *n.* a horny hardening or thickening of the skin, esp. on the toes or feet, often caused by friction or pressure [M.E. *coorne* fr. O.F. *corn*, L. *cornu*, horn]

Corn Belt a region in the midwestern U.S.A. extending from Ohio to Kansas and Nebraska, where corn and corn-fed livestock are raised

corn borer the larva of a European moth, *Pyrausta nubilalis*, widespread in U.S. fields of corn

corn bread bread made from cornmeal baked in a shallow pan, and usually eaten hot

corn cake johnnycake

corn chandler (*Br.*) a retail dealer in corn

corn chip crisp snack food of cornmeal

corn·cob (kǒrnkɒb) *n.* the center part of the corn ear, from which a pipe bowl can be made ‖ a pipe with such a bowl

corn cockle *n. Agrostemma githago*, fam. *Caryophyllaceae*, an annual red-flowered weed, decreasingly common in wheatfields etc.

corn·crake (kǒrnkreik) *Crex crex*, a bird with a harsh grating note, living in standing wheatfields etc.

corn·crib (kǒrnkrib) *n.* a ventilated cagelike structure for storing corn

corn dodger a bread made of cornmeal

cor·ne·a (kǒrni:ə) *n.* the transparent portion of the external covering of the eyeball lying over the iris and pupil and permitting light to enter

the interior **cór·ne·al** *adj.* [L. *cornea (tela)*, horny (web)]

Cor·neille (kǒrneij), Pierre (1606–84), French poet and dramatist. The main theme of his tragedies is commonly referred to as a conflict between love and honor. But the love itself is honorable: the conflict therefore is almost between two duties, with the more social obligation determining how the conflict is resolved. Corneille creates a masculine world of vigor and positive energy, where self-knowledge breeds self-confidence. The verse (alexandrines) is appropriately vigorous, but sensitive to the dramatic action. 'Le Cid' (1636) shows the love-honor conflict at its most romantic. In 'Polyeucte' (1641) human love conflicts with a Christian call to martyrdom. 'Cinna' (1641) is more human, more ironic and more dramatic. 'Horace' (1640) shows the Roman virtues of stoicism and social obligation at their bleakest

cor·nel (kǒrn'l) *n.* the dogwood

cor·nel·ian (kǒrní:liən) *n.* a carnelian [M.E. *corneline* fr. F.]

Cor·nell (kǒrnél), Ezra (1807–74), U.S. businessman. With a fortune acquired as a founder of the Western Union Telegraph Company, he helped to finance the founding and development of Cornell University

Cornell University a U.S. private educational institution founded (1865) under the Morrill Act at Ithaca, New York

cor·ne·ous (kǒrni:əs) *adj.* like horn, horny [fr. L. *corneus*]

cor·ner (kǒrnər) **1.** *n.* the point or place of meeting of e.g. two converging sides, *corner of a box* or walls, *corner of a room* or edges, *corner of a page* ‖ the area thus contained ‖ the angle formed by the meeting of two streets ‖ an angular projection ‖ a photographic print mount ‖ a protective piece to fit over a corner ‖ a position from which escape is difficult or dangerous, *driven into a corner* ‖ a remote place, *from every corner of the earth* ‖ a secret place, *hidden in odd corners* ‖ an obscure part, *an odd corner of history* (*commerce*) a buying up of the whole available supply of a stock or commodity, or most of it, so as to raise the price ‖ (*loosely*) any monopolistic combination to raise prices ‖ (*soccer, hockey*) a free hit or kick from the corner flag when the ball has been kicked or hit over the goal line by a player of the defending side **to cut corners** to economize money, time, effort **to rub the corners off someone** to make a person socially adjusted by getting rid of his gaucherie, self-centeredness etc. **to turn the corner** to pass the critical or dangerous stage **2.** *adj.* situated at or placed across a corner, *a corner cupboard* ‖ (*football*) of a defensive player on right or left of line **3.** *v.t.* to supply with corners ‖ to set in a corner ‖ to drive into a corner, *to corner an enemy* ‖ to put in a difficult position ‖ to obtain a corner or monopoly in (a stock or product) ‖ *v.i.* to make a financial corner, *to corner in cotton* ‖ to form, come to or drive around a corner [M.E. fr. A.F.]

cor·ner·back (kǒrnərbæk) *n.* (*football*) defensive player in the backfield assigned to cover the receiver of passes

cor·nered (kǒrnərd) *adj.* having corners, *a three-cornered hat* ‖ driven into a corner, *a cornered rat*

corner man (*basketball*) the forward

cor·ner·stone (kǒrnərstoun) *n.* the stone forming the corner of a building foundation (often ceremonially laid by a celebrity) ‖ the essential basis of some plan or program

cor·ner·ways (kǒrnərweiz) *adv.* cornerwise

cor·ner·wise (kǒrnərwaiz) *adv.* diagonally across a corner

cor·net (kǒrnét) *n.* a brass wind instrument of the trumpet class, used mainly in brass and military bands, with three valves to provide a full chromatic range ‖ a cornet player ‖ (kǒrnit, kǒrnét) something shaped like a horn, e.g. paper rolled into a cone for carrying groceries ‖ (*Br.*, kǒrnit, kǒrnét) a cone for holding ice cream ‖ (*naut.*, kǒrnit, kǒrnét) a signal pennant ‖ (kǒrnét) any of several organ stops [O.F.]

cor·net (kǒrnit, kǒrnét) *n.* a large spreading headdress of starched white linen worn by Sisters of Charity [F. *cornette*]

cor·net·à·pis·tons (kǒrnétəpístənz) *pl.* **cornets·à·pis·tons** (kǒrnétsəpístənz) *n.* the cornet (brass wind instrument)

cor·net·ist, cor·net·tist (kǒrnétist) *n.* a cornet player

corn·flakes (kórnfleiks) *pl. n.* a breakfast food consisting of rolled, toasted, flavored flakes of corn, eaten with milk and sugar

corn·flour (kórnflauər) *n.* (*Br.*) cornstarch || (*Br.*) flour of rice or other grain

corn·flow·er (kórnflauər) *n.* the blueflowered *Centaurea cyanus*, fam. *Compositae*, found growing among wheat, oats etc. Cultivated varieties are grown

corn·husk (kórnhʌsk) *n.* the husk enclosing an ear of corn

cor·nice (kórnis) *n.* (*archit.*) a horizontal strip of stone, wood or plaster crowning a building, usually molded and projecting, esp. part of the entablature above a frieze || a molding of the wall of a room just below the ceiling || an overhanging mass of snow above a precipice [ult. fr. Ital.]

Cor·nish (kórniʃ) 1. *adj.* of or pertaining to Cornwall or Cornishmen 2. *n.* the Brythonic Celtic language spoken until about 1800 by the people of Cornwall and now used by a small minority **Cór·nish·man** *pl.* **Cór·nish·men** *n.*

Corn Laws (*Eng. hist.*) a series of laws passed in England from 1436 onwards limiting the export and import of wheat. The Corn Law of 1815 allowed wheat to be imported duty-free only when the price had risen to 80 shillings a quarter. The high price of bread caused widespread distress, and led to the formation (1838) of the Anti-Corn Law League under Bright and Cobden. After much agitation, and following the Irish potato famine (1845–6), the Corn Laws were repealed (1846) by Peel

corn liquor (*pop.*) corn whiskey

corn·meal (kórnmi:l) *n.* meal made from corn

cor·no·pe·an (kornóupi:ən) *n.* a trumpetlike organ stop

corn pone corn bread, esp. made without milk or eggs

corn row braided hairstyle resembling rows of corn on each side of the scalp, sometimes with braids and pigtails —**corn-row** *v.*

corn silk the fresh styles and stigmas of corn

corn·stalk (kórnstɔk) *n.* the stalk on which the ear of corn grows

corn·starch (kórnstɑrtʃ) *n.* (*Am.=Br.* cornflour) fine-ground flour made from corn and used as a thickening agent in foods, and in the manufacture of corn sugar

corn·stone (kórnstoun) *n.* a variety of earthy, concretionary limestone mottled red and green || (*geol.*) a bed found in the lower Old Red Sandstone

corn sugar dextrose prepared by the hydrolysis of cornstarch

corn syrup glucose

cor·nu·co·pi·a (kɔrnəkóupi:ə) *n.* (*mythol.*) the horn of the goat Amalthea that suckled Jupiter, shown in art as overflowing with corn, flowers and fruit, an emblem of plenty **cor·nu·có·pi·an** *adj.* [L.L. fr. *cornu copiae*, horn of plenty]

Corn·wall (kórnwɔl, *Br.* kónwəl) (*abbr.* Corn.) a county (area 1,357 sq. miles, pop. 401,500) of extreme S.W. England, including the Scilly Isles. It has a long, rocky, much indented coastline. County town: Bodmin. Administrative center: Truro

Corn·wal·lis (kɔrnwólis, kɔrnwólis), Charles, 1st Marquis Cornwallis (1738–1805), British soldier and administrator. As general during the Revolutionary War, he was forced to surrender (1781) at Yorktown. He was governor-general of India (1786–93) and viceroy of Ireland (1798–1801)

corn whiskey whiskey distilled mainly from corn

corn·y (kórni:) *comp.* **corn·i·er** *superl.* **corn·i·est** *adj.* trite, lacking in imagination || mawkish || out-of-date || poor in quality

co·rol·la (kərólə) *n.* a whorl of petals, esp. brightly colored, growing from the receptacle of a flower between the calyx and stamens [L.=little crown]

cor·ol·lar·y (kórələri:, kórəteri:, *Br.* kəróləri) 1. *pl.* **cor·ol·lar·ies** *n.* (*math.*) a proposition which can be inferred from one already proved as self-evidently true || a natural consequence or result 2. *adj.* following as a result, consequential [fr. L. *corollarium*, money paid for a chaplet, gratuity]

co·rol·late (kəróleit, kərólit, kórəlit, kórəlit, kórəleit, kórəlit) *adj.* having a corolla **co·rol·lat·ed** (kəróleitid, kórəleitid, kórəleitid) *adj.*

Cor·o·man·del, Coast of (kɔrəmǽnd'l, kɔrəmǽnd'l) the southeast littoral of India on the Bay of Bengal, from the Cauvery delta to the Kistna delta. It was the scene of the Franco-British struggle for supremacy in India during the 18th c.

co·ro·na (kəróunə) *pl.* **co·ro·nas, co·ro·nae** (kəróuni:) *n.* (*astron.*) the upper region of the solar atmosphere, consisting of highly ionized gases. It is of unknown extent, but is observed at the time of total eclipse at a distance of 9 million miles from the sun. Spectroscopic evidence indicates temperatures of the order of 1 million degrees C. in parts of the corona, and this cannot be explained satisfactorily as yet || a similar ring around the moon or stars || a luminous ring formed by reflection on a fogbank or cloud on the opposite side of an observer to the sun || (*archit.*) the projecting part of a cornice || (*bot.*) a cup-shaped body formed by the union of scales on perianth leaves, e.g. in the trumpet of the daffodil, narcissus etc. || (*zool.*) the theca and anus of a crinoid || (*biol.*) the head or upper portion of any structure || (*anat.*) any of various bones etc. shaped like a crown, e.g. in the skull or a tooth, (*elec.*) a visible discharge on the surface of a high-voltage conductor || a circular church chandelier [L=crown]

Co·ro·na·do (kɔrɔnáðo), Francisco Vasquez de (1510–c. 1554), Spanish explorer of the southwestern U.S.A.

co·ro·nal (kəróun'l, kórən'l, kórən'l) *adj.* of the corona of the skull || pertaining to or situated toward the suture between the frontal and parietal bones of the skull [F. or fr. L. *coronalis* fr. *corona*, crown]

cor·o·nal (kórən'l, kórən'l) *n.* a crown, coronet or circlet (esp. of gold or gems) || a wreath or garland for the head [prob. A.F.]

cor·o·nar·y (kórəneri:, kórəneri:) *adj.* of or pertaining to a crown, crownlike || (*anat.*) pertaining to either of two arteries arising from the aorta and supplying blood to the heart muscles [fr. L. *coronarius*]

coronary bypass (*med.*) surgical establishment of a blood supply to organs to which the arteries have been blocked or destroyed *syn.* revascularization

coronary thrombosis the formation of a clot in the coronary arteries, and consequent blockage of them. As a result a part of the heart may cease functioning

cor·o·nate (kórəneit, kórəneit) *adj.* (of the sun or moon) supplied with a corona **cór·o·nat·ed** *adj.* [fr. L. *coronare* (*coronatus*), to crown]

cor·o·na·tion (kɔrənéiʃən, kɔrənéiʃən) *n.* the act or ceremony of crowning a sovereign [O.F.]
—In its fullest form the rite used in Europe includes popular consent publicly given, an oath by the sovereign to govern according to certain principles, consecration by prayer and anointment, investiture with regalia, enthronement and communion

Co·ro·nel O·vie·do (kɔrɔnélɔvjéðo) a city (pop. 44,000) in E. Paraguay

cor·o·ner (kórənər, kórənər) *n.* a public officer whose most usual task is to hold an inquiry into the causes of accidental or suspicious deaths **cór·o·ner·ship** *n.* [A.F. *corouner*, orig. the officer responsible for private property rights of the Crown]

coroner's jury the jury sitting at a coroner's inquest

cor·o·net (kórənit, kórənet, kórənit, kórənet, kɔrənét, kɔrənét) *n.* a small crown worn by nobility, e.g. by dukes, earls and their ladies || a representation of this on arms, a carriage etc. || a woman's ornamental headdress, esp. of jewels or gold, or of flowers || the lower part of a horse's pastern || (*zool.*) a knob at the base of a deer's antler **cór·o·net·ed, cór·o·net·ted** *adj.* wearing or entitled to wear a coronet [O.F. *coronette*, dim. of *corone*, crown]

co·ro·noid (kórənɔid, kórənɔid) *adj.* (*anat.*, of bones) curved like a crow's beak [fr. Gk *korōnē*, crow]

Co·ro·pu·na, Ne·va·do (neváðokɔrɔpú:na) a peak (c. 21,720 ft) in the Andes northwest of Arequipa, Peru

Co·rot (kɔrou), Jean Baptiste Camille (1796–1875), French landscape painter. His early strong, luminous landscapes differ markedly from those of a later period, when he sought to convey the poetry of mysterious shadows and half-lights

co·ro·zo (kəróuzou) *n. Phytelephas macrocarpa*, a tree of South America allied to palms [native name]

corozo nut the hardened albumen of the corozo seed, used as a substitute for ivory, e.g. for buttons, chessmen etc.

cor·po·ral (kórpərəl, kórprəl) *adj.* belonging or relating to the body [O.F.]

corporal *n.* (*eccles.*) a cloth used to cover the consecrated elements during the Mass (Eucharist) [fr. M.L. *corporalis* (*palla*), body (cloth)]

corporal *n.* a noncommissioned officer in the army ranking below sergeant [older F. var. of *caporal* fr. Ital.]

cor·po·ral·i·ty (kɔrpərǽliti:) *n.* the fact of being or having a body || material existence [fr. L.L. *corporalitas*]

corporal punishment a punishing by flogging, birching etc.

cor·po·rate (kórpərit, kórprit) *adj.* united, combined into one, *a corporate effort* || incorporated || belonging to an incorporated body, or corporation, *corporate property* **in a corporate capacity** acting as a body rather than as a number of individuals [fr. L. *corporare* (*corporatus*), to form into a body]

corporate state perception of government as ordered, legalistic, yet insensitive to human values; from Charles Reich's *The Greening of America*, 1970 (Sometimes also descriptive of Fascist Italy in the 1920s and 1930s)

corporate town a town having municipal rights and acting through a corporation

cor·po·ra·tion (kɔrpəréiʃən) *n.* a body or society entitled to act as a single person, esp. a body of municipal authorities || (*law*) an artificial person created by charter etc., made up of many persons (corporation aggregate) or one (corporation sole) [fr. L. *corporatio* (*corporationis*), action of incorporating]

cor·po·ra·tive (kórpəreitiv, kórpərətiv, kórprətiv) *adj.* relating to or consisting of a corporation || of a political system giving supreme authority to representatives from key corporations meeting in one corporate body [fr. L. *corporativus*]

cor·po·re·al (kɔrpóri:əl, kɔrpóuri:əl) *adj.* of the body || material, physical (opp. SPIRITUAL) || (*law*) tangible, palpable, *corporeal hereditaments* (material possessions) **cor·po·re·ál·i·ty** *n.* [fr. L. *corporeus*]

cor·po·re·i·ty (kɔrpərí:iti:) *n.* the state or quality of being or having a physical body || physical substance [fr. M. L. *corporeitas*]

cor·po·sant (kórpəzænt) *n.* St Elmo's fire [fr. Port. *corpo santo*=holy body]

corps (kor, kour) *pl.* **corps** (korz, kourz) *n.* part of an army forming a tactical unit and consisting of two or more divisions || a body of specialist troops, *Medical Corps, Intelligence Corps* || a body of trained people working together, e.g. of nurses in a hospital [F.=body]

corps de bal·let (kɔrdəbæléi, kɔrdəbælei) *n.* the chorus of a company of ballet dancers (i.e. as distinct from principals, soloists)

corps di·plo·ma·tique (kɔrdiplɔmætí:k) *n.* the whole body of ambassadors, secretaries, attachés etc. of foreign states in a capital city or court [F.]

corpse (kɔrps) *n.* the dead body of a human being || anything defunct [M.E. *corps*, var. of *cors* fr. O.F.]

corps·man (kórmən, kóurmən) *pl.* **corps·men** (kórmən, kóurmən) *n.* (*mil.*) an enlisted man in the medical corps

cor·pu·lence (kórpjuləns) *n.* the state or quality of being corpulent **cór·pu·len·cy** *n.*

cor·pu·lent (kórpjulənt) *adj.* having a fat body [F.]

cor·pus (kórpəs) *pl.* **cor·po·ra** (kórpərə) *n.* a body of writings of a particular kind or on a particular subject, *a corpus of Greek inscriptions* || (*rhet.*) a whole, ensemble, *the corpus of opinion was in favor* || (*physiol.*) the main part of the structure of an organ, or any of several bodies, masses or parts with particular functions [L.= body]

Cor·pus Chris·ti (kórpəskrísti:) a port and resort (pop. 231,999) in Texas: oil refining, food processing

Corpus Christi, Feast of the Thursday after Trinity, when Catholics carry the consecrated Host in procession with great pomp

cor·pus·cle (kórpəs'l, kórpʌs'l) *n.* any minute body, esp. one of the free-floating cells found in blood [fr. L. *corpusculum*, dim. of *corpus*, body]

cor·pus·cu·lar (kɔrpʌ́skjulər) *adj.* of or pertaining to corpuscles [fr. L. *corpusculum*]

corpuscular theory a theory in physics that light consists of particles or corpuscles given off by luminous bodies (cf. WAVE THEORY)

cor·pus de·lic·ti (kórpəsdilíktai) *n.* (*law*) the basic fact or facts establishing that a crime or

CONCISE PRONUNCIATION KEY: **(a)** æ, c*a*t; ɑ, c*a*r; ɔ f*aw*n; ei, sn*a*ke. **(e)** e, h*e*n; i:, sh*ee*p; iə, d*ee*r; ɛə, b*ea*r. **(i)** i, f*i*sh; ai, t*i*ger; ə:, b*i*rd. **(o)** o, *o*x; au, c*ow*; ou, g*oa*t; u, p*oo*r; ɔi, r*oy*al. **(u)** ʌ, d*u*ck; u, b*u*ll; u:, g*oo*se; ə, b*a*cillus; ju:, c*u*be. x, lo*ch*; θ, *th*ink; ð, bo*th*er; z, *Z*en; ʒ, cor*s*age; dʒ, sava*g*e; ŋ, orangutan*g*; j, *y*ak; ʃ, *fi*sh; tʃ, fe*tch*; 'l, rabb*le*; 'n, redd*en*. Complete pronunciation key appears inside front cover.

offense has actually been committed [L.=body of the crime]

cor·pus ju·ris (kórpəsdʒúəris) n. a collection of laws, the whole body of law by which a people is governed [L.]

cor·ral (kərǽl, Br. kərál) 1. n. an enclosure for cattle, horses etc. ‖ a defensive enclosure made by placing wagons in a circle ‖ an enclosure for the capture of wild animals 2. v.t. pres. part. **cor·ral·ling** past and past part. **cor·ralled** to form a corral with (wagons) ‖ to put or drive (animals) into a corral ‖ (pop.) to capture and keep hold of [Span.]

cor·rect (kərékt) 1. v.t. to put right, to correct an error ‖ to remove faults from, to correct proof sheets ‖ to admonish, reprove, chastise ‖ to adjust, bring to standard, correct your watch ‖ to adjust for some known or estimated deviation, correct the reading for individual error 2. adj. true, a correct account ‖ accurate, the correct time ‖ conforming to recognized standards, correct grammar ‖ conventional ‖ complying with etiquette [fr. L. corrigere (correctus), to correct]

cor·rec·tion (kərékʃən) n. an emending or an emendation ‖ a rebuking or punishing or an instance of either ‖ an allowance made for something to ensure accuracy, correction for wind velocity ‖ **to speak under correction** to admit the possibility of error **cor·rec·tion·al** adj. [F.]

cor·rect·i·tude (kəréktitu:d, kəréktitu:d) n. correctness, esp. propriety of conduct

cor·rec·tive (kəréktiv) 1. adj. tending or having power to correct 2. n. a corrective agent, a corrective for stomach acidity [F.]

cor·rec·tor (kəréktər) n. a person who corrects, censors or punishes ‖ (Br.) a proofreader [fr. A.F. corectour]

Cor·reg·gio (kərréddʒo), Antonio Allegri (c. 1489–1534), Italian painter. He was in advance of his time in his use of light for emphasis and balance in an unconventional composition, in his use of perspective and foreshortening in the cupola paintings at Parma, and in the softness ('morbidezza') of style which contributes to the sensuality of his mythological paintings

Cor·reg·i·dor (kərégidɔr) an island in Manila Bay, the scene of a battle early in the 2nd world war in which U.S. and Filipino forces capitulated (May 6, 1942) to the stronger Japanese army. U.S. troops regained it in 1945

cor·re·late (kórəleit, kórəleit) 1. n. either of two things or words implying the other, e.g. 'father' and 'son' 2. v. pres. part. **cor·re·lat·ing** past and past part. **cor·re·lat·ed** v.t. to bring into mutual or reciprocal relation, to correlate crime with poverty ‖ to connect systematically, to correlate the study of language and literature ‖ v.i. to have a mutual relation, the two sets of figures correlate **cor·re·la·tion** (kɔrəléiʃən, kɔrəléiʃən) n. the act or state of being correlated ‖ (biol.) mutual relationship ‖ (statistics) degree of relationship [fr. L. cor-, together+relatus fr. referre, to refer]

correlation coefficient (statistics) the ratio between one variable and another, varying from + 1 for perfect positive correlation to - 1 for perfect negative correlation, being zero for complete absence of correlation

cor·rel·a·tive (kərélətiv) 1. adj. mutually or reciprocally related ‖ corresponding, similar ‖ (gram.) expressing a reciprocal relationship, correlative conjunctions (e.g. 'neither... nor', 'both... and') ‖ (biol.) found in correlation with another 2. n. something in a mutual relationship to something else ‖ a correlative word [fr. L. cor-, together+relativus, relative]

cor·re·spond (kɔrispónd, kɔrispónd) v.i. to communicate, esp. by letter ‖ to be similar in function, etc., the French Sûreté corresponds to the British Scotland Yard ‖ to be equivalent or representative, red lines on the map correspond to major roads ‖ to be in agreement or harmony, his job corresponds with his interests **cor·re·spónd·ing** adj. agreeing in any way, e.g. in kind, degree or position ‖ similar ‖ related, privileges with corresponding obligations ‖ communicating by or dealing with letters, corresponding secretary [fr. M.L. correspondere, to respond]

cor·re·spond·ence (kɔrispóndəns, kɔrispóndəns) n. harmony, agreement, the state of having qualities in common ‖ an exchange of letters ‖ letters in general

Correspondence, Committees of originally committees appointed by American colonial

legislatures to correspond with English colonial agents. They served (1772) as agencies of colonial discontent and finally (1773) as committees for intercolonial communication. They promoted colonial unity and played a major role in assembling (1774) the first continental congress

correspondence school an institution offering tuition by mail

cor·re·spond·ent (kɔrispóndənt, kɔrispóndənt) 1. n. a person with whom one exchanges letters ‖ a journalist employed to send regular reports or news items to a newspaper ‖ a person having regular commercial contact with a firm, esp. one distant or overseas 2. adj. corresponding [fr. M.L. correspondens (correspondentis) fr. correspondere, to agree with]

corresponding member an honorary member of a society without a vote, taking part in its proceedings at a distance (commonly abroad) by correspondence

Cor·rèze (kɔrez) a department (area 2,272 sq. miles, pop. 240,400) of S. Central France in the Massif Central (*LIMOUSIN). Chief town: Tulle

cor·ri·da (kɔrí:də) n. a bullfight [Span.]

cor·ri·dor (kɔ́ridər, kɔ́ridər, kɔ́ridɔr, kɔ́ridɔr) n. a long passageway, e.g. in a hotel with doors leading off it into separate rooms ‖ an outdoor passage connecting parts of a building ‖ a narrow strip of land across previously foreign territory, owned by a landbound power thus given access to a seaport [F. fr. Ital. corridore fr. correre, to run]

corridor train (Br.) a train in which the cars have a narrow passage from end to end giving access to all seats and lavatories

cor·rie (kɔ́ri, kɔ́ri) n. (geog.) a circular or semicircular recess on a mountainside [Gael. coire, a cauldron]

cor·ri·gen·dum (kɔridʒéndəm, kɔridʒéndəm) pl. **cor·ri·gen·da** (kɔridʒéndə, kɔridʒéndə) n. a mistake, error to be corrected, in a manuscript or printed work ‖ (pl.) a list of such errors and the corrections to be made, included in a book, or issued separately, often with addenda [L.]

cor·ri·gi·ble (kɔ́ridʒəbəl, kɔ́ridʒəbəl) adj. open to correction, amendment or reform [F.]

cor·rob·o·rant (kərɔ́bərənt) 1. adj. serving to confirm 2. n. a supporting fact [F.]

cor·rob·o·rate (kərɔ́bəreit) pres. part. **cor·rob·o·rat·ing** past and past part. **cor·rob·o·rat·ed** v.t. to confirm by law ‖ to give confirmation of or evidence to support, laboratory tests corroborate the maker's claims [fr. L. corroborare (corroboratus), to strengthen]

cor·rob·o·ra·tion (kərɔbəréiʃən) n. confirmation, support by further evidence [F.]

cor·rob·o·ra·tive (kərɔ́bəreitiv, kərɔ́bərətiv) adj. serving to corroborate

cor·rob·o·ra·tor (kərɔ́bəreitər) n. someone who corroborates

cor·rob·o·ra·to·ry (kərɔ́bərətɔri:, krɔ́bərətɔuri:) adj. corroborative

cor·rob·o·ree (kərɔ́bəri:) n. a dance festival of Australian aborigines [native word]

cor·rode (kəróud) pres. part. **cor·rod·ing** past and past part. **cor·rod·ed** v.t. to eat away by degrees, eat into the surface of, acids corrode metals ‖ to consume, corroding envy and malice ‖ v.i. to become eaten away, this metal corrodes quickly [fr. L. corrodere, to gnaw away]

cor·ro·sion (kəróuʒən) n. the process of wearing away the surface of a solid, esp. of metals and building stone, by converting the compact, cohesive substance into a friable one as the result of chemical action or the surface action of moisture (cf. EROSION, *RUSTING) [O.F.]

cor·ro·sive (kəróusiv) 1. adj. producing corrosion ‖ corroding the mind, corrosive criticism 2. n. a substance which corrodes [F. corrosif]

corrosive sublimate mercuric chloride

cor·ru·gate (kɔ́rəgeit, kúrəgeit) pres. part. **cor·ru·gat·ing** past and past part. **cor·ru·gat·ed** v.t. to form into wrinkles, folds, alternate ridges and grooves, corrugated iron ‖ v.i. to become corrugated **cor·ru·ga·tion** n. the act of corrugating ‖ a single ridge or groove of a corrugated surface [fr. L. corrugare (corrugatus)]

cor·ru·ga·tor (kɔ́rəgeitər, kúrəgeitər) n. each of two muscles on the forehead enabling a person to frown [Mod. L.]

cor·rupt (kərʌ́pt) 1. adj. depraved ‖ changed from a sound to a putrid state ‖ dishonest, open to bribery ‖ not genuine, full of errors, a corrupt text 2. v.t. to pervert, make wicked ‖ to defile, taint ‖ to falsify, to corrupt a text ‖ to bribe, to corrupt a judge ‖ v.i. to become corrupt [fr. L. corrumpere (corruptus), to break completely]

cor·rupt·i·bil·i·ty (kərʌptəbíliti:) n. the state or quality of being corruptible

cor·rupt·i·ble (kərʌ́ptəb'l) adj. open to corruption, esp. to bribes **cor·rúpt·i·bly** adv. [fr. L. corruptibilis]

cor·rup·tion (kərʌ́pʃən) n. a corrupting ‖ the state of being or becoming decayed ‖ a spoiling, deteriorating, the corruption of taste by cheap journalism ‖ corrupt practices ‖ perversion ‖ moral decay ‖ a corrupting influence ‖ a debased form of a word [F.]

cor·rup·tive (kərʌ́ptiv) adj. tending to corrupt [fr. L. corruptivus]

Corrupt Practices Act a U.S. congressional law (1925) which regulates spending in political campaigns. No candidate has ever been convicted of violating it

cor·sage (kɔrsáʒ) n. the bodice of a woman's dress ‖ a spray of flowers to be worn on a dress [O.F., dim. of cors, body]

cor·sair n. (hist.) a privateer or pirate, esp. of the Barbary coast [F. corsaire]

corselet * CORSLET

cor·set (kɔ́rsit) n. a close-fitting, usually stiffened, woman's undergarment extending from the bust to below the hips, worn to support the body and sustain or impose shape [F., dim. of O.F. cors, body]

Cor·si·ca (kɔ́rsikə) an island (area 3,367 sq. miles, pop. 292,000) in the Mediterranean, 100 miles southeast of France and 50 miles west of Italy, near Sardinia. It is a department of France. A quarter of the population lives in the two ports of Ajaccio (the capital) and Bastia, the rest in scattered villages, much of the island being uninhabited. Emigration to the continent is heavy. Official language: French. The majority also speak Corsican, an Italian dialect. The land is mostly mountainous (Monte Cinto 8,891 ft). The climate is mild on the coast, but very cold in the mountains. The soil is fertile, but only 2% is cultivated (citrus fruits, olives). Half of the island is pasture and forest. Sheep, goats, and pigs are raised. Industries: wine, olive oil, cork, paper, cheese, tourism. HISTORY. The island was colonized (6th c. B.C.) by the Greeks, and was conquered by the Romans (c. 260 B.C.), the Vandals (469 A.D.) and the Byzantines (533). It passed to Pisa (1077) and to Genoa (1453). Paoli ruled the interior from 1755 until Genoa sold Corsica to France (1768). Britain occupied the island (1794–6 and 1814) but it was restored to France by the Congress of Vienna (1815)

Cor·si·can (kɔ́rsikən) 1. n. an inhabitant or the dialect of Corsica 2. adj. of Corsica

cors·let, corse·let (kɔ́rslit) n. (hist.) a defensive covering for the body, of armor or leather [F. double dim. of cors, body]

Cort (kɔrt), Henry (1740–1800), British ironmaster. His invention of grooved rolls to remove slag and of a method of puddling iron (1784) contributed to the progress of the Industrial Revolution

cor·tege, cor·tège (kɔrtéʒ, kɔrtéiʒ) n. a procession, esp. a funeral procession ‖ a retinue [F.]

Cor·tés (kɔrtés), Hernán (1485–1547), Spanish conquistador. He invaded Mexico (1519) and conquered the Aztec kingdom ruled by Montezuma. After destroying (1521) the capital, he reorganized the country as a Spanish province

Cortes, the (kɔ́rtes) the legislative assembly in Spain and Portugal

cor·tex (kɔ́rteks) pl. **cor·ti·ces** (kɔ́rtisi:z), **cor·tex·es** n. (anat.) the outer layer of gray matter of the brain ‖ the outer part of certain glands, e.g. the adrenal gland, or certain organisms, e.g. some protozoa ‖ (bot.) a plant tissue of varying thickness with many intercellular spaces, lying between the endodermis (which encloses the vascular system) and the outer skin (epidermis). The outer part of the cortex may eventually develop into bark ‖ (loosely) an outer layer, rind, bark [L.=bark]

cor·ti·cal (kɔ́rtik'l) adj. of or pertaining to the cortex of plants or animals ‖ of or connected with the action of the cerebral cortex, cortical blindness [fr. Mod. L. corticalis fr. cortex, shell]

cortical stimulator (med.) device delivering a measured shock used for mental therapy

cor·ti·cate (kɔ́rtikit, kɔ́rtikeit) adj. having bark or a cortical covering **cór·ti·cat·ed** adj. [fr. L. corticatus fr. cortex, bark]

cor·tin (kɔ́rt'n, kɔ́rtin) n. a hormone containing an extract of the adrenal gland [CORTEX]

cor·ti·sone (kɔ́rtizoun, kɔ́rtisoun) *n.* a hormone derived from the adrenal gland, used in the treatment of rheumatoid arthritis and of some eye diseases and some allergic disorders [fr. *dehydrocorticosterone,* the chemical name of the hormone]

co·run·dum (kərʌ́ndəm) *n.* aluminum oxide occurring as a very hard crystallized mineral and used as an abrasive, in polishing powder etc.: forms include ruby, sapphire, emery [Tamil *kurundam,* ruby]

Co·run·na (kərʌ́nə) *LA CORUNA

Corunna, Battle of a British rearguard action (1809) against the French during the Peninsular War. The British commander, Sir John Moore, was fatally wounded

cor·us·cate (kɔ́rəskeit, kɔ́rəskeit) *pres. part.* **cor·us·cat·ing** *past* and *past part.* **cor·us·cat·ed** *v.i.* to throw off flashes of light, glitter, sparkle ∥ to throw out flashes of intellectual brilliance, *coruscating wit* **cor·us·ca·tion** *n.* [fr. L. *coruscare (coruscatus),* to flash]

cor·vée (kɔrvéi) *n.* (*hist.*) the unpaid labor due to a feudal overlord ∥ (*hist.*) the system of such labor (e.g. by French peasants until at least 1776) [F.]

corves *pl.* of CORF

cor·vette (kɔrvét) *n.* (*hist.*) a war vessel with a single tier of guns and a flush deck ∥ (*navy*) an escort vessel, small, fast and lightly armored, having antisubmarine and antiaircraft weapons [F. fr. Port. *corveta*]

cor·vine (kɔ́rvain, kɔ́rvin) *adj.* crowlike ∥ of or pertaining to ravens, crows etc. [fr. L. *corvinus*]

Corvinus *MATTHIAS CORVINUS

Cor·y·bant (kɔ́ribænt, kɔ́ribænt) *pl.* **Cor·y·ban·tes** (kɔribǽnti:z, kɔribǽnti:z), **Cor·y·bants** *n.* (*Gk mythol.*) a priest of Cybele, whose worship was marked by frenzied music and dances **Cor·y·bán·tic** *adj.* [F. *Corybante* fr. L. fr. Gk *Korubanta*]

cor·ymb (kɔ́rimb, kɔ́rimb, kɔ́rim, kɔ́rim) *n.* (*bot.*) a raceme with the lower pedicels elongated so that the top of the inflorescence is nearly flat, e.g. candytuft **co·rym·bose** (kərímbous) *adj.* [F. *corymbe* fr. L. fr. Gk]

cor·y·ne·bac·te·ri·um (kɔrəni:bæktíəri:əm) *pl.* **cor·y·ne·bac·te·ri·a** (kɔrəni:bæktíəri:ə) *n.* a member of *Corynebacterium,* fam. *Corynebacteriaceae,* a genus of chiefly nonmotile, grampositive, aerobic, rod-shaped bacteria, among which are important parasites (e.g. diphtheria) [Mod. L. fr. Gk *korunē,* club- + BACTERIUM]

cor·y·phée (kɔriféi, kɔriféi) *n.* a leading member of a corps de ballet [F.]

co·ry·za (kəráizə) *n.* (*med.*) the common cold ∥ catarrh in poultry [L. fr. Gk *koruza,* running at the nose]

Cos *Kos

cos (kɒs, kɔs) *n.* (*Br.*) romaine [after Gk *Kōs* (Aegean island)]

'Co·sa Nos·tra' (kóusənóustrə) allegedly a group of the Mafia, operating in the U.S.A.

co·se·cant (kousí:kænt, kousí:kənt) *n.* (*math., abbr.* cosec) the reciprocal of the sine [F. *cosecante*]

co·seis·mal (kousáizməl, kousáizməl) **1.** *adj.* of points of simultaneous shock from an earthquake wave **2.** *n.* the line or curve connecting such points on a chart

cosh (kɒʃ) **1.** *n.* (*Br.*) a blackjack, bludgeon **2.** *v.t.* (*Br.*) to strike with a cosh [origin unknown]

co·sig·na·to·ry (kousígnətɔ:ri, kousígnətɔuri:) **1.** *n.* a person signing a document, treaty etc. jointly with others **2.** *adj.* signing jointly

cosily *COZILY

co·sine (kóusain) *n.* (*math., abbr.* cos) a measure of the magnitude of an angle expressed as the constant ratio of the side adjacent to the angle and the hypotenuse in a right-angled triangle

cosiness *COZINESS

Cos·mas and Ba·mi·an (kɒ́sməs, déimi:ən), Sts (3rd c.), Arabian brothers commemorated in the canon of the Mass. After surviving ordeals of drowning, burning and stoning they were beheaded. Feast: Sept. 27

cos·met·ic (kɒzmétik) **1.** *adj.* designed to beautify the complexion, eyes, hair, lips, nails etc. **2.** *n.* a preparation to enhance beauty, cleanse and improve the skin etc. **cos·me·ti·cian** (kɒzmitíʃən) *n.* a person skilled in the use of cosmetics [fr. Gk *kosmētikos* fr. *kosmein,* to adorn]

cosmetic surgery (*med.*) any operation directed at improving appearance, except when required for the prompt repair of accidental injury or the improvement of the functioning of a malformed body member

cos·mic (kɒ́zmik) *adj.* of or pertaining to the cosmos **cós·mi·cal·ly** *adv.* [fr. Gk *kosmikos* fr. *kosmos,* world]

cosmic dust minute particles of solid matter distributed throughout the universe

cosmic radiation radiation by cosmic rays, consisting chiefly of protons, with some electrons and atomic nuclei. Their collision or reaction with particles in the atmosphere gives rise to a wide variety of secondary radiation known as a cosmic ray shower. The energy of a cosmic-ray particle may be as much as 10^{17} eV

cosmic ray any of a group of very high-energy particles reaching the earth from outer space or produced in the earth's atmosphere by the particles from outer space. The former are heavy nuclei moving at speeds close to that of light, while the latter consist in large part of mesons, positrons, electrons, fast protons etc. The energy of some cosmic rays is in the range 10^{15} to 10^{20} eV, far exceeding that of particles produced by man-made particle accelerators

cos·mo·drome (kɒ́zmədroum) *n.* a U.S.S.R. space-launching center

cos·mo·gen·ic (kɒzmədʒénik) *adj.* affected by cosmic rays

cos·mo·gon·ic (kɒzməgɒ́nik) *adj.* relating to or dealing with cosmogony **cos·mo·gón·i·cal** *adj.*

cos·mog·o·nist (kɒzmɒ́gənist) *n.* someone specializing in cosmogony

cos·mog·o·ny (kɒzmɒ́gəni:) *pl.* **cos·mog·o·nies** *n.* the origin of the universe ∥ a theory of its origin [fr. Gk *kosmogonia*]

cos·mog·ra·pher (kɒzmɒ́grəfər) *n.* someone skilled in cosmography

cos·mo·graph·ic (kɒzməgrǽfik) *adj.* concerned with or relating to cosmography **cos·mo·gráph·i·cal** *adj.*

cos·mog·ra·phist (kɒzmɒ́grəfist) *n.* a cosmographer

cos·mog·ra·phy (kɒzmɒ́grəfi:) *pl.* **cos·mog·ra·phies** *n.* a general description of the world or the universe, its interrelations and materials ∥ the science dealing with the structure of the universe, including astronomy, geography and geology [fr. Gk *kosmographia*]

cos·mo·log·i·cal (kɒzmələ́dʒik'l) *adj.* of or relating to cosmology

cos·mol·o·gist (kɒzmɒ́lədʒist) *n.* someone skilled in cosmology

cos·mol·o·gy (kɒzmɒ́lədʒi:) *pl.* **cos·mol·o·gies** *n.* the branch of metaphysics dealing with the universe as a systematic order ∥ a cosmological theory [fr. Gk *kosmos,* world + *logos* discourse]

cos·mo·naut (kɒ́zmənɔt, kɒ́zmənɒt) *n.* (used esp. in the U.S.S.R.) an astronaut [fr. Gk *kosmos,* world + *nautēs,* sailor]

cos·mo·naut·ics (kɒzmənɔ́tiks) *n.* science of space travel —**cosmonaut** *n.* —**cosmonautic** *adj.*

cos·mo·pol·i·tan (kɒzməpólitən) **1.** *adj.* free from local, provincial or national prejudices ∥ composed of many nationalities, languages etc., *a cosmopolitan city* ∥ (*biol.*) common to all or most of the world **2.** *n.* someone who is cosmopolitan **cos·mo·pól·i·tan·ism** *n.*

cos·mop·o·lite (kɒzmɒ́pəlait) **1.** *n.* a person without national ties or prejudices ∥ a plant or animal common to most of the world **2.** *adj.* international in outlook **cos·móp·o·lit·ism** *n.* [fr. Gk *kosmopolitēs*]

cos·mos (kɒ́zməs, kɒ́zmous) *n.* the universe viewed as an orderly whole ∥ an ordered system of ideas, self-inclusive and harmonious, *the Platonic cosmos* [Gk *kosmos*]

cosmos *pl.* **cos·mos, cos·mos·es** *n.* a member of *Cosmos,* fam. *Compositae,* a genus of garden annuals with disklike flowers of white, pink, red etc. [fr. Gk *kosmos,* ornament]

Cosmos U.S.S.R. satellite series used for observation, research, and other scientific applications

cos·mo·tron (kɒ́zmətrɒn) *n.* a protonsynchrotron [COSMIC RAY + ELECTRON]

Cos·sack (kɒ́sæk, kɒ́sək) *n.* a member of a national group of S. Russia, famous as horsemen and cavalrymen. The descendants of Russian and Ukrainian serfs, the Cossacks settled on the steppes (16th c.), establishing the Ukraine as a separate state [Russ. *kozak,* Turk. *quzaq,* adventurer]

cos·set (kɒ́sit) *v.t.* to pamper [perh.= O.E. *cotsǣta,* cot-sitter (an animal reared in the house)]

cost (kɒst, kɒst) *n.* the price paid or to be paid for something ∥ (*pl.*) expenses of litigation, esp. those payable to counsel etc. by the client ∥ an item in the outlay of time, labor, trouble etc. on a job **at all costs** whatever money, sacrifice etc. it may cost, *determined to win at all costs* **at cost** at cost price, at bare manufacturing price **at the cost of** with the loss of or damage of as a direct result, *he finished the work at the cost of his health* **to count the cost** to reckon up the risks involved **to one's cost** to one's disadvantage, suffering or loss [O.F. *cost, coust*]

cost *pres. part.* **cost·ing** *past* and *past part.* **cost** *v.t.* to require an outlay or expenditure of, *his car costs a lot in upkeep* ∥ to result in (a specified loss), *careless driving cost him his life* ∥ to calculate the outlay on, *to cost a job* [O.F. *coster, couster*]

cos·ta (kɒ́stə, kɔ́stə) *n.* (*zool.*) a rib ∥ (*bot.*) a rib or vein **cós·tal** *adj.* [L.= rib]

cost accounting the recording and analysis of production and overhead expenses in a business

Cos·ta e Sil·va (kɒ́ʃtaesí:lvə), Arthur da (1902–69), Brazilian president. He was a leader of the military coup that deposed (1964) President João Goulart. After serving as War Minister in Brazil's first military regime, he was elected (1966) president by the army-controlled Congress. Despite his promises to 'humanize' the regime, he dissolved (1968) Congress and instituted rule by decree, ending all pretense of civilian government

Cos·ta Ri·ca (kɒ́stəri:kə, kɔ́stəri:kə, kóustərí:kə) a republic (area 19,650 sq. miles, pop. 2,339,800) in Central America. Capital: San José. It includes Cocos (area 12 sq. miles), 300 miles to the southwest. 75% of the population live in the highlands, 20% on the Pacific side and 5% on the Caribbean. People: 48% European descent, 47% Mestizo, and minorities of West Indian origin and Indians. Language: Spanish. State religion: Roman Catholic. The land is 75% forest, 13% pasture and 7% arable. The Continental Divide rises to 12,000 ft in the two great volcanic ranges, the Cordillera Volcanica and the Cordillera de Talamanca, and contains the central highland region (3,000–5,000 ft). The Pacific coast is an area of cattle raising and banana plantations. The Caribbean lowland is swampy. Rainfall: 40–80 ins along the Pacific coast, 76 ins in San José, and 100–200 ins in the Caribbean. Average temperature in San José: 68° F. Livestock: cattle. Agricultural products: coffee, bananas, cacao, abaca, corn, sugar, rice. Mineral resources: silver. Exports: coffee, bananas, cacao. Imports: manufactures, machinery, chemicals, foodstuffs. Ports: Puerto Limón on the Atlantic, Puntarenas on the Pacific. University: San José (1843). Monetary unit: colón (divided into 100 centimos). HISTORY. Costa Rica, sparsely populated by scattered groups of Indians, was visited by Columbus (1502), and colonized by Spain (1562 onward), forming a neglected part of Guatemala until it broke away from Spain (1821). It was part of the Mexican Empire (1821–3), and joined the Central American Federation (1823–38). A new constitution was drawn up (1871). It entered the 1st world war (1918) and the 2nd world war (1941) on the side of the Allies. Despite some revolts (1948, 1955), political stability was maintained. (The army was disbanded in 1948, and after 1948 every election was won by the party in opposition at the time.) José Figueres, of the moderate socialist National Liberation Party, who took control (1948) at the head of a junta, stepped aside (1949) and allowed President-elect Otilio Ulate to take office, but later served (1953–8, 1970–82) as constitutional president. Luis Alberto Monge succeeded him during Costa Rica's worst economic crisis in 30 years

Costa Ri·can (kɒ́stərí:k'n, kɔ́stərí:k'n, kóustərí:k'n) **1.** *n.* a native or inhabitant of Costa Rica **2.** *adj.* of or relating to Costa Rica

cos·tate (kɒ́steit, kɔ́steit) *adj.* having ribs or veins [fr. L. *costatus*]

cost-ben·e·fit (kɒstbénəfit) *n.* benefit relative to the cost involved

cos·tean, cos·teen (kɒstí:n) *v.i.* (*Br.*) to sink pits during mining to find the direction of a seam [fr. Corn. *cothas stean,* dropped tin]

cost-ef·fec·tive or **cost-ef·fi·cient** (kɒstiféktiv) (kɒstifíʃənt) *adj.* (*business*) of the relative benefit for the cost involved: *Is the project cost-effective?* —**cost-effectiveness** *n.* —**cost-efficiency** *n.*

cos·ter (kóstər, kɔ́stər) n. (Br.) a costermonger

Cos·ter·mans·ville (kóstərmənzvil, kɔ́stərmənzvil) *BUKAVU

cos·ter·mon·ger (kóstərmʌŋgər, kɔ́stərmʌŋgər, kóstərmɒŋgər, kɔ́stərmɒŋgər) n. (Br.) a London hawker selling esp. fruit and vegetables from a handcart or a stall in a street market [*costard*, a kind of apple + older *monger*, a dealer, trader]

cos·tive (kóstiv, kɔ́stiv) adj. constipated, having slow bowel movements [perh. O.F. *costivé*, constipated]

cost·li·ness (kóstli:nis, kɔ́stli:nis) n. the state or quality of being costly

cost·ly (kóstli:, kɔ́stli:) comp. **cost·li·er** superl. **cost·li·est** adj. expensive ‖ involving great loss, *a costly battle* ‖ sumptuous, luxurious, *costly furnishings*

cost·mar·y (kóstmɛəri:, kɔ́stmɛəri:) pl. **cost·mar·ies** n. *Chrysanthemum balsamita*, fam. *Compositae*, a European aromatic plant smelling of tansy and used as a potherb, for salads etc. [O.E. *cost*, costmary fr. L. fr. Gk + St *Mary*]

cost of living the prevailing level of what must be paid for the necessities of life

cost-of-liv·ing index (kɔstʌvlívíŋ) (Br.) (economics) 1914 index of prices based on 1904-priced package; replaced by Index of Retail Price in 1947 *CONSUMER PRICE INDEX

cost-plus (kóstplʌ́s, kɔ́stplʌ́s) n. (in buying agreements) the cost price plus an agreed rate of profit

cost-push inflation or **cost inflation** (kɔstpúʃ) (business) pressure for price increases due to increased cost

cost sharing (insurance) provisions of a health insurance policy that require the insured or other covered individual to pay some portion of the covered medical expenses

cos·tume 1. (kóstu:m, kɔ́stju:m) n. style of clothing in general, including ornaments, hairstyles etc., *local peasant costume* ‖ a suit or dress representing a particular period, nationality, personage etc., worn at fancy-dress balls ‖ a woman's tailored suit ‖ (Br.) a bathing suit or swimming shorts **2.** (kɒstú:m, kɒstjú:m) v.t. pres. part. **cos·tum·ing** past and past part. **cos·tumed** to supply with a costume [F. fr. Ital. *costume*]

costume jewelry, Br. **costume jewellery** showy jewelry of no intrinsic value

costume piece a play in which the actors wear historical costumes

cos·tum·er (kostú:mər, kɔstjú:mər) n. a maker of, or dealer in, costumes for plays or for fancy dress etc.

cos·tum·ey (kɔstu:mi:) adj. (slang or colloq.) of overelaborate dressing

cos·tum·i·er (kɒstú:mi:ər, kɒstjú:mi:ər) n. a costumer [F.]

Cos·way (kɔ́zwei), Richard (1742–1821), English painter and miniaturist

cosy *COZY

cot (kɒt) n. a camp bed or other small, narrow bed ‖ (Br.) a crib (bed for a small child) ‖ (navy, hist.) a small swinging bed [fr. Hindi *khāt*, bedstead]

cot 1. n. (in compounds) a shelter, *dovecot*, *sheepcot* ‖ a cover or sheath, *finger cot* **2.** v.t. pres. part. **cot·ting** past and past part. **cot·ted** to put (esp. sheep) in a cot [O.E.]

co·tan·gent (koutǽndʒənt, kóutændʒən) n. (math., abbr. cot) the inverse of the tangent

COTAR (acronym) for correlated orientation tracking and range tracking system for space vehicles. It is based on direction of transmissions relative to receiving station

COTAT (acronym) for correlation tracking and triangulation system for tracing a projectile's trajectory, utilizing bases at various distances

cote (kout) n. (in compounds) a cot (shelter), a dovecote

Côte-d'Or (koutdɔr) a department (area 3,391 sq. miles, pop. 456,100) of E. France (*BURGUNDY, *CHAMPAGNE). Chief town: Dijon

co·ten·an·cy (kouténənsi:) pl. **co·ten·an·cies** n. a joint tenancy

co·ten·ant (kouténənt) n. a joint tenant

co·te·rie (kóutəri:) n. a group of people meeting regularly ‖ an exclusive set or circle, esp. literary or social ‖ a clique dedicated to some current literary or artistic fashion or craze [F.]

co·ter·min·al·ity (koutə:rminǽliti:) n. alignment of various civic, political or administrative jurisdictions, e.g., police, sanitation, education

Côtes-du-Nord (koutdynɔr) a department (area 2,786 sq. miles, pop. 525,600) of N.W. France along the north coast of Brittany (*BRITTANY). Chief town: Saint- Brieuc

co·thur·nus (kouθə́:rnəs) pl. **co·thur·ni** (kouθə́:rnai) n. a high-laced, thick-soled boot worn by actors in Greek tragic plays, a buskin [L. fr. Gk *kothornos*]

co·tid·al (koutáid'l) adj. of high tides occurring at the same time

cotidal lines lines drawn on a map joining coastal areas where tides coincide in time

co·til·lion (koutíljən, kətíljən) n. a ballroom or country dance for couples ‖ music for such dances ‖ a formal ball [fr. F. *cotillon*, petticoat]

Cot·man (kótmən, kɔ́tmən), John Sell (1782–1842), English painter in watercolors and oils, the greatest of the Norwich School

co·to·ne·as·ter (kətouni:ǽstər, kɔt'ni:stər) n. a member of *Cotoneaster*, fam. *Rosaceae*, a genus of shrubs, climbers or small trees of N. Europe, with white blossom and red berries [fr. L. *cotonea*, quince]

Co·to·nou (kɔtɔnu:) the principal port (pop. with agglom. 178,000) of Benin, W. Africa, on the Gulf of Benin: lumber, palm products

Co·to·pax·i (koutəpǽksi:) a mountain of Ecuador in the Andes, southeast of Quito, one of the world's highest active volcanoes (19,612 ft)

Cots·wold Hills (kótswould, kótswɔld) a range of hills (average elevation 600 ft) in the W. Midlands of England running northeast through Gloucestershire and Oxfordshire for about 60 miles: the home of Cotswold sheep, a noted long-wooled breed

cot·ta (kótə, kótə) n. (eccles.) a short surplice worn by choristers [M.L.= tunic]

cot·tage (kótidʒ) n. a small house, esp. in the country, for a farm laborer, miner etc. ‖ any small house, esp. in the country, esp. one used as a secondary residence [prob. fr. A.F.]

cottage cheese a soft cheese made of curd

cottage hospital (Br.) a hospital without resident doctors

cottage industry a system of industrial organization in which the workers (usually whole families) process, at home, material supplied by an entrepreneur (usually a merchant)

cottage loaf (Br.) a bread loaf of two round pieces, a smaller on top of a larger

Cott·bus, Kott·bus (kɔ́tbus) a town (pop. 111,502) on the Spree 64 miles southeast of Berlin, in East Germany, a rail center: textiles ‖ the district (area 3,189 sq. miles, pop. 805,000) which includes it

cot·ter (kótər) n. a wedge-shaped piece of metal or wood for keeping joints etc. tight [origin unknown]

cotter pin a split pin inserted through a slot and having its ends forced open so as to bear against the part which it serves to secure, esp. under vibration

Cot·ton (kót'n), John (1585–1652), Anglo-American Puritan clergyman. He was a leader (from 1633) in church and civil affairs in colonial New England. His works include 'The Keyes to the Kingdom of Heaven and the Power Thereof' (1644) and a book of religious instruction for children (1646)

cot·ton (kót'n) **1.** n. a plant of genus *Gossypium*, fam. *Malvaceac* ‖ the soft, white, wool-like fiber enclosing the seeds of the cotton plant ‖ a thread or textile of this fiber ‖ guncotton **2.** adj. made of cotton [F. *cotoc* fr. Arab. *qutn*, *qutun*]
—The cotton plant is native to the New and Old Worlds. The delicate seed hairs consist of a single long cell, with a thick cellulose cell wall. They resemble a twisted, flattened tube, and this allows cotton to be spun into strong yarn (cf. WOOL). The first process of manufacture, called 'ginning', is the separation of the hairs (lint) from the seeds, the seeds being crushed for oil as cottonseed oil, and for cotton cake. The fiber is then baled (478 lb. or, in Egypt, 750 lb.) and exported in this compressed form for manufacture. Chief cotton growers are the U.S.A., U.S.S.R., China, Egypt, India, Brazil

cotton belt the area of the southern U.S.A. where cotton is grown

Cotton Bowl (football) postseason college football game in Dallas, TX

cotton cake compressed cottonseed used as fodder for cattle

cotton candy (Am.=Br. candy floss) sugar, usually colored pink, formed into a light mass of threads by submitting syrup to rapid centrifugal motion

Cotton Famine the result of an interruption (1861–5) in the U.S. cotton supply during the American Civil War, which ruined the cotton industry in Lancashire, England

cotton gin a machine used to separate cotton fibers from the seeds

cot·ton·mouth (kót'nmauθ) pl. **cot·ton·mouths** (kót'nmauθs, kót'nmauðz) n. the water mocassin [after its whiteness about the mouth]

cot·ton·seed (kót'nsi:d) n. the seed of the cotton plant

cottonseed oil oil obtained from the crushed seeds of the cotton plant and used in soaps, lubricants, cosmetics etc., as a salad oil or cooking oil, and in medicine as a laxative

cotton stainer *Dysdercus suturellus*, a pest which stains the lint of developing cotton bud

cot·ton·tail (kót'nteil) n. a member of *Sylvilagus*, a genus of smallish North American rabbits with a white tail

cotton waste refuse yarn from mills, used for cleaning machinery, cars etc.

Cotton Whigs the Southern, proslavery faction of the U.S. Whig party. It arose after 1848 and opposed the antislavery Conscience Whigs

cot·ton·wood (kót'nwud) n. a member of *Populus*, a genus of trees of eastern North America with a cottonlike growth covering the seeds, esp. *P. deltoides*, fam. *Salicaceae* ‖ the wood of these trees

cotton wool (Br.) absorbent cotton

cot·ton·y (kót'ni:) adj. of or like cotton ‖ covered with down like cotton

cotton yarn cotton prepared for weaving or making thread

CO_2 laser carbon dioxide laser

Co·ty (kɔti:), René (1882–1963), French statesman, president of the Republic (1953–9)

cot·y·le·don (kɒt'lí:d'n) n. a primary leaf of the embryo of seed plants and ferns, supplying stored food to the developing embryo (*ENDOSPERM) **cot·y·le·don·ar·y** (kɒt'lí:d'nɛri:), **cot·y·lé·don·ous** adjs [L. fr.Gk *kotulē*, cup]

couch (kautʃ) n. a piece of upholstered furniture for sitting or lying on, a sofa ‖ the bed in which the grain is sprouted during the malting process in making beer [F. *couche*]

couch v.t. to express in words, *to couch criticisms in tactful language* ‖ to lower (a spear or weapon) into the attacking position ‖ v.i. to lay oneself down (now only past part.), *couched on a bed of straw* ‖ (with 'down') to crouch [F. *coucher*, to lie, lay down]

couch·ant (káutʃənt) adj. (heraldry, of heraldic animals) lying down at full length but with head raised [F. pres. part. of *coucher*, to lie down]

couch·ette (kautʃét) n. **1.** compartment berth in a European train that converts a seat to a bed at night. **2.** the train containing such

couch grass (kautʃ, ku:tʃ) any of various grasses with creeping rootstock and rapid powers of spreading, esp. *Agropyron repens*, fam. *Gramineae* [var. of QUITCH O.E. *cwice*]

Cou·é (ku:ei), Emile (1857–1926), French chemist and psychotherapist, advocate of therapy by autosuggestion

cou·gar (kú:gər) n. *Felis concolor*, a large American quadruped of the cat family, of a uniform brown, formerly found throughout the American continent but now largely extinct in E. Canada and the U.S.A. [F. *couguar* fr. Tupi]

cough (kɔf, kɒf) **1.** v.i. to make a cough ‖ (of an engine) to fire irregularly **to cough out** (or **up**) to eject by coughing (e.g. phlegm, blood) **2.** n. a sudden forced expulsion of air from the lungs, through the partially closed vocal cords, and the noise made by this ‖ a tendency to cough, *to have a cough* [M.E. *coghen*, prob. imit.]

cough drop a tablet to relieve coughing

could past, past conditional and pres. conditional of CAN

could·n't (kúd'nt) contr. of COULD NOT

cou·lee (kú:li:) n. (geol.) a solidified lava stream ‖ a steep ravine (esp. in western U.S.A.) [F. *coulée* fr. *couler*, to flow]

cou·lisse (ku:lí:s) n. (usually pl.) the wings of a theater ‖ a piece of grooved wood in which something slides ‖ an area of access to inside knowledge, *the coulisses of academic life* [F.]

cou·loir (ku:lwár) n. a steep gully on the side of a mountain [F. fr. *couler*, to flow]

Cou·lomb (ku:lɔ̃), Charles-Augustin de (1736–1806), French scientist who was the first to formulate the empirical relation between force, charge and distance for electrical and magnetic fields. He invented the torsion balance and studied frictional forces (*COULOMB'S LAW)

cou·lomb (kú:lɒm, ku:lɔ́m) n. (elec.) a unit of electric charge in the mks system, defined as the amount conveyed by 1 ampere in 1 second [after C. A. de *Coulomb*]

Cou·lomb's law (kúːlɒmz) a law in physics which states that the force of repulsion or attraction between charges or permanent magnetic poles is proportional to the product of the charges or the pole strengths and inversely proportional to the square of the distance between them

cou·lom·e·ter (kuːlómitər) n. (*phys.*) a device that measures the quantity of charge flowing past a point in an electrical circuit by the amount of electrolysis that occurs (e.g. by measuring the amount of silver metal deposited from a solution containing silver ions)

cou·lo·met·ric (kuːləmétrik) adj. relating to coulometry

cou·lom·e·try (kuːlómitriː) n. (*chem.*) the analysis of the composition of solutions by measuring the charge necessary to deposit or produce a given amount of substance

coulter *COLTER

coumaphos [$C_{14}H_{16}ClO_5PS$] (cúːməfous) n. insecticide and deworming drug used for cattle and poultry

cou·ma·rin (kúːmərin) n. a white crystalline sweet-smelling substance ($C_9H_6O_2$) used in perfumery and for flavoring, derived esp. from the tonka bean and now manufactured synthetically [F. *coumarine* fr. Guianese *cumarú*, tonkabean tree]

cou·ma·rone (kúːməroun) n. a coaltar derivative (C_8H_6O), also made synthetically and used for adhesives, varnishes etc.

coun·cil (káunsəl) n. a consultative or advisory assembly, *council of foreign ministers* ‖ a body elected or appointed to advise or legislate for a term of office, *city council* ‖ a meeting of such people ‖ discussion, deliberation in a council ‖ a federation of delegates from labor unions composing a legislative body ‖ (*eccles.*) an assembly of churchmen to consider doctrinal, moral, legal problems etc. ‖ (*New Testament*) an assembly of authorities, esp. the Sanhedrin [O.E. fr. O.F. *cuncile*, L. *concilium*, assembly]

Council for New England a body headed by Sir Ferdinando Gorges which, claiming a prior stake in New England, attempted unsuccessfully to persuade King Charles I to dispossess the colonists. Its colony of Maine was later annexed by Massachusetts

council house (*Br.*) a house built by a local authority and leased, usually at a subsidized rent

coun·cil·lor, coun·ci·lor (káunsələr, káunslər) n. a member of a council **cóun·cil·lor·ship, cóun·ci·lor·ship** n. [var. of older *counsellor*]

coun·cil·man (káunsilmən) pl. **coun·cil·men** (káunsilmən) n. a member of a council, esp. of a city council

Council of Europe *EUROPE, COUNCIL OF

Council of the Americas a group of just over 200 corporations representing more than three-quarters of all U.S. private investment in Latin America

Council of the Indies a Spanish institution founded (1509) by Ferdinand the Catholic and entrusted with the administration of Spanish America

council of war (*pop.*) a discussion about how to meet danger, opposition, a nuisance etc. or to plan some concerted action

coun·sel (káunsəl) n. advice resulting from consultation ‖ a legal adviser ‖ (*Br.*) a barrister ‖ (*collect.*) lawyers involved in a case **to keep one's own counsel** to keep one's plans to oneself [M.E. *conseil* fr. O.F. fr. L. *consilium*]

counsel (káunsəl) pres. part. **coun·sel·ing** esp. Br. **coun·sel·ling** past and past part. **coun·seled,** esp. Br. **coun·selled** v.t. to advise, recommend **cóun·sel·ing** n. a professional guidance service for individuals, applying the techniques of psychological testing [M.E. *consellen* fr. F.]

counsel of perfection an ideal injunction, admirable but impracticable advice

coun·se·lor, coun·sel·lor (káunsələr) n. a person who counsels or advises ‖ an adviser, esp. a legal adviser, at an embassy or legation ‖ a legal adviser who may conduct a case in court for his client ‖ an academic adviser ‖ a person in charge of a group of children at camp [M.E. *counseiller* fr. O.F.]

coun·se·lor-at-law, coun·sel·lor-at-law (káunsələrətlɔ́ː) pl. **coun·se·lors-at-law, coun·sel·lors-at-law** (káunsələrzətlɔ́ː) n. a counselor (legal adviser who may conduct cases in court)

count (kaunt) n. a counting or numbering, or checking by this means ‖ a number, figure reached by counting ‖ (*law*) each charge in an indictment ‖ the counting aloud up to ten seconds while a boxer is floored **out for the count** (*boxing*) knocked out **to keep count of** to know how many have been counted, *keep count of the visitors* **to lose count** to fail to keep count [M.E. *counte* fr. O.F.]

count n. a European title of nobility ‖ a nobleman holding it [A.F. *counte*]

count v.t. to add up (units in a collection), *count the eggs* ‖ to check by this process, *count your change* ‖ to repeat (numbers in order, up to and including a specified number), *count three before jumping* ‖ to include in one's reckoning, *50 not counting the children* ‖ to consider (a thing or person) as belonging to a specified class, *she counts him as a friend* ‖ v.i. to name or add up numbers in order ‖ to be important, have significance ‖ to come properly into a reckoning, *white lies don't count* **to count against** to be reckoned to one's disadvantage, *his age counted against him* **to count for** to be of a specified value or importance, *ability without influence counts for little* **to count in** to include in a count **to count off** to divide into groups by counting ‖ to call out numbers in order **to count on** (or **upon**) to rely on **to count out** to declare (a boxer) defeated after he has been floored for ten seconds ‖ (*pop.*) to exclude, *count me out if you're going swimming* **to count out the House** (*Br.*, of the House of Commons or Lords) to end proceedings by pointing out that a quorum is not present [M.E. *counten* fr. O.F.]

count·down (káuntdaun) n. the counting out loud at a fixed rate (e.g. by seconds) of the diminishing time before an action must be taken. It is done backwards from an arbitrary number, e.g. 10, and is used esp. in preparing rockets for firing ‖ the amount of time that must be counted out in this way ‖ (*rocketry*) the operations to be performed and tests carried out before a missile is launched. The lapse of time to zero hour for the launch is signaled by an audible counting aloud backward from some arbitrary starting number

coun·te·nance (káuntənəns) n. the face ‖ the expression on a face, *a tragic countenance* **to lend countenance** to show open approval **to put out of countenance** to cause (someone) embarrassment [O.F. *contenance*, bearing, aspect]

countenance pres. part. **coun·te·nanc·ing** past and past part. **coun·te·nanced** v.t. to show open approval of, support [fr. F. *contenancer*]

counter- (káuntər) prefix opposite in direction ‖ opposed to, retaliatory ‖ complementary [fr. F. *contre-*, L. *contra*, against]

coun·ter 1. adj. opposite, contrary 2. adv. in the opposite direction **to go** (or **run**) **counter to** to be in opposition to 3. v.i. to answer an attack ‖ v.t. to parry, *to counter a threat* 4. n. the part of a horse's breast between the neck and between the shoulders ‖ the curved part of a ship's stern [M.E. *countre* fr. A.F.]

coun·ter n. a flat-topped piece of shop furniture dividing sales attendants from customers, and over which business is transacted ‖ a similar fitting in a bank ‖ a small disk of bone, plastic etc. used e.g. for scoring in games or in playing a board game ‖ a token or imitation coin (e.g. for some telephones) ‖ (*Br.*) someone or something merely made use of **across the counter** as part of normal retail trade **under the counter** (of selling questionable goods or goods in short supply) secretly, surreptitiously [A.F. *counteour, countour,* a thing used in counting]

coun·ter n. (*fencing*) a circular parry ‖ (*boxing*) the giving of a blow while receiving or parrying one, or the blow so given ‖ (*football*) play in which the carrier first loses ground [fr. F. *contre,* against]

coun·ter n. (*shoemaking*) a stiffener giving form to a boot or shoe upper, above the heel [shortened fr. *counterfort*]

coun·ter n. a computer, device for counting ‖ a Geiger counter

coun·ter·act (kauntərǽkt) v.t. to neutralize, *alkalis counteract acids* ‖ to defeat by contrary action ‖ to act in opposition to **coun·ter·ác·tion** n. **coun·ter·ác·tive** adj.

coun·ter·a·gent (kauntəréidʒənt) n. a force or agent acting counteractively

coun·ter·at·tack (káuntərətæk) 1. n. a military offensive launched just after an attack by the enemy 2. v.t. to make a counterattack on ‖ v.i. to make a counterattack

counter attraction a thing that draws someone away from some other attraction, or is meant to

do so ‖ an attraction running counter to another

coun·ter·bal·ance 1. (káuntərbæləns) n. an equal weight balancing another ‖ a compensating influence, power, agency 2. (káuntərbæləns) v.t. pres. part. **coun·ter·bal·anc·ing** past and past part. **coun·ter·bal·anced** to act as a counterbalance with regard to

coun·ter·blast (káuntərblæst, káuntərblɑst) n. a vigorous retort, esp. an energetic and much publicized statement

coun·ter·charge 1. (káuntərtʃɑrdʒ) n. a retort consisting of throwing back a similar charge or one of equal weight 2. (kauntərtʃɑrdʒ) v.t. pres. part. **coun·ter·charg·ing** past and past part. **coun·ter·charged** to level (a charge) in opposition

coun·ter·check 1. (káuntərtʃek) n. an imposed restraint ‖ an independent checking of another check 2. (kauntərtʃék) v.t. to restrain by counteraction ‖ to control by a second, independent check

coun·ter·claim 1. (káuntərkleim) n. an opposing claim, put forward to counter another 2. (kauntərkléim) v.i. to enter or plead a counterclaim ‖ v.t. to claim in a counterclaim

coun·ter·clock·wise (kauntərklókwaiz) adv. and adj. in a direction opposite to that of the hands of a clock

counter conditioning (*behavioral psych.*) habit or condition substituted for an undesirable condition, e.g., sucking candies to overcome smoking

counter culture mores contrary to the accepted mores of the time and place —**counter culturist** n.

coun·ter·es·pi·o·nage (kauntəréspiːənɑʒ, kauntəréspiːənidʒ) n. espionage directed against the enemy's espionage system

coun·ter·feit (káuntərfit) 1. adj. spurious, copied or made in imitation and pretending to be genuine ‖ feigned, *counterfeit grief* 2. n. a counterfeit object 3. v.t. to imitate, esp. with fraudulent intent, to forge ‖ to feign **cóun·ter·feit·er** n. a person who makes false money [O. F. *contre·faire* (*contrefet, contrefait*), to imitate]

coun·ter·foil (káuntərfɔil) n. the part of a check, receipt etc. retained as a record by the drawer and showing details of sum, date etc.

coun·ter·force (káuntərfɔrs) n. (*mil.*) force with the ability to deliver accurate strategic attacks against military targets, e.g., missile silos

counter insurgency action against a rebellion, esp. by guerrillas —**counter insurgent** n.

coun·ter·in·tel·li·gence (kauntərintélidʒəns) n. the activity of identifying and thwarting the plans of an enemy's intelligence agents, or the organization charged with this activity

coun·ter·ir·ri·tant (kauntəríritənt) n. a substance producing surface irritation, for relieving more deep-seated pain, e.g. a liniment used to relieve muscle and joint pain ‖ something which relieves worry, pressure etc. by substituting another source of worry etc. **cóun·ter·ir·ri·tá·tion** n.

coun·ter·mand 1. (kauntərmǽnd, kauntərmánd) v.t. to cancel or revoke (a command) ‖ to recall (a person, troops etc.) by a contrary order ‖ to cancel (e.g. an order) 2. (káuntərmænd, kauntərmɑnd) n. a command etc. revoking a previous one [O.F. *contremander*]

coun·ter·march 1. (káuntərmɑrtʃ) n. a march in the reverse direction to a march just made, esp. for tactical reasons 2. (kauntərmártʃ) v.i. to make a countermarch ‖ v.t. to cause to countermarch

coun·ter·meas·ure (káuntərmeʒər) n. a retaliatory measure

coun·ter·mine 1. (káuntərmain) n. (*mil.*) a mine made to blow up an enemy mine prematurely ‖ a counterplot 2. v. (kauntərmáin) pres. part. **coun·ter·min·ing** past and past part. **coun·ter·mined** v.t. to destroy with countermines ‖ to thwart by countermeasures ‖ v.i. to lay countermines

coun·ter·of·fen·sive (kauntərəfénsiv) n. (*mil.*) a large-scale counterattack

coun·ter·pane (káuntərpein) n. a coverlet for a bed, a bedspread [older *counterpoint* fr. O.F. *contrepointe*]

coun·ter·part (káuntərpɑrt) n. a person fulfilling a role similar to another's, *who is his counterpart in their firm ?* ‖ a person or thing almost exactly resembling another ‖ a thing complementary to, or completing, another ‖ (*law*) the opposite part of an indenture

coun·ter·phobic (kauntərfóubik) adj. of action that ignores fears

coun·ter·plot 1. (káuntərplɒt) *n.* a plot intended to counter another **2.** (káuntərplɒt, kɑuntərplót) *v.i. pres. part.* **coun·ter·plot·ting** *past* and *past part.* **coun·ter·plot·ted** to make such plots

coun·ter·point (káuntərpɔint) *n.* (*mus.*) the art of combining two or more independent melodies simultaneously ‖ a melody composed to accompany another melody [O.F. *contrepoint*]
—Invertible counterpoint (esp. used in fugue) is so written that the melodies can change their relative positions above or below each other. Double (triple, quadruple) counterpoint involves two (three, four) melodies in this particular technique, and so on. In each case all the melodies are interchangeable. Strict counterpoint obeys academic rules based on 16th-c. contrapuntal writing. Free counterpoint does not follow these. Counterpoint originated in Gregorian chant and until the 18th c. it was also the main basis of orchestral music

coun·ter·poise (káuntərpɔiz) *n.* an equal and balancing weight, force or influence ‖ a state of balance or equilibrium [O.F. *contrepeis*]

counterpoise *pres. part.* **coun·ter·pois·ing** *past* and *past part.* **coun·ter·poised** *v.t.* to counterbalance ‖ to compensate for ‖ to put or keep in equilibrium [M.E. *contrepese* fr. O.F.]

coun·ter·pro·gram·ming (kɑuntərpróugræmiŋ) *n.* system of scheduling activities based on what competitors are doing

counter pulsation action to reduce systemic blood pressure by raising diastolic blood pressure

Coun·ter-Ref·or·ma·tion (kɑuntərrefɔrméiʃən) the Roman Catholic reform movement which followed (16th and 17th cc.) the Protestant Reformation

coun·ter·rev·o·lu·tion (kɑuntərrevəlú:ʃən) *n.* a revolution intending to undo the results of a revolution **cóun·ter·rev·o·lú·tion·ar·y** *adj.* and *n.* **cóun·ter·rev·o·lú·tion·ist** *n.*

coun·ter·scarp (káuntərskɑrp) *n.* the exterior wall of a fortified ditch surrounding a fort etc., opposite to the scarp and nearest to the besiegers, often with a covered way beneath [fr. F. *contrescarpe*]

coun·ter·shaft (káuntərʃæft, káuntərʃɑft) *n.* an intermediate shaft transmitting motion from the main shaft to the working parts of a machine

coun·ter·sign (káuntərsain) *n.* a secret sign or word given in reply to a sentry's challenge, in order to pass ‖ a countermark, extra signature on a document, esp. one made by a witness to the main signature [O.F. *contresigne*]

coun·ter·sign (káuntərsain, kɑuntərsáin) *v.t.* to add a ratifying signature to (a signed document) [F. *contresigner*]

coun·ter·sig·na·ture (kɑuntərsígnətʃər) *n.* a signature on a document witnessing to the authenticity of the main signature

coun·ter·sink 1. (káuntərsiŋk, kɑuntərsíŋk) *v.t. pres. part.* **coun·ter·sink·ing** *past* **coun·ter·sank** (káuntərsæŋk, kɑuntərsæŋk) *past part.* **coun·ter·sunk** (káuntərsʌŋk, kɑuntərsʌ́ŋk) to adapt (a screw hole) by chamfering to receive the head of the screw and leave it level with the surface ‖ to sink (a screw) thus **2.** (káuntərsiŋk) *n.* a hole prepared thus for a screw or bolt ‖ a tool for countersinking

coun·ter·spy (káuntərspai) *pl.* **coun·ter·spies** *n.* someone spying on a spy, in military or industrial service

coun·ter·ten·or (kɑuntərténər) *n.* the male singing voice higher than tenor, male alto ‖ a singer with such a voice ‖ a part for such a voice [fr. obs. F. *contreteneur*]

coun·ter·vail (káuntərvéil) *v.t.* to compensate for ‖ *v.i.* (with 'against') to avail against [A.F. *countrevaloir*]

countervailing duty a duty imposed on foreign goods helped by subsidy, so as to give an equal or better chance to home-produced goods

coun·ter·weigh (káuntərwéi) *v.t.* to counterbalance ‖ *v.i.* to act as a counterpoise

coun·ter·weight (káuntərwəit) **1.** *n.* an equivalent or counterbalancing weight **2.** *v.t.* to counterweigh

coun·ter·word (káuntərwə:rd) *n.* a word so often used in various contexts that it has become almost meaningless, e.g. 'nice', 'awful'

coun·tess (káuntis) *n.* the wife or widow of an earl or a count ‖ a lady having equivalent rank in her own right [O.F. *contesse*]

count·ing·house (káuntiŋhaus) *pl.* **count·ing·**

hous·es (káuntiŋhauziz) *n.* an office, room or building where accounts are kept

count·less (káuntlis) *adj.* too many to be counted, innumerable

coun·tri·fied (kʌ́ntrifaid) *adj.* characteristic of rural life, unsophisticated [past part. of older *countrify v.*]

coun·try (kʌ́ntri:) *pl.* **coun·tries 1.** *n.* a region, district, tract of land, esp. with reference to geographical or esthetic features, *mountainous country* ‖ the land in which one was born or to which one owes allegiance ‖ a political state ‖ regions of woods and fields, esp. as opposed to towns, *to live in the country* ‖ the people of a country, nation, *the country is opposed to war* **to appeal** (or **go**) **to the country** (*Br.*) to hold a general election **2.** *adj.* of or relating to the country as opposed to the town [M.E. *contre, contree* fr. O.F.]

coun·try-and-west·ern (kʌntri:ændwéstərn) *adj.* of country music, esp. in western U.S., usu. played with guitars *abbr.* C&W

country cousin a countrified relative regarded patronizingly by sophisticated members of the family

coun·try-dance (kʌ́ntri:dæns, kʌ́ntri:dɑns) *n.* any of various native English dances for several couples which depend on the formation of changing patterns rather than on individual movements **cóun·try-dánc·ing** *n.*

coun·try·folk (kʌ́ntri:fouk) *pl. n.* people whose mode of life is determined by the fact that they live in the country and are not city dwellers

country house a house in the country, esp. when it is a secondary residence ‖ (*Br.*) a large house and grounds in the country, owned by a gentleman

coun·try·man (kʌ́ntri:mən) *pl.* **coun·try·men** (kʌ́ntri:mən) *n.* a compatriot ‖ a person of a specified country, *a north countryman* ‖ (esp. *Br.*) a man who lives in the country, not the town

country music popular music, principally vocal, accompanied by stringed instruments, with southern or western roots and adapted from 18th-century English and Scottish ballads

country rock combination of rock and hillbilly music and country-and-western styles *syn.* rockabilly music

coun·try·side (kʌ́ntri:said) *n.* a rural area, esp. as contrasted with an urban area ‖ its inhabitants, *the countryside is solidly behind him*

coun·try·wom·an (kʌ́ntri:wumən) *pl.* **coun·try·wom·en** (kʌ́ntri:wimən) *n.* a woman who lives in the country ‖ a female compatriot

count·ship (káuntʃip) *n.* (*hist.*) a count's rank, domain or territory

coun·ty (káunti:) *pl.* **coun·ties** *n.* the largest local government division within a state (excluding Louisiana, where 'parish' corresponds) ‖ a territorial division into which the British Isles, and some other countries, are divided for administrative, judicial and political purposes ‖ (*Br.*) the socially privileged of such a county ‖ (*hist.*) the area ruled over by a count [A.F. *counté*]

county borough (*Br.*) a town possessing a municipal organization, having the right to elect one representative (or more) to parliament, with administrative and judicial powers similar to those of a county

county council the elected body governing a county

county court a judicial tribunal in some states ‖ (*Br.*) a local magistrates' court

county family (*Br.*) a family with its ancestral seat in a given county

county seat (*Am.*=*Br.* county town) a town which is the seat of county administration or which retains the title because it formerly was this

county town (*Br.*) a county seat

coup (ku:) *pl.* **coups** (ku:z) *n.* a sudden successful stroke, blow or stratagem [F. fr. L. fr. Gk]

coup de grace (kú:dəgrás) *n.* a decisive or finishing stroke, the death blow [F.]

coup d'e·tat (kú:deitá) *n.* an attempt to overthrow a government by sudden, violent, illegal means [F.]

coup de the·atre (kú:dəteiátr) *n.* a sudden sensational turn in a play ‖ any dramatically sudden and astonishing change of situation in real life [F.]

coupe (ku:p) *n.* a closed automobile, esp. a two-seater, with a body shorter than the corresponding sedan

cou·pé (kú:pei) *n.* a coupe ‖ (*hist.*) a four-wheeled carriage to seat two, with an outside seat for the driver [F.]

Cou·pe·rin (ku:pərē), François (1668–1733), French composer and court musician. He wrote principally for the harpsichord, but also wrote concertos, organ works, church music etc. His father, Charles (1638–79), and his uncle, Louis (1626–61), were also composers and performers

cou·ple (kʌ́p'l) *n.* a pair, *a couple of friends* ‖ (*pop.*) roughly two, *a couple of drinks* ‖ an engaged or married pair ‖ partners in a dance ‖ (*phys.*) a pair of parallel forces of equal magnitude but acting in opposite directions on the same body ‖ a coupler ‖ two hounds on a leash ‖ a pair of collars linked by a leash for holding a couple of hounds [O.F. *cople*]

couple *pres. part.* **cou·pling** *past* and *past part.* **cou·pled** *v.t.* to join, fasten, esp. in pairs ‖ to connect (railroad cars) by a coupling ‖ to bring together, pair off ‖ to associate, *her name was coupled with his* ‖ *v.i.* to unite sexually ‖ to associate in pairs ‖ (*radio*) to join by means of a coupler **cóu·pler** *n.* a device for joining two things, esp. an apparatus for making two manuals (or manual and pedals) of an organ act together, or single notes with their related octaves ‖ (*radio*) a device for connecting electric circuits ‖ (*rail.*) a coupling [O.F. *copler*]

cou·plet (kʌ́plit) *n.* two consecutive lines of verse, esp. when rhyming [F., dim. of *couple*]

cou·pling (kʌ́pliŋ) *n.* a joining or uniting ‖ a device for connecting railroad cars etc. ‖ an appliance for transmitting power or motion in machinery

cou·pon (kú:pɒn, kjú:pɒn) *n.* a detachable slip of paper giving entitlement to a payment of interest or to some service ‖ a ration voucher for food, clothing etc. in time of war or national austerity ‖ a sales promotion voucher ‖ part of a printed advertisement to be cut out as an order form, entry for a competition etc. [F.=piece cut off, fr. *couper*]

cour·age (kə́:ridʒ, kʌ́ridʒ) *n.* the capacity to meet danger without giving way to fear to have **the courage of one's convictions** to be willing to put one's opinions into practice **to lose courage** to despair **to pluck up courage** to begin to be brave **to take courage** to become brave **to take one's courage in both hands** (esp. *Br.*) to summon up all one's courage [M.E. *corage* fr. O.F.]

cou·ra·geous (kəréidʒəs) *adj.* possessing or marked by courage [A.F. *corageous*]

cou·rante (kurᾱnt) *n.* (*mus.*) a quick dance in triple time in a classical suite [F. = running (dance)]

Cou·ran·tyne (kɔ́rəntain, kóurəntain) a river of South America (c. 300 miles long) rising in the Serra Acarahy, and flowing to the Atlantic to form the Guyana-Surinam boundary

Cour·bet (ku:rbei), Gustave (1819–77), French realist painter of portraits, landscapes and genre subjects, who led the reaction against the pseudoclassicism of David and Ingres

cour·i·er (kə́:ri:ər, kúəri:ər) *n.* a person employed by a firm of travel agents etc. to make arrangements abroad for travelers ‖ a special messenger [M.E. *corour, currour* and later *courier* fr. O.F.]

Courier an experimental, delayed repeater communication satellite that has the capability of storing and relaying communications using microwave frequencies

cour·lan (kúərlən) *n.* a member of *Armaus*, fam. *Aramidae*, a genus of tropical American rail-like wading birds with a long bill and a dismal cry [F.]

Cour·nand (kúərnænd), André Frédéric (1895–), U.S. physician and Nobel prize winner (1956) in medicine (with Dickinson W. Richards and Werner Forssmann) for his contribution to heart research

course (kɔrs, kours) **1.** *n.* a moving from one point to another ‖ the direction of travel or path taken ‖ ordinary sequence, *course of events* ‖ a line of conduct, *several courses are open to us* ‖ a racecourse ‖ a golf links ‖ a channel in which water flows ‖ a series of lectures, seminars etc. ‖ a scheme of study leading to a degree, diploma etc. ‖ a series of remedial treatments ‖ any of the successive parts of a meal ‖ a continuous layer of cement or row of bricks, stone etc., e.g. in a wall ‖ the lowest sail on a square-rigged mast **a matter of course** something to be expected as quite usual or habitual **by course of** in accordance with, *by course of law* **in course of** in the

CONCISE PRONUNCIATION KEY: **(a)** æ, c*a*t; ɑ, c*a*r; ɔ f*aw*n; ei, sn*a*ke. **(e)** e, h*e*n; i:, sh*ee*p; iə, d*ee*r; ɛə, b*ea*r. **(i)** i, f*i*sh; ai, t*i*ger; ə:, b*i*rd. **(o)** o, *o*x; au, c*ow*; ou, g*oa*t; u, p*oo*r; ɔi, r*oy*al. **(u)** ʌ, d*u*ck; u, b*u*ll; u:, g*oo*se; ə, b*a*cillus; ju:, c*u*be. x, lo*ch*; θ, *th*ink; ð, bo*th*er; z, *Z*en; ʒ, cor*s*age; dʒ, sava*g*e; ŋ, orangutan*g*; j, *y*ak; ʃ, *f*ish; tʃ, fe*tch*; 'l, rabb*le*; 'n, redd*en*. Complete pronunciation key appears inside front cover.

process of, *in course of construction* **in due course** at the proper time in the future **in the course of** during, *in the course of discussion* **of course** naturally, certainly **to stay the course** (of competitors in a race, or of someone undergoing a test or ordeal) to keep going to the end **to take** (or **run**) **its course** to be allowed to evolve naturally **2.** *v. pres. part.* **cours·ing** *past and past part.* **coursed** *v.t.* to hunt by sight and not by scent, *to course hares* || to cause greyhounds to hunt thus || *v.i.* to move or flow quickly, *the blood coursed through his veins* [F. *cours* and *course*]

cours·er (kórsər, kóursər) *n.* (*rhet.*) a swift horse, charger [F. *corsier*]

courser *n.* a member of *Cursorius*, fam. *Glareolidae*, a genus of small, swift-running, plover-like birds of Asia and Africa [fr. L. *cursorius*]

court (kort, kourt) **1.** *n.* an uncovered area surrounded by walls or buildings and planned as a unit, e.g. an entrance space or area in front of stables, a courtyard || a college quadrangle || a subdivision of a large, multiple-unit building (e.g. a museum) || a short street enclosed at the far end, a dead end || an enclosed space, open or covered, marked off for certain games, *a tennis court* || a division of this || the residence of a sovereign, a palace || a sovereign's family and his retinue of courtiers || the sovereign and state officials regarded as the ruling power || a formal assembly or reception by a sovereign || a place or hall where justice is administered || the judges, magistrates, coroners and other officials acting as a tribunal to administer justice || a meeting of such officials || a body of directors, managers etc. of some corporations or councils etc. || a meeting of such a body || behavior calculated to win favors or to win affection, *to pay court to someone* **to bring** (or **take**) **to court** to have (a case) or a dispute with (someone) tried by law **to settle out of court** to reach agreement about by mutual consent, not by court judgment **2.** *v.t.* to try to gain the favor or affection of, by flattery or attention || to seek in marriage || to allure, attract, entice || to behave as though seeking (harm, a disaster etc.) || *v.i.* to be sweethearts [M.E. *curt, court* fr. O.F.]

court card (*Br.*) a face card

court circular (*Br.*) the daily report of what happens at the royal court, published in certain newspapers, together with other information affecting socially prominent people

court dress a man's formal costume which includes silk knee breeches and stockings

cour·te·ous (kə́:rti:əs) *adj.* polite, civil, considerate in manner [O.F. *corteis, curteis*]

cour·te·san, cour·te·zan (kórtiz'n, kóurtiz'n, kúərtiz'n) *n.* (*hist.*) a prostitute, esp. of Renaissance Italy, often a cultivated and influential woman [F. *courtisane* fr. Ital.]

cour·te·sy (kə́:rtisi:) *pl.* **cour·te·sies** *n.* polite, kind, considerate behavior or an instance of it **by courtesy of** by consent of || under financial advertising arrangement with [O.F. *curtesie, cortesie*]

courtesy light light in a motor vehicle that operates while the door is open

courtesy title a title given by polite customary usage (e.g. to certain relatives of peers) and not held by legal right

courtezan *COURTESAN

court hand (*Eng. hist.*) a handwriting used in characters and deeds from the 16th c. until abolished in 1731

court·house (kórthaus, kóurthaus) *pl.* **court·hous·es** (kórthauziz, kóurthauziz) *n.* a building in which law cases are heard

cour·ti·er (kórti:ər, kóurti:ər) *n.* an attendant at the court of a sovereign [prob. fr. O.F. *cortoyer*, to be at the court]

court·li·ness (kórtli:nis, kóurtli:nis) *n.* the quality of being courtly

court·ly (kórtli:, kóurtli:) *comp.* **court·li·er** *superl.* **court·li·est** *adj.* having or showing very polished, formal manners

courtly love (amour courtois, a term used specifically of the Middle Ages, esp. in literature, though the belief it represents comes from Plato, or from Neoplatonism) the belief that human love, the affinity of two souls, is an ennobling pursuit, even a paradigm of heavenly love. In medieval chivalric society the theory became codified into an etiquette: its cardinal doctrines were humility, courtesy, adultery (Plato notwithstanding, the sexuality of the relationship was generally taken for granted), and the religion of love. This was the classical formulation of the 12th c. represented

in the treatise 'De arte honeste amandi' of Andreas Capellanus and in the Provencal and French society of the time

court-mar·tial (kórtmɑrʃəl, kóurtmɑrʃəl, kərtmɑ́rʃəl, kəurtmɑ́rʃəl) **1.** *pl.* **courts-mar·tial, court-mar·tials** *n.* a judicial court of military or naval officers to try soldiers' or sailors' offenses **2.** *v.t. pres. part.* **court-mar·tial·ing, court-mar·tial·ling** *past* and *past part.* **court-mar·tialed, court-mar·tialled** to try by court-martial

Court of Cassation the supreme court of the judicial system of many countries. Its chief function is to decide, at the request of the litigants or the government, whether or not a final decision previously handed down has been in violation of the law or has been a false interpretation of it

Court of Exchequer (*Br. hist.*) a court of law dealing with matters that affected the revenue. It became (1875) a division of the Supreme Court of Judicature and was merged (1881) with the King's Bench division

court of inquiry a military court which investigates charges against officers etc.

Cour·trai (ku:rtrei) (*Flem.* Kortrijk) a town (pop. 76,072) in N.W. Belgium. Products: linen, cotton and lace. Medieval and Renaissance monuments

court roll (*hist.*) a register of tenants' holdings kept by a manorial court

court·room (kórtru:m, kóurtru:m, kórtrum, kóurtrum) *n.* a room in which sessions of a court of law are held

court·ship (kórtʃip, kóurtʃip) *n.* the wooing of a person one wishes to marry || (of birds etc.) the sequence of song, display etc. preparatory to mating

court shoe (*Br.*) a pump (ladies' high-heeled shoe)

court tennis (*Am.=Br.* real tennis) an ancient game thought to have originated in French ecclesiastical circles in the 11th c., and much in fashion with royalty in the 16th and 17th cc. It is played with a racket and cloth-covered ball in a walled court

cous·cous (kú:sku:s) *n.* a N. African dish of granulated 'flinty' wheat, steamed in the vapor of broth or meat || this and the meat, vegetables and piquant sauce with which it is eaten [F. fr. Arab.]

Cou·sin (ku:zɛ̃), Victor (1792–1867), French philosopher, and minister of education under Guizot and Thiers. His enthusiasm inspired a revival of interest in the history of philosophy in 19th-c. France. His best known work, reflecting his eclectic philosophy, is 'Du Vrai, du bien, et du beau' (1858)

cous·in (kʌ́z'n) *n.* a first cousin || a first cousin once removed, second cousin, second cousin once removed etc., or any distant relative || (*pl.*) people of a group with whom one acknowledges special ties (though blood relationship is not involved), *we must respect the interests of our Canadian cousins* [F.]

cous·in-ger·man (kʌ́z'ndʒə́:rmən) *pl.* **cous·ins-ger·man** (kʌ́z'nzdʒə́:rmən) *n.* one's first cousin, the child of one's uncle or aunt [F. *cousin germain*]

cous·in·hood (kʌ́z'nhud) *n.* the relationship of cousins || the state or quality of being a cousin

cous·in·ly (kʌ́z'nli:) *adj.* like or suitable to a cousin

cous·in·ship (kʌ́z'nʃip) *n.* cousinhood

cou·tu·ri·er (ku:túəri:ei, ku:túəri:ər, ku:túərjei) *n.* a dress designer of a highclass fashion house [F.]

cou·vade (ku:vád) *n.* a primitive custom in which the husband of a wife in childbed himself goes to bed and suffers a symbolic parturition [obs. F. fr. *couver*, to hatch]

co·va·lence (kouvéiləns) *n.* the sharing of a pair of electrons between two atoms to form a bond, one valence being provided by each atom (cf. IONIC BOND) **co·vá·lent** *adj.*

covalent bond a chemical bond formed by covalence

cove (kouv) **1.** *n.* a small sheltered bay, creek or inlet of the sea || a cavern or recess || (*archit.*) a concave molding or arch, esp. connecting a wall and ceiling **2.** *v.i. pres. part.* **cov·ing** *past* and *past part.* **coved** to arch, esp. at a junction of ceiling and wall || (e.g. of the sides of a fireplace) to slope inwards [O.E. *cofa*, a room]

cove *n.* (*Br., pop.*) a chap, a fellow [etym. doubtful, perh. fr. Romany *kova*, person]

cov·e·nant (kʌ́vənənt) **1.** *n.* an agreement, bargain || a sealed contract or clause of such a

contract || (*Bible*) the agreement between God and his chosen people, the Israelites **2.** *v.t.* to agree to by covenant || *v.i.* to enter into formal agreement [O.F. orig. pres. part. of *convenir*, to agree]

Cov·e·nan·ter (kʌ́vənəntər, kʌ́vənæntər) *n.* (*Br. hist.*) a Scottish Presbyterian, esp. one who struggled (1557–1688) for religious liberty and who adhered to the National Covenant (1638)

cov·e·nan·tor (kʌ́vənəntər) *n.* someone who makes a covenant

Cov·ent Garden (kʌ́vənt, kóvənt) an area of central London which was formerly the main fruit and vegetable market || the opera house in this area

Cov·en·try (kʌ́vəntri:, kóvəntri:) an ancient county borough (pop. 340,500) in Warwickshire, England, manufacturing small arms, bicycles, automobiles and textiles. Its medieval cathedral was destroyed in 1940, and a new one dedicated in its place in 1962. University of Warwick (1965) **to send (someone) to Coventry** (*Br.*) to ostracize, boycott, refuse to have social dealings with (someone)

cov·er (kʌ́vər) **1.** *v.t.* to place a cover on or over || to hide, *to cover one's face* || to protect, *rifle fire covered the advance* || to command or dominate (territory), *enemy guns covered the valley* || to keep under aim, *to cover someone with a revolver* || to stand or march immediately behind (another man) || to bring upon (oneself), *to cover oneself with glory* || to spread over, *snow covered the ground* || to extend over, occupy, *the wood covers 20 acres* || to stake a bet equal to (one's opponent's bet) || to accept (a bet) || to protect financially, *covered by insurance* || to be enough to defray the costs of || to have as one's territory or area of work, *our salesman covers the west coast* || (*cricket, baseball*) to stand by (a player) to stop any ball he misses || (*football* etc.) to mark, concentrate on neutralizing (an individual opponent) || (*cards*) to play a higher card than (one's opponent's) || to deal with, embrace, *this book covers the whole subject* || to pass over, travel (a certain distance) || (*journalism*) to report (proceedings, events etc.) || (of an animal) to serve (a female) || to sit on (eggs) so as to hatch them **to cover up** to cover thoroughly || to conceal **2.** *n.* something which extends over a thing, e.g. a top or lid || the binding of a book || a loose or fitted covering on a seat to protect it against dust, dirt or wear || (*Br.*) the outer surface of a tire || the wrapper of a parcel || (*philately*) a stamped envelope that has passed through the mail || a concealing shelter || protecting force, *air cover* || a screen, veil, *under cover of friendship* money to meet liabilities, *the business has adequate cover* || insurance to protect against loss || linen, cutlery etc. for a person at the table || (*cricket*) cover point || (*pl.*) bedclothes || (of an animal) the act of covering **from cover to cover** (of a book etc.) from beginning to end **to break cover** (of game) to emerge from the undergrowth **to take cover** to hide in a place which conceals or shelters **under cover of** protected or concealed by, *under cover of darkness* **under separate cover** in a different parcel or envelope **under the same cover** in the same envelope **cóv·er·age** *n.* a covering || the number of people, or area, reached by a particular medium or e.g. by a television program || money available to meet liabilities || the total range of risks covered by an insurance policy [O.F. *cuvrir, covrir*]

cov·er·all (kʌ́vərɔl) *n.* (often *pl.*) a garment put on at work over ordinary clothes to keep them clean, consisting of overalls and shirt combined

cover charge an extra charge in a restaurant for the use of table linen and cutlery

Cov·er·dale (kʌ́vərdeil), Miles (1488–1568), English bishop. His translation of the Bible (1535) was much used by the translators of the 1611 Authorized Version. The psalter of the 'Book of Common Prayer' is also his

covered wagon, *Br.* also **covered waggon** a large wagon with a canvas cover supported by curved arches, esp. (*hist.*) a prairie schooner

cover girl a model who poses for the covers of popular magazines

cov·er·ing (kʌ́vəriŋ) *n.* that which covers, protects, or conceals

covering letter a letter sent with an invoice, application, goods etc. to explain or modify the enclosures, or sent separately

cov·er·let (kʌ́vərlit) *n.* a bedspread, outer covering for a bed [earlier *coverlite* perh. fr. O.F. *couvre-lit*, lit. *cover-bed*]

cover point a playing position in cricket (behind point and to the bowler's side of him) and lacrosse (just in front of point) ‖ the player occupying this position

cov·ert (kávərt, kóuvərt) 1. *n.* a thicket or copse ‖ (*pl.*) the small feathers covering the base of the wing and tail feathers of birds **to draw a covert** to search it for foxes, game etc. 2. *adj.* hidden, secret, disguised, *a covert glance* [O.F. past part. of *covrir,* to cover]

covert cloth a fine twilled material of wool with cotton or rayon, used for coats and suits

cov·er·ture (kávərtʃər) *n.* a decorative cover, packaging ‖ shelter ‖ a concealment ‖ (*law*) the status of a married woman under her husband's protection [O.F.]

cov·et (kávit) *v.t.* to long to possess (something belonging to another person) **cóv·et·ous** *adj.* strongly desiring another person's property [O.F. *cuveitier, coveiter*]

cov·ey (kávi:) *pl.* **cov·eys** *n.* a hatch of wild birds, esp. partridge and quail [M.E. fr. O.F. *covée* fr. *couver,* to hatch]

cov·ings (kóuviŋz) *pl. n.* the vertical splayed sides of a fireplace

cow (kau) *pl.* **cows,** *archaic pl.* **kine** (kain) *n.* a fully grown female animal of the ox family (*CATTLE), usually kept in herds by farmers for milk ‖ the female of any animal whose male is known as a bull, e.g. the elephant, rhinoceros, whale seal, moose [O.E. *cū*]

cow *v.t.* to intimidate, browbeat [perh. O.N. *kūga,* to force]

cow·age, cow·hage (káuidʒ) *n.* a member of *Mucuna,* fam. *Papilionaceae,* a genus of tropical and subtropical woody vines with stinging hairs on the pods [fr. Hindi *kawāuch*]

cow·ard (káuərd) *n.* a person without courage [O.F. *coart*]

cow·ard·ice (káuərdis) *n.* a lack or failure of courage [O.F. *couardise*]

cow·ard·li·ness (káuərdli:nis) *n.* the state or quality of being a coward

cow·ard·ly (káuərdli:) 1. *adj.* of or befitting a coward 2. *adv.* in a cowardly manner

cow·bell (káubel) *n.* a bell hung around the neck of a free-grazing cow to make her easy to locate

cow·bird (káubə:rd) *n.* a member of *Molothrus,* a genus of birds native to North America, which frequent cattle pens for food. They lay their eggs in other birds' nests

cow·boy (káubɔi) *n.* a cattle herder on a ranch, esp. one who works on horseback

cow·catch·er (káukætʃər) *n.* a metal frame on the front of a railroad engine for throwing aside cattle or other obstacles on the track

cow·er (káuər) *v.i.* to crouch or shrink back, esp. from fear [etym. doubtful]

Cowes (kauz) a seaport, resort and sailing center (pop. 17,000) in the Isle of Wight, England: boatbuilding, marine engineering

cow·fish (káufiʃ) *pl.* **cow·fish·es, cow·fish** *n.* the sea cow or manatee ‖ any of various fishes having strong spines like horns over each eye

cow·girl (káugə:rl) *n.* a girl who helps to herd cattle on a ranch

cowhage *COWAGE

cow·hand (káuhænd) *n.* a person employed on a cattle ranch

cow·herd (káuhə:rd) *n.* a farmhand in charge of the cows

cow·hide (káuhaid) *n.* leather made from the hide of a cow ‖ a whip or thong made from such leather

cowl (kaul) *n.* the hood of a monk's habit ‖ a covering (often hood-shaped) fitted to a chimney or ventilating shaft to prevent wind from blowing down ‖ part of an automobile to which are fitted the windshield and dashboard ‖ a cowling [O.E. *cuhle, cugele*]

Cow·ley (káuli:, kú:li:), Abraham (1618–67), English poet and essayist, author of 'The Mistress' (1647), 'Davideis' (1656), 'A Proposition for the Advancement of Experimental Philosophy' (1661) and 'Essays' (edited by Thomas Sprat, 1668)

cow·lick (káulik) *n.* a tuft of scalp hair which grows in a different direction from the surrounding hair

cowl·ing (káuliŋ) *n.* a protective metal covering over an airplane engine

cow·man (káumən) *pl.* **cow·men** (káumən) *n.* a cowherd ‖ a cattle owner

co-work·er (kóuwə́:rkər, kóuwə̀:rkər) *n.* a person working in collaboration with another

cow·pat (káupæt) *n.* a dropping of cow dung before it has dried

cow·pea (káupi:) *n. Vigna sinensis,* fam. *Papilionaceae,* a plant native to Asia and used in southern U.S.A. for forage and green manure ‖ the edible seeds of this plant

Cow·per (kú:pər, káupər), William (1731–1800), English poet and letter writer. He wrote quiet reflective verse and many hymns. The simplicity and apparent lack of artificiality in his style brought a new spirit into English poetry. He had a rare gift of humor ('John Gilpin'), and lightness of touch

cow·pox (káupɒks) *n.* an eruptive disease on the teats of cows which, when conveyed to human beings by vaccination, gives immunity (whole or partial) from smallpox

cow·punch·er (káupʌntʃər) *n.* a cowboy

cow·rie, cow·ry (káuri:) *pl.* **cow·ries** *n. Cypraea moneta,* a small gastropod of the Indian ocean, whose shell has been used as currency in parts of Africa and S. Asia ‖ any of certain small gastropods of the same genus found on the British Isles [Hindi]

cow·slip (káuslip) *n.* the marsh marigold ‖ (*Br.*) *Primula veris,* fam. *Primulaceae,* a primrose with fragrant yellow flowers, which blooms in early spring [O.E. *cū-slyppe,* cow dung]

Cox (kɒks), David (1783–1859), English watercolorist, and author of 'A Treatise on Landscape Painting and Effect in Water-Colours' (1814) etc.

Cox, Jacob Dolson (1828–1900), U.S. general in the Civil War and secretary of the interior (1869–70) under President U.S. Grant. As a military authority he contributed (from 1874) to 'The Nation' and his books include 'Atlanta' (1882) and 'The March to the Sea: Franklin and Nashville' (1898)

Cox, James Middleton (1870–1957), U.S. publisher and politician. As governor (1913–15, 1917–21) of Ohio he introduced valuable reform legislation, and won the Democratic presidential nomination (1920) to run against Warren G. Harding

cox 1. *n.* the coxswain of a racing boat 2. *v.t.* to act as coxswain to ‖ *v.i.* to act as coxswain

cox·a (kɒksə) *pl.* **cox·ae** (kɒksi:) *n.* the hip or hip joint ‖ (*zool.*) the first joint of the leg of insects **cóx·al** *adj.* [L.=hip]

cox·al·gi·a (kɒksǽldʒi:ə, kɒksǽldʒə) *n.* a pain in the hip **cox·ál·gic** *adj.* [fr. COXA + Gk *-algia,* pain]

cox·comb (kɒkskoum) *n.* (*archaic*) a conceited, silly man [=*cock's comb,* the cap of the professional jester]

Cox·ey's Army (kɒksi:z) a group of unemployed persons led by Jacob S. Coxey, a businessman, who marched (Mar. 25–May 1, 1894) from Massillon, Ohio to Washington, D.C. to advertise the need for economic reform. It disbanded when Coxey and several other members were arrested for trespassing

Cox·sack·ie virus (kɒksǽki:) (*med.*) a group of picornaviruses that destroy striated muscles and cause aseptic meningitis; a disease mimicking poliomyelitis, myocarditis, etc., named after Coxsackie, N.Y.

cox·swain (kɒksən, kɒkswein) *n.* the helmsman, and person in charge, of a ship's boat

coy (kɔi) *adj.* coquettishly bashful [O.F. *coi,* quiet]

coy·o·te (kaióuti:, káiout) *n. Canis latrans,* a small wolf of North America [Nahuatl *coyotl*]

coyotes smugglers of aliens into U.S. esp. via Mexican border

coy·pu (kɔipu:) *n. Myocastor coypus,* fam. *Capromyidae,* a South American aquatic beaverlike rodent, valued for its fur (nutria) [native name]

coz·en (kʌz'n) *v.t.* and *i.* (*rhet.*) to cheat, defraud [etym. doubtful]

coz·en·age (kʌzənidʒ) *n.* (*rhet.*) a cheating or defrauding or being cheated or defrauded

Cozi (acronym) for communication zone indicator, system designed to check long-distance, high-frequency broadcasts by measuring propagation characteristics of the atmosphere from different angles

co·zi·ly, co·si·ly (kóuzili:) *adv.* in a cozy manner

co·zi·ness, co·si·ness (kóuzi:nis) *n.* the state or quality of being cozy

co·zy, co·sy (kóuzi:) 1. *comp.* **co·zi·er, co·si·er,** *superl.* **co·zi·est, co·si·est** *adj.* nicely relaxing, comfortable, *a cozy armchair* ‖ (of people) lovable and easy to get on with 2. *n.* a cover placed over a teapot etc. to keep it warm

Coz·zens (kʌz'nz), James G. (1903–78), U.S. novelist. His works, usually dealing with the

lives of professional men, include 'By Love Possessed' (1957)

C.P.A. certified public accountant, i.e. an accountant legally qualified

CPI (*economics acronym*) for consumer price index (which see)

cpl. corporal

CPM (*acronym*) for cost per thousand, a media unit used to measure cost of advertising in terms of the viewing or reading audience

CPR (*med. acronym*) for cardio-pulmonary resuscitation

CPU (*computer acronym*) for central processing unit

crab (kræb) 1. *n.* the popular name for the 10-legged, short-tailed crustaceans, esp. of *Brachyura* (*HERMIT CRAB, *LAND CRAB, *KING CRAB) ‖ the flesh of the larger edible species ‖ an ill-tempered person ‖ a crab louse **to catch a crab** (*rowing*) to fail to make a proper stroke, esp. by plunging the oar too deeply into the water 2. *v.i. pres. part.* **crab·bing** *past* and *past part.* **crabbed** to hunt crabs, fish for crabs [O.E. *crabba*]

crab *pres. part.* **crab·bing** *past* and *past part.* **crabbed** *v.t.* (of hawks) to scratch or pull to pieces ‖ *v.i.* (*pop.*) to find fault [L.G. *krabben,* to scratch]

crab apple (*Br.*) *Malus sylvestris,* a wild apple with bitter fruit, or its fruit ‖ any cultivated variety of this or its fruit ‖ any of various trees of genus *Malus* or their fruit [origin unknown]

Crabbe (kræb), George (1754–1832) English poet. He maintained the Augustan tradition, which combines irony with serious moral evaluation. His later work unites delicate analysis of nature with realistic description of poverty, injustice and pain. His reputation rests on the art of his verse tales (e.g. 'The Borough' 1810, 'Tales in Verse' 1812)

crab·bed (kræbid) *adj.* ill-tempered, morose, peevish ‖ (of books and other writings) intricate and difficult to follow, deliberately obscure ‖ (of handwriting) cramped, irregular and badly formed

crab·ber (kræbər) *n.* someone who lives by crab fishing ‖ a boat used in crab fishing

crab·by (kræbi:) *comp.* **crab·bi·er** *superl.* **crab·bi·est** *adj.* crabbed (ill-tempered, morose, peevish)

crab·grass (kræbgræs, kræbgrɑs) *n. Digitaria sanguinalis,* an annual grass with creeping stems which root into the soil. It is native to warm and temperate regions

crab louse *Phthyrus pubis,* a parasite found on the pubic hairs of the human body

Crab Island *VIEQUES

crab pot a wicker basket used as a trap for crabs

crack (kræk) 1. *v.t.* to cause to make a sudden, sharp sound, *to crack a whip* ‖ to hit with a sudden, sharp blow, *to crack someone over the head* ‖ to break open (a nut) ‖ (*pop.*) to break into a safe) ‖ to convert (an oil of high boiling point) into an oil or oils of lower boiling point, by breaking down large molecules into smaller ones under heat ‖ to break down (chemical compounds) into simpler ones, often with the help of heat ‖ *v.i.* to fracture without complete separation ‖ to make a sudden, sharp sound, *the rifle cracked* ‖ (of the voice) to break abruptly ‖ (*pop.*) to fail, give way, *to crack under the strain* ‖ (*pop.*) to hurry **crack a joke** to make a joke **to crack down** to inflict sudden punishment, particularly so as to make an example of someone or enforce regulations with renewed strictness in respect of something specified **to crack up** to break down physically or mentally ‖ (*pop.*) to praise highly (a person or thing) 2. *n.* a sudden, sharp sound, *the crack of a whip* ‖ a sharp but not violent blow, *a crack on the head* ‖ a partial breakage without complete separation, *a cup with a crack in it* ‖ a fissure in the ground or in ice ‖ a narrow opening, a chink ‖ a break in the voice ‖ a highly potent and addictive cocaine distillate in rock form ‖ (*pop.*) a joke **to have a crack at** (*pop.*) to make an attempt at 3. *adj.* first-class, of the highest quality, *a crack driver* [O.E. *cracian*]

crack·back (krǽkbæk) *n.* (*football*) a block on a backfield player by a pass receiver who cuts back after the play begins

crack·brained (krǽkbreind) *adj.* crazy

crack·down (krǽkdaun) *n.* (*pop.*) an enforcing of regulations with renewed strictness

cracked (krækt) *adj.* having a crack, fractured ‖ (of the voice) broken and apt to change register ‖ (*pop.*) crazy

crack·er (krækər) *n.* (*Am.=Br.* biscuit) a flat, dry, crisp cake or a piece of unleavened bread ‖ a firework that explodes with a sharp crack ‖ a small paper cylinder containing (along with a novelty, paper hat etc.) an explosive which discharges when its ends are pulled

crack·er-bar·rel (krækərbærəl) *adj.* as unsophisticated as talk in a country general store [fr. the barrel of soda crackers often featuring in such stores]

crack·er·jack (krækərdʒæk) 1. *adj.* (*pop.*) very fine, first-rate 2. *n.* (*pop.*) a first-rate person or thing

crack·ers (krækərz) *adj.* (*Br., pop.*) crazy [prob. fr. CRACKER infl. by CRACKED *adj.*]

crack·ing (krækiŋ) *n.* a process of breaking down petroleum into finer products (e.g. gasoline) by the use of heat, and usually pressure or catalysis, or some combination of these

crack·le (kræk'l) 1. *n.* a slight, sharp, cracking sound, as made by burning twigs ‖ a network of surface cracks in some glazes and in some glassware 2. *v.i. pres. part.* **crack·ling** *past* and *past part.* **crack·led** to make little cracking sounds ‖ to form a crackle (in glaze)

crack·ling (krækliŋ) *n.* the making of little cracking sounds ‖ the skin of pork roasted until it is crisp ‖ (*esp. pl.*) greaves

crack·ly (krækli:) *comp.* **crack·li·er** *superl.* **crack·li·est** *adj.* having a tendency to crackle

crack·nel (kræknəl) *n.* a light, curved biscuit, crisp outside and floury inside ‖ crisply fried fat pork in small pieces [perh. fr. F. *craquelin*]

crack·pot (krækpɒt) 1. *n.* (*pop.*) an eccentric or crazy person 2. *adj.* (*pop.*) crazy

crack-up (krækʌp) *n.* (of a vehicle or aircraft) a breaking up or disintegrating ‖ (of people) a mental breakdown ‖ (of societies, governments, marriages etc.) collapse, disintegration

crack·y (kræki:) *comp.* **crack·i·er** *superl.* **crack·i·est** *adj.* full of cracks ‖ (of ice) liable to crack

Cracow *KRAKOW

cra·dle (kréid'l) 1. *n.* a small bed or cot for a baby, sometimes mounted on rockers ‖ a place where something begins or is nurtured, *the cradle of civilization* ‖ a framework of wood or metal to support a ship during construction or repair ‖ a basketlike device which moves along a rope and carries people up mountains, off wrecked ships etc. ‖ a frame for protecting a broken leg ‖ a moving platform used when painting a ship or the side of a house etc. ‖ a frame fastened to a scythe to make the grass or wheat etc. fall evenly ‖ (*cricket*) a curved framework of wood on which a ball is thrown, used in practicing slip catching ‖ (*engraving*) a serrated chisel ‖ (*mining*) a rocking device used for washing goldbearing earth 2. *v.t. pres. part.* **cra·dling** *past* and *past part.* **cra·dled** to place (a baby) in a cradle ‖ to hold (esp. a baby) in one's arms as if in a cradle ‖ to mow with a scythe fitted with a cradle ‖ to wash in a miner's cradle [O.E. *cradol*, origin unknown]

cra·dle-song (kréid'lsɒŋ, kréid'lsɔŋ) *n.* a gentle song to put a child to sleep, a lullaby

craft (kræft, krɑft) *n.* a trade or occupation that requires skill in the use of the mind and hands, *the craft of painting* ‖ an art viewed as a making that requires developed skills, *the craft of fiction* ‖ the members of a trade collectively, a guild ‖ cunning, deceit, guile ‖ (*pl.* craft) a boat or vessel or aircraft [O.E. *crœft*, strength, skill]

craft guild *GUILD

craft·i·ly (kræftili:, krɑftili:) *adv.* in a crafty manner

craft·i·ness (kræfti:nis, krɑfti:nis) *n.* the state or quality of being crafty

crafts·man (kræftsmən, krɑftsmən) *pl.* **crafts·men** (kræftsmən, krɑftsmən) *n.* a skilled worker practicing a particular craft ‖ an artist with respect to the technical side of his art **crafts·man·ship** *n.*

craft union a union of skilled as opposed to unskilled workers, all of whom practice the same craft

craft·y (kræfti:, krɑfti:) *comp.* **craft·i·er** *superl.* **craft·i·est** *adj.* cunning, wily, deceitful [O.E. *crœftig*, strong, cunning]

crag (kræg) *n.* a steep, rugged rock or cliff ‖ a piece of rock projecting from a surface [perh. fr. Irish *creag*]

crag and tail a long hill with a steep drop at one end and a gentle slope at the other

crag·ged (krægid) *adj.* craggy

crag·gi·ness (krægi:nis) *n.* the quality of being craggy

crag·gy (krægi:) *comp.* **crag·gi·er** *superl.* **crag·gi·est** *adj.* having many crags

Craig (kreig), Edward Gordon (1872–1966), English actor, stage designer and producer, influential in the development of modern theatrical scenic design and stage lighting

Cra·io·va (krɑjóva) a town (pop. 243,117) in the western part of the Walachian plain, S. Rumania: grain trade, textile industry

crake (kreik) *pl.* **crakes, crake** *n.* a member of *Porsana*, fam. *Rallidae*, a genus of somewhat chicken-shaped marsh birds of secretive habits and distinctive cry (*CORNCRAKE) [perh. O.N. *kraka*, crow, *krakr*, raven]

cram (kræm) *pres. part.* **cram·ming** *past* and *past part.* **crammed** *v.t.* to fill very full ‖ to force, *to cram one's clothes into a case* ‖ to stuff with food ‖ to stuff (food) into ‖ to eat (something) greedily ‖ to teach intensively for examination purposes ‖ *v.i.* to eat greedily ‖ to learn hurriedly without prolonged study, *to cram for an examination* [O.E. *crammian*]

cram·bo (krǽmbou) *pl.* **cram·boes** *n.* a game in which one player gives a word to which the others must find a rhyme (cf. DUMB CRAMBO) [etym. doubtful]

cram·full (krǽmfúl) *adj.* full up as a result of cramming

cram·mer (krǽmər) *n.* (*Br.*) a teacher who crams students for an examination

cramp (kræmp) 1. *n.* a metal bar bent at the ends used for temporarily holding together parts of a brick wall, house timbers etc. ‖ a tool for pressing together, a clamp ‖ a restraining or restricting force, *poverty put a cramp on his ambitions* 2. *v.t.* to steer (the wheel of a vehicle) so as to turn it sharply to right of left [perh. fr. Du. or L.G.]

cramp 1. *n.* a sudden painful contraction of the muscles often caused by cold or strain ‖ a temporary paralysis in the muscles caused by excessive use, *writer's cramp* ‖ (*pl.*) severe pains in the stomach 2. *v.t.* to hinder, restrict, *poverty cramped his early development* ‖ to cause to have a cramp ‖ to fasten or secure with a cramp **to cramp someone's style** to hinder someone from showing his full ability, or from showing off **cramped** *adj.* restricted, without room to move ‖ not properly spaced out ‖ narrow-minded **in cramped circumstances** in genteel poverty [M.E. *crampe, craumpe* fr. O.F. fr. O.L.G.]

cramp iron a metal bar bent at the ends, a cramp

cram·pon (krǽmpən) *n.* a metal grappling hook ‖ (*pl.*) climbing irons [F.]

cran (kræn) *n.* (*Br.*) a measure for fresh herrings=37½ imperial gallons [origin uncertain, perh. Gael. *crann*, lot]

Cra·nach (krɑ́nɑx), Lucas (1472–1553), German painter and etcher. His fame rests on his portraits (notably of Luther) but he also painted religious and mythological paintings and nudes, and made woodcuts

cran·ber·ry (krǽnberi:, krǽnbəri:) *pl.* **cran·ber·ries** *n.* the tart, red, edible berry produced by some members of the genus *Vaccinium*, fam. *Ericaceae*, esp. *V. macrocarpon* and *V. oxycoccus* ‖ any of these plants [perh. fr. G. *kranbeere*]

Crane (krein), Harold Hart (1899–1932), American poet, author of 'The Bridge' (1930) and 'White Buildings' (1926)

Crane, Stephen (1871–1900), American author of a realistic novel of the American Civil War, 'The Red Badge of Courage' and of stories and poems

crane (krein) 1. *n.* a member of *Gruidae*, a family of tall, wading birds related to herons and storks, of considerable size and remarkable for their long stiltlike legs. They live in marshes and nest among bushes, laying two eggs. Some migrate for long distances and fly at a great height ‖ a machine for raising and lowering heavy weights ‖ a water siphon with a long, flexible tube for supplying water to railroad engines ‖ an axle fixed to a fireplace for hanging a pot or kettle on 2. *v. pres. part.* **cran·ing** *past* and *past part.* **craned** *v.t.* to raise by a crane ‖ to stretch (one's neck) ‖ *v.i.* to stretch one's neck [O.E. *cran*]

crane fly *Tipula oleracea*, a dipteran insect, characterized by very long legs, body and antennae. The larvae live in soil and often do damage in vegetable gardens and fields and lawns

cranes·bill (kréinzbil) *n.* a popular name given to the geranium, from the long slender beak of the fruit

cra·ni·al (kréini:əl) *adj.* of or belonging to the cranium

cranial nerve one of the major paired nerves originating in the vertebrate brain. They pass out through the openings of the skull to the periphery of the body, particularly the head, and control various actions and sensations, such as sight, smell, swallowing, chewing

cra·ni·ate (kréini:it, kréini:eit) 1. *adj.* having a cranium ‖ vertebrate 2. *n.* a vertebrate [fr. L. *cranium*, skull]

cra·ni·o·log·i·cal (kreini:əlódʒik'l) *adj.* of or relating to craniology

cra·ni·ol·o·gist (kreini:ɒ́lədʒist) *n.* someone who specializes in craniology

cra·ni·ol·o·gy (kreini:ɒ́lədʒi:) *n.* the science which treats of the variations in shape and size of the skull in the different races of man [fr. CRANIUM+Gk *logos*, discourse]

cra·ni·om·e·ter (kreini:ɒ́mitər) *n.* an instrument for measuring skulls

cra·ni·o·met·ric (kreini:əmétrik) *adj.* of or relating to craniometry **cra·ni·o·mét·ri·cal** *adj.*

cra·ni·om·e·try (kreini:ɒ́mitri:) *n.* the science of measuring skulls, esp. in determining racial characteristics [fr. CRANIUM+Gk *metron*, measure]

cra·ni·um (kréini:əm) *pl.* **cra·ni·ums, cra·ni·a** (kréini:ə) *n.* the skull of any vertebrate, esp. that part enclosing the brain [L. fr. Gk *kranion*, a skull]

crank (kræŋk) 1. *n.* an arm set at right angles to a shaft or axle, used for converting reciprocal (to-and-fro) motion into circular motion ‖ an odd or eccentric person 2. *v.t.* to set going with a crank (esp. an automobile engine) ‖ to provide with a crank 3. *adj.* (of machinery) weak, loose, shaky, unreliable [M. E. = yarn reel fr. O.E. *cranc*]

crank·case (kræŋkkeis) *n.* (of an internal combustion engine) the casing enclosing the crankshaft and connecting rods

crank·i·ly (kræŋkili:) *adv.* in a cranky manner

crank·i·ness (kræŋki:nis) *n.* the state or quality of being cranky

crank·pin (kræŋkpin) *n.* (*engin.*) a pin fitted to a crank, and securing a connecting rod

crank·shaft (kræŋkʃæft, kræŋkʃɑft) *n.* (*engin.*) the main shaft of an engine, having a crank (or cranks) for the attachment of connecting rods

crank·y (kræŋki:) *comp.* **crank·i·er** *superl.* **crank·i·est** *adj.* irritable, crotchety ‖ capricious ‖ crazy ‖ (of machinery) loose or liable to break down

Cran·mer (krænmər), Thomas (1489–1556), the first Protestant archbishop of Canterbury (1533–53), appointed by Henry VIII. He annulled (1533) the king's marriage to Catherine of Aragon and supported the Act of Supremacy (1535). He ordered (1539) a revised English Bible to be placed in every church, and compiled much of the Books of Common Prayer of 1549 and 1552. He was burned as a heretic (1556) after the accession (1553) of Mary I

cran·nied (kræni:d) *adj.* having crannies

cran·nog (krænəg) *n.* an ancient lake dwelling in Scotland or Ireland, consisting of an artificial island used as a refuge, dating from the late Bronze Age to the 16th c. A.D. [Irish *crannog*, Gael. *crannag* fr. *crann*, tree]

cran·ny (kræni:) *pl.* **cran·nies** *n.* a small cleft, a chink, crevice, in a wall or rock face [etym. doubtful]

crap (kræp) 1. *n.* craps ‖ a throw at craps (2, 3, or 12) which makes the thrower lose unless he has a point 2. *v.i. pres. part.* **crap·ping** *past* and *past part.* **crapped** (with 'out') to throw a 7 at craps while attempting to make a point [CRAPS]

crape (kreip) *n.* crepe [fr. older F. *crespe*]

crape myrtle *Lagerstroemia indica*, fam. *Lythraceae*, an ornamental flowering shrub native to the East Indies and widely cultivated in the southern U.S.A. for its white, pink, red or purplish flowers

crap·pie (kræpi:) *n. Pomoxis nigromaculatus*, the black crappie, or *P. annularis*, the white crappie, small North American sunfishes [Canad. F. *crapet*]

craps (kræps) *n.* a gambling game with two dice. The bet is won if the first throw is 7 or 11. It is lost if the first throw is 2, 3 or 12. If it is any other total the thrower throws again either until he repeats it (and wins) or turns up a 7 (and loses) **to shoot craps** to play this [fr. F.

crabs fr. Eng. *crabs*, the lowest throw in the old game hazard]

crap·u·lence (krǽpjuləns) *n.* gross drunkenness [fr. L. *crapula*, intoxication]

crap·u·lous (krǽpjuləs) *adj.* drunken ‖ suffering from drunkenness [fr. L. *crapulosus*]

crash (kræʃ) **1.** *n.* a sudden, violent noise ‖ a collision of vehicles or of a vehicle with an obstacle, or a falling to earth of aircraft ‖ the collapse of a business or speculative enterprise **2.** *v.i.* to make a violent noise ‖ to come into collision ‖ (of an aircraft) to fall to earth ‖ to fail in business ‖ *v.t.* to attend (a party) without being invited [imit.]

crash *n.* a coarse linen or cotton fabric, used for towels, lightweight suits etc. [origin unknown]

Crash·aw (krǽʃɔ), Richard (c. 1613–49), English metaphysical poet. In his expression of religious feeling in terms of earthly love it is the earthly which predominates

crash-dive (krǽʃdaiv, krǽʃdaiv) *pres. part.* **crash-div·ing** *past* **crash-dove** (krǽʃdouv, krǽʃdouv) *past part.* **crash-dived** *v.i.* (of submarines) to dive with the utmost speed in an emergency

crash helmet a protective head covering worn by motorcyclists, racing drivers etc.

crash-land (krǽʃlænd) *v.i.* (of aircraft) to land hurriedly in an emergency on the best terrain that offers itself, often with damage to the aircraft

crash pad (*slang or colloq.*) a free place to sleep

crash·wor·thy (krǽʃwəːrði) *adj.* able to protect passengers of a vehicle against the effect of a crash —**crashworthiness** *adj.*

crass (kræs) *adj.* gross ‖ extremely stupid [fr. L. *crassus*, thick, dense]

Cras·sus (krǽsəs), Marcus Licinius (c. 115–53 B.C.), Roman statesman, member of the 1st Triumvirate with Caesar and Pompey (60 B.C.). He was ignominiously defeated by the Parthians and died at Carrhae

crate (kreit) **1.** *n.* a framework of wooden boards for protecting something during transport **2.** *v.t. pres. part.* **crat·ing** *past and past part.* **crat·ed** to pack in a crate [perh. fr. L. *cratis*, a hurdle]

cra·ter (kréitər) *n.* the mouth of a volcano ‖ a hole in the ground made by the explosion of a shell or bomb ‖ any bowl-shaped depression or cavity ‖ a krater [L. fr. Gk *kratēr*, a mixing bowl]

cra·vat (krəvǽt) *n.* an elaborate silk necktie worn with formal morning dress ‖ a trade term for any necktie [F. *cravate*]

crave (kreiv) *pres. part.* **crav·ing** *past and past part.* **craved** *v.t.* to desire strongly, urgently and persistently, *to crave alcohol* ‖ (*Br., old-fash.*) to beg, *to crave a boon* ‖ *v.i.* (with 'for') to long [O.E. *crafian*]

cra·ven (kréivən) **1.** *adj.* (*rhet.*) cowardly, abject, fearful **2.** *n.* (*rhet.*) a coward [M.E. *crauant*, etym. doubtful]

crav·ing (kréiviŋ) *n.* a strong, urgent and persistent desire

craw (krɔ) *n.* (*zool.*) the crop of a bird or insect ‖ the stomach of an animal [M.E. *crawe* fr. O.E.]

craw·fish (krɔ́fiʃ) *pl.* **craw·fish, craw·fish·es** *n.* a crayfish

Craw·ford (krɔ́fərd), Thomas (1814–57), U.S. sculptor. His best-known work is the 'Statue of Freedom' on the capitol dome in Washington, D.C.

Crawford, William Harris (1772–1834), U.S. political leader. He was appointed (1815) secretary of war and (1816) secretary of the treasury by President Madison. He received only 11 fewer votes than James Monroe in the presidential caucus of 1816

crawl (krɔl) **1.** *v.i.* to move forward on hands and knees ‖ to make one's way slowly and painfully ‖ to abase or humiliate oneself ‖ (of plants) to creep along the ground or up a wall ‖ to be as though alive (with crawling insects), *the lawn was crawling with ants* ‖ (of flesh) to register unpleasant, creepy sensations ‖ to swim the crawl ‖ (of paint or glaze) to spread unevenly, form puddles **2.** *n.* the act of crawling ‖ a powerful overarm stroke in swimming, with a thrashing movement of the legs [M.E. *crawlen* fr. O.N.]

crawl *n.* an enclosure in shallow water for confining fish, turtles etc. [Du. *kraal* fr. Span.]

crawling peg money exchange rate maintained within a small range, with parameters established for fixed periods

crawl·way (krɔ́lwei) *n.* **1.** a low-ceilinged passageway **2.** road designed to move large equipment **3.** space under a porch or elevated house

cray·fish (kréifiʃ) *pl.* **cray·fish, cray·fish·es** *n.* any of various long-tailed, freshwater edible crustaceans of the tribe *Astacura*, miniatures of the lobster, and resembling lobsters in appearance and habits. They inhabit Europe, Asia and North America [M.E. *crevice* fr. O.F. fr. O.H.G.]

cray·on (kréiən, kréiɑn) **1.** *n.* a stick of colored chalk or chalk and wax for drawing with **2.** *v.t.* to draw with crayons [F. fr. *craie*, chalk]

craze (kreiz) **1.** *n.* a great or fashionable enthusiasm for something, *a craze for jazz* **2.** *v. pres. part.* **craz·ing** *past and past part.* **crazed** *v.t.* (*rhet.*) to make mad ‖ *v.i.* (*pottery*) to show crackle in the glaze [M.E. *crasen*, to break, perh. of Scand. origin]

cra·zies (kréizi:s) *n.* political extremist group in California led by Ken Kesey in the 1960s

cra·zi·ly (kréizili:) *adv.* in a crazy manner

cra·zi·ness (kréizi:nis) *n.* the state or quality of being crazy

cra·zy (kréizi:) *comp.* **cra·zi·er** *superl.* **cra·zi·est** *adj.* foolish ‖ insane ‖ unsound, full of defects and imperfections ‖ (*pop.*) very enthusiastic, *crazy about stamp collecting* ‖ in love with, *crazy about Harry*

crazy bone the funny bone

Crazy Horse (c. 1849–77), a Sioux Indian chief and tactician in the Sioux War (1875–7). After refusing to settle on government reservations, he was arrested for suspected conspiracy and killed while trying to escape

crazy pavement (*Br.*) a path made of irregularly shaped, flat pieces of stone set in mortar

crazy quilt a quilt sewn from bits of material of different colors and sizes, without regularity of pattern (cf. PATCHWORK)

C reactive protein (*med.*) globulin that precipitates C carbohydrate found in blood of patients with inflammation. It is a property used to test for rheumatic fever

creak (kri:k) **1.** *n.* a harsh grating or Squeaking sound, made e.g. by a loose floorboard or layers of dry leather rubbing together **2.** *v.i.* to make such a sound **créak·i·ly** *adv.* **créak·y** *comp.* **creak·i·er** *superl.* **creak·i·est** *adj.* [imit.]

cream (kri:m) **1.** *n.* the rich, fatty part of milk which gathers on the top ‖ a food or confection containing cream or resembling it, *ice cream* ‖ a creamlike cosmetic ointment, *face cream* ‖ the best part of anything, *the cream of society* ‖ the color of cream, a pale yellow **2.** *v.t.* to beat to a light, smooth consistency ‖ to skim the cream from (milk) ‖ to rub a cosmetic cream into (the skin) ‖ *v.i.* (of milk) to form a cream [F. *crème*]

cream cheese any of various kinds of fresh, soft white cheese

cream·er (krí:mər) *n.* a separator, a machine for separating cream from milk ‖ a small jug or pitcher for cream

cream·er·y (krí:məri:) *pl.* **cream·er·ies** *n.* a shop for the sale of milk, cream, butter etc. ‖ a place where butter and cheese are made [prob. fr. F. *crèmerie*]

cream·i·ness (krí:mi:nis) *n.* the state or quality of being creamy

creaming *SKIM

cream of tartar potassium bitartrate, KH(C₄O₆H₄), found as a deposit in wine vats. Mixed with sodium bicarbonate it is used as baking powder

cream·y (krí:mi:) *comp.* **cream·i·er** *superl.* **cream·i·est** *adj.* having the consistency or color of cream

crease (kri:s) **1.** *n.* a wrinkle or fold mark, whether intended (e.g. along the length of the trouser leg) or not ‖ (*cricket*) the line, in continuation of the stumps, from behind which the bowler bowls, *bowling crease* ‖ (*cricket*) the line, 4 ft in front of this, behind which the batsman takes up his position, *popping crease* **2.** *v. pres. part.* **creas·ing** *past and past part.* **creased** *v.i.* to wrinkle ‖ to become creased ‖ *v.t.* to make creases in [earlier *creaste*, ridge fr. O.F. *creste*]

creas·y (krí:si:) *comp.* **creas·i·er** *superl.* **creas·i·est** *adj.* having creases

cre·ate (kri:éit) *pres. part.* **cre·at·ing** *past and past part.* **cre·at·ed** *v.t.* to bring into being ‖ to make by applying the imagination in some ar-

tistic technique ‖ to produce, *to create a bad impression* ‖ to invest with rank, *the king created four new peers* ‖ (of an actor) to incarnate (a character), esp. playing it for the first time, or in a particularly effective manner ‖ (*Br., pop.*) to go into a tantrum [fr. L. *creare (creatus)*]

cre·a·tine (krí:əti:n, krí:ətin) *n.* an organic base, C₄H₂N₃O₂, found in the muscles of vertebrates, and in the blood, brain etc. [fr. Gk *kreas*, flesh]

cre·a·tion (kri:éiʃən) *n.* the act of creating ‖ everything that has been created, the universe ‖ something that has been created with imagination, e.g. by an author, actor or fashion designer ‖ a bringing into being, *the creation of a fuss* ‖ an investing with rank or title etc., *the creation of new peers* ‖ the Creation (*Bible*) the creation of the world by God described in Genesis [F.]

cre·a·tive (kri:éitiv) **1.** *adj.* having the quality or power of creating ‖ imaginative **2.** *n.* (*slang*) one who is creative, esp. a writer in the advertising field

cre·a·tiv·i·ty (krI:eitíviti:) *n.* creativeness

cre·a·tor (kri:éitər) *n.* someone who creates **the Cre·a·tor** God as maker of the universe and of all life [M.E. *creatour* fr. L.]

crea·ture (krí:tʃər) *n.* a living human or animal ‖ something created, *a creature of the imagination* ‖ a servile tool of someone else [F.]

creature comforts the things that make for bodily comfort (warmth, good food, hot baths, clean linen etc.)

crèche (kreʃ, kreiʃ) *n.* a nursery where infants are looked after when their mothers are at work ‖ a model of the Nativity scene [F.= crib fr. O.H.G.]

Cré·cy, Battle of (kreisi:, krési:) an English victory (1346) over the French in the Hundred Years' War, important in the history of warfare. The English used the longbow (against the French crossbow), small bombards (an early type of artillery), and dismounted men-at-arms

cre·dence (krí:d'ns) *n.* belief, *give no credence to such stories* ‖ credentials (only in), *letters of credence* ‖ (*eccles.*) a small table on which the bread and wine are placed at the Communion service before consecration [F. or fr. M.L. *credentia*]

cre·den·tials (kridénʃəlz) *pl. n.* a letter establishing the authority of the bearer [fr. M.L. *credentia*, credence]

cred·i·bil·i·ty (krɛdəbíliti:) *n.* the state or quality of being credible

credibility gap unbelievability

cred·i·ble (krédəb'l) *adj.* believable **créd·i·bly** *adv.* [fr. L. *credibilis*]

cred·it (krédit) **1.** *n.* the system of buying and selling without immediate payment or security ‖ the power to obtain goods without immediate payment ‖ time allowed for payment ‖ a favorable balance of an account ‖ (*bookkeeping*) the right-hand side of an account where payments received are recorded ‖ belief, *to give credit to a story* ‖ good reputation ‖ a source of honor, *his behavior is a credit to his parents* ‖ an acknowledgment of merit ‖ a credit line ‖ (*Br.*) a standard well above the pass mark attained in an examination ‖ a unit of time (counting towards a required total) recorded as spent attending a course of instruction ‖ the record of such units **2.** *v.t.* to believe ‖ to trust ‖ to enter (a sum of money) upon the credit side of an account ‖ to enter a sum of money in (an account etc.) ‖ to attribute to (a student or his record) the units of time spent in following a course of instruction **cred·it·a·ble** *adj.* quite good, more than just satisfactory **cred·it·a·bly** *adv.* [F. *crédit*]

credit line a printed acknowledgment of the source of copyright material used in a book, play etc.

Créd·it Mo·bil·ier of America (kréditmoubí:liər, kreidi:mɔbi:liei) a U.S. construction company, formed (1867) to build the Union Pacific Railroad, providing the worst scandal of President Grant's administration. It gave company shares to certain Congressmen in return for political favors and charged the Union Pacific exorbitantly for its services. Two Representatives were formally censured by Congress

cred·i·tor (kréditər) *n.* someone to whom a debt is owing ‖ (*bookkeeping*) the right-hand side of an account [older *creditour* fr. A.F.]

cred·it·wor·thy (kréditwəːrði:) *adj.* of one who is a good risk as a borrower —**creditworthiness** *n.*

CONCISE PRONUNCIATION KEY: **(a)** æ, c*a*t; ɑ, c*a*r; ɔ f*aw*n; ei, sn*a*ke. **(e)** e, h*e*n; i:, sh*ee*p; iə, d*ee*r; ɛə, b*ea*r. **(i)** i, f*i*sh; ai, t*i*ger; əː, b*i*rd. **(o)** o, *o*x; au, c*ow*; ou, g*oa*t; u, p*oo*r; ɔi, r*oy*al. **(u)** ʌ, d*u*ck; u, b*u*ll; uː, g*oo*se; ə, *ba*cillus; juː, c*u*be. x, lo*ch*; θ, *th*ink; ð, *b*o*th*er; z, *Z*en; ʒ, cor*s*age. dʒ, sa*v*age; ŋ, oranguta*ng*; j, *y*ak; ʃ, *f*ish; tʃ, fe*tch*; 'l, rabb*le*; 'n, redd*en*. Complete pronunciation key appears inside front cover.

cre·do (krí:dou, kréidou) *pl.* **cre·dos** *n.* a creed **Cré·do** a Christian liturgical Creed, esp. a musical setting of the Nicene Creed [L.=I believe]

cre·du·li·ty (krədú:liti:, krədjú:liti:) *n.* the state or quality of being credulous

cred·u·lous (krédʒuləs) *adj.* gullible, ready to believe without proof [fr. L. *credulus*]

Cree (kri:) *n.* a North American Indian of an Algonquian tribe ‖ his language

creed (kri:d) *n.* a set of beliefs or opinions **Creed** one of the formal summaries of Christian beliefs used liturgically [O.E. *crēda* fr. L.]

Creek (kri:k) *n.* a member of a confederacy of American Indians originally in Alabama and Georgia and now centered in Oklahoma. They number about 10,000 ‖ the Muskogean language of the Creeks

creek (kri:k, krik) *n.* a short arm of a river ‖ a small tributary river or stream ‖ (*Br.*) a small inlet or bay [M.E. *creke, crike*]

Creel (kri:l), George Edward (1876–1953), U.S. journalist and author. During the 1st world war he was appointed (1917) civilian chairman of President Wilson's committee on public information and served as his personal representative at important conferences

creel (kri:l) *n.* a wicker basket for holding fish (esp. as used by an angler) ‖ a wicker trap to catch lobsters etc. ‖ a bar for holding bobbins from which thread is being used in spinning [M.E. *crelle* fr. older F. *crille*, var. of *grille*]

creep (kri:p) 1. *v.i. pres. part.* **creep·ing** *past· and past part.* **crept** (krept) to move along with the body prone and close to the ground ‖ (of babies) to crawl on all fours before learning to walk ‖ to move quietly and stealthily ‖ to move or act in a servile manner ‖ (of time etc.) to go slowly ‖ (of plants) to grow along the ground or up walls, trees etc. ‖ (of the skin) to prickle in fear or disgust ‖ (*Br.*) to drag the bottom of a river, lake etc. with a creeper ‖ to slip very gradually out of place ‖ (of metal rails under traffic) 2. *n.* the act or pace of creeping ‖ (*geol.*) a gradual slipping of disintegrated rock due to stress, atmospheric changes etc., e.g. in a scree ‖ (*phys.*) the slow movement of a solid under stress, due to its rigidity breaking down momentarily, to be replaced by viscosity. The stress is thereby reduced and rigidity is restored, only to break down again, and so on. This occurs more readily if the temperature is high, since the solid is able to exhibit viscosity more easily **the creeps** a sensation of fear or horror [O.E. *crēopan*]

creep·er (krí:pər) *n.* anything that creeps, esp. a plant that creeps along the ground or climbs up walls, trees etc. ‖ any of several birds which run along trees etc. searching the crevices for insects ‖ a grapnel for dragging the bottom of rivers, lakes etc.

creep·i·ly (krí:pili) *adj.* in a creepy way

creep·i·ness (krí:pi:nis) *n.* the quality of being creepy

creeping *adj.* gradual, *a creeping inflation*

creeping barrage a barrier of shellfire, advancing as a protection in front of attacking troops

creep·y (krí:pi:) *comp.* **creep·i·er** *superl.* **creep·i·est** *adj.* having a physical sensation of fear or disgust ‖ producing such a sensation, *creepy stories*

creese *KRIS

cre·mains (kriméinz) *n.* cremated remains of a corpse

cre·mate (krí:meit) *pres. part.* **cre·mat·ing** *past and past part.* **cre·mat·ed** *v.t.* to burn, incinerate (a dead body) **cre·ma·tion** (kriméiʃən) *n.* [fr. L. *cremare (crematus)*, to burn]

cre·ma·tor (krí:meitər) *n.* someone who cremates corpses ‖ an incinerator [L. fr. *cremare*, to burn]

cre·ma·to·ri·um (kri:mətɔ́ːriəm, kri:mətóuriəm, krɛmətɔ́ːriəm) *pl.* **cre·ma·to·ri·a** (kri:mətɔ́ːriə, kri:mətóuriə, krɛmətɔ́ːriə, krɛmətóuriə), **cre·ma·to·ri·ums** *n.* a place where corpses are cremated [Mod. L. fr. *cremare*, to burn]

cre·ma·to·ry (krí:mətɔ:ri, krí:mətóuri, krémətɔ:ri:, krɛmətóuri:) 1. *pl.* **cre·ma·to·ries** *n.* a crematorium 2. *adj.* of or pertaining to cremation

Cré·ma·zie (kreimæzi:), (Joseph) Octave (1827–79), French-Canadian poet and a founder (1860) of the first literary school in Quebec. He wrote patriotic poems and strove to preserve the folklore of French Canada

---

créme Chantilly (krem) whipped cream

Cre·mo·na (krimóunə) an industrial city (pop. 82,500) on the Po in Lombardy, N. Italy, founded in 218 B.C. The great violin makers of the 16th–18th cc. lived here (*STRADIVARIUS, *AMATI)

cre·mo·na (krimóunə) *n.* a cromorne

cre·nate (krí:neit) *adj.* (*biol.*) having a toothed edge, with scalloped margin **cré·nat·ed** *adj.* **cre·ná·tion** *n.* [fr. Mod. L. *crenatus*]

cren·a·ture (krénətʃər, krénətʃər) *n.* (*bot.*) a rounded tooth [fr. Mod. L. *crenatus*, notched]

cren·el (krén'l) *n.* a notched opening in a battlemented parapet [O.F., dim. of *cren*, notch]

cren·el·late, cren·el·ate (krén'leit) *pres. part.* **cren·el·lat·ing, cren·el·at·ing** *past and past part.* **cren·el·lat·ed, cren·el·at·ed** *v.t.* to furnish with battlements **cren·el·lá·tion, cren·el·á·tion** *n.* [F. *créneler*]

cre·nelle (krinél) *CRENEL

cren·u·late (krénjuleit, krénjulit) *adj.* (*bot.*) finely notched with small rounded teeth on the margin **crén·u·lat·ed** *adj.* **cren·u·lá·tion** *n.* [fr. Mod. L. *crenulatus*, dim. of *crenula*, dim. of *crena*, notch]

Cre·ole (krí:oul) 1. *n.* a person of European blood born in the West Indies or Spanish America ‖ a white person descended from French or Spanish settlers in Louisiana and the Gulf states ‖ a person of mixed European and African blood in Louisiana and the Gulf states ‖ the French patois spoken in these states ‖ Haitian Creole 2. *adj.* of or relating to the Creoles ‖ of Creole blood ‖ (*cookery*) cooked in sauce containing tomatoes, peppers and onions [F. *créole* fr. Span.]

cre·o·sote (krí:əsout) 1. *n.* an oily liquid mixture of organic chemicals (esp. phenol and cresol) obtained during the destructive distillation of coal or wood, its main source being the coal tar produced in gas works and coke ovens. The lighter constituents are used as disinfectants and in the manufacture of sheep dips. The heavier fraction, ordinary creosote oil, is used to preserve wood against attack by fungi, white ants and marine borers 2. *v.t. pres. part.* **cre·o·sot·ing** *past and past part.* **cre·o·sot·ed** to treat with creosote [fr. Gk *kreas*, flesh+*sōzein*, to save]

crepe, crêpe, crape (kreip) *n.* a thin fabric, usually of silk, with a wrinkled surface [fr. older F. *crespe*]

crepe de Chine (kréipdəʃí:n) a silk crepe

crepe hair (*cosmetology*) hair confusion created by permanent waving, baking, or oiling

crepe paper thin, crinkled, usually brightly colored paper, used for decorations etc.

crepe rubber a durable crinkled rubber used esp. for the soles of shoes

crep·i·tant (krépit'nt) *adj.* having or making a crackling or rustling sound

crep·i·tate (krépiteit) *pres. part.* **crep·i·tat·ing** *past and past part.* **crep·i·tat·ed** *v.i.* to make a crackling or rustling sound ‖ (*med.*, of rheumatic joints) to move with this sound ‖ (*zool.*, of some beetles) to discharge a fluid with the sound of a sharp crack **crep·i·tá·tion** *n.* [fr. L. *crepitare (crepitatus)*]

crep·on (kréipɒn) *n.* (*cosmetology*) woven-frontlet hairpiece, usu. in pompadour extended to tops of ears

crept *past and past part.* of CREEP

cre·pus·cu·lar (kripʌ́skjulər) *adj.* of twilight ‖ (*zool.*) appearing or active before sunrise, or at dusk [fr. L. *crepusculum*, twilight]

cre·scen·do (kriʃéndou) 1. *adj. and adv.* (*mus.*) increasing in loudness 2. *pl.* **cre·scen·dos, cre·scen·di** (kriʃéndi:) *n.* a gradual increase in sound ‖ a musical passage so played ‖ a buildup towards a climax [Ital., *pres. part.* of *crescere*, to grow]

cres·cent (krés'nt) 1. *n.* the waxing moon ‖ the moon in its first or last quarter ‖ any crescent-shaped object, esp. (*Br.*) such a row of houses ‖ the crescent moon as an emblem of the Turkish or Turkish power or of the Moslem religion 2. *adj.* crescentshaped [M.E. *cressant* fr. O.F.]

cre·sol (krí:sɔl, krí:soul, krí:sɒl) *n.* (*chem.*) a disinfectant substance resembling phenol and obtained from coal tar [fr. CREOSOTE]

cress (kres) *n.* *Lepidium sativum*, fam. *Cruciferae*, a widely cultivated salad plant whose pungent cotyledonary leaves, hypocotyl and shoot are all edible ‖ any of several similar plants of fam. *Cruciferae* (* WATERCRESS) [O.E. *cresse*]

---

cres·set (krésit) *n.* (*hist.*) an iron holder for a burning torch, usually mounted on a pole as a lantern or beacon [O.F.]

crest (krest) 1. *n.* the comb or tuft on the head of a bird or animal ‖ a plume of feathers or other ornament on top of a helmet ‖ the ridge of a helmet ‖ the top of a hill or wave ‖ a mane ‖ (*archit.*) the ridge of a roof or canopy etc. ‖ (*anat.*) a ridge along a bone surface ‖ (*heraldry*) an armorial device placed above the shield, or used separately on a letter heading, silver etc. 2. *v.t.* to furnish with a crest ‖ to serve as a crest to ‖ to reach and pass the top of (a hill, wave etc.) ‖ *v.i.* to rise or form into a crest [O.F. *creste*]

crest·fall·en (kréstfɔlən) *adj.* dejected, dispirited

cre·syl·ic (krisílik) *adj.* relating to, or made from, cresol, creosote etc.

cre·ta·ceous (kritéiʃəs) *adj.* of or like chalk **Cre·ta·ceous** *adj.* of the latest period or system of the Mesozoic era. The many rock types include chalk. Reptiles were dominant on land and in the sea (*GEOLOGICAL TIME) **the Cretaceous** the Cretaceous period or system of rocks [fr. L. *cretaceus*]

Cre·tan (krí:t'n) 1. *n.* an inhabitant of Crete 2. *adj.* of Crete or its inhabitants

Crete (kri:t) (*Gk* Kriti) a mountainous and almost treeless island (area 3,200 sq. miles, pop. 456,642) of Greece, in the E. Mediterranean. Chief town: Canea. Products: olives, raisins, wine, citrus fruits, cereals. HISTORY. A Minoan civilization developed around Knossos (c. 3000–c. 1400 B.C.), but declined under invasions from the mainland. Crete was conquered by the Romans (67 B.C.), and was ruled by the Byzantines (961–1204) and the Venetians (1204–1669). The Turks invaded (1645–9) and by 1669 had virtually conquered the whole island. After many risings during the 19th c., they were forced to withdraw (1898). Crete then became an autonomous state, but, after another rising (1904–5), was annexed (1913) to Greece. Captured (1941) by German airborne forces, it was liberated (1944) by the Allies

cre·tin (krí:t'n, krí:tin) *n.* a mentally and physically retarded person whose condition results from severe thyroid deficiency in early infancy **cré·tin·ism** *n.* [F.]

cre·tonne (kritón, krí:tɒn) *n.* a strong, (usually) unglazed, printed cotton material [F., after *Creton* in Normandy]

Creuse (krə:z) a department (area 2,163 sq. miles, pop. 146,200) of central France in the northwest Massif Central (*LIMOUSIN, *BERRY, *AUVERGNE). Chief town: Guéret

cre·vasse (krəvǽs) *n.* a deep crevice, esp. in a glacier ‖ a breach in a river bank [F.]

Crève·coeur (krevkə:r), Michel Guillaume Jean de (1735–1813), Franco-American author known as J. Hector St John and the 'American Farmer'. His essays 'Letters From an American Farmer' (1782) made him the most widely read commentator on the America of his time

crev·ice (krévis) *n.* a narrow crack or split [M.E. *crevace* fr. O.F.]

crew (kru:) *n.* (a collective term for) a ship's company, or ship's company with the officers ‖ the men manning an aircraft ‖ a body of men working together at a task, *a gun crew* ‖ a band, mob ‖ a rowing team ‖ the sport of rowing in races [fr. O.F. *creue*, growth]

crew *alt. past* of CROW

crew cut a man's closely cropped haircut, worn without a parting

crew·el (krú:əl) *n.* a loosely twisted worsted yarn used for embroidery and tapestry [etym. doubtful]

crew·el·work (krú:əlwə:rk) *n.* a design worked with crewel

crew sock short, heavy, ribbed stocking used by rowers

crib (krib) 1. *n.* a barred wooden manger for animal fodder ‖ (*Am.*=*Br.* cot) a bed, usually with high sides, for a small child ‖ a crèche (model of the Nativity) ‖ a literal prose translation of a literary work in another language, used esp. by young students ‖ plagiarism, a theft of other people's ideas etc. ‖ cards discarded at cribbage for the dealer to use in scoring ‖ a wicker basket, esp. one used as a salmon trap ‖ the framework lining a mine shaft ‖ (*mining*) heavy timbers used as a foundation on a yielding bed, or as a retaining wall ‖ a bin for corn, salt etc. 2. *v. pres. part.* **crib·bing** *past and past part.* **cribbed** *v.i.* to use a crib in one's work ‖ *v.t.* to

---

copy unfairly ‖ to plagiarize ‖ to line with timbers or planks [O.E. *crib, cribb*]

crib·bage (kríbidʒ) *n.* a game played by two, three or four people with playing cards. The score is kept with pegs on a special board

crib death (*med.*) the sudden death of an infant in apparent good health, for undiagnosed causes *also* sudden infant death syndrome

crib·ri·form (kríbrəfɔrm) *adj.* (*anat., bot.*) perforated, sievelike [Mod. L. *cribriformis* fr. *cribrum*, sieve]

crib·work (kríbwəːrk) *n.* a structure of logs built with the layers at right angles to one another ‖ concrete-filled boxes used to carry bridge foundations

Crick (krik) Francis (1916–), English physicist and biochemist who collaborated with James D. Watson and Maurice Wilkins to determine the molecular (double helix) structure of DNA, for which they shared the 1962 Nobel Prize for physiology/medicine

crick (krik) **1.** *n.* a sudden sharp pain or cramp in the muscles, esp. of the neck **2.** *v.t.* to twist or strain (a muscle), causing a crick [prob. imit.]

crick·et (kríkit) *n.* a member of *Gryllidae*, a family of insects allied to the cicada, distinguished by long cerci and filamentous antennae. The males 'chirp' by rubbing their fore wings together and, like the females, have structures (tympanal organs) for perceiving sound [O.F. *criquet*]

cricket *n.* the outdoor team game described below **not cricket** (*pop.*) not fair or sportsmanlike [O.F. *criquet*, a stick to aim at]
—Cricket is played between two teams of 11 players on a prepared turf field having a central pitch 22 yards long, with wickets (3 stumps with transverse bails) in the ground at either end. The bat is of willow with a bound cane handle (not more than 38 ins in length overall, 4½ ins in width). The ball is leather-covered (about 5½ ounces and about 9 ins in circumference). The batting side sends in two batsmen, who score runs by hitting the ball and running the length of the pitch, or by hitting the ball over the boundary line. A batsman may be put out in many ways: bowled, caught, stumped, run out, l.b.w. (leg before wicket). Each batsman is replaced, until 10 men have been put out, or the captain has declared. The other team then goes in to try to score more runs than the first did. The game consists of either one or two innings by each team. Test matches are played between the national teams of England, Australia (since 1877), South Africa, the West Indies, New Zealand, India, Pakistan

cri·coid (kráikɔid) **1.** *adj.* (*anat.*) ring-shaped **2.** *n.* a ring of cartilage in the larynx [fr. Mod. L. *cricoides* fr. Gk]

cri·du·chat syndrome (kri:du:ʃa) genetic form of mental retardation in which one symptom is a mewing cry

cried *past* and *past part.* of CRY

cri·er (kráiər) *n.* an official who makes public announcements in a court ‖ a town crier [M.E. *criere* fr. O.F.]

crime (kraim) *n.* a violation of the law, esp. a serious one ‖ such acts in general, *an increase in crime* ‖ (*loosely*) a foolish or ill-considered action, *it's a crime to waste that whiskey* [F.]

Cri·me·a (kraimí:ə, krimí:ə) a peninsula (area 10,136 sq. miles) of the S. Ukraine, U.S.S.R., with mountains on the south coast. There are many resorts. Towns: Simferopol, Sevastopol, Kerch, Yalta

Cri·me·an (kraimí:ən, krimí:ən) *adj.* of or relating to the Crimea

Crimean War (kraimí:ən, krimí:ən) the war (1853–6) declared on Russia by Turkey (Oct. 1853) by Britain and France (Mar. 1854), and by Sardinia (Jan. 1855). The causes were Russian expansion in the Balkans and the dispute over the guardianship of the Holy Places in Palestine. Battles included Balaclava (the Charge of the Light Brigade) and Inkerman (1854). Sevastopol was taken by the Allies (1855) and the war was ended by the Treaty of Paris (1856). Florence Nightingale organized medical services. The first Victoria Crosses were awarded

crim·i·nal (krímin'l) **1.** *adj.* relating to crime ‖ guilty of crime **2.** *n.* someone who has committed a crime **crim·i·nal·i·ty** (krimináeliti:) *n.* the quality or state of being criminal [F. *criminel*]

crim·i·nal·iza·tion (kriminˈlizéiʃən) *n.* making subject to criminal penalties, e.g., smoking marijuana

crim·i·nate (krímineit) *pres. part.* **crim·i·nat·ing** *past* and *past part.* **crim·i·nat·ed** *v.t.* to accuse of crime ‖ to prove guilty of crime, (more usually) incriminate **crim·i·na·tion** *n.* **crim·i·na·tive, crim·i·na·to·ry** (kríminətɔri, krímineitɔuri:) *adjs* [fr. L. *criminatus* fr. *crimen* (*criminis*), crime]

crim·i·no·log·i·cal (krimin'lódʒik'l) *adj.* of or relating to criminology

crim·i·nol·o·gist (kriminólədʒist) *n.* someone skilled in criminology

crim·i·nol·o·gy (kriminólədʒi:) *n.* the scientific study of crime, criminals and penal treatment etc. (*FORENSIC SCIENCE) [fr. L. *crimen* (*criminis*), crime + Gk *logos*, discourse]

crimmer *KRIMMER

crimp (krimp) **1.** *v.t.* to pinch into waves or ridges, *to crimp a pie crust* ‖ to make flutings in ‖ to gash (the flesh of newly killed fish) so that it contracts ‖ to form into shape, esp. (*shoemaking*) to mold (leather) into shape ‖ to put a crimp in **2.** *n.* a wave or undulation (e.g. in the hair) ‖ a corrugation ‖ the act or result of crimping, e.g. the warping of wood from drying too fast **to put a crimp in** (*pop.*) to cramp or hinder **crimp·y** *comp.* **crimp·i·er** *superl.* **crimp·i·est** *adj.* crimped in appearance [fr. M. Du. *krimpen*, to contract]

crim·son (krímzən, krímsən) **1.** *n.* a deep red color **2.** *adj.* of this color **3.** *v.t.* to cause to become crimson ‖ *v.i.* to become crimson [fr. Span. *cremesin*]

cringe (krindʒ) *pres. part.* **cring·ing** *past* and *past part.* **cringed** *v.i.* to cower, shrink in fear ‖ to behave servilely [O.E. *cringan*, to fall in battle]

crin·gle (kríng'l) *n.* (*naut.*) a small piece of rope with a metal eyelet to take another rope for fastening a sail [Du. or L.G. *kringel* dim. of *kring*, ring]

cri·nite (kráinait) *adj.* (*biol.*) hairy [fr. L. *crinitus*]

crin·kle (kríŋk'l) **1.** *v. pres. part.* **crin·kling** *past* and *past part.* **crin·kled** *v.i.* to wrinkle ‖ *v.t.* to cause to wrinkle **2.** *n.* a crease, wrinkle **crin·kly** *comp.* **crin·kli·er** *superl.* **crin·kli·est** *adj.* [M.E. *crenklen, crynklen* fr. O.E. *crincan*, to sink in a heap]

cri·noid (kráinɔid, krínɔid) **1.** *n.* a member of *Crinoidea*, a large class of tropical and fossil echinoderms that may be sessile and that have five or more feathery arms and a centrally placed ventral mouth **2.** *adj.* of or relating to crinoids **cri·nói·dal** *adj.* [fr. Gk *crinoeidēs*, lily-like]

crin·o·line (krín'lin, krín'li:n) *n.* a petticoat hooped to make a skirt bell out all around ‖ a stiff fabric originally made of flax and horsehair [F.]

cri·ol·lo (kri:óulou, *Span.* kri:ójɔ) *n.* a Spaniard born in the Americas [Span.]

crip·ple (kríp'l) **1.** *n.* a badly lamed or disabled person **2.** *v.t. pres. part.* **crip·pling** *past* and *past part.* **crip·pled** to disable, lame ‖ to frustrate, hinder [O.E. *crypel*]

Cripps (krips), Sir Stafford (1889–1952), British statesman, barrister and Labour M.P. He was ambassador to Russia (1940–2), lord privy seal and leader of the Commons (1942), minister of aircraft production (1942–5), president of the board of trade (1945–7) and chancellor of the exchequer (1947–50)

cri·sis (kráisis) *pl.* **cri·ses** (kráisi:z) *n.* the turning point in a disease ‖ the decisive moment, esp. in a tragedy ‖ a time of danger or suspense in politics etc. **to bring to a crisis** to bring (affairs) to a culminating point [L. fr. Gk *krisis*, decision]

crisis center antisuicide establishment available for advice by telephone to anyone in a depression crisis

crisis theology theology whose point of departure is man's awareness of the inner contradiction in his nature. It is particularly associated with Barth

crisp (krisp) **1.** *adj.* firm and fresh, *crisp lettuce* ‖ fresh and bracing, *a crisp frosty night* ‖ concise, clear and direct, *a crisp style* ‖ (of hair etc.) curly, crinkled **2.** *n.* (*Br.*) potato chip **3.** *v.t.* to make crisp ‖ *v.i.* to become crisp [O.E. *crisp, cyrps* fr. L.]

cris·pate (kríspeit) *adj.* (*bot.*) crisped or wavy in appearance [fr. L. *crispatus*]

cris·pa·tion (krispéiʃən) *n.* the puckering of the skin caused by the erection of the hairs through cold, fright etc. ‖ a curling or being curled [fr. L *crispare*, to curl]

crisp·y (kríspi:) *comp.* **crisp·i·er** *superl.* **crisp·i·est** *adj.* crisp

criss·cross (krískrɔs, krískrɒs) **1.** *n.* a pattern of crossed lines ‖ crossing currents **2.** *adj.* having or consisting of crossing lines **3.** *adv.* crosswise, in different directions **4.** *v.t.* to mark with crossing lines ‖ *v.i.* to cross repeatedly ‖ to move crosswise [orig. *Christ's cross* (from the cross written before the alphabet in 16th and 17th-c. children's books)]

crista (kríste) *n.* (*zool.*) an inward longitudinal fold in the membrane of some bacteria

cris·tate (krísteit) *adj.* (*biol.*) crested [fr. L. *cristatus* fr. *crista*, crest]

cris·te·ros (kri:stéros) *n.* a Mexican political movement and revolt, esp. in Jalisco, during the presidency (1924–8) of Elias Calles, in opposition to the anticlerical provisions in the Constitution which he enforced. No church services were held in Mexico for three years (1926–9), although churches were kept open for private worship [Span.]

cri·te·ri·on (kraitíəri:ən) *pl.* **cri·te·ri·a** (kraitíəri:ə), **cri·te·ri·ons** *n.* a standard or principle by which a thing is judged [Gk *kritērion*, a means for judging]

Cri·thid·i·a (kriθídi:ə) *n.* (*zool.*) genus of flagellate protozoan parasites that attacks invertebrate animals

crit·ic (krítik) *n.* a person skilled in forming opinions and giving a judgment, esp. on literature, art, music etc. ‖ a professional reviewer ‖ a fault finder [fr. L. *criticus* fr. Gk]

crit·i·cal (krítik'l) *adj.* given to expressing severe judgments or passing unfavorable comment ‖ fond of pointing out shortcomings or error, censorious ‖ of a crisis, *the critical moment* ‖ of critics or criticism, *critical essays* ‖ involving danger or suspense, *a critical operation* ‖ discerning, based on thorough knowledge, *a critical opinion* ‖ (*phys., math.*) denoting a point or state at which a change in properties, characteristics etc. takes place [fr. L. *criticus*, discerning]

critical angle (*phys.*) the smallest angle of incidence at which total internal reflection occurs when a ray of light, or other electromagnetic radiation, travels through a medium to its boundary with a less refracting medium

critical constant (esp. *pl.*) the critical temperature, pressure or density of a substance

critical density the density of a substance in its critical state

critical idealism the Kantian doctrine that the mind impresses its forms of sensibility on the original data of the senses and orders them according to the categories of thought (*KANT)

critical mass (*nuclear phys.*) the point in an accumulation of plutonium at which it could explode a nuclear weapon; by extension, the point of any accumulation that could become explosive

critical path analysis system of operational control that uses computer technology to review utilization of resources at each critical point in a program *acronym* CPA *syn.* critical path

critical point critical state

critical pressure the vapor pressure of a liquid at its critical temperature

critical state the condition of a substance when its liquid and vapor phases have the same density

critical temperature the temperature above which a gas cannot be liquefied by the application of pressure alone

critical velocity the velocity of flow of a fluid above which turbulent motion occurs instead of smooth flow

critical volume the volume of 1 gram of a substance in its critical state

crit·i·cism (krítisizəm) *n.* the art of judging merit ‖ a spoken or written judgment concerning some matter resting on opinion ‖ censure, unfavorable comment (*FORM CRITICISM, *HIGHER CRITICISM, *LOWER CRITICISM, *PRACTICAL CRITICISM, *TEXTUAL CRITICISM)

crit·i·cize (krítisaiz) *pres. part.* **crit·i·ciz·ing** *past* and *past part.* **crit·i·cized** *v.t.* to assess the merits and demerits of ‖ to censure ‖ *v.i.* to find fault

cri·tique (krití:k) *n.* a critical essay or review [F.]

Crit·ten·den (krít'ndən), John Jordan (1787–1863), U.S. statesman, known for his unsuccessful 'Crittenden Resolutions' (1860) designed to placate the South by advocating positions favorable to slavery

CONCISE PRONUNCIATION KEY: **(a)** æ, c*a*t; ɑ, c*a*r; ɔ, f*aw*n; ei, sn*a*ke. **(e)** e, h*e*n; i:, sh*ee*p; iə, d*ee*r; ɛə, b*ear*. **(i)** i, f*i*sh; ai, t*i*ger; ə:, b*ir*d. **(o)** o, *o*x; au, c*ow*; ou, g*oa*t; u, p*oo*r; ɔi, r*oy*al. **(u)** ʌ, d*u*ck; u, b*u*ll; u:, g*oo*se; ə, b*a*cillus; ju:, c*u*be. x, lo*ch*; θ, *th*ink; ð, bo*th*er; z, *Z*en; ʒ, cor*s*age; dʒ, sava*g*e; ŋ, oranguta*ng*; j, *y*ak; ʃ, *fi*sh; tʃ, fe*tch*; 'l, rabb*le*; 'n, redd*en*. Complete pronunciation key appears inside front cover.

Cri·vel·li (kri:véli:), Carlo (c. 1430–c. 1493), Venetian painter, influenced by Mantegna, and much given to ornament and decoration. His 'Annunciation' (1486) is in the National Gallery, London

croak (krouk) **1.** *v.i.* (e.g. of a frog or raven) to utter a deep hoarse sound ‖ to talk dismally ‖ *v.t.* to speak or say in a low, hoarse voice **2.** *n.* a hoarse, harsh sound **cróak·i·ly** *adv.* **cróak·y** *adj.* [prob. imit.] **Cro·at** (króuæt) *n.* a native of Croatia ‖ the Slavic language of Croatia

Cro·a·tia (krouéiʃə, krouéiʃi:ə) a constituent republic (area 21,701 sq. miles, pop. 4,530,000) of Yugoslavia, extending from the Hungarian border to the Adriatic between Slovenia and Bosnia-Herzegovina and including Slavonia and Dalmatia. Capital: Zagreb. Croatia proper, the region bounded by these four, is mountainous, with forest and karst. Crops: cereals, sugar beet, figs, olives. Livestock: hogs, cattle. Industries: forestry, mining (lignite, bauxite), engineering, brewing, food processing. Settled by Slav Croats (6th–8th cc.), the country was united with Hungary (1102) but most of it was under Turkish rule (1526–1699). With the collapse of Austria-Hungary (1918), the Croats united with the Serbs and Slovenes in the kingdom renamed (1929) Yugoslavia

Cro·a·tian (krouéiʃən, krouéiʃi:ən) **1.** *n.* a native of Croatia, a Croat **2.** *adj.* of Croatia, the Croats, or their language

Cro·ce (krótʃe), Benedetto (1866–1952), Italian critic and politician whose humanism and political activity helped to revive liberalism in postwar Italy. He published over 80 works. As a critic he denounced all schools of thought based on the irrational, and he affirmed the artist's independence of politics, propaganda or doctrine. His review 'La Critica' (founded in 1903) influenced the literary thought of the Western world

cro·chet (krouʃéi) **1.** *n.* a kind of needlework done with a hook. Thread or yarn is worked into patterns of intertwined loops **2.** *v.t. pres. part.* **cro·chet·ing** (krouʃéiiŋ) *past* and *past part.* **cro·cheted** (krouʃéid) to make (something) by working thread in this way ‖ *v.i.* to work thread in this way [F., dim. of *croche*, hook]

crock (krok) *n.* an earthenware pot or jar [O.E. *croc, crocca*]

crock 1. *n.* (*Br., pop.*) an injured person ‖ (*slang*) nonsense, esp. insincere nonsense ‖ in a hospital, a patient diagnosed by the nonmedical staff as having an unreal, nonphysical, or insignificant illness ‖ a wretched worn-out person, horse, car etc. **2.** *v.t.* (often with 'up') to injure or impair ‖ *v.i.* (often with 'up') to become injured [perh. rel. to CRACK]

crock·er·y (krókəri:) *n.* earthenware vessels [fr. obs. *crocker*, potter]

crock·et (krókit) *n.* (*archit.*) an ornamental carving (usually resembling curled foliage) on the sloping edge of a gable, pinnacle etc. [A.F. *croket*, a curl]

Crock·ett (krókit), Davy (1786–1836), American frontiersman, soldier and politician of Tennessee, killed defending the Alamo (1836)

Crock Pot tradename for the electric crockery stewing pot for slow cooking manufactured by Rival

croc·o·dile (krókədail) *n.* a member of the order *Crocodilia*, amphibious reptiles found in the waters of all warm regions of the world, esp. a member of genus *Crocodylus*. They are the largest living reptiles (up to 30 ft) ‖ (*Br.*) a group of people, e.g. schoolchildren, walking in double file [M.E. *cocodrille* fr. O.F.]

crocodile bird *Pluvianus aegypticus*, an African bird resembling a plover. It alights on crocodiles to pick their teeth and devour their leeches

crocodile tears insincere grief [from the old belief that crocodiles weep while luring or devouring their prey]

croc·o·i·site (króukouizait) *n.* crocoite

cro·co·ite (króukouait) *n.* a red mineral, basic lead chromate, also called chrome orange and chrome red when used as a pigment [fr. Gk *krókos*, saffron]

cro·cus (króukəs) *pl.* **cro·cus·es** *n.* a member of *Crocus*, fam. *Iridaceae*, a genus of low-growing herbaceous plants of which there are some 75 Mediterranean and European species, cultivated for their variously colored spring flowers. The dried stigmas and part of the style of *C. sativus* form saffron [L. fr. Gk *krókos*, saffron]

Croe·sus (krí:səs) (*d. c.* 546 B.C.) the last king of Lydia (560–546 B.C.), of proverbial wealth, overthrown by Cyrus II of Persia (546 B.C.)

croft (kroft, kraft) *n.* (*Br.*) a small holding rented and worked by a tenant (esp. in Scotland) ‖ (*Br. hist.*) a small enclosed piece of arable land, esp. adjoining a cottage **cróft·er** *n.* a farmer working a croft [O.E.=enclosed field]

Cro-Mag·non man (kroumǽgnən, kroumǽgnon, kroumǽnjən) a Paleolithic race of tall, long-skulled men associated with the Aurignacian culture [after *CroMagnon* in S.W. France]

Crome (kroum), John (1768–1821), English painter. With Cotman he led the Norwich School. Most of his subjects were East Anglian landscapes. He is called 'Old Crome' to distinguish him from his son John Bernay Crome (1794–1842)

crom·lech (krómlek) *n.* (in Britain) a prehistoric structure consisting of a large flat stone resting on three or more upright stones ‖ (in France) a dolmen [Welsh fr. *crom*, bent + *llech*, flat stone]

cro·morne (kroumɔ́rn, krəmɔ́rn) *n.* an organ reed stop [F. fr. G. *krummhorn*, crooked horn]

Cromp·ton (krómptən), Samuel (1753–1827), English inventor of the spinning mule (1779)

Crom·well (krómwəl, krómwel, krámwəl, krámwel), Oliver (1599–1658), lord protector of England (1653–8). A Huntingdon yeoman, he was elected (1640) to the Long Parliament, where he became the leader of the Puritans. With the outbreak (1642) of the Civil War, he led his 'ironside' troops to victory over the royalists. He supported the Independent faction of Puritans against the Presbyterians, and urged the execution (1649) of Charles I. With the House of Lords and the Church of England abolished, he became the effective ruler of England. He crushed (1649) the radical Levellers, and subdued Ireland (1649–50) with great cruelty. He defeated (1651) an invasion by the future Charles II, and dissolved (1653) the Long Parliament by force. The council of army officers appointed him lord protector of the Commonwealth (1653). Under his dictatorship, peace was made with Holland (1654), and commercial treaties were signed with Sweden, Denmark, Portugal (1654) and France (1653). Cromwell's authority was delegated (1655) to regional commanders known as major-generals, but he declined (1657) the title of king. In alliance with France, he defeated Spain at sea (1657) and on land (1658). On his death (1658), he was succeeded by his son Richard Cromwell. A great general and administrator, Oliver Cromwell developed the navy and commerce. He had a single-minded biblical faith, and he was relatively tolerant in an intolerant age

Cromwell, Richard (1626–1712), lord protector of England (1658–9), son of Oliver Cromwell. After eight months' rule, he was dismissed (1659) by parliament and the army, and retired to France at the time of the Restoration (1660)

Cromwell, Thomas, earl of Essex (c. 1485–1540), English statesman. Ruthlessly efficient as collector of revenues (1514) for Wolsey, he became chancellor of the exchequer (1533) and secretary (1534) to Henry VIII. He organized the Reformation acts (1532–9) and the dissolution of the monasteries (1536–9). He was executed (1540) when the king tired of Anne of Cleves, whose marriage Cromwell had negotiated

crone (kroun) *n.* an old woman, esp. one of witchlike appearance [prob. fr. O.N.F. *carogne*, cranky old woman]

Cro·nus (króunəs) (Gk *mythol.*) one of the Titans, overthrown by his son, Zeus. The Romans identified him with Saturn

cro·ny (króuni:) *pl.* **cro·nies** *n.* an intimate friend ‖ a drinking companion [orig. Br. university slang perh. fr. Gk *chronios*, contemporary]

cro·ny·ism (króuni:izəm) *n.* favoritism toward friends in business or government

crook (kruk) **1.** *n.* a hooked staff used by a shepherd ‖ a crosier ‖ anything hooked or bent, *the crook of an arm* ‖ a hook ‖ (*pop.*) a thief, criminal ‖ (*mus.*) a device on some wind instruments for changing pitch **2.** *v.t.* to bend into a crook ‖ to grasp with a crook ‖ *v.i.* to bend or curve **crook·ed** (krúkid) *adj.* not straight, twisted ‖ bent or stooping with age or illness ‖ dishonest, *crooked*

dealings [M.E. *crōk* perh. fr. O.N. *krōkr*, crook]

Crookes' rays (kruks) (*phys.*) cathode rays [after Sir William *Crookes* (1832–1919), Eng. physicist]

croon (kru:n) **1.** *v.i.* to sing or hum in an undertone ‖ (of entertainers) to hum or sing with the technique of a crooner ‖ (of babies) to hum or sing softly, abstractedly and contentedly ‖ *v.t.* to hum or sing (a song) in an undertone or with the technique of a crooner **2.** *n.* the sound made by crooning **cróon·er** *n.* a singer of sentimental songs sung in a low, intimate, breathy style, often into a microphone held at the lips [etym. doubtful]

crop (krop) **1.** *n.* harvested grain, fruit etc. ‖ cultivated produce while growing ‖ a group of things coming together, *a crop of difficulties* ‖ the pouchlike dilation of a bird's gullet where food is broken up for digestion ‖ a hunting whip with a loop instead of a lash ‖ the handle of a whip ‖ hair cut short ‖ the style of wearing hair so cut ‖ a complete, tanned animal hide **2.** *v. pres. part.* **crop·ping** *past* and *past part.* **cropped** *v.t.* (of animals) to eat off short, *geese will crop your lawn* ‖ to cut (hair) short and often unevenly ‖ to cut off (ends, parts of a photograph unwanted for printing etc.) ‖ to clip (ears) ‖ to reap, harvest ‖ to cultivate in, *to crop a field with clover* ‖ *v.i.* to bear a crop ‖ (*geol.*) to crop out **to crop out** (*geol.*) to come to the surface **to crop up** to occur unexpectedly (in conversation etc.) [O.E. *cropp*, bunch]

crop-eared (krópiərd) *adj.* with the ears cropped

crop·per (krópər) *n.* a plant, tree etc. with relation to the quality of its yield, *a heavy cropper* ‖ a machine that removes loose ends from linen **to come a cropper** (*pop.*) to fall heavily ‖ (*pop.*) to fail conspicuously

cro·quet (kroukéi) **1.** *n.* a game in which wooden balls are knocked with long-handled wooden mallets through a series of wickets ‖ the act of croqueting a ball **2.** *v.t. pres. part.* **cro·quet·ing** (kroukéiiŋ) *past* and *past part.* **cro·queted** (kroukéid) to drive away (an opponent's ball) by striking one's own placed up against it [North F. for *crochet* fr. *croche*, crook]

cro·quette (kroukét) *n.* a ball of minced meat, fish etc. coated with crumbs and fried [F. fr. *croquer*, to crunch]

cro·sier, cro·zier (króuʒər) *n.* a bishop's or abbot's staff, usually shaped like a shepherd's crook, as a symbol of pastoral office [O.F. *crocier*, bearer of a cross]

cross (krɔs, kros) **1.** *n.* a figure or mark made by placing one line across another (x, +, †) ‖ such a mark made on a document instead of a signature by someone who cannot write ‖ (*hist.*) an upright wooden stake with a horizontal crossbar to which criminals were tied or nailed, esp. the one on which Jesus Christ was crucified ‖ a model or image of this, the chief emblem of Christianity ‖ a staff surmounted by a cross carried in religious processions ‖ a movement of the right hand making the sign of a cross as a sacramental act ‖ suffering, tribulation one has to bear ‖ a decoration in certain orders of knighthood ‖ a decoration awarded for bravery, *the Victoria Cross* ‖ (*heraldry*) a cross-shaped emblem ‖ any of various forms of monument or symbol, *Maltese cross, Celtic cross* ‖ a line or stroke forming part of a letter, e.g. the bar of a 't' ‖ a mark used, esp. at the end of a letter, to signify a kiss ‖ interbreeding ‖ the product of mixed breeding, *a mule is a cross between a mare and a donkey* ‖ (*astron.*) a constellation, *the Southern Cross* ‖ (*plumbing*) a four-way joint in the form of a cross, used at the intersection of two pipes **on the cross** diagonally across the grain or weave **2.** *v.t.* to go across ‖ to place crosswise, *to cross one's arms* ‖ to put the bar on (the letter 't') ‖ (with 'off' or 'out') to draw a line through or across (written matter) to cancel it ‖ to thwart, frustrate ‖ to meet and pass ‖ to mark with a cross ‖ to make the sign of the cross over as a sacramental act ‖ (*Br.*) to draw two parallel lines across (a check) with the words '& Co' between them so that the check is payable only through a bank ‖ *v.i.* to go across something ‖ to lie across something ‖ to interbreed ‖ to cross-fertilize **to cross one's mind** to occur to one **to cross someone's palm** to give money to someone **to cross someone's path** to happen to meet him **to cross swords** to exchange angry or sharp words (with someone) **3.** *adj.* transverse, *crossbeams* ‖ contrary, opposite, *at cross-purposes* ‖ conflicting, *crosscurrents* ‖ peevish, annoyed [M.E. *cros, crosse* fr. O.E. fr. O.N. or O. Ir. fr. L.]

cross assembler (*computer*) a program processed to translate a program to one compatible with another computer

cross·bar (krósbɑr, krósbɔr) *n.* a bar fixed across two others, esp. the transverse wooden bar joining the uprights of a goalpost ‖ the horizontal bar strengthening the frame of a man's bicycle

cross·beam (krósbɪːm, krósbɪːm) *n.* a large beam stretching across a building as a main support

cross·bear·er (krósbɛərər, krósbɛərər) *n.* the person who carries the cross in a Christian religious procession

cross·bench (krósbentʃ, krósbentʃ) *n.* (*Br.*) a bench in parliament reserved for independent members who belong neither to the government nor to the opposition **cross·bench·er** *n.*

cross·bill (krósbɪl, krósbɪl) *n. Loxia curvirostra,* fam. *Fringillidae.* The upper and lower bill halves cross each other when closed, enabling the bird to tear open pine cones for seeds

cross·bones (krósbounz, krósbounz) *pl. n.* a representation on a flag etc. of two thigh bones laid one across the other, usually under a skull, as an emblem of piracy or death

cross·bow (krósbou, krósbou) *n.* a medieval weapon for shooting arrows, stones etc.: the bow was placed crosswise on a grooved wooden stock, and the string was held and released mechanically

cross·bred (krósbred, krósbred) *adj.* produced by crossbreeding

cross·breed (krósbrɪːd, krósbrɪːd) **1.** *v. pres. part.* **cross·breed·ing** *past* and *past part.* **cross·bred** (krósbred, krósbred) *v.t.* to mate (parents of different breeds, or two varieties of the same species) ‖ *v.i.* to practice this kind of breeding **2.** *n.* a plant or animal produced by crossbreeding

crossbusing *BUSING

cross·but·tock (krósbʌtək, krósbʌtək) **1.** *n.* a throw over the hip in wrestling **2.** *v.t.* to throw (one's opponent) with this throw

cross·check (króstʃek) *n.* (*lacrosse*) purposely hitting an opponent's stick

cross·coun·try (króskʌntri, króskʌntri) **1.** *adj.* across fields rather than by roads, *a cross-country race* ‖ through the countryside **2.** *adv.* going over fields etc. or through the countryside

cross·cur·rent (króskərənt, króskərənt, krós·kʌrənt, króskʌrənt) *n.* current going across the general direction of flow ‖ (*pl.*) a body of opinion etc. that goes counter to official or majority opinion or policy

cross·cut (króskʌt, króskʌt) **1.** *n.* a diagonal cut across ‖ a path etc. running crosswise ‖ (*mining*) a cutting across the vein or main working **2.** *adj.* made for crosscutting, *a crosscut saw* **3.** *v.t. pres. part.* **cross·cut·ting** *past* and *past part.* **cross·cut** to cut across the grain of

cross·dis·ci·pli·nar·y (krosdísiplineri) *adj.* involved in two or more academic disciplines, e.g., psychology and history

cross·dress (krosdrés) *v.* to dress in clothing traditionally appropriate to the opposite sex

crosse (krɔs, krɒs) *n.* a lacrosse stick [F.]

cross·ex·am·i·na·tion (krósigzæmiéiʃən, krós·igzæminéiʃən) *n.* the act of someone who cross-examines

cross·ex·am·ine (krósigzæmin, krósigzæmin) *pres. part.* **cross·ex·am·in·ing** *past* and *past part.* **cross·ex·am·ined** *v.t.* to question closely (esp. a witness in a law court) in order to check answers given previously or to elicit fresh information

cross·eyed (krósaid, krósaid) *adj.* squinting, having internal strabismus (i.e. with the eyes turning towards each other)

cross·fer·ti·li·za·tion (krósfə:rt'lizéiʃən, krós·fə:rt'lizéiʃən) *n.* a cross-fertilizing

cross·fer·ti·lize (krósfə:rt'laiz, krósfə:rt'laiz) *pres. part.* **cross·fer·ti·liz·ing** *past* and *past part.* **cross·fer·ti·lized** *v.t.* (*bot.*) to fertilize by cross-pollination ‖ (*zool.*) to fertilize the eggs of a hermaphroditic animal with the spermatozoa of another individual of the species ‖ *v.i.* to undergo cross-fertilization

cross·fire (*mil.*) a firing from two or more points so that the lines of fire cross ‖ any comparable attack, *a cross fire of questioning*

cross·grain intercrossing grain in wood **cross·grained** (krósgréind, krósgréind) *adj.* with the grain intercrossing or running irregularly ‖ perversely ill-tempered

cross hair one of a pair of fine lines at right angles in some surveying or other instruments, for leveling and sighting on an object

cross·hatch (króshætʃ, króshætʃ) *v.t.* to show conventionally by intersecting sets of parallel lines usually set off obliquely, *the property has been crosshatched on this map* ‖ to shade (a drawing) to give the effect of depth by straight crisscrossing lines

cross·head (króshed, króshed) *n.* a beam across the end of a rod, esp. a piston rod ‖ a subordinate heading in the body of reading matter giving an indication of the contents of the following passage

cross·ing (krósiŋ, krósiŋ) *n.* the act of crossing, esp. by a sea voyage ‖ an intersection ‖ a place with special arrangements for the traversing of a road, river etc.

cross·ing·o·ver (krósiŋóuvər, krósiŋóuver) *n.* the interchange of corresponding chromosome segments by homologous pairs of chromosomes during maturation division of a nucleus

crossing sweeper (*Br., hist.*) someone who sweeps the streets

cross·leg·ged (króslégid, króslégid, króslégd, króslégd) *adj.* with one leg crossed over the other at the ankles or knees

cross·let (króslit, króslit) *n.* a small cross, esp. in heraldry [A.F. *croisellette,* dim. of O.F. *crois, cross*]

cross·link·age (króslíŋkidʒ, króslíŋkidʒ) *n.* (*chem.*) a transverse bond linking together chain molecules or other polymers ‖ the process of joining by such bonds or of forming such bonds

cross·mod·al (krósmóud'l) *adj.* relating to information received from two different senses, e.g., sight and sound in television

cross·o·ver (krósouvər, krósouvər) *n.* a crossing from one side, level etc. to another ‖ a place where such a crossing is made ‖ (*biol.*) a chromatid formed as a result of crossing-over

crossover state U.S. state that permits voters registered in one political party to vote in primary elections for candidates of another party

cross·patch (króspætʃ, króspætʃ) *n.* an ill-tempered person

cross·piece (króspiːs, króspiːs) *n.* a piece placed across something ‖ a crossbar

cross ply tire rubber tire built by placing supports of rubber across the base *Cf* RADIAL PLY TIRE

cross·pol·li·na·tion (króspplinéiʃən, króspplinéiʃən) *n.* (*bot.*) the depositing of pollen from one flower on to the stigma of another of the same species

cross·pur·pos·es (króspə́:rpəsiz, króspə́:rpəsiz) *pl. n.* accidentally conflicting purposes **to be** (or **talk**) **at cross-purposes** to be opposed in action (or conversation) through misunderstanding

cross·ques·tion (króskwéstʃən, króskwéstʃən) **1.** *v.t.* to question closely ‖ to cross-examine **2.** *n.* a question asked in cross-examining

cross·ref·er·ence (krósréfərəns, krósréfərəns) *n.* a reference from one part of a book to another

cross·road (krósroud, krósroud) *n.* a road that crosses another, esp. a main road ‖ a road that goes across country, between main roads ‖ (*pl.*) an intersection of two or more roads **at the crossroads** at a decisive point (in a situation), involving a choice between mutually exclusive possibilities

cross·ruff (krósrʌf, krósrʌf, krósrʌf, krósrʌf) *n.* (*bridge*) an alternate trumping by partners of each other's leads

cross section a transverse section, a piece cut off at right angles to the length ‖ a representative sample ‖ (*math.*) the area of a section at right angles to the axis of a cylinder (e.g. a wire, circular rod or tube) ‖ (*phys.*) a measure of the probability of an encounter between particles that will result in some specific effect, usually given as the effective area that one particle presents to another in a scattering experiment (*BARN)

cross·stitch (krósstitʃ, krósstitʃ) *n.* two stitches forming an x ‖ needlework made of such stitches

cross talk (*Br.*) comic rapid dialogue in a variety act ‖ (*Br.*) talk in which one conversation is carried on over others

cross·tie (króstai, króstai) *n.* a transverse beam or rod that acts as a support ‖ (*rail.*) a tie

cross·trees (króstriːz, króstriːz) *pl. n.* (*naut.*) two horizontal pieces of wood or metal fastened

to the top of the lower mast to support the upper mast

cross·walk (króswɔk, króswɔk) *n.* a pedestrians' marked crossing-place over a street or highway

cross·way (króswei, króswei) *n.* (often *pl.*) a crossroad

cross·ways (króswei z, króswei z) *adv.* crosswise

cross·wise (króswaiz, króswaiz) *adv.* crossing, in the form of a cross ‖ across, so as to cross

cross·word (króswə:rd, króswə:rd) *n.* a puzzle in which a checkered square with blank spaces must be filled in with interlocking words (reading horizontally and vertically) deduced from clues

crotch (krotʃ) *n.* a fork, e.g. of a tree ‖ the bifurcation of the human body [etym. doubtful]

crotch·et (krótʃit) *n.* (*mus.*) (*Br.*) a quarter note ‖ an idea clung to obstinately **crótch·et·i·ness** *n.* **crótch·et·y** *adj.* obstinate and rather ill-tempered [F. *crochet,* hook]

Cro·ton (króut'n) a Greek settlement founded by Achaeans (c. 700 B.C.) on the gulf of Tarentum in S. Italy. Pythagoras founded (late 6th c.) a school of philosophy here. It was the home of Milo

cro·ton (króut'n) *n.* a member of *Croton,* fam. *Euphorbiaceae,* a genus of plants and shrubs of which there are 600 tropical and subtropical species [Mod. L. fr. Gk *krotōn,* a tick]

Croton bug *Blettella germanica,* a cockroach found in ships and houses [after *Croton River,* N.Y.]

crouch (krautʃ) **1.** *v.i.* to have the tense posture of an animal preparing to spring ‖ to stand with knees slightly bent, muscles tensed, and shoulders thrust forward, ready to give or receive a blow ‖ to stoop or bend for lack of head room **to crouch down** to squat on one's haunches **2.** *n.* a crouching position [perh. O.F. *crochir*]

croup (kruːp) *n.* inflammation of the larynx and trachea in children, accompanied by a sharp cough and difficulty in breathing [fr. obs. *croup,* to croak]

croup, croupe *n.* the hindquarters of a horse [F. *croupe* of Gmc origin]

crou·pade (kruːpád) *n.* (*equestrianism*) maneuver in which horse throws its hind legs high

crou·pi·er (krúːpiər, krúːpiei) *n.* the person who rakes in the stakes and pays out the winnings at a gaming table [F., orig.=rider on the croup]

croup·y (krúːpi) *comp.* **croup·i·er** *superl.* **croup·i·est** *adj.* of or relating to croup, indicating croup

crou·ton (krúːton, kruːtón) *n.* a small piece of toasted or fried bread served with soup, or used as a garnishing [F. fr. *croûte,* crust]

Crow (krou) *n.* a member of a tribe of Siouan Indians of North America ‖ their Siouan language

crow (krou) *n.* a member of *Corvus,* fam. *Corvidae,* a genus of passerine, mainly vegetarian birds. They have a long black bill and black feet and the tail is nearly covered by the wings (cf. RAVEN, cf. ROOK) **as the crow flies** (of distances) in a straight line, i.e. not following the road etc. **to eat crow** to eat humble pie, to admit humbly that one was wrong [O.E. *crāwe*]

crow 1. *v.i. pres. part.* **crow·ing** *past* and *past part.* **crowed** (*Br. past also* **crew** (kruː)) to utter the loud shrill cry of a cock ‖ (esp. of a baby) to utter a cry of delight ‖ to boast **to crow over** to praise one's own success and mock (the loser) **2.** *n.* the cry of a cock ‖ a happy sound made by babies [O.E. *crāwan,* imit.]

crow·bar (króubɑr) *n.* an iron bar with a wedge at the working end used as a lever

crow·ber·ry (króuberi, króubəri) *pl.* **crow·berries** *n. Empetrum nigrum,* fam. *Empetraceae,* a small, creeping heathland shrub ‖ its small black berry

crowd (kraud) **1.** *n.* a large number of people collected together ‖ (*pop.*) a clique, set, *a rough crowd* ‖ (*pop.*) a large number, *a crowd of things to do* ‖ (*naut.*) a large number (of hoisted sails) **to go with the crowd** to conform weakly, without deliberation **2.** *v.i.* to throng together ‖ to press forward ‖ *v.t.* to press upon, deprive of space ‖ to fill, cram (a space etc.) **to crowd out** to exclude by crowding **to crowd** (or **crowd on**) **sail** to hoist many sails so as to increase speed [O.E. *crudan,* to press]

crow·foot (króufut) *pl.* **crow·foots** *n.* a member of *Ranunculus,* fam. *Ranunculaceae,* a genus of annual and perennial plants, esp. *R. arvensis* ‖

pl. **crow·feet** (króufi:t) (*naut.*) a number of small ropes threaded through a wooden block supporting an awning ‖ *pl.* **crow·feet** (*mil.*) a caltrop

crown (kraun) **1.** *n.* a royal headdress of precious metal or jewels ‖ an emblem resembling this, used as a badge of rank ‖ the monarch himself ‖ (*rhet.*) a wreath or garland, *the victor's laurel crown* ‖ (*rhet.*) a reward, *the martyr's crown* ‖ the top part of the head ‖ the top of a hat ‖ the highest part of an arch ‖ the crest of a road ‖ the crest of a bird ‖ a British coin, at first made of silver and then of cupronickel, first struck in 1551 and latterly issued on special occasions. It is worth 25 pence ‖ a size of paper 15 ins x 19 ins or (*Br.*) 15 ins x 20 ins ‖ (*anat.*) the exposed part of a tooth, esp. the grinding surface ‖ (*zool.*) the cup and arms of a crinoid ‖ (*bot.*) the junction of root and stem ‖ the leafy upper part of a tree ‖ a perfecting touch, completion, *the crown of his achievements* ‖ (*naut.*) the junction of the arms and stem of an anchor ‖ the top part of a bell **the Crown** the supreme power in a monarchy **2.** *v.t.* to place a crown on (someone's head) ‖ to complete, perfect, put the finishing touch to ‖ to be at the top of, surmount ‖ to put a top on (a broken tooth) ‖ (*checkers*) to place a man on (another piece) to make it into a king ‖ (*pop.*) to deal (someone) a blow on the top of the head **to crown all** to complete a series of events (good or bad) and be even better (or worse) than what has gone before [O.E. *corona*, wreath fr. L.]

Crown Colony a British colony over which the Crown retains a certain measure of control in internal affairs

crown glass glass containing potassium or barium (sometimes with boron) instead of sodium. It has a higher melting point than sodium glass, has a refractive index of 1.5, and is used in making lenses etc.

crown lens a convex lens made of crown glass

crown prince the male next in succession to a throne

crown wheel a wheel with cogs set at right angles to the plane, being the larger wheel of a bevel reduction gear

crow's-foot (króuzfut) *pl.* **crow's-feet** (króuzfi:t) *n.* a tiny crease or wrinkle in the skin, esp. at the outer corner of the eye, caused by aging, or by smiling, or by screwing up the eyes against strong light ‖ (*mil.*) a caltrop

crow's nest (*naut.*) a shelter for the lookout man at the masthead

Croy·don (króid'n) a county borough (pop. 252,000) in Surrey, England, on the southern outskirts of London

crozier *CROSIER

c.r.u. or **cru** (*abbr., acronym*) for collective reserve monetary unit; used as a measure of a central bank's reserve *also* **kru**

cruces *alt. pl.* of CRUX

cru·cial (krú:ʃəl) *adj.* decisive, critical ‖ fundamental, *crucial problems* ‖ (*anat.*) cross-shaped [F.]

cru·ci·ate (krú:ʃi:it, krú:ʃi:eit) *adj.* (*bot.*) with leaves or petals in the form of a cross ‖ (*zool.,* of insects' wings) crossing diagonally [fr. M.L. *cruciatus* fr. *crux* (*crucis*), cross]

cru·ci·ble (krú:səb'l) *n.* a vessel for melting substances requiring extreme heat ‖ (*rhet.*) a severe test [fr. M.L. *crucibulum*, night lamp, earthen pot]

crucible steel finely tempered steel used esp. in toolmaking

cru·ci·fer (krú:sifər) *n.* (*eccles.*) crossbearer ‖ (*bot.*) a cruciferous plant [L.L. fr. *crux* (*crucis*), cross+-fer, bearing]

cru·cif·er·ous (kru:sífərəs) *adj.* adorned with or bearing a cross ‖ (*bot.*) of fam. *Cruciferae*, the mustard family, whose flowers have petals arranged in the shape of a cross [fr. L. L. *crucifer*]

cru·ci·fix (krú:sifiks) *n.* a cross with a figure of Christ on it [O.F.]

cru·ci·fix·ion (kru:sifíkʃən) *n.* a **cru·ci·fy·ing** ‖ the state or penalty of being crucified ‖ a representation of the death of Christ [fr. L. *crucifigere*, to fasten to the cross]

cru·ci·form (krú:sifɔrm) *adj.* shaped like a cross [fr. L. *crux* (*crucis*), cross]

cru·ci·fy (krú:sifai) *pres. part.* **cru·ci·fy·ing** *past and past part.* **cru·ci·fied** *v.t.* to put to death by fastening or nailing to a cross ‖ to torment ‖ to mortify (the passions etc.) [O.F. *crucifier*]

crude (kru:d) *comp.* **crud·er** *superl.* **crud·est** *adj.* raw, in a natural state, untreated, *crude oil* ‖ unpolished, graceless, *crude manners* ‖ unfinished, rough, *crude furniture* ‖ undisguised,

---

blunt, *in crude terms* ‖ vulgar, *crude jokes* [fr. L. *crudus*, raw]

Cru·den (krú:d'n), Alexander (1701–70), English compiler of the biblical concordance (1737) on which later concordances are based

cru·di·ty (krú:diti:) *pl.* **cru·di·ties** *n.* something crude ‖ the state or quality of being crude

cru·el (krú:əl) *adj.* liking to inflict pain and suffering ‖ showing pleasure at the suffering of others, *cruel laughter* ‖ causing suffering, *a cruel blow of fate* **crú·el·ty** *pl.* **cru·el·ties** *n.* the quality of being cruel ‖ something cruel done, said, written etc. [F.]

cru·et (krú:it) *n.* a small, glass, stoppered bottle for oil or vinegar used at the table ‖ (*Br., pop.*) a stand holding vinegar and (sometimes) oil bottles and salt and pepper castors ‖ (*eccles.*) a small jug for wine or water used at the Eucharist [M.E. *cruete* fr. O.F.]

cruise (kru:z) **1.** *v.i. pres. part.* **cruis·ing** *past and past part.* **cruised** to make a sea voyage for pleasure ‖ to sail about with no special destination ‖ (*navy*) to be on the search for enemy ships ‖ (of an automobile) to go at the speed most economical for gas consumption in top gear and suitable for long-distance driving ‖ (*slang or colloq.*) to search for a sexual partner at bars or by driving or walking along the streets ‖ to drive slowly about (e.g. of a taxi looking for fares) **2.** *n.* a sea voyage for pleasure [fr. Du. *kruisen*, to cross]

cruise control automobile device that maintains the speed of the car at a level set by the operator

cruise missile (*mil.*) U.S. 1,500-mi.-range missile launched from an aircraft, with flying speed of 500 mph, and altitude of 200 to 600 ft.; proposed as alternative to MX missile

cruis·er (krú:zər) *n.* a warship designed for speed, less heavily armed than a battleship ‖ a motorboat with living accommodation ‖ a squad car

cruis·er·weight (krú:zərweit) *n.* (*Br., pop., boxing*) a light heavyweight

cruising speed (of cars and aircraft) an economic speed from the point of view of fuel consumption

crul·ler, krul·ler (králər) *n.* a small sweet cake given a twisted or ring-shaped form and fried in deep fat [prob. fr. Du. *cruller*]

crumb (krʌm) **1.** *n.* a small fragment, esp. of bread ‖ a small amount, *crumbs of comfort* ‖ the soft inside of a loaf of bread **2.** *v.t.* to coat with crumbs ‖ to break into crumbs [O.E. *cruma*]

crum·ble (krámb'l) *pres. part.* **crum·bling** *past and past part.* **crum·bled** *v.t.* to break into small pieces ‖ *v.i.* to fall to pieces (esp. through age and decay) ‖ to fail, *crumbling hopes* **crúm·bly** *comp.* **crum·bli·er** *superl.* **crum·bli·est** *adj.* easily crumbled [earlier *crimble* fr. M.E. *kremelen*]

crumb·y (krámi:) *comp.* **crumb·i·er** *superl.* **crumb·i·est** *adj.* covered with crumbs ‖ (*pop.*) poor in quality, performance etc.

crump (krʌmp, krump) *n.* (*Br.*) a hard hit ‖ the dull thudding sound of exploding bombs or shells [imit.]

crum·pet (krámpit) *n.* (*Br.*) an English muffin [etym. doubtful]

crum·ple (krámp'l) **1.** *v. pres. part.* **crum·pling** *past and past part.* **crum·pled** *v.t.* to crush into a mass of creases ‖ *v.i.* to become creased ‖ (sometimes with 'up') to collapse **2.** *n.* an untidy crease [fr. older *crump*, crooked]

crunch (krʌntʃ) **1.** *v.t.* to crush noisily with the teeth ‖ to crush underfoot with a similar noise ‖ to make with a crushing noise, *to crunch one's way through snow* ‖ *v.i.* to make a crushing noise by chewing, grinding etc. **2.** *n.* the act of crunching ‖ high-pressure situation ‖ the point in a situation where decision or action is necessary ‖ the noise produced [imit.]

crup·per (krápər, krúpər) *n.* a strap fastened to the back of a saddle and passing under the horse's tail ‖ the hindquarters of a horse [O. F. *cropiere*]

cru·ral (krúərəl) *adj.* (*anat.*) of the leg [L. *cruralis* fr. *crus* (*cruris*), leg]

cru·sade (kru:séid) **1.** *n.* any war undertaken in the name of religion ‖ any energetic movement to remove an evil or improve a situation, *a crusade for road safety* **Cru·sáde** (*hist.*) one of the Christian holy wars described below or the Children's Crusade **2.** *v.i. pres. part.* **cru·sad·ing** *past and past part.* **cru·sad·ed** to take part in a crusade [F. *croisade* and Span. *cruzada*]
—The Crusades were a series of military expeditions made by Christians of W. Europe

---

13th cc.) to recover Jerusalem and the Holy Land from the Moslems. They were a continuous movement, with a constant stream of pilgrims setting out for the Holy Land, but the following main campaigns may be distinguished. The 1st Crusade (1096–9), inaugurated by Pope Urban II at the Council of Clermont (1095), and preached by Peter the Hermit, was made up of two groups: unorganized bands of peasants, many of whom were killed on the overland journey to Constantinople, and organized companies under French nobles. Nicaea surrendered (1097), Antioch fell (1098), Jerusalem was captured (1099), and four Crusader states were established: the Latin Kingdom of Jerusalem, the principality of Antioch, and the counties of Edessa and Tripoli. The 2nd Crusade (1147–9), preached by St Bernard on the fall of Edessa to the Turks (1144), was led by Louis VII of France and Emperor Conrad III of Germany. The siege of Damascus failed and the two groups returned home. The 3rd Crusade (1189–92), preached by the pope after Saladin took Jerusalem (1187), was led by Philippe II of France, Richard I of England and Frederick Barbarossa of Germany. The emperor was drowned on the journey. The French and English could not agree and Philippe returned to France (1196) after the capture of Acre. Richard secured a three-year truce (1193) guaranteeing free access to Jerusalem for pilgrims. The 4th Crusade (1202–4), instigated by Pope Innocent III, was dominated by the Venetians. Constantinople was taken and the Latin Empire of Constantinople established (1204–61). The 5th Crusade (1218–21), proclaimed by Innocent III (1215) against the Saracens in Egypt, failed. The 6th Crusade (1228–9) was led by Emperor Frederick II, who secured Jerusalem, Bethlehem and Nazareth by treaty. The 7th Crusade (1248–54) was proclaimed by Pope Innocent IV (1245) after the capture of Jerusalem by the Saracens (1244). Louis IX of France led an expedition to Egypt, was taken prisoner and lost Damietta. The 8th Crusade (1270) was led again by Louis IX of France, who died on a preliminary expedition in Tunis.

The Crusades failed in their military objective. The Moslems retained the Holy Land, and the Turks overran the Byzantine Empire after the Crusader Latin kingdoms had weakened it. They helped to strengthen the power and prestige of the papacy, and to build up the Italian city-states by increasing Eastern trade

crush (krʌʃ) **1.** *v.t.* to maim, damage or spoil by pressure ‖ to crease, *to crush a dress* ‖ to reduce to a powder or to small pieces under pressure ‖ to squash ‖ to subdue, *to crush a rebellion* ‖ to silence (a critic or opponent) in a humiliating way ‖ *v.i.* to hug violently ‖ to squeeze, *hundreds crushed into the hall* ‖ to become crumpled **2.** *n.* a crushing or being crushed ‖ a large crowd of people ‖ an infatuation, *to have a crush on someone* ‖ the object of such an infatuation ‖ (*Austral.*) a fenced passage narrowing at one end so that animals can be driven down it and received singly for branding [perh. fr. O.F. *croissir*, to crash fr. Gmc]

crust (krʌst) **1.** *n.* the crisp outer part of bread ‖ a hard dry piece of bread ‖ the pastry cover of a pie ‖ a hard outer surface or covering, e.g. of snow, ice etc. ‖ (*geol.*) the light, thin mantle of the earth ‖ (*med.*) a scab ‖ a deposit of tartar on the inside of a wine bottle or barrel ‖ outer appearance masking true character or feelings ‖ (*pop.*) impertinence, nerve **2.** *v.t.* to cover with a crust ‖ *v.i.* to form into, or become covered with a crust [O.F. *crouste*]

crus·ta·cean (krʌstéiʃən) **1.** *n.* a member of *Crustacea*, a class of mostly aquatic and gill-breathing arthropods, including crabs, lobsters and shrimps. They are characterized by a hard exoskeleton, a segmented body divided into head, thorax and abdomen (with fused head and thorax in higher forms) and pairs of highly modified appendages with each segment (for protection, feeding, walking, swimming etc.) **2.** *adj.* of this class [fr. L. *crustaceus*, having a shell]

crus·ta·ceous (krʌstéiʃəs) *adj.* having a hard crust or shell ‖ (*zool.*) with crustacean characteristics [fr. L. *crusta*, shell]

crust·ed (krástid) *adj.* covered with a crust ‖ (of wine) having formed or deposited a crust of tartar

crust·i·ly (krásti:li:) *adv.* in a crusty manner

---

crust·i·ness (krásti:nis) n. the state or quality of being crusty

crust·y (krásti:) comp. **crust·i·er** superl. **crust·i·est** adj. hard, crustlike ‖ (of bread) having a crisp crust ‖ (of persons, esp. men) gruff, hard to approach

crutch (krʌtʃ) n. a wood or metal support to help a lame person to walk ‖ (rhet.) a support, something one relies upon ‖ the crotch, fork of the human body ‖ the forked leg rest of a side-saddle ‖ (naut.) any of various devices used as supports [O.E. crycc, a staff]

Crutch·ed Friars (krátʃid) (hist.) a minor order of friars (1169–1656) wearing a cross ‖ the site of their convent in London

crux (krʌks) pl. **crux·es, cru·ces** (krú:si:z) n. the essential point ‖ an acknowledged puzzling or difficult matter, esp. in major works of literature, a Dante crux [L.=cross]

crux an·sa·ta (krʌksænséitə) pl. **cru·ces an·sa·tae** (krú:si:zænséiti:) n. an ankh

Cruz (kru:s), Sor Juana Iñéz de la (1651–95), Mexican poet nun, best known for her 'Redondillas', a poem castigating men for their unfair treatment of women. Her works include 'Inundación castálida' (1689), 'Poesias' (1691), and 'Obras póstumas' (1700)

cru·zei·ro (kru:zérou) n. unit of currency in Brazil

cry (krai) pres. part. **cry·ing** past and past part. **cried** v.i. to call out (in pain, anger, fear, delight etc.) ‖ to weep ‖ (of an animal) to utter its call ‖ v.t. to shout ‖ to announce for sale by shouting **to cry down** to belittle **to cry for** (rhet.) to beg for ‖ to need urgently, the situation cries for a remedy **to cry for** the moon to yearn for or demand the impossible **to cry off** (Br.) to withdraw from an agreement [F. crier]

cry pl. **cries** n. a shout or wail ‖ a vendor's street call ‖ a watchword or battle cry ‖ a fit of weeping **a far cry from** a great distance from ‖ a great contrast to **in full cry** in full pursuit [F. cri]

cry·ba·by (kráibeibi:) pl. **cry·ba·bies** n. someone who cries often and for no good reason

cry·ing (kráiiŋ) adj. (esp. of a need, shame or evil) calling urgently for attention, flagrant

cry·o·bi·ol·o·gy (krɑiəbaiólədʒi:) n. study of effect of very low temperatures on living things —**cryobiological** adj. —**cryobiologically** adv. —**cryobiologist** n.

cry·o·bi·o·sis (krɑiəbaióusis) n. system and practice of freezing living organisms for future revival Cf CRYONICS

cry·o·chem·is·try (krɑiəkémistri:) n. study of chemistry materials at extremely low temperatures —**cryochemical** adj. —**cryochemically** adv. —**cryochemist** n.

cry·o·e·lec·tron·ics (krɑiouilektróniks) n. study or practice of electronics involving effects of extreme cold, e.g., superconductivity under extremely low temperatures

cry·o·gen (kráiodʒən) n. (chem.) a freezing mixture, refrigerant **cry·o·gen·ic** (krɑioudʒénik) adj. relating to the production of very low temperatures **cry·o·gén·ics** n. a branch of chemistry concerned with the production and effects of very low temperatures [fr. Gk kruos, frost]

cryogenic gyro (phys.) device involving spin of electrons at extremely low temperatures

cryogenic liquid liquified gas at very low temperature, e.g., liquid oxygen, nitrogen, argon

cryogenics study of physical phenomena occurring at temperatures, i.e., from −50°C to near absolute temperatures —**cryogenic** adj. —**cryogenically** adv.

cry·o·lite (kráiolait) n. Na₃AlF₆, a natural fluoride of aluminum and sodium found in Greenland, used for the preparation of soda and pure aluminum [fr. Gk kruos, frost]

cry·om·e·ter (kraiómətər) n. device for measuring extremely low temperatures

cry·on·ics (kraióniks) n. system and practice of freezing organisms for storage in expectation of future revival and use —**cryonic** adj. cryonic sperm

cry·o·pe·xy (cráioupeksi:) n. (med.) surgical procedure for repairing retinas under extremely low temperatures

cry·o·plank·ton (kráiəplæŋktən) n. (biol.) algae adapted for life on polar ice or other locations with extremely low temperatures

cry·o·pre·cip·i·tate (krɑiəprəsípiteit) n. (med.) concentrate of blood-clotting protein obtained by very low-temperature processing —**cryo·precipitation** n. the process

cry·o·probe (kráiəproub) n. device for examining tissue by freezing to very low tempera-

cry·o·pro·tec·tive (krɑiəprətéktivn) adj. designed to protect from low temperatures

cry·o·sar (kráiəsar) n. (electr.) a cryogenic semiconductor used as a switch operable at extremely low temperatures with on-off changing time of nanoseconds Cf CRYOTRON

cry·o·scope (kráiəskoup) n. (chem.) an instrument used to determine freezing points

cry·o·scop·ic (krɑiəskópik) adj. (chem.) of a method of determining molecular weight, by noting the depression of freezing point of a solvent caused by a known concentration of a solute [fr. Gk kruos, frost+skopein, to look at]

cry·o·stat (kráiəstæt) n. (chem.) a device, often in the form of a bath of a low boiling liquid (e.g. liquid nitrogen), used to maintain a constant low temperature

cry·o·sur·ger·y (krɑiəsɔ́:rdʒəri:) n. use of very low temperatures in surgery —**cryosurgeon** n. —**cryosurgical** adj. Cf CRYOPEXY

cry·o·ther·a·py (krɑiəθérəpi:) n. (med.) treatment utilizing very low temperatures syn. cryomotherapy

cry·o·tron (kráiətron) n. (electr.) switch operating in a liquid helium, based on the principle that a magnetic field induced into a control wire will cause a main wire to change from conductive to resistive. A cryotron is used as a short-access-time memory Cf CRYOSAR

cry·o·tron·ics (krɑiətróniks) n. study of electronic devices operating at very low temperatures

crypt (kript) n. an underground room or cell, esp. one underneath a church ‖ (anat.) a simple gland or gland cavity ‖ a follicle [fr. L. crypta, cavern fr. Gk]

crypt·a·nal·y·sis (kriptənǽlisis) n. the deciphering of codes or ciphers **crypt·an·a·lyst** (kriptǽn'list) n. [fr. Gk kruptos, hidden, secret+ANALYSIS]

cryp·tic (kríptik) adj. enigmatic **crýp·ti·cal·ly** adv. [fr. L. crypticus fr. Gk]

crypto- (kríptou) combining form secret ‖ unavowed [fr. Gk kruptos, hidden]

cryp·to·gam (kríptəgæm) n. a plant having no stamens or pistils and producing no flowers or seeds, e.g. ferns, mosses, algae. Reproduction is by spores (cf. PHANEROGAM) **cryp·to·gám·ic**, **cryp·tog·a·mous** (kriptógəmes) adjs [F. cryptogame fr. Gk kruptos, secret, hidden+gamos, marriage]

cryp·to·gram (kríptəgræm) n. something written in code or cipher or in a mystical pattern [fr. Gk kruptos, hidden+gramma, letter]

cryp·to·graph (kríptəgræf, kríptəgraf) n. a cryptogram **cryp·tog·ra·pher** (kriptógrəfər) n. someone who invents codes or ciphers or who breaks them **cryp·to·graph·ic** (kriptəgrǽfik) adj. [fr. Gk kruptos, hidden+graphos, written]

cryp·tog·ra·phy (kriptógrəfi:) n. the art of writing in code or cipher [fr. Mod. L. cryptographia]

crys·tal (krístəl) 1. n. the solid state of a pure substance or mixture, characterized by a regular ordered arrangement of the constituent atoms, usually having external plane faces meeting at angles characteristic of the substance ‖ a substance having some of the properties of a crystal, usually as a result of the ordered arrangement of its molecules ‖ transparent quartz, often cut for ornamental use ‖ a very clear and transparent kind of glass ‖ (Am.=Br. watch glass) a concavo-convex cover of glass or plastic over the face of a watch 2. adj. of or using a crystal ‖ perfectly clear [O.F. cristal fr. L. fr. Gk]

crystal ball radarscope

crystal detector a crystal of galena (or other substance) in contact with a fine wire (the 'cat's whisker') through which an electric current passes, the crystal being a good conductor in one direction only and so rectifying an alternating current. This was the basis of the first radio receivers

crystal gazer a person professing to foretell future events by gazing into a crystal ball

crys·tal·lif·er·ous (kristəlífərəs) adj. producing or bearing crystals [fr. CRYSTAL+L. -fer, bearing]

crys·tal·line (krístəlin, krístəlain) adj. consisting of, or similar to, crystal ‖ extremely clear [F. cristallin and L. crystallinus fr. Gk]

crystalline heavens two transparent spherical surfaces which Ptolemy supposed to lie between the revolving sphere in which the sun and its planets are situated and the firmament in which the fixed stars lie

crystalline laser solid laser that utilizes a pure crystal (ruby, neodymium-doped yttrium-aluminum garnet)

crystalline lens a firm, gelatinous lens-shaped body, consisting of many layers of slightly different refractive indices, behind the pupil of the eye. Its focal length is variable between limits by muscular control of its thickness and shape, and it can thus focus on the retina clear images of objects at different distances (*ACCOMMODATION)

crystalline spheres the crystalline heavens

crys·tal·liz·a·ble (krístəlaizəb'l) adj. able to be crystallized

crys·tal·li·za·tion (kristəlizéiʃən) n. the process of crystallizing ‖ a crystallized form

crys·tal·lize (krístəlaiz) pres. part. **crys·tal·liz·ing** past and past part. **crys·tal·lized** v.i. to assume the form of a crystal ‖ (of ideas) to become clear and definite ‖ v.t. to cause to assume the form of a crystal or crystals ‖ to cause to become clear **to crystallize out** to come out of solution in the form of crystals

crys·tal·lo·graph·ic (kristəlográfik) adj. of or relating to crystallography

crys·tal·log·ra·phy (kristəlógrəfi:) n. the study of the form, symmetry and structure and classification of crystalline substances [fr. Mod. L. crystallographia]

crys·tal·loid (krístəloid) 1. adj. like a crystal 2. n. (chem.) a substance which forms a true solution and can pass through a semipermeable membrane (cf. COLLOID)

crystal oscillator a quartz crystal used to give very constant electrical oscillation, e.g. in a quartz electric clock

Crystal Palace the first large structure of iron and glass, erected by Paxton in Hyde Park, London, to house the Great Exhibition of 1851, and later moved out to Sydenham. Destroyed (1936) by fire

CS symbol for riot-control tear gas

C scan (acronym) carrier system for controlled approach of naval aircraft, an all-weather instrument landing system used on aircraft carriers, utilizing two crossing beams indicating the glide path, shown on the aircraft's instrument indicating the relative position of the aircraft

CSGN *STRIKE CRUISER

CSM (acronym) corn, soy, and milk, a symbol of a U.S. Department of Agriculture powdered food supplement made of these products

CST, C.S.T. Central standard time

ct. cent ‖ carat

CT (med. acronym) cell therapy

cte·noid (tí:noid, ténoid) adj. (zool.) e.g. of fish scales) having a comblike margin [fr. Gk kteis (ktenos), comb]

cten·o·phore (ténəfor, ténəfour, tí:nəfor, tí:nəfour) n. a member of Ctenophora, a phylum of marine transparent animals with eight rows of fused, comblike cilia. Their outward symmetry is radial, the inward is bilateral [fr. Gk kteis (ktenos), comb+-phoros, bearing]

Ctes·i·phon (tésəfon) a city on the Tigris, now ruins. It was the capital of Parthia (c. 250 B.C.– c. 226 A.D.) and of the Sassanid Empire (c. 226– c. 641)

CTOL (acronym) conventional take-off and landing Cf QSTOL, STOL, VTOL

cu. cubic

cuar·to (kwártou) n. (bullfighting) matador's body movement preceding a kill over the bull's horns

Cuauh·té·moc (kwautémɔk) (c. 1495–1525), the last emperor of the Aztecs of Mexico, conquered (1521) by Cortés

cub (kʌb) n. a young bear, fox, lion, tiger, wolf etc. ‖ a novice, a cub reporter ‖ a junior boy scout [origin unknown]

Cu·ba (kjú:bə) the largest island (area 44,206 sq. miles) of the West Indies (Greater Antilles group, *ANTILLES), comprising with the Isle of Pines (area 1,180 sq. miles) and smaller off-shore islands (area 1,350 sq. miles) a republic (pop. 9,995,000). Capital: Havana. Language: Spanish. Religion: Roman Catholic. The land is 17% arable, 11% forest and 34% pasture. Cuba is mostly low and flat, save for the Sierra Maestra (highest point 6,560 ft) in the east, Sierra Trinidad (3,335 ft) in the center and Sierra de los Organos (2,500 ft) in the west. The south coast is swampy. The island has a tropical trade-wind climate with dry warm winters and hot wet summers. Rainfall: 45 ins (more in the interior, less in the east). Average temperatures (F.) in Havana: 71° (Jan.), 82° (July). It is hotter in the east. Cattle are raised. Agricultural products: sugar and tobacco (the world's largest producer), henequen, coffee, cocoa, corn, rice, fruit. Fisheries are important. Forest products: cedar, mahogany. Minerals: copper, manganese, nickel, chromite, oil. Manufactures: rayon, cigars, cement. Exports (72% to the U.S.A. in 1958, mainly to the U.S.S.R. and Soviet bloc since 1960): sugar, tobacco. Imports: machinery, manufactures. Ports: Havana, Matanzas. University: Havana (1712). Monetary unit: peso (divided into 100 cents). HISTORY. Cuba was discovered by Columbus (1492). It was a Spanish colony (1492–1898), except for a brief British occupation (1762–3). Revolts for independence (1868–78, 1895) led to the intervention of the U.S.A. (Spanish-American War, 1898) and the withdrawal of Spain. Cuba was under U.S. military government (1899–1902). It took over government from the U.S.A. (1902), although all military and diplomatic decisions had to have U.S. agreement. The U.S.A. intervened in Cuban affairs (1906–9, 1912, 1917). Cuba became a sovereign state (1934), drew up a new constitution (1940), and entered the 2nd world war with the Allies (1941). General Batista seized power (1952) but was opposed by guerrilla warfare (1953, 1956–8) led by Fidel Castro. Batista was forced to flee and Castro became prime minister (1959). Cuba was declared a people's republic (1960) and within the year the government gained control of the nation's entire resources: land, industry and commerce. Its policy was now oriented toward the socialist countries and against U.S. interests. In 1961, with secret support from Washington, an anti-Castro commando force landed at the Bay of Pigs but was routed by the revolutionary militia. The presence of Russian nuclear missile bases on Cuban soil provoked (1962) a world crisis, which Washington and Moscow resolved peacefully. The decision (1962) by the Organization of American States to exclude Cuba from OAS activities and to sever diplomatic relations (with the exception of Mexico, which retained diplomatic relations) was followed by another (1964) to condemn Cuba for supplying weapons to Venezuelan revolutionary groups, and to suspend trade. Cuba countered this blockade by entering into longterm economic agreements with the U.S.S.R. Cuba adopted its socialist constitution in 1976. Its relations with the U.S.A. were severely strained by the exodus of 125,000 Cubans from the port of Mariel to the U.S.A. (1980). During the mid-1980s relations remained relatively static as both governments refused to compromise

cub·age (kjúːbidʒ) n. cubic content, volume or displacement

Cu·ban (kjúːbən) 1. n. an inhabitant of Cuba 2. adj. of Cuba or its inhabitants

Cu·ban·go (kuːbáŋguː) *OKOVANGO

cu·ba·ture (kjúːbətʃər) n. the determining of cubic content

cub·bing (kʌ́biŋ) n. (Br.) cub-hunting

cub·by·hole (kʌ́biːhoul) n. a little closet or storage place ‖ a very small workroom [fr. older cub, stall, pen]

cube (kjuːb) n. a geometrical solid bounded by six plane faces of equal area and making right angles with one another ‖ the product of three identical factors (the third power), e.g. $a^3 = a \times a \times a$ [F. fr. L. fr. Gk]

cu·be (kjúːbei) n. any of several shrubs or small trees of genus *Lonchocarpus*, fam. *Papilionaceae*, of tropical South America, producing rotenone [Span. *quibey*]

cube (kjuːb) pres. part. **cub·ing** past and past part. **cubed** v.t. to raise to the third power ‖ to cut into cubes [F. *cuber*]

cu·beb (kjúːbeb) n. *Piper cubeba*, fam. *Piperaceae*, a shrub cultivated in the East Indies. The oil distilled from its unripened fruits is used in soaps and medically. The dried fruit is used as a condiment [F. *cubèbe* fr. Arab.]

cube root (kjuːb) a number which, multiplied twice by itself, makes a cube

cub-hunt·ing (kʌ́bhʌntiŋ) n. the hunting of fox cubs

cu·bic (kjúːbik) adj. having the properties of a cube ‖ being the volume of a cube whose edge is a specified unit, *a cubic yard* ‖ (math.) of the third power or degree **cú·bi·cal** adj. cube-shaped [F:. *cubique*]

cu·bi·cle (kjúːbikᵊl) n. a small, separate sleeping division within a dormitory etc. ‖ a partitioned, screened area for changing clothes [fr. L. *cubiculum*]

cubic measure a system of units of volume (*MEASURES AND WEIGHTS)

cu·bi·form (kjúːbifɔrm) adj. cube-shaped

cub·ism (kjúːbizəm) n. the theory and works of a group of artists working in Paris from 1906, led by Braque and Picasso, influenced by primitive sculpture and the work of Cézanne. They painted familiar, easily identifiable objects, not as they saw them, but as they understood them structurally. They reorganized the simplest constituent forms of the object into a geometric composition of flat, interrelated planes, depicting different aspects of the object simultaneously. By 1912 the cubists were painting simplified abstract compositions still further removed from natural appearances, and were including materials other than paint (e.g. sand, wallpaper). Gris, Leger and Delaunay initiated further developments. Archipenko, Laurens, Lipchitz and Zadkine created cubist sculpture **cúb·ist** n. and adj. [F. *cubisme*]

cu·bit (kjúːbit) n. (hist.) a measure of length, 18–22 ins (orig. from the elbow to the tip of the middle finger) [fr. L. *cubitus*, elbow]

cu·bi·tal (kjúːbit'l) adj. of the forearm or the corresponding part in animals [fr. L. *cubitalis*]

cu·boid (kjúːbɔid) 1. adj. cube-shaped 2. n. (anat.) a cube-shaped bone on the outer side of the foot ‖ (geom.) a rectangular parallelepiped **cu·bói·dal** adj. [fr. Gk *kuboeidēs*]

cub scout (Am.=Br. wolf cub) a junior boy scout

cu·chi·fri·to (kuːtʃifríːtou) n. American Spanish dish of cubed pork dipped in batter and deep-fried

cuck·old (kʌ́kəld) 1. n. a man whose wife has committed adultery 2. v.t. to make (one's husband) a cuckold **cúck·old·ry** n. [M.E. *cokewold, cukeweld* fr. O.F.]

cuck·oo (kúːkuː, kúːkuː) pl. **cuck·oos** 1. n. *Cuculus canorus*, a European bird which deposits its eggs in the nests of other birds, for them to hatch 2. adj. (pop.) foolish, crazy [imit. of the male's mating call on two notes]

cuckoo clock a wooden clock containing a mechanical bird which announces the hours with a cuckoo's cry

cuck·oo·pint (kúːkuːpaint, kúːkuːpaint) n. *Arum maculatum*, a perennial plant with a purple-tipped spadix, common in Europe, esp. in the Mediterranean region

cuckoo spit a protective froth exuded by the larvae of certaine insects, and often seen on plants in spittlelike blobs

cu·cul·late (kjúːkəleit, kjuːkʌ́leit) adj. (bot.) with hoodlike sepals or petals ‖ (zool.) with hood-shaped prothorax **cu·cul·lat·ed** (kjúːkəleitid, kjuːkʌ́leitid) adj. [fr. L.L. *cucullatus* fr. *cucullus*, hood]

cu·cum·ber (kjúːkʌmbər) n. a member of *Cucumis*, fam. *Cucurbitaceae*, a genus of annual trailing vines ‖ the long green fleshy fruit of *C. sativus* eaten in salads etc. [O.F. *cocombre*]

cu·cur·bit (kjuːkə́rbit) n. a member of *Cucurbita*, fam. *Cucurbitaceae*, a genus of plants incl. the melon, pumpkin, gourd etc. **cu·cur·bi·tá·ceous** adj. [fr. L. *cucurbita*, a gourd]

Cú·cu·ta (kúːkuːta) a city (pop. 358,240) in N. Colombia, near the Venezuelan border. It was severely damaged by an earthquake (1875) and rebuilt

cud (kʌd) n. the food brought back by a ruminating animal from the first stomach into the mouth to be chewed again **to chew the cud** (of people) to mull over past events [O.E. *cwidu*]

cud·bear (kʌ́dbɛər) n. a red or purple dye obtained from lichens and used as a coloring in pharmaceutical preparations [after Dr *Cuthbert* Gordon, 18th-c. Scots chemist]

cud·dle (kʌ́d'l) 1. v. pres. part. **cud·dling** past and past part. **cud·dled** v.t. to hold closely and fondly ‖ v.i. to curl up comfortably, nestle 2. n. an embrace **cud·dle·some** adj. **cúd·dly** adj. [origin unknown]

cud·dy (kʌ́di) pl. **cud·dies** n. a small room or cabin on a ship [origin unknown]

cudg·el (kʌ́dʒəl) 1. n. a short, stout stick used as a weapon **to take up the cudgels for** to defend strongly (in argument) 2. v.t. pres. part. **cudg·el·ing**, esp. Br. **cudg·el·ling** past and past part. **cudg·eled**, esp. Br. **cudg·elled** to beat with a cudgel [O.E. *cycgel*, a club with rounded head]

Cud·worth (kʌ́dwəːrθ), Ralph (1617–88), leader of the Cambridge Platonists. His chief work is 'The True Intellectual System of the Universe' (1678)

cue (kjuː) 1. n. (theater) an agreed signal, usually a line or word of dialogue, for some action

or speech on or off stage, *lighting cue* ‖ a similar guide to a musical performer ‖ a hint meant to guide behavior etc. 2. pres part. **cu·ing** past and past part. **cued** v.t. to give a cue to [origin unknown]

cue n. a long leather-tipped rod for striking the ball in billiards and related games ‖ a queue of hair ‖ a queue of people 2. pres. part. **cu·ing** past and past part. **cued** to strike with a cue ‖ to form (hair) into a cue [var. of F. *queue*, tail]

cue ball (billiards, pool) the ball (usually white) which is struck by the cue

Cuenca a city and cultural center (pop. 210,280) in S. Ecuador: cathedral, university. Panama hats are made

Cuen·ca (kwéŋka) a province (area 6,636 sq. miles, pop. 315,000) of E. central Spain ‖ its capital (pop. 104,470). Cathedral (13th c.) (*NEW CASTILE)

cuff (kʌf) n. the part of a sleeve which is turned back at the wrist, or which touches the wrist ‖ (Am.=Br. turnup) the turned-up end of a trouser leg ‖ a handcuff **off the cuff** (of an answer, speech) impromptu, given immediately without time for checking [M.E. *coffe, cuffe*, origin uncertain]

cuff 1. v.t. to strike with the open palm or back of the hand 2. n. the blow given in this way [origin unknown]

cuff link one of a pair of linked decorative buttons for fastening the cuffs of a shirt

Cu·fic, Ku·fic (kjúːfik) 1. n. a primitive form of the Arabic alphabet 2. adj. relating to this form [fr. *Cufa*, a city south of Baghdad]

cui·rass (kwiræs) n. (hist.) a piece of armor consisting of a breastplate and backplate (orig. of leather) joined together ‖ (zool.) a hard shell or plate forming a protective cover [F. *cuirasse*]

cui·ras·sier (kwiːrəsíər) n. (hist.) a mounted soldier wearing a cuirass [F.]

cui·sine (kwiːzíːn) n. cooking with reference to quality or style [F.=kitchen]

cuisine minceur *NOUVELLE CUISINE

Cui·tlá·huac (kwiːtláhwak) (d. 1520), tenth and penultimate Aztec emperor who succeeded (1520) his brother Moctezuma II. He defeated the Spaniards on the Noche Triste (1520). He died of a disease (teotlazáhuatl, either smallpox or venereal) introduced into America by the white man

cul-de-sac (kʌ́ldəsæk, kúldəsæk) n. a street or passage with a blind end, a dead end ‖ a situation offering no escape ‖ (anat.) a tube etc. with only one opening [F.=bottom of a sack]

cu·let (kjúːlit) n. the small flat face at the bottom of a gem cut as a brilliant [O.F., dim. of *cul*, bottom, ass]

cu·lex (kjúːleks) pl. **cu·li·ces** (kjúːlisiːz) n. a member of *Culex*, a genus of insects including gnats and the common mosquito of Europe and North America [L.=a gnat]

cu·li·nar·y (kjúːlineri, kʌ́lineri) adj. relating to cooking or the kitchen ‖ suitable for or used in cooking, *culinary plants* [fr. L. *culinarius* fr. *culina*, kitchen]

cull (kʌl) v.t. (rhet.) to pick, gather (flowers, facts etc.) 2. n. something picked out as substandard, e.g. an old or weak animal taken from a flock [O.F. *cuillir*]

cul·len·der (kʌ́lindər) 1. n. a colander 2. v.t. to colander

cul·let (kʌ́lit) n. (glassblowing) refuse glass for remelting [fr. F. *collet* dim. of *col*, neck]

Cul·lod·en, Battle of (kəlɔ́d'n) a victory (1746) by the duke of Cumberland over Charles Edward Stuart. It ended Jacobite attempts to regain the British throne for the Stuarts, and was the last battle fought on British soil

culm (kʌlm) n. (bot., of grasses and sedges) a jointed stem **cul·mif·er·ous** (kʌlmífərəs) adj. bearing culms [fr. L. *culmus*, stalk]

culm n. coal dust ‖ a shaly variety of anthracite [etym. doubtful]

Cul·mide (kʌ́lmaid) adj. of a European mountain-making episode during the Carboniferous period [fr. *Culm*, an epoch of the Carboniferous period]

cul·mi·nant (kʌ́lmənənt) adj. culminating at or forming the top ‖ (of a heavenly body) on the meridian [fr. L. *culminans* (*culminantis*) fr. *culminare*, to culminate]

cul·mi·nate (kʌ́lməneit) pres. part. **cul·mi·nat·ing** past and past part. **cul·mi·nat·ed** v.i. to reach a climax ‖ (astron.) to be on the meridian **cul·mi·ná·tion** n. a climax ‖ (astron.) the highest or lowest altitude of a heavenly body in meridian transit [fr. L.L. *culminare* (*culminatus*) fr. *culmen*, top]

culm measures (*geol.*) a Devonian formation in which beds of culm alternate with grits

cul·pa·bil·i·ty (kʌlpəbíliti) *n.* the state or quality of being culpable

cul·pa·ble (kʌlpəb'l) *adj.* guilty, blameworthy **cúl·pa·bly** *adv.* [M.E. *coupable* fr. O.F.]

cul·prit (kʌlprit) *n.* a guilty person ‖ (*law*) a person accused of an offense, prisoner at the bar [A.F. *cul. prit* short for *Culpable: prest d'averrer*, (you are) guilty: (I am) ready to prove it (a formula which used to be put to a prisoner on a charge of high treason or felony)]

cult (kʌlt) *n.* a system of religious worship ‖ admiration of, or devotion to, a person or thing, esp. as a form of intellectual snobbery ‖ a passing craze or fashion ‖ a creed or sect [F. *culte* and fr. L. *cultus*, worship]

cul·ti·va·ble (kʌltivəb'l) *adj.* able to be cultivated

cul·ti·vate (kʌltiveit) *pres. part.* **cul·ti·vat·ing** *past* and *past part.* **cul·ti·vat·ed** *v.t.* to prepare (land) for crops, till ‖ to raise (crops) by farming, gardening etc. ‖ to improve, refine, *to cultivate the mind* ‖ to foster, cause to develop, *to cultivate an acquaintance* **cúl·ti·vat·ed** *adj.* (of land) prepared for, or planted with, crops, not left to grow wild ‖ (of people) cultured [fr. L.L. *cultivare* (*cultivatus*), to till]

cul·ti·va·tion (kʌltivéiʃən) *n.* a cultivating or being cultivated ‖ refinement, development (of the mind, taste etc.) [F.]

cul·ti·va·tor (kʌltiveitər) *n.* someone who cultivates ‖ an implement for loosening the soil around growing crops and for uprooting weeds

cult of personality rule by unquestioned devotion to the leader, esp. of the Stalin era in the U.S.S.R.

cul·tur·al (kʌltʃərəl) *adj.* of, or relating to, culture or a culture ‖ produced by breeding, *a cultural variety*

cultural anthropology social anthropology

cultural configuration (*anthropology*) the basic, integrative, thematic elements of a culture

cultural determinism (*anthropology*) the view that culture is the basic determinant of social behavior

cultural eutrophication increasing the rate at which bodies of water are destroyed by pollution caused by human activities

cultural focus the tendency in every culture to develop certain institutions or parts more fully than others

cultural imperative *FUNCTIONAL REQUISITE

cultural relativity (*anthropology*) the view that cultural traits or complexes cannot be understood or evaluated without reference to their function in the culture as a whole

Cultural Revolution a movement in China launched (1966) to effect an ideological purge and to restore fidelity to the ideas of Mao Tsetung. A militant organization of young Red Guards, supported by the army, denounced revisionist activities by elements hostile to the communist party. Local struggles for power continued into 1969 before Mao ended the movement. Later Chinese regimes harshly criticized the movement's excesses

cul·tur·a·ti (kʌltʃəráti) *n.* in a community, a culture-centered group of people

cul·ture (kʌltʃər) 1. *n.* the training and development of the mind ‖ the refinement of taste and manners acquired by such training ‖ the social and religious structures and intellectual and artistic manifestations etc. that characterize a society ‖ the rearing of bees, fish, oysters, silkworms etc. ‖ the cultivation of tissues or microorganisms in prepared media, or a product of this 2. *v.t. pres. part.* **cul·tur·ing** *past* and *past part.* **cul·tured** to make a culture of ‖ to grow in a prepared medium [F.]

culture area area in which a similar culture and social values exist

cultured pearl a natural pearl formed by oysters in oyster farms, induced by the insertion of a piece of grit into the oyster

cul·ture-free test (kʌltʃərfrí:) (*psych.*) intelligence test that claims its results are unaffected by cultural or subcultural differences among those tested

culture gap the radical differences in life-style between the U.S.A. and underdeveloped nations

culture shock the traumatic effect of disorientation caused by a major change in milieu experienced by new inhabitants (e.g., by Peace Corps personnel, refugees, missionaries) and sometimes by their hosts (via an invasion)

cul·vert (kʌlvərt) *n.* a drain carrying water under a road, railroad etc. ‖ an underground channel for electric wires or cables [origin unknown]

Cu·man (ku:mán, kju:mán) *n.* a member of a nomadic Turkic people who occupied S. Russia and Walachia (11th c.), were defeated by the Mongols (mid-13th c.), entered Hungary, and merged with the Magyars

Cu·ma·ná (ku:maná) a seaport city (pop. 148,000) in N. Venezuela, the oldest existing European settlement in South America. Exports: tobacco, cacao, fish, cotton textiles, coffee

cum·ber (kʌmbər) *v.t.* to hinder or burden, encumber [O.F. *combrer*]

Cum·ber·land (kʌmbərlənd), William Augustus, duke of (1721–65), English soldier, son of George II. He put down the 1745 Jacobite rebellion, defeating Charles Edward Stuart at Culloden (1746). He is known as 'Butcher' Cumberland

Cumberland (*abbr.* Cumb.) a former county (area 1,520 sq. miles) of N.W. England

Cumberland a navigable river (690 miles long) flowing west through S. Kentucky, turning south into N. Tennessee and looping northward to join the Ohio River in W. Kentucky

Cumberland Gap a natural passage (height 1,314 ft) cutting through N.E. Tennessee and followed by a railroad and highway. The Wilderness Road (blazed and cleared by Daniel Boone, 1775) ran through it

Cumberland Mtns the western range (average height 2,000 ft) of the Appalachian Mtns, mainly in Kentucky and Tennessee

Cumberland Plateau the Cumberland Mtns

cum·ber·some (kʌmbərsəm) *adj.* burdensome ‖ (of objects) unwieldy, apt to get in the way

Cum·bri·an (kʌmbri:ən) 1. *adj.* of or relating to Cumberland ‖ of or relating to Cumbria 2. *n.* a native of Cumberland

cum·brous (kʌmbrəs) *adj.* cumbersome

cum·in, cum·min (kʌmin) *n. Cuminum cyminum*, fam. *Umbelliferae*, a plant native to the Mediterranean area, cultivated for its aromatic seeds, which are used for flavoring [O.E. *cymen* fr. L. fr. Gk]

cum·mer·bund (kʌmərbʌnd) *n.* a broad waist sash [Urdu *kamar-band*, loincloth]

cummin *CUMIN.

cum·mings (kʌmiŋz), (Edward Estlin) e.e. (1894–1962), American poet, whose attempts to discover new forms of expression were important in the development of modern American poetry. His works include the novel 'The Enormous Room' (1922) and numerous poetry collections from 'Tulips and Chimneys' (1923) to '95 Poems' (1958)

'Cummings v. Missouri' a decision (1867) of the U.S. Supreme Court which, after a former Confederate testified that as such he had been excluded from his profession, declared loyalty oaths unconstitutional

cumquat *KUMQUAT

cu·mu·late (kju:mjuleit) *pres. part.* **cu·mu·lat·ing** *past* and *past part.* **cu·mu·lat·ed** *v.t.* to accumulate, heap up, amass ‖ *v.i.* to become massed **cu·mu·la·tion** *n.* **cu·mu·la·tive** (kju:mjulɛitiv, kju:mjulətiv) *adj.* gradually increasing by successive additions, *cumulative effect* ‖ tending to accumulate [fr. L. *cumulare* (*cumulatus*) fr. *cumulus*, a heap]

cumulative evidence (*law*) evidence which reinforces evidence already given

cumulative preference shares shares which entitle a holder to arrears of interest before interest for the current year is distributed to other holders

cu·mu·lo·cir·rus (kju:mjulousírəs) *pl.* **cu·mu·lo·cir·ri** (kju:mjulousírai) *n.* cirrocumulus (*CLOUD FORMS) [Mod. L.]

cu·mu·lo·nim·bus (kju:mjulounímbəs) *pl.* **cu·mu·lo·nim·bi** (kju:mjulounímbai), **cu·mu·lo·nim·bus·es** *n.* a low-based heavy mass of cumulus clouds having considerable vertical development (*CLOUD FORMS) [Mod. L.]

cu·mu·lo·stra·tus (kju:mjuloustréitəs, kju:mjuloustréitai) *pl.* **cu·mu·lo·stra·ti** (kju:mjuloustréitai, kju:mjuloustréitai) *n.* stratocumulus (*CLOUD FORMS) [Mod. L.]

cu·mu·lous (kju:mjuləs) *adj.* of or relating to or like a cumulus

cu·mu·lus (kju:mjuləs) *pl.* **cu·mu·li** (kju:mjulai, kju:mjuli:) *n.* a heaped mass of low-lying

rounded clouds on a flat base (*CLOUD FORMS) [L. = heap]

cu·ne·ate (kjú:ni:it, kjú:ni:eit) *adj.* wedge-shaped [fr. L. *cuneatus*]

cu·ne·i·form (kjú:ní:ifɔrm, kjú:ni:ifɔrm) 1. *adj.* (of a form of writing used in the ancient inscriptions of Babylonia, Assyria, Persia, Akkadia etc.) composed of wedge-shaped strokes which were impressed with a stylus in soft clay ‖ made up of or written in these cuneiform characters ‖ (of certain bones) wedge-shaped 2. *n.* cuneiform characters [prob. fr. F. *cunéiforme*]

Cu·nha (kú:nja), Euclides da (1866–1909), Brazilian novelist, author of 'Os sertões' (1902, trans. 'Rebellion in the Backlands')

cun·ner (kʌnər) *n.* (*Am.*) *Tautogolabrus adspersus*, fam. *Labridae*, a food fish found on the Atlantic coast of North America ‖ (*Br.*) *Crenilabrus melops*, fam. *Labridae*, a food fish [etym. doubtful]

cun·ning (kʌniŋ) 1. *adj.* crafty, full of deceit ‖ skillful, ingenious ‖ sweet, charming 2. *n.* guile, deceit ‖ artfulness ‖ skill, dexterity [O.E. *cunnan*, to know, be able]

cup (kʌp) 1. *n.* a small bowl-shaped vessel, usually with a handle, for drinking tea, coffee etc. from, and usually matched with a saucer ‖ an ornamental vessel, often with a stem of gold or silver, offered as a sports trophy etc. ‖ a cupful, *a cup of tea* ‖ a measure in cookery ‖ the wine of the Eucharist, or the chalice containing it ‖ (*rhet.*) one's portion or fate, *cup of happiness* ‖ wine or cider etc. with fruit flavorings ‖ a rounded hollow, e.g. the socket of certain bones or the calyx of some flowers ‖ (*med.*) a glass vessel used in cupping **in one's cups** drunk **one's cup of tea** (esp. *Br.*) what pleases or suits one 2. *v.t. pres. part.* **cup·ping** *past* and *past part.* **cupped** to form into a cup, *to cup one's hands* ‖ (*med.*) to bleed by cupping [O.F. *cuppe*, perh. fr. L.]

cup·bear·er (kʌpbɛərər) *n.* (*hist.* and *rhet.*) an attendant with the job of pouring out the wine

cup·board (kʌbərd) *n.* a cabinet or small closet, usually with shelves, for china, linen or brooms etc.

cupboard love a display of love in the hope of a reward, esp. food

cup·cake (kʌpkeik) *n.* a small cake baked in a cup-shaped tin

cu·pel (kjú:pel, kju:pél) 1. *n.* a small, shallow cup used in extracting and assaying precious metals 2. *v.t. pres. part.* **cu·pel·ing**, esp. *Br.* **cu·pel·ling** *past* and *past part.* **cu·peled**, esp. *Br.* **cu·pelled** to assay in a cupel **cu·pel·la·tion** (kju:pəléiʃən) *n.* the refinement of precious metals by exposing them to an air blast so that any included base metals are oxidized and sink into the porous cupel or are swept away in the blast [F. *coupelle*]

cup·ful (kʌpful) *pl.* **cup·fuls** *n.* (*cookery*) as much as a cup will hold

Cu·pid (kjú:pid) the Roman god of love, the son of Venus and Mercury, identified with the Greek Eros ‖ a representation of Cupid as a naked, winged boy, usually with a bow and arrows

cu·pid·i·ty (kju:píditi) *n.* avarice, greed, esp. for wealth [F. *cupidité*]

cu·po·la (kjú:pələ) *n.* a rounded roof or ceiling ‖ a small dome-shaped superstructure on a roof, often carrying a weathervane, clock etc. ‖ a furnace for melting metals ‖ a revolving dome protecting guns on battleships ‖ (*anat.*) a domed organ or process, esp. the extremity of the canal of the cochlea [Ital.]

cup·pa (kʌpə) *n.* (*Br.*) a cup of tea

cup·ping (kʌpiŋ) *n.* (*med.*) the application of a cup-shaped instrument to the skin to draw the blood to the surface for bloodletting

cu·pram·mo·ni·um (kju:prəmóuni:əm, kju:prəmóunjəm, kju:prəmóuni:əm, kju:prəmóunjəm) *n.* any of certain complexes containing copper and ammonia, particularly the blue bivalent cation $Cu(NH_3)_4^{2-}$ ‖ cuprammonium solution [fr. L. *cupro-* fr. *cuprum*, copper +AMMONIUM]

cuprammonium solution a blue aqueous solution containing the cuprammonium complex, used as a solvent for cellulose in the manufacture of certain kinds of rayon

cu·pre·ous (kú:pri:əs, kjú:pri:əs) *adj.* containing or resembling copper [fr. L. *cupreus* fr. *cuprum*, copper]

cu·pric (kú:prik, kjú:prik) *adj.* of or containing copper ‖ of compounds of bivalent copper [fr. L. *cuprum*, copper]

cu·prif·er·ous (ku:prífərəs, kju:prífərəs) *adj.* containing copper [fr. L. *cuprum*, copper+-*fer*, bearing]

cu·prite (kú:prait, kjú:prait) *n.* red copper ore, cuprous oxide (Cu₂O) [fr. L. *cuprum*, copper]

cu·prous (kú:prəs, kjú:prəs) *adj.* (*chem.*) of or containing copper ‖ being a compound of univalent copper [fr. L. *cuprum*, copper]

cuprous oxide [Cu₂O] (*electr.*) the usual material base for a semiconductor applied by heat

cu·pule (kjú:pju:l) *n.* the involucre of the female flower of the oak which persists around an acorn ‖ the gemmae-bearing cup of the genus *Marchantia* of liverworts ‖ a small sucker on various animals [fr. L. *cupula*, dim. of *cupa*, cask]

cur (kə:r) *n.* a mongrel dog, esp. a snappish, bad-tempered one ‖ (*old-fash.*) a bad-tempered, despicable fellow [M.E. *curre*, perh. rel. to O.N. *kurra*, to grumble]

cur·a·bil·i·ty (kjuərəbíliti) *n.* the state or quality of being curable

cur·a·ble (kjúərəb'l) *adj.* able to be cured

Cu·ra·çao (kjuərəsóu) an island (area 210 sq. miles, pop. 160,625) and political division of the Netherlands Antilles. Capital: Willemstad (pop. 45,000). Industry: oil refining

cu·ra·çao (kjuərəsóu) *n.* a liqueur flavored with the bitter peel of an orange grown in Curaçao [after the island, where it was first made]

cu·ra·cy (kjúərəsi) *pl.* **cu·ra·cies** the office or employment of a curate

cu·ra·re, cu·ra·ri (kjurúri) *n.* a poison (strychnine) extracted from the vine *Strychnos toxifera*, fam. *Loganiaceae*, and used by South American Indians to tip their arrows, and in medicine to alleviate suffering by relieving paralysis and stimulating the central nervous system [corrup. of *wurali*, the native name for the plant]

cu·ras·sow (kjúərəsou, kjurásou) *n.* a member of *Crax*, a genus of turkeylike birds of Central and South America. They are dark violet, with a purplish-green gloss, white abdomen and golden crest (*GUAN) [CURACAO]

cu·rate (kjúərit) *n.* an assistant to a vicar or a rector [fr. M.L. *curatus*, someone having a charge (*cura*)]

cu·rate-in-charge (kjúəritintʃárdʒ) *n.* (*Br.*) an assistant to a priest, having the responsibility of a subsidiary church, chapel of ease etc.

curate's egg (*Br.*) a thing containing both good and bad qualities, from the story of a curate asked about a stale egg given by his bishop

cu·ra·tive (kjúərətiv) 1. *adj.* having remedial properties, helping to cure 2. *n.* a remedy [F.]

cu·ra·tor (kjuréitər, kjúəreitər) *n.* a person in charge of a museum, art gallery or department of such an institution ‖ (*Br.*) a member of a board managing property, or supervising other matters (e.g. in some universities) **cu·ra·to·ri·al** (kjuərətɔ́ri:əl, kjuərətóuri:əl) *adj.* **cu·rá·tor·ship** *n.* [A.F. *curatour* and L. *curator* fr. L. *curare*, to take care of]

curb (kə:rb) 1. *n.* a chain or strap passing under a horse's lower jaw and used to restrain ‖ a restraint, control ‖ a protective barrier, e.g. around a hearth or the top of a well ‖ (*Br.* also **kerb**) an edging bordering a street sidewalk ‖ (*stock exchange*) a market in stocks not listed on the exchange (orig. on the street after the closing of the exchange) ‖ a hard swelling on a horse's leg 2. *v.t.* to put a curb on (a horse) ‖ to restrain [fr. F. *courbe*. curved]

curb·ing (kə́:rbiŋ) *n.* material for a curb ‖ a curb

curb roof a roof which has a double slope on each side, the lower one being steeper (cf. MANSARD ROOF)

curb·side (kə́:rbsaid) *n.* the side of a curbed sidewalk

curb·stone, Br. also kerb·stone (kə́:rbstoun) *n.* one of the stones forming a curb

cur·cu·li·o (kə:rkjú:li:ou) *pl.* **cur·cu·li·os** *n.* a member of *Curculio*, a genus of weevils, esp. the common fruit weevil which injures plums [L.=corn weevil]

cur·cu·ma (kə́:rkjumə) *n.* a member of *Curcuma*, fam. *Zingiberaceae*, a genus of plants grown in the Far East. Their powdered rhizomes yield arrowroot starch and turmeric [M.L. or Mod. L. fr. Arab. *kurkum*, saffron]

curd (kə:rd) *n.* (esp. *pl.*) the smooth, thickened part of sour milk (cf. WHEY) sometimes used to make cheese ‖ the fatty matter between flakes of salmon flesh [M.E. *crud*, origin unknown]

cur·dle (kə́:rd'l) *pres. part.* **cur·dling** *past* and *past part.* **cur·dled** *v.t.* to cause to clot, congeal ‖

v.i. to form into curds ‖ to thicken, congeal, *the story made my blood curdle*

curd·y (kə́:rdi:) *comp.* **curd·i·er** *superl.* **curd·i·est** *adj.* having the consistency or appearance of curd ‖ coagulating into curd ‖ (of salmon) having a great deal of curd

cure (kjuər) *n.* a remedy ‖ a course of treatment ‖ a successful treatment ‖ (*eccles.*) the pastorate, *cure of souls* ‖ an agent for curing hides [O.F. *cure*]

cure *v.t. pres. part.* **cur·ing** *past* and *past part.* **cured** to restore to health ‖ to remedy ‖ to preserve by smoking, salting, pickling etc. ‖ to treat (hides) with salt or chemicals so as to stop decomposition ‖ *v.i.* (of hides) to become cured [F. *curer*]

cu·ré (kjuréi, F. kyrei) *n.* a French priest in French-speaking countries

cure-all (kjúərɔl) *n.* a panacea

cu·ret·tage (kjurétidʒ, kjuəritáʒ) *n.* the operation performed with a curette

cu·rette (kjurét) 1. *n.* (*surg.*) an instrument for scraping growths etc. from a cavity wall, esp. from the uterus 2. *v.t. pres. part.* **cu·ret·ting** *past* and *past part.* **cu·ret·ted** to scrape with this [F.]

cur·few (kə́:rfju:) *n.* in places under martial law, a fixed time after which (or period during which) no citizen may re-main outdoors ‖ (*hist.*) a medieval rule that all lights and fires should be covered at a certain time in the evening, when a bell was rung ‖ the time for this [fr. A.F. *coeverfu* fr. O.F. *couvrir*, cover+*feu*, fire]

cu·ri·a (kjúəri:ə) *pl.* **cu·ri·ae** (kjúəri:i:) *n.* (*hist.*) one of the 10 divisions of a Roman tribe ‖ (*hist.*) the Roman senate building **Cu·ri·a** the papal court **cú·ri·al** *adj.* [L.]

cu·ri·age (kju:ri:áʒ) *n.* radioactivity expressed in terms of curies

Cu·rie (kyri:, kjúəri:, kjuri:), Pierre (1859–1906), and Marie (1867–1934), French physicists, husband and wife, who together with Becquerel shared a Nobel prize (1903) for researches into radioactivity which included their discovery of radium and polonium. Marie Curie received a second Nobel prize in 1911

cu·rie (kjúəri:, kjuri:) *n.* the unit of measurement of activity of a radioactive material, namely the amount of an isotope which decays at the rate of 3.7 x 10¹⁰ disintegrations per second

curie point the temperature above which a given ferromagnetic material loses its ferromagnetism

cu·ri·o (kjúəri:ou) *pl.* **cu·ri·os** *n.* an interesting object valued for its appearance or associations [shortened fr. *curiosity*]

cu·ri·os·i·ty (kjuəri:ɔ́siti:) *pl.* **cu·ri·os·i·ties** *n.* eagerness to know ‖ inquisitiveness ‖ strangeness ‖ a rare or curious object [O.F. *curioseté*]

cu·ri·ous (kjúəri:əs) *adj.* odd, unusual, *curious behavior* ‖ inquisitive, prying ‖ anxious to learn [O.F. *curius*]

Cu·ri·ti·ba (ku:ri:tí:bə) a trading center (pop. 765,700) of E. Brazil, 70 miles inland from the port of Paraneguá: lumber, coffee, maté

cu·ri·um (kjúəri:əm) *n.* a radioactive element (symbol Cm, at. no. 96) made artificially by bombarding plutonium with high-energy helium nuclei [after Pierre and Marie *Curie*]

curl (kə:rl) 1. *v.t.* to cause to form into curls ‖ to cause to bend around ‖ *v.i.* to form into curls ‖ to assume the shape of a curl ‖ to move in spirals ‖ to play at curling **to curl up** to roll up into a curl ‖ to sit or lie with the legs drawn up 2. *n.* a lock of hair growing in a curved or coiled shape, a ringlet ‖ anything shaped like a curl, twist or spiral **cúrl·er** *n.* a pin etc. for curling the hair ‖ a player at curling ‖ (*football*) crossing pattern of play in which two receivers cross [M.E. *curlen* fr. *croll, crull adj.*, curly]

cur·lew (kə́:rlu:) *n.* a member of *Numenius*, fam. *Scolopacidae*, a genus of shy, long-legged European and North American wading birds with a long, curved, slender bill [perh. imit.]

cur·li·cue (kə́:rlikju:) *n.* a fanciful curl or flourish in writing

curl·i·ness (kə́:rli:nis) *n.* the state or quality of being curly

curl·ing (kə́:rliŋ) *n.* a game played on ice by sliding curling stones across a rink towards a target circle

curling iron tongs heated and used for curling the hair

curling pin (*Br.*) a hair curler

curling stone a round stone up to 36 ins. in circumference, weighing up to 50 lbs., with the

curve flattened at the top and bottom and a handle on the top, used in curling

curl·y (kə́:rli:) *comp.* **curl·i·er** *superl.* **curl·i·est** *adj.* curling ‖ having curls ‖ (of wood) having a wavy grain

cur·mudg·eon (kərmʌ́dʒən) *n.* (*rhet.*) a bad-tempered, churlish man **cur·múdg·eon·ly** *adj.* [origin unknown]

cur·rant (kə́:rənt, kʌ́rənt) *n.* a member of *Ribes*, fam. *Saxifragaceae*, a genus of cold-climate bush fruits, with red, black or white berries, according to species ‖ a small dried grape, or from Greece, once called 'raisin of Corauntz' (Corinth)

cur·ren·cy (kə́:rənsi:, kʌ́rənsi:) *pl.* **cur·ren·cies** *n.* the coins, notes or other tokens in circulation as a means of exchange ‖ the state of being in general use, *words no longer in currency* ‖ general acceptance, prevalence, *the rumor gained currency* ‖ the time during which something is current [fr. L. *currere*, to run]

Currency Act of 1764 an act of the British Parliament, during the ministry of George Grenville, which prohibited the issue of colonial paper money. It increased colonial resentment against the government

cur·rent (kə́:rənt, kʌ́rənt) *adj.* in general use ‖ prevalent, *current gossip* ‖ of the present time, *the current issue of a magazine* [M.E. *corant*, *current*, pres. part. of O.F. *corre*, to run]

current *n.* a mass of air, water or other fluid moving in a certain direction ‖ the stream thus formed ‖ the most rapidly moving part of a river etc. ‖ electric current ‖ a general trend or direction or course of events [O.F. *corant*]

current account (*Br.*) a checking account

current balance an instrument measuring electric current, using the principle of a torsion balance to measure the mechanical force exerted by two conductors on each other when each has a current passing through it

current density the electric current per unit area of conductor perpendicular to the direction of flow

cur·rent·ly (kə́:rəntli:, kʌ́rəntli:) *adv.* at present

current yield (*securities*) the rate of interest based on the price of a bond, regardless of the discount or premium gained or lost at its maturity

cur·ri·cle (kə́:rik'l) *n.* (*hist.*) a two-wheeled open carriage drawn by two horses abreast [fr. L. *curriculum*, a running, a light chariot]

cur·ric·u·lar (kəríkjulər) *adj.* of or relating to a curriculum

cur·ric·u·lum (kəríkjuləm) *pl.* **cur·ric·u·lums, cur·ric·u·la** (kəríkjulə) *n.* a course of study, esp. at a school or college ‖ a list of the courses offered at a school, college or university [L.=a running, a race]

cur·ric·u·lum vi·tae (kəríkjuləmváiti:) *pl.* **cur·ric·u·la vi·tae** (kəríkjuləváiti:) an outline of one's career listing relevant achievements, education, positions held etc.

Cur·rie (kə́:ri:, kʌ́ri:), Sir Arthur William (1875–1933), Canadian general and educator. He was (1917) commander of Canada's overseas forces in the 1st world war, and became (1920) vice-chancellor of McGill University

cur·ri·er (kə́:ri:ər, kʌ́ri:ər) *n.* someone who curries or dresses tanned leather [fr. O.F. *corier*]

Cur·ri·er and Ives (kə́:ri:ər, kʌ́ri:ər) (Nathaniel Currier, 1813–88, and James Merritt Ives, 1824–95), a partnership of U.S. lithographers who produced (c. 1840–90) prints depicting 19th–c. American life

cur·rish (kə́:riʃ) *adj.* (*rhet.*) curlike, bad-tempered, mean

cur·ry (kə́:ri:, kʌ́ri:) 1. *pl.* **cur·ries** *n.* a hot-tasting powder made from turmeric and other spices and used in meat dishes etc., esp. in India ‖ a dish flavored with this powder 2. *v.t. pres. part.* **cur·ry·ing** *past* and *past part.* **cur·ried** to cook with curry [Tamil *kari*, sauce]

curry *pres. part.* **cur·ry·ing** *past* and *past part.* **cur·ried** *v.t.* to rub down and comb (a horse) ‖ to dress (tanned leather) **to curry favor** (*Br. favour*) to seek favor by flattery [O.F. *correier*]

cur·ry·comb (kə́:ri:koum, kʌ́ri:koum) 1. *n.* a metal comb for currying horses 2. *v.t.* to rub down with a currycomb

curse (kə:rs) *n.* an invocation or prayer for divine punishment or harm to come upon someone ‖ an oath or blasphemous imprecation ‖ an evil or source of misery [O.E. *curs*]

curse *pres. part.* **curs·ing** *past* and *past part.* **cursed, curst** *v.t.* to call for divine punishment of or utter a curse or curses on (someone) ‖ to bring harm upon ‖ to swear at ‖ *v.i.* to swear or blaspheme **curs·ed** (kə́:rsid, kə:rst), **curst** *adj.* under a curse ‖ evil, hateful ‖ (*pop.*, kə́:rsid) damned, *a cursed nuisance* [O.E. *cursian*]

cur·sive (kə́:rsiv) **1.** *adj.* (of writing) flowing, written without raising the pen (cf. UNCIAL) **2.** *n.* a flowing script [fr. M.L. *cursivus*]

cur·sor (kə́:rsər) *n.* the sliding part of an instrument, e.g. of a slide rule ‖ an etched transparent plastic sheet that is placed over a radar screen with diameter aligned with the target echo, thus showing on 360-degree screen the angle of the echo source [L.= runner fr. *currere*, to run]

cur·so·ri·al (kə:rsɔ́ri:əl, kə:rsɔ́uri:əl) *adj.* (*zool.*) adapted to running ‖ having limbs etc. adapted to running [fr. L. *cursorius*, of a runner]

cur·so·ri·ly (kə́:rsərili:) *adv.* in a cursory manner

cur·so·ri·ness (kə́:rsəri:nis) *n.* the state or quality of being cursory

cur·so·ry (kə́:rsəri:) *adj.* hurried, superficial [fr. L. *cursorius*, hasty]

curst *CURSED

curt (kə:rt) *adj.* short in speech ‖ abrupt, impolitely brief [fr. L. *curtus*, short]

cur·tail (kərtéil) *v.t.* to cut short, to *curtail a visit* ‖ to cut off (a part) **cur·táil·ment** *n.* [etym. doubtful]

cur·tain (kə́:rt'n, kə́:rtin) **1.** *n.* a hanging cloth used esp. to screen or adorn windows ‖ something like this, *a curtain of rain* ‖ the hanging drape dividing a theater stage from the auditorium ‖ the raising of this at the beginning of a play or its lowering at the end, or at the end of an act ‖ (*Br.*) a curtain call ‖ something that conceals, *hiding the truth behind a curtain of rumors* ‖ (*fortification*) the part of a rampart connecting two towers **2.** *v.t.* to supply with curtains **to curtain off** to screen off with a curtain [M.E. *cortine, curtine* fr. O.F.]

curtain call a call to actors to return to the stage to acknowledge applause

curtain raiser a short one-act play or other entertainment performed in a theater before the main play

curtain wall a wall that is not load-bearing, often a prefabricated section mainly of glass ‖ (*fortification*) a curtain

Cur·tin, (kə́:rtin, kə:rt'n), Andrew Gregg (1817–94), governor of Pennsylvania (1860–7) and loyal supporter of President Lincoln during the Civil War. He organized a volunteer reserve corps, the 'Pennsylvania Reserves', and assembled a governors' meeting to promote the Union cause, which, immediately following the Emancipation Proclamation, strengthened Lincoln's hand

Curtin, John (1885–1945), Australian Labour prime minister (1941–5)

Cur·tis (kə́:rtis), Cyrus Hermann Kotzschmar (1850–1933), U.S. philanthropist and publisher. He founded (1879) 'The Ladies Home Journal', organized (1890) the Curtis Publishing Company, and purchased the 'Saturday Evening Post', the 'Philadelphia Inquirer', and other papers

Curtis, George Ticknor (1812–94), U.S. lawyer. In 'The Constitutional History of the United States from their Declaration of Independence to their Civil War', he voiced the classical Federalist-Whig viewpoint

Cur·tiss (kə́:rtis), Glenn Hammond (1878–1930), U.S. aviation pioneer. He designed and developed the seaplane and supplied military planes to the U.S.A., Great Britain, and Russia during the first world war

curt·sy, curt·sey (kə́:rtsi:) **1.** *pl.* **curt·sies, curt·seys** *n.* an inclination made by women and girls (in many countries only on very formal occasions) as a respectful greeting, the body being allowed to sink gracefully for a moment over the bent knee as one foot is placed behind the other **to drop a curtsy** to curtsy **2.** *v.i. pres. part.* **curt·sy·ing, curt·sey·ing** *past* and *past part.* **curt·sied, curt·seyed** to make a curtsy [var. of COURTESY]

cur·va·ceous (kərvéiʃəs) *adj.* (*pop.*, of a woman) having a shapely figure

cur·va·ture (kə́:rvətʃər) *n.* the extent to which a curve departs from the straight ‖ (*math.*) the rate of change of the slope per unit of arc length ‖ a curved condition, often abnormal, *curvature of the spine* [fr. L. *curvatura* fr. *curvus*, curved]

curve (kə:rv) **1.** *n.* a line or direction subject to continuous deviation from the straight ‖ a thing or part shaped thus ‖ a curving ‖ an amount of

curving ‖ (*baseball*) a ball pitched with spin so that it curves before passing the plate ‖ an unfair act or statement, from baseball's "to throw a curve ball" ‖ (*math.*) any line defined precisely in terms of a series of coordinates which are functions of a given equation **2.** *v. pres. part.* **curv·ing** *past* and *past part.* **curved** *v.i.* to take on the shape of a curve ‖ to move in a curved path ‖ *v.t.* to make (something) assume the shape of a curve or move in a curved path [fr. L. *curvus,* bent]

cur·vet 1. (kə́:rvit) *n.* a horse's tense prancing, its forelegs being raised together and then its hindlegs raised together before the forelegs have quite touched the ground again **2.** (kərvét, kə́:rvit) *v.i. pres. part.* **cur·vet·ing, cur·vet·ting** *past* and *past part.* **cur·vet·ed, cur·vet·ted** to make a curvet [fr. Ital. *corvetta,* dim. of *corvo,* curve]

cur·vi·lin·e·ar (kə:rvilíni:ər) *adj.* bounded by, or consisting of, curved lines [fr. L. *curvus,* curved+*linea,* line]

Cur·zon (kə́:rz'n), George Nathaniel, 1st marquess Curzon of Kedleston (1859–1925), British Conservative statesman, viceroy of India (1899–1905). As foreign secretary (1919–24), he suggested an ethnic boundary (the 'Curzon Line') between Russia and Poland (1919)

Cusa, Nicholas of *NICOLAS OF CUSA

cus·cus (kʌ́skʌs) *n. Andropogon zizamoides,* an Indian grass used for weaving fans, baskets, screens etc. Its aromatic roots yield an oil used in perfumery [fr. Pers. *khas khas*]

cuscus *n.* a member of *Phalanger,* a genus of marsupial quadrupeds found in New Guinea [Mod. L. fr. native name]

cu·sec (kjú:sek) *n.* (of the flow of a fluid) a unit equal to 1 cubic foot per second [CUBIC+SECOND]

Cush·ing (kúʃiŋ), Caleb (1800–79), U.S. politician and diplomat. As U.S. commissioner to China he negotiated the Treaty of Wanghia (1844) which established the principle of extraterritoriality. He served (1853–7) as U.S. attorney general in the Pierce administration

cush·ion (kúʃən) **1.** *n.* a cloth case stuffed with down or feathers, kapok, foam rubber etc. for sitting on or leaning against ‖ something that resembles or serves as this, *a cushion of moss* ‖ something that serves as a shock absorber, e.g. the resilient lining of the sides of a billiard table ‖ the steam left in a cylinder to act as a buffer to the piston ‖ (of a pig etc.) the buttocks ‖ the soft part of a horse's foot protected by the horny hoof **2.** *v.t.* to supply with cushions ‖ to protect with cushions so as to diminish or absorb shock ‖ to shield (a person) e.g. from the full force of hostile criticism ‖ to suppress (criticism) discreetly ‖ to lean as if against a cushion, *she cushioned her head against his shoulder* ‖ (*billiards*) to leave (a ball) placed up against a cushion [M.E. *cuisshin* fr. O.F. *coissin,* etym. doubtful]

cushion craft vehicle that travels on a cushion of air between the vehicle and surface, e.g., Hovercraft *Cf* AIR-CUSHION VEHICLE

Cush·it·ic (kəʃítik) *n.* one of a subfamily of Afro-Asiatic languages spoken in East Africa, Ethiopia and Somaliland [fr. *Cushite,* an inhabitant of ancient Cush in the Nile valley]

cush·y (kúʃi:) *comp.* **cush·i·er** *superl.* **cush·i·est** *adj.* (esp. *Br., pop.,* of a job) well paid, easy, and entailing little work [orig. Br. army slang fr. Hindi *khush,* pleasant]

CUSIP (*acronym*) for Committee on Uniform Security Identification Procedure of The American Bankers Association

cusp (kʌsp) *n.* an apex, e.g. of the crown of a tooth ‖ a sharp point ‖ (*geom.*) the point formed by two converging curves ‖ (*ice skating*) point in a turn when a skater shifts from one edge of a skate blade to the other edge ‖ (*archit.*) a triangular projection between the small arcs in Gothic tracery **cusped** (kʌspt) *adj.* [fr. L. *cuspis* (*cuspidis*), point]

cus·pid (kʌ́spid) *n.* one of the canine teeth [fr. L. *cuspis* (*cuspidis*), a point]

cus·pi·dal (kʌ́spid'l) *adj.* of or like a cusp [fr. L. *cuspis* (*cuspidis*), a point]

cus·pi·date (kʌ́spideit) *adj.* having a cusp ‖ (of a leaf) ending in a point **cús·pi·dat·ed** *adj.* [fr. Mod. L. *cuspidatus*]

cus·pi·dor (kʌ́spidɔr) *n.* a spittoon [Port. = spitter fr. *cuspir,* to spit]

cuss (kʌs) *n.* (*pop.*) a curse ‖ (*pop.*) a fellow, *a funny old cuss* **cuss·ed** (kʌ́sid) *adj.* perverse, pigheaded

cuss·word (kʌ́swə:rd) *n.* (*pop.*) a swearword ‖ (*pop.*) a derogatory term or term of abuse

cus·tard (kʌ́stərd) *n.* a sweetened mixture of eggs and milk baked or steamed ‖ a liquid form of this served as a sauce ‖ a sweetened mixture of milk and a thickening powder as a substitute for the above [fr. older *crustade* fr. F. *croustade*]

custard apple *Annona reticulata,* fam. *Annonaceae,* a tropical succulent fruit

custard glass a light buff colored glass

Cus·ter (kʌ́stər), George Armstrong (1839–76), U.S. cavalry officer. At the Battle of the Little Bighorn (1876), Montana Territory, against the Sioux Indians, his force of 267 was annihilated

cus·to·di·al (kʌstóudi:əl) *adj.* relating to guardianship [fr. L. *custodia,* custody]

cus·to·di·an (kʌstóudi:ən) *n.* a guardian or keeper, esp. of some public building **cus·tó·di·an·ship** *n.* [fr. L. *custodia,* custody]

cus·to·dy (kʌ́stədi:) *n.* guardianship, care ‖ imprisonment [fr. L. *custodia*]

cus·tom (kʌ́stəm) **1.** *n.* a generally accepted practice or habit, convention, *the dictates of custom* ‖ the support given to a shop or firm by dealing with it regularly ‖ (*pl.*) duties levied on imported goods ‖ (*law*) a long-established practice having the force of law **2.** *adj.* made-to-order ‖ dealing in made-to-order goods [O.F. *custume, costume*]

cus·tom·ar·i·ly (kʌ́stəmerili:, kʌstəméǝrili:) *adv.* in a customary manner

cus·tom·ar·i·ness (kʌ́stəmeri:nis) *n.* the state or quality of being customary

cus·tom·ar·y (kʌ́stəmeri:) **1.** *adj.* usual, according to custom **2.** *pl.* **cus·tom·ar·ies** *n.* a written collection of a society's customs [fr. M.L. *custumarius*]

cus·tom-built (kʌ́stəmbilt) *adj.* made-to-order, e.g. of a car body

cus·tom·er (kʌ́stəmər) *n.* a person wishing to make a purchase from a store or firm ‖ someone who buys regularly from a particular store or firm ‖ (*pop.*) a person with respect to the dealings one has or may have with him, *an awkward customer*

cus·tom-house (kʌ́stəmhaus) *pl.* **cus·tom-hous·es** (kʌ́stəmhauziz) *n.* a building where customs duties are collected

cus·tom-made (kʌ́stəmmeid) *adj.* made-to-order

Cus·toms (kʌ́stəmz) *pl. n.* the government department which collects customs duties

cus·toms-house (kʌ́stəmzhaus) *pl.* **cus·toms-hous·es** (kʌ́stəmzhauziz) *n.* a customhouse

Cu·stoz·za, Battle of (ku:stɔ́tsa) a battle (1848) in N. Italy, in which the Austrian army under Radetzky defeated Sardinia

cus·tu·mal (kʌ́stʃuməl) *n.* a customary [fr. M.L. *custumalis*]

cut (kʌt) **1.** *v. pres. part.* **cut·ting** *past* and *past part.* **cut** *v.t.* to make an incision in ‖ to wound with or on something sharp ‖ to sever ‖ to separate into slices or pieces ‖ to reap ‖ to make smaller or shorter by trimming with a sharp instrument ‖ to cross, intersect ‖ to reduce, *to cut prices* ‖ to shorten, *to cut a speech* ‖ to excavate, *to cut a trench* ‖ to hurt (someone) in his feelings ‖ to strike (a ball) so as to put a spin on it ‖ to make, appear as, *to cut a ridiculous figure* ‖ to refuse to recognize (an acquaintance) ‖ to stay away from (what should be attended), *to cut lectures* ‖ to divide (a pack of playing cards) ‖ to castrate ‖ to have (a tooth) grow up through the gum ‖ *v.i.* to make a cut, *this knife cuts badly* ‖ to be capable of being cut, *this stone cuts easily* ‖ to make thrashing strokes, *to cut at nettles with a stick* ‖ (*movies*) to cut back **to cut a caper** to jump about playfully **to cut a dash** (*Br.*) to look smart **to cut along** (*Br.*) to hurry off **to cut and run,** to cut away to run away **to cut back** to shorten, prune ‖ (*movies*) to return for dramatic effect (to a scene which would have taken place earlier in strict narrative sequence) **to cut both ways** to have both favorable and unfavorable effects **to cut down** to cause to fall by cutting, fell ‖ to reduce, *to cut down smoking* ‖ to make smaller, *to cut down a coat* ‖ to economize **to cut in** to interrupt ‖ to enter a moving line of traffic from the side, esp. to overtake another motorist and pull in again too soon ‖ to interrupt a dancing couple so as to claim a partner **to cut it fine** (or close) to allow oneself hardly any margin (e.g. of time or money) **to cut no ice** to have little influence or effect **to cut off** to bring to an end, *death cut him off in his prime* to separate, *cut off from his supplies* ‖ to break the telephone connection of (someone) ‖ to disinherit **to cut one's coat according to one's cloth** to spend within one's income **to cut one's losses** to abandon an unprofitable course of action **to cut out** to remove by cutting ‖ to shape (a figure, design etc.) by cutting it from paper, wood etc. ‖ to supplant (a rival) ‖ to contrive, *to cut out a comfortable job for oneself* ‖ to dispense with, *cut out the nonsense* ‖ to delete, omit, *to cut out the jokes from a speech* ‖ (*pass.*) to be naturally suited for, *he is not cut out to be a farmer* ‖ to remove from the herd ‖ to leave a moving line of traffic suddenly, esp. so as to overtake another vehicle **to cut (someone) short** to interrupt (someone) abruptly and prevent him from continuing to speak **to cut up** to cut into pieces ‖ to destroy ‖ to criticize harshly ‖ to distress ‖ to be a nuisance or cause a disturbance **to cut up rough** (*Br.*) to become angry and menacing **to have one's work cut out** to have as much work as one can manage **2.** *n.* a gash, incision or wound ‖ a reduction, *a cut in wages* ‖ an excision ‖ (*pop.*) a share, *his cut was 10%* ‖ a piece of meat for cooking ‖ a thrashing stroke (e.g. with a whip) ‖ a sharp glancing stroke at a ball ‖ a railroad cutting ‖ a style of fashioning clothes, hair etc. ‖ (*pop.*) a social degree, *he thinks he's a cut above us* ‖ a verbal attack, *that remark was a cut at you* ‖ (*printing*) a process block set in the text ‖ a woodcut **3.** *adj.* having been cut, *cut flowers* ‖ castrated ‖ reduced, *cut prices* [M.E. prob. fr. Gmc]

cut·a·bil·i·ty (kʌtəbíliti:) *n.* proportion of salable meat in a carcass

cut-and-dried (kʌtəndráid) *adj.* definite, worked out in full detail, leaving nothing to chance, improvisation etc.

cu·ta·ne·ous (kju:téiniəs) *adj.* of the skin [fr. Mod. L. *cutaneus* fr. *cutis*, skin]

cut·a·way (kʌtəwei) *n.* a man's formal daytime coat that tapers from the waist to form tails at the back

cutaway coat a cutaway

cut·back (kʌtbæk) *n.* a marked reduction, *a cutback in expenditure* ‖ a flashback in a movie or novel etc. ‖ (*football*) a sudden reversal of direction by the ball-carrier ‖ (*surfing*) maneuver to turn back toward a wave crest

cutch (kʌtʃ) *n.* a tanning extract from various mangrove barks of Borneo and the Philippines [Malay]

cute (kju:t) *comp.* **cut·er** *superl.* **cut·est** *adj.* (*pop.*) attractive, charming ‖ (*pop.*) sharp-witted ‖ deceptively straightforward [ACUTE]

cute·sy or **cute·sie** (kjú:tsi:) *adj.* of an act coyingly cute

cut glass glass with a pattern or ornament cut in it and polished, so that it catches light in the cut as well as on the plane surfaces

Cuth·bert (kʌ́θbərt), St (c. 637–87), bishop of Lindisfarne. Bede wrote his life. Feast: Mar. 20

cu·ti·cle (kjú:tik'l) *n.* the skin, esp. the outer layer or epidermis ‖ the hardened skin around the edges of fingernails and toenails ‖ (*bot.*) the superficial covering of the outer layer of epidermal cells **cu·tic·u·lar** (kju:tíkjulər) *adj.* **cu·tic·u·lar·i·za·tion** *n.* the state of being cuticularized or the process of becoming so **cu·tic·u·lar·ized** *adj.* covered with cuticle or changed to cuticle [fr. L. *cuticula*, dim. of *cutis*, skin]

cu·tie pie (kjú:ti:) (*phys.*) instrument used to measure radiation levels

cu·tin (kjú:tin) *n.* a substance allied to cellulose found in the external layers of thickened epidermal cells [fr. L. *cutis*, skin]

cu·tis (kjú:tis) *pl.* **cu·tes** (kjú:ti:z), **cu·tis·es** *n.* the dermis [L. = skin]

cut·lass (kʌ́tləs) *n.* a short, broad, often slightly curving sword, with one sharp edge, esp. such as were formerly used by sailors [F. *coutelas*]

cut·ler (kʌ́tlər) *n.* someone who makes, sells or repairs knives and other edged instruments [F. *coutelier*]

cut·ler·y (kʌ́tləri:) *n.* knives, forks and spoons used at table ‖ knives and other edged instruments (shears, razors etc.) ‖ the trade or business of a cutler [O.F. *coutelerie*]

cut·let (kʌ́tlit) *n.* a small chop cut from the best end of mutton, lamb, veal or pork, for grilling or frying ‖ a croquette of flaked fish etc. made up into this shape [F. *côtelette*, double dim. of *côte*, rib]

cut·off (kʌ́tɔf, kʌ́tɒf) *n.* a device to prevent cartridges from being fed from a rifle magazine ‖ a shutting off of the driving power from an engine cylinder, or the device used for shutting it off ‖ a

channel formed by a river cutting through the neck of an oxbow ‖ the water cut off in this way ‖ a road, path etc. providing a shortcut

cut·out (kʌ́taut) *n.* a design or figure made by, or prepared for, cutting out from paper, cardboard etc. ‖ a valve in the exhaust pipe of an engine for releasing gas directly into the air instead of through the muffler, thus gaining extra power ‖ a device for disconnecting the battery of a car from the generator ‖ a device for interrupting automatically the flow of electricity to avoid too great a load ‖ an intermediary or device used to obviate direct contact between members of a clandestine organization ‖ a discontinued item, e.g., an out-of-stock record album

cutout box a fireproof box containing the main fuses of an electrical wiring system

cut·purse (kʌ́tpə:rs) *n.* (*hist.*) a pickpocket

cut-rate (kʌ́tréit) *adj.* offered for sale at a price below the general market price, or dealing in goods offered at such prices

Cut·tack (kʌ́tək) a trading town (pop. 138,000) in Orissa, India, on River Mahanadi. Utkal University (1943)

cut·ter (kʌ́tər) *n.* a person or thing that cuts ‖ a single-masted sailing boat rigged fore and aft ‖ a small boat belonging to a warship ‖ a small armed boat used by coast guards

cut·throat (kʌ́tθrout) **1.** *n.* an assassin, a murderer ‖ (*Br.*) a straight razor **2.** *adj.* ruinous, *cutthroat competition* ‖ (of certain card games) three-handed

cut·ting (kʌ́tiŋ) **1.** *n.* a passage or tunnel cut through high ground for a road or railroad etc. ‖ a small shoot bearing leaf buds and used for propagation ‖ (*Br.*) a clipping (paragraph etc. cut from a newspaper) **2.** *adj.* sharp ‖ piercing, *a cutting wind* ‖ sarcastic, unkind, *cutting remarks*

cut·tle (kʌ́t'l) *n.* a 10-armed marine cephalopod mollusk possessing a bony internal shell and the ability to eject a black fluid from a sac and so darken the water for concealment [O.E. *cudele*, origin unknown]

cut·tle·bone (kʌ́t'lboun) *n.* the internal calcareous shell of the cuttle used for polishing and as a mineral supplement to the diet of cage birds

cut·tle·fish (kʌ́t'lfiʃ) *pl.* **cut·tle·fish**, **cut·tle·fish·es** *n.* a cuttle

cut·up (kʌ́tʌp) *n.* someone who makes people laugh by his clowning and joking

cut·wa·ter (kʌ́twɔtər, kʌ́twɒtər) *n.* the foremost part of a ship's prow, that cleaves the water

cut·worm (kʌ́twə:rm) *n.* a caterpillar which cuts off young plants (esp. cabbage, corn, melons) by eating through the stem close to the ground

Cux·ha·ven (kukshá:fən) the outer port (pop. 50,000) of Hamburg, West Germany at the mouth of the Elbe: fishing, holiday resort

Cuyp (kɔip), Aelbert (1620–91), Dutch painter, esp. of animals, and of landscapes suffused with golden light (e.g. 'The Large Dort', 'View of Dordrecht') depicting the summer countryside of the Meuse

Cuz·co (kú:sko) a city (pop. 67,658) of S. Peru in the Andes, at 11,024 ft founded by the Incas (11th c.)

cwt hundredweight [fr. c. = L. *centum*, a hundred + WEIGHT]

-cy *suffix* used mainly to form abstract nouns as in 'aristocracy', or to indicate rank as in 'colonelcy', or function as in 'chaplaincy' [fr. L. *-cia, -tia*, Gk *-kia, -keia, -tia, -teia*]

cy·an (sáiən) *n.* one of a group of greenish blues, esp. one of the subtractive primaries [Gk *kuanos*, a dark blue mineral]

cy·an·ic (saiǽnik) *adj.* (*chem.*) relating to or containing cyanogen ‖ blue [fr. Gk *kuanos* n., a dark blue mineral and *kuaneos* adj., dark blue]

cyanic acid an acid composed of cyanogen, oxygen and hydrogen

cy·a·nide (sáiənaid, sáiənid) *n.* a compound of cyanogen and a metal [fr. Gk *kuanos* n., a dark blue mineral and *kuaneos* adj., dark blue]

cyanide process a method of extracting the gold from crushed ore by means of potassium cyanide solution, the resulting potassium auricyanide being reduced with zinc, filtered and cupeled

cy·a·nite (sáiənait) *n.* a mineral containing aluminum silicate, Al_2SiO_5, usually blue, occurring in blunt prisms in gneiss and mica schist [fr. G. *zyanit*]

cy·an·o·ac·ry·late (saiənouǽkrileit) *n.* (*chem.*) acrylic monomer used to close a wound and as an industrial adhesive

cy·an·o·gen (saiǽnədʒən) *n.* a univalent radical consisting of one atom of nitrogen and one of carbon (CN) forming a colorless, diatomic poisonous gas (C_2N_2). Chemically it resembles the halogen elements, forming direct compounds (*CYANIDE) with metals, of which potassium cyanide (KCN) is one of the most familiar [fr. F. *cyanogène* fr. Gk]

cyanogen agent *BLOOD AGENT

cy·a·no·sis (saiənóusis) *n.* a condition in which the body acquires a blue tinge because of insufficient oxygen in the blood **cy·a·not·ic** (saiənótik) *adj.* [Gk *kuanōsis*, dark blue color]

cy·an·o·type (saiǽnətaip) *n.* a blueprint [fr. Gk *kuanos* n., a dark blue mineral and *kuaneos* adj., dark blue]

Cyb·e·le (síbəli:) (*mythol.*) Phrygian nature goddess whose cult passed to Greece (c. 430 B.C.) and to Rome (c. 204 B.C.). The Greeks identified her with Rhea

cy·ber·cul·ture (sáibərkʌ̀ltʃər) *n.* a social structure dominated by computers

cy·ber·net·ics (saibərnétiks) *n.* the study of the operation of control and communication systems. It deals with both biological systems and man-made machinery [fr. Gk *kubernētēs*, steersman]

cy·borg (sáibɔrg) *n.* a living organism some of whose vital parts have been substituted by electronic or mechanical devices

cy·cad (sáikæd) *n.* a plant of the order *Cycadales*, ancient tropical gymnosperms that have an unbranched trunk of variable height and bear a terminal crown of long leaves and one or more large cones. There are many fossils dating from the Mesozoic [fr. Mod. L. *Cycas* (*Cycadis*) fr. Gk]

cy·ca·sin [$C_8H_{16}N_2O_7$] (sáikəsin) *n.* a carcinogenic and toxic product of a sugar-yielding tropical ornamental fern

Cyc·la·des (síklədi:z) a group of mountainous Greek islands (total area 996 sq. miles, pop. 86,337) in the Aegean, southeast of Attica. Naxos, in the center, is the largest. Crops: vines, olives, citrus fruit, wheat, tobacco. Chief town: Hermoupolis (on Syros)

cyc·la·men (síkləmən, síkləmen) *n.* a member of *Cyclamen*, fam. *Primulaceae*, a genus of plants having a stout corm formed from a thickened hypocotyl, petals bent backwards and pendulous flowers [Mod. L., etym. doubtful]

cy·clase (sáikleis) *n.* (*chem.*) a cyclic phosphodiesterase that acts as a catalytic enzyme

cy·cla·zo·cine [$C_{18}H_{25}NO$] (saiklazóusen) *n.* (*pharm.*) azobenzine derivative used as an analgesic to inhibit effects of morphine and other drugs in drug-addiction therapy

cy·cle (sáik'l) **1.** *n.* a series of recurring events or phenomena, *the cycle of the seasons* ‖ a period of time occupied by a set of events which will go on recurring in similar periods of time, *5-year cycles* ‖ a series of poems or songs with a central theme ‖ an orbit in the heavens ‖ (*biol.*) an ordered series of phenomena in which some process is completed, *life cycle* ‖ (*econ.*) a fluctuation showing a regular pattern, *price cycles* ‖ the circulation of a fluid through a series of vessels ‖ (*phys.*) a ring ‖ (*phys.*) any series of changes which restores a system to its original state ‖ the period of an alternating electric current ‖ a bicycle or tricycle **2.** *v.i. pres. part.* **cy·cling** *past* and *past part.* **cy·cled** to move in cycles ‖ to ride a bicycle [F. or fr. L. *cyclus* fr. Gk]

cycle AMP [$C_{10}H_{14}N_5O_7P$] (*biochem.*) compound believed to be the intercellular messenger controlling hormones and biogenic amines, thus regulating metabolism and the nervous system *abbr.* AMP

cy·cler·y (sáikləri:) *n.* bicycle garage

cy·clic (sáiklik, síklik) *adj.* recurring in cycles ‖ of or related to a cycle ‖ (*bot.*, of a flower) with its parts arranged in a whorl ‖ (*chem.*) having some or all of the constituent atoms in ring formation ‖ (*math.*) of a figure all of whose vertices lie on a circle (e.g. a cyclic quadrilateral) [fr. L. *cyclicus* fr. Gk]

cy·clist (sáiklist) *n.* someone who rides a bicycle

cyclo- (sáiklou) *combining form* of a circle or wheel, circular [fr. Gk *kuklos*, circle, wheel]

cy·clo (sáiklou) *n.* a three-wheel taxi

cy·clo·al·i·phat·ic (saiklouæ̀lifǽtik) *adj.* alicyclic

cy·clo·ben·za·prine [$C_{20}H_{21}N$] (saikləbénzəpri:n) *n.* (*pharm.*) a tricyclic amine used to relieve some types of skeletal muscle spasms caused by diseases of the central nervous system; marketed as Flexeril

cy·clo·cross (sáikləkrɔs) *n.* the sport of bicycling plus cross-country running

cy·clo·di·ene (saiklədáij:n) *n.* (*chem.*) an insecticide with a chlorinated methylene group forming a bridge across a six-membered carbon ring

cy·clo·graph (sáikləgræf) *n.* (*eng.*) electronic device to measure metallurgical properties (hardness, carbon content, etc.) of steel samples, utilizing a cathode-ray screen on which shaped patterns indicate values

cy·cloid (sáiklɔid) *n.* (*math.*) a curve described by a point on a circle which rolls in a straight line **cy·cloi·dal** *adj.* [fr. Gk *kukloeidēs*, like a circle]

cycloidal pendulum a pendulum whose bob swings in a cycloid

cy·clom·e·ter (saiklómitər) *n.* a device for recording the revolutions of a wheel, esp. a bicycle wheel, and so measuring the distance covered ‖ a device for measuring the arcs of circles [fr. Gk *kuklos*, circle + *metron*, measure]

cy·clone (sáikloun) *n.* a region of low atmospheric pressure characterized by rotating winds, in middle and high latitudes called a depression or low. The term usually refers to the violent storms which accompany it, with winds rotating up to 130 m.p.h., often causing havoc [fr. Gk *kuklōn*, moving in a circle]

cyclone cellar an underground refuge from cyclones

cyclone collector device that uses centrifugal force to pull large particles from polluted air

cy·clon·ic (saiklónik) *adj.* of or relating to a cyclone

cy·clo·nite (sáiklənait, síklənait) *n.* a high explosive, $C_3H_6N_3O_6$, used in detonators, bombs and shells [cyclotrimethylene-trinitramine]

cyclopaedia *CYCLOPEDIA

Cy·clo·pe·an (saiklopí:ən) *adj.* like a Cyclops **cy·clo·pe·an** gigantic ‖ of a style of building in stone using large blocks untrimmed and set without mortar

cy·clo·pe·di·a, cy·clo·pae·di·a (saikləpí:di:ə) *n.* an encyclopedia **cy·clo·pe·dic, cy·clo·pae·dic** *adj.* all-embracing like an encyclopedia, *cyclopedic knowledge*

cy·clo·phon (sáikləfon) *n.* switch created by a beam of electrons emitted from a vacuum tube

cy·clo·pousse (sáikləpu:s) *n.* Southeast Asian pedaled or motorized rickshaw; a pedicab

Cy·clops (sáiklops) *pl.* **Cy·clops, Cy·clo·pes** (saiklóupi:z) *n.* (*Gk mythol.*) one of a race of one-eyed giants visited by Odysseus

cyclops *n.* a small freshwater crustacean of genus *Cyclops*, suborder *Copepoda* [L. fr. Gk *kuklōps*, round-eyed]

cy·clo·ram·a (saiklərǽmə, saiklərámə) *n.* a spectacle painted or projected on a screen surrounding the spectator **cy·clo·rám·ic** *adj.* [fr. Gk *kuklos*, circle + *horama*, sight]

cy·clo·spor·in (sáikləspɔrin) *n.* (*pharm.*) drug used following organ transplants to disarm body's immune system

cy·clos·to·mate (saiklóstəmit, saiklóstəmeit) *adj.* (*zool.*) having a circular mouth **cy·clo·stom·a·tous** (saiklóstóumətəs, siklóstómətəs, sịklóstóumətəs) *adj.* [fr. Gk *kuklos*, circle + *stoma* (*stomatos*), mouth]

cy·clo·stome (sáikləstoum, síkləstoun) *n.* a member of *Cyclostomi*, a class of primitive and degenerate aquatic vertebrates. They are eel-like, jawless, limbless animals, and include the lamprey [fr. Gk *kuklos*, round + *stoma*, mouth]

cy·clo·style (sáikləstail, síkləstail) **1.** *n.* an apparatus for duplicating copies of writing or drawing cut on a stencil sheet by a pen with a small sharp wheel **2.** *v.t. pres. part.* **cy·clo·styl·ing** *past* and *past part.* **cy·clo·styled** to duplicate by this means [fr. Gk *kuklos*, circle + L. *stilus*, pen]

cy·clo·tron (sáiklətron, síklətron) *n.* a device used to produce and focus a beam of high-energy positive ions by subjecting them to successive accelerations in a region of constant-frequency alternating electric field. The ions are caused to move in roughly circular paths of increasing radius by the repeated passing of a constant magnetic field through the accelerating field. Particles of energy 10^8 eV can be produced in this manner, the limit being set by the relativistic mass change as the speeds of the

particles approach the speed of light (*SYNCHROTRON) [fr. Gk *kuklos*, circle + ELECTRON]

cyg·net (sígnit) *n.* a young swan [dim. of F. *cygne* or L. *cygnus*, swan]

cyl·in·der (sílindər) *n.* a solid figure traced out when a rectangle rotates using one of its sides as the axis of rotation ‖ a solid or hollow body having this form (esp. the chamber in which a piston is propelled by the expansion of steam or a gas mixture) ‖ the revolving part of a revolver, containing the cartridge chambers [fr. L. *cylindrus* fr. Gk]

cylinder press a printing press in which the paper is brought into contact with the type on a flat bed by the action of a cylinder (cf. ROTARY PRESS)

cy·lin·dri·cal (silíndrik'l) *adj.* cylinder-shaped [fr. Mod. L. *cylindricus* fr. Gk]

cyl·in·droid (sílindroid) *n.* (*math.*) a cylinder with elliptical right sections [fr. Gk *kulindros*, cylinder]

cy·ma (sáima) *pl.* **cy·mae** (sáimi:), **cy·mas** *n.* a concave line and a convex line joined to form a double curve ‖ a doucine [Mod. L. fr. Gk *kuma*, wave]

cymagraph *CYMOGRAPH

cym·bal (símb'l) *n.* (*mus.*) one of a pair of shallow brass plates clashed together to make a ringing clang **cým·bal·ist** *n.* [fr. L. *cymbalum* fr. Gk]

cyme (saim) *n.* (*bot.*) an inflorescence in which the peduncle terminates in a single flower. Other flowers grow later, on lateral shoots [F. *cym*, *cime*, summit]

cy·mo·gene (sáimədʒi:n) *n.* a gaseous product of petroleum used for producing low temperatures [fr. *cymene*, a hydrocarbon fr. Gk *kuminon*, cumin]

cy·mo·graph, cy·ma·graph (sáiməgræf, sáiməgraf) *n.* a device for tracing the outline of moldings **cy·mo·graph·ic, cy·ma·graph·ic** (saiməgrǽfik) *adj.* [fr. Gk *kuma*, wave + *graphos*, written]

cy·mose (sáimous, saimóus) *adj.* (*bot.*) of, like or derived from a cyme ‖ bearing a cyme [fr. L. *cymosus*]

Cym·ric (kímrik, símrik) *adj.* Welsh [fr. Welsh *Cymru*, Wales]

Cyn·e·wulf (kínəwulf) an Anglo-Saxon (probably Northumbrian) poet of the late 8th c. His poems are extant in two early 11th-c. manuscripts. The Exeter Book, Codex Exoniensis, includes 'Crist', 'Guthlac', 'Harrowing of Hell', 'Juliana'. The Vercelli Book, Codex Vercellensis, contains 'Andreas', 'Elene', 'Fates of the Apostles' and 'The Dream of the Rood' (which is attributed to him)

cyn·ic (sínik) **1.** *n.* someone who believes that self-interest is the motive of all human conduct ‖ (*loosely*) a habitual scoffer **Cýn·ic** (*hist.*) a member of a school of Greek philosophers (*DIOGENES) founded by Antisthenes. The Cynics taught that virtue is the only good and that it is to be won by self-control and austerity, not by social conventions **2.** *adj.* cynical **Cý·nic** of the doctrines of the Cynics **cýn·i·cal** *adj.* thinking like a cynic or revealing such thoughts **cyn·i·cism** (sínisịizəm) *n.* the quality of being cynical ‖ an expression of this quality **Cýn·i·cism** the doctrine of the Cynics [fr, L. *cynicus* fr. Gk *kynikos*, doglike]

Cy·no·sceph·a·lae, Battles of (sąinəséfəli:) two battles fought in Thessaly, Greece. In the first (364 B.C.), Alexander of Pherae as defeated by the Thebans under Pelopidas. In the second (197 B.C.) the Romans under Flaminius defeated Philip V of Macedon

cy·no·sure (sáinəʃuər, sínəʃuər) *n.* (*rhet.*) a strong center of interest and attraction [F. fr. L. fr. Gk]

cypher *CIPHER

cy·press (sáipris) *n.* a member of *Cupressus*, a genus of coniferous trees. The general habit is xerophytic, the leaves being much reduced and closely pressed to the stem. *C. funebris* is the funereal cypress of China. *C. macrocarpa* of California is planted for lumber and shade in warm countries ‖ the hard wood of these trees [O.F. *ciprès* fr. L. fr. Gk]

cypress vine *Quamoclit pennata*, fam. *Convolvulaceae*, a cultivated plant of tropical America with red or white tubular flowers

Cyp·ri·an (sípri:ən), St (c. 200–58), bishop of Carthage, one of the Latin Fathers of the Church, and a martyr. Feast: Sept. 16

cyp·ri·noid (síprinoid, sipráinoid) *adj.* of, like, or relating to a carp [fr. Gk *kuprinos*, carp]

Cyp·ri·ot (sípri:ət) **1.** *adj.* of or relating to Cyprus or an inhabitant or the language of Cyprus **2.** *n.* an inhabitant or the language of Cyprus

Cyp·ri·ote (sípri:out, sípri:ət) *adj.* and *n.* Cypriot

cy·pro·hep·ta·dine $[C_{21}H_{21}N]$ (saiprəhéptadi:n) *n.* (*pharm.*) antihistamine and antiserotonim used to relieve itching; marketed as Periactin

cy·pro·ter·one $[C_{22}H_{27}ClO_3]$ (saiprótəroun) *n.* (*pharm.*) synthetic steroid drug used to inhibit male-hormone secretions

Cy·prus (sáiprəs) an island (area 3,572 sq. miles, pop. 662,000) in the E. Mediterranean. It is a republic. Capital: Nicosia. Nationalities and religion: 80% Greeks (Orthodox), 18% Turks (Moslem). Languages: Greek and Turkish, English. The land is 47% arable and 19% forest. The central plain (Messaoria) lies between the Kyrenia Mtns to the north and the Olympus Mtns (Mt Troodos 6,406 ft, snow-capped in winter) in the southwest. Winters are mild, summers are hot and dry in the Messaoria, damp along the coast. Rainfall (chiefly in winter): 14 ins in the Messaoria, 40 ins in the mountains. Mean annual temperature: 69° F. Livestock: sheep, goats. Exports: copper, iron pyrites, oranges, wine, grapes, olives. Other products: cereals, vegetables, asbestos, chromite, gypsum. Imports: metals, manufactured goods, vehicles, fuel oils, meat. Port: Famagusta. Monetary unit: pound (1,000 mils). HISTORY. Cyprus was colonized by the Greeks and fell to the Phoenicians (9th c. B.C.), Assyrians (704 B.C.), Egyptians (560 and 323 B.C.), Persians (525 B.C.), and Macedonians (333 B.C.). It was annexed as a Roman province (58 B.C.) and became part of the Byzantine Empire (395 A.D.). It was frequently attacked by Arabs (7th–10th cc.), was captured by Richard I of England (1191), who sold it to the Lusignan dynasty of Jerusalem (1192). It passed to the Venetian republic (1489), was captured by the Turks (1571), ceded by Turkey to Britain for administration (1878), annexed by Britain on the outbreak of war with Turkey (1914) and became a British Crown Colony (1925). Cyprus was an important Middle East base for the British in the 2nd world war and the postwar period. Archbishop Makarios, who advocated union with Greece, led a struggle for independence (1954–60). Bitter conflicts also took place (1958) between Turkish and Greek Cypriot communities. After agreement had been reached (1959) in London, Cyprus became an independent republic (Aug. 16, 1960) and a member of the British Commonwealth (1961). Fighting began again (1963) between Greeks and Turks, and a U.N. force was sent (1964) to the island. Turkish forces invaded Cyprus (1974), fearing that Greece was preparing to annex it. The island was forcibly partitioned (1975) as a result, with the Greek zone (Republic of Cyprus) led from 1977 by Pres. Spyros Kyprianou, and the Turkish zone under Rauf Denktash declaring itself the Turkish Republic of Northern Cyprus (1983)

cyp·se·la (sípsələ) *pl.* **cyp·se·lae** (sípsəli:) *n.* an achene formed by the fusion of an inferior bicarpellary ovary within the calyx tube, e.g. in composites [Mod. L. fr. Gk *kupselē*, hollow vessel]

Cyr·e·na·ic (sị·rənéiik, sạirənéiik) *n.* a member of the hedonistic school of philosophy founded by Aristippus of Cyrene [fr. L. *Cyrenaicus* fr. Gk fr. **Kurēnē**, Cyrene]

Cyr·e·na·i·ca (sịrənéiikə, sạirənéiikə) the eastern region of Libya. Chief town: Benghazi. Originally Berber territory, it was captured by Arabs in 643 A.D. and passed successively into Turkish (1517) and Italian (1912) hands. It became (1951) part of the newly created kingdom of Libya

Cy·re·ne (sairí:ni:) an ancient Greek city and colony founded in N. Africa, to the west of Egypt. It was annexed (96 B.C.) by the Romans. Important ruins (agora, Temple of Apollo, baths)

Cy·ril (síral), St, of Alexandria (c. 376–444), champion of orthodoxy against Nestorianism. Feast: Jan. 28

Cyril, St, of Jerusalem (c. 315–86), bishop and theologian, one of the Greek Fathers of the Church. Feast: Mar. 18

Cyril and Me·tho·di·us (məθóudi:əs), Sts, brothers from Salonica, the apostles of the Slavs in the 9th c. Feast: Mar. 9

Cy·ril·lic (sirílik) *adj.* of or relating to the Slav alphabet from which Russian, Bulgarian and

---

CONCISE PRONUNCIATION KEY: **(a)** æ, c*a*t; ɑ, c*a*r; ɔ f*aw*n; ei, sn*a*ke. **(e)** e, h*e*n; i:, sh*ee*p; iə, d*ee*r; ɛə, b*ea*r. **(i)** i, f*i*sh; ai, t*i*ger; ə:, b*i*rd. **(o)** o, *o*x; au, c*ow*; ou, g*oa*t; u, p*oo*r; ɔi, r*oy*al. **(u)** ʌ, d*u*ck; u, b*u*ll; u:, g*oo*se; ə, b*a*cillus; ju:, c*u*be. x, lo*ch*; θ, *th*ink; ð, bo*th*er; z, *Z*en; ʒ, corsa*g*e; dʒ, sava*g*e; ŋ, oranguta*ng*; j, *y*ak; ʃ, *fi*sh; tʃ, fe*tch*; 'l, rabb*le*; 'n, redd*en*. Complete pronunciation key appears inside front cover.

Serbian derive [after St *Cyril*, apostle of the Slavs]

Cy·rus (sáirəs) *KURA

Cyrus II 'the Great' (c. 600–529 B.C.), king of Persia (c. 550–529 B.C.), founder of the Achaemenid dynasty. He defeated Croesus of Lydia (546 B.C.) and conquered Babylonia (539 B.C.) and Syria

Cyrus 'the Younger' (c. 424–401 B.C.), son of Darius II. He revolted unsuccessfully against his brother Artaxerxes II

cyst (sist) *n.* (*med.*) a sac containing fluid or semifluid morbid matter or parasitic larvae etc. ‖ a nonliving membrane enclosing a cell or cells ‖ (*biol.*) a hollow organ or cavity containing a liquid secretion [fr. Mod. L. *cystis* fr. Gk *kustis*, bladder]

cys·ta·mine [$C_4H_{12}N_2S_2$] (sístəmi:n) *n.* (*pharm.*) drug formed from distilled cystice used to mitigate radiation sickness

cyst·ic (sístik) *adj.* of or like a cyst ‖ relating to the gallbladder or urinary bladder [F. *cystique*]

cys·ti·cer·cus (sistisə́:rkəs) *pl.* **cys·ti·cer·ci** (sistisə́:rsai) *n.* a tapeworm larva possessing a well-developed bladder, with one colex [Mod. L. fr. Gk *kustis*, bladder + *kerkos*, tail]

cystic fibrosis a congenital, chronic disease of the mucous glands which affects the pancreas and causes digestive and pulmonary disorders

cys·tine (sísti:n, sístin) *n.* an amino acid indispensable in the diet of animals [fr. Gk *kustis*, bladder]

cys·ti·tis (sistáitis) *n.* inflammation of the bladder [fr. Gk *kustis*, bladder]

cys·to·cele (sístəsi:l) *n.* a prolapse of the urinary bladder into the vagina [fr. Gk *kustis*, bladder + *kēlē*, tumor]

cyst·oid (sístɔid) **1.** *adj.* like a bladder **2.** *n.* a mass like a cyst but without a membrane

Cyth·er·a (síθərə, siθíərə) (Kythera, Cerigo) a Greek island (area 110 sq. miles, pop. 10,000) off the Peloponnese, formerly famous for its cult of Aphrodite

Cyth·er·e·a (siθərí:ə) one of the names under which Aphrodite was worshipped [after Cythera, her supposed birthplace]

cy·to·blast (sáitəblæst) *n.* a cell nucleus [fr. Gk *kutos*, cell + *blastos*, germ]

cy·to·chrome (sáitəkroum) *n.* (*biochem.*) a chromoprotein essential for oxidation-reduction processes in plant and animal cells [fr. Gk *kutos*, cell + *chrōma*, color]

cy·to·dif·fer·en·ti·a·tion (saitədifərentʃi:éiʃən) *n.* (*genetics*) development of specialized cells from ordinary cells

cy·to·e·col·o·gy (saitouikólədʒi:) *n.* study of single cells in their environment — **cytoecological** *adj.*

cy·to·ge·net·ics (saitoudʒənétiks) *n.* the cytological aspect of genetics [fr. Gk *kutos*, cell + GENETICS]

cytogenics the branch of genetics that deals with changes in chromosomes

cy·to·ki·nin (saitəkáinin) *n.* plant hormone affecting distribution of root and stem cells

cy·to·log·i·cal (saitlódʒik'l) *adj.* of or relating to cytology

cy·tol·o·gist (saitólədʒis) *n.* someone specializing in cytology

cy·tol·o·gy (saitólədʒi:) *n.* the branch of biology concerned with the structure, function and life history of cells [fr. Gk *kutos*, cell + *logos*, discourse]

cy·to·meg·a·lic (saitəməgǽlik) *adj.* of enlarged cells

cy·to·meg·a·lo·vi·rus (saitəmegɑləváirus) *n.* (*med.*) virus that causes cell enlargement resulting in diseases of brain, kidneys, liver, lung, and salivary glands, esp. in newborn infants

cy·to·plasm (sáitəplæzəm) *n.* that part of the protoplasm of any living cell outside the nucleus (cf. NUCLEOPLASM) **cy·to·plás·mic** *adj.* [fr. Gk *kutos*, cell + PLASM]

cy·to·plast (sáitəplæst) *n.* the unit of protoplasm contained in a cell **cy·to·plás·tic** *adj.* [fr. Gk *kutos*, cell + *plastos*, formed]

cy·to·sine (sáitəsi:n, sáitəzi:n, saitəsin) *n.* a crystalline pyrimidine base ($C_4H_5N_3O$) obtained by the hydrolysis of deoxyribonucleic acid [after G. *zytosin*]

cy·to·skel·e·ton (saitəskélətən) *n.* hypothetical framework to account for the orderliness of biochemical processes in the cell, conceived by biochemist R. A. Peters

cy·to·stat·ic (saitəstǽtik) *n.* a cell-activity retardant — **cytostatic** *adj.* — **cytostatically** *adv.*

cy·to·tech·nol·o·gist or **cytotech** (saitəteknólədʒist) *n.* cell identification technician, e.g., of malignant cells

cy·to·vi·rin (saitəváirin) *n.* a bacteria produced compound used to combat some plant viruses, e.g., tobacco mosaic

C.Z. Canal Zone

czar, tsar, tzar (zɑr, tsɑr) *n.* (*hist.*) the emperor of Russia [Russ. fr. L. *Caesar*]

czar·e·vitch, tsar·e·vitch (zɑ́rəvitʃ, tsɑ́rəvitʃ) *n.* (*hist.*) the son of a czar [Russ.]

cza·rev·na, tsa·rev·na (zɑrévnə, tsɑrévnə) *n.* (*hist.*) the daughter of a czar [Russ.]

cza·ri·na, tsa·ri·na (zɑríːnə, tsɑríːnə) *n.* (*hist.*) the wife of a czar [fr. G. *czarin* fr. *czar*]

czar·ism, tsar·ism (zɑ́rizəm, tsɑ́rizəm) *n.* the autocratic rule of the czars

Czech (tʃek) **1.** *n.* a native of Bohemia, Moravia or Silesia ‖ the West Slavic language of the Czechs **2.** *adj.* of or pertaining to the Czechs or their language

Czech·o·slo·vak (tʃékəslóuvæk, tʃékəslóuvɑk) **1.** *n.* a native of Czechoslovakia ‖ the West Slavic language of the Czechoslovaks **2.** *adj.* of or pertaining to the Czechoslovaks or their language

Czech·o·slo·va·ki·a (tʃekəsləvɑ́ki:ə, tʃekəsləvǽki:ə) a federal republic (area 49,366 sq. miles, pop. 15,500,000) in central Europe. Capital: Prague. People: 68% Czech, 28% Slovak, with small Magyar, German, Polish, Ukrainian and Russian minorities. Languages: Czech (66%), Slovak (28%), Hungarian (3%). Religion: mainly Roman Catholic, 10% Protestant minority, small Orthodox and Jewish minorities. The land is 43% cultivated, 16% pasture and 32% forest. The Bohemian plateau in the west drains to the North Sea and is surrounded by mountain ranges. It is separated from the Moravian depression by a low unproductive divide. In the east the folded ranges of the Carpathians drain to the Black Sea. Annual rainfall: 20 ins in W. Bohemia, 50 ins in the Carpathians. Average temperature in Prague (F.): 30° (Jan.), 67° (July). Agriculture is very largely carried out in cooperatives and collective farms. Livestock: cattle, pigs, poultry. Agricultural products: cereals, potatoes, sugar beet, hops. The timber industry is important. Minerals: coal, iron, graphite, silver, copper, lead, salt, aluminum, uranium, radium, kaolin, oil (refined at Bratislava, which is connected by pipeline to Brody, near Kiev). Industry was nationalized in 1948. Manufactures: rolled-steel and engineering products, textiles, paper, fertilizers, cement, shoes, beer, electricity, glass and porcelain, musical instruments, jewelery. Exports: machinery, manufactures. Imports: iron ore, cotton, wool, oil. There are four universities, the oldest at Prague (1348). Monetary unit: koruna (divided into 100 haler). HISTORY. Czechoslovakia was created out of the dual monarchy of Austria-Hungary from the old Slav kingdoms of Bohemia, Moravia and Slovakia (1918) under the leadership of T. G. Masaryk and Eduard Beneš. Sudetenland was annexed to Germany after the Munich conference (1938). Germany invaded and created the protectorate of Bohemia and Moravia (1939–45), and the independent states of Slovakia and Ruthenia. An underground resistance movement was organized. The republic was recreated and divided into the three provinces of Bohemia, Moravia with Silesia, and Slovakia, after liberation by the U.S.S.R. (1945). The Communists gained control (1948) and drew up a new constitution for a people's republic, the provinces being replaced by administrative regions (1949). A new constitution was promulgated establishing a socialist republic (1960). About one million Warsaw Pact troops, largely from the U.S.S.R., invaded (Aug. 1968) to put an end to the growing liberalization of the regime, and the country remained occupied. Czechoslovakia became (Jan. 1, 1969) a federation of the Czech states (Bohemia and Moravia) and Slovakia. A dissident group known as the Charter 77 movement was founded (1977) to protest the suppression of human rights and it continued to function during the 1980s as an unofficial political opposition in Czechoslovakia

Cze·sto·cho·wa (tʃestɔxóvɑ) a rail center (pop. 237,700) on the upper Warta, S. Poland: textiles. It is a great pilgrimage center, for its miraculous image of the Virgin Mary

CONCISE PRONUNCIATION KEY: (a) æ, c*a*t; ɑ, c*a*r; ɔ f*aw*n; ei, sn*a*ke. **(e)** e, h*e*n; i:, sh*ee*p; iə, d*ee*r; ɛə, b*ea*r. **(i)** i, f*i*sh; ai, t*i*ger; ə:, b*i*rd. **(o)** o, *o*x; au, c*ow*; ou, g*oa*t; u, p*oo*r; ɔi, r*oy*al. **(u)** ʌ, d*u*ck; u, b*u*ll; u:, g*oo*se; ə, b*a*cill*u*s; ju:, c*u*be. x, lo*ch*; θ, *th*ink; ð, *b*other; z, *Z*en; ʒ, cor*s*age; dʒ, sava*g*e; ŋ, oranguta*n*g; j, *y*ak; ʃ, *f*ish; tʃ, fe*tch*; 'l, rab*ble*; 'n, redd*en*. Complete pronunciation key appears inside front cover.

D

	EARLY NORTH SEMITIC	PHOENICIAN	EARLY HEBREW	EARLY GREEK	CLASSICAL GREEK	EARLY ETRUSCAN	EARLY LATIN	CLASSICAL LATIN
	△	◁	◁	△	△	◁	◐	D

	CURSIVE MAJUSCULE (ROMAN)	CURSIVE MINUSCULE (ROMAN)	ANGLO-IRISH MAJUSCULE	CAROLINE MINUSCULE	VENETIAN MINUSCULE (ITALIC)	N. ITALIAN MINUSCULE (ROMAN)
	ꝺ	ꝺ	δ	d	ꝺ	d

A. C. SYLVESTER, CAMBRIDGE, ENGLAND

Development of the letter D, beginning with the early North Semitic letter. Evolution of both the majuscule, or capital, letter D and the minuscule, or lowercase, letter d are shown.

D, d (di:) the fourth letter of the English alphabet ‖ (*mus.*) a note and the key of which it is the tonic ‖ the sign for an English penny or pennies (*abbr.* of Latin denarius) **D** a buckle on military equipment or other D-shaped metal fastening ‖ the symbol for the Roman number 500 ‖ **D** day

'd colloquial elision of 'had' and 'would' as auxiliaries (I'd=I had or I would)

D.A. District Attorney

dab (dæb) 1. *adj.* (*Br., pop.*) adept, expert at doing practical things, esp. (*Br.*) *a dab hand* (*a skillful person*) 2. *n.* (*Br.*) such a person [origin unknown]

dab *n.* the common name for any small flatfish, esp. the European *Limanda limanda* and the North American *L. ferruginea* [origin unknown]

dab 1. *v. pres. part.* **dab·bing** *past* and *past part.* **dabbed** *v.t.* to touch lightly and quickly, *to dab a stain with a wet cloth* ‖ to apply (a substance) by light strokes, *to dab antiseptic on a wound* ‖ *v.i.* to make a weak, ineffective striking movement 2. *n.* a light, quick blow ‖ an applying of light, gentle pressure, esp. with a damp cloth, sponge, brush etc., the material dabbed on a surface, *a dab of paint* [prob. imit.]

dab·ble (dæb'l) *pres. part.* **dab·bling** *past* and *past part.* **dab·bled** *v.t.* to splash about, *to dabble one's toes in water* ‖ *v.i.* to take up a pursuit without serious and consistent effort, *to dabble in politics* **dáb·bler** *n.* a person who takes only superficial interest in some subject, a dilettante [prob. imit.]

dab·chick (dæbtʃik) *n. Podiceps novae-hollandiae*, the smallest grebe, a water bird noted for its diving ‖ *Podilymbus podiceps*, a medium-sized grebe whose whitish bill has a black band around it

dab·ster (dæbstər) *n.* a dabbler

Dac·ca (dækə) the capital (pop. 3,000,000) of Bangladesh on the Ganges delta: rice, jute and hide processing. University (1921)

dace (deis) *pl.* **dace, dac·es** *n. Leuciscus leuciscus*, fam. *Cyprinidae*, a European freshwater fish rarely exceeding 1 lb. in weight ‖ any of various other freshwater fish of fam. *Cyprinidae* [fr. O.F. *dars*, dart]

da·cha (dákə) *n.* in U.S.S.R., a country home, symbol of privileged class

Da·chau (dáxau) a town (pop. 34,100) in Bavaria, West Germany, 11 miles northwest of Munich. It was the site of a Nazi concentration camp (1933–45)

dachs·hund (dækshund) *n.* a small dog of a breed with a long body, long ears, very short legs and a smooth or long-haired bronze (or black and bronze) coat [G.=badger dog]

Da·cia (déiʃə) an ancient region of S.E. Europe, corresponding to Rumania and Transylvania, conquered (c. 106) by the Romans under Trajan

da·coit (dəkɔ́it) *n.* a member of an Indian or Burmese gang of armed robbers [Hindi *dakait* fr. *dākā* gang robbery]

da·coit·y (dəkɔ́iti:) *pl.* **da·coit·ies** *n.* armed robbery by dacoits [Hindi *dakaitī*]

Da·cron (déikrɒn, dækrɒn, déikrən, dækrən) *n.* a strong synthetic fiber that does not wrinkle easily [Trademark]

dac·tyl (dæktil) *n.* a metrical foot of one heavy and two light beats (— ◡ ◡) [fr. L. *dactylus* fr. Gk *daktulos*, a finger, dactyl]

dac·tyl·ic (dæktílik) 1. *adj.* written in dactyls 2. *n.* a line written in dactyls [fr. L. *dactylicus* fr. Gk]

dad (dæd) *n.* (*pop.*) father

da·da (dáda) *n.* an antibourgeois movement in art and literature which spread through Europe after the 1st world war. It carried rejection of traditional moral and esthetic values to the point of nihilism and absurdity, but its advocation of freedom and spontaneity in artistic creation opened the way for new modes of expression, esp. for surrealism. Originated by Tzara in 1916 at Zürich, it was put forward by Arp, Breton, Aragon, Ernst, Duchamp, Picabia, Schwitters and others **dá·da·ism** *n.* [fr. F. *dada*, child's word for a hobbyhorse, or (*pop.*) a boring pet topic]

dad·cap (dádkap) *n.* (*mil. acronym*) for dawn and dusk combat air patrol

dad·dy (dædi:) *pl.* **dad·dies** *n.* (children's word for) father ‖ (*pop.*) a sugar daddy

daddy long·legs (lɔ́ŋlegz, lɔ́ŋlegz) *pl.* **daddy long·legs** the harvestman (arachnid) ‖ (*Br.*) the crane fly

da·do (déidou) *pl.* **da·does, da·dos** *n.* (*archit.*) the smooth-faced rectangular block of a pedestal between its base and cornice ‖ the lower part of an interior wall painted or faced differently from the upper part ‖ a decorated border below (or in place of) the picture rail [Ital.=die, cube]

Da·dra and Na·gar Ha·ve·li (dʌ́dra, nágərhə·véli:) a Union territory (area 189 sq. miles, pop. 74,170) of India, formerly two Portuguese territories

Daed·a·lus (déd'ləs, *Br.* esp. dí:d'ləs) (*Gk mythol.*) a craftsman who built the labyrinth of Crete for the Minotaur, and who made wings for himself and his son, Icarus

dae·mon (dí:mən) *n.* a supernatural being or force not specifically evil ‖ a demon (indwelling compulsive force) **dae·mon·ic** (dimɔ́nik) *adj.* [L.]

daf·fo·dil (dæfədil) *n. Narcissus pseudo-narcissus*, fam. *Amaryllidaceae*, a species of narcissus with a large bell-shaped corona growing from the perianth, cultivated for its ornamental yellow flowers [older *affodill* fr. L. fr. Gk *asphodelus* (initial *d* is unexplained)]

daf·fy (dæfi:) *adj.* silly, weak in the head [obs. *daff*, simpleton, rel. to DAFT]

daft (dæft, dɑft) *adj.* (*pop.*) foolish, crazy [M.E *daffte*=O.E. *gedæfte*, mild, gentle]

da Gama *GAMA

dag·ger (dægər) *n.* a short, knifelike weapon for stabbing, with a sharp-edged, pointed blade ‖ (*printing*, symbol [†]) a reference mark **at daggers drawn** on the point of an open quarrel ‖ **to look daggers** to look murderously angry [etym. doubtful]

Da·ghe·stan A.S.S.R., Da·ge·stan A.S.S.R. (dɒgistán) an autonomous republic (area 13,124 sq. miles, pop. 1,627,000) of the R.S.F.S.R., U.S.S.R. in W. Caucasia, inhabited by many mall Caucasian tribes. Capital: Makhachkala

dag·lock (dæglɒk) *n.* a long lock of hair on a sheep or dog, clotted with mud etc.

Dag·o·bert I (dægəbə:rt) (c. 600–39), Merovingian king of the Franks (628–39)

Da·guerre (dæger), Louis Jacques Mandé (1787–1851), French inventor. After collaborating with Niepce he devised the first practicable photographic process (1838). A polished layer of silver (on a copper plate) was exposed to iodine vapor, which formed a layer of light-sensitive silver iodide. The plate was exposed to light in a camera and then developed with mercury vapor, which formed a white amalgam with the liberated silver. The image was then fixed with sodium thiosulfate, which removed undeveloped silver iodide to give a unique positive

da·guerre·o·type (dəgérətaip, dəgéri:ətaip) *n.* the photographic process invented by Daguerre ‖ a photograph made by this process

dah (dɑ) *n.* a term of endearment for a true love

Dahl·gren (dælgrən), John Adolphus Bernard (1809–70), U.S. admiral. As commander of the South Atlantic Blockading Squadron during the Civil War, he cooperated in the capture of Savannah and Charleston

dahl·ia (dæljə, dúljə, *Br.* esp. déiljə) *n.* a member of *Dahlia*, fam. *Compositae*, a genus of perennial plants with tuberous roots and ornamental rayed flower heads [after Anders *Dahl*, Swedish botanist]

Da·ho·man (dəhóumən) 1. *adj.* of or belonging to an inhabitant of Dahomey ‖ pertaining to Dahomey 2. *n.* an inhabitant of Dahomey

Da·ho·mey *BENIN

CONCISE PRONUNCIATION KEY: **(a)** æ, c*a*t; ɑ, c*a*r; ɔ f*a*wn; ei, sn*a*ke. **(e)** e, h*e*n; i:, sh*ee*p; iə, d*ee*r; ɛə, b*ea*r. **(i)** i, f*i*sh; ai, t*i*ger; ə:, b*i*rd. **(o)** o, *o*x; au, c*o*w; ou, g*oa*t; u, p*oo*r; ɔi, r*oy*al. **(u)** ʌ, d*u*ck; u, b*u*ll; u:, g*oo*se; ə, b*a*cillus; ju:, c*u*be. x, lo*ch*; θ, *th*ink; ð, bo*th*er; z, *Z*en; ʒ, corsa*g*e; dʒ, sava*g*e; ŋ, oranguta*ng*; j, *y*ak; ʃ, *f*ish; tʃ, fe*tch*; 'l, rabb*le*; 'n, redd*en*. Complete pronunciation key appears inside front cover.

Dáil Eir·eann (dailéərən) the lower house in the legislature of the Irish Republic, elected by proportional representation [Irish=assembly of Ireland]

dai·ly (déili:) 1. *adj.* happening or recurring every day 2. *adv.* every day 3. *pl.* **dai·lies** *n.* a newspaper appearing every weekday ‖ (*Br.*) a charwoman who comes in each day to do housework [O.E. *dæglic*]

dai·mon (dáimoun) *n.* a demon (an indwelling force) [Gk]

dain·ty (déinti) 1. *pl.* **dain·ties** *n.* a delicacy 2. *comp.* **dain·ti·er** *superl.* **dain·ti·est** *adj.* small and pretty, delicate ‖ (*rhet.*) choice, fine, *a dainty morsel* [O.F. *deintié, dainté*]

Dai·ren (dairén) *TALIEN

dair·y (déəri) *pl.* **dair·ies** *n.* the part of a farm given over to milk, cream, butter, cheese etc. ‖ a shop where milk, butter and cream etc. are sold [M.E. *deierie* fr. *deie*, female servant]

dairy cattle cows reared for milk rather than meat

dairy farm a farm specializing in dairy produce

dair·y·man (déəri:mən) *pl.* **dair·y·men** (déəri:mən) *n.* a man who works in a dairy ‖ a person who owns a dairy farm

dairy produce milk, butter, cream, cheese, eggs

da·is (déiis, dáiis) *pl.* **da·is·es** *n.* a raised platform in a hall or large room, e.g. for a lecturer's desk [O.F. *deis*, a high table]

dai·sy (déizi) *pl.* **dai·sies** *n.* any of several composite plants having flower heads that consist of a whorl or several whorls of ray florets, e.g. *Bellis perennis*, the common small field flower with small white or pink ray florets, and the oxeye daisy [O.E. *dægeséage*, day's eye]

daisy chain a necklace of linked daisies

dai·sy-wheel printer (déizi:wi:l) (*computer*) printout device surrounding a plastic hub on which radial spokes, each containing a character, are affixed. The wheel rotates to the required character and moves horizontally to the required space, with the character then striking an inked ribbon

Da·kar (dækɑr) the capital (pop. 850,000) of Senegal, on Cape Verde peninsula, the country's main port, trading and industrial center, also serving Mali. International airport. University (1957)

Da·ko·ta (dəkóutə) *n.* a former territory of the U.S.A. (*NORTH DAKOTA, *SOUTH DAKOTA) ‖ a Siouan Indian people inhabiting the northern plains of the U.S.A. ‖ a member of this people ‖ their language

Da·la·dier (dælædjei) Edouard (1884–1970), French radical socialist politician. As premier of France (1938–40), he signed the Munich Agreement (1938)

Da·lai La·ma (dálailámə) the Grand Lama, head of Tibetan Lamaism. Chosen by oracular revelation when a boy, he is regarded in Tibet and in some other parts of China and in Mongolia as the vice-regent of the Buddha and the reincarnation of the previous Dalai Lama. The Potala palace at Lhasa was the official residence until the present (14th) Dalai Lama fled to India (1959) after the Chinese infiltration of Tibet (1950)

dal·a·pon, 2.2 [C₄H₄Cl₂O₂] (dæləppn) *n.* (*chem.*) water-soluble herbicide used esp. against crabgrass and other monocotyledonous plants *also* dichloropropionic acid

da·la·si (dɒlɒsi:) *n.* monetary unit of Gambia, equal to 100 butut or ¼ pound

dale (deil) *n.* (*rhet.*) a valley [O.E. *dæl*]

Dal·e·car·li·a (dæləkárliə) (*Swed.* Dalarna), a region of mountains and hills in central Sweden

dales·man (déilzmən) *pl.* **dales·men** (déilzmən) *n.* (*Br.*) an inhabitant of the Dales, a hilly district in parts of Yorkshire, Cumberland, Westmorland and Derbyshire

Dal·hou·sie (dælháuzi) James Andrew Broun Ramsay, 1st marquis of (1812–60), British governor-general of India (1848–56). He annexed the Punjab, Oudh and Pegu (Burma), improved communications and reformed the administration of India

Daley, (défli:) Richard J. (1902–76), U.S. politician, Democratic mayor of Chicago (1955–76). The last of the political bosses, he ran Chicago with a tight hand and drew national attention for his methods of handling anti-Vietnam War riots during the Democratic Convention in 1968

Da·li (dáli:), Salvador (1904–), Spanish painter, associated with surrealism. He paints fantastic dream images in a style of trompe l'œil realism

Dal·las (dæləs), Alexander James (1759–1817), U.S. financier. As secretary of the treasury (1814–16) under President James Madison, he influenced the establishment of the Second Bank of the U.S.A. and the enactment of the Tariff Act of 1816

Dallas, George Mifflin (1792–1864), U.S. statesman and vice-president under James Polk. He was responsible for the Dallas-Clarendon Convention (1856), called to resolve Central American difficulties. He secured from Great Britain a disavowal of the right of search

Dallas a city and river port (pop. 904,078 with agglom. 2,974,878) in N. Texas, a leading cotton market and oil center, manufacturing machinery

Dallas-Clarendon Treaty a Treaty (1856) signed between George Mifflin Dallas and Lord Clarendon (1800–70), British foreign secretary, which reversed the decision (1853) of John M. Clayton and recognized the British Territory of Honduras

dalles (dælz) *pl. n.* rapids flowing over a flat bottom in a narrow part of a river [F. *dalle*, a slab of stone]

dal·li·ance (dæliəns, dæljəns) *n.* (*rhet.*) amorous byplay ‖ (*rhet.*) frivolous spending of time [fr. DALLY]

dal·ly (dæli) *pres. part.* **dal·ly·ing** *past* and *past part.* **dal·lied** *v.i.* to waste time ‖ to loiter ‖ to toy, play [O.F. *dalier*, to chat]

Dal·ma·tia (dælméiʃə) a region of Croatia, Yugoslavia, extending along the Adriatic from Žadar to Montenegro. Its coast and islands attract many tourists. Dalmatia was conquered by the Romans (12 A.D.), the Goths and Avars (6th c.), Slavs (7th c.) and Byzantines (11th c.). Venice controlled its coast (1420–1797). An Austrian crown land and titular kingdom (1815–1918), it became (1918) part of the kingdom later called Yugoslavia

Dal·ma·tian (dælméiʃən) *n.* an inhabitant of Dalmatia ‖ an extinct Romance language that was spoken on the Dalmatian coast and some Adriatic islands ‖ a large dog of a breed with a white coat spotted black

dal·mat·ic (dælmætik) *n.* (*eccles.*) a sleeved liturgical vestment worn by officiating deacons and bishops ‖ a similar robe worn by kings at their coronation [fr. L. *dalmatica* (*vestis*), a Dalmatian robe]

Dal·ton (dɔ́ltən), John (1766–1844), English scientist. He developed atomic theory, and formulated the law of partial pressures for gases (*DALTON'S LAW). He was the first to describe color blindness accurately (*DALTONISM)

dal·ton·ism (dɔ́ltənizəm) *n.* color blindness, esp. the inability to distinguish between red and green [after John *Dalton*]

Dalton's Law (*phys.*) the statement that the total pressure of a mixture of gases which do not combine chemically is the sum of their partial pressures. The partial pressure is that pressure which each gas would exert if it alone occupied the volume of the mixture, at the same temperature. Thus each gas in a mixture exerts its own pressure, independently of the others [after John *Dalton*]

dam (dæm) 1. *n.* a barrier constructed to hold back a flow of water in order to raise its level ‖ a reservoir of water held back by such a barrier (and used for controlling navigation, supplying towns and villages, irrigating the land, or producing electrical energy) ‖ (*dentistry*) a rubber guard to keep a tooth dry during an operation 2. *v.t. pres. part.* **dam·ming** *past* and *past part.* **dammed** to hold back (water) by constructing a dam **to dam up** to obstruct as though by a dam [M.E. *damm*, of Gmc origin]

dam *n.* (only of animals) a female parent [var. of DAME]

dam·age (dæmidʒ) 1. *v. pres. part.* **dam·ag·ing** *past* and *past part.* **dam·aged** *v.t.* to injure physically (usually objects) ‖ *v.i.* to incur damage, *china damages easily* 2. *n.* injury or harm ‖ (*pl., law*) a money compensation for harm sustained **dám·age·a·ble** *adj.* [O.F. *damagier, damager*]

Dam·an (dəmán) *GOA

Da·man·hur (dæmænhúər) a town (pop. 124,000) in lower Egypt, capital of Beheira province: textiles

Dam·a·scene (dæməsi:n, dæməsi:n) *adj.* pertaining to Damascus or an inhabitant of Damascus

dam·a·scene (dæməsi:n, dæməsi:n) 1. *v.t. pres. part.* **dam·a·scen·ing** *past* and *past part.* **dam·a·scened** to ornament (steel) with a surface pattern made by special welding of steel and iron ‖ to ornament (metal) with an inlaid pattern of gold or silver 2. *adj.* pertaining to these arts [fr. L. *Damascenus*, of Damascus, where the art of damascening steel originated]

Da·mas·cus (dəmǽskəs) the capital (pop. 1,156,000) of Syria, continuously inhabited since before 1000 B.C., a commercial center in the Ghuta oasis, on the main route to Iraq and Iran. Traditional products: brass and copper ware, silks, carpets, carving. Manufactures: textiles, glass, cement. Under Roman rule (63 B.C.–635 A.D.), it was evangelized by St Paul. It was the capital of the Umayyad caliphate (661–750), and was under Ottoman rule (1516–1918). Great Mosque (8th c.). University (1924)

Damascus steel steel with a wavy pattern on its surface, produced by the forging together of steel and iron

dam·ask (dæməsk) 1. *n.* a figured fabric of silk or linen with the pattern woven into it, used esp. for table linen, curtains etc. ‖ Damascus steel 2. *adj.* of the color of a damask rose ‖ made of damask linen or silk ‖ made of Damascus steel 3. *v.t.* to damascene ‖ to weave into (a fabric) ornamental patterns which are picked out by the play of light [after *Damascus*]

Da·mas·ki·nos (ðaməskinɔs), Papandreou (1891–1949), Greek archbishop and politician, a resistance leader during the German occupation (1941–4) and regent (1944–6)

damask rose *Rosa damascena*, a rose widely cultivated for attar of roses in Eastern countries

Dam·a·sus I (dæməsəs), St (c. 305–84), pope (366–84). He encouraged St Jerome to produce the Vulgate

dame (deim) *n.* (*Br.*) the title of a woman who has received an order of knighthood, used before the Christian name ‖ (*Br., pantomime*) a comic female role traditionally played by a male actor [O.F.]

Damian, St *COSMAS AND DAMIAN

Damian, St Peter *PETER DAMIAN

Dam·i·et·ta (dæmi:étə) a port (pop. 113,200) of Lower Egypt on the eastern Nile delta. It was a Saracen fortress during the Crusades

DAMIT (acronym) for Data Analysis Massachusetts Institute of Technology, a computer program for analyzing data by recreating test runs; used by Kansas City Air Defense Sector

damn (dæm) 1. *v.t.* to condemn, *to damn a play* ‖ to bring ruin upon, *to damn someone's chances* ‖ to condemn to eternal punishment ‖ to curse **to damn with faint praise** to express such tepid or qualified approval of (someone or something) as to suggest that there is much more to condemn 2. *n.* 'damn' said as a curse **not worth a damn** worthless **not to give a damn** not to care 3. *adv.* damned [O.F. *damner*]

dam·na·ble (dæmnəb'l) *adj.* deserving condemnation ‖ detestable ‖ annoying

dam·na·tion (dæmnéiʃən) 1. *n.* (*theol.*) a condemning or being condemned to eternal punishment ‖ a complete critical condemnation (of a play etc.) 2. *interj.* an expression of annoyance [F.]

dam·na·to·ry (dæmnətɔri:, dæmnətouri:) *adj.* expressing or conveying condemnation or disapproval ‖ causing condemnation [fr. L. *damnatorius*]

damned (dæmd) 1. *adj.* doomed ‖ condemned to eternal punish (pop.) confounded, tiresome 2. *n.* **the damned** (*theol.*) those condemned to everlasting punishment 3. *adv.* (pop.) very, extremely, *damned difficult* **dámned·est** *n.* (in phrases) **to try one's damnedest** to try as hard as one can **to do one's damnedest** to stop at nothing

damn·ing (dæmiŋ) *adj.* strongly implying or proving guilt, *damning evidence*

Dam·o·cles (dæməkli:z) a courtier (5th c. B.C.) of Dionysius I. Dionysius invited him to a feast and seated him under a sword suspended by a hair. Damocles had excessively praised the tyrant's lot, and Dionysius meant him to see how precarious it was

damp (dæmp) 1. *n.* moisture in a permeable object, esp. a fabric ‖ moisture on the surface of a solid object ‖ moisture in the air ‖ any of various gases dangerous in mining 2. *adj.* slightly wet ‖

impregnated with moisture **3.** *v.t.* to make slightly wet, moisten ‖ to stifle or check (a fire) by heaping on ashes etc. ‖ (*phys.*) to reduce the amplitude of (successive vibrations or waves) ‖ (*mus.*) to stop the vibration of (a string) ‖ to discourage **dámp·en** *v.t.* (esp. *Am.*) to make slightly wet, moisten ‖ to depress, discourage ‖ *v.i.* (esp. *Am.*) to become damp **dámp·er** *n.* a depressing or discouraging person or circumstance ‖ (*mus.*) the felt pad which prevents a piano string from vibrating until the pad is raised by depression of a key or the sustaining pedal ‖ a small sponge for moistening postage stamps, envelopes etc. ‖ a movable metal plate in the flue of a stove for controlling the draft ‖ (*phys.*) any device which decreases the amplitude of vibration or oscillation of a body or a wave motion [rel. to Du. and Dan. *damp*]

damp course (*archit.*) a layer of slate etc. in a wall intended to prevent damp from rising

damper *n.* (*electr.*) in a television receiver, the diode controlling the horizontal deflection circuit, used to smooth the current decrease

dam·sel (dámzəl) *n.* (*old-fash.*) a young unmarried woman [M.E. *dameisele* fr. O.F.]

damsel bug a brown insect (family Nabidae) that feeds on other insects

dam·son (dámzən) *n. Prunus insititia,* a variety of plum tree, introduced into Europe from Damascus. It has a small, oval, black, bluish or yellow fruit (drupe) ‖ the fruit [M.E. *damascene,* of Damascus, fr. L.]

damson cheese a stiff jam of damson purée and sugar

Dan (dæn) Hebrew patriarch, son of Jacob ‖ the Israelite tribe of which he was the founder

dan (dæn) *n.* (sometimes initial capital) **1.** in Oriental self-defense techniques, an expert **2.** an expert level, in which the 9th dan is the highest

Da·na (déinə), Charles Anderson (1819–97), U.S. journalist. As editor (from 1868) of the 'New York Sun,' he popularized the 'human interest story' and influenced post-Civil War politics, moving from an early liberalism to a disillusioned conservatism

Dana, Richard Henry (1815–82), U.S. author and lawyer. His novel 'Two Years Before the Mast' (1840) depicts the hardships of a sailor's life at sea

Dan·a·ë (dǽnəi:) the daughter of Acrisius, king of Argos, and mother of Perseus by Zeus. Zeus came to her, in the tower where her father kept her locked up, in the form of a shower of gold

Da·na·ids (dǽneiidz) (*Gk mythol.*) the 50 daughters of Danaus, king of Argos. They married the 50 sons of Aegyptus, twin brother of Danaus. With the exception of Hypermnestra, they all killed their husbands on the wedding night, in obedience to their father's order. They were condemned to pour water into a bottomless pitcher in Hades

Dan·a·kil (dǽnəki:l) *n.* (Afar) an African Moslem people inhabiting the Danakil desert in Eritrea, Somaliland and Ethiopia, speaking a Cushitic language ‖ a member of this people

Da Nang (dánáŋ) (formerly Tourane) a port and naval base (pop. 492,194) in northern South Vietnam: cotton, silk, soap

da·na·zol [C₂₂H₂₇NO₂] (dǽnəzɔl) *n.* (*pharm.*) a synthetic androgen used to treat endometrial lesions which cause some suppression of ovarian function; marketed as Danocrine

dance (dæns, dɑns) *n.* the act of dancing ‖ a series of set movements to music, either alone or with a partner or partners ‖ a party or social gathering at which the guests dance **to lead someone a dance** to be tiresomely demanding of someone ‖ to lead someone on, intending to let them down later [O.F. *dance, danse*]

dance *pres. part.* **danc·ing** *past* and *past part.* **danced** *v.i.* to move rhythmically, alone or with a partner or other dancers, esp. to music or drumming ‖ to move in a lively or excited way, *to dance with rage* ‖ to move quickly up and down, bounce, *hail danced on the streets* ‖ *v.t.* to dandle **to dance attendance on** to be excessively attentive to (someone) [O.F. *dancer, danser*]

dance of death an allegorical portrayal of Death as a skeleton leading people of all ranks and types in a ritual dance. It was common in the art of the 15th and 16th cc. It was a reminder that all human actions have two contexts, one temporal and one eternal

danc·er (dǽnsər, dánsər) *n.* a person dancing ‖ a person who makes his/her living by dancing in public, in ballet, musical comedy etc.

dan·de·li·on (dǽnd'laiən) *n. Taraxacum officinale,* fam. *Compositae,* a perennial, almost cosmopolitan plant with a thick primary root and a very short sympodial stem. The flowers are yellow and each fruit has a white pappus of hairs. The whole plant contains bitter milky latex. The young leaves are eaten in salad [F. *dent de lion,* lion's tooth]

dan·der (dǽndər) *n.* (*pop.*) bad temper (esp. in phrase) **to get (someone's) dander up** to annoy (someone) [origin unknown]

Dan·die Din·mont (dǽndidínmɒnt) *n.* a terrier of a breed with a rough coat, short legs, and long ears and body [from the character in Scott's 'Guy Mannering']

dan·dle (dǽnd'l) *pres. part.* **dan·dling** *past* and *past part.* **dan·dled** *v.t.* to hold (a child) on one's knee or in one's arms and move him up and down to amuse him [perh. fr. Ital. *dandolare,* to swing up and down]

dan·dri·cide (dǽndrisạid) *n.* any antidandruff chemical

dan·druff (dǽndrəf) *n.* small scales of dead skin on the scalp, scurf [etym. doubtful]

dan·dy (dǽndi:) *pl.* **dan·dies** *n.* (*naut.*) a sloop with a mizzen-lugsail on a jigger aft [Hindi *dandi* fr. *dand,* oar]

dandy 1. *pl.* **dan·dies** *n.* a man who shows exaggerated concern for the elegance of his dress or appearance **2.** *comp.* **dan·di·er** *superl.* **dan·di·est** *adj.* excellent **dán·dy·ism** *n.* the male cult of dressing well, with admirable discretion (*BEAU BRUMMELL) ‖ this exquisite refinement taken up into a generalized social or literary attitude [Scot. *Dandy*+Andrew]

dandy roll a roller which impresses a watermark into paper when it is being made

Dane (dein) *n.* a native of Denmark ‖ (*hist.*) one of the Scandinavian invaders of England of the 9th and 10th cc. (*VIKING) [O.E. *Dene* (pl.)]

Dane·geld (déingeld) *n.* (*hist.*) an English tax levied (991–1012) to buy peace from the Danes, and revived until 1163 as a regular land tax by the Normans [O.E.=Dane payment or tribute]

Dane·law (déinlɔ) *n.* the code of laws established in N. and E. England by the Norse invaders in the 9th and 10th cc. ‖ the section of England ruled by these laws [O.E. *Dena lagu,* Danes' law]

dan·ger (déindʒər) *n.* peril, exposure to harm, injury, loss, esp. loss of life ‖ a thing or circumstance that constitutes a peril ‖ (*rail.*, of a signal) the position directing a train to stop **in danger of** exposed to a risk of, *in danger of falling* **no danger of** no likelihood of **dán·ger·ous** *adj.* [O.F. *dangier, danger*]

dan·gle (dǽŋg'l) *pres. part.* **dan·gling** *past* and *past part.* **dan·gled** *v.i.* to be hanging loosely ‖ *v.t.* to cause to swing lightly to and fro **to keep someone dangling** to keep someone waiting for an answer [of Scand. origin]

Dan·iel (dǽnjəl) a Hebrew prophet (6th c. B.C.) ‖ the book of the Old Testament bearing his name, placed among the Hagiographa by the Hebrew Bible, but included in the Major Prophets by Christian versions of the Old Testament. It was probably written (2nd c. B.C.) to encourage the Jews in their struggle against Syria. It relates how Daniel in captivity in Babylon interpreted the dreams of Nebuchadnezzar, became adviser to the king and emerged unscathed when cast into the lions' den

Dan·iell cell (dǽnjəl) a primary electric cell in which the negative pole is zinc in an electrolyte of dilute sulfuric acid or zinc sulfate solution, and the positive pole is copper in a saturated copper sulfate solution. The poles are separated by a porous partition which allows the flow of electricity but prevents mixture of the electrolytes, and reduces polarization. The cell gives a constant electromotive force of 1.1 volts [after John Frederic *Daniell* (1790–1845), English scientist who invented it in 1836]

Dan·ish (déiniʃ) **1.** *n.* the North Germanic language of Denmark, also spoken in parts of Greenland ‖ (with 'the') the people or inhabitants of Denmark **2.** *adj.* coming from or pertaining to Denmark [O.E. *Denisc*]

dank (dæŋk) *adj.* cold and damp ‖ smelling unpleasantly of damp [M.E. rel. to Swed. *dank,* marshy ground]

D'Annunzio, (dɒnuːntsiou) Gabriele (1863–1938), Italian poet and writer whose adventures and liaisons with well-known women greatly influenced his writing. His poetry includes 'New Song' (1882), 'Laudi cycle' (1903–12), and 'Alcione' (1904). He wrote plays, some expressly for Eleonora *DUSE, including 'The

Dead City' (1902), 'La Gioconda' (1902), and 'The Daughter of Jorio' (1907). Among his novels are 'The Triumph of Death' (1896), 'The Intruder' (1898), and 'The Child of Pleasure' (1898); some of his short stories are collected in 'Virgin Land' (1882)

dan runner (*mil.*) a ship running a line of dan buoys, temporary buoys set up during mine sweeping

danse ma·ca·bre (dānsmækɑbr) *n.* the dance of death [F.]

Dan·te A·li·ghie·ri (dǽnti:æligjéɑri:) (1265–1321), great Italian poet. He came from a noble Florentine family. He probably fought in the Guelf-Ghibelline wars. In 1301, while absent from Florence, he was fined on political charges and later sentenced to death if captured. He spent the rest of his life in exile, at times under the care and protection of sympathetic noblemen, notably Guido da Polenta. His 'Commedia' (c. 1308–c. 1320, not called 'Divina' until the 16th c.), in terza rima, constructed to an elaborate plan of 100 cantos, reflects his faith, his love, his great learning and his concern for political good. The imaginary journey through Hell, Purgatory and Paradise presents a complex moral, political and religious system of the universe and symbolizes the path of the soul from sin and darkness to purification. Dante's other works include 'La Vita Nuova' (c. 1292–4), in which he commemorates his love for Beatrice and the spiritual knowledge that the love brought him, and announces the imaginative work (i.e. the 'Commedia') that it inspired

Dan·te·an (dǽnti:ən) *adj.* pertaining to Dante or his writings ‖ Dantesque [after *Dante* Alighieri]

Dan·tesque (dæntésk) *adj.* resembling the style of Dante, esp. the verse of the 'Divine Comedy', allegorical, full of imagery, and learned [after *Dante* Alighieri]

Dan·ton (dɑ̃tɔ̃), Georges-Jacques (1759–94), French revolutionist. A founder of the Club des Cordeliers (1790) and of the Committee of Public Safety (1793) he organized the defense of France against the Prussians. As minister of justice (1792–4) by his eloquence and political skill he became a rival to Robespierre, who overthrew him (1794). He was guillotined

Dan·ube (dǽnju:b) (G. *Donau, Czech.* Dunaj) Europe's second largest river (1,725 miles). Rising in the Black Forest, it flows east through S.W. Germany, Austria, and Hungary, where it receives the Drava, the Sava and the Tisa. It cuts between the Carpathians and the Balkan Mtns, runs along the Rumanian-Bulgarian border, then curves up into Rumania and flows into the Black Sea in a huge, three-armed delta. Less developed than the Rhine or Elbe, it carries less traffic

Dan·zig *GDANSK

dap (dæp) *pres. part.* **dap·ping** *past* and *past part.* **dapped** *v.t.* to dip quickly in water ‖ *v.i.* to fish by letting the bait or fly touch only the surface of the water [var. of DAB]

Daph·ne (dǽfni:) (*Gk mythol.*) a nymph pursued by Apollo. She was changed into a laurel to escape from him

daph·ne (dǽfni:) *n.* a member of *Daphne,* fam. *Thymelaeaceae,* a genus of shrubs and small trees of Europe and subtropical Asia. Several species are cultivated for their ornamental, fragrant flowers [Gk *daphnē,* the laurel or bay tree]

dap·per (dǽpər) *adj.* (esp. of short, middle-aged men) neat and spruce in appearance [perh. fr. Flem. or L.G.]

dap·ple (dǽp'l) *n.* a dappled color effect [perh. rel. to Icel. *depill,* spot, dot]

dapple 1. *adj.* dappled **2.** *pres. part.* **dap·pling** *past* and *past part.* **dap·pled** *v.t.* to mark with irregular spots or patches of color

dap·pled (dǽp'ld) *adj.* marked with irregular spots or patches of color [prob. fr. O. E. *æppled,* formed into apples]

Dap·sang (dǽpsæŋ) *K2

dap·sone [C₁₂H₁₂N₂O₂S] (dǽpsoun) *n.* (*pharm.*) antimicrobial drug used in malaria and leprosy therapy

dar·af (dǽræf) *n.* unit of elastance, the reciprocal of farad capacitance *ant* farad *Cf* CAPACITANCE

Dar·by (dárbi:), Abraham (1677–1717), English engineer and iron manufacturer. He was the first to use coke to smelt iron (c. 1709)

Dar·da·nelles (dɑrd'nélz) the ancient Hellespont, a narrow strait (42 miles long, 1–4 miles wide) between Europe and Asia Minor, connect-

CONCISE PRONUNCIATION KEY: **(a)** æ, c*a*t; ɑ, c*a*r; ɔ f*aw*n; ei, sn*a*ke. **(e)** e, h*e*n; i:, sh*ee*p; iə, d*ee*r; ɛə, b*ea*r. **(i)** i, f*i*sh; ai, t*i*ger; ə:, b*i*rd. **(o)** o, *o*x; au, c*ow*; ou, g*oa*t; u, p*oo*r; ɔi, r*oy*al. **(u)** ʌ, d*u*ck; u, b*u*ll; u:, g*oo*se; ə, b*a*cillus; ju:, c*u*be. x, lo*ch*; θ, *th*ink; ð, bo*th*er; z, *Z*en; ʒ, cor*s*age; dʒ, sava*ge*; ŋ, orangutan*g*; j, *y*ak; ʃ, *fi*sh; tʃ, fe*tch*; 'l, rabb*le*; 'n, redd*en*. Complete pronunciation key appears inside front cover.

ing the Aegean with the Sea of Marmara. It is the entrance to the Black Sea. It was used by the Persians (480 B.C.) and the Ottoman Turks (1354) in invasions of Europe, and by Alexander (334 B.C.) in the conquest of Asia. Control of it became an important part of the Eastern Question

Dar·da·ni·an (dɑrdéini:ən) 1. *adj.* Trojan 2. *n.* a Trojan [fr. L. *Dardanus*]

Dar·da·nus (dárd'nəs) (*Gk mythol.*) the son of Zeus and Electra, ancestor of the Trojan royal house

dare (dɛər) 1. *v.i. pres. part.* **dar·ing** past and past part. **dared** to have enough courage, *jump if you dare* ‖ to have enough impudence, *deny it if you dare* ‖ *v.t.* to challenge (someone) to do something as a test of courage ‖ (*rhet.*) to brave (e.g. someone's wrath) ‖ (as a verbal auxiliary) to have the courage to, *he dare not tell the truth* or be impudent enough to, *how dare you say that!* 2. *n.* a challenge to do something as a test of courage [O.E. *durran*]

dare·dev·il (dɛ́ərdevəl) 1. *n.* a person who is recklessly daring, esp. in order to show off 2. *adj.* daring in this way **dáre·dev·il·try, dáre·dev·il·ry** *n.* ostentatious recklessness

dare·say (dɛ́ərséi) *v.i. and t.* (in the expression) **I daresay** (*Br.* **dare say**) perhaps

Dar-es-Sa·laam (dɑressəlám) the chief port and capital (pop. 510,000) of Tanzania on the Indian Ocean, a rail terminus. University College of the University of East Africa (1963)

Dar·ién (dɑrjén, dɛɑri:én) (originally called Santa María de la Antigua del Darién) the area comprising the easternmost part of the Isthmus of Panama, situated chiefly within the republic of Panama, but also including a region of Colombia. It was a colony and settlement established by the Spaniards (1510) and a center of early exploration

Darién, Gulf of an inlet of the Caribbean Sea between Panama and Colombia. The Gulf of Urabá forms its inner section

dar·ing (dɛ́əriŋ) 1. *n.* bravery 2. *adj.* adventurous ‖ boldly unconventional

Da·rí·o (dɑrí:ɔ), Rubén (1867–1916), the leading poet of Nicaragua and of all Spanish America, noted esp. for his metrical innovations. His earlier works, 'Azul' (1888) and 'Prosas profanas' (1896), were concerned purely with art for art's sake, but his 'Cantos de Vida y esperanza' (1905) explored the threat of imperialism, the unity and progress of Spanish-speaking peoples, and the problems of human existence

Da·ri·us I (dəráiəs) 'the Great' (c. 550–c. 485 B.C.), king of Persia (c. 521–c. 485 B.C.). He reorganized and consolidated the empire as far as Egypt and India, crushed the Ionian revolt (499 B.C.) and invaded Greece, but was defeated at Marathon (490 B.C.)

Darius II (d. 404 B.C.), king of Persia (424–404 B.C.), son of Artaxerxes I. In his reign the Persian Empire was weakened by revolts and political intrigue

Darius III (c. 380–330 B.C.), king of Persia (336–330 B.C.), cousin of Artaxerxes III. He was defeated by Alexander the Great at Issus (333 B.C.) and Arbela (331 B.C.)

Dar·jee·ling (dardʒí:liŋ) a town (pop. 42,662) in W. Bengal, India, on the slopes of the Himalayas, a health resort and a center of the tea industry

dark (dɑrk) 1. *adj.* partly or totally devoid of light ‖ dispiriting, gloomy ‖ (of color) of a deep shade ‖ (of people) having dark hair, eyes and (often) skin ‖ angry, *a dark look* ‖ very unpromising, *the prospects look dark* ‖ occult and possibly evil, *dark practices* ‖ (*rhet.*) obscure, *a dark prophecy* ‖ mysterious ‖ (*pop.*) secretive, *he's a dark one* 2. *n.* a total absence of light ‖ bad light ‖ night ‖ dark color, esp. in painting **to be in the dark** to be ignorant, not informed **dárk·en** *v.i.* to become dark ‖ *v.t.* to make dark **to darken counsel** to make a hard problem worse by giving confusing advice [O.E. *deorc*]

Dark Ages the period (5th–8th cc.) of European history following the fall of Rome

dark comedy black comedy; pessimistic comic drama *Cf* COMÉDIE NOIRE

dark horse a horse that wins a race unexpectedly ‖ a person revealing unexpected talents ‖ a person thought of (though not on any real evidence) as potentially a strong candidate, rival etc.

dark·ling (dárkliŋ) 1. *adj.* (*rhet.*) dark ‖ (*rhet.*) done in the dark 2. *adv.* (*rhet.*) in the dark [M.E. *darkeling* fr. DARK]

dark·room (dárkru:m, dárkrʊm) *n.* (*photog.*) a room free from light or illuminated only by light which does not affect photosensitive materials

Dar·ling (dárliŋ) a river in New South Wales, Australia, the main tributary (1,700 miles long) of the Murray. Parts are seasonally navigable

dar·ling (dárliŋ) 1. *n.* a beloved person 2. *adj.* loved dearly ‖ lovable [O.E. *deorling* fr. *dēor*, dear]

Darm·stadt (dármstat) a town (pop. 136,200) in Hesse, W. Germany: chemical industries

darn (dɑrn) 1. *v.t.* to mend (worn fabric, or a hole) by weaving wool or thread across the worn part or hole 2. *n.* a worn patch or hole mended in this way [perh. M. F. *darner*]

darn 1. *v.t.* to damn 2. *interj.* damn! 3. *n.* a damn **not to give a darn** to be completely indifferent 4. *adj.* confounded, damnable **darned** 1. *adj.* confounded, damnable 2. *adv.* extremely, *darned glad* [fr. DAMN]

dar·nel (dárn'l) *n.* any of several grasses of genus *Lolium* [fr. Walloon *darnelle*]

darning needle a long needle used in darning

Darn·ley (dárnli:), Henry Stuart, Lord (1545–67), Scottish nobleman, second husband of Mary queen of Scots and father of James I. After murdering (1566) Rizzio, his wife's secretary, he was himself assassinated in mysterious circumstances near Holyrood

Dar·row (dǽrou), Clarence Seward (1857–1938), U.S. lawyer, famous as defense counsel in labor disputes, notably the Pullman Strike of 1895, and in criminal trials, notably the Scopes 'monkey' trial

dart (dɑrt) 1. *n.* (*hist.*) a sharply-pointed light missile, a javelin, arrow etc. ‖ a feathered and pointed object thrown in the game of darts ‖ a sudden swift movement ‖ (*archit.*) an element of the ancient egg and dart pattern ‖ (*mil.*) a target towed by a jet aircraft and fired at by fighter aircraft; used for training only ‖ (*sewing*) a short, tapering tuck made to fit a garment to the figure 2. *v.i.* to move swiftly and suddenly ‖ *v.t.* to aim (a glance, look) swiftly and suddenly [O.F.]

dart·er (dártər) *n.* a member of *Anhinger*, a genus of fish-eating, web-footed birds of tropical Africa and America ‖ any of various freshwater American fish related to the perch

dar·tle (dárt'l) *pres. part.* **dar·tling** past and past part. **dar·tled** *v.t. and i.* (*rhet.*) to dart repeatedly

Dart·moor (dártmʊər) an upland area (mean altitude 1,500 ft) in S.W. Devon, England, bleak moorland in the higher parts with many prehistoric remains. Prison (at Princetown)

Dart·mouth (dártməθ) a port and municipal borough (pop. 6,000) in Devonshire, England, site of the Royal Naval College (1905)

Dartmouth College a U.S. privately operated nonsectarian college chartered (1769) in Hanover, Conn. (now in New Hampshire). It was originally established as an Indian charity school, Eleazar Wheelock serving (1769–79) as its first president

Dartmouth College Case a decision (1819) of the U.S. Supreme Court, headed by John Marshall, which declared that a corporation charter was a contract which could not be impaired by a state law

darts (dɑrts) *pl. n.* an indoor game popular in clubs, public houses etc. Players throw three feathered darts a number of times at a circular board divided into segments, each of which counts a different amount towards the score

Dar·win (dárwin), Charles Robert (1809–82), English naturalist. As official naturalist on the survey vessel H.M.S. 'Beagle' he sailed around the world (1831–6). This started his work of observation, investigation and correlation that led to his theory of evolution by natural selection. (A. R. Wallace reached similar conclusions independently.) Darwin's 'Journal of Researches into the Geology and Natural History of the Various Countries visited by H.M.S. Beagle' was published in 1839 and his 'On the Origin of Species by means of Natural Selection' in 1859

Darwin, Erasmus (1731–1802), British physician, philosopher and poet, grandfather of Charles Darwin. His works include 'The Botanic Garden' (1791) and 'Zoonomia, or the Laws of Organic Life' (1794–6), which ad-

vanced theories of generation important in the history of evolutionary theory (*EVOLUTION)

Darwin the capital (pop. 39,193) of Northern Territory, Australia, a port

Dar·win·i·an (dɑrwíni:ən) 1. *adj.* pertaining to Charles Darwin or his theories 2. *n.* a follower of Darwin

Dar·win·ism (dárwinzəm) *n.* the body of Charles Darwin's teachings (*EVOLUTION)

das (dɒs) *n.* (*abbr.*) for dekastere, 10 cubic meters

dash (dæʃ) 1. *v.t.* to smash, shatter ‖ to throw violently, *to dash a vase to the floor* ‖ to splash, *dash some cold water on him* ‖ *v.i.* (of people and vehicles) to go in a great hurry ‖ to discourage, disappoint ‖ (*Br., pop.*) to damn **to dash off** to write or draw (something) quickly 2. *interj.* (*Br., pop.*) damn! 3. *n.* a rush, sudden movement ‖ a sprint ‖ a punctuation mark (—) used to denote a break or an omission or (in pairs) parentheses ‖ a small amount, *tea with a dash of milk* ‖ the sound of water striking a solid object violently, e.g. waves on a cliff ‖ verve, spirited attack or stylish vigor in behavior or public performance ‖ (*telegraphy*) a long buzzing sound on a Morse transmitter (cf. DOT) ‖ a dashboard ‖ a quick stroke (of the pen) [M.E. *daschen, dassen* prob. fr. O.N.]

dash·board (dǽʃbɔrd, dǽʃbourd) *n.* the instrument panel of a car, boat etc. ‖ a panel at the front or sides of a boat, carriage etc. to protect against splashing

dash·er (dǽʃər) *n.* someone or something that dashes ‖ the plunger of an ice-cream freezer or churn

da·shi·ki (dəʃí:ki:) *n.* men's brightly colored, loose pullover shirt worn in Africa, usu. with short sleeves

dash·ing (dǽʃiŋ) *adj.* having or showing the quality of dash (verve, spirited attack) ‖ (of a person) attractive in a way that combines stylishness with verve

das·tard (dǽstərd) 1. *n.* a coward ‖ a cad 2. *adj.* cowardly and mean **dás·tard·ly** *adj.* [etym. doubtful]

das·y·ure (dǽsi:juər) *n.* a member of *Dasyurus*, a genus of nocturnal carnivorous marsupials of Australia and Tasmania [Mod. L. fr. Gk *dasus*, hairy + *oura*, tail]

data *pl.* of DATUM

data bank (*computer*) a compilation of homogenous information esp. when not stored in a computer, e.g., stored on tapes, discs, drums, etc. —**data-bank** *v. syn.* data base

data base data bank (which see)

dat·a·ble, date·a·ble (déitəb'l) *adj.* to which a date can be ascribed ‖ who can be dated

data cartridge (*computer*) removable magnetic tape in a cartridge, processed or for processing, used in small digital devices

data center (*computer*) central point for receiving, analyzing, processing, etc., of information, e.g., from spacecraft

data circuit (*computer*) a means of receiving digital computer data effectively

data concentrator (*computer*) a device that receives data from several sources and inputs to a speedier processor

da·ta·cy·cle (dǽtəsaik'l) *n.* (*computer*) process of moving data through sequences to increase their utility

data element (*computer*) a unit of information *syn.* data item

data encryption (*computer*) scrambling data so that it is incomprehensible until unscrambled by the receiver

data item *DATA ELEMENT

da·ta·ma·tion (deitəméiʃən) *n.* (*computer*) 1. the computer industry 2. automation using data processing —**data processor** *n.*

Da·ta-Phone (déitəfoun) *n.* Bell System trade name of a device for high-speed telephone transmission of data for conversion to digital processing

Dataphone 50 Service telephone exchange for both voice communication and for transmission and reception of computer-taped data

data processing (*computer*) operation on data according to a set of instructions, e.g., computation, assembling, compiling, interpreting, translating, storing, retrieving, selecting, sorting

data processing center (*computer*) a computer installation available for public use for a fee

da·ta·ry (déitəri:) *pl.* **da·ta·ries** *n.* an officer of the papal Curia who executes matters settled by the pope not in consistory (dispensations etc.) ‖ his chancellery [fr. Mod. L. *datarius* fr. *datum*, date]

da·ta·sink (déitəsink) *n.* (*computer*) a device for receiving data transmissions that is sometimes used for checking or for adding error controls

data switching center (*computer*) installation that relays data based on information contained in the message *also* message switching center

data under voice system used by AT&T to permit digital data to be transferred on low-frequency microwave radio systems (*abbr.* DUV)

date (deit) *n.* the small, very sweet fruit of the date palm ‖ the date palm [O.F. *date* fr. L. fr. Gk]

date 1. *n.* the day of the month and year, or sometimes the year only ‖ this as written or printed information on a letter, newspaper etc. ‖ the period of time to which things or people belong, *of medieval date* ‖ (*pl.*) the years of birth and death of a person, or the length of rule of a king etc. ‖ an appointment, esp. with a person of the opposite sex ‖ (*pop.*) a person of the opposite sex with whom an appointment is made **to date** up to the present **2.** *v. pres. part.* **dat·ing** *past and past part.* **dat·ed** *v.t.* to write a date on ‖ to assign a date to ‖ to make an appointment with (someone of the opposite sex) ‖ to cause to look old-fashioned ‖ to reveal the full age of ‖ *v.i.* to make a reckoning from some point in time, *dating from the birth of Christ* ‖ to extend back in time, *a friendship dating from before the war* ‖ to become old-fashioned **date·a·ble** *adj.* *DATABLE **dat·ed** *adj.* bearing a date ‖ outmoded **date·less** *adj.* undated ‖ so ancient as to be undatable ‖ without a partner of the opposite sex [F.]

date·line (déitlain) *n.* the line in a letter setting out the date of writing, or that in a periodical setting out the place of origin and date of dispatch of an article etc.

date line *INTERNATIONAL DATE LINE

date palm *Phoenix dactilfera*, fam. *Palmae*, a tall tree native to N. Africa. It is widely cultivated in groves in tropical and subtropical regions. The flowers are dioecious. The fruit is an edible berry with a hard endosperm, and is highly nutritious. Sugar is obtained by tapping the stems. The tree also yields fibers used in making mats, thatch, hats etc.

dating bar a place where unmarried persons congregate *syn.* singles bar

da·tive (déitiv) **1.** *adj.* (*gram.*) of the case of a substantive (or word in agreement) or pronoun as an indirect object, or as the object of certain prepositions, found e.g. in Latin and Greek **2.** *n.* the dative case ‖ a word in the dative case [fr. L. *dativus*]

dative bond (*chem.*) a coordinate bond

da·tum (déitəm, dætəm, dátəm) *pl.* **da·ta** (déitə, dǽtə, dátə) *n.* a known fact ‖ the assumption which forms the basis for an inference or conclusion ‖ (*pl.* **da·tums**) a starting point from which e.g. a survey is made [L.=given]

da·tu·ra (dətúərə, dətjúərə) *n.* a member of *Datura*, fam. *Solanaceae*, a genus of plants yielding strong narcotics, atropine and hyoscyamine (*THORN APPLE) [Mod. L. fr. Hindi *dhatura*]

daub (dɔb) **1.** *v.t.* to apply a coating of (soft, sticky material), *to daub whitewash on a wall* ‖ to coat thickly and unevenly, *to daub a wall with clay* ‖ to apply (color or coloring matter) carelessly or insensitively, esp. too thickly, *to daub some lipstick on* ‖ *v.i.* to paint a picture unskillfully **2.** *n.* any soft sticky material for coating an object ‖ a smear ‖ an unskillfully painted picture [O.F. *dauber*]

Dau·bi·gny (doubí:nji:), Charles François (1817–78), French landscape painter, a precursor of Impressionism

Dau·det (doudei), Alphonse (1840–97), French novelist. The most popular of his works, set in his native Provence, are 'Lettres de mon moulin' (1866) and the three Tartarin burlesques

Dau·ga·va (dáugəvə) *DVINA, WESTERN

daugh·ter (dɔtər) *n.* a female human being in relation to her parents ‖ (*rhet.*) the females of a race or country, *daughters of France* ‖ (*rhet.*) a woman whose character has been molded by a particular event or set of circumstances, *a daughter of the revolution* [O.E. *dohter*]

daugh·ter-in-law (dɔtərinlɔ) *pl.* **daugh·ters-in-law** *n.* a son's wife

daugh·ter·ly (dɔtərli) *adj.* of, like or proper in a daughter

Daughters of the American Revolution

(*abbr.* D.A.R.), a U.S. hereditary, patriotic society organized (1890) and chartered (1895) to preserve the U.S. national heritage, to promote Americanization, and to guard against suspected threats to American society. Its organs include 'Daughters of the American Revolution Magazine' and 'The National Defense News'

Dau·mier (doumjei), Honoré (1808–79), French painter, lithographer and sculptor, esp. notable for nearly 4,000 lithographed social and political caricatures

dau·no·my·cin [C₂₇H₂₉NO₁₀] (dɔnəmáisin) *n.* (*pharm.*) experimental antibiotic used in cancer therapy

daunt (dɔnt, dɑnt) *v.t.* to intimidate, fill with dismay **daunt·less** *adj.* fearless, intrepid ‖ (of courage) unshaken [O.F. *danter*]

dau·phin (dɔ́fin, F. doufɛ̃) *n.* (*hist.*) the title given to the eldest son of the king of France from the 14th c. to 1830 [F., fr. the ceding of *Dauphiné* to the house of Valois on condition that the king's eldest son should bear this title]

Dau·phi·né (doufi:nei) a former province of S.E. France, in the Rhône valley and the Alps, comprising the departments of Isère, Hautes-Alpes and Drôme. Lower Dauphiné is a plateau producing cereals, sugar beet, tobacco, fruit, and dairy goods. Dauphiné was detached (11th c.) from the Holy Roman Empire, its rulers, the Counts of Vienne, assuming the title of dauphin. When the French crown bought it (1349), title and lands passed to the crown princes. Historic capital: Grenoble

Da·vao (dávau) a port (pop. 611,311) in the Philippines, on Mindanao, market for abacá, rubber, tobacco, sugar

dav·en·port (dǽvənpɔrt, dǽvənpourt) *n.* a large sofa often designed to serve as a bed ‖ (*Br.*) a small writing desk [etym. doubtful]

Da·vid (déivid) (*d. c.* 972 B.C.), king of the Hebrews (c. 1012–c. 972 B.C.). A shepherd boy, son of Jesse, he killed the Philistine giant Goliath, became king of Israel, and rallied the Hebrew tribes against the Philistines. He established his political and religious capital at Jerusalem (I Samuel xvi–I Kings ii). A poet and musician, he is thought to have composed several of the Psalms. Israel's Messianic hope centered on his descendants, the house of David (from which Jesus came)

David, St (6th c.), patron saint of Wales. He was a leader of the 6th-c. monastic revival. Feast: Mar. 1

David I (1084–1153), king of Scotland (1124–53). He intervened unsuccessfully on behalf of Matilda in her struggle with Stephen for the English throne, made peace (1141), and feudalized administration and land tenure in Scotland

David II (1324–71), king of Scotland (1329–71), son of Robert I. In exile (1333–41), he invaded (1346) England on behalf of the French, was captured, and was ransomed (1357)

Da·vid (dǽvi:d), Jacques Louis (1746–1825), French painter. His classical and historical work was very popular in his day, esp. his portraits of Napoleon and Mme Récamier. Though a neoclassicist, he was a forerunner of the Romantics, often using classical compositions to express Romantic fervor. His rich colors anticipate Delacroix and Géricault

Da·vies (déivi:z), Arthur Bowen (1862–1928), U.S. painter. He founded (1908) the 'Ash Can' school of modern artists and helped organize (1913) the Armory show of works by European and American modernists

Davies, William Henry (1871–1940), Welsh lyric poet. 'The Autobiography of a Super-Tramp' (1908) describes his early wandering life

da Vinci *LEONARDO DA VINCI

Davis (déivis), Bette (1908–), U.S. actress who received Academy Awards for 'Dangerous' (1935) and 'Jezebel' (1938). Her most notable movies include 'Dark Victory' (1939), 'The Little Foxes' (1941), 'All About Eve' (1950), and 'Whatever Happened to Baby Jane' (1962)

Davis, David (1815–86), U.S. Supreme Court associate justice (1862–77). Pres. Abraham Lincoln, for whom Davis had managed the presidential nomination campaign in 1860, appointed him to the Supreme Court in 1862. He wrote the majority opinion for 'Ex parte Milligan' (1866). He served in the U.S. Senate (1877–83)

Davis, Henry Winter (1817–65), U.S. Congressman, known for his 'Wade-Davis manifesto' published in the 'New York Tribune' of Aug. 5, 1864, in which he charged President Lincoln with political opportunism and condemned his Reconstruction policy

Davis, Jefferson (1808–89), president of the Confederate states in the American Civil War (1861–5). Educated at West Point, Davis served in the Black Hawk War and the Mexican War, was elected to the U.S. House of Representatives, was appointed secretary of war under Franklin Pierce (1853–7), and twice represented Mississippi in the U.S. Senate (1847, 1858)

Davis, John (c. 1550–1605), English navigator. In the search for the Northwest Passage, he discovered much of the coast of Baffin I. (1585–7). He discovered the Falkland Is (1592)

Davis, Stuart (1894–1964), American painter. His abstractions, composed of large geometric areas of strong color, derive from cubism

Davis apparatus an escape mechanism to allow a crew to get out of a submerged disabled submarine

Da·vis·son (déivis'n), Clinton Joseph (1881–1958), U.S. experimental physicist. His discovery of the diffraction of electrons won him (and G. P. Thompson of England) the 1937 Nobel prize in physics

Davis Strait a strait (400 miles long, 180–400 miles wide) between S.W. Greenland and Baffin I., Northwest Territories, connecting Baffin Bay with the Atlantic

dav·it (dǽvit, déivit) *n.* a swiveling metal arm with a pulley wheel at the tip. It is used esp. in raising and lowering a ship's boats over the side [fr. the name *David*]

Dav·itt (dǽvit), Michael (1846–1906), Irish nationalist leader. A Fenian, he worked with Parnell to promote Irish land reform

Da·vos (davóus) a resort (pop. 11,500) in a high valley (5,100 ft) of Grisons, Switzerland

Da·vy (déivi:), Sir Humphry (1778–1829), British scientist. His work greatly advanced the study of chemistry in the early 19th c. He discovered the electric arc, isolated sodium and other elements by electrolysis, and invented the Davy lamp

Davy Jones (*naut.*) the spirit of the sea

Davy Jones's locker the bottom of the sea as the grave of drowned sailors

Davy lamp the miners' safety lamp, invented (1815) by Sir Humphry Davy, in which a wire gauze encloses the flame. Air circulates freely and any explosive gases will burn inside the gauze, but the flame does not pass out through it. The heat of the flame is conducted away and dissipated so that the temperature of the gauze does not rise sufficiently to ignite any surrounding explosive gases (*DAMP). This is the principle of all modern flame safety lamps

daw (dɔ) *n.* the jackdaw [M.E. fr. O.E. *dawe*]

daw·dle (dɔ́d'l) *pres. part.* **daw·dling** *past and past part.* **daw·dled** *v.i.* to walk, or do a job, very slowly and lazily ‖ *v.t.* (with 'away') to waste (time) in idling [var. of older *daddle*, imit.]

Dawes (dɔz), Charles Gates (1865–1951), U.S. politician and financier. The Dawes Plan won him (and Sir Austen Chamberlain) the 1925 Nobel prize for peace. He served (1925–9) as vice-president of the U.S. under Calvin Coolidge, and (1929–32) as U.S. ambassador to Great Britain

Dawes Plan a plan drawn up (1924) by Charles Gates Dawes which temporarily solved the problem of Germany's inability to pay 1st world war reparations by providing a reorganization of German finances through loans from mainly U.S. private investors

dawk (dɔk) *n.* (*slang*) **1.** one who is politically neither hawk nor dove **2.** one who approves of peace but does not become involved in campaigning for it

dawn (dɔn) **1.** *n.* the first light of day, daybreak ‖ the first sign of something, *the dawn of civilization* **2.** *v.i.* (of day) to begin to grow light **to dawn on** (or **upon**) to become suddenly clear to the mind of [M.E. *dawen* prob. fr. O.N.]

Daw·son (dɔ́s'n) the receiving and distributing center (pop. 838) of the Klondike mining region, on the right bank of the Yukon River near its junction with the Klondike, in N. Canada. It thrived in the Klondike gold rush (1896) and was the former capital (1898–1951) of the Yukon

Day (dei), Clarence Shepard (1874–1935), U.S. author, known for his 'Life with Father' (1935) depicting family life in a late Victorian household

day (dei) *n.* the time during which the sun is above the horizon (opp. NIGHT) ‖ a day as a point of time or date ‖ a day as marking some event, *Independence Day* ‖ (esp. *pl.*) a period of time, *in days to come* ‖ (*pl.*) one's whole lifetime, *to end one's days* or a period or activity in it, *his dancing days are over* ‖ (with possessive adj.) a time when things go well, *it's not his day today* **by day** during hours of daylight **day after day** for a long wearisome period **day and night** all the time, constantly **day by day** on every day **day in and day out** constantly, without change or respite **from day to day** each day (esp. suggesting rapid progress) ‖ without seeking to plan ahead, *to live from day to day* **one day, one fine day** at some unspecified time either past or future **one of these days** at some unspecified day in the future **the other day** on some unspecified recent day **this day week** (*Br.*) a week from today **to a day** exactly, *three years ago to a day* **to call it a day** to stop working (with the feeling of having done enough) **to win (lose) the day** (*rhet.*) to gain (lose) a battle or a game [O.E. dǣg]

Dayak *DYAK

Dayan (dɑján), Moshe (moh′-shuh) (1915–81), Israeli military and political leader. He commanded troops in the Arab-Israeli war of 1948, was Israeli General Staff Chief in 1953, and fought in the war of 1956. He later served in the Knesset and was minister of agriculture (1959–64), minister of defense (1964–74), and foreign minister (1977–9)

day·bed (déibɛd) *n.* a narrow bed serving as a couch by day ‖ a chaise longue of a style current in the late 17th and 18th cc.

day·book (déibʊk) *n.* (*bookkeeping*) a book in which business transactions are entered immediately, for later transfer to a ledger ‖ a diary or journal

day boy (*Br.*) a boy who attends a boarding school for classes but lives at home (cf. BOARDER)

day·break (déibreik) *n.* dawn

day care away-from-home daytime care of children, usu. of preschool age, e.g., for working mothers —**day-care center** *n.*

day·dream (déidri:m) 1. *n.* a reverie ‖ a wish or plan not likely to be realized 2. *v.i.* to indulge in such fancies

day girl (*Br.*) a girl who attends a boarding school for classes but lives at home

Day-Glo trade name of a fluorescent ink and paint

day·glow (déiglou) *n.* daytime airglow

day laborer, *Br.* **day labourer** a workman employed by the day

Day-Lewis (déilú:is), Cecil (1904–72), English poet and critic, England's poet laureate (1968–72). His early works, such as 'A Hope for Poetry' (1934) and 'Revolution in Writing' (1935), reflected his concern with the changed post-1st world war social order. His poetry is collected in 'Collected Poems' (1929–33; 1954), 'Pegasus' (1957), and 'The Whispering Roots' (1970)

day·light (déilait) *n.* the light of day ‖ dawn **in broad daylight** openly **to let in some daylight on** to expose to publicity or open examination **to see daylight** to understand ‖ to come into existence, esp. to be published

daylight saving time time adjusted by putting forward the clock usually one hour (generally in summer) in some countries, in order to lengthen the period of daylight at the end of the normal working day

day lily a member of *Hemerocallis*, fam. *Liliaceae*, a genus of plants with ornamental, short-lived, orange or brownish flowers resembling lilies

day·long (déilɔŋ, déilɒŋ) *adj.* and *adv.* lasting or continuing all day

day nursery a nursery school ‖ (*Br.*) a room in a house set aside for the children, but where they do not sleep

Day of Atonement Yom Kippur

day of obligation (*Roman Catholic*) one of certain days of outstanding importance which a faithful Catholic is obliged to observe by hearing Mass and abstaining from servile work. They are: all Sundays, and the feasts of Circumcision, Epiphany, St. Joseph, Ascension, Corpus Christi, SS. Peter and Paul, Assumption, All Saints, Immaculate Conception, Christmas

day of reckoning the time when one must face the consequences of one's misdeeds ‖ Judgment Day

days (deiz) *adv.,* (*pop.*) repeatedly or regularly by day

day school a school for pupils who live at home (cf. BOARDING SCHOOL)

days of grace the lapse of time allowed after a payment is due

day·star (déistɑr) *n.* the morning star

day·time (déitaim) *n.* the hours of daylight

Day·ton (déit'n) a city (pop. 203,588, with agglom. 830,070) in Ohio: atomic research, precision instruments (esp. computers)

day trade (*securities*) speculative transaction completed in a single day —**day trade** *n.* —**day trader** *v.*

daze (deiz) 1. *v.t. pres. part.* **daz·ing** *past* and *past part.* **dazed** to bewilder, confuse or stun, by a blow, fear, surprise or grief 2. *n.* a dazed state [M.E. *dasen* fr. O.N.]

daz·zle (dǽz'l) 1. *v.t. pres. part.* **daz·zling** *past* and *past part.* **daz·zled** to confuse the vision of (a person) with bright light ‖ to blind mentally ‖ to impress by brilliant display 2. *n.* light that dazzles, *the dazzle of headlights* **dáz·zle·ment** *n.* [earlier *dasel, dasle* fr. *dase, daze*]

DBCP (*chem.*) dibromochloropropane (which see)

D.C. District of Columbia ‖ (*elec.*) direct current

DC-8 McDonnell-Douglas jet transport with four turbofan engines able to carry passengers or freight; introduced in 1974

DC-9 Super 80 short to medium-range fuel-efficient jetliner manufactured by Douglas Aircraft Co., division of McDonnell-Douglas, launched 1980

DC-9 Super 10 jet transport able to carry 172 passengers or a 147,000-lb load

DC-130 *HERCULES

DC-10 jet transport made in various versions and capable of carrying 270–380 passengers. It has a speed of Mach 0.88, a 3,600-mi. range, and was introduced in 1970

D day (*mil.*) the planners' designation of the day on which to start an operation, the actual date of which will be fixed later ‖ (*hist.*) the day (June 6, 1944) on which the Allied forces landed in N. France in the 2nd world war

DDD (*chem.*) dichlorodiphenyldichloroethane, an insecticide similar to DDT

DDE [$C_{15}H_8Cl$] (*chem.*) a persistent toxic material produced by degraded DDT

DDT (dí:di:tí:) *n.* a white powder used as an insecticide ($C_6H_4Cl)_2CHCCl_3$ [*abbr.* dichlorodiphenyltrichloroethane]

DDVP [$C_4H_7O_4Cl_2P$] (*chem.*) dichlorvosdimethyldichlorovinyl phosphate, an insecticide and miticide used to protect cattle and stored food

de- (di) *prefix* down, away ‖ un- (i.e. countering the action of the verb to which it is prefixed) [L. *de,* from]

de·ac·ces·sion (dɪ:æksɛ́ʃən) *n.* sale of items acquired by an institution, e.g., the sale of art objects by a museum *Cf* ACCESION

dea·con (dí:kən) 1. *n.* (*eccles.*) a member of the clergy next in order below a priest, whom he assists ‖ (*eccles.*) a layman acting as deacon at the Mass or Eucharist ‖ (*nonconformist Churches*) a layman who assists with the Church's secular business 2. *v.t.* to read aloud each verse of (a hymn or psalm) before singing it ‖ (*pop.*) to pack (fruit etc.) with the best on top, giving a false idea of quality ‖ (*pop.*) to treat with some comparable mild dishonesty **déa·con·ess** *n.* (*eccles.*) a woman who assists in the work of a parish [fr. L. *diaconus* fr. Gk]

dead (ded) 1. *adj.* (of animals and plants) in a state of complete and permanent cessation of vital functions ‖ inanimate, having no life, *dead matter* ‖ having no feeling, movement or activity ‖ insensitive, hardened, *dead to feelings of remorse* ‖ no longer used, *a dead language* or usable, *a dead match* ‖ inert, *a dead weight* ‖ lacking resonance, *a dead sound* ‖ (*pop.*) very tired ‖ (*elec.*) uncharged, *a dead wire* ‖ sure, *a dead shot* ‖ not in play or in operation, *a dead ball, a dead microphone* ‖ exact, complete, *a dead halt, dead loss, dead certainty* ‖ (*golf,* of the ball) so close to the hole as to be certainly holed ‖ (*law*) deprived of civil rights (esp. the rights of property) 2. *n.* **the dead** all dead persons or a dead person **the dead of night** the middle of the night when all is quiet and still **the dead of winter** the very middle of winter 3. *adv.* completely, thoroughly, *dead sure, dead on the target* [O.E. *dēad*]

dead·beat (dɛ́dbi:t) *n.* (*pop.*) a person who exploits generosity, a sponger ‖ (*pop.*) a person who habitually does not pay his debts

dead·beat (dɛ́dbi:t) *adj.* (*mech.*) making a stroke without recoil

dead center, *Br.* **dead centre** either of the two positions in which a crankshaft is in line with the connecting rod to which it is hinged ‖ the exact center of any flat surface

dead drop a place for the delivery and pick up of material, arranged so that the parties do not meet, esp. for espionage, ransom

dead·ee (dédi:) *n.* a painted portrait from photograph of a dead person

dead·en (déd'n) *v.t.* to deprive of feeling, *to deaden a nerve* ‖ to deprive of force, reduce, *to deaden a noise* ‖ to reduce the sensitivity to vibration, echo etc. of, *deaden the walls with thick curtains*

dead end a road closed at one end, a cul-de-sac ‖ a job or any situation without hope of betterment **dead-énd** *adj.* of such a road or job ‖ characteristic of, or living in, the slums

dead·eye (dédai) *pl.* **dead·eyes** *n.* (*naut.*) a wooden block having three holes, joining shrouds to stays

dead·fall (dédfɔl) *n.* a trap having a heavy object which falls on the trapped animal and kills or disables it

dead·head (dédhɛd) *n.* a nonpaying member of an audience ‖ an ineffectual person who does not contribute much to the group

dead heat a race in which two or more competitors tie

dead letter a letter which cannot be delivered and is destroyed or returned to the sender ‖ a law that has become obsolete but which has not been repealed

dead·light (dédlait) *n.* (*naut.*) a porthole shutter to prevent light from showing outside, and to keep water out ‖ a heavy glass plate set into a bulwark to admit light ‖ a fixed skylight

dead·line (dédlain) *n.* a set time limit for completing a piece of work ‖ a line around a prison which a prisoner crosses at the risk of being shot

dead load the inert weight of a machine or structure (cf. LIVE LOAD)

dead·lock (dédlok) 1. *n.* the state existing when neither of two opposing parties will give way 2. *v.t.* to bring to a deadlock ‖ *v.i.* to reach a deadlock

dead·ly (dédli:) 1. *comp.* **dead·li·er** *superl.* **dead·li·est** *adj.* causing or capable of causing death or serious injury ‖ implacable, *deadly enemies* ‖ deathlike, *a deadly pallor* ‖ (*pop.*) boring ‖ causing spiritual death, *deadly sin* 2. *adv.* intensely, *deadly dull*

deadly nightshade the belladonna

dead·man (dédmæn) *n.* (*mountaineering*) a pointed plate with a center loop used for belaying in the snow

dead march a slow march for funeral processions

dead nettle a member of *Lamium*, fam. *Labiatae*, a genus of nettles without the irritant property of the stinging nettle, esp. L. *album*, the white dead nettle

dead-on-ar·ri·val (dédonəraivəl) (*adj.*) 1. of one brought to a medical center already deceased 2. of electronic equipment that does not operate on delivery (*abbr.* DOA)

dead·pan (dédpæn) 1. *adj.* expressionless, showing no emotion ‖ (of comedy or humor) played with complete gravity 2. *adv.* in a deadpan manner

dead point dead center

dead reckoning the method of estimating the position of an aircraft or ship without astronomical sightings. The calculation is made using the log and the known or estimated drift [deduced reckoning]

Dead Sea a salt lake (area 393 sq. miles, depth to 1,308 ft) between Israel and Jordan, a source of potash, bromine and magnesium salts

Dead Sea Scrolls Hebrew and Aramaic documents dating from the 2nd c. B.C. to 70 A.D., discovered (1947 and 1952) in the Qumran caves west of the Dead Sea. They include fragments of almost all the books of the Old Testament, and works written by and for an ascetic community (possibly the Essenes). The scrolls have thrown new light on the text of the Old Testament, and on the history, literature and religion of the time of Jesus

dead space 1. (*mil.*) area within the maximum range of a weapon, radar, or observer, that cannot be covered by fire or observation because of

CONCISE PRONUNCIATION KEY: **(a)** æ, c*a*t; ɑ, c*ar*; ɔ f*aw*n; ei, sn*a*ke. **(e)** e, h*e*n; i:, sh*ee*p; iə, d*eer*; ɛə, b*ear*. **(i)** i, f*i*sh; ai, t*ig*er; ə:, b*ir*d. **(o)** o, *o*x; au, c*ow*; ou, g*oa*t; u, p*oor*; ɔi, r*oy*al. **(u)** ʌ, d*u*ck; u, b*u*ll; u:, g*oo*se; ə, b*a*cillus; ju:, c*u*be. x, lo*ch*; θ, *th*ink; ð, bo*th*er; z, *Z*en; ʒ, cor*s*age. dʒ, sava*g*e; ŋ, oranguta*n*g; j, *y*ak; ʃ, *fi*sh; tʃ, fe*tch*; 'l, rabb*le*; 'n, red*den*.   Complete pronunciation key appears inside front cover.

intervening obstacles, the nature of the ground, or the characteristics of the trajectory, or the limitations of the weapons' pointing capabilities **2.** (*electr.*) area or zone within the range of a radio transmitter, but in which a signal is not received **3.** (*mil.*) the volume of space about and around a gun or guided missile system into which the weapon cannot fire because of mechanical or electronic limitations *syn.* dead zone

dead stock goods not producing turnover
dead·weight (dédwéit) *n.* (often **dead weight**) the weight of an inert mass ‖ the weight of rolling stock (cf. LOAD) ‖ the difference (in tons) between what a ship displaces with its full cargo, stores etc. (at load draft) and what it displaces without them (at light draft) ‖ a person making himself a burden to someone without trying to help himself ‖ a totally ineffectual person
dead·wood (dédwụd) *n.* a dead branch on a tree ‖ something that is not useful, e.g. unsalable stock, redundant employees or useless information ‖ solid timbers built in at the bow and stern of a boat when the lines are too narrow to admit framing
dead zone dead space (which see)
deaf (def) **1.** *adj.* wholly or partly deprived of the sense of hearing ‖ unwilling to listen, obstinate, *deaf to all compromise* **to turn a deaf ear** to choose not to hear something **2.** *n.* **the deaf** deaf people [O.E. *déaf*]
deaf-and-dumb alphabet (défəndʌm) a system of signs made with the hands for letters and some words
deaf·en (défən) *v.t.* to deprive permanently or temporarily of the sense of hearing ‖ to make soundproof ‖ *v.i.* to be overwhelmingly noisy
deaf-mute (défmjúːt) *n.* a person who is deaf and dumb
De·ak (déak), Ferencz (1803–76), Hungarian statesman. Together with Andrassy, he was responsible for the establishment of the dual monarchy of Austria-Hungary (1867)
Dea·kin (díːkin), Alfred (1856–1919), Australian Liberal prime minister (1903–4, 1905–8, and 1909–10)
deal (diːl) *n.* a large amount, *a deal of trouble* **a good deal** a fairly large amount **a great deal** a very large amount [O.E. *dǽl*, a part, a share]
deal *n.* a board of soft wood, fir, pine or spruce, measuring (*Am.*) over 7 ins wide and 6 ft long, (*Br.*) 9–11 ins wide, less than 3 ins thick and at least 6 ft long ‖ a number of such boards. Deal is used for making crates etc. and also for furniture, often covered with a veneer of better-quality wood [L.G. *dele*, a plank]
deal 1. *v. pres. part.* **deal·ing** *past* and *past part.* **dealt** (delt) *v.t.* to apportion, distribute among a number, esp. to distribute (cards) among cardplayers ‖ *v.i.* to distribute cards to players ‖ (with 'in') to engage in buying and selling some commodity ‖ (with 'with') to make a business transaction, have business relations ‖ (with 'with') to do what is necessary to meet a situation ‖ (with 'with') to treat a topic, have as subject ‖ (with 'with') to treat a person, esp. to punish him ‖ (with 'with') to behave in a specified way towards others, *to deal justly with someone* **to deal** (someone) **a blow** to hit (someone) hard ‖ to cause suffering or misfortune to (someone) **2.** *n.* the distribution of cards, before a game ‖ a turn to distribute cards, *your deal* ‖ treatment measured out to a person, by someone else or by fate ‖ a business transaction ‖ an illegal transaction advantageous to all transacting parties ‖ *NEW DEAL* **déal·er** *n.* someone who buys and sells some commodity ‖ a cardplayer dealing the cards [O.E. *dǽlan*]
deal·ing (díːliŋ) *n.* treatment of others, *fair dealing* ‖ (*pl.*) business or other (e.g. social) association
dealt *past* and *past part.* of DEAL
dean (diːn) *n.* (*eccles.*) the head of the chapter of a cathedral or collegiate church ‖ the senior member (in length of service) of a body, the doyen ‖ (in some universities) the head of a department or faculty ‖ (*Br.*) in some university colleges) a fellow responsible for discipline [M.E. *deen* fr. O.F. *deien*]
Deane (diːn), Silas (1737–89), the first U.S. diplomat to be sent abroad. He helped to negotiate the treaties of commerce and alliance (1778) with France which contributed to U.S. independence, but was later discredited by unproved charges of embezzlement and disloyalty

dean·er·y (díːnəri) *pl.* **dean·er·ies** *n.* (*eccles.*) the office of dean ‖ (*eccles.*) a dean's house
Dean, Forest of (diːn) an area in W. Gloucestershire, England (Severn and Wye valley), formerly a royal forest: coal and iron deposits
dear (diər) **1.** *n.* a loved or lovable person **2.** *adj.* a polite form of address for beginning letters, *Dear Sir* ‖ (*Br.*) a sometimes ironic form of address in conversation, *don't talk nonsense, my dear man* ‖ precious, cherished, *one's dearest wish* ‖ (esp. *Br.*) costly, expensive ‖ won at great cost, *a dear victory* ‖ (esp. *Br.*) charging high prices **to run for dear life** to flee as fast as possible **3.** *adv.* (*rhet.*) at a high price, *he got his experience dear* ‖ (*rhet.*) very affectionately **4.** *inter.* an exclamation of surprise, dismay or mild sympathy **déar·ly** *adv.* very affectionately ‖ expensively or at a great cost ‖ keenly, earnestly, *we would dearly love to know* [O.E. *déore*]
Dear·born (díərbərn, díərbərn), Henry (1751–1829), U.S. general, and secretary of war (1801–9) under President Jefferson. He established (1803) Fort Dearborn, which developed into the city of Chicago
dearie *DEARY
dearth (dəːrθ) *n.* lack, scarcity [M.E. *derthe* fr. O.E. *déore*, dear]
dear·y, dear·ie (díəri) *n.* (*pop.*, as a breezy term of address to men or women) my dear
death (deθ) *n.* a dying, the end of life ‖ the state of being dead ‖ an end, destruction, *the death of one's hopes* ‖ a cause of death *drink will be the death of him* ‖ the killing of an animal in the hunting field **to catch one's death of cold** to contract a bad cold **to death** so that death results, *to freeze to death* ‖ exceedingly, *bored to death* **to do to death** to kill **to the death** while life lasts, with death as the only outcome, *a fight to the death* [O.E. *déath*]
death·bed (déθbed) **1.** *n.* the bed in which a person dies or is dying **2.** *adj.* done, made etc. just before dying
death·blow (déθblou) *n.* a blow that kills ‖ a blow of fate which ends hopes, ambitions etc.
death camas a member of *Zigadenus*, fam. Liliaceae, a genus of plants whose bulbs are very poisonous to cattle and sheep. They are common in western U.S.A. [Am. Ind. *camass, quamash*]
death certificate the certificate signed by a doctor attesting the cause of a person's death
death count (*Am.=Br.* death roll) the number of people killed in a disaster, accident etc., *the death count stands at 87*
death duty *pl.* **death duties** (*Br.*) death tax
death·less (déθlis) *adj.* (*rhet.*) living for ever, eternal, *deathless glory*
death·ly (déθli) **1.** *adj.* like death, *a deathly hush, deathly pale* **2.** *adv.* exceedingly, *deathly afraid*
death mask a cast taken of a person's face after death
death rate the number of deaths per 1,000 people in a given population over a certain time
death rattle the sound heard in the throat of a dying person, caused by the collection of mucus, which impedes breathing
death roll a list of dead, persons, esp. as the result of a battle or other disaster ‖ (*Br.*) death count
death's-head (déθshed) *n.* the image of a skull as the emblem of death ‖ a moth with wing markings which resemble a human skull
death tax (*Am.=Br.* death duty) a tax on the estate of a dead person, sometimes determined strictly by the size of the estate, sometimes by the degree of consanguinity of the inheritors, or other factors. Death taxes may be legally avoided under some governments, e.g. by making outright gifts to close kin a specified length of time before death
death·trap (déθtræp) *n.* a very dangerous building, place, machine etc.
Death Valley a deep, dry valley (130 miles long, 3–25 miles wide) reaching 276 ft below sea level, between the Panamint and Amargosa mountain ranges in California, one of the hottest places in the world
death warrant an official order for an execution
death·watch (déθwɒtʃ) *n.* a watch kept over a dead or dying person ‖ the guard kept over a person about to be executed
deathwatch beetle any of several small beetles of fam. Anobiidae which bore through wood with a clicking sound and do great damage to buildings

deb (deb) *n.* a debutante [by shortening]
de·bâ·cle, *Br.* also **dé·bâ·cle** (deibák'l, deibǽk'l, dəbák'l, dəbǽk'l) *n.* a disastrous confusion, e.g. a complete military defeat, collapse ‖ the breaking up of ice in a river ‖ the rush of water which follows this, or any comparable flood [F. *débâcle*]
de·bar (dibár) *pres. part.* **de·bar·ring** *past* and *past part.* **de·barred** *v.t.* to exclude from entry, esp. to some privilege, position or right [F. *débarrer*]
de·bark (dibárk) *v.t.* and *i.* to disembark **de·bar·ká·tion** *n.* the act or time of leaving a ship and going ashore ‖ (*mil.*) the operation of getting assault troops ashore [F. *débarquer*]
de·base (dibéis) *pres. part.* **de·bas·ing** *past* and *past part.* **de·based** *v.t.* to lessen the value of (coinage) by using more cheap metal etc. ‖ to lower the standard or character of **de·báse·ment** *n.*
de·bat·a·ble (dibéitəb'l) *adj.* not decided, questionable, *a debatable point* ‖ subject to dispute, *debatable territory*
de·bate (dibéit) **1.** *v. pres. part.* **de·bat·ing** *past* and *past part.* **de·bat·ed** *v.t.* to discuss (a question) thoroughly, esp. at a public meeting or in government ‖ to consider (something requiring a decision) in one's mind ‖ *v.i.* to hold a formal discussion under rules of procedure **2.** *n.* discussion or a discussion, esp. a public one ‖ controversy [O.F. *debatre*]
debating society a society for the holding of formal debates for pleasure
de·bauch (dibótʃ) **1.** *v.t.* to corrupt (a person) **2.** *n.* a bout of excessive self-indulgence in sensual pleasures [F. *débaucher*, orig. to entice away from work]
deb·au·chee (debɔtʃíː, debɔʃíː) *n.* a person who often indulges in sensual excesses [F. *débauché*, debauched]
de·bauch·er·y (dibótʃəri) *pl.* **de·bauch·er·ies** *n.* excessive indulgence in sensual pleasures
deb·by or **deb·bie** (débi) *adj.* in the style of a debutante
de·ben·ture (dibéntʃər) *n.* a certificate issued by a company or corporation, acknowledging a loan upon which interest is payable until the loan is repaid [prob. L. *debentur*, these are due]
debenture stock debentures treated as stock. The total sum is not repaid, interest only being paid to the creditor as a perpetual annuity
de·bil·i·tate (dibíliteit) *pres. part.* **de·bil·i·tat·ing** *past* and *past part.* **de·bil·i·tat·ed** *v.t.* to weaken (the body) [fr. L. *debilitare* (*debilitatus*) fr. *debilis*, weak]
de·bil·i·ty (dibíliti) *pl.* **de·bil·i·ties** *n.* physical weakness, feebleness, or an instance of this [F. *débilité*]
deb·it (débit) **1.** *n.* the account book entry of a sum owed ‖ the left-hand page of an account book where debts are recorded **2.** *v.t.* to charge up (goods or an account) [fr. L. *debitum*, owed]
deb·o·nair, deb·o·naire (debənéər) *adj.* (esp. of young men) having attractive manners and vitality [O.F. *debonaire*=*de bonne aire*, of good stock]
de·boost (dəbúːst) *v.* to reduce the thrust of a missile or spacecraft in flight —**deboost** *n.* the process
de·bouch (dibúːʃ, dibáutʃ) *v.i.* (of people) to emerge, e.g. from a ravine or subway station ‖ (of a stream) to flow from a narrow course into a lake, the sea etc. **de·bóuch·ment** *n.* the act or fact of debouching ‖ an outlet or mouth (e.g. of a river) [F. *déboucher*]
De·bre·cen (débretsen) a town (pop. 196,000) in the E. Hungarian plain (Alföld), a farm and livestock center (cattle and horses) and rail junction. University (1912)
de·brief·ing (dibríːfiŋ) *n.* **1.** practice of extracting information about an experience from its participants **2.** the results
de·bris (dəbríː, déibri) *n.* the remnants of something broken to pieces ‖ broken pieces of rock detached, transported and then deposited by a rush of water, or detached from a cliff and accumulating where they fall [F. *débris*]
Debs (debz), Eugene Victor (1855–1926), American labor leader and a founder of the Socialist party of the U.S.A.
debt (det) *n.* something, esp. money, owed to another ‖ the state of owing ‖ *NATIONAL DEBT* [M.E. *det, dette* fr. O.F.]
debt of honor, *Br.* **debt of honour** a debt the repayment of which cannot be enforced at law, esp. a gambling debt

CONCISE PRONUNCIATION KEY: (**a**) æ, c*a*t; ɑ, c*a*r; ɔ f*aw*n; ei, sn*a*ke. (**e**) e, h*e*n; iː, sh*ee*p; iə, d*ee*r; ɛə, b*ea*r. (**i**) i, f*i*sh; ai, t*i*ger; əː, b*i*rd. (**o**) o, *o*x; au, c*ow*; ou, g*oa*t; u, p*oo*r; ɔi, r*oy*al. (**u**) ʌ, d*u*ck; u, b*u*ll; uː, g*oo*se; ə, b*a*cillus; juː, c*u*be. x, lo*ch*; θ, *th*ink; ð, bo*th*er; z, *Z*en; ʒ, cor*s*age; dʒ, sava*g*e; ŋ, oranguta*ng*; j, *y*ak; ʃ, *fish*; tʃ, fe*tch*; 'l, rabb*le*; 'n, redd*en*. Complete pronunciation key appears inside front cover.

debt·or (détər) n. a person who owes money or service || (bookkeeping) the left-hand side of an account [M.E. dettour fr. O.F.]

debt relief release of the obligation of developing countries to repay loans

de·bug·ging (di:bʌ́giŋ) n. **1.** removal of problems in the operation of an apparatus, esp. in a computer program **2.** removal of concealed devices for monitoring telephone and room-area conversations **—debug** v. **—debugger** n. **— debug program** n.

de·bunk (dibʌ́ŋk) v.t. (pop.) to strip (a person, institution etc.) of fictitious merit, false sentiment, or pretension || to attack the established reputation of (a person of genuine merit) through malice, ignorance, envy etc.

De·bus·sy (dəbysi:), Claude-Achille (1862–1918), French impressionist composer. His 'Préludes' for the piano exploited new techniques of composition. His many orchestral works include 'Prélude à l'après-midi d'un faune' (1892) and 'la Mer' (1903–5). He wrote the lyrical drama 'Pelléas et Mélisande' (1902), and song settings of poems by Verlaine, Baudelaire etc. His subtle, evocative melodies, recitative, harmonies and orchestration all worked a profound change in composition and in musical sensibility. He was also an influential critic

de·but, dé·but (déibju:, deibjú:) n. the first public appearance of someone (esp. an actor) || the first formal presentation of a debutante in society [F. début]

deb·u·tante, déb·u·tante (débjutɑnt, débjutænt) n. a girl making her first appearances at formal social functions [F. débutante]

De·bye-Hü·ckel theory (dəbáihýk'l) the theory that the increased conductivity of an electrolyte which results from dilution is due to a decrease in electrostatic forces and a consequent increase in the mobility of the ions, rather than to further ionization [after P. J. W. Debye (1884–1966), Du. physicist, and E. Hückel (1896–   ), Swiss physicist]

Dec. December

deca- (dékə) prefix ten [fr. Gk deka, ten]

dec·ade (dékeid) n. a period of 10 years || a series or group of 10 || a set of 10 beads, with their corresponding prayers, on a rosary [F.]

dec·a·dence (dékədəns, dikéid'ns) n. a falling away, decline || (hist.) the last years of the Roman Empire, or its literature || (in art and literature) a recurrent attitude esp. characterized by preoccupation with the beauty of corruption and by nostalgia for lost innocence (often presented as an idealizing of vanished youth). The decadent movement at the end of the 19th c. in Europe is known as 'fin-de-siècle' (*WILDE) **déc·a·dent 1.** adj. deteriorating || falling to lower standards || **2.** n. a person of low moral standards || a person excessively civilized, at the cost of moral energy || a writer or other artist in the tradition of decadence [F. décadence]

dec·a·gon (dékəgon) n. a two-dimensional figure with 10 sides and 10 angles **de·cag·o·nal** (dekǽgən'l) adj. [fr. M.L. fr. Gk deka, ten+gonos, angled]

dec·a·gram, Br. also **dec·a·gramme** (dékəgræm) n. 10 grams

de·cal (dí:kæl, dikǽl) n. decalcomania [by shortening]

de·cal·co·ma·ni·a (dikælkəméini:ə, dikælkəméinjə) n. the process of transferring specially prepared colored images from paper to porcelain, paper, glass, metal etc. || such an image [fr. F. décalcomanie]

de·cal·ci·fy (di:kǽlsifai) pres. part. **de·cal·ci·fy·ing** past and past part. **de·cal·ci·fied** v.t. to remove calcium or its compounds from (a substance)

de·ca·les·cence (di:kəlés'ns) n. a decrease in temperature marking the sudden increase in absorption of heat which occurs when metals are heated through critical temperatures **de·ca·les·cent** adj. [fr. L. decalescens fr. decalescere, to grow warm]

dec·a·li·ter, Br. **dec·a·li·tre** (dékəli:tər) n. 10 liters

Dec·a·logue, Dec·a·log (dékəlog, dékəlog) n. the Ten Commandments (Exodus xx and Deuteronomy v). They express the ideal of man's duty to God and his neighbor by which Moses organized and led the Israelites into nationhood, and are the basic tenets of the Jewish religion. Christians accept the Decalogue, together with Christ's example and teaching, as the basis of their morality [F. décalogue fr. L. fr. Gk]

dec·a·me·ter, Br. **dec·a·me·tre** (dékəmi:tər) n. 10 meters

de·camp (dikǽmp) v.i. to go away suddenly and secretly || to break up camp, esp. secretly [F. aécamper]

dec·a·nal (dékən'l, dikéin'l) adj. pertaining to a dean, his office or duties || of the south side of a cathedral, chapel or church choir [fr. L. decanus, dean]

de·cant (dikǽnt) v.t. to pour (wine) from a bottle into a decanter || to pour (liquid) from one vessel into another in such a way as not to disturb any sediment at the bottom **de·cánt·er** n. a long-necked vessel, typically of cut glass or crystal, from which wine is served [F. décanter]

decapitate v. (biol.) to inhibit capacitation in sperm

de·cap·i·tate (dikǽpiteit) pres. part. **de·cap·i·tat·ing** past and past part. **de·cap·i·tat·ed** v.t. to behead **de·cap·i·ta·tion** n. [F. décapiter]

dec·a·pod (dékəpod) n. a member of Decapoda, an order including the most highly organized crustaceans, having five pairs of thoracic appendages modified into pincers, mouthparts and walking legs, and a fused head and thorax. The order includes crabs, lobsters, crayfish, prawns and shrimps [fr. Mod. L. Decapoda fr. Gk deka, ten+pous (podos), foot]

de·car·bon·ize (di:kɑ́rbənaiz) pres. part. **de·car·bon·iz·ing** past and past part. **de·car·bon·ized** v.t. to remove carbon from (e.g. a gasoline engine)

de·car·bu·rize (di:kɑ́rbjəraiz, di:kɑ́rbəraiz) pres. part. **de·car·bu·riz·ing** past and past part. **de·car·bu·rized** v.t. to decarbonize

dec·a·stere (dékəstiər) n. a unit of volume equaling 10 cubic meters

dec·a·syl·lab·ic (dekəsilǽbik) **1.** adj. having 10 syllables **2.** n. a line of 10 syllables **dec·a·syl·la·ble** (dékəsiləb'l) n. and adj.

de·cath·lete (dikæθli:t) n. one who participates in the decathlon event

de·cath·lon (dikǽθlon) n. an athletic contest consisting of 10 different events. That of the Olympic Games includes the 100-meter, 400-meter and 1,500-meter track events, the 110-meter high hurdles, the javelin, discus, putting the shot, pole vault, high jump and broad jump [fr. Gk deka, ten+athlon, contest]

De·ca·tur (dikéitər), Stephen (1779–1820), U.S. naval captain during the War of 1812. He commanded the 'United States', which captured (1812) H.M.S. 'Macedonian' and fought (1815) corsairs in the Mediterranean. He composed the toast: 'Our country! In her intercourse with foreign nations may she always be in the right: but our country, right or wrong'

de·cay (dikéi) **1.** v.i. (of a substance) to lose gradually its original form, quality or value, esp. (e.g. of a rock) by breaking up into pieces or (e.g. of rotten wood, or a diseased tooth) by chemical change || to decrease in activity, force or quality, as in the spontaneous breakdown of radioactive material || to fall into disrepair or great shabbiness || to lose strength or quality **2.** n. the state or process of decaying [O.F. decair]

decay constant the constant ratio of radioactive atoms disintegrating in a given short time interval to the total of those intact at the beginning of the interval

Dec·ca (dékə) n. **1.** radio phase-comparison system that uses a master and slave station to establish a hyperbolic lattice and provide accurate ground position-fixing facilities **2.** short-range navigation, medium-frequency system based on time differences in signals from ground transmitters at various points, used in heavily traveled coastal areas

Dec·can (dékən) the peninsula of India south of the Narbada River, sometimes restricted to the plateau between the Narbada and the Kistna

de·cease (disí:s) **1.** n. (in legal or formal contexts) death **2.** v.i. pres. part. **de·ceas·ing** past and past part. **de·ceased** to die **the de·ceased** n. the dead person or persons [M.E. deces fr. F.]

de·ce·dent (disí:d'nt) n. (law) the dead person [L. decedens (decedentis), departing]

de·ceit (disí:t) n. a deceiving || deception, guile || a trick, fraud **de·céit·ful** adj. [M.E. deceite fr. O.F.]

de·ceive (disí:v) pres. part. **de·ceiv·ing** past and past part. **de·ceived** v.t. to make (someone) believe what is false || to mislead || to break faith with (wife or husband) by committing adultery **to deceive oneself** to persuade oneself to believe something that is not true [O.F. deceveir]

de·cel·er·ate (di:séləreit) pres. part. **de·cel·er·at·ing** past and past part. **de·cel·er·at·ed** v.i. to slow down || v.t. to diminish the speed of **de·cel·er·a·tion** n. [DE+ACCELERATE]

De·cem·ber (disémbər) (abbr. Dec.) n. the 12th and last month of the year, having 31 days [O.F. decembre fr. L. decem, ten (being the tenth month of the Roman year)]

De·cem·brist (disémbrist) n. (Russ. hist.) a member of a conspiracy among certain nobles and army officers for constitutional reform. Their coup against Nicholas I failed (Dec. 1825)

de·cem·vir (disémvər) pl. **de·cem·virs, de·cem·vi·ri** (disémvərai) n. (Rom. hist.) a member of a council of 10 executives, esp. that appointed in 451 B.C. to formulate the first Roman code of law **de·cem·vi·rate** (disémvərit) n. [L. sing. fr. decem, ten+viri, men]

de·cen·cy (dí:sənsi:) pl. **de·cen·cies** n. the quality or state of being decent || accepted standards as regards propriety in language, behavior or modesty **the decencies** the conditions necessary for a decent style of living [fr. L. decentia]

de·cen·na·ry (disénəri:) **1.** pl. **de·cen·na·ries** n. a period of 10 years **2.** adj. pertaining to a period of 10 years [fr. L. decennis fr. decem, ten+annus, year]

de·cen·ni·al (diséni:əl) **1.** adj. happening every 10 years || lasting 10 years || relating to a period of 10 years **2.** n. a 10th anniversary [fr. L. decennium, ten-year period]

de·cent (dí:sənt) adj. observing propriety || fairly good but not outstanding, a decent result || (pop.) likable, a decent chap || (pop.) understanding, taking a humane view || [F. décent]

de·cen·tral·i·za·tion (di:sentrəlizéifən) n. a decentralizing or being decentralized || in an urban community, removal of certain centralized power or control to various areas, usu. to the area where operations take place

de·cen·tral·ize (di:séntrəlaiz) pres. part. **de·cen·tral·iz·ing** past and past part. **de·cen·tral·ized** v.t. to diminish central control of authority in (administration) so as to increase the authority of groups at a lower level || v.i. to pursue this policy

de·cep·tion (disépfən) n. a tricking, deceiving || the state of being deceived || something that deceives or tricks, a hoax, imposture [F. déception]

de·cep·tive (diséptiv) adj. misleading [F. déceptif]

deci- (dési:) prefix one tenth of (the unit specified, in the metric system) [fr. L. decimus, tenth]

dec·i·bel (désəb'l) n. (abbr. db.) a unit of power output expressed by the ratio of the amounts of power (e.g. acoustical or electric) emitted by two sources and equal to 10 times the common logarithm of the ratio || a similar unit for expressing the relative magnitude of two electric currents or voltages || a unit for measuring relative loudness of sounds, equal to the smallest difference of loudness detectable by the human ear. The range of sensitivity of the human ear based on this unit is 130 decibels (the average pain threshold), where 1 decibel is the faintest audible sound

de·cide (disáid) pres. part. **de·cid·ing** past and past part. **de·cid·ed** v.i. to choose, to decide between two candidates || to determine, to decide against a trip to Europe || v.t. to bring to a decision, what decided you to go? || to settle (a question or dispute) **de·cíd·ed** adj. clearly marked, distinct, a decided difference || (of personality or opinions) vigorous and determined **de·cíd·ed·ly** adv. [F. décider]

de·cid·ing (disáidiŋ) adj. of the marginal voice in a balanced decision, e.g., the deciding vote

de·cid·u·a (disídʒu:ə) pl. **de·cid·u·ae** (disídʒu:i:) n. the part of the lining of the uterus which undergoes special changes before and during pregnancy and which is cast off at birth || the part of the lining of the uterus which is cast off during menstruation **de·cíd·u·al** adj. [fr. L. deciduus fr. decidere, to fall away]

de·cid·u·ous (disídʒu:əs) adj. (of trees) shedding their leaves annually at the end of the growth period or at maturity || (of antlers, wings etc.) falling at the end of the growth period or at maturity [fr. L. deciduus fr. decidere, to fall down, away]

dec·i·gram (désigræm) n. one tenth of a gram

dec·ile (désail, dés'l) 1. *n.* (*math.*) any quality of a series of variables that divides it into 10 groups of equal value or frequency 2. *adj.* pertaining to such a quality or to such a group [fr. L. *decem*, ten]

dec·i·li·ter, *Br.* **dec·i·li·tre** (désəli:tər) *n.* one tenth of a liter

de·cil·lion (disíljən) *n.* *NUMBER TABLE [fr. L. *decem*, ten+MILLION]

dec·i·mal (désəməl) 1. *adj.* relating to 10 ‖ of a number scale based on 10, and using multiples and submultiples of 10, *the decimal system* 2. *n.* a group of digits which express number or measurement in units, tens and multiples of 10, tenths and other submultiples of 10. The digits for units and multiples of 10 are followed by a decimal point and then by the digits for tenths, hundredths etc. (Thus 14.26 represents 10+4 units+2 tenths+6 hundredths). A recurring decimal is a number in which the digits of the decimal fraction repeat, singly or in groups, to infinity (e.g. 1 ⅓=1.333...), the digits that repeat being marked by a dot above them (thus 1.3) [fr. M.L. *decimalis* fr. *decima*, tenth part]

decimal fraction a proper fraction in which the denominator is a power of 10. This is indicated by a decimal point placed to the left of the numerator. The number of digits after the point gives the power of 10 in the denominator. (Thus 0.7=7/10, 0.77 = 77/100, 0.777=777/1000)

dec·i·mal·ize (désəməlaiz) *pres. part.* **dec·i·mal·iz·ing** *past* and *past part.* **dec·i·mal·ized** *v.t.* to apply the decimal system to

dec·i·mal·ly (désəmali:) *adv.* by decimals ‖ by tens

decimal point the dot placed to the left of a decimal fraction

dec·i·mate (désəmeit) *pres. part.* **dec·i·mat·ing** *past* and *past part.* **dec·i·mat·ed** *v.t.* to destroy one tenth or (more generally) a large part of, *plague decimated the population* ‖ to put to death one in 10 of **dec·i·ma·tion** *n.* [fr. L. *decimare* (*decimatus*) fr. *decimus*, tenth]

dec·i·me·ter, *Br.* **dec·i·me·tre** (désəmi:tər) *n.* one tenth of a meter

de·ci·pher (disáifər) *v.t.* to put (a text transmitted in cipher) into plain writing ‖ to find out the meaning of, interpret (bad writing, hieroglyphics etc.) **de·ci·pher·a·ble** *adj.* **de·ci·pher·ment** *n.*

de·ci·sion (disíʒən) *n.* a making up of one's mind ‖ the result of making up one's mind, *the judge's decision is final* ‖ resoluteness, *a man of decision* [F. *décision*]

decision table (*management*) tabular summary of factors involved in a problem and alternatives

decision theory 1. (*statistics*) technique of comparing costs of possible courses of action with risks involved, to arrive at a course of action involving minimum-maximum costs with maximum probability of success 2. body of concepts dealing with making rational choices and evaluating risks

de·ci·sive (disáisiv) *adj.* conclusive, settling, *decisive proof* ‖ showing resoluteness, *a decisive personality* [M.L. *decisivus*]

De·cius (dí:ʃəs), Gaius Messius Quintus Trajanus (201–51), Roman emperor (249–51), under whom Christians were violently persecuted

deck (dek) *n.* a floor in a ship, most often wooden, running from side to side, sometimes from end to end ‖ (*Br.*) the floor of a bus ‖ (*printing*) a line of displayed titling, *the second deck of the title* ‖ (*computer*) means of storing information for future use, e.g., magnetic tape ‖ strip of material on which data can be recorded (magnetically, by punching or on optically sensitive material), sometimes in several channels ‖ (*Am.*) a pack of playing cards **on deck** above the lower decks, in the open air [prob. M.Du. *dec*, roof]

deck *v.t.* to array, *to deck a street with flags* ‖ (often with 'out') to dress (oneself) in a fine or fancy way ‖ (*naut.*) to provide with a deck or decks [prob. fr. M.Du. *deken*, to cover]

deck chair a light, collapsible reclining chair of canvas on a wooden or metal frame

deck·hand (dékhænd) *n.* a sailor who cleans the decks and does other manual jobs on ships

deck·house (dékhaus) *pl.* **deck·hous·es** (dékhauziz) *n.* a cabin built on the deck of a ship

deck·le (dék'l) 1. *n.* the edges of a papermaker's hand mold, or the restriction along the wire of a papermaking machine to control the stock ‖ the width of the paper between these deckles ‖ a

deckle edge 2. *v.t. pres. part.* **deck·ling** *past* and *past part.* **deck·led** to give a deckle edge to [G. *deckel* dim. of *decke*, cover]

deckle edge the rough edge of paper before trimming ‖ an imitation of this

deck tennis a game in which a rubber quoit is thrown back and forth over a net dividing a court laid out like a much-reduced tennis court

de·claim (dikléim) *v.t.* to recite (a poem etc.) publicly in a theatrical manner ‖ to pronounce (a discourse) seeking rhetorical effect ‖ *v.i.* to speak with too much emphasis ‖ (with 'against') to protest violently in speech [fr. L. *declamare*, to cry aloud]

dec·la·ma·tion (dɛkləméiʃən) *n.* the art or act of declaiming ‖ an impassioned speech ‖ an exercise in rhetorical speaking **de·clam·a·to·ry** (diklǽmətɔːri:, diklǽmətouri:) *adj.* [fr. L. *declamatio* (*declamationis*)]

de·clar·ant (dikléərənt) *n.* someone who makes a legal declaration [fr. L. *declarare*, to make clear]

dec·la·ra·tion (dɛkləréiʃən) *n.* an act of declaring, *a declaration of war* ‖ a manifesto ‖ a document formalizing matters to be made known publicly ‖ an announcement or affirmation ‖ a solemn statement made by the plaintiff or witnesses instead of the oath, but equally binding ‖ a statement to a customs officer of possessions liable to duty, or other disclosure for tax purposes ‖ (*cricket*) a captain's termination of an inning before all batsmen are out [fr. L. *declaratio* (*declarationis*)]

Declaration of Independence the document of July 4, 1776 in which the American colonies declared themselves independent of Britain. The text is as follows:

When in the Course of human events it becomes necessary for one people to dissolve the political bands which have connected them with another, and to assume among the powers of the earth, the separate and equal station to which the Laws of Nature and of Nature's God entitle them, a decent respect to the opinions of mankind requires that they should declare the causes which impel them to the separation.

We hold these truths to be self-evident, that all men are created equal, that they are endowed by their Creator with certain unalienable Rights, that among these are Life, Liberty and the pursuit of Happiness.—That to secure these rights, Governments are instituted among Men, deriving their just powers from the consent of the governed,—That whenever any Form of Government becomes destructive of these ends, it is the Right of the People to alter or to abolish it, and to institute new Government, laying its foundation on such principles and organizing its powers in such form, as to them shall seem most likely to effect their Safety and Happiness. Prudence, indeed, will dictate that Governments long established should not be changed for light and transient causes; and accordingly all experience hath shewn that mankind are more disposed to suffer, while evils are sufferable, than to right themselves by abolishing the forms to which they are accustomed. But when a long train of abuses and usurpations, pursuing invariably the same Object evinces a design to reduce them under absolute Despotism, it is their right, it is their duty, to throw off such Government, and to provide new Guards for their future security.—Such has been the patient sufferance of these Colonies; and such is now the necessity which constrains them to alter their former Systems of Government. The history of the present King of Great Britain is a history of repeated injuries and usurpations, all having in direct object the establishment of an absolute Tyranny over these States. To prove this, let Facts be submitted to a candid world.

He has refused his Assent to Laws, the most wholesome and necessary for the public good.

He has forbidden his Governors to pass Laws of immediate and pressing importance, unless suspended in their operation till his Assent should be obtained; and when so suspended, he has utterly neglected to attend to them.

He has refused to pass other Laws for the accommodation of large districts of people, unless those people would relinquish the right of Representation in the Legislature, a right inestimable to them and formidable to tyrants only.

He has called together legislative bodies at places unusual, uncomfortable, and distant from the depository of their Public Records, for the sole purpose of fatiguing them into compliance with his measures.

He has dissolved Representative Houses repeatedly, for opposing with manly firmness his invasions on the rights of the people.

He has refused for a long time, after such dissolutions, to cause others to be elected; whereby the Legislative Powers, incapable of Annihilation, have returned to the People at large for their exercise; the State remaining in the mean time exposed to all the dangers of invasion from without, and convulsions within.

He has endeavored to prevent the population of these States; for that purpose obstructing the Laws for Naturalization of Foreigners; refusing to pass others to encourage their migrations hither, and raising the conditions of new Appropriations of Lands.

He has obstructed the Administration of Justice, by refusing his Assent to Laws for establishing Judiciary Powers.

He has made Judges dependent on his Will alone, for the tenure of their offices, and the amount and payment of their salaries.

He has erected a multitude of New Offices, and sent hither swarms of Officers to harass our people, and eat out their substance.

He has kept among us, in times of peace, Standing Armies without the Consent of our legislatures.

He has affected to render the Military independent of and superior to the Civil Power.

He has combined with others to subject us to a jurisdiction foreign to our constitution, and unacknowledged by our laws; giving his Assent to their Acts of pretended Legislation:

For quartering large bodies of armed troops among us:

For protecting them, by a mock Trial, from punishment for any Murders which they should commit on the Inhabitants of these States:

For cutting off our trade with all parts of the world:

For imposing Taxes on us without our Consent:

For depriving us in many cases, of the benefits of Trial by Jury:

For transporting us beyond Seas to be tried for pretended offences:

For abolishing the free System of English Laws in a neighbouring Province, establishing therein an Arbitrary government, and enlarging its Boundaries so as to render it at once an example and fit instrument for introducing the same absolute rule into these Colonies:

For taking away our Charters, abolishing our most valuable Laws and altering fundamentally the Forms of our Governments:

For suspending our own Legislatures, and declaring themselves invested with power to legislate for us in all cases whatsoever.

He has abdicated Government here, by declaring us out of his Protection and waging War against us.

He has plundered our seas, ravaged our Coasts, burnt our towns, and destroyed the lives of our people.

He is at this time transporting large Armies of foreign Mercenaries to compleat the works of death, desolation and tyranny, already begun with circumstances of Cruelty & Perfidy scarcely paralleled in the most barbarous ages, and totally unworthy the Head of a civilized nation.

He has constrained our fellow Citizens taken Captive on the high Seas to bear Arms against their Country, to become the executioners of their friends and Brethren, or to fall themselves by their Hands.

He has excited domestic insurrections amongst us, and has endeavoured to bring on the inhabitants of our frontiers, the merciless Indian Savages, whose known rule of warfare, is an undistinguished destruction of all ages, sexes and conditions.

In every stage of these Oppressions We have Petitioned for Redress in the most humble terms: Our repeated Petitions have been answered only by repeated injury. A Prince, whose character is thus marked by every act which may define a Tyrant, is unfit to be the ruler of a free people.

Nor have We been wanting in attentions to our British brethren. We have warned them from time to time of attempts by their legislature to extend an unwarrantable jurisdiction over us. We have reminded them of the circumstances of our emigration and settlement here. We have appealed to their native justice and magnanimity, and we have conjured them by the ties of our common kindred to disavow these usurpations, which would inevitably interrupt our connections and correspondence. They too have been deaf to the voice of justice and of consanguinity. We must, therefore, acquiesce in the necessity, which denounces our Separation, and hold them, as we hold the rest of mankind, Enemies in War, in Peace Friends.

WE THEREFORE, the Representatives of the UNITED STATES OF AMERICA, in General Congress, Assembled, appealing to the Supreme Judge of the world for the rectitude of our intentions, do, in the Name, and by Authority of the good People of these Colonies, solemnly publish and declare, That these United Colonies are, and of Right ought to be FREE AND INDEPENDENT STATES; that they are Absolved from all Allegiance to the British Crown, and that all political connection between them and the State of Great Britain, is and ought to be totally dissolved; and that as Free and Independent States, they have full Power to levy War, conclude Peace, contract Alliances, establish Commerce, and to do all other Acts and Things which Independent States may of right do. — And for the support of this Declaration, with a firm reliance on the protection of Divine Providence, we mutually pledge to each other our Lives, our Fortunes and our sacred Honor

Declaration of Indulgence *INDULGENCE, DECLARATION OF

Declaration of Lima *INTERNATIONAL CONFERENCE OF AMERICAN STATES, EIGHTH

Declaration of the Rights of Man *RIGHTS OF MAN, DECLARATION OF THE

de·clar·a·tive (diklǽrǝtiv) *adj.* in the nature of a declaration, declaratory [fr. L. *declarativus*]

de·clar·a·to·ry (diklǽrǝtɔri:, diklǽrǝtǝuri:) *adj.* in the nature of a declaration || (*law*) explaining what the existing law is, *a declaratory act* [fr. L. *declarare (declaratus)*, to declare]

Declaratory Act a British act of parliament (1766), passed simultaneously with the repeal of the Stamp Act. It asserted that the colonies were subordinate to and dependent upon the Crown and parliament and that the king and parliament could bind the colonies in all cases

de·clare (diklέǝr) *pres. part.* **de·clar·ing** *past and past part.* **de·clared** *v.t.* to make known explicitly or formally, announce, *to declare war* || to cause to be paid or, *to declare a dividend* || to pronounce (a person) to be (something), *to declare someone the winner* || to affirm or protest strongly, *to declare one's innocence* || to state (dutiable goods) in one's possession || to give particulars of (income liable to tax etc.) || (*bridge*) to name (the trump suit) or call ('no trump') || (*other card games*) to announce the holding of (certain combinations of cards) || *v.i.* (*cricket*) to decide to stop batting before the whole side is out || (with 'against' or 'for') to take sides, vote **de·clárred** *adj.* stated, *declared profits* || professed, *declared intentions* **de·clár·er** *n.* (esp. at cards) [F. *déclarer*]

de·clen·sion (diklénʃǝn) *n.* (*gram.*, in some languages) the inflection of nouns, adjectives, pronouns by means of desinences indicating case, gender and number || (*gram.*) a class of noun etc., as distinguished according to its set of inflections || a declining from a standard, quality etc. || a slope, inclination [perh. F. fr. L. *declinatio (declinationis)*, a bending aside]

de·clin·a·ble (diklάinǝb'l) *adj.* able to be declined grammatically [F. *déclinable*]

dec·li·na·tion (deklinéiʃǝn) *n.* a refusal || the angular distance of a star etc. north or south of the celestial equator, celestial latitude || the compass angle (which varies with the place and time of year) between the direction of a magnetic needle and the true or geographical meridian (cf. DIP) **dec·li·ná·tion·al** *adj.* [O.F. *déclinacion*]

de·cline (diklάin) 1. *v. pres. part.* **de·clin·ing** *past and past part.* **de·clined** *v.t.* to refuse || (*gram.*) to inflect (a noun, adjective, pronoun) || *v.i.* to lose vigor, deteriorate || to refuse || to fall off, diminish (e.g. of prices or numbers) || to slope downwards || (*rhet.*, of the sun or of the day) to begin to go down or draw toward the close 2. *n.* a falling off, loss of vigor, sinking or deterioration || a fall in price or number || a downward slope || a refusal || (*rhet.*, of the sun or

the day) a progress downward or toward a close [F. *décliner*]

de·clin·ing-bal·ance method (diklάiniŋbǽlǝnts) system of calculating depreciation at a decreasing rate, based on a percentage of the previous depreciated cost

dec·li·nom·e·ter (deklinómitǝr) *n.* an instrument for measuring magnetic declination [fr. L. *declinare*, to turn aside+METER]

de·cliv·i·tous (diklívitǝs) *adj.* sloping steeply downwards

de·cliv·i·ty (diklíviti:) *pl.* **de·cliv·i·ties** *n.* a downward slope [fr. L. *declivitas* fr. *de-, away+clivus*, slope]

de·clutch (di:klʌtʃ) *v.i.* to disengage the clutch of a vehicle

de·coct (dikɔ́kt) *v.t.* to extract or prepare a substance from (herbs etc.) by boiling [fr. L. *decoquere (decoctus)*, to boil down]

de·coc·tion (dikɔ́kʃǝn) *n.* a boiling to extract some substance || the resultant liquor [O.F.]

de·code (di:kóud) *pres. part.* **de·cod·ing** *past and past part.* **de·cod·ed** *v.t.* to translate from code into ordinary language

dé·col·le·tage, de·colle·tage (deikɔltáʒ, dekǝlǝtáʒ) *n.* the low-cut neck of a dress || the exposure of neck and shoulders by such a dress [F.]

dé·col·le·té; de·colle·te (deikɔltéi, dekǝlǝtéi) **1.** *adj.* (of a dress) cut low at the neck **2.** *n.* décolletage [F.]

de·col·or·ize, Br. also de·col·our·ize (di:kʌ́lǝraiz) *pres. part.* **de·col·or·iz·ing, Br. also de·col·our·iz·ing** *past and past part.* **de·col·or·ized, Br. also de·col·our·ized** *v.t.* to deprive of color

de·com·pose (di:kǝmpóuz) *pres. part.* **de·com·pos·ing** *past and past part.* **de·com·posed** *v.i.* to break up into component parts or elements || to disintegrate, rot || *v.t.* to cause to break up into component parts or elements || to cause to rot **de·com·po·si·tion** (di:kɔmpǝzíʃǝn) *n.* [F. *décomposer*]

de·com·pos·er (di:kǝmpóuzǝr) *n.* (*biol.*) any organism (bacteria, fungi) that degrades organic substances to their chemical constituents

de·com·pound 1. (dí:kɔ́mpaund, di:kǝmpáund) *adj.* compounded of what is already compounded || (*bot.*, of leaves) having divisions which are themselves compounded **2.** (di:kǝmpáund) *v.t.* to decompose, break down into component parts

de·com·press (di:kǝmprés) *v.t.* to decrease pressure on or reduce compression in **de·com·pres·sion** (di:kǝmpréʃǝn) *n.*

de·con·se·crate (di:kɔ́nsikreit) *pres. part.* **de·con·se·crat·ing** *past and past part.* **de·con·se·crat·ed** *v.t.* to make over (a consecrated building or plot of ground) to secular use

de·con·tam·i·nate (di:kǝntǽmineit) *pres. part.* **de·con·tam·i·nat·ing** *past and past part.* **de·con·tam·i·nat·ed** *v.t.* to free from contamination, esp. to rid (clothes, buildings etc.) of poison gas || to remove classified portions from a secret document **de·con·tam·i·na·tion** *n.*

de·con·trol (di:kǝntróul) **1.** *v.t. pres. part.* **de·con·trol·ling** *past and past part.* **de·con·trolled** to release from control **2.** *n.* a release from control

de·cor, dé·cor (déikɔr, deikɔ́r) *n.* stage scenery || the furnishings and decoration of a room, house etc. [F.]

dec·o·rate (dékǝreit) *pres. part.* **dec·o·rat·ing** *past and past part.* **dec·o·rat·ed** *v.t.* to add something ornamental to, adorn || to honor (someone) with a medal, ribbon etc. || (*Br.*) to paint or put new paper on the walls of (a room etc.) [fr. L. *decorare (decoratus)* fr. *decus*, beauty]

Dec·o·rat·ed (dékǝreitid) *adj.* of the English Gothic style of architecture of the 14th c., distinguished by floral decoration and geometrical tracery

dec·o·ra·tion (dekǝréiʃǝn) *n.* a decorating || something decorative || a ribbon or medal etc. awarded for bravery, service etc. [fr. L. *decoratio (decorationis)*]

Decoration Day Memorial Day

dec·o·ra·tive (dékǝrǝtiv, dékrǝtiv) *adj.* serving to decorate

dec·o·ra·tor (dékǝreitǝr) *n.* someone who professionally plans interior decoration schemes (colors, materials etc.) || (*Br.*) a painter and paperhanger

dec·o·rous (dékǝrǝs, dikɔ́rǝs, dikɔ́urǝs) *adj.* observing propriety [corresponding to L. *decorus* fr. *decor*, beauty]

de·cor·ti·cate (di:kɔ́rtikeit) *pres. part.* **de·cor·ti·cat·ing** *past and past part.* **de·cor·ti·cat·ed** *v.t.* to peel, husk, remove the outer coating from

de·cór·ti·ca·tor *n.* a machine for doing this [fr. L. *decorticare (decorticatus)* fr. *cortex*, bark]

de·co·rum (dikɔ́rǝm, dikɔ́urǝm) *n.* conformity with conventional social manners in speech, writing, dress, behavior [L. neut. of *decorus*, fitting]

de·cou·page (deiku:páʒ) *n.* (*television*) the breakdown of action in a scene into separate shots

de·coup·le (dǝkʌ́pǝl) *v.* **1.** (*electr.*) to reduce a common impedance in a circuit, e.g., bypassing **2.** (*nuclear eng.*) to reduce the effect of a nuclear shock wave, esp. by exploding underground — **decoupler** *n.*

de·coy (dikɔ́i, dí:kɔi) **1.** *n.* a real or imitation bird or animal used to lure other birds or animals to a place where they may be trapped or shot || the place into which animals are lured || a person or thing used as a trap **2.** *v.t.* to lure successfully [earlier *coy* fr. Du. *kooi*, a wildfowl trap fr. L. *cavea*, cage (*de-* unexplained)]

decoy ships (*mil.*) warships or other ships camouflaged as merchantmen or converted commerce raiders, with their armament and other fighting equipment hidden and with special provisions for unmasking their weapons quickly

decoy transponder device for confusing radar signals by returning a large, misleading signal when exposed to a radar pulse

de·crease (dí:kri:s, dikrí:s) *n.* a diminishing || the amount by which something is diminished **on the decrease** lessening [O.F. *decreis*]

de·crease (dikrí:s) *pres. part.* **de·creas·ing** *past and past part.* **de·creased** *v.i.* to grow less, diminish, dwindle || *v.t.* to make less or smaller || (*knitting*) to narrow by casting off or knitting two stitches together [O.F. *descreistre (descreiss-)*]

de·cree (dikrí:) **1.** *n.* an order made by a ruling body or other authority || a judicial decision or sentence given by a court of equity, admiralty, probate or divorce **2.** *pres. part.* **de·cree·ing** *past and past part.* **de·creed** *v.t.* to appoint or order by decree || (of fate) to ordain || *v.i.* to issue a decree [O.F. *decré*]

decree ni·si (nάisai) *n.* a conditional decree of divorce, subject to being made absolute at a later date

dec·re·ment (dékrǝmǝnt) *n.* a decrease, lessening, loss || the quantity lost by wastage etc. || (*radio*) the speed of damping out waves || (*math.*) a negative increment [fr. L. *decrementum* fr. *decrescere*, to decrease]

de·crep·it (dikrépit) *adj.* made dilapidated or extremely weak by age or illness [F. *décrépit*]

de·crep·i·tate (dikrépiteit) *pres. part.* **de·crep·i·tat·ing** *past and past part.* **de·crep·i·tat·ed** *v.t.* to heat (crystals) so as to cause crackling or until crackling ceases || *v.i.* to make a crackling sound, e.g. when crystals are heated **de·crep·i·ta·tion** *n.* [fr. Mod. L. *decrepitare (decrepitatus)*, to crackle]

de·crep·i·tude (dikrépitu:d, dikrépitju:d) *n.* extreme physical weakness || extreme dilapidation

de·cre·scen·do (di:kriʃéndou, deikriʃéndou) *adv. and adj.* (*mus.*) decreasing in loudness [Ital.]

de·cres·cent (dikrésǝnt) *adj.* (of the moon) waning [fr. L. *decrescens (decrescentis)* fr. *decrescere*, to grow smaller]

de·cre·tal (dikrí:t'l) *n.* (*hist.*) a papal decree, settling some doctrinal point or matter of ecclesiastical law || (*pl.*) the collection of such decrees forming part of canon law **de·cré·tal·ist** *n.* a decretist [F. *décrétal*]

de·cre·tist (dikrí:tist) *n.* someone specializing in canon law [fr. M.L. *decretista*]

de·cre·tive (dikrí:tiv) *adj.* with the force of a decree [fr. L. *decernere (decretus)*, to decree]

de·cri·al (dikrάiǝl) *n.* a disparagement, depreciation

de·crim·i·nal·ize (di:kríminǝlaiz) *v.* to remove an action from penal-code penalties —**decriminalization** *n.*

de·cry (dikrάi) *pres. part.* **de·cry·ing** *past and past part.* **de·cried** *v.t.* to disparage, attack in speech [F. *décrier*]

de·crypt (di:krípt) *v.* to convert cipher (encrypted) text into its equivalent plain text by means of a cryptosystem instead of by cryptoanalysis [The term "decrypt" covers the meanings of decipher and decode.]

de·cum·bent (dikʌ́mbǝnt) *adj.* (*bot.*, of stems) trailing on the ground, but rising at the apex || (*zool.*, of bristles etc.) lying flat [fr. L. *decumbere*, to lie down]

de·cur·rent (dikérǝnt, dikʌ́:rǝnt) adj. (bot., of a leaf) having the base prolonged down the stem below the place of insertion [fr. L. decurrens (decurrentis), running down]

de·cus·sate (dikʌ́sit, dikʌ́seit) adj. (bot., of leaves) arranged in pairs, each pair being at right angles to the pairs next to it [fr. L. decussare (decussatus), to cross like an X]

de·dans (dǝdã́) pl. **de·dans** (dǝdã́) n. an open gallery at the service end of the tennis court [F.=inside]

ded·i·cate (dédikeit) pres. part. **ded·i·cat·ing** past and past part. **ded·i·cat·ed** v.t. to devote to a sacred purpose ‖ to devote to any serious purpose, inscribe (a book etc.) in someone's honor **ded·i·ca·tee** (dedikǝtí:) n. the person to whom a thing is dedicated [fr. L. dedicare (dedicatus), to devote]

ded·i·ca·tion (dedikéiʃǝn) n. the act or rite of dedicating ‖ an inscription in a book or on a building etc. as a tribute to a person or persons [O.F. dédication]

ded·i·ca·tive (dédikeitiv) adj. in the nature of a dedication

ded·i·ca·tor (dédikeitǝr) n. someone who dedicates **ded·i·ca·to·ry** (dédikǝtɔri:, dédikǝtouri:) adj.

de·duce (didú:s, didjú:s) pres. part. **de·duc·ing** past and past part. **de·duced** v.t. to infer by reasoning from known facts ‖ to trace the descent or derivation of [fr. L. deducere, to lead away]

de·duct (didʌ́kt) v.t. to subtract, take (an amount) away **de·duct·i·ble** adj. able to be deducted, esp. as a tax allowance [fr. L. deducere (deductus), to lead away]

de·duc·tion (didʌ́kʃǝn) n. a subtracting or taking away ‖ the amount deducted ‖ reasoning from the general to the particular ‖ reasoning in which the conclusion follows necessarily from given premises (cf. INDUCTION) ‖ the conclusion reached in this way [fr. L. deductio (deductionis)]

de·duc·tive (didʌ́ktiv) adj. of reasoning by deduction [fr. L. deductivus]

deed (di:d) 1. n. something done, an act ‖ a brave or otherwise outstanding feat ‖ actual performance as opposed to mere words, guerrillas are soldiers in deed if not in name ‖ (law) a sealed written or printed agreement containing some transfer or other contract, e.g. in the conveyance of real estate 2. v.t. (law) to convey or transfer by deed [O.E. dǣd]

deed poll pl. **deeds poll** (law) a deed executed by one party only, (hist.) on paper not indented, but polled or cut even

deem (di:m) v.t. to consider as true in the impossibility of proving, he was deemed to be the father of the child ‖ to come to believe, he deemed it his duty to go [O.E. dēman, to judge]

deem·ster (dí:mstǝr) n. one of the two justices of the Manx common-law courts, each having jurisdiction over half the Isle of Man [M.E. dēmestre fr. dēmere, someone who judges]

deep (di:p) 1. adj. extending far down below the surface ‖ extending to a specified extent downwards, a well 20 feet deep ‖ (baseball) beyond the normal area covered ‖ plunged in, hands deep in pockets, deep in debt ‖ wide, extending back, lined up six deep ‖ completely absorbed, deep in thought ‖ heartfelt, deep sorrow ‖ well concealed, a deep secret ‖ thorough, deep learning ‖ profound, deep sleep ‖ overwhelming, deep disgrace ‖ (of colors) dark and intense, a deep blue ‖ low-pitched, a deep voice ‖ (of a person) hard to make out, inscrutably clever and perhaps cunning ‖ (of a remark etc.) suggesting aspects of truth not at once apparent **to go off the deep end** to lose all sense of caution ‖ (Br.) to lose one's temper 2. adv. profoundly, deeply, to drink deep ‖ far down, to dig deep 3. n. the intervening unmarked point between two consecutive fathom marks on a lead line ‖ a deep part of a body of water, esp. an ocean channel over 3,000 fathoms **the deep** (rhet.) the sea **deep·en** v.t. to make deep or deeper ‖ v.i. to become deep or deeper [O.E. dēop, dīop]

deep field (cricket) the part of the field near the boundary, esp. behind the bowler, or the player fielding there

Deep-freeze (dí:pfrí:z) n. a freezer enabling food to be stored over a long period [Trademark]

deep freezer a freezer

deep kneading (cosmetology) massage technique grasping and squeezing large portions of flesh

deep minefield an antisubmarine minefield that is safe for surface ships to cross

deep-root·ed (dí:prú:tid, dí:prútid) adj. very hard to do away with, a deep-rooted dislike

deep-sea (dí:psí:) adj. of or pertaining to the deep parts of the sea, not the offshore waters

deep-seat·ed (dí:psí:tid) adj. deep-rooted

deep snow special section in CIA

deep space or **deep sky** (astron.) space beyond the earth and the moon

deep structure (generative grammar) abstract structure in phrase making based on sounds that permit intuitive understanding of ambiguous sentences, applying certain transformational rules ant. surface structure syn. underlying structure

deer (diǝr) pl. **deer**, **deers** n. any of several hoofed, ruminant mammals of fam. Cervidae, found almost universally except in much of Africa and in Australia. The males of most species have solid, branched horns, shed each year. They include elk, moose and reindeer [O.E. dīor, dēor]

Deere (diǝr), John (1804–86), U.S. manufacturer of agricultural implements and a pioneer in the steel plow industry

deer·hound (díǝrhaund) n. a large, rough-haired, long-tailed greyhound, originally used in Scotland for hunting deer

deer lick a damp, salty place or spring where deer come to lick

deer mouse any of various North American mice of genus Peromyscus, esp. P. leucopus of the eastern U.S.A.

deer·skin (díǝrskin) n. the skin of a deer, esp. for clothing ‖ a garment made from it

deer·stalk·er (díǝrstɔkǝr) n. someone who stalks deer for sport ‖ a cloth cap with peaks at front and back, and earflaps

deer·stalk·ing (díǝrstɔkiŋ) n. the sport of approaching deer without being scented or seen, in order to shoot them

de·es·ca·late (di:éskǝleit) pres. part. **de·es·ca·lat·ing** past and past part. **de·es·ca·lat·ed** v.i. (of something that has been escalated) to decrease gradually but steadily ‖ v.t. to decrease gradually but steadily (something, e.g. a war, that has been escalated)

deet [$C_{12}H_{17}ON$] (di:t) n. diethyltoluamide, an insect repellant also DET

def. definition

de·face (diféis) pres. part. **de·fac·ing** past and past part. **de·faced** v.t. to disfigure, spoil the appearance of ‖ to make illegible **de·face·ment** n. [obs. F. defacer]

defac·to (di:fǽktou) 1. adv. actually, in reality 2. adj. maintaining effective control although not permanently and constitutionally established, or not fully recognized by other states, the de facto government ‖ lacking certain formalities of incorporation, a de facto corporation [L.]

defaecate *DEFECATE

defaecation *DEFECATION

de·fal·cate (difǽlkeit, difɔ́lkeit) pres. part. **de·fal·cat·ing** past and past part. **de·fal·cat·ed** v.i. to commit defalcations [fr. M.L. defalcare (defalcatus), to cut off]

de·fal·ca·tion (di:fælkéiʃǝn, di:fɔlkéiʃǝn) n. a misappropriation of entrusted money ‖ the amount misappropriated [fr. M.L. defalcatio (defalcationis), a cutting off]

def·a·ma·tion (defǝméiʃǝn) n. the act of defaming someone's reputation

de·fam·a·to·ry (difǽmǝtɔri:, difǽmǝtouri:) adj. containing defamations ‖ liable to injure a reputation

de·fame (diféim) pres. part. **de·fam·ing** past and past part. **de·famed** v.t. to attack the good reputation of (someone) [O.F. diffamer]

de·fault (difɔ́lt) 1. n. a failure to carry out an obligation, e.g. failure to appear in court when required ‖ failure to pay a debt ‖ (sports) failure to take part in or finish a contest **in default of** in the absence or lack of 2. v.t. to declare (someone) in default and enter judgment against him ‖ (sports) to fail to take part in or finish (a contest) ‖ to forfeit (a contest) by such a failure ‖ v.i. to be guilty of default, e.g. to fail to pay a debt or appear in court **de·fault·er** n. someone who defaults ‖ a soldier guilty of a military offense [O.F. defaute, defaillir (3rd person sing. default)]

de·fea·sance (difí:z'ns) n. (law) a rendering null and void ‖ (law) the conditions in accordance with which a deed is made void ‖ (law) the collateral deed expressing such conditions [O.F. defesance, undoing]

de·fea·si·ble (difí:zǝb'l) adj. (law) capable of being annulled or made void [A.F.]

de·feat (difí:t) 1. n. an overcoming or being overcome in war, sport or argument ‖ frustration, prevention from success 2. v.t. to conquer in war, sport or argument ‖ to frustrate ‖ (law) to make null and void [fr. O.F. desfaire (desfeit), to undo]

de·feat·ism (difí:tizǝm) n. mental acceptance of defeat before the real test takes place (thus making real defeat more likely) **de·feat·ist** adj. and n. [fr. F. défaitisme]

def·e·cate, Br. also **def·ae·cate** (défikeit) pres. part. **def·e·cat·ing**, Br. also **def·ae·cat·ing** past and past part. **def·e·cat·ed**, Br. also **def·ae·cat·ed** v.i. to empty the bowels **def·e·ca·tion**, Br. also **def·ae·ca·tion** n. [L. defecare (defecatus) fr. faex (faecis), dregs]

de·fect (dífekt, difékt) 1. n. a shortcoming, inadequacy ‖ a fault, blemish 2. v.i. (difékt) to desert ‖ to fall away from a cause or party (and usually switch allegiance to another) [fr. L. deficere (defectus), to fail]

de·fec·tion (difékʃǝn) n. a falling or breaking away, e.g. from a party, allegiance or religion [fr. L. defectio (defectionis), a failure]

de·fec·tive (diféktiv) 1. adj. having faults ‖ incomplete ‖ (of intelligence) noticeably subnormal ‖ (gram.) lacking some of the usual forms of declension or conjugation 2. n. a person noticeably subnormal either physically or mentally ‖ (gram.) a word lacking some of the usual forms of declension or conjugation [F. défectif]

de·fec·tor (diféktǝr) n. someone who defects [L.]

defence *DEFENSE

defence mechanism *DEFENSE MECHANISM

de·fend (difénd) v.t. to protect from danger, slander, criticism etc. ‖ to justify ‖ (law) to plead in court on behalf of (someone) ‖ v.i. to plead for the defense [O.F. defendre, to ward off]

de·fend·ant (diféndǝnt) 1. n. (law) the accused person in a case 2. adj. (law) being the accused, a defendant company [F. défendant, defending]

de·fend·er (diféndǝr) n. someone who protects from attack ‖ (sport) the holder of a championship or other title, defending it against the challenger

Defender of the Faith ('Fidei Defensor') the title given by Pope Leo X (1521) to Henry VIII for his writings against Luther. It was withdrawn (1534), but conferred anew by parliament (1544) and has been held ever since by English monarchs

de·fen·es·tra·tion (di:fenistréiʃǝn) n. the act of throwing a person or thing out of a window [DE-+L. fenestra, window]

Defenestration of Prague the throwing of the Emperor's deputy governors out of the window at Prague (May 23, 1618) by Protestant Bohemians in protest at Catholic repression. It touched off the Thirty Years' War

de·fense, Br. **de·fence** (diféns) n. the act of resisting attack ‖ preparation to meet attack ‖ something which defends ‖ (pl., mil.) fortifications ‖ an answer, e.g. to a charge, in self-justification ‖ (law) the defendant's denial or plea and proceedings in court **de·fense·less**, Br. **de·fence·less** adj. [M.E. defens fr. O.F., a forbidden thing and M.E. defense, prohibition fr. L.]

Defense, Department of, U.S. federal department organized in 1949 to direct the armed forces. It is headed by the secretary of defense and operated by the secretary and the Joint Chiefs of Staff, which consists of a chairman and the Army, Navy, Air Force, and when necessary Marine, chiefs of staff. Formed as directed in the National Security Act (1947), the department is headquartered in the Pentagon

defense mechanism, Br. **defence mechanism** a defensive reaction by an organism, e.g. against disease ‖ (psychoanal.) an unconscious protective reaction of the mind to cope with unconscious, personally unacceptable drives

de·fen·si·ble (difénsǝb'l) adj. justifiable ‖ easily defended, in argument or war **de·fen·si·bly** adv. [fr. L. defensibilis]

de·fen·sive (difénsiv) 1. adj. used, done or serving for defense ‖ (securities) of an investment that is not subject to great cyclical change 2. n. the state or position of defense **on the defensive** resisting attack ‖ prepared to resist attack ‖ answering back to what one interprets as criticism [F. défensif]

de·fer (difǝ́:r) pres. part. **de·fer·ring** past and past part. **de·ferred** v.t. to postpone ‖ v.i. to put off taking action **deferable** adj. *DEFERRABLE [M.E. differen fr. O.F.]

defer pres. part. **deferring** past and past part. **deferred** v.i. (followed by 'to') to allow someone else's opinion, judgment etc. to have more weight than one's own, willingly or politely, I defer to your greater experience [F. déférer, to carry down or away]

def·er·ence (défərəns) n. polite regard for someone else's wishes, ideas etc. ∥ respectful submission in deference to out of submissive respect for [F. déférence]

def·er·ent (défərənt) adj. (of a conduit, duct etc.) serving to carry away [F. déférent]

def·er·en·tial (defərénʃəl) adj. showing deference

de·fer·ment (difə́:rmənt) n. postponement, esp. of compulsory military service

de·fer·ra·ble, de·fer·a·ble (difə́:rəb'l) adj. able to be deferred

de·ferred (difə́:rd) adj. put off, postponed ∥ on which interest, dividend etc. is withheld until a stated time

deferred annuity an annuity under which the first payment is made at some date after the end of the first year following purchase

deferred gratification a generally middle-class value or attitude that calls for postponement of immediate gratification or satisfaction of needs in order to achieve long-term education and/or economic goals

deferred income revenues to be paid and received at a later date, e.g., after retirement, in lieu of present payment

Def·fand (defɑ̃), Marie de Vichy-Chamrond, marquise du (1697–1780), French noblewoman and letter writer whose salon attracted philosophers and writers, notably Horace Walpole, Voltaire and d'Alembert

de·fi·ance (difáiəns) n. a deliberate challenge (to authority) by disobedience ∥ an attitude or action designed to provoke hostility ∥ a fierce, contemptuous opposition ∥ a deliberate disregarding in defiance of going deliberately counter to [O.F. defiance]

de·fi·ant (difáiənt) adj. showing defiance [F. défiant]

de·fib·ril·late (di:fíbrileit) v. to restore twitching heart rhythm to normal —**defibrillation** n. —**defibrillative** adj. —**defibrillator** n. electronic device, sometimes implanted —**defibrillatory** adv. —**minidefibrillator** n.

de·fi·cien·cy (difíʃənsi:) pl. **de·fi·cien·cies** n. a lack ∥ a shortage ∥ the amount by which something falls short, esp. revenue ∥ the quality or state of being deficient [fr. L.L. deficientia fr. deficere, to be lacking]

deficiency disease a disease, e.g. scurvy, caused by lack of necessary elements in the diet

de·fi·cient (difíʃənt) adj. lacking something which should be present ∥ below essential requirements ∥ below normal standards [fr. L. deficiens (deficientis) fr. deficere, to be lacking]

def·i·cit (défisit) n. a financial accounting loss [F. déficit]

def·i·lade (defəléid) 1. v.t. pres. part. **def·i·lad·ing** past and past part. **def·i·lad·ed** (mil.) to arrange (fortifications) against enfilading fire 2. n. the precaution of defilading [F.]

de·file (dí:fail, difáil) 1. n. (mil.) a marching in file ∥ a narrow way through which troops can pass only in a narrow column ∥ a narrow steep valley, gorge 2. v.i. pres. part. **de·fil·ing** past and past part. **de·filed** to march in file [F. défiler]

de·file (difáil) pres. part. **de·fil·ing** past and past part. **de·filed** v.t. to desecrate or make ritually unclean, to profane ∥ to corrupt morally **de·file·ment** n. [earlier defoul fr. O.F. defouler rel. to O.E. fūl, foul]

de·fin·a·ble (difáinəb'l) adj. able to be precisely stated or delimited

de·fine (difáin) pres. part. **de·fin·ing** past and past part. **de·fined** v.t. to state the precise meaning of ∥ to be what characterizes (something) ∥ to formulate (e.g. a scientific principle) or describe precisely (e.g. a doctor's duties) ∥ to mark the limits of ∥ to outline clearly, a well-defined image [O.F. definer]

def·i·nite (définit) adj. clear, not vague ∥ limiting, definite bounds ∥ limited, a definite area ∥ (gram., of a modifier) designating an identifiable person or thing, e.g. 'this' and 'that' or the article 'the' **déf·i·nite·ly** 1. adv. exactly 2. interj. (pop.) yes, certainly [fr. L. definitus, having fixed limits]

def·i·ni·tion (definíʃən) n. an act of defining ∥ a set of words explaining the meaning e.g. of a word, scientific principle or property ∥ clearness of detail, esp. of the image given by a lens in a photograph, or on a television screen [O.F.]

de·fin·i·tive (difínitiv) adj. serving to define ∥ decisive, final, a definitive verdict ∥ most authoritative, a definitive biography ∥ (biol., of the host of an adult parasite) fully grown or developed [O.F. definitif]

def·la·grate (défləgreit) pres. part. **def·la·grat·ing** past and past part. **def·la·grat·ed** v.i. to burn rapidly or vigorously ∥ to undergo a vigorous exothermic chemical reaction evolving flame or sparks, and spreading through the material at a speed under that of sound (cf. DETONATE) ∥ v.t. to cause to undergo such a reaction [fr. L. deflagrare (deflagratus), to burn down]

de·flate (diféit) pres. part. **de·flat·ing** past and past part. **de·flat·ed** v.t. to let air or gas out of ∥ (fig.) to cause to shrink suddenly, to deflate someone's self-esteem ∥ to reduce (currency or prices) from an inflated condition ∥ v.i. to lose shape or rigidity through the escape of air or gas **de·fla·tion** n. **de·fla·tion·ar·y** (difléiʃəneri:) adj. [fr. L. deflare (deflatus), to blow away]

de·flect (diflékt) v.t. to bend or turn aside ∥ v.i. (of an arrow, light rays etc.) to deviate from a course [fr. L. deflectere]

de·flec·tion, Br. also **de·flex·ion** (diflékʃən) n. a deviation, a turning or bending aside or down ∥ the amount of deviation of a magnetic needle, or of the moving system of a galvanometer or other instrument, from its zero position ∥ the deviation of radiation from a straight course [fr. L. deflexio (deflexionis)]

de·flec·tive (difléktiv) adj. causing deflection

de·flec·tor (difléktər) n. something that causes deflection

deflexion *DEFLECTION

de·flow·er (difláuər) v.t. to deprive of virginity ∥ to strip (a plant) of its flowers [O.F. desflorer]

def·lu·ent (déflu:ənt) 1. adj. flowing down, e.g. of the lower part of a glacier 2. n. that which flows down [fr. L. defluere, to flow down]

de·fo·cus (difóukəs) v. (optics) 1. to deflect a beam off focus 2. to lose accurate focus —**defocus** n. the lost focus

De·foe (dəfóu), Daniel (1661–1731), English journalist and novelist. A prolific pamphleteer, esp. on political subjects, he was imprisoned, fined and pilloried for his satirical 'Shortest Way with the Dissenters' (1702). 'Robinson Crusoe' (1719) was his most famous novel. Others include 'Moll Flanders' (1722) and 'A Journal of the Plague Year' (1722)

defog (difɔg) v. 1. to remove condensation, e.g., from an auto windshield 2. to remove fog, e.g., from a highway —**defogger** n.

de·fo·li·ate (di:fóuli:eit) pres. part. **de·fo·li·at·ing** past and past part. **de·fo·li·at·ed** v.t. to strip of leaves ∥ v.i. to become stripped of leaves **de·fo·li·a·tion** n. [fr. M.L. defoliare (defoliatus)]

de·fo·li·at·ing agent (di:fóuli:eitiŋ) a chemical that causes trees, shrubs, and other plants to shed their leaves prematurely —**defoliate** v. Cf AGENT ORANGE

De For·est (difɔ́rist, difɔ́rist), Lee (1873–1961), U.S. inventor. He developed the audion (1906), an elementary form of the radio tube, and was a pioneer in radio broadcasting

de·for·est (di:fɔ́rist, di:fɔ́rist) v.t. to cut down trees in (an area) and not replant **de·for·est·a·tion** n. the policy or act of doing this

de·form (difɔ́rm) v.t. to disfigure ∥ to spoil the form or essential quality of ∥ (phys.) to subject to deformation ∥ v.i. to become deformed, changed in shape [O.F. deformer]

de·for·ma·tion (di:fɔrméiʃən, defərméiʃən) n. a deforming or being deformed ∥ (phys.) an alteration of size or shape ∥ the process by which this occurs [fr. L. deformatio (deformationis) fr. deformare, to deform]

de·formed (difɔ́rmd) adj. not having, or no longer having, its true form

de·form·i·ty (difɔ́rmiti:) pl. **de·form·i·ties** n. the state or quality of being deformed ∥ a misshapen part of the body [O.F. déformité]

de·fraud (difrɔ́d) v.t. to cheat (someone) of some right or property [O.F. defrauder]

de·fray (difréi) v.t. to pay or settle (costs or expenses) **de·fráy·al, de·fráy·ment** ns [F. défrayer]

de·frock (di:frɔ́k) v.t. to unfrock, deprive (a priest) of his orders

de·frost (difrɔ́st, difrɔ́st) v.t. to rid of ice or frost ∥ v.i. to become free of ice or frost **de·fróst·er** n.

a device for freeing (esp. a windshield) from frost or ice

deft (deft) adj. quick and neat, a deft movement ∥ clever, quick-witted, a deft answer [var. of DAFT]

de·funct (difʌ́nkt) 1. adj. (of people) dead ∥ (of things) extinct, defunct laws 2. n. the defunct the dead person [fr. L. defungi (defunctus), to perform completely]

de·fuse (di:fjú:z) v. to alleviate a tense or dangerous situation —**defusor** n. the person

de·fy (difái) pres. part. **de·fy·ing** past and past part. **de·fied** v.t. to challenge (someone) to do or prove something, implying that it can't be done ∥ to disobey openly ∥ to resist successfully, to defy attempts at capture [O.F. defier]

De·gas (dəgǽ), Hilaire Germain Edgar (1834–1917), French Impressionist painter and sculptor. He excelled in the portrayal of movement and the effect of light, esp. artificial light, on the human body revealed in 'occupational' postures. (Ballet dancers, circus performers, women ironing etc. were typical subjects.) His compositions are casual and unexpected, often cutting off part of the body or an object with a freedom learned from Japanese prints. Degas painted as though he had no bonds of sympathy with his subjects, but was merely an observer. He also made some fine bronzes, esp. of dancers and horses

De Gas·pe·ri (degáspəri:), Alcid (1881–1954), Italian statesman, prime minister of Italy (1945–53)

de Gaulle *GAULLE

de·gauss (di:gáus) v.t. to neutralize the magnetization of (a ship's hull) by encircling it with a current-carrying coil, esp. as a protection against magnetic mines ∥ to erase a magnetic tape, disc, etc. (*GAUSS)

de·gauss·ing (di:gáusiŋ) n. process of demagnetizing iron objects by running an electric current through an encircling coil, used to protect ships from magnetic mines or laboratory apparatus from effects of nearby magnetic influences

de·gen·er·a·cy (didʒénərəsi:) n. the quality of being or becoming physically or morally degenerate ∥ (genetics) the coding in an amino acid of more than one codon ∥ (quantum mechanics) condition in a system in which several stationary states have the same energy with the same or different wave systems

de·gen·er·ate 1. (didʒénəreit) v.i. pres. part. **de·gen·er·at·ing** past and past part. **de·gen·er·at·ed** to lose former or characteristic qualities to one's detriment, to decline mentally or morally ∥ to grow much worse, the situation degenerated into chaos ∥ (biol.) to change to a less specialized or functionally less active form ∥ (med.) of a tissue or organ) to become enfeebled or impaired 2. (didʒénərit) adj. having lost former or characteristic qualities, degraded ∥ having or being a codon ∥ (math) having more than one subdivision ∥ (biol., pathol.) showing degeneration 3. (didʒénərit) n. a degenerate person, animal, tissue etc. [fr. L. degenerare (degeneratus)]

de·gen·er·a·tion (didʒénəréiʃən) n. intellectual or moral deterioration ∥ the process of becoming degenerate ∥ morbid disintegration or structural change of a tissue or organ ∥ (biol.) change to a less specialized or functionally less active form, retrospective evolution [F. dégénération]

de·gen·er·a·tive (didʒénərətiv, didʒénəreitiv) adj. characterized by degeneration ∥ tending to degenerate or to cause degeneration

de·grad·a·ble (dəgréidəb'l) adj. decomposable —**degradability** n.

deg·ra·da·tion (degrədéiʃən) n. a degrading or being degraded

de·grade (digréid, di:gréid) pres. part. **de·grad·ing** past and past part. **de·grad·ed** v.t. to lower esp. in rank or degree ∥ to debase morally ∥ (geol.) to wear down by erosion ∥ (chem.) to convert to a less complex form by breakdown, or by removal of component parts ∥ v.i. (chem.) to change in this way ∥ to become lower in grade **de·grád·ing** adj. [O.F. dégrader]

de·gran·u·la·tion (di:grænju:léiʃən) n. process of dissolving granules, usu. chemicals

de·gree (digri:) n. a step or stage in an ascending or descending series or process, to improve by degrees ∥ a step in line of descent, degrees of kinship ∥ a relative amount, he must accept some degree of responsibility ∥ a measure of intensity or gravity, a second-degree burn ∥ (rhet.) social rank, men of low degree ∥ (law) a gradation of criminality, murder in the first

degree ‖ a grade or title conferred by universities (and most U.S. colleges) to mark academic achievement ‖ masonic rank ‖ (*gram.*) one of three grades (positive, comparative, superlative) in the comparison of adjectives and adverbs ‖ (*phys.*, symbol °) a division of a scale of measurement, e.g. a unit of temperature on any thermometric scale ‖ (*math.*, symbol °) 1/360 of the angle that the radius of a circle describes in a full revolution ‖ (*algebra*) the power to which a term is raised (e.g. x^n is x to the nth degree) ‖ (*geog.*, symbol °) 1/360 of the circumference of the earth, measured for latitude from the equator, for longitude from the meridian. One degree of latitude or longitude is about 69 miles [O.F. *degre*]

degree day unit of measurement of the average deviation of the mean daily temperature from a given standard (65°F) during one day

degree of freedom any of the set of independent variables which totally define the state or behavior of a system (e.g. temperature, pressure and concentration, or rotational, translational and vibrational energy)

de·gres·sion (digréʃən) *n.* a going down by degrees (opp. PROGRESSION), esp. applied to rates of taxation on sums below a certain limit [fr. L.L. *degressio* (*degressionis*)]

de·hir·ing (di:háiəriŋ) *n.* dismissing, esp. in reverse order of hiring

de·hisce (dihís) *pres. part.* **de·hisc·ing** *past* and *past part.* **de·hisced** *v.i.* (*biol.*) to burst open [fr. L. *dehiscere*, to gape]

de·his·cence (dihísəns) *n.* (*biol.*) the spontaneous opening of a closed structure, along certain lines or in a definite direction, to release the contents **de·his·cent** *adj.* [fr. Mod. L. *dehiscentia* fr. *dehiscere*, to gape]

Deh·ra Dun (déirədú:n) a town (pop. 166,073) in Uttar Pradesh, India, at 2,300 ft: forestry

de·hu·man·ize (di:hjú:mənaiz) *pres. part.* **de·hu·man·iz·ing** *past* and *past part.* **de·hu·man·ized** *v.t.* to divest or deprive of human characteristics

de·hu·mid·i·fy (dj:hju:mídifai) *pres. part.* **de·hu·mid·i·fy·ing** *past* and *past part.* **de·hu·mid·i·fied** *v.t.* to remove moisture from

de·hy·drase or **de·hy·dra·tase** (di:háidreis)/(di:háidrəteis) (*biochem.*) enzyme that speeds transfer of hydrogen (or oxygen) from organisms to other substances, usually creating water

de·hy·drate (di:háidreit) *pres. part.* **de·hy·drat·ing** *past* and *past part.* **de·hy·drat·ed** *v.t.* to remove water from (esp. foodstuffs) ‖ to remove chemically combined water or water of hydration from, or to remove hydrogen and oxygen in the appropriate proportions from **de·hy·dra·tion** *n.* [fr. DE-+Gk *hudōr*, water]

de·hyp·no·tize (di:hípnətaiz) *pres. part.* **de·hyp·no·tiz·ing** *past* and *past part.* **de·hyp·no·tized** *v.t.* to rouse from a hypnotic state

de·ice (di:áis) *pres. part.* **de·ic·ing** *past* and *past part.* **de·iced** *v.t.* to rid of ice ‖ to keep free of ice **de·ic·er** *n.* any physical or chemical means of deicing or any device used for this

de·i·cide (dí:isaid) *n.* the killer or the killing of a god [fr. L. *deus*, god+*caedere*, to kill]

de·i·fi·ca·tion (dj:ifikéiʃən) *n.* a deifying or being deified

de·i·form (dí:ifɔrm) *adj.* godlike in nature or form [fr. M.L. *deiformis*]

de·i·fy (dí:ifai) *pres. part.* **de·i·fy·ing** *past* and *past part.* **de·i·fied** *v.t.* to make a god of, treat as a god [F. *déifer*]

deign (dein) *v.i.* (with 'to') to condescend, *to deign to answer* ‖ *v.t.* (*rhet.*) to condescend to give, *to deign no reply* [O.F. *degnier*]

de·in·sti·tu·tion·al·i·za·tion (di:institu:ʃənəlizéiʃən) *n.* releasing marginal patients from mental institutions —**deinstitutionalize** *v.*

de·i·on·ize (di:áiənaiz) *pres. part.* **de·i·on·iz·ing** *past* and *past part.* **de·i·on·ized** *v.t.* to remove ions from ‖ *v.i.* to recombine ions

de·ism (dí:izəm) *n.* belief in God reached through natural and scientific observation (cf. THEISM). This rationalistic religion, first prevalent in the 17th and 18th cc. and expounded especially by Montesquieu, Voltaire and Rousseau, accepted the idea of God as creator of the universe, but rejected the notion that God might break the laws governing the universe **dé·ist** *n.* **de·is·tic** *adj.* [fr. L. *deus*, god]

de·i·ty (dí:iti) *n. pl.* **de·i·ties** *n.* a god or goddess ‖ the state of being divine **the Deity** God [F. *déité*]

de·ject (didʒékt) *v.t.* to dishearten, depress [fr. L. *dejicere* (*dejectus*), to cast down]

de·jec·ta (didʒéktə) *pl. n.* excrements [L. fr. *dejicere* (*dejectus*), to cast down]

de·ject·ed (didʒéktid) *adj.* cast down in spirits

de·jec·tion (didʒékʃən) *n.* depression, lowness of spirits [O.F.]

de ju·re (di:dʒúəri:) **1.** *adv.* legally, by right **2.** *adj.* lawful [L.]

Dek·ker (dékər), Thomas (c. 1572–1632), English dramatist and pamphleteer. 'The Shoemaker's Holiday', his best-known play, and 'The Gull's Hornbook' (1608), his most famous prose work, show sympathetic understanding of London life and people, humorous satire and vigorous style

de Kooning (dikú:niŋ), Willem (1904–   ), U.S. painter. An abstact expressionist, he emigrated to the U.S. from the Netherlands in 1926. During the 1930s and early 1940s he painted nonfigurative as well as figurative subjects. By the 1950s his works were mainly of women, but by the early 1960s he had turned to landscapes

Del. Delaware

De·la·croix (dələkrwa), Ferdinand Victor Eugène (1798–1863), French painter, the leader of the Romantic school. He consciously rejected the classical formal elements present e.g. in the art of J. L. David. His composition is free, indeed turbulent. His color is powerful and an essential part of the picture's structure. He found inspiration in exotic subjects: Arab life, fierce wild animals, warfare. He was an excellent portrait painter. His 'Journal' is a source of Romantic ideas

Del·a·goa Bay (dələgóuə) a large bay in Mozambique, on the Indian Ocean, on which stands Maputo

De la Mare (dələméər), Walter John (1873–1956), English poet. His sensibility expressed itself in visionary images of flowers, night and magic, and delicately sensual enchantment or trance, passing naturally to a preoccupation with death. He also wrote novels of delicate fantasy

De·lau·nay (dəlounei), Robert (1885–1941), French painter, one of the first to produce nonobjective works. Associated with the cubists, but rejecting their austerity, he painted rhythmic, curvilinear compositions of spectral color harmonies

Delaware a river (280 miles long) in the northeast U.S.A. It rises in the Catskills, and flows into Delaware Bay

Delaware (*abbr.* Del.) a state (area 2,399 sq. miles, pop, 602,000) on the Atlantic Coast of the U.S.A. Capital: Dover. Chief town: Wilmington (pop. 96,000). It is almost entirely formed by a coastal plain. Agriculture: corn, wheat, dairy products, poultry, vegetables. Industries: chemicals, textiles, food processing. State university (1833) at Newark. One of the Thirteen Colonies, Delaware was settled by Dutch and Swedes (early 17th c.), and was ceded (1682) to William Penn. It became (1787) the 1st state of the U.S.A.

Del·a·ware (déləwєər) *pl.* **Del·a·ware, Del·a·wares** *n.* an Indian of an Algonquian tribe, formerly of the Delaware Valley [after Lord *De la Warr*]

Delaware Bay an estuarine inlet (52 miles long) between the New Jersey and Delaware coasts. It receives the Delaware River in the north

De la Warr, Del·a·ware (déləwєər), Thomas West, 12th Baron (1577–1618), first governor of Virginia (1610–18)

de·lay (diléi) *n.* an unexpected lapse of time ‖ lateness ‖ (*football*) pause by a ball carrier to confuse opposition as to next play tactic [O.F. *delai*]

delay *v.t.* to cause to be late ‖ to hinder the progress of ‖ to postpone ‖ *v.i.* to fail to make haste [O.F. *delaier*]

de·lay-Dop·pler mapping (dəléidɒplər) (*astron.*) examination of a planet by measuring the Doppler shift in a radar beam caused by the planet's rotation

de·lec·ta·ble (diléktəb'l) *adj.* (*rhet.*) delightful to the mind or the senses [O.F.]

de·lec·ta·tion (dj:lektéiʃən) *n.* (*rhet.*) delight ‖ enjoyment [O.F.]

del·e·ga·cy (déligəsi:) *pl.* **del·e·ga·cies** *n.* a body of delegates ‖ a delegating or being delegated

del·e·gate (déligeit) *pres. part.* **del·e·gat·ing** *past* and *past part.* **del·e·gat·ed** *v.t.* to appoint as a representative ‖ to give up (some degree of one's powers) to another [fr. L. *delegare* (*delegatus*)]

del·e·gate (déligit, déligeit) *n.* an official representative of some larger body, e.g. at a conference ‖ someone given power to act for another ‖ a representative of a territory in the House of Representatives, with the right to debate but not vote ‖ a member of the lower house of the legislature of Maryland, Virginia or West Virginia [O.F. *delegat*]

del·e·ga·tion (deligéiʃən) *n.* the entrusting of authority ‖ a delegacy, body of delegates [fr. L. *delegatio* (*delegationis*), legation]

de·lete (dilí:t) *pres. part.* **de·let·ing** *past* and *past part.* **de·let·ed** *v.t.* to cross out, erase [fr. L. *delere* (*deletus*), to destroy]

del·e·te·ri·ous (delitíəri:əs) *adj.* harmful physically or morally [fr. Mod. L. *deleterius* fr. Gk]

de·le·tion (dilí:ʃən) *n.* the act of deleting ‖ the thing deleted

Delft (delft) a town (pop. 85,200) in South Holland, the Netherlands, between Rotterdam and The Hague, famous for its earthenware, with food, chemical, electrical and engineering industries

delft *n.* a tin-glazed earthenware made at Delft, usually showing a blue pattern on the white

delft·ware (délftwєər) *n.* delft

Del·ga·do (delgáðo), José Matías (1768–1833), Salvadorian priest, champion of the independence of Central America. He proclaimed (1811) the independence of El Salvador and presided (1823) over its constituent assembly

Del·hi (déli) municipality (pop. 5,227,730) of India, on the Jumna River, comprising Old Delhi, a walled city begun by Shah Jahan (1639), and New Delhi, a modern city and the capital of India (pop. 301,801) south of it, founded in 1931 (*LUTYENS). Traditional crafts: gold, silver and ivory work, embroidery, jewelry. Industries: textiles, engineering, chemicals. University (1922). Monuments, esp. the Fort and Great Mosque

deli or **delly** (déli:) *n.* shortened form for "delicatessen"

De·li·an Confederacy (dí:li:ən, dí:ljən) a maritime alliance of over 200 Greek cities and islands founded 478 B.C. to fight the Persians, under the leadership of Athens. It became an Athenian empire (454–404 B.C.)

de·lib·er·ate (dilíbərit) *adj.* made or done intentionally ‖ slow and careful, *a deliberate manner* [fr. L. *deliberare* (*deliberatus*), to consult]

de·lib·er·ate (dilíbəreit) *pres. part.* **de·lib·er·at·ing** *past* and *past part.* **de·lib·er·at·ed** *v.i.* to think out a matter with proper care, often in committee ‖ *v.t.* to think (something) out in this way [fr. L. *deliberare* (*deliberatus*)]

de·lib·er·a·tion (dilibəréiʃən) *n.* careful consideration, a weighing of reasons for and against ‖ formal discussion or consultation ‖ the quality of being unhurried and in full self-possession [F.]

de·lib·er·a·tive (dilíbərətiv, dilíbəreitiv) *adj.* of or appointed for debate or deliberation [fr. L. *deliberativus*]

de·lib·er·a·tor (dilíbəreitər) *n.* someone who deliberates

De·libes (dəli:b), Clément Philibert Léo (1836–91), French composer, known for his ballets (e.g. 'Coppélia', 1870) and one or two operas ('Lakmé', 1883)

del·i·ca·cy (délikəsi:) *pl.* **del·i·ca·cies** *n.* fineness of quality, *delicacy of texture* ‖ sensitivity, *delicacy of touch* ‖ mechanical sensitivity, fineness of adjustment etc. ‖ fine fragility ‖ susceptibility to disease, constitutional weakness ‖ exquisite consideration for others' feelings ‖ the avoidance of anything offensive to modesty ‖ the need for tactful handling, *the delicacy of the situation* ‖ something to eat of rare or fine quality

del·i·ca·sy (délikəsi:) *n.* (*linguistics*) the subtle degree of difference that distinguishes secondary classes in a primary class

del·i·cate (délikit) *adj.* finely made ‖ very fragile ‖ needing careful handling, *a delicate plant* ‖ easily bruised or made ill ‖ requiring great tact and reflection, *a delicate decision* ‖ requiring fine technique, *a delicate brain operation* ‖ (of colors) soft or subdued ‖ subtle, *a delicate hint* ‖ sensitive, *a delicate sense of smell* ‖ deft, *delicate brushwork* ‖ exquisitely considerate, *delicate reticence* ‖ (of distinctions) finely graduated, *a delicate nuance* ‖ (of mechanisms or instruments) of great precision ‖ sheltered, *a delicate upbringing* ‖ tending to become tired or ill easily ‖ (of health) weak, precarious ‖ (of food) choice [fr. L. *delicatus*, pleasing the senses]

del·i·ca·tes·sen (dęlikətés'n) *n.* a shop selling prepared foods, e.g. hors d'œuvres, cooked meats, liver sausage ‖ the foods sold there [G. *delikatessen* fr. F. *délicatesse*, delicacy]

de·li·cious (dilíʃəs) *adj.* delightful, giving pleasure esp. to the taste, smell, or sense of humor [O.F.]

de·light (diláit) *v.t.* to please very much ‖ *v.i.* (with 'in') to take great pleasure [O.F. *delitier*]

delight *n.* great pleasure ‖ something which gives such pleasure [O.F. *delit*]

de·light·ed (diláitid) *adj.* very pleased **de·light·ed·ly** *adv.* **de·light·ful** (diláitfəl) *adj.* causing delight **de·light·ful·ly** *adv.*

Delilah (dəláilə), Biblical woman, betrayer of Samson. She had his hair, the source of his strength, shaved off, thus paving the way for his capture by the Philistines

de·lim·it (dilímit) *v.t.* to fix the limits or boundaries of [F. *délimiter*]

de·lim·i·tate (dilímiteit) *pres. part.* **de·lim·i·tat·ing** *past and past part.* **de·lim·i·tat·ed** *v.t.* to delimit **de·lim·i·ta·tion** *n.* [fr. L. *delimitare* (*delimitatus*)]

de·lim·it·er (dilímitər) *n.* (*computer*) symbol to mark the end of a unit of information

de·lin·e·ate (dilíini:eit) *pres. part.* **de·lin·e·at·ing** *past and past part.* **de·lin·e·at·ed** *v.t.* to show by drawing, or by outlining in words, *to delineate a plan*

de·lin·e·a·tion, de·lin·e·a·tor *ns* [fr. L. *delineare* (*delineatus*) fr. *linea*, line]

de·lin·quen·cy (dilíŋkwənsi:) *pl.* **de·lin·quen·cies** *n.* wrongdoing ‖ an action going against the law ‖ guilt ‖ a fault, e.g. with respect to duty [fr. L. *delinquentia* fr. *delinquere*, to fail]

de·lin·quent (dilíŋkwənt) **1.** *adj.* guilty of wrongdoing ‖ guilty of a fault, e.g. in respect of duty **2.** *n.* a delinquent person [fr. L. *delinquens* (*delinquentis*) fr. *delinquere*, to fail]

de·li·quesce (dęlikwés) *pres. part.* **del·i·quesc·ing** *past and past part.* **del·i·quesced** *v.i.* (of a substance) to absorb water vapor from the air and dissolve in it because the vapor pressure of the saturated solution of the substance at room temperature is less than the water-vapor pressure in the air (cf. EFFLORESCE) **del·i·qués·cence** *n.* **del·i·qués·cent** *adj.* [fr. L. *deliquescere*, to melt]

de·lir·i·ous (dilíəri:əs) *adj.* in a state of delirium, raving ‖ (*loosely*) wildly excited, in an ecstasy of joy [fr. L. *delirium*, madness]

de·lir·i·um (dilíəri:əm) *pl.* **de·lir·i·ums, de·lir·i·a** (dilíəri:ə) *n.* a temporary disorder of the mind marked by incoherent speech, ravings, hallucinations ‖ wild excitement or ecstasy [L. fr. *delirare*, to go mad]

delirium tre·mens (dilíəri:əmtrí:mənz) *n.* (*pop. abbr.* **d.t.'s**) a violent form of delirium, characterized by trembling and terrifying hallucinations, usually brought on by chronic alcoholism [Mod. L.=trembling madness]

De·li·us (dí:li:əs, dí:ljəs), Frederick (1862–1934), English composer. His works for orchestra and choir include 'A Mass of Life' (1904–5), 'Requiem' (1914–18) and 'Sea Drift' (1904). His operas include 'A Village Romeo and Juliet' (1900–2)

de·liv·er (dilívər) *v.t.* to distribute (mail) ‖ to transport (goods purchased) free to an address as instructed ‖ to convey (something) to the person to whom it is destined, *to deliver a message* ‖ to fulfill a promise ‖ to assist the birth of ‖ to assist (a woman) to give birth ‖ to rescue ‖ to utter, pronounce (a speech, etc.) to an audience ‖ to declaim in a specified manner, *a badly delivered sermon* ‖ to aim, strike (a blow, attack, etc.) ‖ (with 'up', 'over') to yield, *to deliver oneself up to justice* **to deliver oneself of** to speak out, get off one's chest [F. *délivrer*]

de·liv·er·ance (dilívərəns) *n.* a rescuing or setting free ‖ the state of being rescued or set free ‖ a pompous and emphatically expressed opinion [O.F. *delivrance*]

de·liv·er·y (dilívəri:) *pl.* **de·liv·er·ies** *n.* the act of giving birth ‖ a distribution, esp. of mail ‖ the transporting, often free, of merchandise on purchasers' instructions ‖ the declaiming of a speech, lecture, etc. ‖ the manner of doing this ‖ a delivering, handing over or surrendering ‖ a rescuing or setting free ‖ the act or technique of (*baseball*) pitching or (*cricket*) bowling a ball ‖ something delivered **to take delivery of** to have (a purchase) delivered to one [A.F. *delivrée*]

delivery boy a boy who runs errands and delivers goods

dell (del) *n.* a small valley or natural hollow in a grassy hillside or in woods [O.E.]

della Robbia *ROBBIA

De Long (dəlóŋ), George Washington (1844–81), U.S. explorer. He led (1879–81) a disastrous arctic expedition which confirmed the theory of transarctic drift

De·los (dí:lɒs) a tiny island of the Cyclades, site of the sanctuary of Apollo and the treasury of the Delian Confederacy (478–454 B.C.)

de·louse (di:láus, di:láuz) *pres. part.* **de·lous·ing** *past and past part.* **de·loused** *v.t.* to rid of lice

Del·phi (délfai) (ancient Pytho, modern Delphoi) a town (pop. 1,000) on the slopes of Mt Parnassus, Greece. It was the site of Apollo's temple and oracle

Del·phic (délfik) *adj.* pertaining to Delphi or the oracle there ‖ as obscure as the Delphic oracle

Delphic oracle Apollo's oracle at Delphi (8th c. B.C.–4th c. A.D.). The god spoke through a female medium, the Pythia, and a priest delivered the oracular replies. The oracle had very great authority

del·phin·i·um (delfíni:əm) *pl.* **del·phin·i·ums, del·phin·i·a** (delfíni:ə) *n.* a member of genus *Delphinium*, fam. *Ranunculaceae*, esp. any cultivated, perennial species, widely grown for its ornamental, usually blue flowers borne on long racemes [L. fr. Gk *delphinion*, larkspur]

del·ta (déltə) *n.* the fourth letter (Δ, δ) of the Greek alphabet ‖ a low tract of alluvial land formed by the precipitation of river mud when the river water meets the tidal seawater, shaped roughly like a Δ by continually changing channels and deposition **del·ta·ic** (deltéiik) *adj.* [Gk]

Delta Dagger *n.* (*mil.*) a single-engine turbojet interceptor (F-102) employed in air defense, having supersonic speed and the AIM-4 series and AIM-26A (Falcon) armament. It has an all-weather intercept capability

Delta Dart *n.* (*mil.*) a supersonic single-engine turbojet interceptor (F-106) aircraft, F-102 in appearance, with Falcon (AIM-4 series) missiles with nonnuclear warheads and Genie (AIR-2A) rockets with nuclear warheads. It has an all-weather intercept capability

del·ta-9-tet·ra·hyd·ro·can·nib·in·ol (dęltənain-tętrəhaidroukǽnibinɒl) *n.* synthetic marijuana known as THC, used in treating glaucoma

Delta II NATO term for U.S.S.R. submarines with 4,000-mi. range, each carrying 16 missiles

delta ray an electron moving with low velocity, originating from the interaction of an ionizing particle with matter

delta wave brain wave during deepest period of sleep, recorded as a large, slow wave on the encephalograph *Cf* ALPHA WAVE, THETA WAVE

DEL·TIC (déltik) *n.* (*electr.* acronym) for delay line time compression, device for compressing the time of sample waveforms (radar, sonar, seismic, speech, etc.), thus reducing their complexity in order to compare them by autocorrelation

del·toid (déltɔid) **1.** *adj.* triangular **2.** *n.* the large shoulder muscle lifting the arm [fr. Gk *deltoeidēs*, delta-shaped]

de·lude (dilú:d) *pres. part.* **de·lud·ing** *past and past part.* **de·lud·ed** *v.t.* to cause (someone, oneself) to believe wrongly, e.g. by blinding to the truth [fr. L. *deludere*, to play]

del·uge (délju:dʒ) **1.** *n.* a flood ‖ an overwhelming rush of water ‖ a heavy fall of rain ‖ a rush of anything (e.g. words, mail) **2.** *v.t.* *pres. part.* **del·ug·ing** *past and past part.* **del·uged** to flood ‖ to overwhelm as if with a flood [F. *déluge*]

de·lu·sion (dilú:ʒən) *n.* a deluding or being deluded ‖ a false opinion or idea ‖ a false, unshakable belief indicating a severe mental disorder, *delusions of grandeur* **de·lu·sion·al** *adj.* [fr. L. *delusio* (*delusionis*)]

de·lu·sive (dilú:siv) *adj.* deceptive, false **de·lu·so·ry** (dilú:səri:, dilú:zəri:) *adj.* [fr. L. *deludere* (*delusus*), to mock]

de luxe (dəlúks, dəlʌ́ks) *adj.* especially lavish or elegant, *a de luxe edition* [F.]

delve (delv) *pres. part.* **delv·ing** *past and past part.* **delved** *v.i.* to search as if burrowing, *to delve into a problem* ‖ (of a road etc.) to dip suddenly [O.E. *delfan*, to dig]

de·mag·net·ize (di:mǽgnitaiz) *pres. part.* **de·mag·net·iz·ing** *past and past part.* **de·mag·net·ized** *v.t.* to deprive of magnetic properties

demagog *DEMAGOGUE

dem·a·gog·ic (demǝgɒ́dʒik, demǝgógik) *adj.* of or like a demagogue **dem·a·góg·i·cal** *adj.* [fr. Gk *dēmagogikós*]

dem·a·gogue, dem·a·gog (démǝgɒg) *n.* a political speaker or leader who plays upon the passions etc. of the people to win their support for himself or his party ‖ a factious orator ‖ (*hist.*) a leader of the popular faction **dém·a·gogu·er·y** *pl.* **dem·a·gogu·er·ies** *n.* demagogism **dém·a·gog·ism, dém·a·gogu·ism** *n.* the principles or practices of demagogues [fr. Gk *dēmagogós*, a leader of the mob]

dem·a·go·gy (démǝgɒdʒi:, démǝgɒgi:) *n.* demagogism [fr. Gk *dēmagōgia*]

de·mand (dimǽnd, dimánd) *n.* a peremptory request ‖ the thing requested ‖ an urgent claim, *demands on one's time* ‖ an economic need or call, *a big demand for cotton dresses* **in demand** sought after **on demand** when presented for payment [F. *demande*]
—Demand in economics means effective demand, i.e. the amount which potentially would be bought at a certain price at a certain time. This amount will change if the supply or the price changes. When demand is constant and cannot be satisfied by alternatives (as in the case of necessities, e.g. bread) it is said to be 'inelastic'. When many substitutes are available, demand is 'elastic'. Factors which affect demand include changes in population, income and taste, competition of substitutes, expectation about the future (e.g. with regard to inflation or deflation), and such factors as advertising, weather, or social and educational change

demand *v.t.* to ask for peremptorily, claim as one's due ‖ to require, call for, *his job demands great skill* ‖ to inquire with authority, *the policeman demanded the man's business* ‖ *v.i.* (with 'of') to make a demand [F. *demander*]

demand bill a sight draft

demand deposit a bank deposit which may be withdrawn without notice ‖ a bank deposit payable within 30 days

demand draft a sight draft

de·mand·ing (dimǽndiŋ, dimándiŋ) *adj.* requiring a great deal of service or attention

demand loan a call loan

demand note a note payable on demand

de·mand-pull inflation (dimǽndpul) (*economics*) pressure for price increases due to increased demand rather than increased cost of production *Cf* COST-PUSH INFLATION, WAGE-PUSH INFLATION

de·mar·cate (dí:mɑrkeit, dimárkeit) *pres. part.* **de·mar·cat·ing** *past and past part.* **de·mar·cat·ed** *v.t.* to mark the boundaries of [DEMARCATION]

de·mar·ca·tion, de·mar·ka·tion (di:mɑrkéiʃən) *n.* the marking of boundaries, a delimiting [fr. Span. *demarcación*]

de·marche, *Br.* **dé·marche** (deimárʃ) *n.* a move or procedure in an effort to achieve some end, esp. diplomatic [F. *démarche*= proceeding]

demarkation *DEMARCATION

de·mas·cu·lin·ize (di:mǽskju:linaiz) *v.* to make less masculine **demasculizator** *n.*

de·ma·te·ri·al·ize (di:mətíəri:əlaiz) *pres. part.* **de·ma·te·ri·al·iz·ing** *past and past part.* **de·ma·te·ri·al·ized** *v.t.* to deprive of material form or qualities ‖ *v.i.* to lose material form or qualities

de·mean (dimí:n) *v. refl.* to lower in standing or dignity, degrade

demean *v.t.* to behave (oneself) in a specified way [O.F. *demener*, to conduct, manage]

de·mean·or, *Br.* **de·mean·our** (dimí:nər) *n.* outward bearing, behavior, manner [perh. fr. O.F. *demener*, to conduct]

de·ment·ed (diméntid) *adj.* mad, insane ‖ indicating madness [fr. older *dement* v. fr. L. *dementare*, to drive mad]

de·men·tia (dimén ʃə, dimén ʃi:ə) *n.* insanity [fr. L. *demens* (*dementis*), mad]

dementia prae·cox, dementia pre·cox (dimén ʃəprí:kɒks, dimén ʃi:əprí:kɒks) *n.* schizophrenia [Mod. L.=precocious dementia]

Dem·er·a·ra (demǝréərə, demirárə) a river (c. 200 miles long) of Guyana, flowing parallel to the Essequibo River and emptying into the Atlantic near Georgetown: navigable for over 100 miles

dem·er·a·ra (demǝréərə) *n.* a brown sugar from raw, unrefined cane [after *Demerara*, Guyana]

de·mer·it (dimérit) *n.* a quality deserving blame ‖ a fault or defect ‖ (in some systems of authoritative control, e.g. in schools or traffic regulation) a point against an offender [F. *démérite*]

de·mer·sal (dimɜ́:rs'l) *adj.* found in deep water or on the bottom of the sea (cf. PELAGIC) [fr. L. *demergere* (*demersus*), to immerse]

de·mesne (diméin, dimí:n) *n.* (*law*) the holding of land as one's own property ‖ (*law, hist.*) all of an estate, land and buildings, occupied by the owner, i.e. that part not rented to tenants [F. *demeine*]

De·me·ter (dimí:tər) (*Gk mythol.*) the goddess of grain and agriculture, identified with the Roman Ceres

dem·e·tom-S-meth·yl sul·fox·ide (démətomes-méθəl sʌlfóksaid) [C₆H₁₅O₄PS₂] *n.* insecticide and miticide of orgophosphoric compounds used on crop and tree pests

De·me·tri·us I Pol·i·or·ce·tes (dimí:tri:əspplior-sí:ti:z) (c. 337–283 B.C.), king of Macedon (c. 294–287 B.C.), son of Antigonus I

Demetrius II Do·son (dóuson) (c. 278–229 B.C.), king of Macedon (239–229 B.C.), father of Philip V

Demetrius II Ni·ca·tor (naikéitor) (c. 164–125 B.C.), king of Syria (145–140 B.C. and 129–125 B.C.), captured by the Parthians and finally murdered by a pretender

Demetrius I So·ter (sóutər) (c. 187–150 B.C.), Seleucid king of Syria (162–150 B.C.). He defeated and killed Judas Maccabaeus (161 B.C.)

Demetrius of Pha·ler·um (fæléːrum) Greek statesman and historian (c. 350–c. 283 B.C.), governor of Athens (317–307 B.C.)

demi- (démi:) *prefix* half, semi- [F.=half, L. *dimidius*]

dem·i·god (démi:gpd) *n.* the son of a god and a mortal ‖ a deified man

dem·i·john (démi:dʒɒn) *n.* a large, bulging, narrow-necked bottle cased in wickerwork [corrup. of F. *dame-jeanne*, Dame Jane]

de·mil·i·ta·ri·za·tion (di:militərizeiʃən) *n.* a demilitarizing or being demilitarized

de·mil·i·ta·rize (di:mílitəraiz) *pres. part.* **de·mil·i·ta·riz·ing** *past* and *past part.* **de·mil·i·ta·rized** *v.t.* to free from military character or purposes ‖ to free from military control

De Mille (dəmíl), Agnes (1908–   ), U.S. choreographer and dancer, who created (1938) the first important U.S. ballet, 'Rodeo'. She brought ballet technique to musical comedy in, notably, 'Oklahoma.' Some of her many writings include 'Dance to the Piper' (1952) and 'Reprieve' (1981)

De Mille, Cecil Blount (1881–1959), U.S. film producer-director, known for film spectaculars with historical and religious themes, including 'The King of Kings' (1927), 'The Greatest Show on Earth' (1952), and 'The Ten Commandments' (1956)

dem·i·min·i (démi:mɪni) *adj.* less than mini — **demi-mini** *n.* a shorter than miniskirt

dem·i·mon·daine (démi:mɒndéin) *n.* a woman of the demimonde [F.]

dem·i·monde (démi:mɒnd) *n.* a class of women on the fringes of respectable society, depending on money from rich and usually upper-class lovers [F.]

dem·i·pen·sion (démi:penʃən) *n.* hostelry arrangement for some but not all meals

de·mise (dimáiz) **1.** *n.* death ‖ (*law*) the conveyance of an estate by will or lease ‖ the transfer of sovereignty by death, abdication or deposition of the sovereign **2.** *v. pres. part.* **de·mis·ing** *past* and *past part.* **de·mised** *v.t.* (*law*) to convey by will or lease ‖ to transfer (sovereignty) by death or abdication ‖ *v.i.* (*law*) to pass by bequest or inheritance [fr. O.F. *desmettre*, to put away]

dem·i·sem·i·qua·ver (démi:sémi:kwei̯vər) *n.* (*Br., mus.*) a thirty-second note

dem·i·tasse (démi:tæs, démi:tɑs) *n.* a small coffee cup for serving coffee after dinner ‖ a cup of this coffee [F.]

Dem·i·urge (démi:əːrdʒ) *n.* (in Platonic philosophy) the creator of the world ‖ (in Gnosticism) an assistant to the Supreme Being in the act of creation, sometimes thought of as the creator of evil [fr. Gk *dēmiourgos*, craftsman, maker]

dem·i·world (démi:wəːrld) *n.* the fringe of conventional society

dem·o (démou) *n.* short for demonstration

de·mo·bi·li·za·tion (di:məubəlaizéiʃən) *n.* a demobilizing or being demobilized

de·mo·bi·lize (di:móubəlaiz) *pres. part.* **de·mo·bi·liz·ing** *past* and *past part.* **de·mo·bi·lized** *v.t.* to disband (troops), release from military service

de·moc·ra·cy (dəmókrəsi) *pl.* **de·moc·ra·cies** *n.* government by the people, usually through

elected representatives ‖ a state so governed ‖ (*pop.*) social equality **De·moc·ra·cy** the principles of the Democratic party [F. *démocratie* fr. L. fr. Gk]

Democracy Wall wall in Peking on which propaganda posters may be placed by Chinese citizens

dem·o·crat (déməkræt) *n.* someone who believes in democracy **Dem·o·crat** a member of the Democratic party [F. *démocrate*]

dem·o·crat·ic (déməkrǽtik) *adj.* pertaining to, characterized by, believing in, or practicing the principles of, political democracy ‖ (*loosely*) egalitarian **Dem·o·crát·ic** of or belonging to the Democratic party **dem·o·crát·i·cal·ly** *adv.* [F. *démocratique* fr. L. fr. Gk]

democratic centralism theory of flow of power from bottom to top

Democratic Kampuchea *KAMPUCHEA

Democratic party one of the two main political parties of the U.S.A. (cf. REPUBLICAN PARTY). Its origins are traditionally linked with Jefferson's anti-Federalists, who supported states' rights and the interests of workers and small farmers. The party took its present name and developed its organization during the presidency (1829–37) of Jackson. The Democrats won all presidential elections except three in the period 1800–60. They were split (1854) over slavery, became associated with the slave-owning South, and were out of office after the Civil War. Campaigning for lower tariffs, they were again in power (1885–9 and 1893–7) under Cleveland, and (1913–21) under Woodrow Wilson. Under Franklin D. Roosevelt (1933–45), the Democrats were identified as the reform party with the New Deal. They remained in office until 1953, and regained the presidency in 1961, but lost it again (1968). At the 1972 convention George McGovern gained the nomination, stressing an end to the Vietnam War and party reform; he lost to Richard Nixon. In 1976, Democrat Jimmy Carter won a close race against incumbent president Gerald Ford. Carter had a difficult term, with poor congressional relations, stalled energy initiatives, high inflation rates, and an indifferent reputation in foreign affairs. Republican Ronald Reagan won a landslide victory in 1980, and brought the first Republican majority to the Senate since 1954. In 1984, Walter Mondale and his running mate, Geraldine Ferraro, were unable to unseat Reagan, although the Democratic party gained ground with black voters

Dem·o·crat·ic-Re·pub·li·can (déməkrǽtikripʌ́b-likən) *n.* (*Am. hist.*) a member of the political party known (after 1829) as the Democratic party

Democratic-Republican Societies a network of political clubs, serving as the organs of farmers and laborers, that became the chief strength of the Jeffersonian political party

Democratic Study Group members of Congress especially concerned about liberal causes

de·moc·ra·ti·za·tion (dimɒkrətizéiʃən) *n.* a making or becoming democratic

de·moc·ra·tize (dimókrətaiz) *pres. part.* **de·moc·ra·tiz·ing** *past* and *past part.* **de·moc·ra·tized** *v.t.* to make democratic ‖ *v.i.* to become democratic [F. *démocratiser*]

De·moc·ri·tus (dimókritəs) (460–370 B.C.), Greek philosopher who developed still further the atomist theory of his teacher Leucippus

de·mog·ra·pher (dimógrəfər) *n.* someone whose profession is demography

de·mo·graph·ic (di:məgrǽfik, deməgrǽfik) *adj.* of or relating to demography

demographic gap (*social science*) difference between birth and death rates during a demographic transition

de·mo·graph·ics (deməgrǽfiks) *n.* (*social science*) characteristics of a population, e.g., size, sex, age, and marital-status statistics, as well as the number of children, educational level, fertility rate, and other social and economic factors —**demographic** *adj.*

demographic transition (*social science*) period of demographic change occurring concomitantly with industrialization, usu. beginning with traditionally high birth and death rates and a resulting slow rate of population growth; with death rate declining due to developments in public health and medicine, creating a demographic gap and expanding population; and finally, followed by falling birth rate, restoring the pattern of moderate growth

de·mog·ra·phy (dimógrəfi:) *n.* the statistical study of populations (birth rate, death rate, structure by age and sex etc.) through census returns and records of births, marriages, deaths etc. [fr. Gk *dēmos*, people +*graphos*, written]

dem·oi·selle (dəmwazél) *n. Anthropoides virgo*, the Numidian crane found in Asia, N. Africa and S.E. Europe ‖ a member of *Agrion, Calopteryx* and allied genera of slender dragonflies [F.=young lady]

de·mol·ish (dimɒ́liʃ) *v.t.* to destroy the structure of (a building etc.) ‖ to reduce to nothing, overthrow ‖ to refute conclusively (a theory, opponent etc.) ‖ (*pop.*) to eat up quickly [F. *démolir* (*démoliss-*)]

dem·o·li·tion (deməlíʃən, di:məlíʃən) *n.* a demolishing or being demolished [F. *démolition*]

demolition derby (*sports*) contest in which participants demolish each other's motor vehicles until only one car remains mobile

de·mon (dí:mən) *n.* an evil spirit or devil ‖ a wicked, destructive creature ‖ a person relentless in some specified respect, *a demon for work* ‖ an indwelling compulsive force, *driven by a demon of avarice* [L. *daemon*, a spirit and L. *daemonium*, an evil spirit, fr. Gk]

de·mon·e·tize (di:mʌ́nitaiz, di:mɒ́nitaiz) *pres. part.* **de·mon·e·tiz·ing** *past* and *past part.* **de·mon·e·tized** *v.t.* to stop using (a specific metal) for money ‖ to deprive (a note, coin etc.) of value as legal tender [fr. F. *démonétiser*]

de·mo·ni·ac (dimóuni:æk) **1.** *adj.* possessed by a demon ‖ fiendish ‖ frenzied **2.** *n.* someone possessed by a demon **de·mo·ni·a·cal** (di:mənáiə-k'l) *adj.* [fr. L.L. *demoniacus*]

de·mon·ic (dimónik) *adj.* possessed or inspired by a demon or as if by a demon [fr. L. *demonicus* fr. Gk]

de·mon·ism (dí:mənizəm) *n.* the belief in the existence and power of demons

de·mon·o·la·ter (di:mənólətər) *n.* a demon worshipper **de·mon·ól·a·try** *n.* the worship of demons and demonic powers [fr. Gk *daimono-*, demon+*atrēs*, worshipper]

de·mon·ol·o·gy (di:mənóladʒi:) *n.* the study and classification of demons, and of beliefs about them [fr. Gk *daimon*, spirit+ *logos*, discourse]

de·mon·stra·bil·i·ty (dimpnstrəbíliti:, demənstrəbíliti:) *n.* the ability to be demonstrated

de·mon·stra·ble (dimónstrəb'l, démənstrəb'l) *adj.* capable of being clearly shown or logically proved **de·món·stra·bly** *adv.* [fr. L. *demonstrabilis*]

dem·on·strate (démənstreit) *pres. part.* **dem·on·strat·ing** *past* and *past part.* **dem·on·strat·ed** *v.t.* to show clearly and openly by action the existence of, *to demonstrate one's loyalty* ‖ to prove the truth of, by logical or scientific processes ‖ to show how, or how well, (something) works ‖ *v.i.* to explain and teach by performing experiments and showing examples ‖ to be a demonstrator in a laboratory ‖ to make a public display of sympathies, grievances or opinions, e.g. by holding meetings or organizing marches etc. ‖ to make a display of military force [fr. L. *demonstrare* (*demonstratus*)]

dem·on·stra·tion (demənstréiʃən) *n.* an expression of public feeling for or against something through meetings, marches etc. ‖ an outward display of feelings ‖ a logical proving ‖ the manifestation of a process at work, *fruit falling offers a simple demonstration of gravity* ‖ the use of practical experiments for purposes of teaching ‖ a display of the way of working or merits of something ‖ a show of military force to intimidate, confuse or deter a potential enemy **dem·on·strá·tion·al** *adj.* [fr. L. *demonstratio* (*demonstrationis*), a showing]

de·mon·stra·tive (dəmɒ́nstrətiv) **1.** *adj.* serving to point out, prove or show clearly ‖ (of persons) given to open display of feelings, esp. of affection ‖ (*gram.*) pointing out, *demonstrative adjectives and pronouns* **2.** *n.* a demonstrative adjective or pronoun [F. *demonstratif*]

dem·on·stra·tor (démənstreitər) *n.* someone who demonstrates ‖ a participant in a public protest meeting ‖ someone who teaches by practical demonstration, esp. in a laboratory ‖ someone employed to show how (or how well) an article or appliance works [L.]

de·mor·al·i·za·tion (dimɒrəlaizéiʃən, dimɒrəlaizéiʃən) *n.* a demoralizing or being demoralized

de·mor·al·ize (dimɔ́rəlaiz, dimɒ́rəlaiz) *pres. part.* **de·mor·al·iz·ing** *past* and *past part.* **de·mor·al·ized** *v.t.* to destroy or weaken the morale of, undermine the confidence of ‖ to corrupt the morals of, deprave [F. *démoraliser*]

De·mos·the·nes (dimósθəni:z) (384–322 B.C.) Athenian orator and statesman. He saw the danger to Greek liberty from the rising power of Philip of Macedon, against whom he delivered his Philippic orations. He unsuccessfully indicted Aeschines for his conduct of an embassy to Philip (344 B.C.), but vindicated his own political record when he defended Ctesiphon against Aeschines's charges in the trial 'On the Crown' (330 B.C.). He poisoned himself to avoid falling into the hands of Antipater of Macedon

de·mote (dimóut) *pres. part.* **de·mot·ing** *past and past part.* **de·mot·ed** *v.t.* to reduce to a lower rank or class **de·mó·tion** *n.* [DE-+PRO-MOTE]

de·moth·ball (di:móθbɔl) *v.* to remove from deep storage, e.g., old ships

de·mot·ic (dimótik) *adj.* of the people, popular, *demotic speech* ‖ (*archaeol.*) in the simplified popular form of ancient Egyptian writing (cf. HIERATIC) **de·mót·ics** *n.* the study of people, sociology in its broadest sense (a term used in library cataloging) [fr. Gk *dēmotikos*]

Demp·sey (démpsi), Jack (William Harrison Dempsey, 1895–1983), U.S. heavyweight boxing champion of the world (1919–26). He was the first fighter to draw a million-dollar gate

de·mul·cent (dimʌ́lsənt) **1.** *adj.* (*med.*) soothing **2.** *n.* (*med.*) a preparation for soothing raw, inflamed patches of skin [fr. L. *demulcens* (*demulcentis*)]

de·mur (dimə́:r) **1.** *v.i. pres. part.* **de·mur·ring** *past and past part.* **de·murred** to raise objections or scruples, hesitate, show reluctance ‖ (*law*) to put in a demurrer **2.** *n.* an objecting, a protesting, *the design was accepted without demur* [F. *demeurer*, to linger, stay]

de·mure (dimjúər) *comp.* **de·mur·er** *superl.* **de·mur·est** *adj.* modest, quiet and serious-looking (esp. of a girl or her dress) ‖ affectedly modest, coy [*de-* (obscure)+ O.F. *meur*, ripe]

de·mur·ra·ble (dimə́:rəb'l) *adj.* open to legal objection

de·mur·rage (dimə́:ridʒ) *n.* the payment made to a shipowner by the charterer for exceeding the time allowed for loading or unloading ‖ the charge for detaining a freight car or truck beyond the time needed for loading or unloading ‖ the detention or delay which necessitates such payments ‖ a storage fee on goods in transit not collected within a reasonable or predetermined time ‖ (*Br.*) the charge per ounce made by the Bank of England when giving coin or notes for bullion [O.F. *demorage*, delay]

de·mur·ral (dimə́:rəl) *n.* a demurring, raising of objections ‖ an objection raised

de·mur·rant (dimə́:rənt) *n.* (*law*) someone who puts in a demurrer

de·mur·rer (dimə́:rər) *n.* (*law*) an objection to an opponent's evidence on the basis, not of truth, but of relevance or sufficiency in law (which delays the action until the point is settled) [O.F. *demourer*, to stay (infin. as n.)]

De·muth (dəmú:θ), Charles (1883–1935), U.S. watercolor painter, best known for his flower studies

de·my (dimái) *pl.* **de·mies** *n.* a size of paper usually (*Am.*) 16 x 21 ins, (*Br.*) 17½ x 22½ ins (printing), 15½ x 20 ins (writing) ‖ a foundation scholar at Magdalen College, Oxford [F. *demi*, half]

de·my·e·lin·a·tion (di:maiələnéifən) *n.* (*med.*) destruction of the white fatty substance that forms the sheath of nerve fibers

de·mys·ti·fy (di:místifai) *v.* to remove the mystery from

de·myth·i·cize (di:míθisaiz) *v.* to remove the myths

de·my·thol·o·gize (di:miθólədʒaiz) *pres. part.* **de·my·thol·o·giz·ing** *past and past part.* **de·my·thol·o·gized** *v.t.* to present (the Christian gospel) in 20th-c. terms, in the belief that the terminology of the New Testament is largely mythological in the sense that it derives from a world view now proved to be false (*BULTMANN)

den (den) *n.* a wild beast's lair ‖ a gang hideout ‖ a cramped, dirty little room ‖ a snug, secluded room where a person may retire to study or doze in peace [O.E. *denn*, lair]

de·nar·i·us (dinéəriəs) *pl.* **de·nar·i·i** (dinéəriai) *n.* a Roman silver coin current 187 B.C.-274 A.D. The symbol 'd' for penny is an abbreviation of this [L.]

den·a·ry (dénəri, dí:nəri) *adj.* of or based on 10, by tens, tenfold [fr. L. *denarius*, orig. worth 10 asses, fr. *deni*, ten each]

de·na·tion·al·ize (di:næʃən'laiz) *pres. part.* **de·na·tion·al·iz·ing** *past and past part.* **de·na·tion·al·ized** *v.t.* to return (a nationalized industry) to private ownership ‖ to deprive (a nation) of its independent national status or character ‖ to deprive (a person) of his national rights or nationality [F. *dénationaliser*]

de·nat·u·ral·ize (di:nǽtʃərəlaiz) *pres. part.* **de·nat·u·ral·iz·ing** *past and past part.* **de·nat·u·ral·ized** *v.t.* to change the nature of, make unnatural ‖ to deprive of rights as citizen of a state (cf. NATURALIZE)

de·na·tur·ant (di:néitʃərənt) *n.* a denaturing agent, esp. a substance added to fissionable material to make it suitable for use in a reactor but not for a bomb

de·na·ture (di:néitʃər) *pres. part.* **de·na·tur·ing** *past and past part.* **de·na·tured** *v.t.* to change the nature or natural qualities of ‖ to modify (a protein) through some agent (e.g. heat, acid) so that it loses certain of its original properties ‖ to treat with a denaturant [F. *dénaturer*]

denatured alcohol ethyl alcohol made unfit for drinking by the addition of toxic or nauseating substances such as methanol, benzene and sometimes pyridine

Den·bigh·shire (dénbi:ʃər) a county (area 670 sq. miles, pop. 174,000) in N. Wales. County town: Ruthin

den·drite (déndrait) *n.* the natural markings in the form of treelike figures in or on a mineral or stone ‖ the mineral or stone so marked ‖ any of the usually branching processes of a nerve cell which carry impulses towards the cell body (cf. AXON) **den·drit·ic** (dendrítik) *adj.* [fr. Gk *dendritēs*, of or pertaining to a tree]

den·droid (déndrɔid) *adj.* treelike ‖ having many branches [fr. Gk *dendroeidēs*]

den·drol·o·gy (dendrólədʒi:) *n.* the study of trees [fr. Gk *dendron*, tree+*logos*, discourse]

den·gue (déŋgi:, déŋgei) *n.* a common, rarely serious tropical disease spread by mosquitoes, giving rise to fever, limb pains and general malaise, commonly with recurrence a few days later [ult. fr. Swahili *dinga*, *dyenga*, a cramplike seizure]

de·ni·a·ble (dináiəb'l) *adj.* capable of being denied

de·ni·al (dináiəl) *n.* an assertion that something is not true ‖ a refusal to acknowledge, disavowal ‖ a refusal of a request ‖ self-denial

den·ier (dénjər, dəníər) *n.* a unit for measuring the fineness of silk, rayon or (esp.) nylon yarn, expressed as weight in grams per 9,000 meters of thread [O.F. very small coin used as the type of a very small sum or weight]

den·i·grate (dénigreit) *pres. part.* **den·i·grat·ing** *past and past part.* **den·i·grat·ed** *v.t.* to defame, blacken (someone's character) **den·i·grá·tion**, **dén·i·gra·tor** *ns* [fr. L. *denigrare* (*denigratus*)]

den·im (dénəm) *n.* a strong, coarse, twilled cotton fabric used for overalls, jeans etc. ‖ (*pl.*) overalls for rough or dirty work [fr. F. (*serge*) *de Nîmes*]

Den·is (dénis), St (3rd c.), by tradition the apostle of France and first bishop of Paris. Feast: Oct. 9

de·ni·trate (di:náitreit) *pres. part.* **de·ni·trat·ing** *past and past part.* **de·ni·trat·ed** *v.t.* to free from nitrogen or its compounds (e.g. nitric acid, nitrates) **de·ni·trá·tion** *n.* **de·ni·tri·fi·ca·tion** (di:naitrifikéifən) *n.* the process of denitrifying, esp. of liberating elementary nitrogen by denitrifying bacteria

de·ni·tri·fy (di:náitrifai) *pres. part.* **de·ni·tri·fy·ing** *past and past part.* **de·ni·tri·fied** *v.t.* to remove or liberate nitrogen from ‖ to reduce (nitrogen compounds)

den·i·zen (déniz'n) *n.* (*rhet.*) an inhabitant (person, animal or plant) of a place [A.F. *deinzein*]

Den·mark (dénmark) a kingdom (area 16,650 sq. miles, pop. 5,119,150 excluding Greenland and the Faroe Is) in N. Europe. It comprises the mainland of Jylland (Jutland) and 100 inhabited islands of which the most important are Zealand, Lolland, Funen, Falster, Langeland and Bornholm (plus the Faroe Is in the N. Atlantic and Greenland). Capital: Copenhagen. People and language: Danish, with very small German and Swedish minorities. State religion: Lutheran. The land is 75% arable, 10% forest and 9% pasture. Denmark is low and flat, mostly under 100 ft (highest point Ejer Bavnehøj, 565 ft) with indented coasts, no large rivers and few lakes. The climate is temperate. Annual rainfall: 24 ins. Average temperature

(F.): 32° (Jan.), 62° (July). Livestock: cattle, pigs, poultry. Agricultural products: barley, oats, rye, wheat, fodder, sugar beet, bacon, milk, butter, cheese, eggs, fruit. Mineral resources: peat, lignite. Fishing is important. Manufactures: cement, food processing, engineering, agricultural machinery, shipbuilding, porcelain, silverware, furniture. Exports: meat, livestock, dairy products, fish, machinery. Imports: machinery, metals, fuels, fertilizers, cattle feeding stuffs. Ports: Copenhagen, Helsingør, Frederikshavn, Aarhus, Esbjerg. Universities: Copenhagen (1479), Aarhus (1933). Monetary unit: krone (divided into 100 øre). HISTORY. Denmark emerged as a kingdom (9th c.), and the Vikings raided England and France. The Danish kings ruled also in England (1016–42), Norway (1028–47, 1380–1814), Sweden (1397–1532) and Schleswig-Holstein (1460–1864). The Union of Kalmar (1397) brought about the effective union of Denmark, Sweden, Norway, the Faroes, Iceland and Greenland, under King Eric of Pomerania. The Danish crown was elective but remained in the Oldenburg line (1448–1863), and became hereditary (1660) and absolute. Denmark adopted Lutheranism (1536). It was involved in war with Sweden (16th and 17th cc.). Greenland was administered by Denmark (1729) and became a Danish colony (1814). Norway was ceded to Sweden (1814). A liberal constitution with a limited monarchy was adopted in 1849. Schleswig-Holstein was lost in the war with Austria and Prussia (1864). Denmark remained neutral in the 1st world war. Iceland became self-governing (1918) and an independent republic (1944). Denmark was occupied by the Germans (1940–5), and organized a strong resistance movement. Greenland was incorporated as a province of the kingdom (1953) and received home rule in 1979. In 1973, Denmark became a member of the European Economic Community. A center-right coalition government took over in 1982

Denmark Strait a channel (c. 300 miles long, 130 miles wide) between S.E. Greenland and Iceland, connecting the Arctic Ocean with the N. Atlantic. The German battleship 'Bismarck' sank the British 'Hood' (1941) in these waters

Den·nis v. U.S.A. (dénis) a decision (1951) of the U.S. Supreme Court led by Chief Justice Frederick M. Vinson, which upheld the constitutionality of the Smith Act as applied to Communist party leaders

de·nom·i·nate (dinómineit) *pres. part.* **de·nom·i·nat·ing** *past and past part.* **de·nom·i·nat·ed** *v.t.* to give a name to [fr. L. *denominare* (*denominatus*)]

de·nom·i·na·tion (dinɔminéifən) *n.* the act of denominating ‖ a name, esp. one given to a class or category ‖ one of a series of units in numbers, weights or money ‖ a religious sect, *Protestant denominations* **de·nom·i·ná·tion·al** *adj.* pertaining to a religious sect, esp. used by Episcopal Protestants as a collective for other Protestant Churches, (*Br.*) used of sects outside the established Church **de·nom·i·ná·tion·al·ism**, **de·nom·i·ná·tion·al·ist** *ns* [O.F. *denominacion*]

de·nom·i·na·tive (dinóminətiv) **1.** *adj.* acting as a name, or giving one ‖ (*gram.*) derived from a noun **2.** *n.* a word (esp. a verb) derived from a noun [fr. L. *denominativus*]

de·nom·i·na·tor (dinómineitər) *n.* the part of a fraction written below the numerator and separated from it by a usually horizontal line. It denotes the number of equal parts into which the whole is divided [M.L. fr. *denominare* (*denominatus*), to give a name to]

de·no·ta·tion (di:noutéifən) *n.* a denoting, marking off ‖ something which denotes, a designation ‖ an explicit meaning (of a word) ‖ (*logic*) that which a word denotes or designates as opposed to what it connotes or implies (cf. CONNOTATION) [fr. L. *denotatio* (*denotationis*)]

de·no·ta·tive (dínóutətiv, di:nóutéitiv) *adj.* designating ‖ (*logic*) simply naming, not implying associated qualities (cf. CONNOTATIVE)

de·note (dinóut) *pres. part.* **de·not·ing** *past and past part.* **de·not·ed** *v.t.* to be the distinguishing sign of ‖ to indicate, *dark clouds denote a coming storm* ‖ to signify, stand for ‖ (*logic*) to be a name of, designate (cf. CONNOTE) [F. *dénoter*]

de·noue·ment, *Br.* **dé·noue·ment** (deinu:má, deinú:má) *n.* the unraveling or resolution of the complications of a play or a story ‖ the final outcome of a complex situation [F.]

CONCISE PRONUNCIATION KEY: **(a)** æ, c*a*t; ɑ, c*a*r; ɔ f*aw*n; ei, sn*a*ke. **(e)** e, h*e*n; i:, sh*ee*p; iə, d*ee*r; ɛə, b*ea*r. **(i)** i, f*i*sh; ai, t*i*ger; ə:, b*i*rd. **(o)** o, *o*x; au, c*ow*; ou, g*oa*t; u, p*oo*r; ɔi, r*oy*al. **(u)** ʌ, d*u*ck; u, b*u*ll; u:, g*oo*se; ə, b*a*cill*u*s; ju:, c*u*be. x, lo*ch*; θ, *th*ink; ð, bo*th*er; z, *Z*en; ʒ, cor*s*age; dʒ, sava*g*e; ŋ, orangutan*g*; j, *y*ak; ʃ, *f*ish; tʃ, fe*tch*; 'l, rabb*le*; 'n, redd*en*. Complete pronunciation key appears inside front cover.

de·nounce (dináuns) *pres. part.* **de·nounc·ing** *past* and *past part.* **de·nounced** *v.t.* to inform against ‖ to censure, esp. publicly, inveigh against ‖ to announce formally the end of (a treaty, agreement etc.) **de·nóunce·ment** *n.* [O.F. *denoncier*]

denounce *n.* mediating term in the U.S. Senate between "censure," which is the strongest condemnation of a member, and "condemnation," a less harsh term used for censuring members for improper conduct

dense (dens) *comp.* **dens·er** *superl.* **dens·est** *adj.* massed closely together ‖ thick, *dense fog* ‖ (of the expression of thought, images) rich in texture, requiring mental effort to appreciate ‖ stupid, slow-witted ‖ (*phys.*) of a medium which has a relatively large retarding effect on radiation and hence a high refractive power ‖ (*photog.*) tending to be opaque [fr. L. *densus*]

den·sim·e·ter (densímitər) *n.* any instrument for measuring density or specific gravity

den·si·tom·e·ter (dɛnsitómitər) *n.* a densimeter ‖ an instrument for measuring optical density, esp. that of a photographic image

den·si·ty (dénsiti:) *pl.* **den·si·ties** *n.* the quality of being dense ‖ (*phys.*) mass per unit volume ‖ (of a static charge) the quantity of electricity per unit area or unit volume ‖ (*optics*) the degree of opacity of a translucent substance, or of darkening of a photographic image ‖ the amount of anything per unit of volume or area, *population density* ‖ (*pop.*) stupidity [F. *densité*]

dent (dent) *n.* a slight hollow made in a surface by pressure or a blow 2. *v.t.* to make a dent in ‖ *v.i.* to become dented [var. of DINT]

dent *n.* a toothlike notch, e.g. in a lock or gearwheel [F.]

den·tal (dént'l) 1. *adj.* of or relating to the teeth or dentistry ‖ (*phon.*) formed with the tip of the tongue against the teeth or the alveolar ridge, e.g. 't' and 'd' 2. *n.* a dental consonant [fr. Mod. L. *dentalis* fr. *dens* (*dentis*), tooth]

dental floss waxed thread used for cleaning between the teeth

den·tal·ize (dént'laiz) *pres. part.* **den·tal·iz·ing** *past* and *past part.* **den·tal·ized** *v.t.* (*phon.*) to make (a speech sound) dental

den·tate (dénteit) *adj.* (*biol.*) toothed ‖ having a sharp, sawlike edge **den·ta·tion** (dentéiʃən) *n.* [fr. L. *dentatus* fr. *dens* (*dentis*), tooth]

Denticare Canadian government program of free dental care for children

den·ti·cle (déntik'l) *n.* a small tooth or tooth-shaped projection ‖ the scales of certain elasmobranch fish **den·tic·u·lar** (dentíkjulər), **den·tic·u·late, den·tic·u·lat·ed** *adjs* **den·tic·u·lá·tion** *n.* [fr. L. *denticulus*, little tooth]

den·ti·frice (déntifris) *n.* a paste or powder for cleaning the teeth [F.]

den·til (dént'l) *n.* one of a row of small rectangular blocks used as an ornamental design, esp. under a cornice in classical architecture [obs. F. *dentille*]

den·tin (déntin) *n.* dentine

den·tine (dénti:n) *n.* a hard, elastic substance, chemically resembling bone, composing the main part of teeth [fr. L. *dens* (*dentis*), tooth]

den·tist (déntist) *n.* someone professionally qualified to treat ailments of the teeth **den·tist·ry** (déntistri:) *n.* the science of the care of the teeth ‖ the work of a dentist [fr. F. *dentiste*]

den·ti·tion (dentíʃən) *n.* the development of teeth, teething ‖ the number and kind of teeth and the way they are arranged in an animal [fr. L. *dentitio* (*dentitionis*)]

den·ture (déntʃər) *n.* a set of artificial teeth [F.]

den·tur·ist (déntʃərist) *n.* dental technician who provides dentures for patients without benefit of a dentist's professional services

de·nu·clear·ize (di:nú:kli:əraiz) *v.* to make free of nuclear arms —**denuclearization** *n.*

de·nu·cle·ate (di:nú:kli:eit) *v.* to remove the nucleus, esp. of cells

den·u·da·tion (dɛ:nudéiʃən, dɛ:njudéiʃən, dɛnjudéiʃən) *n.* the process of erosion and transportation continually affecting the surface of the earth. The principal agents are water (rivers, rain), frost, glaciers, wind, change in temperature [F. *dénudation*]

de·nude (dinú:d, dinjú:d) *pres. part.* **de·nud·ing** *past* and *past part.* **de·nud·ed** *v.t.* to strip, make bare ‖ to lay bare (rock etc.) by erosion of the strata above [fr. L. *denudare*]

de·nun·ci·a·tion (dinʌnsi:éiʃən) *n.* the act of denouncing ‖ an instance of censure, esp. publicly [fr. L. *denunciatio* (*denunciationis*)]

de·nun·ci·a·tor (dinʌnsi:eitər) *n.* someone who denounces **de·nun·ci·a·to·ry** (dinʌnsi:ətɔri:, dinʌnsi:ətouri:) *adj.* [F. *dénonciateur* fr. L.]

Den·ver (dénvər) the capital (pop. 506,000, with agglom. 1,768,000) of Colorado, center of an agricultural and mining region (gold, silver, coal). Industries: canning, meat packing, mining machinery. City has regional federal offices, branch of U.S. mint, and several military installations

de·ny (dinái) *pres. part.* **de·ny·ing** *past* and *past part.* **de·nied** *v.t.* to declare to be untrue, *to deny a charge* ‖ to repudiate, *Peter denied Christ* ‖ to refuse (someone something or something to someone) **to deny oneself** to practice self-denial [F. *dénier*]

de·o·dand (dí:ædænd) *n.* (*Eng. hist.*) something confiscated by the crown, because it had been the immediate cause of a man's death. The proceeds were used for alms [A.F. *deodande*]

de·o·dar (dí:ədɑr) *n. Cedrus deodara*, fam. *Coniferae*, a very large Himalayan cedar yielding valuable wood and noted for its beauty [Hindi *dě'odār* fr. Skr. *deva-dāra*, divine tree]

de·o·dor·ant (di:óudərənt) *n.* an agent for neutralizing unpleasant odors, esp. of perspiration [fr. DE-+L. *odorans* (*odorantis*) fr. *odorare*, to smell]

de·o·dor·i·za·tion (di:ɔudərizéiʃən) *n.* a deodorizing

de·o·dor·ize (di:óudəraiz) *pres. part.* **de·o·dor·iz·ing** *past* and *past part.* **de·o·dor·ized** *v.t.* to neutralize a bad odor in (a room, clothes etc.) [fr. DE-+L. *odor*, smell]

de·on·to·log·i·cal (di:ɒntəlódʒik'l) *adj.* of or relating to deontology

de·on·tol·o·gist (di:ɒntólədʒist) *n.* a philosopher concerned with deontology

de·on·tol·o·gy (di:ɒntólədʒi:) *n.* the science of duty or moral obligation [fr. Gk *deon* (*deontos*), obligation + *logos*, discourse]

de·or·bit (di:úərbit) *v.* to remove from or depart from orbiting, e.g., of a spacecraft —**deorbit** *n.* the process

de·ox·i·dize (di:óksidaiz) *pres. part.* **de·ox·i·diz·ing** *past* and *past part.* **de·ox·i·dized** *v.t.* to remove oxygen from ‖ to reduce from the state of an oxide

de·ox·y·gen·ate (di:óksidʒəneit) *pres. part.* **de·ox·y·gen·at·ing** *past* and *past part.* **de·ox·y·gen·at·ed** *v.t.* to remove oxygen, esp. free oxygen, from

de·ox·y·ri·bo·nu·cle·ic acid (di:ɒksiráibounu:klí:ik, di:ɒksiráibounju:klí:ik) (*abbr.* DNA) the nucleic acid found in the nuclei of all cells. It is considered as a gene. The chemical structure of DNA is characterized by sequences of four nitrogen bases (adenine, thymine, guanine and cytosine) occurring in one of two nucleic acid chains and in a complementary fashion in the other. The sequence of bases in a gene constitutes a code that determines the nature of the quality conferred on the organism inheriting that gene. It is believed that the sequence of bases determines the sequence of amino-acid residues in a protein synthesized in the cell under the influence of the gene. The process is thought to occur in two steps: the gene serves as a template for the production of some thousands of molecules of ribonucleic acid. This ribonucleic acid then, with the genic master code transmitted to it, combines the molecules of the various amino acids (there are twenty in all) in the proper sequence, each ribonucleic-acid molecule producing some ten thousand protein molecules. In addition to controlling the manufacture of other molecules, DNA can serve as a template for its own reduplication during mitosis

de·ox·y·ri·bo·nu·cle·o·tide (di:ɒksiraibounu:klí:ətaid) *n.* a nucleotide constituent of DNA containing deoxyribose, a structural sugar derivative

de·part (dipárt) *v.i.* to go away ‖ to set off or out ‖ to deviate, *to depart from routine* [O.F. *departir*]

de·part·ed (dipártid) 1. *adj.* bygone 2. *n.* **the departed** the dead person or persons

de·part·ment (dipártmənt) *n.* a distinct branch of a whole, e.g. of a complex business organization, a big store, or municipal, state, college or university administration ‖ an administrative district in France of the largest category **de·part·men·tal** (dipártmént'l, dɛ:partmént'l) *adj.* **de·part·men·tal·ize** *pres. part.* **de·part·men·**

tal·iz·ing *past* and *past part.* **de·part·men·tal·ized** *v.t.* [M.E. fr. O.F.]

Department of State (the correct name for) the State Department of the U.S.A.

department store a large store with many departments, organized for selling many different kinds of goods

de·par·ture (dipártʃər) *n.* a going away ‖ a deviation ‖ a fresh course of action ‖ (*naut.*) the amount by which a ship has changed its longitude in sailing **to take one's departure** to say goodbye and go [O.F. *departeüre*]

de·pend (dipénd) *v.i.* (with 'on' or 'upon' in all senses) to rely for livelihood, support etc., *he depends on his pen for a living* ‖ to rely trustfully, count, *don't depend on his cooperation* ‖ to be contingent, *the plan depends on the weather* [O.F. *dependre*]

de·pend·a·bil·i·ty (dipɛndəbíliti:) *n.* the quality of being dependable

de·pend·a·ble (dipéndəb'l) *adj.* reliable, trustworthy **de·pénd·a·bly** *adv.*

dependance *DEPENDENCE

de·pend·ant, de·pend·ent (dipéndənt) *n.* someone who relies upon another for financial support [F. *dépendant*]

de·pend·ence, de·pend·ance (dipéndəns) *n.* a depending on another for material or emotional support ‖ trust, reliance ‖ the state of being contingent [F. *dépendance*]

de·pend·en·cy (dipéndənsi:) *pl.* **de·pend·en·cies** *n.* the state of being dependent ‖ something depending on or subordinate to another, esp. a country controlled by another

de·pend·ent (dipéndənt) 1. *adj.* (of a person) being a financial charge ‖ (of lands or peoples) subject ‖ (*gram.*, of a clause) subordinate ‖ forced to rely, *dependent on a friend for a lift to town* ‖ (*bot.*) hanging down, *dependent branches* ‖ contingent 2. *n.* *DEPENDANT [F. *dépendant*, spelling altered after L. *dependens* (*dependentis*)]

dependent clause a subordinate clause

de·phos·pho·rize (di:fósfəraiz) *pres. part.* **de·phos·pho·riz·ing** *past* and *past part.* **de·phos·pho·rized** *v.t.* to remove the phosphorus from (ore etc.)

de·pict (dipíkt) *v.t.* to represent by drawing or painting ‖ to describe verbally **de·píc·tion** *n.* [fr. L. *depingere* (*depictus*), to paint]

dep·i·late (dépəleit) *pres. part.* **dep·i·lat·ing** *past* and *past part.* **dep·i·lat·ed** *v.t.* to remove hair from **de·pil·a·to·ry** (dipílətɔri:, dipílətouri:) 1. *adj.* able to remove unwanted hair 2. *pl.* **de·pil·a·to·ries** *n.* a chemical preparation for removing unwanted hair [fr. L. *depilare* (*depilatus*)]

de·plen·ish (dipléniʃ) *v.t.* to reduce considerably the contents of [DE-+REPLENISH]

de·plete (diplí:t) *pres. part.* **de·plet·ing** *past* and *past part.* **de·plet·ed** *v.t.* to reduce or empty by destroying or using up, *depleted capital* **de·plé·tion** *n.* [fr. L. *deplere* (*depletus*), to empty out]

de·plor·a·ble (diplórəb'l, diplóurəb'l) *adj.* much to be regretted ‖ wretched, *deplorable living conditions* **de·plór·a·bly** *adv.*

de·plore (diplór, diplóur) *pres. part.* **de·plor·ing** *past* and *past part.* **de·plored** *v.t.* to regret very much or express conventional regret for, *to deplore someone's absence* ‖ to be grieved and appalled by, *to deplore the torturing of prisoners* [fr. L. *deplorare*, to bewail]

de·ploy (diplói) *v.t.* to spread out (troops) ‖ to cause (ships, tanks etc.) to move into battle formation ‖ *v.i.* (of troops) to spread out ‖ (of a fighting force) to take up battle formation **de·plóy·ment** *n.* [F. *déployer*]

de·plume (di:plú:m) *pres. part.* **de·plum·ing** *past* and *past part.* **de·plumed** *v.t.* to pluck the feathers from ‖ (*rhet.*) to strip honors, possessions etc. from [fr. F. *déplumer*]

de·po·lar·ize (di:póuləraiz) *pres. part.* **de·po·lar·iz·ing** *past* and *past part.* **de·po·lar·ized** *v.t.* to deprive of polarity ‖ to prevent polarization of (e.g. an electrode)

de·po·lit·i·ci·za·tion (di:pplitisizéiʃən) *n.* removal from partisan politics —**depoliticize** *v.* —**depoliticized** *adj. Cf* POLITICIZATION

de·pol·lute (di:pəlú:t) *v.* to remove pollution —**depollution** *n.*

de·po·nent (dipóunənt) 1. *adj.* (*gram.*, of verbs in certain languages) passive or middle voice in form but active in meaning 2. *n.* a deponent verb ‖ someone who gives evidence, esp. in writing, for use in court [fr. L. *deponens* (*deponentis*) fr. *deponere*, to put down, testify]

de·pop·u·late (di:pópjuleit) *pres. part.* **de·pop·u·lat·ing** *past* and *past part.* **de·pop·u·lat·ed** *v.t.*

to reduce the number of inhabitants of **de·pop·u·lá·tion** n. [fr. L. depopulari (depopulatus)]

de·port (dipórt, dipóurt) v.t. to send away from a country, exile **to deport oneself** to conduct oneself, behave in a specified way **de·por·tá·tion** (di:portéiʃən, di:pourtéiʃən) n. banishment (esp. of an alien) [F. déporter, to behave or to carry away]

de·por·tee (di:portí:, di:pourtí:) n. a person deported or sentenced to deportation [F. déporté]

de·port·ment (dipórtmənt, dipóurtmənt) n. bearing, way of walking or holding oneself ‖ behavior, manners [O.F. deportement]

de·pose (dipóuz) pres. part. **de·pos·ing** past and past part. **de·posed** v.t. to dethrone ‖ to remove from office ‖ to say on oath ‖ v.i. to give evidence [F. déposer]

de·pos·it (dipózit) 1. v.t. to store for safety ‖ to put (something) down ‖ to leave a layer or coating of ‖ to pay (a sum) as a security 2. n. something entrusted for safekeeping, esp. money in a bank ‖ a sum paid as a security or as a first installment ‖ anything put down or left to settle, a deposit of dust and grime ‖ a sediment ‖ a coating (of metal, by electrolysis) ‖ a natural accumulation, deposits of iron ore [fr. L. deponere (depositus), to lay down]

deposit account (Br.) a savings account

de·pos·i·tar·y (dipóziteri:) pl. **de·pos·i·tar·ies** n. a person receiving a deposit, a trustee ‖ a depository (storehouse) [fr. L. depositarius]

dep·o·si·tion (depəzíʃən, di:pəzíʃən) n. the act of removing from sovereignty or office ‖ a statement given as evidence ‖ the act of depositing ‖ something deposited ‖ the taking down of Christ from the Cross or a representation of this [O.F.]

de·pos·i·tor (dipózitər) n. someone who deposits money etc.

de·pos·i·to·ry (dipózitȯri:, dipózitȯuri:) pl. **de·pos·i·to·ries** n. a storehouse ‖ a depositary (person) [fr. M.L. depositorium]

de·pot (dí:pou, dépou) n. a storage place (civil or military) ‖ a place where things are deposited before distribution ‖ (mil.) a station for recruiting, training or holding soldiers not sent to a unit ‖ a railroad station ‖ the place from which a bus service is run ‖ (Br.) a regimental headquarters ‖ (Br.) the part of a regiment not on foreign service [F. dépôt]

dep·ra·va·tion (deprəvéiʃən) n. a depraving or being depraved

de·prave (dipréiv) pres. part. **de·prav·ing** past and past part. **de·praved** v.t. to corrupt, pervert, esp. morally [fr. L. depravare]

de·prav·i·ty (dipræviti:) pl. **de·prav·i·ties** n. moral corruption, perversion, wickedness ‖ a particular manifestation of this [fr. older pravity fr. L. (after DEPRAVE)]

dep·re·cate (déprikeit) pres. part. **dep·re·cat·ing** past and past part. **dep·re·cat·ed** v.t. to express disapproval of **dep·re·cá·tion** n. **dep·re·ca·tive** (déprəkeitiv, déprəkətiv), **dep·re·ca·to·ry** (déprəkətȯuri) adjs [fr. L. deprecari (deprecatus), to pray against]

de·pre·ci·ate (diprí:ʃi:eit) pres. part. **de·pre·ci·at·ing** past and past part. **de·pre·ci·at·ed** v.t. to diminish the value of ‖ to belittle ‖ v.i. to diminish in value **de·pre·ci·á·tion** n. a depreciating or being depreciated **de·pre·ci·a·to·ry** (diprí:ʃi:ətȯri:, diprí:ʃi:ətȯuri:) adj. [fr. L. depretiare (depretiatus)]

dep·re·da·tion (depridéiʃən) n. a laying waste ‖ (pl.) ravages **dép·re·da·tor** n. [F. déprédation]

de·press (diprés) v.t. to make gloomy, dispirit ‖ to press down, lower, to depress a lever ‖ to lessen the activity of (trade, a market etc.) **de·prés·sant** 1. adj. (med.) lowering activity 2. n. a medicine which lowers activity, a sedative **de·préssed** adj. dispirited, miserable ‖ (bot.) flattened ‖ (bot.) sunken so that the central part is lower than the margin ‖ substandard in economic activity ‖ having a very low standard of living [O.F. dépresser]

de·pres·sion (dipréʃən) n. a depressing or being depressed ‖ a natural hollow or low-lying place ‖ a state of low mental vitality, dejection ‖ the condition of being less active than usual, a trade depression ‖ an operation to remove cataract from the eye ‖ a region of low atmospheric pressure (cyclonic disturbance) ‖ a lowering of the muzzle of a gun ‖ (survey.) the angle made by an object below the horizontal plane of the viewer ‖ the angular distance of a heavenly body below the horizon ‖ a pressing down, depression of an organ pedal [fr. L. depressio (depressionis)]

Depression of 1929 the result of the collapse of the U.S. stock market (Wall Street crash), brought about by a speculative boom during the administrations of Presidents Harding and Coolidge. The Hoover administration, believing that the prosperity of the nation's business enterprises determines national prosperity, did not provide adequate relief measures to revive the distressed country

de·pres·sor (diprésər) n. any muscle that lowers or depresses a structure ‖ a nerve that controls heart rate and blood pressure ‖ (surg.) an instrument that holds a part down during an examination or operation [L.=that which presses down]

de·pres·sur·ize (di:préʃəraiz) v. to decrease the level of air pressure, e.g., in the cabin of an airplane —**depressurization** n.

de·priv·al (dipráivəl) n. a depriving or being deprived

dep·ri·va·tion (deprivéiʃən) n. deprival ‖ an instance of this [fr. M.L. deprivatio (deprivationis)]

de·prive (dipráiv) pres. part. **de·priv·ing** past and past part. **de·prived** v.t. (with 'of') to withhold or take away something desirable or necessary from (someone), age deprived him of his sight [O.F. depriver]

de·pro·gram·ming (di:próugræmiŋ) n. process of eliminating an attitudinal or thinking process inculcated by a course of intensive indoctrination, e.g., from a religious cult

depth (depθ) n. deepness ‖ an extent of deepness downwards or inwards ‖ the representation of deepness in perspective ‖ the innermost part ‖ the most intense point, the depth of winter ‖ the quality of being profound, depth of feeling ‖ (of color) intensity ‖ (pl., rhet.) a low moral condition, what made him sink to such depths? **in depth** (mil.) of defense) organized in successive lines from front to rear ‖ (of a study, criticism etc.) with thorough rigor, taking the many elements of the whole into account **to be out of one's depth** to find that something is beyond one's knowledge or grasp [fr. DEEP (like 'length', 'breadth')]

depth charge a missile that will explode underwater at a given depth, used esp. against submarines

depth-de·vi·a·tion indicator (depθdi:ví:eiʃən) (mil.) a device used to regulate underwater aiming of a missile, taking into account the bending of sonar beams due to water temperature

dep·u·rate (dépjureit) pres. part. **dep·u·rat·ing** past and past part. **dep·u·rat·ed** v.t. to free from impurities **dep·u·rá·tion**, **dép·u·ra·tor** ns [fr. M.L. depurare (depuratus)]

dep·u·ta·tion (depjutéiʃən) n. a group of representatives chosen to speak or act on behalf of others [fr. L. deputare, to appoint]

de·pute (dəpjú:t) pres. part. **de·put·ing** past and past part. **de·put·ed** v.t. to appoint or send (someone) as one's deputy or agent ‖ to entrust or commit (something) to a deputy [F. députer]

dep·u·tize (dépjutaiz) pres. part. **dep·u·tiz·ing** past and past part. **dep·u·tized** v.i. to act as a deputy ‖ v.t. to appoint as a deputy

dep·u·ty (dépjuti:) pl. **dep·u·ties** n. someone appointed to act on behalf of another ‖ a second-in-command who takes control in his superior's absence ‖ a member of a deputation ‖ a member of certain legislative bodies, e.g. the French Chamber of Deputies [F. député]

De Quin·cey (dikwínsi:), Thomas (1785–1859), English critic and essayist. He is best known for his 'Confessions of an English Opium Eater' (1821). His recollections of his literary contemporaries (esp. Wordsworth, Coleridge, Southey) are valuable

de·rac·in·ate (diræsineit) pres. part. **de·rac·in·at·ing** past and past part. **de·rac·in·at·ed** v.t. to uproot, extirpate **de·rac·i·ná·tion** n. [fr. F. déraciner]

de·rail (diréil) v.t. to cause (a train etc.) to run off the rails ‖ v.i. to run off the rails **de·ráil·ment** n. [F. dérailler]

de·rail·leur (diréilər) n. gear mechanism on a bicycle, usu. 5- or 10-speed, that moves the chain from one speed sprocket to another

De·rain (dərɛ̃), André (1880–1954), French painter. From 1899 he worked with Vlaminck, then Matisse, and for a short time exhibited with the Fauves. Although an associate of Braque and Picasso, he was never a cubist. During the surrealist ferment he retired into solitude, and painted in a spirit wholly in the

Mediterranean tradition. He was also an engraver, designed sets and costumes, and made a small number of remarkable sculptures

de·range (diréindʒ) pres. part. **de·rang·ing** past and past part. **de·ranged** v.t. to make insane ‖ to throw into confusion ‖ to cause to go out of order **de·ránge·ment** n. [fr. F. déranger, to disturb]

de·rate (di:réit) pres. part. **de·rat·ing** past and past part. **de·rat·ed** v.t. (Br.) to lower or abolish the rates levied on (property)

Der·by (dárbi:), Edward George Geoffrey Smith Stanley, 14th earl of (1799–1869), British Conservative statesman. A protectionist, he was prime minister (1852, 1858–9 and 1866–8)

Derby the county town (pop. 215,400) of Derbyshire, England, a county borough: engineering, textiles, porcelain

Der·by (dárbi:) n. (Br.) a race for three year-old horses held annually on Epsom Downs. The name comes from the Derby stakes instituted by the 12th earl of Derby in 1780 ‖ (dɔ́:rbi:) a U.S. race of similar importance, esp. the Kentucky Derby **der·by** (dɔ́:rbi, Am.=Br. bowler) a hard, round, curly-brimmed hat, usually black

Der·by·shire (dárbi:ʃər) (abbr. Derby) a county (area 1,012 sq. miles, pop. 878,000) in the Midlands of England. County town: Derby. Administrative center: Matlock

Derbyshire spar fluorspar

der·e·lict (dérəlikt) 1. adj. abandoned, neglected, left to fall to ruin 2. n. abandoned property, esp. a ship abandoned at sea ‖ a human wreck [fr. L. derelictus]

der·e·lic·tion (derəlíkʃən) n. an abandoning or being abandoned ‖ neglect (of duty) ‖ new land gained from a change in the waterline of the sea, or the process by which such land is won [fr. L. derelictio (derelictionis)]

de·req·ui·si·tion (di:rekwizíʃən) v.t. to return from central or local government to private control

de·ride (diráid) pres. part. **de·rid·ing** past and past part. **de·rid·ed** v.t. to laugh at in scorn, mock [fr. L. deridere]

de·ri·sion (diríʒən) n. mockery, ridicule [F. dérision]

de·ri·sive (diráisiv) adj. scornful, mocking ‖ contemptible, a derisive effort [fr. L. deridere (derisus), to laugh at]

de·ri·so·ry (diráisəri:, diráizəri:) adj. scornful, mocking ‖ such as to cause derision, a derisory offer [fr. L. derisorius]

der·i·va·tion (derivéiʃən) n. a deriving or being derived ‖ an origin, source ‖ a statement of the source of a word, or the act of tracing it ‖ the formation of a word from a root (plus prefix or suffix etc.) ‖ (math.) the deduction of one function from another according to a fixed law [F.]

de·riv·a·tive (dirívətiv) 1. adj. derived from something else 2. n. something derived ‖ a word formed from another, e.g. by the addition of a prefix or suffix ‖ (chem.) a substance structurally related to another that can in theory be obtained from it and that is often used to verify the structure of the original substance ‖ (math., of a function) the limit (if it exists) of the ratio of the increment of a function to the increment in the independent variable as the latter increment tends to zero [F. dérivatif]

de·rive (diráiv) pres. part. **de·riv·ing** past and past part. **de·rived** v.t. to receive, obtain, to derive benefit ‖ to deduce ‖ (chem.) to obtain (a compound) from another ‖ v.i. to stem, take its origin [F. dériver]

derived unit (phys.) any of the units of physical measurement (e.g. a dyne) derived from the fundamental units of length, mass and time

derm (dərm) n. the skin ‖ the dermis [fr. Gk derma, skin]

der·ma (dɔ́:rmə) n. (anat., zool.) the dermis [mod. L. fr. Gk derma, skin]

derma n. beef or poultry intestine used as a casing for food [Yiddish derme, pl. of darm, intestine fr. M.H.G.]

der·ma·bra·sion (dɔ́:rməbreiʒən) (med.) n. technique utilizing chemical and mechanical abrasives for removing a layer of skin in order to remove blemishes

der·mal (dɔ́:rməl) adj. of or relating to the skin, esp. the dermis [fr. DERMA (dermis)]

dermal toxicity ability of a substance, esp. a pesticide or industrial product, to poison people or animals by contact

der·ma·ti·tis (də:rmətáitis) n. a diseased or abnormal condition of the skin [fr. Gk *derma* (*dermatos*), skin]

der·mat·o·gen (də:rmǽtədʒin) n. the young or embryonic epidermis in plants [fr. Gk *derma* (*dermatos*), skin+-*gen*, producing]

der·ma·tol·o·gist (də:rmətɔ́lədʒist) n. a specialist in dermatology

der·ma·tol·o·gy (də:rmətɔ́lədʒi:) n. the branch of medicine dealing with the skin and its diseases [fr. Gk *derma* (*dermatos*), skin+*logos*, discourse]

der·ma·to·phyte (də:rmǽtəfait) n. a fungus living parasitically on the skin of people or animals **der·mat·o·phyt·ic** (də:rmætəfítik) adj. **der·mat·o·phy·to·sis** (də:rmætəfitóusis) n. [fr. Gk *derma* (*dermatos*), skin+*phuton*, plant]

der·mis (də́:rmis) n. the inner layer of the skin, consisting of a vascular connective tissue, the cutis [M.L.]

dé·robe·ment (déroubmənt) n. (*fencing*) evasion maneuver of the hilt to avoid opponent's blade without withdrawing

der·o·gate (dérəgeit) pres. part. **der·o·gat·ing** past and past part. **der·o·gat·ed** v.i. (with 'from') to detract || (with 'from') to fall away, go astray (esp. in a moral context) [fr. L. *derogare* (*derogatus*), to repeal a law]

der·o·ga·tion (derəgéifən) n. a lessening or impairing (of power, authority etc.) || detraction [F.]

de·rog·a·tive (dirɔ́gətiv) adj. derogatory

de·rog·a·to·ry (dirɔ́gətɔ:ri:, dirɔ́gətɔuri:) adj. disparaging [fr. L. *derogatorius*]

der·rick (dérik) n. a hoisting apparatus consisting of a boom carrying a tackle at its outer end and pivoted at the other, often to the foot of a central mast, used (esp. aboard ship) for unloading, etc. and in construction work || (*baseball*) to remove a pitcher during a game || a tower or framework over an oil drilling etc. for supporting and manipulating drilling tackle [after the London hangman *Derick* (c. 1600)]

derrick lift (*weight lifting*) lift of a dead weight without bending legs

der·ring-do (dériŋdú:) deeds of stirring courage, esp. such as typify costume drama [M.E. fr. *durran, dorren,* to dave and *don, do,* to do]

der·ris (déris) n. a member of *Derris,* fam. *Papilionaceae,* a genus of Far Eastern plants whose roots are a source of rotenone || an insecticide prepared from this [Gk *derris,* a covering]

der·vish (də́:rvif) n. a member of any of various Moslem ascetic religious orders. Many are named after their religious exercises, e.g. 'howling' dervishes, 'whirling' dervishes [ult. fr. Pers. *darvēsh, darvīsh,* poor, a friar etc.]

DES (*pharm. abbr.*) for diethylstilbestrol (which see)

DESC (*acronym*) for Defense Electronic Supply Center

des·cant (déskænt) n. (*mus.*) an independent treble melody sung above the main song || a discourse on a theme (suggesting tedious improvisation) [fr. O.F. *deschant*]

des·cant (diskǽnt, deskǽnt) v.i. to discourse at large, elaborate (often tediously) || to sing a descant [fr. O.F. *deschanter*]

Des·cartes (deikært), René (1596–1650), French philosopher, physicist and mathematician. He founded the science of analytical geometry ('la Géometrie', 1637) and discovered the laws of geometric optics. While in his scientific work he reasoned as a materialist, in metaphysics he appears as an idealist. He founded modern metaphysics, rejecting Scholasticism and providing the method of reasoning generally called Cartesianism. In 'Discours de la méthode' (1637) he divests himself of all previously held beliefs, to rebuild on his own basis of certitude, i.e. the fact of his self-conscious existence: 'dubito ergo cogito: cogito ergo sum' (I doubt, therefore I think: I think, therefore I am). By intuition and deduction he both reveals the truth of his own existence and restates the ontological argument for the existence of God. His thought is further developed principally in 'Méditations métaphysiques' (published in Latin 1641, and in French 1644), 'Principia philosophiae' (Latin 1644, French 1647) and 'les Passions de l'âme' (1649), as well as in a vast correspondence

de·scend (disénd) v.i. to go downwards, *steps descending to the lower lawn* || to debase oneself, *would he descend to such methods?* || (with 'on') to make a sudden attack, *wolves descended on the flock* || to be transmitted by inheritance || to proceed (in a narration) from earlier to later

time || to proceed (in an argument) from the more important to the less important, or from the general to the particular || v.t. to go down, *to descend a staircase* to be descended from to come from (a stock or source) [F. *descendre*]

de·scend·ant, de·scend·ent (diséndənt) n. someone or something descended [F. *descendant*]

de·scent (disént) n. a descending || a downward slope || a way down || a moral stooping || lineage, ancestry || (*law*) the transmission of property or title by inheritance [F. *descente*]

Des·champs (deifã̃), Eustache (c. 1346–c. 1406), French poet. Besides many ballades and rondeaux he wrote the 'Miroir de mariage' (unfinished in 13,000 lines), full of comedy and satire

de·school (di:skú:l) v. to lessen the availability of schools

de·scram·bler (di:skrǽmblər) n. device for interpreting scrambled messages, e.g., in radio or telephone communication

de·scribe (diskráib) pres. part. **de·scrib·ing** past and past part. **de·scribed** v.t. to give a description of || (with 'as') to qualify, *would you describe him as brilliant?* || to draw, trace (esp. a geometrical figure) || to move in the outline of, *the arrow described a parabola* [fr. L. *describere*]

de·scrip·tion (diskrípfən) n. a verbal account or portrayal of a person, scene, event etc. || a technical account, definition, *a botanical description* || sort, kind, *toys of every description* **to answer a description** to correspond in appearance to a verbal account [F.]

de·scrip·tive (diskríptiv) adj. serving to describe [fr. L. *descriptivus*]

descriptive botany the science concerned with the systematic description of plants

descriptive geometry the representation on planes of geometric figures, and the geometric determination of angles, distances, intersections etc.

descriptive linguistics the branch of linguistic science which describes languages in their existing state without reference to their history or to related languages

de·scrip·tor (diskríptər) n. (*computer*) a significant word or symbol used to identify and classify data to facilitate retrieval

de·scry (diskrái) pres. part. **de·scry·ing** past and past part. **de·scried** v.t. (*rhet.*) to catch sight of || (*rhet.*) to manage to see, make out (a distant object) [perh. O.F. *descrier*]

des·e·crate (désikreit) pres. part. **des·e·crat·ing** past and past part. **des·e·crat·ed** v.t. to outrage the sanctity of, profane **des·e·cra·tion, des·e·cra·tor** ns [DE-+CONSECRATE]

de·seg·re·gate (di:ségrigeit) pres. part. **de·seg·re·gat·ing** past and past part. **de·seg·re·gat·ed** v.t. to free from the practice of segregation (esp. racial) || to abandon the practice of segregation **de·seg·re·ga·tion** n.

de·se·lect (di:səlékt) v. to dismiss a person from a program or position for which he or she has been selected

de·sen·si·tize (di:sénsitaiz) pres. part. **de·sen·si·tiz·ing** past and past part. **de·sen·si·tized** v.t. (esp. *med.*) to reduce the abnormal sensitivity of (the body) to a substance || (*photog.*) to render insensitive to light

de·sert (dizə́:rt) v.t. to abandon, forsake, and so break faith with (someone) || to leave entirely unoccupied, *deserted classrooms* || v.i. to run away from service in the armed forces [F. *déserter*]

des·ert (dézərt) n. a large area of land where there is not enough vegetation to support human life [O.F.]
—Deserts cover nearly one third of the earth's land surface, including the icy wastes of the Arctic and Antarctic. The term is popularly restricted, however, to the hot deserts. These are, in the northern hemisphere: N. Africa (Sahara), Libya, Saudi Arabia, Syria, Iran, Turkmenistan (Kara Kum), Uzbekistan (Kyzyl Kum), Mongolia (Gobi), North America (Mojave) and, in the southern hemisphere: South Africa (Kalahari), Australia (Great Sandy Desert, Great Victorian Desert etc.), Patagonia and Chile (Atacama)

de·sert (dizə́:rt) n. (esp. *pl.*) a fit reward or punishment, *to get one's deserts* || (esp. *pl.*) worthiness of reward or punishment, *treat him according to his deserts* || merit, *promotion is seldom purely on desert* [O.F. fr. *deservir,* to

de·sert·er (dizə́:rtər) n. someone who deserts, esp. from the armed forces

de·ser·tion (dizə́:rfən) n. a deserting or being deserted || the act or crime of running away from service in the armed forces

de·serve (dizə́rv) pres. part. **de·serv·ing** past and past part. **de·served** v.t. to be worthy of, merit || to have a claim on, *the refugees deserve your help* || v.i. to show worthiness, *she was praised as she deserved* **de·sérved** adj. **de·serv·ed·ly** (dizə́rvidli:) adv. **de·sérv·ing** adj. [O.F. *deservir*]

des·ha·bille (dezəbí:l, dezəbí:) n. dishabille

dés·ha·bi·llé (deizəbí:jei) n. (Br.) dishabille

des·ic·cant (désikənt) 1. adj. drying 2. n. a drying agent

des·ic·cate (désikeit) pres. part. **des·ic·cat·ing** past and past part. **des·ic·cat·ed** v.t. to dry up, *desiccated coconut* || v.i. to become dried up **des·ic·ca·tion** n. **des·ic·ca·tive** (desíkətiv) adj. [fr. L. *desiccare* (*desiccatus*)]

des·ic·ca·tor (désikeitər) n. (*chem.*) a vessel containing a drying agent and used to dry substances or to provide a dry atmosphere || an apparatus for desiccating fruit etc. [fr. L. *desiccare,* to make dry]

de·sid·er·a·tive (disídərətiv, disídəreitiv) adj. (*gram.,* in some languages) of a secondary conjugation signifying a desire for the action or condition denoted by the simple verb, e.g. Skr. *pibāmi* 'to drink', *pibāsāmi* 'I wish to drink' [fr. L.L. *desiderativus,* pertaining to desire]

de·sid·er·a·tum (disidəréitəm) pl. **de·sid·er·a·ta** (disidəréitə) n. anything missing and felt to be needed [L.]

de·sign (dizáin) n. a decorative pattern || instructions for making something which leave the details to be worked out || the formal structure of a picture || the arrangement of forms, colors, materials etc. that go to make a 'style' (in furniture etc.) || the combination of parts in a whole || a plan conceived in the mind || a purpose, intention || (*pl.*) an intention to get possession of, *to have designs on someone's money* [F. *dessein*]

design v.t. to invent and bring into being || to prepare plans or a sketch or model etc. of (something to be made) || to plan in the mind || to intend for a particular purpose || v.i. to make designs [F. *désigner*]

des·ig·nate (dézignit, dézigneit) 1. adj. (always placed after its noun) appointed to an office but not yet in possession of it, *bishop designate* 2. v.t. (dézigneit) pres. part. **des·ig·nat·ing** past and past part. **des·ig·nat·ed** to show, identify, *churches are designated on the map by crosses* || (often with 'as') to name, describe, *designated as depressed areas* || to appoint to office [fr. L. *designare* (*designatus*), to point out]

designated hitter (*baseball*) a player designated at the beginning of a game to substitute at bat for the pitcher (*abbr.* DH)

des·ig·na·tion (dezignéifən) n. a designating or being designated || a name or conventional sign serving to identify || nomination to office [fr. L. *designatio* (*designationis*), a pointing out]

de·sign·ed·ly (dizáinidli:) adv. intentionally

de·sign·er (dizáinər) n. someone who designs e.g. clothes, theater sets, industrial products

de·sign·ing (dizáiniŋ) 1. n. the making of designs 2. adj. scheming, artful

des·i·nence (désinəns) n. (*gram.,* in some languages) an inflectional ending that expresses case and number in the noun and adjective, and person, number and voice in the verb [F.]

des·ip·ra·mine [$C_{18}H_{22}N_2$] (desíprami:n) n. (*pharm.*) antidepressant drug; marketed as Pertofrane and Norpramine *also* desmethylimipramine

de·sir·a·bil·i·ty (dizaiərəbíliti:) n. the quality of being desirable

de·sir·a·ble (dizáiərəb'l) adj. inspiring the wish to possess, *a desirable property* || that one hopes to find in oneself, in others, or in things, *desirable qualities* **de·sír·a·bly** adv. [F. *désirable*]

de·sire (dizáiər) n. yearning, longing || strong sexual attraction || wish, request, *this was done at his desire* || (*rhet.*) the thing desired [O.F. *désir*]

desire pres. part. **de·sir·ing** past and past part. **de·sired** v.t. to want to have, acquire or bring about (something) || to want (to do something) [O.F. *desirer*]

de·sir·ous (dizáiərəs) adj. wishful, desiring [O.F. *desireus*]

de·sist (dizíst, disíst) v.i. to cease (from doing something) [O.F. *desister*]

desk (desk) n. a piece of furniture with a flat or sloping surface for writing or reading at, often fitted with drawers, esp. for office use ‖ a lectern ‖ a division of a big organization, esp. in journalism, *the city desk* [M.E. *deske* prob. fr. M.L. *desca*, table]

des·man (désmən) pl. **des·mans** n. *Galemys pyrenaica*, fam. *Talpidae*, an aquatic mammal about 10 ins long found in mountain streams of S.W. France and in Spain. It has webbed toes and a long snout ‖ *Desmana moschata*, a related mammal about 16 ins long found in streams in the southeast U.S.S.R. It has a musk gland near the root of the tail. The tail is laterally compressed [F. and G. fr. Swed. *desman* (råtta), musk (rat)]

desmethylimipramine *DESIPRAMINE

des·mid (désmid) n. any of many unicellular or colonial algae related to the diatoms but lacking a siliceous cell wall [fr. Mod. L. *Desmidium* fr. Gk fr. *desmos*, bond]

Des Moines (dəmɔ́in) the capital (pop. 191,003) of Iowa, a market center of the corn belt: coal mining, meat packing, flour milling

des·mol·o·gy (dezmɔ́ləʒi:) n. (*med.*) the study of ligaments

Des·mou·lins (deimu:lɛ̃), Camille (1760–94), French revolutionary, orator and propagandist. His speeches and his journal 'les Révolutions de France et de Brabant' made him a leading instigator of the French Revolution. He opposed the tyranny of the Committee of Public Safety, and was executed

des·o·late (désəleit) 1. v.t. pres. part. **des·o·lating** past and past part. **des·o·lat·ed** to make desolate ‖ to depopulate ‖ to lay waste, ravage ‖ to make wretched 2. (désəlit) adj. lonely ‖ forlorn ‖ wasted, barren, *a desolate landscape* ‖ uninhabited [fr. L. *desolare* (*desolatus*), to forsake]

des·o·la·tion (desəléiʃən) n. a desolating ‖ a laying waste ‖ a barren, neglected state or area ‖ extreme loneliness, misery, unhappiness [F.]

de·sorb (di:zúərb) v. to restore an absorbed substance

De So·to (dəsóutou), Hernando (c. 1496–1542), Spanish explorer of the region now comprising the southeastern United States, and discoverer of the Mississippi River. His expedition (from 1539) opened the area to European colonization

de·sox·i·met·a·sone [C$_{22}$H$_{29}$FO$_4$] (dəsɒksimétəsoun) n. (*pharm.*) a synthetic corticosteroid used to control inflammation, itching, and vasoconstrictive symptoms; marketed as Topicort

des·ox·y·ri·bo·nu·cle·ic acid (desóksiráibounu:klí:ik, desóksiráibounju:klí:ik) deoxyribonucleic acid

de·spair (dispéər) 1. v.i. to lose hope 2. n. hopelessness ‖ the cause of despair, *his recklessness is her despair* **de·spair·ing** adj. [fr. O.F. *desperer*]

des·pa·re·ci·do (dəspareisí:dou) n. (*Sp.*) literally, "to be disappeared," a desaparecido is a victim of a government-approved kidnapping, esp. in Argentina

despatch *DISPATCH

De·spen·ser (dispénsər), Hugh le, 'the Elder' (1262–1326), earl of Winchester. With his son Hugh 'the Younger' (c. 1290–1326), he acquired immense power at the court of Edward II. Hated by the barons, they were banished (1321), restored (1322) and put to death (1326)

des·per·a·do (despərádou, despəréidou) pl. **des·per·a·does, des·per·a·dos** n. a criminal who stops at nothing [prob. altered fr. DESPERATE]

des·per·ate (déspərit, désprit) adj. beyond, almost beyond, hope ‖ frantic ‖ reckless and violent ‖ extremely bad, *finances in a desperate state* [fr. L. *desperare* (*desperatus*), to despair]

des·per·a·tion (despəréiʃən) n. a despairing ‖ a state of recklessness caused by despair [F.]

des·pi·ca·ble (dispíkəb'l, déspikəb'l) adj. fit to be despised, contemptible, mean **des·pi·ca·bly** adv. [fr. L. *despicabilis*]

de·spin (di:spín) v. to revolve in an opposite direction to offset the effects of a spinning motion

des·pise (dispáiz) pres. part. **de·spis·ing** past and past part. **de·spised** v.t. to look down upon, feel contempt for [M.E. *despisen* fr. O.F.]

de·spite (dispáit) 1. prep. notwithstanding 2. n. (only in) **in despite of** (*rhet.*) in spite of [M.E. *despit* fr. O.F.]

de·spoil (dispɔ́il) v.t. to plunder, pillage ‖ to strip (a person, institution etc.) of possessions, esp.

by the arbitrary use of force ‖ to ruin (land etc.) by stripping away its valuable products or putting it to wrong use **de·spoil·ment** n. [M.E. *despuilen* fr. O.F.]

de·spo·li·a·tion (dispouli:éiʃən) n. a despoiling or being despoiled [fr. L. *despoliatio* (*despoliationis*)]

de·spond (dispɔ́nd) v.i. to become very disheartened, be dejected **de·spond·ence, de·spond·en·cy** ns **de·spond·ent** adj. [fr. L. *despondere*, to give up]

des·pot (déspɒt, déspət) n. an absolute ruler, a tyrant **des·pot·ic** adj. **des·pot·i·cal·ly** adv. **des·pot·ism** n. [O.F. fr. Gk *despotēs*]

de·spun antenna (di:spʌ́n) aerospace antenna that rotates in the opposite direction of a satellite's rotation, pointing toward the earth at all times

des·qua·mate (déskwəmeit) pres. part. **des·qua·mat·ing** past and past part. **des·qua·mat·ed** v.i. (*med.*) to peel off in scales **des·qua·ma·tion** n. **des·qua·ma·tive** (déskwəmeitiv, diskwǽmətiv), **des·qua·ma·to·ry** (déskwəmətɔri:, déskwəmətɔ̌uri:, diskwǽmətɔ̌ri:, diskwǽmətɔ̌uri:) adjs [fr. L. *desquamare* (*desquamatus*)]

Des·sa·lines (desæli:n), Jean-Jacques (c. 1758–1806), emperor of Haiti (1804–6). An African slave, he freed Haiti from the French (1803), but ruled with great cruelty and was assassinated

Des·sau (désau) a communications center (pop. 101,000) on the River Mulde near the Elbe in former Saxony-Anhalt, E. Germany: engineering industries

des·sert (dizə́:rt) n. a sweet course served at the end of a meal, (*Br.*) esp. fruit and nuts [F. fr. *desservir*, to clear the table]

des·sert·spoon (dizə́:rtspu:n) n. a spoon between a teaspoon and a tablespoon in size

de·Sta·lin·i·za·tion (di:stɑlinizéiʃən) n. process of reversing programs and policies of the Stalin era in the U.S.S.R. and its satellites, e.g., freeing some political prisoners

des·ti·na·tion (destinéiʃən) n. the place to which a person or thing is going [fr. L. *destinatio* (*destinationis*)]

des·tine (déstin) pres. part. **des·tin·ing** past and past part. **des·tined** v.t. (usually *pass.*) to set apart (for a specified purpose) ‖ (of fate) to foreordain **destined for** on its (or his/her) way to [F. *destiner*]

des·ti·ny (déstini:) pl. **des·ti·nies** n. the power of fate ‖ one's predetermined lot [O.F. *destinée*]

des·ti·tute (déstitju:t, déstitu:t) adj. so poverty-stricken as to be without the necessities of life **destitute of** entirely lacking **des·ti·tu·tion** n. [fr. L. *destituere* (*destitutus*), to forsake]

de·stress (di:strés) v. to remove or lessen stress

de·stroy (distrɔ́i) v.t. to smash the structure of, break past mending, demolish ‖ to put an end to (hopes etc.) [M.E. *destruyen* fr. O.F.]

de·stroy·er (distrɔ́iər) n. a small, fast warship armed with guns, depth charges and other weapons and used as an escort or submarine hunter ‖ someone who destroys ‖ something which destroys

destroyer escort (*Am.*=*Br.* frigate) a ship smaller and slower than a destroyer, used against submarines

de·struct (di:strʌkt) adj. of an order to destroy, e.g., a destruct order for a spacecraft

de·struct·i·bil·i·ty (distrʌktəbíliti:) n. the quality of being destructible

de·struct·i·ble (distrʌ́ktəb'l) adj. capable of being destroyed [fr. L. *destructibilis*]

de·struc·tion (distrʌ́kʃən) n. a destroying or being destroyed ‖ the cause of ruin, something which destroys [O.F.]

de·struc·tive (distrʌ́ktiv) adj. causing or liable to cause destruction ‖ negative, not constructive, *destructive criticism* [O.F.]

destructive distillation distillation at a temperature high enough to convert one or more of the substances present into a different substance or substances

des·ue·tude (déswitu:d, déswitju:d) n. the state of being used no longer [F. *désuétude*]

de·sul·fu·rize, Br. de·sul·phu·rize (di:sʌ́lfəraiz, di:sʌ́lfjəraiz) pres. part. **de·sul·fu·riz·ing, Br. de·sul·phu·riz·ing** past and past part. **de·sul·fu·rized, Br. de·sul·phu·rized** v.t. to rid of sulfur

des·ul·to·ri·ly (désəltɔrili:, désəltɔ̌urili:) adv. in a desultory way

des·ul·to·ri·ness (désəltɔrinis, désəltɔ̌urinis) n. the quality of being desultory

des·ul·to·ry (désəltɔri:, désəltɔ̌uri:) adj. jumping from one object of attention to another, without concentration or clear order, *to read in a desultory fashion* [fr. L. *desultorius* fr. *desultor*, trick rider]

DET *DEET

de·tach (ditǽtʃ) v.t. to separate, remove ‖ to send (a regiment, ships etc.) on a special mission away from the main body **de·tách·a·ble, de·táched** adjs (of the mind, opinions etc.) independent, uninfluenced by other people or by prejudice etc. ‖ separate ‖ standing apart [F. *détacher*]

de·tach·ment (ditǽtʃmənt) n. a detaching, separation ‖ troops, ships etc. sent away from the main body on special service, or the sending away of them, or the state of being sent away ‖ cool independence of judgment ‖ freedom from involvement ‖ indifference to worldly ambitions [F. *détachement*]

de·tail (dí:teil, ditéil) n. a small part, an item ‖ (*archit.*) the treatment in full of an element of a plan or construction, or such an element ‖ (*fine arts*) a part of a composition or construction considered in isolation ‖ (*mil.*) a detachment for a special job, or the job itself **to go into detail** to expatiate [F. *détail*]

de·tail (ditéil) v.t. to itemize, list ‖ (*mil.*) to assign to a special duty [F. *détailler*]

de·tailed (dí:teild, ditéild) adj. giving minute particulars, full of detail

detail person sales representative of a pharmaceutical manufacturer who promotes prescription drugs for use by physicians, dentists, and pharmacists

de·tain (ditéin) v.t. to keep from leaving ‖ to keep in custody [M.E. *deteine* fr. O.F.]

de·tain·er (ditéinər) n. (*law*) the detaining of what belongs to someone else ‖ a writ authorizing a prison officer to go on keeping a prisoner in custody [A.F. *detener* v. used as n.]

de·tect (ditékt) v.t. to find out, discover betraying signs of, *did you detect anything suspicious in his manner?* ‖ to discover the presence of, *to detect radioactive material* **de·téct·a·ble** adj. **de·téc·tion** n. **de·téc·tive** 1. adj. serving to detect or concerned with detection 2. n. a policeman whose work is to investigate crime ‖ a private crime investigator [fr. L. *detegere* (*detectus*), to uncover]

detective story a narrative involving the detection by a detective of an apparently perfect crime, the reader being kept informed of the stages so that his own puzzle-solving faculty is in play and the suspense heightened

de·tec·tor (ditéktər) n. an instrument for detecting something, e.g. the presence of radiation [L.]

de·tent (ditént) n. a catch for controlling the motion of machinery, esp. one used in horology [F. *détente*]

dé·tente (deitánt) n. an easing of tension, esp. between nations [F.]

de·ten·tion (diténʃən) n. a detaining or being detained ‖ arrest or confinement ‖ the keeping of a child in school during free time as a punishment [fr. L. *detentio* (*detentionis*)]

detention barracks (*Br.*) a military prison

de·ter (ditə́:r) pres. part. **de·ter·ring** past and past part. **de·terred** v.t. to discourage from some action by making the consequences seem frightening etc. [fr. L. *deterrere*, to frighten from]

de·ter·gent (ditə́:rdʒənt) 1. adj. cleansing 2. n. soap ‖ an alkali, a basic salt, or a mixture of basic salts, used for cleaning metals ‖ one of a large number of cleansing agents that are either solid and soluble in water or organic liquid, that are synthetic and surface-active, and that resemble soaps in emulsifying and solubilizing properties but differ from them in chemical composition. They can be used with hard water [fr. L. *detergens* (*detergentis*) fr. *detergere*, to wash out]

de·te·ri·o·rate (ditíəri:əreit) pres. part. **de·te·ri·o·rat·ing** past and past part. **de·te·ri·o·rat·ed** v.t. to make worse ‖ v.i. to become worse **de·te·ri·o·rá·tion** n. **de·té·ri·o·ra·tive** adj. [fr. L. *deteriorare* (*deterioratus*)]

de·ter·ment (ditə́:rmənt) n. a deterring ‖ a deterrent

de·ter·mi·na·ble (ditə́:rminəb'l) adj. (esp. *law*) liable to be terminated ‖ able to be determined

de·ter·mi·nant (ditə́:rminənt) 1. adj. determining, decisive 2. a determining factor, element etc. ‖ (*math.*) a square matrix [fr. L. *determi-*

nans (*determinantis*) fr. *determinare*, to bound]

de·ter·mi·nate (ditə́:rminit) *adj.* limited, defined ‖ (*rhet.*) definite, resolved, decided, *a determinate answer* ‖ (*bot.*) having the edge well marked ‖ (*bot.*) having an inflorescence ending in a flower, e.g. forget-me-not [fr. L. *determinare* (*determinatus*), to bound]

de·ter·mi·na·tion (ditə:rminéiʃən) *n.* firmness of purpose or character, resolution ‖ the act of determining, fixing, deciding ‖ the act of finding out exactly, *the determination of a quantity by measurement* ‖ (*law*) the settling of a controversy by a judicial decision ‖ a coming to a decision ‖ (*logic*) the defining of terms or concepts by the addition of attributes [F.]

de·ter·mi·na·tive (ditə́:rminətiv, ditə́:rminéitiv) **1.** *adj.* serving to determine, direct or limit **2.** *n.* a characteristic that serves to determine ‖ a sign in hieroglyphic or cuneiform writing attached to a word so as to distinguish it from homographs or otherwise make its meaning clear [F. *déterminatif*]

de·ter·mine (ditə́:rmin) *pres. part.* **de·ter·min·ing** *past* and *past part.* **de·ter·mined** *v.t.* to settle, fix, *eye color is determined by genes* ‖ to cause (someone) to resolve, *what determined her to go?* ‖ to regulate, *the sale of ice cream is partly determined by the weather* ‖ to find out precisely, *to determine distances by trigonometry* ‖ (*law*) to limit, define, *the property is determined by a stream* (*esp. law*) to bring to an end, terminate ‖ to settle by judicial decision ‖ *v.i.* (with 'on') to make up one's mind, resolve ‖ (*esp. law*) to come to an end, terminate ‖ to come to a judicial decision **de·tér·mined** *adj.* resolved, decided ‖ resolute **de·tér·min·ism** *n.* the theory that human actions are controlled by antecedent causes and not by the exercise of free will **de·tér·min·ist** *n.* **de·ter·min·ís·tic** *adj.* [O.F. *determiner*]

de·ter·rence (ditə́:rəns, ditʌ́rəns, ditérəns) *n.* a deterring ‖ (*mil.*) policy of maintaining a high level of military strength to deter an enemy attack ‖ the effect of this policy

de·ter·rent (ditə́:rənt, ditʌ́rənt, ditérənt) **1.** *adj.* meant to deter **2.** *n.* something which deters or is meant to deter

de·ter·sive (ditə́:rsiv) *n.* a cleansing agent, detergent [F. *détersif*]

de·test (ditést) *v.t.* to hate, abhor **de·tést·a·ble** *adj.* **de·tést·a·bly** *adv.* [F. *détester*]

de·tes·ta·tion (di:testéiʃən) *n.* hatred, abhorrence ‖ a loathed person or thing [F.]

de·throne (di:θróun) *pres. part.* **de·thron·ing** *past* and *past part.* **de·throned** *v.t.* to depose (a monarch) ‖ to remove from authority or a position of influence **de·thróne·ment** *n.*

det·o·nate (dét'neit) *pres. part.* **det·o·nat·ing** *past* and *past part.* **det·o·nat·ed** *v.i.* to explode with a loud report ‖ to undergo a vigorous exothermic chemical reaction evolving flame or sparks, and spreading through the material at a speed greater than the speed of sound (cf. DEFLAGRATE) ‖ *v.t.* to cause to explode with a loud report ‖ to cause to undergo a vigorous exothermic chemical reaction **det·o·ná·tion, dét·o·na·tor** *ns* a small cap containing a charge, fixed to the end of a fuse, and used to initiate an explosion in dynamite, gelignite, guncotton etc. [fr. L. *detonare* (*detonatus*), to thunder]

de·tour (dí:tuər, ditúər) **1.** *n.* a deviation from the usual route of course ‖ a circuitous path taken to avoid some obstacle, danger etc. **2.** *v.i.* to make a detour ‖ *v.t.* to make a detour around ‖ to cause to make a detour [F.]

dé·tour (déituə) *n.* (*Br.*) a detour

de·tract (ditrǽkt) *v.i.* (with 'from') to lessen in value or estimation **de·trác·tion** *n.* **de·trác·tive** *adj.* **de·trác·tor** *n.* [fr. L. *detrahere* (*detractus*), to take away from]

de·train (di:tréin) *v.i.* to alight from a train ‖ *v.t.* to cause (troops) to alight or (supplies) to be unloaded from a train

det·ri·ment (détrəmənt) *n.* harm, damage **det·ri·mén·tal** *adj.* harmful, injurious [F.]

de·tri·tal (ditráit'l) *adj.* of or resulting from detritus

de·tri·ted (ditráitid) *adj.* worn down ‖ formed by rock disintegration [fr. L. *deterere* (*detritus*), to wear away]

de·tri·tion (ditríʃən) *n.* (*geol.*) a wearing away [fr. L. *deterere* (*detritus*), to wear away]

de·tri·tus (ditráitəs) *pl.* **de·tri·tus** *n.* any loose matter, e.g. stones, sand, silt, formed by rock disintegration [L. fr. *deterere* (*detritus*), to wear away]

De·troit (ditrɔ́it) a port (pop. 1,088,973, with agglom. 4,352,762) in Michigan, on the Detroit River between Lakes Huron and Erie, connected to Windsor, Canada, by tunnels and a suspension bridge. It is the world's greatest car manufacturing center, a leading steel producer and a great grain market

Det·ting·en, Battle of (détiŋən) a battle (1743) during the War of the Austrian Succession in which George II led an Anglo-Hanoverian army to victory over the French

Deu·ca·li·on (du:kéili:ən, dju:kéili:ən) (*Gk mythol.*) son of Prometheus, and king of Thessaly. He took refuge in an ark with his wife Pyrrha when Zeus flooded the earth. They landed on Mount Parnassus. In obedience to an oracle they threw stones behind them, and these became the new men and women of Greece

deuce (du:s, dju:s) *n.* a playing card bearing the number 2 or the side of a die marked with two spots ‖ (*tennis*) the score of 40-all, when either side must gain two consecutive points to win the game [F. *deux* fr. older *deus*, two]

deuce *n.* (*old-fash., pop.,* used as a mild oath) the devil **deuc·ed** (dú:sid, djú:sid) **1.** *adj.* (*old-fash., pop.*) confounded **2.** *adv.* (*old-fash., pop.*) damnably ‖ very great [prob.=DEUCE, the 2 on a die, this being the worst throw]

de·us ex ma·chi·na (déiəsẹksmǽkinə) *n.* (in a story or play) someone or something artificially introduced to solve a difficulty ‖ (in a situation) someone or something coming providentially to solve a difficulty [L.=god from a machine (a reference to the manner of presenting a god in the ancient Greek theater)]

deu·ter·ate (djú:tiəreit) *v.* (*nuclear phys.*) to add an isotope of hydrogen to any solution

deu·te·ri·um (du:tíəri:əm, dju:tíəri:əm) *n.* an isotope of hydrogen, having twice the mass of a hydrogen atom (symbol D, at. no. 1, at. mass 2.0158). It occurs in small quantities as the oxide D_2O (heavy water) in water, from which it can be obtained by fractional electrolysis [Mod. L. fr. Gk *deuteros*, secondary]

deu·ter·on (dú:tərɒn, djú:tərɒn) *n.* the nucleus of the atom of deuterium [Mod. L. fr. Gk *deuteros*, secondary]

Deu·ter·on·o·my (du:tərɒ́nəmi:, dju:tərɒ́nəmi:) the fifth book of the Old Testament. It contains the final teachings of Moses, and was doubtless inspired by the 8th-c. prophetic movement in Israel. It is usually identified with the book that inspired Josiah's reforms in 621 B.C. (II Kings xxii–xxiii)

deut·sche mark (dɔ́itʃəmárk) either of two units of currency: the basic monetary unit of West Germany, or that of East Germany, in each case consisting of 100 pfennigs ‖ a coin of the value of three of these units [G.]

deux-che·vaux (dú:ʃəvʊ) *n.* (*Fr.*) an automobile with a two-horsepower engine

Deux-Sè·vres (də:sevr) a department (area 2,337 sq. miles, pop. 335,800) of W. France (*POITOU). Chief town: Niort

De Va·le·ra (dəvəléərə) Eamon (1882–1975), Irish statesman. He was elected president (1917) of Sinn Féin, imprisoned in England (1918–9), and became president (1918–22) of the Dáil. He refused to accept the treaty (1921) creating the Irish Free State, and formed (1926) Fianna Fáil, the republican opposition party. As premier (1937–48) of the Irish Free State, he pursued an intensely nationalistic policy aimed at removing British influence and at incorporating N. Ireland within Eire. His policy during the 2nd world war was one of neutrality. He was again premier (1951–4, 1957–9) and was then president of the Irish Republic (1959–73)

de·val·u·ate (di:vǽlju:eit) *pres. part.* **de·val·u·at·ing** *past* and *past part.* **de·val·u·at·ed** *v.t.* to lower the legal value of (a depreciated currency) in a crisis ‖ to lessen the value of **de·val·u·á·tion** *n.*

de·val·ue (di:vǽlju:) *pres. part.* **de·val·u·ing** *past* and *past part.* **de·val·ued** *v.t.* to devaluate

De·va·na·ga·ri (deivənǽgəri:) *n.* an alphabet having long, horizontal strokes at the top of most characters, used in writing Sanskrit and Hindi [Skr.]

dev·as·tate (dévəsteit) *pres. part.* **dev·as·tat·ing** *past* and *past part.* **dev·as·tat·ed** *v.t.* to lay waste, ravage **dev·as·tá·tion, dév·as·ta·tor** *ns* [fr. L. *devastare* (*devastatus*)]

de·vel·op (divéləp) *v.t.* to cause to grow or expand ‖ to elaborate on, *to develop a theory* ‖ to begin to have, *to develop a wobble* ‖ to realize (what was potential) ‖ to expand by putting money into, *to develop a business* ‖ (*photog.*) to treat (an exposed plate or film) chemically so that the image appears (*PHOTOGRAPHY) ‖ (*math.*) to expand to completion ‖ (*mus.*) to elaborate (a theme) ‖ *v.i.* (of mind, body or species) to evolve ‖ to come into being ‖ to expand **de·vél·op·er** *n.* (*photog.*) a chemical reagent used to develop an exposed film **de·vél·op·ment** *n.* the act of developing ‖ evolution (of an organism) ‖ a new factor or situation ‖ (*Am.=Br.* estate) a tract of land developed as a unit by public or private enterprise for residential or industrial purposes, with the houses, factories, shops etc. built on it **de·vel·op·mén·tal** *adj.* relating or incidental to growth, *developmental diseases* [F. *développer*]

developed nations countries with a per capita annual income of more than $2,000 and consequent higher standards of living than in so-called developing, or underdeveloped, nations

developing nations countries with a per capita annual income of less than $2,000 and a commensurate poor standard of living among most of the population *Cf* LESS DEVELOPED COUNTRIES, THIRD WORLD

developmental disability disability constituting a substantial handicap to a person's ability to function normally in society, originating before age 18 and expected to continue indefinitely; esp. those attributable to mental retardation, cerebral palsy, epilepsy, autism, and other neurological impairments (*abbr.* DD)

development area (*Br.*) an area suffering industrial decline and unemployment, where the government actively encourages greater industrial diversity

Dev·e·reux (dévəru:), Robert *ESSEX, EARL OF

de·vi·ate (dí:vi:eit) **1.** *v. pres. part.* **de·vi·at·ing** *past* and *past part.* **de·vi·at·ed** *v.i.* to turn aside (from a course, custom, topic etc.) ‖ *v.t.* to cause to turn aside or diverge, *to deviate a stream* **2.** (dí:vi:it) *n.* someone sexually perverted [fr. L. *deviare* (*deviatus*)]

de·vi·a·tion (di:vi:éiʃən) *n.* a turning aside ‖ a deflection of a compass needle because of the magnetic influence of the aircraft or ship in which it is mounted (cf. DECLINATION) ‖ (*statistics*) the algebraic difference between one of a set of observed values and their mean or average value **de·vi·á·tion·ism** *n.* departure from party orthodoxy, esp. within the Communist party **de·vi·á·tion·ist** *n.* [fr. M.L. *deviatio* (*deviationis*)]

de·vi·a·tor (dí:vi:eitər) *n.* someone who deviates or something which deviates

de·vice (diváis) *n.* a scheme, trick, stratagem ‖ something designed or adapted for a special purpose, *a device for trimming hedges* ‖ a heraldic design ‖ a motto **to leave someone to his own devices** to allow someone to do as he pleases ‖ to leave someone to fend for himself [M.E. *devis* fr. O.F.]

dev·il (dévəl) **1.** *n.* an evil spirit, a demon (*DEMONOLOGY) ‖ a cruel or vicious person ‖ (*pop.*) someone full of spirit and daring, *a devil with the girls* ‖ (*pop.*) a fellow, person, *you lucky devil!* ‖ a junior legal counsel working for experience without pay ‖ (*Br.*) a literary hack whose employer takes the credit and the profits ‖ a printer's devil ‖ any of various implements or machines, esp. one for shredding rags or paper ‖ a mild expletive, *who the devil...?* **the Devil** (in Jewish and Christian theologies) the spirit of evil, Satan **a devil of a** very great, *a devil of a mess* **between the devil and the deep blue sea** in a dilemma, faced with two choices which are both unwelcome **devil a one** (*Br.*) not one **devil take the hindmost** look after your own interest and don't worry about those in a worse position **go to the devil!** be damned! **it's the devil** (*Br.*) it's very awkward or difficult **speak** (*Br.* **talk**) **of the devil** here comes the person of whom we were just talking **the devil to pay** trouble ahead **to give the devil his due** to be just, even to someone one dislikes **to play the devil with** to upset, wreak havoc with **2.** *v. pres. part.* **dev·il·ing**, esp. *Br.* **dev·il·ling** *past* and *past part.* **dev·iled**, esp. *Br.* **dev·illed** *v.t.* to prepare (food) with hot seasoning ‖ to tease, torment ‖ *v.i.* to serve as a devil, e.g. to a lawyer [O.E. *dēofol* fr. Gk]

dev·il·fish (dévəlfiʃ) *pl.* **dev·il·fish, dev·il·fish·es** *n.* the angler (fish) ‖ the octopus, or any large cephalopod ‖ *Manta birostris*, a gigantic species of ray up to 20 ft wide inhabiting American waters, or any of various very big rays

CONCISE PRONUNCIATION KEY: (**a**) æ, c*a*t; ɑ, c*a*r; ɔ f*aw*n; ei, sn*a*ke. (**e**) e, h*e*n; i:, sh*ee*p; iə, d*ee*r; ɛə, b*ea*r. (**i**) i, f*i*sh; ai, t*i*ger; ə:, b*i*rd. (**o**) o, *o*x; au, c*ow*; ou, g*oa*t; u, p*oo*r; ɔi, r*oy*al. (**u**) ʌ, d*u*ck; u, b*u*ll; u:, g*oo*se; ə, b*a*cillus; ju:, c*u*be. x, lo*ch*; θ, *th*ink; ð, bo*th*er; z, *Z*en; ʒ, cor*s*age; dʒ, sava*g*e; ŋ, oranguta*n*g; j, *y*ak; ʃ, *f*ish; tʃ, fe*tch*; 'l, rabb*le*; 'n, redd*en*. Complete pronunciation key appears inside front cover.

dev·il·ish (dévəliʃ, dévliʃ) **1.** adj. like or characteristic of the devil, devilish cunning **2.** adv. (intensive) damnably, devilish hard

dev·il-may-care (dévəlmeikéər) adj. reckless and gay ‖ reckless and proud

dev·il·ment (dévəlmənt) n. mischievousness ‖ wickedness

dev·il·ry (dévəlri) pl. **dev·il·ries** n. black magic ‖ evil ‖ devils collectively ‖ mischievousness, high spirits

Devil's Island a French penal colony (late 19th c.–1946) on an island off the coast of French Guiana

devil's tattoo a drumming with the fingers or feet, as an unconscious habit or as a sign of impatience or boredom

Devil's Tower National Monument the first U.S. national monument (c. 1,347 acres), established in 1906 in N.E. Wyoming and containing a flat-topped, fluted, natural rock tower (856 ft high) resting on a circular ridge (415 ft high) above a river

dev·il·try (dévəltri:) pl. **dev·il·tries** n. mischief ‖ mischievousness

dev·il·wood (dévəlwʊd) n. Osmanthus americanus, fam. Oleaceae, a small North American tree having extraordinarily tough, heavy wood

De Vin·ne (dəvíni:), Theodore Low (1828–1914), U.S. printer, and authority on the history of typography. His works include 'The Invention of Printing' (1876), 'The Practice of Typography' (1900–4) and 'Notable Printers of Italy during the Fifteenth Century' (1910)

de·vi·ous (dí:vi:əs) adj. roundabout, very winding, a devious path ‖ underhanded, shifty, devious means [fr. L. devius, out of the way]

de·vis·a·ble (diváizəb'l) adj. able to be devised

de·vise (diváiz) **1.** v.t. pres. part. **de·vis·ing** past and past part. **de·vised** to contrive, think up (e.g. a method, plot) ‖ (law) to bequeath (realty) by will **2.** n. (law) a giving or leaving (of realty) by will ‖ (law) realty given by will ‖ (law) the will (or part of the will) by which realty is left **de·vi·see** (divaizí:, devizí:), **de·vi·sor** ns [O.F. deviser]

de·vi·tal·i·za·tion (di:vait'lizéiʃən) n. a devitalizing or being devitalized

de·vi·tal·ize (di:váit'laiz) pres. part. **de·vi·tal·iz·ing** past and past part. **de·vi·tal·ized** v.t. to deprive of vitality

de·vit·ri·fi·ca·tion (di:vitrifikéiʃən) n. a devitrifying or being devitrified

de·vit·ri·fy (di:vítrifai) pres. part. **de·vit·ri·fy·ing** past and past part. **de·vit·ri·fied** v.t. to change from the glassy state to a crystalline state ‖ v.i. to lose vitreous nature by deferred crystallization

de·void (divóid) adj. (with 'of') lacking in, completely without, devoid of pity [past part. of older devoid v., to cast out fr. O.F.]

dev·o·lu·tion (devəlú:ʃən) n. the handing down, or passing down, of property to a successor ‖ the transfer of work or authority to a deputy ‖ political process of separating or loosening regions from the nation as a whole (esp. of United Kingdom) by peaceful means, e.g., by legislation ‖ (biol.) degeneration [fr. M.L. devolutio (devolutionis) fr. devolvere, to roll down]

Devolution, War of a war (1667–8), also called the Queen's War, which arose out of Louis XIV's claim to Spanish territory in the Netherlands, ownership being said to have 'devolved' upon his wife, Maria-Theresa. After a series of sieges by the French under Turenne and the formation of the Triple Alliance (1668) the war was ended by the Treaty of Aix-la-Chapelle (1668)

de·volve (divólv) pres. part. **de·volv·ing** past and past part. **de·volved** v.t. to transfer, hand over (e.g. a measure of authority) ‖ v.i. to fall as an obligation, the responsibility devolved upon his successor ‖ to pass by succession or transmission, the residue devolved on his youngest son [fr. L. devolvere, to roll down]

Dev·on (dévən) *DEVONSHIRE

De·vo·ni·an (devóuni:ən) **1.** adj. relating to Devonshire, England ‖ of the period or system of the Paleozoic era characterized by ferns and lower fishes (*GEOLOGICAL TIME) the Devonian Devonian period or system of rocks **2.** n. an inhabitant of Devonshire

Dev·on·shire (dévənʃər) (abbr. Devon) a county (area 2,612 sq. miles, pop. 942,100) in the southwest peninsula of England. County town: Exeter

de·vote (divóut) pres. part. **de·vot·ing** past and past part. **de·vot·ed** v.t. to give wholly, dedi-

cate, she devotes herself to the children ‖ to earmark or make a gift (of money) for a particular use ‖ (rare) to consign to destruction **de·vot·ed** adj. bound by strong affection ‖ loyal, zealous ‖ expressing devotion **de·vot·ed·ly** adv. [fr. L. devovere (devotus)]

dev·o·tee (devəti:) n. an ardent supporter (of a cause, a sport etc.) ‖ someone wholly devoted (esp. in religion)

de·vo·tion (divóuʃən) n. love given with the whole heart and will ‖ ardent addiction, devotion to football ‖ devoutness ‖ (pl.) prayers, worship **de·vo·tion·al** adj. [O.F.]

de·vour (diváuər) v.t. (of or like an animal) to eat up hungrily ‖ to take in eagerly with the senses, to devour with one's eyes or with the mind, to devour a book ‖ to consume, destroy, flames devoured the building [O.F. devorer]

de·vout (diváut) adj. worshiping ‖ attending to religious duties ‖ sincere, earnest, devout hopes [M.E. devot fr. O.F.]

dew (du:, dju:) **1.** n. small drops of moisture condensed from the atmosphere, forming esp. on cool surfaces during the night ‖ droplets resembling this, e.g. tears, sweat **2.** v.t. to wet with or as if with dew [O.E. dēaw]

Dew·ar flask (dú:ər, djú:ər) a vacuum flask [after its inventor, Sir James Dewar (1842–1923), Scottish chemist and physicist]

dew·ber·ry (dú:beri, djú:beri) pl. **dew·ber·ries** n. any of several sweet edible berries related to the blackberry. The loganberry is a developed variety ‖ a plant of the genus Rubus bearing dewberries

dew·claw (dú:klɔ, djú:klɔ) n. the rudimentary inner toe, not reaching the ground, sometimes present on a dog's foot ‖ the false hoof of deer and other ungulates

dew·drop (dú:drop, djú:drop) n. a drop of dew

De Wet (dəvét), Christiaan (1854–1922), Boer general who used successful guerrilla tactics in the Boer War (1899–1902)

Dew·ey (dú:i, djú:i), George (1837–1917), U.S. naval commander. He defeated (May 1, 1898) the Spanish fleet at the battle of Manila Bay, and was promoted admiral of the navy (1899)

Dewey, John (1859–1952), U.S. philosopher and educator. A pragmatist, he was against authoritarian methods, arguing for learning through experience and necessity rather than by rote, and it was this principle that served as a cornerstone for modern progressive education. His publications include 'School and Society' (1900), 'Democracy and Education' (1916), 'Human Nature and Conduct' (1922)

Dewey, Melvil (1851–1931), U.S. librarian, and creator (1876) of the Dewey decimal system of classification. He founded (1883) what became the State Library school in Albany, New York, the first instruction center for librarians. He directed (1889–1906) the New York State library, establishing the system of traveling libraries and picture collections

Dewey, Thomas Edmund (1902–71), U.S. lawyer and political leader. He served (1942–54) as governor of New York and was twice (1944, 1948) the Republicans' presidential nominee

Dewey decimal classification a system of classifying books in libraries, devised (1876) by the U.S. librarian Melvil Dewey (1851–1931)

dew·i·ly (dú:ili:, djú:ili:) adv. in a dewy way

dew·i·ness (dú:i:nis, djú:i:nis) n. the quality or state of being dewy

De Wint (dəwínt), Peter (1784–1849), English landscape painter, of Dutch-American descent, one of the outstanding watercolorists of the 19th c.

dew·lap (dú:læp, djú:læp) n. the pendulous fold of skin under the throat of cattle and certain other animals [dew- (obscure)+O.E. læppa, lobe]

DEW line (mil. acronym) for distant early warning line, automated ring of radar stations near the Arctic Circle from Greenland to Alaska, designed to warn the U.S. of approaching enemy aircraft

dew point (of the condensation of atmospheric water vapor) the temperature at which a vapor reaches saturation and starts to condense

dew pond a shallow pond, natural or artificial, fed by condensation, not by a spring

dew·y (dú:i:, djú:i:) comp. **dew·i·er** superl. **dew·i·est** adj. of, like, covered in or marked by the presence of dew

dew·y-eyed (dú:i:aid, djú:i:aid) adj. sentimentally idealistic

dex or **dex·ie** (deks) n. short term for Dexedrine, trade name of sulfate of dextroamphetamine, a nervous-system stimulant

dex·a·meth·a·sone [$C_{22}H_{29}FO_5$] (deksəméθəsoun) n. (pharm.) potent synthetic adrenocortical steroid cortisone congener used as an antiallergic and anti-inflammatory drug

dex·ter (dékstər) adj. belonging to or located on the right side (cf. SINISTER ‖ (heraldry) on the right-hand part of a shield (the viewer's left) [L.=right]

dex·ter·i·ty (dekstériti) n. manual skill, deftness ‖ mental adroitness [fr. L. dexteritas]

dex·ter·ous (dékstərəs, dékstrəs) adj. dextrous

dex·tral (dékstrəl) adj. on the right-hand side ‖ turned or moving towards the right [fr. L. dextra, right hand]

dex·tran (dékstrən) n. (pharm.) water-soluble polysaccharide polymer used to increase the volume of blood and to maintain blood pressure in shock; marketed as Gentran, Expandex, and Plavolex

dex·tran·ase (dékstrəneiz) n. anti-dental-plaque-formation enzyme related to penicillum

dex·trin (dékstrin) n. any of a number of gummy carbohydrates made by the partial hydrolysis of starch and used as adhesives etc. [F. dextrine]

dex·tro·ro·ta·ry (dekstrouróutəri) adj. dextrorotatory

dex·tro·ro·ta·to·ry (dekstrouróutətɔri, dekstrouróutɔuri) adj. (esp. of a substance which rotates the plane of linearly polarized light) rotating to the right or in a clockwise direction (*OPTICAL ROTATION, cf. LEVOROTATORY) [fr. L. dexter, right-hand+ROTATORY]

dex·trorse (dékstrɔrs) adj. turning in a spiral from left to right, e.g. of a stem or gastropod shell (opp. SINISTRORSE) [fr. L. dextrorsus]

dex·trose (dékstrous) n. an optical isomer of glucose which is dextrorotatory [fr. L. dexter, right-hand]

dex·trous (dékstrəs) adj. physically deft ‖ mentally agile and skillful ‖ made or performed with dexterity [fr. L. dexter, right-hand]

Dhau·la·gi·ri (dauləgíəri) a massif (26,795 ft) of the Himalayas in N.W. Nepal, west of Annapurna

dhow, dow (dau) n. an Arab lateen-rigged vessel [fr. Arab. dōw]

di- (dai) prefix (before a vowel) dia

di- prefix twice, double ‖ (chem.) having two (atoms etc.) [Gk fr. dis, twice]

dia- (dáiə) prefix through, throughout ‖ apart, between [Gk dia, through, across]

di·a·base (dáiəbeis) n. a partly crystalline rock ‖ (Br.) an altered basalt or dolerite **di·a·ba·sic** adj. fr. Gk diabasis, a crossing over]

di·a·be·tes in·sip·i·dus (daiəbí:ti:zinsípidəs, daiəbí:tisinsípidəs) n. a rare disease, characterized by the passage of large amounts of urine, that is caused by a disorder of the pituitary gland [L. diabetes fr. Gk diabētēs, a siphon+L. insipidus, insipid]

diabetes mel·li·tus (daiəbí:ti:zməlaitəs) n. a disease, characterized by the presence of excessive amounts of sugar in the urine and manifested by various metabolic disorders, that is caused by an insulin deficiency or by faulty utilization of insulin. It is occasionally hereditary [L. diabetes fr. Gk diabētēs, a siphon+L. mellitus, honeysweet]

di·a·bet·ic (daiəbétik) **1.** adj. of diabetes ‖ suffering from diabetes **2.** n. a person suffering from diabetes [fr. F. diabétique]

di·a·bol·ic (daiəbólik) adj. wicked, evil ‖ of or like the devil ‖ having to do with sorcery ‖ fiendish in cunning or astuteness **di·a·bol·i·cal** adj. [F. diabolique fr. L. fr. Gk]

di·a·bo·lism (daiæbəlizəm) n. sorcery ‖ devil worship [fr. Gk diabolos, devil]

di·a·bo·lo (di:ábəlou) n. the game of tossing and catching a double cone on a string tied between two sticks, held one in either hand ‖ the cone [Ital.=devil]

di·a·caus·tic (daiəkɔ́stik) **1.** adj. of a curve formed by crossing rays of refracted light **2.** n. a curve thus formed [fr. Gk dia-, through+kaustikos, burnt]

di·a·chron·ic (daiəkrónik) adj. (linguistics) of or being a linguistic study which considers change and development in a language over a period of time (opp. SYNCHRONIC) [fr. DIA-+Gk chronos, time]

di·ac·id (daiæsid) **1.** adj. (chem.) esp. of bases) able to replace two acid hydrogen atoms ‖ (chem., esp. of acid salts) containing two replaceable hydrogen atoms **2.** *n.* acid having two acid hydrogen atoms

di·a·co·nal (daiəkən'l) *adj.* of or concerning a deacon [fr. L.L. *diaconalis*]

di·ac·o·nate (daiǽkənit) *n.* the office of deacon ‖ a period of deaconship ‖ a body of deacons [fr. L.L. *diaconatus*]

di·a·crit·ic (daiəkrítik) **1.** *n.* a mark used to distinguish, e.g. to distinguish uses of the same letter for different sounds (é, è, etc.) **2.** *adj.* serving as a diacritic ‖ serving to distinguish ‖ (*med.*) diagnostic **di·a·crit·i·cal** *adj.* [fr. Gk *diakritikos* fr. *diakrinein*, to distinguish]

di·ac·tin·ic (daiæktínik) *adj.* (*phys.*) able to transmit actinic rays of light [fr. DI-+Gk *aktis* (*aktinos*), ray]

diad *DYAD

di·a·del·phous (daiədélfəs) *adj.* (*bot.*) having stamens in two bundles, owing to fusion of filaments, as in many legumes [fr. DI-+Gk *adelphos*, brother]

di·a·dem (dáiədem) *n.* a crown (as a symbol of royalty) ‖ something resembling a crown [O.F. *dyademe* fr. L. fr. Gk]

di·aer·e·sis, di·er·e·sis (daiérisis) *pl.* **di·aer·e·ses, di·er·e·ses** (daiérisi:z) *n.* two small dots placed over the second of two consecutive vowels to show that it is separately pronounced ‖ the division of one syllable into two esp. by the separation of two adjacent vowels (opp. SYNERESIS) [L. fr. Gk *diairesis*, separation]

Dia·ghi·lev (djágilef), Sergei Pavlovich (1872–1929), Russian ballet impresario. His greatness lay in his grasp of the composite nature of ballet (the interplay of dance, mime, music, decor, costumes and lighting) and in his recognition of genius and his receptivity to good new ideas. The famous Russian Ballet which he developed made use of the greatest available talent in choreography (e.g. Fokine, Massine, Balanchine), dancing (e.g. Nijinsky, Pavlova), decor (e.g. Picasso, Rouault, Braque, Bakst) and music (e.g. Stravinsky, Debussy, Prokofiev)

di·ag·nose (dáiəgnous, dáiəgnouz) *pres. part.* **di·ag·nos·ing** *past* and *past part.* **di·ag·nosed** *v.t.* to determine the nature of (a disease) from its symptoms

di·ag·no·sis (daiəgnóusis) *pl.* **di·ag·no·ses** (daiəgnóusi:z) *n.* the recognition of a disease from its symptoms ‖ a formal statement of the decision reached in identifying a disease [L. fr. Gk *diagnōsis* fr. *diagignōskein*, to distinguish]

di·ag·nos·tic (daiəgnɒstik) **1.** *adj.* of diagnosis **2.** *n.* a diagnosis **di·ag·nós·ti·cal·ly** *adv.* **di·ag·nos·ti·cian** (daiəgnɒstíʃən) *n.* the art of making a diagnosis [fr. Gk *diagnōstikos*]

di·ag·o·nal (daiǽgən'l) **1.** *adj.* joining two non-adjacent vertices of a polygon or two vertices of a polyhedron not in the same face ‖ running from corner to corner in a slanting direction ‖ having oblique markings or weave **2.** *n.* a diagonal straight line or direction ‖ a solidus (diagonal stroke) [fr. L. *diagonalis* fr. Gk]

di·a·gram (dáiəgræm) *n.* a figure or sketch designed to give a broad explanation ‖ a graph or chart ‖ a geometrical figure used to illustrate a theorem **di·a·gram·mát·ic** *adj.* **di·a·gram·mát·i·cal·ly** *adv.* **di·a·gram·ma·tize** (daiəgrǽmətaiz) *pres. part.* **di·a·gram·ma·tiz·ing** *past* and *past part.* **di·a·gram·ma·tized** *v.t.* [F. *diagramme* fr. L. fr. Gk]

di·a·graph (dáiəgræf, dáiəgrɑf) *n.* an instrument used for the mechanical drawing of perspectives and enlargements **di·a·gráph·ic** *adj.* [F. *diagraphe* fr. Gk]

di·al (dáiəl, dáil) **1.** *n.* a circle around or on which a scale is marked, so that the position of one or more pointers, rotating about the center of the circle, can be stated ‖ the numbered disk of an automatic telephone instrument **2.** *v.t. pres. part.* **di·al·ing**, esp. *Br.* **di·al·ling**, *past* and *past part.* **di·aled**, esp. *Br.* **di·alled** to compose (a desired number) with the finger on a telephone [fr. M.L. *dialis*, daily]

di·a·lect (dáiəlekt) *n.* a form of a language distinguished from other forms of the same language by pronunciation, grammar or vocabulary. It may be regional, social, or occupational ‖ a regional form of a language esp. as distinguished from the standard or literary language ‖ a language in relation to the family to which it belongs **di·a·léc·tal** *adj.* [fr. L. *dialectus* fr. Gk]

di·a·lec·tic (daiəléktik) **1.** *n.* the art of examining the truth or validity of a theory or opinion, esp. (*SOCRATES, *PLATO) by question and answer ‖ formal rhetorical argumentation or debate ‖

putation ‖ (*hist.*) logic ‖ (*Kantian philos.*) criticism concerned with metaphysical contradictions when scientific reasoning is applied to objects beyond experience (e.g. the soul, God) ‖ (*Hegelian philos.*) logical subjective development in thought, from a thesis through an antithesis to a synthesis, or logical objective development in history by a continuous unification of opposites **2.** *adj.* proper to the art of reasoning **di·a·léc·ti·cal** *adj.* skilled in or relating to logical disputation ‖ dialectal [O.F. *dialectique*]

dialectical materialism the Marxist theory, based on Hegelian dialectic, affirming that matter exists independently of thought, and that it develops by successive oppositions or negations

di·a·lec·ti·cian (daiəlektíʃən) *n.* someone skilled in dialectic ‖ a dialectologist [F. *dialecticien*]

di·a·lec·tics (daiəléktiks) *pl. n.* (often constr. as *sing.*) any play of ideas bringing together opposites or apparent contradictions and attempting to resolve them ‖ any logical disputation

di·a·lec·tol·o·gist (daiəlektólədʒist) *n.* someone skilled in dialectology

di·a·lec·tol·o·gy (daiəlektólədʒi:) *n.* the study of dialects, including the mapping of local characteristics to establish isoglosses [fr. DIALECT+Gk *logos*, discourse]

dialling tone (*Br.*) dial tone

dialog *DIALOGUE

di·al·o·gist (daiǽlədʒist, dáiələgist, dáiəlɒgist) *n.* a writer of dialogue ‖ one of the speakers in a dialogue [fr. L. *dialogista*]

di·a·logue, di·a·log (dáiəlɒg, dáiəlɔg) *n.* a literary work in conversational form ‖ conversation in a novel, play, movie etc. [O.F. *dialogue*, discourse fr. L. fr. Gk]

dial tone (*Am.=Br.* dialling tone) the sound heard when a telephone line is clear and able to take a new number

di·al·y·sis (daiǽlisis) *pl.* **di·al·y·ses** (daiǽlisi:z) *n.* the separation of substances in solution, esp. of colloids from crystalloids by means of selective diffusion through certain semipermeable membranes **di·a·lyt·ic** (daiəlítik) *adj.* **di·a·lyze**, *Br.* esp. **di·a·lyse** (dáiəlaiz) *pres. part.* **di·a·lyz·ing**, *Br.* esp. **di·a·lys·ing** *past* and *past part.* **di·a·lyzed**, *Br.* esp. **di·a·lysed** *v.t.* to subject to dialysis ‖ to obtain by dialysis **dí·a·lyz·er**, *Br.* esp. **dí·a·lys·er** *n.* (*chem.*) an arrangement for effecting dialysis [L. fr. Gk *dialusis* fr. *dialuein*, to separate completely]

di·a·mag·net·ic (daiəmægnétik) *adj.* relating to, or possessing, diamagnetism

di·a·mag·net·ism (daiəmǽgnitizəm) *n.* a magnetic property of all substances (but one often masked by other magnetic effects such as paramagnetism or ferromagnetism): because of it a substance shows a magnetic permeability smaller than 1 in an external magnetic field. A diamagnetic substance is repelled in proportion to the strength of the external magnetic field and if freely suspended assumes a direction normal to the magnetic meridian (cf. PARAMAGNETISM, cf. FERROMAGNETISM)

di·a·man·tane (daiəmantein) *n.* a hydrocarbon with a molecular arrangement similar to that of a diamond

di·a·man·té (daiəmántei) **1.** *adj.* scattered with glittering particles **2.** *n.* material covered with glittering particles [F. fr. *diamant*, diamond]

di·am·e·ter (daiǽmitər) *n.* a straight line passing through the center of a circle or other curvilinear figure and ending at the boundary of the figure ‖ this measure through or across ‖ (*optics*) a unit of linear magnifying power, *a lens magnifying 50 diameters* **di·am·e·tral** (daiǽmitrəl) *adj.* [fr. L. *diametrus* fr. Gk]

di·a·met·ric (daiəmétrik) *adj.* diametrical **di·a·mét·ri·cal** *adj.* of or pertaining to a diameter ‖ (of opposition) complete **di·a·mét·ri·cal·ly** *adv.* [fr. Gk *diametrikos*]

di·a·mond (dáiəmənd, dáimənd) **1.** *n.* a very valuable precious stone of pure carbon crystallized in the cubic system, and harder than almost any other known substance ‖ a rhombus ‖ a playing card marked with one or more red lozenges ‖ (*pl.*) the suit so marked ‖ a tool fitted with a diamond for cutting glass ‖ a small diamond used as a needle for playing records ‖ a very small size of printing type ‖ (*baseball*) the infield ‖ (*baseball*) the playing field **2.** *adj.* made of or set with diamonds ‖ sparkling ‖ lozenge-shaped ‖ (of a jubilee or wedding or other anniversary) sixtieth or seventy-fifth **3.** *v.t.* to adorn

with diamonds or diamondlike objects [M.E. *diamant* fr. O.F.]

di·a·mond·back (dáiəməndbæk, dáiməndbæk) *n. Crotalus adamanteus*, a rattlesnake found in southern U.S.A. It is the biggest (up to 8 ft) and deadliest snake of North America ‖ *Plutella maculipennis*, the cabbage moth ‖ a terrapin of genus *Malaclemys*, found in salt marshes along the Atlantic and Gulf of Mexico coasts

diamond drill a drill fitted with a diamond for boring hard substances

diamond field a region yielding diamonds

diamond in the rough a person of fine qualities whose lack of social grace tends to keep them from being appreciated ‖ (*pop.*) something, e.g. an idea, of great potential but not fully developed

di·a·mond·oid (dáiəməndɔujd) the shape of a diamond

diamond pane a small, lozenge-shaped windowpane set in lead

diamond point a stylus fitted with a diamond for engraving

Di·an·a (daiǽnə) (*Rom. mythol.*) the goddess of the hunt, of the moon, and of chastity, identified with the Greek Artemis

di·an·drous (daiǽndrəs) *adj.* (*biol.*) having two stamens [fr. Gk fr. *di-*, twice+ *anēr* (*andros*), man, a male]

di·an·thus (daiǽnθəs) *n.* a member of *Dianthus*, fam. *Caryophillaceae*, a genus of plants including carnations and pinks [Mod. L. fr. Gk *Zeus* (*Dios*)+*anthos*, flower]

di·a·pa·son (daiəpéiz'n, daiəpéis'n) *n.* the basic tone of the organ, normally from the 8-ft pipes. In open diapason the ends of the pipes are clear, and the tone louder than in stopped diapason (where the ends of the pipes are plugged). Double diapason uses 16-ft pipes ‖ a swelling burst of harmony ‖ the full compass of an instrument or voice, or of an activity etc. [L. fr. Gk *dia pasōn* (*chordōn symphōnia*), (concord) through all (the notes)]

diapason normal (*mus.*) pitch set by fixing A above middle C at 435 vibrations per second, as compared with the international standard of 440

di·a·pause (dáiəpɔz) *n.* a state of dormancy during development, e.g. in insects ‖ a sexually dormant period in an adult insect

di·a·per (dáiəpər, dáipər) **1.** *n.* (*Am.=Br.* napkin) a piece of absorbent cloth or other material for catching a baby's urine and feces, worn so as to cover the buttocks and crotch ‖ a linen material woven with a diamond pattern or similar repetitive geometrical figure ‖ a repetitive ornamental, often geometrical, pattern **2.** *v.t.* to ornament with a diaper pattern ‖ to put a diaper on (a baby) [O.F. *diapre* fr. Gk]

di·aph·a·nous (daiǽfənəs) *adj.* transparent [fr. M.L. *diaphanus* fr. Gk]

di·a·pho·re·sis (daiəfərí:sis) *n.* (*med.*) perspiration, esp. artificially induced **di·a·pho·ret·ic** (daiəfərétik) **1.** *adj.* inducing perspiration **2.** *n.* an agent with this property [L. fr. Gk]

di·a·phragm (dáiəfræm) *n.* a septum or partition, esp. the muscular partition which separates the cavity of the chest from the abdominal cavity in mammals, the midriff ‖ a thin partition in shellfish, plant tissues etc. ‖ a partition in a tube ‖ (*optics*) the physical element of an optical system that regulates the quantity of light (brightness) traversing the system ‖ (*chem.*) a porous partition for separating solutions ‖ (*phys.*) a metal plate with a central hole, excluding all radiant energy except that which passes through the opening ‖ (*photog.*) an iris diaphragm ‖ a contraceptive in the form of a thin rubber cap fitted over the uterine cervix **di·a·phrag·mat·ic** (daiəfrægmǽtik) *adj.* [fr. L.L. *diaphragma* fr. Gk]

di·a·pos·i·tive (daiəpɒzitiv) *n.* a positive photograph on a transparent medium *Cf* TRANSPARENCY

diarchy *DYARCHY

di·a·rist (dáiərist) *n.* someone who writes a diary, esp. as a literary form

di·ar·rhe·a, esp. *Br.* **di·ar·rhoe·a** (daiərí:ə) *n.* unusually frequent passage of loose, watery stools [L. fr. Gk]

di·a·ry (dáiəri:) *pl.* **di·a·ries** *n.* a daily written account of events, experiences or observations ‖ a book for keeping such an account ‖ a calendar with a space for each day's engagements and memoranda [fr. M.L. *diarius*, daily]

Di·as (dí:əs), Bartolomé (1466–1500), Portuguese navigator who discovered (1487) the Cape of Good Hope

CONCISE PRONUNCIATION KEY: **(a)** æ, c*a*t; ɑ, c*a*r; ɔ f*aw*n; ei, sn*a*ke. **(e)** e, h*e*n; i:, sh*ee*p; iə, d*ee*r; ɛə, b*ea*r. **(i)** i, f*i*sh; ai, t*i*ger; əː, b*i*rd. **(o)** o, *o*x; au, c*ow*; ou, g*oa*t; u, p*oo*r; ɔi, r*oy*al. **(u)** ʌ, d*u*ck; u, b*u*ll; uː, g*oo*se; ə, b*a*cill*u*s; juː, c*u*be. x, lo*ch*; θ, *th*ink; ð, bo*th*er; z, *Z*en; ʒ, corsa*g*e; dʒ, sava*ge*; ŋ, orangutan*g*; j, *y*ak; ʃ, *fi*sh; tʃ, fe*tch*; 'l, rabb*le*; 'n, redd*en*. Complete pronunciation key appears inside front cover.

Di·as·po·ra (daiǽspərə) *n.* the dispersed Jews after the Babylonian Captivity ‖ their dispersion [Gk fr. *diaspeirein*, to scatter]

di·a·stase (dáiəsteis) *n.* an enzyme, derived from malt, which converts starch into sugar in the process of germination, e.g. starch becomes maltose during the brewing of beer **di·a·sta·sic** (dɑiəstéisik), **di·a·stat·ic** (dɑiəstǽtik) *adjs* [F. fr. Gk]

di·as·to·le (daiǽstəli:) *n.* the rhythmical expansion of the heart (opp. SYSTOLE) or other organ **di·as·tol·ic** (daiəstólik) *adj.* [M.L. fr. Gk]

di·as·tro·phism (daiǽstrəfizəm) *n.* the process of upheaval which has wrinkled the earth's crust, forming mountains, ocean beds etc. [fr. Gk *diastrophē*, a turning aside, distortion]

di·a·tes·sa·ron (dɑiətéssərɒn) *n.* a harmony of the four Gospels into a single, fifth narrative [O.F. fr. L. fr. Gk]

di·a·ther·man·cy (dɑiəθə́:rmənsi:) *n.* transparency to radiant heat **di·a·thér·man·ous, di·a·thér·mic** *adjs* permeable by radiant heat [fr. F. *diathermansie* fr. Gk]

di·a·ther·my (dáiəθə:rmi:) *n.* heat treatment of the deeper body tissues by electric currents [fr. Gk *dia*, through+*thermē*, heat]

di·ath·e·sis (daiǽθisis) *pl.* **di·ath·e·ses** (daiǽθisi:z) *n.* (*med.*) a constitutional predisposition to a disease) [Mod. L. fr. Gk *diatithenai*, to dispose]

di·a·tom (dáiətəm) *n.* any of the single-celled or colonial yellow-brown algae which form an important part of marine and freshwater plankton. Diatomite is formed from the siliceous cell walls of dead organisms [fr. Mod. L. *diatoma* fr. Gk *diatomos*, cut through]

di·a·to·ma·ceous earth (dɑiətəméiʃəs) diatomite

di·a·tom·ic (dɑiətómik) *adj.* of a molecule which has two atoms [fr. DI+Gk *atomos*, atom]

di·a·tom·ite (daiǽtəmait) *n.* a light, siliceous, friable deposit derived from the remains of diatoms. Its physical and chemical properties enable it to be used as a filter aid, refractory, insulator, absorbent etc.

di·a·ton·ic (dɑiətónik) *adj.* (*mus.*) pertaining to a given major or minor key, *diatonic scale* (any major or minor scale), *diatonic harmony* (harmony going little outside the notes of the prevailing key) (cf. CHROMATIC) **di·a·tón·i·cal·ly** *adv.* [F. *diatonique* fr. L. fr. Gk]

di·a·tribe (dáiətraib) *n.* a fulminating piece of invective [F. fr. L. fr. Gk]

di·at·ro·pism (daiǽtrəpizəm) *n.* (*biol.*) the tendency of some organs or organisms to take a position at right angles to the line of action of an external stimulus

Díaz, Porfirio (1830–1915), Mexican general and politician. He seized power by force (1876), became president (1877–80, 1884–1911), and centralized the government, developed communications and fostered foreign business connections. He was overthrown (1911) by a radical nationalist revolution

Dí·az del Cas·til·lo (dí:aθðelkɑstí:ljo), Bernal (c. 1492–c. 1581), Spanish soldier and historian, author of 'The True History of the Conquest of New Spain', a first-hand account of the conquest of Mexico by Cortés

di·az·e·pam [C₁₆H₁₃ClN₂O] (daiǽzəpæm) *n.* (*pharm.*) a tranquilizer marketed as Valium

di·az·i·non [C₁₂H₂₁N₂O₃PS] (daiǽzinɒn) *n.* a toxic insecticide used against household pests and plant parasites

di·az·o (daiǽzou) *adj.* of organic compounds containing two nitrogen atoms, each satisfying two valencies of the other, the third valency of each being satisfied by another radical, thus R·N:N·R'. Diazo compounds are intermediates for dyestuffs [fr. DI+*azote*, old name for nitrogen]

Dí·az Or·daz (dí:as órðas), Gustavo (1911–79), Mexican president (1964–70)

dib (dib) *pres. part.* **dib·bing** *past* and *past part.* **dibbed** *v.i.* to fish by letting the bait bob up and down at the surface of the water [var. of DAB, DAP]

di·ba·sic (daibéisik) *adj.* of an acid which has two replaceable hydrogen atoms ‖ (of bases and basic salts) containing two replaceable hydroxyl groups

dib·ber (díbər) *n.* a dibble, the tool used for dibbling

dib·ble (díb'l) 1. *n.* a pointed instrument for making holes in the soil for planting seeds or plants 2. *v.i. pres. part.* **dib·bling** *past* and *past part.* **dib·bled** to use a dibble

dib·bler (díblər) *n.* a species of mammal believed extinct but rediscovered in Australia in 1967

di·bran·chi·ate (daibrǽŋki:it, daibrǽŋki:eit) 1. *adj.* belonging to *Dibranchia*, the group of two-gilled cephalopod mollusks including squids and octopuses 2. *n.* a member of *Dibranchia* [fr. Mod. L. *Dibranchiata* fr. Gk]

di·bro·mo·chlo·ro·pro·pane [C₃H₅Br₂Cl] (daibroumǝkluǝrǝpróupein) *n.* a toxic, carcinogenic pesticide, esp. used against plant parasitic worms. It is said to cause sterility in humans (*abbr.* DBCP)

dibs (dibz) *pl. n.* (*Br.*) jacks (*JACK)

dice (dais) 1. *n. pl.* of DIE ‖ a gambling game played with these ‖ (*sports*) intense contest for position in an auto race 2. *v. pres. part.* **dic·ing** *past* and *past part.* **diced** *v.i.* to play dice ‖ *v.t.* to cut up (vegetables, meat etc.) into small cubes ‖ to mark into squares

di·cen·tra (daiséntrə) *n.* a member of *Dicentra*, fam. *Fumariaceae*, a genus of erect plants with much-divided leaves. They are cultivated for their ornamental flowers, esp. *D. spectabilis* (bleeding heart) [Mod. L. fr. Gk *dikentros* fr. *di-*, twice+*kentron*, spur]

di·cha·si·um (daikéizi:əm, daikéiʒi:əm) *pl.* **di·cha·si·a** (daikéizi:ə, daikéiʒi:ə) *n.* (*bot.*) a cymose inflorescence in which two main axes are produced [Mod. L. fr. Gk *dichasis* fr. *dichazein*, to divide in half]

di·chla·myd·e·ous (daikləmídi:əs) *adj.* having both calyx and corolla [fr. Gk *di-*, twice+*chlamus*, cloak]

di·chlo·ric mirror (daiklúərik) television-camera device consisting of a metal-film-covered glass that permits only some colors to pass through

di·chlo·ride (daiklóraid, daiklóuraid) *n.* a compound of two atoms of chlorine with a divalent metal or positive ion, e.g. HgCl₂

di·chlo·ro·di·phen·yl·di·chlo·ro·eth·ane (daiklúərədaifénəldaiklúəroueθein) *n.* toxic insecticide similar to DDT (*abbr.* DDD)

di·chlo·ro·di·phen·yl·tri·chlo·ro·eth·e·lyne (daiklúərədaifénəltraiklúəroueθəlin) *n.* toxic hydrocarbon insecticide (*abbr.* DDT)

di·chlor·vos [C₄H₇Cl₂O₄P] (daiklúərvɒs) *n.* biodegradable, slightly toxic, organophosphorous pesticide used esp. to eliminate parasitic worms *also* dimenthyl dichlorovinyl phosphate (*abbr.* DDVP)

di·chog·a·mous (daikógəmǝs) *adj.* (*bot.*, of hermaphrodite plants) characterized by the maturing of different sexual elements at different times, ensuring cross-fertilization (cf. PROTANDRY, cf. PROTOGYNY) **di·chóg·a·my** *n.* [fr. Gk *dicho-*, separate+*gamos*, married]

di·chot·ic (daikótik) *adj.* of a sound that is heard differently by each ear **dichotically** *adv.*

di·chot·o·mize (daikótəmaiz) *pres. part.* **di·chot·o·miz·ing** *past* and *past part.* **di·chot·o·mized** *v.t.* to separate into two distinct, esp. opposing, parts ‖ *v.i.* to form a dichotomy

di·chot·o·mous (daikótəmǝs) *adj.* relating to or exhibiting dichotomy

di·chot·o·my (daikótəmi:) *pl.* **di·chot·o·mies** *n.* a division into two opposing parts ‖ (*astron.*) the phase of the moon, or of the inferior planets, when half the disk is seen from the earth to be illuminated ‖ (*biol.*) a repeated forking into two [fr. Gk *dichotomia*, a cutting in two]

di·chro·ic (daikróuik) *adj.* differing in color with the thickness or concentration of the transmitting medium ‖ reflecting light of one color and transmitting light of another ‖ (e.g. of some crystals) showing unlike colors in light transmitted along two different axes ‖ **di·chro·mat·ic**

di·chro·ism *n.* [fr. Gk *dichroos*, two-colored]

di·chro·mat·ic (daikroumǽtik, daikrəmǽtik) *adj.* with two color varieties ‖ exhibiting dichromatism [fr. Gk *di-*, twice+*chromatikos* fr. *chrōma* (*chrōmatos*), color]

di·chro·ma·tism (daikróumətizəm) *n.* limited color blindness, in which only two of the three primary colors are perceived

di·chro·mic (daikróumik) *adj.* containing two atoms of chromium [fr. Gk *dichrōmos*, two-colored]

Dick·ens (díkinz), Charles (1812–70), English novelist. His first book, 'Sketches by Boz' (1836), was a collection of essays written while he was a reporter in the House of Commons. 'Pickwick Papers' (1837) made him famous. A score of novels followed, at almost yearly intervals, first published serially and including 'Oliver Twist' (1841), 'David Copperfield' (1850), 'A Tale of Two Cities' (1859) and 'Great Expectations' (1861). They are remarkable for their abundance of memorable characters (humorous, grotesque or sinister), and for the variety of the humanity (mainly lower-class) which they portray. His attacks on certain abuses in orphanages and schools, courts and prisons, contributed to their reform. He reserved his grimmest satire for the inhumanity of commercialism and industrialism: and in 'Hard Times' (1854) he attacked their underlying concepts

dick·ens (díkinz) *n.* (in interjections) the deuce, the devil [origin unknown]

dick·er (dikər) *v.i.* to barter, haggle [fr. obs. *dicker*, a lot of ten (hides or skins) fr. L.]

dick·ey, dick·y (díki:) *pl.* **dick·eys, dick·ies** *n.* a false front on a shirt or blouse ‖ (*Br.*) a rumble seat [perh. fr. *Dick*, man's name]

Dick·in·son (díkinsən), Emily (1830–86), American poet. She was a recluse and was virtually unknown in her lifetime. She wrote mainly of death and immortality in short, intense, mostly unrhymed lyrics, in which the skillful use of assonance often gives the illusion of rhyme

Dickinson, John (1732–1808), American statesman, known as the author of 'Letters from a Farmer in Pennsylvania' (1767–8), which inveighed against the Townshend Acts, and of many pre-Revolutionary War petitions and declarations. He was instrumental in preparing the first draft of the Articles of Confederation

dicky *DICKEY

di·cli·nous (daikláinəs) *adj.* with stamens and pistils in separate flowers [fr. F. *dicline* fr. Gk *di-*, twice+*klinē*, bed]

di·cot·y·le·don (daikɒt'lí:d'n) *n.* a plant with two cotyledons, a member of the subclass *Dicotyledoneae* of angiosperms, incl. most of the deciduous woody plants of temperate zones and the majority of herbaceous flowering plants (cf. MONOCOTYLEDON) **di·cot·y·lé·don·ous** *adj.* [fr. Mod. L. *Dicotyledones*]

Dic·ta·phone (díktəfoun) *n.* a machine (used esp. in offices for dictation) which records and subsequently reproduces at a chosen speed what is spoken into it [Trademark fr. DICTATE+*-phone* as in 'Gramophone']

dic·tate 1. (dikteit, diktéit) *v. pres. part.* **dic·tat·ing** *past* and *past part.* **dic·tat·ed** *v.t.* to read or say (something) aloud that is to be written down ‖ to prescribe, *to dictate terms of surrender* ‖ *v.i.* to behave like an autocrat 2. (díkteit) *n.* (usually *pl.*) an order, a compelling impulse, *the dictates of conscience* [fr. L. *dictare* (*dictatus*), to speak]

dic·ta·tion (diktéiʃən) *n.* a dictating ‖ something dictated ‖ something written from dictation ‖ a command [fr. L. *dictatio* (*dictationis*) fr. *dictare*, to speak]

dic·ta·tor (díkteitər, diktéitər) *n.* an autocrat, an absolute ruler ‖ someone who acts like a petty tyrant [L.]

dic·ta·to·ri·al (diktətóri:əl, diktətóuri:əl) *adj.* imperious, autocratic ‖ of a dictator [fr. L. *dictatorius*, pertaining to a dictator]

dic·ta·tor·ship (diktéitərʃip) *n.* the office or period of power of a dictator ‖ a form of government in which power is held by a dictator without effective constitutional checks

dictatorship of the proletariat domination by the proletariat, the stage of the Marxist revolution after the destruction of capitalism, leading to the establishment of the communist classless society

dic·tion (díkʃən) *n.* a way of speaking, enunciation or delivery in public speaking ‖ the selection and control of words to express ideas (command of vocabulary, grammatical correctness, effective word order etc.) [F.]

dic·tion·ar·y (díkʃəneri) *pl.* **dic·tion·ar·ies** *n.* a book containing the words or a choice of the words of a language arranged in alphabetical order, with their definitions, and often indicating their pronunciation, part of speech, common usage, provenance etc. ‖ (*computer*) a listing of code words used in a program and their meanings in that program ‖ a compilation of such words limited to a particular subject, *a gardening dictionary* ‖ a work of informative character arranged alphabetically, *a dictionary of quotations* [fr. M.L. *dictionarium*] —The first standard dictionaries of modern tongues were the 'Vocabulario degli Accademici della Crusca' (1612) and the 'Dictionnaire de l'Académie française' (1638–94). Dr. Johnson's

CONCISE PRONUNCIATION KEY: (a) æ, c*a*t; ɑ, c*a*r; ɔ f*aw*n; ei, sn*a*ke. **(e)** e, h*e*n; i:, sh*ee*p; iə, d*ee*r; ɛə, b*ea*r. **(i)** i, f*i*sh; ai, t*i*ger; ə:, b*i*rd. **(o)** o, *o*x; au, c*ow*; ou, g*oa*t; u, p*oor*; ɔi, r*oya*l. **(u)** ʌ, d*u*ck; u, b*u*ll; u:, g*oo*se; ə, b*a*cillus; ju:, c*u*be. x, lo*ch*; θ, *th*ink; ð, bo*th*er; z, *Z*en; ʒ, cor*s*age; dʒ, sa*v*age; ŋ, ora*ng*uta*ng*; j, *y*ak; ʃ, *f*ish; tʃ, fe*tch*; 'l, rabb*le*; 'n, red*den*. Complete pronunciation key appears inside front cover.

dictionary, perhaps the most famous of all English dictionaries, was published in 1755. Noah Webster's 'American Dictionary of the English Language' (1828) was the first to insist primarily on words in current usage and to distinguish between American and English forms and senses. The first dictionaries giving detailed etymologies were compiled by Jacob and Wilhelm Grimm (1854 ff.) and by E. Littré (1863–73). The first encyclopedic dictionary was produced by Pierre Larousse (1866–76)

dic·tum (díktəm) pl. **dic·ta** (díktə), **dic·tums** n. an authoritative saying ‖ a maxim ‖ (law) an opinion expressed by a judge not binding because on a matter incidental to the judgment [L. fr. dicere, to say]

did past of DO

Did·a·che (dídəki:) a 2nd-c. Christian document, 'The Teaching of the Twelve Apostles', giving details of Eastern Church order and liturgy in the 1st c. The text was rediscovered at Constantinople in 1875

di·dac·tic (daidæktik) adj. intending to teach, a didactic poem ‖ having a pedagogic manner (usually pejorative) **di·dác·ti·cal·ly** adv. **di·dác·ti·cism** n. [fr. Gk didaktikos]

di·dap·per (dáidæpər) n. the dabchick or little grebe [for dive-dapper fr. earlier divedap fr. O.E. dúfedoppa, a pelican]

did·dle (díd'l) pres. part. **did·dling** past and past part. **did·dled** v.t. (pop.) to cheat, swindle ‖ (pop.) to move rapidly up and down or back and forth ‖ (with 'away') to fritter (time) away [etym. doubtful]

Di·derot (di:drou), Denis (1713–84), French writer. His direction of the 'Encyclopédie' (from 1745 onwards) was among his greatest achievements. With his powerful intelligence, wide interests and verve, he incarnated the spirit of the 18th c.: with his lively imagination and keen sensibility, he was a precursor of Romanticism. His writings include philosophical essays, plays and novels ('Jacques le fataliste', 1773, and 'le Neveu de Rameau', 1762)

didn't contr. of DID NOT

Di·do (dáidou) legendary daughter of a king of Tyre. She founded Carthage and became its queen. In Virgil's 'Aeneid' she falls in love with Aeneas and throws herself on a funeral pyre when he deserts her

di·do (dáidou) pl. **di·does**, **di·dos** n. (pop.) prank, caper [origin unknown]

didst archaic 2nd person sing. past of DO

did·y·mous (dídəməs) adj. (biol.) growing in pairs [fr. Gk didumos, twin]

die (dai) n. (pl. **dice**, dais) a small cube marked on its faces with 1–6 spots and used in playing dice ‖ (archit., pl. **dies**) the cubic part of a pedestal ‖ (pl. **dies**) any of various tools for cutting, shaping or embossing **the die is cast** the choice has been irrevocably made *CHIP [M.E. de fr. O.F.]

die pres. part. **dy·ing** past and past part. **died** v.i. to cease to live, to die of cancer, by violence, through neglect, for love, from wounds ‖ to fade away, be forgotten, the memory will never die ‖ to fade to nothing, the sound died on the air ‖ to become feeble or cease to be, don't let the fire die ‖ to wither **never say die** don't give in **to die hard** to be difficult to suppress, malicious rumors die hard **to die in harness** to die while still working (not in retirement) **to die in one's bed** to die of age or illness **to die off** to die one by one **to die out** to become extinct [M.E. degen fr. O.F.]

die·back (dáibæk) n. a condition found in shrubs and trees in which branches wither from the tip downwards. It is caused by disease, injury or wrong pruning

die-cast (dáikæst, dáikɒst) pres. part. **die-cast·ing** past and past part. **die-cast** v.t. to make by pouring molten metal into a metal mold **díe-cast·ing** n. the process of molding in this way ‖ a casting so made

Die·fen·ba·ker (dí:fənbeikər), John George (1895–1979), Canadian statesman, Conservative prime minister (1957–63)

Dié·go-Sua·rez (djéigɔswáreθ) (formerly Antsirane) a port (pop. 45,487) and military base at the northern tip of Madagascar, an excellent harbor

die·hard (dáihɑrd) 1. adj. uncompromisingly conservative 2. n. such a person

die-in (dáiin) n. a group protest against construction of nuclear energy plants

di·e·lec·tric (daiiléktrik) 1. n. a nonconductor of electricity 2. adj. of, or having the properties of, a dielectric

dielectric constant a number associated with a nonconducting material that measures its ability to reduce the electric field intensity between charged parallel conducting plates (*CAPACITOR). The dielectric constant is equal to the ratio of the capacitance of a standard capacitor with the material as dielectric to its capacitance with a vacuum as dielectric

dielectric strength the maximum electric field intensity that a given insulating material can sustain without losing its nonconducting properties

Diem *NGO DINH DIEM

Diemen, Anton van *VAN DIEMEN

Dien Bien Phu, Battle of (djénbjénfú:) a battle fought in N. Vietnam, near the Laos border, in which a successful 55-day nationalist siege of French forces (Mar.–May 1954) marked the end of French attempts to regain control of Indochina. It was followed by a Geneva conference (July 21, 1954), which partitioned Vietnam

di·en·ceph·a·lon (daienséfəlɒn) n. the anterior part of the brainstem (*BRAIN), differentiated into the thalamus and hypothalamus [Mod. L. fr. Gk di-, between + enkephalon, brain]

Dieppe (djep) a town (pop. 25,800) in E. Normandy, France, a seaside resort and fishing and commercial port with cross-Channel traffic: shipbuilding

dieresis *DIAERESIS

die·sel (dí:z'l) 1. n. a diesel engine ‖ a ship, locomotive etc. driven by a diesel engine 2. adj. powered by or fitted with a diesel engine ‖ relating to the diesel cycle or engine [after Rudolf Diesel (1858–1913), German inventor of the diesel engine]

diesel cycle an ideal heat-engine cycle in four stages in which the working substance successively undergoes adiabatic compression, constant pressure heating, adiabatic expansion, and constant volume cooling

die·sel·e·lec·tric (dí:z'liléktrik) adj. relating to or using the combination of a diesel engine driving an electric generator to provide electric power

diesel engine an internal-combustion engine in which air is compressed in a cylinder so that its temperature is sufficiently high to ignite fuel injected directly into the cylinder, where combustion and expansion take place and actuate a piston

die·sink·er (dáisiŋkər) n. (mech.) someone who cuts dies **die·sink·ing** n.

di·e·sis (dáiisis) pl. **di·e·ses** (dáiisi:z) n. (printing) the double dagger (symbol [‡]) used in references [L. fr. Gk diesis, a musical interval]

die·stock (dáistɒk) n. a handle or stock for holding screw-cutting dies

di·et (dáiit) n. the food and drink normally taken by an individual or a group, a diet of bread and cheese, a balanced diet ‖ a prescribed course of what is to be eaten and what is not [O.F. diete fr. L. fr. Gk]

diet v.t. to put on a diet ‖ v.i. to eat special food (for health reasons, athletic training etc.) ‖ to eat less so as to become thinner [O.F. dieter]

Di·et (dáiit) n. the law-making assembly of certain nations ‖ (hist.) a national or international conference [fr. M.L. dieta, assembly fr. Gk]

di·e·tar·y (dáiiteri) 1. pl. **di·e·tar·ies** n. a course of diet ‖ an allowance or ration of food 2. adj. relating to diet [fr. L. dietarius]

dietary laws (Jewish religion) laws prohibiting certain foods, or combinations of foods, or prescribing the mode of preparation

di·e·tet·ic (daiitétik) adj. of or relating to diet **di·e·tét·i·cal·ly** adv. **di·e·tét·ics** n. the study of the principles of nutrition [fr. L. diaeteticus fr. Gk]

diethyl ether *ETHER

di·eth·yl·stil·bes·trol (daieθəlstilbéstrɔl) n. (pharm.) a synthetic non-steroid estrogen, once used to avoid miscarriage, sometimes used as morning-after contraceptive; held to cause cancer in offspring at maturity abbr. DES

di·eth·yl·tol·u·a·mide [$C_{12}H_{17}NO$] (daieθəltɒlú:əmaid) n. an insect repellant used esp. against mites, ticks, and spiders abbr. EET

di·e·ti·tian, di·e·ti·cian (daiitíʃən) n. a specialist in dietetics

Diet of Worms *WORMS, DIET OF

diet pill drug capable of reducing appetite or speeding metabolism, usu. a hormone or diuretic

diet soda soda prepared with no sugar, usu. sweetened with saccharine or other cyclamates

DIFAR (acronym) for directional finding and ranging, a U.S. Navy system used to locate submarines in which sonobuoys pick up and broadcast sounds of submarines

dif·fer (dífər) v.i. to be different ‖ to disagree in opinion [F. différer]

dif·fer·ence (dífərəns, dífrəns) n. a differing ‖ an instance of differing ‖ a distinction, make no difference in your treatment of them ‖ the result obtained by subtracting one quantity, function or number from another of the same kind ‖ a disagreement in opinion, quarrel ‖ (heraldry) a change or addition made to a coat of arms to distinguish a junior member or branch of a family from the chief line **it makes a great difference** it is important **it makes no difference** it doesn't matter **to split the difference** to compromise (in a settlement about sums of money, totals etc.) by agreeing on a midway figure [F. différence]

dif·fer·ent (dífərənt, dífrənt) adj. (with 'from', Br. also 'to') dissimilar ‖ not the same, we go to different butchers ‖ (pop.) out of the ordinary, unusual [F. différent]

dif·fer·en·tial (difərénʃəl) 1. adj. showing a difference or differences, varying according to a set of factors ‖ constituting a difference, distinguishing, differential characteristics ‖ having or producing different motions, pressures etc., a differential pulley 2. n. (math.) an arbitrary increment of an independent variable ‖ (math.) the product of the derivative of a function of one variable and the increment of the variable. For functions of more than one variable the differential is the sum of the products of the partial derivatives and the increment of the variable that is not held constant ‖ a differential gear ‖ a wage difference for comparable work applied so as to reflect particular circumstances ‖ a difference in transport rates for goods going over different routes to the same destination or to different destinations, as a means of distributing traffic fairly to competing carriers [fr. M.L. differentialis]

differential calculus a branch of mathematical analysis dealing with the dependence of the rate of change of functions upon changes in the functions' variables

differential equation an equation containing one or more differentials or derivations of functions

differential gear an arrangement of gears connecting two shafts in the same line and enabling one of them to rotate faster than the other when required

differential operator (math.) a specific set of operations involving differentiation

differential screw a screw having two threads of unequal pitch, so that when the screw is turned the threads have a relative motion

dif·fer·en·ti·ate (difərénʃi:eit) pres. part. **dif·fer·en·ti·at·ing** past and past part. **dif·fer·en·ti·at·ed** v.t. to constitute the difference between ‖ to distinguish between ‖ (math.) to form the derivative of ‖ v.i. to make discrimination ‖ to develop separate distinguishing characteristics **dif·fer·en·ti·á·tion** n. [fr. M.L. differentiare (differentiis)]

dif·fi·cult (dífikəlt, dífikʌlt) adj. hard to do ‖ hard to understand or solve ‖ hard to deal with or to please, obstinate ‖ troublesome, worrying [prob. fr. DIFFICULTY] **dif·fi·cul·ty** (dífikəlti:, dífikʌlti:) pl. **dif·fi·cul·ties** n. the quality of being difficult ‖ something which cannot easily be done, understood or believed ‖ an obstacle or hindrance ‖ an objection, demurral, please don't raise difficulties ‖ a disagreement or cause of hostility or estrangement ‖ (often pl.) trouble, esp. financial trouble [M.E. difficultee fr. O.F.]

dif·fi·dence (dífidəns) n. lack of self-confidence ‖ excessive modesty or shyness [fr. L. diffidentia, distrust]

dif·fi·dent (dífidənt) adj. lacking in self-confidence ‖ modest ‖ too modest or shy [fr. L. diffidens (diffidentis) fr. diffidere, to distrust]

dif·fract (difrækt) v.t. to cause to undergo diffraction ‖ v.i. to undergo diffraction [fr. L. diffringere (diffractus), to break apart]

dif·frac·tion (difrækʃən) n. the phenomenon in which electromagnetic or other waves are modified during their propagation. The effect is bending the waves around objects in their path. In the case of light this occurs when it passes by the edge of an opaque body or through a narrow slit, or is reflected from a closely ruled surface. Part of the light appears to be deflected (this deflection is directly proportional to its wavelength) to the region of geometrical shadow, and parallel light and dark (or colored) fringes or lines are produced. Diffraction effects are due to interference and are common to all wave motions [fr. Mod. L. *diffractio* (*diffractionis*) fr. *diffringere*, to break apart]

diffraction grating (*phys.*) a translucent screen upon which are ruled numerous fine opaque lines very close together that act like many parallel slits. They are used to obtain light of a very narrow range of wavelengths by selecting a small portion of the diffracted beam

dif·frac·tive (difrǽktiv) *adj.* tending to diffract

dif·fuse 1. (difjú:z) *v. pres. part.* **dif·fus·ing** *past and past part.* **dif·fused** *v.t.* to spread widely, *to diffuse wisdom* || *v.i.* (*phys.*) to undergo diffusion **2.** (difjú:s) *adj.* widely spread, dispersed || not concise, wordy || (*phys.*, of reflection, or the thing reflected) not coherent (cf. SPECULAR) **dif·fus·i·ble** (difjú:zəb'l) *adj.* [fr. L. *diffundere* (*diffusus*), to pour out]

dif·fu·sion (difjú:ʒən) *n.* a diffusing or being diffused || the reflection of light by a mat surface or transmission of light through frosted glass etc. or the scattering caused by particles in the atmosphere || the random movement of constituent particles caused by thermal agitation that results eventually in the uniform mixing of gases, miscible liquids or suspended solids (*GRAHAM'S LAW) || the spread of cultural elements from one people or district to others [fr. L. *diffusio* (*diffusionis*)]

diffusion pump a pump for producing a very high vacuum by the diffusion of residual gas into a jet of mercury or oil vapor. The gas is carried off and separated from the jet by condensation

dif·fu·sive (difjú:siv) *adj.* tending to diffuse

dig (dig) **1.** *v. pres. part.* **dig·ging** *past and past part.* **dug** (dʌg) *v.t.* to break up or turn (soil) with a spade, fork, paws etc. || to excavate, make (a hole etc.) by digging || to remove from the ground by digging, *to dig potatoes* || to thrust, poke, *to dig spurs into a horse* || *v.i.* to perform the action of digging **to dig for** to look for by digging in the earth **to dig in** to mix into the soil **to dig oneself in** (*mil.*) to make a protective trench || to establish oneself safely in a job || to make oneself thoroughly familiar with a subject **to dig out** to find out by research, inquiry etc. **2.** *n.* a poke or thrust, *a dig in the ribs* || a sarcastic remark || a piece of digging, esp. an archaeological excavation [prob. fr. F. *diguer*]

di·gas·tric (daigǽstrik) **1.** *adj.* (of a muscle) fleshy at each end and tendinous in the middle || of or relating to the digastrics **2.** *n.* one of the muscles which serve to open the jaw [fr. Mod. L. *digastricus* fr. Gk *di-*, twice + *gastēr* (*gasteros*) belly]

Dig·boi oilfield (dígbɔi) an important source of natural oil in Lakhimpur district, Upper Assam, India

di·gen·e·sis (daidʒénisis) *n.* alternation of generations **di·ge·net·ic** (daidʒinétik) *adj.* [Mod. L. fr. Gk *di-*, twice + *genesis*, birth, creation]

di·gest (dáidʒest) *n.* a synopsis of information, usually set out under headings || a body of laws || a form of popular anthology, superficially serious **the Digest** the Pandects [fr. L. *digesta*, things digested]

di·gest (didʒést) *v.t.* to convert (food) into a form that can be assimilated (*DIGESTIVE SYSTEM) || to study and master the significance of in one's mind and store in the memory || to make a digest of || *v.i.* (of food) to admit of or undergo digestion **di·gest·i·bíl·i·ty** *n.* **di·gést·i·ble** *adj.* [fr. L. *digerere* (*digestus*)]

di·ges·tion (didʒéstʃən, daidʒéstʃən) *n.* the conversion of food into chyme in the stomach and the separation from the chyme of the chyle which is absorbed into the bloodstream || the assimilation of ideas || (*chem.*) the changing of the nature of a substance by various means, e.g. by the influence of physical conditions, by extraction of soluble constituents, or by chemical decomposition [F.]

di·ges·tive (didʒéstiv, daidʒéstiv) *adj.* relating to digestion (*DIGESTIVE SYSTEM) || promoting digestion **2.** *n.* a substance aiding digestion [F. *digestif*]

digestive system the alimentary or gastrointestinal tract, the body's apparatus for breaking food particles down by juices and enzymes.

Food, after being partially broken down in the mouth, passes through the esophagus to the stomach, where the process of breakdown continues. It then passes to the small intestine, where further breakdown occurs, and the useful particles are absorbed into the bloodstream. The remaining particles pass through the large intestine and are ultimately expelled as feces

dig·ger (dígər) *n.* someone who digs or something which digs || a gold miner || (*pop.*) an Australian or New Zealand soldier of the 1st world war

dig·gings (díginz) *pl. n.* mines, esp. gold mines || (*Br.*, *pop.*) lodgings

Dig·i·nalt (dídʒinɔlt) *n.* an altimeter based on a digital computer designed by Computer Equipment Corporation

dig·it (dídʒit) *n.* a finger or a toe || a finger's breadth || any of the numbers from 0 to 9 || (*astron.*, in measuring an eclipse) the twelfth part of the diameter of the sun or moon [fr. L. *digitus*, finger]

dig·it·al (dídʒit'l) *adj.* pertaining to a finger or the fingers || having digits || like a digit || (*computer*) of an instrument that accepts data and produces output in the form of characters or digits [fr. L. *digitalis*]

digital computer *COMPUTER

dig·i·tal·is (dídʒitǽlis, dídʒitéilis) *n.* a member of *Digitalis*, fam. *Scrophulariaceae*, a genus of European wild flowers with long racemes of showy flowers || a poisonous mixture of glucosides obtained from the purple foxglove, used as a heart stimulant and diuretic [M.L. = foxglove]

digital lock an automobile security device that requires pressing of numbered buttons in sequence to open doors

digital multimeter service on which measured value of voltage, etc., is shown in a digital display, using an analog to digital converter (*abbr.* DDM)

digital recording (*acoustics*) reproduction of sound fed into a computer through an amplifier, converted to numbers, and stored with recording *Cf* ANALOG RECORDING

digital speech communication system of transmitting voiced messages by wire in digital form

digital switch a device activated by processing specific numbers

digital watch wristwatch or pocket watch that displays the time in digits

dig·i·tate (dídʒiteit) *adj.* (*biol.*) having parts arranged like the fingers on a hand || having fingers || having deep divisions **díg·i·tat·ed** *adj.* **dig·i·tá·tion** *n.* [fr. L. *digitatus* fr. *digitus*, finger]

dig·i·ti·grade (dídʒitigreid) *adj.* (*zool.*) walking with only the digits (toes) touching the ground (cf. PLANTIGRADE) [F.]

dig·i·to·nin [C₅₆H₉₂O₂₉] (dídʒitóunən) *n.* (*pharm.*) an irritant steroid glycoside derived from digitalis; used in treating heart conditions

di·glos·si·a (diglósi:ə) *n.* the use of different languages or dialects for different occasions — **diglossic** *adj.*

dig·ni·fied (dígnifaid) *adj.* showing dignity

dig·ni·fy (dígnifai) *pres. part.* **dig·ni·fy·ing** *past and past part.* **dig·ni·fied** *v.t.* to confer dignity upon || to add an air of distinction to || to give a pretentious name to [O.F. *dignifier*]

dig·ni·tar·y (dígnitəri) *pl.* **dig·ni·tar·ies** *n.* someone who holds high office, esp. ecclesiastical [fr. L. *dignitas*]

dig·ni·ty (dígniti) *pl.* **dig·ni·ties** *n.* worth, excellence, *the dignity of labor* || nobility of manner or bearing || the quality of commanding esteem || high office or rank **to stand on one's dignity** to insist on being treated with respect [O.F. *digneté*]

dig·o·troph·ic (digətróufik) *adj.* of deep lakes that have a low supply of nutrients

di·graph (dáigræf, dáigraf) *n.* two letters representing one sound, e.g. 'ea' in 'heat' [fr. Gk *di-*, two + *graphe*, writing]

di·gress (daigrés, digrés) *v.i.* to wander from the main subject in speaking or writing [fr. L. *digredi* (*digressus*), to deviate]

di·gres·sion (daigréʃən, digréʃən) *n.* a wandering from the subject in speaking or writing || a deliberate turning aside from the main track [fr. L. *digressio* (*digressionis*)]

di·gres·sive (daigrésiv, digrésiv) *adj.* tending to digress, digressing [fr. L. *digressivus*]

digs (digz) *pl. n.* (*Br.*, *pop.*) diggings (lodgings)

di·he·dral (daihí:drəl) *adj.* having or formed by two plane faces || (of aircraft wings) inclined at an angle to each other [fr. Gk *di-*, twice + *hedra*, seat, base]

dihedral angle (*math.*) the angle between two intersecting planes || (*aeron.*) the angle between an airfoil and the horizontal

di·hy·drog·y·ac·e·tone [C₃H₆O₃] (daihaidrɔdʒi:ǽsətoun) *n.* a compond used to produce an artificial tan and contained in fungicides and plasticizers *also* dihydrolypropane (*abbr.* DHA)

diihydroxyquin *IODOQUINO

Di·jon (di:ʒɔ̃) the former capital (pop. 146,000) of Burgundy, France, at the foot of the Côte d'Or, a rail center with metallurgy, mechanical engineering and food industries. Palace of the dukes of Burgundy, church of Notre-Dame (13th c.) and other fine churches. University (1722)

dike, dyke (daik) **1.** *n.* a raised bank constructed to prevent flooding, esp. (as in Holland) to prevent the encroachment of the sea || (*Br.*) a small natural waterway || a low wall, esp. of turf or unmortared stones || a causeway || a crack in a rock stratum filled with igneous matter || the igneous matter itself (cf. VEIN) **2.** *v. pres. part.* **dik·ing, dyk·ing** *past and past part.* **diked, dyked** *v.i.* to construct dikes || *v.t.* to provide or protect with dikes [O.E. *dīc*, a ditch]

di·lap·i·date (dilǽpideit) *pres. part.* **di·lap·i·dat·ing** *past and past part.* **di·láp·i·dat·ed** *v.i.* to fall into disrepair || *v.t.* to cause to fall into ruin or disrepair **di·láp·i·dat·ed** *adj.* [fr. L. *dilapidare* (*dilapidatus*), to waste, to scatter like stones]

di·lap·i·da·tion (dilæpidéiʃən) *n.* a falling, or a causing to fall, into disrepair || (*Br.*, *pl.*) the money paid by an incumbent for wear and tear during his incumbency || the falling away of cliffs etc. or the resulting debris [fr. L. *dilapidatio* (*dilapidationis*)]

di·lat·an·cy (dailéit'nsi:, diléit'nsi:) *n.* the property of being dilatant

di·lat·ant (dailéit'nt, diléit'nt) *adj.* having the property of increasing in volume when subjected to stress because of a wider spacing of particles [fr. L. *dilatans* (*dilatantis*) fr. *dilatare*, to dilate]

di·la·ta·tion (dailətéiʃən, dilətéiʃən) *n.* the quality of being dilatant || a dilating, esp. an enlargement of the pupil of the eye, heart chamber, or other organ [O.F.]

di·late (dailéit, diléit) *pres. part.* **di·lat·ing** *past and past part.* **di·lat·ed** *v.i.* to expand, become wide || to enlarge upon a subject by relating the details of it || *v.t.* to cause to expand || to stretch (something contracted) **di·lá·tion** *n.* [F. *dilater*]

dil·a·tom·e·ter (dailətómitər, dilətómitər) *n.* an instrument to measure thermal expansion, used to determine the expansion coefficients of liquids and solids

di·la·tor (dailéitər, diléitər) *n.* a muscle which expands or dilates an organ [fr. DILATE]

dil·a·to·ri·ly (dílətɔrili:, dílətɔurili:) *adv.* in a dilatory way

dil·a·to·ri·ness (dílətɔri:nis, dílətɔuri:nis) *n.* the quality of being dilatory

dil·a·to·ry (dílətɔri:, dílətɔuri:) *adj.* tending to put off a decision or to prolong a process || meant to cause delay and win time, *dilatory tactics* [fr. L. *dilatorius*, delaying]

Dilaudid (*pharm.*) trade name for dihyromorphinone, an analgesic and respiratory sedative similar to morphine

di·lem·ma (dilémə) *n.* a situation in which one is faced with a choice between equally unsatisfactory alternatives || (*logic*) an argument which forces an opponent to accept one of two propositions both of which contradict his former contention [L. fr. Gk *dilēmma*, assumption]

dil·et·tan·te (dilitǽnti:, dílitant) **1.** *pl.* **dil·et·tan·ti** (dilitánti:), **dil·et·tan·tes** *n.* someone who genuinely loves the fine arts without being a professional || someone who dabbles in art, literature, music etc., without any deep knowledge or application **2.** *adj.* superficial || amateur **dil·et·tánt·ism** *n.* [Ital.]

dil·i·gence (dílidʒəns) *n.* the quality of being diligent [F.]

dil·i·gent (dílidʒənt) *adj.* hard-working, industrious || conscientious, not negligent [F.]

dill (dil) *n.* *Anethum graveolens*, fam. *Umbelliferae*, an annual whose seeds are used as a carminative, and also as a flavoring in pickles etc. [O.E. *dili, dile*]

---

dil·ly-dal·ly (díli:dæli:) *pres. part.* **dil·ly-dal·ly-ing** *past* and *past part.* **dil·ly-dal·lied** *v.i.* (*pop.*) to dawdle ‖ (*pop.*) to vacillate

dil·u·ent (dílju:ənt) **1.** *adj.* diluting ‖ dissolving **2.** *n.* a substance that dilutes or dissolves [fr. L. *diluens* (*diluentis*) fr. *diluere*, to wash away, dilute]

di·lute (dailú:t, dilú:t) **1.** *v. pres. part.* **di·lut·ing** *past* and *past part.* **di·lut·ed** *v.t.* to lessen the concentration of (a mixture) by adding more water or a thinner etc. ‖ to reduce the strength or brilliance of (a color etc.) ‖ to weaken, water down (a story, doctrine etc.) ‖ *v.i.* to become diluted **2.** *adj.* diluted, weakened **di·lú·tion** *n.* [fr. L. *diluere* (*dilutus*), to wash away]

di·lu·tive (dailú:tiv) (*adj.*) (*securities*) effecting a dilution, e.g., of the value of a stock by the issuance of additional shares

di·lu·vi·al (dailú:vi:əl, dilú:vi:əl) *adj.* of or relating to a flood, esp. the flood referred to in the Bible (Genesis vii and viii) ‖ (*geol.*) caused by a deluge [fr. L. *diluvialis* fr. *diluvium*, deluge]

di·lu·vi·um (dailú:vi:əm, dilú:vi:əm) *pl.* **di·lu·vi·ums, di·lu·vi·a** (dailú:vi:ə, dilú:vi:ə) *n.* (*geol.*) glacial drift [L.=deluge]

dim (dim) **1.** *comp.* **dim·mer** *superl.* **dim·mest** *adj.* not bright or clear ‖ indistinct, not clearly visible ‖ vague ‖ (of sound) muffled, faint ‖ (of vision) blurred ‖ (*pop.*) stupid **to take a dim view** (*pop.*) to think poorly (of someone or something) **2.** *v. pres. part.* **dim·ming** *past* and *past part.* **dimmed** *v.t.* to make dim ‖ (*Am.=Br.* dip) to lower the beam of (headlights) ‖ *v.i.* to become dim [O.F.]

dime (daim) *n.* (U.S.A. and Canada) a coin worth 10 cents, one-tenth of a dollar [O.F.=tenth]

dime novel (*old-fash.*) a cheaply produced, paperbacked, melodramatic novel

di·men·sion (diménʃən) *n.* a measurement in a single direction (e.g. length, breadth, thickness or circumference) ‖ (*pl.*) size, *a house of generous dimensions* ‖ (*pl.*) extent or scope, *the dimensions of a task* ‖ (*phys.*) the powers to which the fundamental units of mass, length and time are raised in a derived unit (thus the gram, the centimeter, and the second raised to the power of −2 are the dimensions of the dyne) **di·mén·sion·al** *adj.* [F.]

dim·er·ous (dímərəs) *adj.* (*entom.*) having two-jointed tarsi ‖ (*bot.*) having two parts to each whorl [fr. Mod. L. *dimerus*, ult. fr. Gk *di-*, twice+*meros*, part]

dime store a store selling many kinds of cheap goods

di·me·ter (dímitər) *n.* a verse of two feet or two measures [fr. L. *dimetrus* fr. Gk]

di·meth·o·ate [C₅H₁₂NO₃PS₂] (daiméθəweit) *n.* an organophosphorous insecticide often used to protect livestock

1,1-di·meth·yl·hy·dra·zine [CH₃₂NNH₂] (dɑimé́θəlháidrəzi:n) *n.* a high-energy propellant used in rockets

di·meth·yl·ni·tros·a·mise (daimeθəlnaitrósəmaiz) *n.* a carcinogenic element in tobacco smoke *Cf* NITROSOMES

di·meth·yl sulfoxide [CH₃SO] (daiméθəl) (*pharm.*) pain reliever, anti-inflammatory agent and industrial solvent derived in wood pulp processing (*abbr.* DMSO)

di·meth·yl·tryp·ta·mine [C₁₂H₁₀N₂] (daimeθəltríptəmain) *n.* (*pharm.*) a hallucinogenic similar to psilocybin (*abbr.* DMT)

di·mid·i·ate (dimídi:it, dimídi:eit) *adj.* (*bot.*, of an anther) having one lobe lacking or abortive ‖ (*bot.*, of a pileus) having one side larger than the other ‖ (*bot.*, of the perithecium of a lichen) having the upper part only enclosed in a wall [fr. L. *dimidiare* (*dimidiatus*), to halve]

di·min·ish (dimíniʃ) *v.t.* to make less ‖ (*mus.*) to reduce (a perfect or minor interval) by a chromatic semitone, *a diminished fifth* ‖ *v.i.* to become less [fr. L. obs. *diminue* fr. F. *diminuer*, to lessen+obs. *minish* fr. O.F. *menusier*, to lessen]

di·min·u·en·do (diminju:éndou) (*abbr.* dim., symbol >) **1.** *adj.* (*mus.*) becoming gradually softer **2.** *n.* a diminuendo passage [Ital.]

dim·i·nu·tion (diminú:ʃən, diminjú:ʃən) *n.* the act of diminishing ‖ a decrease ‖ (*mus.*, e.g. in some fugues) a passage repeated but in notes with smaller time values [F.]

di·min·u·tive (dimínjutiv) **1.** *adj.* very small ‖ (*gram.*) expressing diminution, *'booklet'* is the diminutive form of *'book'* **2.** *n.* a word expressing diminution (in English, the chief diminutive suffixes are -cule, -el, -et, -ette, -ie, -in, -kin, -let, -ling, -ock, -ule, -y, and are used to express

---

smallness in size, or sometimes as endearments) [F.]

dim·i·ty (dímiti:) *pl.* **dim·i·ties** *n.* a strong cotton fabric, woven with raised stripes by taking two threads or more as one [fr. Gk *dimitos* fr. *di-*, twice+*mitos*, warp thread]

dim·mer (dímər) *n.* a device for controlling the intensity of illumination (esp. of stage lighting) or (*Am.=Br.* dipper) for lowering the beam of car headlights

di·mor·phic (daimórfik) *adj.* having, or occurring in, two distinct forms **di·mór·phism** *n.* **di·mór·phous** *adj.* [fr. Gk *dimorphos*, two-formed]

dim·ple (dímp'l) **1.** *n.* a small hollow, esp. in the cheek or chin **2.** *v. pres. part.* **dim·pling** *past* and *past part.* **dim·pled** *v.t.* to cause or produce dimples in ‖ *v.i.* to show dimples ‖ (of a stream) to break into little ripples [M.E. *dimpul*, etym. doubtful]

din (din) **1.** *n.* a clamor of discordant, deafening noises **2.** *v. pres. part.* **din·ning** *past* and *past part.* **dinned** *v.t.* (with 'into') to drive home by constant repetition, *to din the facts into a boy* ‖ (of noise) to assail (the ears) ‖ *v.i.* to make a din [O.E. *dyne*]

di·nar (dí:nɑr) *n.* the main monetary unit of Algeria, Iraq, Jordan, Tunisia, Yugoslavia and Kuwait ‖ a coin or note representing one dinar [Arab. and Pers. fr. Gk fr. L.]

dinch (dintʃ) *v.* to crush out, e.g., a cigar

d'Indy *INDY

dine (dain) *pres. part.* **din·ing** *past* and *past part.* **dined** *v.i.* to have dinner ‖ *v.t.* to entertain to dinner ‖ to provide dining accommodation for **to dine out** to eat away from home, college etc. **dín·er** *n.* someone who dines ‖ a dining car on a train ‖ a restaurant built to resemble a dining car on a train [F. *dîner*]

di·ner·ic (dainérik, dinérik) *adj.* (*phys.*) being, or related to, the interface between two immiscible liquids in a single container [fr. Gk *di-*, twice+*néros*, liquid]

Dinesen (dí:nəsən), Isak (ee'-sahk) (1885–1962), Danish writer and pseudonym of Baroness Karen Blixen-Finecke. She wrote of coffee plantation life in Kenya, where she lived (1914–31). Her best-known work was 'Out of Africa' (1937; film, 1985); others included 'Seven Gothic Tales' (1934), 'Winter's Tale' (1942), and 'Last Tales' (1957)

di·nette (dainét) *n.* a small informal dining room, usually just off the kitchen ‖ a small table and chairs styled for use in this room

ding (diŋ) **1.** *v.i.* to ring persistently ‖ to talk with insistence and much repetition ‖ *v.t.* to cause to ring ‖ to say (something) over and over in order to make it understood and remembered **2.** *n.* the sound of a bell, or of metal being struck [imit.]

Din·gaan (díngɑn) (*d.* 1840), king of the Zulus (1828–40). He allowed British missionaries and Boers from the Great Trek to settle in Zululand (1835–8), but retracted. He was defeated by the Boers (1838 and 1840)

Dingaan's Day a public holiday (Dec. 16) in the Republic of South Africa, celebrating the defeat (1838) of the Zulus under Dingaan by the Boers

ding-a-ling (díŋəliŋ) *n.* (*slang*) a flighty, senseless person *syn.* dingbat

ding-dong (díŋdɒŋ, díŋdɒŋ) **1.** *n.* the noise made by a clapper bell or bells **2.** *adj.* (*Br.*, of a battle, argument etc.) very closely contested, with the advantage now on one side, now the other **3.** *adv.* with zest, energy or desperate efforts [imit.]

din·ghy (díŋgi:, diŋi:) *pl.* **din·ghies** *n.* a ship's small boat ‖ a small rowboat (roughly 8–10 ft long), often fitted for sailing ‖ a small inflatable rubber boat carried on an aircraft [fr. Hindi *dingī*, a little boat]

din·gi·ly (díndʒili:) *adv.* in a dingy way

din·gi·ness (díndʒi:nis) *n.* the quality or state of being dingy

din·gle (díŋ'l) *n.* a wooded dell [M.E. *dingel*, abyss]

din·go (díŋgou) *pl.* **din·goes** *n. Canis dingo*, a fierce, wolflike wild dog of Australia [native name]

din·gy (díndʒi:) *comp.* **din·gi·er** *superl.* **din·gi·est** *adj.* drab, dull-colored, dirtylooking [etym. doubtful]

dining car a railroad car equipped as a restaurant

dining room the room in a house, hotel etc. specially used for meals

---

Din·ka (díŋkə) *pl.* **Din·ka, Din·kas** *n.* a pastoral people living in the Nile valley south of Khartoum ‖ a member of this people ‖ their language

dink·y (díŋki:) *comp.* **dink·i·er** *superl.* **dink·i·est** *adj.* (*pop.*) very small and insignificant ‖ (*Br.*) very small and attractively neat [fr. older *dink*, trim]

din·ner (dínər) *n.* the main meal of the day whether taken at midday or in the evening ‖ a festive but formal evening meal with guests, *they are giving a dinner for him* [F. *dîner* v. used as n.]

dinner hour (*Br.*) the midday break from work or school, however long

dinner jacket a tailless dress coat

dinner wagon a wheeled table with shelves for use in the dining room

di·noc·er·as (dainósərəs) *n.* an extinct hoofed elephant-sized mammal of the *Dinocerata* with three pairs of horns [Mod. L. fr. Gk *deinos*, terrible+*keras*, horn]

di·no·saur (dáinəsɔr) *n.* a group of fossil lizards of the Triassic to the Mesozoic. They were terrestrial reptiles of immense size but little brain, e.g. the brontosaur, diplodocus and stegosaur [fr. Gk *deinos*, terrible+*sauros*, lizard]

Dinosaur National Monument a U.S. monument (200,000 acres) established (1915) in N.W. Colorado and N.E. Utah to preserve rich fossil beds containing dinosaur remains and to protect the surrounding canyons and geological formations

dint (dint) **1.** *n.* a dent **by dint of** by the exertion of, by means of **2.** *v.t.* to dent [O.E. *dynt*]

di·oc·e·san (daiósis'n) **1.** *adj.* of a diocese **2.** *n.* the bishop in charge of a diocese [F. *diocesain*]

di·o·cese (dáiəsis, dáiəsi:s) *n.* the district under a bishop's authority [O.F. *diocise* fr. L. fr. Gk]

Di·o·cle·tian (daiəklí:ʃən) (Gaius Aurelius Valerius Diocletianus, 245–313), Roman emperor (284–305), who reestablished order after the military revolts of the 3rd c. He shared his power with Maximian (286–305), and further subdivided his power (293). Diocletian reformed the administration, the finances and the army of the empire, began a bitter persecution of Christians (303) and abdicated (305)

di·ode (dáioud) *n.* a valve or electron tube with two electrodes (anode and cathode) used as a rectifier and as a detector of wireless signals ‖ a semiconductor device with two electrodes, sometimes called a crystal diode

Di·o·do·rus Sic·u·lus (daiədɔ́rəssíkjuləs, daiədóurəssíkjuləs) Greek historian who wrote (c. 20 B.C.) a universal history

di·oe·cious (daiíʃəs) *adj.* (*bot.*) having male and female flowers on different plants of the same species ‖ (*zool.*) having the sexes separate [fr. Mod. L. *Dioecia* (a class in former classifications) fr. Gk *di-*, twice+*oikos*, house]

Di·og·e·nes (daiɔ́dʒəni:z) (c. 412–c. 323 B.C.), Greek philosopher of the Cynic sect, who praised self-sufficiency and despised social conventions

Diogenes La·er·ti·us (leiə́rʃi:əs) (3rd c. A.D.), Greek author of the 'Lives and Opinions of Eminent Philosophers', an important source of biographical material

Di·o·me·des (daiəmí:di:z) (*Gk mythol.*) Thracian king, who fed his horses on human flesh. Hercules killed him and threw his body to the horses. They were then tamed and Hercules was able to catch them (*HERACLES)

Di·on of Syracuse (dáiən) (c. 408–354 B.C.), Greek politician. He was a disciple of Plato, but he governed Syracuse tyrannically (357–354 B.C.) and was assassinated

Di·o·ny·si·a (daiənísi:ə, daiəníʃi:ə) *pl. n.* any of the festivals of Dionysus, esp. those in Attica out of which Greek drama developed [Gk]

Di·o·nys·i·ac (daiənísi:æk) *adj.* of Dionysus or the Dionysia

Di·o·ny·sian (daiəníʃən, daiənísi:ən) *adj.* Dionysiac

Di·o·ny·si·us I (daiənísi:əs, daiəníʃi:əs) (c. 430–367 B.C.), tyrant of Syracuse (405–367 B.C.), who drove the Carthaginians out of Sicily (*DAMOCLES)

Dionysius Ex·ig·u·us (eksígu:əs) (*d.* c. 545), Roman biblical scholar. He established the method of calculating the Christian era, mistakenly considering 1 A.D. as the date of the Incarnation. His collection of ecclesiastical canons began the study of canon law

Dionysius the Areopagite (1st c. A.D.), the chief convert of Paul in Athens (Acts xvii, 34)

---

and traditionally the first bishop of Athens ‖ the pseudonym of a Christian disciple (c. 500) of the Neoplatonist philosopher Proclus, for a long time identified with the first bishop of Athens and with St Denis. A convert from paganism, he became a Syrian bishop. In his four treatises he assimilated the theories and practice of Neoplatonic mysticism into an ecclesiastically disciplined orthodox asceticism. These treatises ('On the Divine Names', 'Mystical Theology', 'The Hierarchy of Heaven', 'The Hierarchy of the Church') were translated into Latin in the 9th c. (*ANGEL)

Di·o·ny·sus, Di·o·ny·sos (daiənáisəs) (*Gk mythol.*) god of the vine, identified with Bacchus and the Roman Liber

Di·o·phan·tus (daiəfǽntəs) (c. 250 A.D.), Greek mathematician of Alexandria, author of important works on the theory of numbers

di·op·side (daiópsaid) *n.* (*mineral.*) a pyroxene containing little or no aluminum [F. fr. Gk]

di·op·tase (daiópteis) *n.* (*mineral.*) an emerald-green copper silicate [F. fr. Gk]

di·op·ter, di·op·tre (daióptər) *n.* a unit of measurement of the refractive power of a lens, the reciprocal of the focal length in meters, given a positive sign for a convergent lens [F. *dioptre* fr. L. fr. Gk]

di·op·tom·e·ter (daioptómitər) *n.* an instrument to measure the accommodation and refraction of the eye [fr. DIA-+OPTIC+METER]

dioptre *DIOPTER

di·op·tric (daióptrik) *adj.* refractive, *a dioptric telescope* **di·óp·trics** *n.* the branch of optics dealing with refraction [fr. Gk *dioptrikos* fr. *dioptra,* an instrument for leveling]

di·o·ram·a (daiərǽmə, daiərámə) *n.* a partly translucent picture seen through an opening and caused by reflected and transmitted light to seem to undergo change (esp. as regards sunset or cloud effects etc.) ‖ a small scenic model with lighting effects **di·o·rám·ic** *adj.* [fr. Gk *dia,* through+*horama,* sight, spectacle]

di·o·rite (daiərait) *n.* a crystalline, granular, igneous rock composed of feldspar and hornblende **di·o·rit·ic** (daiərítik) *adj.* [F. fr. Gk *diorizein,* to distinguish]

Di·os·cu·ri (daiəskjúərai) (*Gk mythol.*) 'sons of Zeus', the title of Castor and Polydeuces, the sons of Leda and Zeus (or of Leda and Tyndareus) and brothers of Helen and Clytemnestra. After death, they became the constellation of Gemini and were worshipped by the Greeks as the gods of mariners. The Romans worshipped them (as Castor and Pollux) before battle

di·ox·ide (daióksaid) *n.* an oxide with two atoms of oxygen linked with another element in the molecule, e.g. carbon dioxide, CO_2

di·ox·in (daióksin) *n.* (*chem.*) 2,3,7,8-tetrachlorodibenzo-p-dioxin, a poisonous impurity present in some herbicides (*abbr.* TCDD)

dip (dip) 1. *v. pres. part.* **dip·ping** *past* and *past part.* **dipped** *v.t.* to immerse momentarily in a liquid ‖ to dye by immersing in a liquid ‖ to immerse (esp. sheep) in a vermin-killing liquid ‖ to make (candles) by immersing a wick in hot tallow ‖ to take up with a ladle, hand, scoop etc. ‖ to lower momentarily (a flag, sail etc.) ‖ (*Br.*) to dim (headlights) ‖ *v.i.* to reach into something, *to dip into a jam jar* ‖ to sink, drop down, *the sun dipped behind the hill* ‖ (of a bird or airplane) to drop suddenly before climbing ‖ to slope downwards ‖ (with 'into') to make a cursory appraisal of a book or subject etc. 2. *n.* a dipping ‖ a quick swim ‖ a hollow to which higher ground dips ‖ a downward slope ‖ a liquid into which something may be dipped ‖ a tallow candle ‖ (*geol.*) the downward slope of a stratum ‖ a sudden drop in flight before climbing ‖ (*mil.*) in naval mine war, the amount by which a moored mine is carried beneath its set depth by a current or tidal stream ‖ (*survey.*) the apparent depression of the horizon below the horizontal plane of the observer, due to his elevation ‖ the angle at a given place between the direction of the earth's magnetic field and the horizontal (*DIP NEEDLE). It can be measured using a magnetic needle free to rotate in the vertical plane (*DIP CIRCLE). It is 90° at the magnetic poles and 0° on the magnetic equator (cf. DECLINATION) [O.E. *dyppan*]

DI particle defective viral particle, made up of mutants that have lost much of their nucleic acid, capable of interfering with normal virus infection, produced when many virus particles of the same kind infect one cell at the same time

dip circle a dip needle

di·phase (dáifeiz) *adj.* having two phases ‖ (*elec.*) carrying, producing or operated by two alternating currents differing in phase, usually by a quarter cycle

di·phos·pho·gly·cer·ic acid [$C_3H_8O_9P_2$] (daifɔsfouglisɛ́ərik) (*biochem.*) essential element in oxidation reduction used in photosynthesis, fermentation, and the conversion of lactose into lactic acid (*abbr.* DPN)

diph·the·ri·a (difθíəri:ə, dipθíəri:ə) *n.* an acute infectious disease, chiefly of children, caused by *Corynebacterium diphtheriae* and characterized by severe inflammation of the throat, heart and nervous system. It is preventable by inoculation **diph·thé·ri·al** *adj.* [fr. F. *diphtérie* fr. Gk]

diph·thong (dífθɔŋ, dífθɒŋ, dípθɔŋ, dípθɒŋ) *n.* a speech sound consisting of two vowels pronounced glidingly in one syllable (as in 'house') **diph·thón·gal** *adj.* **diph·thong·ize** *pres. part.* **diph·thong·iz·ing** *past* and *past part.* **diph·thong·ized** *v.t.* and *i.* [F. *diphthongue* fr. L. fr. Gk]

di·piu·frin (daipjú:frin) *n.* (*pharm.*) drug used to control intraocular pressure in treatment of glaucoma; marketed as Propine

dip·lo·coc·cus (dipləkókəs) *pl.* **dip·lo·coc·ci** (dipləkóksai) *n.* a member of *Diplococcus,* a genus of gram-positive bacteria forming endospores that occur in pairs and are parasites. It includes the pneumonia pathogen [Mod. L. fr. Gk *diploos,* double+*kokkos,* seed]

dip·lod·o·cus (diplódəkəs) *pl.* **di·plod·o·cus·es** *n.* a member of *Diplodocus,* a genus of gigantic extinct North American herbivorous dinosaurs, up to 80 ft in length. They had a very small brain [fr. Gk *diplo-,* double+*dokos,* beam]

dip·loid (díploid) 1. *adj.* (*biol.*) having homologous pairs of chromosomes in the nucleus of a cell, so that twice the haploid number are present 2. *n.* (*crystall.*) an isometric solid with 24 similar quadrilateral surfaces in pairs ‖ (*biol.*) a cell, usually a somatic cell, having a diploid number of chromosomes. This number is typical of the species [fr. Gk *diploos,* double+*eidos,* form]

dip·lo·lin·go (diploulíŋou) *n.* (*slang*) the language of diplomacy

di·plo·ma (diplóumə) *n.* a document conferring some honor or privilege, esp. one recording successful completion of a course of academic study ‖ a state document or charter [L. fr. Gk]

di·plo·ma·cy (diplóuməsi:) *pl.* **di·plo·ma·cies** *n.* the science of international relations ‖ the conduct of negotiations between nations ‖ a tactful dealing with people [F. *diplomatie*]

dip·lo·mat (dípləmæt) *n.* someone officially employed in international diplomacy ‖ a tactful person skilled in handling people [F. *diplomate*]

dip·lo·mat·ic (dipləmǽtik) *adj.* relating to diplomacy ‖ tactful **dip·lo·mát·i·cal·ly** *adv.* [F. *diplomatique*]

diplomatic *n.* diplomatics

diplomatic corps the body of expert functionaries (ambassadors, secretaries, attachés etc.) making up the foreign legations at a seat of government

diplomatic immunity freedom from taxation and payment of customs duty, from liability to arrest, and from the need to observe minor police regulations, usually enjoyed by diplomats and the members of their households on foreign soil under international law

dip·lo·mat·ics (dipləmǽtiks) *n.* the critical study of public and private documents of an administrative, legal, juridical and diplomatic character (charters, laws, treaties, title deeds etc.) [fr. Mod. L. *diplomaticus* fr. Gk]

di·plo·ma·tist (diplóumətist) *n.* a diplomat

di·plo·pi·a (diplóupi:ə) *n.* a disorder of the eyes causing double vision **di·plo·pic** (diplópik) *adj.* [fr. Gk *diploos,* double+*ōps* (*ōpis*), eye]

di·plo·sis (diplóusis) *n.* doubling of the chromosome number, in syngamy [fr. Gk *diplōsis,* a doubling]

dip·lo·tene (díplouti:n) *n.* the stage in meiosis at which bivalent chromosomes split longitudinally [fr. Gk *diploos,* double+*tainia,* band]

dip needle an instrument for measuring the magnetic dip. It consists of a magnetized needle free to rotate in the vertical plane of the magnetic meridian and pointing in the direction of the earth's magnetic field

dip net a long-handled net in the form of a bag, used for scooping up fish

dip·no·an (dípnouən) 1. *n.* a member of *Dipnoi,* an order of fish having gills but also true lungs, formed by a modified swim bladder. Surviving

genera are *Lepidosiren, Protopterus* and *Neoceratodus* 2. *adj.* belonging to, pertaining to or resembling the *Dipnoi* [fr. Mod. L. fr. Gk *di-,* twice+*pnoē,* breath]

di·pole (dáipoul) *n.* a pair of equal and opposite point electric charges or magnetic poles a short distance apart ‖ a molecule having the effective centers of the positive and negative charges separated

dipole moment a vector quantity equal to the product of the charges or poles of a dipole and the distance between them

Dip·per (dípər) *n.* a Dunker

dip·per (dípər) *n.* a member of *Cinclus,* a genus of European birds about 7 ins long, allied to thrushes. They frequent streams and live on aquatic insects and larvae. Species are also found in Asia and America ‖ a kind of ladle ‖ the scoop or grab of an excavator ‖ (*photog.*) an apparatus for handling negatives in the developer ‖ (*Br.*) a dimmer for lowering the beam of car headlights ‖ the Big Dipper (*URSA MAJOR) ‖ the Little Dipper (*URSA MINOR) ‖ someone or something that dips

dipping *n.* use of specially prepared tobacco for sucking (not chewing) **dipper** *n.*

dipping needle a dip needle

dip pipe a pipe with a sunken outlet, e.g. one from a gas main having its end sealed by dipping into a liquid

dip·so·ma·ni·a (dipsouméini:ə) *n.* a morbid craving for alcohol **dip·so·má·ni·ac** *n.* [fr. Gk *dipsa,* thirst+*mania,* madness]

dip·stick (dípstik) *n.* a measure for determining the depth of liquid in a tank, e.g. of oil in the oil reservoir of a car engine

dip·ter·al (díptərəl) *adj.* (*archit.*) having a double colonnade [fr. L. *dipteros* fr. Gk]

dip·ter·an (díptərən) 1. *n.* a member of *Diptera,* an order of insects including the housefly, blowfly, gnat, mosquito etc., having only the front wings developed, and with sucking mouthparts 2. *adj.* relating to *Diptera* [fr. Mod. L. *Diptera* fr. Gk *diptera,* two wings]

dip·ter·ous (díptərəs) *adj.* (*entom.*) belonging to the order *Diptera* ‖ (*bot.*, of seeds, stems etc.) having two winglike appendages [fr. Mod. L. *dipterus* fr. Gk]

dip·tych (díptik) *n.* a painting, or carving, esp. an altarpiece, made on two hinged screens ‖ (*hist.*) a double, hinged writing tablet folding inwards [fr. L. *diptycha* fr. Gk]

di·py·rid·a·mole [$C_{24}H_{40}N_8O_4$] (daipirídəmoul) *n.* (*pharm.*) a drug used to increase coronary blood flow to relieve angina pain

di·quat [$C_{12}H_{12}Br_2N_2$] (dáikwat) *n.* a biodegradable herbicide used to control weeds in water

Di·rac (dirǽk), Paul Adrien Maurice (1902–84), English physicist awarded a Nobel prize (1933) for his work on quantum mechanics and electron spin

dire (dáiər) *comp.* **dir·er** *superl.* **dir·est** *adj.* dreadful, terrible, *in dire peril* ‖ most pressing, *in dire need* ‖ extreme, *to take dire measures* [fr. L. *dirus*]

di·rect (dirékt, dairékt) 1. *v.t.* to explain or point out the way to (someone) ‖ to address, aim (e.g. a criticism or remark) ‖ to address (a parcel etc.) ‖ to turn (something) in a certain direction ‖ to supervise, *to direct excavations* ‖ to control the making of (a film), guiding the actors, cameramen etc. ‖ (*Am.*=*Br.* produce) to direct the actors in and supervise the presentation of (a play) ‖ (of priests, counselors) to advise, guide ‖ to order, instruct ‖ *v.i.* to give orders 2. *adj.* straight, without detours ‖ straightforward, candid, blunt ‖ immediate ‖ not turned aside, *direct rays* ‖ (of descent) in unbroken line from parent to child ‖ (of a descendant) lineal ‖ diametrical, *the direct opposite* ‖ (*astron.*, of a planet's motion when moving with the sun in relation to the fixed stars) from west to east ‖ (of a dye) able to fix itself without a mordant ‖ (*mus.*, of an interval, chord) not inverted 3. *adv.* by the direct way or in a direct manner [fr. L. *dirigere* (*directus*), to put straight]

direct current (*abbr.* D.C.) an electric current of constant magnitude flowing in one direction only (cf. ALTERNATING CURRENT)

direct discourse (*gram.,* *Am.*=*Br.* direct speech) words actually spoken as distinct from a report of words spoken (cf. INDIRECT DISCOURSE)

direct distance dialing telephone system that permits direct dialing outside the local area (*abbr.* DDD)

CONCISE PRONUNCIATION KEY: **(a)** æ, c*a*t; ɑ, c*a*r; ɔ f*aw*n; ei, sn*a*ke. **(e)** e, h*e*n; i:, sh*ee*p; iə, d*ee*r; ɛə, b*ea*r. **(i)** i, f*i*sh; ai, t*i*ger; ə:, b*i*rd. **(o)** o, *o*x; au, c*ow*; ou, g*oa*t; u, p*oo*r; ɔi, r*oy*al. **(u)** ʌ, d*u*ck; u, b*u*ll; u:, g*oo*se; ə, b*a*cillus; ju:, c*u*be. x, lo*ch*; θ, *th*ink; ð, bo*th*er; z, *Z*en; ʒ, corsa*g*e; dʒ, sava*g*e; ŋ, ora*n*gutang; j, *y*ak; ʃ, *fi*sh; tʃ, fe*tch*; 'l, rabb*le*; 'n, red*den*. Complete pronunciation key appears inside front cover.

directed energy weapons (*mil.*) laser beams capable of destroying missiles and other objects

di·rec·tion (dirékʃən, dairékʃən) *n.* the act of directing, aiming or managing ‖ a command ‖ instruction, esp. moral or spiritual ‖ (*pl.*) instructions, esp. about how to use or make something or how to go somewhere ‖ the course which something is taking or is pointed towards ‖ a channel of activity, *to interest oneself in a new direction* ‖ (*pl., Br.*) the address on a letter or parcel **di·réc·tion·al** *adj.* (*radio*) depending upon direction for a good performance [fr. L. *directio* (*directionis*)]

direction finder a wireless receiving device for finding the direction of a source of radio waves

direction indicator (*aeron.*) a compass having an indicator which can be set for a desired course so that the pilot, by comparing his actual course with the desired one, can adjust accordingly

di·rec·tive (diréktiv, dairéktiv) 1. *adj.* directing or to do with directing 2. *n.* an order or instruction, esp. a formal order by state, military or business authority [fr. M.L. *directivus*]

direct labor, *Br.* **direct labour** labor applied directly to the production of something, thus allowing easy assessment of its cost ‖ labor employed directly for maintenance or construction work, esp. by central or local government without subcontraction

di·rect·ly (diréktli:, dairéktli:) 1. *adv.* in a direct manner ‖ not obliquely, *directly overhead* ‖ at once, immediately ‖ presently 2. *conj.* (*Br.*) as soon as, *she came directly she heard*

direct method the method of teaching a foreign language without relying on use of the pupil's own language for making explanations etc.

direct object (*gram.*) the word or words denoting the receiver of an action (*TRANSITIVE VERB, cf. INDIRECT OBJECT)

Di·rec·toire (di:rektwɑr) *adj.* of a style (esp. in women's clothes and in furniture) prevalent in France during the Directory [F.]

di·rec·tor (diréktər, dairéktər) *n.* someone who administers or directs, esp. a member of the board of a commercial company ‖ a priest whom a person or society takes as spiritual adviser ‖ (*Br.*) someone responsible for the making of a film, controlling the actors, cameramen etc. ‖ (*Am.=Br.* producer) someone who directs the actors and supervises the presentation of a play

Di·rec·to·ry (diréktəri:, diréktri:, dairéktəri:, dairéktri:) *n.* (*F. hist.*) the body of five which held executive power 1795–9 during the French Revolution

di·rec·to·ry (diréktəri:, diréktri:, dairéktəri:, dairéktri:) *pl.* **di·rec·to·ries** *n.* a book listing the names and addresses of the inhabitants of a place alphabetically, or according to profession etc. ‖ something which serves to direct, e.g. a codified set of rules [fr. Mod. L. *directorium*, a book of directions]

direct primary an election within a political party in which its candidates are chosen by direct vote

di·rec·tress (diréktris, dairéktris) *n.* a woman director

di·rec·trix (diréktriks, dairéktriks) *pl.* **di·rec·tri·xes**, **di·rec·tric·es** (diréktrisi:z, dairéktrisi:z) *n.* (*plane geom.*) a fixed line used to determine the motion of a point whose distance from a fixed point (the focus) has a constant ratio (the eccentricity) to its perpendicular distance from the directrix, thus generating a conic section ‖ (*solid geom.*) any straight or curved line which a moving line must touch in describing a surface [Mod. L.]

direct speech (*Br.*) direct discourse

direct tax a tax (e.g. income tax) levied directly upon the person who is to pay (as distinct from indirect tax, e.g. a hidden addition in the price of tobacco)

di·rect-vi·sion spectroscope (diréktvíʒən, dairéktvíʒən) a spectroscope using a combination of opposed prisms of different refractive indices, giving no deviation for the middle of the spectrum

dire·ful (dáiərfəl) *adj.* arousing dread

di·ret·tis·si·ma (di:retísi:ma) *n.* direct ascent in mountaineering

dirge (də:rdʒ) *n.* a funeral song of lament ‖ a lament [orig. L. *dirige* fr. *dirigere*, to direct, beginning the antiphon sung in the Office for the Dead]

dir·ham (də:rhǽm) *n.* the basic monetary unit of Morocco ‖ a coin or note of the value of one dirham [Arab. fr. L. *drachma*]

Di·ri·chlet (dirikléi), Peter Gustav Lejeune (1805–59), German mathematician who contributed to the theory of numbers and to the establishment of Fourier's theorem

dir·i·gi·ble (dírdʒəb'l, dirídʒəb'l) 1. *adj.* (of balloons and airships) capable of being guided or steered 2. *n.* a balloon with this quality or an airship [fr. L. *dirigere*, to direct]

dir·i·ment impediment (dírəmənt) (*law*) a disability nullifying marriage from the beginning [fr. L. *dirimere*, to interrupt]

dirk (də:rk) *n.* a dagger, esp. of the Scottish Highlands [earlier *dork, durk,* etym. doubtful]

dirn·dl (dé:rnd'l) *n.* an Alpine peasant dress with close-fitting bodice and full skirt (usually colorful or worked) gathered in at the waist ‖ a full skirt with a tight, gathered waistband [G., dim. of *dirne,* girl]

dirt (də:rt) *n.* any unclean substance, anything that soils ‖ soil ‖ mud ‖ excrement **to treat like dirt** to treat with the utmost contempt [M.E. *drit.* prob. fr. O.N. *drit,* excrement]

dirt cheap very inexpensive ‖ at a very low price

dirt·i·ly (dé:rtili:) *adv.* in a dirty way

dirt·i·ness (dé:rti:nis) *n.* the quality or state of being dirty

dirt road a road with an earth surface

dirt track a track made of rolled cinders, earth etc. for motorcycle racing

dirt·y (dé:rti:) 1. *comp.* **dirt·i·er** *superl.* **dirt·i·est** *adj.* soiled, not clean ‖ indecent, *dirty stories* ‖ mean, despicable, *a dirty trick* ‖ dishonorable, *dirty work* ‖ (of color) murky, tending to black or brown ‖ (*naut.*) stormy, *a dirty night* ‖ (*pop.*) resentful, or likely to be resented, *a dirty look* ‖ (of nuclear explosions) generating excessive fallout 2. *v. pres. part.* **dirt·y·ing** *past and past part.* **dirt·ied** *v.t.* to soil ‖ *v.i.* to become dirty

dirty bomb (*mil.*) a nuclear weapon that purposefully leaves a larger than necessary radioactive residue *syn.* dirty weapon *Cf* NEUTRON BOMB

dirty pool unsportsmanlike or unethical conduct *Cf* DIRTY TRICKS

dirty tricks unethical, sometimes illegal, tactics used to promote a cause or disconcert a political opponent, e.g., hate mail, anonymous press releases, false notices

dirty weapon *DIRTY BOMB

dis- (dis) *prefix* away, apart, asunder ‖ not, the opposite of, un- [L.]

dis·a·bil·i·ty (dɪsəbíliti:) *pl.* **dis·a·bil·i·ties** *n.* a being physically or mentally disabled ‖ a cause of this ‖ a legal disqualification or incapacity

dis·a·ble (diséib'l) *pres. part.* **dis·a·bling** *past and past part.* **dis·a·bled** *v.t.* to incapacitate physically or mentally ‖ to incapacitate legally **dis·á·ble·ment** *n.*

dis·a·buse (dɪsəbju:z) *pres. part.* **dis·a·bus·ing** *past and past part.* **dis·a·bused** *v.t.* to undeceive, free from false ideas

dis·ac·cord (dɪsəkórd) 1. *n.* a disagreement 2. *v.i.* (*rhet.*) to disagree

dis·ad·van·tage (dɪsədvǽntidʒ, dɪsədvántidʒ) 1. *n.* an unfavorable circumstance, drawback, handicap ‖ loss, detriment 2. *pres. part.* **dis·ad·van·tag·ing** *past and past part.* **dis·ad·van·taged** *v.t.* to place at a disadvantage [F. *désavantage*]

disadvantaged *adj.* of economically deprived or handicapped people or groups of people **dis·advantaged** *n.*

dis·ad·van·ta·geous (dɪsædvəntéidʒəs, dɪsædvəntéidʒəs) *adj.* unfavorable

dis·af·fect·ed (dɪsəféktid) *adj.* alienated in feeling or loyalty, nursing a grievance against the authorities [past part. of *disaffect,* obs. v.]

dis·af·fec·tion (dɪsəfékʃən) *n.* discontent, disloyalty (esp. political)

dis·af·for·est (dɪsəfórist, dɪsəfórist) *v.t.* (*Eng. law*) to remove from the protection of forest laws [fr. M.L. *disafforestare*]

dis·ag·gre·gate (dɪsǽgrəgeit) *v.* to separate **dis·aggregate** *n.*

dis·a·gree (dɪsəgrí:) *v.i. pres. part.* **dis·a·gree·ing** *past and past part.* **dis·a·greed** to differ in opinion or total ‖ to quarrel, squabble ‖ (with 'with') to be harmful or unsuitable, *this climate disagrees with him* ‖ to upset the digestion [fr. F. *désagréer*]

dis·a·gree·a·ble (dɪsəgrí:əb'l) *adj.* unpleasant ‖ ill-natured [F. *désagréable*]

dis·a·gree·ment (dɪsəgrí:mənt) *n.* a disagreeing ‖ a being opposed or at variance

dis·al·low (dɪsəláu) *v.t.* to refuse to admit, to deny the truth or validity of, *to disallow a protest* [O.F. *desalouer*]

dis·am·big·u·ate (dɪsæmbígju:eit) *v.* to remove ambiguity **disambiguation** *n.*

dis·ap·pear (dɪsəpíər) *v.i.* to vanish, cease to be visible ‖ to be lost **dis·ap·péar·ance** *n.*

dis·ap·point (dɪsəpóint) *v.t.* to fail to come up to the expectations of ‖ to thwart, frustrate, *disappointed in love* ‖ to break a promise to (someone) **dis·ap·póint·ed** *adj.* unhappy because of frustrated hopes etc. **dis·ap·póint·ing** *adj.* **dis·ap·póint·ment** *n.* someone who or something which disappoints ‖ the state of distress resulting from being disappointed [fr. F. *désappointer*]

dis·ap·pro·ba·tion (dɪsæprəbéiʃən) *n.* disapproval, condemnation **dis·ap·pro·ba·tive** (dɪsæprəbeitiv, dɪsəpróubətiv), **dis·ap·pro·ba·to·ry** (dɪsəpróubətɔri:, dɪsəpróubətɔuri:) *adjs*

dis·ap·prov·al (dɪsəprú:vəl) *n.* moral condemnation ‖ administrative rejection, *disapproval of building plans*

dis·ap·prove (dɪsəprú:v) *pres. part.* **dis·ap·prov·ing** *past and past part.* **dis·ap·proved** *v.t.* to have or express an unfavorable opinion of ‖ to refuse to sanction ‖ *v.i.* to withhold approval **dis·ap·próv·ing·ly** *adv.*

dis·arm (disárm) *v.t.* to deprive of weapons ‖ to deprive of the power to harm ‖ to allay the wrath or suspicion of, or turn aside the criticism of ‖ *v.i.* to cut down armaments, or renounce them [F. *désarmer*]

dis·ar·ma·ment (disárməmənt) *n.* the relinquishment, reduction or limitation of military strength [modification of F. *désarmement*]

dis·arm·ing (disármiŋ) *adj.* tending to allay vexation, *a disarming smile*

dis·ar·range (dɪsəréindʒ) *pres. part.* **dis·ar·rang·ing** *past and past part.* **dis·ar·ranged** *v.t.* to alter the arrangement of ‖ to make untidy **dis·ar·ránge·ment** *n.*

dis·ar·ray (dɪsəréi) 1. *n.* a lack of order ‖ a state of confusion ‖ disorderly dress 2. *v.t.* to throw into disorder [perh. O. F. *desareer*]

dis·as·sem·ble (dɪsəsémb'l) *pres. part.* **dis·as·sem·bling** *past and past part.* **dis·as·sem·bled** to take to pieces

dis·as·so·ci·ate (dɪsəsóuʃi:eit, dɪsəsóusi:eit) *pres. part.* **dis·as·so·ci·at·ing** *past and past part.* **dis·as·so·ci·at·ed** *v.t.* to dissociate **dis·as·so·ci·a·tion** (dɪsəsóuʃi:éiʃən, dɪsəsóusi:éiʃən) *n.* a dissociation

dis·as·ter (dizǽstər, dizástər) *n.* an event causing great loss, hardship or suffering to many people ‖ a great or sudden misfortune ‖ a fiasco **dis·ás·trous** *adj.* [fr. F. *désastre*]

dis·a·vow (dɪsəváu) *v.t.* to refuse to acknowledge or accept responsibility for, disclaim **dis·a·vów·al** *n.* [F. *désavouer*]

dis·band (disbǽnd) *v.t.* to end the existence of (an organization, e.g. a theatrical company) ‖ *v.i.* to disperse, break up **dis·bánd·ment** *n.* [fr. earlier F. *desbander*]

dis·bar (disbár) *pres. part.* **dis·bar·ring** *past and past part.* **dis·barred** *v.t.* (*law*) to expel from the bar, to deprive of the status of (*Am.*) attorney, (*Br.*) barrister **dis·bár·ment** *n.*

dis·be·lief (dísbilí:f) *n.* a refusal to give mental assent ‖ lack of belief, esp. religious belief

dis·be·lieve (dɪsbilí:v) *pres. part.* **dis·be·liev·ing** *past and past part.* **dis·be·lieved** *v.i.* (with 'in') to refuse to believe ‖ (with 'in') to lack faith ‖ *v.t.* to refuse to accept as true **dis·be·líev·er** *n.*

dis·bud (disbʌd) *pres. part.* **dis·bud·ding** *past and past part.* **dis·bud·ded** *v.t.* to remove superfluous buds from

dis·bur·den (disbé:rd'n) *v.t.* to rid of a burden

dis·burse (disbí:rs) *pres. part.* **dis·burs·ing** *past and past part.* **dis·bursed** *v.t.* to pay out (money) ‖ (*rhet.*) to defray (expenses **dis·búrse·ment** *n.* a disbursing ‖ the money paid out [older *disbourse* fr. O. F. *desbourser*]

disc *DISK

DISC (*acronym*) U.S. Domestic International Sales Corporation, government agency for export stimulation offering tax abatement to exporters

disc·aire (dɪskéər) *n.* one who selects records to be played at a discotheque

dis·cal·ce·ate (diskǽlsi:it, diskǽlsi:eit) *adj.* (of religious) barefooted, or wearing sandals [fr. L. *discolceatus* fr. *discalceare*, to remove the shoes from]

dis·calced (diskǽlst) *adj.* discalceate [trans. of L. *discalceatus*]

CONCISE PRONUNCIATION KEY: (**a**) æ, c**a**t; ɑ, c**a**r; ɔ f**aw**n; ei, sn**a**ke. (**e**) e, h**e**n; i:, sh**ee**p; iə, d**ee**r; ɛə, b**ea**r. (**i**) i, f**i**sh; ai, t**i**ger; ə:, b**i**rd. (**o**) o, **o**x; au, c**ow**; ou, g**oa**t; u, p**oo**r; ɔi, r**oy**al. (**u**) ʌ, d**u**ck; u, b**u**ll; u:, g**oo**se; ə, bacill**u**s; ju:, c**u**be. x, lo**ch**; θ, **th**ink; ð, **b**other; z, **Z**en; ʒ, cor**s**age; dʒ, sava**g**e; ŋ, orangutan**g**; j, **y**ak; ʃ, **f**ish; tʃ, fe**tch**; 'l, rabb**le**; 'n, redde**n**. Complete pronunciation key appears inside front cover.

dis·card 1. (diskárd) *v.t.* to get rid of as being of no further use or affording no pleasure ‖ (*card games*) to throw out (a card or cards) from a hand ‖ *v.i.* (*card games*) to throw out a card or cards from a hand 2. (dískord) *n.* (*card games*) the act of discarding ‖ the card or cards thrown out ‖ something gotten rid of or rejected

disc brake or **disk brake** a brake that applies friction against a rotating wheel by two pads closed by a caliper action *Cf* DRUM BRAKE

dis·cern (disə́:rn, dizə́:rn) *v.t.* to see, or make out through any of the senses ‖ to perceive with the mind **dis·cérn·i·ble** *adj.* **dis·cérn·i·bly** *adv.* **dis·cérn·ing** *adj.* discriminating, perceptive **dis·cérn·ment** *n.* a discerning ‖ discrimination, insight, perception [F. *discerner*]

dis·cerp·ti·ble (disə́:rptəb'l, dizə́:rptəb'l) *adj.* (*rhet.*) that can be torn apart [fr. L. *discerpere* (*discerptus*), to pluck apart]

dis·charge 1. (distʃárdʒ) *v.t. pres. part.* **dis·charg·ing** *past* and *past part.* **dis·charged** to unload, *to discharge a cargo* ‖ to send forth, give out, *the factory discharges its waste into the river* ‖ to absolve, free oneself from (an obligation or debt) by an act or payment ‖ to release (an arrow or bullet etc.), fire (a gun) ‖ to rid of an electric charge ‖ to dismiss (a servant, employee) ‖ to release (e.g. a prisoner or patient) ‖ to remove the dye from (a fabric) ‖ (*med.*) to emit (e.g. pus) ‖ *v.i.* (*med.*) to emit pus etc. ‖ (of a gun) to go off, fire ‖ to lose a charge of electricity ‖ to shed a load, *the sewers discharge out at sea* 2. (dístʃardʒ) *n.* an unloading of a ship or cargo ‖ a sending forth or thing sent forth, *a discharge of burnt gases* ‖ the fulfilment of an obligation, esp. the payment of a debt ‖ the firing of a gun etc. ‖ a release ‖ a dismissal ‖ (*law*) an acquittal ‖ (*law*) a dismissal of a court order ‖ a certificate of release or payment etc. ‖ (*med.*) the emission of matter ‖ the process of removing dye ‖ the chemical used in removing dye ‖ (*elec.*) the equalization of a potential difference at two points in an electric field by the flow of charge from one point to the other **dis·chárg·er** *n.* someone who discharges ‖ an apparatus for discharging electricity [O.F. *descharger*]

discharge abstract (*med.*) a summary description of a health facility admission prepared upon a patient's discharge. It records selected data about the patient's diagnosis, treatment and payment

discharge tube (*elec.*) a tube containing gas at very low pressure, in which conduction takes place under the influence of an applied potential difference. Discharge tubes are used for control purposes or to produce some forms of radiant energy

dis·ci·ple (disáip'l) *n.* someone who accepts the doctrine or teachings of another, esp. an early follower of Christ ‖ one of the 12 Apostles **dis·ci·ple·ship** *n.* [O.E. *discipul* fr. L.]

Disciples of Christ a Protestant congregationalist sect, founded in the U.S.A. (1832). It adheres to the New Testament, commemorates the Lord's Supper weekly and strives for the unity of the Christian Church

dis·ci·pli·nal (dísəplin'l, disəplən'l) *adj.* relating to discipline ‖ in the nature of discipline

dis·ci·pli·nar·i·an (disəplinéəri:ən) 1. *n.* someone who maintains or advocates strict discipline **Dis·ci·pli·nar·i·an** (*Eng. hist.*) an early English Puritan who favored the Calvinistic polity 2. *adj.* of or pertaining to the enforcing of strict discipline [fr. M.L. *disciplinarius*, relating to discipline]

dis·ci·pli·nar·y (dísəplineri:) *adj.* of or relating to discipline ‖ concerned with mental training [fr. M.L. *disciplinarius*]

dis·ci·pline (dísəplin) 1. *n.* the training of the mind and character ‖ a branch of learning ‖ a mode of life in accordance with rules ‖ self-control ‖ control, order, obedience to rules ‖ (*eccles.*) a system of practical rules for the members of a Church or an order ‖ punishment, esp. mortification of the flesh by way of penance ‖ a scourge for religious penance 2. *v.t. pres. part.* **dis·ci·plin·ing** *past* and *past part.* **dis·ci·plined** to bring under control ‖ to train ‖ to punish [F.]

di·scip·u·lar (disípjulər) *adj.* of or relating to a disciple

disc jockey a person who presents a radio program of recorded music with comments or chat interspersed

dis·claim (diskléim) *v.t.* to refuse to acknowledge (e.g. responsibility) ‖ (*law*) to renounce a legal claim to ‖ *v.i.* (*law*) to make a disclaimer [A.F. *disclamer, disclaimer*]

dis·claim·er (diskléimər) *n.* a renunciation, e.g. of a legal claim ‖ a disavowal, e.g. of statements made in one's praise ‖ a repudiation, e.g. of someone's selfcriticism [A.F. *disclamer,* infin. as n.]

dis·cli·max (diskláimæks) *n.* (*envir.*) a normally stable ecological community altered by continuous or repeated activities by humans or by other influences

dis·close (disklóuz) *pres. part.* **dis·clos·ing** *past* and *past part.* **dis·closed** *v.t.* to reveal (e.g. a secret) ‖ to expose to view **dis·clo·sure** (disklóuʒər) *n.* the act of disclosing ‖ the thing disclosed [M.E. *disclosen* fr. O.F.]

disc-mem·o·ry (diskmémori:) *n.* (*computer*) data storage device using plastic floppy discs

dis·co (dískou) *n.* music with a strong beat. 1. short for discotheque 2. popular music

dis·coid (dískɔid) *adj.* disk-shaped [fr. L. *discoides* fr. Gk]

dis·col·or, *Br.* **dis·col·our** (diskʌ́lər) *v.t.* to spoil the color of, stain ‖ *v.i.* to become changed or spoiled in color **dis·col·or·á·tion,** *Br.* also **dis·col·our·á·tion** *n.* **dis·cól·or·ment,** *Br.* **dis·cól·our·ment** *n.* [O.F. *descolorer*]

dis·com·fit (diskʌ́mfit) *v.t.* to disconcert, embarrass **dis·com·fi·ture** (diskʌ́mfitʃər) *n.* [M.E. *desconfit* fr. O.F.]

dis·com·fort (diskʌ́mfərt) *n.* physical or mental uneasiness [M.E. *disconfort* fr. O.F.]

dis·com·mode (diskəmóud) *pres. part.* **dis·com·mod·ing** *past* and *past part.* **dis·com·mod·ed** *v.t.* (*rhet.*) to cause inconvenience to

dis·com·pose (diskəmpóuz) *pres. part.* **dis·com·pos·ing** *past* and *past part.* **dis·com·posed** *v.t.* to disturb the composure of **dis·com·po·sure** (diskəmpouʒər) *n.*

dis·con·cert (diskənsə́:rt) *v.t.* to give a mental jolt to, confuse ‖ to upset, spoil (e.g. plans) **dis·con·cért·ment** *n.* [obs. F. *disconcerter*]

dis·con·form·i·ty (diskənfɔ́rmiti:) *pl.* **dis·con·form·i·ties** *n.* (*geol.*) a break between parallel rock strata involving no angular discordance of dip (*UNCONFORMITY)

dis·con·nect (diskənékt) *v.t.* to cause to be no longer connected **dis·con·néct·ed** *adj.* disjoined, not connected ‖ (of speech, writing) disjointed, incoherent **dis·con·nec·tion,** *Br.* also **dis·con·nex·ion** (diskənékʃən) *n.* a disconnecting or being disconnected

dis·con·so·late (diskónsəlit) *adj.* cast down in spirits, utterly dejected [fr. M.L. *disconsolatus*]

dis·con·tent (diskəntént) 1. *n.* dissatisfaction 2. *v.t.* to make dissatisfied **dis·con·tént·ed** *adj.* **dis·con·tént·ment** *n.*

dis·con·tin·u·ance (diskəntínju:əns) *n.* a discontinuing ‖ (*law*) the discontinuing of an action because the plaintiff has not observed the formalities needed to keep it pending [A.F.]

dis·con·tin·u·a·tion (diskəntinju:éiʃən) *n.* a discontinuing [F.]

dis·con·tin·ue (diskəntínju:) *pres. part.* **dis·con·tin·u·ing** *past* and *past part.* **dis·con·tin·ued** *v.t.* to stop, give up, *to discontinue a practice* ‖ *v.i.* to cease [F. *discontinuer*]

dis·con·ti·nu·i·ty (diskɔntinú:iti:, diskɔntinjú:iti:) *pl.* **dis·con·ti·nu·i·ties** *n.* lack of continuity ‖ a break in continuity

dis·con·tin·u·ous (diskəntínju:əs) *adj.* not continuous, interrupted, intermittent [fr. M.L. *discontinuus*]

dis·cord (dískɔrd) *n.* disagreement, quarreling ‖ a jarring combination of sounds **dis·córd·ance** *n.* **dis·córd·ant** *adj.* [O. F. *descord*]

discotheque place for dancing to recorded music; from the French word meaning 'record library'

dis·co·theque, dis·co·thèque (dískoutek) *n.* a nightclub in which people dance to recorded music

dis·count (dískaunt) *n.* a sum deducted (by courtesy, not by right) from an account, e.g. if it is paid immediately or in advance ‖ a sum deducted from the value of a bill of exchange etc. if exchanged before the due time ‖ a discounting ‖ a reduction in price offered to the public for sales promotion **at a discount** at a reduced price ‖ (*Br.*) less esteemed than formerly [O.F. *descompte*]

dis·count (dískaunt) *v.t.* to refuse to accept as being wholly true, *you can discount much of what he says* ‖ to lend money on (e.g. negotiable paper) and deduct a discount or allowance for interest ‖ to sell at a reduced price ‖ to leave out of account deliberately as being of small importance, dismiss as negligible ‖ to take (some

future event of probability) into account in advance and so lessen its effect [O.F. *desconter*]

dis·coun·te·nance (diskáuntənəns) *pres. part.* **dis·coun·te·nanc·ing** *past* and *past part.* **dis·coun·te·nanced** *v.t.* to refuse support or approval of ‖ to abash, put out of countenance

discount house a firm selling brand name goods at prices lower than list prices ‖ (*Br.*) bill broker

dis·cour·age (diskə́:ridʒ, diskʌ́ridʒ) *pres. part.* **dis·cour·ag·ing** *past* and *past part.* **dis·cour·aged** *v.t.* to sap or take away the courage of ‖ to deter ‖ to lessen enthusiasm for and so restrict or hinder, *inflation discourages saving* ‖ to tend no encouragement to ‖ to seek to prevent (by homily etc., not by law) **dis·cóur·age·ment** *n.* a discouraging or being discouraged ‖ something which discourages [fr. O.F. *descoragier*]

dis·course 1. (diskɔ́rs, diskóurs, dískɔrs, dískours) *n.* a speech or lecture ‖ a written dissertation ‖ (*rhet.*) talk, conversation 2. *v.i.* (diskɔ́rs, diskóurs) *pres. part.* **dis·cours·ing** *past* and *past part.* **dis·coursed** to talk rather lengthily or pompously [F. *discours*]

dis·cour·te·ous (diskə́:rti:əs) *adj.* unmannerly, impolite

dis·cour·te·sy (diskə́:rtisi:) *pl.* **dis·cour·te·sies** *n.* incivility, rude behavior ‖ an act of rudeness

dis·cov·er (diskʌ́vər) *v.t.* to find out, *to discover the facts* ‖ to find by exploration, *Columbus discovered America* ‖ to come across, *to discover a bird's nest* ‖ *v.i.* to make a discovery **dis·cóv·er·y** *pl.* **dis·cov·er·ies** *n.* a discovering ‖ the thing discovered [O.F. *descouvrir*]

discovered check (*chess*) the position resulting from a move by a piece or pawn which exposes the king to check by another piece

Discovery Day Columbus Day

discovery rule (*law*) a legal rule in use in some jurisdictions under which the statute of limitations does not commence to run until the wrongful act is discovered or, with reasonable diligence, should have been discovered

disc pack (*computer*) an easily removable unit of connected discs as a package

dis·cred·it (diskrédit) 1. *v.t.* to destroy the trustworthiness of (someone or something) ‖ to refuse to believe or have confidence in 2. *n.* disesteem ‖ a cause of loss of repute ‖ doubt, disbelief, *his past lies threw discredit on his evidence*

dis·cred·it·a·ble (diskréditəb'l) *adj.* injurious to reputation, shameful **dis·créd·it·a·bly** *adv.*

dis·creet (diskrí:t) *adj.* circumspect in word or deed ‖ able to keep silent about matters where prudence requires it ‖ tactful ‖ quietly tasteful, not showy [M.E. *discret* fr. O.F.]

dis·crep·an·cy (diskrépənsi:) *pl.* **dis·crep·an·cies** *n.* the state of being discrepant ‖ an instance of this

dis·crep·ant (diskrépənt) *adj.* inconsistent, at variance [fr. L. *discrepans* (*discrepantis*) fr. *discrepare*, to differ in sound]

dis·crete (diskrí:t) *adj.* separate, distinct, disjoined ‖ (*philos.*) abstract, not concrete [fr. L. *discernere* (*discretus*), to distinguish]

discrete sound system a quadrophonic system of sound reproduction in four channels separated in both input and output

dis·cre·tion (diskréʃən) *n.* prudence, discerning caution, esp. in speech ‖ freedom to make one's own decisions **at discretion** according to one's own choice or judgment **dis·cre·tion·ar·y** (diskréʃəneri:) *adj.* [O.F. *discrecion*]

discretionary account (*finance*) an investment account in which the adviser or broker may buy or sell securities held without consulting the principal

discretionary income (*economics*) income available for personal spending after taxes and use for basic necessities *Cf* DISPOSABLE PERSONAL INCOME

dis·crim·i·nant (diskrímínənt) *n.* (*math.*) a mathematical expression that indicates the behavior of another more complicated function, relation or set of relations

dis·crim·i·nate (diskrímineit) *pres. part.* **dis·crim·i·nat·ing** *past* and *past part.* **dis·crim·i·nat·ed** *v.i.* to use good judgment in making a choice ‖ to observe or make distinctions ‖ (in syllogistic argument) to draw a distinction ‖ *v.t.* to distinguish (one thing) from another, *to discriminate good from bad* ‖ to serve to distinguish **to discriminate against** to single out for unfavorable treatment **dis·crím·i·nat·ing** *adj.* having fine judgment or taste ‖ treating differently, making distinctions, *a discriminating*

CONCISE PRONUNCIATION KEY: **(a)** æ, c*a*t; ɑ, c*a*r; ɔ f*aw*n; ei, sn*a*ke. **(e)** e, h*e*n; i:, sh*ee*p; iə, d*ee*r; ɛə, b*ea*r. **(i)** i, f*i*sh; ai, t*i*ger; ə:, b*i*rd. **(o)** o, *o*x; au, c*ow*; ou, g*oa*t; u, p*oo*r; ɔi, r*oy*al. **(u)** ʌ, d*u*ck; u, b*u*ll; u:, g*oo*se; ə, b*a*cill*u*s; ju:, c*u*be. x, lo*ch*; θ, *th*ink; ð, bo*th*er; z, *Z*en; ʒ, corsa*g*e. dʒ, sava*g*e; ŋ, orangutan*g*; j, *y*ak; ʃ, *fi*sh; tʃ, fe*tch*; 'l, rabb*le*; 'n, redd*en*. Complete pronunciation key appears inside front cover.

tariff [fr. L. *discriminare* (*discriminatus*), to distinguish]

dis·crim·i·na·tion (diskriminéiʃən) *n.* a choosing with care ‖ good taste, discernment ‖ the making of distinctions (often unfair) in meting out treatment, service etc. [fr. L. *discriminatio* (*discriminationis*)]

dis·crim·i·na·tive (diskríminətiv, diskrímineitiv) *adj.* distinctive ‖ discerning [fr. L. *discriminare* (*discriminatus*), to discriminate]

dis·crim·i·na·to·ry (diskríminətɔri:, diskrímətɔuri:) *adj.* preferential, showing favoritism

dis·cur·sive (diskə́:rsiv) *adj.* rambling, going from one point to another with no planned sequence ‖ treating many subjects broadly ‖ proceeding by reasoning or argument (cf. INTUITIVE) [fr. L. *discurrere* (*discursus*), to run about]

dis·cus (dískəs) *pl.* **dis·cus·es, dis·ci** (dísai) *n.* (*athletics*) a heavy disk (4 lbs 6.4 ozs), thrown as far as possible as a trial of strength and skill from a circle 8 ft 2 ½ ins in diameter [L. fr. Gk *diskos*, quoit]

dis·cuss (diskʌ́s) *v.t.* to exchange ideas about (e.g. a problem, plan) ‖ to debate (a set theme) ‖ to gossip about ‖ to allow one's opinions on (a matter) to be questioned **dis·cúss·i·ble,** *Br.* esp. **dis·cúss·a·ble** *adjs* [fr. L. *discutere* (*discussus*), to strike apart]

dis·cus·sion (diskʌ́ʃən) *n.* verbal exchange of ideas ‖ a written or spoken orderly treatment of any subject ‖ argument ‖ idle speculation [O.F.]

dis·dain (disdéin) **1.** *v.t.* to scorn, *to disdain to answer* ‖ to have contempt for (e.g. subterfuge) ‖ to dismiss as not to be taken into consideration **2.** *n.* contempt, scorn **dis·dáin·ful** *adj.* [O.F. *desdeign-ier*]

dis·ease (dizí:z) *n.* an unhealthy condition ‖ a particular malady **dis·éased** *adj.* [M.E. *desese* fr. O.F.]

dis·em·bark (disimbárk) *v.i.* to go ashore ‖ *v.t.* to put ashore **dis·em·bar·ká·tion** *n.* [F. *désembarquer*]

dis·em·bar·rass (disimbǽrəs) *v.t.* (*rhet.,* with 'of') to rid, relieve

dis·em·bod·y (disimbódi) *pres. part.* **dis·em·bod·y·ing** *past* and *past part.* **dis·em·bod·ied** *v.t.* to separate or take away from the body, *a disembodied spirit* ‖ to separate (an idea) from the concrete, *disembodied theories*

dis·em·bogue (disimbóug) *pres. part.* **dis·em·bogu·ing** *past* and *past part.* **dis·em·bogued** *v.i.* (of a stream, river etc.) to empty ‖ *v.t.* (of a stream, river etc.) to pour forth (its waters) [older *disemboque* fr. Span. *desembocar*]

dis·em·bow·el (disimbáuəl) *pres. part.* **dis·em·bow·el·ing,** esp. *Br.* **dis·em·bow·el·ling** *past* and *past part.* **dis·em·bow·eled,** esp. *Br.* **dis·em·bow·elled** *v.t.* to eviscerate, take the innards out of, or cut open so that the bowels hang out **dis·em·bów·el·ment** *n.* [DIS-+obs. *embowel*]

dis·en·chant (disintʃǽnt, disintʃ́ánt) *v.t.* to disillusion, free from enchantment **dis·en·chánt·ment** *n.* [fr. F. *désenchanter*]

dis·en·cum·ber (disinkʌ́mbər) *v.t.* to free from encumbrance

dis·en·dow (disindáu) *v.t.* to take away an endowment from (esp. the Church) **dis·en·dów·ment** *n.*

dis·en·gage (disingéidʒ) *pres. part.* **dis·en·gag·ing** *past* and *past part.* **dis·en·gaged** *v.t.* to free, detach ‖ to free (oneself) from an engagement ‖ to cause (the clutch of a vehicle) to stop binding ‖ to cause (the gears of a vehicle) to stop meshing ‖ (*mil.*) to take (troops) out of a zone of fighting ‖ *v.i.* (of combatants) to break loose, separate **dis·en·gáged** *adj.* freed ‖ without engagement ‖ no longer engaged to marry **dis·en·gáge·ment** *n.*

dis·en·tail (disintéil) *v.t.* (*law*) to free from entail

dis·en·tan·gle (disintǽŋg'l) *pres. part.* **dis·en·tan·gling** *past* and *past part.* **dis·en·tan·gled** *v.t.* to free from entanglement, unravel ‖ to restore order to (e.g. accounts) ‖ *v.i.* to become unraveled **dis·en·tán·gle·ment** *n.*

dis·en·tomb (disintú:m) *v.t.* to remove from the tomb, disinter ‖ (*rhet.*) to unearth, dig out by research

dis·e·qui·lib·ri·um (disi:kwilíbri:əm) *n.* a loss of or lack of balance or stability

dis·es·tab·lish (disistǽbliʃ) *v.t.* to deprive (an established Church) of the position and privileges granted to it by the State ‖ to end (an established state of affairs) **dis·es·táb·lish·ment** *n.*

dis·fa·vor, *Br.* **dis·fa·vour** (disféivər) **1.** *n.* the state of being out of favor ‖ dislike or disapproval **2.** *v.t.* to look upon with disfavor

dis·fea·ture (disfí:tʃər) *pres. part.* **dis·fea·tur·ing** *past* and *past part.* **dis·fea·tured** *v.t.* to spoil the appearance of (cf. DISFIGURE)

dis·fig·u·ra·tion (disfigjuréiʃən) *n.* disfigurement

dis·fig·ure (disfígjər, *Br.* esp. disfígə) *pres. part.* **dis·fig·ur·ing** *past* and *past part.* **dis·fig·ured** *v.t.* to spoil the appearance of **dis·fíg·ure·ment** *n.* a disfiguring or being disfigured ‖ something which disfigures [fr. O.F. *desfigurer*]

dis·fran·chise (disfrǽntʃaiz) *pres. part.* **dis·fran·chis·ing** *past* and *past part.* **dis·fran·chised** *v.t.* to deprive of a citizen's rights ‖ to deprive of voting rights ‖ to deprive of any franchise, privilege or voting right **dis·fran·chise·ment** (disfrǽntʃizmənt) *n.* [DIS-+obs. *franchise*]

dis·ger·mi·no·ma or **dys·ger·mi·no·ma** (disdʒə:rminóumə) *n.* (*med.*) an ovarian tumor similar to, but not as malignant as, seminoma of the testis

dis·gorge (disgɔ́rdʒ) *pres. part.* **dis·gorg·ing** *past* and *past part.* **dis·gorged** *v.t.* to throw up, vomit ‖ (of rivers etc.) to discharge (their waters) ‖ to give up (what one has seized or otherwise dishonestly come by) [fr. O.F. *desgorger*]

dis·grace (disgréis) **1.** *n.* loss of honor or esteem ‖ shame, ignominy ‖ someone or something causing shame or discredit **2.** *v.t. pres. part.* **dis·grac·ing** *past* and *past part.* **dis·graced** to bring shame or discredit upon ‖ to remove from favor or position **dis·gráce·ful** *adj.* [F. fr. Ital.]

dis·grun·tled (disgrʌ́nt'ld) *adj.* peeved, made discontented [DIS-+obs. *gruntle*]

dis·guise (disgáiz) **1.** *v.t. pres. part.* **dis·guis·ing** *past* and *past part.* **dis·guised** to change the normal appearance, sound etc. of, so as to conceal identity, *to disguise one's voice* ‖ to hide, conceal, *to disguise one's disappointment* **2.** *n.* an altering of appearance to conceal identity ‖ the clothing etc. used to work this change **dis·gúise·ment** *n.* [M.E. *desgisen*]

dis·gust (disgʌ́st) *n.* strong aversion, loathing [fr. F. *desgoust*]

dis·gust *v.t.* to fill with loathing ‖ to make indignant ‖ to offend the modesty of (someone) **dis·gúst·ing** *adj.* [fr. F. *desgouster*]

dis·gust·ed (disgʌ́stid) *adj.* (with 'at', 'with' or 'by') feeling or showing disgust **dis·gúst·ed·ly** *adv.*

dish (diʃ) **1.** *n.* a shallow vessel, typically of glass or earthenware, esp. for serving or holding food at meals ‖ the food served in such a dish ‖ the quantity a dish will hold **2.** *v.t.* to put (food) into a dish ‖ (*pop.*) to frustrate (hopes), put an end to (chances) **to dish up** to serve (food) ‖ to rehash (old familiar arguments etc.) [O.E. *disc* fr. L.]

dis·ha·bille (disəbí:l) *n.* the state of being only partly, or carelessly, dressed [fr. F. *déshabillé,* past part. of *déshabiller,* to undress]

dis·ha·bit·u·ate (dishæbítʃu:eit) *v.* to break a habit

dis·har·mo·ni·ous (disharmóuni:əs) *adj.* lacking in harmony

dis·har·mo·nize (dishármənaiz) *pres. part.* **dis·har·mo·niz·ing** *past* and *past part.* **dis·har·mo·nized** *v.t.* to cause to be out of harmony

dis·har·mo·ny (dishárməni:) *n.* discord lack of harmony

dish·cloth (díʃklɔθ, díʃklɔθ) *pl.* **dish·cloths** (díʃklɔθs, díʃklɔθs, díʃklɔðz, díʃklɔðz) *n.* a cloth for washing dishes

dis·heart·en (dishárt'n) *v.t.* to discourage, dispirit **dis·héart·en·ing** *adj.* **dis·héart·en·ment** *n.*

di·shev·el (diʃévəl) *pres. part.* **di·shev·el·ing,** esp. *Br.* **di·shev·el·ling** *past* and *past part.* **di·shev·eled,** esp. *Br.* **di·shev·elled** *v.t.* to make (the hair) tousled or loose and untidy or (the clothes) rumpled, torn etc. [DISHEVELED]

di·shev·eled, esp. *Br.* **di·shev·elled** (diʃévəld) *adj.* with disordered hair ‖ untidy in appearance [fr. O.F. *deschevelé*]

di·shev·el·ment (diʃévəlmənt) *n.* the state of being disheveled

dis·hon·est (disónist) *adj.* not honest, lacking integrity ‖ insincere [fr. O.F. *deshoneste,* dishonest]

dis·hon·es·ty (disónisti:) *pl.* **dis·hon·es·ties** *n.* lack of honesty ‖ a dishonest act, fraud [O.F. *deshonesté,* dishonor]

dis·hon·or, *Br.* esp. **dis·hon·our** (disónər) *n.* disgrace ‖ something which brings disgrace ‖ someone who causes disgrace [O.F. *deshonor*]

dis·hon·or, *Br.* esp. **dis·hon·our** *v.t.* to treat disrespectfully ‖ to bring shame or disgrace on ‖ (of a bank) to refuse to pay or accept (a check etc.) [O.F. *deshonnorer*]

dis·hon·or·a·ble, *Br.* esp. **dis·hon·our·a·ble** (disónərəb'l) *adj.* not honorable, disgraceful **dis·hón·or·a·bly,** *Br.* esp. **dis·hón·our·a·bly** *adv.*

dish·pan (díʃpæn) *n.* (*Am.*=*Br.* washing-up bowl) a utensil in which dishes are washed

dish towel a cloth for drying dishes

dish·ware (díʃwɛər) *n.* containers in which food is served

dish·wash·er (díʃwɔʃər, díʃwɒʃər) *n.* a person or machine that washes dishes

dish·wa·ter (díʃwɔtər, díʃwɒtər) *n.* the water used for washing dishes ‖ (*pop.*) very weak tea, coffee, soup etc. ‖ (*pop.*) discourse having little substance

dis·il·lu·sion (disilú:ʒən) **1.** *v.t.* to free from illusion, disenchant **2.** *n.* the state of being disillusioned **dis·il·lú·sion·ment** *n.*

dis·in·cli·na·tion (disinklinéiʃən) *n.* unwillingness

dis·in·cline (disinkláin) *pres. part.* **dis·in·clin·ing** *past* and *past part.* **dis·in·clined** *v.t.* to make unwilling or not wishful **dis·in·clíned** *adj.*

dis·in·fect (disinfékt) *v.t.* to free from infection by destroying harmful microorganisms

dis·in·fec·tant (disinféktənt) **1.** *n.* an agent used to kill harmful microorganisms, esp. a chemical used for such a purpose **2.** *adj.* suitable for use in disinfecting [fr. F. *désinfectant*]

dis·in·fec·tion (disinfékʃən) *n.* a disinfecting ‖ this process

dis·in·fest (disinfést) *v.t.* to free from vermin etc. **dis·in·fes·tá·tion** *n.*

dis·in·for·ma·tion (disinfuərméiʃən) *n.* false information, designed to confuse or mislead, leaked to an antagonist

dis·in·gen·u·ous (disindʒénju:əs) *adj.* insincere, lacking frankness

dis·in·her·it (disinhérit) *v.t.* to deprive of an inheritance **dis·in·hér·i·tance** *n.* [DIS-+INHERIT, (obs.) to make someone an heir]

dis·in·sec·tion (disinsékʃən) *n.* process of removing insects, esp. from a train or aircraft

dis·in·te·grant (disíntəgrənt) *n.* substance that causes a tablet to disintegrate

dis·in·te·grate (disíntigreit) *pres. part.* **dis·in·te·grat·ing** *past* and *past part.* **dis·in·te·grat·ed** *v.t.* to separate or break up into fragments ‖ *v.i.* to break up, lose unity, go to pieces **dis·in·te·grá·tion, dis·in·te·gra·tor** *ns*

dis·in·ter (disintə́:r) *pres. part.* **dis·in·ter·ring** *past* and *past part.* **dis·in·terred** *v.t.* to take from the grave, exhume ‖ to unearth, dig up [fr. F. *aésenterrer*]

dis·in·ter·est (disíntərist, disíntrist) *n.* absence of partiality because of personal interest ‖ (*pop.*) lack of interest

dis·in·ter·est·ed (disíntristid, disíntərestid) *adj.* impartial, not biased by personal feelings or personal interest ‖ (*pop.*) uninterested

dis·in·ter·me·di·a·tion (disintə:rmi:di:éiʃən) *n.* (*economics*) flight of funds from savings institutions to securities markets providing higher yields

dis·in·tox·i·cate (disintóksikeit) *v.* to remove poisonous material, e.g., in a drug user *also* detoxify, detoxicate **disintoxication** *n.*

dis·join (disdʒóin) *v.t.* to disconnect, separate, unfasten [M.E. *desjoyne* fr. O.F.]

dis·joint (disdʒóint) *v.t.* to separate at the joints ‖ to dislocate **dis·jóint·ed** *adj.* (esp. of talk) disconnected, incoherent [fr. O.F. *desjoindre*]

dis·junct (disdʒʌ́ŋkt) *adj.* disconnected, disjoined ‖ (*zool.*) having the tagmata separated by deep constrictions [fr. L. *disjungere* (*disjunctus*), to disconnect]

dis·junc·tion (disdʒʌ́ŋkʃən) *n.* a disjoining or being disjoined [O.F. or fr. L. *disjunctio* (*disjunctionis*)]

dis·junc·tive (disdʒʌ́ŋktiv) **1.** *adj.* disjoining, separating ‖ (*gram.*) connecting words or clauses expressing alternative or adversative ideas, *disjunctive conjunction* (e.g. 'either... or'), *disjunctive adverb* (e.g. 'otherwise') ‖ (*logic*) expressing alternatives **2.** *n.* a disjunctive conjunction ‖ (*logic*) a disjunctive proposition [fr. L. *disjunctivus*]

disk, disc (disk) *n.* a flat circular plate ‖ (*computer*) magnetic disc round, magnetic coated plastic record for storing data ‖ (*printing*) grid

CONCISE PRONUNCIATION KEY: (**a**) æ, c*a*t; ɑ, c*a*r; ɔ f*aw*n; ei, sn*a*ke. (**e**) e, h*e*n; i:, sh*ee*p; iə, d*ee*r; ɛə, b*ea*r. (**i**) i, f*i*sh; ai, t*i*ger; ə:, b*i*rd. (**o**) o, *o*x; au, c*ow*; ou, g*oa*t; u, p*oo*r; ɔi, r*oy*al. (**u**) ʌ, d*u*ck; u, b*u*ll; u:, g*oo*se; ə, b*a*cillus; ju:, c*u*be. x, lo*ch*; θ, *th*ink; ð, bo*th*er; z, *Z*en; ʒ, cor*s*age; dʒ, *s*avage; ŋ, orangutan*g*; j, *y*ak; ʃ, *fi*sh; tʃ, fe*tch*; 'l, rabb*le*; 'n, red*den*. Complete pronunciation key appears inside front cover.

in a phototypesetting apparatus ‖ (esp. **disc**) a phonograph record ‖ anything which is, or appears, round and flat, *the sun's disk* ‖ any such structure in a plant or in the body, esp. the gristly pads cushioned between the vertebrae [fr. L. *discus* fr. Gk]

disk harrow, disc harrow a harrow which breaks up the earth with a row of disks set at an angle to the line of draft

disk jockey an entertainer who presents record programs on the radio with bright chat between items

dis·like (disláik) **1.** *v.t. pres. part.* **dis·lik·ing** *past and past part.* **dis·liked** to feel an antipathy for **2.** *n.* an aversion, antipathy

dis·lo·cate (dísloukeit) *pres. part.* **dis·lo·cat·ing** *past and past part.* **dis·lo·cat·ed 1.** *v.t.* to put out of joint, displace ‖ to upset (e.g. plans) ‖ (*geol.*) to break the continuity of (strata) **2.** *n.* (*gymnastics*) movement on the rings from an inverted pike position, thrusting legs up and out, body arched, with arms out and rotating on the down swing **dis·lo·cá·tion** *n.* [fr. M.L. *dislocare* (*dislocatus*)]

dis·lodge (dislódʒ) *pres. part.* **dis·lodg·ing** *past and past part.* **dis·lodged** *v.t.* to remove (something) from a position where it is wedged, stuck, clinging etc. ‖ (*mil.*) to drive (an enemy) out of a position **dis·lódg·ment**, esp. *Br.* **dis·lódge·ment** *n.* [O. F. *desloger*]

dis·loy·al (dislóial) *adj.* not loyal **dis·lóy·al·ty** *n.* [O.F. *desloial*]

dis·mal (dízmal) *adj.* gloomy, dreary, depressed ‖ depressing [perh. fr. O.F. *dis mal*, unlucky days]

Dismal Swamp, or **Great Dismal Swamp**, U.S. water, grass, and bog area along the Virginia and North Carolina coast from Norfolk (Va.) to Elizabeth City (N.C.), about 37 mi (60 km) long and 10–15 mi (16–24 km) inland. Centrally located in the Dismal Swamp is freshwater Lake Drummond. A canal runs through the swamp and connects Chesapeake Bay with Albermarle Sound

dis·man·tle (dismánt'l) *pres. part.* **dis·man·tling** *past and past part.* **dis·man·tled** *v.t.* to take to pieces ‖ to strip of furniture and equipment ‖ to deprive (a fortification etc.) of defenses, guns etc. [fr. obs. F. *desmanteller*, to divest of a coat or mantle]

dis·mast (dismást, dismást) *v.t.* to deprive of a mast or masts

dis·may (disméi) **1.** *v.t.* to fill with consternation or alarm **2.** *n.* consternation, alarm [M.E. *dismayen*, prob. fr. O.F.]

dis·mem·ber (dismémbər) *v.t.* to divide limb from limb ‖ to divide, partition (esp. a country) **dis·mém·ber·ment** *n.* [O.F. *desmembrer*]

dis·miss (dismís) *v.t.* to send away, tell to go ‖ to discharge from employment, office etc. ‖ to discard mentally, put out of one's thoughts ‖ to treat briefly, *to dismiss a subject in a few words* ‖ (*law*) to refuse further hearing to (a case) ‖ (*cricket*) to put (a batsman or a team) out of play **dis·míss·al** *n.* a dismissing or being dismissed [prob. fr. L. *dimittere* (*dimissus*)]

dis·mount (dismáunt) *v.i.* to alight from a horse, bicycle etc. ‖ *v.t.* to force (a rider) from a horse etc. ‖ (*mech.*) to take to pieces, dismantle ‖ to take (a jewel) from its setting or (a gun) from its mount

Dis·ney (dízni:), Walt (1901–66), American film cartoonist and director. He created Mickey Mouse (1927), Donald Duck etc. 'Snow White and the Seven Dwarfs' (1938) was the first full-length animated cartoon. He also made animal documentary films and children's adventure films. Two vast amusement parks, Disneyland in California and Disneyworld in Florida, perpetuate his influence in the entertainment world

Dis·ney·esque (dizni:ésk) *adj.* resembling Disneyland

dis·o·be·di·ence (disəbí:di:əns) *n.* failure or refusal to obey **dis·o·bé·di·ent** *adj.* failing or refusing to obey [O.F. *desobedience*]

dis·o·bey (disəbéi) *v.t.* to refuse or fail to obey (a person, orders etc.) ‖ *v.i.* to be disobedient [F. *désobéir*]

dis·o·blige (disəbláidʒ) *pres. part.* **dis·o·blig·ing** *past and past part.* **dis·o·bliged** *v.t.* (*commerce*) to be unable, or fail, to oblige (someone) ‖ to go against the wishes of **dis·o·blíg·ing** *adj.* rather offensive, uncooperative [fr. F. *désobliger*]

dis·o·pyr·a·mide [$C_{21}H_{29}N_3O$] (disoupí:ramaid) *n.* a drug to counteract abnormal heart action (arrythmia) that acts like procainamide and quinidine; marketed as Norpace

dis·or·der (disórdər) **1.** *n.* a state of confusion ‖ disarray, untidiness ‖ riot, lawlessness ‖ a disease, ailment **2.** *v.t.* to confuse, disarrange ‖ to upset the health of **dis·ór·der·ly** *adj.* unruly, wild ‖ untidy ‖ (*law*) violating public order [prob. after F. *désordre*]

disorderly house (*law*) a brothel ‖ (*Br., law*) premises used illegally for gambling

disorderly market *n.* (*securities*) in a securities market, erratic price performance, esp. where no buyers or sellers are readily available *Cf* ORDERLY MARKET

dis·or·gan·i·za·tion (disɔrgənizéiʃən) *n.* a disorganizing or being disorganized

dis·or·gan·ize (disɔrgənaiz) *pres. part.* **dis·or·gan·iz·ing** *past and past part.* **dis·or·gan·ized** *v.t.* to upset the planned scheme of (things) ‖ to bring about a state of disorder in [fr. F. *désorganiser*]

dis·o·ri·ent (disóri:ent, disóuri:ent) *v.t.* to confuse (a person) about his bearings ‖ to make (a person) unsure of where he belongs, make (him) ill-adjusted [fr. F. *désorienter*]

dis·o·ri·en·tate (disóri:enteit, disóuri:enteit) *pres. part.* **dis·o·ri·en·tat·ing** *past and past part.* **dis·o·ri·en·tat·ed** *v.t.* to construct (a church) with the chancel not to the east ‖ (*Br.*) to disorient **dis·o·ri·en·tá·tion** *n.*

dis·own (disóun) *v.t.* to deny authorship of ‖ to repudiate ‖ to disclaim, deny

dis·par·age (dispáriʤ) *pres. part.* **dis·par·ag·ing** *past and past part.* **dis·par·aged** *v.t.* to talk to the detriment of (a person etc.) ‖ to belittle, deprecate **dis·pár·age·ment** *n.* **dis·pár·ag·ing** *adj.* [O.F. *desparagier*, to marry unequally]

dis·par·ate (dísparit, dispárit) *adj.* utterly different in kind, incommensurable [fr. L. *disparatus*, separate]

dis·par·i·ty (dispáriti) *pl.* **dis·par·i·ties** *n.* inequality, great difference [fr. F. *disparité*]

dis·pas·sion·ate (dispáʃənit) *adj.* cool, impartial, without emotion

dis·patch, des·patch (dispátʃ) **1.** *v.t.* to send off (a letter etc.) ‖ to put to death, kill ‖ to put a quick end to, finish off promptly (a piece of work, business etc.) **2.** *n.* a sending off (e.g. of a letter or messenger) ‖ a putting to death ‖ a discharging (of business or a duty) ‖ promptitude ‖ a message, esp. one sent in to a newspaper ‖ an official report, esp. military or diplomatic [fr. Ital. *dispacciare* or Span. *despachar*, to expedite]

dispatch box a box for carrying military or diplomatic papers etc.

dis·patch·er, des·patch·er (dispátʃər) *n.* someone who dispatches ‖ a person whose job is to make sure that the trucks, buses etc. of a transport company go out according to schedule

dispatch rider a messenger carrying military dispatches, esp. by motorcycle

dis·pel (dispél) *pres. part.* **dis·pel·ling** *past and past part.* **dis·pelled** *v.t.* to drive away, disperse (e.g. mists, gloom) [fr. L. *dispellere*]

dis·pen·sa·ble (dispénsəb'l) *adj.* capable of being done without, not necessary ‖ capable of being given out or distributed [fr. L. *dispensabilis*]

dis·pen·sa·ry (dispénsəri) *pl.* **dis·pen·sa·ries** *n.* a place where medical or veterinary prescriptions are made up and given out, and (often) advice or minor treatment provided at little cost or none

dis·pen·sa·tion (dispenséiʃən, dispənséiʃən) *n.* the act of meting out, *dispensation of justice* ‖ an arrangement or management, esp. of the world by nature or providence ‖ a particular fate ordained by providence ‖ a religious economy prevailing at a given time, *the Mosaic dispensation* ‖ an exemption from a rule, penalty or law [F. or fr. L. *dispensatio* (*dispensationis*)]

dis·pense (dispéns) *pres. part.* **dis·pens·ing** *past and past part.* **dis·pensed** *v.t.* to distribute, give out ‖ to prepare and give out (medicine) ‖ to administer (justice) ‖ to grant a dispensation to ‖ to exempt (from a rule) ‖ *v.i.* (with 'with') to do without **dis·pén·ser** *n.* someone who dispenses or something which dispenses ‖ a person who makes up medical prescriptions [O.F. *dispenser*]

dis·peo·ple (dispí:p'l) *pres. part.* **dis·peo·pling** *past and past part.* **dis·peo·pled** *v.t.* to depopulate [fr. O.F. *despeupler*]

dis·per·sal (dispə́:rs'l) *n.* a dispersing or being dispersed, esp. (*biol.*) the spreading of organisms from one place to others

dis·per·sant (dispə́:rsənt) *n.* chemical agent used to break up concentrations of organic material, e.g., spilled oil

dis·perse (dispə́:rs) *pres. part.* **dis·pers·ing** *past and past part.* **dis·persed** *v.t.* to scatter, disseminate ‖ to cause to break up and go away, *to disperse a mob* ‖ to put in position at separate points, *to disperse troops along a bank* ‖ (*optics*) to separate (wavelengths) usually by their different velocities in a refracting medium, but also by diffraction ‖ *v.i.* to break up, go away in different directions ‖ to become dispersed **dis·pér·sive** *adj.* [F. *disperser*]

dis·per·sion (dispə́:rʒən, dispə́:rʃən) *n.* a dispersing or being dispersed ‖ (*statistics*) the scatter of values of a variable around the mean of frequency distribution ‖ (*phys.*) the separation of nonhomogeneous radiation or some other emission (light, X rays, ions etc.) into its components according to some characteristic (wavelength, mass etc.), esp. the dispersion of light into its spectrum ‖ (*phys., chem.*) a system in which one substance is dispersed in another **the Dispersion** the scattering of the Jews without a homeland after the Captivity [F. or fr. L. *dispersio* (*dispersionis*)]

dispersive power (of glass etc.) the difference in refractive indices for two wavelengths, divided by the mean or other specified index minus one ‖ (of a diffraction grating) the rate of change of angular deviation with the wavelength

dis·pir·it, dis·spir·it (dispírit) *v.t.* to dishearten

dis·place (displéis) *pres. part.* **dis·plac·ing** *past and past part.* **dis·placed** *v.t.* to take the place of, oust ‖ to remove from office ‖ to remove from its usual place [fr. O.F. *desplacer*]

displaced person (*abbr.* DP) someone unable to live in his own country because of war or political persecution

dis·place·ment (displéismənt) *n.* a displacing or being displaced ‖ (*phys.*) the vector, drawn between two successive points on the trajectory of a moving object, representing the magnitude and direction of the motion ‖ the amount of fluid displaced by an object placed in it ‖ the volume displaced in a cylinder by one stroke of the piston ‖ (*psychol.*) the transfer of an emotion from one object to another

dis·play (displéi) **1.** *v.t.* to exhibit ‖ (of birds) to exhibit (plumage) in courtship, or aggressively ‖ to reveal, show (qualities etc.) ‖ to set out in large or distinctive printing type ‖ to show ostentatiously ‖ *v.i.* (of birds) to exhibit plumage **2.** *n.* a show, *a display of roses* ‖ (of birds) the characteristic behavior (e.g. the exhibition of plumage etc.) of a male bird before the female while courting or to protect his own territory ‖ a showing, *a display of ill temper* ‖ an ostentatious showing ‖ (*electr.*) device for communicating visually, e.g., a cathode-ray tube ‖ an arrangement of printing type (usually large) to set out titles etc. or command attention [O.F. *despleier*]

dis·please (displí:z) *pres. part.* **dis·pleas·ing** *past and past part.* **dis·pleased** *v.t.* to annoy, offend [M.E. *displesen* fr. O.F.]

dis·pleas·ure (displéʒər) *n.* annoyance, disapproval [O.F. *desplaisir*, v. used as n. and assimilated to PLEASURE]

dis·port (dispórt, dispóurt) *v.t.* to amuse (oneself) by frolicking, *lambs were disporting themselves in the meadow* ‖ (*Br., pop.*) to make (oneself) ridiculous by one's antics ‖ *v.i.* to frolic [M.E. *disporten* fr. O.F.]

dis·pos·a·ble (dispóuzəb'l) **1.** *adj.* that can be disposed of, got rid of ‖ available for use **2.** *n.* something that is to be thrown away after use, e.g., beer cans

disposable personal income (*economics*) personal income available for spending or saving

dis·pos·al (dispóuz'l) *n.* an arrangement (e.g. of furniture in a room) ‖ a getting rid of something, *sewage disposal* ‖ a settlement (of affairs) ‖ a distributing or bestowing (of property) **at someone's disposal** available for use at will ‖ ready to fit in with someone else's plans

dis·pose (dispóuz) *pres. part.* **dis·pos·ing** *past and past part.* **dis·posed** *v.t.* to place in position, arrange ‖ to incline, *his manners disposed her in his favor* ‖ *v.i.* to determine the outcome, *man proposes but God disposes* **to dispose of** to get rid of ‖ to deal as one wishes with ‖ to make final arrangements about ‖ to demolish (arguments etc.) ‖ to stow ‖ to eat (food, a meal) ‖ to sell [O.F. *disposer*]

dis·po·si·tion (dispəzíʃən) *n.* a being disposed ‖ temperament ‖ a placing, arrangement ‖ the power to dispose of something ‖ a making over of property, bestowal ‖ a dispensation, *a dispo-*

CONCISE PRONUNCIATION KEY: **(a)** æ, c*a*t; ɑ, c*a*r; ɔ f*aw*n; ei, sn*a*ke. **(e)** e, h*e*n; i:, sh*ee*p; iə, d*ee*r; ɛə, b*ea*r. **(i)** i, f*i*sh; ai, t*i*ger; ə:, b*i*rd. **(o)** o, *o*x; au, c*ow*; ou, g*oa*t; u, p*oo*r; ɔi, r*oy*al. **(u)** ʌ, d*u*ck; u, b*u*ll; u:, g*oo*se; ə, b*a*cillus; ju:, c*u*be. x, lo*ch*; θ, *th*ink; ð, bo*th*er; z, *Z*en; ʒ, corsa*ge*; dʒ, sava*ge*; ŋ, orangutan*g*; j, *y*ak; ʃ, *fi*sh; tʃ, fe*tch*; 'l, rabb*le*; 'n, redd*en*. Complete pronunciation key appears inside front cover.

sition of fate ‖ a plan or preparatory counter-measure [F.]

dis·pos·sess (dispəzés) v.t. to deprive of property ‖ to oust **dis·pos·sés·sion, dis·pos·sés·sor** ns [fr. O.F. despossesser]

dis·praise (dispréiz) 1. v.t. pres. part. **dis·prais-ing** past and past part. **dis·praised** to disparage 2. n. disparagement [O. F. despreisier]

dis·prod·uct (dísprodʌkt) n. product that has a negative utility or causes more harm in production than it is worth

dis·proof (disprú:f) n. a refutation, refuting ‖ evidence which refutes

dis·pro·por·tion (disprəpórʃən, dísprəpóurʃən) n. lack of proportion **dis·pro·pór·tion·al** adj.

dis·pro·por·tion·ate (dísprəpórʃənit, dísprə-póurʃənit) adj. lacking proportion

dis·pro·por·tioned (dísprəpórʃənd, dísprəpóur-ʃənd) adj. marked by lack of proportion

dis·prove (disprú:v) pres. part. **dis·prov·ing** past and past part. **dis·proved** v.t. to prove to be false

dis·put·a·ble (dispjú:təb'l, díspjutəb'l) adj. questionable, open to dispute **dis·pút·a·bly** adv. [fr. L. disputabilis]

dis·pu·tant (dispjú:t'nt) 1. n. someone involved in a fight ‖ someone involved in a controversy 2. adj. disputing

dis·pu·ta·tion (dispjutéiʃən) n. an argument ‖ an exercise in syllogistic debate **dis·pu·tá·tious** adj. [fr. L. disputatio (disputationis)]

dis·pute (dispjú:t) 1. v. pres. part. **dis·put·ing** past and past part. **dis·put·ed** v.i. to quarrel, argue ‖ v.t. to question the truth of ‖ (rhet.) to fight hard for, they disputed every inch of ground 2. n. a quarrel ‖ a controversy beyond (or without) dispute unquestionably in dispute being argued about [M.E. despute fr. O.F.]

dis·qual·i·fi·ca·tion (diskwolifikéiʃən) n. a disqualifying or being disqualified ‖ something which disqualifies

dis·qual·i·fy (diskwólifai) pres. part. **dis·qual·i-fy·ing** past and past part. **dis·qual·i·fied** v.t. to render unfit, age disqualified her for the job ‖ (sport) to judge ineligible to continue a game, or receive a prize, etc., because of infringement of rules ‖ to take a legal right or privilege from

dis·qui·et (diskwáiit) 1. v.t. to make uneasy, worry 2. n. uneasiness, anxiety **dis·qui·e·tude** (diskwáiitu:d, diskwáiitju:d)

dis·qui·si·tion (diskwiziʃən) n. a formal, careful, rather heavy treatment (written or oral) of a subject [fr. L. disquisitio (disquisitionis)]

Dis·rae·li (dizréili:), Benjamin, 1st earl of Beaconsfield (1804–81), British statesman and novelist, prime minister (1868 and 1874–80). Of Jewish family, he was baptized an Anglican (1817). He gained a reputation as a novelist with 'Vivian Grey' (1826), and entered parliament (1837) as a Tory radical, becoming the leader of the 'Young England' movement. This aimed at creating a new Toryism, based on the aristocracy, the queen and the Church, but also protecting the working class. These views are expressed in his novels 'Coningsby' (1844) and 'Sybil' (1845). He opposed Peel over Free Trade (1846) and got the Reform Bill (1867) passed, giving the vote to all householders. Disraeli became prime minister for 10 months (1868) and then for six years led the opposition to Gladstone. As prime minister (1874–80), he was noted for his tact in his dealings with Queen Victoria, whom he proclaimed empress of India (1877). His vigorous foreign policy included purchasing on his own initiative a major interest in the Suez Canal (1875), and attending the Congress of Berlin (1878). Colonial failures in Afghanistan and S. Africa contributed to his electoral defeat (1880)

dis·re·gard (disrigárd) 1. v.t. to pay no heed to, ignore ‖ to treat as not mattering 2. n. a lack of proper regard, disregard for others' feelings ‖ indifference ‖ neglect

dis·re·pair (disripéər) n. the state of needing repair

dis·rep·u·ta·ble (disrépjutəb'l) adj. not respectable ‖ discreditable ‖ in shabby condition

dis·re·pute (disripjú:t) n. bad repute, discredit

dis·re·spect (disrispékt) n. lack of respect, incivility **dis·re·spéct·ful** adj.

dis·robe (disróub) pres. part. **dis·rob·ing** past and past part. **dis·robed** v.i. to take off one's robes ‖ v.t. to remove robes or garments from

dis·rupt (disrʌpt) v.t. to tear apart, shatter, this quarrel disrupted the home ‖ to interrupt or cause to cease entirely, floods disrupted river traffic [fr. L. disrumpere (disruptus)]

dis·rup·tion (disrʌpʃən) n. a disrupting or being disrupted [fr. L. disruptio (disruptionis)]

dis·rup·tive (disrʌptiv) adj. causing disruption, or likely to do so

dis·sat·is·fac·tion (dissætisfækʃən, dissætisfæk-ʃən) n. a being dissatisfied

dis·sat·is·fied (dissætisfaid) adj. not satisfied ‖ discontented

dis·sat·is·fy (dissætisfai) pres. part. **dis·sat·is-fy·ing** past and past part. **dis·sat·is·fied** v.t. to fail to satisfy ‖ to make discontented

dis·sect (disékt, daisékt) v.t. to cut up ‖ to cut open in order to display and examine the parts of (a plant, animal, etc.) ‖ to examine in detail, to dissect an argument **dis·séc·ted** adj. cut in pieces, cut open ‖ (bot.) having laminæ cut into lobes, the incisions reaching nearly to the midrib [fr. L. dissecare (dissectus)]

dis·sec·tion (disékʃən, daisékʃən) n. the act of dissecting a specimen ‖ something that has been dissected ‖ a minute breaking down of a subject for analysis [fr. L. dissectio (dissectionis)]

dis·sei·sin, dis·sei·zin (dissí:zin) n. (law) the wrongful seizure of property from someone else [M.E. disseisne fr. O.F.]

dis·sem·ble (disémb'l) pres. part. **dis·sem·bling** past and past part. **dis·sem·bled** v.t. to conceal, disguise (e.g. thoughts, feelings, intentions) ‖ v.i. to give a false impression, be hypocritical [earlier dissimule fr. O.F. dissimuler, re-formed like RESEMBLE]

dis·sem·i·nate (disémineit) pres. part. **dis·sem-i·nat·ing** past and past part. **dis·sem·i·nat·ed** v.t. to spread abroad, scatter, disperse (wisdom, beliefs etc.) **dis·sem·i·ná·tion, dis·sém·i·na·tor** ns [fr. L. disseminare (disseminatus), to sow seed]

dis·sen·sion (disénʃən) n. a difference of opinions, discord, strife [F.]

dis·sent (disént) 1. v.i. to withhold assent ‖ to be in positive opposition, hold a declared contrary opinion ‖ to refuse to conform to the doctrines or practices of orthodoxy or the established Church **dis·sént·er** n. someone who dissents, esp. a member of a Protestant dissenting body 2. n. disagreement, difference of opinion ‖ nonconformity in religion [fr. L. dissentire, to differ]

dis·sen·tient (disénʃənt) 1. adj. disagreeing (esp. with the official or majority opinion) 2. n. someone who disagrees or declares his dissent [fr. L. dissentiens (dissentientis) fr. dissentire, to differ]

dis·ser·tate (dísərteit) pres. part. **dis·ser·tat·ing** past and past part. **dis·ser·tat·ed** v.i. to hold forth, discourse **dis·ser·tá·tion** n. a formal discourse, written or spoken ‖ a treatise, esp. an original piece of research written for a doctorate [fr. L. disserere (dissertus), to discuss and dissertarere (dissertatus), to debate]

dis·serv·ice (dissó:rvis) n. a well-meant but in fact harmful attempt to be of service

dis·sev·er (dissévər) v.t. to sever ‖ to cut up in pieces ‖ v.i. to divide [A.F. deseverer]

dis·si·dence (dísidəns) n. disagreement [fr. L. dissidentio]

dis·si·dent (dísidənt) 1. adj. disagreeing, esp. contentiously 2. n. someone who is dissident [fr. L. dissidens (aissidentis) fr. dissidere, to sit apart, to disagree]

dis·sil·i·ent (dissíli:ənt) adj. (bot., of capsules of plants) dehiscing explosively [fr. L. dissiliens (dissilientis) fr. dissilire, to leap apart]

dis·sim·i·lar (dissímələr, dissímilər) adj. unlike **dis·sim·i·lar·i·ty** (disiməlǽriti:) pl. **dis·sim·i·lar·i·ties** n. a being dissimilar ‖ an instance of being dissimilar

dis·sim·i·la·tion (disiməléiʃən, disiməléiʃən) n. (phon.) the change of one sound which resembles another in the same word to a sound less like the other (e.g. earlier 'laurer' to 'laurel') ‖ (biol.) katabolism [DIS- + ASSIMILATE]

dis·si·mil·i·tude (dissimílitu:d, dissimílitju:d) n. lack of similarity, unlikeness [fr. L. dissimilitudo]

dis·sim·u·late (dissímjuleit) pres. part. **dis·sim-u·lat·ing** past and past part. **dis·sim·u·lat·ed** v.t. to conceal, disguise (cf. SIMULATE) ‖ v.i. to dissemble, deceive **dis·sim·u·lá·tion, dis·sím·u·la·tor** ns [fr. L. dissimulare (dissimulatus), to dissemble]

dis·si·pate (dísəpeit) pres. part. **dis·si·pat·ing** past and past part. **dis·si·pat·ed** v.t. to break up and drive away, dispel ‖ to waste, squander ‖ v.i. to disperse, vanish **dís·si·pat·ed** adj. dissolute ‖ squandered, wasted ‖ dispersed [fr. L. dissipare (dissipatus), to scatter]

dis·si·pa·tion (disəpéiʃən) n. a dissipating or being dissipated ‖ frivolous amusement ‖ dissolute pleasures [fr. L. dissipatio (dissipationis)]

dis·so·ci·ate (disóuʃi:eit, disóusi:eit) pres. part. **dis·so·ci·at·ing** past and past part. **dis·so·ci·at-ed** v.t. to keep apart in one's mind, separate ‖ (psychol.) to subject to dissociation ‖ (chem., of a compound) to separate into simpler constituents which are capable of recombining under other conditions ‖ v.i. to become dissociated **to dissociate oneself from** to declare that one has no part in (e.g. a political party, an action or a decision) [fr. L. dissociare (dissociatus), to disunite]

dis·so·ci·a·tion (disousi:éiʃən, disouʃi:éiʃən) n. a dissociating or being dissociated ‖ (chem.) the separation (of a compound) into simpler constituents which are capable of recombining under other conditions (cf. DECOMPOSITION). Dissociation is a reversible change, as when molecules dissociate into ions $HCl \rightleftharpoons H^+ + Cl^-$ ‖ (psychol.) a defense mechanism whereby ideas are divorced from the emotions proper to them (e.g. in hysteria) [fr. L. dissociatio (dissociationis)]

dis·so·ci·a·tive (disóuʃi:eitiv, disóuʃətiv) adj. of, relating to or causing dissociation [DISSOCIATE]

dis·sol·u·bil·i·ty (disoljubíliti:) n. the quality of being dissoluble

dis·sol·u·ble (disóljub'l) adj. capable of being dissolved or separated [fr. L. dissolubilis]

dis·so·lute (dísəlu:t) adj. debauched, dissipated [fr. L. dissolvere (dissolutus), to loosen, dissolve]

dis·so·lu·tion (disəlú:ʃən) n. a breaking up of some cooperative enterprise, esp. a partnership ‖ (chem.) solution ‖ the dismissal of an assembly, esp. (Br.) the ending of a parliament before a general election ‖ a passing away, disappearance, the dissolution of the body after death ‖ (finance) the liquidation of a business [F. or fr. L. dissolutio (dissolutionis)]

dis·solve (dizólv) 1. v. pres. part. **dis·solv·ing** past and past part. **dis·solved** v.t. to cause to pass into a solution ‖ to put an end to, to dissolve a partnership ‖ to disperse, to dissolve parliament ‖ v.i. to pass into solution ‖ (fig., with 'into') to break, melt, to dissolve into tears ‖ (movies, of a sequence) to fade gradually (into another shot) 2. n. (movies) the fading of one shot into another **dis·sól·vent** 1. adj. capable of dissolving something 2. n. a dissolving agent, a solvent [fr. L. dissolvere, to loosen]

dis·so·nance (dísənəns) n. (mus.) discord ‖ disagreement ‖ inconsistency between words and actions, or words and beliefs, or between beliefs [fr. L. dissonantia]

dis·so·nant (dísənənt) adj. discordant, harsh in sound ‖ incongruous [F. or fr. L. dissonans (dissonantis) fr. dissonare, to be discordant]

dispirit *DISPIRIT

dis·suade (diswéid) pres. part. **dis·suad·ing** past and past part. **dis·suad·ed** v.t. to change the intention of (a person) by persuasion **dis·sua·sion** (diswéiʒən) n. **dis·sua·sive** (diswéisiv) adj. [fr. L. dissuadere]

dissyllabic *DISYLLABIC

dissyllable *DISYLLABLE

dis·sym·met·ri·cal (dissimétrik'l, dissimétrik'l) adj. lacking symmetry

dis·sym·me·try (disímitri:, dissímitri:) n. absence of symmetry

dis·taff (dístæf, dístɑf) 1. n. a cleft staff or stick on which wool or flax is wound for spinning by hand ‖ the corresponding part of a spinning wheel 2. adj. (rhet.) relating to a woman or women, female, the distaff side of the family [O.E. distæf]

dis·tal (dístəl) adj. (biol., of bristles etc.) standing far apart, distant ‖ (anat., of the end of any structure) farthest from the middle line of the organism or from the point of attachment (opp. PROXIMAL) [fr. DISTANT (like 'proximal')]

dis·tance (dístəns) 1. n. an interval in space, the shops are a short distance away ‖ the remoter part of a view ‖ an interval of time, things look different at a distance of 10 years ‖ reserve, aloofness ‖ (sports) the specified length of a race, a distance of five furlongs **no distance** quite near **the middle distance** between the foreground and the background **to keep one's distance** to keep a certain interval away (e.g. of vehicles in a convoy) ‖ to remain aloof **within walking distance** near enough to walk to 2. v.t. pres. part. **dis·tanc·ing** past and past part. **dis·tanced** to put or maintain at a distance ‖ to outstrip [O.F.]

dis·tant (dístənt) adj. far away ‖ remote in time, a distant recollection ‖ far removed in relationship, likeness etc., a distant cousin, a distant resemblance ‖ standoffish, reserved, aloof, a distant manner [F.]

dis·taste (distéist) n. dislike ‖ aversion **dis·táste·ful** adj. disagreeable to the taste ‖ causing aversion

dis·tem·per (distémpər) n. a contagious and sometimes fatal disease of animals esp. common among young dogs

distemper 1. n. a preparation made from coloring and size etc., soluble in water, for painting inside walls, mural decoration etc. **2.** v.t. to paint with this mixture [fr. O.F. destemprer, to soak]

dis·tend (disténd) v.t. to cause to swell through internal pressure ‖ to cause to be larger than is normal, reasonable etc., distended profits ‖ to cause to appear more important than is really the case v.i. to swell through internal pressure [fr. L. distendere]

dis·ten·si·ble (disténsəb'l) adj. able to be distended [fr. L. distendere (distensus)]

dis·ten·tion (disténʃən) n. a distending or being distended [F.]

dis·tich (dístik) n. two lines of verse, connected, and usually complete in sense, a couplet [fr. L. distichon fr. Gk]

dis·ti·chous (dístikəs) adj. (bot., of alternate leaves) so arranged that the first is directly below the third [fr. L. distichus, two-ranked fr. Gk]

dis·till, dis·til (distíl) pres. part. **dis·till·ing, dis·til·ling** past and past part. **dis·tilled** v.i. (of a liquid or solid) to undergo a process of evaporation and condensation for purification or fractionation ‖ v.t. to cause to undergo this process‖ to extract the pure essence of (something) **dis·til·late** (dístəlit, dístəleit, distílit) n. the product of distillation [fr. L. distillare, to fall down in drops]

dis·til·la·tion (distəléiʃən) n. a distilling or being distilled [fr. L. distillatio (distillationis)]

dis·till·er (distílər) n. someone who makes spirits by distillation

dis·till·er·y (distíləri:) pl. **dis·till·er·ies** n. a building where spirits are manufactured by distilling (cf. BREWERY)

dis·tinct (distíŋkt) adj. clear, plain, distinct enough to read ‖ marked, definite, a distinct difference between the twins ‖ separate, individual, serving to distinguish, distinct markings [fr. L. distinguere (distinctus), to distinguish]

dis·tinc·tion (distíŋkʃən) n. the making of a difference, discrimination ‖ a difference so made ‖ a being different ‖ modest fame, a poet of distinction ‖ breeding or eminence ‖ a mark of honor, a decoration or award [F.]

dis·tinc·tive (distíŋktiv) adj. distinguishing, marking a difference [fr. L. distinguere (distinctus), to distinguish]

dis·tin·guish (distíŋgwiʃ) v.t. to recognize (something) as distinct from other things ‖ to tell the difference between, can you distinguish one twin from the other? ‖ to make distinct, characterize ‖ to make out, perceive, he heard voices but couldn't distinguish the words ‖ to win honor for (oneself etc.) ‖ v.i. to draw distinctions, discriminate ‖ to point out a difference (esp. in syllogistic disputation) **dis·tín·guish·a·ble** adj. **dis·tín·guished** adj. famous, eminent ‖ showing distinction, a distinguished nose [fr. F. distinguer]

dis·tort (distórt) v.t. to twist out of shape ‖ to give a false significance to, misrepresent, to distort facts **dis·tór·tion** n. a distorting or being distorted ‖ (radio) the alteration of wave form during transmission or reception ‖ (optics) the lens aberration due to the variation of magnification with distance from the lens axis. It results in a sharp but dimensionally inaccurate image **dis·tór·tion·al** adj. [fr. L. distorquere (distortus), to twist to one side]

dis·tract (distrǽkt) v.t. to divert (attention) ‖ to divert the attention of ‖ to disturb, confuse ‖ to bewilder (e.g. with conflicting advice) ‖ to drive nearly mad, distracted with grief [fr. L. distrahere (distractus), to draw apart]

dis·tract·er or **dis·tract·or** (distrǽktər) n. an incorrect option in a multiple-choice test

dis·trac·tion (distrǽkʃən) n. a distracting or being distracted ‖ an interest that provides relaxation ‖ a diversion, interruption ‖ something which prevents concentration ‖ perplexity, bewilderment ‖ frenzy, near madness [fr. L. distractio (distractionis), a drawing apart]

dis·train (distréin) v.i. (law) to seize a person's goods so as to compel him to pay a debt ‖ v.t. (law) to seize and sell (a person's goods) in lieu of receiving payment of a debt ‖ to seize the goods of (someone) in this way **dis·train·ee** (distreiní:) n. someone whose goods are distrained **dis·tráin·er, dis·tráin·or** n. someone who distrains **dis·tráint** n. the action of distraining [fr. O.F. destreindre, to constrain]

dis·traught (distrót) adj. almost crazy with anxiety etc., frantic [var. of obs. adj. distract, distracted]

dis·tress (distrés) n. considerable mental or physical discomfort or pain ‖ acute financial hardship ‖ being in great difficulty or danger ‖ (law) the act of distraining ‖ (law) that which is seized in distraining [O.F. destresse]

distress v.t. to cause considerable mental or physical discomfort or pain [O. F. destresser]

dis·trib·ute (distríbju:t) pres. part. **dis·trib·ut·ing** past and past part. **dis·trib·ut·ed** v.t. to deal out, divide out ‖ to spread, scatter, put at different places ‖ (bot., used passively) to occur geographically ‖ to put (esp. statistical information) into groups or classes ‖ (logic) to use (a term) to include every individual to which the term applies ‖ (printing) to break up (composed type) and put it back into its compartments, or set it aside for melting down and recasting [fr. L. distribuere (distributus), to allot]

dis·tri·bu·tion (distrəbjú:ʃən) n. a distributing or being distributed ‖ the marketing of industrial products ‖ (biol.) the geographical range of an organism or group ‖ a classification or arrangement (esp. of statistical information) ‖ concentration or diffusion, distribution of wealth ‖ (logic) the application of a term to all the individuals within it ‖ (printing) the breaking up of type that has been composed and the return of it to the case or the setting aside of it for melting ‖ (statistics) the number of values at each variable ‖ the probability of any value at any interval ‖ the interval for any range of values **dis·tri·bú·tion·al** adj. [F.]

dis·trib·u·tive (distríbjutiv) 1. adj. of or to do with distribution ‖ (of a word) referring to each and every individual of a group rather than to the group itself **2.** n. a word (e.g. 'each', 'every') referring to individuals of a group separately [F. distributif]

distributive education schooling integrated with an on-the-job training in distribution industries (abbr. D&E)

dis·trib·u·tor (distríbjutər) n. someone who distributes ‖ an agent who markets goods ‖ a device which distributes electric power to the plugs of an internal-combustion engine

dis·trict (dístrikt) 1. n. a region ‖ a political or geographical division of a city, county, state etc. marked off for administrative or other purposes **2.** v.t. to divide into districts [F.]

district attorney (Am.) the prosecutor for a specified district, appointed in federal districts by the president but usually elected in counties

district heating heating from a single community source

District of Columbia (abbr. D.C.) a federal district and seat of the national government of the U.S.A., coextensive with the city of Washington (area 69 sq. miles, pop. 637,681). The land was ceded in 1790 by Maryland

dis·trust (distrÁst) 1. n. a lack of trust **2.** v.t. to have no trust in ‖ to regard with suspicion **dis·trúst·ful**

dis·turb (distə́:rb) v.t. to upset the peace of, bother ‖ to worry ‖ to move out of place [M.E. destorben fr. O.F.]

dis·turb·ance (distə́:rbəns) n. a disturbing or being disturbed ‖ public disorder, tumult ‖ (law) an interfering with rights or property [O.F. destorbance]

di·sul·fate, Br. di·sul·phate (daisÁlfeit) n. a compound containing two sulfate groups

di·sul·fide, Br. di·sul·phide (daisÁlfaid) n. a compound with two atoms of sulfur combined with another element or radical

di·sul·fi·ram [$C_{10}H_{20}N_2S_4$] (daisÁlfərəm) n. (pharm.) drug used in alcoholism therapy that creates sensitivity to alcohol and produces extreme discomfort if alcohol is ingested; marketed as Antabuse

di·sul·fo·ton [$C_8H_{19}O_2PS_3$] (daisÁlfətɒn) n. organophosphorous pesticide used to destroy mites and insects on plants

dis·un·ion (disjú:njən) n. lack of unity, disagreement ‖ separation

dis·u·nite (disju:náit) pres. part. **dis·u·nit·ing** past and past part. **dis·u·nit·ed** v.t. to destroy the harmony or solidarity of (a number of people) ‖ v.i. to fall apart, separate **dis·u·ni·ty** (disjú:niti:) pl. **dis·u·ni·ties** n.

dis·use (disjú:s) n. the state of being no longer used, to fall into disuse

di·syl·lab·ic, dis·syl·lab·ic (disilǽbik, daisilǽbik) adj. having two syllables

di·syl·la·ble, dis·syl·la·ble (disíləb'l, daisíləb'l) n. a word or foot of two syllables [fr. F. dissyllabe fr. L. fr. Gk]

ditch (ditʃ) 1. n. a narrow, shallow trench, esp. for drainage or irrigation **2.** v.i. to make or repair ditches ‖ v.t. to provide with a ditch or ditches ‖ to drive (a vehicle) into a ditch ‖ (pop.) to abandon, get rid of [O.E. díc]

ditch·wa·ter (dítʃwɒtər, dítʃwɔtər) n. stagnant water found in ditches

dith·er (díðər) 1. n. a confused, indecisive state of mind **2.** v.i. to be in a confused state of indecision [var. of obs. didder, to tremble, imit]

dith·y·ramb (díθiræmb, díθiræm) n. a Greek hymn in honor of Bacchus ‖ a poem of a similar character ‖ (rhet.) any wildly rapturous speech or writing **dith·y·rám·bic** adj. and n. [fr. L. dithyrambus fr. Gk]

dit·ta·ny (dít'ni:) pl. **dit·ta·nies** n. fraxinella [M.E. ditane, detany fr. O.F. fr. L. fr. Gk]

dit·to (dítou) 1. pl. **dit·tos** n. (abbr. do.) the same thing as above or as aforesaid (in lists etc., used to avoid repetition) ‖ a ditto mark, two small marks (") to indicate repetition, tabulated under the repeated word **2.** adv. in the same way, as before, likewise [Ital. ditto, detto, said, aforesaid]

dit·tog·ra·phy (ditógrəfi:) n. (paleography) the unintentional repetition of a symbol, letter, syllable or word by a copyist [fr. Gk dittos, twofold+-graphie, writing]

dit·ty (díti:) pl. **dit·ties** n. a short, very simple song or poem [M.E. dite fr. O.F.]

ditty bag a bag used by sailors for odds and ends, esp. needle and thread [etym. doubtful]

Di·u (dí:u:) *GOA

di·u·ret·ic (daijurétik) 1. adj. promoting the excretion of urine **2.** n. a food, medicine etc. having this property [fr. L. diureticus fr. Gk]

di·ur·nal (daié:rn'l) adj. (astron.) completed once in one day ‖ daily, diurnal routine ‖ (zool.) active mainly in the daytime (cf. NOCTURNAL) [fr. L. diurnalis]

di·u·ron [$C_9H_{10}Cl_2N_2O$] (dáijərən) n. a nonbiodegradable weed killer

di·va (dí:və) pl. **di·vas, di·ve** (dí:ve) n. a prima donna, any celebrated woman operatic singer [Ital.]

di·va·gate (dáivəgeit) pres. part. **di·va·gat·ing**, past and past part. **di·va·gat·ed** v.i. to ramble, digress **di·va·gá·tion** n. [fr. L. divagari (divagatus), to wander about]

di·va·lent (daivéilənt) adj. (chem.) having a valency of two (cf. BIVALENT) [fr. DI-+ L. valens (valentis) fr. valere, to be worth]

di·van (divǽn, divǽn, dáivæn) n. a long low couch without ends, generally usable as a bed ‖ an Oriental council of state ‖ an Oriental court of justice ‖ a collection of Persian or Arabic poems by a single author [Pers. dēvān, diwān, brochure, account book, customhouse etc.]

di·var·i·cate (daivǽrikeit, divǽrikeit) pres. part. **di·var·i·cat·ing** past and past part. **di·var·i·cat·ed** 1. v.i. (biol.) to divide into two branches, fork ‖ to diverge **2.** adj. (daivǽrikit, daivǽrikeit, divǽrikit, divǽrikeit) (biol.) widely diverging **di·var·i·cá·tion** n. [fr. L. divaricare (divaricatus)]

dive (daiv) 1. pres. part. **div·ing** past **dived, dove** (douv) past part. **dived** v.i. to plunge headfirst into water, esp. with controlled grace ‖ (of a submarine, water bird etc.) to go underwater ‖ (of an airplane, bird of prey etc.) to plunge down steeply through the air ‖ to dart quickly, esp. so as to hide or flee ‖ (with 'into') to plunge one's hand, she dived into her handbag and produced a tract ‖ to immerse oneself (e.g. in a subject) **2.** n. a diving into water ‖ any of the graceful classical figures of the art of diving ‖ a sudden swift plunge of the body ‖ (of a submarine or aircraft) a plunging ‖ (pop.) a low-class establishment for drinking, gambling etc. [O.E. dūfan, to sink and dýfan, to immerse]

dive-bomb (dáivbɒm) v.t. to attack by dive bomber

dive bomber an airplane designed to dive sharply at its target and bomb from close quarters before coming out of the dive

div·er (dáivər) n. someone who dives, esp. for pearls || someone who works below water in a diving bell or diving suit to examine wrecks etc. || a member of *Colymbus*, fam. *Colymbidae*, a genus of fish-eating seabirds confined to northern latitudes. They are esp. adept at diving and swimming|| a bird of allied genera, e.g. grebe, penguin

di·verge (daivə́:rdʒ, divə́:rdʒ) pres. part. **di·verg·ing** past and past part. **di·verged** v.i. to go in branching directions, *our paths diverge here* || (with 'from') to turn aside, *to diverge from the truth* || to deviate from the normal, differ **di·vér·gence** n. **di·vér·gen·cy** pl. **di·vér·gen·cies** n. **di·vér·gent** adj. diverging || (of a lens) causing a change in the direction of rays away from a common direction or point || (*math.*, of a series) not tending toward a finite limit as the number of terms tends toward infinity [fr. Mod. L. *divergere*, to bend apart]

di·verg·er (dạivə́:rdʒər) n. one capable of thinking imaginatively beyond the ordinary *Cf* CONVERGER; LATERAL THINKING; VERTICAL THINKING

di·vers (dáivərz) adj. (*archaic*) several || (*archaic*) sundry [M.E. *divers, diverse* fr. O.F.]

di·verse (divə́:rs, daivə́:rs, dáivə·rs) adj. different, unlike in character or qualities || various [M.E. *divers, diverse* fr. O.F. (influenced by 'diversity')]

di·ver·si·fi·ca·tion (divə·rsifikéiʃən, daivə·rsifikéiʃən) n. a diversifying or being diversified

di·ver·si·fy (divə́:rsifai, daivə́:rsifai) pres. part. **di·ver·si·fy·ing** past and past part. **di·ver·si·fied** v.t. to make varied [O.F. *diversifier*]

di·ver·sion (divə́:rʒən, divə́:rʃən, daivə́:rʒən, daivə́:rʃən) n. a turning aside, deviating || something which brings pleasant mental distraction || (*mil.*) a ruse to divert the attention of an enemy **di·ver·sion·ar·y** (divə́:rʒəneri:, divə́:rʃəneri:, daivə́:rʒəneri:, daivə́:rʃəneri:) adj. (*mil.*) intended to create a diversion [fr. M.L. *diversio diversionis*)]

di·ver·si·ty (divə́:rsiti:, daivə́:rsiti:) pl. **di·ver·si·ties** n. the state or quality of being diverse || an instance of this || variety [O.F. *diverseté, diversité*]

di·vert (daivə́:rt, divə́:rt) v.t. to turn aside, *to divert traffic* || to distract, *to divert someone's attention* || to amuse, entertain **di·vért·ing** adj. [O.F. *divertir*]

di·ver·tic·u·lum (dạivərtíkjuləm) pl. **di·ver·tic·u·la** (dạivərtíkjulə) n. (*anat., zool.*) an abnormal growth or sac branching off from a hollow organ, or a blind tube branching from a tube or cavity [L.=a bypath]

di·ver·tisse·ment (divə́:rtismənt) n. an entertainment or diversion || a piece of light instrumental music || a short interlude of dancing or singing etc. between the acts of a play or in the course of it || a short ballet, usually of miscellaneous virtuoso dances [F.]

di·vest (divést, daivést) v.t. to deprive (e.g. of honors) || to strip (of clothing) **di·ves·ti·ture** (divéstitʃər, daivéstitʃər), **di·vést·ment** ns [fr. M.L. *disvestire*, to unclothe]

di·vide (diváid) 1. v. pres. part. **di·vid·ing** past and past part. **di·vid·ed** v.t. to separate, *to divide a road into four traffic lanes* || to deal out, share, *divide the work between you* || to put into separate groups || to cause a disagreement between || to mark out, graduate || (*math.*) to find out how many times one number is contained in (another), *divide 100 by 10* || v.i. to do mathematical division || (*math.*, of one number) to be contained a specified number of times in another number, *5 divides into 20 four times* || to separate, branch || (*Br.*) to separate into two groups for voting 2. n. a watershed || a line of division **di·vid·ed** adj. [fr. L. *dividere*]

div·i·dend (dívidend) n. the interest or share of profits payable to shareholders on stock or bonds || the share due to creditors of an insolvent estate || the individual's share of a sum divided || (*math.*) the number to be divided by another (cf. DIVISOR) || a bonus or share of surplus given to a policyholder by an insurance company [F. *dividende*]

di·vid·ers (diváidərz) pl. n. measuring compasses (for dividing lines or angles)

div·i·di·vi (dívi:dívi:) n. the fruit of *Calesalpinia coriaria*, fam. *Papilionaceae*, a small tropical American tree, with short curled pods containing up to 50% tannin. It gives the yellowish tone to leather || the tree itself [Carib.]

div·i·na·tion (dívənéiʃən) n. a divining or foretelling of the future or the unknown by supernatural means || guessing by intuition [O.F.]

di·vine (diváin) 1. adj. of God or a god, *divine wisdom* || addressed to God, *divine worship* || coming from God, *divine grace* || having the nature of a god, *Caligula had himself declared divine* || (*pop.*) superlatively good or beautiful, *divine music* 2. n. a theologian || a priest or clergyman 3. v. pres. part. **di·vin·ing** past and past part. **di·vined** v.t. to guess || to foretell || v.i. to detect the presence of water or metals underground by means of a forked,esp. hazel,twig or rods || to practice divination **di·vín·er** n. [M.E. *devine, divine* fr. O.F. and F. *deviner*]

divine right the political theory that a king governs under unlimited authority given directly by God, to whom alone he is responsible

diving bell a diving apparatus, open at the bottom. It is lowered into the water and a supply of compressed air controls the water level, enabling men to work in the free space

diving suit a pressurized, watertight garment worn by divers

divining rod a forked stick, usually of hazel, used by diviners in looking for underground water, oil, metals etc.

di·vin·i·ty (divíniti:) pl. **di·vin·i·ties** n. the quality of being divine || a god || theology || the study in schools etc. of the Bible and of Church doctrine **the Di·vin·i·ty** God [M.E. *devinite, divinite* fr. O.F.]

divinity circuit binding (*Am.=Br.* yapp) a style of bookbinding, used esp. for leatherbound Bibles, where the cover projects at the edges and is bent to form protective flaps

di·vis·i·bil·i·ty (divizəbíliti:) n. the quality of being divisible

di·vis·i·ble (divízəb'l) adj. capable of being divided || (*math.*) capable of being divided without a remainder **di·vís·i·bly** adv. [fr. L. *divisibilis*]

di·vi·sion (divíʒən) n. a dividing or being divided || a distribution, *a division of tasks* || a sharing, *a division of labor* || something which divides || a section of a larger group || (*math.*) the process of finding out how many times one number is contained in another || lack of harmony, disagreement || the separation of the members of a debating chamber for voting || (*mil.*) a section of a corps, grouping a number of regiments || a special-purpose formation, *the accounting division* **di·vi·sion·al** adj. [M.E. *devisioun, divisioun* fr. O.F.]

division sign the symbol ÷ placed between two numerical expressions: the first is to be divided by the second

di·vi·sor (diváizər) n. (*math.*) the number by which another (*DIVIDEND) is divided [L.]

di·vorce (divórs, divóurs) n. a legal dissolution of marriage || any marked or total separation, *a divorce between ideas and practice* [F.]

divorce pres. part. **di·vorc·ing** past and past part. **di·vorced** v.t. to repudiate (one's wife or husband) by divorce || to end a marriage between (two people) legally by divorce || to sever, separate || v.i. (of a couple) to obtain a divorce

di·vor·cee (divɔrséi, divourséi, divɔ́rsi:, divóursi:) n. a divorced person, esp. a divorced woman **di·vórce·ment** n. [F. *aivorcer*]

div·ot (dívət) n. (*golf*) a piece of turf accidentally sliced out in making a stroke [etym. doubtful]

div·ul·ga·tion (dạivəlgéiʃən, dịvəlgéiʃən) n. a divulging || the thing divulged

di·vulge (daiváldʒ, diváldʒ) pres. part. **di·vulg·ing** past and past part. **di·vulged** v.t. to make known, reveal **di·vúlge·ment, di·vúl·gence** ns [fr. L. *divulgare*, to publish]

di·vul·sion (daivá29lʃən, divá29lʃən) n. (*med.*) a tearing away, rending apart [F. or fr. L. *divulsio* (*divulsionis*)]

di·wan (diwán, diwɔ́n) n. a divan (collection of Persian or Arabic poems) || an Oriental council of state || an Oriental court of justice [Pers.]

Dix (diks), Dorothea (1802–87), U.S. reformer. She crusaded to help improve conditions for the mentally insane and to establish mental hospitals. She also served as head of nurses for the Union army during the Civil War

Dix·i·can (díksi:kən) n. a southern Republican

Dix·ie (díksi:) 1. adj. relating to the Southern states of the U.S.A. 2. n. the Southern states of the U.S.A. || Dixieland jazz [perh. fr. *Dixie*, pop. name for a 10-dollar bill ('dix' was printed on it) issued in Louisiana]

Dix·ie·crat·ic party (dịksi:krǽtik) a faction of the U.S. Democratic party that supported Strom Thurmond and Southern interests in the presidential election of 1948

dix·ie, dix·y (díksi:) pl. **dix·ies** n. (Br., *mil.*) a large iron cooking pot or tea urn [fr. Hind. *degachi*]

Dix·ie·land (díksi:lænd) n. the Southern states of the U.S.A. || the classic jazz style originating in New Orleans before 1914

Dix·i·fi·ca·tion (diksifikéiʃən) n. the process of creating an antediluvian image of the South, e.g., with magnolias, plantations, mockingbirds, etc.

Dix·on (díksən), Roland Burrage (1875–1934), U.S. cultural anthropologist. He organized one of the largest libraries in anthropology, at Harvard University's Peabody museum

dixy *DIXIE

D.I.Y. (*Br. abbr.*) do-it-yourself

diz·zi·ly (dízili:) adv. in a dizzy way || in a dizzying way

diz·zi·ness (dízi:nis) n. the state of being dizzy

diz·zy (dízi:) 1. adj. comp. **diz·zi·er** superl. **diz·zi·est** experiencing a sensation of vertigo || mentally confused || such as to cause vertigo or mental turmoil, *dizzy prospects of wealth* 2. v.t. pres. part. **diz·zy·ing** past and past part. **diz·zied** to make dizzy [O.E. *dysig*, foolish]

Dja·ja·pu·ra, Jajapura (dʒạjapúərə) (formerly Sukarnapura) the capital, chief port and trade center (pop. 45,786) of Irian Barat, Indonesia. During the 2nd world war it served as a major Japanese air base until captured (1944) by U.S. forces in the first liberation of Japanese-held territory in the East Indies. It subsequently became the headquarters of Gen. Douglas MacArthur in the final period of the war

Dja·kar·ta, Ja·kar·ta (dʒəkártə) (formerly Batavia) the capital (pop. with agglom. 4,576,009) of Indonesia, on Djakarta Bay, Java, a commercial and cultural center and port: textiles, leather and rubber goods, machinery, chemicals, shipbuilding

Djam·bi (dʒámbi:) a province of Indonesia in S.E. Sumatra

Djer·ba (dʒérbə) an island (area 198 sq. miles, pop. 60,000) off S. Tunisia, irrigated by thousands of springs, producing olives, dates, fruit and vegetables. It was the lotus-eater's isle of Greek myth

djibbah *JIBBAH

Djibouti (dʒibú:ti:) (formerly Territory of the Afars and of the Issas and Côte française des Somalis or French Somaliland), a French territory (area 8,494 sq. miles, pop. 81,000) in N.E. Africa. Capital: Djibouti. People: 37% Danakil, 29% Somali, with smaller European and Arab minorities. Religion: Moslem and local religions. Inland are the Gonda Mtns, rising to 5,500 ft. Rainfall: 2–10 ins. Temperatures (F.): Oct.–May 77°–95°, May–Oct. up to 113°. The people are mainly nomadic herdsmen. The country's economy depends on the use of Djibouti as a reshipment base: it has been a free port since 1949. Exports (from Ethiopia): hides, cattle, coffee. Imports: cotton goods, sugar, cement, flour. Monetary unit: Djibouti franc. A French settlement was established (1862) and complete possession formalized as French Somaliland (1885). The colony was given overseas territorial status (1946), which it voted to retain (1958). It became independent in 1977. Hassan Gouled Aption was elected president in June of that year || its capital and main port (pop. 150,000) at the entrance to the Red Sea on the Gulf of Aden, terminus of the only railroad into Ethiopia

D layer (*geophys.*) layer of ionized air directly above earth, existing in D region during the daytime, from which radio waves of 1–100 MHz are reflected *Cf* D REGION

DME-COTAR a single-site navigation system that can provide a trajectory course of a missile from a single ground station using distance measuring equipment and COTAR

DMM (*acronym*) digital multimeter

DMSO (*acronym*) dimethylsulfoxide

DMT (*acronym*) dimethyltryptamine

DMZ (*acronym*) demilitarized zone

DNA *DEOXYRIBONUCLEIC ACID

DNA polymerase (*genetics*) an enzyme that stimulates DNA (deoxyribonucleic acid nucleotides), which is the carrier of the genetic code *Cf* RNA POLYMERASE

DN-ase or DNA-ase (*genetics*) an enzyme that converts DNA to nucleotides by hydrolosis

DNF (*acronym*) did not finish

Dnie·per (ní:pər) a river of the U.S.S.R., flowing 1,400 miles from the Valdai hills through Byelorussia and the Ukraine to the Black Sea. It feeds the immense Dnieprostroy hydroelectric plant

Dnie·pro·dzer·zhinsk (dnjeprɔdzərʒíːɲsk) a town (pop. 257,000) in the Ukraine, U.S.S.R., on the Dnieper: chemical and electrometallurgical industries

Dnie·pro·pe·trovsk (dnjeprɔpətrɔ́fsk) a city (pop. 1,066,000) of the Ukraine, U.S.S.R., on the Dnieper: iron and steel

Dnies·ter (níːstər) a river of the U.S.S.R. rising in the Carpathians and flowing 850 miles to the Black Sea

D notice (Br.) request by British government to newspapers that certain information not be published in the national interest

do (duː) 1. v. 1st and 2nd pers. sing. pres. do 3rd pers. sing. pres. does (dʌz) 1st, 2nd and 3rd pers. pl. pres. do pres. part. do·ing past did (did) past part. done (dʌn) v.t. to perform (an action or activity), to do housework ‖ to work at, have as occupation, to do dressmaking for a living ‖ to deal with in required fashion, to do one's hair ‖ to accomplish, finish, when day is done ‖ to have a mechanical performance of, it does 25 miles to the gallon ‖ to cook, do it in the oven ‖ to render, ruin, now you've done it (=spoiled things) ‖ to translate, to do Horace into English verse ‖ v.i. to act, behave, do as I do ‖ to progress, she is doing nicely ‖ to be suitable ‖ to suffice ‖ used as a substitute verb to avoid repetition, the others don't see it as you do ‖ used as an auxiliary verb in negation, you didn't hurt him, in interrogation, did you see him?, in emphasis, he did look foolish, in urgent imperatives, do stop that noise, and in inversions, little do you know it doesn't do to it is unwise to to do away with to get rid of ‖ to kill to do battle to fight to do by to behave towards to do down (Br., pop.) to cheat, swindle to do duty as to serve as to do for (Br.) to domestic work for ‖ (Br.) to ruin (e.g. someone's chances) to do in (pop.) to kill ‖ (pop.) to exhaust, to be really done in to do one's best (utmost etc.) to put forth one's best efforts to do one's bit to make one's contribution to do out (Br.) to clean out to do (someone) out of (something) to diddle (someone) so that he loses (something) to do over to do again ‖ to repaint to do something to to affect to do time (or a specified period) to be in prison (or serve a specified sentence) to do up to fasten ‖ to refurbish ‖ to wrap up to do well to prosper, flourish ‖ (with 'to') to be wise, you would do well to get out of here to do with (pop.) to make use of ‖ (Br.) to tolerate, I can't do with her silliness to do without to manage without to do wonders to produce wonderful results 2. pl. do's, dos n. (Br., pop.) a celebration, entertainment ‖ (pl., Br., pop.) shares, fair do's ‖ a rule to follow, do's and don'ts ‖ (Br., pop.) a swindle [O.E. dōn]

do, Br. also **doh** (dou) pl. **dos, dohs** n. (mus.) the note C in the fixed-do system of solmization ‖ the first note of any diatonic scale in movable-do solmization

do·a·ble (dúːəb'l) adj. able to be done, practicable

doat *DOTE

dob·bin (dóbin) n. (old-fash.) a docile, plodding draft horse [dim. of proper name Dob, var. of Rob, Robin]

Do·ber·man pin·scher (dóubərmənpíntʃər) n. a strong, smooth-coated terrier of a breed much used as watchdogs [after Ludwig Dobermann, 19th-c. German dog-breeder]

Do·bru·ja (dóubruːdʒə) a region in E. Rumania between the Black Sea and the Danube, a fertile, loess-covered plateau, with a continental climate, growing wheat and barley ‖ a province of Rumania, 1913–40. Southern Dobruja was ceded to Bulgaria (1940)

do·bu·ta·mine [C₁₈H₂₃NO₃] (doubjúːtəmiːn) n. (pharm.) synthetic catecholamine used as a cardiac stimulant; marketed as Dobutrex

do·cent (dousént) n. (in some U.S. colleges and universities) a teacher or lecturer not on the regular faculty **do·cént·ship** n. [G.=teacher]

Do·ce·tism (dousíːtizəm) n. a feature of several early Christian heresies which proceeded from dualistic thought to attribute to the person of Christ only an apparent manhood and an illusory suffering [fr. M. L. Docetae, name of these heretics fr. Gk]

doc·ile (dós'l, Br. dóusail) adj. tractable, amenable, easy to manage **do·cil·i·ty** (dosíliti:, Br. dousíliti) n. [F.]

dock (dok) n. a member of Rumex, fam. Polygonaceae, a genus of coarse weeds with large leaves and long roots ‖ any of several other weeds, e.g. coltsfoot and burdock [O.E. docce]

dock 1. n. the solid part of an animal's tail as distinct from the hair ‖ the part of a tail left after cutting ‖ the crupper of a saddle 2. v.t. to cut short (an animal's tail) ‖ to deduct (a sum of money) from someone's wages ‖ to deduct a sum of money from (someone's wages) ‖ to deduct from the wages of (someone) [etym. doubtful]

dock 1. n. an enclosure or artificial basin in which ships may be loaded, unloaded, repaired etc. ‖ (Br.) a platform enclosure in which a railroad line terminates ‖ (pl.) a number of such enclosures with offices, sheds, wharves etc. ‖ a pier 2. v.t. to bring or receive (a ship) into dock ‖ v.i. to come into dock [etym. doubtful]

dock n. the enclosure in court for the accused [perh. Flem. dok, docke, hutch, pen]

dock·age (dókidʒ) n. docking facilities ‖ dock charges ‖ the docking of ships

dock brief (Br.) a brief undertaken gratis by a barrister chosen from those in court by an offender in the dock unable to pay for his defense

dock dues dock charges, dockage

dock·er (dókər) n. a man who works as a dockyard laborer

dock·et (dókit) 1. n. a brief statement on a letter or document of what it contains ‖ (law.) a list register of cases in court ‖ an agenda of business to be dealt with at a meeting ‖ (Br.) a document attached or referring to goods, giving details or instructions about them, a label ‖ (Br.) a document used by a foreman for giving instructions about a job and for registering details of completion ‖ (Br.) a warrant certifying that customs dues have been paid 2. v.t. to label ‖ to abstract and enter (a legal judgment) in the register ‖ to attach a docket to (goods etc.) ‖ to write on (a letter or document) a summary of its contents [origin unknown]

dock·mas·ter (dókmæstər, dókmɑstər) n. the man in charge of a dockyard

dock·yard (dókjɑrd) n. an enclosure containing the docks and equipment for repairing and building ships

doc·tor (dóktər) 1. n. a person qualified to practice medicine ‖ (abbr. Dr) the title of a medical practitioner ‖ (abbr. Dr) the title of the holder of the highest university degree, a Doctor of Divinity ‖ a means (e.g. a metal blade or jet of air) for spreading or controlling a coating 2. v.t. to give first aid to ‖ to adulterate, doctored drink ‖ to alter so as to improve ‖ to alter so as to falsify ‖ (Br., pop.) to castrate ‖ to patch up (machinery etc.) ‖ v.i. to practice medicine **doc·tor·al** adj. **doc·tor·ate** (dóktərit) n. the degree or rank of doctor **doc·to·ri·al** (doktóːriːəl, doktóuriːəl) adj. [O.F.]

Doctorow (dóktərou), E(dgar) L(awrence) (1931–), U.S. writer, who successfully incorporates history into his fiction. His novels include 'The Book of Daniel' (1971), 'Ragtime' (1975), 'Loon Lake' (1980), and 'World's Fair' (1985)

doc·tri·naire (doktrinéər) 1. n. someone apt to apply theories without proper grasp of practical considerations 2. adj. dogmatic, theoretic and unpractical [F.]

doc·tri·nal (dóktrin'l, doktráin'l) adj. of or relating to doctrine [perh. fr. L.L. doctrinalis]

doc·tri·nar·i·an (doktrinéəriːən) n. and adj. doctrinaire

doc·trine (dóktrin) n. the tenets of a literary or philosophical school or of a political or economic system, or the dogma of a religion [F.]

Doctrine of the Faith, Sacred Congregation for the *INQUISITION

doc·u·dram·a (dókjuːdrɑmə) n. motion picture dramatizing a real-life situation

doc·u·ment 1. (dókjumənt) n. an official paper, a certificate ‖ anything written that gives information or supplies evidence 2. (dókjument) v.t. to support or supply with documents, a well-documented case **doc·u·men·ta·rist** (dokjuméntərist) n. **doc·u·men·ta·ry** (dokjuméntəri:) 1. adj. set down in writing, documentary evidence ‖ fully supported by documents ‖ having the validity of a document, a story of documentary interest 2. pl. **doc·u·men·ta·ries** n. a documentary film [O.F.]

documentary film a nonfiction film composed of camera images taken exclusively from real-

ity, later cut etc., given a sound track, and treated as an art film

doc·u·men·ta·tion (dokjumentéiʃən) n. the assembling of documents ‖ the using of documentary evidence to support original written work, or the technique of referring to such evidence in footnotes, appendices etc., or the evidence itself ‖ the classifying and making available of knowledge as a procedure

DOD (acronym) the U.S. Department of Defense

Dodd (dod), Thomas J. (1907–71), U.S. lawyer and Democratic senator from Connecticut (1959–70). He was chief U.S. trial counsel at the Nuremberg trials (1945–6)

dod·der (dódər) n. a member of Cuscuta, fam. Convolvulaceae, a genus of leafless and rootless total parasites, with a twining stem, sending haustoria into the host. The flowers are in heads or short spikes. The fruit (capsules) split and shed four seeds [M.E. doder, perh. of Gmc origin]

dodder v.i. to shake, tremble (from age or weakness) ‖ to totter along [origin unknown]

dod·dered (dódərd) adj. (of a tree) having lost its branches through age or decay [prob. fr. obs. dod fr. M.E. dodden, to lop, poll, clip]

dod·der·ing (dódəriŋ) adj. feeble, tottering, esp. in old age

do·dec·a·gon (doudékəgən, doudékəgɒn) n. a plane figure having 12 sides [fr. Gk dōdeka, twelve+gōnia, angle]

do·dec·a·he·dron (doudekəhíːdrən, doudekəhíː-drən) pl. **do·dec·a·he·drons, do·dec·a·he·dra** (doudekəhíːdrə, doudekəhíːdrə) n. a solid figure with 12 equal plane faces, either all pentagonal or all rhombic [fr. Gk dōdeka, twelve+hedra, base]

Do·dec·a·nese (doudekəníːz, doudek-əníːs) a group of mountainous islands (total area 1,035 sq. miles, pop. 145,071, mainly Greek) in the S.E. Aegean, originally including 12 major islands and many small ones. They are included in the S. Sporades. Rhodes was added when Italy took the group from Turkey (1912). The Dodecanese were united to Greece (1948)

do·dec·a·syl·la·ble (doudekəsíləb'l) n. a line of 12 syllables [fr. Gk dōdeka, twelve+SYLLABLE]

dodge (dodʒ) 1. v. pres. part. **dodg·ing** past and past part. **dodged** v.i. to move suddenly in order to avoid a blow, being seen etc. ‖ to be constantly on the move from place to place with no clear line of progress ‖ to be evasive ‖ (campanology) to ring one place backward out of the usual order ‖ v.t. to avoid by trickery, to dodge income tax ‖ to get quickly out of the way of ‖ to evade (a difficulty or choice) 2. n. a quick evasive movement ‖ a trick, a dodge to evade a problem ‖ (campanology) the sounding of a bell displaced by one number **dódg·er** n. someone who dodges ‖ a person full of subterfuge ‖ a handbill ‖ *CORN DODGER [origin unknown]

Dodg·em (dódʒəm) n. (often pl.) a mechanical amusement consisting of small electric cars which drivers steer about in an enclosure, bumping into other cars and trying not to be bumped [after Dodg'em, trademark]

Dodg·son (dódʒsən), Charles Lutwidge *CARROLL, Lewis

do·do (dóudou) pl. **do·dos, do·does** n. Raphus cucullatus or Didus ineptus, a heavy, flightless bird which formerly inhabited Mauritius but became extinct in the 17th c. It had a large hooked beak, small, down-covered wings and tail, and short thick legs. It was killed for eating ‖ a related species which inhabited the island of Réunion until it also became extinct, in the 18th c. ‖ an eccentric person completely behind the times dead as a dodo completely out of fashion or obsolete [Port. doudo, fool]

doe (dou) pl. **does, doe** n. a female deer, hare or rabbit [O.E. dā]

DOE (acronym) the U.S. Department of Energy

do·er (dúːər) n. someone who doesn't confine himself to thought or talk but takes effective action, habitually

does (dʌz) 3rd pers. sing. pres. of DO

doe·skin (dóuskin) n. the skin of the female deer ‖ the soft leather made from this skin ‖ a fine cloth resembling it

does·n't (dʌz'nt) contr. of DOES NOT

doff (dof, dɔf) v.t. to take off (one's hat) in salutation [=do off]

dog (dɔg, dog) 1. n. Canis familiaris, order Carnivora, a common quadruped of many breeds ‖ a male of the species (cf. BITCH) ‖ a male wolf (cf. BITCH) or fox (cf. VIXEN) ‖ (pop.) a fellow, *a lucky dog* ‖ a term of contempt or abuse ‖ a mechanical gripping device ‖ an iron bar spiked at each end for joining timbers together ‖ (pl.) a pair of metal supports for logs burning on an open hearth **Dog** one of two constellations, the Great Dog (Canis Major, of the Southern hemisphere) and the Little, Dog (Canis Minor, of the northern hemisphere) **not a dog's chance** not the least chance **to go to the dogs** to become ruined or demoralized **to let sleeping dogs lie** not to raise issues that might cause trouble **the dogs** (pop.) greyhound racing 2. *v.t. pres. part.* **dog·ging** *past* and *past part.* **dogged** to track like a hound, *to dog someone's footsteps, dogged by bad luck* ‖ (mech.) to grip with a dog [O.E. *docga*]

dog·ber·ry (dɔ́gbɛri, dɔ́gbɛri) pl. **dog·ber·ries** n. the fruit (drupe) of the dogwood, or the shrub itself ‖ (in Nova Scotia) the mountain ash

dog·cart (dɔ́gkɑrt, dɔ́gkɑrt) n. a twowheeled horsedrawn light carriage with seats placed back to back. Originally the rear seat folded down to make a box for dogs

dog days the period of four to six weeks roughly between early July and mid-August when the Dog Star rises and sets with the sun ‖ (pop.) the hot, stifling days of summer

doge (doudʒ) n. the chief magistrate in the former republics of Venice and Genoa [F. fr. Ital.]

dog-ear (dɔ́giər, dɔ́giər) 1. n. the corner of a page turned down accidentally or to mark a place 2. v.t. to turn down the corners of (a book's pages)

do·gey (dóugi:) pl. **do·geys** n. a dogie

dog·fight (dɔ́gfait, dɔ́gfait) n. a fight between dogs ‖ a confused fight, a free-for-all, esp. in aerial warfare

dog·fish (dɔ́gfiʃ, dɔ́gfiʃ) pl. **dog·fish, dog·fish·es** n. any of various cartilaginous, mostly coastal fish closely related to sharks

dog·ged (dɔ́gid, dɔ́gid) adj. obstinate, pertinacious, persistent

dog·ger (dɔ́gər, dɔ́gər) n. a Dutch fishing boat with two masts and broad bows [M.E. *doggere* perh. fr. DOG]

Dog·ger Bank (dɔ́gər, dóugər) a sandbank (about 170 miles long, 65 miles wide) in the North Sea between England and Denmark, a famous fishing ground

dog·ger·el (dɔ́gərəl, dóugərəl) 1. n. worthless verse ‖ irregular verse measures 2. adj. (of verse) trivial and composed in loose form [origin unknown]

dog grass *Agropyron repens,* fam. *Gramineae,* a couch grass

dog·grel (dɔ́grəl, dóugrəl) n. doggerel

dog·gy (dɔ́gi:, dóugi:) comp. **dog·gi·er** superl. **dog·gi·est** adj. of or like dogs, *a doggy smell* ‖ concentratedly fond of dogs

doggy bag or **doggie bag** a container used to carry home leftovers from a restaurant, ostensibly for the family dog

dog·house (dɔ́ghaus, dóughaus) pl. **dog·hous·es** (dɔ́ghauziz, dóughauziz) n. a man-made shelter for a dog **in the doghouse** (pop.) in disgrace

do·gie, do·gy (dóugi:) pl. **do·gies** n. a motherless calf [origin unknown]

dog in the manger someone who keeps what he doesn't want in order that no one else shall enjoy it

dog Latin bad Latin

dog·ma (dɔ́gmə, dóugmə) pl. **dog·mas, dog·ma·ta** (dɔ́gmətə, dóugmətə) n. a basic doctrinal point in religion or philosophy ‖ such basic points collectively [L. fr. Gk]

dog·mat·ic (dɔgmǽtik, dɔgmǽtik) adj. of or relating to dogma, doctrinal ‖ asserting views as if they were facts, esp. in an arrogant way **dog·mát·i·cal** adj. **dog·mát·ics** n. [fr. L. *dogmaticus* fr. Gk]

dog·ma·tism (dɔ́gmətizəm, dóugmətizəm) n. the assertion of opinion as though it were fact [F. *dogmatisme* fr. M.L.]

dog·ma·tist (dɔ́gmətist, dóugmətist) n. someone who makes dogmatic pronouncements [F. *dogmatiste* fr. M. L.]

dog·ma·tize (dɔ́gmətaiz, dóugmətaiz) pres. part. **dog·ma·tiz·ing** past and past part. **dog·ma·tized** v.i. to state one's opinion as if it were fact ‖ to speak authoritatively [fr. F. *dogmatiser* fr. L. fr. Gk]

do-good·er (dú:gúdər) n. (pop.) someone earnestly bent on doing good (but often too obtuse to see what harm may result from interfering)

dog rose *Rosa canina,* fam. *Rosaceae,* a variable European wild hedge rose with curved or hooked prickles and single pink, white or cream flowers

dog's age (Am., pop.=Br., pop. donkey's years) a very long time, *I haven't seen him in a dog's age* (Br. for donkey's years), *it's a dog's age* (Br. *it's donkey's years) since I saw him*

dog·shore (dɔ́gʃɔr, dɔ́gʃour, dɔ́gʃɔr, dɔ́gʃour) n. a wooden prop (used in pairs) to support a vessel before launching

dog·sled (dɔ́gslɛd, dóuglsɛd) n. a sled drawn by a team of dogs

dogs·tail (dɔ́gzteil, dóugzteil) n. a member of *Cynosurus,* fam. *Gramineae,* a genus of grasses commonly found on acid and basic soils

Dog Star *SIRIUS

dog's-tongue (dɔ́gztʌŋ, dóugztʌŋ) n. hound's-tongue

dog's-tooth violet (dɔ́gztu:θ, dóugztu:θ) dog-tooth violet

dog tag (pop.) a small metal identification plate worn around the neck by members of the armed forces

dog-tired (dɔ́gtáiərd, dóugtáiərd) adj. utterly fatigued

dog·tooth (dɔ́gtu:θ, dóugtu:θ) pl. **dog·teeth** (dɔ́gti:θ, dóugti:θ) n. a pointed molding in Norman and Early English architecture

dogtooth violet *Erythronium denscanis,* fam. *Liliaceae,* a European plant with two mottled leaves at the base and one drooping purple flower

dog·trot (dɔ́gtrɒt, dóugtrɒt) n. the determined pace people use when they must walk rather a long way rather quickly or in unpleasant weather

dog violet *Viola canina,* fam. *Violaceae,* a wild, scentless Old World violet

dog·watch (dɔ́gwɒtʃ, dóugwɒtʃ, dóugwɒtʃ, dɔ́gwɒtʃ) n. (naut.) either of two two-hour watches (4–6 p.m. and 6–8 p.m.)

dog·wood (dɔ́gwud, dóugwud) n. a member of *Cornus,* fam. *Cornaceae,* a genus of shrubs or small trees. *C. sanguinea* has beautiful red autumn foliage. *C. florida* (North America) and some others provide a wood with the qualities of boxwood. *C. mascula* (the cornelian cherry of Europe and Asia) yields fruit which makes good preserves

doh (dou) n. (Br., mus.) do

Doh·ná·nyi (dɔxnánji:), Ernö or Ernst von (1877–1960), Hungarian pianist and composer of orchestral and chamber music etc.

doi·ly, Br. also **doy·ley** (dɔ́ili:) pl. **doi·lies,** Br. also **doy·leys** n. a small, usually round, ornamental mat of lace, paper or plastic placed on a cake plate or under a vase, ornament etc. or on the arms and backs of chairs to protect the material [after *Doiley* or *Doyley,* a London haberdasher]

do·ings (dú:iŋz) pl. n. activities

do-it-your·self (dú:itjərsélf) adj. designed for the use of amateurs, not requiring special knowledge

do·jo (dóudʒou) n. school for training in Oriental (esp. Japanese) techniques of self-defense, e.g., karate, judo

Dol·by System (Dóulbi:) device to eliminate noise from recordings, utilizing extra amplification for higher audio frequencies during recording and adjustments during playback

dol·ce vi·ta (dóultʃei ví:ta) n. (It.) a life style of self-indulgence, esp. in opulent, sensuous living

dol·cy·cline [C$_{22}$H$_{24}$N$_2$O$_8$H$_2$O] (dóulsiklain) n. (pharm) a form of tetracycline said to protect against traveler's diarrhea

dol·drums (dɔ́ldrəmz, dóuldrəmz) pl. n. areas of low pressure in equatorial waters where the weather is generally sultry. Sailing ships were often becalmed there for long periods ‖ low spirits, depression [origin unknown, perh. rel. to DULL]

Dole (doul), Robert J. (1923–), U.S. Republican senator (1969–). From Kansas, he served in the state legislature and was elected to the U.S. House of Representatives in 1960. As senator he was chairman of the Senate Finance Committee (1981–5) and majority leader (1985–). In 1976, he ran unsuccessfully for the vice presidency with Gerald Ford

Dole, Sanford Ballard (1844–1926), the first president (1893–1900) of the Republic of Hawaii and negotiator of Hawaii's annexation to the U.S.A., after which he served (1900–3) as the first governor of the Territory of Hawaii

dole (doul) 1. n. a weekly relief payment made by a government to the unemployed ‖ a share ‖ a charitable distribution (esp. a stingy one) **on the dole** receiving unemployment relief 2. v.t. pres. part. **dol·ing** past and past part. **doled** (with 'out') to give out in small portions, often grudgingly [O.E. *dāl*]

dole·ful (dóulfəl) adj. sad, mournful ‖ dreary, dismal [fr. obs. *dole,* grief fr. F.]

dol·er·ite (dɔ́lərait) n. a medium-grained igneous rock ‖ (Br.) diabase ‖ any igneous rock which cannot be classified without microscopic examination **dol·er·it·ic** (dɔlərítik) adj. [F. fr. Gk *doleros,* deceptive (because it is easily mistaken for diorite)]

dol·i·cho·ce·phal·ic (dɒlikousəfǽlik) adj. longheaded (of a skull whose breadth is less than four-fifths of its length) ‖ of a person or race characterized by such a skull (opp. BRACHYCEPHALIC, *CEPHALIC INDEX) [fr. Gk *dolichos,* long+*kephalē,* head]

doll (dɒl) 1. n. a miniature human figure, usually of a child, made as a toy ‖ a pretty, empty-headed woman 2. v.t. and i. (pop., with 'up') to dress or make up too conspicuously [shortened pet name from *Dorothy*]

dol·lar (dɔ́lər) n. the basic monetary unit of the U.S.A., containing 100 cents ‖ a monetary unit containing 100 cents used also in Canada and some other countries ‖ the symbol ($) of the dollar ‖ a note of the value of one dollar ‖ a U.S. silver coin issued 1794–1935 [earlier *daller, daler* fr. L.G. and Du.]

dollar area a region comprising the U.S.A., Canada, and certain Latin American countries (Cuba, Mexico and Venezuela) in which the dollar is the form of exchange currency

dollar diplomacy diplomacy concerned with furthering a country's financial and commercial interests abroad

Doll·fuss (dɔ́lfu:s), Engelbert (1892–1934), chancellor of Austria (1932–4). His dictatorship ended with his assassination by Austrian Nazis

doll·house (dɔ́lhaus) pl. **doll·hous·es** (dɔ́lhauziz) n. (Am.=Br. doll's house) a toy house

dol·lop (dɔ́ləp) n. (pop.) a shapeless lump, esp. a doled-out portion of mushy food [origin unknown]

doll's house (Br.) a dollhouse

doll·y (dɔ́li:) pl. **doll·ies** n. a child's word for doll ‖ a stout wooden pole, often with a rubber or metal suction cup, and having a cross-handle, used for thumping clothes up and down in a washtub ‖ an object placed between a pile and the head of a pile driver to prevent damage to the latter ‖ a tool with a cupped head for securing the head of a rivet while the other end is being headed ‖ a small wheeled trolley for carrying beams etc. ‖ (movies) such a trolley for moving the camera about the set

dol·man (dɔ́lmən, dóulmən) pl. **dol·mans** n. a Turkish robe worn open at the front ‖ a hussar's jacket worn like a cloak with the sleeves hanging loose [Turk. *dōlāmān*]

dolman sleeve a sleeve not fitted under the armpit, so as to give a loose capelike line

dol·men (dɔ́lmen, dóulmen) n. (in Britain) a stone circle of prehistoric monoliths placed around another, larger one ‖ (in France) a cromlech [F. prob. fr. Corn.]

do·lo·mite (dɔ́ləmait, dóuləmait) n. the double carbonate of calcium and magnesium, CaMg(CO$_3$)$_2$ [after Déodat de *Dolomieu* (1750–1801), French geologist]

Do·lo·mites (dɔ́ləmaits, dóuləmaits) a range of the S.E. Alps, between the Adige and Piave in N. Italy, composed of dolomitic limestone formed into fantastic shapes by erosion. The highest peak is Marmolada (10,965 ft)

dol·o·mit·ic (dɒləmítik) adj. containing dolomite

Do·lo·res, Gri·to de (grí:tɔðeðɔlɔ́res) (Cry of Dolores), the cry: 'Long live America! Long live independence! Death to bad government!' which was shouted (Sept. 16, 1810) by Father Miguel Hidalgo y Costilla and which opened the struggle for Mexican independence. Each year on Sept. 16 the president of Mexico repeats the cry from the national palace balcony

dol·or·ous (dɔ́lərəs, dóulərəs) adj. (rhet.) sad, mournful ‖ (rhet.) distressing [O. F. *doleros*]

dol·phin (dɔ́lfin, dólfin) n. a member of fam. *Delphinidae,* marine mammals of order *Cetacea,* resembling the porpoise. Dolphins are gregarious, fast and strong swimmers, intelligent, inhabiting every sea. They measure up to 10 ft long, and have a pointed snout and a conspicuous dorsal fin. They feed principally on fish ‖ the dorado [earlier *delphin* fr. L. fr. Gk]

dol·phin·a·ri·um (dɔlfinέəriːəm) *n.* an aquarium for dolphins

dolt (doult) *n.* a dull, stupid person, an oaf **dólt·ish** *adj.* [perh. rel. to DULL]

Dom (dom) *n.* a title prefixed to the names of members of the Benedictine and Carthusian monastic orders ‖ (in Portugal and Brazil) a title prefixed to the Christian names of members of the royal family, certain ecclesiastics etc. [short for L. *dominus*, lord]

-dom *suffix* indicating rank as in 'dukedom', domain as in 'kingdom', condition as in 'boredom' or people collectively as in 'officialdom'

DOM [C₁₂H₂₀NO₂] (*acronym*) 2,5-D methoxy-4-methylamphetamine, also known as STP, a psychedelic drug producing effects similar to amphetamine mixed with mescaline

do·main (douméin) *n.* an estate or territory over which authority is exerted ‖ a sphere of action or thought ‖ *EMINENT DOMAIN* **do·mái·nal, do·má·ni·al** *adjs* [F. *domaine*]

dome (doum) **1.** *n.* a large, hemispherical structure surmounting the highest part of a roof ‖ anything thought of as resembling the dome of a building **2.** *v. pres. part.* **dom·ing** *past* and *past part.* **domed** *v.t.* to cover with, or shape like, a dome ‖ *v.i.* to rise in a dome [F. fr. Ital.]

dome car a passenger vehicle with a raised viewing section

Do·me·ni·chi·no (dɔmeniːkíːnɔ) (Domenico Zampieri, 1581–1641), Italian artist. He designed villas in Rome and painted frescos in Naples. His work also included landscapes, altarpieces and devotional pictures

Do·me·ni·co Ve·ne·zia·no (dɔméniːkɔveneːtsjáːnɔ) (d. 1461), Italian painter. The few surviving works show a noble serenity of spirit and a mastery of color, esp. as it is modified by light. The St Lucy altarpiece, whose main panel is in the Uffizi, Florence, is his masterpiece. Piero della Francesca acted as his assistant in Florence (c. 1439)

Do·men·i·kos The·o·to·co·pou·los (douméniːkɔsθiːóutoukɔ́puːlɔs) *EL GRECO*

Domes·day Book (dúːmzdei, dóumzdei) a detailed survey of English counties compiled (1086–7) by order of William I, in two volumes, one covering Essex, Suffolk, and Norfolk, the other covering the rest of England (excluding Northumberland, Durham, Cumberland and N. Westmorland). It records the extent, value and ownership of estates, local customs, and a census of householders

do·mes·tic (dɔméstik) **1.** *adj.* belonging to the home or house, *domestic duties* ‖ relating to family affairs, *a domestic quarrel* ‖ home-loving and capable in household matters ‖ tame, *domestic animals* ‖ of one's own country, not foreign **2.** *n.* a household servant **do·més·ti·cal·ly** *adv.* in a domestic way ‖ as regards a country's home affairs [fr. L. *domesticus*]

do·mes·ti·cate (dɔméstikeit) *v.t. pres. part.* **do·mes·ti·cat·ing** *past* and *past part.* **do·mes·ti·cat·ed** to tame (animals) and teach them to live with man and under his control ‖ to make fond of home and skilled in household affairs **do·mes·ti·cá·tion** *n.* [fr. M. L. *domesticare* (*domesticatus*)]

do·mes·tic·i·ty (dɔumestísitiː, dɔmestísitiː) *pl.* **do·mes·tic·i·ties** *n.* the domesticated state ‖ home life ‖ (*pl.*) domestic matters

domestic prelate priest with rank above chamberlain and holding honorary membership in the papal household

domestic science the branch of study concerned with household management

dom·i·cile (dómisail, dómis'l, dóumisail, dóumis'l) **1.** *n.* a home, dwelling place ‖ a principal place of residence as fixed for legal purposes (taxation, etc.) **2.** *v.t. pres. part.* **dom·i·cil·ing** *past* and *past part.* **dom·i·ciled** to establish in a domicile **dom·i·cil·i·ar·y** (dɔmisíliːˈeriː) *adj.* [F.]

dom·i·cil·i·ate (dɔmisíliːeit) *pres. part.* **dom·i·cil·i·at·ing** *past* and *past part.* **dom·i·cil·i·at·ed** *v.t.* to domicile ‖ *v.i.* to establish residence **dom·i·cil·i·á·tion** *n.* [fr. L. *domicilium*, residence]

dom·i·nance (dóminəns) *n.* the quality of being dominant ‖ a dominating influence

dom·i·nant (dóminənt) **1.** *adj.* controlling, ruling ‖ most noticeable ‖ commanding by position, *a dominant site* ‖ (*biol.*) of a character possessed by one parent which in a hybrid masks the corresponding alternative character derived from the other parent (opp. RECESSIVE). The parental allele is manifested in the first filial generation (heterozygote) ‖ of a species of plant or animal prevalent in a particular ecological community or at a given period of time ‖ (*mus.*) of or related to the dominant **2.** *n.* (*mus.*) the fifth note of the scale relative to the tonic ‖ (*biol.*) a dominant character or species [F.]

dom·i·nate (dómineit) *pres. part.* **dom·i·nat·ing** *past* and *past part.* **dom·i·nat·ed** *v.t.* to exert authority over, control ‖ to tower above ‖ to have a position which commands (e.g. a valley, view) ‖ *v.i.* to exercise domination ‖ to be predominant [fr. L. *dominari* (*dominatus*)]

dom·i·na·tion (dɔminéiʃən) *n.* authority, control ‖ tyranny ‖ predominance

dom·i·neer (dɔminíər) *v.i.* to force one's wishes, opinions or commands overbearingly on others ‖ to tyrannize **dom·i·néer·ing** *adj.* [prob. fr. Du. *domineren* fr. F.]

Dom·i·nic (dóminik) St (Domingo de Guzmán, c. 1170–1221), Spanish founder of the Dominicans (c. 1212). Feast: Aug. 4

Dom·i·ni·ca (dɔminíːkə, dɔmíːnikə) a state in the West Indies. It is a mountainous island (area 290 sq. miles, pop. 81,000), in the Windward Is. Capital: Roseau (pop. 20,000). People: mainly of African descent. The banana trade dominates the economy. Other exports include citrus products, copra, cocoa and bay oil. Currency: East Caribbean dollar. Originally inhabited by Carib Indians, Dominica was discovered (1493) by Columbus, and was ceded to Britain by France (1783). It was a member of the Federation of the West Indies (1958–62), and became a separate colony in 1960. It became a state in association with Britain (Mar. 1, 1967) and in 1978 became independent. Dominica remains a member of the Commonwealth of Nations

do·min·i·cal (dəminik'l) *adj.* of the Lord ‖ of the Lord's day, of Sunday [fr. M.L. *dominicalis*]

dominical letter one of the first seven letters in the alphabet used to mark the Sundays in church calendars and in determining the date of Easter

Do·min·i·can (dəmínikən) **1.** *adj.* of or pertaining to the Dominican Republic **2.** *n.* a native or inhabitant of the Dominican Republic

Dominican 1. *adj.* of or relating to St Dominic or the religious order founded (c. 1212) by him **2.** *n.* a friar of this order [fr. L. *Dominicanus* fr. *Dominicus*, L. for *Domingo* de Guzmán]
—Founded to convert the Albigenses, the Dominican order attaches special importance to theological study and preaching. It has promulgated the teaching of St Thomas Aquinas, who was a member of the order. There are an order of nuns and a lay order

Dominican Republic an independent state (area 19,129 sq. miles, pop. 5,812,900) in the West Indies (Greater Antilles group, *ANTILLES*). It occupies the eastern two thirds of the island of Hispaniola. Capital: Santo Domingo. People: 60% mulatto, 28% of European (Spanish) descent, 12% of African origin. Language: Spanish. Religion: predominantly Roman Catholic. The land is 70% forest and 14% arable. The Cordillera Central (highest point Mt Tina, 10,300 ft) crosses the country from east to west in four parallel ranges. The tropical trade wind climate is marked by dry winters, wet summers and frequent earthquakes and hurricanes. Annual rainfall: 60 ins in the northeastern lowlands, 50–100 ins along the north coast, 40–50 ins in the southeast plains, 20 ins in the southwest interior. Average temperature (F.) at Santo Domingo: 76° (Jan.), 81° (Sept.). It is cooler inland. There is periodic snow in the mountains. Livestock: cattle, hogs, goats. Agricultural products: sugar (esp. in the southeast), coffee, cacao, rice, tobacco, molasses, corn. Mineral resources: gold, copper, high-quality iron ore, gypsum, silver, platinum. Manufactures: rum, textiles, cement, paper, glass. Exports: sugar, molasses, cocoa, coffee. Imports: machinery, iron and steel, foodstuffs, oil, vehicles. Ports: Santo Domingo, Puerto Plata. University: Santo Domingo (1538). Monetary unit: peso oro (divided into 100 centavos). HISTORY. Spain settled the eastern part of Hispaniola as the colony of Santo Domingo (the western part being colonized by France, *HAITI*). It became independent of Spain (1821) but was subjected to Haitian Negro domination (1822–44). The independent Dominican Republic was established (1844), followed by a long period of anarchy and tyranny. U.S. Marines occupied it (1916–24). The U.S.A. controlled the customs (1907–40), and dominated the sugar industry. Gen. Rafael Trujillo established a dictatorship (1930). He was assassinated (1961), and his death led to some liberalization of the régime. Constitutional government was restored when Juan Bosch was elected president (1962), but he was deposed (1963) by the military. When a pro-Bosch faction of the army staged (1965) a coup d'état it led to the intervention of U.S. Marines, later incorporated in an OAS force to which Brazil, Honduras, Nicaragua, Paraguay (themselves all under military government) and Costa Rica contributed. The OAS contingent was withdrawn (1966) after elections in which Joaquin Balaguer defeated Bosch. Balaguer remained in office until 1978 when he was defeated by Antonio Guzman. In 1986, Salvador Jorge Blanco was elected president

do·min·ion (dəmínjən) *n.* sovereignty, supreme authority (*Br., law*) the right of possession ‖ (*hist.*) the lands belonging to a feudal landlord ‖ (*pl.*) an order of angels (*ANGEL*) **Do·min·ion** the title of some self-governing, independent countries within the Commonwealth [F.]

Dominion Day a Canadian public holiday, July 1, commemorating the grant of Dominion status in 1867

do·min·i·um (dəmíniːəm) *n.* (*Br., law*) ownership ‖ political authority [L.]

dom·i·no (dóminou) *pl.* **dom·i·noes, dom·i·nos** *n.* one of the pieces in the game of dominoes ‖ a long, loose cloak with a mask to hide the face, worn at fancy-dress balls and parties, masquerades etc. [F. and Ital.=hooded cloak]
—The game of dominoes probably originated in Italy in the 18th c. It is played with a set of 28 pieces which are marked in two sections in combinations of dots and blanks from double six to double blank. The dominoes are distributed face down to the players. One piece is exposed and the chance to match one or other end of it (or either end of the line that forms as play proceeds) passes from player to player in turn. The first player to lay down all his pieces is the winner

domino effect the effect upon another issue or region resulting from a current action or political policy

domino theory political view that the fall or change of allegiance of one nation precipitates the fall of the governments of its neighbors. It was originally articulated by President Dwight D. Eisenhower in 1945

Do·mi·tian (dəmíʃən) (Titus Flavius Domitianus, 51–96), Roman emperor (81–96), brother and successor of Titus. His provincial administration was efficient, but after 89 he ruled cruelly and despotically and tyrannized the senate

domsat (*acronym*) domestic satellite, a communication satellite in a stationary orbit 22,300 mi. over the equator, used for transmitting television programs and telephone conversations

Don (don) a river of the U.S.S.R. rising in the central Russian plateau and flowing 1,230 miles to the Sea of Azov. It is linked by a canal to the Volga

don (don) *n.* a courtesy title for a Spaniard of high rank, and used by Spanish-speaking people prefixed to a man's Christian name ‖ a form of address to an Italian priest ‖ (*Br.*) a fellow of a college ,or (*broadly*) a teacher in a university [Span. =lord, sir]

don *pres. part.* **don·ning** *past* and *past part.* **donned** *v.t.* (*rhet.*) to put on (robes, armor etc.) [=do on]

do·nate (dounéit, dóuneit) *pres. part.* **do·nat·ing** *past* and *past part.* **do·nat·ed** *v.t.* to give or present (esp. money) to a society, institution etc. [fr. L. *donare* (*donatus*), to give]

Don·a·tel·lo (dɔnətélou) (Donato di Betto Bardi, 1386–1466), Italian sculptor, one of the great early figures of the Italian Renaissance. He sought realism in depicting the human form, and grandeur, forcefulness and drama in the composition of his statues and bronze reliefs. He was one of the first artists to seek help from classical sculpture in realizing these aims. His genius was first fully revealed in the statue of St George (at Orsanmichele, Florence, 1416–20). The tomb of Cardinal Brancacci (1426–7) includes a remarkable relief of the Assumption, while his bronze David, many reliefs, bronze doors etc. mark the height of his powers from the 1430s. He spent 10 years at Padua (1443–53) where his greatest work was executed: the massive bronze altar of the Santo, and the Gattamelata equestrian statue

CONCISE PRONUNCIATION KEY: **(a)** æ, c*a*t; ɑ, c*a*r; ɔ f*aw*n; ei, sn*a*ke. **(e)** e, h*e*n; iː, sh*ee*p; iə, d*ee*r; ɛə, b*ea*r. **(i)** i, f*i*sh; ai, t*i*ger; əː, b*i*rd. **(o)** o, *o*x; au, c*ow*; ou, g*oa*t; u, p*oo*r; ɔi, r*oy*al. **(u)** ʌ, d*u*ck; u, b*u*ll; uː, g*oo*se; ə, b*a*cillus; juː, c*u*be. x, lo*ch*; θ, *th*ink; δ, *b*other; z, *Z*en; ʒ, cor*s*age; dʒ, sava*g*e; ŋ, ora*n*guta*ng*; j, *y*ak; ʃ, fi*sh*; tʃ, fe*tch*; 'l, rabb*le*; 'n, redd*en*. Complete pronunciation key appears inside front cover.

donation   279   Dorion

do·na·tion (dounéiʃən) n. a gift, esp. of money, to a society or institution ‖ the act of making such a gift [F.]

Don·a·tism (dóunətizəm, dónətizəm) a 4th-c. schism in the N. African Church following the apostasies during the Diocletian persecutions. Donatists held that sacraments were invalid outside the one visible Church, that sinners should be excommunicated, and that the State had no rights in ecclesiastical matters. The schism drew from St Augustine his lasting definition of the nature of the ministry and sacraments of the Church **Dón·a·tist** n. [after *Donatus*, bishop of Carthage, one of the leaders]

Do·nau (dóunau) *DANUBE

Don·bas (dɒnbás) the Donets basin, a highly industrialized, densely populated region in the plain of the Donets and lower Dnieper rivers in the Ukraine and the R.S.F.S.R., U.S.S.R. It yields over a third of the U.S.S.R.'s anthracite and coal production

done (dʌn) past part. of DO ‖ adj. finished, completed ‖ cooked as long as thought desirable **done for** doomed without a hope of survival ‖ ruined ‖ filled with a sense of personal failure **done in** utterly exhausted ‖ murdered **done with** quite finished and relegated to the past **to have done with** to put an end to ‖ to have finished with

do·nee (douní:) n. the person who receives a gift ‖ someone who receives a blood transfusion, skin graft etc. [DONOR]

Don·e·gal (dónigɔl) the northern county (area 1,865 sq. miles, pop. 108,344) of Ulster province, Irish Republic. County seat: Lifford

Don·el·son, Fort (dónəlsən) a Confederate camp during the Civil War on the Cumberland River in Tennessee. It surrendered (Feb. 16, 1862) to General Grant's Union forces, opening the river to Union penetration and forcing the eventual evacuation of Nashville and Columbus

Do·nets (dɒnéts) a river of the S. central U.S.S.R., about 670 miles long, rising in the Kursk steppe, and flowing southeast into the Don

Donets basin *DONBAS

Do·netsk (dɒnétsk) (formerly Stalino) a city (pop. 1,047,000) of the Ukraine, U.S.S.R. With Makayevka it forms the largest industrial conurbation in the Donbas: iron and steel, coal mining and chemical industries

dong (dɒŋ) n. one-time monetary unit in Kampuchea, formerly Cambodia

Don·go·la (dóŋgələ) a region (area 27,520 sq. miles, pop. 152,000) of the Northern province of the Republic of the Sudan. It extends on both sides of the Nile above the third cataract. The old town of Dongola was the capital of the ancient Christian kingdom of Nubia

Don·go·lese (dɒŋgəlí:z) n. a native or inhabitant of Dongola the Nubian language spoken by natives of Dongola

Dön·itz (dé:nits), Karl (1892–1980), German admiral. He was a submarine expert in both world wars. In 1945, on Hitler's presumed death, he became head of state for three weeks, signing Germany's surrender. At the Nuremberg Trials he was sentenced to 10 years' imprisonment

Don·i·zet·ti (dɒnizéti:), Gaetano (1797–1848), Italian composer. His 75 operas include 'la Fille du régiment' (1840), 'Lucia di Lammermoor' (1835) and 'Don Pasquale' (1843) and are marked by a flowing melodic style

don·jon (dɒndʒən, dʌndʒən) n. the heavily defended central tower of a medieval castle ‖ a dungeon [O.F.]

Don Juan (dɒnwán) n. a playboy amorist [after a legendary Spanish nobleman philanderer created by Tirso de Molina in 'El burlador de Sevilla' (1630)]

don·key (dóŋki:, dʌŋki:) pl. **don·keys** n. the ass, *Equus asinus* ‖ (pop.) a stupid person [perh. rel. to DUN, brownish]

donkey engine a small auxiliary engine

donkey's years (Br., pop.) dog's age

Donne (dʌn, dɒn), John (c. 1571–1631), English metaphysical poet. His direct, vigorous poetry—amorous in early life, religious and mystical later—is argumentative in method and colloquial in tone, with dramatic immediacy. Its combination of agile thought and intense feeling is best seen in the metaphysical conceit, where feeling and thought fuse in an image that is always ingenious and appropriate,

though it may disconcert at first in the shock of bringing incongruities together. Donne was brought up a Roman Catholic, became a fervent Anglican, was ordained in 1615 and made dean of St Paul's (1621). He was a celebrated preacher. His 'XXVI Sermons', published in 1660, display the same passionate strength of intellect and imagination as his poems do

don·nish (dóniʃ) adj. (Br.) erudite, but apt to be pedantic, and excessively mild or quirky

do·nor (dóunər) n. someone who makes a gift, esp. to a church ‖ a person giving some of his blood for transfusion or skin for grafting etc. (cf. DONEE) [A.F. *donour*]

Don Quix·o·te (dɒnki:hóuti:, dɒnkwíksət) n. a charming and lovable idealist without worldly sense (*CERVANTES)

don't (dount) 1. v. contr. of DO NOT 2. n. (pl.) instructions or advice not to do something, *a list of do's and don'ts*

doo·dle (dú:d'l) pres. part. **doo·dling** past and past part. **doo·dled** v.i. to draw or scribble aimlessly, absent-mindedly or while preoccupied [perth. rel. to DAWDLE]

doo·dle·bug (dú:d'lbʌg) n. (Am.) the larva of the ant lion ‖ (Br., pop.) the V-1 flying bomb (guided missile) used by the Germans against London and S. England (1944)

Doo·ley (dú:li:), Thomas Anthony (1927–61), U.S. physician and author of 'Deliver Us from Evil' (1956), describing the plight of Vietnamese refugees. He was co-founder (with Peter D. Comanduras, 1957) of Medico, Inc., a medical aid corporation providing hospitals etc. to underdeveloped countries

doom (du:m) 1. n. a calamitous fate ‖ ruin, complete destruction ‖ the Last Judgment 2. v.t. to destine to a fate involving death, suffering or unhappiness ‖ to destine to be destroyed, *the village is doomed* [O.E. *dōm*, judgment]

doom painting a medieval painting of the Last Judgment

dooms·day (dú:mzdei) n. the day of the Last Judgment **till doomsday** forever

Doomsday Book the Domesday Book

door (dɔr, dour) n. a solid barrier, swinging on hinges or sliding, to close the entrance of a building, a room, a cupboard etc. ‖ a means of obtaining something, *the door to success* **at death's door** so ill as to be likely to die **from door to door** by calls on householders, *sold from door to door* ‖ from point of departure to point of arrival, *a 10-minute journey from door to door* **next door** to very close to ‖ almost, *next door to impossible* **to get** (or **have**) **a foot in the door** to make (or have) an opening (e.g. a social contact) which may lead to something useful or desirable [O.E. *duru*]

door·bell (dórbel, dóurbel) n. a bell in a house rung from outside by callers

door·case (dórkeis, dóurkeis) n. the frame in the opening of a wall to which the door is fixed

door·frame (dórfreim, dóurfreim) n. the framework into which the panels of a door are mounted ‖ a doorcase

door·jamb (dórdʒæm, dóurdʒæm). n. a vertical side of the frame to which a door is fixed

door·keep·er (dórki:pər, dóurki:pər) n. a man stationed at the entrance of an establishment to control admittance and help visitors ‖ (Roman Catholicism) a member of the lowest of the minor orders

door·knob (dórnɒb, dóurnɒb) n. a round or roundish door handle

door·man (dórmæn, dórmən, dóurmæn, dóurmən) pl. **door·men** (dórmen, dórmən, dóurmen, dóurmən) n. an attendant at the entrance of a hotel, nightclub etc. who opens the door, hails taxis etc.

door·mat (dórmæt, dóurmæt) n. a rough mat, of coconut fiber etc., for wiping mud off the shoes before entering a house ‖ an abject or docile person who is constantly imposed on or made use of

door money entrance money taken at the door of a place of entertainment (as distinct from money taken for tickets sold in advance)

door·post (dórpoust, dóurpoust) n. one of the two upright jambs of a doorcase

door·step (dórstep, dóurstep) n. a broad step outside a house door

door·stop (dórstɒp, dóurstɒp) n. a device for holding a door open ‖ a small rubber block fastened e. g. to the floor to prevent a door from being opened too far

door·way (dórwei, dóurwei) n. the passageway which a door opens or shuts off

door·yard (dórjard, dóurjard) n. a yard near a house door or beside a house

do·pa·mine [$C_8H_{11}NO_2$] (dóupəmi:n) n. an adrenal hormone stimulated by L-dopa (which see) that increases systolic and pulse pressure without affecting diastolic pressure. Used to lessen tremors experienced in Parkinson's disease, heart failure, trauma, etc.; marketed as Intropin *also* hydroxytyramine

dop·ant (dóupənt) n. an impurity in a semiconductor that improves its electrical conductivity *also* dope, doping agent

dope (doup) 1. n. (pop.) a narcotic ‖ a lubricant ‖ an additive used to produce a desired quality ‖ a coating used to give a fabric certain qualities (e.g. used in model aircraft construction) ‖ a drug to stimulate racehorses or dogs ‖ (photog.) a developer, or a preparation used in blocking out or retouching ‖ (pop.) information that lets one into a secret ‖ (pop.) a very stupid person 2. v.t. pres. part. **dop·ing** past and past part. **doped** to drug ‖ to apply dope to [fr. Du. *doop*, sauce]

dope fiend (pop.) a drug addict

dop·ey (dóupi:) comp. **dop·i·er** superl. **dop·i·est** adj. stupid ‖ sleepy ‖ fuddled

Dop·pler effect (dóplər). (phys.) the apparent change of frequency and wavelength due to the relative motion of the source of a wave disturbance and the observer: an approaching source results in an increase of frequency and shortening of wavelength, a receding source has the opposite effect. This principle is used e.g. in astronomy to determine the motion, relative to the earth, of a heavenly body, by observing the shift in the lines of its spectrum [after Christian *Doppler* (1803–53), Austrian mathematician and physicist]

DOPS (acronym) digital optical projector system, used for plotting radar data on a projected target (with grease pencil) with distinctive input devices Cf POPS, TOPS

dor (dɔr) n. *Geotrupes stercorarius*, the black dung beetle‖ any of various beetles making a loud humming noise [O.E. *dora*, origin unknown]

do·ra·do (dərádou) pl. **do·ra·do, do·ra·dos** n. *Coryphaena hippuris*, a brightly colored fish of tropical and temperate seas [Span.=gilded]

DORAN (mil. acronym) doppler range, a system for determining missile range using comparison of wave frequency from three points

Dor·dogne (dɔrdɔnj) a department (area 3,550 sq. miles, pop. 373,200) of S.W. France between Bordeaux and the Massif Central (*LIMOUSIN, *PÉRIGORD). Chief town: Périgueux

Dordogne a river of S.W. France (300 miles). It rises in the Puy-de-Dôme and joins with the Garonne north of Bordeaux to form the Gironde. There are several hydroelectric plants. It runs through beautiful high plateau country, forested with oaks and chestnuts and broken by deep valleys where wheat, corn, tobacco and vines are grown

Dor·drecht (dórdrext) a port (pop. 102,700) on the Maas (Meuse) delta in South Holland, the Netherlands: shipbuilding, chemical, engineering and glassmaking industries

Do·ré (dorei), Gustave (1832–83), French artist. His dramatic style was best suited to the art of illustration, e.g. Dante's 'Inferno' (1861), the Bible (1866), 'Paradise Lost' (1866), 'Don Quixote' (1863) and Rabelais (1851 and 1873). He used chiefly wood engraving

dorey *DORY

Do·ri·an (dóri:ən, dóuri:ən) 1. n. a native of Doris, a division of ancient Greece. The Dorians invaded Thessaly and Boeotia (12th c. B.C.) and settled in Doris between Mt Parnassus and Mt Oeta. They conquered Argos, the Achaean kingdoms, Mycenae and Corinth (12th—11th cc. B.C.) and established colonies in Crete, Halicarnassus and Rhodes (11th c.—8th c. B.C.) 2. adj. pertaining to this race or their home, Doric

Dorian mode a medieval authentic mode represented by the white piano keys ascending from D ‖ the ancient Greek mode represented by the white piano keys descending from E

Dor·ic (dórik, dóurik) 1. adj. of, relating to, or resembling one of the classical orders of Greek architecture, characterized by pillars having no ornament on their capitals, and being 8 times their diameter in height ‖ Dorian 2. n. a dialect of ancient Greek [fr. L. *Doricus* fr. Gk]

Do·rion (dɔrjɔ̃), Sir Antoine Aimé (1816–91), Canadian statesman and judge. He served as

---

CONCISE PRONUNCIATION KEY: (a) æ, cat; ɑ, car; ɔ fawn; ei, snake. **(e)** e, hen; i:, sheep; iə, deer; ɛə, bear. **(i)** i, fish; ai, tiger; əː, bird. **(o)** o, ox; au, cow; ou, goat; u, poor; ɔi, royal. **(u)** ʌ, duck; u, bull; u:, goose; ə, bacillus; juː, cube. x, loch; θ, think; ð, bother; z, Zen; ʒ, corsage; dʒ, savage; ŋ, orangutang; j, yak; ʃ, fish; tʃ, fetch; 'l, rabble; 'n, redden. Complete pronunciation key appears inside front cover.

joint premier of United Canada for 4 days (Aug. 2–5, 1858) in the Brown-Dorion administration and (1863–4) in the Dorion-Macdonald administration, promoting a liberal policy

dor·man·cy (dórmənsi:) *n.* (*bot.*, of seeds) a reduction in protoplasmic activity due to carbon dioxide concentration ‖ (*zool.*) the state of hibernation

dor·mant (dórmənt) *adj.* quiescent ‖ sleeping, or as if sleeping, *a dormant volcano* ‖ (*bot.*) inactive, resting, *a dormant plant* ‖ (*zool.*) hibernating ‖ (*heraldry*) in a sleeping position [O.F.]

dor·mer (dórmər) *n.* a projecting window built out from the slope of a roof [fr. O.F. *dormeor*, a dormitory]

dor·mie, dor·my (dórmi:) *adj.* (*golf*) ahead by as many holes as still remain to be played [origin unknown]

dor·mi·to·ry (dórmitọri:, dórmitọuri:) *pl.* **dor·mi·to·ries** *pl.* a communal sleeping room with a number of beds ‖ a suburban or country district from which many of the inhabitants go daily to work in a nearby town [fr. L. *dormitoriuin*, sleeping place]

dor·mouse (dórmaus) *pl.* **dor·mice** (dórmais) *n.* a rodent of fam. *Myoxidae*, small, arboreal, nocturnal mammals inhabiting temperate and warm countries. They feed on fruit, nuts and acorns, sitting upright to eat. They hibernate through winter in northern countries [M.E. *dormous* prob. rel. to F. *dormir*, to sleep]

dormy *DORMIE

Dor·pat (dórpat) *TARTU

dor·sal (dórsəl) 1. *adj.* (*anat.*) on or lying near the back, in human anatomy sometimes posterior (opp. VENTRAL) ‖ (*bot.*) away from the axis 2. *n.* a dossal [fr. M. L. *dorsalis*]

Dor·set·shire (dórsitʃər) (*abbr.* Dorset) a county (area 973 sq. miles, pop. 572,900) in S.W. England. County town: Dorchester

dor·ter, dor·tour (dórtər) *n.* (*hist.*) a monastery dormitory [O.F. *dortoiir*]

Dor·ti·cós Tor·ra·do (dortiːkóstərráδο), Osvaldo (1919–), Cuban president (1959–) after the Cuban revolution

Dort·mund (dórtmənd) one of W. Germany's oldest towns (pop. 627,000), in the N.E. Ruhr, a large port, connected to the Dortmund-Ems and Rhine-Herne canals, and rail center. Industries: steel, heavy machinery, rolling stock, chemicals, brewing

dortour *DORTER

do·ry, do·rey (dóri:, dóuri:) *pl.* **do·ries, doreys** *n.* a small, flat-bottomed fishing boat [Central Am. Ind. *dori*, dugout]

dory *pl.* **dories** *n. Zeus faber*, a bony fish of the mackerel family, celebrated for the delicacy of its flesh. It is yellow-green with a black spot on each side. It inhabits the Atlantic shores of Europe and the Mediterranean ‖ *Z. capensis*, a related species of southern seas [F. *dorée*, gilded]

dos·age (dóusidʒ) *n.* the amount and frequency in which a medicine is administered ‖ the administration of medicine in doses ‖ the adding of an ingredient to a mixture so as to secure some quality in it, e.g. sugar added to wine to increase the alcoholic content

dose (dous) 1. *n.* the amount of medicine to be taken at one time ‖ (*pop.*) an amount of punishment or anything else one can stand in limited quantities ‖ (of gamma or X-radiation) one roentgen, not necessarily one rad 2. *v.t. pres. part.* **dos·ing** *past* and *past part.* **dosed** to administer medicine to ‖ to treat (wine) with another ingredient, e.g. sugar [F. fr. M.L. fr. Gk]

do·sim·e·ter (dousímitər) *n.* any device for measuring doses of radioactivity or X rays

Dos Pas·sos (dospǽsos), John Roderigo (1896–1970), American novelist, author of 'Manhattan Transfer' (1926) and 'U.S.A.' (1930–6)

doss (dɒs) *v.i.* (*Br.*, with 'down') to lie down to sleep in an improvised bed or no bed at all [perh. rel. to F. *dos*, back]

dos·sal, dos·sel (dós'l) *n.* a hanging of drapery behind an altar, or along the sides of the chancel in a church [fr. M. L. *dossale*]

doss house (*Br.*, *pop.*) a flophouse

dos·si·er (dósi:ei, dósjei) *pl.* **dos·si·ers** (dósi:eiz, dósjeiz) *n.* a set of papers giving information about one particular subject, esp. one person's personal record [F.=a bundle of papers]

dost (dʌst) archaic *2nd pers. sing. pres.* of DO

Dos·to·yev·sky (dɒstɔijévski:), Fyodor Mikhailovich (1821–81), Russian novelist. His greatest works, written in his last 17 years, include 'Crime and Punishment' (1866), 'The Idiot'

(1868–9) and 'The Brothers Karamazov, (1880). The setting of his novels is contemporary Russia, but his themes are universal: good and evil, guilt and redemptive suffering, and the conflict between faith and intellectualism. The peculiarly Dostoyevskian situation is the anguish of a character suspended between systems of belief calling for separate courses of action

dot (dɒt) 1. *n.* a small spot or point, usually round ‖ a point in printing or writing, e.g. a period, or over an *i* or *j* ‖ (*mus.*) a point placed after a note denoting the lengthening of the note by half its value ‖ (*mus.*) a point placed over a note, denoting staccato ‖ a short sound as part of a letter on a Morse transmitter (cf. DASH) **on the dot** absolutely punctual 2. *v.t. pres. part.* **dot·ting** *past* and *past part.* **dot·ted** to mark with a dot or dots ‖ to mark as though with dots, *farms dotted the landscape* **to dot the i's and cross the t's** to leave nothing unsaid, make a matter perfectly clear **dót·ted** *adj.* (*mus.*) increased by half its time value, *a dotted minim* [perh. O.E. *dott*, head of a boil]

dot·age (dóutidʒ) *n.* feeblemindedness as a result of old age **in one's dotage** senile

do·tard (dóutərd) *n.* an old man becoming weak-minded

dote, doat (dout) *pres. part.* **dot·ing, doat·ing** *past* and *past part.* **dot·ed, doat·ed** *v.i.* (with 'on' or 'upon') to lavish ridiculous and inordinate affection ‖ to lavish very great affection **dót·ing, doát·ing** *adj.* [M.E. *doten*]

doth (dʌθ) archaic *third pers. sing. pres.* of DO

dot matrix printer an impact printer output device that prints from needles in a serial or line format

dottel *DOTTLE

dot·ter·el (dótərəl, dótrəl) *n. Eudromias morinellus*, fam. *Charadriidae*, a bird with a grayish back and chestnut and black breast, found in the uplands of Europe and Asia [fr. *dote*, to be foolish (because easily caught)]

dot·tle, dot·tel (dót'l) *n.* smoked tobacco caked in a pipe [DOT]

dot·ty (dóti:) *comp.* **dot·ti·er** *superl.* **dot·ti·est** *adj.* full of dots ‖ (*pop.*) silly or slightly mad ‖ (*pop.*, with 'about') infatuated

Dou·ai Bible, Dou·ay Bible (dúːei) an English translation of the Bible made from the Latin Vulgate and used in the Roman Catholic Church. The New Testament was published in 1582 at Reims and the Old Testament in 1609–10, by the seminary at Douai, France (*ALLEN)

Dou·a·la (duála) the chief port (pop. 250,000) and rail center of Cameroun, and its former capital

dou·ble (dʌb'l) *pres. part.* **dou·bling** *past* and *past part.* **dou·bled** *v.t.* to make double, multiply by two ‖ (*bridge*) to modify (an opponent's contract) with the effect of increasing what stands to be gained or lost ‖ (*mus.*) to duplicate (a melody), *the soprano doubles the violins* ‖ (*mus.*) to play (a second instrument) when needed, *the second flute doubles the recorder* ‖ to sail around, *to double the Cape* ‖ (*Br.*, *billiards*) to make (a ball) rebound ‖ *v.i.* (*Br.*) to break into a run, hurry up ‖ (*Br.*, *billiards*) to rebound **to double back** to fold over ‖ to turn back on one's tracks **to double up** to bend or fold (something over upon itself), *to double up one's fist* ‖ to cause (someone) to bend suddenly in two, esp. in pain ‖ to sleep (two people) in one room ‖ to bend suddenly in two because of pain or helpless laughter ‖ (of two people who would not normally share) to share a room ‖ (*Br.*) to break into a run, hurry up [M.E. *dublen*, *doblen*, fr. O. F.]

double 1. *adj.* having two parts, layers, decks, etc. ‖ forming a pair, *double six* ‖ of twice the usual speed, number or quantity, *a double whiskey* ‖ (of a bed or room) for two people ‖ (*bot.*, of a flower) having more than the normal number of floral leaves (cf. SINGLE) ‖ (*bot.*, of a plant) bearing such flowers **to live a double life** to have two ways of living: one under a usual social front and the other secret and private, esp. involving misconduct 2. *adv.* twice over, two together, *to see double* 3. *n.* something twice as much ‖ a person or thing that resembles another extremely closely ‖ (*mil.*) a running pace, *on the double*, (*Br.*) *at the double* ‖ (*bridge*) the doubling of a bid ‖ one bet placed on two contests, with very high odds ‖ a sharp backward turn ‖ (*baseball*) a hit which enables a batter to reach second base ‖ (*horse racing*) a wager on horses to win two races in the same day; also **daily double** (*movies*) an actor who substi-

tutes for the star, esp. in dangerous scenes ‖ (*pl.*, *tennis*) a game between two pairs [M.E. *duble*, *doble* fr. O.F.]

double bar (*mus.*) a pair of vertical lines across a staff marking the end of a movement or piece

dou·ble-bar·reled, esp. *Br.* **dou·ble-bar·relled** (dʌb'lbǽrəld) *adj.* (of a gun) having two barrels ‖ (*pop.*, of a surname) made up of two names, often hyphenated

double bass the largest and lowest-pitched stringed instrument in an orchestra, roughly of the same shape as a cello but much larger

double bassoon a bassoon larger and an octave lower in pitch than the ordinary type

double bind (*psych.*) dilemma faced by a dependent in which any response will result in disparagement or reprimand. A double bind is often due to conflicting instructions

double blind condition to ensure objectivity in an experiment where neither the person giving instructions nor the subjects are aware of the factors involved *Cf* SINGLE BLIND

double boiler a saucepan having two parts fitting one above the other so that the food in the upper one is cooked by water boiling in the lower

dou·ble-book (dʌb'lbúk) *v.* to accept reservations twice for the same accommodations

dou·ble-breast·ed (dʌb'lbréstid) *adj.* (of a coat) overlapping in front, with a double row of buttons

double chin a roll of fatty tissue below the chin

dou·ble-cov·er (dʌb'lkʌvər) *n.* (*football*, *basketball*) assignment of two defensive players to one offensive player

dou·ble-cross (dʌb'lkrɔ́s, dʌb'lkrós) 1. *v.i.* to cheat or betray (an associate) 2. *n.* such a betrayal

double dagger a diesis

Dou·ble·day (dʌb'ldei), Abner (1819–93), U.S. military officer who is often credited as the inventor of baseball. Although the myth perpetuates, it has been disproved

dou·ble-deal·er (dʌb'ldíːlər) *n.* a person who deceives someone by pretending one thing but doing another

dou·ble-deal·ing (dʌb'ldíːliŋ) 1. *n.* the deception practiced by a double dealer 2. *adj.* of or pertaining to a double-dealer or his deception

dou·ble-deck·er (dʌb'ldékər) *n.* a vehicle with two decks ‖ a sandwich with two layers of filling, three layers of bread

double decomposition a reaction between two molecules in which part of the first combines with part of the second, and the remainder of the first combines with the remainder of the second. Such a reaction may be represented by $AB + CD \rightarrow AD + CB$

dou·ble-dig·it (dʌb'ldídʒit) *adj.* of a number between 10 and 99

dou·ble-dip·per (dʌb'ldípər) *n.* 1. a pensioner who works for another employer and so receives two incomes 2. a government employee who receives income from two separate government sources

double Dutch unintelligible gibberish

dou·ble-edged (dʌb'lédʒd) *adj.* (of a blade) having two cutting edges ‖ (of a remark) apparently charitable but with hidden malice

dou·ble-end·er (dʌb'lendər) *n.* (*surfing*) board built in the same shape at both ends

dou·ble en·ten·dre (duːblātādr) *n.* a remark which can be interpreted in two ways, one of them usually indecent [F.]

double entry a method of bookkeeping in which every transaction is recorded in two books, or two sections of a ledger, as a debit to one account and credit to another

dou·ble-faced (dʌb'lféist) *adj.* two-faced, hypocritical

dou·ble·head·er (dʌb'lhédər) *n.* a train drawn by two engines ‖ (*baseball*) two games played by the same teams on the same day, one right after the other

double helix (*biol.*) two intertwined coils that form the crystalline structure of DNA. The term became popularized by book published in 1953 called *The Double Helix*, by J. D. Watson and F. H. C. Crick **double-helical** *adj.* *Cf* ALPHA HELIX

dou·ble-joint·ed (dʌb'ldʒɔ́intid) *adj.* having extremely flexible joints which permit fingers and toes etc. to bend back much further than is usual

dou·ble-knit (dʌb'lnít) *n.* process or product of knitting with two sets of needles to create interlocked double thickness **double knit** *v.*

dou·ble-lock (dʌb'llók) *v.t.* to lock by turning the key twice in the lock of (a door) ‖ to shut with two bolts

double meaning a double entendre

double negative a statement involving two negatives which together are equivalent to an affirmative. Thus, 'there is nobody here who has no food'='everyone here has some food'

double obelisk (*Br.*) a diesis

double ordering practice of placing orders for a product, esp. during period of short supply, with two sources to ensure delivery in minimum time, canceling one of the orders at a strategic time

double or nothing (*Am.=Br.* double or quits) a gamble on a throw of dice, a hand of cards or a toss of a coin to decide whether a debt already contracted shall be wiped out or doubled

dou·ble-park (dʌb'lpárk) *v.i.* to park an automobile in the road alongside one parked already at the curb ‖ *v.t.* to park (an automobile) in this way

double play (*baseball*) a play by which two players are put out

double precision (*computer*) use of two computer words for one number to achieve greater definition in the result, e.g., more decimal places **multiple precision** *n.* **single precision** *n.* **triple precision** *n.*

double-quick (dʌb'lkwík) 1. *adj.* very quick 2. *adv.* very quickly 3. *n.* (*mil.*) double time

dou·ble-reed (dʌb'lrí:d) *adj.* (*mus.*, of an instrument) having two reeds which beat against each other to set the column of air vibrating, e.g. in the oboe

dou·ble-reef (dʌb'lrí:f) *v.t.* (*naut.*) to take in two reefs of (a sail)

double refraction birefringence

double salt a salt containing two anions or cations ‖ a salt that is the result of the molecular combination of two distinct salts rather than of their coordination

double speak ambiguous language created by involved, bombastic, or circumlocutory semantics

double star two stars rotating about their common center of mass. When the orbital plane is oriented edgewise at some angle with respect to the terrestrial observer the stars eclipse one another in a regular period (cf. VARIABLE STAR) ‖ two stars virtually in the same line of sight though a great distance apart

dou·blet (dʌb'lit) *n.* (*hist.*) a man's close-fitting bodice or jacket with or without sleeves, usually decorated and padded, worn in W. Europe 14th–17th cc. ‖ (*optics*) two associated lines in a spectrum, e.g., in alkali metals ‖ (*electr.*) two elevated antennas in a straight line, with power provided from the center ‖ (*phys.*) two similar particles with different charges, e.g., neutron and proton ‖ (*pl.*) the same number on a pair of dice at a throw ‖ a counterfeit jewel, made by cementing a layer of colored glass between two crystals ‖ (*linguistics*) one of two words derived from the same source but differing in form, e.g. 'legal', 'loyal' [O.F. dim. of *double*, doublet]

double take a quick second reaction to a situation, remark etc., the meaning or implications of which did not at first occur to one ‖ a second look

dou·ble-talk (dʌb'ltɔk) 1. *n.* language empty of meaning or sincerity although superficially it seems meant sensibly ‖ deliberately ambiguous language, or inflated jargon 2. *v.i.* to use such language

dou·ble-think (dʌb'lθiŋk) *n.* the conscious holding of mutually exclusive opinions simultaneously ‖ vocalizing ideas in terms that do not mean what people generally accept them to mean, e.g., "peaceful coexistence"

double time quick time (*mil.*) the fastest rate of marching (180 yard-long paces to the minute), or a slow run, in step ‖ payment at twice the normal rate, for hours worked overtime or on holidays

dou·ble-ton (dʌb'ltən) *n.* (*cards*) two cards only of a suit held in a hand [after SINGLETON]

dou·ble-tongue (dʌb'ltʌŋ) *pres. part.* **dou·ble-tongu·ing** *past* and *past part.* **dou·ble-tongued** *v.i.* to play staccato notes on a wind instrument, esp. a flute, by rapidly moving the tongue alternately to teeth and hard palate

dou·ble-tree (dʌb'ltri:) *n.* the crosspiece of a plow etc., to which the singletrees are fixed when two horses are working together

double whole note (*mus.*) a breve

dou·bloon (dʌblú:n) *n.* (*hist.*) an old type of Spanish gold coin [F. *doublon* or Span. *doblón*]

dou·blure (dəblúər, du:blyr) *n.* the ornamental lining of a book cover, of silk, tooled leather or painted paper [F.=lining]

dou·bly (dʌbli:) *adv.* in a twofold manner, twice over

Doubs (du:) a department (area 2,052 sq. miles, pop. 471,100) of France in the N. Jura, bordering Switzerland. Chief town: Besançon (*FRANCHE-COMTE)

doubt (daut) *n.* a feeling of uncertainty ‖ (esp. *pl.*) misgivings **no doubt** it is probable to **be in doubt about** to be uncertain about **without doubt, without a doubt** certainly [O.F. *doute*]

doubt *v.t.* to disbelieve ‖ to distrust ‖ to be in doubt about ‖ *v.i.* to be in a state of doubt [O.F. *douter*]

doubt·ful (dáutfəl) *adj.* full of doubt ‖ of an uncertain but probably bad character, *a doubtful reputation* ‖ open to doubt

doubting Thomas an inveterate skeptic [after the Apostle *Thomas* (John xx, 24–9)]

doubt·less (dáutlis) 1. *adv.* without doubt, certainly 2. *adj.* (*rhet.*, with 'of') entertaining no doubt

douche (du:ʃ) 1. *n.* a jet (e.g. of water) for cleansing an internal or external part of the body ‖ an instrument for directing such a jet of water 2. *v. pres. part.* **douch·ing** *past* and *past part.* **douched** *v.t.* to give a douche to ‖ *v.i.* to take a douche [F. =stream of water]

dou·cine (du:sí:n) *n.* (*archit.*) an S-shaped molding, i.e. convex and concave in an unbroken curve, with the upper part concave [F.]

dough (dou) *n.* a mass of slightly moistened flour or meal, sometimes with yeast or fat added, esp. for making bread or pastry ‖ (*pop.*) money [O.E. *dāh*]

dough·boy (dóubɔi) *n.* (1st world war) an infantryman, GI

dough hook an attachment in some food processors utilizing a strong beater to knead dough

dough·nut (dóunʌt, dóunət) *n.* a ring or ball of sweetened dough fried in deep fat and often coated with sugar

dough·ti·ly (dáutili) *adv.* (*rhet.*) in a doughty way

dough·ti·ness (dáuti:nis) *n.* (*rhet.*) the quality of being doughty

Dough·ty (dáuti:), Charles Montagu (1843–1926), English traveler and writer. 'Travels in Arabia Deserta' (1888), his masterpiece, is written in a mannered, quasi-Elizabethan prose

dough·ty (dáuti:) *comp.* **dough·ti·er** *superl.* **dough·ti·est** *adj.* (*rhet.*) valiant, courageous [O.E. *dohtig*]

Doug·las (dʌgləs), Clifford Hugh (1879–1952), British social economist. He devised the theory of Social Credit

Douglas, Gavin (c. 1475–1522), medieval Scottish poet. His translation of Virgil's 'Aeneid' into Scots was the first translation of any classical author into any form of English vernacular

Douglas, Stephen Arnold (1813–61), U.S. political leader. As a senator (from 1847), he developed the doctrine of 'popular sovereignty', and drafted the bills giving territorial government to New Mexico and Utah (1850) and the Kansas-Nebraska bill (1854). He participated in the Lincoln-Douglas debates, defeating Lincoln in the Illinois senatorial election but losing to him in the 1860 presidential election

Douglas, William O. (1898–1980), U.S. Supreme Court associate justice (1939–75). Appointed to the Court by Pres. Franklin D. Roosevelt, Douglas championed individual rights and, privately, conservation measures. He was instrumental in such Supreme Court decisions as 'Griswold v. Connecticut' (1965), which abolished a state law against birth control. He wrote 'Of Men and Mountains' (1950), 'A Living Bill of Rights' (1961), 'Go East, Young Man' (1974), and 'The Court Years' (1980)

Douglas Democrats a faction of the U.S. Democratic party which supported Stephen Douglas's Kansas-Nebraska act (1854), and his concept of popular sovereignty

Douglas fir *Pseudotsuga taxifolia*, fam. *Pinaceae*, a very tall coniferous tree grown for timber, native to western North America [after David *Douglas*, Scottish botanist in the U.S.A. (1798–1834)]

Doug·las-Home (dʌgləshjú:m), Sir Alexander Frederick (1903–), formerly 14th earl of Home, British Conservative statesman. He renounced (1963) his peerage to become prime minister (1963–4). He became (1970–74) foreign secretary in the Heath government. In 1974 he was made a life peer as Baron Home of the Hirsel

Doug·lass (dʌgləs), Frederick (originally Frederick Augustus Washington Bailey, c. 1817–95), U.S. black journalist and orator who effectively campaigned (1841–60) at home and abroad for the abolition of slavery. He advocated the use of black troops in the Union Army during the Civil War and later worked in several capacities for the U.S. government

Dou·kho·bor, Du·kho·bor (dú:koubɔr) *n.* a member of a fanatical Russian religious sect, dating from the second half of the 18th c. Their rejection of the Christian sacraments, and of the dogmas of the Trinity and the divinity of Christ, led to their persecution and exile (1843) to the remote Caucasus. Many communities emigrated to W. Canada after 1898, where their religious attitudes (similar to those of the Quakers) continued to bring them into conflict with the authorities [Russ. *dukhobortsy* fr. *dukh*, spirit + *bortsy*, wrestlers]

dour (duər, dáuər) *adj.* sullen, sour ‖ stern, harsh [fr. L. *durus*, hard]

Dou·ro (dúərou) (*Span.* Duero) a river (485 miles long) of the Iberian Peninsula. Rising in N. central Spain, it flows west across Old Castile, along part of the Portuguese-Spanish frontier, then through N. Portugal into the Atlantic at Oporto. Sand bars prevent the entrance of large vessels

douse, dowse (daus) *pres. part.* **dous·ing, dows·ing** *past* and *past part.* **doused, dowsed** *v.t.* to drench with water ‖ to immerse in water ‖ (*naut.*) to lower (sail) ‖ (*pop.*) to extinguish (a light) [origin unknown]

DOVAP (*acronym*) doppler velocity and position, a method of tracking space vehicles and missiles computing the Doppler effect of echoes from several stations

dove (dʌv) *n.* any of several pigeons ‖ the symbol of peace (Genesis viii, 8–12) ‖ the Holy Spirit in Christian symbolism ‖ one who advocates a peaceful solution to international conflicts [M.E. fr. O.N. *dúfa*]

dove (douv) *alt. past* of DIVE

dove·cot (dʌvkɒt) *n.* a dovecote

dove·cote (dʌvkout) *n.* a structure for pigeons to roost or breed in

dove hawk the hen harrier

Do·ver (dóuvər) a port (pop. 100,751) in Kent, England, one of the Cinque Ports, and a popular resort: Norman castle (ruins), built over ancient fortifications

Dover the capital (pop. 23,507) of Delaware

Dover, Straits of the narrow part (about 22 miles long) of the English Channel, 21 miles across at the narrowest point. Ports: Dover and Folkestone in England and Boulogne and Calais in France

Dover, Treaty of *CHARLES II, king of England

dove·tail (dʌvteil) 1. *n.* (*carpentry*) a method of fitting two pieces of wood together, esp. at a right angle, by cutting wedge-shaped pieces out of each and fitting the projections of one into the recesses of the other ‖ a joint made in this way 2. *v.t.* to fix together by means of a dovetail ‖ to cause to fit well together ‖ *v.i.* to fit well together

Dow (dau), Charles Henry (1851–1902), U.S. financial authority and journalist. He was a founder (1882) of Dow, Jones & Company, a financial news service. He compiled (1884) the first average of U.S. stock prices, which developed into the Dow-Jones averages. He served (from 1889) as the first editor of the 'Wall Street Journal', forming a method of stock market analysis which became known as the Dow theory

Dow, Herbert Henry (1866–1930), U.S. chemist and pioneer in the chemical manufacturing industry. He studied the usefulness of brines, produced the first synthetic indigo in the U.S.A., and was granted more than 100 patents

dow *DHOW

CONCISE PRONUNCIATION KEY: (a) æ, cat; ɑ, car; ɔ fawn; ei, snake. (e) e, hen; i:, sheep; iə, deer; ɛə, bear. (i) i, fish; ai, tiger; ə:, bird. (o) o, ox; au, cow; ou, goat; u, poor; ɔi, royal. (u) ʌ, duck; u, bull; u:, goose; ə, bacillus; ju:, cube. x, loch; θ, think; ð, bother; z, Zen; ʒ, corsage; dʒ, savage; ŋ, orangutang; j, yak; ʃ, fish; tʃ, fetch; 'l, rabble; 'n, redden. Complete pronunciation key appears inside front cover.

dow·a·ger (dáuədʒər) n. a widow whose title derives from her dead husband ‖ (*loosely*) a formidably dignified elderly lady [O.F. *douagere*]

dow·di·ly (dáudili) adv. in a dowdy way

dow·di·ness (dáudi:nis) n. the state of being dowdy

dow·dy (dáudi:) 1. *comp.* **dow·di·er** *superl.* **dow·di·est** adj. (of a woman or her clothes) shabby, drab and unfashionable 2. *pl.* **dow·dies** n. a dowdy woman [origin unknown]

dow·el (dáuəl) 1. n. a metal or wooden headless pin for keeping a piece of metal or wood in position 2. *v.t. pres. part.* **dow·el·ing**, esp. *Br.* **dow·el·ling** past and past part. **dow·eled**, esp. *Br.* **dow·elled** to keep in position with a dowel [etym. doubtful]

dow·er (dáuər) 1. n. the part of her husband's property retained by a widow (often attrib., *dower house*) ‖ a dowry ‖ (*rhet.*) a natural gift 2. *v.t.* to give to (someone) as dower or dowry [O.F. *douaire*]

Dow·land (dáulənd), John (c. 1563–c. 1626), English lutenist, composer of songs and instrumental music

Down (daun) the southeastern county (area 952 sq. miles, pop. 246,624) of Northern Ireland. County town: Downpatrick

down (daun) n. the soft fluff on very young birds before they are fledged ‖ the fluff under the feathers of fully-fledged birds ‖ the breast feathers of certain birds, used for stuffing cushions etc. ‖ any fluffy growth resembling down, e.g. soft, very fine hair on the cheeks, or the fuzz on a peach or on some leaves (*PUBESCENCE) [O.N. *dun*]

down n. a stretch of open, treeless, upland ‖ a hillock of sand near the sea cast up by the wind, a dune ‖ *DOWNS [O.E. *dūn*, hill, perh. of Celtic origin]

down 1. adv. from a higher to a lower position, *pull the blind down* ‖ in a direction or place thought of as lower, *let's go down to the club* ‖ in a lower position, on the ground, *fallen down* ‖ below the horizon, *the sun went down* ‖ from generation to generation, or from ancestor to descendant, *traditions handed down* ‖ into a low mental or emotional state, *his morale has gone down* ‖ into a low physical condition, *to go down with a cold* ‖ to a smaller amount, *to dwindle down* ‖ to a fine consistency, *grind the flour down* ‖ into a more concentrated form, *he got his thesis down to 80 pages* ‖ in writing, *take his name down* ‖ in check, *you can't keep a good man down* ‖ to a less active condition, *the fire has died down* ‖ less in value, *their shares are down* ‖ very much, *loaded down with boxes* ‖ as an initial cash payment, *10 dollars down* 2. *prep.* in a lower position on, *further down the hill* ‖ further along, *down the street* ‖ descending toward, through, into ‖ towards the mouth or outlet of 3. adj. descending, *a down current* ‖ in a low or lower place or at a low or lower level, *the river is down* ‖ brought, gone, fallen, pulled, paid, written etc. down ‖ (*Br.*) away from London, *a down train* ‖ ill, *he is down with flu* ‖ depressed, *down in the dumps* ‖ (*games*) behind an opponent in points, *three down* ‖ (*football, of the ball*) out of play ‖ (*baseball*) put out ‖ (*of a boxer*) with a part of the body other than the feet touching the floor ‖ (*of a boxer*) in a position excluding self-defense and acknowledged as such by the referee **down on** ill-disposed towards **down on one's luck** having a series of misfortunes, esp. financial 4. n. *UPS AND DOWNS ‖ (*football*) one of four plays in which the team having the ball must score or advance the ball at least 10 yds in order to keep it ‖ the declaring of the ball as down or the play just before this **to have a down on someone** (*Br.*) to show persistent disfavor or antagonism towards someone 5. *v.t.* to knock, throw, put, bring or drink down, *to down someone with one blow, to down a glass of beer* [O.E. *dūn, dūne* fr. *adune* fr. of, away from + *dun*, hill]

down-and-out (dáunənáut, dáunəndáut) 1. n. a destitute person ‖ a person who is incapacitated or broken down in health 2. adj. destitute ‖ incapacitated, broken down in health

down-at-heel (dáunəthí:l) adj. very shabbily dressed

down·beat (dáunbi:t) n. the accented beat in music ‖ the first beat in the bar ‖ the downward movement of the conductor's baton marking the beat

down-bow (dáunbou) n. (in playing a bowed instrument) a stroke from the heel to the tip of the bow (cf. UP-BOW)

down calver (*Br.*) a cow almost ready to calve

down-calv·ing (dáunkæviŋ, dáunkɑviŋ) adj. (*Br.*) almost ready to calve

down·cast (dáunkæst, dáunkɑst) adj. depressed, dispirited ‖ directed downward, *downcast eyes*

Down Easter a person from New England, esp. Maine

down·er (dáunər) n. (*colloq.*) 1. a depressant drug, e.g., a barbiturate 2. a depressing experience *ant* upper

down·fall (dáunfɔl) n. a heavy fall of rain or snow ‖ a fall from greatness or prosperity ‖ a cause of ruin, *pride will be his downfall* ‖ a deadfall

down·grade (dáungreid) 1. n. a downward slope **on the downgrade** heading for ruin 2. adj. and adv. downhill 3. *v.t. pres. part.* **down·grad·ing** past and past part. **down·grad·ed** to reduce to a status carrying less salary, or put in a lower category

down·haul (dáunhɔl) n. a rope used to help in hauling down a sail

down·heart·ed (dáunhártid) adj. depressed, dejected

down·hill (dáunhíl) 1. adj. describing a downward slope 2. adv. moving down a slope ‖ sloping down ‖ declining, failing in health, energy etc.

down·hill·er (dáunhílər) n. (*skiing*) one who races downhill

down-home (daunhóum) adj. (*colloq.*) homey

down·i·ness (dáuni:nis) n. the quality of being downy

Down·ing Street (dáuniŋ) the street in Westminster, London, where the prime minister and the chancellor of the exchequer have their official residences (sometimes used elliptically to mean the British government or cabinet)

down-in-the-mouth (dáuninðəmáuθ) adj. depressed, dejected

down-mouth (dáunmauθ) v. to make less of a thing or person in conversation. *syn.* bad-mouth

down-play (dáunplei) v. to deemphasize

down·pour (dáunpɔr, dáunpour) n. a heavy shower of rain

down range adv. along the course of a rocket testing range **down-range** adj.

down·right (dáunrait) 1. adj. straightforward, blunt ‖ utter, *a downright lie* 2. adv. thoroughly, *downright rude*

Downs (daunz) any of certain grass-covered ranges of chalk hills in S. England, esp. the North Downs (Surrey and Kent) and the South Downs (Sussex) ‖ a roadstead (about 9 miles long, 6 miles wide) in the English Channel, off E. Kent

Down's syndrome (*med.*) mongolism, a type of congenital mental retardation. An afflicted person typically has a broad face, slanting eyes, and a short fifth finger. Down's syndrome is named for J. L. H. Down, English physician

down·stage (dáunsteidʒ) 1. adv. (*theater*) at or towards the front of the stage 2. (dáunsteidʒ) adj. (*theater*) located or occurring downstage (cf. UPSTAGE)

down·stair (dáunstɛ̱ər) adj. downstairs

down·stairs (dáunstɛ̱ərz) 1. adv. on or to a lower floor, esp. the ground floor 2. (dáunstɛ̱ərz) adj. situated on the floor below, esp. on the ground floor 3. (dáunstɛ̱ərz) n. the ground floor of a building, *the downstairs is still to be painted*

down·stream (dáunstrí:m) adv. and adj. in the direction of the flow of a river or stream, relatively nearer to the mouth of a river

down·throw (dáunθrou) n. (*geol.*) the subsidence of rock strata on one side of a fault

down tick (*securities*) 1. a drop in the price of a security on trading market 2. the transaction *Cf* up tick

down-to-earth (dáuntuɛ́:rθ) adj. realistic and practical

down to the ground (*Br.*, following the verb 'to suit') completely

down·town (dáuntáun, dáuntaun) 1. adv. and adj. to or in the business area of a city or town ‖ to or in the lower part of a town or city 2. n. the main business area of a city or town

down·trod·den (dáuntrɒd'n) adj. kept in subjection, oppressed ‖ trodden down, *downtrodden grass*

down under (*pop.*) Australia or New Zealand

down·ward (dáunwərd) 1. adj. from a higher to a lower level ‖ towards an inferior state 2. adv. in a downward direction [O.E. *adūnweard*]

down·wards (dáunwərdz) adv. downward

down·wind (dáunwind, dáunwind) adj. and adv. on the leeward side ‖ in the same direction as the wind

down·y (dáuni:) *comp.* **down·i·er** *superl.* **down·i·est** adj. covered with any soft fluffy substance ‖ resembling down

dow·ry (dáuri:) *pl.* **dow·ries** n. the money, land or other possessions which a woman brings to her husband under a marriage contract [A.F. *dowarie*]

dowse (dauz) *pres. part.* **dows·ing** past and past part. **dowsed** *v.i.* to search for water or minerals by means of a divining rod [origin unknown]

dowse *DOUSE

dowsing rod a divining rod

Dow·son (dáus'n), Ernest (1867–1900), English fin-de-siècle poet, best known for his 'Cynara'

dox·ol·o·gy (dɒksɒlədʒi:) *pl.* **dox·ol·o·gies** n. a short formula of praise to God, esp. Trinitarian [fr. M.L. *doxologia* fr. Gk *doxa*, giving glory + *logos*, word]

dox·o·ru·bi·cin [C$_{27}$H$_{29}$NO$_{11}$] (dɒksərú:bisin) n. (*pharm.*) cytotoxic antibiotic used in treating tumors, esp. in breast, lymph glands, and ovaries; marketed as Adriamycin

dox·y·cy·cline [C$_{22}$H$_{24}$N$_2$O$_8$H$_2$O] (dɒksisáikli:n) n. (*pharm.*) a broad-spectrum antibiotic derived from tetracycline; sold under the trade name Vibramycin

doy·en (dɔ́iən, dɔién) n. the senior member of a body by length of service, sometimes by age [F. = dean]

Doyle (dɔil), Sir Arthur Conan (1859–1930), English author. His fame rests on the Sherlock Holmes detective stories (1887–1927), and related novels

doyley *DOILY

doz. abbreviation

doze (douz) 1. *v.i. pres. part.* **doz·ing** past and past part. **dozed** to sleep lightly ‖ to be half asleep **to doze off** to fall lightly asleep 2. n. a short sleep, catnap [etym. doubtful]

doz·en (dʌ́z'n) *pl.* **doz·ens, doz·en** n. a group of 12, *a dozen eggs, three dozen* ‖ a small but unspecified number, *a dozen lines would be enough* **to talk nineteen to the dozen** (*Br.*) to chatter fast and incessantly **dóz·ens** *pl.* n. a large but unspecified number, *dozens of times* [O.F. *dozeine, dosaine*]

doz·y (dóuzi:) *comp.* **doz·i·er** *superl.* **doz·i·est** adj. drowsy

DP (*abbr.*) data processing

DP, D.P. displaced person

Dr Doctor

drab (dræb) *comp.* **drab·ber** *superl.* **drab·best** adj. dull brown in color ‖ dull, monotonous, *a drab existence* [fr. F. *drap*, cloth]

Drabble (dræb'l), Margaret (1939–), English writer known for her novels depicting present day English society. She wrote 'The Millstone' (1965), 'The Realms of Gold' (1975), 'The Genius of Thomas Hardy' (1976), 'The Ice Age' (1977), 'A Writer's Britain; Landscape in Literature' (1979), and 'The Middle Ground' (1980)

dra·cae·na (drəsí:nə) n. a member of *Dracuena*, fam. *Liliaceae*, a genus of tropical trees. The stem branches and grows in thickness by the making of secondary cambium. Red resin (dragon's blood), collected from stem incisions, was used as a varnish by the great Italian violin makers (*CREMONA) [Mod. L. fr. Gk *drakaina*, she-dragon]

drachm (dræm) n. a drachma ‖ a dram [F. *drachme*]

drach·ma (drǽkmə) *pl.* **drach·mas, drach·mae** (drǽkmi:) n. an ancient Greek silver coin ‖ a modern Greek monetary unit or a coin representing it ‖ any of several modern measures of weight, esp. a dram [L. fr. Gk]

Dra·co (dréikou) Athenian lawgiver who drew up a code of laws prescribing fixed penalties (621 B.C.). Because of their severity most were revised (594 B.C.) by Solon

Dra·co·ni·an (dreikóuniən) adj. pertaining to Draco, or the code of laws drawn up by him ‖ (of other laws) exceedingly harsh [fr. L. *Draco* fr. Gk]

Dra·con·ic (dreikónik) adj. Draconian

draff (dræf) n. the remains of malt left after brewing [M.E. *draf* prob. fr. Gmc]

draft, draught (dræft, drɑft) 1. n. (*Br.* esp. **draught**) a rough plan of a work to be executed ‖ a writing, drawing, plan etc. as first put on paper and intended to be revised later ‖ the payment of money from an account held for this purpose, esp. by a bank ‖ the written order for this payment ‖ a number of men selected for service with the armed forces or for performing a particular task ‖ conscription ‖ the selection for any compulsory service of one individual, or more than one, from a group ‖ the slight taper given to the sides of a pattern for molding so that it may be withdrawn easily from the mold ‖ (*masonry, Br.* also **draught**) a narrow border chiseled along the edge of a stone to serve as a guide for the stonecutter ‖ (*Br.* esp. **draught**) a current of air in a room, chimney etc ‖ a device for controlling the flow of air in a chimney, fireplace etc. ‖ (*Br.* esp. **draught**) the act of dragging with a net ‖ (*Br.* esp. **draught**) the quantity of fish caught in a net ‖ (*Br.* esp. **draught**) the act of drinking ‖ (*Br.* esp. **draught**) a quantity of liquid drunk ‖ (*Br.* esp. **draught**) the depth of water which a ship requires for floating **2.** *adj.* (*Br.* esp. **draught**) used for pulling loads, *draft animals* ‖ (*Br.* esp. **draught**) drawn from a barrel, *draft ale* **3.** *v.t.* to call up for military service ‖ to detail (esp. troops) for a particular purpose ‖ (*auto racing*) to tailgate a car in order to lessen air pressure in front of one's car ‖ (*baseball, football*) to select new professional players ‖ (*Br.* esp. **draught**) to make a rough, preliminary version of (a document, letter etc.) ‖ (*Br. esp.* **draught**) to draw up (a statute etc.) ‖ (*masonry, Br.* also **draught**) to chisel or dress on (stone) **draftee** (dræfti:) *n.* a conscript **dráft·i·ly, dráught·i·ly** *adv.* **dráft·i·ness, dráught·i·ness** *n.* [M.E. *draht* of Gmc origin]

draft board a group of civilians from a community who select men for military service

drafts·man, *Br.* also **draughts·man** (dráftsmən, drúftsmən) *pl.* **drafts·men, draughts·men** (dráftsmən, drúftsmən) *n.* a person who makes plans or drawings ‖ a person who draws up documents ‖ an artist with particular reference to his skill at drawing ‖ (*Br.,* **draughtsman**) a checker (piece used in the game of checkers)

draft·y, esp. *Br.* **draught·y** (dræfti:, drúfti:) *comp.* **draft·i·er, draught·i·er** *superl.* **draft·i·est, draught·i·est** *adj.* exposed to currents of air, *a drafty room*

drag (dræg) **1.** *v. pres. part.* **drag·ging** *past* and *past part.* **dragged** *v.t.* to pull or haul along, esp. with an effort ‖ to move (one's feet) in walking without completely lifting them from the ground, esp. through tiredness ‖ to search the bottom of (a river, lake etc.) with a grapnel or net in order to recover a body, lost object etc. ‖ to break (land) with a drag or harrow *v.i.* (*mus.*) to go too slowly, or fail to keep up with the conductor's beat ‖ to be dragged, pulled or trailed ‖ to use a drag ‖ (of time) to pass slowly **to drag in** to introduce (a topic etc.) into a discussion unnecessarily **to drag on** to continue for a wearisomely long time **to drag out** to protract **to drag the anchor** (of a ship) to pull the anchor along the sea bottom **2.** *n.* (*agric.*) a heavy harrow ‖ a device, such as a grapnel, for searching the bottom of a river or lake etc. ‖ a strongly scented lure dragged over the ground to leave a trail for hounds, or the hunt that works this way ‖ something or someone that hinders ‖ (*aeron.*) the total air resistance to the flight of an aircraft ‖ (*colloq.*) a boring activity ‖ (*pop.*) women's clothes worn by a man [O.E. *dragan* or O.N.]

drag anchor a floating frame covered with canvas, trailed on the end of a hawser, to lessen drifting and keep the boat head on. It is used when it is not possible to cast the usual type of anchor

drag bunt (*baseball*) a bunt in which the bat is dropped in front of the ball

drag·gle (dræg'l) *pres. part.* **drag·gling** *past* and *past part.* **drag·gled** *v.t.* to make (something) wet and dirty by trailing it on the ground ‖ *v.i.* to become wet and dirty through trailing ‖ to lag behind

drag link a link joining the cranks of two shafts

drag·net (drægnet) *n.* a large net for dragging along the bottom of a river etc. to catch fish, or over a field to enclose small game ‖ a police network for catching criminals

Dra·go (drágɔ), Luis María (1859–1921), Argentine jurist and Foreign Minister, author of the doctrine (1907) which bears his name. Directed against the Platt Amendment, the doctrine repudiated the claim that the collection of foreign debts justifies the use of armed intervention

drag·o·man (drægəmən) *pl.* **drag·o·mans, drag·o·men** (drægəmən) *n.* (in the Near East)

an interpreter in Turkish, Arabic or Persian [F. fr. Gk fr. O. Arab.]

drag·on (drægən) *n.* a mythical, winged animal with a huge scaly body, enormous claws and sharp teeth ‖ a formidably fierce person, esp. a woman ‖ (*zool.*) a lizard having on each flank a broad wing, found in the East Indies and S. Asia [F. fr. L. fr. Gk]

drag·on·et (drægənit, drægənét) *n.* a member of *Callionymus,* fam. *Callionymidae,* a genus of small fish widely distributed in temperate seas. In the breeding season the male has blue and violet markings

drag·on·fly (drægənflai) *pl.* **drag·on·flies** *n.* a member of *Odonata,* an order of neuropterous insects, useful to man. They have four membranous, iridescent wings, a long slender body, huge compound eyes, and strong mouthparts for chewing. They generally fly near water, feeding on insects which they catch in flight. They lay their eggs in water, the larvae feeding voraciously on aquatic insects

drag·on·nades (drægənéidz) *pl. n.* (F. *hist.*) the persecution (1681–5) of the Huguenots under Louis XIV by dragoons quartered in Protestant towns and villages [F.]

dragon's blood red resin from the surface of immature fruits of the jungle palm of Malaya and East Indies, genus *Daemonorops,* fam. *Palmaceae.* In earlier times dragon's blood was collected from stem incisions on the dracaena

dragon tree the dracaena

dra·goon (drəgú:n) **1.** *n.* (*hist.*) a mounted infantryman armed with a carbine ‖ a member of certain cavalry regiments that were formerly mounted infantry **2.** *v.t.* (F. *hist.*) to persecute by setting dragoons upon (*DRAGONNADES) ‖ to bully or harry into a course of action [fr. F. *dragon,* carbine]

drag queen (*slang*) male transvestite

drag racing (*sports*) a type of automobile racing from a standing start covering a straightaway one-quarter mile distance **drag strip** *n.* site for a drag race

drag·rope (drǽgroup) *n.* a rope on a gun carriage used for dragging it or for locking the wheels ‖ a rope attached to an aerostat as a mooring, brake or ballast

drag sail a drag anchor made from a sail

drag sheet a drag sail

drain (drein) **1.** *v.t.* to conduct water away from (land) by means of drains, conduits, canals etc. ‖ (of a river or stream) to carry away the water from (a district) ‖ to remove surplus water from by sieving, standing in racks etc. ‖ to empty (a vessel) of liquid, esp. by drinking ‖ to exhaust of energy, wealth etc. ‖ *v.i.* (of liquid) to flow or trickle away ‖ (often with 'away') to disappear slowly, *his fortune drained away* **2.** *n.* a pipe or channel carrying away water or sewage from a street or a building ‖ a channel for draining off water from flat land ‖ the metal grating and stone or concrete edging surrounding the inlet of a house drain ‖ (*med.*) a tube or catheter for drawing off the discharge from an abscess or open wound ‖ a constant or protracted demand on wealth, energy or other resources ‖ (*Br.,* pop.) a very small amount of liquid, esp. for drinking **to go down the drain** to be lost, wasted or thrown away **drain·age** *n.* the draining of land etc. ‖ a system of drains or water courses [O.E. *dreahnian,* dry]

drain·pipe (dréinpaip) *n.* a pipe (usually of stoneware) carrying off soil or waste for disposal ‖ a vertical (usually metal) pipe on the outside of a house for conveying rainwater to a drain

Drake (dreik), Sir Francis (c. 1540–96), English sailor. After several slave-trading expeditions to W. Africa and the Spanish Main (1566–73), he circumnavigated the globe (1577–80) in the 'Golden Hind'. He delayed the Spanish Armada by raiding Cadiz (1587), and helped to defeat (1588) the Spanish attempt to invade England. He was a kinsman of Sir John Hawkins

drake (dreik) *n.* a male duck (of any species) as distinct from the female [M.E. of Gmc origin]

drake *n.* a mayfly, sometimes used in fishing [O.E. *draca* fr. L. *draco,* dragon]

Dra·kens·berg Mtns (drákənzbə:rg) a chain of mountains in S.E. South Africa, running about 600 miles parallel to the coast between Cape Province and the Vaal River. Highest peak: Mont-aux-Sources (10,761 ft)

Drake Passage (or Drake Strait) a strait (c. 500 miles long, 400 miles wide) between Cape Horn and the South Shetland Is, connecting the South Atlantic and the Pacific

dram (dræm) *n.* a measure of weight: (avoirdupois) 27 1/3 grains or 1/16 oz., (apothecaries') 60 grains or 1/8 oz. ‖ a small shot of liquor, esp. whiskey [O.F. *dragme*]

dra·ma (drámə, dræmə) *n.* a play written for actors to perform ‖ a play which in general is serious, not comic, but which does not rise to tragedy ‖ plays for acting as a literary genre ‖ a slice of real life with the intensity of a play [L.L. fr. Gk]

dra·mat·ic (drəmætik) *adj.* pertaining to drama or the theater ‖ as striking as a play ‖ (of people) inclined to give falsely heightened emphasis to ordinary events, conversation etc. **dra·mát·i·cal·ly** *adv.* [fr. L.L. *dramaticus* fr. Gk]

dramatic irony the ironic effect produced in a play when the characters' behavior is seen by the audience to be out of keeping with the situation being developed, because of the characters' ignorance of the full situation

dra·mat·ics (drəmætiks) *pl. n.* the performance of plays by amateurs ‖ the technique of acting as a branch of study ‖ dramatic behavior

dram·a·tis per·so·nae (drú:mətispər:sóunai) *pl. n.* the characters in a play, or a list of these (cf. CAST) [L.]

dram·a·tist (drǽmətist, drámətist) *n.* a playwright [fr. Gk *drama (dramatos),* drama]

dram·a·ti·za·tion (dræmətizéijən, drəmətizéi-jən) *n.* a turning into a play ‖ a rendering vivid by acting

dram·a·tize (drǽmətaiz, drámətaiz) *pres. part.* **dram·a·tiz·ing** *past* and *past part.* **dram·a·tized** *v.t.* to put (a novel etc.) into the form of a play ‖ to behave dramatically over (an ordinary situation) ‖ to exaggerate histrionically [fr. Gk *drama (dramatos),* drama]

dram·a·tur·gy (drǽmətə:rdʒi:, drámətə:rdʒi:) *n.* the art of writing plays ‖ the technical devices proper to this art [fr. Gk *dramatourgia,* dramatic composition]

drame à clef (dram a klei) *n.* (*Fr.*) a play with characters and/or situations from reality

drame à thèse (dram a tez) *n.* (*Fr.*) a play designed to promote a doctrine or theory

drank *past* of DRINK

drape (dreip) **1.** *v.t. pres. part.* **drap·ing** *past* and *past part.* **draped** to cover or ornament with material, hangings, flags etc. ‖ to arrange (materials) in decorative folds **2.** *n.* a draped tapestry or curtain ‖ the manner of hanging, *the drape of a gown* [F. *draper,* to weave]

drap·er (dréipər) *n.* (*Br.*) a retailer who sells cloths and sometimes clothes [A.F.]

dra·per·y (dréipəri:) *pl.* **dra·per·ies** *n.* the representation of clothes etc. in sculpture, painting etc. ‖ (esp. *pl.*) material hanging in folds ‖ (*Br.*) dry goods ‖ (*Br.*) a draper's business [O.F. *draperie*]

dras·tic (dræstik) *adj.* acting violently, having extreme effects, *a drastic punishment* ‖ rigorous, thoroughgoing, *a drastic overhaul* **drás·ti·cal·ly** *adv.* [fr. Gk *drastikos*]

draught *DRAFT

draught·board (dræftbɔrd, dræftbourd, dráftbɔrd, dráftbourd) *n.* (*Br.*) a checkerboard

draughtily *DRAFTILY

draughtiness *DRAFTINESS

draughts (dræfts, drafts) *n.* (*Br.*) the game of checkers

draughtsman *DRAFTSMAN

draughty *DRAFTY

Dra·va, Dra·ve (drávə) a river (450 miles) which rises in the Austrian Tyrol, and passes through S. Austria and N. Yugoslavia, forming part of the latter's frontier with Hungary, before it flows into the Danube north of Belgrade

Dra·vid·i·an (drəvídi:ən) **1.** *adj.* pertaining to a group of mixed races mainly in S. India and in N. Ceylon, or their languages **2.** *n.* a member of the Dravidian groups of peoples ‖ the family of non-Indo-European agglutinative languages, spoken by about 95 million people in India and Ceylon, including Tamil, Malayalam and Telugu

draw (drɔ) **1.** *v. pres. part.* **draw·ing** *past* **drew** (dru:) *past part.* **drawn** (drɔn) *v.t.* to pull, *a cart drawn by a horse* ‖ to attract, *to draw an audience* ‖ to pull out, extract, *to draw a cork* ‖ to remove the entrails from (a chicken etc.) ‖ to make a picture or plan of with pencil, pen and ink, charcoal, crayon etc. ‖ to delineate in words, *the book's characters are well drawn* ‖ to deduce and formulate, *to draw conclusions* ‖ to inhale, *to draw a deep breath* ‖ to try to get information out of (someone) ‖ to stretch out to greater length, *to draw wire* ‖ to cause to dis-

CONCISE PRONUNCIATION KEY: **(a)** æ, c*a*t; ɑ, c*a*r; ɔ f*aw*n; ei, sn*a*ke. **(e)** e, h*e*n; i:, sh*ee*p; iə, d*ee*r; ɛə, b*ea*r. **(i)** i, f*i*sh; ai, t*i*ger; ə:, b*i*rd. **(o)** o, *o*x; au, c*ow*; ou, g*oa*t; u, p*oo*r; ɔi, r*oy*al. **(u)** ʌ, d*u*ck; u, b*u*ll; u:, g*oo*se; ə, b*a*cillus; ju:, c*u*be. x, lo*ch*; θ, *th*ink; ð, bo*th*er; z, *Z*en; ʒ, cor*s*age; dʒ, sa*v*age; ŋ, ora*n*gutang; j, *y*ak; ʃ, *fi*sh; tʃ, fe*tch*; 'l, rabb*le*; 'n, redd*en*. Complete pronunciation key appears inside front cover.

drawback   284   dressily

charge, *a poultice draws an abscess* ‖ to obtain from a source of supply, *to draw one's wages* ‖ to write out (a check) ‖ (of a boat) to need (a certain depth of water) in order to float ‖ (*Br.*) to search (woods etc.) for game ‖ to get in a lottery, *to draw a winning ticket* ‖ (*Br.*) to cause to swell, *to draw the feet* ‖ *v.i.* to infuse, *let the tea draw* ‖ to make a pastime or profession of drawing pictures etc. ‖ to end a match or game without either side winning ‖ to make the same score as, or arrive level with, another competitor ‖ (with 'on') to obtain something from a reserve, store etc., *to draw on one's imagination* ‖ to draw lots ‖ (of smoking, with 'on') to inhale (through a pipe etc.) ‖ to have a draft, *the chimney draws well* **to draw apart** to grow less intimate, fall away in affection **to draw aside** to take or move aside from others, usually in order to speak privately **to draw away from** to increase one's lead over (people, vehicles etc.) **to draw back** to move back, recoil **to draw in** (*Br.*, of a train) to arrive at the station ‖ (of a vehicle) to come in to the curb or side of the road and halt ‖ (of the period of daylight) to become shorter **to draw on** (*Br.*, of a point in future time) to come nearer **to draw oneself up** to straighten one's back and stand very erect **to draw out** (of a train) to move away ‖ to protract (a speech, explanation etc.) ‖ to encourage (a reticent person) to talk **to draw up** to make a draft of (plans, maps etc.) ‖ to arrange (troops etc.) in formation ‖ (of a vehicle) to come to a halt ‖ to bring one s chair closer **2.** *n.* a stunt, personality etc. that attracts customers or an audience ‖ a game or match that ends without either side winning ‖ the drawing of lots ‖ a raffle ‖ the pulling of a revolver out of its holster to shoot, *quick on the draw* ‖ the movable part of a drawbridge ‖ (*card games*) the choosing of a card from the pack ‖ a deal of cards to improve the hands of players after discarding in draw poker [O.E. *dragan*]

draw·back (drɔ́bæk) *n.* a disadvantage, esp. in something otherwise satisfactory ‖ a withdrawal ‖ an amount of customs or excise duty on imported goods that is paid back when the goods are exported again or if they are used in the manufacture of export items or destroyed in the manufacturing process ‖ a tax refund on products used for certain purposes ‖ money refunded, esp. secretly as a bribe or favor ‖ compensation payment (*KICKBACK)

drawback lock a lock with a spring bolt that can be drawn back by a knob on the inside of a door

draw·bridge (drɔ́brɪdʒ) *n.* a bridge hinged at one end so that it can be pulled up with chains, etc., to prevent passage over it or to allow passage under it

draw-down (drɔ́daun) *n.* a decrease in level of water behind a dam by allowing some water to escape **drawdown** *v.*

draw·ee (drɔɪ́:) *n.* the person on whom a draft or bill of exchange is drawn

draw·er (drɔ́ər) *n.* someone who draws ‖ (drɔr) a boxlike receptacle for clothes, papers etc. which slides in and out of a table, cabinet etc. or on a special frame ‖ (*pl.*, *old-fash.*, drɔrz) underpants

draw·ing (drɔ́ɪŋ) *n.* a sketch, picture or plan in pencil, charcoal, crayon, etc. ‖ the art of producing these ‖ a gathering at which lots are drawn in order to reach some decision

drawing account a current account ‖ an expense account, esp. one recording money advanced to a salesman for his traveling expenses or against his future sales or commission

drawing block a pad of drawing paper

drawing board a wide, straightedged, right-angled, wooden board to which the paper is pinned while a drawing is made

drawing compass a pair of compasses having a pencil or pen on one leg and a point on the other

drawing pin (*Br.*) a thumbtack

drawing room a formal sitting room, esp. the room in which guests are received ‖ a formal reception (e.g. at court) [earlier *withdrawing room*]

draw·knife (drɔ́naɪf) *pl.* **draw·knives** (drɔ́-naɪvz) *n.* a straight metal blade with a handle set at right angles to it at each end, used for planing off surfaces by drawing it towards one

drawl (drɔl) **1.** *v.i.* to speak indistinctly, lengthening the vowels, and slurring one word into the next in a slow, lazy way ‖ *v.t.* to utter in this

way **2.** *n.* this manner of speech [prob. fr. DRAW, to protract]

drawn *past part.* of DRAW

drawn-thread work (drɔ́nθrɛd) linen embroidery in which some of the threads of warp and weft are pulled out of the material to make patterns, the rest of the material then being worked

drawn·work (drɔ́nwə:rk) *n.* drawn-thread work

draw poker (*cards*) the most usual variety of poker, played with five cards dealt face down

draw·shave (drɔ́ʃeiv) *n.* a drawknife

draw shot (*pool*) a shot in which backspin is imparted to the cue ball

draw-string (drɔ́strɪŋ) *n.* a string or cord that runs through eyes or a hem in e.g. a purse or a hood. It gathers the material when it is pulled so as to close an opening or make it smaller

draw stroke (*canoeing*) paddle stroke into the side of a canoe to steer the canoe in the direction of the stroke

draw weight *n.* **1.** (*archery*) the force required to pull the string of a bow **2.** (*curling*) the force necessary to deliver a stone to the opposite side

draw well a deep well from which water is drawn by a bucket on a rope

dray (drei) *n.* a low, flat cart, without sides or with very low sides, used, e.g. by brewers, for very heavy loads [M.E. *dreie* fr. O.E. *dragan*, to draw]

dray horse a powerful cart horse used for pulling drays

dray·man (dréimən) *pl.* **dray·men** (dréimən) *n.* the driver of a dray

Dray·ton (dréit'n), Michael (1563–1631), English poet known for his pastorals and sonnets and for 'Polyolbion' (1612), a long poetical description of the geography and lore of Britain

dread (dred) **1.** *v.t.* to be very much afraid of, esp. to anticipate with great apprehension **2.** *n.* apprehension ‖ great fear ‖ something that is greatly feared *in dread of* greatly afraid of **3.** *adj.* (*rhet.*) feared, dreaded [M.E. *dreden*, *drǣden* of Gmc origin]

dread·ful (drédfəl) *adj.* inspiring dread ‖ very bad, *a dreadful play* **dréad·ful·ly** *adv.*

dread·nought (drédnɔt) *n.* (*hist.*) an early 20th-c. heavily armed battleship, with its main armament consisting of big guns all of the same caliber

dream (dri:m) **1.** *n.* an idea or image present in the sleeping mind ‖ a reverie, daydream ‖ something greatly desired ‖ (*pop.*) something excellent or very beautiful, *a dream of a hat* ‖ an extravagant fancy, *space travel used to be just a dream* **2.** *v. pres. part.* **dream·ing** *past and past part.* **dreamt** (dremt), **dreamed** (dremt, dri:md) *v.t.* to experience mentally while asleep ‖ *v.i.* to have experience of ideas and images during sleep ‖ to indulge in reverie or imagination, usually of a pleasant kind, esp. to daydream **to dream of** (in negative constructions) to contemplate, imagine, *she wouldn't dream of doing such a thing* ‖ to long for (something) or be very desirous of (doing or obtaining something) **to dream up** to conceive, think up (an idea) **dréam·er** *n.* an impractical person who tends to live in a world of fantasy [M.E. *dream*, *drem* fr. O.E. *drēam*, joy and O.N. *draum*, dream]

dream·land (drí:mlænd) *n.* an imaginary land of perfect delight ‖ (a child's word for) sleep

dream·like (drí:mlaɪk) *adj.* as strangely beautiful as something in a dream ‖ as vague or insubstantial as something in a dream

dream·scape (drí:mskeip) *n.* an unreal scene

dream·world (drí:mwə:rld) *n.* a world of fantasy

dream·y (drí:mi:) *comp.* **dream·i·er** *superl.* **dream·i·est** *adj.* (of people) inclined to indulge in daydreams, not energetic or practical ‖ (of things) vague, dreamlike

drear·i·ly (dríərili) *adv.* in a dreary way

drear·i·ness (dríəri:nis) *n.* the state or quality of being dreary

drear·y (dríəri:) *comp.* **drear·i·er** *superl.* **drear·i·est** *adj.* dull and gloomy ‖ depressing ‖ uninteresting [O.E. *drēorig* fr. *drēor*, gore]

dredge (dredʒ) **1.** *v. pres. part.* **dredg·ing** *past and past part.* **dredged** *v.t.* to clear mud etc. from (a harbor or riverbed) with a dredge ‖ *v.i.* to use a dredge **2.** *n.* an apparatus, such as a crane and grab, for clearing mud etc. from a riverbed or harbor, to increase the depth ‖ a device for collecting oysters from the sea bottom or a river [perh. fr. DRAG]

dredge *pres. part.* **dredg·ing** *past and past part.* **dredged** *v.t.* to sprinkle (food) with flour, sugar etc. **drédg·er** *n.* a container with a perforated lid, used for sprinkling flour, sugar etc. over food [fr. older *dredge*, sweetmeat, fr. O.F. *dragee*]

Dred Scott Decision (*Am. hist.*) a decision (1857) of the U.S. Supreme Court that the Missouri Compromise was unconstitutional (obiter dictum) and that Congress had no power to prohibit slavery. The court's verdict increased the controversy between North and South and was nullified (1868) by the Thirteenth and Fourteenth Amendments of the Constitution

D region the lowest region of the ionosphere, extending from 35 to 40 miles. The degree of ionization of this region causes the refraction of the long wavelength radio waves

dregs (dregz) *pl. n.* sediment in a liquid, esp. that which collects at the bottom of a wine bottle ‖ what is worthless or degenerate, *the dregs of humanity* ‖ (*sing.*) a small remnant or small quantity [M.E., rel. to Icel. *dreggiar* and Swed. *drägg*]

Drei·kai·ser·bund (dráikáizərbunt) the Three Emperors' League, an alliance formed (1872) by Franz Joseph of Austria, Alexander II of Russia, and Wilhelm I of Germany. It lapsed in 1879 but was renewed 1881–7

Drei·ser (dráisər, dráizər), Theodore Herman Albert (1871–1945), American novelist, author of 'Sister Carrie' (1900), 'An American Tragedy' (1925) etc.

drench (drentʃ) *n.* a dose of medicine administered to an animal [O.E. *drenc*, a drink]

drench *v.t.* to wet thoroughly, soak ‖ to force (an animal) to take a medicinal dose ‖ to steep (leather) for tanning ‖ to put (a sheep) in a sheep-dip **drénch·er** *n.* (*Br.*) a drenching shower of rain ‖ a device for administering a medicinal dose to an animal [O.E. *drencan*, to make drink, to drown]

Dren·the, Dren·te (drénte) a province (area 1,029 sq. miles, pop. 421,528) in N.E. Netherlands. Capital: Assen

Dres·den (drézdən) an industrial center (pop. 513,387) of East Germany, the old capital of Saxony, on the Elbe: engineering, chemical and metallurgical industries ‖ the surrounding district (area 2,602 sq. miles, pop. 1,876,000)

Dres·den china a fine porcelain made in Meissen, E. Germany, esp. softly pretty figures and elaborately decorated pieces

Dresden, Treaty of the treaty signed Dec. 25, 1745 by Austria, Saxony and Prussia, under which Prussia was allowed to retain Silesia

dress (dres) **1.** *v.t.* to put clothes on ‖ to provide with clothes, *she is expensive to dress* ‖ to arrange decoratively for display, *to dress a window* ‖ to decorate (streets or a ship) with flags ‖ to draw up (soldiers or companies of soldiers) into alignment ‖ to clean and bandage (a wound) ‖ to treat the surface of (stone, leather, textiles etc.) ‖ to groom (a horse) ‖ to clean and truss (poultry, game) ‖ to garnish (a dish) ‖ to treat (soil) with manure or other fertilizer ‖ to style, arrange (hair) ‖ to prepare (ore) for smelting by removing impurities ‖ *v.i.* to put on or change one's clothes, esp. to put on formal or evening clothes ‖ (*mil.*) to get one's dressing or alignment **to dress down** to scold severely **to dress up** to dress formally or elaborately ‖ to put on fancy costume (for charades etc.) **to dress well** to be in the habit of wearing smart clothes **2.** *n.* attire ‖ a woman's frock or gown [O.F. *dresser*, to make straight or right]

dres·sage (drəsáʒ) *n.* the smooth management of a horse in figures or exercises, without obvious use of reins or hands [F.]

dress circle the lowest balcony or circle in a theater

dress coat a black, long-tailed coat worn by men for formal evening occasions

dress code standards established for proper attire, esp. by schools, businesses, and restaurants

dress·er (drésər) *n.* a chest of drawers, often with a mirror ‖ a long, low cupboard or sideboard with extra shelves fitted to a high back above the cupboard, for holding china and kitchen utensils [F. *dressoir*.]

dresser *n.* a person who looks after an actor's costumes and helps him to dress for the stage ‖ (*Br.*) someone who assists a surgeon in the operating theater ‖ any of various tools used for dressing stone, leather etc. [DRESS V.]

dress·i·ly (drésili) *adv.* in a dressy manner

CONCISE PRONUNCIATION KEY: **(a)** æ, cat; ɑ, car; ɔ fawn; ei, snake. **(e)** e, hen; i:, sheep; iə, deer; ɛə, bear. **(i)** i, fish; ai, tiger; ə:, bird. **(o)** o, ox; au, cow; ou, goat; u, poor; ɔi, royal. **(u)** ʌ, duck; u, bull; u:, goose; ə, bacillus; ju:, cube. x, loch; θ, think; ð, bother; z, Zen; ʒ, corsage; dʒ, savage; ŋ, orangutang; j, yak; ʃ, fish; tʃ, fetch; 'l, rabble; 'n, redden. Complete pronunciation key appears inside front cover.

dress·i·ness (drési:nis) n. the quality of being dressy

dress·ing (drésiŋ) n. the act of putting on clothes ‖ the ointments and bandages applied to an injury ‖ any of certain kinds of sauce, esp. for salads ‖ stuffing for poultry etc. ‖ a substance used for stiffening in the finishing of fabrics ‖ manure or other fertilizer ‖ (mil.) alignment

dressing case a small case used, esp. when traveling, for toilet articles

dressing down pl. **dressing downs** a severe and lengthy rebuke

dressing gown a long loose garment worn in the house over pajamas or while dressing or resting

dressing room a small room attached to a bedroom, for keeping clothes in and for dressing in ‖ a room at a theater in which actors dress and make up for performances

dressing station (mil.) a medical post in a battle area for giving first aid to the wounded before they are sent to a hospital

dressing table a chest of drawers or small table with drawers for toilet articles, fitted with a mirror

dress·mak·er (drésmeikər) n. a woman who makes women's clothes to order

dress·mak·ing (drésmeikiŋ) n. the process of making women's clothes ‖ the occupation of a dressmaker

dress parade (mil.) a parade of troops in dress uniform

dress rehearsal a final rehearsal for a play, ceremony etc. made under the conditions of actual performance

dress shield a piece of material sewn on the inside of a woman's dress under the arms to protect the dress from perspiration

dress shirt a man's white shirt with a starched front for evening wear ‖ a man's shirt for wearing with a tie, as distinguished from a sports shirt

dress uniform (mil.) uniform for formal wear

dress·y (drési:) comp. **dress·i·er** superl. **dress·i·est** adj. (of men or women) fond of dressing well ‖ (of clothes) stylish, smart ‖ (of occasions) requiring smart clothes

drew past of DRAW

Drey·er (dráiər), Carl (1889–1968), Danish film director. Among his films are 'la Passion de Jeanne d'Arc' (1930), 'Dies Irae' (1945), 'Ordet' (1956)

Drey·fus (dréifəs, dráifəs), Alfred (1859–1935), French Jewish soldier, imprisoned (1894) on Devil's Island, Guiana, for alleged espionage. He was pardoned in 1899 but finally cleared only in 1906 after a campaign which produced long-lasting political and social division in France

drib·ble (dríb'l) 1. v. pres. part. **drib·bling** past and past part. **drib·bled** v.i. (esp. of babies) to drool ‖ to flow, in a small trickle ‖ v.t. to cause to flow in a trickle ‖ to squeeze (paint) directly on to a canvas without using a brush ‖ (sports) to control (a ball or puck) while running or riding, in such a way that it advances by a series of short kicks (or pats, hits etc.) 2. n. slaver ‖ a small trickle ‖ an instance of dribbling a ball, puck etc. [fr. obs. drib variant of DRIP]

drib·let, drib·blet (dríblit) n. a small amount **by** (or **in**) **driblets** little by little

dried past and past part. of DRY

dried fruit fruit dried either in the sun or in a dehydrating plant. The most important commercial dried fruits are apples, apricots, bananas, dates, figs, grapes (*CURRANT, *RAISIN, *SULTANA), peaches, pears, plums (*PRUNE) and greengages

drier comp. of DRY

dri·er, dry·er (dráiər) n. that which dries ‖ a component of paints, varnishes and inks which makes for quick drying ‖ a machine for dehydrating by direct heat, drafts of hot air, centrifugal action, etc. ‖ a machine for drying the hair ‖ a rack or machine for drying clothes

driest superl. of DRY

drift (drift) 1. n. the process of being driven, usually slowly, in a certain direction by wind, water etc. in motion ‖ a phenomenon compared with this, a drift of population ‖ the distance moved when driven ‖ the thing driven (snow, sand etc.) ‖ the general meaning of a statement, speech etc. as distinct from the details ‖ (naut.) deviation due to current ‖ a round, tapering steel bar for an aircraft due to air currents ‖ (gunnery) the deviation of a projectile due to rotation and for which a correction is applied ‖ (archit.) the horizontal thrust of an arch on its supports ‖ (geol.) a loose mass of debris accumulated by ice, water or wind ‖ (mining) a horizontal passage following a lode or vein ‖ (naut.) the rate of flow (in knots) of an ocean current ‖ a round, tapering steel bar for drawing rivet holes into line, enlarging holes in metal etc. 2. v.i. to be carried along by a current of water or by wind or as if by these ‖ to be piled up by wind ‖ to live without any apparent aim ‖ to move aimlessly ‖ (pop.) to walk slowly ‖ to make or shape a hole in (metal) ‖ to fish with a drift net ‖ v.t. (of a current of water or wind) to carry along or pile up **drift·age** n. the action of drifting ‖ the distance drifted ‖ material washed up on the shore **drift·er** n. a fishing boat, used in fishing with a drift net ‖ someone who drifts, esp. a rather unstable, aimless person who changes jobs constantly etc. [M.E. drift fr. O.E. drífan, to drive]

drift ice floating masses of ice carried by a current in the sea

drift net a large fishing net held open by weights at the bottom and floats at the top and allowed to drift with the tide

drift·wood (dríftwud) n. pieces of wood floating in the sea or cast up on the shore

drill (dril) n. a series of exercises in physical training, in the use of weapons or equipment, or in procedure ‖ training in such exercises ‖ a mental exercise, regularly repeated ‖ a tool or machine for making holes in wood, metal, stone etc. ‖ Urosalpinx cinerea, a sea snail which bores into the shells of oysters ‖ (Br., pop.) the correct way of doing something, what is the drill for filling in this form? [Du. dril, drille, a boring instrument and DRILL V.]

drill v.t. to train in physical or military exercises ‖ to teach by making (a pupil) repeat a set of facts etc. frequently ‖ to bore (holes) through or in something with a drill or as if with a drill ‖ to break up or remove with a drill ‖ v.i. to use a drill ‖ to perform exercises in physical or military training [prob. fr. Du. drillen, to bore a hole]

drill 1. n. a narrow, shallow furrow in which seeds are sown ‖ a row of seeds or plants sown in such a furrow ‖ an agricultural machine which makes a furrow, sows seeds and covers them with earth 2. v.t. to sow (seeds) in a drill ‖ to cultivate (ground) in drills ‖ v.i. to sow seeds in drills [perh. fr. DRILL n., a boring instrument]

drill n. a strong fabric of cotton or linen with a diagonal weave [fr. older drilling fr. G. fr. L.]

drill n. Mandrillus leucophaeus, a W. African baboon, somewhat smaller than a mandrill [perh. fr. native name]

drill ship a ship designed for underwater drilling

dri·ly (dráili:) adv. in a dry way

drin·a·myl (drinəmil) n. (Br.) (pharm.) a drug containing a barbiturate and an amphetamine; colloquially known as purple heart

drink (driŋk) n. a liquid to be swallowed or (by plants) absorbed ‖ alcoholic liquor ‖ excessive drinking of alcohol **to take to drink** to form the habit of drinking too much alcohol [O.E. drinc, drinca]

drink (driŋk) pres. part. **drink·ing** past. **drank** (dræŋk) past part. **drunk** (drʌŋk) v.t. to swallow (a liquid) or the contents of (a cup) ‖ (of plants) to absorb (moisture) ‖ to join in (a toast) by drinking ‖ v.i. to swallow liquid or absorb moisture ‖ to be in the habit of taking alcoholic liquors, esp. to excess ‖ **to drink in** to give close and delighted attention to (e.g. music) **to drink to** to pledge the success or health of **to drink** (someone) **under the table** to drink from the glass with (a person) and get him drunk before one becomes drunk oneself **drink·er** n. [O.E. drincan]

drip (drip) 1. v. pres. part. **drip·ping** past and past part. **dripped** v.i. (of liquid) to fall in drops ‖ (of a solid object) to allow liquid to fall off in drops, hang the shirt up to drip ‖ to be so saturated that liquid exudes ‖ v.t. to cause to fall in drops, to drip paint everywhere 2. n. the falling of liquid in drops ‖ the sound of dripping ‖ a drop of liquid falling or about to fall from something **drip·ping** n. the act of falling in drops, or of allowing something to fall in drops ‖ (also pl.) the fat drained off roasting meat [O.E. dryppan]

drip-dry 1. (drípdrai) adj. (of a garment) made of a material that is washed but not wrung out and that dries quickly without having to be ironed 2. v.i. (drípdrái) pres. part. **drip-drying**

past and past part. **drip-dried** to dry out after washing in this way

drip·line (dríplain) n. (biol.) the approximately circular area directly beneath the leaf canopy of a tree, where most of the tree's feed roots are located

drip painting form of painting in which paint is dropped or dribbled onto the canvas

drip·stone (drípstoun) n. a projecting ledge or molding of stone on the outside of a building, esp. above a window or door, as protection from rainwater running down the wall, and as a decorative feature

drive (draiv) 1. v. pres. part. **driv·ing** past **drove** (drouv) past part. **driv·en** (drívən) v.t. to control the course of (a car, bus, truck etc.), or an animal drawing a vehicle) ‖ to convey in a vehicle ‖ to impel by force, violence, threats, shouts etc., to drive cattle, to drive on idea out of one's mind ‖ to hit or push in some direction, to drive a stake in, drive a ball into the net ‖ to cause to tend to be in a specified state, the noise was driving him crazy ‖ (of power) to activate (a piece of machinery) ‖ to cause to work very hard ‖ to conclude (a bargain) ‖ to frighten (game) on to the guns ‖ to force into a course of action, compel ‖ (of wind) to impel ‖ (golf) to strike (a ball) from the tee with a driver ‖ (mining and engin.) to cut (a tunnel, road or mine gallery) ‖ v.i. to travel by car or in a carriage ‖ to know how to drive a car or be in the habit of driving a car ‖ to advance with great force, driving rain ‖ to hit a golf ball from the tee **to drive at** to mean, intend to convey **to drive into a corner** to force into a difficult position, esp. in an argument **to drive off** (golf) to hit a ball from the first tee with a driver **to drive to distraction** to madden (someone) 2. n. an excursion in a car or bus ‖ the driving of animals or game ‖ a concerted effort by a number of people, e.g. to raise money for a charity etc. ‖ a major military offensive ‖ (computer) mechanism that moves the magnetic tape or disc, including motors, reel hubs, etc. ‖ energy and willpower ‖ (psychol.) a source of motivation, the sex drive ‖ (sport) the act or manner of hitting a ball, a forehand drive ‖ (in vehicles) a system of transmitting power, front-wheel drive ‖ (mech.) the part driving a piece of machinery ‖ a private road through the grounds of a house ‖ a large number of logs floating down a river ‖ a progressive game (e.g. of whist) [O.E. drífan]

drive-in (dráivin) 1. adj. (of a restaurant, movie house etc.) catering to clients who do not get out of their cars 2. n. a drive-in restaurant or movie house

driv·el (drívəl) 1. v. pres. part. **driv·el·ing**, esp. Br. **driv·el·ling** past and past part. **driv·eled**, esp. Br. **driv·elled** v.i. to allow saliva to run from the mouth ‖ (pop.) to talk foolishly ‖ v.t. (pop.) to utter (inanities) 2. n. foolish talk, nonsense [M.E. drevelen fr. O.E. dreflian]

driven past part. of DRIVE

driv·er (dráivər) n. someone who drives a car, bus etc. ‖ a person who drives animals, a drover ‖ (mech.) a driving wheel, or other part of a machine that receives the power directly ‖ (golf) a wood for driving the ball a long distance from the tee

driver ant a member of Dorylus and other genera of African and Asian ants. They travel in armies, driving every living creature before them and doing great damage to vegetation etc.

drive·way (dráivwei) n. a passage along which vehicles or animals may be driven ‖ a private approach to a building, e.g. from the road to one's garage

drive wheel a driving wheel

driving wheel a wheel that receives the power and transmits movement to other parts of a piece of machinery ‖ the wheel of a bicycle that is worked by the pedals ‖ one of the large wheels of a locomotive

driz·zle (dríz'l) 1. v.i. pres. part. **driz·zling** past and past part. **driz·zled** (of rain) to fall in very small drops ‖ to rain slightly 2. n. a slight, very fine rain **driz·zly** adj. [perh. fr. O.E. drēosan, to fall]

drogue (droug) n. a drag anchor ‖ a buoy at the end of a harpoon line ‖ a wind sock [perh. fr. DRAG]

droit (droit, drwa) n. (Br., only in certain legal contexts) a right or due [F.]

droll (droul) adj. amusing ‖ odd, surprising, but humorous, a droll expression [fr. F. drôle, a funny fellow]

droll·er·y (dróuləri:) pl. **droll·er·ies** n. a jesting, humor ‖ a droll remark ‖ amusing behavior ‖ the quality of being droll [F. *drôlerie*]

Drôme (droum) a department (area 2,532 sq. miles, pop. 361,800) of S.E. France between the Rhône and the Alps (*DAUPHINÉ) Chief town: Valence

drom·e·dar·y (drómidəri:, drámədəri:) pl. **drom·e·dar·ies** n. *Camelus dromedarius*, a swift variety of one-humped camel used in the Arabian and African deserts for riding or for carrying burdens (cf. BACTRIAN CAMEL) [fr. F. *dromedaire* fr. L. fr. Gk *dromas*, runner]

drone (droun) 1. n. the male of the honeybee, which does no work in the hive. One drone mates with the queen on her nuptial flight ‖ a very lazy man, esp. one who lives like a parasite ‖ a pilotless aircraft or boat guided by remote control ‖ the bass pipe of bagpipes, which emits a steady humming note below the melody ‖ the sound emitted by this pipe ‖ a monotonous speaker ‖ low, monotonous speech, humming or singing 2. v. pres. part. **dron·ing** past and past part. **droned** v.t. to hum or utter monotonously at a low pitch ‖ v.i. to make a monotonous, low-pitched humming noise [O.E. *drān*, *drǣn*]

drool (dru:l) 1. v.i. to drivel 2. n. drivel [altered fr. DRIVEL]

droop (dru:p) 1. v.i. to hang down ‖ to be lowered, *drooping eyelids* ‖ to slouch ‖ to go limp ‖ to flag, weary or begin to give up hope ‖ v.t. to allow to hang down, slouch etc. 2. n. the act or state of drooping [O.N. *drūpa*]

droop snoop lowered front of an aircraft designed to provide greater visibility *also* droop nose

droop·y (drú:pi:) comp. **droop·i·er** superl. **droop·i·est** adj. hanging over flaccidly ‖ feeling dispirited and weary

drop (drop) n. a very small amount of liquid in a round or pear-shaped mass, either falling or clinging to a surface ‖ (pl.) medicine measured in a number of such drops ‖ (pop.) a small amount of liquid, esp. to drink, *a drop of rum* ‖ a small pendant ornament, *ear drops* ‖ a dropping or falling or the amount by which something falls, *a drop in temperature* ‖ a very steep slope, *a sharp drop* ‖ a sheer fall ‖ a thing that drops or falls, esp. (theater) a piece of cloth scenery not on a frame ‖ the trapdoor of a gallows or the fall a hanged man makes when this opens ‖ a parachute descent ‖ men or materials or supplies dropped by parachute **a drop in the ocean** (or **the bucket**) an insignificant amount **at the drop of a hat** on the least pretext ‖ very readily **to get** (or **have**) **the drop on** to draw and aim a gun at (an adversary) before he can himself draw ‖ to get (or have) at a disadvantage **to take** (or **have had**) **a drop too much** to become (or be) drunk [O.E. *dropa*]

drop pres. part. **drop·ping** past and past part. **dropped** v.t. to allow to fall, accidentally or on purpose ‖ to make (a remark, hint) casually or with studied unconcern ‖ (knitting) to fail to prevent (a stitch) from sliding off the needle ‖ (shooting) to cause to fall by hitting, *to drop a bird* ‖ to give up, *to drop a habit* ‖ (slang) to take orally, esp. drugs ‖ to cease to discuss (a subject) ‖ to cease to be friendly with ‖ to write (a short note, postcard etc.) and mail it ‖ to land (men, supplies or material) by parachute ‖ to lower (the voice) ‖ to set down from a car, ship etc. ‖ (of an animal) to give birth to ‖ (math.) to draw (a line) from a point to a line, plane etc. ‖ v.i. to fall ‖ to let oneself fall ‖ to fall from exhaustion ‖ to become less or lower, *the temperature dropped* ‖ to assume a lower position, *to drop to tenth place* ‖ to go to a position thought of as lower, *to drop downstream* ‖ (mus.) to become lower or flat **to drop astern** (naut.) to fall behind another vessel **to drop away** (of stationary objects) to appear to recede, *the mountains dropped away to the south* **to drop behind** to fail to keep abreast of (a moving object or person) **to drop in** (on someone) to pay a casual or brief visit **to drop off** to become fewer or less ‖ to fall asleep **to drop out** to withdraw from an undertaking [O.E. *dropian*]

drop curtain (theater) a proscenium curtain let down from above (not drawn across)

drop-forge (drópfɔrdʒ, drópfourdʒ) pres. part. **drop-forg·ing** past and past part. **drop-forged** v.t. to forge on an anvil or a die with a drop hammer

drop hammer a power-driven weight which is raised and allowed to fall back on to metal resting on an anvil or a die, in order to shape it

drop-in (drópin) n. 1. an unexpected visitor 2. an informal gathering with a range in time **drop in** v.

drop-kick (drópkik) n. (football, rugby) a kick made by bouncing the ball and kicking it just as it rises

drop leaf a leaf attached to the side of a table by hinges. It is swung up to the table level and supported by a bar when in use

drop·let (dróplit) n. a very small drop of liquid

droplet infection infection spread by airborne droplets of sputum

drop letter a letter collected from the office at which it was mailed ‖ (typography) a displayed initial descending over two lines or more

drop-out (drópaut) n. (Am. = Br. early leaver) a pupil who stops before completing the full course of study ‖ portion of a record that has been eliminated

drop pass (ice hockey) a tactic in which a dribbler leaves the puck for a teammate close behind

drop·per (drópər) n. a tube for measuring or administering liquids by drops ‖ (angling) the top flies (of usually three) in a wet-fly fishing cast

drop·pings (drópiŋz) pl. n. a substance fallen in drops or small pieces, e.g. candle grease or food ‖ the dung of birds and animals

drop press a drop hammer

drop·scone (drópskon, drópskoun) n. (Br.) a small thick pancake cooked on a griddle

drop shot (racket games) a shot which causes the ball or shuttlecock to drop sharply after it has cleared the net

drop·si·cal (drópsik'l) adj. affected with dropsy

drop·sonde (drópsond) n. an instrument dropped by parachute to measure and report atmospheric conditions in areas where ground stations cannot be placed

drop·sy (drópsi:) n. the accumulation of fluid in the tissues of the body, esp. the legs (*EDEMA) [M.E. *ydropsy* fr. O.F. fr. L. fr. Gk]

drosh·ky (dróʃki:) pl. **drosh·kies** n. a Russian horse-drawn, open, four-wheeled carriage [Russ.]

dro·soph·i·la (drousófilə, drəsófilə) n. a member of *Drosophila*, a genus of tiny dipteran insects including the fruit fly. They have been used for experiments on mutation because of their speed of reproduction and their four large, paired chromosomes [Mod. L. fr. Gk *drosos*, dew +*philos*, loving]

dross (drɔs, drɒs) n. the scum that rises to the surface of molten metal ‖ anything worthless [O.E. *drōs*]

drought (draut) n. a prolonged period of dry weather, a lack of rain **drought·y** adj. [O.E. *drūgath*]

drove (drouv) 1. n. a herd of cattle, sheep or other animals being driven from one place to another ‖ (often pl.) a large number of people moving together, *droves of tourists* ‖ a broad chisel used by masons, esp. for grooving or roughly finishing surfaces ‖ a stone surface grooved by this 2. v. pres. part. **drov·ing** past and past part. **droved** v.t. to work (a stone surface) with a drove ‖ to drive (cattle) from one place to another ‖ to make a living by doing this

dro·ver (dróuvər) n. someone who drives cattle, sheep or other animals from one place to another, esp. to market [O.E. *drāf*, the action of driving]

drove past of DRIVE

drown (draun) v.i. to die of suffocation by immersion in a liquid ‖ v.t. to kill by suffocation in a liquid ‖ to submerge or flood, *eyes drowned in tears* ‖ to make inaudible because of greater sound, *words drowned in applause* **to drown one's sorrows** to try to forget one's troubles by getting drunk [M.E. *drounen*, origin unknown]

drown-proof·ing (dráunpru:fiŋ) n. a technique for remaining afloat in water

drowse (drauz) 1. v.i. pres. part. **drows·ing** past and past part. **drowsed** to be half-asleep, doze ‖ v.t. (with 'away') to pass (time) sleepily 2. n. the condition of being half asleep [perh. fr. O.E. *drūsian*, to be sluggish]

drow·si·ly (dráuzili:) adv. in a drowsy way

drow·si·ness (dráuzi:nis) n. the state of being drowsy

drow·sy (dráuzi:) comp. **drow·si·er** superl. **drow·si·est** adj. half-asleep, sleepy ‖ inducing sleep, lulling [prob. rel. to O.F. *drūsian*, to be sluggish]

drub (drʌb) pres. part. **drub·bing** past and past part. **drubbed** v.t. to beat with a stick or cudgel ‖ to hit repeatedly ‖ to defeat overwhelmingly in a fight or competition **drúb·bing** n. a severe defeat ‖ a beating [perh. fr. Arab. *daraba*, to beat]

drudge (drʌdʒ) 1. n. someone who has to work hard at uninteresting tasks, esp. domestic work 2. v.i. pres. part. **drudg·ing** past and past part. **drudged** to work very hard at uninteresting tasks **drudg·er·y** (drʌdʒəri:) n. uninteresting work or any time-consuming work one has no wish to do [origin unknown]

drug (drʌg) 1. n. a substance used as or in a medicine ‖ a chemical substance used to alter the state of the body or the mind ‖ a narcotic substance, esp. one which induces addiction, such as opium ‖ a commodity for which there is little or no demand, *a drug on the market* 2. v. pres. part. **drug·ging** past and past part. **drugged** v.t. to administer drugs to ‖ to act on as though a drug, *heat and weariness drugged his senses* ‖ v.i. to be a drug addict [F. *drogue*, etym. doubtful]

drug·get (drʌ́git) n. a tough, coarse cloth, often of wool and cotton, used esp. for a floor covering, or laid over a carpet to protect it [F. *droguet*, origin unknown]

drug·gist (drʌ́gist) n. a dealer in medicinal drugs ‖ (Am. and Scot.=Eng. pharmaceutical chemist) someone who dispenses or sells medical drugs, toiletries etc.

drug-push·er (drʌ́gpuʃər) n. one who sells illegal drugs *also* pusher

drug-store (drʌ́gstɔr, drʌ́gstour) n. a pharmacist's shop ‖ a store where medicines, toiletries and various other small articles (soft drinks, cosmetics, magazines etc.) are sold

Dru·id (drú:id) n. (hist.) a member of an ancient pre-Christian Celtic order of priests and wizards in Britain, Ireland and Gaul ‖ an officer of the Welsh Gorsedd **Dru·id·ess** (drú:idis) n. **Dru·id·ic, Dru·id·i·cal** adjs. **Drú·id·ism** n. [F. *druide* fr. L. fr. O. Celt.]

drum (drʌm) 1. n. any of various types of percussive musical instrument consisting of a hollow cylinder or hemisphere of wood, metal etc., usually with a skin stretched tightly over the end or ends. The skin is struck to produce a sound ‖ the sound made by such an instrument, or a similar sound ‖ something resembling a drum in shape, e.g. a cylindrical container, or a cylinder or barrel on which cable is wound, e.g. in a capstan ‖ a cylindrical stone block forming part of a pillar or its capital ‖ (zool. and anat.) an organ of the body which gives resonance ‖ a drumfish 2. v.i. pres. part. **drum·ming** past and past part. **drummed** to play a drum ‖ to make a rhythmic beating sound **to drum in** to instill (something) forcibly by repetition **to drum out** to drive out or expel ignominiously **to drum up trade** to go out to get business energetically [etym. doubtful]

drum·beat (drʌ́mbi:t) n. the sound of a drum

drum brake (mech. eng.) braking device consisting of two curved, heat-resistant shoes forced onto the surface of a rotating drum Cf DISC BRAKE

drum·fire (drʌ́mfaiər) n. continuous artillery fire, so rapid as to resemble the beating of a drum

drum·fish (drʌ́mfiʃ) pl. **drum·fish, drum·fish·es** n. any of several species of fish, fam. *Sciaenidae*, that make a drumming noise. Some are found on the east coast of the U.S.A. and others in the Great Lakes and the Mississippi

drum·head (drʌ́mhed) n. the membrane on a drum ‖ the top of a capstan into which bars for turning it are inserted

drumhead court-martial a court-martial dealing summarily with offenders during military operations

drum·lin (drʌ́mlin) n. (geol.) a long narrow mound or hillock formed by glacial drift [Gael. and Ir. *druim*, ridge+-*lin*, perh. = dim. -*ling*]

drum major the leader of a band who marches in front and twirls a baton

drum majorette a female baton twirler who accompanies a marching band

drum·mer (drʌ́mər) n. someone who plays the drums or a drum ‖ a traveling salesman

Drum·mond of Haw·thorn·den (drʌ́məndəv-hɔ́θɔrndən), William (1585–1649), Scottish poet and man of letters. His 'Conversations' with Jonson give useful glimpses of contemporary critical opinion (1618–19)

CONCISE PRONUNCIATION KEY: (a) æ, cat; ɑ, car; ɔ fawn; ei, snake. (e) e, hen; i:, sheep; iə, deer; ɛə, bear. (i) i, fish; ai, tiger; ə:, bird. (o) o, ox; au, cow; ou, goat; u, poor; ɔi, royal. (u) ʌ, duck; u, bull; u:, goose; ə, bacillus; ju:, cube. x, loch; θ, think; ð, bother; z, Zen; ʒ, corsage; dʒ, savage; ŋ, orangutang; j, yak; ʃ, fish; tʃ, fetch; 'l, rabble; 'n, redden. Complete pronunciation key appears inside front cover.

drum printer printing device in which the type or printing plate is on a rotating drum, e.g., a multigraph

drum·stick (drʌ́mstĭk) *n.* a stick for beating a drum. Those used for the bass drum have a padded head covered with chamois leather ‖ the leg bone of a chicken or other fowl

drum store (*computer*) a magnetized rotating cylinder for information storage on the surface with many stationary read/write heads *also* hoisting drum

drunk (drʌŋk) 1. *adj.* intoxicated by alcoholic drink ‖ elated, *drunk with success* **to get drunk** to become intoxicated 2. *n.* a person who is drunk ‖ a drinking bout **drunk·ard** (drʌ́ŋkərd) *n.* a person habitually drunk.[past part. of DRINK (earlier *drunken*)]

drunk·en (drʌ́ŋkən) *adj.* (rarely predicative) in the habit of becoming intoxicated, frequently drunk, *a drunken sot* ‖ caused, by or showing the effects of drunkenness, *a drunken brawl* [old past part. of DRINK]

drunk tank detention center for recuperating inebriates

dru·pa·ceous (dru:péiʃəs) *adj.* bearing drupes ‖ of or relating to a drupe

drupe (dru:p) *n.* a fleshy fruit with one or more seeds each surrounded by a hard layer, e.g. the peach [fr. M.L. *drupa, druppa* (*oliva*), overripe (olive)]

dru·pel (drú:p'l) *n.* a drupelet

drupe·let (drú:plit) a small drupe, usually occurring in groups forming a larger fruit, e.g. the raspberry [dim. fr. L. *drupa*, overripe]

Druse, Druze (dru:z) *n.* a member of a political and heretical Moslem sect dating from the 11th c. The Druses live in the mountains of S.W. Syria and Lebanon. They regard the caliph of Egypt Al Hakim (996–1020) as the 10th and last incarnation of God [fr. Arab. *Durūz* after *Darazi*, the Persian missionary of the creed]

druse (dru:z) *n.* a crust of crystals lining a natural cavity in rock ‖ a cavity encrusted with crystals [G. fr. Bohemian *druza*]

dry (drai) 1. *adj.* comp. **dri·er** superl. **dri·est** free from moisture ‖ lacking moisture, *this cake is rather dry* ‖ needing rain ‖ dried up, *a dry river course* ‖ having little or no rain, *a dry climate* ‖ not underwater, *dry land* ‖ (of a poet etc.) temporarily not creative ‖ not yielding milk, *the cow has gone dry* ‖ (of bread) served without butter ‖ (of masonry) built without mortar ‖ (of wines) not sweet ‖ thirsty ‖ having laws prohibiting the manufacture and sale of alcoholic liquors, *a dry state* ‖ written without an effort to win the reader's attention, *a dry book* ‖ given to making humorous remarks in a matter-of-fact way ‖ quietly ironic, *a dry wit* ‖ bare, plain, *the dry facts of the case* ‖ (of a cough) unaccompanied by mucus in the throat 2. *v. pres. part.* **dry·ing** past and past part. **dried** *v.t.* to make dry ‖ *v.i.* to become dry **to dry up** to make or become quite dry ‖ to stop talking ‖ to run out of ideas 3. *n.* someone who opposes the sale of intoxicating liquors [O. E. *dryge*]

dry·ad (dráiəd, dráiæd) *n.* (*Gk mythol.*) a nymph living in a tree [fr. L. *dryas* (*dryadis*) fr. G k]

dry battery *pl.* **dry batteries** (*elec.*) a battery of dry cells ‖ a dry cell

dry cell a primary cell, usually of the Leclanché type, with the electrolyte in paste form to prevent spilling (*PRIMARY CELL)

dry-clean (dráiklí:n) *v.t.* to clean (fabrics, esp. clothes) with trichlorethylene, benzene etc. instead of water **dry cleaner** someone who does such work ‖ a substance used in such work

dry-cure (dráikjúər) *pres. part.* **dry-cur·ing** *past and past part.* **dry-cured** *v.t.* to cure (meat, fish etc.) without the use of pickling liquids, c.g. in the sun or by smoke

Dry·den (dráid'n), John (1631–1700), English poet and dramatist. His first works of note were court poems, in rhymed couplets or quatrains, He wrote some (mainly undistinguished) comedies, of which 'Marriage à la Mode' (1673) is the best, then turned to tragedy with great success in 'All for Love' (1677). At 50 he turned satirist ('MacFlecknoe', 1682 and 'Absalom and Achitophel', 1681–2) and didactic poet ('Religio Laici' and 'The Hind and the Panther', 1687). In the 18th c. Dryden was credited with having 'reformed' English poetry, banning its metaphysical wildness and metrical irregularity and reducing it to the order and polite wit of the heroic couplet (though his satire has a metaphysical grotesqueness, and is today regarded as a continuer of the line of wit rather than its destroyer). His prose is usually considered the

earliest 'modern' English prose, easy, lucid and polished ('Essay of Dramatick Poesie', 1668 and preface to 'Fables, Ancient and Modern', 1700)

dry dock a dock from which the water can be pumped out, to allow ships to be examined or repaired below the waterline **dry-dock** (dráidɒk) *v.t.* to place in dry dock ‖ *v.i.* to enter a dry dock

dryer *DRIER

dry farming crop production without irrigation on dry land, by conserving soil moisture and growing crops which resist drought

dry fly an artificial fly that floats

dry gap bridge a fixed or portable bridge used to span a gap that does not normally contain water, e.g., antitank ditch, road crater

dry goods (*Am.=Br.* drapery) fabrics, haberdashery etc., as distinguished from hardware, groceries etc.

dry ice solid carbon dioxide, used as a refrigerant and coolant

dry kiln a heated chamber for the controlled drying of lumber

dry law a prohibition law

dry·ly, dri·ly (dráili:) *adv.* in a dry way

dry measure a measure of volume for dry commodities (fruit, grain etc.), e.g. pecks and bushels

dry nurse a nurse who looks after a baby but does not suckle it (cf. WET NURSE)

dry out 1. to recover from, or cause to recover from, drunkenness 2. detoxify

dry·point (dráipɔint) *n.* a needle for engraving on copper plate without the use of acids ‖ the art of doing this ‖ a print from a plate engraved in this way and inked

dry rice rice grown without irrigation on upland ground

dry rot a disease affecting wood, caused by various fungi which penetrate it and destroy it ‖ hidden social or moral deterioration

dry run a tryout, rehearsal ‖ (*mil.*) an exercise without ammunition

dry-shod (dráiʃɒd) *adj.* and *adv.* with dry feet or shoes, without getting the feet or shoes wet

dry-stone wall (dráistɒun) (*Br.*) a wall built without mortar, usually of natural stone

dry wash linen or garments washed and dried but not ironed

DSR (*acronym*) dynamic spatial reconstructor

DSRV (*abbr.*) deep submergence rescue vehicle

D.S.T. daylight saving time

du·ad (dú:æd, djú:æd) *n.* a dyad

du·al (dú:əl, djú:əl) *adj.* double [fr. L. *dualis*]

Dual Alliance the Franco-Russian alliance (1893–4) ‖ the secret Austro-German alliance (1879) negotiated by Bismarck which became (1882) the Triple Alliance with the inclusion of Italy

du·al·ism (dú:əlizəm, djú:əlizəm) *n.* the quality of being twofold ‖ the division of reality into two irreconcilable substances, *the Cartesian mind-matter dualisms, Platonic dualism* ‖ the doctrine that human nature is divided against itself (soul and body, angel and beast) ‖ the doctrine that two distinct principles, good and evil, govern the universe **dú·al·ist** *n.* **du·al·ís·tic** *adj.*

du·al·i·ty (du:æliti:, dju:æliti:) *pl.* **du·al·i·ties** *n.* the quality or state of being dual [fr. F. *dualité* fr. L.L.]

dual number (*gram.*) an inflected form expressing two (cf. SINGULAR, cf. PLURAL), e.g. in ancient Greek

du·al-pur·pose (dú:əlpɜ:rpəs, djú:əlpɜ:rpəs) *adj.* serving two functions

dual-purpose fund (*securities*) mutual fund with shares in two classes in order to share in dividend income and in capital appreciation

Duar·te (dwárte), Juan Pablo (1813–76), Dominican patriot. He freed (1844) his compatriots from Haiti's yoke and founded the Dominican Republic

dub (dʌb) *pres. part.* **dub·bing** past and past part. **dubbed** *v.t.* to make (a man) ceremonially a knight by lightly touching his shoulder with a sword ‖ to give (someone) a nickname ‖ to fit a new sound track to (a film) ‖ (often with 'in') to add (sound effects) to a television program etc. ‖ to rerecord ‖ to treat (leather) by smearing with grease [O.E. *dubban*, etym. doubtful]

du Barry, Comtesse *BARRY

Du·bawnt (du:bɔ́nt) a river (580 miles long) flowing northward from lakes in the S.E. Mackenzie District, Canada, to the central Keewatin District

dub·bin (dʌ́bin) *n.* grease used for treating leather to make it pliable and waterproof [DUB]

dub·bing (dʌ́biŋ) *n.* a new sound track fitted to a film ‖ dubbin [DUB]

Dub·ček (dúbtʃek), Alexander (1921–), Czech statesman. He was First Secretary of the Czech Communist party at the time of the Soviet military intervention (1968). He was expelled (June 1970) from the Czech Communist party

du Bellay *BELLAY

du·bi·e·ty (du:báiəti:, dju:báiəti:) *pl.* **du·bi·e·ties** *n.* doubtfulness, doubt ‖ a matter of doubt [fr. L.L. *dubietas*]

du·bi·ous (dú:biəs, djú:biəs) *adj.* doubtful, having doubts ‖ of questionable value or truth ‖ of questionable character, shady ‖ of uncertain outcome, *a dubious undertaking* [fr. L. *dubiosus*]

du·bi·ta·ble (dú:bitəb'l, djú:bitəb'l) *adj.* open to doubt, open to question [fr. L. *dubitabilis*]

du·bi·ta·tion (du:bitéiʃən, dju:bitéiʃən) *n.* (*rhet.*) doubt [F.]

du·bi·ta·tive (dú:biteitiv, djú:biteitiv) *adj.* (*rhet.*) to do with, given to, or expressing doubt [fr. L. *dubitativus*]

Dub·lin the capital (pop. 525,360) of the Irish Republic and of Dublin County (area 356 sq. miles, pop. 862,219), a port of W. Leinster. It is the country's chief manufacturing and commercial center. Industries: brewing, distilling, textiles, fishing, food processing. Castle (13th c., rebuilt in the 17th c.), St Patrick's Cathedral (1190), Christ Church Cathedral (1038). Trinity College, and University College, National University of Ireland (1854)

Du Bois (du:bɔ́is), William Edward Burghardt (1868–1963) U.S. author, editor, and black civil rights leader. He founded the Niagara movement (1905) which became (1910) the National Association for the Advancement of Colored People (NAACP) and edited (1910–32) its organ 'Crisis'. He campaigned for the emancipation of African colonies

Du·brov·nik (dú:brɔvnik) (*Ital.* Ragusa) a walled town (pop. 66,131) founded in the 7th c., on a rocky peninsula in S. Dalmatia, Yugoslavia, a port and vacation resort

Du·buf·fet (dybyfei), Jean (1901–85), French painter. Influenced by the art of children and of the insane, he paints weirdly distorted figures, rather like graffiti and expressing a sardonically humorous view of contemporary life. He has experimented with media, producing unusual colors and textures

du·cal (dú:k'l, djú:k'l) *adj.* of or belonging to a duke ‖ fit for a duke [F.]

duc·at (dʌ́kət) *n.* (*hist.*) a gold or silver coin once current in several parts of Europe, e.g. Venice [F. fr. Ital.]

Duc·cio di Buo·nin·se·gna (dú:ttʃɔdi:bwɔnin-sénja) (c. 1255–1319), Italian painter. He was the first great Sienese artist, and the last in the calm, grave Byzantine tradition. His greatest work is the Maestà (1311) for the high altar of Siena cathedral

Du·ce (dú:tʃei) *MUSSOLINI

Du·champ (dyʃã), Marcel (1887–1968), American artist, born in France, an originator of dada and surrealism. He is esp. known for his painting 'Nude Descending a Staircase' (1912), which reveals affinities with futurism and cubism. He gave up painting in 1923 and thereafter mainly made sculptures devised from manufactured articles

duch·ess (dʌ́tʃis) *n.* a duke's wife or widow ‖ a woman holding a duchy in her own right [F. *duchesse*]

duch·y (dʌ́tʃi:) *pl.* **duch·ies** *n.* the land ruled by a sovereign duke or duchess ‖ (*Br.*) either of the royal dukedoms of Cornwall (vested in the sovereign's eldest son) or Lancaster [O.F. *duché*]

duck (dʌk) *n.* any of the smallest webfooted swimming birds of fam. *Anatidae*. They are widely distributed, and in the wild state are often migratory. They feed on both vegetable and animal food, retaining morsels caught in the water in the lamellae of their broad, sensitive bills. The mallard is the original of the domestic duck ‖ the female of the species (cf. DRAKE) ‖ the flesh of the bird as food ‖ (*Br., pop.*) a term of affection or empty familiarity ‖ (*cricket*) a batsman's score of 0 **like water off a duck's back** (of a reprimand or criticism) producing no effect **to take to (something) like a duck to water** to master (a job, subject, game)

CONCISE PRONUNCIATION KEY: **(a)** æ, c*a*t; ɑ, c*a*r; ɔ f*aw*n; ei, sn*a*ke. **(e)** e, h*e*n; i:, sh*ee*p; iə, d*ee*r; ɛə, b*ea*r. **(i)** i, f*i*sh; ai, t*i*ger; ə:, b*i*rd. **(o)** o, *o*x; au, c*ow*; ou, g*oa*t; u, p*oo*r; ɔi, r*oy*al. **(u)** ʌ, d*u*ck; u, b*u*ll; u:, g*oo*se; ə, b*a*cillus; ju:, c*u*be. x, lo*ch*; θ, *th*ink; ð, bo*th*er; z, *Z*en; ʒ, cor*s*age; dʒ, sa*v*age; ŋ, orangutan*g*; j, *y*al; ʃ, *f*ish; tʃ, fe*tch*; 'l, rabb*le*; 'n, redd*en*. Complete pronunciation key appears inside front cover.

with the greatest ease [M.E. *duk* fr. O. E. *duce*, diver]

duck *n.* a strong linen or cotton cloth ‖ (*pl.*) trousers or shorts of this cloth [prob. Du. *doek*, linen]

duck 1. *v.i.* to bob or bend down quickly ‖ to dart off quickly in a new direction so as to avoid someone or something ‖ to make a brief curtsy ‖ to plunge the head under the water and come up quickly ‖ to miss a turn or not score in certain games deliberately ‖ *v.t.* to lower abruptly ‖ to dodge, avoid, *to duck responsibility* ‖ to push and hold (someone) under the water for a moment **to duck out** to take French leave **2.** *n.* a quick forcing of someone else's head underwater ‖ a quick plunge ‖ a sudden lowering of the head [M.E. *duken, douken,* to dive]

duck·bill (dʎkbil) *n.* the platypus

duck bill man's haircut with flap of hair at neck

duck·board (dʎkbɔrd, dʎkbourd) *n.* a narrow flat structure of slatted boards laid in quantity in a line over wet or muddy ground, for walking on, or singly on a cold floor, for standing on

duck·er (dʎkər) *n.* any of certain diving birds, e.g. the dabchick, dipper, water ouzel

ducking stool (*hist.*) a seat on the end of a seesaw in which nagging or troublesome women or cheating shopkeepers etc. were tied, and ducked in the village pond. The practice was discontinued c. 1800

duck·ling (dʎkliŋ) *n.* a young duck

duck·pins (dʎkpinz) *n.* (*bowling*) a game using three small balls without finger holes for each game

ducks and drakes a game of skimming flat stones in jumps over water **to play ducks and drakes with** to treat carelessly, squander (money)

duck soup (*pop.* = *Br., pop.* money for jam) (of a test) not at all difficult

duck·weed (dʎkwi:d) *n.* any of several small floating plants of fam. Lemnaceae, esp. of genus Lemna, consisting of a flattened green leaf and stem from which a long root hangs down into the water [Mod. L. fr. Gk]

duck·y (dʎki) **1.** *n. pl.* **duck·ies** (*Br., pop.*) a term of affection or empty familiarity **2.** *adj. comp.* **duck·i·er** *superl.* **duck·i·est** (*pop.*) attractive, charming ‖ (*pop.*) nice, pleasant

duct (dʎkt) *n.* a tube which conveys fluid or some other substance ‖ (*biol.*) a tube formed by a series of cells which have lost their walls at the point of contact ‖ a pipe or conduit for electric cables etc. [fr. L. *ductus,* leading, conduit]

duc·tile (dʎktil) *adj.* (of metals) capable of being drawn out into wire ‖ (of clay) plastic, easily molded ‖ (of persons) easily led or influenced

duc·til·i·ty *n.* [F.]

ductless glands endocrine glands

dud (dʎd) **1.** *n.* a shell, bomb etc. that fails to explode, or a bullet that fails to fire ‖ a person or plan turning out a failure or an object that turns out to be no good ‖ (*pl., pop.*) personal belongings, esp. clothes **2.** *adj.* counterfeit ‖ not sound, useless [origin unknown]

dude (du:d, dju:d) *n.* a dandy, a man of affected speech, dress and manners [origin unknown]

dude ranch a ranch operated partly for the entertainment of tourists, e.g. as a holiday resort

dudg·eon (dʎdʒən) *n.* (in the phrase) **in high dudgeon** deeply offended and aggrieved [origin unknown]

Dud·ley (dʎdli), John *WARWICK, EARL OF

Dudley, Robert *LEICESTER, EARL OF

Dudley, Thomas (1576–1653), Colonial governor of Massachusetts (from 1634). His aristocratic prejudice and stern Puritanism dominated the community during his time

due (du:, dju:) **1.** *adj.* payable, *this bill is now due* ‖ morally owing, *thanks are due to our helpers* ‖ proper, fitting, adequate, *with all due respect, in due time* ‖ expected to arrive (at a given time), *the train is due at 4* ‖ (with 'on') scheduled to speak, sing, perform etc., *due on in 10 minutes* ‖ justified in expecting, *due for promotion* ‖ (*pop.*) about (to), *he is due to find out* ‖ owing, attributable, *damage due to negligence* **2.** *adv.* directly, exactly, *to travel due north* **3.** *n.* that which is morally owed to someone, *give a man his due* ‖ (*pl.*) fees, charges [M.E. *dewe* fr. O.F. *deü, du,* past part. of *devoir,* to owe]

due bill (*commerce*) a written acknowledgment of a debt, not made payable to order like a promissory note

du·el (dú:əl, djú:əl) **1.** *n.* (*hist.*) a fight, arranged and conducted according to a code of honor, between two gentlemen armed as agreed between them, in the presence of two seconds (witnesses), to settle a quarrel over a point of honor ‖ any contest between two antagonists, esp. where they are very evenly matched, *a duel of wits* **2.** *v.i. pres. part.* **du·el·ing,** esp. *Br.* **du·el·ling** *past and past part.* **du·eled** esp. *Br.* **du·elled** to fight a duel or duels **dú·el·ist,** esp. *Br.* **dú·el·list** *n.* someone who fights a duel [F.]

du·en·de (du:éndei) *n.* (*Sp.*) charisma; irresistible charm

Due·ro (dwérɔ) *DOURO

du·et (du:ét, dju:ét) *n.* a piece of music for two singers or performers **du·ét·tist** *n.* [fr. Ital. *duetto* dim. of *duo,* duet]

Du·fay (dyfei, dyfai), Guillaume (c. 1400–74), Flemish-Burgundian composer. He was an early exponent of polyphony, notable for his masses and chansons

duff (dʎf) *n.* a boiled or steamed flour pudding, esp. with raisins etc. [var. of DOUGH]

duff *n.* the decaying leaves and vegetation on the forest floor ‖ fine coal, slack [origin unknown]

duf·fel, duf·fle (dʎfəl) *n.* a coarse woolen cloth with a thick nap [after *Duffel,* a town in Belgium]

duffel bag (*Am.* = *Br.* kit bag) a long canvas bag in which a soldier, airman etc. carries his gear ‖ any small canvas bag closed by a drawstring

duffel coat *DUFFLE COAT

duf·fer (dʎfər) *n.* (*pop.*) a stupid or incompetent person [origin unknown]

duffle *DUFFEL

duffle coat, duffel coat a loose hooded coat of heavy wool, fastened by string loops over peg buttons

Du·four-spit·ze (dyfú:rʃpitzə) *ROSA

Du·fy (dy:fi:), Raoul (1877–1953), French painter. His graceful, gay works, chiefly watercolors, are brilliant in coloring and show deft outline drawing with the brush or pen. He also designed textiles, theater and ballet decor etc.

dug (dʎg) *n.* an udder or teat of female mammals and (*rhet.*) of old hags [origin unknown]

dug *past and past part.* of DIG

du·gong (dú:gɔŋ) *pl.* **du·gongs, du·gong** *n. Dugong dugon,* fam. *Dugongidœ,* a large herbivorous sea mammal of the order *Sirenia* (*SEA COW) [Malay *duyong*]

dug·out (dʎgaut) *n.* a canoe hollowed out from a tree trunk, a pirogue ‖ a shelter dug in the ground, esp. for troops in battle ‖ (*baseball*) a low shelter containing a players' bench and facing the diamond

du Guesclin *GUESCLIN, BERTRAND DU

Du·ha·mel (dyæmel), Georges (1884–1966), French poet, playwright and novelist, author of 'la Chronique des Pasquier'

dui·ker (dáikər) *pl.* **dui·kers, dui·ker** *n.* a small African antelope of genus *Cephalophus,* with short straight horns [Afrik.]

Duis·burg (dýsburk) a West German city (pop. 582,000) at the confluence of the Rhine and the Ruhr, on the Rhine-Herne canal, a large inland port and rail center importing iron ore and other raw materials, and exporting coal and the products of the Ruhr heavy industries. It has textile, chemical and electrical plants

Du·kas (dykæ), Paul (1865–1935), French composer and teacher. He wrote 'l'Apprenti sorcier' (1897), an orchestral scherzo, the opera 'Ariane et BarbeBleue', the dance-poem 'le Péri', and many piano works

duke (du:k, dju:k) *n.* (in some parts of Europe and in former times) a sovereign prince ruling a duchy ‖ (in Great Britain and some other European countries) a nobleman holding the highest hereditary title outside the royal family **dúke·dom** *n.* a territory (duchy) ruled by a duke ‖ the office or rank of a duke [M.E. *duc, duk* fr. F.]

Dukhobor *DOUKHOBOR

dulce *DULSE

dul·cet (dʎlsit) **1.** *adj.* (of sounds) sweet, soothing **2.** *n.* (*mus.*) an organ stop like the dulciana, but an octave higher [fr. F. *doucet*]

dul·ci·an·a (dʎlsi:ǽnə, dʎlsi:ánə) *n.* (*mus.*) an organ stop having a metal pipe and a sweet stringlike tone [M.L.]

dul·ci·fy (dʎlsifai) *pres. part.* **dul·ci·fy·ing** *past and past part.* **dul·ci·fied** *v.t.* to rid of acidity or bitterness [fr. L. *dulcificare*]

dul·ci·mer (dʎlsəmər) *n.* a medieval stringed instrument, having wires of graduated length stretched over a sounding board. The wires are struck with hammers [O.F. *doulcemer*]

du·li·a (du:láiə, dju:láiə) *n.* (*Roman Catholicism*) the veneration of angels and saints (*HYPERDULIA, cf. LATRIA) [M.L. fr. Gk]

dull (dʎl) **1.** *adj.* stupid, slow in understanding ‖ lacking sensitivity, *dull perception* ‖ tedious ‖ uninteresting, colorless in personality ‖ blunt, *a dull blade* ‖ (of pain) not sharp ‖ (of colors and lights) dim, not bright or vivid ‖ (of sounds) muffled, not clear and ringing ‖ (of trade) sluggish ‖ (of weather) cloudy, overcast ‖ without vitality, depressed **2.** *v.t.* to make dull ‖ *v.i.* to become dull **dull·ard** (dʎlərd) *n.* a slow, stupid person [M.E. *dul, dull* fr. O.E. *dol,* foolish]

Dul·les (dʎlis), John Foster (1888–1959), U.S. statesman and international lawyer. As Republican secretary of state (1953–9), he made atomic weapons the mainstay of the West's defense against the spread of communism. He accepted the partition of Vietnam (1954), halted the Anglo-French and Israeli attack on Egypt (1956), and committed the U.S.A. to defend the Nationalist Chinese islands of Quemoy and Matsu (1958)

dull·ness, dul·ness (dʎlnis) *n.* the quality or state of being dull

dul·ly (dʎli) *adv.* in a dull way

Du·long and Pet·it's law (dylɔ̃, pəti:) (*phys., chem.*) a law stating that atomic mass × specific heat = 6.4 (approx.) for solid elements. This approximate law tends to become more exact at high temperatures [after Pierre Louis *Dulong* (1785–1838) and Alexis Thérèse *Petit* (1791–1820), F. scientists]

dulse, dulce (dʎls) *n. Rhodymenia palmata,* and edible seaweed with bright red, deeply divided fronds [fr. Gael. *duileasg*]

Du·luth (dəlú:θ) a port (pop. 92,811, with agglom. 273,000) in Minnesota, on Lake Superior. Exports: iron ore, flour, dairy products, lumber

du·ly (djú:li:, dú:li:) *adv.* in a due and proper manner or degree ‖ at the proper time

du·ma (dú:mə) *n.* (*Russ. hist.*) an elective council, esp. the lower house of the legislature established by czarist decree in 1905 and overthrown by the Bolsheviks in 1917 [Russ.]

Du·mas (dymɑ), Alexandre ('Dumas père', 1802–70), French novelist. He wrote immensely popular historical novels, e.g. 'The Three Musketeers' (1844), 'The Count of Monte Cristo' (1846), and stage melodramas

Dumas, Alexandre ('Dumas fils', 1824–95), French author, natural son of Dumas père. He wrote mainly comedies and social dramas. His 'la Dame aux camélias' first appeared as a novel (1848)

dumb (dʎm) *adj.* permanently unable to speak, mute ‖ without the faculty of speech, *be kind to dumb animals* ‖ temporarily unable to speak, speechless, *struck dumb with amazement* ‖ unwilling to speak, *the prisoner remained dumb* ‖ without the use of words, soundless, *dumb insolence* ‖ inarticulate, *the dumb masses* ‖ (*pop.*) stupid [O.E.]

Dum·bar·ton Oaks Conference (dʎmbɑrt'n) a meeting (1944) in Washington, D.C., of U.S., British, Russian and Chinese delegates, one of the preliminaries to the forming of the U.N. (*YALTA CONFERENCE, *SAN FRANCISCO)

dumb·bell (dʎmbel) *n.* a short bar with a spherical weight at each end, used, one in each hand, to exercise the muscles ‖ (*pop.*) a stupid person

dumb cram·bo (kræmbou) an acting and guessing game. One team chooses a word to be acted by the other, but tells them not the word itself but one which rhymes with it. The actors then act rhymes until they have the word originally chosen

dumb·found, dum·found (dʎmfáund) *v.t.* to shock with amazement, utterly astonish [DUMB+CONFOUND]

dumb show signs and gestures without words ‖ (*hist.*) a part of a play where the action was represented on the stage without words (as in 'Hamlet' iii, 2)

dumb·wait·er (dʎmweitər) *n.* a portable table or stand with revolving shelves, to help with the serving of food ‖ a small elevator for food and dishes, or one for small goods

dum·dum (dʎmdʎm) *n.* a soft-nosed bullet which expands on impact and inflicts a very ugly wound [after *DumDum,* an arsenal near Calcutta, where such bullets were first made]

dumfound *DUMBFOUND

Dum·fries (dʎmfrí:s) a former county (area 1,073 sq. miles) in S.W. Scotland on the English border

dum·my (dʌ́mi:) 1. *n. pl.* **dum·mies** an imitation of, or substitute for, something, esp. a dressmaker's or tailor's figure for fitting clothes or mannequin for displaying clothes ‖ a straw figure for bayonet practice, a silhouette of a man for shooting at, or a sham package for a window display ‖ someone pretending to act for himself but really acting for another ‖ a person put up as a figurehead who plays no real part, a puppet ‖ (*pop.*) a stupid person ‖ (*Br.*) a pacifier (rubber teat for a baby to suck) ‖ (*cards*) an exposed hand played by one of the players in addition to his own ‖ (*cards*) the player who lays his hand down to be so played ‖ (*publishing*) a pattern volume, usually of blank pages, made in advance of an edition for designing or publicity purposes **to sell the dummy** (*rugby*) to trick a would-be tackler by pretending to pass the ball 2. *adj.* sham ‖ simulating real conditions 3. *v.i. pres. part.* **dum·my·ing** *past and past part.* **dum·mied** (*rugby*) to sell the dummy esp. repeatedly [DUMB]

dummy variable (*computer*) an artificial quantity inserted solely to fulfill prescribed conditions, such as fixed word length or block length, but otherwise not significant

Du·mou·riez (dymu:rjei), Charles François (1739–1823), French general who led the Revolutionary armies to victory at Valmy and Jemappes (1792). Removed from his command by the republican government, he deserted to the enemy (1793)

dump (dʌmp) 1. *v.t.* to unload, tip, *to dump coal* ‖ to let fall with a bump ‖ to set down temporarily, *dump your luggage here* ‖ to get rid of, dispose of ‖ (*computer*) to transfer storage contents from an internal to an external storage ‖ the printout when an error is made ‖ (*commerce*) to sell in quantity at a very low price, esp. to sell (surplus goods) abroad at much less than the market price at home, so as to capture a new market and keep home prices up ‖ to land (surplus immigrants) in a foreign country 2. *n.* a scrap heap ‖ a shabby, untidy house, room or place ‖ an unexciting place where there is nothing going on ‖ a place where military supplies are temporarily stored, *an ammunition dump* ‖ a cache of supplies for an expedition [prob. fr. Scand.]

dump·ling (dʌ́mpliŋ) *n.* a lump of dough boiled esp. with stew ‖ a baked pudding of fruit (esp. a whole apple) wrapped in pastry ‖ a short, fat, dumpy person (esp. a child) [prob. rel. to L.G. *dump*, damp]

dump on *v.* (*slang*) to badmouth or denigrate

dumps (dʌmps) *pl. n.* low spirits [prob. fr. Du. *domp*, haze]

dump truck (*Am.=Br.* tip lorry) a truck whose contents are emptied by tilting the truck bed upward and opening the tailgate

dump·y (dʌ́mpi:) *comp.* **dump·i·er** *superl.* **dump·i·est** *adj.* short and podgy

dumpy level (*survey.*) a spirit level with a short telescope and compass (cf. THEODOLITE)

dun (dʌn) 1. *adj.* dull gray-brown 2. *n.* this color ‖ a horse of this color [O.E. *dunn*]

dun 1. *v.t. pres. part.* **dun·ning** *past and past part.* **dunned** to pester with demands for payment of a debt etc. 2. *n.* someone who duns ‖ a debt collector [perh. var. of DIN]

Du·naj (dú:nai) *DANUBE

Du·nant (dynã) Jean Henri (1828–1910) Swiss philanthropist. He founded (1864) the International Red Cross and was awarded (1901) the first Nobel peace prize

Dun·bar (dʌnbár), William (c. 1460–c. 1520), Scottish poet. He wrote satirical and humorous verse, as well as imaginative elegiac verse

Dun·bar·ton (dʌnbárt'n) a former county (area 244 sq. miles) in W. Scotland

Dun·can (dʌ́nkən), Isadora (1878–1927), American expressionist dancer. She danced barefoot, in flowing draperies, in a style opposed to the traditional ballet forms, and interpreted music not written for dancing. She founded schools in France, Germany and Russia

dunce (dʌns) *n.* a very backward child at school ‖ a stupid person [after Duns Scotus, whose followers, called Dunsmen or Dunses, were ridiculed by 16th-c. humanists for the 'useless' subtlety of their reasoning]

dunce cap a conical paper cap formerly put on a dunce's head to humiliate him

dunce's cap a dunce cap

Dun·dee (dʌndí:) a port (pop. 192,760) in Angus, Scotland on the Firth of Tay: jute and textiles, food processing, shipbuilding

dun·der·head (dʌ́ndərhed) *n.* a blockhead, a stupid person **dun·der·head·ed** *adj.* [origin unknown]

Dun·don·ald (dʌndónəld), Thomas Cochrane, 10th earl of (1775–1860), British naval officer and adventurer. He took a leading part (1817–21) in the struggle for independence of Chile and Peru, transporting (1817) the Army of the Andes northward from Chile. He served (1823–5) the cause of Brazilian independence

dune (du:n, dju:n) *n.* a mound or ridge of loose sand piled up by the wind on coasts or in deserts [F. fr. O.Du.]

dune buggy large-wheeled, lightweight motor vehicle for travel on loose sand

Dun·e·din (dʌní:din) the chief city (pop. 114,000) of Otago province, South Island, New Zealand, a port on Otago Harbour. Industries: textiles, engineering. University of Otago (founded 1869)

Dun·ferm·line (dʌnfé:rmlin) a town (pop. 53,400) in Fife, Scotland, on the Firth of Forth, a naval dockyard. Industries: textiles, shipbuilding. Dunfermline Abbey is the burial place of Scottish kings, including Robert the Bruce

dung (dʌŋ) 1. *n.* animal excrement ‖ manure 2. *v.t.* to manure (land) [O.E. *dung*]

dun·ga·ree (dʌŋgərí:) *n.* a coarse Indian calico ‖ (*pl.*) overalls or trousers of dungaree or strong cotton cloth, jeans [Hindi *dungri*]

dung beetle any of various coleopterous insects, e.g. the dor, which make elaborate burrows and bury their eggs in dung

Dunge·ness Point (dʌ́ndʒnis) a cape in S. Argentina, at the north entrance to the Strait of Magellan

dun·geon (dʌ́ndʒən) *n.* (*hist.*) an underground prisoners' cell, esp. in a castle ‖ a donjon [F. *donjon*]

dung fly *pl.* **dung flies** a member of *Scatophaga*, fam. *Scatophagidae*, a genus of flies feeding on dung and breeding in it

dung·hill (dʌ́ŋhil) *n.* a heap of dung or refuse in a farmyard

dunk (dʌŋk) *v.t.* to dip (doughnuts etc.) in tea, coffee etc. before eating them [fr. G. *tunken*, to dip]

Dunk·er (dʌ́ŋkər) *n.* (*pop.*) a member of the Church of the Brethren, a religious sect of German Baptist origin that sprang from pietism. Persecuted in Germany, its members went to the U.S.A. (1719) and settled in various parts of Pennsylvania. They practice trine immersion. They are pacifists and are opposed to all worldly amusements

Dun·kerque (dœ̃kerk) (*Br.* Dunkirk) a French port (pop. 83,163) on the North Sea near Belgium, with textile mills, oil refineries and shipyards. A heroic evacuation of 345,000 British and French troops in the face of the Germans took place May 29–June 4, 1940

Dun·kirk (dʌ́nkə:rk) *DUNKERQUE

dunk shot (*basketball*) basket throw made from above the basket

Dun Laoghai·re (dʌnlé:ərə) (Dunleary, formerly Kingstown), the port (pop. 53,171) of Dublin, Irish Republic, on the Irish Sea, a resort. Chief export: cattle

dun·nage (dʌ́nidʒ) *n.* loose mats, rags, brushwood etc. packed around cargo to keep it dry and undamaged [origin unknown]

Duns Sco·tus (dʌnzskóutəs), John (c. 1265–1308), Scottish Franciscan priest and philosopher who taught in Oxford and Paris. He was called the 'doctor subtilis'. He championed scholasticism based on the Augustinian tradition of the Franciscans, criticizing the philosophy of Aristotle and deviating on certain points from the teachings of St Thomas Aquinas

Dun·sta·ble (dʌ́nstəb'l), John (d. 1453), one of the great pre-Tudor English composers. He influenced the development of polyphonic music

Dun·stan (dʌ́nstən), St (c. 910–88), archbishop of Canterbury (959–88). He helped to revive monasticism on Benedictine lines and promoted a revival of education and learning. He was chief adviser to several English kings. Feast: May 19

dunt (dʌnt) *v.i.* (*pottery*) to crack in the biscuit firing or through too sudden cooling

du·o (dú:ou, djú:ou) *pl.* **du·os** *n.* a piece of music for two instruments, a duet ‖ a pair of performers, esp. in vaudeville [Ital. = two]

du·o·de·cil·lion (du:oudisíljən, dju:oudisíljən) *n.* *NUMBER TABLE [fr. L. *duodecim*, twelve+MILLION]

du·o·dec·i·mal (du:ədésiməl, dju:ədésiməl) 1. *adj.* relating to 12 ‖ of a number scale based on 12 and using multiples and submultiples of 12 2. *n.* a twelfth [fr. L. *duodecimus*, twelfth]

du·o·dec·i·mo (du:ədésimou, dju:ədésimou) *n.* (*abbr.* 12mo, 12°) a small book or page size, each printed sheet being folded to make 12 leaves (about 5 ¼ x 8 1/8 ins each) [L. (*in*) *duodecimo*, ablative of *duodecimus*, twelfth]

du·o·de·nal (du:ədí:n'l, dju:ədí:n'l, du:ód'n'l, dju:ód'n'l) *adj.* relating to the duodenum

du·o·den·a·ry (du:ədí:nəri:, dju:ədí:nəri:, du:ədénəri:, dju:ədénəri:) *adj.* proceeding by twelves ‖ containing 12 [fr. L. *duodenarius*]

du·o·de·num (du:ədí:nəm, dju:ədí:nəm, du:ód'nəm, dju:ód'nəm) *pl.* **du·o·de·na** (du:ədí:nə, dju:ədí:nə, du:ód'nə, dju:ód'nə), **du·o·de·nums** *n.* (*anat.*) the part of the small intestine opening off the stomach (*JEJUNUM, *ILEUM) [L. *duodenum digitorum*, of twelve fingers (breadth)]

du·o·logue (dú:əlɔg, dú:əlɔg, djú:əlɔg, djú:əlɔg) *n.* a play for two actors [fr. Gk *duo*, two+-*logue*, like 'monologue', 'dialogue']

Du·parc (dypærk), Henri (1848–1933), French composer, noted esp. for his songs, though he preserved only a dozen. The melody follows the natural phrasing of the words and yet retains its own freedom, and is sustained by an incomparable interweaving accompaniment

dupe (du:p, dju:p) 1. *n.* someone easily deceived or tricked 2. *v.t. pres. part.* **dup·ing** *past and past part.* **duped** to deceive, cheat, make a fool of **dúp·er·y** *n.* a duping or being duped [F.]

du·ple (dú:p'l, djú:p'l) *adj.* (*mus.*) with two beats to the bar, as in 2/2 or 2/4 time ‖ (*math.*) in the ratio of 2 to 1 [fr. L. *duplus*, double]

Du·pleix (dypleks), Joseph François, marquis (1697–1764), French colonial administrator. His attempt to conquer India for the French was defeated by Clive

Du·ples·sis (dyplesi:), Maurice Le Noblet (1890–1959), Canadian politician, founder of the conservative Union Nationale, and prime minister of Quebec (1936–9, 1944–59)

du·plex (dú:pleks, djú:pleks) 1. *adj.* (*technology*) double, twofold, *duplex drill* ‖ (*telephony*) allowing communication in both directions at once 2. *n.* a duplex house ‖ a duplex apartment [L. *duplex*, double]

duplex apartment an apartment on two floors, arranged as a self-contained dwelling

duplex house a house, divided either horizontally or vertically, containing separate apartments for two families

du·pli·cate 1. *v.t.* (dú:plikeit, djú:plikeit) *pres. part.* **du·pli·cat·ing** *past and past part.* **du·pli·cat·ed** to do or cause to be done twice over ‖ to make in duplicate ‖ to be a copy of ‖ to make several copies of 2. (dú:plikit, djú:plikit) *adj.* double, twofold ‖ exactly like another or several others ‖ (*cards*) of a game in which identical hands are dealt at two or more tables to allow comparison of play and scores 3. (dú:plikit, djú:plikit) *n.* a thing that is exactly like another or others ‖ a second copy of a form or document ‖ (*cards*) duplicate bridge, whist etc. **in duplicate** in two copies **du·pli·ca·tion** *n.* a duplicating or being duplicated ‖ a duplicate **dú·pli·ca·tive** *adj.* **dú·pli·ca·tor** *n.* a machine which quickly makes many copies of a document [fr. L. *duplicare* (*duplicatus*), to double]

du·pli·ca·tion (du:plikéiʃən) *n.* (*genetics*) deviation from normal chromosome formation resulting in repetition of material

du·plic·i·ty (du:plísiti:, dju:plísiti:) *pl.* **du·plic·i·ties** *n.* double-dealing, deceitfulness, deceiving by thinking one thing and saying another or by willfully saying different things at different times ‖ an instance of this [F. *duplicité*]

du Pont de Ne·mours, E.I., & Company (du:póntdənəmúərz, dju:póntdənəmúərz) originally a U.S. gunpowder works founded (1802) by Eleuthère Irénée du Pont (1771–1834) in Wilmington, Delaware. It was purchased (1902) by Pierre Samuel du Pont (1870–1954), under whose presidency (1915–20) it developed scores of chemical products and acquired substantial interests in many other industries, incl. General Motors

Du·pré (dyprei), Marcel (1884–1971), French organist and composer

Du·puy de Lôme (dypyi:dəloum), Enrique (1815–1904), Spanish minister to the United States immediately prior to the Spanish-American War. A letter he wrote (1898) which was scornful of President McKinley was stolen and published in William Randolph Hearst's New

York 'Journal'. He was forced to resign, and U.S.-Spanish relations deteriorated

du·ra·bil·i·ty (dúərəbíliti:, djùərəbíliti:) *n.* the quality of being durable

du·ra·ble (dúərəb'l, djúərəb'l) *adj.* lasting, enduring ‖ not likely to wear out or decay for a long time **dúr·a·bly** *adv.* [F. *durable*]

durable goods consumer merchandise designed to last more than three years

durable press method of textile manufacture that makes pleats or creases more permanent and fabric wrinkle-resistant **durable-press,** *adj. also* permanent press

Du·ra-Eu·ro·pus (dúərəjuəróupəs) an ancient Syrian city on the Euphrates. Excavations have yielded much information about Mesopotamian culture in Hellenistic and Roman times

Du·ral·u·min (duəræljumin, djuəræljumin) *n.* an aluminum alloy containing approx. 95% aluminum, 4% copper and small percentages of manganese and magnesium. It is strong, hard and light and used esp. in aircraft [a trademark, after *Düren*, Prussia, where it was first made in 1910,+ALUMINUM]

du·ra ma·ter (dúərəméitər, djúərəméitər) *n.* a tough, fibrous membrane, outermost of those which envelop the brain and spinal cord (*MENINGES) [M.L.=hard mother, trans. fr. Arab.]

du·ra·men (duəréimən, djuəréimən) *n.* the hard, central region of a tree stem [L.= hardness]

dur·ance (dúərəns, djúərəns) *n.* (*rhet.,* in the phrase) **in durance vile** in prison [O.F.=duration[

Durand (duránd), Asher Brown (1796–1886), U.S. painter, a leader in the Hudson River School of painting. His landscapes, like 'Monument Mountain in the Berkshires' (1850s), used light to convey an almost mystical sense of the union of man with nature. 'Kindred Spirits' (1849) depicts his friends Thomas Cole and William Cullen Bryant observing nature

Du·ran·go (du:ráŋɡɔ) a state (area 47,691 sq. miles, pop. 1,160,300) in north central Mexico. Capital: Durango (pop. 228,686). Agriculture depends on irrigation: cotton, wheat, corn, tobacco, sugar cane, vegetables and fruits. Silver, gold, sulfur, tin, coal, and other deposits are mined. The Cerro del Mercado, a solid hill of iron north of the capital, is one of the world's largest deposits

Du·rão (du:rau), José de Santa Rita (c. 1737–84), Brazilian poet, known for his epic 'Camamúru: poema épico do descubrimento da Bahia' (1781), a poem treating the discovery of southern Brazil by Diego Alvarez

du·ra·tion (duəréiʃən, djuəréiʃən) *n.* continuance in time, *a stay of short duration* ‖ the time that something lasts, *for the duration of the war* [O.F.]

dur·a·tive (dúərətiv, djúərətiv) **1.** *adj.* (*gram.,* of verbal aspect) expressing continuing action **2.** *n.* a durative aspect ‖ a durative verb [fr. L. *durare,* to last]

dup·bar (dʌ́:rbər) *n.* the court of an Indian prince ‖ (*hist.,* in imperial India) a state ceremony of great pomp [Pers. and Urdu *darbār,* court]

Du·raz·zo (du:ráttsɔ) *DURRÈS

Dur·ban (dɔ́:rbən) the main port (pop. 505,963), highly mechanized, of Natal, South Africa, on an inlet of the Indian Ocean. Chief exports: coal, grain. It is also a manufacturing center and a resort. University of Natal (1909)

Dü·rer (dýrər), Albrecht (1471–1528), German artist. He traveled in Italy (1494–5, 1505), and led the Renaissance in Germany. His copper engravings, e.g. 'The Knight, Death and the Devil' (1513) and 'St Jerome in his Study' (1514), are unsurpassed. He was also a master of woodcut, e.g. 'Great Passion' (1511) and the 92 blocks known as 'The Triumphal Arch of the Emperor' in glorification of the emperor Maximilian (1512–15). His watercolors of animals and plants are exceedingly sensitive. He painted and he engraved portraits (e.g. Erasmus, 1526), made marginal drawings for a prayer book, and wrote treatises on a variety of subjects

du·ress (duərés, djuərés) *n.* compulsion, threats, esp. as used illegally to force someone to do something [O.F. *duresse,* severity]

Dur·ham (dɔ́:rəm), John George Lambton, 1st earl of (1792–1840), British statesman, governor-general of Canada (1838). Sent to Canada to investigate rebellions, he was recalled after six months of arbitrary government, but his Durham Report (1839) radically changed the

British idea of empire by recommending responsible government for the colonies

Durham a county (area 1,015 sq. miles, pop. 604,728) of N.E. England ‖ its county town (pop. 85,190). Norman cathedral and castle. University (1832)

du·ri·an (dúəri:ən) *n.* the very large, oval fruit of *Durio zibethinus,* fam. *Bombaceae,* grown in Malaya and the East Indies. The flavor is delicate but the smell is disagreeable ‖ the tree bearing this fruit [Malay=thorn]

dur·ing (dúəriŋ, djúəriŋ) *prep.* throughout (time), *he slept during the sermon* ‖ in the course of [pres. part. of obs. *dure,* to last fr. F.]

Durk·heim (dyrkem), Emile (1858–1917), French sociologist, one of the founders of modern sociology. His writings include 'de la Division du travail social' (1893) and 'le Suicide, étude de sociologie' (1897)

dur·ra (dúərə) *n. Sorghum vulgare,* millet grown for food in N. Africa and S. Asia [Arab.]

Dur·rës (dú:res) (*Ital.* Durazzo) the chief port (pop. 60,000) of Albania, on the Adriatic, with oil-storage wells, food and tobacco industries. It was the site of the battle of Dyrrhachium between Caesar and Pompey in 48 B.C.

durst (dɔ:rst) archaic *past* of DARE

Duse (dú:zə), Eleonora (1858–1924), Italian actress. She toured in such plays as 'La Locandiera' (1893) and 'Magda' (1893) and Gabriele *D'ANNUNZIO's 'La Gioconda' (1898) and 'Francesca da Rimini' (1902)

dusk (dʌsk) *n.* the time of day just before it gets quite dark ‖ shade, gloom **dúsk·i·ly** *adv.* **dúski·ness** *n.* **dúsk·y** *comp.* **dusk·i·er** *superl.* **dusk·i·est** *adj.* shadowy, rather dark ‖ dark-skinned [perh. fr. O.E. *dox* adj., dark]

Düs·sel·dorf (dýsəldɔrf) a port (pop. 615,500) in West Germany on the Rhine, capital of N. Rhine-Westphalia: iron, steel and engineering industries, chemicals, textiles, paper

dust (dʌst) **1.** *n.* minute particles of mineral or plant material, lying on the ground or on the surfaces of things, or suspended in the atmosphere. The sources of dust are meteoric disintegration, volcanic eruptions, desert storms, soil erosion, spores and pollen of trees and plants, and industrial and domestic smoke ‖ other matter in the form of powder, *coal dust* ‖ turmoil, commotion, row, *let the dust settle before you bring the subject up again* ‖ pollen ‖ gold dust ‖ (*rhet.*) a dead person's remains **to throw dust in a person's eyes** to deceive or mislead someone by lying ‖ to prevent someone from finding something out by diverting his attention **2.** *v.t.* to remove dust from ‖ to sprinkle with powder ‖ *v.i.* to remove the dust from furniture etc. [O.E. *düst,* vapor]

dust·bin (dʌ́stbin) *n.* (*Br.*) an ash can

dust bowl land from which the eroded topsoil is blown away in dry weather, esp. the Great Plains desert region of the U.S.A.

dust cart (*Br.*) a garbage truck

dust·cloth (dʌ́stklɔθ, dʌ́stklɒθ) *pl.* **dust-cloths** (dʌ́stklɔðs, dʌ́stklɒθs, dʌ́stklɔðz, dʌ́stklɒðz) *n.* a duster (cloth)

dust cover a paper wrapper in which a bound book is issued to keep it clean and for display ‖ a loose covering put over furniture to keep off dust when rooms are not in use

dust devil a whirling pillar of sand, only a few yards broad but up to 3,000 ft high, moving forward at up to 30 m.p.h. It arises over tropical deserts as a result of very strong convection

dust·er (dʌ́stər) *n.* a cloth for removing dust from furniture etc. ‖ an apparatus for sprinkling dry insecticides on plants ‖ (*baseball*) a pitch deliberately placed high and inside ‖ a woman's short, beltless housecoat

dust·fall jar (dʌ́stfɔl) open container used to collect particles from the air for measurement and analysis

dust·ing (dʌ́stiŋ) *n.* a small quantity of something lightly sprinkled over a surface ‖ (*pop.*) a beating, thrashing

dust jacket a dust cover of a bound book

dust·man (dʌ́stmən) *pl.* **dust·men** (dʌ́stmən) *n.* (*Br.*) a garbage man ‖ (*Br.*) the sandman, a children's personification of sleep

dust off a medical helicopter, used to evacuate casualties

dust·pan (dʌ́stpæn) *n.* a shallow container with a short handle into which dust is swept from the floor

dust sheet a dust cover for furniture

dust shot the smallest size of gunshot, .04 in. in diameter

dust storm a violent dust-laden wind in arid regions, accompanied by hot, parched air and high electrical tension

dust·up (dʌ́stʌp) *n.* (*pop.*) a fight, brawl ‖ (*pop.*) a quarrel

dust·y (dʌ́sti:) *comp.* **dust·i·er** *superl.* **dust·i·est** *adj.* covered with, full of, or like dust **not so dusty** (*Br., pop.*) quite good

Du·sun (dú:s'n) *pl.* **Du·sun, Du·suns** *n.* a member of a Dyak people of Sabah ‖ the language of this people [Malay]

Dutch (dʌtʃ) **1.** *adj.* of, from or characteristic of the Netherlands or its people, language or customs ‖ (*hist.*) of the region now comprising Germany, the Netherlands and Flanders, *High Dutch* (of S. and central Germany), *Low Dutch* (of the N. German coast and the Low Countries) **2.** *n.* the Germanic language of the Netherlands, spoken by about one million (*AFRIKAANS) ‖ (*hist.*) the language of the larger Germanic-speaking region, including High Dutch and Low Dutch (more commonly 'High German' and 'Low German') **the Dutch** the people of the Netherlands **in Dutch** (*pop.*) in disgrace, in trouble **to beat the Dutch** to be surprising or of surpassing excellence **to go Dutch** to share expenses when going out [M. Du. *dutsch,* German in the historical sense of Germany, the Netherlands and Flanders]

Dutch auction an auction in which the auctioneer starts at a high price and brings it down by stages until a bid is made

Dutch barn a barn without sidewalls

Dutch clover *Trifolium repens,* a valuable pasture plant found in all temperate regions

Dutch courage empty courage acquired by drinking (not by resolution)

Dutch door a door divided horizontally in the middle, so that the upper half can be opened separately

Dutch East India Company *EAST INDIA COMPANY, DUTCH

Dutch East Indies *INDONESIA

Dutch elm disease a disease of elm trees, caused by the fungus *Ceratostomella ulmi* carried by bark beetles. The leaves turn yellow and fall off, and the tree dies

Dutch Guiana *SURINAM

Dutch hoe a scuffle hoe

Dutch·man (dʌ́tʃmən) *pl.* **Dutch·men** (dʌ́tʃmən) *n.* a native of the Netherlands ‖ (*hist.*) a Dutch ship, esp. a warship **I'm a Dutchman** (*Br.*) a patently absurd assertion used for emphasis, *if that picture's genuine I'm a Dutchman*

Dutch metal tombac, an alloy of copper and zinc, used for cheap gilding

Dutch oven a three-walled tin box used for roasting meat etc. before an open fire ‖ a brick oven in which food is cooked by the heat radiating from the brick ‖ a heavy iron pot with a closefitting lid, used for stewing meat etc. ‖ a three-legged iron pot, with a flat top for holding live coals, used for cooking in a fireplace

Dutch treat an entertainment where everyone pays for himself

Dutch uncle someone who gives stern, blunt criticism

Dutch Wars (*hist.*) three wars between England and the Netherlands. The 1st Dutch War (1652–4) was a naval war caused by mercantile rivalry. After battles between the Dutch fleet under Tromp and the English fleet under Blake, the Dutch were forced to accept (1654) the terms of the Navigation Act (1651). The 2nd Dutch War (1665–7) was also fought at sea. In the course of it the Dutch fleet raided (1667) the Thames and Chatham. England gained New Netherland, and restrictions on Dutch trade were modified. The 3rd Dutch War (1672–8) was waged jointly by France and England against the Netherlands, but England withdrew (1674) because the war was unpopular. It was ended by the Treaties of Nijmegen (1678–9)

du·te·ous (dú:ti:əs, djú:ti:əs) *adj.* (*rhet.*) dutiful, obedient

du·ti·a·ble (dú:ti:əb'l, djú:ti:əb'l) *adj.* (of imports etc.) subject to customs or other duties

du·ti·ful (dú:tifəl, djú:tifəl) *adj.* mindful of one's duties, properly respectful and obedient ‖ showing a sense of duty, *dutiful attendance at lectures*

du·ty (dú:ti:, djú:ti:) *pl.* **du·ties** *n.* obligations of behavior or conduct in relation to others or to God which have a stronger claim on a person than his self-interest ‖ the work someone is expected to do because of his vocation ‖ (*pl.*) the

CONCISE PRONUNCIATION KEY: **(a)** æ, c*a*t; ɑ, c*a*r; ɔ f*a*wn; ei, sn*a*ke. **(e)** e, h*e*n; i:, sh*ee*p; iə, d*ee*r; ɛə, b*ea*r. **(i)** i, f*i*sh; ai, t*i*ger; ə:, b*i*rd. **(o)** o, *o*x; au, c*o*w; ou, g*oa*t; u, p*oo*r; ɔi, r*oy*al. **(u)** ʌ, d*u*ck; u, b*u*ll; u:, g*oo*se; ə, b*a*cillus; ju:, c*u*be. x, lo*ch*; θ, *th*ink; δ, bo*th*er; z, *Z*en; ʒ, cor*s*age; dʒ, sa*v*age; ŋ, oranguta*ng*; j, *y*ak; ʃ, *f*ish; tʃ, fe*tch*; 'l, rabb*le*; 'n, redd*en*. Complete pronunciation key appears inside front cover.

detailed content of this work, *the duties are not very heavy* ‖ payment due to the government for import, export, manufacture or sale of goods, *customs duties*, for transfer of property, *stamp duty* or for legal recognition of documents etc. ‖ (*mech.*) a machine's effectiveness measured as a ratio of work done to input energy, *a heavy-duty engine* **to be on** (*off*) **duty** to be retained by (free from) the duties of one's occupation **to do duty for** (of an inferior substitute) to be made to serve the same purpose as, *a straw mat did duty for a bed* [A.F. *dueté* fr. *dû*, past part. of *devoir*, to owe]

du·ty-free (dú:ti:fri:, djú:ti:fri:) *adj.* and *adv.* free of customs or excise duty

duty of water the quantity of water needed to irrigate a given area of a given crop

du·ty-paid (dú:ti:péid, djú:ti:péid) *adj.* and *adv.* paid up as regards customs or excise duty

Du·va·lier (dyvǽljei), François ('Papa Doc', 1909–71), Haitian president (1957–71). He reversed Haitian tradition by forming an elite of the black majority and excluding the 5% mulatto minority from political office. He ruled dictatorially, with the tontons macoutes ('bogeymen') as his terror organization. He was succeeded by his son Jean-Claude (1951–   ), who reigned in lavish style until his overthrow in 1986

Du·ver·gier de Hau·ranne (dyverʒieidəourǽn), Jean (1581–1643), abbé de Saint-Cyran, French Roman Catholic theologian, a friend and associate of Jansen. He opened the controversy with the Jesuits, became spiritual director of Port Royal (1636), and was imprisoned (1638–42) by Richelieu (*JANSENISM)

Du Vi·gneaud (dju:ví:njou, du:ví:njou), Vincent (1901–78), U.S. biochemist. He was awarded (1955) the Nobel prize in chemistry for his synthesis of the hormones oxytocin and vasopressin

Dvi·na, Northern (dviná) a river of northern U.S.S.R., 1,000 miles long, flowing into the White Sea near Archangel

Dvina, Western a river of the U.S.S.R. rising near the sources of the Volga and Dnieper and flowing for 640 miles into the Gulf of Riga

DVM (*abbr.*) digital voltmeter

Dvo·řák (dvórʒæk, dvórʒak), Antonín (1841–1904), Czech composer. He wrote operas, symphonies, concertos, choral and chamber works, and songs. His symphony 'From the New World' (1893), reflecting the spirit of national American music, was composed (1892–5) while he was director of the National Conservatory of Music in New York. Some of his music is strongly Czech in rhythm and melody. He was influenced by Smetana and Brahms

dwarf (dwɔrf) **1.** *n.* a freakishly small person. The condition in human beings other than such racial dwarfs as the pygmies of central Africa may be due to disease of the hormones, bones, heart or digestive system ‖ someone made by comparison to seem of relatively little capacity or achievement, *they are dwarfs beside Shakespeare* ‖ a plant or animal far below the usual size of its species ‖ a dwarf star ‖ (*Teutonic and Norse mythol.*) a small being with supernatural powers and esp. skill in working metal **2.** *adj.* undersized, deliberately stunted, esp. of plant varieties, *dwarf peas* **3.** *v.t.* to stunt or inhibit in growth ‖ to make small by comparison ‖ *v.i.* to become dwarf ‖ to seem small by comparison **dwárf·ish** *adj.* dwarflike [O.E. *dweorg, dweorh*]

dwarf dud (*mil.*) a nuclear weapon that, when launched at or emplaced for launching, fails to provide an explosive yield within a reasonable range of that which could be anticipated with normal operation of the weapon; a relative dud

dwarf star any of a large group of dense stars of relatively small volume, more numerous than the giant stars

dwell (dwel) *pres. part.* **dwell·ing** *past* and *past part.* **dwelt** (dwelt), **dwelled** *v.i.* (*rhet.*) to reside **to dwell on** to linger over or concentrate upon (a subject) ‖ to prolong (e.g. a note in music, or a syllable in verse-speaking) **dwéll·er** *n.* (usually in compounds) an inhabitant, a *cave-dweller* **dwéll·ing** *n.* the place where one lives, a house, esp. a primitive one [O.E. *dwellan, dwelian*, to mislead, hinder, delay, be delayed]

dwelling house (*administration*) a residence not used as a shop, office, etc.

dwelt *alt. past* and *past part.* of DWELL

dwerg·er (dwɔ́:rdʒər) *n.* one who has special ability in answering questions involving unconventional or imaginative situations

dwin·dle (dwínd'l) *pres. part.* **dwin·dling** *past* and *past part.* **dwin·dled** *v.i.* to grow gradually less in size, extent, quality or importance [dim. of M.E. *dwinen* fr. O.E. *dwīnan*]

dy·ad, di·ad (dáiæd) *n.* a group of two, a couple ‖ (*chem.*) a divalent element or radical ‖ serious dialogue or relationship ‖ (*biol.*) the half of a tetrad group, a bivalent chromosome **dy·ád·ic, di·ád·ic** *adj.* [fr. L.L. *dyas* (*dyadis*), two fr. Gk]

Dy·ak, Day·ak (dáiæk) *n.* a member of one of the peoples of Borneo. Sea Dyaks, br Ibans, are the most numerous race in Sarawak and also live in Brunei and North Borneo. Land Dyaks are confined to Sarawak

dy·ar·chy, di·ar·chy (dáiɑrki:) *pl.* **dy·ar·chies, di·ar·chies** *n.* a form of government in which two persons or bodies share the power [fr. Gk *di*-, twice+-*archia*, power]

dye (dai) *n.* a substance capable of coloring materials (e.g. textiles, paper, plastics) and generally applied in solution or dispersion, sometimes with the aid of a mordant. Dyes may be of natural origin but nowadays are usually synthetic ‖ a color produced by dyeing **of the deepest dye** of an extreme kind, *a villain of the deepest dye* [O.E. *dēag*]

dye *pres. part.* **dye·ing** *past* and *past part.* **dyed** *v.t.* to give a (specified) color to, or change the color of, by the use of dyes ‖ *v.i.* (of materials) to take color from dye, *this cloth dyes well* [O.E. *dēagian*]

dyed-in-the-wool (dáid'nðəwúl) *adj.* diehard, uncompromising

dye laser a tunable laser utilizing fluorescent dyes for amplification of light

dy·er (dáiər) *n.* someone whose job is dyeing cloth

dy·er's-weed (dáiərzwi̱:d) *n.* any of several plants yielding a yellow to green dye, e.g. woodwaxen

dye·stuff (dáistʌf) *n.* a substance used as, or yielding, a dye [prob. trans. of G. *farbstoff*]

dye·wood (dáiwud) *n.* any wood from which dye is extracted

dy·ing (dáiiŋ) *adj.* about to die ‖ going out of use, *dying customs* ‖ relating to the deathbed, *dying wishes* ‖ (*pop.*) eager or very anxious, *dying to know*

dyke *DIKE

dy·max·i·on (daimǽksi:ɒn) *n.* concept used in construction of maximum net performance per gross energy input based on parts of spheres; conceived by Buckminster Fuller, American engineer and inventor *Cf* GEODESIC DOME

dy·nam·ic (dainǽmik) **1.** *adj.* (*phys.*) pertaining to dynamics ‖ active, forceful, energetic, capable of giving a sense of power and transmitting energy, *a dynamic personality* ‖ (*med.*) to do with the function of an organ rather than its structure **2.** *n.* a moving or driving force **dy·nám·i·cal** *adj.* dynamic ‖ (*theol.*) endowing with divine power, *dynamical inspiration* [fr. F. *dynamique* fr. Gk]

dynamic friction the lesser force into which static friction develops once movement has begun

dynamic pressure pressure resulting from some medium in motion, such as the air, following the shock front of a blast wave

dy·nam·ics (dainǽmiks) *n.* the branch of mechanics (opp. STATICS) that deals with matter in motion (*KINEMATICS) and the forces that produce or change such motion (*KINETICS) ‖ the branch of any science dealing with forces ‖ (*pl.*) the moving moral, as well as physical, forces in any sphere, *the dynamics of social change*

dynamic spacial reconstructor a computer-based X-ray device that records images and projects body organs in three dimensions taking 28 images in 1/160 of a second (*abbr.* DSR)

dy·na·mism (dáinəmizəm) *n.* a theory (e.g. that of Leibniz) which regards matter and mind as involving immanent force ‖ personal dynamic power **dý·na·mist 1.** *n.* an adherent of the theory of dynamism **2.** *adj.* pertaining to dynamism [fr. Gk *dunamis*, power]

dy·na·mite (dáinəmait) **1.** *n.* a powerful explosive invented by Nobel in 1866. It consists essentially of nitroglycerine made stable by mixing with some absorbent such as kieselguhr ‖ a personality, or an element in a situation, likely to produce violent reactions **2.** *v.t. pres. part.* **dy·na·mit·ing** *past* and *past part.* **dy·na-** mit·ed to blow up or destroy with dynamite [fr. Gk *dunamis*, power]

dy·na·mo (dáinəmou) *n.* a generator ‖ a person of boundless energy [short for *dynamoelectric machine*]

dy·na·mom·e·ter (dainəmómitər) *n.* any instrument for measuring the power of a machine, a mechanical force or a draft animal **dy·na·mom·e·try** (dainəmómitri:) *n.* [fr. F. *dynamomètre* fr. Gk]

dy·nap·o·lis (dainǽpəlis) *n.* a metropolis planned to grow along a highway in units of self-sufficient communities

dy·nast (dáinæst, dáinəst, *Br.* also dínəst) *n.* a ruler, member of a dynasty **dy·nás·tic** *adj.* [fr. L.L. *dynastes* fr. Gk]

dy·nas·ty (dáinəsti:, *Br.* also dínəsti:) *pl.* **dy·nas·ties** *n.* a line of rulers of the same family ‖ its period of rule [F. *dynastie* fr. L. fr. Gk]

dy·na·tron (dáinətrɒn) *n.* (*elec.*) a tetrode valve in which the secondary emission of electrons from the plate results in a decrease in the anode current as the anode voltage increases. It may be used as an oscillator [fr. Gk *dunamis*, power+ELECTRON]

dyne (dain) *n.* a unit of force in the cgs system: that force which, applied to a mass of one gram, produces an acceleration of 1 centimeter per second per second [F. fr. Gk *dunamis*, power]

dy·on (dáion) *n.* (*particle phys.*) a hypothetical particle in matter that carries an electric and magnetic charge and quarks

dys- (dis) *prefix* bad, difficult, ill [Gk *dus*]

dys·au·to·no·mi·a (disɔtənóumi:ə) *n.* (*med.*) genetic nervous system disorder affecting automatic functions and sensory perception, carried principally by Jews of European descent **dys·autonomic** *adj.*

dys·bar·ism (dísbarizəm) *n.* (*med.*) popularly known as the bends, a disorder caused by sudden change of air pressure, symptomized by paralyzing cramps *also* caisson disease

dys·en·ter·ic (disentérik) *adj.* relating to, or having, dysentery

dys·en·ter·y (dísənteri:) *n.* a usually endemic disease of the colon characterized by diarrhea and the passage of blood, pus and mucus in the stools, which are highly infectious. Dysentery may be caused by protozoans or pathogenic bacteria that are spread chiefly in water or food [O.F. *dissenterie* fr. L. fr. Gk]

dys·gen·e·sis (disdʒénisis) *n.* (*med.*) a disorder causing underdevelopment of the gonads, e.g., in Turner's syndrome

dys·gen·ic (disdʒénik) *adj.* detrimental to the (human) race (opp. EUGENIC) **dys·gén·ics** *n.* the study of racial degeneration (opp. EUGENICS) [fr. DYS-+-*genic*, producing]

dys·ger·mi·no·ma *DISGERMINOMA

dys·lex·i·a (disléksi:ə) *n.* a nervous trouble interfering with the ability to read or comprehend what is read [Mod. L. fr. DYS-+-*lexia* fr. Gk *lexis*, word, speech]

dys·lo·gis·tic (dislədʒístik) *adj.* disapproving, indicating disfavor **dys·lo·gis·ti·cal·ly** *adv.* [fr. DYS- + EULOGISTIC]

dys·men·or·rhe·a, dys·men·or·rhoe·a (dismenərí:ə) *n.* painful menstruation [Mod. L. fr. DYS-+Gk mēn, month + Gk *rhoia*, a flow]

dys·pep·si·a (dispépsi:ə, dispépʃə) *n.* difficult or painful digestion, indigestion **dys·pép·tic 1.** *adj.* pertaining to or having dyspepsia ‖ bad-tempered ‖ depressed **2.** *n.* someone subject to dyspepsia **dys·pép·ti·cal·ly** *adv.* [L. fr. Gk]

dys·pha·gia (disféidʒə, disféidʒi:ə) *n.* difficulty in swallowing **dys·phag·ic** (disfædʒik) *adj.* [Mod. L. fr. DYS-+Gk *phagein*, to eat]

dys·pha·sia (disféiʒə, disféiʒi:ə) *n.* an impairment or loss of speech or ability to understand language, caused by brain disease or injury (cf. APHASIA) **dys·pha·sic** *adj.* [Mod. L. fr. DYS-+Gk *phasis*, utterance]

dys·pho·ni·a (disfóuni:ə) *n.* difficulty in articulating vocal sounds **dys·phon·ic** (disfónik) *adj.* [Mod. L. fr. DYS-+Gk *phōnos*, sounding]

dysp·ne·a, dysp·noe·a (dispní:ə) *n.* (*med.*) difficulty in breathing **dysp·né·ic dysp·nóe·ic** *adj.* [L. fr. Gk *duspnoia* fr. *duspnoos*, short of breath]

dys·pro·si·um (dispróuzi:əm) *n.* a trivalent, rare-earth element (symbol Dy, at. no. 66, at. mass 162.50) that forms highly magnetic yellowish compounds [Mód. L. fr. Gk *dusprositos*, hard to get at]

dys·to·pi·a (distóupi:ə) *n.* a place where everything is bad **dystopian** *adj. ant.* utopia *Cf* KAKOTOPIA

dys·tro·phic (distróufik) *adj.* (*envir.*) of shallow bodies of water that contain excess humus and plant organic matter, usu. with few fish

dys·tro·phi·ca·tion (dɪstroufikéiʃən) *n.* (*envir.*) pollution of interior waters by industrial and agricultural wastes **dystrophic** *adj.* dystrophic lakes *Cf* EUTROPHICATION

dys·tro·phy (dístrəfi:) *n.* any of several neuromuscular disorders, e.g muscular dystrophy [Mod. L. *dystrophia*]

dys·u·ri·a (disjúəri:ə) *n.* (*med.*) pain in urinating **dys·ú·ric** *adj.* [O.F. *dissurie* fr. L. fr. Gk]

Dyu·sham·be (djuʃámbe) (formerly Stalinabad) the capital (pop. 493,000) of Tadzhikistan, U.S.S.R., a communications center, terminus of the railway from Bukhara: textiles, leather, machinery, tobacco. University

dz. dozen

Dzau·dzhi·kau (djaudʒí:kau) *ORDZHONIKIDZE

Dzer·zhinsk (dzərʒí:nsk) a town (pop. 263,000) of the R.S.F.S.R., U.S.S.R., in central Russia on the Oka River: fertilizers, chemical products, insecticides

Dzun·ga·ri·a (zungéəri:ə) a region of Sinkiang-Uighur, W. China, a depression between the Altai Mtns and the Tien-Shan, consisting of a sandy desert bordered by steppe lands inhabited by nomads. It communicates with Soviet Kazakhstan on the west by the pass known as the Dzungarian Gates

CONCISE PRONUNCIATION KEY: **(a)** æ, c*a*t; ɑ, c*ar*; ɔ f*aw*n; ei, sn*a*ke.   **(e)** e, h*e*n; i:, sh*ee*p; iə, d*ee*r; ɛə, b*ea*r.   **(i)** i, f*i*sh; ai, t*i*ger; ə:, b*i*rd. **(o)** o, *o*x; au, c*ow*; ou, g*oa*t; u, p*oo*r; ɔi, r*oy*al.   **(u)** ʌ, d*u*ck; u, b*u*ll; u:, g*oo*se; ə, b*a*cill*u*s; ju:, c*u*be.   x, lo*ch*; θ, *th*ink; ð, bo*th*er; z, *Z*en; ʒ, cor*sa*ge; dʒ, sa*va*ge; ŋ, ora*ng*uta*ng*; j, *y*ak; ʃ, fi*sh*; tʃ, fe*tch*; 'l, rabb*le*; 'n, redd*en*.   Complete pronunciation key appears inside front cover.

EARLY NORTH SEMITIC	PHOENICIAN	EARLY GREEK	CLASSICAL GREEK	ETRUSCAN		EARLY LATIN	CLASSICAL LATIN
				Early	Classical		
∃	⅂	⅂	Ε	⅂	⅂	⅂	E

CURSIVE MAJUSCULE (ROMAN)	CURSIVE MINUSCULE (ROMAN)	ANGLO-IRISH MAJUSCULE	CAROLINE MINUSCULE	VENETIAN MINUSCULE (ITALIC)	N. ITALIAN MINUSCULE (ROMAN)
Є	£	e	e	e	e

A. C. SYLVESTER, CAMBRIDGE, ENGLAND

Development of the letter E, beginning with the early North Semitic letter. Evolution of both the majuscule, or capital, letter E and the minuscule, or lowercase, letter e are shown.

E, e (i:) the fifth letter in the English alphabet ‖ (*mus.*) a note and the key of which it is the tonic
E the symbol for second-class in Lloyd's register of shipping
E. east, eastern
each (i:tʃ) **1.** *adj.* every one of two or more, *each child had a toy* **2.** *pron.* every one of two or more, *choose one of each, divide it so that each has the same amount* **3.** *adv.* for or to everyone, *give them each a dollar* ‖ apiece, *they cost one franc each* [O.E. ǣlc]
each other referring to two persons or things mutually, *we said good-bye to each other*
each way (*Br.*, betting) for a win or a place
ea·ger (í:gər) *adj.* keen, *an eager appetite* ‖ having a strong desire (to attain some end), *he is eager to meet you* [O.F. *aigre*, sharp]
eager *EAGRE
ea·gle (í:g'l) *n.* a large diurnal bird of prey of fam. *Accipitidrae*, of cosmopolitan distribution ‖ a representation of this bird, as an emblem. In mythology the eagle represents might and courage, and since Roman times has been used as an emblem of empire or sovereign power ‖ the constellation Aquila ‖ (*golf*) a hole played in two below par [M.E. *egle* fr. O. F. *egle, aigle*]
eagle eye observation esp. directed to criticizing or faultfinding, *nothing escapes his eagle eye* **éa·gle-éyed** *adj.*
eagle owl *Bubo bubo*, the biggest European owl. It has large orange eyes and prominent ear tufts
ea·glet (í:glit) *n.* a young eagle [F. *aiglette*]
ea·gre, ea·ger (í:gər) *n.* a bore (tidal wave) [origin unknown]
Ea·kins (éikinz), Thomas (1844–1916), U.S. painter, known for his 'The Gross Clinic' (1875), a large canvas which depicts medical students observing a surgical operation. He emphasized the study of anatomy and perspective in painting and experimented in the photography of motion
ear (iər) **1.** *n.* the compound spike or inflorescence of most cereals, esp. of the mature fruit **2.** *v.i.* to form ears, come into ear [O.E. *ēar*]
ear *n.* the organ of hearing in men and animals, esp. the external part ‖ the power of hearing correctly or of distinguishing and appreciating sounds, *to have no ear for music* ‖ something resembling the external ear, *the ears of a pitcher* **in one ear and out the other** completely unheeded **to be all ears** to listen eagerly **to bring a storm (or a hornet's nest) down about one's ears** to stir up trouble for oneself **to have the ear of** to be in a position to speak about a matter to (someone) knowing that he will pay attention **to keep one's (or have an) ear to the ground** to make sure one gets early information or warning about new

developments **to send someone away with a flea in his ear** (*Br.*) to tell someone just how little one thinks of him ‖ to refuse someone's request roughly **up to the ears in** overwhelmed or overburdened by, *up to the ears in debt* [O.E. *ēare*]
—The ear's function is to convert sound waves into nervous impulses which are conveyed via the auditory nerve to the brain, where they give rise to the sensation of hearing. Sound waves are collected by the pinna, the externally visible part of the ear, and pass down the channel of the external ear to the drum, a membrane which they cause to vibrate. These vibrations are transmitted across the cavity of the middle ear by a system of small interlocking bones, the hammer, anvil and stirrup; and are then conveyed to the cochlea, a spiral organ in the inner ear, which translates them into nervous impulses. The inner ear also contains the labyrinth, a system of channels filled with fluid and projecting in all three dimensions. Movement of the head causes movement of the fluid inside the labyrinth, thus setting up other nervous impulses, which are important for balance. The organs of the inner and middle ear are contained inside the skull. The middle ear is connected with the mastoid air cells and, via the Eustachian tube, with the mouth
ear·ache (íəreik) *n.* a pain inside the ear
ear·drop (íərdrɒp) *n.* a small ornament made to hang from the lobe of the ear ‖ (*pl.*) a fluid medicament inserted into the ear in drops
ear·drum (íərdrʌm) *n.* the membrane in the ear which receives sound impulses
Ear·hart (éərhart), Amelia (1898–1937), U.S. aviation pioneer, the first woman to cross (1928) the Atlantic by air. She attempted (1937) a round-the-world trip during which her plane vanished in the South Pacific
ear·ing (íəriŋ) *n.* (*naut.*) one of the small lines by which the corner of a sail is attached to a yard or gaff
earl (ə:rl) *n.* (in the peerages of Great Britain and Northern Ireland) a nobleman ranking between a viscount and a marquess (*COUNTESS)
éarl·dom *n.* [O.E. *eorl*, a nobleman]
earlier on (*Br.*) at some previous time or stage
ear·li·ness (ə́:rliːnis) *n.* the quality of being early
Ear·ly (ə́:rliː), Jubal Anderson (1816–94), Confederate general during the Civil War, noted for his successful raids (1864) around the Shenandoah Valley and near Washington, D.C. He was defeated (1865) by Gen. Sheridan
ear·ly (ə́:rliː) *comp.* **ear·li·er** *superl.* **ear·li·est 1.** *adj.* at or near the beginning of a period of time, piece of work, series etc. ‖ belonging to a distant

or comparatively distant time in the past, *the early history of Canada, an early model of a car* ‖ in the near future, *please answer at your earliest convenience* ‖ coming or happening before the usual or expected time, *early frosts* **2.** *adv.* at or near the beginning of a period of time, piece of work, series, etc., *we started early in the morning* ‖ long ago, *man learned early to use tools* ‖ unusually or unexpectedly soon, or soon by comparison with others of a comparable kind, *the bus left early, early flowering shrubs* [O.E. *ǣrlice, ǣrlice* adv.]
Early American (of buildings, furniture etc.) dating from the colonial period
early bird (*pop.*) an early arrival ‖ (*pop.*) someone who gets up in the morning early
Early English the pointed Gothic church architecture predominant in England from the second half of the 12th c. to the second half of the 13th c.
early leaver (*Br.*) a dropout
Early Spring (*mil.*) an antireconnaissance satellite weapons system
ear·mark (íərmɑrk) **1.** *n.* a nick in the ear or a tattooed mark or metal tag inside the ear of livestock, identifying ownership **2.** *v.t.* to put an earmark on (livestock) ‖ to set aside for a particular purpose, *to earmark money for a special fund*
ear·muff (íərmʌf) *n.* one of a pair of ear coverings of fur, etc., worn on a headband to protect the ears from frost
earn (ə:rn) *v.t.* to get as a payment, reward or yield in return for work or services ‖ to deserve or obtain by merit or wrongdoing, *the theft earned him three months in jail* ‖ (of money, shares etc.) to bring in, *the investment should earn you 5%* ‖ *v.i.* to be doing paid work ‖ to bring in money from investment **earned** *adj.* (of income) worked for, not derived from investments ‖ deserved [O.E. *earnian*]
earned run (*baseball*) a score not due to an error, made before the first put-out in an inning
earned run average *n.* average runs per inning charged to a pitcher, multiplied by 9
ear·nest (ə́:rnist) *n.* a token or pledge, *an earnest of good faith* ‖ money paid as a deposit to confirm a sale or agreement [M.E. *ernes* fr. F. fr. L. fr. Gk fr. Heb.]
earnest *adj.* heartfelt, *an earnest appeal for help* ‖ serious and diligent, *an earnest student of economics* ‖ emotionally intense and solemn **in earnest** serious, determined, *are you joking or in earnest?* [O. E. *eorneste*]
earn·ing (ə́:rniŋ) *n.* the act of earning or the thing earned ‖ (*pl.*) money earned by work or commerce
earning power the capacity (of a person, machine, investment, etc.) to earn money

CONCISE PRONUNCIATION KEY: **(a)** æ, cat; ɑ, car; ɔ fawn; ei, snake. **(e)** e, hen; iː, sheep; iə, deer; ɛə, bear. **(i)** i, fish; ai, tiger; əː, bird. **(o)** o, ox; au, cow; ou, goat; u, poor; ɔi, royal. **(u)** ʌ, duck; u, bull; uː, goose; ə, bacillus; juː, cube. x, loch; θ, think; δ, bother; z, Zen; ʒ, corsage; dʒ, savage; ŋ, orangutang; j, yak; ʃ, fish; tʃ, fetch; 'l, rabble; 'n, redden. Complete pronunciation key appears inside front cover.

Earp (ə:rp), Wyatt (1848–1929) U.S. gunfighter, gambler and lawman in the West. He came to Tombstone, Ariz. (1880) with his brothers Morgan and Virgil and 'Doc' (John) Holliday; they became involved in a quarrel with the Clanton family that led to a famous shootout (1881) at the OK Corral. Three men on the Clanton side were killed. Later, when Earp's brother Morgan was killed by the Clantons, Wyatt retaliated by killing three men

ear·phone (fərfoun) n. a device converting electrical waves into sound waves and held against the ear or inserted into it

ear·ring (íəriŋ) n. a small ring, often of gold and set with a stone, or a hook supporting an ornament, worn on the earlobe, which is pierced to receive it ‖ a small ornament screwed or clipped to the lobe

ear shell a haliotis

ear·shot (íərʃɒt) n. the distance within which a shout or call can be heard

ear·split·ting (íərsplitiŋ) adj. piercingly shrill or loud

earth (ə:rθ) 1. n. the fifth largest planet of the solar system (mass= 5.87x 10²¹ tons), and the third in order from the sun, about which it moves in an elliptical orbit of mean radius c. 93 million miles, completing one revolution in 365.26 days. The earth has a polar radius of c. 3,950 miles and is almost spherical, being flattened slightly at the poles. It rotates with a 24-hour period on an axis that is tilted slightly with respect to the plane of its orbit. The composition of the earth varies from a dense molten core (thought to consist of nickel and iron and to explain the magnetic field surrounding it) to a light, thin, frangible mantle ‖ the planet on which we live (cf. HEAVEN) ‖ land and sea as opposed to the sky, *the earth is divided into continents* ‖ the topsoil of the earth's crust, *to firm the earth around a plant* ‖ a hole in the ground made e.g. by a fox or badger and used as its shelter ‖ (*Br., elec.*) a ground (electrical conductor) ‖ a natural pigment (e.g. ocher) found in the earth and used by artists **on earth** emphatic substitute for 'ever', *where on earth have you been?* **to come down to earth** to face facts as they are **to move heaven and earth** to make a prodigious effort **to run to earth** to pursue (e.g. a fox) to its earth ‖ to find after prolonged or difficult searching 2. v.t. (with 'up') to heap earth around ‖ (*Br., elec.*) to ground (connect with the ground) [O.E. *eorthe*]

earth closet (*Br.*) a simple privy in which the excreta are covered by earth or ashes

earth dam a dam constructed of compacted soil materials

Earth Day celebration of antipollution efforts by environmentalists, usu. in April

earth·en (ə:rθən) adj. made of earth or baked clay

earth·en·ware (ə:rθənwęər) n. glazed or unglazed pots, plates, crockery, etc., made of clay fired at a lower temperature than that at which its particles would fuse (cf. STONEWARE)

earth·i·ness (ə:rθiːnis) n. the quality of being earthy

earth·light (ə:rθlait) n. earthshine

earth·li·ness (ə:rθlinis) n. the quality of being earthly

earth·ling (ə:rθliŋ) n. (*folktales, science fiction* etc.) a person who lives on the earth

earth·ly (ə:rθli) adj. worldly as opposed to spiritual, *earthly passions* ‖ possible or imaginable, *no earthly reason to make a fuss* **not an earthly** (*Br., pop.*) no chance at all

earth·nut (ə:rθnʌt) n. the edible fruit of any number of tuberous plants, e.g., the peanut ‖ the truffle

earth·quake (ə:rθkwęik) n. a pressure wave in the earth's crust caused by a deep-seated disturbance. Major earthquakes result from fractures, usually along existing faults, in the underlying rock strata which have been subject to cumulative strain. Mild tremors can be caused by movement of the tides and variations in atmospheric pressure. Earthquakes occur most frequently in a circum-Pacific belt and in the recent mountain systems of the Alpine-Himalayan-Indonesian regions. Some notable earthquakes: Lisbon (1755); San Francisco (1906), Tokyo (1923), N. Iran (1957), Agadir, Morocco (1960)

Earth Resources Experiment Package NASA project (acronym EREP) utilizing Skylab to study agriculture and land use, geology, and hydrology on the earth

earth·rise (ə:rθraiz) n. view of the appearance of the earth over the horizon as seen from the moon

earth satellite a satellite that orbits the earth

earth science any of various sciences, esp. geology, concerned with the composition, structure, etc. of the earth

earth sciences the total of sciences concerned with the earth, its origins, movement, composition, oceans, atmosphere, destiny, etc.

earth·shine (ə:rθʃain) n. the faint light sometimes seen illuminating the dark part of the moon (esp. after the new moon), caused by sunlight reflected from the earth

earth station receiving point of messages from satellites *Cf* SATCOM

earth·ward (ə:rθwərd) 1. adj. directed towards the earth, *a satellite on its earthward journey* 2. adv. towards the earth **éarth·wards** adv. earthward

earth·work (ə:rθwə:rk) n. (esp. *archaeol.*) a bank of earth built up to fortify or protect ‖ (*engin.*) the removal or building up of earth in the course of work ‖ art created directly from natural materials, e.g., sand rock

earth·worm (ə:rθwə:rm) n. a worm esp. of genus *Lumbricus*, phylum *Annelida*, elongated, limbless animals of 150 segments, covered with a shiny cuticle, and darker on the dorsal surface, living in the ground. They are hermaphrodite but are always cross-fertilized. Their burrows, which are prevented from crumbling by the worm's exuded mucus, help to aerate, loosen and drain the soil (*WORMCAST)

earth·y (ə:rθi:) comp. **earth·i·er** superl. **earth·i·est** adj. of or like earth ‖ unspiritual, robust and pleasure-loving ‖ gross or bawdy

earth year a mean solar year

ear trumpet an old-fashioned, trumpet-shaped hearing aid

ear·wax (íərwæks) n. cerumen, the waxlike substance which forms in the ear

ear·wig (íərwig) n. a member of *Forficula*, a genus of widely distributed orthopteran insects (¾ in. in length). The anterior wings are short and horny, and the posterior pair are folded transversely and longitudinally. Earwigs avoid the light. They are vegetarian and cause damage in gardens ‖ a small centipede, esp. of genus *Geophilus* [O.E. *ēarwicga*, ear beetle]

ease (i:z) 1. n. physical comfort and relaxation, *to take one's ease* ‖ mental calm, *ease of mind* ‖ freedom from awkwardness or shyness ‖ freedom from difficulty, *ease of access* **to stand at ease** (*mil.*) to stand still and upright (less stiffly than at attention) but with the feet apart (cf. EASY) 2. v. pres. part. **eas·ing** past and past part. **eased** v.t. to lessen the discomfort or anxiety of, relieve ‖ to loosen (e.g. a bolt) ‖ to make less difficult, trying, or tense, *a meeting might ease the situation* ‖ to handle (something) carefully and move it gradually, *ease the cupboard into the corner* ‖ v.i. to become less difficult, trying or tense ‖ (of stocks or the stock market) to fall in price **to ease off** to become less, *sales are sure to ease off after Christmas* ‖ to exert oneself less **to ease springs** (*Br., mil.*) to work the bolt of a rifle to and fro so as to make sure that no round is left in the breech or magazine **to ease the helm** (*naut.*) to bring the wheel back gradually after an alteration of course **éase·ful** adj. [O.F. *eise, aise*, origin unknown]

ea·sel (i:z'l) n. an adjustable frame of wood or metal to support esp. an artist's canvas [fr. Du. *ezel*, ass]

ease·ment (í:zmənt) n. (*law*) a right to make use of another's property (e.g. a right of way over his land) ‖ a building adjoining another, or attached to it, which serves some secondary purpose [O.F. *aisement*]

eas·i·ly (í:zili) adv. in an easy way ‖ without strain or exertion, *to win easily* ‖ comfortably, *to breathe more easily* ‖ smoothly, *to slide easily into place* ‖ by far, *easily our best sprinter* ‖ very possibly, *it could easily happen*

eas·i·ness (í:zinis) n. freedom from difficulty ‖ the state of being comfortable or free from care ‖ (*econ.*) a state of economic weakness involving falling prices and diminished trade

EA-6A *INTRUDER

EA-6B *PROWLER

East (i:st), Edward Murray (1879–1938), U.S. geneticist. He contributed to the development of hybrid corn and advocated, in 'Heredity and Human Affairs' (1927), population control

east (i:st) 1. adv. towards the east 2. n. (usually with 'the') one of the four cardinal points of the compass (*abbr.* E., *COMPASS POINT) ‖ the direction of the rising sun at the equinox **the East** that part of a country which is in this direction from the observer ‖ that part of the world which is in this direction from Europe (*MIDDLE EAST, *FAR EAST) ‖ the states of the U.S.A. east of the Mississippi, esp. the northern states on the Atlantic seaboard 3. adj. of, belonging to or situated towards the east ‖ facing east, *an east window* ‖ (of winds) blowing from the east ‖ (*eccles.*) of the end of a church where the chancel is [O.E. *ēast, ēastan*]

East African Economic Community an organization to promote their economic prosperity formed (Dec. 1967) by Kenya, Tanzania and Uganda, and open to membership of other African states

East Africa, University of a university (inaugurated 1963) supported jointly by the governments of Kenya, Tanzania and Uganda, with colleges in Nairobi, Dar-es-Salaam and Kampala

East An·gli·a (æŋgli:ə) a geographical region of E. England, south of the Wash and north of Essex, including Norfolk, Suffolk and the Isle of Ely. University (1963, at Norwich) ‖ (*hist.*) the Anglo-Saxon kingdom (6th–9th cc.) in the same region. It rose to brief ascendancy (early 7th c.), was subject to the Danes (9th c.) and became an earldom (10th c.)

East Berlin *BERLIN

east·bound (í:stbaund) adj. going east

east by north N. 78° 45' E., one point north of due east (*abbr.* E. b. N., *Br.* esp. E. by N., *COMPASS POINT)

east by south S. 78° 45' E., one point south of due east (*abbr.* E. b. S., *Br.* esp. E. by S., *COMPASS POINT)

East China Sea *CHINA SEA

East End the eastern part of London, containing the docks

East·er (í:stər) 1. n. the chief Christian feast, which celebrates the Resurrection of Christ, on the first Sunday after the first full moon that coincides with, or comes after, the spring equinox (taken as Mar. 21) 2. adj. coming at or near Easter [O.E. *ēastre* perh. from *Eostre*, goddess of dawn, whose festival was celebrated at the spring equinox]

Easter egg a colored, hard-boiled hen's egg, or a chocolate or other candy egg, given as an Easter present, or hidden about the house or garden for children to find

Easter Eve the day before Easter, Holy Saturday

Easter Island a Pacific island (area 55 sq. miles, pop. 1,598) near Chile, remarkable for hundreds of stone colossi probably built by a people massacred (c. 1680) by the ancestors of the present Polynesian inhabitants. The island was annexed (1888) by Chile

east·er·ly (í:stərli) 1. adj. and adv. in or towards the east ‖ (of winds) from that direction 2. n. pl. **east·er·lies** a wind blowing from the east

Easter Monday the day after Easter, a public holiday in many countries

east·ern (í:stərn) adj. situated, facing or moving towards the east **Eastern** of or relating to the East [O.E. *ēasterne*]

Eastern Church (*hist.*) the eastern patriarchates of the Catholic Church before the schism with Rome: Constantinople, Alexandria, Antioch and Jerusalem ‖ the Orthodox Eastern Church ‖ the heretical Eastern Churches (Nestorian, Jacobite etc.) ‖ any of the Uniate Eastern Churches (in communion with Rome, but following the Eastern rite)

Eastern Empire the Byzantine Empire

East·er·ner (í:stərnər) n. a native of the eastern U.S.A.

Eastern Ghats *GHATS

eastern hemisphere the part of the earth lying to the east of the Atlantic Ocean, comprising Asia, Africa, Europe and Australia

east·ern·most (í:stərnmoust) adj. furthest east

Eastern Nigeria *NIGERIA, *BIAFRA

Eastern Orthodox Church *ORTHODOX EASTERN CHURCH

Eastern Question (*hist.*) the international problem caused by the disintegration of the Ottoman Empire in the Balkans and the E. Mediterranean in the 19th c. Russia attempted to take advantage of Turkey's weakness in order to gain territory, continuing the policy of Catherine II. The Serbs revolted against Turkey (1804 and 1815), followed by the Greeks (1821–30). Russia fought Turkey (1806–12), intervened in Greece (1828), gained concessions

CONCISE PRONUNCIATION KEY: (**a**) æ, c*a*t; ɑ, c*a*r; ɔ f*aw*n; ei, sn*a*ke. (**e**) e, h*e*n; i:, sh*ee*p; iə, d*ee*r; ɛə, b*ea*r. (**i**) i, f*i*sh; ai, t*i*ger; ə:, b*i*rd. (**o**) o, *o*x; au, c*ow*; ou, g*oa*t; u, p*oo*r; ɔi, r*oy*al. (**u**) ʌ, d*u*ck; u, b*u*ll; u:, g*oo*se; ə, b*a*cill*u*s; ju:, c*u*be. x, lo*ch*; θ, *th*ink; ð, bo*th*er; z, *Z*en; ʒ, cor*s*age; dʒ, sava*g*e; ŋ, orangutan*g*; j, *y*ak; ʃ, *fi*sh; tʃ, fe*tch*; 'l, rabb*le*; 'n, redd*en*. Complete pronunciation key appears inside front cover.

in the Treaty of Adrianople (1829), precipitated the Crimean War (1853–6) and fought the Russo-Turkish War (1877–8). Russia's diplomatic triumph in the Treaty of San Stefano (1878) was rapidly undone by the Congress of Berlin (1878). The Bulgarians revolted (1875) and gained full independence (1908), and the Balkan Wars (1912–13) broke out. Austria's annexation (1908) of Bosnia-Herzegovina helped to spark off the 1st world war (1914–18). Although many problems remained unsolved, the Eastern Question may be said to have ended with the Treaty of Lausanne (1923), under which Turkey abandoned her claim to all nonTurkish territories of the Ottoman Empire (*STRAITS QUESTION)

Eastern Roman Empire the Byzantine Empire

Eastern Standard time (*abbr.* E.S.T.) Eastern time in the U.S.A.

Eastern time (*abbr.* E.T.) the mean local time of the 75th meridian west of Greenwich, five hours behind Greenwich mean time

Easter Sunday the Sunday on which the Easter festival is celebrated (*EASTER for the method of calculating the date)

East·er·tide (íːstərtaid) *n.* the period from the Saturday before Easter to the Saturday after Whitsunday

Easter week the week that begins on Easter Sunday (cf. HOLY WEEK)

East Flanders *FLANDERS

East Frisian Islands *FRISIAN ISLANDS

East Germany *GERMAN DEMOCRATIC REPUBLIC

East India Company, British a company chartered (1600) by parliament for the monopoly of trade with the eastern hemisphere. Driven from the East Indies (1623) by the Dutch, it concentrated on trade with India, where it clashed with the French (1745–61). Clive's victories enabled it to develop enormous political and economic power in India (18th c.), but after the Indian Mutiny (1857) the Crown assumed the government of India (1858) and the company was dissolved (1874)

East India Company, Dutch a company chartered (1602) by the Netherlands government to trade with the East Indies. It colonized (1652–70) Cape Colony, and captured Ceylon and the Malabar coast from the Portuguese (1658–63). In the face of increasing British competition, it was dissolved (1798)

East Indian a native of the East Indies

East In·dies (índi:z) (*hist.*) India and S.E. Asia ‖ (*hist.*) the whole Malay archipelago ‖ the former Netherlands East Indies, now Indonesia

east·ing (íːstiŋ) *n.* (*naut.*) a sailing towards the east ‖ (*naut.*) the distance thus sailed

East London a port (pop. 130,000) and resort in Cape Province, S. Africa, at the mouth of the Buffalo River, with food, shipbuilding and chemical industries. Exports: wool, citrus fruits

East Lo·thi·an (lóuði:ən) a coastal county (area 267 sq. miles, pop. 52,000) in S.E. Scotland. County town: Haddington

East·man (íːstmən), George (1854–1932), U.S. inventor and manufacturer of the Kodak camera (1888), monopolizing (1927) the U.S. photographic industry. He donated (1924) more than \$75 million, principally to the University of Rochester and the Massachusetts Institute of Technology

east-north-east (íːstnɔrθíːst) 1. *adv.* towards east-northeast 2. *n.* N. 67° 30′ E., a compass point midway between east and northeast (*abbr.* E.N.E., *COMPASS POINT) 3. *adj.* of or situated towards east-northeast ‖ (of winds) blowing from east-northeast

East Prussia (*hist.*) a German province created by the Treaty of Versailles (1919), separated by the Polish Corridor from the rest of Germany. It was divided between Poland and Russia at the Potsdam Conference (1945)

East Riding an administrative district (area 1,172 sq. miles) in Yorkshire, England

East River a strait separating Manhattan from the New York boroughs on Long I.

east-south-east (íːstsauθíːst) 1. *adv.* towards east-southeast 2. *n.* S. 67° 30′ E., a compass point midway between east and southeast (*abbr.* E.S.E., *COMPASS POINT) 3. *adj.* of or situated towards east-southeast ‖ (of winds) blowing from east-southeast

east·ward (íːstwərd) 1. *adv.* and *adj.* towards the east 2. *n.* the eastward direction or part **east·wards** *adv.*

eas·y (íːzi) *comp.* **eas·i·er** *superl.* **eas·i·est** 1. *adj.* not difficult ‖ obtained without difficulty ‖ free from hardship, anxiety or worry ‖ gentle and comfortable, smooth, *an easy pace* ‖ not demanding or oppressive, not strict, *easy hours of work* ‖ not stiff or awkward, *easy prose* ‖ not at all tight, *an easy fit* ‖ not difficult to get the better of, *an easy victim* ‖ (*Br., pop.*) openminded with respect to a course of action, *I'm easy whether we stay or go* ‖ (of buying and selling, or of money) showing plentiful supply, *dairy cows were easy at \$160* **easy on the eyes** (*Br.* eye) (*old-fash.*) good-looking **on easy terms** (*commerce*) by installments 2. *adv.* **easy does it!** go gently, be very careful **to stand easy** (*mil.*) to relax while keeping the feet in the position taken on the order to stand at ease **to go easy with** not to waste or use too much of ‖ to treat carefully **to take it easy** to relax, not to work too hard or go too fast ‖ not to get excited 3. *n.* (*Br.*) a short rest, esp. in rowing [O.F. *aisié* past part. of *aisier*, to put at ease]

easy chair a comfortably upholstered armchair

easy game (esp. *Br.*) easy mark

eas·y·go·ing (íːzi:gouiŋ) *adj.* not strict, very tolerant, *to be too easygoing to keep good discipline* ‖ lazy, not diligent or methodical

easy mark someone easily swindled or otherwise taken advantage of

easy money money got without much effort

eat (íːt) *pres. part.* **eat·ing** *past* **ate** (eit) *past part.* **eat·en** (íːtn) *v.t.* to take as food, *to eat a peach* ‖ to feed on, *horses eat oats* ‖ to include habitually in one's diet, *she never eats fat* ‖ to consume great quantities of, *an old car eats oil* ‖ to corrode, *acids eat metals* ‖ *v.i.* to have a meal ‖ to be of a specified quality when eaten ‖ (with 'into') to reduce something gradually as if by eating it, e.g., by corrosion, *rust has eaten into the fender* ‖ to begin to use something up, *to eat into one's savings* **to eat humble pie** to apologize humbly, climb down from a high and mighty attitude **to eat one's heart out** to fret and give oneself up to self-pity **to eat one's words** to take back an assertion and admit having been wrong **to eat out** to go to a restaurant instead of eating at home **to eat out of someone's hand** to be completely submissive to someone **to eat someone out of house and home** to eat so inordinately as to threaten the provider with ruin **to eat through** to make a way through by gnawing **to eat up** to eat all of ‖ to consume rapidly, *the car ate up the miles* **éat·a·ble** 1. *adj.* fit, but hardly pleasant, to eat 2. *n.* (*pl.*) things to eat **éat·er** *n.* someone who or something which eats as specified, *a slow eater* ‖ (esp. *Br.*) a fruit good to eat uncooked (opp. COOKER) [O.E. *etan*]

Ea·ton (íːtn), Theophilus (1590–1658), Puritan leader and a founder (1637) of New Haven, Connecticut. As colonial governor (from 1638), he was the chief drafter of New Haven's law code of 1656

Eaton agent (íːtən) toxic agent intermediate between virus and bacterium, e.g., mycoplasma pneumoniae, responsible for a form of pneumonia

eau de Co·logne (óudəkəlóun) *n.* cologne [F.=water of Cologne, where it was invented in the 18th c.]

eau-de-nile, *Br.* **eau de nil** (óudəni:l) *adj.* Nile green [F.= water of the Nile]

eau-de-vie (óudəvíː) *n.* a liquor distilled from wine or cider, marc, cereals, etc. (*BRANDY) [F. = water of life]

eaves (íːvz) *pl. n.* the part of a roof which projects over the top of a wall and allows rain to fall clear of the wall or into a gutter [O.E. *efes*, a clipped edge of thatch (orig. sing.)]

eaves·drop (íːvzdrɒp) *pres. part.* **eaves·dropping** *past* and *past part.* **eaves·dropped** *v.i.* to listen to what is not meant for one's own ears, without letting oneself be seen **éaves·dropper**, **éaves·drop·ping** *ns* [earlier *eavesdrip* fr. EAVES+DRIP (i.e., to stand where the eaves drip)]

ebb (eb) 1. *n.* the drawing back of tidal water from the shore ‖ decline, *his fortunes are at a low ebb* 2. *v.i.* (of the tide) to draw back from the shore ‖ to decline, worsen, diminish [O.E. *ebba*]

ebb and flow the movement of the tide ‖ the declines and advances characteristic of business or of any activity in which luck plays a part

Ebbinghaus (ébiŋhaus), Hermann (1850–

1909) German psychologist, noted for approaching the study of memory by using the experimental method. He demonstrated the rate at which things are forgotten and related quantity of things learned to learning time. His works include 'Memory: A Contribution to Experimental Psychology' (1885)

ebb tide a falling tide or low tide (opp. FLOOD TIDE) ‖ a state of near or complete decline

EBCDIC (*acronym*) extended binary-coded decimal intercharge code

E·bert (éibɛərt), Friedrich (1871–1925), German Social Democratic statesman, first president (1919–25) of the Weimar Republic

EB-57 (*mil.*) *CANBERRA

eb·on·ite (ébənait) *n.* a hard black vulcanized rubber used as an insulating material

eb·on·ize (ébənaiz) *pres. part.* **eb·on·iz·ing** *past* and *past part.* **eb·on·ized** *v.t.* to stain or dye (furniture etc.) to make it resemble ebony [EBONY]

eb·on·y (ébəni) 1. *n.* the wood of many trees of fam. *Ebanaceae*, esp. genus *Diospyros*, blackened by a deposition of gum resin in the heartwood ‖ any of these trees 2. *adj.* black as ebony ‖ made of ebony [older *ebene* fr. F. fr. L. fr. Gk] —Ebony grows in tropical forests of Asia and Africa. The wood is hard, heavy, durable and polishes brightly. It is used for cabinetmaking, mosaic and inlaid work, and figure carving

e·brac·te·ate (ibrǽkti:it) *adj.* (*bot.*) without bracts **e·brac·te·at·ed** (ibrǽkti:eitid) *adj.* [fr. Mod. L. *ebracteatus* fr. *e*, without + *bractea*, thin leaf]

E·bro (íːbrou, ébrou) a river (480 miles long) of N.E. Spain, flowing southeast from the Cantabrian Mtns. It is navigable for small vessels in its middle course, through the valley which forms the core of Aragon. Breaking through the S. Catalonian coast range, it waters the huerta at Tortosa, and enters the Mediterranean in a delta

e·bul·lience (ibʌljəns) *n.* the state or quality of being ebullient **e·búl·lien·cy** *n.*

e·bul·lient (ibʌljənt) *adj.* bubbling over with high spirits or enthusiasm [fr. L. *ebulliens* fr. *ebullire*, to boil up]

e·bul·lism (ébu:lizəm) *n.* (*med.*) bubbling in the blood resulting from sharp change in air pressure, e.g., in cases of bends

eb·ul·li·tion (ebulíʃən) *n.* the act or state of boiling ‖ a sudden outburst of feeling [fr. L. *ebullitio* (*ebullitionis*) fr. *ebullire*, to boil up]

E·ça de Que·i·roz (ésədəkɛr5ʃ), José Maria (1845–1900), Portuguese novelist, author of 'O primo Basilio' (1878, Eng. trans. 'Dragon's Teeth', 1889) and other realistic novels

é·car·té (eikɑrtéi, *Br.* eikátei) *n.* a card game for two players. Each player is dealt five cards, and the hands are played somewhat like whist, except that cards may be exchanged. Cards below the 7 are not used [F.]

ec·cen·tric (ikséntrik) 1. *adj.* (of circles, etc.) not having a common center (cf. CONCENTRIC) ‖ with its axle not at the center, *an eccentric wheel* ‖ not conforming to conventions, odd, *eccentric behavior* ‖ (*astron.*, of an orbit) deviating from circular motion 2. *n.* someone who behaves unconventionally ‖ (*engin.*) a device for converting circular motion into to-and-fro rectilinear motion **ec·cén·tri·cal·ly** *adv.* **ec·cen·tric·i·ty** (éksentrisiti) *pl.* **ec·cen·tric·i·ties** *n.* the state of being eccentric ‖ oddness of behavior ‖ an example of such behavior ‖ the distance of an axis or point of rotation from the center of an orbit, e.g., from the sun to the center of a planet's orbit [fr. L. *eccentricus* fr. Gk]

ec·chy·mo·sis (ekimóusis) *n.* an oozing of blood into the tissues. The blood goes from red to blue then becomes yellowish, through alteration of the hemoglobin [Mod. L. fr. Gk]

ec·cle·si·al (iklíːzi:əl) *adj.* of a church; variation of ecclesiastical

Ec·cle·si·as·tes (ikliːzi:ǽsti:z) a book of the Old Testament purporting to be the work of King Solomon but probably written in the late 3rd c. B.C. It considers what is the purpose of life [Gk=preacher]

ec·cle·si·as·tic (ikliːzi:ǽstik) *n.* a priest, clergyman **ec·cle·si·ás·ti·cal** *adj.* of or relating to the Christian Church or clergy ‖ of or used in churches **ec·cle·si·as·ti·cism** (ikliːzi:ǽstisizəm) *n.* the principles that govern the organization of the Church and its well-being ‖ interest in, and support of, such principles [fr. Gk *ekklēsiastikos*, belonging to an assembly or church]

Ec·cle·si·as·ti·cus (ikliːzi:ǽstikəs) a Hebrew book (2nd c. B.C.) of moral proverbs and maxims,

ecclesiological — 296 — ecotone

verses in praise of God and or wisdom, and short essays which celebrate wisdom. It is included in the Roman Catholic canon, but is placed in the Apocrypha in the Authorized Version

ec·cle·si·o·log·i·cal (ikli̯:zi:əlódʒik'l) *adj.* of or relating to ecclesiology

ec·cle·si·ol·o·gist (ikli̯:zi:ólədʒist) *n.* a student of ecclesiology

ec·cle·si·ol·o·gy (ikli̯:zi:ólədʒi:) *n.* the study of churches, their origins, building, development and decoration [fr. Gk *ekklesia*, church + *logos*, word]

ec·dy·sis (ékdisis) *pl.* **ec·dy·ses** (ékdisi:z) *n.* the act of molting a cuticular layer, e.g., in crustaceans and insects [Mod. L. fr. Gk *ekdusis* fr. *ekduein*, to shed]

ec·dy·sone (ékdəsoun) *n.* the insect hormone that controls molting

e·ce·sis (isí:sis) *pl.* **e·ce·ses** (isí:si:z) *n.* (*biol.*) the successful establishment of an immigrant species in a new environment [fr. Gk *oikēsis*, the act of inhabiting]

E·che·ga·ray (eṯ∫egarái), José (1832–1916), Spanish dramatist and mathematician

ech·e·lon (é∫əlon) **1.** *n.* an arrangement of ships, troops, aircraft, etc., in line, such that individuals are regularly stepped back and to the side of the one in front ‖ each successive element of a fighting unit disposed in depth, the first echelon being the one nearest the enemy ‖ a division of any very big organization ‖ a level or grade, *the higher echelons of industry* **2.** *v.t.* to form in an echelon or echelons ‖ *v.i.* to be arranged in echelon [F. *échelon, échelonner* fr. *échelle*, ladder]

E·che·ver·rí·a (eṯ∫everrí:α), Esteban (1805–51), Argentinian Romantic novelist and poet, and lyric voice of the opposition to the tyranny of Rosas

Echeverría Ál·va·rez (álvαres), Luis (1922–), Mexican politician, member of the Revolutionary Institutional party (PRI), and president of the Republic (1970–76)

e·chid·na (ikídnə) *n. Tachyglossus aculeatus*, order *Monotremata*, a toothless, egg-laying mammal of Australia, Tasmania and New Guinea. Echidnas are nocturnal, burrowing animals, feeding on insects by means of a sticky, extensile tongue [Mod. L. fr. Gk *echidna*, viper]

ech·i·nite (ékinait) *n.* a fossil sea urchin [fr. Mod. L. *echinita* fr. *echinus*, sea urchin fr. Gk]

e·chi·no·derm (ikáinədə:rm) *n.* a member of *Echinodermata*, a marine invertebrate phylum characterized by radial symmetry (usually fivefold), a calcareous exoskeleton, a coelom, a nervous system, and a vascular blood and water system, this latter being connected with tentacles or other organs of locomotion. The phylum includes starfish, feather stars, sea urchins, sea cucumbers and sea lilies [fr. Gk *echinos*, hedgehog + *derma* (dermatos), skin]

e·chi·noid (ikáinoid) *n.* a sea urchin [ECHINUS]

e·chi·nus (ikáinəs) *n.* an echinoderm belonging to *Echinus*, a genus of sea urchins ‖ (*archit.*) a molding between the abacus and the column in the Doric and other orders [L. fr. Gk *echinos*, hedgehog, sea urchin]

Ech·o (ékou) (*mythol.*) a nymph who helped Zeus to deceive his wife Hera by distracting her with chatter. Echo was punished by being deprived of the power to say anything except the last syllable of whatever she heard

ech·o (ékou) **1.** *pl.* **ech·oes** *n.* a second reception of sound waves, etc., when these return after reflection from a surface at some distance ‖ a repetition or close imitation, *his last book was an echo of the one before* ‖ an answering sympathetic effect, *his words aroused no echoes in their hearts* ‖ (*mus.*) the soft repetition of a phrase ‖ (*prosody*) the repetition, at the beginning of a new verse, of the last syllables of the preceding verse **to cheer to the echo** to cheer loudly and repeatedly **2.** *v.i.* to produce an echo ‖ *v.t.* to reflect back and so cause an echo ‖ to imitate, esp. weakly ‖ to agree completely with (another's opinions) [L. fr. Gk]

echo·car·di·og·ra·phy (ekoukardi:ágræfi:) *n.* (*med.*) technique utilizing ultrasonics for diagnosing lesions or tumors in the heart

echo chamber a room with walls which reflect sound. It is used in recording, etc., to give echoing effects

echo·en·ceph·a·log·ra·phy (ekouinsefəlógrafi:) *n.* use of ultrasonic waves in medical diagnosis on the brain, measurement of ocean bottoms,

etc. **echoencephalograph** *n.* the instrument

echogram *n.* the record

e·cho·ic (ekóuik) *adj.* onomatopoeic

ech·o·ing (ékouiŋ) *n.* (*cosmetology*) hair-coloring style imitating sun bleaching of blond hair

ech·o·ism (ékouizəm) *n.* onomatopoeia

ech·o·la·li·a (ekouéili:ə) *n.* the pathological repetition of words or phrases said by other people [fr. ECHO + Gk *lalia*, loquacity]

ech·o·lo·ca·tion (ekouloukéi∫ən) *n.* process of determining location by echoes of sonar waves **echolocate** *v.*

echo sounding calculation of the depth of water by measuring the time taken for a sound at the surface to return after reflection by the sea bed

echo virus (*med.*) enteric cytopathogenic human orphan virus, a type associated with, but not necessarily causing, some forms of meningitis, intestinal and respiratory illnesses

Eck (ek), Johann (1486–1543), German Catholic theologian. He was the leading opponent of Luther, notably in the public disputation at Leipzig (1519)

Eck·er·mann (ékαrmαn), Johann Peter (1792–1854), German author, famous for his 'Conversations with Goethe' (1836–48)

Eck·hart (ékhαrt), Johann ('Meister Eckhart', c. 1260–1327), German Neoplatonic philosopher, mystic and celebrated preacher. He is regarded as one of the forerunners of Protestantism

é·clair (eiklɛ́αr, éiklɛ́αr) *n.* a small, finger-shaped cake of chou pastry filled with cream and covered with chocolate or coffee icing [F.=lightning flash]

ec·lamp·si·a (iklǽmpsi:ə) *n.* convulsions or coma, esp. during pregnancy, particularly in the last months and with a first baby [Mod. L. fr. Gk *eklampein*, to shine out]

é·clat (eiklá, F. eiklǽ) *n.* (of performance or display) manifest brilliance

ec·lec·tic (ikléktik) **1.** *adj.* taking from different sources what seems most suitable for one's purpose (esp. in the philosophy of those who, like the Neoplatonists, combined the essentials of other schools of thought, or, in the arts, of those who combine different styles) ‖ not confined to one source or to one point of view, *an eclectic editorial policy* **2.** *n.* an eclectic philosopher, thinker, writer, scientist, etc. **ec·léc·ti·cal·ly** *adv.* **ec·lec·ti·cism** (ikléktisizəm) *n.* [fr. Gk *eklektikos* fr. *eklegein*, to choose]

e·clipse (iklíps) **1.** *n.* the total or partial cutting off of light received from a celestial body, due to another celestial body's moving into an intercepting position ‖ a loss of brightness, reputation, etc. **2.** *v. pres. part.* **e·clips·ing** *past* and *past part.* **e·clipsed** *v.t.* to cause an eclipse of ‖ to diminish the brightness, glory, etc., of, esp. by excelling, *this triumph eclipsed even his father's fame* ‖ *v.i.* (*astron.*) to be eclipsed [O.F. *eclipse* fr. L. fr. Gk]
—An eclipse of the moon occurs when the earth is between the moon and the sun, thus depriving the moon of the sun's light. An eclipse of the sun occurs when the moon is between the sun and the earth. An eclipse of a moon of Jupiter occurs when Jupiter is between this moon and the earth

e·clip·tic (iklíptik) **1.** *n.* the apparent circular path relative to the fixed stars followed by the sun in one year, as seen from the earth **2.** *adj.* of or relating to the position of a heavenly body ‖ relating to the ecliptic [fr. L. *eclipticus* fr. Gk]

ec·logue (éklɔg, éklɔg) *n.* a short, esp. pastoral poem in which a setting is described and sentiments are expressed in conversation or soliloquy [fr. L. *ecloga* fr. Gk *eklogē*, a selection]

eco- (ékou, i:kóu) prefix meaning of the ecology, esp. relating to pollution; e.g. eco-activity, ecometabolic, ecopathogenic, ecopolitical, ecotheological

e·co·ca·tas·tro·phe (ekoukətǽstrəfi:) *n.* catastrophe to the ecological balance caused by man

e·co·cide (ékosaid) *n.* willful destruction of a natural environment, e.g., by herbicides in war

e·co·ge·o·graph·ic or **e·co·ge·o·graph·ic·al** (ekoudʒi:əgrǽfik) *adj.* of geographical aspects of the ecology **ecogeographer** *n.* **ecogeographically** *adv.*

e·co·law (ékolɔ) *n.* legislation dealing with the environment

E co·li or **Esch·er·i·chi·a co·li** (e∫eríki:ə koúlai) *n.* bacillus found in the intestinal system,

which a pure gene has been isolated. It is used in protein synthesis experiments and experiments with immunity factors and enzymes

ec·o·log·i·cal (ekəlódʒik'l) *adj.* of or relating to ecology

ecological art (ekoulódʒik'l) art created from natural forms

ecological balance the stability of an eco-system resulting from interacting processes of its components

e·col·o·gist (ikólədʒist) *n.* a specialist in ecology

e·col·o·gy, oe·col·o·gy (ikólədʒi:) *n.* the branch of biology concerned with the relation between organisms and their environment ‖ the set of relationships between an organism and its environment ‖ a balanced environment used for a natural or artificial environment [fr. Gk *oikos*, house + *logos*, word]

e·con·o·met·rics (ikɒnəmétriks) *n.* the technique of applying methods of mathematical analysis to economic research [ECONOMY + METRIC]

e·co·nom·ic (i̯:kənómik, ekənómik) *adj.* relating to or concerned with economics ‖ financially sound, reasonably profitable ‖ useful in the production of wealth or promotion of commercial prosperity, *the economic applications of hydraulic power* **e·co·nóm·i·cal** *adj.* thrifty, not wasteful ‖ cheap, costing little, *a car economical to run* (esp. in titles of learned societies, journals, etc.) of or relating to economics **e·co·nóm·i·cal·ly** *adv.* **e·co·nóm·ics** *n.* the study of the way in which natural resources are used and how the wealth they produce is divided, and of the application of the underlying principles to the needs and prosperity of society ‖ this science as applied to the financial structure of an organization, industry, etc., *the economics of advertising* [fr. L. *oeconomicus*]

economic growth (i̯:kənómik) (ekənómik) (*economics*) **1.** increase in production of goods per capita **2.** in real terms, increase in economic activity

economic imperialism domination of a foreign nation by domination of its economy

economic scale (*economics*) cost savings resulting from aggregation of resources and/or mass production, esp. decreases in average cost when all factors of production are expanded proportionately

economic warfare aggressive use of economic means to achieve national objectives

e·con·o·mism (ekónəmizəm) *n.* among Marxists, activity for personal gain at the expense of the socialist movement

e·con·o·mist (ikónəmist) *n.* an expert in economics **E·con·o·mist** (*hist.*) a physiocrat [fr. Gk *oikonomos*, steward]

e·con·o·mize (ikónəmaiz) *pres. part.* **e·con·o·miz·ing** *past* and *past part.* **e·con·o·mized** *v.t.* to refrain from wasting ‖ to reduce the amount normally used of ‖ *v.i.* to reduce expenses [fr. Gk *oikonomos*, a steward]

e·con·o·my (ikónəmi:) *pl.* **e·con·o·mies** *n.* thrift, avoidance of waste ‖ a means of saving money or avoiding waste ‖ part of a system that deals with man's material needs, *industrial economy* ‖ a system of producing and distributing the material needs of society, *a capitalist economy* ‖ the interaction of the parts or functions of any organized system, *reforms which dislocate the country's educational economy* [older *oeconomy* fr. F. fr. L. fr. Gk *oikonomia*, household management]

e·co·phys·i·ol·o·gy (ekoufi:zi:ólədʒi:) *n.* study of relationship involving physiology and the environment **ecophysiologically** *adv.* **ecophysiologist** *n.*

ec·o·spe·cies (ékouspi̯:∫i:z, í:kouspi:∫i:z) *n.* (*biol.*) a subdivision of a cenospecies within which a free exchange of genetic material may occur without loss of fertility, but whose members are less capable of fertile crosses with other subdivisions of the cenospecies. It is usually coextensive with the taxonomic species [fr. Gk *oikos*, home + SPECIES]

e·co·sphere (í:kousfiər) *n.* the portion of the universe sustaining life **ecospheric** *adj.*

e·co·sys·tem (í:kousistəm) *n.* the interacting system of a biological community and its non-living surroundings

e·co·te·lem·e·try (ekoutəlémitri) *n.* measurement and transmission of vital information **syn** biotelemetry

ec·o·tone (ékətoun, í:kətoun) *n.* a transitional area between two ecological communities [fr.

CONCISE PRONUNCIATION KEY: (a) æ, *c*at; α, *c*ar; ɔ *faw*n; ei, sn*a*ke. **(e)** e, h*e*n; i:, sh*ee*p; iə, d*ee*r; ɛə, b*ea*r. **(i)** i, f*i*sh; ai, t*i*ger; ə:, b*i*rd. **(o)** o, *o*x; au, c*ow*; ou, g*oa*t; u, p*oo*r; ɔi, r*oy*al. **(u)** ʌ, d*u*ck; u, b*u*ll; u:, g*oo*se; ə, *ba*cillus; ju:, c*u*be. x, lo*ch*; θ, *th*ink; ð, bo*th*er; z, *Z*en; ʒ, corsa*g*e; dʒ, sava*g*e; ŋ, orangutan*g*; j, *y*ak; ∫, *fi*sh; t∫, *fe*tch; 'l, rabb*le*; 'n, red*den*. Complete pronunciation key appears inside front cover.

Gk *oikos*, home + *tonos*, a thing stretched out]

ec·o·type (ékɐtɑip, íːkɐtɑip) *n.* (*biol.*) a subdivision of an ecospecies whose members are generally fertile in crosses both within the ecotype and between ecotypes, but which retain their individuality because of particularly suitable environmental adaptation [fr. Gk *oikos*, home + TYPE]

ec·ru, esp. *Br.* **é·cru** (ékruː, éikruː) **1.** *n.* a light tan color **2.** *adj.* of this color [F. ecru, unbleached]

ECS (*acronym*) European Coal and Steel Community, a free market for coal and steel set up by the European Economic Community. Founded on May 5, 1950

ec·sta·sy (ékstɐsiː) *pl.* **ec·sta·sies** *n.* a state in which reason yields to intense (generally delighted) feeling and one is beside oneself ‖ a state in which an overpowering spiritual influence takes charge of one ‖ a state of contemplative union with God in which the bodily senses cease to function **to go into** (or **be in**) **ecstasies over** to praise with rapture ‖ to gush about [O.F. *extasie* fr. M.L. fr. Gk *ekstasis*, displacement, a trance]

ec·stat·ic (ikstǽtik) **1.** *adj.* feeling, expressing, or causing ecstasy **2.** *n.* someone experiencing mystical joy **ec·stát·i·cal·ly** *adv.* [fr. Gk *ekstatikos* fr. *ekstasis*, trance]

ECT (*acronym*) electroconvulsive therapy, shock treatment

ec·to·derm (éktɐdɐːrm) *n.* the outermost layer of an embryo possessing three germ layers. It is the source of neural tissues, sense organs and skin in the adult ‖ the outer layer of an embryo possessing two germ layers **ec·to·dér·mal, ec·to·dér·mic** *adjs* [fr. Gk *ektos*, outside + *derma*, skin]

ec·to·gen·ic (ektɐdʒénik) *adj.* ectogenous

ec·tog·e·nous (ektɒdʒɐnɐs) *adj.* (of bacteria) able to live and develop outside the host [fr. Gk *ektos*, outside + *genēs*, born]

ec·to·hor·mone (ektɐhúɐrmoun) *n.* a substance produced by a living thing to stimulate others of the same species to specific responses, e.g., sexual attraction **ectohormonal** *adj.*

ec·to·mere (éktɐmiɐr) *n.* (*embry.*) a blastomere from which the ectoderm is developed **ec·to·mer·ic** (ektɐmérik) *adj.* [fr. Gk *ektos*, outside + *meros*, part]

ec·to·morph (éktɐmɔːrf) *n.* an ectomorphic person **ec·to·mór·phic** *adj.* having the physique associated with a predominance in bodily development of organs and tissues derived from the ectodermal layer of the embryo (e.g. brain, nerves and hair), of an asthenic type of body build **éc·to·mórph·y** *n.* [fr. Gk *ektos*, outside + *morphē*, shape]

ec·to·par·a·site (ektoupǽrɐsait) *n.* (*zool.*) a parasite which lives on the outside of its host (cf. ENDOPARASITE) [fr. Gk *ektos*, outside + PARASITE]

ec·to·plasm (éktɐplæzɐm) *n.* the external differentiated layer of cytoplasm in a cell, next to the cell wall ‖ (*spiritualism*) the luminous substance supposed to emanate from a medium in a trance **ec·to·plás·mic** *adj.* [fr. Gk *ektos*, outer + *plasma*, form, mold]

ec·to·sark (éktɐsark) *n.* (*biol.*) the external layer of protoplasm in a protozoan, e.g. amoeba [fr. Gk *ektos*, outside + *sarx* (*sarkos*), flesh]

ec·tos·to·sis (ektɒstóusis) *n.* ossification under or replacing the membranous covering of cartilage [fr. Gk *ektos*, outside + *ostosis*, formation of bone]

ECU (*acryonym*) European Currency Unit, proposed European currency

Ec·ua·dor (ékwɐdɔr) a republic (area, incl. the Galapagos Is, 104,510 sq. miles, pop. 9,251,000) of N.W. South America. Capital: Quito. People: 40% Mestizo, 30% Indian, 10% of European origin, with minorities of Africans, mulattos and others (mainly on the coast). Language: Spanish (official), Quechua, Jivaro (in the east). Religion: mainly Roman Catholic. The land is 75% forest, exploited only in the west (balsa, tropical hardwoods, dyewood), 5% arable, 5% pasture. The Andes run through the center, forming two cordilleras, east and west, separated by an irregular plateau, the Sierra (7,500–10,000 ft), containing half the population and most of the farmland (cereals, root vegetables, fruit). It also contains 30 active volcanoes. Highest peaks: Chimborazo (eastern cordillera) 20,702 ft, and Cotopaxi. In the west is the coastal plain (Costa) with forests and plantations. In the east (the Oriente) is the

upper Amazon basin (rain forest). Average temperatures (F.): Costa and Oriente 75°, Quito (Sierra) 55 °, colder in the mountains, without seasonal variation. Rainfall: Costa 5–20 ins, Andes 20–40 ins, Oriente 40–80 ins. Livestock: cattle, sheep. Minerals: gold, silver, oil. Exports: bananas, coffee, cacao, balsa wood (world's chief supply), shrimps, straw hats. Other products: rice, corn, potatoes and barley, textiles, chemicals, fish. Imports: manufactures, machinery, wheat. Port: Guayaquil. There are six universities. Monetary unit: sucre (100 centavos). HISTORY. The old Indian kingdom of Quito was conquered by the Indians of Peru (15th c.). A Spanish colony was founded by Pizarro (1532) and was included as a presidency in the viceroyalty of Peru, later of New Granada. It became independent of Spain, after uprisings (1808–9) and a revolutionary war (1822) and formed part of Greater Colombia (1822–30). It seceded and became the Republic of Ecuador (1830). Its political history has been marked by many revolutions. It has been involved in many boundary disputes, esp. with Peru. Velasco Ibarra was deposed four times. His 1961 successor Arosemena Monroy (1961–3) was similarly ousted by the military, whose junta (1963–6) was itself forced by popular unrest to resign. Constitutional government returned with the election of Arosemena Gómez (1966) and Velasco Ibarra (1968), but the latter then accepted (1970) dictatorial powers from the military and dissolved Congress. He was deposed (1972) by a military junta headed by army chief Rodríguez Lara. A civilian government was elected (1979) in the first national elections in 11 years. By the 1984 election 18-year-olds and illiterates had been given the vote

ec·u·men·ic, oec·u·men·ik (ękjumének, esp. *Br.* iːkjumének) *adj.* ecumenical **ec·u·mén·i·cal, oec·u·mén·i·cal** *adj.* of or encouraging universal Christian unity ‖ of, pertaining to or being a movement toward universal Christian unity (*WORLD COUNCIL OF CHURCHES) ‖ of a council representative of the whole Roman Catholic Church ‖ worldwide **ec·u·mén·i·cal·ism, oec·u·mén·i·cal·ism** *n.* the principles of the ecumenical movement **ec·u·men·i·cism, oec·u·men·i·cism** (ękjuménisizɐm) *n.* ecumenicalism **ec·u·men·i·cist, oec·u·men·i·cist** (ękjuménisist) *n.* [fr. L. *oecumenicus* fr. Gk]

ec·u·me·nic·i·ty, oec·u·me·nic·i·ty (ękjumɐnísiti, esp. *Br.* iːkjumɐnísiti) *n.* the quality or state of being ecumenical [fr. M. L. *oecumenicitas*]

ec·u·men·op·o·lis (ękjumɐnópɐlis) *n.* the world viewed as a single city

ec·ze·ma (éksɐmɐ, igzíːmɐ) *n.* a skin disease, characterized in the acute stage by red, 'weeping' areas, which may later become dry, rough, scaly and irritable. It is often caused by an allergic reaction to various substances and is rarely contagious (*ALLERGY) **ec·zem·a·tous** (eksémɐtɐs, igzémɐtɐs) *adj.* [fr. Gk *ekzema* fr. *ek*-out+ *zeein*, to boil]

-ed *suffix* used to form the past tense of weak verbs [O.E. *-de, -ede, -ode, -ade*, etym. doubtful]

-ed *suffix* used to form the past participle of weak verbs and participial adjectives expressing the quality resulting from the action of the verb, as in 'distressed parents' [O.E. *-ed, -od, -ad*, etym. doubtful]

-ed *suffix* used to form adjectives from nouns, as in 'wheeled vehicles'

E·dam (íːdɐm, íːdæm) *n.* a round, red-skinned, pressed cheese of yellow color [made near *Edam* in the Netherlands]

e·daph·ol·o·gy (edɐfólɐdʒiː) *n.* study of the soil as the medium for plant growth

E-day the day of Great Britain's entry into the European Common Market, January 22, 1972

Ed·da (édɐ) a collection of Old Norse mythological and heroic poems, written in Iceland in the 9th–12th cc., and known as the 'Elder Edda' or 'Poetic Edda' ‖ a treatise on the poet's art attributed to Snorri Sturluson in which he summarizes the Old Norse legends and a number of prose epics (*ICELANDIC SAGAS) known as the 'Younger Edda' or 'Prose Edda' [O.N.]

Ed·ding·ton (édintɐn), Sir Arthur Stanley (1882–1944), British astronomer. He made many discoveries about the internal constitution of the stars and contributed to the theory of general relativity. He also tried to formulate a basic mathematical theory of the universe

ed·do (édou) *pl.* **ed·does** *n.* the tuberous stem of any of several plants of fam. *Araceae*, esp. taro [prob. fr. African name]

Ed·dy (édiː), Mary Baker (1821–1910), the American founder of Christian Science

ed·dy (édiː) **1.** *pl.* **ed·dies** *n.* a whirling movement, such as that seen when water runs out of a bath or is checked by the bank of a river ‖ a similar movement of air or of some things that float, *eddies of foam* **2.** *v. pres. part.* **ed·dy·ing** *past* and *past part.* **ed·died** *v.t.* to cause to move with a circular or eddying motion ‖ *v.i.* to move in eddies [origin unknown]

eddy current an electrical current induced in a massive conductor, e.g., in the core of a transformer, by an alternating magnetic field

e·del·weiss (éidʹlvais, éidʹlwais) *n.* a member of *Leontopodium*, fam. *Compositae*, a genus of plants native to the Alps, the Andes and the Pyrenees, often growing in places hard to reach. They are xerophytes, growing in low dense tufts and covered with white woolly hairs. They bear small yellowish-white flowers [fr. G. *edel*, noble+*weiss*, white]

e·de·ma, oe·de·ma (idíːmɐ) *pl.* **e·de·mas, oe·de·mas, e·de·ma·ta, oe·de·ma·ta** (idíːmɐtɐ, oe-dé-ma·ta (oe·dé·mɐtɐ) *n.* (*med.*) a local swelling due to the accumulation of serous fluid in the cellular tissue, caused by defective circulation (blood or lymph) ‖ a swelling of plant tissue caused by excessive moisture or unfavorable light and temperature conditions **e·dem·a·tous, oe·dem·a·tous** (idémɐtɐs) *adj.* [Mod. L. fr. Gk *oidēma* (*oidēmatos*), a swelling]

E·den (íːdʹn), Sir Anthony *AVON, 1st Earl of

E·den (íːdʹn) *n.* the biblical garden, or earthly paradise, which was the home of Adam and Eve before the Fall ‖ any lovely or delightful place [Heb.=delight]

e·den·tate (idénteit) **1.** *adj.* without teeth **2.** *n.* a member of *Edentata*, an order of toothless mammals including armadillos, giant anteaters and sloths [fr. L. *edentare* (*edentatus*), to render toothless]

E·des·sa (idésɐ) *URFA

Ed·gar (édgɐr) (c. 944–75), king of Mercia and Northumbria (957–9) and of England (959–75), son of Edmund. Aided by St Dunstan, he initiated monastic reforms. He was crowned (973) in great splendor at Bath, and received the homage of the kings of the Cumbrians, the Scots and the Welsh

Edgar 'the Atheling' (c. 1050–c. 1130), English prince, grandson of Edmund II. Prospective heir to Edward the Confessor, he was ousted (1066) by William I, against whom he led two unsuccessful risings (1068 and 1069)

edge (edʒ) **1.** *n.* the extreme (generally horizontal) limit, e.g., of a table, cliff, wood, sheet of paper, pond, coin ‖ the fringe, region of the outer limit, *the edge of the crowd* ‖ the line formed by the meeting of two surfaces, *a cube has 12 edges* ‖ the sharp side or end of a cutting tool ‖ either of the two sharp sides of the blade of a skate, or a figure performed with the body balanced on one or other side of the blade, *outside edges* **to be on edge** to be tense, nervous, jumpy **to give the sharp** (or **rough**) **edge of one's tongue** to speak sharply or roughly to **to have** (or **give**) **the edge on** to have (or give) an advantage over, *his greater reach gave him the edge on his opponent* **to put an edge on** to sharpen **to set one's teeth on edge** to give a painful feeling of physical or nervous repulsion to **to take the edge off** to take the first keenness from, lessen (e.g. appetite) **2.** *v. pres. part.* **edg·ing** *past* and *past part.* **edged** *v.t.* to make, or serve as, an edge or border for, *reeds edge the lake* ‖ to sharpen, *to edge a chisel* ‖ to move gradually in a confined or awkward place, *to edge a cabinet into a corner* ‖ to make (one's way) sideways, cautiously or stealthily ‖ *v.i.* to advance sideways cautiously, e.g. along a cliff ledge ‖ (with 'away', 'towards', etc.) to move in such a way as not to be noticed ‖ (with 'out of') to take avoiding action by stealth [O.E. *ecg*]

EDGE (*computer acronym*) for electronic data gathering equipment, a computer system for gathering data from various locations for processing; designed by Radio Corporation of America

edge-bone (édʒbɒun) *n.* an aitchbone

Edge-hill, Battle of (édʒhil) the indecisive first engagement (Oct. 23, 1642) in the English Civil War

edge tool any tool with a sharp edge

edge·ways (édʒweiz) *adv.* sideways, *ease the table in edgeways* ‖ standing on edge, *stand the*

CONCISE PRONUNCIATION KEY: (a) æ, c*a*t; ɑ, c*ar*; ɔ f*aw*n; ei, sn*a*ke. (e) e, h*e*n; iː, sh*ee*p; iɐ, d*eer*; ɛɐ, b*ear*. (i) i, f*i*sh; ai, t*i*ger; ɐ:, b*ir*d. (o) o, *o*x; au, c*ow*; ou, g*oa*t; u, p*oor*; ɔi, r*oy*al. (u) ʌ, d*u*ck; u, b*u*ll; uː, g*oo*se; ɐ, b*a*cill*u*s; juː, c*u*be. x, lo*ch*; θ, *th*ink; δ, bo*th*er; z, *Z*en; ʒ, corsa*g*e; dʒ, sava*g*e; ŋ, oranguta*ng*; j, *y*ak; ʃ, *fi*sh; tʃ, fe*tch*; 'l, rabb*le*; 'n, redd*en*. Complete pronunciation key appears inside front cover.

plates edgeways on the rack **not to be able to get a word in edgeways** to have no chance of saying something oneself because someone else talks so much

edge·wise (édʒwaiz) *adv.* edgeways

Edge·worth (édʒwə:rθ), Maria (1767–1849), Anglo-Irish novelist whose 'Castle Rackrent' (1800), 'The Absentee' (1812) and other novels called for a sense of responsibility among Irish landlords. She was influenced by Rousseau

edg·ing (édʒiŋ) 1. *n.* a border, *an edging of lace* 2. *adj.* serving to make edges, *edging shears* [EDGE]

edg·y (édʒi:) *comp.* **edg·i·er** *superl.* **edg·i·est** *adj.* nervous, jumpy, easily annoyed or upset

ed·i·bil·i·ty (ędəbíliti:) *n.* the quality of being edible

ed·i·ble (édəb'l) 1. *adj.* wholesome to eat, eatable 2. *n.* (*pl.*) things to eat, eatables [fr. L.L. *edibilis* fr. *edere*, to eat]

e·dict (í:dikt) *n.* an official order published by a ruler or by authority **e·dic·tal** *adj.* [fr. L. *edictum* fr. *edicere*, to proclaim]

Edict of Nantes *NANTES, EDICT OF

ed·i·fi·ca·tion (ędifikéiʃən) *n.* enlightening of ignorance, or moral or spiritual instruction [fr. L. *aedificatio* (*aedificationis*)]

ed·i·fice (édifis) *n.* a building, esp. an imposing one ‖ an organized system, *the whole edifice of his thought rests on these principles* [F. *édifice*]

ed·i·fy (édifai) *pres. part.* **ed·i·fy·ing** *past* and *past part.* **ed·i·fied** *v.t.* to improve spiritually or morally by instruction or example [F. *édifier*]

edile *AEDILE

Ed·in·burgh (éd'nbə:rou, éd'nbʌrou, esp. *Br.* éd'nbərə), Prince Philip Mountbatten, duke of (1921–), consort of Queen Elizabeth II of Great Britain. He is the son of Prince Andrew, son of King George I of Greece

Edinburgh the capital (pop. 436,936) of Scotland since the 15th c. and its second largest city, built around the rocky ridge on which its fortified castle stands. Its adjoining port, Leith, lies on the south shore of the Firth of Forth. Industries: banking, insurance, printing, publishing, shipbuilding, chemicals, distilling, brewing. University (1583). International festival of music and the arts

E·dir·ne (edírnə) *ADRIANOPLE

Ed·i·son (édis'n), Thomas Alva (1847–1931), American inventor of the phonograph in 1877, and a major contributor to the development of the telephone, electric lamp and other electrical and electronic devices

ed·it (édit) *v.t.* to prepare (literary or musical work) for publication, esp. to establish or prepare a commentary on (a text) ‖ to prepare (a film, radio or television material) in the form in which it is to be seen or heard ‖ to alter (matter for publication) so as to make it more suitable for one's purpose, *the news has been edited to bolster morale* ‖ to be in charge of (a newspaper or periodical) and decide its policy and contents [fr. L. *edere* (*editus*), to give out]

e·di·tion (idíʃən) *n.* a published literary or musical text (esp. with reference to such aspects as reliability, annotation, typography, etc.), *the standard edition of Bach's organ works* ‖ a particular form (selected on commercial or aesthetic grounds) in which a book is produced for sale, *an abridged edition, a paperback edition* ‖ the copies of a version of a text printed at one time, *the third edition* or the total number of such copies, *an edition of 50,000* ‖ one of the several issues of a daily newspaper ‖ a thing or person closely resembling another of the same type, *he is a smaller edition of his brother* [F. *édition*]

e·di·tion·al·ize (idíʃənəlaiz) *v.* to create several editions of a periodical for differing localities

e·di·ti·o prin·ceps (idíʃi·óu prínseps) *pl.* **e·di·ti·o·nes prin·ci·pes** (idíʃi·óuni:z·prínsipi:z) *n.* the first printed edition of a book (usually of early printed books rather than modern ones) [Mod. L.]

ed·i·tor (éditər) *n.* someone who edits a manuscript, book or series of books, newspaper, periodical, film, radio or television material, etc. ‖ someone who is in charge of a particular section of a newspaper or periodical **ed·i·to·ri·al** (editó·ri:əl,editóuri:əl) 1. *adj.* of or relating to an editor, *editorial policy* 2. *n.* an article in a newspaper or periodical which gives the views of those who decide its policy **ed·i·tor·ship** (éditər·ʃip) *n.* [L. fr. *editare*, to give out]

Ed·mon·ton (édməntən) the capital (pop. 532,246) of Alberta, Canada, on the N. Sas-

katchewan River, center of a great wheat and cattle region. Since 1947 oil fields discovered nearby have given rise to oil refineries, petrochemical and plastic industries. University (1906)

Ed·mund (édmənd), St (c. 840–70), king of East Anglia (855–70). He was martyred by Danish invaders for refusing to submit as a vassal or to renounce Christianity. Feast: Nov. 20

Edmund I (c. 922–46), king of the English (940–6), son of Edward the Elder. He defeated (944) the Danes of Northumbria and ravaged (945) Strathclyde

Edmund II 'Ironside' (c. 980–1016), king of the English (1016). On the death of his father, Ethelred II, his succession was contested by Cnut, who controlled the Danelaw. After a short war, they partitioned (1016) England between them, but on Edmund's death soon after Cnut succeeded to the whole kingdom

Edmund Rich, St (c. 1175–1240), archbishop of Canterbury (1233–40). His zeal for reform caused him to quarrel with Henry III over appointments to bishoprics and revenues from vacant sees. He finally withdrew to France (1240). Feast: Nov. 16

Ed·munds (édməndz), George Franklin (1828–1919), U.S. political leader. As chairman (1872–91, except for two years) of the Senate judiciary committee, he helped to establish the electoral commission for the disputed 1876 presidential election. He shared responsibility for the act suppressing polygamy (1882) and for the Sherman Anti-trust act (1890)

E·do (í:dou) *pl.* **E·do, E·dos** *n.* a people of mid-western Nigeria ‖ a member of this people ‖ their language (*KWA)

E·dom (í:dəm) an ancient region between the Dead Sea and the Gulf of 'Aqaba

EDP (*computer*) *abbr.* electronic data processing

Ed·red (édrəd) (d. 955), king of the English (946–55), son of Edward the Elder. He conquered (954) Northumbria, thus ending the last independent Scandinavian kingdom in England

ed·u·ca·ble (édʒukəb'l, édjukəb'l) *adj.* capable of being educated

ed·u·cate (édʒukeit, édjukeit) *pres. part.* **ed·u·cat·ing** *past* and *past part.* **ed·u·cat·ed** *v.t.* to instruct and train, esp. in such a way as to develop the mental, moral and physical powers of ‖ to provide or obtain such training or instruction for ‖ to train or develop (a particular power or skill, etc.), *to educate one's palate* ‖ to train for a particular end, *educated for the law* **éd·u·cat·ed** *adj.* properly taught or trained ‖ showing signs of a good education, *educated speech* [fr. L. *educare* (*educatus*), to bring up]

ed·u·ca·tion (edʒukéiʃən, ędjukéiʃən) *n.* instruction or training by which people (generally young) learn to develop and use their mental, moral and physical powers ‖ the art of giving such training ‖ a gaining of experience, either improving or harmful ‖ a branch, system, or stage of instruction ‖ the fruit of training or instruction **ed·u·ca·tion·al** *adj.* concerned with training and teaching ‖ instructive **ed·u·cá·tion·al·ist, ed·u·cá·tion·ist** *ns* (*Am.*, often used disparagingly) a theorist in educational matters ‖ (*Br.*) an educator (person distinguished for his educational work) [fr. L. *educatio* (*educationis*)]

educational television television programs that teach, esp. regular study courses, sometimes on closed circuit

ed·u·ca·tion·ese (edʒukęiʃəní:z) *n.* the technical jargon of educators

education park group of public schools of different levels or types within a single complex

Education, U.S. Department of (1979) a cabinet-level agency that administers assistance to and sets policies for elementary, secondary, higher and continuing education in state and local institutions. Formerly the Office of Education (1867) in the Department of the Interior (1869–1939), the Federal Security Agency (1939–53) and the Department of Health, Education and Welfare (1953–79), it also renders aid to occupational, vocational and adult education, as well as to Indians, the handicapped and education overseas

ed·u·ca·tive (édʒukeitiv, édjukęitiv) *adj.* serving to educate ‖ to do with education

ed·u·ca·tor (édʒukęitər, édjukęitər) *n.* a teacher ‖ (*Am.*=*Br.* educationalist) a person distinguished for his educational work

e·duce (idú:s, idjú:s) *pres. part.* **e·duc·ing** *past* and *past part.* **e·duced** *v.t.* to bring to light (a truth) by building up the evidence (cf. DEDUCE) [fr. L. *educere*, to lead out]

ed·u·crat (édʒukræt) *n.* bureaucrat of the education system

e·duct (í:dʌkt) *n.* (*chem.*) a substance isolated by decomposing a compound (cf. PRODUCT) [fr. L. *eductum* fr. *educere*, to lead out]

e·duc·tion (idʌ́kʃən) *n.* the act, process or result of educing

e·duc·tive (idʌ́ktiv) *adj.* serving to educt ‖ to do with eduction

e·dul·co·rate (idʌ́lkəreit) *pres. part.* **e·dul·co·rat·ing** *past* and *past part.* **e·dul·co·rat·ed** *v.t.* (*chem.*) to purify, esp. by washing away any acid in **e·dul·co·ra·tion** *n.* **e·dul·co·ra·tive** (idʌ́lkəreitiv) *adj.* [fr. L. *edulcorare* (*edulcoratus*), to sweeten]

Ed·ward I (édwərd) (1239–1307), king of England (1272–1307), son of Henry III. An astute soldier, he led royalist troops to victory in the Barons' War (1264–6), and conquered Wales in two campaigns (1277 and 1282–3). He placed John de Baliol on the throne of Scotland (1292), but deposed him (1296) after Baliol had formed an alliance with Philippe IV of France. While intermittently at war with France, Edward defeated (1298) a Scottish revolt under Wallace, invaded Scotland again (1303), but had to face another revolt (1306) under Robert the Bruce. Edward's greatest achievements were in administration. He issued writs and laws to restrict the jurisdiction of feudal and Church courts. His parliament (1295) was later quoted as a precedent, and became known as the Model Parliament

Ed·ward·i·an (edwɔ́rdi:ən, edwɔ́rdi:ən) *adj.* of the time of Edward VII of England ‖ of the style of this period

Edward II (1284–1327), king of England (1307–27), son of Edward I. Totally inept as a ruler, he left the government largely to his favorites Gaveston, who was murdered (1312) by a baronial faction, and the Despensers, who were put to death (1326). Edward's one attempt to continue his father's conquest of Scotland ended in failure at Bannockburn (1314). The barony strongly opposed the king's incompetent rule, attempting (1311) to subject Edward to a committee of 'lords ordainers'. His queen, Isabella, in alliance with Roger Mortimer, invaded (1326), deposed Edward and put him to death (1327)

Edward III (1312–77), king of England (1327–77), son of Edward II. Having freed himself (1330) from subjection to his mother, Isabella, and to Roger Mortimer, he renewed the war with the Scots, defeating them in 1333 and 1346. With the outbreak (1337) of the Hundred Years' War, he destroyed the French fleet at Sluis (1340), invaded France and, with his son, the Black Prince, won notable victories at Crécy (1346), Calais (1347) and Poitiers (1356). The Treaty of Brétigny (1360) gave Edward half of France south of the Loire. Meanwhile, the king had gone bankrupt (1345) and the economy was suffering from the effects of the Black Death (1348–9, 1361–2 and 1368–9). The war with France was resumed (1369), but by 1375 Edward had lost all his French possessions except Calais, Bordeaux, Bayonne and Brest. At the end of his reign, the king left the government in the hands of his son, John of Gaunt

Edward IV (1442–83), king of England (1461–83), son of Richard, duke of York. With the aid of Warwick 'the kingmaker' he defeated the Lancastrians (1461) and won the throne. Warwick led an unsuccessful rebellion (1469). Edward was driven into exile (1470–1) when Warwick restored Henry VI to the throne. Edward retaliated (1471), killing Warwick in battle, and murdering Henry in prison. A brief war (1475) in France resulted in an annual subsidy from Louis XI, which freed Edward from financial dependence on parliament. He took a personal interest in promoting trade, and was the patron of Caxton

Edward V (1470–83), king of England (1483), son of Edward IV. Under the protection of his uncle, the duke of Gloucester, he was placed in the Tower of London, where he was murdered, together with his brother Richard, duke of York, probably at the instigation of Gloucester, who succeeded as Richard III

Edward VI (1537–53), king of England and Ireland (1547–53), son of Henry VIII. A sickly youth, he was a pawn in the struggle for power between Edward Seymour, duke of Somerset, and John Dudley, earl of Warwick. Neither protector could solve the economic problem of inflation. The reign marked a swing to extreme Protestantism, with the second Book of Common Prayer (1552) and the Forty-two Articles of the Church of England (1553)

Edward VII (1841–1910), king of Great Britain and Ireland (1901–10), son of Victoria. He played an active part in public life in the later years of his mother's reign, traveling widely, and he was particularly popular because of his interest in the theater and sport. His love of pageantry made his reign a reaction against the austerity of Victorianism. He took an active interest in foreign affairs, notably in the signing of the Entente Cordiale with France (1904), and of an agreement with Russia (1907)

Edward VIII (1894–1972), king of Great Britain and Ireland (1936), son of George V. As prince of Wales he demonstrated his interest in foreign trade and social problems, and won popularity. He abdicated, after a reign of 10 months, in order to marry Wallis Simpson, a twice-divorced American. He was made duke of Windsor and was governor of the Bahamas (1940–5)

Edward (1453–71), prince of Wales, son of Henry VI. The Lancastrian candidate for the throne at the start of the Wars of the Roses, he was defeated and killed by Edward IV at Tewkesbury (1471)

Edward, 'the Black Prince' (Edward of Woodstock) *BLACK PRINCE

Edward 'the Confessor' (c. 1002–66), saint and king of England (1042–66), son of Ethelred II. He devoted himself to religion and the rebuilding of Westminster Abbey. A weak ruler, he was unable to control the nobility, notably Earl Godwin, whose son Harold claimed the succession on Edward's death, in opposition to William of Normandy, who claimed that Edward had made him his heir. Feast: Oct. 13

Edward 'the Elder' (c. 870–924), king of Wessex (899–924), son of Alfred. He continued his father's wars with the Danes, driving them back from East Anglia and the E. Midlands (910–17). He annexed Mercia (918) and by 920 was ruler of all England south of the Humber, as well as being the recognized overlord of Scotland, Northumbria and part of Wales

Edward 'the Martyr' (c. 963–78), king of England (975–8), son of Edgar. After his murder, which was probably instigated by his stepmother, he was widely regarded as a saint. Feast: Mar. 18

Edward, Lake (formerly Albert Edward Nyanza) a lake (length 44 miles, area 830 sq. miles) at 3,000 ft in the Albertine rift valley of Uganda on the Zaïre boundary. Crater lakes on the northern shores yield salt, exploited industrially

Ed·wards (édwərdz), Jonathan (1703–58), American theologian and metaphysician. He was a strict Calvinist and a leader of American revivalism. His best-known work is 'The Freedom of the Will' (1754)

Edwards Plateau a highland region (height 2,000–5,000 ft) in S.W. Texas, an extension of the Great Plains

Ed·win (édwin) (c. 585–633), king of Northumbria (617–633), under whose reign Paulinus established a Christian see at York. His supremacy was recognized in all the other English kingdoms except Kent

Ed·wy (édwi) (c. 938–59), king of the English (955–9), son of Edmund I. He drove St Dunstan into exile (957) and quarreled with the Church and the nobles

-ee *suffix* used to indicate someone to whom something is done, given, etc., as 'in trainee' [fr. A.F. -é, past participial ending]

E.E.C. *EUROPEAN ECONOMIC COMMUNITY

eel (i:l) *n.* any of several genera of teleostean fish of the order *Apodes.* They are characterized by a smooth, serpent-like body, devoid of ventral fins and with a continuous dorsal fin. In autumn, adult eels migrate from rivers in Europe and America to lay their eggs in deep Atlantic waters southeast of Bermuda. After a year the young fish begin to swim to the rivers of the two continents. European eels arrive only in the third spring after hatching, compared with the single year's sea journey of U.S. eels before they begin their freshwater development. They may live up to 19 years [O.E. *œl*]

eel·grass (í:lgræs, í:lgrɑs) *n. Zostera marina,* a marine grass which grows along the N. Atlantic coast

eel·pout (í:lpaut) *n.* a marine fish of fam. *Zoarcidae* resembling the blenny [O.E. *œlepūta*]

eel·worm (í:lwə:rm) *n.* a tiny parasitic nematode worm. Different species live in wheat flowers (stimulating gall formation), on flower bulbs, on the roots of certain plants, and in insects and animal dung

EEO (*acronym*) Equal Employment Opportunity

EEOC (*acronym*) Equal Employment Opportunity Commission

ee·rie, ee·ry (íəri:) *comp.* **ee·ri·er** *superl.* **ee·ri·est** *adj.* mysteriously frightening, uncanny **ée·ri·ly** *adv.* **ée·ri·ness** *n.* [M.E. *eri,* timid]

ef·face (iféis) *pres. part.* **ef·fac·ing** *past and past part.* **ef·faced** *v.t.* to rub or wipe out, obliterate ‖ to cause to be as though canceled or forgotten, *this success effaced the memory of his earlier failures* ‖ to outshine **to efface oneself** to stay modestly in the background **ef·fáce·a·ble** *adj.* **ef·fáce·ment** *n.* [F. *effacer*]

ef·fect (ifékt) **1.** *n.* the result produced by a cause ‖ influence, power to change, *his words have no effect on her* ‖ general meaning or purport, *she called him a coward or words to that effect* ‖ a specific scientific phenomenon, usually named after its discoverer, *the Compton effect* ‖ a general appearance or impression, *the picture gives an effect of space and sunlight* ‖ an impression (often false) deliberately produced, *clothes creating an effect of youthfulness* ‖ (*pl.*) artistic contrivances, *lighting effects* ‖ (*pl.*) possessions, assets, *personal effects* **for effect** in order to produce a calculated impression **in effect** virtually, practically speaking, *in effect you mean he is wrong* ‖ in actual fact, *theoretically it does 110 m.p.h. but in effect it seldom goes over 100* **to come into effect** to begin to be operative **to give effect to,** to put into effect to cause to become operative **to good (little, no** etc.) **effect** with good (little, no etc.) results **to take effect** to become operative **with effect from** (*Br.*) so as to be operative on and after, *bus fares will go up with effect from Jan. 1* **2.** *v.t.* to cause to happen, to bring about, *to effect a meeting between two people* ‖ to accomplish, *the crossing was effected without difficulty* [O.F.]

ef·fec·tive (iféktiv) **1.** *adj.* causing or capable of causing a desired or decisive result ‖ in use, in force or in operation ‖ causing a telling or striking effect, *an effective speaker* ‖ (*mil.*) actually available for service **2.** *n.* (*pl., mil.*) men ready and fit to fight [F. *effectif*]

ef·fec·tor (iféktər) *n.* an organ which reacts effectively to the stimulus of a nervous impulse ‖ the mechanical components of a robot used for manipulation of objects [L. fr. *efficere* (*effectus*), to work out]

ef·fec·tu·al (iféktʃu:əl) *adj.* capable of, or successful in, bringing about a desired effect [O.F. *effectuel*]

effectual demand (*econ.*) a demand where there is both the will and the power to purchase

ef·fec·tu·ate (iféktʃu:eit) *pres. part.* **ef·fec·tu·at·ing** *past and past part.* **ef·fec·tu·at·ed** *v.t.* to bring about, cause to happen **ef·fec·tu·á·tion** *n.* [fr. F. *effectuer*]

ef·fem·i·na·cy (iféminəsi:) *n.* the quality in a man or boy of being womanish or girlish

ef·fem·i·nate (iféminit) **1.** *adj.* (of men or boys) womanish or girlish, not virile **2.** *n.* a womanish man or girlish boy [fr. L. *effeminare* (*effeminatus*), to make womanish]

ef·fer·ent (éfərənt) *adj.* leading or bearing away from something, e.g. an organ ‖ (*physiol.*, of nerves) carrying impulses away from a nerve center (opp. AFFERENT) [fr. L. *efferre,* to carry away]

ef·fer·vesce (efərvés) *pres. part.* **ef·fer·vesc·ing** *past and past part.* **ef·fer·vesced** *v.i.* to produce a great number of bubbles (esp. of carbon dioxide), which rise to the surface and burst with a fizzing sound ‖ to manifest high spirits or great excitement **ef·fer·vés·cence, ef·fer·vés·cen·cy** *ns.* **ef·fer·vés·cent** *adj.* [fr. L. *effervescere,* to begin to boil]

ef·fete (ifí:t) *adj.* worn out, without any vitality left ‖ become ineffectual, degenerate [fr. L. *effetus,* exhausted by breeding]

ef·fi·ca·cious (efikéiʃəs) *adj.* useful or successful in bringing about a desired result, *an efficacious remedy* [fr. L. *efficax* (*effcacis*), powerful]

ef·fi·ca·cy (éfikəsi:) *n.* the power to bring about a desired result, effectiveness [fr. L. *efficacia* fr. *efficax,* powerful]

ef·fi·cien·cy (ifíʃənsi:) *n.* the degree of effectiveness with which something is done, or of the person who does it ‖ (of a machine) the ratio of the work done to the work needed to operate the machine ‖ (of an engine) the ratio of the work done by the engine to the work equivalent of the energy supplied to it [fr. L. *efficiens* fr. *efficere,* to effect]

efficiency expert a consultant who advises the management of a business where it could secure increased efficiency

ef·fi·cient (ifíʃənt) *adj.* competent, working properly ‖ (of a machine) producing nearly as much work as it uses (in the form of fuel, etc.) [fr. L. *efficiens* fr. *efficere,* to effect]

efficient cause (*Aristotelian logic*) the immediate producer of a change

Ef·fie (éfi:) *n.* annual award for creative and effective advertising sponsored by N.Y. Chapter of American Marketing Association

ef·fi·gy (éfidʒi:) *pl.* **ef·fi·gies** *n.* a statue, image or dummy of a person **to burn (or hang) in effigy** to burn (or hang) a dummy of (an unpopular character) [F. *effigie*]

ef·fi·lat·ing (éfileitiŋ) (*cosmetology*) technique of cutting hair to graduated lengths from the underside

ef·fi·la·tion (efileíʃən) *n.* light, stroking massage movement **syn** effleurage

ef·flo·resce (eflərés) *pres. part.* **ef·flo·resc·ing** *past and past part.* **ef·flo·resced** *v.i.* (*chem.,* of crystals with water of crystallization) to lose water because the water vapor pressure of the crystals is greater than that of the water vapor in the air, and become powdery on the surface (cf. DELIQUESCE) ‖ (of stonework, brickwork) to become covered with salt particles, due to evaporation at the surface of a salt solution with which bricks, etc., are impregnated [fr. L. *efflorescere,* to blossom out]

ef·flo·res·cence (eflərés'ns) *n.* a bursting into flower or as if into flower ‖ a period of flowering ‖ (*chem.*) the process or result of efflorescing [F.]

ef·flu·ence (éflu:əns) *n.* an outflow or outpouring, e.g. of a liquid, gas, or light ‖ radiance [fr. L. *effluens* fr. *effluere,* to flow out]

ef·flu·ent (éflu:ənt) **1.** *adj.* pouring out, flowing away **2.** *n.* a stream or river flowing out of a body of water (cf. TRIBUTARY) ‖ the waste liquid flowing out of sewage filter, etc. [fr. L. *effluens* (*effluentis*) fr. *effluere,* to flow out]

ef·flu·vi·um (iflú:vi:əm) *pl.* **ef·flu·vi·a** (iflú:vi:ə), **ef·flu·vi·ums** *n.* an emanation unpleasant to breathe or smell, e.g., from marshy ground or rotting vegetation [L. = a flowing out]

ef·flux (éflʌks) *n.* an outflow or escape of liquid or gas ‖ the action of flowing out ‖ (of time) a passing away [fr. L. *effluere* (*effluxus*), to flow out]

ef·fort (éfərt) *n.* an expense of bodily or mental energy to achieve a desired end ‖ the thing achieved by such an expense of energy, *his spurt was a magnificent effort* ‖ a force as distinct from the movement caused by its application [F. fr. *efforcer,* to make an effort]

ef·fort·less (éfərtlis) *adj.* making or appearing to make no effort, easy and graceful

ef·fron·ter·y (ifrʌ́ntəri:) *n.* shameless impudence [fr. F. *effronterie*]

ef·ful·gence (ifʌ́ldʒəns) *n.* radiant light or splendor

ef·ful·gent (ifʌ́ldʒənt) *adj.* radiating light or splendor [fr. L. *effulgere,* to shine forth]

ef·fuse 1. (ifjú:z) *pres. part.* **ef·fus·ing** *past and past part.* **ef·fused** *v.t.* to pour out or forth ‖ *v.i.* (of gases) to issue from a hole in the thin wall of a container (cf. DIFFUSE) **2.** *adj.* (ifjú:s) (of inflorescences) spreading loosely ‖ (of bacterial cultures) spreading thinly ‖ (of shells) open, having a gap between the lips [fr. L. *effundere* (*effusus*), to pour out freely]

ef·fu·sion (ifjú:ʒən) *n.* a pouring out, a shedding, *an effusion of blood* ‖ an extravagant or uncontrolled expression of thought or emotion ‖ (*med.*) the abnormal flow of fluid into a body cavity, e.g., the knee joint ‖ the escape of a gas into a vacuum through an opening that is small in relation to the interparticle distance. The velocities of effusion of different gases at the same temperature obey Graham's law [fr. L. *effusio* (*effusionis*), outpouring]

ef·fu·sive (ifjú:siv) *adj.* unduly demonstrative, gushing ‖ (*geol.,* of rocks) formed by the solidi-

---

CONCISE PRONUNCIATION KEY: **(a)** æ, c*a*t; ɑ, c*a*r; ɔ f*aw*n; ei, sn*a*ke. **(e)** e, h*e*n; i:, sh*ee*p; iə, d*ee*r; εə, b*ea*r. **(i)** i, f*i*sh; ai, t*i*ger; ə:, b*i*rd. **(o)** o, *o*x; au, c*ow*; ou, g*oa*t; u, p*oo*r; ɔi, r*oy*al. **(u)** ʌ, d*u*ck; u, b*u*ll; u:, g*oo*se; ə, b*a*cillus; ju:, c*u*be. x, lo*ch*; θ, *th*ink; ð, bo*th*er; z, *Z*en; ʒ, corsa*g*e; dʒ, sava*g*e; ŋ, oranguta*ng*; j, *y*ak; ʃ, *fi*sh; tʃ, fet*ch*; 'l, rabb*le*; 'n, redd*en*. Complete pronunciation key appears inside front cover.

fication of an outpouring of lava (cf. INTRUSIVE) [fr. L. *effundere* (*effusus*), to pour out]

Ef·ik (ĕfĭk) *n*. a member of a people of S.E. Nigeria ‖ the language of the Efiks

eft (eft) *n*. a newt, esp. *Triton cristatus*, the greater water newt [O.E. *efeta*, origin unknown]

EFT (*banking acronym*) electronic funds transfer, the use of electronically recorded, preauthorized debits and credits in a bank clearinghouse to replace paper checks, e.g., for mortgages, payrolls, dividends, etc.

EFTA *EUROPEAN FREE TRADE ASSOCIATION

EFTA (*acronym*) European Free Trade Association, regional organizaton established in 1959 to create a free-trade area for industrial products among member countries without the political implications of a customs union. The original members (the United Kingdom, Austria, Denmark, Norway, Portugal, Sweden, and Switzerland) were referred to as The Seven (or The Outer Seven), as a counterpart to The Six, the original members of the European Common Market

e.g. for example [fr. L. *exempli gratia*]

e·gal·i·tar·i·an (igælĭtéəri:ən) **1**. *adj*. holding the view that all men have equal social and political rights **2**. *n*. someone who holds this view **e·gal·i·tar·i·an·ism** *n*. [fr. F. *égalitaire*]

Eg·bert (égbə:rt) (c. 775–839), king of Wessex (802–39), who was acknowledged as king by Kent, Cornwall, Surrey, Sussex, Essex, East Anglia, Northumbria and, for a time (828–30), by Mercia

E·ger·i·a (idʒíəri:ə) *n*. a wise female adviser [L. fr. Gk *Egeria*, a nymph, said to have been the adviser of Numa Pompilius]

e·gest (idʒést) *v.t.* to expel (waste material) from the body (cf. INGEST) [fr. L. *egerere* (*egestus*)]

e·ges·ta (idʒéstə) *pl. n.* material egested from the body (cf. INGESTA) [L., neuter pl. of *egestus*]

egg (eg) *n.* the female gamete, ovum ‖ an animal reproductive body consisting of an ovum with its protective coverings or membranes ‖ the egg of the domestic hen, esp. as human food ‖ (*pop.*) the pupa of ants and some other insects **to kill the goose that lays the golden egg** to lose a steady source of gain in order to win an immediate temporary benefit **to put** (or **have**) **all one's eggs in one basket** to stake everything on one possibility, have no alternative plan, etc. [M.E. fr. O.N. *egg*]
—Birds' eggs (the largest of all eggs) have a minute ovum, a food store (yolk) and white (albumen), enclosed in a hard shell (mostly calcium carbonate). The food store nourishes the embryo until it is strong enough to break the shell and emerge

egg *v.t.* (with 'on') to urge or encourage (someone) persistently [O.N. *eggja* fr. *egg*, edge]

egg and dart a pattern, used esp. in architectural carving, in which an egg-shaped ornament alternates with an ornament like an arrowhead (*FRIEZE)

egg·beat·er (égbi:tər) *n* (*Am.=Br.* egg-whisk) a kitchen utensil for beating eggs or liquids by hand ‖ (*pop.*) a helicopter

egg·cup (égkʌp) *n*. a small cup for holding a boiled egg

egg·head (éghĕd) *n*. (*pop.*) a highbrow

egg·nog (égnɒg) *n*. cream, sugar, brandy, wine, etc. with raw egg beaten up in the mixture, drunk hot or cold

egg·plant (égplɑnt, égplɔnt) *n. Solanum melongena*, fam. *Solanaceae*, the aubergine, a slow-growing plant requiring a long, warm season. The fruits are purple and are used as a vegetable

egg-shaped (égʃeipt) *adj*. oval

egg·shell (égʃel) **1**. *n*. the hard outer covering of an egg **2**. *adj*. very thin or delicate, *eggshell china*

egg tooth a small structure on the tip of the upper jaw or beak by which an embryo bird or reptile breaks its shell

egg-whisk (éghwĭsk, égwĭsk) *n*. (*Br.*) an egg-beater

egis *AEGIS

eg·lan·tine (égləntĭn, églənti:n) *n. Rosa eglanteria* or *R. rubiginosa*, fam. *Rosaceae*, a wild rose with sweet-smelling single flowers, found in Europe, W. Asia and North America [F.]

Eg·mont (éxmɔnt), Lamoral, count of (1522–68), Flemish general and statesman whose arbitrary execution by the duke of Alba provoked the rebellion of the Netherlands against Spanish rule

e·go (í:gou, égou) *n.* (*philos.*) a term, associated primarily with the German philosopher Fichte, for the 'I', the subject which is conscious of itself, thinks, has experience of and determines the outside world ‖ (*pop.*) one's image of oneself, *to bolster up one's ego* ‖ (*psychoanal.*) the conscious personality as opposed to the unconscious (cf. ID, cf. SUPEREGO) [L.=I]

e·go·cen·tric (i:gouséntrik, égouséntrik) **1**. *adj*. looking at everything only to see how it affects oneself, or from one's own selfish point of view ‖ (*philos.*) centered in the ego **2**. *n*. a self-centered person **e·go·cen·tric·i·ty** (i:gousentrísiti:, égousentrisiti:) *n.*

e·go·ism (í:gouizəm, égouizəm) *n.* egotism ‖ (*ethics*) the doctrine that man's concern with his own good is the basis of morality (cf. ALTRUISM) **é·go·ist** *n.* **e·go·is·tic, e·go·is·ti·cal** *adjs* [fr. F. *egoïsme*]

e·go·tism (í:gətizəm, égətizəm) *n.* the frame of mind which causes a person to pay too much attention to himself, to be conceited and selfish or refer to himself frequently in writing **é·go·tist** *n.* **e·go·tis·tic, e·go·tis·ti·cal** *adjs*

ego trip (*colloq.* or *slang*) a course of thinking or action to promote one's opinion of oneself **ego-trip** *v.* **ego-tripper** *n.*

e·gre·gious (igrí:dʒəs) *adj*. flagrant, *an egregious breach of conduct* ‖ outstanding for some bad quality, *an egregious fool* [fr. L. *egregius*, prominent]

e·gress (í:grəs) *n.* a way out, exit ‖ the act of going out ‖ the right to go out ‖ (*astron.*) the reappearance of a heavenly body (except the moon) at the end of an eclipse or transit [fr. L. *egredi* (*egressus*), to emerge]

e·gres·sion (igréʃən) *n.* the act or state of emerging [fr. L. *egressio* fr. *egredi*, to go out]

e·gret (í:gret) *n.* a member of *Egretta*, fam. *Ardeidae*, a genus of tall, elegant, snowy white birds related to herons, certain of whose long, thin feathers are used for aigrettes and ospreys [F. *aigrette*]

E·gypt (í:dʒipt) (officially Arab Republic of Egypt) a republic (area 386,198 sq. miles, pop. 44,000,000) occupying the northeast corner of Africa and the Sinai peninsula, cut by the Gulf of Suez and by the Suez Canal (101 miles), which connects the Gulf with the Mediterranean. People and language: Arabic, with Greek, Nubian, Berber, Jewish, Italian and Armenian minorities. Religion: 91% Moslems, 8% Christians (mainly Copts), 1% Jews and others. The Nile runs the length of the mainland. The population is concentrated along its valley and on its delta, at the head of which is Cairo, the capital. West of the Nile is the Libyan Desert, east is the Arabian Desert, rising to 7,165 ft near the Red Sea. The highest mountains are on Sinai (Katherina, 8,662 ft). The country divides into Lower Egypt (Wagh-el-Bahari) north of Cairo and Upper Egypt (El-Saïd) south of Cairo. The Nile rises between June and Sept. and is lowest in May. Flood level: 40 ft in Asyut, 22 ft in Cairo. Climate: Mediterranean in the north, desert elsewhere. Annual rainfall: Alexandria 8 ins, Cairo 1 in, the south nil. Average winter temperatures (F.): 66° along the Mediterranean, 75° in Aswan. Average maximum summer temperatures: Alexandria 87°, Cairo 96°, Aswan 108°. A hot, dry dusty wind (the khamsin) blows Mar.–June. Livestock: cattle, water buffaloes, sheep, donkeys, poultry, goats, camels. Agricultural products: cotton (2nd world producer), cereals, rice, beans, sugarcane, dates, onions. Minerals (chiefly in the Arabian Desert): oil, phosphates, iron ore, gypsum, salt, manganese. Manufactures: textiles, foodstuffs, cement, glass, metals, sugar. Hydroelectricity and irrigation are derived from the Aswan High Dam and other barrages. Exports: cotton. Imports: machinery, wheat, iron and steel, oil, vehicles, fertilizers. Ports: Alexandria, Port Said, Suez. There are five universities, the oldest being El Azhar (Cairo, 972) and Cairo (1925). Monetary unit: Egyptian pound (100 piastres). HISTORY. The recorded history of Egypt is one of the longest known. (Dates before about 1500 B.C. are much disputed.) The ancient kingdoms of Upper and Lower Egypt were united (c. 3110 B.C.) by Menes, who founded the first of the thirty dynasties. The Archaic period (dynasties 1 and 2, c. 3110–c. 2665 B.C.) is little known. The Old Kingdom (dynasties 3–6, c. 2614–c. 2181 B.C.) saw the building of the pyramids of Giza. The capital was probably at

Memphis. The power of the pharaoh was at its height, but it then disintegrated into feudal anarchy (dynasties 7–10, c. 2180–c. 2052 B.C.). The Middle Kingdom (dynasties 11 and 12, c. 2052–c. 1786 B.C.), centered on Thebes, was the classic period of ancient Egyptian art. Economic progress led to expansion abroad. The Hyksos, who had invaded the delta, overran Egypt (dynasties 13–17, c. 1785–c. 1570 B.C.). Under the New Kingdom (dynasties 18–20, 1570–1075 B.C.) the Hyksos were expelled and a strong central government was set up with a large bureaucratic administration. A great empire was established from Nubia to the Euphrates, but it collapsed under the invasion of the Hittites. The Late New Kingdom (dynasties 21–25, 1075–657 B.C.) saw Egypt under foreign rule, begun by the Libyan Sheshonq I of the 22nd dynasty (940–730 B.C.) and continued by the Ethiopians. Egypt was occupied by the Assyrians (670–654 B.C.). After the native rule of the Saite period (26th dynasty, 664–525 B.C.), Egypt was occupied by the Persians (525–332 B.C.) who were expelled (332 B.C.) by Alexander the Great. After his death (323 B.C.) the Ptolemies ruled as his successors, extending their empire to Palestine and Syria, and making Alexandria a center of Hellenistic culture. After the death of Cleopatra (30 B.C.) Egypt became a Roman province (30 B.C.–395 A.D.). Christianity was introduced (3rd c.). Egypt passed to the Byzantine Empire (395–642), which repressed the Monophysite Coptic Christians, and was conquered by the Moslems (640). As part of Islam (642–1517), it was governed first as a province of the Caliphate (646–968), then by the Fatimid rulers (969–1171), who founded Cairo (969), and then by the Ayyubid rulers (1171–1249), who united Egypt and Syria. The rule of the Mamelukes (1249–1517) was notable for its architecture. With the discovery of the route around the Cape of Good Hope, Egypt lost its commercial importance and became an impoverished province of the Ottoman Empire (1517–1879), administered by Turkish pashas. Napoleon invaded Egypt (1798), but the French were defeated by the British and Turkish forces (1801). The Albanian Mohammed Ali became pasha (1805–48), began to modernize Egypt and conquered Arabia (1818) and the Sudan (1822). His son Ibrahim occupied Syria (1832–40) but was forced by Britain and France to withdraw (1841). Ismail governed as pasha (1863–7) and as khedive (1867–79). He opened the Suez Canal (1869), but had to accept Anglo-French financial control when his government became bankrupt. His abdication (1879) was followed by a revolt (1882) led by Arabi Pasha. This was crushed by the British, who occupied Egypt (1882–1914). Under Abbas Hilmi II (1892–1914) an Anglo-Egyptian Condominium of the Sudan was established (1899). At the start of the 1st world war, Turkish suzerainty was abolished and a British protectorate was declared (1914–22) until an independent kingdom was formed (1922) under Fuad I (1922–36). His son Farouk (1936–52) signed the Anglo-Egyptian Treaty (1936), which made Britain and Egypt allies and limited British forces to the canal zone for 20 years. Egypt was a British base in the 2nd world war, and declared war on Germany and Japan in Feb. 1945. The Arab League was set up (1945). Egypt fought Israel unsuccessfully (1948–9). Gen. Neguib seized power (1952) and Farouk abdicated. A republic was established (1953). Col. Nasser took over as premier (1954). When Anglo-American financial support for the Aswan High Dam was withdrawn, Nasser nationalized the Suez Canal (July 26, 1956). Israel, claiming she was subject to border raiding, attacked Egypt (Oct. 29, 1956). British and French forces invaded the canal zone (Oct. 31, 1956) but the U.N. ordered a cease-fire (Nov. 6, 1956). Egypt and Syria formed the United Arab Republic (1958). Yemen joined (1958) the United Arab Republic, creating the United Arab States. Syria and the Yemen withdrew (1961). Egypt again fought Israel (June 1967) but was defeated. The Suez Canal remained closed. Nasser was followed (Oct. 1970) by Anwar Sadat as president. Sadat expelled 20,000 Soviet military advisers and experts (1972), and gained wide popular support when Egypt regained a strip of the Sinai from Israel during the October War (1973) and the Suez Canal was reopened (1975). He concluded a peace treaty with Israel (1979) after the Camp David talks with Israeli Prime Min-

CONCISE PRONUNCIATION KEY: **(a)** æ, c*a*t; ɑ, c*a*r; ɔ f*aw*n; ei, sn*a*ke. **(e)** e, h*e*n; i:, sh*ee*p; iə, d*ee*r; ɛə, b*ea*r. **(i)** i, f*i*sh; ai, t*i*ger; ə:, b*i*rd. **(o)** o, *o*x; au, c*ow*; ou, g*oa*t; u, p*oo*r; ɔi, r*o*yal. **(u)** ʌ, d*u*ck; u, b*u*ll; u:, g*oo*se; ə, b*a*cillus; ju:, c*u*be. x, lo*ch*; θ, *th*ink; ð, bo*th*er; z, *Z*en; ʒ, cor*s*age. dʒ, sava*ge*; ŋ, oranguta*ng*; j, *y*ak; ʃ, *f*ish; tʃ, fe*tch*; 'l, rabb*le*; 'n, redd*en*. Complete pronunciation key appears inside front cover.

ister Begin. He was assassinated (1981) by Muslim fundamentalists and was succeeded by Hosni Mubarak, who tried to improve relations with the rest of the Arab world

E·gyp·tian (idʒípʃən) **1.** *adj.* of or pertaining to the inhabitants of Egypt or their language, culture, etc. **2.** *n.* an inhabitant of Egypt ‖ the Egyptian language ‖ (*printing*) a heavy typeface, with squared serifs

Egyptian language a Hamitic language, now extinct, related to Semitic tongues. Hieroglyphic inscriptions of the 1st dynasty are known. Its last phase was Coptic, which died out as a spoken language in the 16th c., but survives as a liturgical language

E·gyp·tol·o·gist (i:dʒiptólədʒist) *n.* a specialist in Egyptology

E·gyp·tol·o·gy (i:dʒiptólədʒi:) *n.* the study of the archaeological remains of the civilization of ancient Egypt (*PETRIE) [*Egypto-* fr. EGYPT+Gk *logos*, word]

eh (ei, e) *interj.* used to reinforce a question, *what do you think of that, eh?* or simply to announce a question, *eh? what's that you said?*

Eh·ren·fels (éirənfels), Christian von (1859–1932), Austrian philosopher. He influenced the development of Gestalt psychology

Ehr·lich (éərlix), Paul (1854–1915), German bacteriologist. He discovered arsenical compounds used in the treatment of syphilis and his work led to major advances in chemotherapy

EHV *abbr.* extra high voltage

Ei·chen·dorff (áixəndɔrf), Joseph, Baron von (1788–1857), German Romantic writer. Many of his lyrics were set to music by Schumann and Wolf

ei·der (áidər) *n.* a sea duck of genus *Somateria* and related genera, restricted to northern regions. The female plucks the gray down from her breast to cover her eggs [Icel. œð (gen. of pǒr)] **ei·der-down** (áidərdaun) *n.* the soft breast feathers of the eider ‖ a bed covering filled with these feathers ‖ a bed covering filled with inferior feathers, kapok etc.

ei·det·ic (aidétik) *adj.* (of voluntarily produced visual images) coming from the imagination but projected with extreme sharpness and accuracy, as in hallucinations [fr. Gk *eidos*, shape] **ei·det·ic image** (aidétik) a detailed image of something previously seen

ei·do·lon (aidóulən) *pl.* **ei·do·lons, ei·do·la** (aidóula) *n.* an apparition, a ghostly shape or figure [Gk=ghost]

Ei·fel (áifəl) a wooded highland area north of the Mosel and west of the Rhine, West Germany

Eif·fel (áifəl), Alexandre Gustave (1832–1923), French engineer. He designed and built many large iron frameworks, including the Eiffel tower at Paris (985 ft in 1899, raised to 1,052 ft in 1959)

eight (eit) **1.** *adj.* being one more than seven (*NUMBER TABLE) **2.** *n.* twice four ‖ the cardinal number representing this (8, VIII) ‖ eight o'clock ‖ a playing card marked with eight symbols ‖ a team of eight members, esp. in rowing ‖ (*pl*) races for eight-oared boats [O.E. *ahta, eahta, œhte*]

eight ball a black ball marked '8' used in the game of pool **behind the eight ball** (*pop.*) in a tough or dangerous position

eight bells (*naut.*) the eight strokes of a bell that mark the end of a four-hour watch (4, 8 and 12 o'clock)

eight·een (éiti:n) **1.** *adj.* being one more than 17 (*NUMBER TABLE) **2.** *n.* ten plus eight ‖ the cardinal number representing this (18, XVIII) [O.E. *eahtatȳne, eahtatēne*]

eight·een·mo (éití:nmou) *n.* (*abbr.* 18mo) octodecimo [EIGHTEEN + DUODECIMO]

eight·eenth (éití:nθ) **1.** *adj.* being number 18 in a series (*NUMBER TABLE) ‖ being one of the 18 equal parts of anything **2.** *n.* the person or thing next after the 17th ‖ one of 18 equal parts of anything (1/18) ‖ the 18th day of a month [O.E. *eahtatēotha*]

Eighteenth Amendment (1919) an amendment to the U.S. Constitution that prohibited the manufacture and sale of liquor, an enforcement of the Volstead Act (1919), also known as the Prohibition amendment. Largely a result of crusading by temperance movements, the law was blatantly disobeyed by Americans and provided organized crime with a new venture—the manufacture and sale of illegal liquor. The 18th Amendment was repealed in 1933 by the passage of the 21st Amendment

888 Weteye (*mil.*) nerve gas containing toxic agent GB

eight·fold way (éitfould) (*nuclear phys.*) a symmetrical pattern among eight different elementary interacting particles with similar mass, isospin, and hypercharge

eighth (eitθ) **1.** *adj.* being number eight in a series (*NUMBER TABLE) ‖ being one of the eight equal parts of anything **2.** *n.* the person or thing next after the seventh ‖ one of eight equal parts of anything (1/8) ‖ the eighth day of a month ‖ (*mus.*) an octave **3.** *adv.* in the eighth place ‖ (followed by a superlative) except seven, *the eighth biggest* [O.E. *eahtotha*]

Eighth Amendment (1791) an amendment to the U.S. Constitution that prohibits cruel and unusual punishment and the setting of excessive bail or unreasonable fines, part of the Bill of Rights. It has been further defined by the Supreme Court as punishment in relation to the crime committed. In 'Furman v. Georgia' (1972) capital punishment was declared a violation of the 8th Amendment. This was modified by later decisions, and some states reinstated capital punishment for certain serious crimes

eighth note (*mus., Am.=Br.* quaver, symbol ♪) half a quarter note, or one-eighth of a whole note

eight·i·eth (éiti:iθ) **1.** *adj.* being number 80 in a series (*NUMBER TABLE) ‖ being one of the 80 equal parts of anything **2.** *n.* the person or thing next after the 79th ‖ one of 80 equal parts of anything (1/80) [M.E.]

eight·some reel (éitsəm) a Scottish dance for eight dancers

eight·y (éiti:) **1.** *adj.* being ten more than 70 (*NUMBER TABLE) **2.** *pl.* **eight·ies** *n.* eight times ten ‖ the cardinal number representing this (80, LXXX) **the eighties** (of temperature, a person's age, a century, etc.) the span 80–9 [O.E. *hundeahtatig*]

Ei·lat, E·lath (eilát, éilæ, í:læθ) Israel's outlet to the Red Sea, at the head of the Gulf of 'Aqaba. It is the terminus of the pipeline from Haifa. Nasser's attempt to deprive Israel of use of the port was a contributory cause of war (June 1967) between Israel and the Arab states

Eind·ho·ven (áinthouvən) a town (pop. 192,600) in North Brabant, S. Netherlands, a rail center: radio, electrical, metal and textile industries

Ein·hard (áinhart) (c. 770–840), Frankish scholar. He wrote 'Vita Karoli Magni' (c. 820), a biography of Charlemagne

Ein·horn (áinhɔrn), David (1809–79), U.S. Jewish liberal theologian and leader of the U.S. Jewish reform movement. During the Civil War he campaigned against slavery

Ein·sie·deln (áinzi:deln) the site of a Benedictine abbey in Schwyz, Switzerland, containing a famous image of the Virgin and valuable manuscripts and incunables

Ein·stein (áinstain), Albert (1879–1955), mathematical physicist of German birth, naturalized American (1940). He profoundly influenced science in many fields, but is best known for his enunciation of the theory of relativity (generalized theory stated in 'Die Grundlage der Allgemeinen Relativitätstheorie', 1916). He is also distinguished for his work for peace and justice

Einstein equation the mass-energy equation

ein·stein·i·um (ainstáini:əm) *n.* a transuranic element (symbol E or Es, at. no. 99, mass of isotope of longest known half-life 254) [after Albert *Einstein*]

Ei·rann (éərən) *adj.* relating to Eire

Ei·re (éərə) *IRISH REPUBLIC

Ei·sen·how·er (áizənhauər), Dwight David ('Ike') (1890–1969), U.S. general and statesman. He served (1943–5) as Supreme Allied Commander in Europe and (1953–61) as 34th president of the U.S.A., a Republican. He was appointed (June 1942) commander of U.S. forces in Europe and (Nov. 1942) chief of all Allied forces in the North African landings. He directed the invasions of Sicily (July 1943) and Italy (Sept. 1943). In Dec. 1943 he began coordinating plans for the invasion of continental Europe (June 6, 1944). After commanding (1945) U.S. occupation forces in Germany and serving (1945–8) as U.S. army chief of staff, he retired (1948–50) to the presidency of Columbia University. He was recalled to serve (1950–2) as supreme commander of the Allied Powers in Europe, when he organized NATO defense forces. During his presidency Congress ap-

proved (1954) the construction of the St Lawrence Seaway, together with some of the highest peacetime budgets in U.S. history. He presided over the end (1953) of the Korean War, the flow and ebb of the McCarthy 'Red scare', and the formation (1954) of SEATO. He attended (1955) the Geneva summit conference, the first meeting since Potsdam of leaders of the former Allied powers. He proclaimed (1956) the Eisenhower Doctrine, providing for military and economic aid to Middle East nations beset by Communism. He ordered (1958) U.S. marines into Lebanon. A relaxation of the cold war tension ended at a summit conference in Paris (1960) when Nikita Khrushchev accused him of perfidy in the U-2 incident. To enforce racial desegregation in schools in Little Rock, Ark., he federalized (1957) the National Guard

Ei·sen·stein (áizənstain), Ferdinand Gotthold (1823–52), German mathematician, best known for his contributions to the theory of complex numbers

Eisenstein, Sergei Mikhailovich (1898–1948), Russian film director. He perfected the techniques of cutting and close-up in 'Strike' (1923), 'The Battleship Potemkin' (1925) and 'October' (1928). His most famous sound films are 'Alexander Nevsky' (1938) and 'Ivan the Terrible' (1942–5)

Ei·ser·nes Tor (áizɛərnestór) *IRON GATE

eis·tedd·fod (aistéðvɔd) *n.* a Welsh congress, national or local, to foster the national arts by competitions in music, vernacular drama and literature. The modern eisteddfod is a revival of the medieval congresses of Welsh bards, which died out in the Tudor period [Welsh=a formal gathering]

ei·ther (í:ðər, áiðər) **1.** *adj.* each one of two, *on either side of the road* ‖ one or other of two, *no goals were scored in either half* **2.** *pron.* each one of two, *either of the plans is equally dangerous* ‖ one or other of two, *you may take either of the roads* **3.** *conj.* used with 'or' to connect two or more alternatives, *either hurry or miss the concert* **4.** *adv.* (in a negative sentence or one which is given a partly negative sense by such words as 'hardly', 'scarcely', 'little', etc.) used preceded by 'or' to draw particular attention to the last of two or more alternatives, indicating that what is said of the earlier alternatives applies equally, or even more, to the last, *we don't like him, or his family, or his friends, either*. Similarly, without a preceding 'or', it emphasizes that what is denied or asked is in addition to some statement or denial already made or to be undestood, *I can't find the carbon either* [O.E. *p̄ghwœther*]

e·jac·u·late (idʒækjuleit) *pres. part.* **e·jac·u·lat·ing** *past* and *past part.* **e·jac·u·lat·ed** *v.t.* to say in a sudden utterance ‖ to eject (semen) ‖ *v.i.* to eject semen **e·jac·u·lá·tion** *n.* **e·jac·u·la·to·ry** (idʒǽkjulətɔri:, idʒǽkjulətouri:) *adj.* [fr. L. *ejaculari (ejaculatus),* to cast out]

e·ject (idʒékt) *v.t.* to throw out, *the cartridge is ejected automatically* ‖ to turn out, force to leave, *to eject demonstrators* ‖ (*law*) to evict from property, *to eject a tenant* [fr. L. *ejicere (ejectus)*]

e·jec·ta (idʒéktə) *pl. n.* matter thrown out by a natural force. e.g. ash from a volcano [L.=things thrown out fr. *ejicere,* to throw out]

e·jec·tion (idʒékʃən) *n.* an ejecting or being ejected

e·jec·tive (idʒéktiv) *adj.* of ejection ‖ causing ejection

e·ject·ment (idʒéktmənt) *n.* an ejecting ‖ (*law*) an action for the recovery of possession of property

e·jec·tor (idʒéktər) *n.* something which ejects. esp. the mechanism in a firearm which ejects the spent cartridge

e·ji·do (ehí:ðɔ) *n.* an agrarian property, held and worked in common, belonging to the peasants of a village in Mexico. Various governmental reforms since 1917 have given protection against the seizure of ejidos by landowners and financiers, not always successfully ‖ a system of land-tenure reform introduced in Mexico by President Lázaro Cárdenas, under which the haciendas were transferred to the community [fr. Span.]

e·ka·haf·ni·um (ɛkəhǽfni:əm) *n.* (*chem.*) element 104, so-named tentatively; alternatively called kurchatovium. Having a mass number 260, it is produced by irradiating plutonium-242 with neo-22 ions in a heavy ion cyclotron

ek·a·lead (ékəled) *n.* hypothetical element 114

CONCISE PRONUNCIATION KEY: **(a)** æ, c*a*t; ɑ, c*a*r; ɔ f*aw*n; ei, sn*a*ke. **(e)** e, h*e*n; i:, sh*ee*p; iə, d*ee*r; ɛə, b*ea*r. **(i)** i, f*i*sh; ai, t*i*ger; əː, b*i*rd. **(o)** o, *o*x; au, c*ow*; ou, g*oa*t; u, p*oo*r; ɔi, r*oy*al. **(u)** ʌ, d*u*ck; u, b*u*ll; uː, g*oo*se; ə, bacill*u*s; juː, c*u*be. x, lo*ch*; θ, *th*ink; ð, bo*th*er; z, *Z*en; ʒ, cor*s*age; dʒ, sava*g*e; ŋ, oranguta*ng*; j, *y*ak; ʃ, *fi*sh; tʃ, fe*tch*; 'l, rabb*le*; 'n, redd*en*. Complete pronunciation key appears inside front cover.

E·ka·te·rin·burg (ikɑterinbúːrx) *SVERDLOVSK

eke (iːk) *pres. part.* **ek·ing** *past* and *past part.* **eked** *v.t.* (with 'out') to make last longer, *to eke out supplies* ‖ (with 'out') to make small but necessary additions to, *to eke out one's salary* ‖ (with 'out') to make (a living, etc.) with difficulty and hardship [M.E. *eken* fr. O.E. *īecan, ēcan*]

e·kis·tics (ikístics) *n.* study of problems of human communities including economics, geography, sociology, government, coined by Greek planner C. A. Doxiades **ekistic** *adj.* **ekistician** *n.*

Ek·man dredge (Ékmæn) underwater shovel, named for V. Wolfried Ekman, Swedish oceanographer, capable of sampling the bottom of a body of water

el (el) *n.* elevated railroad

e·lab·o·rate 1. (iláebərit) *adj.* made with care and much fine detail, *an elaborate carving* ‖ complicated, *an eloborate tangle of truth and lies* **2.** (iláebəreit) *v. pres. part.* **e·lab·o·rat·ing** *past* and *past part.* **e·lab·o·rat·ed** *v.t.* to make or develop (a complicated thing) with care, to work out in detail ‖ (of a living organism) to change the chemical structure of (a foodstuff) so as to make it more readily assimilable, etc., esp. to cause (a complex organic compound) to come into being from simple substances ‖ *v.i.* to add extra complication or ornament, esp. to go into details about a matter **e·lab·o·ra·tion** *n.* **e·lab·o·ra·tive** (iláebəreiriv, iláebərativ) *adj.* **e·láb·o·ra·tor** *n.* [fr. L. *elaborare (elaboratus),* to work out]

El·a·gab·a·lus (ęlǝgáebǝlǝs) *HELIOGABALUS

El Alamein *ALAMEIN

E·lam (íːlɑm) an ancient kingdom at the head of the Persian Gulf, founded before 4000 B.C., frequently at war with its neighbors until conquered (642–639 B.C.) by Assyria

e·land (íːlǝnd) *n. Taurotragus oryx,* the largest antelope of Central, S. and E. Africa. It stands about 6 ft high. Both sexes are horned [Du. *eland,* elk]

é·lan vi·tal (eilávi:tæl) *n.* the vital force or spontaneous urge which according to Bergson is inherent in the material world and lies behind the evolution of all organisms [F.]

e·lapse (iláeps) *pres. part.* **e·laps·ing** *past* and *past part.* **e·lapsed** *v.i.* (of time, or an equivalent) to pass by [fr. L. *elabi (elapsus),* to glide away]

e·las·mo·branch (iláezmǝbræŋk) *n.* a member of *Elasmobranchii* or *Chondrichthyes,* a class of fish including most cartilaginous types, e.g. sharks, skates, rays, dogfish [Mod. L. fr. Gk *elasmos,* beaten metal + *branchia,* gills]

e·las·tic (iláestik) **1.** *adj.* having the ability to recover its original size or shape after deformation ‖ springy, with the power to give or bend without snapping or breaking ‖ adaptable to circumstances, *a plan elastic enough to allow for alternatives* ‖ (of persons) recovering quickly after a setback, *an elastic temperament* ‖ made of (or partly of) elastic, *an elastic band* **2.** *n.* vulcanized rubber thread, often covered with or woven into fabric, which can be stretched and which returns to its original size when released ‖ (*pop.*) a rubber band **e·lás·ti·cal·ly** *adv.* **e·las·tic·i·ty** (iláestísiti:, ịːlæstísiti:) *n.* the ability to resume the original size or shape after deformation. The deformation may be change of length, change of volume or change of shape and is called the 'strain', the force per unit area which causes the strain being called the stress (*HOOKE'S LAW*). A substance may lose its elasticity if the stress exceeds the elastic limit, or as a result of fatigue due to prolonged stress ‖ the capacity to recover after emotional or other stress, *the elasticity of the stock market* **e·las·ti·cized** (iláestisaizd) *adj.* woven with elastic thread ‖ made with elastic insertions [fr. Mod. L. *elasticus* fr. Gk]

elastic limit the greatest stress to which a body which has elasticity can be subjected without being permanently deformed

e·las·tin (iláestin) *n.* (*biochem.*) an albuminoid from which ligaments are largely formed [ELASTIC+*-in*]

e·las·to·hy·dro·dy·nam·ics (iláestouhaidroudainæmiks) *n.* study of elasticity of water under pressure **elastohydrodynamic** *adj.*

e·las·tos·er (ęlæstóusǝ) *n.* (*biochem.*) an enzyme from the pancreas that makes elastin, a protein made up of soluble elastic fibers

e·late (iléit) *pres. part.* **e·lat·ing** *past* and *past part.* **e·lat·ed** *v.t.* to fill with joy, cause to be

jubilant **e·lát·ed** *adj.* [fr. L. *efferre (elatus),* to raise up]

e·lat·er (élǝtǝr) *n.* (*bot.*) a cell with spiral thickening, which assists in dispersing the spores from the sporogonium (capsule) in liverworts and from sporophylls in equisetums ‖ a member of *Elateridae,* a family of beetles commonly known as click beetles. By vigorous muscular action they are able to leap high into the air. When alarmed they simulate death. They feed on flowers, grasses and decaying wood. The larvae (wireworms) damage the roots of herbaceous plants. Some tropical genera are phosphorescent (*FIREFLY*) **e·lat·er·id** (iláetǝrid) *adj.* [Mod. L. fr. Gk *elatēr,* driver]

e·lat·er·ite (iláetarait) *n.* a dark brown elastic bitumen [ELATER]

Elath *EILAT

e·la·tion (iléiʃǝn) *n.* the quality or state of being filled with joy or jubilation

E layer (*meteor.*) strata of ionized air in the E region of the atmosphere, 100–120 km above sea level, sometimes the cause of bending in the radio waves reflected to earth **syn** Heaviside layer, Kennelly-Heaviside layer

El·ba (élbǝ) a mountainous Italian island (area 86 sq. miles, pop. 26,830) in the Mediterranean between Corsica and Tuscany, where Napoleon was exiled (1814–15)

El·be (élbǝ) (*Czech.* Labe) a river flowing for 725 miles from the mountains of N.E. Bohemia through N. Germany into the North Sea. It is a great waterway, navigable for cargo vessels most of its length, and connected by canals to the Rhine and Oder river systems and to the Baltic. Since the conclusion of WWII it has served as part of the border between East and West Germany

El Bei·da (ælbéidǝ) a town (pop. 31,000) of Libya, in Cyrenaica. It was the capital 1963–4

El·bert, Mt (élbǝːrt) the highest point, (14,431 ft) of the Rocky Mtns

El·blag (élblɔ̄g) (G. Elbing) a port (pop. 92,600) in N. Poland, east of Danzig: shipbuilding, engineering

el·bow (élbou) **1.** *n.* the joint connecting the forearm and upper arm ‖ the point formed at this joint when the arm is bent ‖ a bend or corner resembling a bent arm, e.g. in a pipe **out at elbows** shabby ‖ poor, without money **2.** *v.t.* to jostle with the elbow ‖ to make (one's way) in this manner ‖ *v.i.* to make one's way in this manner [M.E. *elbowe* fr. O.E. *elboga, elnboga*]

elbow grease vigorous physical effort, esp. in rubbing or polishing

el·bow·room (élbouruːm, élbourụm) *n.* room to move or turn around in

El·brus (elbrúːs) the highest peak (18,470 ft) in the Caucasus Mtns, U.S.S.R., and the highest in Europe

El·burz Mtns (élburz) a range (650 miles long, average altitude 5,000 ft) in N. Iran, between the Caspian and the central plateau, rich in coal, lead and iron. Highest point: Mt Demavend (18,600 ft)

El Ca·ney (elkɑnéi:) a region in Oriente province, Cuba, site of an engagement (1898) in the Spanish-American War in which U.S. troops, led by Gen. William Shafter, routed the Spanish forces

El·che, the Lady of (éltʃei) a colored bust in stoneware of a young woman with fine features, and having her hair very curiously dressed, found at Elche in Alicante province, Spain. It shows strong Greek influence and dates from the early 5th c. B.C.

eld·er (éldǝr) **1.** *adj.* (of one of two persons) born at an earlier date, *the elder son* ‖ of higher rank, dignity, validity or other seniority, by virtue of an earlier origin, *the elder title to a property* **2.** *n.* a person who is respected, and whose authority is recognized, because of his age or worthiness, *a village elder* ‖ (in Presbyterian Churches) a lay official who shares with the minister the responsibility for running a church ‖ (in the Mormon Church) a grade of the high, or Melchizedek, order of priesthood ‖ (*hist.*) a member of the Jewish Sanhedrin or of the board which governed the affairs of a synagogue ‖ (in the early Christian Church) a presbyter or priest ‖ (*pl.*) people older than oneself, *she often shocks her elders* [O.E. *eldra,* comp. of *ald, eald,* old]

el·der (éldǝr) *n.* a member of *Sambucus,* fam. *Caprifoliaceae,* a genus of compound-leaved, pithy shrubs or trees growing wild in northern temperate areas. The small white flowers are

strongly scented. The berries grow in large cymes [O.E. *allærn*]

el·der·ber·ry (éldǝrberi:) *pl.* **el·der·ber·ries** *n.* the fruit of the elder ‖ the elder tree

eld·er·ly (éldǝrli:) *adj.* approaching old age, past middle age

eld·er·ship (éldǝrʃip) *n.* the office of an elder in a church

elder statesman a man eminent in public life, and respected for his long service to the nation or a political party, esp. a retired statesman who plays the role of an unofficial adviser

eld·est (éldist) *adj.* (of three or more persons, generally of the same family) oldest

El Do·ra·do (ęldǝrádou) a legendary country or city in South America, between the Amazon and Orinoco, said to be rich in gold and treasure ‖ any place or source of fabulous wealth [Span.=the gilded man (from its legendary ruler)]

El·ea·nor of Aquitaine (élinǝr, élinɔr) (c. 1122–1204), queen of France (1137–52) by her marriage to Louis VII, and queen of England (1154–89) by her marriage (1152) to Henry II. The latter marriage added her vast possessions in France to the English crown, precipitating an Anglo-French struggle which was to last several centuries. Imprisoned after helping her sons in an unsuccessful revolt (1173) against Henry II, she exercised considerable influence during the reign (1189–99) of her son Richard I

El·e·at·ic (eliːætik) *n.* a philosopher of the school possibly founded by Xenophanes (6th c. B.C.) at Elea in Lucania, and later represented by Parmenides and Zeno (5th c. B.C.). The Eleatics believed that all things are one and denied the existence of plurality and change

el·e·cam·pane (ęlikæmpéin) *n. Inula helenium,* fam. *Compositae,* a plant native to central Asia, but naturalized in Europe, W. Asia, North America and Japan. Its rootstock yields a diuretic and expectorant [prob. fr. M.L. *enula campana,* enula of the fields]

e·lect (ilékt) **1.** *adj.* chosen, esp. (*theol.*) chosen by God, predestined to salvation ‖ (following the noun to which it applies) chosen or elected for, but not yet filling, an office or position, *the president-elect* **2.** *pl. n.* **the elect** those chosen by God, those predestined to salvation ‖ a group of people specially privileged in some way **3.** *v.t.* to choose by voting, *to elect a chairman* ‖ (*rhet.*) to decide on (a certain course of action) or choose (to do something), *he elected to withdraw* ‖ to choose (an optional course of study) in high school or college [fr. L. *eligere (electus)*]

e·lec·tion (ilékʃǝn) *n.* the act or process of electing, esp. of choosing by vote ‖ (*theol.*) God's choice of those who are to be saved, or the state of those whom God has chosen for salvation. The nature of such election and the conditions necessary for salvation were fundamental issues between the Reformed Churches, particularly the Calvinists, and the Roman Catholic Church, esp. by contrast with the Augustinian teaching of the evidence and power of good works **e·lec·tion·eer** *v.i.* to try to obtain votes for a political candidate [fr. L. *electio (electionis),* choice]

e·lec·tive (iléktiv) **1.** *adj.* chosen by election or voting, *an elective office* ‖ with the power to choose by vote, *an elective body* ‖ relating to election by vote, *an elective system* ‖ (of a course of studies) optional **2.** *n.* an optional course of studies [F. *electif*]

elective affinity a natural sympathy or attraction between two people

elective surgery (*med.*) surgery that need not be performed on an emergency basis, because reasonable delays will not affect the outcome of surgery unfavorably

e·lec·tor (iléktǝr) *n.* someone who has the right to vote, esp. in the election of representatives in a national assembly ‖ a member of the electoral college ‖ (*hist.*) one of the ecclesiastical and temporal princes who elected the Holy Roman Emperor. There were originally, in the 13th c., six electors. From 1356 to 1547 there were seven, the archbishops of Mainz, Trier and Cologne, the king of Bohemia, the count palatine, the duke of Saxony, and the duke of Brandenburg. By the time the Holy Roman Empire came to an end in 1806 there were 10 **e·léc·tor·al** *adj.* [L.]

electoral college a body of representatives elected by the voters of each state. The electoral college casts the formal vote for the president of the U.S.A. and, separately, for the vice-presi-

CONCISE PRONUNCIATION KEY: (**a**) æ, cat; ɑ, car; ɔ fawn; ei, snake. (**e**) e, hen; iː, sheep; iǝ, deer; ɛǝ, bear. (**i**) i, fish; ai, tiger; ǝː, bird. (**o**) o, ox; au, cow; ou, goat; u, poor; ɔi, royal. (**u**) ʌ, duck; u, bull; uː, goose; ǝ, bacillus; juː, cube. x, loch; θ, think; ð, bother; z, Zen; ʒ, corsage; dʒ, savage; ŋ, orangutang; j, yak; ʃ, fish; tʃ, fetch; 'l, rabble; 'n, redden. Complete pronunciation key appears inside front cover.

dent. Each state has the same number of members of the college as it has representatives in both houses of Congress. All the electoral votes of a state go for a single candidate. Many attempts have been made to reform or eliminate the college

Electoral Commission *COMPROMISE OF 1877

e·lec·tor·ate (iléktərit) n. the whole body of those who have the right to vote in a political election ‖ (hist.) the office or dominions of an elector of the Holy Roman Empire

E·lec·tra (iléktrə) (Gk mythol.) the daughter of Agamemnon. She helped her brother Orestes to avenge their father's death by killing his murderers: their mother, Clytemnestra, and her lover, Aegisthus ‖ a daughter of Oceanus, mother of Iris and the Harpies

Electra complex (Freudian psychol.) a complex in girls or women resulting from an attachment to the father that involves unconscious rivalry with the mother (cf. OEDIPUS COMPLEX)

e·lec·tric (iléktrik) adj. of or pertaining to electricity, containing, produced by, producing or worked by electricity ‖ extremely tense, nervously excited, the mood of the audience was electric **e·léc·tri·cal** adj. [fr. Mod. L. electricus fr. Gk ēlektron, amber (which acquires a charge when rubbed)]

electrical conductivity the reciprocal of the resistivity of a substance

electric arc *ARC

electric arc furnace steelmaking device using high-quality scrap or ore with polluting elements eliminated

electric blackboard telephone-connected display board that receives and enlarges transmitted data in graphic or digital form

electric blue a harsh, bright, slightly greenish blue

electric chair an electrified chair used to electrocute a condemned criminal ‖ this as a penalty

electric charge the property of certain elementary particles which causes them to exert forces on one another and which can be characterized as either negative (like that on an electron) or positive (like that on a proton), according to whether an unknown charge is repelled by or attracted to an electronic-type charge (since charges of the same type repel and those of opposite types attract one another) ‖ Mks unit: coulomb = 6.242×10^{18} elementary electronic charges ‖ a particle or particles having this property

electric circuit any arrangement of conductors through which an electric current can flow, usually including one or more devices (batteries, generators, etc.) that supply current, those that operate on the current, and various types of control for the resistance, voltage, current, etc. of the circuit

electric current a flow of charged particles (e.g., electrons or protons) accompanied by the fields that they generate (mks unit: ampere)

electric eel Electrophorus electricus, a large South American eel (*ELECTRIC ORGANS)

electric eye a device that includes a photoelectric cell used as an automatic controlling mechanism

electric field the field surrounding an electric charge or a moving magnet, being defined at any point by the force acting on a unit positive test charge placed at that point

electric furnace a furnace which, by using the heating effect of an electric current, allows very high temperatures to be reached

electric guitar a guitar whose sound is magnified by an electronic pickup which transmits the tone to an amplifier and loudspeaker

e·lec·tri·cian (ilektríʃən) n. someone whose t.ade is making, installing, maintaining or repairing electrical equipment

e·lec·tric·i·ty (ilektrísiti:) n. a basic form of energy that is a property of certain fundamental particles of matter and consists of mutually attractive positively and negatively charged particles (protons and electrons, respectively, or positrons and electrons). It is characterized by magnetic, chemical and radiant properties, measured in electrostatic or electromagnetic units ‖ an electric current, or stream of electrons ‖ static electricity ‖ the science or study of electricity

electric light light produced by an electric current in any one of several devices, e.g., a fluorescent lamp, an arc lamp, an incandescent lamp

electric organ a musical instrument (typically with two manuals and a pedal keyboard) producing a great range of tones, incl. tones similar to those of the pipe organ

electric organs modifications in muscle tracts in some fish, giving them the property of communicating an electric shock. They are found in electric eels, electric rays and the African catfish

electric potential a scalar quantity equal to the value of the potential function at some point in an electric field compared to its value at some standard point (e.g., infinitely far from all charges). It gives the energy change in moving a unit positive charge from the standard location to the point

electric ray any of various rays of fam. Tropedinidae having electric organs. They inhabit warm seas

electric shock the painful spasm occurring when a current of electricity passes through the body. It may be lethal

electric storm a meteorological condition marked by an intense electric field within a cloud or clouds

e·lec·tri·fi·ca·tion (ilektrifikéiʃən) n. an electrifying or being electrified ‖ the change from the use of some other power to that of electric power, the electrification of a railroad

e·lec·tri·fy (iléktrifai) pres. part. **e·lec·tri·fy·ing** past and past part. **e·lec·tri·fied** v.t. to produce an electric charge or current in ‖ to cause to function by electric power ‖ to thrill or startle as though by an electric shock

e·lec·tro (iléktrou) n. an electrotype [Gk]

electro- (iléktrou) combining form electric ‖ electrically ‖ electricity ‖ electrolysis [fr. Gk ēlektron, amber]

e·lec·tro·a·nal·y·sis (ilektrouənǽlisis) n. the use of electrolysis for chemical analysis

e·lec·tro·car·di·o·gram (ilektroukárdi:əgræm) n. the tracing made by an electrocardiograph

e·lec·tro·car·di·o·graph (ilektroukárdi:əgræf, ilektroukárdi:əgraf) n. an apparatus that detects and records the electric activity of the cardiac muscle, and that is used to diagnose abnormal heart action **e·lec·tro·car·di·og·ra·phy** (ilektroukardi:ɔ́grəfi:) n.

e·lec·tro·chem·i·cal (ilektroukémik'l) adj. of or relating to electrochemistry

electrochemical equivalent the mass of a substance reacting when a specified quantity of charge is passed during electrolysis. It is often expressed in grams per coulomb, the value for silver (the usual standard) being 0.01118 gm/coulomb (*FARADAY)

electrochemical series electromotive series

e·lec·tro·chem·is·try (ilektroukémistri:) n. the science dealing with chemical changes produced by the flow of electric currents and with the energy relations of those changes. It has applications in the production of aluminum or chlorine, in the purification of copper, etc.

e·lec·tro·chrom·ism (ilektroukróumizəm) n. the property of changing color in response to an electrical impulse, e.g., as iridium can **electrochromic display** n.

e·lec·tro·con·vul·sive therapy (ilektroukənvʌ́lsiv) therapeutic electroshock treatments used in mental health programs to relieve depression abbr. ECT syn electroconvulsive shock electroshock therapy (EST)

e·lec·tro·cor·ti·cog·ra·phy (ilektroukourtəkógrəfi:) n. the measurement and recording of brain waves through electrodes placed at the cerebral cortex **electrocorticographer** n. **electrocorticographic** adj. **electrocorticographically** adv.

e·lec·tro·cute (iléktrəkju:t) v.t. pres. part. **electrocuting** past and past part. **electrocuted** to administer a fatal electric shock to ‖ to put (a criminal) to death in this way **e·lec·tro·cú·tion** n. [fr. ELECTRO- + -cute as in 'execute']

e·lec·trode (iléktroud) n. one of the two conductors (anode or cathode) by which an electric current is passed through a device such as an electrolytic cell or a discharge tube by an electrical circuit (electrons being emitted by the cathode) [fr. ELECTRO-+ Gk hodos, way]

e·lec·tro·del·ic (ilektroudélik) adj. of psychedelic effects produced electrically

e·lec·tro·de·pos·it (ilektroudipózit) 1. n. the deposit or plating which is produced at an electrode by electrolysis 2. v.t. to deposit by electrolysis **e·lec·tro·dep·o·si·tion** (ilektroudépəziʃən, ilektroudí:pəziʃən) n.

e·lec·tro·der·mal (ilektroudé:rmal) adj. of the electrical properties of the skin

e·lec·trode·sweep (iléktroudswi:p) n. (mil.) a magnetic cable sweep in which the water forms part of the electric circuit

e·lec·tro·di·al·y·sis (ilektroudaiǽlisis) n. a process that uses electrical current applied to permeable membranes to remove minerals from water, e.g., to desalinate salt water or brackish water

e·lec·tro·duct (iléktrədʌkt) n. system for carrying high-voltage electricity

e·lec·tro·dy·nam·ic (ilektroudainǽmik) adj. of or relating to electrodynamics **e·lec·tro·dy·nám·ics** n. the science which studies electrical forces (electrical current and magnetism) in interaction

e·lec·tro·dy·na·mom·e·ter (ilektroudainəmómitər) n. an instrument for measuring electric current, activated by the torque due to the reaction of two current-carrying coils in series

e·lec·tro·en·ceph·a·lo·gram (ilektrouinséfələgræm) n. the tracing made by an electroencephalograph

e·lec·tro·en·ceph·a·lo·graph (ilektrouinséfələgræf, ilektrouinséfələgraf) n. an instrument which measures and records brain waves. It is used as an aid in the diagnosis of certain brain disorders, e.g., epilepsy

e·lec·tro·fil·ter (iléktroufilter) n. antipollution chimney device that removes particles by electrostatic action

e·lec·tro·fish·ing (iléktroufiʃiŋ) n. technology of catching fish by utilizing their tendency to seek the source of a direct electric current

e·lec·tro·gas·dy·nam·ics (ilektrougæsdainǽmiks) n. use of flow of high-pressure combustion gas to generate electricity, esp. in high-voltage electric-power generation, air-pollution control, and paint spraying **electrogasdynamic** adj.

e·lec·tro·gen·e·sis (ilektroudʒénisis) n. creation of electricity, esp. by living organisms **electrogenic** adj.

e·lec·tro·hy·drau·lics (ilektrouhaidróliks) n. system of producing pulsating discharges of electricity under a liquid, creating shock waves and certain chemical reactions **electrohydraulic** adj. **electrohydraulically** adv.

e·lec·tro·ki·net·ics (ilektroukinétiks, ilektroukainétiks) n. the branch of physics dealing with the steady motion of charge and the behavior of charged particles in electric and magnetic fields (cf. ELECTROSTATICS)

e·lec·trol·y·sis (ilektrólisis) n. the passing of an electric current through an electrolyte to produce chemical changes in it. The current is carried in the electrolyte by ions that migrate to the electrodes where they may react, forming new substances ‖ depilation by means of an electric current applied to the body with a needle-shaped electrode [fr. ELECTRO-+ Gk lusis, loosening, dissolution]

e·lec·tro·lyte (iléktrəlait) n. a liquid solution or fused salt that conducts electricity, the charge being carried by the movement of ions (cf. the movement of electrons in metallic conductors) ‖ a solid substance that when fused or dissolved in a suitable solvent becomes an ionic conductor **e·lec·tro·lyt·ic** (ilektrəlítik) adj. [fr. ELECTRO-+ Gk lutos, soluble]

e·lec·tro·lyze (iléktrəlaiz) pres. part. **e·lec·tro·lyz·ing** past and past part. **e·lec·tro·lyzed** v.t. to cause to undergo electrolysis [fr. ELECTRO-+ Gk lusis, loosening, dissolution]

e·lec·tro·mag·net (ilektroumǽgnit) n. a coil of magnetic material (e.g., soft iron) about which is wound a coil of wire that produces a strongly directed magnetic field only when a current is allowed to flow through the wire. Electromagnets are widely used in electric devices **e·lec·tro·mag·net·ic** (ilektroumægnétik) adj.

electromagnetic field the region surrounding a moving electric charge that consists of magnetic and electric force fields specially related, e.g., as to orientation and strength, and that possesses a definite amount of energy

electromagnetic induction the generation of an electromotive force in a conductor or circuit due to the relative motion of the conductor and a magnetic field, or by a change in the magnetic field strength in the neighborhood of a conductor or circuit

electromagnetic wave a wave propagated through space or a medium by simultaneous periodic variation in the electric and magnetic-field intensity at right angles to each other and to the direction of propagation. The electromagnetic spectrum includes radio waves, microwaves, infrared, visible and ultraviolet radiation, X rays, gamma rays and cosmic rays (in order of decreasing wavelength) and each wavelength is associated (*WAVE-PARTICLE DUALITY) with a photon whose energy increases with decreasing wavelength. The speed of electromagnetic waves is 2.998 x 10^8 m/sec. in a vacuum. This is regarded in relativistic physics as being a universal constant and the theoretical limit to the speed attainable by a particle or body, even one with a rest mass of 0

e·lec·tro·mag·ne·tism (ilẹktroumǽgnitịzəm) *n.* the magnetic force produced by an electric current (e.g., in an electromagnet) ‖ the science which studies the interrelation of electricity and magnetism

e·lec·tro·met·al·lur·gy (ilẹktroumét'lə:rdʒi:, ilẹktroumətǽlərdʒi:) *n.* the science of the electrical processes or methods used industrially for separating metals from alloys, or for refining or shaping metals

e·lec·trom·e·ter (ilektrómitər) *n.* any of several types of instrument that are actuated by the forces between charged bodies and are used to indicate the presence of ionizing radiation and to measure potential differences, e.g., an electroscope **e·lec·tro·met·ric** (ilẹktroumétrik) *adj.* **e·lec·tro·mét·ri·cal·ly** *adv.* **e·lec·trom·e·try** (ilektrómitri:) *n.*

e·lec·tro·mo·tive (ilẹktroumóutiv) *adj.* producing electric current

electromotive force (*abbr.* emf) potential difference

electromotive force series electromotive series

electromotive series the chemical elements or ions arranged according to their standard electrode potential, the order usually showing the tendency of any given element to reduce the ones below it in the series (*OXIDATION-REDUCTION POTENTIAL)

e·lec·tro·my·o·graph (ilẹktroumáiəgræf) *n.* device to record electrical voltage generated by body muscles **electromyogram (EMG)** *n.*

e·lec·tron (iléktron) *n.* a lepton of rest mass 0.511 x 10^6 eV (9.107+ 10^{-28} gm) and electric charge —1 (the electron's charge is the fundamental unit of electric charge equal to 1.602 x 10^{-19} coulomb). The electron is a constituent of the atom [ELECTRIC + -*on*, fundamental particle]

electron affinity the energy required to remove an electron from an ion possessing a single negative charge (cf. IONIZATION POTENTIAL)

e·lec·tro·nar·co·sis (ilẹktrounarkóusis) *n.* (*med.*) semiconsciousness, sometimes passing to unconsciousness, created by electric shock, used in mental therapy, sometimes by anesthesia *Cf* ELECTROCONVULSIVE THERAPY

e·lec·tron-beam laser (ilẹktronbíːm) a laser controlled by an electron beam, used in presenting graphic data on a video screen

electron diffraction an effect due to the fact that a beam of electrons behaves as a wave of very high frequency (*WAVE-PARTICLE DUALITY) and can therefore be diffracted by slits that are roughly of the order of the atomic dimensions (1 -5 Å) of crystals and dense gases. Electron diffraction is used to study the structure of crystals, surface layers of solids and the molecular structure of gases, by allowing a beam of electrons of known energy (and wavelength) to traverse a material of unknown structure, calculating the atomic dimensions from the diffraction pattern

electron diffraction (*optics*) the creation of a lattice by the diffraction of atoms in a crystal

e·lec·tro·neg·a·tive (ilẹktrounégativ) *adj.* carrying a negative electric charge, and then tending to move to the anode in electrolysis ‖ having a tendency to become negative by gaining electrons

e·lec·tro·neg·a·tiv·i·ty (ilẹktrounegətíviti:) *n.* the state, quality or degree of being electronegative

electron gun a cathode and the assembly used to control and focus a stream of thermal electrons emitted from it, used esp. in a cathode ray tube or X-ray tube

e·lec·tron·ic (ilektrónik) *adj.* of or relating to electronics ‖ working or produced by the action of electrons **e·lec·trón·i·cal·ly** *adv.* **e·lec·trón·ics** *n.* the branch of physics dealing with the behavior of electrons in vacuums and gases, with their conduction, with effects in semiconductors, and with the utilization of these properties for the design of electronic devices

electronic art art form utilizing flashing light displays

electronic banking use of magnetically encoded plastic cards at terminals outside a regular bank location for check cashing, deposits, and other money transfer functions *Cf* EFT

electronic calculator a calculator that utilizes integrated electronic circuits to perform arithmetic functions

electronic compositor a device for setting type electronically with characters generated by laser beams

electronic computer a device capable of performing systematic sequences of operation upon data, including numerous arithmetic and logic procedures, without intervention by a human operator during the run

electronic countermeasure (*mil.*) a device designed to misdirect guidance system of an attacking missile

electronic games devices, e.g., electronic tennis, that enable players to manipulate electronic impulses viewed on a display screen (usu. a television set)

e·lec·tron·i·cize (ilektrónisaiz) *v.* to install electronic systems

electronic larynx a device used by those without vocal cords to simulate speech through the use of an electronically controlled artificial larynx inside tube or outside the voice box

electronic lock a security device that responds to a magnetically encoded plastic card

electronic mail system of electronic transmission of postal messages between post offices, e.g., Mailgram, Intelpost

electronic music musical compositions created for tape recording by electronic devices in a laboratory

electronic position indicator a device used to measure ship-to-shore distances by measuring the time elapsed for a radio echo **acronym** EPI

electronic profilometer a device for measuring roughness by the changing voltage in a stylus passed over a surface

electronic watch a timepiece utilizing battery-powered electronic circuits to activate a tuning fork or quartz crystal to sustain movement

electronic warfare (*mil.*) military action involving the use of electromagnetic energy to determine, exploit, reduce, or prevent hostile use of the electromagnetic spectrum, and at the same time retaining its friendly use

electron lens a device for converging or diverging a beam of electrons by means of electric and/or magnetic fields. It is used in the electron microscope, cathode ray tube, etc.

electron microprobe (*med.*) X-ray device that focuses a stream of electrons on a point and measures the backscattered electrons, the resulting radiation fluorescence, etc.

electron microscope a microscope of extremely high magnification and resolving power in which a beam of electrons, focused by means of an electron lens, is made to form an enlarged image of an object on a fluorescent screen or photographic plate. It is used to examine the structure of bacteria, viruses, colloidal particles, etc.

e·lec·tron·o·graph (ilektrónəgræf) *n.* a device that produces images on a photographic emulsion through the use of an accelerated beam of electrons **electronograph** *n.* the image produced **electronography** *v.* the process

e·lec·tron·og·ra·phy (ilẹktronógrəfi:) *n.* production of photographic images using a cathode ray tube

electron synchroton a device designed to accelerate electrons by striking them against a target that will produce gamma rays

electron telescope (*optics*) a telescopic device that focuses the infrared light on a photosensitive cathode that converts and enlarges the image *Cf* ELECTRON MICROSCOPE, SNIPERSCOPE, SNOOPERSCOPE

electron transport system (*biochem.*) biological oxidizing agents arranged in a sequence of increasing strength to form compounds of oxygen and ultimately, oxygen

electron tube an electronic device that consists of a glass or metal container either evacuated or filled with an inert gas, that contains a cathode or filament emitting a stream of electrons, and one or more grids that regulate the stream on its path to the anode or plate. Electron tubes have many uses in modern electronics, the most common being to amplify the energy of an elec-

trical signal or to convert a direct current to an alternating current and vice versa

electron valve an electron tube

electron volt (*phys.*, symbol eV) a unit of energy equal to that gained by an electron in passing through a difference in potential of one volt. 1eV=1.6x 10^{-12} erg

e·lec·tro·nys·tag·mog·ra·phy (ilẹktrɒnistægmógraːi:) *n.* (*med.*) process of recording eye movements used in assessing abnormal eye movements **electronystagmogram** *n.* the record

e·lec·tro·oc·u·lo·gram (ilẹktrouókjuləgræm) *n.* (*med.*) record of measurement of voltage between front and back of eye, used esp. in studying eyeball movement, esp. in sleep *Cf* REM

e·lec·tro·op·tics (ilẹktrouóptiks) *n.* the interaction between optics and electronics leading to the transformation of electrical energy into light or vice versa

e·lec·tro·phone (iléktrəfoun) *n.* a musical instrument that produces electronic music

e·lec·tro·pho·re·sis (ilẹktroufərí:sis) *n.* the movement of suspended particles in a fluid under the influence of an electric field. The separation and identification of proteins and other colloids and the coating of objects with rubber and synthetic polymers are widely used applications [ELECTRO-+ Gk *phorēsis*, being carried]

e·lec·troph·o·rus (ilẹktrófərəs) *pl.* **e·lec·troph·o·ri** (ilẹktrófərai) *n.* a simple device for the production of an electrostatic charge by induction [fr. ELECTRO- + Gk *phoros*, carried]

e·lec·tro·phren·ic respiration (ilẹktrɒfrénik) a device that stimulates the nerve that controls breathing by electrodes placed appropriately. It was designed as a means of artificial respiration and is often so used

e·lec·tro·plate (iléktrəpleit) 1. *v.t. pres. part.* **e·lec·tro·plat·ing** *past* and *past part.* **e·lec·tro·plat·ed** to plate by electrodeposition 2. *n.* something electroplated ‖ such articles collectively

e·lec·tro·pos·i·tive (ilẹktroupózitiv) *adj.* carrying a positive electric charge, tending to move toward the cathode in electrolysis ‖ having a tendency to become positive by releasing electrons, esp. in redox reactions

e·lec·tro·ret·i·nog·ra·phy (ilẹktrourẹtinógræfi:) *n.* the measurement and recording of electrical activity in the retina **electroretinograph** *n.* the instrument **electroretinographic** *adj.*

e·lec·tro·scope (iléktrəskoup) *n.* (*phys.*) an instrument which detects the presence of an electric charge by means of the motion of a charged indicator brought in the neighborhood of the unknown charge. It can be used to determine whether the charge is positive or negative and to indicate the presence of ionizing radiation **e·lec·tro·scop·ic** (ilẹktrəskópik) *adj.* [fr. ELECTRO-+ Gk *skopein*, to observe]

e·lec·tro·shock therapy (iléktrəʃpk) therapy using an electric current to induce coma

e·lec·tro·sleep (iléktrəsli:p) *n.* sleep state induced by low-voltage electricity passed through the brain

e·lec·tro·stat·ic (ilẹktroustǽtik) *adj.* relating to static electricity or to electrostatics

e·lec·tro·stat·ic copier (ilẹktroustǽtik) device for making copies of written material utilizing a charged powdered carbon toner received as an image from material oppositely charged; e.g., the Xerox and Electrofax processes

electrostatic induction the development of a localized charge on a body due to the presence (without contact) of a charged object

electrostatic precipitator air-pollution control device that imparts an electrical charge to particles in a gas stream, causing them to collect on an electrode

electrostatic printer device that prints lines by projecting images onto a drum in electrostatic patterns that attract a powdered ink. These in turn are transferred and fused onto the paper **electrostatic printing** *n.*

e·lec·tro·stat·ics (ilẹktroustǽtiks) *n.* a branch of physics dealing with the study of the forces of interaction of nonmoving electrical charges (cf. ELECTRODYNAMICS)

electrostatic unit (*abbr.* esu) one of a system of units based on the forces between two charged particles, e.g., in the cgs system of units the fundamental electrostatic unit is the statcoulomb

e·lec·tro·steth·o·phone (ilẹktrəstéthəfoun) *n.* (*med.*) a stethoscope equipped with microphone and amplifier

e·lec·tro·ther·a·py (ilɛktrouθérəpi:) *n.* the treatment of disorders by electricity (electric current, radiation etc.)

e·lec·trot·o·nus (ilɛktrót'nəs) *n.* the state of a nerve subjected to the passage of an electric current [Mod. L. fr. ELECTRO-+ Gk *tonos*, tension]

e·lec·tro·type (ilɛ́ktrətaip) 1. *n.* a printing plate made by coating a wax impression (e.g., of standing type) with graphite and then depositing copper on it by electrolysis, the product being backed by a lead alloy ‖ a copy made by this process 2. *v. pres. part.* **e·lec·tro·typ·ing** *past* and *past part.* **e·lec·tro·typed** *v.t.* to print (copies) from an electrotype ‖ *v.i.* to make an electrotype **e·léc·tro·typ·er** *n.*

e·lec·tro·va·lence (ilɛktrouvéiləns) *n.* the transfer of one or more electrons from one atom to another, with the formation of ions, resulting in an ionic bond (cf. COVALENCE) ‖ the number of charges acquired by an atom during compound or ion formation **e·lec·tro·va·lent** *adj.*

electrovalent bond a chemical bond formed by electrovalence

e·lec·trum (ilɛ́ktrəm) *n.* an alloy of gold and silver (from about half to about three-quarters gold) used in ancient times [L. fr. *Gk ēlektron*, amber]

e·lec·tu·ar·y (ilɛ́ktʃuːəri:) *pl.* **e·lec·tu·ar·ies** *n.* (*old-fash.*) a medicine mixed with honey or syrup to make a sweet, soothing paste [fr. L.L. *electuarium*]

e·le·doi·sin [C₅₄H₈₅N₁₃O₁₅S] (elɛdóisin) *n.* (*pharm.*) protein drug, derived from salivary glands of octopuses, that causes dilation of blood vessels and reduction of blood pressure

e·lee·mos·y·nar·y (ɛlimósinɛri:, ɛli:imósinɛri:) *adj.* relating to the giving of alms or to charitable works ‖ supported by, or devoted to, such purposes, charitable [fr. M.L. *eleemosynarius* fr. Gk]

e·le·gance (éligəns) *n.* the state or quality of being elegant [F. *élégance*]

e·le·gant (éligənt) *adj.* gracefully refined ‖ neatly and beautifully made or constructed, e.g., of a mathematical proof ‖ showing good taste, refined, polite, *elegant manners* ‖ fashionable, smart ‖ (*pop.*) very good of its kind [F. élégant]

e·le·gi·ac (ɛlidʒáiək) 1. *adj.* in the form or mood of an elegy, or in elegiacs ‖ mournful, sadly remembering the past 2. *n.* an elegiac couplet ‖ (*pl.*) a poem in elegiac couplets **e·le·gí·a·cal** *adj.* [fr. L. *elegiacus*]

elegiac couplet a meter, used in Greek and Latin verse, in which dactylic hexameters alternate with pentameters

e·le·gist (élidʒist) *n.* a writer of elegies

e·le·gize (élidʒaiz) *pres. part.* **e·le·giz·ing** *past* and *past part.* **e·le·gized** *v.t.* to lament the death of (someone) in an elegy ‖ *v.i.* to write an elegy

el·e·gy (élidʒi:) *pl.* **el·e·gies** *n.* a poem which laments the death of someone ‖ a poem written in a nostalgic or melancholy mood ‖ (*Greek and Latin poetry*) a poem in elegiac meter [fr. F. élégie fr. L. fr. Gk]

el·e·ment (éləmənt) *n.* one of the simplest parts into which something can be divided, or a component of a composite whole ‖ something which is present in small quantity in a larger whole, *there is an element of truth in what he said* ‖ (*pl.*) the simplest and most basic parts of a branch of knowledge, *the elements of mathematics* ‖ (*pl., rhet.*) atmospheric forces, *to brave the elements* (to force oneself to go out into the storm) ‖ (*pl.*) earth, air, fire and water, formerly regarded as the basic constituents of the material universe ‖ (*biol.*) the natural habitat of an organism (water, dry land etc.) ‖ (*chem.*) any of more than 100 substances that never have been separated into simpler substances by ordinary chemical means (cf. COMPOUND). Each is considered to contain atoms all of the same atomic number. All matter consists of elements, either individually or in combination. When arranged in order of increasing atomic number the elements display a characteristic periodic variation in chemical and physical properties (*PERIODIC TABLE*). Most elements lighter than and including uranium occur in nature, the heavier ones being produced artificially (*RADIOELEMENT*) ‖ any distinct part of a composite device, e.g., each of the individual lenses of an objective ‖ (*eccles.*) the matter of a sacrament (i.e. the material thing or action, e.g., the water in baptism or the imposition of hands in holy orders, which take on a Sacramental significance), esp.

(*pl.*) the bread and wine of the Eucharist ‖ (*elec.*) the resistance coil, wire, of an electric heater, kiln, etc., **to be in (out of) one's element** to feel utterly at ease (lost, constrained), *he is in his element playing with children* **el·e·men·tal** (ɛlɛmént'l) 1. *adj.* pertaining to the primitive forces of nature ‖ (*hist.*) of one of the four elements (earth, air, fire, water) ‖ elementary 2. *n.* a spirit identified with one of the primitive forces of nature [O.F.]

el·e·men·ta·ry (ɛləméntəri:, ɛləméntri:) *adj.* very simple, basic, *elementary good manners* ‖ consisting of the simplest parts of a branch of knowledge, *elementary physics* ‖ consisting of a single chemical element [fr. L. *elementarius* fr. *elementum*, a component part]

elementary particle a fundamental particle

elementary school a school of eight grades teaching basic subjects ‖ (in systems with a junior high school) a similar school of six grades

el·e·mi (élɛmi:) *n.* any of several fragrant oleoresins obtained from tropical trees of fam. *Burseraceae* and used in inks, varnishes, lacquers, etc. Manila elemi is obtained by gashing the trunk of *Canarium luzonicum*, a large Philippine tree [F. *élémi*, prob. fr. Arab. *al-lami*]

e·len·chus (ilénkəs) *pl.* **e·len·chi** (ilénkai) *n.* (*logic*) the refutation of another's argument, esp. syllogistically **e·lénc·tic, e·lénc·ti·cal** *adjs* [L. fr. Gk *elenchos*, cross-examination]

el·e·phant (élifənt) *n.* the Indian *Elephas indicus* or the African *Loxodonta africana*, both fam. *Elephantidae*, the largest living land animals, standing 9-12 ft high and weighing 5-6 tons. The nose is an elongated and prehensile trunk. *Loxodonta africana* differs from *Elephas indicus* by its greater height, larger ears, less elevated head, heavier bones and ivory tusks ‖ a size of drawing paper, commonly 28 × 23 ins [M.E. *olifaunt* fr. O.F. fr. L. fr. Gk]

El·e·phan·ta (ɛlifǽntə) (Gharapuri) a small island in the Gulf of Bombay famous for its temple caves (first half of the 6th c. A.D.) adorned with figures of Hindu deities

elephant grass a member of *Pennisetum*, fam. *Gramineae*, a genus of savanna grasses, widely grown for forage ‖ *Typha elephantina*, fam. *Typhaceae*, a tall marsh plant found from S. Europe to the East Indies. Its leaves are used for mats, baskets etc.

el·e·phan·ti·a·sis (ɛlifǽntáiəsis) *n.* filariasis, a tropical disease caused by the multiplication of worms in the body. It is spread by mosquitoes. The worms do little harm when alive, but when dead they block the lymphatic ducts and glands (*LYMPH*), thus causing gross swelling of various parts of the body, esp. the legs and genitals [L. fr. Gk *elephas*, elephant (because of the tough texture of the skin caused by this disease)]

el·e·phan·tine (ɛlifǽnti:n, ɛlifǽntain) *adj.* of or like an elephant ‖ huge and clumsy, *elephantine buk* ‖ pompous and heavy-handed, *elephantine humor* [fr. L. fr. Gk *elephantinos*]

elephant seal *Mirounga leonina*, a large seal (up to 20 ft) of the southern hemisphere, with a long proboscis. Hunters have almost eliminated it ‖ *Mirounga angustirostris*, a smaller seal surviving in a protected herd

elephant shrew a shrew of genus *Macroscelides*, leaping, long-legged, long-nosed insectivores, native to Africa

E·leu·sin·i·an (ɛlju:síni:ən) *adj.* of Eleusis

E·leu·sis (ilú:sis) an ancient city of Attica, Greece, on the Bay of Eleusis, 12 miles northeast of Athens, where the Eleusinian Mysteries, centered on the worship of Demeter, were celebrated. The modern town (pop. 11,000) is one of Greece's few industrial centers: olive oil, distilleries, cement, aluminum

el·e·vate (éliveit) *pres. part.* **el·e·vat·ing** *past* and *past part.* **el·e·vat·ed** *v.t.* to raise to a higher level ‖ to raise in rank or dignity ‖ to raise in price, value, importance, etc. ‖ to raise to a higher moral or intellectual level ‖ to encourage (hopes) or raise (spirits) ‖ (*eccles.*) to raise (the Host) in adoration ‖ to raise the axis of (a gun) or the sights of (a rifle) [fr. L. *elevare* (*elevatus*), to raise]

el·e·vat·ed (éliveitid) 1. *adj.* raised up, lofty ‖ high in rank or dignity ‖ morally or intellectually lofty, *elevated style* ‖ (of importance, value, price etc.) very high or too high 2. *n.* an elevated railroad [past part. of ELEVATE]

elevated railroad (*Am.*) an urban transport system above street level

elevated railway elevated railroad

el·e·va·tion (ɛlivéiʃən) *n.* an elevating or being elevated ‖ height above sea level ‖ loftiness, grandeur ‖ (*archit.*) a side or end view of a building, etc. or a drawing of this view (cf. PLAN) ‖ a hill or piece of rising ground ‖ (*ballet*) a leap, the dancer appearing to hang for a moment in the air ‖ (*astron.*) the angular distance of a heavenly body above the horizon ‖ the angle with the horizontal at which a gun is laid **the Elevation** (*eccles.*) the lifting up of the Host in adoration [fr. L. *elevatio* (*elevationis*)]

el·e·va·tion tint *HYPOSEMETRIC TINTING*

el·e·va·tor (éliveitər) *n.* a machine that can raise or carry a weight from one level to another ‖ (*Am.=Br.* lift) a mechanical apparatus for raising or lowering people or things from floor to floor in a building ‖ a tall building or tower into which grain is mechanically hoisted for storage ‖ (*wrestling*) maneuver in which a wrestler places his leg behind one of his opponent's legs and raises it to cause an imbalance ‖ one of the control surfaces of an aircraft (situated in the tail assembly) which governs climb and descent ‖ a muscle which controls the lifting of a part of the body (cf. DEPRESSOR) [L. = one who, or that which, elevates]

e·lev·en (ilévən) 1. *adj.* being one more than 10 (*NUMBER TABLE*) 2. *n.* 10 plus one ‖ the cardinal number representing this (11, XI) ‖ 11 o'clock ‖ a team of 11 members, e.g., in field hockey [O.E. *endleofon*]

e·lev·en·plus examination (ilévənplʌs) (*Br.*) a test taken at the age of 10 or 11 by children attending primary schools in some localities, to determine which type of secondary school (grammar, technical or secondary modern) they will attend

e·lev·enth (ilévənθ) 1. *adj.* being number 11 in a series (*NUMBER TABLE*) ‖ being one of the 11 equal parts of anything **at the eleventh hour** at the last possible moment ‖ in the nick of time 2. *n.* the person or thing next after the tenth ‖ one of 11 equal parts of anything (1/11) ‖ the 11th day of a month [O.E. *endlyfta, œllefta*]

Eleventh Amendment (1798) an amendment to the U.S. Constitution that limits citizens of one state, or foreign subjects, from bringing suit in federal court against the government of another state unless that state consents. It also applies to citizens of a state bringing suit against their own state. It may not be used by state officers to protect against suits based on individual performance

el·e·von (élɛvɒn) *n.* an aircraft control surface that functions both as an elevator and as an aileron [ELEVATOR+AILERON]

elf (elf) *pl.* **elves** (elvz) *n.* a little creature of folklore with magic power, often mischievous or malicious, but sometimes kind and helpful ‖ an elflike child or person [O.E. *œlf*]

El Fer·rol (elferról) (El Ferrol del Caudillo) a town and naval station (pop. 82,000) with a fine natural harbor in the northwest corner of Spain (Galicia): shipbuilding, fishing, linen and leather industries

elf·in (élfin) 1. *adj.* of or relating to elves, elflike ‖ fey 2. *n.* an elf

elf·ish (élfiʃ) *adj.* of or relating to elves ‖ mischievous

El·gar (élgɑr, élgɑr, Sir Edward (1857–1934), English composer, best known for his cello concerto (1919), two symphonies (1908, 1911), the 'Enigma' variations (1899) and the oratorio 'The Dream of Gerontius' (1900)

El·gin marbles (élgin) a collection of ancient Greek sculptures and inscriptions salvaged from the Acropolis in Athens after its bombardment by the Turks, conveyed to England by Lord Elgin (1766–1841), and bought by the British government (1816) for the British Museum

El·gin·shire (élginʃiər, élginʃər) *MORAYSHIRE*

El·gon, Mt (élgɒn) an extinct volcano (14,178 ft) on the boundary of Kenya and Uganda. The crater is 5 miles across

El Greco *GRECO*

el·hi (élhai) *n.* school for grades 1–12

E·li·a (í:li:ə, í:ljə) *LAMB, Charles*

e·lic·it (ilísit) *v.t.* to draw forth in response, *to elicit a protest* ‖ to arrive at (the truth, etc.) by questioning or other logical process [fr. L. *elicere* (*elicitus*), to entice]

e·lide (iláid) *pres. part.* **e·lid·ing** *past* and *past part.* **e·lid·ed** *v.t.* to drop (a vowel or syllable) in pronunciation ‖ to suppress, strike out (figures, words, etc.) [fr. L. *elidere*]

E·lié·cer Gai·tán (eljésergaitán), Jorge (*d.* 1948), Colombian politician, leader of the Liberal party. His assassination in Bogotá triggered a political war between liberals and conservatives, causing casualties estimated at 200,000

el·i·gi·bil·i·ty (ęlidʒəbíliti:) n. the state or quality of being eligible

el·i·gi·ble (élidʒəb'l) adj. qualified to be chosen, *eligible for reelection* ‖ entitled to receive, *eligible for a pension* ‖ desirable, suitable, esp. having the advantages looked for by prospective mothers-in-law [F. *éligible*]

E·li·jah (iláidʒə) (c. 870–840 B.C.), a prophet of Israel. He bravely resisted the recrudescence of heathenism under Ahab and Ahaziah. His influence was so great that he was cast in the role of herald of the Messiah. St Matthew correlates John the Baptist with him (I Kings, xvii–xxi and II Kings, i, ii)

e·lim·i·nate (ilímineit) *pres. part.* **e·lim·i·nat·ing** *past and past part.* **e·lim·i·nat·ed** v.t. to get rid of, *to eliminate error* ‖ to cause to be no longer included, *to eliminate from a competition* ‖ (*physiol.*) to get rid of by expelling, excrete ‖ (*math.*) to remove (a quantity) from an equation **e·lim·i·na·tion, e·lím·i·na·tor** ns **e·lim·i·na·to·ry** (ilíminətɔ̣ri:, ilíminətouri) adj. [fr. L. *eliminare* (*eliminatus*), to thrust out of]

el·in·var (élinvɑr) n. a nickel-chromium alloy, the elasticity of which is unaffected by changes of temperature, used for the hairsprings of watches [ELASTICITY + INVARIABLE]

El·i·ot (éli:ət, éljət), Charles William (1834–1926), U.S. educator, and president (1869–1909) of Harvard University. He championed the elimination of required courses and raised Harvard's entrance requirements, strongly influencing national secondary education. He edited (1909–10) the 50-volume 'Harvard Classics'

Eliot, George (Mary Ann Evans, 1819–80), English novelist. Her earlier group of novels ('Adam Bede', 1859, 'The Mill on the Floss', 1860, and 'Silas Marner', 1861) are the most popular, but 'Middlemarch' (1872) is considered her greatest work. She was a rationalist, with a strong sense of morality, concerning herself with problems of ethical behavior as well as the social and psychological conflicts arising from the impact of the Industrial Revolution on the middle class. She portrayed faithfully the life and character of the Midlands over a wide range of social levels

Eliot, John (1604–90), New England colonial minister. He led a missionary movement to convert the Algonquian Indians to Christianity and introduce them to the English way of life. He translated (1661–3) the Bible into an Algonquian language. This was the first version in any language to be printed in America

Eliot, Sir John (1592–1632), English statesman, one of the leaders of parliamentary opposition to Charles I

Eliot, Thomas Stearns (1888–1965), poet and critic. American by birth, he became a British subject in 1927. 'The Waste Land' (1922) and other early poems brought him wide recognition. During the 1920s and '30s his poetry (esp. 'Ash Wednesday', 1930), his first play ('Murder in the Cathedral', 1935) and his extremely influential criticism ('The Sacred Wood', 1920, and later volumes, together with his work as editor of 'The Criterion', 1922–39), were largely responsible for a revolution in English and American taste. He emerged as the leading writer in English of his generation. Other plays are 'The Family Reunion' (1939), 'The Cocktail Party' (1950) and 'The Confidential Clerk' (1954). His early poetry was thought to express the disillusion of the postwar generation: it could more accurately be taken as the poetic examination of a bereft world, without belief. Most of his work is a prolonged exploration of the linguistic, cultural and philosophical means of restoring or creating the possibility of positive belief. Perhaps his greatest work is 'Four Quartets' (1936–42)

E·lis (í:lis) a region in the N.W. Peloponnesus, Greece, and its ancient capital, now ruins. The region included Olympia and was powerful in the 6th c.

E·lis·a·beth·ville (ilízəbəθvíl) *LUBUMBASHI

E·li·sha (iláiʃə) (c. 850 B.C.–795 B.C.), Old Testament prophet. He inherited the prophetic mantle of Elijah, but was of greater political than religious importance (I Kings xix, 19–21 and II Kings ii–ix and xiii, 14–19)

e·li·sion (ilíʒən) n. the dropping of a vowel or syllable in pronunciation (e.g., 'I'm' for 'I am') [fr. L. *elisio* (*elisionis*)]

e·lite, *Br.* **é·lite** (ilí:t, eilí:t) n. the few who are considered socially, intellectually or professionally superior to the rest in a group or society ‖ a typewriter face of 12 characters to the inch, 6 lines to the vertical inch [F.]

e·lix·ir (ilíksər) n. a substance sought by alchemists for converting base metals into gold ‖ (*pharm.*) an aromatic preparation, often sweetened and containing alcohol, used for flavoring drugs [M.L. fr. Arab. *al-iksir* prob. fr. *al,* the + Gk *xērion,* a powder used to treat wounds fr. *xēron,* dry]

E·liz·a·beth (ilízəbəθ), mother of John the Baptist, wife of the high priest Zacharias, and cousin of the Virgin Mary

Elizabeth, St (1207–31), daughter of Andrew II, king of Hungary. She married (1222) Louis, landgrave of Thuringia. After his early death (1227) she devoted her life to asceticism and charity. Feast: Nov. 19

Elizabeth (1709–62), empress of Russia (1741–62), daughter of Peter I. A shrewd politician, she gained power by overthrowing Ivan VI, and brought Frederick II of Prussia near to ruin in the Seven Years' War. She was a patron of learning and French culture

Elizabeth I (1533–1603), queen of England (1558–1603), daughter of Henry VIII and Anne Boleyn. Imprisoned in the reign of her sister Mary I, Elizabeth came to the throne (1558) to face problems of religious strife, unstable finances and war with France. With Burghley as her adviser, she tackled the economic problem, ended the war (1559), and reestablished the Church of England on the moderate basis of the Acts of Supremacy and Uniformity (1559) and the Thirty-nine Articles (1563). The queen offers of marriage from Philip II of Spain and others to further her policy of playing off the Catholic powers of Europe against one another, while taking care to remain single. But Catholic plots at home necessitated increasingly severe measures against Catholics as well as the imprisonment (1568) of Mary queen of Scots, whom Elizabeth finally executed (1587) after the Babington plot. Mary's death led Philip II to send the Spanish Armada (1588) in a vain attempt to conquer England. The end of the reign was marked by the growth of Puritan opposition in parliament, where the questions of monopolies and of the succession to the throne caused bitter disputes with the queen. Ireland, in revolt since 1569, was pacified (1600–3), and a rising (1601) under Elizabeth's former favorite Essex was put down. The Elizabethan age saw the beginnings of social legislation in the Poor Laws of 1563 and 1601. Abroad, it was an age of maritime expansion under such adventurers as Hawkins, Raleigh, Frobisher and Drake. In literature, it was the age of Shakespeare, Sidney, Spenser and Marlowe, and there was also a flowering of music, architecture and art. Elizabeth's autocratic vanity and obstinacy were in keeping with a new mood of ebullient nationalism

Elizabeth II (1926–), queen of the United Kingdom of Great Britain and Northern Ireland, and head of the Commonwealth, since 1952, daughter of George VI. Although her duties as a constitutional monarch are largely ceremonial she is conscientious about conducting them. She celebrated the 25th anniversary of her accession in 1977

elk (elk) n. *Alces alces,* the largest of the deer family inhabiting N. Europe and Asia. Adults stand 6 ft high and the male bears very broad, heavy antlers ‖ *Cervus canadensis,* the wapiti ‖ a member of the Elks, a prominent fraternal society [prob. fr. M.H.G. *elch*]

El Kerak *KERAK

El Kha·lil (elkæli:l) *HEBRON

elk·hound (élkhaund) n. a Norwegian dog of a breed bred originally for hunting elks or bears. It is of medium build (height about 20 ins, weight up to 50 lbs). It has a thick close coat and short curled tail

ell (el) n. a former measure of length (Babylonian ell about 39 ins, English ell about 45 ins, Flemish and Dutch ell about 27 ins) [O.E. *eln*]

Elles·mere Island (élzmiər) the northernmost island (area 76,000 sq. miles), mountainous and ice-covered, of the Canadian archipelago, west of N. Greenland, part of Canada's Northwest Territories

El·lice Islands *TUVALU

El·ling·ton (élintən), Edward Kennedy ('Duke' Ellington, 1899–1974), U.S. jazz pianist, composer and conductor

el·lipse (ilíps) n. (*geom.*) a plane figure obtained when a plane intersects a cone obliquely. The sum of the distances of any point on its perimeter from either of two points (foci) within it is constant [L. fr. Gk *elleipsis,* a shortcoming defect]

el·lip·sis (ilípsis) *pl.* **el·lip·ses** (ilípsi:z) n. (*gram.*) a construction leaving out one or more words which must be understood for the grammatical completeness of a sentence, or an instance of this, as in 'it's a book I would like to read' ‖ (*printing*) the use of dots or dashes to indicate that a word or more, or part of a word, has been omitted, e.g., 'd ... d' for 'damned' [L.]

el·lip·soid (ilípsɔid) n. (*geom.*) the surface produced by the rotation of an ellipse around of its axes ‖ the corresponding solid. The earth, for example, is an oblate ellipsoid **el·lip·sói·dal** adj.

el·lip·so·me·ter (ilípsəmi:tər) n. (*electr.*) a device for measuring thickness of films of semiconductors

el·lip·tic (ilíptik) adj. having the form of an ellipse ‖ characterized by ellipsis **el·líp·ti·cal** adj.

El·lis Island (élis) an island in Upper New York Bay, about 1 mile southwest of Manhattan I. It was the chief U.S. immigration station (1892–1943)

El·lo·ra (elɔ́rə, elóurə) a village in Maharashtra, India, near which are Buddhist, Hindu and Jain temples (4th–8th cc.), many carved out of the solid rock of the hillside

El·lore (elɔ́r) *ELURU

Ells·worth (élzwərθ), Lincoln (1880–1951), U.S. explorer, the first person to complete a trans-Arctic (1926) and trans-Antarctic (1935) air crossing. He claimed 300,000 sq. miles of Antarctic terrain for the U.S.A.

elm (elm) n. a member of *Ulmus,* fam. *Ulmaceae,* a genus of tall, graceful, deciduous trees of temperate regions with simple, asymmetrical leaves and hermaphrodite flowers which open before the leaves. The fruit is a samara. The wood is so cross-grained as to be nearly unsplitable, and has many uses. Elms are threatened by Dutch elm disease [O.E.]

El O·beid (eloubéid) a market town (pop. 57,000) of central Sudan: cattle, cereals, gum

el·o·cu·tion (eləkjú:ʃən) n. the art of speaking or reading correctly, clearly, pleasantly and forcefully, esp. in public **el·o·cú·tion·a·ry** adj. **el·o·cú·tion·ist** n. someone skilled in, or who teaches, the art [fr. L. *elocutio* (*elocutionis*)]

E·lo·him (elóuhim,elouhí:m) n. one of the Old Testament names for 'deity'. When used with a definite article it is the personal name of Yahweh, the God of Israel [Heb. = gods, but often taken as sing.]

e·lon·gate (ilɔ́ngeit, ilɔ́ŋgeit, i:lɔ́ngeit, í:lɔngeit) **1.** v. *pres. part.* **e·lon·gat·ing** *past and past part.* **e·lon·gat·ed** v.t. to make longer ‖ v.i. to increase in length **2.** adj. (*biol.*) long and slender [fr. L. *elongare* (*elongatus*)]

e·lon·ga·tion (ilɔngéiʃən, ilɔŋgéiʃən, i:lɔŋgéiʃən, i:lɔŋgéiʃən) n. a lengthening or being lengthened ‖ something elongated ‖ (*astron.*) the angular distance of a planet from the sun or of a satellite from its primary [fr. L.L. *elongatio* (*elongationis*) fr. *elongare,* to remove further]

e·lope (ilóup) *pres. part.* **e·lop·ing** *past and past part.* **e·loped** v.i. (of a lover or pair of lovers) to run away with the intention of getting married ‖ (*Br., law,* of a married woman) to leave one's husband and go off with a lover **e·lópe·ment** n. [A.F. *aloper,* to run away]

el·o·quence (éləkwəns) n. the fluent, skillful use of words to persuade or move hearers or readers [F. *éloquence*]

el·o·quent (éləkwənt) adj. speaking or writing with eloquence ‖ spoken or written with eloquence ‖ (*rhet.*) clearly and movingly indicative, *the ruins were eloquent of some sudden tragedy* [F. *éloquent*]

El Pas·o (elpǽsou) an industrial and commercial city (pop. 277,000) in W. Texas, on the Rio Grande opposite Ciudad Juárez, Mexico

El·phege (élfidʒ), St (954–1012), archbishop of Canterbury (1006–12). He was taken prisoner when the Danes sacked the city, and murdered at Greenwich on his refusal to pay ransom. Feast: Apr. 19

El Sal·va·dor (elsælvədór, elsælvədər) a republic (area 8,260 sq. miles, pop. 4,940,000) of Central America. Capital: San Salvador. People: Mestizo and of European origin, Indian minority. Language: Spanish. Religion: Roman Catholic. The land is 34% forest, 33% pasture and 25% cultivated. Between the east-west chains of volcanic highlands (rising to over 7,000 ft) lie the fertile basins of the center (at 2,000 ft). The north is savanna lowland. Earthquakes are frequent. Average temperature (center) 70–75° F. Annual rainfall: 80 ins. Livestock: cattle, horses. Minerals: gold, silver. Manufactures: textiles, hydroelectricity. Exports: coffee, balsam (main world source). Other products: cotton, rice, corn, sugar, lumber, dyes. Imports: manufactures, machinery, wheat, fuel oils. Ports: La Unión, La Libertad, Acajutla. University at San Salvador. Monetary unit: colón (100 centavos). HISTORY. El Salvador, inhabited by Aztec Indians, was conquered by Spain in 1526, joined the Central American Federation in 1823, and became independent in 1839. From 1931 it was ruled by a succession of military juntas. Undeclared war with Honduras broke out briefly in 1969. Civil war erupted (1979) between leftists and rightists and continued despite the naming of José Napoléon Duarte, a moderate, as president (1980). He was reelected in 1984 but the war continued. U.S. aid to the government prompted denunciations by leftist groups who charged the U.S. with interference in Salvadoran affairs

else (els) **1.** *adv.* in a different way, *how else could they win?*‖ at a different time, *when else would suit you?* ‖ in a different place, *where else could they be?* ‖ otherwise, if not (usually proceded by 'or'), *speak up or else you won't be heard* **2.** *adj.* (after an indefinite or interrogative pronoun) other, different, *what else should I have said?*, *it was his concern and nobody else's* ‖ additional, *is there something else to follow?* [O.E. *elles*]

else·where (élshwɛər, élswɛər) *adv.* in, to or at another or a different place

El·si·nore (élsinôr, elsinóur) (*Dan.* Helsingör) a town (pop. 55,404) in Zealand, Denmark, at the narrowest point of the Sound, a transit port between Sweden and the Continent. Industry: shipbuilding. Its castle, Kronborg (1574–85), is the setting of Shakespeare's 'Hamlet'

E·luard (eilyær), Paul (Eugène Grindel, 1895–1952), French poet. He was one of the early exponents of surrealism, esp. in 'Capitale de la Douleur' (1926). His love poems establish him as a lyric poet, and he also wrote political poems about the Spanish Civil War and the French Resistance

e·lu·ci·date (ilú:sideit) *pres. part.* **e·lu·ci·dat·ing** *past* and *past part.* **e·lu·ci·dat·ed** *v.t.* to make easier to understand, give an explanation of **e·lú·ci·dá·tion**, **e·lú·ci·da·tor** *ns* [fr. *elucidare* (*elucidatus*)]

e·lude (ilú:d) *pres. part.* **e·lud·ing** *past* and *past part.* **e·lud·ed** *v.t.* to slip away from, avoid capture by, dodge away from ‖ to escape the notice, understanding or memory of [fr. L. *eludere*, to deceive]

E·lu·ru (elúəru:) (Ellore) a town (pop. 108,000) of Andhra Pradesh, India, at the head of the irrigation system linking the Godavari and Kistna Rivers: carpets, electrical goods

e·lu·sive (ilú:siv) *adj.* hard to catch, find, pin down or keep hold of ‖ hard to grasp with the mind, remember exactly or define precisely [fr. L. *elusus*, to deceive]

e·lu·so·ry (ilú:səri:, ilú:zəri:) *adj.* elusive, deceptive [fr. L.L. *elusorius*]

e·lu·tri·ate (ilú:tri:eit) *pres. part.* **e·lu·tri·at·ing** *past* and *past part.* **e·lu·tri·at·ed** *v.t.* to separate substances from (a mixture) by washing and decanting, esp. to separate the lighter particles in (a mixture) from the heavier particles by washing **e·lu·tri·á·tion** *n.* [fr. L. *elutriare* (*elutriatus*), to wash out]

e·lu·vi·al (ilú:vi:əl) *adj.* relating to a deposit of eluvium

e·lu·vi·um (ilú:vi:əm) *n.* (*geol.*) a deposit of gravel, soil, etc., formed from disintegration of rocks originating in the place where found (cf. ALLUVIUM) [Mod. L.]

el·ver (élvər) *n.* a young eel [var. of EEL+obs. *fare*, brood or litter of young]

elv·ish (élviʃ) *adj.* elfish [ELF]

E·ly, Isle of (í:li:) an administrative county (area 372 sq. miles, pop. 89,000) within Cambridgeshire, England. Administrative center:

March. The town of Ely (pop. 10,000) has an 11th–c. cathedral

El·y·ot (éli:ət, éljət), Sir Thomas (c. 1490–1546), English humanist and diplomat. He wrote 'The Boke named the Governour' (1531), a philosophical treatise for the education of princes. He also translated several works and published a Latin-English dictionary (1538)

E·ly·sian (ilíʒən, ilí:ʒən) *adj.* of or pertaining to Elysium ‖ (of joy, happiness) perfect

E·lys·i·um (ilíizi:əm) *pl.* **E·lys·i·ums, E·lys·i·a** (ilizi:ə) *n.* (*Gk mythol.*) the Elysian Fields, the abode after death of the brave and good ‖ a place or state of ideal happiness [L. fr. Gk *Elusion*]

el·y·tron (élitron) *pl.* **el·y·tra** (élitrə) *n.* (*zool.*) the anterior wing of certain insects, hard and caselike ‖ one of the scales or shieldlike plates found on the dorsal surface of some worms [Gk *elutron*, a sheath]

el·y·trum (élitrəm) *pl.* **el·y·tra** (élitrə) *n.* an elytron [Mod. L. fr. Gk]

El·ze·vir (élzivior) *n.* a book printed by the Elzevirs ‖ a typeface much used by them. The Elzevirs were a Dutch family of printers 1583–1712, established at Leyden, Amsterdam, The Hague and Utrecht, and famous esp. for their editions of French and Latin classics, considered as typographical masterpieces

em (em) *n.* the letter M, m ‖ (*printing*) a unit of measurement in any size of type that is equal to the width of the letter M (roughly square) ‖ (*printing*) a measure equivalent to 12 points

em- (em) *prefix* (before b, m, p) to put into or on ‖ to go into or on ‖ to cause to be or have [M.E. fr. O.F. fr. L.]

em- *prefix* (before b, m, p) in, within, inside [M.E. fr. L. fr. Gk]

'em (əm) *pron.* (*pop.*) them [M.E., form of *hem*, dative and accusative third person plural]

e·ma·ci·ate (iméiʃi:eit) *pres. part.* **e·ma·ci·at·ing** *past* and *past part.* **e·ma·ci·at·ed** *v.t.* to make thin and worn, to waste by, or as if by, hunger and want **e·má·ci·at·ed** *adj.* **e·ma·ci·á·tion** *n.* [fr. L. *emaciare* (*emaciatus*), to make thin]

em·a·lan·ger·i (eməlændʒéri:) *n.* unit of currency of Swaziland

em·a·nate (éməneit) *pres. part.* **em·a·nat·ing** *past* and *past part.* **em·a·nat·ed** *v.i.* to come, arise (from a source or origin), *the rumor emanated from the village shop* [fr. L. *emanare* (*emanatus*), to flow from]

em·a·na·tion (emənéiʃən) *n.* an emanating ‖ something which issues from a source of origin ‖ the theory exemplified in Neoplatonism and other mystical systems, according to which all things emanate from a supreme principle, of which they are partial and inferior copies ‖ (*chem.*, symbol Em) one of the radioactive gases (esp. radon) produced by the disintegration of a radioactive substance, e.g., radium, thorium and actinium **em·a·ná·tion·ism** *n.* [fr. L. *emanatio* (*emanationis*)]

e·man·ci·pate (imǽnsəpeit) *pres. part.* **e·man·ci·pat·ing** *past* and *past part.* **e·man·ci·pat·ed** *v.t.* to set free from oppression or slavery ‖ to free from restrictive rules or conventions **e·man·ci·pa·to·ry** (imǽnsəpətɔri:, imǽnsəpətóuri:) *adj.* [fr. L. *emancipare* (*emancipatus*), to free (originally a son, from paternal authority)]

e·man·ci·pa·tion (imænsipéiʃən) *n.* a setting free or being set free, esp. from slavery ‖ freedom from political, moral, intellectual or social restraints offensive to reason or justice [F.]

—The emancipation movement set out to end the institution of slavery (cf. ABOLITION). Emancipation was first achieved in England (and throughout the British Empire) in 1839, largely through the efforts of Thomas Foxwell Buxton, parliamentary spokesman for the Antislavery Society. It was achieved in France in 1848, under the leadership of Schoelcher and in the U.S.A. by the Emancipation Proclamation (1863) and the 13th amendment (1865)

Emancipation Proclamation (*Am. hist.*) the declaration issued (Jan. 1, 1863) by Pres. Abraham Lincoln abolishing slavery in the states in rebellion in the Civil War

e·mar·gi·nate (imárdʒinit) *adj.* (*biol.*, esp. of a leaf or petal) having the tip or margin notched [fr. L. *emarginare* (*emarginatus*), to remove the edge of]

e·mas·cu·late 1. (imǽskjuleit) *pres. part.* **e·mas·cu·lat·ing** *past* and *past part.* **e·mas·cu·lat·ed** *v.t.* to weaken, deprive of full force or vigor, *some editors emasculate Shakespeare's dialogue* ‖ to castrate **2.** (imǽskjulit) *adj.* emasculated **e·mas·cu·lat·ed** (imǽskjuleitid) *adj.*

weakened, made feeble **e·mas·cu·la·tion** (imæskjuléiʃən) *n.* [fr. L. *emasculare* (*emasculatus*), to castrate]

em·balm (imbám) *v.t.* to preserve (a corpse) from decay by the application of ointments, resins etc. or by injections **em·bálm·ment** *n.* [M.E. *enbaume* fr. F.]

em·bank (imbǽŋk) *v.t.* to enclose or protect with a raised bank of earth, stone etc. **em·bánk·ment** *n.* a raised bank built to confine a river or canal, or to carry a road or railroad

embarcation *EMBARKATION

em·bar·go (imbárgou) **1.** *pl.* **em·bar·goes** *n.* a government order forbidding foreign ships to enter or leave its ports (esp. before an outbreak of war) ‖ an order forbidding the import, export or carriage of certain commodities ‖ a prohibition (generally in an industrial or commercial context), *the unions put an embargo on the employment of foreign workers* **2.** *v.t.* to lay under an embargo [Span.]

Embargo Act a U.S. Congressional act (1808) in retaliation against Napoleon's Continental System and Britain's orders-in-council of 1807, designed to curtail all foreign trade. Ineffective against both French and British trade and resented in U.S. shipping circles, it was replaced (1809) by the Nonintercourse Act

em·bark (imbárk) *v.t.* to put or take on board ship ‖ *v.i.* to go on board ship ‖ (*rhet.*) to make a start (on something long, difficult or dangerous) [F. *embarquer*]

em·bar·ka·tion, em·bar·ca·tion (embɑrkéiʃən) *n.* the act or process of embarking [F. *embarcation*]

em·bar·rass (imbǽrəs) *v.t.* to cause to feel self-conscious, awkward, shy or ashamed ‖ to make things difficult or complicated for ‖ to hinder, *wearing a sword embarrassed his movements* ‖ (esp. *pass.*) to involve in debt **em·bár·rass·ing** *adj.* **em·bár·rass·ment** *n.* an embarrassing or being embarrassed ‖ something which embarrasses [fr. F. *embarrasser*]

em·bas·sy (émbəsi:) *pl.* **em·bas·sies** *n.* an official mission or delegation, esp. one which represents one country in another at the highest diplomatic level ‖ the residence or offices of the head of such a body ‖ the office or function of an ambassador ‖ (*rhet.*) the mission of a private person who acts as an intermediary [O.F. *ambassee*]

em·bat·tle (imbǽt'l) *pres. part.* **em·bat·tling** *past* and *past part.* **em·bat·tled** *v.t.* to furnish with embattlements [M.E. *embatailen*]

em·bat·tled (imbǽt'ld) *adj.* having battlements ‖ (*heraldry*) having edges like battlements, crenellated [M. E. *embatailed*]

em·bay·ment (embéimənt) *n.* (*geol.*) a large open bay formed by a depression in the shoreline or by the bend of a river

em·bed (imbéd) *pres. part.* **em·bed·ding** *past* and *past part.* **em·bed·ded** *v.t.* to fix (something) firmly into a surrounding substance

em·bel·lish (imbéliʃ) *v.t.* to make more decorative, to add flourishes or ornament to ‖ to add made-up details to (a story) so as to increase the pleasure of telling it or listening to it **em·bél·lish·ment** *n.* [O.F. *embelir* (*embelliss-*)]

em·ber (émbər) *n.* a hot or red-hot fragment of burning coal or wood ‖ (*pl.*) the hot remains of a fire [O.E. *æmerge*]

ember day one of the days specified for fasting and special prayer by Christians for those about to be ordained, being the Wednesday, Friday and Saturday after the first Sunday in Lent, Whitsunday, Holy Cross Day (Sept. 14) and St Lucy's Day (Dec. 13). They are ancient in origin, though not prescribed for the whole Church until 1095 [O.E. *ymbren* fr. *ymbrene*, period of time]

em·ber·goose (émbərgu:s) *pl.* **em·ber·geese** (émbərgi:s) *n. Gavia immer*, a northern, short-legged, web-footed, aquatic bird, the size of a small goose [Norw. *emmer*]

em·bez·zle (imbéz'i) *pres. part.* **em·bez·zling** *past* and *past part.* **em·bez·zled** *v.t.* to steal or use for one's own purposes (money or other property which has been entrusted to one as an employee, servant or agent) **em·béz·zle·ment** *n.* [fr. A.F. *enbesilier*, to make away with]

em·bit·ter (imbitər) *v.t.* to cause to have hard feelings or to bear rancor **em·bít·ter·ment** *n.*

em·bla·zon (imbléizən) *v.t.* to adorn, esp. with heraldic coats of arms or devices ‖ (*rhet.*) to extol, perpetuate the fame of **em·blá·zon·ment**, **em·blá·zon·ry** *ns*

em·blem (émbləm) *n.* an object, or the representation of an object, which serves as a recognized

CONCISE PRONUNCIATION KEY: **(a)** æ, c*a*t; ɑ, c*ar*; ɔ f*aw*n; ei, sn*a*ke. **(e)** e, h*e*n; i:, sh*ee*p; iə, d*ee*r; ɛə, b*ear*. **(i)** i, f*i*sh; ai, t*i*ger; ə:, b*ir*d. **(o)** o, *o*x; au, c*ow*; ou, g*oa*t; u, p*oor*; ɔi, r*oy*al. **(u)** ʌ, d*u*ck; u, b*u*ll; u:, g*oo*se; ə, b*a*cillus; ju:, c*u*be. x, lo*ch*; θ, *th*ink; ð, bo*th*er; z, *Z*en; ʒ, corsa*g*e; dʒ, sava*g*e; ŋ, oranguta*ng*; j, *y*ak; ʃ, *f*ish; tʃ, *f*etch; 'l, rabb*le*; 'n, redd*en*. Complete pronunciation key appears inside front cover.

symbol ‖ a design (which may represent an object), e.g. a publisher's device, used to show who owns or has produced the thing in or on which it appears ‖ a heraldic device in a coat of arms or crest ‖ (*hist.*) a picture illustrating an improving poem, tale or saying, common in 17th-c. books (emblem books) made up of a collection of such pictures and short texts **em·blem·at·ic**, **em·blem·át·i·cal** *adjs* **em·blem·a·tist** (imblémǝtist) *n.* **em·blém·a·tize** *pres. part.* **em·blem·a·tiz·ing** *past and past part.* **em·blem·a·tized** *v.t.* to symbolize, represent by an emblem or serve as an emblem of [O.F. *embleme* fr. L. fr. Gk]

em·ble·ments (émblǝmǝnts) *pl. n.* (*law*) the profits of worked land [O.F. *emblaement* fr. *emblaer*, to sow (with grain)]

em·bod·i·ment (imbódi:mǝnt) *n.* an embodying or being embodied ‖ a person in whom or thing in which a particular quality is embodied

em·bod·y (imbódi:) *pres. part.* **em·bod·y·ing** *past and past part.* **em·bod·ied** *v.t.* to give clear and effective form or expression to, *to embody one's views in a memorandum* ‖ to include as an essential part, *the new model embodies the latest refinements* ‖ to include in a larger whole ‖ to be the concrete expression of

em·bold·en (imbáuldǝn) *v.t.* (*old-fash.*) to give boldness or courage to

embole *EMBOLY

em·bo·lism (émbǝlizǝm) *n.* an obstruction in a blood vessel caused by an embolus carried from another part of the circulatory system ‖ the inserting in the calendar of an extra day or other period of time (e.g. in leap year) to adjust for accuracy ‖ the period inserted [fr. L. *embolismus* fr. Gk]

em·bo·lus (émbǝlǝs) *pl.* **em·bo·li** (émbǝlai) *n.* any foreign object in the bloodstream (e.g. a clot, a bubble of air) which may block a blood vessel and so cause an embolism [L. fr. Gk *embolos*, stopper]

em·bo·ly, **em·bo·le** (émbǝli:) *pl.* **em·bo·lies**, **em·bo·les** *n.* (*embry.*) the process of gastrula formation by invagination of the blastula, typical of embryos with holoblastic cleavage (cf. EPIBOLY) [Gk *embolē* fr. *emballein*, to insert]

em·bos·omed (imbúzǝmd) *adj.* (*rhet.*) surrounded, enveloped

em·boss (imbós, imbós) *v.t.* to produce a raised design, pattern or lettering on (a plain surface, e.g. metal, leather, cloth, paper), esp. by stamping or impressing on it an engraved die ‖ to produce (a raised design etc.) on such a surface [prob. O.F.]

em·bou·chure (ɒmbuʃúǝr) *n.* the mouth of a river ‖ the place where a river valley spreads out over a plain ‖ the mouthpiece of a wind instrument, or the way in which the mouth, lips and tongue are used in playing it [F.]

em·bour·geoise·ment (embuǝrʒwàzmǝnt) *n.* (*Fr.*) the change in the attitudes of a class, usu. working class, to a bourgeois mentality

em·bow·er (imbáuǝr) *v.t.* (*rhet.*) to cover or enclose as though in a bower

em·brace (imbréis) **1.** *v. pres. part.* **em·brac·ing** *past and past part.* **em·braced** *v.t.* to put one's arms lovingly around ‖ to accept gladly, seize, *to embrace an opportunity* ‖ to adopt (a faith, opinion etc.) ‖ to include, incorporate, *'democracy' embraces many concepts* ‖ to encompass, take in with the eye or understanding ‖ *v.i.* to join in an embrace, hug one another **2.** *n.* a clasping or folding in the arms, a hug ‖ a tight grip ‖ an adoption (of a faith, opinion etc.) [fr. O.F. *embracer*]

em·bra·sure (imbréiʒǝr) *n.* a recess in a wall to take a door or window ‖ an opening in a wall or in the parapet of a trench etc., widening toward the outer face, through which fire can be directed at the enemy [F.]

em·bro·cate (émbroukeit) *pres. part.* **em·bro·cat·ing** *past and past part.* **em·bro·cat·ed** *v.t.* to rub with a lotion that relieves pain or muscular stiffness **em·bro·cá·tion** *n.* such a lotion [fr. M.L. *embrocare* (*embrocatus*)]

em·bro·glio (imbróuljou) *n.* an imbroglio

em·broi·der (imbróidǝr) *v.t.* to ornament (cloth, silk, leather etc.) with needlework ‖ to carry out (a design) in needlework ‖ to add to (a story etc.) details that are interesting or entertaining but not true [M.E. fr. EM- + obs. *broider* fr. F. *broder*, to embroider]

em·broi·der·y (imbróidǝri:) *pl.* **em·broi·der·ies** *n.* the art or process of embroidering cloth etc. ‖ the work so produced ‖ the embroidering of a story, or the details so added [M.E. *embrouderie*]

em·broil (imbróil) *v.t.* to involve or entangle in a quarrel or fight ‖ to confuse, muddle or entangle with complications **em·bróil·ment** *n.* [fr. F. *embrouiller*]

em·bry·o (émbri:ou) *pl.* **em·bry·os** *n.* an animal organism during the early stages of growth and development merging in higher animals into fetal stages or ending (as in primitive species) with the larva ‖ a human individual from the time of implantation to the eighth week after conception ‖ a young sporophyte in seed plants, usually consisting of a rudimentary plant embedded in endosperm ‖ in anything in the initial stages of formation, *a criminal in embryo* **em·bry·on·ic** (embri:ónik) *adj.* [M.L. fr. Gk]

em·bry·og·e·ny (embri:ódʒeni:) *n.* the formation and growth of the embryo ‖ its study [EMBRYO+Gk *geneia*, act of being born]

em·bry·oid (émbri:ɔid) *n.* an organism that serves as an embryo in reproduction

em·bry·o·log·ic (embri:ǝlódʒik) *adj.* embryological **em·bry·o·lóg·i·cal** *adj.* of or relating to embryology

em·bry·ol·o·gist (embri:óledʒist) *n.* a specialist in embryology

em·bry·ol·o·gy (embri:óledʒi:) *n.* the branch of biology concerned with the formation of the embryo and its development from the egg to birth ‖ the collective features of the formation and development of the embryo [F. *embryologie*]

em·bry·o·phyte (émbri:ǝfait) *n.* a member of *Embryophyta*, a subkingdom of the plant kingdom including all plants except thallophytes [EMBRYO+Gk *phuton*, plant]

embryo sac (*bot.*) the macrospore, a large single cell within the ovule in angiosperms. Germination results in the division of its nucleus into eight, which form two groups of four, one at each end of the sac. Together these consist of: two polar nuclei, one oosphere or egg cell, two synergidae and three antipodal cells

em·bry·o transfer (émbri:ou) (*med*) technique of placement into the uterus of an egg extracted from the body and fertilized in a petri dish

em·cee (émsí:) *n.* a master of ceremonies [fr. M.C.]

e·mend (iménd) *v.t.* to correct (a text) ‖ to suggest a new reading for (a word or passage in a text) **e·men·da·tion** (i:mendéiʃǝn) *n.* the act of emending ‖ a textual correction **e·men·da·tor** (i:mendeitǝr) *n.* **e·men·da·to·ry** (i:méndǝtǝri:, iméndǝtouri:) *adj.* [fr. L. *emendare*]

em·er·ald (émǝrǝld) **1.** *n.* a bright green precious stone, the green beryl (a silicate of beryllium and aluminum) ‖ the color of an emerald ‖ (*Br. printing*) minionette **2.** *adj.* of or like an emerald ‖ of the color of an emerald [M.E. *emeraude* fr. O.F. fr. L. fr. Gk]

e·merge (imǝ́:rdʒ) *pres. part.* **e·mer·ging** *past and past part.* **e·merged** *v.i.* to come out (from), to appear (from), *the car emerged from a side street* ‖ to come out from a less desirable or less developed state to one more desirable or more advanced ‖ to be brought out in discussion or investigation as a fact or logical conclusion ‖ to come to light, be discovered, *snags are bound to emerge when we start production* **e·mér·gence** *n.* the act of emerging ‖ (*bot.*) subepidermal tissue, e.g. a rose prickle [fr. L. *emergere*, to rise from the sea]

e·mer·gen·cy (imǝ́:rdʒǝnsi:) *pl.* **e·mer·gen·cies** *n.* a situation, often dangerous, which arises suddenly and calls for prompt action ‖ an immediate need [fr. L.L. *emergentia*, a rising up fr. *emergere*]

e·mer·gent (imǝ́:rdʒǝnt) *adj.* coming out, developing, becoming noticeable ‖ (*biol.*) appearing in the course of evolution as a new form [L. *emergens* (*emergentis*) fr. *emergere*, to rise from the sea]

e·mer·i·tus (iméritǝs) *adj.* retired from active duty but retaining honorary rank, *professor emeritus* [L. fr. *emeriri*, to earn by service]

e·mersed (imǝ́:rst) *adj.* protruding out of water [fr. L. *emergere* (*emersus*), to emerge]

e·mer·sion (imǝ́:rʒǝn, imǝ́:rʃǝn) *n.* (*astron.*) the reappearance of a heavenly body after eclipse or occultation [fr. L. *emergere* (*emersus*), to emerge]

Em·er·son (émǝrs'n), Ralph Waldo (1803–82), American philosopher, essayist and poet. His philosophy was known as transcendentalism. The values he particularly stressed were intellectual freedom, integrity, self-reliance and realism. He was strongly influenced by Thomas Carlyle. The best known of his essays, published in two series (1841, 1844) are 'Self-Reliance', 'Compensation' and 'The Over-Soul'. Other volumes are 'English Traits' (1856) and 'The Conduct of Life' (1860)

em·er·y (émǝri:) *pl.* **em·er·ies** *n.* a very hard, granular corundum, intimately mixed with hematite and magnetite, used as an abrasive [F. *émeri* fr. L. fr. Gk]

em·er·y ball (émǝri:) (*baseball*) an illegally roughened ball (usu. accomplished by use of an emery cloth)

emery board a strip of wood covered with powdered emery for filing the fingernails

E·me·sa (emésǝ) *HOMS

E meter (*electr.*) a device for measuring changes in electrical resistance

e·met·ic (imétik) **1.** *adj.* causing vomiting **2.** *n.* a mixture or medicine that induces vomiting [fr. Gk *emetikos* fr. *emeein*, to vomit]

em·e·tine (émǝtin) *n.* an alkaloid powder obtained from ipecacuanha root, used in the treatment of amoebic dysentery [fr. Gk *emetos*, vomiting]

emf *ELECTROMOTIVE FORCE

e·mic (í:mik) *adj.* (*linguistics*) have structurally significant characteristics

em·i·grant (émigrǝnt) **1.** *n.* a person emigrating or who has emigrated **2.** *adj.* emigrating ‖ of or relating to emigration or emigrants [fr. L. *emigrans* (*emigrantis*)]

em·i·grate (émigreit) *pres. part.* **em·i·grat·ing** *past and past part.* **em·i·grat·ed** *v.i.* to leave one's own country or home and settle in another ‖ *v.t.* to cause or help (a person) to emigrate (cf. IMMIGRATE) **em·i·grá·tion** *n.* **em·i·gra·to·ry** (émigrǝtǝri:, émigrǝtouri:) *adj.* [fr. L. *emigrare* (*emigratus*), to wander forth]

é·mi·gré (émigrei) *n.* someone having left his country, generally for political reasons, esp. at the time of the French or Russian revolutions [F.]

E·mi·lia-Ro·ma·gna (imí:ljǝroumánjǝ) a region (area 8,542 sq. miles, pop. 3,948,100) of N. Italy, consisting of the rich southern Po valley and the northern slopes of the Etruscan Apennines. It contains Parma, Reggio, Modena, Bologna, Ferrara, Ravenna etc.

em·i·nence (éminǝns) *n.* distinction in society or in a profession etc. ‖ a piece of high ground ‖ **Em·i·nence** the title of a cardinal [fr. L. *eminentia*]

é·mi·nence grise (eimi:nãsgri:z) *GRAY EMINENCE

em·i·nent (éminǝnt) *adj.* distinguished, widely thought of as superior in some way, *an eminent lawyer* ‖ outstanding, conspicuous, *a man of eminent tact* [fr. L. *eminens* (*eminentis*), pres. part. of *eminere*, to stand out]

eminent domain (*U.S. and internat. law*) the superior right of the sovereign power which entitles it, when necessary, to take possession of any property within its frontiers and use it for the public good, compensation being paid to the owner

em·i·nent·ly (éminǝntli:) *adv.* to an eminent degree

e·mir, **a·mir** (ǝmíǝr) *n.* (in Moslem countries) a native ruler, chieftain, chief officer or nobleman **E·mir**, **A·mir** the title of such a man **e·mir·ate** (ǝmí:rit, ǝmí:reit) *n.* the province ruled by an emir [Arab. *amīr*]

em·is·sar·y (émiseri:) **1.** *pl.* **em·is·sar·ies** *n.* an agent sent on a mission, sometimes in secret, sometimes with great pomp **2.** *adj.* of, or serving as, an emissary [fr. L. *emissarius* fr. *emittere*, to send out]

e·mis·sion (imíʃǝn) *n.* a sending out or giving out, e.g. of light, heat, gas, smoke ‖ that which is given out ‖ an involuntary discharge of semen ‖ an issuing and putting into circulation of paper money ‖ (*elec.*) the throwing off or sending out of electrons, esp. from a heated cathode ‖ the electronic current so produced [fr. L. *emissio* (*emissionis*)]

e·mis·sion control (imíʃǝn) (*mil.*) **1.** selective control of emitted electromagnetic or acoustic energy to minimize its detection by enemy sensors or to improve the performance of installed friendly sensors **also** emcon **2.** system of inspection of motor vehicles for emission of polluting lead and sulphur waste control esp. as applied to manufacturers

emission spectrum an electromagnetic spectrum that is characteristic of the substance acting as a source of radiation and of the method of excitation of this source (*ABSORPTION SPECTRUM, *SPECTROSCOPY)

emission standard maximum permissible pollution from a source

e·mis·sive (ɪmísiv) *adj.* pertaining to the emission of energy [fr. L. *emittere (emissus)*, to send forth]

emissive power (*phys.*) the total thermal energy emitted per second from unit area of a surface at a fixed temperature

em·is·siv·i·ty (ɛmɪsíviti:) *n.* (*phys.*) the ratio of the emissive power of a body to that of a black body at the same temperature

e·mit (ɪmít) *pres. part.* **e·mit·ting** *past* and *past part.* **e·mit·ted** *v.t.* to give out, give off, *to emit a sigh* ‖ to put (currency etc.) in circulation [fr. L. *emittere*, to send forth]

Emmanuel *IMMANUEL

em·me·tro·pi·a (ɛmətróupi:ə) *n.* normal refraction of light in the eye, the condition of normal eyesight **em·me·trop·ic** (ɛmətrópik) *adj.* [Mod. L. fr. Gk *emmetros*, in measure + *-opia*]

Em·my Award (émi:) annual best-in-class statuette award for television performances and technical functions to advance the arts and sciences of broadcasting. Made since 1949, the award was named for emmy, the image orthicon camera tube

e·mol·lient (ɪmóljənt) **1.** *adj.* soothing, softening **2.** *n.* a soothing ointment or lotion [fr. L. *emolliens (emollientis)* fr. *emollire*, to soften]

e·mol·u·ment (ɪmóljumənt) *n.* (often *pl.*) the payment attached to an office or undertaking, *a judge's emoluments* [fr. L. *emolumentum* fr. *emoliri*, to work out or *emolere*, to grind out]

e·mote (ɪmóut) *pres. part.* **e·mot·ing** *past* and *past part.* **e·mot·ed** *v.i.* (*pop.*) to display or affect emotion, esp. in a film or play ‖ (*pop.*) to behave histrionically [EMOTION]

e·mo·ti·cism (ɪmóutɪsɪzəm) *n.* (*ethics*) theory that value judgments are emotionally influenced and not statements of fact or truth

e·mo·tion (ɪmóuʃən) *n.* a strong feeling (such as fear, wonder, love, sorrow, shame) often accompanied by a physical reaction (e.g. blushing or trembling) **e·mó·tion·al** *adj.* of or relating to the emotions ‖ showing deep feeling or emotion, *an emotional farewell* ‖ aimed at the arousing of emotion, *his patriotic argument is purely emotional* ‖ ruled by emotion rather than by reason **e·mó·tion·al·ism** *n.* a tendency to delight in, give way to, display or appeal to emotion **e·mó·tion·al·ist** *n.* **e·mo·tion·ál·i·ty** *n.* the quality or state of being too emotional **e·mo·tion·al·ize** (ɪmóuʃən'laiz) *pres. part.* **e·mo·tion·al·iz·ing** *past* and *past part.* **e·mo·tion·al·ized** *v.t.* to adopt an emotional attitude toward [F. *émotion*]

e·mo·tive (ɪmóutiv) *adj.* exciting emotion or recalling the memory of emotion [fr. L. *emovere (emotus)*, to move]

EMP (*acronym*) electromolecular propulsion, a hypothetical process for precise separation of materials at high speeds. EMP is based on the charge-transfer theory advanced by Robert S. Mulliken

em·pa·na·da (empənáda) *n.* pastry filled with meat, black olives, raisins and eggs, native to Chile and Argentina

empanel *IMPANEL

em·paqu·e·tage (empǽketaʒ) *n.* art form in which packaging of a wrapped object is the distinctive feature

em·pa·thy (émpəθi:) *n.* the power to enter into emotional harmony with a work of art and so derive aesthetic satisfaction ‖ (*psychol.*) the power to enter into the feeling or spirit of others **em·pa·thet·ic** (empəθétik), **em·path·ic** (impǽθik) *adjs* [orig. trans. of G. *einfühlung*, infeeling, after Gk *empatheia*]

Em·ped·o·cles (empédəkli:z) (c. 493–433 B.C.), philosopher and scientist of Acragas (Agrigento) in Sicily. He considered the world to be composed of four elements, air, fire, earth and water, combined and separated by the contrary forces of love and strife

em·pen·nage (ɑmpənáʒ, *Br.* empénidʒ) *n.* tail unit of an aircraft ‖ the set of stabilizing fins on a projectile [F. = the feathers of an arrow]

em·per·or (émpərər) *n.* the ruler of an empire **Em·per·or** (*hist.*) the Holy Roman Emperor **ém·per·or·ship** *n.* [fr. O.F. *empereor*]

em·pha·sis (émfəsis) *pl.* **em·pha·ses** (émfəsi:z) *n.* a special stress or deliberate accent laid on a word or syllable in order to make a meaning or intention unmistakable ‖ a special vigor or deliberation given to an action so as to convey an attitude of mind, *to nod one's head with emphasis* ‖ a special importance given to a thing, or place too much emphasis on examinations ‖ sharpness, esp. of contrast, *the trees stood out with emphasis against the snow* **em·pha·size** (émfəsaiz) *pres. part.* **em·pha·siz·ing** *past* and

past part. **em·pha·sized** *v.t.* to lay emphasis on, stress [L. fr. Gk=declaration]

em·phat·ic (imfǽtik) *adj.* expressed in words or action with emphasis ‖ (of words) adding emphasis or intensifying meaning ‖ strongly marked, strikingly noticeable, *an emphatic decline in unemployment* ‖ having a firm opinion and expressing it, *he is quite emphatic about it* **em·phát·i·cal·ly** *adv.* [fr. Gk *emphatikos*, significant]

em·phy·se·ma (emfisí:mə) *n.* (*med.*) a condition, often a complication in bronchitis, in which the lungs and their constituent air cells are distended with air to the point of inefficiency. It is accompanied by coughing and labored breathing and may affect the heart **em·phy·sem·a·tous** (emfisémətəs) *adj.* [Mod. L. fr. Gk *emphusēma*, inflation]

em·pire (émpaiər) **1.** *n.* a sovereign state whose possessions have been extended by military or economic conquest, colonization, or federation, to include countries or territories originally independent of it ‖ supreme power or sovereignty ‖ an organization (commercial, industrial, financial) having great wealth and power **the Empire** the Holy Roman Empire ‖ the first French Empire under Napoleon, 1804–15 ‖ the British Empire **2.** *adj.* **Empire** (of style in furniture, dress etc.) characteristic of the period of the first French Empire, or imitating that style [F.]

Empire State Building a skyscraper (1,250 ft high, without its television tower) in Manhattan, New York City (1930–1), formerly the world's tallest building

em·pir·ic (empírik) **1.** *n.* someone who believes that in science and philosophy there is no truth other than that obtained by sense observation and experiment ‖ someone who acquires knowledge or practices a science by methods of trial and error without constructing an ordered or scientific system **2.** *adj.* **em·pír·i·cal** making use of, or based on, experience, trial and error, or experiment, rather than theory or systematized knowledge ‖ derived from the senses and not by logical deduction **em·pir·i·cism** (empírisizəm) *n.* the scientific method of proceeding by inductive reasoning from observation to the formulation of a general principle, which is then checked by experiment ‖ the philosophical system, esp. that of the British philosophers Locke, Berkeley and Hume, which confines knowledge to what can be perceived by the senses and rejects what cannot be verified **em·pír·i·cist** *n.* [fr. L. *empiricus* fr. Gk]

empirical formula a chemical formula giving the simplest ratio of the elements in a compound but not its molecular composition or mass (cf. MOLECULAR FORMULA, cf. STRUCTURAL FORMULA)

em·pir·i·cal generalization (empírik'l) a proposition, supported by empirical data, stating a general relationship between variables

em·place·ment (impléismənt) *n.* a gun emplacement, a place or position (platform, gun pit etc.) prepared for a gun [F.]

em·ploy (implói) **1.** *v.t.* to pay (a person) to work for one ‖ to require the work of, keep busy, *the farm employs six men* ‖ to use, make use of, *to employ one's time in reading* **2.** *n.* (in the phrase) **in** (someone's) **employ** working for (someone) **em·plóy·a·ble** *adj.* [F. *employer*]

em·ploy·ee (implói:, emplói:) *n.* someone paid to work esp. on a regular rather than a casual basis [F. *employe*, *past part.* of *employer*]

Employee Stock Ownership Plan IRS-approved employee pension plan under which employers contribute shares of company's stock or funds to buy such shares **acronym** ESOP

em·ploy·er (implóiər) *n.* someone who pays another or others to work for him ‖ a user

em·ploy·ment (implóimənt) *n.* the state of being employed ‖ work done, or to be done, by someone employed, work as livelihood ‖ work as vocation, profession or occupation, *he needs employment that suits his temperament* ‖ work as activity, *employment is one cure for boredom* ‖ the act of using, *employment of force*

employment agency a voluntary or commercial organization for finding work for workers or workers for employers

employment bureau one of the offices initiated (1933) under the U.S. Employment Service to find work for workers and workers for employers

employment exchange (*Br.*) any of the offices established under the Labour Exchanges Act

(1909) to provide a free service for workers wanting jobs and employers wanting workers

em·po·ri·um (empóri:əm, empóuri:əm) *pl.* **em·po·ri·ums, em·po·ri·a** (empóri:ə, empóuri:ə) *n.* a big market or trade center ‖ (*old-fash.*) a big store with lots of departments [L. fr. Gk]

em·pow·er (impáuər) *v.t.* to delegate legal power to, authorize ‖ to enable

em·press (émpris) *n.* the wife of an emperor ‖ a woman ruler of an empire in her own right [M.E. *emperesse* fr. O.F.]

emp·ti·ly (émptili:) *adv.* in an empty way

emp·ti·ness (émpti:nis) *n.* the state of being empty

emp·ty (émpti:) **1.** *comp.* **emp·ti·er** *superl.* **emp·ti·est** *adj.* with nothing in it, *an empty bottle* ‖ unoccupied, *an empty chair* ‖ without substance, *an empty boast* ‖ (with 'of') totally without, *arguments empty of meaning* ‖ without foundation, doomed to failure or disappointment, *empty hopes* ‖ silly, without seriousness, *an empty mind* ‖ (*agric.*) not in calf, pig or foal ‖ (*pop.*) hungry **2.** *pl.* **emp·ties** *n.* an empty packing case, bottle, or other container **3.** *v. pres. part.* **emp·ty·ing** *past* and *past part.* **emp·tied** *v.t.* to cause to become empty, take the contents out of ‖ to transfer (something) from one container to another, *empty the flour into the mixing bowl* ‖ to dismiss all thought or emotion from, *to empty one's mind* ‖ *v.i.* to flow or discharge ‖ to become empty [O.E. *æmitig*]

empty band (*nuclear phys.*) in an atom, a hypothetical band of energy not accounted for by the known electrons in the substance

emp·ty-hand·ed (émpti:hǽndid) *adj.* with no present to give ‖ having failed to obtain what was asked for, *to send someone away empty-handed*

emp·ty-head·ed (émpti:hédid) *adj.* silly, frivolous

em·py·e·ma (empaií:mə) *pl.* **em·py·e·ma·ta** (empaií:mətə), **em·py·e·mas** *n.* an accumulation of pus in a cavity of the body, esp. in the pleural cavity [Mod. L. fr. Gk]

em·py·re·al (empairí:əl, empíri:əl) *adj.* of the empyrean **em·py·re·an** (empairí:ən, empíri:ən) *n.* the vault of the sky ‖ (in medieval cosmology) the highest heaven, containing the element fire [fr. Mod. L. *empyreus* fr. Gk]

Ems (ems) a river (230 miles long) in West Germany flowing into the North Sea near Emden, linked to the Ruhr by the Dortmund-Ems Canal (167 miles)

Ems Telegram a communication from Wilhelm I of Prussia to Bismarck (July 13, 1870) about French demands for the withdrawal of Hohenzollern candidacy for the Spanish throne, which, edited by Bismarck and released in this form to the press, precipitated the Franco-Prussian War (1870–1)

e·mu (í:mju:) *n. Dromiceius novaehollandiae*, a flightless deep-feathered ratite bird of Australia, about 6 ft tall, closely related to the ostrich [fr. Port. *ema*, crane]

em·u·late (émjuleit) *pres. part.* **em·u·lat·ing** *past* and *past part.* **em·u·lat·ed** *v.t.* to try to do as well as **em·u·lá·tion** *n.* **em·u·la·tive** (émjuleitiv, émjulətiv) *adj.* [fr. L. *aemulari (aemulatus)*, to rival]

em·u·lous (émjuləs) *adj.* trying hard to equal or surpass a rival ‖ arising from the desire to emulate, *emulous competition* [fr. L. *aemulus*]

e·mul·si·fy (imálsifai) *pres. part.* **e·mul·si·fy·ing** *past* and *past part.* **e·mul·si·fied** *v.t.* to make into an emulsion [fr. L. *emulgere (emulsus)*, to milk out]

e·mul·sion (imálʃən) *n.* a colloidal dispersion of two incompletely miscible liquids, one of which is in the form of fine droplets, or of a finely divided insoluble solid in a liquid ‖ (*photog.*) the coating, sensitive to light, of a photographic plate or film, consisting of finely divided silver halide crystals in a viscous liquid (e.g. gelatin) [fr. Mod. L. *emulsio* fr. *emulgere (emulsum)*, to milk out]

e·mul·sive (imálsiv) *adj.* having the nature of an emulsion [L. *emulsus*, emulsified]

en- *prefix* in, within, inside [M.E. fr. L. fr. Gk]

en- *prefix* to put into or on ‖ to go into or on ‖ to cause to have or to be ‖ thoroughly [M.E. fr. O.F. fr. L.]

en (en) *n.* (printing) a unit of measurement of type width, half an em [the letter N]

en·a·ble (inéib'l) *pres. part.* **en·a·bling** *past* and *past part.* **en·a·bled** *v.t.* to make it possible for or to allow (a person or thing to do something), *its speed enabled it to get away*

en·act (ináekt) v.t. to make (a bill) into a law ‖ to play out, perform as though on the stage, a ritual enacted before the assembled clan **en·ác·tive** adj. **en·áct·ment** n. an enacting or being enacted ‖ an order, decree, regulation

e·nam·el (ináməl) **1.** n. a glass rendered opaque or translucent by an admixture of tin oxide or other infusible substance and often strongly colored ‖ something worked with this ‖ enamel paint ‖ the hard, white, calcareous substance which coats the crown of a tooth ‖ a cosmetic applied to the nails to give a hard shiny coating **2.** v.t. pres. part. **e·nam·el·ing**, esp. Br. **e·nam·el·ling** past and past part. **e·nam·eled**, esp. Br. **e·nam·elled** to coat with enamel [fr. A.F. enamayller, enameler, to inlay ult. fr. Gmc]
—In the art of enameling the enamel is generally fused on to the surface to be covered. In cloisonné enamel the design is outlined by thin bands of metal soldered to the surface, the spaces between them being filled with the colored enamels. The article is then fired, smoothed and polished, and the thin dividing bands are often gilded. In champlevé enamel the parts to be filled with enamel are hollowed out with a graving tool
enamel paint paint in which the pigment is mixed with special oils which oxidize to give a very hard surface
e·nam·el·ware (ináməlwεər) n. jugs, bowls etc. made of thin sheet steel coated with fired-on enamel
e·nam·ored, Br. esp. **e·nam·oured** (inámərd) adj. (rhet., with 'of') in love [past part. of older enamour v. fr. O.F. enamourer]
en·an·ti·o·morph (inánti:əmɔrf) n. (chem.) either form of a substance which crystallizes in two structural arrangements, one being the mirror image of the other [fr. Gk enantios, contrary + morphē, form]
en·an·ti·o·troph·ic (inánti:ətrófik) adj. (phys.) of a substance which can exist in two stable forms that change reversibly into one another at a certain temperature [fr. Gk enantios, contrary + tropos, turn]
en·ar·chist or **en·arch** (énərkist; énark) n. a French civil service administrator selected from graduates of the Ecole Nationale d'Administration [F.]
en bloc (ãblɔk) adj. as a whole, not individually [F.]
en·cae·ni·a (ensí:ni:ə) n. an anniversary festival of dedication (of a church etc.) ‖ the annual June ceremony at Oxford University in honor of founders and benefactors [L. fr. Gk enkainia, renewal]
en·caged (inkéidʒd) adj. in a cage or cages ‖ as if in a cage, encaged in plaster
en·camp (inkámp) v.i. (of troops) to set up a camp ‖ v.t. to quarter (troops) in a camp **en·cámp·ment** n. a camp ‖ the act of setting up a camp or of quartering troops in a camp
en·cap·su·lent (enkápsəlent) n. the material holding a capsule together
en·case, in·case (inkéis) pres. part. **en·cas·ing, in·cas·ing** past and past part. **en·cased, in·cased** v.t. to enclose in an outer cover or case
en·caus·tic (enkɔ́stik) **1.** n. a method of painting used by the Ancients in which colored waxes were applied to a surface and the color was then fixed by heat ‖ a wax paint used in this process **2.** adj. of or relating to encaustic [fr. Gk enkaustikos, fr. en, in+kaiein, to burn]
encaustic tile a tile decorated with inlays of colored clay and then fired
-ence suffix used to form nouns from adjectives ending in -ent to indicate a state or act [F. -ence fr. L. -entia]
en·ceinte (ãsε̃t) n. the outer wall or enclosure of a castle or fort [F.]
en·ce·phal·ic (ensəfálik) adj. concerned with the encephalon or brain ‖ situated inside the skull [fr. Gk enkephalos, brain]
en·ceph·a·li·tis (ensəfəláitis) n. inflammation of the brain caused by viruses or other microorganisms commonly transmitted by insect bites. It is accompanied esp. by fever, torpor and progressive lethargy, delirium or coma (e.g. sleeping sickness) [Mod. L.]
en·ceph·a·lo·gram (enséfələgræm) n. an X-ray photograph of the cavities of the brain obtained by filling them with air [fr. Gk. enkephalos, brain+gramma, writing]
en·ceph·a·lo·graph (enséfələgræf, inséfələgraf) n. an encephalogram ‖ an electroencephalograph [fr. Gk enkephalos, brain+GRAPH]
en·ceph·a·lo·my·e·li·tis (ensefəloumaiəláitis) n. an inflammation of the brain and spinal cord ‖ a

virus disease in horses affecting the central nervous system. The virus is carried by insects [fr. Gk enkephalos, brain + MYELITIS]
en·ceph·a·lo·my·o·car·di·tis (insefəloumaioukardáitis) n. (med.) brain and heart viral disease characterized by degeneration of heart muscles, lesions of the nervous system, inflammation of the skeletal system, and high fever
en·ceph·a·lon (inséfalon) pl. **en·ceph·a·la** (inséfələ) n. (physiol.) the vertebrate brain [Mod. L. fr. Gk enkephalos, brain]
en·chain (intʃéin) v.t. to bind with chains ‖ (rhet.) to hold captive, control, hold fast [O.F. enchainer]
en·chant (intʃǽnt, intʃánt) v.t. to cast a spell on ‖ to fill with delight **en·chánt·ed** adj. under a spell **en·chánt·er** n. a magician ‖ someone who fascinates **en·chánt·ing** adj. delightful ‖ fascinating **en·chánt·ment** n. a magic spell or charm ‖ the state of being under a spell ‖ delight‖ delightfulness **en·chánt·ress** n. [F. enchanter]
en·chase (intʃéis) pres. part. **en·chas·ing** past and past part. **en·chased** v.t. to set (e.g. a diamond in a ring) ‖ to chase (designs etc.) ‖ to ornament by engraving, embossing, cutting, setting with precious stones etc. [F. enchâsser]
en·ci·na (insí:nə) n. Quercus agrifolia, the evergreen oak of the southern coastal zone of W. North America ‖ Quercus virginiana, the common evergreen oak of E. North America [Span.]
en·cir·cle (insə́rk'l) pres. part. **en·cir·cling** past and past part. **en·cir·cled** v.t. to surround, police encircled the house ‖ to move in a circular path around **en·cir·cle·ment** n. a surrounding or being surrounded
en·clave (énkleiv) n. a territory belonging to one country but surrounded by that of another ‖ a cultural or linguistic group similarly surrounded [F.]
en·clit·ic (inklítik) **1.** adj. pronounced with so little stress that it becomes part of the preceding word, e.g. 'not' in 'cannot' (cf. PROCLITIC) ‖ (Gk gram.) without accent but modifying the accent of the preceding word **2.** n. an enclitic word or particle **en·clit·i·cal·ly** adv. [fr. L. encliticus fr. Gk]
en·close, in·close (inklóuz) pres. part. **en·clos·ing, in·clos·ing** past and past part. **en·closed, in·closed** v.t. to shut in with a wall or other protection ‖ to put (something) into an envelope or parcel with something else ‖ to surround on all sides, hem in ‖ to contain (within a boundary), the frontiers enclose an area of 50,000 sq. miles ‖ (hist.) to fence in (land) that was formerly under open-field cultivation, or common land appropriated by rich landowners ‖ to seclude (religious, a religious order) by rule ‖ to reserve (part of a convent) entirely for the religious of the community
en·clo·sure, in·clo·sure (inklóuʒər) n. something enclosed in a letter or parcel ‖ a place shut in, fenced in or otherwise marked off for a special purpose ‖ a fence or other boundary that encloses an area ‖ (religion) the state of being enclosed ‖ the part of a convent reserved strictly for the religious of a community ‖ (hist.) the enclosing of land, or the land enclosed. In England, enclosure began in the 12th c., was legalized by statutes (1235 and 1285), and increased with the development of the wool trade (after the 14th c.). In the Tudor period it was blamed for vagrancy and social unrest, and there was a final spate of enclosures in the 18th and 19th cc. [O.F.]
en·code (inkóud) pres. part. **en·cod·ing** past and past part. **en·cod·ed** v.t. to put into code
en·co·men·de·ro (eŋkɔmendéro) *ENCOMIENDA
en·co·mi·ast (inkóumi:æst) n. someone who praises highly, esp. a writer of panegyric **en·co·mi·ás·tic, en·co·mi·ás·ti·cal** adjs [fr. Gk enkomiastēs fr. encomion, eulogy]
en·co·mi·en·da (enkoumi:éndə) n. a Spanish colonial institution functioning in America up to the 18th c. Under it the Indians on the estates distributed among the colonists by Crown grant were obliged to work for, or pay tribute to, their master (encomendero), who in turn had to protect them and instruct them in Christian doctrine. The distribution was theoretically a Crown grant [Span.]
en·co·mi·um (inkóumi:əm) pl. **en·co·mi·ums, en·co·mi·a** (inkóumi:ə) n. an expression of high praise [L. fr. Gk enkomion, eulogy]

en·com·pass (inkámpəs) v.t. to surround or enclose, hem in on every side ‖ to embrace within its scope etc.
en·core (áŋkɔr,áŋkour) **1.** interj. the cry of an audience when it is pleased and wants a performer to play (or sing etc.) again **2.** n. the additional performance called for in this way **3.** v.t. pres. part. **en·cor·ing** past and past part. **en·cored** to call on (a performer) to play (or sing etc.) again ‖ to call on the performer of (a song etc.) to perform it again [F.=yet, again]
en·coun·ter (inkáuntər) **1.** v.t. to come upon, meet ‖ to come up against, meet in conflict or battle, or as rivals in sport **2.** n. a meeting by chance, not by design ‖ a conflict, battle, or match or game between rival teams ‖ in health care, any contact between a patient and health professional in which care is given, sometimes excluding telephone contacts [fr. O.F. encontrer, encontre]
encounter group (psych.) therapeutic group designed to increase sensitivity and create physical and emotional awareness of members through body contact and emotional expression. Some utilize marathon sessions, one or two days without sleep, etc., to break down members' resistance **syn** sensitivity group, T-group Cf GROUP THERAPY
en·cour·age (inkə́:ridʒ, inkʌ́ridʒ) pres. part. **en·cour·ag·ing** past and past part. **en·cour·aged** v.t. to give courage or confidence to ‖ to raise the hopes of ‖ to help on by sympathetic advice and interest, to encourage a boy's interest in music ‖ to advise and make it easy for (someone to do something), we encourage our apprentices to attend technical school ‖ to promote, stimulate, high wages encourage early marriage ‖ to strengthen (a belief or idea), his disappearance encouraged the belief that he was guilty **en·cóur·ag·ing** adj. **en·cóur·age·ment** n. a heartening or being heartened ‖ something that cheers and helps on ‖ an inducement, when money falls in value there is no encouragement to save [O.F. encoragier]
en·croach (inkróutʃ) v.i. (with 'on' or 'upon') to overstep the limits of what belongs or is due to one, to encroach on someone's privacy ‖ (with 'on' or 'upon') to make gradual inroads **en·cróach·ment** n. [O.F. encrochier, to catch with a hook]
en·croach·ing (enkróutʃiŋ) n. (football) **1.** body movement over the scrimmage line **2.** making contact with an opponent before the ball is put into play
en·crust, in·crust (inkrást) v.t. to cover with a coating or crust, hands encrusted with dirt ‖ to inlay jewels into, a ring encrusted with rubies [fr. F. incruster]
en·cum·ber (inkámbər) v.t. to hamper, impede, encumbered with parcels ‖ to burden, encumbered with debts ‖ to litter, block up, needlessly encumbered with footnotes [F. encombrer]
en·cum·brance (inkámbrəns) n. any burden, difficulty, responsibility or obligation that encumbers one or restricts one's movement or freedom ‖ (law) a claim on property, e.g. the payment of interest on a mortgage ‖ (law) a dependent child or other person [O.F. encombrance]
-ency suffix used like -ence [fr. L. -entia]
en·cyc·li·cal (insíklik'l) **1.** n. (eccles.) a circular letter, esp. from the pope to the archbishops and bishops of the Roman Catholic Church (occasionally to those of one country only), dealing with ecclesiastical, moral, theological or social questions **2.** adj. (eccles.) intended for many, an encyclical letter [L. fr. Gk enkuklios, all round, general]
en·cy·clo·pe·di·a, en·cy·clo·pae·di·a (insaikləpí:di:ə) n. a book or series of books giving information (generally arranged alphabetically) on all subjects or on all aspects of one subject, an encyclopedia of gardening the **En·cy·clo·pe·di·a** (hist.) the 'Encyclopédie ou dictionnaire raisonné des sciences, des arts et des métiers' edited (1751-72) by the French writers d'Alembert and Diderot, a powerful expression of the new rationalism of prerevolutionary France **en·cy·clo·pé·dic, en·cy·clo·pǽ·dic** adj. in or like an encyclopedia ‖ covering a wide range of knowledge or all aspects of a subject **en·cy·clo·pé·di·cal, en·cy·clo·pǽ·di·cal** adj. **en·cy·clo·pé·dism, en·cy·clo·pǽ·dism** n. the possession of wide and exact knowledge **en·cy·clo·pé·dist, en·cy·clo·pǽ·dist** n. someone who writes, edits or contributes to an encyclopedia **En·cy·clo·pe·dist, En·cy·clo·pae·dist** (hist.) one of the editors or contributors to the (French)

Encyclopedia [L.L. fr. Gk *enkuklios,* all round+*paideia,* education]

en·cyst (insíst) *v.t.* (*biol.*) to enclose in a cyst or sac ‖ *v.i.* (*biol.*) to become enclosed in a cyst or sac **en·cýst·ment** *n.*

end (end) **1.** *n.* the last part of a thing, i.e. the furthest in distance, latest in time, or last in sequence or series ‖ a part of a building, region etc. with respect to position, *the chancel end of a church* or with respect to some distinguishing quality, *the fashionable end of town* ‖ the limit beyond which a thing cannot be extended, *his patience is at an end* or beyond which there is no more, *that's the end of the jam* ‖ that part of a thing which defines or bounds its length, *the ends of a table* (cf. SIDE) ‖ the tip or extremity of a thing, *the end of a cigar* ‖ a piece that is left over, a remnant, *the stub end of a pencil* ‖ the conclusion of what has gone before ‖ a final result or ultimate state ‖ death, *his end came suddenly* ‖ finish, destruction, that which finishes or destroys, *this latest defeat was the end of him* ‖ aim or purpose, *he used the firm's money for his own ends* ‖ the reason for which someone or something exists, *man's end is joy in heaven* ‖ (*football*) the player at either end of the forward line, or his position **at loose ends** *Br.* **at a loose end** at leisure but having nothing particular to do **in the end** finally, after all **no end of** very great, very many **on end** one after another without a break, *for days on end* ‖ on its end, upright **the end** the worst instance or example of something bad, *she was always extravagant but buying all twelve was the end* **to be at** (or **come to**) **an end** to finish, be exhausted **to be on one's beam ends** (*Br.*) to have hardly any money left **to make an end of** to bring to an end, finish ‖ to kill **to make both ends meet** to manage to subsist on one's income **to put an end to** to stop, often by force **to turn end for end** to turn so that the position of the ends is reversed **2.** *adj.* final, *the end result* [O.E. *ende*]

end *v.t.* to stop, *to end a quarrel* ‖ to conclude, *to end a story* ‖ *v.i.* to come to an end ‖ to result in, *the match ended in a draw* **to end off** to conclude, *to end off a story, the path ends off abruptly* **to end up** to reach a final position or situation, *the car ended up in the ditch, he ended up as a major* [O.E. *endian*]

en·da·moe·ba, en·da·me·ba (endəmí:bə) *pl.* **en·da·moe·bae, en·da·me·bae** (endəmí:bi:), **en·da·moe·bas, en·da·me·bas** *n.* a member of *Endamoeba,* a genus of parasitic organisms, some species of which can live in the intestines and liver of man or some of the higher animals. *E. histolytica* causes amoebic dysentery [fr. Gk *end,* within+AMOEBA]

en·dan·ger (indéindʒər) *v.t.* to cause danger to or constitute a cause of danger to

en·dan·gered (endéindʒərd) *adj.* threatened with extinction, e.g., endangered species

endangered species mammals, birds, reptiles and amphibians that are in danger of extinction, usually because of environmental changes and human activity. Humans have exploited land; hunted, trapped or killed for safety, food and research; and polluted the atmosphere for their own needs, thus depriving animals of their habitats and conditions necessary for survival. Endangered species include the peregrine falcon, the bald eagle, some whales, the egret, the bird of paradise, the Atlantic salmon and sturgeon and the orangutan, among many others. The Endangered Species Act (1973) protects the vital habitat of an endangered species. The International Union for the Conservation of Nature and Natural Resources in Morges, Switzerland, publishes a list of threatened species

end around (*football*) tactic in which the ball is carried by an end, taking the ball behind the scrimmage line around the opposite flank

end·ar·ter·ec·to·my or **en·dar·ter·i·ec·to·my** (endɑːrtəréktəmi:) *n.* (*med.*) surgical removal of obstruction plaque, etc., inside an artery

en·dear (indíər) *v.t.* to cause to be held in affection **en·déar·ment** *n.* a word, phrase, act, gesture etc. which expresses affection

en·deav·or, esp. *Br.* **en·deav·our** (indévər) **1.** *v.i.* to make a determined effort **2.** *n.* a determined effort [M.E. *endever* fr. EN- (in)+ O.F. *dever,* duty]

en·dem·ic (endémik) **1.** *adj.* restricted to a particular region or people **2.** *n.* an endemic disease, e.g. silicosis among miners (cf. EPIDEMIC) **en·dém·i·cal** *adj.* [fr. EN- (in)+ Gk *dēmos,* people]

En·ders (éndərz), John Franklin (1897–1985), U.S. microbiologist. He helped to cultivate the poliomyelitis virus in tissue culture, for which he shared (with F. C. Robbins and T. H. Weller) the 1954 Nobel prize in physiology and medicine

end·grain (éndgrein) *adj.* and *adv.* with the ends of the fibers exposed when the wood is cut across its length

end·ing (éndiŋ) *n.* the action of coming or bringing to an end ‖ conclusion, finish, *the story has a happy ending* ‖ (*gram.*) a morpheme added to a word to make inflectional forms, e.g. in English '-s' for the plural of most nouns, or '-ed' for the past of most verbs

en·dive (éndaiv, ɑndi:v) *n. Cichorium endivia,* fam. *Compositae,* a salad plant closely related to chicory [F.]

end·leaf (éndli:f) *pl.* **end·leaves** (éndli:vz) *n.* an endpaper

end·less (éndlis) *adj.* never coming to an end ‖ too great to count ‖ a great deal of, *endless confusion* ‖ (of a driving belt or chain etc.) continuous, with no gap between the joined ends [O.E. *endelēas*]

end man the man at the end of each line in a minstrel show who engages in comic or ribald repartee with the interlocutor

end·most (éndmoust) *adj.* furthest, nearest the end

endo- (éndou) *prefix* within [fr. Gk *endon,* within, at home]

en·do·blast (éndəblæst) *n.* the hypoblast **en·do·blás·tic** *adj.* [ENDO-+ Gk *blastos,* cell]

en·do·car·di·al (endoukɑ́rdi:əl) *adj.* (*anat.*) inside the heart ‖ of or relating to the endocardium

en·do·car·di·um (endoukɑ́rdi:em) *pl.* **en·do·car·di·a** (endoukɑ́rdi:ə) *n.* the membrane lining the cavities of the heart (*MYOCARDIUM, *PERICARDIUM) [Mod. L. fr. Gk *endon,* within + *kardia,* heart]

en·do·carp (éndəkɑrp) *n.* the innermost layer of the pericarp when it is differentiated [F. *endocarpe* fr. Gk *endon,* within+ *karpos,* fruit]

en·do·crine (éndəkrin, éndəkrain) **1.** *adj.* producing secretions that are distributed by means of the bloodstream rather than specialized ducts ‖ relating to the endocrine glands, or their secretions or to the system of endocrine glands **2.** *n.* any endocrine gland or its secretion **en·do·cri·nal** (endəkráin'l), **en·do·crin·ic** (endəkrínik), **en·doc·ri·nous** (endókrinəs) *adjs* [ENDO-+ Gk *krinein,* to separate]

endocrine gland one of a group of glands found in higher animals that produce hormones and secrete them into the bloodstream. Organs which have hormonal function and so belong to the class of endocrine glands are the pituitary body, the thyroid, parathyroid and adrenal glands, the pancreas, and the testicles in the male and ovaries in the female. Other glands whose hormonal function is uncertain are the thymus, the pineal body and the liver, kidneys and spleen

en·do·cri·nol·o·gy (endoukrinólədʒi:) *n.* the study of the endocrine glands, their secretions and their physiological relations to one another and to the organism as a whole **en·do·cri·nól·o·gist** *n.* [ENDOCRINE+Gk *logos,* word]

en·do·cy·to·sis (endousaitóusis) *n.* (*biol.*) process by which cells absorb phagocytes (cells that destroy other cells) or liquids from cell membranes **endocytatic** or **endocytic** *adj.*

en·do·derm (éndədə:rm) *n.* the innermost germ layer in an embryo possessing three layers. It is the source of the lining of the digestive and respiratory organs and of the glands appended to the digestive tract **en·do·dér·mal, en·do·dér·mic** *adjs.* **en·do·dér·mis** *n.* the innermost layer of the cortex of most roots and stems, consisting usually of a single layer of living cells. It is thought to act as a control on the movement of liquids into and out of the stele [F. *endoderme* fr. Gk *endon,* within+ *derma,* skin]

end-of-day glass product resembling something made of scraps of various colors, left over at the end of the day of glass making Cf SPAT-TER GLASS

en·do·gam·ic (endəgǽmik) *adj.* endogamous **en·dog·a·mous** (endógəməs) *adj.* of or relating to endogamy

en·dog·a·my (endógəmi:) *n.* a customary or legally required marriage within the tribe or other social group (cf. EXOGAMY) ‖ (*zool.*) zygote formation by the union of female gametes ‖ (*bot.*) self-pollination [fr. ENDO-+Gk *gamos,* marriage]

en·do·gen (éndədʒən) *n.* a plant which develops by endogenous growth, e.g. most monocotyledons (cf. EXOGEN) **en·dog·e·nous** (endódʒənəs) *adj.* originating within the organism ‖ (*biol.*) developing from a deep-seated layer ‖ (*biol.*) developing within the cell ‖ (*metabolism*) concerned with tissue waste and growth (cf. EXOGENOUS) **en·dóg·e·ny** *n.* (*biol.*) development from a deep-seated layer [F. *endogéne*]

en·do·lymph (éndəlimf) *n.* the fluid in the labyrinth of the ear **en·do·lym·phat·ic** (endoulimfǽtik) *adj.*

en·do·morph (éndəmɔrf)*n.* (*mineral.*) a crystal enclosed in one of a different species ‖ an endomorphic person **en·do·mór·phic** *adj.* ‖ (*mineral.*) of or related to an endomorph ‖ of a pyknic type of body build, having the physique associated with a predominance in bodily development of organs derived from the endodermal layer of the embryo, e.g. the digestive glands and alimentary lining (cf. ECTOMORPHIC, cf. MESOMORPHIC) **en·do·mór·phism** *n.* (*geol.*) a change occurring in an intrusive rock, caused by reaction with the walls of the cavities into which it has flowed or been forced [ENDO-+ Gk *morphē,* form]

end on with their ends facing, *to collide end on* ‖ with an end toward the viewer

en·do·nu·cle·ase (endounú:kli:eis) *n.* (*biochem.*) an enzyme that breaks down deoxyribonucleic acid, or RNA, to produce two or more shorter nucleotide chains Cf EXONUCLEASE

en·do·par·a·site (endoupǽrəsait) *n.* (*zool.*) a parasite which lives inside the body of its host (cf. ECTOPARASITE) **en·do·par·a·sit·ic** (endoupǽrəsítik) *adj.*

en·do·phyte (éndəfait) *n.* (*bot.*) a plant which grows inside another parasitically or otherwise [ENDO- + Gk *phuton,* plant]

en·do·plasm (éndəplæzəm) *n.* the inner part of the protoplasm of a cell (cf. ECTOPLASM) **en·do·plás·mic** *adj.*

en·do·pleu·ra (endouplúərə) *n.* (*bot.*) the inner seed coat

en·do·ra·di·o·sonde (endoureidi:ousónd) *n.* a device implanted in the body to trasmit data on body functions, e.g., for gastrointestinal diagnosis

end organ (*physiol.*) the peripheral termination of a nerve, which either receives sensation or stimulates a response (e.g. a muscular one)

en·dor·phin (endórfin) *n.* morphinelike substance secreted in the pituitary gland to control pain and pleasure Cf ENKEPHALIN

en·dorse, in·dorse (indórs) *pres. part.* **en·dors·ing, in·dors·ing** *past* and *past part.* **en·dorsed, in·dorsed** *v.t.* to sign one's name on the back of (a check etc.) in order to obtain the cash it represents ‖ to make (a check etc.) payable to another by writing his name on the back and signing ‖ in South Africa, to banish blacks from an urban area with regulations designed to restrain emigration to cities ‖ to sign or initial, or add a comment or qualification to (a document) ‖ (*Br.*) to write on (esp. a driving license) particulars of an offense for which the holder has been convicted ‖ to confirm, sanction, show approval of or agreement with (an option, action, proposal etc.) **en·dórse·ment, in·dórse·ment** *n.* [M.E. *endosse* fr. O.F.]

en·do·sarc (éndəsɑrk) *n.* (*biol.*) endoplasm [ENDO-+ Gk *sarx* (*sarkos*), flesh]

en·do·scope (éndəskoup) *n.* (*med.*) an instrument for examining the inside of an organ, e.g. the bladder **en·dos·co·py** (endóskəpi:) *pl.* **en·dos·co·pies** *n.* an examination with this [ENDO-+Gk *skopein,* to observe]

en·do·skel·e·ton (endouskélitən) *n.* an internal skeleton or structurally similar unit in an animal (cf. EXOSKELETON)

en·dos·mo·sis (endɔzmóusis, endɔsmóusis) *n.* (*chem.*) the movement of a substance through a membrane from a region of lower concentration to one of higher concentration ‖ the transfer of material by osmosis into a cell (cf. EXOSMOSIS) **en·dos·mot·ic** (endɔzmótik, endɔsmótik) *adj.*

en·do·sperm (éndəspə:rm) *n.* (*bot.*) the nutritive tissue within the seeds of seed plants **en·do·spér·mous** *adj.* [F. *endosperme* fr. Gk *endon,* within+*sperma,* seed]

en·do·spore (éndəspɔr, éndəspour) *n.* an asexual spore produced within a cell ‖ the endosporium ‖ the inner coat of a sporocyst in some protozoans **en·dos·por·ous** (endóspərəs, endouspórəs, endouspóurəs) *adj.*

en·do·spo·ri·um (endəspóri:əm, endəspóuri:əm) *pl.* **en·do·spo·ri·a** (endəspóri:ə, endəspóuri:ə)

CONCISE PRONUNCIATION KEY: **(a)** æ, c*a*t; ɑ, c*a*r; ɔ f*aw*n; ei, sn*a*ke. **(e)** e, h*e*n; i:, sh*ee*p; iə, d*ee*r; ɛə, b*ea*r. **(i)** i, f*i*sh; ai, t*i*ger; ə:, b*i*rd. **(o)** o, *o*x; au, c*ow*; ou, g*oa*t; u, p*oo*r; ɔi, r*oy*al. **(u)** ʌ, d*u*ck; u, b*u*ll; u:, g*oo*se; ə, *a*bacillus; ju:, c*u*be. x, lo*ch*; θ, *th*ink; ð, bo*th*er; z, *Z*en; ʒ, corsa*g*e. dʒ, sava*g*e; ŋ, orangutan*g*; j, *y*ak; ʃ, *fi*sh; tʃ, fe*tch*; 'l, rabb*le*; 'n, redd*en*. Complete pronunciation key appears inside front cover.

(*bot.*) the inner of two layers of a spore wall [Mod. L.]

en·dos·te·um (endósti:əm) *pl.* **en·dos·te·a** (endósti:ə) *n.* (*anat.*) a vascular, connective layer of tissue lining the large cavities of bones [Mod. L. fr. Gk *endon*, within+*osteon*, bone]

en·dos·to·sis (endostóusis) *pl.* **en·dos·to·ses** (endostóusi:z) *n.* (*anat.*) ossification starting inside cartilage (cf. ECTOSTOSIS) [Mod. L. fr. Gk *endon*, within+*ostōsis*, formation of bone]

en·do·sul·fan [C₉H₆Cl₆O₃S] (endəsálfən) *n.* (*chem.*) toxic insecticide and miticide containing chlorinated sulfate used on vegetables, flowers, and forage crops and to control termites and tsetse flies

en·do·tes·ta (endoutéstə) *n.* (*botany*) the inner layer of the outer covering of a seed

en·do·the·li·um (endouθí:li:əm) *pl.* **en·do·the·li·a** (endouθí:li:ə) *n.* a serum producing epithelium of mesoblastic origin that lines blood vessels and internal body cavities [Mod. L. fr. Gk *endon*, within +*thēlē*, nipple]

en·do·ther·mal (endouθé:rməl) *adj.* endothermic

en·do·ther·mic (endouθé:rmik) *adj.* (of a chemical reaction) accompanied by absorption of heat (cf. EXOTHERMIC)

en·do·tox·in (endoutóksin) *n.* a toxin that remains within the bacterial protoplasm which produces it (cf. EXOTOXIN)

en·dow (indáu) *v.t.* to give money or other property for the permanent upkeep or benefit of (an institution, organization etc.) ‖ (with 'with') to provide with a natural gift, attribute etc., *endowed with intelligence* **en·dów·ment** *n.* the act of endowing (with money or other property) ‖ the money or property so given ‖ a natural gift or ability, *mental endowments* [O.F. *endouer*]

endowment insurance a policy providing for the payment to the person insured of an agreed sum at the end of an agreed period, or at the death of the person insured (if this occurs in the interval) to a person designated

end·pa·per (éndpeipər) *n.* a sheet of paper at the beginning and end of a book, folded to make two leaves, one of which is pasted to the inside of the cover

end play 1. *n.* (*bridge*) a carefully prepared maneuver by the declarer, in the final stages of play, by which the defender is forced to win a trick and make a lead which then permits the declarer to win the decisive trick 2. *v.t.* (*bridge*) to force (a defender) into an end-play situation

end product the object or substance into which raw material is finally changed in a process of manufacture

en·drin [C₁₂H₈OCl₆] (éndrən) *n.* toxic pesticide said to cause irreversible damage to the human central nervous system

en·droph·i·ly (endrófili:) *n.* humanity's ecological dependence on human beings **endophilic** *adj. Cf* EXOPHILY

en·due (indú:, indjú:) *pres. part.* **en·du·ing** *past* and *past part.* **en·dued** *v.t.* to provide with a talent, ability etc., endow [fr. O.F. *enduire*]

en·dur·a·ble (indúərə'l, indjúərəb'l) *adj.* that can be endured

en·dur·ance (indúərəns, indjúərəns) *n.* the capacity to keep going or put up with pain, hardship etc. for a long time ‖ the act of doing this ‖ the length of time that an aircraft can remain in the air under specified conditions without refueling

en·dure (indúər, indjúər) *pres. part.* **en·dur·ing** *past* and *past part.* **en·dured** *v.t.* to bear, stand ‖ to suffer patiently ‖ to put up with, tolerate, *why do you endure his rudeness?* ‖ *v.i.* to remain set in purpose, hold out, under suffering, trial etc. ‖ to last for a long time, *built to endure* **en·dúr·ing** *adj.* [O.F. *endurer*]

en·du·ro (endú:rou) *n.* a sport race stressing endurance, e.g., for motorcycles

end·ways (éndweiz) *adv.* with the end toward one ‖ on end ‖ end to end

end·wise (éndwaiz) *adv.* endways

En·dym·i·on (endími:ən) (*Gk mythol.*) a shepherd loved by Selene. He was permitted by Zeus to keep his beauty forever, in an eternal sleep

en·e·ma (énəmə) *n.* a liquid pumped into the bowels through the rectum, as a purgative or for nourishment ‖ the pumping in of this liquid ‖ the instrument used [Gk=injection]

enemies list a list of enemies, esp. one compiled by Richard M. Nixon while President

en·e·my (énəmi:) 1. *pl.* **en·e·mies** *n.* a hostile nation, or a member of it ‖ (*collect.*) the nation's armed forces or part of them ‖ a person who bears another ill will and actively works or fights against him ‖ someone who opposes, disapproves, or works against (ideas, beliefs etc.), *an enemy of privilege* ‖ something harmful or troublesome, *slugs are among the gardener's worst enemies* 2. *adj.* being or pertaining to an enemy [O.F. *enemi*]

en·er·get·ic (enərdʒétik) *adj.* active, showing great physical or mental energy ‖ requiring great physical effort ‖ forceful, vigorous, *energetic protests* **en·er·gét·i·cal·ly** *adv.* **en·er·gét·ics** *n.* the study of the production of energy and its transformations [fr. Gk *enegētikos*]

energetics (*chem.*) study of the overall picture of energy and its chemical changes in an ecological unit

en·er·gize (énərdʒaiz) *pres. part.* **en·er·giz·ing** *past* and *past part.* **en·er·gized** *v.t.* to give energy to ‖ to cause electricity to flow in, *to energize the core of a magnet*

en·er·giz·er (énərdʒaizər) *n.* a stimulant drug, esp. to relieve psychological depression

en·er·gy (énərdʒi:) *pl.* **en·er·gies** *n.* forcefulness and vigor in actions or words ‖ (often *pl.*) busy activity, *to devote one's energies to making a success of an enterprise* ‖ (*phys.*) the unifying concept of all physical science that associates with any system a capacity for work either as a result of the motion of mass in the system (kinetic energy), the configuration of masses or charges in the system (potential energy) or the presence of photons in the system (radiant energy). Energy is a scalar quantity with dimensions $\frac{mass \times length^2}{time^2}$ that possesses the properties of mass according to the theory of relativity, assigning to a mass M an energy such that $\frac{C^2}{E}$ = M where E is the energy and C² is the speed of light [fr. L.L. *energia* fr. Gk fr. *ergon*, work]

energy agriculture cultivating plants for the purpose of creating energy, e.g., grain for distillation into alcohol

energy efficiency ratio measurement of electrical efficiency of an appliance relative to heat output computed as BTU per hr. output divided by watts used

energy paper fiber impregnated with potassium persulfate and powdered carbon; energy paper is a replaceable active material for a dry cell battery

energy structure a form of kinetic art with motorized, mechanical, or electronic parts

Energy, U.S. Department of (*abbr.* DOE) (1977) a cabinet-level department that oversees energy prices, conservation, fuel allocation and research on new energy sources and nuclear weapons. It was established to consolidate the functions of mainly the Energy Research and Development Administration, the Federal Power Commission and the Federal Energy Administration

en·er·vate (énərveit) *pres. part.* **en·er·vat·ing** *past* and *past part.* **en·er·vat·ed** *v.t.* to lower the vitality of ‖ to sap the willpower of or weaken the mental vigor of **en·er·vá·tion** *n.* [fr. L. *enervare* (*enervatus*), to cut out the tendon of]

en·fee·ble (infí:b'l) *pres. part.* **en·fee·bling** *past* and *past part.* **en·fee·bled** *v.t.* to make feeble **en·fée·ble·ment** *n.* [O.F. *enfeblir*]

en·feoff (infí:f) *v.t.* (*hist.*) to invest with a fief **en·féoff·ment** *n.* the act of so investing ‖ the document recording it [O.F. *enfeffer, enfieffer*]

en·fi·lade 1. (enfəléid, énfəleid) *n.* fire from guns directed straight down the length of a line of troops, a trench, valley etc. 2. (enfəléid) *v.t. pres. part.* **en·fi·lad·ing** *past* and *past part.* **en·fi·lad·ed** to subject to fire of this kind, or cover so as to be able to bring down such fire [F. fr. *enfiler*, to thread]

en·fold (infóuld) *v.t.* (with 'in' or 'with') to wrap up in the folds of ‖ to clasp, *to enfold in an embrace* ‖ to surround, enclose, *hanging woods enfold the lake*

en·force (infɔ́rs, infóurs) *pres. part.* **en·forc·ing** *past* and *past part.* **en·forced** *v.t.* to impose by force, compel, *to enforce obedience* ‖ to give strength to, *statistics would enforce your argument* ‖ to press home, *to enforce a claim by strike action* ‖ to put into force, *to enforce a rule* **en·fórce·a·ble** *adj.* **en·fórce·ment** *n.* [O.F. *forcer*]

en·fran·chise (infrǽntʃaiz) *pres. part.* **en·fran·chis·ing** *past* and *past part.* **en·fran·chised** *v.t.* to give (someone) political rights, esp. the right to vote ‖ to give political rights to (a town or city) ‖ to free from slavery **en·fran·chise·ment** (infrǽntʃizmənt) *n.* [fr. O.F. *enfranchir* (*enfranchiss-*), to set free]

Eng. English ‖ England

En·ga·dine (éngədi:n) a valley of the upper Inn, Switzerland, with a mild, dry climate: resorts (*GRAUBÜNDEN)

en·gage (ingéidʒ) *pres. part.* **en·gag·ing** *past* and *past part.* **en·gaged** *v.t.* to take into one's employment ‖ to reserve in advance, *to engage a table at a restaurant* ‖ to make a promise binding on (oneself), a promise of marriage ‖ to occupy the time of or compel the attention of, *to engage someone in conversation* ‖ (in warfare or other dispute) to come to grips with, to attack, *to engage the main enemy force* ‖ (of mechanical devices) to fit into, mesh with, *the notches of a key engage the wards of a lock* ‖ *v.i.* to join battle ‖ (*mech.*, with 'with') to interlock, mesh ‖ (with 'in') to busy oneself, *to engage in politics* **en·gáged** *adj.* pledged to marry, *an engaged couple* ‖ busy, already occupied, and so not free ‖ (of a gear) meshed ‖ (*archit.*, e.g. of a pillar) set into a wall **en·gáge·ment** *n.* an undertaking or obligation, esp. a promise to marry ‖ an agreement to employ or be employed ‖ an appointment for a fixed time ‖ a battle ‖ (*mech.*) the state of being meshed **en·gág·ing** *adj.* attractive, charming [F. *engager*]

En·gels (éŋəls), Friedrich (1820–95), German socialist and political philosopher. He spent most of his adult life in England as the manager of cotton mills. He met (1844) Karl Marx, and collaborated with him on many works, notably 'The Communist Manifesto' (1848). After Marx's death, he edited (1885–94) volumes II and III of 'Das Kapital'. His own works include 'The Condition of the Working Classes in England in 1844' (1845), 'Landmarks of Scientific Socialism' (1878) and 'The Origin of the Family, Private Property and the State' (1884)

'Engel v. Vitale' (éŋəl; vi:táli:) (1962) a U.S. Supreme Court case that prohibited prayer in public schools. Citing the Constitution's Establishment Clause that religion is too sacred to be administered civilly, Justice Hugo Black wrote the decision in favor of Steven Engel, a New York parent who maintained that prayer in school violated the 1st Amendment's guarantee of freedom of religion

en·gen·der (indʒéndər) *v.t.* to give rise to, *bad conditions of work engender industrial disputes* [F. *engendrer*]

En·ghien, Louis Antoine Henri de Bourbon-Condé, duc d' (1772–1804), French émigré, unjustly executed at Napoleon's orders on suspicion of conspiracy

en·gine (éndʒin) *n.* a device used to transform one form of energy into another, esp. into kinetic energy, *heat engine, internal-combustion engine* ‖ a locomotive ‖ (*hist.*) a war machine, e.g. a catapult [O.F. *engin*, a tool]

engine driver (*Br.*) an engineer (driver of a locomotive)

en·gi·neer (endʒiníər) 1. *n.* an expert in the design and construction of engines, *mechanical engineer* or of electrical equipment, *electrical engineer* or expert in the organization of civil works (roads, bridges etc.), *civil engineer* ‖ a person qualified in any branch of engineering ‖ (*Am.*=*Br.* engine driver) the driver of a locomotive ‖ (*Br.*) a fitter, mechanic or other skilled worker concerned with engines ‖ the man in charge of a ship's engines ‖ (*mil.*) one of a corps trained for roadmaking, bridge-building etc. ‖ someone active behind the scenes in achieving something, *who was the real engineer of their success?* 2. *v.t.* to carry out (a piece of engineering work) ‖ to manage, by using tact, craft or ingenuity, to achieve (a result), *to engineer an election victory* **en·gi·néer·ing** *n.* the science of applying knowledge of the properties of matter and the natural sources of energy to the practical problems of industry (e.g. the construction of industrial plant or machines) [M.E. *engyneour* fr. O.F.]

engineer's chain a measuring device that consists of 50 or 100 1-ft links joined by rings. It is used in surveying

Eng·land (íŋglənd) a country (area 50,331 sq. miles, pop. 45,771,956) occupying the largest, southern part of Great Britain. Capital: London. Language: English. Religion: 80% Church of England, 10% Roman Catholic, with Methodist, Jewish, Congregational, Baptist, Presbyterian and other minorities. The land is 30% arable, 48% pasture, 12% grazing and 6% for-

CONCISE PRONUNCIATION KEY: **(a)** æ, c*a*t; ɑ, c*a*r; ɔ f*aw*n; ei, sn*a*ke. **(e)** e, h*e*n; i:, sh*ee*p; iə, d*ee*r; ɛə, b*ea*r. **(i)** i, f*i*sh; ai, t*i*ger; ə:, b*i*rd. **(o)** o, *o*x; au, c*ow*; ou, g*oa*t; u, p*oo*r; ɔi, r*oy*al. **(u)** ʌ, d*u*ck; u, b*u*ll; u:, g*oo*se; ə, b*a*cillus; ju:, c*u*be. x, lo*ch*; θ, *th*ink; ð, bo*th*er; z, *Z*en; ʒ, cor*s*age; dʒ, sava*g*e; ŋ, oranguta*ng*; j, *y*ak; ʃ, *fi*sh; tʃ, fe*tch*; 'l, rabb*le*; 'n, redd*en*. Complete pronunciation key appears inside front cover.

est. The southwest and west, except for the Severn valley and the Cheshire-Lancashire plain (around Liverpool), are largely a plateau, with rolling plains and downs culminating in hills, chalk ridges and occasional moors. The Pennines, running from the N. Midlands to the Scottish border, are the principal mountain chain, but the highest peaks (Sca Fell, 3,210 ft) are in the Lake District. The east is mainly an open, cultivated plain, narrowing in N. Yorkshire to a passage (Vale of York) between coastal moors and the Pennines, and in Northumberland to a coastal strip. Average temperatures: (Jan.) 40°, (July) 61°. Rainfall: under 30 ins in the east and the Midlands, over 60 ins in the Lake District, Pennines, Exmoor and Dartmoor, 30–60 ins elsewhere. Ports: London, Liverpool, Hull, Manchester, Southampton, Bristol. HISTORY. The earliest known settlers in England were of Iberian stock. They were mingled (after 600 B.C.) with two successive invasions of Celts, who worked bronze and iron, and established a Druid priesthood. The Romans sent expeditions (55–54 B.C.) under Julius Caesar and invaded (43 A.D.) under Claudius. They made England the Roman province of Britannia, quickly conquering the south, putting down the revolt (c. 62 A.D.) of Boadicea, and building roads and fortified towns. The north was not subdued until the end of the 2nd c., despite the fortifications built by Agricola (c. 80) and Hadrian's wall (122–8). Trade prospered and Christianity was introduced. The withdrawal (early 5th c.) of the Roman legions to defend Rome from the barbarians left England exposed to the attacks of the Picts and Scots in the north, and of Germanic invaders on the east coast. THE ANGLES, SAXONS AND JUTES drove the Celts back to Wales and Cornwall, and founded settlements (mid-5th c.) which developed into the kingdoms of Kent, Sussex, Essex, Wessex, East Anglia, Mercia and Northumbria. Christianity was reintroduced, partly by a mission from Rome under Augustine, who landed (597) in Kent, and partly by the Celtic Church centers on Iona and Holy Island. Differences between the two Churches were settled (664) at the synod of Whitby, in favor of the Roman Church. Out of sporadic fighting among the kingdoms, Northumbria emerged dominant (7th c.), and became (late 7th c.) a brilliant center of learning, with Bede and Alcuin, while a native Anglo-Saxon literature developed. Mercia rose to supremacy (8th c.), notably under Offa, who claimed to rule all England. The Danes raided the coasts (late 8th c.), landed an army (865) and began to settle. Wessex, by then the dominant English kingdom, resisted them with little success until Alfred forced the Danes to agree (878) to confine their settlement to the Danelaw in the north and east. Edward the Elder and Athelstan conquered the Danelaw (early 10th c.), and Edgar received the homage of all the kings of Britain at his coronation (973). The Danes renewed their raids (980), overcame Ethelred II, and ruled England (1016–42) under Cnut and his sons. The weak reign (1042–66) of Edward the Confessor left the throne disputed between Harold, son of Earl Godwin, and William, Duke of Normandy, who defeated Harold at Hastings (1066) and ruled (1066–87) as William I. THE NORMANS (1066–1135) added military feudalism to the social and economic organization of Anglo-Saxon England. The English Church remained subservient under William I's nominee, Lanfranc, but friction with the monarchy developed in the reign (1087–1100) of William II, and became serious when Anselm quarreled openly with Henry I. The land was surveyed in Domesday Book (1086–7), and the administrative system was centralized, notably in the reign (1100–35) of Henry I. After William I had dealt severely with English rebellions, the chief threat to the Norman monarchy lay in the risk of baronial revolt. The barons were kept in check by Henry I, whose victory at Tinchebrai (1106) secured them their estates in Normandy. but anarchy broke loose on Henry's death (1135). The barons and the Church took advantage of the civil war (1139–53) between Stephen and Matilda to increase their own power. THE PLANTAGENETS (1154–1399). Royal control was reestablished in the reign (1154–89) of Henry II, despite an unsuccessful baronial rising (1174), and despite the difficulty of ruling an empire that included Normandy, Anjou, Aquitaine and Ireland. Henry failed in his attempt to control the Church by the Constitutions of Clarendon (1164), and the problem was not solved by the murder (1170) of Becket. The Crown was impoverished by Richard I's participation (1190–2) in the 3rd Crusade, his captivity in Germany (1192–4) and his war with France (1194–9). Resultant heavy taxation aroused baronial opposition, which was increased in the reign (1199–1216) of John by the loss of Normandy (1204) and his defeat by the French at Bouvines (1214). John was forced to agree to the barons' demands in Magna Carta (1215), and his successor, Henry III, was forced to agree to the Provisions of Oxford (1258). During the Barons' War (1264–6), Henry was imprisoned (1265) and briefly replaced by a council of barons under Simon de Montfort. Henry's son Edward I restored royal authority, carried out legal reforms, and conquered Wales (1277–83), but financial difficulty led to the summoning of the Model Parliament (1295). His attempt to subdue Scotland collapsed at Bannockburn (1314) under his son, Edward II, whose incompetent reign (1307–27) ended with his deposition by a baronial faction. The Hundred Years' War with France (1338–1453) was begun victoriously by Edward III, but reverses followed. The economy had prospered with the wool trade, but heavy war expenditure and the Black Death (1348–9) precipitated an economic crisis which was followed by a century of economic recession (mid-14th c.–mid-15th c.). The manorial and feudal system, long in decay, began to break up rapidly. Meanwhile, the English language was taking shape in the writings of Langland and Chaucer. Amid the social upheaval, characterized by Lollardry and the Peasants' Revolt (1381), barons acquired private armies. After a troubled reign (1377–99), Richard II was deposed by Henry, duke of Lancaster. THE HOUSE OF LANCASTER. The weakness of Henry IV's title to the throne increased the royal dependence on the barony and parliament, and most of his reign (1399–1413) was spent in putting down rebellions, notably in Wales under Glendower. Henry V diverted attention from the dynastic dispute with the house of York by his renewal of the war with France and his crushing victory at Agincourt (1415). But Henry VI lost all the English possessions in France except Calais by 1453. These reverses, and the misgovernment of England, prompted Cade's rebellion (1450) and contributed to the Wars of the Roses (1455–85). Amid sporadic warfare by baronial armies, Henry was deposed (1461) by Edward of York and, after a brief restoration (1470–1), he was murdered (1471). THE HOUSE OF YORK. Edward IV restored the royal finances, and so avoided the necessity of frequent parliaments. On his death (1483), his sons Edward V and Richard, duke of York, were imprisoned and murdered, almost certainly at the instigation of their uncle, who reigned (1483–5) as Richard III. He was overthrown and killed (1485) at Bosworth Field by a Lancastrian army under Henry Tudor, who ended the feud between Lancaster and York by marrying (1486) the daughter of Edward IV. THE TUDORS. Despite his weak title to the throne, Henry VII strengthened the monarchy, bringing the barony to order in the Court of Star Chamber and, by shrewd economic policy, building up vast financial reserves which freed him from dependence on parliament. Economic revival was aided by his avoidance of war and his encouragement of trade. This financial advantage was squandered by the flamboyant foreign policy of Henry VIII and Wolsey. The new learning of the Renaissance spread to England. Henry VIII's reign (1509–47) saw the separation of the Church of England from papal authority, prompted by the king's need to acquire the wealth of the monasteries, and by the hope that a divorce from Catherine of Aragon might enable Henry to obtain a male heir by a subsequent marriage. His only son, Edward VI, in a reign (1547–53) marked by a severe economic crisis, made the Church of England truly Protestant but, after the brief interlude of Lady Jane Grey (1553), Catholicism was restored by Mary I. The accession (1558) of Elizabeth I marked a return to moderate Protestantism, though Catholic plots continued until the execution (1587) of Mary queen of Scots, and the defeat (1588) of the Spanish Armada. Elizabeth's reign (1558–1603) was a period of economic expansion, maritime exploration, and great developments in literature, music and architecture. The end of the reign saw the growth of a vociferous Puritan opposition among the gentry in the House of Commons. THE STUARTS. The accession (1603) of James VI of Scotland as James I of England marked the personal union of the two crowns. In James's reign (1603–25), and in that of his son Charles I (1625–49), the breach widened between monarch and parliament. Against the Stuart doctrine of the divine right of kings, the Commons claimed the right to control royal policy by withholding supplies. They were angered by James's grants of monopolies, his arbitrary taxation, his pro-Spanish policy and by his worthless favorites such as Buckingham. Charles I was forced to sign (1628) the Petition of Right, but his unparliamentary rule (1629–40) through his minister Strafford and the High Church policy of Laud precipitated the Civil War (1642–52). After Charles's execution (1649), the Commonwealth was set up (1649), and Cromwell was appointed lord protector (1653–8). He was succeeded (1658–9) by his son. THE RESTORATION. A parliament summoned by Monk recalled (1660) Charles II from exile, on the terms of the Declaration of Breda. The Anglican Church was restored, and the civil liberties of Catholics and dissenters were restricted by the Clarendon Code (1661–5) and the Test Act (1673). After the unpopularity of Clarendon and the Cabal, and of the Dutch Wars (1665–7 and 1672–4), Charles obtained (1670) a secret subsidy from Louis XIV. Fear of a reversion to Catholicism caused the beginnings of the division between Whigs and Tories. Discontent grew in the reign (1685–8) of James II on account of his attempts to suspend anti-Catholic legislation and to make Catholic appointments. THE GLORIOUS REVOLUTION. A group of Whigs and Tories invited James's son-in-law, William of Orange, to invade and to redress grievances. James fled to France as William advanced on London (1688), and parliament declared William III and Mary II king and queen (1689). The Bill of Rights (1689) firmly established the supremacy of parliament and made Anne heir to the throne. Protestantism was reaffirmed, with toleration for nonconformist sects. There began a long period of rivalry with France, in the War of the Grand Alliance (1689–97) and the War of the Spanish Succession (1701–14). Trade prospered, and, with the establishment of the Bank of England (1694) and the national debt, London became the leading commercial and financial center of Europe. The Act of Settlement (1701) fixed the succession after Anne on the house of Hanover, and the Act of Union (1707) united England and Scotland. (For subsequent history *GREAT BRITAIN)

England, Church of *CHURCH OF ENGLAND

Eng·lish (ĭngliʃ) **1.** *adj.* of, relating to or characteristic of the country, state or people of England ‖ of the official language spoken in Great Britain, Northern Ireland, the U.S.A., Canada, Australia and other Commonwealth countries **2.** *n.* the English language ‖ this in a particular period of its development, *Middle English* or local or other variation, *American English, Basic English* **the English** (*pl.*) the people of England or its representatives (e.g. armed forces, or a team in international sport) **to put English on** (*Am., billiards*) to put sidespin on a ball **3.** *v.t.* to translate into English [O.E. *englisc, œnglisc*]

English Channel the strait (21–140 miles wide) between England and France, stretching 280 miles southwest from the Straits of Dover to the Atlantic

English Civil War *CIVIL WAR, ENGLISH

English daisy *Bellis perennis* (*DAISY)

English disease economic malaise supposedly caused by Britain's labor-management problems, esp. of excessive application of work rules **also** English sickness

English horn a woodwind instrument like a lower-pitched oboe ‖ an organ stop of similar tone

English language a language of the Germanic branch of the Indo-European family of languages. It is divided by scholars into Old English or Anglo-Saxon (700–1150), Middle English (1150–1450) and Modern English (sometimes called New English, 1450 to the present). About 275 million use it as their mother tongue, and hundreds of millions use English as their second language, i.e. in public affairs. It is the vehicle of a great world literature, and the main language of commerce

CONCISE PRONUNCIATION KEY: **(a)** æ, c*a*t; ɑ, c*a*r; ɔ f*aw*n; ei, sn*a*ke. **(e)** e, h*e*n; i:, sh*ee*p; iə, d*ee*r; ɛə, b*ea*r. **(i)** i, f*i*sh; ai, t*i*ger; ə:, b*i*rd. **(o)** o, *o*x; au, c*ow*; ou, g*oa*t; u, p*oo*r; ɔi, r*oy*al. **(u)** ʌ, d*u*ck; u, b*u*ll; u:, g*oo*se; ə, b*a*cillus; ju:, c*u*be. x, lo*ch*; θ, *th*ink; δ, bo*th*er; z, *Z*en; ʒ, cor*s*age; dʒ, sava*g*e; ŋ, oranguta*ng*; j, *y*ak; ʃ, *fi*sh; tʃ, fe*tch*; 'l, rabb*le*; 'n, redd*en*. Complete pronunciation key appears inside front cover.

Eng·lish·man (íŋgliʃmən) *pl.* **Eng·lish·men** (íŋgliʃmən) *n.* a man who is a native of England or an English subject

English muffin (*Am.*=*Br.* crumpet) a flat, leavened round of batter baked on an iron plate. It is toasted and eaten hot with butter

English sparrow *Passer domesticus,* the house sparrow

Eng·lish·wom·an (íŋgliʃwʊmən) *pl.* **Eng·lish·wom·en** (íŋgliʃwimən) *n.* a woman who is a native of England or an English subject

en·gobe (aŋgóub) *n.* (*pottery*) slip [F.]

en·gorge (ingɔ́rdʒ) *pres. part.* **en·gorg·ing** *past and past part.* **en·gorged** *v.t.* (*med.*) to congest with blood, secretions etc. **en·górge·ment** *n.* [F. *engorger*]

en·graft (ingrǽft, ingráft) *v.t.* to graft in ‖ to plant (principles, habits etc.)

en·grail (ingréil) *v.t.* (*esp. heraldry*) to give a scalloped or serrated edge to, *an engrailed cross* [M.E. *engrele* fr. O.F.]

en·grain, in·grain (ingréin) *v.t.* to instil (habits, tastes etc.) so that they become deep-rooted [M.E. *engreinen* prob. fr. F. *engrainer,* to dye]

en·gram (éngræm) *n.* (*psychol.*) a trace [fr. EN-(in)+ Gk *gramma,* writing]

en·grave (ingréiv) *pres. part.* **en·grav·ing** *past and past part.* **en·graved** *v.t.* to cut a design or lettering on (a hard surface, e.g. copper, glass, the end grain of boxwood, steel, gems etc.) by hand with a burin or other sharp tool, either for decoration or to produce a plate from which the image can be printed ‖ to cut (a design or lettering) on a hard surface with a burin or other sharp tool ‖ to cut a design in (a hard surface) or cut (a design) in a hard surface by a process using photography and etching ‖ to fix deeply in the mind, memory etc. **en·gráv·er** *n.* **en·gráv·ing** *n.* the hand engraver's art or the allied mechanical process ‖ an impression or print taken from an engraved surface [EN-(in)+GRAVE v. after F. *engraver*]

en·gross (ingróus) *v.t.* to occupy (a person or his attention) to the exclusion of everything else ‖ to make a fair copy of (a legal document) in careful, formal handwriting ‖ to draw up in proper legal form **en·gróss·ing** *adj.* holding one absorbed in interest **en·gróss·ment** *n.* [A.F. *engrosser,* to write in large letters and F. *engrosser,* to make gross]

en·gulf (ingʌ́lf) *v.t.* (of a flood, the sea etc.) to swallow up, *the swollen river engulfed the island* ‖ to surround completely, overwhelm, bury, *engulfed in a flood of telegrams*

en·hance (inhǽns, inháns) *pres. part.* **en·hanc·ing** *past and past part.* **en·hanced** *v.t.* to increase, add to (a quality, price or value) **en·hánced** *adj.* heightened, intensified ‖ (*heraldry*) placed higher than is usual (cf. ABASED) **en·hánce·ment** *n.* [A.F. *enhauncer*]

en·hanced radiation weapon (enhǽns'd) (*mil.*) neutron bomb, a nuclear weapon designed to minimize explosive force and maximize radiation

en·har·mon·ic (enharmónik) *adj.* (*mus.,* of notes on the piano and other fixed-note instruments) identical in pitch but differing in notation, e.g. C♯ and D♭ ‖ (of other instruments and the voice) of this same notation difference, but involving a possible slight change of pitch **en·har·món·i·cal·ly** *adv.* [fr. L. *enharmonicus* fr. Gk]

e·nig·ma (inígmə) *n.* something hard to define or understand fully ‖ an unfathomable person ‖ an obscure saying, riddle [L. *aenigma* fr. Gk fr. *ainissesthai,* to speak in riddles]

en·ig·mat·ic (enigmǽtik) *adj.* puzzling, deliberately veiled in meaning, *an enigmatic smile* **en·ig·mát·i·cal** *adj.* [fr. L.L. *enigmaticus*]

En·i·we·tok (eniwítɔk, enímwitɔk) a circular atoll (area 2 sq. miles) of the Marshall Is in the western central Pacific, seized (1914) by Japan from Germany and later administered by Japan as a mandate from the League of Nations. During the 2nd world war it was captured (1944) by a U.S. Marine force. After the war it was made a center for U.S. atomic bomb experiments

en·jamb·ment, en·jambe·ment (indʒǽmmənt) *n.* (in verse) a running over of a sentence from the end of one line to the beginning of the next, or from the end of a rhyming couplet into the next couplet [F. *enjambement* fr. *enjamber,* to encroach]

en·join (indʒɔ́in) *v.t.* to impose as a rule, order or duty, *to enjoin obedience* ‖ to command, urge authoritatively ‖ (*law*) to forbid or restrain (an action) by an injunction [fr. F. *enjoindre*]

en·joy (indʒɔ́i) *v.t.* to take pleasure or delight in, be pleased by ‖ to have the use, benefit or advantage of, *to enjoy a private income* **to enjoy oneself** to have a pleasant time **en·jóy·a·ble** *adj.* pleasant, giving pleasure **en·jóy·ment** *n.* the pleasure or satisfaction given by what is enjoyed, *to their great enjoyment* ‖ something enjoyed, *the theater is his chief enjoyment* ‖ the right to possess and use, *to have the enjoyment of an estate for one's lifetime* [O.F. *enjoier*]

en·keph·a·lin (enkéfalin) *n.* one of two naturally secreted chemicals in the human brain that affect sensations of pleasure and pain *Cf* ENDORPHIN

en·kin·dle (inkínd'l) *pres. part.* **en·kin·dling** *past and past part.* **en·kin·dled** *v.t.* (*rhet.*) to kindle

en·lace (inléis) *pres. part.* **en·lac·ing** *past and past part.* **en·laced** *v.t.* to bind ‖ to entwine **en·láce·ment** *n.*

en·large (inlárdʒ) *pres. part.* **en·larg·ing** *past and past part.* **en·larged** *v.t.* to make bigger, *to enlarge a shop* ‖ to expand. *to enlarge the scope of one's activities* ‖ (*photog.*) to print (a negative) in a larger size ‖ *v.i.* to become bigger, *the business is enlarging* ‖ to widen in scope, *his interests have recently enlarged* ‖ (with 'on' or 'upon') to speak or write more fully about ‖ (*photog.*) to be capable of being printed satisfactorily in a larger size **en·lárge·ment** *n.* the act of enlarging or state produced by enlarging ‖ the part by which something is enlarged, *the enlargement contrasts with the rest of the building* ‖ (*photog.*) a print larger than the original negative **en·lárg·er** *n.* (*photog.*) an apparatus for enlarging photographs, consisting of a source of light, an optical condenser, and a lens or lens system for projecting an enlarged image (reversed as to the intensity of distribution of light with respect to the negative) on a piece of photographic paper [O.F. *enlarger*]

en·light·en (inláit'n) *v.t.* to give (someone) information about, or help him to understand, what is obscure or difficult ‖ to shed light on (a problem) ‖ to civilize by freeing from ignorance, superstition etc. ‖ to give spiritual light to **en·light·en·ment** *n.* an enlightening or being enlightened ‖ something which enlightens **the En·light·en·ment** an intellectual movement of 18th-c. Europe which questioned traditional beliefs and prejudices, esp. in religion, and emphasized the primacy of reason and strict scientific method. It was represented in Germany esp. by Lessing, in England by Locke, Hume and Newton, in France by Voltaire, Diderot, d'Alembert and the Encyclopedists

en·list (inlíst) *v.i.* to enter the armed forces (in the ranks, not as a commissioned officer) ‖ *v.t.* to take into the armed forces, *they are not enlisting men over 35* ‖ to recruit (persons to help), to enlist helpers for a mission ‖ to call in (help or support)

enlisted man a man in the armed forces below the rank of warrant officer

en·list·ment (inlístmənt) *n.* an enlisting or being enlisted ‖ the period for which someone enlists

en·liv·en (inláivən) *v.t.* to make more lively, give animation to ‖ to make gayer or brighter

en masse (anmǽs, amǽs) *adv.* all together, in a group [F.]

en·mesh (inméʃ) *v.t.* to catch as if in a net

en·mi·ty (énmiti) *n.* a state or feeling of hatred or hostility (either shared by two parties. or confined to one) [fr. O.F. *enemistié*]

En·ni·us (éniəs), Quintus (239–169 B.C.), one of the earliest Roman poets, highly esteemed by later Latin writers. Only fragments of his epic and dramatic works survive

en·no·ble (inóub'l) *pres. part.* **en·no·bling** *past and past part.* **en·no·bled** *v.t.* to make spiritually, intellectually or morally elevated, *Christianity adopted and ennobled many pagan customs* ‖ to raise to the ranks of the nobility **en·nó·ble·ment** *n.*

en·nui (ánwi) *n.* boredom, weariness and discontent [F.]

e·nol·o·gy, oe·nol·o·gy (i:nɔ́lədʒi:) *n.* the science or study of wines and wine making [fr. Gk *oinos,* wine+*logos,* discourse]

e·nor·mi·ty (inɔ́rmiti:) *pl.* **e·nor·mi·ties** *n.* shocking wickedness ‖ a shocking crime or offense ‖ a terrible blunder ‖ huge size [fr. F. *énormité*]

e·nor·mous (inɔ́rməs) *adj.* huge, very great **e·nór·mous·ly** *adv.* to a very great degree ‖ an intensive form of 'very', *enormously rich* [fr. L. *enormis*]

E·no·sis (enóusis) *n.* (*Gr.*) union or unification, esp. of all Greek-speaking people, including Greeks living in Cyprus, which is now ruled by Turkey

e·no·tec·a (enoutéka) *n.* a library of wines

e·nough (inʌ́f) **1.** *adj.* as much (in number, quantity or degree) as is needed, *are there enough eggs for all of us?* **2.** *adv.* (invariably placed after the word it modifies, in all senses) sufficiently, in the degree or quantity that is needed, *if you run fast enough you will catch him* ‖ quite, at least as much as is needed or desirable, *he has told you often enough he likes his coffee black* ‖ fairly, tolerably, *he's honest enough, no doubt, but can you really trust him?* ‖ as an intensive of a positive, *oddly enough, he's keen enough on going* **3.** *n.* a sufficient quantity, *have you had enough to eat?* ‖ as much as one can put up with or manage, *that's enough of this nonsense* **4.** *interj.* stop!, no more! [O.E. *genog*]

e·nounce (ináuns) *pres. part.* **e·nounc·ing** *past and past part.* **e·nounced** *v.t.* to utter clearly, enunciate ‖ to state (a proposition) **e·nóunce·ment** *n.* the stating of a proposition [F. *énoncer*]

en pas·sant (ɑ̃pæsɑ̃) *adv.* (*chess,* in phrase) **to take en passant** to capture an enemy pawn that has initially moved two squares with a pawn controlling the first of those squares [F.]

enquire *INQUIRE

enquiry *INQUIRY

en·rage (inréidʒ) *pres. part.* **en·rag·ing** *past and past part.* **en·raged** *v.t.* to make furiously angry ‖ to torment to madness, *enraged by thirst* [fr. O.F. *enrager*]

en·rap·ture (inrǽptʃər) *pres. part.* **en·rap·tur·ing** *past and past part.* **en·rap·tured** *v.t.* to fill with rapture

en·rich (inrítʃ) *v.t.* to make rich or richer in money or goods ‖ to improve the quality of, *to enrich the mind* ‖ to add fullness of flavor or richness to ‖ to add a precious or costly ornament to, *a crown enriched with jewels* ‖ to make a valuable addition to (a collection, museum etc.) **en·rích·ment** *n.* [F. *enrichir*]

En·ri·que (enrí:kei) (kings of Castile and León) *HENRY

En·ri·qui·llo (enri:kí:jɔ) chief of the Indians of Hispaniola, who fought the Conquistadores until he won (1533) freedom for the natives

en·robe (inróub) *pres. part.* **en·rob·ing** *past and past part.* **en·robed** *v.t.* to put a robe on

en·roll, en·rol (inróul) *pres. part.* **en·roll·ing, en·rol·ling** *past and past part.* **en·rolled** *v.t.* to include (a person's name) in a list, *to be enrolled in a register of electors* ‖ to enter (a document) in an official or legal register ‖ *v.i.* to enlist (in the armed forces) ‖ to join a particular body of persons **en·róll·ment, en·ról·ment** *n.* [M.E. *enrolly* fr. O.F. *enroller*]

en·roll·ment period (enróulmənt) period during which individuals may enroll for insurance or health maintenance organization benefits, usu. the initial period between three months before and three months after eligibility, and an annual three months general enrollment period

en route (anrú:t, ɑ̃ru:t) *adv.* on the way, *we met en route* (often with 'to' or 'for' and a named destination) [F.]

ens (enz) *pl.* **en·ti·a** (énʃi:ə) *n.* (*Scholastic philos.*) being in the abstract (cf. ESSE) ‖ something which has existence, an entity [invented as pres. part. of L. *esse,* to be]

En·sche·de (énskədei) a town (pop. 144,346) in Overijssel, the Netherlands: cotton and linen industry

en·sconce (inskóns) *pres. part.* **en·sconc·ing** *past and past part.* **en·sconced** *v.t.* (often *refl.*) to tuck (oneself) away in, install (oneself) in some snug or desirable place, *the cat was ensconced in the workbasket* [prob. fr. O.F. *enconce,* hiding place]

en·sem·ble (ansámb'l, ɑ̃sɑ̃bl) *n.* a thing looked at or judged as a whole or from the point of view of the general effect ‖ (*mus.*) a performance or passage in which all the players or singers take part together ‖ a chamber orchestra ‖ (*theater*) the whole company or cast ‖ a complete matching outfit of clothes [F.]

en·shrine (inʃráin) *pres. part.* **en·shrin·ing** *past and past part.* **en·shrined** *v.t.* to place in a shrine or honored place of safety ‖ to keep dear or sacred (in one's heart, mind, memory etc.) **en·shrine·ment** *n.*

en·shroud (inʃráud) *v.t.* (*rhet.*) to cover completely, hide, *mist enshrouded the hills*

CONCISE PRONUNCIATION KEY: (a) æ, c*a*t; ɑ, c*a*r; ɔ f*aw*n; ei, sn*a*ke. **(e)** e, h*e*n; i:, sh*ee*p; iə, d*ee*r; ɛə, b*ea*r. **(i)** i, f*i*sh; ai, t*i*ger; ə:, b*i*rd. **(o)** o, *o*x; au, c*ow*; ou, g*oa*t; u, p*oo*r; ɔi, r*oy*al. **(u)** ʌ, d*u*ck; u, b*u*ll; u:, g*oo*se; ə, b*a*cillus; ju:, c*u*be. x, lo*ch*; θ, *th*ink; ð, bo*th*er; z, *Z*en; ʒ, corsa*ge*; dʒ, sava*ge;* ŋ, orangutan*g;* j, *y*ak; ʃ, *fi*sh; tʃ, fe*tch;* 'l, rabb*le;* 'n, redd*en.* Complete pronunciation key appears inside front cover.

en·si·form (énsifɔrm) *adj.* (*biol.*) shaped like a sword, xiphoid [fr. L. *ensis*, sword+FORM]
ensiform cartilage the xiphisternum
en·sign (énsain, énsən) *n.* (esp. *naut.*) a flag, standard ‖ an emblem, badge, etc., esp. a symbol of office ‖ (énsən) a U.S. naval officer ranking immediately below a lieutenant junior grade **én·sign·ship** *n.* [O.F. *enseigne*, a sign]
en·si·lage (énsəlidʒ) 1. *n.* silage 2. *v.t. pres. part.* **en·si·lag·ing** *past* and *past part.* **en·si·laged** to ensile
en·sile (insáil, énsail) *pres. part.* **en·sil·ing** *past* and *past part.* **en·siled** *v.t.* to make into silage [fr. F. *ensiler*]
en·slave (insléiv) *pres. part.* **en·slav·ing** *past* and *past part.* **en·slaved** *v.t.* to make a slave of **en·slave·ment** *n.*
en·snare (insnéər) *pres. part.* **en·snar·ing** *past* and *past part.* **en·snared** *v.t.* to catch in or as though in a snare
En·sor (énsɔr), James Sidney (1860–1949), Belgian expressionist painter. His works are macabre fantasies, populated with skeletons and masked figures incongruously rendered in an impressionistic style. Their closest affinities are with the works of Bosch and Pieter Bruegel the Elder
en·sue (insú:) *pres. part.* **en·su·ing** *past* and *past part.* **en·sued** *v.i.* to happen or come afterwards or as a result [fr. O.F. *ensuivre*]
en·sure (inʃúər) *pres. part.* **en·sur·ing** *past* and *past part.* **en·sured** *v.t.* to make certain of getting or achieving, *to ensure victory* (cf. INSURE)
-ent *suffix* used to form adjectives from verbs, corresponding to present participles, as in 'persistent' ‖ used to form agent nouns from verbs, like *-ant*, as in 'superintendent'
en·tab·la·ture (intæblətʃər) *n.* (*archit.*) a structure, supported by columns. consisting of the architrave, frieze and cornice ‖ a raised support for parts of a machine [fr. Ital. *intavolatura*, something laid flat]
en·ta·ble·ment (intéib'lmənt) *n.* the platform at the top of a pedestal or column on which a statue rests (above the dado) [F.]
en·tail (intéil) 1. *v.t.* to bring as a necessary consequence, *any resistance will entail the use of force* ‖ (*law*) to settle (landed property) in such a way that it cannot be sold and must be inherited and bequeathed in a certain way (generally passing from father to eldest son) 2. *n.* such a legal settlement ‖ an entailed estate **en·táil·ment** *n.* [O.F. *entailler*]
en·ta·moe·ba (entəmí:bə) *pl.* **en·ta·moe·bae** (entəmí:bi:), **en·ta·moe·bas**, **en·ta·me·bae** (entəmí:bi:), **en·ta·me·bas** *n.* an endamoeba, esp. one parasitic in vertebrates [fr. Gk *entos*, inside+AMOEBA]
en·tan·gle (intǽng'l) *pres. part.* **en·tan·gling** *past* and *past part.* **en·tan·gled** *v.t.* to catch up in, seemingly inextricably, *to entangle in a net* ‖ to make into a tangle or complicated muddle ‖ to involve in difficulties, complications or undesirable circumstances **en·tán·gle·ment** *n.* an entangling or being entangled ‖ an obstacle meant to delay an enemy
en·ta·sis (éntəsis) *pl.* **en·ta·ses** (éntəsi:z) *n.* (*archit.*) the slight swelling which a column is given toward its center so as to make it look cylindrical [Mod. L. fr. Gk]
En·teb·be (entébə) a town (pop. 21,000) of Uganda on the northwest edge (at 3,850 ft) of Lake Victoria
en·tel·e·chy (entéləki:) *pl.* **en·tel·e·chies** *n.* (*Aristotelian philos.*) act or form as opposed to potency or matter, i.e. the actual realization of what before was only potential ‖ (*vitalist philos.*) an innate vital principle, not physical or mechanical, which purposefully directs the development of an organism [fr. Gk *entelechia* fr. *en telei echein*, to be perfected]
en·tel·lus (entéləs) *n.* *Presbytis entellus*, a sacred Indian langur monkey, gray or yellowish in color, about 2 ft in height, with black hands, feet and face [L., proper name of a boxer in Virgil, 'Aeneid' V]
en·tente (ɑtɑ̃t) *n.* a friendly agreement (short of an alliance) between two or more countries, or the countries so linked [F. = understanding]
Entente Cor·diale (ɑtɑ̃tkɔrdʒæl) the agreement (1904) between Britain and France, settling various colonial disputes. It was joined (1907) by Russia, to form the Triple Entente
Entente, Little *LITTLE ENTENTE
en·ter (éntər) *v.t.* to go or come in or into, *to enter a room, to enter a harbor, ideas enter the mind through the senses* ‖ to penetrate into, *the bullet*

entered *his lung* ‖ to begin (a new period, series etc.), *to enter the age of space travel* ‖ to take up, adopt (an occupation, profession etc.), *to enter politics* ‖ to join (a body or organization), *to enter a firm as a young man* ‖ to admit or cause to be admitted to a body or organization ‖ to put (oneself, someone else, something) down for a competition, *to enter a car for a race* ‖ to add or cause (one's name or a name) to be added to a list, *to enter a heifer in a herdbook* ‖ to make a note or record of (in the appropriate book, list, or other record), *to enter invoices in a ledger* ‖ (*law*) to bring (a writ etc.) before a court in proper form ‖ (*law*) to record (a judgment etc.) ‖ *v.i.* to go in ‖ to come in ‖ (*theater*) to come on stage **to enter into** to start upon, begin to take part in, *to enter into conversation* ‖ to discuss, explain, *to enter into details* ‖ to bind oneself by, *to enter into an agreement* ‖ to share sympathetically, take part sympathetically in, *to enter into someone's feelings* ‖ to form part of, have a bearing or influence upon, be a factor in, *this never entered into the original plan* **to enter an appearance** (*law*) to come into court as attorney for one of the parties concerned in an action **to enter a protest** to make a protest and see that it is recorded in the minutes **to enter religion** to become a monk or a nun **to enter upon** (or **on**) to come into, start, begin to discuss or deal with, *to enter upon a new phase* **to enter up** to record as an entry (e.g. in accounts) [O.F. *entrer*]
en·ter·ic (entérik) *adj.* relating to the intestines [fr. Gk *enterikos* fr. *enteron*, intestine]
enteric fever a disease of the typhoid and paratyphoid group, caused by specific disease bacteria, and spread through the contamination of food and water supplies by feces or urine of people who have the disease or who have had it. An attack runs a severe course for a month or more, and causes a high fever, weakness, alteration of consciousness, and sometimes internal bleeding or perforation of the intestine. It is treated by antibiotics
en·ter·i·tis (entəráitis) *n.* (*med.*) inflammation of the small intestine, with diarrhea and (when acute) vomiting [fr. Gk *enteron*, intestine]
En·ter·o·bac·te·ri·a·ce·ae (entəroubækt::ri:éisi:i:) (*microbiol.*) family of gram-negative rod-shaped bacteria, some parasitic, some living on dead matter, that forms nitrites from nitrates, e.g., *E coli*, salmonella
en·ter·o·bac·tin (entəroubǽktin) *n.* (*microbiol.*) product of enterobacteria that inhibits other bacteria
en·ter·on (éntərɒn) *n.* the alimentary tract, esp. of an embryo or fetus, or (in coelenterates) the single enteric cavity [Gk=intestine]
en·ter·o·path·o·gen·ic (entəroupæθoudʒénik) *adj.* (*med.*) causing intestinal disease **enteropathy** *n.* the diseased condition
en·ter·o·vi·rus (entərouváirʌs) *n.* (*med.*) any of various viruses that exist in the gastrointestinal tract and that may cause neurological or brain diseases **enteroviral** *adj.*
en·ter·prise (éntərpraiz) *n.* a venture, esp. one calling for determination, energy and initiative ‖ the character needed for such a venture ‖ a commercial or industrial undertaking **én·ter·pris·ing** *adj.* with plenty of initiative, ready to undertake new ventures or try new methods or ideas [O.F. *entreprise*, an undertaking]
enterprise zone (éntərpraiz) urban area of high unemployment and poverty for which government undertakes concentrated stimulation through real estate tax freezes, income tax benefits, grants for jobs created, etc.
en·ter·tain (entərtéin) *v.t.* to receive as a visitor or guest ‖ to give interest and pleasure to, amuse ‖ to have in one's mind, *to entertain doubts* ‖ to give thought or consideration to, *not even to entertain the possibility of failure* ‖ *v.i.* to show hospitality **en·ter·táin·er** *n.* a person who entertains professionally, esp. by telling funny stories **en·ter·táin·ing** *adj.* **en·ter·táin·ment** *n.* an entertaining or being entertained ‖ any interesting or diverting performance or spectacle, usually public ‖ hospitality meant to amuse and divert a guest [M.E. *entertene* fr. F.]
en·thal·py (énθælpi) *n.* (*phys.*, symbol H) a thermodynamic quantity defined as the sum of the internal energy of a body and the pressure-volume product [fr. Gk *enthalpein*, to warm up]
en·thrall, en·thral (inθrɔ́l) *pres. part.* **en·thrall·ing, en·thral·ling** *past* and *past part.* **en·thralled** *v.t.* to capture the interest or attention of, hold as if spellbound, delight **en·thráll·**

ing, **en·thrál·ling** *adj.* **en·thráll·ment, en·thrál·ment** *n.*
en·throne (inθróun) *pres. part.* **en·thron·ing** *past* and *past part.* **en·throned** *v.t.* to place (a sovereign or a bishop) upon his throne **en·thróne·ment** *n.*
en·thuse (inθú:z) *pres. part.* **en·thus·ing** *past* and *past part.* **en·thused** *v.i.* to express enthusiasm ‖ *v.t.* to inspire with enthusiasm [back-formation fr. ENTHUSIASM]
en·thu·si·asm (inθú:zi:æzəm) *n.* passionate admiration or interest, *enthusiasm for football* ‖ an object of such feelings, *football is his enthusiasm* ‖ (esp. *hist.*) religious emotion extravagantly manifested [fr. L.L. *enthusiasmus* fr. Gk fr. *enthousia*, a being possessed by a god]
en·thu·si·ast (inθú:zi:æst) *n.* an ardent fan, supporter or admirer, someone passionately interested in something, *a golf enthusiast* ‖ (esp. *hist.*) a person who feels intense religious emotion and who manifests it extravagantly **en·thu·si·ás·tic** *adj.* **en·thu·si·ás·ti·cal·ly** *adv.* [fr. Gk *enthousiastes* fr. *enthousia*, a being possessed by a god]
en·thy·meme (énθəmi:m) *n.* (*logic*) a syllogism in which one premise is left to be understood (e.g. in 'he is only human and therefore liable to make mistakes' the premise 'all men make mistakes' is omitted) [fr. L. *enthymema* fr. Gk]
entia *pl.* of ENS
en·tice (intáis) *pres. part.* **en·tic·ing** *past* and *past part.* **en·ticed** *v.t.* to cause (a person or animal) to cease resisting and to do as one wishes, by offering some inducement **en·tíce·ment** *n.* [O.F. *enticier*, to excite]
en·tire (intáiər) *adj.* whole and complete, absolute and unqualified, *in entire agreement* ‖ not broken or damaged, intact, *the stocks are still entire* ‖ (*bot.*, of leaves) with an unbroken outer edge ‖ (of male animals) not castrated **en·tíre·ly** *adv.* wholly and completely ‖ solely, *we deal entirely with one printer* [O. F. *entier*]
en·tire·ty (intáiərti:, intáirəti:) *pl.* **en·tire·ties** *n.* completeness ‖ (*law*) sole and undivided possession, *to hold a property in entirety* **in its entirety** as an undiminished whole [O.F. *entierté*]
en·ti·tle (intáit'l) *pres. part.* **en·ti·tling** *past* and *past part.* **en·ti·tled** *v.t.* to give (someone) a right, *this ticket entitles you to a seat, his position entitles him to be heard* ‖ to give a title to [A.F. *entitler*]
en·ti·tle·ments (entáit'lmənts) *pl. n.* benefits that one may receive upon request, esp. from a government agency
en·ti·ty (éntiti:) *pl.* **en·ti·ties** *n.* something existing complete in itself, by its own right, *each creature is a separate entity* ‖ (*Scholastic philos.*) a subject having existence (cf. ENS) [fr. L.L. *entitas* as though fr. *ens* (*entis*) pres. part. of *esse*, to be]
en·tomb (intú:m) *v.t.* to enclose or bury in, or as though in, a tomb [O.F. *entoumber*]
en·to·mo·log·ic (entəmələdʒik) *adj.* entomological **en·to·mo·lóg·i·cal** *adj.* to do with entomology
en·to·mol·o·gist (entəmólədʒist) *n.* a specialist in entomology
en·to·mol·o·gy (entəmólədʒi:) *n.* the branch of zoology dealing with the study of insects [fr. F. *entomologie* fr. Gk *entomon*, insect+*logos*, word]
en·to·mos·tra·can (entəmóstrəkən) *n.* (*zool.*) a member of *Entomostraca*, a loosely defined subclass of crustaceans comprising the branchiopods, ostracods, copepods and cirripeds, now used as a convenient term without taxonomic significance [fr. Gk *entomon*, insect+*ostrakon*, pot, shell]
en·tou·rage (ɒnturáʒ) *n.* the companions or servants who attend or surround a person ‖ surroundings [F.]
en·tr'acte (ɑ̃trǽkt) *n.* the interval between two acts or parts of a play or performance, an intermission ‖ a short piece of music, or other short performance, given in this interval [F.]
en·trails (éntreilz, éntrəlz) *pl. n.* bowels or intestines (of men or animals) ‖ (*rhet.*) the inmost or deepest parts, *deep in the entrails of the earth* [O.F. *entraille*]
en·train (intréin) *v.i.* (of troops) to get into a train ‖ *v.t.* to put (troops) into a train ‖ (*eng.*) to add particles or bubbles in a moving liquid
en·tram·mel (intrǽməl) *pres. part.* **en·tram·mel·ing**, esp. *Br.* **en·tram·mel·ling** *past* and *past part.* **en·tram·meled**, esp. *Br.* **en·tram·melled** *v.t.* to entangle, *the offer was entram-*

meled with conditions which we could not fulfill

en·trance (éntrəns) *n.* a door or other opening by which one can enter a building or other place ‖ the act of coming or going in ‖ the act of starting, being admitted etc., *entrance into negotiations* ‖ the right to come or go in or to be admitted, *to be refused entrance* ‖ a fee paid for the right to be admitted ‖ the coming on stage of a player ‖ (*naut.*) the bow of a ship below the waterline [O.F.]

en·trance (intræns, intréns) *pres. part.* **en·tranc·ing** *past and past part.* **en·tranced** *v.t.* to overcome with joy, delight or wonder ‖ to put into a trance **en·tranc·ing** *adj.* delightful **en·trance·ment** *n.*

en·trant (éntrənt) *n.* a candidate in a competition, examination, election etc. ‖ someone newly joining or starting, *new entrants report here* ‖ someone entering a room, building etc., *late entrants are a nuisance in a theater* [F. *pres. part.* of *entrer*, to enter]

en·trap (intræp) *pres. part.* **en·trap·ping** *past and past part.* **en·trapped** *v.t.* to catch (a person) as though in a trap

en·treat (intrí:t) *v.t.* to plead with, *he entreated her to listen* ‖ (*rhet.*) to plead for, implore, *entreat someone's sympathy* **en·treat·y** *pl.* **en·treat·ies** *n.* an entreating, pleading, beseeching [fr. O.F. *entraiter*]

en·tre·chat (ɑ̃trəʃá) *n.* (*ballet*) a leap during which the legs crisscross rapidly at the lower calf [F. fr. Italic. *intrecciata*, interlaced]

en·trée, en·tree (ɑ́ntrei) *n.* freedom of entry, *to be given the entrée into local society* ‖ a dish served between the fish and the meat ‖ the main course of a dinner [F.]

en·trench (intrénʃ) *v.t.* to surround or protect with a trench, *the enemy entrenched themselves on the hill* ‖ to settle (oneself) securely e.g. in a job or some other position thought of as safe ‖ *v.i.* to dig protective trenches ‖ (with 'on') to encroach, *the work is beginning to entrench on his leisure* **en·trench·ment** *n.*

en·tre·pôt (ɑ́ntrəpou) *n.* a big commercial center importing and reexporting commodities [F.]

en·tre·pre·neur (ɑntrəprənə́:r, ɑntrəprənúər) *n.* someone who runs a business at his own financial risk ‖ a middleman [F.]

en·tre·sol (ɑ́ntrəsɒl) *n.* a mezzanine [F.]

en·tro·py (éntrəpi) *n.* (*phys.*, symbol φ) a thermodynamic quantity that measures the fraction of the total energy of a system that is not available for doing work. The change in the entropy of a given system is determined from the ratio dQ/T, where dQ is an infinitesimal quantity of heat transferred to or from the system at the absolute temperature T ‖ (*statistical mechanics*) the logarithm of the probability of occurrence of a given state, i.e. arrangement of constituent particles, which in turn depends upon the relative energies of the possible states [fr. EN- (in)+Gk *tropē*, a turning]

en·trust (intrást) *v.t.* to give for safekeeping or to be looked after, *to entrust a child to a nurse* ‖ to give a task or duty to, *to entrust a soldier with a mission*

en·try (éntri) *pl.* **en·tries** *n.* entrance ‖ the part of a building, around the door, which leads to the interior ‖ (*Br.*) a narrow passage or lane leading to a building or place ‖ someone or something entered for a competition, race etc. ‖ (*law*) the actual taking possession of a property by setting foot in it ‖ the noting, recording or registering of something in a book, list, or other record, or the thing so recorded ‖ (*bridge*) the winning of a trick with respect to its giving the lead in the playing of the next trick **to force an entry** to break in (to a building) [F. *entrée*]

en·twine (intwáin) *pres. part.* **en·twin·ing** *past and past part.* **en·twined** *v.t.* to weave or plait (one thing with another), to twine or wrap around

en·twist (intwíst) *v.t.* to twist about, together etc.

e·nu·cle·ate (inú:kli:eit, injú:kli:eit) **1.** *v.t. pres. part.* **e·nu·cle·at·ing** *past and past part.* **e·nu·cle·at·ed** to extract the stone from (a fruit), the kernel from (a nut) etc. ‖ (*biol.*) to remove or destroy the nucleus of ‖ to remove (a carbuncle, tumor etc.) whole by surgery **2.** *adj.* (*biol.*) without a nucleus **e·nu·cle·a·tion e·nú·cle·a·tor** *ns* [fr. L. *enucleare* (*enucleatus*)]

E·nu·gu (enú:gu:) *n.* a town (pop. 187,000) in the East Central State, Nigeria: tin and coal mining

e·nu·mer·ate (inú:məreit, injú:məreit) *pres.*

part. **e·nu·mer·at·ing** *past and past part.* **e·nu·mer·at·ed** *v.t.* to state or name one by one **e·nu·mer·á·tion** *n.* **e·nú·mer·a·tive** *adj.* [fr. L. *enumerare* (*enumeratus*), to count off]

e·nun·ci·ate (inʌ́nsi:eit) *pres. part.* **e·nun·ci·at·ing** *past and past part.* **e·nun·ci·at·ed** *v.t.* to pronounce (sounds, syllables etc.) ‖ to state, give expression to, *to enunciate a proposition* ‖ *v.i.* to articulate **e·nun·ci·á·tion** *n.* the act or way of pronouncing ‖ the stating (of a proposition, theory, doctrine etc.) **e·nún·ci·a·tive** *adj.* **e·nún·ci·a·tor** *n.* [fr. L. *enuntiare* (*enuntiatus*), to declare]

en·u·re·sis (enjurí:sis) *n.* involuntary urination, bedwetting **en·u·ret·ic** (enjurétik) *adj.* [Mod. L. fr. Gk *enourein*, to urinate in]

en·vel·op (invéləp) *v.t.* to wrap up, esp. in a garment ‖ to cover completely, shroud, *smoke enveloped the warehouse, enveloped in mystery* ‖ (*mil.*) to surround **en·vél·op·ment** *n.* [O. F. *enveloper*]

en·ve·lope (énvəloup, ɑ́nvəloup) *n.* a paper cover with a gummed or tuck-in flap, to hold a letter etc. ‖ the outer skin of an airship or balloon ‖ (*biol.*) a membrane, shell or other covering ‖ (*astron.*) the mass of incandescent gas surrounding the sun, the nucleus of a comet etc. ‖ (*geom.*) a curve or surface tangential to a number of other curves or surfaces [fr. F. *enveloppe* fr. *envelopper*, to wrap up]

en·ven·om (invénəm) *v.t.* (*rhet.*) to poison, embitter [M.E. *envenime* fr. O.F. *envenimer*]

en·vi·a·ble (énvi:əb'l) *adj.* highly desirable **én·vi·a·bly** *adv.*

en·vi·ous (énvi:əs) *adj.* feeling, showing or prompted by envy [O.F. *envieus*]

en·vi·ron (inváirən, inváiərn) *v.t.* (*rhet.*) to surround, *the vineyards environing the city are steadily receding* [F. *environner*]

en·vi·ron·ics (envairóniks) *n.* the use of a combination of various types of equipment (including electronic equipment) to accomplish the control of an environment, e.g., suppression or radio interference, air and water pressure, and temperature control

en·vi·ron·ment (inváirənmənt, inváiərnmənt) *n.* surroundings, esp. the material and spiritual influences which affect the growth, development and existence of a living being **en·vi·ron·mén·tal** *adj.*

en·vi·ron·men·tal art (envairənmént'l) involving the viewer, e.g., in a specially conceived and constructed space or theatrical event **environment** *n.* the work

en·vi·ron·men·tal·ist (envairənméntelist) *n.* one devoted to protecting the ecological balance of the earth

Environmental Protection Agency (*abbr.* EPA) (1970) an independent U.S. government agency that controls solid waste, pesticide, noise and radiation pollution through research, development and training programs

Environmental Study Conference group of members of Congress especially concerned with protection of the environment

en·vi·rons (inváirənz, inváiərnz, énvərənz) *pl. n.* the neighborhood or district surrounding a place [F. fr. *environ*, round about]

en·vis·age (invízidʒ) *pres. part.* **en·vis·ag·ing** *past and past part.* **en·vis·aged** *v.t.* to make a mental picture of, *how do you envisage the finished work?* ‖ to foresee the possibility of, *to envisage complications* [F. *envisager*]

en·vi·sion (invíʒən) *v.t.* to see in the mind's eye (esp. some future occurrence)

en·voy, en·voi (énvɔi) *n.* the closing stanza of a poem, esp. a ballade, repeating the meter and rhymes of the previous half stanza, and beginning by naming the person to whom the poem is addressed [O.F. fr. *envoiier*, to send]

envoy *n.* someone sent on a mission or with a message, usually official ‖ an envoy extraordinary [fr. F. *envoyé*, past part. of *envoyer*, to send]

envoy extraordinary *pl.* **envoys extraordinary** a minister plenipotentiary to a foreign country next in rank to an ambassador

en·vy (énvi) *pres. part.* **en·vy·ing** *past and past part.* **en·vied** *v.t.* to feel malicious envy of or for ‖ to affirm the goodness of (something) by wishing to share it [fr. O.F. *envier*]

envy *pl.* **en·vies** *n.* a feeling of antagonism towards someone because of some good which he is enjoying but which one does not have oneself ‖ a coveting for oneself of the good which someone else is enjoying (traditionally one of the seven deadly sins) ‖ an innocent desire to share

another's good ‖ something which arouses this desire [M.E. *envie* fr. F.]

en·wrap (inræp) *pres. part.* **en·wrap·ping** *past and past part.* **en·wrapped** *v.t.* (*rhet.*) to enfold, *sleep enwrapped the little town* ‖ to absorb mentally, engross

en·wreathe (inrí:ð) *pres. part.* **en·wreath·ing** *past and past part.* **en·wreathed** *v.t.* (*rhet.*) to surround with, or as though with, a wreath, *mist enwreathed the hilltops*

en·zo·ot·ic (enzouótik) **1.** *adj.* (of animal disease) restricted to a certain locality, climate or season **2.** *n.* an enzootic disease [fr. EN- (in)+Gk *zōon*, animal]

en·zy·mat·ic (enzaimætik) *adj.* of, relating to or derived from an enzyme

en·zyme (énzaim) *n.* one of a large class of complex proteinaceous substances of high molecular weight formed in and produced by living matter which are responsible for promoting the chemical reactions upon which life depends (e.g. digestion, respiration, reproduction). They accomplish this by acting like catalysts while themselves undergoing little or no change. Their action is often specific and reversible and may be dependent upon temperature, pH, and the presence of various coenzymes and activators (metallic salts, vitamins etc.) [fr. G. *enzym* fr. Mod. Gk *enzumos*, leavened]

enzyme detergent (énzaim) *n.* detergent with an enzyme derived from bacteria that breaks down proteins. This type of detergent is sometimes regarded as dangerous to skin and lungs

E·o·cene (í:əsi:n) *adj.* of the second epoch or series of the Tertiary (sometimes used of the whole division of the Tertiary before the Miocene. *GEOLOGICAL TIME*) **the E·o·cene** the Eocene epoch or series of rocks [fr. Gk *ēōs*, dawn+*kainos*, new]

e·o·hip·pus (i:ouhípəs) *n.* an extinct horse of the genus *Hyracotherium* of the Eocene of the western U.S.A. [Mod. L. fr. *Gk ēōs*, dawn+*hippos*, horse]

e·o·lith (í:əliθ) *n.* a crude stone implement thought to have been used, and possibly shaped, by man in the earliest period of the Stone Age **E·o·lith·ic** (i:ouliθik) *adj.* of this period ‖ characterized by the use of eoliths, the earliest known stage of human culture [fr. Gk *ēōs*, dawn+*lithos*, stone]

e·o·lo·trop·ic (i:əloutrópik) *adj.* anisotropic

eon *AEON

E-1 (*mil.*) *TRACER

E·os (í:ɒs) (*Gk mythol.*) the goddess of dawn, identified with the Roman Aurora

e·o·sin (í:əsin) *n.* (*chem.*) a red dye, potassium salt of tetrabromofluorescein, used in making red ink and to stain slides in microscopy ‖ one of a number of similar dyes [fr. Gk *ēōs*, dawn]

e·o·sine (í:əsi:n) *n.* eosin

E·o·zo·ic (i:əzóuik) **1.** *adj.* Precambrian **2.** *n.* the Precambrian [fr. Gk *ēōs*, dawn+*zōon*, animal]

EPA 1. *abbr.* Environmental Protection Agency **2.** *abbr.* Equal Pay Act (for women)

e·pact (í:pækt) *n.* the age (in days) of the moon on Jan. 1, by which the dates of Easter and other feasts are determined in the ecclesiastical calendar. This figure represents the difference between the solar and lunar years [fr. F. *épacte* fr. L. fr. Gk *epaktos*, added]

E·pam·i·non·das (ipæminóndəs) (c. 418–362 B.C.), Greek statesman and general. He restored the power of Thebes and broke the military supremacy of the Spartans, defeating them at Leuctra (371) and Mantinea (362)

ep·arch (éparrk) *n.* the governor, or bishop, of an eparchy [fr. Gk *eparchos*, ruler]

ep·ar·chy (éparki:) *pl.* **ep·ar·chies** *n.* an administrative subdivision of a province of modern Greece ‖ a diocese of the Orthodox Eastern Church [fr. Gk *eparchia* fr. *epi-*, over+*archein*, to rule]

ep·au·let, ep·au·lette (epəlét, épələt) *n.* a shoulder ornament (often with a gilt fringe) worn with full-dress uniform [F. *epaulette* dim. of *épaule*, shoulder]

é·pée (eipéi) *n.* a light, long, narrow sword used in fencing. The blade is flexible, triangular or quadrilateral in section, and pointed. There is a round guard for the hand (cf. FOIL, cf. SABER) [F.=sword]

ep·ei·rog·e·ny, ep·i·rog·e·ny (epairódʒəni:) *n.* the distortion of the earth's crust which produced the great land masses [fr. Gk *ēpeiros*, mainland+*-geneia*, manner of production]

ep·en·ceph·a·lon (epenséfələn) *pl.* **ep·en·ceph-**

CONCISE PRONUNCIATION KEY: (**a**) æ, c**a**t; ɑ, c**a**r; ɔ f**aw**n; ei, sn**a**ke. (**e**) e, h**e**n; i:, sh**ee**p; iə, d**ee**r; ɛə, b**ea**r. (**i**) i, f**i**sh; ai, t**i**ger; ə:, b**i**rd. (**o**) o, **o**x; au, c**ow**; ou, g**oa**t; u, p**oo**r; u:, g**oo**se; ə, b**a**cillus; ju:, c**u**be. x, lo**ch**; θ, **th**ink; ð, bo**th**er; z, **Z**en; ʒ, cor**s**age; dʒ, sava**g**e; ŋ, ora**ng**utan**g**; j, **y**ak; ʃ, **fi**sh; tʃ, fe**tch**; 'l, rabb**le**; 'n, redd**en**. Complete pronunciation key appears inside front cover.

a·la (epenséfələ) *n.* (*anat.*) the hindbrain [fr. EPI-+ENCEPHALON]

ep·en·the·sis (epénθisis) *pl.* **ep·en·the·ses** (epénθisi:z) *n.* the occurrence of a letter or sound which is not historical in origin but appears in a word as a result of the articulation of neighboring sounds **ep·en·thet·ic** (epənθétik) *adj.* [L.L. fr. Gk fr. *epi-*, upon+*en-*, in+*tithenai*, to put]

e·pergne (ipə́:rn) *n.* an ornamental dish, often of silver, placed in the center of a dinner table, to hold flowers, fruit, sweets etc. [perh. fr. F. *épargne*, saving]

ep·ex·e·ge·sis (epeksidʒí:sis) *pl.* **ep·ex·e·ge·ses** (epeksidʒí:si:z) *n.* the adding to a word of others which make the meaning more obvious ‖ the words so added **ep·ex·e·get·ic** (epeksidʒétik), **ep·ex·e·gét·i·cal** *adjs* [Gk fr. *epexēgeisthai*, to recount in detail]

e·phed·rine (ifédrin, éfidri:n) *n.* a white crystalline alkaloid $C_6H_5CH\ OHCH(CH_3)·NHCB_3$ used to relieve asthma, nasal congestion etc. [fr. Mod. L. *Ephedra* (name of a plant genus) fr. L. *ephedra*, horsetail+ -INE]

e·phem·er·a (ifémərə) *pl.* **e·phem·er·as, e·phem·er·ae** (iféməri:) *n.* a mayfly of genus *Ephemera* ‖ something short-lived **e·phém·er·al 1.** *adj.* short-lived, of only passing interest or value ‖ (of plants and insects) with a mature or adult life of a few days or less **2.** *n.* something ephemeral [Mod. L. fr. Gk *ephēmerē*, fem. of *ephēmeros*, for one day]

e·phem·er·id (ifémərid) *n.* (*zool.*) a mayfly, order *Plectoptera* [fr. Mod. L. *Ephemerida* fr. Gk]

e·phem·er·is (ifémaris) *pl.* **eph·e·mer·i·des** (efəméridi:z) *n.* a collection of tables giving the position of the sun, moon, planets etc. at regular intervals (usually daily) throughout the year ‖ an astronomical almanac [Mod. L. fr. Gk *ephēmeris*, diary]

e·phem·er·on (ifémərɒn) *pl.* **e·phem·er·a** (ifémərə), **e·phem·er·ons** *n.* an ephemera [Mod. L. fr. Gk fr. *ephēmeros*, for one day]

E·phe·sians, Epistle to the (ifí:ʒənz) the tenth book of the New Testament. It was probably written in the late 1st c. as a circular letter to the churches of Asia on the Person of Christ and the nature of the Church, and is traditionally ascribed to St Paul

Eph·e·sus (éfisəs) an ancient seaport (now ruins) of Ionia, site of a famous temple of Artemis, one of the Seven Wonders of the World. The Church council here condemned Nestorius (431)

e·phod (í:fɒd, éfɒd) *n.* (*Jewish hist.*) a vestment worn by the high priest [Heb. *ēphód*]

eph·or (éfɔr) *pl.* **eph·ors, eph·o·ri** (éfərai) *n.* (*Gk hist.*) a magistrate in any of several Dorian city-states, esp. one of five in Sparta whose authority was a check on that of the two kings [fr. Gk *ephoros*, overseer]

Eph·ra·em Sy·rus (éfreiemsáirəs), St (c. 306–73), of Nisibis, an orator and hymn writer of the Syrian Church. Feast: June 18

E·phra·im (í:freiəm) Hebrew patriarch, son of Joseph ‖ the Israelite tribe of which he was the ancestor

epi- (épi) *prefix* on, upon ‖ over ‖ close to ‖ beside ‖ outer ‖ anterior [Gk]

ep·i·blast (épəblæst) *n.* the ectoderm of an embryo **ep·i·blás·tic** *adj.* [EPI+ Gk *blastos*, sprout]

e·pib·o·ly, e·pib·o·le (ipíbəli:) *pl.* **e·pib·o·lies, e·pib·o·les** *n.* (*embry.*) the overgrowth of the ectodermal layer of some types of blastula about a large, yolk-filled portion of an egg forming a gastrula (cf. EMBOLY). It is typical of embryos with meroblastic cleavage [fr. Gk *epibolē*, a throwing or laying on, something thrown on or laid on]

ep·ic (épik) **1.** *n.* a long narrative poem conceived on a grand scale, telling a story of great or heroic deeds. Originally of folk origin, as in 'Beowulf', it later became linked with literary legends and conventions, as in Milton's 'Paradise Lost' ‖ an account of any enterprise conspicuous for courage and endeavor, *the epic of Arctic exploration* **2.** *adj.* of or having the nature of an epic [fr. L. *epicus* fr. Gk]
—The scale of epic is larger than life. Its heroes are taken up into events that set them apart for celebration by their fellow men, and so each detail (however trivial in itself) is invested with gravity. Epic art consists in this raising of storytelling to the plane where it has this gravity, on this scale. History remote in time, warfare and the courts of kings often provide its mate-

rial. The style of the epic is marked by a diction rich in circumlocutions, epithets, speechmaking and formulas

ep·i·ca·lyx (epikéiliks) *pl.* **ep·i·ca·lyx·es, ep·i·ca·ly·ces** (epikéilisi:z) *n.* a cluster of bracts or bracteoles below the calyx of a flower ‖ an apparent outer or extra calyx of stipules fused in pairs

ep·i·carp (épikarp) *n.* the outermost layer of the pericarp (e.g. the skin of a drupe) [F. *épicarpe* fr. Gk *epi*, upon+*karpos*, fruit]

ep·i·ce·di·um (episí:dí:əm) *pl.* **ep·i·ce·di·a** (episí:dí:ə) *n.* a poem written for a funeral or to lament a death [L. fr. Gk *epikēdeion* fr. *epi*, upon+*kēdos*, grief, funeral rites]

ep·i·cene (épisi:n) **1.** *adj.* having characteristics of both sexes (e.g. of an effeminate youth) ‖ (*gram.*) having the same form for both the masculine and feminine gender (as in some Latin and Greek nouns) **2.** *n.* an epicene person [fr. L. *epicoenus* fr. Gk fr. *epi*, on, to+*koinos*, common]

ep·i·cen·ter, *Br.* **ep·i·cen·tre** (épisentər) *n.* the point on the earth's surface immediately above the focus of an earthquake **ep·i·cén·tral** *adj.* [fr. Mod. L. *epicentrum* fr. Gk *epi*, upon+*kentron*, center]

ep·i·cle·sis, ep·i·kle·sis (epiklí:sis) *pl.* **ep·i·cle·ses, ep·i·kle·ses** (epiklí:si:z) *n.* a prayer to God to send down the Holy Spirit upon the bread and wine offered in the Eucharist that they may be changed into the body and blood of Christ. In the Orthodox Eastern Church it is held that the bread and wine are consecrated not at the words of consecration but at the epiclesis [Gk *epiklēsis* fr. *epikalein*, to invoke]

Ep·ic·te·tus (epiktí:təs) (c. 50–120), Stoic philosopher. He was born the slave of Epaphroditus, a freedman of Nero. His lectures and a 'Manual' ('Enchiridion') of his philosophy were published posthumously by Arrian. They greatly influenced Marcus Aurelius

ep·i·cure (épikjuər) *n.* a discriminating person, esp. one who cultivates and enjoys his taste for the best in food and drink [after *Epicurus*, wrongly taken to be devoted to bodily pleasures]

Ep·i·cu·re·an (epikjuri:ən) **1.** *adj.* pertaining to Epicurus and his followers **ep·i·cu·ré·an** of or appealing to an epicure **2.** *n.* **Epicurean** a follower of Epicurus or his philosophy **epicurean** an epicure **Ep·i·cu·ré·an·ism** *n.* the philosophic system of Epicurus **ep·i·cu·ré·an·ism** the cultivation of epicurean tastes [fr. L. *epicureus* fr. Gk]

ep·i·cur·ism (épikjurizəm) *n.* epicureanism [fr. EPICURUS and EPICURE]

Ep·i·cu·rus (epikjúrəs) (341–270 B.C.), Athenian atomist philosopher. He regarded sense perception as the only basis of knowledge and believed that material objects throw off images which enter our senses. He considered the highest good to be pleasure, but this meant freedom from pain and emotional upheaval, achieved not through sensual indulgence but through the practice of virtue. His teaching formed the basis of the 'De rerum natura' of Lucretius

ep·i·cy·cle (épisaik'l) *n.* (*geom.*) a circular path, the center of which moves along the circumference of a larger circle. Ptolemy used it to describe the motion of the planets **ep·i·cy·clic** (episáiklik, episíklik) *adj.* [fr. L. *epicyclus* fr. Gk *epi*, upon+*kuklos*, circle]

ep·i·cy·cloid (episáikloid) *n.* (*geom.*) the curve traced by a point on the small circle of an epicycle as it rolls on the circumference of a fixed circle **ep·i·cy·clói·dal** *adj.* [EPICYCLE+-*oid* ult. fr. Gk *eidos*, form]

Ep·i·dau·rus (epidɔ́rəs) an ancient port of Argolis, Greece, famous in antiquity for its temple of Asclepius. Greek theater

ep·i·dem·ic (epidémik) **1.** *n.* a disease which becomes widespread in a particular place at a particular time ‖ an occurrence, generally unpleasant, which is widespread or intense, *epidemics of delinquency* **2.** *adj.* widespread, esp. of disease (cf. ENDEMIC) **ep·i·dém·i·cal** *adj.* [fr. F. *épidémique* fr. L. fr. Gk *epi*, upon+*dēmos*, people]

ep·i·de·mi·ol·o·gy (epidi:mi:ɒ́dʒi:) *n.* the branch of medicine studying the transmission and control of epidemic disease [EPIDEMIC+Gk *logos*, word]

ep·i·der·mal (epidə́:rməl) *adj.* of or relating to the epidermis

ep·i·der·mic (epidə́:rmik) *adj.* epidermal

ep·i·der·mis (epidə́:rmis) *pl.* **ep·i·der·mis·es, ep·i·der·mes** (epidə́:rmi:z) *n.* the outer protec-

tive monocellular layer of plants ‖ the protective external skin of vertebrates, consisting of thin layers of horny cells which are sometimes modified to hair and nails etc. ‖ a nonvascular stratified epithelium of epiblastic origin **ep·i·dér·moid, ep·i·der·mói·dal** *adjs* resembling epidermis [Mod. L. fr. Gk *epi*, upon+*derma*, skin]

ep·i·di·a·scope (epidáiəskoup) *n.* a device for projecting on a screen the reflected, enlarged image of an opaque or transparent object [fr. Gk. *epi*, upon+*dia*, through+*skopein*, to observe]

ep·i·did·y·mal (epidídəməl) *adj.* of or relating to the epididymis

ep·i·did·y·mis (epidídəmis) *pl.* **ep·i·di·dym·i·des** (epididímidi:z) *n.* (*anat.*) a coiled tube attached to the upper surface of the testicle through which spermatozoa pass from the testicle to the vas deferens [fr. Gk fr. *epi*, on+*didumos*, testicle]

ep·i·fau·na (epəfɔ́nə) *n.* animal life on the hard bottom of the sea **epifaunal** *adj. Cf* INFAUNA

ep·i·gam·ic (epigǽmik) *adj.* serving to attract a mate [fr. Gk *epigamos* fr. *epi*, for+*gamos*, marriage]

ep·i·gas·tric (epigǽstrik) *adj.* of or relating to the epigastrium ‖ lying upon or over the stomach

ep·i·gas·tri·um (epigǽstri:əm) *pl.* **ep·i·gas·tri·a** (epigǽstri:ə) *n.* an abdominal region lying between the sternum and the diaphragm ‖ the ventral side of the metathorax and mesothorax of insects [Mod. L. fr. Gk fr. *epi*, upon+*gastēr*, stomach]

ep·i·ge·al (epidʒí:əl) *adj.* (*bot.*, of plant parts) growing above ground ‖ (of some insects) living on or close to the ground **ep·i·gé·an** *adj.* [fr. Gk *epigaios* fr. *epi*, on+*gē*, earth]

ep·i·gene (épidʒi:n) *adj.* (*geol.*) formed on the surface of the earth ‖ (*geol.*) of a crystal which is not natural to the substance in which it is found [F. *épigéne* fr. Gk fr. *epi*, upon+-*genēs*, born]

ep·i·gen·e·sis (epidʒénisis) *n.* (*biol.*) a theory of embryonic development holding that the embryo is gradually formed by differentiation of initially unspecialized cells rather than by the unfolding of preformed structures ‖ (*geol.*) metamorphism **ep·i·ge·net·ic** (epidʒənétik) *adj.* [fr. Gk *epi*, upon+*genesis*, creation]

e·pig·e·nous (ipídʒənəs) *adj.* (*biol.*) developing or growing on the surface of an organism [fr. Gk *epi*, upon+-*genēs*, born]

ep·i·ge·ous (epidʒí:əs) *adj.* epigeal

ep·i·glot·tis (epiglótis) *n.* (*anat.*) a fold of cartilage at the back of the tongue that covers the glottis during swallowing [Gk fr. *epi*, upon+*glottis*, tongue]

ep·i·gram (épigræm) *n.* a neat, witty, often paradoxical remark ‖ a short poem on some event or person, often with a satirical point **ep·i·gram·mat·ic** (epigrəmǽtik), **ep·i·gram·mát·i·cal** *adjs* **ep·i·gram·ma·tist** (epigrǽmətist) *n.* **ep·i·grám·ma·tize** *pres. part.* **ep·i·gram·ma·tiz·ing** *past* and *past part.* **ep·i·gram·ma·tized** *v.i.* and *t.* [fr. F. *epigramme* fr. L. fr. Gk *epi*, upon+*graphein*, to write]

ep·i·graph (épigræf, épigraf) *n.* an inscription cut in stone or metal or stamped on a coin or medal ‖ a quotation at the beginning of a book, chapter etc. **e·pig·ra·pher** (ipígrəfər) *n.* **ep·i·gráph·ic** (epigrǽfik), **ep·i·gráph·i·cal** *adjs* **e·pig·ra·phist** (ipígrəfist) *n.* **e·píg·ra·phy** *n.* the study of inscriptions ‖ inscriptions in general, esp. of a particular country or period [fr. Gk *epigraphē* fr. *epi*, upon+*graphein*, to write]

e·pig·y·nous (ipídʒənəs) *adj.* (of petals, stamens and sepals) growing on top of the ovary **e·pig·y·ny** *n.* the condition of being epigynous [EPI-+-*gynous* fr. Gk *gunē*, woman]

epiklesis *EPICLESIS

ep·i·la·tion (epiléiʃən) *n.* the removal of hair, including roots **epilate** *v.* **epilatory** *adj.* **epilatory** *n.* the substance used

ep·i·lep·sy (épəlepsi:) *n.* a chronic nervous disorder of the brain of man and other animals affecting consciousness and muscular control with various degrees of severity. It may be congenital or the result of damage to the brain caused by tumor, injury, glandular imbalance or toxic substances, and may result in convulsions and loss of consciousness **ep·i·lép·tic** *n.* and *adj.* [O.F. *epilepsie* fr. L. fr. Gk *epilambanein*, to take hold of]

ep·i·lim·ni·on (epilímni:ən) *n.* (*envir.*) in a lake, the warm upper water zone from the surface to the thermocline *Cf* HYPOLIMNION

CONCISE PRONUNCIATION KEY: **(a)** æ, *cat*; ɑ, *car*; ɔ *fawn*; ei, *snake*. **(e)** e, *hen*; i:, *sheep*; iə, *deer*; ɛə, *bear*. **(i)** i, *fish*; ai, *tiger*; ə:, *bird*. **(o)** ɒ, *ox*; au, *cow*; ou, *goat*; u, *poor*; ɔi, *royal*. **(u)** ʌ, *duck*; u, *bull*; u:, *goose*; ə, *bacillus*; ju:, *cube*. x, *loch*; θ, *think*; ð, *bother*; z, *Zen*; ʒ, *corsage*; dʒ, *savage*; ŋ, *orangutang*; j, *yak*; ʃ, *fish*; tʃ, *fetch*; 'l, *rabble*; 'n, *redden*. Complete pronunciation key appears inside front cover.

ep·i·logue, ep·i·log (épələg, épəlog) *n.* the concluding part of, or a final note added to, a literary work ‖ a short final speech or scene after the end of a play (cf. PROLOGUE) [F. *épilogue* fr. L. fr. Gk fr. *epilegein*, to say in addition]

ep·i·nas·ty (épinæsti:) *n.* (*bot.*) the more rapid growth of the upper surface of a dorso-ventral organ, e.g. a leaf, causing unrolling or downward curvature [fr. EPI-+-*nasty* fr. Gk *nastos*, close-pressed]

ep·i·neph·rin (epinéfrin) *n.* epinephrine

ep·i·neph·rine (epinéfrin,epinéfri:n) *n.* a hormone produced by the medulla of the adrenal gland that raises the blood pressure by heart muscle stimulation and vasoconstriction, and that regulates blood sugar level. It occurs in three optically isomeric forms, of which the levorotatory form is the most active (*ADRENALIN, *NOREPINEPHRINE) [EPI-+Gk *nephros*, kidney]

ep·i·neu·ri·um (epinúəri:əm, epinjúari:əm) *pl.* **ep·i·neu·ri·a** (epinúəri:ə, epinjúari:ə) *n.* (*anat.*) the sheath of connective tissue surrounding a nerve trunk [Mod. L. fr. Gk *epi*, upon+*neuron*, nerve]

Ep·i·pha·ni·us (epiféini:əs), St (c. 315–403), a Palestinian Jew who became bishop of Salamis in Cyprus (367). He inveighed against Origen and Arianism in his 'Panarion'. Feast: May 12

E·piph·a·ny (ipífəni:) *n.* the feast (Jan. 6) celebrating the manifestation of Christ's divinity to the Gentiles, represented by the Magi **e·piph·a·ny** *pl.* **e·piph·a·nies** a similar manifestation of a divine or superhuman person, e.g. of Vishnu [O.F. *epiphanie* fr. L. fr. Gk fr. *epi*, upon+*phainein*, to show]

ep·i·phe·nom·e·nal·ism (epi:fənómən'lizəm) *n.* (*philos.*) the doctrine that consciousness is purely a product of physical and physiological brain processes, which determine it [EPIPHENOMENON]

ep·i·phe·nom·e·non (epi:fənómənən, epi:fənóm-ənən) *pl.* **ep·i·phe·nom·e·na** (epi:fənómənə) *n.* a secondary or concomitant phenomenon [Mod. L.]

ep·i·phys·e·al (epifízi:əl) *adj.* of or relating to an epiphysis

e·piph·y·sis (ipífisis) *pl.* **e·piph·y·ses** (ipífisi:z) *n.* (*anat.*) any part or process of a bone which is formed from a separate center of ossification and later fuses with the bone ‖ the pineal body ‖ a process on the tibia of certain insects [fr. Gk fr. *epi*, upon+*phusis*, growth]

ep·i·phyte (épifait) *n.* a plant that grows on another plant or some other object (e.g. a stone) but is not parasitic, usually gaining its nourishment from the air. Epiphytes are abundant in wet tropics, esp. in South America **ep·i·phyt·ic** (epifítik), **ep·i·phýt·i·cal** *adjs* [EPI-+-*phyte* fr. Gk *phuton*, plant]

ep·i·phy·tot·ic (epifaitótik) *adj.* (of plant diseases) epidemic

E·pi·rus (ipáirəs) a mountainous region of N.W. Greece

e·pis·co·pa·cy (ipískəpəsi:) *pl.* **e·pis·co·pa·cies** *n.* government of a Church by bishops who have authority over priests and lower clergy, and alone have the power to confer the sacraments of holy orders and confirmation ‖ the office or period of office of a bishop ‖ the body of bishops (of a country etc.) [fr. L.L. *episcopatus* fr. *episcopus*, bishop]

e·pis·co·pal (ipískəp'l) *adj.* of or belonging to bishops or a bishop, *episcopal authority* ‖ accepting the authority and government of bishops **E·pis·co·pal** referring to the Protestant Episcopal Church of the U.S.A. or the Episcopal Church in Scotland [F.]

e·pis·co·pa·lian (ipískəpéiljən) **1.** *adj.* of, concerned with or supporting Church government by bishops **2.** *n.* a supporter of Church government by bishops **E·pis·co·pa·lian** a member of the Protestant Episcopal Church of the U.S.A. or of the Episcopal Church in Scotland **E·pis·co·pá·lian·ism** *n.* [fr. L.L. *episcopalis* fr. *episcopus*, bishop]

e·pis·co·pal·ism (ipískəp'lizəm) *n.* (*hist.*) the doctrine held by the Gallicans that supreme authority in the Church lies with the bishops assembled in council and not (as laid down by the Vatican Council of 1870) with the pope

e·pis·co·pate (ipískəpit) *n.* the office of a bishop, his see, or the period during which he occupies it ‖ a body of bishops [fr. L. *episcopatus* fr. *episcopus*, bishop]

ep·i·sode (épisoud) *n.* a part of a story subordinate to the main theme and generally self-contained ‖ a similar passage in a musical work ‖ a self-contained part of a serial story ‖ an isolated event or instance, separate from the run of events, *the rioting died down save for minor episodes* ‖ (*hist.*) the part of a Greek tragedy between two songs of the chorus, constituting an act **ep·i·sod·ic** (episódik), **ep·i·sód·i·cal** *adjs* consisting of linked episodes ‖ spasmodic [Gk *epeisodion* fr. *epi*, upon+*eisodos*, entrance]

ep·i·spas·tic (epispæstik) **1.** *adj.* causing a blister **2.** *n.* a blistering agent [fr. Mod. L. fr. Gk *epispastikos*, drawing to oneself]

e·pis·ta·sis (ipístəsis) *n.* (*genetics*) the dominance of a nonallelic gene over another gene **ep·i·stat·ic** (epistǽtik) *adj.* [Mod. L. fr. Gk ult. fr. *epi*, upon+*histanai*, to place]

ep·i·stax·is (epistǽksis) *n.* (*med.*) bleeding from the nose [Mod. L. fr. Gk *epistazein*, to fall drop by drop]

e·pis·te·mo·log·i·cal (ipistəmolódʒik'l) *adj.* relating to epistemology

e·pis·te·mol·o·gy (ipistəmóladʒi:) *n.* the branch of philosophy dealing with the study of the nature of knowledge, its origin, foundations, limits and validity [fr. Gk *epistēmē*, knowledge+*logos*, word]

ep·i·ster·nal (epistə́:rn'l) *adj.* of or relating to the episternum

ep·i·ster·num (epistə́:rnəm) *pl.* **ep·i·ster·na** (epistə́:rnə) *n.* a lateral piece attached to one of the hard longitudinal divisions of the exoskeleton in insects ‖ (*anat.*) an anterior cartilaginous part of the sternum, e.g. the interclavicle

E·pis·tle (ipís'l) *n.* one of the 21 letters written by Apostles to individuals or churches and included in the New Testament ‖ a similar letter of instruction written by one of the Church Fathers, e.g. that of St Clement to the church of Corinth ‖ a passage from Scripture (usually from the Epistles in the New Testament) read or sung during Mass or the Eucharist **e·pis·tle** (*rhet.*) a letter ‖ a literary work (prose or poetry) cast in the form of a letter [O.F. fr. L. fr. Gk]

Epistle side the right-hand side of the altar as the priest faces it

e·pis·to·lar·y (ipístəleri:) *adj.* relating to or used in letters, *an epistolary style* ‖ contained or expressed in or carried on by letters, *an epistolary friendship* [fr. F. *epistolaire*]

E·pis·to·ler (ipístələr) *n.* (*eccles.*) the reader of the Epistle in the Anglican liturgy [fr. F. *epistolier*]

ep·i·stom·ics (epistómiks) *n.* the scientific study of knowledge, esp. by construction of formal models of perception, etc., by which knowledge is attained; coined at Edinburgh University in 1969 **ant** epistemology

e·pis·tro·phe (ipístrəfi:) *n.* the repetition of the same word at the end of several consecutive phrases or sentences, e.g. 'we'll work for freedom, we'll fight for freedom, we'll die for freedom' [Mod. L. fr. Gk fr. *epi*, upon+*strophē*, turning]

ep·i·style (épistail) *n.* (*archit.*) an architrave [fr. L. *epistylium* fr. Gk *epi*, upon+*stulos*, pillar]

ep·i·taph (épitæf, épitaf) *n.* words inscribed on a gravestone or other monument in memory or in praise of a dead person or persons ‖ a short, pithy tribute to a dead person, sometimes in verse **ep·i·táph·ic** *adj.* [fr. L. *epitaphium* ult. fr. Gk *epi*, upon+*taphos*, tomb]

e·pit·a·sis (ipítəsis) *pl.* **e·pit·a·ses** (ipítəsi:z) *n.* that part of a play (following the protasis) where the conflict is intensified and the action hastens towards the catastrophe [Mod. L. fr. Gk fr. *epiteinein*, to stretch over]

ep·i·tha·la·mi·on (epəθəléimi:ən) *pl.* **ep·i·tha·la·mi·a** (epəθəléimi:ə) *n.* an epithalamium

ep·i·tha·la·mi·um (epəθəléimi:əm) *pl.* **ep·i·tha·la·mi·ums, ep·i·tha·la·mi·a** (epəθəléimi:ə) *n.* a marriage song or poem praising the bride and bridegroom (cf. PROTHALAMIUM) [L. fr. Gk *epi*, upon+*thalamos*, bridal chamber]

ep·i·the·li·al (epəθí:li:əl) *adj.* of or relating to the epithelium

ep·i·the·li·um (epəθí:li:əm) *pl.* **ep·i·the·li·a** (epəθí:li:ə), **ep·i·the·li·ums** *n.* (*anat.*) an animal tissue that covers external surfaces and lines the tubes and cavities of the body and that consists of one or more layers of cells variously modified to serve as protection, provide sense organs or aid in the excretion of waste products and the assimilation of nutriment [Mod. L. fr. Gk *epi*, upon+*thēlē*, nipple]

ep·i·thet (épəθet) *n.* a word or phrase, adjectival

in force, which serves to characterize, as in 'The Wily Ulysses', 'Jack the Giant Killer' **ep·i·thet·ic, ep·i·thét·i·cal** *adjs* [fr. L. *epitheton*, ult. fr. Gk *epi*, upon+*tithenai*, to put]

e·pit·o·me (ipítəmi:) *n.* a summary of the contents of a book or other writing or piece of exposition, *the Sermon on the Mount is an epitome of Christ's teaching* ‖ a person or thing typical of, or serving as a model of, something larger or wider, *he is the epitome of the self-made man* **e·pit·o·mist** *n.* **e·pit·o·mize** *pres. part.* **e·pit·o·miz·ing** *past* and *past part.* **e·pit·o·mized** *v.t.* to make or serve as an epitome of [L. fr. Gk *epitomē* ult. fr. *epi*, upon+ *temnein*, to cut]

ep·i·tro·choi·dal engine (epitroukóidəl) *WANKEL ENGINE

ep·i·trop·ic fiber (epitrópik) synthetic fiber capable of conducting electricity developed in Great Britain by ICI Fibres. It is produced by embedding tiny particles of carbon powder into the surface of the polymer or nylon fiber

ep·i·zo·on (epizóupn, epizóuən) *pl.* **ep·i·zo·a** (epizóuə) *n.* (*zool.*) an animal living on another, an external parasite [Mod. L. fr. Gk *epi*, upon+*zōon*, animal]

ep·i·zo·ot·ic (epizouótik) **1.** *adj.* (of a disease) attacking many animals of the same kind at the same time and place **2.** *n.* an epizootic disease, e.g. foot-and-mouth disease [fr. F. *épizootique* fr. L. fr. Gk]

e plu·ri·bus u·num (i:plúərəbəsjú:nəm) out of many, one (the motto of the U.S.A.) [L.]

ep·och (épək, *Br.* esp. í:ppk) *n.* a period of time characterized by momentous events or changes ‖ the beginning of such a period, *its publication marked an epoch in scientific thought* ‖ (*geol.*) a division of geological time shorter than a period **ép·och·al** *adj.* [fr. L.L. *epocha* fr. Gk *epochē*, a pause, fixed date]

ep·och-mak·ing (épəkmeikiŋ, *Br.* esp. í:ppk-meikiŋ) *adj.* significant by virtue of ensuring historical developments

ep·ode (époud) *n.* (*hist.*) a type of short poem, lyrical or satirical, written in one of a number of meters, often with a shorter line following a longer, used by Horace ‖ the third part of a Greek ode, following the strophe and antistrophe [O.F. fr. L. fr. Gk *epōidos*, sing after]

ep·o·nych·i·um (epəníki:əm) *n.* (*physiol.*) **1.** the wall of the fingernail **2.** extension of the cuticle at the edges of the nail

ep·o·nym (épənim) *n.* the mythical or historical person or thing after which a tribe, city, country etc. is named, *Pelops is the eponym of the Peloponnesus* **e·pon·y·mous** (ippnəməs) *adj.* [fr. Gk *epōnumos*]

ep·os (épps) *n.* early folk-epic poetry, either recited or written ‖ an epic of this kind [fr. Gk *epos*, song, speech]

E-prime version of English language omitting use of the verb to be; coined by D. Davis Bourlard, Jr.

ep·si·lon (épsələn, épsələn, *Br.* esp. epsáilən) *n.* the fifth letter (E,ε=e) of the Greek alphabet ‖ (*particle phys.*) an elementary particle with positive charge, G-parity, and mass of 1,200 MEV that decays to two pions

Ep·som salts (épsəm) hydrated magnesium sulfate ($MgSo_4$·$7H_2O$), a white, crystalline, soluble salt, used esp. as a laxative [after *Epsom* in Surrey, England]

Ep·stein (épstain), Sir Jacob (1880–1959), American sculptor, of Russo-Polish parentage, who worked mainly in England. His symbolic works, in a simplified or primitive style, reveal influences of cubism and African sculpture. In bronze busts, often of famous subjects, he made subtle use of abstract elements to intensify the expressiveness of essentially representational portraits. He produced many monumental works, e.g. 'St Michael overcoming Satan' on the outer wall of Coventry Cathedral

Ep·stein-Barr virus (epstain bar) (*med.*) virus associated with Burkitt's lymphoma, some human cancers, infectious mononucleosis, etc. It was isolated in 1964 by Michael A. Epstein and Y. M. Barr, English pathologists

Ep-3 (*mil.*) *ORION

ep·u·lot·ic (epu:lótik) *adj.* of ancient Roman sacrificial banquets or the priests that directed them

eq·ua·bil·i·ty (ekwəbíliti:) *n.* the state or quality of being equable

eq·ua·ble (ékwəb'l) *adj.* not changing much, steadily even, without extremes, *an equable climate* ‖ calm, not easily upset or excited, *an* *equable disposition* **éq·ua·bly** *adv.* [fr. L. *aequabilis* fr. *aequare*, to make even]

e·qual (í:kwəl) **1.** *adj.* the same in number, degree, value, rank or other standard of comparison, *equal shares* ‖ with no advantage on either side, even, *an equal match* ‖ impartial, *with equal justice* ‖ without subservience or domination, *on equal terms* ‖ (with 'to') the same in number, degree, value, rank etc. as, *her share is equal to his* ‖ (with 'to') able to face up to, *do you feel equal to seeing him yet?* ‖ (with 'to') equivalent to, *an egg is equal to half a pound of steak in protein value* **2.** *n.* someone or something equal in some point of comparison to another **3.** *v.t. pres. part.* **e·qual·ing** past and past part. **e·qualed**, esp. *Br.* **e·qualled** to be or become equal to ‖ to come up (or sink) to the standard of, *he almost equals your speed, could anything equal such poverty?* [fr. L. *aequalis* fr. *aequus*, even, just]

e·qual-ar·e·a (í:kwəléəri:ə) *adj.* (of a map projection) so drawn as to show the area of all parts correctly to the same scale. (Towards the center of the map shapes also are shown correctly, towards the edges they are distorted)

e·qual·i·tar·i·an (ikwɒlitéəri:ən) *adj.* egalitarian **e·qual·i·tár·i·an·ism** *n.* egalitarianism

e·qual·i·ty (ikwɒliti:) *pl.* **e·qual·i·ties** *n.* the state or an instance of being equal in number, amount, rank, meaning etc. [O.F. *équalité*]

e·qual·i·za·tion (i:kwəlizéiʃən) *n.* an equalizing or being equalized

e·qual·ize (í:kwəlaiz) *pres. part.* **e·qual·iz·ing** past and past part. **e·qual·ized** *v.t.* to make equal ‖ to make regular or even, *to equalize the temperature in all parts of a kiln* ‖ *v.i.* (sports) to score a goal which makes the scores equal **e·qual·iz·er** *n.* (sports) a goal which makes the score equal ‖ (*elec.*) a conductor connecting two points, normally of the same potential, on the armature of an electrical machine

e·qual·ly (í:kwəli:) *adv.* to the same degree, *equally important* ‖ in equal shares or parts

e·qual-op·por·tu·ni·ty (i:kwəlɒpərtú:niti:) *adj.* of employment that does not discriminate between men and women or white and minority race applicants *Cf* AFFIRMATIVE ACTION

equal pay the principle of the same rate for the same work, irrespective of the sex, race etc. of the worker

Equal Rights Amendment (*abbr.* ERA) a proposed 27th amendment to the U.S. Constitution that stated that 'equality of rights under the law shall not be denied or abridged by the United States nor by any State on account of sex.' First introduced in 1923, it was not until 1970 that it received national attention and was approved by the House of Representatives (1971) and Senate (1972). The ratification deadline of 1978 was extended to 1981, but it failed to pass with 35 of the 38 states needed voting in favor. It was reintroduced in 1982, but was defeated in the House in 1983

equal temperament (*mus.*) the system of tuning, now used for the piano and other fixed-pitch instruments, in which there are equal intervals between successive semitones, enabling a performer to play in all keys with equal facility and to modulate freely (cf. MEANTONE TEMPERAMENT)

equal time radio or television time provided for those who disagree with an opinion (usu. political) expressed over the air; by extension, an equal opportunity to present one's case *Cf* FAIRNESS DOCTRINE

e·qua·nim·i·ty (i:kwənímiti:, ɛkwənímiti:) *n.* steady calmness, the state of being unperturbed [fr. L. *aequanimitas* fr. *aequus.* even + *animus*, mind]

e·quate (ikwéit) *pres. part.* **e·quat·ing** past and past part. **e·quat·ed** *v.t.* (*math.*) to state the equality of ‖ to regard as equal in value or as mutually interdependent, *to equate freedom with happiness* [fr. L. *aequare* (*aequatus*) fr. *aequus*, equal]

e·qua·tion (ikwéiʒən, ikwéiʃən) *n.* the act of making equal ‖ (*math.*) a statement of the equality between mathematical expressions ‖ (*chem.*) a quantitative statement of chemical change, using the symbol → to represent the process **e·quá·tion·al** *adj.* [fr. L. *aequatio* (*aequationis*) fr. *aequare*, to equate]

equation of state an equation relating the pressure, temperature, and volume of a fluid, e.g. the van der Waals equation

e·qua·tor (ikwéitər) *n.* the great circle of the earth, in a plane perpendicular to the axis of the earth and equidistant from the poles, divid-

ing the northern and southern hemispheres, 24,903.16 miles in circumference **e·qua·to·ri·al** (i:kwətóri:əl, i:kwətóuri:əl, ɛkwətóri:əl, ɛkwətóuri:əl) **1.** *adj.* on or near or pertaining to the equator **2.** *n.* an astronomical telescope free to revolve on an axis parallel to that of the earth, so that a star is kept in view despite the earth's rotation [L.L. *aequator*, someone who or that which equalizes]

equatorial climate the climate of regions close to the equator, characterized by consistently high temperature and abundant, regular rainfall with maxima corresponding to the equinoxes

Equatorial Guinea (formerly Spanish Guinea) a state (area 10,821 sq. miles, pop. 300,000) on the W. African coast, comprising Rio Muni and 5 islands including Ćioko and Pagalu. Capital: Santa Isabel. Cocoa, coffee and tropical woods are exported. Formerly a Spanish colony, it became self-governing in 1964 and independent in 1968. It became a one-party state (1969–79) under Pres. Nguema, who was overthrown and executed in a military coup. The new government sought ties with the West, principally Spain and the U.S.A.

equatorial plate a group of chromosomes lying at the equator of the spindle during cell division, being the locus of the new cell wall in plant cells after mitosis

eq·uer·ry (ékwəri:, ikwéri:) *pl.* **eq·uer·ries** *n.* an official of the British royal household in attendance on a member of the royal family [F. *écurie*, stable fr. L. fr. O.H.G.]

e·ques·tri·an (ikwéstri:ən) **1.** *adj.* concerned with or representing horseback riding, *an equestrian statue* ‖ (*Rom. hist.*) of or pertaining to the Equites, the class of knights **2.** *n.* (esp. of acrobats) a horseback rider **e·ques·tri·enne** (ikwéstri:én) *n.* a female horseback rider [fr. L. *equester* (*equestris*)]

equi- (í:kwi) *prefix* equal [fr. M.F. fr. L. *aequus*]

e·qui·an·gu·lar (i:kwiǽŋgjulər) *adj.* having all or corresponding angles equal **e·qui·an·gu·lár·i·ty** *n.*

e·qui·dis·tant (i:kwidístənt) *adj.* (with 'from') at the same distance in space or time [F.]

e·qui·lat·er·al (i:kwilǽtərəl) **1.** *adj.* having all sides the same length **2.** *n.* (*geom.*) a figure with all its sides the same length [fr. L.L. *aequilateralis*]

e·quil·i·brant (ikwíləbrənt) *n.* (*mech.*) the force necessary to produce, or capable of producing, equilibrium when added to any system of other forces (equal in magnitude but opposite in direction to their resultant) [F. *équilibrant* fr. *équilibrer*, to equilibrate]

e·quil·i·brate (ikwílabreit, i:kwəláibreit) *pres. part.* **e·quil·i·brat·ing** past and past part. **e·quil·i·brat·ed** *v.t.* to balance (two or more things, e.g. weights, forces) against one another ‖ *v.i.* to be in equilibrium [fr. L.L. *aequilibratus*, level fr. *aequus*, equal + *libra*, balance]

e·qui·li·bra·tion (i:kwələbréiʃən, ikwiləbréiʃən) *n.* an equilibrating or being equilibrated [fr. L.L. *aequilibratus*, level fr. *aequus*, equal]

e·quil·i·brist (ikwíləbrist) *n.* an acrobat who does balancing feats, esp. a tightrope walker **e·quil·i·brís·tic** *adj.* [F. *équilibriste* fr. *équilibre*, equilibrium]

e·qui·lib·ri·um (i:kwəlíbri:əm) *n.* a state of balance between opposing forces or effects, the system involved undergoing no total change. The balance may be stable, recovering rapidly from a change in one of the factors involved, or unstable, destroyed by even a small change in one of those factors ‖ (*chem.*) a dynamic state attained in any reversible reaction or process when the rate of the forward reaction or process is equal to the rate of the reverse reaction or process ‖ (*phys.*) the state of a system in which the net force is zero and which may be either static or dynamic ‖ (*phys.*) uniformity of temperature or pressure throughout a system [L. *aequilibrium* fr. *aequus*, equal + *libra*, balance]

e·quine (í:kwain, ékwain) **1.** *adj.* of or like a horse **2.** *n.* a horse or any other member of fam. *Equidae* [fr. L. *equinus* fr. *equus*, horse]

e·qui·noc·tial (i:kwinɒ́kʃəl, ɛkwinɒ́kʃəl) *adj.* pertaining to the equinox ‖ happening at the time of an equinox ‖ at or near the equator [EQUINOX]

equinoctial circle the celestial equator

equinoctial line the celestial equator

equinoctial point one of the two points of intersection of the celestial equator and the ecliptic

e·qui·nox (í:kwinɒks, ékwinɒks) *pl.* **e·qui·nox·es** *n.* the moment or point at which the sun crosses the equator during its apparent annual motion from north to south, about Sept. 23 (the autumnal equinox), or from south to north, about Mar. 21 (the vernal equinox). At the equinoxes day and night are of equal length [fr. L. *aequinoctium* fr. *aequi-*, equal + *nox* (*noctis*), night]

e·quip (ikwíp) *pres. part.* **e·quip·ping** past and past part. **e·quipped** *v.t.* to provide with what is needed to carry out a particular purpose or function [F. *équiper* prob. fr. O.N. *skipa*, ship]

eq·ui·page (ékwəpidʒ) *n.* a fine car (or carriage), often with attendants and outriders mounted on motorcycles (or horses) ‖ the materials needed for an expedition, long journey etc. [F. *équipage*]

e·qui·par·ti·tion of energy (i:kwəpɑrtíʃən) the postulate that for a system consisting of atoms, molecules or ions in the gaseous state the total thermal energy at equilibrium is equally distributed among the degrees of freedom of motion of the constituent particles. The postulate is accurate only at higher temperatures, the quantization of energy restricting occupation of certain energy levels at lower temperatures (*STATISTICAL MECHANICS)

e·quip·ment (ikwípmənt) *n.* what is needed or is provided to carry out a particular purpose or function ‖ the personal gear, arms, kit etc. carried by troops ‖ a person's knowledge, training, skill, experience etc., *higher mathematics is not part of the ordinary man's equipment* ‖ (*rail.*) rolling stock ‖ the act or process of equipping

e·qui·poise (í:kwəpɔiz, ékwəpɔiz) *n.* a counterweight ‖ the state of equilibrium

e·qui·pol·lence (i:kwəpɒ́ləns) *n.* the state or quality of being equipollent, esp. equality of significance in two logical propositions [O.F. *equipolence*]

e·qui·pol·lent (i:kwəpɒ́lənt) **1.** *adj.* the same or practically the same in force, importance, weight, meaning or effect, equivalent **2.** *n.* something that is equipollent [O.F. *equipolent*]

e·qui·pon·der·ant (i:kwəpɒ́ndərənt) *adj.* counterbalancing ‖ evenly balanced [fr. L. *aequiponderans* (*aequiponderantis*), weighing equally]

e·qui·pon·der·ate (i:kwəpɒ́ndəreit) *pres. part.* **e·qui·pon·der·at·ing** past and past part. **e·qui·pon·der·at·ed** *v.t.* to make equal in weight ‖ to counterbalance ‖ *v.i.* to be equal in weight or force [fr. L. *aequiponderare* (*aequiponderatus*). to weigh equally]

e·qui·po·ten·tial (i:kwəpəténʃəl) *adj.* (*phys.*) having the same potential at all points, *an equipotential surface*

é·quippe (eikí:p) *n.* a sporting team and its equipment [F.]

eq·ui·se·tum (ɛkwisí:təm) *pl.* **e·qui·se·tums**, **eq·ui·se·ta** (ɛkwisí:tə) *n.* a horsetail [L. fr. *equus*, horse + *saeta*, a bristle]

eq·ui·ta·ble (ékwitəb'l) *adj.* fair and just ‖ (*law*) relating to, or valid in, equity as distinct from statute law **éq·ui·ta·bly** *adv.* [F. *équitable*]

eq·ui·ta·tion (ɛkwitéiʃən) *n.* the art of riding on horseback (chiefly of show-riding) [fr. L. *equitatio* (*equitationis*)]

eq·ui·ty (ékwiti:) *pl.* **eq·ui·ties** *n.* fairness and justice, esp. the common fairness that follows the spirit rather than the letter of justice ‖ a legal system (e.g. in the U.S.A., England) which supplements statute or common law and corrects, if necessary, its failure to accord with what is morally just and fair ‖ (*law*) an equitable claim or right ‖ (*law*) an equity of redemption ‖ the value of a property after deducting any charges to which it is liable ‖ (*pl.*, *Br.*) stocks and shares which (unlike debentures and preference shares) do not pay a fixed rate of interest **Eq·ui·ty** (*Br.*) the actors' trade union [O.F. *équité*]

equity of redemption (*law*) the right, granted by a court of equity, of a mortgager to redeem his forfeited estate by payment of capital and interest within a reasonable time after the term of the mortgage has expired

e·quiv·a·lence (ikwívələns) *n.* the state of being equivalent **e·quív·a·len·cy** *n.* [F. fr. M.L. *aequivalentia*]

e·quiv·a·len·cy test (ikwívələnsi:) examination intended to equate an individual's knowledge, experience, and skill, however acquired, with the knowledge, experience, and skill acquired

CONCISE PRONUNCIATION KEY: **(a)** æ, c*a*t; ɑ, c*a*r; ɔ f*aw*n; ei, sn*a*ke. **(e)** e, h*e*n; i:, sh*ee*p; iə, d*ee*r; ɛə, b*ea*r. **(i)** i, f*i*sh; ai, t*i*ger; ə:, b*i*rd. **(o)** o, *o*x; au, c*ow*; ou, g*oa*t; u, p*oo*r; ɔi, r*oy*al. **(u)** ʌ, d*u*ck; u, b*u*ll; u:, g*oo*se; ə, b*a*cillus; ju:, c*u*be. x, lo*ch*; θ, *th*ink; ð, bo*th*er; z, *Z*en; ʒ, cors*a*ge; dʒ, sav*age*; ŋ, orangutan*g*; j, *y*ak; ʃ, *fi*sh; tʃ, fe*tch*; 'l, rabb*le*; 'n, redd*en*. Complete pronunciation key appears inside front cover.

by formal education or training, e.g., high school equivalency test

e·quiv·a·lent (ikwívələnt) **1.** *adj.* (with 'to') equal, having the same effect or value, *his evasiveness was equivalent to lying* **2.** *n.* that which is equivalent to something else, *to change dollars for the equivalent in francs* ‖ (*chem.*) an equivalent weight [fr. L.L. *aequivalere* fr. *aequi-*, equal+*valere*, to be worth]

equivalent weight (*chem.*) the mass (usually on the metric scale) of an element, compound or radical that will combine with or replace or that has the same combining capacity as 8 grams of oxygen (i.e. the atomic mass divided by the usual valence of oxygen) or a specified quantity of some other standard compound or radical (cf. ELECTROCHEMICAL EQUIVALENT, *FARADAY)

e·quiv·o·cal (ikwívək'l) *adj.* capable of being understood in more than one way ‖ suspect, of doubtful validity, honesty or sincerity, *an equivocal reputation* **e·quiv·o·cál·i·ty** *n.* [fr. L.L. *aequivocus*, ambiguous]

e·quiv·o·cate (ikwívəkeit) *pres. part.* **e·quiv·o·cat·ing** *past* and *past part.* **e·quiv·o·cat·ed** *v.i.* to avoid a plain statement or answer and so evade the truth **e·quiv·o·cá·tion, e·quív·o·ca·tor** *ns* [fr. M.L. *aequivocare* (*aequivocatus*), to sound the same]

-er *suffix* used to form agent nouns, as in 'singer' ‖ used to form nouns designating persons according to their trade or occupation, as in 'confectioner', 'first-nighter' or according to their place of origin, as in 'Northerner' [O.E. *-ere*]

-er *suffix* used to form the comparative degree of adjectives, as in 'greener' [O. E. *-ra, -re*]

-er *suffix* used to form the comparative degree of adverbs, as in 'sooner' [O.E. *-or*]

ER *abbr.* emergency room

e·ra (íərə) *n.* a system of dating events from one particular event or moment, *the Christian era starts from the birth of Christ* ‖ a period of time in history or any relatively prolonged stage of development, *the Elizabethan era, the era of the silent film* ‖ a date or event which is taken as the beginning of an era, *the invention of the jet engine marks an era in aircraft development* ‖ (*geol.*) one of the major divisions of geological time [L.L. *aera*, a number expressed in figures prob. fr. *aera* pl. of *aes*, money]

ERA *abbr.* proposed Equal Rights Amendment to the U.S. Constitution

e·ra·di·ate (iréidi:eit) *pres. part.* **e·ra·di·at·ing** *past* and *past part.* **e·ra·di·at·ed** *v.i.* to send out rays of light, radiate **e·ra·di·á·tion** *n.*

e·rad·i·ca·ble (irǽdikəb'l) *adj.* able to be eradicated

e·rad·i·cate (irǽdikeit) *pres. part.* **e·rad·i·cat·ing** *past* and *past part.* **e·rad·i·cat·ed** *v.t.* to stamp out or destroy utterly, *to eradicate disease* **e·rad·i·cá·tion** *n.* **e·rád·i·ca·tor** *n.* a chemical substance for removing ink or stain [fr. L. *eradicare* (*eradicatus*), to uproot]

e·rase (iréis, *Br.* iréiz) *pres. part.* **e·ras·ing** *past* and *past part.* **e·rased** *v.t.* to rub out, efface, to erase *a typing error, erase a tape recording* **e·rás·er** *n.* something used for erasing marks, e.g. a piece of rubber for pencil or a cloth pad for chalk [fr. L. *eradere* (*erasus*), to scrape out]

E·ras·mus (irǽzməs), Desiderius (c. 1469–1536), Dutch scholar, exemplar of the New Learning of the Renaissance, a tolerant, radical Christian humanist opposing religious and political fanaticism and tyranny. In 1516 he published the first Greek edition of the New Testament, with an accompanying Latin version, as an essential preparation for his biblical criticism. His 'Colloquies' were published in 1519. He taught in Paris, Oxford, Cambridge, Bologna and Louvain, and was the intimate friend of John Colet and Sir Thomas More. He finally settled in Basle, where Froben printed a complete edition of his works in 1521. His 'De libero arbitrio' (1523) attacked the theology of Luther. His other works include 'Adagia' (1500 and 1508), 'Enchiridion militis christiani' (1503), and 'Encomium moriae' (1511)

E·ras·tian (irǽstʃən, irǽsti:ən) **1.** *adj.* pertaining to the doctrine, ascribed to Erastus, which holds that the function of the clergy is to teach, not to legislate, and which subordinates the authority of the Church to that of the State even in ecclesiastical affairs **2.** *n.* an upholder of this doctrine **E·rás·tian·ism** *n.* [after *Erastus*]

E·ras·tus (irǽstəs), Thomas (Thomas Lüber, 1524–83), German-Swiss theologian and physician. He was a follower of the Swiss reformer Zwingli. He held that the sole authority to

enforce religious conformity, but not to define doctrine, belonged to the civil powers

e·ra·sure (iréiʃər, *Br.* iréiʒə) *n.* the act of erasing ‖ what has been erased, or the place from which something has been erased

Er·a·to (érətou) the Muse of love poetry

Er·a·tos·the·nes of Cyrene (erətəsθəni:zəvsairí:ni:) (c. 276–c. 196 B.C.), Greek mathematician, astronomer, geographer and philosopher. A versatile scholar, appointed head of the Alexandrian library, he devised a method of finding prime numbers, calculated the circumference of the earth and magnitude of the sun, and was the first systematic geographer

er·bi·um (ə́:rbi:əm) *n.* a chemical element (symbol Er, at. no. 68, at. mass 167.26) in the group of rare earths [after *Ytterby* in Sweden]

Er·ci·lla y Zú·ñi·ga (erθí:lja:i:θú:nji:ga), Alonso de (1533–94), Spanish poet. Much of his epic 'La Araucana' (1569–89) was written while he was a soldier in South America

Erd·man Act (ə́:rdmən) a U.S. Congressional act (1898) which provided for mediation in labor disputes. A positive result was the mediation of the coal strike of 1902, against the will of the operators

ere (eər) **1.** *prep.* (*archaic*) before, *ere sunset* **2.** *conj.* (*archaic*) before ‖ (*archaic*) rather than [O.E. *ær*]

Er·e·bus (érəbəs) (*Gk mythol.*) a gloomy place between the earth and Hades [L. fr. Gk *Erebos*]

E·rech·the·um (irékθi:əm, erəkθí:əm) one of the three principal buildings on the Acropolis of Athens, built 421–407 B.C., famous for its caryatid columns

E·rech·the·us (irékθi:əs, irékθju:s) (*Gk mythol.*) legendary king of Attica

e·rect (irékt) **1.** *adj.* upright, without stooping or bowing, *to stand erect* ‖ (of a dog's hair etc.) on end, bristling ‖ (of the penis or clitoris) stiff and swollen from being distended with blood ‖ (*bot.*) growing vertically, growing at right angles to the stem or branch **2.** *v.t.* to cause to have built or put up, *to erect a monument* ‖ to put in place, *to erect a fence, to erect emotional barriers* ‖ to set upright ‖ to cause to become erect ‖ (*geom.*) to draw, construct, *to erect a perpendicular* ‖ *v.i.* (of the penis or clitoris) to become erect [fr. L. *erigere* (*erectus*), to set up]

e·rec·tile (iréktəl, iréktail) *adj.* capable of standing on end, *the erectile hairs on a dog's back* ‖ capable of becoming erect, *erectile tissues* [F. *érectile*]

e·rec·tion (irékʃən) *n.* an erecting or being erected ‖ a building or other similar structure ‖ a hardening and swelling of the penis or clitoris when distended with blood [fr. L.L. *erectio* (*erectionis*)]

e·rec·tor (iréktər) *n.* a workman on erection work ‖ a machine which erects ‖ a muscle which raises an organ or part of the body

E region a portion of the ionosphere that extends from 40 miles to 90–180 miles above the earth and that refracts radio waves of medium length

er·e·mite (érəmait) *n.* (*hist.*) a hermit, esp. a religious living alone in a secluded place **er·e·mit·ic** (erəmítik), **er·e·mít·i·cal** *adjs* [fr. L.L. *eremita* fr. Gk fr. *erēmia*, a desert]

e·rep·sin (irépsin) *n.* (*biochem.*) an enzyme in the intestinal juice [fr. L. *eripere*, to take away]

er·e·thism (érəθizəm) *n.* (*physiol.*) excessive irritability either of a muscle or other part of the body or (a symptom of mercurial poisoning) of the mind **er·e·this·mic** *adj.* [fr. F. *éréthisme* fr. Gk]

E·re·van (erevɑ́n) (Yerevan) the capital (pop. 1,019,000) of Armenia, U.S.S.R., center of a fertile agricultural lowland. Industries: food processing, cognac, synthetic rubber, light manufactures. University (1921)

Er·furt (érfurt) an industrial city (pop. 206,960) of East Germany. Gothic cathedral, university (1392) ‖ the district (area 2,820 sq. miles, pop. 1,256,000) which includes it (*THURINGIA, *SAXONYANHALT)

erg (ə:rg) *n.* (*phys.*) the unit of work and energy in the cgs system equal to the work done by a force of 1 dyne acting through a distance of 1 centimeter [fr. Gk *ergon*, work]

er·gas·tic (ə:rgǽstik) *adj.* (*biol.*) of intracellular deposits of starch and fat or extracellular secretions) produced as nonliving material by protoplasmic activity [fr. Gk *ergastikos*, able to work]

er·go (ə́:rgou, éərgou) *conj.* and *adv,*. therefore [L.]

er·gom·e·ter (ə:rgómətər) *n.* (*physiol.*) a device for measuring the energy expended by specific body muscles in a controlled task **ergometrics** *n.*

er·go·nom·ics (ə:rgənómiks) *n.* the study of the mental and physical capacities of persons in relation to the demands made upon them by various kinds of work **er·gon·o·mist** (ə:rgónəmist) *n.* [fr. Gk *ergon*, work+*nomos*, law]

er·go·sphere (ə́:rgousfiər) *n.* (*astron.*) hypothetical area surrounding a black hole

er·gos·ter·ol (ə:rgóstərɔl, ə:rgóstəroul) *n.* (*biochem.*) a steroid alcohol found in ergot and the fats of animals, from which (by irradiation with ultraviolet rays) vitamin D is produced [ERGOT+STEROL]

er·got (ə́:rgət) *n. Claviceps purpurea*, a disease of rye and other cereals or grasses ‖ the fungus which produces the disease ‖ a drug made from the dried sclerotium of *Claviceps*, which causes the uterine muscle to contract and is used to control bleeding and to assist childbirth by contracting the womb **ér·got·ism** *n.* a disease characterized either by gangrene or by violent nervous disorders, at one time epidemic in Europe, caused by eating ergot-infected rye or bread made from the infected flour [O.F. *argot*, spur, from the shape of the growth]

Er·ic (érik) 'the Red' (c. 940–c. 1010), Norse chieftain who explored (982–5) the southwest coast of Greenland

Eric IX, St (*d.* 1160), king of Sweden (c. 1150–60). He introduced Christianity into Finland (c. 1155), and is the patron saint of Sweden. Feast: May 18

Eric XIV (1533–77), king of Sweden (1560–8), son of Gustavus I. He waged war (1563–70) with Denmark, and was a suitor of Elizabeth I of England

Eric of Pomerania (1382–1459), king of Denmark (as Eric VII), of Sweden (as Eric XIII, 1396–1439) and of Norway (1389–1442), first king to rule the three countries under the terms of the Union of Kalmar (1397)

Er·ic·son, Er·ics·son (ériksən), Leif (c. 1000 A.D.), Norse explorer, son of Eric the Red. He discovered Vinland, identified as a part of the Newfoundland coast

Er·ics·son (ériksən), John (1803–89), Swedish-U.S. naval engineer. He designed (1862) the first armored-turret ship, the 'Monitor', which gained fame during the Civil War

E·rie (íəri) a city and port of entry (pop. 119,123) on Lake Erie in the northwest corner of Pennsylvania. Manufactures: boilers and engines, stoves, machinery, electric locomotives, flour and gristmill products

Erie the fourth largest lake (area 9,940 sq. miles) of the Great Lakes, between Lakes Ontario and Huron. Chief ports: Detroit, Cleveland, Buffalo. Lake Erie was the site of a naval engagement (1813) during the War of 1812, in which a U.S. naval force commanded by Oliver Perry defeated a British naval force, securing U.S. command of the Great Lakes (*ST LAWRENCE SEAWAY)

Erie Canal the main waterway (340 miles long, 150 ft wide, 12 ft deep) of the New York State barge canal system, between Albany and Buffalo, connecting the Hudson River with Lake Erie

E·rig·e·na (erídʒənə), Johannes Scotus, Irish theologian of the 9th c. He produced the first medieval philosophical and theological synthesis of reason and faith ('De divisione naturae', c. 865)

Erikson (ériksən), Erik Homburger (1902–) a German-American psychoanalyst whose theory of personality development encompassed environment as well as private emotions. He taught at several U.S. universities—Harvard (1934–5, 1960–70), Yale (1936–9) and California (1939–51)—where he emphasized identity, identity crisis and psychosexual development. He later studied psychohistory and wrote about the personality development of historical figures. His works include 'Childhood and Society' (1950), 'Young Man Luther' (1958) and 'Gandhi's Truth' (1970)

Er·in (érin, íərin) an old name for Ireland

E·rin·y·es (i:ríni:z) (*Gk mythol.*) the three Furies (in Latin literature given the names Tisiphone, Megaera and Alecto) who punished sin, esp. the murder of kin. They were pictured as

CONCISE PRONUNCIATION KEY: **(a)** æ, c*a*t; ɑ, c*a*r; ɔ f*a*wn; ei, sn*a*ke. **(e)** e, h*e*n; i:, sh*ee*p; iə, d*ee*r; ɛə, b*ea*r. **(i)** i, f*i*sh; ai, t*i*ger; ə:, b*i*rd. **(o)** ɔ, *o*x; au, c*o*w; ou, g*oa*t; u, p*oo*r; ɔi, r*oy*al. **(u)** ʌ, d*u*ck; u, b*u*ll; u:, g*oo*se; ə, b*a*cillus; ju:, c*u*be. x, lo*ch*; θ, *th*ink; ð, bo*th*er; z, *Z*en; ʒ, corsa*ge*; dʒ, sava*ge*; ŋ, orangutan*g*; j, *y*ak; ʃ, *fish*; tʃ, fe*tch*; 'l, rabb*le*; 'n, redd*en*. Complete pronunciation key appears inside front cover.

winged women with snakes for hair (*EUMENIDES)

ERISA (acronym) Employee Retirement Income Security Act of 1974, providing for control of business pension funds

er·is·tic (erístik) **1.** n. the art of arguing ‖ a controversialist **2.** adj. relating to, used in, or fond of, arguing (esp. arguing for the pleasure of arguing rather than to get at the truth) [fr. Gk eristikos fr. eris, dispute]

E·ri·tre·a (eritrí:ə, ẹritréiə) the coastal province (area 45,754 sq. miles, pop. 2,426,200) of Ethiopia on the Red Sea. Capital: Asmara. Products: cotton, hides. Formerly part of Abyssinia, it was captured by Italy (1890) and became part of Italian East Africa (1936). It was taken by Allied forces (1941), was federated with Ethiopia (1952) and became a province (1962). Secessionists opposed to the central government have waged a rebellion since that time

er·lang (ə́:ræŋ) n. unit of traffic density in communications, based on the average number of calls during a basic hour

Er·lang·en (érlʊ̈ŋən) an industrial town (pop. 100,900) in Bavaria, W. Germany. University (1743)

er·mine (ə́:rmin) n. Mustela erminea, fam. Mustelidae, a savage, carnivorous European animal about 15 ins. long. In summer the fur is reddish brown except for a white belly. In winter (in northern latitudes) its fur turns white except for the black tip of its tail ‖ this fur ‖ wraps or trimming made of this fur ‖ the white fur, with the black tips of the tails, worn by British peers and judges ‖ (heraldry) white, with conventional representations of the tails [O.F. hermin]

erne, ern (ə:rn) n. Haliaetus albicilla, the sea eagle [M.E. ern, arn fr. O.E. earn, eagle]

Ernst (ernst), Max (1891–1976), French painter and engraver, born in Germany, an originator of dada and surrealism. Using the methods of automatism, he developed images as they were suggested to him by the convolutions of textured surfaces, esp. wood grains, or by the chance, incongruous combination of objects

e·rode (iróud) pres. part. **e·rod·ing** past and past part. **e·rod·ed** v.t. to eat away, acid erodes metal ‖ to wear away (land) ‖ v.i. to become eroded [F. éroder]

e·rog·e·nous (iród͡zənəs) adj. of or arousing sexual desire ‖ capable of being sexually stimulated, erogenous zones of the body [fr. Gk erōs, sexual love+genous, producing]

E·ros (íərɒs, érɒs) (Gk mythol.) the god of love, son of Aphrodite, corresponding to the Roman Cupid

e·ros (íərɒs, érɒs) n. sexual love (cf. AGAPE) ‖ sexual tendencies and desires considered as a whole from a psychoanalytical point of view [Gk erōs]

e·ro·sion (iróuʒən) n. an eroding or being eroded, esp. (geol.) the wearing away of land by water, wind or ice [F. fr. L. erosio (erosionis)]

e·ro·sive (iróusiv) adj. causing erosion [fr. L. erodere (erosus), to erode]

e·rot·ic (irótik) adj. of or relating to sexual love ‖ licentious, erotic engravings [fr. Gk erōtikos fr. erōs, sexual love]

e·rot·i·ca (irótikə) pl. n. books or drawings dealing with or illustrating sexual love [Mod. L. fr. Gk erōtika]

e·rot·i·cal·ly (irótikli:) adv. in an erotic way

e·rot·i·cism (irótisizəm) n. sexual excitement or desire ‖ the character of being erotic

er·o·tism (érətizəm) n. eroticism [fr. Gk erōs (erōtos), sexual love]

er·o·tol·o·gy (erətóləd͡ʒi:) n. study of erotic art and literature **erotological** adv. **erotologist** n.

err (ə:r, er) v.i. to make a mistake, to be wrong, to err in judgment ‖ to contain a relative amount of error, to err by less than a thousandth [M.E. erren fr. F. errer]

er·ran·cy (érənsi:) pl. **er·ran·cies** n. the state of erring ‖ an instance of erring

er·rand (érənd) n. a short journey to carry out some particular task or to take a message ‖ the task itself [O.E. ærende, a message]

er·rant (érənt) adj. erring, tending to do wrong ‖ straying ‖ (rhet.) roving [O.F. pres. part. of errer, to wander]

er·rant·ry (érəntri:) n. (hist.) the way of life of a knight-errant

er·ra·ta slip (irúːtə, iréitə) a list of mistakes or misprints in a printed or written book or document [L. fr. errare, to go wrong]

er·rat·ic (irǽtik) **1.** adj. not fitting into any regular pattern of events or behavior, erratic attendance ‖ uneven in quality, his writings are brilliant but erratic ‖ unstable, unbalanced, an erratic genius ‖ (geol., of boulders) transported from their place of origin ‖ (med.) moving from one place in the body to another **2.** n. (geol.) a boulder transported from its place of origin **er·rat·i·cal·ly** adv. [fr. L. erraticus fr. errare, to wander]

er·ro·ne·ous (iróuni:əs) adj. (of a statement, opinion, doctrine etc.) mistaken, wrong [fr. L. erroneus, wandering about fr. errare, to go wrong]

er·ror (érər) n. departure from the truth in a statement or in a belief ‖ a mistake, a typing error ‖ departure from right conduct, to see the error of one's ways ‖ (math.) the difference between the correct result and the computed one ‖ (law) a legal or factual mistake in court proceedings, giving grounds for review upon a writ of error ‖ (baseball) a misplay by the fielding team of a chance that should have led to an out for the batting team or that lets a runner advance **in error** by mistake [M.E. errour fr. O.F.]

er·satz (éərzats, éərsats) **1.** adj. (of a product) synthetic **2.** n. a synthetic product replacing a natural one [G. = substitute]

Erse (ə:rs) **1.** adj. of, written or spoken in Irish ‖ (formerly) of, written or spoken in Scottish Gaelic **2.** n. the Irish language ‖ (formerly) Scottish Gaelic [Scot. var. of IRISH]

Er·skine (ə́:rskin), Thomas, 1st Baron (1750–1823), Scottish jurist whose speeches in defense of Lord George Gordon (1781), Tom Paine (1792) and others are fine examples of forensic oratory

erst·while (ə́:rsthwail,ə́:rstwail) adj. (rhet.) former, operative or existing until then or until now, he began to neglect his erstwhile friends [fr. obs. erst, first, earlier +WHILE]

ERTs (acronym) earth resource technology satellites, U.S. space program charting earth's resources; the satellites themselves

er·u·bes·cent (erubés'nt) adj. becoming red ‖ reddish [fr. L. erubescere, to grow red]

e·ruct (irʌ́kt) v.i. to belch ‖ v.t. to spew out, a volcano eructs molten lava **e·rúc·tate** pres. part. **e·ruc·tat·ing** past and past part. **e·ruc·tat·ed** v.i. and t. to eruct **e·ruc·tá·tion** n. [fr. L. eructare (eructatus)]

er·u·dite (érjudait, érudait) adj. (of a man or a work) learned **er·u·di·tion** (erjudíʃən, erudíʃən) n. scholarly learning [fr. L. erudire (eruditus), to polish]

e·rupt (irʌ́pt) v.i. (of a volcano) to pour forth rocks, lava etc. ‖ (of a geyser) to shoot forth steam ‖ to break or burst out violently from restraint, or as if from restraint ‖ (of teeth) to cut through the gums ‖ (of a rash) to break out on the skin ‖ v.t. (of a volcano or geyser, or of someone or something compared to these) to throw out violently, eject [fr. L. erumpere (eruptus), to break out]

e·rup·tion (irʌ́pʃən) n. an outbreak, explosion (of a natural force) ‖ an outbreak (of violence, passion, disease etc.) ‖ a breaking out in a skin rash ‖ the rash itself [fr. L. eruptio fr. erumpere, to break out]

e·rup·tive (irʌ́ptiv) adj. breaking out violently or tending to do so ‖ produced or formed by volcanic eruption ‖ relating to a skin eruption **e·rup·tiv·i·ty** n. [F. éruptif]

-ery suffix used to form nouns indicating trade, activity or condition, as in 'grocery', place or establishment, as in 'bindery', things collectively, as in 'pottery', qualities, as in 'chicanery' etc. [M.E. fr. F.]

Er·y·man·thus (erəmǽnθəs) a mountain in Arcadia where Hercules had to kill a wild boar (*HERACLES)

er·y·sip·e·las (erisípələs) n. a contagious skin disease caused by Streptococcus erysipelatus. It is marked by inflammation, fever and formation of large blisters, which break and dry into a hard crust [fr. Gk erusipelas fr. eruthros, red+pella, skin]

e·ryth·rism (iríθrizəm, érəθrizəm) n. (of hair, plumage) a condition characterized by unusual redness [fr. Gk eruthros, red]

e·ryth·ro·blast (iríθrəblæst) n. (biol.) any of the nucleated cells, of mesodermal origin (e.g. red bone marrow), which later develop into red blood corpuscles **e·ryth·ro·blás·tic** adj. **e·ryth·ro·blas·to·sis** (iriθroublæstóusis) n. an increase in the number of erythroblasts in the fetus, usually associated with Rh-factor incompatibility [fr. Gk eruthros, red+blastos, bud]

e·ryth·ro·cyte (iríθrəsait) n. a microscopic biconcave disk-shaped enucleate cell containing hemoglobin. They are present in extremely large numbers in vertebrate blood, transporting oxygen from the lungs to the tissues of the body (cf. LEUCOCYTE) **e·ryth·ro·cyt·ic** (iriθrəsítik) adj. [fr. Gk eruthros, red+kutos, a hollow vessel, a cell]

e·ryth·ro·poi·e·tin (əriθroupoíi:tin) n. (physiol.) kidney hormone that stimulates production of red blood cells

e·ryth·ro·leu·kem·i·a (ə:riθroulu:kí:mi:ə) n. (med.) malignant disorder affecting red blood cells and bone marrow

e·ryth·ro·poi·e·sis (əriθroupoiésis) n. (physiol.) the creation and growth of red blood corpuscles

Erz·ge·bir·ge (értsgəbirgə) a range of mountains along the E. German-Czechoslovakian frontier, rich in minerals (esp. coal, uranium, cobalt, bismuth, arsenic and antimony). Highest peak: Mt Klinovec (Keilberg, 4,080 ft), in Czechoslovakia

Er·zu·rum (érzərum) a Turkish city (pop. 190,241) in the center of the Armenian plateau. On the frontier with the U.S.S.R., it has been the scene of much fighting

E·sar·had·don (i:sɑːrhǽd'n) (d. 669 B.C.), king of Assyria (680–669 B.C.), son of Sennacherib. He conquered Egypt (673–670 B.C.), subdued the Chaldeans and rebuilt Babylon

E·sau (í:sɔ) son of Isaac. He was tricked out of his birthright by his younger twin, Jacob (Genesis xxv, 21–34, xxvii)

Es·bjerg (ésbjer) Denmark's chief North Sea port (pop. 76,694) in W. Jutland: fishing, food packing, shipbuilding

es·ca·lade (eskəléid) **1.** n. (hist.) an attack on a stronghold, using scaling ladders to climb the walls **2.** v.t. pres. part. **es·ca·lad·ing** past and past part. **es·ca·lad·ed** to attack by escalade ‖ to climb by using ladders [F.]

es·ca·late (éskəleit) pres. part. **es·ca·lat·ing** past and past part. **es·ca·lat·ed** v.t. and i. to increase gradually but steadily **es·ca·lá·tion** n. [ESCALATOR]

es·ca·la·tion (eskəléiʃən) n. raising the scale of activity, esp. military **escalate** v. **escalatory** adj.

es·ca·la·tor (éskəleitər) n. a moving staircase working on the principle of an endless chain [Mod. L. fr. F. escalader, to scale]

escalator clause a clause allowing for variation in pay, e.g. according to the rise or fall of the cost of living, incorporated in an agreement between an employer and a union

es·cal·lop (iskóləp, iskǽləp) **1.** n. the scallop shellfish ‖ its shell ‖ (heraldry) a scallop shell **2.** v.t. (cooking) to scallop [O.F. escalope, shell fr. Gmc]

es·ca·pade (éskəpeid, eskəpéid) n. a wild, often innocent, adventure involving a throwing over of restraints [F. fr. Span. escapada, escape]

es·cape (iskéip) **1.** v. pres. part. **es·cap·ing** past and past part. **es·caped** v.i. to get free by flight (from prison or other confinement or restraint), regain one's liberty ‖ to leak, flow, or otherwise issue from a container ‖ to find release or relief from worries, troubles or responsibilities ‖ v.t. (of words or sounds) to be uttered or released involuntarily by, a cry of pain escaped him ‖ to get away from (pursuit or restraint) ‖ to avoid, keep or be kept safe from, get away from (death, danger, disaster, punishment etc.) ‖ to elude the memory, understanding or notice of **2.** n. the act of getting free from prison or other confinement, from pursuit or from a pursuer etc. ‖ a way out, a means of getting free from confinement or danger ‖ a leak, flowing out or overflow ‖ avoidance of, preservation from, or getting away from death, danger, punishment etc. ‖ (with a negative or a word, phrase or question implying a negative) a rejecting of something that is obviously true, there is no escape from the evidence ‖ a release or relief from misery, worries or responsibilities ‖ (bot.) a garden plant growing wild **es·cap·ee** n. someone who has escaped **es·cápe·ment** n. a device for checking and regulating the movements of the wheels in a clock or watch ‖ a device for regulating the movement of the carriage of a typewriter [O.N.F. escaper]

escape velocity the minimum velocity that would enable an object attaining it to escape the gravitational field of the earth or of a celestial body

escape wheel (*horology*) a revolving wheel, the teeth of which transmit impulses to the pallets

es·cap·ism (iskéipizəm) *n.* a detaching of the mind from unpleasant facts of reality in favor of a more pleasant world of fancy **es·cáp·ist** *adj.* and *n.*

es·cap·ol·o·gy (iskeipólədʒi:, ȩskeipólədʒi:) *n.* techniques of escaping as a department of knowledge, *the literature of escapology* [fr. ESCAPE+Gk *logos*, word]

es·ca·role (éskəroul) *n.* a crisp, broadleaved variety of endive, used in salads [F.]

es·carp (iskárp) **1.** *v.t.* to cut or shape into an escarpment, or strengthen with an escarpment **2.** *n.* an escarpment **es·cárp·ment** *n.* a natural slope or cliff mounting to a ridge ‖ (*mil., hist.*) a similar slope, often artificially constructed, making a fortress difficult to approach [F. *escarper, escarpe* fr. Ital. *scarpa*, a steep bank]

esch·a·lot (éʃələt) *n.* a shallot [fr. F. *eschalotte*]

es·cha·tol·o·gy (ȩskətólədʒi:) *n.* the branch of theology which deals with the final end of man and of the world [fr. Gk *eschatos*, last+*logos*, word]

es·cheat (istʃí:t) **1.** *n.* (*law*) the return to the State, or (*hist.*) to a feudal lord, or to the Crown, of land left by a person who has died intestate and without heirs ‖ the land so returned **2.** *v.t.* to return (land) as an escheat ‖ *v.i.* to revert as an escheat [M.E. *eschete* fr. O.F.]

Esch·er·i·chi·a coli (eʃəríki:ə) *n.* (*biol.*) bacterium found in the human intestine 1/10,000 in. long, often used in gene-splicing research **also** E COLI

es·chew (istʃú:) *v.t.* (*rhet.*) to do without, refrain from using, avoid **es·chéw·al** *n.* [O.E. *eschiver* fr. Gmc]

esch·scholt·zi·a (eʃóultsi:ə, iskóltsi:ə) *n.* a member of *Eschscholtzia*, fam. *Papaveraceae*, esp. *E. californica*, the California poppy, an annual plant native to western North America, much cultivated for its flowers. In dull weather each petal rolls up on itself, enclosing some stamens. The ripe capsule explodes and scatters seeds [Mod. L. after J. F. von *Eschscholtz* (1793-1831), G. botanist]

'Es·co·be·do v. Illinois' (ȩskəbéidou) a decision (1964) of the U.S. Supreme Court which held that a suspect may not be prevented from seeing his lawyer during a police interrogation

Es·con·di·do, Rio (ȩskondí:dou) *NICARAGUA

Es·co·rial (ȩskorjál) a set of buildings about 30 miles northwest of Madrid, Spain, built (1563-84) by Philip II. It includes a palace, a monastery, a church, a college and the mausoleum of most Spanish sovereigns after Charles V, and houses a famous library and art collection. The Renaissance church is one of the finest in Europe

es·cort 1. (éskort) *n.* a person or group accompanying another person or group out of politeness, for company, to give protection, by way of ceremonial etc. ‖ warships or aircraft acting in a protective or ceremonial role ‖ an accompanying by a person, group or formation ‖ a man accompanying a woman on some social occasion ‖ a guard responsible for a prisoner in transit **under escort** accompanied by guards **2.** (iskórt) *v.t.* to accompany as an escort ‖ to accompany as a courtesy or protection [F. *escorte* fr. Ital. *scorta*, guide, guard]

es·cri·toire (eskritwár) *n.* a writing desk, esp. an antique one [F.]

es·crow (éskrou) *n.* (*law*) a formal contract or deed which does not come into effect until some specified condition has been fulfilled. (Until that time it is held by a third person.) **in escrow** on trust as an escrow [A.F. *escrowe* O.F. *escroe*, scroll]

es·cu·do (eskú:dou) *n.* the basic monetary unit of Portugal and Portuguese territories ‖ a coin of the value of one escudo [Port.=a shield]

es·cu·lent (éskjulənt) *adj.* edible [fr. L. *esculentus* fr. *esca*, food]

es·cutch·eon (iskátʃən) *n.* a shield bearing a coat of arms ‖ the part of a ship's stern bearing her name ‖ a decorative plate, e.g. a keyhole plate or cover [O.N.F. *escuchon*]

Es·dras (ézdrəs) the name given in the Roman Catholic canon to the books of Ezra and Nehemiah ‖ two books placed in the Apocrypha in the Authorized Version and not regarded as canonical by Roman Catholics. The first (c. 2nd c. B.C.) is largely a compilation from Chronicles, Ezra and Nehemiah. The second (c. 2nd c. A.D.) is a collection of apocalyptic visions

-ese *suffix* used to indicate a native or inhabitant, as in 'Chinese' or a language or dialect, as in 'Cantonese', or style, as in 'officialese'

Esfahan *ISFAHAN

eskar *ESKER

Es·ke·naz·ic (ȩskənázik) Ashkenazic

es·ker, es·kar (éskər) *n.* (*geol.*) a long ridge of drift deposited by a receding glacier [Irish *eiscir*, a ridge]

Es·ki·mo, Es·qui·mau (éskəmou) **1.** *pl.* **Es·ki·mos, Es·ki·mo, Es·qui·mau, Es·qui·maux** *n.* one of a group of peoples living in the Arctic and subarctic regions from Greenland westward to Siberia ‖ a member of these peoples ‖ their language **2.** *adj.* of or pertaining to the Eskimos or their language **Es·ki·mó·an** *adj.* Eskimo [Dan. *Eskimo*, F. *Esquimau*, perh. fr. *Algonquian*]
—The Eskimos number about 40,000 and are largely confined to the coastal areas of Greenland, N. Canada and Alaska. They live by hunting, trapping and fishing, and lead a nomadic life. They speak a basically common language, live in small closely-knit social groups and are skilled in handcrafts, such as carving

Eskimo dog a dog of a tough breed used in the Arctic for pulling sledges and hunting. They are heavily built (up to 80 pounds or more), carry the tail curled over the back, and have a double coat of shaggy, usually gray hair over soft, thick, woolly hair

Es·ki·şe·hir (eski:ʃehí:r) a city (pop. 153,000) of central Turkey: sulfur baths, meerschaum deposits

ESOP (*acronym*) employee stock ownership plan

e·soph·a·gus, oe·soph·a·gus (isófəgəs) *pl.* **e·soph·a·gi, oe·soph·a·gi** (isófədʒai) *n.* (*anat.*) the tube through which food passes from the mouth to the stomach [Mod. L. fr. Gk *oisophagos*, the gullet]

es·o·ter·ic (ȩsətérik) *adj.* (of religious, mystical or philosophical teaching or practice) with a meaning that is understood only by those who have received the necessary instruction or training ‖ trained to understand such teaching or practices ‖ difficult to understand ‖ with a private or secret meaning or purpose, *the esoteric language of schoolboys* **es·o·tér·i·cal·ly** *adv.* [fr. Gk *esōterikos* fr. *esōterō*, further within]

ESP, E.S.P. extrasensory perception, e.g. in telepathy

esp. especially

es·pal·ier (ispæljər) **1.** *n.* a fruit tree trained to grow flat along a wall or trellis ‖ a trellis for training such trees **2.** *v.t.* to grow as an espalier [F. fr. Ital. *spalliera* fr. *spalla*, shoulder]

es·par·to (espártou) *n. Stipa tenacissima*, fam. *Gramineae*, a grass grown in N. Africa and Spain. It grows in tufts up to 4 ft. in height and has long flat gray-green leaves. The light fiber is used for making ropes, mats, baskets etc., and for high-quality paper [Span. fr. L. fr. Gk]

es·pe·cial (ispéʃəl) *adj.* particular ‖ outstanding, exceptional **in especial** in particular ‖ especially **es·pé·cial·ly** *adv.* particularly ‖ exceptionally [O.F.]

Es·pe·ran·to (ȩspərántou, ȩspərǽntou) *n.* an artificial language, invented in 1887 by Dr L. L. Zamenhof, based on the Latin roots common to most of the Romance languages [Doktoro *Esperanto* (fr. L. *sperare*, to hope), Zamenhof's pen name]

es·pi·o·nage (éspi:ənɑʒ,ȩspi:ənáʒ) *n.* spying or the use of spies to obtain military, political, scientific, industrial etc. secrets [fr. F. *espionnage* fr. *espion*, spy]

Espionage Act of 1917 a U.S. Congressional act passed as the U.S.A. entered the 1st world war, which penalized spoken and written opposition to the war. Its provisions were reinforced by the Sedition Act of 1918

es·pla·nade (esplənéid, esplənád) *n.* a wide road, generally running along a seafront and raised above the level of the beach [F. fr. Span.]

es·pous·al (ispáuz'l) *n.* (*rhet.*) an adoption or taking up (of a cause, doctrine or line of action etc.) [O.F. *espousailles*, betrothal]

es·pouse (ispáuz) *pres. part.* **es·pous·ing** *past and past part.* **es·poused** *v.t.* to adopt, take up, support (a cause, doctrine, line of action etc.) [O.F. *espouser*, to betroth]

es·pres·so (esprésou) *n.* strong coffee prepared by forcing steam through very finely ground

coffee beans ‖ an establishment where this is drunk [Ital.]

es·prit (esprí:) *n.* wit [F. fr. L. *spiritus*, spirit]

es·prit de corps (espri:dəkór) the common feeling of purpose, pride, loyalty and responsibility that unites a disciplined group [F.= corps spirit]

Es·pron·ce·da (espronθéða), José de (1808-42), Spanish lyric poet and revolutionary

es·py (ispái) *pres. part.* **es·py·ing** *past* and *past part.* **es·pied** *v.t.* (*rhet.*) to catch sight of, notice [O.F. *espier*, to spy out]

Esq. Esquire

Esquimau *ESKIMO

Es·quire (iskwáiər, éskwaiər) *n.* (esp. *Br.*, abbr. Esq.) a courtesy title written after a commoner's surname in an address, no other title (e.g. 'Mr') being used [O.F. *esquier*, shield bearer to a knight]

-ess *suffix* denoting female nouns, as in 'lioness' [F. *-esse* fr. L.L. *-issa* fr. Gk]

es·say (eséi) *v.t.* to test, try out, esp. to assay (metals) ‖ *v.i.* to attempt [ASSAY, respelled after F. *essayer*, to try]

es·say (éséi) *n.* a writing (often quite short) dealing with a particular subject ‖ (*rhet.*, also eséi) a trial or experiment, *an essay in democratic living* ‖ a proof of a rejected design for a stamp or for paper money **és·say·ist** *n.* a writer of essays [O. F. *essai*, attempt]

es·se (ési:) *n.* (*Scholastic philos.*) actual existence (cf. ENS) ‖ essential being [L.= to be]

Es·sen (és'n) the largest city (pop. 670,220) in the Ruhr, West Germany, site of the Krupp works: mining, steel, heavy mechanical engineering, metallurgy, coke production, glass, chemicals, textiles, plastics, furniture

es·sence (és'ns) *n.* the most significant part of a thing's nature ‖ (*philos.*) the sum of the intrinsic properties without which a thing would cease to be what it is, and which are not affected by accidental modifications ‖ (*philos.*) the subject in which attributes adhere ‖ a concentrated extract, e.g. of vanilla **in essence** in fundamental respects, *the account is true in essence though details are invented* [F.]

Es·sene (ési:n, esí:n) *n.* a member of a Jewish sect or brotherhood which flourished from about the 2nd c. B.C. to the 2nd c. A.D., and was centered in isolated communities near the Dead Sea. The Essenes practiced asceticism, held property in common, and sought to practice mystical communion with God [fr. L. *Esseni* fr. Gk, of Heb. origin]

es·sen·tial (isénʃəl) **1.** *adj.* necessary, such that one cannot do without it ‖ of the utmost importance ‖ relating to, or arising from, the real nature of a thing or person, basic, fundamental, *nothing can disguise his essential selfishness* ‖ ideal, as perfect as the mind can conceive, *essential goodness* ‖ containing all that is best or most important in a thing, *the essential flavor* **2.** *n.* something that one cannot do without ‖ (esp. *pl.*) the basic or fundamental part or element in a thing, *to reduce a problem to essentials* **es·sen·ti·al·i·ty** (isenʃi:ǽliti:) *n.* [fr. L.L. *essentialis*]

essential oil one of a class of volatile odoriferous substances obtained by the distillation or extraction of certain plant products. Some are single substances, while others are complex mixtures of organic chemicals. They are used chiefly in medicine and perfumery and as flavorings, e.g. camphor, eucalyptus, lavender, peppermint

essential proposition (*logic*) a statement in which what is said of a subject is already implied in its very definition, e.g. 'A rational being should be judged by the use he makes of his reason'

es·sen·tic (əséntik) *adj.* of an outward expression of an emotion

Es·se·qui·bo (ȩsəkwí:bou) the chief river of Guyana, flowing 600 miles from the Brazilian border to the Atlantic, navigable for 50 miles above its 50-mile estuary

Es·sex (ésiks), Robert Devereux, 2nd earl of (1566-1601), English soldier and favorite of Elizabeth I. His inefficiency as governor-general of Ireland (1599-1600) incurred the queen's displeasure, and he was executed after an unsuccessful attempt to raise a revolt in London (1601)

Essex a county (area 1,419 sq. miles, pop. 1,425,900) in S.E. England. County town: Chelmsford. University (1964, at Colchester) ‖ (*hist.*) the kingdom of the East Saxons. It devel-

---

CONCISE PRONUNCIATION KEY: **(a)** æ, cat; ɑ, car; ɔ fawn; ei, snake. **(e)** e, hen; i:, sheep; iə, deer; ɛə, bear. **(i)** i, fish; ai, tiger; ə:, bird. **(o)** o, ox; au, cow; ou, goat; u, poor; ɔi, royal. **(u)** ʌ, duck; u, bull; u:, goose; ə, bacillus; ju:, cube. x, loch; θ, think; ð, bother; z, Zen; ʒ, corsage; dʒ, savage; ŋ, orangutang; j, yak; ʃ, fish; tʃ, fetch; 'l, rabble; 'n, redden. Complete pronunciation key appears inside front cover.

oped (6th c.) and was incorporated (8th c.) in Mercia

Es·sonne (esɔn) a department (area 699 sq. miles, pop. 923,100) in N. central France, south of Paris (*ILE-DE-FRANCE). Chief town: Evry

-est *suffix* used to form the superlative degree of adjectives and adverbs, as in 'strangest' 'slowest' [O.E. *-est, -ost*]

-est *suffix* formerly used to form the second person singular of the present and past indicative [M.E.]

E.S.T. Eastern Standard Time

EST 1. *abbr.* electroshock therapy **2.** (*acronym*) Erhard Seminar Training, psychological therapy program developed by Werner Erhard

es·tab·lish (istǽbliʃ) *v.t.* to set up, found, *to establish a university* ‖ to place on a firm basis, *to establish law and order* ‖ to bring into being, *to establish communication, establish a precedent* ‖ to set up (oneself or another) in a profession or trade or cause to settle in a locality etc. ‖ to achieve, secure, *to establish control* ‖ to make clear, prove, win general recognition for, *to establish one's innocence* ‖ to make into the official national Church ‖ to eliminate the possibility of losing any tricks left to play in (a suit of cards) **es·táb·lished** *adj.* firmly based, settled, *an established custom* ‖ (of a Church) official, national ‖ (of a post in the civil service, a large corporation etc.) permanent and carrying full benefits (cf. TEMPORARY) ‖ beyond question, *an established fact* **es·táb·lish·ment** *n.* an establishing or being established ‖ a place of business or a residence ‖ the servants of a household ‖ a body of people employed in one organization ‖ an organization as a whole ‖ (*Br.*) the schedule of numbers, ranks and occupations of a public service, or in a large corporation, or of units of the armed services, *the establishment does not allow any more drivers* ‖ an official national Church, e.g. in England the Church of England, in Spain the Church of Rome **the Es·tab·lish·ment** the people established in positions of authority, esp. the ruling class, bound closely together by intermarriage or interest and popularly regarded as having excessive privileges and power [M.E. *establissen* fr. O.F.]

es·tan·cia (estánsjə) *n.* a latifundio (Argentina, Uruguay) devoted to raising cattle on a big scale, esp. in the Rio de la Plata region [fr. Span.=room, dwelling]

es·tate (istéit) *n.* a landed property ‖ the whole of a person's property, incl. real estate and personal estate ‖ (*Br.*) a development (tract of land developed as a unit) ‖ a class in society sharing in the government of a country. In medieval Europe there were usually three estates (nobles, clergy and commons). In modern Britain the three estates are generally taken to be the lords spiritual and the lords temporal (both sitting in the House of Lords) and the Commons ‖ (*rhet.*) condition, *to come to man's estate* [O.F. *estat*]

estate agent the manager of an estate ‖ (*Br.*) a realtor

Es·te (ésti:, éste) an illustrious Italian family, the governors of Ferrara (13th–16th cc.), and Modena and Reggio (13th–18th cc.). They were the patrons of Ariosto and of Tasso

es·teem (istí:m) **1.** *n.* good opinion, regard **2.** *v.t.* to have a high opinion of, value ‖ (*rhet.*) to value (something) as being (something), *to esteem it a privilege* ‖ to consider (oneself) as being (something), *to esteem oneself lucky* [fr. O.F. *estimer*]

es·ter (éstər) *n.* one of a class of compounds that on hydrolysis yield one or more molecules of an acid and one or more molecules of an alcohol and that are often fragrant liquids used as constituents of perfumes and as flavoring materials [coined from G. *äther*, ether+ *säure*, acid]

Es·ter·há·zy (éstərhɑːzi:) a great landowning family of Hungary from the 16th c. until their vast estates were finally sequestered (1860)

es·ter·i·fy (éstérifai) *pres. part.* **es·ter·i·fy·ing** *past* and *past part.* **es·ter·i·fied** *v.t.* (*chem.*) to change into an ester ‖ *v.i.* to be changed into an ester

Es·ther (éstər) the niece of Mordecai and queen of Ahasuerus of Persia. She turned the tables on Haman, the organizer of an attempted Jewish pogrom ‖ the book of the Old Testament relating her story. It was probably written in the Maccabean period (2nd c. B.C.)

es·thete (és0i:t) *n.* an aesthete

es·thet·ic (es0étik) *adj.* aesthetic

Es·tienne (estjén) a family of French Huguenot scholars and illustrious printers of the 16th and 17th cc.

Est·i·gar·ri·bia (ẹsti:gɑrríːbjɑ), José Félix (1888–1940), Paraguayan general, commander of Paraguayan forces in the Chaco War, and president (1939–40)

es·ti·ma·ble (éstəməb'l) *adj.* worthy of esteem ‖ capable of being estimated **és·ti·ma·bly** *adv.* [F.]

es·ti·mate 1. (éstəmit) *n.* a judgment of size, number, quantity, value, distance, quality etc., esp. of something which needs calculation or assessment. An estimate can vary, according to context, from a rough guess to close determination ‖ a statement of the cost or charge which would be involved in a given piece of work, or a tender to carry it out for a certain sum **2.** (éstəmeit) *v. pres. part.* **es·ti·mat·ing** *past* and *past part.* **es·ti·mat·ed** *v.t.* to make an estimate of ‖ *v.i.* to submit an estimate [fr. L. *aestimare* (*aestimatus*), to appraise]

es·ti·ma·tion (estəméiʃən) *n.* an opinion ‖ an assessing of value or importance, *after careful estimation of the risks he accepted* ‖ an estimate ‖ esteem, *to rise in someone's estimation* [M.E. *estimacion* fr. O.F.]

es·ti·ma·tive (éstəmẹitiv, *Br.* éstimətiv) *adj.* capable of estimating ‖ for purposes of estimate, *an estimative figure* [M.E. fr. M.F. or M.L.]

es·ti·ma·tor (éstəmẹitər) *n.* someone who works out cost estimates in a firm ‖ (*statistics*) one who makes a conclusion from a sampling

es·ti·val (éstivəl) *adj.* aestival

es·ti·vate (éstiveit) *pres. part.* **es·ti·vat·ing** *past* and *past part.* **es·ti·vat·ed** *v.i.* to aestivate **es·ti·vá·tion** *n.* aestivation

Es·to·ni·a (estóuni:ə) a constituent republic (area 17,410 sq. miles, pop. 1,466,000) of the U.S.S.R., in N.E. Europe on the Baltic Sea. Capital: Tallinn. It is mostly lowland plain, with many lakes. Agriculture: dairy farming, potatoes, cereals. Industries: shale mining and refining (for the production of gas), lumber, superphosphates. Estonia was ruled by the Teutonic Order (1346–1521), by Sweden (1561–1721) and by Russia (1721–1918). It was independent (1918–40), was incorporated in the U.S.S.R. (1940), occupied by the Germans (1941–4), and reestablished as a constituent republic (1944)

Es·to·ni·an (estóuni:ən) **1.** *adj.* of or pertaining to Estonia or its people **2.** *n.* an inhabitant of Estonia ‖ the language of Estonia

es·top (istɔ́p) *pres. part.* **es·top·ping** *past* and *past part.* **es·topped** *v.t.* (*law*) to prevent or stop, bar, esp. by estoppel **es·tóp·page** *n.* [O.F. *estoper*, to bung or block]

es·top·pel (istɔ́p'l) *n.* (*law*) a being estopped or prevented from denying or asserting something, on the ground that to do so contradicts what has already been admitted or denied, either explicitly in words or implicitly by actions [prob. fr. O.F. *estoupail*, bung]

es·to·vers (istóuvərz) *pl. n.* (*law*) any essential supplies which a tenant is legally allowed to make use of ‖ alimony allowed to a wife divorced from her husband [O.F. *estovoir*, to be necessary, what is necessary]

Es·tra·da (estráðɑ), Genaro (1887–1937), Mexican diplomat and Foreign Minister (1930–2)

Estrada Ca·bre·ra (kɑbrérɑ), Manuel (1857–1924), Guatemalan president (1898–1920). Although his dictatorship brought improvements in education, it ended in revolution

Estrada Pal·ma (pálmɑ), Tomás (1835–1908), Cuban politician, president (1876–7) of the Republic in Arms, and first president (1902–6) of the Free Republic. During his term Cuba was known as the 'model republic', but at the end of that term the U.S.A. felt obliged to intervene under the terms of the Platt Amendment

es·trange (istréindʒ) *pres. part.* **es·trang·ing** *past* and *past part.* **es·tranged** *v.t.* to cause (a person or persons) to become unloving or unfriendly **es·tránge·ment** *n.* [fr. O.F. *estranger*]

es·treat (istrí:t) **1.** *v.t.* (*law*) to extract the record of (a fine etc.) from court records in order to have it prosecuted or enforced **2.** *n.* (*law*) a true copy of a record, esp. of a fine, extracted from court records [A.F. *estrete*, O.F. *estraite*, extract]

Es·tre·ma·du·ra (estremadú:rɑ) (*Span.* Extremadura) a region of Spain on the central plateau bordering Portugal, forming Badajoz and Cáceres provinces. Except for the Tagus and Guadiana valleys (grain, olives, figs) it is arid and depopulated. Sheep and pigs are

raised. Industry: some mining. Chief town: Badajoz. It was reconquered from the Moors in the 13th c.

es·tro·gen, oes·tro·gen (éstrədʒən) *n.* one of a group of female sex hormones that is produced by the ovaries and is responsible for initiating estrus and for the development of secondary sexual characteristics in the female **es·tro·gen·ic, oes·tro·gen·ic** *adj.* [fr. ESTRUS]

es·trone, oes·trone (éstroun) *n.* a specific estrogenic hormone [ESTRUS]

es·trous, oes·trous (éstrəs) *adj.* of the estrus ‖ being in estrus [ESTRUS]

estrous cycle, oestrous cycle the complete sequence of changes involved in the onset and subsidence of estrus

es·tru·ate, oes·tru·ate (éstru:eit) *pres. part.* **es·tru·at·ing, oes·tru·at·ing** *past* and *past part.* **es·tru·at·ed, oes·tru·at·ed** *v.i.* to be in the state of estrus [back-formation fr. *estruation*, the state of being in estrus fr. M.L. *oestrum*, estrum]

es·trum, oes·trum (éstrəm) *n.* estrus [L. *oestrum*, var. of *oestrus*, estrus]

es·trus, oes·trus (éstrəs) *n.* a state of intense sexual activity and receptivity in female mammals other than humans and higher apes ‖ an occurrence of this state [L. *oestrus* fr. Gk *oistros*, gadfly, frenzy]

es·tu·ar·i·al (estʃu:ɛ́ari:əl) *adj.* of or relating to an estuary

es·tu·a·rine (éstʃu:əri̯:n, éstʃu:ərin) *adj.* estuarial

es·tu·a·ry (éstʃu:eri:) *pl.* **es·tu·a·ries** *n.* the tidal mouth of a river [fr. L. *aestuarium*, tidal]

e·su·ri·ence (isuári:əns) *n.* avidity for food **e·sú·ri·en·cy** *n.* esurience

e·su·ri·ent (isuári:ənt) *adj.* avid for food [fr. L. *esurire*, to be hungry]

ET *abbr.* elapsed time

e·ta (éitə) *n.* the seventh letter (H, ŋ =e) of the Greek alphabet

e·ta-par·ti·cle (eitəpártik'l) *n.* (*particle phys.*) elementary particle with no charge, no spin, and a mass of 549 MEV that quickly decays into pions or gamma rays through electromagnetic interactions

etc. *ET CETERA

et cet·er·a (etsétərə, etsétrə) (*abbr.* etc., used to indicate the incompleteness of a list) and others, and so on, *abstract notions such as beauty, truth, goodness etc.* **et·cet·er·as** *pl. n.* sundry items, extras, *a charge of $20 for etceteras* [L. = and the rest]

etch (etʃ) *v.t.* to engrave (a design etc.) on glass or a metal plate, esp. copper, from which a picture or design can be printed. It is usually done by coating a plate with wax, then cutting lines through the wax to expose the metal, then placing the plate in a bath of acid which eats into the exposed metal ‖ to engrave (a plate) in this way ‖ *v.i.* to practice this art **étch·ing** *n.* the art of producing such plates ‖ a print from an etched plate [Du. *etsen*, G. *ätzen*]

e·ter·nal (itə́rn'l) *adj.* never ending, lasting for ever, *the eternal motion of the stars* ‖ without beginning or end in time, *the eternal majesty of the Creator* ‖ ceaseless, or constantly repeated ‖ annoyingly incessant, *stop this eternal arguing* ‖ seemingly limitless, *the eternal wastes of the desert* **e·tér·nal·ize** *pres. part.* **e·tér·nal·iz·ing** *past* and *past part.* **e·tér·nal·ized** *v.t.* to eternize [O.F.]

Eternal City, the Rome, Italy

eternal triangle a situation of conflict in which two men desire the same woman, or two women the same man

e·ter·ni·ty (itə́rniti:) *pl.* **e·ter·ni·ties** *n.* time or existence without beginning or end ‖ the endless state after death ‖ a seemingly endless time or distance [M.E. *eternite* fr. O.F.]

e·ter·nize (itə́rnaiz) *pres. part.* **e·ter·niz·ing** *past* and *past part.* **e·ter·nized** *v.t.* to perpetuate, cause to last forever ‖ to make famous forever [F. *éterniser*]

e·te·sian wind (ití:ʒən) a local wind in the E. Mediterranean blowing for about six weeks in the summer, usually from the north [fr. L. *etesius*, annual fr. Gk]

eth·a·cryn·ic acid [$C_{13}H_{12}Cl_2O_4$] (e0əkrínik) (*pharm.*) diuretic drug used in edema therapy; marketed as Edecrin

e·tham·bu·tol [$C_{16}H_{24}N_2O_2$] (e0ǽmbu:tɔl) *n.* (*pharm.*) synthetic antitubercular drug

eth·am·i·van [$C_{12}H_{17}NO_3$] (e0əmáivən) *n.* (*pharm.*) respiratory stimulant used in cases of intoxication or overdose of sedatives and in lung disease therapy

CONCISE PRONUNCIATION KEY: (**a**) æ, c*a*t; ɑ, c*a*r; ɔ f*aw*n; ei, sn*a*ke. (**e**) e, h*e*n; i:, sh*ee*p; iə, d*ee*r; ɛə, b*ea*r. (**i**) i, f*i*sh; ai, t*i*ger; ə:, b*i*rd. (**o**) o, *o*x; au, c*ow*; ou, g*oa*t; u, p*oo*r; ɔi, r*oy*al. (**u**) ʌ, d*u*ck; u, b*u*ll; u:, g*oo*se; ə, bacill*u*s; ju:, c*u*be. x, lo*ch*; θ, *th*ink; ð, bo*th*er; z, *Z*en; ʒ, cor*s*age; dʒ, sava*g*e; ŋ, oranguta*ng*; j, *y*ak; ʃ, *fi*sh; tʃ, fe*tch*; 'l, rabb*le*; 'n, redd*en*. Complete pronunciation key appears inside front cover.

eth·ane (éθein) *n.* a gaseous paraffin hydrocarbon (C_2H_6) found in natural gas, and formed as a by-product in the cracking of petroleum. It burns with a clear flame. It has neither color nor smell and is used as a fuel and a source of ethylene [ETHER]

eth·a·nol (éθənɔl, éθənoul) *n.* alcohol ‖ solvent and reagent alcohol additive said to raise gasoline octane rating, eliminate engine knock, and sometimes reduce exhaust emissions [ETHANE]

eth·a·ver·ine [$C_{24}H_{29}NO_4$] (eθəvə́:ri:n) *n.* (*pharm.*) vasodilator drug; marketed as Cebral

Eth·el·bald, Aeth·el·bald (éθəlbɔld) (*d.* 860), king of Wessex (856–60). He seized the kingdom while his father Ethelwulf was on a pilgrimage to Rome

Eth·el·bert, Aeth·el·bert (éθəlbə:rt) (*d.* 616), king of Kent (c. 560–616). He was converted to Christianity by St Augustine, and made Canterbury, his capital, a great religious center. He issued the earliest known body of English law

Ethelbert, Aethelbert (*d.* 866), king of Kent (858–66) and of Wessex (860–8), son of Ethelwulf. He spent his reign trying to fight off the Danes

Eth·el·red I, Aeth·el·red I (éθəlred) (*d.* 871), king of Wessex and Kent (866–71), son of Ethelwulf. Helped by his brother Alfred, he spent his entire reign fighting the Danes

Ethelred II, Aethelred II 'the Unready' (c. 968–1016), king of England (978–1016). His policy of buying off the Danes, who renewed their attacks on England at this time, was a total failure. The successes of Swein Forkbeard forced him to flee (1013) to Normandy. He came back (1014) on Swein's death

Eth·el·wulf, Aeth·el·wulf (éθəlwulf) (*d.* 858), king of Kent (828–58) and of Wessex (839–56), son of Egbert. He won a victory over the Danes (851) and subdued the North Welsh (853)

e·ther, ae·ther (í:θər) *n.* a hypothetical substance proposed in the wave theory of light as being the medium of propagation of electromagnetic waves ‖ (*chem.*) one of a class of organic compounds of the general constitution R-O-R' ‖ (*chem.*) a volatile, inflammable colorless liquid, ($C_2H_5)_2$O, diethyl ether, with a sweet, pungent smell, used as an anesthetic and as a solvent ‖ (*rhet.*) the upper regions of the sky ‖ (*ancient and medieval philos.*) the quintessence [L. *aether* fr. Gk *aithēr* fr. *aithein,* to burn]

e·the·re·al (iθíəri:əl) *adj.* light, airy and intangible, *ethereal grace* ‖ heavenly, *an ethereal messenger* ‖ (*chem.*) pertaining to ether **e·the·re·ál·i·ty** *n.* **e·the·re·al·ize** *pres. part.* **e·the·re·al·iz·ing** *past* and *past part.* **e·the·re·al·ized** *v.t.* [fr. L. *aetherius,* like the ether, fr. Gk]

Eth·e·rege (éθəridʒ), Sir George (1635–91), English Restoration comic dramatist, author of 'The Comical Revenge' (1664), 'She Wou'd If She Cou'd' (1668), and 'The Man of Mode' (1676)

e·ther·i·fy (iθérifai) *pres. part.* **e·ther·i·fy·ing** *past* and *past part.* **e·ther·i·fied** *v.t.* to convert into ether

e·ther·ize (í:θəraiz) *pres. part.* **e·ther·iz·ing** *past* and *past part.* **e·ther·ized** *v.t.* to anesthetize with ether

eth·ic (éθik) **1.** *n.* a system of ethics **2.** *adj.* ethical **éth·i·cal** *adj.* dealing with ethics, *an ethical theory* ‖ relating to morality of behavior, *ethical standards* ‖ conforming with an accepted standard of good behavior, *e.g. in a profession or trade* **éth·i·cal·ly** *adv.* in an ethical way ‖ so far as ethics is concerned **éth·ics** *n.* moral philosophy or moral science, i.e. that branch of philosophy which studies the principles of right or wrong in human conduct ‖ a treatise on this science ‖ the moral principles which determine the rightness or wrongness of particular acts or activities [fr. L. *ethicus* fr. Gk *ēthikos,* customary fr. *ēthos,* customary behavior, morals]

eth·i·cal drugs (éθikəl) drugs sold by a doctor's prescription

Ethical Movement (Ethical Culture Movement) a movement initiated (1878) in the U.S.A. by Felix Adler (1851–1933). It aimed at creating a society based on moral and not religious values. Ethical societies existing in Britain and the U.S.A. united (1952) with worldwide Humanist organizations to form the International Humanist and Ethical union

eth·i·on [$C_9H_{22}O_4P_2S_4$] (éθi:ɒn) *n.* organophosphorous insecticide and miticide against aphids, scales, thrips, and mites on food, fibers, and crops

e·thi·on·a·mide [$C_8H_{10}N_2S$] (eθi:ɒnəmaid) *n.* (*pharm.*) tuberculostatic drug used in cases resistant to other antitubercular drugs and in leprosy therapy

E·thi·o·pi·a (i:θi:óupi:ə) (formerly Abyssinia) a republic (area 395,000 sq. miles, pop. 31,995,000) in N.E. Africa. Capital: Addis Ababa. It includes the autonomous province of Eritrea. People: Galla (half the total), Amhara (the most influential) and Somali, with several minorities. Official languages: Amharic, English. Religion: Coptic, with large Moslem and local religious minorities and a small Jewish one. The land is 10% arable, 47% pasture and 3% forest. The central plateau (7,000–8,000 ft) stretches from Eritrea to the Kenya border, and is crossed by mountain ranges (Ras Dashan, 15,160 ft) and cut by deep river valleys. The Sudanese slope is covered with forests and savanna. The steeper eastern slopes drop to the Danakil desert in the northeast (below sea level) and to the Ogaden desert in the southeast. South of Addis Ababa lies a chain of lakes in a depression which is part of the Great Rift Valley. Annual rainfall: northern highlands 40–60 ins, southwest highlands 60–80 ins., Somali plateau 20–30 ins, lowlands 5–10 ins. Mean temperatures (F.) highlands 65°, lowlands 87°. Livestock: sheep, cattle, horses, goats. Crops: coffee, teff, durra. Minerals: iron, marble, mica, salt. Exports: coffee (65% of exports), hides, skins. Imports: textiles, fuel oils, vehicles, machinery. Ports: Massawa, Assab. Much trade goes through Djibouti. University: Addis Ababa. Monetary unit: Ethiopian dollar (100 cents). HISTORY. The kingdom of Axum flourished from the 1st to the 6th cc. Coptic Christianity was adopted in the 4th c. The rulers (from 1270) claimed descent from Solomon and the Queen of Sheba, and extended their territory. Attacked and threatened by Arabs and Turkish Moslems (16th c.) and by the Gallas, Ethiopia suffered from a period of tribal anarchy. The Portuguese made contact with the Negus in 1490, gave military help (1541) and tried unsuccessfully to spread Catholicism (17th c.). Theodore defeated the other chiefs and was crowned emperor (1855), but killed himself because of the defeat inflicted by Sir Robert Napier's British expedition (1867–8). Italy occupied Eritrea (1889) and invaded Ethiopia, but was defeated at Adua (1896) in the reign (1889–1913) of Menelik II, who consolidated the empire, introduced administrative reform, and built the new capital, Addis Ababa (1894). Tafari defeated and expelled the pro-Turkish Lij Yasu (1916) and became regent (1917), Negus (1928), and was crowned Emperor Haile Selassie (1930). Italy invaded (1935) and occupied Ethiopia (1936–41). The British liberated Ethiopia (1941) and the emperor was restored. Eritrea was federated with Ethiopia (1952) and became a province in 1962. In 1974 a military coup overthrew the emperor and a 2,000-year-old monarchy ended. By 1977 communist-backed Lt. Col. Mengistu Haile-Mariam emerged as the leader, and in 1984 the Ethiopian Communist party became Ethiopia's sole political party. Eritrean rebels continued their fight for independence, and the Somalis continued to push the Ethiopians out of the Ogaden, but the new regime had recovered most of those areas by 1981. Drought in the 1980s complicated further Ethiopia's refugee problem that drew worldwide attention as hundreds of thousands fled the north

E·thi·o·pi·an (i:θi:óupi:ən) **1.** *adj.* of Ethiopia or its inhabitants ‖ of or relating to the Monophysite Ethiopian Church, founded in the 4th c. and autocephalous since 1949. It has about five million members and uses Ethiopic for its liturgy **2.** *n.* a native of Ethiopia

E·thi·op·ic (i:θi:ópik, i:θi:óupik) *n.* the ancient language of Ethiopia

eth·moid (éθmɔid) **1.** *adj.* (of the bone forming the walls of the cavity at the root of the nose through which pass the olfactory nerves) like a sieve **2.** *n.* this ethmoid bone **eth·mói·dal** *adj.* [fr. Gk *ēthmoeidēs*]

eth·narch (éθnɑrk) *n.* (*hist.*) the governor of a province or of a people within an empire **éth·nar·chy** *pl.* **eth·nar·chies** *n.* the office or rank of an ethnarch [fr. Gk *ēthnarchēs* fr. *ethnos,* nation + *archos,* rule]

eth·nic (éθnik) *adj.* of or relating to a people whose unity rests on racial, linguistic, religious or cultural ties ‖ deriving from or belonging to such racial etc. ties of a people or country ‖

(*hist.*) Gentile or pagan, as opposed to Christian or Jewish **éth·ni·cal** *adj.* **éth·ni·cal·ly** *adv.* according to ethnic grouping [fr. Gk *ethnikos* fr. *ethnos,* nation]

eth·no·cen·trism (eθnouséntrizəm) *n.* the tendency to regard one's own group and culture as intrinsically superior to all others [fr. Gk *ethnos,* nation + CENTER]

eth·nog·ra·pher (eθnógrəfər) *n.* a specialist in ethnography

eth·no·graph·ic (eθnougræfik) *adj.* of or relating to ethnography **eth·no·gráph·i·cal** *adj.* **eth·no·gráph·i·cal·ly** *adv.* from the ethnographic point of view

eth·nog·ra·phy (eθnógrəfi:) *n.* the description of the races of mankind [fr. Gk *ethnos,* nation + *graphos,* written]

eth·no·lin·guis·tics (eθnouliŋwístiks) *n.* (*linguistics*) study of ethnic influence on languages

eth·no·log·ic (eθn'lódʒik) *adj.* ethnological **eth·no·lóg·i·cal** *adj.* of or relating to ethnology **eth·no·lóg·i·cal·ly** *adv.* from the ethnological point of view

eth·nol·o·gist (eθnólədʒist) *n.* a specialist in ethnology

eth·nol·o·gy (eθnólədʒi:) *n.* the science dealing with the races of mankind, their distribution, relationships and activities [fr. Gk *ethnos,* race + *logos,* word]

eth·no·mu·si·col·o·gy (eθnoumu:sikóloudʒi:) *n.* study of music developed by people in various cultures and subcultures **ethnomusicological** *adj.* **ethnomusicologist** *n.*

eth·no·my·col·o·gy (eθnoumaikóloudʒi:) *n.* study of the use of hallucinogenic mushrooms and other plants in religious or culture groups **ethnomycological** *adj.* **ethnomycologist** *n.*

eth·no·sci·ence (eθnousaiəns) *n.* study of folklore involving the nature of primitive people

e·thol·o·gy (i:θólədʒi:) *n.* the scientific study of animal behavior, esp. with reference to habitat [L. *ethologia,* art of depicting character, fr. Gk]

e·thos (í:θɒs, éθós) *n.* the spirit of a people, a civilization or a system, as expressed in its culture, institutions, ways of thought, philosophy and religion ‖ the universal element that informs a literary work (its irony, sadness etc.) as distinct from the subjective details of its making [Mod. L. fr. Gk *ēthos,* character]

eth·o·sux·i·mide [$C_7H_{11}NO_2$] (eθousʌ́ksimaid) *n.* (*pharm.*) anticonvulsant drug used in epilepsy therapy; marketed as Zarontin

eth·yl (éθil) *n.* (*chem.*) the group C_2H_5, a monovalent alkyl radical derived from ethane [ETHER]

ethyl alcohol *ALCOHOL, ETHANOL

eth·yl·ben·zene (eθəlbénzi:n) *n.* a liquid hydrocarbon, $C_6H_5C_2H_5$, made esp. from ethylene and benzene and used to make styrene

eth·yl·ene (éθəli:n) *n.* the simplest member, $CH_2=CH_2$, of the olefine series of hydrocarbons, a colorless, inflammable gas obtained from petroleum and used chiefly as a raw material in the manufacture of alcohol and plastics [ETHYL]

ethylene dichloride $C_2H_4Cl_2$, an oily liquid used as a solvent and fumigant

ethylene glycol *GLYCOL

eth·yl·par·a·ni·tro phenyl [$C_{14}H_{14}NO_4PS$] (eθəlpærənáitrou) (*chem.*) toxic organophosphorus insecticide and miticide used with malathion on cotton and fruit trees

e·tid·o·caine [$C_{17}H_{28}N_2O$] (etídokein) *n.* (*pharm.*) local anesthetic that stabilizes the neuronal membrane thus preventing conduction of nerve impulses; marketed as Duranest

e·tid·ro·nate [$C_2H_8O_7P_2$] (etídrouneit) *n.* (*pharm.*) drug used in treatment of Paget's bone disease; marketed as Didronel

e·tid·ron·ic acid [$C_2H_8O_7P_2$] (etidrónik) *n.* (*pharm.*) drug used in some bone diseases, esp. Paget's disease, to regulate calcium; marketed as Didronel

e·ti·o·late (í:ti:əleit) *pres. part.* **e·ti·o·lat·ing** *past* and *past part.* **e·ti·o·lat·ed** *v.t.* to blanch (plants) by depriving them of sunlight ‖ to give an unhealthy, pale appearance to **e·ti·o·lá·tion** *n.* [F. *étioler*]

e·ti·o·log·i·cal, esp. *Br.* **ae·ti·o·log·i·cal** (i:ti:əlódʒik'l) *adj.* of or relating to etiology

e·ti·ol·o·gy, esp. *Br.* **ae·ti·ol·o·gy** (i:ti:ólədʒi:) *n.* the branch of philosophy which deals with factors of causation ‖ (*med.*) the factors associated with the causation of disease [fr. L. *aetiologia* fr. Gk]

CONCISE PRONUNCIATION KEY: **(a)** æ, c*a*t; ɑ, c*a*r; ɔ f*aw*n; ei, sn*a*ke. **(e)** e, h*e*n; i:, sh*ee*p; iə, d*ee*r; ɛə, b*ea*r. **(i)** i, f*i*sh; ai, t*i*ger; ə:, b*i*rd. **(o)** o, *o*x; au, c*ow*; ou, g*oa*t; u, p*oo*r; ɔi, r*oy*al. **(u)** ʌ, d*u*ck; u, b*u*ll; u:, g*oo*se; ə, b*a*cill*u*s; ju:, c*u*be. x, lo*ch*; θ, *th*ink; ð, bo*th*er; z, *Z*en; ʒ, cor*s*age; dʒ, sava*g*e; ŋ, ora*ng*uta*ng*; j, *y*ak; ʃ, *fish*; tʃ, fe*tch*; 'l, rabb*le*; 'n, redd*en.* Complete pronunciation key appears inside front cover.

e·ti·o·path·o·gen·e·sis (i:ti:oupæθoudʒénəsis) *n.* (*med.*) the underlying cause of a disease

et·i·quette (étikit, étiket) *n.* the rules of behavior standard in polite society ‖ the rules governing professional conduct, *medical etiquette* ‖ court ceremonial or conventions of official life [F. *étiquette*, ticket, label]

Et·na, L. **Aetna** (étnə) Europe's largest active volcano (about 10,850 ft), on the east coast of Sicily. The fertile soil on the slopes is intensively cultivated

E·ton College (i:t'n) England's most famous private secondary school for boys, founded by Henry VI in 1440

E·to·ni·an (i:tóuniən) 1. *n.* a member of Eton College 2. *adj.* relating to Eton College ‖ typical of Etonians

e·tor·phine (etórfi:n) *n.* (*pharm.*) synthetic sedative drug related to morphine, sometimes used to immobilize wild animals

E·tru·ri·a (itrúəri:ə) an ancient country in central Italy, north of the Tiber, south of the Magra, and west of the Apennines (*TUSCANY) ‖ a kingdom, set up by Napoleon (1801), incorporated in the French Empire (1808), and made into the Grand Duchy of Tuscany in 1809 (*ETRUSCAN)

E·trus·can (itráskən) 1. *adj.* of ancient Etruria 2. *n.* a member of ancient Etruria ‖ the language of ancient Etruria [fr. L. *Etruscus*]
—The Etruscans established themselves in Etruria about the 8th c. B.C. and were at the zenith of their power in the 7th c. B.C. Their fine art is best seen in their statues, pottery, tomb decorations, engraved mirrors and architecture. By the 3rd c. B.C. the Romans had expelled the Etruscan kings and made themselves masters of all the country they had ruled

-ette *suffix* indicating a diminutive, as in 'dinette' ‖ indicating a substitute, as in 'leatherette' ‖ indicating female, as in drum 'majorette' [fr. O.F.]

Et·ty (éti), William (1787–1849), British painter, esp. of the nude. His manner is opulently sensual, within the canons of idealism

é·tude (éitu:d, éitju:d) *n.* (*mus.*) a short composition, written either as an exercise or to demonstrate technique, or to develop a particular limited theme or mood [F. = study]

ETV *abbr.* educational television

E-2 (*mil.*) *HAWKEYE

et·y·mo·log·i·cal (etəməlódʒik'l) *adj.* of or relating to etymology **et·y·mo·lóg·i·cal·ly** *adv.* as regards etymology, according to etymology

et·y·mol·o·gist (etəmólədʒist) *n.* a specialist in etymology

et·y·mol·o·gize (etəmólədʒaiz) *pres. part.* **et·y·mol·o·giz·ing** *past* and *past part.* **et·y·mol·o·gized** *v.t.* to look for or state the etymology of (a word) ‖ *v.i.* to study etymology [fr. L.L. *etymologizare*]

et·y·mol·o·gy (etəmólədʒi:) *pl.* **et·y·mol·o·gies** *n.* the branch of the study of language dealing with the origin, derivation and development of words ‖ the derivation of a word [O.F. *ethimologie* fr. L. fr. Gk fr. *etumos*, true+*logos*, word]

et·y·mon (étəmɒn) *pl.* **et·y·mons**, **et·y·ma** (étəmə) *n.* the root word from which others are derived (e.g. 'hippos', a horse, and 'dromos', a racetrack, are the etymons of 'hippodrome') [L. fr. Gk *etumon*, the real form (neuter of *etumos*, real, true)]

eu- (ju:) *prefix* well [fr. Gk *eus*, good]

Eu·boe·a (ju:bí:ə) (*Gk* Evvoia) a large Greek island (area 1,586 sq. miles, pop. 165,400) in the Aegean off the southeast mainland coast. Chief town: Chalcis. It is largely mountainous (Delphi, 5,718 ft) but the plains produce grain, wine, oil, lemons, honey and figs. Minerals: lignite, magnesite, marble

eu·ca·lyp·tus (ju:kəlíptəs) *pl.* **eu·ca·lyp·ti** (ju:kəlíptai), **eu·ca·lyp·tus·es** *n.* a member of *Eucalyptus*, fam. *Myrtaceae*, a genus of trees native to tropical E. Australia. They are used for afforestation, esp. in N. Africa, S. Brazil and Argentina, because of their rapid growth and great size (up to 300 ft in Australia, and to about 90 ft in S. France). The oil obtained by distillation of the foliage of some species is used esp. medicinally. The trees also yield useful wood, gums and resins [Mod. L. fr. Gk *eu-*, well+*kaluptos*, covered (from the covering of the buds)]

eu·car·y·ote or **eu·kar·y·ote** (ju:kǽri:ɒut) *n.* (*biol.*) an organism in which a true nucleus is visible *Cf* PROCARYOTE

Eu·cha·rist (jú:kərist) *n.* the sacrament in which the body and blood of Christ are presented under the form of bread and wine in thanksgiving to God for the redemption of the world by the death of Christ. Its origins are found in the Gospels and in I Corinthians x, xi ‖ the consecrated bread (and, in some Churches, wine) received at Communion **Eu·cha·rís·tic**, **Eu·cha·rís·ti·cal** *adjs* [O.F. *euchariste* fr. L.L. fr. Gk *eucharistia*, thanksgiving, from Christ's giving thanks to his Father at the Last Supper]

eu·chre, **eu·cher** (jú:kər) 1. *n.* a card game for two, three or four players similar to whist but played with a reduced deck 2. *v.t. pres. part.* **euchring, eu·cher·ing** *past* and *past part.* **euchred, eu·chered** to beat (the trump-making hand) by winning three out of the five tricks [origin unknown]

eu·chro·ma·tin (ju:króumətin) *n.* (*biol*) the portion of chromatin making up the bulk of chromosomes and including active genes

eu·chro·mo·some (ju:króuməsoum) *n.* (*biol.*) a typical chromosome, or autosome

Eu·clid (jú:klid) (3rd c. B.C.), Greek mathematician of Alexandria, virtually the founder of plane geometry. In his 'Elements', of which 13 books survive, he was the first mathematician to give rigorous demonstrations of his theorems

Eu·clíd·e·an (ju:klídi:ən) *adj.* pertaining to the principles of Euclid's geometry

Euclid the Socratic (c. 450–c. 380 B.C.), Greek philosopher. He was a disciple of Socrates and the founder of the Megarian school

eu·dae·mon·ism, **eu·de·mon·ism** (judí:mənizəm) *n.* an ethical system teaching that what is morally good should be chosen because it leads to happiness (cf. HEDONISM) [fr. Gk *eudaimonia*, happiness]

Eudes (ə:d) (Odo, c. 860–98), French king (888–98). As count of Paris, he defended Paris against the Normans (885–7). He was elected to the throne by the nobility, and fought (893–7) the legitimate Carolingian heir, Charles the Simple

eu·di·om·e·ter (ju:di:ómitər) *n.* (*chem.*) a glass tube used for measuring the volume changes when gases interact **eu·di·o·met·ric** (ju:di:oumétrik) *adj* **eu·di·o·mét·ri·cal** *adj* **eu·di·om·e·try** (ju:di:ómitri:) *n.* [fr. Gk *eudios*, clear, pure+*metron*, measure]

Eu·dist (jú:dist) *n.* a member of a teaching society (Congregation of Jesus and Mary) of secular Catholic priests founded at Caen in 1643 by St John Eudes. Their educational work is mainly in Canada

Eu·dox·us of Cni·dus (ju:dóksəs, knáidəs) (c. 406 B.C.–355 B.C.), Greek astronomer and mathematician and student of Plato. He is thought to have been the first to describe the constellations, and is credited with calculating the length of the solar year

Eu·gène (ə:ʒen, ju:dʒí:n), Prince (Eugène de Savoie-Carignan, 1663–1736), Austrian general whose cooperation with Marlborough in the War of the Spanish Succession (1701–14) resulted in great victories over the French at Blenheim (1704), Oudenarde (1708) and Malplaquet (1709)

eu·gen·ic (ju:dʒénik) *adj.* of, concerned with, or encouraging the production of healthy children **eu·gén·i·cal·ly** *adv.* **eu·gén·ics** *n.* the study of methods of protecting and improving the quality of the human race by selective breeding **eu·ge·nist** (jú:dʒənist) *n.* [fr. Gk *eu*, well+*genēs*, born]

Eu·gé·nie (ə:ʒeini:), Eugénie-Marie de Montijo de Guzman, Comtesse de Téba (1826–1920), wife of Napoleon III and empress of the French (1853–70)

Eu·ge·ni·us III (ju:dʒí:ni:əs, ju:dʒí:njəs) (d. 1153), pope (1145–53). With St Bernard of Clairvaux he organized the 2nd Crusade

Eugenius IV (1383–1447), pope (1431–47). He succeeded in briefly reuniting Christendom by the Decree of Union (1439). Papal authority was recognized by the Greeks (1439), the Armenians (1439), the Jacobites (1443) and the Nestorians (1445)

eu·gle·na (ju:glí:nə) *n.* a member of *Euglena*, a genus of flagellate green algae, found in freshwater standing ponds. They have a trace requirement for Vitamin B_{12} and are used as an assay for its presence [Mod. L. fr. Gk *eu-*, good+*glēnē*, pupil of the eye]

eu·he·mer·ism (ju:hí:mərizəm) *n.* the theory that the gods of mythology were originally heroic mortals ‖ the interpretation of myths and legends as glorified accounts of historical events **eu·hé·mer·ist** *n.* **eu·he·mer·ís·tic** *adj.* **eu·hé·mer·ize** *pres. part.* **eu·he·mer·iz·ing** *past* and *past part.* **eu·he·mer·ized** *v.t.* [after *Euhemerus*, 4th–c. B.C. Greek Sicilian philosopher]

Eu·len·spie·gel (ɔ́ilənʃpi:g'l), Till, a traditional comic rogue hero of 14th–c. Germany celebrated in a collection of tales published in 1519. His pranks were the subject of a tone poem (1895) by Richard Strauss

Eu·ler (ɔ́iler), Leonhard (1707–83), Swiss mathematician and friend of the Bernouillis. He was responsible for the revision of nearly all the branches of pure mathematics then known and the foundation of new methods of analysis. He also did important work in other branches of science

eu·lo·gi·a (ju:lóudʒi:ə) *pl.* **eu·lo·gi·ae** (ju:lóudʒi:i:) *n.* (*hist.*) blessed bread distributed to those unable to receive Holy Communion. It survives in the Eastern Orthodox Church as the 'antidoron', the remains of the blessed bread from which the consecrated bread was taken, distributed at the end of the Eucharist to those who did not communicate [L. fr. Gk=praise, blessing]

eu·lo·gist (jú:lədʒist) *n.* someone who eulogizes **eu·lo·gís·tic** *adj.* **eu·lo·gís·ti·cal·ly** *adv.*

eu·lo·gize (jú:lədʒaiz) *pres. part.* **eu·lo·giz·ing** *past* and *past part.* **eu·lo·gized** *v.t.* to praise highly in speech or writing [EULOGY]

eu·lo·gy (jú:lədʒi:) *pl.* **eu·lo·gies** *n.* a written or spoken expression of high praise [fr. Gk *eulogia*, praise]

Eu·men·i·des (ju:ménidi:z) (*Gk mythol.*) 'the gracious ones', a euphemistic name for the Erinyes

eu·my·co·phyte (ju:máikəfait) *n.* a member of *Eumycophyta*, a phylum of thallophytes comprising the true fungi and the fungi imperfecti [fr. Gk *eu*, good+*mukēs*, fungus +*phuton*, plant]

E unit a measurement of the ratio of signal to noise in radar: e.g., E1 = 1:1, E3 = 4:1, E5 = 16:1, at saturation point

eu·nuch (jú:nək) *n.* a castrated man or boy [fr. L. *eunuchus* fr. Gk fr. *eunē*, bed +*echein*, to keep]

eu·on·y·mus (ju:ónəməs) *n.* a member of *Euonymus*, fam. *Celastraceae*, a genus of small evergreen trees or shrubs of which the best known are E. *europaeus*, the spindle tree, and E. *atropurpureus*, a North American wahoo or burning bush [fr. Gk *euonymos*, of good or lucky name fr. *eu-*, good+*onoma*, name]

eu·pa·to·ri·um (ju:pətóri:əm, ju:pətóuri:əm) *n.* a member of *Eupatorium*, fam. *Compositae*, a genus of plants or shrubs, mainly tropical but including the European hemp agrimony [Mod. L. fr. Gk *eupatorion*, agrimony, hemp agrimony]

eu·pep·sia (ju:pépʃə, ju:pépsi:ə) *n.* good digestion (opp. DYSPEPSIA) [Mod. L. Gk fr. *eu-*, well+*peptein*, to digest]

eu·pep·tic (ju:péptik) *adj.* having, or caused by, good digestion (opp. DYSPEPTIC) [fr. Gk *eupeptos* fr. *eu-*, well+ *peptein*, to digest]

eu·phe·mism (jú:fəmizəm) *n.* the use of a pleasant, polite or harmless-sounding word or expression to mask harsh, rude or infamous truths, e.g. to 'pass away' for 'to die' ‖ the word or phrase so used **eu·phe·mís·tic** *adj.* **eu·phe·mís·ti·cal·ly** *adv.* [fr. Gk *euphemismos* fr. *eu-*, good+*phēmē*, speech, fame]

eu·phe·mize (jú:fəmaiz) *pres. part.* **eu·phe·miz·ing** *past* and *past part.* **eu·phe·mized** *v.i.* to use a euphemism ‖ *v.t.* to express by a euphemism [fr. Gk *euphēmizein*, to speak well of]

eu·phen·ics (ju:féniks) *n.* (*genetics*) 1. science of improving the human race by genetic engineering and/or transplants 2. science of biological improvement (of the observable characteristics of the members of a group)

eu·phon·ic (ju:fónik) *adj.* euphonious **eu·phón·i·cal·ly** *adv.*

eu·pho·ni·ous (ju:fóuni:əs) *adj.* having euphony

eu·pho·ni·um (ju:fóuni:əm) *n.* (*mus.*) the brass band equivalent of the tuba in an orchestra [L. fr. Gk *euphōnia*, pleasant sound]

eu·pho·nize (jú:fənaiz) *pres. part.* **eu·pho·niz·ing** *past* and *past part.* **eu·pho·nized** *v.t.* to cause to have euphony

eu·pho·ny (jú:fəni:) *pl.* **eu·pho·nies** *n.* a pleasant concordance of sound ‖ (*phon.*) a tendency towards ease of pronunciation, e.g. the use of 'an' instead of 'a' before words beginning with a vowel [F. *euphonie* fr. Gk]

eu·phor·bi·a (ju:fɔ́rbiːə) *n.* a member of *Euphorbia*, fam. *Euphorbiaceae*, a genus of xerophytic shrubs or trees and a few plants (*SPURGE), mainly tropical. All possess latex, and many are poisonous. Some produce gums and oils. Medicinal plants of the family yield castor oil and croton oil. The cassava is of this family [L. *euphorbea*, after *Euphorbus*, physician to King Juba of Mauretania]

eu·pho·ri·a (ju:fɔ́ri:ə, ju:fóuri:ə) *n.* a feeling of well-being or elation (often, as in drunkenness, deceptive) **eu·phor·ic** (ju:fɔ́rik, ju:fóurik) *adj.* [Mod. L. fr. Gk *euphoria* fr. *eu*, well +*pherein*. to bear]

eu·phor·i·gen·ic (ju:fɔ́ridʒénik) *adj.* inducing euphoria

eu·pho·tic (ju:fóutik) *adj.* (*envir.*) of upper layers of water where light is sufficient to permit growth of green plants

eu·phra·sia (ju:fréiʒə) *n.* a member of *Euphrasia*, fam. *Scrophulariaceae*, a genus of hemiparasitic plants of temperate regions [M.L. fr. Gk *euphrasia*, cheerfulness]

Eu·phra·tes (ju:fréiti:z) one of the two great rivers of Mesopotamia, birthplace of the ancient civilizations of Babylonia and Assyria. It flows 1,700 miles from the mountains of E. Turkey through Syria and Iraq (where its lower course is navigable) to the Shatt-al-Arab and thence 100 miles to the Persian Gulf. Along its alluvial flood plain dates, cereal grains and livestock are raised. The river floods twice yearly

eu·phu·ism (jú:fju:izəm) *n.* an elaborate, highly artificial style of writing and speaking, fashionable in late 16th- and early 17th-c. England, characterized by antithesis, far-fetched simile, and alliteration [after *Euphues*, hero of two prose romances (1579, 1580) by John Lyly]

Eu·rail Pass (júəreil) ticket for virtually unlimited travel on European railroads. It is available for various periods of time at a lower-than-ordinary price

Eur·a·sia (juəréiʒə, juəréiʃə) the land mass of Europe and Asia as a unit

Eur·a·sian (juəréiʒən, juəréiʃən) **1.** *adj.* with one European and one Asian parent ‖ of or relating to Eurasia **2.** *n.* someone having one European parent and one Asian parent

Eu·rat·om (jurǽtəm) (*acronym*) for European Atomic Energy Community

Eure (ə:r) a department (area 2,330 sq. miles, pop. 423,000) of N. France, southwest of the lower Seine (*NORMANDY). Chief town: Evreux

Eure-et-Loir (ə:reilwɑr) a department (area 2,291 sq. miles, pop. 335,200) of N. central France, southwest of Paris (*BEAUCE, *PERCHE). Chief town: Chartres

eu·re·ka (jurí:kə) *interj.* (*rhet.*) an expression of intense pleasure on thinking suddenly of the answer to some knotty problem [Gk *heurēka*=I have found (it). Archimedes is supposed to have uttered this on thinking of a way to measure the purity of gold, by stumbling on the principle of specific gravity]

eurhythmic *EURYTHMIC

Eu·ric (júərik) (*c.* 420–*c.* 484), king of the Visigoths (466–*c.* 484). He conquered and ruled a large part of Spain and Gaul

Eu·rip·i·des (juərípidi:z) (*c.* 480 B.C.–406 B.C.), Greek poetic dramatist, author of about 92 plays. His plays were less grandiose than those of Sophocles and Aeschylus, and contemporaries regarded them as inferior. His plots still came from mythology, but his characters were drawn with great vividness and insight, as if they had been contemporary men and women. Eighteen tragedies survive, among them 'Alcestis', 'Medea', 'Hippolytus', 'Andromache', 'Trojan Women', 'Iphigenia at Aulis', 'Iphigenia in Tauris' and 'The Bacchae', and one satyr play ('Cyclops')

Eu·ro·bond (júəroubɒnd) *n.* (*banking*) bonds of European Investment Bank (EIB) available in yen denominations, German marks, or Swiss francs, etc. Eurobonds are issued by a non-European company for sale in Western Europe

Eu·ro·cap·i·tal (juəroukǽpitəl) *adj.* of money markets in Europe

Eu·ro·cen·tric (juərəséntrik) *adj.* principally concerned with Europe

Eu·ro·cheque (júəroutʃek) *n.* (*Br.*) a credit card for use in Western Europe

Eu·ro·com·mu·nism (juəroukɔ́mu:nizəm) *n.* the independent and diverse policies of West European Communist leaders, esp. with relation to

policies of the Communist Party in the U.S.S.R.

Eu·roc·ra·cy (juərɔ́krəsi:) *n.* the administrators of European Economic Community (the European Common Market) **Eurocrat** *n.*

Eu·ro·cur·ren·cy (juərouké:rensi:) *n.* (*banking*) cash on deposit in the European money market and available for loans outside the country of its origin, e.g., Euromarks, Eurodollars **syn** Eurofunds, Euromoney

Eu·ro·dol·lars (júəroudɒlərs) *pl. n.* American dollars deposited in banks outside U.S.A., esp. in Europe, which serve as short-term capital and flow where interest rates are highest *Cf* EUROCURRENCY

Eu·ro·mar·ket (júəroumɑrkit) *n.* the international money market in currencies of nations outside the locality

Eu·ro·pa (juróupə) (*Gk mythol.*) daughter of Agenor, king of Tyre. She was loved by Zeus who, in the form of a white bull, carried her off to Crete

Eu·rope (júərəp) the fifth largest continent (area 3,800,000 sq. miles, pop. c. 683,000,000) forming the western extension of Eurasia. Political units: Albania, Andorra, Austria, Belgium, Bulgaria, Czechoslovakia, Denmark, Finland, France, German Democratic Republic (East Germany), Federal Republic of Germany (West Germany), Great Britain, Greece, Hungary, Iceland, Irish Republic, Italy, Liechtenstein, Luxembourg, Monaco, the Netherlands, Norway, Poland, Portugal, Rumania, San Marino, Spain, Sweden, Switzerland, part of the U.S.S.R., the Vatican City, Yugoslavia. HISTORY (see also separate countries). Caves in France and Spain show traces of occupation by Cro-Magnon man (c. 50,000–10,000 B.C.). Civilization in Europe developed first in the area of the Aegean Sea, notably the Minoan civilization of Crete (c. 3000–c. 1400 B.C.) and the Mycenean civilization of the Greek mainland (c. 1400–c. 1200 B.C.). Greece was invaded by Aeolians, Ionians and Dorians, and developed an empire extending along the Mediterranean, and a city-state civilization which flourished c. 500–400 B.C. Greece fell (338 B.C.) to Philip II of Macedon, whose son, Alexander the Great, spread Hellenistic culture into Asia. The Italian peninsula was settled (c. 8th c. B.C.) by the Etruscans, but Rome revolted against them and founded a republic (509 B.C.). The Romans dominated the whole peninsula by 300 B.C., drove the Carthaginians from Sicily in the 1st Punic War (264–241 B.C.) and overran Spain in the 2nd Punic War (218–201 B.C.). Rome completed the conquest of Greece (146 B.C.) and, by the 2nd c. A.D., extended its empire around the Mediterranean, through Spain and Gaul to Britain, the Rhine, the Danube and the Balkans. Christianity became legal (313) in the Roman Empire, which split (395) into the Byzantine Empire and the West Roman Empire. The latter fell (476) to the Vandals and Visigoths, who also invaded Spain, while other Germanic tribes, the Franks and Burgundians overran Gaul, and the Angles, Saxons and Jutes conquered England (5th c.). The kingdom of the Franks expanded (6th–8th cc.), to cover what is now France, the Low Countries, Austria, Switzerland, most of Germany and part of Italy, and Charlemagne was crowned emperor of the West (800). On his death (814), his empire split up, but Otto I attempted to revive it (962) as the Holy Roman Empire. Spain was conquered (8th c.) by the Moors, and remained part of Islam until the 13th c. Northern Europe was ravaged by Viking raids (8th–10th cc.) and central Europe by the Hungarians (late 9th c.). Feudalism spread throughout the continent (9th–11th cc.), and its ideals of knighthood found expression in the Crusades (1096–1270). Church and State came into conflict, notably in the Investiture Controversy (1075–1122). Papal power reached its height (early 13th c.) under Innocent III, but then declined (14th c.) with the growth of national monarchies. The population increased (11th–13th cc.), towns, crafts and trade revived, and Flanders and Italy became the centers of the cloth industry (13th c.). But the Black Death (mid-14th c.) ushered in a century of economic recession, during which England and France fought sporadically in the 'Hundred Years' War (1337–1453). The Byzantine Empire fell (1453) with the capture of Constantinople by the Ottoman Turks. Classical learning revived in Europe during the Renaissance (14th–16th cc.), and its spread was furthered by

the invention of printing by movable type (mid-15th c.). Voyages of discovery, notably by the Portuguese (late 15th c.), to India and the New World were followed by European expansion in these areas and wars over trade and colonies (16th c.). The Reformation (early 16th c.) led to religious wars in Germany (1546–54), France (1562–98) and the Low Countries (1572–1648), culminating in the Thirty Years' War (1618–48). Meanwhile, the Ottoman Empire extended through the Balkans and up the Danube. Dominance in Europe passed from Spain and Portugal (16th c.) to the Netherlands (early 17th c.) and France (late 17th c.). France was exhausted by the wars of Louis XIV's reign (1643–1715), and England emerged as the leading naval and economic power in Europe (early 18th c.). England, with a parliamentary monarchy and religious tolerance from 1689 onwards, was the center of the Industrial Revolution (mid-18th c.) and acquired a vast empire. The 18th c., the century of Enlightenment, saw the growth of Russia and Prussia under benevolent despots and the decline of the Ottoman Empire. The constitutional balance of power, previously based on the rivalry between France and the Hapsburgs, now centered on Austria, Russia and Prussia. The French Revolution (1789–99) overturned government and society in France, setting up a limited monarchy (1789–92) and then a republic (1792–9). Napoleon I, who became first consul of France (1799) and emperor (1804), led French armies across Europe in the French Revolutionary Wars (1792–1802) and the Napoleonic Wars (1803–15). By 1812 he controlled almost all of continental Europe, but his final defeat at Waterloo (1815) was followed by the restoration of the monarchies of Europe by the Congress of Vienna (1815). The forces of absolutism crushed liberal revolts in Spain and Naples (1820) but there were more serious revolutions in 1830 in France and Belgium, and in 1848 in France, Italy, Austria, Hungary and in many of the German states. By a mixture of war and diplomacy, national unity was achieved by Italy (1861) and by Germany (1871). The Hapsburg Empire, shaken by nationalist movements in the Balkans, was formed into the Dual Monarchy of Austria-Hungary (1867). Russia, one of the few countries to have made no constitutional progress in the 19th c., underwent a revolution (1905) and obtained certain reforms before the Bolshevik revolution (1917) set up a communist government. The last quarter of the 19th c. had seen the growth of heavy industry in many continental countries, which took part in a worldwide scramble for colonies to find raw materials and markets. The resultant rivalries contributed to the 1st world war (1914–18). After the defeat of Germany (1918), the war was ended by the Treaty of Versailles (1920), and Czechoslovakia, Estonia, Latvia, Lithuania, Poland and what was later called Yugoslavia all became independent. Hungary was separated from Austria. Economic recession (1929–30) brought widespread unemployment and was followed by the rise of fascist dictatorships in Italy and Germany. These countries, rearming despite the ineffectual League of Nations, intervened successfully in the Spanish Civil War (1936–9). Italy, having seized Ethiopia (1935), annexed Albania (1939), while Germany invaded Austria (1938), Czechoslovakia (1939) and Poland (1939), thereby sparking off the 2nd world war (1939–45). Germany overran successively (1939–41) Denmark, Norway, the Netherlands, Belgium, Luxembourg, France, Yugoslavia and Greece. The Germans were driven back from Russia (1943), Italy surrendered to the Allies (1943) and, after Allied landings in northern France (1944), Germany surrendered (1945). After the war, the Soviet Union dominated eastern Europe, extending its control to Albania (1945), Bulgaria and Rumania (1946), Hungary and Poland (1947), Czechoslovakia (1948), and, for a time (1945–8), to Yugoslavia. Elsewhere in Europe, economic aid was provided by the U.S.A., through the Marshall Plan (1948–51). Germany was partitioned and remained a source of disagreement between the Soviet Union and the West. Most W. European nations joined NATO (1949) and those on the other side of the Iron Curtain joined the Warsaw Pact (1955). The cultural, social and economic unity of western Europe was furthered by the formation of the Council of Europe (1949), the European Coal and Steel Community (1952) and the

CONCISE PRONUNCIATION KEY: **(a)** æ, c*a*t; ɑ, c*a*r; ɔ f*aw*n; ei, sn*a*ke. **(e)** e, h*e*n; i:, sh*ee*p; iə, d*ee*r; ɛə, b*ea*r. **(i)** i, f*i*sh; ai, t*i*ger; ə:, b*i*rd. **(o)** o, *o*x; au, c*ow*; ou, g*oa*t; u, p*oo*r; ɔi, r*oy*al. **(u)** ʌ, d*u*ck; u, b*u*ll; u:, g*oo*se; ə, b*a*cillus; ju:, c*u*be. x, lo*ch*; θ, *th*ink; ð, bo*th*er; z, *Z*en; ʒ, corsa*g*e; dʒ, sava*g*e; ŋ, oranguta*ng*; j, *y*ak; ʃ, *f*ish; tʃ, fe*tch*; 'l, rabb*le*; 'n, red*den*. Complete pronunciation key appears inside front cover.

European Monetary Agreement (1958). The European Economic Community and the European Atomic Energy Community (both effective since 1958) and the European Free Trade Association (1959) were formed. Eighteen European countries joined the U.S.A. and Canada in the Organization for Economic Cooperation and Development (1961). The collapse of dictatorships in Portugal and Greece (1974) and the death of Franco (1975) in Spain ended the last repressive regimes in Western Europe, but the imposition of martial law in Poland (1981), Soviet military intervention in Afghanistan (1979) and U.S. deployment of additional nuclear missiles in Western Europe (1983) increased tension between East and West

Eu·ro·pe·an (juərəpí:ən) 1. *adj.* native to or inhabiting Europe ‖ of, relating to, like, situated in, spoken in, happening in or extending throughout Europe ‖ affirming the essential unity of Europe, *a European outlook* ‖ (of a plant or animal) native to Europe (used either to indicate a form introduced into North America or to distinguish the European from the native form having the same name) 2. *n.* a native or inhabitant of Europe

European Atomic Energy Community (*abbr.* EURATOM) part of the European Community. The Treaty of Rome (1958) established EURATOM as a coordinated effort by European countries to regulate and research nuclear energy's potential among the member nations. In 1967 it merged with the EEC (European Economic Community or Common Market)

European Communities (preceded by *the*) three distinct European communities exist: the European Economic Community, usu. called the Common Market or the EEC; the European Coal and Steel Community; and the European Atomic Energy Community, usu. referred to as Euratom. The Communities share five major institutions: the Commission, the Council of Ministers, the European Parliament, the Court of Justice, and the European Council

European Economic Community (*abbr.* EEC) an organization usually called the 'Common Market', arising from the Treaty of Rome and effective since 1958, consisting initially of Belgium, France, the Federal Republic of Germany, Italy, Luxembourg and the Netherlands. Seat: Brussels. It aims at securing increased productivity, free mobility of labor, control of restrictive practices, and coordinated transport and commercial policies in member countries. Cooperation in coal, iron ore and steel has been effective since 1952 and in nuclear research since 1958. A full customs union and common external tariff became effective on July 1, 1968. Overseas territories linked with the Community are associated members. The entry (Jan. 1, 1973) of Denmark, Ireland and Britain and Norway was fully negotiated (1972), but Norway's voters rejected membership (1972). Greece became a full member (1979) and Spain and Portugal joined (1986)

European Free Trade Association (*abbr.* EFTA) an organization consisting of Austria, Denmark, Norway, Portugal, Sweden, Switzerland and Great Britain, effective 1960–72. Finland became an associate member (1961) and Iceland a full member (1970). It aimed at the progressive abolition of tariffs on imports of goods originating in the area. Great Britain and Denmark (1973) and Portugal (1986) withdrew when they joined the EEC. In 1973 the remaining members arranged with the enlarged EEC to remove tariffs on all industrial products by January 1984. An economic cooperation agreement was also reached with Yugoslavia (1983)

Eu·ro·pe·an·ism (juərəpí:ənizəm) *n.* the quality or spirit that gives a special character to European peoples and their cultures ‖ an interest in, or love of, what is specially characteristic of Europe ‖ a sense of European unity

Eu·ro·pe·an·ize (juərəpí:ənaiz) *pres. part.* **Eu·ro·pe·an·iz·ing** *past and past part.* **Eu·ro·pe·an·ized** *v.t.* to impose a European form or forms on

European Monetary Agreement an agency of the Organization for Economic Cooperation and Development which in 1958 replaced the European Payments Union (1950). It operates a multilateral system of settlements between member countries and provides short-term credits from a European Fund

European Monetary System (*banking*) organization of central bankers of Germany,

France, Italy, and Britain to control currency prices, *abbr.* **EMS**

European plan a system of payments in hotels where the price includes room and service but not meals (cf. AMERICAN PLAN)

European Recovery Program *MARSHALL PLAN

eu·ro·pi·um (juróupi:əm) *n.* a rare-earth element, Symbol Eu, at. no. 63, at. mass 151.96 [Mod. L. after EUROPE]

Eu·ro·poort (í:roupʉrt) a new port to the west of Rotterdam for the importation of oil, coal, minerals etc.

Eu·ro·port (júəroupʉort) *n.* a port in Britain or on the continent advantageous for importing into the European Common Market or other continental nations

Eu·ro·ster·ling (juərousta:rliŋ) *n.* (*banking*) British pounds held by nationals of continental Europe *Cf* Eurocurrency, Eurodollars

Eu·ry·bi·a·des (juərəbáiədi:z) Spartan admiral (early 5th c. B.C.), who commanded the Greek fleet in its operations against Xerxes, winning a decisive victory at Salamis (480 B.C.)

Eu·ryd·i·ce (jurídisi:) (*Gk mythol.*) *ORPHEUS

Eu·rym·e·don (jurímidən) a river in Pamphylia, where Cimon decisively defeated the Persians (468 B.C.)

Eu·rys·the·nes (jurísθəni:z) son of Aristodemus and twin of Procles, with whom he ruled Sparta. From them originated the dual kingship of Sparta

Eu·rys·the·us (jurísθi:əs, juərísθju:s) (*Gk mythol.*) a king of Argos for whom Hercules carried out his 12 labors (*HERACLES)

eu·ryth·mic, eu·rhyth·mic (juriðmik) *adj.* (esp. of architecture) harmoniously proportioned **eu·ryth·mi·cal, eu·rhyth·mi·cal** *adj.* **eu·ryth·mics, eu·rhyth·mics** *n.* the training of the body in graceful and harmonious movement by exercise, often to the accompaniment of music, a method devised by the Swiss composer Emile Jaques-Dalcroze (1865-1950) [fr. L. *eurythmia* fr. Gk fr. *eu-*, good+*rhuthmos*, proportion]

Eu·se·bi·us (ju:sí:bi:əs) (c. 265–340), bishop of Caesarea. His 'History of the Church' was the first scholarly work on this subject

Eusebius of Nic·o·me·di·a (nįkoumidí:ə) (*d. c.* 342), Arian leader who supported Arius at the Council of Nicaea (325), baptized Constantine (337) and became patriarch of Constantinople (339)

Eu·sta·chian tube (ju:stéiʃən) (*anat.*) the tube connecting the middle ear and the upper part of the pharynx, permitting the equalization of pressure on each side of the tympanum [after Bartolommeo *Eustachio* (c. 1500-74), Ital. anatomist]

Eustachian valve a fold of the lining membrane of the heart which in the fetus directs the blood from the vena cava inferior to the left auricle

eu·tec·tic (ju:téktik) 1. *adj.* of an alloy or solution whose proportions are such that its melting point is the lowest for any mixture of the same components 2. *n.* a eutectic solution or alloy [fr. Gk *eutēktos*, easily fused]

eu·tec·toid (ju:téktɔid) 1. *n.* a eutectic formed in the solid state 2. *adj.* like a eutectic

Eu·ter·pe (ju:tá:rpi) the Muse of music

eu·tha·na·sia (ju:θənéiʒə, ju:θənéizi:ə) *n.* the deliberate, painless killing of persons who suffer from a painful and incurable disease or condition, or who are aged and helpless [Gk fr. *eu-*, good+*thanatos*, death]

eu·then·ics (ju:θéniks) *n.* a science which aims at improving the race by bettering environmental conditions [fr. Gk *euthenein*, to flourish]

eu·tro·phi·ca·tion (ju:trəfikéiʃən) *n.* (*envir.*) the aging process of a body of water choked by plant life: evolution into a marsh, with the depletion of available oxygen, followed by eventual disappearance. Eutrophication is often speeded by human activities that add too many nutrients **eutrophicate** *v.* **eutrophied** *adj.*

Eu·tro·pi·us (ju:tróupi:əs) (4th c. A.D.), Latin historian. He wrote a survey of Roman history to 364 A.D.

Eu·ty·ches (jú:tiki:z) (c. 375–c. 454), archimandrite of Constantinople. At the Council of Chalcedon (451) the heresy of Monophysitism, which he propounded, was condemned

EVA *abbr.* extravehicular activity

e·vac·u·ant (ivǽkju:ənt) *n.* a purgative or emetic

e·vac·u·ate (ivǽkju:eit) *pres. part.* **e·vac·u·at·ing** *past and past part.* **e·vac·u·at·ed** *v.t.* (*mil.*) to abandon (a town or position) ‖ to empty (a

dangerous place) of troops, civilians, material etc. ‖ to remove (troops, civilians, material etc.) from a dangerous place ‖ to empty, *to evacuate air from a cylinder* ‖ to discharge the contents of (a bodily organ, the bowels) **e·vac·u·á·tion** *n.* **e·vac·u·ee** (ivǽkju:í:) *n.* an evacuated person [fr. L. *evacuare* (*evacuatus*), to empty out]

e·vad·a·ble (ivéidəb'l) *adj.* able to be evaded **e·vade** (ivéid) *pres. part.* **e·vad·ing** *past and past part.* **e·vad·ed** *v.t.* to escape from by skill, cunning, deception, dexterity etc. ‖ to find a way of getting out of (something demanded, asked or expected of one), dodge, *to evade income tax* ‖ to be too difficult, puzzling or baffling for, *the flavor evades definition* ‖ *v.i.* to be evasive [F. *évader*]

e·vad·er (ivéidər) *n.* one who has become isolated in hostile or unfriendly territory and eludes capture by an enemy

e·vag·i·nate (ivǽdʒineit) *pres. part.* **e·vag·i·nat·ing** *past and past part.* **e·vag·i·nat·ed** *v.t.* (*physiol.*) to turn (a tubular organ) inside out ‖ *v.i.* (of such an organ) to protrude in such a way that the inner surface is exposed **e·vag·i·ná·tion** *n.* [fr. L. *evaginare* (*evaginatus*), to unsheathe]

E·vag·o·ras I (ivǽgərəs) (c. 435–c. 374 B.C.), king of Salamis in Cyprus (c. 410–c. 374 B.C.). Isocrates's biography of him (c. 365 B.C.) is the earliest biography extant in Greek

e·val·u·ate (ivǽlju:eit) *pres. part.* **e·val·u·at·ing** *past and past part.* **e·val·u·at·ed** *v.t.* to determine or assess the value of ‖ (*math.*) to express the value of (a quantity) numerically **e·val·u·á·tion** *n.* [fr. F. *évaluer*]

E·van·der (ivǽndər) (*Gk mythol.*) a prince from Arcadia who settled in Latium. He entertained and helped Aeneas and his followers

ev·a·nesce (evənés) *pres. part.* **ev·a·nesc·ing** *past and past part.* **ev·a·nesced** *v.i.* to fade away, disappear like smoke or as though by evaporation [fr. L. *evanescere*]

ev·a·nes·cence (evənés'ns) *n.* the quality of being evanescent ‖ the fact of evanescing

ev·a·nes·cent (evənés'nt) *adj.* fading or disappearing quickly [fr. F. *évanescent*]

e·van·gel·i·cal (i:vænd3élik'l) 1. *adj.* concerned with, or relating to, the preaching of the Christian gospel, *the evangelical mission of St Paul* ‖ contained in, or in accordance with, the teaching of the Gospels, *the evangelical counsels of perfection* ‖ of, like, or relating to the Gospels ‖ of or relating to the school of theology within the Protestant Church which teaches that men are saved or justified by faith, denies that good works and sacraments are in themselves efficacious for salvation, avoids ritual, and recognizes no authority in religious matters other than the Bible 2. *n.* someone who preaches, teaches or holds this theological position **e·van·gél·i·cal·ism** *n.* [fr. L.L. *evangelicus* fr. Gk]

Evangelical Church the name given to the united Lutheran and Reformed Church in Germany. The German Evangelical Church (E.K.I.D.) was forcibly united in 19th-c. Prussia, and voluntarily in 1946. It has a membership of 41 million, the majority of Lutheran origin (*LUTHERANISM, *REFORMED CHURCH)

e·van·ge·lism (ivǽnd3əlizəm) *n.* the preaching of the Christian gospel, missionary activity [fr. archaic evangel, the gospel+*-ism*]

e·van·ge·list (ivǽnd3əlist) *n.* an author of one of the four Gospels (Sts Matthew, Mark, Luke, John) ‖ a preacher of the Christian gospel, an evangelizer or missionary **e·van·ge·lis·tic** *adj.* of, relating to, or like the Christian gospel or one of the four Gospels ‖ of or relating to preaching the Christian gospel ‖ tending towards the evangelical in theology [F. *évangeliste* fr. L. fr. Gk]

e·van·ge·lize (ivǽnd3əlaiz) *pres. part.* **e·van·ge·liz·ing** *past and past part.* **e·van·ge·lized** *v.t.* to teach Christianity to or spread the Christian gospel in [fr. L.L. *evangelizare* fr. Gk]

Ev·ans (évənz), Mary Ann *ELIOT, George **Evans**, Sir Arthur John (1851–1941), British archaeologist. He excavated the palace of Knossos in Crete (1900–8 and post-1918). His published works include 'Cretan Pictographs and Pre-Phoenician Script' (1896) and 'The Palace of Minos' (1921–35)

Ev·ans·ville (évənzvil) a city (pop. 130,496) in S.W. Indiana: automobile bodies, foundry products, gas engines, breweries. Evansville College (1854)

e·vap·o·rate (ivǽpəreit) *pres. part.* **e·vap·o·rat·ing** *past and past part.* **e·vap·o·rat·ed** *v.i.* (of a liquid or solid) to assume the vapor state by a gradual physical change to which all solids and liquids are subject, at all temperatures, though the rate of change may be very slow ‖ to disappear, leaving no trace, *their enthusiasm evaporated* ‖ *v.t.* to cause to evaporate, by raising the temperature or reducing the pressure of [fr. L. *evaporare* (*evaporatus*)]

evaporated milk unsweetened whole milk reduced to a thick consistency by evaporation

evaporating dish (*chem.*) a porcelain dish in which a solution may be evaporated to leave the dissolved substance as a residue

e·vap·o·ra·tion (ivæpəréiʃən) *n.* an evaporating or being evaporated ‖ disappearance without trace [F. fr. L. *evaporatio* (*evaporationis*)]

e·vap·o·ra·tor (ivǽpəreitər) *n.* an apparatus for evaporating

e·vap·o·tran·spi·ra·tion (ivæpoutrænspiréiʃən) *n.* (*envir.*) loss of water from a land area due to the transpiration of plants and evaporation from soil

e·vap·o·tran·spire (ivæpoutrænspáiər) *v.* (*envir.*) to stimulate water evaporation and transpiration from soil **evapotranspiration** *q.v.*

Ev·arts (évərts), William Maxwell (1818–1901), U.S. statesman and lawyer. He served as counsel for President Andrew Johnson in the impeachment trial (1868), as counsel for the U.S.A. in the 'Alabama' arbitration (1872), and as Republican chief counsel in the disputed Hayes-Tilden presidential election (1876)

e·va·sion (ivéiʒən) *n.* the act or a means of evading (a danger, a duty, the law etc.) ‖ a dodging or avoiding e.g. of a question, the truth, a point under discussion etc. [F. *évasion*]

e·va·sive (ivéisiv) *adj.* not candid, evading or dodging the material point, *an evasive answer* ‖ serving to avoid trouble or danger, *evasive tactics* ‖ not easily caught [fr. F. *évasif*]

Eve (i:v) (*Bible*) the first woman, created by God to be the wife of Adam (Genesis iii, 20)

eve (i:v) *n.* the day before some named day, esp. a Church festival, *Christmas Eve* ‖ before a day important for some event, *on the eve of the wedding* ‖ the brief period before some momentous or culminating event, *the eve of victory* ‖ (*rhet.*) evening, dusk [short for EVEN *n.*]

e·vec·tion (ivékʃən) *n.* an inequality in the motion of the moon in its orbit caused by the gravitational pull of the sun [fr. L. *evectio* (*evectionis*) fr. *evehere,* to carry away]

Eve·lyn (í:vlin), John (1620–1706), English diarist. Like Pepys, his contemporary, Evelyn lived a full public life. His diary covered 65 years, compared with Pepys's 10. It is of greater historical importance but less personal interest

e·ven (í:vən) *adj.* (of a surface) smooth, without irregularities, *an even coat of paint* ‖ steady, constant, uniform, not jerky or irregular, *an even flow of work* ‖ (of temper, disposition, mental state) equable, not easily ruffled ‖ of equal height, *the river rose till it was even with the windows* ‖ equal, *an even balance between opposing forces* ‖ exact, exactly whole, without a fraction, *an even 10 seconds* (of bets, chances, odds etc.) equally balanced, with the odds or probability neither for nor against, *it is even money that he will keep his title* ‖ giving a whole number when divided by two (opp. ODD), *2, 4, 6, 8, 10 are even numbers* **of even date** (*Br.*, in business letters) of the same date as that on which the writer is writing, *we have received your letter of even date* **to break even** to finish neither as a winner nor a loser **to get even** to be revenged, *to get even with someone* [O.E. *efen, efn*]

even *adv.* exactly, precisely, just (emphasizing the exact time or manner of an event or action), *even as he opened the door he sensed the thieves' presence*‖ (intensifying a negative) *he didn't even attempt three of the questions* ‖ (intensifying a positive) *even the authorities disagree* ‖ (intensifying a comparative) *it is even colder than yesterday* (emphasizing a conditional or concessive clause) *I'll finish it even if it takes me all night* ‖ (emphasizing an incongruity) *she wears a coat even when it is hot* ‖ indeed, *though well off, even rich, he is happy* [O.E. *efne*]

even *v.t.* (often with 'out', 'up', 'off') to make even, equal or level ‖ *v.i.* (often with 'out', 'up', or 'off') to become even [O.E. *efnan*]

even *n.* (*rhet.*) evening, dusk [O.E. *æfen, ēfen*]

eve·ning (í:vniŋ) *n.* the later part of the day as darkness approaches ‖ the interval between sunset and bedtime ‖ (*rhet.*) the later or closing years (of a man's life, a nation's history, a civilization etc.) ‖ an entertainment or other func-

tion or occupation taking place in the evening [O.E. *æfnung*]

evening dress formal evening clothes, traditionally white bow tie and tails or black bow tie and tuxedo for men and a full-length dress for women

evening primrose a member of *Oenothera,* fam. *Onagraceae,* a large genus of plants native to America. *O. biennis* is cultivated for its long-tubed yellow flowers which open in the evening and give off scent

evening star a planet, esp. Venus, shining brightly at evening in the western sky in the northern hemisphere

e·vens (í:vənz) *pl. n.* (*Br.*) even odds, *the favorite started at evens*

even so nevertheless

e·ven·song (í:vənsɒŋ, í:vənsɒŋ) *n.* the evening service of the Anglican Church, corresponding to the Roman Vespers (to which the word is still sometimes applied)

e·vent (ivént) *n.* an occurrence, esp. one regarded as having importance, *the event made a great impression on him* ‖ an occurrence notable as being an exception to routine, *going to the opera is quite an event for us* ‖ a separate item in a program of games, athletic contests, racing etc. ‖ (*math.*) one of several independent probabilities **at all events** having regard to all possible occurrences **in any event** whatever may occur **in either event** whichever of two possible occurrences takes place **in the event of** in case of **the normal** (or **natural**) **course of events** the expected succession of cause and effect, *in the normal course of events he will be head of the firm* **e·vent·less** *adj.* without any notable happenings, *an eventless journey* [O.F.]

e·ven-tem·pered (í:vəntempərd) *adj.* not easily perturbed or vexed, calm

e·vent·ful (ivéntfəl) *adj.* full of important, exciting or interesting events, *an eventful career* ‖ important because associated with an important event, *on that eventful morning...*

e·ven·tide (í:vəntaid) *n.* (*rhet.*) evening

e·ven·tu·al (ivéntʃuəl) *adj.* final, occurring as a final result or end, *confident of eventual victory* **e·ven·tu·al·i·ty** *pl.* **e·ven·tu·al·i·ties** *n.* something that may possibly occur **e·vén·tu·al·ly** *adv.* in the end [F. *éventuel,* pertaining to events]

e·ven·tu·ate (ivéntʃueit) *pres. part.* **e·ven·tu·at·ing** *past* and *past part.* **e·ven·tu·at·ed** *v.i.* to come as a result, *did any good eventuate from their talks?* ‖ to happen in the end [fr. L. *eventus, event*]

ev·er (évər) *adv.* (with a negative, a partial negative, a doubt, a question or a condition) at any time, *no man has ever doubted my word, they hardly ever go to bed before midnight, I doubt whether there ever was any such person, have they ever met? if you are ever in the neighborhood you must visit us* ‖ (with a comparison) *it is hotter than ever* ‖ (to intensify a comparison or emphasize a question) *why ever didn't you write to me?* ‖ (with 'before', to add emphasis) *before airplanes were ever thought of* ‖ always, *he came late—as ever* **ever after, ever since** for all subsequent time [O.E. *æfre*]

Ev·er·est (évərist) the highest mountain in the world (29,028 ft), in the Himalayas on the Nepal-Tibet border. Attempted by many expeditions, the peak was first reached by Sir Edmund Hillary and Tenzing Norkay on May 29, 1953. It is named for Sir George Everest (1790–1866), who completed the trigonometrical survey of India

Ev·er·ett (évərit), Edward (1794–1865), U.S. statesman, educator and orator. He delivered (1863) the principal oration at the dedication of the national cemetery at Gettysburg, Pa., preceding Lincoln's Gettysburg Address, and raised $70,000 for the preservation of Mt Vernon as a national shrine by his nation-wide oration on George Washington

ev·er·glade (évərgleid) *n.* a marsh or swamp, partly covered in tall grass *EVERGLADES, THE* **E·ver·glades, the** (évərgleidz) a large tract of swampland in Florida, part of which is a national park

ev·er·green (évərgri:n) 1. *adj.* bearing green leaves throughout the year, e.g. laurel, holly (cf. DECIDUOUS) ‖ (*rhet.*) always fresh, *evergreen memories* 2. *n.* an evergreen tree, shrub or plant

ev·er·last·ing (evərlǽstiŋ, everlá:stiŋ) 1. *adj.* lasting for ever ‖ seemingly without end ‖ unlikely to wear out ‖ constantly and infuriatingly

repeated, a *child's everlasting 'why?'* 2. *n.* an everlasting flower

everlasting flower a member of several genera of fam. *Compositae,* and certain other plants whose flower heads retain their shape and color for a long time after being dried, an immortelle

ev·er·more (évərmɔr, évərmɔur) *adv.* henceforth forever [fr. obs. *evermo* fr. O.E. *aefre má*]

e·ver·sion (ivə́:rʒən, ivə́:rʃən) *n.* an everting or being everted [O.F. fr. L. *eversio* (*eversionis*)]

ever so (*pop.,* esp. intensifying an adjective or adverb) very, *he is ever so much better*

e·vert (ivé:rt) *v.t.* (*med.*) to turn (an organ) inside out ‖ to turn outwards **e·vért·ed** *adj.* (*bot.*) turned sharply outwards **e·vér·tor** *n.* a muscle which gives an outward movement to a part of the body, esp. the foot [fr. L. *evertere,* to overturn]

ev·ery (évri) *adj.* each and all (followed by a singular noun and verb), *every Monday we go to market,* (or used with a possessive pronoun) *he anticipates my every wish* each possible or conceivable, *he has had every advantage* ‖ strong or well founded, *you have every reason to fear him* **every now and again, every now and then, every once in a while, every so often** from time to time, occasionally [O.E. *æfre,* ever + *ælc,* each]

every bit to an equal extent, quite, *she is every bit as pleased as you are*

eve·ry·bod·y (évri:bɒdi:) *pron.* every person (of people in general), *not everybody would volunteer for such work* ‖ every person (in a particular group), *no one answers the phone—everybody must be out*

eve·ry·day (évri:dɛi) *adj.* ordinary, part of normal day-to-day routine ‖ common, familiar, *accidents are an everyday occurrence at this corner* ‖ for ordinary daily wear or use, *an everyday jacket*

every inch in all respects, through and through, *every inch a patriot*

Eve·ry·man (évri:mæn) *n.* the ordinary common man, the man in the street [after the central character, typifying man, in the 15th-c. English morality play 'The Summoning of Everyman']

eve·ry·one (évri:wʌn) *pron.* everybody

every other each alternate, *every other Saturday is a holiday*

eve·ry·thing (évri:θiŋ) *pron.* all things, or all relevant things, *the strike brought everything to a standstill* ‖ something supremely important, *success is everything*

eve·ry·where (évri:hwɛər, évri:wɛər) 1. *adv.* in or to every place ‖ in all its parts, *his evidence is everywhere coherent* ‖ wherever, *you see it everywhere you look* 2. *pron.* every place

every which way (*pop.*) in complete disorder, *things were lying around every which way*

Eve·sham, Battle of (í:vʃəm) a battle (1265) in which Simon de Montfort was defeated and killed by royalist forces led by the future Edward I, during the Barons' War

e·vict (ivíkt) *v.t.* to turn (a person) out, esp. to turn (a tenant) out of a house or land ‖ (*law*) to recover (property, a right or title) by legal proof and judgment, of or from the person who holds it **e·víc·tion, e·víc·tor** *ns* [fr. L. *evincere* (*evictus*), to conquer]

ev·i·dence (évidəns) 1. *n.* anything that provides material or information on which a conclusion or proof may be based, an indication, *there was some evidence of foul play but no clue* ‖ (*law*) information, given by a witness in court (oral), contained in documents (documentary), or provided by things (real), used to prove or disprove the point at issue or to arrive at the truth ‖ (*theol.*) the certainty of an undeniable truth, *the evidences of divine revelation* **in evidence** present, to be seen, noticeably present, prominent 2. *v.t. pres. part.* **ev·i·denc·ing** *past* and *past part.* **ev·i·denced** to be evidence for, show, *his confused answers evidenced a guilty conscience* [F. *évidence*]

ev·i·dent (évidənt) *adj.* clear, obvious to the eye or the mind **év·i·dent·ly** *adv.* clearly, obviously [O.F.]

ev·i·den·tial (evidénʃəl) *adj.* constituting or relating to evidence

e·vil (í:vəl) 1. *adj.* wicked, *an evil man, evil counsels* ‖ arising from or caused by real or supposed wickedness, *evil stories are told about her* ‖ indicating wickedness, *an evil gleam in his eye* ‖ foul, disgusting, *an evil stench* ‖ (*rhet.*) disastrous, ill-omened 2. *n.* what is morally wrong,

---

what hinders the realization of the good ‖ what is materially, very harmful, *the evils of famine and disease* [M.E. *uvel, eville, ivel* fr. O.E. *yfel*]

e·vil·do·er (íːvəldúː·ər, iːvəldúː·ər) *n.* (*rhet.*) someone whose actions are evil

evil eye a supposed power bestowed on a person whereby his glance brings sickness, bad luck or death

e·vil-mind·ed (íːvəlmáindid) *adj.* someone set on doing evil

e·vince (ivíns) *pres. part.* **e·vinc·ing** *past* and *past part.* **e·vinced** *v.t.* to show, manifest (some quality, e.g. gratitude) [fr. L. *evincere,* to conquer]

e·vis·cer·ate (ivísəreit) *pres. part.* **e·vis·cer·at·ing** *past* and *past part.* **e·vis·cer·at·ed** *v.t.* to disembowel (a fowl, rabbit etc.) ‖ to weaken seriously by cutting out, e.g. on grounds of propriety, what was the vital content of (a book, play etc.) [fr. L. *eviscerare (evisceratus)*]

ev·o·ca·tion (evəkéiʃən) *n.* a calling forth, evoking [fr. L. *evocatio (evocationis)*]

e·voc·a·tive (ivókətiv) *adj.* tending to evoke memories, images or associations [fr. Mod. L. *evocativus*]

e·voc·a·to·ry (ivókətɔːri, ivókətɔuriː) *adj.* evocative [fr. Mod. L. *evocatorius*]

e·voke (ivóuk) *pres. part.* **e·vok·ing** *past* and *past part.* **e·voked** *v.t.* to cause to be expressed or made manifest in response, *his words evoked laughter* ‖ to bring to mind, cause to be felt, *the music evoked a stream of associated ideas* ‖ to summon (a spirit) by the use of magic [fr. F. *évoquer*]

ev·o·lute (évəluːt, esp. *Br.* íːvəluːt) **1.** *n.* (*geom.*) a curve traced by the free end of a thread of finite length when it is wound upon another curve ‖ thus tracing the locus of the latter's centers of curvature **2.** *adj.* (*bot.*) with edges rolled outwards [fr. L. *evolvere (evolutus),* to roll out]

ev·o·lu·tion (evəlúːʃən, esp. *Br.* iːvəlúːʃən) *n.* a continuous change from a simple to a more complex form ‖ the gradual development e.g. of an idea, argument, plot, institution or social group ‖ (*pl.*) changes in military or naval or airplane formations ‖ (*pl.*) changes in the relative positions of dancers, football players etc. ‖ (*math.*) the extraction of roots from an expression ‖ (*phys.*) continuous emission, *evolution of heat* (cf. ABSORPTION) ‖ the theory that all living things have changed in response to environmental conditions by the natural selection of randomly occurring mutations, developing from the simplest forms to complex forms which are more prolific and stronger, due to their better adaptation to their environment **ev·o·lú·tion·al, ev·o·lú·tion·ar·y** *adjs* **ev·o·lú·tion·ist** *n.* someone who accepts the theory of evolution [fr. L. *evolutio (evolutionis),* an opening out, unfolding]

e·volve (ivólv) *pres. part.* **e·volv·ing** *past* and *past part.* **e·volved** *v.i.* to change continuously from the simple to the more complex ‖ *v.t.* to cause to unfold or develop, *to evolve a plan* ‖ (*phys.*) to emit **e·vólve·ment** *n.* [fr. L. *evolvere,* to unfold, open out]

e·von·y·mus (ivónəməs) *n.* the euonymus

E·vo·ra (évurə) a town (pop. 50,235) in Upper Alentejo, S. Portugal: Roman ruins, cathedral (12th c.)

Ev·ros (évrɒs) *MARITSA

e·vul·sion (iválʃən) *n.* a pulling out or tearing out [fr. L. *evulsio (evulsionis)*]

E·wald (éval), Johannes (1743–81), Danish poet and dramatist. His many plays include 'The Fishers' (1778)

E·we (éiwei, éivei) *pl.* **E·we, E·wes** *n.* a people of S. Ghana, S. Togo and S.W. Benin, speaking a Kwa language ‖ a member of this people ‖ their language

ewe (juː) *n.* a female sheep [O.E. *eowu*]

ew·er (júːər) *n.* a widemouthed pitcher [fr. A.F. *ewiere,* O. F. *eviere*]

Ew·ing (júːiŋ), James (1866–1943), U.S. pathologist, known for his research in cancer and in classifying tumors. His works include 'Neoplastic Diseases' (1919, 4th ed., 1940) and 'Cancer' (1931)

ex (eks) *prep.* (of stocks and shares) without, *ex dividend* (i.e. without the right to receive the pending dividend) ‖ (*commerce*) out of, from, *the price is $20 ex dock* (i.e. any further charges, such as transport, must be paid by the buyer) [L.]

ex- (eks) *prefix* out, forth ‖ deprived of, without ‖ thoroughly ‖ former, as in 'ex-president' [M.E. fr. Mod. L. fr. L.]

exa- (*prefix*) standard international combining prefix meaning 10^{18}

ex·ac·er·bate (iksæsərbeit, igzǽsərbeit) *pres. part.* **ex·ac·er·bat·ing** *past* and *past part.* **ex·ac·er·bat·ed** *v.t.* to make (a quarrel) more violent ‖ to irritate or provoke (someone) to anger ‖ to make (a disease) more serious **ex·ac·er·bá·tion** *n.* [fr. L. *exacerbare (exacerbatus)*]

ex·act (igzǽkt) **1.** *adj.* completely correct or accurate ‖ precise, *an exact fit* ‖ (used to intensify) very, *the exact opposite* ‖ precisely determined, *no exact time was fixed* ‖ meticulous, *exact in following out orders* ‖ calling for precision and accuracy, *engraving is an exact art* ‖ (of numbers, measures etc.) neither more nor less **2.** *v.t.* to insist upon having, demand, *to exact unswerving obedience* ‖ to enforce payment of (a penalty, debt, tax etc.), *to exact retribution* **ex·áct·a·ble** *adj.* **ex·áct·ing** *adj.* making great, trying or continual demands ‖ difficult to satisfy or please [fr. L. *exigere (exactus),* to weigh out]

ex·act·a (igzǽktə) *n.* (*horse racing*) method of betting on a horse race in which first- and second-place horses are picked in order *Cf* PERFECTA

ex·ac·tion (igzǽkʃən) *n.* the enforcing of a payment, esp. when burdensome or unjust ‖ the payment enforced ‖ a burdensome or unreasonable demand or duty [F.]

ex·act·i·tude (igzǽktituːd, igzǽktitjuːd) *n.* the quality of being exact [F.]

ex·act·ly (igzǽktli) *adv.* in an exact manner ‖ wholly, entirely, far from, by no means, *not exactly pleased* ‖ (used to confirm what has just been said or as a positive answer to a question) quite correct

exact science a science, such as physics, in which data can be obtained by direct measurement and can be treated mathematically, under simple conditions of physical control

ex·ag·ger·ate (igzǽdʒəreit) *pres. part.* **ex·ag·ger·at·ing** *past* and *past part.* **ex·ag·ger·at·ed** *v.t.* to go beyond the truth in describing, estimating or representing, *to exaggerate difficulties* ‖ to lay increased emphasis upon, *her hairstyle exaggerates the roundness of her face* ‖ to make larger than normal, *in their pictures children exaggerate heads and arms* **ex·ag·ger·á·tion** *n.* **ex·ag·ger·a·tive** (igzǽdʒərətiv, igzǽdʒərətiv) *adj.* **ex·ag·ger·a·tor** (igzǽdʒəreitər) *n.* [fr. L. *exaggerare (exaggeratus),* to pile up]

exaggerated stereoscopy *HYPERSTEREOSCOPY

ex·alt (igzɔ́ːlt) *v.t.* (*rhet.*) to raise up (in position or dignity) ‖ to praise highly, give glory to ‖ to fill with elation [fr. L. *exaltare,* to lift up]

ex·al·ta·tion (egzɔːltéiʃən) *n.* a state of mental or spiritual elation or excitement ‖ a raising or being raised to a high position or dignity [F.]

Exaltation of the Holy Cross (the feast of Holy Cross Day, Sept. 14) a commemoration of the return to Jerusalem of the Holy Cross, after the Byzantine Emperor Heraclius had recaptured it from the Persians early in the 7th c.

ex·am (igzǽm) *n.* an examination (testing of knowledge) [by shortening]

ex·am·i·na·tion (igzæminéiʃən) *n.* an inspection, *a medical examination* ‖ a considering, *an examination of the relationship between science and religion* ‖ a questioning, *under examination the prisoner broke down* ‖ (often shortened to 'exam') a testing of knowledge or capabilities **ex·am·i·ná·tion·al** *adj.* [F.]

examination paper the questions which a candidate has to answer in writing ‖ his written answers

ex·am·ine (igzǽmin) *pres. part.* **ex·am·in·ing** *past* and *past part.* **ex·am·ined** *v.t.* to look carefully and closely at, inspect (in order to discover the facts, carry out a test, detect a mistake or fraud etc.) ‖ to inquire into, give careful thought to, *to examine a problem* ‖ to question, *to examine a witness* ‖ to test the knowledge or capabilities of ‖ *v.i.* to act as examiner **ex·am·i·nee** (igzæminíː) *n.* a student who is examined **ex·ám·in·er** *n.* [F. *examiner*]

ex·am·ple (igzǽmpʼl, igzáːmpʼl) *n.* a specimen or instance ‖ a mode of behavior to imitate ‖ a punishment meant also as a warning, or a victim of this, *to make an example of an offender* ‖ something which illustrates the working of a general rule or principle, or which helps to make a meaning clearer **for example** (*abbr.* e.g.) as an instance [O.F. *example, exemple*]

ex·an·them (igzǽnθəm, eksǽnθəm) *n.* exanthema

ex·an·the·ma (ẹgzǽnθíːmə, ẹksǽnθíːmə) *pl.* **ex·an·them·a·ta** (egzænθémətə, egzænθíːmətə, eksænθémətə, eksænθíːmətə), **ex·an·the·mas** *n.* (*med.* and *vet.*) an eruption or rash, e.g. the spots in measles or the eruption on the skin and mucous membrane in foot and mouth disease [L.L. fr. Gk *exanthēma* fr. *ex,* out+*antheein,* to blossom]

ex·arch (éksɑrk) *n.* the civil and military governor of a province of the Byzantine Empire ‖ (in the Orthodox Eastern Church) the head of a self-governing Church (e.g. that of Bulgaria), ranking in dignity between a patriarch and a metropolitan **ex·ar·chate** (éksɑrkeit) *n.* the province ruled by an exarch ‖ his office [fr. L. *exarchus* fr. Gk]

ex·as·per·ate (igzǽspəreit) *pres. part.* **ex·as·per·at·ing** *past* and *past part.* **ex·as·per·at·ed** *v.t.* to annoy or irritate beyond endurance ‖ to make more violent or bitter, *a conflict exasperated by tribal jealousies* **ex·as·per·á·tion** *n.* [fr. L. *exasperare (exasperatus),* to make rough]

Ex·cal·i·bur (ekskǽləbər) King Arthur's magic sword, in the Arthurian legend. According to one version, Arthur drew it from a stone, and this was a proof of his royal descent

ex ca·the·dra (ékskəθíːdrə) *adj.* and *adv.* with authority [L.= from the chair]

ex·ca·vate (ékskəveit) *pres. part.* **ex·ca·vat·ing** *past* and *past part.* **ex·ca·vat·ed** *v.t.* (*archaeol.*) to expose by digging away the covering earth etc. from, *they excavated whole streets at Pompeii* ‖ to hollow out by digging, *to excavate a trench* [fr. L. *excavare (excavatus),* to hollow out]

ex·ca·va·tion (ekskəvéiʃən) *n.* a digging out or being dug out ‖ a hole made by excavating ‖ (esp. *pl.*) a site where excavating has been done [fr. L. *excavatio (excavationis)*]

ex·ca·va·tor (ékskəveitər) *n.* someone who excavates ‖ a mechanical digger

ex·ceed (iksíːd) *v.t.* to go beyond (a given or proper limit) ‖ to be greater than in number or degree **ex·céed·ing** *adj.* (*rhet.*) very great in quality, *exceeding kindness* **ex·céed·ing·ly** *adv.* very [M.E. *exceden* fr. F. *exceder*]

ex·cel (iksél) *pres. part.* **ex·cel·ling** *past* and *past part.* **ex·celled** *v.t.* to be superior to in quality, degree, performance etc. ‖ *v.i.* to be outstandingly skilled or gifted, *she excels as a cook* **to excel oneself** to do outstandingly well [fr. F. *exceller*]

ex·cel·lence (éksələns) *n.* very great merit, quality or ability [F.]

Ex·cel·len·cy (éksələnsiː) *pl.* **Ex·cel·len·cies** *n.* the title given to ambassadors, governors general, the governors of certain states of the U.S.A., high commissioners for Commonwealth countries, and some other officials [fr. L. *excellentia,* excellence]

ex·cel·lent (éksələnt) *adj.* extremely good [F.]

ex·cel·si·or (eksélsiːər) *n.* very fine wood shavings used for packing, stuffing upholstery etc. [L. comp. of *excelsus,* high]

ex·cept (iksépt) *v.t.* to exclude from a list, rule, statement, classification etc. ‖ *v.i.* (with 'to' or 'against') to take exception [fr. F. *excepter*]

except 1. *prep.* apart from, excluding **2.** *conj.* (often with 'that') only, but, *the car is in good order except that the brakes need relining* [fr. L. *excipere (exceptus),* to omit]

ex·cept·ing (ikséptiŋ) *prep.* and *conj.* except [fr. M.E. fr. *pres. part.* of *excepten*]

ex·cep·tion (iksépʃən) *n.* an excluding or being excluded ‖ someone or something excepted from a general rule, class etc. ‖ (*law*) an objection against a decision made by the judge during the course of an action **to take exception to** to object to ‖ to be offended by **with the exception of** except, except for **with the exception that** except that **ex·cép·tion·a·ble** *adj.* open to objection **ex·cép·tion·al** *adj.* unusual, outstanding [fr. L. *exceptio (exceptionis)*]

ex·cep·tive 1. (ikséptiv) *adj.* of a word or phrase expressing omission or exclusion, e.g. 'excluding', 'apart from', 'not counting' **2.** *n.* such a word or phrase [fr. L.L. *exceptivus*]

ex·cerpt 1. (éksərpt) *n.* a selected passage from a written work or musical composition **2.** (iksə́ːrpt) *v.t.* to pick out (pieces or passages) from literary or other compositions **ex·cérp·tion** *n.* [fr. L. *excerpere (excerptus),* to pluck out]

ex·cess 1. (iksés) *n.* the state of being greater than something else, *excess of income over ex-*

penditure ‖ the amount by which something is greater than what is usual or permitted etc., *a 10% excess of rejects* ‖ (*pl.*) acts which are more violent than accepted standards of conduct allow, *the troops committed many excesses* ‖ (*pl.*) inordinate indulgence in sensual pleasure ‖ (*chem.*) an amount of one substance greater than is necessary to complete reaction with another ‖ **in excess of** over, *luggage in excess of 40 lbs. is taxed* **to excess** beyond normal limits, immoderately **2.** (ékses, iksés) *adj.* of something greater than what is usual or permitted, *excess weight* [fr. F. *excès*]

ex·ces·sive (iksésiv) *adj.* going beyond the limit of what is needed, tolerable, desirable etc., *to drive at excessive speed* ‖ very great, *excessive kindness* [F. *excessif*]

ex·cess-prof·its tax (éksesprófits) a tax levied, esp. in wartime, on business profits in excess of the average of a specified period

ex·change (ikstʃéindʒ) *pres. part.* **ex·chang·ing** *past and past part.* **ex·changed** *v.t.* to give or receive (one thing in return for something else) ‖ to interchange, take or receive from another (the same thing as that which one gives, or its equivalent), *to exchange greetings, exchange addresses* ‖ to change over from (one thing to another), to substitute (one for another), *to exchange London fog for Riviera sunshine* ‖ to change (money) from one currency to another ‖ *v.i.* (of money, with 'at' or 'for') to have a specified value in another currency ‖ to change places, holidays, jobs etc. with someone [O.F. *eschangier*]

exchange *n.* the giving or receiving of one thing in return for something else ‖ a reciprocal giving and receiving of things of the same kind, *an exchange of letters* ‖ an interchange of visits, jobs etc. ‖ a changeover from one thing to another, *a welcome exchange of poverty for comfort* ‖ a thing given in return for something else, *would this phonograph be a fair exchange for your tape recorder?* ‖ the conversion of the money of one country into that of another ‖ the price of one country's money in the currency of another ‖ a central place of business for merchants, brokers or financiers, *a wool exchange* (*STOCK EXCHANGE) ‖ (*telephone*) the local center to which subscribers are connected and through which they make and receive calls ‖ (*pl., banking*) checks etc. sent to a central clearinghouse **ex·change·a·bil·i·ty** *n.* the state of being exchangeable **ex·change·a·ble** *adj.* capable of being exchanged [M.E. *eschaunge* fr. A.F.]

exchange control control by a country of the exchange of its money against foreign money, with the ability to devalue or revalue when necessary, in the interests of stable international trade. It can limit the amounts made available for buying imports, for foreign travel or emigration, for foreign investments etc. and can claim foreign money earned, giving domestic currency in return, as a safeguard against 'hot' money (speculative money moving between countries for quick profits). The I.M.F. provides a pool of world currencies for countries to borrow in crisis (*FOREIGN EXCHANGE)

exchange theory a theory of social behavior that holds that the actions of individuals, particularly in formal organizations, are motivated by the expectation of having their favors returned, although the obligation so created is diffuse, rather than specific as in economic exchange

exchange, theory of (*phys.*) the theory formulated by Pierre Prévost that all material bodies are continually absorbing, emitting and reflecting radiant energy, the energy flux depending on the temperature

ex·cheq·uer (ikstʃékər) *n.* a state treasury ‖ the finances of a person or group **Ex·cheq·uer** the British government department which receives and takes care of public revenue ‖ the office of the chancellor who has this charge ‖ *COURT OF EXCHEQUER [M.E. *escheker* fr. O.F. *eschequier*, a chessboard, from the checkered cloth which in Norman times covered the table at which payments were made, and which served as an abacus]

ex·ci·mer (éksimer) *n.* (*chem.*) a molecular species formed by two identical molecules excited by an energy source

excimer laser (*optics*) a laser utilizing a noble gas, e.g., helium, neon, operating during an excimer transition

ex·ci·plex (éksipleks) *n.* the excited state complex that forms when molecules of a dye

are electrically stimulated, immediately before emission of light, and leading to the creation of another form of the dye

ex·cise 1. (éksaiz) *n.* a tax duty levied on the manufacture, sale or consumption within a country of certain commodities, or the charge for a license to manufacture or sell them (cf. CUSTOMS) **2.** (iksáiz) *v.t. pres. part.* **ex·cis·ing** *past and past part.* **ex·cised** to lay excise duty on [prob. fr. M. Du. *excijs*]

ex·cise (iksáiz) *pres. part.* **ex·cis·ing** *past and past part.* **ex·cised** *v.t.* to cut away by surgery ‖ to remove, strike out, *the footnotes have been excised from the popular edition* **ex·ci·sion** (iksíʒən) *n.* a cutting out ‖ the thing cut out [fr. L. *excidere* (*excisus*)]

ex·cite (iksáit) *pres. part.* **ex·cit·ing** *past and past part.* **ex·cit·ed** *v.t.* to cause the emotions of (a person) to be intense ‖ to arouse (admiration, jealousy etc.) ‖ to stir up (the imagination etc.) ‖ to incite (a mob) to collective action or hysteria ‖ (*biol.*) to stimulate, cause to respond ‖ (*elec.*) to cause to be electrically active or magnetic **ex·cit·a·bil·i·ty** *n.* **ex·cit·a·ble** *adj.* able to be excited ‖ emotionally unbalanced, quickly enraged or worked up **ex·cit·ant** (iksáit'nt, éksitənt) *n.* something which excites ‖ (*med.*) a stimulant **ex·ci·ta·tion** (eksaitéiʃən) *n.* **ex·ci·ta·to·ry** (iksáitətɔri, iksáitətɔuri) *adj.* (*med.*) stimulating **ex·cite·ment** *n.* an exciting or being excited ‖ a thing or event that causes excitement **ex·cit·ing** *adj.* [F. *exciter*]

ex·ci·ton (éksətɒn) *n.* (*electr.*) a specially excited state of electrons in an insulator or semiconductor that permits transmission of energy without an electric charge, sometimes described as an electron and a hole in a bound state

ex·ci·ton·ics (eksətóniks) *n.* (*electr.*) study of solid state physics dealing with excitons in dielectrics and semiconductors **excitonic** *adj.*

ex·claim (ikskléim) *v.i.* to cry out in emotion or excitement ‖ *v.t.* to utter under the stress of sudden thought or emotion [fr. F. *exclamer*]

ex·cla·ma·tion (ekskləméiʃən) *n.* the act of exclaiming ‖ the words exclaimed ‖ an interjection [F.]

exclamation point, exclamation mark the punctuation mark (!) which follows an exclamation

ex·clam·a·to·ry (iksklǽmətɔri, iksklǽm ətɔuri) *adj.* of or relating to exclamation ‖ fond of using exclamations

ex·clave (ékskleiv) *n.* a part of a country geographically separated from the main part and surrounded by foreign territory (of which it is an enclave) [fr. EX-+L. *clavis*, key]

ex·clude (iksklú:d) *pres. part.* **ex·clud·ing** *past and past part.* **ex·clud·ed** *v.t.* to keep out, prevent or forbid the entry of ‖ to leave out, *exclude from blame* ‖ to make impossible, prevent, *to exclude the possibility of error* ‖ to leave out of account, *they exclude the possibility of murder* **ex·clud·ing** *prep.* except, excepting [fr. L. *excludere*]

ex·clu·sion (iksklú:ʒən) *n.* an excluding or being excluded **to the exclusion of** in such a way as to exclude, *he plays chess to the exclusion of other interests* **with the exclusion of** except for [fr. L. *exclusio* (*exclusionis*)]

ex·clu·sion·a·ry rule (iksklú:ʒənɛri:) (*law*) the barring of evidence unlawfully obtained

ex·clu·sive (iksklú:siv) **1.** *adj.* sole, not shared with any others, *exclusive rights* ‖ confined to a selected few (esp. the rich or snobbish), *an exclusive neighborhood* ‖ fastidiously selective, *exclusive in one's choice of friends* ‖ having the effect of excluding, *mutually exclusive choices* ‖ (*Br.*, of terms charged) limited to what is specified **2.** *adv.* (of dates, numbers etc.) not counting the first and last mentioned, *8 to 16 exclusive* **exclusive of** excluding, not allowing for, *sales, exclusive of this month's, have reached a million* [fr. M.L. *exclusivus* fr. *excludere*, to leave out]

ex·cog·i·tate (ekskódʒiteit) *pres. part.* **ex·cog·i·tat·ing** *past and past part.* **ex·cog·i·tat·ed** *v.t.* to think out or puzzle out **ex·cog·i·ta·tion** *n.* [fr. L. *excogitare* (*excogitatus*)]

ex·com·mu·ni·cate 1. (ekskəmjú:nikeit) *v.t. pres. part.* **ex·com·mu·ni·cat·ing** *past and past part.* **ex·com·mu·ni·cat·ed** (*eccles.*) to exclude partially or totally from communion with the Church **2.** (ekskəmjú:nikit) *adj.* excommunicated **3.** (ekskəmjú:nikit) *n.* an excommunicated person **ex·com·mu·ni·ca·tion** *n.* an excommunicating or being excommunicated. Lesser excommunication excludes from the sacraments, greater excommunication from all the

benefits of the Church [fr. L. *excommunicare* (*excommunicatus*), to excommunicate]

ex·co·ri·ate (ikskɔ́ri:eit, ikskóuri:eit) *pres. part.* **ex·co·ri·at·ing** *past and past part.* **ex·co·ri·at·ed** *v.t.* to remove the skin from by tearing, rubbing, grazing, scalding etc. ‖ (*rhet.*) to criticize savagely **ex·co·ri·a·tion** *n.* [fr. L. *excoriare* (*excoriatus*), to flay]

ex·cre·ment (ékskrəmənt) *n.* waste matter expelled from the bowels **ex·cre·men·tal** (ekskrəmént'l) *adj.* [F. *excrément*]

ex·cres·cence (ikskrés'ns) *n.* an abnormal growth (on a plant, an animal or the human body, e.g. a wart) ‖ a normal external growth, e.g. an elephant's trunk [fr. L. *excrescentia* fr. *ex*, out+*crescere*, to grow]

ex·cres·cent (ikskrés'nt) *adj.* forming or like an excrescence ‖ (*gram.*) epenthetic [fr. L. *excrescens* (*excrescentis*) fr. *excrescere*, to grow out]

ex·cre·ta (ikskrí:tə) *pl. n.* urine and feces, the nonnutritive material taken in with food and passed out of the alimentary canal ‖ (*bot.*) deleterious substances formed within a plant [L.]

ex·crete (ikskrí:t) *pres. part.* **ex·cret·ing** *past and past part.* **ex·cret·ed** *v.t.* to eliminate (waste matter) from the plant or animal system **ex·cré·tive** *adj.* **ex·cre·to·ry** (ékskrətɔri, ékskrətɔuri:) **1.** *adj.* of or for excretion **2.** *n. pl.* **ex·cre·to·ries** an excretory organ [fr. L. *excernere* (*excretus*), to separate out]

ex·cre·tion (ikskrí:ʃən) *n.* the act of excreting ‖ the matter excreted [fr. L. *excretio* (*excretionis*)]

—Some end products of animal metabolism, often nitrogenous compounds, are useless or harmful to the organism. They are excreted from the body, indigestible matter being excreted as feces and urea and other compounds as urine, or they are made harmless within it. Excretion also takes place through the skin (expelling water, salts, fat) and from the lungs (carbonic acid gas). Invertebrates have various means of getting rid of waste products, e.g. the contractile vacuole in the amoeba and other protozoa, nephridia in the earthworm, Malpighian tubules in insects etc. Plants produce few waste products: these are usually excreted in gaseous form or stored as harmless solids

ex·cru·ci·at·ing (ikskrú:ʃi:eitiŋ) *adj.* exceedingly painful or hard to bear [pres. part. of obs. verb *excruciate*]

ex·cul·pate (ékskʌlpeit, ikskʌ́lpeit) *pres. part.* **ex·cul·pat·ing** *past and past part.* **ex·cul·pat·ed** *v.t.* to declare free from blame **ex·cul·pa·tion** *n.* **ex·cul·pa·to·ry** (ikskʌ́lpətɔri:, ikskʌ́lpətɔuri:) *adj.* [fr. EX-+L. *culpa*, fault]

ex·cur·rent (ikskɔ́:rənt, ikskʌ́rənt) *adj.* (*zool.*) of ducts, channels or canals in which there is an outgoing flow, as in sponges ‖ (*bot.*) having the midrib of the leaf projecting beyond the apex ‖ (*bot.*) having a single, straight, undivided main stem, as in some coniferous trees [fr. L. *excurrens* (*excurrentis*) fr. *excurrere*, to run out]

ex·cur·sion (ikskɔ́:rʒən, ikskɔ́:rʃən) *n.* a short pleasure trip to and from a place, esp. one at reduced rates on public transport ‖ a wandering from the subject, a digression ‖ the attempting of an activity other than one's usual one, *an excursion into politics* ‖ (*astron.*) a deviation from the normal path of a heavenly body **ex·cúr·sion·ist** *n.* [fr. L. *excursio* (*excursionis*), a running out]

ex·cur·sive (ikskɔ́:rsiv) *adj.* of or characterized by digression, *an excursive treatment of a subject* [fr. L. *excurrere* (*excursus*), to go forth]

ex·cur·sus (ikskɔ́:rsəs) *pl.* **ex·cur·sus·es, ex·cur·sus** *n.* a special note or appendix in a learned work dealing with a particular point or subject [L.]

ex·cus·a·ble (ikskjú:zəb'l) *adj.* that can be excused or pardoned ‖ justified **ex·cús·a·bly** *adv.*

ex·cus·a·to·ry (ikskjú:zətɔri:, ikskjú:zətouri:) *adj.* serving or intended to excuse, apologetic

ex·cuse (ikskjú:z) *pres. part.* **ex·cus·ing** *past and past part.* **ex·cused** *v.t.* to free (oneself or someone else guilty of a fault) from blame ‖ to be a reason for not blaming, *nothing can excuse such carelessness* ‖ to forgive, overlook, *to excuse a fault* ‖ to release (someone) from an obligation, undertaking or duty, *your ill-health will excuse you from night duties* ‖ to give exemption from, *he is excused night duty* ‖ to permit (someone) to leave a classroom etc. [M.E. *escusen*, *excusen* fr. O.F.]

ex·cuse (ikskjú:s) *n.* the act of excusing ‖ something which serves to excuse ‖ a pretext, *his backache is only an excuse for not gardening* ‖ (*pl.*) apologies [O.F. *escuse*]

ex·di·rec·to·ry (ɛksdəréktəri:) n. (Br.) unlisted telephone numbers

ex·dis (ɛksdəs) n. code word for limited distribution of documents to Cabinet-level personnel

ex·e·at (éksi:æt) n. (Br.) a permission to be absent (e.g. from a college) ‖ a letter authorizing a priest to leave one diocese and take up duty in another [L.=let him go out, 3rd pers. sing. pres. subjunctive of *exire*]

ex·e·cra·ble (éksikrəb'l) adj. arousing horror and detestation, *an execrable crime* ‖ very bad, *in execrable taste* **éx·e·cra·bly** adv. [fr. L. *execrabilis*]

ex·e·crate (éksikreit) pres. part. **ex·e·crat·ing** past and past part. **ex·e·crat·ed** v.t. (rhet.) to condemn as hateful or abominable ‖ to loathe ‖ v.i. to utter curses **ex·e·crá·tion, éx·e·cra·tor** ns **ex·e·cra·to·ry** (éksikrətɔ:ri:, éksikrətouri:) adj. [fr. L. *execrari (execratus)*, to declare sacred or accursed]

ex·ec·u·tant (igzékjutənt) n. a performer, esp. a musical performer [F. *exécutant* pres. part. of *exécuter*, to execute]

ex·e·cute (éksikju:t) pres. part. **ex·e·cut·ing** past and past part. **ex·e·cut·ed** v.t. to carry out, put into effect, *to execute an order* ‖ to perform, *to execute a dance routine* ‖ to make, esp. as a craftsman, *to execute a pair of candlesticks.* ‖ (law) to draw up and complete in correct legal form ‖ to fulfill, *to execute the duties of chairman* ‖ to meet (a trade order) ‖ to put (a condemned person) to death [fr. F. *exécuter*]

ex·e·cu·tion (ɛksikjú:ʃən) n. a carrying out, putting into effect or fulfilling ‖ a performance, esp. of a musical work ‖ the inflicting or suffering of the death penalty ‖ the act of completion in a legally valid form, *the execution of a legal instrument* **ex·e·cú·tion·er** n. someone who carries out the death sentence [M.E. *execucion* fr. A.F.]

ex·ec·u·tive (igzékjutiv) 1. adj. concerned with, or relating to, the putting into effect of orders, plans or policies, *executive power* 2. n. the executive branch of a government ‖ a person holding an executive position in a business firm etc. [EXECUTE]

executive privilege the legally nonbinding practice by the U.S. President or his presidential assistants of refusing to answer questions posed by Congressional committees by claiming separation of powers

ex·ec·u·tor (igzékjutər) n. a person appointed by a testator to carry out the provisions of his will ‖ someone who puts something into execution, esp. a craftsman or artist **ex·ec·u·to·ry** (igzékjutɔ:ri:, igzékjutouri:) adj. administrative ‖ designed to have effect at some future time or in a certain contingency, *an executory contract* **ex·ec·u·trix** (igzékjutriks) pl. **ex·ec·u·tri·ces** (igzékjutráisi:z), **ex·ec·u·trix·es** n. a woman executor [A.F. *exécutour*]

ex·e·ge·sis (ɛksidʒí:sis) pl. **ex·e·ge·ses** (ɛksidʒí:si:z) n. an explanation or commentary on the meaning of a text, esp. of the Scriptures **ex·e·gete** (éksidʒi:t) n. someone who explains or expounds Scripture **ex·e·get·ic** (ɛksidʒétik), **ex·e·gét·i·cal** adjs **ex·e·gét·ics** n. the science of exegesis, esp. the interpretation of Scriptural texts [Gk *exēgēsis*, explanation]

ex·em·plar (igzémplər) n. a model to be imitated ‖ a typical specimen of a class [M.E. *exemplaire* fr. O. F.]

ex·em·pla·ry (igzémpləri:) adj. without fault, worthy to be copied ‖ serving as a warning example ‖ typical, serving as an example or illustration [fr. L.L. *exemplaris* fr. *exemplum*, example]

ex·em·pli·fi·ca·tion (igzɛmplifikéiʃən) n. an exemplifying ‖ an example ‖ (law) a properly witnessed and sealed copy

ex·em·pli·fy (igzémplifai) pres. part. **ex·em·pli·fy·ing** past and past part. **ex·em·pli·fied** v.t. to serve as an illustration or example of, illustrate ‖ to give an example of, *to exemplify the use of a phrase* ‖ (law) to make a properly witnessed and sealed copy of [fr. M.L. *exemplificare*]

ex·empt (igzémpt) 1. adj. (with 'from') not liable to, free from, a duty, law, tax etc. 2. v.t. to cause to be exempt **ex·émpt·i·ble** adj. [fr. F. *exempt, exempter*]

ex·emp·tion (igzémpʃən) n. an exempting ‖ immunity from some obligation, e.g. military service [F.]

ex·e·qua·tur (éksikwéitər) n. a document recognizing a consul, issued by the government of the country to which he is sent ‖ (hist.) the authorization by the civil power of the publication of papal bulls, decrees etc., or the right (denied by the papacy) to decide whether they should be published [L.=let him perform, 3rd pers. sing. pres. subjunctive of *exequi*]

ex·e·quies (éksikwi:z) pl. n. (rhet.) funeral ceremonies [O.F.]

ex·er·cise (éksərsaiz) 1. n. the use or practice of a quality, power, right, *exercise of tact* ‖ the use of a bodily power, *he freed himself by the exercise of sheer strength* ‖ physical exertion for the sake of bodily health ‖ training or practice to develop skill, aptitude, mental or spiritual powers, or something designed to do this ‖ a task set for students, to give practice or to test knowledge ‖ a training operation for troops ‖ (pl., Am.) a program of songs, speeches etc. given at a school or college, *graduation exercises* ‖ a work of art that is in the nature of a trial or practice attempt, *the new work is an interesting exercise in 12-tone technique* 2. v. pres. part. **ex·er·cis·ing** past and past part. **ex·er·cised** v.t. to use, practice (a quality, power etc.), *to exercise discretion, exercise the right to vote* ‖ to give exercise to, *to exercise a horse* ‖ to train, give practice to, *to exercise children in mental arithmetic* ‖ to carry out (duties, a function) ‖ to make demands on, *to exercise someone's patience* ‖ to be a difficulty to, *this problem has exercised the best brains in the industry* ‖ v.i. to take bodily exercise ‖ (mil.) to take part in practice operations [O.F. *exercice*]

ex·ergue (igzó:rg, éksə·rg) n. the space on a coin or medal below the main design, usually on the reverse, for an inscription, date etc. ‖ what is engraved there [F. fr. Gk *ex*, outside+*ergon*, work]

ex·ert (igzó:rt) v.t. to make effective use of, bring into operation, *to exert one's influence* to **exert oneself** to make an effort **ex·ér·tion** n. **ex·ér·tive** adj. [fr. L. *exserere (exsertus)*, to put forth]

Ex·e·ter (éksitər) the county town (pop. 95,621) of Devonshire, England. Cathedral (12th–14th cc.). University (1955)

ex·e·unt (éksi:ənt) a stage direction for actors to go off [L. 3rd pers. pl. pres. indicative of *exire*, to go out]

ex·fil·tra·tion (ɛksfiltréiʃən) n. removal of personnel or units from areas under enemy control

ex·fo·li·ate (eksfóuli:eit) pres. part. **ex·fo·li·at·ing** past and past part. **ex·fo·li·at·ed** v.i. (bot., of leaves or scales) to come off ‖ (geol., of rocks subjected to weathering) to split off in flakes or scales ‖ v.t. (bot.) to shed (leaves or scales from a bud) **ex·fo·li·á·tion** n. **ex·fo·li·a·tive** (eksfóuli:eitiv, eksfóuli:ətiv) adj. [fr. L. *exfoliare (exfoliatum)*]

ex·ha·la·tion (ɛkshəléiʃən) n. the act of exhaling ‖ evaporation of water ‖ something breathed out ‖ a mist or emanation (fr. L. *exhalatio (exhalationis)*]

ex·hale (ekshéil, igzéil) pres. part. **ex·hal·ing** past and past part. **ex·haled** v.i. to breathe out ‖ to be given off, *steam exhaled from the sodden haystack* ‖ v.t. to give off (a scent) ‖ to breathe out (air, tobacco smoke etc.) [fr. F. *exhaler*]

ex·haust (igzóst) 1. v.t. to use up completely, come to the end of (one's patience, ammunition etc.) ‖ to tire out, drain of strength ‖ to empty (a container) ‖ to draw out (contents), *to exhaust air from the lining of a vacuum bottle* ‖ to destroy the fertility of (soil) ‖ to treat or discuss (a subject) so thoroughly that no more is left to be said 2. n. the expulsion of steam or spent gases from the cylinder of a heat engine after their expansion ‖ the steam or spent gases expelled ‖ the pipe through which the spent gases are expelled **ex·haust·i·bil·i·ty** n. **ex·háust·i·ble** adj. **ex·haus·tion** (igzóstʃən) n. **ex·háus·tive** adj. thorough, painstaking, searching, *exhaustive inquiries* [fr. L. *exhaurire (exhaustus)*, to draw out]

ex·hib·it (igzíbit) 1. v.t. to show, display, *to exhibit symptoms of hysteria* ‖ to show (paintings etc.) to the public in a specially assembled collection ‖ to display (goods) for sale 2. n. a thing or collection put on show, *exhibits in a zoo* ‖ something produced as evidence in a court of law **on exhibit** out on view ‖ away on view [fr. L. *exhibere (exhibitus)* fr. *ex*, out+*habere*, to have, hold]

ex·hi·bi·tion (ɛksəbíʃən) n. an exhibiting or being exhibited ‖ a display of something beautiful, valuable, salable, or of historic or other interest ‖ a performance meant to show off skill for the pleasure of an audience, *an exhibition of acrobatics* ‖ a person who makes himself look ridiculous in public ‖ (Br.) a school or university

bursary **ex·hi·bi·tion·er** n. (Br.) the holder of an exhibition at a school or university **ex·hi·bi·tion·ism** n. a form of sexual gratification in which a man displays his genitals or a woman her naked body ‖ the tendency to show off or make oneself the center of interest **ex·hi·bí·tion·ist** n. and adj. [O.F. *exhibicion*]

ex·hib·i·tor (igzíbitər) n. someone who exhibits at an exhibition ‖ a movie house owner or manager

ex·hil·a·rate (igzíləreit) pres. part. **ex·hil·a·rat·ing** past and past part. **ex·hil·a·rat·ed** v.t. to fill with strong feelings of delight or of well-being **ex·hil·a·rant** adj. exhilarating **ex·hil·a·rá·tion** n. **ex·hil·a·ra·to·ry** (igzíləreitɔ:ri:, igzíləreitouri:) adj. tending to exhilarate [fr. L. *exhilarare (exhilaratus)*, fr. *ex (intensive)+hilaris*, gay]

ex·hort (igzó:rt) v.t. to urge or advise strongly, seek earnestly to persuade [fr. L. *exhortari* fr. *ex (intensive)+hortari*, to encourage]

ex·hor·ta·tion (ɛgzɔrtéiʃən, ɛksɔrtéiʃən) n. an earnest persuading ‖ a persuasive sermon or speech addressed to the minds and hearts of its hearers [fr. L. *exhortatio (exhortationis)*]

ex·hor·ta·tive (igzó:rtətiv) adj. hortatory

ex·hor·ta·to·ry (igzó:rtətɔ:ri:, igzó:rtətouri:) adj. hortatory, exhorting

ex·hu·ma·tion (ɛkshju:méiʃən) n. an exhuming or being exhumed

ex·hume (ekshjú:m, igzú:m) pres. part. **ex·hum·ing** past and past part. **ex·humed** v.t. to disinter (a body) after burial ‖ to bring to notice again (what was long forgotten), *he exhumed some of the master's early works* [F. *exhumer*]

ex·i·gence (éksidʒəns) n. exigency [F. *exigence*]

ex·i·gen·cy (éksidʒənsi:) pl. **ex·i·gen·cies** n. a pressing need, requirement, *the exigencies of wartime* ‖ the state or quality of being urgently needed [fr. L. *exigentia*]

ex·i·gent (éksidʒənt) adj. demanding a great deal, exacting ‖ urgent, pressing [fr. L. *exigens (exigentis)* fr. *exigere*, to drive out]

ex·i·gi·ble (éksidʒəb'l) adj. that may be demanded or charged [fr. L. *exigere*, to drive out]

ex·i·gu·i·ty (ɛksigjú:iti:) n. meagerness, smallness [fr. L. *exiguitas*]

ex·ig·u·ous (igzígju:əs, iksígju:əs) adj. very small, meager, generally implying that something is much smaller than it should be, *exiguous supplies of ammunition* [fr. L. *exiguus*, exactly weighed or measured, scanty]

ex·ile (égzail, éksail) pres. part. **ex·il·ing** past and past part. **ex·iled** v.t. to send into exile or as if into exile [O.F. *exilier*]

exile n. banishment or expulsion from one's home or country ‖ a voluntary living outside one's country ‖ long absence from one's home or country or from some place or activity dear to one, *years of provincial exile* ‖ a person banished from, or suffering long absence from, his home or country **the Exile** the Babylonian Captivity of the Jews (586–538 B.C.) **ex·il·ic, Ex·il·ic** (egzílik, eksílik) adjs [O.F. *exil*]

ex·ist (igzíst) v.i. to have real being, *do angels exist?* ‖ to live, *the work will continue after we have ceased to exist* ‖ to be able to maintain life, *to exist on very little money* ‖ to have life but no more than life, *a slave may be said to exist but hardly to live* [F. *exister*]

ex·ist·ence (igzístəns) n. real being, *the five classic proofs of the existence of God* ‖ the state of being in the world of actuality, *this points to the existence of a secret treaty* ‖ a way of life, *to lead a miserable existence* ‖ a life, *she was sure she had had a previous existence* (philos.) a thing that has immediate and concrete reality **ex·íst·ent** adj. and n. **ex·is·ten·tial** (egzisténʃəl, ɛksisténʃəl) adj. relating to existence, *an existential theory* [O. F.]

ex·is·ten·tial·ism (egzisténʃəlizəm, ɛksisténʃəlizəm) n. the doctrine deriving from Kierkegaard that man is not part of an ordered metaphysical scheme, but that individuals must create their own being, each in his own specific situation and environment. The principal exponents of existentialism are Sartre, Jaspers and Heidegger **ex·is·tén·tial·ist** adj. and n. [F. *existentialisme*]

ex·it (égzit, éksit) a stage direction for an actor to go off [L., 3rd pers. sing. pres. indicative of *exire*, to go out]

exit n. a way out (from a public building or enclosure) ‖ an actor's leaving of the stage [fr. L. *exitium* fr. *exire*, to go out]

Ex·moor (éksmuər) a moorland belt, about 40 miles long and 14 wide, in N. Somerset and W.

Devon, England, supporting wild ponies, red deer and sheep. It is a national park

exo- *prefix* outside, outer, outer part [Gk *exō-*, outside]

ex·o·at·mo·sphere (ɛ̀ksouǽtməsfiər) *n.* (*meteor.*) outermost region of the atmosphere, 300–600 mi. above the earth's surface. **syn** region of escape, exosphere

ex·o·bi·ol·o·gy (ɛ̀ksoubaióləʤi:) *n.* study of life outside the earth **exobiological** *adj.* **exobiologist** *n.*

ex·o·carp (ɛ́ksəkɑrp) *n.* the epicarp [fr. EXO-+Gk *karpos.* fruit]

ex·o·crine (ɛ́ksəkrin) *adj.* (*physiol.*, of glands) secreting externally (opp. ENDOCRINE) [fr. EXO-+Gk *krinein*, to separate]

exocrine gland one of the glands that discharge their secretions through ducts. The exocrine glands include the sweat, salivary, mucous and tear glands, and those glands in the stomach, intestine and pancreas which produce the digestive fluids (cf. ENDOCRINE GLAND)

ex·o·crin·ol·o·gy (ɛ̀ksoukrinóləʤi:) *n.* (*biol.*) study of external gland secretions, including those that attract other organisms *Cf* PHEROMONE

ex·o·cy·to·sis (ɛ̀ksousaitóusis) *n.* (*cytol.*) hypothetical process by which cellular substances that transmit impulses are released from the nerve cells

ex·o·dus (ɛ́ksədəs) *n.* a departure in great numbers **Ex·o·dus** the departure of the people of Israel led by Moses from Egypt in the 14th or 13th cc. B.C. || the second book of the Old Testament, which describes this, and includes the Ten Commandments [L. fr. Gk *exodos* fr. *ex*, out + *hodos*, road]

ex of·fi·ci·o (ɛ̀ksəfíʃiːou) *adv.* and *adj.* by virtue of the office held, *the treasurer is an ex officio member of the council* [L.]

ex·o·gam·ic (ɛ̀ksəgǽmik) *adj.* exogamous

ex·og·a·mous (ɛksógəməs) *adj.* of or relating to exogamy

ex·og·a·my (ɛksógəmi:) *n.* a customary or legally required marriage outside the tribe, clan or other social group (cf. ENDOGAMY) [fr. EXO-+Gk *gamos*, marriage]

ex·og·e·nous (ɛksóʤənəs) *adj.* (*biol.*) originating outside the organism (cf. ENDOGENOUS) [F. *exogène* fr. Gk *exō*, outside+*genēs*, produced]

ex·o·hor·mone (ɛ̀ksouhórmoun) *n.* (*biochem.*) hormonal secretion that affects the olfactory organ of another, e.g., odor of a child to its mother

ex·on·er·ate (igzónəreit) *pres. part.* **ex·on·er·at·ing** *past* and *past part.* **ex·on·er·at·ed** *v.t.* to free from blame || to release from a duty or obligation **ex·on·er·a·tion** *n.* [fr. L. *exonerare* (*exoneratus*), to disburden]

ex·o·nu·cle·ase (ɛksonú:kli:eiz) *n.* (*biochem.*) enzyme that detaches a nucleotide from nucleic acid in DNA to break it down by hydrolysis *Cf* ENDONUCLEASE

ex·o·nu·mi·a (ɛksonú:mi:ə) *n.* the study and collection of tokens, medals, coupons, etc. **exonumist** *n.*

ex·o·phil·y (ɛksófili:) *n.* the environment not dependent on humans **exophilic** *adj.* *Cf* ENDOPHILY

ex·oph·thal·mus, ex·oph·thal·mos (ɛksɒfθǽlməs) *n.* protrusion of the eyeballs, a condition often associated with goiter and hyperthyroidism [Mod. L. fr. Gk *ex*, out+*ophthalmos*, eye]

ex·or·bi·tance (igzórbitəns) *n.* the quality of being exorbitant **ex·or·bi·tan·cy** *n.*

ex·or·bi·tant (igzórbitənt) *adj.* much greater than is justified, greatly excessive [fr. L. *exorbitare*, to deviate, go astray]

ex·or·cize, ex·or·cise (ɛ́ksɔrsaiz) *pres. part.* **ex·or·cis·ing, ex·or·ciz·ing** *past* and *past part.* **ex·or·cised, ex·or·cized** *v.t.* to drive out or ward off (an evil spirit) by commanding it, in the name of God, to depart, or by using incantations, charms etc. || to free (a person or place) from the possession of evil spirits [fr. L. *exorcizare* fr. Gk]

ex·or·cism (ɛ́ksɔrsizəm) *n.* the act or process of exorcising || the words etc. used [M.E. fr. L.L. *exorcismus*]

ex·or·cist (ɛ́ksɔrsist) *n.* someone who exorcises evil spirits || the second highest of the minor orders of the Roman Catholic Church [M.E. fr. L.L. *exorcista*]

exorcize *EXORCISE

ex·or·di·um (ɛksɔ́rdiːəm, iksɔ́rdiːəm) *pl.* **ex·or·di·ums, ex·or·di·a** (ɛksɔ́rdiːə, iksɔ́rdiːə) *n.* a beginning or introduction to a formal speech,

---

sermon or literary work (cf. PERORATION) [L. fr. *exordiri*, to begin to weave]

ex·o·skel·e·ton (ɛ̀ksouskélitən) *n.* an external, hard, supporting structure, ectoderm or skin, e.g. in crustaceans and insects || the bony or horny parts (nails, scales or hooves) of vertebrates (cf. ENDOSKELETON)

ex·os·mo·sis (ɛ̀ksɒzmóusis, ɛ̀ksɒsmóusis) *n.* (*biol.*) the movement of a substance through a membrane from a region of higher concentration || the transfer of material by osmosis from a cell (cf. ENDOSMOSIS)

ex·o·sphere (ɛ́ksousfiər) *n.* the outer region of the atmosphere

ex·os·to·sis (ɛ̀ksɒstóusis) *n.* the formation of a knoblike outgrowth on a bone or the root of a tooth || the formation of knots on the surface of wood **ex·os·tot·ic** (ɛ̀ksɒstótik) *adj.* [Mod. L. fr. Gk]

ex·o·ter·ic (ɛ̀ksətérik) *adj.* (of teaching, rites, doctrines) suitable for, or easily understood by, those who are not within an inner circle of initiates (cf. ESOTERIC) || outside the inner circle of initiates **ex·o·ter·i·cal** *adj.* [fr. L. fr. Gk *exōterikos*, fr. *exōterō*, comp. of *exō*, outside]

ex·o·ther·mic (ɛ̀ksouθə́rmik) *adj.* (*chem.*) pertaining to the production (as opposed to absorption) of heat, *an exothermic process* (cf. ENDOTHERMIC) [fr. EXO-+Gk *thermē*, heat]

ex·ot·ic (igzótik) **1.** *adj.* brought in from a foreign country (e.g. of non-native plants) or from a foreign language || like or imitating the foreign, *exotic cooking* || (*pop.*) very unusual, attractively strange, *an exotic scent* **2.** *n.* a plant, word etc. introduced into a country from outside || an exotic-looking person **ex·ot·i·cal·ly** *adv.* **ex·ot·i·cism** (igzótisizəm) *n.* [fr. L. fr. Gk *exōtikos* fr. *exō*, outside]

ex·o·tox·in (ɛ̀ksoutóksin) *n.* a soluble toxin excreted by bacteria (cf. ENDOTOXIN)

ex·pand (ikspǽnd) *v.t.* to make larger, swell, *heat expands metal* || to cause to increase, *to expand trade* || to express in detail (a formula, an algebraic expression etc.) || to enlarge on, treat (a topic) more fully || *v.i.* to become larger, swell || to increase in scope, *the society expanded into a worldwide organization* || to spread out, open out, *the valley expands into a wide plain* || to grow genial, unbend [fr. L. *expandere*, to spread out]

ex·pand·ed cinema (ikspǽndəd) combined cinema and live entertainment

expanding universe, theory of the the theory, as suggested by astronomical observation and relativity theory, that all galaxies may be receding from one another at velocities which are greatest for those furthest apart

ex·panse (ikspǽns) *n.* a wide, open stretch of earth, sky or water [fr. L. *expansum* fr. *expandere* (*expansus*), to spread out]

ex·pan·sile (ikspǽnsəl, ikspǽnsail) *adj.* capable of expansion || of or relating to expansion

ex·pan·sion (ikspǽnʃən) *n.* an expanding or being expanded || the extent to which something expands or has expanded **ex·pán·sion·ism** *n.* a belief in, or policy of, expansion (e.g. of territory, influence, economic production, currency) **ex·pán·sion·ist** *n.* [fr. L. L. *expansio* (*expansionis*)]

ex·pan·sive (ikspǽnsiv) *adj.* happy to communicate thoughts and feelings, *an expansive mood* || broad, wide, *an expansive stretch of lawn* || tending to expand or relating to expansion, *the expansive energy of steam* || working by expansion **ex·pan·siv·i·ty** (ɛkspænsíviti:) *n.* capacity to expand || coefficient of expansion [fr. L. *expandere* (*expansus*), to spread out]

ex par·te (ɛkspɑ́rti:) *adj.* and *adv.* in support of one side only, *an ex parte argument, to argue ex parte* [L.=from one side]

ex·pa·ti·ate (ikspéiʃi:eit) *pres. part.* **ex·pa·ti·at·ing** *past* and *past part.* **ex·pa·ti·at·ed** *v.i.* to speak or write at great length **ex·pa·ti·a·tion** *n.* **ex·pa·ti·a·to·ry** (ikspéiʃi:ətɔri:, ikspéiʃi:ətouri:) *adj.* [fr. L. *expatiari* (*expatiatus*), to walk about]

ex·pa·tri·ate 1. (ikspéitri:eit) *v.t. pres. part.* **ex·pa·tri·at·ing** *past* and *past part.* **ex·pa·tri·at·ed** to force (oneself or someone else) to live away from one's own or his own country **2.** (ikspéitri:it, ikspéitri:eit) *n.* a person living outside his own country **ex·pa·tri·a·tion** *n.* [fr. L. *expatriare* (*expatriatus*)]

ex·pect (ikspékt) *v.t.* to think likely, *I expect the train will be late* || to anticipate the coming of, either with pleasure, *we're all expecting you* or with none, *he's expecting the bill any day* || to hope for, *you can't expect any money* || to require

---

(something) of somebody, *a speech will be expected of you* || to require (someone) to do something, *you are expected to work late if need be* || to suppose, *I expect there are some cigarettes in the house somewhere* **to be expecting** (*pop.*) to be pregnant [fr. L. *expectare*]

ex·pect·an·cy (ikspéktənsi:) *pl.* **ex·pect·an·cies** *n.* a state of expectation || the quality of hopefulness, *youthful expectancy* || an amount that is actuarially probable, *life expectancy* [fr. L. *expectantia*]

ex·pect·ant (ikspéktənt) *adj.* expressing pleasurable hope or anticipation, *an expectant hush* || having prospects, *the expectant heir* || pregnant, *an expectant mother* [O.F.]

ex·pec·ta·tion (ɛkspektéiʃən) *n.* an expecting, *he was proved correct in his expectation* || something anticipated, *his worst expectations did not materialize* || a looking forward with hope or pleasure || a reasonable chance, *is there any expectation of getting away early?* || something regarded as almost certain or fit and proper, *it disappointed their expectations* || (*pl.*) prospects of inheriting || an amount that is actuarially probable, expectancy **to come up to expectation** (or **expectations**) not to disappoint [fr. L. *expectatio* (*expectationis*)]

ex·pec·to·rant (ikspéktərənt) **1.** *adj.* that helps one to spit out phlegm **2.** *n.* a medicine which does this [fr. L. *expectorans* (*expectorantis*) fr. *expectorare*, to expel from the mind]

ex·pec·to·rate (ikspéktəreit) *pres. part.* **ex·pec·to·rat·ing** *past* and *past part.* **ex·pec·to·rat·ed** *v.t.* to cough up and spit out (phlegm etc.) || *v.i.* to cough up and spit out phlegm etc. || to spit **ex·pec·to·ra·tion** *n.* the act of expectorating or an instance of this || that which is spat out [fr. L. *expectorare* (*expectoratus*), to expel from the mind]

ex·pe·di·ence (ikspí:di:əns) *n.* the quality of being expedient || regard for what is advantageous rather than right or just, *to act from expedience* [F. *expédience*]

ex·pe·di·en·cy (ikspí:di:ənsi:) *pl.* **ex·pe·di·en·cies** *n.* expedience || an expedient [EXPEDIENT]

ex·pe·di·ent (ikspí:di:ənt) **1.** *adj.* suitable for the end in view, advisable || bringing a particular limited (often selfish or material) advantage, but one which is not right or just **2.** *n.* a way or means of achieving an end in view, a device **ex·pe·di·en·tial** (ikspi:di:énʃəl) *adj.* [F. *expédient*]

ex·pe·dite (ɛ́kspidait) *pres. part.* **ex·pe·dit·ing** *past* and *past part.* **ex·pe·dit·ed** *v.t.* to hasten, *to expedite an order* || to send, dispatch [fr. L. *expedire* (*expeditus*), to rid of difficulties]

ex·pe·di·tion (ɛkspidíʃən) *n.* a journey or voyage to a particular place or for a particular purpose, *a scientific expedition* || the people taking part in this, with their equipment || a pleasure trip || promptness, quickness **ex·pe·di·tion·ar·y** *adj.* (*mil.*) of or being an expedition **ex·pe·di·tious** *adj.* prompt, quick and effective [fr. L. *expeditio* (*expeditionis*), a freeing from impediments]

ex·pel (ikspél) *pres. part.* **ex·pel·ling** *past* and *past part.* **ex·pelled** *v.t.* to deprive of membership (of a school, political party etc.) || to eject by force, force out, *burned gases are expelled through the exhaust* **ex·pel·la·ble** *adj.* **ex·pel·lent, ex·pel·lant** *n.* and *adj.* [fr. L. *expellere*, to drive out]

ex·pend (ikspénd) *v.t.* to spend (time, money, mental or physical effort etc.) || to use up (ammunition etc.) **ex·pend·a·ble** *adj.* (of equipment etc.) meant to be used up in the normal course of work || (of a person) that can be sacrificed as of no further usefulness [fr. L. *expendere*, to pay out]

ex·pen·di·ture (ikspénditʃər) *n.* an expending || the amount or amounts expended [fr. M.L. *expenditus* fr. *expendere*, to pay out]

ex·pense (ikspéns) *n.* cost in terms of money || cost in terms of anything else paid or sacrificed to achieve an end, e.g. in casualties || a source of expense, *an old car can be a great expense to run* || (*pl.*) money paid out in running a business or household, doing a job etc. **at the expense of** at the cost of, *speed at the expense of accuracy* **to go to any expense** to be unswayed by consideration of what money, time, effort etc. would be involved **to go to expense** to spend money **to put to expense** to oblige to spend money [A.F.]

ex·pen·sive (ikspénsiv) *adj.* costly in money or damage, or in whatever is sacrificed to achieve an end || highpriced or making a high charge

ex·pe·ri·ence (ikspíəri:əns) **1.** *n.* the knowledge or feeling obtained through direct impressions,

---

experience of pain ‖ an instance of direct knowledge, *he has had more than one experience of prison* ‖ the skill or judgment gained by practice, *experience showed in every move he made* ‖ an interesting or remarkable event in a person's life, or something suffered by a person ‖ all that has happened to a person, in his life or in a particular sphere of activity, *in all his professional experience he had never met such a case* **2.** *v.t. pres. part.* **ex·pe·ri·enc·ing** *past* and *past part.* **ex·pé·ri·enced** to have experience of, undergo, feel, *to experience a sense of loss* **ex·pé·ri·enced** *adj.* endowed with experience, with the knowledge and skill derived from experience, *an experienced sailor* [F. *expérience*, a putting to the test]

ex·pe·ri·en·tial (ekspiəri:énʃəl) *adj.* concerned with or provided by experience [fr. L. *experientia*, a putting to the test]

ex·per·i·ment (ikspériment) **1.** *n.* an operation carried out under determined conditions to discover, verify or illustrate a theory, hypothesis or fact ‖ a method or procedure adopted without knowing just how it will work, *an experiment in social living* ‖ experimentation **2.** *v.i.* to make experiments **ex·per·i·men·tal** (iksperəmént'l) *adj.* based on or derived from experiences or experiment ‖ making use of experiment, *experimental psychology* ‖ made or designed as a trial or for use in experiment, *an experimental model* ‖ a lease ‖ breathing out [fr. L. *expiratio (expiartionis)*, a breathing out] **ex·per·i·mén·tal·ism, ex·per·i·mén·tal·ist** *ns* **ex·per·i·men·ta·tion** (iksperəmentéiʃən) *n.* the use of experiment as a method of obtaining or confirming knowledge [O.F.]

ex·pert (ékspə:rt) **1.** *n.* someone whose knowledge or skill is specialized and profound, esp. as the result of much practical experience ‖ (*U.S. Army*) the highest proficiency rating for marksmanship ‖ a soldier with this rating (cf. MARKSMAN, cf. SHARPSHOOTER) **2.** (ékspə:rt, ikspé:rt) *adj.* pertaining to such knowledge or skill ‖ provided by an expert [fr. L. *experiri (expertus*), to put to the test]

ex·per·tise (ekspərti:z) *n.* expert knowledge [F.]

ex·pi·a·ble (ékspi:əb'l) *adj.* that can be expiated

ex·pi·ate (ékspi:eit) *pres. part.* **ex·pi·at·ing** *past* and *past part.* **ex·pi·at·ed** *v.t.* to atone for and so wipe out the guilt of (sin or wrongdoing) **ex·pi·á·tion** *n.* atonement ‖ the means of atonement **éx·pi·a·tor** *n.* **ex·pi·a·to·ry** (ékspis:ətɔ:ri, ékspiːətəuri:) *adj.* [fr. L. *expiare (expiatus)*]

ex·pi·ra·tion (ekspəréiʃən) *n.* a coming to an end (of what is limited in time), *the expiration of a lease* ‖ breathing out [fr. L. *expiratio (expirationis)*, a breathing out]

ex·pire (ikspáiər) *pres. part.* **ex·pir·ing** *past* and *past part.* **ex·pired** *v.i.* (of a period of time, or of what is limited to a period of time) to come to an end ‖ to die ‖ (of a patent etc.) to become void at the end of a term of years ‖ (of a title) to become extinct ‖ to breathe out ‖ *v.t.* to breathe out (carbon dioxide etc.) **ex·pi·ry** (ikspáiəri:, ékspəri:) *n.* a coming to an end, expiration [fr. F. *expirer*]

ex·plain (ikspléin) *v.t.* to make clear, *to explain what one means* ‖ to give a detailed exposition of, *to explain how a machine works* ‖ to give a reason that accounts for or justifies (an event or action), *explain your absence to the manager* ‖ (with 'away') to account for completely, show that no problem or difficulty exists, *you can't explain away the rise in unemployment by denying the statistics* ‖ *v.i.* to give an explanation to **explain oneself** to justify one's conduct ‖ to clarify one's meaning **ex·pláin·a·ble** *adj.* [fr. L. *explanare*, to make flat or plain]

ex·pla·na·tion (eksplənéiʃən) *n.* a making clear, *the figures call for careful explanation* ‖ something which makes clear, *you'll find the explanation in the encyclopedia* ‖ an accounting for or justifying of an event or action ‖ the facts put forward in justification ‖ an attempt on the part of the persons involved to settle a dispute or clear up a misunderstanding by defining terms, stating motives etc. [fr. L. *explanatio (explanationis)*]

ex·plan·a·tive (iksplǽnətiv) *adj.* explanatory [fr. L. *explanare (explanatus)*, to explain]

ex·plan·a·to·ry (iksplǽnətɔ:ri, iksplǽnətəuri:) *adj.* serving or intended to explain, make clear, or account for, *a book with explanatory notes* [fr. L. *explanare (explanatus)*, to explain]

ex·plant (iksplǽnt, iksplánt) *v.t.* (*zool.*, of tissue culture) to take (a living organism, or part of one) and grow it in an artificial medium **ex-**

plan·ta·tion (eksplæntéiʃən, eksplɑntéiʃən) *n.* a tissue culture away from the organism of its origin

ex·ple·tive (ékspliuv) **1.** *adj.* expressing strong emotion, using expletives ‖ used to pad out a sentence or a line of verse **2.** *n.* an exclamation, often an oath, expressing strong emotion ‖ a word or phrase used to pad out a sentence, line of verse etc. **ex·ple·to·ry** (éksplitɔ:ri, éksplitəuri:) *adj.* [fr. L. *expletivus*, serving to fill out]

ex·pli·ca·ble (éksplikəb'l, iksplíkəb'l) *adj.* capable of being explained or accounted for [fr. L. *explicabilis*]

ex·pli·cate (éksplikeit) *pres. part.* **ex·pli·cat·ing** *past* and *past part.* **ex·pli·cat·ed** *v.t.* to explain in detail, bring out the full meaning of [fr. L. *explicare (explicatus)*, to unfold]

ex·pli·ca·tion (eksplikéiʃən) *n.* a bringing out of the full meaning (of a complex or difficult idea, sentence, principle etc.) [F.]

ex·pli·ca·tive (éksplikeitiv, iksplíkətiv) *adj.* serving to explicate

ex·pli·ca·to·ry (éksplikətɔ:ri, éksplikətəuri:) *adj.* explicative

ex·plic·it (iksplísit) *adj.* clearly and openly stated or defined, not left to be understood (cf. IMPLICIT) ‖ direct and unambiguous in speech or writing [F. *explicite*]

ex·plode (iksplóud) *pres. part.* **ex·plod·ing** *past* and *past part.* **ex·plod·ed** *v.i.* to undergo a large sudden increase of volume (usually accompanied by the production of heat, light and sound) resulting in destructive pressures on the surrounding materials ‖ (of a container) to fly to pieces as the result of the sudden large increase in volume of its contents ‖ to release emotional tension suddenly, *to explode into laughter* ‖ *v.t.* to cause to explode ‖ (*pop.*) to destroy (a myth, theory etc.) [fr. L. *explodere*, to drive off the stage by noises of disapproval]

ex·ploit (ikspláit) *v.t.* to derive unjust profit from (the work of another), *to exploit cheap labor* ‖ to use for one's own selfish ends or profit ‖ to develop the use of, make the best use of, *to exploit an invention* **ex·plóit·a·ble** *adj.* **ex·ploi·ta·tion** (eksplɔitéiʃən) *n.* **ex·plóit·a·tive** *adj.* [fr. F. *exploiter*]

ex·ploit (ékspláit) *n.* a heroic or remarkable deed [O.F. *esploit*]

ex·plo·ra·tion (eksplɔréiʃən) *n.* the act of exploring ‖ a journey of exploration ‖ (*med.*) an examination of a wound or part of the body [fr. F. *explorer*]

ex·plor·a·tive (ikspló:rətiv, ikspló:urətiv) *adj.* exploratory [fr. obs. verb *explorate*, to explore fr. L. *explorare (exploratus)*]

ex·plor·a·to·ry (ikspló:rətɔ:ri, ikspló:urə touri:) *adj.* of or relating to exploration [fr. L. *exploratorius*]

ex·plore (ikspló:r, ikspló:ur) *pres. part.* **ex·plor·ing** *past* and *past part.* **ex·plored** *v.t.* to travel in or voyage through (an unknown or little known region) in order to add to man's knowledge ‖ to conduct a search into, investigate, *hydrographers explore the bed of the ocean* ‖ to consider carefully (a possible course of action) ‖ (*med.*) to probe or examine (a wound etc.) ‖ *v.i.* to make a voyage of exploration **ex·plór·er** *n.* someone who explores ‖ (*med.*) an instrument for exploring [fr. F. *explorer*]

Ex·plor·er *n.* unmanned research satellite of which 29 were launched between 1958 and 1965. Explorer was designed to note and telemeter to receiving stations data on atmosphere and space surrounding the earth

ex·plo·sion (iksplóuʒən) *n.* a violent expansion, usually accompanied by noise, caused by a sudden release of energy from a very rapid chemical or nuclear reaction or by the release of highly compressed fluids ‖ an outburst of violent emotion or energy ‖ (*phon.*) the sharp puff of breath sometimes accompanying a stop (e.g. p, t) [fr. L. *explosio (explosionis)*, a driving off the stage by noises of disapproval]

ex·plo·sive (iksplóusiv) **1.** *adj.* used or designed to explode or to cause an explosion, *an explosive charge* ‖ liable to explode, *alcohol vapor is highly explosive* ‖ very dangerous, *an explosive situation* ‖ suddenly violent, *an explosive outburst of temper* ‖ (*phon.*) pronounced with a sudden output of breath **2.** *n.* a substance which is capable of undergoing very rapid decomposition to more stable products (releasing energy in the form of heat, light and sound), accompanied by a rapid expansion of these products. Explosives are used e.g. for propelling projectiles and during blasting (e.g. tunneling, min-

ing and quarrying) ‖ (*phon.*) an explosive consonant [fr. L. *explodere (explosus)*, to drive off the stage by noises of disapproval]

ex·po *abbr.* an exposition, e.g., Expo 70

ex·po·nent (ikspóunənt) *n.* someone who expounds, *an exponent of Zen Buddhism* or interprets, *an exponent of Bach's keyboard music* or advocates, *an exponent of aid to underdeveloped countries* or who is a practitioner, *a well-known exponent of the art of engraving* ‖ (*math.*) an index, a symbol indicating to what power a quantity is to be raised. It is printed as a superior figure or letter, following and above the quantity (in 3^2, ^{2} is the exponent, indicating that 3 is to be squared) **ex·po·nen·tial** (ekspounénʃəl) *adj.* serving to expound, explain or interpret ‖ (*math.*) of an expression involving exponents which are variable quantities [fr. L. *exponere*, to set out]

exponential smoothing *n.* (*management*) technique of forecasting that gives greater weight to more recent information, utilizing index numbers for identifying data

ex·po·nen·ti·a·tion (ekspounenʃi:éiʃən) *n.* (*math.*) the raising of a quantity by the power of its exponent, e.g., increasing geometrically

ex·port **1.** (ikspɔ:rt, ikspóurt, ékspɔ:rt, ékspourt) *v.t.* to send from one country to another in return for goods, money or services (opp. IMPORT) **2.** (ékspɔ:rt, ékspóurt) *n.* the act or trade of exporting ‖ an article or commodity exported **3.** (ékspɔ:rt, ékspóurt) *adj.* pertaining to what is exported or to exportation, *an export license* **ex·pórt·a·ble** *adj.* [fr. L. *exportare*, to carry off]

ex·por·ta·tion (eksportéiʃən, ekspourtéiʃən) *n.* the act or business of exporting ‖ an export [F.]

Export-Import Bank of the United States the principal international financial agency of the U.S. government. It was originally established (1934) to open more foreign markets to U.S. products. It helps to promote the economic development of underdeveloped countries, esp. in Latin America. It is authorized to have up to $40 billion outstanding in the form of loans, guarantees and insurance. It has $1 billion in capital stock and may borrow up to $6 billion from the U.S. Treasury

ex·pose (ikspóuz) *pres. part.* **ex·pos·ing** *past* and *past part.* **ex·posed** *v.t.* to leave uncovered, bare, without clothing or other protection or shelter, *to expose oneself to the sun* ‖ (*hist.*) to abandon outdoors, *the Spartans used to expose babies who were born sickly* ‖ to leave open to attack, danger etc., *an exposed flank* ‖ to subject to, allow to be affected by, *statues exposed to the wind and rain* ‖ to allow light to fall upon (a photographic plate or film) ‖ to display to view, *the dealer exposes the top card* ‖ (*eccles.*) to display for veneration or adoration ‖ to bring to light, uncover, *excavations have exposed a Roman pavement* ‖ to reveal (something secret) ‖ to show up (a crime, fault, mistake etc.), *to expose the fallacy in an argument* **to be exposed** (of a house) to face (a given direction) [F. *exposer*]

ex·po·sé (ekspouzéi) *n.* an exposition (of a theme etc.) ‖ an exposure, esp. of something shameful [F., past part. of *exposer*, to expose]

ex·po·si·tion (ekspəzíʃən) *n.* an explaining and interpreting of a theme, writing etc. ‖ the words which do this ‖ (*mus.*) the statement of a theme in a sonata, symphony or fugue ‖ an exposing, displaying in public ‖ (*eccles.*) the displaying of the consecrated Host for adoration, or of relics for veneration ‖ an exhibition of works of art, industry, commerce etc. [F.]

ex·pos·i·tive (ikspɔ́zitiv) *adj.* expository

ex·pos·i·tor (ikspɔ́zitər) *n.* someone who explains and interprets (a theme, passage in a book etc.) **ex·pos·i·to·ry** (ikspɔ́zitɔ:ri, ikspɔ́zitəuri:) *adj.* descriptive and explanatory [O.F. *expositeur*]

ex·pos·tu·late (ikspɔ́stʃuleit) *pres. part.* **ex·pos·tu·lat·ing** *past* and *past part.* **ex·pos·tu·lat·ed** *v.i.* to remonstrate **ex·pos·tu·la·to·ry** (ikspɔ́stʃulatɔ:ri, ikspɔ́stʃulatouri:) *adj.* [fr. L. *expostulare (expostulatum)*, to demand]

ex·pos·tu·la·tion (ikspɔstʃuléiʃən) *n.* the act of expostulating ‖ a remonstrance [fr. L. *expostulatio (expostulationis)*]

ex·po·sure (ikspóuʒər) *n.* an exposing or being exposed (to light, heat, cold, sickness etc.) ‖ the period during which something or someone is exposed ‖ (*photog.*) any piece of a roll of film or of cut film that is exposed for a single photograph or (as a measure of amount of film) that is intended to be so exposed, *a roll of 36 exposures* ‖

the act of making something shameful publicly known || the aspect (of a house)

exposure meter (*photog.*) a device based on a photoelectric cell which measures the intensity of light falling on a subject and reflected from it, and indicates the proper exposure settings to be applied to the camera

ex·pound (ikspáund) *v.t.* to explain and interpret (e.g. the Scriptures) || to state with great detail [M.E. *expounen* fr. O.F.]

ex·press (iksprés) 1. *adj.* explicitly stated or laid down, *express orders* || particular, special, *he left with the express intention of calling* || specially fast, *an express cleaning service* || concerned with the specially fast transport of goods or delivery of money 2. *n.* an express train || an express rifle|| a fast service for transporting goods or delivering money || a firm which undertakes such work || the goods or money sent by express 3. *adv.* by express train || by an express delivery service || (*Br.*) by express mail [fr. F. *exprés*]

ex·press *v.t.* to state explicitly in words || to indicate by gesture or behavior || to convey implicitly, *the work expresses his attitude towards life* || (*math.*) to represent by using symbols || to send by express delivery || to press out, squeeze out || to put under pressure so as to yield an extract **to express oneself** to communicate one's meaning or feelings **ex·press·age** (iksprésidʒ) *n.* the sending of goods by express delivery || the charge made for this **ex·préss·i·ble** *adj.* [M.E. *expresse* fr. O. F. *espresser, expresser*]

ex·pres·sion (ikspréʃən) *n.* the act of expressing something thought or felt || something expressed, *expressions of gratitude* || a squeezing out || an idiom, *'give way' is a nautical expression meaning 'start rowing'* || (*math.*) a representation by symbols || (*mus.*) subjective interpreting of a passage || a look, or tone of voice, revealing what a person thinks or feels [F.]

ex·pres·sion·ism (ikspréʃənɪzəm) *n.* a mode of artistic expression in which direct communication of feeling or emotion is the main intention. Expressionist works tend to reflect feelings of despair and anxiety, and tormented or exalted states of mind. In them, images of the real world are transformed so that they correspond with these feelings or states of mind by subjective, often intense coloring, distortion of form, strong lines and dramatic contrasts. Expressionism is associated with the art of Germany and the northern countries in the late 19th and 20th cc., esp. that of Munch, Ensor, Nolde, and the Brücke and Blaue Reiter groups, though the tendency can be traced back to such masters as Bosch and Grünewald, and to medieval art. The works of van Gogh, Kokoschka and Soutine are expressionist, as are those of Rouault and others of the Fauve group. Kandinsky's work links the mode to abstract expressionism. There are expressionist elements in the drama, esp. of Strindberg, Kaiser, Brecht and O'Neill, in the music of Schönberg and Berg, and in movies, esp. 'The Cabinet of Dr Caligari' (1919) **ex·prés·sion·ist** *n. and adj.* **ex·pres·sion·ís·tic** *adj.*

ex·pres·sive (iksprésiv) *adj.* of or relating to expression || showing what a person thinks or feels [F.]

express letter (*Br.*) a special delivery letter

ex·press·ly (iksprésli:) *adv.* explicitly, *expressly forbidden* || specially, with a special or avowed intention, *he came expressly to warn you*

ex·press·man (iksprésmæn) *pl.* **ex·press·men** (iksprésmen) *n.* someone employed on express delivery work

express post (*Br.*) special delivery

express rifle a sporting rifle with a high muzzle velocity used in big-game hunting

express train a fast train making few stops

ex·press·way (ikspréswei) *n.* a wide divided road which has several lanes and limited access, and which crosses other roads at a different level, for high-speed through traffic

ex·pro·pri·ate (ekspróupri:eit) *pres. part.* **ex·pro·pri·at·ing** *past* and *past part.* **ex·pro·pri·at·ed** *v.t.* (esp. of state action) to take over (property belonging to someone else) with or without compensation || to take the ownership of property from, *to expropriate a farmer for neglect* **ex·pro·pri·á·tion**, **ex·pró·pri·a·tor** *ns* [fr. L. *expropriare* (*expropriatus*), to dispossess]

ex·pul·sion (ikspʌlʃən) *n.* an expelling or being expelled **ex·púl·sive** *adj.* serving to expel [F.]

ex·punc·tion (ikspʌ́ŋkʃən) *n.* an expunging or being expunged [fr. L. *expunctus*, marked for deletion]

ex·punge (ikspʌ́ndʒ) *pres. part.* **ex·pung·ing** *past* and *past part.* **ex·punged** *v.t.* to wipe out, erase, *to expunge a resolution from the records* [fr. L. *expungere*, to mark (a word) for deletion]

ex·pur·gate (ékspərgeit) *pres. part.* **ex·pur·gat·ing** *past* and *past part.* **ex·pur·gat·ed** *v.t.* to cut out from (a book, play, film, speech etc.) anything thought by the expurgator unsuitable for readers or an audience || to cut out (some of the text) from a book etc. **ex·pur·ga·tion**, **ex·pur·ga·tor** *ns* **ex·pur·ga·to·ri·al** (ikspə:rgətóri:əl, ikspə:rgətóuri:əl), **ex·púr·ga·to·ry** *adjs* [fr. L. *expurgare*, to clean out]

ex·qui·site (ékskwizit, ikskwízit) 1. *adj.*, showing perfection in taste or workmanship of a delicate though often elaborate kind, *exquisite embroidery* || highly sensitive to quality, *exquisite taste* 2. *n.* a mannered young man displaying overrefined taste in his dress [fr. L. *exquirere* (*exquisitus*), to seek out]

ex·san·guine (ekssǽŋgwin) *adj.* anemic, bloodless [fr. EX·+L. *sanguis*, blood]

ex·sert (ekssə́:rt) *v.t.* (*bot.*) to push out **ex·sért·ed** *adj.* (*bot.*, of a part which protrudes from the containing or surrounding part of a plant, e.g. of a stamen beyond the corolla) protruding **ex·ser·tile** (ekssə́:rt'l, ekssə́:rtil) *adj.* **ex·sér·tion** *n.* [fr. L. *exserere* (*exsertus*), to stretch out]

ex·serv·ice (ekssə́:rvis) *adj.* (*Br.*, of equipment) army or navy surplus

ex·serv·ice·man (ekssə́:rvismæn, ékssə́:rvismən) *pl.* **ex·serv·ice·men** (ekssə́:rvismen, ékssə́:rvismən) *n.* (esp. *Br.*) someone who has done service in the armed forces

ex·sic·cate (éksikeit) *pres. part.* **ex·sic·cat·ing** *past* and *past part.* **ex·sic·cat·ed** *v.t.* to dry up, make desert, by excessive cutting down of forests or by continual cultivation of land exposed to wind || to remove moisture from, dessicate or dehydrate **ex·sic·cá·tion** *n.* [fr. L. *exsiccare* (*exsiccatus*)]

ex·stip·u·late (eksstípjulit, eksstípjuleit) *adj.* (*bot.*) without stipules [fr. EX·+L. *stipula*, stalk]

ex·stro·phy (ékstrəfi:) *n.* (*med.*) the extension of an organ or part of an organ, esp. congenital malformation of the bladder [fr. EX·+Gk *strophein*, to turn]

ex·tant (ikstǽnt, ékstənt) *adj.* still in existence, esp. of books or documents not lost or destroyed in the course of time [fr. L. *exstans* (*exstantis*) *pres. part.* of *exstare*, to stand forth]

ex·tem·po·ra·ne·ous (ikstempəréini:əs) *adj.* extempore [fr. L.L. *extemporaneus* fr. *ex*, outside+*tempus* (*temporis*), time]

ex·tem·po·rar·i·ly (ikstempəréərili:) *adv.* extempore

ex·tem·po·rar·y (ikstémpərəri) *adj.* extempore [EXTEMPORE]

ex·tem·po·re (ikstémpəri:) 1. *adv.* without advance preparation, on the spur of the moment 2. *adj.* made or done on the spur of the moment **ex·tem·po·ri·za·tion** (ikstempərizéiʃən) *n.* an extemporizing or something extemporized **ex·tém·po·rize** *pres. part.* **ex·tem·po·riz·ing** *past* and *past part.* **ex·tem·po·rized** *v.i.* to speak or act without advance preparation || *v.t.* to compose, speak, act etc. (something) extempore [L. *ex tempore*, out of time, without time]

ex·tend (iksténd) *v.t.* to lengthen in space or time, *to extend a road, extend a holiday* || to make wider, greater or more inclusive, *to extend the meaning of a word by analogy* || to stretch (one's body) at or to full length || to hold out, *arms extended in supplication* || (*mil.*) to spread out with a regular distance between (men), *troops thinly extended along a riverbank* || to tax the powers of, stretch || to write out (notes etc.) in a full or fuller form || (with 'to') to offer, *to extend an invitation to someone* || (with 'to') to make available, *to extend financial help to someone* || (*bookkeeping*) to carry forward (figures, an entry) || (*Br., law*) to assess || (*Br., law*) to seize (land etc.) by a writ of extent || *v.i.* to stretch out *in* space or time || to reach, *his knowledge of mathematics does not extend to calculus* **ex·ténd·ed** *adj.* lengthened || relatively long || stretched out || compelled to put forth a great effort || enlarged in scope, meaning etc. || widespread || (*printing*, of type) having a wider face than is normal for the height **ex·ténd·er** *n.* a substance used to adulterate, dilute or otherwise modify a product **ex·ténd·i·**

ble, **ex·ténd·a·ble** *adj.* capable of being extended **ex·ten·si·ble** (iksténsəb'l) *adj.* extendible || (of the tongue) capable of being protruded [fr. L. *extendere* (*extensus*), to stretch out]

Extended Binary Coded Decimal Interchange Code (*computer*) a code for alphanumeric information using eight binary positions for each character

extended care facility term used by Medicare at one time to mean a skilled nursing facility qualified for participation in Medicare; amended in 1972 to mean a generic skilled nursing facility for both Medicare and Medicaid **extended care services** *n. pl. abbr.* ECF

extended family family unit consisting of three or more generations living together

ex·ten·sile (iksténsəl, *Br.* iksténsail) *adj.* extensible [fr. L. *extensus* fr. *extendere*, to stretch out]

ex·ten·sion (iksténʃən) *n.* an extending or being extended || something added so as to make longer or bigger, *a canal extension, a hotel extension* || an extra allowance of time, e.g. for paying a debt, finishing a game, or deferring army service || (*logic*) the class of things which a general term can designate, denotation || (*phys.*) the state of having magnitude in three-dimensional space || (*med.*) the stretching of a limb to enable the ends of a broken bone to fit accurately together || a telephone subconnection to a particular room in a building || the making available of resources or services (e.g. of a central library) to people to whom they are not immediately available, or the system which achieves this [fr. L. *extensio* (*extensionis*)]

extension ladder a set of ladders which can either be used independently or linked lengthwise

extension spring a spring of close tight coils which resist a force pulling along the length

ex·ten·sive (iksténsiv) *adj.* covering a wide area, *extensive forests* || great in scope, *extensive documentation* || (*farming*) based on the use of a big area of land with minimum upkeep and expenses (e.g. cattle ranching or sheep farming, cf. INTENSIVE) [fr. L.L. *extensivus* fr. *extendere*, to stretch out]

ex·ten·sor (iksténsər) *n.* a muscle which straightens or stretches a limb (opp. FLEXOR) [L.L. fr. *extendere*, to stretch out]

ex·tent (ikstént) *n.* the length to which a thing stretches or reaches or the area it covers || a very large area, *the whole extent of the kingdom* || amount or degree, *to what extent is Ghana industrialized?* || compass, *within the extent of a person's jurisdiction* || limit, *to the full extent of a person's allowance* [M.E. *extente* fr. A.F.]

ex·ten·u·ate (iksténju:eit) *pres. part.* **ex·ten·u·at·ing** *past* and *past part.* **ex·ten·u·at·ed** *v.t.* to lessen the gravity of (a crime, fault, mistake etc.) by allowing or suggesting a mitigating circumstance **ex·tén·u·at·ing** *adj.* **ex·ten·u·á·tion** *n.* **ex·ten·u·a·to·ry** (iksténju:ətɔri:, iksténju:ətouri) *adj.* [fr. L. *extenuare* (*extenuatus*), to make thin]

ex·te·ri·or (ikstíəri:ər) 1. *adj.* outer (opp. INTERIOR) || visible from or on the outside, *no exterior signs of injury* 2. *n.* the outside, e.g. of a building (opp. INTERIOR) || outward appearance or manner, *a forbidding exterior* || (*movies*) a background or scene filmed outdoors [L., comp. of *exterus*, outside]

exterior angle (*math.*) the angle between any side of a polygon and the extension of an adjacent side || (*math.*) the angle made by a transversal outside either of a pair of straight lines which it intersects

ex·te·ri·or·ize (ikstíəri:əraiz) *pres. part.* **ex·te·ri·or·iz·ing** *past* and *past part.* **ex·te·ri·or·ized** *v.t.* to externalize

ex·ter·mi·nate (ikstə́:rmineit) *pres. part.* **ex·ter·mi·nat·ing** *past* and *past part.* **ex·ter·mi·nat·ed** *v.t.* to destroy, wipe out, get rid of completely, *to exterminate weeds, to exterminate poverty* **ex·ter·mi·ná·tion** *n.* **ex·ter·mi·na·tive** (ikstə́:rmineitiv, ikstə́:rminətiv) *adj.* **ex·tér·mi·na·tor** *n.* **ex·ter·mi·na·to·ry** (ikstə́:rminətɔri:, ikstə́:rminətouri) *adj.* [fr. L. *exterminare* (*exterminatus*), to drive beyond the boundaries]

ex·tern (ékstə:rn) *n.* a person who works in an institution and does not live in it, e.g. a nonresident doctor in a hospital [F. *externe*]

ex·ter·nal (ikstə́:rn'l) 1. *adj.* situated on, pertaining to, or derived from the outside (opp. INTERNAL) || merely superficial, not backed by feeling or conviction || on the outside of the body, *alcohol for external use only* || (of state

---

affairs) foreign ‖ of what lies outside the mind, *external reality* **2.** *n.* (*pl.*) outward appearances **ex·ter·nal·i·ty** (ɛkstəːrnǽliti:) *n.* [fr. L. *externus*]

external angle (*math.*) an exterior angle **ex·ter·nal·ize** (ikstə́ːrnˈlaiz) *pres. part.* **ex·ter·nal·iz·ing** *past and past part.* **ex·ter·nal·ized** *v.t.* to attribute external reality to, *to externalize one's fears* ‖ to express in outward form

extern sister a lay sister of a strictly enclosed order (e.g. Carmelites) who lives in the convent but outside the enclosure, and so can attend to outside business

ex·ter·o·cep·tive (ɛkstərəséptiv) *adj.* (*physiol.*) capable of receiving impressions or stimuli from outside, used in receiving these, or concerned with receiving these. e.g. through the senses (cf. INTEROCEPTIVE, cf. PROPRIOCEPTIVE) [fr. L. *exter*, outside+RECEPTIVE]

ex·ter·o·cep·tor (ɛkstərəséptər) *n.* (*physiol.*) a nerve ending or end organ which responds to impressions or stimuli outside the organism [Mod. L. fr. *exter*, outside+RECEPTOR]

ex·ter·ri·to·ri·al (ɛksteritóːriːəl, ɛkstitóuriːəl) *adj.* extraterritorial **ex·ter·ri·to·ri·al·i·ty** *n.*

ex·tinct (ikstíŋkt) *adj.* (of a fire, flame etc.) put out, burnt out ‖ (of a volcano) no longer active ‖ (of passions, hopes) no longer entertained ‖ (of species) died out, no longer found ‖ (of a title or office) no longer existing, either because abolished or because there is no one to carry it on [fr. L. *exstinguere* (*exstinctus*), to put out]

ex·tinc·tion (ikstíŋkʃən) *n.* (of fire etc.) an extinguishing or being extinguished ‖ a making or becoming extinct ‖ an annihilating or being annihilated **ex·tinc·tive** *adj.* serving or tending to extinguish [fr. L. *extinctio* (*extinctionis*)]

ex·tin·guish (ikstíŋgwiʃ) *v.t.* to put out (a fire, light etc.) ‖ to put an end to, destroy (hope etc.) ‖ to outshine completely (another person or thing) ‖ to silence (an opponent) ‖ to wipe out (a debt) ‖ (*law*) to make null **ex·tin·guish·er** *n.* a fire extinguisher ‖ a small hollow metal cone, sometimes attached to a rod, for putting out candles ‖ someone who extinguishes [fr. L. *extinguere*]

ex·tir·pate (ɛkstərpeit) *pres. part.* **ex·tir·pat·ing** *past and past part.* **ex·tir·pat·ed** *v.t.* to root out, get rid of, utterly destroy **ex·tir·pa·tion**, **ex·tir·pa·tor** *ns* [fr. L. *exstirpare* (*exstirpatus*)]

ex·tol, ex·toll (ikstóul, ikstɔ́l) *pres. part.* **ex·tol·ling, ex·toll·ing** *past and past part.* **ex·tolled** *v.t.* to praise enthusiastically [fr. L. *extollere*, to raise up]

ex·tort (ikstɔ́rt) *v.t.* to obtain by force, threats, deception etc., *to extort money by blackmail* ‖ to force (a meaning, conclusion etc.) from words which cannot reasonably yield it [fr. L. *extorguere* (*extortus*), to twist out]

ex·tor·tion (ikstɔ́rʃən) *n.* an extorting, esp. of money, overcharging **ex·tór·tion·ate** *adj.* using extortion ‖ (of prices or charges) much greater than is fair or reasonable **ex·tór·tion·er, ex·tór·tion·ist** *ns* [fr. L. *extortio* (*extortionis*)]

ex·tra (ɛkstrə) **1.** *adj.* over and above what is usual or normal ‖ (*commerce*) of superior quality **2.** *n.* an extra charge ‖ something for which an extra charge is made ‖ (*movies*) a person hired to take part in crowd scenes etc. ‖ a special (esp. a late) edition of a newspaper ‖ (*cricket*) a run (a bye, leg bye, no ball or wide) conceded by the fielding side but not scored by a batsman **3.** *adv.* more than usually, very [shortened from EXTRAORDINARY and fr. L. *extra*, more than, outside]

extra- (ɛkstrə) *prefix* outside or beyond a thing, not coming within its scope [fr. L. adv. and prep.]

ex·tra·chro·mo·som·al (ɛkstrəkroumə́soumәl) *n.* (*genetics*) affected by elements in addition to the chromosomes

ex·tra·cor·po·re·al (ɛkstrəkɔrpvɔ́riːəl) *adj.* of elements outside the body **extracorporeally** *adv.*

extra cover (*cricket*) a position between cover point and mid off ‖ the fielder in this position

ex·tract 1. (ɛkstrækt) *n.* a passage taken from a book, speech, letter etc. ‖ a concentrated essence, used esp. for flavoring, *coffee extract* ‖ the solid or semisolid matter which remains of a substance after evaporation of moisture or the use of solvents **2.** (ikstrækt) *v.t.* to draw, pull or otherwise take out, *to extract a tooth* ‖ to obtain (an essence, juice etc.) by pressure, distillation, evaporation, treatment with a solvent etc. ‖ to obtain esp. by force or with difficulty, *to extract a subscription* ‖ to obtain (a substance) from the raw materials in which it is contained, *to* *extract copper from ore* ‖ to pick out (a passage from a book, speech, document etc.), to extract figures from a balance sheet ‖ (*math.*) to find (the root of a number) **ex·tráct·a·ble** *adj.* **ex·trác·tor** *n.* a device for extracting, esp. one which extracts the spent round from a gun [fr. L. *extrahere* (*extractus*)]

ex·trac·tion (ikstrǽkʃən) *n.* the act or process of extracting, esp. the pulling out of a tooth ‖ something extracted, *rennet is an extraction from the lining of a cow's stomach* ‖ descent, lineage, *Welsh by extraction* [fr. L. *extractio* (*tractionis*)]

extraction rate the proportion of flour obtained from 100 lbs. of grain ‖ the proportion of mineral or metal obtained from an ore

ex·trac·tive (ikstrǽktiv) **1.** *adj.* serving to extract ‖ based on extraction, *an extractive process* ‖ like or of the nature of an extract ‖ capable of being extracted **2.** *n.* something extracted, *oil of almonds is an extractive* [L. *extrahere* (*extractus*), to extract]

ex·tra·cur·ric·u·lar (ɛkstrəkəríkjulər) *adj.* (of debating, dramatics etc.) outside the regular courses of academic studies

ex·tra·dit·a·ble (ɛkstrədáitəbˈl) *adj.* (of a crime) for which a person may be extradited ‖ (of a person) liable to extradition

ex·tra·dite (ɛkstrədait) *pres. part.* **ex·tra·dit·ing** *past and past part.* **ex·tra·dit·ed** *v.t.* to hand over for extradition ‖ to obtain the extradition of (a criminal suspect or fugitive) from another country or state [back-formation fr. EXTRADITION]

ex·tra·di·tion (ɛkstrədíʃən) *n.* the handing over by a country or state, usually in accordance with a treaty, of a criminal suspect or fugitive, to the country or state having jurisdiction in his case [F. fr. L. *ex-*, out of + *traditio* (*traditionis*), a delivering up]

ex·tra·dos (ɛkstréidɒs, ɛkstrɑdɒs) *n.* the outer surface of an arch or vault (cf. INTRADOS) [F.]

ex·tra·ju·di·cial (ɛkstrədʒuːdíʃəl) *adj.* outside the authority of a legal court ‖ extraneous to the case being tried ‖ (of a confession) not made in court ‖ (of an opinion) unofficial, not given in the speaker's judicial capacity

ex·tra·life·e·con·o·mat·ic (ɛkstrəlaifɛkənoumǽtik) *adj.* (*insurance*) of ordinary life insurance that provides additional ordinary and term insurance from normally accumulating dividends

ex·tra·mar·i·tal (ɛkstrəmǽritˈl) *adj.* of sexual relations outside marriage

ex·tra·mun·dane (ɛkstrəmʌ́ndein, ɛkstrəmʌndéin) *adj.* outside the material world [fr. L.L. *extramundanus*]

ex·tra·mu·ral (ɛkstrəmjúərəl) *adj.* (of university courses and lectures) for students not resident members of the university ‖ existing outside the walls (of a city or fortress) [fr. L. *extramuros*, outside the walls]

ex·tra·ne·ous (ikstréiniːəs) *adj.* coming from outside, *extraneous influences* ‖ not essentially belonging to the matter in question, *to cut out extraneous detail* [fr. L. *extraneus*, external, foreign]

ex·traor·di·nar·i·ly (ikstrɔ́rdˈnerili:) *adv.* to an extraordinary degree ‖ in an extraordinary way

ex·traor·di·nar·y (ikstrɔ́rdˈneri:) *adj.* beyond what is normal or ordinary, *he called for extraordinary powers* ‖ bizarre ‖ astonishing, *extraordinary good luck* ‖ (of an official) specially appointed, serving in addition to the officials regularly appointed and usually for some particular mission [fr. L. *extraoroinarius* fr. *extra ordinem*, outside the usual order]

ex·tra·pa·ro·chi·al (ɛkstrəpəróuki:əl) *adj.* (*Br.*) outside the parish

ex·tra·phys·i·cal (ɛkstrəfízik'l) *adj.* not subject to physical laws or methods

ex·trap·o·lat·a·bil·i·ty (ɛkstrǽpələitəbíliti:) *n.* capable of extrapolating or of being extrapolated

ex·trap·o·late (ikstrǽpəleit) *pres. part.* **ex·trap·o·lat·ing** *past and past part.* **ex·trap·o·lat·ed** *v.t.* to determine from known values (other values), making the assumption that what applies to known data would apply to similar unknown data **ex·trap·o·la·tion** *n.* [fr. EXTRA-+INTERPOLATE]

ex·tra·sen·so·ry (ɛkstrəsénsəri:) *adj.* outside the senses, involving a source other than the senses, *extrasensory perception*

ex·tra·so·lar (ɛkstrəsóulɒr) *adj.* from outside the solar system

ex·tra·ter·res·tri·al (ɛkstrətərréstri:əl) **1.** *adj.* outside the earth or its atmosphere **2.** *n.* one from outside the earth

ex·tra·ter·ri·to·ri·al (ɛkstrəteritóːriːəl, ɛkstrəteritóuriːəl) *adj.* relating to the fiction which considers an embassy as detached from the country in which it is situated and frees the diplomats sent there from the jurisdiction of that country **ex·tra·ter·ri·to·ri·al·i·ty** *n.*

ex·trav·a·gance (ikstrǽvəgəns) *n.* a being extravagant or an instance of this [F.]

ex·trav·a·gant (ikstrǽvəgənt) *adj.* spending more money than one can afford, or spending foolishly, carelessly or wastefully ‖ using too much of anything involving expense, *she is a good cook but extravagant with butter* ‖ going beyond what is reasonable, justified or normal, *extravagant praise for such second-rate acting* ‖ exaggerated, overemphatic, *extravagant language* [F.]

ex·trav·a·gan·za (ikstrævəgǽnzə) *n.* a freely imaginative or fanciful musical stage entertainment, esp. farce or burlesque [fr. Ital. *estravaganza*]

ex·trav·a·sate (ikstrǽvəseit) *pres. part.* **ex·trav·a·sat·ing** *past and past part.* **ex·trav·a·sat·ed** *v.t.* (*med.*) to cause to flow from its proper vessel, esp. to cause (blood) to flow from a blood vessel into the surrounding tissues ‖ to cause (lava etc.) to erupt ‖ *v.i.* (*med.*) to flow out of a proper vessel ‖ (*geol.*) to issue from a fissure **ex·trav·a·sá·tion** *n.* [fr. L. *extra*, outside+*vas*, vessel]

ex·tra·ver·sion (ɛkstrəvɔ́ːrʒən, ɛkstrəvɔ́ːrʃən) *n.* extroversion

ex·tra·vert (ɛkstrəvəːrt) *n.* an extrovert

ex·tra·vert·ed (ɛkstrəvəːrtid) *adj.* extroverted

ex·treme (ikstríːm) **1.** *adj.* furthest out, furthest from the center, *the girl on the extreme right* ‖ utmost, maximum, *the extreme limit of endurance* ‖ very great, with as great a degree as possible of whatever is referred to, *extreme danger, extreme cold* ‖ (of views, opinions etc. and those who hold them) not moderate, esp. far to the left or right ‖ as severe and forcible as possible, *extreme measures* **2.** *n.* (esp. *pl.*) the highest or extreme degree (generally of two opposites), *extremes of heat and cold* ‖ either end of a whole range, *extremes of temperature* ‖ (*pl.*) extreme measures, actions, views etc., *to drive someone to extremes* ‖ (*math.*) the first or last term of a series or ratio ‖ (*logic*) the subject or predicate of a proposition ‖ the major or minor term of a syllogism **in the extreme** in the highest degree, extremely, *boring in the extreme* **to go to extremes** to adopt extreme measures or views or take extreme action **ex·tréme·ly** *adv.* very, exceedingly [O.F.]

Extreme Unction (*Catholic and Eastern Churches*) the sacrament administered by a priest to a sick person in danger of death. It consists of anointing and prayer. It is called 'extreme' because it is the last sacrament in the series which begins with baptism

ex·trem·ism (ikstríːmizəm) *n.* the quality, state or habit of going to extremes (in views or actions)

ex·trem·ist (ikstríːmist) **1.** *adj.* going or inclined to go to extremes in views or actions **2.** *n.* someone of this nature

ex·trem·i·ty (ikstrémiti:) *pl.* **ex·trem·i·ties** *n.* the very end, the tip ‖ (*pl.*) the most distant parts, *the utmost extremities of the earth* ‖ (*pl.*) the hands and feet, esp. the fingers and toes, sometimes the tip of the nose, ears and chin ‖ a situation involving great trouble, difficulty or danger, *for use in an extremity* ‖ extremeness (of views or actions) ‖ (*rhet.*) the utmost degree of emotion, *in the extremity of his anguish* ‖ the limit, *the extremity of one's endurance* ‖ (esp. *pl.*) an extreme measure, *both sides were guilty of extremities* [fr. F. *extrémité*]

ex·tri·cate (ɛkstrikeit) *pres. part.* **ex·tri·cat·ing** *past and past part.* **ex·tri·cat·ed** *v.t.* to disentangle or free (a person or thing) from some tangle, difficulty, danger or muddle **ex·tri·cá·tion** *n.* [fr. L. *extricare* (*extricatus*) fr. *ex*, out+*tricae*, worries]

ex·trin·sic (ikstrínsik) *adj.* working from outside, *extrinsic factors in an illness* ‖ not part of the essential nature of a thing, *considerations extrinsic to a problem* ‖ (*anat.*, of muscles, e.g. the tongue muscles) not completely contained in the organs which they move (cf. INTRINSIC) **ex·trín·si·cal·ly** *adv.* [fr. F. *extrinsèque*]

ex·trorse (ɛkstrɔ́rs) *adj.* (*bot.*, esp. of an anther) turned away from the center of the plant (cf. INTRORSE) [F.]

ex·tro·ver·sion (ˌɛkstrəvə́ːrʒən, ˌɛkstrəvə́ːrʃən) *n.* the psychological state of an extrovert ‖ a manifestation of this (opp. INTROVERSION) [fr. EXTRA-+L. *vertere (versus)*, to turn]

ex·tro·vert (ékstrəvəːrt) *n.* a person interested and taking pleasure more in what happens outside him than in his own emotions or states of mind (opp. INTROVERT) [fr. EXTRA-+L. *vertere (versus)*, to turn]

ex·tro·vert·ed (ékstrəvəːrtid) *adj.* having the characteristics of an extrovert [alt. of G. *extrovertiert*]

ex·trude (ikstrúːd) *pres. part.* **ex·trud·ing** *past and past part.* **ex·trud·ed** *v.t.* to form (a tube, rod or other object) by forcing hot or soft metal, rubber or plastic through an aperture ‖ to cause to protrude, stick out ‖ to cause to emerge ‖ *v.i.* to undergo shaping by being extruded ‖ to stick out, protrude **ex·tru·sive** (ikstrúːsiv) *adj.* (*geol.*, of rocks) formed above ground by the solidification of lava [fr. L. *extrudere* fr. *ex*, out+*trudere*, to thrust]

ex·tru·sion (ikstrúːʒən) *n.* the process of extruding (metal, rubber or plastic) ‖ the shape or object so made ‖ (*geol.*) a substance, e.g. lava, extruding from a fissure [fr. L. *extrudere (extrusus)*, to thrust out]

ex·u·ber·ance (igzúːbərəns) *n.* the state or quality of being exuberant, or an instance of it [F. fr. L. *exuberantia*]

ex·u·ber·ant (igzúːbərənt) *adj.* bubbling over with joy, high spirits, enthusiasm, health etc. ‖ abundant in growth, *exuberant vegetation* ‖ unrestrainedly inventive, *an exuberant imagination* [fr. L. *exuberans (exuberantis)* fr. *exuberare*, to be fertile]

ex·u·date (éksjudeit) *n.* exuded matter, esp. the mixture of serum, fibrin and white corpuscles exuding from blood vessels into an inflamed or damaged area **ex·u·da·tion** *n.*

exudation sweating

ex·ude (igzjúːd, iksúːd) *pres. part.* **ex·ud·ing** *past and past part.* **ex·ud·ed** *v.t.* to ooze with, to cause to ooze ‖ to give off, emit, *the old chest exuded a smell of camphor* ‖ *v.i.* to ooze out in small drops [fr. L. *exudare, exsudare*, to sweat]

ex·ult (igzʌ́lt) *v.i.* to feel and express tremendous joy ‖ (with 'over') to rejoice in the defeat of a rival **ex·ult·an·cy** *n.* **ex·ult·ant** *adj.* **ex·ul·ta·tion** (ˌegzʌltéiʃən, ˌeksʌltéiʃən) *n.* [fr. F. *exulter*]

ex·u·vi·ae (igzúːviːiː) *pl. n.* anything that an animal sloughs or casts off, e.g. a snake's skin or a crab's shell **ex·u·vi·al** (igzúːviːəl) *adj.* **ex·u·vi·ate** (igzúːviːeit) *pres. part.* **ex·u·vi·at·ing** *past and past part.* **ex·u·vi·at·ed** *v.t.* to cast off or slough ‖ *v.i.* to molt **ex·u·vi·a·tion** *n.* fr. L. *exuviae*, things stripped off]

ex·vo·to (eksvóutou) *n.* a tablet, inscription or other votive offering put up in a chapel out of gratitude for a favor granted or in fulfillment of a vow [L.= after a vow]

-ey *suffix* a variant of -y, esp. after y

ey·as (áiəs) *n.* a young hawk or falcon taken from its nest for training [alt. fr. *nias* fr. F. *niais*]

Eyck *VAN EYCK

eye (ai) **1.** *n.* an organ of sight that converts light impinging on it into nervous impulses. In vertebrates the impulses travel from the eye via the optic nerve to the brain, where they produce the sensation of seeing ‖ the iris or colored part of the eyeball, *hazel eyes* ‖ the part around the eyes, *eyes swollen from sleeplessness* ‖ the power of seeing, *she is slowly losing her eyes* ‖ the power of judging and appreciating what one sees, *a good eye for country, an eye for a pretty girl* ‖ a thing like an eye in shape, e.g. the hole for the thread in a needle, the marking on a peacock's tail, the leaf bud of a potato ‖ (often *pl.*) judgment, *in the eyes of the law* ‖ (*meteor.*) the low-pressure center of e.g. a hurricane ‖ an aperture allowing the entry of light, esp. the lens of a camera **all eyes** intently looking, *they were all eyes as the presents were opened* **an eye for an eye** full revenge **by eye** on an estimate made by just looking and not by using an instrument, *to measure a piece of wood by eye* **in the eye of the wind** (*naut.*) in the direction of the wind **my eye!** nonsense! **to catch a person's eye** to attract a person's attention by

intercepting his glance, *catch the chairman's eye* or by being noticeable, *the window display caught her eye* **to close** (or **shut**) **one's eyes to** to pretend not to see, purposely overlook **to cry one's eyes out** to weep bitterly **to get one's eye in** (*Br.*, ball games) to become accustomed to judging the flight of the ball in play **to have an eye to** to be on the lookout for, *to have an eye to a quick profit* **to have** (or **use**) **half an eye** to be not entirely blind or stupid, *if you had half an eye you would see that it won't go through the doorway* **to have one's eye on** to watch with interest and approval ‖ to keep under observation (as being suspicious) **to keep an eye on** to remember to think about, *keep an eye on the time or we'll be late* ‖ to take responsibility for, *keep an eye on the children* ‖ to keep under observation **to keep an eye out for** to be on the lookout for **to keep one's eye on** to look steadily at **to keep one's eyes open** (or **peeled** or **skinned**) to keep a good lookout **to make eyes at** to try to attract (a girl) by a show of interest **to make someone's eyes open** to astonish someone **to open someone's eyes to (something)** to make someone understand or realize (something) **to run one's eye over** (or **through**) to look quickly at, examine quickly (a letter, accounts etc.) **to see eye to eye** to agree **to set eyes on** to catch sight of **to the eye** superficially **to turn a blind eye** to choose not to notice **under one's very eyes** right in front of one, openly **up to the eyes in** wretchedly busy with, *up to the eyes in reading proofs* ‖ overwhelmed by, *up to the eyes in debt* **with an eye to** (or **for**, or **on**) with (something specified) in mind, *designed with an eye to comfort* **with one's eyes open** with full understanding of what is involved **2.** *v.t. pres. part.* **ey·ing**, **ey·ing** *past and past part.* **eyed** to look attentively at ‖ to make an eye in (a rope) ‖ to remove the leaf buds of (a potato) [O.E. *ēage*]

—The human eye is an approximately spherical ball, the muscles which move it being attached to the tough outer lining (the sclera or 'white of the eye'). The sclera is replaced in front by the transparent cornea, and has a central aperture (pupil) surrounded by a colored iris. Light travels through the cornea and then through a lens which focuses it on the inner lining of the sphere (the retina). The light falling upon the retina stimulates nerve impulses that are transmitted along sensory paths of the optic nerve to the brain. Different cells in the retina function so as to provide color vision and vision in dim light. The shape of the lens may be altered by the degree of contraction of its suspensory muscles. The amount of light entering is controlled by the size of the pupil in the center of the iris. These mechanisms allow for optimum vision of objects at varying distances and in varying degrees of brightness

eye·ball (áibɔl) *n.* the globe of the eye of vertebrates, made up of the sclera and cornea and the structures they contain ‖ the eye itself

eye·ball-to·eye·ball (áibɔltuːáibɔl) *adj.* direct, in close confrontation **eyeball to eyeball** *adv.*

eye·bath (áibæθ, áibɑθ) *n.* (*Br.*) an eyecup

eye·bolt (áiboult) *n.* a bolt with a ring or hole in the shaft, instead of the normal flat head, used for lifting

eye·bright (áibrait) *n.* a plant of the genus *Euphrasia*, esp. *E. officinalis*, formerly used for treating eye ailments (*EUPHRASIA)

eye·brow (áibrau) *n.* the curved ridge over the eye ‖ the hair which grows along it **to raise one's eyebrows** to show surprise (esp. at a moral or social slip)

eye·catch·er (áikætʃər) *n.* something that cannot fail to attract attention **éyecatch·ing** *adj.*

eye contact looking directly into people's eyes

eye·cup (áikʌp) *n.* (*Am.*=*Br.* eyebath) a small cup for bathing the eyes

eye·ful (áiful) *pl.* **eye·fuls** *n.* a quantity of something thrown in the eyes **to get an eyeful** to get a good look

eye·glass (áiglæs, áiglɑs) *n.* a monocle ‖ the eyepiece of an optical instrument ‖ (*pl.*) spectacles

eye·hole (áihoul) *n.* a hole, e.g. in a door, through which one can peep ‖ a hole made to take a thread, rope, hook etc., an eyelet

eye·lash (áilæʃ) *n.* one of the hairs growing on the edge of the eyelid

eye·less (áilis) *adj.* (*rhet.*) without sight

eye·let (áilit) *n.* a small hole, often with a metal rim, through which a thread, lace, line etc. can be passed ‖ the metal rim [M.E. *oilet* fr. F. *oeillet* dim. of *oeil*, eye]

eye·lid (áilid) *n.* one of the skins that can be moved to cover the eye

eye·o·pen·er (áioupənər) *n.* something that astonishes one by a sudden revelation of the truth

eye·piece (áipiːs) *n.* (*phys.*) the lens or lens system of an optical instrument (e.g. telescope, microscope) that magnifies the image formed by the objective

eye rhyme a rhyme in which two words appear from their spelling to rhyme, but do not in fact do so, e.g. 'cough' and 'tough', 'warm' and 'harm'

eye·shade (áiʃeid) *n.* a shield for the eyes against strong light worn on the forehead and held in place by a band around the back of the head

eye shadow a cosmetic cream made in various colors and applied to the eyelids to enhance eye beauty

eye·shot (áiʃɒt) *n.* range of vision, eyesight

eye·sight (áisait) *n.* the power of vision, *good eyesight* ‖ range of vision *within eyesight*

eyes only code word on classified or private documents limiting their distribution to the one person to whom they are addressed

eye·sore (áisɔr, áisour) *n.* something that offends by its ugliness

eye splice a loop made by turning back the end of a rope and splicing this into itself

eye·spot (áispɒt) *n.* (*biol.*) a pigment spot in many lower plants, e.g. chlamydomonas, supposed to have a visual function ‖ an ocellus

eye·stalk (áistɔk) *n.* (*zool.*) one of the peduncles which carry the eyes of such animals as lobsters or crabs

eye·strain (áistrein) *n.* tiredness or strain of the eyes, caused by untreated faulty vision or excessively hard usage of the eyes

eye·tooth (áituːθ) *pl.* **eye·teeth** (áitiːθ) *n.* one of the two upper canine teeth

eye·wall (áiwɔl) *n.* (*meteor.*) turbulent clouds in the shape of a funnel, surrounding the calm center of a storm **also** wall cloud

eye·wash (áiwɔʃ, áiwɒʃ) *n.* a lotion for bathing the eyes ‖ words or actions intended to hoodwink a person and conceal the true state of affairs ‖ superficial cleaning or similar pretense calculated to create a good impression merely, or ward off unfavorable comment

eye·wit·ness (áiwítnis) **1.** *n.* a person who actually saw a crime, accident etc. take place **2.** *adj.* emanating from such a person, *an eyewitness account*

eye worm a member of *Thelazia*, a parasitic nematode worm found under the eyelid and in the tear duct of men and certain domestic animals, sometimes causing blindness ‖ *Loa loa*, an African filarial worm found in the human eyeball ‖ a nematode worm found under the nictitating membrane of birds, including fowls

Ey·lau, Battle of (áilau) a bloody but indecisive battle (1807) between the French and the allied Russian and Prussian armies in E. Prussia during the Napoleonic Wars

Eyre (eər) a shallow salt lake (area 3,430 sq. miles) in South Australia, 39 ft below sea level and often dried up

eyrie *AERIE

E·ze·ki·el (izíːkiːəl) a Major Prophet (early 6th c. B.C.) of the Old Testament. He prophesied the overthrow of Judah and, during the Babylonian Captivity, he inspired the Jews with hope of the moral and social revival of Israel and Judah ‖ the book of the Old Testament which contains his prophecies

Ez·ra (ézrə) a Hebrew priest and scribe who returned (c. 400 B.C.) to Jerusalem from exile in Babylon ‖ the book of the Old Testament which bears his name. It describes the return of the Jews from captivity (c. 538 B.C.–400 B.C.) and the rebuilding of the Temple (and city) of Jerusalem, and records the decree barring marriage with Gentiles

CONCISE PRONUNCIATION KEY: **(a)** æ, c**a**t; ɑ, c**a**r; ɔ f**aw**n; ei, sn**a**ke. **(e)** e, h**e**n; iː, sh**ee**p; iə, d**ee**r; ɛə, b**ea**r. **(i)** i, f**i**sh; ai, t**i**ger; əː, b**i**rd. **(o)** o, **o**x; au, c**ow**; ou, g**oa**t; u, p**oo**r; ɔi, r**oy**al. **(u)** ʌ, d**u**ck; u, b**u**ll; uː, g**oo**se; ə, b**a**cillus; juː, c**u**be. x, lo**ch**; θ, **th**ink; ð, bo**th**er; z, **Z**en; ʒ, corsa**g**e; dʒ, sava**g**e; ŋ, orangutan**g**; j, **y**ak; ʃ, **f**ish; tʃ, fe**tch**; 'l, rabb**le**; 'n, redd**en**. Complete pronunciation key appears inside front cover.

EARLY NORTH SEMITIC	PHOENICIAN	EARLY HEBREW (GEZER)	EARLY GREEK	CLASSICAL GREEK	ETRUSCAN		EARLY LATIN	CLASSICAL LATIN
					Early	Classical		
(w)	(w)	(w)	(w)	(w)	(w)	(w)		

CURSIVE MAJUSCULE (ROMAN)	CURSIVE MINUSCULE (ROMAN)	ANGLO-IRISH MAJUSCULE	CAROLINE MINUSCULE	VENETIAN MINUSCULE (ITALIC)	N. ITALIAN MINUSCULE (ROMAN)

A. C. SYLVESTER, CAMBRIDGE, ENGLAND

Development of the letter F, beginning with the early North Semitic letter. Evolution of both the majuscule, or capital, letter F and the minuscule, or lowercase, letter f are shown.

F, f (ef) the sixth letter of the English alphabet ‖ (*mus.*) a note and the key of which it is the tonic **F. Fahrenheit**

fa (fa) *n.* (*mus.*) the note F in the fixed-do system of solmization ‖ (*mus.*) the fourth note of any diatonic scale in movable-do solmization

Fa·bi·an (féibi:ən) **1.** *adj.* of or resembling the tactics of Fabius Maximus Verrucosus ‖ of or relating to the Fabian Society **2.** *n.* a member of that society

Fabian Society a British socialist society founded (1883–4) to promote socialism by gradual reforms. It was influential in setting up (1900) the Labour party. Early members included Sidney and Beatrice Webb, Bernard Shaw and H. G. Wells

Fa·bi·us Max·i·mus Ver·ru·co·sus (féibi:əsmæksəməsveru:kóuzəs), Quintus 'Cunctator' (c. 275–203 B.C.), Roman statesman and general. He was called 'Cunctator' ('the delayer') on account of his tactics of harrying the Carthaginians while avoiding pitched battles, during the 2nd Punic War (218–201 B.C.)

Fa·bi·us Pic·tor (féibi:əspíktɔr), Quintus (*b.* c. 254 B.C.), one of the first Roman historians. His annals traced the history of Rome from its origins, and were used as a source by Livy. He wrote in Greek

fa·ble (féib'l) *n.* a fanciful, epigrammatic story, usually illustrating a moral precept or ethical observation. The characters are often animals, gifted with speech, and possessing the human traits commonly attributed to them (*AESOP, *LA FONTAINE), or they may be gods, persons, or things ‖ (*pop.*) a falsehood [F.]

fa·bled (féib'ld) *adj.* celebrated in legend ‖ fictitious, falsely boasted, *so much for his fabled prowess on skis!* [fr. obs. *fable* v., to tell stories about]

fab·li·au (fǽbli:ou) *pl.* **fab·li·aux** (fǽbli:ouz) *n.* a short story in verse, often coarsely satirical, in French poetry of the 12th and 13th cc., treating comically some scene from middle-class life [fr. O. F. *fabliaux*, pl.]

Fa·bre (fæbr), Jean Henri (1823–1915), French entomologist and writer. His chief work was 'Souvenirs entomologiques' (10 vols, 1870–99). Nobel prize for literature (1910)

fab·ric (fǽbrik) *n.* woven stuff, *textile fabric* ‖ a framework, structure, *the fabric of the roof is affected, the fabric of society* ‖ the texture of a textile [F. *fabrique*]

fab·ric·a·ble (fǽbrikəbəl) *adj.* capable of being made into a useful product **fabricability** *n.*

fab·ri·cate (fǽbrikeit) *pres. part.* **fab·ri·cat·ing** *past* and *past part.* **fab·ri·cat·ed** *v.t.* to construct, esp. to put together standard parts of ‖ to make up, invent (nonexistent facts), *to fabricate evidence* [fr. L. *fabricari* (*fabricatus*)]

fab·ri·ca·tion (fæbrikéiʃən) *n.* a fabricating or being fabricated ‖ something fabricated ‖ a structure of falsehoods [fr. L. *fabricatio* (*fabricationis*)]

Fa·bric·i·us Lus·ci·nus (fəbríʃi:əs luskáinəs), Gaius (*d.* c. 250 B.C.), Roman consul (282 and 278 B.C.). He was famous for his simplicity and probity, esp. when negotiating peace terms with Pyrrhus

Fa·bry's disease (fábrəz) *n.* (*med.*) congenital disorder of the metabolic process in the breakdown of urea, resulting in a rash in the penial area and defects in the cornea. It was named for Johannes Fabry, German dermatologist

fab·u·list (fǽbjulist) *n.* an inventor of fables [fr. F. *fabuliste*]

fab·u·lous (fǽbjuləs) *adj.* belonging to the realm of fable ‖ extraordinary, *fabulous wealth* [fr. L. *fabulosus*]

fa·cade, fa·çade (fəsád, fæsád) *n.* the main front of a building ‖ an appearance or manner intended as a pretense or mask [F. fr. Ital.]

face (feis) **1.** *n.* the front part of the head from forehead to chin, including the features (eyes, nose, mouth etc.) ‖ the expression of a person's countenance ‖ a grimace ‖ (*pop.*) impudence, *he had the face to ask for more* ‖ an outward show of self-possession, *to put the best face one can on a situation* ‖ a mask ‖ the front or main side of a building, monument etc. ‖ a surface, *wipe them off the face of the earth* ‖ the working surface of a tool ‖ any of the planes of a many-sided object or of a crystal ‖ (*printing*) the part of a type, or other raised printing surface, which takes the ink ‖ (*printing*) the collective types of a single design (e.g. of an alphabet), which may be available in many sizes, *a face not suitable for display work* ‖ a dial of a clock etc. ‖ the area of immediate operations in mining, quarrying or climbing, *coal face, rock face* **in the face of, in face of** directly confronting, *in the face of the enemy* ‖ in defiance of, *in the face of authority* **on the face of it** judging only by appearances **to lose face** to suffer a fall in the esteem in which one is held, to drop in prestige and thus in self-esteem **to make** (or **pull**) **a face** to grimace **to make a long face** to show that one is disagreeably afflected **to put a new face on** to change the way a person looks at (a situation) radically **to someone's face** directly to a person (not behind his back) **2.** *v. pres. part.* **fac·ing** *past* and *past part.* **faced** *v.t.* to be opposite to, *our house faces the park* ‖ to turn or have one's face towards, *he turned to face the orchestra* ‖ to put a visible covering on (a surface), *to face a wall with stucco* ‖ to confront, *faced with the evidence, he confessed* ‖ (often with 'up to') to meet resolutely, *to face facts, face up to the future* ‖ (*mil.*) to cause (troops) to turn in a certain direc-

tion ‖ *v.i.* to be situated so as to have the front in a specified direction, *the kitchen faces north* **to face (something) out** (*Br.*) to endure to the end (some embarrassing or otherwise unpleasant trial) and not try to evade it [F.]

face card (*Am.* = *Br.* court card) the king, queen or jack of playing cards

face-cloth (féisklɔθ, féisklɒθ) *pl.* **face-cloths** (féisklɔðs, féisklɒðs, féisklɔðz, féisklɒðz) *n.* a cloth for washing oneself with ‖ a woolen cloth with one smooth surface

face down *v.* to confront to a decision point, esp. from a poor position

face fly *Musca autumnalis,* a fly that clusters on the face of cattle

face-hard·en (féishɑrd'n) *v.t.* to harden the surface of (steel etc.)

face-lift (féislift) *n.* a facial operation meant to rejuvenate by tightening sagging skin, removing wrinkles etc. **face-lift·ing** *n.*

face-off (féisɔf) *n.* a showdown

face·plate (féispleit) *n.* a disk fixed at right angles to the spindle of a lathe, to which the material to be worked is attached

fac·er (féisər) *n.* a blow on the face ‖ an unexpected difficulty for which no solution is at once clear

face-sav·ing (féisseiviŋ) *adj.* allowing one's prestige or self-esteem to be preserved, esp. in a defeat or compromise of some sort

fac·et (fǽsit) *n.* any of the small planes which constitute the surface of a crystal or cut gem ‖ any of the single surface segments of the many simple ocelli of a compound eye ‖ any of the separate aspects of an involved problem, situation etc. [F. *facette* dim. of *face, face*]

fa·ce·ti·ae (fəsí:ʃi:i:) *pl. n.* trivial witticisms, pleasantries ‖ (in book catalogs) items of a coarse or obscene nature [L. fr. *facetus,* witty]

fa·ce·tious (fəsí:ʃəs) *adj.* (of a person) given to sly or pointless joking ‖ (of a remark) characterized by such joking [fr. F. *facétieux*]

face-to-face (féistəféis) *adv.* in the presence of each other ‖ (with 'with') in inescapable confrontation, *face-to-face with a problem*

face value the value as stated on a coin, note, bond etc. ‖ apparent worth, reliability etc., in the absence of other information

fa·cia (féiʃə, fǽʃə) *n.* a fixture over a shop window, displaying the proprietor's name ‖ (*Br.*) the dashboard of a motor vehicle [var. of FASCIA]

fa·cial (féiʃəl) **1.** *adj.* of or pertaining to the face **2.** *n.* a face massage [F.]

facial angle the angle formed by the intersection of the lines from nostril to ear and nostril to forehead, used esp. in describing racial features

facial index the ratio of the breadth of the face to its length

---

CONCISE PRONUNCIATION KEY: **(a)** æ, cat; ɑ, car; ɔ fawn; ei, snake. **(e)** e, hen; i:, sheep; iə, deer; εə, bear. **(i)** i, fish; ai, tiger; ə:, bird. **(o)** o, ox; au, cow; ou, goat; u, poor; ɔi, royal. **(u)** ʌ, duck; u, bull; u:, goose; ə, bacillus; ju:, cube. x, loch; θ, think; ð, bother; z, Zen; ʒ, corsage; dʒ, savage; ŋ, orangutang; j, yak; ʃ, fish; tʃ, fetch; 'l, rabble; 'n, redden. Complete pronunciation key appears inside front cover.

fa·ci·es (féiʃi:i:z) n. (bot.) the general form and appearance of a plant or makeup of a natural group || (geol.) the entire petrologic character of sedimentary deposits, e.g. their composition, color, texture, nature of stratification, esp. as distinguished from other beds of the same age [L.=face]

fac·ile (fæsil, esp. Br. fæsail) adj. performing or performed easily, without great effort || easily won, a facile success || fluent, even if lacking qualities of greater worth , merely superficial [F.=easy]

fa·cil·i·tate (fəsíliteit) pres. part. **fa·cil·i·tat·ing** past and past part. **fa·cil·i·tat·ed** v.t. to make easy or easier **fa·cil·i·ta·tion** (fəsiliteíʃən) n. [fr. F. faciliter]

fa·cil·i·ty (fəsíliti) pl. **fa·cil·i·ties** n. an aptitude for doing some specified thing easily || the quality of being easy to do || dexterity or apparent lack of effort in performing something relatively difficult || (pl.) things that make some specified activity, task etc. easier, facilities for study [F. facilité]

fac·ing (féisiŋ) n. (pl.) a trimming of a different material from the rest on military uniforms or other garments || an extra piece, esp. of the same material, applied at the edge of a garment etc. and turned either in (e.g. for stiffening) or out (e.g. for cuffs) || an outer layer of a different material on a wall, a marble facing

fac·sim·i·le (fæksímili:) n. an exact reproduction of a picture, document, coin, print etc. || the process of long-distance reproduction of print or pictures by telegraph or radio [L. fac, imper. of facere, to make +simile, neuter of similis, like]

facsimile transmitter a device that scans and translates copy into signals for wire transmission, e.g., by telephone **facsimile transmission** n. Cf TELEFACSIMILE

fact (fækt) n. a thing known to be true || a statement about something which has occurred, he got the facts distorted || (law, in certain phrases only) a crime **as a matter of fact, in point of fact, the fact of the matter is...** (introductory phrases used to emphasize an explanation or confession) to tell you the truth **in fact** (usually in contradistinction to some supposed state of affairs) in truth, actually [fr. L. factum, a thing done]

fac·tion (fækʃən) n. a small opposition group within a larger group, or one tending to split off from the larger group, generally with a suggestion of unscrupulous self-interest || excessive liking for political strife or troublemaking, he is too much given to faction to make a party leader **fac·tion·al** adj. of, relating to or characteristic of a faction || tending to create a faction **fac·tion·al·ism** n. [F.]

fac·tious (fækʃəs) adj. contentious, given to raising dissension || of or characteristic of faction [fr. L. factiosus fr. factio, a doing]

fac·ti·tious (fæktíʃəs) adj. artificial, fabricated || deliberately worked up, not natural, factitious gaiety [fr. L. facticius, made by art]

fac·ti·tive (fæktítiv) adj. (gram.) describing verbs which take an object and a complement, with the sense of making ('we made him captain', considering ('I consider her dangerous') or calling ('she called him a coward') [fr. Mod. L. factitivus]

fac·tor (fæktər) 1. n. (math.) a number or term which, divided into a larger number or expression, has an integral remainder, the factors of 12 are 1, 2, 3, 4, 6, 12 || any of the facts or circumstances which, taken together, constitute a result or situation, luck was the biggest factor in his success (biol.) a causative agent in heredity, a Mendelian factor || (biol.) any agent (biotic, climatic, nutritional etc.) contributing to a result || someone who acts as agent for, or is appointed to conduct the affairs of, another 2. v.t. to factorize [fr. F. facteur]

fac·tor·age (fæktəridʒ) n. the business of a factor or agent || his commission

fac·to·ri·al (fæktóri:əl, fæktóuri:əl) 1. n. the function of a positive integer n given by the product of the integer and all the integers between it and unity, denoted by n!, and with the convention that 0!= 1 2. adj. relating to factors or factorials

fac·tor·ize (fæktəraiz) pres. part. **fac·tor·iz·ing** past and past part. **fac·tor·ized** v.t. (math.) to break down (a product) into its factors

factor of safety (engin.) the ratio between the breaking stress of a material and the greatest stress to which it will be subjected

fac·to·ry (fæktəri:) pl. **fac·to·ries** n. a building or group of buildings where goods are manufactured by collective production [F. factorie]

Factory Acts (Br. hist.) laws relating to working hours, safety precautions etc. in industry, first introduced in 1802 and 1819 in the cotton industry, and extended after 1833

factory farming (agriculture) intensive standardized production of fowl and food animals indoors. The animals' movements are highly restricted **also** confinement farming

factory ship floating factory that follows fishing and whaling catcher boats to butcher and process a catch while still on the high seas

fac·to·tum (fæktóutəm) n. someone used in a household, small business etc. for jobs of many kinds [L. fac, imper. of facere, to do+ totum, neuter of totus, whole]

facts of life, the (pop.) the basic facts, esp. as explained to children, about human reproduction || (pop.) basic factors to be reckoned with

fac·tu·al (fæktʃu:əl) adj. concerned with facts || full of facts

fac·u·la (fækjulə) pl. **fac·u·lae** (fækjuli:) n. (astron.) a bright spot or streak on the surface of the sun [L., dim. of fax, a torch]

fac·ul·ta·tive (fækəlteitiv) adj. relating to an authority or permission granted for the exercise of a privilege || optional || (biol.) capable of existing under different sets of conditions, a facultative parasite (cf. OBLIGATE) [F. facultatif]

fac·ul·ty (fækəlti:) pl. **fac·ul·ties** n. a mental or physical power, the faculty of speech || a gift for some special activity, a faculty for languages || a branch of studies (law, medicine etc.) in a university || the teachers of a school, college or university || the members of a particular profession, esp. medicine || (eccles.) a permission or license, esp. (Anglican Church) one required for structural changes in a church [F. faculté]

fad (fæd) n. a short-lived fashion or craze || (Br.) an exaggeratedly fussy attitude, esp. about eating or not eating certain kinds of food **fad·dish** adj. inclined to take up fads || (Br.) fussy about likes and dislikes **fad·dist** n. **fad·dy** comp. **fad·di·er** superl. **fad·di·est** adj. **faddish**, esp. (Br.) about food or hygiene [origin unknown]

fadayeen *FEDAYIN

fade (feid) pres. part. **fad·ing** past and past part. **fad·ed** v.i. to lose color || to lose freshness or vigor || (of a sound) to lose intensity gradually || (of an image, memory or dream) to become gradually less and less distinct || v.t. to cause to lose color, freshness, intensity or distinctness gradually **to fade in** (movies, television, radio) to become gradually clearer until normal clarity is reached, or to cause to do this **to fade out** (movies, television, radio) to become gradually less and less distinct and finally disappear, or to cause to do this **fade·less** adj. not liable to fade [O.F. fader, to wither]

faecal *FECAL

faeces *FECES

Fa·en·za (fáentsa) a town (pop. 54,703) in Emilia, Italy, southwest of Ravenna, famous, esp. in the 15th and 16th cc., for its earthenware

Faeroe Islands *FAROE ISLANDS

fag (fæg) 1. v. pres. part. **fag·ging** past and past part. **fagged** v.t. (often with 'out') to make weary || v.i. to work laboriously, toil away || (Br., of a younger boy in some boarding schools) to be at the call of an older boy for certain menial tasks 2. n. (Br.) an exhausting or boring task || (Br., at some boarding schools) a younger boy who performs tasks for an older boy || (pop.) a cigarette [etym. doubtful]

fag end the last and coarse end of a web of cloth || the untwisted end of a rope || the last remnant of anything

fag·ot, fag·got (fægət) 1. n. a bundle of sticks for firewood bound together || a bundle of pieces of wrought iron for rolling or hammering into bars || chopped pig's liver, lights etc., onions and seasoning, made up into balls or sticks for frying 2. v.t. to make (sticks) into a bundle || to ornament with fagoting || v.i. to make fagots **fag·ot·ing, fag·got·ing** n. ornamental embroidery made by drawing the horizontal threads from a woven fabric and then tying the remaining vertical threads in the middle, making waisted bunches, or this process [F. fagot. origin unknown]

Fahd ibn Abd al-Aziz (fádibnæbdalazí:z) (1922–), king of Saudi Arabia (1982–). He served as minister of education and the interior and deputy prime minister before succeeding King Khalid, his half-brother

Fahr·en·heit (færənhạit), Daniel Gabriel (1686–1736), German physicist who established (1715) the Fahrenheit scale

Fahrenheit scale (abbr. F.) a temperature scale on which the freezing point of water is 32° and its boiling point 212°. A temperature of x°F. corresponds to 5/9 (x–32)°C.

fai·ence (faiáns) n. glazed earthenware [orig. made in Faenza, Italy]

fail (feil) n. (only in) **without fail** for certain [O.F. faile, faille]

fail v.i. to omit or forget to do something required || (of supplies etc.) to become exhausted, give out || (of someone old or seriously ill, or of the mental faculties) to grow feeble || to die out, cease to function, the engine failed || to crash financially, go bankrupt || to be unsuccessful, the attack failed || to be inadequate or deficient, the crop failed two years running || v.t. to be unsuccessful in (an exam etc.) || to declare (a candidate) to be unsuccessful || to let (someone) down completely, to disappoint utterly || to be lacking to, words fail me to describe the scene || to abandon suddenly. his courage failed him **fail·ing** 1. n. a weakness in character 2. prep. in the absence of, in default of, failing wine we will make do with beer [O.F. faillir, to be lacking]

faille (fail, feil) n. a ribbed silk fabric of plain weave used for dresses, ties etc. [F.]

fail·ure (féiljər) n. lack of success || lack or sudden end of performance, engine failure || the fact of failing, failure to be heard || an unsuccessful person, thing or project || neglect or omission, failure to comply || a financial crash, a bank failure || a running short, failure of supplies [earlier failer fr. A.F.]

fain (fein) 1. adj. (archaic) willing, content, eager || (archaic) obliged, compelled 2. adv. (archaic) willingly [O.E. fœgen, fœgn]

faint (feint) 1. adj. likely to faint, weak, feeble || pale, dim, indistinct || slight, a faint resemblance 2. n. a sudden loss of consciousness from shock, exhaustion, loss of blood etc. 3. v.i. to lose consciousness in a faint [M.E. feint fr. O.F. fr. feindre, to pretend]

faint·heart·ed (féinthártid) adj. lacking courage or resolution

faints *FEINTS

fair (fεər) adj. (of the hair or complexion) light-colored, blond || just, equitable, a fair share || according to the rules, a fair fight || (of a wind) favorable || (of weather) cloudless || (of a chance or probability) quite good || of medium quality, his game is only fair || (rhet.) beautiful, fair to behold || (pop.) complete, thorough, it was a fair scramble getting away **fair to middling** good enough but not very good **in a fair way** likely, in a fair way to win $100 [O.E. fœger]

fair adv. according to the rules, to play fair || squarely, it caught him fair between the eyes **to bid fair** to seem likely to (do or become something) [O.E. fœger]

fair v.t. (shipbuilding) to make smooth and regular || to join one thing to (another) in a structure so that the two surfaces run smoothly into one another || v.i. (often with 'up') to begin to clear up and become cloudless [O.E. fœgrian]

fair n. a traveling collection of sideshows and amusements || a large-scale exhibition to promote trade || a traditional market held on a specific date, with amusements and sideshows || a specialized market, a cattle fair [O.F. feire]

fair and square correct, honest, correctly, honestly

fair ball (baseball) a batted ball that first strikes the ground beyond first or third base and within the foul lines, or that comes to rest before passing first or third base and within the foul lines, or that passes first or third base after striking the ground within the foul lines

Fair·banks (fέərbæŋks) a commercial town (pop. 22,645) of Alaska, terminus of the Pan-American Highway. Construction of the Alaskan oil pipeline in the 1970s brought growth to the town

fair catch (football) a catch of a punted ball made by a player on side who makes a signal to indicate that he will not attempt to advance the ball when caught, so as to be immune to interference by opponents

fair copy a neat copy of a draft or corrected text

Fair Deal the social and economic program introduced by President Harry Truman. It increased the minimum wage, extended social security benefits, and allocated federal funds for slum clearance. Conservative elements de-

---

CONCISE PRONUNCIATION KEY: **(a)** æ, cat; ɑ, car; ɔ fawn; ei, snake. **(e)** e, hen; i:, sheep; iə, deer; εə, bear. **(i)** i, fish; ai, tiger; ə:, bird. **(o)** o, ox; au, cow; ou, goat; u, poor; ɔi, royal. **(u)** ʌ, duck; u, bull; u:, goose; ə, bacillus; ju:, cube. x, loch; θ, think; ð, bother; z, Zen; ʒ, corsage; dʒ, savage; ŋ, orangutang; j, yak; ʃ, fish; tʃ, fetch; 'l, rabble; 'n, redden. Complete pronunciation key appears inside front cover.

feated its attempt to repeal the Taft-Hartley Act, to extend federal power projects, and to introduce civil rights and national health programs

Fair Employment Practices Commission a U.S. commission established (1941) to thwart racial discrimination in employment on federal contracts, and to make the most efficient use of skilled manpower during the 2nd world war. Several states enacted the idea in statutes

Fair·fax (féərfæks), Thomas Fairfax, 3rd Baron (1612–71), English soldier and statesman. He commanded the New Model army (1645–50) until replaced by Cromwell, and defeated Charles I at Naseby. As one of the king's judges (1649) he was against the death penalty, and was responsible with Gen. Monk for the return of Charles II (1660)

fair game the animals a hunter is permitted to kill in sport ‖ a legitimate target for ridicule

fair·ground (féərgraund) n. a site where fairs are held or where a fair is in progress

fair-haired (féərheərd) adj. blond, having light-colored hair

fair-haired boy (Am=Br. blue-eyed boy) a favorite, someone looked on with special indulgence

fair·ing (féəriŋ) n. a structure whose main function is to streamline and smooth the surface of an aircraft [fr. FAIR v.]

Fair Isle an island (pop. 100) off N. Scotland, producing jerseys knit in colors and designs said to be Moorish and traceable to survivors of the Spanish Armada

fair·ly (féərli) adv. in a just and equitable manner ‖ moderately, *he plays fairly well* ‖ positively, *he fairly bellowed across the hall* [FAIR adj.]

fair-mind·ed (féərmáindid) adj. unprejudiced, just

fairness doctrine (broadcasting) principle and practice of allowing equal air time to opposing candidates with differing viewpoints on controversial issues

fair play equitable dealings between contending parties ‖ respect for others' rights according to one's own ideas of social justice

fair-trade agreement (féərtréid) a contract between a manufacturer and a distributor fixing a minimum price for the resale of a commodity bearing the manufacturer's trademark

fair·way (féərwei) n. a navigable channel for vessels entering or leaving a harbor ‖ any unobstructed course ‖ (golf) a prepared strip of turf between the tee and the green

fair·y (féəri) **1.** n. pl. **fair·ies** (folklore) a small supernatural being, capable of intervening in human affairs, usually in order to help **2.** adj. of or relating to fairies [O. F. faerie]

fairy lamps (Br.) small colored lamps used for decoration

fair·y·land (féəri:lænd) n. a region inhabited by fairies, an enchanted region ‖ a delicately beautiful scene

fairy lights (Br.) fairy lamps

fairy ring a ring of darker grass in a patch of turf, caused by proliferation of the spores of fungi

fairy tale a story for children about fairies, or about magic and enchantment ‖ a very improbable story ‖ a lie

Fai·sal (fáis'l), (1905–75), king of Saudi Arabia (1964–75), son of ibn Saud. He was assassinated by his nephew and succeeded by his brother

Faisal I (1885–1933), the first king of Iraq (1921–33)

Faisal II (1935–58), the last king of Iraq (1953–8), assassinated in a coup [*KASSEM]

Faisalabad (fáis'ləbəd), a city, formerly Lyallpur, (pop. 1,092,000) of N.E. Pakistan: food processing, cotton milling, engineering

fait ac·com·pli (féitækɔmpli:) pl. **faits accomplis** (féitsækɔmpli:) n. an action completed and, for this reason only, not a matter for argument [F.=an accomplished fact]

faith (feiθ) n. trust, confidence, *have no faith in his assurances* ‖ complete acceptance of a truth which cannot be demonstrated or proved by the process of logical thought, *religious faith* ‖ a religion based upon this ‖ the virtue by which a Christian believes in the revealed truths of God **in good (bad) faith** with honest (dishonest) intentions **to keep (break) faith with** to remain (cease to remain) loyal to **faith·ful** (féiθful) **1.** adj. steadfast in faith ‖ loyal ‖ accurate, true to the original, *a faithful account of what happened* **2.** n. **the faithful** conscientious

adherents to a system of religious belief [fr. O. F. feid, feit]

faith healer someone who practices faith healing **faith healing** the treating of diseases through faith in God

faith·less (féiθlis) adj. disloyal, breaking pledges ‖ having no religious faith

Fai·yum, Fa·yum (fáiju:m) a trade and communications center (pop. 167,000) of N. Egypt in an irrigated agricultural region of the same name: cotton spinning

Faiyum portraits paintings on wood of the first four centuries A.D., first discovered in 1820 in Egyptian tombs, the work of Greek artists. They are painted in distemper colors or in natural pigments mixed with beeswax and burnt into the wood, or in a combination of these techniques. They combine Oriental plastic conceptions with Western realism, and may be thought of as a prelude to Byzantine art

fake (feik) **1.** n. (naut.) one loop of a rope coiled for free running **2.** v.t. pres. part. **fak·ing** past and past part. **faked** (naut.) to coil (a rope) in fakes [origin unknown]

fake 1. v. pres. part. **fak·ing** past and past part. **faked** v.t. to make a false imitation of, counterfeit ‖ to contrive (something) so as to deceive ‖ (with 'up') to contrive (something) as a working substitute ‖ v.i. to pretend, sham **2.** n. something faked **3.** adj. artificial, false, *fake pearls* [etym. doubtful]

fake book (music) unauthorized publication of melodies or shortened versions of melodies

fa·kir (fəkíər) n. a Moslem religious beggar ‖ a Hindu ascetic [Arab. faqir, poor, a poor man]

fa·la·fel (fəlófəl) n. a Middle Eastern dish of fava bean, chick peas, parsley, and often green peppers, onions, radishes, and seasoning

Fa·lan·gism (fəlǽndʒizəm) n. a Spanish fascist movement founded (1933) by J. A. Primo de Rivera. It triumphed in the Spanish Civil War under Franco **Fa·lán·gist** adj. and n. [fr. Span. Falange (Española), (Spanish) Phalanx]

fal·cate (fǽlkeit) adj. hooked, crescent-shaped, *falcate claws* **fál·cat·ed** adj. (astron., of the waxing or waning moon etc.) in the form of a crescent [fr. L. falcatus fr. falx, sickle]

fal·chion (fɔ́ltʃən) n. a broad, short, medieval sword with a slightly curved blade [M.E. fauchoun fr. O.F.]

fal·ci·form (fǽlsifɔrm) adj. (anat.) sickle-shaped [fr. L. falx (falcis), a sickle]

fal·con (fɔ́lkən, fǽlkən) n. a diurnal bird of prey esp. of genus *Falco*, that has a very strong, compact body with powerful, long, pointed wings, a large head and a sharp, hooked beak. It is carnivorous, and cosmopolitan in distribution ‖ the female of *Falco peregrinus*, the peregrine, used in falconry (cf. TERCEL) [M.F. faucon fr. O.F.]

Falcon n. (mil.) a U.S. air-to-air guided missile (AIM-4A), with homing device, semiactive radar guidance, and a range of 5 mi. Some Falcons are equipped with nuclear warheads. The Falcon family (AIM-4 series, AIM-26A, and AIM-47A) can be carried on interceptor aircraft and used on the F-101B, F-102, F-104, and F-106

fal·con·er (fɔ́lkənər, fǽlkənər) n. someone who keeps and trains hawks or falcons for hunting [O.F. faulconnier]

fal·con-gen·tle (fɔ́lkəndʒént'l, fǽlkəndʒént'l) n. (falconry) the female peregrine falcon [F. faucon-gentil]

fal·con·ry (fɔ́lkənri:, fǽlkənri:) n. the art of hunting game with birds of prey, and the training of these birds. The sport originated in the Far East and was widely popular in Europe in medieval times [F. fauconnerie]

fald·stool (fɔ́ldstu:l) n. a folding stool or chair without arms, provided e.g. for a bishop in Christian churches, or for the English monarch at his coronation ‖ a desk from which, in Anglican churches, the litany is sung or said [fr. M.L. faldistolium fr. O.H.G. fr. faldan, to fold+stuol, chair]

Fa·ler·ni·an (fəlɔ́:rni:ən) n. a famous wine of Roman times made in Campania, in S. Italy [fr. L. (vinum) Falernum, Falernian (wine)]

Falk·land Islands and Falkland Islands Dependencies (fɔ́lklənd) (Span. Islas Malvinas) a group of islands (area 4,618 sq. miles, pop. 1,800) in the S. Atlantic, 400 miles northeast of Cape Horn. Capital: Stanley (pop. 1,100). People: of European origin. Language: English. Religion: Christian. There are two main islands and 200 small ones. Average temperature: 43° F. Rainfall: 26 ins. Products: wool, meat, vegetables, hides and skins, fish. The Falkland

Islands Dependencies are South Georgia and South Sandwich. Products: whale and seal oil. The Falklands were discovered in 1592, settled by the French (1764), sold to Spain (1766) and occupied by the British (1833). They are also claimed by the Republic of Argentina. Argentine troops seized the islands in April 1982. The British launched several thousand troops, and on June 14, 1982, the Argentines surrendered

Falkland Sound a channel (c. 50 miles long, 2–20 miles wide) in the South Atlantic separating the two principal islands of the Falkland Is (East and West Falkland)

Falkner *FAULKNER

Fall (fɔl), Albert Bacon (1861–1944), U.S. secretary of the interior (1921–3). He was involved in the 'Teapot Dome' affair and sentenced to one year's imprisonment for accepting a $100,000 bribe

fall (fɔl) **1.** pres. part. **fall·ing** past **fell** (fel) past part. **fall·en** (fɔ́lən) v.i. to drop by gravity ‖ to lose balance and drop to the ground ‖ to allow oneself to drop to the ground or to one's knees ‖ to decrease, *prices have fallen* ‖ to lose position, *to fall from favor* ‖ (of temperature) to become lower in degree ‖ to decline in value or in price level ‖ (of clothes, curtains etc.) to hang, *to fall in thick folds* ‖ to be killed, *to fall in battle* ‖ to be captured, *the fort fell without a shot being fired* ‖ (of a government) to be voted out of office ‖ (cricket, of a wicket) to be taken ‖ to slope downwards, *the land falls gently away from the house* ‖ (of wind, floodwater, sound etc.) to subside, diminish ‖ (of the face) to take on an expression of disappointment or dismay ‖ (of the eyes) to be suddenly lowered ‖ to seem to descend *night fell, a silence fell on them* ‖ to happen by way of obligation, *it fell to his brother to do the job* ‖ to pass by right, *the inheritance fell to the nephew* ‖ to pass into some state, *to fall asleep* ‖ to occur, *his birthday falls on a Tuesday* ‖ to cease to resist a temptation ‖ to have its position, *the accent falls on the last syllable* ‖ to divide analytically, *it falls into three periods* ‖ (of the young of some animals, esp. sheep and hares) to be born **to fall back** to retreat **to fall back on** to retire to (a reserve or defensive position) ‖ to turn through force of circumstances to (something which serves as a substitute) **to fall behind** to fail to keep pace with schedule ‖ to fail to keep up with the person or group setting the pace **to fall down on** to fail to accomplish (a job) or keep to (a schedule) **to fall due** to be liable for settlement **to fall for** to be deceived by (a trick) ‖ to be captivated by (a person) **to fall flat** (of a joke or a proposition) to make no impression **to fall in** (mil.) to get into parade formation **to fall in with** to agree to cooperate with ‖ to meet by accident and sign up with **to fall into line with** to adapt one's ideas or actions to (an agreed course of action) **to fall in love with** to experience or suffer an obsessive passion for **to fall foul of** (naut.) to collide, get entangled, with ‖ to quarrel with **to fall off** to start to decrease, degenerate **to fall on** to discover by accident **to fall out** (mil.) to disperse from, or leave, parade formation ‖ (mil.) to drop out of the line or ranks **to fall out with** to quarrel with **to fall over oneself, to fall over backwards** to show excessive eagerness (to do some action) **to fall short** (of expectations, a total etc.) to disappoint, fail to fulfill requirements **to fall through** (of plans or arrangements) to fail to materialize **to fall to** to start (eating, working, fighting) with eagerness ‖ to start eating, working or fighting with eagerness **to fall under** (a heading) to be classified under **to fall upon** to attack savagely **to let fall** to reveal casually (a piece of information, esp. secret or confidential) **2.** n. the act or an instance of falling ‖ a distance fallen ‖ falling matter, *a light fall of snow* ‖ the way a thing falls, *the fall of a dress* ‖ autumn ‖ a descent to a lower level ‖ a decrease, decline, *a fall in purchasing power* ‖ an amount by which something drops ‖ a downfall, collapse ‖ the taking or surrendering of a stronghold after a siege or attack ‖ (wrestling) a scoring throw ‖ the rope of a hoisting tackle ‖ a quantity of timber cut down ‖ (pl.) a cascade, waterfall ‖ (of animals) a birth or the number of young born **the Fall** (theol.) the transition of Adam from primal innocence to a knowledge of evil (Genesis iii) [O.E. feallan]

Fal·la (defáljə), Manuel Maria de (1876–1946), Spanish composer and pianist. He is well known for his popular songs, his opera 'La vida breve' (1905), and the ballet 'The Three-Cornered Hat' (1919)

CONCISE PRONUNCIATION KEY: **(a)** æ, c*a*t; ɑ, c*ar*; ɔ, f*aw*n; ei, sn*a*ke. **(e)** e, h*e*n; i:, sh*ee*p; iə, d*ee*r; ɛə, b*ear*. **(i)** i, f*i*sh; ai, t*i*ger; ə:, b*ir*d. **(o)** o, *o*x; au, c*ow*; ou, g*oa*t; u, p*oor*; ɔi, r*oy*al. **(u)** ʌ, d*u*ck; u, b*u*ll; u:, g*oo*se; ə, b*a*cillus; ju:, c*u*be. x, lo*ch*; θ, *th*ink; ð, bo*th*er; z, *Z*en; ʒ, cor*s*age; dʒ, sa*v*age; ŋ, ora*ng*uta*ng*; j, *y*ak; ʃ, *f*ish; tʃ, fe*tch*; 'l, rabb*le*; 'n, redd*en*. Complete pronunciation key appears inside front cover.

fal·la·cious (fəléi∫əs) adj. based on error ‖ misleading [fr. L. fallacia fr. fallax, deceptive]

fal·la·cy (fǽləsi:) pl. **fal·la·cies** n. a false notion, a popular fallacy ‖ a piece of false reasoning ‖ the quality in reasoning of being false or unsound ‖ *PATHETIC FALLACY [fr. L. fallacia fr. fallax, deceptive]

fall·en (fɔ́lən) past part. of FELL

Fallen Timbers, Battle of an engagement (1794) in N.W. Ohio, in which the U.S. forces under Gen. Anthony Wayne defeated the Indians, who surrendered (1795) their lands

fall guy (pop.) someone easily exploited and victimized ‖ (pop.) a person made to take the blame

fal·li·bil·i·ty (fælǝbíliti) n. the quality of being fallible

fal·li·ble (fǽləb'l) adj. subject to the possibility of erring or being mistaken [fr. L. L. fallibilis]

falling star a meteor

Fal·lo·pi·an tubes (fəlóupi:ən) the two ducts by which ova pass from the ovary to the uterus in female mammals [after Fallopius, Latinized name of Gabriele Fallopio (1523-62), Italian anatomist]

fall·out (fɔ́laut) n. the radioactive material produced by a nuclear explosion, which is distributed through the atmosphere and settles on the earth ‖ the settling of this material ‖ an unexpected byproduct of a process

fal·low (fǽlou) 1. adj. (of land) plowed and harrowed but left without crops for a season 2. n. land so treated 3. v.t. to break up (land) with plow and harrow, but without seeding [M.E. falow, plowed land]

fallow deer a small yellowish-brown European deer of genus Dama, spotted with white in summer, dark brown in winter [O.E. falu, fealu, fealo, pale yellow]

F.A.L.N. abbr. Fuerzas Armadas de Liberación Nacional (Armed Forces of National Liberation), a Puerto Rican revolutionary organization dedicated to the establishment of an independent Puerto Rico

false (fɔls) 1. adj. untrue, a false accusation ‖ logically wrong, a false conclusion ‖ incorrect, mistaken, a false alarm ‖ not genuine, artificial, false teeth ‖ deceitful, lying, a false tax return ‖ disloyal, a false friend ‖ meant to deceive ‖ fake, a false door ‖ (archit.) not structurally necessary or not permanent, a false ceiling ‖ (mus.) off pitch ‖ not natural, straining for effect ‖ misconceived, mistaken, false economies ‖ (bot.) incorrectly so-named, the false acacia **to make a false move** to make a tactical mistake in a critical situation **to put someone in a false position** to compromise someone so that his motives and actions are liable to be misunderstood or so that he may be compelled to act against his own convictions **to sail under false colors** (Br. colours) to pretend to be what one is not 2. adv. not honestly, to play false ‖ not on the note, to sing false [O.E. fals fr. L. falsus]

false acacia Robinia pseudoacacia, the North American locust tree

false consciousness 1. identification with, and support of, the interests of a social class other than one's own **2.** failure to recognize one's true class membership and interests

false·hood (fɔ́lshud) n. falsity ‖ a lie ‖ lying

false imprisonment imprisonment without legal justification

false negative in health care, an incorrect diagnosis that the patient does not have a disease or condition

false positive in health care, an incorrect diagnosis that the patient has a disease or condition

false pretenses, false pretences (law) the crime of representing oneself or one's situation as other than is true in order to acquire money or credit

false pride unjustified fear of indignity

false quantity an incorrect length given to a vowel sound in scanned verse

fal·set·to (fɔlsétou) 1. pl. **fal·set·tos** n. a man's voice produced in a register above its normal range 2. adv. in this register [Ital., dim. of false]

fals·ie (fɔ́lsi:) n. padded bra to create the impression of larger breasts

fal·si·fi·ca·tion (fɔlsifikéi∫ən) n. a falsifying or being falsified ‖ something falsified [fr. L.L. falsificare, to falsify]

fal·si·fy (fɔ́lsifai) pres. part. **fal·si·fy·ing** past and past part. **fal·si·fied** v.t. to alter with intent to defraud, to falsify accounts ‖ to misrepresent,

to falsify an issue ‖ to pervert, to falsify the course of justice [fr. F. falsifier]

fal·si·ty (fɔ́lsiti) pl. **fal·si·ties** n. the quality of being false, deceitfulness ‖ an untrue assertion [O.F. falseté]

Fal·ster (fɑ́lstər) a Danish island (area 198 sq. miles, pop. 44,467) south of Zealand

fal·ter (fɔ́ltər) 1. v.i. to stumble in movement, action or speech ‖ to begin to lose one's determination ‖ v.t. (often with 'out') to say in a hesitant or feeble way 2. n. a faltering ‖ a faltering sound [etym. doubtful]

Fa·ma·gus·ta (fæmǝgústǝ) (Gk Ammochostos) the chief port (pop. 39,400) of Cyprus, on the east coast

fame (feim) n. the state of being widely known and esteemed or acclaimed, renown ‖ (rhet.) reputation, of evil fame [F.]

famed (feimd) adj. renowned, celebrated ‖ (rhet.) generally reported, she is not so beautiful as she is famed to be [past part. of obs. v. fame fr. O.F.]

fa·mil·ial (fəmíljəl, fəmíli:əl) adj. of or relating to a family ‖ (of a disease) abnormally frequent in a family [fr. L. familia, family]

fa·mil·iar (fəmíljər) 1. adj. knowing intimately, familiar with every detail ‖ accustomed, well known by frequently repeated experience, a familiar routine ‖ much seen, a familiar figure at concerts ‖ (of personal relations) close and pleasantly free from formality ‖ presumptuous, impudent 2. n. a familiar spirit ‖ (Roman Catholic Church) a member of a pope's or bishop's household rendering certain domestic services, though not menial ones [O.F. familier]

fa·mil·i·ar·i·ty (fəmili:ǽriti) pl. **fa·mil·i·ar·i·ties** n. close knowledge or acquaintance ‖ the state of being well known ‖ an unjustified presumption of intimacy in speech or behavior ‖ (pl.) unwelcome gestures of affection [F. familiarité]

fa·mil·iar·i·za·tion (fəmiljərizéi∫ən) n. a familiarizing or being familiarized

fa·mil·iar·ize (fəmíljəraiz) pres. part. **fa·mil·iar·iz·ing** past and past part. **fa·mil·iar·ized** v.t. to cause (someone, oneself) to get to know something well

familiar spirit a demon who comes at the call of a witch or wizard

fam·i·ly (fǽmili:) pl. **fam·i·lies** n. a group consisting of parents and their children ‖ the children of two parents ‖ a group of people closely related by blood, e.g. children and their parents, their cousins, their aunts and uncles ‖ a group consisting of individuals descended from a common ancestry, an old army family ‖ a household ‖ unit of a crime syndicate usu. in a specific geographic area ‖ a group of related genera of animals, plants, languages etc. ‖ (rhet.) a harmonious group bound together by common interest, the family of nations [fr. L. familia, household]

family allowance a sum of money allowed by some governments to mothers to help them feed and clothe their children ‖ a grant made by an employer to a worker according to the number of his dependent children

family circle the close group relationship of a household

Family Compact (Eur. hist.) any of three alliances of 1733, 1743 and 1761 between the Bourbon rulers of France and Spain ‖ (Canad. hist.) the nickname given to the powerful clique of ultra-Tories who dominated the government of Upper Canada c. 1791-1840

family ganging in health care, the unethical practice of requiring or encouraging a patient to return for care to a publicly paid health program with other members of the family, e.g., with other children, so that the program can charge for care given to each family member

family name a surname

family planning the attempt, using birth-control methods, to time pregnancies in the best interests of the parents and the children

family room a family recreation room in a home

family therapy (psych.) treatment technique for interpersonal problems involving interviews with the whole family in behavioral and systems-based approaches

family tree a genealogical chart of the generations of a family, or a chart showing the relationships of languages sharing a common ancestry

fam·ine (fǽmin) n. extreme scarcity of food ‖ starvation, to die of famine ‖ a scarcity of something, a coal famine [F.]

fam·ished (fǽmi∫t) adj. hungry to the point of starvation ‖ (pop.) feeling very hungry [fr. older famish v. fr. L. fames, hunger]

fa·mous (féiməs) adj. celebrated ‖ (pop.) excellent **fa·mous·ly** adv. excellently [A.F. famous, O.F. fameux]

fam·u·lus (fǽmjuləs) pl. **fam·u·li** (fǽmjulai) n. an attendant on a magician or alchemist [L.=servant]

fan (fæn) n. a devotee of a particular sport, pursuit, entertainer, entertainment etc. [shortened fr. FANATIC]

fan 1. n. a manually operated device for agitating the air before one's face so as to make one feel cooler. Fans are commonly of silk or paper mounted on ribs which radiate from a pivot to open out into a sector of a circle, and which fold back on themselves compactly when the device is not in use ‖ a mechanically operated propeller setting up currents of air for cooling rooms or attached to water-cooled engines for the same purpose ‖ a small sail on a windmill to keep it in the wind ‖ the blade of a propeller ‖ (hist.) a device for winnowing 2. v. pres. part. **fan·ning** past and past part. **fanned** v.t. to agitate the air in front of (a person, with cooling effect, or a fire, with heating effect) with or as if with a fan ‖ to agitate (the air) in this way ‖ (of a breeze) to blow gently upon ‖ (hist.) to winnow (grain) or winnow away (chaff) with a fan ‖ to knock back the hammer of (a revolver) rapidly and repeatedly with the edge of one hand while keeping the trigger depressed with the first finger of the other, for more rapid firing ‖ to cause (cards etc.) to spread out like a fan ‖ (baseball) to strike (a batter) out ‖ v.i. (with 'out') to open like a fan or (mil.) in fan-shaped formation [O.E. fann fr. L. vannus, a winnowing fan]

fa·nat·ic (fənǽtik) 1. adj. overenthusiastic, zealous beyond the bounds of reason 2. n. an inordinately zealous adherent or supporter, esp. in politics or religion **fa·nát·i·cal** adj. **fa·nat·i·cism** (fənǽtisizəm) n. wild and often dangerous enthusiasm, esp. in politics or religion [fr. L. fanaticus fr. fanum, temple]

fan cameras an assembly of three or more cameras systematically disposed at fixed angles relative to each other so as to provide wide lateral coverage with overlapping images Cf SPLIT VERTICAL PHOTOGRAPHY

fan·cied (fǽnsi:d) adj. favorite, the fancied horse came in second ‖ imagined, fancied affronts [past part. of FANCY]

fan·ci·er (fǽnsi:ər) n. a person specially interested in the breeding of a certain kind of animal or plant in order to establish particular characteristics in the breed

fan·ci·ful (fǽnsifəl) adj. produced by fancy, unreal ‖ arranged in an unusual or odd way

fan·ci·ly (fǽnsili:) adv. in a fancy way

fan·cy (fǽnsi:) 1. pl. **fan·cies** n. the faculty of forming mental images, esp. the light, superficial play of this faculty (contrasted with imagination) ‖ a product of this faculty ‖ a whim, caprice ‖ a delusion ‖ a vague intuition ‖ a liking, to take a fancy to someone 2. adj. comp. **fan·ci·er** superl. **fan·ci·est** (of artifacts) ornamental, not plain ‖ (of prices) unreasonably high ‖ (of birds and animals) bred for particular characteristics, a fancy pigeon ‖ (of canned goods) of superior quality **the fancy** enthusiastic followers of some pastime, or narrow interest, or of boxing as a sport 3. v.t. pres. part. **fan·cy·ing** past and past part. **fan·cied** to call up a mental picture of, can you fancy him in uniform? ‖ (used imperatively as an exclamation of surprise) imagine, fancy that! ‖ to suppose, suspect, I fancy he is annoyed ‖ to be attracted to, she fancies that green one ‖ to wish to have, do you fancy a glass of beer? ‖ to have a high opinion of, he fancies himself as a swimmer [contr. of FANTASY]

fancy diving the execution of ornamental dives into water, performing set evolutions

fancy dress a masquerade costume worn for a party

fan·cy-free (fǽnsi:frí:) adj. not committed in love

fancy goods (commerce) objects of small value, primarily decorative

fan·cy·work (fǽnsi:wə:rk) n. ornamental needlework ‖ fussy display of skill at the expense of attack, e.g. in boxing, cut out the fancywork

fan·dan·go (fændǽngou) n. a vigorous Spanish dance in triple time [Span.]

fan·fare (fǽnfɛər) n. a flourish of trumpets, bugles or other brass instruments [F.]

Fang (fæŋ) *n.* a member of a Bantu-speaking people of N. Gabon and Rio Muni ‖ this people ‖ their language

fang (fæŋ) *n.* a long, pointed tooth, esp. in dogs or wolves, or one of the long, hollow or grooved teeth of poisonous snakes through which venom is passed ‖ one of the prongs in the root of a tooth ‖ the spike of a tool driven into the handle or stock **fanged** (fæŋd) *adj.* having fangs [O.E.]

fan jet jet engine designed to attain additional thrust by drawing air through a ducted fan

fan·leaf palm (fǽnlị:f) a fan palm

fan·light (fǽnlait) *n.* a window in the shape of an open fan with radiating bars, over a door

fan mail letters received by a famous person, esp. someone in the entertainment field, from admirers

fan·on (fǽnən) *n.* (*eccles.*) a maniple ‖ a short cape worn by the pope at solemn pontifical Mass [M.E. *fanoun* fr. M.F. *fanon* fr. Gmc]

fan palm any palm with fanshaped leaves, e.g. the talipot or Washingtonia

fan·tail (fǽnteil) *n.* a tail in the shape of a fan ‖ a variety of domestic pigeon having such a tail ‖ a member of *Rhipidura*, a genus of flycatchers of Asia and Australia

fan·tan (fǽntæn) *n.* a gambling game in which gamblers bet on how many beans, counters etc. will be left over from a quantity counted out in fours by the banker [Chin.]

fan·ta·sia (fæntéiʒə, fæntəzí:ə) *n.* a musical composition not in a set form ‖ (*mus. hist.*) a contrapuntal work in several sections for one keyboard instrument or e.g. for viols ‖ a medley of well-known airs [Ital. = fantasy]

fan·tas·tic (fæntǽstik) *adj.* belonging to the realm of fancy, *fantastic visions* ‖ very peculiar, *fantastic notions* ‖ wilfully elaborated, *fantastic convolutions* ‖ (*pop.*) incredible **fan·tás·ti·cal·ly** *adv.* [fr. M.L. *fantasticus* fr. Gk]

fan·ta·sy, phan·ta·sy (fǽntəsi:) *pl.* **fan·ta·sies, phan·ta·sies** *n.* playful imagination, fancy ‖ a grotesque mental image ‖ (*numismatics*) a pseudocoin sometimes created as a proposal for minting, sometimes by an unauthorized agency, for collectors ‖ (*psychol.*) a daydream satisfying some desire ‖ (*pop.*) thinking, planning etc. not based on sound reason or prudence [O.F. *fantasie* fr. L. fr. Gk]

Fan·ti (fǽnti:) *pl.* **Fan·ti** *n.* a people of Ghana ‖ a member of this people ‖ the Akan dialect spoken by this people ‖ the literary language based on this dialect

Fan·tin-La·tour (fɑ̃tἐlætu:r), Ignace Henri Jean Théodore (1836–1904), French painter. He excelled in still life and flower painting, and in portraits

fan tracery (*archit.*) ornamental tracery on fan vaulting

fan vaulting (*archit.*) ribbed vaulting springing from a few shafts and spreading fanwise delicately

fan·wort (fǽnwə:rt) *n. Cabomba caroliniana*, fam. *Nymphaeaceae*, a water plant with peltate floating leaves and much-divided submerged leaves, commonly used in aquariums

F.A.O. *FOOD AND AGRICULTURAL ORGANIZATION*

far (fɑr) *comp.* **far·ther** (fɑ́rðər), **fur·ther** (fə́:rðər) *superl.* **far·thest** (fɑ́rðist), **fur·thest** (fé:rðist) **1.** *adv.* at a considerable distance or to a great extent (in space or time), *far from the shore, far back in history, far from agreeing* ‖ very much, *far better at painting than at writing* **as far as** to but not beyond, *let's go as far as the river* ‖ to the extent that, *as far as he is concerned* **by far** by a large degree **far from it** not at all **how far** to what extent, *how far can he be trusted?* **so far** up to now ‖ to a certain extent, *he is patient with her so far but then he begins to shout* **so far so good** up to this point all is well **thus far** up to this point or moment **to go far** to be eminently successful **to go too far** to overstep the bounds of truth or politeness **2.** *adj.* very distant, remote, *the far horizon* ‖ the more distant of two, *the far side of the lake* [O.E. *feorr*]

far·ad (fǽrəd) *n.* (*elec.*) the mks unit of electrical capacitance: the capacitance of a capacitor which when charged with 1 coulomb maintains a difference in potential of 1 volt between its plates **far·a·da·ic** (færədéiik) *adj.* faradic [after Michael *Faraday*]

Far·a·day (fǽrədei), Michael (1791–1867), English physical scientist. He discovered electromagnetic induction and many other important electrical and magnetic phenomena. He was,

early in his career, assistant to Sir Humphry Davy

far·a·day (fǽrədei) *n.* (*phys.*) the quantity of electricity (=96,500 coulombs) needed to deposit or evolve 1 equivalent weight of an element or ion during an electrochemical reaction [after Michael *Faraday*]

Faraday effect the rotation of plane-polarized light as it traverses an isotropic transparent medium along the lines of force of a magnetic field

fa·rad·ic (fərǽdik) *adj.* of or pertaining to induced asymmetric alternating currents of electricity (cf. GALVANIC)

fa·ra·dism (fǽrədizəm) *n.* (*cosmetology*) use of electric current to stimulate body tissue

Faraketen Panzer Roland *n.* (*mil.*) armored infantry carrier of the German Federal Republic

far and away by a big lead or margin, *he is far and away our best swimmer*

far and near everywhere

far·an·dole (fǽrəndoul) *n.* a Provençal dance in 6/8 time accompanied by pipe and tabor [F. fr. Prov.]

far and wide over a relatively large area, *to search far and wide*

far·a·way (fɑ́rəwẹi) *adj.* remote, *faraway parts of the world* ‖ (of a facial expression) dreamy

farce (fɑrs) *n.* a dramatic representation intended only to amuse (cf. COMEDY) ‖ the class of such dramas ‖ any event with a futile or absurd outcome **far·ci·cal** *adj.* **far·ci·cál·i·ty** *n.* the quality of being farcical [F.]

far·cy (fɑ́rsi:) *pl.* **far·cies** *n.* a contagious, sometimes fatal, disease of horses, mules etc., a form of glanders [fr. F. *farcin*]

fare (feər) *n.* the cost of a journey (by train, bus, airplane, ship etc.) ‖ (*commerce*) a passenger in a hired vehicle ‖ food, diet, *good plain fare* [O.E. *fær* and *faru*]

fare *pres. part.* **far·ing** *past* and *past part.* **fared** *v.i.* to manage, get along ‖ (with 'well' or 'ill') to experience luck of the kind indicated ‖ (with 'well' or 'ill') to be fed with the amount and quality of food indicated [O.E. *faran*, to travel]

Far East the region of E. and S.E. Asia including China, Korea and Japan, and sometimes the Malay Archipelago and Indochina **Far Eastern** *adj.*

Fa·rel (færel), Guillaume (1489–1565), French religious reformer. With Calvin he took an active part in the Reformation in Geneva (1534–5)

fare·well (feərwél) **1.** *interj.* (*rhet.*) goodbye **2.** *n.* a leavetaking, *to make one's farewells* **3.** (fέ:rwel) *adj.* last, parting, *a farewell glance* [M.E. *farewell*]

far·fetched (fɑ́rfétʃt) *adj.* (of jokes, comparisons, excuses etc.) laboriously contrived, not plausible

far-flung (fɑ́rflʌ́ŋ) *adj.* (*rhet.*) of huge extent ‖ (*rhet.*) remote

Far·go (fɑ́rgou), William George (1818–81), U.S. businessman. He cofounded (1850, with Henry Wells) the American Express company and organized (1852) the Wells, Fargo company

far-gone (fɑ́rgɔ́n, fɑ́rgɑ́n) *adj.* (esp. in mental or physical illness or moral corruption) in a very bad state

fa·ri·na (fərí:nə) *n.* flour or meal made from wheat, nuts, starchy roots, sea moss etc. ‖ (*Br.*) starch, esp. potato starch [L.=flour]

far·i·na·ceous (færinéiʃəs) *adj.* starchy ‖ like meal [fr. L. *farinaceus*]

fa·ri·nose (fǽrinous) *adj.* yielding farina ‖ (*biol.*) producing or covered with a whitish powder or fine dust [fr. L. *farinosus*]

farm (fɑrm) **1.** *n.* an area of land used for cultivation or animal breeding under individual or collective management ‖ a tract of water for cultivating fish, oysters etc. ‖ (*baseball*) a minor-league team attached to a major-league team and providing it with recruits for training **2.** *v.t.* to raise (crops, stock, poultry etc.) on a farm for the market ‖ to use (land) for this purpose, *he farms 500 acres* ‖ (*hist.*, often with 'out') to lease for a fixed sum or fixed percentage (the right to collect taxes etc.) to someone ‖ (*hist.*) to pay a certain sum for (the right to collect taxes etc.) ‖ (often with 'out') to delegate (work) to outside workers, *to farm out a contract* ‖ *v.i.* to be a farmer, cultivate the land **fárm·er** *n.* a person who owns or rents a farm [F. *ferme*]

Far·mer (fɑ́rmər), James Leonard (1920–　), U.S. black civil rights leader and founder of the

Congress of Racial Equality (CORE). Elected (1961) its full-time national director, he became a major spokesman for the black nonviolent cause

Farmer, John (late 16th c.), English composer of madrigals and church music, esp. 'First Set of English Madrigals' (1599)

farm·er-gen·er·al (fɑ́rmərdʒénərəl) *pl.* **farm·ers-gen·er·al** *n.* (*F. hist.*) one of the members of a corporation authorized to farm taxes (1697–1789) [trans. of F. *fermier-général*]

Farmers Union (National Farmers union, Farmers Educational and Cooperative union), a union founded (1902) at Point, Texas, to promote education in marketing, credit and tenure for farmers and to establish cooperative marketing enterprises. Originally based in the south, it became active (1920) in the plains states. It differs from other farmers' organizations in that it engages in more informal cooperative activities with organized labor, caters more to the small farmer, and advocates greater market reform

farm·hand (fɑ́rmhænd) *n.* a paid worker on a farm

farm·house (fɑ́rmhaus) *pl.* **farm·hous·es** (fɑ́rmhauziz) *n.* the dwelling on his land in which a farmer lives

farm laborer, *Br.* **farm labourer** a farmhand

farm·stead (fɑ́rmsted) *n.* the land and buildings making up a small farm

farm team *n.* (*baseball*) a minor-league club formed to provide training for players groomed for a major-league team

farm·yard (fɑ́rmjɑrd) *n.* the space adjoining or enclosed by farm buildings, generally serving as a run for chickens etc.

Farne Islands (fɑrn) a group of some 17 islets on N.E. Northumberland, England. Inner Farne contains a 14th-c. chapel on the site of a hermitage of St Cuthbert (late 7th c.)

Far·ne·se (fɑrnéze) an Italian family which ruled (1545–1731) Parma and Piacenza, a duchy created (1545) by Pope Paul III (Alessandro Farnese)

Farnese, Alessandro (1545–92), duke of Parma and Piacenza (1586–92), general and diplomat in the service of Philip II of Spain. As governor of the Netherlands (1578–92), he put down revolts against Spanish rule, and intervened in France (1590–2) against Henri IV

far·o (féərou) *n.* a gambling game played with cards [fr. F. *pharaon*, pharaoh, perh. because of a picture on one of the cards]

Far·oe Islands, Faer·oe Islands (féərou) (Dan. Faeroerne, Faroese Föroyar) a group of self-governing Danish islands (area 540 sq. miles, pop. 43,000) in the N. Atlantic between Iceland and the Shetlands. Capital: Thorshavn (pop. 11,586). Products: wool, fish, root vegetables. The Faroes were settled by Vikings (9th c.), became Danish (1380) and were granted home rule (1948)

Far·o·ese (féərouí:z, féərouí:s) **1.** *pl.* **Far·o·ese** *n.* a native of the Faroe Islands ‖ a Norse dialect close to Icelandic spoken in the Faroe Islands **2.** *adj.* relating to the inhabitants or language of the Faroe Islands

far-off (fɑ́rɔ́f, fɑ́rɑ́f) *adj.* remote in space or time

Fa·rouk (fərú:k) (1920–65), the last king of Egypt (1936–52). He was forced into exile (1952) by a military coup (*NEGUIB)

far-out (slang) **1.** *adj.* beyond extreme **2.** used as an exclamation, wonderful

Far·quhar (fɑ́rkwər, fɑ́rkər), George (1677–1707), Anglo-Irish dramatist. 'The Recruiting Officer' (1706) and 'The Beaux' Stratagem' (1707) were his most popular plays. His work was more sentimental and less cynical than that of Restoration dramatists before him

far·ra·go (fərɑ́gou) *pl.* **far·ra·goes** *n.* a confused jumble, *his story was a wild farrago of nonsense* [L. = mixed fodder]

Far·ra·gut (fǽrəgət), David Glasgow (1801–70), U.S. admiral. During the Civil War he secured the surrender (1862) of Confederate-held New Orleans, assisted Grant in the capture of Vicksburg, and, after crossing the mine-infested Mobile Bay, seized (1864) the 'Tennessee' and the forts within the channel

Far·rar (fǽrər), Frederic William (1831–1903), English clergyman and writer. His works range from a 'Life of Christ' (1874, in answer to Renan's) to sentimental and highly moral stories or boarding schools, e.g. 'Eric, or Little by Little' (1858). He became dean of Canterbury in 1895

CONCISE PRONUNCIATION KEY: (**a**) æ, c*a*t; ɑ, c*a*r; ɔ f*aw*n; ei, f*a*ce.　(**e**) e, h*e*n; i:, sh*ee*p; iə, d*ee*r; εə, b*ea*r.　(**i**) i, f*i*sh; ai, t*i*ger; ə:, b*i*rd. (**o**) o, *o*x; au, c*ow*; ou, g*oa*t; u, p*oo*r; ɔi, r*oy*al.　(**u**) ʌ, d*u*ck; u, b*u*ll; u:, g*oo*se; ə, b*a*cillus; ju:, c*u*be.　x, lo*ch*; θ, *th*ink; ð, bo*th*er; z, *Z*en; ʒ, corsa*g*e; dʒ, sava*g*e; ŋ, orangutan*g*; j, *y*ak; ʃ, *f*ish; tʃ, fet*ch*; 'l, rabb*le*; 'n, redd*en*.　Complete pronunciation key appears inside front cover.

far-reach-ing (fárrí:tʃiŋ) adj. having wide range, scope, influence or effect

far red n. at the extreme part of the infrared color spectrum with wave lengths 30–1000 microns

Far-rell (fǽrəl), James Thomas (1904–79), U.S. novelist, known for his trilogy 'Young Lonigan' (1932), 'The Young Manhood of Studs Lonigan' (1934) and 'Judgement Day' (1935), which depict the life of the lower-middle-class Irish on Chicago's south side

far-ri-er (fǽri:ər) n. (Br.) a smith who shoes horses **fár-ri-er-y** n. (Br.) the farrier's craft [O.F. ferrier]

far-row (fǽrou) 1. n. a litter of pigs 2. v.i. (of a sow) to give birth to a litter ‖ v.t. (of a sow) to give birth to (a litter) [O.E. fearh]

farrow adj. (of cows) not calving in a given year or season [origin unknown]

far-see-ing (fársi:iŋ) adj. able to see a long chain of consequences

far-sight-ed (fársáitid) adj. hypermetropic (opp. NEARSIGHTED) ‖ prudent

fart (fart) 1. v.i. (not in polite usage) to break wind, let wind fly from the anus 2. n. (not in polite usage) such an emission of wind [M.E.]

far-ther (fárðər) alt. comp. of FAR ‖ adv. and adj. further [M.E. ferther]

far-ther-most (fárðərmoust) adj. most distant, most remote

far-thest (fárðist) alt. superl. of FAR ‖ adj. and adv. furthest [M.E. ferthest]

far-thing (fárðiŋ) n. a very small British coin, of the value of a quarter of a penny, no longer current ‖ the least little bit, not to care a farthing [O.E. feorthing]

far-thin-gale (fárðiŋgeil) n. (hist., 16th and 17th cc.) a petticoat with whalebone hoops, or a pad forming a roll around the waist, worn to make a skirt stand out at the hips [fr. O.F. verdugale fr. Span.]

fart-lek (fártlək) n. (sports) training program of jogging, running, and walking

Far West the U.S.A. west of the Great Plains

f.a.s. *FREE ALONGSIDE SHIP

fas-ces (fǽsi:z) pl. n. (hist.) a bundle of rods bound together with the blade of an axe projecting, used as the insignia of the magistrates of ancient Rome ‖ (hist.) this as a symbol of Italian Fascism [L., pl. of fascis, a bundle]

fas-ci-a (fǽʃi:ə, féiʃə) pl. **fas-ci-ae** (fǽʃi:i:, féiʃi:) n. (archit.) a long band of wood or stone under eaves or cornices, esp. in the Ionian order ‖ (anat.) an ensheathing band of connective tissue ‖ (zool.) a broad, well-defined band of color ‖ (Br.) a dashboard **fás-ci-al** adj. [L.= band]

fas-ci-ate (fǽʃi:it) adj. (bot., of stems, branches etc.) coalescing and thus abnormally thick and flattened ‖ (zool.) marked by bands of color **fas-ci-at-ed** (fǽʃi:eitid) adj. fasciate **fas-ci-á-tion** n. [fr. L.L. fasciare (fasciatus), to bind]

fas-ci-cle (fǽsik'l) n. (bot.) a bunch, bundle, cluster ‖ (anat.) a bundle of nerve fibers ‖ a single part of a book published in sections **fás-ci-cled**, **fas-cic-u-lar** (fəsíkjulər), **fas-cíc-u-late** (fəsíkjuléit, fəsíkjulit), **fas-cic-u-lat-ed** adjs. (bot.) arranged in clusters **fas-cic-u-lá-tion** n. [fr. L. fasciculus dim. of fascis, a bundle]

fas-ci-cule (fǽsikjuːl) n. a fascicle of a book [F. fr. L. fasciculus]

fas-ci-nate (fǽsineit) pres. part. **fás-ci-nat-ing** past and past part. **fás-ci-nat-ed** v.t. to compel delighted interest in ‖ (pop., of snakes, stoats etc.) to paralyze by ocular hypnosis ‖ to hold (someone) as if under a spell **fás-ci-nat-ing** adj. **fas-ci-ná-tion**, **fás-ci-na-tor** ns. [fr. L. fascinare (fascinatus), to enchant]

fas-cine (fæsíːn) n. a long bundle of sticks bound together and used chiefly in war for emergency engineering operations, e.g. to facilitate the passage of tanks and other vehicles [F.]

Fas-cism (fǽʃizəm) n. (hist.) the ideological outlook and its extremist manifestations in Mussolini's Italian counterrevolutionary movement (1919-22) and in his dictatorship (1922-43). The Roman fasces were taken as a renewed symbol of law and order, but violence in putting down opposition characterized the régime **fas-cism** any political or social ideology of the extreme right which relies on a combination of pseudoreligious attitudes and the brutal use of force for getting and keeping power [fr. Ital. fascismo fr. fascio, a political group]

Fas-cist (fǽʃist) 1. n. an adherent or supporter of Fascism ‖ a member of the Fascist political party **fas-cist** a someone who holds fascist views 2. adj. of or pertaining to Fascist ideas or to the Fascist régime **fas-cist** characterized by or advocating fascism [fr. Ital. fascista]

fash-ion (fǽʃən) 1. n. way, manner, entertained in magnificent fashion ‖ the style of clothes worn at a particular period, Elizabethan fashions ‖ modishness, a slave to fashion ‖ social prominence, women of fashion ‖ a prevailing mode in speech, personal adornment, social behavior etc. ‖ dress in its aspect of changing style, a history of fashion **after a fashion** in a rough-and-ready or slipshod way **after one's usual fashion** in one's customary way **all the fashion** fashionable **in fashion** currently the mode **out of fashion** no longer stylish **to set the fashion** to introduce a new style which others copy 2. v.t. to mold, shape **fásh-ion-a-ble** adj. currently in style, modish ‖ being the object of a modish interest, a fashionable painter **fásh-ion-a-bly** adv. [O.F. façon]

fashion plate an illustration of a new style of dress ‖ (pop.) someone dressing in the height of fashion

Fa-sho-da (fəfóudə) a town (now Kodok) of the Sudan. It was the scene of a diplomatic incident (1898) when it was occupied by Marchand on behalf of France, while Kitchener claimed the territory for Britain. After several months of crisis, France withdrew (1899)

fast (fæst, fast) 1. v.i. to abstain from food, either entirely or partly 2. n. an act of abstinence from food ‖ a period of time during which adherents of a faith are required to abstain from food **to break one's fast** to resume eating after a period of abstinence [O.E. fæstan, to observe]

fast adj. swift, a fast runner ‖ speedy, a fast worker ‖ lasting a short time, a fast trip ‖ allowing rapid progress, a fast racetrack ‖ (of a clock or watch) in advance of the real time ‖ loyal, fast friends ‖ firmly fixed, the pole is fast in the ground ‖ (of dyes) that will not wash out or fade ‖ (photog.) having a high shutter speed ‖ gay and dissipated, to lead a fast life ‖ (bacteriol.) resistant to destruction or staining **to make fast** to tie (a boat) up ‖ to lock, bar or bolt [O.E. fæst]

fast n. (naut.) a mooring rope, hawser or chain [M.E. fest fr. O.N. festr, a rope]

fast adv. quickly, hurriedly, to drive fast ‖ fixedly, securely, stuck fast ‖ soundly, fast asleep ‖ wildly, in a dissipated way, living fast **to be fast and furious** (of fun, a game etc.) to be hectic **to hold fast** to keep secure hold of, or keep constantly in mind **to play fast and loose** to be deceitful and inconstant or reckless and irresponsible **to stand fast** to hold one's ground, be firm ‖ (mil.) to cease to move (because of an emergency) and await new orders [O.E. fæste]

fast-back (fǽstbæk) n. 1. automobile designed with rear section sloping downward in an unbroken line 2. the roof of such a vehicle Cf HATCH BACK, NOTCH BACK

Fastback n. breed of lean pigs, first produced in Britain in 1971

fast-breed-er reactor (fǽstbri:dər) (nuclear phys.) nuclear plant that produces fissionable material from high-energy neutrons as a byproduct in excess of the amount it uses

fast day (eccles.) a day appointed for fasting

fas-ten (fás'n, fæs'n) v.t. to make secure ‖ to fix firmly, tie, attach ‖ (with 'on') to fix (thoughts, attention) ‖ to get firm hold with (the teeth) ‖ v.i. (with 'on') to get firm hold, the dog fastened on the seat of his pants ‖ (with 'on') to fix one's attention, the magistrate fastened on one detail in the evidence ‖ to close securely **to fasten upon** to grasp (an excuse etc.) ‖ to single out and attack **fás-ten-er** n. a device for attaching one thing to another, a snap fastener **fás-ten-ing** n. a device for securing something, e.g. a jewel case, dress, necklace [O.E. fæstnian]

fast-food adj. of restaurants, usually of a chain, that serve quickly prepared foods, esp. frankfurters, hamburgers, French fries, sandwiches **fast food** n. the type of food available in fast-food restaurants

fas-tid-i-ous (fæstídi:əs) adj. having highly developed taste ‖ fussily particular, too fastidious to stay at a cheap hotel ‖ meticulous, check with fastidious care [fr. L. fastidiosus, distasteful]

fas-tig-i-ate (fæstídʒi:it, fæstídʒi:eit) adj. narrowing to a pointed top ‖ (bot.) having erect and clustered branches ‖ (zool.) united in a tapering bundle [fr. L. fastigatus fr. fastigium, the top of a gable, summit]

fast-ness (fǽstnis, fástnis) n. fixedness, irremovability, e.g. of dyes ‖ (hist. and rhet.) a fortress or stronghold [FAST, fixed]

fast tape n. (trading) term inserted in reports when transactions on the trading floor take place in such volume and with such rapidity that price quotation reports are behind

fast-track adj. extremely aggressive

fast tracking n. building technique to speed completion of a structure by beginning work early, e.g., laying a foundation before plans are completed and approved

fat (fæt) 1. n. the greasy material constituting the largest portion of the cells of adipose tissue and occurring in other parts of animals and in plants ‖ one of a class of neutral compounds which may be solid or liquid, and insoluble in water, and which are glycerides of one or more fatty acids. They are obtained industrially from the adipose tissue of animals, or from certain seeds and fruits (e.g. linseed, cottonseed, soya bean). Fats have the highest calorific value of all classes of food and are an important source of energy for warm-blooded animals. They are also used industrially, chiefly for the manufacture of soaps and lubricants ‖ a solid or semi-solid fat as distinguished from a fatty oil ‖ the best part of something, living on the fat of the land **the fat is in the fire** trouble is imminent 2. adj. (of the body) bulky due to fat rather than to bone or muscle ‖ thick, a fat wad of bank notes ‖ financially rewarding, a fat job ‖ (of animals) made fat for slaughtering, fat stock ‖ (esp. of meat) containing a high proportion of fat ‖ (of clay) sticky ‖ (of coal) bituminous ‖ (printing, of type) broadfaced ‖ (of a printed page) with large spaces [O.E. fætt]

Fatah *AL-FATAH

fa-tal (féit'l) adj. resulting in death, a fatal illness ‖ calamitous ‖ fateful **fá-tal-ism** n. the belief that all events are naturally or supernaturally predetermined ‖ the mental attitude of submission to the inevitability of the power of fate **fá-tal-ist** n. someone who adopts a fatalistic attitude, or believes in fatalism **fa-tal-ís-tic** adj. accepting one's fate with stoicism or lethargy [fr. L. fatalis, fr. fatum, fate]

fa-tal-i-ty (fətælíti:, feitælíti:) pl. **fa-tal-i-ties** n. subjection to the power of fate ‖ the quality of being predestined to disaster ‖ the quality of causing death or calamity ‖ fate ‖ a disaster, esp. one causing death ‖ a person killed in an accident or disaster [fr. F. fatalité]

fa-ta mor-ga-na (fátəmɔrgánə) pl. **fa-ta mor-ga-nas** n. a mirage, esp. that seen in the Strait of Messina [Ital.=Morgan le Fay]

fat city n. (slang) the state of being in luxury

fate (feit) n. a power that supposedly predetermines events, fate stepped in and prevented our meeting (cf. CHANCE) ‖ the history of an individual or of a social group (family, tribe, country etc.) considered as predetermined ‖ the future of a person or persons, it took the jury five minutes to settle his fate ‖ doom, destruction ‖ one's ultimate end **fát-ed** adj. predetermined, destined **fáte-ful** adj. controlled by fate ‖ critical, decisive in effect [fr. L. fatum, that which has been spoken]

Fates (feits) (Gk mythol.) three female figures believed to have control of human destiny. Clotho (Gk 'spinner') spun the thread of life, Lachesis (Gk 'caster of lots') determined its length, and Atropos (Gk 'the inflexible') lopped it off

fat farm (colloq.) a health spa, esp. for dieters

fat-head (fǽthed) n. (pop.) a stupid person

fa-ther (fáðər) 1. n. the male parent ‖ (rhet.) an ancestor, our fathers before us ‖ an originator, the father of modern astronomy ‖ a venerable person ‖ the oldest member of an institution or community **Fa-ther** a title of reverence for a priest **the Father** (theol.) the first person of the Trinity 2. v.t. to be the father of ‖ to originate and guide through the early stages, to father a bill in Congress ‖ (with 'on') to fix the original responsibility for (an idea etc.) [O.E. faeder]

Father Christmas (Br.) Santa Claus

fa-ther-hood (fáðərhud) n. the state of being a father

fa-ther-in-law (fáðərinlɔ) pl. **fa-thers-in-law** n. a husband's or wife's father

fa-ther-land (fáðərlænd) n. (esp. German usage) one's native country

fa-ther-less (fáðərlis) adj. having no living father ‖ having no acknowledged father

fa-ther-ly (fáðərli:) adj. characteristic of a loving father

father of the chapel the senior member of the association of workers in a printing house

Father of the Christian Church one of those theologians whose writings helped to define the faith in the first five centuries of the Christian Church

Father's Day an annual day (usually the third Sunday in June) when fathers are made much of, with presents etc.

fath·om (fǽðəm) **1.** *n.* a measure of depth of water equal to 6 ft ‖ (*Br.*) a quantity of wood measuring 6 sq. ft. in section **fáth·om·less** *adj.* (*rhet.*) too deep to measure, *fathomless oceans* ‖ too profound to understand, *fathomless wisdom* **2.** *v.t.* to measure the depth of, to sound ‖ to get to the bottom of, to comprehend, *to fathom someone's intentions* [O.E. *fœthm*, the extent of the arms outstretched]

fath·om·e·ter (fæðómətər) *n.* device to measure ocean depth using sonar

fathom line a nautical line with a weighted end for taking depth soundings ‖ a contour line of the ocean bed

fa·tigue (fətíːg) **1.** *n.* weariness after exertion or hard work ‖ (*zool.*) a condition of cells, tissues or organs which, as a result of excessive activity, temporarily lose the power to respond to further stimulation ‖ a condition of a material, esp. a metal, causing loss of elasticity and tendency to fracture after long or repeated stress, even though the stress may be less than that which would cause failure under static conditions ‖ (*mil.*) a noncombatant task for soldiers ‖ (*pl., mil.*) clothing worn while doing fatigue duty **2.** *v.t. pres. part.* **fa·ti·guing** *past* and *past part.* **fa·tigued** to make weary [F. *fatigue, fatiguer*]

Fat·i·mid (fǽtəmid) *n.* someone claiming descent from Fatima, daughter of Mohammed, and Ali ‖ a member of the Moslem dynasty (909–1171) which ruled in N. Africa, Egypt and Syria

Fat·i·mite (fǽtəmait) *n.* a Fatimid

fat·ling (fǽtliŋ) *n.* a young animal, esp. a calf, fattened for slaughter [fr. FAT V.+ -*ling*]

fat·ten (fǽt'n) *v.t.* to make fat ‖ to make (animals) fat for slaughtering ‖ to make (soil) fertile or rich ‖ *v.i.* to grow fat

fat·ty (fǽti:) *comp.* **fat·ti·er** *superl.* **fat·ti·est** *adj.* containing fat, adipose, *fatty tissues* ‖ caused by an accumulation of fat, *fatty degeneration of the heart*

fatty acid one of a series of monocarboxylic acids which occur naturally as glycerides or esters in fats or oils. They may be manufactured by saponification of fats or by synthesis and are used in the production of soaps and detergents

fa·tu·i·tous (fətúːitəs, fətjúːitəs) *adj.* fatuous

fa·tu·i·ty (fətúːiti:, fətjúːiti:) *pl.* **fa·tu·i·ties** *n.* foolishness ‖ something foolish [fr. F. *fatuité*]

fat·u·ous (fǽtʃuːəs) *adj.* foolish, esp. empty-headed or vacuously self-satisfied, *a fatuous smile* [fr. L. *fatuus*]

fau·ces (fɔ́ːsiːz) *pl. n.* (*anat.*) the upper part of the throat, from the root of the tongue to the pharynx ‖ (*bot.*) the throat of a corolla [L.]

fau·cet (fɔ́ːsit) *n.* a device for controlling the flow of a fluid from a pipe or container [F. *fausset, spigot*]

Faulk·ner, Falk·ner (fɔ́knər), William Harrison (1897–1962), American novelist. His novels and short stories are set in the imaginary Yoknapatawpha County, based on his own native region in Mississippi. His themes, drawn from the life mainly of poor people and oppressed blacks in the post-Civil War Southern states of the U.S.A., are usually of hardship, violence, suffering, decadence and injustice. 'Sanctuary' (1931), 'Light in August' (1932), 'As I Lay Dying' (1930) and 'The Sound and the Fury' (1929) are among the best-known. He won the Nobel prize for literature (1949)

fault (fɔlt) **1.** *n.* something for which one is rightly open to blame ‖ a mistake, *a fault in addition* ‖ a blemish, *a slight fault in the rim* ‖ a moral failing ‖ (*geol.*) a fracture within the earth's crust caused by vertical slipping or folding, distinguished from a simple crack by the break in continuity of the rock strata ‖ an imperfect insulation or leakage in a telecommunications line ‖ (*tennis* etc.) a failure to serve the ball correctly **at fault** responsible for a mistake or a breach of good manners etc. **to find fault with** to complain about **to a fault** excessively, to the point of imprudence **fáult·i·ly** *adv.* **fáult·less** *adj.* not to blame ‖ without blemish **fáult·y** *comp.* **fault·i·er** *superl.* **fault·i·est** *adj.* imperfect, defective ‖ *v.t.* to criticize (someone) with justice, *you can't fault him in matters of*

grammar ‖ (*geol.*) to cause a fault in [M.E. *faut* fr. O.F.]

fault·find·er (fɔ́ltfaindər) *n.* a tiresome person constantly finding fault with things or people **fáult·find·ing** *n.*

faun (fɔn) *n.* (*Rom. mythol.*) one of a class of lustful, benevolent rural deities, represented as men with the horns, legs and tail of a goat and sharply pointed ears. They personified the fertility of nature [fr. L. *Faunus*, identified with Gk Pan]

fau·na (fɔ́nə) *pl.* **fau·nas, fau·nae** (fɔ́niː) *n.* animal life in general, as distinguished from flora, esp. the indigenous animals of a certain region, environment or period ‖ a classification of the animals of a region, environment or period **fáu·nal** *adj.* [Mod. L. fr. *Fauna*, goddess sister of Faunus]

Faure (fɔr), Francois Félix (1841–99), French statesman, president of France (1895–9)

Fau·ré (fourei), Gabriel Urbain (1845–1924), French composer. He was a great teacher (e.g. of Ravel) and his exquisite songs are important in the history of French music. The best known are settings of the works of the poets of late 19th-c. France, esp. Verlaine. His last great song cycle,'L'horizon chimérique' (1922), and his 'Requiem' for solo voices, chorus and orchestra (1882) indicate his range. Besides the songs, he wrote many works for the piano, chamber music, incidental music for the stage etc.

Faure (fɔr), François Félix (1841–99), French statesman, president of France (1895–9)

Faust legend (faust) a German legend about an astrologer who made a pact with the devil, surrendering his soul in return for youth, knowledge and magical power. The legend inspired Marlowe and Goethe and others, and provided the material for operas by Berlioz (1846) and Gounod (1859), and for a symphony by Liszt (1857)

Fau·tri·er (foutri:ei), Jean (1898–1964), French painter. His compositions of free forms in impasto reveal affinities with abstract expressionism

Fauve (fouv) *n.* a painter who worked in the spirit of Fauvism **Fáuv·ism** *n.* an early 20th-c. liberating movement in painting in France. Essentially the Fauves sought to achieve expression by a violent effort at the orchestration of pure color, and to paint nature not with formal imitation but in purely pictorial terms. Matisse, Marquet, Rouault, Friesz, Dufy, Vlaminck, Derain and (for a short time) Braque were associated with Fauvism [F.=wild animal]

faux pas (foupá) *pl.* **faux pas** (foupáz) *n.* a social blunder [F.=false step]

fa·ve·la (favélə) *n.* a Brazilian shantytown, esp. a Rio de Janeiro slum [Port.]

fa·ve·o·late (fəvíːəleit, fəvíːəlit) *adj.* (*biol.*) honeycombed or alveolate [fr. Mod. L. *faveolus* fr. *favus,* honeycomb]

fa·vor, *Br.* **fa·vour** (féivər) *v.t.* to be to the advantage of ‖ to suit, *yellow favors her complexion* ‖ (*commerce*) to oblige, *please favor us with an early reply* ‖ to show partiality towards ‖ to resemble in looks ‖ to be in favor of [O.F. *favorer*]

favor, *Br.* **favour** *n.* approbation, *to look on someone with favor* ‖ an act of kindness going beyond what could normally be expected ‖ advantage, *evidence in our favor* ‖ the condition of being approved or liked, *no longer in favor* ‖ unfair partiality ‖ an emblem or mark of support for some cause or individual, e.g. a rosette or ribbon ‖ a decorative trinket or knick-knack such as party guests may be given ‖ (*commerce*) a letter **in favor of** in support of **in someone's favor** to someone's advantage **without fear or favor** impartially, uninfluenced by threats or personal likings [M.E. *favor* fr. O.F.]

fa·vor·a·ble, *Br.* **fa·vour·a·ble** (féivərəb'l) *adj.* giving or expressing approval ‖ auspicious ‖ (of a wind) following ‖ (of business or bargaining terms) attractive, *favorable conditions* **fá·vor·a·bly,** *Br.* **fá·vour·a·bly** *adv.* [fr. F. *favorable*]

fa·vored, *Br.* **fa·voured** (féivərd) *adj.* granted special concessions

fa·vor·ite, *Br.* **fa·vour·ite** (féivərit) **1.** *n.* an object or person regarded with esteem or affection above others ‖ (*racing*) the animal generally backed to win **2.** *adj.* most or very much liked, regarded with special affection **fá·vor·it·ism,** *Br.* **fá·vour·it·ism** *n.* the showing of a special liking for one person or a few individuals in a group by acts of partiality where impartiality is called for [O.F. *favorit*]

favorite son the favored candidate of a state delegation of a political party for presidential nomination

favour *FAVOR

favourable *FAVORABLE

favoured *FAVORED

favourite *FAVORITE

fa·vus (féivəs) *n.* (*med.*) a contagious skin disease caused by a fungus [L. *favus,* honeycomb]

Fawkes (fɔks), Guy (1570–1606), English conspirator. With other Catholics he formed the Gunpowder Plot to blow up James I and parliament (Nov. 5, 1605). The plot, which may have been the work of government agents provocateurs, was discovered (Nov. 4, 1605), and Fawkes and others were executed. Guy Fawkes Day (Nov. 5) is celebrated in Britain with bonfires, fireworks and the burning of Guys

fawn (fɔn) **1.** *n.* a deer less than one year old **2.** *adj.* light yellowish-brown **3.** *v.i.* (of a doe) to give birth to a fawn [O.F. *faon*]

fawn *v.i.* (of animals, esp. dogs) to show affection or seek attention by hand-licking, rubbing up against one etc. ‖ (of persons) to seek favor by servile and flattering behavior **fáwn·ing** *adj.* [M.E. *fauhnen, fahnen*]

FAX (*abbr.*) short for facsimile, process for transmitting documents by telephone or radio

fax units *pl. n.* offices that have facsimile-transfer equipment for private or public use

fay (fei) *n.* (*rhet.*) a fairy [fr. O.F. *fae, faie*]

Fayum *FAIYUM

faze (feiz) *pres. part.* **faz·ing** *past* and *past part.* **fazed** *v.t.* to disconcert, daunt [etym. doubtful]

fa·zen·da (fazéndə) *n.* a Brazilian form of latifundio, esp. a coffee plantation [Port. fr. L. *facienda,* things to be done]

F.B.I. *FEDERAL BUREAU OF INVESTIGATION

FB-111 (*mil.*) strategic bomber version of the F-111

F clef the bass clef

fe·al·ty (fíːəlti:) *pl.* **fe·al·ties** *n.* (*hist.*) a feudal vassal's or tenant's acknowledgment of loyalty and obligation to his lord [fr. O. F. *fealte*]

fear (fiər) **1.** *n.* the instinctive emotion aroused by impending or seeming danger, pain or evil ‖ likelihood, *no fear of forgetting* ‖ danger, *fear of infection* ‖ (*pl.*) anxiety ‖ awe, reverence, *in the fear of God* **for fear** lest **for fear** because of the risk or danger of **in fear of one's life** fearing one may be killed **no fear!** (*pop.*) certainly not! **2.** *v.t.* to be afraid of, *to fear someone's anger* ‖ to imagine or assume in fear ‖ to regret politely or conventionally, *I fear I must go* ‖ to revere with awe, *to fear God* ‖ *v.i.* to be afraid, feel fear **féar·ful** *adj.* causing fear, *fearful to contemplate* ‖ reluctant through misgiving, *they were fearful of tackling him on his own ground* ‖ (*pop.*) appalling, extreme, *a fearful muddle* ‖ (*rhet.*) frightened or showing fear, *fearful entreaties* **féar·ful·ly** *adv.* (*pop.*) extremely, *they arrived fearfully late* **féar·less** *adj.* having no fear **féar·some** *adj.* causing fear ‖ daunting ‖ (*pop.*) very great, *fearsome hard luck* [O.E. *fœr,* danger, *fœran,* to terrify]

fea·si·bil·i·ty (fiːzəbíliti:) *n.* the quality of being feasible

fea·si·ble (fíːzəb'l) *adj.* possible to do or achieve ‖ possible to believe **féa·si·bly** *adv.* [O. F. *faisable*]

feast (fiːst) **1.** *n.* a fine, elaborate meal designed for celebration ‖ a date in the calendar appointed for the celebration of some religious anniversary ‖ an abundance of anything giving enjoyment, *a feast for the eyes* **2.** *v.t.* to provide with a feast ‖ *v.i.* to enjoy a feast **to feast oneself on** to enjoy (something giving pleasure) hugely [O.F. *feste, fester*]

Feast of Lanterns a Chinese festival for the final part of the new year, on the 15th of the first month

Feast of Tabernacles *SUKKOTH

feat (fiːt) *n.* a deed (physical, intellectual or moral) out of the ordinary, *a feat of balancing, feat of memory, feat of endurance* [O. F. *fait, fet,* fact]

feath·er (féðər) *v.t.* to furnish with feathers ‖ to shave down the edge of (something) so that it is very fine ‖ (*rowing*) to turn (the oar) so that its blade is horizontal and skims the water's surface lightly ‖ (*aeron.*) to turn (the propeller) so that its blades move with minimum resistance through the air ‖ (*shooting*) to knock feathers out of (a bird) but not kill it ‖ *v.i.* to grow or sprout feathers ‖ to move like feathers ‖ to feather an oar or propeller ‖ (of a hound) to

CONCISE PRONUNCIATION KEY: **(a)** æ, c*a*t; ɑ, c*a*r; ɔ f*aw*n; ei, sn*a*ke. **(e)** e, h*e*n; iː, sh*ee*p; iə, d*ee*r; ɛə, b*ea*r. **(i)** i, f*i*sh; ai, t*i*ger; əː, b*i*rd. **(o)** o, *o*x; au, c*ow*; ou, g*oa*t; u, p*oo*r; ɔi, r*oy*al. **(u)** ʌ, d*u*ck; u, b*u*ll; uː, g*oo*se; ə, b*a*cillus; juː, c*u*be. x, lo*ch*; θ, *th*ink; ð, bo*th*er; z, *Z*en; ʒ, corsa*g*e; dʒ, sava*g*e; ŋ, orangutan*g*; j, *y*ak; ʃ, *fish*; tʃ, fe*tch*; 'l, rabb*le*; 'n, redd*en*. Complete pronunciation key appears inside front cover.

make quivering movements of the stern and tail when searching for the scent **to feather one's nest** to accumulate money or property [O.E. *gefithrian*]

feather *n.* one of the epidermal outgrowths that cover the body of a bird, comprising a hollow quill and shaft from which develops the vane, composed of barbs and barbules. Feathers are light, impervious to water and, being bad conductors of heat, they help to preserve the high body temperature of birds, besides being essential for flight || (usually *pl.*) plumage || the vane of an arrow || a plume worn in a hat || a flaw marked like a feather, e.g. in an eye or a gem || (*rowing*) the action of feathering **a feather in one's cap** a personal success to be proud of **birds of a feather** people of one kind, interest or nature **in fine** (or **high, full**) **feather** in high spirits [O. E. *fether*]

feather bed a bed with a soft, thick, feather-filled mattress **feath·er·bed** (féðerbed) *pres. part.* **feath·er·bed·ding** *past* and *past part.* **feath·er·bed·ded** *v.i.* to impose a featherbed rule or work under a featherbed rule || *v.t.* to make conditions unduly easy for, *farmers are featherbedded by the new subsidies*

featherbed rule a union rule forcing employers to slow down the pace of work, employ more workers than are needed etc., when work is short

feath·er·brained (féðerbreind) *adj.* (*pop.*) stupidly frivolous

feath·er·edge (féðeredʒ) **1.** *n.* a fine edge || a board thinner at one edge than the other, used for clapboards etc. **2.** *v.t. pres. part.* **feath·er·edg·ing** *past* and *past part.* **feath·er·edged** *v.t.* to give a featheredge to, esp. to prepare (boards) for weatherboarding etc.

feath·er·grass (féðergræs, féðergrɑs) *n.* a grass of the genus *Stipa,* esp. *S. pennata* of Europe || *Leptochloa filiformis,* a grass of southern U.S.A. and tropical America

feath·er·i·ness (féðeri:nis) *n.* the quality of being feathery

feath·er·ing (féðeriŋ) *n.* the plumage of birds || feathery tufts or fringes of an animal's coat, e.g. a spaniel's || the feathers of an arrow || a featherlike structure or marking, e.g. in flowers || (*archit.*) the points of intersection of foils in window tracery, cusps

feather star a free-swimming crinoid echinoderm found in deep marine waters. It has 10 radial arms

feath·er·stitch (féðerstitʃ) **1.** *n.* a decorative zigzag stitching used in embroidery **2.** *v.t.* to embroider with this stitch

feath·er·weight (féðerweit) *n.* a professional boxer whose weight does not exceed 126 lbs. || an amateur boxer whose weight does not exceed (*Am.*) 125 lbs. or (*Br.*) 126 lbs. || somebody who does not matter much || something very light

feath·er·y (féðeri:) *adj.* light or soft as a feather, featherlike

fea·ture (fí:tʃer) **1.** *n.* a part of the face, esp. as regards appearance, *her mouth is her best feature* || (*pl.*) the face in general || the distinctive part, trait or characteristic of a thing, *geographical features, the story has some unusual features* || a distinctive article, picture etc. in a newspaper or periodical || (*Am.*= *Br.* feature film) the main item in a movie program **2.** *v.t. pres. part.* **fea·tur·ing** *past* and *past part.* **fea·tured** to give prominence to, *the magazine is featuring his articles* || (of a film) to present as the star actor or actress **féa·tured** *adj.* displayed, advertised as a special feature **féa·ture·less** *adj.* lacking distinctive features [O.F. *faiture*]

feature film (*Br.*) a movie feature

feb·re·ris·ta (febreríːsta) *n.* a supporter of Paraguay's Partido Revolucionario Febrerista, which gave (Feb. 1936) Paraguayans important social laws, incl. an agrarian reform

fe·brif·u·gal (fibrífjugl, febrifjú:g'l) *adj.* relieving fever

feb·ri·fuge (fébrifju:dʒ) **1.** *adj.* antifebrile **2.** *n.* a medicine used to relieve fever [F. *fébrifuge*]

fe·brile (fí:bril, fébril, Br. fí:brail) *adj.* of fever || feverish [F.]

Feb. February

Feb·ru·ar·y (fébru:eri:, fébju:eri:) *n.(abbr.* Feb.) the 2nd month of the year, having 28 days except in leap year, when it has 29 [M.E. *feverer* fr. O.F.]

fe·cal, fae·cal (fí:k'l) *adj.* of or relating to feces

fe·ces, fae·ces (fí:si:z) *pl. n.* bodily waste discharged through the anus [L. *faeces* pl. of *faex.* dregs]

Fech·ner (féknər), Gustav Theodor (1801–87), German philosopher and physicist. He is famous for his theories of mind-body relationships, developed in 'Elemente der Psychophysik' (1860) and 'In Sachen der Psychophysik' (1877)

feck·less (féklis) *adj.* shiftless and inefficient [Scot. *feck* perh. for EFFECT]

fec·u·lence (fékjuləns) *n.* the state of being feculent

fec·u·lent (fékjulənt) *adj.* foul, fecal [F. *féculent*]

fe·cund (fí:kənd, fékʌnd) *adj.* prolific, fertile || rich in inventive power, *a fecund imagination* [F. *fecond*]

fe·cun·date (fí:kəndeit, fékʌndeit) *pres. part.* **fe·cun·dat·ing** *past* and *past part.* **fe·cun·dat·ed** *v.t.* to make fruitful or prolific || to fertilize, pollinate, impregnate **fe·cun·da·tion** *n.* [fr. L. *fecundare* (*fecundatus*)]

fe·cun·di·ty (fikʌnditi:) *n.* the quality or state of being fecund [fr. L. *fecunditas*]

fed *past* and *past part.* of FEED **fed up** disgusted, annoyed

fe·da·yin or **fe·da·yeen** (fədæjí:n) *pl. n.* Arab guerrilla fighters

fed·er·a·cy (fédərəsi:) *pl:* **fed·er·a·cies** *n.* an alliance, federation of states [fr. L. L. *foederatus,* federated]

fed·er·al (fédərəl) **1.** *adj..* characterizing an agreement between states to unite, forgoing some sovereignty but remaining independent in internal affairs, *a federal union* || pertaining to this consolidated state, *the federal government* || relating to the central government of the U.S.A. || (*Am. hist.*) of or supporting the Union in the Civil War (1861–5) **Fed·er·al** (*Am. hist.*) favoring strong centralized government, esp. as advocated by the Federalists **2.** *n.* **Federal** (*Am. hist.*) a supporter or soldier of the Union in the Civil War (1861–5) [F. *fédéral*]

Federal Bureau of Investigation (*abbr.* F.B.I.) the investigating branch of the U.S. Department of Justice

Federal Communications Commission an independent agency of the U.S. government which regulates radio, television and interstate telephone services

federal district an area set aside by a country as the seat of its capital, e.g. the District of Columbia in the U.S.A.

Federal Emergency Relief Act (*abbr.* FERA), a U.S. Congressional act (1933), part of President Franklin Roosevelt's New Deal program. It provided outright grants to local authorities for unemployment allowances, under the direction of Harry L. Hopkins

federal funds *pl. n.* (*banking*) bank reserves in excess of the Federal Reserve Bank requirement that are available for loans to other banks

fed·er·al·ism (fédərəlizəm) *n.* the federal principle of government || the support of this principle **Fed·er·al·ism** (*Am. hist.*) the principles of the Federalists [fr. F. *fédéralisme*]

fed·er·al·ist (fédərəlist) *n.* a supporter of federalism **Fed·er·al·ist** (*Am. hist.*) a member of the political party (c. 1787–c. 1823) which favored strong centralized government during the controversy (1787–8) over the adoption of the Constitution, and which was in power 1789–1800 || (*Argentinian hist.*) a federalista [fr. F. *fédéraliste*]

fe·de·ra·lis·ta (feðeralíːsta) *n.* (*Argentinian hist.*) a supporter of regional autonomy and a loose confederation of the provinces. The conflict between federalistas and unitarios was the cause of civil war in Argentina in the 19th c. [Span.]

Federalist Papers, The a series of essays written (1787–8) by Alexander Hamilton, James Madison, and John Jay to persuade the voters of New York to support ratification of the new U.S. Constitution. Their insight into the problems of a federal system gave the Constitution its system of checks and balances. The 10th essay argues that republican institutions can succeed in a large area with a heterogeneous population

Federalist Party a U.S. political party formed (1789) by those who championed the views of Alexander Hamilton and opposed the views of Thomas Jefferson. The Federalists, generally conservative and rich, favored a strong centralized government and the promotion of industry. Their pro-British opposition to the War of 1812 led to the decline of the party outside its New England base and to its dissolution (1824)

fed·er·al·ize (fédərəlaiz) *pres. part.* **fed·er·al·iz·ing** *past* and *past part.* **fed·er·al·ized** *v.t.* and *i.* to unite in a federation

Federal Republic of Germany *GERMANY, FEDERAL REPUBLIC OF*

Federal Reserve System the central banking system of the U.S.A., consisting of 12 Federal Reserve banks, in 12 districts, with a central board. The 12 banks serve as banks of reserve and discount for more than 10,000 affiliated banks, including all national banks. The system was established in 1913

Federal Theater Project an organization established (1935) by the U.S. government to provide employment for actors and to provide the disadvantaged with a nationwide theater. It developed the 'Living Newspaper', which presented controversial events using a loose, disconnected dramatic form. The project was branded communistic by the federal government and suppressed (1939)

Federal Trade Commission (*abbr.* FTC), a U.S. commission established (1914) to police interstate commerce in order to eliminate 'unfair competition', including false or misleading advertising

fed·er·ate (fédəreit) **1.** *v. pres. part.* **fed·er·at·ing** *past* and *past part.* **fed·er·at·ed** *v.i.* to come together in federation || *v.t.* to organize (states) into a federation **2.** *adj.* federated [fr. L. *foederare* (*foederatus*)]

Federated Malay States *MALAYA*

fed·er·a·tion (fedəréiʃən) *n.* the act of uniting with a league for common purposes, esp. in forming a sovereign power with control of foreign affairs, defense etc., while each member state retains control of internal matters || a group of states so united || a sovereign state so produced || a federated society, e.g. a league of clubs, societies, trade unions (cf. CONFEDERACY) **fed·er·a·tion·ist** *n.* an advocate of federation [F.]

Federation of Arab Emirates *UNITED ARAB EMIRATES*

Federation of Rhodesia and Nyasaland the Central African Federation

fed·er·a·tive (fédərətiv, fédəreitiv) *adj.* of or relating to federation

fe·do·ra (fidɔ́ːrə, fidóurə) (*Am.*=*Br.* trilby) a man's brimmed felt hat with the crown creased lengthwise [after Sardou's play *Fédora* (1882)]

fee (fi:) **1.** *n.* a payment for the services of a professional man (e.g. a doctor or lawyer) or a public body (e.g. a library or professional body) || the entrance charge for an examination etc. || (usually *pl.*) money paid terminally to a private school || (*law*) inheritable land or estate || (*hist.*) land held in feud **2.** *v.t. pres. part.* **fee·ing** *past* and *past part.* **feed, fee'd** (*Br.*) to give a fee to [A.F. *fie, fee,* O.F. *fieu, fiu, fief*]

fee·ble (fí:b'l) *adj.* lacking in energy or strength, weak || lacking in character or intelligence || lacking in effectiveness, *a feeble speech* || dim, unclear, indistinct, *a feeble light* [O.F. *feble, foible*]

fee·ble-mind·ed (fí:b'lmáindid) *adj.* mentally deficient || silly, foolish

feed (fi:d) **1.** *v. pres. part.* **feed·ing** *past* and *past part.* **fed** (fed) *v.t.* to give food to, *to feed the dog* || to suckle (a baby) || to put food into the mouth of, *the baby can almost feed himself* || to fortify, *to feed one's hopes on horoscopes* || to supply food for, *to feed a big family* || to supply (material) to, *the conveyor belt feeds boxes into the machine* || to feed material to, *the conveyor belt feeds the machine with boxes* || to supply as fuel to, *to feed coal into a furnace* || to supply fuel to || to supply (electrical energy) to || to supply electrical energy to || to be a source of supply of, *two rivers feed the reservoir* || to supply as food, *to feed cream to cats* || (*theater*) to supply (esp. a comedian) with cue lines, improvising material on which he makes jokes || (*games,* e.g. field hockey) to give a pass to || *v.i.* (esp. of animals) to eat **to feed on** to consume, live on **to feed up** to give plenty of food to, *a convalescent needs feeding up* || to fatten (stock) **2.** *n.* food, esp. for livestock, fodder etc. || a meal, esp. (*Br.*) a feeding for a baby || the process of feeding a machine with raw material etc. || the material thus supplied || the mechanism for such feeding || (*Br.*) a straight man (actor) || the part of the action of a firearm which moves up the cartridge from the clip or magazine to the chamber **on the feed** (esp. of fish) feeding or searching for food **out at feed** turned out to graze [O.E. *fēdan*]

feed, fee'd *past* and *past part.* of FEE

feed·back (fí:dbæk) n. the return to a system, process or device of part of its output ‖ (elec.) the return to the input of an amplification system of part of the output in order to control amplification, e.g. to increase (positive feedback), decrease (negative feedback) or otherwise change the quality of amplification ‖ the use of part of the output of a system to control and correct discrepancies in the operation of the system ‖ response following an action, e.g., comments after a speech, esp. when designed to correct a situation ‖ a partial return of the end products of any process to its source, esp. in biology, psychology or sociology ‖ (med.) return to input that stimulates the proper adjustment, e.g., biofeedback

feedback inhibition (genetics) inhibition of an enzyme at the beginning of a series of reactions, resulting from a critical indication in the end product

feed·er (fí:dər) n. (entom.) an organ for feeding ‖ a device, apparatus etc. for feeding material to a machine ‖ a source of supply, e.g. a tributary to a river, branch railway to a main line, or minor road to a main one ‖ (games, e.g. rounders) the player who throws the ball to the striker ‖ a wire conductor supplying electricity ‖ (Br.) a child's feeding bottle ‖ (Br.) a child's bib worn for meals ‖ someone who or something which feeds, this rose is a gross feeder

feed-in n. an event designed to provide free food to those who attend

feed·ing (fí:diŋ) n. the act or process of feeding or being fed, esp. (Am.= Br. feed) a meal for a baby

feeding bottle a bottle containing milk etc. with a nipple, for feeding babies

feeding ground the area where a herd or group of animals customarily feeds

feed through n. (electr. eng.) the conductor connecting the two sides of a board or metal screen containing printing circuits on both sides

feed tube n. a plastic tube used to insert food into a processor bowl

feel (fí:l) 1. pres. part. **feel·ing** past and past part. **felt** (felt) v.t. to perceive, learn, explore by touching, feel the water and see how warm it is ‖ to become aware of through the senses, to feel the blast of an explosion ‖ to experience (an emotion), to feel sympathy ‖ to sense, we feel he is telling the truth, she felt things were about to go wrong ‖ to resent, she felt the slight bitterly ‖ to experience the effects of, the whole country felt the earthquake ‖ v.i. to be, or become aware of being, do you feel better now? ‖ to affect one's senses as being, it feels velvety ‖ to have sympathy or compassion, we feel with you in your loss **to feel for** to look for blindly with the hand or hands ‖ to sympathize with, we feel for you in your loss **to feel in one's** bones to know instinctively, she felt in her bones that the decision was wrong **to feel like** to be inclined to (to want(a drink etc.) **to feel oneself** to be in good health **to feel one's way** to find the way forward by groping ‖ to proceed cautiously **to feel up to** to feel fit for 2. n. the sense of touch, soft to the feel ‖ the effect on the sense of touch, to judge by the rough feel ‖ atmosphere, the room had an eerie feel ‖ an instinctive understanding of, esp. as manifesting an aptitude, a feel for clay **féel·er** n. someone who or something that feels, esp. an organ for testing by touch, e.g. the tentacle of an octopus or antenna of an insect ‖ a remark, hint, proposal etc. put out to sound the opinions of others **feel·ing** (fí:liŋ) 1. n. the act or state of someone who feels ‖ the effect conveyed by the sense of touch, a feeling of roughness ‖ sensation in general, a feeling of discomfort ‖ bodily power to feel, he has lost all feeling in the leg ‖ an emotion, feelings of gratitude ‖ resentment, antagonism, during the crisis feeling ran high ‖ (pl.) susceptibilities, emotions, to hurt someone's feelings ‖ emotional solidarity, strong family feeling ‖ sympathy, a man of feeling ‖ an intuitive belief, conviction based on other grounds than reason ‖ opinion, the general feeling was against it ‖ (with 'for') sensitive understanding or response, feeling for nature ‖ the ability to use sensitively, a feeling for language 2. adj. that feels sensitive, a feeling heart **feel·ing·ly** adv. in a way that shows the speaker's sympathy, self-pity, prejudice etc. [O.E. fēlan]

feel·ie (fí:li:) n. an artwork designed to be touched and felt **feelie** adj.

fee simple pl. **fees simple** (law) inheritable land or estate with no restriction to a particular class of heirs

feet pl. of FOOT (abbr., as a measure, ft.) **on one's feet** standing up ‖ standing up in order to make a speech ‖ recovering from illness ‖ financially independent or out of difficulty **to fall on one's feet** to be lucky, and materially successful as a result **to sit at the feet of** (rhet.) to be a pupil of **to sweep someone off his** (or her) **feet** to be instantly and overwhelmingly attractive to someone **to stand on one's own feet** to be independent as a result of one's own efforts

fee tail pl. **fees tail** (law) inheritable land or estate, restricted to certain inheritors

feet dry n. (mil.) in air intercept, close air support and air interdiction, a code meaning I am, or that contact designated is over land

feet of clay a hidden weakness discovered in someone idealized [after Nebuchadnezzar's dream, Daniel ii, 33]

Feh·ling's solution (féiliŋz) a solution of copper sulfate, caustic soda and sodium potassium tartrate, used in the detection and estimation of certain sugars [after Herman Fehling (1812–85), G. chemist]

Fehr·bel·lin, Battle of (fεərbelí:n) the Brandenburg victory (1675) over Sweden, which lost most of its German possessions

F-8 *CRUSADER

F-18 *HORNET

feign (fein) v.t. to represent by false appearance, simulate, to feign death ‖ to pretend, to feign indifference **feigned** (feind) adj. sham, fictitious, a feigned enthusiasm ‖ fraudulent, feigned documents [M.E. feinen, feignen fr. O.F.]

Fein·ing·er (fáiniŋgər), Lyonel (1871–1956), American painter. His geometric abstractions transformed objects into crystalline reflections of color and light

feint (feint) 1. n. a false appearance, pretense, to make a feint of working ‖ a mock attack meant to deceive an opponent about the attack proper, e.g. in military strategy or in boxing ‖ a deceptive movement, e.g. in fencing 2. v.i. to make a feint [F. feinte]

feints, faints (feints) pl. n. the first and last crude spirit obtained in distilling e.g. whiskey [FAINT adj.]

feld·spar (féldspɑr) n. any of a rock-forming group of crystalline minerals, white or pink in color and consisting of aluminosilicates of potassium, sodium, calcium and barium. They are used in the manufacture of porcelain and glass and as a source of semiprecious stones, e.g. moonstone **feld·spath·ic** (féldspæθik) adj. [fr. older G. feldspath fr. feld, field+spath, spar]

fe·lic·i·tate (filísiteit) pres. part. **fe·lic·i·tat·ing** past and past part. **fe·lic·i·tat·ed** v.t. to congratulate **fe·lic·i·tá·tion** n. congratulation [fr. L. felicitare (felicitatus) fr. felix, happy]

fe·lic·i·tous (filísitəs) adj. notably apt, happily expressed, well chosen [FELICITY]

fe·lic·i·ty (filísiti) pl. **fe·lic·i·ties** n. marked aptness or grace of language ‖ a well-chosen expression ‖ a state of great happiness [O.F. felicité]

fe·lid (fí:lid) n. a carnivorous animal (e.g. lion, tiger) of fam. Felidae, having soft fur and characterized by sharp teeth, sheathed, retractile claws, quick sight, keen scent and acute hearing [fr. Mod. L. Felidae fr. feles, cat]

fe·line (fí:lain) 1. adj. of cats, a feline species ‖ catlike, feline grace ‖ cunningly spiteful, a feline remark 2. n. an animal of the cat family **fe·lin·i·ty** (filíniti) n. [fr. L. felinus]

fell (fel) 1. v.t. to cut down, to fell an oak ‖ to cause to fall, to knock down ‖ (sewing) to stitch down the folded back projection of (a seam) 2. n. an amount of timber cut ‖ a seam formed by felling **féll·er** n. someone who fells timber [O.E. fellan, fiellan, fyllan]

fell n. a stretch of moorland, esp. in N. Britain ‖ (Br., in place-names) a craggy mountain [O.N. fiall]

fell n. the skin of an animal, a hide with the hair on it, pelt [O.E. fel, fell]

fell adj. (rhet.) fierce, cruel, deadly **at one fell swoop** with a single vigorous concerted attack or at a single blow [O.F. fel]

fell past of FALL

fel·lah (féla) pl. **fel·la·heen, fel·la·hin** (félahi:n), **fell·ahs** n. a peasant in Arab-speaking countries [Arab.]

fel·late (fəléit) v. to perform fellatio on **fellator** n.

Fellini (felí:ni:), Federico (1920–   ), Italian film director, known for his use of neorealism. His works include 'The White Sheikh' (1952), 'La Strada' (1954; Academy Award, 1956), 'La Dolce Vita' (1960), '8½' (1963), 'City of Women' (1981), and 'Ginger and Fred' (1986)

fel·loe (félou) n. a felly [O.E. felg]

fel·low (félou) n. a man, esp. a man of whom one speaks with familiarity or condescension ‖ a person, one, a fellow has to eat ‖ (often pl.) a companion, associate, separated from his fellows ‖ a counterpart, one of a pair, here is one but where is its fellow? ‖ (in combination with nouns) one of the same class, a fellow sufferer ‖ an elected graduate holding endowment for a period of research etc., or a member of the governing body of a college, in some (esp. British) universities **Fel·low** a member of a learned society [O.E. fēolaga, someone who lays down money in partnership, fr. O.N.]

fellow feeling sympathy arising esp. from shared experience

fel·low·man (féloumæn) pl. **fel·low·men** (féloumén) n. another human being thought of as being like oneself by virtue of his humanity

fel·low·ship (félouʃip) n. the companionship and comradeship characteristic of group solidarity or the friendly exchange between individuals that springs from shared work, shared religious practices etc. ‖ (in titles) a guild, association, fraternity etc. ‖ communion between church members etc. ‖ the position, status or salary of a college fellow

fellow traveler, esp. Br. **fellow traveller** someone supporting the aims of an organization, esp. the Communist party, without being fully committed and active

fel·ly (féli:) n. the rim of a wheel, held in place by spokes and bounded by a tire ‖ a segment of this rim [O.E. felg]

fe·lo-de-se (fí:loudisí:) pl. **fe·lo-nes-de-se** (fílóuni:zdisí:), **fe·los-de-se** (fí:louzdisí:) n. (law) a person who has committed suicide ‖ (law, sing. only) the act of suicide [L. felo, felon+de se, about himself]

fel·on (félən) n. (law) someone guilty of a felony [O.F.]

felon n. an abscess, esp. under or near the nail of a finger or toe [perh. O. F. felon, a villain]

fe·lo·ni·ous (filóuni:əs) adj. wicked, criminal ‖ (law) of the nature of a felony, a felonious act

fel·o·ny (féləni) pl. **fel·o·nies** n. (law) a grave crime (e.g. murder, arson) more serious than a misdemeanor [fr. F. félonie]

fel·site (félsait) n. feldspar and quartz in the form of a compact mass [FELSPAR]

fel·spar (félspɑr) n. (Br.) feldspar **fel·spath·ic** (felspæθik) adj. (Br.) feldspathic

felt (felt) 1. n. a fabric made by pressing and rolling (wool, hair, fur etc.) with size or lees ‖ an undercarpet or stair tread etc. made of this ‖ material like felt ‖ (papermaking) the fabric web carrying the newly formed paper over the rollers etc. 2. v.t. to make into felt ‖ to cover with felt ‖ to put felt under ‖ v.i. to mat together, e.g. after repeated washings [O.E.]

felt past and past part. of FEEL ‖ adj. experienced, admitted, a felt need

fe·luc·ca (fəlʌkə, fəlú:kə) n. a small Mediterranean coastal merchant vessel, lateen-rigged, sometimes having oars [Ital. feluca perh. fr. Arab.]

fe·male (fí:meil) 1. adj. of the sex in animals or plants that produces or is capable of producing eggs or bearing young (symbol ♀) ‖ (bot.) pertaining to any reproductive structure that contains elements to be fertilized by male elements ‖ pertaining to women, female suffrage ‖ (engin.) describing a hollow part, tool etc. fitted to take a corresponding male part, a female socket 2. n. a female person, animal or plant [M.E. femelle fr. O.F.]

female screw a hollow cylinder or cone with a spiral groove on its inner surface, into which a male screw fits

fem·i·nine (féminin) 1. adj. of the female sex ‖ of women, feminine fashions ‖ characteristic of women, feminine curiosity ‖ having qualities thought of as proper to women ‖ (gram.) having female gender 2. n. the feminine gender ‖ a word in this gender [O.F. feminin]

feminine caesura a caesura not immediately after a stressed syllable

feminine ending the ending of a line of verse with an unstressed syllable ‖ (gram.) a termination or final syllable that marks a feminine word

feminine rhyme a rhyme of two syllables, the second unstressed, e.g. 'gaily, daily'

fem·i·nin·i·ty (feminíniti) n. the quality of being feminine

fem·i·nism (féminizəm) n. the policy, practice or advocacy of political, economic and social equality for women **fém·i·nist** n. an advocate of feminism [fr. L. *femina*, woman]

fem·i·ni·za·tion (feminizéiʃən) n. the transformation of a male into a female

fem·i·nize (féminaiz) pres. part. **fem·i·niz·ing** past and past part. **fem·i·nized** v.t. to cause (a male) to become female [fr. L. *femina*, woman]

femme (fem) n. one who assumes the female role in a lesbian relationship Cf BUTCH

fem·o·ral (fémərəl) adj. of, relating to or near the femur

femto- (femtou-) combining form meaning 1 quadrillion

fem·tom·e·ter (femtómətər) *FERMI

fe·mur (fí:mər) pl. **fe·murs, fem·o·ra** (fémərə) n. the thighbone ‖ the corresponding part of an insect's leg [L.]

fen (fen) n. low marshy land, partially covered with water if not drained, or often flooded **the Fens** the low-lying alluvial flats of Cambridgeshire, Lincolnshire and Norfolk in England occupying the basins of the Nene, Great Ouse, Witham and Welland. Drainage works (begun by the Romans but dating mainly from the 17th c.) have transformed once waterlogged land into a rich fruit, vegetable and flower-growing area [O.E. *fen, fenn*]

fence (fens) 1. n. a railing (of wood, wire etc.) enclosing a field, garden etc. to keep beasts in or intruders out or simply to mark a boundary ‖ an artificial obstacle for a horse to jump over in show jumping or steeplechasing ‖ fencing with saber, épée etc. as an art ‖ a person receiving stolen goods ‖ a place where stolen goods are received ‖ a guard or guide in various machines **on the fence** not yet committed **to sit (or be) on the fence** to wait and see where the advantage lies before one commits oneself 2. v. pres. part. **fenc·ing** past and past part. **fenced** v.i. to fight in contest with a saber, épée etc. ‖ to practice fencing as a sport ‖ to avoid answering questions in debate by shifting ground or parrying ‖ to deal in stolen goods ‖ v.t. to enclose, provide or surround with a fence **to fence in** to restrict within an enclosure ‖ to restrict (a person) with controls **to fence off** to isolate by means of a fence **fénc·er** n. someone skilled in fencing ‖ someone who builds, erects or repairs fences **fénc·ing** n. the art of attack, defense etc. with sword or foil ‖ the art of parrying etc. in debate ‖ fences collectively ‖ material for making fences [M.E. *fens* short for *defens*, defense]

fence-mend·ing (fénsmendiŋ) n. restoring good political relationships

Fencer *SUKHOI

Fencer aircraft (fénsər) (mil.) U.S.S.R. fighter plane (SU-24) capable of carrying 5 tons of missiles

fend (fend) v.t. (with 'off') to repel, parry, *to fend off a blow* ‖ v.i. (with 'for') to struggle to look after, *a large family to fend for* **to fend for oneself** to manage without help **fénd·er** n. a device to defend or protect, esp. (Br.) a guard in front of an open fireplace ‖ a bundle of rope or a log of wood etc. to protect the side of a ship against the quayside or another ship ‖ (Am.=Br. bumper) a shock absorber on a locomotive ‖ (Am.=Br. mudguard, wing) a metal cover or guard over the wheel of a vehicle to deflect or catch splashes of mud from the wheels [DEFEND]

Fé·ne·lon (feinl5), François de Salignac de La Mothe- (1651–1715), French prelate and writer. He was appointed tutor to the duke of Burgundy (1689), and wrote for him 'Dialogues des morts' (published 1700) and 'les Aventures de Télémaque' (1699). These thinly-veiled criticisms of Louis XIV's policies brought him into political disfavor. His 'Explication des maximes des saints' (1697) was condemned by the Church as being favorable to quietism. Fénelon submitted, and withdrew to the archbishopric of Cambrai, to which he had been appointed in 1695. There he revised and published 'le Traité de l'existence et des attributs de Dieu' (1712). In Fénelon may be seen at work the beginnings of the new liberal outlook that was to characterize the 18th c.

fen·es·tel·la (fenəstélə) n. (archit.) a niche in the chancel wall of a church, on the south side of the altar, containing the piscina and sometimes the credence [L., dim. of *fenestra*, window]

fe·nes·tra (finéstrə) pl. **fe·nes·trae** (finé stri:) n. a small windowlike opening in a bone or between two bones, esp. one of two openings in the bone between the middle and the inner ear ‖ a transparent spot on the wings of certain insects ‖ the pit on the head of a cockroach **fe·nés·tral** adj. [L.=window]

fe·nes·trate (finéstreit) adj. having numerous openings ‖ (biol.) having small perforations or transparent spots [fr. L. *fenestrare (fenestratus)* fr. *fenestra*, window]

fen·es·tra·tion (fenistréiʃən) n. (archit.) the arrangement of windows in a building, their size, placing, style, etc. ‖ (med.) the making of an opening in a bone to replace an obstructed fenestra [fr. L. *fenestrare (fenestratus)*, to make a window in]

Feng-yang (fʌ́ŋján) (formerly Pengpu) a town (pop. 253,000) of Anhwei, China, 100 miles northwest of Nanking: iron and steel, textiles, food processing

Fen·ian (fí:njən) n. a member of the Fenian Society, or Irish Republican Brotherhood, a secret organization formed (1858) in the U.S.A. and Ireland with the aim of ending British rule in Ireland. Fenians organized raids in Canada (1866 and 1870) and England (1867), which focused attention on the Irish problem. The movement declined (1868), and disappeared with the establishment (1921) of the Irish Free State [modification of Gael. *Fiann*, a legendary band of Irish warriors]

fen·man (fénmən) pl. **fen·men** (fénmən) n. (Br.) an inhabitant of the Fens

fen·nec (fénik) n. *Fennecus zerda*, a small, fawn-colored desert fox of N. Africa with very big ears [Arab. *fenek*]

fen·nel (fén'l) n. a member of *Foeniculum*, fam. *Umbelliferae*, a genus of aromatic plants native to Europe. The bulbs and young leaves are eaten raw or cooked [O.E. *finugle, finule, fenol*]

fen·o·pro·fen [$C_{15}H_{14}O_3$] (fenəpróufən) n. (pharm.) nonsteroidal anti-inflammatory drug used as a pain reliever, esp. for arthritics; marketed as Nalfon

fen·ta·nyl [$C_{22}H_{28}N_2O$] (féntənil) n. (pharm.) analgesic drug used in postoperative periods for prevention of restlessness, emergence delirium, and excessive frequency of respiration; marketed as Sublimaze

fen·thi·on [$C_{10}H_{15}O_3PS_2$] (fénθi:ɒn) n. an organophosphorous insecticide

fen·u·greek (fénjugri:k) n. *Trigonella foenum-graecum*, fam. *Papilionaceae*, an Asiatic plant cultivated for making curry and for veterinary medicine [O.E. *fenogræcum* fr. L. *faenum graecum*, Greek hay]

feoff (fef, fi:f) 1. v.t. (hist.) to enfeoff 2. n. a fief **feoff·ee** (feffi:, fi:fi:) n. (law) someone to whom a feoffment is made [fr. O.F. *feoffé*]

feoffee in (or **of**) **trust** (law) a trustee invested with a feoffment

feoffer *FEOFFOR

feoff·ment (féfmənt, fi:fmənt) n. (law) a mode of conveying freehold land etc. ‖ the gift of a fief [A.F. *feoffement*]

feoff·or, feoff·er (féfər, fi:fər) n. (law) someone who makes a feoffment to another [fr. A.F. *feoffour*]

fe·ral (fiərəl, férəl) adj. wild ‖ like a wild beast, brutal [fr. L. *fera*, wild beast]

Fer·ber (fə́:rbər), Edna (1887–1968), U.S. writer of best-selling novels, notably 'Show Boat' (1926, musical version 1927), 'Saratoga Trunk' (1941), and 'Giant' (1952)

fer-de-lance (ferd'læns, ferd'láns) pl. **fer-de-lance** n. *Bothrops atrox*, a large poisonous snake of South and Central America, related to the rattlesnake [F.=iron head of lance]

Ferdinand I (c. 1379–1416), king of Aragon and Sicily, and count of Barcelona (1412–16)

Ferdinand II king of Aragon and Sicily *FERDINAND V OF CASTILE

Ferdinand I (1793–1875), emperor of Austria (1835–48), son of Francis I. Suffering from fits of insanity, and faced with revolts in Vienna (1848), he abdicated in favor of his nephew Franz Josef I

Ferdinand (1861–1948), ruling prince (1887–1908) and czar (1908–18) of Bulgaria. After defeats in the 2nd Balkan War and the 1st world war, he was forced to abdicate, and retired to his native Germany

Ferdinand I 'the Great' (c. 1016–65), king of Castile (1035–65) and León (1037–65). He drove the Moors from Toledo, Saragossa and Seville

Ferdinand III, St (c. 1199–1252), king of Castile (1217–52) and León (1230–52). He permanently united the crowns of Castile and León, and confined the Moors to Granada. Feast: May 30

Ferdinand V 'the Catholic' (1452–1516), king of Castile (1474–1504), (as Ferdinand II) king of Aragon and Sicily (1479–1516) and (as Ferdinand III) king of Naples (1504–16), son of John II of Aragon. His marriage (1469) to Isabella I of Castile, and his conquest (1492) of the Moorish kingdom of Granada, united Spain. He established (1478) the Inquisition in Spain, and attempted to expel the Jews (1492) and the Moors (1502). He sponsored Columbus's voyage (1492) to the New World, intervened in the Italian Wars, and bequeathed a large empire to his grandson, the future Emperor Charles V

Fer·di·nand I (fə:rdinænd) (1503–64), Holy Roman Emperor (1558–64), king of Hungary and Bohemia (1526–64). As ruler of the Hapsburgs' German possessions (1521–64), he was responsible for the compromise Peace of Augsburg (1555) between Catholics and Protestants

Ferdinand II (1578–1637), Holy Roman Emperor (1619–37), king of Bohemia (1617–27) and of Hungary (1618–26), grandson of Ferdinand I. His reign was spent in fighting Protestantism during the Thirty Years' War, a policy which met with failure in the Treaty of Prague (1635)

Ferdinand III (1608–57), Holy Roman Emperor (1637–57), king of Hungary (1626–57), and of Bohemia (1627–57), son of Ferdinand II. He led the imperial forces in the Thirty Years' War, but had to assent to the Treaty of Westphalia (1648), which virtually ended the central power of the Holy Roman Empire

Ferdinand I (c. 1423–94), king of Naples (1458–94). His autocratic rule provoked revolts (1462 and 1485)

Ferdinand III king of Naples *FERDINAND V OF CASTILE

Ferdinand IV king of Naples *FERDINAND I OF THE TWO SICILIES

Ferdinand I (Port. Fernando) (1345–83), king of Portugal (1367–83). He fought a series of disastrous wars (1370–82) against Castile, in which John of Gaunt intervened (1372) on behalf of Portugal

Ferdinand (1865–1927), king of Rumania (1914–27). He brought Rumania into the 1st world war on the side of the Allies

Ferdinand VI (c. 1713–59), king of Spain (1746–59), son of Philip V

Ferdinand VII (1784–1833), king of Spain (1808–33), son of Charles IV. He was deposed by Napoleon a month after his accession (1808), but restored in 1814. The Spanish-American colonies became independent during his reign

Ferdinand I (1751–1825), king of the Two Sicilies (1816–25) and (as Ferdinand IV) of Naples (1759–1806). He was dispossessed of Naples (1806) by Napoleon, but continued to reign in Sicily under English protection until he was proclaimed king of the Two Sicilies. His reactionary rule provoked a revolt (1820)

Ferdinand II (1810–59), king of the Two Sicilies (1830–59). A reactionary despot, he gained the nickname 'Bomba' from the bombardments with which he crushed revolts (1848–9)

fer·e·to·ry (féritɔri:, féritouri:) pl. **fer·e·to·ries** n. a shrine, usually portable, for a Christian saint's relics ‖ the chapel for keeping such a shrine, often behind the high altar [M.E. *fertre* fr. O.F.]

Fer·gha·na (fərgúnə) a fertile valley (area 10,500 sq. miles) in Uzbekistan and Tadzhikstan, U.S.S.R., watered by the Syr Darya: cotton, fruit, silk

fe·ri·al (fiəri:əl) adj. (eccles.) of a day in the calendar which is not a festival or fast day ‖ of a service appointed for such a day [F. *férial*]

fe·rine (fiərain) adj. feral [fr. L. *ferinus* fr. *fera*, wild beast]

Fer·man·agh (fərmǽnə) the southwestern county (area 714 sq. miles, pop. 50,900) of Northern Ireland. County town: Enniskillen

Fer·mat (fermǽ), Pierre de (1601–65), French mathematician and founder of the modern theory of numbers. His 'last theorem', still lacking a general proof, stated that if n, x, y and z are integers, $x^n + y^n = z^n$ cannot be true if n is greater than 2. With Pascal he developed the theory of probability. He formulated the general principle (called Fermat's principle) concerning the behavior of light, stating that in traveling from one point to another a ray of light will take the path of minimum or maximum time as compared with adjacent arbitrary paths. The laws of reflection and refraction may be shown to be direct consequences of this (*GEOMETRICAL OPTICS)

fer·ma·ta (fermátə) n. (mus.) a pause [Ital.]

fer·ment (fə́rment) v.i. to undergo fermentation ‖ v.t. to cause fermentation in ‖ to inflame, excite, stir with anger etc. [F. fermenter]

fer·ment (fə́:rmənt) n. any agent able to produce fermentation by enzyme action ‖ fermentation ‖ commotion, unrest, tumult [F.]

fer·men·ta·tion (fə:rmentéifən) n. a chemical change produced by enzymes, particularly an energy-producing transformation of carbohydrate material yielding esp. alcohols, acids and carbon dioxide. The process of fermentation is widely used industrially in the production of alcoholic beverages and certain pharmaceuticals ‖ restless excitement **fer·men·ta·tive** (fə:rméntətiv) adj. able to ferment or to cause to ferment [fr. L. fermentatio (fermentationis)]

Fer·mi (férmi:), Enrico (1901–54), Italian physicist. He migrated to the U.S.A. (1939) and worked on the first controlled release of nuclear energy (1942). This led to the manufacture of the atomic bomb. Nobel prize for physics (1938)

fer·mi (fə́:rmi:) n. unit of length equal to 10^{-13} cm used in measuring nuclear distances

Fer·mi-Di·rac statistics (férmi:diræk) a quantum mechanical statistical system which analyzes the permitted distribution of particles among the allowed energy states of a system and which demonstrates that two identical fundamental particles having nonintegral spin quantum number cannot exist in the same energy state (cf. BOSE-EINSTEIN STATISTICS)

fer·mi·on (férmi:ɒn) n. (phys.) any fundamental particle having nonintegral spin quantum number (e.g. 1/2, 3/2, 5/2 etc.) and that obeys Fermi-Dirac statistics [after Enrico Fermi]

fer·mi·um (férmi:əm) n. an artificial, radioactive element (symbol Fm, at. no. 100, mass of isotope of longest-known half-life 253) [after Enrico Fermi]

fern (fə:rn) n. a member of Felicineae, a class of vascular, nonflowering plants characterized by alternation of generations. The sporophyte is the conspicuous generation, possessing a vascular root and stem and large, pinnately compound fronds bearing sori on the margin or undersurface. Spores released by the sori give rise on germination to the gametophyte generation, consisting of a small flat thallus producing antheridia and archegonia. Fern species are numerous, grow in tropical and temperate zones, and exhibit wide variations in structure (* PTEROPSID) [O.E. fearn]

Fer·nán·dez de Li·zar·di (fernándesðeli:sárði:), José Joaquín (1776–1827), Mexican novelist, known as 'El pensador mexicano'. His 'El Periquillo Sarniento' (1816), in the Spanish picaresque tradition, describes Mexican society shortly before independence and the longings of the mestizo for national and spiritual freedom. 'La Quijotita y su prima' (1818) treats of the education of women. The autobiographical 'Noches Tristes' (1818) introduced Romanticism to Mexico. 'Don Catrín de la Fachenda' (1832) presented a new picaresque type, the fallen aristocrat

Fernández de Oviedo, Gonzalo (1478–1557), Spanish historian and naturalist, author of the 50-volume 'Historia general y natural de las Indias' (1535–57)

Fer·nan·do de No·ron·ha (fernándudənərɔ́njə) a group of islands (area 10 sq. miles, pop. 1,400) about 225 miles off the east coast of Brazil; penal colony

Fer·nan·do Poo (or **Po**) (fernándoupóu), or Bioko, a mountainous, volcanic island (area 779 sq. miles, pop. 62,000) in the Gulf of Guinea, comprising, with Annobón (area 6 sq. miles, pop. 1,400), part of Equatorial Guinea. Capital: Santa Isabel. People: Bubi (Bantuspeaking), with Nigerian and various European minorities. Highest point: 10,190 ft. Exports: cocoa, coffee, sugar, cotton, palm oil, hardwoods. Discovered by the Portuguese (1470), it was ceded to Spain (1778) and became part of Equatorial Guinea (1959)

Fer·nel (fernel), Jean (1497–1558) French physician, astronomer and mathematician

fe·ro·cious (fəróufəs) adj. savage, fierce, a ferocious animal ‖ cruel, violent, a ferocious attack ‖ intense, ferocious energy [fr. L. ferox (ferocis), fierce]

fe·roc·i·ty (fərósiti:) pl. **fe·roc·i·ties** n. the quality of being ferocious ‖ an act of intense cruelty [fr. F. férocité]

Fer·rar (férər), Nicholas (1592–1637), English theologian. He founded (1625) a religious community at Little Gidding, Huntingdonshire, disbanded (1647) by parliament

Fer·ra·ra (ferárə) a city (pop. 150,265) near the Po in Emilia, Italy, center of a rich agricultural area, with sugar refineries, textile and shoe factories. It was a brilliant capital under the house of Este. Castello Estense (1385), Renaissance palaces, cathedral (begun 1135). University (1391)

Ferraro, (fərárou), Geraldine Anne (1935–), U.S. politician, who was the first major-party female vice presidential candidate (Democratic party, 1984). A lawyer, she represented the borough of Queens in New York City in the U.S. House of Representatives (1979–84) before being selected to run (1984) with Democratic presidential candidate Walter Mondale; they were defeated by Republicans Ronald Reagan and George Bush. Her campaign was plagued by allegations of corruption in her family's business dealings

Fe·rre (fére), Luis Alberto (1904–), Puerto Rican politician, founder (1967) of the New Progressive party, which favors statehood for Puerto Rico. As governor (1969–73), he respected the 1967 referendum ratifying the constitution of 1952, which established Puerto Rico as an Associated Free State

fer·re·dox·in (ferədóksin) n. (biochem.) plant protein containing iron that transfers electrons in anaerobic bacteria cells or in organisms depending on photosynthesis

fer·ret (férit) 1. n. Mustela furo, an albino variety of the European polecat, often kept half-tamed for use in netting rabbits ‖ Mustela nigripes, a related variety 2. v.i. to hunt with ferrets ‖ v.t. to clear (an area, burrow etc.) by using ferrets **to ferret out** to search out, esp. by close questioning or guile, to ferret out a secret **fér·ret·y** adj. (of people) shifty, ferretlike [O.F. furet, fuiret]

fer·ri·age, fer·ry·age (féri:idʒ) n. a ferry charge ‖ conveyance over a ferry

fer·ric (férik) adj. pertaining to, or containing iron, esp. describing compounds having a higher valency (usually 3) of iron, e.g. ferric oxide (Fe_2O_3) (*FERROUS) [fr. L. ferrum, iron]

fer·rif·er·ous (férífərəs) adj. (of rocks etc.) iron-bearing [fr. L. ferrum, iron+ -fer, producing]

fer·ris·tor (féristər) n. (electr.) a miniature high-frequency reactor used as a coincidence gate, oscillator, etc., in computers

Fer·ris wheel (féris) an immense revolving power-driven wheel with seats for passengers suspended from its rim, set up in amusement parks etc. [after G. W. G. Ferris (1859–96), U.S. engineer]

fer·rite (férait) n. (mineral.) any of several iron ores [fr. L. ferrum, iron]

Fer·rol del Cau·di·llo, El (ferróldelkauðí:ljo) a naval base (pop. 82,000) in La Coruña, N.E. Spain: shipyards

fer·ro·mag·net·ic (féroumægnétik) adj. of a substance possessing ferromagnetism **fer·ro·mag·ne·tism** (féroumǽgnitizəm) n. the property possessed by iron, nickel and cobalt, as well as certain alloys, of having a very large magnetic permeability, of retaining a residual magnetism in the absence of an external magnetic field (*HYSTERESIS), and of having a characteristic response to a magnetic field, the flux density increasing with increasing magnetic intensity up to a saturation point (cf. PARAMAGNETISM, cf. DIAMAGNETISM) [fr. L. ferrum, iron+MAGNETIC]

fer·ro·man·ga·nese (féroumǽngəni:z, ferou-mǽngəni:s) n. an alloy of iron and manganese used in steelmaking

fer·ro·pseu·do·brook·ite (ferousu:doubrúkait) n. titanium iron oxide rock from the moon brought to earth by Apollo II crew Cf KREEP

fer·ro·type (férətaip) n. a tintype

fer·rous (férəs) adj. of or containing iron, esp. describing compounds containing or derived from divalent iron (cf. FERRIC) [fr. L. ferrum, iron]

ferrous sulfate the salt $FeSO_4$, used as a mordant, in ink, and as a tonic

fer·ru·gi·nous (fərú:dʒinəs) adj. of or containing iron or iron rust ‖ reddish brown, like rust in color [fr. L. ferrugo (ferruginis), rust]

fer·rule (féru:l, férəl) n. a cap fitted to the end of a stick or umbrella to prevent wear or slipping ‖ a metal ring serving to fasten the handle to a tool, or to join sections of a fishing rod, tent pole etc. [older verrel, verril fr. O.F.]

Fer·ry (feri:), Jules (1832–93), French statesman, prime minister of France (1880–1 and 1883–5). He introduced (1882) secular, compulsory and free primary education. He pursued a policy of colonial expansion in Tunisia, Madagascar and Indochina

fer·ry (féri:) 1. pres. part. **fer·ry·ing** past and past part. **fer·ried** v.t. to transport in a boat, to ferry passengers ‖ to deliver (an automobile, aircraft, naval craft, etc.) under its own power, esp. from the factory to the purchaser ‖ to transport (troops etc.) by aircraft which shuttle back and forward between two points 2. pl. **fer·ries** n. a ferryboat ‖ a place where passengers or goods are ferried, or the service which ferries them ‖ (law) the right to ferry for a fee ‖ the regular service route of aircraft [O.E. ferian, to convey]

ferryage *FERRIAGE

fer·ry·boat (féri:bout) n. a boat working a ferry service

fer·ry·man (féri:mən) pl. **fer·ry·men** (féri:mən) n. a man who works a ferry

fer·tile (fə́:rt'l, Br. fə́:rtail) adj. highly productive, fertile soil, a fertile variety of bean ‖ (of seeds, eggs etc.) capable of developing ‖ capable of breeding or reproducing ‖ productive, creative, a fertile imagination [O. F. fertil]

Fertile Crescent an area of fertile land extending in a semicircle from Israel to the Persian Gulf. It was the cradle of Sumerian, Babylonian, Assyrian, Phoenician and Hebrew civilization

fer·til·i·ty (fərtíliti:) pl. **fer·til·i·ties** n. the state or quality of being fertile ‖ (demography) birthrate [F. fertilité]

fertility drug n. a drug designed to stimulate ovulation, thus promoting fertility in women

fer·til·i·za·tion (fə:rt'lizéifən) n. a fertilizing or being fertilized ‖ the union of haploid gametes, restoring the diploid chromosome complement and initiating the development of a new individual. The process in animals involves penetration of the usually large sessile egg by a small motile spermatozoon, completion of the maturation process of the ovum, and fusion of the nuclei to form the zygote nucleus. In seed plants the process is accomplished by penetration of the pollen tube into the ovule and embryo sac, permitting the introduction of a nonmotile male gamete (cf. CONJUGATION, cf. PARTHENOGENESIS)

fer·ti·lize (fə́:rt'laiz) v.t. pres. part. **fer·ti·liz·ing** past and past part. **fer·ti·lized** to make (an egg, ovum) capable of developing by the union of sperm with it ‖ to make fertile or productive ‖ to make (soil) productive by enriching it with nitrogen compounds, phosphorus, potassium etc. **fér·ti·liz·er** n. a preparation containing the elements essential to plant growth [FERTILE]

fer·u·la (férjulə) n. a member of Ferula, fam. Umbelliferae, a genus of Old World plants (*ASAFETIDA) [L.=giant fennel, a rod]

fer·ule (féru:l, féru:l) 1. n. a cane or stick for punishing children 2. pres. part. **fer·ul·ing** past and past part. **fer·uled** v.t. to punish with a ferule

fer·ven·cy (fə́:rvənsi:) n. the quality of being fervent

fer·vent (fə́:rvənt) adj. ardent, emotionally intense [F.]

fer·vid (fə́:rvid) adj. fervent [fr. L. fer vidus, hot]

fer·vor, Br. fer·vour (fə́:rvər) n. intensity of feeling, passion, devotion [M.E. fervor, fervour fr. O.F.]

Fès *FEZ

fes·cue grass (féskju:) a member of Festuca, fam. Gramineae, a genus of grasses incl. some perennial pasture grasses [O.F. festu, a straw]

fess, fesse (fes) pl. **fess·es** n. (heraldry) a bar across the middle of the field of an escutcheon (shield) [O.F.]

fes·tal (féstəl) adj. of or pertaining to a feast ‖ gay, festive, a festal occasion [O.F.]

fes·ter (féstər) 1. v.i. (of a wound etc.) to produce pus ‖ to produce bitter feelings, rankle, festering resentment ‖ to rot, putrefy, festering corpses 2. n. a festering sore, pustule [fr. obs. n. fester fr. O.F. festre]

fes·ti·val (féstivəl) 1. n. a joyful celebration or occasion, the Christmas festival ‖ a local season of entertainment, often annual, when cultural works are produced or performed 2. adj. of a feast day ‖ of a festival [O.F.]

fes·tive (féstiv) adj. of feasts or festivals ‖ gay, a festive party [fr. L. festivus]

fes·tiv·i·ty (festíviti:) *pl.* **fes·tiv·i·ties** *n.* merry-making, gaiety ‖ (*pl.*) festive activities [O.F. *festivité*]

fes·toon (festú:n) 1. *n.* a garland of flowers, leaves, ribbons etc. hanging in a curve between two points ‖ a carved or molded ornament representing this 2. *v.i.* to form festoons ‖ *v.t.* to decorate with festoons **fes·tóon·er·y** *pl.* **fes·toon·er·ies** *n.* [F. *feston* fr. Ital. *festone*]

FET *abbr.* federal excise tax

fe·tal, foe·tal (fí:t'l) *adj.* of or relating to a fetus

fetal circulation, foetal circulation the blood-exchange system of the fetus, incl. the umbilical arteries and vein

fetal hemoglobin *n.* (*med.*) a dominant variant of hemoglobin in newborns that causes a form of anemia if it persists excessively **also** hemoglobin F

fetalization *NEOTENY

fe·tal·o·gy (fi:tǽlədʒi:) *n.* (*med.*) study of the growth, development, and disorders of the fetus

fetologist *n.* **fetoscopy** *n.* technique for examining the fetus by taking tissue samples from the uterus *Cf* AMNIOCENTESIS

fetal position *n.* womb position with knees and arms drawn to chest, head forward, body curved

fe·ta·tion, foe·ta·tion (fi:téiʃən) *n.* the formation of a fetus [fr. L. *fetare*, to produce young]

fetch (fetʃ) 1. *v.t.* to go and get, bring, *fetch the doctor!* ‖ to obtain as its price, to sell for, *to fetch a record sum* ‖ to deal (a blow) ‖ (*Br.*) to fetch up (a sigh, groan) **to fetch and carry** to run around and be attentive as if one were a servant **to fetch up** (*Br.*) to vomit ‖ (*Br.*) to and oneself at last (in a place, without having had a clear intention of getting there), *to fetch up in jail* ‖ to heave, utter (a sigh) 2. *n.* (*naut.*) a continuous line or course from point to point (e.g. of a bay)

fétch·ing *adj.* attractive [O.E. *feccan, feccean*]

fete, fête (feit) 1. *n.* a festival, entertainment, esp. an outdoor sale for charity ‖ the day dedicated to the saint after whom a child is named commemorated by Roman Catholics as a second birthday 2. *v.t.* to entertain (a person, in celebration of some event or exploit) ‖ to celebrate (a success etc.) [F. *fête, fêter*]

fe·ti·cide, foe·ti·cide (fí:tisaid) *n.* the killing of a fetus, abortion

fet·id, foet·id (fétid) *adj.* having a strong offensive smell [fr. L. *fetidus*]

fet·ish (fétiʃ, fí:tiʃ) *n.* an object believed by certain primitive peoples to embody a spirit and exert magical powers, e.g. to protect its owner, cure diseases etc. ‖ an idea, practice etc. regarded with excessive or irrational reverence, *she makes a fetish of punctuality* **fét·ish·ism** *n.* the worship of fetishes ‖ excessive or irrational reverence for some idea, practice etc. ‖ (*psychol.*) the centering of strong sexual emotion in objects (e.g. shoes or furs) or parts of the body not normally associated with such emotion **fét·ish·ist** *n.* **fet·ish·ís·tic** *adj.* [F. *fétiche* fr. Port. *fetiço*, charm]

fet·lock (fétlok) *n.* a projection behind and above the hoof in members of the horse family ‖ the tuft of hair growing on this joint [M.E. *fetlak, fytlok*]

fet·ter (fétər) 1. *n.* a chain or shackle for the feet of a prisoner ‖ a tether for an animal ‖ (*pl., rhet.*) captivity, *a mind in fetters* 2. *v.t.* to put fetters on ‖ to restrain, hamper [O.E. *feter*]

fet·tle (fét'l) 1. *v.t. pres. part.* **fet·tling** *past* and *past part.* **fet·tled** to put in order, esp. (*pottery*) to brush off (excess glaze) or clean up the joints of (molded ware) before firing ‖ to cover (the hearth of a furnace) with loose material to protect it from heat 2. *n.* physical or mental condition, *in poor fettle* **fét·tling** *n.* loose material, e.g. sand, strewn on the hearth of an iron-ore furnace [M.E. *fetlen, fettlen*, to make ready, prob. fr. O.E. *fetel*, belt]

fe·tus, foe·tus (fí:təs) *n.* a vertebrate that has passed the early stages of development (*EMBRYO) and attained the basic final form prior to parturition. In humans this period is from about the third to the ninth month [L. *fetus*]

feud (fju:d) *n.* (*hist.*) an estate held by a tenant on condition of services being rendered to an overlord in feud held in this way (cf. ALODIUM) [fr. M.L. *feudum, feodum*]

feud 1. *n.* a long-standing quarrel, esp. deadly enmity between families, clans, tribes etc. (*BLOOD FEUD) 2. *v.i.* to wage a feud [M.E. *fede* fr. O.E.]

feu·dal (fjú:d'l) *adj.* pertaining to feuds, fiefs or fees, *feudal tenure* ‖ pertaining to the feudal

system, *feudal law*, ‖ of ideas of social relations characteristic of the feudal system **féu·dal·ism** *n.* the feudal system **féu·dal·ist** *n.* **feu·dal·ís·tic** *adj.* [M.L. *feudalis*]

feu·dal·i·ty (fju:dǽliti:) *pl.* **feu·dal·i·ties** *n.* feudal practices or theory ‖ a feudal holding of land [fr. F. *feudalité, feodalité*]

feu·dal·i·za·tion (fju:d'lizéiʃən) *n.* a feudalizing or being feudalized

feu·dal·ize (fjú:d'laiz) *pres. part.* **feu·dal·iz·ing** *past* and *past part.* **feu·dal·ized** *v.t.* to make feudal

feudal system (*hist.*) the system of economic, political and social organization which flourished in Europe (9th–4th cc.). It was based on the relation of lord to vassal and the holding of land in feud. Vassals held land from a seigneur, and ultimately from the king, in return for homage and military service. The economic unit was the manor: villeins and serfs held land from the lord of the manor, rendering in return labor services and dues

feu·da·to·ry (fjú:dətɔri:, fjú:dətɔuri:) 1. *adj.* standing in feudal relation to another, as vassal to lord ‖ (of kingdoms or persons) subject 2. *pl.* **feu·da·to·ries** *n.* a vassal ‖ a state subject to the overlordship of another [fr. M.L. *feudare*, enfeoff]

feud·ist (fjú:dist) *n.* a party to a feud

Feu·er·bach (fɔ́iərbáx), Ludwig Andreas (1804–72), German philosopher who defected from Hegelian idealism to a materialist view of man and history. His 'Essence of Christianity' (1841), translated into English by George Eliot (1854), had a strong influence on Marx and Engels

Feuil·lants, Club des (klybdeifaːjã) a political club (July 1791–Aug. 1792) of the French Revolution. Led by Lafayette, it was formed from the right wing of the Jacobins, and advocated a limited monarchy and the constitution of 1791

Feul·gen stain (fɔ́ilgən) *n.* (*organic chem.*) a stain used for studying the nucleus of cells of higher plants and animals and other chromatinic material; named for R. Feulgen, German physiologic chemist

fe·ver (fí:vər) 1. *n.* human body temperature above the normal 98.6° F. or 37.0 C., usually accompanied by rapid pulse and general malaise ‖ a disease causing such high temperature, *typhoid fever* ‖ a high state of excitement, agitation, *a fever of anticipation* ‖ a wave of irrational enthusiasm 2. *v.t.* to put in a state of great excitement and agitation [O.E. *fefor*] —Fever usually results from infectious disease of some sort, but is sometimes a response to chemical, thermal or other injury, or mental disturbance. To a certain extent it may be regarded as a useful reaction of the body in attempting to clear itself of a noxious agent, but above 103° F. (39.5° C.) the febrile reaction may itself become dangerous. Above 107° F. (41.7° C.) it is frequently fatal

fe·ver·few (fí:vərfju:) *n. Chrysanthemum parthenium*, fam. *Compositae*, a perennial European herb formerly used as a febrifuge [O.E. *fēferfuge* fr. L.]

fe·ver·ish (fí:vəriʃ) *adj.* having a fever ‖ marked by fever, *a feverish condition* ‖ caused by fever, *feverish dreams* ‖ causing fever, *feverish swamps* ‖ restlessly excited, *feverish activity*

fe·ver·ous (fí:vərəs) *adj.* feverish

fever strip *n.* (*med.*) a blackened plastic band imbedded with heat-sensitive liquid crystals that will denote body temperature (sometimes N for normal, F for fever) when placed on a patient's forehead

few (fju:) 1. *adj.* consisting of a small, indefinite number, *few people have read the book* ‖ (with 'a') a small number of, *only a few people understood him* **every few** at intervals of a small number of specified units, *every few days he visits them* **few and far between** scarce in number **no fewer than** (used emphatically) as many as, *no fewer than 50 people competed* 2. *n.* a small number of people, things etc. **the few** the minority of people **the happy few** the privileged minority ‖ (*mil.*) in air intercept usage, seven or less aircraft 3. *pron.* a small, indefinite number of people or things [O.E. *fēawe, fēawa*]

fey (fei) *adj.* slightly mad, crazy ‖ attuned to the supernatural world ‖ elfin [O.E. *fǣge*]

Fey·deau (feidou), Georges (1862–1921), French playwright, author of many clever farces including 'la Dame de chez Maxim' (1899) and 'Occupe-toi d'Amélie' (1908)

Fez (fez) (*F*. Fès) an agricultural trading center (pop. 325,327) in N. Morocco 100 miles east of Rabat. Industries: textiles, carpets, light manufacturing. There are over 100 mosques. Two universities (859, 1961). Fez was the capital of Morocco (808–1062, 1269–1548 and 1662–1912)

Fez·zan (fezán) an area in southwestern Libya. It was a province until 1963

fez (fez) *pl.* **fez·zes** *n.* a brimless felt cap, usually red and tasselled, shaped like a truncated cone, worn by many Moslems [Turk. *fes* perh. after Fès (Fez), in Morocco]

ff. following, *pages 365-6 ff.* ‖ folios

FF *FRIGATE

F-15 *n.* (*mil.*) U.S. single-seat fighter plane carrying Sidewinder and Sparrow missiles to a total weight of 16,000 lbs, with a speed of mach 2.5 and a range of 2,875 to 3,450 mi.

F-5E *TIGER II

F-4 *PHANTOM II

F-14 *TOMCAT

fi·an·cé (fi:ãséi, fi:ánsei) *n.* a man in relation to the woman to whom he is engaged to be married **fi·an·cée** (fi:ãséi) *n.* a woman in relation to the man to whom she is engaged [F.]

Fi·an·na Fail (fí:ənəfáːl) an Irish nationalist political party, founded (1926) by De Valera with the aim of removing British influence from Ireland [Ir.= Fenians of Ireland]

fi·as·co (fi:ǽskou) *pl.* **fi·as·cos, fi·as·coes** *n.* an absurd or complete failure [Ital.=bottle]

fi·at (fáiæt) *n.* (*law*) a formula expressing sanction ‖ an authorization ‖ a command, decree, order [L.=let it be done]

fiat money paper money not based upon specie, and made legal tender by law or fiat

fib (fib) 1. *n.* a trivial lie 2. *v.i. pres. part.* **fib·bing** *past* and *past part.* **fibbed** to tell such a lie [perh. fr. obs. *fible-fable*, nonsense]

fi·ber, fi·bre (fáibər) *n.* a fine thread, *a fiber of wool* ‖ a threadlike structure of animal or vegetable tissue ‖ (*bot.*) an elongate cell typical of some sclerenchymas that is found in wood, leaves, phloem, cortex and dry fruits (cf. SCLEREID) ‖ a substance made of threads, *cotton fiber* ‖ a fibrous structure, *a textile of rough fiber* ‖ a substance, natural or man-made, that can be spun, woven, felted etc. ‖ a threadlike root for twig ‖ moral strength [F.] —The principal animal fibers are built up from long-chain protein molecules. They include silk, which is extruded by the larvae of moths, and a group including wool, hair and fur, which grow outwards from depressions (follicles) in the skin of animals. Vegetable fibers consist mainly of cellulose and lignin. They are isolated from the seeds and fruits (coir, cotton, kapok), stems (flax, hemp, jute) or leaves (manila hemp, sisal, raffia) of plants. Man-made fibers are of two kinds. Regenerated fibers such as rayons are made by dissolving a natural fibrous material and extruding it. Rayon was first produced at the end of the 19th c. and is now manufactured by three main processes (viscose, cellulose acetate and cuprammonium). Synthetic fibers are made by polymerizing comparatively simple chemical compounds. A major industry has resulted from the invention of nylon by the American chemist W. H. Carothers in 1937. Nylon is a generic term covering a range of fibers built up from amides which react at both ends to form long chains. The raw material, benzene, is readily obtained from coal tar or petroleum

fi·ber·board, *Br.* fi·bre·board (fáibərbɔrd, fáibərbourd) *n.* a material made by the compression of fibers, e.g. of wood, into sheets which may be sawn, nailed, etc. ‖ one of the boards so made

fi·ber·fill (fáibərfil) *n.* synthetic fibers used to pad cushions, quilted jackets, sleeping bags, clothing, quilts, pillows, etc.

fiber glass, *Br.* fibre glass the trade name for fine glass fibers used for textile manufacture, and for material made from these which is used for the bodies of light cars, boats etc. and in felted form for insulation

fiber optics *n.* (*optics*) study and technique of light and image transmission via flexible transparent fibers (glass, plastic, etc.) **fiber-optic** *adj.*

fi·ber·scope (fáibərskoup) *n.* (*med.*) an instrument applying fiber optics used in medical examinations and other situations when a light source must be bent to enable direct viewing

Fi·bo·nac·ci number (fi:bənátʃi:) (*math.*) any number in the infinite series in which each number after 1 is the sum of the two preceding numbers, e.g., 1, 1, 2, 3, 5, 8. It is named for Leonardo Fibonacci, Italian mathematician

fi·bril (fáibrəl) n. a small threadlike structure ‖ the component part of a fiber ‖ (bot.) the smallest subdivision of a root, a root hair ‖ (zool.) a minute thread of muscle tissue **fi·bril·lar, fi·bril·lar·y** adjs **fi·bril·lá·tion** n. the act or process of making fibrils ‖ (med.) the irregular action of part of the heart **fí·bril·lose** adj. [fr. Mod. L. fibrilla]

fi·brin (fáibrin) n. a white insoluble protein formed from fibrinogen and precipitated as a tangle of threads when blood clots [FIBER]

fi·brin·o·gen (faibrínədʒin) n. a globulin converted by thrombin to fibrin during blood clotting **fi·brin·o·gen·ic** (faibrinoudʒénik) adj.

fi·bri·no·pep·tide (faibrinoupéptaid) n. (org. chem.) protein formed in the blood-clotting process

fi·brin·ous (fáibrinəs) adj. accompanied by fibrin

fi·bro·car·ti·lage (faibroukárt'lidʒ) n. cartilage in which the matrix, except immediately about the cells, is composed mainly of fibers ‖ a part composed of this cartilage [fr. FIBER+CARTILAGE]

fi·broid (fáibroid) 1. adj. formed of or resembling fibrous tissues 2. n. a benign tumor of the wall of the uterus [FIBER]

fi·bro·in (fáibrouin) n. an albuminoid substance, the chief constituent of silk, cobwebs etc. [FIBER]

fi·bro·ma (faibróumə) pl. **fi·bro·ma·ta** (faibroumátə), **fi·bro·mas** n. a benign tumor consisting mainly of fibrous tissue [Mod. L.]

fi·bro·sis (faibróusis) n. excessive formation of fibrous connective tissue in a part or organ [Mod. L.]

fi·bro·si·tis (faibrousáitis) n. any of various disorders of muscular tissue, esp. of rheumatic origin [Mod. L.]

fi·brous (fáibrəs) adj. containing fibers, a fibrous loam ‖ like fibers, a fibrous texture [fr. Mod. L. fibrosis]

fi·bro·vas·cu·lar (faibrouvǽskjulər) adj. (bot.) consisting of fibers and conducting (vascular) tissue [fibro-, fibrous+VASCULAR]

fib·u·la (fíbjulə) pl. **fib·u·lae** (fíbjuli:), **fib·u·las** n. the outer of two bones in the shank (below the knee) of the hind limb of most vertebrates (*TIBIA) ‖ (hist.) a Greek or Roman clasp or brooch **fíb·u·lar** adj. [L.=brooch]

fiche (fi:ʃ) n. filmstrip used in recording and filing information Cf FILM CARD, MICROFICHE

Fich·te (fíxtə), Johann Gottlieb (1762–1814), German philosopher, disciple of Kant and teacher of Schelling. His system, derived at first from Kant, resolved itself into an absolute idealism recognizing no other reality than the ego

fich·u (fíʃu:) n. a woman's three-cornered scarf worn over the shoulders [F.]

Fi·ci·no (fi:tʃi:no), Marsiglio (1433–99), Italian humanist philosopher. Leader of the Florentine Academy, he translated the complete works of Plato into Latin (1463–77). He expressed Christianity in Neoplatonist terms, harmonizing reason and revelation.

fick·le (fík'l) adj. inconstant, capricious, a fickle lover [O.E. ficol]

Fick's law (fiks) the law of chemistry and physics stating that the diffusion of one material in another is proportional to the negative of the gradient of the concentration of the first material [after Adolf Fick (1829-1901), G. physiologist]

fic·tile (fíktəl, Br. fíktail) adj. made by a potter ‖ relating to pottery [fr. L. fictilis, able to be shaped]

fic·tion (fíkʃən) n. literature consisting of invented narrative, esp. the novel and short story ‖ a false story or statement ‖ a pretense, invention ‖ a falsehood (e.g. that there exists a 'man in the street') conventionally accepted as true because it is useful to make the assumption **fíc·tion·al** adj. pertaining to fiction ‖ not restricted to fact, a fictional account [F.]

fic·ti·tious (fíktíʃəs) adj. imagined, not factual, a fictitious narrative ‖ (of a name or character) assumed ‖ imaginary, feigned, fictitious emotions ‖ pertaining to or like fiction ‖ existing by virtue of a legal or polite fiction [fr. L. ficticius]

fic·tive (fíktiv) adj. capable of or relating to imaginative creation, fictive powers ‖ imaginary, not genuine [F.]

fid (fid) n. a tapering pin of wood or iron used to separate the strands when splicing a rope ‖ a square bar of wood or iron supporting the topmast of a sailing boat etc. ‖ a thick piece or wedge [origin unknown]

fid·dle (fíd'l) 1. n. a violin ‖ (in an orchestra) a violin player ‖ (naut.) a rack or railing, often of cord, to prevent dishes etc. from sliding off the table in rough weather ‖ (Br., pop.) a piece of petty financial trickery **fit as a fiddle** in good health and spirits **to play second fiddle** to accept a subordinate position 2. v. pres. part. **fid·dling** past and past part. **fid·dled** v.i. (often familiar or contemptuous) to play the violin ‖ to make aimless, interfering, indecisive or annoyingly distracting movements, to fiddle with a pencil ‖ v.t. to play (a tune) on a violin ‖ (Br., pop.) to cheat, he was fiddled into buying it ‖ (Br., pop.) to falsify, to fiddle one's income tax **to fiddle away** to waste (time) [M.E. fithele]

fid·dle·back (fíd'lbæk) adj. (of a chasuble or a chair) shaped like a fiddle

fid·dle·fad·dle (fíd'lfæd'l) 1. n. nonsense, foolish talk 2. v.i. pres. part. **fid·dle·fad·dling** past and past part. **fid·dle·fad·dled** to fuss, trifle 3. interj. nonsense!

fid·dler (fídlər) n. someone who plays the fiddle, esp. someone hired to do so ‖ a fiddler crab ‖ (Br., pop.) someone who engages in petty fraud [O.E. fithelere]

fiddler crab a small crab of the genus Uca, the males of which have one of the claws greatly enlarged

fid·dle·sticks (fíd'lstiks) interj. nonsense! rubbish!

fid·dley, fid·ley (fídli:) n. the metal framework surrounding the hatch leading to the stokehole of a steamship [origin unknown]

fid·dling (fídliŋ) adj. trifling, futile

Fi·del·is·mo (Spanish; usu. capitalized) Fidelism or Castroism, i.e., principles and activities promoting political policies associated with Fidel Castro and the Cuban government, esp. in Latin America **Castroist, Castroite, Fidelist, Fidelista** n. one loyal to Fidel Castro

fi·del·ist·a (fi:deli:sta) n. a supporter of Fidel Castro [Span.]

fi·del·i·ty (fidéliti) pl. **fi·del·i·ties** n. the faithful performance of duty ‖ loyalty, fidelity to one's principles ‖ adherence to the contract of marriage, marital fidelity ‖ exactness, a portrait of great fidelity ‖ (elec., in radio, television etc.) the degree of accuracy in the reproduction of the sound or picture (*HIGH FIDELITY) [F. fidélité]

fidg·et (fídʒit) 1. v.i. to be constantly making restless little movements ‖ to be uneasy, worry ‖ v.t. to make (someone) disturbed or worried 2. n. (also pl.) restlessness, accompanied by frequent nervous movements ‖ someone who fidgets or disturbs others **fidg·et·i·ness** n. **fidg·et·y** adj. [fr. obs. fidge, to twitch, origin unknown]

fidley *FIDDLEY

fi·do (fáidou) n. (numismatics) a coin with a minting error

fi·du·cial (fidú:ʃəl, fidjú:ʃəl) adj. based on faith or trust ‖ (phys., survey.) of a point or line taken as reference basis [fr. L. fiducialis]

fiducial marks *COLLIMATING MARKS

fiducial point n. (optics) a reference point in the reticule of an optical instrument **also** fiduciary

fi·du·ci·a·ry (fidú:ʃi:eri:, fidjú:ʃi:eri:) 1. adj. of the nature of a trust or trusteeship ‖ held or given in trust ‖ (of paper money etc.) having a value depending on public confidence (*FIAT MONEY) 2. pl. **fi·du·ci·ar·ies** n. someone acting in a fiduciary capacity, a trustee [fr. L. fiduciarius]

fie (fái) interj. (old-fash.) for shame! [O.F.]

fief (fi:f) n. (hist.) land held in feud [F.]

Field, Cyrus West (1819–92), U.S. businessman, a founder (1854) of the telegraph company that laid (1866) the first transatlantic cable

Field, David Dudley (1805–94), U.S. lawyer. He led the movement to codify common-law procedure in New York. It resulted (1848) in the 'Civil Code of Procedure', widely adopted within the U.S.A. and (1873) in England and Ireland

Field, Eugene (1850–95), U.S. journalist and children's poet. He wrote (1883–95) a humor column for the 'Chicago Record' satirizing the pretensions of the Chicago meat barons

Field, John (1782–1837), Irish composer. His compositions include 18 nocturnes, the first of the kind

Field, Marshall (1834–1906), U.S. department store owner. He organized (1881) Marshall Field & Company, for which he created many of the now current retail selling practices. He made very large donations to child welfare and educational institutions

field (fi:ld) 1. n. an area of land, usually enclosed, devoted to pasture or the cultivation of crops ‖ (pl.) meadows or arable land, the footpath runs through the fields ‖ (rhet.) a battleground ‖ (in compounds) an area of land yielding minerals, a coalfield or covered with snow etc., a snowfield ‖ an area of land set aside and made suitable for a particular use, a playing field ‖ the area on which something is drawn, painted etc., e.g. the ground color of a flag, the background of a picture or coin, or (heraldry) the surface of a shield ‖ (computer) position on a punched card or an area in a record always used to record the same type of data ‖ data in adjacent core positions, designated by a flag bit, to be treated as a unit ‖ (phys.) a space within which electric, gravitational or magnetic etc. effects exist and can be, in principle, specified at each point ‖ a particular body of interest, study, knowledge or thought, in the field of medicine ‖ (racing) the competing horses, a big field for the last race ‖ all runners except the favorite, 10-1 the field! ‖ all those taking part in a sport or contest outof-doors ‖ (baseball, cricket) the nonbatting side ‖ (baseball, cricket) the ground in which the fielders stand 2. v.t. (baseball, cricket) to stop or catch (the ball) ‖ v.i. (cricket) to play against the batting side ‖ to answer without previous preparation, e.g., to field questions 3. adj. of or relating to a field ‖ growing in fields [O.E. feld]

field allowance (Br.) additional money paid to an officer when in the field (on campaign) to meet increased expenses

field ambulance (Br.) a mobile hospital which follows an army into action

field artillery guns other than antitank or antiaircraft artillery, firing shells, used by armies in the field. There are three categories: light, medium and heavy

field book a book used esp. by a surveyor for note-taking during research

field day a day of maneuvers by troops ‖ a day spent working outdoors e.g. by a naturalist searching for specimens ‖ (Am.) a day of athletic events outdoors ‖ a gala day, big occasion ‖ an occasion marked by some great success

field dressing (Br.) an appliance for dressing wounds, carried by soldiers on active service

field-ef·fect transistor (fi:ldifekt) (electr.) a nonrectifying transistor with a circuit application like that of a vacuum tube, with principal conduction path through a bar of N-type semiconductor. Control is accomplished through depletion layers on each side

field·er (fi:ldər) n. (baseball, cricket) a player stationed in the field

fielder's choice (baseball) an attempt by a fielder, when handling a batted ball, to put a base runner other than the batter out, when a play to first base would have put the batter out

field event an athletic contest (e.g. throwing the javelin) other than a track event

field·fare (fi:ldfɛər) n. Turdus pilaris, a bird (about 10 in long) related to the thrush, with an ash-colored head and black tail, the upper back and wing coverts being chestnut. It spends the summer in N. Europe and W. Asia and winters in Britain and central and S. Europe [M.E. feldefare]

field glasses a pair of binoculars

field goal (football) a goal scored by a placement or drop kick not immediately following a touchdown ‖ (basketball) a basket thrown while the ball is in play

field gun a piece of mobile artillery other than antiaircraft or antitank artillery

field hockey (Am.=Br. hockey) a game played on a field (100 x 60 yds) divided into four zones, between two teams of 11 players. The aim is to score goals by driving a hard white leather ball into the opponent's goal, using a flat-faced, curved stick (cf. ICE HOCKEY)

field hospital a temporary hospital in the field staffed by army surgeons, nurses, orderlies etc.

field house a building at an athletic field where players dress and equipment is stored

Field·ing (fi:ldiŋ), Henry (1707–54), English novelist. His first published novel, 'Joseph Andrews' (1742), which he described as 'a comic epic poem in prose', began as a parody of Richardson's 'Pamela'. The History of Tom Jones, a Foundling' (1749) is his best and most popular work. It is a lively, rambling, picaresque novel, jocular and sentimental by turns. But Fielding saw much of the suffering beneath the surface of the London society of his time, and his 'The Life of Mr. Jonathan Wild the Great' (1743) is a powerful satire

field intensity (*phys.*) the force acting on a unit electric charge or unit magnetic pole placed at a given point

field-i·on microscope (fi:ldəion) *n.* microscope that translates positive-ion electron emissions to produce an image on a fluorescent screen

field judge *n.* (*football*) an official who observes and judges kicks, forward passes, time intervals, etc.

field kitchen (*mil.*) a cooking place set up in the field for fighting troops ‖ the portable cooking equipment used

field magnet a magnet used for producing or maintaining a magnetic field, e.g. the magnet of a dynamo

field marshal the highest rank of officer in the British army, ranking immediately above a general

field mouse a mouse, esp. of genera *Apodemus* (Old World) or *Microtus* (New World), living in open fields

field officer an army officer with the rank of colonel, lieutenant colonel or major

Field of the Cloth of Gold the field near Guînes, France, where Henry VIII of England met François I of France (1520), an occasion famous for its spectacular pageantry

field of view the whole area visible to a person, esp. to someone looking through an optical instrument

field punishment (*Br.*) the summary punishing of soldiers while actively on campaign

Fields (fi:ldz), W. C. (c. 1879–1946), U.S. entertainer, born William Claude Dukenfield. He created the image of a cynical, pompous, hard drinker or con man who hated children, wives, mothers-in-law, dogs, and policemen, among others. His films include 'David Copperfield' (1935), 'You Can't Cheat an Honest Man' (1939), 'My Little Chickadee' with Mae West (1940), and 'Never Give a Sucker an Even Break' (1941)

fields·man (fi:ldzmən) *pl.* **fields·men** (fi:ldzmən) *n.* (*cricket*) a fielder

field sports (*Br.*) outdoor sports, esp. hunting, shooting, fishing

field strength field intensity

field trial a trial of sporting dogs or working sheepdogs

field trip a group visit by students to a factory, museum etc. in order to learn by direct observation

field·work (fi:ldwə;rk) *n.* (*mil.*) an earthwork fortification thrown up by troops in the field ‖ the work of collecting original data or information on the spot, e.g. by archaeologists, botanists, social scientists etc. **field·work·er** *n.* a person doing such work

fiend (fi:nd) *n.* the Devil, Satan ‖ any demon or evil spirit ‖ a person actuated by intense wickedness, esp. by cruelty ‖ (with an attributive noun etc.) an addict, *a dope fiend* or devotee, *a fresh-air fiend* **fiend·ish** *adj.* devilish [O.E. *feond*]

fierce (fiərs) *comp.* **fierc·er** *superl.* **fierc·est** *adj.* savage, violently hostile, *a fierce dog* ‖ raging, violent, *a fierce wind* ‖ intense, passionate, *a fierce attachment* [O.F. *fers, fiers*]

fi·er·y (fáiəri:) *comp.* **fi·er·i·er** *superl.* **fi·er·i·est** *adj.* flaming with fire, *a fiery furnace* ‖ looking like fire, blazing red, *a fiery sunset* ‖ (of eyes) glowing, flashing ‖ seeming to burn, *a fiery curry* ‖ vehement, *a fiery speech* ‖ passionate, *a fiery temper* ‖ (*hist.*, of arrows etc.) bearing fire ‖ (*rhet.*, of horses) mettlesome

fiery cross the emblem of a burning cross used by the Ku Klux Klan to strike terror ‖ (*Scot. hist.*) a charred or blood-stained wooden cross used by Highlanders as an emblem to rally the clans for war

Fie·sole (fjézole) (*Rom.* Faesulae) a town (pop. 114,111) in Tuscany, Italy, near Florence: Roman theater and baths, Romanesque cathedral

fi·es·ta (fi:ésta) *n.* a festival, esp. a religious holiday, in Spain and Latin America [Span.]

Fife (faif) a former county, now an administrative region (area 505 sq. miles, pop. 339,180), in E. Scotland. County town: Cupar

fife (faif) **1.** *n.* a small shrill-noted flute used in some military bands to accompany the drum **2.** *v. pres. part.* **fif·ing** *past* and *past part.* **fifed** *v.i.* to play a fife ‖ *v.t.* to play (a tune) on a fife [perh. G. *pfeife*, pipe or fr. F. *fifre*]

fife rail a rail around a ship's mast, near the deck, with belaying pins to which running gear is belayed

FIFO (*accounting acronym*) first in, first out. FIFO is a chronological inventories accounting method *Cf* LIFO

fif·teen (fifti:n) **1.** *adj.* being one more than 14 (*NUMBER TABLE) **2.** *n.* 10 plus five ‖ the cardinal number representing this (15, XV) ‖ a team of 15 members, esp. in Rugby Union [O.E. *fiftēne, fiftyne*]

fif·teenth (fifti:nθ) **1.** *adj.* being number 15 in a series (*NUMBER TABLE) ‖ being one of the 15 equal parts of anything **2.** *n.* the person or thing next after the 14th ‖ one of 15 equal parts of anything (1/15) ‖ the 15th day of a month [O.E. *fītēotha*]

15th Amendment (1870), provision of the U.S. Constitution that assured the right to vote to those qualified regardless of 'race, color, or previous condition of servitude,' and prevented state or federal governments from infringing upon that right. It provided for the federal government to legislate voting qualifications and disallowed specific restrictions imposed by the states

fifth (fifθ) **1.** *adj.* being number five in a series (*NUMBER TABLE) ‖ being one of the five equal parts of anything **2.** *n.* the person or thing next after the fourth ‖ one of five equal parts of anything (1/5) ‖ the fifth day of a month ‖ (*mus.*) the note five steps above or below a given note in a diatonic scale, inclusive of both notes ‖ (*mus.*) the interval between these notes ‖ (*mus.*) a combination of these notes **3.** *adv.* in the fifth place ‖ (followed by a superlative) except four, *the fifth biggest* [O.E. *fīfta*]

5th Amendment (1789), provision of the Bill of Rights of the U.S. Constitution that assures accused criminals of certain rights. It protects against double jeopardy and self-incrimination; requires indictment by grand jury when a federal offense is involved; and guarantees due process of law and just compensation for taking of private property for public use

fifth column a group within a nation or faction secretly working to help the enemies of that nation or the opponents of that faction **fifth columnist** a member of such a group [name given by a rebel general to Franco's supporters inside the government-held Madrid in the Spanish Civil War, as four columns approached to attack the city]

Fifth Monarchy Men (*Eng. hist.*) a fanatical sect during the Commonwealth advocating establishment by force of Christ's kingdom on earth, as the last of the five kingdoms prophesied by Daniel

fifth pathway *n.* (*med.*) one of the several ways enabling an individual who obtains all or part of his or her medical education abroad to enter postgraduate medical education in the U.S.A., by providing supervised clinical training, a screening examination, and AMA-approved internship or residency

fif·ti·eth (fifti:iθ) **1.** *adj.* being number 50 in a series (*NUMBER TABLE) ‖ being one of the 50 equal parts of anything **2.** *n.* the person or thing next after the 49th ‖ one of 50 equal parts of anything (1/50) [O.E. *fiftigotha*]

fif·ty (fifti:) **1.** *adj.* being 10 more than 40 (*NUMBER TABLE) **2.** *pl.* **fif·ties** *n.* five times 10 ‖ the cardinal number representing this (50, L) **the fifties** (of temperature, a person's age, a century etc.) the span 50-9 [O.E. *fiftig*]

fif·ty-fif·ty (fifti:fifti:) **1.** *adv.* (*pop.*) equally **2.** *adj.* (*pop.*) shared equally ‖ (*pop.*, of a division) equal, half-and-half

fig (fig) *n.* a member of *Ficus*, fam. *Moraceae*, a genus of tropical trees and shrubs of most varied habit, commonly having adventitious and aerial roots, and including the banyan and the india rubber tree. *F. carica*, growing wild and domesticated in the Mediterranean region and in California, is valued for its fruits ‖ the fruit of the fig tree ‖ the least little bit, *she doesn't care a fig for him* [O.F. *figue* fr. Port.]

fig. figure

fight (fait) *pres. part.* **fight·ing** *past* and *past part.* **fought** (fɔt) *v.i.* to give mutual blows ‖ to

take part in a war ‖ to be one of two or more combatants in physical combat ‖ to strive, struggle ‖ to engage in a legal contest ‖ *v.t.* to win (one's way) by fighting ‖ to try to stop, prevent or overcome, *to fight disease* ‖ to make war upon ‖ to oppose by legal action ‖ to defend one's interests in (a legal case) ‖ to engage in (a war or battle) ‖ to box against ‖ to engage in (a boxing contest) ‖ to cause to fight, *to fight cocks* **to fight it out** to settle a difference by fighting **to fight on** to continue to fight **to fight to a finish** to continue fighting until a decision is reached [O.E. *feohtan*]

fight *n.* a physical struggle for victory ‖ a battle ‖ single combat ‖ an effort to overcome something, *a fight against illiteracy* ‖ fighting spirit, a will to fight, *to be full of fight* **to give** (or **show**) **fight** to show willingness to fight **to put up a good** (**poor**) **fight** to fight with (without) courage and persistence **fight·er** *n.* someone who fights, esp. someone full of determination to win ‖ an aircraft designed mainly for aerial combat [O.E. *feohte, feoht, gefeoht*]

fighting chair *n.* (*fishing*) a seat attached to the boat deck from which an angler pulls in a hooked fish

fighting chance a possibility of winning sufficient to give an incentive to try hard, although the margin is very small

fighting cock a gamecock

fig marigold a carpeting plant of genus *Mesembryanthemun*, esp. *M. edule*, with fleshy leaves and showy flowers

fig·ment (figmənt) *n.* something made up with no basis of truth [fr. L. *figmentum*]

Fi·gue·res Fer·rer (fi:géresferrér), José (c. 1908–), Costa Rican president (1953–8, 1970–74). As founder of the National Liberation Party, he became a leader of democratic reform in Latin America, opposed to dictatorship and advocating moderate socialism

fig·u·ra·tion (figjuréiʃən) *n.* the act or mode of giving form or shape ‖ a shape or outline ‖ an emblematical or allegorical representation ‖ ornamentation, esp. (*mus.*) the ornamental treatment of a passage, esp. the decoration of a bass part [F.]

fig·u·ra·tive (figjurətiv) *adj.* expressed by means of metaphor or other figure of speech, *figurative language* ‖ addicted to or abounding in figures of speech, *a figurative style* ‖ representing by means of a figure, *figurative art* [F.]

fig·ure (fígjər, *Br.* fígə) **1.** *n.* the written or printed symbol for a number ‖ (*pl., pop.*) addition, accounting etc., *good at figures* ‖ price, *sold at a low figure* ‖ a diagram, esp. a plane geometrical form enclosed by lines, e.g. a triangle ‖ a three-dimensional form enclosed by surfaces e.g. a cylinder ‖ any such plane or solid form ‖ a drawing of a form ‖ a diagram in a printed text ‖ the human form, *she has a good figure* ‖ a piece of sculpture, esp. a representation of the human form ‖ a person dimly perceived, *a figure loomed up out of the mist* ‖ a personage, *the great figures of history* ‖ a decorative pattern or design ‖ a movement in a dance (esp. a folk dance or country dance) ‖ a set pattern cut by the skates in display skating ‖ (*gram.*) a permitted deviation from the rules, e.g. ellipsis ‖ (*mus.*) a short succession of notes or harmonies, a brief melodic or harmonic passage from which a phrase, a theme or a whole movement may be developed **to cut a fine** (**poor**) **figure** to make a good (poor) impression **to keep one's figure** to stay slim **2.** *v. pres. part.* **fig·ur·ing** *past* and *past part.* **fig·ured** *v.t.* to represent by means of a figure, diagram, picture etc., *St John is figured as a lion* ‖ to decorate with patterns or designs ‖ to employ figures of speech in, *figured language* or represent by a figure of speech ‖ (*pop.*) to consider ‖ *v.i.* to work out figures, do arithmetic ‖ to be a personage of some note, *to figure briefly in history* to appear, *his name figured among the guests* **to figure on** (*pop.*) to intend ‖ to count on ‖ to take account of, *have you figure on there being a transport strike the day you leave?* **to figure out** to solve ‖ to arrive at an understanding of **to figure out at** to work out to (a specified total) **fig·ured** *adj.* represented by a painted or sculpted figure ‖ ornamented, patterned ‖ shaped, fashioned [F.=form, shape]

figured bass (*mus.*) a bass part, esp. for an accompanying keyboard instrument, in which the basic overlying harmony is shown by numbers under the notes, indicating which intervals above these notes should be included in the upper voices, while leaving their relative posi-

---

tion to the performer's discretion. Thus $\frac{6}{4}$ under a C indicates an F and an A are to be sounded

figure eight the shape of the figure 8, esp. as performed by an ice skater

fig·ure·head (fígjərhęd, *Br.* fígəhęd) *n.* (*hist.*) a carved figure, often a head or bust only, on the bow of a sailing ship ‖ a person nominally in authority but having no real power

figure of speech an unusual, essentially metaphorical mode of expression, used for effect in speech and writing and to clarify or deepen meaning by suggesting similitudes which provoke thought

fig·ur·ine (fígjuri:n) *n.* a small statue, carved or molded [F. fr. Ital.]

fig wasp *Blastophagus psenes*, fam. *Agaontidae*, an insect which breeds in the caprifig and is the agent in caprification

fig·wort (fígwə:rt) *n.* a member of *Scrophularia*, fam. *Scrophulariaceae*, a genus of annual and perennial plants with quadrangular stems and opposite leaves, e.g. foxglove, snapdragon

Fi·ji (fí:dʒi:) an independent state (area 7,055 sq. miles, pop. 700,000) in the S.W. Pacific, consisting of two large islands (Viti Levu and Vanua Levu) and about 800 smaller ones, of which about 100 are permanently inhabited, incl. Rotuma (area 18 sq. miles, pop. 6,000), 225 miles north-northwest. Capital: Suva. People: 50% Indian, 42% Fijian (Melanesian) with European, Rotuman and Chinese minorities. Religion: 38% Protestant (mainly Methodist), c. 40% Hindu, with Roman Catholic, Moslem, Sikh and Confucian minorities. The islands are volcanic, with dense forests in the mountains (summit: Mt Victoria, 4,341 ft, on Viti Levu). The climate is oceanic with frequent tropical storms Nov.-Apr. Cattle are raised. Crops: sugarcane, coconuts, rice, bananas. Exports: sugar, gold, bananas, coconut oil. Imports: cereals, clothing, fuel oils, machinery, iron and steel. Monetary unit: Fijian dollar. HISTORY. Little is known of the early Melanesian civilization. The islands were sighted by Tasman (1643) and later visited by Cook (1774) and Bligh (1789). Traders and missionaries penetrated them in the 1830s, and they became a British colony (1874). Indians immigrated as indentured labor (1879–1917). Fiji became independent (Oct. 10, 1970), within the Commonwealth.

Fi·ji·an (fí:dʒi:ən, esp. *Br.* fi:dʒí:ən) **1.** *adj.* of or relating to Fiji **2.** *n.* a native of Fiji

fil·a·gree (fíləgri:) *n.* filigree

fil·a·ment (fíləmənt) *n.* a fine threadlike body or fiber ‖ (*elec.*) a thin thread of metal, carbon etc. heated or made incandescent in some electric lamps etc. ‖ a thin metallic fiber that serves as the cathode in electron tubes ‖ (*bot.*) the stalk of a stamen, bearing the anther ‖ a hypha, a threadlike string of cells or a long single cell in certain fungi, bacteria etc. **fil·a·men·ta·ry** (fìləméntəri:), **fil·a·men·tous** (fìləméntəs) *adjs* [fr. Mod. L. *filamentum* fr. *filare*, to spin]

fi·lar (fáilər) *adj.* relating to threads or lines ‖ having threads stretched across the field of view, *a filar microscope* [fr. L. *filum*, thread]

fi·lar·i·a (filéəri:ə) *pl.* **fi·lar·i·ae** (fi- léəri:i:) *n.* a parasitic nematode, esp. of genus *Wuchereria*. *W. Bancrofti* causes elephantiasis. The larva is parasitic in mosquitoes, and the adult in man **fi·lar· i·al** *adj.* **fil·a·ri·a·sis** (filəráiəsis) *n.* elephantiasis [Mod. L. fr. L. *filum*, a thread]

fil·a·ture (fílətʃər) *n.* the process of reeling silk from cocoons ‖ a machine for this ‖ an establishment for this [F.]

fil·bert (fílbərt) *n.* the nut of the cultivated hazel ‖ *Corylus avellana* or *C. maxima*, fam. *Corylaceae*, the European shrubs on which these nuts grow [prob. because ripe about St Philibert's Day, Aug. 22]

filch (filtʃ) *v.t.* to steal, pilfer [origin unknown]

file (fail) **1.** *n.* a steel instrument with a surface of cutting ridges or teeth used for smoothing, cutting through or abrading surfaces of metal etc. **2.** *v.t. pres. part.* **fil·ing** *past* and *past part.* **filed** to cut or smooth with or as if with a file [O.E. *fēol*]

file **1.** *n.* a device of various kinds for keeping papers, or for organizing them for ease of reference etc. ‖ a set of papers so kept ‖ a series of issues, e.g. of a newspaper or periodical, kept in order ‖ (*chess*) one of the eight rows of squares from player to player vertically across the board ‖ a row of persons or things arranged one behind the other ‖ a soldier in the front rank of a formation and the man (or men) behind him **in**

file (esp. *mil.*) one behind the other **2.** *v. pres. part.* **fil·ing** *past* and *past part.* **filed** *v.t.* to place (a paper) in or on a file ‖ to place (a document) with others so as to be available for reference ‖ (with 'off' or 'out') to cause (soldiers) to move in file ‖ (*law*) to submit (a petition), e.g. for divorce ‖ *v.i.* to march or move in file ‖ to apply, *to file for a pension* [F. *fil*, thread and *file*, rank, file fr. L. *filum*, thread]

fi·let (filéi, *Br.* also filít) *n.* a lace or net with a geometrical pattern worked on a square mesh [F.=thread]

fil·i·al (fíli:əl) *adj.* of, relating to or appropriate to a son or daughter, *filial duty* [fr. L.L. *filialis*]

filial generation (*biol.*) a generation after the parental one, *second filial generation*

filial piety devotion and dutifulness to one's parent or parents

fil·i·a·tion (fìli:éiʃən) *n.* the relationship of child to parent, esp. son to father ‖ the branching or forming of offshoots ‖ an offshoot ‖ a genealogical relationship or line of descent, e.g. of a language or culture ‖ (*law*) the fixing of the legal paternity of an illegitimate child [F.]

fil·i·bus·ter (fíləbʌstər) **1.** *n.* (*hist.*) a freebooter ‖ the obstruction of legislative action by delaying tactics, e.g. by making long speeches to consume time (esp. in the U.S. Senate) **2.** *v.i.* to act as a filibusterer **fil·i·bus·ter·er** *n.* someone who filibusters [Span. *filibustero* fr. F. fr. Du. *vrijbuiter*, freebooter]

fil·i·cide (fílisaid) *n.* the crime of killing one's son or daughter ‖ someone guilty of this crime [fr. L. *filius*, son, *filia*, daughter+*caedere*, to kill]

fi·lif·er·ous (failífərəs) *adj.* having threadlike parts [fr. L. *filum*, thread+*fer*, bearing]

fil·i·form (fílifɔrm) *adj.* (*biol.*) threadlike, thread-shaped [fr. L. *filum*, thread]

fil·i·gree (fíligri:) *n.* lacy ornamental work, formerly of metal beads, now of fine wire (gold, silver, copper etc.) ‖ any delicate or fragile openwork **fil·i·greed** *adj.* [fr. obs. *filigreen* fr. F. *filigrane* fr. Ital.]

fil·ing (fáiliŋ) *n.* the act or process of filing ‖ (*pl.*) the minute pieces of metal rubbed on in filing, *copper filings*

filip *FILLIP

Fil·i·pi·no (fìləpí:nou) **1.** *adj.* of a native of the Philippine Is ‖ of a citizen of the Philippine Republic **2.** *n.* a native of the Philippine Is or citizen of the Philippine Republic

fill (fil) *v.t.* to make full, *to fill a glass, fill one's pockets* ‖ to distend to the full extent, *wind filled the sails* ‖ to occupy the whole space of, *smoke filled the room* ‖ to stock lavishly, *to fill a garden with flowers* (*Am.=Br.* stop) to plug up a cavity in (a tooth) with metal etc. in order to arrest decay ‖ to plug (a crack or hole) ‖ to occupy (an office) ‖ to appoint someone to (a vacant post) ‖ to treat (fabrics, leather etc.) so as to block the crevices, pores etc. ‖ to occupy (time), *to fill every minute of the day* ‖ to satisfy, glut ‖ to dispense (a prescription etc.) ‖ to fulfill (an order) ‖ *v.i.* to become full **to fill a need** (or **want**) to provide something recognized as being useful or necessary **to fill away** (*naut.*) to trim the sails to catch the wind **to fill in** to complete (an outline) or color etc. (an area) ‖ to complete (entries to a document) ‖ to put material into (a hole) up to the surrounding level ‖ to do something to occupy a period of (time) **to fill out** to enlarge to some appropriate limit ‖ to distend ‖ to complete (a document) to become plumper **to fill the bill** to be a person or thing of the kind needed for some task, function etc. **to fill up** to make quite full ‖ (*Br.*) to complete (a document) ‖ to supply deficient parts of ‖ to silt up [O.E. *fyllan*]

fill *n.* a full supply, enough to satisfy one's needs, *to eat one's fill* (*Br.*) enough to fill something, *a fill of tobacco* ‖ enough to satiate, *to have had one's fill of entertainment* ‖ (*securities*) a trading order that demands immediate execution or cancellation [O.E. *fyllo, fyllu*]

fill·er (fílər) *n.* one hundredth of a forint ‖ a coin worth this [Hung. *fillér*]

fill·er (fílər) *n.* a substance added to increase bulk, weight etc. ‖ tobacco used for the interior of cigars ‖ a substance used to mend cracks in plaster, plug screw holes etc. ‖ something printed in a newspaper etc. to fill up a column ‖ inferior material used to fill a casing of a more valuable substance ‖ a device used for filling, e.g. on a fountain pen ‖ a substance (inert, chemical, or explosive) carried in an ammunition container such as a projectile, mine, bomb,

or grenade ‖ one of a number of individuals required to bring a unit, organization, or approved allotment to authorized strength

fil·let **1.** *n.* (filéi) a boneless piece of meat, fish or esp. of beef from the loin ‖ (filít) a narrow band to bind the hair ‖ a thin narrow strip of material, e.g. cotton, leather ‖ (*archit.*) a flat band separating two moldings or between flutings of a column ‖ (*heraldry*) a horizontal division of a shield, quarter of the chief in depth (*bookbinding*) a plain or ornamental line stamped on a book cover ‖ the tool used for this **2.** (filéi) *v.t.* to remove the bone from (fish or meat) and divide it into long, thin slices [F. *filet*]

fil·ling (fíliŋ) *n.* the act of filling ‖ a substance used in filling, esp. cement used to fill a decayed tooth ‖ the woof or weft in woven fabrics ‖ yarn as prepared for the shuttle

filling station (*Br.*) a gas station

fil·lip (fílip) **1.** *n.* (also **fil·ip**) a flick of the fingernail tensed against the thumb and suddenly released ‖ an encouragement or stimulus ‖ a quick little blow **2.** *v.t.* to flick with a fillip ‖ to encourage, stimulate ‖ to strike with a quick little blow [FLIP]

fil·lis·ter (fílistər) *n.* an adjustable plane for rabbeting ‖ the groove in the bar of a window sash where the glass is fitted [origin unknown]

Fill·more (fílmɔr, fílmour), Millard (1800–74), 13th president (1850–3) of the U.S.A., following the death of Zachary Taylor. A Whig, he sponsored and signed the Compromise of 1850. He tried unsuccessfully to unite the Whig party on the basis of compromise over the slavery issue, but was forced to join the Know-Nothing movement, running (1856) unsuccessfully as its presidential candidate

fil·ly (fíli:) *pl.* **fil·lies** *n.* a young mare [perh. O.N. *fylja*]

film (film) **1.** *n.* a thin layer, *a film of dust* ‖ a growth on the eye ‖ a haze dimming the sight ‖ a sheet or strip of celluloid or other material that has been coated with a light-sensitive emulsion which, when exposed to an optical image in a camera and chemically treated, gives negative or positive, black and white or colored photographs ‖ (esp. *Br.*) a movie with an accompanying soundtrack **2.** *v.t.* to make a movie of ‖ to cover with or as if with a film ‖ *v.i.* to be in the process of making a movie ‖ to be suitable for making into a movie [O.E. *filmen*, a membrane]

film badge *n.* a piece of masked photographic film worn by workers exposed to radiation to monitor their exposure. Radiation darkens the film

film card *n.* microfiche mounted on a card

film·let (fílmlət) *n.* a very short (3–15 minutes) film

film noir *n.* (usu. italics) French film of somber tones and pessimistic mood

film·og·ra·phy (filmógrəfi:) *n.* study of, or writings about, motion pictures, their history or personalities

film·set (fílmset) *n.* **1.** set for a motion picture **2.** composed type by photography **filmset** *adj.* **filmsetter** *n.* filmsetting *v.*

film·strip (fílmstrip) *n.* a strip of film consisting of a sequence of frames (pictures) with captions or accompanying script. Projected on a screen, they are used by teachers, lecturers etc. as visual aids

film·y (fílmi:) *comp.* **film·i·er** *superl.* **film·i·est** *adj.* hazy, misty ‖ like gauze

fi·lose (fáilous) *adj.* threadlike ‖ ending in a threadlike form (*biol.*, of the pseudopodia of protozoa) slender [fr. L. *filum*, a thread]

fils (fils) *pl.* **fils** *n.* a unit of currency of Iraq and Kuwait worth one thousandth of a dinar [Arab.]

fil·ter (fíltər) **1.** *n.* a device for separating solids from liquids, or suspended particles from gases, consisting of a porous substance through which only the liquid or gas can pass ‖ (*phys.*) a device for removing or reducing waves or oscillations of certain frequencies without affecting other vibrations passing through it ‖ (*photog.*) a lens screen which has different absorptive powers for different wavelengths of light **2.** *v.t.* to pass (something) through or as if through a filter ‖ *v.i.* to go through or as if through a filter, *the truth filtered into his mind* ‖ (*Br.*) to turn off at a junction or controlled crossing along a road on one's driving (near) side **to filter out** (of facts, information etc.) to issue slowly, become gradually known [M.E. *filtre* fr. O.F.]

CONCISE PRONUNCIATION KEY: (a) æ, c*a*t; ɑ, c*a*r; ɔ, f*aw*n; ei, sn*a*ke. (e) e, h*e*n; i:, sh*ee*p; iə, d*ee*r; ɛə, b*ea*r. (i) i, f*i*sh; ai, t*i*ger; ə:, b*i*rd. (o) o, *o*x; au, c*ow*; ou, g*oa*t; u, p*oo*r; ɔi, r*oy*al. (u) ʌ, d*u*ck; u, b*u*ll; u:, g*oo*se; ə, b*a*cill*u*s; ju:, c*u*be. x, lo*ch*; θ, *th*ink; ð, bo*th*er; z, *Z*en; ʒ, cor*s*age; dʒ, sava*g*e; ŋ, orangutan*g*; j, *y*ak; ʃ, *fi*sh; tʃ, fe*tch*; 'l, rabb*le*; 'n, redd*en*. Complete pronunciation key appears inside front cover.

fil·ter·a·ble (fíltərəbəl) adj. able to be filtred ‖ (of a virus) able to pass through a filter for retaining bacteria

filth (filθ) n. foul matter, esp. of a nauseating character ‖ obscene language or thoughts ‖ anything that corrupts or defiles, physically or morally **filth·y** comp. **filth·i·er** superl. **filth·i·est** adj. extremely dirty ‖ obscene [O.E. fȳlth]

filthy lucre money

fil·trate (fíltreit) 1. n. a fluid which has passed through a filter 2. v.t. and i. pres. part. **fil·trat·ing** past and past part. **fil·trat·ed** to filter

fil·tra·tion (filtréiʃən) n. the act or process of filtering [F.]

fim·bri·ate (fímbri:it) adj. (biol.), of petals, tubes, ducts, antennae etc.) fringed at the margin **fim·bri·at·ed** (fímbri:eitid) adj. **fim·bri·a·tion** (fimbri:éiʃən) n. [fr. L. fimbriatus]

fin (fin) n. one of the paired membranous limbs or unpaired dermal outgrowths used by a fish to propel and steer itself ‖ anything resembling this, e.g. the limb of a seal or whale, or the ridge left on a metal casting ‖ (aeron.) an external rib, parallel to the axis of symmetry, preserving balance and direction by dividing the airflow ‖ a rib to provide a cooling surface, e.g. on a car radiator [O.E. finn]

fin·a·ble, fine·a·ble (fáinəb'l) adj. (of an offense) subject to a fine ‖ (of a person) liable to be fined

fi·na·gle (finéig'l) pres. part. **fi·na·gling** past and past part. **fi·na·gled** v.i. (pop.) to practice guile, wangle ‖ v.t. (pop.) to get (something) by guile [etymn. doubtful]

fi·nal (fáin'l) 1. adj. the last of a series, the final performance ‖ coming at the end, the final chapter ‖ ultimate, final defeat ‖ decisive, conclusive, a final judgment ‖ concerned with the end product or purpose, what is his final objective? ‖ (gram.) describing a clause of purpose (starting 'in order that', 'lest' etc.) 2. n. a deciding race, game, contest etc. ‖ (often pl.) the last of a series of examinations or an examination at the end of a course ‖ the latest edition of a newspaper in any one day, the late night final ‖ (mus.) the note on which an ecclesiastical mode ends **fi·nal·ist** n. a competitor in a deciding game, competition etc. **fi·nal·ly** adv. lastly, in conclusion ‖ completely, once for all, judgment was finally delivered [F.]

final cause (Aristotelian logic) the end or purpose of a thing

fi·nal·e (finǽli:, fináli:) n. the last movement of a musical composition ‖ the last aria, chorus etc. of an act of an opera ‖ the last piece performed at a concert ‖ the last scene of a play ‖ the last event in a dramatic series of events [Ital.]

fi·nal·ism (fáin'lizəm) n. (philos.) the doctrine of final causes (cf. TELEOLOGY)

fi·nal·i·ty (fainǽliti) pl. **fi·nal·i·ties** n. the state or quality of being final ‖ teleology [F. finalité]

fi·nal·ize (fáin'laiz) pres. part. **fi·nal·iz·ing** past and past part. **fi·nal·ized** v.t. to put into final form

fi·nance (fainǽns, fáinæns, finǽns) 1. n. monetary affairs ‖ the management of public or company revenue ‖ (pl.) monetary resources 2. v.t. pres. part. **fi·nanc·ing** past and past part. **fi·nanced** to provide with money or provide money for ‖ to raise the money for **fi·nan·cial** (fainǽnʃəl, finǽnʃəl) adj. pertaining to financiers or financial operations [O.F.]

finance company a company specializing in the financing of installment plan sales

financial disclosure n. requirement that a person provide information on assets and income, often asked of candidates for, or employees in, public office

financial service n. an investment advisory company and its publications, e.g., Standard & Poor's

financial year the period of a calendar year (not necessarily Jan. 1-Dec. 31) for accounting purposes

fin·an·cier (fainənsí:r, finənsí:r, Br. fainǽnsjə, finǽnsjə) n. a large-scale investor, capitalist ‖ someone skilled in financial matters, esp. those of a public concern [F.]

fi·nan·ism (fáinənizəm) n. a financial management simulation

finch (fintʃ) n. a small, seed-eating bird of fam. Fringillidae. They are widely distributed, and have a strong, sharply pointed, conical beak, suitable for crushing seeds [O.E. finc]

find (faind) 1. v. pres. part. **find·ing** past and past part. **found** (faund) v.t. to discover (what was lost) ‖ to discover by seeking, to find one's way ‖ to discover by experiment or study, to find the answer to a problem ‖ to discover by trial or experience, they found life difficult in that climate ‖ to discover by the feelings, he found them a trial or the intellect, you won't find it easy to define ‖ to discover by chance, we found him abandoned by the roadside ‖ to arrive at, liquids find their own level ‖ to make (a way) somehow, the statement found its way into print ‖ to obtain, to find acceptance ‖ to succeed in getting or raising, to find the capital for a house ‖ to summon up, to find courage to continue ‖ to perceive (oneself) to be as specified, to find oneself outwitted ‖ to declare (a verdict) ‖ to declare (a person) as specified (guilty, insane etc.) ‖ to provide, the employer finds accommodation ‖ to discover (the scent) or start (game) in hunting ‖ v.i. to discover the scent or start game in hunting ‖ to reach and deliver a verdict **to be found** to be, exist, emus are found in Australia **to find oneself** to discover one's potentialities and begin to realize them ‖ (Br.) to furnish oneself, to find oneself in clothes **to find out** to learn, discover ‖ to detect (someone) in wrongdoing, subterfuge etc. 2. n. a finding ‖ something valuable that is found ‖ a starting of game or picking up of the scent in hunting ‖ someone discovered to be of great quality, esp. when this is not expected **find·er** (fáindər) n. someone who or something which finds ‖ a small telescope attached to a large one, to simplify directing it on to a particular object ‖ a lens in a microscope for a similar purpose ‖ (photog.) a viewfinder [O.E. findan]

fin-de-siè·cle (fɛdəsjékl) adj. belonging to the end of the 19th c., esp. implying a certain refined decadence [F.=end of century]

find·ing (fáindiŋ) n. the act of someone who finds ‖ (pl.) something found by research, he published his findings in the trade journal ‖ (often pl.) the result of an inquiry or of judicial examinaton ‖ (pl.) equipment, tools etc. provided by a workman at his own expense

fine (fain) 1. adj. highly satisfactory, excellent, a fine performance ‖ very skilled and delicate, fine workmanship ‖ made or worked with delicacy, fine lace ‖ consisting of small particles, fine sand ‖ made of slender threads, fine sik ‖ highly refined, fine silver ‖ (of gold and silver) containing a specified proportion of pure metal, 18 carats fine ‖ thin, sharp, a fine point ‖ highly accomplished, a fine violinist ‖ (of athletes or animals) trained to perfection ‖ dressy, fine clothes ‖ subtle, a fine distinction ‖ able to see and appreciate subtleties, a fine sense of justice ‖ refined, fine taste ‖ uplifted, the praise gave him a fine feeling ‖ mannered, ornate, fine writing ‖ (old-fash.) excessively refined and proud, she has become a fine lady ‖ complimentary, fine phrases ‖ (used as an intensive) tremendous, he made a fine mess of it ‖ (of the weather) bright and clear, or (Br.) simply not raining **one** (or **some**) **fine day** at some time in the distant future 2. adv. very well **to cut** (Br. also **run**) it **fine** to leave only just enough time (for something that has to be done) **to cut a corner fine** to manage just to get around a corner 3. v. pres. part. **fin·ing** past and past part. **fined** v.t. (often with 'down') to make (beer, wine) clear ‖ (often with 'down') to make finer, thinner or less coarse ‖ (often with 'away') to remove gradually until fineness is achieved ‖ v.i. (of beer, wine, often with 'down') to become clear ‖ (often with 'down') to taper [F. fin]

fine 1. n. a sum of money paid as an imposed penalty for an offense 2. v.t. pres. part. **fin·ing** past and past part. **fined** to punish by imposing a fine on **fine·a·ble** adj. *FINABLE [M.E. fin, settlement of a dispute, fr. O.F.]

fine arts those arts concerned with beauty rather than utility, i.e. usually including poetry and music but sometimes limited to painting, sculpture and architecture

fine chemical a chemical produced in a relatively pure state, usually in small amounts, e.g. for photographic purposes (cf. HEAVY CHEMICAL)

fine-draw (fáindrɔ́) pres. part. **fine-draw·ing** past **fine-drew** (fáindrú:) past part. **fine-drawn** (fáindrɔ́n) v.t. to repair (torn edges of material) by drawing them together with fine stitches ‖ to draw out (wire) to extreme fineness **fine-drawn** adj. (of features) refined, not coarse ‖ (of distinctions in analysis) subtle

fine·ness (fáinnis) n. the quality of being fine ‖ (metall.) the amount of pure metal in an alloy, often expressed in parts per thousand by weight

fin·er·y (fáinəri:) pl. **fin·er·ies** n. a refinery [F. finerie]

finery n. showy, elaborate clothing, ornaments etc.

fines (fainz) pl. n. very finely powdered material (e.g. ore or fiber)

fines herbes (fi:nzerb) pl. n. a mixture of herbs (e.g. parsley, thyme, chives) used as a seasoning or garnish [F.=fine herbs]

fine-spun (fáinspʌn) adj. (of silk etc.) spun finely, delicate ‖ (of theories etc.) unpractical, tenuous

fi·nesse (finés) 1. n. subtlety of contrivance, judgment etc. ‖ a skillful strategic maneuver ‖ (cards) an attempt at taking a trick by choosing to play a card lower than some as yet unplayed card, taking the chance that this unplayed card is in a hand whose turn has passed 2. v. pres. part. **fi·ness·ing** past and past part. **fi·nessed** v.i. (cards) to make a finesse ‖ v.t. to make or achieve by subtlety, to finesse one's way into a position [F.=fineness]

fine-tune (faintú:n) v. to regulate with great exactness

fine-tuned out adj. carefully screened

Fin·gal's Cave (fíŋ'lz) a cave (227 ft long, 117 ft high) on Straffa, Inner Hebrides, Scotland, lined with basaltic pillars

fin·ger (fíŋgər) 1. n. a terminal digit of the hand, esp. other than the thumb ‖ something shaped like, or as thin as, a finger, a finger of cake ‖ the breadth of a finger, two fingers of whiskey ‖ the part of a glove into which a finger is inserted ‖ a pointer on a dial **to have a finger in the pie** to take part in something, participate, esp. in a way that is too forward or meddlesome **to lay a finger on** to hit so as to hurt **to let slip through one's fingers** to lose hold of or allow to escape or pass one by **to lift a finger** (in negative and interrogative constructions) to make the slightest effort **to put one's finger on** to identify, diagnose exactly (esp. something wrong) **to turn** (or **twist** or **wind**) **someone around one's (little) finger** to coax someone with ease into doing as one wishes ‖ (taboo slang) an obscene gesture of contemptuous rejection 2. v.t. to touch with the fingers, handle ‖ to perform (a piece of music) with a certain fingering ‖ to mark (notes of printed or written music) so as to indicate which fingers are to be used [O.E.]

fin·ger·board (fíŋgərbɔrd, fíŋgərbourd) n. the part of a stringed instrument against which the fingers press to alter the note ‖ the keyboard of a piano, organ etc.

finger bowl a vessel holding water for rinsing the fingers at table

finger food snacks that can be eaten politely without utensils, e.g., hors d'oeuvres, small cakes

fin·ger·ing (fíŋgəriŋ) n. (Br.) thick woolen yarn for stockings [earlier fingram, perh. fr. F. fin grain]

fingering n. the method of using the fingers in performing a piece of music, or the notation indicating this [FINGER]

finger mark (esp. Br.) a stain made by the fingers **fin·ger·mark** (fíŋgərmɑrk) v.t. (esp. Br.) to stain by handling

fin·ger·nail (fíŋgərneil) n. the nail growing on a finger

finger painting painting by putting color on wet paper with the finger ‖ a painting made by this mehod

finger plate a plate of china, metal etc. fastened above or below the handle of a door to prevent finger marks

fin·ger·print (fíŋgərprint) 1. n. an impression of a fingertip left on a surface ‖ such an impression taken in ink to record or check identification 2. v.t. to take an impression of the fingerprints of (a person)

fin·ger·stall (fíŋgərstɔl) n. a protective cover of rubber, plastic or leather for an injured finger

fin·ger·tip (fíŋgərtip) n. the tip of a finger ‖ a protective covering for the end of a finger **at one's fingertips** immediately available ‖ present in one's mind as the result of mastering detail **to one's fingertips** utterly, a cynic to his fingertips

fin·i·al (fíni:əl) n. (archit.) an ornament at the apex of a spire, gable, pinnacle etc. ‖ any crowning or finishing architectural feature [var. of FINAL]

fin·i·cal (finik'l) adj. finicky [perh. fr. FINE]

fin·ick·ing, fin·nick·ing (fínikiŋ) adj. finical [origin unknown]

fin·ick·y, fin·nick·y (fíniki:) *adj.* overfastidious, unduly exacting or exact, esp. giving too much finish to the details of an artifact ‖ having such finish

fin·ish (fíniʃ) **1.** *v.t.* to cause to come to an end, *to finish a story* ‖ to arrive at the end of, *to finish a journey* ‖ to complete (esp. the remainder of something), *he finished the book last night* ‖ to consume entirely, *to finish a chicken* ‖ to cause the death of, *the fever almost finished him* ‖ to exhaust completely ‖ to put the final touches to, *to finish a scenario* ‖ (esp. *Br.*) to complete the social education of, *she went to Switzerland to be finished* ‖ *v.i.* to come to an end **to finish off** to complete ‖ to have or provide with an ending ‖ to consume completely **to finish up** to find oneself or itself in the end, *the car finished up in the ditch* **to finish with** to break off relations with ‖ to conclude with, to be rounded off by **2.** *n.* conclusion, end ‖ a manner or style of finishing, *a mat finish to the paintwork* ‖ the material used for a decorative surface, *a veneer finish* ‖ (*fine arts*) surface refinement (often excessive) ‖ social polish, cultivated manners, speech etc. **to be in at the finish** (*hunting*) to be present at the kill **to fight to a finish** to fight till one side is defeated or gives in **fin·ished** *adj.* concluded, *a finished era* ‖ perfected, *a finished work of art* ‖ thorough, *a finished education* ‖ incapable of further achievement, *he is finished as a leader* **fin·ish·er** *n.* someone or something which finishes, esp. a craftsman, machine or substance involved in some final process of manufacture ‖ (*pop.*) a crushing blow [M.E. *fenys, finisch* fr. O. F. *fenir* (*feniss-*)] **finishing school** a private school putting emphasis on social and cultural accomplishments for girls

Fin·is·tère (fīni:stɛɛr) a department (area 2,729 sq. miles, pop. 769,000) of N.W. France at the western extremity of Brittany (*BRITTANY). Chief town: Quimper

Fin·is·terre, Cape (fīnistéər) the northwest point of Spain

fi·nite (fáinait) *adj.* having definable bounds ‖ (of numbers) able to be counted, not infinite or infinitesimal ‖ (*gram.*) of a verb which is limited by tense, number and person, *'we went', 'they are going'* are finite forms of the verb *'to go'* (cf. INFINITIVE) [fr. L. *finitus*]

Fink (fiŋk), Mike (c. 1770–1823), U.S. frontiersman. His rough, adventurous career as a keelboat king on the Mississippi and Ohio Rivers ended in his violent death but made him a legend

fink (fiŋk) *n.* (*slang*) one who tells tales; a betrayer

fink out *v.* (*slang*) to cop out, to quit

Fin·land (fínlənd) (*Finn.* Suomi) a republic (area 130,160 sq. miles, incl. Ahvenanmaa and inland water, pop. 4,816,000) in N. Europe. Capital: Helsinki. People and language: nine tenths Finnish, one tenth Swedish, with some Lapps in the north. Religion: Lutheran, with an Orthodox minority. The land is 70% forest, 10% lakes, 8% arable and 1% pasture. Only the extreme northwest is mountainous (highest point: Haltiatunturi, 4,340 ft). Forests are found up to 68° N. There are 50,000 lakes, many linked by canals. Rainfall: 30 ins in the south, 20 ins in the north. Average temperatures (F.) for Feb. and July: 8° and 56° in Lapland, 22° and 66° in the southwest. Livestock: cattle, poultry. Crops: cereals (wheat in the southwest, rye to 66° N., barley to 68° N.), potatoes (to the Arctic Circle). Exports: lumber, paper, wood pulp. Other products: furs, fish (esp. herring and salmon), wood products (esp. furniture and prefabricated houses), textiles, matches, glass, porcelain. Minerals: copper, zinc, iron, nickel. Imports: metals, machinery, fuel oils, chemicals. Ports: Helsinki and Kotka, (in winter) Hangö and Turku. There are five universities. Monetary unit: markka (100 pennia). HISTORY. The Finns, nomadic tribes of the north, settled the country (1st c. A.D.). It was conquered and Christianized by Sweden (12th–14th cc.), and ceded to Russia (1809), becoming an autonomous grand duchy (1809–1917). It declared itself an independent state (1917). Civil war broke out between the Red Guards, supported by the Russians, and the White Army, under Gen. Mannerheim, supported by the Germans (Jan.-May 1918). The latter took power until the end of the 2nd world war. The republic was established (1919). It was invaded by Russia (1939) and surrendered the Karelian Isthmus (1940). It joined the German attack on Russia (1941) but signed an armistice (1944), losing

Petsamo to Russia. Dr. Kekkonen was president (1956–82) and was succeeded by Mauno Koivisto. Finland signed agreements with the European Economic Community (1973) and with the U.S.S.R. (1977)

Finland, Gulf of the eastern arm of the Baltic Sea, south of Finland

Fin·land·i·za·tion (finlændizéiʃən) *n.* process of becoming a small, weak neighbor because of the military might and political power of a superpower neighbor. Finlandization results in the concession of a nation's sovereign liberties

Fin·lay (fínlei), Carlos Juan (1833–1915), Cuban physician and research scientist in the field of tropical disease. He discovered the transmitting agent of yellow fever

Finlay River *MACKENZIE RIVER

Finn (fin) *n.* a native or inhabitant of Finland ‖ a person speaking a Finnish language

fin·nan had·die (finənhædi:) finnan haddock

finnan haddock (fínənhædək) smoked haddock [after R. *Findharn* or the village of *Findon*, Scotland]

fin·ner (fínər) *n.* the rorqual whale, the dorsal fin of which shows above water

Fin·ney (fíni:), Charles Grandison (1792–1875), U.S. evangelist and theologian, known for his spectacular revivalist meetings in New York

Finn·ic (fínik) *adj.* Finnish ‖ of or being a branch of the Finno-Ugric subfamily of Uralic languages

finnicking *FINICKING

finnicky *FINICKY

Finn·ish (fíniʃ) **1.** *adj.* of the people of Finland or their language ‖ of peoples allied to the Finns **2.** *n.* the language of the Finns. It belongs to the Finno-Ugric group, which comes under the general heading of Uralic languages, and is related to Hungarian. It is spoken by about three million people living in Finland proper and in small population pockets in Norway, Sweden and the U.S.S.R. It has been influenced by the Slavic and Germanic languages

Finn·mark (fínmark) Norway's largest, northernmost, easternmost and least populated province (area 18,106 sq. miles, pop. 72,000). Capital: Vadsö

Fin·no-U·gri·an (fínoujú:gri:ən, finouú:gri:ən) Finno-Ugric

Fin·no-U·gric (fínoujú:grik, finouú:grik) **1.** *n.* a subfamily of the Uralic family of languages including Finnish, Estonian, Hungarian and Lapp **2.** *adj.* belonging to or pertaining to this subfamily

fi·no (fí:nou) *n.* type of sweet sherry created when flour yeasts develop on surface of wine in cask, extracting sugar and other materials

fiord, fjord (fjɔrd, fjourd) *n.* a narrow inlet of the sea enclosed by high cliffs, e.g. on the Norwegian and Alaskan coasts [Norw.]

fir (fə:r) *n.* an evergreen tree of genus *Abies*, fam. *Pinaceae*. Firs have needle leaves borne directly on the stem, and large cones which are wind-pollinated and ripen in one year. *A. balsamea* yields Canada balsam. Many others yield useful timbers and resins ‖ the wood of such trees [M.E. *firr, firre*]

Fir·bank (fə:rbæŋk), Ronald (1886–1926), English novelist. His works include 'The Flower Beneath the Foot' (1923), 'Sorrow in Sunlight' (1924,) 'Concerning the Eccentricities of Cardinal Pirelli' (1926). He sets out to please the reader by telling comic stories with brevity and grace. The comedy is grotesquely imbued with tragic tones, and compassion stems from the mingling. In technique Firbank made a significant contribution to the novel

Fir·dau·si (fiərdáusi:) (Abdul Kasim Hasan, c. 930–1020), Persian poet. His epic 'Shah-nama' ('Book of Kings') is a history of Persia to his own day

fire (fáiər) **1.** *n.* a chemical change accompanied by the emission of heat and light, and often flame, usually a change consisting in the combination of carbon compounds with the oxygen of the air ‖ a mass of material undergoing this change or gotten ready for this ‖ the act of undergoing this chemical change, *to go through fire* ‖ a conflagration ‖ (*Br.*) a gas or electric heater for a room ‖ the discharge of a gun or guns ‖ passion, *there is no fire in the work* **to be on fire** to be burning ‖ to be passionately eager **to be under fire** to be within the range of hostile gunfire ‖ to be the object of criticism **to catch fire** to begin to burn **to play with fire** to treat potentially dangerous things too lightly **to set fire to, set on fire** to cause to begin to burn **to set the world** (*Br.* also **the Thames**)

on fire to achieve fame by spectacular achievements **2.** *v. pres. part.* **fir·ing** *past* and *past part.* **fired** *v.t.* to discharge (a gun etc.) ‖ to cause (bullets, rounds etc.) to be propelled from a gun ‖ to make by gunfire, *to fire a salute* ‖ to ask (questions) or make (remarks etc.) in rapid succession ‖ to set fire to, esp. so as to destroy ‖ (*pop.*) to dismiss, discharge (an employee) ‖ to stimulate, *to fire someone with enthusiasm* ‖ to bake (bricks, pottery etc.) in a kiln ‖ to cure (tobacco, tea etc.) by heat ‖ to cauterize (horses' hooves etc.) ‖ to supply with fuel, *to fire a kiln* ‖ to light the fuse of (an explosive) ‖ *v.i.* to shoot a gun or guns etc. ‖ (of a gun etc.) to go off ‖ to be detonated, *the explosives fired spontaneously* ‖ to be affected by fire, *the clay fires a rosy red* ‖ (of an internal-combustion engine) to have the compressed mixture in the cylinders ignited ‖ (of wheat etc.) to turn yellow prematurely, e.g. in a drought **to fire away** to go on firing ‖ to begin putting questions or making remarks, criticisms etc. [O.E. *fyr*]

fire alarm an apparatus for giving notice of the outbreak of a fire

fire·arm (fáiərɑrm) *n.* any portable weapon firing shot or bullets by gunpowder

fire·ball (fáiərbɔl) *n.* a large meteor ‖ lightning shaped like a ball of fire ‖ (*hist.*) a ball of sacking etc. filled with inflammable materials and hurled into the enemy lines

fire·base (fáiərbeis) *n.* (*mil.*) military establishment designed to deliver heavy gunfire

Fire·bee (fáiərbi:) *n.* (*mil.*) a remote-controlled air- or ground-launched target drone (BOM-34) powered by a turbojet engine, capable of achieving high subsonic speeds. The Firebee is used to test, train, and evaluate weapon systems employing surface-to-air and air-to-air missiles

fire boat a boat equipped for fighting fires

fire bomb an incendiary bomb

fire·box (fáiərbɔks) *n.* the chamber of a boiler in which the fire is made, esp. this in a steam locomotive

fire·brand (fáiərbrænd) *n.* someone who stirs up strife ‖ a brand (piece of burning wood)

fire·break (fáiərbreik) *n.* a barrier, e.g. of cleared land, to prevent the spread of fires, esp. in forests

fire·brick (fáiərbrik) *n.* a refractory brick made of fireclay

fire brigade a body of men trained and equipped to fight fires ‖ (*Br.*) the fire department

fire·bug (fáiərbʌg) *n.* (*pop.*) a pyromaniac

fire·clay (fáiərklei) *n.* clay resistant to high temperatures, used for firebrick, crucibles etc. It is made of almost pure aluminum silicate

fire company a body of men trained and equipped to fight fires

fire control the system in a ship, fort etc. of regulating the firing of guns at targets ‖ civil defense against fire

fire·crack·er (fáiərkrækər) *n.* a small, cylindrical firework which goes off with a sharp, cracking noise when its fuse is lit

fire-cure (fáiərkjuər) *pres. part.* **fire-cur·ing** *past* and *past part.* **fire-cured** *v.t.* to cure (tobacco) in the smoke of an open wood fire

fire·damp (fáiərdæmp) *n.* a combustible gas consisting mainly of methane formed in mines by the decomposition of coal ‖ the explosive mixture formed by this and air

fire department (*Am.=Br.* fire brigade) the public fire-fighting organization

fire·dog (fáiərdɔg, fáiərdɒg) *n.* an andiron

fire drill the organized practice of what must be done in the emergency of an outbreak of fire

fire-eat·er (fáiəri:tər) *n.* an entertainer who pretends to eat fire ‖ a violently aggressive person, esp. in talk

fire engine a vehicle carrying men and equipment to fight fires

fire escape a permanent stairway on the outside of high buildings for escape in case of fire ‖ (*Br.*) an extension ladder used by firemen

fire extinguisher a portable metal container ejecting chemicals, or water and chemicals, for putting out fires

fire-flood·ing (fáiərflʌdiŋ) *n.* process of sending steam or air under pressure into an exhausted oil well to revive oil production **fire flood** *v.*

fire·fly (fáiərflai) *pl.* **fire-flies** *n.* any of several winged, nocturnal insects emitting light by the oxidation of luciferin, e.g. the male of beetles of fam. *Lampyridae* (*GLOWWORM) or any of several tropical click beetles

CONCISE PRONUNCIATION KEY: **(a)** æ, c*a*t; ɑ, c*a*r; ɔ f*aw*n; ei, sn*a*ke. **(e)** e, h*e*n; i:, sh*ee*p; iə, d*ee*r; ɛə, b*ea*r. **(i)** i, f*i*sh; ai, t*i*ger; ə:, b*i*rd. **(o)** o, *o*x; au, c*ow*; ou, g*oa*t; u, p*oo*r; ɔi, r*oy*al. **(u)** ʌ, d*u*ck; u, b*u*ll; u:, g*oo*se; ə, b*a*cillus; ju:, c*u*be. x, lo*ch*; θ, *th*ink; δ, bo*th*er; z, *Z*en; ʒ, corsa*g*e; dʒ, sava*g*e; ŋ, ora*ng*utan*g*; j, *y*ak; ʃ, fi*sh*; tʃ, fe*tch*; 'l, rabb*le*; 'n, redd*en*. Complete pronunciation key appears inside front cover.

fire-guard (fáiərgard) n. a fire screen (protective metal screen) || a man employed to watch for and deal with forest fires || a firebreak

fire-house (fáiərhaus) pl. **fire-hous-es** (fáiərhauziz) n. a fire station

fire irons metal fireside utensils, e.g. poker, shovel and tongs

fire-light (fáiərlait) n. light from a fire, esp. one in an open hearth or a campfire

fire-light-er (fáiərlaitər) n. (Br.) a readily combustible preparation used to get a coal fire going quickly

fire-lock (fáiərlɒk) n. (hist.) an old form of gun in which the priming was discharged by a lock with steel and flint

fire-man (fáiərmən) pl. **fire-men** (fáiərmən) n. a member of a fire department || the man responsible for feeding the fire, e.g. of a steam engine, furnace etc.

fireman's carry (wrestling) maneuver placing opponent's arm over one's shoulder and grasping a crotch hold, usu. followed by a hoist and a kneel to force opponent to the mat

fire opal a girasol (opal)

fire-place (fáiərpleis) n. the hearth or grate for an open fire in a room

fire-plug (fáiərplʌg) n. a hydrant for supplying mains water to hoses in case of fire

fire-pow-er (fáiərpauər) n. the total number and weight of bullets, shells, missiles etc. able to be fired by a military unit in a given time

fire-proof (fáiərpruːf) 1. adj. incombustible, a fireproof fabric 2. v.t. to make incombustible, esp. by impregnating with chemicals

fire-rais-ing (fáiərreiziŋ) n. (Br.) arson

fire screen a protective metal screen or grid placed in front of an open fire, stove etc. against sparks or falling embers etc. || (Br., old-fash.) a light, portable screen to shield a person (esp. his face) from the direct heat of an open fire

fire ship (hist.) a vessel carrying combustible or explosive substances set adrift among enemy ships to fire them

fire-side (fáiərsaid) 1. n. the part of a room in a house nearest the fire or hearth 2. adj. for people in their homes, informal

fire station the building housing fire engines and firemen on call

Fire-stone (fáiərstoun), Harvey Samuel (1868–1938), U.S. pioneer rubber manufacturer who founded (1900) the Firestone Tire and Rubber Company

fire-stone (fáiərstoun) n. (esp. Br.) sandstone used for lining kilns and in the building of fireplaces etc.

fire tower a lookout tower for a person watching for outbreaks of fire

fire-trap (fáiərtræp) n. a building etc. specially dangerous to be in in the event of a fire because of its construction, or one specially liable to the risk of fire

fire walking the ordeal of walking barefoot over hot stones, embers etc.

fire warden an official empowered to take measures against fires

fire-wa-ter (fáiərwɔtər, fáiərwɒtər) n. (pop.) rough, very strong alcoholic liquor [name formerly given by North American Indians to whiskey, gin or rum]

fire-wood (fáiərwud) n. wood for burning on a fire

fire-work (fáiərwəːrk) n. a device used in quantity for entertainment by effects of colored light, smoke, noise etc. caused by combustion or explosion || (pl.) a display of fireworks || (pl.) a verbal display of wit or anger

fir-ing (fáiəriŋ) n. the act of discharging a gun, mine etc. || the act of feeding or keeping burning a furnace etc. || the process of baking ceramic ware in a kiln || the scorching of plants as a result of unfavorable soil conditions || fuel for a fire

firing line the line of troops in active contact with the enemy

firing party a firing squad

firing pin a pin-shaped device striking the detonator in the cartridge head in the breech mechanism of a gun, rifle etc.

firing squad a group of men detailed to carry out an execution by shooting || a group detailed to fire a salute at a funeral with military honors

fir-kin (fəːrkin) n. a small cask for beer, butter, fish etc. || an indeterminate measure equal to the fourth part of a barrel (e.g. the equivalent of 9 imperial gallons of liquid or 56 lbs of butter) [older ferdekyn, perh. fr. M. Du. vierde, a fourth part]

firm (fəːrm) 1. adj. compact, solid, firm muscles || stable, a firm foundation || steady, a firm voice || steadfast, resolute, a firm decision || exercising authority with discipline || not liable to cancellation or modification, a firm offer || (of prices, stock market etc.) steady, not fluctuating much 2. adv. firmly, to stand firm 3. v.t. to make firm || v.i. to become firm [O.F. firme]

firm n. a partnership or business house || the name under which such a partnership (not having the legal status of a company) conducts business [fr. Ital., Span., Port. firma, signature]

fir-ma-ment (fəːrməmənt) n. the whole vault of the sky with its myriad stars etc. [fr. L. firmamentum]

fir-man (fəːrmán) n. (in some Oriental countries) a royal decree, edict etc. [Pers.]

firmer chisel a woodworker's short chisel, thin in relation to breadth

firmer gouge a woodworker's short gouge

firm-ware (fəːrmwɛər) n. (computer) 1. software and hardware component so integrated as to make function of each indistinguishable 2. a handwired logic circuit to perform functions of a program

firn (fiərn) n. névé [G.=last year's (snow)]

first (fəːrst) 1. adj. being number one in a series (*NUMBER TABLE) earliest in time, a first edition || nearest the front, the first row || foremost in importance, rank etc., first secretary || earliest available, we caught the first train home || earliest with relation to an unspecified time, the first snow || fundamental, first principles || rudimentary, he hasn't the first idea of drawing || (mus., of an instrument or voice) having a part generally higher in pitch than that of the second instrument or voice of the same kind, first violin, first soprano || of low gear in a vehicle at first hand directly, from personal knowledge at first sight instantaneous, instantaneously, love at first sight || judging by first impressions, a risky plan at first sight **first thing** at the earliest moment, do it first thing tomorrow **in the first place** firstly, to begin with **not to know the first thing about** to be completely ignorant about 2. n. the first person or thing mentioned or the first of a series, the first of the speakers || (Br.) a grading in the first class of an examination || a first prize or a victory in a race or other contest || the first day of a month || low gear in a vehicle || (pl.) certain products (lumber, flour, butter etc.) of the highest quality **from the first** from the beginning **to be the first to** to do without reluctance, he would be the first to admit it 3. adv. before any other person or thing, to finish first || for the first time, we first went there last year || before anything else, you must finish your work first [O.E. fyrst]

first aid the emergency treatment of someone wounded or taken ill

first base (baseball) the base that must be touched first by the base runner || (baseball) the player placed at this base **to get to first base** (pop.) to make headway

first blood drawing first blood in a duel; hence, a victory in the first encounter, seen to be an advantage

first-born (fəːrstbɔrn) 1. adj. eldest 2. n. (rhet.) the first child of a family

first cause (philos.) the prime mover || (theol.) God as the source of all causality

first-class (fəːrstklǽs, fəːrstklɑ́s) 1. adj. of the highest class, or the best quality || of or traveling in the most luxurious accommodation in a railroad train, aircraft or passenger vessel divided into various classes || (Br.) of the highest division in certain examinations or of a grading in this division 2. adv. by the first class

first cost (Br.) prime cost

first cousin the child of one's uncle or aunt

first cousin once removed one's first cousin's child || one's parent's first cousin

first day the day on which new postage stamps of a particular issue are available || a first-day cover **First Day** Sunday (used esp. by the Society of Friends)

first-day cover (fəːrstdei) (philately) an envelope or wrapper bearing a stamp of a new issue, posted from the town of issue on the day of issue

first-de-gree burn (fəːrstdigríː) a mild burn not involving blistering or charring of the tissues

first-dol-lar coverage (fəːrstdɒlər) (insurance) coverage under a policy that begins with the first dollar of expense incurred by the insured for the covered benefits, i.e., with no deductible, although coinsurance may be in effect

first finger forefinger

first floor the ground floor || (Br.) the story above the ground floor

first-fruits (fəːrstfrúːts) pl. n. the earliest produce, crops etc. of the season, esp. those offered in a church thanksgiving || first profits, gains or effects

first-hand (fəːrsthǽnd) adv. and adj. from the original sources or by personal experience

first in, first out *FIFO

first intention (med.) the healing of a wound quickly and with little scar formation

First Lady the wife of the president of the U.S.A. or of the governor of a state of the U.S.A., or whoever presides for him at social functions if the man has no wife

first lieutenant an officer in the U.S. army, air force or marine corps ranking above a second lieutenant and below a captain

first-ling (fəːrstliŋ) n. (rhet.) offspring or products held in special regard as being the first of their kind

first-ly (fəːrstliː) adv. to begin with, in the first place

first mortgage a mortgage having priority over all subsequent mortgages

first name the given name (as compared with the surname)

first night the first performance of a play in a theater **first-night-er** (fəːrstnáitər) n. someone who habitually attends such performances

First Nonimportation Act of 1806 a U.S. Congressional act (effective 1808), barring the importation of goods from Britain that could be imported from elsewhere. It reflected the mounting Anglo-U.S. hostility prior to the War of 1812

first offender someone convicted for the first time of an offense

first papers papers declaring intention to seek naturalization, filed by an applicant for citizenship

first person (gram.) the speaker in a sentence, indicated by the form of a verb or pronoun, 'me' is a first person pronoun

first principles the fundamental assumptions on which a chain of reasoning may be based

first quarter the phase of the moon, a week after new moon, when half its disk is illuminated by the sun

first-rate (fəːrstréit) 1. adj. of the finest quality || of the highest efficiency || of the largest or most important class, a first-rate power 2. adv. very well

First Reconstruction Act a U.S. Congressional act passed (1867) after the Civil War, over President Johnson's veto. It divided the South into five military districts and denied the Southern states readmittance to the Union unless they permitted black suffrage and ratified the Fourteenth Amendment. It led to other reconstruction acts, under which the major generals commanding the occupying forces were placed under the authority of Congress

first sergeant (mil.) a senior noncommissioned officer of a company acting as administrative assistant to the commander

first-strike (fəːrststráik) adj. (mil.) of nuclear weapons suitable for a first strike attack on the enemy, but vulnerable to first strike by the enemy

first-strike capability n. (mil.) capacity of a nuclear power to destroy an enemy's ability to retaliate

first water *WATER

First World the rich, industrialized nations such as the U.S., the nations of Western Europe, and Canada, Australia, New Zealand, and Japan

firth (fəːrθ) n. a narrow arm of the sea, esp. a river mouth [perh. O.N. fiorthr]

Firth-i-an adj. (linguistics) of linguistic principles of J. R. Firth of the University of London. Firthian linguistics are based on polysystemicism in which the context of a situation changes its meanings. The neo-Firthian approach is propounded by M. A. K. Halliday

fis-cal (fiskəl) adj. of or pertaining to the public treasury or revenue, fiscal reforms || financial, fiscal control [F.]

fiscal agent a financial representative, esp. a trust company employed by a corporation

fiscal year any yearly period established as the accounting period for business purposes

Fisch-er (fíʃər), Emil Hermann (1852–1919), German chemist, famous esp. for his work on sugars and the purine group. Nobel prize (1902)

CONCISE PRONUNCIATION KEY: (a) æ, cat; ɑ, car; ɔ fawn; ei, snake. (e) e, hen; iː, sheep; iə, deer; ɛə, bear. (i) i, fish; ai, tiger; əː, bird. (o) o, ox; au, cow; ou, goat; u, poor; ɔi, royal. (u) ʌ, duck; u, bull; uː, goose; ə, bacillus; juː, cube. x, loch; θ, think; ð, bother; z, Zen; ʒ, corsage; dʒ, savage; ŋ, orangutang; j, yak; ʃ, fish; tʃ, fetch; 'l, rabble; 'n, redden. Complete pronunciation key appears inside front cover.

Fisch·er von Er·lach (fíʃərfɔnéɑrlax), Johann Bernhard (1656–1723), Austrian baroque architect. His masterpiece is the 'Karl-Borromäus-Kirche' (1716–37) in Vienna

Fish (fiʃ), Hamilton (1808–93), U.S. statesman. As secretary of state (1869–77) under President Grant, he successfully negotiated in critical Anglo-American and Spanish-American disputes

fish (fiʃ) *pl.* **fish, fish·es** *n.* a member of *Pisces*, a class of backboned aquatic animals, many of which yield flesh that is highly nutritious, and some yielding oil for food or industrial use ‖ the flesh, whether raw or cooked **to drink like a fish** to drink a great deal of alcohol habitually **to feel like a fish out of water** to feel uncomfortable or ill at ease because of strange surroundings **to have other fish to fry** to have more important business in hand [O.E. *fisc*] —The cartilaginous fishes (*Chondrichthyes*, incl. sharks, rays, skates) are covered with placoid scales. Their gills have separate openings. They have no swim bladder. The rudimentary notochord persists. The bony fishes (*Osteichthyes*, incl. most freshwater and marine fish), are covered with bonelike scales. Their gills are covered by an operculum. Most have a swim bladder

fish *v.i.* to try to catch fish, e.g. with a net or line ‖ to search for something underwater by dredging, hooking etc., *to fish for sunken treasure* ‖ to try to get something, usually by indirect methods, *to fish for compliments* ‖ *v.t.* to fish in, *to fish a river* ‖ to draw up or out from water or as if from water, *he fished a coin out of his pocket* **to fish in troubled waters** to profit from disturbances or others' difficulties **to fish out** to exhaust the fish of **to fish the anchor** to draw up the flukes of the anchor to the gunwale [O.E. *fiscian*]

fish 1. *pl.* **fish** *n.* (*naut.*) a piece of timber convex on one side and concave on the other, used to strengthen a spar etc. ‖ a fishplate 2. *v.t.* to mend (a spar, mast etc.) by means of a fish ‖ to join (rails etc.) with a fishplate [perh. F. *fiche* or perh. FISH]

fish-and-chips (fíʃəntʃíps) *pl. n.* (esp. *Br.*) portions of fish (usually filleted) fried in batter, with French fries

fish ball a ball of shredded whitefish and mashed potatoes, usually fried

fish·bolt (fíʃbǫult) *n.* (*Br., rail.*) a bolt for fastening fishplates and rails

fish·bowl (fíʃbǫul) *n.* a spherical glass vessel for keeping live goldfish etc. in

Fish·er (fíʃər), Andrew (1862–1928), Australian Labours statesman. He was prime minister (1908–9, 1910–13, 1914–15) and high commissioner in London (1915–21)

Fisher, Irving (1867–1947), U.S. political economist and statistician who strongly influenced monetary theory. He advocated the adoption of a 'compensated dollar' containing a given value of gold, instead of the conventional given weight of gold, to prevent extreme price-level fluctuation

Fisher, St John (c. 1469–1535), English humanist scholar, bishop of Rochester (1504–34). He was executed for refusing to acknowledge Henry VIII as supreme head of the Church of England. Feast: June 22

Fisher, John Arbuthnot, 1st Baron Fisher of Kilverstone (1841–1920), British admiral, first sea lord (1904–10 and 1914–15). He introduced the dreadnought into the British navy and prepared the fleet for the 1st world war

fish·er (fíʃər) *n. Martes pennanti*, a North American carnivorous mammal of the weasel family, extinct in much of its territory through overhunting [O.E. *fiscere*]

Fisher exact probability test (*statistics*) a test of statistical significance for normal variables, used instead of the chi-square test when the sample size and cell frequencies are small

fish·er·man (fíʃərmən) *pl.* **fish·er·men** (fíʃərmən) *n.* someone who lives by fishing ‖ someone who fishes for pleasure

fisherman's bend a kind of knot used, e.g. to secure a boat

fish·er·y (fíʃəri:) *pl.* **fish·er·ies** *n.* the fishing industry ‖ an area where fishing is carried on, *deep-sea fisheries* ‖ a place where fish are bred ‖ (*law*) the right to fish in particular waters

fish-eye (fíʃai) *n.* 1. (*photography*) an extremely wide angle (180°) view, often a distorted one 2. (*photography*) a photograph made with a fisheye lens 3. the use of such a lens

fish glue isinglass ‖ a liquid glue made by heating the fins, bones and skin of fish with water

fish hawk the osprey

fish·hook (fíʃhuk) *n.* a hook, usually barbed, used for catching fish ‖ a part of the tackle used to raise a ship's anchor

fish-in (fíʃin) *n.* group participation in illegal fishing to protest unwanted regulations

fish·ing (fíʃiŋ) *n.* the occupation, sport, or process of catching fish ‖ a place where fish are to be caught

fishing line (*Br.*) a fishline

fishing rod a long tapered rod, often jointed and with a reel attached, for catching fish

fish joint a joint held by fishplates

fish kettle a long narrow utensil for boiling fish

fish ladder a series of pools stepped one above another that allow fishes to get over a dam on their journey upstream

fish·line (fíʃlain) *n.* (*Am.=Br.* fishing line) a length of linen or nylon cord used esp. with a rod for fishing

fish meal dried fish or fish waste, used for animal food and as fertilizer

fish·mon·ger (fíʃmʌŋgər) *n.* (*Br.*) a tradesman who sells fish [fr. FISH+*monger*, a dealer]

fish·plate (fíʃpleit) *n.* one of a pair of metal plates holding rails in position at a joint or overlapping the ends of heavy timbers joined end to end

fish·pond (fíʃpɒnd) *n.* a pond stocked with fish, for commerce or ornament

fish protein concentrate a flour of powdered dried fish designed as a tasteless, odorless, dietary supplement *abbr.* FPC

fish slice (*Br.*) a kitchen implement used for turning fish over in the frying pan ‖ (*Br.*) a fish knife for serving at the table

fish tackle (*naut.*) tackle used to fish the anchor

fish-tail (fíʃteil) 1. *v.i.* to swing an aircraft from side to side as a means of reducing speed 2. *n.* an object or part of an object with an end shaped like the cleft tail of a fish ‖ the maneuver of fishtailing

fishway *FISH LADDER

fish·wife (fíʃwaif) *pl.* **fish·wives** (fíʃwaivz) *n.* a woman who sells fish from a market stall, esp. such a person as a criterion of skill in swearing

fish·y (fíʃi:) *comp.* **fish·i·er** *superl.* **fish·i·est** *adj.* of, relating to or like fish, *a fishy taste* ‖ dull, lusterless, *a fishy eye* ‖ doubtful, unreliable, suspicious, *a fishy story* ‖ rich in fish

Fisk (fisk), James (1834–72), U.S. stock broker and speculator, known for his questionable business tactics and manipulations. He was best known for his role in the 'Erie War' (1868), an attempt to prevent Cornelius Vanderbilt from taking full control of the Erie Railroad, and in 'Black Friday' (1869), a result of an attempt to corner the gold market. He was killed by a disgruntled business associate

Fiske (fisk), Bradley Allen (1854–1942), U.S. admiral. He invented numerous naval warfare instruments, incl. the turbine-driven torpedo and the electric range-finder

Fiske, John (1842–1901), U.S. historical writer. In 'Outlines of Cosmic Philosophy' (1874), he demonstrated the compatibility of Darwin's theory of evolution with religion

Fisk University (fisk), a coeducational college at Nashville, Tenn., chartered (1867) by the American Missionary Society to provide education for blacks. It still has a large black enrollment

fis·sile (fís'l) *adj.* able to be split (esp. of wood in the direction of the grain) ‖ fissionable [fr. L. *fissilis*]

fis·sion (fíʃən) *n.* the act or process of splitting into parts, esp. (*biol.*) asexual reproduction by means of division into two equal parts (binary fission) or more than two (multiple fission), e.g. in bacteria, corals etc. ‖ (*phys.*) the splitting of an atomic nucleus into approximately equal parts, e.g. by bombardment with neutrons (cf. RADIOACTIVITY). This may take place with an overall loss in mass, resulting in the release of enormous amounts of energy, esp. when heavy elements are used, as in the atomic bomb or in a controlled process in a reactor to produce energy for industrial and scientific purposes (*NUCLEAR ENERGY) **fis·sion·a·ble** *adj.* [fr. L. *fissio* (*fissionis*)]

fis·sion-track dating (fíʃəntræk) (*geol.*) technique for determining the date of a geological formation by measuring tracks left by the spontaneous fission of uranium 2.38 that are proportionate to the age of the formation

fis·si·ros·tral (fisirɔ́strəl) *adj.* (of birds) having a deeply cleft beak [fr. L. *fissus*, split+*rostrum*, beak]

fis·sure (fíʃər) 1. *n.* a narrow opening or cleft made by splitting, esp. in rock ‖ a cleaving or cleavage ‖ (*anat.*) a narrow opening in an organ, a groove separating certain skull bones or a cleft in the lobes of the brain 2. *v.t.* and *i. pres. part.* **fis·sur·ing** *past* and *past part.* **fis·sured** to split into fissures [F.]

fist (fist) *n.* the hand when clenched, with the fingers folded tightly into the palm [O.E. *fȳst*]

fist·i·cuffs (fístikʌfs) *pl. n.* (*old-fash.*) fighting with bare fists, *a bout of fisticuffs*

fis·tu·la (fístʃulə) *pl.* **fis·tu·las, fis·tu·lae** (fístʃuli:) *n.* (*med.*) an abnormal channel leading from an internal organ to the exterior of the body, the result of injury or inflammation ‖ (*vet.*) inflammation of a horse's withers **fís·tu·lar, fís·tu·lous** *adjs* [L.=pipe, flute]

fit (fit) 1. *adj.* suited to a particular end, *fit to eat, not fit for publication* ‖ (with 'for') good enough, *fit for a king* ‖ proper, right, *do what you think fit* ‖ competent or suitably endowed by nature, *he is not fit io govern* ‖ brought into a specified condition, ready, *she worked till she was fit to drop* ‖ in good physical condition, healthy 2. *v. pres. part.* **fit·ting** *past* and *past part.* **fit·ted, fit** *v.t.* to suit, *a present to fit the occasion* ‖ to qualify, make competent, *his experience fits him for the job* ‖ to answer to, correspond with, *he fits the description* to bring into harmony with, *to fit a policy to a new situation* ‖ to be the right size or shape for ‖ to adjust the size or shape of so as to be right ‖ (with 'for') to measure (someone or something), *to fit a room for curtains* ‖ to insert into a position where there is just enough room, *fit the cupboard under the stairs* ‖ to install, put in as equipment etc., *to fit fog lights* ‖ *v.i.* to be correct in size or shape to be in harmony or agreement ‖ (of statistical data) to correspond with a standard **to fit in** to make time for between other activities, *to fit in a visit* ‖ to find room or a place for, *we can fit you in at the corner table* ‖ to place where there is just enough room, *fit the bookcase in between the windows* ‖ to occupy such a position, *it fits in nicely* ‖ to go well with, *he doesn't fit in with their other friends* ‖ to adjust one's plans to suit others **to fit out** to equip **to fit up** to equip, esp. lavishly 3. *n.* the manner or degree of fitting ‖ the degree of correspondence of statistical data with a standard ‖ something which fits [origin unknown]

fit *n.* a seizure, convulsion ‖ a short sudden attack or outburst, e.g. of depression or coughing ‖ a short spell, *a fit of idleness* **by fits and starts** in irregular bursts of activity **to have** (or **throw**) **a fit** to become suddenly and violently angry or upset [O.E. *fitt*, conflict]

Fitch (fitʃ), John (1743–98), U.S. metal craftsman. He designed an early version of the steamboat which operated successfully (1787), for which he was granted a U.S. and French patent (1791)

fitch (fitʃ) *n.* the fitchew

fitch·et (fítʃit) *n.* the fitchew

fit·chew (fítʃu:) *n.* the polecat, *Mustelia putorius* ‖ its fur [O.F. *fissel* dim. of M. Du. *fisse*, polecat]

fit·ful (fítfəl) *adj.* spasmodic

fit·ly (fítli) *adv.* properly, in a fit manner

fit·ment (fítmənt) *n.* a piece of furniture or equipment, esp. built-in furniture ‖ (*pl.*) fittings

fit·ness (fítnis) *n.* the state of being fit, suitable, appropriate ‖ good health

fit·ter (fítər) *n.* someone who fits things, *a tailor's fitter* ‖ a qualified mechanic who assembles finished parts of machinery or equinpment

fit·ting (fítiŋ) *n.* (esp. *pl.*) a piece of fixed equipment or furnishing ‖ a small part for a piece of apparatus or an installation ‖ a trying-on of tailor-made clothes, *a second fitting* ‖ (*Br., commerce*) a size and shape, e.g. of shoes, *a narrow fitting*

fitting (*pres. part.* of FIT) *adj.* appropriate, *a fitting reply*

Fitz·ger·ald (fitsdʒérɑld), Edward (1809–83), English writer and scholar. He is best known for his free translation of the 'Rubáiyát of Omar Khayyám' (1859)

Fitz·ger·ald (fitsdʒérɑld), F. Scott (1896–1941), American novelist. He portrayed, without complete detachment, the hectic disillusionment of what he called the Jazz Age (the years after

CONCISE PRONUNCIATION KEY: **(a)** æ, c*a*t; ɑ, c*a*r; ɔ f*aw*n; ei, sn*a*ke. **(e)** e, h*e*n; i:, sh*ee*p; iə, d*ee*r; ɛə, b*ea*r. **(i)** i, f*i*sh; ai, t*i*ger; ə:, b*i*rd. **(o)** o, *o*x; au, c*ow*; ou, g*oa*t; u, p*oo*r; ɔi, r*oy*al. **(u)** ʌ, d*u*ck; u, b*u*ll; u:, g*oo*se; ə, b*a*cillus; ju:, c*u*be. x, lo*ch*; θ, *th*ink; ð, bo*th*er; z, *Z*en; ʒ, cor*s*age. dʒ, sava*g*e; ŋ, orangutan*g*; j, *y*ak; ʃ, fi*sh*; tʃ, fe*tch*; 'l, rabb*le*; 'n, redd*en*. Complete pronunciation key appears inside front cover.

1918) in such novels as 'The Great Gatsby' (1925) and 'Tender is the Night' (1934)

FitzGerald, Garret (1926–), Irish politician, prime minister (1981–2; 1982–). Leader of the Fine Gael party from 1977, he was elected prime minister in 1981, served until Feb. 1982 and was elected again in Dec. 1982. His efforts to achieve peace in Northern Ireland have been unsuccessful, but he concluded an agreement with Britain regarding the administration of Northern Ireland (1985)

FitzGerald contraction a phenomenon predicted by the theory of relativity, involving the apparent change in length with respect to an observer of a moving body. The size of the change which occurs in a body moving with velocity v is related to its length at rest by the ratio

$$\sqrt{1 - \frac{v^2}{c^2}} \cdot 1,$$

where c is the velocity of light [after George FitzGerald (1851–1901), Ir. physicist]

Fitz·wil·liam Virginal Book (fitswíljəm) one of the earliest and most important collections of Elizabethan keyboard music

Fiu·me (fjú:me) *RIJEKA

five (faiv) **1.** *adj.* being one more than four (*NUMBER TABLE) **2.** *n.* four plus one ‖ the cardinal number representing this (5, V) ‖ five o'clock ‖ a playing card (domino etc.) marked with five symbols ‖ a team of five members, esp. in basketball [O.E. fīf]

five-and-ten (fáivəntén) *n.* a dime store

five-day week (fáivdẹi) a working week of five working days

five-fin·ger exercise (fáivfiŋgər) a composition for practice on the piano so as to work the muscles of all the fingers

five-o'clock shadow (fáivouklɒk) the beginnings of a beard

five·pence (fáivpəns, fáifpəns) *n.* (Br.) the sum of five pennies

five-pen·ny (fáivpəni:, fáifpəni:) *adj.* (Br.) costing fivepence

fiv·er (fáivər) *n.* (pop.) a five-dollar bill ‖ (Br. pop.) a five-pound note ‖ (games) anything scoring or counting five points, runs etc.

fives (faivz) *n.* a game in which a small, hard, leather-covered ball is struck with gloved hands against the walls of a court. It is popular mainly in British schools and universities, and can be played by two or four players. There are two versions, Rugby fives and Eton fives, each having its particular type of court and slightly different rules (cf. HANDBALL)

five-year plan (fáivjiər) a national economic plan for execution within five years, esp. to control the rate of industrialization of a country. The first (1928) was applied in the U.S.S.R.

fix (fiks) **1.** *v.t.* to fasten firmly, make fast ‖ to make as if rigid, *a fixed smile* to direct (one's eyes or attention) with concentration ‖ to look or stare steadily at (something or someone) ‖ (of an object) to seize and hold (one's attention) ‖ to commit (details) to one's mind or memory ‖ to determine, establish, *to fix a price, fix a day for a meeting* ‖ to place (oneself), establish (one's residence etc.) with a degree of permanency ‖ to arrange, *to fix one's hair* ‖ to prepare, *to fix a salad* ‖ to repair ‖ (chem.) to convert (a gas) into a solid compound ‖ (dyeing) to make (a color) fast ‖ (microscopy) to preserve for examination ‖ (photog.) to make (a negative or print) permanent by dissolving and washing away unreduced bromide etc. ‖ (pop.) to influence the result of (a race, fight, election etc.) by bribery etc. ‖ (pop.) to deal with (someone) so as to punish, reduce to silence, counter etc. ‖ (mil.) to attach (bayonets) to rifles as a parade drill ‖ *v.i.* to become fixed, *his eyes fixed on the hole in the ceiling* **to fix on** to select as a final choice **to fix up** to supply (someone) with what he wants ‖ to make definite arrangements about, *to fix up a return match* ‖ to set up (something temporary or improvised) ‖ to arrange and equip, *he fixed up the garage as a workshop* ‖ to repair, restore to good condition **2.** *n.* a difficult situation, dilemma ‖ the position of a ship or aircraft, as determined by bearings, radio etc. ‖ the process of finding such a position [fr. L. *figere* (*fixus*), to fasten]

fix·ate (fíkseit) *pres. part.* **fix·at·ing** *past* and *past part.* **fix·at·ed** *v.t.* (psychol.) to arrest or attach (the libido) at an infantile stage of psychosexual development ‖ to direct and focus the eyes on ‖ *v.i.* (psychol.) to undergo fixation ‖ to

concentrate one's attention or gaze [fr. L. *figere* (*fixus*), to pierce + -*ate*]

fix·a·tion (fikséiʃən) *n.* the act of fixing ‖ (chem.) the conversion of a gas, esp. atmospheric nitrogen, into a solid compound ‖ the preparation of specimens for study by treating them with formaldehyde ‖ (psychol.) the partial arrest of psychosexual development at an infantile stage with consequent immaturity of sexual or other relationships ‖ the accurate direction and focusing of the eyes, for optimum vision [fr. M.L. *fixatio* (*fixationis*)]

fix·a·tive (fíksətiv) **1.** *adj.* able to fix or make permanent **2.** *n.* any of various substances used to make something more permanent, e.g. to keep the hair tidy, preserve a specimen for display, prevent a photographic print or film from fading

fixed (fikst) *adj.* fastened, *fixed seating* ‖ not volatile, *a fixed acid* ‖ (of colors) fast, permanent ‖ formed into a compound, *fixed nitrogen* ‖ settled, definite, *a fixed income* ‖ (of a look) steadily directed ‖ controlled by bribery, *a fixed election*

fixed capital durable capital goods used over a period of time, e.g. buildings, machinery, tools

fixed charge (commerce) a charge that occurs regularly and does not alter in accordance with the volume of business done, e.g. rent, rates, insurance

fixed idea an obsessive idea

fix·ed·ly (fíksidli:) *adv.* in a fixed manner

fixed point (phys.) the melting temperature of ice, or the boiling point of water (under standard conditions), used in constructing a thermometric scale ‖ (math.) a decimal point that is in a fixed position, e.g., on a calculator

fixed star a true star such a vast distance away that its position in relation to other stars does not appear to change appreciably

fix·ings (fíksiŋz) *pl. n.* (pop.) accessories or trimmings, esp. of a meal

fix·i·ty (fíksiti:) *pl.* **fix·i·ties** *n.* the state of being fixed ‖ stability ‖ (phys.) the capacity to endure heat without becoming gaseous or losing weight [fr. L. *fxus*, fixed]

fix·ture (fíkstʃər) *n.* a thing fixed permanently in position ‖ any of the fixed items bought or sold with a building (e.g. gas pipes, electric fittings) or with land (e.g. a greenhouse, fencing) ‖ the date fixed in advance for a game or athletics meeting, or the meeting itself ‖ (pop.) someone or something thought of as invariably present [fr. obs. *fixure*, fixed condition fr. L.L. *fixura*]

Fi·zeau (fi:zou) Armand Hippolyte Louis (1819–96), French physicist. He devised and used (1849) the first terrestrial method of measuring the velocity of light. He also used the principle of the Doppler effect in measuring the velocity of the stars in relation to the earth

fizz (fiz) **1.** *n.* a hissing or spluttering sound ‖ (pop.) champagne, or any effervescent drink **2.** *v.i.* to make a hissing or spluttering sound [imit.]

fiz·zle (fiz'l) **1.** *v.i. pres. part.* **fiz·zling** *past* and *past part.* **fiz·zled** to hiss or splutter feebly **to fizzle out** to come to nothing, esp. after a good start **2.** *n.* (pop.) a complete failure, fiasco

fizz·y (fízi:) *comp.* **fizz·i·er** *superl.* **fizz·i·est** *adj.* effervescent

fjord *FIORD

fl. fluid

Fla. Florida

flab·ber·gast (flǽbərgæst) *v.t.* to shock with overwhelming surprise [origin unknown]

flab·bi·ly (flǽbili:) *adv.* in a flabby way

flab·bi·ness (flǽbi:nis) *n.* the state or quality of being flabby

flab·by (flǽbi:) *comp.* **flab·bi·er** *superl.* **flab·bi·est** *adj.* lacking firmness, *flabby muscles* ‖ having soft, slack flesh ‖ hanging loosely, *flabby sails* ‖ feeble, *a flabby character* [var. of FLAPPY]

fla·bel·late (fləbélit) *adj.* (zool.) fanshaped [fr. L. *flabellinn*, fan]

fla·bel·li·form (fləbélifɔrm) *adj.* flabellate

fla·bel·lum (fləbéləm) *pl.* **fla·bel·la** (fləbéla) *n.* (zool.) a fan-shaped organ or structure ‖ the fan carried in front of the pope on ceremonial occasions ‖ a fan used in religious processions [L.=fan]

flac·cid (flǽksid) *adj.* limp, flabby, *flaccid muscles* ‖ feeble, *a flaccid will* **flac·cid·i·ty** *n.* [F. *flaccide*]

flag (flæg) *n.* (pl.) the quill feathers of a bird's wing [etym. doubtful]

flag *n.* the popular name of many monocotyledonous plants with ensiform leaves, esp. *Iris pseudacorus* [etym. doubtful]

flag 1. *n.* a fine-grained rock that splits into slabs suitable for paving ‖ a paving stone of this ‖ any paving stone, e.g. of concrete ‖ (pl.) a pavement or roadway made of paving stones **2.** *v.t. pres. part.* **flag·ging** *past* and *past part.* **flagged** to pave with flagstones [etym. doubtful, perh. rel. to FLAKE]

flag 1. *n.* a piece of cloth or bunting, usually with a pattern or a device, generally oblong or square in shape, attached to a pole or staff, and used to denote nationality, party or ownership, to mark a position, or to exchange information ‖ the admiral's flag hoisted on his flagship when he is in command at sea ‖ the tail of a setter or Newfoundland dog ‖ the 'for hire' signal of a taxi **to dip the flag** to lower it as a salute or sign of surrender **to hoist (strike) one's flag** (of an admiral) to raise (lower) his flag at sea, and thus assume (relinquish) command **2.** *v.t. pres. part.* **flag·ging** *past* and *past part.* **flagged** to signal (orders etc.) by means of flags (with 'down') to bring to a stop by means of flags, *the driver was flagged down on the third lap* ‖ to put flags on or over (something) ‖ to mark out with flags ‖ to draw attention to, e.g. attach markers to (selected documents in a file etc.) ‖ to convey a message to with flag signals or with motions of the hand [origin unknown]

flag *pres. part.* **flag·ging** *past* and *past part.* **flagged** *v.i.* (e.g. of a plant) to hang down limply, droop ‖ (of a person) to show signs of exhaustion ‖ (of attentive interest) to begin to fail [etym. doubtful]

flag-boat (flǽgbout) *n.* (Br.) a boat serving as a marker in yachting contests, etc.

Flag Day June 14, the anniversary of the adoption (1777) of the national flag of the U.S.A.

flag day (Br.) tag day

flag·el·lant (flǽdʒələnt, fladʒélənt) **1.** *n.* someone who whips himself (or others), esp. as an ascetic discipline or a sexual aberration **2.** *adj.* practicing flagellation [fr. L. *flagellans* (*flagellantis*) fr. *flagellare*, to whip]

flag·el·late (flǽdʒəlit, flǽdʒəleit, fladʒélit, fladʒéleit) **1.** *adj.* shaped like a flagellum ‖ having a flagellum or flagella **2.** *n.* a member of *Flagelata*, a class of algae, single-celled or colonial microorganisms, having one flagellum. Most have chlorophyll and are holophytic. Some are colorless and may be classed as protozoa **flág·el·lat·ed** *adj.* flagellate [fr. L. *flagellum*, a whip]

flag·el·late (flǽdʒəleit, fladʒéleit) *pres. part.* **flag·el·lat·ing** *past* and *past part.* **flag·el·lat·ed** *v.t.* to whip or scourge **flag·el·lá·tion**, **flág·el·la·tor** *n.* **flag·el·la·to·ry** (flǽdʒələtɔri:, flǽdʒələtɔuri, fladʒélətɔri:, fladʒélətɔuri:) *adj.* [fr. L. *flagellare* (*flagellatus*) to whip]

fla·gel·lum (fladʒéləm) *pl.* **fla·gel·la** (fladʒéla), **fla·gel·lums** *n.* (biol.) a whiplike extension from the free surface of some cells, responsible for movement by lashing, in many zoospores, bacteria, protozoans etc. ‖ (bot.) the creeping runner or shoot of a plant [L.=whip]

flag·eo·let (flǽdʒəlɛt) *n.* an obsolete instrument of the flute class [F.]

flag football touch football in which the tug-off of a flag substitutes for a tackle

flag·ging (flǽgiŋ) *adj.* beginning to peter out, *flagging enthusiasm* [fr. pres. part. of FLAG, to droop]

flagging *n.* flagstones ‖ an area covered with flagstones

fla·gi·tious (fladʒíʃəs) *adj.* (rhet.) grossly wicked ‖ (rhet.) guilty of enormous crimes [fr. L. *flagitiosus*]

flag·man (flǽgmən) *pl.* **flag·men** (flǽgmən) *n.* someone who carries or signals with flags, e.g. at races

flag officer a naval officer entitled to display a flag showing his rank (admiral, vice admiral, rear admiral)

flag·on (flǽgən) *n.* a vessel for holding liquor, esp. one with a handle, spout and lid, for serving wine etc. at table ‖ a vessel for holding wine at the Eucharist ‖ a large globular glass bottle [M.E. *flakon* fr. O.F.]

flag·pole (flǽgpoul) *n.* a tall pole from which a flag is flown, flagstaff

fla·gran·cy (fléigrənsi:) *n.* the state or quality of being flagrant

fla·grant (fléigrənt) *adj.* conspicuously evil, *a flagrant crime* ‖ glaringly wrong, *a flagrant error* [fr. L. *flagrare*, to blaze]

CONCISE PRONUNCIATION KEY: **(a)** æ, c*a*t; ɑ, c*a*r; ɔ f*aw*n; ei, sn*a*ke. **(e)** e, h*e*n; i:, sh*ee*p; iə, d*ee*r; ɛə, b*ea*r. **(i)** i, f*i*sh; ai, t*i*ger; ə:, b*i*rd. **(o)** o, *o*x; au, c*ow*; ou, g*oa*t; u, p*oo*r; ɔi, r*oy*al. **(u)** ʌ, d*u*ck; u, b*u*ll; u:, g*oo*se; ə, b*a*cillus; ju:, c*u*be. x, lo*ch*; θ, *th*ink; ð, bo*th*er; z, *Z*en; ʒ, corsa*g*e; dʒ, sava*g*e; ŋ, ora*ng*utang; j, *y*ak; ʃ, *fi*sh; tʃ, fet*ch*; 'l, rabb*le*; 'n, redd*en*. Complete pronunciation key appears inside front cover.

flag·ship (flǽgʃip) *n.* the ship in a fleet which bears the flag indicating that the admiral is on board ‖ the showpiece of a group, e.g., a flagship hotel of a chain

flag·staff (flǽgstæf, flǽgstɑf) *n.* a pole for hoisting a flag on

flag·stone (flǽgstoun) *n.* a paving stone

Fla·her·ty (flɑ́ərti:), Robert Joseph (1884–1951), U.S. film maker. His 'Nanook of the North' (1920–2), an on-the-spot portrayal of Eskimo life, set a high standard for documentary film. Other films include 'Elephant Boy' and 'Louisiana Story'

flail (fleil) **1.** *n.* an implement used for threshing grain etc. by hand, consisting of a wooden handle attached by a hinge of leather to a heavier stick (the swingle or swipple) which swings from it **2.** *v.t.* to beat with, or as if with, a flail ‖ to thresh (grain) by hand ‖ to lash around, *to flail one's arms* ‖ *v.i.* to wave like a flail [O.E. *fligel*]

flair (flɛər) *n.* an intuitive gift of discrimination, *to rely on flair, a flair for picking winners* ‖ a natural ability, aptitude, *a flair for acting* [F.]

flak (*colloq.*) complaints ‖ criticism difficult to handle. From the exploded bullets of antiaircraft fire

flake (fleik) *n.* a rack, e.g. for drying fish ‖ *mining*) a framework designed for shelter [perh. O.N. *flake*, a hurdle]

flake 1. *n.* a small, thin, loose-textured fragment, *flakes of snow* ‖ a thin but broad piece that scales off, *flakes of rust* or something resembling these, *soap flakes* ‖ (*pl.*) pieces into which the flesh of certain fish separates ‖ a flake tool ‖ (*slang*) an eccentric person **2.** *v. pres. part.* **flak·ing** *past* and *past part.* **flaked** *v.i.* to fall as or like snow ‖ to come away in flakes ‖ to separate into flakes ‖ *v.t.* to cover with flakes ‖ to make flaky ‖ to work (flint) into flake tools or to chip (flake tools) from flint [etym. doubtful]

flake·board (fleikbuərd) *n.* a structural board of sawdust and resin

Flakenpanzer I Gepard (*mil.*) mobile defense vehicle of German Democratic Republic carrying two 35-mm automatic cannons

flake tool a Stone-Age tool which was a flake off a larger stone core. It was then itself sometimes worked on

flake white white lead in the form of scales, used as a pigment

flak jacket (flǽk) apparel designed to protect the torso from bullets or shrapnel by means of steel plates sewn into the padding *Cf* BULLET-PROOF VEST

flak·y (fléiki:) *comp.* **flak·i·er** *superl.* **flak·i·est** *adj.* consisting of flakes or tending to break up into flakes

flam·beau (flǽmbou) *pl.* **flam·beaux, flam·beaus** (flǽmbouz) *n.* a flaming torch [F.]

flam·boy·ance (flæmbɔ́iəns) *n.* the state or quality of being flamboyant

flam·boy·ant (flæmbɔ́iənt) **1.** *adj.* florid, ornate, vivid in color, *a flamboyant shrub* ‖ ostentatious, overelaborate, showy, *flamboyant clothing* **Flam·boy·ant** of French Gothic architecture of the 15th and early 16th cc., e.g. the west front of Rouen cathedral, characterized by flamelike curves and ornate carving **2.** *n. Poinciana regia,* a tropical tree widely cultivated for its flaming red racemes of flowers [F.]

flame (fleim) *n.* a body of glowing, burning gas ‖ the state of burning with a blaze, *to burst into flame* ‖ a blaze of red, *the flames of sunset* ‖ (*rhet.*) intense feeling, passion ‖ (*old-fash., pop.*) a sweetheart, an *old flame* ‖ a strong reddish orange color like a flame [O.F. *flambe*]

flame (fleim) *pres. part.* **flam·ing** *past* and *past part.* **flamed** *v.i.* to burst into flame or burn with flames ‖ to look as though in a blaze, *the garden flamed with color* ‖ *v.t.* to treat with a flame, pass through a flame e.g. so as to sterilize **to flame up** to break out in angry passion [O. F. *flamber*]

flame laser a gas laser utilizing an ignited mixture of carbon disulfide and oxygen to produce carbon monoxide laser emissions

fla·men (fléimen) *pl.* **fla·mens, flam·i·nes** (flǽmini:z) *n.* (in ancient Roman religion) a priest serving one of certain gods of the pantheon (cf. PONTIFEX) [L.]

fla·men·co (floménkou) *n.* a dance style of Andalusian gypsies ‖ the music or song accompanying this [Span. *flamingo* fr. M.Du. *Vláming* Fleming]

flame·out (fléimaut) *n.* a failure of proper combustion in a jet-engined aircraft

flame stitch a needlepoint stitch resembling a flame

flame-throw·er (fléimθrɔuər) *n.* a device expelling burning oil in a stream from a nozzle, used in warfare to attack tanks, pillboxes etc. and in agriculture to destroy weeds, pests etc. [trans. of G. *flammenwerfer*]

flam·ing (fléimiŋ) *adj.* in flames ‖ blazing, very hot, *a flaming sun* ‖ violent, *a flaming temper* ‖ flagrant, *a flaming lie* ‖ (*Br.,* pop.) damned, *a flaming nuisance* ‖ flamelike in color

fla·min·go (flomíŋgou) *pl.* **fla·min·gos, fla·min·goes** *n.* a social, web-footed wading bird of fam. Phoenicopteridae. They are characterized by extraordinarily long, thin legs, neck and bill, rose or scarlet plumage, and a small head. They are powerful in flight and are able to swim. They are widely distributed in tropical and subtropical regions [Port.]

Flam·i·ni·nus (flæmínáinəs), Titus Quinctius (c. 229–c. 174 B.C.), Roman statesman, general, and consul (198 B.C.). He defeated Philip V of Macedon at Cynoscephalae (197), and proclaimed the freedom of Greece at the Isthmian games (196)

Fla·min·i·us (flomíni:əs), Gaius (*d.* 217 B.C.), Roman statesman and general. He was tribune of the plebs (232 B.C.) and consul (223 B.C.) He began the Flaminian Way, the great road in N. Italy from Rome to cisalpine Gaul. He was killed at Trasimeno when his army was ambushed by Hannibal

flam·ma·bil·i·ty (flæməbíliti:) *n.* degree of proneness to catch fire

flam·ma·ble (flǽmob'l) *adj.* (in technical contexts) liable to ignite [fr. L. *flammare,* to set on fire]

Flam·steed (flǽmsti:d), John (1646–1720), English astronomer, the first astronomer royal. He devised a new and more reliable way of determining longitude at sea

flan (flæn, flɑn) *n.* an open pie typically containing fruit and glazed [F.]

Flan·ders (flǽndərz) a former countship of Europe on the North Sea, now included in the Belgian provinces of East and West Flanders, the Netherlands province of Zeeland, and the French department of the Nord. It is an intensely cultivated plain laced by canals, perfectly flat in the coastal polder region, broken by occasional sandy hills (200–300 ft) inland. Ports: Dunkerque, Ostend, Zeebrugge. Chief inland towns: Ghent, Bruges, Lille. Products: vegetables, cereals, processed foods, textiles, coal. HISTORY. Flanders was part of Roman Gaul and of the Frankish Empire (5th–9th cc.) It became (862) a feudal countship, increased its power and prosperity (11th and 12th cc.), and by the 13th c. dominated the European cloth industry. Flanders became subject to France (14th c.), but sided with England in the Hundred Years' War. It passed (1384) to the house of Burgundy, under whose rule commerce and art flourished, though the cloth industry declined, then passed to the Hapsburgs (1482), revolted (1576), but was regained by Spain (1584). Louis XIV annexed the western part (1659–78), and the remainder passed to Austria (1714), to the Netherlands (1815), and to Belgium (1830). On account of its strategic position, Flanders has been a major battleground in many wars, esp. both world wars

Flanders, East a province (area 1,147 sq. miles, pop. 1,306,000) of N. Belgium. Capital: Ghent

Flanders, West a province (area 1,248 sq. miles, pop. 1,043,000) of N.W. Belgium. Capital: Bruges

flange (flændʒ) **1.** *n.* a projecting edge or rib, e.g. of a metal wheel or beam, for strengthening, guiding, attaching or securing **2.** *v.t. pres. part.* **flang·ing** *past* and *past part.* **flanged** to furnish with a flange [fr. older *flanche* perh. fr. O.F. *flanc,* flank]

flank (flæŋk) **1.** *n.* the side of an animal between the ribs and thigh, *a flank of bacon* ‖ the side of a hill, mountain, building etc. ‖ the right or left side of an army, fleet etc. **2.** *v.t.* to be situated on the flanks of, *a road flanked with trees* ‖ (*mil.*) to guard on the flank ‖ (*mil.*) to attack from the flank ‖ to pass around the flank of [F. *flanc*]

flank·er or **flank·er back** (flǽŋkər) *n.* (football) player positioned far to the right or left of the formation. The position of flanker is generally assumed by the pass receiver

flan·nel (flǽn'l) **1.** *n.* a soft, twilled woolen material with little nap ‖ (*pl.*) pants made of this ‖ (*Br.*) a washcloth **2.** *v.t. pres. part.* **flan·nel·ing,** esp. *Br.* **flan·nel·ling** *past* and *past part.* **flan-**

neled, esp. *Br.* **flan·nelled** to rub with a flannel [perh. fr. Welsh *gwlanen* fr. *gwlân,* wool]

flannel board an audio-visual aid or instructional game for the very young in which flannel units (letters, numbers, construction pieces) adhere merely by contact to a flannel-covered board

flan·nel·ette (flæn'lét) *n.* a soft, warm, napped cotton material resembling flannel, used esp. for pajamas

flap (flæp) **1.** *n.* something broad and flat that is attached on one side only and hangs down from the attachment or can be moved freely around it, e.g. the part for sealing an envelope or the cover of a coat pocket ‖ the movement made by a bird's wing or by a sail in the breeze or by something comparable, e.g. a shirt hung out to dry ‖ the sound accompanying such a movement ‖ a sudden unreasoning loss of self-confidence resulting in confused and often foolish actions or words ‖ (*aeron.*) a movable airfoil on the trailing edge of an aircraft wing ‖ (*med.*) a piece of skin or bone partly separated from the adjoining tissue ‖ a group of sightings of unidentified flying objects at a similar time and place **2.** *v. pres. part.* **flap·ping** *past* and *past part.* **flapped** *v.i.* (with 'at') to strike out weakly with something broad and flat, *he flapped at it with his paper* ‖ (of a bird's wings) to move up and down, esp. while the bird remains perched or standing ‖ to lose self-confidence suddenly and say or do silly things as a result ‖ *v.t.* to move (the wings) up and down ‖ to cause to move lightly one way and another with a dry, slapping sound, *the breeze flapped the sails* [imit.]

flap·jack (flǽpdʒæk) *n.* a griddlecake ‖ (*Br.*) a flat circular powder compact

flap·pa·ble (flǽpəbəl) *adj.* (*colloq.*) of one capable of being disconcerted easily **ant** unflappable

flap·per (flǽpər) *n.* something that flaps ‖ a device for scaring birds ‖ a device for swatting flies ‖ a young partridge or duck ‖ a broad fin or flipper ‖ the tail of a lobster etc. ‖ the forelimb of a turtle ‖ (*hist.*) an emancipated young woman in the 1920s

flare (flɛər) **1.** *n.* a sudden emission of bright flame ‖ a spurt of flame, e.g. from an acetylene burner in the open air ‖ a device used esp. by ships and aircraft to illuminate a position, target etc. a gradual spreading and widening, *the flare of a skirt* ‖ (*photog.*) a defect caused by too great a local concentration of light ‖ (*football*) a short lateral pass **2.** *v. pres. part.* **flar·ing** *past* and *past part.* **flared** *v.i.* (of a fire) to emit flames which are bright and fierce but unsteady ‖ to become wider, *her skirt flares from the waist* ‖ *v.t.* to cause to flare **to flare up** to emit bright flame suddenly ‖ to become suddenly angry [origin unknown]

flare·back (flɛ́ərbæk) *n.* a burst of flame towards the source of the fuel e.g. in a furnace

flare path the area illuminated brightly to guide aircraft on a landing strip

flares *n.* slacks with cuffs wider than the leg

flare-up (flɛ́ərʌp) *n.* a sudden outburst of flame ‖ a sudden outburst of anger or excitement

flar·ing (flɛ́əriŋ) *adj.* flaming, very bright

flash (flæʃ) **1.** *v.i.* to give out a momentary, intensely bright light ‖ to give out flames or sparks ‖ to emit light suddenly, *a spotlight flashed in his face* ‖ to reflect light brilliantly ‖ to move quickly, *a figure flashed across the screen* ‖ to come into the mind as quick as lightning ‖ (*glassmaking*) to spread out in a sheet ‖ *v.t.* to send (signals etc.) by flashes of light ‖ to make known over great distances in little time, *the news was flashed around the world* ‖ to allow to be seen briefly, *to flash a smile at someone* ‖ (*glassmaking*) to cause to spread out in a sheet ‖ to cover (glass) with a film of color ‖ to coat (glass) with a thin layer of colored glass or metal ‖ (*building*) to protect against rain by laying sheet metal on (joints, roof valleys etc.) ‖ to fill or flood (a stream, river etc.) with water, esp. suddenly and rapidly ‖ (of water) to rush along ‖ to give out in flashes, *to flash fire* ‖ to display ostentatiously, *he flashed a wad of banknotes at him* **2.** *n.* a sudden burst or gleam of light, *the flash of a spotlight* ‖ a photograph taken by flashbulb ‖ flame, *the flash of guns* ‖ an instant of time, *everything happened in a flash* ‖ a sudden, short-lived feeling, *a flash of hope* ‖ a sudden manifestation, *a flash of genius* ‖ (*Br., mil.*) a small piece of colored cloth worn on uniform as a unit emblem ‖ a short news dispatch, esp. by radio ‖ a chute of water down a weir to carry a boat over, or the mechanism for producing this chute 3. *adj.* (*Br., pop.*) flashy, gaudy, *flash clothes* ||(*Br., pop.*) sporty, fast, *a flash car* || pertaining to thieves etc., *flash language* [imit.]

flash·back (flǽʃbæk) *n.* a short insertion in the plot sequence e.g. of a film or novel to relate events prior to the time of the narrative || a sudden recurrence in the memory of an incident or emotion from the past || (*drug culture*) recurrence of a hallucination and accompanying emotional disturbance

flash·board (flǽʃbɔrd, flǽʃbourd) *n.* a board placed alongside a dam to increase its depth of water and used to release water to the mill

flash·bulb (flǽʃbʌlb) *n.* a small electric bulb for taking pictures indoors or at night

flash burn a burn caused by momentary exposure to a source of intense radiant heat, e.g. an explosion

flash card a card used in mental drill, as an aid to memorizing e.g. vocabulary or spelling || a card which a judge of e.g. a skating performance displays to declare his score

flash-cook (flǽʃkuk) *v.* to cook rapidly under intense heat, e.g., by infrared radiation

flash-cube (flǽʃkjub) *n.* (*photography*) disposable flash bulb with capability of four exposures

flashed glass (flæʃd) layered glass with a veneer of colored glass or with metallic oxide flashed onto it

flash·er (flǽʃər) *n.* (*colloq.*) male who briefly exposes genitals in public **flash** *v.*

flash flood a sudden violent flood after a heavy rain

flash-for·ward (flæʃfɔ́wərd) *n.* storytelling technique of presenting future events before the contemporary story line *Cf* FLASHBACK

flash·i·ly (flǽʃili:) *adv.* in a flashy way

flash·i·ness (flǽʃi:nis) *n.* the quality of being flashy

flash·ing (flǽʃiŋ) *n.* a strip of metal used to waterproof joints in masonry, roofing etc.

flash in the pan a hard effort or sudden brilliant performance which leads to nothing for lack of being sustained || a person who briefly gives promise of being brilliant but who does not fulfill the promise

flash·light (flǽʃlait) *n.* (*Am.= Br.* torch) a small, portable container fitted with an electric light bulb and dry-cell battery || the light that flashes from a lighthouse || (*photog.*) a sudden bright light used for taking photographs at night or indoors

flash·o·ver (flǽʃouvər) *n.* (*elec.*) a discharge through the air from a high potential source to the ground, or around or over a solid or liquid insulator

flash photolysis method of examining transient molecular fragments by causing a chemical to decompose under an intense flashing light

flash point the lowest temperature at which vapor (e.g. of an inflammable liquid) catches fire in the air when a small flame is applied

flash-print·ing (flǽʃprintiŋ) *n.* technique of making an electronic record of protein patterns used to trace fish migrations, etc

flash·y (flǽʃi:) *comp.* **flash·i·er** *superl.* **flash·i·est** *adj.* showy but worthless, *flashy jewelry* || given to empty display, *a flashy writer*

flask (flæsk, flɑsk) *n.* a narrow-necked vessel, normally of blown glass, used in laboratories || a flat broad bottle, often of metal, for carrying liquor in one's pocket || (*Br.*) a Thermos || a frame for holding the sand forming the mold in foundries [O.E. *flasce, flaxe*]

flat (flæt) **1.** *adj.* (of a surface) even and level || unbroken by depressions or projections, *flat country* || (*racing*) uninterrupted by jumps || stretched out, *to fall flat on the ground* || spread out, *he hit it with his flat hand* || completely in ruins || broad, smooth and lacking thickness, e.g. like a coin || uniform, *a flat tint of red* || without gloss || outright, *a flat refusal* || dull, monotonous, *a flat tone of voice* || without energy or zest || lacking sparkle or effervescence, stale, *flat beer* || inactive, *a flat market* not funny, *flat jokes* || (of feet) having the instep arch fallen (*FLATFOOT) || (of a tire) deflated || (of a sail) taut || (of a curve) shallow || (*mus.*) lower by half a tone, thus B flat (B♭) is half a tone lower than B natural (B) || (*mus.*) below the correct pitch **that's flat** (*pop.*) that's my last word on the subject **to fall flat** (of a joke) to fail to amuse **2.** *adv.* absolutely, precisely, *he went flat against his promise* || in a downright way, *she told him flat she wouldn't* **flat out** (*Br.*) at maximum speed ||

(*Br.*) exhausted, *he was flat out after the race* **3.** *n.* the flat part of something, *the flat of the hand* || level ground, *on the flat* || (*pl.*) low-lying ground over which the tide flows, *mud flats* || (*theater*) a section of scenery mounted on a wooden frame || a punctured tire || a flat-bottomed boat || a flat basket || a flat box for growing seedlings || a flatcar|| (*mus.*) a note lowered a semitone below the note named || (*mus.*) a sign (♭) indicating this lowering **4.** *v. pres. part.* **flat·ting** *past and past part.* **flat·ted** *v.t.* to cause to have a nonglossy surface, or to remove the gloss from (a surface) || to lower (a note) by a semitone || to plant or transplant in a flat || *v.i.* (*mus.*) to go flat [O.N. *flatr*]

flat *n.* an apartment (set of rooms) on one floor [altered fr. Scot. *flet* fr. O.E. *flet, floor*]

flat·boat (flǽtbout) *n.* a square-ended flat-bottomed (i.e. keelless) boat, esp. for transport in shallow water

flat·car (flǽtkɑr) *n.* (*rail.*) a freight car with no sides or roof

flat·fish (flǽtfiʃ) *pl.* **flat·fish, flat·fish·es** *n.* a member of *Heterosomata*, an order of bony marine fish incl. turbot, flounder, sole, halibut. The adults have laterally compressed bodies, swim on one side, and have both eyes on the upper side

flat·foot (flǽtfut) *pl.* **flat·feet** (flǽtfi:t) *n.* a foot in the condition in which the instep arch has fallen so that the entire sole rests on the ground || this condition flatfoot || (*pop.*) clumsy, (*pop.*) determined, forthright

flat·iron (flǽtaiərn) *n.* an iron which is heated externally on the base and is used for pressing clothes, linen etc.

flat maternity (*insurance*) a single, all-inclusive maternity benefit *Cf* SWAP MATERNITY, SWITCH AND FLAT MATERNITY

flat race a race over level ground in athletics or horse racing

flat rate an unvarying charge, e.g. one not proportional to consumption

flat silver silver cutlery, as distinguished from silver bowls, jugs etc.

flat spin (*aeron.*) the movement of an aircraft out of control when spinning towards ground level with its body parallel to the ground || (*pop.*) a state of acute, hysterical nervousness

flat·ten (flǽt'n) *v.t.* to make flat || to make dull, dispirit || to knock down, *he flattened him with one blow* || *v.i.* to become flat **to flatten out** (*aeron.*) to change the flying position of an aircraft so as to bring its body parallel with the ground after a dive, climb or spin

flat·ter (flǽtər) *v.t.* to praise excessively, esp. in a calculating way || to gratify the vanity of, *he was flattered by your invitation* || to cause to look more handsome (e.g. in a painting) or seem to have more quality (e.g. in a description) than is really the case **to flatter oneself** to delude oneself into a hope or belief, *you flatter yourself if you think she isn't after your money* || to venture to think, *I flatter myself that I can deal with the matter best* **flat·ter·y** *n.* insincere or excessive praise [etym. doubtful]

Flat·ter·y, Cape (flǽtəri:) a high promontory at the northwest extremity of Washington state, at the entrance to Juan de Fuca Strait

flat·top (flǽttɒp) *n.* an aircraft carrier

flat·u·lence (flǽtʃuləns) *n.* the quality or state of being flatulent **flat·u·len·cy** *n.* flatulence [F.]

flat·u·lent (flǽtʃulənt) *adj.* causing stomach or alimentary gases, *a flatulent diet* || afflicted with such gases || inflated, pretentious, *a flatulent style of writing* [F.]

flat·ware (flǽtwɛər) *n.* cutlery and flat vessels for the table, esp. of silver or silver plate (cf. HOLLOW WARE)

flat water calm water

flat·ways (flǽtweiz) *adv.* flatwise (cf. EDGEWAYS)

flat winding (*cosmetology*) the spiral winding of hair on a rod without twisting

flat·wise (flǽtwaiz) *adv.* with the flat side presented to the receiver, or placed downwards (cf. EDGEWISE)

flat·work (flǽtwə:rk) *n.* (*laundering*) articles (e.g. sheets, towels) that do not need hand ironing

flat·worm (flǽtwə:rm) *n.* a worm of the phylum *Platyhelminthes*. They are invertebrate animals, divided into three classes: *Turbellaria* (mostly free-living and aquatic), *Trematoda* (parasitic flukes) and *Cestoidea* (parasitic tapeworms)

Flau·bert (floubeər), Gustave (1821–80), French novelist. 'Madame Bovary' (1857) is the tale of a Romantic bourgeoise whose infidelities lead to her death. 'L'Education sentimentale' (1869) is an account of the aspirations and eventual failure of a conventionally Romantic young idealist student. Both are realist in that Romantic attitudes are shown in action in French 19th–c. bourgeois society, but they deal ambiguously with human life, with a disturbing irony. 'La Tentation de Saint Antoine' (1874) and 'Salammbô' (1862), with their fantasies of violence and eroticism, and 'Bouvard et Pécuchet', an uncompleted onslaught of pathological ferocity on the bourgeois mentality, also give insights into the turbulence of Flaubert's mind. Thus although Flaubert's work is usually regarded as the origin of realism in the modern world, it was anything but merely realistic. Stylistically he toiled for perfection, and his technical achievements were deeply influential: Henry James, Conrad and Joyce all acknowledged his influence

flaunt (flɔnt) **1.** *v.t.* to display proudly or brazenly || to flout, *to flaunt the regulations* || *v.i.* to wave brightly, *a flag flaunting in the wind* || to display oneself **2.** *n.* the act of flaunting, a display [origin unknown]

flau·tist (flɔ́tist, flɑ́utist) *n.* a flute player [fr. Ital. *flautista*]

fla·ves·cent (flavés'nt) *adj.* yellowish or turning yellow [fr. L. *flavescere,* to become yellow]

fla·vin (fléivin) *n.* one of a group of yellow pigments obtained from quercitron bark or made synthetically || a yellow acridine dye used as an antiseptic [fr. L. *flavus,* yellow]

fla·vo·pro·tein (fleivoupróuti:n) *n.* a conjugated protein containing riboflavin, important as hydrogen carriers in biological oxidization [fr. L. *flavus,* yellow +PROTEIN]

fla·vor, *Br.* **fla·vour** (fléivər) **1.** *n.* the quality belonging to food, drink etc. that is experienced through the combined senses of taste and smell || flavoring || a characteristic quality, *the book has a decadent flavor* **2.** *v.t.* to give flavor to **flá·vor·ing,** *Br.* **flá·vour·ing** *n.* a substance for adding flavor, esp. an essence to give a particular taste to food, *vanilla flavoring* [prob. O.F. *flaur, fleiur, fraor,* smell]

flaw (flɔ) *n.* a sudden brief spell of rough weather, squall [etym. doubtful]

flaw 1. *n.* a crack or gap, *a flaw in concrete* || a blemish, defect, *a flaw in character* || a weakness that invalidates, *a flaw in the title to a property* **2.** *v.t.* to cause a defect in, *the story is flawed by a weak ending* || to crack, *ice had flawed the new concrete* || *v.i.* to become cracked **fláw·less** *adj.* perfect [perh. O.N. *flaga,* slab]

flax (flæks) *n.* a plant of the genus *Linum,* fam. *Linaceae,* esp. *L. usitatissimum* || its fibers, raw or dressed [O.E. *fleax*]
—Flax, an annual plant, is grown either for fibers or for seed. Flax for fiber is typically grown in a cool, moist (summer) climate, and good, porous soil. The seeds are sown close together to produce long slender stems, up to 4 ft in height. The crop is used for the manufacture of linen, for tensile thread, twine, writing paper, sailcloth etc. Different strains are grown (mainly in tropical countries) for seed yielding linseed oil

flax·en (flǽksən) *adj.* like flax or of flax || of the color of dressed flax, blond

Flax·man (flǽksmən), John (1755–1826), English neoclassical artist and sculptor. He supplied designs for the Wedgwood pottery (1775–87), illustrated the 'Iliad' and other classical works, and made memorial sculpture for tombstones

flax·seed (flǽkssi:d) *n.* a seed of flax || linseed

flay (flei) *v.t.* to strip the skin or flesh from, *to flay hides* || to peel off the skin or bark from, *to flay willows* || to fleece, charge (a person) extortionately || to criticize harshly [O.E. *flēan*]

F layer (*meteor.*) a two-part region in the ionosphere 90–200 mi. above earth that reflects radio waves earthward at 50 MHz, F1 effective both day and night, and F2 (Appleton layer) only at night and certain times and places *Cf* D and E LAYERS

flea (fli:) *n.* a small, wingless insect of the order *Siphonaptera,* esp. *Pulex irritans,* attacking humans, and *Ctenocephalus canis,* attacking dogs [O.E. *flēah, flēa*]
—Fleas are tiny external parasites with a siphonlike sucking tube. They lack wings but are capable of leaping several inches. Metamorphosis is complete. They number from 900 to 1,000

CONCISE PRONUNCIATION KEY: (**a**) æ, c*a*t; ɑ, c*ar*; ɔ f*aw*n; ei, sn*a*ke. (**e**) e, h*e*n; i:, sh*ee*p; iə, d*eer*; ɛə, b*ear*. (**i**) i, f*i*sh; ai, t*i*ger; ə:, b*i*rd. (**o**) o, *o*x; au, c*ow*; ou, g*oa*t; u, p*oo*r; ɔi, r*oy*al. (**u**) ʌ, d*u*ck; u, b*u*ll; u:, g*oo*se; ə, b*a*cillus; ju:, c*u*be. x, lo*ch*; θ, *th*ink; δ, bo*th*er; z, *Z*en; ʒ, cor*s*age; dʒ, sava*g*e; ŋ, ora*n*gutan*g*; j, *y*ak; ʃ, *fi*sh; tʃ, fet*ch*; 'l, rabb*le*; 'n, red*den*. Complete pronunciation key appears inside front cover.

species and are most abundant in tropical and warm regions, but are found even in polar regions (*BUBONIC PLAGUE)

flea·bane (flíːbeɪn) *n.* any of various composite plants reputed to keep fleas away

flea beetle any of various coleopteran insects with chewing mouthparts and hind legs adapted for leaping. *Altica* species are destructive to grapevines, hops, turnips etc.

flea·bite (flíːbaɪt) *n.* the bite of a flea ‖ the red discoloration caused by it ‖ a petty annoyance ‖ an insignificant sum or item of expense

flea·bit·ten (flíːbɪtˈn) *adj.* bitten by fleas ‖ infested with fleas ‖ (of a gray horse) flecked with darker markings

flea collar an animal collar containing an insecticide that destroys fleas while worn

flea-flick·er (flíːflɪkər) *n.* (football) 1. play starting as a double reverse, with the ball going to quarterback for a long pass 2. a forward pass followed by a lateral pass

fleam (fliːm) *n.* a surgical instrument for bleeding (esp. cattle and horses) [O.F. *flieme*]

flea market a street market where sundry secondhand articles are for sale

flèche (fleʃ) *n.* (archit.) a slender spire, esp. one above the intersection of the nave and a transept

fleck (flek) 1. *n.* a small mark or speck ‖ a freckle or other colored mark on the skin ‖ a patch of light or color, *flecks of sunlight* 2. *v.t.* to spot with flecks **fléck·er** *v.t.* to mark in patches, dapple, fleck [etym. doubtful]

Fleck·er (flékər), James Elroy (1884–1915), English poet. 'Hassan' (1922), an Oriental fantasy of mingled cruelty and love, with perverse undertones, is his best-known work

flec·tion, flex·ion (flékʃən) *n.* a bending or flexing ‖ a part bent ‖ (gram.) inflection **fléc·tion·al, fléx·ion·al** *adj.* [fr. L. *flexio* (*flexionis*)]

fled *past* and *past part.* OF FLEE

fledge (fledʒ) *pres. part.* **fledg·ing** *past* and *past part.* **fledged** *v.i.* (of birds) to grow the feathers needed for flight ‖ *v.t.* to provide with feathers, *to fledge an arrow* ‖ to bring up (a bird) until it is ready for flight [fr. obs. adj. *fledge*, feathered, cf. O.E. *unflycge*, unfledged]

fledg·ling, fledge·ling (flédʒlɪŋ) *n.* a bird just fledged ‖ an immature or inexperienced person

flee (fliː) *pres. part.* **flee·ing** *past* and *past part.* **fled** (fled) *v.i.* (rhet.) to run away, esp. from danger or evil ‖ (rhet.) to pass swiftly away, vanish, *the snow had fled* ‖ *v.t.* (rhet.) to run away from ‖ (rhet.) to shun, *to flee temptation* [O.E. *fléon*]

fleece (fliːs) 1. *n.* the coat of wool covering a sheep or similar animal ‖ the amount of wool taken from sheep etc. at one shearing ‖ a thick and woolly hair or covering ‖ something resembling wool, *a fleece of snow* ‖ a thin sheet of cotton or wool fiber ‖ a fabric with a silky pile 2. *v.t. pres. part.* **fleec·ing** *past* and *past part.* **fleeced** to rob (someone) by overcharging, or by cheating at cards **fléec·y** *comp.* **fleec·i·er** *superl.* **fleec·i·est** *adj.* covered with, consisting of or resembling wool [O.E. *fléos*]

fleet (fliːt) *n.* a number of warships under one command ‖ any naval force ‖ a national navy ‖ a number of ships sailing together, *a whaling fleet* ‖ a group of vehicles under one control, *a fleet of taxis* or of aircraft, *a fleet of bombers* ‖ (Br.) a row of fishing nets [O.E. *fléot*, a ship, a number of ships]

fleet *adj.* (rhet.) swift and agile ‖ (rhet.) transient [etym. doubtful]

fleet admiral the highest rank of officer in the U.S. navy, ranking immediately above an admiral

fleet·ing (flíːtɪŋ) *adj.* transient, passing swiftly away [O.E. *fléotan*, to flow]

Fleet Street the London press [fr. the street off the Strand where many newspapers have their publishing offices]

Flem·ing (flémɪŋ), Sir Alexander (1881–1955), British bacteriologist. He was best known for his discovery of penicillin. Nobel prize for medicine (1945)

Fleming, Ian (1908–64), English writer best known for his creation of James Bond, Agent 007, the spy whose bizarre exploits foil international conspiracies. His novels, most of which were made into films, include 'Casino Royale' (1954), 'Moonraker' (1955), 'From Russia with Love' (1957), 'Dr. No' (1958), 'Goldfinger' (1959), 'Thunderbird' (1961), 'The Spy Who Loved Me' (1962), and 'You Only Live Twice' (1964). He also wrote 'Chitty-Chitty-Bang-Bang' (1964), a children's story

Fleming, Sir John Ambrose (1849–1945), English electrical engineer. He invented the thermionic valve (1904)

Fleming, Sir Sandford (1827–1915), Canadian engineer responsible for surveying and constructing the Intercolonial, Canadian Pacific, and Newfoundland railways, and for the international agreement (1884) to implement a worldwide standard time

Fleming *n.* a Flemish-speaking Belgian, esp. one living in Flanders [M.Du. *Vlâming*]

Flem·ish (flémɪʃ) 1. *adj.* of or belonging to the people, country or language of Flanders 2. *n.* the language of Flanders [fr. M. D u. *Vlaemisch*]

Flemish bond a method of bonding brickwork by alternating longitudinal brick faces (stretchers) with brick ends (headers) in each course

flench (flentʃ) *v.t.* to flense

Flens·burg (fléntsburk) a town (pop. 95,000) of Schleswig-Holstein, West Germany, on the Danish frontier, on the Baltic: shipbuilding, engineering, fishing, brewing

flense (flenz) *pres. part.* **flens·ing** *past* and *past part.* **flensed** *v.t.* to strip the skin or blubber from (a whale, seal etc.) [Du. *flense*]

flesh (fleʃ) 1. *n.* the muscular substance, together with the fat and connective tissues, of man and animals ‖ the human body as distinct from mind, soul or spirit ‖ the part of an animal body that is considered food ‖ the pulpy part of a fruit. ‖ sensual human nature, *sins of the flesh* **in the flesh** in bodily form, in real life **to make someone's flesh creep** (or **crawl**) to terrify someone, esp. with mingled horror and repugnance **to put on** (**lose**) **flesh** to grow plumper (thinner) 2. *v.t.* to train (hounds) for hunting by giving them flesh from the kill to eat ‖ to remove the flesh from (skin, hides etc.) [O.E. *flaésc*]

flesh and blood human nature, *more than flesh and blood could stand* ‖ factual development, food for thought, *the exposition needed more flesh and blood* **one's own flesh and blood** one's blood relatives

flesh·ette (fleʃét) *n.* (mil.) a barbed antipersonnel dart-shape projectile delivered through an explosive container

flesh·i·ness (fléʃiːnɪs) *n.* the quality of being fleshy

flesh·ings (fléʃɪŋz) *pl. n.* flesh-colored tights worn on the stage to represent skin ‖ scraps of flesh from scraped skins, hides etc. used for making glue

flesh·ly (fléʃliː) *adj.* (rhet.) carnal, sensual, *fleshly lusts* [O.E. *flaésclic*]

flesh·pots (fléʃpɒts) *pl. n.* luxury, high living [Exodus xvi, 3]

flesh wound a wound injuring the tissues without touching a vital organ or bone

flesh·y (fléʃiː) *comp.* **flesh·i·er** *superl.* **flesh·i·est** *adj.* (of a person) plump ‖ (of a chicken etc.) yielding more than average meat for eating ‖ succulent, pulpy, *fleshy leaves*

fletch (fletʃ) *v.t.* to feather (an arrow) [perh. rel. to FLEDGE]

Fletch·er (flétʃər), Alice Cunningham (1838–1923), U.S. ethnologist. Her anthropological studies, incl. 'The Omaha Tribe' (1911), and her personal efforts, contributed to the improvement of American Indian life

Fletcher, Giles, the Younger (c. 1586–1623), English poet. His principal work is the epic poem 'Christ's Victorie and triumph over and after death' (1610)

Fletcher, John (1579–1625), English Jacobean playwright, best known for romantic tragedies written in collaboration with Francis Beaumont, e.g. 'The Knight of the Burning Pestle' (1613) and 'The Maide's Tragedy' (1619)

Fletcher, Phineas (1582–1650), English poet. His best-known work is 'The Purple Island' (1633), an elaborate allegorical description of the human body

'Fletcher v. Peck' a decision (1810) of the U.S. Supreme Court led by Chief Justice John Marshall. It ruled that an act of the Georgia legislature rescinding a land grant was unconstitutional because it violated the right of contract. The decision was the first to declare a state legislative act unconstitutional

fleur-de-lis, fleur-de-lys (fləˈrdəliː) *pl.* **fleurs-de-lis, fleurs-de-lys** (fləˈrdəliː) *n.* (heraldry) a conventionalized iris or lily ‖ the former French royal emblem ‖ the emblem of the Scouts [F.=lily flower]

fleu·ret (fləˈrit) *n.* a small ornament resembling a flower [fr. F. *fleurette* dim. of *fleur*, flower]

fleu·ron (fléˈrɒn) *n.* an ornament shaped like a flower, used in architecture, decorative printing etc. ‖ a printer's type ornament [F. fr. *fleur*, flower]

Fleu·rus, Battle of (fláˈrys) a French victory (1794) in the French Revolutionary Wars, which saved France from invasion by the Austrians

Fleu·ry (fləˈriː), André Hercule de (1653–1743), French cardinal and statesman. As chief adviser (1726–43) to Louis XV he was the virtual ruler of France. He stabilized the finances, but was drawn into the Wars of the Polish Succession and of the Austrian Succession

flew *past* of FLY

flews (fluːz) *pl. n.* the hanging chaps of the upper lip in certain breeds of dog, e.g. the bloodhound [origin unknown]

flex (fleks) *n.* (Br.) electric cord [shortened fr. FLEXIBLE]

flex *v.t.* to bend (a joint) by the flexors ‖ to move (a muscle) so as to bend a joint [fr. L. *flectere* (*flexus*), to bend]

flex·a·gon (fléksəgɒn) *n.* a paper so folded that when exposed in several ways, it creates a variety of views

flex·i·bil·i·ty (fleksəbíliː) *n.* the quality of being flexible

flex·i·ble (fléksəbˈl) *adj.* easily bent, not rigid, *a flexible metal* ‖ pliable, *a flexible plastic sheet* (cf. RIGID) ‖ adaptable, capable of being modified, *a flexible plan* ‖ responsive to changing conditions, *a flexible mind* ‖ open to influence, *a flexible character* [F.]

flexible response (mil.) strategy designed to provide reaction to aggressive action short of massive retaliation, esp. with a view to providing suitable conventional forces to contain an enemy force at lowest possible level of conflict

flexion *FLECTION

flex·i·time (fléksitaɪm) *n.* a system of optional work times (within limits) to permit staggered work hours

flex·or (fléksər) *n.* a muscle which causes a joint to bend (cf. EXTENSOR) [Mod. L.]

flex·u·os·i·ty (flekʃuːɒsitiː) *pl.* **flex·u·os·i·ties** *n.* the quality or state of being flexuous ‖ a sinuosity, winding

flex·u·ous (flékʃuːəs) *adj.* sinuous, having turns or windings ‖ adaptable [fr. L. *flexuosus*]

flex·ure (fléksər) *n.* the state or process of being flexed or bent ‖ a turn, bend or curve ‖ (geol.) the bending of strata etc. under pressure ‖ (math., in the theory of elasticity) the curving of a line or surface [fr. L. *flexura*]

flib·ber·ti·gib·bet (flíbərtidʒíbit) *n.* a restless, flighty and frivolous girl or young woman [imit. of chatter]

flick (flik) 1. *n.* a quick light stroke, e.g. with a whip ‖ a flip with the finger end against the thumb ‖ a deft, swift turn of the wrist ‖ a sudden jerk ‖ a hasty applying of something, *a flick of the duster, a flick of paint* 2. *v.t.* to strike with a flick, e.g. of a whip ‖ to move with a flick of the finger ‖ *v.i.* to make a flick with a whip, a finger etc. [imit.]

flick·er (flíkər) 1. *v.i.* to waver, quiver, *flickering shadows* ‖ to burn fitfully, *a light flickered in the distance* ‖ (with 'out') to waver and then become extinguished, *the lights began to flicker out* 2. *n.* a flickering movement, light or flame, *the flicker of firelight* ‖ a momentary stir of feeling, *a flicker of hope* [O.E. *flicorian*]

flicker *n.* any of several North American woodpeckers of genus *Colaptes*, often brightly marked with red or reddish yellow [imit.]

flicker photometer (phys.) a device for comparing the illuminating powers of two sources of light regardless of their qualities. A screen is illuminated directly by one source, the light from the other reaching it between the vanes of a rotating wheel. The flickering effect ceases when the intensities of illumination are equal

flick-knife (flíknaɪf) *n.* (British) a switchblade knife

fli·er, fly·er (fláɪər) *n.* a bird or insect with reference to the quality of its flight, *a strong flier* ‖ an aviator ‖ an animal, vehicle etc. that is exceptionally fast ‖ a flying jump ‖ a widely distributed handbill ‖ (pop.) a reckless gamble, esp. in the stock market ‖ (Br.) someone unusually gifted and a hard worker ‖ the part which twists the thread on a spinning machine as it winds on to the bobbin ‖ one of the steps in a flight of identical, rectangular steps (cf. WINDER)

flight (flaɪt) 1. *n.* the act or mode of flying ‖ the power of flying ‖ a journey by air ‖ the distance that an aircraft, rocket etc. can fly ‖ a journey on the schedule of an airline, *three flights a week to Hong Kong* || a flock of birds, insects etc., *a flight of sparrows* || (*pl.*) a bird's flight feathers || a volley, *a flight of arrows* || (of time) a swift passing || (of stairs) a unit block, *walk up three flights* || a set of hurdles for athletics or rails for steeplechasing || a soaring or sally, *a flight of fancy* || a small unit of aircraft, *a flight of bombers* || (*angling*) a device enabling the bait to spin rapidly || (*archery*) a light, low-feathered arrow for shooting long distances, or a contest with these **in the first** (or **highest**) **flight** (*Br.*) in the first rank, of the highest quality **in flight** while flying **2.** *v.t.* to vary the pace and trajectory of (a cricket ball) so as to deceive the batsman [O.E. *flyht*]

flight *n.* the act of fleeing || a sudden hastening away, *the flight of the middle-aged from the cities* **to put to flight** to cause to run away **to take flight, take to flight** to run away [M.E. fr. O.E. *flyht*]

flight bag a zippered canvas carrying bag capable of fitting beneath an aircraft seat

flight deck the deck of an aircraft carrier for takeoff and landing

flight feather one of the wing or tail feathers supporting a bird in flight

flight·less (fláitlis) *adj.* incapable of flight

flight lieutenant an officer in the British Royal Air Force ranking below a squadron leader and above a flying officer

flight·wor·thy (fláitwəːrði:) *adj.* suitable for safe flight

flight·y (fláiti:) *comp.* **flight·i·er** *superl.* **flight·i·est** *adj.* capricious, frivolous, irresponsible

flim·si·ly (flímzili) *adj.* in a flimsy way

flim·si·ness (flímzi:nis) *n.* the state or quality of being flimsy

flim·sy (flímzi:) **1.** *comp.* **flim·si·er** *superl.* **flim·si·est** *adj.* lacking substance || poorly made, or made of poor material, and lacking requisite strength || easily torn, *flimsy paper* || unsound, weak, *a flimsy excuse* **2.** *pl.* **flim·sies** *n.* a carbon copy of a typescript, invoice etc. made on thin paper [origin unknown]

flinch (flintʃ) **1.** *v.i.* to shrink or draw back, *to flinch from an unpleasant duty* || to wince, to bear pain without flinching **2.** *n.* the act or process of flinching [etym. doubtful]

Flin·ders (flíndərz), Matthew (1774–1814), English navigator. He charted the coasts of Australia (1795–9 and 1801–3), and is said to have been the first to correct compass errors caused by iron in ships

fling (fliŋ) **1.** *v.t. pres. part.* **fling·ing** *past* and *past part.* **flung** (flʌŋ) to throw or hurl from the hand || to move violently, *to fling out one's arms* || to put summarily, *to fling someone into prison* || to throw to the ground, *the wrestler flung his opponent* || to send (troops etc.) into attack || *v.i.* to go violently or in a temper, *to fling out of the room* || (of a horse etc., esp. with 'out') to kick and plunge **to fling oneself into** to engage keenly and energetically in, *to fling oneself into a job* **to fling (something) in someone's teeth** to reproach someone with (something), *to fling someone's failures in his teeth* **to fling out** to utter (a remark) with forceful suddenness **2.** *n.* the act or an instance of flinging || a lively, esp. Scottish, dance with quick arm and leg movements || the music for this || a sarcastic attack || a period of going all out for sensual pleasure || a sudden violent movement, *a fling of the rope caught him unawares* **in full fling** going full force **to have a fling at** (*pop.*) to make an attempt at [M.E. *flingen*]

Flint (flint) a town (pop. 159,611) in Michigan, a center of the automobile industry

flint (flint) *n.* a heavy and hard variety of silica which emits sparks when struck with steel and is easily chipped to a cutting edge. It usually has a steel-gray or nearly black interior, encrusted with white. Flint is found in nodules of chalk, often in layers, and may have been formed in the silicification of sponge skeletons || a stone of this material used in building || a prehistoric tool of knapped flint || anything hard and unyielding, *a heart of flint* || (*hist.*) a piece of flint used with steel for striking fire, e.g. in a flintlock gun || a small piece of metal alloy used to produce a spark in a cigarette lighter || a pebble made of flint [O.E.]

flint corn *Zea mays indurata*, a type of corn (maize) with kernels of hard starch

flint glass a heavy, high-quality glass containing lead silicate, originally made from powdered flint, used in optical instruments by reason of its high refractive index

flint-heart·ed (flínthártid) *adj.* hardhearted, not to be moved

flint·lock (flíntlɒk) *n.* (*hist.*) the lock of a firearm in which the cock or hammer holds a flint for igniting a charge || (*hist.*) a gun or pistol discharged in this way

Flint·shire (flíntʃər) a former county (area 256 sq. miles), in N. Wales. It became part of the new county of Clwyd (1974)

flint·y (flínti) *comp.* **flint·i·er** *superl.* **flint·i·est** *adj.* made of or abounding in flint || as hard as flint

flip (flip) **1.** *v. pres. part.* **flip·ping** *past* and *past part.* **flipped** *v.t.* to toss or flick with a quick movement of the fingers, esp. so as to cause (e.g. a coin) to turn over in midair || to lose control of oneself, creating either a good or bad response || to cause (a pancake) to do this and land back in the pan reverse side up || to strike lightly || to flick (the fingers) together || to move with a flick or jerk || *v.i.* to make a flipping motion **2.** *n.* a light blow || a flick || a short aircraft flight || (*banking*) flexible loan insurance plan, in which a down payment is made to a savings account, drawn upon to supplement interest and amortization when the loan is due **3.** *adj.* (*pop.*) flippant [imit.]

flip *n.* (*hist.*) a spiced drink of beer and liquor, sweetened, and heated with a poker || an iced drink of liquor, sugar, egg and nutmeg [perh. fr. FLIP, to toss]

flip chip (*electr.*) a transistor-circuiting chip with an adhesive pad

flip flop 1. *v.* (*colloq.*) to turn about in viewpoint **2.** *n.* (*computer*) bistable trigger circuit with two output lines and two input lines, capable of assuming either of two stable states, with output depending on the input line **3.** *n.* any device capable of operating in either of two stable states

flip·pan·cy (flípənsi) *pl.* **flip·pan·cies** *n.* the state or quality of being flippant || a flippant remark

flip·pant (flípənt) *adj.* treating serious matters with levity or lack of respect [perh. fr. FLIP, to toss]

flip·per (flípər) *n.* a limb for swimming with, e.g. in seals and walruses || a penguin's wing || (*pl.*) rubber swimming fins attached to the feet by frogmen, skin divers etc.

flip side 1. the second side of a record **2.** extension, a counterpart

flip-top box (flíptɒp) packaging (usu. cardboard) that can be closed after portion of contents have been removed, e.g., for cigarettes

flirt (fləːrt) **1.** *v.t.* to move, esp. to open and close, with quick little movements, *to flirt a fan* || *v.i.* to show amorous interest without any depth of feeling || (with 'with') to take a superficial or half-serious interest, *to flirt with an idea* **2.** *n.* someone who flirts || a quick little movement || (esp. *horol.*) a lever or other mechanical device for controlling periodic motion **flir·tá·tion** *n.* the act of flirting or an instance of it **flir·tá·tious** *adj.* fond of amorous flirting [origin unknown]

flit (flit) **1.** *v.i. pres. part.* **flit·ting** *past* and *past part.* **flit·ted** to make sudden, brief flights from place to place || to come or go swiftly, *an idea flitted through his mind* || (*Br., pop.*) to move, to change one's residence, esp. (*Br., pop.*) to do this secretly so as to avoid paying debts **2.** *n.* the act or motion of flitting || an instance of flitting [O.N. *flytja*]

flitch (flitʃ) **1.** *n.* a side (of bacon) || a piece of fish for smoking || a slice cut from a tree trunk, esp. an outside slice **2.** *v.t.* to cut into flitches or strips [O.E. *flicce*]

flitch beam a compound beam of flitches strengthened by a metal plate between them

flit·ter (flítər) *v.i.* to fly in apparently haphazard, unhasting zigzags

float (flout) *n.* something that floats on a fluid, or itself enables something else to float || a cork or quill on a fishing line || a cork or hollow ball supporting a fishing net in the water || an inflated part helping to support a fish or aircraft || the hollow metal ball at the end of a lever controlling the water level in a tank, cistern etc., or a similar device in a carburetor controlling the gasoline level || (*Br.*) a low cart, *a milk float* || a low-wheeled movable platform for displays etc. in a procession or carnival, or the display itself and its movable platform || (*weaving*) the passing of part of the weft over the warp without interweaving, or the thread thus passed || a mass of floating ice or weeds || (*theater, pl.*) footlights || any of various tools for

smoothing surfaces used by masons, plasterers etc. || a single-cut file for filing metal || a raft || (*banking*) the total of outstanding checks in the process of collection at any given time || money kept in a cash register for making change [O.E. *flot*, floating state, and O.E. *flota*, ship, fleet]

float *v.i.* (of a body which displaces its own weight of a fluid and therefore becomes weightless) to rest on or near the surface of a fluid || to be held up by air, gas or fluid, *balloons floated in the sky* || to be suspended in a fluid || to move gently, drift, *ideas floated through my mind* || to wander aimlessly, *floating around town* || to hover in front of the eyes || (*weaving*, of a thread) to pass over or under two or more threads before being woven in || (of a boat) to get afloat || *v.t.* (of liquid) to support (a buoyant object) || to set afloat || to start and obtain support for (a scheme or company) || to negotiate (a loan) || to circulate (a rumor) || (*weaving*) to pass (a thread) over or under two or more threads before weaving it in || (*weaving*) to work (a pattern) by floating threads || (*plastering* etc.) to level or smooth with a float || to grind and wash (pigments) in running water **float·a·ble** *adj.* capable of floating || (of a river etc.) able to float rafts, logs etc. || (of ores) suitable for treatment by flotation [O.E. *flotian*]

floatage *FLOTAGE

floatation *FLOTATION

float banking funds held while transfer instruments are being processed, e.g., by checks not yet cleared **playing the float**

float bridge (*Br.*) a floating bridge (bridge of rafts)

float·er (flóutər) *n.* someone who floats or drifts || something that floats || a person who illegally casts a vote in more than one polling place || (*Br.*) a government or other stock recognized as security [FLOAT v.]

float·ing (flóutiŋ) *adj.* that floats || concerned with cargoes at sea, *floating rates* || not fixed in one place, form, use etc., fluctuating, *a floating population* || (*med.*) abnormally attached, *a floating kidney* || (*mech.*) housed or connected to operate smoothly as though floating, *a floating axle* || (*finance*, of capital) not permanently invested, used for current expenditure || (*finance*, of a debt) due for payment within the financial year and usually not funded [FLOAT v.]

floating anchor a drag anchor

floating bridge a bridge supported on pontoons || part of a bridge that can be moved on pontoons || a flat-bottomed ferryboat propelled across a river or harbor on underwater chains || (*Am.=Br.* float bridge) a bridge of rafts

floating decimal decimal-point placement in a calculator to provide maximum number of places in the result *Cf* FIXED POINT

floating dock a dock floating on the water, able to be submerged for the entry of a ship and then floated, thus raising the ship as if in dry dock

floating light a lightship or lighted buoy

floating ribs either of the two lowest pairs of ribs (in man the 11th and 12th), not attached to the sternum nor to the cartilages of the upper ribs

floating vote that part of the electorate not permanently committed or loyal to a particular party

floating voter or **floater** a voter committed to no political party; an independent

float·stone (flóutstoun) *n.* a builder's rubbing block of iron, for removing marks from curved brickwork || (*mineral.*) a very light porous variety of opal

float tank (*therapy*) apparatus of 250-gal tubs of saltwater at 93.5°F temperature set in total darkness to provide sensory deprivation; used for relief from tension and pain

floc (flɒk) *n.* (*chem.*) a small light mass e.g. of smoke, or a fine flaky precipitate [fr. L. *floccus*, flock of wool]

floc·cose (flɒkous) *adj.* (*bot.*, of bacterial growth) covered with woollike tufts [fr. L. L. *floccosus*, tufted]

floc·cu·late 1. *adj.* (flɒkjulit) having little tufts of hair **2.** *v.* (flɒkjuleit) *pres. part.* **floc·cu·lat·ing** *past* and *past part.* **floc·cu·lat·ed** *v.t.* to cause (soil, sediment etc.) to gather into tufted masses || *v.i.* to gather into tufted masses **floc·cu·lá·tion** *n.* [FLOCCULUS]

floc·cu·la·tion (flɒkjuléiʃən) *n.* separation of suspended solids during waste water treatment by chemically created clumps of flocs

floc·cule (flɒkjuːl) *n.* (*chem.*) a floc [fr. L. *flocculus*, tuft]

CONCISE PRONUNCIATION KEY: **(a)** æ, c*a*t; ɑ, c*a*r; ɔ f*aw*n; ei, sn*a*ke. **(e)** e, h*e*n; i:, sh*ee*p; iə, d*ee*r; ɛə, b*ea*r. **(i)** i, f*i*sh; ai, t*i*ger; əː, b*i*rd. **(o)** o, *o*x; au, c*ow*; ou, g*oa*t; u, p*oo*r; ɔi, r*oy*al. **(u)** ʌ, d*u*ck; u, b*u*ll; uː, g*oo*se; ə, b*a*cillus; juː, c*u*be. x, lo*ch*; θ, *th*ink; ð, bo*th*er; z, *Z*en; ʒ, cor*s*age; dʒ, sava*g*e; ŋ, orangutan*g*; j, *y*ak; ʃ, *fi*sh; tʃ, fet*ch*; 'l, rabb*le*; 'n, redd*en*. Complete pronunciation key appears inside front cover.

floc·cu·lence (flókjuləns) *n.* the state of being flocculent **flóc·cu·len·cy** *n.*

floc·cu·lent (flókjulənt) *adj.* woolly ‖ (*chem.*) consisting of or containing flocs ‖ showing or covered in tufts [fr. L. *floccus*, flock of wool]

floc·cu·lose (flókjulous) *adj.* flocculent

floc·cu·lous (flókjuləs) *adj.* flocculent

floc·cu·lus (flókjuləs) *pl.* **floc·cu·li** (flókjulai) *n.* a small tuft of wool, hairs etc. ‖ (*anat.*) a small lobe on the undersurface of each half of the cerebellum ‖ (*astron.*) one of the cloudlike shapes in the solar atmosphere [Mod. L., dim. of *floccus*, flock of wool]

floc·cus (flókəs) *pl.* **floc·ci** (flóksai) *n.* a tuft of wool or hairs, esp. at the end of a tail ‖ a floccule [L.=flock of wool]

flock (flok) **1.** *n.* a number of birds living, feeding or moving together, *a flock of starlings* ‖ a number of goats or sheep herded together ‖ a crowd of people ‖ the body of Christians in relation to Christ, or a church congregation in relation to its pastor **2.** *v.i.* to come together in a flock or large crowd ‖ to move like a flock, *the crowd flocked into the stadium* [O.E. *flocc*]

flock 1. *n.* a lock, tuft of wool, cotton, hair etc. ‖ shredded wool or cotton refuse used as a filling for cushions, mattresses etc. ‖ material for flocked paper **2.** *v.t.* to fill (a mattress etc.) with flock ‖ to cover (a wallpaper) with flock [prob. O.F. *floc*]

flock paper (*Br.*) flocked paper

Flod·den Field, Battle of (flód'n) a battle (1513) in which the English repulsed a Scottish invasion. The Scots suffered heavy losses, and their king, James IV, was killed

floe (flou) *n.* an ice floe [prob. Norse *flo*, layer]

flog (flog, flɔg) *pres. part.* **flog·ging** *past* and *past part.* **flogged** *v.t.* to beat or strike hard and repeatedly with a cane etc. ‖ (*fishing*) to cast time and again into (a stream) ‖ to drive too hard, obtain exhausting effort from, *to flog an engine* ‖ (*Br., pop.*) to appropriate (something) and sell (it) **to flog a dead horse** to waste one's efforts trying to stir up enthusiasm for something people have lost interest in [perh. Br. school slang fr. L. *flagellare*, to whip]

flo·ka·ti, *pl* **-es** (flóukati:) *n.* Greek high-pile handwoven rug

flong (floŋ, flɔŋ) *n.* (*printing*) a papier-mâché matrix used for stereotyping [fr. F. *flan*, a flan, flong]

flood (flʌd) **1.** *n.* a large quantity of water covering what is usually dry land, as the result of a river or sea's flowing over its usual limits, the breaking of a dam, a tidal wave, or a strong wind which drives waves inland ‖ the state of a river that is very full of water, *in flood* ‖ the point of high tide, *at the flood* ‖ an abundance of something which seems to flow, *floods of tears*, *a flood of oratory* **the Flood** (*Bible*) the flood in the time of Noah (Genesis vi, 9) **2.** *v.t.* to cover with a flood ‖ to cause (a river) to be in spate ‖ to irrigate ‖ to fill (e.g. a carburetor) to overflowing ‖ (*pop.*) to add a lot of water to (whiskey etc.) ‖ to overwhelm, e.g. with work or orders ‖ *v.i.* to be in a state of flood ‖ to be subject to submersion by a flood **to flood in** to arrive in great abundance, *offers of help flooded in* **to flood out** to force to leave a dwelling or place because of floods [O.E. *flōd*]

flood control the regulation of river flow by floodgates etc. so as to prevent unwanted flooding or to promote irrigation

flood·gate (flʌ́dgeit) *n.* a gate in a waterway which is opened when the water reaches a certain level, to prevent flooding upstream ‖ the lower gate of a river or canal lock ‖ a sluice

flood·light (flʌ́dlait) **1.** *n.* a powerful lamp used, generally in quantity, e.g. for stage illumination or to show off building exteriors etc. at night ‖ the light provided by such lamps **2.** *v.t. pres. part.* **flood·light·ing** *past* and *past part.* **flood·light·ed, flood·lit** (flʌ́dlit) to light with floodlights

flood·mark (flʌ́dmark) *n.* the highest level reached by a flood

flood tide the incoming or rising tide (opp. EBB TIDE) ‖ a tide at its highest point

flood·wa·ter (flʌ́dwɔtər, flʌ́dwɒtər) *n.* the uncontained water of a flood

floor (flor, flour) **1.** *n.* the lower horizontal surface of a room, on which one stands ‖ the bottom of a sea, river, cave, mine, gallery or platform of a bridge etc. ‖ the space for dancing in a restaurant or nightclub ‖ a structure dividing a building horizontally into stories ‖ a story ‖ a level surface ‖ a minimum level, e.g. of prices (cf. CEILING) ‖ (*shipbuilding*) a timber or metal

plate across the keel between the inner and outer bottoms ‖ (in a legislative or debating chamber) the part where members speak from **to have the floor** to have the right to speak or to go on speaking in a legislative or debating assembly **to take the floor** to speak in debate **2.** *v.t.* to fit with a floor ‖ to knock down, *to floor an opponent* ‖ to nonplus, reduce to silence for want of a rejoinder or a solution [O.E. *flōr*]

floor·age (flóridʒ, flóuridʒ) *n.* floor space

floor·board (flórbɔrd, flóurbourd) *n.* a fixed board in the floor of a room ‖ a movable board laid in the bottom of a boat

floor·cloth (flórklɔθ, flóurklɔθ, flórklɒθ, flóurklɒθ) *n.* (*Br.*) a cloth for washing floors

floor exercise competitive gymnastics event including tumbling, somersaults, handstands, ballet movement

floor·ing (flóriŋ, flóuriŋ) *n.* material for floors ‖ floors, esp. with reference to the material of which they are made ‖ the process of spreading and airing the germinating grain on the floor of a malthouse

floor leader a party representative chosen to control party tactics etc. in a legislative assembly

floor·man (flórmæn) *n.* (*wagering*) a bookmaker's runner

floor partner (*securities*) member of a securities dealing firm who holds membership on the trading exchange and is thus entitled to trade at a lower commission rate

floor·scape (flórskeip) *n.* (*architecture*) overall overhead view of patterns and textures in an area designed for visual appeal, emphasizing space or used to direct traffic flow *Cf* CITYSCAPE, TOWNSCAPE

floor show an entertainment, e.g. in a nightclub, presented informally to customers while they eat or drink

floor·through (flórθru:) *n.* an apartment consisting of an entire floor of a building **floorthrough** *adj.*

floor·walk·er (flórwɔkər, flóurwɔkər) *n.* (*Am.=Br.* shopwalker) a person employed in a big store to act as overseer and to ensure that customers' requirements are met

flop (flop) **1.** *v. pres. part.* **flop·ping** *past* and *past part.* **flopped** *v.i.* to move clumsily, *frogmen flopped about on deck* ‖ to let oneself drop (into a chair, on to a bed, to the ground etc.) in an ungainly way ‖ (of a fish taken out of the water) to make convulsive movements ‖ (of a bird) to flap its wings clumsily ‖ to be a conspicuous failure (e.g. of a novel or play, or of a person) ‖ *v.t.* to throw with a flop ‖ (of a bird) to move (its wings) up and down with a loud flapping sound **2.** *n.* a flopping motion or sound ‖ a failure **3.** *adv.* with a flop, *to fall flop on one's face* **flóp·py** *comp.* **flóp·pi·est** *superl.* **flop·pi·est** *adj.* lacking firmness and tending to bob about in a limp way [var. of FLAP]

flop-eared (flópiərd) *adj.* having floppy ears

flop·house (flóphaus) *n.* (*Am., pop.= Br., pop.* doss house) a common lodging house

floppy disc (*computer*) **1.** flexible magnetic coated plastic (Mylar) disk used for storing data **2.** a protective envelope containing a slot through which a magnetic unit can read or record **syn** diskette

Flo·ra (flórə, flóurə) (*Rom. mythol.*) the goddess of flowers and gardens

flo·ra (flórə, flóurə) *pl.* **flo·ras, flo·rae** (flóri:, flóuri:) *n.* plant life in general, esp. plants of a certain region, environment or period (cf. FAUNA) ‖ a classification of the plants of a region, environment or period [after the goddess FLORA]

flo·ral (flórəl, flóurəl) *adj.* of flowers, *a floral painting* ‖ like flowers, *floral decorations in stone* ‖ of floras [fr. L. *floralis*, of the goddess FLORA]

Flor·ence (flórəns, flórəns) (*Ital.* Firenze) a city (pop. 460,924) of Tuscany, Italy, on the Arno, N. central Italy. Among its magnificent buildings are the cathedral (1296–1436), the baptistry (11th c.), the churches of Santa Croce (1294–1442) and Santa Maria Novella (1278–1360), the Palazzo Vecchio (1314) and the Ponte Vecchio (1345). The Palazzo degli Uffizi (1560) houses one of the world's great art collections. Manufactures: textiles, straw hats, jewelry, porcelain, machinery. University (1924). A Roman town, Florence became capital of a dukedom under the Lombards, then a free republic (1250) under the Guelphs. In the 13th and 14th cc. the textile trade and banking made it a thriving commercial center. The Florentine

school of painters, which developed here at the end of the 13th c. and in the 14th c., was to be the center of that renewal of Italian art which culminated in the Renaissance of the 15th c. Florence was ruled (1434–1737) by the Medici. It became capital of the grand duchy of Tuscany (1569) and of Italy (1865–70). It was devastated by a flood (1966). Restoration of its art treasures was supported by contributions from all over the world

Flor·en·tine (flórənti:n, flórənti:n, flórəntain, flórəntain) **1.** *adj.* belonging to Florence in Tuscany (Italy), *Florentine painters* ‖ characteristic of the architecture or art of Florence **2.** *n.* an inhabitant of Florence ‖ the Florentine dialect [fr. L. *Florentinus*]

Flo·res (flóres), Juan José (1800–64), Ecuadorian revolutionary general and first president (1830–4, 1839–45). He separated (1830) Quito from Gran Colombia and gave it the name of Ecuador, establishing the capital at Quito and promulgating the constitution of 1843

Flo·res (flóris, flóuris) a mountainous island (area 5,511 sq. miles, pop. 900,000) in the Lesser Sunda group, Indonesia. The Flores Sea lies to the north, separating the island from the Celebes

flo·res·cence (florés'ns, flourés'ns) *n.* the state or period of being in flower ‖ a bursting into flower **flo·rés·cent** *adj.* [fr. L. *florescere*, to flower]

flo·ret (flórit, flóurit) *n.* one of the small individual flowers of a composite flower [fr. O.F. *floret*]

flo·ri·at·ed (flóri:eitid, flóuri:eitid) *adj.* made in flowerlike patterns, *floriated lace* [fr. L. *flos* (*floris*), flower]

flo·ri·cul·ture (flórikʌltʃər, flóurikʌltʃər) *n.* the cultivation of ornamental flowering plants **flo·ri·cúl·tur·ist** *n.* [fr. L. *flos* (*floris*), flower]

flor·id (flórid, flórid) *adj.* heavily ornate, *florid architecture* ‖ flowery in style ‖ flushed, a *florid complexion* [fr. L. *floridus*, flowery]

Flor·i·da (flórida, flórida) (*abbr.* Fla) a state (area 58,560 sq. miles, pop. 10,416,000) formed by a low-lying peninsula at the southeastern tip of the U.S.A. Capital: Tallahassee. Chief city: Miami. Agriculture: citrus fruits, sugarcane, tobacco, vegetables, beef cattle. Fisheries. Resources: timber, phosphate (30% world supply). Industries: food processing, pulp and paper, chemicals, aircraft and missiles, tourism. Chief universities: University of Miami (1926) at Coral Gables and University of Florida (1905) at Gainesville. Florida was controlled by Spain (1513–1763), ceded to Britain (1763), returned to Spain (1783), and purchased (1819) by the U.S.A., of which it became (1845) the 27th state

Flo·ri·da·blan·ca (flɔri:ðablánka), José Moñino, conde de (1728–1808), Spanish statesman. As chief minister (1776–92) to Charles III, he carried out beneficial economic reforms

Florida Keys an arc of small islands extending southwest from the tip of Florida for over 100 miles: fisheries and sponge fisheries

Florida Strait (or Straits of Florida) a channel (c. 110 miles wide) between the Florida Keys and the northern coast of Cuba, joining the Gulf of Mexico with the Atlantic

flo·rid·i·ty (flɔriditi:) *n.* the state or quality of being florid

flo·rif·er·ous (flɔrifərəs) *adj.* bearing flowers, esp. bearing flowers profusely [fr. L. *florifer*]

flo·ri·le·gi·um (flɔrilí:dʒi:əm, flourilí:dʒi:əm) *pl.* **flo·ri·le·gi·a** (flɔrilí:dʒi:ə, flourilí:dʒi:ə) *n.* an anthology [Mod. L. fr. *florilegium*, trans. Gk *anthologia*]

flor·in (flórin, flórin) *n.* a British coin, originally of silver, worth two shillings ‖ the gulden (monetary unit of the Netherlands) ‖ (*hist.*) a gold coin first struck (1252) in Florence ‖ (*Eng. hist.*) a gold coin, worth about six shillings, of Edward III [F.]

Flo·ri·o (flóri:ou, flóuri:ou), John (c. 1553–1626), English writer and lexicographer, esp. famous for his translation 'The Essayes of Montaigne' (1603)

flo·rist (flórist, flóurist, flórist) *n.* someone who sells flowers ‖ someone who cultivates and breeds flowers [fr. L. *flos* (*floris*), flower]

florists' flower a flower produced by crossing, selective breeding etc. (cf. SPECIES)

floss (flos, flɔs) *n.* the outside loose pieces of silk of a cocoon, or other waste fibers unable to be spun ‖ (*bot.*) corn silk ‖ silk embroidery thread [etym. doubtful]

floss silk short silk fibers used for making cheap silk fabrics

floss·y (flɔ́si:, flɔ́si:) *comp.* **floss·i·er** *superl.* **floss·i·est** *adj.* of or like floss ‖ soft as down

flo·tage, float·age (flóutidʒ) *n.* the act or state of floating ‖ buoyancy ‖ the part of a ship above the waterline ‖ flotsam ‖ (*Br.*, **floatage**) the right of taking flotsam

flo·ta·tion, float·a·tion (floutéiʃən) *n.* the act or state of floating ‖ (*mineral.*) the separation of mineral particles from a crushed ore by stirring with a heavy oil, the separation being due to large differences of surface tension [FLOAT v.]

flo·til·la (floutílə) *n.* a small fleet ‖ a fleet of small vessels [Span.]

flot·sam (flɔ́tsəm) *n.* the wreckage of a ship or its cargo found floating on the sea (cf. JETSAM ‖ people who are drifters ‖ accumulated objects of little value [fr. A.F. *floteson*]

flounce (flauns) 1. *n.* a brusque, self-conscious movement of the body, usually expressing petulance or high rage, sometimes merely to attract attention 2. *v.i. pres. part.* **flounc·ing** *past* and *past part.* **flounced** to go with such movements ‖ (of a horse) to plunge, make struggling movements [etym. doubtful]

flounce 1. *n.* a strip of cloth or lace gathered and sewn (e.g. on a woman's skirt) by the upper edge only 2. *v.t. pres. part.* **flounc·ing** *past* and *past part.* **flounced** to trim or adorn with a flounce or flounces [earlier *frounce* fr. O.F. *fronce*, fold]

floun·der (fláundər) *n. Pleuronectes flesus*, a small, edible flatfish ‖ any of various flatfish, esp. of fam. *Pleuronectidae* and fam. *Bothidae* [A.F. *floundre*, a kind of fish]

flounder *v.i.* to struggle, stumble about (in mud etc.) ‖ to do things badly, blunder [etym. doubtful]

flour (fláuər) 1. *n.* a finely ground and sieved wheat meal ‖ the ground meal of rye, barley or other cereals ‖ the ground meal of other food products, e.g. potato or cassava ‖ any fine, soft powder 2. *v.t.* to make into flour ‖ to sprinkle with flour, *to flour pastry* [FLOWER, original sense 'finest part']

flour·ish (flɔ́riʃ, flʌ́riʃ) 1. *v.i.* to grow well ‖ to succeed, do well, *he is flourishing in his new job* ‖ (used to indicate a person's date or a main period of literary or artistic activity) to live, work, be in its developed stage, *he flourished in the early 18th c., Impressionism flourished in the late 19th c.* ‖ *v.t.* to display ostentatiously ‖ to cause to move with a sweeping, wavelike motion 2. *n.* a calculated showiness of manner ‖ an ostentatious gesture, a waving (of hands, handkerchiefs) or brandishing (of a weapon or the fist) ‖ a curving, decorative stroke of the pen around a letter or word in calligraphy ‖ (*mus.*) a showy passage, impromptu addition etc. ‖ a fanfare [fr. O.F. *florir* (*floriss-*)]

flour·y (fláuəri) *comp.* **flour·i·er** *superl.* **flour·i·est** *adj.* of or like flour ‖ covered with flour ‖ (of potatoes) tending to break up into light particles when cooked

flout (flaut) *v.t.* to treat with contempt, set aside brazenly, *to flout someone's orders, flout tradition* ‖ *v.i.* (with 'at') to mock, jeer [etym. doubtful]

flow (flou) 1. *v.i.* (of matter, esp. fluids) to move with a continuous change in shape, as a result of the absence of forces of interaction between the constituent particles of a substance ‖ to move like a stream contained by banks, *crowds flowed down the avenue* ‖ (of a liquid, or something that behaves comparably, e.g. grain) to run or spread freely, *the wine flowed over the table* ‖ (of the blood) to circulate ‖ (of blood) to be spilled, esp. in violence ‖ (of the tide) to rise (cf. EBB) ‖ (of a stream etc.) to be full and running fast ‖ to run smoothly and effortlessly, *talk flowed freely* ‖ (of hair, draperies etc.) to hang with graceful freedom ‖ to be dispensed abundantly, *the champagne flowed all night* ‖ to gush forth in a spring ‖ to issue from, *wisdom flows from experience* 2. *n.* the act of flowing ‖ the rate of flowing, e.g. of a current ‖ a quantity of substance passing a given point in a flowing system in unit time, e.g. 1 ampere equals 1 coulomb of charge flowing past a point in 1 second ‖ the rising of the tide ‖ a smooth falling in waves or folds, *the flow of drapery* ‖ a steady, copious, progressive movement of goods, ideas, talk etc., *the flow of production* **flow·age** (flóuidʒ) *n.* a flooding or being flooded [O.E. *flōwan*]

flow chart a diagram or chart analyzing the flow of work, materials etc. through a factory, workshop or plant ‖ (*computer*) representation of a program or algorithm, esp. in commercial data processing

flow·er (fláuər) 1. *n.* a flowering plant ‖ its blossom only ‖ (*bot.*) the part of a sporophyte of a higher plant bearing sporophylls which is capable of reproduction, esp. when it bears a perianth differentiated into a calyx and corolla, an androecium and a gynoecium ‖ (*pl., chem.*) the powdery substance left after sublimation, *flowers of sulfur* ‖ (*pl.*) the scum on wine etc. formed by fermentation ‖ (*pl.*) rhetorical ornament, *flowers of speech* ‖ a printer's ornament, fleuron ‖ (*rhet.*) the choicest part or specimen, *the flower of the country's youth* **in flower** blooming 2. *v.i.* to blossom, produce flowers ‖ (*rhet.*) to develop and flourish ‖ *v.t.* to bring into flower ‖ to decorate with flowers or a floral design **flow·er·er** (fláuərər) *n.* a flowering plant with respect to its time or manner of flowering, *a late flowerer* **flow·er·et** (fláuərit) *n.* a floret [M.E. *flour, flur* fr. O.F.]

flower child a hippie of the 1960s, esp. one carrying, wearing, or offering a flower expressing love of peace, beauty, etc. **flower people** *n. pl.* **flower power** *n.*

flower girl (esp. *Br.*) a woman or girl who sells flowers in the street ‖ a little girl who carries flowers at a wedding

flower head (*bot.*) a capitulum

flow·er·i·ly (fláuərili) *adv.* in a flowery manner

flow·er·i·ness (fláuəri:nis) *n.* (esp. of language) the state or quality of being flowery

flower piece a painting of flowers ‖ a flower arrangement

flow·er·pot (fláuərpɔt) *n.* a container for growing plants, usually of unglazed earthenware

flow·er·y (fláuəri) *adj.* ornate in style or language ‖ given to using ornate language ‖ full of flowers, *flowery meadows*

flowing sheet (*sailing*) a sheet with the lee clews eased off when the wind is nearly across the boat's course

flown *past. part.* of FLY

flow sheet a flow chart

flow soldering method of soldering printed circuits by immersing board into a wave of molten solder to attain precise depths **syn** wave soldering

flu·ence (flú:ens) *n.* (*phys.*) unit of measurement of particle flux in terms of particles per sq cm in a time period

flu, flue (flu:) *n.* (*pop.*) influenza

fluc·tu·ate (flʌ́ktʃueit) *pres. part.* **fluc·tu·at·ing** *past* and *past part.* **fluc·tu·at·ed** *v.i.* to change constantly, esp. between opposites ‖ to show irregular variation *a fluctuating market* **fluc·tu·a·tion** *n.* [fr. L *fluctuare* (*fluctuatus*), to wave]

flue (flu:) *n.* down or fluff, *cotton flue* [etym. doubtful]

flue *n.* a type of fishing net, esp. a dragnet [M.E.]

flue *n.* a pipe or vent for carrying off smoke, gases, etc. to the outside air ‖ (*engin.*) a channel for conveying a current of hot or cold air for heating, air conditioning etc. [origin unknown]

flue *FLU

flu·en·cy (flú:ənsi) *n.* the quality of being fluent [fr. L *fluentia*]

flu·ent (flú:ənt) *adj.* having or showing ease of command of speaking in public, writing, using a foreign language etc. [fr. L *fluere*, to flow]

flue pipe an organ pipe sounded by air under pressure impinging on a fixed edge (cf. REED PIPE)

flue stop an organ stop consisting of flue pipes

fluff (flʌf) 1. *n.* soft down worn off blankets etc. ‖ any soft downy mass of feathers, fur, hair etc. ‖ (*pop.*) a stumble in a speech or misplay in a game 2. *v.t.* to shake so as to make plump, *to fluff a pillow* ‖ to shake out into a fluffy mass ‖ (*pop.*) to make an error in (spoken lines in a play) or misplay (a shot) in a game ‖ to smooth and whiten (the flesh side of leather) ‖ to become fluffy **fluff·i·ness** *n.* **fluff·y** *comp.* **fluff·i·er** *superl.* **fluff·i·est** *adj.* of or like fluff [etym. doubtful]

flu·gel·man (flú:gəlmən) *pl.* **flu·gel·men** (flú:gəlmən) *n.* a fugleman

flu·id (flú:id) 1. *n.* a substance (e.g. a liquid or gas) that under the influence of small forces flows and is capable of assuming the shape of its container (cf. SOLID, *KINETIC THEORY) 2. *adj.* able to flow ‖ able or likely to change, *his opinions are fluid, a fluid situation* [F. *fluide*]

fluid dram a unit of liquid capacity equal to 1/8 fluid ounce (in U.S. measures = 0.225 cu. in., in Br. measures = 0.2167 cu. in.)

fluid drive the power coupling for a car etc., operating on a hydraulic turbine system: one set of turbine blades (impellers), driven in oil and connected to the flywheel of the engine, turns another set of turbine blades (runners) attached to the transmission gears

flu·id·ex·tract (flu:idékstrækt) *n.* (*pharm.*) an alcoholic solution of a vegetable drug, one cubic centimeter of which corresponds in active ingredients to one gram of the dry drug

flu·id·ics (flu:ídiks) *n.* the technology concerned with the use of the flow of fluids to accomplish sensing, computation, amplification and control functions [FLUID]

flu·id·i·fy (flu:ídifai) *pres. part.* **flu·id·i·fy·ing** *past* and *past part.* **flu·id·i·fied** *v.t.* to make fluid ‖ *v.i.* to become fluid

flu·id·i·ty (flu:íditi) *n.* the state or quality of being fluid

fluid mechanics the mechanics of the properties of gases and liquids

fluid ounce a unit of liquid capacity equal to 1/16 pint (1.8047 cu. ins) in U.S. measures and to 1/20 imperial pint (1.7339 cu. ins) in Br. measures

fluke (flu:k) *n.* the triangular plate on the arm of an anchor which buries itself fast in the ground ‖ the barb or barbed head of a harpoon, arrow or lance ‖ (*pl.*) the lobe of a whale's tail [perh. FLUKE, flatfish]

fluke *n.* a flatworm of class *Trematoda*, having a complicated life cycle in which the larvae are parasitic on invertebrates and the adults on vertebrates (*LIVER FLUKE) ‖ a flatfish, esp. a flounder [O.E. *flōc*]

fluke 1. *n.* a stroke of luck, an accidentally successful or lucky stroke, esp. at billiards 2. *v. pres. part.* **fluk·ing** *past* and *past part.* **fluked** *v.i.* to make a fluke, esp. at billiards ‖ *v.t.* to get by a fluke, *he fluked his way into the championship* [origin unknown]

fluk·i·cide (flú:kisaid) *n.* a substance that kills flukes

fluk·y, fluk·ey (flú:ki:) *comp.* **fluk·i·er** *superl.* **fluk·i·est** *adj.* infested with flukes

fluk·y (flú:ki:) *comp.* **fluk·i·er** *superl.* **fluk·i·est** *adj.* lucky, done or won by luck ‖ (of a breeze) light and veering often

flume (flu:m) 1. *n.* a sloped artificial channel made to convey water over some distance for irrigation, or to a mill or ore-washing plant etc., or to transport logs, etc. ‖ a gorge containing a stream 2. *v.t. pres. part.* **flum·ing** *past* and *past part.* **flumed** to convey (water or logs etc.) down a flume [M.E. *flum, flun* fr. O.F.]

flum·mer·y (flʌ́məri) *pl.* **flum·mer·ies** *n.* hocus-pocus, humbug ‖ empty compliments ‖ any of various desserts made of milk, flour, eggs etc. [Welsh *llymru*, a kind of food]

flum·mox (flʌ́məks) *v.t.* (*pop.*) to baffle, disconcert, perplex [origin unknown]

flung *past* and *past part.* of FLING

flunk (flʌŋk) *v.t.* (*pop.*) to fail (esp. an examination) ‖ (*pop.*) to fail (someone) in an examination **to flunk out** (*pop.*) to be dismissed, esp. from college, for failure [perh. rel. to FUNK]

flun·key, flun·ky (flʌ́ŋki:) *pl.* **flun·keys, flun·kies**, *n.* a liveried servant, footman ‖ a toady ‖ a subordinate [etym. doubtful]

flu·o·cin·o·lone acetonide [$C_{24}H_{30}F_2O_6$] (flu:ousínouloun) *n.* (*pharm.*) anti-inflammatory, anti-itching salve; marketed as Synalar

flu·o·cin·o·nide [$C_{26}H_{32}F_2O_1$] (flu:ousínounaid) *n.* (*pharm.*) glue corticosteroid anti-inflammatory, anti-itching, vasoconstrictor drug; marketed as Lidex R

flu·o·ra·cet·a·mide (fluərasétəmaid) *n.* (*chem.*) fluoracetic acid, a pesticide used in Great Britain

flu·o·resce (flurés, flɔrés, flourés) *pres. part.* **flu·o·resc·ing** *past* and *past part.* **flu·o·resced** *v.i.* to show fluorescence

flu·o·res·ce·in (flurési:in, flɔrési:in, flourési:in) *n.* a yellowish-red crystalline dye, $C_{20}H_{12}O_5$, that is widely used as an indicator or tracer since it gives a green fluorescence under ultraviolet light, even in extreme dilution. It is also an intermediate for the synthesis of other dyes (*EOSIN) [FLUORESCE]

flu·o·res·cein (fluərési:in) *n.* (*med.*) fluorescent fluorene dye used intravenously to gauge circulation and lesions in retina, optic nerve, iris, and choroid

fluo·res·cence (flurés'ns, flɔrés'ns, flourés'ns) *n.* (*phys.*) a luminescence which may or may not persist after removal of the excitation but whose decay does not depend on temperature (cf. PHOSPHORESCENCE) ‖ the property of emitting such radiation ‖ the radiation so emitted, often in the visible region **fluo·res·cent** *adj.* [FLUORSPAR, after 'opalescence']

fluorescent lamp a tubular glass electric lamp containing mercury vapor and equipped with an electron gun and anode, whose inner surface is coated with fluorescent substances. These give off visible light when subjected to ultraviolet radiation, produced when the mercury vapor is bombarded by a stream of electrons

fluorescent microscope an ultraviolet microscope

fluor·i·date (flúərideit, flɔ́rideit, flóurideit) *pres. part.* **fluor·i·dat·ing** *past* and *past part.* **fluor·i·dat·ed** *v.t.* to subject to fluoridation [back-formation fr. FLUORIDATION]

fluor·i·da·tion (fluəridéiʃən, flɔrideíʃən, flouridéiʃən) *n.* the addition of fluorides to (drinking water) so as to combat tooth decay [FLUORIDE]

fluo·ride (flúəraid, flɔ́raid, flóuraid) *n.* a binary compound of fluorine ‖ a salt or ester of hydrofluoric acid [fr. Mod. L. *fluor*, mineral of group incl. fluorspar]

flu·or·i·diz·er (flúəridaizər) *n.* compound of fluorine used as liquid repellant textile finish or to prevent dental caries **fluoridize** *v.*

fluo·rine (flúəri:n, flɔ́ri:n, flóuri:n) *n.* a nonmetallic toxic monovalent element of the halogen group (symbol F, at. no. 9, at. mass 18.9984). It is normally a yellowish gas. It is highly reactive and a most powerful oxidizing agent [F. fr. Mod. L. *fluor*, mineral of group incl. fluorspar]

fluo·rite (flúərait, flɔ́rait, flóurait) *n.* fluorspar [Ital.]

flu·o·ro·car·bon (flúəroukɑrbən) *n.* a gas used as a propellant in aerosols, thought to be modifying the ozone layer in the stratosphere, thereby allowing more harmful solar radiation to reach the earth's surface

flu·or·o·plas·tic (fluərəplæstik) *n.* any of various fluorine plastics suitable for molding or coating

fluo·ro·sis (fluróusis, flɔróusis, flouróusis) *n.* an abnormal condition produced by a greatly excessive intake of fluorine, e.g. spotting of tooth enamel through excessive fluorine in drinking water [Mod. L.]

fluor·o·ur·a·cil (fluərəúərəsil) *n.* (*pharm.*) a fluorine pyramidine drug used in cancer chemotherapy; marketed as Etudex

flu·or·spar (flú:ərspɑr, flú:ərspɑr) *n.* native calcium fluoride, occurring in cubic crystals which are either colorless or colored by impurities. It is a source of fluorine compounds [fr. L. *fluor*, flux+SPAR (mineral)]

flur·ry (flɔ́:ri:, flʌ́ri:) 1. *pl.* **flur·ries** *n.* a sharp sudden gust of wind ‖ a sudden gusty shower of rain or snow ‖ a fit of nervous excitement, *a flurry of alarm* ‖ the struggles of a dying whale 2. *v.t. pres. part.* **flur·ry·ing** *past* and *past part.* **flur·ried** to fluster, esp. by causing to hasten, divide attention, etc. [imit.]

flush (flʌʃ) 1. *v.t.* to startle (a game bird) and cause it to fly up ‖ *v.i.* (of a game bird) to start up suddenly, fly up 2. *n.* a number of game birds flushed at once [perh. imit.]

flush 1. *v.i.* to blush ‖ to flow and spread suddenly and freely, *the blood flushed into his cheeks* ‖ to glow suddenly red, e.g. with reflected sunset ‖ *v.t.* to cause (water etc.) to flow ‖ to cleanse by sending a rush of water over or through ‖ to redden, inflame, *anger flushed his cheeks* ‖ to cause a rush of emotion in, *flushed with pride* ‖ to make level, *to flush brickwork by pointing* 2. *n.* a sudden flow (esp. of water or blood) ‖ a rush of emotion ‖ a feverish rush of heat ‖ (*rhet.*) a state of fresh and confident vigor, *the first rush of youth* ‖ a fresh growth of grass or leaves etc. 3. *adj.* (of a river) in flood ‖ (*pop.*) affluent ‖ level with adjoining surfaces, *doors flush with the walls* ‖ immediately adjacent and in line, *are the edges flush?* ‖ (*printing*) level with the left edge of the printed matter of the page, not indented 4. *adv.* so as to be level, *plaster flush to the window* ‖ so as to be adjacent and in line [etym. doubtful]

flush *n.* (*card games*) a hand or run of cards belonging to one suit [perh. fr. L. *fluxus*, flow]

Flush·ing (flʌ́ʃiŋ) (*Du.* Vlissingen) a Channel port (pop. 29,250) at the mouth of the W. Scheldt, on the island of Walcheren, S.W. Netherlands. Industries: shipbuilding, fishing, petrochemicals

flus·ter (flʌ́stər) 1. *v.t.* to make nervous, agitate and confuse ‖ *v.i.* to be in such a state 2. *n.* a state of confused agitation, flurry [etym. doubtful]

flute (flu:t) 1. *n.* a woodwind instrument consisting of a hollow wooden (sometimes metal) cylinder, played by blowing through a lateral blowhole and stopping other holes with fingers or keys. It has a range of three octaves upwards from middle C ‖ an organ stop of flutelike quality ‖ (*archit.*) a long vertical rounded groove in a column, esp. in classical orders ‖ a similar groove cut into the walls of a pot, glass etc. or fashioned in cloth 2. *v. pres. part.* **flut·ing** *past* and *past part.* **flut·ed** *v.i.* to play on a flute ‖ *v.t.* to utter in a soft, clear, high-pitched voice ‖ to form rounded grooves in (a pillar, pot etc.) **flut·ing** *n.* decorative flutes on a column etc. **flút·ist** *n.* a flute player [M.E. *flowte, fluite* fr. O.F.]

flut·ter (flʌ́tər) 1. *v.i.* to flap the wings in a short flight, *to flutter to the ground* or without flying at all ‖ to flit, *butterflies fluttered over the cabbages* ‖ to wave with flapping motions, *the curtain fluttered in the wind* ‖ to vibrate or beat irregularly, *his pulse fluttered feebly* ‖ to tremble, to be thrown into confusion or uncertainty ‖ *v.t.* to flap (the wings) in a short flight or without flying ‖ to cause to wave with flapping motions ‖ to make agitated little movements with (a fan) ‖ to throw into a state of agitation or confusion 2. *n.* a quick irregular movement, *the flutter of an eyelid* ‖ an irregular pulse or vibration ‖ a state of agitated excitement ‖ an effect of surprise causing comment or stir, *his speech made quite a flutter* ‖ the rapid alternate beating of the legs in swimming the crawl and backstroke ‖ (*Br., pop.*) a mild gamble ‖ rapid changes in pitch on a recording, due to variations in speed ‖ (*med.*) an abnormal cardiac vibration ‖ (*aeron.*) an abnormal oscillation or up-and-down movement in a wing or tail, occurring at a critical speed [O.E. *flotorian*, to float about]

flut·y (flú:ti:) *comp.* **flut·i·er** *superl.* **flut·i·est** *adj.* flutelike in sound, sweet and soft but clear

flu·vi·al (flú:vi:əl) *adj.* of, caused by, found in or relating to rivers [F.]

flu·vi·a·tile (flú:vi:ətail) *adj.* fluvial [F.]

flux (flʌks) 1. *n.* the act of flowing ‖ the condition of continuously changing ‖ a substance added to another in order to give a lower melting point and promote fusion, or (as in soldering) to remove a film of oxide ‖ (*phys.*) the rate of transfer of energy (e.g. light) or matter (e.g. a liquid) across a given surface area 2. *v.t.* to make more fusible by adding a flux to ‖ to cause to flow or melt ‖ *v.i.* to become fluid, melt ‖ to fuse [F.]

flux·ion (flʌ́kʃən) *n.* (*hist., math.*) the rate of change of a variable [F.]

Fly (flai) the longest river (800 miles long, navigable for 500) of New Guinea, flowing from the mountains through S. Papua and New Guinea and forming part of the territory's western frontier

fly (flai) 1. *v. pres. part.* **fly·ing** *past* flew (flu:) *past part.* **flown** (floun) *v.i.* to move through the air by means of wings, jets, propellers etc. ‖ to travel by air ‖ (of bullets etc.) to be impelled through the air ‖ (of kites, flags etc.) to float or wave in the air ‖ to operate an aircraft, *he has flown for years* ‖ to rush, *to fly out of the room, to fly into a temper* ‖ (*pop.*) to hasten away ‖ (of time) to pass quickly ‖ (of money) to be quickly spent ‖ to run away, flee ‖ (*baseball, past and past part.* **flied**) to hit a fly ‖ (*hawking, with 'at'*) to hunt with a hawk ‖ *v.t.* to cause to float or move through the air, *to fly kites* ‖ to hoist (a flag) or keep (a flag) hoisted ‖ to operate (an aircraft) ‖ to pass over in an aircraft, *to fly the Atlantic* ‖ to transport in an aircraft ‖ to flee from, *to fly the country* ‖ (*theater, past and past part.* **flied**) to raise (scenery) from the stage to the flies ‖ (*hawking*) to send (a hawk) up after game **to fly a kite** (*Br.*) to make a proposal or gesture intended to test how things stand, e.g. before making a commitment **to fly at** to attack suddenly and violently **to fly high** to be ambitious **to fly in the face (or teeth) of** to flout, act in a way that shows disdain or defiance **to let fly at** to attack with words in a burst of anger 2. *pl.* **flies** *n.* the act of flying or the course or distance flown, *a long fly* ‖ the flap covering the fastening up the front of trousers ‖ (*pl., Br.*) the buttons of this fastening ‖ the flap at a tent entrance ‖ the outer canvas of a double-topped tent ‖ the part of a flag farthest from the staff ‖ the breadth of a flag extended ‖ the flyleaf of a book ‖ (*pl., theater*) the space over the stage for storing and operating scenery, lights etc. ‖ (*baseball*) a fly ball ‖ (*football*) forward pass tactic in which the receiver moves directly past the line of scrimmage ‖ a device for regulating speed in clockwork etc. ‖ a flywheel ‖ (*Br., hist.*) a covered one-horse carriage **on the fly** (*pop.*) terribly busy ‖ while still in the air before bouncing, *to catch a ball on the fly* [O.E. *flēogan*]

fly *comp.* **fli·er** *superl.* **fli·est** *adj.* (*Br., pop.*) alert and astute, and esp. quick to see financial advantage [origin unknown]

fly *pl.* **flies** *n.* almost any dipteran insect, esp. the housefly ‖ (*angling*) a hook dressed with feathers, used as bait ‖ (*bot.*) any of several plant diseases caused by minute insects or the insects collectively which cause the disease ‖ (*printing*) a vibrating frame with fingerlike attachments for taking printed sheets from a power press **a fly in the ointment** some minor difficulty spoiling or standing in the way of a plan or undertaking [O.E. *flēoge, flȳge*]

fly agaric *Amanita muscaria.* a poisonous mushroom

fly·a·way (fláiəwei) *adj.* (of clothing) cut full, loose ‖ (of persons) flighty, unreliable ‖ (of aircraft for sale) ready to fly, *what is the flyaway price?*

fly·a·way (fláiəwei) *n.* (*gymnastics*) horizontal-bar dismount method with a backward somersault

fly·back (fláibæk) *n.* (*television*) the return of a cathode ray beam between the tracings of two images

fly ball (*baseball*) a ball which is hit high enough off the ground to be caught (cf. GROUNDER)

fly·belt (fláibelt) *n.* an area infested with the tsetse fly

fly·blow (fláiblou) *n.* the egg or young larva deposited by a blowfly **fly·blown** *adj.* containing eggs or larvae of blowflies, *flyblown meat* ‖ dirty and shabby, *a flyblown hotel* ‖ soiled, *a flyblown reputation*

fly-by-night (fláibainait) 1. *adj.* inadequately financed, not credit-worthy, *a fly-by-night company* 2. *n.* someone who flees his creditors

fly·catch·er (fláikætʃər) *n.* any of several passerine birds of the Old World order *Muscicapidae* and the New World order *Tyrannidae.* The bill is short, strong and slightly hooked, with bristles on the broad, flat, lower portion ‖ an insect-eating plant of genus *Drosophyllum*

fly-cruise (fláikru:s) *n.* vacation cruise package in which participants fly to the port of embarkation

flyer *FLIER

fly-fish·ing (fláifiʃiŋ) *n.* the sport of casting for fish with artificial flies

fly half (*rugby*) standoff half

fly·ing (fláiiŋ) *adj.* that flies or can fly ‖ moving through the air with wings or as if with wings ‖ hanging loose, streaming, *a flying sail* ‖ very brief, *a flying visit* ‖ temporary, *a flying bridge* ‖ designed for or capable of rapid movement, *police flying squad* ‖ of or designed for aircraft or airmen, *a flying suit*

flying boat a seaplane in which the fuselage is adapted to serve as a float

flying bomb a pilotless jet-propelled aircraft with an explosive warhead. An early type, the V.1, was used by the Germans in the 2nd world war to bombard England

flying buttress (*archit.*) an elegant buttress arched out from a wall, used esp. in Gothic architecture to carry roof pressure outwards and downwards

flying crane a crane-equipped cargo-handling helicopter

Flying Dutchman a phantom ship of ill omen alleged to appear to sailors in the waters surrounding the Cape of Good Hope

flying fish any of several fishes of fam. *Exocoetidae.* They have large pectoral fins like parachutes which enable them to glide in the air for short flights after they have thrust themselves from the water. Flying fish are found mainly in tropical or warm seas

flying fox any of several large fruit-eating bats, suborder *Megachiroptera*, of the southern hemisphere. They have elongated snouts and foxlike ears, and a wingspread up to 5 ft.

flying gurnard any of several fishes, fam. *Dactylopteridae*, which have large pectoral fins enabling them to make short gliding flights above the water

flying jib a light triangular sail set before the jib on an extension of the jib boom

flying lemur either of two cat-sized, arboreal, nocturnal mammals, *Cynocephalus volans* of the E. Indies and *C. philippinensis* of the Philippines, having folds of skin from neck to tail on each side which act like a parachute, so that they can make long, gliding leaps

flying mare a throw in which a wrestler seizes his opponent's wrist, turns around, and throws him over his back

flying officer an officer in the British Royal Air Force ranking below a flight lieutenant and above a pilot officer

flying phalanger a phalanger native to Australia, esp. of the genera *Petaurus* and *Acrobates*. They have a patagium

flying pickets (British) mobile groups of strikers whose intent is to block deliveries of parts to plants that are being struck

flying saucer any of several large saucer-shaped flying objects which many people claim to have observed in the sky

flying squad (*Br.*) a detachment of motorized police, on a radio network, with a headquarters

flying squirrel any of several squirrels having folds of skin between the fore and hind legs which enable them to take gliding leaps

flying start a start of a race in which the starting post is passed at full speed ‖ a very good beginning

Flying Tigers a volunteer group of U.S. pilots organized (1941) by General Claire Chennault to fight for the Chinese, especially in defense of the Burma road, during the 2nd world war

fly·leaf (fláilịːf) *pl.* **fly·leaves** (fláilịːvz) *n.* a blank leaf at the beginning or end of a book ‖ a blank sheet in a circular, program etc.

fly nut a butterfly nut

fly·o·ver (fláiọuvər) *n.* (*Am.*=*Br.* flypast) a formation flight by aircraft at low altitude over spectators ‖ (*Br.*) an overpass

fly·pa·per (fláipẹipər) *n.* paper coated with a sticky or poisonous substance for hanging up in rooms to kill flies

fly·past (fláipæst, fláipɑst) *n.* (*Br.*) a flyover (formation flight)

fly sheet a loose circular, handbill ‖ (*Br.*) the fly (outer canvas) of a double-topped tent

fly·speck (fláispẹk) 1. *n.* a spot of excrement made by a fly ‖ a small dirty mark 2. *v.t.* to mark with flyspecks

fly·swat·ter (fláiswɒtər) *n.* a flat piece of wire mesh or rubber mounted on a handle, for killing flies

fly·way (fláiwẹi) *n.* an air route followed by migrating birds

fly·weight (fláiwẹit) *n.* a professional or amateur boxer whose weight does not exceed 112 lbs ‖ a professional or amateur weightlifter whose weight does not exceed 114.5 lbs

fly·wheel (fláihwịːl, fláiwịːl) *n.* a solid heavy disk mounted on a shaft, serving to offset fluctuations of the speed of the associated machinery by its inertia, esp. on an engine crankshaft, where it counteracts torque and carries the engine over dead center

FM frequency modulation

FNMA 1. *abbr.* Federal National Mortgage Association, which issues bonds (Fannie Mae's) to the public to finance mortgages provided to farmers 2. the bonds

f-num·ber (éfnʌmbər) *n.* (*photog.*) the number obtained by dividing the focal length of a lens by its effective diameter. It is usually written after the symbol f/, and gives the relative aperture of the camera lens. The lower the f-number, the brighter the image and the shorter the exposure needed [=focal number]

foal (foul) 1. *n.* the young of a horse, donkey or other member of fam. *Equidae*, esp. under one year of age **in** (or **with**) **foal** (of a horse etc.) pregnant 2. *v.t.* to give birth to (a foal) ‖ *v.i.* to give birth to a foal [O.E. *fola*]

foam (foum) 1. *n.* a mass of whitish bubbles formed on liquid by agitation, fermentation etc. ‖ a dispersion of a gas or vapor in a liquid ‖ froth formed in an animal's mouth by saliva or on its skin by perspiration ‖ a lightweight cellular material, e.g. of rubber 2. *v.i.* to foam or gather foam ‖ to rage, *to foam with anger* ‖ *v.t.* to produce a lightweight cellular material by forming air bubbles in (a plastic etc.) [O.E. *fām*]

foam rubber sponge rubber, made from latex by foaming it, used for pillows, upholstery etc.

foam·y (fóumiː) *comp.* **foam·i·er** *superl.* **foam·i·est** *adj.* consisting of foam or like foam ‖ covered with foam

fob (fob) *n.* a small pocket in the trouser waist for a watch ‖ a chain or ribbon ‖ a small ornament worn at the end of a fob chain or ribbon [origin unknown]

fob *pres. part.* **fob·bing** *past and past part.* **fobbed** *v.t.* (with 'off') to pass (something) off as better than it is, or genuine when it is false ‖ to talk or otherwise fool (someone) into accepting an imitation as genuine or an inferior article as having quality ‖ to put (someone) off by guile, *he fobbed her off with vague promises* [etym. doubtful]

f.o.b. *FREE ON BOARD

fob chain the short chain or ribbon worn dangling from a pocket watch

FOBS (*mil.*) (acronym) fractional orbital bombardment system

fo·cal (fóukļ) *adj.* of, pertaining to or situated at a focus [fr. Mod. L. *focalis*]

focal infection a chronic or persistent infection of a region or organ of the body, e.g. a tooth or tonsil, which may cause disease elsewhere in the body

fo·cal·i·za·tion (fọukļizéiʃən) *n.* a focalizing or being focalized

fo·cal·ize (fóukļaiz) *pres. part.* **fo·cal·iz·ing** *past and past part.* **fo·cal·ized** *v.t.* to focus ‖ (*med.*) to limit (an infection) to one small area ‖ *v.i.* to become adjusted to a focus ‖ (*med.*, of an infection) to become limited to one small area

focal length the distance between the principal focus and the optical center of a lens, mirror etc.

focal plane a plane perpendicular to the axis of a lens system, containing one of the principal foci

focal-plane shutter (*photog.*) a camera shutter that is essentially a screen with an aperture (usually adjustable) that moves across the film near the focal plane for very short exposures

Foch (foʃ), Ferdinand (1851–1929), French marshal. He directed the Battle of the Somme (1916) and was Allied supreme commander (1918) of the victorious armies in the 1st world war

fo·co (fóukou) *n.* a focal center of guerrilla power

fo'c'sle *FORECASTLE

fo·cus (fóukəs) 1. *pl.* **fo·cus·es, fo·ci** (fóusai) *n.* (*phys.*) a point to which waves from a distant source converge, or from which they appear to diverge, after reflection or refraction ‖ focal length ‖ adjustment for, or the condition of, distinct vision or sharpness ‖ (*math.*) one of the two fixed points to which any point on a curve has a definite distance relationship ‖ a center of interest, importance etc. ‖ (*seismology*) the point of origin of an earthquake ‖ (*med.*) the part of the body where a disease is centered 2. *v. pres. part.* **fo·cus·ing, fo·cus·sing** *past and past part.* **fo·cused, fo·cussed** *v.t.* to cause to converge to a focus ‖ to adjust (a mirror, lens etc.) so that waves from each point of an extended source converge to a point image ‖ to concentrate and direct (the attention etc.) ‖ *v.i.* to come to a focus [L.=hearth]

focused beam *PENCIL BEAM

focused interview an interview pertaining to a specific event, e.g., a riot, common to the experience of the respondents

fod·der (fódər) 1. *n.* dried food (hay, straw etc.) for cattle, sheep, horses etc. 2. *v.t.* to feed with fodder [O.E. *fōdor*]

foe (fou) *n.* (*rhet.*) an enemy, adversary [O.E. *fāh, fāg*, hostile]

foehn, föhn (fəːn) *n.* a warm dry wind characteristic of the valleys of the European Alps [G.]

foetal *FETAL

foetal circulation *FETAL CIRCULATION

foetalization *NEOTENY

foetation *FETATION

foeticide *FETICIDE

foetus *FETUS

fog (fog) 1. *n.* water vapor condensed on fine suspended particles, forming a dense opaque cloud at or just above the earth's surface ‖ (*Br., meteor.*) the condition of the atmosphere when visibility is less than 1,100 yds. ‖ (*photog.*) cloudiness or opaqueness obscuring a film or print **in a fog** bewildered, mentally at a loss 2. *v. pres. part.* **fog·ging** *past and past part.* **fogged** *v.t.* to cover or surround with fog ‖ to confuse or perplex (the mind) ‖ to cause (a matter for thought) to be obscure for lack of clear presentation ‖ (*photog.*) to cause (a film or print) to become cloudy, esp. through being exposed to stray light ‖ *v.i.* (often with 'up') to become covered or obscured by fog or as if by fog ‖ (*photog.*) to become cloudy, esp. through being exposed to stray light [etym. doubtful]

fog *n.* a second growth of grass, aftermath [origin unknown]

fog·broom (fógbruːm) *n.* fog disperser

fogey *OLD FOGY

Fog·gia (fɔddʒa) a city (pop. 153,300), market and rail center in N. Apulia, S. Italy

fog·gi·ly (fógiliː) *adv.* in a foggy manner

fog·gi·ness (fóginis) *n.* the state or quality of being foggy

fog·gy (fógiː) *comp.* **fog·gi·er** *superl.* **fog·gi·est** *adj.* misty, thick with fog, *a foggy morning* ‖ (*photog.*) fogged ‖ muddled, indistinct, *a foggy memory* [prob. fr. FOG, second growth of grass]

Foggy Bottom U.S. Department of State (used pejoratively)

fog·horn (fóghɔrn) *n.* a device for sounding deep warning blasts to ships in fog

fog lamp a fog light

fog light a low-set vehicle headlight (usually yellow) designed to penetrate fog

fogy *OLD FOGY

föhn *FOEHN

foi·ble (fɔibļ) *n.* an odd feature or mild failing in a person's character ‖ a fad ‖ (*fencing*) the weaker part of a sword blade, between the middle and the point (cf. FORTE) [F. *foible, faible*, weak]

foie gras (fwɑgrɑ) *n.* the fatted liver of a goose prepared as a pâté [F.]

foil (fɔil) 1. *n.* a leaf or very thin sheet of metal, such as is used to protect packaged cigarettes or food against moisture ‖ a thin metallic coat, e.g. of silver, tin or tin amalgam, used as a mirror backing ‖ a thin polished leaf of metal, sometimes colored, placed under paste or inferior stones or clear enamels to increase brilliancy ‖ (*archit.*) a rounded leaf-shaped segment between cusps, esp. in Gothic window tracery etc. ‖ something that sets off or enhances something else, esp. a character in a play or novel who serves to bring out the qualities of another 2. *v.t.* to back or cover with foil ‖ (*archit.*) to decorate with foils [O. F. *foil, foille*]

foil (*fencing*) a light, thin, blunt-edged sword with a button on its point to prevent injury [etym. doubtful]

foil *v.t.* to frustrate (efforts etc.) or wreck (schemes etc.), by countering with guile ‖ to thwart (a person) in his designs ‖ (of animals) to cross over or run back on (their scent or trail) so as to throw off pursuit [fr. O.F. *fuler, foler, fouler*, to full cloth, trample]

foist (fɔist) *v.t.* to get rid of (something) by fraud or deception, *to foist inferior goods on a customer* [prob. fr. Du. dial. *vuisten*, to take in the hand]

Foix (fwæ) a former countship of S. France in the lower Pyrenees, forming most of modern Ariège. Its hills and valleys support mixed farming. Historic capital: Foix. A countship from the 11th c., it gained, by marriages, Béarn and Navarre, but passed to the Bourbons (1548) by marriage and was attached to the crown (1607)

Fo·kine (foukíːn), Michel (1880–1942), Russian dancer and choreographer. He worked in St Petersburg and Paris with Diaghilev and after 1925 in the U.S.A. He created the modern ballet. His compositions include 'les Sylphides', 'Scheherazade', 'Firebird', 'le Spectre de la rose', 'Petrouchka'

Fok·ker (fókər), Anthony Herman Gerard (1890–1939), Dutch-U.S. designer and manufacturer of aircraft for military and commercial use

fo·late [$C_{19}H_{19}N_2O_6$] (fóuleit) *n.* (*pharm.*) a folic acid (B complex) derivative used in the treatment of sprue and anemia

fold (fould) 1. *n.* an enclosure, often of movable hurdles, to contain and protect sheep ‖ a flock of sheep ‖ (*rhet.*) the community of those who subscribe to some organized religious or pseudoreligious system 2. *v.t.* to enclose (sheep) in a fold ‖ to put sheep enclosed in this way on (land) to crop and manure it by sections [O.E. *fald*]

fold 1. *v.t.* to cause one part of (something) to lie on another, *to fold a blanket* ‖ to clasp around, embrace and draw close to one, *to fold someone in one's arms* ‖ to reduce into a small space, by making folds in, *to fold a tent* ‖ to cross and hold (the arms) close to the body ‖ to clasp (the hands) together in a relaxed way ‖ (of birds or

CONCISE PRONUNCIATION KEY: (**a**) æ, c*a*t; ɑ, c*a*r; ɔ f*aw*n; ei, sn*a*ke. (**e**) e, h*e*n; iː, sh*ee*p; iə, d*ee*r; ɛə, b*ea*r. (**i**) i, f*i*sh; ai, t*i*ger; əː, b*i*rd. (**o**) o, *o*x; au, c*ow*; ou, g*oa*t; u, p*oo*r; ɔi, r*oy*al. (**u**) ʌ, d*u*ck; u, b*u*ll; uː, g*oo*se; ə, b*a*cillus; juː, c*u*be. x, lo*ch*; θ, *th*ink; ð, bo*th*er; z, *Z*en; ʒ, cor*s*age; dʒ, sa*v*age; ŋ, ora*ng*utan; j, *y*ak; ʃ, *f*ish; tʃ, fe*tch*; 'l, rabb*le*; 'n, redd*en*. Complete pronunciation key appears inside front cover.

aircraft) to bring (the wings) in close to the body ‖ (*cooking*) to work in to a mixture gently without stirring ‖ *v.i.* to be able to be folded **to fold up** to reduce to a small space by closing, bending etc., *to fold up a map* ‖ to be made of hinged or jointed parts, so as to be able to be made to occupy less space when not in use ‖ (*pop.*, esp. of a contest or enterprise) to fail, collapse **2.** *n.* the arrangement or crease caused by folding ‖ a little undulation in a fabric, *the folds of a dress* ‖ (*geol.*) a bending back of strata (*FOLDING) ‖ (*Br.*) a hollow between hills etc. [O. E. *feal-dan*]

-fold *suffix* multiplied a specified number of times, *fiftyfold* ‖ differentiated in a specified number of aspects, *a threefold problem* [O.E. *-feald*, M.E. *-fald*]

fold·er (fóuldər) *n.* a paper or cardboard holder for loose papers ‖ a folded printed leaflet ‖ a paper-folding machine

fold·ing (fóuldiŋ) **1.** *n.* (*geol.*) a bending of rock strata, caused by compression of the earth's crust ‖ (*Br.*) the progressive cropping and manuring of land by putting sheep in folds on it and moving them at intervals **2.** *adj.* designed to fold away or fold into a compact shape

fo·li·a·ceous (fouli:éiʃəs) *adj.* having the form, texture or mode of growth of a foliage leaf [fr. L. *foliaceus*, leafy]

fo·li·age (fóuli:idʒ) *n.* the leaves of a plant or tree ‖ sprays of leaves ‖ (*archit.*) the representation of leaves, branches and flowers as ornamentation [fr. *foillage* fr. F. *feuillage*]

fo·li·ar (fóuli:ər) *adj.* pertaining to or consisting of leaves [fr. Mod. L. *foliaris*]

fo·li·ate (fóuli:eit) *pres. part.* **fo·li·at·ing** *past* and *past part.* **fo·li·at·ed** *v.t.* to spread over with foil, esp. tinfoil ‖ to number (the leaves of a book) ‖ (*archit.*) to ornament with foils or foliage ‖ *v.i.* to put forth leaves ‖ to split into leaflike layers [fr. L. *folium*, leaf]

fo·li·ate (fóuli:it) *adj.* composed of leaves ‖ leaflike **fo·li·a·tion** (fouli:éiʃən) *n.* the production of leaves, leafing ‖ a covering with a thin sheet of metal or an amalgam ‖ (*archit.*) ornamentation with foils (trefoils etc.) ‖ (*art*) leaflike decoration ‖ (*bot.*) the arrangement of leaves in a leaf bud ‖ the act of beating metal into foil ‖ the applying of tin amalgam to glass, e.g. in the making of mirrors ‖ (*geol.*) a structure in certain rocks of more or less parallel layers of different mineralogical character [fr. L. *foliatus*, leaved]

fo·li·o (fóuli:ou) **1.** *n.* a leaf of a book or manuscript numbered only on the front ‖ the leaf number of such a leaf ‖ a large sheet of paper folded once ‖ a very large book made of sheets folded once ‖ (*bookkeeping*) the facing pages of a ledger when used concurrently, or one page only when used for both sides of an account ‖ (*law*) a certain number of words (100 in the U.S.A., 72 or 90 in Great Britain) used as a unit in assessing the length of a document ‖ (*printing*) the page number of a book **in folio** on folio paper **2.** *adj.* being of once-folded sheets, *a folio edition* [L. ablative of *folium*, leaf]

fo·li·ose (fóuli:ous) *adj.* with many leaves ‖ like a leaf [fr. L. *foliosus*]

folk (fouk) **1.** *pl.* **folk, folks** *n.* people as belonging to a class, *farmhands, cowmen and such folk* ‖ the great mass of common people that make up a nation, produce its unsophisticated art and continue its traditions, *the Russian folk* ‖ (*pl.*, *Am.* **folks**, *Br.* **folk**) relatives **2.** *adj.* used by or springing from the mass of common people as distinguished from the individual or the few, *folk art* [O.E. *folc*]

folk crime a violation of the law not considered a serious breach of the moral code, e.g., a traffic offense, tax evasion

folk dance a traditional dance of country people

Folke·stone (fóukstən) a port (pop. 43,760) for cross-Channel traffic and a vacation resort near Dover, England

folk etymology the transformation of a word or part of a word so as to give a seeming relation to some other, more familiar word

folk·lore (fóuklɔr, fóuklour) *n.* the stories, sayings, local customs, songs, dances etc., handed down from generation to generation among the unsophisticated members of a race or nation ‖ the science and study of these

folk mass a religious mass based on a folk-music liturgy

folk rock folk music with overtones of rock 'n' roll **folk rock** *adj.* **folk rocker** *n.*

folk·say (fóuksei) *n.* the local ways in which natives speak

---

folk song a popular song handed down orally, of unknown origin and often existing in more than one version

folk·sy (fóuksi:) *comp.* **folk·si·er** *superl.* **folk·si·est** *adj.* (esp. of people in or from small communities) zealously sociable

folk tale an anonymous traditional story, orally transmitted, the subject rarely being tied to a particular time or place

folk·ways (fóukweiz) *pl. n.* the unconscious patterns of living, thinking and acting in a human society

fol·li·cle (fólik'l) *n.* (*bot.*) a dry, one-celled, monocarpellary fruit with several seeds dehiscing along a ventral suture only (e.g. peony, larkspur) ‖ (*anat.*) a small cavity, e.g. that in which a hair root grows **fol·lic·u·lar** (fəlíkjulər), **fol·lic·u·late** (fəlíkjulit), **fol·lic·u·lat·ed** *adjs* [fr. L. *folli-culus*, small bag]

fol·low (fólou) **1.** *v.t.* to go or come after ‖ to go in pursuit of, *follow that car!* ‖ to succeed in order of time, *Tuesday follows Monday* ‖ to succeed (someone) in a position, *he will follow his father as chairman* ‖ to result from, be a necessary consequence of, *ill health often follows a poor diet* ‖ to proceed along, *to follow a path* ‖ to imitate, *it follows the original faithfully* ‖ to act in accordance with, *to follow the rules* ‖ to accept as an authority or guide, *to follow the fashion* ‖ to pay attention to, watch, *to follow someone's progress* ‖ to take an interest in and make a study of, *to follow racing form* ‖ to understand, *to follow an explanation* ‖ (*old-fash.*) to practice (a profession), *to follow the law* ‖ *v.i.* to come or go after a person or thing in time, sequence or place ‖ to occur as a consequence, *what follows from this?* ‖ to pay attention so as to understand **as follows** as is written below ‖ as is about to be said **to follow on** (*cricket*) to go in to bat again as a team immediately after the first innings, because the score is more than 150 runs behind the opponent's first-innings score **to follow out** to carry out to the end, *follow out these instructions faithfully* **to follow through** (*golf, tennis, billiards etc.*) to continue the stroke after striking the ball ‖ to carry (an action) through to completion **to follow up** to consolidate by supporting action, *to follow up hospital treatment* ‖ to continue to keep up interest in, *to follow up a news item* **2.** *n.* (*billiards*) a stroke in which the player hits his ball above center so that it continues to roll on after hitting the opponent's ball ‖ (*billiards*) the spin imparted by this stroke **fól·low·er** *n.* an adherent, disciple ‖ a part of a machine that is not driven but receives its motion from another part **fól·low·ing 1.** *n.* a group of adherents or disciples **2.** *adj.* succeeding, next, *the following morning* ‖ about to be mentioned ‖ moving in the same direction, *a following wind* **3.** *prep.* immediately after [fr. O.E. *folgian, fylgan*, to follow]

fol·low-my-lead·er (fóloumilí:dər) *n.* (esp. *Br.*) follow-the-leader

fol·low-on (fólouɒn) *n.* (*cricket*) a second innings batted by a team straight after its first innings, when its first-innings score falls more than 150 runs behind that of the first team

fol·low-the-lead·er (fólouðəlí:dər) *n.* a game in which each player, one behind the other, imitates the leader's actions

fol·low-through (fólouθru:, fólouθrú:) *n.* (in certain ball games) the smooth continuing of the movement of a stroke after the ball has been hit

follow shot (*billiards*) a shot made with follow

fol·low-up (fólouʌp) *n.* the act of following up ‖ a business or advertising letter sent soon after the first one, to put more pressure on the recipient

fol·ly (fóli:) *pl.* **fol·lies** *n.* behavior arising from stupidity ‖ misguided behavior liable to end disastrously ‖ a foolish act or idea ‖ a lapse from moral rectitude ‖ a contrived ruin or decorative temple, common in the 18th and 19th cc. as part of the picturesque landscaping of an estate ‖ (*pl.*) a light theatrical revue [M.E. *folye* fr. O.F.]

Fol·som man (fóulsəm) a member of a North American race, supposedly dating from the last glacial age, who lived to the east of the Rocky Mtns [after *Folsom*, New Mexico]

fo·ment (foumént) *v.t.* to excite, foster or instigate (disorder, hatred, revolt) ‖ to treat with warm water or hot moist cloths **fo·men·ta·tion** *n.* [fr. F. *fomenter*]

fond (fond) *adj.* affectionate, loving ‖ foolishly tender, indulgent, *spoiled by a fond father* ‖ fool-

---

ishly cherished, *fond hopes* **to be fond of** to hold in affection ‖ to take pleasure in, *to be fond of music* (with pres. part.) ‖ to have the habit of, *to be fond of giving advice* [M.E. *fonned* fr. *fon*, to befool]

fon·dant (fóndənt) *n.* a soft sugar confection [F. fr. *fondre*, to melt]

fon·dle (fónd'l) *pres. part.* **fon·dling** *past* and *past part.* **fon·dled** *v.t.* to handle lovingly, caress ‖ *v.i.* (with 'with') to play amorously [fr. obs. *fond*, to dote]

fond·ly (fóndli:) *adv.* affectionately ‖ credulously

fon·due (fondú:) *n.* a dish of hot melted cheese cooked in white wine [F.]

fondue fork a long, single-tined fork used for eating cheese or meat fondue

F-100 *SUPER SABRE

F-101-B *VOODOO

F-102 *DELTA DAGGER

F-105 *THUNDERCHIEF

F-106 *DELTA DART

F-111 (*mil.*) U.S. twin-engine, supersonic turbofan, all-weather tactical fighter, capable of employing nuclear and nonnuclear weapons and operating from very short, relatively unprepared air strips: made by General Dynamics

Fon·se·ca (fɔséka), Manuel Deodoro da (1827–92), Brazilian general, leader of the revolt which overthrew (1889) the monarchy, and first president (1889–91) of the republic

Fonseca, Gulf of (or Fonseca Bay) a large inlet on the Central American Pacific coast with El Salvador on the north, Honduras on the east, and Nicaragua on the south

font (font) *n.* (*printing*) a complete set of types of a particular size and face [fr. F. *fonte*]

font *n.* a receptacle for water used in Christian baptism ‖ a receptacle for holy water ‖ a source, origin [O.E. *font, fant* fr. L. *fons* (*fontis*), a fount]

Fon·taine·bleau (fɔ̃tenblou) a French town (pop. 16,778) about 35 miles southeast of Paris ‖ its palace (now a museum), built (16th c.) for François I by the architects Gilles le Breton, Philibert Delorme and Serlio, and decorated by a group of Italian and French artists known as the Fontainebleau School, notably Il Rosso, Francesco Primaticcio and Niccoló dell' Abbate

font·al (fónt'l) *adj.* (*rhet.*) original, primary ‖ (*rhet.*) baptismal ‖ relating to a font [fr. M.L. *fontalis*]

Fon·tan·a (fɔntána), Domenico (1543–1607), Italian architect. His works include the Lateran palace and the Vatican library at Rome, and the royal palace at Naples

fon·ta·nel, fon·ta·nelle (fɒntanél) *n.* a membranous space esp. on top of an infant's skull, where the bones of the skull have not yet fused [F., dim. of *fontaine*, fountain]

Fon·te·nelle (fɔtnel), Bernard le Bovier de (1657–1757), French writer. He was a supporter of the 'modern' scientific outlook in opposition to the 'ancient' supernatural or religious beliefs regarding the universe. His most important works were 'Entretiens sur la pluralité des mondes' (1686) and 'Histoire des oracles' (1687)

Fon·te·noy, Battle of (fɔtnwæ) a French victory, under Marshal de Saxe, against the English, the Austrians and the Dutch during the War of the Austrian Succession (1745)

Foo·chow (fú:dʒóu) (Minhow) the capital (pop. 1,650,000) of Fukien, S.E. China, a seaport: sawmills, silk, cotton, lacquer and paper industries. It was China's foremost tea market until the late 19th c.

food (fu:d) *n.* any substance which, by a process of metabolism, a living organism can convert into fresh tissue, energy etc. ‖ a solid substance eaten for nourishment (opp. DRINK), esp. this as served at a meal ‖ something which can be put to constructive use, *food for thought* [O.E. *fóda*]

Food and Agriculture Organization (*abbr.* F.A.O.) a specialist agency of the U.N. set up on Oct. 16, 1945. Administrative center: Rome. It advises on techniques of agriculture, fisheries and forestry, and aims at securing higher nutritional standards throughout the world

food poisoning an intestinal disorder (*GASTROENTERITIS) due to eating foodstuffs (esp. meat or milk dishes, ice cream etc.) which have been contaminated by bacteria, or to eating substances unfit for human consumption, e.g.

CONCISE PRONUNCIATION KEY: **(a)** æ, c*a*t; ɑ, c*a*r; ɔ, f*aw*n; ei, sn*a*ke. **(e)** e, h*e*n; i:, sh*ee*p; iə, d*ee*r; ɛə, b*ea*r. **(i)** i, f*i*sh; ai, t*i*ger; ə:, b*i*rd. **(o)** o, *o*x; au, c*ow*; ou, g*oa*t; u, p*oo*r; ɔi, r*oy*al. **(u)** ʌ, d*u*ck; u, b*u*ll; u:, g*oo*se; ə, b*a*cillus; ju:, c*u*be. x, lo*ch*; θ, *th*ink; ð, bo*th*er; z, *Z*en; ʒ, corsa*g*e; dʒ, sava*g*e; ŋ, orangutan*g*; j, *y*ak; ʃ, *f*ish; tʃ, *f*etch; 'l, rab*ble*; 'n, red*den*. Complete pronunciation key appears inside front cover.

poisonous mushrooms, or foodstuffs which have been affected by chemicals

food processor an electrified mechanical device that mixes, chops, and liquifies food

food pyramid the ecological food relationship with primitive green plants at the base and increasingly developed fauna eating the lesser developed species

food stamp certificate redeemable at retail food stores, issued by the U.S. Department of Agriculture to low-income families and individuals

food·stuff (fú:dstʌf) n. a basic substance used as food

fool (fu:l) 1. n. someone lacking common sense or judgment ‖ (hist.) a jester, a professional clown ‖ someone made to appear stupid ‖ a dessert of crushed stewed fruit thickened with milk, eggs or cream **to be no** (or **nobody's**) **fool** to be intelligent and have one's wits about one **to make a fool of** to make (someone) appear stupid ‖ to deceive (someone) by a joke 2. adj. (pop.) foolish, silly, that fool woman 3. v.i. to trifle, not be serious ‖ v.t. to deceive ‖ to cheat, trick **to fool around** (Br. also **about**) to behave like a clown for fun ‖ to play stupidly or irresponsibly, don't fool around with that gun **fóol·er·y** n. foolish behavior [M.E. fol fr. O.F.]

fool·har·di·ness (fú:lhɑrdi:nis) n. the quality of being foolhardy

fool·har·dy (fú:lhɑrdi:) comp. **fool·har·di·er** superl. **fool·har·di·est** adj. fearless but taking thoughtless, unnecessary risks [O.F. fol hardi, foolish, bold]

fool·ish (fú:liʃ) adj. silly, ridiculous, a foolish person, a foolish hat ‖ lacking in good sense, prudence or judgment or showing such a lack

fool·proof (fú:lpru:f) adj. absolutely safe against misinterpretation or misuse ‖ guaranteed never to go wrong

fools·cap (fú:lzkæp) n. folio printing or writing paper varying roughly between 12 x 15 ins and 13½ x 17 ins ‖ (pop.) paper 13 x 8 ins, often lined [fr. the watermark on some 17th-c. papers]

fool's cap, foolscap n. (hist.) a jester's cap with bells on it ‖ (hist.) a dunce's conical paper hat

fool's errand a pointless or fruitless task or journey

fool's gold iron or copper pyrites, like gold in color

fool's paradise a fondly illusory state of security or happiness

foot (fut) 1. pl. **feet** (fi:t) n. the part at the end of the leg usually below the ankle joint on which vertebrates stand or walk ‖ any of various organs of locomotion in invertebrates ‖ that part of something which covers the human foot, the foot of a stocking ‖ a step, tread, to walk with a light foot ‖ the lowest part, the foot of the page ‖ a base, a teapot with a round foot ‖ the low end of a leg of a piece of furniture ‖ the end of a bed etc. furthest from the head ‖ a unit of length used in English-speaking countries equal to 12 ins, one third of the standard yard ‖ (hist., mil.) soldiers who fight on foot, a regiment of foot ‖ (printing) the lowest part of the body of a type on either side of the groove ‖ (refining, pl. **foots**) sediment, dregs, e.g. in oil refuse or coarse sugar ‖ that part of a sewing machine which keeps the cloth steady ‖ (poetry) a group of measured syllables constituting a metrical unit **on foot** walking (as distinct from using transportation) ‖ (of plans etc.) in an early stage of development **to change foot** to change instantaneously in marching from one foot to the other without breaking rhythm **to have one foot in the grave** to be old or sick and failing **to put one's best foot forward** (Am.) to create the best possible impression ‖ (Br.) to make an effort to walk quickly **to put one's foot down** to be firm in exercising authority **to put one's foot in it** (or **in one's mouth**) to make a tactless blunder **to set (something) on foot** to start (a rumor etc.) **to tread under foot** to oppress 2. v.t. to make or renew a foot for (a stocking or sock) **to foot it** to go on foot **to foot the bill** to bear the expense **fóot·age** n. length in feet ‖ (movies) the total length of a film ‖ frontage [O.E. fōt]

foot-and-mouth disease (fut'nmáuθ) a highly infectious virus disease of cattle etc., characterized by fever, excessive salivation and ulcerating lesions in the mouth and on the feet. In Europe, animals within a 10-mile radius are immunized when an outbreak of the disease occurs. In Great Britain and North America all infected animals are slaughtered. In many tropical countries the disease is endemic but

milder than in Great Britain and North America

foot·ball (fútbɔl) n. any of various team games played with a ball (round or elliptical according to the game played) consisting of an inflated rubber bladder in a leather case, esp. (Am.=Br. American football) a game developed since 1876, played by two teams each of 11 players with an oval-shaped ball on a rectangular field (100 yds by 53 1/3 yds) having an H-shaped goal, and a 10-yd end zone beyond, at either end. The object is to run or pass the ball by a series of plays into the opponents' end zone and score a touchdown (6 points). Handling, kicking and throwing the ball in any direction, tackling and blocking are permitted. There are specific rules concerning the number of downs, yards gained and the position of players. Points may also be scored by a field goal (3 points), a safety (2 points) and a conversion after a touchdown (1 point) ‖ the ball itself (*SOCCER, *RUGBY FOOTBALL) **fóot·ball·er** n. someone who plays football or (Br.) soccer

foot·board (fútbɔrd, fútbourd) n. a sloping board on which the foot-operated pedals of a vehicle are mounted ‖ an upright section across the foot of a bed

foot brake a brake operated by the foot

foot·bridge (fútbridʒ) n. a bridge for pedestrians only

foot·can·dle (fútkænd'l) n. (phys.) a unit of illumination, equal to that on a square foot of surface that is everywhere 1 foot from a uniform 1-candle point source, being equal to 1 lumen/ft²

foot·ed (fútid) adj. having a foot or feet, a footed bowl ‖ having a specified number of feet, four-footed animals ‖ having a specified kind of foot, a claw-footed table

foot·er (fútər) n. (in hyphenated compounds) a person or thing measuring a specific number of feet, a six-footer

foot·fall (fútfɔl) n. the sound of a footstep

foot fault (tennis) the fault of stepping over the base line, or walking, running or jumping, while serving ‖ (volleyball) the fault of stepping over the end line while serving or over the center line while playing **foot·fault** (fútfɔlt) v.i. to make a foot fault ‖ v.t. to call a foot fault against (a player)

foot·gear (fútgiər) n. footwear

Foot Guards the Brigade of Guards, British crack infantry regiments: the Coldstream, Grenadier, Irish, Scots and Welsh Guards

foot·hill (fúthil) n. a hill at the foot of a range of mountains ‖ (pl.) the approaches to a mountain

foot·hold (fúthould) n. a place to put one's foot where it will bear one's weight when climbing ‖ an initial position of advantage, to get a foothold in a rival market

foot·ing (fútiŋ) n. a firm placing of the feet, he lost his footing and fell ‖ a secure place to stand on ‖ a basis of organization, a sound business footing ‖ (Br.) jogging a social relationship, on a friendly footing ‖ (archit.) a projecting course at the lower end of a wall, column etc. used for distributing the load

foot·lights (fútlaits) pl. n. (theater) the lights along the front of a stage, screened from the audience, and used to illuminate actors and decor from floor level ‖ the acting profession, the lure of the footlights **to get over** (or **across**) **the footlights** to succeed in making a desired effect on the audience

foot·ling (fú:tliŋ) adj. trivial

foot·loose (fútlu:s) adj. having no responsibilities, free to go where one wants to and do as one pleases

foot·man (fútmən) pl. **foot·men** (fútmən) n. a uniformed manservant who waits on the table, answers the door and sees people into or out of their cars etc.

foot·mark (fútmɑrk) n. a footprint

foot·note (fútnout) 1. n. a note at the bottom of a printed page to elucidate a minor point raised in the text without burdening the narrative, or to give a reference 2. v.t. pres. part. **foot·not·ing** past and past part. **foot·not·ed** to add a footnote to

foot·pad (fútpæd) n. (hist.) a highwayman operating on foot ‖ a large, flat landing device, e.g.,

of a spacecraft, that distributes the weight of a vehicle to avoid sinking into soft surfaces

foot·path (fútpæθ, fútpɑθ) pl. **foot·paths** (fútpæðz, fútpɑðz, fútpæθs, fútpɑθs) n. a narrow path across fields, through woods etc. for walkers ‖ (Br.) a sidewalk

foot·plate (fútpleit) n. (Br.) the platform for the driver and fireman in a steam locomotive

foot·pound (fútpaund) n. a unit of work in the foot-pound-second system, being the work done when a pound-force acts through a distance of 1 foot in the direction of the force ‖ a unit of torque

foot·pound·al (fútpáund'l) n. the absolute unit of work in the foot-pound-second system, being the work done when a force of 1 pound acts through a distance of 1 foot in the direction of the force

foot·pound·sec·ond (fútpáundsékənd) adj. (abbr. fps) of a system of units based on the foot as unit of length, the pound as unit of weight or mass, and the second as unit of time

foot·print (fútprint) n. a mark made by the foot ‖ (electr.) an area that receives signals from a downlink

foot reflexology nonmedical therapy based on manipulation of the foot

foot·rest (fútrest) n. a cushion, stool, bar etc. to rest the feet on

foot rot an infectious skin ulcer, common in sheep and cattle, affecting the foot and caused by the bacterium Fusiformis necrophorus

foot rule a measure one foot long

foot·slog (fútslɒg) pres. part. **foot·slog·ging** past and past part. **foot·slogged** v.i. to go a long, weary way on foot

foot soldier (mil. hist.) an infantryman

foot·sore (fútsɔr, fútsour) adj. having sore feet from walking or marching

foot·stalk (fútstɔk) n. (bot.) the pedicel or petiole of a flower ‖ a peduncle ‖ (zool.) a muscular attachment of certain animals (e.g. a barnacle)

foot·step (fútstep) n. a footfall ‖ a footprint **to follow in someone's footsteps** to mirror in one's own career the earlier career of someone else

foot·stock (fútstɒk) n. the tailstock of a lathe containing the dead center

foot·stool (fútstu:l) n. a low stool to rest the feet on when sitting

foot·ton (fúttʌn) n. a unit of work or energy in the fps system equal to the work done in lifting against standard gravity 1 ton through a distance of 1 foot

foot·way (fútwei) n. a sidewalk ‖ a pathway

foot·wear (fútwɛər) n. things to wear on the feet other than socks or stockings

foot·well (fútwel) n. space in an automobile where foot pedal, brake, etc., are housed

foot·work (fútwə:rk) n. control of the feet in boxing, football etc.

foot·worn (fútwɔrn, fútwourn) adj. worn away by the feet, a footworn path ‖ footsore

fop (fɒp) n. a man excessively interested in his dress **fóp·per·y** pl. **fop·per·ies** n. **fóp·pish** adj. [origin unknown]

for (fɔr) 1. prep. as a representative of, on behalf of, the lawyer acted for them during the trial ‖ in honor of, a parade was staged for the new president ‖ in support of, in favor of, they declared they were for a negotiated peace ‖ with the purpose of, I bought the book for studying at home ‖ with the aim of going to, they left for London ‖ for the benefit of, I exercise for my figure ‖ given over to, a darkroom for photography ‖ destined to (a specific person or thing), a gift for our mother, a stamp for a letter ‖ to allow of, too many for separate mention ‖ (of feelings or capacities) towards, affection for one's parents ‖ in its or their effect on, the medicine is good for you ‖ as being, to take for granted ‖ in place of, she used a cup for a soup bowl ‖ considering the usual nature of, a clever remark for David, warm for December ‖ in spite of, you are a poor musician for all your training ‖ as the effect of, she wept for boredom ‖ as a result of, he felt better for having said it ‖ to set against, we have 10 sunny days for each rainy one (but indicating equality when preceded and followed by the same subject, pound for pound) ‖ to the amount of, a bill for $10 ‖ at the amount of, the clock sold for 100 dollars ‖ to the extent or duration of, it lasts for eight hours ‖ at (a certain time), a date for 10 o'clock ‖ regarding, for my part I prefer to remain here ‖ in order to have, get etc., will you go for the laundry? ‖ because of, he was punished for cheating **for all that** nevertheless **for**

oneself without help, *I can do it for myself* ‖ for one's own benefit **2.** *conj.* (used to introduce an explanation or proof of something previously stated) because, since, seeing that, *he couldn't attend, for it would make him appear in agreement* [O.E. *for*]

for·age (fɔ́ridʒ, fóridʒ) **1.** *n.* food for horses and cattle ‖ the act of foraging, a hunt for provisions **2.** *v. pres. part.* **for·ag·ing** *past* and *past part.* **for·aged** *v.t.* to collect forage from ‖ to supply with forage ‖ to get by making a forage ‖ *v.i.* to go out in search of forage ‖ to search [fr. O. F. *fourrage, fourrager*]

foraging ant any of several ants that forage for food in groups, esp. the driver ant

For·a·ker (fɔ́rəkər), Joseph Benson (1846–1917), U.S. politician. As U.S. senator from Ohio, he drafted the Foraker Act of 1900

For·a·ker Act of 1900 (fɔ́rəkər, fórəkər) a U.S. Congressional act of the McKinley administration, which provided for civil government in Puerto Rico

fo·ra·men (fɔréimən, fouréimən) *pl.* **fo·ram·i·na** (fɔræminə, fourǽminə), **fo·ra·mens** *n.* a small opening or perforation, esp. through a bone or membranous structure [L. fr. *forare*, to bore]

foramen mag·num (mǽgnəm) *n.* the opening in the occipital region of the skull through which the spinal cord passes to become the medulla oblongata, part of the brainstem [L.=great opening]

for·a·min·i·fer (fɔrəmínifər, fɔrəmínifər) *n.* a protozoan of order *Foraminifera*, class *Rhizopoda*. These microorganisms secrete around themselves a calcareous shell, coiled like a snail's and perforated by very many tiny holes, through each of which a pseudopod extends. They are found, usually sessile, in salt water, and their skeletal remains form much of the ooze on the ocean floor, often consolidating as chalk [fr. L. *foramen* (*foraminis*), opening]

for·ay (fɔ́rei, fórei) **1.** *n.* a raid to get food, capture booty, or just pillage **2.** *v.i.* to make a raid, pillage [etym. doubtful]

forbad *alt. past* of FORBID

forbade *alt. past* of FORBID

forbear *FOREBEAR

for·bear (fɔrbéər) *pres. part.* **for·bear·ing** *past* **for·bore** (fɔrbór, fɔrbóur) *past part.* **for·borne** (fɔrbórn, fɔrbóurn) *v.i.* to control one's patience, not give way to anger ‖ to abstain ‖ *v.t.* to refrain from (using, doing etc.), *you must forbear taking advantage of your strength* **for·béar·ance** *n.* [O.E. *forberan*, to endure]

for·bid (fɔrbíd, forbíd) *pres. part.* **for·bid·ding** *past* **for·bade** (fərbéid, forbéid), *past* **for·bad** (fərbǽd, forbǽd) *past part.* **for·bid·den** (fərbíd'n, forfíd'n) *v.t.* to command (someone) not to do something, *I forbid you to leave the house* ‖ to put an interdiction against (something), *he forbids smoking during office hours* ‖ to put (a place) out of bounds ‖ to make impossible, prevent, *the weather forbade all idea of a picnic* **for·bíd·dance** *n.* **for·bíd·ding** *adj.* frighteningly difficult, *a forbidding task* ‖ angry, *forbidding looks* ‖ unlovely, *a forbidding country* ‖ lowering, *forbidding cliffs* **for·bíd·den** *adj.* [O.E. *forbēodan*]

forbore *past* of FORBEAR

forborne *past part.* of FORBEAR

force (fɔrs, fours) **1.** *n.* the exertion of physical strength, *we had to use force to restrain him* ‖ physical vigor, *the force of manhood* ‖ mental or moral strength, esp. in the overcoming of opposition, *by force of argument* ‖ the power and might of a ruler or state, *the force of the Roman Empire* ‖ the capacity to convince, influence or affect, *force of character* ‖ (*law*) violence exerted on a person or thing, *the burglar opened the desk by brute force* ‖ (*phys.*) any influence or agency that produces a change in the velocity of an inelastic object, whether it be in speed or direction. Force is defined in classical physics as the product of the mass of an object and its acceleration, or in a system where mass is not conserved as the time rate of change of momentum (*LAW OF MOTION) ‖ (esp. *pl.*) an organized body of men, troops, warships, etc., *a labor force, armed forces* **by force** by using force or by being forced **in force** required by law or regulation, *a curfew was in force at the time* ‖ in large numbers **to come into force** to become required by law or regulation, *the new tax comes into force next week* **2.** *v.t. pres. part.* **forc·ing** *past* and *past part.* **forced** to compel by using physical or moral strength ‖ to produce with difficulty, *to force a smile* ‖ to cause to open by using physical strength, *to force a door* ‖ to drive

or impel against physical resistance, *the water was forced to the top of the cliff* ‖ (*cards*) to compel (a player) to use a trump card, or to play a particular card, or to reveal by his play the strength of his hand ‖ (*baseball*) to put out (a man on base) by compelling him to make room for another runner ‖ (*baseball*, of a pitcher) to allow (a run) to be scored when the bases are full by giving a base on balls which automatically brings home the player on third base ‖ (*hort.*) to hasten the growth of (plants etc.) by artificial means **to force someone's hand** to compromise someone in such a way that he is obliged to take an action whether he wishes to or not **to force the pace** to cause to speed up more than would seem reasonable or normal

forced (fɔrst, fourst) *adj.* compelled by force ‖ opened by force ‖ insincere, *a forced laugh* [F. *force, forcer*]

forced draft, esp. *Br.* **forced draught** a current of air driven forward by pressure to bring about combustion

force de frappe (fɔrsdəfrǽp) *n.* (*Fr.*, often italics) a nuclear deterrent force

forced landing an emergency landing of an aircraft

forced march (*mil.*) a march made rapidly and with few halts, calling on the endurance of the troops

force feed a pressure lubricating system in internal-combustion engines **force-feed** (fɔ́rsfiːd, fóursfiːd) *pres. part.* **force-feed·ing** *past* and *past part.* **force-fed** (fɔ́rsfíd, fóursféd) *v.t.* to compel to accept food

force·ful (fɔ́rsfəl, fóursfəl) *adj.* forcible

force main (*envir.*) power-driven sewage system

force·meat (fɔ́rsmiːt, fóursmiːt) *n.* seasoned chopped meat, used for stuffing or for making meatballs [fr. F. *farce*, stuffing]

force of habit the effect of sheer repetition in making behavior virtually automatic, *we said 'no' from force of habit*

for·ceps (fɔ́rseps) *pl.* **for·ceps** *n.* a two-pronged instrument, esp. surgical and obstetrical pincers, for taking hold of delicate or minute things ‖ (*anat.*) a limb shaped like a forceps, e.g. one of the pair of appendages of the earwig [L.]

force pump a pump which delivers liquid well above its own level or under considerable pressure (cf. SUCTION PUMP)

for·ci·ble (fɔ́rsəb'l, fóursəb'l) *adj.* made or done by using force, *a forcible entry* ‖ convincing, impressive, powerful, *a forcible argument* **fór·ci·bly** *adv.* [O.F.]

Ford (fɔrd, fourd), Ford Madox (Ford Madox Hueffer, 1873–1939), English novelist, editor and critic. He founded 'The English Review' (1908–37) and edited it until 1911. His novels include 'The Good Soldier' (1915) and the tetralogy 'Parade's End' (1924–8)

Ford, Gerald Rudolph, Jr. (1913–), U.S. statesman, 38th president (1974–7). After graduating from the University of Michigan (1935) and Yale Law School (1941), he served in the Navy during World War II, married Elizabeth (Betty) Bloomer Warren (1948), and served as a Republican in the U.S. House of Representatives (1949–73). In 1973, when Vice Pres. Spiro T. Agnew resigned, Ford was nominated for the vice presidency by Pres. Richard M. Nixon. He assumed the presidency in Aug. 1974 when Nixon, threatened with impeachment, resigned. Faced with economic crises, deteriorating conditions in Southeast Asia, and the stigma of following in Nixon's footsteps—he granted Nixon full pardon in 1975—he lost the 1976 election to Democrat Jimmy Carter and retired from public office

Ford, Henry (1863–1947), American engineer. He founded the Ford Motor Company at Detroit in 1903, and was a pioneer of standardization, mass production and the assembly line. By adopting these techniques he was able to produce reliable, low-cost cars and other motor vehicles. He made his first 'gasoline buggy' in 1893 and produced farm tractors in 1915

Ford, John (1586–c. 1640), English dramatist. His plays usually have a strongly tragic theme, sensationally handled, e.g. 'Tis Pity She's a Whore' (1633), which treats of incest. 'The Witch of Edmonton' (1621), in which he collaborated with Dekker and Rowley, was lively and popular

Ford, John (Sean O'Fearna, 1895–1973), American film director. Among his films are: 'The

Informer' (1936), 'Stagecoach' (1940), 'The Quiet Man' (1953)

ford (fɔrd, fourd) **1.** *n.* a place where a river is shallow and can be crossed by wading **2.** *v.t.* to cross by wading [O.E.]

Ford Foundation philanthropic organization, established in 1936. It received the main part of the fortunes of Henry Ford, his wife, and his son Edsel

Ford Motor Company a U.S. automobile manufacturing company founded (1903) by Henry Ford in Detroit, Mich., and controlled since 1907 by the Ford family. By gaining control of raw materials and the means of distribution, by adapting the assembly line method to automobile production, and by producing an inexpensive, standardized car, it soon became the world's largest automobile producer. It featured (1908–28) the Model T, the first car designed for a mass market

fore (fɔr, four) **1.** *n.* the bows of a ship **at the fore** (*naut.*) on the foremast masthead **to the fore** (of personalities) in the public eye, conspicuous ‖ (of money) ready and available **2.** *adj.* placed in front, forward, advanced, *the fore edge* **3.** *adv.* (*naut.*) in or towards the bows [O.E.]

fore *interj.* (*golf*) a warning to people in the line of flight of a ball that is about to be played [BEFORE]

fore- (fɔr, four) *prefix* in front ‖ beforehand, in advance ‖ anticipatory [O.E.]

fore and aft from one end of a ship to the other, from stem to stern

fore-and-aft rig a sailing-ship rig in which all the sails, or most of them, are set on the masts or on stays in the midship line, i.e. not attached to yards (cf. SQUARE RIG)

fore-and-aft sail a sail carried on a gaff or stay, not set to yards

fore·arm (fɔrárm, fourárm) *v.t.* to arm in advance, *to forearm oneself against criticism*

fore·arm (fɔ́rɑrm, fóurɑrm) *n.* the part of the arm between the elbow and the wrist

fore·bay (fɔ́rbei) *n.* (*envir.*) the water impounded above a dam

fore·bear, for·bear (fɔ́rbɛər, fóurbɛər) *n.* (usually *pl.*) an ancestor other than an immediate ancestor [FORE+obs. *beer* (BE +-er), someone who is before]

fore·bode (fɔrbóud, fourbóud) *pres. part.* **fore·bod·ing** *past* and *past part.* **fore·bod·ed** *v.t.* to betoken, portend (usually evil or trouble) ‖ to have a presentiment of (disaster etc.) **fore·bód·ing** *n.* a sign of something to come ‖ a presentiment, esp. of evil

fore·brain (fɔ́rbrein, fóurbrein) *n.* the front section of a vertebrate's developing brain ‖ in the adult, the part which develops from this section, i.e. the diencephalon and telencephalon

fore·cast (fɔ́rkæst, fóurkæst, fɔ́rkɑst, fóurkɑst) **1.** *v.t. pres. part.* **fore·cast·ing** *past* and *past part.* **fore·cast, fore·cast·ed** to predict on the basis of scientific observation and applied experience (e.g. in meteorology), or by simple estimate of probability **2.** *n.* something predicted

fore·cas·tle, fo·c'sle (fóuksəl) *n.* the forward part of a merchant ship ‖ the sailors' quarters in this ‖ (*hist.*) a small raised bow deck on old warships, for observation and command

fore·close (fɔrklóuz, fourklóuz) *pres. part.* **fore·clos·ing** *past* and *past part.* **fore·closed** *v.t.* (*mortgage law*) to deprive (a person) of the equity of redemption for nonpayment of money due ‖ to bar, remove (the right of redemption) ‖ *v.i.* to take away the right to redeem a mortgage **fore·clos·ure** (fɔrklóuʒər, fourklóuʒər) *n.* [fr. O.F. *forclore* (*forclos-*)]

fore·con·scious (fɔrkɒnʃəs, fóurkɒnʃəs) *n.* the preconscious

fore·court (fɔ́rkɔrt, fóurkourt) *n.* a court or enclosed space in front of a building ‖ (*tennis, badminton* etc.) the part of the court between the net and the service line, divided in two by the center line

fore·doom (fɔrdúːm, fourdúːm) *v.t.* to destine to an unfortunate fate, *a plot foredoomed to failure*

fore edge the outer edge of a book or of a leaf of a book

fore·fa·ther (fɔ́rfɑðər, fóurfɑðər) *n.* (esp. *pl.*) an ancestor, esp. a remote ancestor [M.E. *forfader, forefader*]

fore·fin·ger (fɔ́rfiŋgər, fóurfiŋgər) *n.* the finger next to the thumb

fore·foot (fɔ́rfut, fóurfut) *pl.* **fore·feet** (fɔ́rfiːt, fóurfiːt) *n.* one of the front feet of a quadruped ‖ (*naut.*) the forward part of a ship at the junction of stem and keel

fore-front (fórfrʌnt, fóurfrʌnt) n. a position of leadership, *in the forefront of research* ‖ a conspicuous position, *to come to the forefront*

foregather *FORGATHER

forego *FORGO

fore-go-ing (fɔrgóuiŋ, fourgóuiŋ) adj. mentioned above, *the foregoing clause* [fr. obs. *forego*, to precede]

foregone conclusion a result that could be foreseen ‖ a decision reached before a matter could be properly considered

fore-ground (fórgraund, fóurgraund) n. the part of a scene nearest the viewer ‖ the most noticeable position, *to put oneself in the foreground*

fore-hand (fórhænd, fóurhænd) 1. adj. (*racket games*, of a stroke) made with the palm of the hand turned in the direction of the stroke (opp. BACKHAND) 2. adv. with a forehand stroke 3. n. (*tennis* etc.) a forehand stroke or the capacity to play forehand strokes ‖ the part of a horse in front of a rider

fore-hand-ed (fórhændid, fóurhændid) adj. prudent with respect to the future ‖ made or done in good time, timely ‖ (*racket games*) forehand

fore-head (fórid, fórid, fórhed, fórhed) n. the front of the vertebrate head, in man above the eyebrows to where the hair begins to grow

for-eign (fórin, fórin) adj. not of one's own country or race ‖ coming from or typical of some country outside one's own, *foreign produce* ‖ having to do with other countries, *foreign travel* ‖ relating to or coming from a district, province or society other than one's own ‖ introduced from outside, *our foreign population is growing* ‖ outside one's knowledge, *the subject is foreign to me* ‖ unrelated, extraneous, *a question foreign to the topic* ‖ (*law*) outside the jurisdiction of the governmental unit in question (opp. DOMESTIC) [M.E. *forein, foreyn* fr. O.F.]

foreign affairs external relations with other countries

foreign body an object, e.g. a swallowed pin, that is inside a person's body but ought not to be ‖ any unwanted object in something, e.g. a fly in the soup

foreign correspondent a journalist employed to transmit news from some country other than that in which the newspaper or magazine concerned is published

for-eign-er (fórinər, fórinər) n. someone whose nationality is other than one's own ‖ a ship from another country

foreign exchange the currency of countries other than one's own, or current and short-term credit instruments payable in such currency ‖ payments made between residents of different countries

foreign legion a volunteer corps of foreigners serving within the framework of a regular army, esp. that founded (1831) by France for service in Algeria

foreign relations the conduct of affairs between sovereign states

for-eign-trade zone (fórintréid, fórintréid) a free port

fore-judge (fordʒʌdʒ, fourdʒʌdʒ) pres. part. **fore-judg-ing** past and past part. **fore-judged** v.t. to make a judgment or decision about, before hearing the evidence

fore-know (fornóu, fournóu) pres. part. **fore-know-ing** past **fore-knew** (fornú:, fornjú:, fournú:, fournjú:) past part. **fore-known** (fornóun, fournóun) v.t. to have prior knowledge of, foresee **fore-knowl-edge** (fórnɒlidʒ, fóurnɒlidʒ) n. knowledge of an event or thing before it happens

Fo-rel (fɔrél) a mountain (11,100 ft) in E. Greenland, near the coast

fore-la-dy (fórleidi:, fóurleidi:) pl. **fore-la-dies** n. a forewoman

fore-land (fórlænd, fóurlænd) n. a promontory ‖ a strip of land left fronting a seawall, embankment etc. for strengthening

fore-leg (fórleg, fóurleg) n. either of the front legs of a quadruped

fore-limb (fórlim, fóurlim) n. a foreleg, or anterior fin, wing etc.

fore-lock (fórlɒk, fóurlɒk) n. a cluster or lock of hair just above the forehead **to take time by the forelock** to grasp the chance to anticipate events and not delay action

forelock n. (esp. *naut.*) a wedge or linchpin driven through the shaft of a bolt to keep it in position

fore-man (fórmən, fóurmən) pl. **fore-men** (fórmen, fóurmən) n. someone who supervises

other workmen ‖ a member of a jury who acts as leader and spokesman

fore-mast (fórmæst, fóurmæst, fɔrmɒst, fóurmɒst) n. the mast nearest a ship's bows

fore-most (fórmoust, fóurmoust) 1. adj. first of several in place or time, rank or status 2. adv. first ‖ most importantly [O. E. *formest, fyrmest*]

fore-name (fórneim, fóurneim) n. the given name as distinct from the family name

fore-named (fórneimd, fóurneimd) adj. named above (in a document)

fore-noon (fórnu:n, fóurnu:n) n. the part of the day from dawn until midday, or between breakfast and lunch

fo-ren-sic (fərénsik) 1. adj. relating to law courts or to public debate 2. n. an oral or written argumentative exercise, e.g. in the teaching of rhetoric **fo-rén-si-cal-ly** adv. [fr. L. *forensis* fr. *forum*, public place]

forensic medicine medical jurisprudence

fo-ren-sics (fərénsiks) n. the art of debate, esp. of legal argument

forensic science the study and application of scientific facts and techniques to legal problems

fore-or-dain (fɔrɔrdéin, fourɔrdéin) v.t. to predestine **fore-or-di-na-tion** (fɔrɔrd'néiʃən, fourɔrd'néiʃən) n.

fore-part (fórpart, fóurpart) n. the front part

fore-paw (fórpɔ, fóurpɔ) n. a foreleg paw

fore-peak (fórpi:k, fóurpi:k) n. the compartment or tank in the angle of a ship's bows

fore-quar-ter (fórkwɔrtər, fóurkwɔrtər) n. the front half of a side of mutton, beef etc.

fore-reach (fɔrrí:tʃ, fourrí:tʃ) v.t. (*naut.*) to overhaul and pass when the sails are close-hauled ‖ v.i. (*naut.*) to gain ground, esp. when going about

fore-run (fɔrrʌn, fourrʌn) pres. part. **fore-run-ning** past **fore-ran** (fɔrræn, fourræn) past part. **fore-run** v.t. to be the precursor of, to come before as a token of what is to follow **fóre-run-ner** n. a predecessor

fore-sail (fórseil, fóurseil, fórs'l, fóurs'l) n. the principal and lowest sail on the foremast of a square-rigged vessel ‖ the lower sail abaft the foremast on a schooner

fore-see (fɔrsí:, foursí:) pres. part. **fore-see-ing** past **fore-saw** (fɔrsɔ́, foursɔ́) past part. **fore-seen** (fɔrsí:n, foursí:n) v.t. to have a vision of (a future event), e.g. in a dream ‖ to arrive at a reasonable estimate of (what is probable), esp. with a view to taking measures in advance **fore-sée-a-ble** adj. of what can be anticipated ‖ of the future that lies sufficiently close to allow forecasting

fore-shad-ow (fɔrʃædou, fourʃædou) v.t. to indicate, prefigure (some future event or circumstance)

fore-sheet (fórʃi:t, fóurʃi:t) n. the rope which keeps the sheltered corner of the foresail in place ‖ (*pl.*) the space in the bows of an open boat

fore-shore (fórʃɔr, fóurʃour) n. the part of the shore between the high-water mark and low-water mark ‖ the land lying between the high-water limit and the coastline proper

fore-shor-ten (fɔrʃɔ́rt'n, fourʃɔ́rt'n) v.t. (*fine arts*) to apply the laws of perspective in representing (a person or object) so as to give the illusion of depth

fore-show (fɔrʃóu, fourʃóu) pres. part. **fore-show-ing** past **fore-showed** past part. **fore-shown** (fɔrʃóun, fourʃóun) v.t. to indicate (what is to follow)

fore-sight (fórsait, fóursait) n. prophetic capacity, prevision ‖ provident care for the future ‖ the aiming device at the front of the barrel of a rifle etc. used in conjunction with the backsight **fóre-sight-ed** adj.

fore-skin (fórskin) n. the fold of skin covering the end of the penis

for-est (fórist, fórist) 1. n. a large area of land covered with trees and brush growing thickly ‖ the trees on such land ‖ something which, in its density, is like a forest of trees, *a forest of chimneys* **not to see the forest for the trees** (*Am.=Br.* not to see the wood for the trees) to be so absorbed in or bemused by detail as to lose sight of the main issue 2. v.t. to cause to become forest [O.F.]
—The three principal classes of forest are coniferous, deciduous and equatorial. Coniferous forests are composed of evergreen conifers. They form the world's chief source of softwood. They grow in a vast belt across North America and N. Eurasia, with outcrops in mountainous

areas further south. Deciduous forests supply most of the valuable hardwood lumber: teak from the tropical monsoon forests of India and Burma, and oak, elm and beech from the cool intermediate forests of America and Europe. Equatorial forests are hot, wet evergreen forests in regions such as the Amazon and Congo basins and Indonesia, supplying hardwoods such as mahogany and ebony. Besides wood for fuel, furniture, building etc., forests yield secondary products such as balsams, rubber, dyes, paper and edible oils, and are of value in the preservation of wildlife and the prevention of soil erosion

fore-stall (fɔrstɔ́l, fourstɔ́l) v.t. to frustrate the intentions of (someone) by acting before him ‖ to act in anticipation of (future circumstances or possibilities) [O.E. *foresteall*]

for-est-a-tion (fɔristéiʃən, fouristéiʃən) n. afforestation

fore-stay (fórstei, fóurstei) n. a support for the foremast of a ship running from the foremast head to the deck

for-est-er (fóristər, fóristər) n. someone in charge of a forest ‖ someone who plants and cares for forest trees ‖ *Macropus giganteus*, the giant kangaroo of Australia, esp. the male [fr. O.F. *forestier*]

for-est-ry (fóristri:, fóristri:) n. the science of planting and tending forests ‖ (*rare*) forest land [O.F. *foresterie*]

fore-taste 1. (fórteist, fóurteist) n. a sample of something to come 2. (fɔrtéist, fourtéist) v.t. pres. part. **fore-tast-ing** past and past part. **fore-tast-ed** to sample (something) beforehand

fore-tell (fɔrtél, fourtél) pres. part. **fore-tell-ing** past and past part. **fore-told** (fɔrtóuld, fourtóuld) v.t. to announce (an event) before it happens

fore-thought (fórθɔt, fóurθɔt) n. prudence in thinking ahead and providing for likely contingencies ‖ cool premeditation as opposed to sudden impulse

fore-to-ken 1. (fórtoukən, fóurtoukən) n. an indication of something to come 2. (fɔrtóukən, fourtóukən) v.t. to be a sign of (future events or conduct)

fore-top (fórtɒp, fóurtɒp) n. the top of the foremast of a ship

fore-top-gal-lant mast (fɔrtɒpgǽlənt, fourtɒp-gǽlənt, fɔrtəgǽlənt, fóurtəgǽlənt) the mast above the fore-topmast

fore-top-gallant sail the sail above the fore-topsail

fore-top-mast (fɔrtɒpmæst, fourtɒpmæst, fɔr-tɒpmɒst, fourtɒpmɒst) n. the mast above the foremast

fore-top-sail (fɔrtɒpseil, fourtɒpseil, fɔrtɒpsəl, fourtɒpsəl) n. the sail above the foresail

for-ev-er (fərévər, fɔrévər) adv. eternally, *may you live forever* ‖ without a break or so often as to seem so, *he is forever complaining*

for ever adv. (*Br.*) eternally

for-ev-er-more (fərévərmɔr, fɔrévərmɔr, fərév-ərmóur, fɔrévərmóur) adv. (*rhet.*) for all time

fore-warn (fɔrwɔ́rn, fourwɔ́rn) v.t. to give advance warning to

forewent past of FOREGO

fore-wing (fórwiŋ, fóurwiŋ) n. an anterior wing of an insect

fore-wom-an (fórwumən, fóurwumən) pl. **fore-wom-en** (fórwimən, fóurwimən) n. a woman overseeing the work of other people in a factory ‖ a woman acting as the president of a jury and as its spokeswoman

fore-word (fórwə:rd, fóurwə:rd) n. a preface

fore-yard (fórjɑrd, fóurjɑrd) n. the lowest yard on the foremast of a sailing ship

For-far (fórfər, fɔ́rfər) *ANGUS

for-feit (fórfit) 1. n. a fine for breach of contract or negligence ‖ a small fine for breaking the rules of a club etc. ‖ the act of forfeiting, *the forfeit of voting rights* ‖ something forfeited ‖ (*pl.*) a game in which items taken from players are recovered by the performance of imposed and often ridiculous or embarrassing tasks 2. adj. lost or taken away as a forfeit 3. v.t. to be deprived of as a penalty for a crime, fault, error etc. or as a necessary result or consequence, to surrender, lose [fr. O.F. *forfait*, past part.]

for-fei-ture (fórfitʃər) n. the act of forfeiting ‖ something forfeited [O.F. *forfaiture, forfeture*]

for-gath-er, fore-gath-er (fɔrgǽðər) v.i. to join with others in an assembly, esp. in an informal or casual gathering

forgave past of FORGIVE

forge (fɔrdʒ) *n.* the workshop of a blacksmith, with its furnace, anvil and bellows ‖ the furnace itself, or the hearth used to shape wrought iron ‖ a workshop and furnace where metals are melted and refined [O.F. *forge*]

forge *pres. part.* **forg·ing** *past* and *past. part.* **forged** *v.t.* to heat and hammer (metal) into shape ‖ to form or shape (something) by heating and hammering metal ‖ to imitate (something) and attempt to pass it off as genuine, *to forge a signature* ‖ *v.i.* to commit forgery [fr. O.F. *forgier*]

forge *pres. part.* **forg·ing** *past* and *past. part.* **forged** *v.i.* to move forward with effort, esp. so as to secure an advance, *to forge into the lead* ‖ (with 'ahead') to make rapid progress ‖ (with 'ahead') to increase one's lead over others in a race rapidly [etym. doubtful]

forg·er·y (fɔrdʒəri:, fóurdʒəri:) *pl.* **forg·er·ies** *n.* the act or art of forging or falsifying (documents, signatures etc.) ‖ something counterfeit [FORGE v., to heat]

for·get (fərgét) *pres. part.* **for·get·ting** *past* **for·got** (fərgót) *past part.* **for·got·ten, for·got** *v.t.* to fail to keep in the memory ‖ to overlook unintentionally, neglect, *to forget someone's birthday* ‖ to leave behind unintentionally, *she has forgotten her keys again* ‖ to stop thinking about, *try to forget this affair* ‖ *v.i.* to be apt to forget things ‖ to suffer a lapse of memory, *to forget about answering a letter* **to forget oneself** to act rudely ‖ to lose dignity by unworthy behavior ‖ to escape from self-consciousness, *he forgot himself in the music* **for·gét·ful** *adj.* apt to forget [O.E. *forgietan*]

for·get-me-not (fərgétmi:nɒt) *n.* a low-growing plant of genus *Myosotis*, fam. *Borraginaceae*, esp. *M. palustris*

for·giv·a·ble, for·give·a·ble (fərgívəb'l) *adj.* that may be forgiven or pardoned **for·gív·a·bly** *adv.*

for·give (fərgív) *pres. part.* **for·giv·ing** *past* **for·gave** (fərgéiv) *past part.* **for·giv·en** (fərgívən) *v.t.* to excuse (a wrong or a wrongdoer), *nothing could forgive such rudeness* ‖ to pardon, *the victim forgave his attacker* ‖ to remit or cancel (a debt) ‖ *v.i.* to show or grant forgiveness or pardon **for·gíve·a·ble** *adj.* (Br.) *FORGIVABLE **for·gíve·ness** *n.* a forgiving or being forgiven **for·gív·ing** *adj.* willing to forgive, *a forgiving spirit* [O.E. *forgiefan*]

for·go, fore·go (fɔrgóu) *pres. part.* **for·go·ing, fore·go·ing** *past* **for·went, fore·went** (forwént) *past part.* **for·gone, fore·gone** (fɔrgɔ́n, forgón) *v.t.* to go without, renounce for oneself (e.g. a pleasure or satisfaction), *to forgo a holiday in order to finish a job* [O.E. *forgan*]

forgot *past* of FORGET

forgotten *past part.* of FORGET

for·int (fɔ́rint) *n.* the standard monetary unit of Hungary, consisting of 100 filler [Hung.]

fork (fɔrk) 1. *n.* an agricultural implement consisting of two or more prongs on a long handle and used for digging, carrying, picking up or pitching ‖ a pronged instrument for handling food, in cooking, serving or eating ‖ the place where something divides, e.g. a road into two roads, a tree trunk into branches, or the crotch of the human body ‖ one of the branches into which a river, road, tree etc. is divided ‖ a sharp point (e.g. of an arrow) ‖ a support with two prongs, *a bicycle fork* ‖ (*mus.*) a tuning fork 2. *v.i.* to divide or develop into branches, *we'll meet where the river forks* ‖ *v.t.* to form into the shape of a fork ‖ to pick up or pitch with a fork, *to fork hay* ‖ (*pop.*, with 'out', 'over' or 'up') to pay **forked** *adj.* Y-shaped, cleft, *a forked twig* ‖ zigzag, *forked lightning* [O.E. *forca*]

fork·lift (fɔ́rklift) *n.* a machine for lifting heavy objects by pushing a row of steel fingers under them and then raising them by hydraulic or other means, the steel fingers being withdrawn when the load is deposited

for·lorn (fərlɔ́rn) *adj.* hopeless, *a forlorn cry* ‖ deserted, forsaken, *a forlorn landscape* ‖ wretched-looking, pitiful, *a forlorn appearance* [past part. of O.E. *forlēosan*, to lose]

forlorn hope an undertaking with little chance of success [fr. Du. *verloren hoop*, lost troop]

form (fɔrm) *n.* shape ‖ outward appearance apart from color, esp. the essential structure of a thing, *a table has a very simple form* ‖ a person, animal or thing considered as a shape, *dim forms passed him in the mist* ‖ a variety, manifestation, example, *is tax evasion a form of dishonesty?* ‖ pattern ‖ the relationship of parts of a work of art in the organization of the whole, *Beethoven developed the concerto form* ‖ nature,

his speech was in the form of a bitter attack ‖ a document with blank spaces for information to be written in ‖ a long wooden seat or bench without a back ‖ (esp. *Br.*) a class in a school ‖ that which gives shape, a mold ‖ (*engin.*) a frame for holding assembled parts in place ‖ (*gram.*) one of the varieties of a word in spelling, pronunciation or inflection ‖ state of performance or training (physical or mental), *the swimmer's form was improving* ‖ behavior according to rule, custom, convention or etiquette, *it is polite form to shake hands when meeting a person* ‖ a formula, prescribed order or layout of words, or established practice or ritual ‖ (*philos.*) the formative principle, nature or essence of a thing as distinguished from the matter it is composed of ‖ (*Platonic philos.*) an idea ‖ (*Aristotelian and Scholastic philos.*) the principle which defines the kind or species of a thing ‖ (*logic*) the relation of propositions one to another ‖ (*printing, Br.* also **forme**) a body of type secured in a chase ‖ a hare's nest **a mere matter of form** an action performed for outward appearance only, without feeling or conviction **in due form** in the correct manner, *a document drawn up in due form* **in good form** witty ‖ in good spirits ‖ performing well, *the speaker was in good form tonight* **in top form** in good physical condition [O. F. *fourme*]

form *v.t.* to make, shape ‖ to put together, *to form a sentence* ‖ to mold by instruction or discipline, *to form someone's character* ‖ to develop, *to form a habit* ‖ to conceive, *to form an idea* ‖ to organize into or become arranged as, *to form a double file* ‖ to constitute, *five colleges formed the university* ‖ (*gram.*) to construct (a new word or a variant) by derivation etc. ‖ to assume the form of, *gasoline forms vapor above a certain temperature* ‖ *v.i.* to arise, to take form, *clouds began to form* ‖ (esp. *mil.*) to draw up, to assume formation, *the platoon formed into open order* [O.F. *fourmer*]

for·mal (fɔ́rməl) 1. *adj.* of or pertaining to form, rule or ceremonial, *formal speech, formal logic, formal dress* ‖ having form without spirit, perfunctory, *formal expressions of regret* ‖ explicit, not merely understood, *he gave his formal consent* ‖ (*philos.*) of the essence of a thing rather than its matter 2. *n.* a social event for which one has to wear formal dress [fr. L. *formalis*]

form·al·de·hyde (fɔrmǽldihaid) *n.* the aldehyde HCHO, a pungent colorless gas used in aqueous solution (*FORMALIN) as a disinfectant, as a preservative, and as a curing agent [FORMIC+ALDEHYDE]

For·ma·lin (fɔ́rməlin) *n.* an aqueous solution containing about 40% formaldehyde by volume and a small quantity of methanol [Trademark]

form·al·ism (fɔ́rməlizəm) *n.* strict adherence to prescribed forms, esp. in religion, art and literature **fór·mal·ist** *n.* someone characterized by formalism or who advocates formalism **for·mal·ís·tic** *adj.*

for·mal·i·ty (fɔrmǽliti:) *pl.* **for·mal·i·ties** *n.* conformity or attention to rule, custom or etiquette ‖ (esp. *pl.*) an official or customary requirement, *customs formalities* ‖ a merely formal act ‖ the quality of being formal [F. *formalité*]

form·al·ize (fɔ́rməlaiz) *pres. part.* **form·al·iz·ing** *past* and *past part.* **form·al·ized** *v.t.* to put on a legal, official or regular basis ‖ *v.i.* to act with formality

formal organization a complex social group, e.g., a college or government agency, whose objectives, rules, and roles are formally or specifically defined

for·mat (fɔ́rmæt) *n.* the linear measurements of a publication, often expressed in terms of the number of times the sheet was folded (octavo, quarto) to produce a page of the size chosen ‖ (*loosely*) the general typographical style and physical characteristics of a publication ‖ the general characteristics of organization of something, e.g. a radio program *v.* to produce in a special plan, size, shape, or proportion [F.]

for·ma·tion (fɔrméiʃən) *n.* a forming or being formed ‖ that which has been formed, *a biological formation* ‖ (*geol.*) rock beds sufficiently homogeneous to be regarded as a unit in geological mapping ‖ the form in which something is arranged, e.g. the arrangement of wild ducks on the wing ‖ an arrangement of troops, *battle formation* ‖ an arrangement of aircraft flying at small fixed intervals from one another [fr. L. *formatio (formationis)*]

form·a·tive (fɔ́rmətiv) 1. *adj.* serving to form, *the formative years of life* ‖ (*gram.*, of prefixes,

terminations etc.) serving to form words 2. *n.* (*gram.*) a formative element [O.F. *formatif*]

form book a written guide to racing form consulted before placing bets

form criticism a method of biblical criticism (originating in 19th-c. Germany) which classifies passages of scripture into aesthetic categories (myths, parables, songs, narrative etc.) and relates them to the historical period to which they can be dated

forme (*Br., printing*) *FORM

for·mé, for·mée (fɔ́rmei) *adj.* pattée

for·mer (fɔ́rmər) 1. *adj.* earlier, *in a former existence* ‖ of the first or first mentioned of two ‖ having once held a certain post or office, *the former prime minister* 2. *pron.* the first or first-mentioned of two (opp. LATTER) **fór·mer·ly** *adv.* at a time in the past [M.E. *formere*, comp. fr. O.E. superl. *formest*]

For·mi·ca (fɔrmáikə) *n.* a laminated plastic product used, e.g. for kitchen furniture [Trademark]

for·mic acid (fɔ́rmik) a colorless, volatile, irritant liquid acid, HCOOH, occurring in most ants and in some plants. It is usually produced synthetically and is used chiefly in the textile industry [fr. L. *formica*, ant]

for·mi·car·y (fɔ́rmikeri:) *pl.* **for·mi·car·ies** *n.* an ant nest [fr. M.L. *formicarium*]

for·mi·da·ble (fɔ́rmidəb'l, fɔrmídəb'l) *adj.* likely to prove hard, *a formidable task* or hard to overcome, *a formidable opponent* or hard to deal with, *a formidable mother-in-law* ‖ to be feared, *formidable powers* ‖ impressive, *a formidable display of scholarship* **fór·mi·da·bly** *adv.* [F.]

form·less (fɔ́rmlis) *adj.* without shape, amorphous ‖ needing better arrangement, *a formless essay* ‖ incorporeal, *formless shades*

form letter a stock letter whose wording provides the form to be used whenever the circumstances apply ‖ a printed or duplicated letter sent out in quantity

For·mo·sa (fɔrmóusə) *TAIWAN

for·mu·la (fɔ́rmjulə) *pl.* **for·mu·las, for·mu·lae** (fɔ́rmjuli:) *n.* (*chem.*) a symbolic representation of the composition, constitution or configuration of a substance ‖ (*logic, math.*) a statement expressed in symbols showing the relationships of interrelated facts ‖ a form of words defining a doctrine, principle etc. ‖ a verbal phrase or any set form accepted as conventional ‖ a form of words for ritual or ceremonial usage **for·mu·lar·i·zá·tion** *n.* **fór·mu·lar·ize** *pres. part.* **for·mu·lar·iz·ing** *past* and *past part.* **for·mu·lar·ized** *v.t.* [L., dim. of *forma*, form]

formula grant U.S. Government contract offered to fulfill a national need, usu. to nonprofit organizations

formula plan (*securities*) investment system for investing in equities at the lower level of a cycle and fixed-income securities at the upside of a cycle

for·mu·lar·y (fɔ́rmjuleri:) 1. *pl.* **for·mu·lar·ies** *n.* (*pharm.*) a book of formulas ‖ a collection of set forms of ritual, prayers etc. 2. *adj.* relating to formulas [fr. F. *formulaire*]

for·mu·late (fɔ́rmjuleit) *pres. part.* **for·mu·lat·ing** *past* and *past part.* **for·mu·lat·ed** *v.t.* to express (a doctrine, problem etc.) in a clear or systematic way ‖ to express in a formula **for·mu·lá·tion** *n.* a formulating or being formulated ‖ an expression resulting from formulating

for·mu·lism (fɔ́rmjulizəm) *n.* a strict or blind adherence to formulas **for·mu·lis·tic** *adj.*

for·mu·li·za·tion (fɔrmjulizéiʃən) *n.* a formulation

for·mu·lize (fɔ́rmjulaiz) *pres. part.* **for·mu·liz·ing** *past* and *past part.* **for·mu·lized** *v.t.* to formulate

for·my (fɔ́rmi:) *adj.* pattée

for·myl (fɔ́rmil) *n.* the radical HCO of formic acid

for·ni·cate (fɔ́rnikeit) *pres. part.* **for·ni·cat·ing** *past* and *past part.* **for·ni·cat·ed** *v.i.* to commit fornication [fr. L. *fornicare (fornicatus)* fr. *fornix*, brothel]

for·ni·ca·tion (fɔrnikéiʃən) *n.* voluntary sexual intercourse between an unmarried man and an unmarried woman (cf. ADULTERY) [O.F.]

for·ni·ca·tor (fɔ́rnikeitər) *n.* someone who commits fornication

for·nix (fɔ́rniks) *pl.* **for·ni·ces** (fɔrnisi:z) *n.* (*anat.*) an arch or fold, esp. as found in the cerebral hemispheres in man and in the higher mammals [L.]

For·rest (fɔ́rist, fɔ́rist), John, 1st Baron Forrest (1847–1918), Australian statesman and ex-

CONCISE PRONUNCIATION KEY: **(a)** æ, *cat*; ɑ, *car*; ɔ *fawn*; ei, *snake*. **(e)** e, *hen*; i:, *sheep*; iə, *deer*; ɛə, *bear*. **(i)** i, *fish*; ai, *tiger*; əː, *bird*. **(o)** o, *ox*; au, *cow*; ou, *goat*; u, *poor*; ɔi, *royal*. **(u)** ʌ, *duck*; u, *bull*; uː, *goose*; ə, *bacillus*; juː, *cube*. x, *loch*; θ, *think*; δ, *bother*; z, *Zen*; ʒ, *corsage*; dʒ, *savage*; ŋ, *orangutang*; j, *yak*; ʃ, *fish*; tʃ, *fetch*; 'l, *rabble*; 'n, *redden*. Complete pronunciation key appears inside front cover.

plorer. He led an expedition (1874) across Western Australia, of which he was the first prime minister (1890–1901)

For·res·tal (fɔ́ristəl, fɔ́ristəl, fɔ́ristɔl, fɔ́ristɔl), James Vincent (1892–1949), the first U.S. secretary of defense, a position created by the National Security Act of 1947

Forester (fɔ́ristər, fɔ́ristər), C(ecil) S(cott) (1899–1966), English writer, best known for his novels about Capt. Horatio Hornblower, such as 'A Ship of the Line' (1938). He also wrote 'Payment Deferred' (1926), 'The Gun' (1933), and 'The African Queen' (1935; film, 1952)

for·sake (fɔrséik) *pres. part.* **for·sak·ing** *past* **for·sook** (fɔrsúk) *past part.* **for·sak·en** (fɔrséikən) *v.t.* (*rhet.*) to desert, abandon || (*old-fash.*) to break off from, give up (esp. bad habits) **for·sák·en** *adj.* deserted [O.E. *forsacan*, to oppose, deny]

for·sooth (fɔrsú:θ) *adv.* (*archaic*) in truth, truly [O.E. *forsōth*]

For·ster (fɔ́rstər), Edward Morgan (1879–1970), English novelist. 'Howard's End' (1910) and 'A Passage to India' (1924) are probably the best known of his five novels. Forster belonged to the Bloomsbury group and he shares their attitude of agnostic liberal humanism, placing most value on individual sensitivity, esp. as expressed in personal relations. 'A Room with a View' also shows a satirical wit in the tradition of Jane Austen. His novels all affirm the need to respond freshly, sympathetically and honestly to people and to cultures, and abandon inhibiting prejudices (in particular the insularity, emotional shallowness and self-satisfied philistinism held to characterize the English middle classes). He also wrote short stories ('The Celestial Omnibus', 1911) and essays ('Abinger Harvest', 1936)

for·swear (fɔrswéər) *pres. part.* **for·swear·ing** *past* **for·swore** (fɔrswɔ́r) *past part.* **for·sworn** (fɔrswɔ́rn, fɔrswóurn) *v.t.* to reject or renounce with vehement protestation or on oath || **to forswear oneself** to commit perjury **for·swórn** *adj.* perjured [O.E. *forswerian*]

for·syth·i·a (fərsíθiə, fərsáiθiə) *n.* a cultivated shrub of fam. *Oleaceae*, native to China. Its bright yellow flowers form before the leaves [after W. *Forsyth* (1737–1804), Eng. botanist]

Fort (fɔr), Paul (1872–1960), French symbolist poet, author of 'Ballades françaises' (1897 and after)

fort (fɔrt, fourt) *n.* a fortified place occupied only by troops || (*hist.*) a fortified trading post **to hold the fort** to be responsible during the temporary absence of whoever is usually responsible [F.]

For·ta·le·za (fɔrtəléza) a port (pop. metropolitan area 2,884,000) of N. Brazil. Industries: textiles, food processing, lobster fishing. Exports: rubber, sugar, coffee, cotton, carnauba wax

Fortas (fóurtəs), Abe (1910–82), U.S. Supreme Court associate justice (1965–9). A lawyer, he was appointed to the court by Pres. Lyndon B. Johnson. Noted as a civil liberties activist, he argued for the poor's right to legal counsel in *Gideon v. Wainwright* (1962); his nomination to the chief justiceship in 1969 was thwarted by the Senate, and he resigned from the Court

Fort-de-France (fɔrdəfrɑ́s) the capital (pop. 98,807) and chief port of Martinique, on the west coast

forte (fɔrt, fourt) *n.* something in which a person particularly excels || (*fencing*) the stronger part of a sword blade, from hilt to middle (cf. FOIBLE) [fr. F. *fort*, strong]

for·te (fɔ́rtei, fɔ́rti:) (*mus.*, *abbr.* f, F) **1.** *adj.* loud, powerful **2.** *adv.* loudly, powerfully **3.** *n.* a passage played forte [Ital.]

For·tes·cue (fɔ́rtiskju:), Sir John (c. 1394– c. 1476), English jurist. In his 'The Governance of England' (c. 1471) he advocated that the king should be advised by a permanent staff of councilors. This reflected current Yorkist practice

Forth (fɔrθ, fourθ) a river and firth in E. central Scotland, rising near Aberfoyle and spanned by the Forth Bridge (a cantilever railroad bridge, 5,350 ft long, designed by Sir Benjamin Baker, completed 1889) at Queensferry and by a road bridge (completed 1964). Chief port: Leith

forth (fɔrθ, fourθ) *adv.* out from concealment or as if from concealment **and so forth**, and so on, et cetera **back and forth** backwards and forwards **from this** (or **that, which**) **time forth** from this (or that) time on

forth·com·ing (fɔrθkʌ́miŋ, fourθkʌ́miŋ) *adj.* approaching, *in the forthcoming weeks* || shortly to appear, *forthcoming publications* || made avail-

able when required, *the expected aid was not forthcoming* || (*Br.*) willing to give information or be sociable

forth·right (fɔ́rθrait, fóurθrait) *adj.* direct, frank, decisive

forth·with (fɔ́rθwiθ, fóurθwiθ, fɔ́rθwíθ, fóurθwiθ) *adv.* at once, immediately

for·ti·eth (fɔ́rti:iθ) **1.** *adj.* being number 40 in a series (*NUMBER TABLE*) || being one of the 40 equal parts of anything **2.** *n.* the person or thing next after the 39th || one of 40 equal parts of anything (1/40) [O.E. *fēowertigotha*]

for·ti·fi·ca·tion (fɔrtifikéiʃən) *n.* a fortifying or being fortified || the science of fortifying || something that fortifies || (*mil.*, esp. *pl.*) works constructed so as to fortify [F.]

for·ti·fy (fɔ́rtifai) *pres. part.* **for·ti·fy·ing** *past and past part.* **for·ti·fied** *v.t.* to strengthen structurally || (*mil.*) to strengthen (a defensive position etc.) against attack || to give moral strength to, encourage || to add nutritive value to, enrich || to strengthen (wine) with alcohol || *v.i.* (*mil.*) to build fortifications [fr. F. *fortifier*]

for·tis (fɔ́rtis) **1.** *adj.* (*phon.*, of a consonant) pronounced with strong articulation **2.** *pl.* **for·tes** (fɔ́rti:z) *n.* (*phon.*) such a consonant [L.= strong]

for·tis·si·mo (fɔrtísimou) (*mus.*, *abbr.* ff.) **1.** *adj.* very loud **2.** *adv.* very loudly **3.** *pl.* **for·tis·si·mos, for·tis·si·mi** (fɔrtísimi) *n.* a fortissimo passage [Ital. superl. of *forte*, loud, loudly]

for·ti·tude (fɔ́rtitu:d, fɔ́rtitju:d) *n.* endurance or courage in the face of pain or adversity || moral strength, one of the cardinal virtues [F.]

Fort Knox a military post in Kentucky, site of the U.S. gold bullion depository

Fort La·my (fɔrlæmi:) *N'DJAMENA

fort·night (fɔ́rtnait) *n.* (esp. *Br.*) a continuous period of two weeks **fort·night·ly 1.** *adj.* occurring or appearing once every two weeks **2.** *adv.* once every two weeks **3.** *pl.* **fort·night·lies** *n.* a periodical issued at intervals of two weeks [O.E. *fēowertyne niht*]

FORTRAN (computer acronym) formula translation, a computer programming language translatable into machine language, esp. to solve algebraic problems; designed by IBM

for·tress (fɔ́rtris) *n.* a fortified place, military stronghold [O.F. *forteresse*]

Fort Sum·ter (sʌ́mtər) a fort in Charleston harbor, South Carolina, where troops of the Confederacy fired the shots that began the American Civil War (Apr. 12, 1861)

for·tu·i·tous (fɔrtú:itəs, fɔrtjú:itəs) *adj.* happening by chance or accident **for·tú·i·ty** *pl.* **for·tu·i·ties** *n.* chance, accident || a chance occurrence [fr. L. *fortuitus*]

for·tu·nate (fɔ́rtʃunit) *adj.* owing to good luck or receiving good luck, lucky || favorable, *a fortunate choice* [fr. L. *fortunatus*]

for·tune (fɔ́rtʃən) *n.* the power of chance in mankind's affairs || an instance of how this affects someone, *it was his good fortune to be present at the time* || personal wealth, *to make a fortune* || a large sum of money, *it cost the firm a fortune* || success in general, *to seek one's fortune* || destiny, *to have one's fortune told* **a small fortune** (*pop.*, of the cost of something) a large amount of money [F.]

fortune hunter someone out to become rich without effort, esp. by a rich marriage

for·tune-tell·er (fɔ́rtʃəntelər) *n.* a person who claims to foretell the future and makes money out of the claim

Fort Wayne the third largest city (pop. 172,196) in Indiana, in the northeast part of the state: railroads, electrical equipment, hosiery, car wheels, motor trucks

Fort William *THUNDER BAY

Fort Worth (wə:rθ) a city (pop. 385,164, with agglom. 2,974,805) in Texas. It is the commercial center of the oil fields and agricultural and livestock area of N.W. Texas. Texas Christian University (1873)

for·ty (fɔ́rti:) **1.** *adj.* being ten more than 30 (*NUMBER TABLE*) **2.** *pl.* **for·ties** *n.* four times ten || the cardinal number representing this (40, XL) **the forties** (of temperature, a person's age, a century, etc.) the span 40–9 [O.E. *fēowertig*]

40 Committee a high-level U.S. review group to authenticate sensitive operations of the CIA. The 40 Committee was authorized during the Nixon Administration

'For·ty-five Rebellion (fɔrti:fáiv) (1745), the last Jacobite revolt in Britain

for·ty-nin·er (fɔrti:náinər) *n.* (*Am. hist.*) someone who joined in the California gold rush of 1849

forty winks (*pop.*) a brief sleep, esp. during the day

fo·rum (fɔ́rəm, fóurəm) *pl.* **fo·rums, fo·ra** (fɔ́rə, fóurə) *n.* (*Rom. hist.*) the marketplace or public square of a city, a center of judicial and public business || any place or institution where questions of public concern can be discussed or decided, *the United Nations is a forum of world opinion* **the Forum** an open space in ancient Rome between the Capitoline and Palatine hills, used for public business and political meetings

for·ward (fɔ́rwərd) **1.** *adj.* toward the front, *the forward battle area* || (of seasons) early || (of growth) advanced || precociously developed, *he is forward for his age* || showing substantial progress, *the book is well forward* || progressive, radical, *a forward outlook* || onward, advancing, *the forward march of science* || eager, prompt, *forward with offers of help* || overbold in a too familiar way || (*naut.*, fɔ́rəd) of the front (bow) section of a ship || (*commerce*, of goods etc. not immediately available) of or for the future, *a forward contract* or for future delivery, *forward buying* **2.** *adv.* towards the front, in the direction one is facing, ahead, *to run forward* || towards improvement or progress, *a general movement forward in world health* || in advance, *he sent scouts forward of the main body* || into prominence, into view, to the attention of someone, *to push oneself forward* || onward in time, *from that day forward* || (*naut.*) at the forepart of a ship **3.** *n.* (football, hockey etc.) one of the players positioned near or towards the opponents' goal, having an attacking, scoring function **4.** *v.t.* to send (a letter etc.) to a further destination || to convey, dispatch (goods etc.) || to advance, promote, *to forward a project* || (*bookbinding*) to trim, line and put (a sewn book) into its cover, ready for finishing **fór·ward·er** *n.* someone who forwards || someone who receives goods for transportation and delivers them to the carrier for transmission to the proper destination [O.E. *foreweard*]

forward pass (*football*) a pass in which the ball is thrown from behind the line of scrimmage towards the opponent's goal

for·wards (fɔ́rwərdz) *adv.* (of a direction or movement) forward

forwent *past of* FORGO

for·zan·do (fɔrtsándou) *adj. and adv.* (*mus.*, *abbr.* fz.) sforzando [Ital.]

Fos·co·lo (fɔ́skɔlɔ), Ugo (1778–1827), Italian poet. His works include 'Dei Sepolcri' (1807), 'Sonetti' (1802) and the unfinished 'Le Grazie' (1815). He also wrote the novel 'Ultime Lettere di Jacopo Ortis' (1802) and some excellent criticism. He was a political exile in England from 1816

FOSDIC (computer acronym) film optical scanning device for input to computers, a device that reads forms to produce recorded magnetic tape suitable for computer input; designed by the U.S. Bureau of Standards and Bureau of the Census

fos·sa (fɔ́sə) *pl.* **fos·sae** (fɔ́si:) *n.* (*anat.*) a groove or depression, *the temporal fossa of the skull* [L.=a ditch]

fosse (fɔs, fɔs) *n.* a ditch or moat, esp. in fortification || (*anat.*) a fossa [F.]

fos·sette (fɔsét, fɔsét) *n.* a little hollow || a dimple [F.]

fos·sil (fɔ́s'l) **1.** *n.* the recognizable remains, or an impression left by them, of a plant or animal of the remote, geological past, preserved in the earth's crust || (*pop.*) someone or something out of date, esp. a person holding outworn opinions **2.** *adj.* of the nature of a fossil **fos·sil·á·tion** *n.* **fos·sil·if·er·ous** *adj.* containing fossils, rich in fossils **fos·sil·i·zá·tion** *n.* **fos·sil·ize** *pres. part.* **fos·sil·iz·ing** *past and past part.* **fos·sil·ized** *v.t.* to make a fossil of || *v.i.* to become a fossil || to become set in outworn opinions [F. *fossile*]

fos·so·ri·al (fɔsɔ́riəl, fɔsóuriəl) *adj.* (*zool.*) burrowing || (*zool.*) adapted for digging or burrowing [fr. L. *fossorius*]

Fos·ter (fɔ́stər, fɔ́stər), Stephen Collins (1826–64), American composer. Among his best-known songs are 'Oh! Susannah' (1848), 'My Old Kentucky Home' (1853) and 'Old Black Joe' (1860)

fos·ter (fɔ́stər, fɔ́stər) *v.t.* to rear || to encourage, promote (ideas, feelings, plants etc.) || to harbor, nurse (ambitions etc.) in oneself [O.E. *fostor, fōstrian*]

fos·ter·age (fɔ́stəridʒ, fɔ́stəridʒ) *n.* the act of fostering a child (or an idea etc.) || the state of being a foster child

---

foster brother a boy in relation to his foster parents' child or foster child [O.E. *fóster-bróthor*]

foster care (*administration*) the care of children, sick or aged people in supervised homes or institutions by statutory or voluntary welfare organizations

foster child a boy or girl in relation to his or her foster parents [O.E. *fóstercild*]

foster father a male foster parent [O.E. *fósterfœder*]

foster home (*administration*) a household in which a child or a sick or aged person is placed by a statutory or voluntary organization

fos·ter·ling (fóstərliŋ, fóstərliŋ) *n.* a foster child [O.E. *fóstorling*]

foster mother a female foster parent [O.E. *fóstermódor*]

foster parent a man or woman acting as father or mother to a child who is not his or her offspring, nor a stepchild, and not legally adopted

foster sister a girl in relation to her foster parents' child or foster child

Fou·cauld (fu:kou), Charles Eugène de (1858–1916), French explorer of Morocco and missionary in the Sahara. His writings include a Tuareg-French dictionary and 'Écrits spirituels' (1923). He died by assassination

Fou·cault (fu:kou), Jean Bernard Léon (1819–68), French physicist. He used a method for measuring the velocity of light which enabled him to prove that the velocity is less in water than in air, thus finally disposing (1850) of the corpuscular theory. Using a long, heavy pendulum, he demonstrated the rotation of the earth on its axis (1851). He invented the gyroscope (1852)

Fou·ché (fu:ʃei), Joseph (1759–1820), French minister of police (1799–1802, 1804–10 and 1815–16). An extreme Jacobin, he put down a revolt in Lyon (1793) with great brutality. He served both Napoleon and Louis XVIII as minister of police, establishing an elaborate spy system

Foucquet *FOUQUET, Nicolas

fought *past* and *past part.* of FIGHT

foul (faul) *v.t.* to make foul ‖ to pollute ‖ to bring dishonor on ‖ to block or choke with foreign matter ‖ to jam (e.g. a road crossing) ‖ to tangle ‖ to come into collision with ‖ (*baseball*) to bat (a ball) outside the foul lines ‖ *v.i.* to become foul ‖ to become entangled ‖ to collide ‖ (*sports*) to commit a foul **to foul out** (*baseball*) to be put out by the catch of a foul ball **to foul up** (*pop.*) to make a mess of [O.E *fúlian*]

foul 1. *adj.* extremely offensive to the senses, dirty, disgusting, stinking ‖ polluted with noxious matter, *foul air* ‖ (of a gun barrel, ship's bottom etc.) clogged up or covered with foreign matter ‖ entangled ‖ in collision ‖ indecent or profane, *foul language* ‖ obnoxious, unpleasant, *a foul taste, a foul mood* ‖ morally repulsive, evil ‖ (*sports*) contrary to the rules of the game ‖ (*baseball*) outside the foul lines ‖ (of weather) stormy ‖ (of wind or tide) contrary ‖ defaced by alterations, *a foul text* **to fall foul of** to come into collision with ‖ (of persons) to come into conflict with **2.** *n.* a collision esp. of boats ‖ an entanglement ‖ (*sports*) an act forbidden by the rules ‖ (*baseball*) a foul ball [O.E. *fúl*]

fou·lard (fu:lárd) *n.* a thin soft silk or silk and cotton material used for ties, scarves, trimmings etc. ‖ a scarf or tie of this material [F.]

foul ball (*baseball*) a ball batted outside the foul lines

foul line (*baseball*) either of two straight lines extending from home plate through the outer corners of first and third base and prolonged to the end of the outfield ‖ (*basketball*) the line from where a player who has been fouled takes a free shot ‖ (*bowling*) the line which a player must not step over when releasing the ball

foul·mouthed (fáulmauðd, fáulmauθt) *adj.* swearing frequently or using obscene language

foul play criminal violence ‖ (*sports*) play against the rules

foul shot (*basketball*) a free throw at the basket awarded as a penalty

foul tip (*baseball*) a ball which glances off the bat. The batter is out on a foul tip if he has two strikes against him and the catcher catches the ball

found (faund) *v.t.* to melt and pour (metal) into a mold ‖ to cast (an object) by this process ‖ to

melt or fuse (ingredients for glassmaking) ‖ to make (glass) by doing this [fr. F. *fondre*]

found *v.t.* to originate, *to found a firm* ‖ to establish (an institution) by endowment ‖ to begin the building of ‖ (with 'on' or 'upon') to base [F. *fonder*]'

found *past* and *past part.* of FIND **all** (or **everything) found** with free board and lodging provided

foun·da·tion (faundéiʃən) *n.* a founding or being founded ‖ the solid base, either natural or prepared from concrete etc. on which a building is raised ‖ the lowest courses of a wall, building etc., usually underground ‖ the establishment and endowment of an institution ‖ an endowed institution or endowed charity or fund ‖ a basis, esp. a basis of truthfulness ‖ an underlying principle, *the foundations of evolutionary belief* ‖ the body or ground material on which something is overlaid, e.g. material to stiffen a dress ‖ a foundation garment ‖ a liquid or cream cosmetic used as the base for makeup **on the foundation** (*Br.*) entitled to benefit by the funds or income of an endowed institution [fr. L. *fundatio* (*fundationis*)]

Foundation Day an Australian public holiday (Jan. 26) to commemorate the landing (1788) of the British at Sydney Cove

foun·da·tion·er (faundéiʃənər) *n.* (*Br.*) a student at an endowed school or college who has won an award from its funds

foundation garment a supporting undergarment (girdle or corset)

foundation member (*Br.*) a charter member

foundation stone a stone laid with public ceremony and bearing an inscription, to commemorate the beginning of an important new building

found·er (fáundər) *n.* someone who founded or helped to found an institution

founder *n.* a person who founds or casts metal or glass

founder 1. *v.i.* (of a building etc.) to fall down, collapse ‖ to go lame, stumble ‖ to sink or stick fast in soft ground ‖ to fail, esp. financially ‖ (of a ship) to become filled with water and sink ‖ (of a horse) to have founder ‖ *v.t.* to cause to founder ‖ (*vet.*) to cause (a horse) to become afflicted with founder **2.** *n.* inflammation of sensitive tissue in a horse's hoof [O.F. *fondrer*]

founders' shares (esp. *Br.*) shares issued to the original shareholders of a public company, often carrying special voting privileges and sometimes receiving a special dividend after the payment of an agreed minimum dividend on ordinary shares

Founding Father (*Am. hist.*) a member of the Constitutional Convention of 1787

found·ling (fáundliŋ) *n.* an abandoned infant [M.E. *fundeling* fr. *funden*, to find]

found object an object either discarded by a person or left by nature (sea shells, driftwood) that has collector interest or aesthetic qualities

found poem prose with unintended poetic content, e.g., 'and hence no force, however great, can draw a cord, however fine, into a horizontal line which shall be absolutely straight'

found·ress (fáundris) *n.* a woman founder

found·ry (fáundri:) *pl.* **found·ries** *n.* a building where metal or glass is founded ‖ the art or process of casting metals ‖ metal castings [F. *fonderie*]

fount (faunt) *n.* (*rhet.*) a source, spring or fountain, *a fount of wisdom* [fr. F. *font*]

fount (*Br., printing*) a font

foun·tain (fáuntən) *n.* a water spring ‖ the source or head of a stream etc. ‖ a contrived ornamental jet of water, e.g. in a courtyard, garden or public square ‖ a jet of drinking water, e.g. in a park or station ‖ the structure containing a jet of water ‖ a soda fountain [M.E. *fontayne* fr. O.F.]

foun·tain·head (fáuntənhed) *n.* the main source of a stream ‖ a person or thing regarded as the originator of something

fountain pen a pen containing a reservoir of ink fed to the nib as the pen is used

Fou·quet (fu:kei), Jean (c. 1420–c. 1480), French painter and miniaturist. He visited Italy in his youth, and learned Italian techniques of modeling and the representation of light effects. His miniatures, portraits and altarpieces are remarkable for their realistic treatment of people and landscapes. His Book of Hours for Étienne Chevalier (c. 1457) is one of the masterpieces of illumination. Little of his

work is documented and attributions are on grounds of style

Fou·quet, Fouc·quet (fu:kei), Nicolas (1615–80), French minister of finance (1653–61) and friend of Mazarin, overthrown by Colbert

Fou·quier-Tin·ville (fu:kjætẽvi:l), Antoine Quentin (1746–95), French revolutionist. As public prosecutor (1793–4) under the Terror, he sent hundreds to the guillotine, including Desmoulins, Danton and Marie-Antoinette. He himself was guillotined after the fall of Robespierre

four (fɔr, four) **1.** *adj.* being one more than three (*NUMBER TABLE) **2.** *n.* twice two ‖ the cardinal number representing this (4, IV) ‖ four o'clock ‖ a playing card (domino etc.) marked with four symbols ‖ four people together engaged in a game or sport, *a bridge four, tennis four* ‖ (*cricket*) a hit from which four runs are scored or made ‖ a team of four members, esp. in rowing ‖ (*pl.*) races for four-oared boats **on all fours** with hands and knees on the ground [O.E. *féower*]

four-di·men·sion·al (fɔrdiménʃən'l, fóurdiménʃən'l) *adj.* having four dimensions (*FOURTH DIMENSION)

four-flush (fɔrflʌʃ, fóurflʌʃ) *v.i.* (*pop.*) to make a false claim, bluff **four-flush·er** *n.* a bluffer ‖ a humbug [fr. poker term: to pretend one has five of a suit when in fact one has four]

four-fold table (fɔrfould) (*math.*) a table containing four cells formed by the cross tabulation of two variables, each having two values or categories

four-foot·ed (fɔrfútid, fóurfútid) *adj.* of a quadruped

Four Freedoms, the the four sorts of liberty essential to human dignity proclaimed by F. D. Roosevelt (Jan. 6, 1941): freedom of speech and expression, freedom of worship, freedom from want, freedom from fear

Four-H Club (or **4-H Club**) an organization for teaching modern farming methods to young people. The clubs are sponsored by the U.S. Department of Agriculture [Head, Heart, Hands, Health, all being meant to benefit]

four-hand·ed (fɔrhǽndid, fóurhǽndid) *adj.* (of certain games) requiring four players ‖ (*mus.*) for two players at one keyboard ‖ quadrumanous

Four Hundred a U.S. idiom meaning a select group. It was created (1892) by Samuel Ward McAllister (1827–95), a U.S. socialite, when, in shortening a list for a ball, he boasted that there were 'only about 400 people in New York society'

Fou·rier (fu:rjei), Charles (1772–1837), French philosopher and economist. In place of society as he found it, he advocated small colonies ('phalansteries' of about 1,800, with property held in common) of selected groups of individuals, each contributing to the welfare of all through the harmonious cooperation of their divergent gifts and temperaments, and each assuring his own well-being in this way. He believed that in such conditions men would work willingly. The ideas were enthusiastically taken up outside France, esp. in the U.S.A. after 1840. The colonies started by disciples failed

Fourier, Jean Baptiste Joseph, Baron de (1768–1830), French physicist, mathematician and politician, important for his theorem that any periodic function may be resolved into sine and cosine terms

Fourier analysis a mathematical method used in the solution of physical problems that involves the development of a complex periodic function into a series of sine and cosine functions whose coefficients are computed by integration. The method is widely used for the solution of analytic expressions associated with electrical circuits, heat transfer and atomic vibrations (*HARMONIC ANALYSIS)

Fou·ri·er·ism (fúəri:ərizəm) *n.* the system advocated by Charles Fourier **Fou·ri·er·ist** *n.*

four-in-hand (fɔrinhænd, fóurinhænd) *n.* a vehicle driven by one person and drawn by four horses ‖ a necktie tied with a slipknot

four-leaf clover (fɔrli:f, fóurli:f) a leaf of the clover plant having four lobes instead of three. It is said to bring luck to someone who finds one growing

Fournier, Alain *ALAIN-FOURNIER

four-o'clock (fɔrəklɒk, fóurəklɒk) *n.* *Mirabilis jalapa*, fam. *Nyctaginaceae*, a common American garden plant. Its flowers open in the evening and are protogynous

---

CONCISE PRONUNCIATION KEY: **(a)** æ, c*a*t; ɑ, c*a*r; ɔ f*aw*n; ei, sn*a*ke; i:, sh*ee*p; iə, d*ee*r; ɛə, b*ea*r. **(i)** i, f*i*sh; ai, t*i*ger; ə:, b*i*rd. **(o)** o, *o*x; au, c*ow*; ou, g*oa*t; u, p*oo*r; ɔi, r*oy*al. **(u)** ʌ, d*u*ck; u, b*u*ll; u:, g*oo*se; ə, b*a*cillus; ju:, c*u*be. x, lo*ch*; θ, *th*ink; ð, bo*th*er; z, *Z*en; ʒ, cor*s*age; dʒ, sava*ge*; ŋ, orangutan*g*; j, *y*ak; ʃ, *fi*sh; tʃ, fe*tch*; 'l, rabb*le*; 'n, redd*en*. Complete pronunciation key appears inside front cover.

four·pence (fórpəns, fóurpəns) *n.* the sum of four British pennies or pence ‖ a silver maundy coin of this nominal value

four·pen·ny (fórpəni:, fóurpəni:) 1. *adj.* worth four pennies or pence 2. *n.* a bus ticket or other object priced at this

four·plex (fórpleks) *n.* an apartment on four levels

four·post·er (fórpóustər, fóurpóustər) *n.* an old-fashioned bed with tall posts at the corners used to support a canopy and usually curtains

Four-Power Pact an agreement (1921) reached by Great Britain, France, Japan, and the U.S.A. at the Washington Conference (1921–2), to respect mutually their Pacific island possessions and to consult one another if controversy arose

four·score (fórskór, fóurskóur) *adj.* (*old-fash.*) eighty

four·some (fórsəm, fóursəm) *n.* (*golf*) a game between two pairs of players, each pair sharing a ball ‖ (*pop.*) a group of four persons

four·square (fórskwéər, fóurskwéər) 1. *adj.* square-shaped ‖ correctly aligned ‖ firm and forthright 2. *adv.* squarely and solidly ‖ forthrightly

four·star (fórstər, fóurstər) *adj.* of the rank of general or admiral

four star *adj.* rated as of the highest quality, e.g., *a four-star restaurant*

four·stroke (fórstrouk, fóurstrouk) *adj.* of the type of internal-combustion engine, or its cycle of operations, in which the pistons make four movements corresponding to intake, compression and ignition, combustion and expansion, and exhaust

four·teen (fórtí:n, fóurtí:n) 1. *adj.* being one more than 13 (*NUMBER TABLE) 2. *n.* 10 plus four ‖ the cardinal number representing this (14, XIV) [O.E. *fēowertēne*]

Fourteen Points President Wilson's statement (Jan. 8, 1918) of a liberal basis for a possible peace settlement of the lst world war, founded on democracy and self-determination

14th Amendment (1868), provision of the U.S. Constitution that assured citizenship, personal liberties, and rights to the freed slaves. It guaranteed due process of law and equality under protection of the law. It also was concerned with representation in Congress and the holding of public office by Southerners involved in the Civil War

four·teenth (fórtí:nθ, fóurtí:nθ) 1. *adj.* being number 14 in a series (*NUMBER TABLE) ‖ being one of the 14 equal parts of anything 2. *n.* the person or thing next after the 13th ‖ one of 14 equal parts of anything (1/14) ‖ the 14th day of a month [O.E. *fēowertēotha*]

Fourteenth of July the anniversary of the fall of the Bastille (1789), a national holiday in France (*FRENCH REVOLUTION)

fourth (fɔrθ, fourθ) 1. *adj.* being number four in a series (*NUMBER TABLE) ‖ being one of the four equal parts of anything ‖ of or pertaining to the gear immediately above third in some vehicles 2. *n.* the person or thing next after the third ‖ a quarter, a fourth part (¼) ‖ (*Br.*) a grading in the fourth class of an examination ‖ a fourth prize in a race or other contest ‖ the gear immediately above third in some vehicles ‖ the fourth day of a month ‖ (*mus.*) the note four steps above or below a given note in a diatonic scale, inclusive of both notes ‖ (*mus.*) the interval between these notes 3. *adv.* in the fourth place ‖ (followed by a superlative) except three, *the fourth biggest* [O.E. *feortha*]

4th Amendment (1789), provision of the Bill of Rights of the U.S. Constitution that guarantees the right to privacy and freedom from unreasonable search and seizure. Originally written into the Bill of Rights to protest the Writs of Assistance, it has come to include all forms of invasion of privacy

fourth dimension (*math.*) the dimension (time) added in the space-time continuum to the three spatial dimensions (*RELATIVITY)

fourth·ly (fórθli:, fóurθli:) *adv.* (in enumerations) in the fourth place

fourth market (*securities*) sale of unlisted securities directly to investors *Cf* THIRD MARKET

Fourth of July the anniversary of the Declaration of lndependence (1776), a national holiday in the U.S.A.

Fourth World developing countries with very low per capita incomes, little expectation of economic growth, and few natural resources, esp. the list of 29 least developed countries identi-

fied by the United Nations in 1971 as being the poorest

four-wheel (fórhwí:l, fóurhwí:l, fórwí:l, fóurwí:l) *adj.* functioning on each of the four wheels of a vehicle, *four-wheel drive* ‖ having four wheels

Fou·ta Djal·lon (fóutæ dʒǽlɔn)(Futa Jallon) a mountainous district (Tamgué, 4,200 ft) in W. Guinea. The Niger and Senegal Rivers rise here

fo·ve·a (fóuvi:ə) *pl.* **fo·ve·ae** (fóuvi:i:) *n.* (*anat.*) a small pit or depression [L.]

fo·ve·a cen·tral·is (fóuvi:əsentrǽlis) *n.* a small pit or depression of the retina where vision is most acute

fowl (faul) *pl.* **fowl, fowls** 1. *n.* a domestic cock, hen, duck or turkey 2. *v.i.* to hunt wildfowl [O.E. *fugol*]

fowl cholera an acute contagious disease in domestic poultry and wild birds caused by the bacterium *Pasteurella multocida* (or *P. avicida*)

Fow·ler (fáulər), Henry Watson (1858–1933), English lexicographer. He compiled a number of standard works on the English language, including 'The King's English' (1906) and 'The Concise Oxford Dictionary of Current English' (1911), both works in collaboration with his brother F. G. Fowler, and his outstanding individual work 'A Dictionary of Modern English Usage' (1926)

Fow·liang (fóuljáŋ) (formerly Kingtehchen) a town (pop. 92,000) in N. Kiangsi province, China. The presence of kaolin east of Lake Poyang led to the establishment of its porcelain industry (6th c. A.D.) which flourished under the Sung dynasty. The Ming dynasty established the Imperial porcelain works (1369)

fowl·ing (fáuliŋ) *n.* wildfowling

fowling piece a light gun used esp. for hunting wildfowl

fowl pest an infectious virus disease of domestic poultry and many wild birds

fowl plague fowl pest

fowl pox a virus disease of chickens, turkeys, etc.

Fox (fɔks), Charles James (1749–1806), British statesman. Elected to parliament (1768) as a supporter of North, he joined the Rockingham Whigs (1774) in opposition to North's American policy. Apart from brief periods as foreign secretary (1782–3 and 1806), his long parliamentary career was spent in opposition. A brilliant orator, he upheld the principles of the French Revolution and the cause of parliamentary reform, and attacked slavery

Fox, George (1624–91), English religious leader, founder of the Society of Friends (Quakers). In revolt against Calvinism and against the externals of religious expression, he preached the perfectibility of all men through inward personal experience. His 'Journal' is the classic expression of his faith. After the revelation which came to him in 1647, he began to preach widely in England and, after 1671, in the West Indies, North America, and the Netherlands

Fox, William (1879–1952), U.S. film producer and distributor. His holdings, including a production company, an exhibition company, and a chain of movie theaters, were valued (1929) at $300 million

fox (fɔks) 1. *pl.* **fox·es, fox** *n.* a mammal of fam. *Canidae*, esp. genus *Vulpes*. They are carnivores, closely related to dogs, but with a more elongated body. The muzzle is slender and pointed, the ears are large and erect, and the tail is bushy. Species are found in most parts of the world, except South America, but esp. in the northern hemisphere. They raid farmyards for chickens etc. They also destroy small game ‖ the fur of this animal ‖ someone cunning or full of guile **Fox** *pl.* **Foxes, Fox** an Indian people of the Fox River valley, Wisconsin ‖ a member of this people ‖ their Algonquian language 2. *v.t.* (*pop.*) to trick, baffle, *that foxed you!* ‖ to discolor, stain (manuscripts, prints, leaves of a book) with specks of brown, esp. through dampness ‖ to renew (the upper leather of a shoe) ‖ *v.i.* (of papers, book leaves etc.) to become discolored [O.E.]

fox and geese a board game in which a player with 16 pegs (geese), free only to move forward, tries to corner a solitary peg (the fox) free to move forward or backward ‖ a similar game played on the checkerboard, with four pieces against one

Foxe (fɔks), John (c. 1516–87), English martyrologist. His monumental work 'History of the Acts and Monuments of the Church' (1563), a defense esp. of Protestant reformers, became popular as 'Foxe's Book of Martyrs'

Foxe Basin a body of water (300 miles long, 200–250 miles wide) between Melville Peninsula and Baffin Is., Northwest Territories, Canada, joining the Hudson Bay through the Foxe Channel (200 miles long, 90–200 miles wide)

Foxe Channel *FOXE BASIN

foxed (fɔkst) *adj.* discolored with brown stains, esp. through dampness

fox·glove (fɔksglʌv) *n.* digitalis (flower)

fox·hole (fɔkshoul) *n.* (*mil.*) a hole used as shelter or as a firing point during a battle

fox·hound (fɔkshaund) *n.* a dog of a large, strong, keen-scented, swift breed trained for hunting foxes, hunting in packs

fox hunt the pursuit on horseback of a fox, using hounds **fox-hunt** (fɔkshʌnt) *v.i.* to hunt foxes in this way

fox·i·ly (fɔksili:) *adv.* in a foxy way

fox·i·ness (fɔksi:nis) *n.* the quality of being foxy

fox·ing (fɔksiŋ) *n.* a piece of leather used for mending the upper of a shoe, or for decorating it

Fox-Jet a 4- to 6-seat twin-turbofan transport (St 600 5/8) introduced in 1980 by Foxjet International

fox·tail (fɔksteil) *n.* the tail of a fox ‖ a grass with brushlike spikes, esp. of genus *Alopecurus*, fam. *Gramineae*

fox terrier a small, lively wirehaired or smooth-haired breed of dog used for driving foxes from their earth, but also very popular as a pet

fox-trot (fɔkstrɔt) 1. *n.* a ballroom dance, in duple time, characterized by slow walking and quick running steps ‖ the music for such a dance 2. *v.i. pres. part.* **fox-trot·ting** *past* and *past part.* **fox-trot·ted** to dance the fox-trot

fox·y (fɔksi:) *comp.* **fox·i·er** *superl.* **fox·i·est** *adj.* foxlike, full of guile, wily in ways or looks, *a foxy lawyer* ‖ reddish-brown ‖ mildewy, stained with spots of brown ‖ (of wine or beer) sour ‖ (*sexist slang*) sexy, as describing a woman

foy·er (fɔiər, fɔiei) *n.* an entrance hall esp. in a theater or concert hall [F.]

fps *FOOT-POUND-SECOND

fra·cas (fréikəs, *Br.* frǽkɑ) *pl.* **fra·cas·es**, *Br.* **fra·cas** (frǽkɑz) *n.* a noisy disturbance, brawl, row [F.]

frac·tion (frǽkʃən) 1. *n.* a very small proportion, *only a fraction of the truth* ‖ an amount less than the whole, a part, *a large fraction of the electorate* ‖ (*math.*) a noninteger quantity expressed in terms of a numerator and a denominator (e.g. 3/4) or in decimal form (e.g. 0.75) (*DECIMAL FRACTION, *IMPROPER FRACTION, *PROPER FRACTION, *VULGAR FRACTION) ‖ (*chem.*) a part of a component that may be separated by fractionation 2. *v.t.* to separate into fractions **frác·tion·al** *adj.* (*math.*) pertaining to fractions, *a fractional expression* ‖ of that which is a fraction, esp. a small fraction, *a fractional risk of failure* ‖ (*chem.*) of any process of fractionation, *fractional distillation of petroleum* **frac·tion·ate** (frǽkʃəneit) *pres. part.* **frac·tion·at·ing** *past* and *past part.* **frac·tion·at·ed** *v.t.* to separate (a mixture or substance) into smaller portions having different properties by distillation, precipitation etc. **frac·tion·á·tion** *n.* **frác·tion·ize** *pres. part.* **frac·tion·iz·ing** *past* and *past part.* **frac·tion·ized** *v.t.* to divide into fractions [O.F. *fraccion*, a breaking]

fractional orbital bombardment system strategy for orbiting a nuclear warhead and delivering it by aborting its orbit over the target

fractionation 1. (*mil.*) capability of carrying many small warheads on a single ICBM, limited to 10 per launcher by SALT II 2. (*business*) the practice of charging separately for several services or components of a service that were previously subject to a single charge or free of charge, in order to increase a total fee

frac·tious (frǽkʃəs) *adj.* with frequent outbreaks of temper, peevish, unruly [fr. FRACTION, (*obs.*) a brawling]

frac·ture (frǽktʃər) 1. *n.* a breaking or being broken ‖ a break in a bone or cartilage (*COMPOUND FRACTURE, *SIMPLE FRACTURE) ‖ (*geol.*) the surface revealed in a stone sample broken along other than cleavage planes, *a conchoidal fracture* 2. *v. pres. part.* **frac·tur·ing** *past* and

past part. **frac·tured** *v.t.* to break ‖ *v.i.* to be liable to break ‖ to become broken [F.]
fraenulum *FRENULUM
fraenum *FRENUM
frag (fræg) *v.* to deliver a fragmentation grenade in order to deliberately injure an officer
fragging *v.*
frag·ile (frædʒəl, *Br.* frædʒail) *adj.* easily broken or damaged ‖ (of health) delicate **fra·gil·i·ty** (frədʒíliti) *n.* [F.]
frag·ment (frægmənt) *n.* a piece broken off from the whole ‖ an incomplete or isolated part, *he could remember only fragments of what happened* ‖ the existing part of something unfinished or incomplete, esp. of a writing or work of art **frag·men·tal** (frægmént'l) *adj.* fragmentary ‖ (*geol.*) clastic **frag·men·tar·y** (frægmənteri) *adj.* composed of broken parts ‖ dissociated, broken up, *fragmentary conversation* **frag·men·tá·tion** *n.* a breaking into fragments [F.]
fragmentation bomb a bomb whose rather thick walls splinter upon explosion
Fra·go·nard (frægonær), Jean Honoré (1732–1806) French painter. He showed in much of his painting a delicate but pronounced eroticism. Watteau's idealized outdoor tableaux become in Fragonard less poignant, and more frivolous, while remaining aristocratically ironic
fra·grance (fréigrəns) *n.* sweetness of scent ‖ a sweet scent [O.F.]
fra·grant (fréigrənt) *adj.* having a delicious smell ‖ (*rhet.*, of the past) delectable, *fragrant memories*
frail (freil) *adj.* easily broken, fragile ‖ feeble, *frail arguments* ‖ morally weak, *frail humanity* [fr. O.F. *fraile, frele*]
frail *n.* a rush basket for the shipping of figs or raisins ‖ the quantity held by such a basket [O.F. *frayel*]
frail·ty (fréilti) *pl.* **frail·ties** *n.* moral weakness ‖ an example of this, a shortcoming [fr. O.F. *fraileté*]
fraise (freiz) *n.* a tool for enlarging a circular hole in stone ‖ a tool for cutting or correcting teeth in watch wheels ‖ a style of neck ruff ‖ (*fortification*) a horizontal or inclined defense of pointed stakes around ramparts [F.]
fram·be·sia, fram·boe·sia (fræmbí:ʒə) *n.* yaws [Mod. L.]
frame (freim) **1.** *n.* an arrangement of parts fitted together, holding something in place or keeping the form of something unchanged, e.g. the supporting skeleton of a building or the rigid tubular structure of a bicycle ‖ (*shipbuilding*) any one of the skeletal structures making up the ribs ‖ an ideal or established order, *the frame of society* ‖ the build of a person, *a large frame to feed* ‖ a cold frame ‖ a single exposure in the run of exposures of a film or filmstrip ‖ (*television*) one isolated image in the succession of images transmitted ‖ a border of wood or other material put around a picture or mirror ‖ (*computer*) the time required to transmit a package of data ‖ the basic unit of programmed instruction for a student ‖ a punch position or recording on a tape, etc. ‖ (*embroidery*) an adjustable structure for keeping work taut ‖ (*pool, snooker*) a triangular form used in setting up the balls, or the balls themselves while still arranged in a triangle, or the period of play while the balls are being pocketed ‖ (*bowling*) the period of play from when the pins have been set up to when they are set up again: 10 frames make a game ‖ (*beekeeping*) a structure put in the hive for the bees to build their honeycombs in **2.** *v.t. pres. part.* **fram·ing** *past* and *past part.* **framed** to surround with a frame, or as if with one ‖ to assemble (ideas etc.) in an orderly way, *to frame a plan* ‖ to devise, *to frame a method* ‖ to formulate, *to frame a reply* ‖ to make a structure for, *to frame a roof* ‖ (*pop.*) to place (someone) in an incriminating position by falsifying the evidence ‖ (*movies*) to bring (an image) into register with the projector aperture [O.E. *framian*, to further]
frame house a wooden house, the wooden walls being nailed on a wooden frame
frame of mind a temporary mental attitude
frame of reference a set of references (axes) by which position in space can be described ‖ a set of instructions, rules etc. providing a standard with reference to which some particular matter, situation etc. can be assessed, delimited etc. ‖ context or evaluative presuppositions in which an activity occurs
frame of reference context or evaluative presuppositions within which an activity occurs

frame-shift (fréimʃift) *n.* (*genetics*) mutation in which triplet codons are not correctly translated
frame-up (fréimʌp) *n.* (*pop.*) a machination intended to involve an innocent person in a crime or offense
frame-work (fréimwə:rk) *n.* a basic structure which supports and gives shape, or a broad outline plan etc. thought of as having a similar function
fram·ing (fréimiŋ) *n.* the material out of which picture frames etc. are made ‖ the act or process of providing with a frame ‖ a framework
framing chisel a heavy chisel used in making mortises
franc (fræŋk) *n.* the monetary unit of France, Belgium, Switzerland, Luxembourg and certain African countries which were formerly French or Belgian colonies ‖ a coin worth one franc [F.]
Fran·çaise, Pointe (pwĕtfrãsez) a cape at the northwest tip of French Guiana
franc CFA the basic monetary unit of certain former French colonies in Africa, of the Malagasy Republic, and of some overseas territories of France ‖ a coin of the value of one franc CFA [Communauté Financière Africaine]
franc CFP the basic monetary unit of French Polynesia and New Caledonia ‖ a coin of the value of one franc CFP [Communauté française du Pacifique]
France (fræns, frɑns) a republic (area 212,822 sq. miles incl. Corsica, pop. 54,174,000) in W. Europe. Capital: Paris. Religion: mainly Roman Catholic, 2% Protestant, 230,000 Jewish. The land is 34% arable, 23% pasture, 20% forest and 3% vineyards. It consists of lowland basins separated by mountains. The Paris basin, the Aquitaine basin, the plains of Languedoc and the Saône-Rhône depression form (counterclockwise) a circle around the Massif Central. The frontier lowlands of Alsace and Flanders are joined respectively to the Paris basin by the Belfort gap and the hills of Artois. The mountainous regions are (clockwise): the Ardennes (2,000 ft), the Vosges (4,667 ft), the Jura (5,642 ft), the Alps (Mont Blanc, 15,781 ft), the Pyrenees (11,000 ft) and the Armorican Massif (1,000 ft). The granite plateau of the Massif Central rises to 6,188 ft (Puy de Sancy) and 5,753 ft (Mezenc) in the Cévennes. Annual rainfall: Brest 32 ins, Paris 22 ins, Strasbourg 26 ins, Clermont-Ferrand 25 ins, Bordeaux 30 ins, Marseille 23 ins. Average winter and summer temperatures (F.): Brest 45° and 63°, Paris 36° and 65°, Strasbourg 31° and 66°, Clermont-Ferrand 35° and 66°, Bordeaux 41° and 68°, Marseille 43° and 72°. Livestock: cattle, sheep, hogs, horses. Agricultural products: cereals (esp. wheat in the Beauce), sugar beet, vegetables, fruit, silk, rice, olive oil, lumber. France produces one third of the world's wine (notably in the Midi, Champagne, Bourgogne and around Bordeaux). Resources: iron, coal, oil, lignite, bauxite, potash, fish, hydroelectricity. Main industries: iron and steel, sugar, textiles, chemicals, vehicles, ships, plastics, leather, foodstuffs, printing, aircraft, oil refining, light manufactures, tourism. Exports: machinery, vehicles, textiles, wine and liqueurs, luxury goods, notably tapestries, perfumes, porcelain, glass and crystal ware, furniture, clothes (haute couture), jewelry. Imports: coal, oil, machinery, textiles, iron and steel. Ports: Marseille, Le Havre, Rouen, Dunkerque. The Midi canal (built 1631) links the Atlantic and the Mediterranean. There are 19 universities, the oldest being Paris (1215) and Toulouse (1230). Monetary unit: franc (100 centimes). Overseas departments: Martinique, Guadeloupe, Réunion, French Guiana. Overseas territories: French Polynesia, New Caledonia, French Somaliland, St Pierre and Miquelon, French Southern and Antarctic Territories, Wallis and Futuna. Franco-British condominium: New Hebrides. HISTORY. Caves in S.W. France show signs of occupation by Cro-Magnon and other early races of man. In historic times, the earliest settlers were of Ligurian and Iberian stock, and trading colonies were founded along the Mediterranean coast by Phoenicians and Greeks. The Gauls, a Celtic people, settled (6th c. B.C.), and were divided into many tribes when Rome made the south the province of Transalpine Gaul (121 B.C.). The whole of Gaul was conquered (58 B.C.–51 B.C.) by Julius Caesar, and Christianity was introduced (1st c. A.D.). The Gallo-Roman civilization which developed

was to have a permanent influence on French language and institutions. The country was invaded (3rd–5th cc.) by Germanic tribes, the Burgundians and the Visigoths settling in the south and the Franks in the north. These defeated under Aetius to defeat (451) the Huns under Attila. The Franks were ruled (448–751) by the Merovingians, one of whom, Clovis, extended his rule (481–511) over the whole country, and was converted (c. 496) to Christianity. On his death his kingdom was divided and, during wars between the kings of Austrasia and Neustria, power passed to the mayors of the palace. One of these, Charles Martel, halted the Moorish invasion of Europe at Poitiers (732). His son, Pépin III, founded the Carolingian dynasty (751–987) and was succeeded by Charlemagne, in whose reign (768–814) a strong administration was built up and the arts flourished. He subdued the Lombards, Bavarians, Saxons and Avars, and was crowned Emperor (800) by the pope. His vast empire was divided by the Treaty of Verdun (843) into three parts, one of which, the kingdom of the W. Franks, later evolved into France. The power of the Carolingians declined as a powerful feudal nobility developed, and as the north coast was raided by Vikings, to whom Normandy was ceded (911). Hugh Capet took the throne (987) and established the Capetian dynasty (987–1328). The early Capetians exercised little authority beyond a small area around Paris, but Louis VI strengthened royal power and extended the royal domain during his reign (1108–37). The towns prospered and commerce developed. The marriage (1152) of Henry II of England to Eleanor of Aquitaine, the divorced wife of Louis VII, gave a large part of France to England, but in the reign of Philippe II (1180–1223) it was all regained except Gascony (1204). By his victory at Bouvines (1214) Philippe II made France a dominant military power. France took a leading part in the Crusades, the Sorbonne became a center of theological learning, magnificent Gothic cathedrals were begun and, in the reign (1226–70) of Louis IX high ideals of kingship and justice were established. In the reign (1285–1314) of Philippe IV, the first States General was summoned (1302), the power of the feudal nobility was crushed, royal authority was asserted over the Church, and the papacy was induced to reside at Avignon (1309–78). The direct male line of Capetians died out (1328) and the throne passed to a younger branch, the house of Valois, whose claim was disputed by Edward III of England. In the ensuing Hundred Years' War (1337–1453) France was defeated at Crécy (1346) and Poitiers (1356), was ravaged by the Black Death, was humiliated in the Treaty of Brétigny (1360), and lost her position as the cultural center of Europe. Under Charles V, Bertrand du Guesclin regained (1369–73) all the lost territory except Calais and Gascony, but civil war broke out (1407). Henry V of England renewed the war (1415), and France was again humiliated at Agincourt (1415) and by the Treaty of Troyes (1420). The French cause was revived by Joan of Arc who, after a brilliant campaign, had the dauphin crowned (1429) as Charles VII. By 1453, Calais was the only English possession in France. In the reign (1461–83) of Louis XI, the power of the dukes of Burgundy was crushed, and the royal domain was extended to contain what is nearly all of present-day France except Brittany, which was added in 1491. The latter involved France in the costly Italian Wars (1494–1559), the first phase of a struggle with the Hapsburgs which was to last more than two centuries. François I's reign (1515–47) saw the beginnings of the Renaissance in France and of colonial expansion. The growing absolutism of the court and the increasing numbers of Huguenots precipitated the Wars of Religion, in which Catherine de' Medici, the Guises and the Holy League tried to prevent the succession of the Protestant Henri de Navarre. The latter succeeded as Henri IV on the death (1589) of Henri III, the last of the Valois, but was not recognized as king by the Holy League until he abjured Calvinism (1593). Under Henri IV, the first of the Bourbons, religious toleration was guaranteed in the Edict of Nantes (1598), and prosperity was restored by Sully. During the reign (1610–43) of Louis XIII and the first part (1643–61) of that of Louis XIV, French policy was dictated first by Richelieu and then by Mazarin. France allied herself victoriously

CONCISE PRONUNCIATION KEY: **(a)** æ, cat; ɑ, car; ɔ fawn; ei, snake. **(e)** e, hen; i:, sheep; iə, deer; ɛə, bear. **(i)** i, fish; ai, tiger; ə:, bird.
(o) o, ox; au, cow; ou, goat; u, poor; ɔi, royal. **(u)** ʌ, duck; u, bull; u:, goose; ə, bacillus; ju:, cube. x, loch; θ, think; ð, bother; z, Zen; ʒ, corsage;
dʒ, savage; ŋ, orangutang; j, yak; ʃ, fish; tʃ, fetch; 'l, rabble; 'n, redden. Complete pronunciation key appears inside front cover.

with the Protestant powers against the Hapsburgs in the Thirty Years' War (1618–48). The Huguenots were crushed, the Fronde was defeated and, with the growth of the theory of divine right, royal absolutism reached its height under Louis XIV. Religious toleration ended with the revocation (1685) of the Edict of Nantes, and Jansenism was put down. A brilliant court developed at Versailles, and French classicism, language and manners influenced the whole of Europe. Despite the work of Colbert and Louvois, France was weakened financially by a series of wars: the War of Devolution (1667–8), the Dutch War (1672–8), the War of the Grand Alliance (1689–97) and the War of the Spanish Succession (1701–14). French expansion was halted by the Peace of Utrecht (1713). In the reign (1715–74) of Louis XV, the growing financial crisis was alleviated by Fleury, but the War of the Austrian Succession (1740–8) and the Seven Years' War (1756–63) resulted in the loss of Canada and of most possessions in India. The Encyclopedists and the physiocrats in vain demanded political, social and economic reform of the ancien régime. Turgot attempted reform, but was dismissed (1776) by Louis XVI. Necker was unable to persuade the nobles to abandon their fiscal privileges and, faced with national bankruptcy, advised the summoning of the States General for the first time since 1614. The French Revolution broke out (1789). Louis XVI was executed (1793), the First Republic was established, and the French Revolutionary Wars began (1792–1802). The Directory was set up (1795) and overthrown (1799) by Napoleon, who established the Consulate (1799) and the First Empire (1804). The Napoleonic Code was instituted (1804). The Napoleonic Wars (1803–15) spread French domination throughout the continent of Europe, but Napoleon suffered reverses in the Peninsular War (1808–14) and in the retreat from Moscow (1812). He abdicated (1814) and was exiled to Elba, the monarchy being restored with Louis XVIII. Napoleon returned to France (1815), but, after the Hundred Days (Mar.–June 1815), was defeated by the Allies at Waterloo, and was exiled to St Helena. The Congress of Vienna restored Louis XVIII, and reduced France to her frontiers of 1789. During the reign (1814–24) of Louis XVIII and that (1824–30) of Charles X, the severe limitation of the franchise and the reactionary policy of the government provoked a liberal revolution in Paris (July 27–9, 1830). Charles fled and was replaced by the duc d'Orléans, who was proclaimed king of the French as Louis Philippe. His rule (1830–48) developed into a plutocracy under the guidance of Guizot. The conquest of Algeria was begun, but failed to deflect attention from corruption at home. An economic crisis (1847) was followed by a proletarian revolution (Feb. 22–4, 1848), in which Louis Philippe abdicated. An attempt to put Louis Blanc's socialism into practice was unsuccessful. Louis Napoleon was proclaimed (1848) president of the Second Republic. A coup d'état (Dec. 2, 1851) established the Second Empire, Louis Napoleon becoming emperor (1852) as Napoleon III. His dictatorship was modified after 1859 by liberal reforms, and the beginnings of industrialization brought prosperity. He took France into the Crimean War, gained Nice and Savoy (1860) after a brief intervention in Italy, and sent a disastrous expedition to Mexico (1861–7). Napoleon III's regime collapsed when Prussia invaded during the Franco-Prussian War (1870–1), after which France lost Alsace-Lorraine. The insurrection of the Paris Commune was put down (1871) by the Third Republic (1871–1940) under Thiers. A republican constitution was adopted (1875) and the republicans obtained a majority (1879). Public education was secularized. The regime was shaken by the Boulanger crisis (1889), the Panama Canal scandal (1889) and the Dreyfus affair (1894–1906). The latter was followed by political realignment and a wave of anticlericalism, in which Church and State were separated (1905). Amid growing industrialization, a socialist party emerged under Jaurès, and trade unions developed. Colonial expansion continued in Africa and Indochina, clashing with Britain at Fashoda (1898) and with Germany in Morocco (1905 and 1911). France made an alliance with Russia (1894), the Entente Cordiale with Britain (1904) and the Triple Entente with Britain and Russia (1907).

The 1st world war cost France 1,400,000 dead, and exhausted her economy, but by the Treaty of Versailles (1919) she regained Alsace-Lorraine. Germany refused to pay reparations, and Poincaré sent French troops to occupy the Ruhr (1923–5). The succeeding years were marked by inflation, economic depression (1932) and political instability until Léon Blum formed (1936) a Popular Front government. In the face of the rise of Hitler in Germany, France allied herself with the Little Entente and built the Maginot line. But she remained inactive when Hitler occupied the Rhineland (1936), and she adopted the policy of appeasement at Munich (1938). France declared war (Sept. 3, 1939) when Germany invaded Poland. The Germans invaded France (May 1940) and quickly reached Paris. The government, retreating to Vichy, appointed Pétain as premier, signed an armistice (June 22, 1940) and suspended the constitution. The Germans occupied N. France (1940) and then the rest of the country (Nov. 1942). De Gaulle escaped to London, organized the Free French, and established a provisional government in Algiers (1943). After the Allied invasion of Normandy (June 1944) and the liberation of Paris (Aug. 25, 1944), de Gaulle governed France until the constitution of the Fourth Republic was drawn up (1946). France joined the Organization for European Economic Cooperation (1947), NATO (1949) and the European Economic Community (1957). Postwar reconstruction was hampered by government instability and by war in Indochina (1946–54) and Algeria (1954–62). The Algerian crisis of 1958 restored de Gaulle to power. A new constitution, giving the president greater power, established the Fifth Republic (1958) and the French Community (1959). De Gaulle was elected president (1959). The war in Algeria ended (1962) with the grant of independence. A treaty of cooperation was signed (1963) with West Germany. France created an atomic striking force and pursued a policy of independence in foreign affairs. De Gaulle resigned (Apr. 1969). Georges Pompidou was elected (June 1969) president, followed by Valéry Giscard d'Estaing and François Mitterrand (1981–), a Socialist. He was forced to curtail his social welfare policies because of a deteriorating economy (1982–3). Unrest in New Caledonia and a scandal over French involvement in the sabotaging of a ship belonging to an anti-nuclear group (1985) also marked his presidency

France (frãs), Anatole (Jacques Anatole Thibault, 1844–1924), French novelist and critic. His works have a penetrating irony, reflecting a pervading cynicism in politics and religion. He wrote an elegant, classical French. His works include 'le Crime de Sylvestre Bonnard' (1881), 'Les dieux ont soif' (1912), 'l'Ile des pingouins' (1908)

Francesca, Piero della *PIERO DELLA FRANCESCA

Franche-Com·té (frãʃkõtei) a former province of E. France, forming the departments of Jura and Doubs in the N. Jura Mtns, Haute-Saône in the upper Saône valley and Belfort, a plain between the Vosges and the Jura. Occupations: forestry and dairy farming in the Jura, mixed farming and industry (textiles, metallurgy) in the plains. Historic capitals: Dole (until 1678), Besançon. A countship separated (9th c.) from the kingdom of Burgundy, and a fief (1032) of the Holy Roman Empire, it was contested by Burgundy, France, Austria and Spain for 600 years, until France acquired it (1678)

fran·chise (fræntʃaiz) n. (with 'the') full rights of citizenship, esp. the right to vote in public elections ‖ a privilege or right usually granted by a government charter to a person or company, to exercise an exclusive service or office, or to form a company to do this ‖ the jurisdiction over which a franchise extends [O.F.=freedom]

fran·chi·see (fræntʃaizí:) n. one who is granted a franchise

Fran·ci·a (frãnθi:ɑ), José Gaspar Rodríguez (1766–1840), Paraguayan dictator (1814–40). He led his country's struggle for independence from Spain (1811) and broke relations with the Vatican

Fran·cis·can (frænsískən) 1. adj. of the religious order founded by St Francis of Assisi, a Franciscan monastery 2. n. a member of this order [fr. M.L. Franciscus]
—The Franciscan order comprises the Friars Minor (approved by Pope Innocent III in 1209),

founded to live in poverty and to preach repentance, the Poor Clares for women (founded 1212) and the Tertiaries for laymen (approved 1230). The rule was first written in 1221, revised in 1223 and approved by Pope Honorius III. The Franciscans provided many of the leading medieval scholars, including Alexander of Hales, St Bonaventura, William of Occam, Duns Scotus, St Antony of Padua and Roger Bacon. The Franciscans have been the keepers of the Holy Places since the 15th c., and take an active part in missionary work

Fran·cis I (frænsis) (1708–65), Holy Roman Emperor (1745–65), duke of Lorraine (1729–37), grand duke of Tuscany (1737–65). He married (1736) Maria Theresa, heiress to the Hapsburg lands, and was elected emperor during the War of the Austrian Succession (1740–8)

Francis II (1768–1835), the last Holy Roman Emperor (1792–1805) and, as Francis I, the first emperor of Austria (1804–35), son of Leopold II. After his defeat by Napoleon at Austerlitz (1805), the Holy Roman Empire was dissolved. After the Congress of Vienna (1815), his chancellor, Metternich, made Austria a leading European power

Francis I (1777–1830), king of the Two Sicilies (1825–30), son of Ferdinand I

Francis II (1836–94), the last king of the Two Sicilies (1859–61), son of Ferdinand II. He was forced into exile after Garibaldi's invasion of Sicily (1860)

Francis kings of France *FRANÇOIS

Francis Ferdinand *FRANZ FERDINAND

Francis Joseph *FRANZ JOSEPH

Francis of Assisi, St (Francesco Bernardone, c. 1181–1226), Italian founder of the Franciscan order. He renounced wealth, choosing to follow Christ in humility, poverty and active love of mankind. His love for all creation, esp. the poor and lepers, revealed freshly to men the beauty of Christ's life and the mystery of the Incarnation. He received the stigmata (1224). Feast: Oct. 4

Francis of Sales (seilz, F. sæl), St (1567–1622), Savoyard bishop of Geneva. He was the founder of the Order of Sisters of the Visitation (1610), and author of the classic 'Introduction to the Devout Life' (1604). Feast: Jan. 29

Francis of Sales, Society of St *SALESIAN

Francis Xa·vier (zéivjər), St (1506–52), Spanish Jesuit missionary. He was one of the founders, with St Ignatius Loyola, of the Society of Jesus. He made missionary journeys (1541–52) in Goa, Ceylon, the East Indies, Japan and China, and was called 'Apostle of the Indies'. Feast: Dec. 3

fran·ci·um (frænsi:əm) n. a radioactive alkali-metal element (symbol Fr, at. no. 87, mass of isotope of longest known half-life 223), obtained as a disintegration product of actinium [Mod. L. fr. FRANCE]

Franck (frãk), César Auguste (1822–90), naturalized French composer, organist and teacher, of Belgian birth. He wrote many organ works and many songs, but is chiefly known for certain deep, passionate works written well after he was 50: the 'Symphonic Variations for Piano and Orchestra' (1885), 'Symphony in D minor' (1886–8), 'Sonata for Piano and Violin' (1886), 'String Quartet in D major' (1886–8) and three chorales for the organ (1890). His rich chromatic harmony and melodic purity influenced many modern composers

Fran·co (fræŋkou), Francisco (1892–1975), Spanish general and head of state. He organized the revolt in Morocco (July 1936) which precipitated the Spanish Civil War (1936–9), and was proclaimed commander in chief (1936) and 'El Caudillo' (1937) of the Falangists. In 1939 he became dictator. He was named regent of Spain for life (1947). The Cortes approved (1969) his proposal that on his death or retirement Prince Juan Carlos of Bourbon should become king of Spain, which he did in 1975 as *JUAN CARLOS I

Fran·çois (frãswæ) (1494–1547), king of France (1515–47), cousin of Louis XII. Most of his reign was occupied in attempts to conquer Italy and in rivalry with the Emperor Charles V. Unable to gain the support of Henry VIII of England (1520), he challenged the power of the Hapsburgs in four Italian Wars (1521–5, 1527–9, 1536, 1542). He finally abandoned his claims to Italy (1544) and made peace with England (1546). Under his patronage of the arts, the French Renaissance reached its height

---

François II (1544–60), king of France (1559–60), son of Henri II. He married (1558) Mary queen of Scots. During his short reign the government was in the hands of his uncles, the Guises, who plunged France into debt and into civil war

fran·co·lin (fræŋkəlin) *n.* a member of *Francolinus* or allied genera, partridges of S. Asia and Africa [F. fr. Ital.]

Fran·co·nia (fræŋkóunjə, fræŋkóuni:ɑ) a medieval duchy of Germany, along the Main and middle Rhine. It was created (9th c.) and partitioned (10th c.) into Rhenish Franconia and Eastern Franconia. The former soon disintegrated, and the latter came to be dominated (15th c.) by the bishops of Würzburg, and passed to Bavaria by 1815

Fran·co·phone (fræŋkəfoun) *adj.* of French-speaking countries, esp. in Africa **Francophone** *n.* one who habitually speaks French while residing in an area where a different language is spoken

Fran·co-Prus·sian War (fræŋkoupráʃən) a war (1870–1) provoked by Franco-Prussian rivalry, esp. over the candidacy of Leopold of Hohenzollern for the Spanish throne (*EMS TELEGRAM). Prussia, led by von Moltke, and in alliance with the S. German states, invaded France, and won victories (Aug.–Oct. 1870) at Wörth, Gravelotte, Sedan, Strasbourg and Metz. The people of Paris demanded the abdication of Napoleon III, and the Third Republic was proclaimed (Sept. 4, 1870). Paris was brought under siege (Sept. 19, 1870) and capitulated (Jan. 28, 1871). King William of Prussia was proclaimed German Emperor at Versailles (Jan. 18, 1871). By the Treaty of Frankfurt (May 1871) France ceded Alsace and E. Lorraine (including Metz) to Germany, and agreed to pay an indemnity of 5 billion francs

franc-ti·reur (frɑ̃ti:rə:r) *pl.* **francs-ti·reurs** (frɑ̃ti:rə:r) *n.* a civilian sniper, guerrilla (fighter) [F.]

fran·gi·ble (frændʒəb'l) *adj.* breakable, brittle, fragile [O.F.]

fran·gi·pane (frændʒəpein) *n.* a dessert made with almonds, cream and sugar ‖ frangipani [F., said to be after a 16th-c. Italian marquis of *Frangipani*]

fran·gi·pan·i (frændʒəpǽni:, frændʒəpɑ́ni:) a member of *Plumeria*, fam. *Apocynaceae*, a genus of tropical trees cultivated for their beautiful and highly perfumed flowers. *P. rubra* is known as red jasmine ‖ a perfume prepared from the flowers of *P. rubra*

Fran·glais (frɒŋgléi) *n.* French misused with much English integrated **franglification** *n.* Cf FRINGLISH

Frank, (fræŋk) Anne (1929–45), Dutch Jewish chronicler of life during the World War II Nazi occupation of the Netherlands. She kept a diary (published, 1947; film, 1959), found after her death in a concentration camp, of the events during the 2 years she and her family were hidden in Amsterdam

Frank (fræŋk) *n.* a member of a group of Germanic tribes dwelling (3rd c.) along the middle and lower Rhine. During the reign (481–511) of Clovis, they conquered and unified Gaul. The Frankish kingdom was ruled by the Merovingians (448–751) and by the Carolingians (751–987). Charlemagne extended the kingdom into an empire (8th c.), but this was divided (843) at the Treaty of Verdun into the kingdoms of the Eastern and Western Franks. The former became Germany and the latter France

frank (fræŋk) *adj.* without guile, open, *a frank face* ‖ stating unwelcome facts or giving critical opinions without trying to soften their impact, *frank to the point of rudeness* ‖ undisguised, *frank rebellion* [O.F. *franc*]

frank 1. *v.t.* to send (mail) free of charge ‖ to mark (mail) for free delivery **2.** *n.* a mark or sign indicating that mail is to be sent free ‖ the right to send mail free ‖ a letter etc. sent free [fr. *frank*, (obs.) free (of charge)]

Frank·fort (fræŋkfərt) the capital (pop. 25,973) of the state of Kentucky

Frank·furt-am-Main (fráŋkfu:rtəmmáin) (Frankfort-on-Main) a great banking, commercial and industrial city (pop. 628,200) in Hesse, West Germany. It is a rail and air center and is connected to the Rhine and Danube river systems. Its political and economic importance dates from the 8th c. The Holy Roman Emperors were elected and (after 1562) crowned here. Most of the old city was destroyed by bombing in 1944–5. It has, chemical, automobile, ma-

chine and clothing industries. University (1914)

Frank·furt an der O·der (fráŋkfu:rtɑnderóudər) (Frankfort-on-the-Oder) a town (pop. 65,644) on the Polish frontier, East Germany, with good rail and water communications and machine, furniture and chemical industries ‖ the district (area 2,721 sq. miles, pop. 666,000) which includes it (*BRANDENBURG)

Frank·furt·er (fræŋkfɑrtər), Felix (1882–1965) associate justice (1939–62) of the U.S. Supreme Court. He held liberal views and was a leading proponent of the New Deal, but he leaned in favor of limiting civil liberties on the grounds that government has the right to protect itself by investigating committees and legislation

frank·furt·er, frank·fort·er (fræŋkfɑrtər) *n.* a smoked beef, or beef and pork, sausage [after *Frankfurt-am-Main*]

Frank·furt Parliament (fráŋkfərt) a constitutional assembly (1848–9) representing the German states. It met in Frankfurt after the 1848 revolution, failed to unify Germany, and was replaced (1851) by the restored German Confederation

Frankfurt, Treaty of the treaty (May 10, 1871) ending the Franco-Prussian War

frank·in·cense (fræŋkinsens) *n.* a fragrant gum resin obtained from various trees of genus *Boswellia*, fam. *Burseraceae*, mainly in E. Africa and S. Asia. It is used for burning as incense [O.F. *franc encens*]

franking machine (*Br.*) a postage meter

Frank·ish (fræŋkiʃ) **1.** *adj.* of the Franks **2.** *n.* the Germanic language of the Franks

Frank·lin (fræŋklin), Benjamin (1706–90), American statesman, scientist and writer. Disillusioned with British rule in America, he helped to draft the Declaration of Independence (1776). He was ambassador to France (1776–85) and took part in the peace negotiations (1781–3) at the end of the Revolutionary War. He gained a worldwide reputation for his scientific work, which included a new theory of the nature of electricity, and for his inventions, which included the lightning rod

Franklin, Sir John (1786–1847), British explorer. In 1819–22 and 1825–7 he explored the coastline of N. Canada. He perished with his crew exploring the Northwest Passage

Franklin a sparsely-populated district (area incl. water: 549,253 sq. miles) in the Northwest Territories, Canada, administered from Ottawa. It includes Baffin Is., the Boothia and Melville Peninsulas, and the islands of the Arctic archipelago

frank·lin (fræŋklin) *n.* a small landowner in England in the 14th and 15th cc., of free but not noble birth [M.E. *frankeleyn, fraunkeleyn* fr. A.F. *fraunclein*]

Franklin stove an iron heating stove with doors which can be shut up for slow burning or opened so that the stove gives out heat and light like a fireplace [after its inventor, Benjamin *Franklin*]

frank·pledge (fræŋkpledʒ) *n.* a system in Anglo-Saxon law by which each male member of a tithing was responsible for the good behavior of every other member ‖ the member himself [A.F. *franc pledge*]

fran·tic (fræntik) *adj.* nearly mad with anger, pain, grief, fear etc. or suggesting such near-madness, *a frantic hurry, frantic flag-waving* **frán·ti·cal·ly** *adv.* [M.E. *frentik, frantik* fr. O.F.]

Franz Ferdinand (frɒnz) (1863–1914), archduke of Austria, nephew and, after 1896, heir to Franz Joseph. His assassination (June 28, 1914) at Sarajevo led to the Austrian ultimatum to Serbia and so touched off the 1st world war

Franz Jo·sef Land (fræntsdʒóuzif) an Arctic archipelago (about 80 islands, total area 8,000 sq. miles) east of Spitsbergen and north of Novaya Zemlya, belonging to the U.S.S.R., which has set up meteorological stations. Bears and foxes are occasionally trapped

Franz Joseph I (1830–1916), emperor of Austria and king of Hungary (1848–1916), nephew of Ferdinand I. Having put down the 1848 revolution, he continued to rule the Hapsburg Empire through the army and the bureaucracy until his defeat by France and Piedmont at Solferino (1859), when some constitutional reforms were introduced (1860–1). He allied with Bismarck's Prussia to defeat Denmark in the war over Schleswig-Holstein (1864), but was defeated by Prussia in the Seven Weeks' War

(1866). Despite the formation (1867) of the Dual Monarchy of Austria-Hungary, the question of racial minorities had considerably weakened the empire when the assassination (1914) at Sarajevo of Franz Joseph's nephew, Franz Ferdinand, touched off the 1st world war

frap (fræp) *pres. part.* **frap·ping** *past* and *past part.* **frapped** *v.t.* (*naut.*) to bind tightly [O.F. *fraper*, to strike]

Fraser (fréizər), John Malcolm (1930–), Australian prime minister (1975–83). He held several government positions before heading the Liberal party and becoming prime minister. Considered a conservative, he curbed inflation, revised the national health administration, and streamlined government expenses, but was unable to reduce the country's unemployment rate. He was succeeded by Robert Hawke

Fra·ser (fréizər), Peter (1884–1950), Scottish-born New Zealand statesman, prime minister of New Zealand (1940–9)

Fraser the main river of British Columbia, Canada, rising in the Rocky Mtns and flowing for about 700 miles into the Pacific

frass (fræs) *n.* (*entomology*) a mixture of sawdust and excrement used by insects in a home-building effort, e.g., of pine beetles

fra·ter (fréitər) *n.* (*hist.*) a refectory of a monastery [O.F. *fraitur*]

fra·ter·nal (frətá:rn'l) *adj.* of a brother or brothers ‖ brotherly, *fraternal affection* ‖ (*biol.*) designating twins from two ova (cf. IDENTICAL) (*Am.*) of or relating to a fraternity **fra·tér·nal·ism** *n.* [fr. L. *fraternus*, brotherly]

fra·ter·ni·ty (frətá:rniti:) *pl.* **fra·ter·ni·ties** *n.* the state of being brothers ‖ brotherliness ‖ men with common professional interests, *the legal fraternity* ‖ a religious brotherhood ‖ (in U.S. colleges) a private, usually residential, social club of male students (cf. SORORITY) [O.F. *fraternité*]

frat·er·ni·za·tion (frætərnizéiʃən) *n.* a fraternizing [F. *fraternisation*]

frat·er·nize (frætərnaiz) *pres. part.* **frat·er·nizing** *past* and *past part.* **frat·er·nized** *v.i.* to be friendly ‖ to behave as friends ‖ (of occupying troops) to be intimate with civilians of the country occupied [F. *fraterniser*]

F ratio or **F test** (*stat.*) in the analysis of variance, a test of statistical significance for the difference in means between two or more groups

frat·ri·cid·al (frætrisáid'l, freitrisáid'l) *adj.* relating to fratricide

frat·ri·cide (frætrisaid, fréitrisaid) *n.* the act of killing one's own brother or (*law*) sister ‖ a person who kills his own brother or (*law*) sister [F.]

fraud (frɔd) *n.* the use of deception for unlawful gain or unjust advantage ‖ something that constitutes a criminal deception ‖ someone who is not what he pretends he is [O.F. *fraude*]

fraud·u·lence (frɔ́dʒuləns) *n.* the quality or state of being fraudulent

fraud·u·lent (frɔ́dʒulənt) *adj.* characterized by fraud, *a fraudulent claim* ‖ obtained by fraud, *fraudulent gains* [O.F.]

fraught (frɔt) *adj.* (with 'with') filled with, *words fraught with hidden meanings* ‖ (with 'with') involving or potentially filled with, *a journey fraught with danger* [fr. M. Du. *vracht*]

Fraun·ho·fer lines (fráunhoufər) dark lines in the spectrum of sunlight attributed to the presence of various elemental substances and their ions in the sun [after Joseph von *Fraunhofer* (1787–1826) German physicist]

frax·i·nel·la (fræksinélə) *n. Dictamnus albus*, fam. *Rutaceae*, a perennial plant of Europe and Asia which secretes a volatile and inflammable ethereal oil [Mod. L., dim. of *fraxinus*, ash]

fray (frei) *n.* (*rhet.*) a fight, brawl [fr. older *affray*, fright]

fray *v.t.* to break threads in (part of a garment, esp. sleeves, collar or elbows) by hard wear ‖ to cause the threads in (a rope or the edge of material) to separate instead of remaining close ‖ to strain (the nerves, temper etc.) almost to breaking point ‖ *v.i.* to become frayed ‖ (of deer) to rub the velvet off new horns against trees [fr. F. *frayer*]

Fra·zer (fréizər), Sir James George (1854–1941), Scottish social anthropologist. His 'The Golden Bough' (1890–1915) attempts to demonstrate, by means of a rich collection of data regarding primitive, classical and modern beliefs and rituals, the existence of a universal primitive religion based on the cycle of the seasons. His other works include 'Totemism and Exogamy' (1910), 'Belief in Immortality' (1913–24) and 'Fear of the Dead' (1933–6)

fra·zil (fréiz'l) *n.* crystals of ice formed on the surface of a fast-flowing river, the flow preventing sheet ice from forming [perh. fr. F. *fraisil*, cinders]

fraz·zle (fréz'l) **1.** *v. pres. part.* **fraz·zling** *past and past part.* **fraz·zled** *v.t.* to wear, fray || to tire, *frazzled with the heat* **2.** *n.* a state of exhaustion **worn to a frazzle** utterly exhausted || very badly frayed [origin unknown]

freak (fri:k) *n.* a person or animal malformed in a way which makes him or it an object of curiosity || (*pop.*) an eccentric person || an inexplicable act or happening, *it was a freak that he passed the test* || combining suffix meaning "addicted to," e.g., drug freak, old-book freak || a sudden, capricious notion, whim, *freaks of fancy* **2.** *adj.* occurring as a freak **fréak·ish** *adj.* [etym. doubtful]

freak out *v.* (*slang*) to hallucinate or otherwise lose rationality, esp. as the result of taking illicit drugs **freaked-out** *adj.* **freak-out** *n.* one who freaks out; a gathering of members of the drug culture; a loss of sense of reality

Fré·chette (freiʃet), Louis Honoré (1839–1908), French-Canadian poet. His patriotic poetry, incl. 'les Fleurs boréales et les Oiseaux de neige' (1879), was the first work by a Canadian to be acclaimed (1880) by the French Academy

freck·le (frék'l) **1.** *n.* a small brownish fleck in the skin caused by exposure to sunlight or ultraviolet light **2.** *v.t. pres. part.* **freck·ling** *past* and *past part.* **freck·led** to cover or mark with freckles || *v.i.* to become covered or marked with freckles **fréck·ly** *adj.* covered with freckles

fred·die (frédi:) *n.* (*mil.*) in air-intercept usage, a controlling unit

Fre·de·gund (fri:digʌnd) (c. 545–97), Frankish queen. She murdered Sigebert I and her own stepchildren, and ruled as regent for her son Clotaire II

Frederick I (1657–1713), elector of Brandenburg (1688–1701), first king of Prussia (1701–13), son of Frederick William 'the Great Elector.' He was a patron of the arts and sciences

Frederick I (1471–1533), king of Denmark and Norway (1523–33), son of Christian I

Frederick III (1609–70), king of Denmark and Norway (1648–70), son of Christian IV. He was at war with Sweden (1657–60), and was forced to cede possessions in S. Sweden

Frederick IV (1671–1730), king of Denmark and Norway (1699–1730). He failed in his attempts to regain S. Sweden, but acquired Schleswig

Frederick VI (1768–1839), king of Denmark (1808–39) and of Norway (1808–14). An ally of Napoleon, he was forced to cede Norway to Sweden (1814)

Frederick VII (1808–63), king of Denmark (1848–63). He put down a revolt in Schleswig-Holstein (1848), and promulgated a more liberal constitution

Frederick IX (1899–1972) king of Denmark (1947–72), son of Christian X

Frederick III 'the Fair' (c. 1286–1330), king of Germany (1314–26), rival king to Louis IV of Bavaria (1314–47), who defeated him in 1322

Fred·er·ick I Barbarossa (frédrik) (Friedrich, c. 1123–90), Holy Roman Emperor (1155–90), German king (1152–90), nephew of Conrad III. Having pacified the quarrels of Guelphs and Ghibellines, he embarked (1154) on a campaign to enforce his feudal rights in Italy. He captured Milan (1162) and Rome (1166), supporting an antipope against Alexander III until he was crushingly defeated at Legnano (1176). He was drowned during the 3rd Crusade

Frederick II (1194–1250), Holy Roman Emperor (1220–50), German king (1212–50) and king of Sicily (1197–1250), son of Henry VI. His almost continual struggle with the Lombard League and the papacy led to his excommunication (1239) and his defeat at Parma (1248). He had led the 6th Crusade, and had given Sicily a code of laws (1231). His court at Palermo attracted Jewish, Moslem and Christian scholars

Frederick III (1415–93), Holy Roman Emperor (1452–93), German king (as Frederick IV, 1440–93). He remained apathetic in the face of revolts among his Swiss, Austrian and Hungarian subjects

Frederick V 'the Winter King' (1596–1632), elector of the Palatinate (1610–23) and king of

Bohemia (1619–20). Routed (1620) at the White Mountain at the start of the Thirty Years' War, he lost all his territories

Frederick II 'the Great' (1712–86), king of Prussia (1740–86), son of Frederick William I. With the army created by his father, he entered the War of the Austrian Succession (1740–8), defeating Austria at Mollwitz (1741), and gaining Silesia. After a final victory at Kesselsdorf (1745) and the Treaty of Dresden (1745), he devoted himself to domestic administration and to legal, financial and army reform. The Seven Years' War (1756–63) enabled him to retain Silesia. In the first partition of Poland (1772) he acquired W. Prussia without Danzig and Thorn. He formed the Fürstenbund (League of German Princes, 1785). An admirer of French culture and patron of writers, he was host to Voltaire (1750–3). He wrote 'l'Antimachiavel' (1740) and 'A History of the House of Brandenburg' (1751)

Frederick III (1831–88), king of Prussia and German emperor (Mar. 9–June 15, 1888), elder son of Wilhelm I

Frederick William 'the Great Elector' (Friedrich Wilhelm, 1620–88), elector of Brandenburg (1640–88). He rehabilitated Brandenburg after the Thirty Years' War, creating a small standing army and a military bureaucracy. He fought France and Sweden (1674), defeating the Swedish army at Fehrbellin (1675), and making peace with France at Nijmegen (1678)

Frederick William I (1688–1740), king of Prussia (1713–40), son of Frederick I. A militarist and a despot, he raised the Prussian army to 83,000 men. By the Treaty of Stockholm (1720) he received most of Pomerania from Sweden

Frederick William II (1744–97), king of Prussia (1786–97), nephew of Frederick the Great. He allowed Prussia's military power to decline. War with France (1792–5) resulted in the loss of all Prussian land west of the Rhine (TREATIES OF BASLE, 1795), although Prussia gained from the second partition of Poland (1793) and the third (1795)

Frederick William III (1770–1840), king of Prussia (1797–1840), son of Frederick William II. Under his indecisive and reactionary rule, Prussia was defeated by Napoleon at Jena (1806), and humiliated in the Treaty of Tilsit (1807). He joined the final offensive against Napoleon (1814–15), regained territory at the Congress of Vienna (1815), and became a convinced member of the Holy Alliance

Frederick William IV (1795–1861), king of Prussia (1840–61), son of Frederick William III. His hatred of democratic constitutions prevented him from accepting the crown of a united Germany from the Frankfurt Parliament (1849). He became insane (1857). His brother Wilhelm I acted as regent (1858–61)

Fred·er·icks·burg, Battle of (frédriksbəːrg) a battle (Dec. 13, 1862) of the Civil War, in which Lee's Confederate army was victorious

Fred·er·ic·ton (frédriktən) the capital (pop. 43,723) of New Brunswick, Canada. University (1800)

Fred·er·iks·na·gar (frédəriksnʌgár) *SERAMPUR

free (fri:) **1.** *adj.* not subject to external constraints or domination, *a free society* || not captive, at liberty || able to move, loose || not having to be paid for, *the refreshments are free* || (with 'from') clear of (a specified condition), *free from pain* || not busy, without prior engagements || not reserved or occupied, *the room will be free in June* || not being used, *he grabbed it with his free hand* || without trade or tariff restrictions, *a free port* || unhampered, *a free flow of traffic* || able to act and choose for oneself, *a free agent* || spontaneous, voluntary, *a free offer* || generous, profuse, *he is free with his money* || unrestrained from the point of view of manners and morality, *he was too free with his secretary* || unconstrained by convention || not literal, not wholly faithful to the original, *a free translation, a free interpretation of the concerto* || open to all without restrictions, *a free market* || unimpeded, *a free road* || not fastened, *the free end of the rope* || (*chem.*) not combined, *free oxygen* || (of power, energy) available || (*naut.*), of a wind) blowing from a direction more than six points from straight ahead **to have one's hands free** to have no commitments that prevent one from doing something one wants to do **to make free with** to treat or use (belongings of others) as if one owned them **to set free** to

release **2.** *adv.* without expense || without penalty || (*naut.*) with the wind blowing more than six points from straight ahead **3.** *v.t.* to release from constraint, set free || to disengage, *to free one's hands* || to relieve, *to free someone from an obligation* [O.E. *frēo, frīo, frīg* and *frēon, frēogean*]

free agent (*baseball, football*) professional athlete not bound by contract who may thus join any team on his own terms

free air anomaly (*geophys.*) the difference between measured gravity and theoretical gravity that has been computed for latitude and corrected for elevation

free alongside ship (*abbr.* f.a.s.) delivered free of charge at the side of the ship (cf. FREE ON BOARD)

Free and Accepted Masons a secret organization for men which developed (17th c.) from the medieval fraternities of stonemasons in England and Scotland. The organization spread rapidly in the early 18th c. and is now established in most countries of the world. Its members, Freemasons, believe in a Supreme Being, profess universal brotherhood, and practice mutual assistance. An elaborate ritual is used

free and clear (*law*) pertaining to real estate unencumbered by mortgages, liens etc.

free and easy without constraint of manner || casual, unexacting in respect of oneself or others

free association the mental process of making associations which the reason does not seek to order, repress, or otherwise control || (*psychoanal.*) the technique of getting a subject to give the words that come at once to his mind in response to a stimulus word, picture etc. or to talk about some topic with a freedom that gives the analyst an insight into unconscious processes of his mind

free-base drugs (fri:beis) cocaine chemically treated with ether, ingested by smoking

free-bee or **free-bie** (fri:bi:) *n.* (*slang*) gift, souvenir, or ticket offered and received without charge

free·board (fri:bɔrd, fri:bourd) *n.* the space between deck and waterline on the side of a ship or boat || the space between the undercarriage of a motor vehicle and the ground || (*envir.*) vertical distance between normal water level and the top of a flume

free·boot·er (fri:bu:tər) *n.* someone who lives by plunder and loot, esp. a pirate [fr. Du. *vrijbuiter*]

free·born (fri:bɔrn) *adj.* born free (not a slave, vassal, bondsman etc.)

Free Church (*Br.*) a Nonconformist Church

Free Church of Scotland the Church of those who seceded from the Presbyterian Church of Scotland in 1843. The two reunited in 1929

free city a self-governing city with sovereign powers, esp. in medieval Italy and Germany

free·dance (fri:dæns) *n.* (*ice skating*) movement to music selected by the skater

freed·man (fri:dmən) *pl.* **freed·men** (fri:dmən) *n.* a liberated male slave, esp. a Negro after the Civil War

Freedmen's Bureau a U.S. federal agency created (1865) after the Civil War in answer to Republican abolitionist demands to safeguard blacks from re-enslavement and to improve their standard of living. It created and nurtured over 1,000 black schools and black teacher-training institutions. It also solicited black support for the Republican party, alienating white Southerners, and was closed (1872) by Congress

free·dom (fri:dəm) *n.* enjoyment of personal liberty, of not being a slave nor a prisoner || the enjoyment of civil rights (freedom of speech, freedom of assembly etc.) generally associated with constitutional government || the state of not being subject to determining forces || liberty in acting and choosing || immunity to or release from obligations, undesirable states of being etc., *freedom from taxation, freedom from fear* || ability to move with ease || excessive familiarity || unrestricted use or enjoyment, *he gave them the freedom of his library* || (with 'from') an absence of, *freedom from controls* || (in the arts) spontaneity unfettered by rules and conventions || a privilege (e.g. honorary citizenship) conferred on someone to do him honor [O.E. *frēodom*]

Freedom of Information Act (1966), U.S. law that makes U.S. government agency records, except those involving national security and other confidential matters (such as trade se-

CONCISE PRONUNCIATION KEY: **(a)** æ, c*a*t; ɑ, c*a*r; ɔ f*aw*n; ei, sn*a*ke. **(e)** e, h*e*n; i:, sh*ee*p; iə, d*ee*r; ɛə, b*ea*r. **(i)** i, f*i*sh; ai, t*i*ger; əː, b*i*rd. **(o)** o, *o*x; au, c*ow*; ou, g*oa*t; u, p*oo*r; ɔi, r*oy*al. **(u)** ʌ, d*u*ck; u, b*u*ll; u:, g*oo*se; ə, b*a*cillus; ju:, c*u*be. x, lo*ch*; θ, *th*ink; ð, bo*th*er; z, *Z*en; ʒ, cor*s*age; dʒ, sava*g*e; ŋ, orangutan*g*; j, *y*ak; ʃ, *fi*sh; tʃ, fe*tch*; 'l, rabb*le*; 'n, redd*en*. Complete pronunciation key appears inside front cover.

crets and investigatory files), available to the public. It was amended by the Privacy Act of 1974, which enables individuals to know what federal agency records apply to them and to ensure that those records are accurate

Freedom of Information Act law passed July 29, 1976, requiring federal agencies to make records available to public scrutiny, to have open meetings and make public any communications that influence decisions. Similar laws are in effect in most states. Known as the Sunshine Law

freedom of the press the right to print and publish without government censorship

freedom ride (sometimes initial capitals) trip to Southern states by civil rights workers to break unconstitutional laws and customs favoring racial segregation in public places —**freedom rider** *n.*

free drop the dropping of equipment or supplies from an aircraft without the use of parachutes

freed·wom·an (fríː·dwʊmən) *pl.* **freed·wom·en** (fríː·dwɪmən) *n.* a liberated female slave

free energy (*phys.*) a thermodynamic quantity that is a measure of the portion of the total energy of a system available for conversion to work, the free energy change for any given process being equal to the maximum work available or the minimum work that must be done in going from the initial to the final state of the process

free enterprise the system of leaving private business to compete and make profit (as opposed to tight state control) || a private business within such a system

free fall the falling of a body through the air without any attempt being made to modify the pull of gravity || the initial stage of a parachute jump, before the parachute is opened

free fight (*Br.*) a free-for-all

free-fire zone (fríːfaiər) (*mil.*) an area where any moving thing can be a target

free-for-all (fríːfərɔl) *n.* a fight without rules in which any number of people join or become involved

Free French the French military formations which, under the orders of de Gaulle, continued the struggle against the Axis after the fall of France in 1940 in the 2nd world war

free·hand (fríːhænd) *adj.* done without the aid of drawing or measuring instruments

free hand complete freedom to make decisions and act on them

free·hand·ed (fríːhændid) *adj.* generous

free·hold (fríːhould) 1. *n.* (*law*) tenure of landed property in absolute possession || (*law*) a landed property so held || a tenure of an office similar to such a freehold 2. *adj.* held in absolute possession **free·hold·er** *n.* the owner of a freehold

free house (*Br.*) a public house not owned by a brewer, and so able to sell drinks of any brand (cf. TIED HOUSE)

free lance someone who works esp. in a liberal occupation at his own risk and not under contract to any one employer, esp. a journalist unattached to any one newspaper, magazine or publishing house || a politician who acts independently of a party line **free-lance** 1. (fríːlæns, fríːlɑns) *adj.* of or relating to a free lance 2. (fríːlæns, fríːlɑns) *v.i. pres. part.* **free-lanc·ing** *past* and *past part.* **free-lanced** to be a free lance

free list a list of people who are to receive complimentary tickets, copies, samples etc. || a list of things exempt from a charge which would otherwise be made, e.g. a schedule of goods not subject to import duties

free-liv·ing (fríːlívin) *adj.* (*biol.*) capable of moving from place to place || (*biol.*) independent with respect to metabolism, not parasitic nor symbiotic

free-load (fríːloud) *v.i.* to sponge, be a social parasite **free-load·er** *n.*

free love the practice of having sexual relations with a member of the opposite sex without being married to the person

free·man (fríːmən) *pl.* **free·men** (fríːmən) *n.* someone having the freedom of a city, borough, company or corporation || a freeborn citizen [O.E. frēoman]

free·mar·tin (fríːmɑrtn) *n.* a sterile or otherwise sexually defective female calf born the twin of a male calf [origin unknown]

Free·ma·son (fríːmeisn) *n.* a member of the Free and Accepted Masons **Free·ma·son·ry** *n.* the institutions and practices of Freemasons **free·ma·son·ry** an instinctive solidarity between numbers of people having some common calling, enthusiasm, way of life etc.

free on board (*abbr.* f.o.b.) delivered at the vendor's charge to and into the train, vessel or other long-distance transport being used (cf. FREE ALONGSIDE SHIP)

free period a period in a school timetable when a student is not being taught but uses the time for private study or some educational activity || a period in a school timetable when a teacher is not giving a lesson

free play exercise (*mil.*) an exercise in which it is desired to test the capabilities of forces under simulated wartime conditions. It is limited only by those artificialities or restrictions required by peacetime safety regulations

free port a port, or district near a port, where exported and imported goods are handled without being subject to duty

Free·port Doctrine (fríːpɔrt, fríːpourt) the principle expounded by Stephen A. Douglas in Freeport, Ill., during the second Lincoln-Douglas debate (Aug. 27, 1858), by which the people of a U.S. territory had the right to determine whether their territory would be slave or free. It was bitterly attacked in the South

free radical (*chem.*) an atom or group of atoms with one or more unpaired electrons, which may enter into chemical-bond formation. Free radicals are usually highly reactive (hence shortlived) and are difficult to prepare in other than low concentration

free-re·turn trajectory (fríːriːtɔ́ːrn) path of a spacecraft that provides for a return to earth

free safety (*football*) team member not assigned to cover any member of his or the opposing team, but to assist wherever needed

free·sia (fríːʒə, fríːʒiːə) *n.* a South African plant of genus *Freesia*, fam. *Iridaceae*, cultivated for its ornamental, scented flowers [Mod. L.]

free soil (*Am. hist.*) territory in which slavery was illegal, esp. before the Civil War **free-soil** *adj.*

Free-Soil·er (fríːsɔílər) *n.* an adherent of the Free-Soil party

Free-Soil party the political organization active (1848–54) in opposing the spread of slavery to newly acquired territories of the U.S.A. It merged (1854) with the Republican party

free-spo·ken (fríːspóukən) *adj.* given to speaking one's mind without restraint

Free State (*Am. hist.*) any state of the U.S.A. in which slavery was prohibited before the Civil War (1861–5)

Free State Party an antislavery political party established (1854) in the territory of Kansas by the Topeka Constitution

free·stone (fríːstoun) 1. *n.* a stone readily cut in any direction, esp. limestone or sandstone || a stone of certain varieties of plum, peach etc. which does not adhere closely to the flesh of the fruit || a fruit having such a stone (cf. CLINGSTONE) 2. *adj.* having a stone which does not adhere closely to the flesh of the fruit

free·style (fríːstail) *n.* a race, esp. in swimming, in which a competitor may use any style he pleases

free·think·er (fríːθiŋkər) *n.* someone who forms his ideas about religion without regard to dogma, usually taking a position of skepticism or denial

free thought thought which does not rest on, and is usually clearly opposed to, authority or tradition in matters of religion

Free·town (fríːtaun) the capital (pop. 274,000) of Sierra Leone, a naval and commercial port, with the country's only good natural harbor

free trade the flow of commerce between nations unrestricted by protective tariffs **free trader** an advocate of free trade

free university a student-run institution for study at will, without faculty restriction and without grades or credits, often emphasizing a point of view on a controversial issue

free verse verse whose structure is without regular meter and is usually without rhyme, but is distinguished from prose by rhythm, a certain heightening of language, poetic intention, or typographical display

free·way (fríːwei) *n.* a usually toll-free expressway

free·wheel (fríːhwiːl, fríːwiːl) 1. *n.* a clutch device connected with the transmission of a motor vehicle, which releases the propeller shaft whenever this revolves faster than the engine shaft || the device on a bicycle by which the back wheel may be disconnected from the driving gear and so revolve freely 2. *v.i.* to drive a motor vehicle with the clutch disengaged || to ride a bicycle without pedaling, i.e. allow it to proceed under its own momentum, or downhill by force of gravity, with the back wheel disengaged || (*pop.*) to behave irresponsibly

free·wheel·ing (fríːwiːliŋ) *adj.* (*automotives*) of the capability of disengaging a motor so that the vehicle may proceed on its own momentum without restraint, saving energy

free will the power and exercise of unhampered choice, *he did it of his own free will* || the doctrine that man is free to control his own actions uncoerced by necessity of fate **free-will** (fríːwil) *adj.* voluntary, *a freewill offering*

freeze (friːz) 1. *v. pres. part.* **freez·ing** *past* **froze** (frouz) *past part.* **fro·zen** (fróuz'n) *v.i.* to change from a liquid to a solid by heat loss, esp. to turn into ice || to be cold enough to turn water into ice || to have the contents turned to ice, *the pipes have frozen* || to suffer intense cold || to die by frost || to become rigid as a result of shock or fright, *the smile froze on his face* || to try to avoid being seen, heard etc. by becoming rigid and silent || (with 'to') to become fixed to by freezing or become as though fixed in this way || *v.t.* to form ice in or on || to preserve (meat, fruit, vegetables, fish etc.) by refrigeration below freezing point || to anesthetize (a part of the body) by artificial freezing || to fix (a price, wage etc.) unchangeably until further authorized adjustment || (*finance*) to immobilize (assets) by governmental authority, prohibiting exchange, withdrawal or expenditure within the country where the assets are **to freeze out** (*pop.*) to get rid of (some objectionable person) by chilly and unfriendly behavior 2. *n.* a freezing or being frozen || a cessation of changes, usu. in economic factors, e.g., a job freeze, a wage freeze || a period of freezing || financial, legislative or administrative action intended to have an immobilizing effect **freez·er** *n.* a machine for freezing ice cream || the part of a refrigerator in which the temperature is below freezing point || a refrigerated room or compartment for quick-freezing perishable food [O.E. frēosan]

freeze-etch·ing (fríːzetʃiŋ) *n.* preparation of a specimen for an electron microscope observation involving freezing and fracturing so that internal structure may be observed **freeze etch** *v.* **freeze etched** *adj.*

freeze-up (fríːzʌp) *n.* a period of freezing weather marking the onset of winter e.g. in subarctic regions

freez·ing (fríːziŋ) *adj.* at or below freezing point || very cold || (of manners) distant, most unfriendly

freezing point the temperature at which a liquid solidifies || the temperature at which liquid and solid phases of a substance are in equilibrium at atmospheric pressure

free zone a free port

F region the uppermost region of the ionosphere, occurring from 90 to 250 miles above the earth's surface

Frei·burg (Switzerland) (fráibuːrk) *FRIBOURG

Frei·burg-im-Breis·gau (fráibuːrkimbráisgau) a city (pop. 174,121) at the foot of the Black Forest in S.W. West Germany: book publishing, textiles, machinery. University (1457)

freight (freit) 1. *n.* the hire of a ship for transporting goods || the transporting of goods by ship, or by other means of transport, esp. ordinary transport service by common carrier, charged at a lower rate than express, and taking longer || a charge for transporting goods, freightage || a shipload, cargo or a load transported by other means || a train carrying goods 2. *adj.* carrying goods rather than passengers, *a freight plane* 3. *v.t.* to load (a ship) with cargo || to load (other transport) with goods for transporting || to transport by freight **freight·age** *n.* the charge for the transportation of goods || transportation of goods || cargo [prob. M. Du. vrecht]

freight car (*Am.*=*Br.* goods wagon) a railroad car for transporting goods

freight·er (fréitər) *n.* a ship which carries cargo || anyone concerned in the transportation of goods by freight || someone who loads a ship || someone who receives and forwards goods || a freight-carrying aircraft

freight train (*Am.*=*Br.* goods train) a railroad train consisting of freight cars

Frei·li·grath (fráiliːgrɑt), Ferdinand (1810–76), German poet, translator and revolutionary

Frei Mon·tal·va (fréimɔntálva), Eduardo (1911–82), Chilean jurist, writer, politician, and president (1964–70). His reform program

---

includes the nationalization of copper resources, agrarian and educational modernization, and increased production, advocating Latin American economic integration

Fre·man·tle (frí:mænt'l) the main seaport (pop. 29,940) of W. Australia, near Perth

Frémont (frí:mɒnt), John Charles (1813–90), U.S. explorer and political leader. He surveyed and mapped the wilderness of the western U.S.A., and led the revolt (1845) against Mexico which resulted in the secession of California. He ran unsuccessfully for president (1856) as the first candidate of the Republican party

French (frentʃ), Daniel Chester (1850–1931), U.S. sculptor, known for his statue of 'The Minuteman' (1875) in Concord, Mass., and the seated Lincoln (1922) in the Lincoln memorial, Washington, D.C.

French, John Denton Pinkstone, 1st earl of Ypres (1852–1925), British field marshal. He commanded (1914–15) the British Expeditionary Force in France and Belgium, and was lord lieutenant of Ireland (1918–21)

French 1. adj. pertaining to, or characteristic of, the country, people or language of France **2.** n. the language of the French people (*FRENCH LANGUAGE) **the French** the French people [O.E. frencisc]

French Academy (F. Académie française) a learned body founded in 1635 by Richelieu. Its members set themselves to codify the language in correct usage and to prune it of provincialism, thereby creating a standard approximating to that of the educated classes. The Academy has a constant membership of 40 men, known as the 'Immortals'. They admit new words or definitions to the Academy's dictionary of the French language (1st edition 1694, 18th edition 1935), and award certain literary prizes (*INSTITUT DE FRANCE)

French and Indian War (1754–63), the American aspect of the Seven Years' War, and the last of the wars between England and France for control of North America (1689–1763). Wolfe's capture of Quebec (1759) was the decisive British victory and was followed by the fall of Montreal (1760). The war was ended by the Treaty of Paris (1763)

French bean (esp. Br.) any bean of genus Phaseolus of which the entire young green pod is eaten

French Canada the areas, chiefly Quebec province, of Canada where French language and culture predominate, the inhabitants being primarily of French descent

French Canadian a Canadian of French descent

French chalk a variety of talc used as a moisture absorbent, a grease remover, and for drawing lines on cloth

French Community the association formed in 1959 by France, her overseas departments and territories, and various independent African countries formerly under French control

French doors a pair of French windows without an intervening panel

French dressing a sauce for a salad etc. consisting of seasoned oil and vinegar

French Equatorial Africa an administrative unit which grouped (1910–58) the French overseas territories of Gabon, the Middle Congo (now the Republic of the Congo), Ubangi-Shari (now the Central African Republic) and Chad

French fry (Am., esp. pl., =Br. chips) a long thin strip of potato fried in deep fat

French Guiana (gi:já:nə) an overseas department (area 35,000 sq. miles, pop. 81,000) of France in N.E. South America. Capital: Cayenne. People: mainly mulatto, with minorities of Bush Negroes and Indians in the interior. Religion: Roman Catholic and local religions. The land is 88% forest (gum and dyewoods, tropical hardwoods) and under 1% cultivated (cereals, cacao, sugarcane, tropical fruits). It rises to 2,300 ft in the far south. Average temperature (F.): 80° on the coast, hotter inland. Rainfall: over 100 ins on the coast, lower inland. Minerals: gold, bauxite (unexploited), tantalite. Exports: gold, lumber, rosewood essence. Imports: coffee, sugar, meat, rice, manioc and manufactured goods. Ports: Cayenne, St-Laurent-du-Maroni, Oyapoc. Monetary unit: metropolitan franc. HISTORY. The area was first settled by the French (c. 1637). It was occupied by the British and Portuguese (1809) and restored to France (1817). Sporadic colonization, the emancipation of slaves (1848) and the establishment of a penal colony (1854–1938)

retarded its growth. It became an overseas department in 1946

French horn a brass wind instrument with a coiled 11-ft tube and valves. It normally has a range of about three and a half octaves upwards from B below the bass staff

French·i·fy (fréntʃifai) pres. part. **French·i·fy·ing** past and past part. **French·i·fied** v.t. to arrange so as to look or seem French

French Indochina (hist.) the union (1887–1954) of the French possessions of Cambodia, Tonkin, Annam and Cochin China, together with Laos (1893–1954) and Chankiang (a part of S. Kwangtung leased from China, 1898–1943). An expedition sent (1858) by Napoleon III captured Saigon (1859). A protectorate was established (1863) over Cambodia, and the colony of Cochin China was created (1867). Annam and Tonkin became (1884) protectorates, and the whole region was combined (1887) in the Union of Indochina. Laos was added (1893) and the territory of Chankiang was leased (1898). After the Japanese occupation (1940–5), the restoration of French control was opposed by nationalist forces who had set up (1945) the independent republic of Vietnam. The ensuing war (1946–54) ended with the French defeat at Dien Bien Phu (1954). The Geneva agreements (1954) ended French Indochina by recognizing the neutrality of Laos and Cambodia and partitioning Vietnam

French knot an embroidery stitch made by winding the thread around the needle once or more than once, and then sending the needle back through the material at the point where it was drawn through

French Language French belongs to the Italic (Romanic) group of the Indo-European family of languages. It developed from the vernacular Latin of the Roman Empire. The French language had a strong influence in W. Europe during the Middle Ages and in the 18th c. For three centuries (following the Norman Conquest) it was the official language of the English court and has had a profound effect on modern English. French borrowed heavily from Italian during the Renaissance and has also many Germanic borrowings. In the 18th c. it was the universal language of European culture. Historically, French is divided into three periods: Old French, before the 14th c., Middle French, 14th–16th cc., and Modern French, from the 16th c. to the present day. It is spoken in France by about 46,500,000, in Belgium by about 3,500,000, in Switzerland by about 1,100,000 speakers, in Canada by about 6,000,000, in Haiti by about 3,500,000, and in other French-speaking countries by about 41,000,000 speakers, in all about 100 million

French leave (in the phrase **to take French leave** to absent oneself without permission or go away without leave-taking

French·man (fréntʃmən) pl. **French·men** (fréntʃmən) n. a man of French birth or nationality ‖ (hist.) a French ship, esp. a warship

French marigold Tagetes patula, an annual bushy plant with strong-smelling orange flowers splashed with red

French mustard a mustard (condiment) made with wine vinegar

French pastry puff pastry baked in fancy shapes and variously filled with custard, cream, jam etc.

French polish a polish of wood alcohol and shellac applied to wooden furniture **French-pol·ish** (fréntʃpóliʃ) v.t. to give a high gloss to (wooden furniture) with French polish

French Polynesia (F. Polynésie française) an overseas territory (area 2,500 sq. miles, pop. 77,000) of France and member of the French Community, comprising several groups of islands in the S. Pacific. Chief island: Tahiti. Chief town: Papeete. Main products: phosphates, copra, coffee, vanilla, mother-of-pearl (*AUSTRAL ISLANDS, *MARQUESAS ISLANDS, *TUAMOTU ARCHIPELAGO, *SOCIETY ISLANDS)

French Revolution the series of violent political and social upheavals in France (1789–99), which overthrew the French monarchy and ended with the establishment of the Consulate. Its causes lay in the many defects of the ancien régime: political power was monopolized by a privileged nobility, the peasants were depressed by the continuance of the feudal system and inefficient agricultural methods, the state was bankrupt after a long series of wars, and there was rapid inflation. Calonne and Necker

tried to reform the antiquated fiscal system (1787–8), but failed when the nobles refused to abandon their privileges. Louis XVI was persuaded to summon the States General for the first time since 1614, but when these met at Versailles (May 5, 1789), the third estate, inspired by the example of the Revolutionary War and by the writings of 18th-c. philosophers (notably Rousseau and Montesquieu), refused to submit to the nobility and upper clergy. Led by Sieyès and Mirabeau, they took the Tennis Court Oath (June 20, 1789), declared themselves to be the National Assembly, and invited the other estates to join them. The king summoned troops to Versailles, and this, together with adverse economic conditions, provoked insurrection in Paris, where the Bastille was stormed (July 14, 1789). Riots followed in towns throughout France, and the National Guard was established under Lafayette. Rural rioting spread panic in the countryside and prompted the deputies at Versailles to vote the abolition of feudalism (Aug. 4, 1789) and to vote the Declaration of the Rights of Man (Aug. 26, 1789). A Paris mob marched to Versailles (Oct. 5, 1789) and ordered the royal family to move to Paris. The Assembly followed (Oct. 15, 1789), and from then on Paris dominated the course of the revolution. The next 18 months were spent in constitutional debate, in the course of which the old provinces of France were replaced by 83 departments, and the Civil Constitution of the Clergy was voted (July 12, 1790). Church land was nationalized and sold, the proceeds forming the security for the assignats. The constitution of 1791 established a limited monarchy and a restricted franchise. Republicanism grew after the royal family had attempted to escape from Paris (June 20, 1791) and were recaptured at Varennes in N.E. France. The Legislative Assembly, which began work Oct. 1, 1791, was suspicious of plots between French émigrés, Marie Antoinette and the Austrian court, and declared war on Austria (Apr. 20, 1792), thus beginning the French Revolutionary Wars. Early reverses in the war led the mob to storm the Tuileries (Aug. 10, 1792) and to commit the September massacres (Sept. 2–6, 1792) in prisons in Paris and the provinces. The Paris Commune, led by Marat, increased its power, and the Legislative Assembly was replaced by the Convention, which abolished the monarchy (Sept. 21, 1792). Political power passed to the Girondists and the king was executed (Jan. 21, 1793). This brought Britain, Holland and Spain into the war against France. Amid military defeats, the treason of Dumouriez and revolt in the Vendée, the extremists of the Mountain organized an armed insurrection (June 2, 1793) which purged the Convention of Girondists and established the emergency government of the Committee of Public Safety. Many Girondists were executed (Oct. 31, 1793). The new government, dominated by Robespierre, represented the dictatorship of the Mountain, and was reinforced by the mass executions of the Terror. With the execution (Mar.–Apr. 1794) of Hébert and Danton and their followers, Robespierre's rule became even more extremist. Maximum wages and prices were fixed. Christianity was replaced by the Cult of the Supreme Being as the official religion. The Convention overthrew Robespierre on 9 Thermidor (July 27, 1794) and a reaction set in. A new constitution was voted (Aug. 22, 1795), and the Vendémiaire insurrection in Paris (Oct. 5, 1795) was put down by Barras and Napoleon Bonaparte. The period of the Directory (1795–9) was marked by economic crises at home and the growth of Napoleon's reputation as a military leader abroad. The Directory was overthrown (Nov. 9, 1799) by the coup d'état of Brumaire, which transferred power to three consuls, Napoleon emerging as the dominant one. Within France, the Revolution had begun to give political power to the bourgeoisie and to distribute land to the peasantry. Its ideals of liberty, equality and fraternity remained as an inspiration to European liberals in the 19th c.

French Revolutionary calendar a calendar beginning Sept. 22, 1792, the date of the inauguration of the 1st French Republic. Twelve months of 30 days each allowed five (or six) days for festivals. The months were: Vendémiaire, Brumaire, Frimaire, Nivôse, Pluviôse, Ventôse, Germinal, Floréal, Prairial, Messidor, Thermidor (Fervidor), Fructidor. The calendar was abolished in 1804

French Revolutionary Wars the wars (1792–1802) in which revolutionary France fought two coalitions of European powers. After the Declaration of Pillnitz (1791), France declared war on Austria (1792). The first coalition was formed (1792) by Austria and Prussia, and was joined by Sardinia (1792) and by Britain, Spain and the Netherlands (1793). Dumouriez won early successes for France at Valmy and Jemappes (1792). France suffered reverses (1793), but Carnot organized a war effort which sent French armies into the Low Countries and many German and Italian states. Prussia, the Netherlands and Spain made peace (1795) with France. As a result of Napoleon's brilliant campaign in Italy (1796–7), Sardinia made peace (1796) and Austria submitted to the Treaty of Campo-Formio (1797). Britain maintained her naval supremacy in the Atlantic and the Mediterranean, and Nelson's victory at the Nile (1798) temporarily isolated Napoleon in Egypt. The second coalition, organized (1798) by Pitt, included Britain, Russia, Austria, Naples, Portugal and Turkey. Russia withdrew (1799). Napoleon's return to Europe (1799) was followed by overwhelming French victories at Marengo and Hohenlinden (1800). Turkey submitted (1800), followed by Austria, Naples and Portugal (1801). Britain made peace with France at Amiens (1802), but the struggle was resumed (1803) in the Napoleonic Wars. The French Revolutionary Wars saw the spread of French influence and of the ideas of the French Revolution over much of Europe. Republics were established in parts of Italy, Switzerland and the Netherlands and Napoleon emerged as the military and political leader of France

French seam a seam made by stitching together the right sides of the material, trimming closely, and turning and stitching on the other side so that all raw edges are enclosed

French Somaliland *DJIBOUTI

French Southern and Antarctic Territories (*F*. les Terres Australes et Antarctiques françaises) a group of territories claimed by France, comprising the islands of St Paul and Nouvelle Amsterdam, and the Kerguelen and Crozet archipelagoes, all (total land area 3,039 sq. miles) in the S. Indian Ocean north of the Antarctic Circle, with Adélie Land, a sector of Antarctica between 136° E. and 142° E., south of 60° S.

French Sudan *MALI

French toast slices of bread dipped in an egg and milk mixture and fried

French Togoland *TOGOLAND, *TOGO

French twist (*cosmetology*) hairstyle in which back is combed up from the neck in smooth rolls with ends covered

French Union the name given by the French constitution of 1946 to the political union of the French Republic (comprising metropolitan France and overseas departments and territories) and associated territories and states. The constitution of 1959 revised the structure of the French Union, which became the French Community

French West Africa (*hist.*) an administrative unit, grouping (1895–1958) the former French overseas territories of Dahomey (now Benin), French Guinea, the French Sudan (now Mali), the Ivory Coast, Mauritania, Niger, Senegal and Upper Volta (now Burkina Faso)

French window a window reaching down to floor level and opening like a door, usually onto a balcony, porch or patio

French·wom·an (fréntʃwʊmən) *pl.* **French·wom·en** (fréntʃwimin) *n.* a woman of French birth or nationality

Fre·neau (frinóu), Philip Morin (1752–1832), U.S. poet and essayist of the American revolution. His patriotic contributions include his essays 'The British Prisonship' and 'American Independence' (1780) and editorials (1791–3) for the 'National Gazette'. His poetry introduced themes and techniques uniquely American, anticipating Poe and Bryant

fre·net·ic, phre·net·ic (frinétik) *adj.* frenzied, frantic, *frenetic haste* [M.E. *frenetik, frenetike* fr. O.F. fr. L. fr. Gk *phrenētikos*, mad]

fre·nu·lum, frae·nu·lum (fríːnjuləm, frénjuləm) *pl.* **fre·nu·la, frae·nu·la** (fríːnjulə, frénjulə) *n.* a frenum, esp. when small [Mod. L.]

fre·num, frae·num (fríːnəm) *pl.* **fre·na, frae·na** (fríːnə) *n.* (*anat., zool.*) a fold of membrane, e.g. of the tongue, clitoris etc. ‖ a process on the hind wing of lepidopterans for attachment to the forewing [L.=a bridle]

fren·zied (frénziːd) *adj.* possessed by or manifesting frenzy ‖ (*pop.*) hectic, *frenzied haste* ‖ violently agitated, *frenzied waves*

fren·zy (frénziː) *pl.* **fren·zies** *n.* a state of tense emotional excitement or mental disturbance close to madness ‖ (*pop.*) intense activity, *a frenzy of work* ‖ a hectic rush, *a frenzy of preparations* [M.E. *frenesie* fr. O.F.]

fre·on (fríːɒn) *n.* any of a group of nonflammable paraffin hydrocarbons containing fluorine atoms used as the working substance in refrigerators [fr. *Freon*, a trademark]

fre·quen·cy (fríːkwənsi) *pl.* **fre·quen·cies** *n.* the quality or condition of occurring repeatedly, *his requests for money come with great frequency* ‖ the number of times a periodic phenomenon or process occurs in a unit of time, e.g. the number of alternations (cycles) per second of an alternating electric current or the number of vibrations of a pendulum per minute (*PERIOD) ‖ the number of objects falling into a single class in a statistical survey of the variation of specified characteristics (*FREQUENCY DISTRIBUTION) [fr. F. *fréquence*]

frequency distribution the organization of statistical data produced by dividing the range of values of the variable into classes and showing the frequency of each class

frequency modulation (*abbr.* FM) a system of radio broadcasting that modulates the frequency of a carrier wave (of constant amplitude) in accordance usually with an audio signal (e.g. one obtained from a microphone) (cf. AMPLITUDE MODULATION)

fre·quent (fríːkwənt) *adj.* occurring often, *frequent headaches* ‖ in close proximity, *there are frequent hotels along that road* ‖ habitual, *a frequent concertgoer* ‖ (*Br.*, of the pulse) rapid [fr. L. *frequens* (*frequentis*) crowded]

fre·quent (frikwént, fríːkwənt) *v.t.* to resort habitually to, go often to **fre·quen·ta·tion** *n.* [fr. L. *frequentare*]

fre·quen·ta·tive (frikwéntətiv) **1.** *adj* (*gram.*) expressing by its form frequent repetition or intensification of an action **2.** *n.* (*gram.*) a frequentative verb ‖ (*gram.*) frequentative aspect [fr. L. *frequentativus*]

fres·co (fréskou) **1.** *pl.* **fres·coes, fres·cos** *n.* a method of painting pictures on plaster, usually on a wall or ceiling, by laying on the color (powdered pigment suspended in water) before the plaster is dry ‖ a picture painted by this method **2.** *v.t.* to paint (a wall etc. or a subject) in this medium [Ital.=cool]

Fres·co·bal·di (frɛskɔbáldiː), Girolamo (1583–1643), Italian composer, an innovator in organ and harpsichord music ('Fiori musicali', 1635)

fresco sec·co (sékou) *n.* painting on dry plaster, using albumen as a binder (cf. FRESCO) [Ital.]

fresh (freʃ) **1.** *adj.* just picked, gathered, made etc., *fresh eggs* ‖ not stale, *fresh air* ‖ not salted, cured or preserved in any way, *fresh fish* ‖ (of water) not salt ‖ brisk and cold, refreshing, *a fresh morning* ‖ (of the wind) fairly strong, of more than breeze force ‖ not tired, in full vigor ‖ not soiled, *a fresh pair of stockings* ‖ further, *a fresh sheet of paper* ‖ new, different, *a fresh start* ‖ opening up a new field of experience, *a fresh line* ‖ having full youthful bloom, *fresh young girls* ‖ healthy-looking, *a fresh complexion* ‖ (with 'from') just come, *fresh from school* ‖ too familiar, impertinent ‖ of a cow that has just recently calved and begun to give milk **to break fresh ground** to try some previously untried sphere of activity **2.** *adv.* freshly, quite recently **3.** *n.* a stream of fresh water, a freshet ‖ the part of a tidal river just above the flow of salt water **fresh·en** *v.t.* to make fresh ‖ (*naut.*) to relieve (a rope) of strain by changing its position ‖ (with 'up') to make (oneself) clean and neat and get rid of strain and fatigue by washing, changing one's clothes etc. ‖ to remove saltiness from (salted meat, fish etc.) the soaking or parboiling ‖ *v.i.* to become fresh ‖ (with 'up') to freshen oneself up ‖ to bear a calf and begin to give milk [O.E. *fersc*]

fresh·et (fréʃit) *n.* a rush of fresh water caused by rain or melted snow ‖ a stream of fresh water flowing into the sea

fresh·ly (fréʃliː) *adv.* in a fresh way ‖ (with *past part.*) just recently

fresh·man (fréʃmən) *pl.* **fresh·men** (fréʃmən) *n.* a student in his first year at a university or college ‖ a student in the first year of a four-year high school

fresh-run (fréʃrʌn) *adj.* (of salmon) newly come from the sea to fresh water again

fresh·wa·ter (fréʃwɒtər, fréʃwɒtər) *adj.* pertaining to, living in or being water that is not salt ‖ located inland and usually of a countrified or provincial nature

Fres·nel (freinél), Augustin Jean (1788–1827), French engineer. He devised methods of obtaining interference of light and, by a zone treatment of a wave front, explained both the apparently rectilinear propagation of light and the phenomenon of diffraction

fres·nel (freinél) *n.* a unit of frequency equal to 10^9 kilocycles/sec [after A. J. *Fresnel*]

Fresnel lens a compound lens having axial symmetry, whose surface is a series of concentric, ring-shaped steps, widely used in headlights and in the optical apparatus of lighthouses

Fres·no (fréznou) a city (pop. 217,289, with agglom. 514,229) of California, in the fertile San Joaquin valley: wine, fruit and vegetable preserving

fret (fret) **1.** *n.* one of a set of narrow ivory, wooden or metal strips across the fingerboard of some stringed instruments. The finger is pressed against it to control the length of string made to vibrate **2.** *v.t. pres. part.* **fret·ting** *past* and *past part.* **fret·ted** to fit with frets [origin unknown]

fret 1. *n.* (esp. *archit.*) a decorative pattern made by the continuous repetition of a figure constructed out of straight lines usually meeting at right angles, as in Greek key patterns **2.** *v.t. pres. part.* **fret·ting** *past* and *past part.* **fret·ted** to ornament (e.g. a ceiling or wooden screen) with interlacing patterns of carved or embossed work ‖ to checker, dapple, *a path fretted with leafy shadow* [perh. O.F. *frete*, latticework]

fret 1. *v.t. pres. part.* **fret·ting** *past* and *past part.* **fret·ted** *v.i.* to be in a state of anxiety, vexation or discontent ‖ to become chafed or rubbed ‖ *v.t.* to cause to be in a state of anxiety, vexation or discontent ‖ to wear away, chafe, rub ‖ to make uneven, ruffle, *the wind fretted the surface of the water* ‖ to make (a hole, channel etc.) by wearing away **2.** *n.* a state of anxiety, vexation or discontent ‖ erosion or an instance of it **fret·ful** *adj.* inclined to fret, e.g. from vexation or illness [O.E. *fretan*, to devour]

fret·saw (frétsɔ) *n.* a fine saw blade stretched on a metal frame, used for cutting out ornamental designs in thin wood

fret·work (frétwɜːrk) *n.* the art of cutting out designs in thin wood with a fretsaw ‖ work so executed ‖ (*archit.*) decoration carved in frets

Freud (frɔid), Anna (1895–1982), Austrian-English psychoanalyst, daughter of Sigmund Freud. She worked especially with children and founded Hampstead Child Therapy Course and Clinic (1938). Her works include 'Introduction to the Technique of Child Psychoanalysis' (1927), 'The Ego and the Mechanisms of Defence' (1936), and 'Normality and Pathology in Childhood' (1965)

Freud, Sigmund (1856–1939), Austrian psychiatrist, founder of psychoanalysis. Studying under J. M. Charcot, Paris (1885–6), and in collaboration with Josef Breuer, Vienna, Freud used hypnosis in the treatment of hysteria. He abandoned this for a method of free association and dream analysis which he called psychoanalysis. At first he placed great emphasis on the role of the unconscious in personality development and discovered the importance of infantile sexuality and the Oedipus complex. Main works of this period are: 'The Interpretation of Dreams' (1900), 'The Psychopathology of Everyday Life' (1904) and 'Three Contributions to the Sexual Theory' (1905). In 'Beyond the Pleasure Principle' (1920) Freud outlined the two dominant principles of the mind as the pleasure-pain complex and the repression-compulsion complex, an instinctive drive of the organism to return to previous states. 'The Ego and the Id' (1923), his last work on psychoanalysis, outlined a new theory of the ego, in which he showed the ego and the superego to be in constant tension, giving rise often to morbid mental attitudes, e.g. inferiority complexes, guilt feelings etc. Four of Freud's most prominent associates, Jung, Adler, Rank and Stekel, founded separate schools of psychoanalysis

Freud·i·an (frɔidiən) **1.** *adj.* pertaining to the work and ideas of Sigmund Freud **2.** *n.* an adherent or advocate of the ideas of Sigmund Freud

Frey (frei) (*Scand. mythol.*) the god of fertility and fruitfulness, of peace and prosperity

Frey·a (fréiə) (*Scand. mythol.*) the sister of Frey and goddess of love and beauty and of fertility

Frey·re (fréirə), Gilberto (1900–), Brazilian sociologist and anthropologist, whose 'Casa grande e senzala' (1946, Eng. trans. 'The Masters and the Slaves', 1956) and 'Sobrados e mucambas' (Eng. trans. 'The Mansions and the Shanties', 1963), are twin anthropological-psychological studies of Brazilian life

Frey·tag (fráitak), Gustav (1816–95), German novelist ('Soll und Haben', 1855) and dramatist ('Die Journalisten', 1854)

Fri. Friday

fri·a·bil·i·ty (fraiəbíliti:) *n.* the state or quality of being friable

fri·a·ble (fráiəb'l) *adj.* (of soil etc.) easily crumbled, apt to crumble [F.]

fri·ar (fráiər) *n.* a member of certain monastic orders, esp. one of the four mendicant orders (under vows of poverty and chastity) known as the Grey Friars (*FRANCISCAN), Austin Friars (*AUGUSTINIAN), Black Friars (*DOMINICAN) and White Friars (*CARMELITE) [M.E. *frere* fr. O.F.]

Friar Minor *FRANCISCAN

friar's balsam a medicinal product, consisting mainly of benzoin, balsam of Tolu, aloes and storax, for application to small wounds and ulcers, or for mixing with hot water and inhaling to clear catarrh etc.

fri·ar·y (fráiəri) *pl.* **fri·ar·ies** *n.* a house of an order of friars ‖ a brotherhood of friars

frib·ble (fríb'l) **1.** *n.* (*old-fash.*) a trifler **2.** *v.i. pres. part.* **frib·bling** *past* and *past part.* **frib·bled** (*old-fash.*) to behave in a frivolous manner, trifle [etym. doubtful]

Fri·bourg (fri:bu:r) (*G.* Freiburg) a French-speaking, mainly Catholic canton (area 647 sq. miles, pop. 185,246) of W. Switzerland ‖ its capital (pop. 39,695). Cathedral (15th–16th c.). University (1889)

fric·as·see (fríkəsi:) **1.** *n.* a dish of meat, poultry or game cut up and cooked in a sauce **2.** *v.t.* to cook (meat etc.) in this way [F. *fricassée*]

fric·a·tive (fríkətiv) **1.** *adj.* of a consonant produced by friction of the breath emitted through the narrow aperture of either lips or teeth, e.g. 'f', 'th', 's' **2.** *n.* such a consonant [fr. Mod. L. *fricativus*]

fric·tion (fríkʃən) *n.* (*mech.*) the force which opposes the movement of one surface sliding or rolling over another with which it is in contact ‖ the act of rubbing the surface of the body, e.g. with a lotion to stimulate the skin after shaving ‖ emotional opposition to the acts or behavior of another person, discord between individuals or within a group **fric·tion·al** *adj.* [F.]

frictional unemployment unemployment produced by merely temporary difficulties, change of work etc.

friction calendering a bright, shiny finish used on lining twills, sateen silesia, messaline, and bind-finish cloths. The effect is brought about by the one calender roller going at a slightly increased speed over the other roller in the set

Fri·day (fráidi:, fráidei) *n.* the sixth day of the week [O.E. *frigedæg*, day of the goddess Frigga]

fried *past* and *past part.* of FRY

Frie·dan (fri:dǽn), Betty (1921–), U.S. writer and feminist, a founder of the National Organization for Women (NOW) (1966). She wrote 'The Feminine Mystique' (1963) and began the contemporary woman's movement. Other works include 'It Changed My Life' (1976) and 'The Second Stage' (1981)

Fried·land, Battle of (frí:dlænd) the French victory (1807) in which Napoleon brought the Russians to terms at Tilsit

Fried·man, (frí:dmən), Milton (1912–), U.S. economist, whose conservative approach often opposes the policies of John Maynard Keynes. A professor (1948–) at the University of Chicago, he favors limits for the federal manipulation of monies, the elimination of price supports and protective tariffs, and a negative income tax. His works include 'Capitalism and Freedom' (1962), 'A Monetary History of the United States (1867–1960)' (with Anna J. Schwartz, 1963), and 'Free to Choose' (with Rose Friedman, 1980). He received in 1976 the Nobel prize for economics

Fried·rich (frí:drix), Caspar David (1774–1840), German painter of Romantic landscapes

friend (frend) *n.* someone on terms of affection and regard for another who is neither relative

nor lover ‖ someone who freely supports and helps out of good will ‖ an acquaintance ‖ an ally, *the friends of France* ‖ (*Br.*) a person who covenants to give financial help over a period of years, e.g. for the upkeep of a cathedral **Friend** a member of the Society of Friends **my honourable friend** (*Br.*) an M.P. in the House of Commons as he is formally referred to in debate by another **my learned friend** (*Br.*) the formal style of reference used by one lawyer of another in court **to have a friend at court** to have someone influential to speak on one's behalf **to make friends with** to strike up a friendship with ‖ to gain the support or goodwill of [O.E. *frēond*]

friend·li·ness (fréndli:nis) *n.* the quality or state of being friendly

friend·ly (fréndli:) **1.** *adj. comp.* **friend·li·er** *superl.* **friend·li·est** showing interest and good will, amiable, *a friendly smile* ‖ manifesting kindness, *a friendly act* ‖ sympathetic, *a friendly interest* ‖ not hostile, *a friendly sheikh* ‖ (*rhet.*) causing feelings of well-being and good will, welcoming, *a friendly fire was burning in the hearth* ‖ (of a game) played for the sport and not as part of a competition or for a prize ‖ (of a legal action) brought merely to get a legal decision **2.** *adv.* amicably, *friendly disposed* [O.E. *frēondlic* adj., *frēondlice* adv.]

Friendly Islands *TONGA

friendly society (*Br.*) a benefit society

friend·ship (fréndʃip) *n.* a relationship of mutual affection and good will ‖ the state of being a friend or of being friends ‖ harmonious cooperation, *friendship between two countries* [O.E. *frēondscipe*]

Friendship Force a reciprocal people-to-people exchange of visiting program between countries, encouraged by the participants' governments

Friends, the Society of a Christian body founded (mid–17th c.) in England by George Fox. Its members, known as Friends or Quakers, believe that the Holy Spirit shines in the heart of every man (inner light). They have few rites and no ordained ministry, and their meetings are characterized by much silent and free prayer. Friends are opposed to war, and most refuse to participate in it. Originally a radical Puritan sect, they suffered violent persecution (17th c.), and many emigrated to form communities abroad, e.g. in New England (1656) and in Pennsylvania (1682). In the 19th c. many Friends were prominent in social reform, e.g. Elizabeth Fry. Friends sponsor much humanitarian and educational work

frier *FRYER

Fries (fri:s), John (1750–1818), U.S. rebel and leader of Pennsylvania Germans opposed to the levying (1798) of Federal property taxes for a possible war with France. Sentenced to death, he was pardoned by President John Adams

Fries·land (frí:zlənd) (*Du.* Vriesland) a province (area 1,323 sq. miles, pop. 589,252) in the northern Netherlands. Capital: Leeuwarden ‖ (*hist.*) the region comprising the above province and the former German districts of E. and N. Friesland

Fri·esz (fri:ez), Othon (1879–1949), French painter, a Fauve

frieze (fri:z) *n.* an ornamental band, e.g. along the top of a wall ‖ (*archit.*) that part of the entablature of a building between the architrave and the cornice, usually decorated with sculpture, or the band of sculpture itself ‖ the decorative border of a wallpaper below the ceiling or cornice [F. *frise*]

frieze *n.* a rough woolen cloth with a shaggy nap usually on one side only [F. *frise* fr. *friser*, to curl]

frig·ate (frígit) *n.* (*Am.*) a warship of 5,000–7,000 tons, smaller than a cruiser ‖ (*Br.*) a destroyer escort ‖ (*hist.*) a fast three-masted sailing ship carrying up to 60 guns, next in size to ships of the line [F. *frégate*]

frigate bird a large swift-flying tropical marine bird of fam. *Fregatidae* with long wings and tail. They feed mainly on fish, often by robbing other birds of fish they have caught

Frig·ga (fríga) (*Scand. mythol.*) queen of the gods and the sky, goddess of the hearth, wife of Odin

fright (frait) *n.* a sudden shock of fear or alarm, a feeling of sudden terror ‖ a grotesque-looking object or person **fright·en** *v.t.* to cause to feel fear ‖ to make loath to run the risk of, *he is frightened of looking silly* **fright·ful** *adj.* causing horror, *a frightful accident* ‖ causing anxi-

ety, *frightful suspense* ‖ (*pop.*) provoking ridicule, *a frightful hat* ‖ (*pop.*) very bad *frightful weather* ‖ (*pop.*) extreme, intense, *a frightful nuisance* **fright·ful·ly** *adv.* in a frightful way ‖ (*pop.*) very, extremely [O.E. *fryhto*]

frig·id (frídʒid) *adj.* extremely cold ‖ forbidding, *a frigid silence* ‖ marked by a chilling formality ‖ of a person not being able to achieve orgasm in sexual intercourse [fr. L. *frigidus*]

fri·gid·i·ty (fridʒíditi:) *n.* the quality or state of being frigid, esp. a person's lack of sexual desire or inability to achieve orgasm [F. *frigidité*]

frigid zones the areas around the North and South Poles within the polar circles

frig·o·rif·ic (frigərífik) *adj.* producing cold, chilling [F. *frigorifique*]

frig·o·rim·e·ter (frigərímitər) *n.* a thermometer designed to measure very low temperatures [fr. L. *frigus* (*frigoris*), coldness+METER]

fri·jol (frí:houl, *Span.* fri:hól) *pl.* **fri·jo·les** (frí:houlz, fri:hóuli:z, *Span.* fri:hóles) *n.* a bean of genus *Phaseolus*, esp. *P. vulgaris*, the kidney bean [Span.]

fri·jo·les refritos (fri:hóuli:s) Latin dish of mashed, cooked, seasoned, refried beans

frill (fril) **1.** *n.* an ornamental edging used to trim clothes, curtains etc., formed by gathering the inner edge and leaving the outer edge loose ‖ a similar decoration made with paper to ornament e.g. the knucklebone of a ham ‖ (*pl.*) superficial embellishments, *a plain story without any frills* ‖ (*biol.*) a natural ruff of feathers, fur or membrane **2.** *v.t.* to ornament with a frill **fril·ly** *comp.* **fril·li·er** *superl.* **fril·li·est** *adj.* adorned with frills ‖ like a frill [etym. doubtful]

fringe (frindʒ) **1.** *n.* an ornamental border of loose or twisted threads made at an edge or made separately for attachment ‖ a border or edge of hair on an animal or plant ‖ an outer margin, *the fringe of the forest* ‖ (*Br.*) bangs (hair cut square across the forehead) ‖ (*optics*) any of the light or dark bands produced by the diffraction or interference of light ‖ a marginal or extremist group of any society, *the anarchist fringe* **2.** *v.t. pres. part.* **fring·ing** *past* and *past part.* **fringed** to form a border for, *trees fringed the lake* ‖ to border on, *the river fringes his land* ‖ to put a fringe on **3.** *adj.* at the limit or border, *a fringe area of clear television reception* [M.E. *frenge* fr. O.F.]

fringe benefit an equivalent to a payment over and above the basic wage, paid by an employer, e.g. paid holiday, pension contribution, meal voucher

Fringlish (fríŋliʃ) *n.* misused English with much French integrated into it *Cf* FRANGLAIS, HINGLISH, JAPLISH, SPANGLISH

frip·per·y (frípəri) *pl.* **frip·per·ies** *n.* cheap finery ‖ trashy ornamentation ‖ affected elegance [O.F. *freperie* fr. *frepe*, rag]

Fris·bee (frízbi:) *n.* (*sports*) trade name for a popular toy circular disc thrown between participants

Fri·sian (fríʒən) **1.** *n.* a native or inhabitant of Friesland or the Frisian Is ‖ (*hist.*) a member of the W. Germanic people who lived (1st c. A.D.) between the mouths of the Scheldt and Ems Rivers, and who were probably associated with the Anglo-Saxon invasion of England (5th c.) ‖ the W. Germanic language of the Frisian people **2.** *adj.* of or relating to Friesland, the Frisians or to their language

Frisian Islands a chain of islands along the Dutch, German and Danish coasts. They have been separated from the mainland by the land's sinking. The West Frisian Is include Texel, Vlieland, Terschelling, Ameland and Schiermonnikoog, and belong to the Netherlands. The East Frisian Is include Borkum, Juist, Norderney, Langedog and Spiekeroog, and belong to Germany. The North Frisian Is consist of Sylt, Föhr, Nordstrand, Pellworm, Amrum (which are German) and Römö, Fanö and Manö (which are Danish)

frisk (frisk) **1.** *v.i.* to scamper and jump about playfully ‖ *v.t.* (*pop.*) to search (a person or his clothes) for weapons or stolen goods, by quickly feeling over his clothing ‖ (*pop.*) to steal from (someone) in this manner **2.** *n.* a frolic, gambol ‖ (*pop.*) a quick search of a person for concealed weapons or stolen goods [fr. older *frisk* adj. fr. O.F. *frisque*, full of life]

fris·ket (frískit) *n.* (*printing*) an iron frame strung with tapes for keeping the sheet in position on the tympan of a hand press during printing ‖ (*printing, photog.*) a masking device [fr. F. *frisquette*]

frisk·i·ly (frískili:) *adv.* in a frisky manner

CONCISE PRONUNCIATION KEY: **(a)** æ, c*a*t; ɑ, c*a*r; ɔ f*aw*n; ei, sn*a*ke. **(e)** e, h*e*n; i:, sh*ee*p; iə, d*ee*r; ɛə, b*ea*r. **(i)** i, f*i*sh; ai, t*i*ger; ə:, b*i*rd. **(o)** o, *o*x; au, c*ow*; ou, g*oa*t; u, p*oo*r; ɔi, r*oy*al. **(u)** ʌ, d*u*ck; u, b*u*ll; u:, g*oo*se; ə, b*a*cillus; ju:, c*u*be. x, lo*ch*; θ, *th*ink; ð, bo*th*er; z, *Z*en; ʒ, cor*s*age; dʒ, sa*v*age; ŋ, orangutan*g*; j, *y*ak; ʃ, *fish*; tʃ, fe*tch*; 'l, rabb*le*; 'n, redd*en*. Complete pronunciation key appears inside front cover.

frisk·i·ness (fríski:nis) *n.* the quality or state of being frisky

frisk·y (fríski:) *comp.* **frisk·i·er** *superl.* **frisk·i·est** *adj.* lively and playful

frit (frit) 1. *n.* a calcined mixture of materials from which glass is made ‖ the composition used for making soft porcelain ‖ glass quenched and ground as a basis for certain glazes and enamels 2. *v.t. pres. part.* **frit·ting** *past* and *past part.* **frit·ted** to make a frit of (material for glass or porcelain manufacture) [fr. Ital. *fritta* fr. *friggere*, to fry]

Frith (friθ), William Powell (1819–1909), English painter. He excelled in the detail of crowd scenes, e.g. 'Ramsgate Sands' (1854), 'Derby Day' (1858)

frith (friθ) *n.* a firth

frit·il·lar·y (frít'lẹri:) *pl.* **frit·il·lar·ies** *n.* a member of *Fritillaria*, fam. *Liliaceae*, a genus of temperate plants of the northern hemisphere cultivated for their ornamental flowers. The buds and fruit are erect, but the open flower is pendulous ‖ any of various butterflies with mottled markings of genus *Argynnis* and related genera [fr. Mod. L. *Fritillaria*]

fri·to·mis·to (fri:toumi:stou) *n.* dish of meat, seafood, or vegetables deep-fried in batter

frit·ter (frítər) *n.* a small lump of batter, containing sliced fruit, vegetables or meat, fried in deep fat [F. *friture*]

fritter *v.t.* (with 'away') to waste (time, money etc.) on too many or frivolous interests ‖ to cause to break into fragments or as if into fragments [O.F. *freture, fraiture*]

Fri·u·li-Ve·ne·zia Giu·lia (fri:ú:li:venétsjadʒú:ljα) an autonomous region (area 3,030 sq. miles, pop. 1,242,987) of Italy, between the Carnic Alps and the Adriatic. Capital: Udine. Products: cereals, fruit, vegetables, wine, silk. Italy recovered the western part (Udine) from Austria in 1866, and gained the eastern part (Gorizia) in 1919

friv·ol (frível) *v. pres. part.* **friv·ol·ing**, esp. *Br.* **friv·ol·ling** *past* and *past part.* **friv·oled**, esp. *Br.* **friv·olled** *v.i.* to behave frivolously ‖ *v.t.* (with 'away') to waste in trifling, spend frivolously [FRIVOLOUS]

fri·vol·i·ty (frivóliti:) *pl.* **fri·vol·i·ties** *n.* the quality of being frivolous ‖ a frivolous piece of behavior [fr. F. *frivolité*]

friv·o·lous (frívələs) *adj.* gay and lighthearted in pursuit of trivial or futile pleasures ‖ lacking in proper seriousness ‖ empty, without importance, *frivolous arguments* [fr. L. *frivolus*]

frizz, friz (friz) 1. *v.t.* (often with 'up') to cause (hair) to form a close mass of short curls ‖ to dress (leather) with pumice or a scraping knife ‖ *v.i.* (of hair) to become frizzed 2. *n.* a close mass of short curls [fr. F. *friser*]

friz·zle (fríz'l) *v. pres. part.* **friz·zling** *past* and *past part.* **friz·zled** *v.i.* to make a sizzling noise, e.g. in frying, roasting, grilling, etc. ‖ *v.t.* to sear and sizzle (meat, etc.) by frying, roasting, etc. ‖ to scorch [imit.]

frizzle l. *v.t. pres. part* and *i.*, **friz·zling** *past* and *past part.* **friz·zled** to curl in small close curls 2. *n.* a mass of frizzed hair **fríz·zly** *adj.* [etym. doubtful]

friz·zy (frízi:) *comp.* **friz·zi·er** *superl.* **friz·zi·est** *adj.* (of hair) curled in a mass of tight curls

fro (frou) *adv.* *TO AND FRO

Frö·bel, Froe·bel (frö:b'l), Friedrich Wilhelm August (1782–1852), German educator. He opened the first kindergarten (1837). He believed that the teacher should further children's natural development by freely encouraging their creative sense through games and exercises

Fro·ben (fróubən), Johann (*L.* Frobenius, c. 1460–1527), German printer. He set up his own printing works in Basle in 1491, and printed over 300 titles, including the works of his friend Erasmus. He introduced roman and italic into Germany. His books are distinguished both for their accuracy and their fine impression

Fro·bish·er (fróubiʃər), Sir Martin (c. 1535–94), English navigator. He visited Labrador and S. Baffin Is. (1576–8) in search of the Northwest Passage

frock (frɒk) *n.* (*Br.*) a woman's light dress for informal occasions ‖ a child's dress ‖ a monk's habit [F. *froc*]

frock coat a man's long-skirted, double-breasted coat, not cut away in front, worn esp. in the 19th c.

FROD (*mil. acronym*) for functionally related observable difference, a reconnaissance bomber

Froebel *FRÖBEL

froe, frow (frou) *n.* a tool with the handle set at right angles to the blade, used for splitting staves for casks and shingles [etym. doubtful]

frog (frɒg, frɔg) *n.* a small, coldblooded, tailless, leaping animal of order *Anura*, esp. genus *Rana*, living both on land and in water. Its larval form is the tadpole **frog in the throat** hoarseness [O.E. *frogga*]

frog *n.* an attachment to a belt for a bayonet or a sword ‖ a coat-fastening consisting of a loop (often of braid) and a spindle-shaped button (sometimes tasselled), used e.g. on duffel coats and in a highly ornamental form on some military full-dress uniforms ‖ a perforated flower holder used to assist with arrangements [etym. doubtful]

frog *n.* a V-shaped pad of elastic, horny but sensitive substance in the middle of the underside of a horse's hoof [etym. doubtful]

frog *n.* a grooved iron device at an intersection of railroad (or streetcar) tracks to allow passage across, or to, another line ‖ a device for supporting and insulating intersecting trolley wires [origin unknown]

Frog *n.* (*mil.*) (NATO) name for a series of U.S.S.R. surface-to-surface battlefield missiles carrier with a 12- to 30-m range

frog·fish (frógfiʃ, frógfiʃ) *pl.* **frog·fish, frog·fish·es** *n.* a fish of fam. *Antennariidae*, e.g. the angler

frogged (frɒgd, frɔgd) *adj.* (of a garment) having frogs as fastenings

frog·man (frógmæn, frógmæn, frógmən, frógmən, frógmən) *pl.* **frog·men** (frógmen, frógmen, frógmən, frógmən) *n.* a diver equipped with flippers, a rubber suit, and a breathing apparatus allowing him to stay underwater for a long period. Frogmen are used in reconnaissance, wreck-searching, underwater demolition etc.

frog·march (frógmα:rtʃ, frógmα:rtʃ) *v.t.* to carry (someone putting up a resistance, e.g. a schoolboy or a criminal) face downwards parallel with the ground, each limb being held by one person

frog spawn eggs of the female frog ‖ certain freshwater algae

Fro·gurt (fróugə:rt) *n.* trade name for frozen yogurt

Frois·sart (frwæsær), Jean (c. 1337–1404), French chronicler and poet. He traveled widely in Europe and lived in the French and English courts. His chronicle, based on the existing chronicle of Jean le Bel, gives a vivid if biased description of feudal life 1326–1400

frol·ic (frólik) 1. *v.i. pres. part.* **frol·ick·ing** *past* and *past part.* **frol·icked** to frisk, gambol 2. *n.* an outburst of high spirits ‖ a bit of gay, harmless fun **fról·ic·some** *adj.* [Du. *vroolijk* adj.]

from (frʌm, frɒm) *prep.* indicating outward movement or distance in relation to a point in space or time, *a radius of 100 miles from London, from 1 o'clock onwards* ‖ indicating a point of departure, or starting point in place or time or abstract calculation, *they saw it from the hill, from midnight to midday* ‖ indicating a place of origin, *creatures from outer space* ‖ indicating cause, *from motives of jealousy* ‖ indicating separation, *they released him from his obligation* ‖ indicating deprivation, *they took her passport from her* ‖ indicating a relationship of distinction, *you cannot tell one twin from the other* ‖ describing a change of amount, state or quality, *it has gone up from 1,000 dollars to 1,500, he changed from a rebel into a conformist* ‖ indicating source or derivation, *a picture copied from an old master* ‖ indicating selection, *he was chosen from 20 candidates* ‖ (with 'to') indicating limits, *cocktails from 6 to 8* ‖ (with 'to' and extreme cases or examples) indicating wide scope, *from A to Z* ‖ sent or given by, *a gift from an uncle* [O.E. *fram, from,* forward, away]

Fro·men·tin (frɔmᾶtɛ̃), Eugène (1820–76), French painter and writer. He painted finely detailed pictures with Oriental themes, and wrote art criticism, travel books and one novel, 'Dominique' (1863)

Fromm (frɔm), Erich (1900–80), German psychoanalyst who maintained that human needs should be fulfilled by society because the personality is shaped by culture. He taught at various universities, including New York University during the 1960s. His works include 'Man for Himself' (1947), 'Psychoanalysis and Religion' (1950), 'The Sane Society' (1955), 'The Art of Loving' (1956), and 'The Anatomy of Human Destructiveness' (1973)

frond (frɒnd) *n.* (*bot.*) the leaf of a palm ‖ the leaf of a fern, often bearing spores ‖ (*bot.*) the thallus of some seaweeds and lichens ‖ (*rhet.*) any leaf or leaflike appendage **frónd·ed** *adj.* having fronds [fr. L. *frons (frondis),* a leaf]

Fronde (frɒ̃d) (*F. hist.*) the revolt (1648–53) against the administration of Mazarin, during Louis XIV's minority. The Paris parliament rebelled against fiscal policy (May 1648), its leaders were imprisoned by Mazarin, Paris rose in revolt, and the rising was suppressed (Jan.–Mar. 1649) by a royal army under Condé. Condé then led a new revolt among the nobility, in alliance with Spain (1650), but this was put down in Paris (1652) and in the provinces (1653)

Fron·di·zi (frondí:si:), Arturo (1908–), Argentinian lawyer and president (1958–62). His austerity program to revitalize the economy irritated the military, and when he allowed the 'Peronista' party to participate in the 1962 Congressional elections, the military deposed him

fron·dose (fróndous) *adj.* covered with or bearing fronds [fr. L. *frondosus,* leafy]

front (frʌnt) 1. *n.* the most forward part or surface of anything, *the front of the train* ‖ the most advanced position, *only those in the front can see* ‖ (in static warfare) the most advanced battle line, where the fighting takes place ‖ the scene of a particular activity, *the home front* ‖ a grouping of separate bodies of people, esp. political parties, for some common objective, *a solid front, a popular front* ‖ (*archit.*) a face of a building, esp. the one having the main entrance ‖ (esp. *Br.*) a seaside promenade ‖ (of land) frontage ‖ a dicky, shirtfront ‖ outward demeanor, *a bold front* ‖ the part of the human body opposite the back, *turn on your front* ‖ a person appointed to a post as a figurehead to bring prestige, or a person or group used to cover up some illegal activity ‖ (*meteor.*) the surface of separation between cold and warm masses of air, usually lying along a trough of low pressure ‖ the auditorium of a theater and all that is in front of the curtain, including the personnel who work there **in front of** before (place) **to change front** to alter abruptly the grounds of argument **to come to the front** to become a leader, come to be in the public eye **to keep up a front** to maintain an appearance of success and prosperity so as to conceal failure or disaster 2. *adj.* of the, or in the, more or most forward position, *front legs* ‖ (*phon.*) articulated with the front of the tongue, *a front vowel* 3. *adv.* at or to the front, esp. in **out front** (*theater*) in the audience **up front** (*mil.*) in the front line [O.F. *front,* forehead]

front *v.t.* to face toward, *the house fronts the lake* ‖ to be in front of, *a rose garden fronts the house* ‖ (*archit.*) to supply a front or face to, *fronted with marble* ‖ to confront ‖ (*phon.*) to pronounce with the tongue in the forward position ‖ *v.i.* to serve as a front ‖ to be facing, *the house fronts on the lake* [fr. O.F. *fronter*]

front·age (frʌ́ntidʒ) *n.* the front of a plot of land, esp. with respect to its length and the direction it faces ‖ the land between the front of a building and the street, road or river which it faces ‖ the front of a building [FRONT *n.*]

frontage road a service road

fron·tal (frʌ́nt'l) *adj.* in or at or relating to the forward part ‖ directly towards the front, *a frontal assault* ‖ (*anat.*) pertaining to the forehead, *a frontal bone* ‖ relating to a meteorological front [fr. Mod. L. *frontalis*]

frontal *n.* the cloth hanging in front of an altar, changed according to the ecclesiastical seasons ‖ the facade of a building [M.E. *frountel* fr. O.F.]

front bench (*Br.*) either of the two rows of seats in the House of Commons occupied by members who are of ministerial or shadow cabinet rank **front bencher** someone who occupies such a seat (cf. BACK BENCH)

front door the main entrance to a house etc. ‖ a frank, open approach towards a desired goal, *to do something through the front door*

Fron·te·nac (frɒ̃tænæk), Louis de Buade, comte de (1620–98), French governor (1672–82 and 1689–98) of New France (Canada)

front-end load (frʌ́ntend) (*banking*) installment payments arranged so that an increased proportion are due at the beginning of the period

fron·ten·is (frənténəs) *n.* (*sports*) a Latin American ballgame played with tennis rackets on four-walled court

fron·tier (frʌntíər) **1.** *n.* the border separating one country from another ‖ (esp. *pl.*) an area of mental activity where much remains to be done, *the frontiers of biochemistry* ‖ a marginal region between settled and unsettled lands **2.** *adj.* at or relating to a frontier [O.F. *frontiere*] —The American frontier moved steadily westward as America expanded. The first frontiers, formed when colonists moved from the Atlantic coast into the Pennsylvania valley and across the Allegheny Mtns deep into the continent, developed chiefly after the War of 1812. First came pioneers engaged in hunting and subsistence farming, then came settlers who bought the pioneers' half-developed land and introduced a simple, community life, and after them came financiers and businessmen who brought the communities to maturity and gave them a voice in national affairs. The last frontiers, from 1840, bringing the greatest hardships to settlers but also the richest rewards, carried Americans to the Pacific coast. Settlement came mostly in rushes accompanied by lawlessness, waste, exaggerated optimism and a 'get-rich-quick' attitude. Although the federal census announced the physical end of the frontier in 1890, the unique frontier experience produced a nation and a people marked by individualism, courage, belief in progress, and love of freedom and opportunity

fron·tiers·man (frʌntíərzmən) *pl.* **fron·tiers·men** (frʌntíərzmən) *n.* (*Am. hist.*) someone living in a frontier territory

Fron·ti·nus (frɒntáinəs), Sextus Julius (c. 30–104), Roman statesman, governor of Britain (c. 74–8), where he was succeeded by Agricola. He was the author of a manual on strategy and a treatise on Rome's water supply

fron·tis·piece (frʌntispi:s) *n.* an introductory illustration to a book, usually facing the title page ‖ (*archit.*) a facade ‖ (*archit.*) a pediment over a window, door etc. [F. *frontispice*]

front·lash (frʌntlæʃ) *n.* reaction to a backlash designed to neutralize it *Cf* BACKLASH

front·let (frʌntlit) *n.* an ornament worn on the forehead, or a band tied around it ‖ a phylactery ‖ an animal's forehead ‖ a short cloth over the upper part of an altar frontal [O.F. *frontelet*]

front matter (*Am.*=*Br.* prelims, *PRELIMINARIES*) the title page and other pages of a book preceding the text proper

front money (*business*) initial investment required to get a speculative project started in anticipation of attracting investment later by others

fron·ton (frɒntɒn) *n.* a pediment [F. fr. Ital. *frontone*]

front-page (frʌntpéidʒ) *adj.* (of news) important or sensational enough to be printed on the front page of a newspaper

front·stall (frʌntstɔl) *n.* (*armor*) a plate having holes for the horse's eyes and nostrils and attached to the bridle

Frost (frɔst, frɒst), Robert Lee (1875–1963), American poet. He wrote of the country ways and life in New England. Among his books are 'A Boy's Will' (1913), 'North of Boston' (1914), 'Mountain Interval' (1916), 'New Hampshire' (1923), 'A Witness Tree' (1942) and 'Collected Poems' (1930)

frost (frɔst, frɒst) **1.** *n.* the crystallization of the water in the atmosphere upon exposed surfaces occurring when their temperature falls below freezing point ‖ the ice thus formed ‖ temperature below freezing point, *10 degrees of frost* ‖ coldness of manner ‖ (esp. *Br.*, *pop.*) a disappointing failure **2.** *v.t.* to damage by frost ‖ to cover with ice crystals ‖ to roughen the surface of (glass) and thus destroy its transparency, though not its translucency ‖ to coat with frosting [O.E. *frost, forst*]

frost·bite (frɔstbit, frɒstbit) **1.** *n.* an injury to the tissues of part of the body caused by exposure to freezing cold **2.** *v.t. pres. part.* **frost·bit·ing** *past* **frost·bit** (frɔstbit, frɒstbit) *past* and *past part.* **frost·bit·ten** (frɔstbit'n, frɒstbit'n), **frost·bit** to injure (a part of the body) by exposure to freezing cold

frostbiting or **frostbite boating** (*sports*) sailboating for sport during the winter **frostbiter** *n.*

frost·bound (frɔstbaund) *adj.* frozen

frost·ed (frɔstid, frɒstid) *adj.* covered with frost ‖ (of glass etc.) given a roughened surface like frost ‖ coated with frosting ‖ frostbitten

frost flower *Milla biflora*, fam. *Liliaceae*, a small plant of southwestern U.S.A. and Mexico

‖ one of the ice crystal whorls formed e.g. on windows when it is freezing

frost·i·ly (frɔstili:, frɒstili:) *adv.* in a frosty manner

frost·i·ness (frɔsti:nis, frɒsti:nis) *n.* the quality or state of being frosty

frost·ing (frɔstiŋ, frɒstiŋ) *n.* a mixture of fine sugar, white of egg etc. used to coat a cake ‖ an unglossed finish on metal or glass ‖ a decorative substance made from powdered glass flakes, varnish and glue ‖ (*cosmetology*) creation of two-tone style by bleaching small sections of hair

frost·y (frɔsti:, frɒsti:) *comp.* **frost·i·er** *superl.* **frost·i·est** *adj.* cold with frost, or producing frost ‖ covered with frost ‖ unfriendly, cold in feeling, *a frosty reception*

froth (frɔθ, frɒθ) **1.** *n.* the mass of small bubbles produced by the agitation or fermentation of a liquid ‖ foam ‖ spume ‖ frivolous or trivial talk or writing **2.** *v.t.* to cause to form froth ‖ to cause to be covered with froth ‖ *v.i.* to foam, *frothing at the mouth* ‖ to cover with something insubstantial **fróth·i·ly** *adv.* **fróth·i·ness** *n.* **fróth·y** *comp.* **fróth·i·er** *superl.* **fróth·i·est** *adj.* light as froth ‖ covered in froth ‖ frivolous, superficial [M.E. *frothe* perh. fr. O.N.]

Froude (fru:d), James Anthony (1818–94), British historian. His biography of Carlyle (1882–4) provoked much criticism

frou-frou (frú:fru:) *n.* a fussy decoration, esp. on clothes ‖ the soft hissing sound made by the movement of petticoats or skirts [F.]

frow *FROE

fro·ward (fróuərd) *adj.* (*old-fash.*) stubbornly self-willed [early M.E. fr. O.N. *frá*, from+ -*ward*]

frown (fraun) **1.** *v.i.* to wrinkle the brow, e.g. in displeasure, puzzlement or deep thought ‖ (with 'on', 'upon', 'at') to be disapproving in attitude, *she frowns on such pleasures* ‖ (*rhet.*, of inanimate things) to look foreboding, *frowning cliffs* ‖ *v.t.* to subdue (someone) with a frown, *she frowned him into silence* **2.** *n.* a wrinkling or drawing together of the brows indicating e.g. displeasure, puzzlement or concentration [M.E. *froune* fr. O.F.]

frowst·y (fráusti:) *comp.* **frowst·i·er** *superl.* **frowst·i·est** *adj.* (*Br.*) musty, stale-smelling, e.g. of the air of a long unused room [origin unknown]

frowz·i·ly (fráuzili:) *adv.* in a frowzy manner

frowz·i·ness (fráuzi:nis) *n.* the state or quality of being frowzy

frowz·y (fráuzi:) *comp.* **frowz·i·er** *superl.* **frowz·i·est** *adj.* (of people or things) unkempt, slovenly ‖ (of the atmosphere) stale, musty [origin unknown]

froze *past* of FREEZE

fro·zen (fróuz'n) *past part.* of FREEZE ‖ *adj.* congealed ‖ injured or killed by freezing ‖ (of food) preserved by freezing ‖ (of assets) not able to be realized except with great loss ‖ (of an account) placed under a ban on withdrawals

frozen frame a cinema image held motionless

Fruc·ti·dor (frykti:dɔr) *FRENCH REVOLUTIONARY CALENDAR

fruc·tif·er·ous (frʌktífərəs) *adj.* fruit-bearing [fr. L. *fructifer*]

fruc·ti·fi·ca·tion (frʌktifikéiʃən) *n.* fruit formation ‖ any spore-producing structure in cryptogams ‖ (*rhet.*) fulfillment, realization [fr. L. *fructificatio* (*fructificationis*) fr. *fructus*, fruit]

fruc·ti·fy (frʌktifai) *pres. part.* **fruc·ti·fy·ing** *past* and *past part.* **fruc·ti·fied** *v.i.* to bear fruit ‖ to have positive results ‖ *v.t.* (*rhet.*) to cause to bear fruit, make fruitful

fruc·tose (frʌktous) *n.* a sweet, optically active sugar, $CH_2OH(CHOH)_3COCH_2OH$, found esp. in fruits, honey etc. in the levorotatory form ‖ one of the optical isomers of this [fr. L. *fructus*, fruit]

fruc·tu·ous (frʌktʃu:əs) *adj.* fruitful [O.F. *fructuous*]

frug (fru:g) *n.* rock 'n roll dance in which hips, arms, head, and shoulders move in rhythm while feet move little or not at all —**frug** *v.*

Frug (preceded by "the") fad dance to rock 'n roll music popular in the 1960s

fru·gal (frú:g'l) *adj.* scanty, *a frugal meal* ‖ economical, *frugal habits* **fru·gal·i·ty** (fru:gǽliti:) *n.* [fr. L. *frugalis*]

fru·giv·o·rous (fru:dʒívərəs) *adj.* (*zool.*) living on fruit [fr. L. *frux* (*frugis*), fruit+ -*vorus*, eating]

fruit (fru:t) **1.** *n.* the enlarged or developed reproductive body of a seed plant, consisting of one or more seeds and usually various protective and supporting structures. Fruits are dry or fleshy, and dehiscent or indehiscent ‖ such a fruit with an edible pulp commonly eaten as dessert, e.g. an orange ‖ dessert fruits collectively, *a diet mainly of salads and fruit* ‖ the result of effort, esp. success **2.** *v.i.* to bear fruit ‖ *v.t.* to cause to bear fruit [O.F.]

fruit bat a flying fox

fruit·cake (frú:tkeik) *n.* a rich cake containing dried and candied fruits, and nuts

fruit·er (frú:tər) *n.* a fruit tree with respect to its yield, *a poor fruiter* ‖ a merchant ship carrying fruit

fruit·er·er (frú:tərər) *n.* (esp. *Br.*) a fruit retailer

fruit fly a small dipteran fly whose larvae live on fruit or rotting vegetable matter (*DROSOPHILA*)

fruit·ful (frú:tfəl) *adj.* fertile, productive in abundance, *a fruitful tract of land* ‖ producing beneficial results, *a fruitful discussion* [FRUIT]

fru·i·tion (fru:íʃən) *n.* the state of bearing fruit ‖ (of plans etc.) a being realized, a coming to fulfillment [O.F. *fruission, fruition*]

fruit·less (frú:tlis) *adj.* yielding no fruit ‖ unprofitable, useless, *fruitless efforts*

fruit machine (*Br.*) a slot machine in which a player wins according to the matching of fruit symbols which are spun by a pull on a lever

fruit sugar fructose

fruit·y (frú:ti:) *comp.* **fruit·i·er** *superl.* **fruit·i·est** *adj.* like fruit in taste, appearance or smell ‖ (of wine) having a rich taste of grapes ‖ (*Br.*, *pop.*) indecent and amusing, *fruity stories* ‖ (of the voice) thickly sweet

fru·men·ta·ceous (fru:məntéiʃəs) *adj.* made of wheat or like wheat or other cereals [fr. L. *frumentaceus*]

Fru·men·ti·us (fru:ménʃi:əs), St (c. 300–380), the apostle of Ethiopia. Feast: Oct. 27

fru·men·ty (frú:mənti:) *n.* mulled wheat boiled in milk and flavored with sugar, spices etc. [M.E. fr. O.F. *frumentée, foumentée*]

frump (frʌmp) *n.* an unattractive woman dowdily dressed **frúmp·ish** *adj.* **frúmp·y** *comp.* **frump·i·er** *superl.* **frump·i·est** *adj.* dull and dowdy [origin unknown]

Frun·ze (frú:nzə) (formerly Pishpek) the capital (pop. 533,000) of Kirghizia, U.S.S.R., in a cotton-growing district: textiles, food processing, tobacco. University (1951)

frus·trate (frʌstreit) *pres. part.* **frus·trat·ing** *past* and *past part.* **frus·trat·ed** *v.t.* to prevent (someone) from achieving an object or prevent (an attempt etc.) from being made successfully, often by foiling ‖ to cause feelings in (someone) of being thwarted or baffled, deprived of what was due, or having some fundamental need unsatisfied [fr. L. *frustrari* (*frustratus*), to disappoint]

frus·trat·ed cargo (frʌstreitəd) any shipment of supplies and/or equipment that while en route to destination is stopped prior to arrival and for which further disposition instructions must be obtained

frus·tra·tion (frʌstréiʃən) *n.* a frustrating or being frustrated ‖ something which frustrates [fr. L. *frustratio* (*frustrationis*), disappointment]

frus·tum (frʌstəm) *pl.* **frus·tums, frus·ta** (frʌstə) *n.* the remaining part of a solid pyramid or cone when its upper part has been cut away along a plane parallel to the base ‖ part of a regular solid intercepted between two planes, usually parallel [L.=a piece broken off]

fru·tes·cent (fru:tésənt) *adj.* shrubby in habit or appearance [fr. L. *frutex* (*fruticis*), a shrub]

fru·ti·cose (frú:tikous) *adj.* (*bot.*) shrubby, like a shrub [fr. L. *fruticosus*]

Fry (frai), Christopher (1907–   ), English playwright. His verse plays, remarkable for their freshness of invention and verbal play, include 'A Phoenix Too Frequent' (1946), 'The Lady's Not for Burning' (1949), 'Venus Observed' (1950), and 'The Dark is Light Enough' (1954)

Fry, Elizabeth (1780–1845), English prison reformer. A Quaker, she worked for the improvement of the conditions for women in Newgate Prison, London (1813 onward)

Fry, Roger (1866–1934), English art critic, painter and potter. He is best known for his championing of the Postimpressionists, esp. Cézanne. His criticism includes 'Bellini' (1899), 'Vision and Design' (1920), 'Transformations' (1926) and 'Cézanne' (1927)

fry (frai) **1.** *n. pl.* **fries** (*pop.*) a dish of fried food ‖ (*pop.*) an outdoor social gathering at which the main dish is fried, *a fish fry* ‖ the heart, liver etc. of an animal, usually eaten fried, *pig's fry* **2.**

v. pres. part. **frying** *past* and *past part.* **fried** (fraid) *v.t.* to cook in hot fat or oil in a shallow open pan ‖ *v.i.* to be cooked in this way [F. *frire*]

fry *pl. n.* freshly hatched fish ‖ salmon of the second year ‖ smaller kinds of adult fish that go in shoals ‖ people regarded as having little importance [O.N. *frió, freõ, frœ*, seed]

fry·er, fri·er (fráiər) *n.* a chicken suitable for frying ‖ a deep vessel used for frying

frying pan a long-handled, shallow, iron or aluminum pan used for frying

F scale (*psych.*) an attitude scale used to measure the elements in the authoritarian personality

F-16 (*mil.*) U.S. fighter plane designed to replace F-104, carrying Sidewinder, Sparrow, and other air-to-air missiles, to a total weight of 15,200 lbs. It has a speed to mach 2.4 and a range of 2,415 mi

f-stop (ɛfstɒp) *n.* the variable f-number setting on a camera lens

ft foot, feet

Fu·ad I (fu:ád) (Ahmad Fu'ad, 1868–1936), sultan (1917) and king (1922–36) of Egypt

Fuchs (fu:ks), Sir Vivian Ernest (1908–), British geologist and explorer. He led the Commonwealth Trans-Antarctic Expedition (1955–8), Hillary joining him at the South Pole

fuch·sia (fjú:ʃə) *n.* a member of *Fuchsia*, fam. *Onagraceae*, a genus of perennial shrubs found mainly in tropical America. They are widely cultivated for their ornamental, pendulous, red, purple or white flowers. Many show two buds in each axil [Mod. L., after Leonhard *Fuchs* (1501–66), G. botanist]

fuch·sine, fuch·sin (fúksin, fúksi:n) *n.* a magenta aniline dye [FUCHSIA]

fu·coid (fjú:kɔid) **1.** *adj.* like or relating to fucus **2.** *n.* a seaweed of the order *Fucales*

fu·cus (fjú:kəs) *pl.* **fu·cus·es, fu·ci** (fjú:sai) *n.* a member of *Fucus*, a genus of green-brown leathery seaweeds of fam. *Fucaceae*, or any of certain other similar seaweeds [L.=rock lichen]

fud·dle (fʌd'l) **1.** *v.t. pres. part.* **fud·dling** *past* and *past part.* **fud·dled** to stupefy or confuse, e.g. with drink **2.** *n.* a state of mental haze, e.g. after too much alcohol [origin unknown]

fud·dy-dud·dy (fʌdi:dʌdi:) *pl.* **fud·dy-dud·dies** *n.* (*pop.*) an old fogy [etym. doubtful]

fudge (fʌdʒ) **1.** *n.* a soft candy made of sugar, chocolate or other flavoring, milk and butter etc. ‖ (*printing*) a last-minute insertion on a newspaper printing machine of a block of print giving news received too late for plating ‖ nonsense ‖ **2.** *v. pres. part.* **fudg·ing** *past* and *past part.* **fudged** *v.i.* to talk nonsense ‖ *v.t.* to fake ‖ to make or do (something) in a makeshift or blurry way, *to fudge arpeggios* [origin unknown]

Fuehrer *FÜHRER

fu·el (fjú:əl) **1.** *n.* combustible material used as a source of heat or energy ‖ food as a source of energy ‖ fissionable material used as a source of atomic energy ‖ anything that makes strong feelings or passions (anger etc.) stronger **2.** *v. pres. part.* **fu·el·ing**, esp. *Br.* **fu·el·ling** *past* and *past part.* **fu·eled**, esp. *Br.* **fu·elled**, to provide with fuel ‖ *v.i.* to take in fuel [O.F. *fowaille, feuaile*]
—The principal solid fuels are formed from decayed vegetable matter and consist mainly of carbon and hydrogen. They include anthracite, coal (which may be converted into coke, coalite or other smokeless fuels), lignite, peat and wood. The principal liquid fuels—diesel oil, gasoline and kerosene—are obtained from petroleum. A gaseous fuel, natural gas, is obtained usually from subterranean wells, and others (coal gas, water gas and producer gas) are manufactured from coal

fuel cell an electrochemical device which converts the chemical energy of fuel oxidation directly to electricity without combustion, and which is a relatively light, efficient and quiet source of power

fuel injection (*mechanics*) use of a pump mechanism to spray fuel into the cylinder of an internal combustion engine at the proper point in the cycle —**fuel injection engine** *n.* —**fuel injector** *n.*

Fuen·tes (fwéntes), Carlos (1929–), Mexican novelist of Marxist sympathies, who uses the stream-of-consciousness method. His 'Las buenas conciencias' (1959) portrays the outcast of society, and his 'La muerte de Artemio Cruz' (1963, Eng. trans. 'The Death of Artemio Cruz',

1964) is a panoramic exposé of the Mexican Revolution and its aftermath

fug (fʌg) *n.* (esp. *Br.*) stuffy air in a room etc. when overheated and full of stale breath and tobacco smoke [origin unknown]

fu·ga·cious (fju:géiʃəs) *adj.* (*rhet.*) evanescent, fleeting ‖ (*bot.*) of sepals, petals etc.) falling off soon after the flower opens (opp. PERSISTENT, cf. CADUCOUS) **fu·gac·i·ty** (fju:gæsiti:) *n.* [fr. L. *fugax (fugacis)*]

fu·gal (fjú:g'l) *adj.* of fugue, in the style of a fugue

Fug·ger (fʌgər) a family of S. German merchants and financiers, associated with Augsburg from 1367, prominent in the 15th and 16th cc. They had a virtual monopoly of central European copper and silver, and acquired vast lands as securities for their loans to kings, emperors and popes. Their money secured the election (1519) of Charles V as Emperor

fug·gy (fʌgi:) *comp.* **fug·gi·er** *superl.* **fug·gi·est** *adj.* (esp. *Br.*, of the atmosphere of a room etc.) stuffy

fu·gi·tive (fjú:dʒitiv) **1.** *n.* someone fleeing from punishment, danger, pursuit, authority etc. **2.** *adj.* in flight, running away ‖ liable to change, not durable, *a fugitive color* ‖ (of literary compositions) scattered, occasional ‖ ephemeral [F. *fugitif*]

fugitive slave laws (*Am. hist.*) federal acts (1793 and 1850) providing for the return between states of escaped slaves. The laws increased the hostility between North and South and were repealed (1864)

fu·gle·man (fjú:g'lmən) *pl.* **fu·gle·men** (fjú:g'l-mən) *n.* a trained soldier formerly used as a guide to his fellows while drilling ‖ a leader, such as the scout bird flying ahead of a formation of wild ducks [fr. G. *flügelmann*, leader of the file]

fugue (fju:g) *n.* a musical composition in which a melody (the subject) is taken up by successive 'voices' in imitation, so that the original melody seems to be pursued by its counterparts. The first voice enters in the tonic, the second in the dominant: this key sequence is repeated for as many voices as the fugue has. In its full elaboration the fugue has further subjects introduced into its structure, and the themes may be elaborated, inverted or otherwise varied (*COUNTERPOINT). Perhaps the most formal or academic of European musical forms, this apparently constricting medium was made the vehicle of utterances of great vigor and splendor esp. by J. S. Bach, e.g. in 'The Art of Fugue' (1749) and 'The Well-Tempered Clavier' (1722, 1744) ‖ (*psychol.*) a disturbed state of mind during which the patient behaves, apparently consciously, in ways of which he has no recollection afterwards [F. fr. Ital. *fuga*, flight]

Füh·rer, Fueh·rer (fjúərər, fýrər) the title assumed by Hitler [G.=leader]

Fu·ji·ta (fu:dʒí:tə), Tsugouharu or Tsuguji (1886–1968), Japanese painter, naturalized French, a member of the École de Paris

Fu·ji·ya·ma (fu:dʒi:jámə) (Fujisan) a nearly symmetrical volcanic cone (12,400 ft) in south-central Honshu, Japan. It is sacred to Buddhists, and often occurs as a subject in Japanese art. The volcano has been dormant since 1707

Fu·kien (fú:kjén) a province (area 45,551 sq. miles, pop. 24,000,000) of S.E. China along the China Sea opposite Formosa

Fu·ku·o·ka (fu:ku:óukə) a port (pop. 1,039,300) on the north coast of Kyushu, Japan, serving Chikuho, a coal-mining area. Industries: paper, electrical goods, silk, pottery. Kyushu University (1910)

Fu·ku·shi·ma (fu:ku:ʃí:mə) a town (pop. 263,000) in N. Honshu, Japan, an agricultural market (rice, soybeans), producing silk textiles. University

-ful *suffix* as much as will fill, as in 'teaspoonful' ‖ tending to, as in 'useful' ‖ characterized by, as in 'resentful' [orig.=FULL *adj.*]

Fu·la·ni (fu:láni:) *pl.* **Fu·la·ni, Fu·la·nis** *n.* a member of a predominantly light-complexioned people inhabiting the Sudan between Senegal and the Upper Niger. They conquered (1805–10) the powerful Hausas, founded the kingdom of Sokoto in Nigeria, and have had great political importance in W. African history ‖ their language

Ful·bert (fylber) (c. 960–1028), scholar and bishop of Chartres (1006–28). His cathedral school attracted scholars from all over Europe. He began the rebuilding of Chartres Cathedral (1020)

Ful·bright (fúlbrait), James William (1905–), U.S. senator (1945–75) from Arkansas and Chairman (1959–74) of the Senate Foreign Relations Committee. His Fulbright Act (1946) provided for an exchange program of students and teachers between the U.S.A. and other countries

ful·crum (fʌlkrəm, fúlkrəm) *pl.* **ful·crums, ful·cra** (fʌlkrə, fúlkrə) *n.* the point about which a lever turns or on which it is supported ‖ (*bot.*) a supporting organ, e.g. a tendril or stipule ‖ (*zool.*) a chitinous structure in the base of the rostrum of insects ‖ (*zool.*) a spinelike scale on the anterior fin rays of many ganoid fish [L.=the foot of a couch]

Ful·da (fú:ldə) a city (pop. 46,000) in Hesse, West Germany, with textile and chemical industries. It grew around a Benedictine abbey founded (8th c.) by St Boniface, who is buried here, and was a medieval center of learning

ful·fill, ful·fil (fulfíl) *pres. part.* **ful·fill·ing, ful·fil·ling** *past* and *past part.* **ful·filled** *v.t.* to carry out (a promise) ‖ to obey (a law, command) ‖ to satisfy (a prayer, desire) ‖ to complete, accomplish (a task) ‖ to answer (a purpose) ‖ to comply with (conditions) ‖ to prove true (a prophecy) ‖ to realize (a destiny) **to fulfill oneself** to realize all one's potentialities as a person **ful·fill·ment, ful·fil·ment** *n.* [O. E. *fullfyllan*]

ful·gent (fʌldʒənt) *adj.* (*rhet.*) shining radiantly [fr. L. *fulgens (fulgentis)*]

ful·gu·rant (fʌlgjərənt) *adj.* (*rhet.*) flashing as in lightning [fr. L. *fulgurans (fulgurantis)* fr. *fulgurare*, to flash]

ful·gu·rate (fʌlgjəreit) *pres. part.* **ful·gu·rat·ing** *past* and *past part.* **ful·gu·rat·ed** *v.i.* (*rhet.*) to flash like lightning [L. *fulgurare (fulguratus)*]

ful·gu·rite (fʌlgjurait) *n.* the fused, usually tubular, substance formed when sand or rock is struck by lightning [fr. L. *fulgur*, lightning]

fu·lig·i·nous (fju:lídʒinəs) *adj.* like soot, sooty ‖ soot-colored [fr. L. *fuliginosus*]

full (ful) *adj.* completely filled ‖ filled with emotion, *a full heart* ‖ crowded ‖ characterized by a pronounced trait, *full of ambition* or by an obsession, *full of his new theory* ‖ well filled with food, *a full stomach* ‖ ample, thoroughly adequate, *a full report* ‖ well supplied, *a full cupboard* ‖ at maximum development, size etc., *at full speed* ‖ (of sounds) having depth or volume, *full tones* ‖ (of light, color) strong, *in full daylight* ‖ (of materials) arranged in gathers or folds, *full curtains* ‖ expanded, *full sails* ‖ well filled out, plump, *a full figure* ‖ unqualified, *full agreement, in full retreat* ‖ (with 'of') having much or many, *full of cracks* ‖ (with 'of') having an abundance, *full of work* ‖ having the same parents, *one full brother and one half brother* ‖ (binding) on spine and boards, *bound in full leather* **full up** (*Br.*) completely filled **2.** *n.* (with 'the') the highest point, *the moon is at the full* **in full** completely without cuts etc., *they played 'Hamlet' in full* **to the full** utterly, *we enjoyed it to the full* **3.** *adv.* exactly *full in the center* ‖ directly, squarely, *full in the face* ‖ (*rhet.*) perfectly, entirely, very, *full well* **4.** *v.t.* to gather or pleat (cloth) for greater fullness ‖ *v.i.* (of the moon) to become full [O.E.]

full *v.t.* to shrink and thicken (cloth) by applying dampness, heat, friction and pressure [fr. O.F. *fuler*]

full·back (fúlbæk) *n.* (soccer, hockey etc.) a defensive player nearest the defended goal or in front of the goalkeeper, or this position of play ‖ (football) a player behind the scrimmage line, used in attack for line plunges and blocking, or this position of play

full binding a book binding entirely of leather (cf. HALF BINDING, cf. QUARTER BINDING, cf. THREE-QUARTER BINDING)

full-blood·ed (fúlblʌdid) *adj.* having ancestors of a single stock, *a full-blooded aborigine* ‖ passionate ‖ vigorous ‖ full of rich detail, *a full-blooded account*

full-blown (fúlblóun) *adj.* (of flowers) completely open ‖ complete, *a full-blown investigation*

full-bod·ied (fúlbódi:d) *adj.* (of wine) having the full flavor of the grape

full-bound (fúlbáund) *adj.* having full binding

full close (*mus.*) a perfect cadence

full disclosure requirement by Securities and Exchange Commission that officers and directors of a public corporation disclose all pertinent information pertaining to operations of the company *Cf* FINANCIAL DISCLOSURE

full dress formal dress, esp. ceremonial military uniform **full-dress** (fúldres) *adj.* pertain-

CONCISE PRONUNCIATION KEY: **(a)** æ, c*a*t; ɑ, c*ar*; ɔ, f*aw*n; ei, sn*a*ke. **(e)** e, h*e*n; i:, sh*ee*p; iə, d*ee*r; ɛə, b*ea*r. **(i)** i, f*i*sh; ai, t*i*ger; ə:, b*i*rd. **(o)** o, *o*x; au, c*ow*; ou, g*oa*t; u, p*oo*r; ɔi, r*oy*al. **(u)** ʌ, d*u*ck; u, b*u*ll; u:, g*oo*se; ə, b*a*cillus; ju:, c*u*be. x, lo*ch*; θ, *th*ink; ð, bo*th*er; z, *Z*en; ʒ, corsa*ge*; dʒ, sava*ge*; ŋ, orangutan*g*; j, *y*ak; ʃ, *fi*sh; tʃ, fet*ch*; 'l, rabb*le*; 'n, redd*en*. Complete pronunciation key appears inside front cover.

ing to this ‖ complete in every particular, *a full-dress inquiry*

Ful·ler (fúlər), Buckminster (1895–1983), American architect and engineer. He is noted for his revolutionary technological designs, and as the inventor of the geodesic dome

Fuller, Thomas (1608–61), English clergyman, antiquarian and wit. He wrote the collection of short biographical studies etc. called 'The History of the Worthies of England' (1662), known as 'Fuller's Worthies'

full·er (fúlər) *n.* someone who fulls cloth [O.E. *fullere*]

fuller l. *n.* a blacksmith's tool used to groove and spread iron ‖ the resulting groove, e.g. in a bayonet 2. *v.t.* to form a groove in (a bayonet) [etym. doubtful]

fuller's earth a claylike material, mainly hydrated aluminum, magnesium and calcium silicates etc., used e.g. for absorbing grease from wool and in the refining of oils and fats

full-fash·ioned (fúlfǽʃənd) *adj.* (esp. of stockings) shaped in the knitting process so as to give perfect fit

full-fledged (fúlflédʒd) *adj.* (of birds) having all their feathers ‖ completely qualified, *a full-fledged lawyer*

full-grown (fúlgróun) *adj.* mature, *a full-grown tree*

full house (*poker*) a hand with three of a kind and a pair

full-length (fúlléŋθ, fúlléŋkθ) 1. *adj.* (of a portrait) showing the complete figure, but not necessarily life-size ‖ (of a book, play etc.) not abridged ‖ (of a mirror) showing the complete figure ‖ (of a skirt) covering the legs entirely 2. *adv.* lying at full length, *full-length on the floor*

full moon the phase of the moon when it gives greatest illumination ‖ the period when the moon is in this phase

full nelson (*wrestling*) a hold in which a wrestler gets both his arms under his opponent's arms from behind and clasps his own hands behind his opponent's neck

full·ness, ful·ness (fúlnis) *n.* the quality or state of being full

full pitch (*cricket*) a full toss

full-rigged (fúlrígd) *adj.* (*naut.*) having three or more masts, each with the full complement of square sails

full stop a period (punctuation mark)

full-term (fúltə́:rm) *adj.* born at the end of the normal gestation period (cf. PREMATURE)

full tilt at top speed

full-time (fúltáim) *adj.* working the standard number of hours per week, *a full-time nurse* ‖ demanding the standard number of hours per week, *a full-time job*

full toss (*cricket*) a ball which reaches the wicket without first hitting the ground

ful·ly (fúli) *adv.* entirely, completely ‖ at least, *fully 1,000 people were there*

ful·ly-fash·ioned (fúli-fǽʃənd) *adj.* full-fashioned

ful·mar (fúlmər) *n. Fulmarus glacialis,* a seabird of the petrel family found in the Arctic and N. Atlantic regions [prob. Scand.]

ful·mi·nant (fʌ́lminənt) *adj.* (*med.*) fulminating [F.]

ful·mi·nate (fʌ́lmineit) 1. *v. pres. part.* **ful·mi·nat·ing** *past* and *past part.* **ful·mi·nat·ed** *v.i.* to flash like lightning or to explode like thunder ‖ *v.t.* to thunder forth (threats, denunciations or commands) 2. *n.* a (usually explosive) salt of fulminic acid, esp. mercury fulminate [fr. L. *fulminare (fulminatus),* to strike with lightning]

fulminate of mercury mercury fulminate

ful·mi·nat·ing (fʌ́lmineitiŋ) *adj.* (*med.,* of a disease) developing quickly and with great severity

ful·mi·na·tion (fʌlminéiʃən) *n.* a violent and menacing denunciation ‖ (*fig.*) a thundered warning or condemnation ‖ a violent explosion [fr. L. *fulminatio (fulminationis),* lightning]

ful·min·ic acid (fʌlmínik) an unstable acid, CNOH, which forms very explosive salts of some metals, esp. mercury

fulness *FULLNESS

ful·some (fúlsəm) *adj.* (esp. of flattery or praise) excessively or offensively exaggerated

Ful·ton (fúltən), Robert (1765–1815), American engineer and inventor. He pioneered inland steam navigation in the U.S.A. with his 'Clermont', the first commercially successful steamboat (1807). He experimented with submarines and torpedoes, and built (1814) the 'Fulton', the first steam warship

ful·vous (fʌ́lvəs) *adj.* dull yellowish brown, tawny [L. *fulvus*]

fu·ma·role (fjú:məroul) *n.* a small hole in the ground in an active volcanic region from which gases and vapors issue [fr. F. *fumerolle*]

fum·ble (fʌ́mb'l) 1. *v. pres. part.* **fum·bling** *past* and *past part.* **fum·bled** *v.t.* to deal with clumsily or awkwardly, bungle ‖ (*sports*) to fail to catch or control (a ball), bungle (a pass etc.) ‖ *v.i.* to grope awkwardly ‖ to speak as though finding it hard to express oneself, *to fumble for words* 2. *n.* a clumsy or groping use of the hands ‖ a bungling of an action [etym. doubtful]

fume (fju:m) 1. *n.* (esp. *pl.*) pungent, often noxious, vapor or smoke ‖ a suspension of particles in gas or air, *factory fumes* ‖ **in a fume** in a furious, pent-up state of mind. 2. *v. pres. part.* **fum·ing** *past* and *past part.* **fumed** *v.i.* to give off fumes ‖ to be angry in a pent-up way *v.t.* to subject (wood) to the action of fumes of ammonia so as to darken it, *fumed oak* [O.F. *fum, fumer*]

fu·mi·gate (fjú:migeit) *v. pres. part.* **fu·mi·gat·ing** *past* and *past part.* **fu·mi·gat·ed** *v.t.* to subject to smoke or fumes, esp. in order to disinfect, kill insects, etc. **fu·mi·ga·tion, fú·mi·ga·tor** *ns* a device for fumigating ‖ someone who fumigates [fr. L. *fumigare (fumigatus)*]

fu·mi·to·ry (fjú:mitɔri:, fjú:mitɔuri:) *pl.* **fu·mi·to·ries** *n.* a plant of genus *Fumaria,* fam. *Fumariaciae,* annuals often climbing by petioles. *F. officinalis* was formerly used as a scorbutic [O.F. *fumeterre*]

fum·y (fjú:mi) *comp.* **fum·i·er** *superl.* **fum·i·est** *adj.* full of fumes ‖ giving off fumes

fun (fʌn) 1. *n.* pleasure and amusement, *to have fun* ‖ gaiety, playfulness, *full of fun* **for fun** for pleasure, not for money ‖ **in fun** as a joke, *to say something in fun* **to make fun of** to ridicule 2. *v.i. pres. part.* **fun·ning** *past* and *past part.* **funned** (*pop.*) to joke 3. *adj.* characterized by or providing fun [etym. doubtful]

fun·a·bout (fʌ́nəbaut) *n.* small motor vehicle used principally for pleasure

fu·nam·bu·list (fju:nǽmbjulist) *n.* a performer on a tightrope [fr. L. *funambulus,* a ropewalker]

fun-and-games nonserious light-hearted activity

Fun·chal (funʃál) the capital and chief port (pop. 48,638) of Madeira, Portugal, on the east coast: cathedral (15th c.)

Fun City sloganeering name for New York City, sometimes used ironically

func·tion (fʌ́ŋkʃən) 1. *n.* a characteristic activity or the activity for which something exists, *to fulfill a function* ‖ end or purpose, *what is the true function of education?* ‖ an official duty, *the functions of a magistrate* ‖ a ceremony or social gathering of some formality ‖ chemical behavior due to the presence of a functional group ‖ a functional group ‖ (*math.*) a relation that associates with every ordered set of numbers (x, y, z . . .) a number f (x, y, z . . .) for all the permitted values of x, y, z . . . ‖ any quantity, trait or fact that depends upon and varies in accordance with another, *the final color is partly a function of the time that the article is left in the vat* 2. *v.i.* to act, perform a function ‖ to be in working order, *to stop functioning* **func·tion·al** (fʌ́ŋkʃən'l) *adj.* pertaining to function ‖ designed primarily in accordance with criteria determined by use, rather than according to canons of taste ‖ (*med.*) affecting the functions but not the substance of an organ, *a functional disorder* ‖ (*math.*) pertaining to a function or functions, *functional analysis* [O.F.]

functional group (*chem.*) an atom, a group of atoms, or type of bonding in a substance that gives to the substance a characteristic behavior, e.g. the basic functional group — NH_2

func·tion·al·ism (fʌ́ŋkʃənəlizəm) *n.* a doctrine or practice stressing that the function of the thing to be designed should dictate the form of the design

functional requisite (*social science*) a basic societal need that must be met if a society is to survive

func·tion·a·ry (fʌ́ŋkʃəneri:) 1. *adj.* (*med.*) functional 2. *pl.* **func·tion·a·ries** *n.* an official

function element (*computer*) logic element; a computer device that performs one or more logic functions

fund (fʌnd) 1. *n.* an available store of immaterial resources, *a fund of knowledge* ‖ an accumulation of money, esp. one set aside for a certain purpose, *a building fund* ‖ (*pl.*) financial resources **in funds** with money to spend **the funds** (*Br.*) the stock of the national debt 2. *v.t.*

to convert (a floating debt) into a long-term debt at fixed interest ‖ to put in a fund *v.i.* (*Br.*) to invest in the funds [fr. L. *fundus,* the bottom]

fun·da·ment (fʌ́ndəmənt) *n.* the anus ‖ the buttocks [M.E. *fondement* fr. O.F.]

fun·da·men·tal (fʌndəmént'l) 1. *adj.* basic, essential, *a fundamental truth* ‖ affecting the foundations of something, *a fundamental change* ‖ deep-rooted in a person or being part of the elementary nature of a thing, *the fundamental silliness of the idea* ‖ (*mus.,* of a tone) being the lowest primary note, determining pitch, in a harmonic series (cf. OVERTONE) 2. *n.* something fundamental ‖ (*mus.*) the fundamental note of a harmonic series [M.E. fr. L.L. *fundamentalis,* of a foundation]

fun·da·men·tal·ism (fʌndəmént'lizəm) *n.* an extreme Protestant position characterized by the belief that the Bible is a verbally accurate recording of the word of God. It holds that the writers were divinely inspired to the smallest detail of revealed truth ‖ adherence to traditional beliefs of any kind **fun·da·mén·tal·ist** *n.*

fundamental particle any of a group of bodies that are at present considered to be the ultimate constituents of matter and that are classified according to such properties as charge, spin, mass, (*BARYON, *MESON, *LEPTON, *PHOTON, *GRAVITON)

fundamental units the units of mass, length and time, in terms of which all other, derived, units can be expressed

fun·do (fʌ́ndou) *n.* a ranch in Chile [Span.]

funds flow (*business*) movement of working capital in and out of an enterprise *Cf* CASH FLOW

fun·dus (fʌ́ndəs) *pl.* **fun·di** (fʌ́ndai) *n.* (*anat.*) the internal bottom surface of a hollow organ or the part furthest from the opening [L.=bottom]

fun·dus·co·py (fʌndʌ́skɒpi:) (*med.*) examination of the interior of the eye **fundusectomy** *n.* removal of a hollow organ, e.g., the uterus **funduscope** *n.* the instrument

fundus photography photography of the bottom of a hollow organ

Fun·dy, Bay of (fʌ́ndi:) an inlet of the Atlantic Ocean separating Nova Scotia from New Brunswick (Canada) and Maine (U.S.A.). There are dangerous tides

Fü·nen (fýnən) (*Dan.* Fyn) the second largest island (area 1,149 sq. miles, pop. 398,255) of Denmark. Chief town: Odense

fu·ner·al (fjú:nərəl) 1. *n.* the ceremony of burial or cremation of a dead person ‖ the procession attending a burial or cremation ‖ the burial service ‖ (*pop.*) problem (concern), *that's your funeral* 2. *adj.* of or pertaining to a funeral or funerals [fr. O.F. *funeraille*]

funeral director an undertaker

funeral home a place where the dead are prepared for burial or cremation

funeral parlor a funeral home

funeral pyre a pile of wood etc. on which a dead body is burned

fu·ner·a·ry (fjú:nəreri:) *adj.* of or to do with a funeral [fr. L.L. *funerarius*]

fu·ne·re·al (fju:níəri:əl) *adj.* mournful, gloomy, *a funereal atmosphere* [fr. L. *funereus*]

fun fair a bazaar organized by a school, church etc. to raise money ‖ (*Br.*) an amusement park

fun fur colorful, inexpensive fur garment for casual wear, often of assembled scrap pieces *Cf* SYNTHETIC FUR

fun·gal (fʌ́ŋg'l) *adj.* of or pertaining to a fungus

fungi *pl.* of FUNGUS

fun·gi·cide (fʌ́ndʒisaid) *n.* a substance which destroys fungi [fr. FUNGUS+L. -*cidium,* killing]

fun·gi·ble (fʌ́ndʒib'l) *adj.* (*law*) of or pertaining to goods (e.g. coal, lumber) of which any unit or part can take the place of another in meeting an order etc. [fr. M.L. *fungibilis*]

fun·gi im·per·fec·ti (fʌ́ndʒaiimpərféktai) *pl. n.* a group of fungi which are not classified usually because the complete life history is not known (e.g. ringworm) but which are considered as eumycophytes [L.]

fun·gi·stat (fʌ́ndʒistæt) *n.* an agent that is fungistatic

fun·gi·stat·ic (fʌndʒistǽtik) *adj.* able to hinder the growth of fungi without killing them

fun·go (fʌ́ŋgou) *pl.* **fun·goes** *n.* (*baseball*) a ball hit for fielding practice by a batter who throws it up in the air and strikes it as it comes down [origin unknown]

fun·goid (fʌ́ŋgɔid) 1. *adj.* funguslike 2. *n.* a fungoid plant

fun·gous (fʌ́ŋgəs) *adj.* funguslike ‖ of or pertaining to fungi [fr. L. *fungosus*]

fun·gus (fʌ́ŋgəs) *pl.* **fun·gi** (fʌ́ndʒai, fʌ́ŋgai) *n.* a member of *Eumycophyta*, a phylum of thallophytes comprising ascomycetes, basidiomycetes, phycomycetes and fungi imperfecti. They are parasitic or saprophytic plants, devoid of chlorophyll. Fungi often exhibit alternation of generations with widely differing sexual and asexual stages, the latter consisting often of a system of hyphae partially differentiated into complex reproductive bodies. Some fungi are harmful to plants or animals (including man) while some are valued as food or for the organic fermentations they produce (*ANTIBIOTIC). They are universally distributed and include molds, mushrooms, mildews, blights, rusts and (in some classifications) yeasts, bacteria and slime molds ‖ a disease caused by a fungus [L.]

fu·ni·cle (fjúːnikʹl) *n.* (*bot.*) an ovule stalk ‖ (*anat.*) a cord or band, e.g. of nerve fibers [FUNICULUS]

fu·nic·u·lar (fjuːníːkjulər) 1. *adj.* pertaining to a rope or cable ‖ pertaining to the tension in a rope or cable ‖ worked by a rope or cable 2. *n.* a funicular railway [L. *funiculus* dim. of *funis*, rope]

funicular railway a railway operated by cables, the ascending and descending cars counterbalancing one another

fu·nic·u·lus (fjuːníːkjuləs) *pl.* **fu·nic·u·li** (fjuːníːk-julai) *n.* a funicle ‖ the umbilical cord ‖ the spermatic duct ‖ one of the ventral, lateral or dorsal columns of the white matter of the spinal cord [L. dim. of *funis*, rope]

funk (fʌŋk) 1. *n.* (*pop.*) a state of fright and self-distrust ‖ (*pop.*) a coward 2. *v.t.* (*pop.*) to avoid or avoid doing because of fright ‖ *v.i.* (*pop.*) to be in a state of fright [etym. doubtful]

funk art pop art formed from assembled household or industrial items **funk artist** *n.*

funk hole a dugout (shelter dug in the ground)

funk·y (fʌ́ŋkiː) *adj.* (*slang*) quaintly unsophisticated, sometimes nostalgic

fun·nel (fʌ́nʹl) 1. *n.* a cone-shaped vessel ending in a tube at the base, used for pouring liquids or powders through a small opening ‖ the metal flue of a ship or steam engine, a smokestack ‖ a lighting or ventilating shaft 2. *v. pres. part.* **fun·nel·ing**, esp. *Br.* **fun·nel·ling** *past* and *past part.* **fun·neled**, esp. *Br.* **fun·nelled** *v.t.* to cause to pass through a funnel or as if through one ‖ *v.i.* to take the shape of a funnel ‖ to pass through a funnel or as if through one [M.E. *fonel* perh. fr. O.F.]

fun·nies (fʌ́niːz) *pl. n.* (*pop.*) comic strips

fun·ni·ly (fʌ́niliː) *adv.* in a funny way ‖ in a strange way **funnily enough** by a strange coincidence ‖ strange to say

fun·ni·ness (fʌ́niːnis) *n.* the state or quality of being funny

fun·ny (fʌ́niː) *comp.* **fun·ni·er** *superl.* **fun·ni·est** *adj.* that makes one laugh, *a funny story* ‖ (*pop.*) puzzling ‖ (*pop.*) ill

funny bone that part of the humerus over which the sensitive ulnar nerve passes at the elbow. When knocked it causes an odd, rather painful, tingling sensation

fun·ny·man (fʌ́niːmæn) *pl.* **fun·ny·men** (fʌ́niː-men) *n.* a comedian (person who tells jokes professionally) or someone full of wisecracks and joking

fur (fəːr) 1. *n.* the dressed pelt of certain animals (mink, beaver, fox, rabbit, seal etc.) ‖ this as an item of apparel, worn loose around the neck and over the shoulders ‖ a coat, wrap, stole etc. made of several such pelts ‖ the soft, fine, thick hair that covers many animals, e.g. a cat ‖ (*pl.*) the skins of animals with the fur attached ‖ a covering or crust, e.g. of carbonate of lime in a kettle ‖ an epithelial coating on the tongue of someone ill **to make the fur fly** to cause a quarrel or fight 2. *adj.* made of, or pertaining to, fur, *a fur coat* 3. *v. pres. part.* **fur·ring** *past* and *past part.* **furred** *v.t.* to provide, cover, trim or clothe (something or someone) with fur ‖ to coat with a deposit ‖ to make (a floor or ceiling) level by inserting strips of wood ‖ *v.i.* to become coated with a deposit [O.F. *forrer*, to line]

fu·ran (fjúəræn) *n.* a colorless, inflammable, liquid, heterocyclic compound, C_4H_4O, used in the preparation of intermediates for the manufacture of nylon [fr. L. *furfur*, bran]

fu·ra·zol·i·done [$C_8H_7N_3O_5$] (fjəːrəzóːlidoun) *n.* (*pharm.*) antibiotic drug used for relief of Trichomonas vaginitis, usu. as a suppository; marketed as Furozoner

fur·be·low (fəːbilou) 1. *n.* a flounce or frill ‖ (*pl.*) fussy trimmings ‖ (*Br.*) the seaweed *Laminaria bulbosa*, with large wrinkled fronds 2. *v.t.* to trim with furbelows [etym. doubtful]

fur·bish (fəːbiʃ) *v.t.* to polish, cause to shine ‖ (with 'up') to give a new look to, renovate ‖ to refresh one's knowledge of [fr. O.F. *forbir* (*forbiss*-)]

fur·cate (fəːkeit) 1. *adj.* forked 2. *v.i. pres. part.* **fur·cat·ing** *past* and *past part.* **fur·cat·ed** to fork, divide **fur·ca·tion** *n.* [fr. M.L. *furcatus*, (of the hoof) cloven]

fur·cu·la (fəːkjulə) *pl.* **fur·cu·lae** (fəːkjuliː) *n.* a forked structure or process, esp. the wishbone [L. dim. of *furca*, fork]

fur·cu·lum (fəːkjuləm) *pl.* **fur·cu·la** (fəːkjulə) *n.* a furcula [Mod. L. dim. of *furca*, fork]

Fu·re·tière (fyrətjer), Antoine (1619–88), French writer. His realistic novel 'Roman bourgeois' (1666) satirizes the behavior of lawyers. He also compiled a 'Dictionnaire universel'

fur·fur (fəːrfər) *pl.* **fur·fur·es** (fəːrfjuriːz) *n.* dandruff, scurf ‖ (*pl.*) flaky scales of epidermis, esp. bits of scurf **fur·fu·ra·ceous** (fəːrfjəréiʃəs) *adj.* covered with dandruff, scurfy ‖ (*bot.*) covered with flaky scales [L.=bran]

fur·fur·al (fəːrfjər   æl) *n.* an oily, sweet-smelling liquid aldehyde, C_4H_3OCHO, obtained by the distillation of bran, wood etc. and used for making furan, in resins, lacquers and dyes, and as a solvent [short for *furfuraldehyde* fr. L. *furfur*, bran+ALDEHYDE]

Fu·ries (fjúəriːz) the Erinyes

fu·ri·ous (fjúəriəs) *adj.* passionately angry ‖ violent, frantic, *furious haste* [O.F. *furieus*]

furl (fəːrl) 1. *v.t.* to roll up (a sail) and tie it to a yard or boom ‖ to fold up, close (a flag, umbrella, fan etc.) ‖ *v.i.* to become furled ‖ (with 'off') to roll off ‖ (with 'away') to roll away 2. *n.* a furling or being furled ‖ a roll of something furled [prob. F. *ferler*]

fur·long (fəːrlɔŋ, fəːrlɒŋ) *n.* a unit of distance equaling one eighth of a statute mile or 220 yds (201.17 meters), used esp. in horse racing and surveying [O.E. *furlang*, the length of a furrow]

fur·lough (fəːrlou) 1. *n.* leave of absence, *on furlough* ‖ a leave of absence, esp. one given to a soldier ‖ the document granting this 2. *v.t.* to grant a furlough to ‖ *v.i.* to spend a furlough [fr. Du. *verlof*]

fur·me·ty (fəːrmitiː) *n.* frumenty

fur·nace (fəːrnis) *n.* an apparatus in chamber form for the production of intense heat to melt metals, reduce ores etc. ‖ the firebox of a hot-water or hot-air heating system in a building [M.E. *forneis* fr. O.F.]

fur·nish (fəːrniʃ) *v.t.* to provide (a house etc.) with furnishings ‖ to supply, equip, *to furnish soldiers with uniforms* ‖ to yield, provide, *one cow furnished milk for all of them* **fur·nish·ings** *pl. n.* furniture and fittings for a house etc. ‖ haberdashery, *men's furnishings* [O.F. *furnir* (*furniss*-)]

fur·ni·ture (fəːrnitʃər) *n.* movable articles (bed, table etc.) put in a room to make it habitable and decorative ‖ accessories or equipment, e.g. the tackle of a ship or the stilts, shelves etc. used in packing a kiln ‖ (*printing*) pieces of metal or wood used to make margins, blank spaces etc. and secure the type in its form or chase [fr. F. *fourniture*]

fu·ror (fjúərɔr) *n.* a furore

fu·rore (fjúərɔr, *Br.* fjuːróːriː) *n.* intense mass enthusiasm ‖ mass rage, uproar [Ital.]

fu·ro·se·mide [$C_{12}H_{11}ClN_2O_5S$] (fjəːróusəmaid) *n.* (*pharm.*) diuretic used in treatment of edema; marketed as Lasir

fur·ri·er (fəːriːər, fʌ́riːər) *n.* a dealer in furs or fur garments ‖ someone who dresses furs ‖ someone who makes fur garments **fur·ri·er·y** (fəːriːəriː, fʌ́riːəriː) *n.* the craft or trade of a furrier

fur·ri·ness (fəːriːnis) *n.* the state or quality of being furry

fur·ring (fəːriŋ) *n.* a lining or trimming with fur ‖ the fur used for lining or trimming ‖ the formation of a coating, esp. on the tongue ‖ the coating itself ‖ (*archit.*) the fixing of brick, wood etc. to a surface for leveling purposes before plastering etc. or to combat dampness, or the material used ‖ the doubling of planks on the side of a ship, or the wood used

fur·row (fəːrou, fʌ́rou) 1. *n.* a trench in the earth made by a plow ‖ the track of a ship ‖ any track, channel or groove ‖ (*rhet.*) a deep wrinkle, *furrows of care* 2. *v.t.* to make a furrow, channel or groove in ‖ to wrinkle deeply ‖ *v.i.* to make a furrow, channel or groove ‖ to become deeply wrinkled [O.E. *furh*]

furrow slice the ridge of earth turned over by the moldboard in plowing

fur·ry (fəːriː) *comp.* **fur·ri·er** *superl.* **fur·ri·est** *adj.* covered with or clothed in fur ‖ resembling fur ‖ (esp. of the tongue) coated with fur

Fur Seal Islands *PRIBILOF IS

Fürth (fyrt) an industrial town (pop. 101,639) adjoining Nuremberg in Bavaria, West Germany

fur·ther (fəːrðər) alt. *comp.* of FAR ‖ *adj.* additional, *a further topic of conversation* ‖ more remote in time, *till further notice* ‖ more distant, *the further side of the mountain* [O.F. *furthra*]

further alt. *comp.* of FAR ‖ *adv.* to or at a greater distance, *you can go no further* ‖ to a greater extent, *to inquire further into a matter* ‖ also, *I shall further prove you were lying* [O.E. *furthor*]

further *v.t.* to advance, promote, *to further the cause of peace* **fúr·ther·ance** *n.* [O. E. *fyrthrian*]

fur·ther·more (fəːrðərmɔr, fəːrðərmour) *adv.* moreover, besides

fur·ther·most (fəːrðərmoust) *adj.* most distant, furthest

fur·thest (fəːrðist) alt. *superl.* of FAR ‖ 1. *adj.* most distant ‖ extreme, *the furthest point of endurance* 2. *adv.* at or to the greatest distance or degree

fur·tive (fəːrtiv) *adj.* stealthy ‖ shifty ‖ done so as not to be noticed [F. *furtif*]

fu·run·cle (fjúərʌŋkʹl) *n.* a boil [fr. L. *furunculus*, little thief]

fu·ry (fjúəriː) *pl.* **fu·ries** *n.* violent rage ‖ a fit of rage, *she flew into a fury* ‖ violence (of weather, mental disease etc.) ‖ a violently angry woman **like fury** in an intense degree, furiously [F. *furie*]

furze (fəːrz) *n.* a papilionaceous plant belonging to the genera *Ulex* or *Genista*, esp. *U. europaeus*, a prickly, xerophytic European shrub with yellow flowers often found on moors and heathland [O.E. *fyrs*]

fu·sain (fjuːzein, fjuːzein) *n.* a fine charcoal made from spindlewood and used by artists ‖ a drawing made with this [F.]

Fusan *PUSAN

fus·cous (fʌ́skəs) *adj.* dusky, brownish gray [L. *fuscus*]

fuse (fjuːz) 1. *v. pres. part.* **fus·ing** *past* and *past part.* **fused** *v.t.* to melt (a solid) ‖ to join by melting together or as if by melting together ‖ *v.i.* to melt ‖ to become joined by being melted together or as if melted together ‖ (of lights etc. in an electric circuit) to fail because the circuit is broken by a melted fuse wire 2. *n.* a short length of wire or metal of low melting point inserted in an electric circuit and melting (thus breaking the circuit) if the current flow heats it above its melting point [fr. L. *fundere* (*fusus*), to pour, melt]

fuse, fuze (fjuːz) 1. *n.* a combustible or detonating tube, piece of cord, metal etc. which ignites or detonates an explosive ‖ a detonating device inserted into an explosive weapon (e.g. a torpedo or shell) designed to set off the charge on impact 2. *v.t. pres. part.* **fus·ing, fuz·ing** *past* and *past part.* **fused, fuzed** to furnish with a fuse [fr. Ital. *fuso*, a spindle]

fuse box a cutout box

fu·see, fu·zee (fjuːzíː) *n.* (*horology, old-fash.*) a conical pulley which unwinds a chain or cord into the cylinder containing the mainspring, the spring's gradual loss of power being counterbalanced by the fusee's increasing diameter ‖ a match with a large head of phosphorus etc., burning even in a wind [F. *fusée*, a spindleful of tow]

fu·se·lage (fjúːsəlɑːʒ, fjúːzəlɑːʒ, fjúːsəlidʒ, fjúːzə-lidʒ) *n.* the body structure of an airplane, to which the wings and tail are attached [F.]

Fu·se·li (fjúːzəliː), Henry (Johann Heinrich Füssli, 1741–1825), Swiss painter, who lived most of his adult life in England. He made his name with scenes from Shakespeare and dramatic pictures full of nightmare and fantasy

fu·sel oil (fjúːzʹl, fjúːsʹl) a liquid obtained as a by-product in the distillation of fermenting liquids that is a mixture mainly of amyl, butyl, and propyl alcohols, and is used as a solvent [G. *fusel*, bad liquor]

CONCISE PRONUNCIATION KEY: (**a**) æ, c*a*t; ɑ, c*a*r; ɔ f*aw*n; ei, sn*a*ke. (**e**) e, h*e*n; iː, sh*ee*p; iə, d*ee*r; ɛə, b*ea*r. (**i**) i, f*i*sh; ai, t*i*ger; əː, b*i*rd. (**o**) o, *o*x; au, c*ow*; ou, g*oa*t; u, p*oo*r; ɔi, r*oy*al. (**u**) ʌ, d*u*ck; u, b*u*ll; uː, g*oo*se; ə, b*a*cillus; juː, c*u*be. x, lo*ch*; θ, *th*ink; ð, bo*th*er; z, *Z*en; ʒ, corsa*g*e; dʒ, sava*g*e; ŋ, orangutan*g*; j, *y*ak; ʃ, *fi*sh; tʃ, fe*tch*; 'l, rabb*le*; 'n, redd*en*. Complete pronunciation key appears inside front cover.

fusel wire wire used for fuses in electric circuits

Fu·shih (fú:ʃi:) *YENAN

Fu·shun (fú:ʃún) a city (pop. 1,700,000) in Liaoning province, N.E. China, center of the country's richest coal fields and of an important oil industry

fu·si·bil·i·ty (fju:zəbíliti:) *n.* the quality of being fusible ‖ the degree to which something is fusible

fu·si·ble (fjú:zəb'l) *adj.* capable of being fused ‖ having a low melting point, easily melted

fu·si·form (fjú:zifɔrm) *adj.* cigar-shaped or spindle-shaped, tapering, at both ends [fr. L. *fusus,* spindle]

fu·sil·ier, fu·sil·eer (fju:zəlíər) *n.* a soldier in one of the British regiments formerly equipped with light muskets (fusils) [F.]

fu·sil·lade (fjú:səleid, fjú:zleid, fjú:səlɑd, fjú:zəlɑd) **1.** *n.* rapid and repeated fire from many firearms ‖ a mass execution by such fire **2.** *v.t. pres. part.* **fu·sil·lad·ing** *past* and *past part.* **fu·sil·lad·ed** to shoot down (persons) or assault (a place) by fusillade [F.]

fu·sion (fjú:ʒən) *n.* a melting together into a fused mass, e.g. of metals ‖ (*phys.*) the union of light atomic nuclei to form heavier ones under extreme conditions of temperature and pressure, taking place with overall loss in mass and resulting in great energy release. This type of reaction takes place in the sun and in hydrogen bombs. The practical control of fusion reactions has not yet been realized (*NUCLEAR ENERGY, cf. FISSION) ‖ the change of a substance from solid to liquid condition ‖ a blending together so that the component parts are not distinguishable ‖ a coalition **fu·sion·ist** *n.* someone joining in a coalition [fr. L. *fusio* (*fusionis*)]

fusion bomb a bomb whose energy is derived from the fusion of light nuclei, esp. a hydrogen bomb

fusion point melting point

fuss (fʌs) **1.** *n.* unnecessary excitement ‖ worry about trifles ‖ complaint, objection **to make a fuss of** to surround (someone) with affectionate or flattering attentions **2.** *v.i.* to be in a state of restless commotion ‖ to worry unduly or about trifles ‖ to raise objections, complain ‖ *v.t.* to bother (someone), esp. with unwanted attentions [etym. doubtful]

fuss·budg·et (fʌsbʌdʒit) *n.* (*pop.*) someone given to fussing

fuss·i·ly (fʌsili:) *adv.* in a fussy way

fuss·i·ness (fʌsi:nis) *n.* the quality or state of being fussy

fuss·pot (fʌspɒt) *n.* (*pop.*) a fussbudget

fuss·y (fʌsi:) *comp.* **fuss·i·er** *superl.* **fuss·i·est** *adj.* given to fussing ‖ hard to please, fastidious, exacting ‖ bustling, *a fussy little fishing port* ‖ (of clothes, ornament etc.) having too many small or unnecessary details

fus·tian (fʌstʃən) **1.** *n.* a cotton fabric with a twill weave and a short nap, e.g. corduroy ‖ (*rhet.*) bombast, pretentious nonsense **2.** *adj.* made of fustian ‖ (*rhet.,* of language) pompous, pretentious [O.F. *fustaigne*]

fus·tic (fʌstik) *n.* a yellowish or olive-colored dye from the heartwood of the tropical American tree *Chlorophora tinctoria,* fam. *Moraceae* ‖ the wood of the tree ‖ *YOUNG FUSTIC [F. *fustoc* fr. Span. fr. Arab. fr. Gk *pistake,* pistachio]

fus·ti·ness (fʌsti:nis) *n.* the state or quality of being fusty

fus·ty (fʌsti:) *comp.* **fus·ti·er** *superl.* **fus·ti·est** *adj.* musty, moldy, rank, *a fusty cellar* ‖ out-of-date, old-fashioned, *fusty ideas* [fr. O.F. *fust,* cask]

Futa Jallon *FOUTA DJALLON

fu·thark (fú:θɑrk) *n.* the runic alphabet [from its first six letters]

fu·tile (fjú:t'l, Br. fjú:tail) *adj.* unavailing, *a futile attempt* ‖ pointless, trifling and wearisome, *futile conversation* **fu·til·i·ty** (fju:tíliti:) *pl.* **fu·til·i·ties** *n.* the quality of being futile ‖ something futile [F.]

fut·tock (fʌtək) *n.* one of the lower, curved, upright framing timbers in a wooden ship [etym. doubtful]

futtock plate an iron plate across the top of a lower mast. The deadeyes of the topmast rigging and the upper ends of the futtock shrouds are attached to it

futtock shroud one of the iron shrouds from the futtock plate to a band around the lower mast, so that the topmast rigging is joined to the lower mast

Fu·tu·na Island (fu:tú:nə) *WALLIS AND FUTUNA ISLANDS

fu·ture (fjú:tʃər) **1.** *adj.* of or in time to come, *future developments* ‖ destined to be, *he met his future wife when they were both students* ‖ (*gram.,* of a tense) relating to time yet to come **2.** *n.* time yet to come, *it lies in the future* ‖ prospects, *the future of space research* ‖ future events, *to foresee the future* ‖ (*gram.*) the future tense or a verb in this tense ‖ (*pl., commerce*)

goods or securities bought or sold on a contract for future delivery [O.F.]

future shock distress caused by inability to adjust to rapid changes in the ways of living, from the 1970 book *Future Shock,* by Alvin Toffler *Cf* CULTURE SHOCK

fu·tur·ism (fjú:tʃərizəm) *n.* a movement in the arts founded (1909) in Italy by the poet Filippo Tommaso Marinetti. In violent reaction against tradition, it exalted dynamic aspects of contemporary life: speed and mechanization. Poets produced experimental works from which all usual form and meaning were eliminated. Artists, led by Boccioni, produced abstract paintings and sculptures, representing objects in motion by means of repetition of forms, emphasis on lines of force, and the dissolving of clear division between objects and space ‖ study of, and interest in, forecasting or anticipating the future or alternative futures, or theorizing on how to impose controls on events **fu·tur·ist** *n.* and *adj.*

fu·tu·ri·ty (fju:túəriti:, fju:tjúəriti:, fju:tʃúəriti:) *pl.* **fu·tu·ri·ties** *n.* time to come, the future ‖ a future condition or event ‖ the quality of being future

futurity race a race, esp. a horse race for two-year-olds, for which competitors are entered at birth or sooner

fuze *FUSE

fuzee *FUSEE

fuzz (fʌz) **1.** *n.* a fluffy mass or coating of fine particles or fibers etc. e.g. on cloth or a peach ‖ a blurred effect **2.** *v.t.* to cover with fuzz ‖ to blur ‖ *v.i.* to become covered with fuzz ‖ to become blurred [etym. doubtful]

fuzz·box (fʌzboks) *n.* (*music slang*) an electric-guitar attachment that creates a fuzzy quality to the sound emitted

fuzz·i·ly (fʌzili:) *adv.* in a fuzzy way

fuzz·i·ness (fʌzi:nis) *n.* the quality or state of being fuzzy

fuzz·y (fʌzi:) *comp.* **fuzz·i·er** *superl.* **fuzz·i·est** *adj.* like fuzz, covered with fuzz, downy, frayed etc. ‖ (of hair) consisting of tightly interlaced curls ‖ indistinct, blurred, not clear

-fy *suffix* to become, as in 'liquefy' or cause to become, as in 'nullify' [fr. F. v. ending *-fier* and fr. M.L. *-ficare,* L. *facere*]

FYI (*acronym*) for your information

fyl·fot (fílfɒt) *n.* a swastika [etym. doubtful]

Fyn (fin) *FÜEN

CONCISE PRONUNCIATION KEY: (a) æ, c*a*t; ɑ, c*a*r; ɔ f*aw*n; ei, sn*a*ke.   **(e)** e, h*e*n; i:, sh*ee*p; iə, d*ee*r; ɛə, b*ea*r.   **(i)** i, f*i*sh; ai, t*i*ger; ə:, b*i*rd.
(o) o, *o*x; au, c*ow*; ou, g*oa*t; u, p*oo*r; ɔi, r*oy*al.   **(u)** ʌ, d*u*ck; u, b*u*ll; u:, g*oo*se; ə, b*a*cillus; ju:, c*u*be.   x, lo*ch*; θ, *th*ink; ð, bo*th*er; z, *Z*en; ʒ, corsa*g*e;
dʒ, sava*g*e; ŋ, oranguta*ng*; j, *y*ak; ʃ, *fi*sh; tʃ, fe*tch*; 'l, rabb*le*; 'n, redd*en*.   Complete pronunciation key appears inside front cover.

	EARLY NORTH SEMITIC	PHOENICIAN	EARLY HEBREW (GEZER)	EARLY GREEK	CLASSICAL GREEK	ETRUSCAN		EARLY LATIN	CLASSICAL LATIN
						Early	Classical		
G	�ↄ	∧	↑	↑	⌐	↿	⟩	⟨	G
	CURSIVE MAJUSCULE (ROMAN)	CURSIVE MINUSCULE (ROMAN)	ANGLO-IRISH MAJUSCULE	CAROLINE MINUSCULE	VENETIAN MINUSCULE (ITALIC)	N. ITALIAN MINUSCULE (ROMAN)
	ך	ᡋ	ᵹ	g	*g*	g

A. C. SYLVESTER, CAMBRIDGE, ENGLAND

Development of the letter G, beginning with the early North Semitic letter. Evolution of both the majuscule, or capital, letter G and the minuscule, or lowercase, letter g are shown.

G, g (dʒi:) the seventh letter of the English alphabet ‖ (*mus.*) a note, and the key of which it is the tonic ‖ (*phys.*) the symbol (G) for the constant of gravitation in Newton's law of gravitation ‖ the symbol (g) for the acceleration due to gravity of a freely falling body

g. gram grams

Ga. Georgia

gab (gæb) **1.** *n.* (*pop.*) chatter ‖ idle talk **2.** *v.i. pres. part.* **gab·bing** *past* and *past part.* **gabbed** to chatter, talk idly [perh. imit.]

GABA (*zool. acronym*) for gamma-aminobutyric acid, an amino acid present in the brain of mammals

gab·ar·dine (gǽbərdi:n) *n.* a fine hard-laid cloth of twill weave used e.g. for raincoats [var. of GABERDINE]

gab·ble (gǽb'l) **1.** *n.* hurried, confused, meaningless chatter **2.** *v. pres. part.* **gab·bling** *past* and *past part.* **gab·bled** *v.t.* to utter rapidly and in a confused or foolish way, *to gabble an excuse* ‖ *v.i.* to speak in this way [imit.]

gab·bro (gǽbrou) *pl.* **gab·bros** *n.* (*geol.*) a group of coarsely crystalline igneous rocks, of deep-seated origin, consisting chiefly of plagioclase feldspar and pyroxene (*HORNBLENDE) [Ital.]

gab·by (gǽbi:) *comp.* **gab·bi·er** *superl.* **gab·bi·est** *adj.* (*pop.*) talkative

ga·belle (gæbél) *n.* a tax, esp. that on salt in France under the ancien régime [F.]

gab·er·dine (gǽbərdi:n) *n.* (*hist.*) a long, loose gown, esp. as worn by Jews and almsmen in the Middle Ages ‖ gabardine [older *gawbardyne* fr. O.F. fr. Gmc]

ga·ble (géib'l) *n.* the triangular upper part of a wall closing the end of a ridged roof ‖ the gable-topped end wall of a building ‖ a triangular architectural decoration, e.g. over a doorway or window **gá·bled** *adj.* [O.F. prob. fr. O.N. *gafl*]

Ga·bo (gábou), Naum (Naum Pevsner, 1890– , brother of Antoine Pevsner), American sculptor, born in Russia, an originator of constructivism

Ga·bon (gæbɔ̃) a republic (area 103,000 sq. miles, pop. 480,000) in W. central Africa. Capital: Libreville. People: Fang, with Mpongwe, Kota, Negrillo and other minorities, 1% European. Language: French, Bantu languages. Religion: 42% Roman Catholic, 15% Protestant, 42% local African religions, 1% Moslem. The heart of Gabon is the forested Ogoué basin bounded on the north by the Cristal Mtns, on the south by the Achango Mtns (M'Bigou, 3,900 ft), and stretching from the coastal plain to the eastern plateaus (1,000–2,000 ft). Average temperature (F.): 79°. Rainfall: 98 ins. Main products: peanuts, millet, manioc, cocoa,

Okoumé lumber for plywood, mahogany, ebony. Minerals: oil, gold and diamonds, manganese, iron ore, uranium. Industries: lumber, palm oil extraction, whaling. Exports: lumber, manganese. Ports: Libreville, Port-Gentil. Monetary unit: franc CFA. HISTORY. Portuguese explorers visited (15th c.) the coast, which later became a main slave-trade center. The French established a settlement (1839) in the Gabon estuary, founded Libreville (1849) and extended their authority along the coast and into the interior. The territory was made part of the French Congo, then in 1910 became a separate colony. Gabon became an autonomous member state of the French Community in 1958 and acceded to full independence on Aug. 17, 1960. Gabon is a constitutional republic with a president and unicameral National Assembly. Leon M'ba was the first president; when he died in 1967, Omar Bongo became president

Gabor (gábour), Dennis (1900–79), British scientist, Nobel prizewinner in physics (1971). He developed holography, a method of taking 3-dimensional photographs without a lens

Gab·o·ro·nes (gæbəróunəs) the capital (since 1965, pop. 38,000) of Botswana, formerly a trading center on the Cape Town–Beira railroad

Ga·bri·el (géibri:əl) the archangel who announced to the Virgin Mary that she would be the mother of Jesus (Luke 1, 26–38). Gabriel is also revered by Moslems as having dictated the Koran to Mohammed

Ga·bri·el (gǽbri:el), Jacques-Ange (1698–1782), French architect, best known for his Petit Trianon at Versailles and the École Militaire in Paris

Ga·bri·e·li (gɑbri:éli:), Giovanni (1577–1612), Italian composer whose works, e.g. the 'Sacred Symphonies' (1579), and other sacred music, for voices with instruments and instrumental groups, make use of dynamic and tonal contrasts in a way that prefigures the baroque

Gad (gæd) Hebrew patriarch, son of Jacob ‖ the Israelite tribe of which he was the ancestor

gad (gæd) **1.** *n.* a pointed iron bar for loosening ore, splitting rock etc. **2.** *v.t. pres. part.* **gad·ding** *past* and *past part.* **gad·ded** to loosen and split with a gad [O.N. *gaddr*, a spike]

gad *v.i. pres. part.* **gad·ding** *past* and *past part.* **gad·ded** (in the phrase) **to gad about** to be constantly going out in search of pleasure [etym. doubtful]

gad·a·bout (gǽdəbaut) *n.* someone constantly moving around, esp. for frivolous reasons

Gad·di (gáddi:), Taddeo (c. 1300–66), Florentine painter. He is thought to have been an assistant of Giotto. His most famous extant works, mostly in Florence, are frescoes, altarpieces and ceilings

gad·fly (gǽdflai) *pl.* **gad·flies** *n.* any of various flies (e.g. the botflies, warble flies, tabanids) that bite cattle ‖ an irritating person, esp. one who goads others into action by persistent criticism

gadg·et (gǽdʒit) *n.* a small, ingenious and useful fitting, e.g. in machinery ‖ a useful device, *kitchen gadgets* ‖ a clever but trivial device that is hardly more than a knickknack [origin unknown]

gad·oid (gǽdɔid, géidɔid) **1.** *n.* a member of *Gadidae*, a family of fish including cod, haddock, pollack, whiting, hake etc. **2.** *adj.* of or resembling the *Gadidae* [fr. Mod. L. *gadus*, cod fr. Gk]

gad·o·lin·i·um (gæd'líni:əm) *n.* one of the rare-earth elements (symbol Gd, at. no. 64, at. mass 157.25) [fr. *gadolinite*, a mineral which is a source of rare earths]

ga·droon (gædrú:n) *n.* (usually *pl.*) a short, wide ornamental fluting in glass, silver etc. ‖ (*archit.*) a notched or carved rounded molding [fr. F. *godron*]

Gads·den Purchase (gǽdzdən) a U.S.-Mexican treaty negotiated (1853) between James Gadsden, U.S. minister to Mexico, and Santa Anna, president of Mexico. Mexico agreed to cede 19 million acres south of the Gila River to enable the U.S. government to construct a southern transcontinental railroad, in return for $15 million in payment. The U.S. Senate ratified (1854) the treaty, but reduced the area and the payment by one third

gad·wall (gǽdwɔl) *pl.* **gad·wall, gad·walls** *n. Anas strepera* or *Chaulelasmus streperus*, a freshwater wild duck of N. Europe and America, about as big as a mallard [origin unknown]

Gael (geil) *n.* a Scottish Celt ‖ an Irish Celt **Gáel·ic 1.** *adj.* of or pertaining to the Gaels or their language **2.** *n.* a branch of the Celtic family of languages comprising Irish (Erse), Scottish Gaelic and Manx. The total of Gaelic speakers outside Ireland does not exceed 100,000 [Scot. Gael. *Gaidheal*, a member of the Gaelic race]

gaff (gæf) **1.** *n.* a barbed fishing spear ‖ an iron hook for lifting heavy fish into a boat ‖ (*cockfighting*) a metal spur replacing a natural spur ‖ (*naut.*) a spar on which the upper edge of a fore-and-aft sail is extended **to stand the gaff** to stand up well to difficulties, ridicule etc. **2.** *v.t.* to strike or catch hold of with a gaff [F. *gaffe*, boathook]

gaff *n.* (*Br.*, only in) **to blow the gaff** to blurt out a secret, give away a plot [origin unknown]

gaffe (gæf) *n.* a social blunder or quite tactless remark [F.]

CONCISE PRONUNCIATION KEY: **(a)** æ, cat; ɑ, car; ɔ fawn; ei, snake.   **(e)** e, hen; i:, sheep; iə, deer; ɛə, bear.   **(i)** i, fish; ai, tiger; ə:, bird. **(o)** o, ox; au, cow; ou, goat; u, poor; ɔi, royal.   **(u)** ʌ, duck; u, bull; u:, goose; ə, bacillus; ju:, cube.   x, loch; θ, think; ð, bother; z, Zen; ʒ, corsage; dʒ, savage; ŋ, orangutang; j, yak; ʃ, fish; tʃ, fetch; 'l, rabble; 'n, redden.   Complete pronunciation key appears inside front cover.

gaf·fer (gǽfər) n. (pop., old-fash.) an old man, esp. (Br.) an old countryman ‖ (Br.) a foreman, boss [contr. of GRANDFATHER]

Gaf·sa (gúfsə) a mining town and oasis (pop. 236,000) of central Tunisia: phosphates

gag (gæg) **1.** v. pres. part. **gag·ging** past and past part. **gagged** v.t. to stop up the mouth of (someone) with a gag ‖ to fasten open the jaws of, e.g. for surgery ‖ to restrict the freedom of speech of ‖ v.i. to retch or choke ‖ (theater) to interpolate jokes into a script **2.** n. something crammed into the mouth to prevent sound ‖ a device used to hold the mouth open, e.g. in dentistry ‖ any suppression of freedom of speech ‖ (Br.) the closure of debate in parliament (*GUILLOTINE) ‖ a joke, esp. one interpolated in a play etc. ‖ a hoax, trick [imit.]

ga·ga (gágə) adj. (pop.) slightly crazy ‖ (pop.) foolishly enthusiastic or infatuated ‖ (pop.) senile [F.]

ga·ga·ku (gágəku:) n. Japanese court ceremonial music

Gage (geidʒ), Thomas (1721–87), British general. Appointed (1774) governor of the Massachusetts Bay Province, he ordered (1775) British troops to raid the ammunition supply of the patriots at Concord. This led to the opening battle of the American Revolution, at Lexington

gage (geidʒ) n. (hist.) a challenge to fight, or the symbol of such a challenge, usually a glove thrown down ‖ something deposited as security [O.F. guage]

gage *GAUGE

gag·gle (gǽg'l) **1.** n. a flock of geese ‖ a little group, a gaggle of housewives **2.** v.i. pres. part. **gag·gling** past and past part. **gag·gled** (of geese) to cackle [imit.]

Gag Laws a series of resolutions passed (1836–40) in the House of Representatives providing that all petitions relating to slavery were to be tabled without being printed, referred to committee, or discussed. No similar action was taken by the Senate. Abolitionists, resentful of the infringements of the constitutional right of petition, gained in national support

gag strip a comic cartoon with no story continuity

Gai·a (gáiə, géiə) (Gk mythol.) Ge

gai·e·ty, gay·e·ty (géiiti:) pl. **gai·e·ties, gay·e·ties** n. the quality of being or looking gay ‖ merrymaking, entertainment [fr. F. gaieté]

gai·ly, gay·ly (géili) adv. in a gay fashion

gain (gein) n. financial profit ‖ (pl.) winnings or profits ‖ an improvement or increase, a gain in prices ‖ the acquiring of wealth ‖ advantage [O.F.]

gain n. a notch in a beam or a wall for a joist, girder etc. [origin unknown]

gain v.t. to acquire, obtain, to gain experience ‖ to obtain as a profit ‖ to earn, to gain a good reputation ‖ to win, to gain a victory ‖ to reach, to gain the summit ‖ to obtain by steady increase, to gain weight ‖ (of clocks and watches) to become increasingly fast by, the clock gains five minutes a day ‖ v.i. to improve, advance, to gain in knowledge ‖ (of clocks and watches) to become increasingly fast **to gain ground** to advance **to gain ground on, to gain on** (or **upon**) to get closer to in pursuit ‖ to leave (pursuers) further behind **to gain the upper hand** to get the mastery in a contest **to gain time** to obtain a desired delay **gáin·er** n. a back-somersault dive made from a front-dive takeoff position **gáin·ful** adj. profitable, money-earning, a gainful occupation **gáin·ings** pl. n. profits, earnings [fr. F. gagner]

Gain·ful (géinfəl) (mil.) U.S.S.R. surface-to-air missile (SA-6) weighing 1,200 lbs, with radio command and radar homing direction

gain·say (geinséi, géinsei) pres. part. **gain·say·ing** past and past part. **gain·said** (geinséid, geinséd, géinseid, géinsed) v.t. (old-fash.) to contradict, deny, there is no gainsaying the evidence [O.E. gegn-, against+SAY]

Gains·bor·ough (géinzbə:rou, géinzbʌrou, Br. géinzbərə), Thomas (1727–88), English painter and foundation member of the Royal Academy. Practically self-taught, he was influenced in his earlier work by the Dutch masters and Vandyke. He broke from tradition by painting his native countryside as he saw it and not as an idealized version of the Roman campagna. His landscape backgrounds to portraits are free, almost impressionistic, with strong feeling for woodland solitude. His portraits typically are images of patrician breeding, elegance and self-assurance

Gai·ser·ic (gaizérik) *GENSERIC

gait (geit) **1.** n. a manner of walking, running etc., a shuffling gait ‖ (of horses) a manner of moving the feet, e.g. a trot, canter **2.** v.t. to train (a horse) to a particular gait [alt. form of gate, a way]

gait·er (géitər) n. a cloth or leather covering for the leg from knee to instep, or for the ankle and instep ‖ (hist.) an overshoe with a cloth upper ‖ an ankle-high shoe with elastic side insertions [F. guêtre]

Gait·skell (géitskəl), Hugh Todd Naylor (1906–63), British politician, leader of the Labour party (1955–63)

Ga·ius (gáiəs, géiəs) (c. 110– c. 180), Roman jurist. His 'Institutes' formed the basis of the Corpus Juris Civilis of Justinian I

ga·la (géilə, gúlə, gúlə) **1.** n. a festival, a grand social occasion ‖ (Br.) an athletic contest, a swimming gala **2.** adj. highly festive, a gala day, gala occasion [F. fr. Ital.]

ga·lac·tan (gælǽktən) n. (chem.) a compound sugar including gums, agar, and fruit pectins found in algae, mosses, and lichens that yield galactose on hydrolysis

ga·lac·tic (gəlǽktik) adj. of or pertaining to a galaxy [fr. Gk galaktikos, milky fr. gala (galaktos), milk]

ga·lac·to·ki·nase (gælæktəkíneis) n. (physiol.) an enzyme that causes the breakdown of some sugars for use by cells

ga·lac·tose (gəlǽktous) n. a white crystalline sugar, $C_6H_{12}O_6$, obtained from lactose by hydrolysis [fr. Gk gala (galaktos), milk]

ga·la·go (gəléigou) n. a member of Galago, fam. Lorisidae, a genus of small, agile arboreal African primates. They are nocturnal in habit [Mod. L.]

Gal·a·had, Sir (gǽləhæd) the purest of the knights, in the Arthurian legend

gal·an·tine (gǽlənti:n) n. a dish of cooked, boned chicken, veal etc., stuffed or spiced, covered in aspic, and served cold [F.]

Ga·lá·pa·gos Islands (gəlúpəgəs) (Span. Archipiélago de Colón) a group of 13 large volcanic islands (area 3,029 sq. miles, pop. 9,000) and many islets in the Pacific, 650 miles west of Ecuador, of which they form a province. Their flora, fauna and geology are unique. The only two inhabited are San Cristóbal and Isabela. The islands were discovered (1535) by the Spanish, and were annexed (1832) by Ecuador. Darwin's studies of the giant tortoises there helped to form his theory of evolution

Ga·la·ta·Pe·ra (gɑlɑtápéərɑ) *ISTANBUL

ga·la·te·a (gælətéiə) n. sturdy, twill cotton fabric used for children's playclothes, named for the Greek sea nymph

Ga·lati (gɑláts) a port (pop. 267,962) in E. Rumania on the Danube: naval base, shipbuilding

Ga·la·tia (gəléiʃə) an ancient country of Asia Minor, now part of Turkey. It was settled (3rd c. B.C.) by Gauls, became subject to Rome (2nd c. B.C.) and was a Roman province (25 B.C.). Chief town: Ancyra (modern Ankara)

Ga·la·tians, Epistle to the (gəléiʃənz) the ninth book of the New Testament, written either c. 48 or c. 55 by St Paul to the churches of Galatia. It enunciates his doctrine of justification by faith and contains a vindication of his mission to the gen-tiles

gal·ax·y (gǽləksi:) pl. **gal·ax·ies** n. one of the vast number of systems containing stars, nebulae, star clusters and interstellar matter that make up the universe. The Milky Way is the local galaxy seen from the earth. Galaxies are classified principally according to shape, ranging from spherical and elliptical through spiral (with or without barred nucleus) to amorphous (*SPIRAL GALAXY) ‖ a brilliant company, a galaxy of talent **Gal·ax·y** the Milky Way [F. galaxie fr. L. fr. Gk]

Galaxy (mil.) a large cargo transport aircraft (C-5A) powered by four turbofan engines, capable of refueling in flight, and with the capacity of carrying a very large payload

Gal·ba (gǽlbə), Servius Sulpicius (c. 5 B.C.–69 A.D.), Roman emperor (68–9) after the murder of Nero

gal·ba·num (gǽlbənəm) n. an aromatic, bitter gum resin obtained from several Asiatic plants, esp. Ferula galbaniflua. It has been used medicinally [M.E. fr. L.]

Gal·braith (gǽlbreiθ), John Kenneth (1908–), U.S. economist and diplomat, author of 'The Affluent Society' (1958), 'The New Indus-trial State' (1967), 'A Life In Our Times: Memoirs' (1981) and 'The Voice of the Poor' (1983)

Galdós, Benito Pérez *PÉREZ GALDÓS

gale (geil) n. (meteor.) a wind having a speed from 32 to 63 m.p.h. ‖ a strong wind ‖ a gust, noisy outburst, gales of laughter [etym. doubtful]

gale n. sweet gale [O.E. gagel, gagol]

ga·le·a (géili:ə) n. (biol.) a helmet-shaped petal or other similarly shaped structure [L.=helmet]

ga·le·a cap·i·tis (géili:əkæpi:tis) n. the thin sheath covering the head of a spermatozoon

ga·le·ate (géili:eit) adj. helmet-shaped ‖ having a galea **gá·le·at·ed** adj.

Ga·len (géilən) (Claudius Galenus, c. 130–c. 200), physician and philosopher of Pergamum. He wrote many works on physiology and anatomy which dominated medical thought until the Middle Ages

ga·le·na (gəlí:nə) n. the chief ore of lead, native lead sulfide, PbS, occurring as bluish-gray cubic crystals [L.]

Ga·len·ic (gəlénik) adj. of Galen, or his teachings **Ga·lén·i·cal** adj. Galenic **ga·lén·i·cal** n. a natural, vegetable, nonsynthetic pharmaceutical preparation

galet *GALLET

Ga·li·ci·a (gəlíʃi:ə, gəlíʃə) a region of Spain at the northwest corner of the Iberian peninsula, forming Lugo, La Coruña, Pontevedra and Orense Provinces. It is mountainous and fertile, with a deeply indented coast. Crops: cereals, fruit, vegetables. Industries: cattle-raising, forestry, fishing, some mining. Chief town: La Coruña. It was a separate kingdom (411–585), was taken from the Moors by Asturias (8th–9th cc.), was independent (1065–72), and merged with the kingdom of Castile and León. Galician is widely spoken

Ga·li·ci·a (gəlíʃi:ə, gəlíʃə, gəlítsjə) a region of E. Europe on the north side of the Carpathians. Chief town: Lvov. Galicia was ruled by Poland (1386–1772) and by Austria (1772–1919), then regained (1919) by Poland. The east was annexed (1945) to the Ukraine

Ga·li·cian (gəlíʃən) **1.** n. a native or inhabitant of Spanish Galicia ‖ the Romance language of a Spanish Galician **2.** adj. of or pertaining to Spanish Galicia, its people or its language

Ga·li·cian (gəlíʃən, gəlítsjən) **1.** n. a native or inhabitant of Polish Galicia, esp. a Polish Jew of the region ‖ (loosely) one of the Yiddish dialects spoken by such a Jew **2.** adj. of or pertaining to Polish Galicia or (loosely) to one of the Yiddish dialects spoken by a Jew of this region

Gal·i·le·an (gælilí:ən, gælili:éiən) **1.** adj. of or pertaining to Galilee **2.** n. someone from Galilee **the Galilean** Jesus

Galilean adj. of the astronomer Galileo Galilei

Galilean telescope a type of refracting telescope, having a convergent objective and a divergent eyepiece. It gives a slightly magnified upright image, has a limited field of view, and is used in opera glasses

Gal·i·lee (gǽlili) the northern region (area 1,800 sq. miles) of Israel, mainly hill country devoted to mixed farming and olive and tobacco plantations. It was the scene of Christ's early ministry

gal·i·lee (gǽlili) n. a chapel or porch at the entrance of certain English churches [O.F. galilée]

Galilee, Sea of a lake (area 112 sq. miles) in Israel through which the Jordan flows. It lies 680 ft below sea level

Gal·i·le·o (gæləléiou) (Galileo Galilei, 1564–1642), Italian astronomer and physicist. His many achievements include the discovery of the isochronism of the pendulum, and the demonstration that the acceleration of a falling body does not depend on its mass. He constructed telescopes, discovered Jupiter's satellites, and observed sunspots and the mountainous nature of the moon. A supporter of Copernican theory, Galileo was forced by the Inquisition to recant (1633)

gal·i·mo·ny (gǽlimouni:) n. payment in lieu of alimony for separated lesbians. Cf PALIMONY

gal·in·gale (gǽlingeil) n. the aromatic rhizome of some E. Asian plants related to ginger, esp. Alpina officinalis and Kaempferia galanga, formerly used in cooking and medicine ‖ Cyperus longus, an Old World sedge with a root having similar properties [fr. O.F. galingal fr. Arab. fr. Chin. Ko-liang-kiang, mild ginger from Ko]

gal·i·pot, gal·li·pot (gǽləpɒt) *n.* a crude turpentine oleoresin which exudes from and hardens on the bark of *Pinus pinaster*, a S. European pine [F.]

gall (gɔl) **1.** *n.* an injury to a horse's skin caused by chronic chafing ‖ a cause of intense irritation, *gall to one's pride* ‖ impertinence ‖ bile ‖ the gallbladder **2.** *v.t.* to chafe so as to cause a sore ‖ to irritate or mortify ‖ *v.i.* to become sore through chafing [O.E. *gealla*, perh. fr. L. *galla*, gallnut]

gall *n.* a growth, which may take many varied forms, on the tissues of plants, caused by plant or animal parasites [F. *galle*]

Gal·la (gǽlə) *pl.* **Gal·la, Gal·las** *n.* any of several peoples of S. Ethiopia and E. Africa ‖ a member of these peoples ‖ their Cushitic language [perh. Arab. *ghalīz*, rough, wild]

gal·lant (gǽlənt) *adj.* showing noble courage ‖ (*Br.*) the conventional epithet used in referring to an ex-service M.P. during parliamentary debate ‖ (gəlánt) showily attentive to women [F. *galant*]

gal·lant·ry (gǽləntri:) *pl.* **gal·lant·ries** *n.* dashing bravery ‖ showily attentive behavior to women ‖ a compliment made to a woman by a man flirting with her [F. *galanterie*]

Gal·la·tin (gǽlətin), Albert (1761–1849), U.S. statesman. As Secretary of the Treasury under President Thomas Jefferson, he changed U.S. financial policy from Federalist to Jeffersonian and, despite the costly Barbary War and the Louisiana Purchase, reduced the national debt. He was a chief negotiator of the Treaty of Ghent

gall·blad·der (gɔ́lblædər) *n.* a muscular sac present in most vertebrates, opening into the bile duct. It stores bile until there is food in the duodenum

Gal·le (gǽlə, gúlə), Johann Gottfried (1812–1910), German astronomer. Guided by the calculations of Le Verrier, he discovered the planet Neptune (1846)

Ga·lle·gos (gɑljégɒs), Rómulo (1884–1969), Venezuelan novelist who served (Feb. 15–Nov. 24, 1948) as president of his country but was ousted for his liberalism. His novels 'Doña Bárbara' (1929) and 'Cantaclaro' (1931) depict respectively the violence and the solitude of life on the vast Venezuelan llanos

gal·le·on (gǽli:ən, gǽljən) *n.* (*hist.*) a sailing ship, often with three or four decks, shorter and higher than a galley and armed with cannon, used (15th and 16th cc.) for war or trade, esp. by the Spaniards in their American trade [F. *galion* and Span. *galeón*]

gal·ler·y (gǽləri:) *pl.* **gal·ler·ies** *n.* an indoor balcony projecting from the wall of a church or hall, providing extra accommodation ‖ (*theater*) the highest balcony, with the cheapest seats ‖ the people who sit there ‖ a long narrow room, e.g. one for exhibiting pictures in stately homes ‖ a room or series of rooms used for exhibiting works of art ‖ an art dealer's premises ‖ a covered passage, partly open at one side, and usually above ground level ‖ an underground passage made by animals, e.g. by moles or ants ‖ (*mining*) a working drift or level ‖ an underground passage [fr. F. *galerie*]

gal·let, gal·et (gǽlit) **1.** *n.* a chip of stone **2.** *v.t.* to garret [F. *galet*, pebble]

gal·ley (gǽli:) *n.* (*hist.*) a long, low, narrow, single-decked ship propelled by sails and oars, usually rowed by condemned criminals, and extensively used in the 16th c. by the Venetians and Genoese ‖ an ancient Greek or Roman warship with one or several banks of oars ‖ a large open rowing boat, such as is used by the captain of a warship ‖ the kitchen of a ship ‖ (*printing*) an oblong tray with upright sides, to hold type which has been set ‖ a galley proof [M.E. *galeie* fr. O.F.]

galley proof a printer's proof taken from type locked in a galley to permit correction before the type is made up in pages

galley slave (*hist.*) a man condemned to row in a galley

gall·fly (gɔ́lflaɪ) *pl.* **gall·flies** *n.* any of several insects that lay their eggs in plant tissues, causing galls

gal·liard (gǽljərd) *n.* a lively dance in triple time popular in Europe during the 16th and 17th cc. [fr. O.F. *gaillard*]

Gal·lic (gǽlik) *adj.* of or pertaining to the Gauls, or France [fr. L. *Gallicus*]

gal·lic acid (gǽlik) a white crystalline acid, $C_6H_2(OH)_3COOH$, found in many plants, e.g. tea, and in galls [fr. F. *gallique*]

Gal·li·can (gǽlikən) **1.** *adj.* of the ancient church of Gaul or France ‖ (*hist.*) having to do with Gallicanism **2.** *n.* an adherent of Gallicanism **Gál·li·can·ism** *n.* (*hist.*) a theory claiming the restriction of papal power over the Roman Catholic Church in France. It originated in the Great Schism and reached its height in the 17th c., in the quarrel between Louis XIV and Innocent XI. The French bishops declared their independence (1682), but Louis abandoned Gallicanism (1693). The issue was submerged in the French Revolution (cf. ULTRAMONTANISM) [fr. L. *Gallicanus*]

Gal·li·cism (gǽlisizəm) *n.* a French idiom or grammatical construction taken over into another language ‖ a characteristically French action, outlook etc. [F. *gallicisme*]

gal·li·cize (gǽlisaiz) *v. pres. part.* **gal·li·ciz·ing** *past* and *past part.* **gal·li·cized** *v.t.* to make French in character, speech or expression ‖ *v.i.* to become French in character etc. [fr. L. *Gallicus*]

Gal·li-Cur·ci (gǽlikə́:rtʃi:), Amelita (1889–1963), Italian-U.S. coloratura soprano. Her U.S. debut (1916) at the Chicago Auditorium as Gilda in Verdi's 'Rigoletto' led to her success (1921–30) with the New York Metropolitan Opera Company

Gal·li·e·nus (gæli:éinəs), Publius Licinius Valerianus Egnatius (218–68), Roman emperor (253–68), son of Valerian, with whom he ruled jointly (253–60)

gal·li·mau·fry (gæləmɔ́fri:) *pl.* **gal·li·mau·fries** *n.* (*rhet.*) a jumble, a confused mixture [fr. F. *galimafrée*]

gal·li·na·ceous (gæli:néiʃəs) *adj.* of or belonging to *Galliformes*, an order of birds including game birds (pheasants, grouse etc.) and domestic poultry [fr. L. *gallinaceus* fr. *gallina*, hen]

Ga·lli·nas, Point (gají:nəs) *GUAJIRA

gall·ing (gɔ́liŋ) *adj.* irritating, exasperating

gal·li·nule (gǽlinju:l, gǽlinu:l) *n.* any of several aquatic birds constituting a subfamily of fam. *Rallidae*, esp. the moorhen [fr. Mod. L. *Gallinula*]

gal·li·ot (gǽli:ət) *n.* (*hist.*) a Dutch sailing boat ‖ (*hist.*) a small galley, usually Mediterranean [F. *galiote*]

Gal·lip·o·li (gəlípəli:) (*Turk.* Gelibolu) a peninsula in Turkey on the European side of the Dardanelles. It was the scene of an unsuccessful Allied expedition (Apr. 1915–Jan. 1916)

gal·li·pot (gǽləpɒt) *n.* (*hist.*) a small earthenware glazed pot, esp. one used by apothecaries [etym. doubtful]

gallipot *GALIPOT

gal·li·um (gǽli:əm) *n.* a soft bluish-white metallic element (symbol Ga, at. no. 31, at. mass 69.72). It has a low melting point (29.75°C.) and expands on solidification [Mod. L. fr. L. *gallus*, cock, trans. of *Lecoq* de Boisbaudran, who discovered it in 1875]

gallium arsenide [GaAs] (*electr.*) a semiconductor material with a maximum operating temperature of 400°C used in transistors

gallium arsenide phosphide [GaAsP] (*electr.*) material used in semiconductors that produces red or amber light

gal·li·vant (gǽlivænt) *v.i.* to gad about [etym. doubtful]

gall midge any of several small, two-winged flies of fam. *Cecidomyiidae*, most of which cause the formation of galls

gall·nut (gɔ́lnʌt) *n.* a gall resembling a nut, esp. on oaks

gal·lon (gǽlən) *n.* (*abbr.* gal.) a liquid measure: the wine gallon, the U.S. standard, is 231 cu. ins (3.785 liters), and the imperial gallon, the British standard, is 277.42 cu. ins (4.546 liters). Both are equal to 4 quarts ‖ a dry measure, one eighth of a bushel [M.E. *galun, golon* fr. O.N.F.]

gal·loon (gəlú:n) *n.* (*hist.*) a narrow, closewoven braid or ribbon for trimming dresses etc. ‖ silk ribbon used in making wigs [fr. F. *galon*]

gal·lop (gǽləp) **1.** *n.* the fastest pace of horses and similar animals, in which all four feet are off the ground in each stride ‖ a ride at this pace **at a gallop, at full gallop** at full speed **2.** *v.t.* to make (a horse) gallop ‖ *v.i.* to go at a gallop ‖ to progress quickly, hurry, *to gallop through a book* [O.F. *galop, galoper*]

Gal·lo-Ro·man (gælouróumən) *adj.* of Gaul under Roman rule

Gal·lo·way (gǽləwei), Joseph (c. 1731–1803), American colonial statesman and loyalist. At the first Continental Congress (1774) he proposed a written constitution for the empire which would unite Great Britain and the colonies. His plan was rejected by only one vote and was later expunged from the record through the vigorous opposition of the radicals

Galloway a district of S.W. Scotland, comprising Wigtown and Kirkcudbright counties, formerly a sovereign territory of much greater extent: cattle- and sheep-raising, fishing, extensive dairy farming

gal·lo·way (gǽləwei) *n.* a horse of a small strong breed originating in Galloway, Scotland

gal·lows (gǽlouz) *pl. n.* (often treated as *sing.*) a wooden structure for the execution of the death sentence by hanging ‖ the punishment of hanging, *condemned to the gallows* [O.E. *galga, gealga*]

gallows bird (*rhet.*) a person who deserves to be hanged

gall·stone (gɔ́lstoun) *n.* a deposit of cholesterol and, occasionally, bile salts, sometimes formed in the gallbladder or bile duct

Gal·lup poll (gǽləp) a sampling of the opinions of a cross section of the general public, from which the general opinion on a topic is deduced [after G. H. Gallup (1901-), U.S. statistician]

gall wasp a member of *Cynipedae*, a family of hymenopterous insects

ga·lop (gǽləp) **1.** *n.* a lively 19th-c. dance in 2/4 time **2.** *v.i.* to dance the galop [F.]

ga·lore (gəlɔ́r, gəlóur) *adj.* (used postpositively) in plenty, *whiskey galore* [fr. Ir. *go leór*, enough]

ga·losh (gəlɒ́ʃ) a waterproof boot worn over the shoe to keep out snow or water ‖ (*Br.*) a rubber (low overshoe) [F. *galoche*, clog fr. L. fr. Gk]

Galosh (*mil.*) Soviet antiballistic missile system surrounding Moscow. Installed in 1964, it has 64 launchers at four sites and consists of missiles with three-stage propulsion and radar command capable of carrying a multimegaton nuclear warhead

Gals·wor·thy (gɔ́lzwə:rði:, gǽlzwə:rði:), John (1867–1933), English novelist and playwright. In 'The Forsyte Saga' (1922) he has left a picture of English Edwardian society and its implicit assumptions: much concern with money and position, deep philistinism, and thwarted emotions. His dramas were usually based on some ethical or social problem (e.g. 'Strife', 1909 and 'Loyalties', 1922)

Galt (gɔlt), Sir Alexander Tilloch (1817–93), Canadian politician. As minister of finance (1858–67, with intervals), he introduced (1858–9) the first Canadian protective tariff, and led the movement which resulted (1867) in the federation of British North America

galt *GAULT

Gal·ton (gɔ́ltən), Sir Francis (1822–1911), English scientist, esp. famous for his pioneer work in eugenics. He was a cousin of Charles Darwin

Gal·va·ni (galvá:ni:), Luigi (1737–98), Italian physiologist. His experiments with animals led him to believe that nerves and muscles generated electricity which resulted in muscular movement. Volta later showed that the current observed had resulted from the contact of two different metals used in Galvani's experiments

gal·van·ic (gælvǽnik) *adj.* of or produced by galvanism ‖ sudden, violent and spasmodic, as though affected by an electric shock, *a galvanic movement* **gal·ván·i·cal** *adj.* [GALVANISM]

gal·va·nism (gǽlvənizəm) *n.* (*phys.*) a direct-current electricity, esp. that produced by chemical changes [F. *galvanis- me*]

gal·va·ni·za·tion (gælvənizéiʃən) *n.* a galvanizing or being galvanized

gal·va·nize (gǽlvənaiz) *pres. part.* **gal·va·niz·ing** *past* and *past part.* **gal·va·nized** *v.t.* to stimulate by electric currents ‖ to coat with metal by electrolysis ‖ to coat (iron or steel) with zinc ‖ to rouse to sudden action through shock or excitement [fr. F. *galvaniser*]

gal·va·nom·e·ter (gælvənɒ́mitər) *n.* an instrument for detecting or measuring a small electric current, by means of the movement of a magnetic needle or coil in the magnetic field exerted by the current

gal·va·no·met·ric (gælvənoumétrik) *adj.* of or pertaining to galvanometry

gal·va·nom·e·try (gælvənɒ́mitri:) *n.* the measurement of galvanic currents

gal·va·no·scope (gǽlvənəskoup) *n.* a galvanometer used only to detect the presence and direction of a current **gal·va·nos·co·py** (gælvənɒ́skəpi:) *n.*

CONCISE PRONUNCIATION KEY: **(a)** æ, c*a*t; ɑ, c*ar*; ɔ f*aw*n; ei, sn*a*ke. **(e)** e, h*e*n; i:, sh*ee*p; iə, d*ee*r; ɛə, b*ea*r. **(i)** i, f*i*sh; ai, t*i*ger; ə:, b*i*rd. **(o)** o, *o*x; au, c*ow*; ou, g*oa*t; u, p*oo*r; ɔi, r*o*yal. **(u)** ʌ, d*u*ck; u, b*u*ll; u:, g*oo*se; ə, b*a*cillus; ju:, c*u*be. x, lo*ch*; θ, *th*ink; ð, bo*th*er; z, *Z*en; ʒ, cor*s*age; dʒ, sava*g*e; ŋ, orangutan*g*; j, *y*ak; ʃ, *fi*sh; tʃ, fe*tch*; 'l, rabb*le*; 'n, redd*en*. Complete pronunciation key appears inside front cover.

Gal·ves·ton (gǽlvistən) a city and port of entry (pop. 61,902) on an island bridged to the southeast coast of Texas. Exports: cotton, sulfur, oil, grain. Manufactures: wire and nails, food products, cement, clothing. Fisheries

Gal·way (gɔ́lwei) a county (area 2,295 sq. miles, pop. 171,836) of W. Connacht, Irish Republic ‖ its county seat

gam (gæm) **1.** *n.* sociable talk between seamen when whalers meet at sea ‖ a school of whales **2.** *v.i. pres. part.* **gam·ming** *past* and *past part.* **gammed** (of whalers) to meet at sea and have sociable talk ‖ (of whales) to form a school [perh. fr. GAME *n.*]

Ga·ma (dəgǽmə, dəgáːmə), José Basílio da (1741–95), Brazilian poet. His 'O Uraguay' (1769) accused the Jesuits of stirring up the Indians against the Portuguese and Spanish governments. It served as propaganda for the expulsion of Jesuits from the Portuguese Empire by the Marquis of Pombal

Ga·ma, Vasco da (c. 1469–1524), Portuguese navigator who discovered the route to India around the Cape of Good Hope (1497–8)

gam·ba (gǽmbə, gámbə) *n.* an organ stop with the tone of a viola da gamba

gam·bade (gæmbéid) *n.* a gambado [F.]

gam·ba·do (gæmbéidou) *pl.* **gam·ba·does, gam·ba·dos** *n.* a horse's caper ‖ a prank ‖ a sudden, fantastic move [Span. *gambada*]

Gam·bet·ta (gæmbétə), Léon (1838–82), French statesman. A republican, he opposed Napoleon III, declared the Third Republic (1870), and, when Paris was besieged by the Prussians, escaped by balloon (1870) to organize resistance in the provinces. After the war, he led the attack on clericalism, and was briefly prime minister (1881–2)

Gam·bi·a (gǽmbiə) a republic (area 4,003 sq. miles, pop. 635,000) in W. Africa. Capital and port: Bathurst. Main ethnic groups: Mandingo, Wolof. Religion: mainly Moslem with a minority of Christians and others professing local African religions. The territory forms a 10-mile-wide strip along the Gambia River and is an enclave in Senegal. Rainfall: 39 ins in Bathurst. Livestock: cattle, goats. Crops: peanuts, rice, millet, cotton, sorghum, corn, beans, palm kernels. Exports: peanuts, palm kernels, dried and smoked fish. Imports: textiles, manufactured goods, machines, foodstuffs, drugs and medicines. Monetary unit: West African pound. HISTORY. Portuguese explorers first visited the mouth of the Gambia River (15th c.), followed by English traders who established a settlement (17th c.). Gambia became a British colony (1843), achieved full internal self-government (1963) and gained independence (Feb. 18, 1965) within the Commonwealth. It became a republic (Apr. 1970) after a national referendum. The prime minister, Sir Dawda Jawara has served as president since independence. Gambia and Senegal inaugurated the confederation of Senegambia in 1982, in which the Senegalese president serves as president, and the Gambian president serves as vice president

Gambia a river (600 miles long) navigable at all seasons, which rises in the Fouta Djallon, W. Guinea, and flows north and west through Senegal and Gambia to the Atlantic at Bathurst

gam·bier, gam·bir (gǽmbiər) *n.* a catechu obtained from the leaves of *Uncaria gambir*, a Malayan woody vine. It is used in tanning and dyeing [Malay]

gam·bit (gǽmbit) *n.* an opening move or series of moves in chess, in which the player risks losing a pawn or a piece, to secure an advantageous position ‖ any purposeful or provocative opening to a conversation, contest etc. [fr. Ital. *gambetto*, a tripping up]

gam·ble (gǽmb'l) **1.** *v. pres. part.* **gam·bling** *past* and *past part.* **gam·bled** *v.i.* to play a game for money ‖ to take risks in the hope of getting better results than by some safer means ‖ to stake one's money or hopes, *to gamble on the weather's being fine* ‖ *v.t.* to risk by staking, *to gamble one's wages* **to gamble away** to lose by gambling **2.** *n.* the act of gambling ‖ a risky undertaking **gam·bler** *n.* [prob. fr. a var. of O.E. *gamenian*, to sport]

Gam·bo·a (gəmbóə), Federico (1864–1939), Mexican writer and diplomat, and the leading exponent of naturalism in the Mexican novel: 'Suprema ley' (1895), 'Santa' (1903), 'Reconquista' (1903), and 'La llaga' (1912)

gam·boge (gæmbúːʒ, gæmbóudʒ) *n.* a gum resin obtained from S.E. Asian trees of the genus *Garcinia*, esp. *G. Hanburyi*, used as a yellow pigment and as a cathartic [fr. Mod. L. *gambogium* fr. CAMBODIA]

gam·bol (gǽmb'l) **1.** *n.* a frisking, playful leaping **2.** *v.i. pres. part.* **gam·bol·ing**, esp. *Br.* **gam·bol·ling** *past* and *past part.* **gam·boled**, esp. *Br.* **gam·bolled** to frisk, leap about [older *gambad*, *gambaude*, *gambolde* fr. F. *gambade*, a leap]

gam·brel (gǽmbrəl) *n.* a piece of bent iron used by butchers for suspending carcasses ‖ a gambrel roof [O.F. *gamberel*]

gambrel roof a roof with its slope broken by an obtuse angle, the lower slope being steeper, and the upper slope gentler

game (geim) **1.** *n.* a contest played for sport or amusement according to rules ‖ the method employed in such a contest, *we played a conventional game* ‖ any playful activity for amusement or diversion ‖ (*pl.*) athletic, musical and dramatic contests and shows in ancient Greece and Rome ‖ (*pl.*) organized outdoor sporting activities, esp. at school ‖ a single round or part of a contest (tennis, bridge etc.) ‖ the number of points that must be scored to win such a round ‖ the state of a sporting contest at a given moment, *the game stands at four-all* ‖ a scheme, plan or intrigue against others, *so that's your game!* ‖ (*collect.*) wild animals or birds hunted for sport or food ‖ the flesh of these used for food ‖ a kept flock (of tame swans) **off one's game** not playing very well, **off form the game is up** the plan has failed, the plot has been exposed to **make game of** to make fun of **to play someone's game** to help someone's plan unintentionally **to play the game** to play according to the rules ‖ to behave honorably **2.** *adj.* pertaining to game (animals), *game laws* **3.** *v.i. pres. part.* **gam·ing** *past* and *past part.* **gamed** to gamble, play for money [O.E. *gamen*, sport, fun]

game *adj.* (of a limb) chronically stiff and painful [origin unknown]

game *adj.* plucky ‖ ready and willing to perform any challenging action [GAMECOCK]

game·cock (géimkɒk) *n.* a cock of a cockfighting breed

game·keep·er (géimkiːpər) *n.* a person employed to look after the protection and breeding of the game on an estate

game plan plan for a course of action, esp. to attain a certain end. *syn.* scenario

games·man·ship (géimzmənʃip) *n.* the art of winning games by talk or behavior designed to demoralize or distract one's opponent [coined by Stephen Potter (1900-), Br. author]

game·some (géimsəm) *adj.* (*rhet.*) gay, sportive

games theory theory of the rational behavior of people in conflicting circumstances based on various formulas, notably minimal solution, in which each party minimizes the maximum loss others may impose. Games theory is utilized in some political, military, and business decision making

games, theory of *THEORY OF GAMES

gam·e·tan·gi·um (gæmitǽndʒiəm) *pl.* **gam·e·tan·gi·a** (gæmitǽndʒiə) *n.* (*bot.*) a specialized cell or structure in which the gametes (esp. of algae) are produced (cf. SPORANGIUM) [fr. Mod. L. *gameta*, gamete + Gk *angeion*, vessel]

gam·ete (gǽmiːt) *n.* a reproductive cell, with a haploid number of chromosomes, capable of fusing with another gamete and thereby producing a new individual (*FERTILIZATION, *ZYGOTE) [fr. Mod. L. *gameta* fr. Gk *gametē*, wife, *gametēs*, husband]

ga·me·to·gen·e·sis (gəmiːtoudʒénisis, gæmiːtoudʒénisis) *n.* the formation of gametes (*SPERMATOGENESIS, *OOGENESIS) [Mod. L.]

ga·me·to·phore (gæmíːtəfɔr, gəmíːtəfour) *n.* (*bot.*) a branch of a gametophyte upon which gametangia are borne [fr. GAMETE + Gk *-phoros*, bearing]

ga·me·to·phyte (gəmíːtəfait) *n.* (*bot.*, in plants exhibiting alternation of generations) the generation which produces gametes and alternates with the sporophyte ‖ an individual of this generation [fr. GAMETE + Gk *phuton*, plant]

gamey *GAMY

game warden an official in a game reserve ‖ an official who sees that game laws are respected on public lands

ga·mic (gǽmik) *adj.* (*biol.*) requiring fertilization in order to develop [fr. Gk *gamikos* fr. *gamos*, marriage]

gam·in (gǽmin) *n.* a street urchin [F.]

gam·ine (gæmíːn) **1.** *n.* a Tomboy ‖ a girl with urchin charm **2.** *adj.* of the air, looks, ways etc. of a gamine [F.]

gam·ing (géimiŋ) *n.* gambling

gam·ma (gǽmə) *n.* the third letter Γ, γ=g) of the Greek alphabet ‖ the gamma moth ‖ (*pl.* **gamma**) a microgram ‖ (*photog.*) the degree of contrast of a developed or printed exposure

gam·ma·di·on, gam·ma·ti·on (gəméidiːən) *pl.* **gam·ma·di·a, gam·ma·ti·a** *n.* a swastika [late Gk dim. of *gamma*, since the figure comprises four capital gammas]

gamma globulin one of several globulins of blood plasma or serum containing most antibodies

gamma moth *Plusia gamma*, a migratory European moth with a gamma-shaped mark on each fore wing

gamma radiation (*nuclear phys.*) a large amount of electromagnetic radiation, e.g., from a nuclear reaction

gamma ray an electromagnetic wave of shorter wavelength (i.e. less than 0.1 Å) and more energetic than an X ray. Gamma rays are produced during the decomposition of some unstable atomic nuclei (*RADIOACTIVITY). They are employed in radiotherapy and are also one of the major hazards of atomic bomb explosions (*SPECTROSCOPY) ‖ (*nuclear phys.*) high-energy proton in transition. The most penetrating radiant nuclear energy, it can be stopped by dense materials like lead

gam·ma·rus (gǽmərəs) *n. Gammarus pulex*, a small freshwater crustacean found in quick-flowing streams [fr. Mod. L. fr. Gk *kammaros*, crayfish]

gam·ma·sonde (gǽməsɒnd) *n.* radio transmission package carried in a balloon. *syn.* radiosonde

gamma surgery (*med.*) bloodless technique utilizing pellets of radioactive cobalt or other isotopes to destroy cancerous cells, also used in treating Parkinson's disease, etc.

gammation *GAMMADION

gam·mer (gǽmər) *n.* (*old-fash.*) an old woman, esp. (*Br.*) an old countrywoman [contr. of GRANDMOTHER]

gam·mon (gǽmən) **1.** *n.* smoked or cured ham ‖ the bottom part of a flitch of bacon including the hind leg **2.** *v.t.* to cure (bacon) [O.N.F. *gambon*]

Gammon (*mil.*) U.S.S.R. long-range antiaircraft and antimissile solid-propellant missile weighing 2,500 lbs, with a 160-mi range and radar guidance

gammon 1. *n.* a victory at backgammon in which the winner bears off all his men before his opponent removes any **2.** *v.t.* to beat (one's opponent) thus [perh. M.E. *gamen*, game]

gammon 1. *v.t.* (*naut.*) to lash (the bowsprit) to the stem of a ship by rope, chain or a band of iron **2.** *n.* (*naut.*) a gammoning **gám·mon·ing** *n.* (*naut.*) a rope, chain or iron band by which the bowsprit is gammoned [origin unknown]

gam·my (gǽmi:) *comp.* **gam·mi·er** *superl.* **gam·mi·est** *adj.* (*Br.*), of a limb) slightly lame [var. of GAME]

gam·o·gen·e·sis (gæmoudʒénisis) *n.* sexual reproduction, reproduction by means of gametes **gam·o·ge·net·ic** (gæmoudʒənétik) *adj.* **gam·o·ge·net·i·cal·ly** *adv.* [fr. Gk *gamos*, marriage + GENESIS]

gam·o·pet·a·lous (gæmopét'ləs) *adj.* (*bot.*) sympetalous, with the petals joined (opp. POLYPETALOUS) [fr. Mod. L. *gamopetalus*]

gam·o·phyl·ious (gæmofíləs) *adj.* (*bot.*) with leaves joined by their edges [perh. fr. (assumed) Mod. L. *gamophyllus*]

gam·o·sep·al·ous (gæmousépələs) *adj.* (*bot.*) with the sepals joined [perh. fr. (assumed) Mod. L. *gamosepalus*]

ga·mut (gǽmət) *n.* the entire range or scope of something, *the gamut of the emotions* ‖ the compass of a voice or musical instrument ‖ the whole series of recognized musical notes ‖ (*mus., hist.*) the great scale or its lowest note [contr. of M.L. *gamma ut* (names of notes)]

gam·y, game·y (géimi:) *comp.* **gam·i·er** *superl.* **gam·i·est** *adj.* having the taste or smell of game when it is high ‖ abounding in game ‖ sensational, scandalous, *a gamy story* [GAME]

gan·der (gǽndər) *n.* the male goose ‖ (*pop.*) a look, glance, *take a gander* [O.E. *gandra*, *ganra*]

Gan·dha·ra (gʌndárə) a district of N. Pakistan, famous for its Greco-Buddhist sculptures (2nd c. A.D.) (*TAXILA)

CONCISE PRONUNCIATION KEY: **(a)** æ, c*a*t; ɑ, c*a*r; ɔ, f*aw*n; ei, sn*a*ke. **(e)** e, h*e*n; iː, sh*ee*p; iə, d*ee*r; ɛə, b*ea*r. **(i)** i, f*i*sh; ai, t*i*ger; əː, b*i*rd. **(o)** o, *o*x; au, c*ow*; ou, g*oa*t; u, p*oo*r; ɔi, r*oy*al. **(u)** ʌ, d*u*ck; u, b*u*ll; uː, g*oo*se; ə, b*a*cill*u*s; juː, c*u*be. x, lo*ch*; θ, *th*ink; ð, bo*th*er; z, *Z*en; ʒ, corsa*g*e. dʒ, sava*g*e; ŋ, orangutan*g*; j, *y*ak; ʃ, *f*ish; tʃ, fe*tch*; 'l, rabb*le*; 'n, red*den*. Complete pronunciation key appears inside front cover.

Gan·dhi (gándi:, gǽndi:), Mohandas Karamchand (1869–1948), Indian nationalist and leader of reform within Hinduism, often called Mahatma ('great soul'). Trained as a lawyer, he went (1893) to South Africa, and fought for legal rights for Indians. Returning to India (1915), he joined in the campaign for independence, leading acts of civil disobedience, for which he was frequently imprisoned. He was president (1924) of the Indian National Congress. He participated (1931–46) in the independence negotiations with Britain, and was regarded as 'the architect of India's freedom'. He is remembered for his advocacy of noncooperation, his use of hunger strikes, his opposition to caste barriers, in particular his championing of the untouchables, and his work for unity between Hindus, Moslems and Sikhs. He was assassinated

Gandhi, Rajiv (1944–), prime minister of India (1984–), son of Indira* GANDHI and grandson of Jawaharlal* NEHRU. An airline pilot, he was elected to parliament (1981) to fill his late brother's seat and became secretary general of the Congress (I) party in 1983. He became prime minister upon the assassination of his mother (1984)

Gandhi, Shrimati Indira (1917–84), Indian stateswoman, daughter of Nehru. Prime minister of India (1966–77, 1980–4) Gandhi maintained India's status as a non-aligned nation while at the same time keeping close ties with the U.S.S.R. She was assassinated in 1984 by Sikhs in her security guard

Ganef (mil.) U.S.S.R. solid-propellant missile weighing 4,000 lbs, with 45-mi range, radio command direction

gang *GANGUE

gang (gæŋ) 1. n. a team of workmen working together ‖ a number of men or boys banding together, esp. lawlessly. Occasionally girls are members ‖ a set of tools etc. arranged to work together 2. v.i. (often with 'up') to band together, join **to gang up on** to band together against **gang·er** (gǽŋər) n. a man in charge of a gang of workmen [O.E. gang, gong, a going]

Gan·ges (gǽndʒi:z) a river (about 1,560 miles long, draining 419,000 sq. miles, including some of India's most densely populated areas) of N.E. India, sacred to Hindus, who make pilgrimages to it to wash away their sins. Rising in the foothills of the S. Himalayas about 100 miles from Hardwar and later joined by the Jumna and other tributaries, it enters the Bay of Bengal in a great delta with the Brahmaputra

gang hook two or three fishhooks with their shanks joined

gang·ing (gǽŋiŋ) n. (mechanics) method providing more than one control of an apparatus with a single knob

ganglia pl. of GANGLION

gan·gli·at·ed (gǽŋgli:eitid) adj. having ganglia

gan·gling (gǽŋgliŋ) adj. lanky and awkward, a gangling youth [etym. doubtful]

gan·gli·on (gǽŋgli:ən) pl. **gan·gli·a** (gǽŋgli:ə), **gan·gli·ons** n. (anat.) a mass of nerve tissue containing nerve cells found either at the junction of two nerves or within the brain ‖ (med.) a small cystic tumor, joined either to a joint membrane or a tendon sheath **gán·gli·on·at·ed** adj. [Gk ganglion, a tumor under the skin]

gan·gli·on·ec·to·my (gæŋgli:ənéktəmi:) pl. **gan·gli·on·ec·to·mies** n. the surgical removal of a ganglion [fr. GANGLION+Gk ektomē, a cutting out]

gan·gli·on·ic (gæŋgli:ónik) adj. pertaining to or composed of ganglia

gan·gli·o·si·do·sis, pl. **-ses** (gæŋgli:ousidóusis) n. (med.) disorder of the biosynthesis or breakdown of the neuronal surface membranes and the spleen

gan·gly (gǽŋgli:) comp. **gan·gli·er** superl. **gan·gli·est** adj. gangling

Gang of Four the leadership of the Cultural Revolution in China, discredited in October 1976 after the death of Mao Zedong. Members include Jiang Qing (Mao's widow), Zhang Chungiao (Deputy Prime Minister), and Chen Buda, Wang Hongwen, and Yao Won-Yuan (Politburo members). With six others, they went on trial for treason in 1980

gang·plank (gǽŋplæŋk) n. a long, narrow movable bridge or plank for going between quay and boat

gan·grene (gǽŋgri:n) 1. n. (med.) the necrosis of part of a living body, e.g. a toe or a single muscle. Gangrene is usually due to blockage of the artery taking blood to that part, caused by disease. injury, or poisoning 2. v. pres. part. **gan·gren·ing** past and past part. **gan·grened** v.t. to affect with gangrene ‖ v.i. to become affected with gangrene **gan·gre·nous** (gǽŋgrənəs) adj. [fr. L. gangraena fr. Gk gangraina, an eating sore]

gang·sa (gáŋsə) n. Indonesian timpani instrument of brass and bamboo

gang·ster (gǽŋstər) n. a member of a gang of criminals or gunmen [GANG]

Gang·tok (gǽŋtók) *SIKKIM

gangue, gang (gæŋ) n. the commercially worthless matter in a metal or mineral deposit [F. fr. G. gang, a vein or lode]

gang·way (gǽŋwei) 1. n. (Br.) a passage, a way between rows of seats in a theater etc. ‖ (naut.) a passageway on a ship ‖ (naut.) a ladder and platform slung over a ship's side ‖ a platform connecting quarterdeck and forecastle ‖ (naut.) a gangplank ‖ (naut.) the opening in the bulwarks through which the gangplank is passed 2. interj. stand aside!, make way! [O.E. gangweg]

gan·is·ter, gan·nis·ter (gǽnistər) n. (geol.) a hard siliceous stone in the lower coal measures ‖ a mixture of ground quartz and fireclay used to line certain metallurgical furnaces [origin unknown]

gan·net (gǽnit) n. any of several large, web-footed sea birds of fam. Sulidae living socially on cliffs and rocky islands [O.E. ganot]

gannister *GANISTER

gan·oid (gǽnoid) 1. adj. (of fish scales) rhomboidal, consisting of a layer of bone covered with an enamel-like substance ‖ (of fish) having such scales 2. n. a fish having ganoid scales [F. ganoï-de fr. Gk]

gant·let (góntlit, gǽntlit) 1. n. (rail.) a section of double track, e.g. at a tunnel or bridge, where the inner rails overlap in order to avoid switching to a single track ‖ the gauntlet (form of punishment) 2. v.t. (rail.) to run (tracks) together in a gantlet [alt. form of GAUNTLET]

gant·line (gǽntlain) n. a girtline

gan·try (gǽntri) pl. **gan·tries** n. a four-footed wooden stand for supporting barrels or for rolling barrels to a higher level ‖ a structure raised on side supports so as to span something, e.g. a platform for a traveling crane, or a structure for rail signals set over several tracks [etym. doubtful]

Gan·y·mede (gǽnəmi:d) (Gk mythol.) a beautiful youth carried off to Olympus by Zeus, to be cupbearer to the gods ‖ one of the satellites of the planet Jupiter

gaol *JAIL

gaoler *JAILER

gap (gæp) n. an opening or breach in a wall, fence, hedge etc. ‖ a breach in defenses ‖ a pass through hills, a defile ‖ a break in continuity, a pause ‖ a wide difference in views or ideas [O.N.=chasm]

gape (geip) 1. v.i. pres. part. **gap·ing** past and past part. **gaped** to open the mouth wide ‖ to be wide open, a deep crevasse gaped before them ‖ to show a gap, be split, the tent gaped at the back ‖ to stare in wonder or surprise 2. n. the act of gaping ‖ an open-mouthed stare ‖ (zool.) the distance between the wide-open jaws of birds, fishes etc. ‖ the part of a bird's beak where it opens ‖ the opening between the shells of a bivalve ‖ a gap or rent **the gapes** a disease of poultry and other birds, of which gaping is a symptom ‖ a fit of yawning [O.N. gapa]

gape·worm (geipwə:rm) n. Syngamus trachealis or S. trachea, a parasitic nematode worm that causes the gapes in birds

gar (gɑr) n. a garfish

ga·rage (gərɑ́ʒ, gərɑ́dʒ, Br. gǽrɑʒ) 1. n. a building in which cars etc. are kept ‖ a commercial enterprise for the repair, and often the sale, of motor vehicles ‖ a place where gasoline and oil are sold 2. v.t. pres. part. **ga·rag·ing** past and past part. **ga·raged** to put (a vehicle) in a garage [F.]

garage sale sale of personal possessions on owner's premises. also tag sale, yard sale

Ga·ra·mond (gærǽmɔ̃), Claude (1480–1561), French type designer. Types based on his designs are still in use

Ga·ray (gɑrái), Juan de (c. 1527–83), Spanish conquistador in Peru and Paraguay. He founded (1573) Santa Fe (in present Argentina) and completed (1580) the second founding of Buenos Aires

garb (gɑrb) 1. n. manner of dress, esp. when distinctive or odd, or the clothes themselves, cleri-cal garb 2. v.t. (esp. pass. and refl.) to dress, esp. in some distinctive or odd way [fr. Ital. garbo, elegance]

gar·bage (gárbidʒ) n. animal or vegetable refuse, kitchen waste, rubbish ‖ (computer) inaccurate or unsuitable data ‖ (basketball) an easy score made from below the basket ‖ (tennis) a shot just over the net ‖ (ice hockey) an easy shot made by a rebound [M.E.]

garbage truck (Am.=Br. dust cart) a vehicle for collecting refuse

gar·ble (gárb'l) pres. part. **gar·bling** past and past part. **gar·bled** v.t. to give a confused version of (a message, facts) ‖ to tell (a story) with the facts mixed up or wrong ‖ to select parts of (a story) and recount them in an incompetent, unfair or malicious way [perh. fr. Ital. garbellare fr. Arab., or fr. L.L. cribellare, to sift]

Gar·bo (gárbou), Greta (Lovisa Gustafsson, 1905–), Swedish-U.S. film star. Her films include 'Mata Hari' (1931), 'Grand Hotel' (1932), 'Anna Karenina' (1935), 'Camille' (1937), and 'Ninotchka' (1939)

gar·board (gárbord, gárbourd) n. the first row of planks or iron plates on a ship's bottom, next to the keel [perh. Du. gaarboard]

garboard strake a garboard

Gar·cí·a (gɑrsí:ɑ), Alejo (d. 1525), Portuguese explorer, who penetrated (1524) the Chaco of Paraguay and Bolivia

García Cal·de·rón (kalderón), Francisco (1883–1953), Peruvian historian, sociologist, and diplomat. His 'Latin America: Its Rise and Progress' (Eng. trans. 1913) advocated government by the élite

Gar·cí·a Lor·ca (gɑrθi:alórka), Federico (1898–1936), Spanish poet and playwright. His most famous book of verse was 'Romancero Gitano' (1928). His plays include the trilogy 'Bodas de Sangre' (1933), 'Yerma' (1934) and 'La Casa de Bernarda Alba' (1936). His poetry is lyrical, free and colorful, marked by the use of striking surrealist imagery

Garcia Marquez, (márkɛəs) Gabriel, (1928–), Colombian writer, Nobel prizewinner for literature (1982). His works, many of which trace Colombia's history, include 'One Hundred Years of Solitude' (1967), 'In Evil Hour' (1968), 'The Autumn of the Patriarch' (1975), and 'Chronicle of a Death Foretold' (1981)

García Mo·re·no (mɔréno), Gabriel (1821–75), Ecuadorian president (1861–5, 1869–75). His religious fanaticism and despotism led to his assassination

Gar·ci·la·so de la Ve·ga (gɑrθi:lásoðelavéga), (c. 1503–36), Spanish poet. He was among the first to utilize Italian Renaissance meter and the pastoral themes of Latin and Italian poets. His settings are artificial and his language is greatly heightened: but he used them with exquisite style to convey the deepest emotion. His relatively few poems, esp. the sonnets and eclogues, had an enormous influence in his own day, as well as on poets up to modern times

gar·con·nière (gɑrsəni:éər) n. (Fr.) a bachelor's home

Gard (gær) a department (area 2,270 sq. miles, pop. 494,600) of S. France (*LANGUEDOC). Chief town: Nîmes

Gar·da (gárda) Italy's biggest lake (area 143 sq. miles), in Lombardy and Veneto, at the foot of the Alps (elevation 213 ft): resorts

gar·den (gárd'n) 1. a. a piece of ground where flowers, fruit and vegetables are grown, usually near a house ‖ (often pl.) a big area of laid-out garden open to the public ‖ (Br., pl. with name prefixed) a street or square of houses, Onslow Gardens ‖ (rhet.) a region of great fertility or beauty, Touraine, the garden of France **to lead up the garden path** to lead on or mislead with vague promises or false information 2. v.i. to work in a garden [O.N.F. gardin]

garden city a planned town with private and public gardens

gar·den·er (gárd'nər) n. a person who makes his living by cultivating gardens ‖ a person who looks after a garden nonprofessionally

gar·de·nia (gɑrdí:njə) n. a member of Gardenia, a genus of tropical trees and shrubs of fam. Rubiaceae, with fragrant white or yellow flowers. The Cape jasmine (G. florida) is the variety most cultivated for its flowers [Mod. L., after Dr Alexander Garden (1730-91), U.S. botanist]

garden party a social gathering held on the lawns of a garden

Gar·di·ner (gárdnər, gárd'nər), Stephen (c. 1483–1555), English bishop and statesman, lord high chancellor (1553–5). After supporting the Reformation under Henry VIII, he reversed his policy under Mary I and was responsible for the persecution of Protestants

Gardner, John Champlain (gárdnər) (1933–82), U.S. writer whose background in medieval history and the classics is evident in his works. Novels include 'The Wreckage of Agathon' (1970), 'Grendel' (1971), 'The Sunlight Dialogues' (1972), 'Nickel Mountain' (1973) and 'October Light' (1976). 'On Becoming a Novelist' (1983) and 'The Art of Fiction' (1984) were published after his death in a motorcycle accident

Garfield (gárfi:ld), James Abram (1831–81), 20th president (1881) of the U.S.A., a Republican. He was influential in settling the disputed presidential contest of 1876. He antagonized the 'Stalwart' faction of the Republican party, led by Roscoe Conkling by appointing James Blaine, his political enemy, as secretary of state. He was assassinated four months after his election

gar·fish (gárfiʃ) n. any of several freshwater ganoid fishes of fam. *Lepisosteidae* of North America ‖ the needlefish [O.E. *gār*, spear+FISH]

gar·gan·tu·an (gɑrgǽntʃu:ən) adj. huge, enormous, *a gargantuan feast* [after *Gargantua*, the giant in Rabelais's satirical romance]

gar·get (gárgit) n. mastitis of domestic animals, esp. an inflammation of cows' udders [perh. fr. obs. *garget*, throat fr. O.F.]

gar·gle (gárg'l) 1. v. pres. part. **gar·gling** past and past part. **gar·gled** v.i. to wash the throat with esp. antiseptic liquid kept in motion in the mouth or throat by breath expelled from the lungs ‖ to make gargling noises ‖ v.t. to wash (the throat) by gargling 2. n. the liquid used in gargling ‖ the act of gargling [fr. F. *gargouiller*]

gar·goyle (gárgɔil) n. a Gothic waterspout projecting from a gutter in the form of a grotesque human or animal, its mouth being the spout ‖ any grotesque figure [O.F. *gargouille*]

Gar·i·bal·di (gǽrəbɔ́ldi:), Giuseppe (1807–82). Italian patriot and soldier. A leader of the Risorgimento, he fought against the Austrians in Lombardy (1848–9) and defended the republic established (1849) in Rome by Mazzini. With 1,000 volunteers, his 'redshirts', he captured (1860) Sicily and Naples from the Bourbons, adding them to the territory acquired in the north by Cavour to form (1861) the kingdom of Italy

gar·ish (géəriʃ, gǽriʃ) adj. harsh, glaring and gaudy in color ‖ vulgarly bright and showy [older *gaurish* perh. fr. *gaure, to* stare]

gar·land (gárlənd) 1. n. a circlet of flowers ‖ a circlet of gold, jewels etc. ‖ (*hist.*) a laurel or other wreath as a festive sign of victory ‖ (*naut.*) a ring of rope lashed to a spar to prevent chafing ‖ (*skiing*) a sideslip on a slope 2. v.t. to deck or crown with a garland [O.F. *garlande, gerlande*]

gar·lic (gárlik) n. any of several plants of the genus *Allium*, fam. *Liliaceae*, esp. *A. sativum*. The bulb is a compound of several small cloves, stronger and more pungent in smell and flavor than an onion, and much used for flavoring **gár·lick·y** adj. [O.E. *gārlēac* fr. *gār*, spear+*lēac*, leek]

gar·ment (gármənt) n. any article of clothing ‖ (*pl.*, esp. *commerce*) clothes [O.F. *garniment*, *garnement*, equipment]

garment bag a long, foldable traveling bag with facilities for hanging garments

Gar·mo Peak (gármou) *COMMUNISM, MT.

gar·ner (gárnər) 1. n. (*rhet.*) a granary, storehouse 2. v.t. (*rhet.*) to collect or gather in or as if in a granary [M.E. *gerner* fr. O.F.]

gar·net (gárnit) n. a hard, brittle, crystalline mineral found in gneiss and mica schist. The precious garnet is a deep red gem. The common garnet, a coarser almandite and andradite, is used as an abrasive (O.F. *grenat*]

gar·nish (gárniʃ) 1. v.t. to decorate (esp. a dish) with something savory or pretty ‖ (*law*) to garnishee ‖ (*law*) to summon (a person) to take part in a litigation pending between others 2. n. a savory or decorative addition, esp. to a dish at table **gar·nish·ee** (gɑrniʃí:) 1. n. (*law*) a person who has in his possession a defendant's money or property and is ordered not to dispose of it pending settlement of the lawsuit 2. v.t. (*law*) to order (someone) not to dispose of a defendant's money or property pending settlement of a lawsuit ‖ (*law*) to attach (wages, property etc.) by court authority in order to pay a debt **gár-**

nish·ment n. (*law*) a summons to a third person to appear in court in connection with a lawsuit between two other parties ‖ (*law*) a warning to a third person to keep possession of property belonging to a defendant in a lawsuit in case it is needed to pay off a debt ‖ a garnish [fr. O.F. *garnir* (*garniss-*), to fortify]

gar·ni·ture (gárnitʃər) n. anything used to garnish [F.]

Ga·ronne (gǽrɔn) a river (400 miles long) in S.W. France, flowing from the Pyrenees to the Atlantic, joining the Dordogne in the Gironde, and connected with the Mediterranean by the Canal du Midi: hydroelectric power

Garonne (Haute-) * HAUTE-GARONNE

garotte *GARROTE

gar·pike (gárpaik) n. a garfish

gar·ret (gǽrit) n. a room in a house directly under the roof, an attic [M.E. *garite* fr. O.F. *garite, guerite*, watchtower fr. Gmc]

garret v.t. (*archit.*) to point (stonework) with small chips of stone in the joints [origin unknown]

gar·ri (gári:) n. ground cassava, a staple food in Nigeria

Gar·rick (gǽrik), David (1717–79), outstanding English actor and theater manager. He did much to increase popular enjoyment of Shakespeare's plays and, as manager of Drury Lane (1747–76), he introduced many changes in acting techniques, costumes and decor, lighting etc.

Gar·ri·son (gǽris'n), William Lloyd (1805–79), U.S. antislavery leader who campaigned for the total and immediate emancipation of the slaves. As founding-editor (1831–65) of the 'Liberator', and as founder of the New England Antislavery Society (1832) and the American Antislavery Society (1833), he strongly influenced Lincoln's proclamation of emancipation and the adoption of the amendment to the U.S. Constitution forever prohibiting slavery

gar·ri·son (gǽris'n) 1. n. the troops stationed in a fort or town 2. v.t. to place a garrison in ‖ to occupy as a garrison ‖ to put on garrison duty [M.E. *garison* fr. O.F. fr. Gmc]

gar·rote, gar·rotte, ga·rotte (gərót, gəróut) 1. n. a device used for strangling ‖ strangulation by garroting ‖ (*hist.*) a Spanish instrument of torture, an iron collar tightened by a screw 2. v.t. pres. part. **gar·rot·ing, gar·rott·ing, ga·rott·ing** past and past part. **gar·rot·ed, gar·rott·ed, ga·rott·ed** to strangle (a person) by leaping on him from behind and throttling him with a wire etc. ‖ (*hist.*) to execute by throttling [Span. *garrote*, the stick or screw used to tighten the collar]

gar·ru·li·ty (gərú:liti:) n. the quality of being garrulous

gar·ru·lous (gǽruləs) adj. given to constant idle, trivial, tedious talking [fr. L. *garrulus* fr. *garrire*, to chatter]

gar·ter (gártər) n. a band of elastic used to keep up one's stocking ‖ a strap of elastic hanging from a girdle etc., with a fastener to keep a woman's stocking up ‖ (*Am.=Br.* suspender) an elastic device with a fastener for keeping a sock or stocking up **the Garter** the highest order of British knighthood, founded in the mid-14th c. ‖ the badge of membership of the order ‖ membership in the order 2. v.t. to put a garter around [O.F. *gartier, jartier*]

garter belt (*Am.=Br.* suspender belt) a woman's undergarment for keeping her stockings up

garter snake a member of *Thamnophis*, fam. *Colubridae*, a genus of harmless American striped snakes

garth (gɑrθ) n. a cloister garth [M.E. fr. O.N. *garð-r*]

Gar·vey (gárvi:), Marcus (1887–1940), British West Indian popular leader, the first to work for solidarity between Caribbean blacks and U.S. blacks

Gar·y (géəri:), Elbert Henry (1846–1927), U.S. jurist who was the chief organizer of the U.S. Steel Corporation. As chairman (from 1901) of U.S. Steel, he introduced stock ownership, profit sharing, higher wages, and safe, sanitary conditions

Gary a city (pop. 151,953) of Indiana on Lake Michigan, adjoining Chicago. It is noted as a steelproducing center

gas (gǽs) 1. n. pl. **gas·es, gas·ses** a fluid substance that fills and thus takes the shape of its container (cf. LIQUID, cf. SOLID) ‖ (*chem. and phys.*) a fluid substance at a temperature above its critical temperature 'cf. VAPOR) ‖ a substance

or mixture of substances in a gaseous state used to produce light and heat (e.g. natural gas), anesthesia (e.g. laughing gas), or a poisonous or irritant atmosphere (e.g. tear gas) ‖ (*pop.*) fluent trivial talk or empty boasting or rhetoric ‖ (*Am.=Br.* petrol) gasoline **to step on the gas** to put one's foot down hard on the accelerator of an automobile etc. ‖ to force oneself to move or act more quickly 2. v. pres. part. **gas·sing** past and past part. **gassed** v.i. to give off gas (esp. of a battery during charging) ‖ (*pop.*) to talk trivially and too much ‖ v.t. to submit (something) to the action of gas, esp. to singe (fabric) so as to remove unnecessary fibers ‖ to harm or kill (someone) by poison gas [coined by Jan Baptista van Helmont (1577–1644), Belgian chemist, after Gk *chaos*, chaos]

gas·bag (gǽsbæg) n. a bag of impervious fabric for containing gas ‖ (*pop.*) someone who talks boastfully or at length but says little of importance

gas bearing (*mechanics*) a bearing that rotates in a shaft containing a viscous gas under pressure, thus avoiding the friction of metal contact

gas black a sooty substance obtained by carbonizing natural gas, used in black paints

gas carbon a hard deposit of fairly pure carbon, formed on the walls of retorts in the distillation of coal

gas chamber a sealed room filled with gas, used for capital punishment in some U.S. states. Gas chambers were also used by the Nazis for mass exterminations

gas chromatography technique for separating a volatile mixture into its components by moving an inert gas over a sorbent. *also* gas-liquid chromatography

gas coal a usually bituminous coal used for making gas by distillation

Gas·cogne (gǽskɔnj) *GASCONY

gas coke coke resulting from the distillation of coal for gas

Gas·con (gǽskən) 1. adj. of Gascony 2. n. a native of Gascony, whose inhabitants are reputed braggarts [F.]

gas constant the general constant R, in the ideal gas equation
= 1.987 calories/°K per mole
= 8.314 x 10^7 ergs/°K per mole ‖ any constant in an equation of state of a gas

Gas·co·ny (gǽskəni:) (F. Gascogne) a former province of S.W. France, reaching from the Pyrenees to the Garonne. It comprises Landes and part of Gironde on the coast, Gers and parts of Lot-et-Garonne, Tarn-et-Garonne and N. Haute-Garonne in the central Aquitaine basin, and parts of S. Haute-Garonne, Ariège and Hautes-Pyrénées in the mountains. Industries: fishing, agriculture (cereals, vines), cattle raising, brandy distilling (Armagnac, in the east). Historic capital: Auch. Chief towns: Biarritz, Bayonne. A Basque duchy from the 6th c., Gascony became a fief of Aquitaine (9th c.), was annexed (llth c.) and shared Aquitaine's history (*AQUITAINE, *GUYENNE)

gas cooker (*Br.*) a gas stove

gas-dy·nam·ic laser (gǽsdainǽmik) a gas laser containing nitrogen, carbon dioxide, and a catalyst that converts thermal energy into radiation; designed to be used for wireless transmission of power

gas engine an internal-combustion engine that uses manufactured or natural gas as fuel

gas·e·ous (gǽsi:əs, gǽʃəs) adj. in the form of a gas ‖ of or pertaining to gas

gas etching (*electr.*) technique for removing excess material from a semiconductor circuit with the use of hydrogen chloride at 1,000°C or other volatile material

gas gangrene gangrene caused by clostridia which enter the body through dirty wounds, producing gas and a liquid discharge

gas guzzler (*colloq.*) a motor vehicle that uses a great deal of fuel

gash (gǽʃ) 1. n. a deep long cut or slash ‖ the act of gashing 2. v.t. to make a gash in [M.E. *garse*, *garsen* fr. O.F. *garser*]

gas·hold·er (gǽshoulder) n. (*Am.=Br.* gasometer) a storage tank for gas

gas·house (gǽshaus) pl. **gas·hou·ses** (gǽshauziz) n. a gasworks

gas·i·fi·ca·tion (gæsifikéiʃən) n. the act or process of gasifying

gas·i·fy (gǽsifai) pres. part. **gas·i·fy·ing** past and past part. **gas·i·fied** v.t. to cause (a solid or liquid) to become a gas ‖ v.i. to become, be converted into, a gas

Gas·kell (gǽskəl), Elizabeth Cleghorn (1810–65), English novelist. 'Mary Barton' (1848) and 'North and South' (1855) describe with realism and sympathy the lives of industrial and agricultural workers. 'Cranford' (1853) depicts with charm a quiet country town

gas·ket (gǽskit) *n.* a thin sheet of rubber, leather or metal placed between two flat surfaces to seal the joint, e.g. between the cylinder block and cylinder head in a car engine ‖ a packing of hemp or tow used to seal a joint ‖ (*naut.*) a rope used to secure a furled sail to a yard [origin unknown]

gas·kin (gǽskin) *n.* a part of the hind leg of a horse or other quadruped between stifle and hock [etym. doubtful]

Gaskin (*mil.*) U.S.S.R. solid-propellant missile (SS-9) with a 5-mi range

gas laser any of several types of laser in which a gas (neon and helium or carbon dioxide and nitrogen) is discharged in a glass or quartz tube with a special glass window at each end. The gas is excited by high-frequency oscillation or a direct current flow between the electrodes

gas laws *BOYLE'S LAW, *CHARLES'S LAW, *GAY-LUSSAC'S LAW, *VAN DER WAAL'S EQUATION, *IDEAL GAS LAW, *AVOGADRO'S LAW

gas·light (gǽslait) *n.* light produced by burning gas ‖ a gas burner used for illumination

gas mantle a roughly hemispherical structure made of filaments of a refractory material. It gives off an intense white light when placed in a gas flame

gas maser a microwave amplifier, utilizing a gas (usually ammonia) interacting with microwave electromagnetic radiation, used in atomic clocks

gas mask a protective device worn over the face, esp. in warfare or industry, to filter out noxious fumes or gases

gas meter an apparatus recording cubic capacity of gas produced or consumed

gas·o·hol (gǽsəhɔl) *n.* mixture of 10% alcohol (ethanol) and 90% gasoline for use by motor vehicles

gas·o·line, gas·o·lene (gǽsəli:n, gǽsəli:n) *n.* (*Am.*=*Br.* petrol) a refined mixture of lower members of the hydrocarbon series, esp. hexane, heptane and octane. It is used, mixed with air and in a fine spray, as the fuel in an internal-combustion engine

gas·om·e·ter, gaz·om·e·ter (gæsɔ́mitər, gæzɔ́mitər) *n.* a vessel for measuring or holding gas ‖ (*Br.*) a gasholder [fr. F. *gazomètre*]

gasp (gæsp, gɑsp) **1.** *v.i.* to catch the breath suddenly in astonishment ‖ to pant, heave through breathlessness ‖ *v.t.* to utter breathlessly **2.** *n.* the act of gasping ‖ a convulsive struggle to draw breath **at one's last gasp** about to die [O.N. *geispa*, to yawn]

GASP (*computer acronym*) for general activity simulation program, a transaction-oriented simulation language based on FORTRAN

Gas·pé Peninsula (gæspéi) a mountainous, thinly populated region (area 11,390 sq. miles) of S.E. Quebec, Canada, south of the St Lawrence estuary

Gasperi *DE GASPERI

gas range a gas stove

gas ring a burner in the form of a circular pipe with small holes from which the gas issues in jets, used for cooking

Gas·sen·di (gæsɔ́di:), (Pierre Gassend, 1592–1655), French astronomer and empiricist philosopher. His attacks on Aristotelian philosophy and his exposition of Epicurus made him the most illustrious of the 17th–c. freethinkers

Gas·ser (gǽsər), Herbert Spencer (1888–1963), U.S. physiologist who shared (with Joseph Erlanger) the 1944 Nobel prize in physiology and medicine for his research in nerve fibers

gas·si·ness (gǽsi:nis) *n.* the quality of being gassy

gas·sing (gǽsiŋ) *n.* the act of a person who or thing which gasses ‖ the affecting, overcoming, or killing by gas of persons, insects etc. ‖ the evolution of gases during electrolysis ‖ the singeing of fabric to remove unnecessary fibers

gas station a roadside filling station for the retail sale of gasoline and oil

gas stove a domestic appliance, often combining burners, grill and oven, for cooking by gas

gas·sy (gǽsi:) *comp.* **gas·si·er** *superl.* **gas·si·est** *adj.* containing gas, esp. when this is easily released, *a gassy beer* ‖ gaseous

gas tar coal tar

Gast·ar·bei·ter (gɑstɑ́rbaitər) *n. s.* and *pl.* (*Gr.*, literally, guest worker; sometimes italics) foreign worker (Yugoslav, Italian, Turkish, Spanish) in Germany, Switzerland, and, by extension, in other northern European countries

Ga·stein, Convention of (gɑʃtáin) a treaty (1865) between Austria and Prussia, under which the former was to administer Holstein and the latter Schleswig

gas·ter·o·pod (gǽstərəpɒd) *n.* a gastropod

gas thermometer a thermometer containing a gas as the working substance, the determination of temperature being based upon the change of pressure at constant volume, or of volume at constant pressure, and possessing the advantage of high sensitivity over conventional liquid thermometers

gas·tight (gǽstait) *adj.* not penetrable by gas

gas·trae·a, gas·tre·a (gæstrí:ə) *n.* a hypothetical gastrulalike animal consisting of two layers of cells, assumed by Haeckel to be the ancestral metazoan [Mod. L. fr. Gk *gastēr*, stomach]

gas·tric (gǽstrik) *adj.* of or relating to the stomach [fr. Gk *gastēr* (*gasteros*), stomach]

gastric juice a thin fluid secreted by the glands in the mucous membrane of the stomach and consisting of dilute hydrochloric and lactic acids with enzymes such as pepsin and rennin. It is the chief agent of digestion

gastric ulcer a stomach ulcer (*PEPTIC ULCER)

gas·trin (gǽstrin) *n.* a hormone secreted by the pyloric mucosa, which stimulates production of gastric juices [fr. Gk *gastēr* (*gasteros*), stomach]

gas·tri·tis (gæstráitis) *n.* inflammation of the stomach, esp. of the mucous membrane lining it [Mod. L. fr. Gk *gastēr* (*gasteros*), stomach]

gas·tro·en·ter·i·tis (gæstrouentəráitis) *n.* a disturbance of the intestines, causing vomiting, diarrhea and cramp. It is usually due to the eating of contaminated food [fr. Gk *gastēr* (*gasteros*), stomach+ENTERITIS]

gas·tro·nome (gǽstrənoum) *n.* a connoisseur of food **gas·tron·o·mer** (gæstrɔ́nəmər) *n.* [F.]

gas·tro·nom·ic (gæstrənɔ́mik) *adj.* of or relating to gastronomy **gas·tro·nóm·i·cal** *adj.* [fr. F. *gastronomique*]

gas·tron·o·mist (gæstrɔ́nəmist) *n.* a gastronome

gas·tron·o·my (gæstrɔ́nəmi:) *n.* good eating as an art or science [fr. F. *gastronomie* fr. Gk]

gas·tro·pod (gǽstrəpɒd) *n.* a member of *Gastropoda*, the largest class of mollusks, including snails and slugs **gas·trop·o·dous** (gæstrɔ́pədəs) *adj.* [fr. Gk *gastēr* (*gasteros*), stomach+*pous* (*podos*), foot]

gas·tro·scope (gǽstrəskoup) *n.* (*med.*) a tubular optical instrument which is inserted into the stomach by way of the mouth and esophagus, and which carries its own source of light, thus permitting visual inspection of the lining of the stomach **gas·tro·sco·pic** (gæstrəskɔ́pik) *adj.*

gas·tros·co·py (gæstrɔ́skəpi:) *n.* [fr. Gk *gastēr* (*gasteros*), stomach+*skopein*, to watch]

gas·tro·trich (gǽstrətrik) **1.** *n.* a member of *Gastrotricha*, a small group of microscopic many-celled freshwater worms, usually classed with the rotifers, having cilia on the ventral side **2.** *adj.* of or pertaining to *Gastrotricha* [fr. Gk *gastēr* (*gasteros*), stomach+*thrix* (*trichos*), hair]

gas·tro·vas·cu·lar (gæstrouvǽskjulər) *adj.* (*zool.*) serving for digestive and circulatory functions [fr. Gk *gastēr* (*gasteros*)+VASCULAR]

gas·tru·la (gǽstrulə) *pl.* **gas·tru·lae** (gǽstruli:) *n.* an early metazoan embryo, consisting of an ectoderm and an endoderm, often in the form of a hollow cup, enclosing the archenteron. It is produced in various ways, e.g. by invagination of part of the blastula or by epiboly of the blastoderm **gás·tru·lar** *adj.* **gas·tru·late** (gǽstruleit) *v.i. pres. part.* **gas·tru·lat·ing** *past* and *past part.* **gas·tru·lat·ed** to undergo gastrulation **gas·tru·lá·tion** *n.* the formation of a gastrula [Mod. L. dim. fr. Gk *gastēr* (*gasteros*), stomach]

gas turbine an internal-combustion engine in which compressed air is fed into a combustion chamber where it is heated by the combustion of a fuel, the hot compressed gases then expanding to drive a turbine

gas·works (gǽswə:rks) *n.* a plant where gas for lighting and heating is manufactured

gat or **gath** (gát) (gɑθ) *n.* final rhymic movement in a traditional Hindu raga

gate (geit) **1.** *n.* a wooden or metal barrier on hinges or pivots, capable of being opened and shut, and filling the opening in a wall or fence ‖ an opening or passageway through any wall or barrier ‖ the structure built about an entrance, *we passed between the gates of the palace* ‖ any means of entrance or exit, *the Straits of Gibraltar are the gate of the Mediterranean* ‖ a mountain pass or defile ‖ a device regulating the passage of water ‖ the slotted guide for the gearshift of an internal-combustion engine ‖ the device which controls the passage of film through a movie camera ‖ the number of people paying to see an athletic contest etc., or the amount of money collected from them ‖ (*computer*) a logic element with outputs under set conditions **2.** *v.t. pres. part.* **gat·ing** *past* and *past part.* **gat·ed** (*Br.*) to punish (boys at boarding school, or students in colleges) by confining them to the premises ‖ to adjust (a loom) for weaving by tying on the warp threads [O.E. *geat*, door]

gate *n.* (*forging*) the channel in the mold through which molten metal streams into the pattern cavity ‖ the waste metal cast in the opening of the gate [perh. fr. O.E. *gyte*, pouring out]

gate-crash (géitkræʃ) *v.t.* (*pop.*) to crash (a party) **gáte-crash·er** *n.* (*pop.*) an intruder at a party

gate·house (géithaus) *pl.* **gate·hou·ses** (géithauziz) *n.* a lodge at the gateway to a park or estate ‖ a room over an old city gate, formerly a prison ‖ a structure at a dam etc. containing the controls regulating flow

gate·keep·er (géitki:pər) *n.* a person in charge of a gate, e.g. at a railroad crossing or at the entrance to a zoo

gate-leg table (géitleg) a table with dropleaves which are supported, when extended, by a pair of hinged legs. The legs fold in under the fixed central leaf when the drop leaves are lowered

gate money the total admission receipts for an athletic event etc.

gate-post (géitpoust) *n.* the post on which a gate is hung or against which it shuts

Gates (geits), Horatio (c. 1727–1806), U.S. general during the Revolutionary War. As commander (1777) in New York, he forced British Gen. John Burgoyne to surrender

Gates·head (géitshed) a county borough (pop. 217,500) in Durham, England, on River Tyne, opposite Newcastle: engineering, chemical and rope manufacture

gate·way (géitwei) *n.* an opening or passage that may be closed with a gate ‖ the structure built around an opening

gath·er (gǽðər) **1.** *v.t.* to collect as harvest ‖ to pluck, *to gather a rose* ‖ to amass, *to gather information* ‖ to gain, *to gather speed* ‖ to cause to collect or come together, *this cloth gathers dust* ‖ to summon up (one's thoughts, strength) for an effort ‖ to draw parts together, *to gather folds in a dress* ‖ (*printing*) to assemble (printed sheets) for binding ‖ to wrinkle, pucker, *his brow was gathered in thought* ‖ to deduce, learn indirectly ‖ to infer **2.** *v.i.* to come together, assemble ‖ to mass, accumulate, *clouds gathered on the horizon* ‖ (of a sore) to generate pus **to gather head** to increase in strength, come to a head **to gather in** to harvest **to gather itself** (of an animal) to draw up the limbs for a spring **to gather one's breath** to pause and rest briefly after a physical effort or emotional shock **to gather oneself together** to compose oneself after emotional or physical disturbance or a fit of absentmindedness **to gather up** to pick up, *he gathered up the child in his arms* ‖ to collect or summon up (one's energies) before exertion ‖ to collect together, accumulate **to gather way** (of a ship) to begin to go fast enough to answer the helm **2.** *n.* (usually *pl.*) part of a dress, cloth etc. that has been gathered in **gáth·er·ing** *n.* an assembly of people ‖ (*printing*) a signature, a number of leaves of a book folded for stitching [O.E. *gaderian*]

Gat·ling (gǽtliŋ), Richard Jordan (1818–1903), U.S. inventor who created (1862) the Gatling machine gun. His sowing machines and other agricultural implements furthered the development of U.S. agriculture

GATT *GENERAL AGREEMENT ON TARIFFS AND TRADE

gauche (gouʃ) *adj.* awkward ‖ lacking in social graces [F.]

gau·che·rie (gouʃərí:) n. awkwardness ‖ tactlessness [F.]

gau·ches·co (gautʃéskou) adj. (Sp.) of the gauchos of Argentina, esp. of a type of poetry

gau·chiste or **gau·chist** (gouʃí:st) n. (Fr.) a leftist. —**gauchiste** adj.

gau·cho (gáutʃou) n. a South American cowboy [Span.]

gaud (gɔd) n. (rhet.) a showy ornament, a trinket [M.E. gaude]

Gau·dí (gaudí:), Antonio (1852–1926), Spanish architect. He developed an intensely personal style inspired by medieval and Islamic art and characterized by sinuous lines of force and asymmetry. The unfinished Church of the Sagrada Familia, Barcelona (1883–1926), is his best-known work

Gau·dier-Brzes·ka (góudjeibréʃka), Henri (Henri Gaudier, 1891–1915), French sculptor. He produced portraits, figures and animal studies, some of which tend toward abstraction. His superb sense of form is also apparent in numerous drawings of animals

gaud·i·ly (gɔ́dili) adv. in a gaudy way

gaud·i·ness (gɔ́dinis) n. the quality of being gaudy

gaud·y (gɔ́di:) comp. **gaud·i·er** superl. **gaud·i·est** adj. showy and cheap, tastelessly ornate [perh. fr. GAUD]

gaudy pl. **gaud·ies** n. an annual college dinner at Oxford University, England, for graduate members etc. [fr. L. gaudium, joy]

gauffer *GOFFER

gauge, gage (geidʒ) 1. n. a standard measure, esp. of the thickness of wire or sheet metal and of the diameter of bullets ‖ the diameter of the bore of a gun ‖ an instrument for measuring quantity of rainfall, force of wind etc. ‖ an instrument for testing and checking the dimensions of tools, wire etc. ‖ a sliding measure used by carpenters for striking a line parallel to the straight side of a piece of wood ‖ the width between the insides of the rails of a railroad track ‖ measure, means of estimating, criterion, this report provides some gauge of his ability ‖ a device attached to a container to show the height of its contents ‖ (printing) a strip to regulate the width of a margin ‖ (naut., usually **gage**) the position of a ship in relation to the wind ‖ (building) the part of a slate or tile exposed to the weather when laid ‖ (plastering) the amount of plaster of paris used with common plaster to make it set more quickly **to take the gauge of** to estimate 2. v.t. pres. part. **gaug·ing, gag·ing** past and past part. **gauged, gaged** to measure with a gauge ‖ to measure the capacity of (a cask etc.) ‖ to estimate, appraise, to gauge an opponent's strength ‖ to make conformable to a standard: to make (bricks, stones etc.) uniform ‖ to mix (plasters) in certain proportions for quick drying **gáuge·a·ble** adj. **gáug·er, gág·er** n. someone who measures the capacity of casks etc. ‖ (Br.) an exciseman [O.N.F. gauge]

gauge theory (phys.) principle unifying the weak and electromagnetic interactions in subatomic matter, hypothesized by Albert Einstein

gauge wheel a wheel fixed to the underside of a plow limiting the depth of furrow

Gau·guin (gougé), Paul (1848–1903), French painter. He worked in isolation, spending his later years in the South Sea Islands, but has been classed with Cézanne and Van Gogh as a Postimpressionist. He retained the Impressionists' use of pure unmixed colors, but chose colors for their vibrancy and expressive power, and laid them out in large flat areas, abandoning the attempt of the Impressionists to reproduce optical processes or illusions. His composition is also non-natural: it is essentially bold pattern-making

Gau·ha·ti (gauháti:) a commercial center (pop. 123,783) of Assam, India, on the Brahmaputra. University (1948)

Gaul (gɔl) the Roman province of Gallia, divided into two regions: Cisalpine Gaul in N. Italy, and Transalpine Gaul, the area now comprising France, Switzerland, Belgium and the Netherlands. The former was conquered by the Romans (222 B.C.). The southern part of Transalpine Gaul became a Roman province (121 B.C.), and the rest was conquered (58–50 B.C.) by Caesar. Transalpine Gaul was ravaged (5th c.) by Visigoths, Burgundians and Franks, was conquered (486) by Clovis, and became part of the kingdom of the Franks

Gaul (gɔl) n. a member of the Celtic people formerly inhabiting Gaul [F. Gaule fr. L. Gallia]

Gaul·ish (gɔ́liʃ) 1. adj. of or relating to Gaul or its people 2. n. the Celtic language of ancient Gaul, extinct since the 5th or 6th c. A.D.

Gaulle (dəgɔ́l, dəgóul), Charles de (1890–1970), French statesman and general. After France's surrender to Germany (1940), he escaped to London, refused to recognize the Vichy government, and organized the Free French forces. He led the French government-in-exile in Algiers (1943–4), and, after the liberation, was head of the provisional government in Paris (1944–6). De Gaulle withdrew from public political life (1953), but was recalled (1958) at the time of the Algerian crisis. After a referendum, he established the Fifth Republic (1958), of which he became the first president (1959). He ended the war in Algeria (1962), restored political and economic stability in France, was reelected president (1965) by popular suffrage, and took an independent line in foreign policy. He quit (Apr. 1969) the presidential office when a referendum on regional and Senate reforms (which he had urged as being essential) received a negative vote

gault, galt (gɔlt) n. (geol.) a stiff, dark clay [origin unknown]

gaul·the·ri·a (gɔlθíəri:ə) n. a member of Gaultheria, fam. Ericaceae, a genus of evergreen shrubs. Oil of wintergreen is obtained from the leaves of G. procumbens, American wintergreen [after JeanFrançois Gaultier (d. 1756), F. botanist in Canada]

Gaunt, John of *JOHN OF GAUNT

gaunt (gɔnt) adj. (of persons) haggard, emaciated, esp. from illness or suffering [origin unknown]

gaunt·let (gɔ́ntlit, gɑ́ntlit) n. a strong glove with a covering for the wrist ‖ (hist.) a steel glove of mail or plate worn with armor from the 14th c. **to fling** (or **throw**) **down the gauntlet** to challenge to combat **to pick** (or **take**) **up the gauntlet** to accept such a challenge [M.E. gantelet fr. F. dim. of gant, glove]

gaunt·let, gant·let (gɔ́ntlit, gɑ́ntlit) n. (hist., in phrase) **to run the gauntlet** to be forced as punishment to run between rows of men and be struck by them [older gantlope corrup. of Swed. gatlopp]

gaun·try (gɔ́ntri:) pl. **gaun·tries** n. (Br.) a gantry

gaur (gáuər) pl. **gaur, gaurs** n. Bibos gaurus, fam. Bovidae, a large wild ox with thick curved horns found in the hill forests of India, Burma and Malaysia [fr. Hind.]

Gauss (gaus), Johann Karl Friedrich (1777–1855), German mathematician. In addition to his work in pure mathematics, he made major contributions to theoretical astronomy, geodesy, terrestrial magnetism and electricity and other branches of physics

gauss (gaus) n. (elec.) a cgs electromagnetic unit of magnetic induction, equal to that which will induce an electromotive force of 1 abvolt in each linear cm. of conductor moving laterally with a speed of 1 cm./sec. perpendicular to the magnetic flux [after J. K. Gauss]

Gauss·i·an distribution (gɔ́si:ən) (statistics) distribution following the usual natural bell-shaped pattern, which increases and decreases gradually and symmetrically to and from the point of greatest probability

Gauss's law a statement in physics equating the total electric flux across any closed surface lying within an electric field with 4 π times the electric charge enclosed by it

Gau·ta·ma (gáutəmə) *BUDDHA

Gau·tier (goutjei), Théophile (1811–72), French poet, journalist and novelist. As a young man he was a violent Romantic, but the Parnassian creed which he evolved had much to do with refining the technique of art until it was capable of meeting any demands made upon it. His best verse appeared in 'Émaux et Camées, (1852) and he wrote several novels and books of travel, as well as literary, dramatic and art criticism

gauze (gɔz) n. a thin, open-woven fabric of silk, cotton or linen ‖ any such semitransparent material, e.g. wire gauze ‖ a thin haze **gáuz·i·ness** n. **gáuz·y** comp. **gauz·i·er** superl. **gauz·i·est** adj. [F. gaze]

gave past of GIVE

gav·el (gǽvəl) n. the hammer with which e.g. the chairman of a meeting calls for attention or silence, or with which an auctioneer marks a sale [origin unknown]

gav·el·kind (gǽvəlkaind) n. (Eng. hist.) a system of land tenure in which intestate property was divided equally among sons or collateral heirs, esp. in Anglo-Saxon Kent [M.E. gavelkynde fr. gavel, rent or tribute paid to a superior+kynde, kinde, kind]

Gav·es·ton (gǽvistən), Piers (d. 1312), favorite of Edward II of England, who appointed him regent (1308). The barons put him to death

ga·vi·al (géivi:əl) n. Gavialis gangeticus, a very long Indian crocodile [F. corrup. of Hind. ghariyāl]

ga·votte (gəvɔ́t) n. a lively old French dance in 4/4 time [F. ult. fr. Mod. Provençal Gavot, an Alpine peasant]

Ga·wain, Sir (gáwin) a nephew of King Arthur in the Arthurian legend, the ideal of knightly courtesy

gawk (gɔk) 1. n. (pop.) a stupid and awkward person 2. v.i. (pop.) to stare stupidly **gáwk·i·ly** adv. in a gawky way **gáwk·i·ness** n. the state or quality of being gawky **gáwk·y** comp. **gawk·i·er** superl. **gawk·i·est** adj. clumsy and stiffly awkward, ungainly [etym. doubtful]

Gay (gei), John (1685–1732), English poet and playwright. His most famous work is the lyrical drama 'The Beggar's Opera' (1728)

gay (gei) adj. merry, cheerful, lighthearted ‖ bright in color, brilliant ‖ pleasure-loving ‖ a homosexual, usu. male [F. gai]

Ga·ya (gáya) a town (pop. 179,884) in Bihar, India, a Buddhist and Hindu pilgrimage place, and a rail junction

gayety *GAIETY

Gay Liberation militant movement for civil rights for homosexuals

Gay-Lus·sac (geiləsǽk), Joseph Louis (1778–1850), French physicist and chemist. He studied such diverse phenomena as the magnetic field of the earth, the relation of combining volumes of reacting gases and the physical and chemical properties of iodine, chlorine and boron (which he discovered)

Gay-Lussac's law (geiləsǽks) the statement that when gases react chemically the volumes measured at constant temperature and pressure of the reactants and products (if they are gases too) are in the ratios to each other of simple whole numbers

gayly *GAILY

gay·o·la (geióulə) n. (slang) illegal payoffs made by homosexuals or homosexual establishments to avoid exposure to the authorities

gay power concept that expresses the united demands of homosexuals, esp. for civil rights

Ga·za (gáza) a Palestinian border town (pop. 120,000), historic gateway between Egypt and the Middle East, once a Philistine city. It is the capital of the Gaza Strip

gaz·ar (gázər) n. a transparent silk fabric, often with shiny sequins or metal beads

Gaza Strip a coastal region (area 100 sq. miles) of S.W. Palestine, administered by Egypt after 1949, with well over 200,000 Arab refugees. Capital: Gaza. It was invaded by Israeli troops during the Suez crisis (1956) and subsequently policed by a U.N. force. It was again occupied by Israeli troops (June 1967)

gaze (geiz) 1. n. a long, intent look 2. v.i. pres. part. **gaz·ing** past and past part. **gazed** to look intently [origin unknown]

ga·ze·bo (gəzi:bou) pl. **ga·ze·bos, ga·ze·boes** n. a summerhouse or roof turret with a fine view [origin unknown]

ga·zelle (gəzél) n. a member of Gazella, fam. Bovidae, a genus of small, swift, graceful antelopes. G. dorcas, the common gazelle, lives in herds in the deserts of N. Africa and Arabia [F. fr. Arab. ghazāl]

ga·zette (gəzét) 1. n. (hist.) a periodical news sheet **Ga·zette** one of three official British biweekly government papers (the 'London Gazette', 'Edinburgh Gazette' and 'Belfast Gazette') with announcements of honors, names of bankrupts, lists of government appointments and promotions, and other public notices 2. v.t. pres. part. **ga·zet·ting** past and past part. **ga·zet·ted** (Br.) to publish in an official gazette, esp. (chiefly pass.) to announce the military appointment etc. of (someone) in a gazette [F. fr. Ital. gazzetta]

gaz·et·teer (gæzitíər) n. a geographical dictionary [fr. F. gazettier, a writer for a newspaper (the dictionary being originally intended for such users)]

Ga·zi·an·tep (gɑzi:ɑntép) (formerly Aintab) a town (pop. 808,697) in S. central Turkey: textiles

gaz·pa·cho (gəzpátʃou) n. soup of cucumbers and tomatoes seasoned with sweet peppers and onions

GB [C₄H₁₀FO₂P] (mil.) symbol for U.S. organic phosphorous nerve gas fluoroisopropoxy methyl phosphine oxide; formerly called sarin in Germany

GBU (mil.) air-to-surface glide bomb family with pivotal wings to increase its range; carries a MK 84 or M 118H1 3,000-lb bomb, and tv guidance; manufactured by Rockwell International and Hughes Aircraft

G clef the treble clef

GD (mil.) U.S. Army nerve gas capable of entering body through skin or lungs to cause sweating, convulsions, vomiting, diarrhea, asphyxia

Gdansk (gədánsk) formerly Danzig, a Polish port (pop. 421,000) on the Baltic near the mouth of the Vistula. It was founded by Germans (1224), later a Hanseatic city, under the Teutonic Order (1309–1466), under Polish suzerainty (1466–1793), and annexed by Prussia (1793). It was established as a free city in 1919 by the Treaty of Versailles. In 1939, German interference in the dispute between Poland and Danzig was an immediate cause of the World War II. After the war it was fully incorporated into Poland and its population, depleted by the Germans who left, was replenished by refugees from the east. Shipbuilding, machinery and distilling industries

GDP (economics acronym) for gross domestic product

Gdy·ni·a (gədíni:ə) a port (pop. 221,000) in Poland, 10 miles northeast of Gdansk. It was constructed (1921) as the chief port on the Polish Corridor, and was annexed by Germany (1939–45)

Ge (dʒi:) (Gk mythol.) the goddess personifying the earth, the mother of Uranus, Cronus etc.

ge·an·ti·cli·nal (dʒi:æntikláin'l) 1. adj. pertaining to an anticlinal fold of strata extending over a large area of the earth's surface 2. n. a geanticline **ge·án·ti·cline** n. a geanticlinal fold [fr. Gk gē, earth + ANTICLINAL]

gear (giər) 1. n. (collect.) the tools, materials etc. needed, and assembled, for a piece of work or particular activity, climbing gear ‖ personal belongings ‖ a combination of moving parts with a specified mechanical function, steering gear ‖ a device for connecting the moving parts of a machine, usually by the engagement of toothed wheels or their equivalent, so that the speed of rotation of one part causes a different speed of rotation of the other part: if the velocity ratio is small the gear is low, and if the ratio is great, the gear is high in gear having the moving parts engaged with one another out of gear having these parts disengaged 2. v.t. to furnish with a gear or apply a gear to ‖ to put into gear ‖ to adjust according to need, to gear one's efforts to an overall plan ‖ v.i. (with 'with') to be in gear ‖ (with 'into') to fit exactly [M.E. gere fr. O.N. gervi]

gear·box (gíərbɒks) n. the unit comprising the gears in a transmission system ‖ a protective case for the gears of a car

gear case a protective case enclosing the chain and gear wheels of a bicycle

gear change (Br.) a gearshift

gear·ing (gíəriŋ) n. the act of fitting a machine with gears ‖ the kind or quality of the gears with which a machine is fitted ‖ power-transmitting toothed wheels or gears, a series of gear wheels

gear·shift (gíərʃift) n. (Am. = Br. gear change) a manually operated device for engaging and disengaging gears

gear wheel a toothed wheel which is part of a gear

Geb·el Ka·the·ri·na (dʒéb'lkæθərí:nə) *KATHERINA GEBEL, *SINAI

Gebel Mu·sa (mú:sə) *SINAI

geck·o (gékou) pl. **geck·os, geck·oes** n. a member of fam. Gekkonidae, small insect-eating lizards, often having adhesive pads on the toes. They are common in warm climates, and harmless [Malay gēkoq, imitating its cry]

Gecko (mil.) U.S.S.R. air-defense, solid-propellant missile (SS-8) with range of 10 mi and radio-command direction

GED (acronym) for General Educational Development, test used in determining high-school equivalency and for other purposes

gee (dʒi:) interj. (often with 'up') a command to a horse to move forward or go faster [origin unknown]

gee interj. an expletive denoting surprise, admiration etc. [contr. of Jesus]

Gee·long (dʒilɔ́ŋ) a port (pop. with agglom., 111,000) in Victoria, Australia: wool industries

geep (gi:p) n. offspring of a goat and a sheep. syn. shoat

geese pl. of GOOSE

geest (gi:st) n. (geol.) old alluvial deposits on the land's surface ‖ loose earth, gravel etc. formed by rock decay [Du. = dry or sandy soil]

Ge·hen·na (gihénə) n. (Bible) hell ‖ a place of torment [eccl. L. fr. Gk fr. Heb. gēhinnōm, hell, originally the valley of Hinnom near Jerusalem where children were once burned in sacrifice]

Gei·ger counter (gáigər) a device for measuring intensity of ionizing radiation consisting of a Geiger-Müller tube and electronic equipment for recording the number of ionizations occurring in the tube [after Hans Geiger (1882-1945) G. physicist]

Gei·ger-Mül·ler counter (gáigərmjú:lər) a Geiger counter

Geiger-Müller tube a device consisting of a tube containing a wire axial anode enclosed in a cylindrical cathode. When high-energy electromagnetic radiation passes through the tube it causes ionization of the low-pressure gas in it which can then conduct a pulse of current [after Hans Geiger and W. Müller, G. physicists]

Geiger tube a Geiger-Müller tube

gei·sha (géiʃə) pl. **gei·sha, gei·shas** n. a Japanese woman trained to entertain men in teahouses and at social functions by dancing, singing, playing an instrument or conversing [Jap.]

Geiss·ler tube (gáislər) a tube containing rarefied gas which becomes luminous when an electric discharge takes place in it [after H. Geissler (1815-79), G. physicist]

gel (dʒel) 1. n. a colloidal dispersion that may be jellylike (e.g. gelatin) or not (e.g. silica gel), usually formed by coagulation of a sol, e.g. by cooling or evaporation 2. v.i. pres. part. **gel·ling** past and past part. **gelled** to form or become a gel ‖ to congeal, crystallize, become more defined, esp. an idea or situation [GELATIN]

Ge·la·si·us I (dʒeléiʃi:əs), St (d. 496), pope (492-6). His theory that the papacy was superior to all secular power dominated the struggle between Church and State for many centuries. Feast: Nov. 21

gel·a·tin, gel·a·tine (dʒélətin, dʒélət'n) n. a brittle, transparent, tasteless colloidal protein, soluble in water, extracted with glue and size from animal hides, skins and bones, and used in foods, photography and the making of sizing, plastic compounds etc. ‖ a substance having physical properties similar to those of gelatin, e.g. agar-agar ‖ blasting gelatin **ge·lat·i·nate** (dʒəlǽtineit) pres. part. **ge·lat·i·nat·ing** past and past part. **ge·lat·i·nat·ed** v.t. and i. to gelatinize **ge·lát·i·nize** pres. part. **ge·lat·i·niz·ing** past and past part. **ge·lat·i·nized** v.t. to make gelatinous ‖ (photog.) to treat or coat with gelatin ‖ v.i. to become gelatinous [F. gélatine]

ge·lat·i·nous (dʒəlǽt'nəs) adj. jellylike ‖ of or containing gelatin [fr. F. gélatineux]

ge·la·tion (dʒəléiʃən) n. the act or process of freezing [fr. L. gelatio (gelationis) fr. gelare, to freeze]

geld (geld) pres. part. **geld·ing** past and past part. **geld·ed, gelt** (gelt) v.t. to castrate (an animal) ‖ to spay [O.N. gelda]

Gel·der·land, Guel·der·land (géldərlænd) a province (area 1,965 sq. miles, pop. 1,708,860) in the east and central Netherlands. Capital: Arnhem

geld·ing (géldiŋ) n. a gelded animal, esp. a gelded horse [O.N. geldingr]

Gel·i·bo·lu (geli:bəlu:) *GALLIPOLI

gel·id (dʒélid) adj. frozen ‖ extremely cold **ge·lid·i·ty** (dʒəlíditi:) n. [fr. L. gelidus]

gel·ig·nite (dʒélignait) n. a mixture of nitroglycerine, nitrocellulose, potassium nitrate and wood pulp, used as an explosive [perh. fr. GELATIN + L. ignis, fire]

Gel·lert (gélərt), Christian Fürchtegott (1715-69), German poet

Gel·li·us (géli:əs), Aulus (c. 130-c. 180), Latin author of 'Noctes Atticae', a miscellaneous anthology, valuable for its quotations from lost works of Greek and Roman writers

Gel·sen·kir·chen (gelzənkírxən) an industrial city and communications center (pop. 320,100) in the central Ruhr, West Germany: coal mining, metal working, machines, glass, chemicals etc.

gem (dʒem) 1. n. a precious stone, esp. when cut and polished for ornament ‖ an engraved precious or semiprecious stone ‖ something treasured particularly, the gem of the collection ‖ someone who ought to be treasured ‖ a work of art that is small and exquisite ‖ an old size of type, between brilliant and diamond 2. v.t. pres. part. **gem·ming** past and past part. **gemmed** to adorn with gems [O.E. gim fr. L. gemma, bud, jewel]

GEM (acronym) for ground effect machine, an air-cushion vehicle. Cf AIR-CUSHION VEHICLE

Ge·ma·ra (gemɑ́rə) n. a rabbinical exposition of the Mishnah. It is written in Aramaic, and forms the second part of the Talmud ‖ the Talmud [Aram. = completion]

gem·i·nate (dʒémineit) 1. adj. (bot.) growing in pairs ‖ twin (applied to corresponding forms of a species or subspecies found in corresponding but separate regions, e.g. reindeer and caribou) 2. v. pres. part. **gem·i·nat·ing** past and past part. **gem·i·nat·ed** v.t. to double ‖ v.i. to occur in pairs **gem·i·ná·tion** n. a doubling ‖ the doubling of a consonant sound ‖ the doubling of a letter in spelling ‖ the formation, from a single tooth germ, of two teeth which grow together [fr. L. geminare (geminatus) fr. geminus, twin]

Gem·i·ni (dʒéminai, dʒémini:) the constellation of Castor and Pollux ‖ the third sign of the zodiac, represented as twins [L. = twins]

gem·ma (dʒémə) pl. **gem·mae** (dʒémi:) n. an asexual unicellular or multicellular outgrowth of a plant or animal which develops into a new organism, as in certain mosses and liverworts [L. = bud]

gem·mate (dʒémeit) 1. adj. bearing, or reproducing by, gemmae 2. v.i. pres. part. **gem·mat·ing** past and past part. **gem·mat·ed** to bear or reproduce by gemmae [fr. L. gemmare (gemmatus), to bud]

gem·ma·tion (dʒeméiʃən) n. asexual reproduction by gemmae ‖ the period of growth or the arrangement of gemmae **gem·ma·tive** (dʒémətiv) adj. [F.]

gem·mu·la·tion (dʒemjuléiʃən) n. the formation of or reproduction by gemmules

gem·mule (dʒémju:l) n. a small plant bud ‖ asexual reproductive body of some sponges ‖ one of the hypothetical particles in Darwin's theory of pangenesis [F.]

gems·bok (gémzbɒk) n. Oryx gazella, a nearly extinct S. African antelope with long, straight horns [Du.]

gen (dʒen) n. (Br., pop.) information [GENERAL INFORMATION]

Gen. General

gen·darme (ʒɑndárm) n. a policeman in some countries, esp. France ‖ (mountaineering) a rock pinnacle on an arête **gen·dár·me·rie, gen·dárm·er·y** pl. **gen·dar·me·ries, gen·darm·er·ies** n. a corps of gendarmes ‖ the building where gendarmes are stationed [F.]

gen·der (dʒéndər) n. (gram.) the classification of words, or the class to which a word belongs by virtue of such classification, according to the sex of the referent (natural gender) or according to arbitrary distinctions of form and syntax (grammatical gender). Modern English has few traces of grammatical gender, but Latin nouns all have gender, masculine, feminine or neuter, often contradicting natural gender. Adjectives and articles have gender insofar as they change form to agree with the noun they qualify ‖ (pop.) sex (male or female) [M.E. gendre fr. O.F.]

gene (dʒi:n) n. a portion of a chromosome which, if further subdivided into parts, would lose the character of a hereditary unit, i.e. the ability to copy itself during the reproductive process of the cell, and the ability to copy itself even after undergoing a mutation. The power to reproduce itself, which can be retained after mutation, is a characteristic possessed only by genes. This makes the gene not only the basic unit of heredity and evolution but also the basis of those characteristic processes of growth, development and reproduction that distinguish each species (*HEREDITY, *DEOXYRIBONUCLEIC ACID) [fr. Gk gen-, root of gignesthai, to be born]

ge·ne·a·log·i·cal (dʒi:ni:əlódʒik'l) adj. of or pertaining to genealogy [fr. F. généalogique]

ge·ne·al·o·gist (dʒi:ni:ólədʒist, dʒi:ni:ǽlədʒist) n. someone who studies, traces or records genealogies

ge·ne·al·o·gy (dʒi:ni:ólədʒi:, dʒi:ni:ǽlədʒi:) pl. **ge·ne·al·o·gies** n. the study of family pedigrees ‖ the descent of a person or family from an ancestor, generation by generation ‖ the record of this descent, a pedigree ‖ the line of development of a plant or animal from earlier forms [O.F. *genelogie, genealogie* fr. L.L. fr. Gk]

gene pool (*genetics*) the overall genetic assets of an interbreeding population

genera *pl.* of GENUS

gen·er·a·ble (dʒénərəb'l) *adj.* capable of being generated [fr. L. *generabilis*]

gen·er·al (dʒénərəl) **1.** *adj.* pertaining to a whole or to most of its parts, not particular, not local, *the general good of the community* ‖ prevalent, widespread, *the general opinion* ‖ customary, usual, *his general practice was to sleep late* ‖ concerned with main features and not with details, *a general survey of English history* ‖ not restricted, *a general amnesty* ‖ indefinite, vague ‖ not specialized, *a general practitioner* ‖ above the rank of colonel, *of general rank* ‖ of top rank, *postmaster general* **2.** *n.* an army officer ranking below (*Am.*) a general of the army or (*Br.*) a field marshal and above a lieutenant general ‖ an officer of the same rank in the U.S. air force or marine corps ‖ (by courtesy) a lieutenant general or major general ‖ any army commander as military strategist ‖ (*eccles.*) the head of a religious order **in general** for the most part [O.F.]

General Abrams (*mil.*) U.S. full-tracked combat tank (XM-1), with 105-mm or 120-mm guns

General Agreement on Tariffs and Trade (*abbr.* GATT) an international treaty signed by 83 nations and observed by an additional 27 countries (1978). GATT went into effect Jan. 1, 1948 and provides standards for international trade, including a non-discriminatory trade policy, multilateral negotiations to reduce tariffs, and consultation over trade disputes. In 1964 GATT founded the International Trade Center, which works with the U.N. Conference on Trade and Development to help developing nations with their export trade. GATT headquarters are in Geneva

General American the standard pronunciation of Americans other than natives of the South or of the eastern seaboard

General Assembly the governing body and highest ecclesiastical court of the Presbyterian Church and certain other Churches ‖ the deliberative body of the United Nations in which each member state is represented and receives one vote ‖ the legislature in certain states of the U.S.A.

general average (*insurance*) apportionment of loss caused by intentional damage to a ship. (In maritime insurance an insurer must compensate for loss or damage to part of a ship or her cargo if such a loss or damage is incurred in order to protect the remainder, though not for negligent loss or damage)

General Certificate of Education (*abbr.* G.C.E.) the certificate awarded in England at any of three levels: ordinary, advanced and scholarship. Results largely control admission to skilled trades, professions and universities

general court-martial a military court for offenses of the most serious kind, with authority to impose dishonorable discharge or capital punishment. It is composed of at least five commissioned officers. Its proceedings are governed by a law officer who is required to be a member of the bar. Prosecution is by a trial counsel and defense by a defense counsel, both required to be members of the bar

general delivery a department of a post office handling letters which are held until called for

general election an election covering the whole country (cf. BY-ELECTION)

General Electric Company the largest electrical company in the U.S.A., incorporated (1892) at Schenectady, N.Y.

gen·er·al·is·si·mo (dʒénərəlísimou) *n.* the supreme commander of a country's armed forces or of several armies acting together (not applied to British or U.S. generals) [Ital., superl. of *generale,* general]

gen·er·al·i·ty (dʒénərǽliti) *pl.* **gen·er·al·i·ties** *n.* a general point, *the meeting discussed generalities only* ‖ a vague statement, *meaningless generalities* ‖ the state of being general ‖ (*old-fash.*) the majority, the main body [F. *généralité*]

gen·er·al·i·za·tion (dʒénərəlizéiʃən) *n.* a general notion or statement (whether true or false) derived from particular instances ‖ the forming of such notions or statements

gen·er·al·ize (dʒénərəlaiz) *pres. part.* **gen·er·al·iz·ing** *past* and *past part.* **gen·er·al·ized** *v.i.* to draw a general rule or statement from particular instances ‖ to use generalities ‖ *v.t.* to draw (a general rule or statement) from particular instances ‖ to base a generalization upon (particular instances) ‖ to bring into general use, popularize

Generalized System of Preferences a system approved by GATT (General Agreement on Tariffs and Trade) in 1971 and by the U.S. in 1976, authorizing developed countries to give preferential tariff treatment to developing countries, in effect waiving the most-favored-nation principle. *abbr.* **GSP**

gen·er·al·ly (dʒénərəli) *adv.* usually, for the most part ‖ widely, *generally welcomed* ‖ in a general sense, without particulars, *generally speaking*

General Motors Corporation (*abbr.* GMC) a U.S. producer of motor vehicles and one of the largest corporations in the world. Incorporated in 1916, with headquarters in Detroit, Mich., it developed the electric self-starter, ethyl gasoline, and crankcase ventilation

general obligation bond debenture of a municipality backed by the full taxing power of the issuing community

general of the air force the highest rank of officer in the U.S. air force

general of the army the highest rank of officer in the U.S. army, ranking immediately above a general

general paralysis general paresis

general paresis a disease of the nervous system, caused by syphilis, that leads to ultimate paralysis, deterioration of the mental faculties and death

general practitioner a nonspecialist medical doctor

gen·er·al-pur·pose (dʒénərəlpɔ́:rpəs) *adj.* of general use, comprehensively useful, *a general-purpose weed killer*

general relativity *RELATIVITY

gen·er·al·ship (dʒénərəlʃip) *n.* military skill ‖ skillful management, leadership ‖ the office of general

general staff a number of officers who assist the commander in administrative and executive duties at army or divisional headquarters

general strike a paralyzing strike, by workers who are members of trade unions, in all or most of a country's industries

gen·er·ate (dʒénəreit) *pres. part.* **gen·er·at·ing** *past* and *past part.* **gen·er·at·ed** *v.t.* to cause to be, produce, *steam is generated in a boiler* ‖ (*biol.*) to procreate ‖ (*math.*) to trace out or produce (a line or figure) by motion (of a point, line or other element) ‖ (*linguistics*) in generative grammar, to produce a sentence from kernels of material [fr. L. *generare* (*generatus*), beget]

gen·er·a·tion (dʒénəréiʃən) *n.* a producing or being produced, *the generation of electricity* ‖ procreation ‖ a whole body of persons, animals or plants removed in the same degree from an ancestor ‖ the whole body of persons thought of as being born about the same time, *the rising generation* ‖ a period of time, about 25 or 30 years, roughly corresponding to the age of parents when their children are born ‖ (*math.*) the formation of a surface or solid figure by the motion of some element, in accordance with a mathematical law, *the generation of a line by a point* [fr. L. *generatio* (*generationis*)]

generation gap difference in mores between one generation and the next

gen·er·a·tive (dʒénəreitiv, dʒénərətiv) *adj.* of the production of offspring ‖ able to produce

generative grammar (*linguistics*) a theory or set of statements for the generation of the possible phrases of a language or part of a language (the well-formed phrases and only these)

gen·er·a·tive-trans·for·ma·tion·al grammar (dʒénəreitivtrænsfuərméiʃən'l) (*linguistics*) technique for deriving grammatical construction in a language from underlying psychological forces, hypothesized by Noam Chomsky, an approach to language that makes possible the generation of an infinite number of sentences in a language and to specify the structure of each —**generative** *adj.* —**generativist** *n.* Cf DEEP STRUCTURE, SURFACE STRUCTURE

gen·er·a·tor (dʒénəreitər) *n.* an apparatus for converting mechanical energy into electricity, a dynamo ‖ an apparatus for producing gas or steam [L.=that which generates]

gen·er·a·trix (dʒénəréitriks) *pl.* **gen·er·a·tri·ces** (dʒénəréitrisi:z) *n.* (*math.*) a point, line or plane whose motion produces respectively a line, plane or solid [L. fem. of *generator,* that which generates]

ge·ner·ic (dʒənérik) *adj.* (*biol.*) of or pertaining to a genus ‖ of or pertaining to a group or class ‖ having a wide or general application, not specific **ge·nér·i·cal·ly** *adv.* [fr. L. *genus* (*generis*), race, class]

gen·er·os·i·ty (dʒénərósiti) *pl.* **gen·er·os·i·ties** *n.* the quality of being generous ‖ an instance of this [fr. L. *generositas* (*generositatis*)]

gen·er·ous (dʒénərəs) *adj.* giving freely, liberal, not stingy ‖ noble-minded, magnanimous ‖ plentiful, copious ‖ (of wine) full and rich ‖ (*rhet.,* of soil) very fertile [fr. F. *généreux*]

gene sequencing technique for rearranging a genetic structure to achieve a purpose, e.g., to have bacteria produce insulin

Gen·e·sis (dʒénisis) the first book of the Old Testament and of the Pentateuch. It describes God's creation of the world, and traces the history of the Hebrews from Abraham to Joseph. The book is generally thought to have been compiled after the Exile, from three main sources of the 9th–6th cc. B.C.

gen·e·sis (dʒénisis) *pl.* **gen·e·ses** (dʒénisi:z) *n.* origin ‖ mode of generation [L. fr. Gk *genesis,* origin, creation]

gene splicing (*genetics*) **1.** injection of genetic material from foreign organisms to change genetic structure of other organisms. **2.** technique of changing inherited characteristics by recombining segments of the genetic material in DNA. Cf GENETIC ENGINEERING, INTERFERON

Ge·nêt (ʒəne), Edmond Charles Edouard (1763–1834), French minister (appointed Apr. 1793) to the U.S.A. He was instructed to encourage hostilities between the U.S.A. and Great Britain, to fit out privateers in American ports to prey on British shipping, and to promote raids against British and Spanish possessions in the Gulf of Mexico. The outraged Federalists under George Washington demanded (Aug. 1793) his recall

Ge·net (ʒəne), Jean (1910–86), French writer and poet. His experimental plays, e.g. 'The Blacks' (1958) and 'The Balcony' (1959), and novels, including 'Our Lady of the Flowers' (1948), are concerned mainly with the play of illusion and reality

gen·et (dʒénit) *n.* a member of *Genetta,* fam. *Viverridae,* a genus of carnivorous Old World mammals, allied to civets, but with the scent glands less developed [O.F. *genete, genette* fr. Arab. *jarnait*]

ge·net·ic (dʒənétik) *adj.* of or relating to the origin or development of something ‖ of or relating to genetics **ge·nét·i·cal·ly** *adv.* **ge·nét·i·cist** (dʒənétisist) *n.* **ge·nét·ics** *n.* the branch of biology concerned with the heredity and variation of organisms ‖ the genetic constitution of an organism, group or kind [fr. GENESIS]

genetic code sequence of a triplet of nucleotides in DNA and messenger RNA molecules that specify the order of assembly of proteins in amino acids, some of which determine inheritance of one or more biological characteristics. Cf DNA, MESSENGER RNA

genetic engineering (*genetics*) the science of alteration of genetic material to produce new traits. —**genetic deletion** *n.* —**genetic engineer** *n.* —**genetic insertion** *n.* —**genetic surgery** *n.* Cf EUPHENICS

genetic epistemology (*psych.*) a group of theories regarding the development of knowledge and understanding in a child as influenced by heredity

ge·net·i·cism (dʒənétisizəm) *n.* (*psych.*) theory that all human character, personality, and national history are determined by genetic factors; coined by P. B. Medawar in 1959

genetic load (*genetics*) the mutations in the gene pool of a species

genetic map (*genetics*) the placement of the genes on a chromosome

genetic marker *MARKER

genetic screening process of selection (of employees, etc.) by determining supposedly inherited weaknesses or strengths

Ge·ne·va (dʒəní:və) (F. *Genève*) a mainly French-speaking canton (area 108 sq. miles, pop. 349,040), around the western end of the Lake of Geneva, Switzerland ‖ its capital (pop. 156,505). Industries: watchmaking, electrical goods, jewelry, chocolate, tourism. University. Geneva was the home (1536–64) of Calvin, and

---

CONCISE PRONUNCIATION KEY: **(a)** æ, c*a*t; ɑ, c*a*r; ɔ f*aw*n; ei, sn*a*ke. **(e)** e, h*e*n; i:, sh*ee*p; iə, d*ee*r; ɛə, b*ea*r. **(i)** i, f*i*sh; ai, t*i*ger; ə:, b*i*rd. **(o)** o, *o*x; au, c*ow*; ou, g*oa*t; u, p*oo*r; ɔi, r*oy*al. **(u)** ʌ, d*u*ck; u, b*u*ll; u:, g*oo*se; ə, b*a*cillus; ju:, c*u*be. x, lo*ch*; θ, *th*ink; δ, *b*other; z, *Z*en; ʒ, cor*s*age; dʒ, sava*g*e; ŋ, ora*n*gutang; j, *y*ak; ʃ, *f*ish; tʃ, *f*etch; 'l, rabb*le*; 'n, redde*n*. Complete pronunciation key appears inside front cover.

became the center of the Reformation. It joined Switzerland in 1815. It was the headquarters of the League of Nations (1920–46), and is the headquarters of the International Red Cross, the World Health Organization and other international bodies

Geneva bands two strips of white cloth hanging at the throat worn by some Protestant clergymen (originally by the Calvinist clergy of Switzerland)

Geneva Bible an English translation of the Bible (Geneva, 1560) made by English Protestant refugees. It was based on Tyndale's version. It was itself succeeded by the King James Authorized Version

Geneva Conventions international humanitarian conventions (1864, 1868 and 1929), formulated by the International Red Cross, to safeguard certain human rights in time of war. They specified that military hospitals were to be regarded as neutral, the wounded respected, and medical services, personnel and supplies protected under the Red Cross emblem. These conventions were extended to sea warfare in 1907, to the treatment of prisoners of war in 1929, and were modernized and further extended in 1949

Geneva cross the Red Cross symbol

Geneva gown a loose black (usually academic) preaching gown worn by some Protestant clergymen (originally by the Calvinist clergy of Switzerland)

Geneva, Lake of (F. Lac Léman) a long lake (area 225 sq. miles) through which the Rhône flows, in the angle of the Alps and the Jura, S.W. Switzerland, part of the French frontier: tourism

Ge·ne·viève (ʒənəvjev), St (c. 422–512), patron saint of Paris. She sustained the population when Attila the Hun threatened to attack Paris. Feast: Jan. 3

Gen·ghis Khan (dʒéŋgiskán) (c. 1162–1227), Mongol conqueror and emperor. After gaining control of Mongolia (1206), he conquered N. China (1211–15), then vast territories in central and S. Asia and Asia Minor. After his death his dominions, which stretched from the Pacific to the Black Sea, were divided among his descendants (*KUBLAI KHAN)

gen·ial (dʒí:njəl) adj. pleasant, cheerful, kindly ‖ (of climate, air etc.) mild, warm [fr. L. genialis]

ge·ni·al (dʒináiəl) adj. (anat.) of the chin [fr. Gk geneion, chin]

ge·ni·al·i·ty (dʒi:ni:ǽliti:) n. the quality of being genial

gen·ic (dʒénik) adj. of a gene ‖ genetic [GENE]

ge·nic·u·late (dʒəníkjulit) adj. (biol.) bent like a bent knee [fr. L. geniculatus fr. geniculum dim. of genu, knee]

ge·nie (dʒí:ni:) pl. **ge·nies, ge·ni·i** (dʒí:ni:ai) n. a jinn [F. génie]

Genie (mil.) unguided missile (AIR-2A) with nuclear warhead having a 10-km range

gen·i·pap (dʒénəpæp) n. Genipa americana, fam. Rubiaceae, a large tree native to South America and the West Indies ‖ its edible fruit [fr. Port. genipapo fr. Tupi]

ge·nis·ta (dʒənístə) n. a member of Genista, fam. Papilionaceae, a genus of small yellow-flowered shrubs, mainly in the Mediterranean region [L.=broom]

gen·i·tal (dʒénit'l) adj. pertaining to the reproductive organs [fr. L. genitalis fr. gignere (genitus), to beget]

gen·i·ta·lia (dʒénitéiljə) pl. n. the genitals [L.]

gen·i·tals (dʒénit'lz) pl. n. the organs of reproduction, esp. the external organs

gen·i·ti·val (dʒénitáivəl) adj. (gram.) having genitive form

gen·i·tive (dʒénitiv) 1. adj. of or in the genitive case 2. n. the genitive case ‖ a word in this case [fr. L. genetivum, genitivum, belonging to birth or generation]

genitive case (in some languages) an inflectional case of substantives showing possession, substance and partition ‖ (loosely) a case considered as resembling the genitive, e.g. the possessive case in English

gen·i·tou·ri·nar·y (dʒénitoujúərineri:) adj. relating to the genital and urinary organs or their functions [fr. L. genitalis, genital+URINARY]

gen·ius (dʒí:njəs) pl. **gen·ius·es, ge·ni·i** (dʒí:ni:ai) n. extraordinary power of intellect, imagination or invention ‖ a person gifted with this ‖ extraordinary aptitude (for some pursuit), a genius for making enemies ‖ the special characteristics or spirit of an age, culture, people or

institution, the genius of Greek civilization ‖ (rhet., pl. **genii**) a guardian spirit of a person, place or institution [L.=tutelary spirit, inborn nature]

ge·ni·us lo·ci (dʒí:ni:əslóusai) n. the guardian spirit of a place ‖ the various associations connected with a place

Gen·nes·a·ret, Lake of (gənézərit) the Sea of Galilee

Gen·o·a (dʒénouə) (Ital. Genova) Italy's chief port (pop. 795,027) on the Mediterranean (Gulf of Genoa) below the Apennines in Liguria. Industries: steel, cement, metallurgy, oil, aircraft supplies, shipbuilding. Genoa was a prosperous trading and banking center in the Middle Ages. University (1243)

gen·o·cid·al (dʒénəsáid'l) adj. of or pertaining to genocide

gen·o·cide (dʒénəsaid) n. the deliberate extermination of a race of people, such as the Nazis attempted against the Jews [fr. Gk genos, race+L. caedere, to kill]

Gen·o·ese (dʒénouí:z, dʒénouí:s) 1. adj. of or pertaining to Genoa or its inhabitants 2. pl. **Gen·o·ese** n. a native or inhabitant of Genoa

ge·nome (dʒí:noum) n. (genetics) the total complement of chromosomes of a species, including all genes and constitutional structure

ge·no·type (dʒí:nətaip, dʒénətaip) n. the genetic constitution of an individual ‖ a group of individuals with the same genetic constitution ‖ the typical species of a genus (cf. PHENOTYPE) **ge·no·typ·ic** (dʒí:nətípik, dʒénətípik) adj. **ge·no·typ·i·cal** adj. [fr. Gk gignesthai, to be born+TYPE]

gen·re (ʒánrə, F. ʒãr) n. a kind ‖ a type or category. esp. of works of art and literature [F.]

genre painting art which treats realistically subjects of everyday life

gens (dʒenz) pl. **gen·tes** (dʒénti:z) n. an ancient Roman family group whose members claimed descent through the male line from a common ancestor ‖ (anthrop.) a tribe or clan tracing descent through the male line [L.]

Gen·ser·ic (génsərik) (or Gaiseric, c. 390–477), king of the Vandals (428–77). He seized most of N. Africa, Sicily, Sardinia, Corsica and the Balearic Is from the Roman Empire (429–75) and plundered Rome (455)

Gent *GHENT

gent (dʒent) n. (pop., short for) gentleman

gen·ta·mi·cin (dʒéntəmaísin) n. (pharm.) broad-spectrum antibiotic in a salve active against many gram-negative pathogens; marketed as Garamycin

gen·teel (dʒentí:l) adj. (of manners or people) excessively refined through social pretension ‖ (old-fash.) of or relating to the upper class [F. gentil]

gen·tian (dʒénʃən) n. a plant of the genus Gentiana, fam. Gentianaceae. Gentians are mostly Alpine plants of tufted growth with conspicuous tubular flowers, usually blue or purple ‖ the rhizome and roots of G. lutea of S. Europe, used in tonics [fr. L. gentiana fr. Gentius (180-167 B.C.), an Illyrian king said to have discovered their medicinal quality]

gentian violet a purple dye made from methyl derivatives, used as an antiseptic and as a stain in microscopy

gen·tile (dʒéntail) 1. adj. not Jewish, esp. Christian ‖ (among Mormons) not Mormon 2. n. a non-Jew, esp. a Christian ‖ (among Mormons) a non-Mormon [F. gentil]

Gen·ti·le da Fa·bria·no (dʒentí:ledafabrjáno) (Gentile di Niccolò di Giovanni Massi, c. 1370–1427), Italian painter. His historical frescos, which influenced Venetian art, are no longer extant. His 'Adoration of the Magi' (1423), in S. Trinità, Florence, particularly influenced the Florentine painters.

gen·til·i·ty (dʒentíliti:) n. refinement in conduct and manners ‖ excessive and affected refinement or delicacy [O.F. and F. gentilité, gentle birth]

gen·tle (dʒént'l) 1. adj. mild, sensitively light, a gentle voice, a gentle touch ‖ moderate, not strong or violent, a gentle breeze ‖ docile, a gentle horse of gentle birth born into the upper class 2. n. a maggot used as bait in fishing [M.E. gentil fr. O.F.]

gen·tle·folk (dʒént'lfouk) pl. n. people of gentle birth (*GENTLE)

gen·tle·man (dʒént'lmən) pl. **gen·tle·men** (dʒént'lmən) n. a man of the wealthy, leisured class ‖ a man of high principles, honorable and courteous (regardless of social position) ‖ (in polite and conventional usage) a man ‖ (hist.) a

man entitled to bear arms, but not a nobleman ‖ (law) a man who does not work for his living but lives on private income [GENTLE+MAN, after O.F. gentil hom]

gen·tle·man-at-arms (dʒént'lmənətármz) pl. **gen·tle·men-at-arms** (dʒént'lmənətármz) n. (mil.) a member of the British sovereign's bodyguard

gentleman farmer a man who runs a farm without being financially dependent on it

gen·tle·man·ly (dʒént'lmənli:) adj. characteristic of or befitting a gentleman

gentleman's agreement an agreement regarded as binding in honor, but not written and not enforceable by law

gentleman's gentleman a valet

gen·tle·wom·an (dʒént'lwumən) pl. **gen·tle·wom·en** (dʒént'lwimən) n. (old-fash.) a woman of good family

gen·tly (dʒéntli:) adv. in a gentle manner

gen·tri·fi·ca·tion (dʒentrəfikéiʃən) n. the process of redeveloping an urban area by inducing an improvement in the economic level of the population, e.g., eliminating slum areas by making properties attractive to a more affluent population

gen·try (dʒéntri:) n. people of good family, esp. those next in rank to the nobility [prob. fr. O.F. genterise var. of gentelise fr. gentil, gentle]

gentry controversy challenge to the hypothesis that the historic changes in England between 1540 and 1640 were the result of the rise of entrepreneur landlords

gen·u·flect (dʒénjuflekt) v.i. to bend the knee as a formalized gesture in worship **gen·u·flec·tion, gen·u·flex·ion** n. [L. genuflectere]

gen·u·ine (dʒénju:in) adj. real, not pretended, genuine affection ‖ authentic, a genuine signature ‖ frank, honest, sincere [fr. L. genuinus, innate, inborn]

ge·nus (dʒí:nəs) pl. **gen·e·ra** (dʒénərə), **ge·nus·es** n. (biol.) a group of animals or plants within a family, closely connected by common characteristics. A genus is divided into species. The generic name (with capital initial) and the specific name together constitute the scientific name of an organism ‖ a class of things [L.=race, sort]

ge·o·cen·tric (dʒi:ouséntrik) adj. measured from or considered as seen from the earth's center ‖ having or representing the earth as a center, the geocentric conception of the universe **ge·o·cén·tri·cal** adj. [fr. Gk gē, the earth+CENTRIC]

ge·o·chem·is·try (dʒi:oukémistri:) n. the study of the chemical composition of, and chemical changes in, the crust of the earth [fr. Gk gē, the earth+CHEMISTRY]

ge·o·chro·nol·o·gy (dʒi:oukrənólədʒi:) n. the science of fixing a time scale for the earth's history before the period covered by written documents, using geological data [fr. Gk gē, the earth+CHRONOLOGY]

ge·o·co·ro·na (dʒi:oukəróunə) n. the earth's outer rim, primarily a layer of hydrogen in the upper atmosphere

ge·ode (dʒí:oud) n. (geol.) a hollow nodule of stone formed in sedimentary rock, and having walls lined with crystals [F. géode]

ge·o·des·ic (dʒi:oudésik, dʒi:oudí:sik) 1. adj. geodetic 2. n. a geodesic line **ge·o·dés·i·cal** adj. [GEODESY]

geodesic dome a spherical dome made of light triangulated parts in tension (*FULLER)

geodesic line the shortest distance between two points on a surface, e.g. a straight line on a plane, or an arc of a great circle on a sphere

ge·od·e·sy (dʒi:ódisi:) n. the science of surveying portions of the earth's surface which are so large that the earth's curvature has to be taken into account **ge·o·det·ic** (dʒi:oudétik), **ge·o·dét·i·cal** adj. [F. géodésie fr. Gk geōdaisiā fr. gē, the earth+daiein, to divide]

geodetic line a geodesic line on the earth's surface

ge·o·det·ics (dʒi:oudétiks) n. geodesy

geodetic satellite satellite that, with three ground stations, accurately maps land masses on earth, utilizing angle measurements and time between echos of electro-magnetic waves

ge·od·ic (dʒi:ódik) adj. of or pertaining to a geode

ge·o·dim·et·er (dʒi:ədímətər) n. device for measuring distances by measuring the time it takes for a beam of light to travel to and return from a distant mirror

GEODSS (acronym) for ground-based electro-optical space surveillance, a system for photo-

---

graphing and surveilling orbiting objects, using Baker-Nunn cameras and the computerized elimination of celestial bodies

ge·o·dy·nam·ic (dʒiːoudainǽmik) adj. of or relating to the forces inside the earth **ge·o·dy·nám·i·cal** adj. **ge·o·dy·nám·ics** n. [fr. Gk gḗ, the earth+DYNAMIC]

Geoffrey of Monmouth (dʒéfri:) (c. 1100–54), English chronicler, bishop of St Asaph (1152–4). His 'Historia regum Britanniae' (c. 1147) is one of the main sources of the Arthurian legend (*ARTHUR)

Geoffrey Plantagenet *PLANTAGENET

ge·og·nos·tic (dʒiːɒgnɒstik) adj. of or pertaining to geognosy **ge·og·nós·ti·cal** adj.

ge·og·no·sy (dʒiːɒgnəsi:) n. the part of geology that deals with the materials and structure of the earth [fr. F. géognosie fr. Gk gḗ, the earth+gnōsis, knowledge]

ge·og·ra·pher (dʒiːɒgrəfər) n. a specialist in geography [fr. M.L. geographus]

ge·o·graph·ic (dʒiːəgrǽfik) adj. of or relating to geography **ge·o·gráph·i·cal** adj. [fr. Gk geōgraphikos]

geographical latitude the angle made at any point by the perpendicular to the earth's surface with the plane of the equator

geographical medicine branch of medicine dealing with effects of climate, altitude, and environmental factors on human beings

geographical mile a nautical mile

ge·og·ra·phy (dʒiːɒgrəfi:) pl. **ge·og·ra·phies** n. the science of the earth, broadly divided into physical geography, which deals with the composition of the earth's surface and the distribution of its features, and human geography, which includes economic, political and social geography and is concerned essentially with the changes wrought by man on his environment. The science is less a body of knowledge than a technique for examining and relating phenomena in terms of their varying distribution over the earth's surface ‖ the data with which this science deals ‖ a treatise or textbook of geography [F. géographie fr. L. fr. Gk geōgraphiā]

ge·oid (dʒiːɔid) n. the earth considered as a geometrical solid with the mean level of the ocean as its surface, which is thus at every point perpendicular to the direction of gravity [fr. Gk geoeidēs, earthlike]

ge·o·log·ic (dʒiːəlɒdʒik) adj. of or pertaining to geology **ge·o·lóg·i·cal** adj.

geological time the period of about 4.5 billion years covering the history of the Earth. Geological time is divided into periods of unequal length called eons, eras, periods, and epochs

ge·ol·o·gist (dʒiːɒlədʒist) n. a specialist in geology

ge·ol·o·gize (dʒiːɒlədʒaiz) pres. part. **ge·ol·o·giz·ing** past and past part. **ge·ol·o·gized** v.i. to study geology ‖ to make a geological survey

ge·ol·o·gy (dʒiːɒlədʒi:) pl. **ge·ol·o·gies** n. the scientific study of the nature, formation, origin and development of the earth's crust and of its layers ‖ these data, the geology of Europe ‖ a treatise on this subject [fr. M.L. geologia fr. Gk gḗ, the earth+logos, discourse]

ge·o·mag·net·ic (dʒiːoumǽgnétik) adj. of or pertaining to terrestrial magnetism **ge·o·mag·net·ism** (dʒiːoumǽgnitizəm) n. [fr. Gk gḗ, the earth+MAGNETIC]

ge·o·man·cer (dʒiːəmǽnsər) n. someone who practices geomancy

ge·o·man·cy (dʒiːəmǽnsi:) n. divination by random figures or lines on the ground, or on paper [F. géomancie fr. L. fr. Gk]

ge·om·e·ter (dʒiːɒmitər) n. any of several large-winged moths of fam. Geometridae ‖ a larva of these moths. They move as if measuring the ground, looping and straightening ‖ a geometrician [fr. M.F. geometre fr. L.]

ge·o·met·ric (dʒiːəmétrik) adj. of or pertaining to geometry ‖ formed of regular lines, curves and angles, a geometric design **ge·o·mét·ri·cal** adj. [fr. L. geometricus fr. Gk]

geometrical isomerism stereoisomerism due to different directional arrangements of specific groups in a molecule which are distinguishable when a substantial energy barrier to free rotation about a bond exists

geometrical optics a branch of optics in which only the empirical laws of the rectilinear propagation of light, of the mutual independence of the rays constituting a beam of light, and of reflection and refraction (*FERMAT'S PRINCIPLE) are employed to describe the behavior of light in optical systems. Geometrical optics cannot

describe the diffraction of light or other purely wave phenomena (cf. PHYSICAL OPTICS)

geometric art any of various art forms in painting and sculpture utilizing rectangles, circles and other forms. Cf HARD EDGE, OP ART, TACHISM

ge·om·e·tri·cian (dʒiːɒmitríʃən, dʒiːəmitríʃən) n. a specialist in geometry

geometric progression a series with a constant ratio between successive quantities, e.g. 1, 3, 9, 27, 81 (cf. ARITHMETIC PROGRESSION)

ge·om·e·trid (dʒiːɒmitrid, dʒiːəmétrid) 1. adj. (biol.) of or relating to a geometer 2. n. a geometer (moth) [L. Geometra, generic name]

ge·om·e·trize (dʒiːɒmitraiz) pres. part. **ge·om·e·triz·ing** past and past part. **ge·om·e·trized** v.i. to work by geometrical methods ‖ v.t. to put into geometric form

ge·om·e·try (dʒiːɒmitri:) pl. **ge·om·e·tries** n. the mathematical study of the properties of, and relations between, points, lines, angles, surfaces and solids in space ‖ a treatise on this subject ‖ the dimensional relations within a composite, the geometry of a figure [F. géométrie fr. L. fr. Gk. geōmetriā] fr. gḗ, the earth+metriā, measuring]

ge·o·mor·phol·o·gy (dʒiːoumɔrfólədʒi:) n. the branch of physical geography, allied to geology, which analyzes and explains the physical form of landscape [fr. Gk gḗ, the earth+MORPHOLOGY]

ge·oph·a·gy (dʒiːófədʒi:) n. the practice of eating earthy matter, esp. clay or chalk, either to compensate for lack of food or as a symptom of mental illness [fr. Gk gḗ, the earth+phagein, to eat]

ge·o·phys·i·cal (dʒiːoufízik'l) adj. of or pertaining to geophysics

Geophysical Year *INTERNATIONAL GEOPHYSICAL YEAR

ge·o·phys·i·cist (dʒiːoufízisist) n. a specialist in geophysics

ge·o·phys·ics (dʒiːoufíziks) n. the application of the methods of physics to the study of the earth and its atmosphere. It includes meteorology, terrestrial magnetism, seismology, hydrology etc. [fr. Gk gḗ, the earth+PHYSICS]

ge·o·pol·i·tics (dʒiːoupólitiks) n. the study of physical, economic and anthropographic features as factors affecting government policies, esp. foreign policy and defense. Unlike political geography, which deals with static conditions, it is dynamic, regarding the State as an organism that grows and develops [G. Geopolitik, coined by Rudolf Kjellen (1864-1922), Swed. political scientist]

ge·o·probe (dʒiːouproub) n. satellite designed to explore the earth and its surrounding area in space

ge·o·ref (dʒiːourɛf) n. (cartography) a worldwide position reference system that can be applied to any map or chart graduated in latitude and longitude regardless of projection. Georef involves a method of expressing latitude and longitude in a form suitable for rapid reporting and plotting; from "The World Geographic Reference System"

George (dʒɔrdʒ), St (3rd–4th cc.), patron saint of England since the time of Edward III. He was, according to legend a Roman officer martyred in 303 under Diocletian for refusal to persecute Christians. The most famous of his exploits was the slaying of a dragon. Feast: Apr. 23

George (dʒɔrdʒ) n. a jewel showing a figure of St George and forming part of the Garter insignia [after St George]

George Cross a British decoration, instituted in 1940, and awarded, primarily to civilians, for heroism

George I (1660–1727), first Hanoverian king of Great Britain (1714–27) under the Act of Settlement (1701), and elector of Hanover (1698–1727). His ignorance of English and absence from meetings of the Cabinet left government in the hands of Whig ministers (Stanhope, Townshend, Walpole). Constitutional control over the Crown thus increased during his reign

George II (1683–1760), king of Great Britain and elector of Hanover (1727–60), son of George I. He supported Austria in the War of the Austrian Succession (1740–8) and was the last British king to fight in battle (Dettingen, 1743). His son Frederick, prince of Wales, became the center of opposition, and forced Walpole's resignation (1742). George reluctantly accepted the elder Pitt as minister during the Seven Years'

War (1756–63), in which Britain sided with Prussia

George III (1738–1820), king of Great Britain (1760–1820), elector (1760–1815) and then king (1815–20) of Hanover. Brought up to favor personal rule, he caused the resignation of the elder Pitt and of Newcastle (1761), and ruled through patronage for over 20 years. The British defeat in the Revolutionary War (1775–83) made him unpopular. He brought the younger Pitt to power (1783) and took a less active role in politics, although he caused a political crisis in 1801 by refusing to sign the Catholic Emancipation Act. His growing insanity led to the regency (1811–20) of the prince of Wales (later George IV)

George IV (1762–1830), king of Great Britain and Hanover (1820–30), after being regent (1811–20) for his father, George III. His reign saw the passage of the Catholic Emancipation Act (1829). The Crown lost power and prestige during his reign, because of his attempt to divorce his wife for adultery (the Queen's Affair, 1820–1) and because of his extravagant dissipation

Georges Bank underwater geological formation 150 mi east of Cape Cod, major fishing ground believed to hold petroleum and natural gas

geor·gette (dʒɔrdʒét) n. a thin silk crape dress material [after Madame Georgette de la Plante, Parisian modiste]

George V (1865–1936), king of Great Britain (1910–36), son of Edward VII. He dealt with crises over the reform of the House of Lords (1911) and Irish Home Rule (1914). He abandoned (1917) all German titles, and changed the name of the royal family from Saxe-Coburg-Gotha to Windsor

George VI (1895–1952), king of Great Britain (1936–52), son of George V. He succeeded on the abdication of his brother, Edward VIII. His reign saw the formation of a multiracial Commonwealth

George I (1845–1913), king of Greece (1863–1913). The son of Christian IX of Denmark, he was elected to the throne after the deposition (1862) of Otto I

George II (1890–1947), king of Greece (1922–3 and 1935–47). He was exiled after the establishment of a republic (1923) and again (1941–5) during the 2nd world war

George, David Lloyd *LLOYD GEORGE

George, Henry (1839–97), American economist. His 'Progress and Poverty' (1879) advocated a single tax based on unearned income. His views influenced many of the founders of the Fabian Society

Ge·or·ge (géiórgə), Stefan (1868–1933), German poet. Influenced by the English Pre-Raphaelites (*ROSSETTI, Dante Gabriel) and the French symbolists, his lyric poetry is esoteric, nonnaturalistic and formally exquisite. His later poetry was prophetic of a German cultural and nationalist revival

George·town (dʒɔ́rdʒtaun) the capital (pop. 188,000) and chief port of Guyana, an industrial and transportation center

George Town *PENANG

Geor·gia (dʒɔ́rdʒə) a constituent republic (area 26,900 sq. miles, pop. 5,016,000) of the U.S.S.R. in S.W. Caucasia, bordering Turkey and the Black Sea. Capital: Tbilisi (Tiflis). Agricultural products: tea, citrus fruits, grapes, corn, silk. Resources: manganese (the leading world producer), coal, oil. Industries: mining, iron and steel, motor vehicles, textile processing. Georgia was subject to Russia (18th and 19th cc.), became a Soviet Republic (1921) and part of the U.S.S.R. (1936)

Georgia (abbr. Ga) a state (area 58,876 sq. miles, pop. 5,639,000) of the southeastern U.S.A. Capital: Atlanta. In the south it forms part of the Atlantic coastal plain, divided from the Appalachians in the north by a piedmont region. Agriculture: cotton, tobacco, peanuts, poultry, livestock. Resources: kaolin, fuller's earth. Industries: cotton textiles, agricultural processing, paper and pulp, transport equipment. State university (1785) at Athens. Georgia, one of the Thirteen Colonies, was settled in the 18th c. and named after George II. It became (1788) the 4th state of the U.S.A.

Geor·gian (dʒɔ́rdʒən) adj. of the period of the first four Georges, kings of Great Britain (1714-1830) ‖ of the early reign of George V, Georgian poetry

Georgian 1. *adj.* of or pertaining to Georgia, U.S.S.R. **2.** *n.* the Caucasian language of Georgia, U.S.S.R. || an inhabitant of Georgia, U.S.S.R.

Georgian 1. *adj.* of or pertaining to Georgia, U.S.A. **2.** *n.* an inhabitant of Georgia, U.S.A.

Georgian Bay an inlet (c. 125 miles long, 50 miles wide) of Lake Huron, S.E. Ontario province, Canada

Georgia, Strait of a channel (c. 150 miles long, 20–40 miles wide) between British Columbia and Vancouver Is. connecting with several sounds and straits to form part of the inland water route from Washington State to Alaska

ge·o·stat·ic (dʒi:oustætik) *adj.* pertaining to the force exerted by a column of earth or of a similar substance [fr. Gk *gē*, the earth + STATIC]

ge·o·sta·tion·a·ry (dʒi:oustéiʃənéri:) *adj.* of a satellite, orbiting over a fixed place on earth in rhythm with it. *syn.* geosynchronous

ge·o·stroph·ic (dʒi:oustrófik) *adj.* depending on the deflective force due to the earth's rotation, *geostrophic winds* [fr. Gk *gē*, the earth + *strophikos*, turned]

geosynchronous *GEOSTATIONARY

ge·o·syn·cli·nal (dʒi:ousinkláin'l) **1.** *adj.* pertaining to a synclinal fold of strata extending over a large area of the earth's surface **2.** *n.* a geosyncline **ge·o·syn·cline** *n.* a great shallow basin or trough in the earth's crust in which marine sediments have accumulated over millions of years to a depth of many thousands of feet (cf. GEANTICLINE) [fr. Gk *gē*, the earth + SYNCLINAL]

ge·o·tac·tic (dʒi:outæktik) *adj.* of or pertaining to geotaxis

ge·o·tax·is (dʒi:outæksis) *n.* (*biol.*) a response by a freely moving organism to the force of gravity [fr. Gk *gē*, the earth + *taxis*, arrangement]

ge·o·tec·ton·ic (dʒi:outektónik) *adj.* (*geol.*) structural || relating to the arrangement, form and structure of rocks in the earth's crust [fr. Gk *gē*, the earth + TECTONIC]

ge·o·ther·mal energy hot water and steam beneath the earth's surface harnessed for use

ge·o·trop·ic (dʒi:outrópik) *adj.* (*biol.*) of or pertaining to geotropism **ge·ot·ro·pism** (dʒi:ótrəpizəm) *n.* (*biol.*) the growth reactions of a plant in response to the force of gravity. Roots are generally positively geotropic (growing downward) and stems negatively geotropic (growing upward) [fr. Gk *gē*, the earth + *tropē*, a turning]

Ge·ra (géirɑ) a town (pop. 128,247) in central East Germany; textiles, machinery and chemicals || the surrounding district (area 1,585 sq. miles, pop. 723,700) (*THURINGIA)

ge·ra·ni·um (dʒiréini:əm) *n.* a plant of genus *Geranium*, fam. *Geraniaceae*, having brightly colored flowers and pungent-smelling leaves. Geraniums are widely distributed, esp. in temperate areas. Perfume oil is extracted from the foliage of many species. Geranium is also the common name of the allied genus *Pelargonium*, to which the common garden geranium of Europe belongs [L. fr. Gk *geranion* fr. *geranos*, crane (from the shape of the fruit, like a crane's bill)]

ger·bil, ger·bille (dʒə́:rb'l) *n.* any of several small burrowing rodents of *Gerbillus* and related genera, having elongated hind legs for leaping, found in sandy parts of Africa and Asia [F. *gerbille*]

gerfalcon *GYRFALCON

ger·i·at·ric (dʒeri:ǽtrik) *adj.* (*med.*) pertaining to geriatrics || (*med.*) of or relating to aging or the aged **ger·i·át·rics** *n.* the branch of medicine dealing with old age and its diseases [fr. Gk *gēras*, old age + *iatrikos*, pertaining to healing]

Gé·ri·cault (ʒeiri:kou), Théodore (1791–1824), French Romantic painter. 'The Raft of the Medusa' (1819) is his best-known work. He is notable also for his paintings of horses and his portraits

ger·i·o·vi·tal (dʒeri:ouváitəl) *n.* (*med.*) antisenility, longevity drug related to procaine; sponsored by Dr. Ana Aslan of Romania

germ (dʒə:rm) *n.* a microorganism, often pathogenic || the earliest stage in the development of an organism, e.g. the formative protoplasm of an egg || a seed or embryo || a thing from which something may develop as if from a seed, *the germ of a plan formed in his mind* [F. *germe*]

Ger·man (dʒə́:rmən), Sir Edward (Edward German Jones, 1862–1936), English composer of light music

Ger·man (dʒə́:rmən) **1.** *adj.* of or relating to Germany, its language, inhabitants and customs **2.** *n.* a native of Germany || the language of Germany (*GERMAN LANGUAGE) [fr. L. *Germanus*, prob. of Celtic origin]

German Baptist Brethren the official name of the Dunkers before 1908

German Confederation a confederation of 34 German sovereign princes under the presidency of Austria, set up (1815) at the Congress of Vienna. It was superseded by the Frankfurt Parliament (1848), reestablished (1851), and dissolved by Prussia after the Seven Weeks' War (1866)

German Democratic Republic (East Germany) a republic (area 41,802 sq. miles, pop. 16,738,000) of central Europe on the Baltic. Capital: East Berlin. Language: German, with a small Sorbian minority in the southeast. Religion: 81% Protestant, 11% Roman Catholic. The land is 49% arable, 27% forest and 12% pasture. Coastal lagoons give way to the N. German plain: this comprises (with N. Poland) the Baltic lake plateau (lakes and glacial valleys, with peat deposits) and further south a fertile loess region. The south is a highland including the Harz Mtns, the Fichtelgebirge and the Thüringer Wald in the west and the Erzgebirge along the Czechoslovak border. The Oder is frozen 80 days a year and there is often sea ice along the Baltic coast and permanent winter snow east of Berlin. Average temperature (F.): 30° (Jan.), 65° (July). Rainfall: 20 ins except in the southern mountains (30–50 ins). Livestock: cattle, hogs, sheep, poultry, horses. Crops: cereals, potatoes, sugar beet. Agriculture is largely organized in collective farms and in cooperatives for machinery and distribution. Minerals: lignite (world's largest producer), rare metals (uranium, cobalt, bismuth, arsenic and antimony in E. Thuringia and W. Erzgebirge), iron ore, coal, copper, potash. The major industries are nationalized. Industries: iron and steel, mining, chemicals, textiles, shipbuilding, diesel engines, machinery and machine tools, shoes, photographic and optical goods, electrical equipment, cement, toys. Exports: manufactures, machines, factories (e.g. prefabricated sugar refineries and shipyards). Imports: iron and steel, foodstuffs, phosphate. Port: Rostock (enlarged to deal with the whole E. German and Czechoslovak hinterland). There is an extensive river system. There are 44 universities and colleges. Monetary unit: deutsche mark (East) (100 pfennigs). In the administrative reorganization of 1952 the five East German states were replaced by 14 districts. Government: Council of State with chairman as head of state; Erich Honecker has served as chairman since 1971. The Council of Ministers heads the government with its chairman acting as prime minister; Willi Stoph has served as chairman since 1964. Most members of the unicameral legislature belong to the communist Socialist Unity party (SED). The general secretary of the SED central committee also serves as Council of State chairman. East Germany became a member of the Warsaw Treaty Organization and Comecon in the 1950's. HISTORY *GERMANY

ger·man·der (dʒərmǽndər) *n.* a plant of the genus *Teucrium*, fam. *Labiatae*, esp. *T. chamaedrys*, the common or wall germander || any of certain species of *Veronica*, fam. *Scrophulariaceae*, esp. *V. chamaedrys*, the germander speedwell [fr. M.L. *germandra* fr. Gk *chamaidrus* fr. *chamai*, on the ground + *drus*, oak]

ger·mane (dʒərméin) *adj.* relevant [var. of older *german*, akin]

German East Africa (*hist.*) a former German colony in E. Africa, comprising Tanganyika, Ruanda-Urundi and Mozambique, acquired (1884) by Germany, and divided (1919) among Great Britain, Belgium and Portugal

Ger·man·ic (dʒərmǽnik) **1.** *adj.* of the Teutonic peoples || (*hist.*) of the Germans **2.** *n.* the language of the early Germanic peoples [fr. L. *Germanicus*]

—Germanic dialects developed from the Indo-European parent language in prehistoric times among the tribes of northern Germany and southern Scandinavia and have formed the basis of three main language groups: North Germanic or Scandinavian (Norwegian, Icelandic, Swedish, Danish and Faroese), East Germanic (Gothic), and West Germanic (English, Frisian, Dutch, High and Low German)

Ger·man·i·cus Caesar (dʒərmǽni:kəs) (15 B.C.–19 A.D.), Roman general, nephew of Tiberius, whose jealousy he provoked by his brilliant German campaigns (14–16 A.D.)

Ger·man·ism (dʒə́:rmənizəm) *n.* a characteristic feature of the German language taken over into another language || a characteristic German action, outlook etc.

ger·ma·ni·um (dʒərméini:əm) *n.* a metallic element (symbol Ge, at. no. 32, at. mass 72.59) occurring in certain zinc and copper ores. It is a semiconducting material and is widely used in the manufacture of transistors [Mod. L. fr. *germanus*, German]

Ger·man·ize (dʒə́:rmənaiz) *pres. part.* **Ger·man·iz·ing** *past* and *past part.* **Ger·man·ized** *v.t.* to make German in character, speech or expression || *v.i.* to become German in character etc.

German language the standardized form of High German, belonging to the Germanic family. It is the official and literary tongue in Germany, Austria and German Switzerland. It is pronounced according to rules set by a commission in 1898 for the guidance of German actors. Taken in a wider sense, it consists of a number of dialects of central and southern Germany, known as High German, and the dialects of the north, known as Low German. The development of a tongue which could be read and understood by the nation as a whole was largely the work of Martin Luther: his use, esp. in his translation of the Bible, of the vocabulary of the common people of Thuringia and of the style employed officially in the Saxony electorate, had a crystallizing influence. Modern German is characterized by a strict word order, a well-preserved system of inflections and an elaborate system of compounding words

German measles a mild, infectious virus disease, occurring chiefly in childhood, and causing glandular swellings, fever and a rash like measles. If it occurs within the first three months of pregnancy it may damage the fetus

German shepherd (*Am.=Br.* Alsatian) a dog of a breed standing up to 26 ins in height. They are powerful and intelligent, and are trained for police work and as guides for blind people

German silver nickel silver

Ger·ma·ny (dʒə́:rməni:) a region of north central Europe divided since 1949 into two states: the German Democratic Republic (East Germany) and the Federal Republic of Germany (West Germany). (For geographical descriptions see separate entries.) HISTORY. The area was overrun by German tribes (5th and 6th cc.) after the collapse of the Roman Empire. Saxony was gradually conquered by the Franks (6th and 7th cc.). The Merovingian dynasty was replaced (751) by the Carolingians under Pépin III. The empire of his son Charlemagne was divided into three by the Treaty of Verdun (843). The eastern part, the Kingdom of the E. Franks, formed the nucleus of a German state, and was enlarged at the Treaty of Mersen (870). While the frontiers were attacked by Magyars, Norsemen and Slavs, great feudal duchies developed: Franconia, Swabia, Bavaria, Saxony, Lorraine. Conrad of Franconia, elected king (911), tried in vain to impose his authority on the dukes. His successor, Duke Henry of Saxony (who reigned 919–36), restored some of the royal power by his victories over the Magyars and Slavs. This policy was continued in the reign (936–73) of Otto I, who intervened in Italy on behalf of the pope (951), and was crowned Holy Roman Emperor (962). Imperial power over the Church reached its peak under Henry III (1039–56), but then declined as a result of the Investiture Controversy, civil disturbances and rebelling dukes. The last German duchy, Saxony, was destroyed (1180) in the reign of Frederick I, and the Slavs were pushed back eastwards (12th and 13th cc.). Germany relapsed into anarchy, however, on the death of Frederick II (1215–50). After the Great Interregnum, the German princes elected Rudolf of Hapsburg as Emperor (1273). The early Hapsburgs (1273–1308) expanded their territories, but could not establish a centralized monarchy. Germany disintegrated into more than 350 warring states. Emperors relied on the prosperous cities and commercial leagues of the 15th c. (*HANSEATIC LEAGUE) for support against the rebellious nobility and peasants. Individual states, esp. Hapsburg Austria under Maximilian I and Charles V, consolidated their power. The Reformation split Germany into a Catholic south and a Lutheran

---

CONCISE PRONUNCIATION KEY: **(a)** æ, c*a*t; ɑ, c*a*r; ɔ f*aw*n; ei, sn*a*ke. **(e)** e, h*e*n; i:, sh*ee*p; iə, d*ee*r; ɛə, b*ea*r. **(i)** i, f*i*sh; ai, t*i*ger; ə:, b*i*rd. **(o)** o, *o*x; au, c*ow*; ou, g*oa*t; u, p*oo*r; ɔi, r*oy*al. **(u)** ʌ, d*u*ck; u, b*u*ll; u:, g*oo*se; ə, b*a*cillus; ju:, c*u*be. x, lo*ch*; θ, *th*ink; ð, bo*th*er; z, *Z*en; ʒ, cor*s*age; dʒ, sava*g*e; ŋ, oranguta*ng*; j, *y*ak; ʃ, *fi*sh; tʃ, fe*tch*; 'l, rabb*le*; 'n, redd*en*. Complete pronunciation key appears inside front cover.

north. The Thirty Years' War completed the devastation of Germany, which was left as a loose confederation of petty principalities under the nominal rule of the Emperor (PEACE OF *WESTPHALIA, 1648). Prussia, under the Hohenzollern Electors of Brandenburg, emerged as a powerful state, and defeated Austria in the Seven Years' War (1756–63). The Hohenzollerns produced three great rulers in one century: the Great Elector Frederick William (who reigned 1640–88), Frederick William I (1713–40) and Frederick II (1740–86). German philosophy, music and literature flourished (*ENLIGHTENMENT). Napoleon finally destroyed (1806) the Holy Roman Empire, and combined all the German states except Prussia and Austria in the Confederation of the Rhine (1806). This was replaced by the German Confederation (1815) with Prussia and Austria. At the Congress of Vienna (1815) Prussia was rewarded for her part in the defeat of Napoleon by important territorial gains along the Rhine. Metternich's Austria enforced a reactionary policy on Germany (*KARLSBAD DECREES, 1819). Prussia formed a customs union, the Zollverein (1834), with the S. German states. The 1848 revolution removed Metternich, but the Frankfurt Parliament failed to unify Germany, and disbanded. Austrian domination was restored by the Treaty of Olmütz (1850). Bismarck, in charge of Prussian policy from 1862, pursued a 'little Germany' policy (i.e. Germany without Austria). Prussia attacked and defeated Schleswig-Holstein (1864), Austria (1866) and then France (1870–1). The S. German states agreed to join a German empire, of which the Prussian king was proclaimed emperor (Jan. 18, 1871). Germany gained Alsace-Lorraine from the Franco-Prussian War, and began to industrialize rapidly. Bismarck, chancellor of the German Federal Empire (1871–90), struggled with Catholic and Socialist opposition (*KULTURKAMPF), and introduced a social insurance plan (1881–9). Conflicting alliances were formed with Austria and Russia (*DREIKAISERBUND, 1873) and with Austria (1879) and Italy (1882). Under Kaiser Wilhelm II (1888–1918), Germany's colonial expansion clashed with British and French interests. German interest in the Balkans (*BAGHDAD RAILWAY) angered Russia. Crises in Morocco (1905 and 1911) increased Germany's isolation. In the 1st world war (1914–18), Germany invaded Belgium and France (1914), Poland, Rumania and Serbia (1915), and defeated Russia (1918). Germany's exhaustion in 1918 was increased by the terms of the Versailles Treaty (1919). Kaiser Wilhelm fled after the outbreak of a Social Democratic revolution, all the German states became republics, and a democratic federal constitution was adopted at Weimar (1919). The Social Democratic government, under Ebert (1919–25) and Hindenburg (1925–34), led the national recovery. But the world economic crisis (1929) created mass unemployment and national bankruptcy. Hitler, leader of the National Socialists, seized power (1933) and instituted a totalitarian state by terrorist methods. He repudiated the Treaty of Versailles, rearmed Germany, occupied the Rhineland (1936), allied with Italy and Japan (1936), intervened in the Spanish Civil War (1936–9), annexed Austria, and demanded parts of Czechoslovakia (1938). Germany's invasion of Danzig and Poland (1939) provoked the 2nd world war (1939–45). Germany invaded Denmark, Norway, the Netherlands, Belgium, France (1940), Yugoslavia, Greece (1941), N. Africa (1940), and much of Russia (1941). Germany finally surrendered to the Allies (May 8, 1945). After the war, Germany was disarmed, and lost her eastern provinces, beyond the Oder-Neisse line, to Poland. The Allies divided Germany into four occupation zones (American, British, French and Russian). The Soviet blockade of Berlin (Apr. 1948–May 1949) led to the division of Germany (1949) into East and West Germany. West Germany became a member of the European Coal and Steel Community (1952), a sovereign state and member of NATO (1955), was rearmed, regained the Saar (1957), and entered the European Economic Community (1958). Rapid economic recovery took place under the government of Konrad Adenauer (1949–63). East Germany remained in the Russian sphere of influence. The East German authorities built (1961) a wall dividing East and West Berlin in an attempt to stop the flow of refugees to West

Germany. The West German government signed (1963) a treaty of cooperation with France. In 1970 W. Germany recognized de facto the eastern frontiers of Poland. West Germany's policy of *Ostpolitik* established a new relationship with East Germany and the Soviet Union, outlined by a series of treaties between West Germany, the U.S.S.R., Poland and East Germany. In 1970, West German Chancellor Brandt met with East German Chairman Willi Stoph; in 1972 a Quadripartite Agreement was signed regarding the status of Berlin, and a Basic Treaty settled relations between the two states, stopping short of reunification. In 1973 both Germanies became full U.N. member nations

Germany, Federal Republic of (West Germany) a republic (area. incl. West Berlin, 95,908 sq. miles, pop. 61,713,000) of central Europe on the North Sea and the Baltic. Capital: Bonn. Language: German, with a small Danish minority. Religion: 51% Protestant, 45% Roman Catholic, with a very small Jewish minority. The land is 36% arable, 28% forest and 23% pasture. The coast, shallow and silted, gives way to salt marshes. Behind it, the north is a plain, with sandy heaths and moors. The center and south are highland, stretching in the west from the Rhine plateau to the Black Forest, and in the east from the Harz Mtns through the Thüringer Wald and the Fichtelgebirge to the Bohemian Forest. West of the N. Rhine are the Eifel and Hunsrück Mtns, separated by the Moselle. East of the Rhine are the Sauerland, Westerwald and Taunus Mtns, separated by the Sieg and Lahn Rivers. The Bavarian Alps, rising to 9,719 ft (Zugspitze), form the frontier with Austria. The Rhine at Cologne is frozen 20 days a year. Average temperature (F.) in the center: 32° (Jan.), 64° (July). Rainfall: 25 ins in the north, 40–50 ins in the southern mountains. Livestock: cattle, horses, sheep, hogs, poultry. Agricultural products: cereals, potatoes, sugar beet, wine. Forestry and fishing are important. Minerals: bituminous coal (the Rhur, the Saar), iron ore (the Harz Mtns), copper ore, oil, lignite, potash, lead, zinc. Industries: mining iron and steel, metal smelting, machines, textiles, electrical engineering, vehicles, chemicals, shipbuilding, electricity, oil refining (Hamburg, Bremen), plastics, toys, aluminum, cement, pottery, photographic cquipment, optical instruments. Exports: manufactures, coal. Imports: foodstuffs, raw materials, fuel oil. Ports: Hamburg, Bremen, Kiel. There is an extensive river and canal system. There are 17 universities. Monetary unit: deutsche mark (West) (100 pfennigs). Government: ceremonial president, bicameral legislature and federal chancellor, who is head of government. West Germany consists of ten individual states each with its own president and parliament. Helmut Schmidt was chancellor 1974–82, when Helmut Kohl took office. West Germany became a full member of the United Nations in 1973. HISTORY *GERMANY

germ cell a gamete (cf. SOMATIC CELL)

germ-free (dʒə́rmfrí:) *adj.* without contamination by micro-organisms

ger-mi-cid-al (dʒə:rmisáid'l) *adj.* of or pertaining to a germicide **gér-mi-cide** *n.* a germ-killing agent [fr. GERM+L. *caedere*, to kill]

ger-mi-nal (dʒə́:rmin'l) *adj.* of or pertaining to a seed, germ cell or reproduction ‖ in the earliest stage of development, *germinal ideas* [fr. Mod. L. *germinalis* fr. *germen*, sprout]

germinal disc a blastodisc

germinal vesicle the enlarged nucleus of a primary oocyte

ger-mi-nate (dʒə́:rmineit) *pres. part.* **ger-mi-nat-ing** *past* and *past part.* **ger-mi-nat-ed** *v.i.* to begin to grow, sprout, develop ‖ *v.t.* to cause to sprout ‖ to produce (ideas, forces etc.) [fr. L. *germinare* (*germinatus*)]

ger-mi-na-tion (dʒə̀:rminə́iʃən) *n.* the beginning of growth. Under suitable conditions of temperature, water and air, seeds increase their rate of metabolism. Absorption of water releases enzymes which transform stored starch, protein or fat into a soluble form for use by the embryo [fr. L. *germinatio* (*germinationis*)]

ger-mi-na-tive (dʒə́:rminei̯tiv, dʒə́:rminəiv) *adj.* having power to bud or develop ‖ of or relating to germination

Ger-mis-ton (dʒə́:rmistən) a town (pop. 145,000) in the Transvaal, South Africa, with the world's largest gold refinery: engineering, smelting, cotton

germ layer one of the three primary layers of cells in the embryos of higher animals that are formed during gastrulation and that eventually give rise to the tissues and organs of the adult (*ECTODERM, *MESODERM, ENDODERM)

germ plasm the part of the cell containing the hereditary materials ‖ (*hist.*, in early biological theories) germ cells and their precursors carrying hereditary material, independent of somatic cells

germ theory the theory that all living organisms develop from germ cells ‖ the theory that infectious diseases are transmitted by germs or microorganisms

germ warfare the controlled use of germs in war to weaken or destroy the enemy by contaminating water supplies, inducing sickness etc.

Gé-rôme (ʒeiróum), **Jean Léon** (1824–1904), French artist and sculptor whose works reflected classicism and conservativism. He is most noted for the paintings 'Cockfight' (1874), 'The Death of Caesar' (1867), and 'Thumbs Down' (1874)

Ge-ro-na (herɔ́na) a province (area 2,264 sq. miles, pop. 467,945) of Catalonia, N.E. Spain ‖ its capital (pop. 87,648). Gothic cathedral (11th–15th cc.)

Ge-ron-i-mo (dʒerɔ́nəmou) (c. 1829–1909), Apache Indian leader. His infamous raids (c. 1858–86) on American settlements in the Southwest led to his capture by the U.S. Army and his military confinement

ger-on-toc-ra-cy (dʒèrəntɔ́krəsi:) *pl.* **ger-on-toc-ra-cies** *n.* government by old men ‖ a governing body composed of old men ‖ a government controlled by such a body [fr. F. *gérontocratie* fr. Gk *gerōn*, old man+*kratia*, government]

ger-on-tol-o-gist (dʒèrəntɔ́lədʒist) *n.* a specialist in gerontology **ger-on-tól-o-gy** *n.* the study of the phenomena of old age [fr. Gk *gerōn*, old man+*logos*, discourse]

Gerry, Elbridge (geári:) (1744–1844), U.S. political leader, vice president (1813–4) under James Madison. He was a Massachusetts delegate to the Continental Congresses (1776–80; 1783–5) and Constitutional Congress (1787), a signer of the Declaration of Independence, a member of the U.S. House of Representatives (1789–93) and governor of Massachusetts (1810–12). The political term 'gerrymander' is named for his redistricting of Massachusetts to ensure his party's majority

ger-ry-man-der, **jer-ry-man-der** (dʒérimændər) 1. *n.* a manipulation of electoral districts in order to give one political party an advantage by concentrating the opposition's voting strength in as few districts as possible ‖ a district or districts so manipulated 2. *v.t.* to arrange (the electoral districts of a region) in such a way ‖ *v.i.* to create a gerrymander [after Elbridge *Gerry* (d. 1814), U.S. statesman+SALAMANDER, from the odd shape of a Massachusetts election district created in 1812 to the Republican advantage under his governorship]

Gers (ʒer) a department (area 2,428 sq. miles, pop. 175,400) of S.W. France between the Garonne and the Pyrenees. (*ARMAGNAC) Chief town: Auch

Gersh-win (gə́:rʃwin), George (Jakob Bruskin Gershvin, 1898–1937), American composer. He used jazz idiom in his works, which include 'Rhapsody in Blue' (1923) and the opera 'Porgy and Bess' (1935)

Ger-son (ʒers5), Jean Charlier de (1363–1429), French nominalist theologian. He held that a Church council might supersede the authority of the pope. He attended the Council of Constance (1414–18), and played an important part in the condemnation of Hus

ger-und (dʒérənd) *n.* (*Latin gram.*) a verbal noun used in all but the nominative case ‖ (*English gram.*) a verbal noun ending in '-ing'. It is used like a noun but retains certain verbal characteristics, e.g. the ability to take an object (e.g. 'cooking' in 'cooking soufflés is difficult') **ge-run-di-al** (dʒərʌ́ndi:əl) *adj.* [fr. L. *gerundium* fr. *gerere*, to carry out]

ger-un-dive (dʒərʌ́ndiv) 1. *adj.* of or like the gerund 2. *n.* (*Latin gram.*) the verbal adjective from the gerund stem, expressing necessity or fitness [fr. L.L. *gerundivus*]

Ger-y-on (géri:ən) (*Gk mythol.*) a winged three-bodied monster killed by Heracles

Ge-samt-kunst-werk (gəzámtkunstverk) *n.* (*Gr.*; literally, total artwork; usu. italics) comprehensive art form including various forms, e.g., drama, poetry, and music

Ges·ner (gésnər), Konrad von (1516–65), Swiss naturalist, physician, biologist, philologist and bibliographer. His 'Historia animalium' (1551–8) is a seminal work of modern zoology

ges·so (dʒésou) n. plaster of paris or gypsum prepared for use in painting ‖ a prepared paste used as a ground for painting on wood or canvas [Ital.]

ge·stalt (gəʃtált) pl. **ge·stalts, ge·stal·ten** (gəʃtáltən) n. an integrated structure or shape considered as an entity whose properties cannot totally be deduced from the sum of its parts (*GESTALT PSYCHOLOGY) [G.=shape, form]

Gestalt psychology the theory of unitary mental organization based on the observation that perception is structural and cannot be resolved as the mere agglomeration of minute definable responses to local stimuli. Our apprehension of visual shapes, for instance, or of melodies in music, is a total and integrated response which merely analytical procedures are inadequate to describe

Ge·sta·po (gəstápou) n. the secret state police of Nazi Germany [G. fr. Geheime Staatspolizei, secret state police]

Ges·ta Ro·ma·no·rum (dʒéstəroumənórəm) a collection of short didactic stories compiled in Latin probably in the 13th c. and printed in the 15th c. They were enormously popular and provided plot material for many writers (e.g. for Shakespeare in 'Pericles' and 'The Merchant of Venice')

ges·tate (dʒésteit) pres. part. **ges·tat·ing** past and past part. **ges·tat·ed** v.t. to carry in the uterus during gestation ‖ to cause to develop slowly in the mind ‖ v.i. to be in the process of gestation [back-formation fr. GESTATION]

ges·ta·tion (dʒestéiʃən) n. the inter-uterine period in the development of the mammalian embryo, which from fertilization to birth is supplied with food and oxygen through the blood system of the parent carrying it. The gestation period varies widely: in dogs and cats about 63 days, in humans about 280 days, in elephants about 624 days ‖ the period of development of a plan etc. [fr. L. gestatio (gestationis) fr. gestare, to carry]

ges·tic·u·late (dʒestíkjuleit) pres. part. **ges·tic·u·lat·ing** past and past part. **ges·tic·u·lat·ed** v.i. to wave the arms about, make expressive gestures while speaking or instead of speech ‖ v.t. to express by gestures, to gesticulate one's approval **ges·tic·u·la·tion** n. **ges·tic·u·la·tive** (dʒestíkjuleitiv, dʒestíkjulətiv) adj. **ges·tic·u·la·tor** n. **ges·tic·u·la·to·ry** (dʒestíkjulətóri:, dʒestíkjulətɔuri) adj. [fr. L. gesticulari (gesticulatus) fr. gesticulus, a little gesture]

Ges·ti·do (hestí:ðo), Oscar (1901–67), Uruguayan soldier and politician. He became president (1967), after elections (1966) which resulted in a new constitution, under which the system of an executive council was replaced by that of a one-man executive

ges·ture (dʒéstʃər, dʒéʃtʃər) 1. n. a movement of the hand or body to express an emotion or intention ‖ some word or deed either intended to convey an attitude or intention or dictated by diplomacy or respect for form 2. v.i. pres. part. **ges·tur·ing** past and past part. **ges·tured** to make gestures, gesticulate [fr. M.L. gestura, bearing]

get (get) pres. part. **get·ting** past got (gɒt) past part. **got, got·ten** (gɒt'n) v.t. to acquire ‖ to procure, to get by-products from coal ‖ to fetch ‖ to buy, you must get some new shoes ‖ to receive, to get a present ‖ to earn ‖ to arrive at by calculation, what answer did you get? ‖ to hit, the bullet got him in the arm ‖ to hit and kill, did you get that pigeon? ‖ to suffer, to get a bump on one's head ‖ to catch, have they got the thief? ‖ to catch (an illness) ‖ to receive as a sentence or fate, to get the worst of it ‖ to make, bring into a certain state or position, to get someone angry, get your things together ‖ to prepare, to get breakfast ‖ (pop.) to grasp the meaning of, understand, to get the point ‖ to secure for oneself, to get one's own way ‖ to establish communication with by radio, telephone etc. ‖ to induce, persuade, get him to keep quiet ‖ to catch the spirit of, reproduce, the painter has got her expression well ‖ to obtain (in answer), to get no reply ‖ (pop.) to baffle, puzzle ‖ (pop.) to irritate ‖ (pop.) to charm, enchant ‖ v.i. (with 'across', 'over', 'here', 'there' etc.) to succeed in moving, arriving etc., to get across a road, to get there on time ‖ to become, to get better, to get acquainted ‖ (with infin.) to

grow, come gradually, you'll get to like him ‖ to go, take oneself off, you should get to bed now ‖ (with pres. part.) to begin, once he gets going he can't stop ‖ (pop., imper.) clear out!, go away! **get along!** be off with you! ‖ rubbish! **to get about** (Br.) to move about, be active ‖ to travel ‖ (Br., of gossip, news) to spread ‖ (naut.) to turn around **to get across** to pass over, cross ‖ (Br.) to annoy, he gets across everyone ‖ to communicate effectively, to get an idea across ‖ to have a desired effect on an audience etc. **to get along** to progress, the patient is getting along well ‖ to manage, we aren't rich but we get along ‖ to agree, be on friendly terms **to get around** to travel a lot ‖ (Am. =Br. **to get round**) to evade, can we get around this last clause? ‖ to persuade, coax, she knows how to get around him ‖ (of gossip, news) to spread ‖ to acquire worldly experience **to get around to** finally to reach or find time to, he never got around to thanking them **to get at** to reach ‖ to obtain access to, he can't get at the money until he is 25 ‖ (Br., pop.) to criticize unkindly, esp. obliquely ‖ to mean, hint at, what are you getting at? **to get away** to escape ‖ (with 'with') to do or say with impunity **to get back** to return, they got back home yesterday ‖ to recover, he never got the money back **to get by** to pass ‖ to manage, we'll get by with a bit of luck **to get by heart** to learn by heart **to get down** to come down, dismount ‖ to deject, oppress, this sultry weather gets her down ‖ to copy down **to get down to** to settle down to, get down to work **to get going** to begin, start moving ‖ to become lively **to get in** to enter, board, get in the car ‖ to collect, bring in, get in the wash ‖ to arrive, my train got in late ‖ to be elected, he got in with a good majority **to get into** to enter, board ‖ to become involved in, to get into trouble **to get (something) through** (esp. Br. **into**) **someone's head** to force to understand or realize (something) **to get in with** to win the favor of **to get off** to dismount ‖ to escape punishment, to get off with a warning ‖ to make a start, they got off this morning ‖ to be allowed time off from work etc. ‖ to dismount from **to get off with** (Br.) to begin to be on amorous terms with **to get on** to board, mount ‖ to progress, to get on well at school ‖ to be on good terms ‖ to begin to grow old ‖ (of time) to grow late **to get on for** (or **towards**) to approach in age, he is getting on for 60 or in time, it is getting on for noon **to get on to** to succeed in finding out ‖ (Br.) to contact **to get out** to leave, depart ‖ to escape ‖ to take out, produce, I got out my passport ‖ to withdraw (a book) from a library **to get out of** to leave, depart from ‖ to avoid, to get out of military service **to get out of hand** to break from control **to get over** to cross over, surmount ‖ to recover from **to get (something) over** to do and finish with (something) ‖ to be persuasively convincing about **to get round** (Br.) to get around (something or someone) **to get somewhere** (**nowhere**) to achieve some (no) result **to get the better of** to defeat **to get there** to achieve one's purpose, succeed **to get through** to finish, we'll never get through all that spaghetti ‖ to spend, she soon got through her allowance ‖ to pass (an exam etc.) ‖ to pass an exam etc. ‖ to establish communication **to get up** to rise from bed, from a sitting position etc. ‖ to mount, ascend ‖ to produce, increase, to get up steam, get up speed ‖ (of the wind, a storm, the sea) to increase, begin to grow rough ‖ to prepare, to get up an entertainment ‖ (Br.) to refurbish, learn again, to get up one's Latin ‖ to decorate, dress up **to get up to** to do mischievously, he gets up to all sorts of tricks **to have got** to have, I've got a new idea **to have got to** to be obliged to, I've got to go now **to tell someone where he gets off** (or **where to get off**) to tell someone off, rebuke him [M.E. geten fr. O.N. geta]

get·a·way (gétəwei) n. an escape ‖ the act of starting, a poor getaway

Geth·sem·a·ne (geθsémani) the garden at the foot of the Mount of Olives near Jerusalem, where Jesus often went with his disciples and which was the scene of the Agony, betrayal and arrest of Jesus (Matthew xxvi, 36)

get on the stick v. (slang) to take hold of a situation

get-to·geth·er (géttəgeðər) n. (pop.) a social gathering, reunion

Get·tys·burg (géti:zbə̩rg) a small town in Pennsylvania, where (July 1–3, 1863) the Confederate army under Lee was defeated by the Federal army under Meade in what proved to be the crucial battle of the American Civil War

Gettysburg Address Lincoln's speech (Nov. 19, 1863) at the dedication of the national cemetery on the Civil War battlefield at Gettysburg, Pa. It is a famous eulogy of American democracy ('government of the people, by the people, for the people shall not perish from the earth')

get·up (gétʌp) n. (pop.) a style of dressing (usually extraordinary) ‖ (pop., of publications) style of production

ge·um (dʒí:əm) n. a member of Geum, fam. Rosaceae, a genus of hardy herbaceous perennials of temperate regions [Mod. L.]

gew·gaw (gjú:gɔ gú:gɔ) n. a showy thing of little worth [origin unknown]

gey·ser (gáizər) n. a spring which throws up jets of hot water and steam from time to time, found in regions that are, or recently have been, volcanic ‖ (Br., gí:zə) a gas-operated apparatus for heating water [Icel. Geysir, a hot spring in Iceland]

gey·ser·ite (gáizərait) n. an opaline silica deposit found near geysers and hot springs

Gha·na (gánə) (former Gold Coast and British Togoland) a republic (area 91,843 sq. miles, pop. 13,804,000) in W. Africa. Capital: Accra. People: Ashanti, Fanti, Dagomba and other African groups, with small European and Levantine minorities. Language: English (official), Akan dialects, tribal languages. Religion: local African religions with 15% Christians (mainly Roman Catholic), Moslem minority. The land is 22% arable and 17% forest (excluding savanna woodland). The Volta River crosses Ghana north-south. A marshy coastal plain gives way to uplands covered with tropical forest: the Togo-Akwapim Mtns (rising to 3,000 ft) east of the Volta, and the Ashanti plateau west of it Annual rainfall (monsoon season Mar.–July): 30 ins in the southeast, 80 ins in the southwest, 58 ins in Kumasi, 43 ins at Tamale. Average temperature (F.): 79°–84°. Livestock: sheep, goats, cattle and poultry. Crops: cocoa (chief world producer), coffee, palm oil, coconuts, rubber, corn, rice, cassava, plantains, peanuts, yams, tobacco, millet. Minerals: gold, manganese, diamonds, bauxite, salt. Manufactures: foodstuffs, leather, jewelry, weaving, pottery. Hydroelectricity is produced from the Volta River. Exports: cocoa, gold, diamonds, manganese, lumber, palm kernels, bauxite. Imports: foodstuffs, textiles, cement, vehicles, machinery, oil, construction materials. Ports: Sekondi-Takoradi, Tema. Universities: Accra, Kumasi. Monetary unit: cedi (100 pesawas). HISTORY. Ghana takes its name from the powerful empire which flourished in the region of the Middle Niger (4th–mid-11th cc.). The first Europeans to visit the region were Portuguese traders (1471) followed by Dutch, English, Danish and Swedish slave merchants who set up forts and settlements. The British gained control of the area, known as the Gold Coast. The coastal states became a Crown colony and the Northern Territories a protectorate (1901). A new constitution (1946) gave Africans a share in government, and the constitution of 1951 gave a large measure of internal self-government. Dr Kwame Nkrumah was named prime minister (1952). British Togoland voted (1956) to become an integral part of an independent Gold Coast. The Gold Coast became the independent dominion of Ghana within the British Commonwealth (Mar. 6, 1957). Ghana became a republic with a presidential régime on July 1, 1961 and a one-party socialist state (1964). The Ghana army removed the civilian government by a coup d'état (Feb. 1966). Civilian government was restored (1969), with Dr Busia as prime minister. Edward Akuto Addo was elected (1970) president. A coup d'état (1972) overthrew Dr Busia's administration. Civilian rule returned to the country in 1979. Hilla Limann became president, but he was deposed in a military coup (1981) led by Jerry Rawlings

ghar·ial (gə́:riəl) n. a gavial

ghast·li·ly (gǽstlili:, gɑ́stlili:) adv. in a ghastly way

ghast·li·ness (gǽstli:nis, gɑ́stli:nis) n. the state or quality of being ghastly

ghast·ly (gǽstli:, gɑ́stli:) 1. adj. comp. **ghast·li·**

er *superl.* **ghast·li·est** horrifying, gruesome, *a ghastly murder* || deathlike, ghostlike, *a ghastly pallor* || (*pop.*) very unpleasant **2.** *adv.* in a ghastly manner, *ghastly pale* [fr. obs. *gast,* to terrify fr. O.E. *gæstan*]

Ghats, Eastern and Western (gɒts) two mountain ranges (average height 1,500–2,000 ft) of S. India, parallel with the southeast and southwest coasts respectively

gha·zal (gəzǽl) *HAFIZ (poet)

Ghaz·na·vid, Ghaz·ne·vid (gǽznəvid) *n.* a member of a Moslem dynasty (c. 977-1155), taking its name from the ancient city of Ghazni in E. Afghanistan. Their empire at its greatest extent, under Mahmud of Ghazni, covered a vast area of central Asia

Ghaz·za·li (gæzáli:), Abu Hamid Mohammed al- (1058–1111), Moslem theologian. His 'The Revival of the Sciences of Religion' combines scholastic dogma and modified Sufi mysticism

ghee (gi:) *n.* clarified semifluid butter made from water buffalo's milk [Hindi *ghi*]

Ghent, *Flem.* **Gent** (gent) an ancient city and port (pop. 241,695), capital of East Flanders, N.W. Belgium, at the confluence of the Lys and Scheldt Rivers, connected to the sea by two canals: textiles, metal, chemical and sugar industries. University (1816)

Ghent, Treaty of (1814), U.S.-British peace treaty, signed at Ghent, Belgium, that ended the War of 1812. Under the treaty of the U.S.A. and Britain agreed to stop fighting, restore occupied territory and negotiate Canadian-U.S. border problems. The Battle of New Orleans (1815) was fought after the treaty because of the slowness of communications

gher·kin (gə́rkin) *n. Cucumis anguria,* fam. *Cucurbitaceae,* a plant yielding a knobbly fruit, like a small cucumber, used mainly for pickles || the fruit of this plant || an immature cucumber selected for pickling [fr. Du. *gurken*]

ghet·to (gétou) *pl.* **ghet·tos, ghet·toes** *n.* (*hist.*) the quarter of a city in which Jews were required to reside || a quarter of a city largely inhabited by Jews || a quarter where members of a minority reside as a result of social or economic pressure [Ital.]

Ghib·el·line (gíbəli:n, gíbəlain) a member of the political faction in Italy which supported the Emperor in the dispute (11th–14th cc.) with the pope (cf. GUELPH) [fr. Ital. *Ghibellino,* corrup. of G. *Waiblingen,* estate of the Hohenstaufen emperors]

Ghib·el·line (gíbəli:n, gíbəlain) *n.* a member of the political faction in Italy which supported the Emperor in the dispute (11th-14th cc.) with the pope (cf, GUELPH) [fr. Ital. *Ghibellino,* corrup. of G. *Waiblingen,* estate of the Hohenstaufen emperors]

Ghi·ber·ti (gi:bérti:), Lorenzo (c. 1378–1455), Florentine goldsmith, painter and sculptor. He made two of the three pairs of bronze doors of the baptistry at Florence. His first pair (1404–24, to match Pisano's) is in a style close to international Gothic. The second pair (1425–52) is on a radically altered plan, in an elegant, classical style. Ghiberti's 'Commentarii' are a main source of information about trecento art in Florence and Siena

Ghir·lan·da·io (gi:rlɑndájɔ), Domenico (Domenico Bigordi, 1449–94), Florentine painter, esp. of frescoes, e.g. that of St Jerome (1480) at the church of Ognissanti, Florence, and 'Christ Calling the First Apostles' (1481) in the Sistine Chapel, Rome

ghost (goust) **1.** *n.* the specter of a person appearing after their death, an apparition || a slight trace, a glimmer, *not the ghost of a chance* || a ghost-writer || (*phys.*) a false line in a line spectrum due to the defective ruling of the diffraction grating || (*optics*) a secondary image or bright spot caused by a defect in the lens of an instrument **to give up the ghost** to die **2.** *v.t.* to be the ghost-writer of (a book) || *v.i.* to act as ghost-writer [O.E. *gāst,* spirit]

GHOST (*meteor. acronym*) for global horizontal sounding techniques for collecting information about the atmosphere through balloons

ghost·li·ness (góustli:nis) *n.* the state or quality of being ghostly

ghost·ly (góustli:) *comp.* **ghost·li·er** *superl.* **ghost·li·est** *adj.* like a ghost || eerie, preternatural || (*archaic*) concerned with spiritual matters, *ghostly counsel* [O.E. *gāstlic,* spiritual]

ghost town a town no longer inhabited, esp. a former boom town

ghost-writ·er (góustraitər) *n.* someone wholly or partly responsible for writing published under another person's name

ghoul (gu:l) *n.* (in Oriental stories) a spirit which robs graves and devours corpses || (*pop.*) a person of weird or macabre appearance or habits **ghóul·ish** *adj.* [Arab. *ghūl* fr. *gh[a]la,* to seize]

G.I. (dʒi:ái) **1.** *n.* an American serviceman, esp. an enlisted man **2.** *aoj.* of, characteristic of or belonging to the U.S. Army [GOVERNMENT ISSUE]

Gia·co·met·ti (dʒɑkɔmétti:), Alberto (1901–66), Swiss sculptor and painter who worked in Paris. In his sculpture he first worked in a cubist style, and he participated briefly in the surrealist movement. His long, attenuated human figures, rigid and rough-textured, create a sense of vast space expressive of individual isolation

Gian·ni·ni (dʒəní:ni:), Amadeo Peter (1870–1949), U.S. financier. He consolidated (1930) many small banks into the Bank of America National Trust and Savings Association, one of the world's largest banks. He bequeathed a large sum to the University of California

gi·ant (dʒáiənt) **1.** *n.* a mythical person of superhuman size, often appearing in children's stories or in folklore || an abnormally tall person || anything large of its kind || someone of exceptional ability, *an intellectual giant* **2.** *adj.* exceptionally big **gí·ant·ess** *n.* [M.E. *geant* fr. O.F.]

giant fulmar *Macronectes giganteus,* a large (up to 3 ft) brownish petrel of the Indian and Antarctic Oceans

gi·ant·ism (dʒáiəntʃizəm) *n.* the state of being very large or too large, *the dangers of giantism in industry*

giant panda *PANDA

Giant's Causeway a promontory of basaltic rock pillars weathered to different heights and presenting a stepped surface, projecting from the Antrim coast in N. Ireland

giant sequoia *Sequoiadendron giganteum,* an evergreen tree of S. California that can grow to over 300 ft

giant star any of a large group of massive stars of enormous volume and extremely low density which are in general cooler than dwarf stars of the same spectral classification

gia·our (dʒáuər) *n.* (for Moslems) a non-Moslem, esp. a Christian [Pers. *gaur, gōr*]

gib *JIB (to stop)

gibb *JIB (*v., naut.*)

gib·ber, jib·ber (dʒíbər) **1.** *v.i.* to mutter quickly and inarticulately, esp. with rage or fright **2.** *n.* gibberish [imit.]

gib·ber·ish (dʒíbəriʃ, gíbəriʃ) *n.* rapid inarticulate chatter || speech that is not understood and therefore sounds like a confused gabble [imit.]

gib·bet (dʒíbit) **1.** *n.* (*hist.*) a gallows || (*hist.*) an upright post with an arm from which the bodies of executed criminals were hung and exposed, as a warning to others **2.** *v.t.* to put to death on the gibbet || to expose to public scorn [M.E. *gibet* fr. O.F.]

Gib·bon (gíbən), Edward (1737–94), English rationalist historian, author of 'The History of the Decline and Fall of the Roman Empire' (1776–88), a work of monumental erudition, dealing with the years 180–1453. Gibbon is renowned for his accuracy of detail and shrewdness of judgment, his gift for irony and epigram, his anticlerical views and the Latinized elegance of his prose

gib·bon (gíbən) *n.* an anthropoid ape of either of two genera, *Hylobates* or *Symphalangus,* fam. *Pongidae,* native to S.E. Asia. Gibbons are tailless, have exceptionally long arms, and give a loud, piercing cry [F.]

Gib·bons (gíbənz), Grinling (1648–1721), English woodcarver and sculptor. He was master carver in wood to the Crown. His sculpture includes the statue of James II outside the National Gallery, London

Gibbons, James (1834–1921), U.S. Roman Catholic cardinal whose works include 'The Faith of our Fathers' (1876). He served (from 1889) as the first chancellor of the Catholic University of America

Gibbons, Orlando (1583–1625), English composer and organist. He wrote madrigals and instrumental music, as well as services and anthems

'Gibbons v. Og·den' (ɔ́gdən, ógdən) a U.S. Supreme Court decision (1824) of Chief Justice John Marshall. It extended the power of Congress over interstate commerce

gib·bos·i·ty (gibósiti:) *pl.* **gib·bos·i·ties** *n.* the quality or state of being gibbous || a protuberance, esp. an abnormal backward curvature of the spine

gib·bous (gíbəs, dʒíbəs) *adj.* rounded out, convex || (of the moon or a planet) above half and less than full || humpbacked, having a hump [fr. L. *gibbus,* hump]

Gibbs (gibz), Joseph Williard (1839–1903), U.S. mathematical physicist whose work 'On the Equilibrium of Heterogeneous Substances' (1876–8) advanced the application of thermodynamics to chemistry

gibe, jibe (dʒaib) **1.** *v. pres. part.* **gib·ing, jib·ing** *past* and *past part.* **gibed, jibed** *v.i.* to jeer, scoff || *v.t.* to mock **2.** *n.* an expression of mockery, a taunt, sneer [etym. doubtful]

gibe *JIBE (to agree)

gib·lets (dʒíblits) *pl. n.* the gizzard and edible innards of a fowl, commonly removed before it is cooked and used for making gravy or soup [M.E. *gibelet* fr. O.F.]

Gi·bral·tar (dʒibrɔ́ltər) a British Crown colony (area 2½ sq. miles, pop. 30,000) and strategic air and naval base occupying the Rock of Gibraltar, a peninsula (summit: 1,396 ft) at the tip of S. Spain. The inhabitants are mainly of Italian, Spanish and Portuguese descent, with some Maltese and English. Languages: Spanish, English. Religion: 87% Roman Catholic, 7% Anglican, 3% Jewish. Average temperature (F.): 64°. It is a free port. Moorish (except 1309–33) from 711, Gibraltar was captured by Castile (1462) and ceded to Britain by Spain under the Treaty of Utrecht (1713). The Strait of Gibraltar (8½–23 miles wide) connects the Atlantic with the Mediterranean. Spain claims possession. The population of Gibraltar, by 12,138 votes to 44, expressed its will to remain British in a referendum (Sept. 1967). In 1969, Spain pressed its claim to the peninsula by closing its border with Gibraltar. The border was partly reopened in 1982 and totally reopened in 1985 although Spain did not relinquish its claim

Gib·son (gíbsən), Charles Dana (1867–1944), U.S. artist and illustrator. He created the 'Gibson girl', his pen-and-ink conception of the ideal American girl, and introduced for 'Collier's Weekly' the popular 'Adventures of Mr. Pipp' series

gid (gid) *n.* a brain disease of sheep caused by coenuri [shortened fr. GIDDY]

gid·di·ly (gídili:) *adv.* in a giddy manner

gid·di·ness (gídi:nis) *n.* the quality or state of being giddy

Gid·dings (gídiŋz), Franklin Henry (1855–1931), a founder of systematic sociology in the U.S.A.

Giddings, Joshua Reed (1795–1864), Congressman (1838–42) and abolitionist. He was censured by Congress for soliciting abolitionist aid from Great Britain

gid·dy (gídi:) *comp.* **gid·di·er** *superl.* **gid·di·est** *adj.* dizzy || making one feel dizzy, *a giddy height* || (*old-fash.*) frivolous [O.E. *gidig,* mad]

Gide (ʒi:d), André (1869–1951), French writer. His novels include 'L'Immoraliste' (1902) and 'les Faux-Monnayeurs' (1925). He founded (1909) the influential 'Nouvelle Revue française'. He also wrote essays, translations, reminiscences, plays, and an autobiography, 'Si le grain ne meurt' (1920–24). His published 'Journal' covers the years 1889–1949

Gid·e·on (gídi:ən) a judge and hero of Israel who saved his people from the Midianites (Judges vi–viii)

'Gideon v. Wain·wright' (wéinrait) a decision (1963) of the U.S. Supreme Court which declared that a man accused of a felony has a right to free counsel if he cannot afford a lawyer

Gier·ek (gírək), Edward (1913–), Polish statesman, first secretary of the Polish communist party (1970–80). He succeeded Gomulka when the latter resigned over food-price riots

gift (gift) **1.** *n.* a thing given || a natural talent || the right to give, *a benefice in the gift of the bishop* || (*Br.,* pop.) something easy to do, a cinch **to look a gift horse in the mouth** to criticize the quality of a present one has been given **2.** *v.t.* to endow with a natural talent || to give as a gift || to bestow gifts upon [O.E.]

gift·ed (gíftid) *adj.* endowed by nature, *gifted with a sense of humor* || talented

gift of gab, *Br.* **gift of the gab** the ability to talk fluently and plausibly

Gi·fu (gí:fú:) a town (pop. 410,000) in Honshu, Japan, on the River Nagara: paper products, other light industries

gig (gig) **1.** *n.* a fish spear ‖ a line with hooks on it, drawn through a shoal to catch fish when they are not biting **2.** *v.i. pres. part.* **gig·ging** *past* and *past part.* **gigged** to fish with a gig [shortened fr. *fishgig* fr. *fizgig*, a kind of fish spear]

gig *n.* a light two-wheeled carriage drawn by one horse ‖ a long, light ship's boat ‖ a rowing boat used mainly for racing ‖ a gig mill (machine) [fr. obs. *gig*, something that whirls]

gig *n.* (*show business*) a professional engagement, a job [origin unknown]

gig- combining prefix meaning one billion, 10⁹. *abbr* G

gig·a·bit (gígəbɪt) *n.* (*computer*) unit of information equal to 1 billion bits. *Cf* KLOBIT, MEGABIT

gigacycle *GIGAHERZ

gig·a·herz (gígəhə́rts) *n.* (*electr.*) frequency unit of 1 billion Hz

gi·gan·tic (dʒaigǽntik) *adj.* giantlike, very large, *a gigantic effort* **gi·gán·ti·cal·ly** *adv.* [fr. L. *gigas* (*gigantis*), a giant]

gi·gan·tism (dʒaigǽntizəm) *n.* giantism ‖ abnormal tallness, often caused by overactivity of the pituitary gland

gig·gle (gíg'l) **1.** *v.i. pres. part.* **gig·gling** *past* and *past part.* **gig·gled** to laugh foolishly or nervously or in an attempt to repress outright laughter **2.** *n.* foolish, nervous or half-suppressed laughter **the giggles** a fit of such laughter **gig·gly** *adj.* [imit.]

gig mill a machine for raising the nap on cloth ‖ a building in which gig mills are used

GIGO (*computer acronym*) for garbage in, garbage out, term for poor programming

gig·o·lo (dʒígəlou, ʒígəlou) *pl.* **gig·o·los** *n.* a man kept by a woman ‖ a professional male dancing partner or paid escort [F.]

gigue (ʒi:g) *n.* a dance in 6/8 or 12/8 time, usually the last movement of the 17th-c. and 18th-c. suite [F. fr. Ital. *giga*, fiddle]

Gi·jón (hi:hón) an ancient seaport (pop. 125,000) in Oviedo, N.W. Spain, on the Bay of Biscay, with an excellent harbor: metallurgy, chemicals and oil refining

Gi·la (hí:lə) a river (c. 630 miles long) flowing from S.W. New Mexico, through S. Arizona to the Colorado River at the southwestern corner of Arizona

Gila monster a member of *Heloderma*, fam. *Helodermatidae*, a genus of large poisonous lizards (esp. *H. suspectum*) inhabiting the sandy deserts of the southwestern U.S.A. and northern Mexico [after the *Gila* River, Arizona]

Gil·bert (gílbərt), Cass (1859–1934), U.S. architect. He designed the Woolworth building, an early skyscraper in semi-Gothic style, in New York City and the neoclassical Supreme Court building in Washington, D.C.

Gilbert, Grove Karl (1843–1918), U.S. geologist. Joining (1879) the U.S. Geographical Survey, he mapped the geology of portions of the Rocky Mountains, becoming one of the first investigators to study the relation between geological structure and surface features

Gilbert, Sir Humphrey (c. 1539–83), English navigator. He tried to discover the Northwest Passage. He founded the colony of Newfoundland (1583)

Gilbert, Sir William Schwenck (1836–1911), English playwright, humorist and librettist. He collaborated (1871–96) with Arthur Sullivan to write the famous, still popular, Gilbert and Sullivan operettas (*SULLIVAN). His poems include 'The Bab Ballads' (1869)

gil·bert (gílbərt) *n.* a cgs unit of magnetomotive force, equal to 10/4π ampere-turns [after William *Gilbert* (1544–1603), English physicist]

Gil·ber·ti·an (gilbə́:rti:ən) *adj.* belonging to or suggesting the whimsical. topsy-turvy world of Gilbert and Sullivan operettas [after W. S. *Gilbert*]

Gil·ber·tine (gílbərti:n, gílbərtain) *n.* a member of an English religious order (12th-16th cc.) founded by Gilbert of Sempringham. It was primarily an order of Benedictine nuns with Augustinian canons ministering spiritually to them

Gilbert Islands *KIRIBATI

Gilbert of Sem·pring·ham (sémprɪŋəm), St (c. 1083–1189), founder of the only medieval religious order of English origin, the Gilbertines

gild (gild) *pres. part.* **gild·ing** *past* and *past part.* **gild·ed, gilt** (gilt) *v.t.* to cover with a fine layer of gold or gold leaf ‖ (*rhet.*) to make golden, *the sun gilded the hilltop* ‖ to give a speciously attractive appearance to **to gild the lily** to praise, eulogize etc. inordinately [O.E. *gyldan*]

gild *GUILD

Gil·das (gíldəs) (c. 516–70), English historian. His 'De excidio et conquestu Britanniae' is the only extant contemporary account of the Anglo-Saxon conquest of Britain (5th c.)

gild·hall (gíldhɔl) *n.* a guildhall

gild·ing (gíldin) *n.* the practice of overlaying with gold or yellow metal ‖ the gold or yellow metal used ‖ the gilded surface produced ‖ a deceptively fine exterior

Gil·e·ad (gíli:əd) a fertile mountainous region of ancient Palestine, northeast of the Dead Sea

Gil·ga·mesh (gílgəmeʃ) a legendary king, hero of an ancient Babylonian epic found inscribed on 12 tablets in the palace of Ashurbanipal at Nineveh

Gill (gil), Eric (1882–1940), English stone and woodcarver, type designer and Roman Catholic apologist. Like Morris, he worked for the revival of crafts. His carvings were monumental and devotional. His type designs include the inscriptional roman Perpetua (1925) and the famous Gill Sans (1927), the most used sans-serif type of this century

gill (gil) **1.** *n.* the vascular respiratory organ in fish and other water-breathing animals ‖ the dewlap of a fowl ‖ one of the vertical radiating plates on the underside of mushrooms or toadstools **2.** *v.t.* to gut (fish) ‖ to catch (fish) by the gill covers in a gill net [origin unknown]

gill (dʒil) *n.* either of two liquid measures: (*Am.*) ¼ of a U.S. liquid pint or 7.218 cu. ins, (*Br.*) a unit equal to ¼ of an imperial pint or 8.669 cu. ins [O.F. *gille, gelle*, a wine measure]

gill cover (gil) a bony projection protecting a fish's gills

gill fungus (gil) a fungus having blade-shaped gills under the cap

gil·lie (gíli:) *n.* a fishing and hunting guide and attendant in Scotland [Gael. *gille*, boy, servant]

gill net (gil) a net which allows a fish's head to pass through its meshes but catches the gill covers when the fish tries to withdraw

Gill·ray (gílrei), James (1757–1815), English caricaturist. His 'Farmer George' series satirized George III and English society

gil·ly·flow·er (dʒíli:flauər) *n.* (*old-fash.*) any of several plants with clove-scented flowers, e.g. the wallflower [O.F. *girofle, gilofre*, clove]

gilt (gilt) **1.** *n.* gilding ‖ superficial glitter **2.** *adj.* gilded [past part. of GILD]

gilt *n.* a young sow [O.N. *gyltr*]

gilt-edged security an investment (e.g. in government stock) which involves little risk and low yield

gim·bals (dʒímbəlz, gímbəlz) *pl. n.* a device for keeping a ship's compass or chronometer level at sea [altered fr. *gimmal* fr. O.F. *gemel*, a double ring]

gim·crack (dʒímkræk) **1.** *n.* a useless, showy knickknack, a gewgaw **2.** *adj.* carelessly or hastily put together ‖ cheap and tawdry [M.E. *gibecrake*]

gim·let (gímlit) *n.* a small tool with a cross handle, used to bore holes for screws [O.F. *guinbelet, guimbelet*]

gimlet eye a piercing, observant eye **gim·let-éyed** *adj.*

gim·mick (gímik) *n.* a gadget ‖ any clever scheme, *a gimmick to attract customers* ‖ a hidden device for controlling a gambling wheel ‖ any deceptive trick or device [etym. doubtful]

gimp (gimp) *n.* a trimming of silk or cotton strengthened with wire ‖ a silk fishing line bound with wire ‖ a coarse thread used in lace making to outline the design [perh. fr. Du. *gimp* or F. *guimpe*]

gin (dʒin) *n.* a strong liquor distilled from grain and flavored with juniper berries or a substitute for them ‖ gin rummy [short for *geneva*, a spirit made in Holland, fr. Du. *genever*]

gin 1. *n.* a spring trap with steel teeth, a snare ‖ a hoisting device, usually a tripod with one hinged leg ‖ a machine for removing seeds etc. from fiber, esp. cotton **2.** *v.t. pres. part.* **gin·ning** *past* and *past part.* **ginned** to trap, snare with a gin ‖ to remove seeds from (cotton) with a gin [shortened fr. O.F. *engin*, engine]

gin·ger (dʒíndʒər) **1.** *n.* a plant of the genus *Zingiber*, esp. *Z. officinale*, a perennial native to Asia but widely cultivated for its aromatic rhizome, which is used as a spice, in sweetmeats and in medicine ‖ the rhizome of *Z. officinale* ‖ (*pop.*), vigor, spirit ‖ a sandy reddish color **2.** *adj.* of a sandy, reddish color **3.** *v.t.* (*pop.*, with 'up') to liven, animate ‖ to add ginger to [O.E. *gingiber* fr. L.L. fr. Gk fr. Skr]

ginger ale a sweetened, carbonated, nonalcoholic drink flavored with ginger extract

ginger beer a nonalcoholic effervescent drink flavored with ginger

gin·ger·bread (dʒíndʒərbred) *n.* cake made with molasses and ginger ‖ cheap, gaudy ornamentation **to take the gilt off the gingerbread** (*Br.*) to make a thing or situation lose its apparent attractiveness and so cause disenchantment

ginger group (*Br.*) a pressure group within a party, urging stronger action

gin·ger·ly (dʒíndʒərli:) **1.** *adv.* very cautiously or warily, so as not to damage or disturb, or so as to avoid close contact **2.** *adj.* very cautious or wary [origin unknown]

ginger nut a gingersnap

gin·ger·snap (dʒíndʒərsnæp) *n.* a crisp, thin, hard cookie flavored with ginger

ginger wine a wine made from bruised ginger, water and fermented sugar

gin·ger·y (dʒíndʒəri:) *adj.* like ginger in taste or color ‖ (esp. of horses) high-spirited, full of vigor

ging·ham (gíŋəm) *n.* an inexpensive cotton fabric, usually checked or striped [F. *guingan* fr. Malay *ginggang*, striped]

gin·gi·val (dʒíndʒivəl, dʒindʒáivəl) *adj.* of or relating to the gums [fr. L. *gingiva*, gum]

gin·gi·vi·tis (dʒindʒiváitis) *n.* inflammation of the gums [Mod. L. fr. *gingiva*, gum]

gink·go, ging·ko (gíŋkou) *pl.* **gink·gos, gink·goes, ging·kos, ging·koes** *n. Ginkgo biloba*, fam. *Ginkgoaceae*, a gymnospermous deciduous tree with dioecious flowers, native to China and Japan. It is the only living representative of its genus. Ginkgos have been preserved as sacred in Japanese temple gardens, and are rarely found wild [Mod. L. fr. Jap. *ginkyo* fr. *gin*, silver+*kyo*, apricot]

gin·ner·y (dʒínəri:) *pl.* **gin·ner·ies** *n.* a mill for ginning cotton

Ginnie Mae *GNMA

gin rummy a variety of rummy in which a player with a total of not more than 10 unmatched points may expose his cards, winning or losing according to his opponent's hand

gin·seng (dʒínsen) *n. Panax schinseng*, fam. *Araliaceae*, a palmate-leaved plant of E. Asia with an aromatic root valued by the Chinese as a panacea ‖ a North American woodland plant, *P. quinquefolius* ‖ the root of either of these plants, used in medicine ‖ the preparation made from the root [Chin.]

Gio·no (ʒounou), Jean (1895–1970), French novelist, famous for his poetic treatment of Provençal life e.g. in 'Colline' (1929), 'Regain' (1930)

Gior·da·no (dʒɔrdánɔ), Luca (1632–1705), Neapolitan painter. His output was enormous and was mainly devotional or biblical

Gior·gio·ne (dʒɔrdʒóne) (Giorgio da Castelfranco, c. 1477–1510), Venetian painter. A pupil of Bellini, he exerted great influence on his contemporaries, notably Titian. His painting is evocative, with mellow coloring and a notable integration of figures and landscape. Only a few extant works can be attributed to him with certainty

Giot·to (dʒɔtta) (Giotto di Bondone, c. 1267–1337), Florentine painter. The gravity and certain stylistic features of his paintings still show the influence of Byzantine art, but he is considered as one of the creators of modern painting, by the amplitude of his vision of the world, by his view of men, and by the dramatic force which he achieved by his use of modeling of solid bodies, representation of draperies, and foreshortening of limbs or objects extended in the imagined depth of the picture space. His first authentic work was the series of frescoes in the Arena Chapel, Padua. His other great cycles of frescoes are at Assisi and in Santa Croce, Florence

Gio·van·ni da Fie·so·le (dʒɔvánni:dafjézɔle) *ANGELICO, Fra

gipsy *GYPSY

gipsy moth *GYPSY MOTH

gi·raffe (dʒirǽf, *Br.* dʒiráf) *n. Giraffa camelopardalis*, fam. *Giraffidae*, an African ruminant quadruped, the tallest living animal (18-20 ft) with an extraordinarily long neck and long forelegs. Giraffes are light fawn in color,

---

CONCISE PRONUNCIATION KEY: **(a)** æ, c*a*t; ɑ, c*ar*; ɔ, f*aw*n; ei, sn*a*ke. **(e)** e, h*e*n; i:, sh*ee*p; iə, d*eer*; ɛə, b*ear*. **(i)** i, f*i*sh; ai, t*ig*er; ə:, b*ir*d. **(o)** o, *o*x; au, c*ow*; ou, g*oa*t; u, p*oor*; ɔi, r*oy*al. **(u)** ʌ, d*u*ck; u, b*u*ll; u:, g*oo*se; ə, b*a*cillus; ju:, c*u*be. x, lo*ch*; θ, *th*ink; ð, bo*th*er; z, *Z*en; ʒ, cor*sag*e; dʒ, sa*v*a*ge*; ŋ, oran*g*utan*g*; j, *y*ak; ʃ, *f*ish; tʃ, *f*e*tch*; 'l, rabb*le*; 'n, redd*en*. Complete pronunciation key appears inside front cover.

marked with darker patches. They live in small herds in the open country south of the Sahara, feeding on leaves [F. *girafe* fr. Arab. *zarāfah*]

Gi·ral·dus Cam·bren·sis (dʒirǽldəskæmbrén-sis) (Gerald de Barri, c. 1147–c. 1223), Welsh churchman and historian. His 'Itinerary' and 'Description of Wales' are the best known of his many lively, personal, occasional writings

gir·an·dole (dʒírəndoul) *n.* an elaborate, branched candle holder ‖ an earring or pendant, with a large jewel set in a circle of smaller ones ‖ a rotating firework ‖ a rotating water jet [F. fr. Ital.]

Gi·rard (dʒirárd, ʒi:rær), Stephen (1750–1831), U.S. merchant, banker and philanthropist. He purchased (1810) the assets of the endangered First Bank of the United States, establishing the Bank of Stephen Girard in Philadelphia, and subscribed (1814) 95% of the U.S. government's war bond issue

gir·a·sol (dʒírəsɔl) *n.* a variety of opal which has a reddish glow in bright light ‖ the Jerusalem artichoke [Ital. fr. *girare*, to turn+*sole*, the sun]

gir·a·sole (dʒírəsoul) *n.* a girasol

Gi·raud (ʒi:rou), Henri Honoré (1879– 1949), French general. He commanded the French army in N. Africa (1942–3), but resigned after disagreements with de Gaulle

Gi·rau·doux (ʒi:roudu:), Jean (1882–1944), French novelist and playwright. His novels include 'Suzanne et le Pacifique' (1921) and 'Siegfried et le Limousin' (1922). His plays include 'Amphitryon 38' (1929), 'La guerre de Troie n'aura pas lieu' (1935), 'Ondine' (1939), 'la Folle de Chaillot' (1945). Satirical wit and verbal coruscation blend in his work with poetic fantasy and reverie

gird (gəːrd) *v.i.* (with 'at') to jeer, gibe, scoff [M.E. *girden*, *gurden*, to strike, move rapidly, thrust]

gird *pres. part.* **gird·ing** *past* and *past part.* **gird·ed**, **girt** (gəːrt) *v.t.* (*rhet.*) to encircle (the waist) with a belt ‖ (*archaic*) to fasten with a belt, *he girt on his sword* ‖ (*rhet.*) to surround, encircle, *girded about with hills* ‖ (*refl.*, *rhet.*) to clothe oneself, equip oneself, *to gird oneself for battle* **gird·er** *n.* an iron or steel (rarely wooden) beam used in building and bridge construction ‖ (in floors) one of the main joist-supporting, horizontal members [O.E. *gyrdan*]

gir·dle (gəːrd'l) 1. *n.* a belt or sash encircling the waist ‖ anything which encircles like a girdle ‖ a usually elastic undergarment worn by women to hold in the waist, hips and buttocks ‖ the ring made around a tree by cutting away the bark ‖ (*anat.*) a bony arch to support a limb, *the pelvic girdle* ‖ the outer rim of a cut gem clasped by the setting 2. *v.t. pres. part.* **gird·ling** *past* and *past part.* **gird·led** to bind with a girdle ‖ to encircle, enclose ‖ to cut a ring around the bark of [O.E. *gyrdel*]

girdle *n.* (*Br.*) a griddle

girl (gəːrl) *n.* a female child ‖ a young unmarried woman ‖ (*pop.*) a single or married woman at any age ‖ a female servant, maid ‖ a girl friend, sweetheart ‖ a present or former member of a girls' school or women's college, *a Vassar girl* [M.E. *girle*, *gurle*, *gerle*, youngster, origin unknown]

Girl Friday (*pop.*) an efficient and reliable female employee, esp. a private secretary or assistant in an office prepared to do jobs outside the usual routine (*MAN FRIDAY)

girl friend a female friend, esp. a sweetheart

girl guide (*Br.*) a girl scout

girl·hood (gəːrlhud) *n.* the years of being a girl ‖ the state of being a girl

girl·ish (gəːrliʃ) *adj.* of, like or suitable to a girl

girl scout (*Am.*=*Br.* girl guide) a member of the World Association of Girl Guides and Girl Scouts, founded (1910) in England by Lord Robert Baden-Powell and his sister Agnes to form character and to teach good citizenship among girls. Stress is laid on open-air activities and domestic skills. The movement, modeled on that of the scouts, has groups throughout the world

gi·ro (dʒáirou) *pl.* **gi·ros** *n.* (*Br.*) a checking account system administered by the post office

Gi·ronde (ʒi:rɔ̃d) a department (area 4,140 sq. miles, pop. 1,061,500) of S.W. France around the Garonne estuary (*GUYENNE). Chief town: Bordeaux ‖ (*hist.*) the party of the Girondists

Gironde an estuary (45 miles long) formed by the junction of the Garonne and the Dordogne, in S.W. France

Gi·ron·dist (dʒirɔ́ndist) 1. *n.* (*F. hist.*) a member of the moderate republican party during the French Revolution. After a long struggle in the Convention, the Girondists were overthrown (June 2, 1793) by their rivals, the Jacobins, and many of them were beheaded Oct. 31, 1793 2. *adj.* relating to this party [fr. GIRONDE, where the leaders came from]

girt *alt. past* and *past part.* of GIRD (to encircle)

girth (gəːrθ) 1. *n.* the band which fastens around the body of a horse or other animal to secure the saddle, pack etc. ‖ the circumference of a thing, *the girth of a tree* 2. *v.t.* to fit or secure with a girth [M.E. *gerthe* fr. O.N.]

Gir·tin (gəːrtin), Thomas (1775–1802), English painter. He was one of the great English watercolor painters, excelling in landscape and architectural work. He brought a new richness of tone to the medium, which he handled with freedom and spontaneity

girt·line (gəːrtlain) *n.* (*naut.*) a line rove through a block, e.g. at the end of a bowsprit, for hoisting rigging

Giscard d'Estaing, Valery (ʒi:skár destɛ̃ vah-lay-ree') (1926–), French president (1974–81). He served in various government positions from 1952, including minister of finance (1962–6; 1969–74). As president he encouraged international cooperation, private enterprise, and nuclear power development. He was succeeded by François Mitterrand

Gis·le·ber·tus (dʒi:z'lbéərtəs) (early 12th c.), one of the great sculptors of the Middle Ages, esp. for his work in Autun cathedral (1125–35)

Gis·sing (gísiŋ), George Robert (1857–1903), English realist novelist, author of 'New Grub Street' (1891) etc.

gist (dʒist) *n.* the main point, the heart of the matter ‖ (*law*) the real ground or point of an action [O.F. fr. *gésir*, to lie, depend (on)]

give (giv) 1. *v. pres. part.* **giv·ing** *past* **gave** (geiv) *past part.* **giv·en** (gívən) *v.t.* to offer as a present ‖ to hand over ‖ to put into someone's hands, *give me my bag* ‖ to pay as price ‖ to make involuntarily, *to give a start* ‖ to provide with, supply ‖ to furnish as product, *sugar gives us energy* ‖ to offer as host or sponsor, *to give a banquet in someone's honor* ‖ to produce, yield, *this seed gives good results* ‖ to show, *to give signs of annoyance* ‖ to grant, confer, *to give someone a scholarship* ‖ to confer ownership of ‖ to inflict, *he gave the offender a stiff sentence* ‖ to cause to have, *the dog has given him fleas* ‖ to pronounce, *they will give their decision today* ‖ to utter, *to give a shout* ‖ to administer, *to give an injection* ‖ to pledge, *to give one's word* ‖ to allow, permit, *give yourself plenty of time* ‖ to concede, admit ‖ to devote, *to give thought to a problem* ‖ to put a caller in communication by telephone with, *give me the police* ‖ to do someone (a free service), *to give someone a lift* ‖ to deliver (a message) ‖ to bestow in charity, by legacy, as alms etc. ‖ to put in temporary keeping, *give me your watch while you swim* ‖ to perform before an audience ‖ to render as being due, *give him the benefit of the doubt, give them three cheers* ‖ to proffer, *he gave him his hand* ‖ to name for a toast ‖ (in physical dealings with someone) to bestow, inflict, *he gave her a kiss, to give someone a blow* ‖ to volunteer or reply as information, *she gave him her telephone number, try to give him all the details* ‖ to sacrifice, *to give one's life for a cause* ‖ to bestow in marriage ‖ *v.i.* to make a gift ‖ to yield to pressure, *the ice gave under his weight* ‖ to open or look out, *the window gives on to a garden* **to give away** to dispose of gratis ‖ to distribute (prizes) ‖ to betray ‖ to reveal (what should be kept secret) ‖ to bestow (a bride) formally **to give back** to restore to ownership **to give forth** to send out, emit **to give ground** (*mil.*) to fall back, retreat ‖ to yield **to give in** to admit defeat, yield ‖ to hand in, *to give in an exam paper* **to give off** to throw off, emit **to give out** to announce, report ‖ to emit ‖ to hand out, distribute ‖ (of supplies etc.) to run short, become exhausted **to give oneself out to be (something)** to claim to be (something) **to give over** to stop being a nuisance ‖ to deliver to the authority or keeping of ‖ to devote (to a specified use) ‖ (with *pres. part.*) to cease from **to give (someone) to understand** to inform, allow to infer **to give tongue** (of hounds) to pick up the scent and bark **to give up** to abandon ‖ to hand over or hand back, *to give a criminal up to the police* ‖ to cease from ‖ to cease to have dealings with ‖ to abandon one's efforts with, *the doctors have given him up*

as incurable ‖ to admit defeat **to give way** to give ground ‖ to yield the right of way ‖ to make concessions ‖ to retire in someone's favor ‖ to break down or collapse under stress ‖ (*rowing*) to start to row or to pull harder 2. *n.* elasticity, springiness, *there is plenty of give in a wooden plank* [O.E. *giefan*]

give-and-take *n.* compromise, the making of mutual concessions ‖ exchange of ideas or conversation

give·a·way (gívəwei) *n.* an inadvertent revealing or betraying of oneself or one's plans etc. ‖ something given away, esp. merchandise, to encourage the sale of a product ‖ (*pop.*) a radio or television contest having as an essential feature the giving of prizes

give·back (gívbæk) *n.* a payment or conceding right previously won, the return of which is asked for in a negotiation

giv·en (gívən) *past part.* of GIVE ‖ *adj.* agreed, fixed, *a given day* ‖ executed, esp. in official documents, *given under my hand ...* ‖ (*math., logic*) granted, admitted as the basis of a calculation, or as data or premises **given to** in the habit of, *given to idling* **given up** to addicted to

given name a person's first name as distinct from his family name

give-up (gívʌp) *n.* (*securities*) 1. a market order executed by a floor broker on behalf of another broker, with shared commission. 2. the share of the commission

Gi·za (gí:zə) an Egyptian town (pop. 1,246,054) on the Nile, near which stand the Sphinx and a group of pyramids including the biggest

giz·zard (gízərd) *n.* the muscular chamber of the alimentary canal of various birds, esp. poultry ‖ the proventriculus of certain insects **to stick in one's gizzard** to be offensive to one's pride, *it stuck in his gizzard to have to apologize* [M.E. *giser* fr. O.F.]

gla·bel·la (gləbélə) *pl.* **gla·bel·lae** (gləbéli:) *n.* (*anat.*) the flat area of bone on the forehead between the eyebrows [Mod. L.]

gla·brate (gléibreit) *adj.* (*biol.*) glabrous ‖ becoming glabrous [fr. L. *glabrare* (*glabratus*), to make smooth]

gla·brous (gléibrəs) *adj.* (*biol.*) hairless, with a smooth even surface [fr. L. *glaber*, smooth]

gla·cé (glæsei) *adj.* (of fruit) covered with sugar, candied ‖ (of fruit etc.) iced, frozen ‖ (of cloth and leather) with a glossy surface [F.]

gla·cial (gléiʃəl) *adj.* icy, frozen ‖ (*geol.*) of or pertaining to glaciers ‖ (*chem.*) having icelike crystals

glacial epoch a glacial period

glacial period a period of geological time when a large part of the earth's surface was covered by glaciers. There have been three major glacial periods. The earliest was in late Precambrian times, 600-700 million years ago, the second in late Palaeozoic times, 250 million years ago (in the southern hemisphere), and the third, to which the term is most often applied, in the Pleistocene period, when an ice sheet covered North America and N. Europe. The best-known existing ice sheets are those of Greenland and Antarctica

gla·ci·ate (gléiʃi:eit) *pres. part.* **gla·ci·at·ing** *past* and *past part.* **gla·ci·at·ed** *v.t.* to cover (land) with glaciers ‖ to affect by glacial action ‖ *v.i.* to become ice ‖ (of land) to become covered with glaciers [fr. L. *glaciare* (*glaciatus*), to freeze]

gla·cier (gléiʃər) *n.* a river of ice in a high mountain valley formed by the consolidation under pressure of snow falling on higher ground. The ice sheets of Antarctica and Greenland are in themselves vast glaciers [F.]

Glacier Bay National Monument a U.S. national monument established in 1925 and comprising an area of 2,274,595 acres in S.E. Alaska. It consists of ice fields and more than 20 glaciers

gla·ci·ol·o·gy (gleiʃi:ɔ́lədʒi:) *n.* the branch of geology dealing with the accumulation on the earth's surface of glaciers, and their effect on animal and vegetable life ‖ the glacial features of a region [fr. GLACIER+ Gk *logos*, word]

gla·cis (gléisis, glǽsis) *pl.* **gla·cis**, **gla·cis·es** *n.* a bank sloping away from a fortification, to expose attacks to firing from ramparts [F., orig.=slippery place]

Glack·ens (glǽkənz), William James (1870–1938), U.S. artist. His illustrations (1898–1908) in the 'New York World' and 'New York Herald' depicted all aspects of contemporary life

---

CONCISE PRONUNCIATION KEY: **(a)** æ, c*a*t; ɑ, c*a*r; ɔ f*aw*n; ei, sn*a*ke. **(e)** e, h*e*n; i:, sh*ee*p; iə, d*ee*r; ɛə, b*ea*r. **(i)** i, f*i*sh; ai, t*i*ger; əː, b*i*rd. **(o)** o, *o*x; au, c*ow*; ou, g*oa*t; u, p*oo*r; ɔi, r*oy*al. **(u)** ʌ, d*u*ck; u, b*u*ll; u:, g*oo*se; ə, b*a*cillus; ju:, c*u*be. x, lo*ch*; θ, *th*ink; ð, bo*th*er; z, *Z*en; ʒ, cor*s*age; dʒ, sava*g*e; ŋ, ora*n*guta*ng*; j, *y*ak; ʃ, *fish*; tʃ, fe*tch*; 'l, rabb*le*; 'n, redd*en*. Complete pronunciation key appears inside front cover.

glad (glæd) comp. **glad·der** superl. **glad·dest** adj. joyful, a glad smile ‖ (used only predicatively) happy about some specific circumstance, pleased, glad to be of service **glad·den** (glǽd'n) v.t. to make glad [O.E. glæd]

glade (gleid) n. a clear, open space in a forest ‖ an everglade [origin unknown]

glad eye (in phrases) **to give (someone) the glad eye** to ogle (someone) flirtatiously **to get the glad eye** to be ogled flirtatiously

glad hand (pop.) a fulsomely effusive, insincere greeting or welcome

glad·i·ate (glǽdi:eit, gléidi:eit) adj. (bot.) sword-shaped [fr. L. gladius, a sword]

glad·i·a·tor (glǽdi:eitər) n. (hist.) a fighter with a sword or other weapon at a Roman circus **glad·i·a·tor·i·al** (glæˌdi:ətɔ́ri:əl, glæˌdi:ətóuri:əl) adj. [L., fr. gladius, sword]

glad·i·o·la (glædi:óulə) n. a gladiolus [L., neut. pl. taken as fem. sing.]

glad·i·o·lus (glædi:óuləs) pl. **glad·i·o·li** (glædi:óulai), **glad·i·o·lus·es**, n. a plant of genus Gladiolus, fam. Iridaceae, having long, sword-shaped leaves and bright, variously colored flowers. Most species are native to Africa, some are Asian, some European [L., dim. of gladius, sword]

glad·ly (glǽdli:) adv. with gladness ‖ willingly

Glad·stone (glǽdstən), William Ewart (1809–98), British statesman, prime minister (1868–74, 1880–5, 1886 and 1892–4). He entered parliament as a Tory (1832), and served under Peel as president of the Board of Trade (1843–5) and colonial secretary (1845–6), resigning with other Peelites after the repeal of the Corn Laws. As chancellor of the exchequer (1852–5 and 1859–65) under Aberdeen and Palmerston, he reduced income tax and many tariffs. He led the newly formed Liberal party to victory (1868) over Disraeli, his lifelong political rival. Gladstone's first ministry (1868–74) disestablished the Irish Church (1869), carried a Land Act to protect Irish tenants (1870), introduced the secret ballot (1872) and carried out military, educational and civil service reforms. His second ministry (1880–5) brought in the Reform Act of 1884, and his third and fourth ministries (1886 and 1892–4) were occupied in unsuccessful attempts to carry a Home Rule Bill for Ireland. Gladstone was preoccupied by home affairs, but used his gifts as an orator to denounce the Turkish massacres in Bulgaria (1876). A scholar and theologian, he failed to gain the same influence with Queen Victoria as Disraeli

Gladstone bag (Br.) a traveling bag hinged so as to open into two equal compartments [after William Ewart Gladstone]

glair (glɛər) 1. n. egg white, esp. as used to make a kind of size for bookbinding ‖ any viscous, transparent substance resembling egg white 2. v.t. to coat with glair **glair·y** adj. [F. glaire]

glamor *GLAMOUR

Gla·mor·gan·shire (gləmɔ́rgənʃər) (abbr. Glam.) a former county (area 813 sq. miles, pop. 1,228,000) in S.E. Wales. County town was Cardiff

glam·or·ize (glǽməraiz) pres. part. **glam·or·iz·ing** past and past part. **glam·or·ized** v.t. to make (something) appear more attractive than it really is ‖ to add glamour to (a person)

glam·or·ous (glǽmərəs) adj. having glamour

glam·our, glam·or (glǽmər) n. dazzling charm, allure and mysterious fascination [corrup. of GRAMMAR: the original meaning 'enchantment' derived from the popular association between learning and magic]

glance (glæns, glans) n. a shiny metallic ore [fr. G. glanz, luster]

glance 1. v. pres. part. **glanc·ing** past and past part. **glanced** v.i. to look briefly, to glance at the headlines ‖ to be deflected obliquely at the point of impact, the ball glanced off his bat ‖ (usually with 'over') to allude with deliberate brevity, to glance over a topic ‖ to flash, gleam ‖ v.t. (cricket) to deflect (the ball) by playing it with the bat oblique 2. n. a brief look, one glance confirmed his worst fears ‖ a sudden gleam of light ‖ (cricket) a deflecting stroke [etym. doubtful]

gland (glænd) n. a single structure of cells, which takes certain substances from the blood and secretes them in a form which the body can use or eliminate. The exocrine glands discharge their secretions through ducts to the skin or internal cavities of the body. The endocrine glands are ductless, and pass their secretions (hormones) into the bloodstream ‖ a similar structure in a plant [fr. F. glande]

gland n. (mech.) a device for preventing leakage of fluids, esp. the part that compresses the packing in a stuffing box [origin unknown]

glan·dered (glǽndərd) adj. affected with glanders

glan·der·ous (glǽndərəs) adj. of or affected with glanders

glan·ders (glǽndərz) pl. n. a highly contagious disease of horses, mules and asses, caused by the bacterium Malleomyces mallei or Pfeifferella mallei, and characterized by fever, swelling of glands beneath the jaw and a heavy mucous discharge from the nose. It can be passed to sheep, goats and man, but not to cattle [O.F. glandre, gland]

glan·du·lar (glǽndʒulər) adj. of, like, consisting of, or containing a gland or gland cells [fr. F. gandulire]

glandular fever infectious mononucleosis

glans (glænz) pl. **glan·des** (glǽndi:z) n. the glans penis ‖ the glans clitoridis [L. glans, acorn]

glans cli·tor·i·dis (klitóridis, klitóuridis) n. the acorn-shaped termination of the clitoris

glans penis n. the acorn-shaped termination of the penis

Glan·ville (glǽnvil), Ranulf de (d. 1190), English jurist, chief justiciar of England (1180–9) under Henry II. He was responsible for 'Tractatus de legibus et consuetudinibus regni Angliae', the earliest treatise on English law

glare (glɛər) 1. v. pres. part. **glar·ing** past and past part. **glared** v.i. to shine brightly and fiercely ‖ to stare fiercely ‖ to be too conspicuous ‖ v.t. to express (anger etc.) with a look, to glare defiance 2. n. a strong, fierce light ‖ a fierce, intense look ‖ (of colors) the quality of being uncomfortably bright **glar·ing** adj. bright and dazzling, a glaring light ‖ staring fiercely ‖ flagrant, a glaring injustice ‖ garish, too vivid, glaring colors [M.E. glaren]

Gla·rus (glúrəs) (F. Glaris) a German-speaking canton (area 267 sq. miles, pop. 36,718) in E. central Switzerland ‖ its capital (pop. 6,000)

glar·y (glɛ́əri:) comp. **glar·i·er** superl. **glar·i·est** adj. glaring

Glas·gow (glǽsgou) a city (pop. 765,915) in Scotland on the River Clyde, a manufacturing and shipping center: iron and steel, machinery, chemicals, textiles, clothing. University of Glasgow (1450), Strathclyde University (1964)

glas·phalt (glǽsfɔlt) n. road surfacing of asphalt and crushed glass

glass (glæs, glas) 1. pl. **glass·es** n. a hard, brittle, transparent or translucent, greenish solid solution made by melting a mixture of silica (esp. sand) and various silicates, with metallic oxides added to give the product special qualities ‖ a drinking vessel made of glass ‖ its contents, to drink a glass of beer ‖ a mirror made of glass backed by a bright film of reflecting metal ‖ a protective cover made of glass ‖ a glass lens ‖ an optical device having a glass lens or lenses, e.g. a telescope or microscope ‖ (pl.) spectacles ‖ (pl.) binoculars ‖ a barometer ‖ an hourglass ‖ a pane of glass ‖ glassware ‖ greenhouses, or greenhouse conditions, grown under glass 2. v.t. to fit with, cover with, or encase in glass 3. adj. made of glass, pertaining to glass [O.E. glæs]
—Colorless glass is obtained by adding manganese, which neutralizes traces of iron in the sand. Different tints are obtained by adding various metallic oxides. Lead oxide gives a softer glass, often used for drinking vessels, etc. Boron makes the glass heat-resistant (*FIBER GLASS, *STAINED GLASS)

glass·blow·er (glǽsblouer, glásblouər) n. a person who blows glass or a machine which does this

glass·blow·ing (glǽsblouiŋ, glásblouiŋ) n. the blowing of a cavity in semimolten glass and the subsequent shaping of the glass article, using the blowpipe flame to make and keep the glass workable

glass cloth a hard-finished, lintless cloth of linen etc. used to dry and polish glassware ‖ a fabric made of woven fiber glass

glass cutter a tool with a point or edge of diamond or very hard steel, able to cut glass ‖ someone who cuts glass professionally

glass eye an artificial eye made of glass ‖ a kind of blindness in horses

glass·ful (glǽsful, glásful) n. as much as a glass can contain

glass harmonica a musical instrument of the 18th and 19th cc. consisting of a series of glass bowls played by rubbing the edges with a moistened finger

glass·house (glǽshaus, gláshaus) pl. **glass·hous·es** (glǽshauziz, gláshauziz) n. (Br.) a greenhouse ‖ a glassworks ‖ (Br., pop.) a military prison

glass·i·ly (glǽsili:, glásili:) adv. in a glassy manner

glass·ine (glæsí:n, glɑsí:n) n. a thin, glazed, nearly transparent paper used for envelope windows, book jackets etc.

glass·i·ness (glǽsi:nis, glási:nis) n. the state or quality of being glassy

glass laser (optics) a solid laser that uses tons of rare-earth elements in a glass host for amplification. also amorphous laser

glass paper thick paper on which powdered glass is made to adhere, used as an abrasive

glass snake Ophisaurus ventralis, fam. Anguidae, a limbless lizard of the southern U.S.A., reaching a length of 3-4 ft. The caudal vertebrae are brittle, loosely connected and easily detached

glas·steel (glǽsti:l) adj. (architecture) of something made of glass and steel, e.g., some skyscrapers

glass·ware (glǽswçər, gláswçər) n. articles made of glass, esp. tableware

glass wool a mass of fine glass threads, used for filtering and as a heat insulator

glass·work (glǽswə:rk, gláswə:rk) n. the making of glass and glassware ‖ glassware **glass·works** pl: n. a factory where glass is made

glass·wort (glǽswə:rt, gláswə:rt) n. a plant of genus Salicornia, esp. S. europoeae, fam. Chenopodiaceae, containing much alkali and formerly used in glassmaking ‖ a saltwort, Salsola kali, of the same family

glass·y (glǽsi:, glási:) comp. **glass·i·er** superl. **glass·i·est** adj. like glass ‖ dull, lifeless, a glassy stare ‖ smooth, calm, the glassy surface of the lake

Glau·ber salt (glǻubər) Glauber's salt

Glauber's salt crystallized sodium sulfate, $Na_2SO_4 \cdot 10H_2O$, used as an aperient [after J. R. Glauber (1604-68), G. chemist]

glau·co·ma (glɔkóumə, glaukóumə) n. a disease of the eye, characterized by an increase of pressure of the fluids within the eyeball, leading to gradual loss of vision and blindness **glau·có·ma·tous** adj. [Gk]

glau·cous (glɔ́kəs) adj. grayish blue or grayish green ‖ (bot.) covered with a powdery or waxy bloom [fr. L. glaucus, bluish green or gray]

glaze (gleiz) 1. v. pres. part. **glaz·ing** past and past part. **glazed** v.t. to fit (a window or picture frame) with glass ‖ to apply a vitreous coating to (pottery etc.) ‖ to give a smooth, glossy coating to (leather, cloth, certain foods etc.) ‖ to cover (a painted surface) with a thin transparent layer so as to modify the underlying color ‖ to polish ‖ v.i. to become glassy, my eyes glazed with boredom **to glaze in** to enclose with glass panels 2. n. the glassy compound fired on pottery etc. to make it watertight or to please the eye ‖ a brightness, sheen ‖ a smooth coating (given to cloth, leather, food etc.) ‖ a glassy film ‖ a transparent coat applied to a painted surface ‖ ice formed by rain falling on objects below freezing temperature ‖ a stretch of icy ground [M.E. glasen fr. glas, glass]

gla·zier (gléiʒər) n. someone who cuts and sets glass in windows professionally **glá·zier·y** n. [GLASS]

glaz·ing (gléiziŋ) n. the using or applying of glaze ‖ material used as glaze ‖ glass to be set as windows

Gla·zu·nov (glázunʌf, glazunɔ́f), Aleksandr Konstantinovich (1865–1936), Russian composer. His 6th symphony, piano and violin music and ballet 'The Seasons' (1901) are among his best-known works

GLCM (mil. acronym) for ground launched cruise missile

gleam (gli:m) 1. n. a glint ‖ a faint light, or something compared to this, a gleam of hope 2. v.i. to glint ‖ to glow, to shine dimly [O.E. glaem]

gleam·er (glí:mər) n. a cosmetic face rouge designed to create a gleaming appearance

glean (gli:n) v.i. to gather leavings of grain after the reaping ‖ v.t. to gather leavings of grain in (a field) after reaping ‖ to collect little by little, to glean bits of information **glean·ing** n. (usually pl.) something gathered by gleaning [M.E. glenen fr. O.F.]

glebe (gli:b) n. land belonging to a clergyman's benefice [fr. L. gleba, clod, soil]

glee (gli:) *n.* effervescent, demonstrative mirth ‖ laughing satisfaction at the misfortunes of others ‖ (*mus.*) an unaccompanied part-song mainly of the 18th c. for three or more voices (usually male) [O.E. *glīw*, *glēo*]

glee club a club for singing glees and other part-songs etc.

glee·ful (glí:fəl) *adj.* filled with glee

gleet (glí:t) *n.* a chronic mucous discharge, e.g. from the urethra in gonorrhea [M.E. *glette* fr. O.F.]

Glei·witz (gláivits) *GLIWICE

glen (glen) *n.* a narrow valley [fr. Gael. *gleaun*]

Glen·coe (glenkóu) a glen in the Scottish Highlands, where the Macdonalds were massacred (1692) by their traditional enemies, the Campbells, on the pretext of disloyalty to William III of England. The incident aroused great ill feeling against England

Glen·dow·er, Glyn Dwr (glendáuər), Owen (c. 1359– c. 1416), Welsh leader of a revolt (1400–9) against Henry IV's rule in Wales

glen·gar·ry (glengǽri) *pl.* **glen·gar·ries** *n.* a man's cap, of Highland origin, creased from front to back and usually with small streamers hanging at the back [after *Glengarry*, Scotland]

Glenn (glen), John Herschel, Jr. (1922–), U.S. astronaut. He was the first American to achieve orbital flight in space. He made (1962) a triple circle of the earth in 4 hrs. 56 min., reaching a maximum altitude of 187.75 miles and a velocity of 17,545 m.p.h., and covering a distance of about 81,000 miles. He served in the U.S. Senate (1975–) and in 1984 ran for the Democratic presidential nomination

gle·noid (glí:nɔid) *adj.* (*anat.*, of a bone) slightly hollowed out to receive the rounded end of another bone, so forming a joint [fr. Gk *glenoeidēs* fr. *glēnē*, socket +*eidos*, form]

glib (glib) *comp.* **glib·ber** *superl.* **glib·best** *adj.* too pat, *glib excuses* ‖ shallow and facile, *a glib tongue* [etym. doubtful]

glide (glaid) 1. *v. pres. part.* **glid·ing** *past and past part.* **glid·ed** *v.i.* to move smoothly forward without apparent effort, *the swan glided downstream* ‖ (*aeron.*) to fly without engine power ‖ to move silently, *to glide about a sickroom* ‖ to pass imperceptibly, *the years glide by* ‖ (*mus.*) to pass from one note to another with a glide ‖ *v.t.* to cause to glide 2. *n.* the act of gliding ‖ a sliding step used in dancing (*mus.*) a slur ‖ (*phon.*) the transitional sound made when changing from one speech position to another ‖ (*cricket*) a delicate deflection, *a leg glide* **glid·er** *n.* an engineless aircraft used for sport and, as a towed transport, esp. for military purposes. Gliders are usually launched by catapult, by winch, or by towing aircraft. They climb by making use of upward air currents and thermals, and gain speed in losing height. The principles of gliding were first accurately demonstrated by Sir George Cayler (1773-1857) in the early 19th c. The knowledge of aerodynamics gained in early gliding experiments by Otto Lilienthal, the Wright brothers and others was of great importance in the evolution of powered flight ‖ a swinging porch seat [O.E. *glīdan*]

glide bomb (*mil.*) an airborne bomb fitted with foils to increase its range

glim·mer (glímər) 1. *v.i.* to shine feebly or intermittently 2. *n.* a feeble or intermittent light ‖ a faint gleam (of hope etc.) ‖ a glimpse **glim·mer·ing** *n.* [M.E. *glimeren*, *glemeren*]

glimpse (glimps) 1. *v.t. pres. part.* **glimps·ing** *past and past part.* **glimpsed** to catch sight of briefly or fleetingly 2. *n.* a brief view, *to catch a glimpse of someone* [M.E. *glysen*]

Glin·ka (glíŋkə), Mikhail Ivanovich (1804–57), Russian composer. He was one of the founders of the Russian nationalist school of music. His works include the operas 'A Life for the Czar' (1836) and 'Russlan and Ludmilla' (1842)

glint (glint) 1. *v.i.* to flash, sparkle, *the windows glinted in the sun* ‖ (of the eyes) to express (an emotion) by flashing, *her eyes glinted malice* 2. *n.* a flash, gleam ‖ a variation in a radar signal due to reflection from the target surface [M.E. *glinten*, *glenten* prob. fr. O.N.]

glis·sade (glisád, gliséid) 1. *n.* (in mountaineering) a controlled slide down a steep slope, usually over ice or snow ‖ a sliding step in dancing 2. *v.i. pres. part.* **glis·sad·ing** *past and past part.* **glis·sad·ed** to execute a glissade [F. fr. *glisser*, to slide]

glis·san·do (glisándou) *pl.* **glis·san·di** (glisándi:), **glis·san·dos** *n.* a rapid succession of notes on a piano, harp etc. played by sliding the fingertip or nail over the keys or strings [prob. an Italianized form fr. F. *glissade*]

glis·ten (glís'n) 1. *v.i.* to sparkle, glitter ‖ to appear bright, usually by reflecting light, *his eyes glistened with tears* 2. *n.* a glitter [O.E. *glisnian*]

glitch (glitʃ) *n.* (*slang*) a misfunction in machinery, esp. in electricity input resulting in a surge in power

glit·ter (glítər) 1. *v.i.* to sparkle very brightly ‖ to be resplendent 2. *n.* sparkle, brilliance ‖ bits of tinsel, glass etc. used for ornamentation **glit·ter·y** *adj.* [M.E. *gliteren* prob. fr. O.N.]

glitter rock a staging of rock music with male participants dressed in absurd female attire

Gli·wi·ce (gliːvíːtsə) (formerly Gleiwitz) a Polish industrial town (pop. 199,200) in Upper Silesia: metalworks, machinery, paper, chemicals

gloam·ing (glóumiŋ) *n.* (*rhet.*) dusk, twilight [O.E. *glōmung*]

gloat (glout) *v.i.* to look at or think about something with malicious, greedy or lustful pleasure [etym. doubtful]

glo·bal (glóub'l) *adj.* spherical ‖ involving the whole world, *global warfare* ‖ comprehensive, total

global tectonics *PLATE TECTONICS

global village a futuristic version of world community as a village created by a high-level of electronic communications; conceived by Marshall McLuhan

glo·bate (glóubeit) *adj.* shaped like a globe

globe (gloub) *n.* a sphere ‖ a spherical model of the earth or the heavens ‖ (*rhet.*) the earth ‖ a spherical or almost spherical glass vessel [F.]

globe artichoke *ARTICHOKE

Globe Theatre a former playhouse in Southwark, London, built (1599) by Cuthbert Burbage. His brother Richard was leading actor in many of the early productions of Shakespeare's plays which took place here

globe-trot·ter (glóubtrɒtər) *n.* someone who travels frequently and widely for pleasure

globe-fish (glóubfiʃ) *pl.* **globe-fish, globe-fish·es** *n.* a member of *Tetraodontidae*, a family of tropical marine fish which can puff themselves up when alarmed

glo·bi·ge·ri·na (gloubidʒəríːnə) *n.* a member of *Globigerina*, fam. *Globigerinidae*, a genus of foraminifers whose shells are found fossilized in tertiary formations and are abundant in calcareous deposits of mud on the ocean bed [Mod. L. fr. L. *globus*, ball+*gerere*, to carry]

glo·bin (glóubin) *n.* a colorless protein occurring in hemoglobin [fr. L. *globus*, globe]

glo·boid (glóubɔid) *adj.* nearly spherical ‖ spherical

glo·bose (glóubous) *adj.* globoid [fr. L. *globosus* fr. *globus*, globe]

glob·u·lar (glɒbjulər) *adj.* globe-shaped ‖ consisting of globules [fr. L. *globulus*, globule]

glob·ule (glɒbjuːl) *n.* a small round particle or drop [F.]

glob·u·lin (glɒbjulin) *n.* any one of a group of simple proteins (e.g. gamma globulin) that coagulate under heat and are insoluble in pure water, widely found in animal or plant tissues, e.g. in blood plasma

glock·en·spiel (glókənʃpiːl) *n.* a musical percussion instrument consisting of a set of metal bars without resonators, struck by two small hammers or arranged on a keyboard ‖ a carillon [G.=bell play]

glomb (glɒm) *n.* (*mil. acronym*) for glide bomb, a bomb-containing glider launched and guided to its target by radio

glom·er·ate (glɒmərit) *adj.* (*biol.*) tightly clustered together **glom·er·a·tion** (glɒməréiʃən) *n.* [fr. L. *glomerare* (*glomeratus*), to form into a ball]

glom·er·ule (glɒməruːl) *n.* a mass of tiny flowers forming a single cymose flowerhead ‖ a glomerulus [F. *glomérule*]

glo·mer·u·lus (glɒmérulɒs, glɒmérjulɒs) *pl.* **glo·mer·u·li** (glɒmérulai, glɒmérjulai) *n.* a cluster of blood vessels, e.g. at the beginning of the kidney tubule, where unconcentrated urine is formed by filtration from the blood [Mod. L.]

Glom·ma (glɒmə) Norway's largest river (375 miles), flowing into the Skagerrak at Fredrikstad

gloom (gluːm) *v.i.* (*rhet.*) to look morose, sullen ‖ (*rhet.*, of the sky, etc.) to look menacing, lower 2. *n.* semidarkness ‖ heavy shadow ‖ melancholy, dejectedness [M.E. *gloumen*, O.E. *glūmian*. to look sullen]

gloom·i·ly (glúːmili) *adv.* in a gloomy way

gloom·i·ness (glúːminis) *n.* the state or quality of being gloomy

gloom·y (glúːmi) *comp.* **gloom·i·er** *superl.* **gloom·i·est** *adj.* dark, obscure, *a gloomy wood* ‖ melancholy ‖ dismal, depressing

glop (glɒp) *n.* (*slang*) a shapeless blob of mush, e.g., food, toothpaste. **gloppy** *adj.*

glo·ri·a (glɔ́ri:ə, glɔ́uriːə) *n.* the Gloria Patri, a doxology ‖ the Gloria Tibi, a response in the Mass etc. ‖ the Gloria in Excelsis Deo, the hymn 'Glory be to God on high' in the Mass etc., or the music for it ‖ (*art*) a halo [L.]

glo·ri·fi·ca·tion (glɔrifikéiʃən, glɔurifikéiʃən) *n.* a glorifying or being glorified [fr. L.L. *glorificatio* (*glorificationis*)]

glo·ri·fy (glɔ́rifai, glɔ́urifai) *pres. part.* **glo·ri·fy·ing** *past and past part.* **glo·ri·fied** *v.t.* to ascribe glory to, praise, *to glorify God* ‖ to make radiantly beautiful ‖ to swell pompously the importance of, esp. by naming pretentiously, *a damp cottage glorified under the name 'The Grange'* [fr. F. *glorifier*]

glo·ri·ole (glɔ́riːoul, glɔ́uriːoul) *n.* (*art*) a halo [F.]

glo·ri·ous (glɔ́riːəs, glɔ́uriːəs) *adj.* full of glory or worthy of glory, illustrious ‖ splendid, thrilling, *a glorious view* ‖ (*pop.*) immensely enjoyable [A.F.]

Glorious First of June, Battle of the a British naval victory (1794) over the French during the French Revolutionary Wars

Glorious Revolution (*Eng. hist.*) the name given to the overthrow (1688–9) of James II and the proclamation of William III and Mary II as joint sovereigns. The resultant Bill of Rights (1689) marked the ascendancy of parliamentary authority over the divine right that had been claimed by the Stuarts

glo·ry (glɔ́ri:, glɔ́uri:) 1. *pl.* **glo·ries** *n.* praise, adoration, *glory be to the Father* ‖ great renown ‖ particular distinction, *her hair was her glory* ‖ magnificence, splendor ‖ sublime beauty, *the glory of a summer dawn* ‖ (*art*) the luminous aureole surrounding the whole body of Christ ‖ the splendor of heaven, beatitude, *the saints in glory* **in one's glory** in a situation which gives intense satisfaction by the opportunity to indulge one's special talents or passions **to cover oneself in** (or **with**) **glory** to distinguish oneself by a conspicuously good performance, brave act etc. 2. *v.i. pres. part.* **glo·ry·ing** *past and past part.* **glo·ried** to exult, rejoice, *he gloried in his new-found freedom* ‖ to take pride (in) [M.E. *glorie* fr. O.F.]

gloss (glɒs) (glɒs) 1. *n.* an interlinear translation ‖ an explanatory interlinear or marginal insertion in the text of a book ‖ a glossary ‖ a verbal interpretation or paraphrase ‖ a sophistical, misleading interpretation 2. *v.t.* to insert glosses in or provide a glossary for (a text) ‖ to comment on or interpret in a misleading or prejudiced way, *to gloss the truth* ‖ *v.i.* to make glosses [fr. O.F. *glose* fr. L. *glossa* fr. Gk *glōssa*, (foreign) tongue, word needing explanation]

gloss 1. *n.* sheen ‖ deceitful appearance 2. *v.t.* to give a gloss to ‖ (with 'over') to cause to seem less serious, difficult, unfavorable etc. than is really the case by specious argument etc. [etym. doubtful]

glos·sa (glɒsə, glɒsə) *pl.* **glos·sae** (glɒsi:, glɒsi:), **glos·sas** *n.* (*entom.*) a tonguelike projection in the middle of the labium of many insects [Mod. L. fr. Gk *glōssa*, tongue]

glos·sa·ri·al (glɒséariːəl, glɒséəriːəl) *adj.* of or in the nature of a glossary

glos·sa·rist (glɒsərist, glɒsərist) *n.* someone who makes glosses ‖ someone who compiles a glossary

glos·sa·ry (glɒsəri:, glɒsəri:) *pl.* **glos·sa·ries** *n.* a list of difficult, old, technical or foreign words with explanations, usually at the end of a text [fr. L. *glossarium*]

glos·sa·tor (glɒséitər, glɒséitər) *n.* a writer of glosses, esp. one of the medieval commentators on law [M.L.]

glos·se·mat·ics (glɒsəmǽtiks, glɒsəmætiks) *n.* linguistic analysis according to the distribution and interrelationship of glossemes

glos·seme (glɒsi:m, glɒsi:m) *n.* the smallest unit that signals a meaning in a language (e.g. a word, an intonation, a grammatical element) [L.=tongue fr. Gk]

gloss·i·ly (glɒsili, glɒsili) *adv.* in a glossy way

gloss·i·ness (glɒsinis, glɒsinis) *n.* the state or quality of being glossy

gloss·y (glɒsi:, glɒsi:) 1. *adj. comp.* **gloss·i·er** *su-*

---

perl. **gloss·i·est** shiny, smooth, highly polished ‖ superficially attractive, specious 2. pl. **gloss·ies** n. a magazine printed on glossy paper

glost firing (glɒst, glɔst) the process of firing a glaze on ware that has already been through the biscuit firing [fr. *glost* var. of GLOSS, sheen]

GLOTRAC (*acronym*) for global tracking, a system for tracking satellites designed by General Dynamics Corporation

glot·tal (glɒt'l) adj. of or pertaining to the glottis ‖ (*phon.*) produced by or in the glottis

glottal stop (*phon.*) a complete momentary closure of the glottis, e.g. in pronouncing 'law officer'

glot·tis (glɒtis) n. the opening between the vocal cords in the throat which controls the modulation of speech sounds [Mod. L. fr. Gk. *glotta*, a form of *glossa*, tongue]

glot·to·chro·nol·o·gy (glɒtoukrɒnɒlədʒi:) n. (*linguistics*) measurement involving lexicostatistics of the change in a language since its origin

Glouces·ter (glɒstər, glɔstər), Gilbert de Clare, 8th earl of (1243–95). He supported first the baronial faction and later the royalists in the Barons' War, and helped Edward I's accession to the throne

Gloucester, Humphrey, duke of (1391–1447), protector of England during Henry VI's minority (1422–9), son of Henry IV. He was a patron of learning and the Church

Gloucester, Thomas of Woodstock, duke of (1355–97), son of Edward III. He led the baronial opposition to Richard II and was imprisoned for treason (1397)

Gloucester the county town of Gloucestershire, England, a county borough (pop. 92,133) on the Severn. Cathedral (1088–1498)

Gloucester (glɒstər, glɔstər) n. a hard cheese originating in the county of Gloucestershire

Glouces·ter·shire (glɒstərʃər, glɔstərʃər) (*abbr.* Gloucester, Glos.) a county (area 1,257 sq. miles, pop. 499,351) in western England. County town: Gloucester

glove (glʌv) 1. n. one of a pair of coverings for the hands, usually with separate divisions for the fingers and for the thumb, worn for warmth, protection or adornment **hand in glove** on terms of complete mutual understanding. esp. where wrongdoing is involved 2. v.t. pres. part. **glov·ing** past and past part. **gloved** to cover with or as if with a glove ‖ to furnish with gloves ‖ (*baseball*) to catch (the ball) in one's gloved hand **glóv·er** n. someone who makes or sells gloves [O.E. *glóf*]

glove box a protective box with extruded gloves through which radioactive, contaminated, germ-free, or other materials can be handled without personal hand contact

glow (glou) 1. v.i. to emit light, esp. red light, without the smoke or flame of rapid combustion ‖ to be radiant, *to glow with pride* ‖ to have a bright, warm color, *the trees glowed in the sunset* 2. n. the emission of light without smoke or flame ‖ warmth produced by physical exertion ‖ warmth of emotion or passion, *the glow of anger* [O.E. *glōwan*]

glow·er (glάuər) 1. v.i. to stare with sullen anger 2. n. a look of sullen anger [perh. fr. GLOW]

glow·ing (glóuiŋ) adj. bright and warm in color ‖ compellingly favorable and attractive, *in glowing terms*

glow·worm (glóuwərm) n. a wingless or rudimentary-winged insect which emits light, esp. one of the females or larvae of beetles of fam. *Lampyridae*, which produce a steady light from the abdomen

glox·in·i·a (glɒksíni:ə) n. a member of *Gloxinia*, fam. *Gesneriaceae*, a genus of tropical American and greenhouse plants, with richly colored leaves and bell-shaped flowers of various shades [Mod. L. after B. P. *Gloxin* (18th c.), G. botanist]

gloze (glouz) pres. part. **gloz·ing** past and past part. **glozed** v.t. (with 'over') to gloss over [O.F. *glose*]

Glubb (glʌb), Sir John Bagot (1897–1986), British general. He commanded the Arab Legion in Transjordan (1938–56), and was known as 'Glubb Pasha'

glu·cin·i·um (glu:síni:əm) n. beryllium [Mod. L. fr. *glucina*, beryllium oxide fr. F. fr. Gk]

glu·ci·num (glu:sáinəm) n. glucinium

Gluck (gluk), Christoph Willibald (1714–87), German operatic composer. He sought to reform opera by making the music serve the

drama more closely. His best-known work is 'Orpheus' (1762)

glu·co·pro·tein (glu:koupróuti:n) n. glycoprotein

glu·cose (glú:kous) n. a sugar, $C_6H_{12}O_6$, found in honey, grapes and sweet fruits, and also made artificially from carbohydrates, esp. starch, by hydrolysis. It is used esp. in the food industry. It is normally the chief source of body energy and in its simple state is the form in which carbohydrate is assimilated by the animal body [fr. Gk *glukus*, sweet]

glu·co·side (glú:kəsaid) n. a glycoside that yields glucose on hydrolysis

glue (glu:) 1. n. a hard, brown, brittle substance obtained from crude gelatin and used as an adhesive when softened by heating or solution ‖ any similar adhesive 2. v. pres. part. **glu·ing** past and past part. **glued** v.t. to attach with glue or as if with glue ‖ v.i. to become glued [fr. O.F. *glu*, birdlime]

glue-sniff·ing (glú:snifiŋ) n. physically harmful practice of inhaling fumes of some forms of glue to achieve intoxication

glue·y (glú:i:) comp. **glu·i·er** superl. **glu·i·est** adj. covered with glue ‖ sticky

glum (glʌm) comp. **glum·mer** superl. **glum·mest** adj. gloomy, morose [fr. obs. v. *glum* fr. M.E. *glomen*]

glu·ma·ceous (glu:méiʃəs) adj. of, consisting of or bearing glumes

glume (glu:m) n. (*bot.*) a bract at the base of a grass inflorescence or spikelet [fr. L. *gluma*, husk]

glu·on (glú:ɒr) n. (*particle phys.*) hypothetical particle believed to hold together the centers of atoms

glut (glʌt) 1. v.t. pres. part. **glut·ting** past and past part. **glut·ted** to fill to excess, oversupply, *to glut the market* ‖ to satisfy utterly, *to glut one's appetite* ‖ to overfeed, gorge, *to glut oneself on oysters* 2. n. oversupply, *a glut of apples* [prob. fr. O.F. *glut*, gluttonous]

glu·ta·ral·de·hyde [$C_5H_8O_4$] (glu:tərældəhaid) n. (*chem.*) disinfectant compound used in tanning

glu·te·al (glú:ti:əl) adj. of or pertaining to the buttock muscles [fr. Mod. L. *glutaeus* fr. Gk *gloutos*, rump, buttock]

glu·ten (glú:t'n) n. an elastic protein substance in grain giving consistency to dough. It remains when starch is extracted [L.=glue]

gluten bread bread made from flour rich in gluten and low in starch

glu·te·nous (glú:t'nəs) adj. of or containing gluten

glu·teth·i·mide [$C_{13}H_{15}NO_2$] (glu:téθəmaid) n. (*pharm.*) a nonbarbiturate hypnotic; marketed as Doriden

glu·ti·nous (glú:t'nəs) adj. like glue, viscous [fr. L. *glutinosus*]

glut·ton (glʌt'n) n. someone who eats excessively ‖ someone with a remarkable willingness to endure or perform something of a specified nature, *a glutton for work* ‖ *Gulo gulo*, a carnivorous mammal of the weasel family found in N. Europe and Asia, closely resembling the wolverene of North America **glút·ton·ous** adj. [M.E. *glutun, gloton* fr. O.F.]

glut·ton·y (glʌt'ni:) n. excessive eating and drinking [M.E. *glutunie, glotonie*]

glyc·er·ide (glísəraid) n. one of a large class of compounds that are esters of glycerol and one or more usually fatty acids, that occur naturally as fats and are also prepared synthetically for the manufacture of soaps and lubricants

glyc·er·in (glísərin) n. glycerol [fr. Gk *glukeros*, sweet]

glyc·er·ine (glísəri:n, glísərin) n. glycerol

glyc·er·ol (glísərɒl, glísəroul) n. a sweet, viscous, hygroscopic alcohol, $CH_2OH \cdot CHOH \cdot CH_2OH$, that occurs naturally in the combined forms as glycerides, and is recovered in the manufacture of soaps from fats. It is an important industrial chemical used chiefly as a solvent, as a lubricant, and as a raw material for the manufacture of nitroglycerin

gly·co·gen (gláikədʒən) n. a white, tasteless polysaccharide, $(C_6H_{10}O_5)n$, occurring esp. in the liver and muscle where it is stored as a sugar-supply reserve, capable of complete conversion into glucose when needed **gly·co·gen·ic** (glaikədʒénik) adj. [fr. Gk *glukos*, sweet+*genes*, producing]

gly·col (gláikɒl, gláikoul) n. (*chem.*) a colorless, thick, sweet liquid, $C_2H_4(OH)_2$, ethylene glycol,

used as an antifreeze and in making plasticizers ‖ any of the group of dihydroxy alcohols **gly·col·ic, gly·col·lic** (glaikólik) adjs [GLYCERIN]

gly·co·pep·tide (glaikoupéptaid) n. a glycoprotein

gly·co·pro·tein (glaikoupróuti:n) n. any of several complex proteins which contain a carbohydrate in combination with a simple protein

gly·co·side (gláikəsaid) n. one of a class of compounds (of both natural and synthetic origin) which, upon hydrolysis by dilute acids or enzymes, yield one or more molecules of a sugar and often a noncarbohydrate

gly·co·sur·i·a (glaikousúəri:ə) n. (*med.*) a condition in which an abnormal amount of sugar is present in the urine, e.g. in diabetes mellitus **gly·co·sur·ic** adj. [fr. F. *glycose*+Gk *ouron*, urine]

gly·cyr·rhet·in·ic acid [$C_{30}H_{46}O_4$] (glisi:-rətinik) hydrocarbon created by hydrolysis of glycyrrhizic acid

Glynde·bourne (gláindbɔrn) a village in E. Sussex, England, where an annual international opera festival has been held since 1934

glyph (glif) n. an ornamental vertical groove in carving ‖ a carved pictograph ‖ short for hieroglyph, a nonverbal sign, e.g., road driving warnings **glýph·ic** adj. [fr. Gk *gluphē*, carving]

glyp·tic (glíptik) adj. relating to carving, usually on gems [fr. Gk *gluptikos* fr. *gluphein*, to carve]

glyp·to·don (glíptədɒn) n. a member of *Glyptodon*, a genus of enormous extinct mammals closely allied to the armadillo. The glyptodon was the size of an ox, with a thick protection of polygonal osseous plates. Its fossil remains are found in the Upper Tertiary strata of South America [Mod. L. fr. Gk *gluptos*, carved+*odous* (*odontos*), tooth]

glyp·to·dont (glíptədɒnt) n. a glyptodon

glyp·tog·ra·phy (gliptógrəfi:) n. the art, study or process of engraving gems [fr. Gk *gluptos*, carved+*graphos*, written]

G-man (dʒí:mæn) pl. **G-men** (dʒí:mɛn) n. (*pop.*) a criminal investigator from the Federal Bureau of Investigation [GOVERNMENT MAN]

gnarl (nɑrl) 1. n. a twisted, knotty outgrowth on a tree 2. v.t. to twist, contort **gnarled** (nɑrld) adj. twisted and knobby, *gnarled fingers* **gnárl·y** comp. **gnarl·i·er** superl. **gnarl·i·est** adj. [earlier *knurled*, origin unknown]

gnash (næʃ) v.t. to grind (the teeth) together, in anger etc. ‖ v.i. to grind the teeth together, in anger etc. [etym. doubtful]

gnat (næt) n. any of various very small, two-winged flies of the order *Diptera* ‖ any very small fly that bites or stings, e.g. the sand fly [O.E. *gnætt*]

gnath·ic (næθik) adj. pertaining to the jaws [fr. Gk *gnathos*, jaw]

gnathic index a measure of the degree of protrusion of the jaw, obtained by multiplying the ratio between the distance from the basion to the nasion and the distance from the basion to the prosthion by 100

gnaw (nɔ) pres. part. **gnaw·ing** past **gnawed** (nɔd) past part. **gnawed, gnawn** (nɔn) v.t. to scrape and wear away with the teeth, *dogs gnaw bones* ‖ (of hunger, worry etc.) to be a continuous inner torment to ‖ v.i. to bite on something continuously, *to gnaw at a chicken leg* **gnáw·ing** n. a persistent fretting discomfort, pain or anxiety [O.E. *gnagan*]

Gnei·se·nau (g'náizənau), August Neithardt, Count von (1760–1831), Prussian field marshal. He helped Stein and Scharnhorst to reorganize the Prussian army after the Treaty of Tilsit (1807) and served as Blücher's chief of staff in the campaigns of 1813 and 1815

gneiss (nais, gnais) n. (*geol.*) a crystalline, metamorphic rock formed by the recrystallization of granite, in which the minerals (e.g. quartz or feldspar, and mica) are separated in characteristic dark and light bands [G.]

Gniez·no (g'njéznɔ) a town (pop. 50,600) in W. central Poland, an ancient capital and crowning place of Polish kings

GNMA (*banking*) pass-through mortgage-backed certificates guaranteed by the Government National Mortgage Association (GNMA or Ginnie Mae). The certificates are backed by pools of FHA-insured and/or VA-guaranteed residential mortgages, with the mortgage and notes held in safekeeping by a custodial financial institution

gnome (noum) n. a member of a race of small, misshapen imaginary beings, originally guardians of the earth's subterranean treasures ‖ a goblin or dwarf [F.]

gnome (noum, nóumi:) *n.* a pithy saying, aphorism [Gk *gnōmē*]

gno·mic (nóumik) *adj.* pithy and sententious, *gnomic poetry* ‖ using aphorisms, *a gnomic writer* [fr. Gk *gnōmikos* fr. *gnōmē*, maxim]

gno·mon (nóumon) *n.* the pin of a sundial ‖ (*geom.*) the part of a parallelogram remaining after a smaller and similar parallelogram has been removed from one of its corners **gno·mon·ic** *adj.* [Gk *gnōmōn*, indicator]

gno·sis (nóusis) *n.* a divinely inspired knowledge [Gk=knowledge]

gnos·tic (nóstik) 1. *adj.* possessing gnosis **Gnos·tic** of or pertaining to Gnosticism 2. *n.* **Gnos·tic** an adherent from Gnosticism

Gnos·ti·cism (nóstisizəm) *n.* a trend of religious thought with Far Eastern origins which flourished in the Hellenistic Near East. There were numerous Gnostic sects, both pagan and Christian. The Christian Gnostics denied the literal meaning of the Scriptures and saw only an esoteric meaning based on gnosis, e.g. they did not believe that a real Jesus was really crucified [fr. Gk *gnōstikos*]

gno·to·bi·ot·ic (noutoubaíotik) *n.* study of a germ-free environment. **—gnotobiologically** *adv.* **—gnotobiotic** *adj.*

GNP deflator (economics) running monthly index compiled by U.S. Department of Commerce to adjust the value of the measured gross national product for changes in the value of the dollar

gnu (nu:, nju:) *pl.* **gnu, gnus** *n.* one of several southern African antelopes of genera *Connochaetes* and *Gorgon*, having a heavy neck, an oxlike head, and a tail like that of a horse. They have long curved horns and are fierce when attacked [Hottentot]

go (gou) 1. *v.i. pres. part.* **go·ing** *past* **went** (went) *past part.* **gone** (gon) *v.i.* to be in motion, *to go along a road, the car is going fast* ‖ to move with a specified purpose, *to go on an errand, go for a walk, go shopping* ‖ to leave, *you must go at noon* ‖ to disappear, *the pain will soon go* ‖ to be lost, *my sight went early* ‖ to be abolished, *compulsory Latin must go* ‖ to extend, reach, *the property goes to the river, the treaty is all right as far as it goes* ‖ to be working, perform its proper function, *this clock doesn't go, this generator is kept going all the time* ‖ to be in a specified state, *to go barefoot* ‖ to become, *to go blind* ‖ (of time) to pass ‖ to sound, *the bell has gone* ‖ to be current, *the story goes that she was once rich* ‖ to be known, *he goes by the name of Charlie* ‖ to be on the average, *she is a good preacher as preachers go* ‖ to have a certain content, run, *the song goes like this* ‖ to be placed, lie, *your left hand should go here* ‖ to make a certain motion, sound etc., *go like this with your head, the firework went bang* ‖ to be determined, *promotion goes by age* ‖ to be guided, *give him some data to go upon* ‖ to take a certain course, *everything went well at the meeting, to go straight, the country has gone Communist* ‖ to remain, *to go unpunished* ‖ to be spent, *all our money goes on women* ‖ to share, *to go fifty-fifty* ‖ to die ‖ to give way, crack, break down, *my ankle's gone again, the clutch has gone* ‖ to become worn, *the trousers have gone at the knees* ‖ to be a regular or frequent attender, *to go to church* ‖ to commit oneself to action or expense, *to go to any lengths* ‖ to have recourse, *to go to war, to go to court* ‖ to fit, be contained, *this luggage won't go in the car, 2 goes into 6 three times* ‖ to belong, *coats go on the coatrack* ‖ (of colors) to harmonize, be compatible ‖ to be sold, *going cheap* ‖ to be applied, *that money goes to charity* ‖ to contribute, *it all goes to show how wrong you can be* ‖ to be allotted, *the prize went to the old man* ‖ to be valid, *what I say goes, that goes for you, too* ‖ (used in the pres. or past continuous tense with an infin.) to be about or intending, *he's going to leave soon* ‖ *v.t.* to travel on, *to go on a journey* ‖ to travel a distance of, *to go 10 miles* ‖ to follow (a way, road etc.), *go the short way* ‖ (*Br.*) to strike, chime etc., *it has just gone 6* ‖ to risk, wager, *go $10 on a horse* ‖ to bid (at cards), *to go three no-trumps* **go along with you!** be off! no more of your nonsense! **it** (or **that**) **goes without saying** it (or that) is self-evident **to be going on** (*Am.=Br.* **to be going on for**) to be almost or approaching (a specified age or time) **to go about** to circulate, *a story is going about* ‖ (*naut.*) to tack ‖ to set to work at, *you are not going about it correctly* **to go after** ‖ to chase ‖ to try to obtain **to go against** to run counter to, *it goes against the*

rules **to go ahead** to start ‖ to make progress ‖ to move into the lead **to go along** to continue, *make up the story as you go along* ‖ to agree ‖ to cooperate ‖ to accompany, *will you go along with me?* **to go around** (or **round**) to make one's way around ‖ to make a detour ‖ to circulate, *the story soon went around* ‖ to pay a visit, *I went around to see him* ‖ to be sufficient to supply everyone **to go at** to work hard at ‖ to attack **to go at it** (*pop.*) to apply oneself with energy **to go away** to leave on one's honeymoon ‖ to leave home (e.g. for a holiday or a weekend) **to go before** to precede in time, *pride goes before a fall* ‖ to proceed in front of ‖ to take precedence over, *he goes before me in seniority* ‖ to be submitted for decision or trial to, *this will have to go before the president* **to go by** to pass, *time goes by, the car went by* ‖ to pass unheeded, *let the world go by* **to go down** to descend ‖ (of the sun, a ship, prices etc.) to sink ‖ (of the wind, sea) to subside ‖ (*Br.*) to be received by an audience, *the comedy went down well* ‖ to be written down or recorded in history and tradition, *Nelson has gone down as an English hero* ‖ to extend, *this history goes down to the 16th century* ‖ to be conquered ‖ (*bridge*) to fail to fulfill one's contract ‖ to be swallowed ‖ (*Br.*, Oxford and Cambridge) to leave the university temporarily or permanently **to go far** to do great things, distinguish oneself ‖ to buy much, *$50 a week doesn't go far these days* **to go for** to fetch ‖ to attack ‖ to produce, *my labors went for nothing* ‖ to try to get ‖ (*pop.*) to like **to go in** to enter ‖ (with 'with') to join as a partner ‖ to be hidden from sight, *the sun has gone in* (behind a cloud) ‖ to begin an innings in cricket **to go in for** to take up, engage in (a pursuit), *to go in for accountancy* ‖ to enjoy, indulge in, *to go in for practical jokes* ‖ to enter for (an examination or competition) **to go into** to enter (a profession etc.), *to go into politics* ‖ to enter (an emotional state), *to go into hysterics* ‖ to examine in detail, *to go into a matter* ‖ to begin to dress in, *to go into mourning* **to go it** (*pop.*) to go at it **to go it alone** to act unilaterally **to go off** to depart ‖ (of a gun) to fire ‖ (of a bomb, firework etc.) to explode ‖ (of an alarm) to sound ‖ (*Br.*, of food etc.) to go bad ‖ (*theater*) to make an exit ‖ (of a performance etc.) to turn out, *did the concert go off well?* ‖ to elope, *she went off with the gamekeeper* ‖ to fall asleep or lose consciousness ‖ (*Br.*) to die away, *the pain soon went off* ‖ (of gas, light, water) to cease to be available for consumption **to go on** to continue, *go on with your work* ‖ to proceed, *I went on to my second argument* ‖ to base one's reasoning on, *do you have facts to go on?* ‖ (*theater*) to make an entry ‖ to take place, *what's going on here?* ‖ (of time) to pass ‖ to chatter, nag, scold ‖ to behave, esp. badly, *to judge by the way she is going on...* ‖ (of gas, light, water) to begin to be available for consumption ‖ to slip over (the foot, hand etc.), *these shoes won't go on* ‖ to start to receive, *to go on half pay* **go on!** rubbish! ‖ (*imper.*) do it, continue **to go one better** to improve on someone else's performance **to go out** to go outdoors ‖ (*Br.*) to leave home, or go abroad (e.g. for employment), *he went out to Australia to farm* ‖ to seek amusement and social life away from home ‖ to be extinguished ‖ to cease to hold office, *the Tories have gone out* ‖ to cease to be popular or fashionable, *long skirts have gone out* ‖ (of workers) to strike ‖ (of the heart) to feel sympathy, *her heart went out to him* **to go out with** to date (a member of the opposite sex) **to go over** to cross ‖ to change one's allegiance, esp. in religion, *to go over to Rome* ‖ to examine, *to go over details* ‖ to revise, *to go over a manuscript* ‖ to rehearse, *let's go over the last scene* ‖ to be received by an audience, *the play went over well* **to go round** to go around **to go through** to go in at one side and come out at the other, *the nail went right through* ‖ (with 'with') to complete, *you'll have to go through with it once you start* ‖ to traverse, *they went through the desert* ‖ to study, examine in detail, *to go through the figures* ‖ to undergo ‖ to spend (money) ‖ to sell out, *the novel went through many editions* **to go under** to succumb, be defeated ‖ to sink **to go up** to rise ‖ to be built ‖ to be reduced to ruins by or as if by an explosion, *the whole shop went up in smoke* ‖ (*Br.*) to enter a university or begin a new term **to go with** to accompany ‖ (*pop.*) to court (as lover) ‖ to be sold together with, *the box goes with the instruments* ‖ to harmonize with, *purple goes well with yellow* **to go without** to make do without, put up with not having, *I can't go without sleep* **to let it go at**

that to accept a stage as final, be willing to cut short what could be taken further **to let oneself go** to cease to take a pride in oneself ‖ to lose one's inhibitions 2. *pl.* **goes** *n.* energy, drive ‖ an attempt, *you have a go at it now* ‖ (*Br.*, games) a turn, *it's your go next* **a near go** (*Br.*, pop.) a close shave **from the word go** right from the start **no go** useless, a useless effort, *the attempt was no go* **on the go** busy, active **to make a go of** to make a success of [O.E. *gān*]

Go *n.* 1. ancient Japanese boardgame played with stones with the objective of gaining territory to gain points. 2. (*aerospace*) in space terminology, "ready to go"

Go·a (góuə) a region (area 1,301 sq. miles, pop. 1,082,117) on the west coast of India administered directly by the central government. Goa was the largest remnant of Portuguese India, first seized (1510) by Alfonso de Albuquerque. It was taken back by force (Dec. 1961) and with the smaller territories of Daman and Diu constituted a Union Territory (Mar. 1962)

go·a (góuə) *n.* *Gazella picticaudata*, the Tibetan gazelle [fr. Tibetan *dgoba*]

Goa (*mil.*) NATO name for U.S.S.R. air-defense, solid-propellant missile (SA-3), with 20-mi range and radio-command direction

goad (goud) 1. *n.* a pointed stick for driving beasts ‖ something that torments or spurs to action 2. *v.t.* to use a goad on ‖ to urge on by continually irritating [O.E. *gād*]

go-a·head (góuəhed) 1. *adj.* active, energetic, enterprising, *a go-ahead manager* 2. *n.* the signal to proceed ‖ permission to start

goal (goul) *n.* (football, ice hockey etc.) the pair of posts etc. between or into which the ball or puck has to be sent to score points ‖ the act of sending the ball or puck between the two posts or into the hoop etc. ‖ the point thus scored ‖ an aim or objective, *his goal is to win back the property* [M.F. *gol* prob. rel. to O.E. *gǣlan*, to hinder]

goal·ie (góuli) *n.* (*pop.*) the goalkeeper

goal·keep·er (góulki:pər) *n.* (*hockey, soccer* etc.) the player assigned to the defense of the goal

goal line the line marking the end of the playing field or the goal in various games

goal mouth (*hockey, soccer*) the entrance to the goal

goal·post (góulpoust) *n.* one of two posts which mark the goal in several games

go around mode in an automatic flight control system, a control mode that terminates an aircraft approach and programs a climb. *Cf* OVERSHOOT

goat (gout) *n.* a wild or domesticated horned ruminant of genus *Capra*, fam. *Bovidae*, closely allied to the sheep. It frequents rocks and mountains, and feeds on scanty, coarse vegetation. The milk is used esp. for cheese. Goats are also valuable for their hair or wool (*ANGORA, *CASHMERE) and for their hides (*MOROCCO) ‖ (*pop.*) a lecher ‖ a scapegoat **to get someone's goat** to irritate someone **to separate the sheep from the goats** to separate the good from the bad [O.E. *gāt*]

goat antelope any of several animals of fam. *Bovidae* resembling the antelope but related to the goat, e.g. the chamois

goat·ee (gouti:) *n.* a small, pointed or tufted beard on the chin [GOAT]

goat·herd (góuthə:rd) *n.* someone who tends goats

goat·ish (góutiʃ) *adj.* like a goat ‖ (*pop.*) lecherous

goat moth a large moth of fam. *Cossidae*, esp. *Cossus cossus* of Europe and Asia, and the American *Prionoxystus robiniae* (*CARPENTER MOTH), whose larvae feed on and develop in the wood of trees

goat·skin (góutskin) *n.* the skin of a goat ‖ a garment or wine bag made from it

goat·suck·er (góutsʌkər) *n.* any of several nocturnal or crepuscular birds of fam. *Caprimulgidae*, e.g. the whippoorwill and nighthawk. The name comes from an old fable that they milk goats

gob (gob) *n.* a mass or lump, *a gob of clay* **gobs of** (*pop.*) lots of, large amounts of [O.F. *gobe*, *goube*, a mouthful]

gob *n.* (*pop.*) a sailor in the U.S. navy [origin unknown]

gob·bet (góbit) *n.* (*Br.*, *pop.*) a short extract from a prepared text set for translation or comment ‖ (*old-fash.*) a hunk, mouthful of food [O.F. *gobet*, mouthful]

CONCISE PRONUNCIATION KEY: **(a)** æ, c*a*t; ɑ, c*a*r; ɔ f*aw*n; ei, sn*a*ke. **(e)** e, h*e*n; i:, sh*ee*p; iə, d*ee*r; ɛə, b*ea*r. **(i)** i, f*i*sh; ai, t*i*ger; ə:, b*i*rd. **(o)** o, *o*x; au, c*ow*; ou, g*oa*t; u, p*oo*r; ɔi, r*oy*al. **(u)** ʌ, d*u*ck; u, b*u*ll; u:, g*oo*se; ə, b*a*cillus; ju:, c*u*be. x, lo*ch*; θ, *th*ink; δ, bo*th*er; z, *Z*en; ʒ, corsa*g*e; dʒ, sava*g*e; ŋ, oranguta*ng*; j, *y*ak; ʃ, *fi*sh; tʃ, fet*ch*; 'l, rabb*le*; 'n, redd*en*. Complete pronunciation key appears inside front cover.

gob·ble (gób'l) *pres. part.* **gob·bling** *past* and *past part.* **gob·bled** *v.t.* and *i.* to eat greedily, quickly and noisily [GOB, a lump]

gobble 1. *v.i. pres. part.* **gob·bling** *past* and *past part.* **gob·bled** (of a turkeycock) to make its characteristic guttural sound **2.** *n.* this sound [imit.]

gob·ble·dy·gook, gob·ble·de·gook (gób'ldi:-guk) *n.* (*pop.*) bureaucratic verbiage ‖ complex, pretentious jargon

gob·bler (góblər) *n.* (*pop.*) a male turkey

Gob·e·lin tapestry (góbəlin) a kind of tapestry made at the state-owned factory in Paris, France, named after the Gobelin brothers, celebrated dyers and weavers of the 15th c.

go·be·tween (góubitwi:n) *n.* an intermediary

Go·bi Desert (góubi:) one of the world's largest deserts (area 600,000 sq. miles), a plateau (average height 3,000 ft) covered with gravel and sand, extending about 1,500 miles from the Great Khingan Mtns in Manchuria to Sinkiang, China, most of it being in Mongolia. A few nomad tribes inhabit it. Rainfall: 5–8 ins. Extremes of temperature (F.): 150° (July),–60° (Dec.)

Go·bi·neau (gɔbi:nou), Comte Joseph-Arthur de (1816–82), French diplomat and author. His theory of the superiority of the Aryan race, expounded in his 'Essai sur l'inégalité des race humaines' (1853–5), was later made use of by Hitler

gob·let (góblit) *n.* (*hist.*) a drinking vessel of glass or metal without handles but with a stem, a stand and sometimes a cover ‖ a wineglass with a foot and a stem [M.E. *gobelet* fr. O.F.]

gob·lin (góblin) *n.* a mischievous, ugly spirit [M.E. *gobelin* fr. F.]

go·by (góubai) *n.* (only in the phrases) **to get the go-by** to be snubbed **to give (someone) the go-by** to ignore or avoid (someone)

go·by (góubi:) *pl.* **go·bies, go·by** *n.* a member of any of 400 species constituting fam. *Gobiidae*, small, bony, carnivorous fish usually found at the bottom of tropical seas or ponds. Most of them have the pelvic fins joined to form sucking disks [fr. L. *gobius, cobius* fr. Gk *kōbios*, gudgeon]

go·cart (góukɑrt) *n.* a stroller (light, wheeled chair) ‖ a homemade toy car ‖ a handcart

god (gɒd) *n.* (in polytheistic religions) a being to whom worship is ascribed ‖ an image of such a deity ‖ an idolized person or thing, *money is his god* **God** (in monotheistic religions) the supreme being, seen as the omnipotent creator and ruler of the universe **the gods** *pl. n.* the theater audience up in the gallery ‖ the gallery itself **for God's sake** an expression of urgency with a request, *for God's sake hurry up* **God knows** I do not know and cannot find out, *God knows where he is* ‖ assuredly, *God knows it's true* [O.E.]

Godard, Jean Luc (goudár, zhawn luek) (1930–), French film director, known for his New Wave movies and innovative camera and plot techniques. His films include 'Breathless' (1959), 'A Married Woman' (1964), 'La chinoise' (1967), 'Detective' (1984) and 'Hail Mary' (1985)

Go·da·va·ri (goudávəri:) a sacred river (about 900 miles) of India, rising in the Western Ghats and flowing into a delta on the Bay of Bengal

god·child (gódtʃaild) *n.* a boy or girl in relation to the godparents

God·dard (gódərd), Calvin Hooker (1891–1955), U.S. military historian and criminologist. He organized (1930) a scientific crime-detection laboratory in Chicago, Ill., in which he developed methods and instruments for identifying the weapon which fired a given bullet

Goddard, Robert Hutchings (1882–1945), U.S. scientist. He achieved (1926) the first flight of a liquid-fuel rocket. The U.S. government appointed him (1942) to direct research on jet-propelled planes. He was granted about 150 patents

Goddard and Town·send (táunzənd) two families of Quaker cabinetmakers of Newport, R.I., who during the 17th and 18th cc. produced furniture in the Queen Anne and Chippendale styles

god·daugh·ter (góddɔtər) *n.* a girl godchild

god·dess (gódis) *n.* a female deity

go·de·tia (goudi:ʃə) *n.* a member of *Godetia*, fam. *Onagraceae*, a genus of hardy, temperate plants with brightly colored flowers [Mod. L. after C. H. *Godet* (d. 1879), Swiss botanist]

god·fa·ther (gódfɑðər) *n.* a man who sponsors a child at baptism, assuming responsibility for the child's religious guidance up to confirmation ‖ chief-of-chiefs in the Mafia and, by extension, other organizations

God-fear·ing (gódfiəriŋ) *adj.* devout

god-for·sak·en (gódfərseikən) *adj.* dismal, joyless, *this town is a godforsaken hole* ‖ wicked, irredeemable, *a godforsaken wretch*

God·frey de Bouil·lon (gódfri:dəbu:jɔ̃) (Godefroi IV de Boulogne, c. 1060–1100), French leader of the 1st Crusade. After the capture of Jerusalem (1099), he was elected the first ruler of the Latin Kingdom of Jerusalem (1099–1100)

God·havn (gódheivən) a town and administrative center (pop. 700) on the Davis Strait in W. Greenland

god·head (gódhed) *n.* the state or quality of being divine, divinity **the Godhead** God

god·hood (gódhud) *n.* divine nature, godhead

Go·di·va, Lady (gədáivə) (c. 1040–c. 1080), the wife of Leofric, earl of Mercia. Legend states that, in order to obtain a reduction of the taxes on the people of Coventry, she accepted her husband's challenge to ride naked through the town. All refrained from looking at her except one, the original Peeping Tom

God·kin (gódkin), Edwin Lawrence (1831–1902), Anglo-U.S. editor. He founded (1865) 'The Nation', a U.S. national weekly review. He served (1883–99) as chief editor of the 'New York Evening Post', in which he fought for civil service and currency reform and attacked Tammany Hall

god·less (gódlis) *adj.* not acknowledging a god ‖ (*pop.*) wicked

god·like (gódlaik) *adj.* like a god ‖ fit for a god

god·li·ness (gódli:nis) *n.* the quality or state of being godly

god·ly (gódli:) *comp.* **god·li·er** *superl.* **god·li·est** *adj.* pious, devout

god·moth·er (gódmʌðər) *n.* a woman who sponsors a child at baptism and assumes responsibility for the child's religious guidance up to confirmation

Go·dol·phin Treaty (gədólfin) a treaty signed (1670) between Great Britain and Spain. Spain allowed Britain to establish settlements in Honduras

go·down (góudaun) *n.* a warehouse in the Far East [fr. Malay *gadong, godong*]

god·par·ent (gódpɛərənt) *n.* a godfather or a godmother

god·send (gódsend) *n.* something received unexpectedly just when needed

god·son (gódsʌn) *n.* a boy godchild

Godt·haab (góthɔp) the capital and oldest Danish settlement (pop. 9,561) of Greenland, on the southwest coast

Go·du·nov (gódunɔf, gʌdu:nóf), Boris Fyodorovich (c. 1551–1605), regent (1585–98) and Czar (1598–1605) of Russia. He extended the empire, limited the freedom of movement of the serfs (1587) and established a Russian patriarchate in Moscow (1589), thus freeing the Russian Church from Greek domination

God·win (gódwin) (d. 1053), earl of Wessex. Chief adviser to Cnut, he wielded immense political power, and secured the election (1042) of Edward the Confessor. Growing Norman influence at court ousted him from favor, but on the king's death (1066), Godwin's son succeeded to the throne as Harold II

Godwin, William (1756–1836), British political philosopher. His social anarchism and belief in human perfectibility through reason, expressed in his 'Enquiry Concerning Political Justice' (1793), influenced Shelley, Wordsworth, Coleridge and Southey. He and his wife, Mary Wollstonecraft Godwin (1759–97), ardently defended the French Revolution

Godwin Austen *K2

god·wit (gódwit) *n.* a member of *Limosa*, fam. *Scolopacidae*, a genus of marsh birds resembling curlews, with long legs, but having the bill slightly curved upwards [origin unknown]

Goeb·bels (gə:b'ls), Joseph Paul (1897–1945), German Nazi leader. As head of Nazi propaganda (1928–45), he made cynical use of psychological methods of swaying the masses. Upon Hitler's suicide, Goebbels and his wife poisoned their children and killed themselves

Goering *GÖRING

Goes *VAN DER GOES

GOES (acronym) for geostationary operational environmental satellite produced by Hughes Aircraft Co.

Goe·thals (góuθəlz), George Washington (1858–1928), U.S. general and engineer. As chief engineer (1907–14) of the Isthmian Canal Commission, he successfully completed the difficult construction of the Panama Canal, becoming (1914) the first civil governor of the Canal Zone

Goe·the (gé:tə), Johann Wolfgang von (1749–1832), German poet, dramatist and novelist. His understanding of literature, art, science and philosophy made him the last of the great 'universal' men. He freed the German language from clumsiness and foreign literary domination in a vast output of easy, natural and personal lyrics, and inspired the great German composers. 'Hermann and Dorothea' (1797) is a narrative poem of beauty and power. As a playwright Goethe is most famous for 'Faust' (1808 and 1832), his masterpiece, though this is only one of several great dramas. As a novelist he influenced German literature for a generation with 'The Sorrows of Werther' (1774) and the 'Wilhelm Meister' novels (1796–1829). Goethe held posts at the court of Weimar, including the directorship of the theater (1791–1817). There, with Herder, Schiller and others, he evolved the classical German ideal of culture as a process of personal spiritual development

go·fer (góufər) *n.* (*business slang*) an assistant often sent on errands, from "go for"

gof·fer, gauf·fer (góufər) *v.t.* to make wavy, crimp (lace edging, frills etc.) with a hot iron **góf·fer·ing** *n.* an ornamental frill [fr. F. *gaufrer*, to stamp a pattern]

Gog and Ma·gog (gog, méigog) two giant statues in Guildhall in London, representing the legendary survivors of a race of giants living in Britain in Roman times. The two names appear sporadically in the Bible as appellations for peoples as well as for countries. In the Apocalypse they signify the future enemies of the Kingdom of God

go-get·ter (góugétər) (*pop.*) *n.* an energetic, determined, often aggressive person

gog·gle (góg'l) **1.** *v. pres. part.* **gog·gling** *past* and *past part.* **gog·gled** *v.i.* to stare with eyes protruding or rolling ‖ (of eyes) to protrude ‖ *v.t.* to roll (the eyes) **2.** *n.* a rolling of the eyes [origin unknown]

gog·gle-eyed (góg'laid) *adj.* having bulging eyes ‖ having the eyes very wide open in astonishment or wonder

gog·gles (góg'lz) *pl. n.* a protective mask for the eyes with transparent eyepieces, worn by skindivers, motorcyclists, welders etc. [GOGGLE v.]

Gogh *VAN GOGH

go-go (góugou) *adj.* **1.** of lively discotheque-type dancing by a demonstrator. **2.** (*securities*) by extension, securities that are highly volatile, particularly on the bullish side. *Cf* A-GO-GO

Go·gol (góg'l), Nikolai Vasilievich (1809–52), Russian novelist and dramatist. His best-known works are the comedy 'The Government Inspector' (1836) and the novel 'Dead Souls' (1842). He also wrote many brilliant short stories

Gog·ra (gógrə) a river (about 570 miles) which rises in S.W. Tibet and flows south through the Himalayas (Nepal) to the Ganges

Goi·del·ic (gɔidélik) **1.** *adj.* of or relating to the Goidels, the northern branch (Irish and Scots) of the Celts, or their languages **2.** *n.* the group of Celtic languages spoken by the Goidels, incl. Irish, Scottish Gaelic and Manx [O. Ir. *Goidel*]

go·ing (góuiŋ) **1.** *n.* departure ‖ the state of a path, racecourse or road, *the going was smooth* ‖ rate of progress, *it was good going to finish in an hour* **2.** *adj.* working, in operation, *is the clock going?* ‖ (*pop.*) available, *is there any coffee going?* ‖ viable, *a going concern* ‖ prevailing, current, *at the going price* [pres. part. of GO]

go·ings-on (góuiŋzon) *pl. n.* (*pop.*) behavior or activities, esp. when not approved by the speaker

goi·ter, goi·tre (gɔitər) *n.* an enlargement of the thyroid gland that often results from deficient iodine in the diet and may be associated with hypothyroidism or, sometimes, with hyperthyroidism **goi·trous** *adj.* [F.]

go-kart (góukɑrt) *n.* (*sports*) miniature open four-wheeled racing vehicle. —**Go-Kart** trademark

Gol·con·da (golkóndə) an ancient diamond-cutting city near Hyderabad, India, renowned for its wealth. It was destroyed (1687) by Aurangzeb

gold (gould) 1. *n.* a yellow, malleable, ductile metallic element (symbol Au, at. no. 79, at. mass 196.967) that occurs naturally in the uncombined state. It is monovalent and trivalent, and resists most chemical attack (save e.g. by chlorine or aqua regia). It is used in coinage, dentistry and jewelry, hardened by being alloyed esp. with copper or silver (*CARAT) || (*collect.*) coins minted from this metal || the color of gold, a deep yellow 2. *adj.* made of gold, or having the color of gold [O.E.]

gold·beat·er's skin (góuldbi:tərz) a membrane prepared from the large intestine of an ox, used for separating the leaves of metal in goldbeating

gold·beat·ing (góuldbi:tiŋ) *n.* the process of hammering gold into thin leaves

Goldberg, Arthur Joseph (góuldbərg) (1908–), U.S. lawyer and associate justice of the Supreme Court (1962–5). A lawyer for the AFL-CIO, he served as secretary of Labor (1961–2) before being appointed to the Supreme Court by Pres. John F. Kennedy. He resigned to become ambassador to the United Nations (1965–8)

gold·brick (góuldbrik) 1. *n.* (*pop.*) a sham (orig. a brick coated thinly with gold) || (*pop.*) a shirker, loafer, esp. a soldier who shirks his assignments 2. *v.i.* (*pop.*) to loaf, shirk an assigned duty **góld·brick·er** *n.*

gold certificate a U.S. Treasury certificate given as receipt for a deposit of gold

Gold Coast *GHANA

gold digger a man mining for gold || (*pop.*) a woman who cultivates a man's society for the money she can get out of him

gold dust fine particles of gold obtained in placer mining

gold·en (góuldən) *adj.* having the color of gold || made of gold || eminently favorable, *a golden opportunity* || having the qualities associated with gold, e.g. purity, splendor, excellence || (of a jubilee, wedding or other anniversary) fiftieth

golden age a flourishing period, *the golden age of English drama*

gold·en·age (góuldəneidʒ) *adj.* of senior citizens (over 65). —**golden-ager** *n.*

golden-age club social and recreational organization for the elderly

Golden Bull *CHARLES IV, Holy Roman Emperor

golden calf any materialistic or unworthy object set up for worship, esp. money [fr. the golden calf made by Aaron for the Israelites, Exodus xxxii]

golden eagle *Aquila chrysaetos,* fam. *Falconidae,* a large eagle frequenting mountainous regions, about 3 ft long, with a wingspread of up to 6 ft

gold·en·eye (góuldənai) *n. Bucephala clangula* or *Glaucionetta clangula,* a North American and Eurasian sea duck, expert at diving

Golden Fleece (*Gk mythol.*) a ram's fleece of gold, guarded by a dragon in a sacred grove on the isle of Colchis, sought by Jason and the Argonauts, and gained with the help of Medea

Golden Fleece, Order of the an order of chivalry founded (1429) by Philippe the Good, duke of Burgundy. The order contained 31 knights and was the principal order of Austria and Spain

Golden Gate a steep-sided channel (1 mile wide and 4 miles long) in California, connecting San Francisco Bay with the Pacific Ocean, spanned by a suspension bridge (1937) with a central span of 4,200 ft

Golden Horde the Mongols who overran E. Europe (mid-13th c.), founding an empire in Russia which lasted until the late 14th c.

Golden Horn a curved inlet of the Bosporus, which forms the harbor of Istanbul, Turkey

Golden Legend the English version, printed by Caxton, of the 'Legenda Sanctorum' (popularly called the 'Legenda Aurea'), a collection of saints' lives and pious legends in Latin compiled by Jacobus de Voragine

golden mean the middle way of wisdom or prudence which avoids extremes

golden number the number given to a year in the Metonic lunar cycle of 19 years, used in calculating the date of Easter

golden oldie a one-time popular recording hit

golden pheasant *Chrysolophus pictus,* a pheasant of China and Tibet, with richly colored head and neck plumage

gold·en·rod (góuldənrɒd) *n.* a common composite plant, esp. a member of genus *Solidago,* having tall, stiff stems and terminal racemes of small, yellow flowers. There are about 100 species in North America. *S. virgaurea* is the only British species

golden rule a guiding principle

gold·en·seal (góuldənsi:l) *n. Hydrastis canadensis,* fam. *Ranunculaceae,* an American perennial plant, the roots and rhizome of which have been used medicinally

golden section the division of a line or geometrical figure so that the ratio of the lesser to the greater part is equal to the ratio of the greater part to the whole

golden wattle *Acacia pycnantha,* fam. *Mimosaceae,* a S.E. Australian tree with very fragant, bright yellow flowers

gold·field (góuldfi:ld) *n.* a gold-mining district

gold·filled (góuldfild) *adj.* (esp. of jewelry) having a thicker coating of gold than that normally deposited by electrolysis

gold·finch (góuldfintʃ) *n. Carduelis carduelis,* a small, brightly colored European finch with yellow-barred black wings. It is a favorite cage bird || the yellowhammer || an American finch of genus *Spinus* [O.E. goldfinc-]

gold·fish (góuldfiʃ) *pl.* **gold·fish, gold·fish·es** *n. Carassius auratus,* fam. *Cyprinidae,* a small, usually golden or orange freshwater fish related to the carp, originally from S. China and Japan

gold foil gold beaten into thin sheets, thicker than gold leaf

Golding, William (góuldiŋ) (1911–), British writer, Nobel prizewinner for literature (1983). Known for his use of allegory, he often wrote of man's barbaric qualities tempered by civilization. His novels include 'Lord of the Flies' (1954), 'The Inheritors' (1955), 'Free Fall' (1959), 'The Spire' (1964), 'Darkness Visible' (1979), 'Rites of Passage' (1980), 'A Moving Target' (1982) and 'The Paper Men' (1984). His essays are collected in 'The Hot Gates and Other Occasional Pieces' (1966)

gold leaf gold beaten into sheets of four to five millionths of an inch in thickness, used for gilding

Gold·man (góuldmən), Emma (1869–1940). Lithuanian-born international anarchist. An immigrant to the U.S.A., she was deported (1919) to Russia but left the country in 1921, disillusioned. Her works include an autobiography, 'Living My Life' (1931)

gold mine a place where gold is mined || a source of great wealth

Gol·do·ni (gɔldóni:), Carlo (1707–93), Italian dramatist. He wrote about 250 plays, including 'The Servant of Two Masters', still frequently performed. Goldoni was the founder of realistic Italian comedy in succession to the commedia dell' arte

gold plate tableware etc. of solid gold || articles coated with gold by electroplating

gold point (in foreign trade) the rate of exchange at which it is no more expensive to settle accounts by shipping gold than by buying exchange

gold points melting point of gold, 1064.43°C, on the Standard International Scale

gold record an award to recorded performers who participated in the creation of a record that has sold no fewer than 500,000 copies. *Cf* GRAMMY

gold reserve the supply of gold kept in a country's central or national bank to maintain the value of governmental promissory notes

Gold Reserve Act of 1934 a U.S. Congressional act of the New Deal, which empowered the president to manipulate the value of the dollar to cause an increase in prices

gold rush a rush of people to a place where goldfields have just been discovered, e.g. California (1849), the Klondike (1896-9)

Gold·smith (góuldsmiθ), Oliver (1728–74), Irish poet and man of letters. His poems include 'The Traveller' (1764) and 'The Deserted Village' (1770). He also wrote the novel 'The Vicar of Wakefield' (1766) and a comedy, 'She Stoops to Conquer' (1773), which is still performed

gold·smith (góuldsmiθ) *n.* a craftsman who works in gold || a dealer in articles of gold [O.E.]

gold standard a monetary system in which the unit of currency is equivalent to a certain quantity of gold

Gold Standard Act of 1900 a U.S. Congressional act which required the U.S. Treasury to maintain a minimum gold reserve of $150 million and authorized the issuance of bonds, if necessary, to protect that minimum

gold stick (*Br.*) the gilt rod carried on state occasions by the colonel of the Life Guards or by the captain of the gentlemen-at-arms **Gold Stick** the person entitled to bear this rod

Gold·wa·ter (góuldwɔtər, góuldwɒtər), Barry Morris (1909–), U.S. Senator from Arizona (1953–64, 1968–). He ran unsuccessfully as Republican presidential candidate in the 1964 contest against Lyndon Johnson. His political philosophy is embodied in his 'The Conscience of a Conservative' (1960)

golf (gɔlf, golf) 1. *n.* an outdoor game, originating in Scotland, in which a small, white, resilient ball is hit with one of a set of long-shafted clubs into a series of 9 or 18 holes up to about 550 yards apart from one another and distributed over a course having natural or artificial hazards (trees, sand-filled bunkers etc.). The object is to hit the ball into each hole in as few strokes as possible. Golf is played by one, two or three persons or two competing pairs 2. *v.i.* to play golf [etym. doubtful]

golf cart a motorized cart for carrying golf equipment and a player on the golf course

golf club a stick with a wooden or iron head, for hitting the ball in golf

golf course an area laid out for golf, having 9 or 18 holes, each with a tee, fairway, green and one or more hazards

golf links *pl.* **golf links** a golf course, esp. one by the sea shore

Gol·go·tha (gɔ́lgəθə) the place near Jerusalem where Jesus was crucified || Calvary (Mark xv, 22)

go·liard (góuljərd) *n.* (*hist.*) one of the medieval wandering scholars who wrote and performed ribald or satirical songs and entertainments in Latin **gol·iárd·ic** *adj.* [O.F.=glutton]

Go·li·ath (gəláiəθ) the Philistine giant killed by David with a stone shot from a sling (I Samuel, xvii)

gol·ly (góli) *interj.* used to express mild surprise, wonder or puzzlement [alteration of GOD]

gol·ly·wog, gol·li·wog (góli:wɒg) *n.* a black, male, grotesquely dressed doll with fuzzy hair [coined by Bertha Upton (*d.* 1912), U.S. writer]

go·losh (gəlóʃ) *n.* a galosh

G.O.M. *GRAND OLD MAN

gombo *GUMBO

Go·mel (góuməl) an old town (pop. 405,000) of Byelorussia, U.S.S.R., a railroad junction: engineering, clothing and chemical industries

Go·me·ra (gɔméra) *CANARY ISLANDS

go metric *v.* to change to the metric system. *Cf* METRICATE

Gó·mez (gɔ́mes), José Miguel (1858–1921), Cuban president (1909–13) of a liberal administration. After an electoral defeat (1912), he led (1917) a revolt against the government, was incarcerated, and after his release left Cuba (1920) for the U.S.A.

Gómez, Juan Vicente (c. 1857–1935), Venezuelan politician. He was dictator of Venezuela (1908–35)

Gómez, Laureano (1889–1965), Colombian politician and president (1950–53). Despite strong liberal opposition, he suspended constitutional guarantees

Gómez, Máximo (1836–1905), Cuban general and patriot. He was appointed (1895) commander in chief of the Army of Liberation by José Martí

Gómez de la Ser·na (gɔ́meθdelasérna), Ramón (1888–1963), Spanish writer. A literary rebel, he is known esp. for sardonic epigrams which he called 'greguerías'

Go·mor·rah (gəmɔ́ra) a Palestinian city destroyed for its vices (*SODOM)

Gom·pers (gómpərz), Samuel (1850–1924), American labor leader. He founded the American Federation of Labor and was its president (1886–94 and 1896–1924). He founded (1920) the International Labor Organization

Go·mul·ka (gəmúlkə), Wladyslaw (1905–82), Polish statesman, first secretary of the Polish Communist party (1956–70). He led the riots (1956) which gained Poland greater independence from the U.S.S.R. He resigned (Dec. 1970) after riots over increased food prices and general economic discontent

go·mu·ti (gəmú:ti) *n. Arenga saccharifera* or *A. pinnata,* a Malayan palm from which palm wine, jaggery and a wiry fiber used for cables are obtained [fr. Malay (*pohon*) *gemuti*]

go·nad (góunæd, gónæd) *n.* a primary sexual gland, the testicle or ovary [fr. Gk *goneos, gon*, generation, seed]

Gon·çal·ves Di·as (gõsálvezðí:ɑs), Antonio (1823–64), Brazilian poet and scholar. His poems 'Canção do Tamoio', 'Maraba', and 'I-Juca-Pirama' exalt the past of his native land and are redolent of tropical nature. He published (1858)' Diccionário de Língua Tupi'

Gon·cha·rov (gʌntʃaróf), Ivan Aleksandrovich (1812–91), Russian novelist, author of 'Oblomov' (1857), a picture of the indolent Russian country gentleman

Gon·court (gõku:r), Edmond Louis Antoine Huot de (1822–96), French novelist of the naturalist school. His fame rests on the journal he kept from 1851 with his brother Jules Alfred (1830–70), full of criticism, information and gossip. Edmond, in his will, founded the Académie Goncourt, a literary society which awards an annual prize for French fiction

Gond (gɔnd) *n.* a member of a central Indian tribe, mostly living in Madhya Pradesh

Gon·dar (góndɑr) a town (pop. 43,000) in N.W. Ethiopia, the capital from the 16th c. until 1868

gon·do·la (góndələ) *n.* a graceful narrow flat-bottomed boat about 30 ft long used on the canals of Venice, propelled by a single oar at the stern, and with upward-curving prow and stern ‖ a car suspended from a dirigible or balloon ‖ a flat-bottomed barge ‖ an open railroad car [Ital.]

gon·do·lier (gɔndə'liər) *n.* the rower of a gondola [F. fr. Ital.]

Gond·wa·na (gɔndwánə) **Gond·wa·na·land** (gɔndwá:nəlænd) *n.* a hypothetical continent which in primeval times linked S. America, Africa, Arabia, India (the Deccan), Australia and Antarctica

gone (gɔn, gɒn) *past part.* of GO ‖ *adj.* past, *those days are gone* ‖ (intensive for) dead, *dead and gone* ‖ (*pop.*) more than (in time), *it is gone six years since they met* ‖ (*pop.*) advanced in pregnancy, *six months gone* ‖ (*pop.*, with 'on') infatuated **far gone in** deeply involved in (crime, vice etc.) **gón·er** *n.* (*pop.*) someone dead or about to die, *make one move and you're a goner*

gon·fa·lon (gónfələn) *n.* a banner with streamers, hanging from a crossbar, carried in processions in Italy **gon·fa·lon·ier** *n.* a standard-bearer ‖ (*hist.*) a chief magistrate in some medieval Italian republics [fr. Ital. *gonfalone*]

gong (gɔŋ, gɒŋ) *n.* a metal disk with its rim turned back. It hangs freely, and when struck gives a muffled, resonant note ‖ a mechanism consisting of a saucer-shaped bell sounded by a hammer [Malay]

Gón·go·ra y Ar·go·te (góŋgɔrɑːɑrgóte), Luis de (1561–1627), one of Spain's great poets (*GONGORISM) renowned esp. for his long later works, including the 'Fábula de Polifemo y Galatea' and 'Las Soledades'

Gon·go·rism (góŋgərɪzəm, góŋgərɪzəm) *n.* the Spanish literary style created by Góngora and imitated by his followers. Highly mannered and witty, it is characterized by Latinized constructions, mythological allusions and the use of far-fetched conceits

gonia *pl.* of GONION ‖ *alt. pl.* of GONIUM

go·nid·i·al (gounídi:əl) *adj.* of or containing a gonidium

go·nid·i·um (gounídi:əm) *pl.* **go·nid·i·a** (gounídi:ə) *n.* an asexual reproductive cell produced upon a gametophyte ‖ the algal constituent of lichen ‖ a supposed minute reproductive body in certain bacteria [Mod. L. fr. Gk *gónos*, offspring]

go·ni·om·e·ter (gouni:ómɪtər) *n.* an instrument for measuring angles, e.g. the interfacial angles of crystals ‖ a direction finder **go·ni·óm·e·try** *n.* [fr. F. *goniomètre* fr. Gk *gonia*, angle + *metron*, measure]

go·ni·on (góuni:ɒn) *pl.* **go·ni·a** (góuni:ə) *n.* a point on the human skull at either of the angles of the lower jaw [Mod. L.]

go·ni·um (góuni:əm) *pl.* **go·ni·a** (góuni:ə), **go·ni·ums** *n.* a primitive sex cell [Mod. L.]

gon·o·coc·cus (gɔnəkókəs) *pl.* **gon·o·coc·ci** (gɔnəkókai, gɔnəkóksai) *n. Neisseria gonorrhoeae*, the bacterium causing gonorrhea [fr. Gk *gónos*, offspring + *kokkos*, a grain]

go·no·go (gounóugo) *adj.* (*slang*) of stop and start, esp. of decisions

gon·o·phore (gónəfɔr, gónəfour) *n.* a sporophyll-bearing extension of the axis in certain

plants ‖ a reproductive zooid in hydrozoans [fr. Gk *gōnos*, offspring + *phoros*, bearing]

gon·or·rhe·a, gon·or·rhoe·a (gɔnərí:ə) *n.* a venereal disease caused by gonococci and characterized by the discharge of pus from the genital organs. It is transmitted by sexual intercourse. It is treated with antibiotics [M.L. fr. Gk *gónos*, seed, offspring + *rhoia*, flux]

Gon·za·ga (gɔndzága) an Italian family which ruled Mantua (1328–1708)

Gon·zá·lez (gɔnθáleθ), Julio (1876–1942), Spanish sculptor. He was among the first to use soldered iron in creating abstract geometric forms

González Dá·vi·la (dávi:la), Gil (d. 1543), Spanish explorer, discoverer (1522) of Nicaragua

González Pra·da (gɔnsálespráðα), Manuel (1848–1918), Peruvian writer in verse ('Minúsculas', 'Libertarias', 'Exóticas', and 'Gráfitos') and in prose ('Horas de lucha', 'Páginas libres'). He opposed all forms of political, social or literary conservatism

Gon·za·lo de Cór·do·ba (gɔnθáloðekórðoba), Hernández (1453–1515), Spanish soldier. He earned the title 'the Great Captain' in wars with the Moors in Spain and the French in Italy. His reform of the infantry made Spain a dominant military power

goo (gu:) *n.* (*pop.*) sticky matter ‖ (*pop.*) cloying sentimentality [perh. fr. *glue*]

goo·ber (gú:bər) *n.* a peanut [of African origin]

good (gud) **1.** *comp.* **bet·ter** (bétər) *superl.* **best** (best) *adj.* serving its purpose well, having desired qualities ‖ morally excellent, virtuous ‖ well behaved, dutiful ‖ kind ‖ agreeable, pleasant, *a good time* ‖ beneficial, *milk is good for your teeth* ‖ sound, wholesome, *will the meat still be good tomorrow?* ‖ worthwhile, serious, *good music* ‖ thorough, *a good workout* ‖ considerable, *a good deal of unpleasantness*, *a good while* ‖ full, rather more than, *it's a good month since you wrote* ‖ efficient, competent, *good at Latin* ‖ sound, reliable, safe, *a good risk*, *a good debt* ‖ orthodox and devout, *a good Catholic* ‖ valid, *the rule holds good* ‖ of the upper middle class, *a good family* ‖ (*Br.*) used in address ironically, *my good girl, that's no way to behave* ‖ used as an intensive, *I've put good money into this business* **a good few** (*Br.*) a fairly large number **as good as** practically, virtually, *it's as good as done* **good afternoon** (**day, evening, morning, night** etc.) forms of address used on meeting or parting **good and** (*pop.*) quite, *come when you're good and ready* **good for** beneficial to the health of ‖ valid for ‖ in a fit state for ‖ to be relied on for, *he's always good for a laugh* ‖ used as an exclamation of approval, *good for you!* **to be as good as one's word** to do as promised **to feel good** (*pop.*) to be conscious of good spirits or health **to make good** to repair ‖ to fill in, *to make good an omission* ‖ to perform, fulfill, effect, *to make good a boast* ‖ to substantiate, *to make good an allegation* ‖ to become prosperous, succeed **2.** *n.* that which is morally right, *good and evil*, *a great power for good*, *up to no good* ‖ profit, benefit, advantage, *he did it for his own good* ‖ use, value, worth, *what's the good of complaining?* **for good** forever **to come to no good** to be unprofitable or unsuccessful ‖ to get into trouble morally **to the good** beneficial, *your efforts are all to the good* ‖ in profit, *10 dollars to the good* **3.** *adv.* very, *a good long time* **4.** *interj.* an exclamation of satisfaction or pleasure [O.E. *gōd*]

good-bye, good-by (gudbái) **1.** *interj.* farewell **2.** *n.* a farewell, *say your good-byes and come* [contracted form of *God be with you*]

good-fel·low·ship (gudféloufɪp) *n.* genial companionship within a group

good-for-noth·ing (gúdfərnʌθɪŋ) **1.** *adj.* worthless, idle **2.** *n.* an idle, worthless person

Good Friday the Friday before Easter, the anniversary of Christ's crucifixion

good-heart·ed (gúdhártɪd) *adj.* kind, quick to offer friendship or help

good hu·mor, *Br.* **good hu·mour** cheerfulness of temperament **góod-hú·mored**, *Br.* **góod-hú·moured** *adj.*

good-look·ing (gúdlúkɪŋ) *adj.* personally attractive ‖ handsome

good·ly (gúdli) *comp.* **good·li·er** *superl.* **good·li·est** *adj.* (*old-fash.*) sizable, *a goodly chunk* [O.E. *gōdlic*]

good nature kindness, readiness to take trouble to help others ‖ willingness to overlook other people's faults **góod-ná·tured** *adj.* character-

ized by good nature ‖ without malice, *good-natured ridicule*

good-neigh·bor policy, *Br.* **good-neigh·bour policy** a policy of friendly political and economic relations between countries, esp. (*Am. hist.*) that evolved (1933) by F. D. Roosevelt toward Latin America

good·ness (gúdnis) **1.** *n.* the quality or state of being good ‖ the good element of something, *the goodness of the beef goes into the gravy* **2.** *interj.* used as a euphemism for 'God' in mild expletives [O.E. *gōdnes*]

good offices friendly services, mediation, *use your good offices to find me a job*

goods (gudz) *pl. n.* possessions ‖ wares, merchandise ‖ (*Br.*) things to be transported by rail, freight **to deliver the goods** to perform the contract undertaken ‖ (*pop.*) to come up to expectations

Good Samaritan a person who compassionately helps someone in distress [after the good Samaritan in Luke x, 30-37]

goods and chattels personal possessions

good sense practical wisdom, reasonableness

Good Shepherd a name by which Jesus is called [John x, 11-12]

good-sized (gúdsáizd) *adj.* reasonably large, large rather than small

goods train (*Br.*) a freight train

goods wagon (*Br.*) a freight car

good-tem·pered (gúdtémpərd) *adj.* not easily ruffled or liable to anger ‖ not angry

good·will (gúdwíl) *n.* the assessable custom built up over a period by a shop or business, *how much is the goodwill worth?* ‖ (used attributively) friendliness, *a goodwill mission*

Good·win Sands (gúdwin) shifting sandbanks off the east coast of Kent, England, treacherous to shipping

good·y (gúdi:) **1.** *pl.* **good·ies** *n.* (*pop.*, usually *pl.*) something good to eat, e.g. a sweet **2.** *interj.* (used by children or in imitation of children) an expression of delight

Good·year (gúdjiər), Charles (1800–60), American inventor of vulcanization

good·y-good·y (gúdi:gúdi:) **1.** *adj.* priggishly virtuous **2.** *pl.* **good·y-good·ies** *n.* a prig **3.** *interj.* (*pop.*) expressing gratification

goo·ey (gú:i:) *comp.* **goo·i·er** *superl.* **goo·i·est** *adj.* (*pop.*) like goo, sticky ‖ (*pop.*) excessively sweet or sentimental

goof (gu:f) **1.** *n.* (*pop.*) a silly or stupid person ‖ (*pop.*) a foolish mistake, blunder **2.** *v.i.* (*pop.*) to make a foolish mistake ‖ (*pop.*, often with 'off') to shirk work ‖ *v.t.* (*pop.*) to make a botch of, bungle **góof·y** *adj.* (*pop.*) foolish, silly [prob. fr. obs. *goff*, a dolt]

goof-off (gúfɔf) *v.* (*colloq.*) to avoid work, esp. work for which one is paid. **—goof off** *n.* the person

goo·gly (gú:gli:) *n.* (*cricket*) an offbreak bowled with a leg-break action

goo·gol (gú:gɒl) *n.* (*math.*) the figure one followed by 100 zeroes [coined by Edward Kasner (d. 1955), U.S. mathematician]

goo·gol·plex (gú:gɒlpleks) *n.* the figure one followed by a googol of zeroes [GOOGOL+DUPLEX]

Goo·kin (gú:kin), Daniel (1612–87), American colonial magistrate and soldier. As superintendent (from 1656) of the Massachusetts Indians, he protected them against maltreatment by white settlers

goon (gu:n) *n.* (*pop.*) a stupid person ‖ a thug, esp. among prison guards or strikebreakers [after a cartoon strip character created by E. C. Segar (d. 1938), U.S. cartoonist]

goose (gu:s) *pl.* **geese** (gi:s) *n.* a waterfowl of fam. *Anatidae*, between a duck and swan in size, esp. a member of one of the domesticated varieties living chiefly on land, feeding on herbage and valued for their meat and feathers ‖ the female goose (opp. GANDER) ‖ the flesh of the goose as food ‖ a silly person ‖ (*pl.* **goos·es**) a tailor's iron **to cook someone's goose** to destroy someone's chances [O.E. *gōs*]

goose·ber·ry (gú:sberi:, gú:zberi:) *pl.* **goose·ber·ries** *n.* a member of *Ribes*, fam. *Saxifragaceae*, a genus of small shrubs native to cool, moist climates ‖ the edible, sour fruit of this shrub, larger than the currant, to which it is closely related **to play gooseberry** (*Br.*, *pop.*) to be an unwelcome third with lovers

goose·flesh (gú:sfleʃ) *n.* a temporary pimply state of the skin produced by the erection of tiny hairs as a result of fear, cold or thrill, and usually accompanied by a little shiver

goose·foot (gú:sfut) *pl.* **goose·foots** *n.* a plant of fam. *Chenopodiaceae*, esp. a member of genus

CONCISE PRONUNCIATION KEY: **(a)** æ, c**a**t; ɑ, c**a**r; ɔ f**aw**n; ei, sn**a**ke. **(e)** e, h**e**n; i:, sh**ee**p; iə, d**ee**r; ɛə, b**ea**r. **(i)** i, f**i**sh; ai, t**i**ger; əː, b**i**rd. **(o)** o, **o**x; au, c**ow**; ou, g**oa**t; u, p**oo**r; ɔi, r**oy**al. **(u)** ʌ, d**u**ck; u, b**u**ll; u:, g**oo**se; ə, b**a**cill**u**s; ju:, c**u**be. x, lo**ch**; θ, **th**ink; ð, bo**th**er; z, **Z**en; ʒ, corsa**g**e; dʒ, sava**g**e; ŋ, oranguta**ng**; j, **y**ak; ʃ, **f**ish; tʃ, **f**et**ch**; 'l, rabb**le**; 'n, redd**en**. Complete pronunciation key appears inside front cover.

Chenopodium, smelling strongly of bad fish [from the shape of its leaves]

goose grass any of several straggling plants, e.g. *Galium aparine*, fam. *Rubiaceae*, an annual plant with a prickly stem, and knotgrass

goose·neck (gú:snɛk) *n.* something (e.g. a pipe) curving in the shape of a goose's neck or flexible and able to hold such a curve

goose pimples gooseflesh

goose quill (*hist.*) a pen made from a goose's feather

goose step a marching step in which the knees are not bent, associated esp. with the Nazi and Fascist armies **góose-step** *pres. part.* **goose-step·ping** *past* and *past part.* **goose-stepped** *v.i.* to march with this step

G.O.P. *GRAND OLD PARTY

go·pher (góufər) *n.* a member of *Geomyidae*, a family of American burrowing rodents about the size of a rat, with large cheek pouches ‖ a member of *Citellus*. *Sciuridae*, a genus of North American burrowing rodents related to the chipmunk ‖ *Gopherus polyphemus*, a burrowing land tortoise of the southern U.S.A., whose eggs and flesh are valued as food [perh. fr. F. *gaufre*, honeycomb (from the shape of their burrows)]

gopher snake *Drymarchon corais couperi*, fam. *Colubridae*, a harmless burrowing snake of the southern U.S.A. It may be up to 8 ft long ‖ a member of *Pituophis*, fam. *Colubridae*, a genus of large, harmless snakes of North America which feed chiefly on rodents

go private (*business*) to restore a public company to private ownership. *also* take private

go public (*business*) to offer stock-ownership participation in a privately owned or closed corporation

Go·rakh·pur (góurəkpu:r) a rail center (pop. 230,911) in Uttar Pradesh, N. India, 100 miles north of Benares

go·ral (góurəl) *n.* a member of *Naemorhedus*, a genus of Asian goat antelopes with small horns

Gorbachev (garbətʃáf), Mikhail Sergeyevich (1931–), Soviet Communist Party general secretary and president (1985–). Educated in law and agriculture, he held regional government positions in Stavropol from 1967 before being appointed to the Central Committee in 1971 and to the Politburo in 1980. He succeeded Konstantin Chernenko as Soviet leader in 1985 and worked toward improved Soviet social and economic conditions and better relations with Western countries. He projected the new image of younger leadership in the U.S.S.R.

Gor·cha·kov (gartʃakóf), Prince Alexander Mikhailovich (1798–1883), Russian statesman, foreign minister (1856–82) and chancellor (1863–83) of Russia. His cooperation with Prussia enabled Russia to free herself by 1870 from the terms of the Treaty of Paris (1856)

Gor·di·an knot (górdiːən) (*Gk mythol.*) the knot tied by King Gordius of Phrygia which, an oracle declared, would be undone only by the man destined to conquer Asia. Alexander the Great cut it (334 B.C.) with his sword and marched on to conquest **to cut the Gordian knot** to settle a complex problem by some single, trenchant decision

Gor·don (górd'n), Charles George (1833–85), British general. His successes in China (1859–65) won him fame as 'Chinese Gordon'. He entered the service of the khedive of Egypt (1873), and, as governor-general of the Sudan (1877–80), helped to suppress slavery and improve communications. The British government sent him back to the Sudan (1884) to evacuate the Egyptian garrisons endangered by the Mahdi's revolt. Gordon's force was surrounded in Khartoum, and he was killed before relief could arrive. The public reaction at his death contributed to the fall of Gladstone's second ministry

Gordon, Lord George (1751–93), British religious agitator. He fomented the Gordon riots (1780), a violent protest against legislation which had lightened the penalties on Roman Catholics. The riots, which took place in London, were put down by troops on the orders of George III

Gordon setter a setter of a black, long-haired breed which originated in Scotland c. 1820, with tan markings on the muzzle, neck and legs [after Alexander, 4th duke of *Gordon*]

gore (gɔr, gour) *pres. part.* **gor·ing** *past* and *past part.* **gored** *v.t.* to pierce or wound with horns or tusks [origin unknown]

gore *n.* (*rhet.*) blood, esp. blood that has been shed [O.E. *gor*, dung, dirt]

gore 1. *n.* a triangular piece of material used to give a flare to a skirt etc. ‖ a triangular panel in an umbrella, sail, balloon etc. **2.** *v.t. pres. part.* **gor·ing** *past* and *past part.* **gored** *v.t.* to vary width with a gore ‖ to cut into a triangular shape [O.E. *gāra*, spearhead-shaped piece of land]

Gor·gas (górgəs), William Crawford (1854–1920), surgeon general of the U.S. Army. His success in combating (1904–6) yellow fever made possible the construction of the Panama Canal

gorge (gɔrdʒ) *n.* a narrow ravine between hills ‖ (*hist.*) the rear entrance into a fortification or outwork ‖ a choking mass, e.g. of ice ‖ the line made where the collar and lapels of a jacket or coat turn over **to make one's gorge rise** to give one a feeling of revulsion [O.F.=throat]

gorge 1. *v. pres. part.* **gorg·ing** *past* and *past part.* **gorged** *v.t.* to eat greedily ‖ *v.t.* to fill (oneself) with food ‖ to fill up, choke, stuff, *ditches gorged with water* **2.** *n.* a gluttonous feed [fr. O.F. *gorger*]

gor·geous (górdʒəs) *adj.* splendid, sumptuous, magnificent ‖ (*pop.*) excellent, fine, nice, good [fr. O.F. *gorgias*, finely dressed]

Gor·ges (górdʒiz), Sir Ferdinando (c. 1566–1647), English soldier. He backed (1607) an early expedition to Maine which formed a colony, and organized many other expeditions to America. He received (1639) a charter from the king creating him lord proprietor of Maine

gor·get (górdʒit) *n.* (*hist.*) a piece of armor protecting the throat ‖ a medieval wimple covering the neck and shoulders ‖ a colored patch on the throat of a bird etc. [O. F. *gorgete*]

Gor·gi·as (górdʒiːəs) (c. 485 B.C.–c. 380 B.C.), Greek orator and Sophist who wrote on rhetoric and was one of the first to introduce cadence into prose. Plato gave the name 'Gorgias' to his dialogue attacking Sophist rhetoric

Gor·gon (górgən) *n.* (*Gk mythol.*) one of three sisters (Euryale, Medusa and Stheno) with snakes instead of hair, whose gaze turned people to stone (*PERSEUS) **gorgon** a fierce-looking woman [fr. L. *Gorgo* (*Gorgonis*) fr. Gk]

Gor·gon·zo·la (gərgənzóulə) *n.* an Italian blue cheese, made of cows' milk [after *Gorgonzola*, a town near Milan, Italy]

go·ri·las (gɔríːləs) *pl. n.* the Argentinian senior military officers who engineered the overthrow of Perón (although he had appointed them) and ruled Argentina (1955-7)

go·ril·la (gərílə) *n. Gorilla gorilla*, fam. *Pongidae*, the largest of the anthropoid apes, native to some equatorial forests of W. Africa. Gorillas stand up to 6 ft, are of magnificent strength, and are ferocious when attacked. They may weigh up to 500 lbs. They move about in families, living in the treetops and feeding on fruit, bamboo shoots, leaves etc. They have very long arms, strong jaws and canine teeth, and the face is covered with shiny black skin [said to be an African word for wild man, in the Greek account of a voyage (c. 500 B.C.) by Hanno, Carthaginian navigator]

gor·i·ly (górili:, góurili:) *adv.* in a gory manner

Gö·ring, Goe·ring (góːriŋ), Hermann Wilhelm (1893–1946), German Nazi leader. As Prussian prime minister and German air minister (1933–45), he founded and led the Gestapo, directed German rearmament before the 2nd world war, planned the German air offensive and was appointed Hitler's successor. He committed suicide in prison after being sentenced to death at Nuremberg

gork (gɔrk) *n.* (*medical slang*) a hospital patient who is, and is likely to remain, comatose. Gork was originally a term for patients with mysterious ailments, and an acronym for "God only really knows." **—gorked** *adj.* stupefied

Gor·ky (górki:), Arshile (1904–48), American painter, born in Armenia, an originator of abstract expressionism. Working from nature, and using methods of automatism, he evolved cryptic images which he rendered with refined lines and vibrant color in nonobjective compositions

Gorky, Maxim (Aleksei Maximovich Peshkov, 1868–1936), Russian author. His humble origins, his enthusiasm for Bolshevism, and his association with Lenin brought him honor after the Revolution. Outside Russia, he is best known for his play 'The Lower Depths' (1902), his short stories, his novel ' Mother' (1907) and his autobiographical works

Gorky (formerly Nizhny Novgorod) a city (pop. 1,344,000) in the R.S.F.S.R., U.S.S.R., on the Volga. Industries: motor vehicles, paper, textiles, shipbuilding, iron and copper. University (1918)

Gor·lov·ka (górləfkə) a city (pop. 338,000) of the Ukraine, U.S.S.R.. in the Donets basin, linked by pipeline with the Grozny oilfields: coal mining, engineering and chemical industries

gor·mand·ize (górməndaiz) *pres. part.* **gor·mand·iz·ing** *past* and *past part.* **gor·mand·ized** *v.i.* to eat greedily [fr. older *n.* fr. F. *gourmandise*]

Gor·rie (góri:, góuri:), John (1803–55), U.S. inventor (1850) of the first practical process for making ice artificially

gorse (gɔrs) *n.* (esp. *Br.*) furze [O.E. *gorst*]

Gor·ton (górtən), John Grey (1911–), Australian statesman. He was elected leader of the Liberal party and was Prime Minister (1968-71)

Gorton, Samuel (1592–1677), colonial founder of Warwick, R.I., which he established (1648) as a haven for the members of his small religious sect (Gortonites), who asserted that true Christians share God's perfection

gor·y (góri: góuri:) *comp.* **gor·i·er** *superl.* **gor·i·est** *adj.* (*rhet.*) covered with blood and horrible to see

gosh (gɔʃ) *interj.* used to express mild surprise or sudden pleasure [alteration of GOD]

gos·hawk (góshɔk) *n. Accipiter gentilis*, a species of accipiter inhabiting North America and Eurasia (*HAWK) [O.E. *gōs-hafoc*, goose-hawk]

Go·shen (góuʃən) a region in Lower Egypt colonized by the Israelites before the Exodus (Genesis xiv, 10), taken as a symbol for a place of comfort and plenty

gos·ling (gózliŋ) *n.* a young goose [M.E. *geslyng* fr. O.N.]

go-slow (góuslóu) *n.* (*Br.*) a slowdown

Gos·pel (góspəl) *n.* one of the first four books (Matthew, Mark, Luke and John) of the New Testament ‖ part of one of these books read at Mass or the Communion Service **gos·pel** the record of Christ's life contained in Matthew, Mark, Luke and John ‖ the message about redemption preached by Christ ‖ the content of Christian preaching, *to spread the gospel* ‖ (*pop.*) anything that is to be firmly believed ‖ a principle that one acts upon, *the gospel of efficiency* **gós·pel·er,** esp. *Br.* **gós·pel·ler** *n.* the reader of the gospel at High Mass [O.E. *godspel*, good tidings, trans. of Gk *euangelion*]
—The sayings of Jesus and accounts of significant events in his life and esp. of the circumstances of his death in 30 A.D. were preserved orally by the early Church, possibly finding some written form c. 50 A.D. (*BIBLE). These traditions were used by Mark in his portrait of Jesus as Messiah (*CHRIST), and Mark's own Gospel was almost certainly used by Luke in his account of the origins and teachings of the Christian Church. Mark's work also probably played a large part in the formation of the local (Syrian) church traditions out of which Matthew's Gospel came to be written. Finally (late 1st c.) the memories and reflections of John were recorded. Other accounts of Jesus's life (the Apocryphal gospels) were produced, but were never accepted by the Church in general

gospel music Afro-American music combining spirituals and blues, and jazz

Gospel side the north side of the altar, at which the gospel is read

gospel song a musical genre characteristic of one aspect of Afro-American music, with its origins in the earliest hymn-singing traditions of slavery. Solo singers normally interpret black-spiritual themes in a bel canto style, whereas cabaret etc. groups stress the hypnotic rhythmic and expressive elements close to jazz. Rock and roll is a development of this and of blues

gos·sa·mer (gósəmər) **1.** *n.* a light film of spiders' threads, such as is seen spread over grass and traced out in sparkling drops of dew ‖ one single such thread ‖ exceedingly light, gauzy material **2.** *adj.* as light and delicate as gossamer ‖ of gossamer [M.E. *gossomer* perh.=goose-summer, i.e. early November when geese are eaten, and gossamer is most frequently seen]

gos·sip (gósip) **1.** *n.* easy, fluent, trivial talk ‖ an instance of this, *she dropped in for a gossip* ‖ talk about people behind their backs ‖ a person who indulges in gossip **2.** *v.i.* to talk idly, chatter, esp. about people **gós·sip·y** *adj.* [O.E. *godsibb*, baptismal sponsor fr. *god*, God+*sibb*, akin]

gossip column a newspaper or magazine column containing chat about well-known personalities

gos·sy·pol [$C_{30}H_{30}O_8$] (gósəpoul) n. **1.** (chem.) toxic phenolic compound from cotton seeds. **2.** (pharm.) basic ingredient of a male contraceptive pill used in China

got past and alt. past part. of GET

Gö·ta·land (jɔ́:tələnd) *SWEDEN

Gö·te·borg (jə:təbɔ́rj) *GOTHENBURG

Goth (gɒθ) n. a member of a powerful Germanic tribe which, occupying a region extending from the Baltic to the Black Sea, attacked (3rd c. A.D.) the Roman Empire, subsequently splitting into the Visigoths and the Ostrogoths

Go·tha (góuθə) an ancient town (pop. 58,660) in Thuringia, central East Germany. It is a center for publishing and insurance. Industries: machinery, rubber products, railroad equipment, aircraft. The Palace of Friedenstein, a 17th–c. ducal residence, is here

Gotha, Almanach de an annual survey of European royal houses, noble families and diplomats, first published in 1764 at Gotha, and edited in French and German

Goth·en·burg (góθənbə:rg) (Swed. Göteborg) a Swedish seaport (pop. 442,410), founded 1619, on the west coast at the mouth of the Göta River: shipbuilding, fishing, ball bearings, automobiles, textiles. University (1887)

Goth·ic (góθik) **1.** adj. of or relating to the Goths or their language ‖ of a form of art, esp. architecture, which flourished in Europe from the late 12th c. to the Renaissance ‖ of or relating to a class of sensational novels of the late 18th and early 19th cc. dealing with macabre or mysterious events in medieval settings ‖ (loosely) medieval ‖ primitive, barbaric **2.** n. the Gothic language, extant mainly in fragments of the Bible translated by Bishop Wulfila (4th c.), the sole representative of East Germanic ‖ Gothic architecture ‖ Gothic type [fr. L. gothicus] —Gothic architecture, a development of the earliest Romanesque, spread from N.W. France to flourish all over Europe in the 12th-15th cc., as far afield as Finland, Portugal and Sicily. Each country tended to produce a national style of Gothic (*DECORATED, *PERPENDICULAR). Its distinguishing features are the pointed or ogival arch, elaborate stone vaulted roofs, clustered columns and rich stone carving. Development of technique led to high buildings with walls consisting very largely of windows, the great stresses being taken by the arches themselves, by pillars, and by buttresses, often flying buttresses. The Gothic church or cathedral, seeming to aspire eternally heavenwards, is naturally taken as a symbol of medieval spirituality. But Gothic is a term applied also to castles, palaces and houses, as well as sculpture, painting and the minor arts (the word is here loosely used to mean 'of the later Middle Ages'). In France, England and Germany, Gothic can be seen mingled with Romanesque or merging into the later Flamboyant style. A renewed appreciation of Gothic appeared in the 18th and early 19th cc. Interest in the Middle Ages became a cardinal doctrine of Romanticism and a symbol of revolt against rationalism. Scholarship developed, and 19th-c. architects in Europe and North America began to produce Gothic buildings of great correctness as well as some of high imagination. Gothic was also applied to municipal and industrial buildings, but by the 1880s the movement gave way to greater eclecticism

Gothic Revival a style of architecture and decoration of the 18th and 19th cc. imitating the Gothic style of the Middle Ages

Gothic type (printing) black letter type ‖ a square-cut type without serifs or other extra strokes

Got·land (gɒ́tlənd) a Swedish island province (area 1,225 sq. miles, pop. 54,447) in the Baltic. Capital: Visby. It is a plateau, 41% forest, with a relatively mild climate. Exports: agricultural produce, cement, limestone

got·ten (gɒ́t'n) alt. past part. of GET

Gott·fried von Strass·burg (gɒ́tfri:tʃɔnʃtrásburx) (late 12th–early 13th cc.), German medieval poet, author of the epic chivalric poem 'Tristan and Isolde'

Göt·tin·gen (gɔ́:tiŋin) a town (pop. 123,600) in Lower Saxony, West Germany: scientific instruments, pharmaceutical products. University (1737)

Gott·lieb (gɒ́tli:b), Adolph (1903–   ), American painter, an originator of abstract expressionism. He paints simple forms arranged in flat, geometric compositions

Gottschalk (gɒ́tʃək), Louis Moreau (1829–69), U.S. composer, conductor, and musician. A pianist, he debuted in Paris in 1849 and New York City in 1853 and continued to perform and conduct his works in the U.S.A., the Caribbean, and South America. His works blend Creole, American black and Spanish techniques

Gott·sched (gɒ́tʃeit), Johann Christoph (1700–66), German poet and critic who upheld (vainly) the application of French classical standards to German literature

Gott·wald (gɒ́tvalt), Klement (1896–1953), Czech Communist leader, president of Czechoslovakia (1948–53)

gouache (gwaʃ, gú:áʃ) n. a method of painting in which watercolors are mixed with gum arabic to make them opaque ‖ a picture painted in this way [F. fr. Ital. guazzo]

Gou·da (gáudə, gú:də) a town (pop. 59,185) in the Netherlands, on the IJssel, 12 miles northeast of Rotterdam. Gothic town hall (founded 1449). Gouda was a center of the medieval cloth trade. It is famous for its cheese, and pottery is also manufactured

Gouda (gáudə, gú:də) n. a mild whole milk cheese shaped like a flattened sphere, usually coated with red wax [after Gouda, Holland, where it originated]

gouge (gaudʒ) **1.** n. a chisel with a concavo-convex cross section for cutting grooves **2.** v.t. pres. part. **goug·ing** past and past part. **gouged** to cut out with a gouge ‖ to scoop or force out, as if with a gouge, he had his eyes gouged out [F.]

Gou·jon (gu:ʒɔ), Jean (c. 1510–c. 1566), French Renaissance sculptor. His style, with elongated, elegant figures, shows classical and Italian influences. He excelled in bas-relief. In Paris he worked on reliefs for the Fontaine des Innocents and for the rood screen of St Germain l'Auxerrois, which are now in the Louvre. He also did many decorations (1550–62) for the Louvre. He illustrated the French edition of Vitruvius

Gou·lart (gu:lár), João (1918–76), president of Brazil (1961–4). His administration held (1963) a plebiscite, which called for a presidential rather than a parliamentary form of government. This allowed him to expropriate oil refineries and farmlands, distributing the latter to landless peasants. He was deposed (1964) by the army and exiled

gou·lash (gú:laʃ, gú:læʃ) n. a stew of beef or veal and vegetables flavored with paprika [fr. Magyar gulyas-(hus) fr. gulyas, herdsman+hus, meat]

goulash communism the aspect of communism stressing greater production of consumer goods. —**goulash communist** n.

Gould (gú:ld), Jay (Jason) (1836–92), U.S. financier and speculator. Allied with the notorious Tweed Ring, he manipulated control (1867–72) of the Erie Railroad, acquiring a fortune estimated at $25 million. His speculation in gold resulted in the panic of 'Black Friday' (Sept. 24, 1869). He developed the 'Gould system' of railroads in the southwestern states as well as elevated railways in New York City, and acquired the 'New York World' and the Western Union Telegraph Company

Gou·nod (gu:nou), Charles François (1818–93), French composer. The opera 'Faust' (1859) was his first great success and 'Romeo and Juliet' (1867) was only slightly less popular. Gounod also wrote songs and church music

gou·ra·mi (gu:rámi:) pl. **gou·ra·mi, gou·ra·mis, gou·ra·mies** n. Osphronemus goramy, fam. Anabantidae, a large freshwater fish, used as food in S.E. Asia ‖ any of several smaller, colorful fish of the same family, often kept in home aquariums [Malay gurami]

gourd (guərd) n. the fruit of any plant of fam. Cucurbitaceae, esp. any of several large, hardrinded, inedible fruits of genus Lagenaria, used for making vessels etc. ‖ a small, ornamental, hard-rinded, inedible variety of pumpkin ‖ a gourd-bearing plant ‖ the hollowed out hard rind of any of these fruits, used for holding liquids etc. [fr. F. gourde]

gour·mand (gúərmənd) n. someone who appreciates good food but without the refinement of taste of a gourmet, and usually with gluttonous excess [F.]

gour·met (gúərmei, guərméi) n. someone who is an expert judge of good food and wine [F.]

Gour·mont (gu:rmɔ̃), Remy de (1858–1915), French critic and novelist. He was the first to draw attention to the importance of the Symbolist writers

gout (gaut) n. an intensely painful form of arthritis affecting the joints, esp. the big toe, and most often found in men. It appears to be due to a disorder of metabolism, as a result of which small, needlelike crystals of uric acid are deposited inside the joints and elsewhere **gout·y** comp. **gout·i·er** superl. **gout·i·est** adj. having or tending to have gout ‖ resulting from or causing gout ‖ resembling gout [O.F. goute]

Gov. Governor

gov·ern (gávərn) v.t. to control and direct, rule ‖ to be dominant in, determine, self-interest governs all her actions ‖ to restrain, control, to govern one's temper ‖ to serve as or constitute a law or rule for, principles governing a case ‖ (gram.) to have depending on it, a preposition governs a noun, or require (a given case or number) ‖ to control the speed or power of (a machine) esp. by an automatic control ‖ v.i. to rule **gov·ern·a·ble** adj. [O.F. governer]

gov·ern·ance (gávərnəns) n. control, authority, a matter outside his governance [O.F. gouvernance]

gov·ern·ess (gávərnis) n. a woman employed to teach children in their own homes [fr. O.F. gouverneresse]

gov·ern·ment (gávərnmənt, gávərmənt) n. a governing, nationwide rule, authoritative control ‖ a system of governing, democratic government ‖ the ministers who govern a country ‖ (gram.) a governing (of the number or case etc. of one word by another) **gov·ern·men·tal** (gʌvərnméntəl, gʌvərmént'l) adj. [fr. M.F. gouvernement]

gov·er·nor (gávərnər) n. someone who governs ‖ the chief executive of each state of the U.S.A. ‖ (Br.) the ruler of a province or colony ‖ (Br.) the person in charge of a fortress or prison ‖ a member of the governing board of an institution, e.g. of a school or hospital ‖ (mech.) a device for keeping the speed of rotation of a driven shaft constant as the load on it varies. In the simple centrifugal type, weights fly outwards as the speed increases. This increases the moment of inertia and may also operate a mechanical link which reduces the fuel supply [fr. O.F. gouverneur]

gov·er·nor-gen·er·al (gávərnərdʒénərəl) pl. **gov·er·nors-gen·er·al, gov·er·nor-gen·er·als** n. a high-ranking governor, esp. (Br.) the Crown's representative in a dominion or colony

gov·er·nor·ship (gávərnərʃip) n. the office of a governor ‖ the term of office of a governor, or his exercise of it

Govt., govt. government

Gow·er (gáuər), John (c. 1330–1408), English poet. His best-known work is the 'Confessio Amantis' (c. 1393), a collection of verse tales

Gower Peninsula a region of S. Wales, west of Swansea, of great beauty: sheep farming

gown (gaun) **1.** n. a woman's dress, esp. a particularly elegant one, wedding gown ‖ a loose robe, esp. worn as official dress by judges, lawyers, aldermen etc. or as academic dress ‖ *NIGHTGOWN **2.** v.t. to clothe in a gown [M.E. goune fr. O.F.]

Gow·on (góuɒn), Yakubu (1934–   ), Nigerian soldier and statesman. He became (Jan. 1966) army chief of staff and a member of Gen. Ironsi's supreme military council. He assumed power as head of state after a coup d'état (July 28, 1966). He ended (Jan. 1970) by force of arms the secession of Biafra, proclaimed an amnesty, and set about the reunification of his country. He was deposed in 1975

gox abbr. for gaseous oxygen

Go·ya y Lu·cien·tes (gɔ́jai:lu:θjéntes), Francisco (1746–1828), Spanish painter and etcher. Goya's brilliant, richly colored portraits of royal and other sitters were remarkably frank. This implicit criticism of the Spanish court was paralleled by his attacks in his series of etchings and aquatints,'los Caprichos', on the cruelty of war, the bigotry of Spanish Catholicism, the Inquisition, and the philistinism of the rich. Social criticism merged into a purely personal vision of horror, cruelty and madness

Goz·zi (gɒ́tsi:), Carlo, Count (1720–1806), Italian dramatist. His many light plays included 'Turandot' (1762), which became the subject of several operas, and his fable 'L'amore delle tre melarance' (1761) inspired Prokofiev's opera 'The Love of Three Oranges' (1921)

CONCISE PRONUNCIATION KEY: **(a)** æ, cat; ɑ, car; ɔ fawn; ei, snake. **(e)** e, hen; i:, sheep; iə, deer; ɛə, bear. **(i)** i, fish; ai, tiger; ə:, bird. **(o)** o, ox; au, cow; ou, goat; u, poor; ɔi, royal. **(u)** ʌ, duck; u, bull; u:, goose; ə, bacillus; ju:, cube. x, loch; θ, think; ð, bother; z, Zen; ʒ, corsage; dʒ, savage; ŋ, orangutang; j, yak; ʃ, fish; tʃ, fetch; 'l, rabble; 'n, redden. Complete pronunciation key appears inside front cover.

Goz·zo·li (gɔ́ttsɔli:), Benozzo (Benozzo di Lese di Sandro, 1420–97), Florentine painter, pupil of Fra Angelico. His famous fresco 'Journey of the Magi' (c. 1459), which depicts the Medici family as the Magi, is in the Medici Chapel of the Palazzo Riccardi, Florence

GPSS-1 (computer) 1. (acronym) for generic problem statement stimulator, class of discrete, transaction-oriented simulation languages, 2. (acronym) for general purpose systems stimulator, a program language

gr. gram, grams ‖ grain, grains

Graaf·i·an follicle (grɑ́fi:ən) one of the small sacs in a mammalian ovary in which an ovum matures [after R. de Graaf (d. 1673), Du. anatomist]

grab (græb) 1. v. pres. part. **grab·bing** past and past part. **grabbed** v.t. to seize suddenly, snatch ‖ (pop.) to capture, they grabbed him before he could escape ‖ to seize illegally, forcibly or greedily ‖ (colloq.) to hold excited attention ‖ v.i. to make a snatching gesture 2. n. the act of grabbing ‖ a sudden snatch or grasp ‖ a forcible or unscrupulous seizure ‖ a mechanical device for grabbing and lifting [Du. or L.G. grabben]

grab bag (Am.=Br. lucky dip) an attraction at a bazaar, fair etc., in which articles are drawn blind from a receptacle, often for a small fee, or a game in which prizes etc. are drawn in this way

grab·ble (græb'l) pres. part. **grab·bling** past and past part. **grab·bled** v.t. to grope about ‖ to sprawl, lie prone [Du. grabbelen]

grab sample (envir.) a sample of soil or water. Cf GRAB SAMPLER

grab sampler open-jawed device for taking samples of substrata soil and organisms, e.g., Ekman Grab, Peterson Grab, etc.

Grac·chus (grǽkəs), Tiberius Sempronius (163 B.C.–133 B.C.), Roman popular leader, tribune in 133 B.C. His brother Gaius Sempronius (153 B.C.–121 B.C.) was tribune in 123–122 B.C. The attempts of the brothers (the Gracchi) to reform the agrarian laws in favor of the poorer citizens led to their violent deaths at the hands of the aristocratic faction

Grace (greis), William Gilbert (1848–1915), English cricketer. He played a leading part in making cricket the English national game

grace (greis) 1. n. charm, elegance, attractiveness, esp. of a delicate, slender, refined, light or unlabored kind ‖ a sense of what is fitting, she received them with natural grace ‖ courtesy, he had the grace to say thank you ‖ delay conceded as a favor, a day's grace ‖ an attractive feature ‖ a social accomplishment ‖ favor, a fall from grace ‖ (theol.) unconstrained and undeserved divine favor or goodwill, God's loving mercy displayed to man for the salvation of his soul ‖ a short prayer of thanksgiving offered before or after a meal ‖ a title used in referring to or addressing a duke, duchess or archbishop **with good (bad, ill) grace** gladly, willingly (reluctantly, grudgingly) **to be in someone's good graces** to enjoy someone's favor 2. v.t. pres. part. **grac·ing** past and past part. **graced** to add grace to, adorn ‖ to honor, do credit to, to grace an occasion [F. grace]

grace·ful (gréisfəl) adj. elegant in proportions or movement, slender or lithe ‖ courteous, charmingly expressed, a graceful compliment ‖ pleasing, attractive

grace·less (gréislis) adj. lacking in grace, inelegant, a graceless style ‖ lacking in propriety, rude, a graceless intrusion

grace note (mus.) a note of embellishment not essential to the harmony

Graces, the (mythol.) the sister goddesses, Euphrosyne, Aglaia and Thalia, personifying beauty

Gra·cián (grɑθján), Baltasar (1601–58), Spanish writer and Jesuit. His work was mainly moralistic and reflective. His masterpiece was 'El criticón' (1651–7)

grac·ile (grǽs'l) adj. thin ‖ gracefully slender ‖ graceful [fr. L. gracilis, slender]

gra·cious (gréiʃəs) 1. adj. showing grace in character, manners or appearance ‖ courteous, a gracious host ‖ condescendingly kind (often used ironically) ‖ having qualities associated with good breeding and refinement of taste, gracious living ‖ (theol.) bestowing divine grace, merciful 2. interj. an exclamation of surprise etc. [O.F.]

grack·le (græk'l) n. any of several Old World birds of fam. Sturnidae ‖ any of several North American blackbirds of fam. Icteridae, having

glossy, iridescent plumage [fr. L. graculus, jackdaw]

gra·date (gréideit) pres. part. **gra·dat·ing** past and past part. **gra·dat·ed** v.i. to pass gradually from one shade of color into another ‖ v.t. to cause to gradate ‖ to arrange in order of size, rank etc. [GRADATION]

gra·da·tion (greidéiʃən) n. a grading or being graded ‖ a stage in the transition from one grade or type to another ‖ the gradual passing of one color into another ‖ (linguistics) an ablaut [fr. L. gradatio (gradationis) fr. gradus, step]

grade (greid) 1. n. a degree or step in rank, quality or value ‖ a class of persons or things of the same rank, quality etc. ‖ a yearly stage in a child's school career ‖ the pupils in such a stage ‖ a mark or rating awarded to a pupil ‖ a cross-bred variety (of cattle etc.) having one purebred parent ‖ a gradient ‖ (linguistics) the position (of a vowel) in the ablaut series **on the upgrade (downgrade)** rising, improving (falling, worsening) **to make the grade** to achieve the required standard 2. v. pres. part. **grad·ing** past and past part. **grad·ed** v.t. to arrange in grades, sort ‖ to gradate, blend ‖ to award a grade or mark to ‖ to level out the gradients of (a road etc.) ‖ (breeding) to cross with superior stock ‖ v.i. to pass from one grade to another **to grade up** to improve (bloodstock) by crossing with superior stock [F.]

grade crossing (Am.=Br. level crossing) a place where a road crosses a railroad at the same level

grade point numerically evaluated school grade multiplied by the number of credits. — **grade-point average, grade-points credits**

grad·er (gréidər) n. a student in a specified grade, third grader

grade school an elementary school

gra·di·ent (gréidi:ənt) n. the degree of slope of a road or railroad ‖ a slope ‖ change (in temperature, pressure etc.) as a function of unit distance traveled in a specified direction [fr. L. gradiens (gradientis) fr. gradi, to advance]

gradient method (math.) method of solving a problem equivalent to selecting the steepest path up a mountain after each step in the direction of the steepest slope. Variations involve step lengths, change of direction

gra·din (gréid'n) n. a ledge at the back of an altar ‖ a low step or seat in a series of these [fr. F. gradin fr. Ital.]

gra·dine (gréidi:n) n. a gradin

Grad·u·al (grǽdʒu:əl) n. an antiphon or responsory sung or said in the Mass between the Epistle and the Gospel ‖ a book containing all that part of the Mass that is sung by the choir [fr. M.L. graduale]

grad·u·al (grǽdʒu:əl) adj. proceeding or taking place slowly, step by step, not steep or abrupt, a gradual improvement [fr. M.L. gradualis fr. gradus, step]

grad·u·ate (grǽdʒu:it) 1. n. someone who has taken a bachelor's degree ‖ someone who has completed a set course of study at school or college and received a diploma ‖ (chem.) a graduated flask or tube 2. v. (grǽdʒu:eit) pres. part. **grad·u·at·ing** past and past part. **grad·u·at·ed** v.i. to become a graduate ‖ to pass by gradations, gradate ‖ v.t. to grant a degree or diploma to ‖ to attach a scale of numbers to (a measuring instrument), or to mark (it) at fixed places of measurement ‖ to graduate according to a certain scale, graduated income tax [fr. M.L. graduare (graduatus), to admit to a degree]

graduated payment mortgage (banking) loan secured by property in which amortization varies in accordance with a formula, usu. based on ability to pay

graduate school a division of a university offering courses leading to a degree above the bachelor's

graduate student a student at a graduate school

grad·u·a·tion (grædʒu:éiʃən) n. a graduating or being graduated ‖ the ceremony of conferring academic degrees etc. ‖ a mark on a vessel, gauge etc. to indicate measurement

Gra·dy (gréidi:), Henry Woodfin (1850–89), U.S. journalist and orator. His address 'The New South' (Dec. 1886) helped to abate post-Civil War animosities

Graecism *GRECISM

Graecize *GRECIZE

Graeco-Roman *GRECO-ROMAN

graf·fi·to (græfí:to) pl. **graf·fi·ti** (græfí:ti:) n. an inscription or design scratched into an ancient wall ‖ a rude scribbling on a wall, e.g. in a pub-

lic toilet ‖ an incised decoration to reveal a second color, e.g. on a pot [Ital.]

'Graf Spee' (gráfʃpei) a German pocket battleship destroyed (1939) by scuttling before two small British vessels in Montevideo harbor. This was the first naval action of the 2nd world war, and the only action in American waters

graft (græft, grɑft) 1. n. (hort.) a shoot or bud from one plant inserted in a slit or groove cut in another plant (the stock) ‖ (med.) a piece of transplanted living tissue ‖ the process of grafting ‖ the place where a stock and scion unite ‖ the dishonest use of public office for private gain ‖ the gains thus secured 2. v.t. (hort.) to insert as a graft ‖ (med.) to transplant (living tissue) ‖ to insert (something) into an alien position so that it is accepted as belonging, new customs grafted on to old traditions ‖ v.i. to become joined in a graft ‖ to make a graft [fr. O.F. grafe, greffe]

Gra·ham (gréiəm), Martha (c. 1895–), U.S. dancer and choreographer, a leader of the Modern Dance movement which stems from Isadora Duncan. Her works include 'Deaths and Entrances' (1943) and 'Cave of the Heart' (1947)

Graham, William Franklin ('Billy') (1918–), U.S. evangelist. His worldwide revival meetings have been attended by hundreds of thousands of people. He developed a large organization to counsel those whom he converted

gra·ham (gréiəm) adj. made of whole wheat flour [after Sylvester Graham (1794–1851), U.S. physician]

Gra·hame (gréiəm), Kenneth (1859–1932), Scottish author. His books for children, notably 'The Wind in the Willows' (1908, dramatized 1929 as 'Toad of Toad Hall' by A. A. Milne), have become classics

Graham Land the northern part of the Antarctic Peninsula

Graham's law (phys.) the statement that the velocities of diffusion of different gases are inversely proportional to the square roots of their densities (when determined under identical conditions) [after Thomas Graham (d. 1869), Scottish chemist]

Gra·hams·town (gréiəmztaun) a town (pop. 24,000) in S.E. Cape Province, South Africa. Rhodes University College (1904)

Grail (greil) n. the cup used by Christ at the Last Supper. According to medieval legend, Joseph of Arimathea caught Christ's blood in the Grail when he was crucified, and later brought the cup to Britain. The legend inspired the quest of the Holy Grail in Arthurian legend, symbolizing spiritual regeneration [fr. O.F. graal, grael]

Grail (mil.) NATO name for U.S.S.R. man-portable air-defense, solid-propellant missile (SS-7), weighing 20 lb. It has a 10-km range and infrared homing

grain (grein) 1. n. the seed of a cereal grass ‖ such seeds collectively, sacks of grain ‖ harvested cereals in general ‖ a minute, hard particle, a grain of salt ‖ the smallest unit of weight, .10023 oz. avoirdupois or .0021 oz. apothecaries or troy ‖ a very small amount, a grain of comfort ‖ the hairy surface of leather ‖ a stamped pattern imitating the grain of leather ‖ the direction and pattern in which wood fibers grow, or the natural arrangement of strata in stone, coal etc. **against the grain** against one's natural tendency or inclination 2. v.t. to paint (something) so that it appears to have the natural grain of wood or marble ‖ to give a granular surface to ‖ v.i. to become granulated [O.F. grain, grein]

grain alcohol ethyl alcohol, made from grain

grain elevator *ELEVATOR

grain·y (gréini:) comp. **grain·i·er** superl. **grain·i·est** adj. granular ‖ showing a strong natural or artificial grain ‖ (photog.) having a mottled appearance due to the presence of large silver bromide particles

gram, esp. Br. **gramme** (græm) n. (abbr. **gm**) the unit of mass in the metric system, defined as the thousandth part of the standard kilogram mass [F. gramme]

gram n. the chick-pea ‖ any pulse used as food for horses [fr. Port. grão]

gram·a·dan (græmədən) n. proposal to have landowners transfer lands to a village assembly to be managed for the benefit of all villages; prepared by Mahatma Ghandi

gram·a, gram·ma (græmə) n. a North American pasture grass of genus Bouteloua, fam. Gramineae [Span. grama]

gram atom the quantity of an element which has a mass in grams equal to its atomic mass (cf. MOLE)

gram atomic mass gram atom

gram atomic weight gram atom

gram equivalent an equivalent weight expressed in grams

gram·i·ci·din (græmisáid'n) n. an antibiotic, obtained from *Bacillus brevis*, a soil bacterium which destroys gram-positive bacteria [fr. GRAM(-POSITIVE)+L. *caedere*, to kill]

gra·min·e·ous (grəmíni:əs) adj. pertaining to fam. *Gramineae* (*GRASS) [fr. L. *gramineus* fr. *gramen* (*graminis*), a grass]

gram·i·niv·o·rous (græminívərəs) adj. grass-eating [fr. L. *gramen* (*graminis*), grass+L. *vorare*, to eat]

gramma *GRAMA

gram·ma·log, gram·ma·logue (græməlog, græməlog) n. a single stroke for a whole word in shorthand [fr. Gk *gramma*, letter+*logos*, word]

gram·mar (græmər) n. the science dealing with the systematic rules of a language, its forms, inflections and syntax, and the art of using them correctly (*PHONOLOGY, *MORPHOLOGY, *SYNTAX) ‖ the applying of these rules ‖ the system of forms and syntactical usages characteristic of any language ‖ a book of grammar ‖ the basic principles of an art or science [M.E. *gramere* fr. O.F. fr. L. fr. Gk]

gram·mar·i·an (grəmέəri:ən) n. someone who specializes in or writes about grammar [M.E. *gramarien* fr. O.F.]

grammar school an elementary school, at a level between primary and high school ‖ (Br.) a secondary school which prepares pupils for the university and the professions

gram·mat·i·cal (grəmætik'l) adj. of or pertaining to grammar, *grammatical gender* ‖ in accordance with the rules of grammar, *that sentence is not grammatical* **gram·mat·i·cal·ly** adv. [fr. L. *grammaticus* fr. Gk]

gram·mat·i·cal·i·ty (grəmætikǽliti:) n. (linguistics) degree of conformity to rules of the grammar of a language

gramme *GRAM

gram molecular mass gram molecule

gram molecular weight gram molecule

gram molecule a mole expressed on the metric scale

Gram·my (græmi:) n. pl. **-s** or **-ies** annual award in 40 categories for recordings; presented by the National Academy of Recording Arts and Sciences since 1950. *Cf* GOLD RECORD

gram·neg·a·tive (græmnégətiv) adj. (esp. of bacteria) not retaining the purple dye when stained by Gram's method

Gram·o·phone (græməfoun) n. (Br.) a phonograph [trademark fr. Gk *gramma*, letter+*phone*, sound]

Gram·pi·ans (græmpi:ənz) the central mountain system (about 150 miles long) which divides the Scottish Highlands from the Lowlands. Ben Nevis (4,406 ft)

gram·pos·i·tive (græmpózitiv) adj. (esp. of bacteria) retaining the purple dye when stained by Gram's method

gram·pus (græmpəs) n. *Grampus griseus*, a cetacean of the northern hemisphere, having teeth only in the lower jaw ‖ any of several other cetaceans, e.g. the killer whale [earlier *graundepose* fr. O.F.]

Gram's method a method for the differential staining of bacteria [after Hans C. J. Gram (1853–1938), Dan. physician]

Gra·na·da (grənádə) a province (area 4,928 sq. miles, pop. 761,734) of Andalusia, S. Spain ‖ its capital (pop. 262,182), situated at the foot of the Sierra Nevada and dominated by the Alhambra. It was the capital (1232–1492) of the last Moslem kingdom in Spain. Cathedral (1523). University (1531)

gran·a·de·ro (grænədérou) n. (Sp.) (usu. italics) in Mexico, a member of the special force used to quell riots

gran·a·dil·la (grænədílə) n. any of various passionflowers, esp. *Passiflora quadrangularis* of South America ‖ its juicy, aromatic, gourdlike fruit [Span. dim. of *granada*, pomegranate]

Gra·na·dos (grənádous), Enrique (1867–1916), Spanish composer, esp. of piano music, incl. 'Goyescas' (1912–14), which formed the basis for his opera (1916) of the same name

gran·a·ry (grænəri:, gréinəri:) pl. **gran·a·ries** n. a storehouse for threshed grain ‖ a region producing or exporting much grain [fr. L. *granarium*]

Gran Ca·na·ria (gránkənárja) *CANARY ISLANDS

Gran Cha·co (grantʃákɔ) (or Chaco) the great plain between the Andes and the River Paraguay, comprising S.E. Bolivia, E. Paraguay and N. Argentina. Despite heavy rainfall in some areas it consists, owing to poor soil, of scrub forest in the east and savanna in the west, with marshes throughout. Products: tannin, lumber (laurel, quebracho, carob), cattle, cotton (mainly in Argentina)

Gran Co·lom·bia (gránkɔlómbja) a republic established (1819) by the Congress of Angostura, comprising Venezuela, Cundinamarca, and Quito. It was dissolved in 1830

grand (grænd) **1.** adj. accompanied by pomp and display, splendid ‖ imposing, distinguished, *grand company* ‖ self-important, *grand airs* ‖ highest, or very high in rank, *grand master of the lodge* ‖ great, *Napoleon's grand army* ‖ main, principal, *the grand staircase* ‖ summing up all the others, final, *the grand total* ‖ noble, dignified, lofty, *grand style* ‖ (pop.) very enjoyable, excellent ‖ (used only in compounds) indicating the second degree of ancestry or descent, as in 'grandparent' **2.** n. a grand piano [O.F.]

grandad *GRANDDAD

Grand Alliance, War of the the war (1689–97) between Louis XIV of France and the Grand Alliance, a coalition comprising the League of Augsburg and the Netherlands, Savoy and England. Louis invaded (1689) the Rhine Palatinate and attempted a counterrevolution in Ireland, but was defeated (1690) at the Boyne. The French were defeated at sea (1692) but were victorious on land (1692–3). The war was ended by the Treaty of Ryswick (1697), but the same belligerents were again at war (1701–14) in the War of the Spanish Succession

Grand Banks a vast extension of the continental shelf off S.E. Newfoundland in the North Atlantic, one of the world's greatest cod-fishing grounds

Grand Canal (*Chin.* Yün-ho) the chief canal (1,200 miles) of China, running north-south from Peking to Hangchow. Begun in the 5th c. B.C., it was almost completed under Yang Ti (605–617) and reconstructed in the late 13th c. by Kublai Khan

Grand Canyon a gorge (217 miles long) cut by the Colorado River through the high plateau of N.W. Arizona. It is over 1 mile deep and 4–18 miles wide

Grand Canyon of the Yellowstone *YELLOWSTONE RIVER

grand·chIld (græntʃaild) pl. **grand·chil·dren** (græntʃildrin) n. a child of one's son or daughter

Grand Coulee Dam a dam (height 550 ft) on the Columbia River, northeast central Washington State. Its reservoir (Franklin D. Roosevelt Lake) extends 146 miles to the Canadian Border. It is used for flood control, irrigation, power and river regulation

grand·dad, gran·dad (grændæd) n. (a child's word for) grandfather

grand·daugh·ter (grændɔtər) n. the daughter of one's child

grand duchess the wife or widow of a grand duke ‖ a woman who governs a grand duchy in her own right ‖ a daughter of the Russian czar

grand duchy a sovereign territory ruled by a grand duke or grand duchess

grand duke the sovereign of a European state who ranks next to a king and is styled royal highness ‖ a son of the Russian czar

gran·dee (grændí:) n. a Spanish or Portuguese nobleman of the highest rank [Span. and Port. *grande*, great (person)]

Grande Terre Is. (grádter) *GUADELOUPE

gran·deur (grændʒər, grændjər) n. sublimity, *the grandeur of mountain scenery* ‖ splendor, magnificence, *the grandeur of the throne room* ‖ nobility, elevation, *moral grandeur* [F.]

grand·fa·ther (grændfɑðər) n. the father of either of one's parents

Grandfather Clause a provision in the Alabama constitution of 1901. This constitution restricted suffrage to literate persons who had been in steady employment for the 12 months prior to registration and who paid taxes on property assessed at $300. The Grandfather Clause extended the franchise to those who had served in the U.S. or Confederate army or navy in time of war, to their lawful descendants, and to those persons of good character who understood 'the duties and obligations of citizenship

under a republican form of government', provided they registered before 1902. Thus it alleviated to a degree the discrimination in Alabama against blacks

grandfather clause a provision of law that permits continued eligibility or coverage for individuals or organizations already receiving benefits under a law, despite a change in the law that would otherwise make them ineligible

grandfather clock a pendulum clock in a wooden case standing on the floor and normally taller than a man

grand·fa·ther·ly (grænfɑðərli:) adj. like a grandfather or with the indulgence befitting a grandfather

Grand Gui·gnol (grági:njól) a macabre and gory stage entertainment ‖ drama so laboriously horrific as to fall into absurdity [after *le Grand Guignol*, a theater in Montmartre, Paris]

gran·dil·o·quence (grændíləkwəns) n. the quality of being grandiloquent

gran·dil·o·quent (grændíləkwənt) adj. pompous and overeloquent in style or delivery [fr. L. *grandiloquus*]

gran·di·ose (grǽndi:ous) adj. grand in an impressive way, imposing ‖ of inflated importance or magnificence [F. fr. Ital.]

grand jury a jury of from 12 to 23 persons which investigates certain indictments in private session and decides whether or not there is sufficient evidence to warrant a trial. The grand jury was abolished (1933) in England, but continues in the U.S.A.

grand larceny (law) theft of property exceeding a value fixed by state law, usually between $25 and $50

grand·ma (grænmɑ) n. (a child's word for) grandmother

grand mal (grǽndmæl) n. a severe epilepsy characterized by violent convulsions and loss of consciousness (cf. PETIT MAL)

grand·moth·er (grænmʌθər) n. the mother of either of one's parents

grand·moth·er·ly adj. like a grandmother or with the indulgence befitting a grandmother ‖ excessively fussy, *grandmotherly legislation*

Grand National a steeplechase held annually in March at Aintree, Liverpool, England, over a 4½-mile course with 30 jumps, one of the main British sporting events

Grand National Consolidated Trades Union (*Br. hist.*) the first union of skilled and unskilled workers, formed (1834) by Robert Owen, and dissolved a few months later after the persecution of the Tolpuddle Martyrs

grand old man (abbr. G.O.M.) a name applied to a respected and well-loved veteran in any field of human activity (orig. to Gladstone)

Grand Old Party (abbr. G.O.P.) the Republican party of the U.S.A.

grand opera opera in which the entire text is sung

grand·pa (grænpɑ) n. (a child's word for) grandfather

grand·par·ent (grænpέərənt) n. a grandfather or grandmother

grand piano a large piano with horizontal strings in a harp-shaped case (cf. UPRIGHT PIANO)

Grand Prix (grápri:) pl. **Grands Prix** (grápri:, grápri:z) an international horse race for three-year-olds run in June at Longchamp, Paris, one of the main annual French sporting events ‖ any of certain international automobile races

Grand Rapids a city (pop. 181,843) in W. Michigan: furniture, metal products, foods, chemicals, paper products, textiles, petroleum refineries. Calvin College (1876), Aquinas College (1923)

Grand Remonstrance (*Eng. hist.*) a list of protests against the arbitrary rule of Charles I, reiterating and expanding the Petition of Right, drawn up (1641) by the Long Parliament. Charles's evasive reply, and his attempt (Jan. 3, 1642) to arrest the five members responsible, precipitated the English Civil War

grand slam (bridge) the taking of all 13 tricks ‖ (baseball) a home run hit when there is a runner on each base

grand·son (grænsʌn) n. the son of one's child

grand·stand (grænstænd) n. a roofed-over stand with tiered seats, commanding the best view at football games etc.

Grand Te·ton National Park (tí:tɒn) a mountainous, forest-covered area (484 sq. miles) in N.W. Wyoming. It was declared (1929) a national park and enlarged (1950) to include most of the contiguous Jackson Hole National Monument

grand tour (*hist.*) an extended tour of Europe, formerly part of the education of young British aristocrats

grange (gréindʒ) *n.* a country house, esp. with associated farm buildings ‖ (*hist.*) an outlying farmhouse with its related buildings, belonging to a monastery or to a feudal lord ‖ a lodge of the Patrons of Husbandry, a farmers' association founded 1867 **The Grange** the popular name for this association [A.F. *graunge*]

gra·nite (grǽnit) *n.* a very hard crystalline igneous rock normally composed of quartz, feldspar and mica, valuable for building **gra·nít·ic** *adj.* [fr. Ital. *granito*]

gra·niv·o·rous (grænívərəs) *adj.* feeding on seeds and grain [fr. Mod. L. *granivorus*]

grann·lax (grǽnlæks) *n.* Swedish lunch of marinated dry-cured salmon with sugar and spices

gran·ny (grǽni:) *pl.* **gran·nies** *n.* (a child's word for) grandmother

granny dress woman's 19th-century style dress reaching from neck to ankles, often with ruffles, sometimes with high waistline and scoop neck

granny glasses *n.* small spectacles with gold or silver rims typical of 1880–1910 era

granny knot a square knot crossed the wrong way and therefore insecure

gra·no·la (grænóulə) *n.* a breakfast food of rolled oat, nut, and raisin mixture

Grant (grænt, grɑnt), Ulysses Simpson (1822–85), 18th president (1869–77) of the U.S.A., a Republican. During the Civil War, he captured (1863) Vicksburg and defeated (1863) Gen. Braxton Bragg at Chattanooga, for which he was appointed (1864) commander-in-chief of the Union army. He cut off Gen. Robert E. Lee's retreat at Appomattox Courthouse, and received (1865) Lee's surrender. He became (1866) the first American since George Washington to hold the rank of full general. His terms as president were marked by partisanship and political corruption

grant (grænt, grɑnt) **1.** *v.t.* to agree to fulfill, *to grant a request* ‖ to allow to have, give ‖ to admit, concede, *he would not grant that he was wrong* ‖ to concede (a proposition) without proof for the sake of argument, *granted your premises, your conclusion is still false* ‖ (*law*) to bestow formally, transfer **to take for granted** to assume ‖ to accept (someone or something) thoughtlessly, without proper appreciation, esp. through familiarity **2.** *n.* the act of granting ‖ something granted, esp. money ‖ (*law*) the formal bestowal of property ‖ (*law*) the property bestowed **gran·tée** *n.* (*law*) someone who receives a grant [A.F. *graunter, granter* O.F. *graanter, greanter*]

Granth Sāhib (grɔnt) *n.* the holy book of the Sikhs [Hind.=book, code]

grant-in-aid (grǽntinéid, grántinéid) *pl.* **grants-in-aid** *n.* a single sum of money paid from public funds by a central government (or by a private organization) to aid esp. some public work undertaken by a local authority

gran·tor (grǽntər, grúntər, græntɔ́r) *n.* (*law*) someone who makes a grant [A.F. *grantor*]

grants·man (grǽntsmæn) *n.* a specialist in obtaining grants from foundations, corporations, and governmental agencies. —**grantsmanship** *v.*

gran·u·lar (grǽnjulər) *adj.* consisting of grains ‖ as if composed of grains in surface or structure [fr. L.L. *granulum* dim. of *granum*, grain]

gran·u·late (grǽnjuleit) *pres. part.* **gran·u·lat·ing** *past* and *past part.* **gran·u·lat·ed** *v.t.* to form into grains ‖ to roughen the surface of ‖ *v.i.* to become granular ‖ (of a wound when forming a scab) to form tiny prominences of fresh tissue **gran·u·lá·tion** *n.* [fr. L.L. *granulum* dim. of *granum*, grain]

gran·ule (grǽnju:l) *n.* a small grain [fr. L.L. *granulum* dim. of *granum*, grain]

gran·u·lo·cyte (grǽnju:lousáit) *n.* (*med.*) a group of leucocytic blood cells

gra·num (gréinəm) *n.* (*botany*) a small drop of chlorophyll pigment in the strama of a chloroplast

Gran·ville (grǽnvil), John Carteret, 1st Earl (1690–1763), British statesman. He successfully led the opposition (1730–42) to Walpole,

and succeeded him as head of the administration (1742–4)

Gran·ville-Bar·ker (grǽnvilbárkər), Harley (1877–1946), English dramatist ('The Voysey Inheritance', 1909), producer and drama critic, also known for his 'Prefaces to Shakespeare' (1927–45)

grape (greip) *n.* a green or purple berry growing in bunches on a vine of genus *Vitis*. Grapes can be eaten fresh or dried (*CURRANT, *RAISIN), or pressed and fermented to make wine ‖ (*pl.*) a growth on the fetlock of a horse [O.F. *grape, grappe*, bunch of grapes]

grape·fruit (gréipfru:t) *n. Citrus paradisi,* fam. *Rutaceae,* a small tree native to the West Indies ‖ the large yellow citrus fruit which it yields

grape hyacinth any of several flowering plants of genus *Muscari,* fam. *Liliaceae,* esp. *M. racemosum,* which produces from a bulb a raceme of small blue flowers, the upper ones neuter and particularly conspicuous

grape·shot (gréipʃɔt) *n.* (*hist.*) a scattering charge for cannon

grape sugar dextrose

grape·vine (gréipvain) *n.* any grape-bearing vine ‖ an unofficial network of communication by which gossip and information are spread ‖ a figure in skating

graph (græf, grɑf) **1.** *n.* a diagram showing the relation of one variable quantity to another, by expressing their values as distances from usually two, sometimes three, axes at right angles to one another **2.** *v.t.* to denote by a graph [short for GRAPHIC FORMULA]

graph·eme (grǽfi:m) *n.* the smallest distinctive unit in a writing system ‖ all the written symbols in a writing system used to represent a single phoneme, taken as one unit

graph·ic (grǽfik) *adj.* concerned with decoration and representation on a flat surface, *graphic arts, graphic methods* ‖ (of descriptive writing, drawing etc.) conjuring up a clear picture in the mind, vivid, *a graphic account* ‖ having to do with graphs or diagrams ‖ (*mineral.*) showing marks like written characters on the surface or in section, *graphic granite* ‖ *n.* a visual, nonalphabetical numerical display, esp. on the cathode ray tube of a computer **graph·i·cal** *adj.* **graph·i·cal·ly** *adv.* [fr. L. fr. Gk *graphikos* fr. *graphē*, writing]

graphic formula (*chem.*) a structural formula

graph·ite (grǽfait) *n.* a naturally occurring form of carbon. It is a softish black material, used in the manufacture of pencils, dry lubricants, paints, in electrical apparatus, and as a moderator in nuclear reactors [G. *graphit* fr. Gk *graphos,* written]

graph·o·ep·i·tax·y (grǽfouépitæksi:) *n.* (*chem.*) crystal-growing process for integrated circuits, utilizing a single crystal silicon in a noncrystalline substrate, e.g., a glass plate with potential use in solar cells

graph·ol·o·gist (grǽfólədʒist) *n.* a specialist in graphology

graph·ol·o·gy (grǽfólədʒi:) *n.* the study of handwriting and the inferring of character or aptitude from it [fr. Gk *graphē,* writing +*logos,* discourse]

graph·o·scope (grǽfouskoup) *n.* (*computer*) cathode-ray screen on which changes may be made by a special stylus

graph·o·ther·a·py (grǽfouθérəpi:) *n.* diagnosis and therapy of personality or emotional problems through handwriting analysis

graph paper paper ruled into small squares for drawing graphs on

grap·nel (grǽpnəl) *n.* a small, clawed anchor or other hooked instrument, used e.g. in dragging ‖ (*hist.*) an instrument with claws used for seizing and holding an enemy ship when boarding ‖ (*mil.*) in naval mine warfare, a device fitted to a mine mooring designed to grapple the sweep wire when the mooring is cut [A.F. *grapenel* assumed dim. of *grapon,* a throwing instrument with iron claws]

grap·ple (grǽpl) **1.** *n.* a grip, grasp ‖ a grapnel **2.** *v. pres. part.* **grap·pling** *past* and *past part.* **grap·pled** *v.i.* to fight at close quarters or hand to hand ‖ to try hard to find a solution, *to grapple with a problem* ‖ *v.t.* to seize or hold with or as if with a grapnel [fr. O.F. assumed *grapelle,* a little hook]

grappling iron a grapnel (instrument with claws)

grap·to·lite (grǽptəlait) *n.* any of several extinct colonial marine organisms, fossilized in the form of markings on Palaeozoic black shales [fr. Gk *graptos,* marked +*lithos,* rock]

GRAS (*acronym*) for "generally recognized as safe," a category used by the U.S. Food and Drug Administration

grasp (græsp, grɑsp) **1.** *v.t.* to seize hold of firmly with the hand ‖ to hold firmly ‖ to understand, comprehend ‖ *v.i.* to reach out eagerly ‖ to try to seize advantage, *to grasp at an opportunity* **2.** *n.* a tight hold, grip ‖ control, *to fall into someone's grasp* ‖ intellectual control, understanding, *a good grasp of grammar* **within (beyond) one's grasp** within (out of) reach **grásp·ing** *adj.* aggressively out for one's own advantage [M.E. *graspen* fr. *grapsen*]

Grass (græs), Günter (1927–), German novelist and playwright. He became famous with his picaresque novel 'The Tin Drum' (1959). Other works include 'Cat and Mouse' (1961, Eng. trans., 1963), 'Dog Years' (1963; trans., 1965), 'Local Anaesthetic' (1969; trans., 1970), 'From the Diary of a Snail' (1972; trans., 1973) and 'The Flounder' (1977; trans., 1978)

grass (græs, grɑs) **1.** *n.* the low green herbage of pastureland and lawns ‖ a member of *Gramineae,* one of the largest and most cosmopolitan of the monocotyledonous families (including cereals, reeds, bamboos, as well as pasture grasses), with fibrous roots, hollow jointed stems, alternate, linear, bladed, sheathing leaves, and fruit in the form of a caryopsis ‖ pasture, grazing, *at grass* ‖ pastureland ‖ grass-covered ground ‖ (*pop.*) marijuana **to let the grass grow under one's feet** to waste time when there is an opportunity to be grasped **2.** *v.t.* to plant with grass ‖ to feed on grass pasture ‖ to lay on the grass for bleaching [O.E. *græs, gærs*]

grass carp herbivorous fish bred in China and the U.S.S.R. to control growth of weeds in water. *also* white amu

grass·hop·per (grǽshopər, grúshopər) *n.* any of several leaping, orthopterous, plant-eating insects of the suborder *Saltatoria,* predominantly nocturnal and allied to locusts

grass·land (grǽslænd, grúslænd) *n.* pasture or grazing land in temperate regions

grass roots the rural and agricultural population of a country ‖ what is basic, fundamental **gráss-roots** *adj.*

grass skiing (*sports*) the sport of sliding down straw-covered hills on specially designed skates

grass snake *Natrix natrix,* a common European harmless snake ‖ *Ophiodrys vernalis,* a bright green North American harmless snake

grass sponge *Spongia graminea,* an inferior coarse sponge from Florida and the Bahamas

grass tree a member of *Xanthorrhea,* fam. *Liliaceae,* a genus of Australian plants yielding a resin used in varnish etc., esp. *X. hastilis,* which has spearlike leaves and a spike of flowers

grass widow a woman whose husband is away from home on business etc. ‖ a woman divorced or separated legally from her husband

grass wrack eelgrass

grass·y (grǽsi:, grúsi:) *comp.* **grass·i·er** *superl.* **grass·i·est** *adj.* planted with grass ‖ of or pertaining to grass, grasslike

grate (greit) *n.* a frame of metal bars to contain fuel in a fireplace or furnace ‖ the fireplace itself ‖ a grating, grill (of a window or over an opening) [M.E. *grate,* lattice fr. M.L. *grata, crata*]

grate *pres. part.* **grat·ing** *past* and *past part.* **grat·ed** *v.t.* to reduce to small pieces by rubbing against a sharp or rough surface, *to grate cheese* ‖ to rub or grind (something) against something else, making a harsh noise, *to grate one's teeth* ‖ *v.i.* to make a harsh sound ‖ to have an irritating effect, *it grates on one's nerves* [O.F. *grater,* to scrape]

grate·ful (gréitfəl) *adj.* feeling or showing gratitude ‖ (*rhet.*) comforting, pleasant, *the grateful warmth of the fire* [fr. older *grate* adj. fr. L. *gratus,* pleasing]

gra·ter (gréitər) *n.* a kitchen utensil for grating food [O.F. *grateor, gratour*]

Gra·tian (gréiʃən, gréiʃi:ən) (Flavius Gratianus, 359–83), Roman emperor (375–83), son of Valentinian I. He ruled jointly with his half brother, Valentinian II. He strongly attacked paganism

grat·i·cule (grǽtikju:l) *n.* a scale in the field of a telescope or microscope superimposed on the eyepiece ‖ a design upon which a grid pattern is marked to facilitate its reproduction on a larger or smaller scale [F.]

grat·i·fi·ca·tion (grǽtifikéiʃən) *n.* a gratifying or being gratified ‖ a source of satisfaction

CONCISE PRONUNCIATION KEY: **(a)** æ, c*a*t; ɑ, c*a*r; ɔ f*aw*n; ei, sn*a*ke. **(e)** e, h*e*n; iː, sh*ee*p; iə, d*ee*r; ɛə, b*ear*. **(i)** i, f*i*sh; ai, t*i*ger; ə:, b*i*rd. **(o)** o, *o*x; au, c*ow*; ou, g*oa*t; u, p*oo*r; oi, r*oy*al. **(u)** ʌ, d*u*ck; u, b*u*ll; uː, g*oo*se; ə, b*a*cillus; juː, c*u*be. x, lo*ch*; θ, *th*ink; δ, bo*th*er; z, *Z*en; ʒ, cor*s*age; dʒ, sava*g*e; ŋ, orangutan*g*; j, *y*ak; ʃ, *fi*sh; tʃ, fet*ch*; 'l, rabb*le*; 'n, redd*en*. Complete pronunciation key appears inside front cover.

grat·i·fy (grǽtifai) *pres. part.* **grat·i·fy·ing** *past and past part.* **grat·i·fied** *v.t.* to do a favor to, please ‖ to indulge, satisfy, *to gratify one's curiosity* [fr. F. *gratifier*]

grat·ing (gréitiŋ) *n.* a partition, frame or cover of bars, parallel or crossed ‖ (*phys.*) a diffraction grating [fr. GRATE n.]

grating *pres. part.* of GRATE ‖ *adj.* harsh, discordant ‖ irritating

G rating (*cinema*) suitable for general viewing according to industry-designated classification administered by the Motion Picture Association of America

gra·tis (gréitis, grǽtis, grútis) 1. *adv.* without charge, *copies can be obtained gratis* 2. *adj.* free, given away [L., contr. fr. *gratiis*, out of kindness]

grat·i·tude (grǽtitju:d, grǽtitu:d) *n.* a feeling of appreciation for a kindness or favor received [F.]

Grat·tan (grǽt'n), Henry (1746–1820), Irish statesman. A fine orator, he advocated independence for Ireland and Catholic emancipation

gra·tu·i·tous (grətú:itəs, grətjú:itəs) *adj.* given or received free ‖ unwarranted, uncalled for, *a gratuitous insult* ‖ (*law*) given without compensation [fr. L. *gratuitus*, spontaneous]

gra·tu·i·ty (grətú:iti:, grətjú:iti:) *pl.* **gra·tu·i·ties** *n.* a tip for services rendered ‖ (*Br.*) a gift of money paid to a soldier on his quitting the service [fr. F. *gratuite*]

grat·u·la·to·ry (grǽtʃələtɔri:, grǽtʃələtʃouri:) *adj.* (*rhet.*) congratulatory [fr. L.L. *gratulatorius*]

Grau·bün·den (graubýndən) (F. Grisons) Switzerland's largest canton (pop. 164,641, speaking German, Romansh and Italian), in the southeast. Capital: Chur (pop. 25,000)

grau·pel (gráup'l) *n.* (*meteor.*) granular snow [G.]

Grau San Mar·tín (gráusɑnmartí:n), Ramón (1889–1969), Cuban physician, politician and president (1933–4, 1944–8)

gra·va·men (grəvéimen) *pl.* **gra·va·mens, gra·vam·i·na** (grəvéimənə) *n.* a grievance ‖ (*law*) the basic substance of a grievance or charge [L.L. fr. L. *gravare*, to load]

grave 1. (greiv) *adj.* warranting anxiety, *grave news* ‖ solemn, thoughtful ‖ important, weighty, *a grave decision* ‖ (grɑv) of, or marked with, an accent (`) used to indicate vowel quality (e.g. in French) or various kinds of stress (*ACCENT) 2. (grɑv) *n.* a grave accent [F.]

grave (greiv) *n.* a trench dug for the burial of a corpse ‖ a burial place, tomb ‖ (*rhet.*) any place that receives the dead, *a watery grave* **to turn in one's grave** to have one's eternal peace destroyed (by words or acts that one would have vehemently disapproved in one's lifetime) [O.E. *græf*]

grave *pres. part.* **grav·ing** *past* **graved** *past part.* **grav·en** (gréivən), **graved** *v.t.* (*rhet.*) to shape by carving, *graven images* ‖ (*rhet.*) to engrave [O.E. *grafan*, to dig, engrave]

grave *pres. part.* **grav·ing** *past and past part.* **graved** *v.t.* to clean (the bottom of a wooden ship) by burning and retarring [prob. fr. O.F. *grave*, shore]

grave·clothes (gréivklɔuðz, gréivklɔuz) *pl. n.* the clothes in which a dead body is buried

grave·dig·ger (gréivdɪgər) *n.* a person who digs graves for a livelihood

grave goods objects sometimes found with the corpse in burials

grav·el (grǽvəl) 1. *n.* a loose mixture of small pebbles and rock fragments, and sometimes sand ‖ (*geol.*) a stratum of this ‖ (*med.*) a collection of granular crystals in the kidneys and bladder (cf. STONE) ‖ the condition characterized by this 2. *v.t. pres. part.* **gra·vel·ing**, esp. *Br.* **gra·vel·ling** *past and past part.* **grav·eled**, esp. *Br.* **gra·velled** to cover with gravel **grav·el·ly** *adj.* [O.F. *gravele, gravelle*, dim. of *grave*, sand, shore, of Celt. origin]

graven *past part.* of GRAVE (to shape by carving) ‖ *adj.* carved or as though carved

grav·er (gréivər) *n.* an engraver's burin ‖ a small prehistoric carving and marking tool

Graves (greivz), Robert Ranke (1895–1985), English poet. He has sought a personal integrity in his poetry, avoiding fashion. He has also written historical novels, incl. 'I, Claudius' (1934) and 'Claudius the God' (1934). His 'The White Goddess' (1948) is based on poetic myth, and 'The Greek Myths' (1955) is a popular exposition of classical mythology

Graves (grǽv) a region of S.W. France, south of Bordeaux and west of the Garonne, producing a light wine, esp. white

Graves's disease (greivz, gréivziz) exophthalmic goiter (*EXOPHTHALMUS)

grave·stone (gréivstoun) *n.* a stone marking a grave, usually inscribed with the name of the dead person and the dates of his birth and death

grave·yard (gréivjɑrd) *n.* a burial ground, cemetery

gra·vid (grǽvid) *adj.* pregnant ‖ heavy and distended with eggs (e.g. of salmon) ‖ (*rhet.*) portentous, *gravid skies* [fr. L. *gravidus*]

gra·vim·e·ter (grəvímətər) *n.* an instrument like a hydrometer for measuring the specific gravity of a liquid or solid **grav·i·met·ric** (grævəmétrik) *adj.* relating to the gravimeter ‖ relating to measurement by weight, esp. relating to a system of quantitative chemical analysis based on the weights of reactants and products of reaction (cf. VOLUMETRIC) ‖ measured by weight **grav·i·met·ri·cal** *adj.* **gra·vim·e·try** (grəvímətri:) *n.* [fr. F. *gravimètre*]

graving dock a dry dock, esp. one in which ships may be cleaned and repaired

graving tool a graver

grav·i·sphere (grǽvisfɪr) *n.* the extent in space in which the gravity of a body is dominant

grav·i·tate (grǽviteit) *pres. part.* **grav·i·tat·ing** *past and past part.* **grav·i·tat·ed** *v.i.* to move under the force of gravity, *the planets gravitate around the sun, water will always gravitate to its lowest level* ‖ to move or be attracted compulsively towards some center of influence, *the crowds gravitated towards the refreshments stand* [fr. Mod. L. *gravitare* (*gravitatus*)]

grav·i·ta·tion (grævitéiʃən) *n.* the act or process of gravitating ‖ (*phys.*) a force of attraction acting between two bodies that is independent of the chemical nature of the bodies or the presence of intervening matter and that is described by the law of gravitation. According to the theory of relativity, gravitation is a fundamental property of space **grav·i·ta·tion·al** *adj.* [fr. Mod. L. *gravitatio* (*gravitationis*)]

grav·i·ta·tion·al collapse (græviténʃənəl) (*astron.*) hypothetical tendency of matter in space to gravitate together to form larger celestial bodies

gravitational constant (*abbr.* G) the proportionality constant in the law of gravitation, equal to $6.670 \times 10^{-11} \frac{\text{newton-m}^2}{\text{kg}^2}$

gravitational field a region of space associated with some configuration of mass in which gravitational forces can be detected

gravitational potential a scalar quantity associated with some point in a gravitational field, whose value is that of the potential function for gravitation at the point compared with some standard (e.g. a point infinitely far away from all mass)

grav·i·ton (grǽvitɒn) *n.* (*phys.*) a gravitational quantum whose existence has not yet been verified by experiment but which is expected to have 0 rest mass and spin quantum number 2 [GRAVITY+-*on*, fundamental particle]

grav·i·ty (grǽviti:) *pl.* **grav·i·ties** *n.* solemn importance, *the gravity of the occasion* ‖ seriousness, *an offense of great gravity* ‖ seriousness of demeanor, *an air of mock gravity* ‖ weight, heaviness ‖ (*phys.*) the gravitational attraction between the earth and bodies at or near its surface ‖ (*phys.*) gravitation in general [fr. F. *gravité*]

gravity feed a supply system of a substance from a higher level to a lower one using force of gravity without power assistance

gravity waves or **gravitational waves** (*phys.*) discrete waves radiated by gravity, hypothicized by Albert Einstein and confirmed in 1969

gra·vure (grəvjúər) *n.* photogravure [shortened fr. PHOTOGRAVURE]

gra·vy (gréivi:) *n.* the juice that comes out of meat while it is cooking ‖ a sauce made from this juice [M.E. *grave, gravey* perh. fr. O.F.]

gravy boat a boat-shaped receptacle for serving gravy in

Gray (grei), Asa (1810–88), U.S. botanist. As professor of natural history (from 1842) at Harvard University, he made Cambridge, Mass., the American center for botanical study, and developed the nation's largest herbarium

Gray, Elisha (1835–1901), U.S. inventor of the telegraphic switch, the annunciator, the tele-

graphic repeater, and the private telegraph line printer. He was involved in a legal battle with Alexander Graham Bell over the invention of the telephone, which he lost

Gray, Thomas (1716–71), English poet and scholar. He is best known for the 'Elegy Written in a Country Churchyard' (1750). With Collins, Gray introduced or reintroduced certain Romantic themes into English literature: the notion (with his Pindaric odes) of inspired poetic frenzy, an interest in the older English poetry, the romantic landscape and the conception of the melancholy, lonely poet

Gray code (*computer*) an error-minimizing code differing one bit from the binary code, e.g., 6 = 100 in the binary code, 101 in the Gray code

gray-col·lar (gréikɒlər) *adj.* of technical workers

gray, grey (grei) 1. *adj.* of a color between white and black ‖ overcast or gloomy, *a gray day* ‖ depressing, cheerless ‖ gray-haired ‖ of the members of a religious order wearing a gray habit ‖ (of fabric) just as it leaves the loom or spinning machine, unbleached and undyed, but not necessarily gray in color 2. *n.* a gray color, pigment, fabric etc. ‖ a dull gray light, *the first gray of dawn* ‖ a white horse ‖ (of cloth) the state of being unbleached and undyed, *in the gray* 3. *v.t.* to make gray ‖ *v.i.* to become gray [O.E. *græg*]

gray·beard (gréibɪərd) *n.* an old man ‖ a bellarmine

gray eminence someone exercising power in the background [fr. *l'Eminence grise*, the nickname for Richelieu's private secretary, Père Joseph]

gray goose a greylag

gray hen the female of the black grouse (cf. BLACKCOCK)

grayhound *GREYHOUND

graylag *GREYLAG

gray·ling (gréiliŋ) *n.* a member of *Thymallus*, fam. *Salmonidae*, a genus of freshwater game fish related to the salmon. They are yellowish-brown with deep brown stripes, and are found in cold streams

gray·mail (gréimeil) *n.* claim in a legal action that a proper defense requires the revelation of classified information

gray market a market using underhand but not strictly illegal methods for selling scarce goods at high prices (cf. BLACK MARKET)

gray matter brownish-gray neural tissue, esp. of the central nervous system, mainly composed of nerve cells and forming the cortex of the cerebrum and cerebellum, the nuclei of the brain and part of the spinal cord (cf. WHITE MATTER) ‖ (*pop.*) brains, intelligence

gray mullet *pl.* **gray mullet, gray mullets** an edible shore fish of fam. *Mugilidae*, found in temperate regions, esp. in the Mediterranean, and occasionally living in brackish or fresh water. They are 1-2 ft long

Gray Panthers (1971), U.S. movement that lobbies against age discrimination on the local, state and federal level

gray people in the U.S.S.R., children of Americans who hold both Soviet and American citizenship

gray power the economic, legal, and social influence of the organized aged

gray propaganda propaganda that does not specifically identify the source of its information

Gray's Inn *INNS OF COURT

gray squirrel *SQUIRREL

gray wolf the timber wolf

Graz (grɑts) Austria's second largest city (pop. 248,500), a former ducal capital, in the southeast: chemicals, iron and steel, leather. University (1586)

graze (greiz) 1. *v. pres. part.* **graz·ing** *past and past part.* **grazed** *v.t.* to touch or rub lightly in passing, *the wheels just grazed the curb* ‖ to rub the skin from, abrade, *the bullet grazed his arm* ‖ to suffer a slight abrasion of, *she grazed her knee* ‖ *v.i.* to come into light scraping contact 2. *n.* a superficial abrasion or rub caused by grazing [perh. fr. GRAZE, to crop]

graze *pres. part.* **graz·ing** *past and past part.* **grazed** *v.i.* to feed on growing grass ‖ *v.t.* to put out to pasture ‖ to put cattle etc. to feed on (a field) ‖ to feed on (growing grass) ‖ to look after (grazing cattle etc.) [O.E. *grasian*]

gra·zier (gréizər) *n.* (esp. *Br.*) someone who grazes cattle for market

graz·ing (gréiziŋ) *n.* pasture

CONCISE PRONUNCIATION KEY: **(a)** æ, c*a*t; ɑ, c*a*r; ɔ f*aw*n; ei, sn*a*ke. **(e)** e, h*e*n; i:, sh*ee*p; iə, d*ee*r; ɛə, b*ea*r. **(i)** i, f*i*sh; ai, t*i*ger; ə:, b*i*rd. **(o)** o, *o*x; au, c*ow*; ou, g*oa*t; u, p*oo*r; ɔi, r*oy*al. **(u)** ʌ, d*u*ck; u, b*u*ll; u:, g*oo*se; ə, b*a*cillus; ju:, c*u*be. x, lo*ch*; θ, *th*ink; ð, bo*th*er; z, *Z*en; ʒ, cor*s*age; dʒ, sava*ge*; ŋ, orangutan*g*; j, *y*ak; ʃ, fi*sh*; tʃ, fe*tch*; 'l, rabb*le*; 'n, redd*en*. Complete pronunciation key appears inside front cover.

grease 1. (griːs) *n.* soft, melted or rendered animal fat ‖ any oily or fatty matter, esp. when used as a lubricant or protective film on cars, machinery etc. ‖ the oily matter in wool ‖ the raw state of wool just after shearing and before being cleaned, *wool in the grease* ‖ a disease of horses producing inflammation of the fetlock and pastern **2.** (griːs, griːz) *v.t. pres. part.* **greas·ing** *past* and *past part.* **greased** to put or rub grease on, lubricate **to grease the hand** (or **palm**) **of** to bribe **to grease the wheels** to make affairs run smoothly (esp. with the aid of money) [M.E. *grece, grees* fr. O.F. *gresse*]

grease gun a small, hand-operated pump for lubricating machinery

grease·paint (gríspeint) *n.* makeup worn by actors on the stage

grease trap a trap in a drain for preventing the passage of grease

greas·i·ly (gríːsili:, gríːzili:) *adv.* in a greasy manner

greas·i·ness (gríːsiːnis, gríːziːnis) *n.* the state or quality of being greasy

greas·y (gríːsiː, gríːziː) *comp.* **greas·i·er** *superl.* **greas·i·est** *adj.* covered with grease ‖ containing, made of or like grease ‖ damp and slippery, *greasy roads* ‖ dirty-looking, unwashed ‖ insinuating, using a veneer of politeness to ingratiate oneself

greasy pole (*Br.*) a sport at fairs in which competitors struggle with one another on a greased pole

great (greit) *adj.* large in size, big ‖ as an intensive, emphasizing a following adjective, *a great big apple* ‖ large in number or extent, *a great deal* ‖ a high degree of, *great generosity* ‖ beyond the ordinary, *great talent* ‖ specially important, memorable, *one's first flight is a great experience* ‖ powerful, important ‖ significant in history, *a great battle* ‖ chief, preeminent, *the great attraction at the exhibition* ‖ favorite, *that's a great trick of his* ‖ eminent, distinguished, having remarkable ability etc., *a great artist* ‖ noble, *great thoughts* ‖ of high rank or position ‖ fully deserving the name of (intensifying the sense of the following noun), *a great friend of mine* ‖ enthusiastic in the pursuing of some interest or activity, *a great football fan* ‖ excellent, satisfactory, very pleasing (amusing, exciting etc.), *we had a great time* ‖ (used only in compounds) one degree further removed in ancestry or descent, e.g. in 'great-grandfather' (cf. GRAND) **great at** very good at, proficient at, *she's great at chess* **great in** (*pop.*) excelling in, *the team is great in attack* **great on** (*pop.*) keen on, knowledgeable about, *she's great on Roman history* [O.E. *grēat*]

great anteater *ANTEATER

Great Artesian Basin a lowland (area c. 670,000 sq. miles) of Australia extending from the Gulf of Carpentaria to New South Wales and containing the world's largest supply of artesian water

great auk *Pinguinus impennis,* a flightless auk extinct since the mid-19th c., exterminated by man

great-aunt (gréitænt, gréitánt) *n.* the aunt of either of one's parents

Great Australian Bight a bay (600 miles wide) on the south coast of Australia, part of the Indian Ocean

Great Awakening (1720–50), American colonial movement, chiefly among clergymen, to revive an interest in religion. Revivalists such as George Whitefield, Theodorus Frelinghuysen, Gilbert Tennent and Jonathan Edwards preached Calvinistic doctrine and encouraged personal religious experiences. A Second Great Awakening, emphasizing free will, occurred from 1795 through the 1840s

Great Barrier Reef a coral reef (1,250 miles long) off the east coast of Queensland, Australia

Great Basin an arid region (area approx. 210,000 sq. miles, elevation mainly 5,000–7,000 ft) of the western U.S.A., between the Rocky Mtns and the Sierra Nevada, and between the Colorado and Columbia River basins. There is no outlet to the sea, and its rivers are lost in saline lakes (*GREAT SALT LAKE) and sinks

Great Bear *URSA MAJOR

Great Bear Lake a large lake (about 175 miles long, area about 12,000 sq. miles) in the Northwest Territories of Canada. There are large deposits of radium and uranium near its shores

Great Britain (or Britain) the largest island (area 88,619 sq. miles) of the British Isles, comprising England, Scotland and Wales

Great Britain and Northern Ireland, the United Kingdom of a kingdom (area 94,500 sq. miles, pop. 54,128,000) in N.W. Europe. Capital: London. It comprises England, Wales, Scotland, Northern Ireland, the Isle of Man and the Channel Islands. Language: English, with Welsh and Gaelic minorities. Religion: 52% Church of England, 9% Roman Catholic, 3% Presbyterian, 2% Methodist (Jewish, Baptist, Congregationalist, Calvinistic Methodist and Quaker minorities). Livestock: sheep, cattle, hogs, poultry. Principal crops: cereals, potatoes, vegetables, fodder, fruit, sugar beet. Principal resources: coal, iron ore, china clay, limestone, granite, fish. Manufactures and industries: iron and steel, nonferrous metals, machinery, machine tools, vehicles, aircraft, plastics, electrical goods, chemicals, cotton, wool, petroleum, shipbuilding, pottery, thread, tweed, bricks, glass, carpets, food and drink, printing and publishing, rubber products, furniture, footwear, clothing. Exports: manufactured goods. Imports: petroleum products, meat, fruit and vegetables, machinery, cereals, metals, oil, chemicals, coffee, cocoa, tea, spices, dairy products, wood and pulp, wool, paper, tobacco, raw cotton, oils and fats. Main ports: London, Liverpool, Hull, Manchester, Southampton, Glasgow, Belfast. Universities: 32 (the oldest being Oxford, Cambridge and St Andrews). Monetary unit: pound sterling (divided into 100 pence). Great Britain has dependencies as follows. Colonies: Bahamas, Bermuda, British Honduras, British Indian Ocean Territories, British Virgin Is, Cayman Is, Falkland Is, Gibraltar, Gilbert and Ellice Is, Hong Kong, Montserrat, Pitcairn, St Helena with Ascension and Tristan da Cunha, Seychelles, Turks and Caicos Is. Protectorate: Solomon Is. Protected states: Brunei, Trucial States. Franco-British condominium: New Hebrides. St Kitts-Nevis-Anguilla, Dominica, Grenada, St Lucia, St Vincent and Antigua-Barbuda-Redonda are states in association with Britain. HISTORY. (For the history of England and Scotland prior to 1707 see separate entries.) The Act of Union (1707) united England and Scotland, and reduced the threat of Scottish Jacobitism at a time when England was involved in the War of the Spanish Succession (1701–14). On the death (1714) of Queen Anne, the Hanoverian line succeeded to the throne, in accordance with the Act of Settlement (1701). After two unsuccessful risings (1715 and 1745), Jacobitism ceased to be an important political force, and a century of internal stability ensued. THE GEORGIAN AGE. In the reigns (1714–27 and 1727–60) of George I and George II, government was dominated by the Whigs, under Stanhope, Townshend and Walpole. The period was marked by the growth of the cabinet and of ideas of party government and ministerial responsibility. With Walpole, the office of prime minister became a regular but unofficial feature of the constitution. Trade, finance and colonialism prospered, but brought Britain into conflict with France and Spain in the War of the Austrian Succession (1740–8) and the Seven Years' War (1756–63). The latter war, shrewdly directed by the elder Pitt, left Britain dominant in Canada and India, and the leading colonial power. Under the Whig oligarchy, the increased wealth brought by commerce was reflected in sumptuous country houses and landscape gardens. Classical taste was manifest in architecture, painting, furniture, music and literature. George III's attempt to take a more active part in politics than his predecessors culminated in the loss of the American colonies after the Revolutionary War (1775–83). Under the younger Pitt, economic expansion continued, with the growth of the Industrial Revolution and of improvements in agriculture and communications. Rapid growth of population, and the drift from the country to the towns, provoked social problems and the beginnings of radicalism. Economic problems were increased by the French Revolutionary Wars (1792–1802), the Napoleonic Wars (1803–15) and the War of 1812. Rebellion in Ireland (1798) led to the union of Great Britain and Ireland in the United Kingdom (1800). The skepticism and moral decadence prevalent in the earlier 18th c. gave way to the growth of Methodism, humanitarianism and evangelicalism. Literature was dominated by the Roman-

tic movement, and economics by the theories of Adam Smith, Malthus and Ricardo. George III became increasingly insane and George IV became regent (1811–20) and then king (1820–30). During this reign, and that of William IV (1830–7), the prestige of the monarchy sank to a low level. The Congress of Vienna (1814–15) gave Britain new colonial possessions, but economic distress and unrest continued at home, while the Corn Laws (1815) kept the price of bread high. The Tory government (1812–27) of Lord Liverpool resorted at first to repression, resulting in the Peterloo Massacre (1819). After Castlereagh's death (1822), Canning introduced a more liberal foreign policy, while Huskisson and Peel began economic and domestic reforms. The Combination Laws were repealed (1824) and Catholic Emancipation was passed (1829). The Whig ministry (1830–4) of Lord Grey passed the Reform Act (1832), abolished slavery in the British Empire (1833), reformed the Poor Law (1834), passed a Factory Act (1833) and gave help to schools for the poor (1832).

THE VICTORIAN AGE. Queen Victoria succeeded to the throne of Great Britain (1837), but Hanover was now separated from the British Crown. Melbourne continued as Whig prime minister until 1841, when he was replaced by a Conservative ministry under Peel. As the result of a campaign by Cobden and Bright, and of the Irish potato famine, Peel repealed (1846) the Corn Laws, thereby splitting his own party, which was then driven into opposition. Free trade, combined with Britain's naval predominance, increased her industrial supremacy over the rest of the world. Under Palmerston, foreign policy took on a jingoistic tone, but war was avoided, except for the Crimean War (1854–6) and the Indian Mutiny (1857–8). As railroads and heavy industry developed, towns grew rapidly, often creating slums, while trade unions began to be more effectively organized. The demands of the lower middle classes for a widening of the franchise failed with Chartism (1848), but were largely achieved by the Reform Acts of 1867 and 1884. Gladstone led a reforming Liberal ministry (1868–74) which carried out sweeping reforms of education (1870), the civil service (1870), local government (1871), the licensing laws (1872) and the army and introduced the ballot in parliamentary elections (1872). Disraeli led a Conservative ministry (1874–80) which carried out further domestic reforms and dealt with the problems of a rapidly expanding empire (*COMMONWEALTH). Queen Victoria was proclaimed empress of India (1877). Gladstone was again prime minister (1880–5, 1886 and 1892–4) and was increasingly occupied by Irish affairs. He had disestablished the Irish Church (1869) and had passed an Irish Land Act (1870), and he now made two unsuccessful attempts to carry an Irish Home Rule Bill (1886 and 1893). This issue split the Liberal party, Joseph Chamberlain leading the Liberal Unionists into alliance with the Conservatives, who were in power (1895–1902) under Salisbury. A growing policy of imperialism, esp. in Africa, led to the Boer War (1899–1902). Britain's policy of 'splendid isolation' was proving untenable, because her industrial lead had been overtaken by Germany and the U.S.A., and because her agriculture had begun to decline in the 1870s. Victoria's death (1901) ended an era which had produced many great writers (e.g. Dickens, Trollope, Carlyle, Tennyson, Hardy), religious reformers (e.g. Newman, Pusey) and scientists (e.g. Faraday, Huxley, Darwin). Art had been influenced by the Pre-Raphaelites and the Gothic Revival. The Fabian Society was drawing attention to social problems, and the Labour party was being formed. The popular press appeared at the end of the century to meet the demands of a population taking an increased part in national life. During Victoria's long reign, the monarchy regained the esteem and the affection of the people.

THE TWENTIETH CENTURY. After Edward VII's accession, Balfour became prime minister (1902–5). His Conservative ministry carried an important Education Act (1902), but was split by Chamberlain on tariff reform. In face of the menace of German armament, Britain signed alliances with Japan (1902), France (1904) and Russia (1907). A strong Liberal administration (1906–15) under Campbell-Bannerman and Asquith brought in many social reforms, in-

CONCISE PRONUNCIATION KEY: **(a)** æ, c*a*t; ɑ, c*a*r; ɔ f*aw*n; ei, sn*a*ke. **(e)** e, h*e*n; iː, sh*ee*p; iə, d*ee*r; ɛə, b*ea*r. **(i)** i, f*i*sh; ai, t*i*ger; əː, b*i*rd. **(o)** o, *o*x; au, c*ow*; ou, g*oa*t; u, p*oo*r; ɔi, r*oy*al. **(u)** ʌ, d*u*ck; u, b*u*ll; uː, g*oo*se; ə, b*a*cill*u*s; juː, c*u*be. x, lo*ch*; θ, *th*ink; ð, bo*th*er; z, *Z*en; ʒ, cor*sa*ge; dʒ, sa*v*age; ŋ, orangutan*g*; j, *y*ak; ʃ, *fi*sh; tʃ, fe*tch*; 'l, rabb*le*; 'n, redd*en*. Complete pronunciation key appears inside front cover.

cluding the protection of trade union funds (1906), military reorganization (1907), the beginning of old-age pensions (1908) and the establishment of employment exchanges (1909). George V succeeded to the throne (1910). The rejection by the House of Lords of Lloyd George's attempt to tax unearned income on land (1909) led to a constitutional crisis which ended with the drastic reduction of the Lords' power by the Parliament Act (1911). The suffragette movement was resorting to violence to obtain votes for women, and the passage of a Home Rule Bill (1914) brought the risk of civil war in Ireland, but domestic strife was submerged in the outbreak of the 1st world war (1914–18). A coalition government was set up (1915) under Asquith, who was replaced (1916) by Lloyd George. The British army, on a voluntary basis until 1917, lost about 800,000 men during the war. The vote was given to women over 30 and the school-dropout age was raised to 14 (1918). Lloyd George's coalition continued in power until 1922, having faced increasing problems of post-war economic settlement and of guerrilla warfare in Ireland. The ensuing Conservative government (1922–3) under Bonar Law and Baldwin gave independence to the Irish Free State (1922). The Labour party, which had grown steadily since the beginning of the century, formed its first government (1924) under MacDonald, but fell from power after nine months. A Conservative ministry (1924–9) under Baldwin faced increasing labor problems and the general strike of 1926. The voting age for women was reduced to 21 (1928). MacDonald again formed a Labour government (1929), but, as the world economic crisis was felt in Britain, this was widened (1931) to become a coalition national government. The gold standard, adopted in 1925, was abandoned (1931), payments on war debts were suspended, and protective tariffs were introduced with preference for empire countries (1932). Popular way of life was profoundly changed by the advent of broadcasting and the movies and the mass production of motor vehicles. A constitutional crisis occurred after the death (1936) of George V, when his successor, Edward VIII, announced his intention of marrying an American divorcee. Baldwin's refusal to give governmental approval to the marriage led to Edward VIII's abdication, and the succession of George VI (1936). Neville Chamberlain became prime minister (1936–40), and continued Baldwin's policy of appeasement toward the aggressions of the Axis powers until Britain entered the 2nd world war (Sept. 3, 1939). After the Germans had invaded Poland, Denmark, Norway, the Netherlands and Belgium, Chamberlain resigned (1940) in favor of Churchill, who led a coalition government until 1945. Thousands of British troops were evacuated from Dunkirk (1940), but the Battle of Britain (1940) prevented a German invasion. German bombs and rockets caused terrible damage, and the war as a whole cost Britain about 400,000 lives, and left her economically exhausted. The postwar Labour government (1945–51) under Attlee attempted to deal with the financial crisis, but had to accept vast sums of U.S. aid, and was forced (1949) to devalue the pound. A large-scale program of nationalization included the Bank of England (1945), air transport (1946), the supply of gas and electricity (1947), road and rail transport (1947) and the iron and steel industry (1949). The Welfare State was brought into being by the National Insurance Act (1946), the Housing Acts (1946 and 1949) and the National Health Service Act (1946), which provided free medical service for all. The Education Act of 1944 raised the school-dropout age to 15. Britain was faced with grave problems of inflation and of balance of payments. Rationing and conscription continued. The Conservative party was returned to power (1951–64) under the leadership successively of Churchill (1951–5), Eden (1955–7), Macmillan (1957–63) and Douglas-Home (1963–4). George VI was succeeded (1952) by Elizabeth II. The steel and road haulage industries were denationalized (1953), rationing was gradually ended, and there was a rapid growth of prosperity. India and many former colonies became independent (*COMMONWEALTH). Britain was involved in the Korean War (1950–3), intervened in Suez (1956) and faced risings in Cyprus (1954–60) and Kenya (1952–9). The Labour party was returned to power (1964) under Wilson. Steel

was renationalized (1967). The pound sterling was devalued (Nov. 1967) by 14.3%, and successive austerity budgets were implemented. After several years of negotiated attempts, Britain joined the European Economic Community in 1973. Racial tensions grew during the 1960's as many nonwhite citizens of the Commonwealth nations sought employment in Britain. In 1968 the Race Relations Bill prohibited racial or ethnic discrimination. In addition, tensions continued in Northern Ireland between British troops and the Irish Republican Army. The Conservative party returned to power in 1970, and Conservative Margaret Thatcher, Britain's first woman prime minister, took office in 1980. Her party enjoyed a brief surge of popularity during Britain's victory over Argentina in the Falkland Islands war (1982). But Thatcher's policy of economic retrenchment came increasingly under attack, sparking riots in some Midlands cities and in London in 1985

great bustard *Otis tarda,* the biggest land bird in Europe. It is also found in Asia and Africa (*BUSTARD)

great circle a circle on the surface of a sphere, whose plane passes through the sphere's center. Thus the shortest distance between any two points on the earth's surface is an arc of a great circle

great-circle route a route following a great circle of the earth, used by ships or planes crossing large expanses of the globe

great-coat (gréitkout) *n.* a heavy overcoat

Great Compromise of 1787 an emendation of the draft of the U.S. Constitution proposed during the Continental Congress of 1787. It gave the states equal representation in the Senate and representation proportionate to population in the House (the slave population being accredited on a three-fifths basis). It also established the electoral college for electing the U.S. president, and forbade Congress to abolish the slave trade before 1808

great council (*Eng. hist.*) an assembly of the tenants-in-chief of any of the Norman kings

Great Dane a dog of a smooth-coated massive, fearless, intelligent breed of German origin. Great Danes may stand up to 3 ft in height at the shoulder

Great Divide the Continental Divide

Great Dividing Range a series of mountain ranges and plateaus running parallel with the eastern coast of Australia. The Australian Alps at the southern end are the highest range (Mt Kosciusko 7,316 ft)

Greater Antilles *ANTILLES

Greater Colombia a former independent state formed (1819) by Bolívar, comprising Colombia, Panama, Venezuela and (after 1822) Ecuador. Venezuela and Ecuador seceded (1830). Panama became part of New Granada (*COLOMBIA) and seceded (1903) from Colombia

greater ku·du (kú:du:) *Strepsiceros strepsiceros,* a large African antelope with very long horns twisted in a spiral

Greater London an administrative area of S.E. England, comprising 32 Inner and Outer London boroughs (*LONDON)

Great Exhibition of 1851 an international exhibition (May 1851) esp. of manufactures in Paxton's Crystal Palace in Hyde Park, London. Prince Albert was very active in the organizing of it. More than half the 13,000 exhibitors were non-British. It was financially a success, was important in the history of art and architecture, and inaugurated the series of international exhibitions held since

great gross a unit of quantity equaling 12 gross

great-heart·ed (gréithártid) *adj.* (*rhet.*) brave || (*rhet.*) magnanimous

great horned owl *Bubo virginianus,* a large North American owl || the eagle owl

Great Interregnum the period in German history from the death of Conrad IV (1254) to the election of Rudolf I of Hapsburg (1273), during which the princes extended their territories and increased their authority

Great Lakes a chain of five freshwater lakes (total area 95,000 sq. miles) along the boundary of the U.S.A. and Canada: Superior (the largest), Michigan (the only one wholly in the U.S.A.), Huron, Erie and Ontario. They form the most important system of inland waterways in the world, being linked to the sea by the St Lawrence Seaway and to many inland industrial centers by connecting waterways

Great Leap Forward program of industrialization initiated by Mao Zedong in China during the years 1958–1961. The plan resulted in two disastrous harvests and brought the nation to the edge of economic ruin, resulting in the according of priority to agriculture and a higher priority to the development of modern technology

great·ly (gréitli:) *adv.* much, to a great degree (esp. with comparatives, participles and certain verbs), *greatly superior, greatly admired, greatly to be preferred*

Great Mogul the ruler of the Mogul Empire

great organ (*mus.*) the principal, most powerful division of an organ having two or more manuals. It comprises the pipes having the loudest tone and the related manual and controls

Great Plains a generally semi-arid grass plateau in the west central U.S.A. and Canada, bounded on the east by the prairies of the Mississippi valley and on the west by the Rocky Mtns

great primer (*printing*) an old size of type, about 18 point

Great Rebellion *CIVIL WAR, ENGLISH

Great Rift Valley a depression stretching from the Jordan valley, W. Asia, to Mozambique, E. Africa, including the Dead Sea, the Gulf of 'Aqaba, the Red Sea, a chain of lakes crossing Ethiopia, Lake Rudolph, the valley of central Tanganyika and (in a western branch) the chain of lakes (Albert, Edward, Kivu and Malawi) curving along the Democratic Republic of the Congo border. From 1,300 feet below sea level at the Dead Sea it rises to 6,000 ft in S. Kenya

Great Russian 1. *n.* a member of the chief ethnic group of the U.S.S.R., inhabiting esp. the center and northeast || the Slavic language spoken by members of this group, the official language of the U.S.S.R. **2.** *adj.* of or relating to the Great Russians or their language

Greats (greits) *pl. n.* the Oxford B.A. final examination, esp. that for honors in Literae Humaniores (classics), or the course of study for it [short for *great go,* the former cant term]

great scale (*mus., hist.*) the scale ascribed to Guido d'Arezzo, including all the notes recognized in medieval church music, and ranging from G on the lowest line of the modern bass staff to E in the top space of the modern treble staff

great seal the principal seal of a state, esp. that of Great Britain in the keeping of the lord chancellor **Great Seal** the lord chancellor || his office

Great Society slogan for social legislation program (1963–1969) of President Lyndon B. Johnson

Great St Bernard *ST BERNARD, GREAT

Great Salt Lake a large shallow salt lake (about 70 miles long, 30 miles wide, average depth about 12 ft) in N.W. Utah. Its area has fluctuated between 1,500 and about 2,200 sq. miles, varying according to changes in the level

Great Sandy Desert (*Arab.* Rub' al Khali) a vast desert region (area 300,000 sq. miles) of S. Arabia

Great Schism a split (1378–1417) in the Catholic Church during which there were rival popes at Rome and Avignon. It arose less from dogma than from the political rivalries of Italy and France. It was ended by the Council of Constance

Great Slave Lake a lake (area 10,719 sq. miles) in the S. Mackenzie District, Canada. It is the source of the Mackenzie River

Great Smoky Mountains *APPALACHIAN MOUNTAINS

Great Trek the mass migration (1835–6) of Boer farmers from Cape Colony to escape British domination. It resulted in the foundation of the new republics of Natal, the Transvaal and the Orange Free State

great-un·cle (gréitʌŋk'l) *n.* the uncle of either of one's parents

Great Victoria Desert a desert region of S. Australia

Great Wall of China a defensive fortification (about 1,500 miles long, average height 22 ft, width 20 ft, with 40-ft towers every 100 yards) running from the coast of N.E. Hopei to W. Kansu. It was built in the reign (246–209 B.C.) of the emperor Shih Huang-ti to defend China's northern frontier, and substantially rebuilt under the Ming Dynasty (1368–1644)

Great War, the *WORLD WAR, the 1st

greave (griːv) *n.* (*hist.*, esp. *pl.*) armor for the shins [O.F. *greve*, shin, greave]

greaves (griːvz) *pl. n.* the refuse of melted tallow, used in prepared dog foods [fr. L.G. *greve*]

grebe (griːb) *n.* a member of *Colymbidae* (or *Podicipedidae*), a widely distributed family of freshwater diving birds which visit the sea when migrating and in winter. They have lobed toes and are excellent swimmers and divers, but are ungainly on land, walking upright like penguins [F. *grèbe*]

Gre·cian (griːʃən) **1.** *adj.* (esp. of architecture and human features) Greek, esp. of ancient Greece **2.** *n.* a Greek scholar [fr. L. *Graecia*, Greece]

Grecian nose a straight nose continuing the line of the forehead without any dent

Gre·cism, esp. *Br.* **Grae·cism** (griːsizəm) *n.* a Greek idiom or other characteristically Greek feature, esp. used in another language ‖ the spirit or style of Greek culture or art [fr. F. *grécisme*]

Gre·cize, esp. *Br.* **Græ·cize** (griːsaiz) *pres. part.* **Gre·ciz·ing**, esp. *Br.* **Grae·ciz·ing** *past and past part.* **Gre·cized**, esp. *Br.* **Græ·cized** *v.t.* to make Greek in attitude, customs etc. ‖ to use characteristically Greek spellings etc. in (a word, language etc.)

Gre·co, El (elgrékou), (Doménikos Theotokopulos, c. 1544–1614), Spanish painter, one of the outstanding artists of the Counter-Reformation. He was born in Crete and worked in Venice and Rome before going to Spain. He achieved great spiritual intensity in his work, through the baroque treatment of line and space (notably in his elongations of the human figure), and through a dramatic use of color and of sudden juxtaposition of dark and light

Gre·co-Ro·man, esp. *Br.* **Grae·co-Roman** (griːkouróumən) *adj.* of or relating to that which is partially Greek and partially Roman, *the Greco-Roman world of the 1st c.*

Greece (griːs) (*Gk* Hellas) a kingdom (area 51,182 sq. miles, pop. 9,706,687) in S.E. Europe. Capital: Athens. People and language: 96% Greek, 2% Turkish, 1% Slav (Macedonian), with small Vlach, Albanian, Bulgarian and Armenian minorities. Religion: 94% Orthodox, 2% Moslem, with small Roman Catholic, Armenian, Jewish and Protestant minorities. The land is 26% arable, 15% forest and 9% pasture. Chief islands: Ionian Is, Euboea, Cyclades, N. Sporades, Crete, Dodecanese, Aegean Is. The cultivated plains of Thrace, Macedonia and Thessaly, and the basins of Boeotia and Arcadia are hemmed in by mountains. The Pindus Mtns run parallel to the coast through Macedonia, Thessaly and Epirus. The eastern mountains (e.g. Olympus) run at right angles to the coast and reappear in the 2,000 islands of the Aegean. The Peloponnese is stony in the east and fertile in the south (Messenia). Annual rainfall: 40 ins in the west, 20 ins in the east. Average winter and summer temperatures (F.): Corfu 50° and 77°, Athens 47° and 80°, lower in the mountains. Livestock: sheep, goats, cattle, donkeys. Agricultural products: olives, wine, fruit, cereals, rice, tobacco, vegetables, cheese. Mineral resources (largely unexploited): iron pyrites, emery, bauxite, zinc, lead, manganese, lignite, magnesite, chromite, antimony, marble. Manufactures: shipbuilding, textiles, chemicals, foodstuffs. Exports: tobacco, dried fruit, olives, olive oil, wine, iron ore, pyrites, bauxite. Imports: machinery, vehicles, manufactures, coal, oil, foodstuffs. Main ports: Piraeus, Patras, Salonica. Universities: Athens (1837), Salonica (1925). Monetary unit: drachma (100 lepta). HISTORY. Greek-speaking Achaeans invaded the Greek peninsula from central Europe c. 2000 B.C., displacing and enslaving the Pelasgians. The earliest highly developed civilization in the Aegean area was the Minoan civilization of Crete (c. 3000–1400 B.C.) which spread to the mainland and gave rise to the Mycenean civilization (c. 1400–1200 B.C.). This is the heroic age described by Homer. This civilization was destroyed (c. 1200 B.C.) by the Dorians, the second great wave of Greek-speaking invaders from the north, who increased the migrations to the islands and to Asia Minor. The early tribal settlements developed (1000–700 B.C.) into small independent city-states. Rising populations and a shortage of land led to overseas colonization on the coast of the Black Sea, in Sicily and in the western Mediterranean (c. 750–500 B.C.). By 500 B.C. most cities were governed by oligarchies or democracies. In spite of their common language, the city-states remained divided and developed separately, with Athens and Sparta emerging as the leading powers. The Greek cities of Asia Minor, which had been absorbed into the Lydian and Persian empires during the 6th c., revolted (499 B.C.) and were crushed, despite help from Athens. This led to the Persian Wars (499–449 B.C.), in which Persia invaded European Greece and was defeated at Marathon (490) and Plataea (479), the Persian fleet being destroyed at Salamis (480). Athenian democracy reached its height under Pericles and Athens became the intellectual and artistic center of Greece. Growing rivalry between Sparta and Athens led to the Peloponnesian War (431–404 B.C.), which ended with the surrender of Athens. Continuing rivalries and conflicts greatly weakened the Greek city-states, and Macedonia, under Philip II, grew in power and dominated Greece (338 B.C.). Through his conquests, Philip's son, Alexander the Great, spread Greek civilization over the known Western world and across Asia to India. After his death (323 B.C.) his empire was divided by quarrels among his generals. Incessant internecine warfare further weakened Greece and it was made a Roman province (146 B.C.). Its culture continued to spread throughout the Near East and greatly influenced Rome (*HELLENISM). When the Roman Empire was divided (395 A.D.), Greece became a province of the Byzantine Empire until it was divided into Latin Crusader Kingdoms (1204). It was conquered by the Turks (1466) and remained under Turkish rule until the successful Greek War of Independence (1821–30). A monarchy was established (1832) under Otto of Bavaria, who abdicated (1862) and was succeeded by George I (1863). Greece continued to absorb Turkish territories—Thessaly (1878), Crete, Macedonia, Epirus and most of the Turkish islands after the Balkan Wars (1912–13), and Thrace and part of N.W. Asia Minor after the 1st world war, in which Greece, after the deposition (1917) of pro-German King Constantine I, had fought on the Allied side. Greece lost its Asian territories in wars with Turkey (1921–3). Greek boundaries were finally settled with large transfers of minority populations. After the banishment (1924) of George II, monarchists and republicans struggled for power and Metaxas finally established a dictatorship (1936). After an abortive Italian invasion (1940), Greece was occupied (1941) by the Germans. Resistance continued until the liberation (1944), when the pro-communist guerrilla army (E.L.A.S.) was prevented from seizing power by British and American intervention, though not finally broken until 1949. A limited monarchy was restored (1946) under George II, succeeded by his brother Paul (1947). Greece joined NATO (1952) and has benefited from American aid. The army seized power (Apr. 21, 1967). King Constantine called (Dec. 13, 1967) upon army units to overthrow the military junta, failed, and went into exile. A republic was proclaimed in 1973 but a military dictatorship ruled until the following year when democracy was restored under Karamanlis. Andreas Papandréou took office in 1981 and was reelected in 1985

greed (griːd) *n.* excessive desire, esp. for food or wealth [GREEDY]

greed·i·ly (griːdili) *adv.* in a greedy manner

greed·i·ness (griːdinis) *n.* the state or quality of being greedy

greed·y (griːdi) *comp.* **greed·i·er** *superl.* **greed·i·est** *adj.* inordinately fond of food, gluttonous ‖ inordinately desirous, avaricious, *greedy for fame* [O.E. *grædig*]

Greek (griːk) **1.** *n.* a native of Greece (ancient or modern) ‖ a member of the Greek Orthodox Church ‖ the Greek language (classical or modern) ‖ the group of Indo-European languages to which Greek belongs **it's all Greek to me** I don't understand any of it **2.** *adj.* of or pertaining to Greece, its people, culture or language [O.E. *Grēcas* pl. fr. L. *Graecus* fr. Gk *Graikos*]

Greek Catholic a member of any Orthodox Eastern Church ‖ a member of a Greek Uniate church

Greek cross a cross having four equal arms at right angles

Greek Father a Father of the Christian Church who wrote in Greek

Greek fire a mixture used by the Byzantine Greeks for setting enemy ships on fire

Greek language the language originally comprising three principal groups: Ionic and Attic, Aeolic, and Doric. The earliest literary language was the Ionic epic of Homer. With Athenian political supremacy Attic became the predominant literary form (c. 500-300 B.C.) and the Koine (common Greek), an adaptation of Attic, later became the language of the Hellenistic world. A more or less classical Greek remained the written language of the Byzantine Empire. Modern Greek has undergone grammatical changes and foreign influences similar to those which produced the Romance languages

Greek Orthodox Church a church which originated in 1833 shortly after Greek independence. It was the first of the autonomous churches in the Balkans, diminishing the authority of Constantinople. It belongs to the Orthodox Eastern Church, which separated from Rome in 1054

Greek War of Independence the struggle (1821–9) in which the Greeks won independence from the Turks. The rebellion began under the leadership of the Ypsilanti brothers, and was supported by most of Europe. Britain, France and Russia destroyed the Turko-Egyptian fleet at Navarino (1827). Russia declared war (1828) on Turkey, which was finally forced to accept full Greek independence (1832)

Gree·ley (griːliː), Horace (1811–72), American newspaper editor. He founded (1841) the 'New York Tribune', through which as an antislavery spokesman he exercised great influence on public opinion before the Civil War. He popularized the phrase 'Go west, young man'

Green (griːn), Duff (1791–1875), U.S. political journalist. After becoming (1826) founding-editor of the 'United States Telegraph', a Jacksonian Democratic organ, he was appointed (1828) printer to Congress and a member of Jackson's 'Kitchen Cabinet'

Green, John Richard (1837–83), British historian, author of a 'History of the English People' (1877–80)

Green, Thomas Hill (1836–82), English moral philosopher. A neo-Hegelian idealist in revolt against contemporary utilitarian ethics, he stressed the spiritual and religious nature of self-fulfillment and of true citizenship in 'Prolegomena to Ethics' (1883) and 'Principles of Political Obligation' (1895)

Green, William (1873–1952), U.S. labor leader, president (1924–52) of the American Federation of Labor

green (griːn) **1.** *adj.* of the color sensation stimulated by the wavelengths of light in that portion of the spectrum between blue and yellow, being the color e.g. of emeralds ‖ covered with herbage or foliage, in leaf ‖ having a pale, sickly complexion, e.g. from fear ‖ vegetable, *green salad* ‖ not yet ripe or mature, *green fruit* ‖ young and flourishing, *green shoots* ‖ not dried, weathered, smoked, tanned, fired etc., *green wood, green bacon, green hide* ‖ (*rhet.*) full of vigor, fresh, *a green old age* ‖ immature, unskilled, inexperienced ‖ gullible, easily fooled **to be green around the gills** to look as though about to be sick **2.** *n.* a green color, pigment, fabric etc. ‖ the green part of something ‖ green vegetation or foliage, verdure ‖ (*pl.*) leafy vegetables, e.g. spinach, beet tops etc. ‖ (*pl.*) leaves or branches of trees used for wreaths, decorations etc. ‖ a stretch of grass for public use, *the village green* ‖ (*golf*) the area of short-cut turf surrounding the hole [O.E. *grēne*]

green *v.i.* to become green ‖ *v.t.* to make green [O.E. *grēnian*]

green·back (griːnbæk) *n.* (*pop.*) any U.S. legal-tender note ‖ one of the nonconvertible bank-notes issued by the U.S.A. during the Civil War ‖ (*surfing*) an unbroken wave

Greenback Labor Party a U.S. political party formed (1878) to promote agricultural as well as labor interests through currency reform. It sponsored the Hatch Act (1887), which granted federal subsidies to promote scientific agriculture, and accorded (1889) Cabinet standing to the Department of Agriculture

Green Bay, a port city (pop. 87,899) in NE Wisconsin on Lake Michigan's Green Bay, settled 1634 as a fur trading post: paper, cheese

Green Bay an inlet (c. 120 miles long, 10–20 miles wide) of Lake Michigan, forming the southeastern boundary of the Upper Michigan Peninsula and N.E. Wisconsin

---

CONCISE PRONUNCIATION KEY: **(a)** æ, c*a*t; ɑ, c*a*r; ɔ f*aw*n; ei, sn*a*ke. **(e)** e, h*e*n; iː, sh*ee*p; iə, d*ee*r; ɛə, b*ea*r. **(i)** i, f*i*sh; ai, t*i*ger; əː, b*i*rd. **(o)** o, *o*x; au, c*ow*; ou, g*oa*t; u, p*oo*r; ɔi, r*oy*al. **(u)** ʌ, d*u*ck; u, b*u*ll; uː, g*oo*se; ə, b*a*cillus; juː, c*u*be. x, lo*ch*; θ, *th*ink; ð, bo*th*er; z, *Z*en; ʒ, corsa*g*e; dʒ, sava*g*e; ŋ, oranguta*ng*; j, *y*ak; ʃ, *f*ish; tʃ, fe*tch*; 'l, rabb*le*; 'n, redd*en*. Complete pronunciation key appears inside front cover.

green bean a French bean

green·belt (grí:nbɛlt) *n.* a belt of fields, commons and undeveloped land around a large town, in which building is prohibited or strictly controlled so as to prevent indiscriminate expansion or speculative development. The original Green Belt encircled Greater London

Green Beret (*mil.*) a member of the U.S. Army Special Forces, especially prominent in Vietnam War, 1964–1965

green card permanent visa permitting foreign nationals to work and reside in the U.S. — **green carder** *n.*

green cheese unmatured cheese, whey cheese, or cheese colored green with sage

Greene (gri:n), Graham (1904–), English novelist and playwright. His many novels, remarkable for their storytelling, and often involving problems of conscience, include 'The Power and the Glory' (1940), 'The Heart of the Matter' (1948), 'The End of the Affair' (1951), 'Travels With My Aunt' (1970), 'The Human Factor' (1978), 'Ways of Escape' (1981), 'Monsignor Quixote' (1982) and 'The Tenth Man' (1985)

Greene, Nathanael (1742–86), American Revolutionary War general. Appointed (1780) commander in the Carolina campaign, he turned British victories, notably Guilford Courthouse, ultimately into British defeats and forced (1782) the British to evacuate Charlestown

Greene, Robert (1558–92), English writer. He wrote euphuistic romances and a few plays, but is perhaps best known for the presumed attack on Shakespeare in his pamphlet 'Greenes Groatsworth of Wit Bought with a Million of Repentance' (1592)

green·er·y (grí:nəri:) *n.* green foliage, esp. used for decoration

green-eyed (grí:naid) *adj.* jealous

green·finch (gri:nfɪntʃ) *n. Chloris chloris,* a common European finch with green and yellow plumage ‖ *Arremonops rufivirgatus,* a green and yellow North American finch

green fingers (*Br.*) green thumb

green·fly (grí:nflai) *n.* (*Br.,* usually *collect.*) aphid

green·gage (grí:ngeidʒ) *n.* a variety of sweet, greenish-yellow plum [introduced into England from France by Sir William *Gage* (*d.* 1820), Br. botanist]

green goddess dressing salad dressing of sour cream, anchovies, chives, parsley, tarragon, vinegar mayonnaise, black pepper, lemon juice, and other seasonings

green·gro·cer (grí:ngrousər) *n.* (*Br.*) a retail seller of fresh fruit and vegetables **green·gro·cer·y** *pl.* **green·gro·cer·ies** *n.* (*Br.*) the business of a greengrocer ‖ (*Br.*) his place of trade ‖ (*Br.*) the articles he sells

green·heart (grí:nhɑrt) *n.* any of several hardwooded tropical American trees, esp. the bebeeru ‖ the wood of any of these trees ‖ a fishing rod of this wood

green·horn (grí:nhɔrn) *n.* a raw, simple, inexperienced person, easily fooled or parted from his money ‖ a newcomer

green·house (grí:nhaus) *pl.* **green·hous·es** (grí:nhauziz) *n.* a building with roof and walls of glass, often heated, and used for growing flowers and plants that need warmth, or for forcing early produce

greenhouse effect (*meteor.*) increase in earth's temperature due to accumulation of carbon dioxide and water vapor in warm air trapped by a mass of cold air. This results in retention of infrared rays from the sun and increased surface temperatures, with the melting of some polar ice

green·ie (grí:ni:) *n.* (*golf*) competition for position on the green nearest the hole. *syn.* oozler

green·ing (grí:niŋ) *n.* the renewal of youthfulness; from a book by Charles A. Reich, *The Greening of America*

Green·land (grí:nlənd) (Danish) the world's largest island (area 839,800 sq. miles, pop. 53,000) lying mostly within the Arctic Circle, politically part of Denmark. Capital: Godthaab. It is largely covered by an ice cap over two miles deep in places. The population (mainly Eskimo with a European minority) is concentrated on the Southwest coast. Industries: fishing, cryolite mining. Greenland was discovered (late 10th c.) by Eric the Red, and colonized by Danes from 1721. It came under direct Danish control (1729) and was made (1953) an integral part of the kingdom. Its air bases have growing strategic importance. Home rule was approved in

1978 and instituted in 1979. Greenland holds two seats in the Danish national assembly. In 1985, Greenland withdrew from the European Economic Community

Greenland Sea the Arctic Ocean lying between Greenland on the west and Spitzbergen and Iceland on the east. It has valuable fishery resources

green laser a gas laser utilizing mercury and argon as basic gases that creates a greenline easily transmitted through seawater

Green·leaf (grí:nli:f), Simon (1783–1853), U.S. legal educator. As professor of law (from 1833) at Harvard University, he published his 'Treatise on the Law of Evidence' (1842–53) and drafted the original constitution of the Republic of Liberia

green light (*pop.*) authoritative permission to go ahead with some project

green·ling (grí:nliŋ) *n.* any of various food fishes of fam. *Hexagrammidae* of the N. Pacific coast [GREEN + *-ling,* suffix denoting condition]

green manure a green crop, esp. clover, plowed back into the soil as a fertilizer

green monkey disease (*med.*) an often-fatal infection characterized by severe internal bleeding transmitted through close contact with green monkeys. It is also called Marburg virus disease for a 1968 case discovered in Marburg, West Germany

Green Mountain Boys (*Am. hist.*) the partisan bands who fought to keep Vermont free of the control of New York. They also fought with some success during the Revolutionary War (1775–83)

Green Mountains *APPALACHIAN MOUNTAINS

green·ness (grí:nnis) *n.* the quality or state of being green

Green·ock (grí:nək) a port (pop. 57,324) in Renfrewshire, S.W. Scotland on the Clyde estuary: shipyards, varied industries

Gree·nough (grí:nou), Horatio (1805–52), U.S. sculptor and author. His statue of George Washington (1832), in the Smithsonian Institution, was the first work by a U.S. sculptor to be commissioned by the U.S. government. His brief essays on art (1852), outlining his theory of functionalism, influenced modern architecture

Green Paper (*Br.*) a governmental study with a proposal for discussion. *Cf* WHITE PAPER

green pepper *SWEET PEPPER

green pound (*economics*) the exchange rate used to convert European Common Market farm prices, fixed under its Common Agricultural Policy (CAP), to the British Pound. Other Common Market countries also have "green" currencies

green power (*colloq.*) the power of money

green revolution (*agriculture*) the dramatic increase in food production from high-yield hybrid seed varieties, control of pests, and scientific farming

green·room (grí:nru:m, grí:nrum) *n.* a room in a theater which actors and actresses use socially

green·sand (grí:nsænd) *n.* a cretaceous rock series like sandstone whose green color is due to the presence of grains of glauconite

Greens·bo·ro (grí:nzbə:rou, grí:nzbʌrou) a city (pop. 155,642) of N. central North Carolina: textile mills, terra-cotta works, foundries, machine shops, lumber mills. Greensboro College (1838)

green·shank (grí:nʃæŋk) *n. Tringa nebularia,* a large sandpiper of N. Europe distinguished from the redshank by its paler gray upper parts and green legs

green·stick fracture (grí:nstik) a type of bone fracture common in children. The bone is partly broken and partly bent

green·stuff (grí:nstʌf) *n.* green vegetables ‖ greenery

green·sward (grí:nswɔrd) *n.* (*rhet.*) a stretch of carefully tended grass

green tack bonding of fabrics where the bond is first created by a wet adhesive process in curing, while the bond is not fully cured and is not ripe

green tea *TEA

green thumb (*Am.=Br.* green fingers) the gift of being successful at gardening, esp. at raising seedlings, taking cuttings etc.

green vitriol copperas

Green·wich (grínidʒ, grénidʒ) a borough (pop. 214,000) of S.E. London on the Thames, site of the Royal Naval College and the National Mar-

itime Museum, and, formerly, of the Royal Greenwich Observatory

Greenwich Mean Time (*abbr.* G.M.T.) the time of day at the Greenwich meridian, as registered by a clock which reads 12 noon when the sun is seen at its maximum altitude. Under Central European Time European clocks are 1 hour ahead of this

Greenwich meridian the prime meridian passing through Greenwich, England

Green·wich Village (grénitʃ) a section of New York City, in lower Manhattan, a center for artists and writers

Greer, Germaine (griər) (1939–), Australian feminist. She was prominent in the U.S. feminist movement of the 1970s and is best known for 'The Female Eunuch' (1970). Other works include 'The Obstacle Race' (1979) and 'Sex and Destiny' (1984)

greet (gri:t) *v.t.* to address with courteous words or gestures on meeting, *to greet someone with a smile* ‖ to salute the arrival of in a specified manner, *he was greeted with catcalls* ‖ to make an impression on the senses of (someone arriving), *the smell greeted him on the stairs* [O.E. *grǣtan*]

greet·ing (grí:tiŋ) *n.* an expression or gesture used when meeting someone ‖ a form of address at the beginning of a letter, e.g. 'Dear Sir' ‖ an expression of goodwill, *birthday greetings*

greg·a·rine (grégərin) **1.** *adj.* of or pertaining to *Gregarinida,* an order of parasitic protozoans that inhabit invertebrates and create cyst-producing spores **2.** *n.* a member of *Gregarinida* [Mod. L. *Gregarina,* the type genus]

gre·gar·i·ous (grigéəri:əs) *adj.* living in or pertaining to flocks or communities ‖ fond of being among other people ‖ (*biol.*) colonial, growing in clusters [fr. L. *gregarius*]

grège, greige (greiʒ) *n.* fabric allowed to remain just as it leaves the loom, unbleached, undyed and untreated (*GRAY) ‖ a color between gray and beige [fr. F. *grège,* raw (silk)]

Gregg (greg), John Robert (1867–1948), Irish-American inventor of a shorthand system first printed (1888) in Liverpool. It was introduced to the U.S.A. in 1893.

Gre·go·ri·an calendar (grigɔ́ri:ən, grigóuri:ən) a system of reckoning time introduced by Pope Gregory XIII in 1582 to correct an error in the Julian calendar, which allowed the year 11 minutes and 10 seconds too much. The regularization was effected by omitting the accumulated deficit of days (11, when the calendar was adopted in England and the English colonies of America in 1752) and establishing that centenary years should be leap years only if divisible by 400 (e.g. 2000)

Gregorian chant a form of plainsong named after Pope Gregory I, in whose time it was introduced

Gregorian Church *ARMENIAN

Greg·o·ry I (grégəri:), St, 'the Great' (c. 540–604), pope (590–604), one of the Church Fathers. At a critical period in the history of the Christian Church he strengthened and reorganized the papacy, extended the primacy of Rome in the West, and spread Benedictine monasticism. He reformed the liturgy and sent St Augustine on his mission of conversion to Britain. Feast: Mar. 12

Gregory VII, St (c. 1021–85), pope (1073–85). As a Benedictine monk he was known as Hildebrand. He vigorously reformed Church law, discipline and administration. He forbade (1075) Henry IV of Germany to conduct lay investitures, thus beginning the Investiture Controversy. Gregory excommunicated Henry (1076), absolved him at Canossa (1077), and was forced into exile when Henry captured Rome (1083). Feast: May 25

Gregory IX (c. 1145–1241), pope (1227–41). He quarreled with Emperor Frederick II and twice excommunicated him (1227 and 1239)

Gregory XI (1331–78), pope (1370–8). He transferred the Holy See back from Avignon to Rome (1377)

Gregory XIII (1502–85), pope (1572–85). He founded many Jesuit colleges and seminaries and made efforts to reconvert to Catholicism countries which had become Protestant. This involved him in unsuccessful plots to depose Elizabeth I of England. His Gregorian calendar superseded the Julian calendar

Gregory, Lady Isabella Augusta (1852–1932), Irish playwright, who helped to found Abbey Theatre (1899). She collected Irish folktales and was a main force behind the renaissance of

CONCISE PRONUNCIATION KEY: **(a)** æ, *cat;* ɑ, *car;* ɔ *fawn;* ei, *snake.* **(e)** e, *hen;* i:, *sheep;* iə, *deer;* ɛə, *bear.* **(i)** i, *fish;* ai, *tiger;* ə:, *bird.* **(o)** o, *ox;* au, *cow;* ou, *goat;* u, *poor;* ɔi, *royal.* **(u)** ʌ, *duck;* u, *bull;* u:, *goose;* ə, *bacillus;* ju:, *cube.* x, *loch;* θ, *think;* ð, *bother;* z, *Zen;* ʒ, *corsage;* dʒ, *savage;* ŋ, *orangutang;* j, *yak;* ʃ, *fish;* tʃ, *fetch;* 'l, *rabble;* 'n, *redden.* Complete pronunciation key appears inside front cover.

Irish literature. As a leader of the Abbey Theatre, she wrote plays performed there, often collaborating with William Butler Yeats and Douglas Hyde. Her works include 'Spreading the News' (1904) and 'The Gaol Gate' (1906)

Gregory of Naz·i·an·zus (næzi:ænzəs), St (c. 329–c. 389), bishop of Constantinople. He championed orthodoxy against the Arian and Apollinarian heresies, and was largely responsible for the reassertion of the Nicene faith. Feast: May 9 (Roman Catholic Church), Jan. 25 and Jan. 30 (Orthodox Church)

Gregory of Nys·sa (nísə), St (c. 335–c. 394), brother of St Basil, one of the Greek Fathers, and a zealously orthodox follower of Origen. Feast: Mar. 9 (Roman Catholic Church), Jan. 10 (Orthodox Church)

Gregory of Tours, St (c. 538–c. 594), Frankish bishop of Tours (573–94) and historian. His 'Historia Francorum' is a valuable source for the events of his time. Feast: Nov. 17

Gregory Thau·ma·tur·gus (θɔmətɔ́:rgəs), St (c. 213–c. 270), bishop, one of the Greek Fathers, and the most distinguished of Origen's pupils. Feast: Nov. 17

Gregory the Illuminator, St (c. 257–c. 337), the patron saint of Armenia. Feast: Sept. 30 (Orthodox Church), Oct. 1 (Roman Catholic Church)

greige *GRÈGE

grei·sen (gráiz'n) n. a crystalline, igneous rock consisting of quartz and white mica [G.]

gre·mi·al (grí:mi:əl) n. a cloth placed on a bishop's lap when he is seated at Mass [fr. L.L. gremialis fr. gremium, lap]

grem·lin (grémlin) n. (pop.) an imaginary mischievous little gnomelike creature blamed esp. by airmen for mishaps [fr. F. dial. grimelin, brat]

grem·mie (grémi:) n. (surfing) a nuisance beginner. syn. gremlin

Gre·na·da (grinéidə) a state (pop. 88,000, mainly of African descent) in the Windward Is, West Indies, including Grenada proper (area 120 sq. miles) with Carriacou and adjacent islets of the Grenadines. Capital: St George's (pop. 7,000). Language: French patois and English. Religion: mainly Roman Catholic. Highest point: 2,756 ft. Products: cocoa, nutmeg, mace, bananas, cotton, spices, vanilla, sugar, coffee, fish, citrus fruit. Monetary unit: East Caribbean dollar. Grenada was discovered (1498) by Columbus, and was ceded to Britain by France (1783). It was a member of the Federation of the West Indies (1958–62) and became a separate colony in 1960. It became a state in association with Britain (Mar. 3, 1967). Independence within the Commonwealth was declared in 1974. In Oct. 1983 the U.S. invaded Grenada to forestall a suspected Cuban/Soviet military build-up there; by Dec. all U.S. troops had been withdrawn. The following year Herbert A. Blaize was elected prime minister

gre·nade (grinéid) n. a small, fused, explosive shell, with a round or oval segmented iron casing, thrown by hand or fired from a rifle ‖ a round glass bottle thrown to put out fires, spread tear gas etc. by dispersing its chemical contents [F. fr. Span. granada, pomegranate]

gren·a·dier (grenədíər) n. (hist.) a soldier who threw grenades ‖ Ploceus oryx (or Pyromelana oryx), a S. African weaverbird with red and black plumage ‖ a member of Macruridae, a family of deep-sea fishes related to the cod, with a tapering body and whiplike tail **Gren·a·dier** a member of the Grenadier Guards, the senior regiment (formed 1685) of the British army

gren·a·dil·la (grenədílə) n. the granadilla

gren·a·dine (grenədí:n, grénədi:n) n. a fabric of loosely woven cotton, wool, silk or rayon [F. perh. after Granada, Spain]

grenadine n. a sweet fruit syrup usually made from pomegranates [F. dim. of grenade, pomegranate]

Gren·a·dines (grenədí:nz) a chain of islets (half are dependencies of St Vincent, half of Grenada) in the Windward group, West Indies. The largest is Carriacou (area 13 sq. miles, pop. 6,400, administered by Grenada (*GRENADA)

Gre·no·ble (grənóbl) an old city (pop. 160,000) of the Isère, S.E. France, below the Grand-Chartreuse massif: electrical engineering, metallurgy, food processing, textiles, leather, tourism. Cathedral (12th–13th cc.). University (1339)

Gren·ville (grénvil), George (1712–70), British statesman, prime minister (1763–5). His

Stamp Act (1765) helped to bring on the Revolutionary War

Grenville, Sir Richard (c. 1541–91), English sea captain. He was mortally wounded on board his ship, the 'Revenge', after a prolonged lone battle with Spanish ships off the Azores

Grenville, William Wyndham, Baron Grenville (1759–1834), British statesman, son of George Grenville. He was prime minister (1800–7) of a coalition known as the 'ministry of all the talents'

grenz ray (grénz) one of the longest of the X-rays; used in skin therapy and research on plants and animals

Gresh·am (gréʃəm), Sir Thomas (c. 1519–79), English financier. His policies restored monetary stability in the early years or Elizabeth I's reign. He was the founder of the Royal Exchange (1568) in London

Gresham's law (econ.) the principle that money of lower intrinsic value tends to drive money of equal denomination but higher intrinsic value out of circulation, due to the hoarding of the latter [after Sir Thomas Gresham]

gres·so·ri·al (gresóri:əl, gresóuri:əl) adj. (zool.) adapted for walking [fr. Mod. L. gresorius fr. gradi (gressus), to walk, go]

Greuze (grə:z), Jean-Baptiste (1725–1805), French painter of sentimental and moralistic works

Grev·ille (grévil), Sir Fulke, Baron Brooke (1554–1628), English minor poet. His 'Life of the Renowned Sir Philip Sidney' (1652) contains valuable information about the period

Gré·vy (greivi:), Jules (1807–91), French statesman, president of France (1879–87)

grew past of GROW

Grey (grei), Charles, 2nd Earl Grey (1764–1845), British statesman. As Whig prime minister (1830–4) he carried the Reform Act of 1832 by persuading William IV to threaten to create enough Whig peers to force it through parliament. His ministry also passed the Factory Act of 1833 and abolished slavery within the British Empire (1833)

Grey, Edward, 1st Viscount Grey of Fallodon (1862–1933), British statesman, foreign secretary (1905–16). In the face of German armament, he sought to maintain peace in Europe by means of ententes with France and Russia. When negotiation failed, he led Britain into the 1st world war

Grey, Sir George Edward (1812–98), British statesman. As governor (1845–52 and 1861–7) and prime minister (1877–9) of New Zealand, he made peace with the Maoris and initiated many liberal reforms. He wrote 'Polynesian Mythology' (1855)

Grey, Lady Jane (1537–54), queen of England (July 10–19, 1553), great-granddaughter of Henry VII. Her father-in-law, John Dudley, earl of Warwick, proclaimed her as queen in an attempt to perpetuate his own power after the death of Edward VI. The usurpation ended when Mary I claimed the throne, and Lady Jane Grey was executed

grey *GRAY

Grey Friar, Gray Friar a Franciscan friar

grey·hound, gray·hound n. a dog of an ancient breed used for chasing hares and for racing. It stands over 2 ft high, has a short smooth coat, long legs, slender body and keen sight [O.E. grighund, etym. doubtful]

grey·lag, gray·lag (gréilæg) n. Anser anser (or A. cinereus), the common gray wild goose of Europe

grib·ble (gríb'l) n. Limnoria lignorum or L. terebrans, a small marine isopod boring crustacean which is very destructive to the submerged timbers of piers, wharves etc. [etym. doubtful]

grid (grid) 1. n. a frame of spaced parallel bars, a grating ‖ (elec.) a lattice or spiral electrode positioned between two others in an electron tube ‖ (Br.) a network of electrical power cables (underground, or overhead on pylons) connecting power stations and enabling high-voltage electricity to be transferred or distributed ‖ a similar system of linked gas supply ‖ a frame of numbered squares superimposed on a map so that exact reference may be made to any point on the map ‖ a gridiron for cooking ‖ (typography) on a phototypesetting machine, the glass screen on which the typeset text is exposed ‖ (auto racing) the starting point 2. v.t. pres. part.

grid·ding past and past part. **grid·ded** to furnish with a grid [shortened fr. GRIDIRON]

grid circuit (elec.) the circuit including the grid and cathode in an electron tube

grid current (elec.) the current passing between the grid and the cathode in an electron tube

grid·dle (gríd'l) n. a circular plate, usually of iron, for cooking pancakes etc. on [M.E. gredil, gredile fr. O.F.]

grid·dle·cake (gríd'lkeik) n. a thin batter pancake cooked on a griddle

grid·i·ron (grídaiərn) n. a framework of metal bars with legs or a handle, used for broiling ‖ (naut.) a frame of parallel beams used to support a ship in dock ‖ (theater) a framework of planks and beams over a stage, supporting the mechanism for curtains and scenery ‖ (football) the playing field, so called from its network of marked lines ‖ (hist.) a framework of iron bars used for torture by fire [M.E. gredire, a griddle, later confused with 'iron']

grid·lock (grídlɒk) n. a massive automobile traffic jam in which no car can move in any direction

grief (gri:f) n. deep sorrow ‖ a cause of sorrow or anxiety **to come to grief** to meet with disaster ‖ to fail [M.E. gref, greve fr. O.F.]

Grieg (gri:g), Edvard Hagerup (1843–1907), Norwegian composer. He combined a natural romanticism with strong feeling for Norwegian folk music in his instrumental music, e.g. the 'Piano Concerto in A Minor' (1868), in his songs, and in the incidental music to Ibsen's 'Peer Gynt'

griev·ance (grí:vəns) n. a real or fancied wrong, hardship, or cause of complaint [M.E. grevance fr. O.F.]

grieve (gri:v) pres. part. **griev·ing** past and past part. **grieved** v.t. to cause deep sorrow to ‖ v.i. to feel grief, mourn [M.E. greve fr. F. grever]

griev·ous (grí:vəs) adj. bringing great suffering and trouble ‖ (of disease, injury etc.) very painful, severe ‖ exciting grief, pitiful, in a grievous state ‖ serious, heinous, grievous sin [M.E. grevous fr. F.]

grif·fin, grif·fon, gryph·on (grifin) n. a fabulous creature with the head and wings of an eagle and the body of a lion [O.F. grifoun fr. L. fr. Gk]

Grif·fith (grifiθ), Arthur (1872–1922), Irish statesman. He founded Sinn Fein (1905), and, with Michael Collins, led the Irish delegation (1921) which negotiated the establishment of the Irish Free State

Griffith, David Lewelyn Wark (1875–1948), pioneer American film director who largely established movies as an independent art. His masterpieces are 'Birth of a Nation' (1914) and 'Intolerance' (1916)

Grif·fiths (grifiθs), John Willis (1809–82), US. naval architect who designed the 'Rainbow' (launched 1845), the first clipper sailing ship

grif·fon (grifin) n. any of several coarse-haired dogs of a European breed existing in several varieties, esp. the Brussels Griffon [F.]

griffon *GRIFFIN

griffon vulture a member of Gyps, a genus of large vultures of S. Europe, Asia Minor and N. Africa, esp. G. fulvus

Gri·jal·va (gri:hálva), Juan de (d. 1527), Spanish explorer of Yucatán (1518)

grill (gril) 1. n. a form of postal cancellation consisting of a rectangular pattern of small dots made by a metal roll with points 2. v.t. to emboss with a grill [GRILLE]

grill 1. v.t. to broil on a gridiron or under the broiling apparatus of a gas or electric stove ‖ to torture with great heat ‖ to interrogate closely, torment by severe questioning ‖ v.i. (Br., pop.) to expose oneself to great heat, grilling in the sun ‖ to be broiled on a gridiron 2. n. a gridiron ‖ a device on gas and electric stoves for radiating an intense direct red heat for cooking meat, making toast, browning the tops of savory dishes etc. ‖ a dish of grilled food ‖ a grillroom ‖ the act or process of grilling [F. griller fr. gril]

grill *GRILLE

gril·lage (grílidʒ) n. a heavy framework of beams and crossbeams as a foundation for building in soft soil [F.]

grille, grill (gril) n. a grating or crosswork of bars, set in a door for observing callers, or in a wall ‖ an ornamental metal radiator cover on an automobile, admitting air for cooling the engine ‖ a barred window ‖ a protective grating or latticed metal screen behind which nuns or

---

prisoners receive visitors or clerks in banks, ticket offices and post offices may deal with customers ‖ (*court tennis*) a square opening on the hazard side of the court at the end opposite the service end, in the corner ‖ a spawn-hatching frame [F. *grille*]

Grill·par·zer (grílpɑrtsər), Franz (1791–1872), Austrian dramatist, author of historical and classical tragedies, e.g. the 'Golden Fleece' trilogy (1819–22)

grill·room (grílru:m, grílrum) *n.* a restaurant where grilled foods are served

grill·work (grílwə:rk) *n.* construction in the form of a grille

grilse (grils) *pl.* **grilse, grils·es** *n.* a salmon in the year after its first return from the sea to the river to spawn (cf. PARR, cf. SMOLT) [origin unknown]

grim (grim) *comp.* **grim·mer** *superl.* **grim·mest** *adj.* stern, severe, *a grim struggle* ‖ unrelenting, *grim determination* ‖ forbidding, threatening, *a grim outlook* ‖ unalleviated by humor or cheerfulness ‖ sinister ‖ mirthless, *a grim smile* [O.E. *grimm*]

gri·mace (griméis, gríməs) **1.** *n.* a twisted expression of the face caused by slight pain or shyness, or to convey disgust, distaste, annoyance etc., or to frighten, irritate or amuse, or as an affectation **2.** *v.i. pres. part.* **gri·mac·ing** *past* and *past part.* **gri·maced** to make a grimace [F.]

Gri·mal·di (griméldi:, grimɑ́ldi:), Joseph (1779–1837), English pantomimist and clown, of Italian parentage. British clowns are still called 'Joey' after him

grime (graim) **1.** *n.* ingrained dirt or soot **2.** *v.t. pres. part.* **grim·ing** *past* and *past part.* **grimed** to cover with dirt, soil [fr. Du. or L.G.]

grim·i·ly (gráimili:) *adv.* in a grimy manner

grim·i·ness (gráimi:nis) *n.* the quality or state of being grimy

Grim·ké (grímki:), Sarah Moore (1792–1873) and Angelina Emily (1805–79), U.S. abolitionist and feminist sisters. They lectured against slavery and for women's rights. Sarah wrote 'Letters on the Equality of the Sexes and the Condition of Women' (1838); Angelina's main work was 'Letters to Catherine Beecher in Reply to an Essay on Slavery and Abolitionism' (1838)

Grimm (grim), Jakob Ludwig Karl (1785–1863), German philologist and mythologist. His 'Deutsche Grammatik' (1819–37) explored the relationship between various Germanic languages (*GRIMM'S LAW). He collaborated with his brother, Wilhelm Karl Grimm (1786–1859), on a collection of German folk tales ('Kinder- und Hausmärchen', commonly known as 'Grimm's Fairy Tales' (1812–15). The brothers did not live to complete their monumental German dictionary

Grimm's law (*phon.*) a statement of sound correspondences, formulated (1822) by Jakob Grimm: Proto-Indo-European voiceless stops became Proto-Germanic voiceless fricatives, Proto-Indo-European voiced stops became Proto-Germanic voiceless stops, and Proto-Indo-European voiced aspirated stops became Proto-Germanic voiced fricatives and then Proto-Germanic voiceless stops became High German affricates or voiceless fricatives and Proto-Germanic voiced stops became High German voiceless stops

Grims·by (grímzbi:) Britain's biggest fishing port (pop. 92,596), in Lincolnshire

grim·y (gráimi:) *comp.* **grim·i·er** *superl.* **grim·i·est** *adj.* covered with grime, dirty

grin (grin) **1.** *v. pres. part.* **grin·ning** *past* and *past part.* **grinned** *v.i.* to smile broadly, showing the teeth, in amusement, pleasure, pain, contempt etc. ‖ (of dogs) to bare the teeth, e.g. when snarling ‖ *v.t.* to express by grinning. *to grin one's delight* **to grin and bear it** to suffer without complaining **to grin like a Cheshire cat** to grin unwaveringly and foolishly in an immensely broad grin **2.** *n.* the act of grinning ‖ a broad or distorted smile [O.E. *grennian*]

grind (graind) **1.** *v. pres. part.* **grind·ing** *past* and *past part.* **ground** (graund) *v.t.* to crush to powder or tiny pieces by friction, e.g. between millstones, or between one's teeth, or in a coffee or pepper mill ‖ to produce by grinding *to grind flour* ‖ (with 'down') to crush with harsh rule or misery, treat cruelly, *ground down by tyranny* ‖ to sharpen, smooth, file down or shape by friction, *to grind knives to a sharp edge, to grind a lens* ‖ (with 'down') to suppress by wearing down, *to grind down the opposition* ‖ to cause to

grate, *to grind one's teeth* ‖ to thrust with a twisting motion, *he ground his knee into his opponent's stomach* ‖ to work by turning a handle, *to grind a hand mill* ‖ to produce (music) by being worked in this way, *the barrel organ ground out a tune* ‖ (with 'out') to produce with toil and (unwilling) effort, force out, *to grind out a song lyric* ‖ to compel by repeated effort to absorb (learning, sense etc.), *to grind some grammar into a person's head* ‖ *v.i.* to perform the activity of reducing something to fine particles by friction ‖ to admit of being ground ‖ (of a vehicle) to move laboriously, *the truck ground slowly up the hill* ‖ to work or study hard (esp. for an examination) ‖ to grate, *the door ground on its hinges* **2.** *n.* a period of unbroken hard work or study to which one forces oneself ‖ (*pop.*) an unremitting student ‖ a long, steady gradient or the effort needed to climb it ‖ the act of grinding [O.E. *grindan*]

grind·er (gráindər) *n.* a person who grinds ‖ a thing used for grinding [M.E. and O.E. *grindere*]

grind·er·y (gráindəri:) *pl.* **grind·er·ies** *n.* (*Br.*) shoemakers' or other leatherworkers' materials ‖ a place where tools etc. are ground

grind·stone (gráindstoun) *n.* a thick stone disk revolving on an axle and used for grinding, sharpening and smoothing ‖ a stone from which grindstones are made **to keep one's nose to the grindstone** to keep steadily at a task by an effort of the will

grin·go (gríŋgou) *n.* (among Latin Americans, usually pejorative) a foreigner, esp. an Englishman or North American [Mexican Span.]

grip (grip) **1.** *n.* a tight hold, strong grasp ‖ the power to grasp, *to test one's grip* ‖ a way of holding, *the right grip for a wrestling throw* ‖ (*fig.*) hold, power, *get a grip on yourself, the grip of winter* ‖ mental grasp, intellectual mastery ‖ the power to hold attention, *the play lost its grip in the third act* ‖ any device that grips ‖ the part of a racket etc. that one holds ‖ a traveling bag **to come to grips** to fight in close struggle ‖ **to make a serious struggle or attempt at mastery**, *to come to grips with a situation* **to lose one's grip** to lose control or mastery, e.g. of affairs or of an art or skill **2.** *v. pres. part.* **grip·ping** *past* and *past part.* **gripped** *v.t.* to take a firm hold of, grasp, seize ‖ to seize the attention of, *his play gripped the audience* ‖ *v.i.* to take hold by friction, *worn tires do not grip on wet roads* [O.E. *gripe*, grasp and O.E. *gripa*, handful]

gripe (graip) **1.** *v. pres. part.* **grip·ing** *past* and *past part.* **griped** *v.i.* (*pop.*) to complain continually ‖ (*naut.*) to tend to veer into the wind ‖ *v.t.* (*naut., past part.* only) to tie up with gripes **2.** *n.* (*pop.*) a bout of complaining, *I enjoy a good gripe* ‖ (*pl., naut.*) lashings securing a boat in position ‖ (*pl.*) pain in the bowels, colic [O.E. *gripan*, to grip]

grippe (grip) *n.* influenza, or a disease resembling influenza [F.]

Gri·qua·land East and West (grí:kwələænd, grí:kwələænd) districts of Cape Province, South Africa. Griqualand East (area 6,602 sq. miles) forms part of the Transkeian Territories. Griqualand West (area 15,197 sq. miles), with rich diamond deposits (*KIMBERLEY), borders the Kalahari desert

Gris (gri:s, gri:), Juan (José Victoriano González, 1887–1927), Spanish cubist painter, in Paris from 1906. He painted still lifes in which he made the subject conform to and evolve from a complex geometric organization of the picture space, and used color purely as an element of design (*CUBISM)

gri·saille (grizéil, grizái) *n.* a form of decorative painting or stained-glass work in gray monochrome, to give the impression of objects in relief [F.]

gris·ly (grízli:) *comp.* **gris·li·er** *superl.* **gris·li·est** *adj.* horrifying, terrifying ‖ ghastly, esp. relating to physical mutilation, wounds etc. [O.E. *grislic*]

gri·son (gríz'n) *n.* a member of *Grison*, a genus of large Central and South American weasel-like mammals, esp. *G. vittatus*. It emits a foul stink when attacked [F. fr. *gris*, gray]

Gri·sons (gri:zɔ̃) *GRAUBÜNDEN

grist (grist) *n.* grain for grinding ‖ malt crushed for brewing ‖ the quantity of grain ground at one time **to bring grist to one's mill** to bring in (a little) revenue **it's all grist to his mill** he turns anything to his profit or advantage [O.E. *grist*]

gris·tle (grís'l) *n.* cartilage, esp. the tough, flexible, whitish tissue in meat **gris·tli·ness** (grísli:nis) *n.* **gris·tly** *adj.* [O.E.]

grist·mill (grístmil) *n.* a mill for grinding grain, esp. grain brought by individual customers for milling

grit (grit) **1.** *n.* tiny particles of stone or sand ‖ a kind of coarse sandstone ‖ the grain or structure of stone ‖ pluck and tenacity **2.** *v. pres. part.* **grit·ting** *past* and *past part.* **grit·ted** *v.t.* to grate or grind, *to grit one's teeth* ‖ *v.i.* to emit a grating sound [O.E. *grēot*]

grits (grits) *pl. n.* oats with the husk removed, but not ground ‖ coarse oatmeal ‖ coarse hominy ‖ loose gravel for road-surfacing [O.E. *grytte*]

grit·ti·ness (gríti:nis) *n.* the quality or state of being gritty

grit·ty (gríti:) *comp.* **grit·ti·er** *superl.* **grit·ti·est** *adj.* like or containing grit ‖ plucky, brave

griv·a·tion (grivéiʃən) *n.* the difference between grid north and magnetic north. *also* grid magnetic angle, grid variation. *Cf* ISOGRIV

griz·zle (gríz'l) *pres. part.* **griz·zling** *past* and *past part.* **griz·zled** *v.i.* (*Br.*) to grumble, gripe ‖ (*Br.*, esp. of children) to fret continually, complain with whining [origin unknown]

grizzle *pres. part.* **griz·zling** *past* and *past part.* **griz·zled** *v.t.* to make gray or gray-haired ‖ *v.i.* to become gray or gray-haired **griz·zled** *adj.* grayish ‖ gray-haired [fr. older *grizzle*, gray, gray hair fr. O.F. *grisel* fr. *gris*, gray]

griz·zly (grízli:) **1.** *comp.* **griz·zli·er** *superl.* **griz·zli·est** *adj.* gray-haired or turning gray **2.** *pl.* **griz·zlies** *n.* a grizzly bear

grizzly bear *Ursus horribilis*, fam. *Ursidae*, a big, fierce bear of W. North America. Grizzlies may grow about 9 ft long and weigh 1,000 lbs

groan (groun) **1.** *v.i.* to make a deep moaning sound through pain, grief or distress ‖ (*rhet.*) to suffer, be oppressed, *the people groaned under the burden of taxes* ‖ (*rhet.*) to be heavily loaded down, *the cart groaned under the weight of the piano* ‖ *v.t.* to utter with a groan **2.** *n.* a deep moaning sound [O.E. *granian*]

groat (grout) *n.* (*hist.*) a small European coin, usually of silver (esp. 13th–16th cc.) ‖ an English silver coin, worth fourpence, first struck in 1351 [M.E. *groot* fr. M. Du. *groot*, great]

groats (grouts) *pl. n.* hulled or hulled and coarsely crushed grain, esp. oats, grits ‖ oatmeal [M.E. *grotes* rel. to O.E. *grot*, fragment and GRITS]

gro·cer (gróusər) *n.* a retailer of common household foods, e.g. tea, coffee, canned food, butter, and of household goods, e.g. soap and matches. U.S. grocers (but not British grocers) also sell meat, milk, fresh fruit and vegetables [M.E. *grosser*, orig. one who sells in gross fr. O.F. *grossier*]

gro·cer·y (gróusəri:) *pl.* **gro·cer·ies** *n.* the grocer's trade ‖ (*pl.*) goods bought at the grocer's ‖ a grocer's store

grocery store a grocer's store

Grock (grɒk) (Adrian Wettach, 1880–1959), Swiss clown famous for his musical virtuosity as well as acrobatic skill

Gro·cyn (gróus'n), William (c. 1446–1519), English humanist. A friend of More, Colet and Erasmus, he was one of the first to teach Greek at Oxford

grog (grɒg) *n.* a drink of rum and hot water mixed ‖ fired clay ground up, and used mixed in with plastic clay esp. to reduce shrinkage [after Edward Vernon (1684–1757), Br. admiral who first had the sailor's ration of neat rum diluted and who was called 'Old Grog' from the grogram cloak he wore]

grog·gi·ly (grógili:) *adv.* in a groggy manner

grog·gi·ness (grógi:nis) *n.* the quality or state of being groggy

grog·gy (grógi:) *comp.* **grog·gi·er** *superl.* **grog·gi·est** *adj.* unsteady, shaky on one's feet, as after an illness, a drinking bout etc. ‖ (of things) shaky, likely to collapse ‖ (of a horse) weak in the forelegs

grog·ram (grógrəm) *n.* a coarse fabric of silk, mohair and wool, often stiffened with gum [older *grograne* fr. F. *gros grain*, large (i.e. coarse) grain]

groin (grɔin) **1.** *n.* the fold or depression between belly and thighs **2.** (*archit.*) the sharp curved edge formed by the intersection of two vaults **2.** *v.t.* to build with groins, *to groin a roof* [M.E. *grynde, grinde* origin unknown]

groin, groyne (grɔin) **1.** *n.* a massive wooden framework or low broad wall of concrete or masonry run out from a shore to combat erosion **2.** *v.t. pres. part.* **groin·ing, groyn·ing**

past and *past part.* **groined, groyned** to supply (a beach) with groins [perh. fr. O.F. *groign,* promontory, lit. snout]

Gro·lier (grɔljei, gróuli:ər), Jean (Jean Grolier de Servières, 1479–1565), French bibliophile. He was a friend of Budé and a patron of Aldus Manutius. His books were bound sumptuously, in calf or morocco tooled in gold

grom·met (grómit) *n.* a grummet

Gro·my·ko (groumí:kou), Andrei Andreyevich (1909–), Russian diplomat, U.S.S.R. foreign minister 1957–85, president of U.S.S.R. (1985–)

Gro·ning·en (gróuniŋən) the northernmost province (area 867 sq. miles, pop. 556,869) of the Netherlands ‖ its capital (pop. 167,866), a trade center, connected by canals to the North Sea and Isselmeer: sugar, textile and other industries. It is the center of a vast field of natural gas. University (1614)

groo·groo *GRUGRU

groom (gru:m, grum) **1.** *n.* a bridegroom ‖ a man or boy who looks after horses ‖ (*Br.*) any of certain titular officers of the royal household, *groom in waiting* **2.** *v.t.* to look after, esp. clean and brush (horses) ‖ to smarten (oneself) up ‖ to prepare, train (someone for a certain job) [M.E. *grom, grome,* origin unknown]

grooms·man (grú:mzmən, grúmzmən) *pl.* **grooms·men** (grú:mzmən, grúmzmən) *n.* (*old-fash.*) the best man at a wedding

groove (gru:v) **1.** *n.* a channel or rut, *the sliding panels move in double grooves* ‖ a routine which makes for dullness ‖ (*colloq.*) a good time **2.** *v.t. pres. part.* **groov·ing** *past* and *past part.* **grooved** to make a groove or grooves in ‖ to enjoy, esp. with excitement along with others [M.E. *grofe* fr. O.N.]

grope (group) *pres. part.* **grop·ing** *past* and *past part.* **groped** *v.i.* to feel about, search blindly, *to grope for a light switch* ‖ to feel or search mentally, with uncertainty and difficulty, *to grope for words* [O.E. *grāpian,* to touch, grope]

Gro·pi·us (gróupi:əs), Walter (1883–1969), architect, designer and teacher, a naturalized American of German origin. A pioneer in the functional application of glass and concrete in factories, schools and houses, he founded and taught at the Bauhaus. His buildings include the Fagus works at Alfeld, Germany (1912), the Bauhaus at Dessau (1926), the Harvard Graduate Center at Cambridge, Mass. (1950), Pan Am building, New York City (1961–3)

gros·beak (gróusbj:k) *n.* any of several European and American finches with thick, conical bills, e.g. *Pinicola enucleator,* the pine grosbeak [fr. F. *grosbec*]

gro·schen (gróuʃən) *n.* an Austrian coin of the value of one hundredth of a schilling [G.]

gros·grain (gróugrein) *n.* a heavy, corded fabric of silk and cotton, often used for ribbons [F.]

gross (grous) *pl.* **gross** *n.* 12 dozen, 144, *a gross of pencils* [F. *grosse* fem. of *gros,* big]

gross 1. *adj.* repulsively fat ‖ outrageous, flagrant, glaring, *gross negligence* ‖ not refined, vulgar, *gross manners* ‖ indecent, obscene, *gross humor* ‖ total, all-inclusive (opp. NET), *gross weight, gross income, gross tonnage* ‖ (of the senses) dull, insensitive, crude, *a gross palate* **2.** *n.* a totality, sum total **in gross, in the gross** in bulk, wholesale **3.** *v.t.* to gain as gross profit [O.F. *gros,* fem. *grosse,* big, thick]

Grosse·teste (gróustest), Robert (c. 1175–1253), English prelate and scholar. He was a lecturer in the Franciscan school at Oxford and taught Roger Bacon. As bishop of Lincoln (1235–53), he fought against abuses, notably the nepotism of Innocent IV. He wrote commentaries on Aristotle, and works on mathematics, physics and theology

gross multiple (*securities*) a factor method of approximating the value of income property based on its potential income

gross out to alienate by being vulgar

Grosz (grous), George (1893–1959), German-U.S. draftsman and painter. Noted in Germany after the 1st world war for his satirical, demonic caricatures of bourgeois society, he turned in the U.S.A. to depicting ravaged figures of the 2nd world war

grosz (grɔʃ) *pl.* **gro·szy** (gróʃi:) *n.* a Polish monetary unit equal to 1/100th of a zloty ‖ a coin of the value of one grosz [Pol.]

gro·tesque (groutésk) **1.** *adj.* (*art*) combining human, animal and plant forms in a fantastic way ‖ (*literary criticism*) combining elements of tragedy and comedy inextricably ‖ (*loosely*) strangely fanciful, bizarre ‖ ludicrously incon-

gruous, absurd ‖ unnaturally distorted, *a grotesque smile* ‖ ridiculously bad, *a grotesque failure* **2.** *n.* (*art*) painting or carving in grotesque style, *a master of the grotesque* ‖ a grotesque figure, design or carving ‖ (*literary criticism*) a genre in which tragedy and comedy are inextricably combined, arousing compassion **gro·tes·que·rie, gro·tes·quer·y** (groutéskəri:) *n.* grotesqueness, usually with reference to the fanciful elaboration of fantastic figures and designs [older *crotesque* fr. M.F. fr. Ital. *grotesca*]

Gro·te·wohl (gróutəvoul), Otto (1894–1964), German Communist leader, prime minister of East Germany (1949–64)

Gro·ti·us (gróuʃi:əs), Hugo (Huigh de Groot, 1583–1645), Dutch scholar and statesman. His treatise 'De iure belli ac pacis' (1625) helped to found the study of international law

grot·to (grótou) *pl.* **grot·toes, grot·tos** *n.* a picturesque cave ‖ an artificial cave once fashionable in gardens [fr. Ital. *grotta* fr. L. fr. Gk *kruptē,* vault]

grouch (grautʃ) **1.** *n.* a bad-tempered, grumbling person ‖ a fit of sulkiness ‖ a fit of grumbling ‖ a cause for grumbling **2.** *v.i.* to complain ‖ to be bad-tempered **gróuch·i·ly** *adv.* **gróuch·i·ness** *n.* **gróuch·y** *comp.* **grouch·i·er** *superl.* **grouch·i·est** *adj.* [var. of obs. *grutch* fr. O.F. *groucier, groucher*]

ground (graund) **1.** *n.* the surface of the earth ‖ the upper soil ‖ a place or area on the earth's surface, *holy ground* ‖ (*pl.*) land, often with lawns, flower gardens etc., attached to a house for ornament and recreation ‖ an area of land devoted to and equipped for some special purpose, *camping ground* ‖ (often *pl.*) a basis for action or belief, motive, sound reason, *grounds for divorce, ground for complaint* ‖ the bottom of the sea or of a body of water, *to touch ground* ‖ (*pl.*) dregs, *coffee grounds* ‖ a basic surface or foundation color in painting, embroidery etc. ‖ (*etching*) the substance that is spread on metal and cut through with a needle where the acid is to act ‖ (*elec., Am.=Br.* earth) an electrical conductor enabling electricity to pass into the earth ‖ (*music*) a ground bass **from the ground up** thoroughly **on grounds of** because of ‖ **on the pretext of to break fresh** (or **new**) **ground** to do something new, open up new fields of inquiry or research **to break ground** to begin work on a building site ‖ **to break fresh ground to cover the ground** to deal with everything required to be dealt with **to cut the ground from under someone's feet** to anticipate someone's arguments or ideas and dispose of them before they are put forward **to fall to the ground** to fail, collapse, *our plans fell to the ground* **to keep one's** (or **both**) **feet on the ground** to be realistic and not idealistic, not forget practical realities **to lose ground** to fall behind or fail to maintain the full extent of a lead in a race ‖ to weaken in any competitive situation, e.g. to lose sales appeal **to shift one's ground** to change the basis of one's arguments or intentions **to suit someone down to the ground** to be exactly fitted to someone's requirements or wishes or personality **2.** *adj.* of, at or near the ground, pertaining to the ground **3.** *v.t.* to run (a ship) aground ‖ to confine (an aircraft, a pilot) to the ground, prevent from flying ‖ to base or establish, *to ground one's arguments on plain facts* ‖ to instill the basic facts into, *to ground a pupil in Latin grammar* ‖ to place on the ground, *to ground rifles* ‖ (*elec., Am.=Br.* to earth) to connect with a ground ‖ to prepare the ground of (embroidery etc.) ‖ *v.i.* (*baseball*) to hit a grounder ‖ to touch bottom, *the boat grounded on a sandbar* [O.E. *grund,* bottom of the sea, earth]

ground *past* and *past part.* of GRIND

ground·age (gráundidʒ) *n.* (*Br.*) a tax on vessels entering a port

ground bait a quantity of bait thrown into the water to attract fish to the place being fished

ground bass (*mus.*) a bass composed of a reiterated musical figure

ground cher·ry (gráundtʃeri:) *n.* a member of *Physalis,* fam. *Solanaceae,* a genus of American plants characterized by an inflated calyx encircling the cherrylike fruit ‖ the fruit of this plant ‖ any of several European dwarf cherries

ground-control approach (*abbr.* G.C.A.) a technique of landing aircraft by radar in bad visibility, solely through guidance from an operations room on the ground

ground-controlled approach ground-control approach

ground cover close growth of low-growing plants e.g. in a rose garden as a foil for the main plantation ‖ the low growth other than young trees under the trees of a forest

ground crew a team of mechanics and technicians who service aircraft between flights

ground effect machine an air-cushion vehicle, *abbr.* GEM. *Cf* AIR-CUSHION VEHICLE, HOVERCRAFT

ground·er (gráundər) *n.* (*baseball, cricket, soccer*) a ball which is struck, bowled, kicked etc. so that it rolls along the ground without rising

ground floor the floor at or nearest to ground level **to get in on the ground floor** to be one of the first to take advantage of a business opportunity

ground frost a frost which affects the surface of the earth and is liable to damage vegetation

ground glass glass with the surface roughened so that it is translucent but not transparent ‖ powdered glass

ground·hog (gráundhɔg, gráundhɒg) *n.* a woodchuck

Groundhog Day Feb. 2 (in some places Feb. 14), on which day the weather is supposed to indicate either the early coming of spring or the continuing of cold weather. The groundhog is said to emerge from his burrow, and if the day is sunny he is frightened back by his shadow: there will be six weeks more of wintry weather

ground ice ice formed on the bed of a stream

ground·ing (gráundiŋ) *n.* basic instruction, *a good grounding in Greek*

ground ivy *Nepeta hederacea,* fam. *Labiatae,* a perennial European and North American creeping plant with a violet flower. It is a common garden weed

ground·keep·er (gráundki:pər) *n.* (*Am.=Br.* groundsman) a person employed to tend grounds

ground landlord the owner of ground leased for building

ground·less (gráundlis) *adj.* without foundation or motive

ground level any plane of the earth's surface (*SEA LEVEL), *the building rises 200 ft above ground level* ‖ (*phys.*) ground state

ground·ling (gráundliŋ) *n.* any of several small fish which live at the bottom of the water, e.g. the gudgeon or roach ‖ a creeping plant, or one of low growth

ground·nut (gráundnʌt) *n.* (*Br.*) *Arachis hypogaea,* fam. *Papilionaceae,* the peanut ‖ (*Br.*) its nutlike seed ‖ *Apios tuberosa,* a North American wild bean

ground pine *Ajuga chamaepitys,* fam. *Labiatae,* a European plant with a resinous smell ‖ any of several club mosses, esp. *Lycopodium clavatum* and *L. complanatum,* fam. *Lycopodiaceae*

ground plan a plan of the ground floor of a building ‖ a basic pattern, *the 'Odyssey' provided the ground plan for Joyce's 'Ulysses'*

ground plate a piece of metal in the ground for grounding an electrical circuit

ground rent rent paid to a ground landlord

ground rule a basic principle of action in a given situation

ground·sel (gráundsəl) *n.* a member of *Senecio,* fam. *Compositae,* a genus of common annual weeds, esp. *S. vulgaris* [O.E. *gundœswelgiœ, grundeswylige*]

ground·sheet (gráundʃi:t) *n.* a waterproof sheet spread on the ground to protect against damp, used by campers and soldiers

grounds·man (gráundzmən) *pl.* **grounds·men** (gráundzmən) *n.* (*Br.*) a groundkeeper

ground speed the speed of an aircraft in relation to the ground (*AIRSPEED)

ground squirrel any of several burrowing rodents of fam. *Sciuridae,* esp. a member of *Citellus,* a genus of W. North American rodents, often striped

ground staff (*Br.*) administrative or other non-flying personnel at a military or civil airfield ‖ men employed to look after grounds or a playing field

ground state (*phys.*) the state of an atom when its orbiting electrons give it minimum energy

ground swell deep, slow, broad waves in a heavy sea, caused by a distant storm, earthquake or explosion

ground-to-ground (gráundtu:graund) *adj.* (*mil.*) of a land-to-land missile

ground·out (gráundaut) *n.* (*baseball*) a put-out resulting from a grounder to infield

ground·wa·ter (gráundwɔtər, gráundwɒtər) n. water beneath the land surface that feeds wells and springs and maintains the level of rivers and lakes in dry weather

ground wave a radio wave transmitted along the earth's surface (cf. SKY WAVE)

ground wire (elec.) a wire making a ground connection

ground·work (gráundwɜːrk) n. a foundation, basis ‖ essential basic labor or study ‖ the background to an embroidered or other pattern etc.

ground zero the point on the surface of the ground or water at which or immediately below or above which an atomic bomb explodes

group (gruːp) 1. n. a number of people or things gathered closely together and considered as a whole, the crowd split up into smaller groups ‖ an organized body of people with a common purpose, a research group ‖ a number of persons or things classed together, a group of languages ‖ (geol.) a system of rocks dating from a specified era ‖ (chem.) a radical, a methyl group ‖ one of eight major divisions of the periodic table (the vertical columns as it is usually constructed) containing elements whose atomic numbers bear a special periodic relation to each other and whose properties are closely related (e.g. halogens, inert gases, cf. PERIOD) ‖ (math.) a set of elements and an operation (e.g. addition, multiplication or a symmetry operation) that obey the axioms of a group (*GROUP THEORY) ‖ (in scientific classification) a cross-division falling outside the regular system ‖ a blood group ‖ (art, photog.) two or more figures or objects forming a compositional whole ‖ an organizational unit in the R.A.F., combining a number of stations ‖ a unit of an echelon in the U.S. Air Force next above a squadron 2. v.t. to put into groups ‖ to arrange artistically, a well-grouped composition ‖ to classify ‖ v.i. to form a group [fr. F. groupe fr. Ital. prob. fr. Gmc]

group captain an officer in the British Royal Air Force ranking below an air commodore and above a wing commander

group·er (gruːpər) pl. **group·ers**, **group·er** n. any of several members of Serranidae, a family of tropical fish common in warm seas (esp. the Caribbean), esp. a member of genera Epinephelus or Mycteroperca [fr. Port. garupa]

group·ie (gruːpiː) n. 1. a follower of famous people, esp. a teenage follower of a rock 'n' roll singer. 2. a woman who follows celebrities for sexual association. Cf TEENY BOPPER

Group of 5 the five major non-Communist economic powers: the U.S., West Germany, Great Britain, Japan, and France

Group of 77 group of developing countries that has its origins in the "Caucus of 75," developing countries organized preparatory to UNCTAD (United Nations Conference on Trade and Development, 1964) and expanded by two members to issue a "Joint Declaration of the 77 Developing Countries"

Group of 20 the Interim Committee of Finance Ministers of the International Monetary Fund (IMF) composed of the finance ministers of the five wealthiest IMF members. Cf GROUP OF FIVE

Group of 24 a group formed in 1971 of finance ministers from the 24 developing-country members of the the International Monetary Fund, representing eight countries from each of the African, Asian, and Latin American country groupings in the Group of 77

group theory 1. (nuclear phys.) method of studying neutron diffusion in a reactor core based on approximating the velocity of a member of a group. 2. (math.) study of classification of finite groups and the structure of all groups

group therapy (psych.) therapeutic technique in which a group of people meet regularly under direction of a trained leader to exchange experiences and interpersonal reactions to aid in understanding themselves

group·think (gruːpθiŋk) n. 1. process of analyzing problems by a group with special talents. 2. accepting without questioning the predominant views on social, political, and ethical matters

grou·pus·cule (gruːpəscjuːl) n. a minor group

grouse (graus) 1. v.i. pres. part. **grous·ing** past and past part. **groused** to grumble 2. n. a fit of grumbling [origin unknown]

grouse pl. **grouse** n. any of several game birds of fam. Tetraonidae, having plump bodies and feathered legs (*CAPERCAILLIE, *PTARMIGAN,

*RED GROUSE, *RUFFED GROUSE) [origin unknown]

grout (graut) 1. n. thin mortar for filling cracks or spaces under pressure 2. v.t. to fill up with grout [O.E. grūt, coarse meal]

grove (grouv) n. a group of trees without undergrowth growing naturally as if arranged by man ‖ (of certain trees) an orchard, an orange grove

grov·el (gróvəl, grávəl) pres. part. **grov·el·ing**, esp. Br. **grov·el·ling** past and past part. **grov·eled**, esp. Br. **grov·elled** v.i. to lie face down or crouch or crawl at someone's feet as if begging for mercy or favor ‖ to abase oneself abjectly ‖ to take pleasure in what is base, wallow **grov·el·ing**, esp. Br. **gróv·el·ling** adj. abject ‖ obsequious [back-formation fr. M.E. grovelynge adv., prob. fr. O.N. á grūfu, on the face]

grow (grou) pres. part. **grow·ing** past **grew** (gruː) past part. **grown** (groun) v.i. to exist or develop as a living plant ‖ to be cultivated, rice grows in China ‖ to increase in size as a living organism ‖ to increase in any way, become larger, support grew steadily for our policies ‖ to become gradually, to grow old, it grew dark, you will grow used to it ‖ (with the infin.) to come to, he grew to like her after a while ‖ v.t. to cause to grow, cultivate, to grow vegetables ‖ to allow to grow, to grow a beard ‖ to develop, he has grown a habit of twitching his nose **to grow into** to become, she grew into a fine girl ‖ to grow to fit (clothes) **to grow on** (or **upon**) to win favor with gradually, you may not like it at first but it grows on you **to grow out of** to become too big for, to grow out of one's clothes ‖ to abandon in the process of maturing, to grow out of childish habits ‖ to stem from, have as source, assertiveness may grow out of feelings of insecurity **to grow together** to become united by growth **to grow up** to reach adulthood ‖ to become prevalent, the custom grew up of sacrificing to a god **grow·er** n. a plant that grows in a specified way, a fast grower ‖ a person who grows vegetables etc., as distinguished from a distributor [O.E. grōwan]

growing pains pains in the limbs of children, popularly associated with growing ‖ early difficulties in the development of an organization, project etc.

growl (graul) 1. v.i. to make the characteristic threatening guttural sound of a dog ‖ v.t. to utter in a gruff, rumbling voice, esp. angrily 2. n. the sound made in growling **grówl·er** n. (Br., pop.) a fourwheeled horse-drawn cab ‖ a small iceberg [imit.]

grown past part. of GROW ‖ adj. having reached full size and maturity

grown-up 1. (gróunʌp) adj. adult, past adolescence 2. (gróunʌp) n. an adult (always in contradistinction to children)

growth (grouθ) n. the process of growing or developing ‖ increase in size, to measure the growth of a plant over a period of a week ‖ origin, development, cultivation, a custom of foreign growth ‖ something growing or grown, a growth of beard ‖ a morbid formation such as a cancer or tumor ‖ adj. (securities) of investments expected to increase in value due to expansion of the industry or the company [GROW]

growth center a place that provides sensitivity training

growth fund (securities) a mutual investment fund with a goal of capital appreciation rather than income, esp. specializing in growth stocks

growth hormone *HUMAN GROWTH HORMONE

groyne *GROIN

Groz·ny (gróznɪ) town in U.S.S.R., the capital (pop. 379,000) of the Checheno-Ingush A.S.S.R., in the N. Caucasus, the center of a great oil field

grub (grʌb) n. a maggot, caterpillar or any similar insect larva ‖ (pop.) food [perh. fr. GRUB v.]

grub pres. part. **grub·bing** past and past part. **grubbed** v.i. to dig or poke in the ground, to grub for roots ‖ to search or work laboriously, grub through the old files ‖ (with 'up' or 'out') to dig up or out ‖ (with 'up' or 'out') to discover by laborious search [M.E. grubben prob. fr. O.E.]

grub·bi·ly (grʌbɪliː) adv. in a grubby manner

grub·bi·ness (grʌbɪnɪs) n. the quality or state of being grubby

grub·by (grʌbiː) comp. **grub·bi·er** superl. **grub·bi·est** adj. dirty, unwashed ‖ grub-infested

grub screw a very short headless screw used to prevent lateral movement

grub·stake (grʌbsteɪk) 1. n. money or supplies given to a mining prospector in return for a share of the profits ‖ a gift or loan for a person in difficult circumstances or for the launching of a business venture 2. v.t. pres. part. **grub·stak·ing** past and past part. **grub·staked** to provide with a grubstake

Grub Street the world of hack writers ‖ hack writers in general [after Grub Street (now Milton Street), London, formerly the home of many hack writers]

grudge (grʌdʒ) 1. v.t. pres. part. **grudg·ing** past and past part. **grudged** to be reluctant to give, grant or allow (something) through envy, spite or meanness, to grudge someone's success ‖ to resent (doing something), he grudges buying drinks for people who earn twice as much as he does 2. n. a feeling of resentment, envy or spite **grudg·ing** adj. reluctant, forced, a grudging admission of responsibility [older grutch fr. M.E. gruce, gruchche fr. O.F. groucier, groucher, to grumble]

gru·el (gruːəl) n. a very thin porridge for invalids and old people [O.F.=ground grain]

gru·el·ing, esp. Br. **gru·el·ling** (gruːəliŋ) 1. adj. severely testing, exhausting, a grueling job 2. n. a harsh testing, questioning or punishing [fr. older gruel v.t., to punish by feeding with gruel]

grue·some (gruːsəm) adj. ghastly, sickening, revolting, esp. associated with blood and mutilation, a gruesome murder [Dan. grusom, cruel]

gruff (grʌf) adj. (of the voice) hoarse, rough and harsh ‖ (of speech or manner) blunt, almost surly, gruff thanks [prob. fr. Du. or L.G.]

gru·gru, **groo·groo** (gruːgruː) n. any of several spiny palm trees of tropical America, esp. Acrocomia sclerocarpa of Brazil and A. aculeata of the West Indies, which yield a yellow palm oil [Span., of Cariban origin]

grum·ble (grʌmb'l) 1. v. pres. part. **grum·bling** past and past part. **grum·bled** v.i. to complain in a persistent, bad-tempered way, show discontent ‖ to make a low growling sound, rumble ‖ v.t. to utter in a sullen complaining way, mutter surlily 2. n. a complaint ‖ something said in a nagging, complaining way ‖ a low growling sound **grúm·bler** n. [prob. fr. Du. gromelen]

grume (gruːm) n. a thick fluid, esp. a clot of blood [fr. L.L. grumus, a little heap]

Grumman Tomcat (mil.) 1969-designed carrier-based, U.S. Navy fighter plane (F-14), used for protecting a strike force, clearing air space, and defending ships at sea

grum·met (grʌmɪt) n. a metal eyelet used in canvas bags, tents, sails etc. to prevent fraying and tearing ‖ (naut.) a ring of twisted rope etc. for fastening, wadding etc. ‖ (fr. F. gromette, curb of a bridle]

gru·mous (gruːməs) adj. (bot.) containing or like grume ‖ consisting of a cluster of grains or granules [fr. Mod. L. grumosus]

grump·i·ly (grʌmpiliː) adv. in a grumpy manner

grump·i·ness (grʌmpinɪs) n. the quality or state of being grumpy

grump·y (grʌmpiː) comp. **grump·i·er** superl. **grump·i·est** adj. bad-tempered, disagreeable [perh. rel. to GRUNT]

Grü·ne·wald (grýnəvalt), Matthias Nithardt Gothardt (c. 1470–1528), German painter. He was the last and probably the greatest painter of the German Gothic school. He had probably seen Italian Renaissance painting. He used some of its techniques of realism to convey a spirituality which is entirely of the late Middle Ages. His greatest work is the Isenheim altar (c. 1515) now in the museum at Colmar

grun·gy (grʌndʒiː) adj. (slang) run down, decrepit

grunt (grʌnt) 1. v.i. (esp. of hogs) to make a low, gruff, snorting sound ‖ (of persons) to make a similar sound, expressing discontent, tiredness, effort, irritation, boredom, self-satisfaction etc. ‖ v.t. to utter as if with grunts 2. n. a low gruff sound made by hogs or like that made by hogs ‖ any of several large edible American marine fishes of fam. Pomadasidae (or Haemulidae), which make grunting sounds when taken from the water ‖ (slang) a private infantryman, esp. in Vietnam [O.E. grunnettan fr. grunian, to grunt]

grunt·work (grʌntwɜːrk) n. (slang) menial labor performed in armed forces

Gru·yère (gru:ʒéər) *n.* a hard Swiss processed whole-milk cheese, pale yellow. It has a sweetish, nutty flavor [after *Gruyère*, a district in Switzerland]

gryphon *GRIFFIN

GSL (*abbr.*) for U.S. Federal government guaranteed student loans

G-string (dʒí:strɪŋ) *n.* a strip of cloth between the legs supported by a cord around the waist ‖ a similar cloth with decoration, worn by striptease performers **G string** a string tuned to G on a musical instrument

G suit an inflatable suit worn by jet pilots to counteract the worst gravitational effects of high-speed maneuvers and to prevent blackouts [GRAVITY SUIT]

gua·cha·ro (gwátʃərou) *n. Steatornis guacharo,* a nocturnal bird of South America and Trinidad which feeds on fruits. An oil extracted from its young is used in place of butter [Span.]

gua·co (gwákou) *n.* either of two tropical American plants, *Mikania guaco* or *Aristolochia maxima,* the dried leaves of which are used as an antidote for snakebite [Span.]

Gua·da·la·ja·ra (gwɑðalɑhɑ́rɑ, gwɑd'ləhárə) a province (area 4,676 sq. miles, pop. 143,124) of central Spain ‖ its capital (pop. 21,000) (*NEW CASTILE)

Guadalajara the second largest city (pop. 1,626,152) of Mexico, founded in 1542, the main rail junction and economic center of the west coast. Industries: textiles, leather. Crafts: furniture, glassware, pottery. Cathedral (16th c.), university

Gua·dal·ca·nal (gwɑd'lkænæl) a small strategically placed island (area 2,509 sq. miles, pop. 46,619) in the Solomons, S.W. Pacific Ocean, the scene of fierce fighting between the Americans and Japanese (1942–3). The American victory was a turning point in the 2nd world war

Gua·dal·qui·vir (gwɑðɑlki:víːr) Spain's most important river (375 miles long), flowing west through Andalusia to the Atlantic, navigable for oceangoing ships as far as Seville

Gua·da·lupe Hi·dal·go, Treaty of (gwɑd'lú:phi:dálgou) the treaty signed (1848) by the U.S.A. and Mexico, ending the Mexican War. The U.S.A. gained a tract of land now forming California, Nevada and Utah, and part of New Mexico, Arizona, Colorado and Wyoming. The Rio Grande was accepted as the boundary between Texas and Mexico, and the U.S.A. paid Mexico $15,000,000

Guadalupe, Virgin of the patron saint since 1910 of all Spanish America. Her basilica is at Tepeyac, on the outskirts of Mexico City

Gua·de·loupe (gwɑd'lú:p) twin islands of the Leeward group, West Indies, forming, with Marie-Galante (area 58 sq. miles, pop. 16,000), La Désiderade, St Barthélemy, Les Saintes and N. St Martin, an overseas department (total area 638 sq. miles, pop. 319,000) of France. Capital: La Basse-Terre. Largest town: Pointe-à-Pitre. People: mainly of African descent and Mulatto, with Creole, European and East Indian minorities. Guadeloupe proper (area 538 sq. miles) consists of Grande-Terre (flat, cultivated) separated by a natural channel from Basse-Terre (mountainous, volcanic, forest-covered). Highest point: 4,900 ft. Mean annual temperature (F.): 78°. Rainfall: 86 ins on the coast, heavier inland. Chief products: bananas, sugar, rum, vanilla, coffee, cocoa. Colonized by the French after 1635, the islands were several times captured by the British, and finally restored to France (1816). They were made an overseas department in 1946

Gua·dia·na (gwɑðjánɑ, gwɑdjɑ́nə) a river (510 miles long), largely unnavigable, rising in central Spain. It flows west to Badajoz, then south, partly through Portugal and along the frontier, to the Atlantic

guai·a·cum (gwáiəkəm) *n.* a member of *Guaiacum,* fam. *Zygophyllaceae,* a genus of Caribbean trees (*LIGNUM VITAE) ‖ the valuable heavy hardwood of any of these trees ‖ a wood resin obtained from *G. officinale* or *G. sanctum,* used in some chemical tests [Mod. L. fr. Span. *guayaco* fr. Haitian]

Guai·cu·rú, Guay·cu·rú (gwɑiku:rú:) *pl.* **Guai·cu·rú, Guai·cu·rus, Guay·cu·rú, Guay·cu·rús** *n.* an Indian people of the Gran Chaco ‖ a member of this people ‖ their language [Span. *guaicuru, guaycuru*]

Guai·ní·a (gwɑiníːə) *RÍO NEGRO

Gua·ji·ra (gwɑhí:rɑ) a peninsula (80 miles long, 30–60 miles wide) in Colombia, between the Gulf of Venezuela and the Caribbean Sea. Its tip, Point Gallinas, is the most northern point of South America

Guam (gwɑm) the principal island (area 209 sq. miles, pop. 105,821) of the Mariana group, N. Pacific, a U.S. naval base since 1898. During the 2nd world war it fell (1941) to a Japanese attack but was recovered (1944) by U.S. forces. It served for the remainder of the war as a major air and sea base. In 1950 it became a territory of the U.S.A. Capital: Agaña

guan (gwɑn) *n.* a member of *Cracidae,* a family of South American gallinaceous game birds allied to the curassow [Span. fr. Cariban]

Gua·na·ba·ra Bay (gwɑnəbárə) a deep bay (approx. 16 miles long, 11 miles wide, 1 mile wide at the entrance) forming the harbor of Rio de Janeiro, Brazil

gua·na·co (gwənákou) *pl.* **gua·na·cos, gua·na·co** *n. Lama guanicoe,* the wild llama of the Andes [Span. fr. Quechua *huanaco, huanacu*]

Gua·na·jua·to (gwɑnɑhwátə) an inland state (area 11,810 sq. miles, pop. 3,045,600) of Mexico, within the central plateau (average elevation 6,000 ft). Capital: Guanajuato (pop. 36,809). Corn, beans, barley and wheat are grown on the fertile plains in the south, and stock raising is important. Mining (silver, gold, tin, lead, mercury, copper and opals) is the main industry. There are flour mills, tanneries, leather factories, cotton and woolen mills, foundries and potteries

guan·eth·i·dine [$C_{10}H_{22}N_4$] (gwɑneθədi:n) *n.* (*pharm.*) drug used to reduce high blood pressure; marketed as Ismelin

gua·nine (gwáni:n, gwánin) *n.* a crystalline purine derivative ($C_5H_5N_5O$), 2-amino-6-hydroxy purine, found in animal excrement (esp. guano) and also obtained by hydrolysis of deoxyribonucleic acid [GUANO]

gua·no (gwánou) *n.* deposits formed from the droppings of seabirds, found esp. on islands off the coast of Peru, rich in nitrogen and phosphates and valuable as fertilizer [Span. fr. Quechua *huanu, dung*]

Guan·tá·na·mo (gwɑntánɑmou) a port (pop. 129,005) of E. Cuba, in Oriente province, a U.S. naval base since 1903

Gua·po·ré (gwɑpuréi) (or Iténez) a river (c. 950 miles long) rising in S.W. Brazil and flowing to unite with the Mamoré River along the Brazil-Bolivia boundary

gua·ra·na (gwɑrɑ́nə) *n.* a paste made from the dried and ground seeds of *Paullinia cupana,* fam. *Sapindaceae,* a liana grown in Brazil, used to make a stimulating drink rich in caffeine and tannin ‖ a drink prepared from this paste [Tupi]

Gua·ra·ni (gwɑrɑni:) *n.* a member of a tribe of Indians of Bolivia, Paraguay and S. Brazil ‖ the language of this tribe

gua·ra·ni the basic unit of currency of Paraguay ‖ a coin or note of the value of one guarani [of native origin]

gua·ra·ni (gwɑráni:) *n.* unit of currency of Paraguay, equal to 100 pesos

guar·an·tee (gærəntí:) **1.** *n.* a pledge given by the makers of an article that they will repair or replace it free if it is unsatisfactory or develops defects within a stated time from the date of purchase ‖ (*law*) a written undertaking made by one person to a second person to be responsible if a third person fails to perform a certain duty, e.g. pay a debt ‖ the person who gives such a guarantee, a guarantor ‖ the person to whom such a guarantee is given ‖ (*law*) a thing given as a security for payment of a loan or fulfillment of a duty ‖ a firm promise, assurance, something that makes another thing seem sure **2.** *v.t. pres. part.* **guar·an·tee·ing** *past* and *past part.* **guar·an·teed** to accept responsibility for the genuineness, proper working or quality of (an article) ‖ to act as guarantor for ‖ to give a security for, secure ‖ to undertake to answer for (the debt or default of another person) ‖ to engage (that something has happened or will happen), *who can guarantee that she will keep her word?* ‖ to promise, assure someone of (something), *can you guarantee me a job when I get there? I can guarantee that you will enjoy yourself* [earlier *garanté* perh. fr. Span. *garante* = F. *garant*]

guaranteed annual income (*economics*) program to provide a minimum annual income for (a) employees or (b) all citizens. *Cf* NEGATIVE INCOME TAX

guar·an·tor (gærəntɔr) *n.* (*law*) a person who gives a guarantee

guar·an·ty (gǽrənti:) *pl.* **guar·an·ties** *n.* (*law*) a guarantee [fr. A.F. *guarantie* fr. *guarant,* warrant]

guard (gurd) *n.* a keeping watch against surprise, attack or theft ‖ watch, control, *keep a close guard on your language* ‖ (*boxing* etc.) a posture of defense ‖ (*boxing* etc.) defense ‖ (*football*) either of two players on each side of the center ‖ (*basketball*) one of two defending players at the rear of the court ‖ a person or body of persons (esp. soldiers) set to keep watch over something or against danger ‖ a ceremonial escort or protective force, *the Imperial Guard, guard of honor* ‖ (*pl.*) regiments of soldiers in the British army attached to the person of the sovereign ‖ a separate part of an army with a special responsibility, *the advance guard* ‖ a prison official or officials with responsibility for the security of prisoners ‖ (*Br.*) a brakeman ‖ that part of the hilt of a sword that protects the hand ‖ any other protective device **off** (**on**) **guard** unprepared (prepared) for surprise, attack, deceit etc. **to keep guard over** to watch over **to mount guard** to take up sentry position **to stand guard** to act as guard [M.E. *garde* fr. F. fr. Gmc]

guard *v.t.* to keep watch over so as to check or control, *guard the prisoner well* ‖ to keep watch over so as to protect from danger, defend ‖ to keep in check, control, *guard your temper* ‖ to provide with a guard, protective device etc. ‖ (*lawn bowling, curling*) to protect (a bowl, stone) by screening it with a second one from a later player ‖ (*chess*) to protect (one piece) with another ‖ (*cards*) to protect (a high card) with another lower one or lower ones ‖ *v.i.* to be cautious or watchful, take precautions, *to guard against infection* [GUARD n. or fr. F. *garder*]

guard·ant (gúrd'nt) *adj.* (*heraldry,* of an animal) looking full face toward the observer [F. *gardant*]

guard·ed (gúrdid) *adj.* cautious, circumspect, *a guarded answer*

guard·house (gúrdhaus) *pl.* **guard·hous·es** (gúrdhauziz) *n.* a building where military prisoners are kept, and where the guard and military police are quartered during their spell of duty

Guar·di (gwárdi:), Francesco (1712–93), Venetian painter. His pictures of Venice, less precise and static than those of Canaletto, have more movement and atmosphere

Guardia Gu·tiér·rez (gu:tjérres), Tomás (1832–82), Costa Rican general and president (1870–6, 1877–82). He constructed the Costa Rican interocean railroad and began to make Costa Rican coffee a worldwide export

guard·i·an (gárdi:ən) *n.* someone who undertakes legal custody of the person and property of someone unable to look after themselves, esp. a person who assumes parental responsibilities for an orphaned child ‖ a protector, keeper, custodian ‖ the superior of a Franciscan convent [M.E. *gardein* fr. A.F.]

guardian angel an angel believed to have charge of a particular individual

guard·i·an·ship (gárdi:ənʃip) *n.* the office and legal responsibility of guardian ‖ protection, keeping

guard·room (gárdru:m, gárdrum) *n.* a guardhouse

guards·man (gárdzmən) *pl.* **guards·men** (gárdzmən) *n.* a member of the National Guard ‖ (*Br., mil.*) a private or officer of the Guards

guard's van (*Br., rail.*) a caboose

Guar·ne·ri (gwɑrnéri:) a famous Italian family of violin makers of 17th and 18th–c. Cremona. A violin made by this family is known as a Guarnerius

Gua·te·ma·la (gwatəmálə) a republic (area 42,042 sq. miles, pop. 7,480,000) in Central America. Capital: Guatemala City. People: Maya-Ouiché (54%) and Ladino (mixed Indian-Spanish), small African and Afro-Carib minorities. Language: Spanish (official), Indian languages. Religion: mainly Roman Catholic, 4% Protestant. The land is 14% arable, 64% forest and 5% pasture. Two branches of the Central American cordillera enclose a plateau (mainly 6,000–9,000 ft) which crosses the country behind a malarial coastal plain (cattle-raising). The plateau, containing large lakes and crossed by volcanic chains (Tajumulco, 13,812 ft), and the Pacific slopes, are fertile and populous. Earthquakes are frequent. The northern lowland (the Petén) is rain forest. Rainfall: 52 ins at Guatemala City. Average temperatures (F.): lowlands 80°, Guatemala City 65°. Agricultural

---

CONCISE PRONUNCIATION KEY: (**a**) æ, c*a*t; ɑ, c*a*r; ɔ, f*aw*n; ei, sn*a*ke. (**e**) e, h*e*n; i:, sh*ee*p; iə, d*ee*r; ɛə, b*ea*r. (**i**) i, f*i*sh; ai, t*i*ger; ə:, b*i*rd. (**o**) o, *o*x; au, c*ow*; ou, g*oa*t; u, p*oo*r; ɔi, r*oy*al. (**u**) ʌ, d*u*ck; u, b*u*ll; u:, g*oo*se; ə, bacill*u*s; ju:, c*u*be. x, lo*ch*; θ, *th*ink; δ, bo*th*er; z, *Z*en; ʒ, cor*s*age; dʒ, sava*g*e; ŋ, orangutan*g*; j, *y*ak; ʃ, *f*ish; tʃ, fe*tch*; 'l, rabb*le*; 'n, redd*en.* Complete pronunciation key appears inside front cover.

products: coffee, bananas, cotton, sugar, corn, rice, beans, wheat, chicle gum, essential oils, rubber, tobacco. Mineral resources: lead, zinc, silver, antimony, chrome, petroleum. Exports: coffee, bananas, cotton, essential oils, tropical hardwoods, chicle. Imports: textiles, foodstuffs, petroleum, manufactured goods, chemicals. Chief port: Puerto Barrios, on the Atlantic. University at Guatemala City. Monetary unit: quetzal (100 centavos). HISTORY. The Maya Indians were defeated by the Spanish general Alvarado (1523). The subsequent kingdom of Guatemala attained independence from Spain (1821) but was annexed by Mexico (1823) into the Central American Federation. Guatemala again became independent (1839) and was ruled by a series of dictators. Economic progress was made between the two world wars. During the presidency (1931–44) of Gen. Jorge Ubico, large concessions were made to U.S. business interests, especially United Fruit. Following a popular revolution, Juan José Arevalo (1945–51) introduced reform, which was continued, esp. in agriculture, by his successor Jacobo Arbenz Guzmán. The support, however, which Arbenz drew from the Communists provoked Col. Carlos Castillo Armas to launch (from exile) a coup d'état. Castillo's term (1954–7) ended in his assassination. Miguel Ydígoras Fuentes, of the National Democratic Reconciliation party, won office (1958) but was also overthrown (1963) by a military junta which installed Col. Enrique Peralta Azurdia. Elections in 1966 were won by Julio Méndez Montenegro of the moderate leftist Revolutionary party. A surge in political violence (1966–8) was checked by Col. Carlos Arana Osorio, whose eradication in Zacapa of one of Latin America's largest guerrilla movements and whose 'law and order' electoral platform won him the presidency (1970). Violence, however, continued, including the murder of two foreign diplomats, U.S. Ambassador John Gordon Mein in 1968 and West German Ambassador Count Karl von Spreti in 1970. A rural guerrilla movement and numerous left- and right-wing terrorist groups disrupted Guatemala's politics from the mid-1960's. The country was governed by a series of military and elected civilian rulers from 1954. Christian Democratic party leader Marco Vinicio Cerezo Arevalo, elected president in Dec. 1985, promised fundamental land and tax reform may be in the offing. Guatemala's dispute with Belize over British Honduras remains unresolved

Guatemala City (*Span.* Guatemala) the capital (pop. 1,180,000) of Guatemala, at 4,877 ft in the central plateau. Founded in 1799, it was largely destroyed by earthquakes (1917–18) and rebuilt. Cathedral, university (1678, reopened 1910). There are light industries

gua·va (gwávə) *n. Psidium guajava*, fam. *Myrtaceae*, a small tropical tree ‖ its gritty, pearlike fruit, used to make a dessert marmalade or guava jelly, or eaten fresh [Span. *guayaba*, of native origin]

Gua·ya·quil (gwɑjɑkíːl) the largest city (pop. 823,219) and chief port of Ecuador at the head of the Gulf of Guayaquil. Cathedral, university

Guayaquil, Gulf of an inlet on the southwest coast of Ecuador, bounded on the south by the tip of N.W. Peru. It contains many islands, the largest being Puná Is.

gua·yu·le (gwɑjúːliː) *n. Parthenium argentatum*, fam. *Compositae*, a southern U.S. and Mexican plant which produces latex [Span. fr. Nahuatl *cuahuli* fr. *quauitl*, plant+*uli*, gum]

gu·ber·na·to·ri·al (guːbərnətóːriəl, gubərnətóuriəl) *adj.* pertaining to a governor or a governor's office [fr. L. *gubernator*, governor]

gudg·eon (gʌ́dʒən) *n. Gobio gobio*, a small European and Asian freshwater fish allied to the carp, used as bait [M.E. *gojon, gogen* fr. F. *goujon*]

gudgeon *n.* a pivot at the end of a beam or axle ‖ a ring on a gate which drops over a hook on the gatepost ‖ the socket in which a rudder turns ‖ a pin holding together two blocks (e.g. of stone) [O.F. *gojon, goujon*]

gudgeon pin (*mech.*) a wrist pin

Guelderland *GELDERLAND

guel·der rose (géldər) *Viburnum trilobum*, fam. *Caprifoliaceae*, an ornamental shrub with round bunched white flowers [after *Guelderland* (Gelderland)]

Guel·ders (géldərz) *GELDERLAND

Guelph, Guelf (gwelf) a German princely family (9th–12th cc.) ‖ a member of the political faction in Italy which maintained (11th–14th cc.) the supremacy of the pope against the claims of the Emperor (cf. GHIBELLINE)

gue·non (gənɔ̃, gənóun) *n.* any of several long-tailed African monkeys belonging to *Cercopithecus* and related genera [F., origin unknown]

guer·don (gə́rd'n) *n.* (*rhet.*) reward, recompense [O.F. fr. M.L. fr. O.H.G.]

Gue·rick·e (gýrikə), Otto von (1602–86), German physicist. He invented the first air pump (1654), and demonstrated the power of a vacuum with the Magdeburg hemispheres, two copper hemispheres joined to form a globe, which were practically inseparable once the air was pumped out of the globe. He also discovered that light could be produced from electricity

guerilla *GUERRILLA

Guer·ni·ca (gerníːkə, gwéːrni:kə) a town (pop. 14,678) in N. Spain. Its destruction (Apr. 27, 1937), caused by indiscriminate fascist bombing during the Spanish Civil War inspired a great painting by Picasso

Guern·sey (gə́rnziː) the second largest of the Channel Is (area 24 sq. miles, pop. 54,381), growing early vegetables for export to England

Guern·sey (gə́rnziː) *n.* a cow of a breed first bred on Guernsey and famous for its yield of rich milk

Guer·re·ro (gerréro), Vicente (1783–1831), Mexican independence leader who kept alive (1810–17) the revolutionary cause through guerrilla warfare. Appointed president (1829), he proved an inept administrator. Following a revolt led by Santa Anna he was overthrown (1829) and executed (1831)

Guerrero a Pacific coast state (area 24,631 sq. miles, pop. 2,013,000) of Mexico. The Sierra Madre del Sur covers its entire surface except for the coastal plain. Principal river: the Balsas. Capital: Chilpancingo (pop. 18,000). Agricultural products: coffee, cotton, tobacco and cereals. Forest products: rubber, vanilla, textile fibers. Mineral resources: silver, gold, mercury, lead, iron, coal, sulfur, precious stones

guer·ril·la, gue·ril·la (gərílə) *n.* someone engaged in harassing, raiding or sabotage operations carried out by small bands of irregulars acting independently. The term was first used of the Spaniards who harassed Napoleon's army during the Peninsular War. This method of warfare has often been used against enemy occupation, esp. where the terrain allows the guerrillas to hide and live off the country. Tito's partisans in Yugoslavia were an outstanding example in the 2nd World War [Span. dim. of *guerra*, war]

guerrilla theater street theater, presenting short dramas or pantomime, usually with an antiestablishment theme, at any location where an audience can be gathered. *Cf* STREET THEATER

Gues·clin (geklɛ̃), Bertrand du (c. 1320–80), French soldier, constable of France (1370–80). He distinguished himself in the service of Charles V, and drove the English almost completely out of France

guess (ges) 1. *v.t.* to hazard an opinion about without full knowledge or detailed reasoning, *guess where he comes from* ‖ to conjecture correctly, *he guessed her age* ‖ to think likely, suppose, *I guess you're tired after your journey* ‖ *v.i.* to conjecture, *I don't really know, I'm just guessing* **to guess at** to attempt to arrive at (an answer) by conjecture **to keep someone guessing** to keep someone in a state of uncertainty 2. *n.* a rough estimate ‖ a conjecture [M.E. *gessen* prob. fr. O.N.]

guess·work (géswə:rk) *n.* the finding of answers to problems by guessing

guest (gest) *n.* someone who receives hospitality ‖ a person staying at a hotel ‖ (*biol.*) a parasitic insect or other organism [O.E. *giest, gæst*]

guest·house (gésthaus) *n.* a boardinghouse, esp. one of some standing

guest of honor, *Br.* **guest of honour** the honored or chief guest at a social function

guest·work·er (géstwə:rkər) *n.* English for the German *Gastarbeiter*, a foreign laborer working in northern European countries

Gue·va·ra (gevára), Ernesto 'Che' (1928–67), Cuban revolutionary, Argentinian by birth. As a guerrilla leader and Fidel Castro's chief lieutenant, he became (1959–61), after Fulgencio Batista's overthrow, president of the national

bank and minister of industry. He helped to sever Cuba's economic ties with the U.S.A. and to direct trade to the Communist bloc. He was killed while waging guerrilla warfare in Bolivia

Gue·var·ist (geivárist) *n.* follower of Ernesto (Che) Guevera, Argentine-born revolutionary in the Cuban revolution, killed in Bolivia

guff (gʌf) *n.* (*pop.*) empty talk, either foolish or meant to deceive [imit.]

guf·faw (gʌfɔ́:) 1. *n.* a loud, coarse laugh 2. *v.i.* to make such a laugh ‖ *v.t.* to utter with such a laugh [imit.]

Gug·gen·heim (gú:gənhaim), a family of U.S. industrialists founded by Meyer Guggenheim (1828–1905) and continued by his seven sons, who controlled (from 1888) international mining interests. Simon Guggenheim (1867–1941) established the 'Guggenheim Memorial Foundation' which grants fellowships to writers and artists. In 1937 Solomon R. Guggenheim (1861–1949) established the Guggenheim Museum for non-objective art, in New York City

Gui·an·a (giːǽnə) a region of N.E. South America bounded by the Amazon and Orinoco Rivers and the Atlantic, incl. Guyana, French Guiana and Suriname, with parts of S. and E. Venezuela and N. Brazil. The interior is largely unexplored

Guic·ciar·di·ni (gwiːtʃɑrdíːniː), Francesco (1483–1540), Italian historian and politician. He was Florentine ambassador to Spain (1512–14), and governor of the Papal States (1516–24). His 'History of Italy' (written 1534–40) is a masterpiece of Renaissance historical writing. It covers the period 1492–1534

guid·ance (gáid'ns) *n.* the act of guiding ‖ direction, advice ‖ leadership

guide (gaid) *pres. part.* **guid·ing** *past* and *past part.* **guid·ed** *v.t.* to go before or with in order to show the way ‖ to direct the course of, steer, *to guide a boat* ‖ to control, direct, influence ‖ *v.i.* to act as a guide [F. *guider*]

guide *n.* a person who shows the way to strangers, esp. to tourists or to mountaineers ‖ a book of information esp. for visitors to a place ‖ a book of rudiments for beginners ‖ an adviser ‖ the principle governing behavior or choice, *let conscience be your guide* ‖ (*mech.*) any device which steadies or directs motion ‖ (*Br.*) a girl scout [F.]

guide·book (gáidbuk) *n.* a book containing information for travelers

guided missile a military missile whose course is controlled remotely or by a target-seeking device

guid·ed·mis·sile cruiser (gáidədmís'l) (*mil.*) warship designed to operate with strike and amphibious forces against air, surface, and subsurface threats, carrying 3-, 5-, and/or 6-in guns, advanced area-defense antiair-warfare missile system and antisubmarine-warfare weapons. acronym CG

guide·line (gáidlain) *n.* a lightly drawn line used as a guide, e.g. in laying out lettering ‖ an outline policy statement

guidelines *pl. n.* officially declared, but not legislated, limitations, usu. on prices or wages or as instructions for a procedure

Guideline/SA-N2 U.S.S.R. air-defense solid-propellant missile (SA-N2), with liquid sustaining fuel, weighing 50 lb with range of 30 mi and radio command direction

guide·post (gáidpoust) *n.* a signpost

Gui·do d'A·rez·zo (gwíːdoːdɑréttsə) (c. 990–c. 1050), Italian Benedictine monk and musical theorist, the inventor of solmization

gui·don (gáid'n) *n.* (*mil.*) a small triangular pennant used as a marker ‖ the person who carries it [F. fr. Ital. *guidone*]

Gui·do Re·ni (gwíːdəréiniː) (1575–1642), Italian painter, famous in the 17th and 18th cc. for his grace, color and drawing, and Raphaelesque style. His paintings treat religious subjects with sentimentality and a mannered show of exaltation. He was a magnificent etcher and a pioneer in the use of colored chalks

Gui·gnol (giːnjɔl) a figure reminiscent of Punch appearing in puppet shows in late 18th-c. France (*GRAND GUIGNOL)

Guild *n.* (*mil.*) U.S.S.R. air-defense weapon (SA-1) with liquid propulsion and a 20-mi range

guild, gild (gild) *n.* (*hist.*) a medieval association of merchants or craftsmen ‖ a society of people with common interests and aims [O.E. *gild, gyld* and *gegyld*, infl. by O.N. *gildi*]

—Medieval guilds were of two main types: merchant guilds and craft guilds. The merchant guilds, which flourished esp. in England in the 12th to 16th cc., comprised the merchants and craftsmen in each town. They monopolized local trade and often dominated municipal corporations. On the Continent, they gave rise to vast organizations, e.g. the Hanseatic League. The craft guilds, which developed in the 12th c., united the workmen engaged in the same craft (e.g. goldsmiths, carpenters) in one town. Their members were divided into masters, journeymen and apprentices, and they aimed at regulating terms and standards of trade and production, and conditions of apprenticeship. They also gave help to needy members. In time they became restrictive and privileged, and declined in England in the 16th c., though some continued on the Continent until the 18th and 19th cc. The London craft guilds survive in ceremonial and charitable form in the livery companies

guil·der (gíldər) *n.* a gulden [corrup. of G. and Du. *gulden*]

guild·hall (gíldhɔl) *n.* the hall where a guild or corporation meets, town hall **Guild·hall** the meeting place (built 1411–23) of the corporation of the City of London

guilds·man (gíldzmən) *pl.* **guilds·men** (gíldzmən) *n.* a member of a guild

guild socialism an economic theory advocating the management of each industry by a council of its own workers, under state control. The theory was popular in Britain in the 1920s

guile (gail) *n.* deceiving trickery, low cunning ‖ wiliness **guile·ful**, **guile·less** *adjs* [O.F. prob. fr. Gmc]

Guil·ford Courthouse (gílfərd) a village in north central North Carolina, site of a battle (1781) in the American Revolutionary War between British forces commanded by Gen. Charles Cornwallis and American patriots under Gen. Nathanael Greene. The Americans, although forced to retreat, inflicted heavy losses that led to the final defeat of the British at Yorktown

Guil·laume de Lor·ris (gi:joumdəlɔri:s) (early 13th c.), French poet, author of the first 4,058 lines of 'Roman de la Rose' (c. 1236). The poem was completed, in a totally alien manner, by Jean de Meung with the addition of 17,772 lines. The first portion effectively combined the pervading theme of courtly love with the popular technique of allegory, in a style subsequently much imitated

guil·le·mot (gílimot) *n.* any of several ducklike auks with stubby necks, of genera *Uria* and *Cepphus*, esp. *C. grylle*, the black guillemot [F. fr. *Guillaume*, William]

Gui·llén (gwi:jén), Nicolás (1904–), Cuban poet. His early poems, notably 'Motivos de son' (1930) and 'Sóngoro cosongo' (1931), express intense racial and political feelings. His later poetry, reflecting his Marxist beliefs, deals with social and economic problems. He served as a deputy in the People's Assembly and as president of the National Union of Writers and Artists of Cuba. 'Obra poetica' (1920–58) appeared in 1972–3

guil·loche (gilóuʃ) *n.* (*archit.*) an ornament composed of lacings of bands of S-shaped curves with the openings filled with round devices ‖ a similar pattern engraved on metal, e.g. in jewelry (watch backs etc.) [F. *guillochis* fr. *guilloche*, the tool used]

guil·lo·tine (gílɔti:n, gilɔtí:n, gí:ɔti:n) **1.** *n.* a machine adopted in the French Revolution (and still used in France) for beheading people, by means of a blade sliding down between grooved posts ‖ a method of fixing a time limit for a parliamentary debate ‖ a surgical instrument for cutting out the tonsils or uvula ‖ a machine for cutting paper **2.** *v.t. pres. part.* **guil·lo·tin·ing** *past* and *past part.* **guil·lo·tined** to use the guillotine on [F. after J. I. *Guillotin* (1738–1814), French doctor, who advocated its use as being more humane than other methods]

guilt (gilt) *n.* the fact of having committed a legal offense ‖ the fact of having transgressed the moral law ‖ a feeling of culpability [O.E. *gylt*]

guilt·i·ly (gílti:li) *adv.* in a guilty manner

guilt·i·ness (gílti:nis) *n.* the state or quality of being guilty

guilt·less (gíltlis) *adj.* innocent

guilt·y (gílti:) *comp.* **guilt·i·er** *superl.* **guilt·i·est** *adj.* having committed an offense, *guilty of*

manslaughter ‖ showing guilt, *a guilty look* ‖ feeling guilt, *a guilty conscience* [O.E. *gyltig*]

Guin·ea (gíni:) a republic (area 100,000 sq. miles, pop. 5,430,000) in W. Africa. Capital: Conakry. People: 38% Peuls (Fulani), 19% Malinke, 9% Susu, 6% Kissi. Language: French, Fulani and Mande dialects. Religion: fetishism, with Moslem and Christian minorities. The land consists of a marshy coastal plain, a sandstone plateau and the granite Fouta Djallon Mtns (over 4,000 ft). Rainfall: 170 ins at Conakry, under 80 ins inland. Average temperature: 79°F. in Conakry, lower inland. Livestock: cattle, sheep, goats. Crops: rice, palm nuts, coffee, fruit, millet, bananas, peanuts. Minerals: diamonds, bauxite, iron ore. Industries: aluminum, food processing. Exports: minerals, aluminum, palm kernels, bananas. Imports: petroleum products, cement, rice, sugar. Port: Conakry. Monetary unit: Guinea franc. HISTORY. The Portuguese explored the coast (15th c.). European commercial interests struggled for control (17th–18th cc.), and the French conquered the Fulani tribes of Fouta Djallon, establishing Guinea as a colony (1890). It joined the French Union (1958) but became an independent republic outside the French Community (Oct. 2, 1958). Sékou Touré was president from independence to 1984, when he died and a military junta took control. The Military Committee for National Recovery appointed a cabinet of military and multi-ethnic civilian members, headed by Pres. Lansana Conté

Guinea (*hist.*) the name given by 15th-c. explorers to that coast of Africa from Gambia to the Congo. The Gulf of Guinea is the part of the Atlantic Ocean extending along this coast from Liberia to Cameroun

guin·ea (gíni:) *n.* (*Br.*) a unit of value of £ 1.05 used in stating professional fees and subscriptions and in pricing paintings, horses etc. ‖ (*Br., hist.*) a gold coin minted 1663–1813, originally worth 20 shillings, but fixed (1717) at 21 shillings [after *Guinea*, where the gold to make them was first obtained]

Guinea Bissau (gini:bisáu), an independent republic (area 13,948 sq. miles, pop. 827,000, incl. offshore islands), formerly an overseas territory of Portugal, in W. Africa. Capital and chief port: Bissau (pop. 109,486). People: Balante, Fulani, Mandingo and other African groups, with small mulatto and European minorities. Religion: 60% Animist, 33% Moslem, 4% Roman Catholic. Official languages: Crioulo, Portuguese. The country is a lowland, laced by river estuaries and gulfs, rising to 650 ft in the southeast. The coast is swampy, the interior mainly savanna. Average temperature (F.): 77 (Jan.), 85 (May). Rainfall: 51–85 ins. Livestock: cattle, goats, hogs, sheep. Agricultural products: peanuts, rice, coconuts, lumber, wax, hides. Exports: peanuts, palm oil and kernels, hides, rice. Imports: textiles, manufactures, food, machinery, vehicles. HISTORY. The area was visited by a Portuguese expedition (1446) and became a separate Portuguese colony in 1879 after disputes between Britain and Portugal. A rebellion by Africans against Portuguese rule, led by a Cape Verdean, Amilcar Cabral, started in 1959 and escalated into large-scale guerrilla warfare until Cabral's assassination (1973). The territory unilaterally declared its independence that same year, and Cabral's brother, Luis Cabral, became president (1974). After the Portuguese revolution (1974), Portugal recognized Guinea Bissau's independence. Cabral was deposed (1980) and a new constitution was adopted (1984) in which the ruling Council of the Revolution was replaced by an indirectly elected National People's Assembly

Guinea corn durra

guinea fowl *Numida meleagris*, a bird with grayish plumage, the size of a small domestic chicken, related to the pheasant. It is native to Africa but widely domesticated for its eggs and meat

guinea hen a female guinea fowl

guinea pig a member of genus *Cavia*, fam. *Caviidae*, esp. *C. cobaya*, a small, tailless, short-eared South American rodent, nocturnal, fast-maturing and prolific, introduced into Europe in the 16th c. Guinea pigs are kept as pets, and are also widely used in medical and biological research ‖ any person or animal used for experiment

Guinea worm *Dracunculus medinensis*, a long, parasitic nematode worm which lodges under the skin of man and some other mammals,

entering the body in drinking water, and which produces ulcers and swelling. It is common in African and other warm countries

Guin·e·vere (gwíniviər) Arthur's queen, in the Arthurian legend. She was unfaithful to Arthur in her love for Sir Lancelot

Guinness (gínəs), Sir Alec (1914–), British actor. Best known for his role in 'The Bridge on the River Kwai' (1957), for which he received an Academy Award, he also played in 'Great Expectations' (1946), 'Oliver Twist' (1948), 'The Lavender Hill Mob' (1951), 'The Man in the White Suit' (1951), 'The Ladykillers' (1955), 'Lawrence of Arabia' (1962) and 'Star Wars' (1977). He was knighted in 1959

gui·pure (gipjúər) *n.* ornamental lace with a large pattern and no mesh background, the pattern being held in place by single threads [F.]

Gui·puz·co·a (gi:pú:θkɔɑ) a province (area 728 sq. miles, pop. 692,986) of N. Spain. (*BASQUE PROVINCES) Capital: San Sebastián

Güi·ral·des (gi:ráldes), Ricardo (1886– 1927), Argentine novelist. In his poetic novel 'Don Segundo Sombra' (1926), depicting the career of an Argentinian gaucho and his youthful apprentice, he evinced both a cosmopolitan spirit and a deep affection for his native land

Guiscard, Robert *ROBERT GUISCARD

Guise (gi:z), Henri de Lorraine, 3rd duc de (1550–88), French nobleman. He was chiefly responsible for planning the murder of Coligny and the Massacre of St Bartholomew (1572). An ardent Catholic, he established (1576) the Holy League. He attempted to gain the throne in opposition to the future Henri IV, but was assassinated at Blois

guise (gaiz) *n.* (*rhet.*) outward appearance, esp. assumed to conceal the truth, *cruel insults in the guise of advice* [O.F. and F. *guise*, manner, style fr. Gmc]

gui·tar (gitár) *n.* a musical instrument, normally with six strings. These are plucked, the tone intervals being controlled by a fret. The Spanish guitar is the most familiar type. It has a range of more than three octaves above E below the bass staff **gui·tar·ist** *n.* [Span. *guitarra* and F. *guitare* fr. Gk *kithara*]

Gui·zot (gi:zóu), François (1787–1874), French historian and statesman. He was the effective head of the government (1840–7) and premier (1847–8). His rigidly conservative policies helped to bring about the revolution of 1848

Gu·ja·rat (gu:dʒərát) a state (area 72,137 sq. miles, pop. 30,930,000) of India on the Arabian Sea, bordering Pakistan. Capital: Ahmedabad. Crops: cotton, cereals, tobacco, peanuts. Minerals: salt (*RANN OF KUTCH), petroleum. Main industry: cotton textiles

Gu·ja·ra·ti (gu:dʒəráti:) *n.* an Indic language spoken in Gujarat and neighboring Indian states

Guj·ran·wa·la (gudʒrənwúlə) a town (pop. 196,000) in N.E. Pakistan, 40 miles north of Lahore: agricultural products, textiles, brassware, jewelry, metallurgy, hydroelectricity

gu·lag (gú:lag) (*acronym*) for Main Administration of Corrective Labor Camps (in U.S.S.R.), the agency of Soviet secret police that administers forced labor camps. The term and phenomenon were publicized by Aleksandr I. Solzhenitsyn in *The Gulag Archipelago*, published in 1974

gulch (gʌltʃ) *n.* a short, steepsided ravine [perh. fr. earlier *gulch*, to swallow]

gul·den (gúldən) *n.* the monetary unit of the Netherlands ‖ (*hist.*) any of several gold or silver coins used in the Netherlands, Germany and Austria, on the pattern of the Florentine florin [G. and Du. *gulden* adj., golden]

gules (gju:lz) *n.* and *adj.* (*heraldry*) red (conventionally represented by vertical hatching) [fr. O.F. *goules*, *gueules* pl., ermine dyed red]

gulf (gʌlf) *n.* an area of sea partly surrounded by coast, larger and with a relatively narrower opening than a bay ‖ (*rhet.*) a great abyss ‖ a huge gap, *the great gulf between theory and practice* [M.E. *golf* fr. O.F. *golfe* ult. fr. Gk]

Gulf Stream a warm and powerful ocean current flowing from the Gulf of Mexico northward along the east coast of North America, merging off Newfoundland with the North Atlantic Drift

gulf·weed (gʌlfwi:d) *n.* a member of genus *Sargassum*, esp. *S. bacciferum*, a tropical brown seaweed found in the Sargasso Sea and in the Gulf Stream

gull (gʌl) **1.** *v.t.* (*old-fash.*) to trick, cheat, deceive **2.** *n.* (*old-fash.*) someone easily cheated or

CONCISE PRONUNCIATION KEY: **(a)** æ, c*a*t; ɑ, c*a*r; ɔ f*aw*n; ei, sn*a*ke. **(e)** e, h*e*n; i:, sh*ee*p; iə, d*ee*r; ɛə, b*ea*r. **(i)** i, f*i*sh; ai, t*i*ger; ə:, b*i*rd. **(o)** o, *o*x; au, c*ow*; ou, g*oa*t; u, p*oo*r; ɔi, r*oy*al. **(u)** ʌ, d*u*ck; u, b*u*ll; u:, g*oo*se; ə, b*a*cill*u*s; ju:, c*u*be. x, lo*ch*; θ, *th*ink; ð, bo*th*er; z, *Z*en; ʒ, corsa*g*e; dʒ, sava*g*e; ŋ, orangutan*g*; j, *y*ak; ʃ, *f*ish; tʃ, fe*tch*; 'l, rabb*le*; 'n, redd*en*. Complete pronunciation key appears inside front cover.

deceived, a dupe ‖ (*mil.*) in electronic warfare, a floating radar reflector used to simulate a surface target at sea for deceptive purposes [etym. doubtful]

gull *n.* a bird of fam. *Laridae*, esp. any of several members of *Larus*, a cosmopolitan genus of web-footed, long-winged seabirds usually found near coasts, where they feed largely on fish and mollusks and scavenge refuse. They have stout, curved bills and strong legs. Their plumage is generally white with gray markings. They have a harsh cry [M.E. perh. fr. Celt.]

gul·let (gʌ́lit) *n.* the esophagus ‖ the throat ‖ (*biol.*) something like the esophagus in appearance or purpose ‖ a channel for water ‖ a gully [M.E. *golet* fr. O.F.]

gul·li·bil·i·ty (gʌləbíliti:) *n.* the state or quality of being gullible

gul·li·ble (gʌ́ləb'l) *adj.* easily deceived or cheated [fr. GULL v.]

gul·ly (gʌ́li:) **1.** *pl.* **gul·lies** *n.* a small steep valley made by water ‖ (*cricket*) the position in the field between point and slips ‖ the player occupying this position **2.** *v.t. pres. part.* **gul·ly·ing** *past* and *past part.* **gul·lied** to make channels in [prob. var. of GULLET]

gulp (gʌlp) **1.** *v.t.* (often with 'down') to swallow (usually a drink) quickly or greedily ‖ (with 'down') to suppress by the action of swallowing convulsively, *to gulp down one's rage* ‖ *v.i.* to swallow food or drink quickly or greedily ‖ to gasp, pant, *to gulp for breath* **2.** *n.* the act of gulping ‖ an action like a swallow, e.g. a suppressed sob ‖ a large mouthful [imit.] ‖ (*computer*) a unit consisting of a number of bytes treated as a word

gum (gʌm) **1.** *n.* a sticky liquid that exudes from some trees and shrubs and is also obtained from some seaweeds, dissolving in water, hardening in air, and used as an adhesive or thickening agent in making emulsions, cosmetics and food preparations, and in calico printing ‖ a substance resembling this ‖ a candy made from gelatin or from some other gumlike substance ‖ chewing gum ‖ a gum tree ‖ the secretion which collects in the corner of the eyes ‖ a disease of fruit trees marked by morbid secretion of gum (* RESIN) **2.** *v. pres. part.* **gum·ming** *past* and *past part.* **gummed** *v.t.* to stick with gum, *to gum a loose page in a book* ‖ to clog with gum ‖ to smear with gum ‖ *v.i.* to exude gum ‖ to become gummy **to gum up the works** to cause great delay or bring things to a halt in confusion [M.E. *gomme* fr. O.F. fr. L. fr. Gk]

gum *n.* the flesh by which the teeth are partly surrounded ‖ (often *pl.*) the alveolar part of the jaw [O.E. *gōma*]

Gu·mal (gəmʌ́l) (or Gomal) a river (150 miles long) flowing from E. Afghanistan to the Indus in Pakistan ‖ the pass (summit 7,500 ft) which it cuts through the Sulaiman Mtns

gum ammoniac a gum resin obtained from *Dorema ammoniacum*, a Persian plant, used in medicine as a cement

gum arabic an odorless, tasteless gum, widely used as an adhesive, derived from a few wild species of acacia, e.g. *Acacia arabica* and *A. senegal*

gum·bo (gʌ́mbou) *n.* the okra plant or its pods ‖ a soup thickened with gummy okra pods and containing vegetables and meat or seafood ‖ fine silty soil, chiefly in the western U.S.A., which becomes waxy when it is saturated with water **Gum·bo** a Creole patois spoken esp. in Louisiana [dialect, of Bantu origin]

gum·boil (gʌ́mboil) *n.* a small abscess or boil on the gums

gum boot a loose, heavy waterproof rubber boot without laces, coming almost to the knee

gum·drop (gʌ́mdrɒp) *n.* (*Am.=Br.* wine gum) a candy made from flavored gelatin etc.

gum elemi elemi

gum·ma (gʌ́mə) *pl.* **gum·mas, gum·ma·ta** (gʌ́mətə) *n.* (*med.*) a syphilitic lump with gummy contents **gúm·ma·tous** *adj.* [Mod. L. fr. *gummi*, gum]

gum·mi·ness (gʌ́mi:nis) *n.* the quality or state of being gummy

gum·my (gʌ́mi:) *comp.* **gúm·mi·er** *superl.* **gúm·mi·est** *adj.* sticky, gumlike ‖ containing gum

gump·tion (gʌ́mpʃən) *n.* (*pop.*) drive and initiative [Scot.]

gum resin a mixture of gum and resin extracted from certain plants. The chief gum resins are gum ammoniac, asafetida, gamboge, myrrh and scammony

gum tree any of several trees that exude gum, esp. certain kinds of eucalyptus **up a gum tree** (*Br.*) in a fix

gun (gʌn) **1.** *n.* any weapon, e.g. a revolver, rifle, machine gun, cannon or piece of artillery, having a metal tube along which a bullet or shell is propelled by explosive force ‖ an air gun ‖ a toy imitation of any such weapon ‖ a tool etc. like a gun in that it ejects some object, substance etc. ‖ (*Br.*) a person taking part in a shoot, *a party of six guns went out* **to blow great guns** to blow at gale force **to go great guns** to be in excellent form **to stick to one's guns** to defend doggedly one's position in argument or refuse to give up in any situation ‖ (*surfing*) a round-nosed board used when waves are high (15 ft plus) **2.** *v. pres. part.* **gun·ning** *past* and *past part.* **gunned** *v.t.* (esp. with 'down') to shoot, *troops were gunning down civilians* ‖ (*pop.*) to accelerate (a motor, engine etc.) ‖ *v.i.* (*pop.*) to go at high speed **to gun for** to hunt for with a gun ‖ to look for in order to harm or reprimand ‖ (*pop.*) to try to get, *gunning for office* [M.E. *gunne, gonne*, etym. doubtful]

gun·boat (gʌ́nbout) *n.* a small but heavily armed vessel of shallow draft for patrol and for shore bombardment

gun carriage a structure on which a gun may be mounted for firing, transportation etc.

gun·cot·ton (gʌ́nkɒt'n) *n.* a cellulose nitrate, esp. a higher-nitrated one used as an explosive

gun·dog (gʌ́ndɒg, gʌ́ndɔg) *n.* a dog trained to work with a hunter out shooting

gun·fire (gʌ́nfaiər) *n.* a firing from guns ‖ (*mil.*) the firing of all guns of a troop, battery etc. on a target, esp. after ranging by one gun only

gun·lock (gʌ́nlɒk) *n.* the mechanism in a gun by which the charge is fired

gun·man (gʌ́nmən) *pl.* **gun·men** (gʌ́nmən) *n.* a thief or killer armed with a gun

gun·met·al (gʌ́nmet'l) *n.* a variety of bronze containing essentially 9 parts of copper to 1 part of tin, from which cannon were formerly cast ‖ any of several dark gray metals or alloys used for belt buckles, toys etc. ‖ the dark gray color of such metals

Gunn effect *n.* (*electr.*) the occurrence of microwave oscillation in a type of gallium arsenide when a constant DC voltage is applied on the opposite face. Used in amplifiers, radar, etc., it was discovered by J. B. Gunn in 1963. —**Gunn amplifier** *n.* —**Gunn diode** *n.* —**Gunn oscillator** *n.*

gun·nel (gʌ́n'l) *n.* any of several small, marine blennies, esp. *Pholis gunnelus* of the N. Atlantic [origin unknown]

gunnel *GUNWALE

gun·ner (gʌ́nər) *n.* an artillery corporal who aims the gun ‖ a naval warrant officer in charge of a ship's guns ‖ (*Br.*) a private in the artillery ‖ (*pop.*) any member of an artillery unit ‖ the member of an aircraft crew who mans the gun ‖ the man who fires the harpoon on a whaler

gun·ner·y (gʌ́nəri:) *n.* (*mil.*) the science of the use of guns

gun·ny (gʌ́ni:) *n.* coarse cloth, usually made from jute, used for sacks [Hindi *gōn, gōnī*]

gun·ny·sack (gʌ́ni:sæk) *n.* a sack made of gunny

gun·pow·der (gʌ́npaudər) *n.* an explosive made from saltpeter, sulfur and charcoal now largely superseded by more powerful explosives, but still used in fireworks

Gunpowder Plot *FAWKES

gun room (*Br.*) a room in a warship for junior officers ‖ a room in a private house where sporting guns are kept

gun·run·ning (gʌ́nrʌniŋ) *n.* the unlawful smuggling of arms and ammunition across frontiers

gun·ship (gʌ́nʃip) *n.* (*mil.*) a heavily armed helicopter

gun·shot (gʌ́nʃɒt) *n.* shot fired from a gun ‖ range of fire, *out of gunshot*

gun-shy (gʌ́nʃai) *adj.* (esp. of hunting dogs) frightened at the noise of a gun

gun·smith (gʌ́nsmiθ) *n.* someone who makes and repairs small firearms

gun·stock (gʌ́nstɒk) *n.* the wooden stock of a shotgun or similar firearm

gun·ter (gʌ́ntər) *n.* a gunter rig ‖ Gunter's scale [after Edmund *Gunter* (1581–1626), Eng. mathematician]

gunter rig (*naut.*) a rig consisting of a topmast which slides up and down the lower mast on rings

Gunter's chain a chain 66 ft long consisting of 100 links, a unit of length used in surveying public lands

Gunter's scale a rule giving the logarithms of chords, sines, tangents etc.

Gun·tur (guntúər) a town (pop. 269,991) and rail center in Andhra Pradesh, E. India: tobacco, cotton

gun·wale, gun·nel (gʌ́n'l) *n.* the upper edge of the side of a ship or boat [fr. GUN+WALE fr. its earlier use to support a ship's guns]

gup·py (gʌ́pi:) *pl.* **gup·pies** *n.* *Lebistes reticulatus*, fam. *Poeciliidae*, a small ornamental freshwater fish popular in home aquariums. Guppies are native to the S. West Indies and N. South America, where they feed on mosquito larvae. The adults are cannibalistic and often eat their young [after R. J. L. *Guppy*, naturalist of Trinidad]

Gup·ta (gúptə) a dynasty of N. India, founded (c. 320) by Chandragupta I, destroyed by the Huns (mid–6th c.)

gur·gi·ta·tion (gə:rdʒitéiʃən) *n.* ebullient motion, esp. of water [fr. L.L. *gurgitare* (*gurgitatus*), to flood]

gur·gle (gə́:rg'l) **1.** *v. pres. part.* **gur·gling** *past* and *past part.* **gur·gled** *v.i.* to make a bubbling sound like water being poured from a bottle or sucked over stones ‖ *v.t.* to utter with such a bubbling sound, *she gurgled her thanks* **2.** *n.* the sound made in gurgling [imit.]

gur·jun (gə́:rdʒən) *n.* any of several members of *Dipterocarpus*, fam. *Dipterocarpaceae*, a genus of E. Indian trees yielding gurjun balsam ‖ gurjun balsam [Bengali *garjan*]

gurjun balsam a thin oleoresin used in varnish, obtained from the gurjun

Gur·kha, Gur·khas *n.* (*hist.*) a member of a race inhabiting the kingdom of Gurkha in Nepal ‖ (since the 18th c.) a native of Nepal ‖ a Nepalese soldier in the Indian army or in the Gurkha Regiment of the British army

gur·nard (gə́:rnərd) *pl.* **gur·nard, gur·nards** *n.* a member of *Triglidae*, a family of marine fishes found in tropical and temperate seas, with large pectoral fins which have feelers used for crawling on the bottom. Gurnard have a nearly round, tapering body, and a spiny head covered with bony plates [prob. fr. F. *grognard*, fr. *grogner*, to grunt]

gur·net (gə́:rnit) *n.* a gurnard

gu·ru (gúəru:, gurú:) *n.* a Hindu religious teacher and spiritual adviser [Hindi] ‖ any leading figure; a great teacher

gush (gʌʃ) **1.** *v.i.* to flow or pour out in torrents, *water gushed from the burst main* ‖ to behave or speak with sloppy or affected excess of feeling, *women gushed over the young painter* ‖ to produce a copious flow of something, *the wound gushed with blood* ‖ *v.t.* to emit suddenly or copiously, *his eyes gushed tears* ‖ to utter too effusively, *'I adore Greece', she gushed* **2.** *n.* an outpour ‖ the fluid etc. emitted in such an outpour ‖ exaggerated display of feeling, esp. insincere, *his welcome was mere gush* **gúsh·er** *n.* an oil well in which the oil spurts from the ground without pumping **gúsh·i·ly** *adv.* in a gushy manner **gúsh·i·ness** *n.* the quality or state of being gushy **gúsh·y** *comp.* **gúsh·i·er** *superl.* **gúsh·i·est** *adj.* fulsomely effusive [M.E. *gosshe, gusche* prob. imit.]

gus·set (gʌ́sit) *n.* a triangular piece of cloth inserted so as to widen or strengthen a garment ‖ a reinforcing device, e.g. a triangular piece of metal in a corner of a structure [O.F. *gouchet, gousset* from a point in a suit of armor]

gust (gʌst) *n.* a strong burst of wind ‖ a sudden brief rush, emission, puff etc., *a gust of smoke* ‖ an outburst of emotion, *a gust of anger* [O.N. *gustr*]

Gus·taf (gʌ́stæf) *GUSTAVUS (kings of Sweden)

gus·ta·tion (gʌstéiʃən) *n.* the act of tasting ‖ (*rhet.*) the sense of taste [fr. L. *gustatio* (*gustationis*)]

gus·ta·to·ry (gʌ́stətɔri:, gʌ́stətouri:) *adj.* pertaining to the act of tasting or sense of taste [fr. L. *gustare* (*gustatus*), to taste]

Gus·ta·vus I Vasa (gʌstávəs) (1496–1560), king of Sweden (1523–60), founder of the Vasa dynasty. He led a successful Swedish revolt against Danish rule (1521). Elected king (1523), he made Sweden a strong, united country, freeing her (1537) from the economic dominance of the Hanseatic League, and establishing Lutheranism as the state religion (1529)

Gustavus II A·dol·phus (ədɒ́lfəs) (1594–1632), king of Sweden (1611–32), grandson of Gusta-

CONCISE PRONUNCIATION KEY: (a) æ, c*a*t; ɑ, c*a*r; ɔ f*aw*n; ei, sn*a*ke. (e) e, h*e*n; i:, sh*ee*p; iə, d*ee*r; ɛə, b*ea*r. (i) i, f*i*sh; ai, t*i*ger; ə:, b*i*rd. (o) o, *o*x; au, c*ow*; ou, g*oa*t; u, p*oo*r; ɔi, r*oy*al. (u) ʌ, d*u*ck; u, b*u*ll; u:, g*oo*se; ə, b*a*cillus; ju:, c*u*be. x, lo*ch*; θ, *th*ink; ð, bo*th*er; z, *Z*en; ʒ, cor*s*age; dʒ, sava*ge*; ŋ, orangutan*g*; j, *y*ak; ʃ, *f*ish; tʃ, fe*tch*; 'l, rabb*le*; 'n, redd*en*. Complete pronunciation key appears inside front cover.

vus I. A great statesman and military genius, he made Sweden powerful, and, fighting for the Protestant cause against the Empire in the Thirty Years' War, he conquered most of Germany. He was killed at the Battle of Lützen

Gustavus III (1746–92), king of Sweden (1771–92). He strengthened royal authority by two coups d'état (1772 and 1789). He was assassinated by a group of nobles

Gustavus IV (1778–1837), king of Sweden (1792–1809). A reactionary, he was deposed and his family was barred from the throne

Gustavus V (1858–1950), king of Sweden (1907–50)

Gustavus VI (Gustaf Adolf) (1882–1973), king of Sweden (1950–73), son of Gustavus V

gust·i·ly (gástili) *adv.* in a gusty manner

gus·to (gástou) *n.* enthusiastic enjoyment, zest [Ital.=taste]

gust·y (gásti:) *comp.* **gust·i·er** *superl.* **gust·i·est** *adj.* coming in gusts, *gusty rain* ‖ marked by gusts of wind, *a gusty day* ‖ characterized by sudden outbursts, *gusty laughter*

gut (gʌt) **1.** *n.* (*pl., pop.*) entrails ‖ (*pl., pop.*) pluck and determination ‖ (*pl., pop.*) forceful content, *the pictures are pretty but lack guts* ‖ (*physiol.*) the alimentary canal or its lower part ‖ a piece of animal intestine used for the strings of musical instruments, fishing lines, tennis rackets and surgical stitching (*CATGUT) ‖ (*angling*) the silken substance taken from silkworms ready to spin their cocoons, used for snoods ‖ a narrow passage of water **2.** *v.t. pres. part.* **gut·ting** *past* and *past part.* **gut·ted** to remove the entrails of ‖ to destroy all but the framework of, *fire gutted the house* ‖ to extract what is essential from, *to gut a book* **3.** *adj.* (*colloq.*) intuitive, *gut reaction* ‖ basic, *gut issues* [O.E. *guttas* pl.]

gut·ate (gáteit) *adj.* shaped like a drop

gut course *n.* (*colloq.*) an easy college course; a snap course

Gu·ten·berg (gú:t'nberk) (Johannes Gensfleisch, c. 1397–1468), German printer. He invented (c. 1436) printing from movable type. The first printed Latin Bible, known as the Gutenberg Bible (1452–5), is attributed to him

gut·fight·er (gátfaitər) *n.* one who fights with all he has; a tough adversary

Guth·rum (gú:rəm) (d. 890), Danish king of East Anglia. He led Danish raids on Wessex (871–8) and reached agreement with Alfred at Wedmore (878). Under this treaty, Guthrum became a Christian and confined Danish settlement to E. England

Gu·tiér·rez Ná·je·ra (gu:tjérresnaherɑ), Manuel (1859–95), Mexican poet who founded (1894) the 'Revista azul', the first modernist journal of Mexico. His poems, notably 'La Duquesa Job' and 'La Serenata de Schubert' illustrate the transition between romanticism and modernism

gut·ta (gátɑ) *pl.* **gut·tae** (gáti:), **gut·tas** *n.* (*archit.*) a droplike ornament forming one of a series, esp. on a Doric entablature [L. =drop]

gut·ta-per·cha (gátəpá:rtʃə) *n.* a substance resembling rubber but more resinous and with less change when vulcanized, obtained from any of several Malayan trees of genera *Payena* and *Palaquium*, fam. *Sapotaceae*. Gutta-percha is used esp. in dentistry and as electrical insulation in submarine cables [Malay *getah*, gum + *percha*, name of tree]

gut·ter (gátər) **1.** *n.* a metal trough along the edge of a roof to catch and carry away rainwater ‖ a channel in a road for draining off rainwater, specifically the channel formed along the sides of town streets by the angle between curb and road surface ‖ slum environment, *he rose from the gutter to become prime minister* ‖ the space formed by the adjoining inside margins at the center opening of a book ‖ (*philately*) the spaces between stamps in sheets to permit perforation ‖ a channel, conduit or groove **2.** *v.t.* to make channels in ‖ *v.i.* (of water) to flow in channels ‖ (of candles) to melt away as the wax runs down at the side and burn fitfully or feebly [O.F. *gutiere, goutiere* fr. *goutte*, drop]

gut·ter·snipe (gátərsnaip) *n.* a street urchin

gut·tur·al (gátərəl) **1.** *adj.* of the throat ‖ (of speech sounds) produced in the throat, e.g. 'k' and 'g' ‖ throaty, harsh, grating **2.** *n.* a guttural sound in speech **gút·tur·al·ize** *pres. part.* **tur·al·iz·ing** *past* and *past part.* **gut·tur·al·ized** *v.t.* (*phon.*) to make guttural [fr. Mod. L. *gutturalis*]

guy (gai) **1.** *n.* a rope or chain to keep something steady or in place, *the guys of a tent* **2.** *v.t.* to fasten with a guy [fr. O.F. *guie*, a guide]

guy 1. *n.* (esp. *Am., pop.*) a man, fellow ‖ (*Br.*) a person of ludicrous appearance **Guy** (*Br.*) an effigy of Guy Fawkes, carried around the streets and burned on Nov. 5 **2.** *v.t.* to ridicule, esp. by burlesque parody [after *Guy Fawkes*]

Gu·ya·na (gaiǽnə, gaiánə) a republic (area 83,000 sq. miles, pop. 834,000) in N.E. South America. People: 42% East Indian, 38% of African descent with Mulatto and Indian minorities. Religion: 60% Christian, with Hindu, Moslem and other minorities. Capital: Georgetown. The land is 4% arable and 87% forest (gum and dyewoods, tropical hardwoods). Behind the coastal agricultural plain (10–60 miles wide) is a forest strip (with mineral deposits) then mountain ranges (Mt Roraima, 8,260 ft) and savanna. Wet seasons: Apr.–Aug. and Nov.–Jan. Annual rainfall: 90 ins along the coast, less in the interior. Average temperatures (F.): 70°–90° along the coast, 86°–103° in the interior. Exports: sugar, rice, rum, lumber, bauxite, manganese, diamonds. Other products: cattle, coconuts, gold. Imports: machinery, fuel oils, foodstuffs. Ports: Georgetown, New Amsterdam. Monetary unit: British West Indian dollar. University (1963, in Georgetown). HISTORY. The Guiana coast, then inhabited by Indians, was first sighted (1498) by Columbus. The Dutch founded settlements (1596, 1625, 1627) which were captured by the British (1796), retaken by the Dutch (1802–3) and finally ceded to Britain (1814) as British Guiana. The colony received full internal self-government (Aug. 1961) with Jagan as premier. Jagan was succeeded (1964) by Burnham, under whom the colony became fully independent (May 26, 1966) and a member of the British Commonwealth. In 1968 Burnham was reelected over Jagan. Guyana became (Feb. 1970) a republic. A constitution was adopted in 1980 providing for a president, prime minister and unicameral legislature. Burnham was the first president and ruled until his death in 1985, when prime minister Hoyte succeeded him

Guy·enne (gyjen) a former province of S.W. France, known before the 13th c. as Aquitaine. It forms most of coastal Gironde, Dordogne and parts of Lot-et-Garonne and Tarn-et-Garonne in the Aquitaine Basin, and Lot and Aveyron in the Massif Central. Industries: agriculture (mainly cereals and vines), wine, livestock (sheep, beef and dairy cattle), food processing, petroleum (concentrated near Bordeaux, historic capital and main port). Regained from the English in 1453, it was attached to the Crown from 1472

Guy Fawkes Day *FAWKES

Guy·on (gyi:jɔ̃), Madame (Jeanne-Marie Bouvier de la Motte Guyon du Chesnoy, 1648–1717), French mystic. Her quietist teaching influenced Fénelon. She was imprisoned for heresy in the Bastille (1695–1702)

Guz·mán Blan·co (gu:smánblángkɔ), Antonio (1829–99), Venezuelan dictator. As dictator (1870–3) and constitutional president (1873–88), he suppressed the news media and attacked the Roman Catholic Church. He maintained absolute power in Venezuela even though he spent much of his time in Europe

guz·zle (gáz'l) *pres. part.* **guz·zling** *past* and *past part.* **guz·zled** *v.t.* and *i.* to drink or eat greedily and rapidly [earlier *gussel* perh. fr. O.F. *gosiller* fr. *gosier*, throat]

GVH disease *n.* (*med.*) a disorder caused by transplanted tissue attacking the tissue of the host (as opposed to being rejected by the host)

Gwa·li·or (gwáli:ɔr) a former principality of central India, incorporated (1948) in Madhya Bharat State (which became (1956) Madhya Pradesh) ‖ its old capital (pop. 384,772), famous for its medieval hill fort. The new industrial town of Lashkar is part of Gwalior

Gwe·lo (gwéilou) a town (pop. 72,000) in Zimbabwe: agricultural and rail center

Gwyn (gwin), Nell (Eleanor Gwyn, c. 1650–87), English actress and mistress of Charles II, by whom she had two children

gybe *JIBE

gym (dʒim) *n.* a gymnasium ‖ gymnastics [GYMNASIUM]

gym·kha·na (dʒimkánə) *n.* a fete with horseback riding and competitions ‖ (*motor racing*) impromptu competition over a twisting course

[GYMNASTICS+Hind. (gend-)khana, racket court]

gym·na·si·um (dʒimnéizi:əm) *pl.* **gym·na·si·a** (dʒimnéizi:ə), **gym·na·si·ums** *n.* a room or building for physical exercise, with ropes, vaulting horses, wall bars etc. and changing rooms, shower baths etc., and sometimes also equipped for indoor sports ‖ a type of secondary school in Europe, esp. in Germany, for students preparing for the university [L. fr. Gk *gumnasion* fr. Gk *gumnazein*, to train (naked) fr. *gumnos*, naked]

gym·nast (dʒimnæst) *n.* a person skilled in gymnastics [fr. Gk *gumnastēs*, a trainer of athletes]

gym·nas·tic (dʒimnæstik) *adj.* having to do with gymnastics **gym·nas·tics** *n.* exercises to teach body control and agility and strengthen the muscles [fr. L. *gymnasticus* fr. Gk *gumnastikē* n., gymnastics]

gym·no·sperm (dʒimnəspə:rm) *n.* a seed plant of the class *Gymnospermae* producing seeds not enclosed in an ovary. The class contains many kinds of plants (e.g. conifers, cycads) (cf. ANGIOSPERM, *PTEROPSID) **gym·no·spér·mous** *adj.* [fr. Mod. L. *gymnospermus* fr. Gk *gumnos*, naked + *sperma*, seed]

gy·nae·ce·um (gainisí:əm) *n.* (*Gk* and *Rom. Antiq.*) the women's apartments in a house ‖ a gynoecium [L. fr. Gk *gunaikeion*]

gy·nan·dro·morph (gainǽndrəmɔrf) *n.* an organism in which the body is of fundamentally different constitution in different parts, male in some, female in others (cf. HERMAPHRODITE) [fr. Gk *gunandros*, of doubtful sex fr. *gunē*, woman + *anēr* (*andros*), man + *morphē*, shape]

gy·nan·drous (gainǽndrəs) *adj.* having stamens fused with pistils, as in some orchids [fr. Gk *gunandros*, of doubtful sex]

gy·ne·coc·ra·cy, gy·nae·coc·ra·cy (gainikɔ́krəsi:) *n.* rule by women [fr. Gk *gunaikokratia* fr. *gunē* (*gunaikos*), woman + *kratos*, power]

gy·ne·col·o·gist, gy·nae·col·o·gist (gainikɔ́lədʒist) *n.* a specialist in gynecology

gy·ne·col·o·gy, gy·nae·col·o·gy (gainikɔ́lədʒi:) *n.* the study of women's diseases, esp. diseases of the female genital organs and urinary disturbances, excluding problems occurring in late pregnancy (cf. OBSTETRICS) [fr. Gk *gunē* (*gunaikos*), woman + *logos*, discourse]

gy·noe·ci·um, gy·ne·ci·um (gainí:si:əm) *pl.* **gy·noe·ci·a, gy·ne·ci·a** (gainí:si:ə) *n.* the female reproductive organ of a flower, composed of one or more carpels [GYNAECEUM, confused with Gk *oikion*, house]

gy·no·phore (gáinəfɔr, gáinəfour) *n.* (*bot.*) the stalk supporting the ovary, an elongation of the thalamus between stamens and pistil [fr. Gk *gunē*, woman + *-phoros*, bearing]

Győr (djə:r) an industrial city and rail center (pop. 124,500) on an arm of the Danube in N.W. Hungary: milling, distilling, leather, textiles, rolling stock

gyp (dʒip) **1.** *n.* (*pop.*) a cheat, swindle ‖ (*pop.*) a swindler ‖ (*Br.*) a college manservant, esp. at Cambridge University **2.** *v.i.* and *t. pres. part.* **gyp·ping** *past* and *past part.* **gypped** (*pop.*) to swindle, cheat [prob. fr. GYPSY]

gy·plure (dʒípluər) *n.* (*entomology*) synthetic sex attractant for a female gypsy moth

gyp·soph·i·la (dʒipsófilə) *n.* a plant belonging to *Gypsophila*, fam. *Caryophyllaceae*, a genus of hardy annuals bearing tiny white flowers on threadlike stalks [Mod. L. fr. Gk *gupsos*, chalk + *philos*, loving]

gyp·sum (dʒípsəm) **1.** *n.* a mineral, hydrated calcium sulfate (CaSO₄·2H₂O), used as a fertilizer, and to make plaster of paris **2.** *v.t.* to treat with gypsum as manure [L. fr. Gk *gupsos*, gypsum, chalk]

gypsum board plasterboard

gypsy cab an unlicensed taxicab, often operating in urban areas considered dangerous

gyp·sy, gip·sy (dʒípsi:) *pl.* **gyp·sies, gip·sies 1.** *n.* a member of a swarthy Caucasoid people believed to have originated in India and to have entered Europe in the 14th or 15th c. Gypsies are found chiefly in Turkey, Russia, Poland, Hungary, Spain, England, and the U.S.A., in dwindling numbers. They are characterized by their itinerant way of life, their refusal to be assimilated into the culture of adopted countries, and their tribal organization and culture. They have made their living as horse dealers, peddlers, musicians (esp. in central Europe before the 2nd World War), makers of brooms and baskets, metalworkers and fortune-tellers. Their language is Romany **2.** *adj.* of or relating

CONCISE PRONUNCIATION KEY: **(a)** æ, c*a*t; ɑ, c*a*r; ɔ f*aw*n; ei, sn*a*ke. **(e)** e, h*e*n; i:, sh*ee*p; iə, d*ee*r; ɛə, b*ea*r. **(i)** i, f*i*sh; ai, t*i*ger; ə:, b*i*rd. **(o)** o, *o*x; au, c*ow*; ou, g*oa*t; u, p*oo*r; ɔi, r*oy*al. **(u)** ʌ, d*u*ck; u, b*u*ll; u:, g*oo*se; ə, b*a*cillus; ju:, c*u*be. x, lo*ch*; θ, *th*ink; ð, bo*th*er; z, *Z*en; ʒ, corsa*g*e; dʒ, sava*g*e; ŋ, oranguta*ng*; j, *y*ak; ʃ, *fi*sh; tʃ, *fe*tch; 'l, rabb*le*; 'n, redd*en*. Complete pronunciation key appears inside front cover.

to a gypsy or gypsies [earlier *gipcyan* for Egyptian]

gypsy moth, gipsy moth *Porthetria dispar*, fam. *Lymantriidae*, a brownish or white European moth, now also common in the U.S.A., whose larvae are destructive to the leaves of trees

gy·rate 1. (dʒairéit, dʒáireit) *v.i. pres. part.* **gy·rat·ing** *past* and *past part.* **gy·rat·ed** to go around in a circle or spiral, whirl, revolve **2.** (dʒáireit) *adj.* (*biol.*) having convolutions **gy·rá·tion** *n.* **gy·ra·to·ry** (dʒáirətɔri:, dʒáirətouri:) *adj.* [fr. L. *gyrare* (*gyratus*)]

gyr·fal·con, ger·fal·con (dʒɜ́:rfɔlken, dʒɜ́:rfælkən) *n.* any large falcon of arctic regions in Europe, Asia or North America [O.F. *gerfaucon*]

gy·ro (dʒáirou) *n.* a gyroscope ‖ a gyrocompass

gy·ro·com·pass (dʒáiroukʌmpəs) *n.* a compass whose essential element is a continuously driven gyroscope, the spinning axis of which is allowed to move only in a horizontal plane. Because of the earth's rotation, this axis aligns itself with that of the earth and so points true north (cf. MAGNETIC COMPASS) [fr. Gk *guros*, ring+ COMPASS]

gy·ro·cop·ter (dʒáirəkɒptər) *n.* single-passenger autogyro with a forward propeller

gy·ro·mag·netic (dʒairoumægnétik) *adj.* having to do with the magnetism of a rotating electrical particle [fr. Gk *guros*, ring+MAGNETIC]

gy·ro·pi·lot (dʒáirəpɑilət) *n.* an automatic pilot [GYROSCOPE+PILOT]

gy·ro·plane (dʒáirəplein) *n.* an aircraft with a horizontal propeller the pitch of whose blades may be varied [GYROSCOPE +AIRPLANE]

gy·ro·scope (dʒáirəskoup) *n.* a rapidly spinning wheel mounted in such a way that its plane of rotation can vary. Its moment of inertia, however, keeps this plane constant in space unless a very large couple is applied. Gyroscopes are used in navigation (e.g. in the gyrocompass), as stabilizers and in scientific instruments **gy·ro·scop·ic** (dʒairəskɔ́pik) *adj.* [F. fr. Gk *guros*, ring+*skopein*, to observe]

gy·rose (dʒáirous) *adj.* (*bot.*) marked with wavy lines [fr. Gk *guros*, ring]

gy·ro·sta·bi·liz·er (dʒairoustéib'l̩aizər) *n.* a gyroscopic mechanism for stabilizing a ship or aircraft [GYROSCOPE+STABILIZER]

gy·ro·stat (dʒáirəstæt) *n.* an instrument for demonstrating the principles of gyrostatics ‖ a gyrostabilizer **gy·ro·stát·ic** *adj.* **gy·ro·stát·ics** *n.* the branch of physics concerned with rotating bodies [fr. Gk *guros*, ring+*statos*, standing]

gy·ro·tron (dʒáirətrɒn) *n.* device used to measure motion of a system, based on a vibrating tuning fork whose movement frequency changes when it moves

EARLY NORTH SEMITIC	PHOENICIAN	EARLY HEBREW	EARLY GREEK	CLASSICAL GREEK	ETRUSCAN		EARLY LATIN	CLASSICAL LATIN
					Early	Classical		
ᛡ	ᛡ	ᛢ	⊟	⊟	ᛢ	⊟	⊟	H

CURSIVE MAJUSCULE (ROMAN)	CURSIVE MINUSCULE (ROMAN)	ANGLO-IRISH MAJUSCULE	CAROLINE MINUSCULE	VENETIAN MINUSCULE (ITALIC)	N. ITALIAN MINUSCULE (ROMAN)
Ᏺ	f	h	b	ƀ	ɧ

A. C. SYLVESTER, CAMBRIDGE, ENGLAND

Development of the letter H, beginning with the early North Semitic letter. Evolution of both the majuscule, or capital, letter H and the minuscule, or lowercase, letter h are shown.

H, h (eitʃ) the eighth letter of the English alphabet. Its sound is the aspiration of the following vowel but it is sometimes (e.g. in heir, honor) not sounded ‖ (chem.) the symbol for the element hydrogen ‖ (engin.) an H-shaped steel girder

Haa·kon I (hɔ́kon) (c. 914–c. 961), king of Norway (c. 935–c. 961)

Haakon VII (1872–1957), king of Norway (1905–57). During the German occupation (1940–5) of Norway, he led a government-in-exile in Britain

Haarlem *HARLEM

Ha·bak·kuk (hǽbəkək) a Minor Prophet (c. 7th c. B.C.) of the Old Testament ‖ the book of the Old Testament which bears his name. The book considers why God permits the good to suffer, and states that the just shall live by faith

hab·e·as cor·pus (héibi:əskɔ́rpəs) n. (law) a writ issued by a judge requiring an imprisoned person to be brought to a stated place at a stated time, usually to a court, for the legality of his imprisonment to be examined. It was made enforceable in England by the Habeas Corpus Act (1679), and it is guaranteed in the Constitution of the U.S.A. In both countries the right of habeas corpus may be suspended only in emergency

hab·er·dash·er (hǽbərdæʃər) n. the keeper of a men's clothing store ‖ (Br.) a dealer in small articles and materials used in sewing, such as needles, buttons, thread, trimmings etc. **hab·er·dash·er·y** (hǽbərdæʃəri) pl. **hab·er·dash·er·ies** n. goods sold by a haberdasher ‖ a shop where these are sold [perh. fr. A.F. hapertas, origin unknown]

hab·er·geon (hǽbərdʒən) n. (hist.) a sleeveless coat of mail protecting the neck and chest [F. haubergeon]

Ha·ber process (húbər) (chem.) a method for synthesizing ammonia by the catalyzed combination of nitrogen and hydrogen at high temperature and pressure [after Fritz Haber (1868-1934), G. chemist]

ha·bil·i·ments (həbíləmənts) pl. n. the distinctive garb of a profession etc. or the garb appropriate to a particular occasion [M.E. abilyment fr. O.F. habillement, abillement, outfit, attire]

hab·it (hǽbit) n. a tendency to repeat an act again and again, he has a habit of scratching his head when thinking ‖ a behavior pattern that has a degree of automatism, smoking is an expensive habit ‖ a monk's or nun's robe ‖ a woman's tailored dress for riding sidesaddle ‖ (biol.) a characteristic mode of growth and appearance or occurrence [M.E. abit, habite fr. O.F.]

hab·it·a·ble (hǽbitəb'l) adj. able to be lived in [F.]

ha·bi·tant (ǽbi:tā, hǽbitənt) pl. **ha·bi·tants** (ǽbi:tā, hǽbit'nts) n. a Canadian, esp. a farmer, of French descent [F.]

hab·i·tat (hǽbitæt) n. a place or region inhabited by an animal or plant in the natural state ‖ underwater housing for researchers [L.=it dwells]

ha·bi·ta·tion (hæbitéiʃən) n. the act of living in a place, fit for human habitation ‖ (rhet.) a place or building lived in [M.E. habitacioun fr. O.F.]

ha·bit·u·al (həbítʃu:əl) adj. (of an act) performed as the result of a habit, habitual theft ‖ (of a person) having a fixed habit, confirmed, a habitual thief ‖ (of a thing) usual, accustomed, in its habitual place [fr. M.L. habitualis fr. habitus, condition]

ha·bit·u·ate (həbítʃu:eit) pres. part. **ha·bit·u·at·ing** past and past part. **ha·bit·u·at·ed** v.t. to make familiar by repetition, to habituate oneself to noise **ha·bit·u·á·tion** n. a habituating or being habituated [fr. L. habituare (habituatus) fr. habitus, condition]

ha·bit·u·é (həbítʃu:ei, həbítʃu:éi) n. someone who assiduously frequents a place, e.g. a particular restaurant [F.]

Habsburg *HAPSBURG

ha·chure (hæʃúər) 1. n. (pl.) short parallel lines used in mapmaking to indicate broadly relief and degree of slope 2. v.t. pres. part. **ha·chur·ing** past and past part. **ha·chured** to mark (part of a map) with hachures or indicate (a feature) by hachures [F. fr. hacher, to cut into small pieces]

ha·ci·en·da (hɑsi:éndə) n. a large property in Latin America (esp. Mexico and Chile), devoted to cash crops or monoculture, or worked as a sheep or cattle ranch. The term is used with inclusive or particular reference to the owner's residence [Span.]

hack (hæk) 1. n. a horse for riding (as distinguished from a hunter etc.) ‖ a horse let out for hire ‖ a worn-out horse ‖ a writer employed to write matter of no originality or no great literary merit ‖ (pop.) a taxi 2. v.i. to ride on a hired horse ‖ to ride out for pleasure ‖ to do the work of a hack writer ‖ (pop.) to drive a taxi 3. adj. (of a writer) employed to write matter of no originality or no great literary merit ‖ (of writing) of no originality nor great literary merit [HACKNEY]

hack n. (falconry) the board on which a hawk's meat is put ‖ (falconry) the state of partial liberty in which a young hawk is kept while untrained but fed at a board, at hack ‖ a frame for drying out bricks before they are fired ‖ a row or pile of unfired bricks put to dry [var. of HATCH]

hack 1. v.t. to cut by using a sharp blow or succession of blows ‖ to cut unskillfully, carve badly ‖ (sports) to kick or otherwise bruise (the shins of another player) ‖ v.i. to cough repeatedly and raspingly ‖ (with 'at') to make cutting blows ‖ (with 'at') to make wild kicks or hits 2. n. (sports) a bruise or wound caused by a kick ‖ a rough cut made by a sharp blow, he made great hacks in the tree with his blunt ax ‖ a tool used for hacking ‖ a harsh, dry cough [M.E. hacken]

hack·a·more (hǽkəmɔr, hǽkəmour) n. a rope halter, passed through the horse's mouth, used in breaking in a horse [perh. fr. Span. jaquima, headstall of a halter]

hack·ber·ry (hǽkbɛri) pl. **hack·ber·ries** n. a North American hardwood tree of genus Celtis, fam. Ulmaceae, esp. C. occidentalis, bearing an edible purple berry ‖ this fruit ‖ the wood of this tree [fr. Scand.]

hack hammer a hammer with a cutting edge used in dressing stone

hack·ing pocket (hǽkiŋ) a garment pocket with a slanted opening

hack·le (hǽk'l) 1. n. one of the long shining feathers on a cock's neck, erected in combat ‖ one of the erectile bristles on a dog's back and neck ‖ a fishing fly made mainly of filaments from hackle feathers ‖ a steel comb used in combing flax or hemp 2. v.t. pres. part. **hack·ling** past and past part. **hack·led** to dress (flax, hemp) with a hackle [M.E., prob. fr. O.H.G.]

hackles 1. (angling) feathers used to tie flies. 2. (hunting) hair along a hound's spine

hack·ma·tack (hǽkmətæk) n. a coniferous tree, esp. Larix laricina, the American larch [Am. Ind.]

hack·ney (hǽkni) 1. pl. **hack·neys** n. a horse of compact, strong build kept for riding or for driving 2. adj. (of a cab) let out for hire [M.E. hakenai fr. O.F. haquenée, an ambling horse]

hack·neyed (hǽkni:d) adj. made tedious or commonplace by frequent repetition [fr. older hackney v., to make commonplace]

hack·saw (hǽksɔ) n. a narrow steel saw with small teeth, kept taut in a bow-shaped frame and used by hand to cut esp. metal [HACK, to cut+SAW]

hack·work (hǽkwə:rk) n. routine work done by a hack (writer)

had past and past part. of HAVE ‖ used with adjectives and adverbs of comparison to indicate necessity, you had better go or (rhet.) preference, I had sooner die

ha·dal (heíd'l) adj. of the ocean below 6,000 meters

had·dock (hǽdək) pl. **had·dock, had·docks** n. Melanogrammus aeglefinus, fam. Gadidae, a food fish with a dark spot on either side of the body behind the head. It breeds in northern seas, and is smaller than the cod [origin unknown]

hade (heid) **1.** *n.* (*geol.*) the angle made with the vertical by the plane of a rock fault or mineral vein **2.** *v.i. pres. part.* **had·ing** *past* and *past part.* **had·ed** (*geol.*) to make an angle with the vertical [etym. doubtful]

Ha·des (héidi:z) *n.* (*Gk mythol.*) the subterranean world where the spirits of men go at death ‖ hell [Gk *Hades*, one name of Pluto, the god of departed spirits]

Ha·dhra·maut (hɑdrəmáut) a plateau region (averaging 4,500 ft) in E. South Arabia, populated by Hadramis (farmers raising cereals, dates, coconuts and coffee) and Beduins

hadj, hajj (hædʒ) *pl.* **hadj·es, hajj·es** *n.* a pilgrimage made by a Moslem to Mecca [Arab. *hajj*]

hadj·i, haj·ji (hædʒi:) *pl.* **hadj·is, haj·jis** *n.* a title earned by a Moslem by making a hadj and often used as a prefix to his name [Arab. *hājī*, a pilgrim]

Had·ley (hædli:), Arthur Twining (1856–1930), U.S. economist and railroad specialist. As president (1899–1921) of Yale University, he published 'Economics: an Account of the Relations between Private Property and Public Welfare', which opposed governmental control of industry. He advocated a cooperative rather than an individualistic approach to society

had·n't (hæd'nt) *contr.* of 'had not' (*HAVE)

Ha·dri·an (héidri:ən) (popes) *ADRIAN

Hadrian (Publius Aelius Hadrianus, 76–138), Roman emperor (117–38), adopted son and successor of Trajan. He abandoned Trajan's expansionist policy in Asia, consolidated the frontiers of the empire and carried out administrative, military and legal reforms. He traveled widely in the provinces, encouraging the introduction of Roman customs and scholarship, and the building of fine public buildings

Hadrian's Wall a Roman defensive frontier wall (about 74 miles long), which crosses N. Britain from the Tyne to the Solway. It was built (122–8) on the orders of the Emperor Hadrian

Haeck·el (hék'l), Ernst (1834–1919), German biologist and philosopher. Under the influence of Darwin he put forward the gastraea theory ('General Morphology', 1866) to bridge the gap between protozoans and metazoans. He developed Darwin's theory of evolution into a mechanistic monism ('Evolution of Man', 1874)

haemacytometer *HEMACYTOMETER
haemal *HEMAL
haematic *HEMATIC
haematite *HEMATITE
haematoblast *HEMATOBLAST
haematocryal *HEMATOCRYAL
haematocyte *HEMATOCYTE
haematocytometer *HEMATOCYTOMETER
haematology *HEMATOLOGY
haematothermal *HEMATOTHERMAL
haematoxylin *HEMATOXYLIN
haemic *HEMIC
haemocyte *HEMOCYTE
haemoglobin *HEMOGLOBIN
haemolysis *HEMOLYSIS
haemophilia *HEMOPHILIA
haemorrhage *HEMORRHAGE
haemorrhoids *HEMORRHOIDS
haemostatic *HEMOSTATIC

haf·fir (hæfi:r) *n.* (*Arabic*) in North Africa, an artificial pond to collect rainwater

Ha·fiz (hafiz) (Shams ad-Din Mohammed, c. 1320–89), Persian poet. He was the master of the ghazal, a form of ode consisting of couplets with a recurring rhyme

ha·fiz (háfiz) *n.* a Moslem title of respect, esp. for someone who knows the Koran by heart [Arab. *hāfiz*, a person who remembers]

haf·ni·um (hæfni:əm) *n.* a rare tetravalent metallic chemical element (symbol Hf, at. no. 72, at. mass 178.49) that readily emits electrons [fr. L. *Hafnia*, Copenhagen]

haft (hæft, hɑft) **1.** *n.* the handle of a cutting tool or weapon, usually shaped from tough, fibrous wood **2.** *v.t.* to fit with such a handle [O.E. *hæft*]

hag (hæg) *n.* an ugly old woman ‖ a hagfish [M.E. *hegge, hagge* fr. *hægtesse, hægtes*, a witch]

Ha·gar (héigɑr) the Egyptian bondswoman by whom Abraham had Ishmael. After the birth of Isaac, Abraham's wife Sarah drove Hagar and Ishmael away. They were saved from death by an angel, for the boy was destined to be the

father of the Arab peoples (Genesis xvi, xvii, xxi)

Ha·gen (hágən) a steel-manufacturing town (pop. 226,301) in the E. Ruhr, West Germany: also textiles, paper, toolmaking

hag·fish (hægfiʃ) *pl.* **hag·fish, hag·fish·es** *n.* a marine cyclostome of order *Hyperotreta*. They are the lowest group of living vertebrates. They are eel-like, jawless animals which secrete quantities of slime. They have four pairs of tentacles by which they attach themselves to fish, invading and eating their flesh. They are hermaphrodites

Hag·ga·dah (həgádə) that part of Jewish civil and religious law (*TALMUD) which embodies principles and injunctions in tales and legends ‖ the narrative of the Exodus read during Passover [Heb.=a story]

Hag·gai (hægi:ai, hǽgai) a Minor Prophet (6th c. B.C.) of the Old Testament. He urged the Jews to rebuild the Temple after their return to Jerusalem from captivity in Babylonia ‖ the book of the Old Testament which contains his prophecies

hag·gard (hægərd) **1.** *adj.* looking worn out by suffering, worry or overexertion ‖ (of a hawk) caught wild in her adult plumage **2.** *n.* a hawk caught wild in her adult plumage [M.F. *hagard*, untamed, untamed hawk, prob. fr. M.H.G.]

hag·gis (hægis) *n.* a Scottish dish made of the heart, liver, lungs etc. of a sheep, minced with oatmeal, suet and onions, packed into a sheep's stomach and boiled [origin unknown]

hag·gle (hæg'l) **1.** *v.i. pres. part.* **hag·gling** *past* and *past part.* **hag·gled** to argue about the price of an article as a process of buying and selling, or about the conditions attached to an agreement etc. **2.** *n.* an argument about price, terms of agreement etc. [frequentative of Scot. *hag*, to chop, cut]

hag·i·oc·ra·cy (hægi:ókrəsi:, heidʒi:ókrəsi:) *pl.* **hag·i·oc·ra·cies** *n.* government by a group of persons looked upon as holy ‖ a state governed by such a group [fr. Gk *hagios*, holy + *-kratia*, rule]

Hag·i·og·ra·pha (hægi:ógrəfə, heidʒi:ógrəfə) *pl. n.* the books of the Old Testament other than the Law and the Prophets. They comprise Psalms, Proverbs, Job, Song of Solomon, Ruth, Lamentations, Ecclesiastes, Esther, Ezra, Nehemiah and Chronicles. The Hebrew Bible also includes Daniel among the Hagiographa [L.L. fr. Gk *hagios*, holy + *graphos*, written]

hag·i·og·ra·pher (hægi:ógrəfər, heidʒi: ógrəfər) *n.* an author of a book of the Hagiographa ‖ the author of a life of a saint **hag·i·óg·ra·phy** *n.* the writing of the lives of saints [fr. M.L. fr. Gk *hagios*, holy + *graphos*, written]

hag·i·ol·a·try (hægi:ólətri:, heidʒi:ólətri:) *n.* the worship of saints [fr. Gk *hagios*, holy + *latreia*, worship]

hag·i·ol·o·gy (hægi:ólədʒi:, heidʒi:ólədʒi:) *pl.* **hag·i·ol·o·gies** *n.* literature consisting of the lives of saints ‖ a book consisting of such lives, or a list of saints [fr. Gk *hagios*, holy + *logos*, word]

hag·i·o·scope (hægi:əskoup, heidʒi:əskoup) *n.* a squint in a church [fr. Gk *hagios*, holy + *skopein*, to watch]

hag·rid·den (hægrid'n) *adj.* suffering from terrifying dreams, or nameless fears, as if cursed by a witch

Hague, The (heig) (Du. 's-Gravenhage or Den Haag) a city (pop. 606,000) on the North Sea in S. Holland, Netherlands, seat of the government and court (palace) but not the capital (*AMSTERDAM), and seat of the International Court of Justice. It has flourishing handicrafts and an international art trade

Hague Conference of 1899 an international conference called by Czar Nicholas II, held at The Hague, Netherlands, and attended by the representatives of 24 countries. It signed conventions covering the pacific settlement of international disputes, the rules of land warfare, and the application to naval warfare of the principles of the Geneva Convention of 1864. It prohibited the launching of projectiles from balloons, the use of poison gases (not ratified by the U.S.A. or Great Britain), and the use of dumdum bullets. It created the Hague Permanent Court of Arbitration, consisting of a list of judges from which the parties in controversy might select the members of an arbitral tribunal for their particular case

Hague Conference of 1907 an international conference called by Czar Nicholas II, held at The Hague, Netherlands, and attended by the

representatives of 44 countries, including all of Latin America, previously (1899) absent. It signed conventions covering, notably, the laws of land and naval warfare and the rights and duties of neutral powers in time of war. A draft convention for a Judicial Arbitration Court, proposed by the U.S. delegate, helped to establish (1920) the Permanent Court of International Justice

ha·ha (háha) *n.* a fence, hedge or wall hidden in a ditch or trench so as not to interrupt a landscape [F. *haha* perh. fr. *haie*, hedge]

Hahn (hɑn), Otto (1879–1968), German physical chemist. He made important contributions in radioactivity and discovered several new elements, including protactinium (with Meitner). With Strassmann he demonstrated (1938) that neutron bombardment can produce the nuclear fission of uranium. Nobel Prize (1944)

Hahn (ɑn), Reynaldo (1875–1947), French composer and conductor of Venezuelan origin, famous esp. for his collections of songs

hahn·i·um (háni:əm) *n.* (*chem.*) transuranic chemical element 105, radioactive, with atomic weight of 260, half-life of 1.6 sec. Hahnium was synthesized in 1970 at Lawrence Radiation Laboratory and named for German chemist Otto H. Hahn

haick *HAIK

Hai·fa (háifə) a port (pop. 229,300) and industrial center of Israel: oil refineries (supplied by pipeline from Eilat), machine, chemical and textile industries

Haig (heig), Alexander Meigs, Jr. (1924–), U.S. Secretary of State 1981–2). A U.S. Military Academy graduate (1947), he served as National Security Advisor, Henry Kissinger's special assistant (1969–72), Pres. Nixon's Army vice-chief of staff (1972–3), White House chief of staff (1973–4), and NATO commander (1974–8). Secretary of State under Pres. Reagan, he was often criticized for his handling of authority and resigned in 1982

Haig Douglas, 1st Earl Haig (1861–1928), British field marshal. He was commander in chief (1915–18) of the British forces in France and Flanders during the 1st world war

Haight-Ash·bur·y (heitǽʃberi:) *n.* section of San Francisco associated with the drug culture in the 1960s

haik, haick (haik) *n.* a strip of cotton or woolen cloth worn by Arabs to cover the head and torso [Arab. *hayk* fr. *hāk*, to weave]

hai·ku (háiku:) *n.* a Japanese verse form comprising three lines of 5, 7 and 5 syllables respectively, unrhymed, and referring to one of the seasons [Jap.]

hail (heil) **1.** *n.* pieces of ice varying in size from a pea to a small ball formed by repeated convectional vertical movements within clouds at low temperature ‖ a thick shower of anything, *a hail of arrows* **2.** *v.i.* (impers., of hail) to fall ‖ to fall like hail [O.E. *hægel, hagol*]

hail **1.** *v.t.* to call out to (a person) ‖ (*rhet.*) to welcome, *he hailed the news with joy* ‖ *v.i.* (with 'from') to be a native or inhabitant of a named place **2.** *n.* a call made to attract attention ‖ a salute **within hail** near enough to hear a shout [O.N. *heill*, healthy]

hail·er (héilər) *n.* an electrified bullhorn

Hai·le Se·las·sie (háili:sələǽsi:, háili:səlási:) (1892–1975), emperor of Ethiopia (1930–74). Born Tafari Makonnen, he became regent (1916–28) and negus (1928–30) of Ethiopia. He was in exile (1936–41) during the Italian occupation of Ethiopia. The army seized control (1974); stripping him of his powers and removing him from the throne. Long a dominant figure in African politics, he was placed under house arrest until his death (1975)

hail-fel·low-well-met (héilfelouwélmét) *adj.* having a friendly, familiar manner, though with more heartiness than depth of feeling behind it

Hail Mary *AVE MARIA

hail·stone (héilstoun) *n.* a single piece of hail

hail·storm (héilstɔrm) *n.* a violent storm during which hail falls

Hai·nan (háinán) an island (area 13,000 sq. miles, pop. 2,900,000) in the South China Sea east of the Gulf of Tonkin, part of Kwantung, S.E. China. Capital and port: Kiungshan. Chinese settlers farm the coastal plains (rice, peanuts etc.). The mountainous interior, possessing valuable forests, is inhabited by aboriginal tribes

---

CONCISE PRONUNCIATION KEY: (a) æ, cat; ɑ, car; ɔ fawn; ei, snake. (e) e, hen; i:, sheep; iə, deer; ɛə, bear. (i) i, fish; ai, tiger; ə:, bird. (o) o, ox; au, cow; ou, goat; u, poor; ɔi, royal. (u) ʌ, duck; u, bull; u:, goose; ə, bacillus; ju:, cube. x, loch; θ, think; ð, bother; z, Zen; ʒ, corsage; dʒ, savage; ŋ, orangutang; j, yak; ʃ, fish; tʃ, fetch; 'l, rabble; 'n, redden. Complete pronunciation key appears inside front cover.

Hai·naut (enou) a province (area 1,436 sq. miles, pop. 1,321,846) in S.W. Belgium. Capital: Mons

Hai·phong (háifɔŋ) the chief port (pop. 1,190,900) of northern Vietnam, on the Red River delta, an industrial center (cotton, cement and chemical industries)

hair (hɛər) n. a threadlike tube of horny, fibrous substance with a core containing pigment cells, rooted in the skin and growing freely outwards, kept pliable by oil from glands in the skin, tending to lose its pigmentation with age or (where protective coloring of animals is concerned) in regions of ice or snow, or because of disease ‖ the covering of these on the human head or an animal body ‖ a threadlike growth on plants ‖ a hairbreadth **not to turn a hair** to remain calm and self-possessed **to get in someone's hair** to get on someone's nerves **to let one's hair down** to release one's hair from pins, ribbons etc. so that it hangs loosely ‖ (pop.) to discard formality and restraint and give free expression to one's feelings ‖ (pop.) to impart confidences without reserve **to make one's hair stand on end** to horrify or terrify one **to split hairs** to draw unimportant distinctions in an argument [O.E. hær, hēr]

hairbrained *HAREBRAINED

hair-breadth (héərbrɛdθ, héərbrɛtθ) **1.** n. a very small margin or distance, to win by a hairbreadth **2.** adj. extremely narrow, a hairbreadth escape

hair-brush (héərbrʌʃ) n. a hand brush for grooming the hair

hair clip (Br.) a bobby pin

hair-cloth (héərklɔθ, héərklɒθ) n. cloth woven from hair ‖ a hair shirt

hair-curl·ing (héərkə:rliŋ) adj. (colloq.) frightening

hair-cut (héərkʌt) n. the act of having the hair cut ‖ the style of cutting it

hair-do (héərdu:) pl. **hair-dos** n. the style in which a person's hair is arranged

hair-dress·er (héərdrɛsər) n. someone who professionally cuts and grooms people's hair ‖ (Br.) a barber

hair-dress·ing (héərdrɛsiŋ) n. the craft or work of a hairdresser or (Br.) a barber ‖ a dressing for the hair

hair grip (Br.) a bobby pin

hair hygrometer (phys.) an instrument indicating the dampness of the air by the effect of dampness on the twist and length of a single hair

hair-i·ness (héəri:nis) n. the state or quality of being hairy

hair-line (héərlain) n. a very thin line (e.g. the upstroke of a pen) or stripe (on cloth) ‖ the line of a person's hair at the forehead

hair-net (héərnɛt) n. a fine net colored to match a person's hair and used to keep it in place ‖ a coarser net used in the process of setting someone's hair

hair-piece (héərpi:s) n. a toupee (small wig)

hair-pin (héərpin) **1.** n. an elongated U-shaped pin used to keep e.g. a chignon in place **2.** adj. sharply turning, a hairpin bend

hair-rais·ing (héərreiziŋ) adj. causing terror or fearful apprehension

hairs·breadth (héərzbrɛdθ, héərzbrɛtθ) **1.** n. a hairbreadth **2.** adj. hairbreadth

hair shirt a haircloth shirt worn by an ascetic or in penance

hair slide (Br.) a barrette

hair space (printing) the thinnest strip of metal used for line spacing

hair-split·ting (héərsplitiŋ) **1.** n. the making of tiresomely subtle or pedantic distinctions in argument **2.** adj. tiresomely subtle in making logical distinctions

hair-spring (héərspriŋ) n. a coiled spring of thin invar controlling the oscillation of the balance wheel of a watch or clock

hair stroke a thin line in lettering ‖ the line drawn by a single inked hair in calibrating a measuring instrument

hair-style (héərstail) n. a way of having the hair arranged

hair-ti·cian (hɛərtíʃən) n. a barber

hair transplant medical process of transferring plugs of a patient's hair and skin from a hirsute head area (usu. the outer ring) to a bald or balding area

hair trigger a trigger releasing the firing mechanism of a gun by very slight pressure
hair-trig·ger (héərtrigər) adj. very finely adjusted ‖ responding instantaneously

hair weaving process of intertwining a person's hair with nylon and human hair to cover baldness. --**hair weaver** n.

hair·y (héəri:) comp. **hair·i·er** superl. **hair·i·est** adj. covered with hair ‖ having more than the usual quantity of hair ‖ like hair

Hai·ti (héiti:) a republic (area 10,700 sq. miles, pop. 5,195,200) in the Greater Antilles (*ANTILLES), occupying the western third of Hispaniola. Capital: Port-au-Prince. People: 90% of African descent, 10% Mulatto. Language: French (official), Creole. Religion: Roman Catholic (official), Protestant minority, voodoo is practiced. The land is 30% arable, 50% forest (hardwoods) and 10% pasture. Three rugged mountain ranges cross the country, separated by plains containing the bulk of the population. Highest point: La Selle (8,790 ft). Average temperatures (F.): 70°–85° at sea level, cooler inland. Rainfall: 55 ins. Livestock: hogs, goats, asses, mules. Manufactures: sugar refining, rum, oils. Exports: coffee, bananas, sugar, bauxite. Non-export crops: sisal, cotton, rice. Imports: cotton goods, foodstuffs, machinery, vehicles, petroleum products. University (Port-au-Prince). Monetary unit: gourde (100 centimes). HISTORY. The western part of Hispaniola was settled (17th c.) by French pirates, and ceded (1697) by Spain to France. This became the rich sugar-producing colony of Saint Domingue, and many African slaves were imported. They revolted (1791) and the whole island was declared independent (1804), but the eastern part seceded in 1844 (*DOMINICAN REPUBLIC). In Haiti, a long period of economic chaos and political anarchy culminated in American occupation (1915–34). American fiscal control continued until 1947. Constitutional changes were made in 1950, at the start of the dictatorship of Paul Magloire (1950–6), and in 1957, at the start of that of François Duvalier, who reversed Haiti's tradition of government by the 5% mulatto élite by championing the black masses. He established a militia to offset any threat from the military, together with a terror squad known as the Tontons Macoutes ('bogeymen'). He was succeeded (1971) by his son Jean-Claude. Foreign aid was restored but economic or political reasons prompted thousands to emigrate. Jean-Claude was forced into exile in 1986, and a junta took control of the government

Hai·tian (héiʃən, héiti:ən) **1.** adj. of or relating to Haiti **2.** n. a native or inhabitant of Haiti

Haitian Creole the French spoken by most Haitians

hake (heik) n. a wooden frame on which bricks, tiles, cheeses etc. are set to dry [etym. doubtful]

hake pl. **hake, hakes** n. a fish of genus Merluccius, related to cod, but with the head flattened, two dorsal fins and one long anal fin. There are American and European species, many being valuable food fishes [perh. fr. O.N. haki, hook]

Ha·kim, Al (ɑlháki:m) *DRUSE

Hak·luyt (hæklu:t), Richard (c. 1552–1616), English geographer. His books 'Divers Voyages Touching the Discoverie of America' (1582) and 'The Principall Navigations, Voiages and Discoveries of the English Nation' (1589) encouraged English colonization in the 16th c.

Ha·ko·da·te (hɑkoudátei) a port (pop. 315,150) at the southern end of Hokkaido, Japan

Ha·laf·i·an (həláfi:ən) adj. of a culture which flourished in parts of Syria and Mesopotamia before 3500 B.C. The culture was characterized by the use of copper and stone, and by the production of burnished polychrome pottery [after Tell Halaf, a site in N.E. Syria]

ha·la·la or ha·la·lah (həlálə) n. monetary unit of Saudi Arabia, equal to 1/100 riyal

ha·la·tion (həléiʃən) n. (photog.) a blurring of a negative due to the light reflection from the emulsion support [HALO]

hal·berd (hælbərd, hólbərd) n. (hist.) a combination of spear and battle-ax with a haft 5-7 ft long, used as a weapon in the 15th and 16th cc.
hal·berd·ier (hælbərdíər) n. a soldier armed with a halberd [O.F. halebard fr. M.H.G.]

hal·cy·on (hælsi:ən) **1.** n. the kingfisher, supposed by the ancients to calm the sea for 14 days at the winter solstice and to build a floating nest on the calm water **2.** adj. calm, peaceful, happy, halcyon days [L. halcyon fr. Gk alkuōn, kingfisher]

Hal·dane (hóldein), Richard Burdon, 1st Viscount Haldane of Cloan (1856–1928), British Liberal statesman. As secretary for war

12), he carried out important army reforms, setting up an imperial general staff, an expeditionary force and a territorial army. He was lord chancellor (1912–15 and 1924)

Hale (heil), George Ellery (1868–1938), U.S. astronomer. After inventing and developing (1888–91) the spectroheliograph, an instrument that photographs the sun in monochromatic light, he discovered magnetic fields in sun spots. He built the world's largest refracting telescope and developed the 200-inch reflecting telescope on Mount Palomar, Calif.

Hale, John Parker (1806–73), U.S. senator from New Hampshire, and the first outspoken critic of slavery (1847–53) in the Senate. He ran (1852) as the presidential candidate for the Free Soil party

Hale, Nathan (1755–76), American hero of the Revolutionary War, hanged by the British for spying. His last words were purportedly 'I only regret that I have but one life to lose for my country'

hale (heil) adj. (esp. of an elderly person) physically sound and well [O.E. hāl]

hale pres. part. **hal·ing** past and past part. **haled** v.t. to force to go, he was haled before the judge [M.E. halen fr. M.F. haler, to haul]

ha·ler (hálər) pl. **ha·lers, ha·le·ru** (háləru:) n. one hundredth of a koruna, or a coin of this value [Czech.]

Ha·lé·vy (ælеivi:), Jacques François Fromental Elie (1799–1862), French composer. The most famous of his many operas is 'la Juive' (1835)

Halévy, Ludovic (1834–1908), French author. In collaboration with Meilhac he wrote many comic operas for which Offenbach composed the music ('la Belle Hélène', 1864, 'la Vie Parisienne', 1866 etc.). With Meilhac he also wrote the libretto for Bizet's 'Carmen' (1875). His novels include 'l'Abbé Constantin' (1882)

half (hæf, hɑf) **1.** pl. **halves** (hævz, hɑvz) n. one of the two equal parts into which something is or may be divided ‖ one of two equal periods in a game divided by a break ‖ (Br.) a half pint ‖ a halfback ‖ a term, semester **to go halves** to share equally **2.** adj. being one half of something, a half pint **3.** adv. to the extent of a half, you only half filled his glass ‖ almost, to feel half dead ‖ partly, he said it half seriously **to be too clever by half** (Br.) to be obnoxiously conceited **to do something by halves** to do something with insufficient attention or energy [O.E. healf, side]

half-a-crown (hæfəkráun, háfəkráun) n. a half-crown

half a dozen six **it's six to one and half a dozen to the other** there is no real difference ‖ the fault is on both sides

half-and-half (hæfənhæf, háfənháf) **1.** adj. half one thing and half something else ‖ involving equal sharing **2.** adv. into equal parts ‖ equally **3.** n. a mixture of two things, esp. of milk and light cream for the table, in equal or nearly equal parts

half-back (hæfbæk, háfbæk) n. (field hockey etc.) a player immediately behind the forward line, or this position ‖ (football) one of the backs near each flank, or this position

half-baked (hæfbéikt, háfbéikt) adj. poorly planned ‖ foolish

half binding a bookbinding in which the spine and about a quarter of the front and back boards next to the spine are covered in one material and the rest of the boards are covered in a different material (cf. FULL BINDING, cf. QUARTER BINDING, cf. THREE-QUARTER BINDING)

half-bound (hæfbáund, háfbáund) adj. bound in a half binding

half-breed (hæfbri:d, háfbri:d) n. someone of mixed breeding, esp. of mixed white and American Indian parentage

half brother a brother through one parent only

half-caste (hæfkæst, háfkɑst) n. someone of mixed racial descent

half cock the position of the hammer (cock) of a gun when held in the first notch so that it cannot be released by the trigger **to go off at half cock, to go off half cocked** to be a failure because of insufficient preparation

half-crown (hæfkráun, háfkráun) n. a British cupronickel coin worth £. 125, made until 1946 of silver

half-dol·lar (hæfdólər, háfdólər) n. a U.S. or Canadian coin worth 50 cents

half gainer a fancy dive starting from a front dive position but executed as a back dive

---

half-har·dy (hǽfhɑrdi:, háfhɑrdi:) *comp.*
half-har·di·er, *superl.* **half-har·di·est** *adj.* (of a plant) able to tolerate a little frost but killed by sharp frost
half-heart·ed (hǽfhártid, háfhártid) *adj.* lacking the enthusiasm that comes of full conviction
half hitch a knot made by passing the end of a rope around itself and through the bend, making a simple noose
half-hol·i·day (hǽfhólidei, háfhólidei) *n.* (Br.) a break from work of half a day's duration
half hour the midpoint between two hours ‖ half an hour **half-hour·ly** (hǽfáuərli:, háfáuərli:) *adj.* and *adv.*
half-land·ing (hǽflǽndiŋ, háflǽndiŋ) *n.* (Br.) a landing breaking a flight of stairs at other than floor level
half-length (hǽfleŋθ, hǽfleŋkθ, háfleŋθ, háfleŋkθ) *adj.* describing a portrait which shows the upper half of the person
half-life (hǽflaif, háflaif) *n.* the time required for the disappearance of one half of the initial quantity of a substance undergoing a chemical or nuclear reaction ‖ the time required for half the amount of a substance to be eliminated, metabolized etc. after it has been introduced into an organism
half-light (hǽflait, háflait) *n.* a dim light hard to see detail in, esp. the grayish light just before nightfall or just before daybreak
half-mast (hǽfmǽst, háfmást) *n.* the middle point of a mast. A flag flown at it is a sign of mourning
half measures actions which are only partly effective, whether through deliberate compromise or through lack of will or energy
half-moon (hǽfmu:n, háfmu:n) **1.** *n.* the appearance of the moon as seen at the quarters, when only one half of it is visible ‖ a shape similar to this ‖ a tool having this shape, esp. one for edging lawns ‖ the whitish area at the base of the fingernail **2.** *adj.* shaped like a half-moon
half mourning mourning costume in which the black is relieved by gray or white etc., worn when the period of full mourning is over or when the person mourned was a distant relative ‖ the period when such mourning is worn
half nelson (*wrestling*) a grip in which an arm is thrust under the corresponding arm of an opponent and the hand is pressed on the back of his neck (cf. FULL NELSON)
half note (*mus., Am.=Br.* minim) a note (symbol ♩) equal to two quarter notes or half a whole note
half-pass (hǽfpæs) *n.* (*equestrianism*) performance sideway and forward in two tracks
half pay (Br.) a pension roughly equal to half the salary previously earned ‖ (Br., hist.) the allowance paid to an officer while temporarily not on active service
half-pen·ny (héipni:, héipəni:) *pl.* **half·pence** (héipəns), **half·pen·nies** *n.* (hist.) a British coin worth half a penny
half plate (Br.) a photographic plate or film of the size 6½ x 4¼ ins
half sister a sister through one parent only
half sole a shoe sole from shank to toe only
half sovereign a British gold coin worth 10 shillings issued until 1916, and subsequently on special occasions
half step (*mus.*) the smallest interval in a diatonic scale, represented on a keyboard instrument by the interval between any two adjacent keys, e.g. between C and D♭
half thickness (*nuclear phys.*) thickness of absorbing material necessary to reduce by one half the intensity of radiation that passes through it
half-tim·bered (hǽftimbərd, háftímbərd) *adj.* (*archit.*) having a framework of timber, the spaces being filled with stonework, brickwork or plaster-covered laths
half time (*sports*) a short interval halfway through a game of football etc. **half-time** (hǽftaim, háftaim) *adj.* pertaining to this interval, *the half-time score* ‖ working regularly half a day, *half-time workers*
half title (*printing*) the short title on the leaf preceding the title page ‖ (*printing*) a similar short title of a part or section of a book, displayed either separately or at the head of the first page of the new part or section
half·tone (hǽftoun, háftoun) **1.** *adj.* (*printing*) of a block, or the impression made from it, in which gradations of light and shade are effected

by varied spacing of dots **2.** *n.* a printed picture obtained from a halftone block ‖ the process using such blocks ‖ (*mus.*) a half step
half-track (hǽftræk, háftræk) *n.* a vehicle traveling on a pair of caterpillar tracks and a front pair of wheels
half-truth (hǽftru:θ, háftru:θ) *n.* a statement which is true so far as it goes but which often omits, deliberately, something vital
half volley (*sports*) the act of striking a ball immediately when it begins to rise from the ground ‖ this stroke
half volte (*equestrianism*) a half-circle figure followed by an oblique
half·way (hǽfwéi, háfwéi) **1.** *adj.* equally distant between two points ‖ (*fig.*) not taken far enough, *halfway measures* **2.** *adv.* half the distance, *he went back with him halfway* ‖ at the point of compromise, *to meet someone halfway*
halfway house sheltered workshop or residence designed to help adjustment of institutionalized persons in the process of release, e.g., mental patients, prisoners
half-wit (hǽfwit, háfwit) *n.* someone of subnormal intelligence **half-wit·ted** *adj.*
half-year·ly (hǽfjíərli:, háfjíərli:) **1.** *adj.* occurring every six months **2.** *adv.* twice a year
hal·i·but (hǽlibət, hólibət) *pl.* **hal·i·but, hal·i·buts** *n.* a food fish of genus *Hippoglossus*, one of the largest flatfish, females sometimes weighing 300 lbs or more. Halibut are caught on both sides of the N. Atlantic and in the Pacific [M.E. *halybutte* fr. *haly*, holy+ *butt*, flat fish]
Hal·i·car·nas·sus (hælikɑrnǽsəs) an ancient city of Asia Minor, famous for the tomb of Mausolus and as the birthplace of the historians Herodotus and Dionysius
hal·ide (hǽlaid, héilaid) *n.* a binary compound of a halogen with a more electropositive element or radical [HALOGEN]
hal·i·eu·tic (hælijú:tik) *adj.* concerned with fishing **hal·i·eu·tics** *n.* the art of fishing [fr. L. fr. Gk *halieutēs*, fisherman]
Hal·i·fax (hǽlifæks), Charles Montagu, 1st earl of (1661–1715). English statesman. His financial measures (esp. the floating of the national debt, 1692, the foundation of the Bank of England, 1694, and the reform of the coinage, 1696–7) helped to found British prosperity in the 18th c.
Halifax, Edward Frederick Lindley Wood, 1st earl (2nd creation) of (1881–1959), British Conservative statesman. He was viceroy of India (1926–31), foreign secretary (1938–40) and ambassador to Washington (1941–6)
Halifax, George Savile, 1st marquis of (1633–95), English statesman. He earned the nickname of 'the Trimmer' by ceasing (1688) to support James II and instead furthering the accession of William III
Halifax the capital (pop. 114,594, with agglom. 277,727) of Nova Scotia, Canada, a rail center, passenger port and Canada's chief winter port: shipbuilding, oil refining
hal·i·o·tis (hæli:óutis) *n.* a member of *Haliotis*, a genus of ear-shaped fossil and recent gastropodous mollusks. They adhere to rocks in littoral zones and are widely distributed [fr. Gk *hals*, sea+ *ous* (ótos), ear]
hal·ite (hǽlait, héilait) *n.* rock salt [fr. Gk *hals*, salt]
hal·i·to·sis (hælitóusis) *n.* bad-smelling breath [Mod. L. fr. *halitus*, breath]
Hall (hɔl), Asaph (1829–1907), U.S. astronomer. As professor of mathematics at the U.S. Naval observatory, Washington, D.C., he discovered (1877) the two satellites of Mars, whose orbits he calculated
Hall, Charles Francis (1821–71), U.S. arctic explorer. While leading the last of three expeditions to the Arctic in the naval ship 'Polaris', he attained (1871) the northernmost point hitherto reached by any vessel
Hall, Charles Martin (1863–1914), U.S. inventor who devised the electrolytic process which forms the basis for industrial mass production of aluminum. As vice-president (from 1890) of what became the Aluminum Company of America, he acquired a fortune which he bequeathed chiefly to educational institutions
Hall, Granville Stanley (1844–1924), U.S. pioneer psychologist. He founded (1887) the 'American Journal of Psychology'. As the first president (1888–1920) of Clark University, he established the first institute of child psychology in the U.S.A. He became (1892) the first president of the American Psychological Association, and published many works

Hall, James (1793–1868), U.S. author of history and fiction who depicted French community life in Illinois and portrayed the typical backwoodsman, voyageur and Indian–hater. His best short stories are found in 'Legends of the West' (1832) and 'Tales of the Border' (1835)
Hall, James (1811–98), U.S. geologist. As the state geologist of New York, he published (1847–94) 'The Palaeontology of New York'
hall (hɔl) *n.* a large or small entrance space into which the main door of a house opens and from which there is access to other rooms ‖ a connecting passage or corridor between rooms ‖ a communally owned building where public business is transacted or where people meet for social or recreative purposes, *town hall* ‖ a large room used for meetings or social occasions, *dance hall, parish hall* ‖ (Br.) a college dining room, or the evening meal served in it to students ‖ (in some universities, in proper names) a college (e.g. Trinity Hall, Cambridge) or building or group of buildings (e.g. Mellanby Hall, Ibadan) ‖ (in some villages, in proper names) a country residence of some importance [O.E. *heall*, a shelter]
hal·lah, chal·lah (xúlə, Heb. xɑlá) *pl.* **hal·lahs, chal·lahs**, *Heb.* **hal·loth, chal·loth** (xɑlót) *n.* a loaf of bread eaten by Jews esp. on the Sabbath. It is leavened with yeast, made with egg, and glazed with egg before being baked. The loaf is often braided
Hal·le (húlə) a port (pop. 232,400) of East Germany on the Saale, a rail and trading center. Industries (based on brown coal deposits): metallurgy, machinery, chemicals, beet sugar etc. University (1694) ‖ the surrounding district (area 3,386 sq. miles, pop. 1,962,000) (*SAXONY-ANHALT)
Hal·leck (hǽlək), Henry Wager (1815–72), U.S. general and jurist. As supreme commander (1861) in the west during the Civil War, he showed administrative skill in organizing the volunteer armies, but a lack of strategical and tactical ability. His 'Elements of Military Art and Science' (1846) was widely read by volunteer officers
Hall effect (*phys.*) the creation of a potential difference across the edges of a metal strip along which current flows placed in a magnetic field perpendicular to its surface [after Edwin H. Hall (d. 1938), U.S. physicist]
hal·le·lu·jah (hælilú:jə) *n.* alleluia [Heb. *halleluyah*, praise Jehovah]
Hal·ley (hǽli:), Edmund (1656–1742), English astronomer and the first to predict the return of a comet. He produced the first catalogue of stars visible in the southern hemisphere after his own observations ('Catalogus stellarum australium', 1679). He observed the great comet of 1682, since known as Halley's comet, calculated its orbit and correctly predicted its return (in 1758) in his 'Synopsis astronomiae cometicae' (1705). He made contributions to the study of the moon, the motion of the stars, and of Venus. Halley's 'Tabulae astronomicae' was published in 1749
halliard *HALYARD
hall·mark (hólmɑrk) **1.** *n.* a set of official marks stamped on a gold or silver article to guarantee the standard of purity of the metal, after assay by government analysts (or, in Britain, the Goldsmiths' Company) ‖ any mark or sign of genuineness, *the hallmark of success* **2.** *v.t.* to stamp with a hallmark [after Goldsmiths' *Hall*, in London, where the marks were first used]
hal·loo (həlú:) **1.** *v.i.* to holler as a way of attracting attention, or (Br.) to indicate to huntsmen that a fox has been sighted or to encourage hounds **2.** *n.* the shout [perh. fr. F. *halloer*, to pursue with shouts]
hal·low (hǽlou) *v.t.* to make holy or sacred ‖ to revere as holy [O.E. *hālgian* fr. *hālig*, holy]
Hal·low·een, Hal·low·e'en (hælloui:n, hɒloui:n) *n.* the evening of Oct. 31 (preceding All Saints Day) [shortened fr. *All-hallow-even* fr. O.E. *ealra hālgena*, of all the saints + *ēfen*, eve]
Hall process an electrolytic process for extracting aluminum from a fused solution of alumina in cryolite [after Charles M. *Hall* (d. 1914), U.S. chemist]
Hall·statt (hólstæt, hálʃtat) *adj.* of an early Iron Age culture in Europe (c. 700–c. 450 B.C.), characterized by the transition from bronze to iron [after *Hallstatt*, a village in Austria]
halluces *pl.* of HALLUX
hallucinant *n.* cause of hallucinations. —**hallucinate** *v.* to see what does not exist. —**hallucinogenic** *n.* a causative drug

hal·lu·ci·nate (həlú:sineit) *pres. part.* **hal·lu·ci·nat·ing** *past* and *past part.* **hal·lu·ci·nat·ed** *v.t.* to cause (a person) to suffer from hallucinations ‖ *v.i.* to experience hallucinations **hal·lu·ci·na·tion** *n.* perception unaccompanied by reality, e.g. hearing voices when no one is present ‖ an object of such perception **hal·lu·ci·na·to·ry** (həlú:sinətɔri:, həlú:sinətɔ:ry) *adj.* [fr. L. *hallucinari* (*hallucinatus*) or *allucinari* (*allucinatus*), to wander in the mind]

hal·lu·cin·o·gen (həlú:sinədʒen) *n.* a drug (e.g. mescaline) which induces hallucinations **hal·lu·cin·o·gén·ic** *adj.* [fr. HALLUCINATION+Gk *genēs*, born]

hal·lu·ci·no·sis (həlu:sinóusis) *n.* a mental condition characterized by hallucinations [Mod. L.]

hal·lux (hæləks) *pl.* **hal·lu·ces** (hæljəsi:z) *n.* the big toe of the human foot ‖ the backward pointing toe of a bird [Mod. L. altered fr. *allex*, the big toe]

hall·way (hɔ́lwei) *n.* an entrance hall ‖ a passage connecting two or more rooms

halm (hɔm) *n.* a haulm

hal·ma (hælmə) *n.* a game played on a board of 256 squares with marked corner areas, by two players each with 19 pieces or by four players each with 13 pieces. These are moved towards the diagonal corner opposite the starting position, and friend or foe can be leapt over. The winner is the first to muster all his men in the opposite corner [fr. Gk *halma*, a leap]

Hal·ma·be·ra (hælməhérə) an island (area 6,870 sq. miles, pop. 88,000) in the Moluccas, E. Indonesia: nutmeg, resin, sago, rice, tobacco, coconuts

ha·lo (héilou) *pl.* **ha·loes, ha·los** *n.* a disk of diffused light surrounding the sun or moon or a lamp etc., caused by the refraction of light in air in which small water drops or ice particles are suspended ‖ (*painting*) a bright disk or ring painted above, or surrounding, the head of a holy person as a symbol of glory ‖ glory investing a person in the eyes of others [fr. Gk *halōs*, a threshing floor, disk of the sun, moon, or a shield]

hal·o·gen (hælədʒen) *n.* (*chem.*) one of the five elements (fluorine, chlorine, bromine, iodine, astatine) belonging to group VII of the periodic table. They are reactive gases or liquids that normally exist as diatomic molecules in the elemental state [fr. Gk *hals* (*halos*), salt+*genēs*, born]

hal·o·per·i·dol [C_{21}H_{23}ClFNO_2] (hæloupéərədɔl) *n.* (*pharm.*) antipsychotic tranquilizer drug; marketed as Haldol

hal·o·phyte (hæləfait) *n.* (*bot.*) a shore plant, i.e. one capable of thriving on salt-impregnated soils [fr. Gk *hals* (*halos*), salt +*phuton*, plant]

hal·o·thane [C_2HBrClF_3] (hælouθein) *n.* (*pharm.*) 1. a noninflammable, nonexplosive gaseous general anesthetic. 2. a general inhalant, nonexplosive anesthetic; marketed as Fluothane

Hals (hɑls), Frans (c. 1580–1666), Dutch painter. He is best known for his portraits, which were perhaps the first 'informal' portraits, using free and bold handling to catch the sitter in a relaxed, characteristic expression

Hal·sey (hɔ́lsi:, hɔ́lzi:), William Frederick ('Bull') (1882–1959), U.S. admiral who commanded (1944–5) the 3rd fleet in the Pacific during the 2nd world war. In the battle for Leyte gulf his fleet sank four Japanese carriers and a battleship

Häl·sing·borg (helsiŋbɔ́rj) a town (pop. 101,323) in S. Sweden, at the narrowest point of the Sound, the main port for motor traffic to the continent and a trade center. Industries: rubber manufactures, shipbuilding

halt (hɔlt) *adj.* (*rhet.*) lame, limping [M.E. fr. O.E. *halt, healt*]

halt 1. *n.* a cessation of movement or action, *to come to a halt* ‖ (*Br., rail.*) a way station 2. *v.i.* to stop suddenly ‖ (*mil.*) to stop marching or marking time ‖ *v.t.* to cause (someone or something) to come to a halt ‖ (*mil.*) to cause (troops) to stop marching or marking time [G. *halt* fr. *halten*, to hold]

halt·er (hɔ́ltər) 1. *n.* a rope or strap fastened at one end around the head of a horse or riding camel and used to lead the animal or to tie it to a firm support ‖ the rope used to hang a criminal ‖ a woman's garment encircling the waist and held in place by straps around the neck, so as to leave the arms and back bare 2. *v.t.* to put a halter on (an animal) [O.E. *hœlftre*]

hal·te·res (hæltiəri:z) *pl. n.* rudimentary posterior wing structures looking like knobbed rods and serving as balancers in dipteran insects [fr. Gk *haltēres* fr. *hallesthai*, to leap]

halt·ing (hɔ́ltiŋ) *adj.* (of steps) dragging, slow ‖ (of rhythm) ragged, uneven ‖ (of utterance, translation etc.) marked by hesitance or awkwardness ‖ (of grammar, argument etc.) betraying imperfect command

halve (hæv, hɑv) *pres. part.* **halv·ing** *past* and *past part.* **halved** *v.t.* to divide into two equal portions ‖ to share equally ‖ to lessen by half ‖ to fit (wooden beams) together at the ends by cutting away half the thickness of each ‖ (*golf*) to win the same number of holes in (a match) as an opponent ‖ (*golf*) to reach (a hole) in the same number of strokes as an opponent [M.E. *halfen, halven*]

halves *pl.* of HALF

hal·yard, hal·liard (hæljərd) *n.* (*naut.*) a rope or tackle used to hoist or lower yards, sails or flags [earlier *halier, hallyer*, associated with YARD]

ham (hæm) 1. *n.* a whole thigh of a hog, salted and smoke-dried, eaten roasted, boiled or fried ‖ the back of an animal's thigh ‖ a ham actor or performer ‖ a licensed amateur operator of a radio station 2. *adj.* of an actor or performer who plays his part without intelligence and with overemphasis of gesticulation or voice ‖ of or relating to amateur radio 3. *v. pres. part.* **ham·ming** *past* and *past part.* **hammed** *v.t.* to play (a part) like a ham actor ‖ *v.i.* to behave like a ham actor [O.E. *ham. hamm*, the back of the thigh]

Ha·ma (hɑ́mɑ) a town (pop. 154,000) of W. Syria on the Orontes, a railroad junction and market

Ha·mad (hɑmád) *SYRIAN DESERT

Ham·a·dan (hæmədæn) a city (pop. 155,848) of W. Iran: carpet making, leatherwork

ham·a·dry·ad (hæmədráiəd, hæmədráiæd) *n.* the king cobra ‖ *Cynocephalus hamadryas*, a large Arabian and Abyssinian baboon ‖ (*Gk mythol.*) a dryad living and dying with the tree she inhabited [L. fr. Gk *Hamadruas* fr. *hama*, together+*drus*, tree]

Ha·ma·mat·su (hɑmɑmɑ́tsu:) a town (pop. 475,552) in Central Honshu, Japan, the rail and agricultural center for W. Shizuoka: textiles, dyeing, plastics

Ham·burg (hæmbə:rg, hámburx) West Germany's largest port city, forming a state (area 288 sq. miles) of West Germany, at the head of the Elbe estuary, handling a vast inland and transatlantic trade. Industries: shipbuilding, oil refineries, engineering, chemicals, food processing. University (1919). It was a leading town of the Hanseatic League. Nearly destroyed in the 2nd world war, it has been largely rebuilt

ham·burg·er (hæmbə:rgər) *n.* chopped beef ‖ a hamburg steak ‖ a bun or bread roll containing fried or grilled chopped steak [HAMBURG STEAK]

hamburger steak a hamburg steak

ham·burg steak (hæmbə:rg) finely chopped beef made up into patties and fried or grilled [after *Hamburg* in Germany]

Ha·mil·car Bar·ca (hæmilkɑrbárkə) (*d.* 228 B.C.), Carthaginian general. He commanded the Carthaginian army in Sicily during the 1st Punic War, and, after the loss of Sicily, began (237 B.C.) to build up an empire in Spain

Ham·il·ton (hæmiltən), Alexander (c. 1756–1804), American statesman. A staunch Federalist, he was Washington's secretary and aide-de-camp (1777–81), and secretary of the treasury (1789–95). His financial proposals, the creation of a national bank and of a federal bank, were opposed by Jefferson

Hamilton, Anthony (c. 1645–1720), French author, born in Ireland of Scottish parents. His 'Mémoires du Comte de Gramont' were published in 1713

Hamilton, Lady Emma (c. 1765–1815), Nelson's mistress (1798–1805). She had a daughter, Horatia, by him

Hamilton, Sir William Rowan (1805–65), Irish mathematician and astronomer. His wide researches include the origination and development of the theory of quaternions

Hamilton the capital (pop. 3,000) of Bermuda, on Bermuda I.

Hamilton a town (pop. 81,600) in North Island, New Zealand, on the Waikato River: lumber, dairy produce. University (1964)

Hamilton a port (pop. 306,434, with agglom. 542,095) of Ontario, Canada, on Lake Ontario: steel, iron, textiles

Ham·ite (hæmait) *n.* a member of a group of African peoples incl. the Berbers of N. Africa, the Tuaregs of the Sudan and the Galla of E. Africa, regarded as of kindred origin and speaking various related languages **Ham·it·ic** (hæmítik, hamítik) 1. *adj.* of or relating to a language of the Hamites 2. *n.* the group of Hamitic languages [after *Ham*, son of Noah]

Ham·it·ic languages two groups of languages related to the Semitic family and spoken in Africa north of the equator. The Eastern group is spoken in Ethiopia and the area between the Nile and the Red Sea. The Northern group is spoken in the Berber districts of N. Africa. The Hamitic languages have also influenced many of the continent's non-Hamitic tongues, including Hottentot. Hamitic inscriptions have been found on ancient Egyptian papyri. Today there are 47 stock languages and 71 dialects

Ham·i·to-Se·mit·ic (hæmitousəmítik) 1. *n.* a family of languages, including the subgroups Hamitic and Semitic, widely spoken from N. and W. Africa to S.W. Asia 2. *adj.* of or belonging to Hamito-Semitic

ham·let (hæmlit) *n.* a small group of dwellings in a rural district, not large enough to warrant a church or school [M.E. *hamelet* fr. O.F. fr. Gmc]

Ham·lin (hæmlin), Hannibal (1809–91), U.S. vice-president (1861–5) under Abraham Lincoln. He favored radical emancipation measures and the arming of blacks

Ham·mar·skjöld (hæmərʃald, hámərʃald), Dag Hjalmar Agne Carl (1905–61), Swedish statesman. As secretary-general of the U.N. (1953–61), he did much to relieve international tension, and was awarded posthumously the Nobel peace prize (1961)

ham·mer (hæmər) 1. *n.* a tool consisting of a short, heavy crosspiece made of a hard substance (often steel) fitted at one end of a handle, different kinds being used for driving nails, beating metals etc. ‖ a hinged lever with a knob at its free end, used as a striker e.g. in a carriage clock or a piano ‖ a gavel ‖ the part of the mechanism of a firearm which strikes the cap of the cartridge ‖ (*anat.*) the malleus ‖ (*athletics*) a spherical weight at one end of a flexible handle, thrown in the 'throwing the hammer' contest ‖ a steam hammer ‖ a drop hammer ‖ (*elec.*) a trembler in a make-and-break mechanism **to come under the hammer** to be put up for sale by auction **to go at it hammer and tongs** to argue (or fight) with great energy 2. *v.t.* to hit with a hammer blow or series of hammer blows, *to hammer a nail in* ‖ to shape (metal) by striking it with a series of hammer blows ‖ (*Br., stock exchange*) to declare (a firm of stockbrokers) insolvent ‖ *v.i.* to deliver a series of blows, *to hammer on a door* **to hammer at** to make a prolonged attack on, *to hammer at the enemy's defenses* **to hammer home** to drive well in, *to hammer a nail home, to hammer home the truth* **to hammer out** to arrive at (what one seeks) by persistent hard work, *to hammer out a solution* [O.E. *hamor*]

hammer and sickle the emblem of a sickle crossed by a hammer, adopted by the U.S.S.R. in 1923 as a symbol of the unity of interest and purpose of worker and peasant ‖ the flag bearing this emblem

hammer beam (*archit.*) a short stout beam projecting horizontally and internally from a wall to support the principal roof timbers without the need of a tie beam

Ham·mer·fest (hámərfest) Europe's northernmost town (pop. 7,500), in Finnmark, Norway: fishing, sealing, whaling

ham·mer·head (hæmərhed) *n.* the head of a hammer ‖ (*zool.*) *Sphyrna zygaena* and related sharks of fam. *Sphyrnidae*, distinguished by the shape of the head, which resembles a doubleheaded hammer laid flat. Some species are fished for their hides and livers ‖ (*pop.*) a blockhead

ham·mer·less (hæmərlis) *adj.* (of a firearm) having the hammer concealed

ham·mer·lock (hæmərlɒk) *n.* (*wrestling*) a hold in which the opponent's arm is twisted and bent behind his back

ham·mer·toe (hæmərtou) *n.* (*med.*) a toe having a permanent angular bend towards the sole of the foot

Hammer v. Dagenhart (hæmər; déigənhart) (1918), U.S. Supreme Court case that declared

CONCISE PRONUNCIATION KEY: **(a)** æ, c*a*t; ɑ, c*a*r; ɔ f*aw*n; ei, sn*a*ke. **(e)** e, h*e*n; i:, sh*ee*p; iə, d*ee*r; ɛə, b*ea*r. **(i)** i, f*i*sh; ai, t*i*ger; ə:, b*i*rd. **(o)** o, *o*x; au, c*ow*; ou, g*oa*t; u, p*oo*r; ɔi, r*oy*al. **(u)** ʌ, d*u*ck; u, b*u*ll; u:, g*oo*se; ə, b*a*cillus; ju:, c*u*be. x, lo*ch*; θ, *th*ink; ð, bo*th*er; z, *Z*en; ʒ, corsa*g*e. dʒ, sava*g*e; ŋ, orangutan*g*; j, *y*ak; ʃ, *fish*; tʃ, fe*tch*; 'l, rabb*le*; 'n, red*den*. Complete pronunciation key appears inside front cover.

the Federal Child Labor Act of 1916 unconstitutional. The law, which prohibited goods made by factories violating child labor laws from entering interstate trade, was knocked down because it did not deal with the commerce clause under the Constitution. The decision was overruled in 'U.S. v. Darby' (1941)

Hammett, (hæmət), Dashiell (1894– 1961), U.S. writer, especially of mysteries, creator of private investigators Sam Spade and Nick and Nora Charles. His works include 'Red Harvest' (1929), 'The Dain Curse' (1929), 'The Maltese Falcon' (1930), 'The Glass Key' (1931), and 'The Thin Man' (1934). 'The Big Knockover and Other Stories' (ed., Lillian Hellman; 1966) and 'The Continental Op' (1974) were published posthumously

Ham·ming code (hæmiŋ) (*computer*) a code used in entering data to help detect errors, containing information bits at 3,5,6, and 7, and check bits for parity at 1,2, and 4. *also* hammer code

ham·mock (hæmək) *n.* a rectangle of canvas or strong net suspended from firm supports by several thin ropes at each end. Hammocks are used to relax in or (commonly by sailors) to sleep in, and they also serve as a shroud for burial at sea [Span. *hamaca* prob. fr. Carib]

Ham·mond (hæmənd), John Hays, Jr. (1888– 1965), U.S. inventor who devised various radio-control systems for coastal defense and navigation, an improvement for pipe-organ mechanisms, and a new type of reflecting modulator for pianos

Ham·mu·ra·bi (hæmurábi:) (c. 18th c. B.C.), king of Babylonia. By a series of campaigns against neighboring peoples, he created a great empire centered on Babylon. He promulgated one of the earliest known comprehensive codes of law

Hamp·den (hæmpdən, hæmdən), John (1594– 1643), English statesman, one of the leaders of the parliamentary opposition to Charles I. His conviction (1638) for refusing to pay ship money made him a hero of the struggle against arbitrary taxation

ham·per (hæmpər) **1.** *v.t.* to make (action or progress) difficult, *hampered by a tight skirt, hampered by lack of French* **2.** *n.* (*naut.*) rigging, equipment or other gear disposed on or below deck and making it difficult for men to move around a ship [M.E. *hampren*]

hamper *n.* a large rectangular basket usually of coarse wickerwork, with a lid ‖ a large basket divided into compartments for packing and transporting bottles of wine etc. or food delicacies [older *hanaper* fr. O.F. *hanapier*, a case for holding a 'hanap' (ciborium)]

Hamp·shire (hæmpʃiər) (*abbr.* **Hants**) a county (area incl. the Isle of Wight 1,650 sq. miles, pop. 1,456,367) of S. England. County town: Winchester

Hamp·ton (hæmptən), Wade (1818–1902), U.S. statesman and Confederate general during the Civil War. He commanded General Lee's army during the defense of Petersburg and attempted to save President Jefferson Davis from capture after General Johnston's surrender, He was the dominant figure (1878–90) in South Carolina politics and was responsible for restoring home rule

Hampton Court Palace a palace near London begun in 1514 by Cardinal Wolsey and given to Henry VIII, who added to it. Sir Christopher Wren made further additions for William III. It was a royal residence until George II's day, and is now a museum. A conference was held there (1604) under the presidency of James I in order to settle differences between the Puritans and the Church of England. It resulted in the expulsion of many Puritan clergy

Hampton Roads a natural harbor connected by a channel in the west to the Chesapeake Bay in S.E. Virginia, and an important naval base. It was the site of the Civil War engagement (1862) between the 'Monitor' and the 'Merrimack', and of the peace conference (1865) between President Lincoln and Confederate representatives

ham·ster (hæmstər) *n.* a member of *Cricetus,* a genus of thick-bodied, short-tailed rodents. They have large cheek pouches in which they carry grain to an underground store. They are also carnivorous. Hamsters breed several times a year, a litter containing 7-12 young, born blind. *C. auratus,* the golden hamster, is often kept as a pet [G.]

ham·string (hæmstriŋ) **1.** *n.* (in man) one of the five tendons of the thigh muscle behind the knee ‖ (in quadrupeds) a large tendon at the back of the joint between the knee and the fetlock in the hind leg **2.** *v.t. pres. part.* **ham·string·ing** *past* and *past part.* **ham·strung** (hæmstrʌŋ) to lame (an animal) by severing the hamstring ‖ to cripple or make inoperative, *hamstrung for lack of money*

Ham·sun (hámsun), Knut (Knut Pedersen, 1859–1952), Norwegian realistic novelist. His most famous novel is 'The Growth of the Soil' (Eng. trans. 1920)

ham·u·lus (hæmjuləs) *pl.* **ham·u·li** (hæmjulai) *n.* (*bot.*) a hooked bristle ‖ (*anat.*) a hooklike part, e.g. at the end of some bones [L. dim. of *hamus,* hook]

Han (hɑn) *n.* a Chinese dynasty, during whose rule (206 B.C.–220 A.D.) Buddhism was introduced into China. The dynasty favored bureaucratic, imperial government, furthered a revival of learning, and extended China's frontiers

Ha·na·fi Moslems (hɑnɑfi:) *n.* nationalist and religious organization of AfroAmericans; rival organization to Black Muslims

hance (hæns, hɑns) *n.* (*naut.*) a curved contour, e.g. the rise of bulwarks ‖ (*archit.*) the arc of smallest radius at the beginning of the curve of an elliptical or many-centered arch [perh. A.F. fr. O.F. *hauce,* a rise]

Han·cock (hænkɒk), John (1737–93), American statesman. His signature comes first on the Declaration of Independence

Hancock, Winfield Scott (1824–86), Union general during the Civil War. As commander (1863–4) of II Corps, Army of the Potomac, he successfully defended Cemetery Ridge. He was nominated (1880) the Democratic presidential candidate against James Garfield

Hand (hænd), Learned (1872–1961), U.S. jurist. As chief judge (1939–51) of the federal court of appeals for the second circuit, he was responsible for some 2,000 opinions in all fields of law, notably the antitrust suit (1945) against the Aluminum Company of America and the conviction (1950) of the top 11 U.S. Communist party leaders on Smith Act charges of conspiracy. His Harvard lectures were published (1958) as 'The Bill of Rights'

hand (hænd) **1.** *n.* the part of the human body from the wrist to the fingertips, or the corresponding part in a tetrapod vertebrate. It is used for grasping, touching, communicating by gesture etc. ‖ a pointer on a dial, *hour hand* ‖ a style of penmanship, *a round hand* ‖ (*card games*) the cards held by a player ‖ a round in a game of cards, *a last hand of bridge* ‖ a pledge of fidelity, *he gave me his hand on it* ‖ (*old-fash.*) a promise to marry, *he asked him for his daughter's hand* ‖ (*pop.*) applause by an audience, *give him a big hand* ‖ the exercise of authority, *by conquest they came under his hand* ‖ four inches (the breadth of a hand) as a unit of measurement for the height of a horse ‖ a member of a ship's crew ‖ an employee on a farm or in a factory ‖ a person with reference to a specified skill, *he is a good hand with a gun* ‖ skill, ability, *he has a good hand with horses* ‖ (*commerce*) a small bundle (of tobacco leaves), a bunch (of bananas) etc. a **free hand** unrestricted powers of decision and action **at first** (**second** etc.) **hand** directly (indirectly as specified) from the person concerned **at hand** near and available ‖ (*rhet.*) very close in future time **at the hands of** by the acts of, *to suffer at the hands of the police* **by hand** with the hands as distinct from by machinery ‖ (of raising animals) by human care and not by the mother ‖ in handwriting **from hand to hand** from person to person **from hand to mouth** without provision beyond the immediate present **hand in hand** holding hands ‖ in close cooperation **hand over fist** (of making money) in great quantity and at great speed **hand over hand** (in rope climbing) with one hand passed over the other alternately **hands down** (of winning) by an easy victory **hands off!** don't touch! **hands up!** raise both arms above the head (so as to be harmless)! ‖ raise one hand above the head (to indicate consent)! **in hand** under control ‖ in progress ‖ owned and available ‖ to spare, *with five minutes in hand* **off one's hands** no longer one's responsibility **on every hand** on all sides **on hand** available **on the one hand... on the other (hand)** from this point of view... from that (point of view) **out of hand** beyond control ‖ summarily **out of one's hands** not in one's

control or sphere of influence **ready to hand** easily and quickly available **show of hands** voting by raising the hand in sign of agreement **the upper hand** (in a contest, argument, struggle etc.) domination **to be able to turn one's hand to anything** to be able to do a wide range of esp. practical work **to do a hand's turn** (in negative and interrogative expressions) to help by doing at least some work **to force someone's hand** to compel someone by oblique methods to do what one wishes him to do **to have a hand in** to participate in to some extent **to have one's hands full** to be fully occupied **to have on one's hands** to be left with the burden of ‖ to have the troublesome responsibility of **to keep one's hand in** to maintain the mastery of an acquired skill by using it **to lay hands on** to get within one's power, capture ‖ to use violence on (someone) ‖ to find (something temporarily mislaid or concealed) **to lend** (or **give**) **a hand** to assist **to lift a hand** (in negative and interrogative expressions) to make an effort to help **to set one's hand to** to begin (a task) **to shake hands** to clasp hands in mutual greeting or in token of agreement or forgiveness **to take a hand in** to share in (an act) **to take in hand** to undertake ‖ to undertake the training of by reforming or disciplining ‖ to regain control of (oneself) **2.** *v.t.* to give with the hand, *he handed her her ticket* ‖ to assist or guide with the hand, *he handed her into the taxi* ‖ (*naut.*) to furl (a sail) **to hand down** from to a successor, *the title is handed down from father to son* **to hand in** to submit, *to hand in one's resignation* ‖ to give up, *small arms must be handed in to stores by noon* **to hand it to (someone)** (*pop.*) to acknowledge some quality in (someone) **to hand off** (*rugby*) to push away (an opponent who is trying to tackle one) with the open hand **to hand on** to pass to another person or to others **to hand out** to distribute **to hand over** to pass over the control of (something), *he handed over the fortress to the enemy* **3.** *adj.* of or pertaining to the hand ‖ worked, used, carried etc. by hand ‖ created by hand [O.E. *hand, hond*]

hand·bag (hændbæg) *n.* a woman's bag held in the hand, chiefly used to carry small necessities

hand·ball (hændbɔl) *n.* a game for two or four players, something like squash, but in which the hard rubber ball is struck with the hand. It is played on either one-wall or four-wall courts (cf. FIVES) ‖ the ball used

hand·bar·row (hændbærou) *n.* a handcart ‖ a workman's stretcher with two handles at each end carried by two men, for shifting loads (cf. WHEELBARROW)

hand·bell (hændbɛl) *n.* a small bell, fitted with a handle, rung by shaking it

hand·bill (hændbil) *n.* a small printed publicity sheet distributed by hand

hand·book (hændbuk) *n.* a book containing summarized information on a particular subject ‖ a guidebook ‖ a book in which a bookmaker records bets

hand·car (hændkɑr) *n.* (*rail., Am.=Br.* trolley) a flat car propelled along a railroad by a hand lever and used to convey tracklayers etc. to their place of work

hand·cart (hændkɑrt) *n.* a small twowheeled cart pushed by its short wooden shafts

hand·clasp (hændklæsp, hændklɔsp) *n.* a clasping of each other's hand by two people to express a strong bond of sympathy, affection, loyalty etc.

hand·craft (hændkræft, hændkrɑftɑ) **1.** *n.* a handicraft **2.** *v.t.* to make or work (something) by hand

hand·cuff (hændkʌf) **1.** *n.* a steel band which can be clamped around the wrist and locked, usually joined by a short chain to a second one so that the wrists of a person under arrest are held close together, often behind his back, or so that his wrist is clamped to a policeman's to prevent escape **2.** *v.t.* to fasten handcuffs on (a person)

Han·del (hænd'l), George Frederick (1685– 1759), musician and composer of German birth, naturalized English. He composed with extreme facility ('Messiah' was written in 21 days), and his immense output includes over 40 operas ('Rinaldo', 1711), about 20 oratorios, sacred and secular ('Messiah', 1741, 'Israel in Egypt', 1738, 'Samson', 1742), orchestral suites (Concerti Grossi), occasional music ('Water Music', 1717, 'Music for the Royal Fireworks', 1748), organ concertos, vocal and choral music

CONCISE PRONUNCIATION KEY: **(a)** æ, c*a*t; ɑ, c*a*r; ɔ f*aw*n; ei, sn*a*ke. **(e)** e, h*e*n; i:, sh*ee*p; iə, d*ee*r; ɛə, b*ea*r. **(i)** i, f*i*sh; ai, t*i*ger; ə:, b*i*rd. **(o)** o, *o*x; au, c*ow*; ou, g*oa*t; u, p*oo*r; ɔi, r*oy*al. **(u)** ʌ, d*u*ck; u, b*u*ll; u:, g*oo*se; ə, b*a*cillus; ju:, c*u*be. x, lo*ch*; θ, *th*ink; ð, bo*th*er; z, *Z*en; ʒ, corsa*g*e; dʒ, sava*g*e; ŋ, orangutan*g*; j, *y*ak; ʃ, *fi*sh; tʃ, fe*tch*; 'l, rabb*le*; 'n, redd*en*. Complete pronunciation key appears inside front cover.

and a great mass of chamber and instrumental music. Even his religious and formal music is dominated by the influence of the theater, and at its best is music of profound psychological subtlety and variety, an expression of the full range of human feeling

hand·ful (hǽndful) *pl.* **hand·fuls** *n.* as much as the hand will hold || a small number, *only a handful of survivors* || (*pop.*) a person or thing that is hard to manage [O.E. *handfull*]

hand gallop an easy, steady, moderate gallop

hand glass a small mirror or magnifying glass mounted on a handle || (*naut.*) a half-minute or quarter-minute sandglass used in timing the running out of a log line

hand grenade a small explosive shell thrown by hand after withdrawing a pin to activate the fuse

hand·grip (hǽndgrip) *n.* a rubber or plastic sheath fitted to the handlebar of a bicycle, the handle of a golf club etc., to prevent slipping of the hand

hand·gun (hǽndgʌn) *n.* a firearm (pistol, revolver) that can be held and fired with one hand

hand·i·cap (hǽndikæp) **1.** *n.* a disadvantage possessed by one person as compared with others, esp. a physical disability which limits the capacity to earn || a contest in which an allowance of distance, weight or time is made to the weaker competitors, or an artificial disadvantage imposed on the stronger ones || the allowance given or disadvantage imposed || (*golf*) the number of strokes by which a player is expected to exceed the standard for the course **2.** *v.t. pres. part.* **hand·i·cap·ping** *past* and *past part.* **hand·i·capped** to allot a handicap to (a competitor) || to put at a disadvantage, esp. a physical disadvantage **hand·i·cap·per** *n.* an official who decides what handicap to allot [formerly *hand in cap.*, a game in which winners were penalized]

hand·i·craft (hǽndikræft, hǽndikrɑft) *n.* a craft (trade or occupation) [for 'handcraft', like 'handiwork']

hand·i·ly (hǽndli:) *adv.* in a handy way || conveniently || easily, *it won the race handily*

hand·i·ness (hǽndinis) *n.* the state or quality of being handy

hand·i·work (hǽndiwə:rk) *n.* the product of handwork, *the curtains were his own handiwork* [O.E. *hand+geweorc*, work]

hand·ker·chief (hǽŋkərtʃif, hǽŋkərtʃi:f) *n.* a usually square piece of fabric carried in a pocket or handbag, used esp. for blowing the nose, weeping into, and waving goodbye with

han·dle (hǽnd'l) *n.* the part of a tool, utensil, weapon etc. designed for the hand or fingers to grasp || something that can be used as a pretext, *don't give him a handle for complaint* **to fly off the handle** to become suddenly very angry indeed [O.E.]

handle *pres. part.* **han·dling** *past* and *past part.* **han·dled** *v.t.* to touch or take in the hands, *do not handle the goods on display* || to deal with (a person, problem) || to be concerned with, treat, *this book handles the problems of old age* || *v.i.* to respond to control, *the new car handles beautifully* [O.E. *handlian*]

han·dle·bar (hǽnd'lbɑr) *n.* a curved bar transverse to the fork of the front wheel of a bicycle or motorcycle, used by hand for steering, and usually having other controls mounted on it

hand·ler (hǽndlər) *n.* someone who handles || someone who professionally exhibits dogs etc. in shows || someone who helps in the training of a boxer, or who acts as his second in a fight

hand·loom (hǽndlu:m) *n.* a loom worked by hand, not by mechanical power

hand·made (hǽndméid) *adj.* made by hand, not by machine

hand·maid (hǽndmeid) *n.* (*rhet.*) something looked on as having a ministering capacity, *science is the handmaid of philosophy* || (*archaic*) a female servant

hand·maid·en (hǽndmeid'n) *n.* (*rhet.* and *archaic*) a handmaid

hand-me-down (hǽndmi:dʌun) **1.** *adj.* (esp. of clothes) passed on, esp. to a younger member of the family **2.** *n. (pl.)* clothes passed on

hand·out (hǽndʌut) *n.* a leaflet or folder of information or publicity supplied by official departments or an agency || an item of clothing or food given to a beggar or tramp, or anything given for nothing

hand·o·ver (hǽndʌuvər) *n.* (*Br.*) the act of transferring the responsibility for an office, together with the relevant documents, moneys etc., to its new holder

hand·pick (hǽndpik) *v.t.* to select with an eye to high quality, *he handpicks his materials* || to select for one's own advantage, *to handpick jurors*

hand·rail (hǽndreil) *n.* a long piece of wood or metal etc. which can be held for support or protection when climbing or descending a steep slope or stairs, or to prevent oneself from falling from a balcony, terrace etc.

hand·saw (hǽndsɔ) *n.* a saw worked by hand, not by mechanical power

hand·set (hǽndset) **1.** *n.* the combined telephone transmitter and receiver mounted as a single unit **2.** *pres. part.* **hand·set·ting** *past* and *past part.* **hand·set** *v.t.* to set (type) by hand **3.** *adj.* (of type) set by hand

hand·shake (hǽndʃeik) *n.* a shake with the right hand of another's right hand in greeting, farewell, congratulation etc.

hand·some (hǽnsəm) *adj.* (of men) good-looking || (of women) beautiful in a way which commands admiration || (of animals) well-shaped and good to look at || ample, generously large, *a handsome reward* || gracious, highly praising, *a handsome compliment* || impressive and pleasing, *a mansion of handsome proportions* [M.E. *handsom*, easily handled]

hands-on (hǽndzɔn) *adj.* of using the hands, e.g., *a hands-on operation*

hand·spike (hǽndspaik) *n.* a lever used for moving heavy weights, e.g. for maneuvering a field gun

hand·spring (hǽndspriŋ) *n.* a feat of agility in which the feet pass right over the head and the body lands in the standing position still facing the original direction. Only the hands and feet touch the floor

hand·stand (hǽndstænd) *n.* a balancing feat in which a person holds his body vertical with the head downwards, arms extended, hands on the ground and legs together in the air

hand-to-hand (hǽndtəhǽnd) *adj.* (of combat) between man and man within arm's reach of one another

hand-to-mouth (hǽndtumáuθ) *adj.* (of existence) improvised constantly and barely adequate for immediate needs

hand·work (hǽndwə:rk) *n.* work done with the hands [O.E. *handweorc*]

hand·writ·ing (hǽndraitiŋ) *n.* writing done by hand || the style of such writing in a particular person

handwriting reader a computer-laser system to convert handwritten characters into machine-readable data

hand·writ·ten (hǽndrit'n) *adj.* in a person's handwriting

Hand·y (hǽndi:), **W**(illiam) **C**(hristopher) (1873–1958), U.S. black composer whose 'Memphis Blues' became (1912) the first blues song ever published. His works include 'St Louis Blues' (1914) and 'Beale Street Blues' (1917)

hand·y (hǽndi:) *comp.* **hand·i·er** *superl.* **hand·i·est** *adj.* conveniently near, *the shops are nice and handy* || able to do useful small manual jobs, esp. about the house || dexterous, *handy with an ax* || convenient and practical, *a handy little gadget*

hand·y·man (hǽndi:mæn) *pl.* **hand·y·men** (hǽndi:men) *n.* a man able to do many useful kinds of work with his hands reasonably well, esp. a man employed to do a variety of jobs

hang (hæŋ) **1.** *v. pres. part.* **hang·ing** *past* and *past part.* **hung** (hʌŋ) *v.i.* to be suspended, *your coat is hanging in the hall* || to have the weight supported, *a door hangs on its hinges* || to await a decision, *the question was left hanging* || (of drapery) to fall in folds or (of a jacket etc.) in an elegant loose fit || (of flowers) to droop for lack of moisture || (*Br.*, of a dress, slip etc.) to be too low at the bottom hem || (*pres. part.* **hanging** *past* and *past part.* **hanged**) to suffer death by being suspended by the neck || *v.t.* to suspend (something) || to attach (wallpaper, a poster etc.) to a wall || to decorate (a room etc.) with festoons etc. || to suspend (game) until it is high or (meat) until it is in good condition for cooking || to display (a picture) on a wall || (*pres. part.* **hanging** *past* and *past part.* **hanged**) to kill by suspending by the neck **to go hang** to become a matter of indifference or neglect, *to let an opportunity go hang* **to hang about** (or **around**) to linger or loiter in a place or near a person **to hang a jury** to prevent a jury from reaching a verdict for want of the required majority for decision **to hang back** to hesitate to commit oneself to

hang fire to be held up in its progress, *his novel is still hanging fire* **to hang in the balance** to be in doubt or suspense **to hang on** (or **upon**) to depend on, *much hangs on his decision* || to pay rapt attention to, *the crowd hung on his words* || (*pop.*) to persevere, continue, *hang on till next summer* || (*pop.*) to wait, *hang on while I fetch the key* **to hang one's head** to let one's head droop in shame **to hang on to** to hold firmly to **to hang out** to put (laundry) out to dry || to display (a flag or signal) || (*pop.*) to reside || to be (at a specified place) more often than not, *he hangs out at the poolroom* **to hang over** to be suspended over || to cover like a cloud || to threaten, *a fearful danger hangs over his head* **to hang together** to be consistent and coherent, *his arguments don't hang together* || (*pop.*) to be a united group, *to hang together in a crisis* **to hang up** to suspend || (*pop.*) to cause delay in || to break off a telephone conversation **2.** *n.* the manner in which something hangs, *the hang of a skirt* || (*pop.*) a very small bit, *she doesn't care a hang* **to get the hang of** to grasp the meaning or way of working of [O.E. *hangian v.i.*, to hang and *hōn v.t.*, to cause to hang]

han·gar (hǽŋər) *n.* a very large shed used to house aircraft [F.]

Hang·chow (hǽŋtʃáu) the capital (pop. 1,105,000) of Chekiang, E. central China, capital of S. China under the Sung dynasty (12th c.). It is a port (terminus of the Grand Canal), with engineering and textile industries (silk). Hangchow Bay is an arm of the East China Sea

hang-dog (hǽŋdɔg, hǽŋdɒg) *adj.* (of a look) showing guilt or shame

hang·er (hǽŋər) *n.* a coat hanger

hang·er-on (hǽŋərɔ́n, hǽŋərɒn) *pl.* **hang·ers-on** *n.* someone attaching himself to an influential person or group in the hope of personal advantage

hang five *v.* (*surfing*) to ride with the body forward and the toes of one foot protruding over the edge of the surfboard. —**hang ten** *v.* to ride a surfboard with both feet at the front edge of the board

hang glide *v.* (*sports*) to glide in harness in a kitelike glider, usually from a hill. —**hang glider** *n.* person and the apparatus. —**hang gliding** *n.*

hang·ing (hǽŋiŋ) **1.** *n.* the act of suspending (e.g. pictures in an exhibition) || execution or killing by suspending by the neck || (*pl.*) curtains or draperies **2.** *adj.* suspended from a support above || situated on a steep slope, *a hanging garden* || meriting death by hanging, *a hanging matter*

hanging buttress a buttress supported by a projection from a wall

hang loose *v.* (*colloq.*) to remain flexible; to relax

hang·man (hǽŋmən) *pl.* **hang·men** (hǽŋmən) *n.* a public executioner who hangs criminals

hang·nail (hǽŋneil) *n.* a piece of loose skin at the side or root of a fingernail or toenail

hang·nest (hǽŋnest) *n.* the Baltimore oriole, whose purselike nest, up to 2 ft in length, hangs from the tip of a tree limb and has the entrance hole near the bottom and to one side

hang·out (hǽŋaut) *n.* (*pop.*) the place (e.g. corner café, drugstore etc.) which someone or some group or some type of person habitually frequents

hang·o·ver (hǽŋʌuvər) *n.* headache and nausea as the result of drinking too much alcohol || something left over from earlier times or circumstances, *shortage of housing was a hangover from the war*

hang-up (hǽŋʌp) *n.* (*colloq.*) an emotional problem

ha·ni·wa (háːniwa) *n.* clay funerary figures left at graves in Japan

hank (hæŋk) *n.* two or more coils of wool, cotton or silk tied together (560 yds of wool, 840 yds of cotton) || (*naut.*) a ring or hoop to which a fore-and-aft sail is fastened || a lanky lock (of hair) [perh. fr. Norse]

han·ker (hǽŋkər) *v.i.* (with 'after' or 'for', or the infinitive) to have a continual nagging desire (for something or to possess or do something) **hán·ker·ing** *n.* [etym. doubtful]

Hán-kiang (hándʒjáŋ) (or Han) a river (900 miles long) flowing from S. central Shensi, China, to the Yangtze at Wuhan

Han Kook (han kuk) South Korea

Han-kow (hǽŋkáu) *WUHAN

CONCISE PRONUNCIATION KEY: **(a)** æ, c*a*t; ɑ, c*a*r; ɔ f*aw*n; ei, sn*a*ke. **(e)** e, h*e*n; iː, sh*ee*p; iə, d*ee*r; ɛə, b*ea*r. **(i)** i, f*i*sh; ai, t*i*ger; əː, b*i*rd. **(o)** o, *o*x; au, c*ow*; ou, g*oa*t; uː, p*oo*r; ɔi, r*oy*al. **(u)** ʌ, d*u*ck; u, b*u*ll; uː, g*oo*se; ə, b*a*cillus; juː, c*u*be. x, lo*ch*; θ, *th*ink; δ, bo*th*er; z, *Z*en; ʒ, cor*s*age; dʒ, sava*g*e; ŋ, orangutan*g*; j, *y*ak; ʃ, *fish*; tʃ, fet*ch*; 'l, rabb*le*; 'n, redd*en*. Complete pronunciation key appears inside front cover.

han·ky-pan·ky (hǽŋki:pǽŋki:) n. (pop.) mild deceit, cheating, or other sly dealing [arbitrary formation, prob. rel. to HOCUS-POCUS]

Han·ni·bal (hǽnəb'l) (247–c. 182 B.C.), Carthaginian general, son of Hamilcar Barca. Commander of the Carthaginian army in Spain, he precipitated the 2nd Punic War by attacking Saguntum, a Roman ally in Spain (219 B.C.). With a vast army and 40 elephants, he made a crossing of the Alps (218 B.C.) and defeated the Romans at Trasimene (217 B.C.) and Cannae (216 B.C.). After further campaigns in Italy he returned to Africa (203 B.C.) to defend Carthage, and was defeated by Scipio Africanus at Zama (202 B.C.). He carried out administrative reforms in Carthage, but went into exile (c. 195 B.C.) when Rome demanded his life, later committing suicide to avoid capture

Han·no (hǽnou) (5th c. B.C.), Carthaginian navigator. He explored the Atlantic coast of Africa as far as Sierra Leone

Hanno 'the Great' (3rd c. B.C.), Carthaginian statesman. He opposed Hannibal, advocating peace with Rome and a Carthaginian empire in Africa

Ha·noi (hænɔ́i, hɑnɔ́i) the capital (pop. 2,570,905) of Vietnam, a port in the N. at the apex of the Red River delta, S.E. Tonkin. Exports: rice, sugar, silk. Industries: textiles, paper, distilling. University (1917). It was the 7th-c. seat of the Chinese rulers of Annam. It became the capital of Annam after the 15th c. It was occupied by the French (1882–1954)

Han·o·ver (hǽnəvər) (G. Hannover) a former province of Prussia, forming (since 1946) most of the W. German state of Lower Saxony. As an electorate (1692–1814) and kingdom (1814–66), it was joined (1714–1837) in a personal union with the British Crown. It was annexed (1866) by Prussia

Hanover the capital (pop. 535,854) of Lower Saxony, on the Leine, chief communications center of northern West Germany. Industries: rubber goods, textiles, machinery, motor vehicles etc.

Hanover the name (1714–1901) of the British royal house. George Louis, elector of Hanover, succeeded to the British throne (1714) as George I under the provisions of the Act of Settlement (1701). His descendants ruled both Hanover and Great Britain until the separation of the two thrones on the accession (1837) of Victoria. The name was changed to Saxe-Coburg-Gotha on the accession (1901) of Edward VII **Han·o·ve·ri·an** (hænouvíəri:ən) adj.

Han·sard (hǽnsərd) the reports of the proceedings of the British parliament. They have been official, and verbatim, since 1909 and are published by H.M. Stationery Office [after Thomas Curson *Hansard* (1776–1833), the first printer of the (unofficial) series begun (1803) by William Cobbett]

Hansberry (hǽnzberi) Lorraine (1930–65), U.S. playwright, the first black woman to have a play performed on Broadway. Her play 'A Raisin in the Sun' (1959; film, 1961; musical, 1973) won the New York Drama Critics Circle Award. She also wrote 'The Sign in Sidney Brustein's Window' (1964) and 'Les Blancs' (1970; adapted for the stage by her husband Robert Nemiroff)

hanse (hǽns) n. (hist.) a medieval merchant guild, **Hanse** the Hanseatic League [O.F. fr. M.H.G., association of merchants fr. O.H.G. *hansa*, a band of men]

Han·se·at·ic League (hænsi:ǽtik) a commercial league of N. German towns, founded in the 13th c. to control trade in the Baltic. Centered on Lübeck, the League included more than 70 towns in the 14th c., and by the 15th c. dominated the trade of N. Europe. It enforced its monopoly by means of boycotting, developed its own system of commercial and maritime laws, and established branches with special privileges in many towns. It declined in the 16th c. as national commerce developed, and was dealt a fatal blow by the Thirty Years' War

han·som (hǽnsəm) n. (hist.) a two-wheeled cab, seating two passengers behind hinged half-doors and under a hood, the driver being on a seat up behind the hood, with his reins passing up over the hood [patented in 1834 by J. A. *Hansom* (1803–82), Eng. architect who designed it]

Han·son (hǽnsən), John (1721–83), American Revolutionary leader. He was elected (1781) president of the Congress of the Confederation by the continental congress under the Articles of Confederation, though he held none of the powers given the first president under the U.S. Constitution

Ha·nuk·kah (hɑ́nəkə, *Heb.* xanu:kɑ́) n. the Jewish festival commemorating the rededication of the Temple after the victory (165 B.C.) by the Maccabees over the Syrians. It lasts eight days, beginning on the 25th day of Kislev. Each night the menorah is lit [Heb., lit.=a dedication]

Han·yang (hánjáŋ) *WUHAN

hap·haz·ard (hǽphǽzərd) **1.** adj. of events occurring by chance or illogically rather than by design, *his choice was made in a purely haphazard way* **2.** adv. according to no set plan or system, *he made his choice haphazard* [O.N. *happ*, luck + HAZARD]

hap·less (hǽplis) adj. (rhet.) unlucky, *a hapless youth* [O.N. *happ*, luck]

hap·log·ra·phy (hæplɔ́grəfi) n. writing a word, syllable or letter only once where correctly it occurs twice, in juxtaposition (cf. HAPLOLOGY) [fr. Gk *haploos*, single + *graphe*, writing]

hap·loid (hǽplɔid) **1.** adj. (biol.) having half the number of chromosomes characteristic of a somatic cell, e.g. having the number of chromosomes characteristic of a gamete (cf. DIPLOID) **2.** n. (biol.) a haploid cell [fr. Gk *haploos*, single, simple + *-eidēs*, like]

hap·lol·o·gy (hæplɔ́lədʒi:) n. pronouncing a syllable only once where correctly it occurs twice, in juxtaposition (cf. HAPLOGRAPHY) [fr. Gk *haploos*, single + *logos*, discourse]

hap·lo·sis (hæplóusis) n. (biol.) the halving of the chromosome number during meiosis [fr. Gk *haploos*, single, simple + *-osis*, morbid condition]

ha'p'orth (héipərθ) n. (Br., hist.) as much as a halfpenny could buy ∥ (Br., pop.) any minute quantity or negligible amount

hap·pen (hǽpən) v.i. to occur, take place ∥ to occur quite by accident or spontaneously ∥ to chance, *if you happen to see him* **to happen on** (or **upon**) (something or someone) to find or meet by chance **to happen to** (someone) to befall [M.E. *happenen*, *hapnen* fr. earlier *hap* fr. O.N. *happ*, luck]

hap·pen·ing (hǽpəniŋ) n. a special or unusual staged event involving many spectators, esp. in the arts

hap·pen·stance (hǽpənstæns) n. a chance circumstance [HAPPEN = (CIRCUM) STANCE]

hap·pi·ly (hǽpəli:) adv. in a happy manner ∥ luckily

hap·pi·ness (hǽpi:nis) n. feelings of joy and pleasure mingled in varying degree, *intense happiness, quiet happiness* ∥ the satisfaction of the deepest desire, *the search for happiness*

hap·py (hǽpi:) comp. **hap·pi·er** superl. **hap·pi·est** adj. experiencing joy and pleasure, *to feel happy* ∥ expressing such feelings, *a happy face* ∥ lucky, fortunate, *a happy coincidence* ∥ apt, *a happy choice of words* ∥ drunk ∥ as though made drunk by (something specified in a preposed, hyphenated noun), *punch-happy* and esp. with the result of being too quick to make use of something specified, *gun-happy* [fr. older *hap* fr. O.N. *happ*, luck]

hap·py-go-luck·y (hǽpi:goulʌ́ki:) adj. cheerfully taking things as they happen, without care for the future ∥ haphazard

happy hour a period during which a bar offers special inducements, e.g., lower prices

Haps·burg, Habs·burg (hǽpsbə:rg, hɑ́psburg) the dynasty which supplied dukes and archdukes of Austria (from 1282), kings of Hungary and Bohemia (from 1526), and emperors of Austria (from 1804). They ruled the Holy Roman Empire (1438–1806) and were kings of Spain (1516–1700). The name was derived from the ancestral castle of Habichtsburg (11th c.) in the Aargau canton of Switzerland. They extended their territories by conquest and marriage to include Austria, Hungary, Bohemia, S. Poland, N. Italy, Naples, Sardinia, Burgundy and the Netherlands. Most of the family possessions were lost in 1918 when Austria became a republic. The dynasty was notable for its support of Catholicism and conservatism

hap·tic lens (hǽptik) a type of contact lens that aligns with white of the eye (sclera). *Cf* MICROCORNEAL LENS

ha·ra-ki·ri (hærəkíəri:) n. a method of suicide in Japan, consisting of disembowelment with a sword. It was originally reserved for men of samurai rank in disgrace or condemned to death [Jap. *hara*, belly + *kiri*, cutting]

Har·ald I (hǽrəld) 'Fairhair' (c. 850–933), first king of Norway (872–c. 930)

Harald III 'Hardrada' (1015–66), king of Norway (1046–66). With Tostig, earl of Northumbria, he invaded England (1066) and was defeated and killed at Stamford Bridge by the army of Harold II of England

Harald 'Bluetooth' (d. c. 985), king of Denmark (c. 940–c. 985). Christianity was introduced into Denmark during his reign

ha·rangue (hərǽŋ) **1.** n. a long and forceful speech made to a gathering of people **2.** v.t. pres. part. **ha·rangu·ing** past and past part. **ha·rangued** to make a harangue to [earlier *arang* fr. O.F. *arenge*, harangue]

Ha·rap·pa (hərǽpə) the site in central Punjab of one of the chief cities of the Indus civilization (*INDIA, *MOHENJODARO)

Ha·rar (hɑ́rər) an ancient walled town (pop. 70,289) in S.E. Ethiopia, capital of Harar province and the chief Moslem center of Ethiopia: coffee trading

Harare (hərɑ́rei) (formerly Salisbury) the capital and largest city (pop. 656,000) of Zimbabwe. It was renamed Harare, the name of a local African chief before European colonization, when Zimbabwe gained its independence (1982). It is the industrial and commercial center of Zimbabwe: metallurgy, building materials, food and tobacco processing. University

har·ass (hǽrəs, hərǽs) v.t. to subject (someone) to continuous vexatious attacks, questions, demands or other unpleasantness ∥ (mil.) to make repeated raids or attacks on **har·ass·ment** n. [F. *harasser* perh. fr. O.F. *harer*, to set a dog on]

Har·bin (hɑ́rbin) (Charbin or Pinkiang), the capital (pop. 2,150,000) of Heilungkiang, N.E. China, the industrial and trade center of N. Manchuria

har·bin·ger (hɑ́rbindʒər) n. (rhet.) a person, object or event heralding the future [M.E. *herbergeour*, someone who provides lodgings fr. O.F. *herbergier*, to lodge]

har·bor, Br. **har·bour** (hɑ́rbər) n. a bay or inlet of quiet water protected from stormy waves by man-made or natural walls permitting ships to enter and leave through a narrow entrance (the harbor mouth) for anchorage or shelter ∥ a place of refuge [O.E. *hereborg* fr. *here*, army + *beorg*, shelter]

harbor, Br. **harbour** v.t. to shelter, *to harbor a fugitive from justice* ∥ to cherish secretly, *to harbor suspicions* ∥ v.i. to take refuge or anchor in a harbor [O.E. *herebeorgian*]

har·bor·age, esp. Br. **har·bour·age** (hɑ́rbəridʒ) n. the shelter provided by a harbor ∥ a harbor

harbor master, Br. **harbour master** the official responsible for seeing that harbor regulations are complied with

Har·burg-Wil·helms·burg (hɑ́rburxvílhelmsburx) *HAMBURG

hard (hɑrd) **1.** adj. (of solid things) difficult to cut, crack or crush ∥ not easy, *hard to understand* ∥ not easy to do, *a hard translation* ∥ not easy to comprehend or accept, *a hard fate* ∥ not easy to bear, *hard punishment* ∥ oppressive, *a hard master* ∥ unkind, *hard feelings* ∥ unfeeling, *a hard heart* ∥ tough, *training has made him hard* ∥ energetic and persistent, *a hard worker* ∥ of nonbiodegradable pesticides ∥ of news of events with immediate importance ∥ of copy for publication readable without video screen ∥ ungenerous, *a hard bargain* ∥ unfavorable, *hard luck* ∥ (of prices) high and tending to stay high ∥ (of currency) backed by large gold reserves or a steady and prosperous economy, so that its value (in terms of commodities which it can buy) does not fluctuate appreciably ∥ (of water) having in solution esp. salts of calcium or magnesium which react with soap and so prevent the soap from lathering ∥ (of liquor) having a high percentage of alcohol ∥ (pop., of 'c' and 'g') pronounced as in 'come' and 'go' ∥ (of wheat) having a rich gluten content ∥ (fine arts) lacking grace, *a hard line* ∥ (phys., of radiant energy) having relatively high penetrating power ∥ **to be hard on** to be stern with ∥ to be an unjust or unlucky burden on **2.** adv. strongly, *to blow hard* **hard by** (rhet.) close beside **hard come by** obtained with great effort **hard up** acutely short of money **hard up for (something)** lacking, *to be hard up for words to express one's feelings* **hard upon** close behind **to be hard put to it** to experience difficulty, e.g. in controlling oneself **to go hard with** to be to one's misfortune [O.E. *heard*]

hard-and-fast (hɑ́rd'nfǽst, hɑ́rd'nfɑ́st) adj. (of rules) unalterable and strictly binding ∥ (of a

CONCISE PRONUNCIATION KEY: **(a)** æ, c*a*t; ɑ, c*a*r; ɔ f*aw*n; ei, sn*a*ke. **(e)** e, h*e*n; i:, sh*ee*p; iə, d*ee*r; ɛə, b*ea*r. **(i)** i, f*i*sh; ai, t*i*ger; ə:, b*i*rd. **(o)** o, *o*x; au, c*ow*; ou, g*oa*t; u, p*oo*r; ɔi, r*oy*al. **(u)** ʌ, d*u*ck; u, b*u*ll; u:, g*oo*se; ə, b*a*cillus; ju:, c*u*be. x, lo*ch*; θ, *th*ink; ð, bo*th*er; z, *Z*en; ʒ, cor*s*age; dʒ, sa*v*age; ŋ, orangutan*g*; j, *y*ak; ʃ, *fi*sh; tʃ, fe*tch*; 'l, rab*ble*; 'n, red*den*. Complete pronunciation key appears inside front cover.

line of conduct) rigidly determined ‖ (of distinctions) clearly fixed

Har·dang·er (hɑrdǽŋgər) a fiord (114 miles long) south of Bergen, Norway

Har·dang·er·vid·da (hɑrdǽŋgərviḋə) a region of mountains and plateaus east of Hardanger fiord, S. Norway

hard-baked (hɑ́rdbéikt) adj. baked until hard ‖ (Br.) disillusioned and made callous by experience

hard beach (mil.) a portion of a beach especially prepared with a hard surface extending into the water. It is employed for the purpose of loading or unloading directly into or from landing craft

hard-bit·ten (hɑ́rdbit'n) adj. tough, steeled by experience ‖ hard and realistic

hard·board (hɑ́rdbɔrd, hɑ́rdbourd) n. material manufactured in sheets from sawdust and chips of wood bound together under heat and pressure by plastic or resin, used in house fittings and furniture

hard-boiled (hɑ́rdbɔ́ild) adj. (of an egg) boiled until the albumen and yolk are both solid ‖ (of people) tough and realistic, without sentimental illusions, esp. to the point of being cynical

hard·bound (hɑ́rdbɑund) adj. of a book bound with boards covered with cloth. —**hardback** n.

hard cash coin or banknotes as contrasted with checks or promises to pay at a future date

hard cider (Am.=Br. cider) an alcoholic drink made from fermented apple juice

hard coal anthracite

hard-core (hɑ́rdkɔ́r, hɑ́rdkóur) n. (Br.) broken bricks, stones, clinker etc., laid down and pounded firm as a foundation for roads, paving etc. **hard core** the central, most determined or most dependable group within a group **hárd·córe** adj. of or pertaining to the hard core ‖ (esp. of pornography) blatant

hard-core adj. 1. of persons whose status is not easily changed, e.g., hard-core unemployed 2. of pornography, explicit

hard court a tennis court with an asphalt or similar surface, not grass

hard drug an addictive drug, e.g., heroin. Cf SOFT DRUG

hard edge n. of abstract painting created with sharply defined geometric forms, usually with strong color. —**hard-edger** n.

hard·en (hɑ́rd'n) v.i. to become hard ‖ (of prices) to rise, or cease to fall, on the market ‖ to become tougher in mind and character ‖ to become callous or intolerant ‖ v.t. to make (something) hard or harder ‖ to make hardy ‖ to make hardhearted, callous or cynical **hárd·en·er** n. a substance added to give a paint or varnish a harder finish

Har·den·berg (hɑ́rd'nberx), Prince Karl August von (1750–1822), Prussian statesman. As chancellor of Prussia (1810–22), he continued Stein's social and political reforms (esp. until 1815), and represented Prussia at the Congress of Vienna (1815)

hard·ened (hɑ́rdənd) adj. especially strengthened to withstand stress

hardened site (mil.) an enclosure or area able to withstand effects of enemy attack, usu. underground, esp. nuclear attack, e.g., for housing nuclear missiles

hard·en·ing (hɑ́rd'niŋ, hɑ́rdniŋ) n. a material turning the surface of iron into steel ‖ (chem.) the conversion of liquid fats or oils into the solid state by hydrogenation

hard-fea·tured (hɑ́rdfi:tʃərd) adj. having unattractive looks which suggest lack of sensitiveness or human sympathy

hard-gloss (hɑ́rdglɔs, hɑ́rdglɒs) adj. (of a paint) drying to give a hard shiny surface

hard-hat (hɑ́rdhæt) n. 1. construction worker 2. by extension, a determined, outspoken conservative; a person strongly antagonistic to nonconformists. —**hardhattism** n.

hard-head·ed (hɑ́rdhéd:d) adj. realistic and practical, unswayed by sentiment

hard-heart·ed (hɑ́rdhɑ́rtid) adj. callous, unfeeling

hard-hit·ting (hɑ́rdhitiŋ) adj. direct, vigorous and effective

Har·di·ca·nute (hɑ́rdikənju:t) *HARTHACNUT

Har·die (hɑ́rdi:), James Keir (1856–1915), British Socialist leader. He became (1892) the first Socialist to be elected to parliament, founded (1893) the independent Labour party, and led the Labour party (1906–15) in the House of Commons. He was a militant writer and speaker

hardie *HARDY n.

har·di·hood (hɑ́rdi:hud) n. (old-fash.) boldness

har·di·ly (hɑ́rd'li:) adv. (old-fash.) in a bold manner

har·di·ness (hɑ́rdi:nis) n. the state or quality of being hardy

Har·ding (hɑ́rdiŋ), Warren Gamaliel (1865–1923), 29th president (1921–3) of the U.S.A., a Republican. His administration was notable only for the calling (1921) of the Washington Naval Conference and for its record of general corruption. Two of his cabinet members were convicted of complicity in the Teapot Dome scandal after his death

hard labor, Br. **hard labour** imprisonment in which the prisoner is made to do strenuous manual work

hard-laid (hɑ́rdléid) adj. (of rope) twisted so that the strands are at an angle of about 45°

hard line rigid adherence to a program or dogma; uncompromising. —**hard-line** adj., v. —**hard-liner** n.

hard·ly (hɑ́rdli:) adv. not to any great degree, scarcely, she hardly knew him ‖ only just, barely, he had hardly started when he fell ill ‖ not quite, not at all, that is hardly true ‖ (rhet.) with effort or difficulty, freedom hardly won ‖ severely, harshly, don't deal hardly with him

hard-mouthed (hɑ́rdmáuðd, hɑ́rdmáuθt) adj. (of a horse) insensitive to handling, not answering well to the bit

hard·ness (hɑ́rdnis) n. the quality of being hard ‖ difficulty ‖ unfeelingness ‖ harshness ‖ physical toughness ‖ resistance of a metal to deformation and indentation ‖ resistance of a mineral to abrasion

hard news reports of actual happenings, esp. of some importance vs. opinion, stunts, etc. Cf HARD COPY

hard-of-hear·ing (hɑ́rdəvhíəriŋ) adj. partly deaf

hard pad a virus disease in dogs, often fatal, similar to distemper. It is characterized by pneumonia and diarrhea, and hardening of the skin on the paws and the nose

hard palate the hard, bony forward part of the palate

hard-pan (hɑ́rdpæn) n. a compacted layer of subsoil consisting of detrital matter ‖ ground that is hard and unbroken ‖ (fig.) rock bottom, bedrock

hard rock hard driving, loud rock 'n' roll music with a regular beat, usu. involving electronically amplified instruments. Cf SOFT ROCK

hard rubber ebonite

hards (hɑrdz) pl. n. the coarse parts of flax or hemp that remain on the fiber after the separation process [O.E. heordan]

hard science a natural or physical science, e.g., chemistry, biology. —**hard scientist** n. Cf NATURAL SCIENCE, SOFT SCIENCE

hard sell a sales technique using an aggressive, high-pressure approach (cf. SOFT SELL)

hard·ship (hɑ́rdʃip) n. suffering or privation difficult to bear, or an instance of either

hardship post a work assignment, usu. abroad, where difficult conditions warrant additional compensation

hard solder a high-melting solder, containing copper, used for brazing

hard state an efficient, well-organized, stable sovereign state. Cf SOFT STATE

Hardt (hɑrt) *RHINELAND-PALATINATE

hard-tack (hɑ́rdtæk) n. a mixture of flour and water without salt baked hard and used formerly on ships as a substitute for bread

hard-top (hɑ́rdtɒp) n. an automobile resembling a convertible but having a rigid plastic or metal roof. The roof is sometimes made so that it can be dismounted and a canvas top substituted ‖ indoor motion picture theater

Hard·war (hɑ́rdwɑr) a holy city (pop. 41,000) in Uttar Pradesh, India. The Ganges is made sacred here by Vishnu's footprint in stone

hard·ware (hɑ́rdwɛər) n. (Am.=Br. ironmongery) metal goods ‖ (electronics) equipment used in computing (cf. SOFTWARE)

hard·wood (hɑ́rdwud) n. any close grained wood from deciduous trees, e.g. oak, beech, ash, and from some tropical trees, e.g. mahogany, logwood (cf. SOFTWOOD)

hard X ray an X ray with great ability to penetrate

Har·dy (hɑ́rdi:), Alexandre (c. 1569–c. 1632), French dramatist. His best plays prepared the way for 17th-c. Classical drama

Har·dy (hɑ́rdi:), Thomas (1840–1928), English novelist and poet. His major novels show with elaborate irony a universe ruled by a pitiless

fate, and the indifference of man to the suffering and misery of his fellow creatures. His native Dorset (which he calls 'Wessex') forms the somber setting for most of his novels. The most important of these are: 'Far from the Madding Crowd (1874), 'The Return of the Native' (1878), 'The Mayor of Casterbridge' (1886), 'Tess of the d'Urbervilles' (1891), and 'Jude the Obscure' (1896). Much of Hardy's poetry is anecdotal. Yet some 20 or so short lyrics, usually about the pain of loss, catch a bleak moment of intense truth. 'The Dynasts' (3 vols: 1904, 1906, 1908) is an elaborate epic drama of the Napoleonic Wars

har·dy, har·die (hɑ́rdi:) pl. **har·dies** n. a blacksmith's chisel which fits into a hole in the anvil [prob. fr. HARD]

hardy comp. **har·di·er** superl. **har·di·est** adj. strong, robust ‖ (of plants) able to flourish outdoors all year without special protection [O.F. hardi fr. hardir, to harden fr. Gmc]

hare (hɛər) 1. pl. **hares, hare** n. a herbivorous lagomorph. Hares are up to 2 ft in length and have long ears, large eyes, short tail, long hind legs and a divided upper lip. They are widely distributed in temperate regions. They have acute sight and hearing, and move with bounding swiftness. The females produce 3–6 young, several times a year. The flesh is edible ‖ the fur or pelt of a hare 2. v.i. pres. part. **har·ing** past and past part. **hared** to run very fast [O.E. hara]

hare and hounds a cross-country race in which two runners (the 'hares') start in advance of other runners (the 'hounds') who try to overtake them. The 'hares' leave a trail of scattered pieces of paper

hare·bell (hɛ́ərbel) n. Campanula rotundifolia, fam. Campanulaceae, the bluebell of Scotland, a small, delicate, blue, bell-flowered, herbaceous plant, growing wild in temperate countries ‖ the wood hyacinth

hare·brained, Br. also **hair·brained** (hɛ́ərbreind) adj. (of a person) stupidly prone to act without thought of the consequences ‖ (of an action) done with a stupid failure to think of the consequences

Hare Krishna (hɑ́ri:kríʃnə), Hindu movement, also known as International Society for Krishna Consciousness, founded by A.C. Bhaktivedanta Swami and brought to the U.S. in 1965. The mantra of the society, 'hare krishna' ('O Lord Krishna') is chanted three times a day by followers

hare·lip (hɛ́ərlip) n. a congenital deformity consisting in a divided upper lip. It can be corrected by surgery

har·em (hɛ́ərəm, hǽrəm) n. the women's apartments in a Moslem household ‖ the wives and servants of the master of the house who live in these apartments [Arab. harām, harīm, sacred, forbidden]

hare's-foot trefoil (hɛ́ərzfut) Trifolium arvense, fam. Papilionaceae, a species of clover

Har·gei·sa (hɑrgéisə) a town (pop. 60,000) of W. Somali, center of a vast livestock-raising region

Har·greaves (hɑ́rgri:vz), James (d. 1778), British millwright who invented (1764) the spinning jenny, enabling a number of threads to be spun by one machine. The invention provoked riots (1768) by spinners who feared for their livelihood

har·i·cot (hǽrikou) n. a member of Phaseolus, fam. Papilionaceae, a genus of edible beans, esp. P. vulgaris ‖ a mutton stew with vegetables [F. perh. fr. Nahuatl ayerotli, bean]

Har·ing·ton (hǽriŋtən), Sir John (1561–1612), English writer and wit. He was popular in his day for his version of Ariosto and for an amusing work on the privy, 'Metamorphosis of Ajax' (1596)

Ha·ri·ri, Al- (alhɑrí:ri:) (1054–1122), Arabian writer. His masterpiece was the 'Maqamat', a collection of rhymed fablelike tales full of wit, imagination and shrewd observation

hark (hɑrk) v.i. (archaic) to listen closely ‖ v.t. (archaic) to listen to ‖ (Br., with 'forward', 'away' etc.) to urge (hounds) to work **to hark back** (with 'to') to refer to (a time in the past), he is always harking back to his college days ‖ (of hounds) to go back in their tracks to try to recover lost scent ‖ (Br.) to call (hounds) back [M.E. herkien]

harken *HEARKEN

harl, harle (hɑrl) n. a fiber of flax or hemp ‖ a herl [perh. M.L.G. herle, harle]

Har·lan (hárlən), John Marshall (1833–1911), associate justice (from 1877) of the U.S. supreme court, best known for his decisions during the Reconstruction period after the Civil War. In the 'Civil Rights Cases' (1883), he urged a broader interpretation of the 13th and 14th amendments, stating in one instance that the 14th amendment provided for punishment of individuals who discriminated against blacks. Many of his views were rejected by the court

Harlan, John Marshall (1899–1971), U.S. associate justice of the Supreme Court (1955–71), grandson of John Marshall HARLAN. A strict constructionist, he was appointed to the Court by Pres. Eisenhower and helped to advance the cause of civil rights and wrote the Court's majority opinion in 'NAACP v. Alabama ex. rel Patterson' (1958)

Har·lem (hárləm) (*Du.* Haarlem) a city (pop. 169,000) in N. Holland, Netherlands, west of Amsterdam: bulb growing, shipbuilding, machinery, printing, textiles, brewing, chemical industries

Har·le·quin (hárlikwin, hárlikin) *n.* a character (partner to Columbine, a dancer) in commedia dell' arte. He survives as a buffoon in European and American pantomime. He plays wearing a mask and dressed in particolored tights, and carrying a wooden wand or sword **har·le·quin** *adj.* of variegated, bright colors [F. *harlequin, arlequin* fr. Ital.]

har·le·quin·ade (hərlikwinéid, hərlikinéid) *n.* a scene in pantomime in which Harlequin and the clown fool about and engage in horseplay

Har·ley (hárli:), Robert (1661–1724), 1st earl of Oxford, English Tory statesman. With Lord Bolingbroke, he negotiated the Treaty of Utrecht (1713). He was the patron of Swift and Pope

har·lot (hárlət) *n.* (*old-fash.*) a prostitute **hár·lot·ry** *n.* (*old-fash.*) prostitution [O.F. *herlot, harlot,* a knave, vagabond]

harm (hárm) 1. *n.* injury, hurt, *to come to no harm* ‖ moral wrong, *there's no harm in trying* 2. *v.t.* to injure, hurt [O.E. *hearm, hearmian*]

HARM (hárm) (*mil. acronym*) for U.S. Navy high-speed antiradiation missile (AGM 88A), with programmable digital processors, for use in F-4 G Wild Weasel and other aircraft; in development by Texas Instruments Corp.

har·mat·tan (hərmətǽn) *n.* a hot, dry, dust-laden wind of W. Africa [fr. Span. *haramatan* fr. Fanti]

harm·ful (hármfəl) *adj.* injurious, hurtful **harm·less** (hármlis) *adj.* not injurious, not hurtful ‖ not likely to cause trouble

Har·mon (hármən), Millard Fillmore (1888–1945), U.S. general during the 2nd world war. He commanded (1942–4) all U.S. forces in the South Pacific and (from 1944) U.S. army air forces in the central Pacific, launching the strategic air war against Japan

har·mon·ic (hármónik) 1. *adj.* (*phys.*) bearing the relation of a harmonic to the fundamental frequency ‖ (*math.* and *phys.*) that can be expressed in terms of sine and cosine functions (*HARMONIC ANALYSIS) ‖ (*mus.*) of or relating to harmony as distinct from melody or rhythm ‖ harmonious ‖ of or relating to harmonics 2. *n.* (*phys.*) one of the components of harmonic motion (*HARMONIC MOTION) that is an integral multiple of the frequency of the fundamental wave on which it is superimposed, e.g. the higher harmonic of a 60-cycle current wave ‖ (*mus.*) a tone in the harmonic series, esp. one of the overtones produced by causing a wire or air column to vibrate in two or more equal portions instead of as a whole ‖ (*elec.*) a frequency simply related to the fundamental frequency of an alternating current or radio wave [fr. L. *harmonicus* fr. Gk]

har·mon·i·ca (hármónikə) *n.* a small rectangular wind instrument in which free reeds are agitated by the exhalation or inhalation of the breath ‖ a glass harmonica [L. fem. of *harmonicus* adj., harmonic]

har·mon·i·cal·ly (hármónikli:) *adv.* (*math.*) in a harmonic relation ‖ (*mus.*) with respect to harmony

harmonic analysis a mathematical method of solving certain physical problems (e.g. the motion of a vibrating string, or the flow of heat in solids) of a kind that takes mathematical expression in a differential equation and that includes a set of known values for the independent variable (called the boundary conditions). The solution takes the form of a finite, conver-

gent series of products of sine and cosine function (*FOURIER ANALYSIS)

harmonic minor scale (*mus.*) a minor scale having semitones between the second and third, the fifth and sixth, and the seventh and eighth steps, the other intervals being whole tones

harmonic motion (*phys.*) a vibratory motion that may be characterized as consisting of one mode or a combination of modes of simple harmonic motion (*SIMPLE HARMONIC MOTION)

harmonic progression (*math.*) a progression consisting of terms whose reciprocals constitute an arithmetic progression e.g. 1/5, 1/7, 1/9)

har·mon·ics (hármóniks) *n.* the theory or science of musical sounds

harmonic series (*mus.*) a series of tones comprising a fundamental tone and those tones above it whose frequencies are integral multiples of the fundamental's frequency

har·mo·ni·ous (hármóuni:əs) *adj.* pleasing to the ear, tuneful ‖ interrelated in a pleasing way, *harmonious proportions* ‖ free from jarring differences of feeling or opinion [fr. F. *harmonieux*]

har·mo·nist (hármənist) *n.* (*mus.*) someone skilled in harmony ‖ someone who reconciles narratives by different authors dealing with the same subject

har·mo·ni·um (hármóuni:əm) *n.* a reed organ, the sounds being produced by forcing air through free reeds of metal, using bellows worked by the feet [F.]

har·mo·ni·za·tion (hərmənizéifən) *n.* a harmonizing or being harmonized

har·mo·nize (hármənaiz) *pres. part.* **har·mo·niz·ing** *past* and *past part.* **har·mo·nized** *v.i.* to be, sing or play in harmony ‖ to be in agreement ‖ to blend tastefully ‖ *v.t.* to provide (a melody) with harmonies ‖ to bring into agreement ‖ to cause to blend tastefully [F. *harmoniser*]

har·mo·ny (hárməni:) *pl.* **har·mo·nies** *n.* a pleasing combination of musical sounds ‖ the relationship between two or more notes sung or played simultaneously (cf. MELODY) ‖ the science of combinations of musical sounds and of their use in composition ‖ a reconciliation of narratives, *a harmony of the Gospels* ‖ agreement, *this story is not in harmony with the facts* ‖ peace, *he disturbs the harmony of the household* ‖ pleasing relationship, *architecture in harmony with the landscape* [F. *harmonie* fr. L. fr. Gk]

harmony of the spheres a theory of Pythagoras stating that the spheres in which heavenly bodies move emit musical sounds depending upon their radii and upon the speed of the bodies

Harms·worth (hármzwə:rθ) *NORTHCLIFFE

Har·nack (hárnæk), Adolf von (1851–1930), German Lutheran theologian. His 'Das Wesen des Christentums' (1900) became the manifesto of modernist theology. His chief work was 'Lehrbuch der Dogmengeschichte' (1886–90)

har·ness (hárnis) 1. *n.* the complete set of leather belts and straps with their metal fittings worn by a draft animal ‖ the working contrivance in some mechanical operations, e.g. in raising or lowering the warp threads in a loom ‖ reins for children learning to walk ‖ (*hist.*) the armor and accessories of a knight or man-at-arms **in double harness** working with a partner, or as partners **in harness** at work to **die in harness** to die before retiring from work 2. *v.t.* to put a harness on (an animal) ‖ to fasten by means of a harness ‖ to control and utilize (a source of power), *to harness the tides* ‖ to tie together as though in harness, *certain conditions are harnessed to the plan* [M.E. *harneis* fr. O.F.]

harness race a trotting race

Harold kings of Norway and Denmark *HARALD

Har·old I (hǽrəld) 'Harefoot' (*d* 1040), king of England (1037–40), son of Cnut. He claimed the throne in opposition to his half brother Harthacnut, and died as the latter was planning to invade England

Harold II (c. 1022–66), king of England (1066), son of Earl Godwin. He succeeded (1053) to his father's earldom, and was chief adviser to Edward the Confessor for the remainder of the reign. He promised (c. 1064) to support the candidacy of William of Normandy to the English throne, but later repudiated the promise, and, on Edward's death, was elected king by the English nobility. He defeated an invasion by his brother Tostig and Harald III of Norway at

Stamford Bridge (Sept. 25, 1066), but was defeated by William of Normandy at Hastings (Oct. 14, 1066), where he was killed

harp (hárp) *n.* a musical instrument consisting of taut wires within a large, roughly triangular, wooden frame, the wires being plucked with the fingertips [O.E. *hearpe*]

harp *v.i.* to play on a harp ‖ (with 'on') to make frequent, boring or annoying reference [O.E. *hearpian*]

Har·pers Ferry (hárpərz) a town (pop. c. 600) in West Virginia, at the confluence of the Potomac and Shenandoah Rivers, and the site of John Brown's raid (1859). A commercial and industrial center at the time of the Civil War, it was captured (1862) by the Confederate General 'Stonewall' Jackson, who took the largest number of Union prisoners (12,500) taken in the war. Most of the town is now Harpers Ferry national monument

Har·pies (hárpi:z) *pl. n.* (*Gk mythol.*) the three daughters of Electra and Thaumas, personified as snatchers of human souls. In appearance they were monstrous birds with the faces of women

har·pist (hárpist) *n.* someone who plays the harp

har·poon (hárpú:n) 1. *n.* a barbed spear with an attached line, hurled from a boat or fired from a gun to bury itself in the flesh of a whale or large fish 2. *v.t.* to spear with a harpoon [F. fr. *harpon* fr. *harpe,* claw]

Harpoon (*mil.*) *n.* a U.S. radar-guided, turbojet, antiship, low-level missile, carrying a 500-lb conventional warhead, capable of being employed from surface ships (RGM-84), aircraft (AGM-84), or submarines (UGM-84)

harp·si·chord (hárpsikɔrd) *n.* a keyboard instrument, the keys operating quills or leather points which pluck taut wires. A forerunner of the piano, it was esp. used from the 16th to the 18th cc. and is still preferred by many performers of keyboard music of this period [fr. obs. F. *harpechorde* fr. *harpe,* harp+*chorde,* string]

har·py (hárpi:) *pl.* **har·pies** *n.* a foul-tempered, domineering woman ‖ a rapacious person [fr. L. *harpyia* fr. Gk]

harpy eagle *Harpia harpyja,* the South American crested eagle, with a fan-shaped tail

har·que·bus (hárkwəbəs) *pl.* **har·que·bus·es** *n.* an arquebus

har·ri·dan (hǽridən) *n.* an evil-tempered old woman, esp. one hideously made up to look young [perh. fr. F. *haridelle,* worn-out mare]

har·ri·er (hǽri:ər) *n.* a hawk of genus *Circus,* having very long wings and tail. They fly close to the ground and subsist chiefly on small mammals. They are widely distributed [HARRY]

harrier *n.* a hound used for hunting hares, closely resembling the foxhound but smaller in size ‖ a cross-country runner [perh. fr. HARE]

Harrier (*mil.*) *n.* British VTOL short-range fighter aircraft

Har·ri·man (hǽrəmən), Edward Henry (1848–1909), U.S. financier and railroad magnate. After purchasing (1898) the Union Pacific railroad, he vied unsuccessfully with James J. Hill for control of the Northern Pacific, which led to a crisis on Wall Street. His methods were denounced (1907) by President Theodore Roosevelt

Har·ring·ton (hǽriŋtən), James (1611–77), English political writer. His 'The Common-Wealth of Oceana' (1656) describes a utopian society, and advocates a written constitution, the ballot, and government by country gentlemen

Har·ris (hǽris), Joel Chandler (1848–1908), U.S. author, who depicted plantation life in the South. As a humor writer for many southern newspapers, esp. the 'Atlanta Constitution', he created the very popular 'Uncle Remus' stories, capturing the black dialect

Harris, Roy (1898–1979), American composer. His works are mainly orchestral or choral and occasionally incorporate American folk themes

Harris, William Torrey (1835–1909), U.S. educator and philosopher. As U.S. commissioner of education (1889–1906), he introduced art, music, science and manual arts into the curriculum, and advocated the professional study of education for teachers in training

Harris a district in the island of Lewis, Outer Hebrides, Scotland, famous for its home-dyed, handwoven tweed

Har·ris·burg (hǽrisbə:rg) the capital (pop. 53,264, with agglom. 345,000) of Pennsylvania,

CONCISE PRONUNCIATION KEY: **(a)** æ, cat; ɑ, car; ɔ *faw*n; ei, *snake.* **(e)** e, *hen;* i:, *sheep;* iə, *deer;* eə, *bear.* **(i)** i, *fish;* ai, *tiger;* ə:, *bird.* **(o)** o, *ox;* au, *cow;* ou, *goat;* u, *poor;* ɔi, *royal.* **(u)** ʌ, *duck;* u, *bull;* u:, *goose;* ə, *bacillus;* ju:, *cube.* x, *loch;* θ, *think;* ð, *bother;* z, *Zen;* ʒ, *corsage.* dʒ, *savage;* ŋ, *orangutang;* j, *yak;* ʃ, *fish;* tʃ, *fetch;* 'l, *rabble;* 'n, *redden.* Complete pronunciation key appears inside front cover.

on the Susquehanna River: iron, steel, textiles

Har·ri·son (hǽris'n), Benjamin (1833–1901), 23rd president (1889–93) of the U.S.A., a Republican, and grandson of William H. Harrison. He was elected over Grover Cleveland in probably the most corrupt campaign in U.S. history. All Republican partisan measures, including the McKinley Tariff Act, received his approval. He convoked (1889) the Pan-American Congress

Harrison, Frederic (1831–1923), English philosopher. He was a pioneer of positivism in England, and author of 'The Meaning of History' (1862), 'Order and Progress' (1875) etc.

Harrison, William Henry (1773–1841), ninth president (1841) of the U.S.A., a Whig. As the Congressional delegate (1799) from the Northwest Territory, he helped to divide the territory into Indiana and Ohio, and as governor (1800–12) of the Indiana Territory, he opened these lands to white settlement by negotiating treaties with the Indians. He led the U.S. forces against Tecumseh in the Battle of Tippecanoe. In the War of 1812 he was commander in the Northwest, capturing (1813) Detroit and winning (1813) the Battle of the Thames. He won the presidency on his slogan 'Tippecanoe and Tyler too', in the first highly publicized campaign in U.S. history. He died after only one month in office

har·row (hǽrou) 1. *n.* an iron frame with spikes or disks in echelon, drawn by a tractor or horse and used after plowing to break up clods of soil into a fine tilth, to cover seed with tilth, or to tear up weeds 2. *v.t.* to work over (a field) with a harrow ‖ to lacerate (the feelings) **hár·row·ing** *adj.* [M.E. *harwe*]

harrowing of hell the conquest and plundering of hell by Christ (when, after his crucifixion and before his ascension into heaven,'he descended into hell') to release the souls of the righteous who died in pre-Christian times [fr. archaic *harrow*, to harry, ravage]

har·ry (hǽri:) *pres. part.* **har·ry·ing** past and past part. **har·ried** *v.t.* to harass, harried by creditors ‖ to make repeated attacks on ‖ to lay waste, ravage [O.E. *hergian*, to ravage]

harsh (harʃ) *adj.* without mercy, a harsh sentence ‖ finding fault with acerbity, a harsh critic ‖ oppressive, a harsh ruler ‖ displeasing to one of the senses, harsh colors ‖ stark, a harsh contrast [M.E. *harsk* prob. fr. O.N.]

Har·sha (hárʃa) (d. 647), the ruler (606–47) of an empire which he created in N. India. He provided political stability here after the disintegration of the Gupta Empire

Har·sha·var·dha·na (hárʃəvárdənə) the ruler Harsha. He assumed the title Vardhana after his early conquests in N. India

Hart, (hart) Gary Warren (1936–), U.S. politician, Democratic senator (1975–1985) from Colorado. He managed George McGovern's presidential campaign (1972) before being elected to the Senate in 1974. He ran for the Democratic presidential nomination in 1984 on a platform of nuclear arms control and budget revamping, but lost to Walter Mondale. He wrote 'A New Democracy' (1983)

hart (hart) *pl.* **harts, hart** *n.* (*Br.*) the male deer (esp. the red deer) esp. from its fifth year onwards [O.E. *heort, heorot*]

Harte, (hart) Bret (Francis Bret Harte, 1836–1902), American author inspired by mining-camp life in mid-19th-c. California. His stories include 'The Luck of Roaring Camp' (1868) and 'The Outcasts of Poker Flat' (1869)

har·te·beest (hártəbi:st, hártbi:st) *pl.* **har·te·beests, har·te·beest** *n. Alcephalus caama*, a large, swift African antelope with ringed, curved horns. It stands about 4 ft at the shoulders [Afrik. fr. Du. *hert*, hart + *beest*, beast]

Hart·ford (hártfərd) the capital (pop. 136,392, with agglom. 525,000) of Connecticut: insurance business, engineering, textile and food-processing industries

Hartford Convention a U.S. convention (1815) of New England Federalists who proposed amending the Constitution to protect states' rights. The distrust it aroused elsewhere hastened the decline of the Federalist party

Har·tha·cnut (hárðəknú:t) (c. 1019–42), king of Denmark (1035–42) and of England (1040–2), son of Cnut. His English inheritance was usurped at first by his half brother Harold I, on whose death he succeeded peacefully. He left the government largely in the hands of Earl Godwin

Hart·ley (hártli:), David (1705–57), English philosopher and psychologist. His 'Observations on Man' (1749) sets forth the principle of associationism

Hart·mann (hártmən), Karl Robert Eduard von (1842–1906), German philosopher, author of 'Philosophy of the Unconscious' (1869 Eng. trans 1884)

Hart·mann von Au·e (hártmənfonáue) (c. 1170–c. 1210), German poet. He wrote mainly epic poems on the Arthurian and other legends, and lyrics on sacred subjects

harts·horn (hártshɔrn) *n.* a substance, largely ammonium carbonate, obtained from shavings or clippings of the horns of a hart. It was formerly the chief source of ammonia

Har·tung (hártuŋ), Hans (1904–), French painter born in Germany. Working in a manner akin to that of abstract expressionism, he paints nonobjective compositions of linear rhythms

har·um-scar·um (héərəmskéərəm, hǽrəmskǽrəm) 1. *adj.* (of people or behavior) wild in a scatterbrained way 2. *adv.* in a harum-scarum way 3. *n.* someone who is harum-scarum [prob. fr. HARE+SCARE]

Ha·run al-Ra·shid (harú:nalraʃí:d) (c. 763–809), Abbasid caliph of Baghdad (786–809). A distinguished military leader, he exacted tribute from the Byzantine Empire. Under his rule, Baghdad became a thriving commercial center, and his court attracted poets, scholars, philosophers and musicians

Har·vard University (hárvərd) the oldest university in the U.S.A., in Cambridge, Massachusetts, founded in 1636 and named after its first benefactor, John Harvard (1607–38), a nonconformist minister born in England. It consists of Harvard College, graduate schools and research institutes

har·vest (hárvist) 1. *n.* the gathering in of ripe crops or fodder ‖ the time of year when crops are gathered in ‖ crops with respect to their yield, a good harvest ‖ the result of action or behavior 2. *v.t.* to gather in (a crop) ‖ to obtain (the result of action or behavior) [O.E. *hærfest*]

harvest bug a larval mite of fam. *Trombiculidae*, the size of a grain of cayenne pepper, scarlet in color. In hot months harvest bugs are found on vegetation. They burrow into the skin of people and domestic animals, causing inflammation and acute irritation

har·ves·ter (hárvistər) *n.* a machine used in harvesting ‖ a harvest worker [HARVEST v.]

harvest festival a religious service of thanksgiving for the harvest

harvest home a secular celebration of the end of a harvest

har·vest·man (hárvistmən) *pl.* **har·vest·men** (hárvistmən) *n.* a member of *Phalangida*, an order of long-legged arachnids. They have a short ovoid body, with stink glands on the cephalothorax. They are nocturnal and omnivorous

harvest mite a harvest bug

harvest moon the full moon nearest to the autumnal equinox (Sept. 22 or 23). For nearly two weeks before, it rises on successive nights at nearly the same hour, in mid-northern latitudes

Har·vey (hárvi:), William (1578–1657), English physician who discovered and convincingly demonstrated the circulation of the blood, unifying previous and fragmentary theories ('Exercitatio anatomica de motu cordis et sanguinis', 1628). He also did important work in embryology ('Exercitationes de generatione animalium', 1651)

Harvey Steel Process a process of hardening steel armor plate by heat treatment in carbon, introduced (1891) by A. H. Harvey, U.S. metallurgist

Har·wich (hǽridʒ) a town (pop. 15,280) in Essex, England, 70 miles northeast of London: a passenger port for the Hook of Holland, Antwerp and Esjberg

Ha·ry·a·na (hari:ána) *PUNJAB

Harz Mtns (harts) a wooded massif between the Weser and the Elbe, central Germany, surmounted by the Brocken (3,747 ft) (*WALPURGIS NIGHT)

has 3rd pers. sing. pres. tense of HAVE

Ha·sa, al- (alhása) a district (area 22,500 sq. miles) of Nejd, Saudi Arabia, on the Persian Gulf, the country's chief oil-producing region. Operating center: Dhahran. Port: Dammam

Ha·san (hás'n) (c. 625–69), fifth caliph, eldest son of Ali and Fatima, and Shi'ite imam

has-been (hǽzbin) *n.* a person whose fame has died or whose powers have diminished ‖ a thing that has grown obsolete, diminished in importance etc.

Has·dru·bal (hǽzdrub'l) (d. 207 B.C.), Carthaginian general, brother of Hannibal. He commanded the Carthaginian army in Spain (218–207 B.C.) and, in an attempt to reinforce Hannibal in Italy, crossed the Alps, but was defeated and killed on the Metaurus

Ha·šek (háʃek), Jaroslav (1883–1923), Czech writer, author of the satirical novel 'The Good Soldier Schweik' (1920–3)

hash (hæʃ) 1. *n.* meat, esp. meat previously cooked, chopped with potatoes and baked or fried **to make a hash of** to make a lamentable failure of **to settle someone's hash** to prevent someone from being a trouble any longer 2. *v.t.* to cut (esp. meat) into small pieces ‖ (pop.) to make a muddle or failure of **to hash over** to talk about in detail, consider minutely the various aspects of [earlier *hache* fr. F. *hacher*, to cut up]

Hash·e·mite Kingdom of Jordan (hǽʃəmait) *JORDAN

hash·ish (hǽʃi:ʃ, hǽʃiʃ) *n.* a narcotic derived from hemp, esp. *Cannabis sativa*, fam. *Moraceae*, that is chewed, smoked or drunk for its intoxicating effects [Arab.]

Has·i·dism (hǽsidizəm) *n.* a Jewish religious and social sect founded in Poland in the 18th c. by Rabbi Israel ben Eliezer (1700-60). The movement was a protest against authoritarian rationalism and emphasized the ecstatic elements of Judaism [fr. Heb. *hasídhīm*, pious ones]

has·let (héizlit, hǽslit) *n.* part of the entrails (heart, liver etc.) of an animal (esp. a pig) roasted for food or made into a pâté [M.E. *hastelet* fr. O.F.]

has·n't (hǽzənt) *contr.* of HAS NOT

hasp (hæsp, hasp) 1. *n.* a bar, usually of metal hinged at one end and pierced near the other end, used with a staple and toggle or padlock as a fastening for a door, window, lid etc. 2. *v.t.* to fasten by means of a hasp [O.E. *hæpse*, fastening and *hæpsian*, to fasten]

Has·san II (hás'n) (1930–), king of Morocco (1961–). He assumed the office of prime minister after a state of emergency was declared (1965)

has·sle (hǽs'l) 1. *n.* (pop.) a wrangle, dispute ‖ (pop.) an annoying struggle 2. *v. pres. part.* **has·sling** past and past part. **has·sled** *v.i.* (pop.) to bicker ‖ *v.t.* to bother, annoy [etym. doubtful]

has·sock (hǽsək) *n.* a small, firm, stuffed cushion, often covered with carpet material, used for kneeling on or as a footrest ‖ a matted tuft of coarse grass [O.E. *hassuc*]

hast (hæst) archaic 2nd pers. sing. pres. tense of HAVE

has·tate (hǽsteit) *adj.* (bot., of leaves) triangular, with two sharp lobes extending at the base, giving the leaf a spear-shaped appearance [fr. L. *hastatus* fr. *hasta*, spear]

haste (heist) *n.* deliberate speediness ‖ an attempt to be more speedy than is reasonable **in haste** hastily **to make haste** to hurry **has·ten** (héis'n) *v.i.* to move with hurry ‖ *v.t.* to bring on sooner than if events were left to run their course, the remark hastened his downfall ‖ to treat as urgent, execute with added speed ‖ to cause (someone) to make haste or be precipitate [O.F. *haste, haster*]

hast·i·ly (héistili:) *adv.* in a hurry ‖ in too great a hurry

hast·i·ness (héisti:nis) *n.* the state or quality of being hasty

Has·tings, Battle of (héistiŋz) the decisive victory (Oct. 14, 1066) of the Norman army under Duke William (later William I) over the English led by King Harold, in Sussex, England. The battle, depicted in the Bayeux Tapestry, was followed by the Norman conquest of England

Hastings, Warren (1732–1818), first governor-general of British India (1774–85). After carrying out financial and legal reforms in India, he was impeached (1788) on charges of corruption, but finally acquitted (1795)

hast·y (héisti:) *comp.* **hast·i·er** *superl.* **hast·i·est** *adj.* impetuous, precipitate, a hasty decision ‖ made or done with haste, a hasty visit ‖ (of the temper) quickly flaring into anger [O.F. *hasti* for *hastif*]

hasty breaching (*mil.*) the creation of lanes through enemy minefields by such methods as blasting, pushing rollers or disabled vehicles through the minefields, deliberate breaching, or bypassing the obstacle. *Cf* BREACHING

hasty pudding a pudding made from cornmeal, often served with molasses ‖ (*Br.*) oatmeal porridge, or a pudding of similar consistency made from flour and milk or water

hat (hæt) 1. *n.* an article designed to protect or adorn the head, and distinguished from a cap esp. by having a brim or by being voluminous in the crown **to keep something under one's hat** to keep something a secret **to take one's hat off to** to affirm one's admiration for **to talk through one's hat** to talk nonsense 2. *pres. part.* **hat·ting** *past* and *past part.* **hat·ted** *v.t.* to put a hat on, supply with a hat [O.E. *hœt*]

Ha·tay (hɑtái) *ALEXANDRETTA

hat·band (hǽtbænd) *n.* a ribbon sewn externally around the bottom of the crown of a hat ‖ an internal strip of leather used to stiffen and keep the crown of a hat in shape

hat block a rounded block used for shaping or ironing a hat

hatch (hætʃ) 1. *v.i.* to emerge from an egg as a result of incubation ‖ (of eggs) to open when incubation is completed ‖ to emerge from a chrysalis ‖ *v.t.* to produce (young) from eggs by incubation ‖ (often with 'up') to produce as a result of scheming 2. *n.* the act or process of hatching ‖ the brood hatched [M.E. *hacchen*]

hatch *n.* an aperture, fitted with a door or lid, in a wall (e.g. a serving hatch between kitchen and dining room), in a floor (e.g. giving access to a wine cellar or vault), in the deck of a ship (e.g. giving access to a hold), in a ceiling (e.g. giving access to a loft), or in a roof ‖ a covering for a ship's hold or stairway ‖ a hatchway ‖ a sliding door in a lock gate or weir controlling the flow of water [O.E. *hœc*]

hatch *v.t.* to mark with numerous fine parallel lines, e.g. in engraving or in delineating an area on a map or drawing [earlier *hach, hache* fr. F. *hacher*, to hack]

hatch·back (hǽtʃbæk) *adj.* in a motor vehicle, a rear sloping roof that swings open upward, to accept luggage and/or passengers. —**hatch-back** *n.* the car. *Cf* FASTBACK, NOTCHBACK

hatched (hætʃt) *v.* dismissed from federally funded employment on the grounds of violating the Hatch Act, which prohibits political activity by federal employees

hatch·el (hǽtʃəl) 1. *n.* an instrument with sharp steel teeth used in dressing flax, i.e. in separating the fiber from the hards 2. *v.t.* to dress (flax) with a hatchel [M.E. *hecchel, hechele*]

hatch·er·y (hǽtʃəri) *pl.* **hatch·er·ies** *n.* a device or place where eggs (e.g. of trout) are hatched under care

hatch·et (hǽtʃit) *n.* a small ax with a short handle for chopping or splitting ‖ a tomahawk **to bury** (**dig up**) **the hatchet** to make peace (war), or end (start) a quarrel [F. *hachette* dim. of *hache*, ax]

hatchet face a narrow face with sharp prominent features **hatch·et·fáced** *adj.*

hatch·ing (hǽtʃiŋ) *n.* shading by fine parallel lines

hatch·ment (hǽtʃmənt) *n.* (*heraldry*) a lozenge-shaped funeral panel bearing the arms of a deceased person and hung for a time on a wall of his dwelling to signalize his death [altered fr. ACHIEVEMENT]

hatch·way (hǽtʃwei) *n.* a large opening in the deck of a ship giving access to the hold ‖ any opening that may be shut by a hatch

hate (heit) 1. *n.* intensely hostile aversion, compounded of anger and fear, and centered on a real or supposed cause of injury 2. *v.t. pres. part.* **hat·ing** *past* and *past part.* **hat·ed** to experience the sensation of hate in relation to (persons or things) ‖ (*pop.*) to dislike strongly, *he would hate to disappoint you, she hates the cold* **hate-ful** *adj.* arousing the sensation of hate ‖ unkind, mean [O.E. *hete, hatian*]

hath (hæθ) archaic *3rd pers. sing. pres.* of HAVE

Hath·a·way (hǽθəwei), Anne (c. 1557–1623), wife of William Shakespeare

Ha·to·ya·ma (hɑtɔjama), Ichirō (1883–1959), Japanese political leader and prime minister (1954–6)

hat·pin (hǽtpin) *n.* a long ornamental pin thrust through a woman's hat and hair to keep the hat in place

ha·tred (héitrid) *n.* the passion of hate [HATE+ *red* fr. O.E. *rœden*, condition]

Hat·shep·sut (hǽtʃépsuːt) (early 15th c. B.C.), Egyptian queen (c. 1489–c. 1469 B.C.) of the 18th dynasty. She married, and ruled jointly with, her half brother, Thutmose III. She built a magnificent temple beside the Nile near Thebes

hat·ter (hǽtər) *n.* someone who makes or sells hats [HAT *n.*]

Hat·ter·as, Cape (hǽtərəs) a promontory, dangerous to shipping, on Hatteras I., off the east coast of North Carolina

hatter's shakes (*med.*) disease due to mercury poisoning characterized by muscular tremors, formerly common among hatters. *Cf* MADHATTER'S DISEASE

hat trick (*cricket*) the feat of taking three wickets with successive balls [from an old custom of presenting a bowler who did this with a new hat]

Hat·tu·sas (xútusas) *BOGAZKOY

hau·berk (hóbərk) *n.* (*hist.*) a coat of interwoven steel rings, often sleeveless [O.F. *hauberc* fr. O.H.G.]

haugh·ti·ly (hót'li:) *adv.* in a haughty manner

haugh·ti·ness (hóti:nis) *n.* the quality or state of being haughty

haugh·ty (hóti:) *comp.* **haugh·ti·er** *superl.* **haugh·ti·est** *adj.* displaying overbearing pride, with disdain for others [fr. F. *haut*, high]

haul (hɔl) 1. *v.t.* to pull with an effort, *to haul a boat up a bank* ‖ to transport by road, railroad etc. ‖ (*naut.*) to alter the course of (a ship), esp. by sailing closehauled ‖ *v.i.* to give a long, steady pull, *haul on the rope* ‖ (*naut.*) to alter course by sailing close-hauled **to haul down the flag** to surrender **to haul over the coals** to reprimand **to haul up** (*pop.*) to bring to trial, *to be hauled up before the judge* 2. *n.* a strong steady pull ‖ a transporting or the distance over which a load is transported ‖ the quantity of fish taken in a net or in a catch ‖ the valuables stolen by a thief on one job **hául·age** *n.* the act of hauling goods ‖ the charge made for this **háuler** *n.* someone who transports goods by road **haul·ier** (hóljər) *n.* (*Br.*) a hauler [M.E. *halen* fr. O.F.]

haulm (hɔm) *n.* (*Br.*) the stem or stalk of a plant ‖ (*Br., collect.*) stalks of plants such as potatoes, peas etc. after harvesting [O.E. *healm*]

haunch (hɔntʃ, hantʃ) *n.* the lateral part of the body between the ribs and the thigh ‖ a leg and loin of meat cut in one piece ‖ (*archit.*) the shoulder of an arch, between the crown and the piers **to squat** (or **sit**) **on one's haunches** to sit resting one's hindquarters on one's upturned heels [O.F. *hanche* perh. fr. Gmc]

haunt (hɔnt, hant) 1. *v.t.* (of ghosts, spirits etc.) to pay frequent visits to, or be continually present in ‖ to visit very frequently, *to haunt a bar* ‖ to follow (someone) about in an unwelcome way ‖ to be always present as a nagging anxiety in the mind of **to be haunted** to be frequented by ghosts, spirits etc. 2. *n.* a place which one frequents, *to visit one's old haunts* ‖ a den or feeding place of an animal [F. *hanter*, to frequent]

Haupt·mann (háuptman), Gerhart Johann (1862–1946), German author. His naturalistic sociological dramas include 'The Weavers' (1892). His later plays and poems are often in a more romantic and symbolic vein

Hau·sa (háusə) *pl.* **Hau·sas, Hau·sa** *n.* a people of mixed Negroid and Berber stock forming the predominant linguistic group in N. Nigeria. The Hausa developed a civilization by the 10th c., became Moslem (14th c.) and prospered esp. in the 17th c. They were conquered by the Fulani (early 19th c.) ‖ a member of this people ‖ the Sudanic language of this people, spoken widely in W. Africa, written in Arabic script

Hauss·mann (ousmæn), Georges Eugène, Baron (1809–91), French administrator. As prefect of the Seine (1853–70), he rebuilt Paris with wide radial boulevards and avenues, laid out parks, and reconstructed the sewerage system

haus·to·ri·um (hɔstóri:əm, hɔstóuri:əm) *pl.* **haus·to·ri·a** (hɔstóri:ə, hɔstóuri:ə) *n.* (*bot.*) a specialized structure of some parasitic plants (e.g. dodder, mistletoe etc.) which penetrates into the vascular bundles of the host plant to obtain nourishment [Mod. L. fr. L. *haustor*]

haut·bois, haut·boy (óuboi, hóuboi) *pl.* **haut·bois, haut·boys** *n.* (*mus.*) the former name for an oboe ‖ an organ stop giving an oboelike quality ‖ *Fragaria moschata*, fam. *Rosaceae*, a tall species of strawberry [F. *hautbois*]

haute cou·ture (outku:tyr) *n.* the art and industry of the leading women's fashion houses [F.]

haute cuisine (outkwizi:n) (*Fr.*) dishes prepared in the grand manner with elaborate sauces. —**haute cuisine** *adj.*

Haute-Ga·ronne (outgærɔn) a department (area 2,457 sq. miles, pop. 777,400) in S. France (*GASCONY, *LANGUEDOC). Chief town: Toulouse

Haute-Loire (outlwær) a department (area 1,930 sq. miles, pop. 205,500) in S. central France (*LANGUEDOC, *LYONNAIS). Chief town: Le Puy

Haute-Marne (outmærn) a department (area 2,420 sq. miles, pop. 212,300) in N.E. France (*CHAMPAGNE). Chief town: Chaumont

Hautes-Alpes (outzælp) a department (area 2,178 sq. miles, pop. 97,400) of S.E. France in the Alps (*DAUPHINÉ, *PROVENCE). Chief town: Gap

Haute-Saône (outsoun) a department (area 2,074 sq. miles, pop. 222,300) in E. France (*FRANCHE-COMTÉ). Chief town: Vesoul

Haute-Sa·voie (outsævwa) a department (area 1,774 sq. miles, pop. 447,800) in E. France (*SAVOY). Chief town: Annecy

Hautes-Py·ré·nées (outpi:reinei) a department (area 1,750 sq. miles, pop. 227,200) in S.W. France (*GASCONY). Chief town: Tarbes

hau·teur (outé:r, houté:r) *n.* haughtiness [F.]

Haute-Vienne (outvjen) a department (area 2,119 sq. miles, pop. 352,100) in W. central France (*LIMOUSIN, *MARCHE, *POITOU). Chief town: Limoges

Haut-Rhin (ourẽ) a department (area 1,354 sq. miles, pop. 635,200) in N.E. France (*ALSACE). Chief town: Colmar

Hauts-de-Seine (oudəsen) a department (area 68 sq. miles, pop. 1,438,900) in N. central France, west of Paris. Chief town: Nanterre (*ILE-DE-FRANCE)

Ha·va·na (həvǽnə) (*Span.* Habana) the capital (pop. 1,981,300) and economic center of Cuba, in Havana province, on the northeast coast, founded in 1519, on a peninsula sheltering one of the best harbors in the western hemisphere. Main industries: sugar refining, rum, tobacco (esp. cigars), meat packing. Spanish castle (16th c.), baroque cathedral (17th–18th cc.), palace (18th–19th cc.). University (1670)

Havana (həvǽnə) *n.* a cigar made in Cuba of local tobacco [after HAVANA (the capital)]

Havana Conference of Foreign Ministers of the American Republics a conference held (1941) in Havana. It pledged to take over any territories in America belonging to European powers which were themselves invaded. Under this agreement Canada occupied St Pierre and Miquelon Is

have (hæv) 1. *v. 1st* and *2nd pers. sing. pres.* **have** *3rd pers. sing. pres.* **has** (hæz) *1st, 2nd* and *3rd pers. pl. pres.* **have** *pres. part.* **hav·ing** *past* and *past part.* **had** (hæd) *v.t.* ('have' is often replaced by 'have got') to hold in the hand, *what have you there?* ‖ to catch and hold, *now I have you* ‖ to own, possess, *they have two cars* ‖ to be in a specified personal relationship to, *I have four brothers, she has many enemies* ‖ to contain, *the house has five rooms, the book has illustrations* ‖ to accept, *will you have another?* ‖ to take, *to have a bath* ‖ to receive, *I have my reward* ‖ to experience mentally, *to have an idea, have a dream* ‖ to experience, undergo, *to have an operation, have a nice time* ‖ to understand suddenly, *I have it!* ‖ to be afflicted with, *to have gout* ‖ to permit, *I won't have it* ‖ to give birth to, *to have a baby* ‖ to assert, insist on, *he will have it that I said so* ‖ to cause to do (with infin.) or suffer (with past part.), *please have him cut the grass, have the house rewired* ‖ to be under an obligation or necessity as regards, *to have a job to do* ‖ to engage in some activity, *to have a quarrel* ‖ to gain control of, *he has the game if he makes no mistakes* ‖ to know, *I have it by heart* ‖ (*pop.*) to trick, deceive, cheat ‖ to hold at a disadvantage ‖ used as an auxiliary with past participles of most verbs to form their perfect tenses, *I have seen my tailor, I had seen him, I shall have seen him, I would have seen him* etc. ‖ (often hæf) used with infinitives to express obligation or necessity, *I have to go now, does it have to be me?* **to have at** (*rhet.*) to attack **to have done with** to have finished with, finished using (or doing etc.) **to have it coming to** deserve what one gets, esp. punishment or bad luck **to have it in for (someone)** to bear (someone) ill will **to have it in one** to have the courage or ability, *I didn't know he had it in him to go on alone* **to have it out** to discuss or fight in order to settle a problem, quarrel etc. **to**

CONCISE PRONUNCIATION KEY: (**a**) æ, c*a*t; ɑ, c*a*r; ɔ f*aw*n; ei, sn*a*ke. (**e**) e, h*e*n; i:, sh*ee*p; iə, d*ee*r; ɛə, b*ea*r. (**i**) i, f*i*sh; ai, t*i*ger; ə:, b*i*rd. (**o**) o, *o*x; au, c*ow*; ou, g*oa*t; u, p*oo*r; ɔi, r*oy*al. (**u**) ʌ, d*u*ck; u, b*u*ll; u:, g*oo*se; ə, b*a*cillus; ju:, c*u*be. x, lo*ch*; θ, *th*ink; ð, bo*th*er; z, *Z*en; ʒ, cor*s*age; dʒ, sava*ge*; ŋ, orangutan*g*; j, *y*ak; ʃ, *f*ish; tʃ, fe*tch*; 'l, rabb*le*; 'n, redd*en*. Complete pronunciation key appears inside front cover.

have it over to be in a better position than (someone) **to have nothing on** to have no information to the discredit of ‖ **to have no advantage over to have something on** to possess information to the discredit of **to have to do with** to be a concern of, *what has this to do with me?* ‖ to be concerned with, deal with **to have up** (*Br.*) to summon **to let someone have it** to hurt someone physically or with words etc. **2.** *n.* (*Br., pop.*) a fraud ‖ (*pop.*) a person or nation with wealth, *the haves and the have-nots* [O.E. *habban*]

ha·ven (héivən) *n.* a small natural bay or inlet providing shelter and anchorage for ships ‖ a refuge [O.E. *hœfen*]

have·n't (hǽvənt) *contr.* of HAVE NOT

ha·ver (héivər) (*Br.*) *v.i.* to hesitate before making a decision [origin unknown]

hav·er·sack (hǽvərsæk) *n.* a bag slung over the shoulder by a strap and used to carry food etc. [F. *havresac* fr. G. *habersack,* sack for oats]

hav·oc (hǽvək) *n.* destruction on a wide and intense scale **to play** (or **make, raise**) **havoc with** to cause intense disturbance in or disruption to, *the weather played havoc with our plans* [A.F. *havok* fr. O.F. *havot*]

haw (hɔ) *n.* the nictitating membrane [origin unknown]

haw *n.* the berry of the hawthorn ‖ the hawthorn [O.E. *haga,* hedge]

haw 1. *v.i.* to make this sound when hesitating for words, esp. *to hem and haw* **2.** *n.* this sound [imit.]

Ha·wai·i (həwáii:, həwáji:) a state (area 6,424 sq. miles, pop. 994,000) of the U.S.A. in the central Pacific (Polynesia), consisting of a group of more than 20 volcanic islands and atolls. Inhabited islands: Oahu, Hawaii, Maui, Kauai, Molakai, Lanai, Niihau. Capital: Honolulu. People: 37% Japanese, 23% of European descent, 17% Hawaiian, 12% Filipino, 7% Chinese, 2% Puerto Rican, 2% Korean. Main language: English. Highest points: Mauna Kea (13,784 ft) and Mauna Loa (13,675 ft), volcanoes on Hawaii. The land is 7% arable, 40% grazing and 25% forest. Average temperature (F.) at Honolulu: 75°. Annual rainfall: from 15 ins on the leeward side of the islands to over 300 ins in the mountains. Agriculture: sugarcane (first state producer), pineapples (first world producer), coffee, flowers, beef cattle. Resources: bauxite, pumice. Industries: sugar processing, canning, tourism, fishing, handicrafts. State university (1907) at Honolulu. Captain Cook discovered the islands (1778), then under the rule of native kings. Trade was developed (19th c.) by the Americans, who annexed the islands (1898) and made them a territory (1900). The Japanese attack (Dec. 7, 1941) on Pearl Harbor brought the U.S.A. into the 2nd world war. Hawaii became (1959) the 50th state of the U.S.A.

Ha·wai·ian (həwáiən, həwájən) **1.** *adj.* of or pertaining to Hawaii **2.** *n.* a native or inhabitant of Hawaii ‖ the Polynesian language of Hawaii

Hawaiian guitar a guitar having 6-8 strings which are plucked with thimbles, and whose pitch is controlled by a metal bar placed across the strings

hawk (hɔk) **1.** *n.* a diurnal bird of prey of suborder *Falcones,* esp. fam. *Accipitridae* (*ACCIPITER, *BUTEO, *HARRIER), fam. *Falconidae* (*FALCON) and fam. *Pandionidae* (*OSPREY). They are found throughout the world. They are smaller than either eagles or vultures ‖ a person who is grasping or who preys on others ‖ a person who advocates a military or bellicose solution to a disagreement **2.** *v.i.* to hunt with hawks trained for this sport [O.E. *heafoc*]

hawk *n.* a small square board for mortar or plaster, with a handle underneath [etym. doubtful]

hawk *v.t.* to carry about for sale, *to hawk a manuscript* ‖ to peddle (goods) in the street by shouting ‖ *v.i.* to be a hawker [HAWKER]

Hawk (*mil. acronym*) for homing-all-the-way killer (MIM-23), a mobile air-defense artillery, radio-guided, surface-to-air missile system that provides nonnuclear, low- to medium-altitude air-defense coverage for ground forces with a 25-mi range, semi-active homing, 45,000-ft ceiling, and speed of Mach 3. *Cf* BAE HAWK

Hawke (hɔk), Edward (1705–81), 1st Baron Hawke of Towton, British admiral. He destroyed the French fleet in Quiberon Bay (1759), saving England from the threat of invasion during the Seven Years' War

Hawke, Robert James Lee (1929–), Australian prime minister (1983–). A labor leader, he led the Australian Council of Trade Unions from 1970 and in 1973 was elected leader of the Australian Labour Party. He was first elected to Parliament in 1980 and served until he replaced Liberal party prime minister J. Malcolm Fraser

Hawke's Bay a region (area 4,260 sq. miles, pop. 120,000) on the eastern coastal plain of North Island, New Zealand. Chief town: Napier. Products: wool, apples, canned fruit and vegetables

Hawk·eye (hɔ́kai) *n.* (*mil.*) a twin turboprop, multicrew, early-warning and interceptor-control aircraft (E-2), with a long-range radar and integrated computer system for the detection and tracking of targets; designed to operate from aircraft carriers

Haw·kins (hɔ́kinz), Sir John (1532–95), English privateer who made a handsome profit out of the slave trade, robbing Portuguese slavers in W. Africa and selling their captives to Spanish colonies in the West Indies. He took part in the defeat of the Armada (1588)

hawk 1. *v.i.* to clear the throat in a noisy manner ‖ to cough up (phlegm) **2.** *n.* an effort to cough up phlegm [imit.]

haw·ker (hɔ́kər) *n.* someone who peddles goods esp. from a cart etc., moving from place to place and shouting out his wares [prob. fr. L.G. *hoker,* huckster]

hawk-eyed (hɔ́kaid) *adj.* having keen vision that misses nothing

hawk-moth (hɔ́kmɔθ, hɔ́kmɒθ) *pl.* **hawk-moths** (hɔ́kmɔθs, hɔ́kmɔðz, (hɔ́kmɒθs, hɔ́kmɒðz) *n.* a member of *Sphingidae,* a family of lepidopterous insects universally distributed. They have a stout body, short thick antennae and a retractable proboscis for extracting nectar [fr. their flight, like a hawk's]

hawk-nosed (hɔ́knouzd) *adj.* having an aquiline nose

hawks·bill turtle (hɔ́ksbil) *Eretmochelys imbricata,* a carnivorous sea turtle whose shell yields fine-quality tortoise shell

Hawks·more, Hawks·moor (hɔ́ksmuər), Nicholas (1661–1736), English architect. He was a pupil and partner of Wren and Vanbrugh, and assisted both on many of their works. His own buildings in Gothic style include the library of Queen's College, Oxford (1700–14) and the baroque churches of St Mary Woolnoth, London (1716–19) and St George's, Bloomsbury (1720–30)

hawk·weed (hɔ́kwi:d) *n.* any of several composites of genera *Hieracium, Picris* or *Erechtites*

hawse (hɔz) *n.* (*naut.*) the part of a ship's bow containing hawseholes ‖ the distance between a ship's head and the anchors which she rides ‖ the arrangement of the cables when a ship is moored with two cables, one from either side of the bow [perh. O.N. *hals,* neck, part of the bows]

hawse·hole (hɔ́zhoul) *n.* (*naut.*) a hole in the bow of a ship for running cables through

haw·ser (hɔ́zər) *n.* (*naut.*) a cable, often of steel, used in mooring or warping a ship [prob. A.F. *hauceour* fr. O.F. *haucier,* to hoist]

haw·thorn (hɔ́θɔrn) *n.* a member of *Crataegus,* fam. *Rosaceae,* a genus of quick-growing shrubs or small trees found in temperate climates. The thorns are modified branches. They have small glossy leaves and strongly scented white or pink flowers, the fruit of which are haws [O.E. *hagathorn, hœguthorn, hœgthorn* fr. *haga,* hedge + *thorn,* thorn]

Haw·thorne (hɔ́θɔrn), Nathaniel (1804–64), American novelist. His most famous works, 'The Scarlet Letter' (1850) and 'The House of the Seven Gables' (1851), present an unusual blend of romance and puritan morality expressed through an elaborate figurative method akin to allegory

Haw·thorne effect (hɔ́θɔn) improvement in performance resulting from the interest expressed by researchers and knowledge that the activity is being measured. *Cf* PLACEBO EFFECT

Hay (hei), John Milton (1838–1905), U.S. secretary of state (from 1898) under Presidents William McKinley and Theodore Roosevelt. His first open-door note (1899) proclaimed that all nations should have equal trading rights in China, his second (1900) that all nations should preserve China's territorial and administrative integrity. He negotiated with Lord Pauncefote, the British ambassador in Washington, the

Hay-Pauncefote treaty of 1901. This modified the Clayton-Bulwer treaty of 1850 and gave the U.S.A. authority to construct and have exclusive control over an isthmian canal connecting the Atlantic and Pacific Oceans. He and President Theodore Roosevelt abetted the revolution which gave (1903) Panama independence from Colombia and facilitated the construction of the Panama Canal. He settled (1903) the Alaska boundary question with Great Britain

hay (hei) **1.** *n.* stems and leaves of grasses etc. as a crop that is cut and dried for fodder **2.** *v.i.* to make hay ‖ *v.t.* to cut and dry (grasses) for hay ‖ to feed with hay **to make hay of** (*Br.*) to demolish ‖ (*Br., sports*) to defeat easily by a wide margin **to make hay while the sun shines** to profit from favorable circumstances, grasp an opportunity [O.E. *hieg, hig,* heg]

Ha·ya·ka·wa (hɑjəkáwə), S(amuel) I(chiye) (1906–), U.S. semanticist, author of 'Language in action' (1941); U.S. Senator (R.—Calif., 1976–84)

Hay-Bu·nau-Va·ril·la Treaty (héibynóuværi:jæ) a U.S.-Panamanian treaty (1903), replacing-the Hay-Herrán treaty, in which Panama granted the U.S.A. exclusive use, occupation and control of the Canal Zone (formally transferred, 1904), in turn receiving $10 million in cash and a $250,000 annuity to begin nine years after ratification

hay·cock (héikɒk) *n.* a mound of fresh-cut hay left in the meadow to dry out before being carted away

Hay·dn (háid'n), Franz Joseph (1732–1809), Austrian composer. His enormous output includes 104 symphonies and 76 quartets. These were the two musical forms in which he achieved his greatest work, for in them he evolved what was in essence the classical sonata form. With Haydn, therefore, European music departed finally from the old contrapuntal forms originally derived from polyphonic choral music. The models he developed were taken up by Mozart and Beethoven. Haydn's oratorios 'The Creation' (1796–8) and 'The Seasons' (1798–1801) are among his finest achievements

Hay·don (héid'n), Benjamin Robert (1786–1846), English painter. He was a friend of Keats and other prominent figures, and gives an interesting insight into the artistic life and temper of his times in his 'Autobiography' (1847)

Hayes (heiz), Isaac Israel (1832–81), U.S. arctic explorer. As a surgeon with Elisha Kent Kane's expedition, he discovered (1854) and explored Grinnell Land, the central section of Ellesmere Is.

Hayes, Rutherford Birchard (1822–93), 19th president (1877–81) of the U.S.A., a Republican. He became president after the controversial election of 1876, when an electoral commission awarded him all disputed returns, thereby alienating his opposition and weakening his administration. His withdrawal (1877) of federal troops from the South marked the end of the post-bellum military occupation

hay fever a condition caused by an allergic reaction to grass pollens or other plant products, and hence of markedly seasonal incidence. The condition is characterized by acute inflammation of the mucous membranes of the eyes and nasal passages (*ALLERGY)

hay·field (héifi:ld) *n.* a meadow in which the grass is allowed to grow for hay ‖ such a field in which haymaking is in progress

hay·fork (héifɔrk) *n.* a long-handled, slender-pronged, light fork for turning, pitching and carrying hay

Hay-Her·rán Treaty (héierrán) a treaty negotiated (1903) by John Hay, U.S. Secretary of State, and Tomás Herrán, Colombian chargé d'affaires in Washington, in which Colombia leased to the U.S.A. for 99 years a strip of land across the Isthmus of Panama for the construction of a canal. Since the Colombian Congress refused to ratify it, a Panamanian junta, supported by U.S. naval forces, revolted and declared Panama's independence from Colombia

hay·lage (héilidʒ) *n.* storage place for dried grass

hay·loft (héilɒft, héilɒft) *n.* a place for storing hay over a stable or under a barn roof

Hay-mar·ket Riot (héimɑ:rkit) a U.S. anarchist demonstration held (1886) in Chicago's Haymarket Square, in which seven policemen were killed. Although the crime was imputed to

CONCISE PRONUNCIATION KEY: **(a)** æ, c*a*t; ɑ, c*a*r; ɔ f*aw*n; ei, sn*a*ke. **(e)** e, h*e*n; i:, sh*ee*p; iə, d*ee*r; ɛə, b*ea*r. **(i)** i, f*i*sh; ai, t*i*ger; ə:, b*i*rd. **(o)** o, *o*x; au, c*ow*; ou, g*oa*t; u, p*oo*r; ɔi, r*oy*al. **(u)** ʌ, d*u*ck; u, b*u*ll; u:, g*oo*se; ə, b*a*cillus; ju:, c*u*be. x, lo*ch*; θ, *th*ink; ð, bo*th*er; z, *Z*en; ʒ, cor*s*age; dʒ, sa*v*age; ŋ, ora*ng*uta*ng*; j, *y*ak; ʃ, *f*ish; tʃ, fe*tch*; 'l, rabb*le*; 'n, redd*en*. Complete pronunciation key appears inside front cover.

anarchists, the reputation of organized labor, especially that of the Knights of Labor, suffered in consequence

hay·mow (héimou) *n.* a part of a barn where hay is stored, or the hay itself

Hayne (hein), Robert Young (1791–1839), U.S. political leader who was a spokesman for the South and a defender of slavery. In his debate (1830) with Daniel Webster, he argued that any state had the right to nullify a federal law which it considered an infringement on its rights under the constitution. He strongly influenced the North Carolina ordinance (1832) which declared federal tariff laws null and void

Hay-Paunce·fote Treaty (pónsfut) *HAY, John Milton

hay·rack (héiræk) *n.* a rack with wide spaces between the bars canted out from the wall inside a coxshed or stable, into which hay is dropped and from which cows and horses can feed

hay·rick (héirik) *n.* a haystack

hay·ride (héiraid) *n.* a ride in an open truck or wagon with some hay in it, esp. at night, by a group, for fun

hay·seed (héisi:d) *n.* a seed of grass shaken from hay ‖ (*pop.,* a city-dweller's term) an unsophisticated person living in the country

hay·stack (héistæk) *n.* a quantity of hay built up outdoors into a compressed mass, with a thatched, ridged or conical top to drain off the rain

Haystack antenna (*mil.*) U.S. Air Force computer-controlled antenna used with 150-ft diameter reflector for tracking orbiting satellites and radio stars

hay·wire (héiwaior) **1.** *n.* a wire used to bind bales of hay, straw etc. **2.** *adj.* (*pop.*) mixed up, out of order ‖ (*pop.*) crazy **to go haywire** (*pop.*) to behave as if crazy or to become crazy

haz·ard (hæzərd) *v.t.* to place (something) in a dangerous or risky situation wittingly or unwittingly ‖ to attempt (an answer, guess etc.) [F. *hasarder* fr. *hasard,* chance]

hazard *n.* a risk or chance associated with danger ‖ (*golf*) a ground obstacle in the direct path of the ball ‖ (*court tennis*) a winning opening in a court ‖ (*billiards, pool*) a stroke which pockets a ball, *a winning hazard* (pocketing the object ball), *a losing hazard* (pocketing the player's own ball off the object ball) **ház·ard·ous** *adj.* risky [O.F. *hasard, hasart,* prob. fr. Arab.]

haze (heiz) *n.* a cloudy, misty appearance of the air, caused by intense heat producing irregular and changing densities of its layers or by a fine suspension of dust or vapor particles, affecting the transmission of light and lessening visibility ‖ a cloudy appearance in a liquid or on a solid surface ‖ obscurity of mental vision [etym. doubtful, perh. fr. HAZE adj.]

haze *pres. part.* **haz·ing** *past* and *past part.* **hazed** *v.t.* (*pop.*) to place (someone, esp. an initiate into a fraternity) in an embarrassing or humiliating situation by forcing him to do menial or foolish tasks [O.F. *haser,* to annoy, irritate]

ha·zel (héiz'l) **1.** *n.* a member of *Corylus,* fam. *Corylaceae,* a genus of hairy-leaved shrubs or small trees found in temperate climates. Its fruit is the hazelnut ‖ the wood of such a tree **2.** *adj.* (esp. of eyes) having the reddish-brown color of hazelnuts [O.E. *hæsel*]

ha·zel·nut (héiz'lnʌt) *n.* the fruit of the hazel, an edible hard-shelled nut [O.E. *hæselhnutu*]

Haz·litt (hæzlit), William (1778–1830), English critic and essayist. His works include 'Lectures on the English Poets' (1818), 'Characters of Shakespeare's Plays' (1817) and 'The Spirit of the Age, or Contemporary Portraits' (1825). He was influential in the early 19th-c. revival of interest in the Elizabethan dramatists. He was a lifelong friend of Lamb and was early influenced by Coleridge

ha·zy (héizi:) *comp.* **ha·zi·er** *superl.* **ha·zi·est** *adj.* (of the air) characterized by haze ‖ indistinct, as if seen through a haze ‖ (of mental processes) not clear, *a hazy recollection* [etym. doubtful]

H-bomb *HYDROGEN BOMB

HC (*abbr.*) for hard copy

HC-130 *HERCULES

he (hi:) **1.** *pron.,* 3rd person sing., nominative case a male person, animal or personified thing already mentioned ‖ (often followed by 'who' or 'that') any person, *he who believes such stories must be weak in the head* **2.** *adj.* (prefixed) male,

---

a *he-goat* **3.** *n.* a male, *is it a he or a she?* ‖ (*Br.*) the game of tag [O.E. *he, hē*]

head (hed) **1.** *n.* the top part of the human body or foremost part of an animal's body. It contains the brain, mouth, nose, eyes and ears and its structure protects these organs ‖ the leading person in a community, institution etc., or the position he holds ‖ the foremost, most effective part of a tool, *the head of an ax* ‖ (*engin.*) the part of a machine containing the cutting tool, *the head of a lathe* ‖ (*slang*) a drug user ‖ the foremost or front part, *the head of a marching column* ‖ the uppermost part, *the head of a river* ‖ the froth on beer etc. ‖ the top of a boil ready to burst ‖ (*bot.*) a compact or rounded mass of flowers, leaves or leafstalks at the top of the stem ‖ the pillow end of a bed ‖ the brain as man's thought center, *a good head for figures,* or center of bodily control, *he has no head for heights* ‖ a section of, or topic within, a speech, essay etc., *a report under three heads* ‖ one individual out of a number of persons or animals, *the charge is a dollar a head* ‖ (*collect.*) individual animals, *30 head of cattle* ‖ a critical stage, *things have come to a head* ‖ a headland ‖ a body of water maintained at a specific height to feed a mill etc. ‖ the height of such a body of water ‖ the force generated by the fall of such a body of water ‖ the pressure per unit area of a contained body of liquid or gas ‖ the height or length of a head, *he is a head taller than she is, the horse won by a head* ‖ (also *pl.*) the obverse side of a coin ‖ (*mus.*) the skin of a drum ‖ (*naut.*) the bow and adjacent parts of a ship ‖ (*mining*) an underground tunnel where coal is being worked ‖ the part of a bell between the crown and the sound bow **head and shoulders** by far **head over heels** deeply, overwhelmingly (in debt, love etc.) **standing on one's head** easily, *he could do that standing on his head* **to act** (or go) **over someone's head** to act without someone's knowledge or consent, esp. by ignoring the proper chain of command **to be on one's head** to be one's responsibility **to be** (or go) **off one's head** (*pop.*) to be (or go) crazy, or apparently crazy **to be** (or go) **out of one's head** (*pop.*) to be (or become) delirious **to be weak in the head** (*pop.*) to be of subnormal intelligence **to eat one's head off** to eat without working, *my horse is eating its head off* **to give a horse** (or a **person**) **his head** to allow (a horse) to go where it likes or as fast as it likes or to allow (a person) to do as he sees fit **to go out of one's head** to be forgotten, *it went completely out of his head* **to go to one's head** (of alcohol) to make one a little drunk ‖ (of praise, success, power etc.) to make one conceited **to keep one's head** to remain calm with the reason under control **to keep one's head above water** to remain solvent or otherwise manage to cope with pressing obligations **to knock on the head** (*Br.*) to put an end to, *she knocked that little scheme on the head* **to lose one's head** to lose one's self-control, to become irrational **to make head** to struggle forward, *he made no head against the current* **to make head or tail of** to understand, make sense of **to promote over someone's head** to ignore the conventional claims of superiority of a person and promote (someone else) instead **to put it into someone's head** to suggest something to someone **to put our** (etc.) **heads together** to consult one another (each other) **to take it into one's head** (to do something) to conceive (a specified plan or idea) whimsically **to talk over someone's head** to talk of matters beyond someone's understanding **to talk someone's head off** (*pop.*) to talk at great length to someone **to turn someone's head** (of flattery, success etc.) to make someone vain **2.** *adj.* chief in authority, *head waiter* **3.** *v.i.* to move in a certain direction, *to head for home* ‖ to grow to a head ‖ *v.t.* to lead, to head a deputation ‖ to be at the top of, *his name heads the list* ‖ to put at the top of, *head your letter with yesterday's date* ‖ to entitle, *how will you head this chapter?* ‖ to remove the head or top from (grain, a tree etc.) ‖ to cause (something) to move in a certain direction ‖ to proceed around the upper part of (a stream) ‖ to propel (a soccer ball) with the head [O.E. *hēafod*]

head·ache (hédeik) *n.* a usually persistent pain in the head ‖ (*pop.*) a vexing problem

head·band (hédbænd) *n.* a band worn around the head, esp. for holding a woman's hair back from the eyes ‖ a decorative band stitched or glued inside the spine of a book at the top and bottom ‖ a band connecting a pair of earphones ‖ (*printing*) a headpiece

---

head·board (hédbord, hédbourd) *n.* a vertical, often decorative board at the head of a bed against which pillows can rest

head·cheese (hédtʃi:z) *n.* meat from a pig's (or calf's) head, boiled and pressed in a mold, in its natural aspic

head·count·er (hédkauntər) *n.* **1.** census taker **2.** pollster

head dip (*surfing*) action in which surfer squats and dips his or her head into a wave

head·dress (héddres) *n.* something worn on the head, esp. as part of an elaborate costume

head·er (hédər) *n.* a dive or jump headfirst, *to take a header* ‖ a brick or stone laid perpendicular to the face of a wall ‖ someone who fits the heads on casks etc. ‖ (*electr.*) the plate of a hermetically sealed device through which electrical terminals pass ‖ (*soccer*) a hitting of the ball with the top of one's head

head·first (hédfə:rst) *adv.* with the head foremost ‖ impulsively, without the least delay, *to plunge headfirst into a fight*

head·fore·most (hédfórmoust, hédfóurmoust) *adv.* headfirst

head·gear (hédgiər) *n.* anything worn on the head ‖ a bridle for a horse ‖ (*mining*) machinery at the top of a shaft or boring

head·hunt (hédhʌnt) *v.i.* to attack enemies in order to secure human heads as ritual trophies **héad·hunt·er** *n.*

head·hunt·er (hédhʌntər) *n.* a professional recruiter for professional personnel. —**head hunt** *v.*

head·ing (hédiŋ) *n.* the title of a piece of writing or of a section of one ‖ (*mining*) a drift ‖ (*mining*) a passageway connecting two larger tunnels

head lamp a headlight

head·land (hédlənd) *n.* a point of land projecting into the sea, a lake etc. ‖ a strip of unplowed land left at either end of a plowed field

head·less (hédlis) *adj.* having no head ‖ lacking a leader ‖ lacking prudence or proper thought

head·light (hédlait) *n.* a powerful light, with reflector and lens, fitted on the front of a motor vehicle, locomotive or aircraft ‖ a light at a ship's masthead

head·line (hédlain) **1.** *n.* the title of a news item in a newspaper, printed in large, bold type ‖ (*printing*) a line at the head of a page giving the title of the book and page number ‖ (*Br., pl.*) a news summary given at the beginning of a news broadcast ‖ the rope along the top of a fishing net **to make the headlines** to be important enough to warrant a newspaper account with headlines **2.** *v.t. pres. part.* **head·lin·ing** *past* and *past part.* **head·lined** to be performing as the headliner in **héad·lin·er** *n.* a starring performer

head·lock (hédlɒk) *n.* (*wrestling*) a hold in which the opponent's head is held between one's arm and body

head·long (hédlɒŋ, hédlɒŋ) **1.** *adv.* headfirst ‖ full tilt ‖ impetuously **2.** *adj.* done or proceeding with the head foremost ‖ done with utmost haste ‖ impetuous

head·man (hédmæn) *pl.* **head·men** (hédmen) *n.* a chief or person in authority esp. in a tribe etc. [O.E. *hēafodman*]

head·mas·ter (hédmæstər, hédmάstər) *n.* (*Am.*) a man who heads the administration of a private school ‖ (*Br.*) the man responsible for the instruction given in a school and for the administration of it

head·mis·tress (hédmistris) *n.* (*Am.*) a woman who heads the administration of a private school ‖ (*Br.*) the woman responsible for the instruction given in a school and for the administration of it

head·most (hédmoust) *adj.* leading, foremost

head·on (hédón, hédòn) *adj.* with the head, or foremost part (e.g. of a ship, vehicle etc.) moving toward or facing another person or thing, *a head-on collision* **head on** *adv.* in a head-on way

head·phone (hédfoun) *n.* (*radio, telephone* etc.) a set of receivers for both ears attached to a headband

head·piece (hédpi:s) *n.* a helmet or other head covering ‖ an ornamental engraving or other decoration at the head of a chapter or page in a book

head·quar·ters (hédkwortərz) *n.* (*mil.,* abbr. H.Q.) the command post of a com- manding officer and his staff ‖ a center from which operations are directed

head·rest (hédrest) *n.* a support for the head, e.g. on a dentist's chair, automobile seat etc.

CONCISE PRONUNCIATION KEY: **(a)** æ, c*a*t; ɑ, c*ar*; ɔ f*aw*n; ei, sn*a*ke. **(e)** e, h*e*n; i:, sh*ee*p; iə, d*ee*r; ɛə, b*ea*r. **(i)** i, f*i*sh; ai, t*i*ger; ə:, b*ir*d. **(o)** o, *o*x; au, c*ow*; ou, g*oa*t; u, p*oor*; ɔi, r*oy*al. **(u)** ʌ, d*u*ck; u, b*u*ll; u:, g*oo*se; ə, b*a*cillus; ju:, c*u*be. x, lo*ch*; θ, *th*ink; ð, bo*th*er; z, *Z*en; ʒ, corsa*g*e; dʒ, sava*g*e; ŋ, orangutan*g*; j, *y*ak; ʃ, *fi*sh; tʃ, fet*ch*; 'l, rabb*le*; 'n, redd*en*. Complete pronunciation key appears inside front cover.

headrest (*automobile*) the head cushion at the top of the seat designed to prevent or minimize whiplash. *syn.* head restraint

head·room (hédrʊːm, hédrʊm) *n.* the clear space above a person's head e.g. in a doorway or an automobile, or above a truck, train etc., e.g. when passing under a bridge

head·set (hédset) *n.* (*radio, telephone* etc.) a headphone, often with a mouthpiece attached

head·ship (hédʃip) *n.* the fact or position of commanding some enterprise or institution etc.

head shop (*slang*) outlet for drug-use accessories and associated artifacts

heads·man (hédzmən) *pl.* **heads·men** (hédzmən) *n.* an executioner who chops heads off

heads or tails the two possible positions in which a tossed coin may fall, i.e. effigy (the head) uppermost or hidden

head·spring (hédsprɪŋ) *n.* the source of a stream || a gymnastic feat similar to a handspring, but with the head and hands touching the floor as the feet pass over the head

head·stall (hédstɔl) *n.* the part of a bridle or halter that goes around a horse's head behind its ears

Head Start, U.S. program sponsored by the Department of Health and Human Services' Administration for Children, Youth and Families that provides educational services to handicapped and low-income family children. Begun in 1965, it also provides medical care

head start an advantage given to or won by an animal in a hunt, a racing opponent etc.

head·stock (hédstɒk) *n.* (*engin.*) the part of a machine supporting a movable part, e.g. the rotating spindle of a lathe or the cutters of a planing machine

head·stone (hédstoun) *n.* a stone erected at the head of a grave || a cornerstone

head·stream (hédstriːm) *n.* a stream forming a source of a river

head·strong (hédstrɒŋ, hédstrɔŋ) *adj.* willful and obstinate || resulting from a determination to have one's own way

heads up (*mil.*) in air intercept, a code meaning "Enemy got through" or "I am not in position to engage target"

head teacher 1. (*Br.*) chief official of a state school, usu. not a teacher **2.** (*U.S.*) one in charge of a school. *syn.* headmaster, headmistress

head-to-head (hédtuhéd) *adj.* in close contact. *Cf* EYEBALL-TO-EYEBALL

head voice the upper register of the voice, in which higher musical tones are produced

head·wait·er (hédwéitər) *n.* a man who supervises the waiters in a restaurant

head·wa·ters (hédwɒtərz, hédwɔtərz) *pl. n.* the source and upper reaches of a river

head·way (hédwei) *n.* progress, *to make rapid headway* || the rate of progression || the time span between movement of successive transportation vehicles, e.g., trains || headroom

head wind a wind blowing head-on

head·word (hédwərd) *n.* a word set out in distinctive type as the subject of an entry in a dictionary, catalogue etc.

head·work (hédwərk) *n.* (*soccer*) use of the head to propel the ball

head·y (hédi) *comp.* **head·i·er** *superl.* **head·i·est** *adj.* (of alcoholic drinks) likely to intoxicate || (of speech, writing etc.) intended to incite or inflame

heal (hiːl) *v.i.* to become well or whole again || *v.t.* to restore (someone) to health || to restore (a diseased or damaged bone or tissue or a wound) to its normal condi- tion || to cause (painful emotions) to be no longer grievous **to heal a breach** to bring about a reconciliation [O.E. *hǣlan*]

health (helθ) *n.* the state of fitness of the body or of the mind, *in poor health* || this state when it is good, *a picture of health* **to drink to the health of, to drink to (someone's) health** to toast (someone) [O.E. *hǣlth*]

Health and Human Services, U.S. Department of, federal agency that administers various responsibilities in the fields of health and social security. Originally the Federal Security Agency (1939–53), it became the Department of Health, Education and Welfare (HEW) from 1953 until that department was divided into the Departments of Education and of Health and Human Services in 1979. It administers the Public Health Service, the Office of Human Development Services, the Social Security Administration, and the Health Care Financing

Administration. The secretary of this department is a member of the President's cabinet

health card an identification card containing basic health record, similar to a credit card; issuance to each covered individual or family unit proposed in several national health-insurance bills

health certificate a certificate stating that the bearer (or plant, animal etc. concerned) is free from disease

health food special food and food supplements believed to be specially healthful, esp. unsprayed, organically grown, and unprocessed foods

health·ful (hélθfəl) *adj.* promoting good health

health·i·ly (hélθəli) *adv.* in a healthy manner

health·i·ness (hélθiːnis) *n.* the state or quality of being healthy

health maintenance organization an entity that provides or otherwise assures the delivery of basic and supplemental health maintenance and treatment services to a voluntarily enrolled group within a geographic area and for which it is reimbursed through a predetermined, fixed, periodic payment. *abbr.* **HMO**

health resort a place where people of delicate health or convalescents go to rest or follow a prescribed cure

health spa a recreational hotel with facilities for weight reduction, massage, exercise, baths, etc. *also* health farm

health·y (hélθi) *comp.* **health·i·er** *superl.* **health·i·est** *adj.* normally having good physical and mental health || conducive to good health, *a healthy climate* || appearing to have, or indicate, good health, *a healthy complexion* || likely to be for one's good, *a healthy regard for the law* || (*pop.*, of appetite etc.) good and large

heap (hiːp) **1.** *n.* any material gathered or thrown together into a pile, *a heap of rubbish* || (*pop.*) a large number or quantity, *a heap of troubles* **heaps of** (*pop.*) many, a lot of, *heaps of times, heaps of money* || plenty of, *heaps of time* **to be struck all of a heap** (*Br.*) to be utterly astonished, taken aback **2.** *v.t.* to gather or throw into a heap || to load, *to heap food on a plate, to heap abuse on* **a heaping** (*Br.* heaped) **spoonful** a spoonful filled to overflowing **to heap coals of fire** to return good for evil **to heap up** to gather together, collect, *to heap up trouble for oneself* [O.E. *hēap*]

heaps (hiːps) *adv.* (*pop.*) much, extremely

hear (hiər) *pres. part.* **hear·ing** *past* and *past part.* **heard** (hɜːrd) *v.t.* to experience or be aware of (sounds), usually as a result of stimulation of the auditory system by sound waves, *he hears the song, he heard her singing* || to apprehend (sound waves) aurally, *a dog can hear higher frequencies than we can* || to listen to so as to check, *to hear a child's multiplication tables* || to listen to so as to consider, *to hear a complaint* || to attend, *to hear Mass, to go to hear an opera* || (*law*) to take evidence from, *to hear a defendant* || (*law*) to conduct the trial of (a case) || *v.i.* to experience or be aware of sounds usually as a result of stimulation of the auditory system by sound waves || to hear 'of' or 'from' || to receive information or news, *he heard from her yesterday* (by letter etc.) || to be informed, *we hear that he has gone away* || (future tense only) to be subject to reprimand **hear! hear!** an interjection by a member of an audience expressing approval **not to hear of** not to permit, *he will not hear of your going so soon* **to hear out** to listen to to the end [O. E. *hīeran, hēran*]

hear·er (híərər) *n.* someone who hears, esp. one of several, *to shock one's hearers*

hear·ing (híəriŋ) *n.* the act of apprehending or the ability to apprehend sounds aurally || an act or instance of listening || (*law*) the listening to evidence and pleas in a law court || (*law*) a trial, esp. one heard only by a judge or judges || the distance over which a sound can be heard, *out of hearing* **hard of hearing** a little deaf **to give fair hearing to** to offer an opportunity to be heard without prejudice

hearing aid an electrical or electronic apparatus for the amplification of sound, worn by those suffering from certain forms of deafness

hark·en, hark·en (hɑrkən) *v.i.* (*rhet.*) to listen, pay attention to what is said) [O.E. *hercnian, heorcnian, hyrcnian*]

Hearn (hɜːrn), Lafcadio (1850–1904), U.S. writer on Japan. His works, notably 'Glimpses of Unfamiliar Japan' (1894), romantically portray the last vestiges of a feudal order

hear·say (híərsei) *n.* that which one has been told but has not directly experienced || the process of acquiring such information, *to know by hearsay* [fr. archaic phrase *to hear say*]

hearsay evidence (*law*) testimony based on hearsay, inadmissible in a court

hearse (hɜːrs) *n.* a vehicle used for conveying a corpse in its coffin to the place of burial etc. [M.F. *herse*, harrow. harrow-shaped frame for holding candles over a coffin]

Hearst (hɜːrst), William Randolph (1863–1951), American newspaper publisher. He created a vast chain of popular newspapers, based on sensational reporting, banner headlines and low price

heart (hɑrt) **1.** *n.* the hollow muscular organ which, by rhythmical contraction and expansion, forces the blood through the circulatory system of vertebrates || the central part of something, *the heart of the city, the heart of a head of lettuce* || the most important part of something, *the heart of the matter* || the fount of man's emotions and deepest feelings || kindness, affection, *to have no heart* || conscience, *to know in one's heart that an action is wrong* || disposition, *a kind heart* || courage and zeal, *to have no heart for a task* || a state of mind or feeling, *with a heavy heart* || (*pl., cards*) a suit marked with a representation of one or more red hearts (♡) || a card of this suit **have a heart!** (*pop.*) be merciful! **not to have the heart to** be unwilling to (do something distressing), *she hadn't the heart to tell him the bad news* **to break one's heart** to be acutely distressed in one's affections or sensitivity **to cry one's heart out** to grieve so much, and for so long, that emotion is exhausted **to do one's heart good** to give one an unexpected feeling of pleasure and satisfaction **to give (or lose) one's heart to** to give all one's affection to **to have a change of heart** to change from being unkind or unsympathetic to being kind or sympathetic **to have one's heart in** to be very fond of (one's work etc.) **to have one's heart in one's boots** to be fearfully apprehensive **to have one's heart in one's mouth** to be very alarmed **to have one's heart in the right place** to be kind and affectionate **to have something at heart** to have great interest in or sympathy for **to have the heart to (do something)** (in negative and interrogative constructions) to have the courage to (do something) **to learn (or know) something by heart** to memorize (or have memorized) something **to lose heart** to be discouraged and ready to give up **to set one's heart on** to desire very strongly **to speak from one's heart** to speak with deep sincerity **to take heart** to be encouraged **to take to heart** to heed with seriousness || to mind so much as to be upset by **to take to one's heart** to take into one's affections **to wear one's heart on one's sleeve** to expose one's feelings to the world **with all one's heart** (*rhet.*) most willingly **2.** *v.i.* (of lettuce etc.) to form a head [O.E. *heorte*]

—In man, the heart comprises four chambers: the right auricle and ventricle and the left auricle and ventricle. The left auricle and ventricle receive oxygenated blood from the lungs and the left ventricle pumps it to all parts of the body through the arteries. In the tissues it passes into minute vessels, the capillaries, which are adjacent to cells of all the tissues. Here the blood exchanges oxygen and nutrients for wastes and carbon dioxide. The blood returns to the heart through veins and passes through the right auricle and ventricle to the lungs, where the carbon dioxide is exchanged for oxygen

heart·ache (hɑrteik) *n.* persistent mental suffering through loss of a loved person or disappointment in love

heart·beat (hɑrtbiːt) *n.* one of the rhythmical muscular movements of the heart

heart·break (hɑrtbreik) *n.* overwhelming sorrow **heart·break·ing** *adj.* causing overwhelming sorrow || tending to crush the spirits, *a heartbreaking task* **heart·bro·ken** (hɑrtbroukən) *adj.* suffering overwhelming sorrow

heart·burn (hɑrtbɜːrn) *n.* a burning sensation felt in the stomach (near the heart), caused by indigestion

heart·burn·ing (hɑrtbɜːrniŋ) *n.* emotional discomfort, esp. caused by envy, disappointment, jealousy, or a sense of guilt

heart·en (hɑrtn) *v.t.* to inspire with fresh determination

heart·felt (hɑrtfelt) *adj.* (*rhet.*) deeply and sincerely felt

CONCISE PRONUNCIATION KEY: **(a)** æ, c*a*t; ɑ, c*ar*; ɔ f*aw*n; ei, sn*a*ke. **(e)** e, h*e*n; iː, sh*ee*p; iə, d*eer*; ɛə, b*ear*. **(i)** i, f*i*sh; ai, t*i*ger; əː, b*ir*d. **(o)** o, *o*x; au, c*ow*; ou, g*oa*t; u, p*oor*; ɔi, r*oy*al. **(u)** ʌ, d*u*ck; u, b*u*ll; uː, g*oo*se; ə, b*a*cillus; juː, c*u*be. x, lo*ch*; θ, *th*ink; ð, bo*th*er; z, *Z*en; ʒ, cor*s*age; dʒ, sava*g*e; ŋ, orangutan*g*; j, *y*ak; ʃ, *fi*sh; tʃ, fe*tch*; l, rabb*l*e; n, redde*n*. Complete pronunciation key appears inside front cover.

hearth (haɑrθ) *n.* the floor of a fireplace or the area immediately in front of a fireplace ‖ (*metall.*) the lowest part of a blast furnace from which molten metal flows ‖ (*metall.*) the part of a reverberatory furnace where the ore is placed [O.E. *heorth*]

hearth·stone (háɑrθstoun) *n.* a stone forming a hearth ‖ a soft stone or a mixture of pipe clay and grit used to scour and whiten doorsteps etc.

heart·i·ly (hártili:) *adv.* very warmly, *to welcome someone heartily* ‖ with a good appetite, *to eat heartily* ‖ enthusiastically, *to applaud heartily* ‖ thoroughly, *to agree heartily*

heart·i·ness (hárti:nis) *n.* the quality of being hearty

heart·land (hártlænd) *n.* (*geopolitics*) a central land area regarded as able to maintain itself in matters of production and defense

heart·less (hártlis) *adj.* devoid of all feelings of affection ‖ cruel, pitiless ‖ showing cruelty or lack of affection, *a heartless remark*

heart·rend·ing (hártrɛndiŋ) *adj.* causing grief and pity, *heartrending cries*

heart·sick (hártsɪk) *adj.* (*rhet.*) depressed and weak with yearning, or marked by such depression

heart·strings (hártstrɪŋz) *pl. n.* (only in phrases) **to play on someone's heartstrings** to appeal to someone's feelings of affection and pity in order to achieve some object **to tug at someone's heartstrings** to move someone deeply to compassion

heart-to-heart (hárttəhárt) *adj.* intimate, without emotional reserve, *a heart-to-heart talk*

heart·warm·ing (hártwɔrmiŋ) *adj.* encouraging

heart·wood (hártwud) *n.* the innermost nonliving portion of the xylem of vascular plants that serves primarily as mechanical support (*SAPWOOD)

heart·y (hárti:) *comp.* **heart·i·er** *superl.* **heart·i·est** *adj.* very warm, *a hearty welcome* ‖ vigorous, *hale and hearty, a hearty kick* ‖ abundant, *a hearty breakfast* ‖ exuberant, genial and energetic to the point of excess

heat (hi:t) *n.* high temperature ‖ the condition of being hot ‖ hot weather ‖ (*phys.*) the energy of a material body associated with the random motions of its constituent particles (i.e. atoms, molecules and smaller structural units), which is proportional to the product of its temperature and mass. The transfer of heat to a body causes a rise in its temperature and changes in most of its properties (e.g. density, reactivity state, solubility) ‖ intensity of emotional feeling, *words spoken in the heat of the moment* ‖ intensity of action, *in the heat of the battle* ‖ excessive bodily temperature associated e.g. with sunburn, a boil etc. ‖ (with 'in', *Br.* 'on') a period of intense sexual excitement in a female animal ‖ pungency of flavor, *the heat of the curry made his hair stand on end* ‖ a preliminary race or other contest to reduce the number of competitors who may compete in the semifinals or finals [O.E. *hætu, hæto*]

heat *v.t.* (often with 'up') to supply heat to, make hot or hotter ‖ *v.i.* (often with 'up') to become hot or hotter [O.E. *hætan*]

heat capacity the quantity of heat needed to raise the temperature of a body through 1°C, equal to the product of the specific heat of the body and its mass

heat content *ENTHALPY

heat·ed (hí:tid) *adj.* subjected to heat ‖ emotionally violent, *a heated argument*

heat engine any device (e.g. a steam engine) for converting heat energy into work (cf. REFRIGERATION CYCLE, *CARNOT CYCLE)

heat·er (hí:tər) *n.* a device that gives off heat, e.g. an electric stove ‖ a device that heats its contents, e.g. a water heater

heat exchanger a device (e.g. the radiator of a motor vehicle, or a condenser) for transferring heat from one fluid to another without allowing them to mix

heat exhaustion a condition marked by fainting, dizziness and nausea. It is caused by excessive sweating and consequent loss of salt and fluid, through too much physical exercise in hot weather

Heath (hi:θ), Edward (1916–), British statesman. He became (1965) leader of the Conservative party and (1970–4) Prime Minister

heath (hi:θ) *n.* a plant of fam. *Ericaceae,* usually found growing on open, barren, poorly drained soil ‖ (esp. *Br.*) an area of mainly level uncultivated land which has poor, coarse undrained soil and which is typically rich in peat or peaty humus [O.E. *hæth*]

hea·then (hí:ðən) **1.** *pl.* **hea·thens, hea·then** *n.* a person who does not worship the God of the Christians, Jews or Moslems **2.** *adj.* of or relating to heathens, their beliefs and practices [O.E. *hiæthen*]

hea·then·dom (hí:ðəndəm) *n.* (*collect.*) heathens [O.E. *hæthendōm*]

hea·then·ish (hí:ðəniʃ) *adj.* characteristic of a heathen [O.E. *hæthenisc*]

hea·then·ism (hí:ðənizəm) *n.* the practices and beliefs of heathens

hea·then·ize (hí:ðənaiz) *pres. part.*

hea·then·iz·ing *past* and *past part.* **hea·then·ized** *v.t.* to make heathen ‖ *v.i.* to become heathen

hea·then·ry (hí:ðənri:) *n.* heathendom ‖ heathenism

heath·er (héðər) *n.* a member of fam. *Ericaceae,* esp. *Calluna vulgaris,* a low evergreen shrub with linear, closely crowded, wiry leaves and racemes of light purple, pink and white flowers. It is found in northern climates, esp. on moorland **heath·er·y** *adj.* [M.E. *hadder*]

heat lightning bright flashes of sheet lightning without thunder, seen near the horizon usually at twilight, and thought to be the reflection by high clouds of far-off lightning

heat of combustion the heat released by the total combustion of a fixed amount of a substance

heat of condensation (*phys.*) the thermal energy released when a substance at its boiling point passes from the vapor to the liquid state. It is equal to the heat of vaporization, but opposite in sign

heat of formation the quantity of heat released or absorbed when a compound is formed by the direct union of its elements

heat of fusion the thermal energy absorbed when a substance at its melting point passes from the solid to the liquid state expressed per unit mass. It is equal to the heat of melting, but opposite in sign

heat of melting the heat absorbed during isothermal melting (*HEAT OF FUSION)

heat of neutralization the quantity of heat released or absorbed when a gram equivalent of an acid or base is exactly neutralized in a dilute solution

heat of reaction the thermal energy absorbed or released during a chemical reaction (usually at constant pressure and temperature), expressed per unit mass of product or reactant

heat of solution the quantity of heat released or absorbed when 1 gram or 1 mole of a substance is dissolved in a large volume of solvent

heat of vaporization the thermal energy absorbed during isothermal vaporization expressed per unit mass of substance (*HEAT OF CONDENSATION)

heat pipe a pipe that uses pressure differences to transfer heat containing fluids

heat pollution heated industrial waste that causes environmental changes. *also* thermal pollution

heat pump a device for extracting heat from a low-temperature source to supply a high-temperature sink by means of a refrigeration cycle operated in reverse. Heat pumps are sometimes used to heat a building, the source of heat being usually outside the building (e.g. the ground or air)

heat shrinkable plastic a thin plastic material with capability of shrinking 50% when heated, used in packaging irregularly shaped objects

heat sink a device or substance for dissipating unwanted heat, e.g., from a transistor or rectifier

heat·stroke (hí:tstrouk) *n.* an acute condition marked by the inactivity of the sweat glands, very high body temperature, fast pulse, delirium and sometimes coma. It is caused by extended exposure to excessive heat

heat transfer printing technique of fabric printing by heat transfer of printed design from paper to fabric, similar to decalcomania

heat treatment the subjection of metals to heat under controlled conditions, in order to produce desired structural changes, with the resultant changes in physical properties (*ANNEAL, *TEMPER)

heat wave a relatively long spell of abnormally hot weather

heave (hi:v) **1.** *v. pres. part.* **heav·ing** *past* and *part part.* **heaved,** (*naut.*) **hove** (houv) *v.t.* to raise with much effort ‖ (*pop.*) to throw (a heavy object) ‖ to emit (a long-drawn-out sigh) ‖ (*naut.*) to move (a ship) or haul, or pull (something on a ship) ‖ (*geol.*) to displace (a stratum) ‖ *v.i.* to rise and fall rhythmically under powerful compulsion, *the horse's flanks were heaving* ‖ (*naut.,* of a ship) to move **to heave around** (*naut.*) to come closer **to heave down** (*naut.*) to careen **to heave in sight** (*naut.*) to come into view **to heave to** (*naut.*) to bring a ship to a standstill heading into the wind **2.** *n.* the act of heaving ‖ (*geol.*) the horizontal component of the slip along a fault [O.E. *hebban, hōf, hafen*]

heave-ho (hí:vhou) to lift forcefully, to be lifted out. **—give the heave-ho** *v.* to lift out of or into

heav·en (hévən) *n.* the upper regions, regarded in many religions as the abode of the deity or deities, and of the blessed ‖ (*pop.*) perfect happiness ‖ (*rhet.*) the upper air ‖ (*pl.*) the space above us seeming to form a vault, *the stars shone in the heavens* **Heav·en** (in exclamations) God, *Heaven protect you!* **to move heaven and earth** to do one's utmost [O.E. *hefen, heofon*]

heav·en·li·ness (hévənli:nis) *n.* the state or quality of being heavenly

heav·en·ly (hévənli:) *adj.* pertaining to heaven or the heavens ‖ (*pop.*) very delightful [O. E. *heofonlic*]

heav·en·ward (hévənwərd) *adj.* and *adv.* directed or moving toward heaven

heav·en·wards (hévənwərdz) *adv.* heavenward

heaves (hi:vz) *pl. n.* (of horses) a disease in which the flanks heave and coughing persists

heav·i·ly (hévəli:) *adv.* in a heavy manner [O.E. *hefiglice*]

heav·i·ness (hévi:nis) *n.* the state or quality of being heavy

Heav·i·side (hévi:said), Oliver (1850–1925), British engineer and physicist who made important contributions to the theory of electromagnetic fields. He predicted the existence of a layer of ionized gases in the upper atmosphere (*KENNELLY, *KENNELLY-HEAVISIDE LAYER, *IONOSPHERE)

Heaviside layer *KENNELLY-HEAVISIDE LAYER

heav·y (hévi:) **1.** *comp.* **heav·i·er** *superl.* **heav·i·est** *adj.* of considerable weight, *a heavy load* ‖ having high specific gravity and considerable weight in relation to volume, *lead is a heavy metal compared with aluminum* ‖ of more than the usual amount, *heavy expenses* or weight, *heavy woolens* or force, *a heavy storm* or size, *heavy guns* ‖ weighing down on one or threatening to do so, oppressive, *a sky heavy with clouds, to rule with a heavy hand* ‖ joyless, *a heavy heart* ‖ clumsy in conception or execution, *a heavy speech* ‖ (of people) uninteresting ‖ (of soil) clayey ‖ lacking in grace, *heavy features* ‖ lacking vitality, *heavy with sleep* ‖ difficult to accomplish, *a heavy task* or to assimilate, *heavy reading* or to digest, *a heavy pudding* ‖ tiresomely grave, *to play the heavy father* ‖ (*rhet.*) nearing parturition, *heavy with young* ‖ steep, *a heavy grade* **to make heavy weather of** (a job) to make a labor of (a light task) **2.** *pl.* **heav·ies** *n.* (*theater*) the actor who plays the part of the villain, or the part or character itself [O.E. *hefig*]

heavy *adv.* heavily **to hang heavy** to be oppressive, *time hangs heavy on his hands* **to lie heavy** to be a burden, *the words lay heavy on his conscience* [O.E. *hefige*]

heavy chain (*org. chem.*) any of the polypeptide subunits in antibodies (immunoglobins) classified as alpha, gamma, delta, epsilon, or mu. *Cf* LIGHT CHAIN

heavy chemical a chemical in a relatively crude state produced and handled in bulk (cf. FINE CHEMICAL)

heav·y-du·ty (hévi:dú:ti:, hévi:djú:ti:) *adj.* able to stand great or continuous stress, *a heavy-duty engine* ‖ (of goods) chargeable at a high tariff

heavy going difficult and tiring conditions of progress, *the mud gave us some heavy going* ‖ dull, hard work, *the lunch party was heavy going*

heav·y-hand·ed (hévi:hændid) *adj.* domineering, oppressive, *a heavy-handed father* ‖ clumsy

heav·y-heart·ed (hévi:hártid) *adj.* worried and sad

heavy hydrogen deuterium

heav·y-lift ship (hévi: lift) a ship specially designed and capable of loading and unloading heavy and bulky items up to 100 tons

---

CONCISE PRONUNCIATION KEY: **(a)** æ, c*a*t; ɑ, c*a*r; ɔ f*aw*n; ei, sn*a*ke. **(e)** e, h*e*n; i:, sh*ee*p; iə, d*ee*r; ɛə, b*ea*r. **(i)** i, f*i*sh; ai, t*i*ger; əː, b*i*rd. **(o)** o, *o*x; au, c*ow*; ou, g*oa*t; u, p*oo*r; ɔi, r*oy*al. **(u)** ʌ, d*u*ck; u, b*u*ll; uː, g*oo*se; ə, b*a*cillus; ju:, c*u*be. x, lo*ch*; θ, *th*ink; ð, bo*th*er; z, *Z*en; ʒ, cor*s*age; dʒ, sa*v*age; ŋ, ora*ng*utang; j, *y*ak; ʃ, *f*ish; tʃ, fe*tch*; 'l, rabb*le*; 'n, redd*en*. Complete pronunciation key appears inside front cover.

heavy missiles (*mil.*) land-based missiles with very heavy payloads, e.g., Soviet SS-18

heavy oil an oil obtained by distilling coal tar and having a high specific gravity

heav·y·set (hévi:sét) *adj.* stocky

heavy water (*chem.*) water containing a high proportion of deuterium in the form of deuterium oxide, D₂O. It is used as a moderator in nuclear reactors

heav·y·weight (hévi:weit) *n.* a professional boxer whose weight is over 175 lbs ‖ an amateur boxer whose weight is over (*Am.*) 178 lbs or (*Br.*) 174 lbs ‖ a person, esp. a rider, who is above average weight

Heb·bel (héb'l), Christian Friedrich (1813–63) German dramatist and poet, one of the pioneers of modern realistic drama. His tragedies include 'Maria Magdalena' (1844) and the trilogy 'Die Niebelungen' (1862)

He·be (hí:bi:) (*Gk mythol.*) the goddess of youth and cupbearer to the gods of Olympus, identified with the Roman Juventas

he·be·phre·ni·a (hi:bifrí:ni:ə) *n.* a group of symptoms of schizophrenia marked by uncontrolled silliness, inappropriate emotional reactions and delusions. These occur chiefly in adolescents **he·be·phren·ic** (hi:bifrénik) *adj.* [fr. Gk *hēbē*, youth+*phrēn*, the mind]

Hé·bert (eiber), Jacques René (1755–94), French revolutionist and journalist. An extreme radical, he was a leader of the Paris Commune during the French Revolution. He was plotting to overthrow Robespierre, whom he accused of being too moderate, when he was arrested and executed

heb·e·tate (hébiteit) 1. *v. pres. part.* **heb·e·tat·ing** *past* and *past part.* **heb·e·tat·ed** *v.t.* to dull or blunt (mental or physical responses) ‖ *v.i.* (of mental or physical responses) to become dull or blunt 2. *adj.* (*bot.*) having a dull or soft point **heb·e·ta·tion** *n.* [fr. L. *hebetare* (*hebetatus*) fr. *hebes*, dull]

heb·e·tude (hébitu:d, hébitju:d) *n.* mental dullness and lethargy [fr. L. *hebetudo*]

He·bra·ic (hibréiik) *adj.* pertaining to the Hebrews, their language, laws etc. **He·brá·i·cal·ly** *adv.* [fr. L. L. *Hebraicus* fr. Gk]

He·bra·ism (hí:breiizəm) *n.* the religion, or system of thought, of the Hebrews ‖ a characteristic of the Hebrews ‖ a characteristic of the Hebrew language or a Hebrew expression [F. *hébraïsme* or fr. Mod. L. *Hebraïsmus*]

He·bra·ist (hí:breiist) *n.* someone learned in the Hebrew language and Hebrew literature [fr. HEBRAIC+*-ist*]

He·brew (hí:bru:) 1. *n.* an Israelite, or member of a related Semitic group (for history *JEW); the language of the ancient Hebrews ‖ the currently spoken and written form of this language 2. *adj.* pertaining to the Jews [M.E. *Ebreu* fr. O.F. fr. L. fr. Gk fr. Aram.]
—The Hebrew language belongs to the Semitic family and is generally divided into three periods: Old Testament Hebrew, Postbiblical, and Modern Hebrew (which developed in the 19th c. and is now used by the Jews in Israel). It has a special script, based on the pictographic alphabet of the ancient Phoenicians. The Hebrew verb assigns priority to aspect rather than tense, e.g. an action is considered more from the standpoint of its completion (perfective aspect) or incompletion (imperfective aspect) than from the standpoint of its chronological relation to the narrator

Hebrews, Epistle to the the 19th book (late 1st c.) of the New Testament, traditionally ascribed to St Paul, though the ascription is now generally doubted. It postulates Christ as the fulfillment of some Old Testament ideas, notably of sacrifice and priesthood

Heb·ri·des, Outer and Inner (hébridi:z) two archipelagoes (land area 2,812 sq. miles), comprising over 500 islands and islets, 92 being inhabited, off N.W. Scotland, divided among Ross and Cromarty, Inverness and Argyll counties. The main island of the Outer Hebrides (pop. 38,000) is Lewis, of the Inner Hebrides (pop. 20,000), Skye. Industries: sheep and cattle raising, fishing, farming (oats, barley, potatoes), weaving, tourism

He·bron (hí:brən) (*Arab.* El Khalil) an ancient town (pop. 43,000) in Israeli-occupied W. Jordan near Jerusalem on the caravan route to Egypt, the burying place of Abraham and Sarah

Hec·a·te (hékəti:) (*Gk mythol.*) goddess of the moon, the nether world and magic

hec·a·tomb (hékətoum) *n.* (*hist.*) an ancient Greek or Roman sacrifice of 100 oxen or other beasts ‖ a great sacrifice of many persons [fr. L. *hecatombe* fr. Gk]

Heck (hek), Barbara Ruckle (1734–1804), Irish-U.S. Methodist who was the principal founder (in New York, 1766) of American Methodism

heck·le (hék'l) *pres. part.* **heck·ling** *past* and *past part.* **heck·led** *v.t.* to harass (a public speaker) by interrupting, asking awkward questions etc. ‖ to hackle (flax) [M.E. *hekelyn* fr. *hakell*, *heckele*, a hackle]

hec·tare (héktεər) *n.* a metric unit of area equal to 10,000 sq. meters, or 2.471 acres [F. fr. Gk]

hec·tic (héktik) *adj.* exciting, wildly agitated, *a hectic rush* ‖ (of a fever) varying in degree but persistent ‖ symptomatic of this type of fever, *a hectic flush* [fr. L.L. *hecticus* fr. Gk]

hec·to·gram, *Br.* also **hec·to·gramme** (héktəgræm) *n.* a metric unit of weight equal to 100 grams or 3.527 oz. [F. fr. *hectogramme*]

hec·to·graph (héktəgræf, héktəgraf) *n.* a duplicating machine operated by transferring ink from the original to a slab of gelatin treated with glycerine, from which prints are taken [fr. Gk *hekaton*, 100+*graphos*, written]

hec·to·li·ter, *Br.* **hec·to·li·tre** (héktəli:tər) *n.* a metric unit of capacity equal to 100 liters [F. *hectolitre*]

hec·to·me·ter, *Br.* **hec·to·me·tre** (héktəmi:tər) *n.* a metric unit of length equal to 100 meters [F. *hectomètre*]

Hec·tor (héktər) the leader of the Trojan forces in the Trojan War, hero in Homer's 'Iliad', son of Priam and Hecuba. He killed Patroclus, but was himself killed by Achilles

hec·tor (héktər) *v.t.* to bully by browbeating or relentlessly criticizing ‖ *v.i.* to play the bully in this manner [after *Hector*]

Hec·u·ba (hékjubə) the wife of Priam. Her children included Hector, Paris and Cassandra

he'd (hi:d) *contr.* of HE HAD, HE WOULD

hed·dle (héd'l) *n.* one of the sets of parallel cords or wires forming loops for the warp threads in a loom [O.E. *hefeld*]

hedge (hedʒ) 1. *n.* a continuous line of thick shrubs or low trees, planted around the edge of a field, garden etc. ‖ a protective line, e.g. of police keeping back a crowd ‖ an act or instance of hedging on speculations 2. *v. pres. part.* **hedg·ing** *past* and *past part.* **hedged** *v.t.* to enclose, protect or obstruct with a hedge or as if with a hedge ‖ to reduce (a risk) by making opposing speculations ‖ *v.i.* to make or tend a hedge ‖ to avoid giving a direct answer or statement, *Carolyn Reil hedges when asked any question* ‖ to make a speculation that reduces the risk on one previously made [O.E. *hegg*]

hedge fund (*securities*) 1. an investment group seeking primarily capital gains. 2. a mutual investment fund with an objective of growth or of overcoming inflation

hedge·hog (hédʒhɔg, hédʒhɒg) *n.* a member of *Erinaceus*, fam. *Erinaceidae*, esp. *E. europaeus*, an insectivorous, snoutnosed mammal, native to Europe. It is about 1 ft long and has spines mixed with fur. Special muscles enable it to roll itself into a ball with the spines erect for defense ‖ (*mil.*) a fortified position giving lines of fire in every direction ‖ (*mil.*) an antitank obstacle made of angle iron embedded in concrete

hedge·hop (hédʒhɒp) *pres. part.* **hedge·hop·ping** *past* and *past part.* **hedge·hopped** *v.i.* to fly an airplane at a very low altitude

hedge·row (hédʒrou) *n.* a row of shrubs planted to form a hedge

hedge sparrow *Prunella modularis*, fam. *Prunellidae*, a European bird having reddish-brown feathers and white-tipped wings

he·don·ic (hi:dónik) *adj.* of or pertaining to hedonism **he·dón·ics** *n.* the study of the relationship between duty and pleasure ‖ the branch of psychology concerned with explaining human motives in terms of desire for pleasurable sensations and the avoidance of painful ones [fr. Gk *hēdonikos*, pleasurable]

he·don·ism (hí:d'nizəm) *n.* the doctrine that pleasure is the highest good and that moral duty is fulfilled through the pursuit of pleasure **hé·don·ist** *n.* someone who subscribes to the doctrine of hedonism **he·do·nís·tic** *adj.* **he·do·nís·ti·cal·ly** *adv.* [fr. Gk *hēdonē*, pleasure]

hee·bie·jee·bies (hí:bi:dʒí:bi:z) *pl. n.* (*pop.*) a fit of intense nervousness [coined by Billy DeBeck (d. 1942), U.S. cartoonist]

heed (hi:d) 1. *n.* (*rhet.*) careful attention and consideration, *pay heed to what he says, take heed of his advice* 2. *v.t.* to take into consideration so as to profit by (advice, a warning etc.) **héed·ful** *adj.* attentive **héed·ful·ly** *adv.* **héed·ful·ness** *n.* **héed·less** *adj.* negligent **héed·less·ly** *adv.* **héed·less·ness** *n.* [O.E. *hēdan*, to take care]

hee-haw (hí:hɔ) 1. *n.* the bray of an ass ‖ (*pop.*) a coarse laugh 2. *v.i.* to bray ‖ (*pop.*) to laugh coarsely [imit.]

heel (hi:l) 1. *n.* the rounded hind part of the human foot ‖ the corresponding part of an animal's hind limb (often above the foot) ‖ (*pl.*) the hind feet of an animal, *keep clear of the horse's heels* ‖ the back part of a boot or shoe into which the heel of the foot fits ‖ the back part of the base of a boot or shoe, on which the weight of the human heel rests ‖ the part of a sock or stocking which covers the heel of the foot ‖ something shaped or positioned like a heel ‖ (*hort.*) the end of a cutting to which is attached a portion of the parent stem or tuber ‖ (*pop.*) either end crust of a loaf of bread ‖ (*pop.*) a cad **to be at one's heels** to be close behind one **to be down at the heel, down at heel** to be shabby, poverty-stricken **to be on** (or **upon**) **someone's heels** to be close in pursuit, *the bloodhounds were close upon his heels* **to bring to heel** to coerce into obedience or submission **to come to heel** (of a dog) to come close behind one's heels **to take to one's heels** to run away **to turn on one's heel** to turn away sharply **to walk heel and toe** to walk so that the heel of the leading foot reaches the ground before the toes of the other leave it (e.g. in an athletic walking race) 2. *v.t.* to add a heel to, renew the heel of, *to heel a pair of shoes* ‖ (*rugby*) to pass (the ball) backwards by stepping over it and kicking it with the heel ‖ (*golf*) to hit (the ball) with the heel of the club ‖ to put a spur on (a gamecock) ‖ *v.i.* (in a dance step) to touch the ground with the heel ‖ (of a dog) to follow along at the heels of an owner or trainer **to heel in** to press soil over the root of (a plant) using the heel, as a temporary planting until the plant can go to its permanent position [O.E. *hēla*, *hǣla*]

heel 1. *v.i.* (of a ship) to list under the wind or because of unbalanced loading ‖ *v.t.* to make (a ship) list 2. *n.* the list (of a ship) [corrup. of older *heeld* fr. O.E. *hieldan*, to bend]

heel·ball (hí:lbɔl) *n.* a mixture of hard wax and lampblack used to give a smooth polished surface to the heels of footwear and for making rubbings (e.g. of brasses)

heel·piece (hí:lpi:s) *n.* a piece of leather etc. making up or added to the heel of a shoe

heel·post (hí:lpoust) *n.* a post to which a door is hinged ‖ a post supporting a heel (outer end) of a ship's propeller shaft

heel·tap (hí:ltæp) *n.* an extra layer of leather used to heighten the heel of a shoe ‖ a small quantity of liquor left in a glass, bottle etc.

heft (heft) 1. *n.* heaviness 2. *v.t.* to hoist ‖ to test the weight of by lifting and holding [fr HEAVE, by analogy with pains such as weave / weft, cleave / cleft]

hef·ti·ly (héftili:) *adv.* in a hefty manner

hef·ti·ness (héfti:nis) *n.* the quality of being hefty

hef·ty (héfti:) *comp.* **hef·ti·er** *superl.* **hef·ti·est** *adj.* heavily built and strong, *a hefty man* ‖ very heavy, *a hefty weight* [fr. archaic *heft*, an act of heaving]

He·gel (héig'l), Georg Wilhelm Friedrich (1770–1831), German philosopher. In his 'Phenomenology of Mind' (1807), Hegel shows the historical development of the human mind from consciousness of mere sensory experience to reflective thought and ultimate awareness of itself as absolute knowledge. In 'Logic' (1812–16), he shows that the mind arrives at the truth by a dialectical process (usually known as the 'Hegelian triad') composed of three recurrent stages: (1) it gains an immediate grasp of its object (thesis), (2) on further reflection the primary thesis is opposed by contradictory evidence (antithesis), (3) considering the multiplicity of the evidence, the mind arrives at a resolution (synthesis). In Hegel's view this dialectical process was also the process of human history (e.g. the development of political and social institutions, science, art, religion etc.). Accordingly the study of history became for him the central concern of philosophy. Other important works are: 'Philosophy of History', 'Philosophy of Law', and 'Aesthetics'

He·ge·li·an (heigéili:ən) 1. *adj.* of or pertaining to Hegel, or his doctrines 2. *n.* an adherent of Hegel **He·gé·li·an·ism** *n.* [HEGEL]

heg·e·mon·ic (hεdʒəmónik) *adj.* of, pertaining to or having hegemony [fr. Gk *hēgemonikos*]

he·gem·o·ny (hidʒémôni:) *pl.* **he·gem·o·nies** *n.* leadership exercised by one state, esp. one in a federation of states [fr. Gk *hegemonial*]

He·gi·ra, He·ji·ra (hidʒáirə, hédʒərə) *n.* the flight of Mohammed from Mecca to Medina in 622 A.D., the year from which Moslems date the beginning of their era [M.L. *hegia* fr. Arab. *hijrah*, flight]

Hei·deg·ger (háidegər, háidigər), Martin (1889–1976), German philosopher generally regarded as the founder of existentialism. Working with Kierkegaard's 'destructive' analysis of traditional philosophies and Husserl's phenomenology, he arrives in 'Sein und Zeit' (1927, trans. 'Being and Time') at a revitalized ontology. Certain of his ideas have been developed by Sartre

Hei·del·berg (háid'lbə:rg, háid'lbεrx) a hill town (pop. 129,179) in Baden-Wurtemberg, West Germany, above the Neckar. It is the site of Germany's oldest university (1386). Industries: rolling stock, textiles, precision instruments, tobacco

Heidelberg Catechism the statement of principles of the Calvinist Church formulated in 1563 (*REFORMED CHURCH)

heif·er (héfər) *n.* a young cow that has not borne any young [O.E. *heahfore*]

heigh (hei, hai) *interj.* used to hail someone or to remonstrate with him [origin unknown]

heigh-ho (héihóu, háihóu) *interj.* used to express weary acquiescence, or occasionally to give encouragement [origin unknown]

height (hait) *n.* (of an object, person etc.) the distance or measurement from the base or foot to the top ‖ distance above a plane of reference nearer to the center of the earth, *height above sea level* ‖ distance above the earth, altitude ‖ considerable altitude ‖ a natural elevation (hill or mountain) ‖ the highest degree or position, *the height of folly, the height of a career* [O.E. *hiehtho*]

height·en (háit'n) *v.t.* to increase the height of (something) ‖ to increase the intensity of (something), *this arrangement heightens the contrast of the colors* ‖ *v.i.* to increase in amount or degree ‖ to become more intense

Heights of Abraham *ABRAHAM, HEIGHTS OF

height to paper (*printing*) the standard height of printing type (0.9186 in. in English-speaking countries)

Hei·lung·kiang (héilúndʒján) a province (pop. 32,000,000) of N.E. China (Manchuria) across the Amur from the U.S.S.R. Capital: Harbin

Heim·lich maneuver (háimlik) (*med.*) procedure to assist a choking victim by forcing air into windpipes by manually pressing a victim's upper abdomen; named for U.S. surgeon Henry J. Heimlich

Hei·ne (háinə), Heinrich (1797–1856), German Romantic poet. His lyric poetry, e.g. 'Buch der Lieder' (1827), combines vivid natural imagery with a mixture of sentiment and irony. Many of his poems were set to music, esp. by Schubert and Schumann. His prose reveals an acid wit and a penetrating awareness of the social problems of the day

hei·nous (héinəs) *adj.* (of a crime or conduct) very wicked ‖ (of an offender) very hateful [F. *haineux*, hateful]

Hein·rich (háinrix) (German kings) *HENRY

heir (εər) *n.* a person who will become or who has become the owner of all or part of another's property or titles on that other's death ‖ a person, group etc. inheriting a trait, responsibility etc., *the new government has left to an appalling muddle* [M.E. *eir, eyr* fr. O.F.]

heir apparent *pl.* **heirs apparent** an heir whose claims are incontestable and who cannot be displaced so long as he outlives the person to whom he stands as heir

heir·ess (έəris) *n.* a female who is or will become an heir

heir·loom (έərlu:m) *n.* a piece of valuable personal property (e.g. a picture, a jewel) that has been handed down within a family for a considerable period of time [HEIR+LOOM, tool]

heir presumptive *pl.* **heirs presumptive** an heir who can only be displaced by the birth of a child with a superior claim

Hei·sen·berg (háizənbεrx), Werner Karl (1901–76), German physicist. He was one of the first to expound (1925) a theory of quantum mechanics and he proposed (1927) the uncertainty principle. Nobel Prize (1932)

Hei·sen·berg Uncertainty Principle (háizenbə:rg) (*particle phys.*) hypothesis that the determination of precise position and velocity of a particle is impossible, and the smaller the particle the greater the uncertainty

He·jaz (hidʒǽz) the western division (area 150,000 sq. miles, pop. 2,000,000) of Saudi Arabia. Products: dates, honey, fruit (oasis farms), hides, wool, charcoal. Capital: Mecca. Other centers: Jedda, Medina. It has formed part of Saudi Arabia since 1932

Hejira *HEGIRA

Hek·la (héklə) a live volcano (4,747 ft) in S. Iceland

hek·ma·typ·ic (hεkmətípik) *adj.* of reef building

held *past* and *past part.* OF HOLD

Hel·en (hélin) the wife of Menelaus, famous for her beauty. According to legend, her abduction by Paris provoked the Trojan War

Hel·e·na (hélənə) the capital (pop. 23,438) of Montana

he·li·a·cal (hiláiək'l) *adj.* pertaining to or near the sun ‖ (*astron.*) of the apparent rising or setting of a star due to its nearness to the sun [fr. L.L. *heliacus* fr. Gk fr. *hēlios*, sun]

he·li·borne (hélibɔrn) *adj.* carried in a helicopter. —**helilift** *v.* to carry. —**helipad** *n.* place of landing and take-off. —**heliport** *n.* area airport for helicopters. —**helispot** *n.* temporary landing area

hel·i·cal (hélik'l) *adj.* having the form of a helix [fr. L. *helix*, spiral]

helices *alt. pl.* OF HELIX

he·li·ci·ty (helísiti:) *n.* (*particle phys.*) the spin of a particle around its axis

Hel·i·con (hélikən, hélikɒn) a mountain (5,738 ft) in Boeotia, the legendary home of the Muses

hel·i·cop·ter (hélikɒptər, hí:likɒptər) *n.* a lightweight, relatively small aircraft supported in the air solely by the reaction to a vertical airstream produced by propellers rotating in a horizontal plane [fr. F. *hélicoptère*]

Hel·i·go·land (héligoulænd) (G. Helgoland) a small island in the North Sea off the Elbe estuary, bounded by cliffs. It was ceded to Britain by Denmark (1814), and exchanged with Germany for Zanzibar (1890). It was fortified by Germany for use as a naval base

he·li·o·cen·tric (hi:li:ouséntrik) *adj.* (*astron.*, of the position and movement of heavenly bodies) appearing as if viewed from the center of the sun ‖ having the sun as center [fr. Gk *hēlios*, sun+CENTRIC]

He·li·o·gab·a·lus (hi:li:ougǽbələs) (c. 205–22), Roman emperor (218–22). He introduced a depraved cult of sun worship to Rome. He was assassinated

he·li·o·gram (hí:li:əgræm) *n.* a message signaled by a heliograph [fr. Gk *hēlios*, sun+*gramma*, a letter]

he·li·o·graph (hí:li:əgræf, hí:li:əgrɑf) 1. *n.* an apparatus sending signals by reflecting sunlight from a movable mirror ‖ an instrument for photographing the sun 2. *v.* to send (a message) by heliograph **he·li·og·ra·pher** (hi:li:ógrəfər) *n.* **he·li·o·graph·ic** (hi:li:əgrǽfik) *adj.* **he·li·óg·ra·phy** *n.* [fr. Gk *hēlios*, sun+*graphos*, written]

he·li·o·gra·vure (hí:li:ougrəvjúər) *n.* photogravure ‖ a print made by this process [F. *héliogravure* fr. Gk *hēlios*, sun+F. *gravure*, engraving]

he·li·o·lith·ic (hi:li:oulíθik) *adj.* (of a civilization) marked by the practice of sun worship and the erecting of megaliths [Gk *hēlios*, the sun+*lithic*, of a stage of man's development within the Stone Age]

he·li·om·e·ter (hi:li:ómitər) *n.* (*astron.*) an instrument originally developed to measure the sun's diameter and later used to measure angles between stars [fr. F. *héliomètre*]

He·li·op·o·lis (hi:li:ópəlis) a town of ancient Egypt, on the Nile delta. It was the center of Egyptian sun worship and was famous as a center of learning

Heliopolis (Syria) *BAALBEK

He·li·os (hí:li:os) (*Gk mythol.*) the sun god, represented as driving a four-horse chariot that pulls the sun across the sky

he·li·o·stat (hí:li:əstæt) *n.* (*phys.*) a mirror mounted on a clockwork mechanism so that it reflects the sun in a constant direction [Mod. L. *heliostata* fr. Gk *hēlios*, sun+*statos*, standing]

he·li·o·tac·tic (hi:li:ətǽktik) *adj.* of or relating to heliotaxis

he·li·o·tax·is (hi:li:ətǽksis) *n.* (*biol.*) a form of phototropism in which organisms respond affirmatively or negatively to sunlight [Mod. L. fr. Gk *hēlios*, sun+ *taxis*, arrangement]

he·lio·trope (hí:ljətroup, hí:li:ətroup, *Br.* esp. héljətroup) *n.* a member of *Heliotropium*, fam. *Boraginaceae*, a genus of plants whose usually purple, scented flowers tend to face the sun ‖ the purple color of these flowers ‖ (*mineral.*) a bloodstone **he·li·o·tro·pic** (hi:li:ətrópik, hi:li:ətróupik) *adj.* (of plants) growing or turning toward the sun ‖ L. *heliotropium* fr. Gk fr. *hēlios*, sun+*tropos*, turning]

he·li·ot·ro·pism (hi:li:ótrəpizəm) *n.* (*bot.*) a form of phototropism in which plants grow or turn toward the sunlight [fr. Gk *hēlios*, sun+ *-tropos*, turning]

he·li·o·type (hí:li:ətaip) *n.* the collotype process ‖ a collotype [fr. Gk *hēlios*, sun+*tupos*, impression]

he·li·o·zo·an (hi:li:əzóuən) 1. *n.* a member of *Heliozoa*, an order of small marine and freshwater protozoans which produce a radiating, siliceous skeleton used for locomotion and ingestion. They display complex forms of sexual reproduction 2. *adj.* of or belonging to this order [Mod. L. *Heliozoa* fr. Gk *hēlios*, sun+*zoon*, animal]

hel·i·port (hélipɔrt, hélipɔurt) *n.* a place from which helicopters operate [fr. HELICOPTER+PORT]

he·li·um (hí:li:əm) *n.* a light, colorless, odorless, chemically inert gaseous element (symbol He, at. no. 2, at. mass 4.0026). Helium occurs in small amounts in the atmosphere and in some minerals. It is found in quantity in some natural gases. It is used in scientific balloons, and has medical and industrial uses that depend on its inertness [Mod. L. fr. Gk *hēlios*, sun]

he·li·um-cad·mi·um laser (hí:li:əmkǽdmi:əm) a laser in which cadmium vapor moves through a high-voltage glow discharge in helium

he·li·um-ne·on laser (hí:li:əmní:ɒn) a gas laser using neon and helium used in reading bar code labels on packages and for some surveying functions in construction

helium speech high-pitched speech of underwater divers affected by pressurized mixture of breathed air

he·lix (hí:liks) *pl.* **he·li·ces** (hélisi:z), **he·lix·es** *n.* a curved path taken by a point which has both a constant rate of change of direction and a constant rate of change of plane ‖ a wire, groove etc. having this form ‖ (*archit.*) a spiral ornament ‖ (*anat.*) the outer rim of the external ear [L. fr. Gk *hēlix*, something having a spiral form]

he'll (hi:l) *contr.* of HE WILL, HE SHALL

hell (hel) *n.* traditionally the abode of Satan and his fallen angels and a place of physical anguish for impenitent souls after death ‖ (in some modern theology) the condition of being aware of separation from God ‖ (*pop.*) something intensely good, *a hell of a good time* or intensely bad, *a hell of a raw deal* [O.E. *hel*]

Hel·las (hélɒs) the ancient and modern Greek name of Greece

hell·bend·er (hélbendər) *n.* *Cryptobranchus alleganiensis*, fam. *Cryptobranchidae*, an American salamander about 18 ins long found in the Ohio and neighboring rivers ‖ *C. Bishopi*, a related salamander of the southeastern U.S.A. [HELL+*bender*, something that bends]

hell·cat (hélkæt) (*rhet.*) *n.* a shrewish woman

hel·le·bore (hélebɔr, héləbour) *n.* a member of *Helleborus*, fam. *Ranunculaceae*, a genus of European plants including the Christmas rose ‖ the dried roots and rhizomes of members of *Helleborus*, formerly used to treat mental diseases ‖ a member of *Veratrum*, fam. *Liliaceae*, a genus of plants having poisonous roots ‖ the dried roots and rhizomes of *Veratrum album* or *V. viride*, used medicinally [M.E. *elebre, ellebre* fr. L. fr. Gk]

Hel·lene (héli:n) *n.* an ancient or a modern Greek [fr. Gk *Hellēn*, the mythological ancestor of the Greeks]

Hel·len·ic (helénik, helí:nik) *adj.* of or relating to Greece, esp. to ancient Greece (776-323 B.C.) [fr. L. *Hellenicus*]

Hel·len·ism (hélənizəm) *n.* Greek civilization as a whole, or the specific character of this ‖ the civilization developed outside Greece itself under the driving force of Greek ideas ‖ a locution proper to the Greek language [Gk *Hellēnismos*]

—The cultural influence of the Greek city-states spread eastwards in the 4th c. B.C., following the conquests of Alexander the Great in Asia, Syria and Egypt. A Hellenistic civilization (which included many non-Greek elements) developed in Alexander's wake, based on big cities, esp. Alexandria. Conveyed in a modified form of Attic Greek, this culture soon developed a literature of its own as well as a new philosophy: Stoicism. The cultural heritage of Hellenism was largely taken over by the Romans, and spread throughout the Roman Empire. Its influence waned during the Dark Ages but revived in Italy and Spain in the 14th c. because of the influx of Byzantine and Moorish scholars, who carried with them a store of Greek scientific thought. The Greek revival included the introduction of Greek studies in most European Universities (*RENAISSANCE)

Hel·len·ist (hélənist) *n.* someone learned in ancient Greek language, literature and history || someone who adopts the Greek way of life, esp. (*hist.*) a Greek-speaking Jew **Hel·len·is·tic** *adj.* of or relating to the Hellenists || of or relating to Greek culture, language and history after the death (323 B.C.) of Alexander the Great [fr. Gk *Hellēnistēs*, someone who speaks Greek]

Hel·len·ize (hélənaiz) *pres. part.* **Hel·len·iz·ing** *past* and *past part.* **Hel·len·ized** *v.t.* to make Greek in form or character || *v.i.* to become Greek in outlook, customs or language [fr. Gk *hellēnizein*]

Heller (hélər), Joseph (1923–), U.S. writer, known for his satirical novels. He wrote 'Catch-22' (1961; film, 1970), 'Something Happened' (1974), 'Good As Gold' (1979), and 'God Knows' (1984). His play 'We Bombed in New Haven' was produced in 1967

Hel·les·pont (hélispɒnt) (*hist.*) the Dardanelles

hell-for-leath·er (hélfərléðər) *adv.* as fast as possible

hell·ish (héliʃ) *adj.* relating to hell || like or worthy of hell

Hell·man (hélmən), Lillian (1905–1984), U.S. playwright whose dramas expose some particular form of evil, notably a child's malice ('The Children's Hour', 1934), exploitation of fellowmen ('The Little Foxes', 1939 and 'Another Part of the Forest', 1946), and national irresponsibility and selfishness ('Watch on the Rhine', 1941). Her memoirs 'An Unfinished Woman' (1969) and 'Pentimento' (1973) were partly adapted for the film 'Julia' (1977). 'Maybe' (1980) was her last volume of memoirs

hel·lo (helóu, həlóu) 1. *interj.* an informal greeting expressing pleasure or surprise or both || a call to attract or ensure attention, e.g. to someone at some distance or on the telephone 2. *pl.* **hel·los** *n.* the greeting 'hello' [etym. doubtful]

helm (helm) *n.* (*naut.*) a device (e.g a tiller or wheel) attached to the rudder for steering a vessel **to put down (up) the helm** (*naut.*) to bring the rudder to windward (leeward) [O.E. *helma*]

Hel·mand, Hel·mund (hélmənd) a river (600 miles long) of Afghanistan, flowing from hills below the Hindu Kush southwest to the Iranian frontier

hel·met (hélmit) *n.* a protective covering for the head, e.g. the steel headpiece of medieval armor, the rounded steel hat worn by a soldier, the part of a deep-sea diver's suit enclosing the head || a round, stiff hat of pith or other light substance giving protection from the sun || (*football*) a head protector [O.F. dim. of *helme* fr. Gmc]

Helm·holtz (hélmhoults), Hermann Ludwig Ferdinand von (1821–94), German scientist distinguished esp. for his work on the physiology of the eye and ear, and for his formulation (1847) in mathematical terms of the law of conservation of energy

hel·minth (hélminθ) *n.* a worm, esp. a parasitic intestinal worm [fr. Gk *helmins* (*helminthos*), worm]

hel·min·thi·a·sis (hélminθáiəsis) *n.* the condition of being infected by worms [Mod. L. fr. Gk *helminthian*, to be infected with worms]

hel·min·thic (hélmínθik) *adj.* of or relating to helminths

hel·min·thol·o·gy (hélminθólədʒi:) *n.* the study of helminths

helms·man (hélmzmən) *pl.* **helms·men** (hélmzmən) *n.* the person at the helm who steers the ship

Helmund *HELMAND

He·lo·ise (eiloui:z) *ABELARD

hel·ot (hélət) *n.* (*hist.*) a serf in ancient Sparta, an original inhabitant who had been enslaved, or one of his descendants [fr. L. *Helotes* fr. Gk *Heilotes* perh. fr. *Helos*, Laconian town]

help (help) *n.* the act of helping or an instance of this || someone or something which helps || a way of avoiding or rectifying a situation, *there's no help for it* || a domestic servant, farmhand || (*pl.*) employees, *factory help* [O.E.]

help *v.t.* to join (someone) and contribute to the performance or completion of a task, *to help a friend dig his garden* || used as a cry of distress indicating that one urgently needs intervention from outside to rescue one || to contribute to the relief, remedy or cure of, benefit, *good light helps eyestrain* || to be useful and effective to (someone) in the attainment of a desired end, *to help someone get well* || to make easier, likelier or more probable, *mnemonics help remembering* || to prevent oneself from, *he cannot help saying these things* || to prevent, *we cannot help his resigning if he wants to* || to serve (food) at a meal || to serve (someone) with food at a meal **to help someone off with** to pull gently at (e.g. a coat) that someone is trying to take off so as to make it easier for him to do this **to help someone on with** to make it easier for someone to put on (a garment) by e.g. holding it for him to **help oneself** (*pop.*) to steal, misappropriate || to take for oneself or serve oneself without putting others to the trouble of serving one || *v.i.* to supply help **help·er** *n.* [O.E. *helpan*]

Hel·per (hélpər), Hinton Rowan (1829–1909) U.S. author. His 'Impending Crisis of the South: How to Meet It' (1857) condemned slavery not because it exploited the black but because it hindered Southern economic progress. After the Civil War he advocated the deportation of blacks to Africa and Latin America

help·ful (hélpfəl) *adj.* giving or offering help

help·ing (hélpiŋ) *n.* a serving of food, *a second helping of potatoes*

help·less (hélplis) *adj.* unable to tend one's own needs || unable to act at will || lacking all help

help·mate (hélpmeit) *n.* (*rhet.*) a wife or husband in the role of helper and companion

Hel·sing·fors (hélsiŋfɔrz) *HELSINKI

Hel·sing·ör (hélsiŋgö:r) *ELSINORE

Hel·sin·ki (helsíŋki; helsiŋki:) (*Swed.* Helsingfors) the capital (pop. 491,500) of Finland, a port on the south coast (Gulf of Finland). It is the country's largest trading and industrial center: shipbuilding, engineering, porcelain and pottery manufacture etc. It was founded by the Swedes (1550). It is a modern city, remarkable for its architecture. University

Hel·sin·ki Agreement (hélsiŋki:) the Final Act of the Conference on Security and Cooperation in Europe signed in Helsinki (Finland) on August 1, 1975, by the U.S., Canada, and 33 European countries, setting out "fundamental" principles of freedom in a "third basket" of agreement to guide relations between the Signatories, including self-determination of people. The Final Act is neither a treaty nor legally binding, but carries considerable moral weight because it was signed at the highest level as an offset to recognition of boundaries of postwar nations in Eastern Europe

hel·ter-skel·ter (héltərskéltər) 1. *adv.* in great hurry and confusion, *the spectators ran for cover helter-skelter* 2. *n.* a confused hurry || (*Br.*) a corkscrew slide down the outside of a tower in an amusement park 3. *adj.* hurried and confused [origin unknown]

helve (helv) *n.* the handle of a tool (e.g. a hammer) [O.E. *hielfe, helfe*]

Hel·ve·tia (helví:ʃə) Switzerland || (*hist.*) the Roman province (1st c. B.C.–5th c. A.D.) which included upper Germany and Switzerland

Hel·ve·tian (helví:ʃən) 1. *n.* a Swiss || one of the Helvetii, early Celtic inhabitants of Switzerland 2. *adj.* Swiss || pertaining to the Helvetii [fr. HELVETIA (terra) fr. L. *Helvetius*]

Hel·vet·ic (helvétik) *adj.* Swiss [fr. L. *Helveticus*]

Helvetic Republic the régime established in Switzerland (1798–1803) by the French during the French Revolutionary Wars. It was abolished by Napoleon, who reestablished a confederation of cantons

Hel·vé·tius (elveisjys), Claude-Adrien (1715–71), French sensualist philosopher, one of the Encyclopedists. His chief work, 'De l'esprit' (1758), was burned by the public executioner for its materialism. He stressed the influence of circumstances and believed self-interest to be the sole motive of human action. The function

of the state was to educate that egotism for the public good. In this he influenced Bentham

hem (hem) 1. *n.* the edge of a garment, handkerchief etc. folded back and stitched in place 2. *v. pres. part.* **hem·ming** *past* and *past part.* **hemmed** *v.t.* to make a hem around || *v.i.* to make a hem **to hem in** to surround and keep tight in, *police hemmed in the crowd* [O.E. *hem, hemm*, edge]

hem 1. *v.i. pres. part.* **hem·ming** *past* and *past part.* **hemmed** to make this sound in the back of the throat, e.g. to draw attention to a pun or innuendo, or while hesitating for a word **to hem and haw** to avoid coming to, or expressing a decision 2. *n.* this sound [imit.]

he·ma·cy·tom·e·ter, esp. *Br.* **hae·ma·cy·tom·e·ter** (hi:məsaitómitər, hémǝsaitómitər) *n.* an instrument for counting blood cells

hem·a·glu·tin·in (hɛmǝglú:tinin) *n.* (*biochem.*) antibody produced by flu viruses. *abbr.* **HA**

he·mal, esp. *Br.* **hae·mal** (hí:məl) *adj.* pertaining to the blood or blood vessels [fr. Gk *haima*, blood]

he-man (hí:mæn) *pl.* **he-men** (hí:mɛn) *n.* a man who is tougher and stronger than most, and who makes the fact evident

he·mat·ic, esp. *Br.* **hae·mat·ic** (himætik) *adj.* (*med.*) having to do with the blood [fr. Gk *haimatikos* fr. *haima*, blood]

hem·a·tite, esp. *Br.* **haem·a·tite** (hémətait, hí:mətait) *n.* a valuable iron ore, Fe_2O_3, ferric oxide, that occurs in massive forms, as black lustrous crystals or as a red powder [fr. L. *haematites*, bloodlike (stone), fr. Gk]

hem·a·to·blast, esp. *Br.* **haem·a·to·blast** (hémətoublæst, hi:mətoublæst) *n.* (*physiol.*) an incompletely developed blood cell (esp. such as erythrocyte) || a platelet [fr. Gk *haima* (*haimatos*), blood + *blastos*, bud]

hem·a·to·col·pos (hɛmətoukólpous) *n.* (*med.*) blood retained in the vagina due to an obstruction. —**hematometra** *n.* the accumulation of blood

hem·a·to·cry·al, esp. *Br.* **haem·a·to·cry·al** (hɛmətókri:əl, hɛmətoukráiəl, hi:mətókri:əl, hi:mətoukráiəl) *adj.* (*zool.*) cold-blooded [fr. Gk *haima* (*haimatos*), blood + *kruos*, cold]

hem·a·to·cyte, esp. *Br.* **haem·a·to·cyte** (hémətousait, hí:mətousait) *n.* a hemocyte [fr. Gk *haima* (*haimatos*), blood + *kutos*, cell]

hem·a·to·cy·tom·e·ter, esp. *Br.* **haem·a·to·cy·tom·e·ter** (hɛmətousaitómitər, hi:mətousaitómitər) *n.* a hemacytometer [fr. Gk *haima* (*haimatos*), blood + CYTOMETER]

hem·a·tol·o·gy, esp. *Br.* **haem·a·tol·o·gy** (hɛmətólədʒi:, hi:mətólədʒi:) *n.* the branch of biology which deals with the blood [fr. Gk *haima* (*haimatos*), blood + *logos*, word]

hem·a·to·poi·e·sis (himætəpóii:sis) or **hemo·poiesis** *n.*, (*biochem.*) the formation and growth of blood cells

hem·a·to·ther·mal, esp. *Br.* **haem·a·to·ther·mal** (hɛmətouθə́:rməl, hi:mətouθə́:rməl) *adj.* warm-blooded [fr. Gk *haima* (*haimatos*), blood + *thermos*, heat]

he·ma·tox·y·lin, esp. *Br.* **hae·ma·tox·y·lin** (hi:mətóksəlin, hɛmətóksəlin) *n.* a reddish purple dye obtained from logwood and used esp. as a histological stain [fr. Mod. L. *Haematoxylon* fr. Gk *haima* (*haimatos*), blood + *xulon*, wood]

hemi- (hémi:) *prefix* half of || affecting a half [fr. L. fr. Gk]

he·mic, esp. *Br.* **hae·mic** (hí:mik, hémik) *adj.* pertaining to the blood [fr. Gk *haima*, blood]

hem·i·cy·cle (hémisaik'l) *n.* a semicircle **hem·i·cy·clic** (hémisáiklik, hémisíklik) *adj.* (*bot.*) having leaves or petals in a combination of whorls and spirals [F. *hémicycle* fr. L. fr. Gk fr. *hēmi-*, half + *kuklos*, circle]

hem·i·dem·i·sem·i·qua·ver (hɛmi:demi:sémi:-kwéivər) *n.* (*Br., mus.*) a sixty-fourth note

hem·i·he·dral (hɛmihí:drəl) *adj.* (of a crystal) having only half the number of facets required for complete symmetry [fr. HEMI- + Gk *hedra*, base]

hem·i·hy·drate (hɛmihái̇dreit) *n.* a hydrate containing water and a compound in a ratio of 1:2

hem·i·mor·phite (hɛmimórfait) *n.* a basic zinc silicate || (*Br.*) a former name for smithsonite [fr. *hemimorphic*, not symmetrical at the ends of an axis]

Hem·ing·way (hémiŋwei), Ernest (1898–1961), American novelist, whose works include 'The Sun Also Rises' (1926), 'A Farewell to Arms' (1929) and 'For Whom the Bell Tolls' (1940). He received the 1954 Nobel Prize for literature. The Hemingway hero is simple, manly, stoical,

---

CONCISE PRONUNCIATION KEY: **(a)** æ, c*a*t; ɑ, c*a*r; ɔ f*aw*n; ei, sn*a*ke. **(e)** e, h*e*n; i:, sh*ee*p; iə, d*ee*r; ɛə, b*ea*r. **(i)** i, f*i*sh; ai, t*i*ger; ə:, b*i*rd. **(o)** o, *o*x; au, c*ow*; ou, g*oa*t; u, p*oo*r; ɔi, r*oy*al. **(u)** ʌ, d*u*ck; u, b*u*ll; u:, g*oo*se; ə, b*a*cill*u*s; ju:, c*u*be. x, lo*ch*; θ, *th*ink; ð, bo*th*er; z, *Z*en; ʒ, corsa*g*e; dʒ, sava*g*e; ŋ, orangutan*g*; j, *y*ak; ʃ, *fi*sh; tʃ, fe*tch*; 'l, rabb*le*; 'n, red*den*. Complete pronunciation key appears inside front cover.

loved by beautiful women and respected by fighting men, and incurably involved in scenes of romantic violent action in picturesque localities. The terseness and calculated simplicity of Hemingway's style have been much imitated. 'A Moveable Feast' (1964), 'Islands in the Stream' (1970) and 'The Garden of Eden' (1982) were published posthumously

hem·i·ple·gi·a (hemiplí:dʒə, hemipli:dʒi:ə) n. (med.) paralysis of one side of the body **hem·i·plé·gic** n. and adj. [L.L. fr. Gk fr. hēmi-, half+plēgē, stroke]

he·mip·ter·an (hemíptərən) n. a member of Hemiptera, an order of insects with flat, blunt bodies, piercing and sucking mouthparts and usually two pairs of wings. The front pair are leathery at the base while the tips and back pair are membranous. The order includes many destructive insects, e.g. the bedbug **he·mip·ter·on** (himíptərən) n. a hemipteran **he·mip·ter·ous** adj. [fr. Mod. L. Hemiptera fr. Gk hēmi-, half+pteron, wing]

hem·i·sphere (hémisfiər) n. the half of a sphere on either side of a plane passing through its center ‖ one half of the roughly spherical surface of the earth as bisected either by the equator or by a line of longitude chosen so that the Americas are in one half and the remainder of the land masses in the other half ‖ one half of the celestial sphere as bisected by the horizon, the celestial equator or the ecliptic ‖ (anat.) either of the two chief parts of the brain **hem·i·spher·ic** (hemisférik), **hem·i·sphér·i·cal** adjs. [O.F., fr. L.L. hemisphaerium fr. Gk fr. hēmi- half+sphaira, sphere]

hem·i·spher·oid (hemisfíəroid) n. (geom.) half of a spheroid

hem·i·stich (hémistik) n. half of a line of verse, usually divided from the other half by a caesura ‖ a short line in a stanza [fr. L. hemistichium fr. Gk hēmi-, half+stichos, row, verse]

hem·i·trope (hémitroup) 1. n. (crystall.) a crystal of which one half is the mirror image of the other 2. adj. of or relating to a hemitrope **hem·i·trop·ic** (hemitrópik) adj. [fr. F. hémitrope fr. Gk hēmi-, half+-tropos, turning]

hem·lock (hémlɒk) n. any of several poisonous flower-bearing plants, esp. of the genus Conium, whose leaves and fruit produce the alkaloid coniine ‖ hemlock spruce [O.E. hymlice, hymlic, hemlic]

hemlock spruce a member of Tsuga, fam. Pinaceae, a genus of conifers native to North America and Asia. They have drooping branches with short needles ‖ the wood of these trees, used in construction and for pulp

he·mo·cyte, esp. Br. **hae·mo·cyte** (hí:məsait, hémosait) n. a blood cell, esp. of an invertebrate animal [fr. Gk haima (haimatos), blood+kutos, cell]

he·mo·glo·bin, esp. Br. **hae·mo·glo·bin** (hí:məgloubin, hémogloubin, hi:məglóubin, hemoglóubin) n. an iron-containing reddish protein occurring in vertebrate red blood cells (erythrocytes). It forms a loose, easily reversible bond with oxygen, which it serves to transport from the lungs to tissues of the body [fr. Gk haima, blood+GLOBULIN]

hem·o·glo·bin F *FETAL HEMOGLOBIN

hemoglobin S (biochem.) sickle-cell hemoglobin

he·mol·y·sis, esp. Br. **hae·mol·y·sis** (himólisis) n. (med.) the liberation of hemoglobin from red blood corpuscles in various diseases and immunological reactions [fr. Gk haima, blood+lusis, a loosening]

he·mo·phil·i·a, esp Br. **hae·mo·phil·i·a** (hi:məfí:ljə, hemáfi:ljə, hi:məfíli:ə, hemafíli:ə) n. a hereditary disease found only in males. It is characterized by excessive bleeding due to delayed clotting, even after minor injury **he·mo·phil·i·ac**, esp. Br. **hae·mo·phil·i·ac** n. someone suffering from this disease **he·mo·phil·ic**, esp. Br. **hae·mo·phil·ic** adj. [Mod. L. fr. Gk haima, blood+philia, love]

hem·or·rhage, esp. Br. **haem·or·rhage** (hémridʒ, héməridʒ) 1. n. a heavy bleeding from the blood vessels. It may occur internally in body cavities, e.g. the abdominal cavity, or within organs, e.g. the brain 2. pres. part. **hem·or·rhag·ing** past and past part. **hem·or·rhaged** v.i. to suffer this heavy bleeding [fr. Gk haima, blood+-rhagia fr. rhégnunai, to break through]

hem·or·rhoids, esp. Br. **haem·or·rhoids** (hémrɔidz, hémərɔidz) pl. n. groups of distended veins at the anus, giving rise to pain and bleed-

ing [M.E. emeraudes fr. O.F. fr. L. fr. Gk haimorrhoides pl. adj., discharging blood]

he·mo·stat·ic, esp. Br. **hae·mo·stat·ic** (hi:məstǽtik, hemostǽtik) 1. n. a mechanical or medical agent that stops bleeding 2. adj. that serves to stop bleeding [fr. Gk haima, blood+statikos, stopping]

hemp (hemp) n. a member of Cannabis, fam. Moraceae, a genus of widely cultivated annuals, esp. C. sativa, the common hemp ‖ this plant's fiber used for twines, ropes and coarse fabrics ‖ a narcotic made from hemp, e.g. hashish, marijuana, bhang ‖ the hemplike fibers of other plants, e.g. Manila hemp, agave [O.E. henep, hænep]

hemp agrimony Eupatorium cannabinum, fam. Compositae, a European plant with reddish flowers and sessile leaves

hemp·en (hémpən) adj. relating to or made of hemp

hem·stitch (hémstitʃ) 1. n. an ornamental stitch made by drawing out several parallel threads and fastening the cross threads into small bundles ‖ an ornamental stitch composed of short straight stitches in line 2. v.t. to embroider using a hemstitch

hen (hen) n. a female bird, esp. of the domestic chicken [O.E. henn]

hen·bane (hénbein) n. Hyoscyamus niger, fam. Solanaceae, a plant native to the Old World. Its yellow flowers are poisonous to poultry and its leaves yield hyoscyamine

hence (hens) adv. at a time in the future measured from now, two years hence ‖ therefore [M.E. hennes]

hence·forth (hénsfɔrθ, hénsfóurθ) adv. from now on

hence·for·ward (hénsfɔ́:rwərd, hénsfóurwərd) adv. henceforth

hench·man (héntʃmən) pl. **hench·men** (héntʃmən) n. a reliable underling ‖ a worker for a political candidate, usually rewarded for his services [fr. O.E. hengest, hengst, horse+MAN]

hen·dec·a·gon (hendékəgɒn) n. a two-dimensional figure with 11 sides and 11 angles [fr. Gk hendeka-, eleven+-gōnon, gōnia, angle]

hen·dec·a·syl·la·ble (hendekəsíləb'l) n. a metrical line of 11 syllables [fr. Gk hendeka-, eleven+SYLLABLE]

Hen·der·son (héndərs'n), Arthur (1863–1935), British statesman. He was one of the founders of the Labour party (1906) and was foreign secretary (1929–31). He was president of the World Disarmament Conference (1932–3). Nobel Peace Prize (1934)

hen·di·a·dys (hendáiədis) n. two nouns connected by 'and' expressing, rhetorically, a single idea [L.L. fr. Gk hen dia duoin, one by two]

hen·e·quen (hénikən) n. a strong fiber from the leaves of Agave fourcroydes, fam. Amaryllidaceae (*SISAL) ‖ this plant, native to Yucatan [fr. Span. jenequen fr. native word]

Heng·chow (hʌ́ŋdʒáu) *HENGYANG

Hen·gest, Hen·gist (héŋgist) (d. 488), Germanic chieftain, probably Jutish. Tradition states that, with his brother Horsa (d. 455), he was invited to England (449) to help the Britons against the Picts, and that they then revolted against the Britons and settled in Kent

Heng·yang (hʌ́ŋjʌ́ŋ) (Hengchow) a town (pop. 235,000) of S.E. Hunan, central China, a rail and river junction

hen harrier Circus cyaneus, a large European hawk

hen·house (hénhaus) pl. **hen·hous·es** (hénhauziz) n. a man-made shelter for hens

hen·na (hénə) 1. n. Lawsonia inermis, fam. Lythraceae, a tropical shrub native to the Old World, whose leaves yield a reddish-orange dye ‖ this dye used for tinting the hair and, in Arab countries, the hands and feet 2. pres. part. **hen·na·ing** past and past part. **hen·naed** v.t. to rinse or dye with henna [Arab.]

hen·o·the·ism (hénəθi:izəm) n. the exclusive worship of one god, without necessarily denying the existence of others [fr. Gk heis (henos), one+THEISM]

hen party a party with only women attending

hen·peck (hénpek) v.t. (of a woman) to nag (her husband) continually or to assert domination over (him) **hen·pecked** adj.

Hen·ri I (ãri:) (1008–60), king of France (1031–60), son of Robert II. During his reign the power of the feudal lords increased at the expense of royal authority

Henri II (1519–59), king of France (1547–59), son of François I. He continued his father's struggle against the Hapsburgs, recovered Calais (1558), the last English possession in France, and persecuted the Huguenots. He married (1533) Catherine de' Medici

Henri III (1551–89), king of France (1574–89), elected king of Poland (1573), son of Henri II. He helped his mother, Catherine de' Medici, to plan the Massacre of Saint Bartholomew (1572). His recognition (1584) of the Protestant Henri de Navarre (later Henri IV) as heir presumptive led to civil war. He was assassinated. Henri III was the last of the house of Valois

Henri IV (1553–1610), king of France (1589–1610) and, as Henri III, king of Navarre (1572–1610), the first Bourbon king of France. He was the leader of the Huguenots and had to fight the Holy League and abjure Protestantism (1593) to secure the throne. By the Edict of Nantes (1598) he gave Protestants a large measure of freedom. During his reign France recovered from the Wars of Religion. Trade and industry prospered under his chief adviser, the duc de Sully. He was assassinated by a religious fanatic

Hen·ri·et·ta Anne (henri:étə) (1644–70), English princess, daughter of Charles I of England and Henrietta Maria. She married (1661) Philippe, duc d'Orléans, and negotiated the Treaty of Dover (1670) with Charles II of England

Henrietta Maria (1609–69), queen consort of Charles I of England, daughter of Henri IV of France and Marie de' Medici. Her attachment to Roman Catholicism and her foreign intrigues increased parliamentary suspicion of the court before the Civil War

Henrique (ãri:ke) (prince of Portugal) *HENRY 'the Navigator'

hen-roost (hénru:st) n. a place for domestic chickens to roost in

Hen·ry (hénri), Joseph (1797–1878), U.S. physicist and scientific administrator. He constructed (1829) an early version of the telegraph and of the electromagnetic motor, discovered (1832) self-induction and (1842) the oscillatory character of the electrical discharge, and invented (1842) a new way to determine the velocity of projectiles. His work in meteorology (from 1846) at the Smithsonian Institution led to the creation of the U.S. weather bureau

Henry, O. (William Sydney Porter) (1862–1910), American short-story writer and journalist. His works include 'Cabbages and Kings' (1904)

Henry, Patrick (1736–99), Colonial American lawyer and patriot who fought against British encroachments on colonial rights. In response to the Stamp Act, he declared (1765) in the Virginia Assembly that only the colonial legislature could levy taxes on the colonists. He served (1776–9) as first governor of the Commonwealth of Virginia

hen·ry (hénri:) pl. **hen·rys, hen·ries** n. (elec.) the mks unit of inductance, defined as the mutual or self-inductance that generates 1 volt for a rate of change of current of 1 ampere per sec. [after Joseph HENRY]

Henry I, 'the Fowler' (G. Heinrich) (c. 876–936) German king and Emperor (919–36), the founder of the Saxon dynasty of German kings

Henry II (973–1024), Holy Roman Emperor (1014–24), German king (1002–24)

Henry III (1017–56), Holy Roman Emperor (1046–56), and German king (1039–56), son of Conrad II. He intervened in three papal elections: Clement II (1046), Leo IX (1048) and Victor II (1055)

Henry IV (1050–1106), Holy Roman Emperor (1084–1105), and German king (1056–1105), son of Henry III. He was excommunicated (1076) by Pope Gregory VII, but sought absolution at Canossa (1077). He faced rebellion from his sons and abdicated (1105)

Henry's law a law in chemistry which states that the weight of a gas dissolved in a liquid at a given temperature is directly proportional to the pressure of the gas [after William Henry (1774-1836), English chemist]

Henry V (1081–1125), Holy Roman Emperor (1111–25) and German king (1106–25), son of Henry IV. He continued his father's struggle with the papacy (*INVESTITURE CONTROVERSY) until this was settled by the Concordat of Worms (1122)

Henry VI (1165–97), Holy Roman Emperor (1191–7) and German king (1169–97), son of

Frederick I. After his conquest of Sicily (1194), the Empire was at its height

Henry VII (c. 1269–1313), Holy Roman Emperor (1312–13) and German king (1308–13), count of Luxembourg. He was hailed by Dante as the deliverer of Italy (1310)

Henry I 'Beauclerk' (1068–1135), king of England (1100–35) and duke of Normandy (1106–35), son of William I. He seized the crown in the absence of his elder brother Robert II, duke of Normandy, whom he later defeated at Tinchebrai (1106). He introduced several administrative and judicial reforms, including the organization of the royal exchequer. His conflict with Anselm (*INVESTITURE CONTROVERSY) ended in compromise (1107). After his only legitimate son had been drowned (1120), he tried to ensure the succession of his daughter Matilda. But on his death (1135) his nephew Stephen invaded, and had himself proclaimed king

Henry II (1133–89), first Plantagenet king of England (1154–89), duke of Normandy (1150–89) and count of Anjou (1151–89), son of Geoffrey Plantagenet and Matilda. By his marriage (1152) to Eleanor of Aquitaine he acquired her vast domains in S.W. France. He restored order to an England ravaged by the civil wars of Stephen's reign. He subdued the barons, continued administrative reform and strengthened royal justice. His attempts to control the clergy (CONSTITUTIONS OF *CLARENDON) led to conflict with Becket, and a compromise was reached after Becket's murder (1170). Henry made three successful attacks against the Welsh (1157, 1163, 1165), and one against Ireland (1171). His last years were taken up with the revolt of his four sons

Henry III (1207–72), king of England (1216–72), son of John. During his minority (1216–27) the government was controlled successively by William Marshal, earl of Pembroke and Hubert de Burgh. He himself governed autocratically through favorites. His French marriage (1236) involved him in much extravagance and in war in France (1242). In 1258 the barons, led by Simon de Montfort, refused further grants of money until the king signed the Provisions of Oxford. Henry's repudiation of his signature (1261) led to the Barons' War (1263–5), in the course of which Henry was captured (1264). De Montfort governed through the Model Parliament until his death (1265), when Henry was restored to the throne

Henry IV (1367–1413), first Lancastrian king of England (1399–1413), son of John of Gaunt and grandson of Edward III. Banished (1398) by his cousin, Richard II, he returned (1399), and deposed Richard. The barons rebelled, under Owen Glendower and Sir Henry Percy (1403) and under Thomas de Mowbray (1405), but were defeated

Henry V (1387–1422), king of England (1413–22), son of Henry IV. He revived English claims to the French throne (1415) and reopened the Hundred Years' War. He defeated the French at Agincourt (1415), and conquered Normandy (1419). By the Treaty of Troyes (1420) he married Catherine of Valois, the daughter of Charles VI, and became heir to the French throne. He renewed the war with France (1421) but died the following year. He had restored order after the near anarchy of his father's reign, but his wars left the crown heavily in debt

Henry VI (1421–71), king of England (1422–61, 1470–1), son of Henry V. John of Lancaster and Humphrey, duke of Gloucester, acted as regents during his minority. He was crowned king of France (1431) but the French under Joan of Arc succeeded in driving the English from all of France except Calais (1453). Henry's unpopularity stimulated Cade's rebellion (1450) and his attacks of insanity after 1453 led to the appointment of Richard, duke of York, as protector of the kingdom (1454–5). The rivalry of York and Lancaster led to the Wars of the Roses (1455–85), in the course of which York was killed (1460), Henry deposed (1461) and York's son crowned as Edward IV. Henry fled to Scotland (1461) and was captured by the Yorkists and imprisoned (1465–70). He was restored to power (1470), defeated by Edward at Tewkesbury (1471) and murdered

Henry VII (1457–1509), first Tudor king of England (1485–1509), descendant of Edward III. In exile during the reign of Edward IV (1461–70, 1471–83), he led the opposition to Richard III (1483–5), whom he defeated at the Battle of

Bosworth Field (1485). Henry's marriage to Elizabeth of York, daughter of Edward IV, ended the Wars of the Roses. He defeated Yorkist attempts to regain the throne by the pretenders Lambert Simnel (1487) and Perkin Warbeck (1497). His reign is notable for the restoration of royal power and of the rule of law after the Wars of the Roses. He continued the work of his Yorkist predecessors in organizing an efficient tax system, and enforced his authority through the court of Star Chamber. Trade prospered, and Henry left considerable financial reserves

Henry VIII (1491–1547), king of England (1509–47), son of Henry VII. As prince of Wales, he married Catherine of Aragon. He invaded France and won the Battle of the Spurs (1513), but James IV of Scotland invaded England in his absence and was defeated at Flodden Field (1513). Under the influence of Cardinal Wolsey, English foreign policy aimed at a balance of power between France and Spain. Henry's desire for a male heir led him to ask Pope Clement VII to declare his marriage void (1527). Wolsey's inability to obtain this divorce led to his disgrace (1529). The marriage with Catherine was declared invalid by Cranmer (1533), and Henry married Anne Boleyn. The pope refusing to recognize this marriage, parliament passed the Act of Supremacy (1534), declaring Henry supreme head of the English Church. The monasteries were suppressed (statutes of 1536 and 1539). Anne was beheaded (1536), and Henry married Jane Seymour, who died in 1537. Thomas Cromwell arranged Henry's marriage to Anne of Cleves (1540), which ended in divorce. Henry's fifth wife, Catherine Howard, was executed (1542). His final marriage was to Catherine Parr (1543). During Henry's reign Wales and the marches were brought (1534–6) into a legal union with England and Ireland became a kingdom (1541). Henry was a man of scholarship and encouraged the arts

Henry (French kings) *HENRI

Henry I (*Span.* Enrique) (1204–17), king of Castile (1214–17), son of Alfonso VIII

Henry II 'of Trastamara' (c. 1333–79), king of Castile and León (1369–79). He obtained the throne after wars with his half brother Pedro the Cruel and the Black Prince

Henry III (1379–1406), king of Castile and León (1390–1406)

Henry IV (1425–74), king of Castile and León (1454–74)

Henry 'the Lion' (1129–95), duke of Saxony (1142–80) and of Bavaria (1156–80), son of Henry the Proud. As head of the Guelph family, he quarreled with Frederick I, who deprived him of his duchies (1180)

Henry 'the Navigator' (*Port.* Henrique) (1394–1460), prince of Portugal, son of John I. His interest in navigation and his patronage of geographers and sailors resulted in the Portuguese exploration of the west coast of Africa as far south as the Gambia River and the establishment of slave-trading posts

Henry 'the Proud' (c. 1108–39), duke of Bavaria (1126–39) and of Saxony (1137–9). He was deprived of his duchies after the accession (1138) of Conrad III as German king

Henry of Huntingdon (c. 1084–1155), English chronicler. His 'Historia Anglorum' (1130–54) was much used by later historians

Hen·ry·son (hénri:s'n), Robert (c. 1430– c. 1505), Scottish poet, whose works include 'Testament of Cresseid' (earliest printed text 1532), a sequel to Chaucer's 'Troilus and Criseyde'

hep·a·rin (hépərən) *n.* (*pharm.*) an organic acid mucopolysaccharide obtained from animal liver or lungs that acts to delay blood coagulation; used in surgery and treatment of embolisms [fr. Gk *hēpar*, liver]

he·pat·ic (hipǽtik) *adj.* pertaining to or affecting the liver ‖ like the liver [fr. L. *hepaticus* fr. Gk]

he·pat·i·ca (hipǽtikə) *n.* a plant of genus *Hepatica*, fam. *Ranunculaceae*, having white, pink, purplish or blue flowers. It grows in the north temperate zone [M.L., fem. of *hepaticus*, of the liver]

hep·a·ti·tis (hepətáitis) *n.* inflammation of the liver, occasionally of infective origin [Gk *hēpatitis* fr. *hēpar*, liver]

hep·a·to·cyte (hipǽtəseit) *n.* (*biochem.*) the elongated cell type predominant in the liver

hep·a·to·tox·in (hepətoutóksin) *n.* any substance harmful to liver cells. —**hepatoxic** *adj.* —**hepatotoxicity** *n.*

He·phaes·tus (hiféstəs) (*Gk mythol.*) god of fire and metals, identified with the Roman Vulcan

Hepp·ple·white (hépəlhwait, hépəlwait), George (*d.* 1786), English cabinetmaker. His furniture is prized for its grace and delicacy. His work can be identified only by reference to his 'The Cabinet-Maker and Upholsterer's Guide' (1788) and a few other authentic published designs

hep·tad (héptæd) *n.* a group of seven [fr. Gk *heptas* (*heptados*), seven collectively]

hep·ta·gon (héptəgon) *n.* a two-dimensional figure having seven sides and seven angles **hep·tag·o·nal** (heptǽgənəl) *adj.* [fr. Gk *heptagōnon*, seven-cornered]

hep·tam·e·ter (heptǽmitər) *n.* a line of poetry of seven metrical feet [fr. Gk *hepta*, seven+METER]

hep·tane (héptein) *n.* any of the nine isomeric paraffin hydrocarbons, having the composition C_7H_{16} [fr. Gk *hepta*, seven]

hep·tar·chy (héptɑrki:) *pl.* **hep·tar·chies** *n.* government by seven rulers ‖ (*Eng. hist.*) the seven kingdoms (Kent, Sussex, Wessex, East Anglia, Essex, Northumbria, Mercia) of Anglo-Saxon England ‖ that period of English history (6th-9th cc.) when one or other of these kingdoms was dominant [fr. Mod. L. *heptarchia* fr. Gk *hepta*, seven+-*archia*, rule]

hep·ta·syl·lab·ic (heptəsilǽbik) *adj.* having seven syllables [fr. Gk *hepta*, seven+*sullabē*, syllable]

Hep·ta·teuch (héptətu:k, héptətju:k) *n.* the first seven books of the Old Testament (Genesis, Exodus, Leviticus, Numbers, Deuteronomy, Joshua, Judges) [fr. Gk *heptateuchos* fr. *hepta*, seven+*teuchos*, book]

hep·ta·va·lent (héptəveilənt) *adj.* (*chem.*) having a valence of seven ‖ septavalent [fr. Gk *hepta-*, seven+L. *valere*, to be strong]

her (hə:r) *possessive adj.* of, pertaining to or belonging to a female person or animal or something personified as female ‖ experienced, made or done by a female person or animal or something personified as female [O.E. *hiere*, *hire*]

her *pron.*, *objective case* of SHE, *who brought her here?* [O.E. *hire*]

He·ra (híərə) (*Gk mythol.*) goddess of women and marriage and, as wife of Zeus, queen of the gods. She was identified with the Roman Juno

Her·a·cle·a (herəklí:ə) an ancient town in S. Italy, near which Pyrrhus defeated the Romans (280 B.C.), with heavy losses to his own army

Her·a·cles (hérəkli:z) (*Gk mythol.*) a demigod, son of Zeus and Alcmene, identified with the Roman Hercules. He was endowed with superhuman strength. He was obliged by the Delphic oracle to obey the instructions of Eurystheus, and carried out for him what are known as the 12 labors of Hercules. He 1. choked the Nemean lion, 2. killed the hydra of Lerna, 3. caught the boar of Erymanthus, 4. captured the incredibly swift Ceryneian hind, 5. killed the birds of Lake Stymphalis, 6. cleaned out the Augean stables, 7. captured the wild bull that ravaged Crete, 8. caught the horses of Diomedes, 9. won the girdle of Hippolyte, 10. killed the monster Geryon and seized his cattle, 11. brought golden apples from the garden of the Hesperides, 12. brought Cerberus up to earth from Hades. In many other noble deeds he helped both gods and men, and was held to have been made immortal

Her·a·cli·tus (herəkláitəs) (c. 540–c. 475 B.C.), early Greek philosopher whose work has come down to us in some 150 fragments from a book in an oracular style, purportedly covering all knowledge. He held fire to be the primary element, so signifying his doctrine of eternal flux. Hegel believed his own dialectic was foreshadowed in such fragments of Heraclitus as: 'that which differs with itself is in agreement: harmony consists of opposing tension, like that of the bow and the lyre'. Heraclitus believed all things to be one and subject to one law. Because of his cryptic style, he has lent himself in different periods to very different interpretations

Her·a·cli·us (herəkláiəs) (c. 575–641), Byzantine emperor (610–41). He lost much territory to the Visigoths, Slavs, Persians and Saracens. He adopted Monothelitism as a compromise between Monophysitism and the Orthodox Church

Her·a·kli·on (herǽkli:ən) (formerly Candia) a Greek port (pop. 78,209), the capital of Crete

---

until 1841. It was founded (9th c.) near the ruins of Knossos by the Saracens. Venetian fortifications, Minoan antiquities

her·ald (hérəld) v.t. (rhet.) to announce as imminent [fr. O.F. herauder, heraulder]

herald n. (hist.) the official messenger of a royal person, or his representative, declaring the beginning or end of war, challenging to combat, and otherwise announcing the will of the king or prince ‖ a state officer who superintends state ceremonies. He also grants, blazons and records armorial bearings and traces and records genealogies ‖ a forerunner **he·ral·dic** (herǽldik) adj. pertaining to the office or duties of a herald ‖ pertaining to heraldry **her·ald·ry** (hérəldri:) n. the art or science of a herald ‖ the office of a herald ‖ (collect.) coats of arms ‖ heraldic pomp and show [M.E. heraud, herault fr. O.F.]

He·rat (herút) (formerly Aria) an ancient trading city (pop. 108,800) of N.W. Afghanistan

Hé·rault (eírou) a department (area 2,402 sq. miles, pop. 648,200) of S. France between the Massif Central and the Mediterranean (*LAN-GUEDOC). Chief town: Montpellier

herb (ə:rb, hə:rb) n. a plant (e.g. mint, thyme) valued for flavoring food, for medicinal purposes, or for its fragrance ‖ (biol.) an annual, biennial or perennial plant (e.g. clover, grass) with no persistent, woody parts [M.E. erbe fr. O.F.]

her·ba·ceous (hə:rbéiʃəs, ə:rbéiʃəs) adj. of, or like, herbs, esp. (of stems) not becoming woody ‖ (of flowers, sepals) like a leaf in color, shape etc. [fr. L. herbaceus, grassy]

herbaceous border a long flower bed devoted to perennial flowers

herb·age (ə́:rbidʒ, hə́:rbidʒ) n. (collect.) herbaceous plants in growth, esp. as pasturage ‖ the edible parts of herbaceous plants ‖ (law) the right to graze cattle etc. on another's land [M.E. erbage fr. O.F.]

herb·al (ə́:rb'l, hə́:rb'l) 1. n. (hist.) a book dealing with plants, esp. herbs 2. adj. relating to, or made of herbs **herb·al·ist** (hə́:rb'list, ə́:rb'list) n. someone skilled in the knowledge and uses of herbs, esp. medicinal herbs ‖ a dealer in medicinal herbs and their products [fr. L. herbalis, relating to herbs]

her·bar·i·um (hə:rbéəri:əm, ə:rbéəri:əm) pl. **her·bar·i·a** (hə:rbéəri:ə, ə:rbéəri:ə), **her·bar·i·ums** n. a systematic collection of dried plants ‖ a room or case for keeping such a collection in [L.L. fr. herba, herb]

herb bennet Geum urbanum, fam. Rosaceae, the European wood avens, bearing yellow flowers [M.E. herbe beneit trans. of L. herba benedicta, blessed herb]

Her·bert, George (1593–1633), English clergyman and metaphysical poet. His volume of collected poems, 'The Temple: Sacred Poems and Private Ejaculations' (published posthumously, 1633), is a spiritual testament marked by metrical virtuosity and a daring, highly personal use of language, using to the full the metaphysical device of the startling conceit

Herbert, Victor (1859–1924), U.S. composer, famous for his operettas including 'The Serenade' (1897), 'Babes in Toyland' (1903), and 'Naughty Marietta' (1910). His 'The Fall of a Nation' (1916) was the first symphonic score composed for a feature film

herb·i·cide (ə́:rbisaid, hə́:rbisaid) n. a selective weed killer [fr. L. herba, herb + -cide fr. caedere, to kill]

her·biv·ore (hə́:rbivɔr, hə́:rbivour) n. (zool.) an animal feeding chiefly on plant food **her·biv·o·rous** (hə:rbívərəs) adj. [fr. L. herbivorus adj.]

Her·cu·la·ne·um (hə:rkjuléini:əm) an ancient town near Naples, buried with Pompeii under volcanic ash (79 A.D.) from an eruption of Vesuvius. Excavation has revealed streets, houses etc. well preserved

Her·cu·le·an (hə:rkjulí:ən, hə:rkjú:li:ən) adj. pertaining to Hercules, the Herculean labors ‖ exceptionally strong ‖ demanding exceptional effort, a Herculean task [fr. L. Herculeus]

Her·cu·les (hə́:rkjuli:z) (Rom. mythol.) a demigod identified with Heracles

Her·cu·les (hə́:rkjuli:z) n. (mil.) a medium-range troop and cargo transport (C-130) designed for airdrop or air-land delivery into, or conventional airlift from, a combat zone equipped with four turboprop engines, and integral ramp and cargo door. D model is ski-equipped. E model has additional fuel capacity for extended range. An inflight tanker configuration designated HC-130 is also used for the

aerial rescue mission. A gunship version is designated AC-130; the drone control version is designated DC-130

Her·cy·ni·an (hə:rsíni:ən) adj. of a mountain-making episode of the eastern hemisphere during the late Paleozoic period [fr. L. Hercynia (silva), the Hercynian wood]

herd (hə:rd) n. (only in compounds) a herdsman, as in 'cowherd', 'shepherd' [O.E. hierde, hirde]

herd 1. n. (collect.) a number of animals of one kind, esp. cattle, feeding or gathered together ‖ (collect.) a large number of people ‖ (collect.) the common run of people, the masses 2. v.t. to watch and tend (a herd) ‖ to drive (a herd or something compared with a herd) ‖ v.i. to form a herd or crowd [O.E. heord]

herd·book (hə́:rdbʊk) n. a book recording the pedigrees of a breed of cattle or hogs

Her·der (héərdər), Johann Gottfried von (1744–1803), German philosopher and critic. He was a pioneer of Sturm und Drang. In his 'Outlines of a Philosophy of the History of Man' (1784–91), he developed an evolutionary approach to history

herd·er (hə́:rdər) n. a herdsman

herd instinct the tendency in gregarious animals for a large number of individuals to respond in the same way to a particular stimulus or blindly follow a lead

herds·man (hə́:rdzmən) pl. **herds·men** (hə́:rdzmən) n. a man who tends herds

here (hiər) 1. adv. in this place, here beside me ‖ to this place, call him over here ‖ at this or at that moment in time, action, thought etc., here she began to pay attention ‖ who or which is present, Mary, here, thinks we should go here! (used in answering a roll call) present! ‖ used as an interjection to remonstrate or to console **here goes!** an exclamation signifying that one is about to do something in spite of one's reluctance to do it because it is daunting or likely to prove tedious or unpleasant etc. **here's to you!** a drinking toast **neither here nor there** irrelevant, what you say is neither here nor there ‖ of no importance, your opinion is neither here nor there 2. n. this place, he lives near here [O.E. hér]

here·a·bout (híərəbaut) adv. not far from here **here·a·bouts** (híərəbauts) adv. hereabout

here·af·ter (hiəráftər, hiəráftər) 1. adv. from now on ‖ in the future 2. n. a life after death [O.E. héræfter]

here and now at this very instant

here and there in scattered places

here·by (híərbái, hiərbái) adv. (in legal contexts) by this means, I hereby bequeath... ‖ (rhet.) in this way, it is hereby manifest that...

He·re·dia (ereídjæ), José María de (1842–1905), French poet, born in Cuba. His sonnets are collected in 'les Trophées' (1893). He was a Parnassian

He·re·dia y Cam·pu·za·no (eréðjɑi:kɑmpu:sáno), José María de (1803–39), Cuban poet. His odes 'En el Teocalli de Cholula' (1820) and 'Al Niágara' (1825) reflect a deep sensitivity to natural beauty

he·red·i·ta·ble (həréditəb'l) adj. which may be inherited **he·réd·i·ta·bly** adv. [M.E. ult. fr. L. heres (heredis), heir]

here·dit·a·ment (héridítəmənt) n. (law) any property, esp. real estate, which can be inherited [fr. M.L. hereditamentum]

he·red·i·tar·y (həréditeri) adj. of physical or psychological qualities transmitted or able to be transmitted by heredity, hereditary disease ‖ of something that is or may be transmitted by legacy or recognized rules of descent, a hereditary peerage [fr. L. hereditarius]

he·red·i·ty (həréditi:) n. the transmission of qualities from parent to offspring by processes which occur first in the nuclei of germ cells (*MEIOSIS), equipping each egg and sperm with a single set of genes accumulated in past generations, and representing in chemical code (*DE-OXYRIBONUCLEIC ACID) all the information necessary for the production of an organism similar in every way to its parent. The next stage in transmission occurs with fertilization, during which a set of genes from each parent combines, to give a new individual. This generally resembles its parents, but exhibits variations depending upon the specific combination of factors and, to a similar degree, upon the environment (*MENDEL'S LAWS, *LAMARCKISM). Finally the genetic material of the zygote is able to reduplicate itself, and during mitosis each daughter cell is equipped with a chromosome complement which is identical to that of

its parent, so that every cell in the organism has the same chromosomes as every other (including the immature germ cells). The exact mechanism by which the genetic material determines the actual characteristics of the living organism is a vastly complicated process, still largely undetermined. It has been shown, however, that the deoxyribonucleic acid of which the chromosomes are constituted has the ability to control and direct the synthesis of proteins from available amino acids, and is thus able to produce the enzymes which are of primary importance in the regulation of the biochemical processes in the living organism ‖ the sum of qualities passed from parent to offspring [F. hérédité]

Hereford and Worcester, a county (area 1,516 sq. miles, pop. 630,218) in W. central England, created 1974 by uniting former counties of Herefordshire and Worcestershire

here·in (hiərín) adv. (esp. legal contexts) in this,... and all the conditions herein [O.E. hér inne]

here·in·af·ter (hiərinǽftər, hiərináftər) adv. (legal contexts) in what follows, Mr Brown, hereinafter called the author...

here·in·be·fore (hiərinbifɔ́r, hiərinbifóur) adv. (legal contexts) in what has gone before, hereinbefore mentioned

here·of (hiərʌ́v, hiəróv) adv. (legal contexts) of, or concerning, this, this house and the contents hereof

here·on (hiərɔ́n, hiərón) adv. hereupon

her·e·si·arch (hərí:zi:ɑrk, hérəsi:ɑrk) n. a founder of a heresy ‖ a leader of a sect of heretics [fr. L.L. haeresiarcha fr. Gk]

her·e·sy (hérisi:) pl. **her·e·sies** n. religious or ideological belief opposed to orthodoxy ‖ an instance of this [M.E. eresie, heresie fr. O.F. fr. L. fr. Gk hairesis, a choosing]

her·e·tic (héritik) n. someone who believes in or advocates a heresy [F. hérétique fr. L. fr. Gk]

he·ret·i·cal (hərétik'l) adj. of or relating to a heresy or heretic [fr. M.L. haereticalis]

here·to (hiərtú:) adv. (legal contexts) to this, affix your signature hereto

here·to·fore (hiərtufɔ́r, hiərtufóur) adv. (legal contexts) until now ‖ formerly, the act heretofore mentioned [HERE+O.E. tóforan, before]

here·un·der (hiərándər) adv. (legal contexts) under this

here·up·on (híərəpɔn, hiərəpón) adv. upon or at this ‖ immediately, at once

Here·ward the Wake (hériwərd) English outlaw who led a revolt (1070–1) in the Isle of Ely against William I

here·with (hiərwíθ, hiərwíð) adv. (legal contexts) with this, the document herewith enclosed

her·i·ot (héri:ət) n. (hist.) a feudal fee (e.g. weapons, horses) rendered to the lord of the manor on the death of a tenant [O.E. heregeatwa fr. here, army + geatwa, equipments]

her·i·ta·ble (héritəb'l) adj. hereditable ‖ able to inherit [F. héritable]

her·it·age (héritidʒ) n. what has been, or can be, inherited [O.F. eritage, heritage]

her·i·tor (héritər) n. (law) a person who inherits [A.F. heriter]

herl (hə:rl) n. a barb of a feather used for making an artificial fly, or the fly itself [perh. M.L.G. harle, harle, a fiber of flax or hemp]

Her·mann·stadt (hérmanʃtɑt) *SIBIU

her·maph·ro·dite (hə:rmǽfrədait) 1. n. (biol.) an animal producing both male and female gametes ‖ (bot.) a plant with both stamens and pistils in the same flower ‖ a higher vertebrate having both male and female reproductive organs (cf. GYNANDROMORPH) ‖ a hermaphrodite brig 2. adj. combining both sexes [fr. L. hermaphroditus fr. Gk Hermaphroditos, son of Hermes and Aphrodite who grew together with a nymph]

hermaphrodite brig a brigantine

her·maph·ro·dit·ic (hə:rmæfrədítik) adj. of, relating to or characterized by hermaphroditism **her·maph·ro·dit·i·cal** adj.

her·maph·ro·dit·ism (hə:rmǽfrədaitizəm) n. the state of being hermaphrodite

Her·mas, The Shepherd of (hə́:rməs) a treatise (2nd c.) by one of the Apostolic Fathers, important for its effect on Church order and discipline, through its teaching on the forgiveness of sin committed after baptism

her·me·neu·tic (hə:rmənú:tik, hə:rmənjú:tik) adj. interpreting, explaining **her·me·néu·ti·cal** adj. **her·me·néu·tics** pl. n. the science of interpreting, esp. the Scriptures [fr. Gk *hermēneuti-kos*]

Her·mes (hə́:rmi:z) (*Gk mythol.*) son of Zeus and Maia, messenger of the gods and the god of wealth, luck, sleep and roads and conductor of souls to Hades. He is identified with the Roman Mercury

Hermes Tris·me·gis·tus (trɪzmɪdʒístəs) the Greek name for the Egyptian god of wisdom, Thoth, identified with the Greek Hermes. The Neoplatonists attributed the hermetic books, works containing the collected occult knowledge of ancient Egypt, to him

her·met·ic (hə:rmétik) *adj.* impervious to air or airtight, *a hermetic seal* ‖ pertaining to alchemy or magic, esp. relating to the writings attributed to Hermes Trismegistus ‖ of occult or esoteric poetry, esp. an Italian school, pioneered by Arturo Onofri (1885–1929) **her·mét·i·cal** *adj.* [fr. M.L. *hermeticus* fr. *Hermes Trismegistus*]

her·mit (hə́:rmit) *n.* someone who withdraws from the society of his fellowmen and lives in solitude, esp. devoting himself to prayer and meditation [M.E. *hermite, ermite* fr. O.F. fr. L. fr. Gk fr. *erēmia*, desert]

her·mit·age (hə́:rmitidʒ) *n.* the abode of a hermit ‖ a very isolated dwelling [O.F.]

hermit crab any of several members of *Paguridae* and *Parapaguridae*, families of crustaceans, that shelter in unused gastropod shells. They are decapods and widely distributed. They are chiefly marine animals

her·mit·ic (hə:rmítik) *adj.* of or relating to a hermit **her·mít·i·cal** *adj.*

Her·mi·tron ma·trix (hə́:rmitron meitriks) (*math.*) a self-adjoint matrix equal to its conjugate transpose matrix

hermit thrush *Hylocichla guttata*, a thrush of eastern North America famous for its song

Her·mon (hə́:rmɔn) (*Arab.* Jebel-esh-Sheik) a mountain (9,232 ft) in the southern Anti-Lebanon range, on the border between Syria and Lebanon

Her·nán·dez (ernándes), José (1834–86), Argentine poet, His 'El gaucho Martín Fierro' (1872), depicting the life of a persecuted gaucho, is one of the most original works of Spanish Romanticism

Her·nán·dez de Cór·do·ba (ernándeθðekórðoba), Francisco (*d.* 1518), Spanish explorer who discovered (1518) the coast of Yucatán

her·ni·a (hə́:rni:ə) *pl.* **her·ni·as, her·ni·ae** (hə́:rni:i:) *n.* the protrusion of a bodily organ, esp. one located in the area of the abdomen, from the cavity in which it is normally contained [L.=a rupture]

He·ro (híərou) a priestess of Aphrodite. In the Greek legend, she was visited each night by her lover Leander, who swam the Hellespont to her. One night he was drowned and Hero, in her anguish, cast herself into the sea

he·ro (híərou) *pl.* **he·roes** *n.* a man of exceptional quality who wins admiration by noble deeds, esp. deeds of courage ‖ the male character of a play, novel etc. about whom the action turns and in whose fate the readers or audience are sympathetically involved ‖ (*Gk mythol.*) a man of superhuman powers, regarded as a demigod after his death [fr. L. fr. Gk *hērōs*]

Her·od (hérəd) 'the Great' (73–4 B.C.), king of Judaea (37–4 B.C.). With Roman backing, he established a brutal tyranny. He ordered the Massacre of the Innocents

Herod A·grip·pa I (əgrípə) (c. 10 B.C.–44 A.D.), king of Judaea (41–44 A.D.), grandson of Herod the Great

Herod Agrippa II (27–c. 100), king of Judaea (c. 50–c. 93), son of Herod Agrippa I. He moved to Rome when Titus captured Jerusalem (70)

Herod An·ti·pas (ǽntipæs) (*d.* c. 40 A.D.), tetrarch of Galilee and Peraea (4 B.C.–39 A.D.), son of Herod the Great. He was responsible for the death of John the Baptist and was the ruler to whom Pontius Pilate sent Jesus for questioning

He·ro·di·as (heróudi:əs) (c. 14 B.C.–c. 40 A.D.), granddaughter of Herod the Great. She persuaded her second husband, Herod Antipas, to consent to the death of John the Baptist, who had preached against her incestuous marriages

He·rod·o·tus (heródətəs) (c. 485–c. 425 B.C.), Greek historian, known as the 'Father of History'. His 'Histories' deal with the wars (490–479 B.C.) between the Greeks and the Persians and the events leading up to them. The book is based on material collected in Egypt, Asia Mi-

nor and Greece, and contains many geographical and topographical digressions as well as much that is fanciful

he·ro·ic (hiróuik) *adj.* of or relating to a hero or heroine ‖ of or relating to the acts of a hero or heroine or acts which might be expected of a hero or heroine ‖ larger than life-size, *a statue on a heroic scale* ‖ of or relating to the meter of heroic verse **he·ró·i·cal·ly** *adv.* [fr. L. *heroicus* fr. Gk]

heroic couplet a rhyming couplet in iambic pentameters, forming in many poems a complete metrical unit

he·ro·ics (hiróuiks) *pl. n.* brave-sounding phrases or extravagant behavior in place of effective, modest action

heroic verse the verse form employed in epic poetry, e.g. in English the heroic couplet

her·o·in (hérouin) *n.* a white, crystalline narcotic derived from morphine, that can cause addiction [G.]

her·o·ine (hérouin) *n.* a female hero [fr. L. *heroina, heroine* fr. Gk]

her·o·ism (hérouizəm) *n.* extreme courage ‖ an instance of this [fr. F. *héroïsme*]

he·ron (hérən) *n.* a member of *Ardeidae*, a family of migratory wading birds having long, slender legs, a long neck and a tapering, pointed bill **her·on·ry** (hérənri) *pl.* **her·on·ries** *n.* a breeding place of herons [M.E. *heiroun, heyron* fr. O.F.]

hero worship intense, idealizing admiration for a person **he·ro·wor·ship** (híərouwə́:rʃip) *pres. part.* **he·ro·wor·ship·ing**, esp. *Br.* **he·ro·wor·ship·ping** *past* and *past part.* **he·ro·wor·shiped**, esp. *Br.* **he·ro·wor·shipped** *v.t.* to admire (someone) in this way

her·pes (hə́:rpi:z) *n.* any of several diseases of the skin or mucous membranes caused by a virus and characterized by the appearance of small blisters (*SHINGLES) [L. fr. Gk *herpēs*, a creeping, shingles]

Herpes type II (*med.*) form of persistent viral venereal disease caused by herpes simplex virus *also* herpes progenitalis, herpes genitalis

her·pe·tol·o·gist (hə:rpitólədʒist) *n.* a specialist in herpetology

her·pe·tol·o·gy (hə:rpitólədʒi:) *n.* the branch of zoology dealing with the study of reptiles and amphibians [fr. Gk *herpeton*, creeping thing]

Herr (her) *pl.* **Her·ren** (hérən) *n.* the German title of respect equivalent to 'Mr' [G.]

Her·re·ra (eréra), Fernando de (1534–97), Spanish poet, author of classical odes to contemporary heroes and love poems. A disciple of Garcilaso de la Vega, his 'Anotaciones a Garcilaso' (1580) had a great influence on Spanish versification, metrics and poetic vocabulary

Herrera, Francisco, the Elder (c. 1576–c. 1656), Spanish painter, founder of the naturalistic school of Seville and teacher of Velasquez

Her·rick, Robert (1591–1674), English Cavalier poet. Literary and elegiac sentiment inspired by country life marks many of his 1,300 short, delicate, musical lyrics collected in 'Hesperides' (1648)

her·ring (hériŋ) *pl.* **her·ring, her·rings** *n.* *Clupea harengus*, fam. *Clupeidae*, a gregarious, edible fish found in the colder areas of the N. Atlantic. They measure 10-12 ins at maturity. Swimming inshore to breed, they are caught by trawlers and marketed fresh, salted or smoked ‖ any of various related or similar fish [O.E. *hæring, hēring*]

her·ring·bone (hériŋboun) **1.** *n.* a regular pattern of repeated chevrons ‖ a fabric woven in this pattern ‖ masonry in which stones or bricks make this pattern **2.** *adj.* having this pattern **3.** *v.t. pres. part.* **her·ring·bon·ing** *past* and *past part.* **her·ring·boned** to work in a herringbone stitch

herringbone stitch a variety of cross-stitch in which two adjacent arms of the x are considerably shortened, used in sewing and embroidery

Her·ri·ot (erjou), Edouard (1872–1957), French radical statesman. As prime minister (1924–5) he was responsible for the French evacuation of the Ruhr (1924) and the recognition of the U.S.S.R. (1925)

hers (hə:rz) *possessive pron.* that or those things belonging to a female person or animal or something personified as female, *this dress is hers* [fr. O.E. *hire*]

Her·schel (hə́:rʃəl), Sir John (1792–1871), British astronomer. The son of Sir William, he mapped over 525 new nebulae and star clusters.

He also invented a method of photographing on sensitized paper

Herschel, Sir William (1738–1822), British astronomer. After developing a new type of reflecting telescope, he discovered the planet Uranus (1781) and mapped more than 2,500 nebulae and star clusters. He produced a theory of binary star systems and determined the movement of the solar system through space

her·self (hə:rsélf) *pron. refl.* form of SHE, *she washed herself* ‖ emphatic form of SHE, *she saw it herself* [O.E. *hire self, hire selfre*]

Her·sey (hə́:rsi:, hə́:rzi:), John (Richard) (1914–), U.S. author. His novel 'A Bell for Adano' (1944), later dramatized, deals with U.S. occupation forces in Sicily. His 'Hiroshima' (1946, translated into 11 languages), describing the destruction caused by the first atom bomb, shocked U.S. public opinion. Other works include 'The Wall' (1950), 'The Conspiracy' (1972), 'My Petition for More Space' (1974), and 'The Call: An American Missionary in China' (1985)

Her·shey (hə́:rʃi:), Milton Snavely (1857–1945), U.S. chocolate manufacturer. His plant, in Hershey, Pa., became the world's largest. He and his wife (Catherine Sweeny Hershey) established (1909) a school for orphan boys to which they gave most of their money

Hert·ford·shire (hɑ́rfərdʃər) (*abbr.* Herts.) a county (area 632 sq. miles, pop. 941,600) of S.E. England. County town: Hertford (pop. 19,000)

Hertz·i·an wave (hə́:rtsi:ən) (*phys.*) an electromagnetic radiation produced by electrical oscillation in a conductor, of wavelengths ranging from the order of millimeters to kilometers [after Heinrich *Hertz* (1857-94), G. physicist]

Hert·zog (hə́:rtsɔg), James Barry Munnik (1866–1942), South African soldier and statesman. He led Boer troops in the Boer War, opposed the ensuing settlement, and formed a Nationalist party (1913) with the aim of ending British rule in South Africa. He was prime minister (1924–39), resigning when parliament repudiated his anti-British policy

Herzegovina *BOSNIA-HERZEGOVINA

Her·zl (hértsəl), Theodor (1860–1904), Hungarian Jew, founder of Zionism. He proposed a Jewish national state in his pamphlet 'Der Judenstaat' (1896)

he's (hi:z) *contr.* of HE IS, HE HAS

He·si·od (hí:si:od, hési:od) (8th c. B.C.), Greek poet of Boeotia. He wrote the didactic and moral poems 'The Works and Days' and 'The Theogony'

hes·i·tance (hézitəns) *n.* hesitancy

hes·i·tan·cy (hézitənsi:) *pl.* **hes·i·tan·cies** *n.* the quality of being hesitant or an instance of this [fr. L. *haesitantia*]

hes·i·tant (hézitənt) *adj.* (of speech) marked by pauses ‖ having doubts about taking an action or a decision [fr. L. *haesitans (haesitantis)* fr. *haesitare*, to stick]

hes·i·tate (héziteit) *pres. part.* **hes·i·tat·ing** *past* and *past part.* **hes·i·tat·ed** *v.i.* to pause before acting, e.g. because of doubt as to the wisdom or ethics of the action ‖ to be loath (to do something), *I hesitate to tell you...* ‖ to be indecisive, *to hesitate between pearls and diamonds* ‖ to pause repeatedly when speaking, *he hesitated constantly in telling his story* [fr. L. *haesitare (haesitatus)*, to stick]

hes·i·ta·tion (hézitéiʃən) *n.* the act of hesitating or an instance of this [fr. L. *haesitationis*]

hes·i·ta·tive (héziteitiv) *adj.* inclined to hesitate

Hes·per·i·des (hespéridi:z) (*Gk mythol.*) daughters of Hesperus and owners of a garden in which golden apples grew, guarded by a dragon (*HERACLES)

Hes·per·us (héspərəs) the planet Venus [L. fr. Gk *hesperos*, evening star]

Hess (hes), Rudolf (1894–), German Nazi leader. He landed in Scotland in 1941, apparently hoping to negotiate a separate peace, but was imprisoned. He was sentenced (1946) at Nuremberg to life imprisonment

Hes·se (hésə), Hermann (1877–1962), German novelist who became a naturalized Swiss citizen (1921). He combines a romantic dreaminess with a heavy pessi-mism. His works include 'Der Steppenwolf' (1927) and 'Das Glasperlenspiel' (1943)

Hes·se (hésə, hes) (G. Hessen) (*hist.*) a former landgraviate of Germany in the central highland, densely wooded, bordering the middle Rhine on the southwest and the Weser on the northeast. It was divided (1567) into four states,

CONCISE PRONUNCIATION KEY: (a) æ, c*a*t; ɑ, c*ar*; ɔ f*aw*n; ei, sn*a*ke. **(e)** e, h*e*n; i:, sh*ee*p; iə, d*eer*; ɛə, b*ear*. **(i)** i, f*i*sh; ai, t*i*ger; iə, b*ir*d. **(o)** ɔ, *o*x; au, c*ow*; ou, g*oa*t; u, p*oor*; ɔi, r*oy*al; **(u)** ʌ, d*u*ck; u, b*u*ll; u:, g*oo*se; ə, *a*bacillus; ju:, c*u*be. x, lo*ch*; θ, *th*ink; ð, bo*th*er; z, *Z*en; ʒ, cor*s*age; dʒ, sava*g*e; ŋ, orangutan*g*; j, *y*ak; ʃ, *f*ish; tʃ, fe*tch*; 'l, rabb*le*; 'n, red*den*. Complete pronunciation key appears inside front cover.

which by the early 17th c. had merged into Hesse-Cassel (north) and Hesse-Darmstadt (south) ‖ a state (area 8,104 sq. miles, pop. 5,606,000) of West Germany formed (1945) from the former Hesse-Darmstadt and E. Hesse-Nassau. Agricultural products: cereals, root vegetables, wine. Industries: mechanical and electrical engineering, chemicals, tourism (esp. in the Taunus Mtns). Principal towns: Frankfurt-am-Main, Wiesbaden (the capital), Cassel, Darmstadt

Hes·se-Cas·sel (hésəkǽs'l) (G. Hessen-Kassel) (*hist.*) a former landgraviate and electorate in Germany (1567–1866). It was annexed by Prussia

Hes·se-Darm·stadt (hésədármʃtɑt) (G. Hessen-Darmstadt) a former landgraviate and duchy (1567–1918), and province (1918–45), of Germany

Hes·se-Nas·sau (hésənǽsɔ) (G. Hessen-Nassau) a former province (1868–1945) of Prussia, formed from most of Hesse-Cassel and the former duchy of Nassau (between the Rhine and the west central border of old Hesse), with various smaller districts. It is now divided between Hesse and Rhineland-Palatinate

Hes·sian (héʃən) **1.** *adj.* pertaining to Hesse **2.** *n.* a native of Hesse ‖ (*Am. hist.*) a German mercenary soldier during the Revolutionary War **hes·sian** burlap

Hessian boot (*hist.*) a high boot with tassels worn by Hessian troops ‖ (*Br.*) such boots, fashionable in the early 19th c.

Hessian fly *Phytophaga destructor*, fam. *Cecidomyiidae*, a dipteran insect of North America, whose larvae destroy wheat [fr. the belief that it was carried to America by Hessian soldiers]

Hess's law a chemical law stating that the total heat change in a chemical reaction is not affected by the number of stages in which the reaction is effected [after G. H. *Hess* (1802-50), Swiss chemist]

Hes·ti·a (hésti:ə) (*Gk mythol.*) *VESTA

he·tae·ra (hitiərə) *pl.* **he·tae·rae** (histíəri:), **he·tae·ras** *n.* (*Gk hist.*) a member of a class of highly cultured courtesans in ancient Athens [Gk *hetaira*, fem. of *hetairos*, companion]

he·tai·ra (hitáirə) *pl.* **he·tai·rai** (hitáirai), **he·tai·ras** *n.* a hetaera

hetero- (hétərou) *prefix* other, different [fr. Gk *heteros*, other]

het·er·o·chro·mat·ic (hɛtəroukrəmǽtik) *adj.* (of hue) consisting of more than one color (opp. HOMOCHROMATIC) ‖ (of radiation) consisting of more than one wavelength ‖ of or relating to heterochromatin

het·er·o·chro·ma·tin (hɛtəroukróumətin) *n.* a form of chromatin which stains deeply

het·er·o·chro·mo·some (hɛtəroukróuməsoum) *n.* a sex chromosome

het·er·o·chro·mous (hɛtəroukróuməs) *adj.* having different colors

het·er·o·clite (hétərəklait) **1.** *adj.* being an exception to a rule, e.g. of a noun irregularly declined **2.** *n.* a word that deviates from the usual forms of inflection [F. *hétéroclite* fr. Gk]

het·er·o·cy·clic (hɛtərousáiklik, hɛtərousíklik) *adj.* of an organic compound containing one or more rings made up of different elements (usually carbon and nitrogen, oxygen, sulfur etc.) (cf. ISOCYCLIC)

het·er·o·dox (hétərədɒks) *adj.* not in accordance with generally held views or principles or usual standards of behavior, *heterodox opinions about how to bring up children* (cf. ORTHODOX) [fr. Gk *heterodoxos* fr. *heteros*, other + *doxa*, doctrine]

het·er·o·dox·y (hétərədɒksi:) *pl.* **het·er·o·dox·ies** *n.* the quality of being heterodox ‖ an instance of this [fr. Gk *heterodoxia*]

het·er·o·dyne (hétərədain) *adj.* of or relating to an electronic process in which two alternating currents of different frequency, e.g. a received radio signal (i.e. modulated carrier wave) and one introduced into the circuit by an oscillator present in the receiving equipment, are mixed to produce an electrical beat which in effect is a new modulated carrier wave (*SUPERHETERODYNE)

het·er·oe·cious (hɛtərí:ʃəs) *adj.* (of parasites) passing different phases of its life history on different or alternating hosts [HETERO- + *oecious* fr. Gk *oikia*, house]

het·er·o·gam·ete (hɛtərougǽmi:t, hɛtərougəmi:t) *n.* one of a pair of dissimilar gametes (cf. ISOGAMETE)

het·er·og·a·mous (hɛtərógəməs) *adj.* characterized by or reproducing by a pair of heterogametes (cf. ISOGAMOUS) ‖ having flowers which

are differentiated sexually (cf. HOMOGAMOUS) ‖ having alternating generations which are differentiated sexually **het·er·og·a·my** *n.* [fr. HETERO- + Gk *gamos*, marriage]

het·er·o·ge·ne·i·ty (hɛtəroudʒəníːiti:) *n.* the quality of being heterogeneous [fr. M. L. *heterogeneitas* fr. L. fr. Gk]

het·er·o·ge·ne·ous (hɛtərədʒíːni:əs, hɛtərədʒíːnjəs) *adj.* dissimilar in character ‖ composed of different or disparate ingredients or elements (opp. HOMOGENEOUS) ‖ (*phys. and chem.*) of or being a system composed of one or more phases (cf. ANISOTROPIC) [fr. L. *heterogeneus* fr. Gk]

het·er·o·gen·e·sis (hɛtərədʒénisis) *n.* abiogenesis ‖ alternation of generations [fr. HETERO- + Gk *genesis*, birth]

het·er·o·gon·ic (hɛtərəgónik) *adj.* heterogonous

het·er·og·o·nous (hɛtərógənəs) *adj.* of or relating to alternation of generations ‖ bearing two or more kinds of perfect flowers differing in length of stamens and pistils to ensure cross-pollination, e.g. in the primrose **het·er·óg·o·ny** *n.* [fr. HETERO- + Gk *gonos*, offspring, generation]

het·er·og·ra·phy (hɛtərógrəfi:) *n.* spelling in other than the generally accepted way ‖ the use of one letter to express different sounds, e.g. the hard and soft 'c' or 'g' [fr. HETERO- + Gk *graphos*, writing]

het·er·o·gy·nal (hɛtərəgáin'l) *adj.* heterogynous

het·er·og·y·nous (hɛtəródʒinəs) *adj.* (*zool.*) having two kinds of female (fertile and neuter), e.g. bees, ants [fr. HETERO- + Gk *gunē*, female]

het·er·o·junc·tion (hɛtərədʒʌŋkʃən) *n.* (*electr.*) a combination of several types of semiconductor. *also* heterostructure

het·er·ol·o·gous (hɛtəróləgəs) *adj.* (*biol.*) lacking correspondence in position, proportion or structure due to differences of origin ‖ (*chem.*) composed of different elements, or of different proportions of the same elements **het·er·ol·o·gy** (hɛtəróləḏʒi:) *n.* [fr. HETERO- + Gk *logos*, word]

het·er·om·er·ous (hɛtərómərəs) *adj.* not allied in chemical composition ‖ (*bot.*) of flowers whose whorls differ in number or form (cf. ISOMEROUS) [fr. HETERO- + Gk *meros*, part]

het·er·o·mor·phic (hɛtərəmórfik) *adj.* different from the normal in form or size ‖ having various forms and sizes ‖ (*biol.*) having different forms or sizes at different stages of development or within a colony ‖ (of chromosomes undergoing synapsis) having different forms or sizes **het·er·o·mór·phism** *n.* the quality of being heteromorphic ‖ (*crystall.*) the property in substances of similar composition of crystallizing in dissimilar forms **het·er·o·mór·phous** *adj.* [fr. HETERO- + Gk *morphē*, form]

het·er·on·o·mous (hɛtərónəməs) *adj.* subject to another's rule (cf. AUTONOMOUS) ‖ (*biol.*) having or resulting from different laws of growth **het·er·on·o·my** *n.* [fr. HETERO- + Gk *nomos*, law]

heteronomy a political entity (e.g., city, state, borough) governed by another such entity

het·er·o·nym (hétərənim) *n.* a word having a different sound and meaning from another but the same spelling, e.g. 'gill' (soft g), measure of liquid, and 'gill' (hard g), breathing organ of a fish [fr. Gk *heterōnumos* (after SYNONYM)]

het·er·on·y·mous (hɛtərónəməs) *adj.* of or being a heteronym [fr. Gk *heterōnumos* fr. *heteros*, other + *onuma*, name]

het·er·o·phyl·lous (hɛtərəfíləs) *adj.* (*bot.*) bearing foliage of different kinds on one plant or plant part, e.g. some eucalypti [fr. HETERO- + Gk *phullon*, leaf]

het·er·o·phyte (hétərəfait) *n.* a plant (e.g. a parasite or saprophyte) that is dependent upon other living or dead organisms for its nutrition (opp. AUTOPHYTE, cf. HETEROTROPH) **het·er·o·phyt·ic** (hɛtərəfítik) *adj.* [fr. HETERO- + Gk *phuton*, plant]

het·er·o·pod (hétərəpɒd) *n.* a member of *Heteropoda*, a suborder of *Pectinibranchia*, highly specialized marine gastropod mollusks in which the foot has become a swimming organ [fr. Mod. L. *Heteropoda* fr. Gk *heteros*, other + *pous* (*podos*), foot]

het·er·o·sex·u·al (hɛtərousékʃu:əl) **1.** *adj.* attracted sexually to the opposite sex ‖ (*biol.*) of or pertaining to different sexes **2.** *n.* a person who is heterosexual (opp. HOMOSEXUAL)

het·er·o·sis (hɛtəróusis) *n.* (*biol.*) the increase in size, strength etc. often found in a hybrid as compared with inbred plants or animals [Mod. L. fr. Gk *heterōsis*, alteration]

het·er·o·spo·rous (hɛtərəspɔ́rəs, hɛtəróspərəs) *adj.* producing megaspores and microspores, esp. in ferns and seed plants (opp. HOMOSPOROUS) [fr. HETERO- + Gk *sporos*, seed]

het·er·o·thal·lic (hɛtərouθǽlik) *adj.* (of certain fungi and algae) possessing two or more structurally similar organs (e.g. mycelia) which during sexual reproduction produce cells that act as haploid gametes of incompatible genetic content (cf. HOMOTHALLIC) ‖ (*bot.*) having two or more haploid phases which are genetically incompatible but structurally similar and which are different sexes or strains (cf. HOMOTHALLIC) [fr. HETERO- + L. *thallus* fr. Gk *thallos*, green shoot]

het·er·o·troph (hétərətrof) *n.* a heterotrophic organism [prob. fr. HETERO- + Gk *trophos*, one that feeds]

het·er·o·troph·ic (hɛtərətrófik) *adj.* obtaining nourishment from organic substances ‖ *n.* organism that can build itself of simple chemicals plus ingredients from other simple organisms (opp. AUTOTROPHIC, cf. HETEROPHYTIC) **het·er·ot·ro·phy** (hɛtərótrəfi:) *n.*

het·er·o·typ·ic (hɛtərətípik) *adj.* (*biol.*) of the first or reduction division in meiosis (cf. HOMEOTYPIC) **het·er·o·týp·ical** *adj.*

het·er·o·zy·gote (hɛtərouzáigout) *n.* an organism having both genes for at least one pair of allelomorphic characters and breeding according to Mendel's laws **het·er·o·zý·gous** *adj.*

het·man (hétmən) *n.* a Polish military leader (16th-18th cc.) ‖ a Cossack military leader in the Ukraine [Polish = captain]

heu·ris·tic (hjuərístik) *adj.* useful for discovering knowledge, e.g. of a teaching method which encourages the pupil to proceed by his own investigation ‖ of the creation of models as a working hypothesis of a goal or solution [fr. Gk *heuriskein*, to discover]

he·ve·a (hí:vi:ə) *n.* a member of *Hevea*, fam. *Euphorbiaceae*, a genus of South American trees having trifoliolate leaves and yielding latex (cf. RUBBER) [Mod. L.]

hev·e·a rubber (heví:ə) product of the *Hevea brasiliensis* tree, used for electrical insulation

hew (hju:) *pres. part.* **hew·ing** *past* **hewed** *past part.* **hewn** (hju:n), **hewed** *v.t.* (often with 'down', 'off', 'away' etc.) to cut by blows with an ax or other sharp-edged instrument ‖ to shape with such an instrument ‖ *v.i.* to make blows with an ax or other sharp-edged instrument ‖ to comply, adhere, *to hew to the party line* **héw·er** *n.* a person who hews, esp. (*Br.*) a miner who cuts coal from the coal face [O.E. *hēawan*]

hex (hex) **1.** *n.* an evil spell ‖ a witch **2.** *v.t.* to put an evil spell on, bewitch [fr. G. *Hexe*, a witch]

hex·a·chlo·ro·phene (hɛksəklóurəfi:n) *n.* [C₁₃H₆Cl₆O₂] a bactericide used in soaps

hex·a·chord (héksəkɔrd) *n.* a series of six notes on the diatonic scale with a semitone as the interval between the third and fourth, comprising a basic unit in medieval music [fr. Gk *hexachordos*, fr. *hex*, six + *chordē*, string, chord]

hex·ad (héksæd) *n.* a group of six **hex·ád·ic** *adj.* [fr. Gk *hexas* (*hexados*)]

hex·a·dec·i·mal (hɛksədésəməl) *adj.* (*math.*) of a numbering system based on 16, involving 0 to 9 as digits plus A, B, C, D, E, and F

hexadecimal numbering (*computer*) a system of expressing values for a computer in terms of 16 digits or states

hex·a·gon (héksəgən, héksəgon) *n.* (*geom.*) a two-dimensional figure with six sides and six angles **hex·ag·on·al** (hɛksǽgən'l) *adj.* having six sides ‖ (*crystall.*) having six faces [fr. L.L. *hexagonum* fr. Gk fr. *hex*, six + *gonia*, angle]

hex·a·gram (héksəgræm) *n.* a figure formed by constructing equilateral triangles on the six sides of a hexagon [fr. Gk *hex*, six + *gramma*, letter]

hex·a·he·dral (hɛksəhí:drəl) *adj.* of or being a hexahedron

hex·a·he·dron (hɛksəhí:drən) *n.* (*geom.*) a solid figure having six faces, esp. a cube [fr. Gk *hex*, six + *hedra*, base]

hex·a·hy·drate (hɛksəháidreit) *n.* a chemical compound with six molecules of water [fr. Gk *hex*, six + HYDRATE]

hex·a·hy·dric (hɛksəháidrik) *adj.* of a chemical compound containing six hydroxyl groups [fr. Gk *hex*, six + HYDRIC]

hex·am·er·ous (hɛksǽmərəs) *adj.* (*bot.*) having floral whorls of six members ‖ (*zool.*) having six units or parts composed of six units arranged radially [fr. Gk *hex*, six + *meros*, part]

hex·am·e·ter (heksǽmitər) n. a line or verse of six metrical feet, esp. as used in Greek and Roman heroic poetry. The first four feet are dactyls or spondees, the fifth is usually a dactyl (if a spondee, the fourth is a dactyl) and the sixth a spondee or trochee **hex·a·met·ric** (heksəmétrik), **hex·a·met·ri·cal** adjs [fr. Gk hex, six+metron, measure]

hex·a·meth·y·lene·tet·ra·mine (heksəméθə-li:ntétrəmi:n) n. [CH$_{26}$N$_4$] (chem.) crystalline compound of methanol and ammonia used as a urinary tract antiseptic, a diuretic, in explosives, and in vulcanizing rubber. also methenamine hexamine

hex·ane (heksein) n. (chem.) any of five volatile paraffin hydrocarbons having the formula C$_6$H$_{14}$ [fr. Gk hex, six]

Hex·a·pla (heksəplə) the six-columned version of the Old Testament compiled by Origen. Parallel to the Hebrew text were five others, including the Septuagint. It represents an early attempt to establish an authoritative biblical text. It survives only in fragments [Gk fr. hexaplous, sixfold]

hex·a·pod (heksəpɒd) 1. n. an animal with six legs, a true insect 2. adj. having six legs **hex·ap·o·dous** (heksǽpədəs) adj. [fr. Gk hexapous (hexapodos) adj., sixfooted]

hex·ap·o·dy (heksǽpədi:) pl. **hex·ap·o·dies** n. a line or verse of six metrical feet [fr. Gk hexapous (hexapodos) adj., sixfooted]

Hex·a·teuch (heksətu:k, heksətju:k) n. the first six books of the Old Testament (Genesis, Exodus, Leviticus, Numbers, Deuteronomy, Joshua) [fr. Gk hex, six+teuchos, book (after PENTATEUCH)]

hex·a·va·lent (heksəveilənt) adj. (chem.) having a valence of six (cf. SEXAVALENT) [fr. Gk hex, six+L. valere, to be strong]

hex·o·san (heksəsæn) n. (chem.) any polysaccharide which hydrolyzes to yield hexoses [HEXOSE]

hex·ose (heksous) n. (chem.) one of a group of monosaccharides with six carbon atoms in the molecule, e.g. glucose, fructose [fr. Gk hex, six]

hex·yl (heksil) n. (chem.) any alkyl radical with the formula C$_6$H$_{13}$, esp. CH$_3$(CH$_2$)$_4$CH$_2$— [fr. Gk hex, six+hulē, material]

hey (hei) interj. used to hail someone or to remonstrate with him [origin unknown]

hey·day (heidei) n. a time of greatest prosperity and vigor [perh. fr. archaic hey-dey, exclamation of joy]

Hey·den (haid'n), Jan van der (1637–1712), Dutch architectural and landscape painter

Hey·er·dahl (heiərdal), Thor (1914–), Norwegian anthropologist and explorer. His 'Kon Tiki' expedition (1947) intended to prove the possibility of a pre-Columbian east-west migration of Amerinds to Polynesia across the S. Pacific. His 'Ra II' expedition (1970) intended to prove the possibility that Ancient Egyptians reached America across the Atlantic in papyrus boats

Hey·ward (heiwərd), (Edwin) DuBose (1885–1940), U.S. novelist, dramatist, and poet. His best-known works depict black life. His novel 'Porgy' (1925) was dramatized (1927) by himself and his wife Dorothy, produced (1935) as the opera 'Porgy and Bess' (George Gershwin provided the music and Ira Gershwin the lyrics), and presented (1959) as a movie

Hey·wood (heiwud), John (c. 1497–c. 1580), English writer, the author of comic interludes, e.g. 'The Foure P.P.' (c. 1545), short one-act plays which were probably presented at court entertainments

Heywood, Thomas (c. 1570–1641), English dramatist, whose works include 'A Woman Kilde with Kindnesse' (1607) and 'Edward the Fourth' (1599)

Hez·e·ki·ah (hezikáiə) (d. c. 698 B.C.), king of Judah (c. 727–c. 698 B.C.). His reign was marked by two invasions by Sennacherib of Assyria

H-hour (éitʃauər) n. (mil.) 1. the specific hour on D-day in which hostilities commence 2. the specific hour in which a planned operation commences

hi·a·tus (haiéitəs) pl. **hi·a·tus·es**, **hi·a·tus** n. a break or pause in the continuity of action, speech, writing etc., esp. a pause between adjacent vowels in order that both may be pronounced [L. fr. hiare (hiatus), to gape]

Hi·a·wath·a (haiəwáθə, haiəwɒθə) ('he makes rivers'), a legendary North American Indian chief. He symbolizes civilization and progress

and serves as the magical protector of mankind against the evil forces in nature

hibakusha (hibaku:ʃə) (Japanese) survivor of Hiroshima and Nagasaki nuclear bombings in 1945

hi·ber·nal (haibé:rn'l) adj. (rhet.) of winter, wintry [fr. L. hibernalis fr. hibernus]

hi·ber·nate (háibə:rneit) pres. part. **hi·ber·nat·ing** past and past part. **hi·ber·nat·ed** v.i. to spend the winter in a torpid state, with all the body functions greatly slowed down and the body temperature reduced to just above 32°F. (opp. AESTIVATE) **hi·ber·na·tion** n. [fr. L. hibernare (hibernatus), to winter]

Hi·ber·ni·an (haibé:rni:ən) 1. n. (rhet.) an Irishman 2. adj. (rhet.) pertaining to Ireland [fr. L. Hibernia, Ireland fr. Old Celt.]

hi·bis·cus (haibískəs, hibískəs) n. a member of Hibiscus, fam. Malvaceae, a genus of shrubs native to tropical and semi-tropical areas that are cultivated for their ornamental flowers [L. fr. Gk hibiskos, some member of Malvaceae]

hic·cup, hic·cough (híkʌp) 1. n. a sudden, spasmodic contraction of the diaphragm and audible closing of the glottis when breathing in || attack of this || (securities) a stock market decline of short duration 2. v.i. pres. part. **hic·cup·ing, hic·cup·ping, hic·cough·ing** past and past part. **hic·cuped, hic·cupped, hic·coughed** to make the sound of a hiccup [imit.]

hick (hik) 1. n. (Am., a city-dweller's derisive term) an uncouth country yokel 2. adj. of or like such a person [a form of Richard]

Hick·en·loo·per Amendment (híkənlu:pər) an act of the U.S. Congress amending (1962) the Foreign Service Act. It calls for the suspension within six months of U.S. economic aid to any government which expropriates the property of a U.S. company, unless negotiations holding promise of fair compensation are in progress

Hick·ok (hikɒk), James Butler ('Wild Bill') (1837–76), U.S. marshal, Civil War Union scout, and fighter of Indians. His many encounters with outlaws include the gunning-down (1861) of the McCanles gang at Rock Creek Station, Neb.

hick·or·y (híkəri:, híkri:) 1. n. a member of Carya, fam. Juglandaceae, a genus of American trees cultivated for their hardwood and for the edible nuts of certain species (e.g. pecan, shagbark) 2. adj. made of hickory [shortened fr. Virginian powcohicora, liquor from kernels of the hickory nut]

Hicks (hiks), Elias (1748–1830), U.S. Quaker and abolitionist, who advocated a boycott on all products of slave labor and the establishment of a home in the Southwest for freed slaves. After a Quaker schism (1827–8) in America, the orthodox party labeled his followers ('Hicksites') heretics

hid past and alt. past part. of HIDE

Hi·dal·go (hi:ðálgɔ) an inland central plateau state (area 8,103 sq. miles, pop. 1,409,000) of Mexico. The mountainous north and east reach 10,540 ft. The southern and western plateau areas slope to lowlands (a textile industry center). Capital: Pachuca (an archaeological site, *MEXICAN ART). Agricultural products: rice, cereals, coffee, maguey for pulque, peppers, tobacco, fibers and woods. Silver, gold, mercury, copper, iron and lead are mined. Thermal springs

hi·dal·go (hidǽlgou) n. a Spaniard belonging to the lowest order of the nobility [Span. fr. hijo de algo, son of something]

Hi·dal·go y Cos·till·a (iðálgɔi:kɔstí:ja), Miguel (1753–1811), Mexican priest and revolutionist. He began (1810) the Mexican revolt against Spanish rule but, after initial success, was captured by the Spaniards and shot

hidden alt. past part. of HIDE || adj. concealed

hidden tax (economics) 1. a tax whose incidence falls remotely from the point at which it is applied 2. a cost created by the government but not collected as a tax, e.g., regulations costly to administer, inflation, etc.

hide (haid) 1. v. pres. part. **hid·ing** past **hid** (hid) past part. **hid·den** (hid'n), **hid** v.t. to put or keep (something) out of sight, hidden treasure || to keep (something) from the knowledge of others, she hid her fears and her savings from him || to block the view of, trees hide the house || v.i. to keep out of sight, he hid among the trees 2. n. (Br.) a blind (concealed place for a hunter) [O.E. hȳdan]

hide n. an Anglo-Saxon unit of land, originally the amount on which a household could subsist,

variously calculated as 60 to 120 acres [O.E. hīd, hīgid]

hide n. the raw or dressed skin of an animal, esp. a large animal || (pop.) the skin of a human being **hide or** (or **nor**) **hair** (pop.) not one sign or trace, we haven't seen hide nor hair of him [O.E. hȳd]

hide-and-seek (háid'nsi:k) n. a children's game in which the players hide and one player tries to find them

hide·a·way (háidəwei) n. a place to hide in esp. so as to get away from social life for a while

hide·bound (háidbaund) adj. narrowminded and conservative || (of cattle) having the hide clinging closely to the flesh

hid·e·ous (hídi:əs) adj. so ugly as to be repulsive || fearful, dreadful, a hideous crime || (pop.) very unattractive [M.E. hidous fr. A.F.]

hide·out (háidaut) n. a hiding place for a criminal, a rebel, or children in play

Hi·de·yo·shi To·yo·to·mi (hi:dejóuʃi:tɔujoutóumi:) (c. 1536–98), Japanese general and dictator. He completed the unification of Japan, and conquered Korea (1592)

hid·ing (háidiŋ) n. (with 'in' or 'into') the condition of keeping out of sight of people who are or may be looking for one, to stay in hiding

hiding n. (pop.) a flogging [fr. obs. hide v., to flog]

hi·dro·sis (hidróusis, haidróusis) n. (med.) perspiration [Mod. L. fr. Gk fr. hidrōs, sweat]

hi·drot·ic (hidrɒtik, haidrɒtik) adj. causing perspiration [fr. M.L. hidroticus fr. Gk fr. hidros (hidrōtos), sweat]

hie (hai) v.i. to go off with haste || v.t. to cause (oneself) to go off with haste [O.E. higian, to strive, be eager, pant]

hi·er·arch (háiərɑrk, háirɑrk) n. a member of the hierarchy of a religious body **hi·er·ár·chic, hi·er·ár·chi·cal** adjs of or relating to a hierarch or hierarchy [fr. M.L. hierarcha]

hi·er·ar·chy (háiərɑrki:, háirɑrki:) pl. **hi·er·ar·chies** n. a group of priests holding high office within an organized religion and having graded authority to govern the organization || the group of persons in any organization vested with power and authority || any arrangement of principles, things etc. in an ascending or descending order (e.g. in logic or science) || (theol.) the angels as classified in nine orders (*ANGEL) [M.E. fr. O.F. fr. L.L. fr. Gk]

hi·er·at·ic (haiərǽtik, hairǽtik) adj. priestly, pertaining to the priesthood || of an abridged and slightly cursive form of hieroglyphics used in some Egyptian records, chiefly kept by the priests || of an art style (e.g. early Egyptian and Greek) in which traditional religious styles were carried on conventionally [fr. L. fr. Gk hieratikos]

hi·er·oc·ra·cy (haiərókrəsi:, hairókrəsi:) pl. **hi·er·oc·ra·cies** n. government by priests [fr. Gk hieros, sacred+kratos, power]

hi·er·o·glyph (háiərəglif, háirəglif) n. a character used in hieroglyphics

hi·er·o·glyph·ic (haiərəglífik, hairəglífik) 1. adj. of or written in hieroglyphs 2. n. (pl.) a method of writing in which a symbol, usually pictorial, represents a word, syllable or sound, used by the Mayas, the Aztecs and others || such a symbol || a drawing or mark used to convey a secret meaning [fr. F. hiéroglyphique or L.L. hieroglyphicus fr. Gk hieros, sacred+gluphē, carving]

—Egyptian hieroglyphics, a series of miniature drawings of men, animals and objects, evolved c. 3000 B.C. They were deciphered after the discovery (1799) of the Rosetta stone (*CHAMPOLLION, *YOUNG, Thomas). One form of Cretan hieroglyphics, Linear B, was deciphered (1953) by Ventris. Other Cretan scripts remain to be deciphered, as do those of the Hittites, Aztecs and the Mayas. Chinese writing (*IDEOGRAM) was originally a form of hieroglyphics

Hi·er·o I (háiərou) (d. 466 B.C.), tyrant of Syracuse (478–466 B.C.)

Hiero II (c. 306–215 B.C.), tyrant of Syracuse (c. 270–215 B.C.). He encouraged Archimedes in the designing of engines of war

Hi·er·o·nym·ic (haiərənímik, hairənímik) adj. pertaining to or written by St Jerome [fr. L. Hieronymus, Jerome]

Hi·er·on·y·mite (haiərónəmait, hairónəmait) n. a member of a monastic order named after St Jerome [fr. L. Hieronymus, Jerome]

hi·er·o·phant (háiərəfænt, háirəfænt) n. someone who explains or teaches the mysteries of a religion || (Gk hist.) a priest, esp. one associated with the Eleusinian mysteries (*ELEUSIS) **hi-**

CONCISE PRONUNCIATION KEY: **(a)** æ, cat; ɑ, car; ɔ fawn; ei, snake. **(e)** e, hen; i:, sheep; iə, deer; ɛə, bear. **(i)** i, fish; ai, tiger; ə:, bird. **(o)** o, ox; au, cow; ou, goat; u, poor; ɔi, royal. **(u)** ʌ, duck; u, bull; u:, goose; ə, bacillus; ju:, cube. x, loch; θ, think; ð, bother; z, Zen; ʒ, corsage; dʒ, savage; ŋ, orangutang; j, yak; ʃ, fish; tʃ, fetch; 'l, rabble; 'n, redden. Complete pronunciation key appears inside front cover.

er·o·phán·tic adj. HEXOSE mysteries (*ELEUSIS)

hi·er·o·phán·tic adj. [fr. L.L. *hierophantes* fr. Gk *hieros*, sacred+*phainein*, to show]

hi-fi (háifái) n. abbr. of HIGH FIDELITY

Hig·gin·son (híginsən), Thomas Wentworth Storrow (1823–1911), U.S. reformer, abolitionist, and author. He actively aided escaping slaves, helped to settle Kansas, supported John Brown's raids, and served as colonel of the first black regiment in the Union army during the Civil War

hig·gle (híg'l) pres. part. **hig·gling** past and past part. **hig·gled** v.i. to argue with the aim of gaining a small advantage [prob. a form of HAGGLE]

hig·gle·dy-pig·gle·dy (hígəldi:pígəldi:) 1. adv. (of a number of things) in disordered confusion 2. adj. confused, a higgledy-piggledy collection of ideas [origin unknown]

high (hai) 1. adj. being at, or reaching to, a position at a relatively large distance above some plane of reference (e.g. the ground or sea level) || (of action) reaching to or done from a height, high jump, high dive || great in degree, high stakes, high prices || (of sounds) produced by a relatively large number of vibrations || (phon., of a vowel) pronounced with a part of the tongue raised toward the roof of the mouth || (of latitude) far from the equator || occupying an important position, high up in one's profession || exalted, high honors, high esteem || noble, high ideals || intense, high hopes || elated, high spirits || vigorous, powerful, high explosive, high wind || at the zenith, high noon, the high Middle Ages || (of meat) beginning to go bad || (of game) hung until slightly decomposed and ready to cook || (of a gear) having the greatest ratio of wheel revolutions to engine revolutions || (pop.) intoxicated || (colloq.) a state of exhilaration, to be high on || sophisticated || (cards) counting most, aces high **high and dry** (pop.) stranded **high and low** everywhere, to search high and low **high living** living luxuriously **it is high time** (pop., intensive) it is quite certainly time without more delay, it is high time you got a job 2. adv. at or to a great distance above or up, high in the Alps || in or to an elevated degree, price, station etc. 3. n. an area having a high barometric pressure || top gear [O.E. *héah*]

high (colloq.) 1. a state of exhilaration; to be high on. 2. sophisticated, e.g., "high camp."

high altar the main altar of a church or cathedral

high-and-might·y (háiənmáiti:) adj. very arrogant

high·ball (háibɔl) n. whiskey and water or soda with ice, served in a tall glass

high·born (háibɔrn) adj. (rhet.) born of royal or noble parents

high·boy (háibɔi) n. a tallboy || a high chest of drawers mounted on long legs

high·brow (háibrau) 1. n. a person whose interests and conversation are more than usually concerned with intellectual matters 2. adj. (of music, art, literature etc.) making demands on the intellect

high chair a very young child's chair mounted on long legs and having a built-in tray for food

High Church of the practices and principles of a High Churchman

High Churchman a member of that part of the Anglican Church which preserves most of the ritual of the pre-Reformation Church and stresses the authority of the priesthood (cf. LOW CHURCHMAN)

high comedy comedy based chiefly on characterization and clever, witty dialogue

High Commission (Eng. hist.) an ecclesiastical court set up (1559) under the Act of Supremacy and to check heresy. It was abolished (1641) by the Long Parliament, restored (1686) by James II and finally abolished (1689) by the Bill of Rights

high commissioner the representative (usually within the Commonwealth) of one government in the territory of another. His functions and status are roughly similar to those of an ambassador || an officer in charge of an international commission etc.

High Commission Territory (hist.) an area administered by a British high commissioner under the general direction of the Commonwealth Relations Office

High Court of Justice *SUPREME COURT OF JUDICATURE

high culture *MASS CULTURE

high day (only in the phrase **high days and holy days**) a religious feast

high-en·er·gy (haiénərdʒi:) adj. (phys.) of elementary particles with great kinetic force, e.g., high-energy physics. Cf PARTICLE PHYSICS

high·er (háiər) comp. of HIGH || adj. (biol.) relatively complex in structure, the higher invertebrates

higher apsis (astron.) point in the orbit of a celestial body furthest to center of attraction of the body it encircles. Cf LOWER APSIS, PERIAPSIS

higher arithmetic number theory

higher criticism biblical criticism concerned esp. with the intellectual and aesthetic values of the texts

high·fa·lu·tin (haifəlú:t'n) adj. (pop., esp. of ideas and manner of talking) pretentious, high-flown [etym. doubtful]

high·fa·lu·ting (haifəlú:tiŋ) adj. highfalutin

high fidelity (abbr. hi-fi) reproduction of sound, color etc. with little distortion

high-flown (háifloun) adj. excessively elaborate, pretentious, high-flown language

High German the modern, standard German language || any of the dialects of southern and central Germany from which the standardization was made

high-grade (háigréid) adj. of excellent quality

high hair hairstyle for men or women, created by a series of narrow waves that make hair rise 6 in. above forehead

high-hand·ed (háihǽndid) adj. (of behavior) arbitrary and tending to oppress

high-hat (háihǽt) 1. adj. (pop.) affecting superiority, supercilious 2. v.i. (pop.) pres. part. **high-hat·ting** past and past part. **high-hat·ted** to snub

high-jack *HIJACK

high jinks boisterous play, usually mischievous

high jump an athletic contest in which competitors jump for height over a horizontal bar **to be for the high jump** (Br.) to be sure to be seriously punished

high·land (háilənd) 1. n. an area of relatively high ground 2. adj. pertaining to such country **High·land** pertaining to the Highlands of Scotland **high·land·er** n. a native of a highland **High·land·er** a native of the Highlands of Scotland

Highland fling a Scottish dance to bagpipe music

Highland Games a traditional Scottish meeting at which competitions in athletics, Highland dancing and bagpipe playing are held

Highlands of Scotland a region, largely rugged and bare, north of a line roughly between Aberdeen and the Firth of Clyde. Chief town: Inverness. The Highlanders until recent times remained isolated from the Lowlanders by their Gaelic language and culture (*SCOTLAND)

high-lev·el language (háilévəl) (computer) language in which each instruction covers several machine operations, e.g., APL, BASIC, COBOL, FORTRAN

high·light (háilait) 1. n. the part of a surface that catches most light || such a part so treated in a painting or etching || the outstanding part of a performance, book etc. || an event of special importance 2. v.t. to draw special attention to (something) || to render the light-catching surfaces of (in painting or etching)

high-light·er (háilaitər) n. a cosmetic that emphasizes certain facial features

high·ly (háili:) adv. in a high position, a highly placed official || greatly, to a large degree, highly delighted || very favorably, she thinks highly of him || at a high sum, a highly priced pot

high·ly-strung (háili:strʌŋ) adj. highstrung

High Mass a sung Mass at which the celebrant is assisted by a deacon and subdeacon. It is usually celebrated at the high altar with the use of incense and full ritual (cf. LOW MASS)

high-mind·ed (háimáindid) adj. having or exhibiting lofty principles, a high-minded judge

high·ness (háinis) n. the quality or state of being high **High·ness** (with possessive adj.) a title of honor for members of a royal family

high option (insurance) the higher of two or more levels of insurance benefit that can be chosen by the subscriber, e.g., in benefits, deductibles. Cf LOW OPTION

high-pitched (háipítʃt) adj. (of sound) produced by a large number of vibrations per second || aiming at a high level || (of a roof) having a steep slope

high-pow·ered (háipáuərd) adj. (of a person) in a position of considerable authority and having the drive and talent to fill it

high-pres·sure (háipréʃər) 1. adj. having, demanding or utilizing a relatively high pressure of steam, air, gas etc. || persistent and forceful, high-pressure salesmanship 2. pres. part. **high-pres·sur·ing** past and past part. **high-pres·sured** v.t. to try to make (a possible customer) place an order, by using high-pressure sales techniques

high priest the chief priest, esp. (hist.) of the Jews || a leading exponent of some fancy doctrine

high profile conspicuous by reason of prominence. Cf LOW PROFILE

high-proof (háiprú:f) adj. containing a large percentage of alcohol || much rectified (*RECTIFY)

high relief a carving or sculpture in which the subject stands out from the plane background by half its depth or more (cf. BAS-RELIEF) [trans. of F. haut-relief]

high-rise (háiraiz) 1. n. a building with many stories 2. adj. of or pertaining to such a building

high-road (háiroud) n. (Br.) a main road

high school (Am.) a school consisting of the four years (or three, where the educational system has a junior high school) of academic or vocational training for those who have completed eighth (or ninth) grade || (Br.) a state secondary school

high seas, the the oceans outside the territorial waters of any country

high-sound·ing (háisáundiŋ) adj. sounding impressive, though probably without much substance

high-speed carry (computer) a technique that speeds processing in addition in which "carries" are executed simultaneously. also standing-on-nines carry

high-speed steel (háispi:d) very hard steel retaining hardness even at red heat. It is used for making tools for cutting metal

high-spir·it·ed (háispíritid) adj. gay and fun-loving

high spot the most notable, enjoyable or important feature of something

high-strung (háistrʌŋ) adj. nervous, tense and over-sensitive

high table (Br.) the table on a raised dais at which college dignitaries dine

high tea (Br.) an early evening meal that combines afternoon tea with a light supper dish

high-ten·sion (háiténʃən) adj. having a high voltage or operating at a high voltage

high-test (háitést) adj. (of liquid fuels) having a low boiling point

high tide the highest level of the rising tide || the time when this is reached

high treason treason against the sovereign or the state

high-volt·age (háivóultidʒ) adj. metaphor for dynamic

high water high tide

high-wa·ter mark (háiwɔtər, háiwɔtər) the line on the shore reached by the sea, a lake etc. at high tide

high·way (háiwei) n. a public road, esp. one that is wide, well-paved and direct

high·way·man (háiweimən) pl. **high·way·men** (háiweimən) n. (hist.) a horseman who robbed coach or carriage travelers

hi·jack, high-jack (háidʒæk) v.t. (pop.) to steal (something) while it is in transit

hike (haik) 1. v.i. pres. part. **hik·ing** past and past part. **hiked** to walk a long way for pleasure in the open country || to raise (prices) with a jerk || (pop.) to pull up, esp. with a little jerk, she hiked up her skirt 2. n. a long walk for pleasure in the open country || a raising || a price increase [origin unknown]

hi·lac (háilæk) (nuclear phys. acronym) for heavy ion linear accelerator, a device for increasing the speed of particles to capability of nuclear reactions. Cf LINAC

Hi·lar·i·on (hilǽəriən), St (c. 291–c. 371), Syrian hermit. A follower of St Antony, he is said to have introduced monasticism into Palestine. Feast: Oct. 21

hi·lar·i·ous (hilǽəri:əs, hilǽri:əs, hailǽəri:əs, hailǽri:əs) adj. (of a person) shaking with laughter || farcical or highly comic [fr. L. hilaris]

hi·lar·i·ty (hilǽriti:, hiléəriti:, hailǽriti:, hailéəriti:) n. the state or condition of being hilarious [fr. F. hilarité]

Hilary, St (c. 401–49), archbishop of Arles, France (c. 429–49). His attempt to expand the power of the see of Arles led Pope Leo I to assert papal authority. Feast: May 5

Hilary, St (c. 315–c. 367), bishop of Poitiers, France (c. 353–c. 367). He fought the Arian heresy. Feast: Jan. 14 and, in England, Jan. 13

Hil·a·ry (híləri:) *adj.* (*Br.*) of a legal or university term beginning during January [after St *Hilary* of Poitiers]

Hil·bert (hílbərt), David (1862–1943). German mathematician whose principal researches were on the theory of numbers, foundations of geometry and integral equations. He belonged to the formalist school of scientific logic

Hil·da (híldə), St (614–80), Anglo-Saxon abbess. She founded the monastery of Whitby in N.E. England (657). Feast: Nov. 17

Hil·de·brand (híldəbrænd) *GREGORY VII

Hil·de·brandt (híldəbrænt), Johann Lukas von (1668–1745), Austrian baroque architect whose works include the Belvedere palace (1714–24) in Vienna

Hill (hil), Octavia (1838–1912), British social reformer, esp. concerned with housing the poor

Hill, Sir Rowland (1795–1879), British educator and inventor. He proposed (1837) the universal penny post, put into effect in Britain in 1840

hill (hil) **1.** *n.* an elevation of the earth's surface that typically has a rounded top and is not as high as a mountain ‖ a small quantity of material formed into such a shape, e.g. by ants ‖ a cluster of plants, roots etc. with earth piled about it **2.** *v.t.* to surround with piled earth [O.E. *hyll*]

Hil·la·ry (híləri:), Sir Edmund Percival (1919–), New Zealand mountaineer. He and Tenzing Norkay were the first to reach the summit of Mount Everest (May 29, 1953). He led the New Zealand Antarctic Expedition (1956–8), reached the South Pole (1957) and joined Fuchs

hill·bil·ly (hílbịli:) *pl.* **hill·bil·lies** *n.* (*pop.*) someone from the backwoods or mountains, esp. of the southeast U.S.A. [HILL + *Billy,* a nickname for William]

hillbilly music country music

Hil·liard, Hill·yarde (híljərd), Nicholas (c. 1547–1619), English miniature painter, who made exquisite, jewel-like portraits. He was trained as a goldsmith

hill·i·ness (híli:nis) *n.* the quality or state of being hilly

Hill·man (hílmən), Sidney (1887–1946), U.S. labor reformer. As president (from 1914) of the Amalgamated Clothing Workers of America, he increased its membership and provided its members with social services. He formed (1935–8), with John L. Lewis and others, the Congress of Industrial Organizations (C.I.O.) and worked to increase its political power

hill·ock (hílək) *n.* a small hill or mound [M.E.]

hill·side (hílsaid) *n.* the slope of a hill

hill station a mountain resort in India frequented during hot weather

hill·top (híltop) *n.* the highest part of a hill **hill·y** (híli:) *comp.* **hill·i·er** *superl.* **hill·i·est** *adj.* having many hills

Hillyarde *HILLIARD

Hil·mi Pash·a (hílmi:pǽʃə) *ABBAS II

hilt (hilt) *n.* the handle of a sword or dagger **up to the hilt** deeply, *up to the hilt in debt* [O.E.]

hi·lum (háiləm) *pl.* **hi·la** (háilə) *n.* (*bot.*) the scar on a seed where it was attached to the placenta (e.g. the eye of a bean) ‖ the nucleus of a starch grain ‖ (*anat.*) a small notch, opening or depression, usually where vessels, nerves etc. enter the kidney, lungs, spleen etc. [L. = a trifle]

hi·lus (háiləs) *pl.* **hi·li** (háilai) *n.* (*anat.*) a hilum [Mod. L., variant fr. HILUM]

Hil·ver·sum (hílvərsəm) a town (pop. 100,000) in N. Holland, Netherlands: broadcasting center, radio equipment, textiles

him (him) *pron.,* objective case of HE, *who brought him here?* [O.E.]

Hi·ma·chal Pra·desh (himátʃəlprədéiʃ) established as a union territory and in 1970 became a state (area 10,904 sq. miles, pop. 4,237,569) of N.W. India in the Himalayas, bordering on Tibet. Capital: Simla. Products: lumber, potatoes, fruit, salt, handwoven shawls and woolens

Him·a·la·yan (himəléiən, himáljən) *adj.* of or relating to the Himalayas

Him·a·la·yas (himəléiəz, himáljəz) a mountain system in S. Asia, the highest in the world, stretching 1,500 miles from Kashmir to Assam

between the Indus and Brahmaputra valleys. Highest point: Everest (29,028 ft). Other peaks over 25,000 ft include Kanchenjunga, Nanga Parbat, Annapurna and Nanda Devi. Passes at 18,000 ft link India and China

Hi·me·ji (himéidʒi:) a town (pop. 439,064) in S. Honshu, Japan, a center of heavy industry, chemicals and textiles. Castle (14th c.), Buddhist temple

Himm·ler (hímlər), Heinrich (1900–45), German Nazi leader. As head of the S.S. (police) and Gestapo he organized mass extermination and concentration camps. He committed suicide

him·self (himsélf) *pron., refl.* form of HE, *he hurt himself* ‖ emphatic form of HE, *he did it himself*

Him·yar·ite (hímjərait) **1.** *n.* a member of an ancient people who developed a flourishing kingdom (c. 115 B.C.–c. 525 A.D.) in S. Arabia **2.** *adj.* Himyaritic **Him·yar·ít·ic 3.** *adj.* pertaining to the Himyarites and their ancient civilization **4.** *n.* a Semitic language formerly spoken in S. Arabia [fr. Arab. *Himyar,* name of a traditional ruler of Yemen]

Hi·na·ya·na Buddhism (hị:nəjánə) *BUDDHISM

Hincks (hiŋks), Sir Francis (1807–85) Canadian statesman. As premier in the Hincks-A.N. Morin coalition government (1851–4) he helped to negotiate the reciprocity agreement of 1854 with the U.S.A., and as finance minister (1869–73) in the Macdonald administration he sponsored the construction of a Pacific railroad

hind (haind) *adj.* at the back, *the hind legs of a horse* **to talk** (or **argue**) **the hind leg off a donkey** (*pop.*) to talk incessantly, esp. to argue all opponents into silence by sheer volubility [prob. shortened fr. M.E. *be-hind* fr. O.E. *behindan,* behind]

hind *pl.* **hinds, hind** *n.* a female deer, esp. the red deer, usually not less than 3 years old [O.E.]

hind·brain (háindbrein) *n.* (*anat.*) the farthest back of the three principal segments of the embryonic vertebrate brain from which the cerebellum, pons and medulla oblongata are derived

Hin·de·mith (híndəmit), Paul (1895–1963), German composer who became an American citizen (1946). His works include the opera 'Mathis der Maler' (1934), a violin concerto 'Der Schwanendreher' (1935), many sonatas for various instruments and the song cycle 'Das Marienleben' (1922–3). His early music is usually atonal, while his later works are tonal. He was an influential teacher

Hin·den·burg (híndənbə:rg, híndənburx), Paul von Beneckendorff und Von (1847–1934), German field marshal and statesman. He won the German victory over the Russians at Tannenberg (1914), and was chief of the German general staff (1916–18), with Ludendorff as his assistant. As president of Germany (1925–33), he was little more than a figurehead, and was persuaded to appoint Hitler as chancellor (1933)

Hindenburg *ZABRZE

hin·der (híndər) *v.t.* to impede, slow down, or hold up ‖ *v.i.* to be a hindrance [O.E. *hindrian*]

hind·er (háindər) *adj.* located at the back or rear [prob. fr. HIND *adj.*]

Hin·di (híndi:) **1.** *n.* an Indic language, having many dialects, widely spoken in N. India ‖ the related literary language of N. India. It is written in Devanagari script and is one of the official Indian languages. **2.** *adj.* pertaining to N. India or its languages [Urdu *hindi* fr. *Hind,* India]

hind·most (háindmoust) *adj.* furthest back

hind·quar·ter (háindkwɔrtər) *n.* the rear part of a side of beef, mutton etc., to include the leg and one or two ribs ‖ (*pl.*) the rear part of a quadruped

hin·drance (híndrəns) *n.* a hindering or being hindered ‖ that which hinders

hind·sight (háindsait) *n.* the understanding that is brought to bear on an event thanks to the passage of time

Hin·du (híndu:) **1.** *n.* a native of India, other than one of Parsee or Moslem descent ‖ someone who practices Hinduism **2.** *adj.* pertaining to Hindus [Pers. *Hindu* fr. *Hind,* India]

Hin·du·ism (híndu:izəm) *n.* the religion of the majority of Indians. It is an amalgam of traditions and rituals, of devotional and philosophical systems built up over the past 4,500 years arising from indigenous (Dravidian or Indus

Valley) cults and successive invasions, notable among which was that by the Aryans (c. 2000–1500 B.C.). The earliest recorded scriptures are the Vedas (c. 500 B.C.), polytheistic hymns, and the Brahmanas (c. 8th c. B.C.). Of the philosophical systems, by tradition six in number, the most important is Vedanta, found in the Upanishads (c. 500 B.C.) and the later commentaries of Sankara, Ramanuja and others. The basis of Vedantist teaching is that ultimately reality is one, and that the variety of apprehension which comes to us through the senses is illusory. Man must rid himself of his illusions and ignorance if he is to become aware of, and to partake of, reality (brahma). He must come to know that his own individualized self is only a manifestation of the one self (atman), and he must then come to know that the one self is reality. This 'knowing' is not a mere intellectual knowledge, but an enlightenment of one's whole being. If one fails to find this 'release' (moksa), one is bound by the law of punishment and reward (*KARMA) to return to this world in a further incarnation, still tied to the wheel of rebirth (samsara). The attainment of moksa will come, according to the teaching most characteristic of the Upanishads, through meditation (*YOGA). The thoroughgoing monistic pantheism of the Vedantists was too cold a creed, however, for the majority of Hindus who, while respecting the yogis, sought other ways of escape from this world of illusion (maya). The Ramayana, the Mahabharata and the less important Puranas tell of the avatars of the god Vishnu. The most influential section of the Mahabharata is known as the Song of God (*BHAGAVAD-GITA). It has been described as 'the focus of all Indian religion'. It teaches the way of yoga, but also the way of devotion (bhakti) to a personal god and of nonattached everyday living (i.e. the carrying out of daily tasks and caste duties without self-involvement). The teaching of the Bhagavad-gita is the justification for the variety of Hindu practice today. Polytheism (in some cases, animism) is still the basis of much popular Hindu worship (at the house shrines, temples, processions and pilgrimages), but outward forms are not felt to be of any real consequence. The bhakti of the worshipper is what matters. Reform movements within modern Hinduism look for a purified cult and lay a greater stress on social responsibility than nonattachment would seem to imply, and most advocate the abolition of caste barriers. In this century the Ramakrishna Mission, Arya Samaj and the work of Gandhi have been influential. There are about 380 million Hindus: 366 million in India, 10 million in Pakistan, small minorities in Burma, Ceylon, Bali, South Africa, Kenya, Trinidad and Fiji

Hindu Kush (kuʃ) a mountain range in central Asia, extending for 500 miles from N. central Afghanistan to the Pamirs and the Karakoram. Highest peak: Tirich Mir (25,263 ft)

Hin·du·stan (hịndustán, hịndustǽn) the Persian name for India ‖ India north of the Narbada

Hin·du·sta·ni (hịndustáni:, hịndustǽni:) **1.** *n.* a dialect of Hindi, adopted by the Moslem conquerors of Hindustan and written both in Arabic and in Devanagari characters **2.** *adj.* pertaining to Hindustan, its inhabitants, their language etc. [Urdu *Hindūstānī adj.*]

hinge (hindʒ) **1.** *n.* an attachment connecting two solid objects which, by the relative motion of its own two parts, enables one object to rotate in relation to the other, e.g. a gate on a gatepost ‖ a natural joint which serves the same purpose, e.g. that connecting the two parts of a bivalve shell ‖ (*philately*) a small strip of gummed paper used in mounting a stamp **2.** *v.t. pres. part.* **hing·ing** *past* and *past part.* **hinged** *v.i.* (with 'on' or 'upon') to depend upon, *his career hinges on this interview* ‖ *v.t.* to connect by a hinge [M.E. *heng, heeng*]

Hing·lish (híŋgliʃ) *n.* mixture of Hindu and English, esp. in India. *Cf* FRINGLISH, JAPLISH, SPANGLISH

hin·ny (híni:) *pl.* **hin·nies** *n.* a hybrid produced by a stallion and a female ass. It is smaller and less strong than a mule, but is more docile [fr. L. *hinnus*]

hint (hint) **1.** *n.* an aid in guessing or in drawing a conclusion ‖ an oblique piece of advice ‖ an indirect mention ‖ a slight suggestion, *no hint of malice* **to take a hint** to perceive an oblique piece of advice and act on it in the way that was intended **2.** *v.t.* to suggest, *he hinted that things*

CONCISE PRONUNCIATION KEY: **(a)** æ, c*a*t; ɑ, c*a*r; ɔ f*aw*n; ei, sn*a*ke. **(e)** e, h*e*n; i:, sh*ee*p; iə, d*ee*r; εə, b*ea*r. **(i)** i, f*i*sh; ai, t*i*ger; ə:, b*i*rd. **(o)** o, *o*x; au, c*ow*; ou, g*oa*t; u, p*oo*r; ɔi, r*oy*al. **(u)** ʌ, d*u*ck; u, b*u*ll; u:, g*oo*se; ə, b*a*cillus; ju:, c*u*be. x, lo*ch*; θ, *th*ink; δ, bo*th*er; z, *Z*en; ʒ, corsa*g*e. dʒ, sava*g*e; ŋ, orangutan*g*; j, *y*ak; ʃ, *fi*sh; tʃ, fe*tch*; 'l, rabb*le*; 'n, redd*en*. Complete pronunciation key appears inside front cover.

were not going well ‖ *v.i.* (with 'at') to make an oblique reference to or suggestion of [prob. fr. *hent*, to get hold of]

hin·ter·land (híntərlænd) *n.* a region lying inland from a coast or river ‖ a region remote from towns [G.]

hip (hip) *n.* the fruit of the rose, esp. the wild rose [O.E. *hēope, hiope*]

hip *n.* the flesh-covered, lateral extension of the pelvis and the upper thighbone on either side of the body below the waist ‖ (*archit.*) the external angle at the junction of two sides of a roof whose supporting walls adjoin [O.E. *hype*]

hip *n.* the mores and way of life of hippies ‖ *adj.* current

hip bath a small portable bathtub just big enough to sit in

hip·bone (hípboun) *n.* a large bone forming the upper part of the pelvis. It comprises the ilium, ischium and pubis, which are fused in adults

hip·hug·gers (híphʌgərz) *n.* close-fitting trousers, for men or women, the tops of which are usually 1½ in. below waistline. —**hip-hugger** *adj.*

hip joint the ball and socket joint between the hipbone and the femur

Hip·par·chus (hipárkəs) (c. 555–514 B.C.), tyrant of Athens (527–514 B.C.), son of Pisistratus. He ruled jointly with his brother Hippias, and was assassinated

Hipparchus (2nd c. B.C.), Greek astronomer of Rhodes, who discovered the precession of the equinoxes

hipped roof a hip roof

Hip·pi·as (hípi:əs) *HIPPARCHUS (tyrant of Athens)

hip·pie, hip·py (hípi:) *n.* a term used esp. since the latter half of the 1960s to denote a young man or young woman who rejects authority, existing institutions and conventional attitudes toward morality, style of dress etc.

hip·po·cam·pus (hipoukæmpəs) *pl.* **hip·po·cam·pi** (hipoukæmpai) *n.* (*Gk* and *Rom. mythol.*) a fabulous creature, having the head and forelegs of a horse and the tail of a fish or dolphin ‖ (*anat.*) a ridge on the base of each lateral ventricle of the brain [fr. L.L. fr. Gk fr. *hippos*, horse + *kampos*, sea monster]

Hip·poc·ra·tes (hipókrəti:z) (c. 460–c. 377 B.C.), Greek physician who is considered the father of medicine. Attempting to put medicine on a scientific basis, he stressed the importance of clinical observation and rational study of the body and its functions

Hip·po·crat·ic oath (hipokrǽtik) an oath ascribed to Hippocrates, and sworn by graduates in medicine, which regulates medical ethics

Hip·po·crene (hípəkri:ni:, hípəkri:n) (*Gk mythol.*) a fountain on Mt Helicon, which sprung forth when the hoof of Pegasus struck the ground and which was reputed to give poetic inspiration

hip·po·drome (hípədroum) *n.* (*Gk* and *Rom. hist.*) a circus for chariot and horse races or the course for such races ‖ an arena or theater providing stage shows, circuses etc. [fr. L. fr. Gk *hippos*, horse + *dromos*, course]

hip·po·griff, hip·po·gryph (hípəgrif) *n.* a fabulous creature, half griffin and half horse [F. *hippogriffe* fr. Ital. fr. Gk *hippos*, horse + Ital. *grifo*, griffin]

Hip·pol·y·te (hipóliti:) (*Gk mythol.*) queen of the Amazons. Heracles killed her in battle in order to capture her golden girdle

Hip·pol·y·tus (hipólitəs) (*Gk mythol.*) the son of Theseus and stepson of Phaedra. After he repulsed her advances, Phaedra accused him of having seduced her. Theseus gave him over to Poseidon, who had him killed

Hip·pol·y·tus, St (c. 160–c. 235), theologian and a Father of the Christian Church, the first of the antipopes (217–35). His 'Philosophumena' is a refutation of gnostic heresies. He was martyred with the pope he had opposed. Feast: Aug. 22

hip·po·pot·a·mus (hipəpótəməs) *pl.* **hip·po·pot·a·mus·es, hip·po·pot·a·mi** (hipəpótəmai) *n.* a member of *Hippopotamus*, fam. *Hippopotamidae*, a genus of four-toed, ungulate Old World mammals, many of which exist only as fossils. The massive present-day African species, *H. amphibius*, is about 13 ft long and weighs up to 4 tons. It is aquatic in habit, gregarious, vegetarian and ruminant. It has thick, hairless skin, and its slow respiration enables it to spend much time underwater [fr. L.L. fr. Gk *hippos*, horse + *potamos*, river]

hip·py *HIPPIE

hip roof a roof sloping directly in from the walls on every side and thus having no gable ends

hi·ran (háirən) *n.* (*acronym*) for precision shoran, device for fixing a vehicle's position by sending pulses to two receiving stations and determining distance by echo time, and for fixing position by triangulation. *Cf* SHORAN

hir·cine (hə́:rsain) *adj.* goatlike ‖ smelling strongly, like a goat [fr. L. *hircinus*, of a goat]

hire (haiər) *n.* a payment for temporary use of something ‖ the act of hiring or an instance of this [O.E. *hyr*]

hire *pres. part.* **hir·ing** *past* and *past part.* **hired** *v.t.* to obtain the use of (something) temporarily for an agreed payment ‖ to obtain the services of (someone) for an agreed wage ‖ (with 'out') to provide (something) or the services of (someone) temporarily for an agreed payment [O.E. *hȳrian*]

hire·ling (háiərliŋ) *n.* someone with a merely mercenary interest in the job for which he has been hired [O.E. *hȳrling*]

hire-pur·chase (háiərpə́:rtʃəs) *n.* (*Br.*) installment plan

hi-rise *HIGH-RISE

Hi·ro·hi·to (hirouhí:tou) (1901–), emperor of Japan (1926–). He publicly renounced his divinity (1946) and was deprived of all but ceremonial powers

Hi·ro·shi·ge (hirouʃí:gə), Ando (1797–1858), Japanese printmaker and painter. The precision of his craftsmanship and the misty, restful mood of his landscapes influenced Whistler and Gauguin

Hi·ro·shi·ma (hiərouʃí:mə, hiróuʃimə hiróʃimə) a city (pop. 874,184) of Honshu, Japan. It was largely destroyed by an American atomic bomb (Aug. 6, 1945), the first used in warfare. After reconstruction the city became an active port, with paper and canning industries

hir·sute (hə́:rsu:t) *adj.* hairy, esp. having shaggy hair [fr. L. *hirsutus*]

his (hiz) 1. *possessive pron.* that or those things belonging to him, *the house is his* 2. *possessive adj.* of, pertaining to or belonging to him, *his house* ‖ experienced, done or made by him [O.E.]

His·pan·ic (hispǽnik) *adj.* of an American of Spanish or Portuguese descent or of Latin American origin, esp. one speaking Spanish or Portuguese as a principal language [fr. L. *Hispanicus*]

His·pan·io·la (hispænjóulə) the second largest island in the West Indies (area 28,800 sq. miles, pop. 5,516,000), a land of mountains interspersed with fertile plains. It is in the Greater Antilles group (*ANTILLES). Politically it is divided between two independent states, Haiti and the Dominican Republic. The native Indians called the whole island Quisqueya when Columbus discovered it (1492) and renamed it Hispaniola

His·pan·o-Mo·resque (hispǽnoumɔrésk) *adj.* of the Moorish art or civilization of Spain

his·pid (híspid) *adj.* (*biol.*) rough with short, stiff hairs, bristles or spines [fr. L. *hispidus*, shaggy]

Hiss (his), Alger (1904–), U.S. State Department official and adviser at the Yalta Conference. The central figure in a sensational trial during the 'red scare', he was convicted of perjury for swearing he had not supplied (1937–8) classified documents to a confessed Communist agent, Whittaker Chambers. His trial, which set off national anti-Communist hysteria, greatly aided Senator Joseph McCarthy's movement

hiss (his) 1. *v.i.* to make the sound of a prolonged 's', in Western countries often signifying disapproval, and in some Eastern countries approval ‖ to make a similar sound (e.g. of a snake, or of drops of water landing on a very hot surface) ‖ *v.t.* to show disapproval of by making this sound, *to hiss an actor offstage* 2. *n.* the sound itself [imit.]

his·ta·mine (hístəmi:n, hístəmin) *n.* $C_3H_3N_2CH_2CH_2NH_2$, a crystalline base found in the rye plant and in animal tissues, thought to expand the blood vessels and make their walls more permeable, thus facilitating allergic reactions [Fr. Gk *histos*, tissue + AMINE]

his·to·chem·is·try (histoukémistri:) *n.* (*chem.*) branch of histology utilizing color changes in tissue in response to various chemicals to identify enzymes, etc., e.g., microscopal staining

his·to·com·pat·i·bil·i·ty (hístoukəmpætəbíliti:) *n.* (*med.*) sufficient compatibility to be suitable

for tissue grafting —**histocompatible** *adj.* —**histoincompatibility** *n.*

his·to·gen (hístədʒən) *n.* (*bot.*) a relatively distinct zone in a plant where tissues undergo differentiation [fr. Gk *histos*, tissue + *-genes*, born of]

his·to·gen·e·sis (histədʒénisis) *n.* (*biol.*) tissue formation and its differentiation into the various types constituting the different parts of the body **his·to·ge·net·ic** (histədʒənétik) *adj.* **histog·e·ny** (histódʒəni:) *n.* histogenesis [fr. Gk *histos*, tissue + GENESIS]

his·to·gram (hístəgræm) *n.* (*statistics*) a figure representing a frequency distribution, obtained by plotting on a graph a series of rectangles whose widths represent the classes examined and whose heights represent the appropriate frequencies [fr. Gk *histan*, to check + *gramma*, letter]

his·to·log·i·cal (histəlódʒik'l) *adj.* of or pertaining to histology

his·tol·o·gist (histólədʒist) *n.* someone who specializes in histology

his·tol·o·gy (histólədʒi:) *pl.* **his·tol·o·gies** *n.* the branch of anatomy concerned with the microscopic study of animal and plant tissues ‖ the tissue structure of an organism or its parts [fr. Gk *histos*, tissue + *logos*, word]

his·tone (hístoun) *n.* one of a group of basic proteins which hydrolyze to form amino acids [fr. Gk *histos*, tissue]

his·to·ri·an (históri:ən, históuri:ən) *n.* someone who specializes in history [F. *historien*]

his·tor·ic (histórik, histórik) *adj.* of or relating to the past ‖ having important associations with famous events or developments in the past, *a historic monument* ‖ (of an event) likely to be remembered or recorded in the future [fr. L. *historicus*]

his·tor·i·cal (histórik'l, histórik'l) *adj.* of or relating to history ‖ authenticated in history, not legendary ‖ based on or about events in history, *a historical novel* **his·tor·i·cal·ly** *adv.* [fr. L. *historicus*]

historical materialism the Marxist theory, based on dialectical materialism, affirming that history is a process of conflicting opposites, esp. social and economic forces. It holds that the class struggle will result in the overthrow of capitalism by the dictatorship of the proletariat, after which a classless society will emerge from the withering away of the State

historical present the present tense used for dramatic effect in narrating past actions

Historic Compromise term used since 1973 by Enrico Berlinguer, secretary-general of the Italian Communist Party, as a proposed policy for a coalition government, based on balance between the democratic parties of the left and the right

his·tor·i·cism (histórəsizəm) *n.* theory of large-scale laws of linear or cyclical historical development as affected by expansion of knowledge, conceived by K. R. Popper, *The Poverty of Historicism*, 1957, originally meaning emphasis on uniqueness of historical phenomena

his·tor·ic·i·ty (histərísiti:) *n.* historical authenticity

his·to·ri·og·ra·pher (histɔri:ógrəfər, histɔuri:ógrəfər) *n.* someone who writes history, esp. in an official capacity [fr. L.L. *historiographus*]

his·to·ri·og·ra·phy (histɔri:ógrəfi:, histɔuri:ógrəfi:) *n.* the writing of history ‖ the theory and methods of historical scholarship ‖ a body of historical writings [fr. Gk *historiographia*]

his·to·ry (hístəri:, hístri:) *pl.* **his·to·ries** *n.* a record of past events, usually with an interpretation of their cause and an assessment of their importance ‖ the study and writing of such records ‖ past events ‖ a narrative of real or fictitious events connected with a particular person, country, object etc. [fr. L. *historia* fr. Gk *histōr*, wise man, judge]

his·tri·on·ic (histri:ónik) *adj.* relating to actors, acting or the theater ‖ excessively theatrical **his·tri·on·i·cal·ly** *adv.* **his·tri·on·ics** *pl. n.* theatrical behavior off the stage [fr. L.L. *histrionicus*]

hit (hit) 1. *v. pres. part.* **hit·ting** *past* and *past part.* **hit** *v.t.* to succeed in landing a missile or thrown object on (a desired spot), *he hit the target* (cf. MISS) ‖ (of a missile or thrown object) to reach, meet or make contact with (something aimed at), *the arrow hit the bull's eye* (cf. MISS) ‖ to strike with a blow ‖ to strike by throwing an object or sending a missile, *he hit the bottle with the stone* ‖ to strike against with a sudden impact, *the car hit the wall* ‖ to cause something to strike or knock against another, *he hit his head on the lamp* ‖ to deliver (a blow) ‖ to hurt emotionally or financially ‖ to criticize adversely ‖ (*backgammon*) to remove (a blot) ‖ (*baseball*) to make (a hit having a particular value) ‖ *v.i.* to make a blow, strike etc. ‖ (with 'against') to come into sudden contact, *she hit against the hot stove* ‖ (of an internal combustion engine) to fire **to be hard hit** to be the victim of very adverse circumstances **to hit a man when he is down** to injure someone already suffering under misfortune **to hit at something** to try to hit something **to hit below the belt** (*boxing*) to foul by hitting low ‖ to take an unfair advantage **to hit it off** to get on well together **to hit one's fancy** to appeal to one suddenly and strongly **to hit out at** to try to combat, *to hit out at one's critics* **to hit someone off** (*Br.*) to mimic someone **to hit the mark** to hit an object aimed at ‖ to reach a standard **to hit the road** to start or resume traveling **to hit the spot** (of food or drink) to be exactly what is wanted at the moment **to hit on** (or **upon**) to discover suddenly or by chance 2. *n.* the act of hitting or an instance of this ‖ a criticism, esp. an oblique one ‖ a popular success, *to be a hit in a play* ‖ (*underworld slang*) a murder committed under a "contract" from the underworld ‖ (*slang*) a dose of a hard drug [O.E. *hyttan*]

hit-and-run (hít'nrán) *adj.* (of a motor vehicle driver) having left the scene of an accident in which he hit a victim without stopping to inquire or report ‖ (of a motor vehicle accident) involving such an offending motorist

hitch (hitʃ) 1. *v.t.* to move (something) by little jerks ‖ to fasten temporarily or loosely, *to hitch a horse to a post* ‖ to attach (something to be towed) firmly by a hook etc., *to hitch a trailer to a car* ‖ *v.i.* to move slowly and jerkily ‖ to become caught by or fastened to something, *her dress hitched on a nail* **to hitch up** to pull up with a little tug ‖ to harness (a draft animal) 2. *n.* an obstacle, impediment ‖ an accident or breakdown, *the wedding went off without a hitch* ‖ a jerky pull ‖ (*naut.*) any of various kinds of knot, *clove hitch, half hitch* [etym. doubtful]

Hitchcock (hítʃkɒk), Sir Alfred (1899–1980), British director, whose British and Hollywood films were known for their wit, suspense and terror. Among his many films are 'The Man Who Knew Too Much' (1934), 'The Thirty-Nine Steps' (1935), 'Rebecca' (1940), 'Lifeboat' (1943), 'Spellbound' (1945), 'Notorious' (1946), 'Dial M for Murder' (1954), 'Rear Window' (1954), 'To Catch a Thief' (1955), 'Vertigo' (1958), 'Psycho' (1960) and 'The Birds' (1963). He made cameo appearances in all of his films and hosted the television series 'Alfred Hitchcock Presents' (1955–65). He was knighted in 1980

hitch·hike (hítʃhaik) *pres. part.* **hitch·hik·ing** *past* and *past part.* **hitch·hiked** *v.i.* to travel by begging free rides in motor vehicles

hith·er (híðər) 1. *adv.* (*rhet.*) to, or towards, this place 2. *adj.* (*rhet.*) on this side ‖ (*rhet.*) toward this side, nearer [O.E. *hider*]

hither and thither in a variety of directions ‖ back and forth

hith·er·to (híðərtú:, híðərtu:) *adv.* up till this time

Hit·ler (hítlər) Adolf (1889–1945), German Nazi dictator. Born in Austria, he moved (1913) to Munich and, after serving in the German army in the 1st world war, joined the National Socialist German Workers' party, which he reorganized on military lines. His unsuccessful attempt to seize power in Bavaria (1923) resulted in a prison sentence. He expounded his theories of the racial superiority of the Aryans and his hatred of the Jews in 'Mein Kampf' (1923). The economic crisis of 1929–30 greatly increased the numbers of Nazis and Hitler was appointed chancellor of Germany (1933), becoming Führer of the Third Reich after the death of Hindenburg (1934). Having established a totalitarian regime in Germany, Hitler began to rearm the country in defiance of the Treaty of Versailles. He sent troops to the Rhineland (1936), allied himself with Mussolini (1936), and invaded Austria (1938) and Czechoslovakia (1938–9). He continued his aggression despite the Munich Agreement (1938), invading Poland (1939) and provoking the 2nd world war. His early military successes were offset by heavy defeats at Stalingrad and in N. Africa (1942–3). Having survived a plot to assassinate him (1944), he committed suicide when Berlin fell to the Russians

hit-or-miss (hítərmís) *adj.* careless, lacking in precision or system

Hit·tite (hítait) 1. *n.* a member of an ancient people who flourished in Asia Minor and Syria c. 2000–c. 1200 B.C. The Hittites built up an empire centered on Bogazkoy which dominated the Middle East in the 14th c. B.C., but which fell to the Assyrians in the late 12th c. B.C. ‖ the language of the Hittites, related to primitive Indo-European and preserved in cuneiform and hieroglyphic inscriptions 2. *adj.* pertaining to the Hittites or their language

hive (haiv) 1. *n.* a man-made shelter for honeybees to live in ‖ a swarm of bees in such a shelter ‖ a building etc. thronged with busy people 2. *v. pres. part.* **hiv·ing** *past* and *past part.* **hived** *v.t.* to cause (a swarm of bees) to enter an empty hive ‖ to store (e.g. honey) in a hive ‖ *v.i.* to live in or go to a hive [O.E. *hyf*]

hives (haivz) *pl. n.* (construed as *sing.* or *pl.*) a temporary skin condition of allergic origin characterized by raised itchy patches of skin and caused by reaction to various agents, e.g. certain foods, inhalants or drugs (*ALLERGY) [origin unknown]

ho (hou) *interj.* used to attract attention, *ho there! get out of the way* ‖ (*old-fash.*) used to express surprise or joy

hoa·gie or **hoa·gy** (hóugi:) *n.* a meat and/or cheese sandwich on a long roll

Hoar (hɔr, hour) Samuel (1778–1856), U.S. lawyer and statesman. A strong advocate of the abolition of slavery, he helped to found (1848) in Mass. the Free-Soil party and (1854) the new Republican party

hoar (hɔr, hour) 1. *adj.* (*rhet.*) hoary 2. *n.* hoarfrost [O.E. *hār*]

hoard (hɔrd, hourd) *v.t.* to collect, keep and store away as a hoard [O.E. *hordian*]

hoard *n.* a number of things, or quantity of material, esp. money or valuables, put together in a safe, usually secret place ‖ a body of ideas, knowledge etc. stored up for future use [O.E. *hord*]

hoard·ing (hórdiŋ, hóurdiŋ) *n.* a temporary board wall placed around construction work ‖ (*Br.*) a billboard [fr. O.F. *hourd*, scaffold]

hoar-frost (hórfrɒst, hórfrost, hóurfrɒst) *n.* ice crystals which become attached to trees and bushes etc. and are formed by the condensation of fog or mist

hoarhound *HOREHOUND

hoar·i·ness (hóri:nis, hóuri:nis) *n.* the quality of being hoary

hoarse (hɔrs, hours) *adj.* (of a voice) rough, scratchy or husky ‖ (of a person) having such a voice **hóars·en** *v.t.* to make hoarse ‖ *v.i.* to become hoarse [M.E. *hoos, hors, hoors* fr. O.E. *hās*]

hoar·y (hóri:, hóuri:) *comp.* **hoar·i·er** *superl.* **hoar·i·est** *adj.* (*rhet.*, of persons, hair etc.) gray or white from age ‖ (*rhet.*) ancient [HOAR]

hoax (houks) 1. *v.t.* to deceive (someone), esp. in fun 2. *n.* a deception, esp. one meant as a joke [etym. doubtful]

hob (hɒb) *n.* a ledge at the top of a fire grate on which things are placed to be kept warm ‖ a tool used in cutting the teeth of a chaser [origin unknown]

hob *n.* (in phrases, often with 'with') **to play hob, raise hob** to make trouble or serious mischief, cause a thorough disturbance [obs.=hobgoblin, fr. M.E. var. of *Rob.*, short for the proper name *Robin*]

Ho·bart (hóubart) the capital (pop. 168,500) of Tasmania, Australia, on the Derwent River near the sea, a trade and export center (fruit, lumber, textiles). University (1890)

Hob·be·ma (hóbəmə), Meindert (1638–1709), Dutch painter. He mainly painted pastoral and wooded landscapes, often including a water mill

Hobbes (hɒbz), Thomas (1588–1679), English philosopher. In his 'Leviathan' (1651) he developed a political philosophy based on the view that men are essentially selfish and that to escape anarchy they have entered into a social contract, by which they submit to the sovereign

hob·ble (hób'l) 1. *v. pres. part.* **hob·bling** *past* and *past part.* **hob·bled** *v.i.* (esp. of an old or lame person) to walk with short, unsteady steps, *to hobble along* ‖ *v.t.* to join the legs of (a horse, camel etc.) by a short rope so that it can take only short steps and will not stray far 2. *n.* a hobbling gait ‖ the rope used in hobbling an animal [M.E.]

hob·ble·de·hoy (hóbəldi:hɔi) *n.* (*old-fash.*) a boy in late adolescence, physically clumsy and awkward in manner [origin unknown]

hobble skirt a skirt very narrow at the hem, necessitating tiny steps

hobbles or **hopples** (*racing*) straps placed on pacer horses to synchronize steps. *also* trammels

hob·by (hóbi:) *pl.* **hob·bies** *n.* a spare time interest or occupation, esp. one taken up just for pleasure [M.E. *hoby, hobyn*, small or ambling horse]

hob·by·horse (hóbi:hɔrs) *n.* a long stick topped by a wooden horse's head. A child straddles the stick and pretends to ride it ‖ a rocking horse ‖ a wicker horse worn in a morris dance by the person portraying a horse ‖ this person **to ride one's hobbyhorse** to talk boringly and frequently about a pet idea [*hobby*, small horse+HORSE]

hob·gob·lin (hóbgɒblin) *n.* a mischievous male sprite [fr. *hob*, a name for Robin Goodfellow+GOBLIN]

hob·nail (hóbneil) *n.* a short, thick nail with a large head, groups of which are driven into the leather sole and heel of a boot to lessen wear and give a better grip [HOB, peg+NAIL]

hob·nob (hóbnɒb) *pres. part.* **hob·nob·bing** *past* and *past part.* **hob·nobbed** *v.i.* (with 'with') to be on familiar terms (esp. with those richer or socially more distinguished than oneself) [earlier *habnab* fr. M.E. *habben*, to have+*nabben*, not to have]

ho·bo (hóubou) *pl.* **ho·boes, ho·bos** *n.* a tramp ‖ a seasonal migratory worker [origin unknown]

Hob·son's choice (hóbsənz) an apparent choice when in reality there is no alternative [after Thomas *Hobson* (1544-1631), English liveryman, who insisted that each client must take the horse nearest the stable door or none]

Ho Chi Minh (hóutʃi:mín) (Nguyên Tat Thanh, 1890–1969), Communist leader and president of North Vietnam (1954–69). He formed (1941) the Vietminh (League for the Independence of Vietnam), a coalition of nationalist and Communist groups, which won the war of independence (1946–54) against the French and afterwards the dominant political party

Ho Chi Minh City (hóuʃi:mín) (formerly Saigon) a city in southern Vietnam and the former capital (pop. with its suburb of Cholon 1,825,297) of South Vietnam; a seaport (Saigon River) and major transportation, commercial and industrial center 60 miles from the sea, European in aspect. It served as U.S. military headquarters during the Vietnam War. After the North Vietnamese overran Saigon (1975), it was renamed Ho Chi Minh City. Much of its population growth resulted from migration during the war. Industries (largely concentrated in Cholon): shipbuilding, food (esp. rice, sugar) and rubber processing, textiles. University

hock (hɒk) *n.* a joint of the hind leg in some quadrupeds which bends backward. It corresponds to the human ankle [O.E. *hog, hoch*]

hock *n.* (*Br.*) a light German white wine, orig. that of Hochheim on Main, Hesse, but now any similar Rhine wine [shortened fr. *hockamore* fr. G. *Hochheimer*]

hock 1. *n.* (*pop.*) in the phrase **in hock** at the pawnshop ‖ in debt 2. *v.t.* (*pop*) to pawn [etym. doubtful]

hock·ey (hóki:) *n.* ice hockey ‖ field hockey [perh. rel. to O.F. *hoquet*, crook, bent stick]

ho·cus-po·cus (hóukəspóukes) *n.* deliberately mystifying nonsense [mock Latin expression (prob. a corruption of the 'hoc est corpus' of the Mass) used by conjurers]

hod (hɒd) *n.* a V-shaped trough mounted on a long staff, used for carrying bricks, mortar etc. up and down scaffolding ‖ a coal scuttle [prob. var. of *hot* fr. O.F. *hotte*, a basket]

ho-dad (hóudæd) *n.* (*surfing*) a surfing enthusiast, esp. a nonsurfer

Hodge (hɒdʒ), Charles (1797–1878), U.S. conservative Presbyterian theologian, an advocate of exegetical systematic theology

hodge-podge (hódʒpɒdʒ) *n.* an ill-assorted mixture, medley [M.E. corrup. of *hotchpotch*, a stew]

hod·o·graph (hódəgræf, hódəgraf) *n.* (*math.*) a curve obtained by joining the ends of straight lines which represent displacements etc. of a moving point (e.g. the wave form derived from lines representing successive transverse displacements) [fr. Gk *hodos*, way+*-graphos*, writing]

ho·do·scope (hódəskoup) *n.* (*phys.*) a battery of Geiger counters used to trace paths of ionizing particles

Hoe (hou), Richard March (1812–86), U.S. inventor of the rotary printing press (patented 1846), which revolutionized printing processes

hoe (hou) **1.** *n.* a hand tool used in cultivation, consisting of a narrow, thin, flat piece of steel with a sharp edge, fixed almost at right angles to the end of a long pole and used for breaking up clods of earth, loosening the topsoil, dragging out or cutting weeds, drawing earth into a ridge etc. **2.** *v. pres. part.* **hoe·ing** *past* and *past part.* **hoed** *v.t.* to take a hoe to (weeds, earth etc.) ‖ *v.i.* to use a hoe **to have a long row to hoe** to have a long grueling task to perform [F. *houe*]

Ho·fei (hʌféi) (formerly Luchow) a town (pop. 1,484,000) in E. central China, west of Nanking: cotton thread

Hoff·mann (hófmən, hofmən), Ernst Theodor Wilhelm (1776–1822), German novelist. His tales of horror and the supernatural include 'The Devil's Elixir' (1815). Three of his stories were used by Offenbach for 'Tales of Hoffmann' (1881)

Hof·mann (hʌfmən, hófmən), Hans (1880–1966), U.S. painter and leader in the development of abstract expressionism. His works, notably 'Germania' and 'Elegy', make use of violent, clashing colors

Hof·manns·thal (hófmənstal), Hugo (1874–1929), Austrian dramatist and poet. He wrote the librettos for 'Der Rosenkavalier' (1911), 'Ariadne auf Naxos' (1912), 'Elektra' (1909) and other Strauss operas. He is also known for his version of the English morality play 'Everyman' (1911), performed annually in Salzburg, Austria

Hof·stadt·er (hófstætər), Richard (1916–70), U.S. political and Social historian who interpreted U.S. politics in cultural and non-economic terms in 'The Age of Reform' (1955) and 'Anti-Intellectualism in American Life' (1964)

hog (həg, hog) **1.** *pl.* **hogs, hog** *n.* a member of *Suidae*, esp. of genus *Sus*, omnivorous mammals having stout bodies with thick, usually bristled skin, long broad snouts and cleft hoofs. All breeds are descended from the European wild boar *S. scrofa* or a crossbreed of this and the Asiatic *S. indicus*. In Europe and North America hogs are raised mainly for meat (pork, bacon) and lard. In Africa and Asia they are primarily scavengers ‖ (*Br.*) a castrated male pig raised for slaughter ‖ (*pop.*) a greedy or filthy person **to go the whole hog** to carry an action to its absolute limit **2.** *v.t. pres. part.* **hog·ging** *past* and *past part.* **hogged** to take more than one's share of [O.E. *hogg*]

ho·gan (hóugən, hóugən) *n.* a Navaho Indian dwelling of logs and branches covered with earth [Navaho]

Ho·garth (hóugarθ), William (1697–1764), English artist. The series of satirical engravings, made after his paintings, include 'The Harlot's Progress' (1732), and 'The Rake's Progress' (1735), portraying the seamier side of London with stark realism. In 'Marriage à la Mode' (1745) he makes savage sport of London high society. He also painted many portraits

hog·back (hógbæk, hógbæk) *n.* a ridge of land having steep slopes at the sides and a sharp crest

hog cholera (*Am.*=*Br.* swine fever) an infectious lung disease of swine, caused by a virus

hog·gish (hógiʃ, hógiʃ) *adj.* (*pop.*, of a person) greedy, gluttonous

hog·ma·nay (hogmənéi) *n.* (*Scot.*) New Year's Eve ‖ (*Scot.*) a gift, usually a cake, which a child collects on that day [perh. of F. origin]

hog's-back (hógzbæk, hógzbæk) *n.* (*Br.*) a hogback

hogs·head (hógzhed, hógzhed) *n.* a large cask holding 63–140 gallons ‖ a liquid measure of capacity, equal to (*Am.*) 63 wine gallons or (*Br.*) 52 ½ imperial gallons (*GALLON)

hog·tie (hógtai, hógtai) *pres. part.* **hog·ty·ing** *past* and *past part.* **hog·tied** *v.t.* to tie all four feet of (an animal) together ‖ to hamper, *production delays hogtied the signing of the contract*

hog·wash (hógwəʃ, hógwoʃ, hógwəʃ, hógwoʃ) *n.* insincere or worthless talk or writing [from older meaning of 'slops fed to pigs']

Ho·hen·lin·den, Battle of (houənlíndən) a French victory (Dec. 3, 1800) over the Austrians during the French Revolutionary Wars. The battle, a complement to Marengo, drove Austria to make peace with France

Ho·hen·lo·he-Schil·lings·fürst (houənlóuəʃílingzfyrst), Chlodwig, prince von (1819–1901), German statesman. After being head of the Bavarian government (1866–70), German ambassador in Paris (1874–85), and governor of Alsace-Lorraine (1885–94), he became chancellor of the German Empire (1894–1900)

Ho·hen·stau·fen (houənʃtáufən) a German royal dynasty which ruled Germany and the Holy Roman Empire (1138–1254) and Sicily (1194–1268). Its reigning members were Conrad III, Frederick I, Henry VI, Otto IV, Frederick II and Conrad IV

Ho·hen·zol·lern (houənzólərn) a royal German dynasty which provided the electors of Brandenburg (1415–1701), kings of Prussia (1701–1918) and emperors of Germany (1871–1918). Frederick William 'The Great Elector' (1640–88) enlarged Brandenburg lands. Frederick William I (1713–40) and Frederick II 'The Great' (1740–86) made Prussia a major European power. Wilhelm I (1861–88) finally defeated the Hapsburgs for control of Germany (*SEVEN WEEKS' WAR, 1866) and was crowned emperor of Germany (1871). Wilhelm II (1888–1918) led Germany into the 1st world war. His flight from Germany (1918) marked the end of the dynasty's power

hoi pol·loi (hóipəloi) *n.* the common people, the masses viewed with condescension [Gk=the many]

hoist (hoist) **1.** *v.t.* to raise esp. by means of ropes, cranes etc., *to hoist a flag* ‖ to lift up, *he hoisted the child on to his shoulders* **2.** *n.* a push up ‖ a mechanical truck, crane etc. for lifting and moving heavy loads [corrup. of obs. *hoise*, origin unknown]

hoist *adj.* carried off (only in) **hoist with one's own petard** made the victim of one's own scheming [past part. of obs. *hoise*, to hoist]

hoisting drum *DRUM STORE

hoi·ty-toi·ty (hóiti:tóiti:) *adj.* petulantly haughty [perh. fr. *hoit*, to frolic noisily]

Hok·kai·do (hókkaidou) the northernmost island (area 30,307 sq. miles, pop. 5,442,000) of the four main islands of Japan. Chief town: Sapporo. The climate is extreme with long, cold winters. Main industry: fishing (*JAPAN)

ho·kum (hóukəm) *n.* (*pop.*) nonsense, bunk ‖ (*pop.*) hollow or false show [perh. fr. HOCUS-POCUS+BUNKUM]

Ho·ku·sai (hókusai), Katsushika (1760–1849), Japanese painter and engraver. He is best known for his colored woodcuts: tender, often humorous glimpses of Japanese landscape and life. He influenced Degas, Toulouse-Lautrec and van Gogh

Hol·bach (dólbæk), Paul Henri, Baron d' (1723–89), French philosopher and Encyclopedist, atheist and materialist, author of 'le Système de la nature'

Hol·bein (hólbain), Hans, the Younger (1497–1543), German painter and engraver. His early works, done mostly in Basel, include religious subjects and occasional portraits. After 1532 he lived in England. He is esp. famous for his portraits, e.g. Erasmus (1530), Anne of Cleves (1539), in 1536, he became court painter to Henry VIII: his court paintings are not idealized and the collective effect of this gallery of calm, watchful portraits of calm, watchful sitters is extremely powerful. Holbein also made many woodcuts

hold (hould) **1.** *v. pres. part.* **hold·ing** *past* and *past part.* **held** (held) *v.t.* to have and continue to have in one's hand or hands ‖ to support or keep in place with some part of one's body, *he held the dog between his knees* ‖ to detain, *to hold a prisoner* ‖ to contain, *this box holds all my clothes* ‖ to retain, *does this pan hold water?* ‖ to consider, regard as having a specified value, quality or nature, *they hold life cheap, he holds gambling to be immoral* ‖ to keep in a certain position or condition, *hold your head up* ‖ to support, keep in position, *this column holds the weight of the roof* ‖ to keep, *to hold someone's attention* ‖ to force (someone) to abide by a promise etc. ‖ (*mil.*) to keep control of, *to hold a fort* ‖ to be in possession of, *to hold an office* ‖ to preside over, *to hold court* ‖ to conduct, carry on, *to hold a meeting* ‖ (*mus.*) to sustain (a note) ‖ *v.i.* to continue, *my offer still holds* ‖ to remain whole under pressure ‖ to remain valid, *the law*

still holds **hold on!** wait! ‖ keep firm hold! **to hold aloof** to keep oneself aloof **to hold back** to suppress (truth) ‖ to keep in reserve ‖ to be reticent ‖ to be slow to attack **to hold by** (or **onto, to**) to continue to have the same feelings for, or ideas about (something), *to hold by one's beliefs, to hold onto one's hopes, to hold to an opinion* **to hold down** to keep under restraint ‖ to keep (a job) **to hold forth** to speak at length to an audience or as if to an audience **to hold good** to remain valid **to hold in one's hands** to have power over **to hold off** to keep at a distance ‖ to keep (someone) from advancing or attacking **to hold one's breath** to keep the breath in one's lungs ‖ to be in a state of sympathetic anxiety, *hold your breath until I get back* **to hold oneself in** to curb the expression of one's feelings **to hold one's ground** (or **one's own**) to keep one's position in fighting or argument **to hold one's hand** to postpone taking action **to hold one's head high** to face the world confidently with one's honor unquestioned **to hold one's tongue** to stop talking ‖ to refrain from speaking out when one should or when one longs to do so **to hold out** to continue to be sufficient to the end or for a specified time ‖ to continue to resist **to hold out on someone** to keep back something (money, information etc.) from someone **to hold over** to postpone **to hold someone's hand** to give moral support to someone **to put on hold** to ask a telephone caller to wait **to hold something against someone** to set something against someone in one's estimate of him **to hold something over someone** to keep something as a constant threat over someone **to hold up** to support ‖ to delay, *the heavy traffic held me up* ‖ to point a gun at and rob ‖ to raise aloft **to hold water** to be valid **to hold with** to agree with, approve of **2.** *n.* the act of holding, *catch hold of the handle* ‖ something providing a grip for the fingers, *that rock is a safe hold* ‖ a controlling influence, *that habit is getting a hold on you* ‖ in a missile-launching countdown, an order to stop; by extension, any order to delay ‖ (*wrestling*) a seizing or holding of an opponent in a particular manner **to take hold** (of ideas etc.) to begin to become established [O.E. *halden, healdan*]

hold *n.* (*naut.*) the space belowdecks in a ship, where the cargo is stored ‖ a compartment in this [corrup. of HOLE and *holl*, a hole]

hold·all (hóuldɔl) *n.* a light traveling bag of canvas or other flexible material

hold·back (hóuldbæk) *n.* a student held back in a school grade on his or her request so as to remain eligible for athletic competition, esp. in a junior high school

hold·er (hóuldər) *n.* someone who holds, *the holder of the winning ticket* ‖ something which holds, *a cigarette holder*

Höl·der·lin (hé:ldərli:n), Johann Christian Friedrich (1770–1843), German poet. A profound Hellenist, he based his works on classical models and themes. In addition to his lyric poems, these include the novel 'Hyperion' (1794–9), and the unfinished tragedy 'The Death of Empedocles' (1798–9)

hold harmless provision (*insurance*) a provision that prevents the insured party from suffering additional covered expenses or loss

hold·ing (hóuldin) *n.* a having or keeping hold ‖ land, shares etc. owned

holding company a company formed to acquire and own a part or a majority of the shares in one or more other companies

holding pattern (*air traffic control*) route undertaken by aircraft waiting to land

holding pattern mode (*air traffic control*) automatic control of an aircraft to fly a programmed holding pattern

holding point (*air traffic control*) a specified location, identified by visual or other means, in the vicinity of which a flying aircraft's position is maintained

holding tank container usu. a boat or tank, for sewage awaiting disposal

hold·o·ver (hóuldouvər) *n.* someone or something left over from earlier times or circumstances

hold time hiatus in a countdown, e.g., in launching of a missile

hold·up (hóuldʌp) *n.* an armed robbery ‖ a delay or stoppage

hole (houl) *pres. part.* **hol·ing** *past* and *past part.* **holed** *v.t.* to make a hole in ‖ (*golf*) to hit (the ball) into its hole ‖ to force (an animal) into its hole **to hole up** to retire, esp. by oneself, from all social contact

---

hole *n.* a small space or cavity partly or wholly surrounded by matter ‖ an empty space made in the earth or other material by an animal, to serve as a home or hiding place ‖ a small, dark, often dirty place ‖ a situation that is embarrassing or from which there is apparently no escape ‖ (*golf*) a small cuplike pit into which the ball must be played ‖ (*golf*) the distance between two such successive pits ‖ (*golf*) the contest between players to play a ball over such a distance in the fewest strokes ‖ (*golf*) a win in such a contest, *two holes up* **to make a hole in** to use up a considerable amount of a large supply of **to pick holes in** to find or draw attention to defects in (an argument etc.) [O.E. *hol*, a hollow place]

hole-and-cor·ner (hóulənkórnər) *adj.* secret, furtive, *hole-and-corner methods*

Hol·guín (ɔlgíːn) a town (pop. 151,938) in N.E. Cuba, in Oriente province, a commercial center for a region producing sugar, coffee, tobacco and cattle

hol·i·day (hólidei) *n.* a day on which one does not go to work, school etc. Such days are religious festivals, or days set apart for commemorating some past event, famous person's birthday etc. ‖ (*Br.*) a vacation **on holiday** (*Br.*) on vacation [O.E. *hǽlingdæg*, holy day]

hol·i·day·ma·ker (hólideimeikər) *n.* (*Br.*) someone on vacation

ho·lid·ic (houlídik) *adj.* composed of defined constituents. *Cf* HOLISM, MERIDIC, OLIGIDIC

ho·li·ly (hóulili) *adv.* in a holy manner

ho·li·ness (hóuliːnis) *n.* the quality of being holy **Holiness** (*Roman Catholicism*, with possessive) a title for the pope [O.E. *hǽlignes, hǽlignys*]

Hol·in·shed (hólinʃed), Raphael (*d. c.* 1580), English historian. His 'Chronicles of England, Scotland and Ireland' (1578) were used by Shakespeare as a source for his historical plays and for 'Macbeth', 'King Lear' and 'Cymbeline'

ho·lism (hóulizəm) *n.* a philosophy so named by Smuts. It belongs to the system of biological thought formulated esp. by Bergson. In dissatisfaction with 19th-c. mechanistic evolutionary theory, it affirms the principle of emergence: life as concerned with the making of larger and larger organic wholes, greater than the sum of their parts ‖ (*med.*) treatment of human ailments by treating the whole person **hó·list** *n.* **ho·lís·tic** *adj.* **ho·lís·ti·cal·ly** *adv.* [fr. Gk *holos*, whole]

holistic *adj.* of a planning approach viewing the situation as a whole. **—holist** *n.* **—holistically** *adv.* **—holistic medicine** *n.* treatment of the whole organism, not just the symptoms of a disease

Hol·land (hólənd), Clifford Milburn (1883–1924), U.S. engineer who constructed the Holland tunnel, connecting New York and Jersey City, N.J., under the Hudson River

Holland, Henry Richard Vassall Fox, 3rd Baron (1773–1840), British Whig statesman, nephew of Charles James Fox. His London residence, Holland House, became a salon for Whig statesmen, and for writers and scientists, in the early 19th c.

Holland, John Philip (1841–1914), U.S. inventor of the modern submarine. His 'Holland' was the first submarine to be purchased (1900) by the U.S. navy

Holland a name often used for the Netherlands, but correctly applied only to a former province (1579–1795) on the W. central coast, divided since 1840 into two: North Holland (area 1,163 sq. miles, pop. 2,201,000, capital Harlem) and South Holland (area 1,212 sq. miles, pop. 2,903,000, capital The Hague). Main industry: dairy farming

hol·land (hólənd) *n.* a coarse, unbleached linen with a glazed surface, used for upholstery etc. [fr. *Holland* (province of the Netherlands) where it was first made]

Hol·lan·di·a (hólændiə) *SUKARNAPURA

hol·lands (hóləndz) *n.* a gin made in the Netherlands [fr. Du. *hollandsch* (*genever*), hollands gin]

hol·ler (hólər) **1.** *v.i.* and *t.* to shout or cry out **2.** *n.* a yell, shout [var. of older *hollo*, to shout]

Hol·ler·ith code or **Hol·ler·ith** (háləriθ) (*computer*) an alphanumeric code used on punched cards, with zone punches in the first three columns, etc., for Herman Hollerith. **—Hollerith card** *n. also* punch card, punched card

hol·low (hólou) **1.** *adj.* having an empty space within (opp. SOLID), *a hollow vessel* ‖ curving inwards, *hollow cheeks* ‖ (of sounds) like sounds made by, or in, empty vessels or rooms, *a hollow ring, a hollow roar* ‖ meaningless or insincere, *hollow promises* **to beat (someone) hollow** to win a victory over (someone) by a very big margin **2.** *v.t.* (with 'out') to make hollow ‖ (with 'out') to make by hollowing [M.E. *holg, holeh*]

hollow *n.* a little hole ‖ a saucer-shaped piece of ground [O.E. *holh*]

hollow ware utensils (e.g. kettles, saucepans, cups, tumblers) which are relatively hollow (cf. FLATWARE)

hol·ly (hóli:) *pl.* **hol·lies** *n.* a member of *Ilex*, fam. *Aquifoliaceae*, a genus of evergreen shrubs and trees usually having prickly leaves with a shiny surface. They bear dioecious flowers and bright red berries. Holly is traditionally associated with Christmas [shortened fr. O.E. *holegn, holen*]

hol·ly·hock (hóli:hɔk, hóli:hɒk) *n.* *Althaea rosea*, fam. *Malvaceae*, a tall, herbaceous plant, cultivated for its variously colored, ornamental flowers, borne on long spikes [HOLY+older *hock*, mallow]

Hol·ly·wood (hóli:wud) a section (pop. 185,000) of Los Angeles, California, and center of the U.S. film industry

holm (houm) *n.* the holm oak [corrup. of *holn* fr. O.E. *holen*, holly]

Holmes (houmz), Oliver Wendell (1809–94). American poet, essayist and physician. His witty, polished essays and many of his poems are contained in 'The Autocrat of the Breakfast Table' (1858), 'The Professor at the Breakfast Table' (1860) and 'The Poet at the Breakfast Table' (1872)

Holmes, Oliver Wendell (1841–1935), American jurist, associate justice of the U.S. Supreme Court (1902–32). A liberal, he interpreted the constitution in such a way as to defend the rights of individuals. Son of the preceding

Holmes, William Henry (1846–1933), U.S. anthropologist. As curator of the Chicago Natural History museum (1894–7) and of the U.S. National museum (1897–1902, 1910–20), he surveyed the ancient cities of southern Mexico and denied the theory of an autochthonous American man

hol·mi·um (hóulmi:əm) *n.* a metallic trivalent rare earth (symbol Ho, at. no. 67, at. mass 164.30) [Mod. L. fr. *Holmia*, Latinized name for Stockholm]

holm oak *Quercus ilex*, fam. *Fagaceae*, an evergreen oak native to Mediterranean regions, with dark green leaves resembling holly

hol·o·blas·tic (hɒləblǽstik, houləblǽstik) *adj.* relating to ova that undergo cleavage throughout the cell (cf. MEROBLASTIC)

hol·o·caust (hóləkɔst, hóuləkɔst) *n.* a large-scale sacrifice or destruction esp. of life, esp. by fire [F. *holocauste* fr. L.L. fr. Gk *holos*, whole+*kaustos*, burned]

Holocaust destruction of European Jewry by the Nazis. (usu. preceded by *The*.)

Hol·o·cene (hóləsiːn, hóuləsiːn) *adj.* of the present geological epoch (*GEOLOGICAL TIME) **the Holocene** the Holocene epoch or series of rocks [fr. Gk *holos*, whole+*kainos*, recent]

ho·lo·cline (hóuloukliːn) *n.* discontinuation of salinity in seawater at about 180 ft

Hol·o·fer·nes (hɒləfɔ́ːrniːz, houləfɔ́ːrniːz) *JUDITH

ho·lo·gram (hóləgræm, hóuləgræm) *n.* an interference pattern (normally on a photographic plate) resolvable into a completely three-dimensional image when illuminated by a laser beam [fr. Gk *holos*, whole+*gramma*, something written]

hol·o·graph (hóləgræf, hóləgraf, hóuləgræf, hóuləgraf) **1.** *n.* a document all of which was written by hand by its author or signatory **2.** *adj.* of such a document [F. *holographe* fr. L. fr. Gk *holos*, whole+*-graphos*, writing]

ho·lo·graph·ic memory (hɒləgrǽfik) three-dimensional thermoplastic photographic film used to store memory in optical computers

holographic one-tube goggle an eye-piece that permits night vision utilizing thin-film diffraction optics and electronics to amplify light and near-infrared radiation

ho·log·ra·phy scanner (houlógrəfi:) a device that utilizes a wraparound field of light to reach out and scan a group of packages by holography, reading imprinted codes, used at supermarket checkout counters; developed by IBM

hol·o·he·dral (hɒləhíːdrəl, houləhíːdrəl) *adj.* (of a crystal) having the complete number of facets required for perfect symmetry [fr. Gk *holos*, whole+*hedra*, base]

ho·lo·phone (hóuləfoun) *n.* a device for recording patterns in time to create an acoustical hologram

hol·o·pho·tal (hɒləfóut'l, houləfóut'l) *adj.* of or having the properties of a holophote

hol·o·phote (hóləfout, hóuləfout) *n.* a device for concentrating all the light from a source into a beam, as in a lighthouse [fr. Gk *holos*, whole+*phōs* (*phōtos*), light]

hol·o·phras·tic (hɒləfrǽstik, houləfrǽstik) *adj.* expressing a complex of ideas by a single word [fr. Gk *holos*, whole+*phrazein*, to tell]

hol·o·thu·ri·an (hɒləθúəriːən, houləθúəriːən) *n.* a member of *Holothurioidea*, a class of echinoderms, comprising the sea cucumbers, with generally elongated forms, bilateral symmetry, a reduced exoskeleton consisting of scattered spicules, and tube feet for creeping [fr. Mod. L. *Holothuria*, the type genus of *Holothurioidea*]

hol·o·type (hólətaip, hóulətaip) *n.* (*biol.*) a single specimen chosen for designation of a new species [fr. Gk *holos*, whole+*tupos*, character]

Holst (houlst), Gustav (1874–1934), English composer. His work includes the orchestral suite 'The Planets' (1915) and choral and ballet music

Hol·stein (hóulʃtain); Friedrich von (1837–1909), German diplomat, who effectively dominated German foreign policy (1890–1906), although only holding the post of counselor. His policies played an important part in isolating Germany before the 1st world war

Holstein *SCHLESWIG-HOLSTEIN

Hol·stein (hóulstain, hóulsti:n) *n.* a dairy cow of a breed originally raised in Friesland. They are black and white, and yield large quantities of milk of low butter fat content

hol·ster (hóulstər) *n.* a pistol case attached to the belt or the saddle or slung from the shoulder and carried under the arm [Du. or fr. O.E. *heolster*, hiding place]

Holt (hoult), Harold Edward (1908–67), Australian Liberal statesman, prime minister of Australia (1966–7)

holt (hoult) *n.* (*Br.*) a burrow or den of an animal, esp. the otter [var. of HOLD *n.*]

ho·ly (hóuli:) *comp.* **ho·li·er** *superl.* **ho·li·est** *adj.* of God or a god, his works, dwelling place, attributes etc. ‖ (of a person) living a life of spiritual purity ‖ (of things) dedicated, set apart, for sacred usage [O.E. *hälig*]

Holy Alliance an agreement concluded Sept. 26, 1815, by which Russia, Prussia and Austria agreed to govern by Christian principles. It was used by Metternich to further his policy of reaction

Holy Communion the Eucharist

holy day a religious feast

Holy Father (*Roman Catholicism*) the pope

Holy Ghost the third person of the Trinity

Holy Grail *GRAIL

Ho·ly·head (hóli:hed) a town (pop. 10,000) on Holyhead I. off the west coast of Anglesey, N. Wales, 260 miles northwest of London, the chief port for mail and passengers between London and Dublin since the early 19th c.

Holy Innocents Day *INNOCENTS, MASSACRE OF THE

Holy Island (Lindisfarne) a small island off the coast of Northumberland, England. After the foundation of a church (635) by St Aidan, it was the center of Celtic missionary work in N. England

Holy Land Palestine

Holy League (*F. hist.*) a coalition of Catholic nobles formed (1576) by Henri, duc de Guise during the Wars of Religion. Its aims were to suppress Huguenot influence and to exclude Henri de Navarre from the throne. When the latter succeeded (1589) as Henri IV, the Holy League continued its resistance until the king abandoned Protestantism (1593)

Holy League (*Ital. hist.*) an alliance formed (1510) by Pope Julius II, comprising Ferdinand V of Spain, Henry VIII of England and Emperor Maximilian I, with the aim of driving Louis XII of France from Italy

Holy Office, Congregation of the *INQUISITION

holy of holies (*Jewish hist.*) the innermost and most sacred room of the Jewish Tabernacle and later of the Temple in Jerusalem. It contained the Ark of the Covenant

holy orders the three major orders in the Roman Catholic Church or Anglican Church ‖

ordination **to take** (or **enter**) **holy orders** to receive ordination

Holy Places various sites in Palestine associated with the life and ministry of Christ

Holy Roman Emperor (*hist.*) the head of the Holy Roman Empire

Holy Roman Empire a loose confederation of central European states formed in 962, when Otto I was crowned Holy Roman Emperor. Ostensibly to protect the papacy, it was designed to revive the imperial power of Charlemagne (crowned 800), which had disintegrated. The empire reached the height of its power under Henry III (1046–56), and became centered on Germany. It was weakened by the Investiture Controversy (1075–1122), and by the death (1125) of Henry V, the last direct descendant of Otto I. For the next two centuries the German princes claimed the right to elect the Emperor. Hohenstaufens were elected from 1138 to the Great Interregnum (1254–73). After this, Emperors ceased to intervene in Italy, and the imperial borders drew back to Germany. The Hapsburg dynasty supplied nearly all the Emperors from Albert II (1438–9) up to 1806, but in 1648 the Treaties of Westphalia robbed the empire of much of its power by recognizing the independence of the German princes. By the time Prussia emerged under Frederick II (1740–86) as the leading German state, the empire was no more than a name. It was finally ended (1806) by Napoleon

Holy Saturday the Saturday of Holy Week, between Good Friday and Easter Day

Holy See the office or authority of the pope ‖ the papacy

Holy Spirit the Holy Ghost

ho·ly·stone (hóuli:stoun) **1.** *n.* (*naut.*) a piece of soft sandstone used to scour the wooden planks of a ship's deck **2.** *v.t. pres. part.* **ho·ly·ston·ing** *past* and *past part.* **ho·ly·stoned** (*naut.*) to scour (the deck) in this way [origin unknown]

holy water water blessed by a priest, used symbolically as a cleanser from sin and for conveying blessing or exorcising evil

Holy Week the week preceding Easter Sunday, during which the last events in the life of Christ, from his triumphal entry into Jerusalem until the eve of his resurrection, are commemorated

Holy Writ the Bible

hom·age (hómidȝ,ómidȝ) *n.* a mark or testimony of esteem, respect or veneration ‖ (*hist.*) the public ceremony by which a vassal acknowledged his relationship to his lord **to do** (or **pay**) **homage** to express homage by word or gesture [O.F. *ommage, homage, humage*]

hom·a·lo·graph·ic (hɒmǝlougrǽfik) *adj.* (of a map or diagram) maintaining correct proportions and relationships between parts of the whole [fr. Gk *homalos*, even + GRAPHIC]

hom·bre (ómbrei, ómbri:) *n.* (*pop.*) a man, fellow [Span.]

hom·bre (hómbər) *n.* (*cards*) ombre

hom·burg (hómbə:rg) *n.* a man's hat made of soft felt, having a stiff, narrow brim and dented crown [fr. *Homburg*, a city in Hesse, W. Germany]

Home (hju:m), 14th earl of *DOUGLAS-HOME

home (houm) **1.** *n.* the private living quarters of a person or family ‖ the place, city etc. where a person lives ‖ the place, city etc. where one was born or reared ‖ a building where orphans, old people etc. are housed and cared for ‖ the native environment of an animal or plant ‖ the place where something originated, developed etc. ‖ (*baseball* etc.) the point to which a player seeks to move or return **at home** in one's own home ‖ willing to receive visitors, *at home on Tuesday and Thursday afternoons* ‖ at ease, as if one were in one's own home, *make yourself at home* **to be at home with** to be familiar with, or used to, *he's quite at home with decimals* **2.** *adj.* of or associated with a home, one's home or native country ‖ (*sports*) played on one's usual field, court etc., not on one's opponent's, *a home game* **3.** *adv.* to or into one's home ‖ all the way, *to drive the nail home* ‖ exactly where intended, *the remark hit home* **to bring** (*something*) **home to** (*someone*) to make (something) fully understood by (someone) **nothing to write home about** (*pop.*) not very good, *her cooking is nothing to write home about* **4.** *v. pres. part.* **hom·ing** *past* and *past part.* **homed** *v.i.* (esp. of some pigeons) to locate and make for home ‖ (of aircraft, guided missiles etc., with 'in') to move directly to a specified target, place etc. ‖ *v.t.* to

guide (an aircraft, missile etc.) to a specific place by radio etc. [O.E. *hām*]

home base (*baseball*) the plate ‖ a place that serves as a working headquarters

Home Box Office a form of cable television for a fee. *abbr.* **HBO**

home·com·ing (hóumkʌmiŋ) *n.* a return home after a considerable absence ‖ an annual celebration for alumni in some colleges and universities or high schools

home computer (*computer*) minicomputer processor programmed for personal problems, home management, and games

home economics the branch of study concerned with household management

home farm (*Br.*) a farm reserved and worked for his own household by the owner of an estate containing other farms

home free *adj.* having achieved comfortable position toward one's goal, from baseball

home-grown (hóumgróun) *adj.* (of animal or vegetable produce) grown by the seller or consumer

home help (*Br.*) a woman registered with local authorities to give temporary domestic help when called upon

home industry piecework done at home for a central selling organization

home·land (hóumlænd) *n.* one's native country

homelands in South Africa, areas of concentrated black settlement in which black people were urged or forced to resettle

home·li·ness (hóumli:nis) *n.* the quality of being homely

home·ly (hóumli:) *comp.* **home·li·er** *superl.* **home·li·est** *adj.* simple, plain, *homely language* ‖ plain-featured, not attractive, *a homely face*

home-made (hóumméid) *adj.* made at home, not in a factory ‖ crudely made by an amateur, not professional

home·mak·er (hóummeikər) *n.* someone responsible for the running of a household

Home Office the British government department responsible for law and order within England and Wales

ho·me·o·mor·phism, *Br.* also **homoe·o·mor·phism** (houmi:ɔ́mrfizəm) *n.* close similarity in crystalline form of substances of unlike chemical composition [fr. Gk *homoios*, of the same kind + *morphē*, shape]

ho·me·o·path, *Br.* also **ho·moe·o·path** (hóumi:-əpæθ) *n.* a practitioner of homeopathy

ho·me·o·path·ic, *Br.* also **ho·moe·o·path·ic** (houmi:əpǽθik) *adj.* pertaining to or practicing homeopathy **ho·me·o·páth·i·cal·ly**, *Br.* also **ho·moe·o·páth·i·cal·ly** *adv.*

ho·me·op·a·thy, *Br.* also **ho·moe·op·a·thy** (houmi:ɔ́pəθi:) *n.* a system of treating disease by administering small doses of a drug which would cause a healthy person to have the symptoms of the disease under treatment [fr. Gk *homoios*, of the same kind + *pathos*, suffering]

ho·me·o·sta·sis (houmi:əstéisis) *n.* a movement within a system, person or group towards equilibrium ‖ the capacity of a government to remain stable in the face of major internal adjustments [fr. Gk *homoios*, of the same kind + *stasis*, condition]

ho·me·o·typ·ic (houmi:ətípik) *adj.* (*biol.*) of the equal or second division in meiosis (cf. HETEROTYPIC) **ho·me·o·týp·ical** *adj.* [fr. Gk *homoios*, of the same kind + TYPIC]

home plate (*baseball*) a piece of rubber set into the ground beside which the batter stands and which a player must touch after completing the round of bases in order to score a run

Ho·mer (hóumər) the poet, supposedly blind, regarded by the Greeks as the author of the 'Iliad' and 'Odyssey'. Modern scholars recognize a fundamental unity of the epics and date them sometime before 700 B.C.

Homer, Winslow (1836–1910), U.S. painter, known especially for his depiction of New England fishermen (e.g. 'The Herring Net', 1885) and of Adirondack hunters (e.g. 'Huntsman and Dogs', 1891)

homer *n.* a homing pigeon ‖ (*baseball*) a home run ‖ (*air traffic control, mil.*) base that locates aircraft and guides them using radio transmissions to provide bearings

Ho·mer·ic (houmérik) *adj.* pertaining to Homer, his poetry or the age of which he wrote ‖ epic, heroic

home·room (hóumru:m, hóumrum) *n.* a school classroom where students of the same grade meet informally for class activities under a teacher's guidance

home rule self-government, esp. in internal matters, by a colony or dependent territory

Home Rule the movement, founded (1870), to obtain self-government for Ireland. It was led in the 1880's by Parnell, who drew attention to the Irish problem by parliamentary obstruction. Gladstone was won over to the cause, and made two unsuccessful attempts (1886 and 1893) to carry a Home Rule Bill in parliament. The Liberals carried a third Home Rule Bill (1912–14) but it roused protests in Ulster, and was delayed by the 1st world war. S. Ireland was given dominion status as the Irish Free State (1921)

home run (*baseball*) a hit which enables the hitter to run all the bases and score a run

home·sick (hóumsik) *adj.* longing for home

home·spun (hóumspʌn) **1.** *n.* cloth woven from yarn spun at home or cloth imitating this **2.** *adj.* of such cloth ‖ plain, unsophisticated, *homespun philosophy*

home stand (*baseball*) games played at a team's own field

Home·stead (hóumsted), a steel-producing borough of Pittsburgh on the Monongahela River in southwest Pa., and in the 1890s the world's most advanced steel production center. It was the site of the unsuccessful strike of 1892, a pitched battle between steelworkers and company guards, which delayed the unionization of U.S. steelworkers for 40 years

home·stead (hóumsted) *n.* a house, esp. a farm, together with the outbuildings ‖ a tract of land granted under the Homestead Act **2.** *v.i.* to settle land and farm it, esp. under the Homestead Act ‖ *v.t.* to settle (land) and claim it, esp. under the Homestead Act **hóme·stead·er** *n.* the owner of a homestead ‖ a settler under the Homestead Act [O.E. *hāmstede*]

Homestead Act a law passed (1862) by the U.S. Congress, under which settlers might each acquire up to 160 acres of public land for a nominal fee, on condition of five years' residence on, and cultivation of, the plot of land. This law was followed by similar legislation in the early 20th c., and was a major factor in bringing settlers to the western U.S.A.

home·stretch (hóumstrétʃ) *n.* the straight of a racecourse

home team (*sports*) the team on whose field, court etc. a match or game is being played

home·ward (hóumwərd) **1.** *adv.* towards home **2.** *adj.* going in the direction of home [O.E. *hāmweard*]

home·wards (hóumwərdz) *adv.* homeward [O.E. *hāmweardes*]

home·work (hóumwə:rk) *n.* work done at home ‖ work required to be done after school hours by a schoolboy or schoolgirl

home·y, hom·y (hóumi:) *comp.* **hom·i·er** *superl.* **hom·i·est** *adj.* appropriately cozy and unpretentious ‖ (*pejorative*) inappropriately lacking a sense of style

hom·i·ci·dal (hɒmisáid'l) *adj.* pertaining to homicide ‖ tending towards homicide

hom·i·cide (hómisáid) *n.* the killing of a human being by another, whether murder or manslaughter ‖ someone who kills another [F.]

hom·i·let·ic (hɒmɪlétik) *adj.* pertaining to a homily **hom·i·lét·ics** *n.* the art of preaching [fr. Gk *homilētikos*, conversable]

hom·i·ly (hómili:) *pl.* **hom·i·lies** *n.* a sermon in which spiritual values are discussed in relation to some practical subject ‖ a wearisome moralizing lecture [O.F. *omelie* fr. L. fr. Gk *homilia*, discourse]

homing adaptor device that, when used with an aircraft radio receiver, produces aural and/or visual signals indicating the direction of a transmitting radio station with respect to the heading of the aircraft

homing mine (*mil.*) in naval mine warfare, a mine fitted with propulsion equipment that homes on to a target

homing pigeon a carrier pigeon

hom·i·ni·za·tion (hóminizéiʃn) *n.* **1.** evolutionary development of human characteristics **2.** causing to act in a humanlike way, e.g., *hominization of machines*. **—hominized** *adj.*

hom·i·ny (hómini:) *n.* hulled corn kernels with the germ removed, often ground, and eaten boiled or fried [fr. N. Am. Ind.]

Ho·mo (hóumou) *n.* the genus of the fam. *Hominidae* whose only species is *Homo sapiens*, including all existing and some extinct humans [L.=man]

homo- (hóumou) *prefix* same [fr. Gk *homos*]

---

ho·mo·cen·tric (houmouséntrik, homouséntrik) *adj.* having a common center (cf. CONCENTRIC) [fr. Mod. L. *homocentricus* fr. Gk *homos*, same+*kentrikos*, centric]

ho·mo·chro·mat·ic (houmoukrəmǽtik, homoukrəmǽtik) *adj.* having one color ‖ having the same color (opp. HETEROCHROMATIC)

ho·mo·cy·clic (houmousáiklik, homousíklik, homousáiklik, homousíklik) *adj.* isocyclic

ho·moe·cious (houmíːʃəs, homíʃəs) *adj.* (*biol.*) of a parasite) dependent on one host throughout its life cycle [fr. HOMO-+Gk *oikia*, house]

homoeomorphism *HOMEOMORPHISM

homoeopath *HOMEOPATH

homoeopathic *HOMEOPATHIC

homoeopathy *HOMEOPATHY

ho·mog·a·mous (houmógəməs) *adj.* relating to homogamy ‖ characterized by homogamy

ho·mog·a·my (houmógəmi) *n.* inbreeding owing to some type of isolation ‖ (*bot.*) the state of having all the florets of a capitulum hermaphrodite ‖ (*bot.*) the state of having pistils and stamens ripe at the same time [fr. HOMO-+Gk -*gamos*, married]

ho·mo·ge·ne·i·ty (houmədʒəníːiti:, homədʒəníːiti:) *n.* the quality of being homogeneous ‖ (*statistics*) equality of a factor distribution in populations [fr. L.L. *homogeneitas*]

ho·mo·ge·ne·ous (houmədʒíːnjəs, houmədʒíːniːəs, homədʒíːnjəs, homədʒíːniːəs) *adj.* similar in character ‖ having at all points the same composition and properties (opp. HETEROGENEOUS) ‖ (*math.*) of an expression in which all the terms are of the same degree, or represent commensurable quantities [fr. L.L. *homogeneus* fr. Gk]

ho·mo·gen·e·sis (houmoudʒénisis, homoudʒénisis) *n.* (*biol.*) reproduction in which like begets like

ho·mo·ge·net·ic (houmoudʒənétik, homoudʒənétik) *adj.* exhibiting homogeny ‖ of homogenesis

ho·mog·e·nize (houmódʒənaiz, həmódʒənaiz) *pres. part.* **ho·mog·e·niz·ing** *past* and *past part.* **ho·mog·e·nized** *v.t.* to make homogeneous (e.g. milk, by breaking down the fat globules and casein) [HOMOGENOUS]

ho·mog·e·nous (houmódʒənəs, homódʒənəs) *adj.* (*biol.*) exhibiting homogeny ‖ homogeneous [fr. HOMO-+Gk *gonos*, kind]

ho·mog·e·ny (houmódʒənəs, homódʒəni:) *n.* (*biol.*) structural correspondence of individuals or of parts, because of a common ancestor (cf. HOMOPLASY) [fr. Gk *homogeneia*, homogeneity]

ho·mog·o·nous (houmógənəs, homógənəs) *adj.* (*bot.*) bearing one kind of flower having stamens and pistils of the same length **ho·móg·o·ny** *n.* [fr. HOMO-+Gk *gonos*, offspring, generation]

ho·mo·graft (houmougrǽft) *n.* a graft from a genetically different person. *also* allograft. Cf XENOGRAFT

hom·o·graph (hóməgræf, hóməgrɔf) *n.* a word which has the same spelling as another but differs in derivation and meaning or pronunciation, e.g. 'minute', the time interval, and 'minute', tiny [fr. HOMO-+Gk -*graphos*, written]

Homo habilis precursor of man that lived two million years ago, identified from fossils in Olduvai Gorge, Tanzania, by Louis Leakey in 1960

homolog *HOMOLOGUE

ho·mo·log·i·cal (houməlódʒik'l) *adj.* characterized by homology

ho·mol·o·gize (houmólədʒaiz, həmólədʒaiz) *pres. part.* **ho·mol·o·giz·ing** *past* and *past part.* **ho·mol·o·gized** *v.t.* to make or show as homologous [HOMOLOGY]

ho·mol·o·gous (houmóləgəs, həmóləgəs) *adj.* being similar or corresponding to others as to structure, value, relationship etc. ‖ (*chem.*) of compounds which, though differing in composition quantitatively, have a similar qualitative structure and can be grouped in a series with a regular difference in composition, e.g. the hydrocarbons: methane CH_4, ethane C_2H_6, propane C_3H_8 etc. ‖ of the relation between elements in the same group in the periodic table, e.g. the alkali metals ‖ (*biol.*) of structures bearing a fundamental similarity due to a common origin, though possibly modified for different functions [fr. Gk *homologos*, agreeing]

ho·mol·o·graph·ic (houmələgrǽfik) *adj.* homalographic [F. *homolographique*]

hom·o·logue, hom·o·log (hóməlɔg, hómələg) *n.* that which is homologous (cf. ANALOGUE) [F. fr. Gk]

ho·mol·o·gy (houmólədʒi:, həmólədʒi:) *n.* the condition of being homologous [fr. L.L. *homologia* fr. Gk]

ho·mol·o·sine projection (houmóləsain, həmóləsain) a method of mapping the earth's land areas whereby the land mass (not the oceans) contained within any pair of parallel lines of latitude and longitude is equal in area to any other land mass similarly contained [fr. Gk *homalos*, even]

ho·mo·mor·phic (houməmɔ́rfik, homəmɔ́rfik) *adj.* of homomorphism ‖ of homomorphy ‖ (of chromosomes undergoing synapsis) having like forms or sizes **ho·mo·mór·phism** *n.* similarity in form ‖ the condition of bearing perfect flowers of only one kind **ho·mo·mór·phous** *adj.* of homomorphism **hó·mo·mór·phy** *n.* similarity of external form, despite differences of structure [fr. HOMO-+Gk *morphē*, shape]

ho·mo·mor·phism (houmoumɔ́rfizəm) *n.* (*math.*) a function that preserves the algebraic operations between two algebraic systems

hom·o·nym (hómənim) *n.* a word having the same sound, or the same spelling and sound, as another which has a different meaning, e.g. 'bare' and 'bear' ‖ a namesake [fr. L.L. *homonymum* fr. Gk]

hom·o·nym·ic (hɔmənímik) *adj.* homonymous

ho·mon·y·mous (houmɔ́nəməs, həmɔ́nəməs) *adj.* being a homonym **ho·món·y·my** *n.* the condition of being homonymous [fr. L.L. *homonymus* fr. Gk]

ho·mo·phile (houmǝfail) *n.* **1.** a homosexual **2.** one positively concerned with homosexuals' being and their welfare. —**homophilic** *adj.* Cf HOMOPHOBE

ho·mo·phobe (hóuməfoub) *n.* one who fears homosexuals. —**homophobia** *v.* —**homophobic** *adj.*

hom·o·phone (hóməfoun, hóuməfoun) *n.* a homonym ‖ a letter having the same sound as another **hom·o·phon·ic** (hɔməfónik, houməfónik) *adj.* (*mus.*) having the same pitch ‖ (*mus.*) of homophony **ho·moph·o·nous** (həmófənəs) *adj.* (*mus.*) having the same pitch ‖ having the same sound, e.g. 'f' in English, 'v' in German ‖ being a homophone [fr. Gk *homophōnos*, having the same sound]

ho·moph·o·ny (həmófəni) *n.* identity of sound ‖ (*mus.*) the movement of parts in accord with a single melody, e.g. in hymns (Opp. POLYPHONY) [fr. Gk *homophōnia*]

ho·moph·y·ly (homófəli:, houmófəli:) *n.* similarity resulting from common origins [fr. Gk *homophulia*]

ho·mo·plas·tic (houmǝplǽstik, hɔmǝplǽstik) *adj.* (*biol.*) of or relating to homoplasy [fr. HOMO-+Gk *plastikos*, fit for molding]

ho·mo·pla·sy (houmǝpléisi:, houmóplǝsi:) *n.* (*biol.*) resemblance in structure between different organs or organisms because of evolution along similar lines (cf. HOMOGENY) [fr. HOMO-+Gk *plasis*, molding]

ho·mo·po·lar (houmǝpóulǝr, hɔmǝpóulǝr) *adj.* of or relating to a chemical bond between atoms of similar electronegativity ‖ having the poles of the primary axis alike

ho·mop·ter·an (houmɔ́ptǝrǝn) *n.* a member of *Homoptera*, an order of insects (e.g. cicadas, leafhoppers, plant lice) usually having four similar wings, though in some the hind wings are reduced or absent. The mouthparts are sucking or piercing. Incomplete metamorphosis is displayed **ho·móp·ter·ous** *adj.* [fr. Mod. L. *Homoptera* fr. Gk *homos*, same+*pteron*, wing]

ho·mo·sex·u·al (houmousékʃuːǝl) **1.** *adj.* of, characterized by or involving sexual attraction felt by a person for another person of the same sex **2.** *n.* a person (esp. male) so attracted (cf. LESBIAN) **ho·mo·sex·u·al·i·ty** (houmousekʃuːǽliti:) *n.*

ho·mo·spo·rous (houmǝspórǝs, houmǝspóurǝs, houmǝspǝrǝs) *adj.* (*bot.*) producing asexual spores of one kind only (opp. HETEROSPOROUS) [fr. HOMO-+Gk *sporos*, seed]

ho·mo·tax·is (houmǝtǽksis, hɔmǝtǽksis) *n.* similarity in order of arrangement ‖ (*geol.*) similarity in different localities of a succession of strata, which may have been deposited at different geological periods **ho·mo·tax·i·al** (houmǝtǽksiːǝl, hɔmǝtǽksiːǝl) *adj.* [fr. HOMO-+Gk *taxis*, arrangement]

ho·mo·thal·lic (houmǝθǽlik, hɔmǝθǽlik) *adj.* (of certain fungi and algae) possessing spore-producing organs that provide compatible haploid gametes for sexual reproduction (cf. HETEROTHALLIC) [fr. HOMO-+Gk *thallos*, young shoot]

ho·mo·tro·pous (houmóutrǝpǝs) *adj.* (*bot.*, of an embryo) having the radicle directed toward the hilum [fr. HOMO-+Gk *tropos*, turning]

ho·mo·type (hóumǝtaip, hómǝtaip) *n.* (*biol.*) one of two or more organs having corresponding structure **ho·mo·typ·ic** (houmǝtípik, hɔmǝtípik) *adj.* [fr. HOMO-+Gk *tupos*, type]

ho·mo·zy·gote (houmouzáigout, hɔmouzáigout) *n.* an organism bearing genes for only one member of at least one pair of allelomorphic characters and that breeds true to type **ho·mo·zý·gous** *adj.*

Homs (hɔms) a city (pop. 267,000) of Syria on the Orontes, trading in textiles (silk) and petroleum. As ancient Emesa it was famous for its Temple of the Sun

ho·mun·cule (houmʎnkjuːl) *n.* a homunculus

ho·mun·cu·lus (houmʎnkjuləs) *pl.* **ho·mun·cu·li** (houmʎnkjulai) *n.* a little being without a body, sexless and endowed with supernatural power, whom the alchemists claimed to create [L., dim. of *homo*, man]

homy *HOMEY

Hon. Honorable (title) **hon.** honorary

Ho·nan (hóunǝn) a province (area 66,676 sq. miles, pop. 74,422,739) of E. central China in the Hwang-ho basin. Capital: Chengchow

hon·cho (hóntʃou) *n.* (*colloq.*) head man

Hon·du·ras (hɔndúǝrǝs, hɔndjúǝrǝs) a republic (area 43,227 sq. miles, pop. 3,820,000) in Central America. Capital: Tegucigalpa. People: 90% Mestizos, with Indian, African, Afro-Carib and European minorities. Languages: Spanish, local languages, some English. Religion: predominantly Roman Catholic. The country is divided into the eastern lowlands (timber), the northern alluvial plains and coastal sierras (bananas), the central highlands, rising to 9,400 ft, and the Pacific lowlands (sesame and cotton). Average temperatures (F.): 79°–82° in the lowlands, 67°–74° in the mountain basins and valleys. Rainfall: 70–110 ins in the north and east, 60–80 ins on the Pacific plains and the mountain slopes, 40–70 ins in the sheltered interior. Livestock: cattle, hogs, horses. Exports: bananas (60% of exports), coffee, lumber, silver, cattle, hogs, meat, cotton, corn, gold, rubber, abaca. Manufactures: Panama hats, cigars, bricks, furniture. Other products: beans, sorghum, rice, sugarcane, tobacco, citrus fruits, zinc, lead, hydroelectricity. Imports: manufactured goods. Ports: Amapala on the Pacific, La Ceiba, Tela and Puerto Cortés on the Atlantic. University of Tegucigalpa (1847). Monetary unit: lempira (100 centavos). HISTORY. Honduras formed (300–900 A.D.) part of the flourishing Maya civilization, but this had declined and been replaced by separate Indian groups when Columbus explored the north coast (1502). Spanish settlement began (1524) and prospered with the establishment of slave estates and the discovery of gold and silver (16th c.). After raids by the Dutch (1643) and the English (17th and 18th cc.), Honduras gained its independence from Spain (Sept. 15, 1821) and joined the Central American Federation (1823–38). There followed 70 years of internal strife, occupation by U.S. marines (1911–33), a civil war (1924) and a dictatorship (1933–49). Honduras joined the Organization of Central American States (1951). The liberal leader Ramón Villeda Morales was elected president (1957) but deposed (1963) by Col. Osvaldo López Arellano, who won (1965) election by the assembly. The 'football war' (1969) with El Salvador resulted in a Colombia-style pact between the two principle parties, National and Liberal, in which all government offices were distributed equally between the two, and in Honduras' withdrawal from the Central American Common Market. Ramón Cruz, the government's nominee, was elected (1971) president in a vote open for the first time to women. Policarpo Paz García served as provisional president until 1982 when a national assembly and president Roberto Suazo Cordova took office. Nicaraguan and Honduran troops saw conflict in mid-1985

Honduras, Gulf of an inlet of the Caribbean Sea between S. British Honduras, E. Guatemala, and N. Honduras

hone (houn) *n.* **1.** a piece of stone with a very fine abrasive surface, used to grind a cutting tool (e.g. razor, scythe) to a sharp edge **2.** *v.t. pres. part.* **hon·ing** *past* and *past part.* **honed** to sharpen by using a hone [O.E. *hán*, a stone]

Ho·neg·ger (hónigǝr), Arthur (1892–1955), Swiss composer. Although he was one of 'Les Six,' his development was away from French traditions. 'King David' (1921), a biblical drama, and 'Joan of Arc at the Stake' (1935) are among his stage works. He wrote five symphonies and much other orchestral music, including 'Pacific 231' (1923)

ho·nest (ónist) *adj.* never deceiving, stealing, or taking advantage of the trust of others ‖ sincere, truthful, *an honest opinion* ‖ sincere in appearance, *an honest face* ‖ obtained by fair means, *honest earnings* **hó·nest·ly** 1. *adv.* with honesty ‖ (used as an intensive) really, *I honestly mean it* 2. *interj.* (used to express mild reproach) *honestly, you're impossible* [O.F. *honeste* fr. L. *honestus*]

Honest John (*mil.*) a surface-to-surface, free-flight, solid-propellant rocket (MGR-1) with nuclear and nonnuclear warhead capability, designed to attack targets in support of ground forces up to a range of 40,000 meters

hon·es·ty (ónisti:) *n.* the act or condition of being honest ‖ a member of *Lunaria*, fam. *Cruciferae*, a genus of European biennials, esp. *L. annua*, having white or purple cruciferous flowers and semi-transparent papery silicles [O.F. *honeste, oneste* fr. L. *honestas*]

hon·ey (hÁni:) 1. *pl.* **hon·eys** *n.* a sweet viscous fluid made by bees, esp. honeybees, from nectar and stored to serve as food during the winter ‖ (*pop.*) a term of endearment 2. *pres. part.* **hon·ey·ing** past and past part. **hon·eyed, hon·ied** *v.t.* (*pop.*, often with 'up') to blandish (someone) ‖ to sweeten with honey, or as if with honey [O.E. *hunig*]

honey badger the ratel

honey bag a bee's sac for containing nectar

honey bear the sloth bear ‖ the kinkajou

hon·ey·bee (hÁni:bi:) *n.* a honeyproducing member of *Apis*, fam. *Apidae*, esp. *A. mellifera* (*BEE)

honey bucket a container, esp. in Japan in towns without sewers, for collecting human excrement. —**honey wagon** *n.* the carrier

honey buzzard *Pernis apivorus*, fam. *Falconidae*, a European hawk which feeds on the larvae of bees and wasps

hon·ey·comb (hÁni:koum) 1. *n.* an aggregate of hexagonal wax cells, made by bees for their eggs, larvae and store of honey ‖ anything having a comparable complex structure, *the old town is a honeycomb of narrow passages* ‖ a small cavity in cast metal 2. *v.t.* to make many holes in, *the hills were honeycombed with caves* ‖ to make a honeycomb pattern on [O.E. *hunigcamb*]

hon·ey·dew (hÁni:dʉ:, hÁni:djʉ:) *n.* a sweet sticky substance excreted by aphids on the leaves and stems of plants ‖ the honeydew melon

honeydew melon a variety of muskmelon having sweet, light greenish flesh and smooth rind

honey eater a member of *Meliphagidae*, a family of large, long-billed birds, native to Australia. They have a long extensile tongue and feed mainly on nectar

hon·eyed, hon·ied (hÁni:d) *adj.* sweetened with honey ‖ sweet to the ear, ingratiatingly persuasive, *honeyed tones*

honey guide a member of *Indicatoridae*, esp. of the genera *Prodotiscus* and *Indicator*, a family of birds native to Africa and Asia. Their monotonous cries guide animals and men to the nests of wild bees ‖ (*bot.*) variously colored marks on petals or on a perianth, indicating the way to the nectary

hon·ey·moon (hÁni:mʉ:n) 1. *n.* a holiday taken by a newly married couple 2. *v.i.* to spend a honeymoon

hon·ey·suck·er (hÁni:sʌkər) *n.* a honey eater

hon·ey·suck·le (hÁni:sʌk'l) *n.* a member of *Lonicera*, fam. *Caprifoliaceae*, esp. the woodbine

Hong Kong (hóŋkoŋ) a British Crown Colony (area 398¼ sq. miles, pop. 5,313,000) on the coast of S.E. China, 90 miles southeast of Canton. It consists of Hong Kong Is. (32 sq. miles), Kowloon peninsula (incl. Kowloon city) and Stonecutters Is. (3¾ sq. miles), and the New Territories (356 sq. miles), on the mainland. Capital: Victoria (pop. 1,000,000). People: Chinese. Languages: Chinese (Cantonese dialect), English, and various Chinese dialects. The land is 13% arable. Hong Kong Is. is hilly, rising to 1,823 ft at Victoria Peak. Kowloon peninsula, separated from the island by a 1-mile harbor, extends into the New Territories. These are mostly mountainous (peaks between 2,000 and 3,000 ft), with a small agricultural lowland in the northwest. Average temperature (F.): (Feb.)

59°, (July) 82°. Rainfall: 85 ins (with great yearly variations). Rainy season: May–Sept. Typhoons occur. Crops: rice, vegetables, fruit. Industries: textiles and clothing, shipbuilding, iron and steel, aircraft engineering, machinery and cement, electrical equipment, paint, food processing, tobacco, wig making, plastics, light manufacturing, printing, fishing, tourism. The natural harbor (area 175 sq. miles) at Victoria is among the world's finest, and Hong Kong is the world's largest entrepôt port. University (1911), Chinese University (1963). Monetary unit: Hong Kong dollar (100 cents). HISTORY. China ceded (1842) Hong Kong to Britain after the Opium War. Kowloon peninsula was added (1860) and, on a 99-year lease, the New Territories (1898). There has been an influx of more than a million refugees from the mainland since 1947. The rapid expansion of Hong Kong's manufacturing industries has compensated for the loss of entrepôt trade with China. The Korean War caused an embargo (1951) on the export of strategic goods to China. Britain and China jointly announced in 1984 that the colony would become a special administrative zone of China in 1997. China agreed to preserve the colony's currency and legal system, as well as specific rights of residents, until 2043. A Chinese-British organization will monitor the agreement until the year 2000

Hong Kong flu (*med.*) virus first identified in Hong Kong and spread worldwide in 1969 and 1970. *also* Mao flu

honied *HONEYED

honk (hoŋk, hoŋk) 1. *n.* the call of the wild goose ‖ a similar sound, e.g. of a car horn 2. *v.i.* to make such a sound [imit.]

hon·ky or **hon·key, hon·kie** (hónki:) *n.* a white person. (Used disparagingly.)

honk·y-tonk (hóŋki:toŋk, hóŋki:toŋk) *n.* (*pop.*) a cheap drinking and dancing place [origin unknown]

Hon·o·lu·lu (honəlú:lu:) the capital (pop. 365,048) and chief port of Hawaii, on S. Oahu: intercontinental airport, sugar refineries, pineapple canneries. University of Hawaii

hon·or, *Br.* **hon·our** (ónər) *n.* moral integrity ‖ (*rhet.*) the esteem accorded to virtue or talent ‖ conventional respect for a person of high rank or public distinction or for a worthy symbol, *to hold the flag in honor* ‖ an award or distinction ‖ (*pl.*) awards or special ceremonies to express public respect ‖ (in formal invitations) privilege, *to request the honor of someone's company* ‖ a person who reflects credit on someone or something, *an honor to his country* ‖ (*old-fash.*) a woman's chastity or good reputation ‖ (*pl.*) academic distinction, *to pass an examination with honors* ‖ (*pl.*) the honors program ‖ (*pl., whist*) ace to jack in a trump suit ‖ (*pl., bridge*) ace to ten in a trump suit ‖ (*pl., bridge, whist*) the scoring value of such cards **Honor** (with possessive) a title of respect used esp. for judges **honor bound** compelled by considerations of upright behavior **on one's honor** put in the position of being trusted, not forced, to behave in a certain way **to do honor to** to make a public show of respect for **to do the honors** to do what is expected of the host [O. F. *onor, onur, honor, honur*]

honor, *Br.* **honour** *v.t.* to feel or show honor for ‖ to confer honor on ‖ (*commerce*) to treat as valid, *to honor a check* [O.F. *onorer, honorer*]

hon·or·a·ble, *Br.* **hon·our·a·ble** (ónərəb'l) *adj.* showing great respect or self-respect, *honorable conduct* ‖ worthy of respect, *an honorable attempt* ‖ (of the details of an agreement) consistent with the honor of all parties, *an honorable peace* ‖ (*Br.*) used in parliamentary language in referring to a member of the House of Commons **Honorable** a U.S. courtesy title of certain government officials, e.g. members of Congress **Honourable** (*abbr.* Hon., *Br.*) a title of younger sons of earls, children of peers below the rank of marquis, maids of honor, justices of the High Court, members of executive councils in the Dominions and Crown Colonies etc. [O.F. *honorable, honurable*]

honorable mention, *Br.* **honourable mention** an acknowledgment of merit short of winning a prize

hon·or·a·bly, *Br.* **hon·our·a·bly** (ónərəbli:) *adv.* in an honorable way

hon·o·rar·i·um (ɒnəréəri:əm) *pl.* **hon·o·rar·i·ums, hon·o·rar·i·a** (ɒnəréəri:ə) *n.* a gift of money made to some person in recognition of voluntary services and as a token of esteem ‖ a

payment to a professional man for his services in lieu of a fixed fee [L.L.]

hon·or·ar·y (ónəreri:) *adj.* of an unpaid office or the person holding it ‖ of duties which are merely nominal ‖ of something intended to do honor, *an honorary degree* [fr. L. *honorarius*]

hon·or·if·ic (ɒnərífik) 1. *adj.* imparting or conferring the highest respect, esp. designating certain forms of speech in many Oriental languages used when addressing a superior 2. *n.* an honorific word, title or expression [fr. L. *honorificus*]

Ho·no·ri·us (hounóri:əs, hounóuri:əs), Flavius (384–423), Roman emperor (395–423). On the death of his father, Theodosius I, the Roman empire was divided (395), and Honorius received the western part

Honorius II (*d.* 1130), pope (1124–30). He reconciled Emperor Henry V and the papacy in the Concordat of Worms (1122)

Honorius III (*d.* 1227), pope (1216–27). He was tutor to Emperor Frederick II, and worked for peace in many European countries

honor roll a list of names of people who served in the armed forces, or who died in such service, as a local memorial ‖ a list of pupils who have won some academic distinction

honors program a university or college program for outstanding students, usually involving research or specialized study, leading to a degree with honors

honour *HONOR

honourable *HONORABLE

honours degree (*Br.*) a university academic degree gained by examination at a higher level than that required for a pass degree. It is now usually the standard degree

Hon·shu (hónʃu:) the largest island (area, with adjacent islets, 87,293 sq. miles, pop. 82,559,580) of Japan. The word means 'mainland'. Chief town: Tokyo. Industries: manufacturing, agriculture (*JAPAN)

Hooch (houx), Pieter de (1629–c. 1684), Dutch painter. His best pictures, in which he showed a mastery of light, were of indoor domestic subjects recording the calm conduct of the average prosperous Dutch household

hooch (hu:tʃ) *n.* (*pop.*) alcoholic liquor, esp. crude or bootleg liquor [abbr. of Alaskan *hoochinoo*, a strong alcoholic drink] ‖ a house, esp. a thatched home in Vietnam

Hood (hud), John Bell (1831–79), Confederate general in the Civil War. After vainly fighting to save Atlanta, his army was defeated at Franklin (1864) and Nashville (1864) and finally destroyed by U.S. General George H. Thomas

Hood, Robin *ROBIN HOOD

Hood, Thomas (1799–1845), English poet and humorist. His comic verse and prose tended, esp. in his day, to eclipse his poems of social protest, e.g. 'The Song of the Shirt' (1843)

hood (hud) 1. *n.* a loose bonnetlike covering for the head and neck, often attached to a coat or cloak ‖ (*Am.*=*Br.*) bonnet) the cover over the engine of a car etc. ‖ a loose cape worn over the upper part of an academic gown ‖ (*falconry*) a loose cover for the falcon's head ‖ (*Br.*) the canvas top of a car or baby carriage 2. *v.t.* to cover, or furnish, with a hood [O.E. *hód*]

hood (hud, hu:d) *n.* a hoodlum [by shortening]

-hood *suffix* denoting state or condition, as in 'fatherhood', or to classify a body of people, as in 'priesthood' [M.E. *-hod, -hode* fr. O.E. *-hád*]

hooded seal *Cystophora cristata*, fam. *Phocidae*, a large seal. The male has an inflatable hoodlike sac on its head

hooded snake a cobra

hood·lum (hú:dləm, húdləm) *n.* (*pop.*) a hooligan ‖ (*pop.*) a gangster [origin unknown]

hoo·doo (hú:du:) 1. *n.* (*pop.*) voodoo ‖ (*pop.*) a spell intended to harm ‖ (*pop.*) a person or thing bringing bad luck 2. *v.t.* (*pop.*) to cause to have bad luck ‖ (*pop.*) to bewitch [of African origin]

hood·wink (húdwiŋk) *v.t.* to deceive by concealing the truth or by trickery

hoo·ey (hú:i:) *n.* (*pop.*) nonsense, humbug [origin unknown]

hoof (huf, hu:f), 1. *pl.* **hooves** (huvz, hu:vz), **hoofs** *n.* the sheath of horn covering the forepart of the foot in a horse, cow, sheep, pig etc. ‖ the foot of such an animal **on the hoof** (of hoofed animals for slaughtering) alive 2. *v.t.* (*pop.*, often with 'it') to walk ‖ *v.i.* to dance [O.E. *hóf*]

hoof·beat (húfbi:t, hú:fbi:t) *n.* the sound of hooves on the ground

CONCISE PRONUNCIATION KEY: (**a**) æ, c*a*t; ɑ, c*a*r; ɔ, f*aw*n; ei, sn*a*ke. (**e**) e, h*e*n; i:, sh*ee*p; iə, d*ee*r; εə, b*ea*r. (**i**) i, f*i*sh; ai, t*i*ger; ə:, b*i*rd. (**o**) o, *o*x; au, c*ow*; ou, g*oa*t; u, p*oo*r; ɔi, r*oy*al. (**u**) ʌ, d*u*ck; u, b*u*ll; u:, g*oo*se; ə, b*a*cillus; ju:, c*u*be. x, lo*ch*; θ, *th*ink; δ, bo*th*er; z, *Z*en; ʒ, corsa*g*e; dʒ, sava*g*e; ŋ, orangutan*g*; j, *y*ak; ʃ, *f*ish; tʃ, fe*tch*; 'l, rabb*le*; 'n, redd*en*. Complete pronunciation key appears inside front cover.

hoof·print (húfprint, hú:fprint) *n.* an impression left by an animal's hoof

Hoogh·ly (hú:gli:) the western arm (160 miles long) of the Ganges delta, India, navigable by ocean vessels up to Calcutta

hook (huk) **1.** *n.* a piece of a durable material, esp. metal, curved or bent sharply and able to support a considerable strain, used for taking hold of or suspending things ‖ a fishhook ‖ something having the shape of a hook, e.g. a curving headland ‖ the terminal curve of a shorthand or written character ‖ (*boxing*) a short swinging blow given with the elbow held bent and rigid ‖ the element in a writing that attracts favorable attention ‖ (*surfing*) the crest ‖ (*cricket*) a stroke deflecting the ball without hitting it at the pitch, from the on to the off side ‖ (*golf*) a drive which sends the ball far to the left (or to the right if the player is left-handed) **by hook or by crook** by fair means or foul **hook, line and sinker** (*pop.*) completely, *he swallowed the excuse hook, line and sinker* **on one's own hook** (*Am.=Br.* off one's own bat) on one's own initiative **2.** *v.t.* to use a hook to catch, fasten or suspend (something) ‖ to form (e.g. one's arm) into a hook ‖ to catch (a fish) on a hook ‖ to make (a rug) by drawing thread or lengths of wool through a canvas using a hook ‖ (*rugby*) to capture and heel (the ball) ‖ (*golf, cricket*) to hit (the ball) with a hook ‖ (*boxing*) to hit with a hook ‖ (*baseball*) to pitch (the ball) so that it curves ‖ (*pop.*) to steal ‖ (*pop.*) to trap (someone) into doing something ‖ *v.i.* to curve like a hook ‖ to be fastened by means of hooks [O.E. *hóc*]

hook·ah (húkə) *n.* an Oriental tobacco pipe in which the smoke is cooled by being drawn through water, often scented, and is inhaled through a long flexible tube [Arab. *huqqah*, vase, cup]

hook and eye a fastening device, e.g. for a dress closing, consisting of a metal hook and corresponding metal loop or bar

Hooke (huk), Robert (1635–1703), English scientist who formulated Hooke's law. He made contributions to astronomy, chemistry, mathematics, mechanics and biology. His 'Micrographia' (1665) contains the results of his observations on plant tissue

hooked (hukt) *adj.* hook-shaped, e.g. of an aquiline nose ‖ furnished with hooks ‖ made using a hook

Hook·er (húkər), Joseph ('Fighting Joe', 1814–79), U.S. general in the Civil War. He was commander (1863) of the Army of the Potomac, when General Lee routed him at Chancellorsville

Hooker, Richard (1554–1600), English theologian. His 'Of the Lawes of Ecclesiastical Politie' (1593–7), in admirable prose, was a defense of the reformed Church of England against Puritan attacks. It did much to clarify the intellectual bases of Anglicanism

Hooker, Thomas (1586–1647), Colonial Puritan minister who argued that 'the choice of public magistrates belongs unto the people by God's own allowance.' He served (1633–6) as pastor of what became Cambridge, Mass., moving (1636) with his congregation to Connecticut, where he founded Hartford

hook·er (húkər) *n.* (*rugby*) the center man in the front row of a scrum who attempts to hook the ball

Hooke's law the statement in physics that the strain produced in an elastic body is proportional to the stress which causes it [after Robert *Hooke*]

Hook of Holland the outer port of Rotterdam, Netherlands

hook·up (húkʌp) **1.** *n.* the constituent parts of an apparatus (e.g. of a radio network, a telephone) ‖ the connection and arrangement of such parts **2.** *v.t.* to install ‖ to arrange and connect the parts of (an apparatus)

hook·worm (húkwə:rm) *n.* a member of *Ancylostomatidae*, a family of nematodes having mouthparts armed with hooks. In the adult stage they are parasitic on mammals, including man, attaching themselves to the intestine wall ‖ ankylostomiasis

hook·y (húki:) *n.* (in phrase) **to play hooky** to play truant [origin unknown]

hoo·li·gan (hú:ligən) *n.* (*pop.*) a rowdy, noisy youth, esp. one belonging to a gang [prob. after an Irish *Hooligan* family of Southwark, London, at the turn of the 19th c.]

hoop (hu:p, hup) **1.** *v.i.* to whoop **2.** *n.* a whoop [F. *houper*]

hoop 1. *n.* a strip of metal, wood etc. bent to form the circumference of a circle, used in binding the staves of a cask ‖ a child's toy consisting of a large circle made of wood, metal or plastic, played with by rolling it ‖ a circle of metal or whalebone giving form to a hoop skirt ‖ a hoop skirt ‖ (*Br., croquet*) a wicket **2.** *v.t.* to fasten with a hoop or hoops ‖ to encircle [O.E. *hóp*]

hooping cough *WHOOPING COUGH

hoo·poe (hú:pu:) *n.* a member of *Upupidae*, a family of birds native to Europe, Asia and Africa, esp. *Upupa epos* having golden-brown and black plumage and a large erect crest [imit. fr. its call]

hoop skirt a skirt or petticoat distended by hoops

hoorah *HURRAH

hooray *HURRAY

hoot (hu:t) **1.** *n.* an aspirated, loud sound of derision or laughter ‖ a similar sound, e.g. of an automobile horn ‖ the call of an owl **not to care (or give) a hoot** (*pop.*) not to care at all **not worth a hoot** utterly worthless or useless **2.** *v.i.* to make a hoot ‖ *v.t.* to make derisive hoots at (someone) **hóot·er** *n.* something that makes a hooting sound, esp. (*Br.*) a car horn or a factory whistle [imit.]

Hoo·ton (hú:t'n), Earnest Albert (1887–1954), U.S. physical anthropologist. As professor (from 1930) at Harvard University, he studied Indian skeletons in New Mexico, and the psychology of American criminals. His works include 'Up from the Ape' (1931) and 'Man's Poor Relations' (1942)

Hoo·ver (hú:vər), Herbert Clark (1874–1964), 31st president (1929–33) of the U.S.A., a Republican. He organized U.S. relief to Europe during and after the 1st world war. Following the economic depression of 1929, he introduced relief measures including the Reconstruction Finance Corporation, the Emergency Relief Act, and Federal home loan banks. He was nevertheless criticized for withholding direct federal aid to the unemployed. When veterans demanding the immediate payment of bonus certificates marched on Washington, he ordered federal troops to oust them. His secretary of state introduced the Stimson Doctrine. He strongly opposed the New Deal and the foreign policy of his successor, Franklin Roosevelt. He was chairman of the Hoover Commission (1947–9, 1953–5), which recommended ways of simplifying and reducing the cost of government administration

Hoover, J. Edgar (1895–1972), U.S. director (1924–72) of the Federal Bureau of Investigation (FBI). He established the FBI National Academy, a highly selective employee training program, a scientific crime-detection laboratory, and the world's largest fingerprint file

Hoover Dam a dam (1936) on the Colorado River between Nevada and Arizona, the highest (726 ft) in the U.S.A.

hop (hɒp) *n. Humulus lupulus,* fam. *Cannabinaceae,* a perennial, lobe-leafed herbaceous climber grown in Europe and the U.S.A. The flowers are dioecious, with the female inflorescence in catkinlike clusters ‖ (*pl.*) these female inflorescences, which are dried and used for flavoring malt liquors, esp. beer and ale, and for medicinal purposes [M. Du. *hoppe*]

hop 1. *v. pres. part.* **hop·ping** *past* and *past part.* **hopped** *v.i.* (of persons) to make a little jump from the ground using only one foot or both feet or to progress by a series of such little jumps ‖ (of birds, animals) to move forward in a series of little jumps from the ground with both or all feet ‖ to move quickly, *to hop out of bed* ‖ (with 'over') to jump quickly over ‖ to make a short flight or a quick short journey, *hop over to the butcher's* ‖ *v.t.* to jump over ‖ to jump into, *to hop a bus* ‖ to obtain (a ride) by hitchhiking **to hop from one thing to another** to change the subject of one's conversation, attention etc. quickly and repeatedly **2.** *n.* an instance of hopping ‖ a short trip, esp. by airplane ‖ (*pop.*) a dance [O.E. *hoppian,* to leap]

hope (houp) *pres. part.* **hop·ing** *past* and *past part.* **hoped** *v.i.* to have hope ‖ *v.t.* to wish and expect, *we are hoping that they will arrive today* **to hope against hope** to cling to one's hopes despite the unlikelihood of their being fulfilled [O.E. *hopian*]

hope *n.* a confident expectation that a desire will be fulfilled ‖ wishful trust, *to place one's hope in someone* ‖ something which one longs to see realized, *peace is the hope of the world* ‖ a person in whom confidence is placed or who

could provide what is wanted, *he is her last hope* ‖ the virtue by which a Christian looks with confidence for God's grace in this world and glory in the next [O.E. *hopa*]

hope chest (*Am.=Br.* bottom drawer) a girl's collection of household linen etc. in preparation for eventual marriage

hope·ful (hóupfəl) *adj.* being full of hope ‖ likely to fulfill hopes

Ho·pei (hóupéi) (former Chihli) a province of N. Central E. China (area 59,341 sq. miles, pop. 43,000,000) bordering the Yellow Sea. Chief cities: Peking, Tientsin (the capital)

hope·less (hóuplis) *adj.* without hope ‖ affording no reason for hope

Hope·well (hóupwel, hóupwəl) the site, in what is now southern Ohio, of a cultural development (c. 500 B.C.–A.D. 500) shared by prehistoric American Indians. Its groups of burial mounds, with extensive enclosures of banked earth, reveal their burial customs, architectural and building practices, technology, economy, and social structure. It influenced related cultural developments, especially across the northern U.S.A.

hop fly *Phorodon humuli,* an aphid destructive to the hop plant

Ho·pi (hóupi:) *pl.* **Ho·pi, Ho·pis** *n.* a member of a Pueblo tribe of N. Arizona ‖ their Shoshonean language

Hop·kins (hópkinz), Esek (1718–1802), the first commodore of the American navy. Appointed (1775) commander of the first U.S. continental fleet, he was suspended (1777) from his command for disobeying orders

Hopkins, Sir Frederick Gowland (1861–1947), British biochemist, noted for his pioneer work in the chemistry of vitamins. Nobel Prize (1929)

Hopkins, Gerard Manley (1844–89), English poet and Jesuit priest. His poems were first published by Robert Bridges in 1918, but they won serious critical acclaim only in the 1930s. They are disconcertingly original, syntactically arresting and full of coined compound words and alliteration. The imagery is dense, sensuous, and mostly drawn with a closely observing eye from nature. The poems convey a sense of energy to the reader, partly by their phrasing and rhythms (*SPRUNG RHYTHM) and partly by their vigorous rejoicing in the created world as a manifestation of the love and glory of God. That Hopkins suffered anguish at times can be seen from the later sonnets. His letters and notebooks make complementary reading to the poems

Hopkins, Harry Lloyd (1890–1946), U.S. social worker and government official. As administrator (1933–8) of the Federal Emergency Relief Administration, a New Deal aid program for the unemployed, he strongly influenced reform enactment, including the Works Progress Administration (WPA). He served (from 1938) as President Franklin Roosevelt's personal adviser and emissary during the 2nd world war

hop·lite (hóplait) *n.* a heavily armed soldier of ancient Greece [fr. Gk *hoplitēs*]

Hopper (hópər), Edward (1882–1967), U.S. painter whose works depict the realism of American life, especially that in New York and New England. His paintings include 'House by the Railroad' (1925), 'From Williamsburg Bridge' (1928), 'Sunday Morning' (1930), 'Gas' (1940) and 'Nighthawks' (1942)

hop·per (hópər) *n.* (esp. in compounds) something that hops ‖ the larva of various insects, e.g. the grasshopper, locust ‖ a container, usually narrow at the bottom and wide at the top, which delivers its contents to something below it, e.g. one delivering fuel to a furnace ‖ a barge with a tilting bottom, used for discharging refuse or mud from a dredger etc. into deep water

hopper car (*rail.*) a freight car with a sloping bottom for discharging sand etc. by gravity

hop·ple (hóp'l) **1.** *v. pres. part* **hop·pling** *past* and *past part.* **hop·pled** *v.t.* to hobble (an animal) **2.** *n.* (esp. *pl.*) a hobble (rope) [origin unknown]

Hopp·ner (hópnər), John (1758–1810), English portrait painter of royal and fashionable personages

hop pole one of the long, stout poles erected to support the strings along which hop plants climb, and to support the plants themselves

hop·scotch (hópskɒtʃ) *n.* a children's game in which the players hop through the compartments of an oblong figure traced on the ground and retrieve a stone previously tossed on the figure

hop, step and jump (*Am.=Br.* hop, skip and jump) an athletic contest consisting of these three movements in uninterrupted succession

hop tree *Ptelea trifoliata,* fam. *Rutaceae,* a North American cultivated ornamental shrub, the bitter fruit of which can be used in brewing as a hops substitute

Hor·ace (hórəs, hórəs) (Quintus Horatius Flaccus, 65–8 B.C.), Roman poet. He fought with Brutus at Philippi (42 B.C.) but was introduced to Maecenas's circle (38) and became a loyal supporter and friend of Augustus. His books of 'Odes' deal elegantly with a wide variety of subjects, imitating the lyrical forms of Sappho and Alcaeus. The 'Satires' and 'Epistles' treat literary, political and moral themes and the 'Ars Poetica' (one of the 'Epistles') gathers together various precepts of literary criticism

Ho·ra·tius Co·cles (hɔréɪʃəskóukliːz), Publius, legendary Roman hero. He and two companions fought off the Etruscan army while the Romans cut down the bridge which lay between the Etruscans and Rome. Having saved Rome from invasion, he swam the Tiber to safety

horde (hɔrd, hourd) *n.* a vast number of people, assembled or loosely associated ‖ (*hist.*) one of various Mongolian tribes of nomadic, often barbaric herdsmen [ult. fr. Turk. *ordă, ordĭ, ordŭ,* camp]

hore·hound, hoar·hound (hórhaund, hóurhaund) *n. Marrubium vulgare,* fam. *Labiatae,* a plant having the stem and leaves covered with soft, thick hair. Its juice is used as a remedy for colds, and as a flavoring for candies [O.E. *hāre hūne* fr. *hār,* hoary+*hūne,* some plant]

Hor·gan (hórgən), Stephen Henry (1854–1941), U.S. editor and newspaper illustrator. He was the first to make halftone illustrations which could be reproduced on newsprint paper

ho·ri·zon (həráɪz'n) *n.* the apparent line of junction of earth or sea with sky (the apparent or visible horizon) ‖ (*astron.*) the plane in which the eye of the observer lies and which is normal to the line joining the observer to the earth's center (the sensible horizon) ‖ (*astron.*) a circle whose plane is parallel to the sensible horizon and passes through the earth's center (the true celestial or geometrical horizon) ‖ (*navigation* etc.) a level mirror (e.g. the surface of a trough of mercury) used as the sensible horizon, e.g. for observing altitudes (known also as an artificial horizon) ‖ (*geol.*) a rock stratum dated by reference to its distinctive fossil remains ‖ the limit of vision, experience etc. [M.E. *orizont* fr. O.F. fr. L.L. fr. Gk]

hor·i·zon·tal (hɔrizónt'l, horizónt'l) **1.** *adj.* at right angles to a radius of the earth (cf. VERTICAL) ‖ (of machinery) having its parts arranged or moving in a plane at right angles to a radius of the earth ‖ of or located at the horizon **2.** *n.* a line, plane etc. that is horizontal [fr. L. *horizon* (*horizontis*)]

horizontal bar a horizontally fixed metal or wooden bar used in gymnastics

horizontal intensity (*phys.,* of the earth's magnetic field) the horizontal component of the earth's magnetic intensity, equal numerically to the total intensity multiplied by the cosine of the magnetic dip

horizontal system (*mil.*) plan for deployment of MX missiles along trenches or roads

hor·mo·nal (hórmoun'l) *adj.* of or relating to hormones

hor·mone (hórmoun) *n.* one of a group of substances of variable composition which are produced in most living systems and are transported by the circulation of the body fluids or sap. Hormones, which in higher animals are produced by the endocrine glands, serve to regulate metabolism, growth and reproduction, by controlling specific chemical processes and by coordinating the function of various groups of organs [fr. Gk *hormōn,* pres. part. of *horman,* to urge on]

hor·mo·nol·o·gy (hɔrmoυnólədʒi:) *n.* the study of hormones

Hor·muz, Straits of (hórmʌz) a strait connecting the Persian Gulf to the Arabian Sea

horn (hɔrn) **1.** *n.* a hard, pointed, permanent outgrowth of epidermis, usually curved and paired, on the head of some animals, e.g. cattle, antelope. They use them as weapons ‖ one of a pair of similar outgrowths which are branched and deciduous, esp. in males of the deer family ‖ the tough, flexible, semitransparent substance,

composed mainly of keratin, of which these growths are made, or an imitation of this substance ‖ (*mus.*) any of various wind instruments (originally made from an animal's horn) ‖ a French horn ‖ an instrument for making loud warning noises, e.g. a foghorn, a car horn ‖ (*hist.*) something fashioned from an animal's horn, e.g. a powder horn ‖ (*zool.*) a hornlike projection, e.g. the eye stem of a snail or the mandible of a stag beetle ‖ something shaped like a horn **to be on** (or **between**) **the horns of a dilemma** to be obliged to choose between unpleasant alternatives **to draw in one's horns** to be less aggressive in manner ‖ to economize ‖ to be less active **2.** *v.t.* to furnish with horns ‖ (of an animal with horns) to pierce with a horn ‖ *v.i.* **to horn in** (with 'on') to intrude [O.E.]

horn·beam (hórnbiːm) *n.* a member of *Carpinus,* fam. *Corylaceae,* a genus of hardwood trees of Europe and North America having simple leaves, smooth bark and catkinlike, usually monoecious, flowers

horn·bill (hórnbil) *n.* a member of *Bucerontes,* a suborder of birds native to Asia and Africa. They have very large bills with a horny excrescence

horn·blende (hórnblend) *n.* a mineral including mixed silicates of calcium, magnesium and iron. It is a constituent of many rocks, e.g. gabbro [G.]

horn·book (hórnbuk) *n.* (*hist.*) a paper with the alphabet, the Lord's Prayer etc. printed on it, mounted on a board and protected by a sheet of transparent horn, in use until the mid-18th c. by children learning to read

Horn, Cape *CAPE HORN

horned (hórnd) *adj.* having a horn or horns or hornlike projections

horned toad a member of *Phrynosoma,* fam. *Iguanidae,* a genus of viviparous lizards native to the western U.S.A. and Mexico. They have broad, flat bodies covered with many spiny protrusions and a more prominent hornlike spine above each eye

horned viper *Aspis cornutus* or *Cerastes cornutus,* fam. *Viperidae,* a desert viper found in Egypt and Asia, having two spiky scales on its head

hor·net (hórnit) *n.* any of various large, strong members of *Vespidae,* a family of wasps. Up to 200 individuals live in a sheltered hollow nest, made of material manufactured from the bark of trees. They are herbivorous and carnivorous and can inflict a severe sting **to stir up a hornets' nest** to arouse the fierce anger of a number of people [O.E. *hyrnetu, hyrnet*]

Hor·net (hórnet) *n.* (*mil.*) proposed U.S. Navy fighter plane (F-18) developed by Northrop Corp.

horn of plenty a cornucopia

horn·pipe (hórnpaip) *n.* (*hist.*) a wooden pipe, fitted with a reed and horn mouthpiece ‖ a lively dance to the music of a hornpipe ‖ this music

horn·y (hórni:) *comp.* **horn·i·er** *superl.* **horn·i·est** *adj.* of or like horn ‖ having horns ‖ calloused

hor·o·log·ic (hɔrəlódʒik, horəlódʒik) *adj.* pertaining to horology **hor·o·log·i·cal** *adj.* [fr. L. *horologicus* fr. Gk *hora,* hour+*-logos,* word]

ho·rol·o·gist (hɔrólədʒist, hourólədʒist) *n.* a clockmaker

ho·rol·o·gy (hɔrólədʒi:, hourólədʒi:) *n.* the science of measuring time by mechanical devices ‖ the art of making timepieces [fr. Gk *hora,* hour+*logos,* word]

hor·o·scope (hórəskoup, hórəskoup) *n.* the configuration of the planets, esp. at the time of a person's birth, from which astrologers predict his future ‖ a diagram representing the configuration of the stars and planets at any given time **to cast a horoscope** to construct such a diagram and use it to make predictions **ho·ros·co·py** (hɔróskəpi:, houróskəpi:) *n.* this practice [F. fr. L. fr. Gk]

Horoscope-by-Phone a 24-hour-a-day, 15-second prerecorded telephone guidance by zodiac signs by astrologer Jeanne Dixon, offered to subscribers in New York

Horowitz (hóurəvits), Vladimir (1904–), U.S. pianist, born in Kiev, Russia. After touring in Europe and Russia, he debuted in the U.S. at Carnegie Hall in 1928. Although he retired in 1953, he returned to the concert stage in 1965. His 1978 Carnegie Hall 50th anniversary and 1986 Moscow concerts brought international acclaim

hor·ren·dous (hɔréndəs, hʊréndəs) *adj.* of a kind to inspire horror, dreadful [L. *horrendus*]

hor·ri·ble (hórəb'l, hórəb'l) *adj.* giving rise to horror ‖ extremely unpleasant or unpleasing **hór·ri·bly** *adv.* [O.F.]

hor·rid (hórid, hórid) *adj.* very unkind ‖ horrible [fr. L. *horridus* fr. *horrere,* to bristle]

hor·rif·ic (hərífik, horífik) *adj.* causing or likely to cause horror **hor·rif·i·cal·ly** *adv.* [fr. F. *horrifique* or fr. L. *horrificus*]

hor·ri·fy (hórifai, hórifai) *pres. part.* **hor·ri·fy·ing** *past* and *past part.* **hor·ri·fied** *v.t.* to cause horror to ‖ to shock [fr. L. *horrificare*]

hor·rip·i·la·tion (hɔrɔpəléiʃən, hɔrɪpəléiʃən) *n.* the bristling of the hairs of the head or body due to fear or disease [fr. L.L. *horripilatio (horripilationis)* fr. *horrere,* to bristle+*pilus,* hair]

hor·ror (hórər, hórər) *n.* intense fear joined with repulsion ‖ something which causes horror ‖ (*pop.*) someone, esp. a child, who behaves in a horrid way [M.E. *orrour* fr. O.F.]

Hor·sa (hórsə) *HENGEST

hors d'oeu·vre (ɔrdə:vr) *pl.* **hors d'oeu·vres, hors d'oeu·vre** (ɔrdə:vr) *n.* various dishes served as appetizers before the principal luncheon or dinner courses [F.]

horse (hɔrs) **1.** *n. Equus caballus,* fam. *Equidae,* a large, herbivorous animal with a flowing mane and a tail of coarse hair, and with the hoof undivided. It has been domesticated since prehistoric times as a beast of burden, a draft animal and for riding ‖ a stallion or gelding as distinguished from a mare, filly, colt or pony ‖ a clotheshorse ‖ a vaulting horse ‖ (*mining*) a mass of rock, clay etc. impeding the extraction of a mineral from a vein or seam **Horse** (in titles) mounted troops **a horse of a different color** quite a different matter **from the horse's mouth** from the source, not from some third person **hold your horses!** don't be impatient, wait a moment! **to be on one's high horse, to ride the high horse** to behave with dogmatic arrogance **2.** *v. pres. part.* **hors·ing** *past* and *past part.* **horsed** *v.t.* to provide a horse for (someone) ‖ *v.i.* **to horse around** (*pop.*) to fool around [O.E. *hors*]

horse·back (hórsbæk) *adv.* on a horse **on horseback** riding on a horse

horse block a wooden step, or large stone, to mount a horse from

horse box a tall closed van used to transport a horse by rail or road

horse·break·er (hórsbreikər) *n.* someone who breaks in or trains young or wild horses

horse·car (hórskɑr) *n.* a railroad car or a truck fitted for transporting horses ‖ (*hist.*) a horse-drawn streetcar

horse chestnut *Aesculus hippocastanum,* fam. *Hippocastanaceae,* a shade tree, widely found in temperate climates, having palmate leaves, ornamental pink or white flowers in erect conical clusters, and a fruit consisting of a prickly capsule containing a large, inedible seed ‖ this seed

horse·cloth (hórsklɔθ, hórsklɒθ) *pl.* **horse·cloths** (hórsklɔθz, hórsklɒθz, hórsklɔðs, hórsklɒðs) *n.* a rug for covering a horse after exercise

horsed (hɔrst) *adj.* (*mil.*) mounted on horseback

horse·flesh (hórsfleʃ) *n.* the flesh of a horse as food ‖ (*collect.*) horses, *a good judge of horseflesh*

horse·fly (hórsflai) *pl.* **horse·flies** *n.* a member of *Tabanidae,* a family of dipterans whose female members suck the blood of horses, cows etc.

horse·hair (hórshɛər) *n.* coarse, long hair from the tail or mane of a horse, used as mattress stuffing and, formerly, woven into upholstery cloth

horse latitudes (*naut.*) one of two regions of calms bordering the tradewind regions, about 30° north and south of the equator [origin unknown]

horse·laugh (hórslæf, hórslɑf) *n.* a loud, coarse laugh

horse·leech (hórsliːtʃ) *n. Haemopis gulo,* fam. *Hirudinidae,* a large aquatic European leech ‖ any of several related North American leeches

horse·man (hórsmən) *pl.* **horse·men** (hórsmən) *n.* someone who rides a horse, esp. with respect to skill ‖ a skillful rider **hórse·man·ship** *n.* skill in riding and managing a horse

horse·play (hórspleï) *n.* rough, boisterous play

horse·pow·er *n.* (*Am.*) a standard unit of power equal to 746 watts ‖ (*Br.*) a standard unit of power equal to 550 foot-pounds per second (nearly equal to 746 watts) ‖ the power of an engine measured in standard horsepower units (cf. BRAKE HORSEPOWER)

horse·rad·ish (hórsrædiʃ) n. Armoracia lapathifolia, fam. Cruciferae, a perennial plant cultivated for its fleshy white root ‖ this root ‖ a pungent condiment made from this root

horse sense (pop.) common sense

horse·shoe (hórsʃuː) n. a curved bar of iron with a flat face, shaped to fit the rim of a horse's hoof, to which it is nailed for protection ‖ (pl.) a game played by trying to throw horseshoes over a stake fixed 40 ft away

Horseshoe Bend a turn on the Tallapoosa River in east central Alabama, site of a battle (1814) in which the militia commanded by Andrew Jackson defeated the Creek Indians, who then surrendered

horseshoe crab Limulus polyphemus, a king crab found off the eastern coast of North America

horse·tail (hórstei̯l) n. a member of Equisetum, fam. Equisetaceae, a genus of perennial plants. The sporophyte possesses a rhizome giving rise to an aerial, jointed, hollow stem which bears scalelike leaves and occasionally branches at the joints. Strobili, borne at the tips of the stem, disseminate spores. These produce the gametophyte, a small lobed prothallus with rhizoids, usually not observed in nature (*ALTERNATION OF GENERATIONS). Horsetails are of wide distribution, principally in moist, temperate regions

horse·whip (hórʃwip, hórswip) 1. n. a whip with a long lash used in driving and managing horses 2. v.t. pres. part. **horse·whip·ping** past and past part. **horse·whipped** to lash (someone) with a horsewhip

horse·wom·an (hórswumən) pl. **horse·wom·en** (hórswimin) n. a woman who rides a horse, esp. with respect to her skill

hors·ey, hors·y (hórsiː) comp. **hors·i·er** superl. **hors·i·est** adj. of or pertaining to a horse or horses, a horsey smell hung about the place ‖ (of a man or woman) heavily preoccupied with the breeding, keeping or riding of horses

Hor·ta (ɔrtæ), Victor (1861–1947), Belgian architect, an originator of art nouveau. His work announced basic 20th-c. principles of design, esp. in combining the structural and decorative use of iron and glass

hor·ta·tive (hórtətiv) adj. giving advice or encouragement [fr. L. hortativus]

hor·ta·to·ry (hórtətɔri, hórtətɔuri) adj. exhorting, urging on with advice [fr. L.L. hortatorius]

Hor·thy de Nagy·bá·nya (hórtiː dənódjbɑnjɔ), Miklós (1868–1957), Hungarian admiral and statesman. He became commander in chief of the Austro-Hungarian navy (1917), organized a counterrevolution (1919) against Bela Kun, and was regent of Hungary (1920–44). He was deposed by the Nazis for seeking an armistice with the Allies

hor·ti·cul·tur·al (hɔrtikʌltʃərəl) adj. pertaining to horticulture

hor·ti·cul·ture (hórtikʌltʃər) n. the art of growing flowers, fruit and vegetables **hor·ti·cul·tur·ist** n. [fr. L. hortus, garden+cultura, cultivation]

hor·tus sic·cus (hórtəssikəs) n. a herbarium (collection) [L.=dry garden]

Ho·rus (hórəs, hóurəs) (Egypt. mythol.) the hawkheaded god of day

Ho·sain A·li (hɔséinɑliː) *BAHA-ULLAH

ho·san·na (houzǽnə) n. a cry of praise and worship [fr. L.L. osanna, hosanna fr. Gk fr. Heb.]

HO scale the standard of model toy measurement based on ⅛ in to the ft

hose (houz) 1. n. a flexible tube used for conveying water ‖ (collect., hist. and commerce) stockings ‖ (hist.) tights or breeches 2. v.t. pres. part. **hos·ing** past and past part. **hosed** to spray with a hose [O.E. hosa]

Ho·se·a (houzíːə) a Minor Prophet (8th c. B.C.) of the Old Testament. He told of God's forgiving love even for unfaithful Israel ‖ the book of the Old Testament containing his prophecies

ho·sier (hóuʒər) n. someone who deals in stockings, socks and (Br.) men's underwear **ho·sier·y** n. (collect.) the goods dealt in by a hosier ‖ his business ‖ (Br.) the place where such goods are made

Hospice, a program, begun in England in 1967, that eases the last days of terminally-ill patients and assures a natural death in as homelike surroundings as possible. There are cur-

rently almost 1,500 hospice programs in the U.S.

hos·pice (hóspis) n. a building, usually kept by a religious order, where travelers can obtain rest and food

hos·pi·ta·ble (hóspitəbˈl, hɒspítəbˈl) adj. gladly and generously receiving guests and attending to their needs and comfort ‖ receptive, hospitable to new ideas **hós·pi·ta·bly, hospít·a·bly** adv. [obs. F. hospitable]

hos·pi·tal (hóspitˈl) n. an institution equipped and staffed to provide medical and surgical and sometimes psychiatric care for the sick and injured ‖ (hist.) a charitable institution e.g. for housing the elderly or educating the young [O.F.]

Hos·pi·tal·er, Hos·pi·tal·ler (hóspitˈlər) n. a Knight Hospitaler

hos·pi·tal·i·ty (hɒspitǽliti) pl. **hos·pi·tal·i·ties** n. the receiving of a guest ‖ the treatment given to or received by a guest ‖ a tendency to, and liking for, the frequent receiving of guests ‖ (Br.) free board and lodging, hospitality will be provided [O.F. hospitalité]

hos·pi·tal·i·za·tion (hɒspit'lizéiʃən) n. a hospitalizing or being hospitalized ‖ the period of being in a hospital as a patient

hos·pi·tal·ize (hóspit'laiz) pres. part. **hos·pi·tal·iz·ing** past and past part. **hos·pi·tal·ized** v.t. to place as a patient in a hospital

Hospitaller *HOSPITALER

Host (houst) n. the bread or wafer which is consecrated in the Eucharist [O.F. oiste, hoiste, sacrifice]

host (houst) n. someone who provides hospitality ‖ (hist.) the landlord of an inn ‖ (biol.) any organism in which a parasite spends part or the whole of its existence and from which it derives nourishment or protection or both ‖ (biol.) an organism which receives grafted or transplanted tissue [O.F. oste, hoste]

host n. a great number, a host of enemies ‖ the angels and archangels, the heavenly host [O.F. ost, host, army]

hos·tage (hóstidʒ) n. a person held as a pledge that certain conditions will be fulfilled, failing which his life or well-being will be forfeited ‖ the condition of being a hostage [O.F. ostage, hostage]

hos·tel (hóstəl) n. (Br.) a residence, usually run by a nonprofit-making organization, providing board and lodging to students, elderly or ill persons etc. at a moderate cost ‖ a youth hostel [O.F. ostel, hostel]

hos·tel·ry (hóstəlri) pl. **hos·tel·ries** n. (archaic) an inn [O.F. ostelerie, hostelerie]

host·ess (hóustis) n. a female host ‖ (hist.) the mistress of an inn ‖ a woman who welcomes and assists clients, e.g. in a restaurant or aircraft [O.F. ostesse]

hos·tile (hóstəl, Br. hóstail) adj. antagonistic, a hostile reception ‖ warlike ‖ of or relating to an enemy, a hostile nation [fr. L. hostilis fr. hostis, enemy]

hos·til·i·ty (hostiliti) pl. **hos·til·i·ties** n. antagonism, unfriendliness ‖ (pl.) acts of war [fr. L.L. hostilitas]

host·ler (hóslər, óslər) n. (hist.) a groom or stableman at an inn [shortened form of hosteler, a person running a hostel]

Hos·tos (óstɔs), Eugenio María de (1839–1903), Puerto Rican author. 'Moral Social' and other works present Puerto Rico as a country under oppression

hot (hɒt) adj. at a high temperature, esp. at a considerably higher temperature than one's body temperature, a hot oven ‖ (of body temperature) above normal ‖ producing a sensation similar to heat, a hot mustard ‖ (of an emotion) causing a sensation of body heat ‖ violent, a hot chase ‖ controversial, a hot issue ‖ following or pressing closely, hot on his heels ‖ (hunting, of the scent) clear and strong ‖ (in guessing games) close to the solution ‖ freshly arrived, news hot from the press ‖ of a communications medium offering much information but requiring minimal attention ‖ electrically charged, a hot wire ‖ radioactive ‖ (pop.) stolen, a hot car ‖ (jazz) characterized by exciting rhythm and tonality and by improvisation **to make it hot for someone** to make conditions difficult for someone [O.E. hāt]

hot adv. hotly [O.E. hāte]

hot air (pop.) empty talk or boasting

hot·bed (hótbed) n. a mound of earth and rotting vegetable matter, kept hot by the heat emitted during rotting, and used for raising tender plants or for accelerating their growth ‖

(rhet.) a place which favors the growth of disease, vice etc.

hot-blood·ed (hótblʌdid) adj. (of people) passionate ‖ (of people) rash, impetuous ‖ (of horses) having Arab blood

hot cake a griddlecake **to sell** (or **go**) **like hot cakes** to sell very fast, be in very strong demand

hot cell (nuclear phys.) a lead-shielded laboratory designed for handling radioactive substances

hotch·potch (hótʃpótʃ) n. a meat stew with lots of vegetables in it ‖ a hodgepodge [M.E. fr. F. hochepot]

hot cross bun a spicy bun marked with a cross, eaten on Good Friday

hot dog a hot, freshly cooked sausage (esp. a frankfurter) sandwiched in a split roll of bread

hot dog v. (skiing) to perform stunts

ho·tel (houtél) n. a large building with a resident staff, providing accommodation and often meals [F. hôtel]

hot·foot (hótfut) 1. adv. hastily 2. v.i. (with 'it') to go in a hurry, hotfoot it over to the house

hot·head·ed (hóthédid) adj. impetuous, rash ‖ apt to flare into a temper or become overexcited

hot·house (hóthaus) pl. **hot·hous·es** (hóthauziz) n. a greenhouse whose temperature is maintained at an artificially high level

hothouse effect *GREENHOUSE EFFECT

Ho·tien (hóutjén) *KHOTAN

hot line 1. a direct telephone or teletype providing immediate communication between leaders of two nations or organizations, esp. for use in an emergency, e.g. between Washington and Moscow 2. a line to a radio or television special broadcast soliciting interviews

hot·ly (hótliː) adv. in a hot manner

hot mooner (astron.) one who believes that moon craters resulted from volcanic action. syn. vulcanist

hot pants very short, close-fitting shorts

hot pepper any of certain plants of genus Capsicum bearing peppers containing large amounts of capsaicin ‖ the fruit itself

hot plate a heated metal shelf or plate for keeping food hot ‖ a small portable cooking stove

hot pot meat stewed with potatoes in a closed pot

hot-press (hótpres) 1. n. a machine consisting of hot plates for smoothing and glossing paper or cloth 2. v.t. to make (paper or cloth) smooth and glossy by pressing in this machine

hot pursuit (mil.) an attack on an enemy force escaping into a neutral country

hot rod a car whose motor has been supercharged for high speed

hot shoe base for camera-synchronized flash attachment

hots (slang or colloq.) state of being sexually aroused

Hot·spur (hótspər) *PERCY, Sir Henry

Hot·ten·tot (hót'ntɒt) n. a member of a nomadic, pastoral people inhabiting the southwestern part of S. Africa. They are similar to the so-called Bushmen in physical features and language ‖ their language, which, together with Bushman, is regarded as forming a separate linguistic family [Afrik.]

hot tub a large wooden tub usually for group bathing

hot water (pop.) trouble, esp. with the authorities

hot water pollution *THERMAL POLLUTION

hot wire (mechanics) a technique for starting an ignition system without a key, e.g., for stealing motor vehicles. —**hot-wire** v.

houdah *HOWDAH

Hou·di·ni (huːdíːniː), Harry (Erich Weiss), 1874–1926), U.S. magician, famous for the sensational way he extricated himself from handcuffs, shackles, locked containers etc.

hound (haund) 1. n. a dog used in hunting or tracking, that follows the prey by scent ‖ a chaser in hare and hounds 2. v.t. to pursue relentlessly, to hound someone out of society ‖ (with 'on') to urge to follow the (or ride to) hounds to take part in hunting with a pack of hounds [O.E. hund]

Hound Dog (mil.) a turbojet-propelled, air-to-surface missile (AGM-28) designed to be carried externally on the B-52, equipped with a nuclear warhead useful for high- or low-altitude attacks, supplementing the internally carried firepower of the B-52

CONCISE PRONUNCIATION KEY: **(a)** æ, cat; ɑ, car; ɔ fawn; ei, snake. **(e)** e, hen; iː, sheep; iə, deer; ɛə, bear. **(i)** i, fish; ai, tiger; əː, bird. **(o)** o, ox; au, cow; ou, goat; u, poor; ɔi, royal. **(u)** ʌ, duck; u, bull; uː, goose; ə, bacillus; juː, cube. x, loch; θ, think; ð, bother; z, Zen; ʒ, corsage; dʒ, savage; ŋ, orangutang; j, yak; ʃ, fish; tʃ, fetch; 'l, rabble; 'n, redden. Complete pronunciation key appears inside front cover.

hound's-tongue (háundztʌŋ) n. a member of *Cynoglossum*, fam. *Boraginaceae*, a genus of coarse plants having a tongue-shaped leaf, esp. *C. officinale*

hound's tooth (also **houndstooth check, hound's-tooth check**) a broken-check pattern or fabric woven in it

Hou·phouët-Boi·gny (u:fweibwɑnji:), Felix (1905–), Ivory Coast statesman, president of the Ivory Coast (1960–). He held office in various French governments (1956–9)

hour (áuər) n. a 24th part of the mean solar day, subdivided into 60 minutes, i.e. 60 minutes of sidereal time ‖ a fixed period of time, *the lunch hour is 45 minutes* ‖ this very moment, *at this hour* ‖ a special moment, or short time, *the hour of danger* ‖ time of day, *at an early hour* ‖ 15 minutes of longitude at the equator, being the angle turned through by the earth in 1 hour ‖ (*pl.*) a working period, esp. within any 24 hrs, *to work long hours* ‖ (*pl.*) times for habitual activities, esp. getting up and going to bed ‖ (*pl.*) canonical hours appointed for devotions ‖ (*pl.*) these devotions ‖ a measure of distance expressed as the amount of time necessary to travel it, *our home is an hour from here* **after hours** after regular working hours or after closing hours **on the hour** precisely at the sixtieth minute of an hour, *the news is broadcast on the hour* **the question of the hour** the most discussed question at a particular time [O.F. *ure, ore*]

hour circle (*astron.*) any of the 12 circles passing through the poles at right angles to the equator

hour-glass (áuərglæs, áuərglɒs) n. a device for measuring the period of one hour, this being the time taken by a measured quantity of fine, dry sand to pass through a narrow tube from an upper glass bulb into a lower one

hour hand the shorter hand of a watch or clock, indicating the hour

hou·ri (húəri) n. a beautiful young girl inhabiting the Moslem paradise [F. fr. Pers. ult. fr. Arab. *hawira*, with black eyes like a gazelle's]

hour·ly (áuərli) **1.** adj. done, or occurring, every hour **2.** adv. every hour ‖ very soon, *we are expecting hourly to hear the news*

'Hou·sa·ton·ic', S.S. (hu:sətónik) a U.S. vessel torpedoed (Feb. 3, 1917) by a German submarine, in violation of the rights of neutrals. On the same day President Wilson broke off diplomatic relations with Germany

House (haus), Edward Mandell (1858–1938) U.S. diplomat and confidential adviser (1912–19) to President Woodrow Wilson. As Wilson's chief agent in foreign affairs during the 1st world war, Col. House drafted (1916) with Sir Edward Grey, the British foreign secretary, an early peace proposal, led (1917) the U.S. mission to the Inter-Allied conference in London and Paris, persuaded (1918) the Allied chiefs of state to accept Wilson's Fourteen Points, and helped compose the covenant of the League of Nations

house (hauz) *pres. part.* **hous·ing** *past* and *past part.* **housed** v.t. to provide or be a home or shelter for (someone or something) ‖ to fix in a secure place, e.g. (*naut.*) to lash (a gun etc.) so that it cannot move ‖ (*carpentry*) to fix in a socket [O.E. *hūsian*]

house (haus) *pl.* **hous·es** (háuziz) n. a building for a person or family to live in ‖ a household, *she canvassed 12 houses* ‖ the ancestors and living members of a family, esp. a noble or royal family, *the house of Windsor* ‖ the audience in a theater, *a responsive house* or the theater itself, *a full house* ‖ a group of persons engaged in a corporate activity, or having a common interest or vocation, *a banking house* ‖ the place where a legislature meets or the legislative body itself, *the upper house* ‖ a residence in a university, college, school etc. or the persons residing there ‖ a religious community or its residence ‖ a sign of the zodiac regarded as the seat of a planet's greatest influence ‖ (*astrology*) one of the 12 equal parts into which the celestial sphere is divided **like a house afire** with great success, *the interview went off like a house afire* **on the house** paid for by the owners or management, not by the customer **to bring down the house** to win an overwhelming ovation from an audience **to clean house** to put a house in order **to keep house** to manage the domestic arrangements of another person, *she keeps house for her cousin* ‖ to do housework **to keep to the house** to stay indoors, because of slight illness **to move house** (*Br.*) to leave one home and set up

another **to set** (**or put**) **one's house in order** to tidy up one's house ‖ to straighten out one's affairs ‖ to place oneself above criticism [O.E. *hūs*]

house agent (*Br.*) a realtor

house arrest the state of being confined to one's house by order of the ruling authorities

house·boat (háusbout) n. a flatbottomed boat, or barge, with a superstructure fitted out for living in

house·bod·y (háusbɒdi:) n. one who stays at home most of the time, esp. while others in the family are active

house·boy (háusbɒi) n. a male domestic servant other than a butler

house·break (háusbreik) *pres. part.* **house·break·ing** *past* **house·broke** (háusbrɒuk) *past part.* **house·bro·ken** (háusbrɒukən) v.i. (*law*) to commit the crime of housebreaking [HOUSEBREAKER]

house·break *pres. part.* **house·break·ing** *past* **house·broke** (háusbrɒuk) *past part.* **house·bro·ken** (háusbrɒukən) v.t. (*Am.=Br.* housetrain) to train (a dog, cat etc.) to live in the house with clean habits [HOUSEBROKEN]

house·break·er (háusbreikər) n. (*law*) someone who breaks into another's house in order to steal ‖ (*Br.*) a wrecker (someone whose business is demolishing buildings) **hóuse·break·ing** n. (*law*) the crime of being a housebreaker (thief)

house·bro·ken (háusbrɒukən) adj. (of a dog, cat etc.) trained to have clean habits in the house

house·coat (háuskout) n. a long, one-piece garment worn by women around the house esp. before dressing for the day

house·fly (háusflai) *pl.* **house·flies** n. *Musca domestica*, fam. *Muscidae*, a dipteran insect found in temperate and tropical zones. Its spindle-shaped eggs are laid in groups in decaying organic material. The larvae hatch in a day and within a fortnight pupate in a dry place. Haircovered disks on the legs enable flies to adhere to any surface. They spread germs with their feet and mouthparts

house·hold (háushould) **1.** n. the family, servants etc. living in one house **House·hold** (*Br.*) the royal domestic establishment **2.** adj. of, or concerned with, a household **House·hold** (*Br.*) of, or concerned with, the Household

house·hold·er (háushouldər) n. the occupier of a house who owns it or pays rent for it

household word a word, name or phrase familiar to everyone

house·hus·band (háushʌzbənd) n. a married man who performs the household chores

house·keep·er (háuski:pər) n. a woman responsible for looking after another's house, a school residence etc.

house·keep·ing (háuski:piŋ) n. the running of a house or home

house·leek (háusli:k) n. a member of *Sempervivum*, fam. *Crassulaceae*, a genus of plants having a thick fleshy rosette of leaves, esp. *S. tectorum*. They grow esp. on old walls, roofs etc.

house·lights (háuslaits) *pl. n.* the lights illuminating the area of a theater where the audience sits

house·maid (háusmeid) n. a living-in woman servant employed to do light housework

housemaid's knee a swelling due to inflammation of the bursal sac covering the kneecap

house manager an employee of a theater responsible for its efficient day-to-day running (e.g. house staff, cleanliness of the auditorium etc.) but having no stage or backstage responsibility (cf. STAGE MANAGER)

house martin *Delichon urbica* (also called *Chelidon urbica*), a common European martin, white below with a blue-black head and back. It likes to nest under the eaves of houses

house·mas·ter (háusmæstər, háusmɑstər) n. a male teacher in charge of a house at a boys' boarding school

house·mate (háusmeit) n. a nonrelative, male or female, who lives in the same house or apartment with another person

house·mis·tress (háusmistris) n. a woman in charge of a house at a girls' boarding school

house·moth·er (háusmʌðər) n. a woman who manages a dormitory at an institution for children (e.g. a boarding school) or a women's dormitory or sorority house at a college

House of Commons *PARLIAMENT

house of correction an institution to which minor offenders, believed capable of being reformed, are sent

House of Keys the representative legislative assembly of the Isle of Man

House of Lords *PARLIAMENT

House of Representatives *CONGRESS

house organ a small newspaper or magazine circulated among the staff of a business etc.

house party an extension of hospitality to guests for a few days esp. in a country house ‖ the guests themselves

house physician the resident physician in a hospital

house-proud (háuspraud) adj. preoccupied with the care, cleanliness and attractiveness of the home ‖ manifesting this virtue to excess, so that ease, comfort and welcome are sacrificed to it

house-room (háusru:m, háusrum) n. (in the phrase) **to make houseroom for** to find room in one's house for

house-sit·ter (háusitər) n. one who is engaged to occupy a house or apartment during the absence of its usual occupant, principally for purposes of security and maintenance

house sparrow *Passer domesticus*, fam. *Fringillidae*, an insectivorous sparrow found in Europe, Asia, North America and Australia, having gray and brown plumage. It nests and lives near houses

house surgeon the resident surgeon in a hospital

house-to-house (háustəhaus) adj. made, calling or done at house after house (in a road, town etc.)

house·top (háustɒp) n. a house roof **from the housetops** publicly, so as to let as many people know as possible

house-train (háustrein) v.t. (*Br.*) to housebreak

house-warm·ing (háuswɔrmiŋ) n. a party to celebrate having just moved into a house or other dwelling

house·wife (háuswaif) *pl.* **house·wives** (háuswaivz) n. the wife of a householder, responsible for the domestic running of the house ‖ (*Br.*) (házif) a small case containing pins, needles, thread etc. **house·wife·ly** adj. [M.E. *huswif* fr. *hūs*, house + *wīf*, woman]

house·work (háuswərk) n. the work involved in looking after a home

house·y-house·y (háusi:háusi:) n. (*Br.*, esp. *mil.*) bingo

hous·ing (háuziŋ) n. a providing of shelter, esp. the organized provision of houses ‖ (*collect.*) houses ‖ (*archit.*) a hole or recess made to receive the end of a beam ‖ (*mech.*) a frame or box for holding a piece of machinery, *a clutch housing* ‖ (*naut.*) the part of the mast which is belowdecks

housing n. a horse's cloth cover, either for protection or as a caparison [fr. older *house*, a covering of cloth material]

Housing and Urban Development, U.S. Department of (*abbr.* HUD), federal agency created in 1965 to direct housing and city development programs. It assists urban renewal efforts, gives mortgage insurance for home buyers, provides low-income rental help, rehabilitates substandard housing, and aids inner city businesses. The secretary of this department is a member of the President's cabinet

Hous·man (háusmən), Alfred Edward (1859–1936), English poet and classical scholar. His poems, esp. in the collection 'A Shropshire Lad' (1896), were immensely popular

Hous·say (u:sái), Bernardo Alberto (1887–1971) Argentine physiologist. His demonstration that the hormone secreted by the anterior lobe of the pituitary gland prevents the metabolism of sugar and that the injection of pituitary extract induces symptoms of diabetes, earned him (with C.F. and G.T. Cori) the 1947 Nobel Prize in medicine

Hous·ton (hjú:stən), Sam (Samuel) (1793–1863), U.S. politician. As commander in chief of the Texas army, he defeated (Apr. 21, 1836) Santa Anna's Mexican forces on the bank of the San Jacinto, winning the independence of Texas. He served (1836–8, 1841–4) as president of Texas and, after Texas was admitted (1845) into the U.S.A., as the state's first U.S. senator. Elected governor of Texas in 1859, he was deposed in 1861 for refusing to join the Confederacy. The city of Houston, Texas, was named after him

---

CONCISE PRONUNCIATION KEY: (a) æ, cat; ɑ, car; ɔ fawn; ei, snake. (e) e, hen; i:, sheep; iə, deer; ɛə, bear. (i) i, fish; ai, tiger; ə:, bird. (o) o, ox; au, cow; ou, goat; u, poor; ɔi, royal. (u) ʌ, duck; u, bull; u:, goose; ə, bacillus; ju:, cube. x, loch; θ, think; ð, bother; z, Zen; ʒ, corsage; dʒ, savage; ŋ, orangutang; j, yak; ʃ, fish; tʃ, fetch; 'l, rabble; 'n, redden. Complete pronunciation key appears inside front cover.

Hous·ton (hjuː:stən) the largest city (pop. 1,595,138) of Texas, a major port, linked with the Gulf of Mexico by the Houston Ship Channel: oil refineries, metallurgy, food processing, chemical industries

hove alt. *past* and *past part.* OF HEAVE

ho·vel (hʌvəl, hóvəl) *n.* a small, squalid dwelling [origin unknown]

hov·er (hʌvər, hóvər) *v.i.* (often with 'over', 'above', 'aloft' etc.) to remain in the same place in the air for a short time as though suspended ‖ (with 'about', 'around', 'near' etc.) to move about, but keep near to, *he is forever hovering around her* [perh. fr. older *hove*, to hover]

Hov·er·craft (hʌvərkræft, hʌvərkrɑft, hóvərkræft, hóvərkrɑft) *n.* a transport vehicle which rides on a cushion of air ejected from an annular ring beneath it without any contact with the land or sea over which it travels [trademark]

how (hau) *adv.* in what way or manner, *to know how to cook, how did it happen?* ‖ in or to what degree, amount, number, *he didn't know how fast he could run, how much does it cost?* ‖ in what condition, *how did you find him?, you know how we found him* ‖ for what reason, why, *how is it that the book is missing?, we know how he came to steal it* ‖ (in a relative construction) in whatever way, *do it how you like* ‖ (pop.) that, *he told me how he had seen you* ‖ (emphatic) to what a great extent, degree, amount etc., *how stupid of me!* **how about** used to introduce a suggestion, *how about a little walk?* **how do you do?** (as a greeting) how are you? [O.E. *hū*]

How·ard (háuərd) *CATHERINE HOWARD

Howard, Bronson Crocker (1842–1908), U.S. playwright, known for his 'Saratoga' (1870) and 'Shenandoah' (1888)

Howard, Charles, 2nd Baron Howard of Effingham and 1st earl of Nottingham (1536–1624), lord high admiral of England (1585–1618), He commanded the English fleet which defeated the Armada (1588)

Howard, Henry *SURREY, EARL OF

Howard, John (1726–90), British prison reformer. He traveled widely in Britain and on the Continent inspecting prison conditions, and wrote 'The State of the Prisons' (1777)

Howard, Oliver Otis (1830–1909), U.S. general during the Civil War who served (1865–72) as head of the Freedmen's bureau. Howard University in Washington, D.C., which he established (1867) for blacks, is named after him

Howard, Thomas *NORFOLK, DUKES OF ‖ *SUFFOLK, EARL OF

Howard University a coeducational university in Washington, D.C., founded (1867) for the education of freed slaves. Its student body is still largely black

how·be·it (háubiːit) *conj.* (archaic) however that may be, nevertheless

how·dah, hou·dah (háudə) *n.* a seat, usually canopied, on the back of an elephant [Pers. and Urdu *haudah* fr. Arab. *haudaj*]

Howe (hau), Elias (1819–67), U.S. inventor of the sewing machine (patented, 1846). After a patent dispute was settled (1854) in his favor, he received royalties on all sewing machines sold in the U.S.A.

Howe, Joseph (1804–73), Canadian statesman who led (1836–48) the successful movement for responsible government in Nova Scotia. As premier (1860–3) of Nova Scotia, he opposed the confederation of Canada

Howe, Julia Ward (1819–1910), U.S. author and reformer, best known for her song 'The Battle Hymn of the Republic' (1862)

Howe, William, 5th Viscount Howe (1729–1814), British general. He commanded (1775–8) the British army in the Revolutionary War. His brother Richard (1726–99), 1st Earl, commanded the fleet (1776–8) in the same war

How·ells (háuəlz), William Dean (1837–1920), U.S. author, critic, and leader of the realistic school of American literature. His early novels, notably 'The Rise of Silas Lapham' (1885), portray everyday American life and the self-made man. His later works, including 'A Traveller from Altruria' (1894), explore American social problems

how·ev·er (hauévər) **1.** *adv.* in whatever way or manner, *however you may decide* ‖ (emphatic) in what way?, *however did you do that?* ‖ in or to whatever degree, amount, number, *however hot it may be, however much I would like to* **2.** *conj.* nevertheless, but, *he does not agree, however, with the rest of the article*

how·itz·er (háuitsər) *n.* a short cannon, lobbing a shell with low muzzle velocity but high trajectory [fr. G. *haubitze* fr. Bohemian *houfnice*, a catapult]

howl (haul) **1.** *v.i.* (of wolves, dogs etc.) to make a prolonged, hollow, wailing call ‖ (of high winds etc.) to make a similar sound ‖ (of a person) to make a similar sound e.g. from grief, fear etc. ‖ to laugh very loudly and unrestrainedly ‖ *v.t.* to utter with a howl **2.** *n.* any of these sounds or cries [M.E. *houlen*, imit.]

howl·er (háulər) *n.* (pop.) a ridiculous, bad mistake ‖ the howler monkey

howler monkey *n.* a member of *Alouatta*, fam. *Cebidae*, a genus of South and Central American monkeys which produce remarkably loud howling sounds because of an enlargement of the hyoid bone and the larynx

howl·ing (háuliŋ) *adj.* of someone or something which howls ‖ (pop.) extreme, *a howling success*

How·rah (háurə) a city (pop. 742,298) in W. Bengal, India, opposite Calcutta on the Hooghly River, a rail center: chemicals, textiles, glass

how·so·ev·er (hausouévər) *adv.* (archaic) in whatever way ‖ to whatever extent

hoy·den (hóid'n) *n.* a noisy, unrestrained girl ‖ a tomboy **hóy·den·ish** *adj.* [origin unknown]

Hoyle (hoil), Sir Fred (1915–), British mathematician, cosmologist, and astronomer who adheres to the controversial steady-state continuous creation of matter theory of the universe. He taught at Cambridge University (1945–72), the Royal Institution of Great Britain from 1972, and wrote 'Frontiers of Astronomy' (1955) and 'Highlights in Astronomy' (1975). His fiction works include 'The Black Cloud' (1957) and 'Ossian's Ride' (1957). He was knighted in 1972

H.P., h.p. horsepower

H.Q. headquarters

Hr·dlič·ka (hə́:rdlitʃkə), Ales (1869–1943), Czech-U.S. physical anthropologist. He asserted that the North American Indian is of Asiatic origin, and that mankind evolved in Europe, not Asia

H.R.H. His (Her) Royal Highness

Hrolf (rolf) *ROLLO

hsien (ʃin) *n.* a Chinese county

Hsing·king (ʃíndʒiŋ) *CHANGCHUN

ht height

Huainan *HWAINAN

Huambo (wámbou) (formerly Nova Lisboa), a trading center (pop. 61,885) of W. central Angola on the Benguela-Beira railroad

hua·na·co (wənákou) *n.* the guanaco

Huas·car (wáskər) (d. 1533), king of the Incas (1525–32). After a civil war with his half brother, Atahualpa, with whom he shared the kingdom, he was overthrown and murdered

Huas·ca·rán (wɑskərán) the highest mountain (22,205 ft) in Peru

hua·si·pun·ge·ro (hwɑsi:pu:nhéro) *n.* a Peruvian or Bolivian day laborer who has a piece of land to work for himself in part-return for his labor [Quechua]

hub (hʌb) *n.* the central part of a wheel from which the spokes radiate ‖ the point of greatest interest and importance, *he talks as if his village were the hub of the universe* [etym. doubtful]

Hub·ble (hʌb'l), Edwin Powell (1889–1953), U.S. astronomer and pioneer cosmologist, famous for his investigations of extragalactic nebulae

hub·ble-bub·ble (hʌb'lbʌb'l) *n.* a type of hookah [imit.]

Hub·ble constant or **Hub·ble's constant** (hʌb'l) (astron.) measure of calculated speed at which galaxies recede, based on the red shift, according to Hubble's law

hub·bub (hʌbʌb) *n.* a noisy confused mingling of sounds ‖ a tumult or uproar, *let the hubbub die down before you impose any new restrictions* [imit.]

hub·cap (hʌbkæp) *n.* a protective or ornamental cap screwed or clamped on the wheel of a motor vehicle

Hu·bert (hjuː:bərt), St (c. 656–c. 728), Frankish bishop of Maastricht and Liège (c. 704–c. 727), the patron saint of hunters. Legend says that he had a vision of a crucifix between the antlers of a stag that he was hunting. Feast: Nov. 3

Hubert de Burgh (dəbə:rg) (d. 1243), chief justiciar of England (1215–32). During Henry III's minority, he shared the regency with Stephen

Langton, and became (1227) Henry III's chief minister

Hu·ber·tus·burg, Treaty of (hjuː:bə́:rtəsbə:rg) a treaty signed (Feb. 15, 1763) at Hubertusburg in Saxony by Prussia, Austria and Saxony at the end of the Seven Years' War. Prussia retained Silesia and was established as a major European power

Hub·li (húbli:) a town (pop. 379,166) in Mysore, S.W. India: textiles, chemicals

hu·bris (hjuː:bris) *n.* scornful, overweening pride ‖ (Gk tragedy) transgression of the divine or moral law through ambition or one of the passions, ultimately causing the transgressor's doom [Gk]

huck (hʌk) *n.* huckaback

huck·a·back (hʌkəbæk) *n.* a strong cloth of linen, or linen and cotton, with a rough surface, used as toweling [origin unknown]

huck·le·ber·ry (hʌkʻlʲbeɾi:) *pl.* **huck·le·ber·ries** *n.* a member of *Gaylussacia*, fam. *Ericaceae*, a genus of North American shrubs which produce an edible, tart, dark blue to black berry ‖ this berry [prob. corrup. of *hurtleberry*, a whortleberry and WHORTLEBERRY]

huck·ster (hʌkstər) *n.* a peddler or market vendor dealing in small articles ‖ (pop.) an advertising man [fr. older *huck*, to haggle]

HUD (acronym) for U.S. Department of Housing and Urban Development, created in 1965

Hud·ders·field (hʌdərzfiːld) a county borough (pop. 130,060) in the West Riding of Yorkshire, England: textiles, engineering, iron, coal

hud·dle (hʌd'l) **1.** *v. pres. part.* **hud·dling** *past* and *past part.* **hud·dled** *v.t.* (Br.) to gather together, pile up or mix together (a number of things) in a slovenly, hurried way ‖ (with 'up') to draw (oneself) in, esp. defensively ‖ *v.i.* (of a number of people or animals) to gather together very close to one another **to huddle up to** to move close up to (someone or something) **2.** *n.* a group of people or animals gathered very close together ‖ (Br.) slovenly confusion ‖ (football) the grouping of a team behind the line of scrimmage where the quarterback (offensive team) or the captain (defensive team) tells his team the secret plan for the next play or plays **to go into a huddle** to get together in order to discuss something privately [etym. doubtful]

Hud·son (hʌdsən), George (1800–71), British railroad financier, nicknamed 'the railway king'. He was responsible, through his financial speculation, for the railroad boom in Britain in the 1840s but was ruined when frauds were disclosed

Hudson, Henry (d. 1611), English navigator. After unsuccessful attempts to find the Northeast Passage (1607–9), he began searching for the Northwest Passage. He explored the Hudson River (1609) and Hudson Bay (1610), where his crew mutinied, setting him adrift in an open boat (1611)

Hudson, William Henry (1841–1922), English naturalist and writer, born in Argentina. He is best known for his books about life in South America, e.g. 'Green Mansions' (1904), 'Far Away and Long Ago' (autobiographical, 1918), and for his books on English country life, e.g. 'Nature in Downland' (1900)

Hudson a river of New York State, flowing 315 miles from the Adirondack Mtns to New York Harbor, navigable by oceangoing vessels to Troy (8 miles above Albany)

Hudson Bay an inland sea (850 miles long, 650 miles wide) in E. central Canada, linked with the Atlantic and the Arctic Oceans, largely ice-bound except July–Oct. Henry Hudson explored it (1610)

Hudson's Bay Company an English company founded by royal charter (1670) to enjoy a fur trade monopoly in the region of Hudson Bay and to search for a Northwest Passage. The land it controlled was ceded (1870) to Canada. It continues as a private trading company in Canada

Hudson Strait a strait (450 miles long, 50–100 miles wide) between Baffin Is. and Quebec province in N.E. Canada, connecting the Hudson Bay to the Atlantic

Hué (hwéi) a town (pop. 209,000) in central Vietnam on the R. Hué, near the coast, the former capital of Annam: royal palace

hue (hjuː:) *n.* that quality of a color which allows it to be classed as red, yellow, green, blue or an intermediate (*COLOR) [O.E. *hīew, hīw*, appearance]

CONCISE PRONUNCIATION KEY: **(a)** æ, c*a*t; ɑ, c*a*r; ɔ f*aw*n; ei, sn*a*ke. **(e)** e, h*e*n; iː, sh*ee*p; iə, d*ee*r; ɛə, b*ea*r. **(i)** i, f*i*sh; ai, t*i*ger; əː, b*i*rd. **(o)** o, *o*x; au, c*ow*; ou, g*oa*t; u, p*oo*r; oi, r*oy*al. **(u)** ʌ, d*u*ck; u, b*u*ll; uː, g*oo*se; ə, b*a*cillus; juː, c*u*be. x, lo*ch*; θ, *th*ink; ð, bo*th*er; z, *Z*en; ʒ, cor*s*age; dʒ, sa*v*a*g*e; ŋ, orangutan*g*; j, *y*ak; ʃ, *fi*sh; tʃ, fe*tch*; 'l, rabb*le*; 'n, redd*en*. Complete pronunciation key appears inside front cover.

hue and cry a noisy protest ‖ shouts and sounds of pursuit through a crowded place [fr. Anglo-Norman *hu e cri*]

hued (hju:d) *adj.* (in hyphenated compounds) having a hue or hues as specified

Huel·va (wélva) a province (area 3,913 sq. miles, pop. 400,000) of Andalusia, S.W. Spain ‖ its capital (pop. 105,625)

Huer·ta (wérta), Victoriano (1854–1916), Mexican dictator (1913–14) who led a coup d'état to depose Francisco Madero. Failure to gain U.S. recognition forced him to resign

huer·ta (wérta) *n.* a highly cultivated, esp. irrigated, piece of land in Spain [Span.=garden, orchard]

Hues·ca (wéska) a province (area 5,848 sq. miles, pop. 234,000) of N.E. Spain ‖ its capital (*ARAGON)

huff (hʌf) **1.** *v.t.* to cause (someone) to be offended ‖ (checkers) to remove (an opponent's piece) from the board when he fails to use it to make a jump **2.** *n.* (only in the phrase) **in** (or **into**) **a huff** in (or into) a fit of bad temper through being offended **húff·i·ly** *adv.* **húff·i·ness** *n.* **húff·y** *comp.* **huff·i·er** *superl.* **huff·i·est** *adj.* [imit.]

hug (hʌg) **1.** *n.* a tight clasp or squeeze with the arms, esp. as an affectionate embrace ‖ a wrestling grip **2.** *v. pres. part.* **hug·ging** *past* and *past part.* **hugged** *v.t.* to clasp tightly between one's arms ‖ to dwell on (a feeling, memory etc.), esp. keeping it a secret, *to hug a grievance* ‖ to keep close to (something), *the ship hugged the coast* **to hug oneself** to congratulate oneself in delight [origin unknown]

huge (hju:dʒ) *adj.* extremely large [M.E. *huge*, *hoge* prob. fr. O.F. *ahuge*, *ahoge*]

Hü·gel (hýg'l), Baron Friedrich von (1852–1925), Austrian philosopher, Roman Catholic theologian (*MODERNISM) and mystic, author of 'Essays and Addresses on the Philosophy of Religion' (1921, 2nd series, 1926), 'The Mystical Element of Religion' (1908, revised 1923)

huge·ly (hjú:dʒli:) *adv.* to a great degree

hug·ger-mug·ger (hʌ́gərmʌ̀gər) **1.** *n.* the act or an instance of keeping secret ‖ a jumble **2.** *adj.* secret ‖ jumbled **3.** *adv.* in a secret manner ‖ in a jumbled manner **4.** *v.t.* to keep secret ‖ *v.i.* to act furtively ‖ to act in a confused manner [origin unknown]

Hugh (hju:) 'the Great' (*d.* 956), French duke, son of Robert I. He was the virtual ruler of France under the later Carolingians. His son was elected king as Hugh Capet

Hugh Ca·pet (kéipit) (F. Hugues Capet, c. 940–96), king of France (987–96), founder of the Capetian dynasty, son of Hugh the Great. He succeeded to his father's lands (956) and was elected king in opposition to the last Carolingian claimant

Hughes (hju:z), Charles Evans (1862–1948), U.S. statesman. As secretary of state (1921–5) under President Warren Harding, he negotiated, at the Washington Conference, the first successful naval arms limitation agreement, the dissolution of the Anglo-Japanese Alliance, and the establishment of Four-Power and Nine-Power treaties for stabilization in the Far East. He was largely responsible for the enactment of the Dawes Plan. As chief justice (1930–41) of the U.S. Supreme Court, he provoked historic debate by declaring the extreme New Deal measures unconstitutional

Hughes, David Edward (1831–1900), Anglo-U.S. inventor. He invented a type-printing telegraph instrument (patented 1855), an early version of the microphone, and the induction balance. He contributed to the theory of magnetism

Hughes, Langston (1902–67), U.S. poet. His works, including 'Shakespeare in Harlem' (1942) and 'One-Way Ticket' (1949), make use of dialect and jazz rhythms. A spokesman for his fellow blacks, he published 'Fight for Freedom; Story of the NAACP' (1962)

Hughes, Sir Sam (1853–1921), Canadian minister of militia and defense (1911–16). He organized (1914) the first Canadian contingent to serve in the 1st world war

Hughes, William Morris (1864–1952), Australian statesman, Labour prime minister of Australia (1915–23)

Hugh of Avalon (hjú:əvǽvələn), St (c. 1135–1200), Burgundian bishop of Lincoln, England (1186–1200). He partially rebuilt Lincoln cathedral. Feast: Nov. 17

Hu·go (ygou, hjú:gou), Victor Marie (1802–85), French poet, novelist and dramatist. In the drama, e.g. 'Hernani' (1830), 'Ruy Blas' (1838), he broke through the classical restrictions. In his lyric poetry, e.g. 'les Feuilles d'automne' (1831), 'les Rayons et les Ombres' (1840), 'Contemplations' (1856), he invented or restored innumerable beauties of meter and harmony. He also wrote epic and satirical poetry. The variety of his prolific genius profoundly enriched French poetry and opened the way for many modern stylistic changes. As a novelist, e.g. in 'Notre-Dame de Paris' (1831) and 'les Misérables' (1862), he influenced Romantic fiction throughout Europe

Hu·gue·not (hjú:gənɒt) a Calvinist Protestant in France during the religious struggles of the 16th and 17th cc. The numbers of Huguenots grew in the late 16th c., and their rivalry with the Catholics led to the Wars of Religion (1562–98). They triumphed when the Protestant Henri IV succeeded to the throne (1589), and obtained toleration under the Edict of Nantes (1598). When this was revoked (1685), many Huguenots fled to Switzerland, England and America, where they often made an important contribution to industry

huh (hʌ) *interj.* used to express disbelief, contempt, surprise etc. or as an interrogative

Hu·he·hot (hú:həhɒt) (formerly Kweisui) the capital (pop. 314,000) of Inner Mongolia, China, an ancient trade center comprising two towns, Kweihwa and Suiyuan. It is the seat of a living Buddha

Huit·zil·o·póch·tli (wɪtzi:loupóutʃtli:) the Aztec god of war and chief of the Aztec pantheon

hu·la (hú:lə) *n.* a native Hawaiian dance [native word]

Hu·la·gu (hu:lágu:) (1217–65), Mongol conqueror, grandson of Genghis Khan. He invaded Persia, destroyed Baghdad (1258) and overthrew the Abbasid dynasty

hula hoop (*sports*) a circle of wood or plastic rotated around the body by physical movements, popular in the 1950s

hula hula the hula ‖ (*Br., pop.*) a hula skirt

hula skirt a grass skirt worn by a hula dancer

hulk (hʌlk) *n.* the body, or hull, of a ship no longer seaworthy, sometimes used for storage ‖ (*pl., hist.*) this used as a prison ‖ a large ship, difficult to maneuver ‖ a big clumsy man **húlk·ing** *adj.* big and clumsy [O.E. *hulc*]

Hull (hʌl), Clark Leonard (1854–1952), U.S. theoretical psychologist who applied quantitative methods to aptitude prognosis and learning mechanisms. His theories appear in 'Aptitude Testing' (1928), 'Principles of Behavior' (1943), and 'A Behavior System' (1952)

Hull, Cordell (1871–1955), American statesman, U.S. secretary of state (1933–44). At the Moscow conference (1943) he established the system of collective security which led to the foundation of the Nobel Peace Prize (1945)

Hull, Isaac (1773–1843), U.S. navy commodore. As commander (1810–12) of the 'Constitution', he defeated (1812) the British frigate 'Guerrière' (*CONSTITUTION)

Hull (officially Kingston-upon-Hull) a county borough (pop. 269,100) in the East Riding of Yorkshire, England, on the Humber, a major port. Industries: textiles, chemicals, iron and steel, food processing. University (1954)

hull (hʌl) **1.** *n.* the body framework of a ship ‖ the framework of an airship ‖ the float of a flying boat **2.** *v.t.* to hit or pierce the hull of (a ship), e.g. with a torpedo [perh. HULL (pod, shell etc.)]

hull **1.** *n.* the pod, shell etc. of a seed or fruit ‖ the calyx of some fruits, e.g. the strawberry **2.** *v.t.* to remove the hull or hulls from [O.E. *hulu*]

hul·la·ba·loo, hul·la·bal·loo (hʌ́ləbəlu:) *n.* loud, confused noise [imit.]

hull down (of a ship) so far away that only the masts, funnel etc. are visible over the horizon

Hul·ly Gul·ly (hʌ́li: gʌ́li:) *n.* fad dance executed to instructions from a caller with dancers in a line behind the caller

Hulme (hju:m), Thomas Ernest (1883–1917), English critic and poet, and one of the founders of Imagism. His book 'Speculations' was published in 1924

hum (hʌm) **1.** *v. pres. part.* **hum·ming** *past* and *past part.* **hummed** *v.i.* to make a continuous sound in the throat, with the mouth closed ‖ (of bees, moving machine parts etc.) to make a similar sound ‖ (*Br., pop.*) to smell unpleasantly ‖ *v.t.* to sing (a song, tune etc.) by humming **to make things hum** to be very active and make others work too **to hum and haw** (*Br.*) to talk with frequent slight pauses which express doubt or irresolution, or to make petty criticisms **2.** *n.* the sound or act of humming ‖ (*Br., pop.*) an unpleasant smell [M.E. *humme*, imit.]

hu·man (hjú:mən) **1.** *adj.* of or characteristic of man ‖ being a person ‖ of people as limited creatures, *human failings* ‖ resembling man **2.** *n.* (*pop.*) a person [M.E. *humayn, humayne, humain, humaine* fr. F.]

human diploid cell vaccine (*med.*) antirabies treatment, involving five injections vs. 21 injections previously required

hu·mane (hju:méin) *adj.* showing kindness, consideration etc. to persons or animals ‖ of or relating to the humanities, *humane studies* [earlier spelling of HUMAN separated after 1700]

human engineering (*genetics*) science of changing human genetic makeup by gene splicing and manipulation, e.g., to eliminate certain hereditary diseases. *also* genetic engineering

human geography *GEOGRAPHY

human growth hormone (*med.*) synthetic somatotropin (pituitary hormone) used to stimulate linear growth, created in 1979 by Dr. Chow Hao Li and Dr. Donald Yamashiro. *abbr.* HGH. *also* growth hormone

hu·man·ism (hjú:mənizəm) *n.* a movement of the 15th and 16th cc. which aspired to restore the universally human values of classical antiquity as opposed to the debased scholasticism of the late Middle Ages, by reviving the languages, philosophy and literature of ancient Greece and Rome ‖ any of several movements purporting to advocate the universally human as against utilitarian science, religious dogma, uncontrolled passion (e.g. Romanticism), political strivings etc.

hu·man·ist (hjú:mənist) **1.** *n.* an adherent of humanism **2.** *adj.* of or pertaining to humanism **hu·man·ís·tic** *adj.* [fr. F. *humaniste*]

humanistic medicine (*med.*) medical practice and culture that respects and incorporates the concepts that (1) the patient is more than his or her disease, and (2) the professional is more than a scientifically trained mind using technical skills

hu·man·i·tar·i·an (hju:mænitéəri:ən) **1.** *n.* someone who actively promotes the welfare of the human race **2.** *adj.* being or characteristic of a humanitarian **hu·man·i·tár·i·an·ism** *n.* [HUMANITY]

hu·man·i·ty (hju:mǽniti:) *pl.* **hu·man·i·ties** *n.* (*collect.*) mankind ‖ kindness to other people, or to animals ‖ (*pl.*, usually with 'the') studies (history, art, literature, classics etc.) emphasizing the cultural aspects of civilization [F. *humanité*]

hu·man·i·za·tion (hju:mənizéiʃən) *n.* a humanizing or being humanized

hu·man·ize (hjú:mənaiz) *pres. part.* **hu·man·iz·ing** *past* and *past part.* **hu·man·ized** *v.t.* to impart desirable human qualities, or interest, to ‖ to make (someone) have more of the affective qualities of a normal human being [fr. F. *humaniser*]

hu·man·kind (hjú:mənkaind, hjú:mənkáind) *n.* mankind

hu·man·ly (hjú:mənli:) *adv.* within the limitations of what man or a man can do, *we will finish it if it is humanly possible* ‖ in a way that is characteristic of normal human beings

human nature the inherent character of mankind

human potential movement (*psych.*) program to improve individual self-respect and human relationships through sensitivity training sessions

Human Rights program enunciated at Helsinki: "the right to be free from governmental violations of the integrity of the person. . . ."; "the right to the fulfillment of such vital needs as food, shelter, health care, and education. . . ."; and "the right to enjoy civil and political liberties. . . ."; released January 1978 by U.S. State Department and urged on all nations. *HELSINKI AGREEMENT

Hum·ber (hʌ́mbər) an estuary (1–8 miles wide, 40 miles long) between Yorkshire and Lincolnshire, England, navigable by large ships to Hull

hum·ble (hʌmb'l) **1.** *comp.* **hum·bler** *superl.* **hum·blest** *adj.* possessing or marked by the virtue of humility ‖ of little worth, of lowly condition or rank, *a humble dwelling, humble origins* **2.** *v.t. pres. part.* **hum·bling** *past* and *past part.* **hum·bled** to cause to feel humble to

CONCISE PRONUNCIATION KEY: (a) æ, c*a*t; ɑ, c*a*r; ɔ f*aw*n; ei, sn*a*ke. (e) e, h*e*n; i:, sh*ee*p; iə, d*ee*r; ɛə, b*ea*r. (i) i, f*i*sh; ai, t*i*ger; ə:, b*i*rd. (o) o, *o*x; au, c*ow*; ou, g*oa*t; u, p*oo*r; ɔi, r*oy*al. (u) ʌ, d*u*ck; u, b*u*ll; u:, g*oo*se; ə, b*a*cill*u*s; ju:, c*u*be. x, lo*ch*; θ, *th*ink; ð, bo*th*er; z, *Z*en; ʒ, corsa*g*e; dʒ, sava*g*e; ŋ, orangutan*g*; j, *y*ak; ʃ, *f*ish; tʃ, fe*tch*; 'l, rabb*le*; 'n, redd*en*. Complete pronunciation key appears inside front cover.

humble oneself to perform an act of submission by way of apology or penitence [M.E. *umble*, *humble* fr. O.F.]

hum·ble-bee (hámb'lbi:) *n.* a bumblebee [origin unkown]

humble pie (only in the phrase) **to eat humble pie** to make an unqualified, abject apology

hum·bly (hámbli:) *adv.* in a humble way

Hum·boldt (húmbolt, hámboult), Baron Alexander von (1769–1859), German explorer and scientist. 'Voyage aux régions équinoxiales du nouveau continent' (1807–39) contains his scientific observations made on an expedition to Central and South America. 'Kosmos' (1845–62) is a physical description of the universe and a history of science

Humboldt, Baron Wilhelm von (1767–1835), German statesman and philologist. As privy councilor (1809), he reformed Prussia's educational system

Humboldt the largest glacier in the world (its front is 60 miles long), in N.W. Greenland

Humboldt Current a marine current flowing northward along the coast of N. Chile and Peru. Its relatively cold waters lower air temperatures and produce much cloud and fog

hum·bug (hámbʌg) 1. *n.* the hiding of falsehood under an appearance of sincerity || insincere talk or writing || a person behaving insincerely || *Br.*) a hard, boiled peppermint candy 2. *v. pres. part.* **hum·bug·ging** *past and past part.* **hum·bugged** *v.t.* to mislead (someone) by a sham || *v.i.* to be a humbug [origin unknown]

hum·drum (hámdrʌm) *adj.* uninspired, flat, *a humdrum speech* [etym. doubtful, perh. fr. HUM]

Hume (hju:m), David (1711–76), Scottish philosopher and historian. He developed Locke's empiricism to the logical conclusion of utter skepticism, and argued that all ideas come from impressions, of which causality was one. His works include 'Philosophical Essays Concerning Human Understanding' (1748), 'An Enquiry Concerning the Principles of Morals' (1751), 'Political Discourses' (1752), and 'History of England' (1754–62)

hu·mer·al (hjú:mərəl) 1. *n.* a priest's vestment, an oblong scarf worn over the shoulders 2. *adj.* of or pertaining to the humerus || of or pertaining to the shoulders [fr. L.L. ult. fr. L. *humerus*, shoulder]

humeral veil a humeral

hu·mer·us (hjú:mərəs) *pl.* **hu·mer·i** (hjú:mərai) *n.* the long bone of the upper arm, articulating with the scapula above, and with the radius and the ulna below || the corresponding bone in the foreleg of a quadruped [L.=shoulder]

hu·mic (hjú:mik) *adj.* of or obtained from humus [fr. L. *humus*, earth]

hu·mid (hjú:mid) *adj.* (of atmosphere) containing a high percentage of water vapor || damp, moist **hu·mid·i·fy** (hju:mídifai) *pres. part.* **hu·mid·i·fy·ing** *past and past part.* **hu·mid·i·fied** *v.t.* to make humid [F.]

hu·mid·i·fi·er (hju:mídifaiər) *n.* a device for humidifying a room or building

hu·mid·i·ty (hju:míditi:) *n.* the state of being humid (*ABSOLUTE HUMIDITY, *RELATIVE HUMIDITY) [fr. F. humidité fr. L.]

hu·mi·dor (hjú:midɔr) *n.* a container for keeping cigars moist and fresh

hu·mil·i·ate (hju:míli:eit) *pres. part.* **hu·mil·i·at·ing** *past and past part.* **hu·mil·i·at·ed** *v.t.* to make (a person) suffer by lessening his dignity or self-esteem [fr. L. humiliare (humiliatus)]

hu·mil·i·a·tion (hju:mili:éiʃən) *n.* a humiliating or being humiliated || an instance of this [F.]

hu·mil·i·ty (hju:míliti:) *n.* the quality of being without pride || voluntary self-abasement, *to practice humility* [F. humilité]

hum·ming (hámiŋ) *adj.* making the sound of a hum || very active, *business is humming*

hum·ming·bird (hámiŋbə:rd) *n.* a member of *Trochilidae*, a family of minute and beautiful birds, found in the Americas. The rapid vibration of their wings produces a humming sound and allows them to feed, on insects and nectar, while on the wing

hum·mock (hámək) *n.* a mound || (*geol.*) a raised portion in an ice field formed by lateral pressure || a raised, dry, wooded spot in a swamp **hum·mock·y** *adj.* [origin unknown]

hu·mor, *Br.* **hu·mour** (hjú:mər) 1. *n.* something which arouses amusement, laughter etc. || the capacity for recognizing, reacting to, or expressing something which is amusing, funny etc. || a mood, frame of mind, *in a good humor, in no humor to be contradicted* || (*hist.*) one of four

---

body fluids supposed to determine temperament and health **out of humor** cross 2. *v.t.* to let (someone) have his own way for the sake of peace and quiet || to keep (someone) in a good temper [A.F. *humour, umour*, O.F. *humor, umor*]

hu·mor·esque (hju:mərésk) *n.* (*mus.*, esp. of certain 19th-c. music) a caprice [fr. G. *humoreske* fr. L. *humor, humor*]

hu·mor·ist (hjú:mərist) *n.* someone who expresses humor in his writing, conversation etc. **hu·mor·is·tic** *adj.* [F. *humoriste* fr. L.L. fr. L.]

hu·mor·ous (hjú:mərəs) *adj.* having, or giving rise to, humor

humour *HUMOR

hump (hámp) 1. *n.* a rounded, raised protrusion **to get** (or **give**) **the hump** (*Br., pop.*) to become (or make) irritated 2. *v.t.* to make (something) hump-shaped, *to hump one's back* || (*Br., pop.*) to carry, *you'll have to hump your suitcase* [origin unknown]

hump·back (hámpbæk) *n.* a person whose spine is so misshapen that his back is humped || such a back **húmp·backed** *adj.* having such a back || having such a shape, *a humpbacked bridge*

humpback whale a member of *Megaptera*, fam. *Balaenopteridae*, a genus of whalebone whales having a small hump on the back

Hum·per·dinck (húmpərdiŋk), Engelbert (1854–1921), German composer. He is known esp. for his operas, esp. 'Hansel and Gretel' (1893)

Humphrey (hámfri:), Hubert Horatio, Jr. (1911–78), U.S. political leader, vice president (1965–9). A Democratic senator from Minnesota (1949–64; 1971–8), he championed labor and civil rights. Vice-president under Pres. Lyndon B. Johnson, he ran for the presidency in 1968, but was defeated by Richard M. Nixon

hu·mus (hjú:məs) *n.* the organic part of soil, formed by the partial decomposition of vegetable or animal matter [L.]

Hun (hʌn) *n.* a member of a nomadic Asian people who invaded Europe (4th and 5th cc.), forcing the Visigoths and Ostrogoths to invade the Roman Empire. Under Attila they controlled most of what is now Germany, Poland and European Russia. They invaded the Byzantine Empire and the Western Roman Empire (early 5th c.) [fr. M.L. *Hunni* prob. fr. *Hun-yü*, a Turkic tribe]

Hu·nan (hú:nán) a mountainous province (area 105,467 sq. miles, pop. 49,000,000) of S.E. China. Capital: Changsha

hunch (hántʃ) 1. *n.* a hump on a person's back or a rounding of the shoulders || a large hunk or piece || (*pop.*) an intuitive feeling about a situation or a coming event 2. *v.t.* to bend into a hump || (with 'up' or 'out') to cause to form a hump [etym. doubtful]

hunch·back (hántʃbæk) *n.* a humpback **hunch·backed** *adj.* humpbacked

hun·dred (hándrid) 1. *pl.* **hun·dred, hun·dreds** *n.* ten times ten (*NUMBER TABLE) || the cardinal number representing this (100, C) || (*pl.*) in mathematical calculations, the column of figures three places to the left of the decimal point || (*Br. hist.*) a subdivision of a county with its own court. The term survives in certain conventional usages || (*Am.*, esp. *hist.*) a similar division of a county, retained only in Delaware **hun·dreds of** very many **ninety-nine times out of a hundred** nearly always 2. *adj.* being ten more than 90 [O.E.]

Hundred Days (*F. hist.*) the period of Napoleonic rule after Napoleon's return to Paris (Mar. 20, 1815) from Elba. It ended with Louis XVIII's restoration (June 28, 1815) after Waterloo

Hundred Days of 1933 a U.S. Congressional session (March–June, 1933) inaugurating President Franklin Roosevelt's New Deal. It enacted intensified programs of relief, recovery, and reform to counteract immediately the effects of the depression

hundreds and thousands (*Br.*) nonpareil (pellets of sugar)

hun·dredth (hándridθ, hándritθ) 1. *adj.* being number 100 in a series (*NUMBER TABLE) || being one of the 100 equal parts of anything 2. *n.* the person or thing next after the 99th || one of 100 equal parts of anything (1/100)

hun·dred·weight (hándridweit) *pl.* **hun·dred·weight, hun·dred·weights** *n.* (*abbr.* cwt.) a measure of weight equal to (*Am.*) 100 lbs avoirdupois or (*Br.*) 112 lbs

---

Hundred Years' War a period of intermittent war (1337–1453) between France and England. It was basically caused by the refusal of the Plantagenet kings of England to do homage to the kings of France for the fief of Aquitaine. Other causes were Anglo-French rivalry for the Flanders wool trade, and a growing sense of national consciousness. The war began (1337) when Edward III of England claimed the French throne. The English won victories at Sluis (1340), Crécy (1346) and Poitiers (1356), and gained more French territory, though most of it was lost again by 1373. Henry V renewed the war (1415), won a crushing victory at Agincourt (1415) and was recognized as heir to the French throne (Treaty of Troyes, 1420). After his death (1422), Joan of Arc rallied the French, and the English were gradually expelled (1423–53) from France, until only Calais remained in their possession

hung *past and alt. past part.* of HANG (*v.i.*, to be suspended)

Hun·gar·i·an (hʌŋgéəri:ən) 1. *adj.* of or pertaining to Hungary or its people 2. *n.* a native of Hungary || the Hungarian language

Hungarian language the Finno-Ugric language of Hungary spoken by about 10,750,000 people including Rumanian, Czechoslovakian and Yugoslav minorities. It has borrowed considerably from Latin, Slavic, German, Bulgarian and Turkish. Hungarian has a well-developed case system and is characterized by an abundant use of suffixes

Hun·ga·ry (hángəri:) a republic (area 35,912 sq. miles, pop. 10,645,000) of central Europe. Capital: Budapest. Language: Hungarian (96%), with a small German minority. People: 93% Magyar, 5% German, with Slovak, Croat and other small minorities. Religion: 62% Roman Catholic, 25% Protestant, 3% Orthodox, 1% Jewish. The Danube bisects the country. East of it a large plain, the Nägy Alföld, itself bisected by the Tisza, stretches beyond the Rumanian border. Hills (rising to 3,336 ft) break it in the far north, where floods are frequent. West of the Danube lies Transnubia, a rolling plain, in the south broken by hills rising to 2,648 ft near Pécs, with Lake Balaton and the Bakony Forest (2,333 ft) in the center. The land is 60% arable, 12% forest and 17% pasture. Climate: continental. Average rainfall: under 20 ins in the Tisza Valley, 20–30 ins in the plains, over 30 ins in the mountains. Livestock: cattle, sheep, hogs, horses. Agricultural products: corn, wheat, barley, sugar beet, potatoes, eggs, milk, wool, wine. Resources: coal (esp. near Pécs), bauxite, oil, hydroelectricity. Industries: fishing, mining, steel, cement, fertilizers, textiles, sugar. Exports: wheat, cattle, metal products, clothing, footwear. Imports: lumber, hides, paper, cotton, machinery. There are four universities. Monetary unit: forint (100 filler). HISTORY. Magyar tribes from the Urals conquered what is now Hungary (late 9th c.). The country was Christianized and unified under St Stephen, the first Hungarian king (1001–38). After a troubled period during which foreign rulers struggled for the Hungarian crown, the country fell to the Turks (Battle of Mohacs, 1526). By 1699, the Turks had been expelled, and the Hapsburgs gained control. Protestantism was repressed and estates confiscated. A series of rebellions followed, until a general amnesty was proclaimed (1687). Hungary became an integral part of the Hapsburg dominions (1722) and was largely ruled from Vienna. A revolutionary movement (1848) under Kossuth and Deak won a measure of self-government and the liberation of the peasants: but the revolution was crushed (1849) by Austrian and Russian forces, and an absolutist régime was imposed. Hungary gained complete internal independence with the establishment (1867) of the dual monarchy of Austria-Hungary. An independent republic was proclaimed (1918) but, after Bela Kun's brief communist rule (1919), Hungary was made a constitutional monarchy (1920) under the regency of Horthy. In an attempt to solve the problem of minorities, Hungary was reduced to the area inhabited by Magyars, involving the loss of over half its territory and population. After occupation by the Germans (1944) and the Russians (1945), a republican constitution was adopted (1946). The Communist party gained full control (1948) and Hungary was declared a republic (1949). A revolution (1956) was crushed by Soviet armed force and a new régime set up under Kádár who con-

---

CONCISE PRONUNCIATION KEY: **(a)** æ, c*a*t; ɑ, c*a*r; ɔ f*aw*n; ei, sn*a*ke. **(e)** e, h*e*n; i:, sh*ee*p; iə, d*ee*r; ɛə, b*ea*r. **(i)** i, f*i*sh; ai, t*i*ger; ə:, b*i*rd. **(o)** o, *o*x; au, c*ow*; ou, g*o*at; u, p*oo*r; ɔi, r*oy*al. **(u)** ʌ, d*u*ck; u, b*u*ll; u:, g*oo*se; ə, b*a*cillus; ju:, c*u*be. x, lo*ch*; θ, *th*ink; ð, bo*th*er; z, *Z*en; ʒ, cor*sa*ge; dʒ, sava*g*e; ŋ, orangutan*g*; j, *y*ak; ʃ, *fi*sh; tʃ, fe*tch*; 'l, rabb*le*; 'n, redd*en*. Complete pronunciation key appears inside front cover.

tinues to rule. Under Kádár economic and political conditions improved

hun·ger (hángər) **1.** *n.* a desire or craving for food ‖ a strong desire for anything, *hunger for adventure* ‖ a condition of physical weakness and distress suffered as the result of a long period of undernourishment **2.** *v.i.* to feel hunger for food or other objects of desire, *to hunger for affection* [O.E. *hungor, hungur*]

hunger strike a refusal to eat by prisoners, political groups etc. trying to force an authority to yield to certain demands

Hung Hsiu-ch'üan (húnʃjú:tʃyán) (1812–64), Chinese Christian mystic and leader of the Taiping Rebellion

hun·gri·ly (hángrili:) *adv.* in a hungry manner

hun·gri·ness (hángri:nis) *n.* the condition of being hungry

hun·gry (hángri:) *comp.* **hun·gri·er** *superl.* **hun·gri·est** *adj.* feeling hunger ‖ characterized by or showing hunger ‖ having a strong desire for, *hungry for news* ‖ (of land or soil) poor, lacking humus or other essentials for plant growth **to go hungry** to go without eating [O.E. *hungrig, hungreg*]

hung up *adj.* being extremely involved with an emotional problem

hunk (hʌŋk) *n.* a large, thick piece of something, *a hunk of bread* [perh. fr. Flem. *hunke*]

hun·kers (hánkərz) *pl. n.* (only in the phrase) **on one's hunkers** on one's haunches [origin unknown]

Hun·kers and Barn·burn·ers (hánkərz, bárnbə:rnərz) two factions of the New York State Democratic party during the 1840s. The conservative Hunkers ('those who seek office for themselves'), led by William L. Marcy, advocated the use of revenues for internal improvements, the chartering of state banks, and the perpetuation of slavery. The radical Barnburners ('farmers who burn their barns to destroy rats'), led by Martin Van Buren, advocated the abolition of slavery and the use of revenues to pay off the state debt. When the slavery issue prompted the Barnburners to join (1848) the Free-Soil Party, it weakened the support for New York's Democratic presidential candidate, and this helped to elect General Zachary Taylor

Hunt (hʌnt), Leigh (James Henry Leigh Hunt, 1784–1859), English poet, critic and journalist and friend of many writers (e.g. Shelley, Keats). His works include 'Autobiography' (1850)

Hunt, Richard Morris (1828–95), U.S. architect. He introduced 19th-c. French traditions into American architecture. His designs include the Vanderbilt mausoleum on Staten Island

Hunt, William Holman (1827–1910), English painter and one of the founders of the Pre-Raphaelite Brotherhood

hunt (hʌnt) **1.** *v.t.* to pursue (game, a person) with the intention of capturing or killing ‖ to pursue (a fox etc.) on horseback with hounds ‖ to cover (an area) in search of game ‖ to use (a horse, hounds) for hunting ‖ to attempt to find by careful and thorough searching ‖ *v.i.* to participate in a hunt ‖ to search ‖ (*campanology*) to alter the order in which a bell is rung so as to shift it 'up' by successive changes from first place to last or 'down' from last place to first ‖ (of machinery, engines etc.) to oscillate about a given mean point or speed as a result of inadequate stability control **to hunt after** (or **for**) to try to discover **to hunt down** to continue to hunt until the capture or kill is effected ‖ to search diligently for until successful **to hunt out** to succeed in finding by searching **to hunt up** to look for (a particular thing among many) **2.** *n.* the act of hunting or an instance of this ‖ the persons engaged in hunting ‖ the district hunted over ‖ (*campanology*) a change rung on from five to 12 bells **hunt·er** *n.* someone who hunts, esp. for game ‖ a horse bred and trained to be ridden for hunting ‖ a dog trained for use in hunting ‖ a watch provided with a hunting case [O.E. *huntian*]

Hun·ter (hántər), Robert Mercer Taliaferro (1809–87), U.S. politician who unsuccessfully campaigned to settle Northern and Southern differences on the eve of the Civil War. He served (1865) as a Confederate commissioner at the unsuccessful Hampton Roads Conference, and he helped to restore Virginia to the Union

hunter's moon the next full moon after the harvest moon

hunt·ing (hántiŋ) *n.* **1.** (*eng.*) the variation from the standard speed in a rotating mechanism because of malfunction of the control system. **2.** (*aerodynamics*) an approximately constant oscillation in the flight of an aircraft

hunting box (*Br.*) a small country lodge used as a residence during the hunting season

hunting case a watch case with a hinged cover to protect the glass

Hun·ting·don (hántiŋdən), Selina Hastings, countess of (1707–91), English Methodist leader and patroness of Whitefield. Her Calvinistic Methodist sect was known as the 'Countess of Huntingdon's Connexion'. Most of the churches are now affiliated to the Congregational Church

Hun·ting·don·shire (hántiŋdənʃər) (*abbr.* **Hunts.**) a county (area 366 sq. miles, pop. 80,000) of central England. County town: Huntingdon

Hun·ting·ton (hántiŋtən) the largest city (pop. 63,684) in West Virginia, in the western part of the state: tobacco and agricultural market (mainly apples), rail terminal, coal-mining center. Manufactures: steel rails, nickel alloys, stoves, glass, shoes

Huntington's chorea (kəri:ə) *n.*, hereditary disease affecting the brain. Symptoms, usually dormant until ages 35–45, are irregular body movements, slurred speech, and deteriorating mental faculties. There is no treatment, but scientists have isolated a factor for determining presence of the gene that causes the disorder

hunt·ress (hántris) *n.* (*rhet.*) a female hunter, esp. as an epithet of Diana

Hunts·man (hántsmən), Benjamin (1704–76), British inventor and steel manufacturer. He devised (c. 1750) the crucible process for making high-quality cast steel

hunts·man (hántsmən) *pl.* **hunts·men** (hántsmən) *n.* a hunter, esp. an official of an organized hunt who helps to control the hounds

Hu·nya·di (húnjɒdi:), János (c. 1387–1456), Hungarian soldier and statesman. His victory at Belgrade (1456) staved off the Turkish conquest of Hungary for 70 years. His son, Matthias Corvinus, became king of Hungary

Hu·pa (hú:pə) *pl.* **Hu·pa, Hu·pas** *n.* an Athapaskan people of N.W. California ‖ a member of this people ‖ their language

Hu·pei, Hu·peh (hú:péi) a province (area 80,169 sq. miles, pop. 47,800,000) of S. central China, containing the Yangtze-Han basin. Capital: Wuhan

hur·dle (hé:rd'l) **1.** *n.* a movable, short section of a fence of light construction used as part of an enclosure, as a gate etc., or as an obstacle to be jumped over by horses ‖ an open frame to be cleared by athletes in a race ‖ (*pl.*) such a race ‖ an obstacle to a course of action **2.** *v. pres. part.* **hur·dling** *past and past part.* **hur·dled** *v.i.* to compete in a hurdles race ‖ *v.t.* to surround with hurdles ‖ to jump (a hurdle) **hur·dler** *n.* someone who competes in a hurdles race [O.E. *hyrdel*]

hurds (hə:rdz) *pl. n.* hards

hur·dy-gur·dy (hé:rdi:gé:rdi:) *pl.* **hur·dy-gur·dies** *n.* a musical instrument equipped with a rosined wheel which when turned plays the strings. A set of keys controls the pitch ‖ a barrel organ [prob. imit.]

hurl (hə:rl) **1.** *v.t.* to throw violently ‖ to utter (threats, abuse etc.) with vehemence **2.** *n.* the act of hurling or an instance of this [etym. doubtful]

Hur·ley (hé:rli:), Patrick Jay (1883–1963), U.S. diplomat and secretary of war (1929–33) under Herbert Hoover. During the 2nd world war he served as General George Marshall's representative and attempted to provide relief for U.S. troops on Bataan. He was (1944–5) U.S. ambassador to China, and tried to reconcile the Kuomintang government and the Communist faction

hurl·ey, hurl·y (hé:rli:) *pl.* **hurl·eys, hurl·ies** *n.* hurling ‖ a stick with a wide blade used in this game [HURL]

hurl·ing (hé:rliŋ) *n.* an old Irish game resembling hockey, played by two teams of 15 players who use a hurley to carry or hit the ball [HURL]

hurly *HURLEY

hurl·y-burl·y (hé:rli:bé:rli:) *n.* rush and confusion, usually noisy [imit.]

Huron the second largest lake (area 23,010 sq. miles) of the Great Lakes of the U.S.A. and Canada, bordering Michigan and Ontario, between Lakes Superior and Erie (*ST LAWRENCE SEAWAY)

Hu·ron (hjúərən, hjúərɒn) *pl.* **Hu·ron, Hu·rons** *n.* a member of a confederation of North American Indian tribes which occupied the territory between Lakes Huron, Erie and Ontario ‖ this tribe ‖ their Iroquoian language

hur·rah, hoo·rah (hərá) **1.** *interj.* used to express triumph, appreciation etc. **2.** *n.* this cry

hur·ray, hoo·ray (həréi) *interj.* and *n.* hurrah

hur·ri·cane (hé:rikein, hárikein, *Br.* hárikən) *n.* a cyclone with wind velocities exceeding 73 and often reaching over 100 miles per hour, usually covering a large area and accompanied by thunder, lightning and heavy rain, occurring esp. in the West Indies and Gulf of Mexico [Span. *huracan* fr. Carib.]

hurricane lamp a lamp designed to keep burning in the wind, its flame being shielded by strong glass

hur·ried (hé:ri:d, hári:d) *adj.* done in a hurry ‖ done in such a hurry as to be jeopardized

hur·ry (hé:ri:, hári:) **1.** *n.* the performing of an action quickly and without delay ‖ the need to act in this way, *is there any hurry for the work?* ‖ excessive haste **in a hurry** quickly ‖ soon, *they won't invite us again in a hurry* ‖ wishing to act without delay, *in a hurry to begin* **2.** *v. pres. part.* **hur·ry·ing** *past and past part.* **hur·ried** *v.i.* (often with 'up') to be quick, waste no time ‖ *v.t.* (often with 'up' or 'along') to make (someone or something) act, move etc. more quickly ‖ to do quickly or too quickly **to hurry off** to go away quickly [etym. doubtful]

hur·ry-scur·ry (hé:ri:ské:ri:, hári:skári:) **1.** *n.* the doing of something very fast and in a confused manner **2.** *v.i. pres. part.* **hur·ry-scur·ry·ing** *past and past part.* **hur·ry-scur·ried** *v.i.* to act quickly and confusedly **3.** *adv.* in a quick and confused manner

hurt (hə:rt) *v. pres. part.* **hurt·ing** *past and past part.* **hurt** *v.t.* to cause bodily or mental pain to ‖ to do physical harm to, *the bad weather hurt his trade* ‖ to damage ‖ to lessen the well-being or status of, *to hurt one's reputation* ‖ *v.i.* to cause or feel pain, *my head hurts* [F. *hurter*]

hurt *n.* something which causes pain, *a hurt to one's pride* [prob. fr. O.F. *hurte*]

hurt·ful (hé:rtfəl) *adj.* causing harm, pain or injury

hur·tle (hé:rt'l) *v. pres. part.* **hur·tling** *past and past part.* **hur·tled** *v.i.* to move with great force and noise ‖ *v.t.* to make (something) move with great force and noise [M.E. *hurtlen*, prob. fr. *hurten*, to hurt]

Hus (hus), Jan (c. 1369–1415), Bohemian religious reformer, commonly called John Huss. Influenced by the teachings of Wyclif, he denounced ecclesiastical abuses and challenged the authority of Rome. He was excommunicated (1410), and accepted the safe-conduct of the Emperor Sigismund to attend the Council of Constance (1414), but at Constance he was summarily condemned and burned at the stake as a heretic

Husák (hu:sak), Gustav (1913–), Czechoslovakian president (1975–). He held regional government posts in Slovakia, was arrested as a 'Slovak nationalist' and was imprisoned (1951–60). In 1968 he was made deputy premier of Czechoslovakia and, after the Soviet invasion in 1968, he succeeded (1969) Alexander Dubcek as leader of his country's Communist party and became president in 1975

hus·band (házbənd) **1.** *n.* the male partner in a marriage (cf. WIFE) **2.** *v.t.* (*rhet.*) to take care of, use sparingly, *to husband one's strength* [O.E. *húsbonda, húsbunda, householder*]

hus·band·ry (házbəndri:) *n.* farming‖ (*rhet.*) management, esp. thrifty management

Hu·sein (huséin) (c. 626–80), Shi'ite imam, second son of Ali and Fatima

Hu·sein ib·n A·li (huséinibənáli:) (1856–1931), sherif of Mecca (1908–16), king of Hejaz (1916–24). He gained power by a successful revolt against the Turks, but was overthrown by ibn Saud

hush (hʌʃ) **1.** *v.i.* to stop making noise ‖ *v.t.* to cause (someone or something) to cease to make a noise **to hush up** to keep from being generally known **2.** *n.* a cessation of noise ‖ silence [M.E. *hussht* adj., silent]

hush-hush (hʌʃhʌʃ) *adj.* very secret

hush money money paid to prevent someone from telling something

husk (hʌsk) **1.** *n.* a dry, outer covering of some seeds and fruits, e.g. corn ‖ (*fig.*) the worthless part of something after the useful or valuable part has been removed **2.** *v.t.* to remove the husk from [M.E. *huske,* possibly fr. O.E. *hūs,* house]

husk·i·ly (hΛskili:) *adv.* in a husky manner

husk·i·ness (hΛski:nis) *n.* the quality of being husky

husk·ing (hΛskiŋ) *n.* a husking bee

husking bee a get-together on a farm for husking corn

Hus·kis·son (hΛskis'n), William (1770–1830), British Tory statesman. As president of the board of trade (1823–7), he abolished many protectionist duties and worked out a sliding scale to modify the Corn Laws

husk·y (hΛski:) *pl.* **hus·kies** *n.* an Eskimo dog [perh. corrup. of ESKIMO]

husk·y *comp.* **husk·i·er** *superl.* **husk·i·est** *adj.* full of husks ‖ husklike ‖ (of speech, or a voice) having a dry, rough sound of lower pitch than normal ‖ tough, strong and heavily built, *a husky boy* [HUSK]

Huss *HUS

hus·sar (huzár) *n.* (*mil.*) a soldier of a light cavalry regiment [Hung. *huszar,* freebooter, light horseman]

Hus·sein (huséin) (1935–   ), king of Jordan (1952–   )

Hus·serl (húserl), Edmund Gustav Albrecht (1859–1938), German philosopher who formulated the doctrine of transcendental phenomenology. He postulated the being of the world as direct personal observation transcendentally constituted by a perceiver. This immediate perception he termed 'the phenomenological reduction', the permanent and only opening to true philosophy. Man with his sensibly perceived body, including the image he sees of himself when reflecting on his past actions or future projects, is not the subject, but an object constituted by the 'I myself' (ich selbst), the pure transcendental subject. Husserl has greatly influenced Sartre, Heidegger and Merleau-Ponty. His central work is 'Ideas: central Introduction to a Pure Phenomenology' (trans. 1913)

Huss·ite (hΛsait) *n.* a follower of Jan Hus. The Hussites fought a series of intermittent wars (1419–78) in Bohemia and Moravia. Their original aim was to prevent the Emperor Sigismund from succeeding to the Bohemian throne. The wars were partially resolved by the Council of Basle, when the moderate Hussites were accepted back into the Church, but they continued as a civil struggle between other Hussite groups

hus·sy (hΛsi:, hΛzi:) *pl.* **hus·sies** *n.* (*old-fash.*) a saucy girl ‖ (*old-fash.*) a shamelessly immoral woman [corrup. of HOUSEWIFE]

hus·tings (hΛstiŋz) *pl. n.* the proceedings of an election ‖ a platform from which election speeches are made ‖ (*Br. hist.*) a platform on which parliamentary candidates were nominated prior to 1872 ‖ an ancient court of the City of London [O.E. *hŭsting* fr. O.N. *hŭs-thing,* house assembly]

hus·tle (hΛs'l) **1.** *v. pres. part.* **hus·tling** *past* and *past part.* **hus·tled** *v.t.* to shove, jostle rudely ‖ to push quickly forward, off, out etc., *they hustled him off the platform* ‖ to force (someone) to act quickly, *we were hustled into agreeing* ‖ *v.i.* to push one's way quickly ‖ to act, or appear to act, quickly and forcefully, esp. in getting things done **2.** *n.* (*pop.*) a hurry, *in a great hustle*
hús·tler *n.* (*pop.*) an energetic, bustling person [fr. Du. *husselen, hutselen,* to shake]

Hustler 500 *AMERICAN HUSTLER

hut (hΛt) *n.* a small, roughly-built single-story and usually one-room building used as a dwelling, office or shelter [F. *hutte* fr. Gmc]

hutch (hΛtʃ) *n.* a box, usually with one side made of slats or wire netting, used to house small animals, e.g. rabbits ‖ (*mining*) a truck for hoisting coal out of a pit ‖ (*mining*) a trough for washing ore ‖ a low cupboard topped by racks for china [M.E. *huche, hucche* fr. F. *huche,* a chest]

Hutch·ins (hΛtʃinz), Robert Maynard (1899–1977) U.S. reform educator. His lectures, including 'Education for Freedom' (1943), 'The Conflict in Education' (1953) and 'University of Utopia' (1953), opposed overspecialized, pragmatic education and advocated nonconformity and protest as a means of improving society

Hutch·in·son (hΛtʃinsən), Anne (c. 1591–1643), Colonial religious enthusiast. She led the 'Antinomians', a religious faction that attacked the authority of the Massachusetts clergy. After

banishment (1638) from the colony, she and her followers helped to found Rhode Island

Hutchinson, Thomas (1711–80), Colonial legislator, jurist, and royal governor (1771–4) of the province of Massachusetts. Although he removed British troops during the Boston Massacre (1770), on the eve of the Revolution he felt impelled to enforce ministerial measures which alienated the patriots

hut·ment (hΛtmənt) *n.* (esp. *mil.*) a collection of huts, often temporary

hut·ted (hΛtid) *adj.* lodged in or consisting of huts, *a hutted camp*

Hut·ten (hút'n), Ulrich von (1488–1523), German humanist, poet and satirist. He wrote virulent attacks on princes and the Roman Catholic Church, and supported Luther

hutzpah or **hulzpah** *CHUTZPAH

Hux·ley (hΛksli:), Aldous Leonard (1894–1963), English novelist and essayist, grandson of T. H. Huxley and brother of Sir Julian. His 'Brave New World' (1932) describes a science-controlled civilization of the future

Huxley, Sir Julian Sorell (1887–1975), British biologist, grandson of T. H. Huxley and brother of Aldous. He was the first director general of UNESCO (1946–8). Among his published works are 'Essays of a Biologist' (1923), 'Evolution, the Modern Synthesis' (1942) and 'Evolution in Action' (1952)

Huxley, Thomas Henry (1825–95), British biologist. He was a leading exponent of Darwin's theory of evolution. His works include 'Zoological Evidences as to Man's Place in Nature' (1863) and 'Science and Culture' (1881)

Huy·gens (háigənz), Christiaan (1629–95), Dutch physicist, mathematician and astronomer. He improved the telescope and discovered Saturn's rings ('Systema Saturnium', 1659). His work on the pendulum ('Horologium Oscillatorium', 1673) led to investigations on the acceleration due to gravity, the shape of the earth, centrifugal force and inertia. He formulated the wave theory of light, for which he had to hypothesize the existence of a medium, the ether ('Traité de la lumière', 1690)

Huys·mans (wi:smäs), Joris-Karl (1848–1907), French novelist, who passed from naturalism to Christian mysticism. His works, marked by an exceedingly rich vocabulary, include 'A Rebours' (1884) and 'La Cathédrale' (1898)

Hwai·nan, Huai·nan (hwáinán) a city (pop. 286,900) of N.W. Anhwei, China: coal mines

Hwai·ning (hwáiniŋ) *ANKING

hwan (hwɔn) *pl.* **hwan** *n.* the basic monetary unit of South Korea, divided into 100 won [Korean]

Hwang-hai (hwɔ́ŋhái) *YELLOW SEA

Hwang-ho (hwɔ́ŋhóu) (*Eng.* Yellow River) China's second largest river (2,700 miles long, draining 55,000 sq. miles). It rises at 14,000 ft in S.E. Tsinghai and after two huge bends, first north, then south, flows across the N. China plain into the Yellow Sea. Silt-laden (6 kg. per cubic meter), the yellow loess giving it its name, it deposits vast quantities of alluvium in its passage over the plain, raising the level of its bed and causing disastrous floods

hy·a·cinth (háiəsinθ) *n.* a member of *Hyacinth,* fam. Liliaceae, a genus of plants native to Asia Minor. They are widely cultivated from bulbs, esp. *H. orientalis,* for their highly scented, bell-shaped, racemose flowers ‖ (*mineral.*) a reddish or orange zircon used as a gem [fr. Gk *huakinthos*]

hyaena *HYENA

hy·a·lin (háiəlin) *n.* *HYALINE

hy·a·line 1. (háiəlin, háiəlain) *adj.* glasslike, glassy **2.** (háiəlin, háiəli:n) *n.* (also **hyalin**) a nitrogenous substance that is the main constituent of the walls of hydatid cysts [L.L. *hyalinus* fr. Gk *hualos,* glass]

hyaline membrane disease (*med.*) respiratory disease in the newborn caused by a glasslike film over lung lining, identified in 1975. *abbr.* **HMD**

hy·a·lite (háiəlait) *n.* (*mineral.*) a clear, glassy variety of opal [fr. Gk *hualos,* glass]

hy·al·o·gen (haiælədʒən, háiəloudʒen) *n.* (*biol.*) any of the insoluble substances found in animal tissues which are related to mucoids and hydrolyze to form hyalines [fr. Gk *hualos,* glass+*genes,* born of]

hy·al·o·plasm (haiǽləplæzəm) *n.* (*biol.*) the clear, relatively fluid ground substance of cytoplasm [fr. Gk *hualos,* glass+PLASM]

hy·brid (háibrid) **1.** *n.* (*biol.*) an offspring resulting from crossbreeding ‖ (*gram.*) a word com-

posed of elements from two or more languages **2.** *adj.* of or being a hybrid [fr. L. *hybrida,* offspring of a domestic sow and a wild boar]

hybrid computer (*computer*) an integrated device combining the memory and logic of a digital computer with the speed and flexibility of an analog computer

hy·brid·ism (háibridizəm) *n.* hybridity ‖ the production of hybrids

hy·brid·i·ty (haibríditi:) *n.* the state of being a hybrid

hy·brid·i·za·tion (háibridizéiʃən) *n.* a hybridizing or being hybridized

hy·brid·ize (háibridaiz) *pres. part.* **hy·brid·iz·ing** *past* and *past part.* **hy·brid·ized** *v.t.* and *i.* to crossbreed

hy·brid·o·mas (haibridóuməz) *n.* (*biol.*) cells used in genetic splicing to produce monoclonal antibodies from antibodies and tumor cells

hybrid perpetual any of various roses mainly derived by crossing the bourbon rose and characterized by a long flowering season

hy·da·tid (háidətid) *n.* a larval tapeworm typically filling a watery cyst ‖ this cyst ‖ the disease produced by such cysts [fr. Gk *hudatis (hudatidos),* a drop of water]

Hyde, Charles Cheney (1873–1952), U.S. international law expert. His treatise 'International Law Chiefly as Interpreted and Applied by the United States' (1922) contended that an international security organization, invested with full military authority, could secure world peace. He drafted (1923) for the U.S. Department of State a model treaty for commerce and navigation

Hyde, Edward *CLARENDON, EARL OF

Hy·der·a·bad (háidərəbæd, háidərəbad) a former principality (1724–1949) in central Deccan, central India, since 1956 mainly part of Andhra Pradesh ‖ a city (pop. 2,093,448) of this region, now capital of Andhra Pradesh: pottery, paper, textiles, antibiotics

Hyderabad the capital (pop. 795,000) of Sind, Pakistan, on the Indus, a rail center: silk weaving, gold and silver work, lacquerwork, pottery

Hy·der A·li (háidərali:) (c. 1722–82), ruler of Mysore (1766–82). He fought two wars (1767–9 and 1780–2) against the British in India

hy·der·gine (háidərdʒin) *n.* (*pharm.*) a drug taken sublingually to stimulate brain activity

Hy·dra (háidrə) a Greek island (area 21 sq. miles, pop. 3,000) in the Aegean, 4 miles off the coast of Argolis

hy·dra (háidrə) *n.* a member of *Hydra* or various other genera of small, freshwater hydrozoan polyps having a basal disk attaching it to a stone or plant. Its slender cylindrical body has threadlike stinging tentacles around the mouth as an aid to catching prey. It is nonmetagenetic and reproduction is typically by asexual budding, though sexual reproduction does occur ‖ (*Gk mythol.*) the manyheaded snake killed by Hercules (*HERACLES) [L. fr. Gk *hudra,* the snake killed by Hercules]

hy·dran·gea (haidréindʒə) *n.* a member of *Hydrangea,* fam. Saxifragaceae, a genus of plants whose showy blue, pink or white flowers are in large cymose corymbs. Most, or in cultivated varieties all, of the flowers are neuter [Mod. L. *Hydrangea* fr. Gk]

hy·drant (háidrənt) *n.* a pipe, fitted with tap and nozzle, by which water may be drawn from a supply main, e.g. for fire fighting, street cleaning etc. [fr. HYDRO-]

hy·dranth (háidrænθ) *n.* (*zool.*) a nutritive zooid in a hydroid colony [fr. HYDRA+Gk *anthos,* flower]

hy·drate (háidreit) **1.** *n.* a compound or other chemical species containing hydrogen and hydroxyl either in the proportion in which they form water or associated (e.g. by adsorption) with one or more molecules of water **2.** *v. pres. part.* **hy·drat·ing** *past* and *past part.* **hy·drat·ed** to cause or allow to form a hydrate (in either of the senses above) [fr. Gk *hudōr,* water]

hy·drau·lic (haidrɔ́lik, haidrɔ́lik) *adj.* of fluids, esp. water, in motion ‖ of the pressure exerted by water when conveyed through pipes ‖ of substances, machinery etc. affected by or operated by fluids in motion, *hydraulic brakes* **hy·dráu·li·cal·ly** *adv.* [fr. L. *hydraulicus* fr. Gk fr. *hudōr,* water+*aulos,* pipe]

hydraulic brake a brake utilizing the resistance of oil both to compression and to flow in a narrow tube

hydraulic cement a cement which sets hard under water

CONCISE PRONUNCIATION KEY: **(a)** æ, c*a*t; ɑ, c*a*r; ɔ f*aw*n; ei, sn*a*ke. **(e)** e, h*e*n; i:, sh*ee*p; iə, d*ee*r; ɛə, b*ea*r. **(i)** i, f*i*sh; ai, t*i*ger; ə:, b*i*rd. **(o)** o, *o*x; au, c*ow*; ou, g*oa*t; u, p*oo*r; ɔi, r*oy*al. **(u)** Λ, d*u*ck; u, b*u*ll; u:, g*oo*se; ə, b*a*cillus; ju:, c*u*be. x, lo*ch*; θ, *th*ink; ð, bo*th*er; z, *Z*en; ʒ, corsa*g*e; dʒ, sava*g*e; ŋ, oranguta*ng*; j, *y*ak; ʃ, *fi*sh; tʃ, fe*tch*; 'l, rabb*le*; 'n, redd*en.* Complete pronunciation key appears inside front cover.

hydraulic press a press in which application is made of the fact that fluid pressure is transmitted equally in all directions (Pascal's law), a force applied to a piston of small area being transmitted as pressure to a piston of large area, this therefore exerting a much greater force

hydraulic ram a pump for raising a smaller amount of water to a higher elevation or pressure by using the energy of a greater amount of falling water

hy·drau·lics (haidrɔ́liks, haidróliks) *n.* the science of controlling and using water pressure or the pressure of other fluids ‖ the application of hydrodynamics and fluid mechanics to engineering problems

hy·dra·zine (háidrəzi:n) *n.* a colorless reducing basic liquid, NH_2NH_2, used in rocket and jet engine fuels [fr. HYDRO-+AZOTE]

hy·dra·zo·ic acid (haidrəzóuik) a colorless, poisonous, foul-smelling explosive liquid, HN_3, whose heavy metal salts are also explosive [HYDRO-+AZOTE]

hy·dric (háidrik) *adj.* characterized by abundance of moisture (cf. XERIC) [fr. HYDRO-]

hy·dride (háidraid) *n.* (*chem.*) a binary compound of hydrogen with another element or radical [fr. HYDRO-]

hy·dri·od·ic acid (haidri:ódik) a strong reducing acid, HI, formed by dissolving hydrogen iodide in water [fr. HYDRO-+IODINE]

hydro- (háidrou) *prefix* relating to water ‖ afflicted with or accompanied by an accumulation of serous fluid ‖ hydrogen or combined with hydrogen [ult. fr. Gk *hudōr*, water]

hy·dro (háidrou) *n.* (*colloq.*) a hydrofoil speedboat

hy·dro·bro·mic acid (haidroubróumik) a strong acid, HBr, formed by dissolving hydrogen bromide in water [HYDRO-+*bromic*, containing bromide]

hy·dro·car·bon (haidroukárbən) *n.* (*chem.*) one of a large class of organic compounds containing only carbon and hydrogen, occurring in many cases in petroleum, natural gas and coal

hy·dro·cele (háidrəsi:l) *n.* (*med.*) an accumulation of fluid in a body organ, esp. the scrotum [L. fr. Gk fr. *hudōr*, water+*kēlē*, tumor]

hy·dro·ce·phal·ic (haidrousəfǽlik) **1.** *adj.* of or having hydrocephalus **2.** *n.* someone who suffers from hydrocephalus

hy·dro·ceph·a·lus (haidrəséfələs) *n.* (*med.*) an excess of cerebrospinal fluid in the cranial cavity causing enlargement of the skull and mental retardation [L. fr. Gk fr. *hudōr*, water+*kephalē*, head]

hy·dro·chlo·ric acid (haidrəklórik, haidrəklɔ́urik) a strong acid, HCl, formed by dissolving hydrogen chloride in water. It has wide industrial and laboratory applications

hy·dro·chlo·ride (haidrəklóraid, haidrəklóuraid) *n.* a compound of hydrochloric acid

hy·dro·chlo·ro·thi·a·zide (haidrəklɔurəθáiəzaid) *n.* [$C_7H_8O_4N_3ClS_2$] (*pharm.*) diuretic drug used to reduce high blood pressure; marketed as Esidrix, HydroDiuril, and Oretic

hy·dro·cy·an·ic acid (haidrousaiǽnik) a weak, intensely poisonous acid, HCN, formed by dissolving hydrogen cyanide in water

hy·dro·dy·nam·ic (haidroudainǽmik) *adj.* of or relating to hydrodynamics **hy·dro·dy·nam·ics** *n.* the branch of hydromechanics that deals with the motion of fluids and of immersed solid bodies (cf. HYDROSTATICS) [fr. Mod L. *hydrodynamicus*]

hy·dro·e·lec·tric (haidrouiléktrik) *adj.* of the production of electricity by water **hy·dro·e·lec·tric·i·ty** (haidrouilektrísiti:, háidroui:lektrísiti:) *n.* electricity produced by hydroelectric conversion

hy·dro·flu·or·ic acid (haidroufluːɔ́rik, haidroufluːɔ́rik) a highly corrosive and poisonous weak acid, HF, formed by dissolving hydrogen fluoride in water, used in etching glass [HYDRO-+*fluoric*, containing fluorine]

hy·dro·foil (háidrəfɔil) *n.* a flat or curved fin attached to a ship's hull and acting as a stabilizer ‖ a plate or fin, e.g. on a speedboat, for lifting the hull clear as the speed mounts ‖ a craft equipped with such hydrofoils

hy·dro·gas·i·fi·ca·tion (haidrəgæsəfəkeiʃən) *n.* (*chem.*) creation of methane gas from coal by use of hydrogen. —**hydrogasifier** *n.* apparatus used for the process

hy·dro·gen (háidrədʒən) *n.* a nonmetallic, monovalent element (symbol H, at. no. 1, at.

mass 1.00797) that is the lightest of all the elements and has the simplest structure (one proton and one electron). It is not normally found in the uncombined state on the earth, but it occurs in a very great number of compounds. It is used in syntheses, reduction and hydrogenation, as a component in rocket fuel, in producing high-temperature flames (by combustion with oxygen) and (in its liquid form) for cooling (cf. DEUTERIUM, cf. TRITIUM) [F. *hydrogène* fr. Gk]

hy·drog·e·nate (haidródʒəneit, haidrədʒəneit) *pres. part.* **hy·drog·e·nat·ing** *past* and *past part.* **hy·drog·e·nat·ed** *v.t.* to cause to combine chemically with, or undergo the action of, hydrogen

hy·dro·ge·na·tion (haidrɒdʒənéiʃən, haidrədʒənéifən) *n.* the chemical process in which hydrogen is either added to an unsaturated molecule (e.g. the hydrogenation of olefines to increase the quality of fuels or of unsaturated vegetable oils to produce margarine) usually in the presence of a catalyst, or the destruction of highly aromatic molecules (e.g. in coal) at high temperature and pressure with the addition of hydrogen [HYDROGEN]

hydrogen bomb (*abbr.* H-bomb) a bomb releasing enormous energy by the fusion at extremely high temperature and pressure of nuclei of isotopes of hydrogen to form helium

hydrogen bond a weak chemical bond formed between covalently bonded hydrogen and a more electronegative element (e.g. oxygen, fluorine) that may be either intermolecular or intramolecular, and that is primarily electrostatic in character

hydrogen bromide HBr, a colorless gas that forms hydrobromic acid when dissolved in water

hydrogen chloride HCl, a colorless, pungent, poisonous gas that forms hydrochloric acid when dissolved in water

hydrogen cyanide HCN, an intensely poisonous volatile liquid or gas that forms hydrocyanic acid when dissolved in water

hydrogen electrode an electrode consisting usually of a spongy, platinum surface bathed in an acidic solution over which hydrogen gas is bubbled. When the partial pressure of hydrogen gas and the concentration of hydrogen ions are adjusted to standard levels the electrode is conventionally assigned a potential of zero and serves as a standard of comparison for all other redox potentials

hydrogen fluoride HF, a colorless, very poisonous, corrosive liquid or gas that forms hydrofluoric acid when dissolved in water

hydrogen iodide HI, a heavy, colorless gas that forms hydriodic acid when dissolved in water

hydrogen ion the positive ion of hydrogen, H^+

hy·drog·e·nize (haidródʒənaiz, háidrədʒənaiz) *pres. part.* **hy·drog·e·niz·ing** *past* and *past part.* **hy·drog·e·nized** *v.t.* to hydrogenate [HYDROGEN]

hydrogen laser (*optics*) a molecular gas laser utilizing hydrogen to generate beams in the ultraviolet range

hydrogen maser (*phys.*) a gas maser utilizing hydrogen to produce its signals

hy·drog·e·nous (haidródʒənəs) *adj.* of, relating to, or containing hydrogen

hydrogen peroxide H_2O_2, a thick, syrupy, explosive, corrosive liquid, usually made available in solution. It decomposes to give oxygen and water. It is used as an oxidizing agent, e.g. in bleaching and antiseptics, and as a component of rocket fuels

hydrogen sulfide, hydrogen sulphide H_2S, a colorless, inflammable, very poisonous, foul-smelling gas. It occurs in some natural springs, volcanic gases and petroleum. It is used in syntheses and as a precipitating agent

hy·drog·ra·pher (haidrógrəfər) *n.* a specialist in hydrography **hy·dro·graph·ic** (haidrəgrǽfik) *adj.* of hydrography [fr. Gk *hudōr*, water, after GEOGRAPHER]

hy·drog·ra·phy (haidrógrəfi:) *n.* the scientific study of the waters of the earth's surface, esp. with regard to their industrial uses and navigability [fr. Gk *hudōr*, water, after GEOGRAPHY]

hy·droid (háidrɔid) **1.** *n.* the polyp phase of a hydrozoan **2.** *adj.* of the *Hydroida*, an order of hydrozoans in which the asexual polyp generation alternates with a generation of medusae or of polyps having medusoid reproductive structures ‖ like a hydra polyp [HYDRA]

hy·dro·ki·net·ic (haidroukinétik, haidroukainétik) *adj.* (*phys.*) of the flow of fluids and the cause and effect of this flow **hy·dro·ki·net·ics** *n.* the scientific study of the flow of fluids

hy·dro·log·i·cal (haidrəlɒdʒik'l) *adj.* of hydrology

hy·drol·o·gist (haidrólədʒist) *n.* a specialist in hydrology

hy·drol·o·gy (haidrólədʒi:) *n.* the scientific study of water, esp. its natural occurrence, characteristics, control and conservation [Mod. L. *hydrologia*]

hy·drol·y·sis (haidrólisis) *n.* a chemical reaction of water in which the reagent other than water is decomposed and hydrogen and hydroxyl are added, usually with the formation of two or more new compounds **hy·dro·lyte** (háidrəlait) *n.* a substance subjected to hydrolysis **hy·dro·lyt·ic** (haidrəlítik) *adj.* **hy·dro·lyze, hy·dro·lyse** (háidrəlaiz) *pres. part.* **hy·dro·lyz·ing, hy·dro·lys·ing** *past* and *past part.* **hy·dro·lyzed, hy·dro·lysed** *v.t.* to submit to hydrolysis ‖ *v.i.* to become hydrolyzed [fr. Gk *hudōr*, water+*lusis*, dissolving]

hy·dro·mag·net·ics (haidroumægnétiks) *n.* study of phenomena in the motion of fluids conducting electricity in a magnetic field

hy·dro·me·chan·ics (haidrouməḱǽniks) *n.* the study of fluids and immersed solid bodies in motion and at rest

hy·dro·me·du·sa (haidroumidú:sə, haidroumidjú:sə) *pl.* **hy·dro·me·du·sae** (haidroumidú:si:, haidroumidjú:si:) *n.* a medusa budded from a hydroid, being the sexual generation of this hydrozoan. It produces polyps from eggs and sperm

hy·dro·mel (háidrəməl) *n.* a mixture of honey and water, becoming mead on fermentation [L. fr. Gk *hudromeli* fr. *hudōr*, water+*meli*, honey]

hy·dro·met·al·lur·gi·cal (haidroumet́lə́:rdʒik'l) *adj.* of or involving hydrometallurgy

hy·dro·met·al·lur·gy (haidroumét'lə:rdʒi:) *n.* the treatment of mineral ores by processes involving the use of water

hy·dro·me·te·or (haidroumí:ti:ər) *n.* any weather phenomenon produced by the condensation of moisture in the atmosphere, e.g. rain, hail, fog

hy·drom·e·ter (haidrómitər) *n.* an instrument for measuring the specific gravity of a liquid, using the principle of flotation

hy·dro·met·ric (haidrəmétrik) *adj.* of hydrometry

hy·drom·e·try (haidrómitri:) *n.* the measurement of specific gravity, esp. of a liquid [fr. Mod. L. *hydrometria*]

hy·dro·nauts (háidrənɔts) *n.* U.S. Navy personnel engaged in undersea search and rescue missions. *Cf* AQUANAUT

hy·dron·ics (haidróniks) *n.* system of heating or cooling by circulation of a fluid in an enclosed system, e.g., hot water heating in a home. — **hydronic** *adj.* —**hydronically** *adv.*

hy·dro·path·ic (haidrəpǽθik) *adj.* of or pertaining to hydropathy

hy·drop·a·thy (haidrópəθi:) *n.* the treatment of disease solely by means of water (used both internally and externally) [fr. HYDRO-, after 'allopathy', 'homeopathy']

hy·dro·phil·ic (haidrəfílik) *adj.* denoting a strong affinity for water [fr. Mod. L. *hydrophilus*]

hy·dro·pho·bi·a (haidrəfóubi:ə) *n.* aversion to water, esp. as a symptom of rabies ‖ rabies, esp. in man **hy·dro·pho·bic** *adj.* of or affected by hydrophobia ‖ (*chem.*) denoting a lack of affinity for water [L. fr. Gk *hudrophobia* fr. *hudōr*, water+*phobos*, fear]

hy·dro·phone (háidrəfoun) *n.* an instrument for detecting sound transmitted through water [fr. HYDRO-+Gk *phonein*, to sound]

hy·dro·phyte (háidrəfait) *n.* an aquatic plant **hy·dro·phyt·ic** (haidrəfítik) *adj.* [fr. Gk *hudōr*, water+*phuton*, plant]

hy·dro·plane (háidrəplein) *n.* a light motorboat which, by means of hydrofoils, can rise partially or completely out of the water at high speed ‖ a seaplane

hy·dro·plan·ing háidrəpleiniŋ) *n.* skidding of a motor vehicle on a wet road

hy·dro·pon·ics (haidrəpóniks) *n.* the growing of plants in water with essential chemicals in solution, instead of in soil [fr. Gk *hudōr*, water+*ponos*, labor]

hy·dro·psy·cho·ther·a·py (haidrəseikouθérəpi:) *n.* (*psych.*) treatment of emotional disorders by immersion in warm baths, etc.

CONCISE PRONUNCIATION KEY: (**a**) æ, c**a**t; ɑ, c**a**r; ɔ f**aw**n; ei, sn**a**ke. (**e**) e, h**e**n; i:, sh**ee**p; iə, d**ee**r; ɛə, b**ea**r. (**i**) i, f**i**sh; ai, t**i**ger; ə:, b**i**rd. (**o**) o, **o**x; au, c**ow**; ou, g**oa**t; u, p**oo**r; ɔi, r**o**yal. (**u**) ʌ, d**u**ck; u, b**u**ll; u:, g**oo**se; ə, b**a**cillus; ju:, c**u**be. x, lo**ch**; θ, **th**ink; ð, bo**th**er; z, **Z**en; ʒ, cor**s**age; dʒ, sava**g**e; ŋ, orangutan**g**; j, **y**ak; ʃ, **fi**sh; tʃ, fe**tch**; 'l, rabb**le**; 'n, redd**en**. Complete pronunciation key appears inside front cover.

hy·dro·scope (háidrəskoup) n. (hist.) a water clock ‖ a device for seeing something deeply submerged in water [fr. Gk hudroskopion, water clock and hudroskopos, water seeker]

hy·dro·skim·mer (háidrəskimər) n. a vehicle that uses an air cushion for travel over water. Cf AIR-CUSHION VEHICLE, HOVERCRAFT

hy·dro·space (háidrəspeis) n. the land beneath the oceans. Cf INNER SPACE

hy·dro·sphere (háidrəsfiər) n. the liquid part of the earth's surface, e.g. oceans, seas, lakes (cf. ATMOSPHERE, cf. LITHOSPHERE)

hy·dro·stat·ic (haidrəstætik) adj. of or pertaining to hydrostatics **hy·dro·stat·ics** n. the branch of hydromechanics that deals with characteristics (esp. the pressure) of fluids, and immersed solid bodies, at rest (cf. HYDRODYNAMICS) [ult. fr. Gk hudōr, water+statikos, causing to stand]

hy·dro·tax·is (haidrətæksis) n. (biol.) the motion of an organism in response to the stimulus of moisture [Mod. L.]

hy·dro·ther·a·peu·tic (háidrouθerepjú:tik) adj. of or pertaining to hydrotherapy

hy·dro·ther·a·py (haidrouθérepi:) n. treatment of disease in which water is used externally, e.g. medicinal baths [fr. Gk hudōr, water+therapeia, healing]

hy·dro·ther·mal (haidrəθə́:rməl) adj. relating to hot water, esp. (geol.) relating to the combined action of water and heat in effecting the metamorphosis of rocks [fr. Gk hudōr, water+thermos, heat]

hydrothermal energy heat derived from underground steam

hy·dro·trope (háidrətroup) n. a cosolvent in a detergent used to hold components in the solution

hy·dro·trop·ic (haidrətrópik) adj. (of roots) turning in response to the stimulus of water **hy·drot·ro·pism** (haidrótrəpizəm) n. this response [fr. Gk hudōr, water+tropos, turning]

hy·drous (háidrəs) adj. containing water [fr. Gk hudōr, water]

hy·drox·ide (haidróksaid) n. a chemical compound containing the hydroxyl (OH) group, and ionizing to liberate hydroxyl (OH−) ions

hy·drox·o·co·bal·a·min (haidróksoukoubáləmin) n. (pharm.) drug used in treating vitamin B₁₂ deficiency in pernicious anemia; marketed as alphaRESIDOL

hydroxy- (haidróksi:) prefix (chem.) containing hydroxyl [HYDROXYL]

hy·drox·y acid a carboxylic acid with one or more hydroxyl groups in the molecule

hy·drox·yl (haidróksil) n. the monovalent (OH) group or radical characteristic of hydroxides, alcohols, oxygen acids etc. [fr. HYDROGEN+OXYGEN]

hydroxytyramine (haidróksi:táirəmi:n) n. *DOPAMINE

hy·drox·y·u·re·a (haidróksi:ju:rí:ə) n. [CH₄N₂O₂] (pharm.) drug used in treating forms of leukemia, melanoma, and carcinoma of the ovary; marketed as Hydrea

hy·dro·zo·an (haidrəzóuən) n. (zool.) a member of Hydrozoa, a class of coelenterates including polyps and jellyfish, usually exhibiting alternation of generations [fr. Mod. L. Hydrozoa fr. HYDRA+Gk zōon, animal]

hy·e·na, **hy·ae·na** (haií:nə) n. a member of Hyaenidae, a family of nocturnal, carnivorous Old World quadrupeds having powerful jaws, strong teeth and well-developed forelimbs. Hyena crocuta or Crocuta crocuta, a black-spotted species of S. Africa, utters laughterlike screams [L. hyaena fr. Gk]

hy·et·o·graph (haiétəgræf, haiétəgrɑf) n. a chart showing average annual rainfall in different regions **hy·e·to·graph·ic** (haiɛtəgræfik) adj. **hy·e·tog·ra·phy** (haiɛtógrəfi:) n. the study and mapping of the distribution of rainfall [fr. Gk huetos, rain+graphos, written]

hy·e·to·log·i·cal (haiɛt'lódʒik'l) adj. of hyetology

hy·e·tol·o·gy (haiitólədʒi:) n. the scientific study of natural precipitation [fr. Gk huetos, rain+logos, word]

hy·e·tom·e·ter (haiitómitər) n. a rain gauge [fr. Gk huetos, rain+METER]

hy·giene (háidʒi:n) n. the science of health, its preservation and the prevention of disease ‖ the practice of measures designed to attain and preserve health **hy·gi·en·ic** (haidʒi:énik, haidʒi:nik), **hy·gi·en·i·cal** adjs **hy·gien·ics** n. the science of hygiene **hy·gien·ist** (haidʒí:nist, haidʒénist) n. [F. hygiène fr. Gk]

---

hy·gric (háigrik) adj. of, relating to or containing moisture [fr. Gk hugros, wet]

hy·gro·graph (háigrəgræf, háigrəgrɑf) n. an instrument which records changes in the humidity of the air [fr. Gk hugros, wet+graphos, written]

hy·grom·e·ter (haigrómitər) n. an instrument used in determining the relative humidity of the air **hy·gro·met·ric** (haigrəmétrik) adj. **hy·grom·e·try** (haigrómitri:) n. [fr. Gk hugros, wet+METER]

hy·gro·phyte (háigrəfait) n. a plant which thrives in plentiful moisture **hygro·phyt·ic** (haigrəfítik) adj. [fr. Gk hugros, wet+phuton, plant]

hy·gro·scope (háigrəskoup) n. an instrument which shows variations in humidity **hy·gro·scop·ic** (haigrəskópik) adj. relating to substances which absorb and retain moisture [fr. Gk hugros, wet+-skopein, to observe]

Hyk·sos (híksɒs, híksous) pl. n. Asian invaders who ruled Egypt between the 13th and 17th dynasties (c. 1785–c. 1570 B.C.)

hy·lo·zo·ism (hailəzóuizəm) n. the doctrine that all matter is endowed with life [fr. Gk hulē, matter+zōē, life]

Hy·men (háimen) (Gk and Rom. mythol.) the god of marriage

hy·men (háimən) n. the thin fold of mucous membrane at the entrance to the vagina [Gk humen (humenos), membrane]

hy·me·ne·al (haiməní:əl) 1. adj. of or pertaining to marriage 2. n. a marriage song [fr. L. hymenaeus]

hy·me·nop·ter·an (haimənóptərən) n. a member of Hymenoptera, an order of insects (e.g. bees, wasps, ants) having usually four membranous wings, chewing and sucking mouthparts and, in the female, an ovipositor. Metamorphosis is complete. They often display colonial social habits [fr. Mod. L. Hymenoptera fr. Gk humen (humenos), membrane+pteron, wing]

hy·me·nop·ter·on (haimənóptərɒn) n. a hymenopteran

hy·me·nop·ter·ous (haimənóptərəs) adj. being or having the characteristics of a hymenopteran ‖ of or pertaining to the order Hymenoptera [Mod. L. hymenopterus, having membranous wings]

Hy·met·tus (haimétəs) a mountain chain (rising to 3,369 ft) in Attica and Boeotia, Greece

hymn (him) 1. n. a song or ode in praise, adoration or supplication of God, esp. one sung at a religious service 2. v.t. (rhet.) to praise or supplicate in a hymn ‖ v.i. (rhet.) to sing a hymn [O.E. ymen fr. L. hymnus fr. Gk]

hym·nal (hímnəl) n. a book containing a collection of hymns [fr. L. hymnus, a hymn]

hymn·book (hímbʊk) n. a hymnal

hym·no·dist (hímnədist) n. someone who writes hymns **hym·no·dy** (hímnədi:) n. the singing or the composition of hymns ‖ the study of hymns ‖ (collect.) hymns [fr. M.L. hymnodia fr. Gk]

hym·nol·o·gist (himnólədʒist) n. someone who studies or composes hymns [HYMNOLOGY]

hym·nol·o·gy (himnólədʒi:) n. the study or the composition of hymns ‖ (collect.) hymns [fr. HYMN+Gk logos, word]

hy·oid (háioid) 1. adj. of a bone at the base of the tongue, shaped like the Greek letter u 2. n. this bone [fr. F. hyoïde fr. L. fr. Gk huoeidēs, shaped like the upsilon]

hy·pae·thral (haipí:θrəl, hipí:θrəl) adj. (archit., e.g. of some classical temples or sanctuaries) not having a roof [fr. L. hypaethrus fr. Gk hupaithros, under the sky]

hype (háip) n. intentional excess verging on deception that creates great popular enthusiasm for a person or product; from hypodermic needle. —**hype** v. —**hyped** adj.

hyper- prefix excessive, overmuch, above [fr. Gk huper- fr. huper prep. and adv., over, beyond]

hy·per·a·cid·i·ty (haipərəsíditi:) n. excessive acidity

hyperaemia *HYPEREMIA

hyperaesthesia *HYPERESTHESIA

hy·per·al·ge·si·a (haipərældʒí:zi:ə) n. abnormally acute sensitivity to pain **hy·per·al·ge·sic** adj. [Mod. L.]

hy·per·bar·ic (haipərbǽrik) adj. of oxygen use under pressure greater than one atmosphere

hy·per·bo·la (haipə́:rbələ) pl. **hy·per·bo·las**, **hy·per·bo·lae** (haipə́:rbəli:) n. a plane curve that is the locus of points whose distance from a fixed point (the focus) divided by its distance from a fixed line (the directrix) is a positive constant greater than 1 (cf. PARABOLA). A hyper-

---

bola is formed by the section of a right circular cone by a plane cutting the cone at an angle at the base greater than the angle formed by the cone's side with its base [Mod. L. fr. Gk huperbolē, excess, exaggeration]

hy·per·bo·le (haipə́:rbəli:) n. a figure of speech which greatly exaggerates the truth [fr. Gk huperbolē, excess, exaggeration]

hy·per·bol·ic (haipərbólik) adj. of hyperbole ‖ of a hyperbola **hy·per·ból·i·cal** adj. [fr. Gk huperbolikos, excessive]

hy·per·bo·loid (haipə́:rbələid) n. a surface that when cut by planes parallel to one coordinate plane gives elliptical sections and when cut by the other two coordinate planes gives hyperbolic sections, providing the axes are properly oriented [HYPERBOLA]

hy·per·charge strangeness (háipərtʃɑrdʒ) (nuclear phys.) a quantum representing a delay in interaction between some elementary particles

hy·per·crit·i·cal (haipərkrítik'l) adj. too critical, esp. of trivial faults

hy·per·du·li·a (haipərdulí:ə, haipərdʒulí:ə) n. (Roman Catholicism) the veneration of the Virgin Mary as superior to the saints (*DULIA, *LATRIA)

hy·per·e·mi·a, **hy·per·ae·mi·a** (haipəri:mjə) n. congestion of the blood **hy·per·e·mic**, **hy·per·á·mic** adj. [Mod. L.]

hy·per·es·the·si·a, **hy·per·aes·the·sia** (haipərisθí:ʒə) n. excessive sensitivity to pain or other forms of sensation [Mod. L.]

hy·per·eu·tec·tic (haipərjutéktik) adj. containing a component in excess of the eutectic composition

hy·per·fo·cal distance (haipərfóuk'l) the nearest distance at which a lens may be focused while giving a satisfactory definition for the image of a very distant object

hy·per·gly·ce·mi·a, **hy·per·gly·cae·mi·a** (haipərglaisí:mi:ə) n. an excess of sugar in the blood [HYPER-+glycemia, presence of glucose]

hy·per·gol·ic fuel (haipərgálik) fuel that will ignite spontaneously with an oxidizer, used as the propulsion agent in certain missile systems, e.g., aniline with fuming nitric acid

hy·per·in·fla·tion (haipərinfléiʃən) n. extreme (doubling or tripling), persistent, daily rise in prices destroying the value of money as an exchange medium, e.g., in Germany, 1923

hy·per·lip·id·e·mi·a (haipərlipədí:mi:ə) n. (med.) a condition of more than normal lipids (fats) in the blood. also hyperlipemia

hy·per·mar·ket (háipərmɑrkit) n. (Br.) assemblage of small shops under a single roof, often in the suburbs, and usu. with a common theme, e.g., antiques; in U.S., a center, e.g., an antique center

hy·per·me·ter (haipé:rmitər) n. a line of poetry having a redundant syllable **hy·per·met·ric** (haipərmétrik), **hy·per·mét·ri·cal** adjs [fr. Gk hupermetros, beyond measure]

hy·per·me·tro·pi·a (haipərmitróupi:ə) n. inability to see near objects distinctly owing to a condition of the eye in which light from such objects is brought to focus behind the retina **hy·per·me·trop·ic** (haipərmitrópik) adj. [Mod. L.]

hy·per·on (háipərɒn) n. (phys.) a baryon other than the proton or neutron [HYPER-+-on, fundamental particle]

hy·per·o·pi·a (haipəróupi:ə) n. hypermetropia **hy·per·op·ic** (haipərópik) adj. [HYPER-+Gk ōps, eye]

hy·per·pha·gi·a (haipərféidʒi:ə) n. (med.) an excessive, sometimes insatiable appetite, symptom of diabetes, seen in some psychoses. —**hyperphagic** adj. also bulimia

hy·per·phys·i·cal (haipərfízik'l) adj. supernatural

hy·per·pi·tu·i·ta·rism (haipərpitú:itərizəm, haipərpitjú:itərizəm) n. overactivity of the pituitary gland, esp. of its growth-controlling hormones ‖ excessive growth resulting from this **hy·per·pi·tu·i·ta·ry** (haipərpitú:iteri:, haipərpitjú:iteri:) adj.

hy·per·pla·sia (haipərpléiʒə, haipərpléiʒi:ə) n. overgrowth of cells in a tissue **hy·per·plas·tic** (haipərplǽstik) adj. [Mod. L.]

hy·per·py·ret·ic (haipərpairétik) adj. of or having hyperpyrexia

hy·per·py·rex·i·a (haipərpairéksi:ə) n. abnormally high temperature [Mod. L.]

hy·per·sen·si·tive (haipərsénsitiv) adj. acutely, excessively or abnormally sensitive **hy·per·sen·si·tiv·i·ty** n.

---

hy·per·son·ic (haipərsónik) *adj.* of speed more than five times that of sound in air

hy·per·ster·e·o·sco·py (haipərstęrióskəpi:) *n.* exaggerated stereoscopy, i.e., stereoscopic viewing in which the relief effect is noticeably exaggerated, caused by the extension of the camera base

hy·per·ten·sion (haipərténʃən) *n.* abnormally high blood pressure in the arteries that may or may not be associated with observable organic disorders (e.g. kidney diseases, obesity, diabetes) ‖ a condition resulting from such abnormally high blood pressure and often accompanied by nervousness, dizziness and headaches

hy·per·thy·roid·ism (haipərθáirɔidizəm) *n.* excessive activity of the thyroid gland ‖ a condition resulting from this, characterized by increased rate of metabolism, loss of weight, and sometimes goiter

hy·per·ton·ic (haipərtónik) *adj.* (*physiol.*, of muscles) having excessive tension ‖ (*chem.*) having a greater osmotic pressure than a control! fluid **hy·per·to·nic·i·ty** (haipərtənsíiti:) *n.*

hy·per·tro·phic (haipərtróufik, haipərtrófik) *adj.* of or affected with hypertrophy

hy·per·tro·phy (haipé:rtrəfi:) *pl.* **hy·per·tro·phies** *n.* abnormal increase in size or overdevelopment of a part of the body [fr. Mod. L.]

hyp·es·the·sia (hipisθí:ʒə) *n.* reduced sensitivity of touch **hy·pes·the·tic** (hipisθétik) *adj.* [Mod. L.]

hypethral *HYPAETHRAL

hy·pha (háifə) *pl.* **hy·phae** (háifi:) *n.* (*bot.*) the threadlike element of the vegetative mycelium of a fungus that may be in the form of a hollow tube (as in most phycomycetes) or may be septate (as in ascomycetes and basidiomycetes) ‖ a filamentous cell in the medulla of an algal thallus (e.g. seaweeds) **hý·phal** *adj.* [Mod. L. fr. Gk *huphē*, web]

hy·phen (háifən) **1.** *n.* a punctuation mark (-) used to join two words or two elements of a word, e.g. in 'counselor-at-law', and to divide a word syllabically, e.g. at the end of a line **2.** *v.t.* to hyphenate [L.L. fr. Gk fr. *hupo*, under+*hen*, one]

hy·phen·ate (háifəneit) *pres. part* **hy·phen·at·ing** *past* and *past part.* **hy·phen·at·ed** *v.t.* to join or divide by a hyphen ‖ to write with a hyphen **hy·phen·a·tion** *n.*

hyp·no·a·nal·y·sis (hipnouænǽlisis) *n.* psychoanalysis while the patient is under hypnosis [Mod. L. fr. Gk *hupnos*, sleep+ANALYSIS]

hyp·no·gen·e·sis (hipnoudʒénisis) *n.* the inducing of a hypnotic state **hyp·no·ge·net·ic** (hipnoudʒənétik) *adj.* [Mod. L. fr. Gk *hupnos*, sleep+GENESIS]

hyp·noid (hípnɔid) *adj.* of or similar to mild hypnosis, but not necessarily induced hypnotically **hyp·nói·dal** *adj.* [fr. Gk *hupnos*, sleep]

hyp·no·log·ic (hipnəlódʒik) *adj.* of hypnology **hyp·no·lóg·i·cal** *adj.*

hyp·nol·o·gist (hipnólədʒist) *n.* a specialist in hypnology

hyp·nol·o·gy (hipnólədʒi:) *n.* the study of the phenomena of normal sleep [fr. Gk *hupnos*, sleep+*logos*, word]

hypnopedia *SLEEP-LEARNING

hyp·no·sis (hipnóusis) *pl.* **hyp·no·ses** (hipnóusi:z) *n.* an artificially induced state, resembling sleep, but characterized by exaggerated suggestibility and continued responsiveness to the voice of the hypnotist. It is used in the medical treatment of a variety of nervous and bodily disorders [fr. Gk *hupnoun*, to put to sleep]

hyp·no·ther·a·peu·tic (hipnouθęrəpjú:tik) *adj.* of hypnotherapy

hyp·no·ther·a·py (hipnouθérəpi:) *n.* treatment of disease by hypnotism [fr. Gk *hupnos*, sleep+THERAPY]

hyp·not·ic (hipnótik) **1.** *adj.* of or inducing hypnosis ‖ inducing normal sleep ‖ susceptible to hypnotism **2.** *n.* a sleep-producing agent ‖ a hypnotized person or someone susceptible to hypnotism **hyp·nót·i·cal·ly** *adv.* [fr. F. *hypnotique* fr. L. fr. Gk fr. *hupnoun*, to put to sleep]

hyp·no·tism (hípnətizəm) *n.* the practice of inducing hypnosis **hýp·no·tist** *n.* someone who practices hypnotism **hyp·no·tize** (hípnətaiz) *pres. part.* **hyp·no·tiz·ing** *past* and *past part.* **hyp·no·tized** *v.t.* to induce hypnosis in (someone) [HYPNOTIC]

hy·po (háipou) *n.* sodium thiosulfate [HYPOSULFITE]

hypo *n.* (*pop.*) a hypodermic syringe or injection

hypo- (háipou) *prefix* below, under, deficient ‖ (*chem.*, of a compound) containing less oxygen

than is usual in its series [fr. Gk *hupo-*, *hup-* fr. *hupo*, prep. and adv., under]

hy·po·blast (háipəblæst) *n.* the endoderm of an embryo [fr. HYPO-+Gk *blastos*, germ]

hy·po·caust (háipəkɔst) *n.* (*hist.*) a heating system used in Roman buildings, comprising an underground furnace and a series of flues and open spaces to conduct the warm air to the rooms [fr. L.L. *hypocaustum* fr. Gk]

hy·po·chlor·ite (haipouklɔ́rait, haipouklóurait) *n.* an ester or salt of hypochlorous acid

hy·po·chlor·ous acid (haipouklɔ́res, haipouklóurəs) a weak, unstable acid, HClO, used as an oxidizing and bleaching agent

hy·po·chon·dri·a (haipəkóndri:ə) *n.* hypochondriasis ‖ a state of mental depression often accompanying hypochondriasis [fr. L.L. *hypochondria* fr. Gk *hupo*, below+*chondros*, cartilage]

hy·po·chon·dri·ac (haipəkóndri:æk) **1.** *n.* a person suffering from hypochondria **2.** *adj.* pertaining to hypochondria or to a hypochondriac ‖ (*anat.*) below the ribs **hy·po·chon·dri·a·cal** (haipəkɔndráiək'l) *adj.* [F. *hypochondriaque*]

hy·po·chon·dri·a·sis (haipoukɔndráiəsis) *n.* (*med.*) excessive (often pathological) preoccupation with real or fancied ailments [HYPOCHONDRIA]

hy·po·chon·dri·um (haipəkóndri:əm) *pl.* **hy·po·chon·dri·a** (haipəkóndri:ə) *n.* one of the two abdominal regions just below the ribs [Mod. L. fr..Gk *hupochondrion*, abdomen]

hy·po·co·ris·tic (haipəkərístik) *adj.* of, used as, or like a pet name ‖ using pet names or euphemisms [fr. Gk *hupokoristikos* fr. *hupokorizesthai*, to play the child]

hy·po·cot·yl (haipəkót'l) *n.* (*bot.*) the part of an embryonic seedling which lies below the cotyledon [HYPO-+*-cotyl*, cuplike fr. Gk *kotylē*, cup]

hy·poc·ri·sy (hipókrəsi:) *pl.* **hy·poc·ri·sies** *n.* pretense of virtue, benevolence or religious devotion ‖ an instance of such pretense [O.F. *ypocrisie* fr. L. fr. Gk]

hyp·o·crite (hípəkrit) *n.* someone guilty of hypocrisy [O.F. *ypocrite* fr. L. fr. Gk]

hyp·o·crit·i·cal (hipəkrítik'l) *adj.* of or characterized by hypocrisy [fr. Gk *hupokritikos*]

hy·po·cy·cloid (haipousáiklɔid) *n.* (*geom.*) the curved path of a point on the circumference of a circle which rolls internally on the circumference of another circle **hy·po·cy·clói·dal** *adj.*

hy·po·der·ma (haipədé:rmə) *n.* (*zool.*) the hypodermis ‖ (*bot.*) a layer of supporting tissue just under the epidermis **hy·po·dér·mal** *adj.* being beneath the epidermis ‖ of the hypoderma or the hypodermis **hy·po·dér·mic 1.** *adj.* of the area just beneath the skin ‖ administered just beneath the skin, *a hypodermic injection* ‖ pertaining to an injection just beneath the skin, *a hypodermic needle* **2.** *n.* a hypodermic syringe ‖ a hypodermic injection **hy·po·dér·mi·cal·ly** *adv.* [Mod. L. fr. Gk *hupo*, below+*derma*, skin]

hypodermic syringe a syringe fitted with a sharp, hollow needle for administering an injection below or into the skin

hy·po·der·mis (haipədé:rmis) *n.* (*bot.*) the hypoderma ‖ (*zool.*) a cellular layer which secretes the horny integument or cuticle of annulates, arthropods etc. ‖ the hypoblast [fr. Gk *hupo*, below+*dermis*, skin]

hy·po·dip·loi·dy (haipoudiplɔ́idi:) *n.* (*genetics*) the condition of having slightly less than the normal number of chromosomes. —**hypodiploid** *adj.*

hy·po·eu·tec·tic (haipoujutéktik) *adj.* containing less of a component than in the eutectic composition

hy·po·gas·tric (haipəgǽstrik) *adj.* of the hypogastrium [fr. F. *hypogastrique* fr. Mod. L. fr. Gk]

hy·po·gas·tri·um (haipəgǽstri:əm) *n.* the lower central region of the abdomen [Mod. L. fr. Gk *hupogastrion*]

hy·po·ge·al (haipədʒí:əl) *adj.* (*bot.*, of plant parts) growing underground ‖ (of some insects) living underground ‖ (*geol.*) of or being in the interior of the earth [fr. L. *hypogeus*, subterranean fr. Gk]

hy·po·gene (háipədʒi:n) *adj.* (of rocks) formed or being beneath the surface of the earth **hy·po·ge·net·ic** (haipədʒənétik) *adj.* [fr. HYPO-+Gk *genes*, born of]

hy·pog·e·nous (haipódʒənəs) *adj.* (*bot.*) growing on the lower surface of something, e.g. a leaf [fr. L. *hypogeus*, subterranean fr. Gk]

hy·po·glos·sal (haipəglɔ́s'l, haipəglɔ́s'l) **1.** *adj.* of a pair of cranial nerves controlling the muscles of the tongue and adjacent structures **2.** *n.* either of these nerves [fr. Mod. L. *hypoglossus*, hypoglossal nerve fr. Gk *hupo*, below+*glōssa*, tongue]

hy·po·gly·ce·mi·a, **hy·po·gly·cae·mi·a** (haipouglaisí:mi:ə) *n.* a deficiency of sugar in the blood [HYPO-+*glycemia*, presence of glucose]

hy·pog·y·nous (haipódʒinəs) *adj.* (of petals, stamens and sepals) growing from below the ovary and not adhering to it **hy·póg·y·ny** *n.* the condition of being hypogynous [fr. Mod. L. *hypogynus* fr. Gk]

hy·po·lim·ni·on (haipoulímni:on) *n.* the colder bottom zone of a stratified lake or ocean

hy·po·na·tre·mi·a (haipnətri:mi:ə) *n.* (*med.*) an abnormally low level of salt in the blood. —**hyponatremic** *adj.*

hy·pon·y·my (haipónimi:) *n.* (*linguistics*) cases under case grammar approach

hy·po·phar·ynx (haipoufǽriŋks) *n.* the lingua of many insects, e.g. mosquitoes, that is a growth on the floor of the mouth. It is either a sensory or a piercing organ **hy·po·pha·ryn·ge·al** (haipoufærindʒí:əl, haipoufárindʒi:əl) *adj.* of the hypopharynx ‖ below the pharynx [F.]

hy·poph·y·sis (haipófisis) *pl.* **hy·poph·y·ses** (haipófisi:z) *n.* the pituitary gland ‖ (*bot.*) the last cell of the suspensor in the embryo of a flowering plant from which the root and root cap develop [Gk *hypophysis*, outgrowth]

hy·po·pla·sia (haipəpléiʒə, haipəpléiʒi:ə) *n.* arrested development of an organ of the body **hy·po·plas·tic** (haipəplǽstik) *adj.* [Mod. L. fr. Gk *hupo*, below+*plasis*, molding]

hy·pos·ta·sis (haipóstəsis) *pl.* **hy·pos·ta·ses** (haipóstəsi:z) *n.* (*philos.*) the substantial essence of things as distinguished from their attributes ‖ (*theol.*) the essence of the Godhead or of a person of the Trinity, esp. Christ ‖ the personification of an essence or principle ‖ (*med.*) the accumulation of blood in a dependent part of the body, e.g. at the base of the lungs **hy·pós·ta·size** *pres. part.* **hy·pos·ta·siz·ing** *past* and *past part.* **hy·pos·ta·sized** *v.t.* to hypostatize [L.L. fr. Gk *hupostasis*, support]

hy·po·stat·ic (haipəstǽtik) *adj.* constituting the unique essence or personality of a thing ‖ (*med.*) of hypostasis [fr. Gk *hupostatikos*, supporting]

hypostatic union (*theol.*) the union in Christ of human and divine natures

hy·pos·ta·tize (haipóstətaiz) *pres. part.* **hy·pos·ta·tiz·ing** *past* and *past part.* **hy·pos·ta·tized** *v.t.* to attribute personality or substantial essence to [Gk *hupostatos*, supporting]

hy·po·style (háipəstail) **1.** *adj.* (*archit.*) having the roof or ceiling supported by pillars **2.** *n.* a building of this kind [fr. Gk *hupostulos* fr. *hupo*, under+*stulos*, pillar]

hy·po·tax·is (haipətǽksis) *n.* (*gram.*) syntactical subordination of clauses etc. by the use of connectives, e.g. 'she came, but stayed only a minute' (cf. PARATAXIS) [Gk=subordination]

hy·po·ten·sion (haipouténʃən) *n.* abnormally low blood pressure

hy·pot·e·nuse (haipót'nu:s, haipót'nju:s) *n.* (*geom.*) the side opposite the right angle of a right-angled triangle [fr. L.L. *hypotenusa* fr. Gk *hupoteinousa*, subtending (line)]

hy·po·thal·a·mus (haipouθǽləməs) *pl.* **hy·po·thal·a·mi** (haipouθǽləmi) *n.* the portion of the diencephalon lying beneath the thalamus (*BRAIN) that coordinates responses of the sympathetic nervous system, e.g. body temperature control

hy·po·thec (haipóθik) *n.* (*Rom.* and *Scot. law*) a security held by a debtor but serving as a guarantee to the creditor, who will assume possession if the debt is not paid **hy·poth·e·car·y** (haipóθəkęri:) *adj.* [F. *hypothèque* or fr. L.L. *hypotheca* fr. Gk]

hy·poth·e·cate (haipóθikeit) *pres. part.* **hy·poth·e·cat·ing** *past* and *past part.* **hy·poth·e·cat·ed** *v.t.* to pledge (property) as security **hy·poth·e·cá·tion** *n.* [M.L. *hypothecare* (*hypothecatus*)]

hy·po·ther·mi·a (haipəθé:rmi:ə) *n.* a subnormal body temperature artificially induced to retard metabolic processes and facilitate surgery [Mod. L. fr. Gk *hupo*, under+*thermē*, heat]

hy·poth·e·sis (haipóθisis) *pl.* **hy·poth·e·ses** (haipóθisi:z) *n.* an idea or proposition not derived from experience but formed and used to explain certain facts (e.g. in science) or to provide the foundation or primary assumption of an argument **hy·poth·e·size** (haipóθisaiz) *pres. part.* **hy·poth·e·siz·ing** *past* and *past part.* **hy·poth·e·sized** *v.i.* to make a hypothesis ‖ *v.t.* to assume [Gk *hupothesis*, foundation]

hy·po·thet·ic (haipəθétik) *adj.* involving a hypothesis ‖ of or based on a hypothesis **hy·po·thét·i·cal** *adj.* [fr. Gk *hupothetikos*]

hypothetical imperative (*philos.*) an imperative which applies only to specific circumstances (cf. CATEGORICAL IMPERATIVE)

hy·po·thy·roid·ism (haipəθáirɔidizəm) *n.* insufficient activity of the thyroid gland ‖ a condition resulting from this, characterized by a reduced rate of metabolism, lethargy, weight increase and sometimes goiter

hy·po·ton·ic (haipətónik) *adj.* (*physiol.*, of muscles) having very low tension ‖ (*chem.*) having a lower osmotic pressure than a control fluid **hy·po·ton·ic·i·ty** (haipoutənisiti:) *n.*

hyp·sog·ra·phy (hipsógrəfi:) *n.* the geography of areas above sea level and the mapping of these [fr. Gk *hupsos*, height+*graphos*, written]

hyp·som·e·ter (hipsómitər) *n.* an instrument for determining altitude above sea level in terms of atmospheric pressure, by finding the boiling temperature of a liquid **hyp·sóm·e·try** *n.* the science of determining altitude above sea level [fr. Gk *hupsos*, height+METER]

hyp·so·met·ric tinting (hipsəmétrik) (*cartography*) a method of showing relief on maps and charts by coloring in different shades those parts which lie between selected levels. —**hyp·sometric map** *n. also* altitude tint, elevation tint, layer tint

hy·rax (háiræks) *pl.* **hy·rax·es, hy·ra·ces** (háirəsi:z) *n.* a member of *Hyracoidea*, an order of small, quadruped African and Asian mammals [Mod. L. ft. Gk *hurax*, shrew]

hy·son (háis'n) *n.* a green tea of China [fr. Chin. *hsi-ch'un*, bright spring]

hys·sop (hisəp) *n. Hyssopus officinalis*, fam. *Labiatae*, a small, bushy European plant with blue flowers. Its leaves have a pungent, mintlike aroma, and were formerly used as a medicine [fr. L. *hyssopus* fr. Gk]

hys·ter·ec·to·my (histəréktəmi:) *pl.* **hys·ter·ec·to·mies** *n.* surgical removal of the womb [fr. Gk *hustera*, womb+*ektomē*, a cutting out]

hys·ter·e·sis (histərí:sis) *n.* (*phys.*) delay in the production of an effect by a cause, as exhibited in the elastic and magnetic behavior of matter. An example is the delay in recovery from the stress on a strained body after the stress has been removed (leaving a residual strain). A similar delay occurs in magnetic induction **hys·ter·et·ic** (histərétik) *adj.* [Gk *husterēsis*, a lagging behind]

—The hysteresis cycle is a cycle of variation in the magnetic field used for magnetic induction. The field is periodically reversed until the magnetic induction is a function only of the strength of the field and of its rate of change. The induction is then plotted against the field and a hysteresis curve is obtained, from which the magnetic properties of the substance can be found (coercive force, remanence etc.)

hys·te·ri·a (histíəri:ə, histéri:ə) *n.* a condition, due to a psychological disturbance, characterized by excessive excitability and anxiety. Symptoms of severe bodily disease, e.g. blindness, paralysis, anesthesia and loss of voice, are often produced, or exaggerated, in the absence of adequate bodily cause ‖ behavior in an individual or group characterized by uncontrolled, excessive anxiety, emotionalism etc. [Mod. L. fr. HYSTERIC]

hys·ter·ic (histérik) **1.** *adj.* of or characterized by hysteria **2.** *n.* a hysterical person ‖ (*pl.*) a fit of uncontrolled laughing, crying etc. **hys·tér·i·cal** *adj.* [fr. L. fr. Gk *husterikos* fr. *hustera*, womb]

hys·ter·on prot·er·on (hístərɒnprótərɒn) *n.* (*gram.*) a figure of speech in which what should follow comes first ‖ an inversion of the natural or logical order [L.L. fr. Gk *husteron proteron*, the latter (placed as) the former]

hys·ter·ot·o·my (histərótəmi:) *pl.* **hys·ter·ot·o·mies** *n.* a surgical opening of the womb, e.g. a Caesarean section [Mod. L. *hysterotomia* fr. Gk *hustera*, womb+*-tomia*, a cutting]

CONCISE PRONUNCIATION KEY: **(a)** æ, c*a*t; ɑ, c*a*r; ɔ f*a*wn; ei, sn*a*ke. **(e)** e, h*e*n; i:, sh*ee*p; iə, d*ee*r; ɛə, b*ea*r. **(i)** i, f*i*sh; ai, t*i*ger; ə:, b*i*rd. **(o)** o, *o*x; au, c*ow*; ou, g*oa*t; u, p*oo*r; ɔi, r*oy*al. **(u)** ʌ, d*u*ck; u:, b*u*ll; u:, g*oo*se; ə, b*a*cill*u*s; ju:, c*u*be. x, lo*ch*; θ, *th*ink; δ, *b*other; z, *Z*en; ʒ, cor*s*age; dʒ, *s*avage; ŋ, oranguta*ng*; j, *y*ak; ʃ, *fi*sh; tʃ, fe*tch*; 'l, rabb*le*; 'n, redd*en*. Complete pronunciation key appears inside front cover.

	EARLY NORTH SEMITIC	PHOENICIAN	EARLY HEBREW	EARLY GREEK	CLASSICAL GREEK	ETRUSCAN		EARLY LATIN	CLASSICAL LATIN
						Early	Classical		
I	⇃	⫪	⫪	⟨	I	I	I	I	I

CURSIVE MAJUSCULE (ROMAN)	CURSIVE MINUSCULE (ROMAN)	ANGLO-IRISH MAJUSCULE	CAROLINE MINUSCULE	VENETIAN MINUSCULE (ITALIC)	N. ITALIAN MINUSCULE (ROMAN)
I	ſ	I	ı	i	ı

A. C. SYLVESTER, CAMBRIDGE, ENGLAND

Development of the letter I, beginning with the early North Semitic letter. Evolution of both the majuscule, or capital, letter I and the minuscule, or lowercase, letter i are shown.

I, i (ai) the ninth letter of the English alphabet ‖ (*math.*) the symbol (i) for the square root of − 1 ‖ (*phys.*) the symbol (I) for moment of inertia

I 1. *pron., 1st person sing., nominative case* oneself, as named by oneself **2.** *n.* the self or ego [O.E. *ic*]

Ia. Iowa

IAEA *INTERNATIONAL ATOMIC ENERGY AGENCY

-ial *suffix* of or pertaining to, as in 'memorial' [fr. L. *-ialis, -iale*]

i·amb (áiæmb) *n.* an iambus

i·am·bic (aiæmbik) **1.** *adj.* of verse using the iambus **2.** *n.* an iambus ‖ (often *pl.*) verse using the iambus ‖ a satirical poem written in iambuses [fr. L. *iambicus* fr. Gk]

i·am·bus (aiæmbəs) *pl.* **i·am·bus·es, i·am·bi** (aiæmbai) *n.* a metrical foot composed of a short syllable followed by a long one (v—), or an unaccented syllable followed by an accented one [L. fr. Gk *iambos*]

-ian *suffix* of or belonging to, as in 'Freudian' [fr. L. *-ianus*]

i·an·thi·na (aiænθinə) *n.* janthina

Ia·si, Jas·sy (jáʃi:, jaʃ) a city (pop. 264,947) of E. Moldavia, Rumania. Industries: hemp and cotton spinning, chemicals, food processing. University (1860)

i·at·ro·gen·ic (aiætrədʒénik) *adj.* (*med.*) resulting from the activity of a physician. Originally applied to a disorder or disorders inadvertently induced in the patient by the manner of the physician's examination, discussion, or treatment (*Cf* HALO EFFECT), it now applies to any condition occurring in a patient as a result of medical treatment, such as a drug reaction

I·ba·dan (ibád'n) the capital (pop. 1,800,000) of the Western State, Nigeria, a market (cotton, palm oil, tobacco): University (1962, founded 1948 as a University College)

I·ba·gué (i:bágé) a city (pop. 263,669) of W. central Colombia on a high plain (c. 4,300 ft) about 60 miles west of Bogotá

I·ban (íban) *DYAK

Ibañez *BLASCO IBAÑEZ

I·ba·ñez del Cam·po (i:bánjesðelkámpɔ), Carlos (1877–1960), Chilean president, inaugurated in 1927. His authoritarianism and ineffective economic policy caused his overthrow (1931) and exile. Appealing to the lower-working-class element, he served again as president (1952–8), but failed to improve the Chilean economy

I·be·ri·an (aibíəri:ən) **1.** *adj.* of the region constituted by the Iberian Peninsula ‖ of ancient Iberia (now transcaucasian Georgia) **2.** *n.* a Spaniard or Portuguese ‖ (*hist.*) a member of the Caucasoid people formerly inhabiting the Iberian Peninsula ‖ the language spoken by this people [fr. L. *Iberia* fr. Gk *Ibēres,* the Spaniards]

Iberian Peninsula the most westerly peninsula of southern Europe, lying between the Atlantic and the Mediterranean, bounded on its land side (northeast) by the Pyrenees, and comprising Spain and Portugal. The Strait of Gibraltar separates it from N. Africa

I·bert (i:ber), Jacques François Antoine (1890–1962), French composer of comic operas, chamber music etc.

I·ber·ville (i:bervi:l), Pierre Le Moyne, Sieur d' (1661–1706), French Canadian explorer. He was the first to explore the delta of the Mississippi (1699), and founded the first white colony in Louisiana (1699)

i·bex (áibeks) *pl.* **i·bex·es, i·bex** *n.* any of several wild mountain goats of Europe and Asia. The male has large horns curved backward [L.]

ibid. (ibid) ibidem

i·bi·dem (ibidəm, ibáidəm) in the same already specified book, chapter etc. [L.=in the same place]

i·bis (áibis) *pl.* **i·bis·es, i·bis** *n.* any of several wading birds of fam. *Threskiornithidae,* allied to the storks, found esp. in tropical regions. They are about 2 ft tall, with long, downward-curving bills. *Threskiornis aethiopica* was venerated by the ancient Egyptians [L. fr. Gk *ibis,* the Egyptian ibis]

I·bi·za (i:ví:θa) *BALEARIC ISLANDS

IBM *INTERNATIONAL BUSINESS MACHINES

ibn A·ra·bi (íbənárabi:) (1165–1240), Arab scholar and reputedly the greatest mystic of Islam. His chief works, 'Fusus al Hikam' and 'Futuhat al Makkiya', form an encyclopedia of Sufic doctrines

ibn Ba·tu·ta (ibənbatú:ta) (c. 1304–c. 1378), Moslem traveler. He dictated (c. 1355) a vivid description of his journeys (1325–54), which had taken him through N. and W. Africa, Asia, India and the Far East

ibn Khal·dun (ibənxaldú:n) (1332–1406), Arab historian. He is most famous for the 'muquaddama' (introduction) to his historical work 'Kitab al Ibar' in which he develops a scientific philosophy of history

ibn Sa·ud, Ab·dul A·ziz (íbənsaú:d, úbdulazí:z) (c. 1880–1953), founder and king (1925–53) of Saudi Arabia. After leading Wahhabi conquests of Nejd (1902–5) and Hejaz (1924–5), he became king of these areas, the country being renamed Saudi Arabia in 1932. Under his rule, the kingdom's vast oil resources were developed with American capital

ibn Si·na (íbənsí:na) *AVICENNA

I·bo (í:bou) *pl.* **I·bo, I·bos** *n.* a people of S.E. Nigeria ‖ a member of this people ‖ their language (*KWA)

Ib·ra·him Pa·sha (ibrahí:mpáʃə) (1789–1848), Egyptian general, son of Mohammed Ali. He occupied Nejd (1817–18), most of Greece (1825–8), and Syria (1832), of which he became governor (1833–9). He served briefly (1848) as viceroy of Egypt

Ib·sen (íbsən), Henrik Johan (1828–1906), Norwegian dramatist. 'Brand' (1866) and 'Peer Gynt' (1867) were his first real successes and the last of his verse plays. His later works, e.g. 'A Doll's House' (1879), 'Ghosts' (1881), 'The Wild Duck' (1884), 'Rosmersholm' (1886) and 'Hedda Gabler' (1890), deal with social problems, while the last plays 'The Master Builder' (1892), 'John Gabriel Borkman' (1896), 'When We Dead Awaken' (1899) etc., are more obviously symbolic. However, in all the prose plays the realistic surface action is symbolic of some deeper psychological situation and serves to reveal the complexities of powerful but often tragically marred characters. Ibsen's realism, and also his practice of using a central symbol to throw light on the action, immensely influenced modern dramatists

ibuprofen (aibjú:prəfin), a nonprescription analgesic drug that reduces swelling and relieves pain and cramps. In the U.S. a prescription for it was necessary until 1984

-ic *suffix* used to form adjectives meaning of, pertaining to, as in 'bardic' [fr. F. *-ique* fr. L. *-icus*]

IC (*electr. abbr.*) for integrated circuit

I·ca (í:ka) *PUTUMAYO

-ical *suffix* used to form adjectives meaning of, pertaining to, and to provide alternative forms for adjectives ending in -ic, as in 'cosmological' [fr. *-ic*+*-al* fr. L. *-alis,* pertaining to]

-ically *suffix* used to form adverbs from adjectives ending in -ic or -ical

ICAO *INTERNATIONAL CIVIL AVIATION ORGANIZATION

Ic·a·rus (íkərəs, áikərəs) (*Gk mythol.*) the son of Daedalus. He escaped from the labyrinth of Crete with wings attached by wax, but flew too near the sun. The wax melted and he was drowned in the Aegean

I·ca·za Co·ro·nel (i:kásakɔrɔnél), Jorge (1906–78), Ecuadorian writer, known for his realistic portrayal of the suffering of the Indians in his novels, notably 'Huasipungo' (1934) and 'En las calles' (1935)

ICBM, I.C.B.M. an intercontinental ballistic missile, having a range of 3,500 nautical miles or more

I.C.C. Interstate Commerce Commission

ice (ais) **1.** *n.* water solidified by freezing || the frozen surface of water || a dessert of frozen, sweetened water flavored with fruit juice etc. || (*Br.*) a serving of ice cream || something looking like ice, *camphor ice* **to break the ice** to break down the formality or reserve in human intercourse || (*slang*) an illegal bonus paid for a ticket to a public event, esp. to a selling employee || to be the first of a group to do some group action **to cut no ice** to be ineffective, make no impression **to skate** (**or be or tread**) **on thin ice** to be dealing with a matter where there is great danger of making a mistake or causing personal offense unless great care is taken **2.** *v. pres. part.* **ic·ing** *past* and *past part.* **iced** *v.t.* to convert into ice || to cover with ice || to cool by adding or applying ice to or by refrigerating, *to ice beer* || to cover with icing, *to ice a cake* || *v.i.* to become coated with ice **3.** *adj.* of or pertaining to ice || used on or for ice [O.E. *īs*]

Ice Age a time of extensive glaciation || the Pleistocene or Glacial epoch

ice ax, *Br.* **ice axe** a small pickax carried by mountaineers esp. for cutting footholds in the ice

ice bag a waterproof bag containing crushed ice, which may be applied to a part of the body for local cooling in certain illnesses

ice·berg (áisbə:rg) *n.* a large, floating mass of ice, only one-ninth projecting above water [prob. fr. Du. *ijsberg*]

ice·blink (áisbliŋk) *n.* the reflection on the horizon of far-off ice fields

ice·boat (áisbout) *n.* a boat built for traveling on ice, with runners resembling those of a sled

ice·bound (áisbaund) *adj.* surrounded or held in by ice, an *icebound ship* || obstructed by ice, an *icebound harbor*

ice·box (áisbɒks) *n.* an insulated box in which the temperature is kept low by ice, used for storing perishable food or for cooling drinks || a refrigerator

ice·break·er (áisbreikər) *n.* a high-powered ship with strongly constructed bow, which breaks a passage through ice by its downward thrust

ice cap a permanent cover of ice over a large area of land, e.g. a glacier on a plateau, sloping down from a central point

ice cream a frozen dessert made of cream, eggs and sugar, and flavored with syrups, fresh fruit etc.

ice-cream cone (áiskri:m) a cone-shaped wafer containing ice cream

ice-cream soda a drink consisting of ice cream, flavored syrup and soda water

iced (aist) *adj.* covered with ice, affected by ice || cooled with ice, chilled || (*cooking*) having a coating or filling of icing

ice·fall (áisfɔl) *n.* the steep part of a glacier, consisting of jagged blocks of ice || a frozen waterfall

ice field a continuous sheet of floating ice || an ice cap

ice floe an extensive mass of floating ice, smaller than an ice field

ice foot the belt or ledge of ice fringing a coast between low-water and high-water marks, esp. in polar regions

ice-free (áisfri) *adj.* (of a sea, river, port etc.) not obstructed by ice

ice hockey a form of hockey played on ice, esp. popular in Canada. The object is to score goals by shooting the puck into the opponents' goal. Teams of six, using flat, angled sticks, play on skates in a rink 200 by 85 ft

ice·kha·na (áiskɒnə) *n.* (*sports*) a place for ice sports events, esp. a frozen lake on which automobile contests are held

Ice·land (áislənd) an island republic (area 39,758 sq. miles, pop. 232,000) in the N. Atlantic. Capital: Reykjavik. Language: Icelandic. Religion: Lutheran. 30% of the land consists of glaciers, snowfields (including Vatnajökull, 3,500 sq. miles) and lava beds. 1% is arable. There are over 100 volcanoes and many geysers. Elevation: mainly 600–3,000 ft. Highest peak: Hvannadalshnútur 6,950 ft. Average temperatures (F.) in Reykjavik: (Jan.) 30°, (July) 52°. Rainfall: 60–90 ins in the mountains and on the south and east coasts, 50 ins in the southwest plains, 10–20 ins in the north. Earthquakes are frequent. Livestock: sheep, cattle, horses. Crops: hay, potatoes, turnips. Chief occupations: fishing (cod, herring, salmon), fish processing. Exports: fish, fish oils, sheepskins. Imports: fuel oil and gasoline, ships, wood, cereals, machinery, paper, coal, vehicles, cement,

foodstuffs. University: Reykjavik (1911). Monetary unit: króna. HISTORY. The island was settled (870–930) by Norse and Irish immigrants, who established (930) a legislative assembly, the Althing. In the age of the sagas, the Icelanders settled Greenland and visited North America (10th c.). Christianity was introduced (11th c.) and the Church gained considerable power (12th c.). Feudal disputes (1262–4) ended in submission to Norway. Royal and Church power increased at the expense of the Althing, and Iceland passed (1380) to Denmark. Natural calamities and a Danish trade monopoly (1602–1787) caused a decline which ended only with the reform of the Althing (1843), the establishment of free trade (1854) and the grant of a constitution (1874). Independence was obtained (1918). Because of its strategic position, Iceland was occupied by the British (1940), who were replaced by the Americans (1941). A republic was established (June 17, 1944). Iceland joined the U.N. (1946) and NATO (1949), and the U.S.A. took over the country's defense (1951). Iceland extended (1958) her coastal fisheries from 4 to 12 nautical miles. Vigdis Finnbogadottir became Iceland's first woman president (1980).

Ice·lan·dic (aisléndik) **1.** *adj.* pertaining to Iceland **2.** *n.* the Icelandic language. Icelandic is spoken by the population of Iceland and by a few people in North America. It belongs, with Norwegian, Danish and Swedish, to the northern branch of the Germanic group of Indo-European languages. Old Icelandic and Old Norse differ only in minor features. During the period of classical Old Icelandic (1150–1350) the sagas, formerly a part of oral tradition, were written down. The use of Latin by the clergy was responsible for the introduction of many Latin borrowings and loan translations during the period 1350–1530, but most of these were later eliminated. The translation of the New Testament (1540) marked the beginning of Modern Icelandic. The number of German loanwords was high because of the influence of Luther's version of the New Testament

Icelandic saga *SAGA

Iceland moss *Cetraria islandica,* an edible lichen found in the Arctic and boreal regions

Iceland poppy *Papaver nudicaule,* a subarctic poppy with yellow or white flowers || *P. alpinum,* an alpine poppy with white, yellow, pink or orange flowers || any of various cultivated poppies derived from these

Iceland spar a transparent calcite found esp. in Iceland

ice·man (áismæn) *pl.* **ice·men** (áismen) *n.* a man who delivers ice || someone who makes or sells ice

ice milk ice cream made with skim milk

ice needle a thin ice crystal floating in the air in cold, clear weather

I·ce·ni (aisí:nai) *pl. n.* (*hist.*) an ancient British tribe inhabiting E. England (1st c. A.D.). Under Boadicea, they revolted against Roman rule (61 A.D.)

ice-out (áisaut) *n.* thawing process of the surface of a body of water. **—ice out** *v.*

ice pack a large expanse of pack ice || crushed ice in a bag or towel for application to a part of the body in certain illnesses

ice pick a sharp, pointed kitchen or bar implement for cracking ice

ice pick scar (*med.*) permanent scar caused by deep internal cysts working skinward

ice plant *Mesembryanthemum crystallinum,* fam. *Aizoaceae,* a xerophyte with hairy, glistening leaves

ice plow, *Br.* **ice plough** a device for cutting ice on a river, lake etc. into blocks

ice point the temperature (0°C. or 32°F.) at which ice and air-saturated water are in equilibrium under standard atmospheric pressure

ice·scape (áisskeip) *n.* a landscape consisting principally of ice caps

ice sheet an ice cap, esp. a glacier covering a very large area for a long period of time, as in the glacial epochs

ice skate a thin bladelike runner which may be clamped to the sole of a boot, used for gliding on ice || a boot fitted with such a runner

ice-skate (áisskeit) *pres. part.* **ice-skat·ing** *past* and *past part.* **ice-skat·ed** *v.i.* to skate on ice

ice-up (áisʌp) *n.* the process of freezing. **—ice up** *v.*

I·chang (í:tʃáŋ) a port (pop. 100,000) in S.W. Hupeh, China, situated just below the Yangtze gorges. It is the terminus for oceangoing vessels

from Shanghai, and the chief entrepôt for the produce of Szechwan and the Yangtze Valley

ich·neu·mon (iknú:mən, iknjú:mən) *n.* a mongoose, esp. *Herpestes ichneumon* found esp. in Egypt, where it was venerated in antiquity as a destroyer of crocodiles' eggs || the ichneumon fly [L. fr. Gk *ichneumōn,* tracker]

ichneumon fly a member of *Ichneumonoidea,* order *Hymenoptera,* a superfamily of parasitic wasps which deposit their eggs either in or on the bodies, eggs or larvae of other insects and ultimately destroy them. They are useful to man in controlling caterpillars etc.

ich·nol·o·gy (iknɒ́lədʒi:) *n.* the study of fossil footprints [fr. Gk *ichnos,* track + *logos,* discourse]

i·chor (áikɔr) *n.* (*Gk mythol.*) a celestial fluid running instead of blood in the veins of gods || a thin discharge from certain ulcers or wounds **i·cho·rous** (áikərəs) *adj.* [Gk *ichōr*]

ich·thus, ich·thys (íkθəs) *n.* a representation of a fish, symbolizing Christ in Christian iconography [Gk, fr. the monogram of Christ: *Iēsous Christos Theou HUios Sōtēr,* Jesus Christ Son of God Savior]

ich·thy·oid (íkθi:ɔid) **1.** *adj.* resembling a fish **2.** *n.* a vertebrate having a fishlike form [fr. Gk *ichthus* (*ichthuos*), fish]

ich·thy·o·log·i·cal (ikθi:əlɒ́dʒik'l) *adj.* of or pertaining to ichthyology

ich·thy·ol·o·gist (ikθi:ɒ́lədʒist) *n.* a specialist in ichthyology

ich·thy·ol·o·gy (ikθi:ɒ́lədʒi:) *n.* the scientific study of fish [fr. Gk *ichthus* (*ichthuos*), fish + *logos,* discourse]

ich·thy·oph·a·gi (ikθi:ɒ́fədʒai) *pl. n.* people subsisting chiefly on fish and seafood **ich·thy·a·gous** (ikθi:ɒ́fəgəs) *adj.* fish-eating **ich·thy·oph·a·gy** (ikθi:ɒ́fədʒi:) *n.* the practice of eating fish [L. fr. Gk *ichthus* (*ichthuos*), fish +*phagein,* to eat]

Ich·thy·or·nis (ikθi:ɔ́rnis) *n.* a genus, fam. *Ichthyornithidae,* of ternlike birds of the Mesozoic era with sharp, socketed teeth and well-developed wings, found fossilized in the Cretaceous rocks of North America [Mod. L. fr. Gk *ichthus* (*ichthuos*), fish + *ornis* (*ornithos*), bird]

ich·thy·o·saur (íkθi:əsɔr) *n.* a member of *Ichthyosauria,* an order of Mesozoic fossil marine reptiles (3–30 ft long), having four paddlelike flippers and a long and powerful tail, dorsal and caudal fins, and conical teeth in grooves (adapted for catching fish). They occurred chiefly in the Lias [Mod. L. fr. Gk *ichthus* (*ichthuos*), fish + *sauros,* lizard]

ich·thy·o·sis (ikθi:óusis) *n.* a congenital skin disease in which the epidermis becomes hard, rough and scaly **ich·thy·ot·ic** (ikθi:ɒ́tik) *adj.* [Mod. L. fr. Gk *ichthus* (*ichthuos*), fish]

ichthys *ICHTHUS

i·ci·cle (áisik'l) *n.* a hanging, tapering piece of ice formed by the successive freezing of drops of water as they prepare to fall from the point of attachment [O.E. *īses gicel*]

i·ci·ly (áisili:) *adv.* in an icy manner

i·ci·ness (áisi:nis) *n.* the quality or state of being icy

ic·ing (áisiŋ) *n.* any sweet coating for cakes etc., esp. frosting

icing sugar (*Br.*) confectioners' sugar

i·con, i·kon (áikɒn) *n.* a painting, mosaic or enamel of Christ, the Virgin Mary or a saint, revered as a sacred object in the Eastern Church [L.L. *icon* fr. Gk *eikōn,* picture]

I·co·ni·um (aikóuni:əm) *KONYA

i·con·ize (áikənaiz) *v.* to idolize

i·con·o·clasm (aikɒ́nəklæzəm) *n.* the practice or beliefs of an iconoclast [fr. Gk *eikōn,* image +*klasma,* a breaking]

i·con·o·clast (aikɒ́nəklæst) *n.* a person who destroys religious images, or who opposes their use in worship || a person who seeks to destroy the established order or accepted beliefs, customs, reputations etc. **I·con·o·clast** (*hist.*) an adherent of the movement within the Byzantine Empire to abolish the veneration of icons (8th and 9th cc.). The movement caused violent controversy, which ended (843) when the veneration of icons was officially authorized, being distinguished from the worship ('latria') offered to God **i·con·o·clás·tic** *adj.* **i·con·o·clás·ti·cal·ly** *adv.* [fr. L.L. *iconoclastes* fr. Gk *eikōn,* image + *-klastēs,* breaker]

i·con·o·graph·ic (aikɒnəgráfik) *adj.* of or pertaining to iconography **i·con·o·gráph·i·cal** *adj.*

i·co·nog·ra·phy (aikənɒ́grəfi:) *n.* the study of the images used in art, their sources, and their

CONCISE PRONUNCIATION KEY: **(a)** æ, c*a*t; ɑ, c*a*r; ɔ f*aw*n; ei, sn*a*ke. **(e)** e, h*e*n; i:, sh*ee*p; iə, d*ee*r; ɛə, b*ea*r. **(i)** i, f*i*sh; ai, t*i*ger; ə:, b*i*rd. **(o)** o, *o*x; au, c*ow*; ou, g*oa*t; u, p*oo*r; ɔi, r*oy*al. **(u)** ʌ, d*u*ck; u, b*u*ll; u:, g*oo*se; ə, *a* bacill*u*s; ju:, c*u*be. x, lo*ch*; θ, *th*ink; ð, bo*th*er; z, *Z*en; ʒ, corsa*g*e; dʒ, sava*g*e; ŋ, oranguta*ng*; j, *y*ak; ʃ, *fish*; tʃ, fe*tch*; 'l, rabb*le*; 'n, redd*en*. Complete pronunciation key appears inside front cover.

meaning ‖ the use of symbolic images in art [fr. M.L. *iconographia* fr. Gk *eikōn*, image +*graphos*, written]

i·co·nol·a·try (ạikənólətri:) *n.* the worship of images (cf. IDOLATRY) [fr. Gk *eikōn*, image + *latreia*, worship]

i·con·ol·o·gy (ạikənóləd3i:) *n.* the study of icons ‖ iconography [fr. Gk *eikōn*, image + *logos*, discourse]

i·con·o·scope (aikónəskoup) *n.* (*elect.*) an electronic device used in television to convert an optical image into electrical impulses [fr. *Iconoscope*, a trademark]

i·con·o·stas (aikónəstæs) *n.* an iconostasis [Russ. fr. Gk *eikonostasis*]

i·co·nos·ta·sis (ạikənóstəsis) *pl.* **i·co·nos·ta·ses** (ạikənóstəsi:z) *n.* (*Orthodox Church*) a screen on which icons are placed. It divides the sanctuary from the rest of the church [eccles. L. fr. eccles. Gk fr. *eikōn*, image + *stasis*, position]

i·co·sa·he·dral (aikousəhí:drəl) *adj.* having the form of an icosahedron

i·co·sa·he·dron (aikousəhí:drən) *n.* (*geom.*) a solid with 20 plane sides [Gk *eikosaedron* fr. *eikosi*, twenty + *hedra*, base]

ic·ter·ic (iktérik) *adj.* pertaining to or affected with jaundice [fr. L. *ictericus* fr. Gk fr. *ikteros*, jaundice]

ic·ter·us (íktərəs) *n.* jaundice ‖ a plant disease which turns the foliage yellow [L. fr. Gk *ikteros*, jaundice]

Ic·ti·nus (iktáinəs) (late 5th c. B.C.), Greek architect. With Callicrates, he designed the Parthenon

ic·tus (íktəs) *n.* (*prosody*) metrical stress ‖ (*med.*) a convulsion or stroke [L.=blow, stroke]

ICU (*med. abbr.*) for intensive care unit

i·cy (áisi:) *comp.* **i·ci·er** *superl.* **i·ci·est** *adj.* covered with ice ‖ so cold that ice forms ‖ very cold in manner

Id. Idaho

id (id) *n.* (*psychoanal.*) the reservoir of man's instinctive drives, as defined by Freud (cf. EGO, cf. SUPEREGO) [Mod. L., trans. of G. *es*, it]

I'd (aid) *contr.* of I HAD, I WOULD

I·da, Mt (áidə) a mountain in central Crete (highest point 8,195 ft)

Ida, Mt (*Turk.* Kazdagi) a mountain (summit 5,180 ft of the Ida Mtns range) in N.W. Asia Minor

I·da·ho (áidəhou) (*abbr.* Id.) a state (area 83,557 sq. miles, pop. 965,000) of the northwestern U.S.A., largely occupied by the Rocky Mtns. Capital: Boise. Agriculture (the leading industry, although very dependent on irrigation): potatoes (first state producer), wheat, fodder crops, beans and peas, beef and dairy cattle. Resources: timber, silver and lead (first state producer of each), zinc, copper, gold, beryllium ore. Industries: lumber and forest products, metal refining, food processing. State university (1889) at Moscow. Idaho became a territory (1863) and the 43rd state (1890)

-ide, -id *suffix* (*chem.*) used to form names of compounds [after OXIDE]

i·de·a (aidíə) *n.* a mental image, conception ‖ an opinion ‖ a plan, *have you any ideas for the future ?* ‖ (*loosely*) knowledge, *have you any idea of the time?* ‖ a vague sense of probability, hunch ‖ appraisal, estimate, *to form an idea of someone's ability* **to get ideas into one's head** to hope for more than will be fulfilled **what's the big idea?** (*pop.*) what is all this nonsense about? [L.L. fr. Gk] —Plato defines an idea as a perfect and eternal pattern of which reality is an imperfect copy. According to Descartes and others an idea is a mental image, while according to Kant it arises independently of sense perception

i·de·al (aidíəl) **1.** *n.* a model of perfection or beauty **2.** *adj.* pertaining to an ideal ‖ supremely good or desirable ‖ existing only in thought [F. *idéal*]

ideal gas (*phys.*) a gas that obeys the ideal gas law exactly [*KINETIC THEORY]

ideal gas law (*phys.*) the equation of state for a hypothetical gas (PV=nRT, where P=pressure of gas, V=volume, n=number of moles, R=gas constant, T=temperature on the Kelvin scale) originally formulated as a combination of Charles's law and Boyle's law, both of which describe approximately the behavior of real gases at moderate conditions of temperature and at low pressures. The ideal gas law is a direct consequence of the kinetic theory and therefore can only be true for a gas whose particles behave as described by the assumptions of that theory

i·de·al·ism (aidíəlizəm, aidí:əlizəm) *n.* the attitude which consists in conceiving ideals and trying to realize them ‖ (*philos.*) any doctrine holding that thought deals with representation and ideas rather than with material objects ‖ (*art*) emphasis on ideal types rather than the faithful representation of reality [fr. F. *idéalisme* or G. *idealismus*]

i·de·al·ist (aidíəlist, aidí:əlist) *n.* a person who accepts and adheres to the concepts of idealism ‖ a person who attaches more importance to ideals than to practical considerations ‖ (*art*) a proponent of idealism as opposed to realism **i·de·al·is·tic** *adj.* **i·de·al·is·ti·cal·ly** *adv.*

i·de·al·i·ty (aidi:ǽliti:) *n.* the quality or state of being ideal rather than real ‖ the ability to form and retain ideals

i·de·al·i·za·tion (aidi:əlizéiʃən) *n.* an idealizing or being idealized ‖ something idealized

i·de·al·ize (aidí:əlaiz) *pres. part.* **i·de·al·iz·ing** *past* and *past part.* **i·de·al·ized** *v.t.* to attribute ideal perfection to ‖ to show something in its ideal form, *an idealized landscape, Whistler idealized all mothers in the portrait of his own mother* ‖ *v.i.* to conceive of or form an ideal

i·de·al·ly (aidí:əli:) *adv.* in an ideal way, perfectly ‖ theoretically

i·de·ate (áidi:eit, aidí:it) *n.* the reality corresponding to an idea [fr. Mod. L. *ideatus*, deriving from an idea]

i·de·ate (áidi:eit, aidí:eit) *pres. part.* **i·de·at·ing** *past* and *past part.* **i·de·at·ed** *v.t.* to construct a mental image of ‖ to imagine (something) not present to the senses ‖ *v.i.* to form ideas [IDEA]

i·de·a·tion (aidi:éiʃən) *n.* the forming of ideas **i·de·a·tion·al** *adj.*

i·dée fixe (i:deifi:ks) *n.* a fixed idea [F.]

i·den·tic (aidéntik) *adj.* of a communication made in precisely the same terms by each of several governments to another (cf. JOINT) [fr. M.L. *identicus* fr. *idem*, the same]

i·den·ti·cal (aidéntik'l) *adj.* (of two or more things) the same in all respects ‖ (*biol.*) designating twins produced from one zygote (cf. FRATERNAL) ‖ (*pop.*) the very same, *this is the identical spot where we stood yesterday* [fr. M.L. *identicus* fr. *idem*, the same]

i·den·ti·fi·ca·tion (aidentifikéiʃən) *n.* an identifying or being identified ‖ something that identifies ‖ (*math.*) the conformity or differences between a model and reality with regard to certain variables and parameters. A model is "identified" if all of its equations are identified

i·den·ti·fy (aidéntifai) *pres. part.* **i·den·ti·fy·ing** *past* and *past part.* **i·den·ti·fied** *v.t.* to recognize the identity of (someone or something) ‖ to establish or demonstrate the identity of, *she identified him as her attacker, can you identify yourself?* ‖ to consider as being the same or as being necessarily associated, *he identifies her happiness with his own* ‖ *v.i.* to think of oneself as being one with another person or thing **to identify oneself with** to show oneself to be committed to, *he refused to identify himself with fascist methods* ‖ to think of oneself as being one with (another person), *he identifies himself with his father* [fr. L.L. *identificare*, to make identical]

i·den·ti·ty (aidéntiti:) *pl.* **i·den·ti·ties** *n.* the fact of being the same in all respects ‖ who a person is, or what a thing is, *his identity was uncertain* ‖ (*math.*) a statement of equality (an equation) which is true under all conditions [fr. F. *identité*]

identity crisis (*psych.*) emotional disturbance, characterized by self-consciousness, uncertainty, and anxiety, common during adolescence

identity hypothesis (*psych.*) identity theory (which see)

identity matrix (*math.*) a square matrix in which the principal diagonal is 1 and all other entities are 0

identity theory (*psych.*) hypothesis that introspective mental states are products of certain physical states of the brain and nervous system. *also* identity hypothesis

id·e·o·gram (ídi:əgræm, áidi:əgræm) *n.* a symbol, or picture which represents and conveys an idea of an object without using its name, *a numeral or a pictorial road sign* ‖ a symbol representing a word but not representing the sounds which constitute it, *as in alphabetic writing* [fr. Gk *idea*, idea + *gramma*, a letter]

id·e·o·graph (ídi:əgræf, ídi:əgrɑf, áidi:əgræf, áidi:əgrɑf) *n.* an ideograph **id·e·o·gráph·ic** *adj.* **id·e·o·gráph·i·cal·ly** *adv.* **id·e·o·gráph·y**

(ídi:ógrəfi:, aidi:ógrəfi:) *n.* [fr. Gk *idea* idea+*graphos*, written]

i·de·o·log·ic (ạidi:əlód3ik,idi:əlód3ik) *adj.* of or pertaining to ideology ‖ of or relating to ideas **i·de·o·lóg·i·cal** *adj.*

id·e·ol·o·gism (idi:óləd3izəm) *n.* extreme loyalty to an ideology

i·de·ol·o·gy (aidi:óləd3i:, ịdi:óləd3i:) *pl.* **i·de·ol·o·gies** *n.* a body of ideas used in support of an economic, political or social theory ‖ the way of thinking of a class, culture or individual ‖ (*philos.*) the science of ideas, esp. those springing from sensory stimulation [fr. F. *idéologie*]

ides (aidz) *pl. n.* (in the ancient Roman calendar) the 15th day of March, May, July and October and the 13th day of all other months [F. fr. L. *Idus*]

id·i·o·blast (ídi:əblæst) *n.* a plant cell containing oil, gum, calcium carbonate or other products and which differs from the surrounding parenchyma ‖ (*biol.*) a hypothetical structural cell unit [fr. Gk *idios*, separate + *blastos*, cell]

id·i·o·cy (ídi:əsi:) *pl.* **id·i·o·cies** *n.* the lowest grade of mental deficiency ‖ very stupid or foolish behavior ‖ an instance of such behavior [IDIOT]

id·i·om (ídi:əm) *n.* the language peculiar to a people, country, class, community or, more rarely, an individual ‖ the structure of the usual patterns of expression of a language ‖ a construction, expression etc. having a meaning different from the literal one or not according to the usual patterns of the language ‖ a writer's characteristic use of words, *the Wodehouse idiom* ‖ a characteristic style in music, art etc., *the cubist idiom* [fr. L. *idioma* fr. Gk fr. *idios*, own, private]

id·i·o·mat·ic (ịdi:əmǽtik) *adj.* peculiar to the patterns of expression of a particular language ‖ of or pertaining to idioms, *idiomatic command of French* ‖ (of a language) having many idioms **id·i·o·mát·i·cal·ly** *adv.* [fr. Gk *idiōmatikos*, particular]

id·i·o·mor·phic (ịdi:əmórfik) *adj.* (*geol.*, of minerals in igneous rock) having the characteristic crystalline form (cf. ALLOTRIOMORPHIC) [fr. Gk *idios*, own+ *morphē*, form]

id·i·o·path·ic (ịdi:əpǽθik) *adj.* of or pertaining to an idiopathy **id·i·o·páth·i·cal·ly** *adv.*

id·i·op·a·thy (idi:ópəθi:) *pl.* **id·i·op·a·thies** *n.* a disease which is not caused or preceded by another disease [fr. Mod. L. *idiopathia* fr. Gk fr. *idios*, separate+ *pathos*, suffering]

id·i·o·plasm (ídi:əplæzəm) *n.* the generative or germinal part of a cell, generally considered equivalent to chromatin **id·i·o·plas·mat·ic** (ịdi:ouplæzmǽtik), **id·i·o·plás·mic** *adjs* [fr. Gk *idios*, separate + PLASM]

id·i·o·syn·cra·sy (ịdi:əsíŋkrəsi:) *pl.* **id·i·o·syn·cra·sies** *n.* a distinguishing habit of thought, feeling or behavior characteristic of an individual, esp. a personal peculiarity **id·i·o·syn·crat·ic** (ịdi:ousinkrǽtik) *adj.* **id·i·o·syn·crát·i·cal·ly** *adv.* [fr. Gk *idiosunkrasia*, a mixing together]

id·i·ot (ídi:ət) *n.* a person afflicted by idiocy, having a mental age of two years or less, and requiring constant care (cf. IMBECILE, cf. MORON) ‖ (*pop.*) a dolt **id·i·ot·ic** (ịdi:ótik) *adj.* [F. fr. L. *idiota* fr. Gk *idiōtes*, layman]

idiot board a teleprompter

id·i·ot·i·cal·ly (ịdi:ótikli:) *adv.* in an idiotic manner [fr. *idiotical* fr. L.L. *idioticus*]

id·i·o·type (ídi:ətaip) *n.* (*immunology*) property of an antibody new to the body that creates anti-genicity and is unique among antigens

i·dle (áid'l) **1.** *adj.* unwilling to work ‖ not working, *the factory was idle for a week* ‖ casual, not serious, *an idle jest* **2.** *v. pres. part.* **i·dling** *past* and *past part.* **i·dled** *v.i.* to let time pass without working ‖ to waste time ‖ (of an engine) to consume fuel without being connected with moving parts ‖ *v.t.* (with 'away') to let (a period of time) pass without working, *to idle away the morning* **i·dler** *n.* someone who is idle ‖ an idler wheel [O.E. *ídel*, empty]

idler wheel a cogged wheel which transmits motion from another wheel to a third wheel without altering the velocity ratio or direction of the revolution

idle wheel an idler wheel

i·dly (áidli:) *adv.* in an idle manner

i·do·crase (áidəkreis, áidəkreiz) *n.* vesuvianite

i·dol (áid'l) *n.* an image of a god constructed of wood, stone etc. and worshipped as if it were the god it represents ‖ a person or object of intense admiration or love [O.F. *idole* fr. L.L. fr. Gk]

CONCISE PRONUNCIATION KEY: **(a)** æ, c*a*t; ɑ, c*a*r; ɔ f*aw*n; ei, sn*a*ke. **(e)** e, h*e*n; iː, sh*ee*p; iə, d*ee*r; ɛə, b*ea*r. **(i)** i, f*i*sh; ai, t*i*ger; əː, b*i*rd. **(o)** o, *o*x; au, c*ow*; ou, g*oa*t; u, p*oo*r; ɔi, r*oy*al. **(u)** ʌ, d*u*ck; u, b*u*ll; uː, g*oo*se; ə, b*a*cillus; juː, c*u*be. x, lo*ch*; θ, *th*ink; ð, bo*th*er; z, *Z*en; ʒ, corsa*g*e; dʒ, sava*g*e; ŋ, orangutan*g*; j, *y*ak; ʃ, *fish*; tʃ, fe*tch*; 'l, rabb*le*; 'n, red*den*. Complete pronunciation key appears inside front cover.

i·dol·a·ter (aidólətər) n. someone who worships idols **i·dól·a·tress** n. a female idolater [fr. O.F. idolatre fr. eccles. L. fr. Gk]

i·dol·a·trize (aidólətraiz) pres. part. **i·dol·a·triz·ing** past and past part. **i·dol·a·trized** v.t. to idolize | v.i. to worship idols [IDOLATRY]

i·dol·a·trous (aidólətrəs) adj. of, pertaining to or having the nature of idolatry | practicing idolatry [IDOLATER]

i·dol·a·try (aidólətri:) n. the worship of an idol or of idols [fr. O.F. idolatrie, ydolatrie fr. eccles. L. idolatria]

i·dol·ize (áid'laiz) pres. part. **i·dol·iz·ing** past and past part. **i·dol·ized** v.t. to treat as an idol, esp. to love with inordinate affection

I·dom·e·neus (aidómənu:s, aidómənu:s) (Gk mythol.) Cretan king. He fought in the Trojan War and, caught in a storm on the return journey, made a rash vow to sacrifice the first living thing he met on landing safely in Crete. It was his son

I·dri·si (idrí:si:) (c. 1099–c. 1166), Arab geographer. He wrote (1154) a description of the earth based on the work of Ptolemy and other geographers, and on his own travels in N. Africa and W. Asia. He made a silver celestial globe for his patron, Roger II of Sicily

i·dyll, i·dyl (áid'l, Br. ídil) n. a short pastoral poem | a verse or prose work, esp. with a rural setting, evoking a mood of ideal contentment | an event, situation etc. suitable as a subject for an idyll **i·dyl·lic** (aidílik) adj. **i·dýl·li·cal·ly** adv. **i·dýl·list, i·dýl·ist** n. [fr. L. idyllium fr. Gk eidullion, dim. of eidos, picture]

i.e. that is, to be precise [fr. L. id est]

Iena *JENA

I·e·ya·su To·ku·ga·wa (i:éiasu:toukugáwa) (1542–1616), Japanese general and founder of the Tokugawa shogunate (1603–1867)

if (if) **1.** conj. in case, in the event that, if it rains we will stay at home | on the assumption that, if x=y and y=z then x=z | granting that, if you are right we are really in trouble | supposing, if it were true it would be monstrous | on condition that, if he apologizes she will forgive him | although, he is kindly, if a bit too impulsive | whether, ask if he can come **2.** n. a condition | a supposition, there are too many ifs in your offer [O.E. gif]

IFC *INTERNATIONAL FINANCE CORPORATION

I·fe (i:fei) a town (pop. 176,000) in W. Nigeria, 45 miles east of Ibadan: palace of the Oni of Ife, and museum of Yoruba antiquities. University (1961)

If·ni (ifni:) a coastal area (741 sq. miles, pop. 45,784) of S.W. Morocco. It was ceded (1860) to Spain, though Spanish rule became effective only in 1934. Spain returned it (Jan. 1969) de jure to Morocco

ig·loo, ig·lu (íglu:) n. an Eskimo dwelling, esp. one in the shape of a dome built of blocks of snow | dome-shaped portable plastic structure designed for protective covering [Esk.=house]

igloo space area in an earth-covered structure of concrete and/or steel designed for the storage of ammunition and explosives

Ig·na·tius (ignéiʃəs), St (d. c. 110), bishop of Antioch. His letters to the Churches in Asia Minor show his great charity. Feast: Feb. 1

Ignatius, St (c. 798–877), patriarch of Constantinople. An opponent of the Iconoclasts, he was elected patriarch (c. 846), deposed (858) in favor of Photius, but restored as patriarch (867). Feast: Oct. 23

Ignatius Loy·o·la (lɔióulə), St (c. 1491–1556), Spanish theologian. He founded the Society of Jesus (1540), was elected its general (1541) and wrote its 'Constitutions', which remain in force unaltered. His 'Spiritual Exercises' are a system of rules, prayers, self-examination etc. to train the whole man for the Christian life. Feast: July 31

ig·ne·ous (ígni:əs) adj. containing, resembling or emitting fire [fr. L. igneus]

igneous rock rock formed by the cooling and recrystallization of molten magma. It is one of the three main types of rock composing the earth's crust (cf. METAMORPHIC ROCK, cf. SEDIMENTARY ROCK). Igneous rock occurs either beneath the earth's surface or extruded as lava or volcanic rock

ig·nis fat·u·us (ígnis fætʃu:əs) pl. **ig·nes fat·u·i** (ígneizfætʃu:ai) n. a will-o'-the-wisp (marsh gas) [M.L. or Mod. L.=foolish fire]

ig·nit·a·ble, ig·nit·i·ble (ignáitəb'l) adj. capable of being ignited

ig·nite (ignáit) pres. part. **ig·nit·ing** past and past part. **ig·nit·ed** v.t. to heat (something) so strongly that it begins to burn | to set on fire | v.i. to begin to burn [fr. ignite obs. adj. fr. L. ignire (ignitus)]

ignitible *IGNITABLE

ig·ni·tion (igníʃən) n. the act of making something begin to burn | the method or process of igniting a fuel mixture, e.g. in an internal-combustion engine [fr. M.L. or Mod. L. ignitio (ignitionis)]

ig·no·ble (ignóub'l) adj. unworthy or degraded in character or quality (opp. NOBLE) [F.]

ig·no·min·i·ous (ignəmíni:əs) adj. disgraceful, characterized by or deserving ignominy | degrading, humiliating [F. ignominieux or fr. L. ignominiosus]

ig·no·min·y (ígnəmini:) n. public disgrace | base conduct leading to disgrace [F. ignominie]

ig·no·ra·mus (ignəréiməs, ignərǽməs) n. someone who has little or no knowledge or education | (law, hist.) an endorsement formerly written by a grand jury on a bill of indictment denoting that the evidence was insufficient to support the charge [L.=we do not know]

ig·no·rance (ígnərəns) n. the state of not knowing, to act in ignorance | a lack of education [F.]

ig·no·rant (ígnərənt) adj. not knowing, ignorant of the facts | lacking education | showing or resulting from ignorance, an ignorant remark [F.]

ig·nore (ignɔ́r, ignóur) pres. part. **ig·nor·ing** past and past part. **ig·nored** v.t. to refuse to take notice of, refuse to consider, he ignored their presence, ignore those threats [fr. F. ignorer or L. ignorare, not to know]

I·gua·la (i:gwálə) a town in S. Mexico in the state of Guerrero, where Iturbide proclaimed (Feb. 24, 1821) the 'Plan of Iguala'. The plan, initiated by Guerrero, guaranteed the political independence of Mexico as a constitutional monarchy, the monarch to be selected from the royal house of Spain. Since Ferdinand VII repudiated the plan, Iturbide proclaimed himself (1822) Emperor Agustin I

i·gua·na (igwánə) n. a member of Iguanidae, a family of edible, herbivorous, usually arboreal, tropical American lizards reaching 5 ft or more in length, having a long tail, a large, wide mouth, denticulate teeth and sharp claws [Span. fr. Carib]

i·gua·no·don (igwánədɒn) n. a genus of herbivorous dinosaurs of the early Cretaceous, 25-30 ft long, having teeth and bones resembling those of the iguana, and a pelvis like that of a bird [fr. IGUANA + Gk odous (odontos), tooth]

I·guas·su Falls (i:gwasú:) (Span. Iguazú) a series of cataracts above the mouth of the Iguassu River on the Argentine-Brazilian border, pouring over a 210-ft precipice, 2½ miles wide

ih·ram (i:rám) n. a two-piece garment of white cotton worn by pilgrims to Mecca, one piece wrapped around the loins, the other worn on the upper part of the body, leaving the right shoulder and arm free | the state of devotion and of being subject to certain rules, concomitant with the wearing of this garment | a pilgrim wearing this garment [Arab.]

IHS a monogram for 'Jesus' often embroidered on church vestments etc. [fr. Gk IHΣ (OYΣ), Jesus]

Ijs·sel·meer (áisəlmeir) a freshwater lake (area 1,125 sq. miles) in the N. Netherlands, formerly part of the Zuider Zee but closed off by a dam (finished 1932)

I·ka·ri·a (i:kɑ́ri:ɑ:) a Greek island (area 99 sq. miles, pop. 10,000) of the Sporades, between Samos and Tinos

i·ke·ba·na (ikeibánə) n. Japanese art of flower arrangement

I·ke·da Hayato (i:keidə) (1899–1965), Japanese statesman, prime minister (1960–4)

Ikh·na·ton (iknát'n) the title taken by Amenhotep IV

ikon *ICON

il- (il) prefix form of IN- before l

i·lang-i·lang, y·lang-y·lang (í:læŋí:læŋ) n. Canangium odoratum, fam. Annonaceae, a tree of Malaysia and the Philippines. Its greenish yellow flowers yield a delicate perfume when distilled | the perfume produced from these flowers [Tagalog álangílang]

il·e·ac (íli:æk) adj. of or relating to the ileum

Ile-de-France (i:ldəfrɑ̃s) a former province of France in the central Paris basin, historically the nucleus of the unified kingdom. It includes the modern departments of Oise, Seine, Essonne, Hauts-de-Seine, Seine-Saint-Denis, Val-

de-Marne, Val-d'Oise, Yvelines and part of Aisne. It is a rich agricultural region (cereals, sugar beets, market produce, dairy foods) as well as a great center of industry (*FRANCE). Center: Paris. Main towns: Beauvais, Versailles, Compiègne, Fontainebleau. Many large forests remain. It grew around the countship of Paris, the domain of the Capetians, and was a province from the 16th c. to 1789

il·e·i·tis (ili:áitis) n. inflammation of the ileum [fr. ILEUM+-ITIS]

I·ler·da (iló:rdə) *LÉRIDA

il·e·um (íli:əm) pl. **il·e·a** (íli:ə) n. the lowest part of the small intestine, opening into the large intestine [L.L.]

il·e·us (íli:əs) n. illness due to obstruction of the intestines [L. fr. Gk ileos or eileos, colic]

i·lex (áileks) n. the holm oak | a holly [L.]

il·i·ac (íli:æk) adj. (anat.) of or pertaining to the ilium or the region near the ilium [F. iliaque or fr. L.L. iliacus]

Il·i·ad (íli:əd) a Greek epic poem in 24 books, probably composed before 700 B.C., attributed to Homer. It describes a group of incidents in the tenth and last year of the Trojan War, telling how Achilles, who had retired to his tents after a quarrel with Agamemnon, returned to avenge his friend Patroclus, killed by Hector. Besides the graphic battle scenes, fine passages include the description of the funeral of Patroclus, the moving farewell between Hector and Andromache, and Priam's request for Hector's body

Il·i·on (íli:ɒn) the Greek name for Troy

Il·i·um (íli:əm) the Latin name for Troy

il·i·um (íli:əm) pl. **il·i·a** (íli:ə) n. the uppermost of the three sections of the hipbone [L.]

ilk (ilk) n. (usu. in the phrase) **of that ilk** of that sort [O.E. ilca, the same]

Ill. Illinois

ill (il) **1.** adj. comp. **worse** (wə:rs) superl. **worst** (wə:rst) in bad health, not well, sick (comp. also **ill·er** superl. also **ill·est**) | causing or tending to cause evil or harm, ill will | far below standard, faulty, ill breeding **ill at ease** uneasy **to be taken ill** to become ill suddenly **2.** n. anything causing evil, harm, pain, trouble etc., social ills **3.** adv. comp. **worse** superl. **worst** adversely, badly, they took our criticisms ill | scarcely or not at all, it ill becomes him to criticize [M.E. fr. O.N. illr]

ill. illustration, illustrated

I'll (ail) contr. of I WILL or I SHALL

ill-ad·vised (ílədváizd) adj. done without proper consideration, not judicious

Il·lam·pu (i:jámpu:) the highest peak (21,490 ft) in Bolivia, rising near Lake Titicaca in W. central Bolivia

il·la·tion (iléiʃən) n. (logic) a deduction | (logic) the act of deducing [fr. L.L. illatio (illationis)]

il·la·tive (iléitiv) adj. (gram.) expressing an inference, 'therefore' is an illative conjunction | (logic) having to do with deducing, the illative faculty [fr. L.L. illativus]

ill-bred (ílbréd) adj. rude or showing rudeness, an ill-bred person, an ill-bred answer

Ille-et-Vi·laine (i:leivi:len) a department (area 2,697 sq. miles, pop. 653,000) in N.W. France (*BRITTANY). Chief town: Rennes

il·le·gal (ilí:g'l) adj. violating the law **il·le·gál·i·ty** pl. **il·le·gal·i·ties** n. the quality or state of being illegal | an illegal act [F. illégal or fr. M.L. illegalis]

il·le·gal·ize (ilí:gəlaiz) pres. part. **il·le·gal·iz·ing** past and past part. **il·le·gal·ized** v.t. to make illegal

il·leg·i·bil·i·ty (iledʒəbíliti:) n. the state or quality of being illegible

il·leg·i·ble (iléGʒəb'l) adj. not legible **il·lég·i·bly** adv.

il·le·git·i·ma·cy (ilidʒítəməsi:) n. the state or quality of being illegitimate

il·le·git·i·mate (ilidʒítəmit) adj. born out of wedlock | contrary to law, an illegitimate interpretation of the constitution | not authorized by the law | not in accordance with the rules of logic, an illegitimate conclusion [fr. L. illegitimus]

ill-fat·ed (ílféitid) adj. destined to have bad luck | causing bad luck, an ill-fated encounter

ill-fa·vored, Br. ill-fa·voured (ílféivərd) adj. not pleasing in appearance | unpleasant, objectionable

ill-found·ed (ílfáundid) adj. not sustained by logical reasons or facts, ill-founded fears

ill-got·ten (ílgɒ́t'n) adj. dishonestly, illegally or evilly obtained, ill-gotten gains

ill humor, Br. ill humour irritability, crossness

of temperament or mood ‖ a cross, sullen mood, in an *ill humor* **ill-hu-mored,** *Br.* **ill-hu-moured** (ilhjú:mərd) *adj.*

il-lib-er-al (ilíbərəl) *adj.* intolerant, narrow-minded **il-lib-er-al-i-ty** (iljbərǽliti:) *n.* [F.]

il-lic-it (ilísit) *adj.* not permitted by law [F. *illicite*]

il-lim-it-a-bil-i-ty (iljmitəbíliti:) *n.* the quality or state of being illimitable

il-lim-it-a-ble (ilímitəb'l) *adj.* having no limits ‖ immeasurable, *illimitable ambition*

Il-li-nois (ilinói) (*abbr.* Ill.) a state (area 56,400 sq. miles, pop. 11,448,000) on the midwestern plains of the U.S.A. Capital: Springfield. Chief city: Chicago. Agriculture (about 90% of the total area is farmed): corn (leading state producer with Iowa), soybeans (leading producer), hogs, beef and dairy cattle. Resources: coal, oil, fluorspar, sand, limestone. Industries: machinery, electrical manufactures, iron and steel, metal products, meat packing, textiles, chemicals, printing and publishing. Principal universities: University of Illinois (1867) at Champaign-Urbana, Northwestern (1851) at Evanston, University of Chicago. Illinois was explored by the French (late 17th c.), was ceded to Britain (1763) and joined (1784) the U.S.A., of which it became (1818) the 21st state

Illinois a navigable river (273 miles long) and principal internal waterway in Illinois, flowing southwest and emptying into the Mississippi River in W. Illinois

Il-li-nois (ilinói) *pl.* **Illinois** *n.* a confederacy of Indian peoples formerly of Illinois, Iowa and Wisconsin ‖ a member of one of these peoples ‖ their Algonquian language

il-lit-er-a-cy (ilítərəsi:) *n.* the quality or state of being illiterate

il-lit-er-ate (ilítərit) **1.** *adj.* unable to read or write ‖ unfamiliar with books ‖ having little knowledge of the correct use of language ‖ (of writing or speech) showing little knowledge of the correct use of language ‖ having little or no knowledge of a specified subject, *musically illiterate* **2.** *n.* a person who is illiterate [fr. L. *illiteratus*, not learned]

ill-man-nered (ílmǽnərd) *adj.* having or showing impolite or coarse manners

ill nature a surly or malevolent disposition **ill-na-tured** (ílnéitʃərd) *adj.*

ill-ness (ílnis) *n.* the state of being ill (in health) ‖ a particular disease

il-log-i-cal (ilódʒik'l) *adj.* contrary to the laws of logic ‖ (of persons) thinking or acting in a way incompatible with logic

ill-o-mened (ílóumənd) *adj.* inauspicious, attended by bad omens

ill-starred (ílstárd) *adj.* ill-fated

ill-tem-pered (íltémpərd) *adj.* having or showing a bad temper

ill-timed (íltáimd) *adj.* inopportune

ill-treat (íltrí:t) *v.t.* to treat cruelly

il-lu-mi-nate (ilú:mineit) *pres. part.* **il-lu-mi-nat-ing** *past* and *past part.* **il-lu-mi-nat-ed** *v.t.* to give light to (a region or space) ‖ to decorate with bright or colored lamps ‖ to light up by floodlighting ‖ to decorate (a manuscript) by means of colored initials, borders, pictures etc. (*ILLUMINATION) ‖ to make clear to the mind, *to illuminate a problem* ‖ to subject to detection by radar, sonar, or other radiation ‖ to enlighten (someone) [fr. L. *illuminare* (*illuminatus*), to light up]

il-lu-mi-na-ti (ilu:mináti:) *pl. n.* persons claiming to have superhuman knowledge [L., pl. of *illuminatus*, enlightened]

il-lu-mi-na-tion (ilu:minéiʃən) *n.* the act of illuminating ‖ the decoration of streets or buildings by bright or colored lights ‖ the lights themselves ‖ the lighting up of buildings etc. with floodlights ‖ the decoration of a manuscript ‖ a decoration in a manuscript ‖ the act of making or becoming clear to the mind ‖ (*phys.*) the amount of light falling on unit area of a surface per second [F.]

—The illumination of manuscripts and books includes the drawing and painting of independent illustrations in the margins, and the embellishment of initial letters, flourishes etc. within the columns of writing, usually in gold and bright color, with great decorative freedom. Initial letters of medieval manuscripts were often incorporated in a comparatively large picture, which might be devotional, domestic or floral, and a whole page of a gospel might be devoted to a single illustration. Illumination was one of the major art forms, esp. in the early Middle Ages, and through this medium impor-

tant traditions of art from classical antiquity were transmitted

il-lu-mi-na-tive (ilú:mineitiv, ilú:minətiv) *adj.* of or producing illumination [fr. L. *illuminare* (*illuminatus*)]

il-lu-mi-na-tor (ilú:mineitər) *n.* someone who or something which illuminates

il-lu-mine (ilú:min) to illuminate [F. *illuminer*]

illus illustration, illustrated

ill-us-age (íljú:sidʒ) *n.* cruel, abusive treatment

il-lu-sion (ilú:ʒən) *n.* a delusion ‖ a false interpretation by the mind of a sense perception, *an optical illusion* ‖ a belief or hope that has no real substance **il-lu-sion-ar-y** *adj.* **il-lu-sion-ism** *n.* the doctrine or theory that the external world is an illusion ‖ the use of trompe l'œil or other illusionary effects in painting or decoration **il-lu-sion-ist** *n.* a conjurer ‖ a supporter of the theory of illusionism [F.]

il-lu-sive (ilú:siv) *adj.* deceptive [fr. L. *illudere* (*illusus*), to mock]

il-lu-so-ry (ilú:səri:, ilú:zəri:) *adj.* illusive [fr. L.L. *illusorius*]

il-lus-trate (íləstreit) *pres. part.* **il-lus-trat-ing** *past* and *past part.* **il-lus-trat-ed** *v.t.* to supplement (a written or verbal account) by pictures or designs ‖ to ornament (a book, periodical etc.) with pictures or designs ‖ to make clear by means of examples, *he illustrated his point by relating his own experiences* ‖ *v.i.* to make something clear with pictures, designs or examples **il-lus-tra-tive** (ilástrətiv, íləstreitiv) *adj.* (esp. of an example or story) serving to illustrate **il-lus-tra-tor** (íləstreitər) *n.* someone who illustrates books etc., esp. for a living [fr. L. *illustrare* (*illustratus*), to light up]

il-lus-tra-tion (iləstréiʃən) *n.* the act of illustrating ‖ an example used to explain or demonstrate ‖ a picture, ornament etc. used to illustrate a book or paper [F.]

—In largely illiterate societies (e.g. the European Middle Ages) illustration was an essential part of instruction. For this reason much medieval art was designed to be 'read' and not merely appreciated as art: every detail yielded information to spectators used to seeing all things as symbolical of some aspect of a divinely ordered universe. Early block books, for instance, had illustrations on which barely literate clergy could base detailed expositions of a scripture text. With the Renaissance, illustration became art instead of teaching. The techniques of composition and draftsmanship developed in major art forms were applied first to woodcut, then to wood and copper engraving. But the old tradition survived in emblem books until the 17th c. In the 19th c., techniques of photographic reproduction by line block, halftone and gravure were added to the lithographic processes. This meant a great increase in technical ability at the time of the rise of popular journalism

il-lus-tri-ous (ilástri:əs) *adj.* held in or conferring the highest public esteem [fr. L. *illustris*, lighted up]

Il-lyr-i-a (ilíəri:ə) an ancient region on the east coast of the Adriatic, corresponding roughly to Albania and W. Yugoslavia. It was a Roman province (1st–5th cc.)

il-men-ite (ílmənait) *n.* an oxide of iron and titanium, $FeTiO_3$, a black crystalline ore [after the *Ilmen* Mtns, in the S. Urals, where it is found]

I.L.O. *INTERNATIONAL LABOR ORGANIZATION

I-lo-i-lo (i:louí:lou) the chief port (pop. 227,374) of the central Philippines (Visayas), on S.E. Panay

I-lo-rin (ilóri:n) the capital (pop. 282,000) of Kwara State, Nigeria on the Lagos-Kano railway. It is the trade center for a vast agricultural area

I.L.P. *INDEPENDENT LABOUR PARTY

I'm (aim) *contr.* of I AM

im- (im) *prefix* form of IN- before b, m,p

im-age (ímidʒ) **1.** *n.* a carved, painted or drawn effigy of a person or thing ‖ a mental picture or concept ‖ the optical counterpart of an object, each of whose points acts as a source of light which is reflected in a mirror or focused by a lens (*VIRTUAL IMAGE, *REAL IMAGE) ‖ a person or thing resembling another person or thing, a likeness, *she is the image of her father* ‖ (*computer*) data from one medium (e.g., a punched card) recorded on another medium ‖ (*television*) reproduction of a view on a receiver ‖ (*psych.*) presentation of a sensory experience **2.** *v.t. pres.*

part. **im-ag-ing** *past* and *past part.* **im-aged** to form an image of [F.]

im-age-build-ing (ímidʒbjldiŋ) *n.* creation of a desired public acceptance through public relations, publicity, and advertising

image orthicon (*television*) a highly sensitive camera tube that focuses images on one side of a storage target, scanned from the reverse side by an electron beam. *Cf* ORTHICON

im-age-ry (ímidʒri:) *pl.* **im-age-ries** *n.* expression rich in images ‖ literary images collectively ‖ the images occurring in someone's mind [O.F. *imagerie*]

im-ag-i-na-ble (imǽdʒinəb'l) *adj.* capable of being conceived by the imagination [fr. L.L. *imaginabilis* fr. *imaginare*, to imagine]

im-ag-i-nal (imǽdʒin'l) *adj.* (*zool.*) of or pertaining to an imago

im-ag-i-nar-y (imǽdʒineri:) *adj.* existing only in the imagination ‖ (*math.*) of or relating to the square root of a negative quantity [fr. L. *imaginarius*]

imaginary quantity (*math.*) a quantity including the square root of a negative number

im-ag-i-na-tion (imædʒinéiʃən) *n.* the power to form mental images of objects not perceived or not wholly perceived by the senses ‖ the power to form new ideas by a synthesis of separate elements of experience, and the ability to define new ideas ‖ the gift of employing images in writing or painting ‖ resourcefulness, *with a little imagination you will find a way* ‖ the tendency to attribute reality to unreal things, situations and states, *his imagination led him to believe he was being persecuted* ‖ intuitive understanding, *his imagination compensates for his lack of experience* [F.]

im-ag-i-na-tive (imǽdʒinətiv, imǽdʒineitiv) *adj.* having, using or showing imagination ‖ having intuitive understanding [O.F. *imaginatif*]

im-ag-ine (imǽdʒin) *pres. part.* **im-ag-in-ing** *past* and *past part.* **im-ag-ined** *v.i.* to use the imagination viably ‖ *v.t.* to picture in the imagination ‖ to conceive of, *imagine his surprise,* ‖ to suppose, *I imagine he will resign* ‖ to form delusory ideas about, invent (something without any basis of truth) [F. *imaginer*]

im-ag-ing photopolarimeter (ímədʒiŋ) an electronic camera used in spacecraft utilizing Nicol prisms

im-ag-ism (ímidʒizem) *n.* the body of theories of a group of anti-Romantic and anti-Georgian British and American poets (c. 1912-18) who aimed at simplicity and detachment in poetic expression by the clear presentation of visual images. T. E. Hulme formulated the ideas, and also wrote a handful of poems. Ezra Pound took up Hulme's ideas for a time and became the leading poet of the movement. Chinese poetry in translation was an important influence **ím-ag-ist** *n.* a member of this movement

i-ma-go (iméigou) *pl.* **i-mag-i-nes** (imǽdʒini:z, iméidʒini:z), **i-ma-gos, i-ma-goes** *n.* an adult insect developing from a pupa or after the last molt of a nymph ‖ (*psychol.*) the unconscious infantile conception of one's parent [L. = image]

i-mam, i-maum (imám) *n.* a Moslem prayer leader officiating in a mosque ‖ any of several spiritual and temporal Moslem leaders **i-mám-ate, i-máum-ate** *n.* the office or title of an imam ‖ the region ruled by an imam [Arab.]

im-bal-ance (imbǽləns) *n.* lack of balance

im-be-cile (ímbisəl, ímbisil, *Br.* esp. ímbisi:l) **1.** *n.* a mentally deficient person having a mental age of about 3-7 years, who requires supervision and help in dressing and feeding himself etc. (cf. IDIOT, cf. MORON) ‖ (*pop.*) a dolt **2.** *adj.* of or relating to an imbecile ‖ stupid [older *imbecille* fr. F. fr. L.]

im-be-cil-i-ty (imbisíliti:) *n.* mental deficiency somewhat less severe than idiocy (*IMBECILE) [older *imbecillitie* fr. F. *imbécillité* fr. L.]

im-bed (imbéd) *v.t. pres. part.* **im-bed-ding** *past* and *past part.* **im-bed-ded** to embed

im-bibe (imbáib) *pres. part.* **im-bib-ing** *past* and *past part.* **im-bibed** *v.t.* to take in (liquid, moisture etc.) ‖ to take into the mind by a gradual process, *to imbibe knowledge* [fr. F. *imbiber* and L. *imbibere*, to drink in]

im-bri-cate 1. (ímbrikit, ímbrikeit) *adj.* (*biol.*, of scales, bracts, plates etc.) having parts overlapping each other like roof tiles **2.** (ímbrikeit) *v. pres. part.* **im-bri-cat-ing** *past* and *past part.* **im-bri-cat-ed** *v.i.* to overlap in the manner of tiles ‖ *v.t.* to overlap or cause to overlap in this

manner **im·bri·ca·tion** n. [fr. L. imbricare (imbricatus), to cover with tiles]

im·bro·glio (imbróuljou) n. a very involved, confused situation [Ital.]

Im·bros (ímbrɒs) *IMROZ

im·bue (imbjú:) pres. part. **im·bu·ing** past and past part. **im·bued** v.t. to fill, esp. with moisture or color ‖ to fill, e.g. with an emotion, imbued with a love of all creation [fr. L. imbuere, to wet, stain]

I.M.F. *INTERNATIONAL MONETARY FUND

IMF (acronym) for International Monetary Fund

Im·hoff Tank (ímhɒf) (eng.) a large, two-story wastewater tank containing an upper chamber for continuous flow with slots for solids to fall through, and a lower chamber for sludge digestion; patented by Karl Imhoff

I·mip·ra·mine (imíprəmi:n) n. [C$_{19}$H$_{24}$N$_2$] (pharm.) slow-acting antidepressant drug; marketed as Tofranil

im·i·ta·bil·i·ty (imitəbíliti:) n. the quality or state of being imitable

im·i·ta·ble (ímitəb'l) adj. capable of being imitated

im·i·tate (ímiteit) pres. part. **im·i·tat·ing** past and past part. **im·i·tat·ed** v.t. to use as a model for one's own actions ‖ to mimic, ape ‖ to resemble externally, the varnish was made to imitate wood grain [fr. L. imitari (imitatus)]

im·i·ta·tion (imitéiʃən) 1. n. the act of imitating ‖ a copy produced by imitating ‖ (mus.) repetition of a phrase or subject in another key or voice 2. adj. made so as to be mistakable for what is genuine [fr. L. imitatio (imitationis)]

imitation milk a synthetic or vegetable dietary milk substitute

im·i·ta·tive (ímiteitiv) adj. of that which imitates, an imitative gesture [fr. L.L. imitativus]

im·i·ta·tor (ímiteitər) n. someone who imitates [fr. F. imitateur]

im·mac·u·late (imækjulit) adj. impeccably clean ‖ having no fault, an immaculate performance ‖ (biol.) without spots or marks of different color [fr. L. immaculatus, without stain]

Immaculate Conception, the (Roman Catholicism) the dogma (promulgated 1854) that the Virgin Mary was free of original sin from the very moment of her conception by St Anne ‖ the feast, Dec. 8, on which this is celebrated

im·ma·nence (ímənəns) n. the quality or state of being immanent **ím·ma·nen·cy** n.

im·ma·nent (ímənənt) adj. inherent, intrinsic ‖ (theol., of God) actually present throughout the material universe (cf. TRANSCENDENT) [fr. L.L. immanens (immanentis) fr. immanere, to dwell within]

Im·man·u·el, Em·man·u·el (imǽnjuːəl) a child prophesied by Isaiah (Isaiah vii, 14) as a deliverer of Judah. The name was applied to Jesus (Matthew i, 23) [fr. Gk fr. Heb. immānūēl, God with us]

im·ma·te·ri·al (imətíəriəl) adj. having no physical substance ‖ having no importance or relevance **im·ma·te·ri·al·ism** n. (philos.) the theory that matter has no existence apart from one's idea of it **im·ma·te·ri·al·i·ty** n. the quality or state of being immaterial [fr. M.L. immaterialis]

im·ma·ture (imətúər,imətjúər,imətʃúər) adj. not mature **im·ma·tu·ri·ty** n. the quality or state of being immature [fr. L. immaturus]

im·meas·ur·a·bil·i·ty (imeʒərəbíliti:) n. the quality or state of being immeasurable

im·meas·ur·a·ble (iméʒərəb'l) adj. incapable of being measured, esp. because too large **im·meas·ur·a·bly** adv.

im·me·di·a·cy (imí:di:əsi:) n. the state or quality of being immediate ‖ (philos.) direct consciousness as distinguished from consciousness involving an intermediate agency such as memory

im·me·di·ate (imí:di:it) adj. without an intervening lapse or interval, instant, an immediate response ‖ (philos.) intuitive, immediate knowledge of God ‖ direct, immediate cause ‖ (loosely) closest, in the immediate neighborhood [fr. M.L. immediatus, having no intermediary member or agent]

im·me·di·ate·ly (imí:di:itli:) 1. adv. at once, with no intervening lapse of time ‖ directly, with no intervening agent, this affects us all immediately ‖ with no intervening space or object, immediately up against the wall ‖ closely, immediately in the area of the farm 2. conj. as soon as, directly

im·med·i·ca·ble (imédikəb'l) adj. (rhet.) irremediable

Im·mel·mann turn (ímɛlmən) (aeron.) a maneuver in which an airplane reverses direction by performing half a loop followed by a roll through half a complete turn [after Max Immelmann (1890-1916), G. aviator]

im·me·mo·ri·al (iməmɔ́riəl, iməmóuriəl) adj. so old as to have its origin beyond the recall of memory or historical record, immemorial tradition

im·mense (iméns) adj. tremendously large [F.]

im·men·si·ty (iménsiti:) pl. **im·men·si·ties** n. the state or quality of being immense ‖ something immense [F. immensité or fr. L. immensitas]

im·men·su·ra·ble (iménʃərəb'l) adj. immeasurable [F.]

im·merse (imɔ́:rs) pres. part. **im·mers·ing** past and past part. **im·mersed** v.t. to put in below the surface level of a liquid or gas, to immerse one's feet in water ‖ (esp. refl. and pass.) to absorb (oneself) in one thing to the exclusion of all others, to immerse oneself in one's studies [fr. L. immergere (immersus), to dip]

im·mer·sion (imɔ́:rʒən, imɔ́:rʃən) n. an immersing or being immersed ‖ baptism by immersing the whole body in water ‖ (astron.) the disappearance of a celestial body behind another or within the shadow of another [fr. L.L. immersio (immersionis)]

immersion heater an apparatus for heating a liquid by immersing an electrically heated rod in it

immersion lens an objective of short focal length dipping into oil or water, resulting in light from a wider field entering the instrument equipped with it

immersion objective an immersion lens

im·mesh (iméʃ) v.t. to enmesh

im·me·thod·i·cal (iməθɒdik'i) adj. not methodical

im·mi·grant (ímigrənt) 1. n. someone who immigrates into a country (cf. EMIGRANT) 2. adj. of or pertaining to immigrants or immigration [fr. L. immigrans (immigrantis)]

im·mi·grate (ímigreit) pres. part. **im·mi·grat·ing** past and past part. **im·mi·grat·ed** v.i. to enter a country of which one is not a native, in order to live in it permanently ‖ v.t. to bring (a foreigner) into a country for this purpose (cf. EMIGRATE) **im·mi·gra·tion** n. the act of immigrating ‖ the rate at which immigrants come into a country over a period of time [fr. L. immigrare (immigratus)]

im·mi·nence (íminəns) n. the quality or state of being imminent ‖ something imminent, esp. danger or evil **im·mi·nen·cy** n. [fr. L.L. imminentia]

im·mi·nent (íminənt) adj. about to happen, his arrival is imminent ‖ threateningly impending, imminent danger [fr. L. imminens (imminentis) fr. imminere, to impend]

im·mis·ci·ble (imísəb'l) adj. incapable of being mixed or blended ‖ (phys.) of certain liquids) incapable of being formed into a homogeneous mixture **im·mis·ci·bly** adv.

im·mit·i·ga·ble (imítigəb'l) adj. not capable of being mitigated **im·mit·i·ga·bly** adv. [fr. L. immitigabilis]

im·mit·tance (imít'ns) n. (electr.) impedance and admittance to networks, transmission lines, etc.

im·mo·bile (imóub'l, imóubi:l) adj. not in motion ‖ inactive ‖ immovable [F.]

im·mo·bil·i·ty (imoubíliti:) n. the quality or state of being immobile [F. immobilité or fr. L. immobilitas]

im·mo·bi·li·za·tion (imoubəlizéiʃən) n. an immobilizing or being immobilized

im·mo·bi·lize (imóubəlaiz) pres. part. **im·mo·bi·liz·ing** past and past part. **im·mo·bi·lized** v.t. to render incapable of movement ‖ to render incapable of action, to immobilize troops ‖ (commerce) to convert (floating capital) into fixed capital [fr. F. immobiliser]

im·mod·er·ate (imɒ́dərit) adj. unreasonably large ‖ going beyond the proper limits [fr. L. immoderatus]

im·mod·est (imɒ́dist) adj. violating conventional standards of decency, immodest dress ‖ lacking humility, immodest claims [fr. L. immodestus]

im·mod·es·ty (imɒ́disti:) n. the quality or state of being immodest [fr. L. immodestia]

im·mo·late (íməleit) pres. part. **im·mo·lat·ing** past and past part. **im·mo·lat·ed** v.t. to offer up, esp. to kill, in sacrifice ‖ (rhet.) to make a sacrificial victim of, he was immolated on the altar of

his father's pride [fr. L. immolare (immolatus), to sprinkle with sacrificial meal]

im·mo·la·tion (iməléiʃən) n. the act of immolating ‖ a sacrifice [fr. L. immolatio (immolationis)]

im·mo·la·tor (íməleitər) n. someone who immolates [L.]

im·mor·al (imɔ́rəl, imɒ́rəl) adj. violating accepted standards of moral (esp. sexual) behavior (cf. AMORAL)

im·mo·ral·i·ty (imɒrǽliti:) pl. **im·mo·ral·i·ties** n. the quality or state of being immoral ‖ an immoral act

im·mor·tal (imɔ́rt'l) 1. adj. not subject to death ‖ everlasting, immortal fame ‖ never to be forgotten, an immortal deed 2. n. (Gk and Rom. mythol.) one of the gods ‖ someone whose fame will never die **Im·mor·tal** a member of the French Academy [fr. L. immortalis]

im·mor·tal·i·ty (imɔrtǽliti:) n. the quality or state of being immortal [F. immortalité fr. L.]

im·mor·tal·ize (imɔ́rt'laiz) pres. part. **im·mor·tal·iz·ing** past and past part. **im·mor·tal·ized** v.t. to give everlasting life to ‖ to confer undying fame on

im·mor·telle (imɔrtél) *EVERLASTING FLOWER

im·mov·a·bil·i·ty (imu:vəbíliti:) n. the quality or state of being immovable

im·mov·a·ble (imú:vəb'l) 1. adj. not subject to being moved ‖ unyielding in attitude, purpose etc. 2. n. (law, usually pl.) property which cannot be moved, e.g. land, buildings etc.

immovable feast a religious feast which occurs on the same calendar day every year

im·mov·a·bly (imú:vəbli:) adv. so as to be unable to move or be moved

im·mune (imjú:n) adj. having immunity (against illness) ‖ protected or safe from a danger etc. ‖ exempt, immune from taxation [fr. L. immunis, exempt]

im·mu·ni·ty (imjú:niti:) pl. **im·mu·ni·ties** n. (med.) the state of being temporarily or permanently able to resist an infection ‖ (law) exemption from a tax, duty or jurisdiction ‖ freedom from danger of penalty [fr. L. immunitas]
—Immunity may be constitutional (e.g., humans are immune to fowl plague) or acquired. Acquired immunity is due to the presence in the body of antibodies which counteract specific pathogenic microorganisms or their products, antigens. These agents may be acquired after the onset of a disease or by inoculation with a vaccine: immunity to smallpox is provided by exposure to the cowpox microorganisms. Other diseases which may be so guarded against include yellow fever, plague, cholera, poliomyelitis, tetanus, typhus, diphtheria and whooping cough. Temporary or partial immunity may also be provided against tuberculosis, typhoid, measles etc. (*SERUM)

im·mu·ni·za·tion (imjunizéiʃən) n. an immunizing or being immunized

im·mu·nize (ímjunaiz) pres. part. **im·mu·niz·ing** past and past part. **im·mu·nized** v.t. to render immune, esp. against a particular disease

imm·u·no·as·say (imjunouǽsei) n. (immunology) assessment of characteristics of a chemical that helps create immunity from disorders

imm·u·no·blas·tic lymphadenopathy (imjunoublǽbstik) n. (med.) a disease of the white blood cells, esp. in liver and spleen

imm·u·no·com·pe·tence (imjunoukɒ́mpətens) n. ability to assist or to create immunity. — **immunocompetent** adj.

imm·u·no·cyte (imjunousáit) n. (immunology) cell that creates immunity by attacking other cells

imm·u·no·de·fic·ien·cy (imjunoudifíʃənsi:) n. (immunology) a lack of immune reaction capability in the body

i·mmu·no·e·lec·tro·pho·re·sis (imjunouəlektrəfərí:sis) n. (immunology) technique for separating and identifying certain proteins (antigens) by their immunological reactions after separation from the host substance. —**immunoelectrophoretic, -poretic** adj. —**immunoelectrophoretically, -poretically** adv.

imm·u·no·flu·o·resc·ence (imjunouflurés'ns) n. (immunology) fluorescent labeling of antibodies for study under ultraviolet light. —**immunofluorescent** adj.

imm·u·no·glob·u·lin (imjunouglǽbjələn) n. (immunology) blood protein that stimulates an antibody, creating immunity

i·mmu·no·hem·a·tol·o·gy (imjunouhi:mətúlədʒi:) n. (immunology) study of immunizing capability of the blood. —**immunohematologic** *adj.*

im·mu·nol·o·gy (imjunólədʒi:) *n.* the study of immunity to disease

imm·u·no·phar·ma·col·o·gy (ímjunoufɑrməkolədʒi:) *n.* (*immunology*) study of chemical substances that provide immunity from disorders

imm·u·no·su·ppress·ant (imjunousəprés'nt) *n.* (*pharm.*) drug used to suppress rejection of transplanted tissue

im·mure (imjúər) *pres. part.* **im·mur·ing** *past and past part.* **im·mured** *v.t.* to shut in behind walls, imprison ‖ to seclude as if in a prison, *immured in the library* **im·múre·ment** *n.* [fr. M.L. *immurare* fr. *im-*, in+*murus*, wall]

im·mu·ta·bil·i·ty (imju:təbíliti) *n.* the quality or state of being immutable

im·mu·ta·ble (imjú:təb'l) *adj.* incapable of being changed **im·mú·ta·bly** *adv.* [fr. L. *immutabilis*]

imp (imp) *n.* a little or young devil ‖ a mischievous sprite ‖ (*Br., pop.*) a mischievous child [O.E. *impa*, young shoot]

imp. imperative

im·pact 1. (ímpækt) *n.* a clash or collision imparting force ‖ the impression made by a person, thing or idea, *the impact of a speech on an audience* **2.** (impækt) *v.t.* to press together, or into a limited space **im·páct·ed** *adj.* (of a fracture) wedged together at the broken ends ‖ (of a tooth) wedged in between the jawbone and another tooth [fr. L. *impingere (impactus)*, to impinge]

im·pac·ted (impæktəd) *adj.* (*substandard*) strongly and adversely affected by unusual circumstances; affected

impacted area a community in which nontaxable property substantially limits tax revenues, e.g., a military base town

im·pac·tion (impækʃən) *n.* an impacting or being impacted [fr. L. *impactio (impactionis)*]

im·pair (impéər) *v.t.* to lessen in quality or strength, damage **im·páir·ment** *n.* [M.E. *empaire, empeire* fr. O.F. *empeirer*, to make worse]

im·pale (impéil) *pres. part.* **im·pal·ing** *past and past part.* **im·paled** *v.t.* to pass a sharp pointed object through, *to impale one's foot on a spike* ‖ to fix (a body) by piercing through with a pointed object ‖ (*hist.*) to torture or kill in this way ‖ (*heraldry*) to arrange (two coats of arms) with a dividing vertical line, on one shield [F. *empaler*]

im·pale·ment (impéilmənt) *n.* an impaling or being impaled [F. *empalement*]

im·pal·pa·bil·i·ty (impælpəbíliti) *n.* the quality or state of being impalpable

im·pal·pa·ble (impælpəb'l) *adj.* not perceptible to the touch ‖ (of powders) so fine that, when pinched between finger and thumb, the grains cannot be felt ‖ not easily apprehended by the mind **im·pál·pa·bly** *adv.* [F.]

im·pa·na·tion (impənéiʃən) *n.* (*theol.*) the doctrine that the body of Christ is present after the consecration in the Eucharistic bread and wine without these changing their substance (cf. CONSUBSTANTIATION, cf. TRANSUBSTANTIATION) [fr. M.L. *impanatio (impanationis)*]

im·pan·el (impæn'l) *pres. part.* **im·pan·el·ing**, esp. *Br.* **im·pan·el·ling** *past and past part.* **im·pan·eled**, esp. *Br.* **im·pan·elled** *v.t.* to list (jurymen) or select for service on a jury.

im·part (impárt) *v.t.* to give a share of (something), *cloves impart their flavor to the food* ‖ to make known, communicate, *to impart information* [O. F. *empartir, impartir*]

im·par·tial (impárʃəl) *adj.* without prejudgment, *an impartial mind* ‖ not favoring one side more than the other, *impartial justice* **im·par·ti·al·i·ty** (impɑrʃiæliti:) *n.*

im·part·i·bil·i·ty (impɑrtəbíliti:) *n.* the quality or state of being impartible

im·part·i·ble (impártəb'l) *adj.* not subject to partition, esp. (*law*) of an estate which cannot be divided [fr. L.L. *impartibilis*, indivisible]

im·pass·a·bil·i·ty (impæsəbíliti:, impɑsəbíliti:) *n.* the quality or state of being impassable

im·pass·a·ble (impæsəb'l, impɑsəb'l) *adj.* incapable of being passed over or through **im·páss·a·bly** *adv.*

im·passe (ímpæs, ímpɑs, ĉpɑs) *n.* a situation from which there appears to be no way out ‖ a road or pathway that has no exit, a dead end [F.]

im·pas·si·bil·i·ty (impæsəbíliti:, impɑsəbíliti:) *n.* the quality or state of being impassible

im·pas·si·ble (impæsəb'l, impɑsəb'l) *adj.* not

subject to pain or suffering ‖ without feeling ‖ incapable of being injured (cf. IMPASSIVE) **im·pás·si·bly** *adv.* [F.]

im·pas·sioned (impæʃənd) *adj.* full of passionate emotion, *an impassioned speech* [fr. Ital. *impassionare*, to fill with passion]

im·pas·sive (impæsiv) *adj.* not giving any outward sign of emotion ‖ not feeling pain, sensation or emotion **im·pás·siv·i·ty** *n.*

im·pas·to (impástou, impæstou) *n.* (*art*) the laying on of a thick layer of paint ‖ (*art*) the layer of paint put on in this way [Ital.]

im·pa·tience (impéiʃəns) *n.* the state or quality of being impatient [O.F. *impacience, impatience*]

im·pa·tient (impéiʃənt) *adj.* lacking or showing a lack of patience, restless and fretful under delay, opposition or difficulty ‖ eagerly desiring and restive at delay, *impatient to go, impatient for news* ‖ (with 'of') unwilling to put up with, *impatient of bureaucratic fuss* [O.F. *impacient, impatient*]

IMPATT diode (*electr. acronym*) for impact avalanche transit-time diode, a solid-state microwave diode used as an oscillator or an amplifier in the very high frequencies

im·peach (impí:tʃ) *v.t.* to charge with a crime, esp. to accuse (a state official) of treason or corruption before a special tribunal ‖ to question the honesty or sincerity of (something), *his honor was impeached, to impeach someone's motives* **im·péach·a·ble** *adj.* **im·péach·ment** *n.* [M.E. *empechen, enpechen*, to hinder fr. O.F.] —Impeachment in Britain took the form of an accusation by the House of Commons, after which the House of Lords pronounced judgment. The procedure fell into disuse in the 19th c. In the U.S.A., impeachment continues as a means of trying complaints against public officials. Charges are brought by the House of Representatives, and trial is by members of the Senate

im·pec·ca·bil·i·ty (impəkəbíliti:) *n.* the quality of being impeccable

im·pec·ca·ble (impékəb'l) *adj.* without fault or flaw **im·péc·ca·bly** *adv.* [fr. L.L. *impeccabilis*]

im·pe·cu·ni·os·i·ty (impəkju:nɔsiti:) *n.* the quality or state of being impecunious

im·pe·cu·ni·ous (impəkjú:ni:əs) *adj.* having very little or no money [fr. IM-(not)+obs. *pecunious, rich*]

im·ped·ance (impí:d'ns) *n.* (*elec.*) the opposition offered by an electrical circuit to the flow of an alternating current, measured by the ratio of the effective applied voltage to the effective current (cf. RESISTANCE) ‖ (*acoustics*) the ratio of the pressure on a surface to the volume-displacement [IMPEDE]

im·pede (impí:d) *pres. part.* **im·ped·ing** *past and past part.* **im·ped·ed** *v.t.* to hamper, obstruct or hold back, *to impede progress* [fr. L. *impedire*, to shackle someone's feet]

im·ped·i·ment (impédəmənt) *n.* something which impedes ‖ a speech defect, e.g. a lisp [fr. L. *impedimentum*]

im·ped·i·men·ta (impédəméntə) *pl. n.* cumbersome baggage or equipment [L.]

im·pel (impél) *pres. part.* **im·pel·ling** *past and past part.* **im·pelled** *v.t.* to drive forward ‖ to urge, *impelled by conscience to confess* [fr. L. *impellere*]

im·pel·lent (impélənt) *n.* something that impels [fr. L. *impellens (impellentis)*]

im·pel·ler (impélər) *n.* someone who or something which impels

im·pend (impénd) *v.i.* (esp. of something feared) to be on the verge of happening [fr. L. *impendere*, to hang over]

im·pen·e·tra·bil·i·ty (impenitrəbíliti:) *n.* the quality or state of being impenetrable

im·pen·e·tra·ble (impénitrəb'l) *adj.* of that which cannot be entered or passed through ‖ impossible to understand, *an impenetrable mystery* ‖ not receptive to impressions, ideas etc., *impenetrable stupidity* **im·pén·e·tra·bly** *adv.* [F.]

im·pen·i·tence (impénitəns) *n.* the quality or state of being impenitent **im·pén·i·ten·cy** *n.* [fr. L.L. *impaenitentia*]

im·pen·i·tent (impénitənt) *adj.* not feeling sorrow for sin ‖ obstinately holding an opinion, *an impenitent socialist* [fr. L. *impaenitens (impaenitentis)*]

imper. imperative

im·per·a·tive (impérətiv) **1.** *adj.* which must at all costs be obeyed or which cannot in any way be ignored, *imperative command, imperative need* ‖ (*emphatic*) necessary, *it is imperative that*

he be there ‖ (*gram.*) of the mood that expresses command (cf. INDICATIVE, cf. SUBJUNCTIVE) **2.** *n.* that which is imperative, an order (*CATEGORICAL IMPERATIVE, *HYPOTHETICAL IMPERATIVE) ‖ (*gram.*) the imperative mood ‖ (*gram.*) a verb in this mood [fr. L.L. *imperativus*]

im·per·cep·ti·bil·i·ty (imparseptəbíliti:) *n.* the quality or state of being imperceptible

im·per·cep·ti·ble (imparséptəb'l) *adj.* not perceptible to the senses ‖ of that which the mind is unable to distinguish, *imperceptible shades of meaning* **im·per·cép·ti·bly** *adv.* [F.]

im·per·cep·tion (imparsépʃən) *n.* lack of or failure in perception

im·per·cep·tive (imparséptiv) *adj.* not perceiving, esp. blind to subtle qualities in people and things

imperf. imperfect

im·per·fect (impá:rfikt) **1.** *adj.* not perfect ‖ not complete ‖ (*mus.*, of an interval) diminished ‖ (*gram.*, of a tense) expressing continuous but unfinished action or state, e.g. 'he was walking' (past imperfect), 'he will be walking' (future imperfect) ‖ (*law*) not legally enforceable **2.** *n.* the imperfect tense ‖ a verb form in this tense [M.E. *imparfit, imperfit* fr. F.]

imperfect cadence (*mus.*) a cadence consisting of a progression to the dominant chord from another chord, e.g. the tonic chord

im·per·fec·tion (imparfékʃən) *n.* the quality or state of being imperfect or defective ‖ a defect [F. or fr. L. *imperfectio (imperfectionis)*]

im·per·fec·tive (impəriéktiv) *adj.* (in Slavonic languages) of aspects of verbs indicating incomplete or continuing action

im·per·fo·rate (impá:rfərit) *adj.* (*philately*) of stamps printed in sheets without perforation or roulettes ‖ (*anat.*) lacking the normal opening [fr. IM- (not)+*perforate* adj., perforated]

im·per·fo·ra·tion (impə:rfəréiʃən) *n.* the quality or state of being imperforate ‖ something that is imperforate

im·pe·ri·al (impíəri:əl) **1.** *adj.* pertaining to an emperor or an empire ‖ of weights and measures defined by British statute, *imperial pint* ‖ (*loosely*) majestic **Im·pe·ri·al** (*hist.*) of or relating to the Holy Roman Empire **2.** *n.* a small tufted beard beneath the lower lip (after Napoleon III) ‖ a size of paper, *Am.* 23 ins x 31 ins, *Br.* 22 ins x 30 ins ‖ (*hist.*) a Russian gold coin of 15 roubles [O.F. *emperial, imperial*]

imperial gallon *GALLON

im·pe·ri·al·ism (impíəri:əlizəm) *n.* the extension by one country of its authority over other lands by political, military or economic means ‖ the policy or doctrine of such extension of authority **im·pé·ri·al·ist** *n. and adj.* **im·pe·ri·al·is·tic** *adj.* **im·pe·ri·al·is·ti·cal·ly** *adv.* —In the ancient world, vast empires were built up by Babylonia, Assyria, Egypt, Persia, Greece and Rome, and in the Middle Ages by the Byzantines and the Ottomans. Imperialism is usually taken to refer, however, to later forms of empire building which followed the rise of national states in Europe (15th c.). Colonies were acquired (mid-15th c.late 18th c.) by Spain, Portugal, France, England and the Netherlands for commercial and religious motives. This movement was helped by the formation of trading companies (17th c.) and by theories of mercantilism (16th-18th cc.), but resulted in colonial wars (17th and 18th cc.). The Revolutionary War (1775-83) and the rise of laissez-faire economic theories lessened the appeal of colonialism (early 19th c.). Interest in imperialism revived sharply (late 19th c.) in Britain, the U.S.A., France, Germany, Belgium, Italy, Russia and Japan. The ensuing scramble for Africa, the Middle East and the Far East was inspired by the need to find raw materials and markets for protectionist industries, as well as by missionary and other ideals. The resultant rivalries helped to cause the 1st world war, after which imperialism again fell into discredit. After the 2nd world war the Italian, German and Japanese empires were broken up. The other imperial powers granted autonomy to increasing numbers of their colonies, notably in Africa and Asia

Imperial Preference an arrangement by which countries of the Commonwealth impose lower tariffs on goods from one another than on those from other countries. The system was first proposed (1897) by Joseph Chamberlain and it split the Conservative party (1906). It was adopted (1931-3)

im·per·il (impérəl) *pres. part.* **im·per·il·ing**, esp. *Br.* **im·per·il·ling** *past and past part.* **im·per**

iled, esp. *Br.* **im·per·illed** *v.t.* to expose to danger, esp. the danger of loss, *drought imperiled the crops*

im·pe·ri·ous (impíəriəs) *adj.* overbearing in manner || imperative, *imperious necessity* [fr. L. *imperiosus,* imperial]

im·per·ish·a·bil·i·ty (imperiʃəbíliti:) *n.* the quality or state of being imperishable

im·per·ish·a·ble (impériʃəb'l) *adj.* of that which will not perish, decay or be destroyed, *imperishable fame* **im·pér·ish·a·bly** *adv.*

im·pe·ri·um (impíəriəm) *n.* supreme authority, empire || (*law*) the right to use the state's power to enforce the law [L.]

im·per·ma·nence (impɔ́ːrmənəns) *n.* the quality or state of being impermanent **im·pér·ma·nen·cy** *n.*

im·per·ma·nent (impɔ́ːrmənənt) *adj.* not permanent

im·per·me·a·bil·i·ty (impəːrmi:əbíliti:) *n.* the quality or state of being impermeable

im·per·me·a·ble (impɔ́ːrmi:əb'l) *adj.* not permeable **im·pér·me·a·bly** *adv.* [F. or fr. L. *impermeabilis*]

im·per·son·al (impɔ́ːrsən'l) *adj.* without personal content, reference or quality, *impersonal criticism, an impersonal letter* || (*gram.,* of verbs) without a specified subject or having a subject which does not indicate an actual agent, e.g. 'it rains' || (*gram.,* of pronouns) having indefinite reference, e.g. 'one', 'people', 'they' etc. **im·per·son·ál·i·ty** *n.* [fr. L.L. *impersonalis*]

im·per·son·ate (impɔ́ːrsəneit) *pres. part.* **im·per·son·at·ing** *past and past part.* **im·per·son·at·ed** *v.t.* to pretend to be (someone else) || to imitate or mimic in order to entertain **im·per·son·á·tion** *n.* an impersonating or being impersonated **im·pér·son·a·tor** *n.* an entertainer who mimics well-known people [fr. L. *im-* +*persona,* person]

im·per·ti·nence (impɔ́ːrt'nəns) *n.* the quality or state of being impertinent || something impertinent **im·pér·ti·nen·cy** *pl.* **im·per·ti·nen·cies** *n.* [F.]

im·per·ti·nent (impɔ́ːrt'nənt) *adj.* acting or speaking disrespectfully or showing an offensive lack of respect || not pertinent [F. Or fr. L. *impertinens* (*impertinentis*), not relevant]

im·per·turb·a·bil·i·ty (impəːrtəːrbəbíliti:) *n.* the quality or state of being imperturbable

im·per·turb·a·ble (impəːrtɔ́ːrbəb'l) *adj.* not susceptible to alarm, agitation etc. **im·per·túrb·a·bly** *adv.* [fr. L.L. *imperturbabilis*]

im·per·vi·ous (impɔ́ːrvi:əs) *adj.* impenetrable, *the walls are impervious to damp* || not open (to reason, persuasion etc.) [fr. L. *impervius*]

im·pe·ti·go (impitáigou) *n.* a contagious pustular skin disease caused by streptococci or staphylococci [L. fr. *impetere,* to attack]

im·pe·trate (ímpitreit) *pres. part.* **im·pe·trat·ing** *past and past part.* **im·pe·trat·ed** *v.t.* (*theol.*) to obtain by entreaty [fr. L. *impetrare,* to obtain]

im·pet·u·os·i·ty (impetʃu:ɔ́siti:) *n.* the quality or state of being impetuous

im·pet·u·ous (impétʃu:əs) *adj.* showing or acting with impulsiveness || (*rhet.*) rushing violently [F. *impétueux*]

im·pe·tus (ímpitəs) *n.* the force which causes a given motion or activity || a stimulus resulting in increased activity || the property a body possesses due to its mass and speed, esp. when moving with violence and suddenness (not used technically) || incentive, driving force [L. fr. *impetere,* to attack]

Imp·hal (ímphʌl) the capital (pop. 100,366) of Manipur, India

im·pi·e·ty (impáiiti:) *pl.* **im·pi·e·ties** *n.* lack of piety || an impious act [F. *impiété*]

im·pinge (impíndʒ) *pres. part.* **im·ping·ing** *past and past part.* **im·pinged** *v.i.* (with 'on', 'against') to come into sharp contact || (with 'on') to make an impression (on the mind, senses etc.) || (with 'on') to encroach, *these decrees impinge on our liberties* [fr. L. *impingere,* to drive in]

im·pi·ous (ímpi:əs) *adj.* lacking piety || wicked [fr. L. *impius*]

imp·ish (ímpiʃ) *adj.* mischievous

im·plac·a·bil·i·ty (implækəbíliti:) *n.* the quality or state of being implacable

im·plac·a·ble (implǽkəb'l) *adj.* not to be placated, deaf to all appeals || inexorable **im·plác·a·bly** *adv.* [F.]

im·plant (implǽnt, implǽnt) *v.t.* to plant deeply or firmly || (*med.*) to insert (e.g. a living tissue, as in grafting, or drugs for gradual absorption) beneath the skin || (*med.*) to intro-

duce (a living embryo) into the uterus of a host mother || to instill firmly in the mind 2. (ímplænt, ímplʌnt) *n.* (*med.*) the tissue, drug etc. used in implanting [F. *implanter*]

im·plan·ta·tion (implæntéiʃən, ˌimplʌntéiʃən) *n.* an implanting or being implanted || the passage of cells (esp. of tumors) from one part of the body to another part where they grow again

im·plau·si·ble (implɔ́zəb'l) *adj.* lacking the appearance of truth, *implausible excuses* **im·pláu·si·bly** *adv.*

im·ple·ment (ímpləmənt) 1. *n.* a tool || a thing or person serving as an instrument 2. *v.t.* to carry into effect, *to implement a promise* **im·ple·men·tal** (impləmént'l) *adj.* serving as an implement, helpful **im·ple·men·tá·tion** *n.* [perh. fr. L. *implementum,* a filling up]

im·pli·cate (ímplikeit) *pres. part.* **im·pli·cat·ing** *past and past part.* **im·pli·cat·ed** *v.t.* to involve, often in an unpleasant, incriminating manner, *to be implicated in a crime* [fr. L. *implicare (implicatus),* to entwine]

im·pli·ca·tion (implikéiʃən) *n.* an implying or being implied || something implied || an implicating or being implicated [fr. L. *implicatio (implicationis),* an entwining]

im·pli·ca·tive (ímplikeitiv, implíkətiv) *adj.* implicating || of or related to an implication

im·plic·it (implísit) *adj.* understood though not stated, *an implicit agreement* || unquestioning, absolute, *implicit confidence* [F. *implicite* or fr. L. *implicitus*]

im·plied (impláid) *adj.* suggested without being stated, involved without being specified

implied powers powers that are not specifically granted to Congress by the Constitution of the U.S.A. but which can legally be exercised as being necessary for the exercise of other specified powers

im·plode (imploúd) *pres. part.* **im·plod·ing** *past and past part.* **im·plod·ed** *v.t.* (*phon.*) to pronounce by implosion || *v.i.* to burst inward [fr. IM-+EXPLODE]

im·plore (implɔ́r, implóur) *pres. part.* **im·plor·ing** *past and past part.* **im·plored** *v.t.* to beseech with great intensity of feeling || to beg for, *to implore mercy* [fr. L. *implorare,* to cry aloud]

im·plo·sion (imploúʒən) *n.* a bursting inwards (opp. EXPLOSION) || (*phon.*) an internal compression of air, e.g. before sounding 'k', 'p' and 't'

im·plo·sive (imploúsiv) *adj.* [IMPLODE]

im·ply (implái) *pres. part.* **im·ply·ing** *past and past part.* **im·plied** *v.t.* to suggest without actually stating, *his questions implied his disbelief* || to involve logically, *lush vegetation implies heavy rainfall* [O.F. *emplier,* to enfold]

im·po·lite (impəláit) *adj.* having or showing bad manners [fr. L. *impolitus,* not polished]

im·pol·i·tic (impólitik) *adj.* lacking in tact or prudence || inexpedient

im·pon·der·a·bil·i·ty (impɒndərəbíliti:) *n.* the state or quality of being imponderable

im·pon·der·a·ble (impóndərəb'l) 1. *adj.* having no measurable weight || having an importance impossible to estimate 2. *n.* (usually *pl.*) a factor in a situation whose importance is unknowable

im·port 1. (impɔ́rt, impóurt) *v.t.* to bring in (goods) from abroad || to introduce (ideas etc.) taken from some outside source || (*rhet.*) to mean, imply || *v.i.* to be of importance 2. (ímpɔrt, ímpourt) *n.* something imported (opp. EXPORT) || (*rhet.*) meaning || (*rhet.*) importance [fr. L. *importare*]

im·por·tance (impɔ́rt'ns) *n.* the quality of being important [F.]

im·por·tant (impɔ́rt'nt) *adj.* producing a great effect, having great influence or significance || mattering greatly, *it is important to find out* || having a high social position || self-important, pompous, *an important manner* [F.]

im·por·ta·tion (impɔrtéiʃən) *n.* an importing or being imported || something imported

im·por·tu·nate (impɔ́rtʃunit) *adj.* persistently demanding, esp. in an annoying or unreasonable way [fr. L. *importunus,* inopportune]

im·por·tune (impɔrtú:n, ˌimpərtjú:n, impɔ́rtʃən) *pres. part.* **im·por·tun·ing** *past and past part.* **im·por·tuned** *v.t.* to vex (someone) by demanding too often or too vehemently or unreasonably || *v.i.* to be importunate [F. *importuner*]

im·por·tu·ni·ty (impɔrtú:niti:, ˌimpɔrtjú:niti:) *pl.* **im·por·tu·ni·ties** *n.* the quality or state of being importunate || an importunate demand [F. *importunité*]

im·pose (impóuz) *pres. part.* **im·pos·ing** *past and past part.* **im·posed** *v.t.* to place (a tax, fine etc.) as a burden || to use superior strength or

authority to secure submission to (one's will etc.) || to force others to receive (esp. oneself) as guest, companion etc. || to fob off, cause to be accepted as genuine, flawless etc. (what is not) || (*printing*) to arrange (pages) in a form || *v.i.* (with 'on') to take unfair advantage || (with 'on') to use deception **im·pós·ing** *adj.* impressive [F. *imposer*]

im·po·si·tion (impəzíʃən) *n.* an imposing or being imposed || a tax or duty || the taking of an unfair advantage || (*printing*) the arranging of pages in a form || (*Br.*) supplementary work given as punishment at school [fr. L. *impositio (impositionis*) fr. *imponere,* to lay on]

imposition of hands (*eccles.*) the laying on of hands in confirmation, ordination etc.

im·pos·si·bil·i·ty (impɒsəbíliti:) *pl.* **im·pos·si·bil·i·ties** *n.* the quality or state of being impossible || something impossible [F. *impossibilité*]

im·pos·si·ble (impósəb'l) *adj.* incapable of occurring or being done || unacceptable, *an impossible suggestion* || hard to tolerate, *an impossible woman* **im·pós·si·bly** *adv.* [F. or fr. L. *impossibilis*]

impossible art conceptual art

im·post (ímpoust) 1. *n.* a tax, esp. a duty on imported goods 2. *v.t.* to classify (imported goods) in order to fix duties [O.F.]

impost *n.* (*archit.*) the upper member of a pillar or entablature on which an arch rests [F. *imposte*]

im·pos·tor, im·post·er (impóstər) *n.* a person pretending to be someone he is not, or pretending to possess a quality he does not have [F. *imposteur-*)]

im·pos·ture (impóstʃər) *n.* deception, esp. by an impostor || an instance of this [F.]

im·po·tence (ímpətəns) *n.* the quality or state of being impotent **ím·po·ten·cy** *n.* [F.]

im·po·tent (ímpətənt) *adj.* having no power or force, *impotent gestures* || (of a male) unable to perform the sexual act (cf. STERILE) [F.]

im·pound (impáund) *v.t.* to take into temporary protective legal custody, *to impound stolen goods* || to confine (stray animals) in a pound || to collect (water) in a reservoir

im·pov·er·ish (impóvəriʃ) *v.t.* to make poor || to exhaust the strength or productivity of (esp. soil) **im·póv·er·ish·ment** *n.* [fr. O.F. *empoverir (empoveriss-)*]

im·prac·ti·ca·bil·i·ty (impræktikəbíliti:) *n.* the quality or state of being impracticable

im·prac·ti·ca·ble (impræktikəb'l) *adj.* (of an idea or plan) not feasible || not usable, *an impracticable road* **im·prác·ti·ca·bly** *adv.*

im·prac·ti·cal (impræktik'l) *adj.* not practical || impracticable

im·pre·cate (ímprikeit) *pres. part.* **im·pre·cat·ing** *past and past part.* **im·pre·cat·ed** *v.t.* to invoke (evil) || to curse || *v.i.* to utter imprecations [fr. L. *imprecari (imprecatus),* to pray for, invoke]

im·pre·ca·tion (imprikéiʃən) *n.* cursing || a curse [fr. L. *imprecatio (imprecationis)*]

im·pre·ca·tor (ímprikeitər) *n.* someone who imprecates

im·pre·ca·to·ry (ímprikətɔri:, imprikətóuri:) *adj.* of or relating to imprecation

im·pre·cise (imprisáis) *adj.* not precise, vague

im·preg·na·bil·i·ty (impregnəbíliti:) *n.* the quality or state of being impregnable

im·preg·na·ble (imprégnəb'l) *adj.* (of an egg etc.) capable of being impregnated

impregnable *adj.* of that which cannot be taken by assault, *an impregnable castle* **im·prég·na·bly** *adv.* [M.E. *imprenable* fr. F.]

im·preg·nate 1. (imprégnit, imprégneit) *adj.* impregnated 2. (imprégneit) *v.t. pres. part.* **im·preg·nat·ing** *past and past part.* **im·preg·nat·ed** to make pregnant || to interpenetrate or saturate || to cause to be interpenetrated or saturated || to imbue (with an idea), *a mind impregnated with mystical doctrine* **im·preg·ná·tion** *n.* an impregnating or being impregnated [fr. M.L. or L.L. *impraegnatus*]

im·pre·sa·ri·o (imprisári:ou, ˌ:mpresárjo) *n.* someone who promotes, manages or organizes concerts, variety shows, plays, boxing tournaments etc. [Ital.]

im·pre·scrip·ti·ble (impriskríptəb'l) *adj.* of that which cannot be taken away by any external authority, *the imprescriptible rights of conscience* **im·pre·scrip·ti·bly** *adv.* [F.]

im·press 1. (imprés) *v.t.* to make a mark on (something), using pressure || to make (a mark) on something, using pressure || to have an effect on (the mind, emotions etc.) || to cause (an idea) to have an effect, *he impressed its importance on* them ‖ *v.i.* to arouse admiration **2.** (ímpres) *n.* an imprint ‖ a characteristic, distinguishing mark, *the printer's impress* ‖ (*rhet.*) an effect on the mind, mode of development, character etc. [fr. L. *imprimere (impressus),* to press upon]

im·press (imprés) *v.t.* to take forcibly (persons or goods) for public service

im·press·i·bil·i·ty (impresəbíliti:) *n.* the state or quality of being impressible

im·press·i·ble (imprésəb'l) *adj.* capable of being impressed ‖ impressionable

im·pres·sion (impréʃən) *n.* an impressing or being impressed ‖ a mark made by impressing ‖ (*printing*) a copy made from type or a plate ‖ (*printing*) the mark made by inked type on paper under pressure, *a clean impression* ‖ (*printing*) the group of copies made at one time without removing the form from the printing press (cf. EDITION) ‖ an effect produced on the feelings or senses ‖ a vague notion or belief ‖ (*dentistry*) an imprint in plastic etc. of the teeth and parts of the jaw [F.]

im·pres·sion·a·bil·i·ty (impreʃənəbíliti:) *n.* the state or quality of being impressionable

im·pres·sion·a·ble (impréʃənəb'l) *adj.* easily affected or influenced [F.]

Im·pres·sion·ism (impréʃənjizəm) *n.* the theory and practice of the French school of painting described below **im·pres·sion·ism** (*mus.*) a style of composition which evokes subtle moods and impressions, characterizing the works of Debussy, Delius, Ravel etc. ‖ its counterpart in literature (cf. SYMBOLISM) [F. *impressionisme*] —Impressionism was a term first used sarcastically in 1874 by a critic referring to a Monet landscape, *'Impression, soleil levant'*. Later it was used to describe the work of a group of artists—chiefly Manet, Monet, Renoir, Pissarro, Cézanne and Degas—who revolted against the official conservatism of the French Salon. They determined to paint things as they appeared to the painter at the moment, not as they are commonly thought or known to be. The movement coincided with scientific analysis of the nature of light diffraction and diffusion and with the development of photography. These discoveries enabled the painters to create new, more natural ways of rendering light effects by making use of natural and optical phenomena. To this extent the technique was analytical. The practical result, in the paintings, was a liberation: palettes became brilliant, as love of the open air and a feeling of immediacy and spontaneity transformed their art. Certain earlier painters (e.g. Constable and Turner, who was obsessed with the free rendering of effects of refracted light) were recognized as precursors. Impressionism, concerning itself with immediacy and the effect of light on surfaces, was always liable to seem insubstantial. Without sacrificing the open-air feeling and the practical knowledge of the ways of light and the eye, certain painters— notably Cézanne—wished also to give a sense of solidity, relationship in space, structure, weight and permanence. The discoveries of Impressionism were subordinated to this new attempt to render other relationships. The more solid Postimpressionist art, concerned with the geometry of form, led to cubism. The painter who especially links Impressionism with Postimpressionism is Seurat

Im·pres·sion·ist (impréʃənist) **1.** *n.* a painter belonging to the school of Impressionism **im·prés·sion·ist** a writer or musician whose work is characterized by impressionism **2.** *adj.* of, belonging to or characterized by Impressionism **im·pres·sion·ist** characterized by impressionism **im·pres·sion·is·tic** *adj.* impressionist ‖ conveying a general impression **im·pres·sion·is·ti·cal·ly** *adv.* [fr. F. *impressioniste*]

impressionist an actor who imitates public figures

im·pres·sive (imprésiv) *adj.* making a strong impression, esp. by arousing awe, admiration etc.

im·press·ment (imprésmənt) *n.* the act of impressing men or goods for public service

im·prest (ímprest) *n.* money loaned, esp. public money loaned to enable someone to discharge government duty [fr. Ital. *impresto,* a loan]

im·pri·ma·tur (imprimátər, imprimáitər) *n.* official license to print or publish ‖ any sanction, approval [L.=let it be printed]

im·print (ímprint) *n.* a mark or design produced by pressure ‖ a characteristic effect, *the work bore the imprint of his personality* ‖ a publisher's imprint ‖ a printer's imprint [M.E. *empreynte, emprinte* fr. F.]

im·print (imprínt) *v.t.* to stamp or fix (a decoration etc.) on something ‖ to fix (in the memory or mind) [M.E. *empreynten, emprenten, emprinten* fr. O.F.]

imprinting (*ethology*) phenomenon of learning process that conditions rapidly to a narrow response, e.g., incubator goslings first led to feeding by a toy will respond thereafter only to that toy

im·pris·on (impríz'n) *v.t.* to confine in a prison ‖ to confine, restrict, *imprisoned by dogmatic beliefs* [O.F. *emprisoner, emprisoner*]

im·pris·on·ment (impríz'nmənt) *n.* an imprisoning or being imprisoned [M.E. *enprisonement, emprisonement* fr. A.F.]

im·prob·a·bil·i·ty (improbəbíliti:) *pl.* **im·prob·a·bil·i·ties** *n.* the state or quality of being improbable ‖ something improbable

im·prob·a·ble (impróbəb'l) *adj.* not probable ‖ hard to believe, *improbable excuses* **im·prób·a·bly** *adv.* [fr. L. *improbabilis*]

im·pro·bi·ty (improúbiti:) *n.* (*rhet.*) dishonesty ‖ lack of principles [fr. L. *improbitas*]

im·promp·tu (imprómptu:, imprómptju:) **1.** *adj.* without preparation, extemporaneous, *an impromptu speech* **2.** *adv.* done without preparation, extemporaneously, *he spoke impromptu* **3.** *n.* (*mus.*) a composition (esp. for piano) which gives the impression of being improvised [fr. L. *in promptu,* in readiness]

im·prop·er (imprópər) *adj.* offending against accepted standards of decency ‖ not conforming to what is conventionally thought suitable ‖ not right, unlawful

improper fraction (*math.*) a fraction in which the numerator is greater than the denominator (cf. PROPER FRACTION)

im·pro·pri·e·ty (imprəpráiiti:) *pl.* **im·pro·pri·e·ties** *n.* the quality of being improper ‖ an improper action ‖ an improper or incorrect use of language [fr. F. *impropriété* or L. *improprietas*]

im·prov·a·bil·i·ty (impru:vəbíliti:) *n.* the state or quality of being improvable

im·prov·a·ble (imprú:vəb'l) *adj.* capable of being improved **im·próv·a·bly** *adv.*

im·prove (imprú:v) *pres. part.* **im·prov·ing** *past and past part.* **im·proved** *v.t.* to make better in quality ‖ to make more productive, *to improve land* ‖ *v.i.* to become better, *his health is improving* (with 'on' or 'upon') to do better (than), *you can improve on your last effort* [older *enprowe, emprowe* fr. A. F.]

im·prove·ment (imprú:vmənt) *n.* an improving or being improved ‖ an instance of this, *his second novel is a great improvement on his first* ‖ an addition to a house etc. which increases its economic value [A.F. *emprowement*]

im·prov·er (imprú:vər) *n.* (*Br.*) someone who works for a low wage or no wage while learning and improving his skill

im·prov·i·dence (impróvidəns) *n.* the quality or state of being improvident [fr. L. *improvidentia*]

im·prov·i·dent (impróvidənt) *adj.* not provident

im·prov·ing (imprú:viŋ) *adj.* constituting or containing a moral lesson or example, *an improving story*

im·prov·i·sa·tion (improvizéiʃən, imprəvizéiʃən) *n.* an improvising or being improvised ‖ something improvised

im·prov·i·sa·tor (impróvizeitər, imprəvizeitər) *n.* someone who improvises poems or songs [fr. *improvisate,* to improvise]

im·prov·i·sa·to·ri·al (improvizətóri:əl, improvizətóuri:əl) *adj.* pertaining to an improvisation or to an improvisator **im·pro·vi·sa·to·ry** (impróvaizətori:, imprəváizətóuri:) *adj.*

im·pro·vise (ímprəvaiz) *pres. part.* **im·pro·vis·ing** *past and past part.* **im·pro·vised** *v.t.* to compose, perform or say extemporaneously ‖ to select, make or provide (a substitute for something not available) ‖ *v.i.* to compose, perform or speak extemporaneously ‖ to select, make or provide a substitute for something not available ‖ (*mus.*, with 'on') to use (a composition) as the basis of free invention [F. *improviser*]

im·pru·dence (imprú:d'ns) *n.* the quality of being imprudent ‖ an imprudent action [fr. L. *imprudentia*]

im·pru·dent (imprú:d'nt) *adj.* lacking or showing a lack of prudence [fr. L. *imprudens (imprudentis)*]

im·pu·dence (ímpjudəns) *n.* the quality of being impudent ‖ impudent behavior [fr. L. *impudentia*]

im·pu·dent (ímpjudənt) *adj.* bold and shameless ‖ disrespectful in a way that avoids plain rudeness [fr. L. *impudens (impudentis)*]

im·pugn (impjú:n) *v.t.* to challenge the integrity, veracity etc. of [fr. L. *impugner*]

im·pulse (ímpʌls) *n.* a force applied suddenly ‖ motion produced by a suddenly applied force ‖ a sudden desire to do something, not arising from reason or passion, *he bought the car on impulse* ‖ (*phys.*) the product of the average force acting on a body and the interval of time during which it acts, being a vector quantity equal to the change of momentum of the body during the same time interval ‖ (*physiol.*) the excitation produced in nerve and muscle tissue by stimuli and resulting in physiological activity [fr. L. *impulsus*]

impulse buying purchasing done on the spur of the moment, usu. by stimulus at the point of sale. **—impulse buyer** *n.*

im·pul·sion (impʌlʃən) *n.* an impelling or being impelled ‖ an impulse [F.]

im·pul·sive (impʌlsiv) *adj.* susceptible to impulse, prone to act on impulse rather than after reflection ‖ motivated by an impulse [O.F. *impulsif* or fr. M.L. *impulsivus*]

im·pu·ni·ty (impjú:niti:) *n.* immunity to or exemption from punishment, *to break the law with impunity* [fr. L. *impunitas*]

im·pure (impjúər) *adj.* not pure ‖ not hygienic ‖ not chaste ‖ lewd, *impure thoughts* ‖ ritually unclean ‖ (*art*) of mixed style ‖ (of language) ungrammatical or containing foreign elements [fr. L. *impurus*]

im·pu·ri·ty (impjúəriti:) *pl.* **im·pu·ri·ties** *n.* the quality or state of being impure ‖ something impure ‖ something which renders a thing impure [O.F. *impurité*]

im·put·a·bil·i·ty (impju:təbíliti:) *n.* the quality or state of being imputable

im·put·a·ble (impjú:təb'l) *adj.* capable of being imputed **im·pút·a·bly** *adv.* [fr. M.L. *imputabilis*]

im·pu·ta·tion (impjutéiʃən) *n.* an imputing or being imputed ‖ an accusation [fr. L.L. *imputatio (imputationis)*]

im·pute (impjú:t) *pres. part.* **im·put·ing** *past and past part.* **im·put·ed** *v.t.* to attribute (esp. blame, misfortune etc.), *she imputed the disaster to his vanity* [F. *imputer*]

Im·roz (imróz) (*Gk* Imbros) a Turkish island (area 110 sq. miles, pop. 6,000) in the N.E. Aegean near the entrance to the Dardanelles. It was occupied by Greece (1912–14) and Britain (1914–23)

in- (in) *prefix* in, into, on, upon, towards, against [L. fr. *in*=in, into]

in- *prefix* not, non-, un- [L.]

in (in) **1.** *prep.* contained by, placed physically so as to be surrounded by, *the car is in the garage* ‖ into, *put the car in the garage* ‖ within, *the castle is still in view* ‖ by groups of, *line up in fours* ‖ affecting, *a cold in the head* ‖ having as a condition or state, *in poor health* ‖ wearing, *soldiers in uniform* ‖ with regard to, *they differ in height* ‖ as a result of, *to jump in surprise* ‖ under the influence of, *in a trance* ‖ within the sphere or realm of, *in my experience* ‖ Working for or as part of, *he is in a law firm* ‖ at, *in school* ‖ during, *he did it in an hour* ‖ at the end of (a period of time), *he'll do it in an hour from now* ‖ while performing the act of, *in crossing the street* ‖ using, *speaking in French, in many colors* ‖ made of, *in oak* ‖ with, *covered in mud* ‖ so as to acquire the shape or form of, *to fall in a heap* ‖ within the capacity of, *she didn't have it in her* ‖ **in that** because, in the respect that, with regard to the fact that **2.** *adv.* from the ouside to the inside, *please come in* ‖ so as to mingle, *mix an egg in with the milk* ‖ so as to agree, *his plans fell in with hers* ‖ within a space, position, situation etc., *his party put him in* ‖ **in and out** alternately in, then out ‖ **in for** competing in (a competition) ‖ shortly destined for, *in for a beating* ‖ **in for it** committed to some action ‖ sure to be punished ‖ **in with** on good terms with **3.** *adj.* reserved for people or things arriving, *the in door, the in tray* ‖ at home ‖ (*colloq.*) currently popular among important people, e.g., the *in-place* ‖ doing or knowing what is currently popular **4.** *n.* (*pop.*) influence, *he has an in with the boss* ‖ **the ins and outs** all the involved facts (of a situation etc.) [O.E.]

In (*chem.*) indium

-in *suffix* compounded with an infinitive to indicate a group activity, esp. one involving protest, passive resistance etc., or mutual encouragement, *a sit-in, a love-in*

CONCISE PRONUNCIATION KEY: **(a)** æ, cat; ɑ, car; ɔ fawn; ei, snake. **(e)** e, hen; i:, sheep; iə, deer; εə, bear. **(i)** i, fish; ai, tiger; ə:, bird. **(o)** o, ox; au, cow; ou, goat; u, poor; ɔi, royal. **(u)** ʌ, duck; u, bull; u:, goose; ə, bacillus; ju:, cube. x, loch; θ, think; ð, bother; z, Zen; ʒ, corsage; dʒ, savage; ŋ, orangutang; j, yak; ʃ, fish; tʃ, fetch; 'l, rabble; 'n, redden. Complete pronunciation key appears inside front cover.

in. inch

in·a·bil·i·ty (inəbíliti:) *n.* the state or quality of being unable [O.F. *inhabilite* or fr. M. L. *inhabilitas*]

in ab·sen·tia (inæbsénʃə) (esp. of an accused person being tried or sentenced, or of someone being given an award) in his or her absence, *sentenced to death in absentia* [L. =in absence]

in·ac·ces·si·bil·i·ty (inæksesəbíliti:) *n.* the quality or state of being inaccessible

in·ac·ces·si·ble (inæksésəb'l) *adj.* which cannot be reached, *the village is inaccessible by car* || (of a person) difficult to approach and make contact with **in·ac·cés·si·bly** *adv.* [F.]

in·ac·cu·ra·cy (inækjurəsi:) *pl.* **in·ac·cu·ra·cies** *n.* the quality of being inaccurate || an instance of this

in·ac·cu·rate (inækjurit) *adj.* not accurate, making or containing errors

in·ac·tion (inækʃən) *n.* lack of action or motion || failure to act when action is called for

in·ac·ti·vate (inæktiveit) *pres. part.* **in·ac·ti·vat·ing** *past* and *past part.* **in·ac·ti·vat·ed** *v.t.* to make inactive || (*biochem.*) to arrest the activity of (certain substances)

in·ac·tive (inæktiv) *adj.* not active || making no effort || (*mil.*) not on actual duty

in·ac·tiv·i·ty (inæktiviti) *n.* the state or quality of being inactive

in·a·dapt·a·bil·i·ty (inədæptəbíliti) *n.* the quality or state of being inadaptable

in·a·dapt·a·ble (inədæptəb'l) *adj.* not able to adapt

in·ad·e·qua·cy (inædikwəsi:) *pl.* **in·ad·e·qua·cies** *n.* the quality or state of being inadequate || an instance of this

in·ad·e·quate (inædikwit) *adj.* not enough, *an inadequate income* || not capable (of fulfilling a requirement)

in·ad·mis·si·bil·i·ty (inədmisəbíliti) *n.* the quality or state of being inadmissible

in·ad·mis·si·ble (inədmísəb'l) *adj.* not admissible **in·ad·mís·si·bly** *adv.*

in·ad·ver·tence (inədvá:rt'ns) *n.* the quality or state of being inadvertent || a mistake due to lack of attention **in·ad·ver·ten·cies** *n.* [fr. M.L. *inadvertentia*]

in·ad·vert·ent (inədvá:rt'nt) *adj.* not intended, accidental [fr. IN- (not)+obs. *advertent*, attentive]

in·ad·vis·a·ble (inədváizəb'l) *adj.* not advisable, not prudent

in·al·ien·a·bil·i·ty (ineiljənəbíliti) *n.* the quality of being inalienable

in·al·ien·a·ble (inéiljənəb'l) *adj.* of that which cannot be given or taken away, *inalienable rights* **in·ál·ien·a·bly** *adv.*

in·al·ter·a·bil·i·ty (inɔltərəbíliti) *n.* the quality of being inalterable

in·al·ter·a·ble (inɔ́ltərəb'l) *adj.* that cannot be altered **in·ál·ter·a·bly** *adv.*

in·and·in (inəndín) **1.** *adv.* (of breeding etc.) repeatedly, generation after generation within the same or closely related stock **2.** *adj.* occurring in this way, *in-and-in breeding*

in·ane (inéin) *adj.* having no meaning or sense, *an inane remark* || silly [fr. L. *inanis*, empty]

in·an·i·mate (inænəmit) *adj.* having no organic life || not having animal life, *inanimate vegetation* || showing no sign of having life || lacking liveliness, *an inanimate performance* [fr. L.L. *inanimatus*, lifeless]

in·a·ni·tion (inəníʃən) *n.* exhaustion due to lack of sufficient food [fr. L. *inanitio* (*inanitionis*) fr. *inanire*, to make empty]

in·an·i·ty (inæniti) *pl.* **in·an·i·ties** *n.* the quality or state of being inane || something inane [fr. L. *inanitas*]

in·ap·peas·a·ble (inəpí:zəb'l) *adj.* of that which cannot be appeased

in·ap·pe·tence (inæpitəns) *n.* lack of appetite || lack of desire **in·áp·pe·ten·cy** *n.*

in·ap·pe·tent (inæpitənt) *adj.* having no appetite or desire

in·ap·pli·ca·bil·i·ty (inæplikəbíliti:, inəplikəbíliti:) *n.* the quality of being inapplicable

in·ap·pli·ca·ble (inæplikəb'l, inəplíkəb'l) *adj.* not applicable **in·áp·pli·ca·bly** *adv.*

in·ap·po·site (inæpəzit) *adj.* not to the point, irrelevant

in·ap·pre·ci·a·ble (inəpri:ʃi:əb'l, inəprí:ʃəb'l) *adj.* too small or unimportant to be taken into account **in·ap·pré·ci·a·bly** *adv.*

in·ap·pre·ci·a·tive (inəprí:ʃi:eitiv, inəprí:ʃətiv) *adj.* not showing or having appreciation

in·ap·pre·hen·si·ble (inæprihénsəb'l) *adj.* not perceptible to the senses || not capable of being grasped by the mind

in·ap·pre·hen·sion (inæprihénʃən) *n.* failure to apprehend

in·ap·pre·hen·sive (inæprihénsiv) *adj.* failing to apprehend || unaware of peril

in·ap·proach·a·bil·i·ty (inəproutʃəbíliti:) *n.* the quality or state of being inapproachable

in·ap·proach·a·ble (inəpróutʃəb'l) *adj.* unapproachable **in·ap·próach·a·bly** *adv.*

in·ap·pro·pri·ate (inəpróupri:it) *adj.* not appropriate

in·apt (inæpt) *adj.* inappropriate || unskillful, clumsy

in·ap·ti·tude (inæptitu:d, inæptitju:d) *n.* lack of aptitude

in·arch (inártʃ) *v.t.* to graft (a scion) into a neighboring stock without separating the scion from the parent tree

in·ar·tic·u·late (inartíkjulit) *adj.* unable to speak intelligibly || (of speech sounds) indistinct || unable to express oneself verbally, *inarticulate with rage* || not good at putting one's thoughts into words || (*biol.*) not hinged or segmented [fr. L. *inarticulatus*, not jointed]

in·ar·tis·tic (inartístik) *adj.* not artistic || not in accord with accepted standards of art or beauty **in·ar·tís·ti·cal·ly** *adv.*

in·as·much (inəzmátʃ) *adv.* (with 'as') insofar as || (with 'as') since, because

in·at·ten·tion (inəténʃən) *n.* lack of attention

in·at·ten·tive (inəténtiv) *adj.* failing to pay attention

in·au·di·bil·i·ty (inɔdəbíliti:) *n.* the state or quality of being inaudible

in·au·di·ble (inɔ́dəb'l) *adj.* not capable of being heard **in·áu·di·bly** *adv.* [fr. L. *inaudibilis*]

in·au·gu·ral (inɔ́gjərəl) **1.** *adj.* pertaining to inauguration **2.** *n.* an address made at an inauguration || an inauguration ceremony [F.]

in·au·gu·rate (inɔ́gjəreit) *pres. part.* **in·au·gu·rat·ing** *past* and *past part.* **in·au·gu·rat·ed** *v.t.* to initiate formally into public use with ceremony || to install in office with ceremony || to begin (an undertaking etc.) [fr. L. *inaugurare* (*inauguratus*), to consecrate after observing omens]

in·au·gu·ra·tion (inɔgjəréiʃən) *n.* an inaugurating or being inaugurated || a formal beginning [fr. L. *inauguratio* (*inaugurationis*)]

Inauguration Day the day on which the newly elected president of the U.S.A. is formally installed in office, Jan. 20 of the year following his election

in·au·gu·ra·tor (inɔ́gjəreitər) *n.* someone who inaugurates

in·aus·pi·cious (inɔspíʃəs) *adj.* not auspicious, unfavorable

in between *adv.* and *prep.* between

in·board (ínbɔrd, ínbourd) **1.** *adv.* (*naut.*) towards the center of a vessel (opp. OUTBOARD) **2.** *adj.* (*naut.*) situated at the center of a vessel

in·born (ínbɔ́rn) *adj.* inherent

in·bound (ínbáund) *adj.* homecoming, inward bound

in·bounds (ínbáundz) *adj.* (*basketball*) of a play started by passing from out of bounds

in·bred (ínbréd) *adj.* bred in-and-in || produced by inbreeding || deeply engrained, *inbred good manners* [past part. of INBREED]

in·breed (ínbrí:d, ínbrí:d) *pres. part.* **in·breed·ing** *past* and *past part.* **in·bred** *v.t.* to breed (closely related plants or animals) || *v.i.* (of members of a community or family) to marry close relations over several generations

inc. incorporated

In·ca (íŋkə) *n.* a member of the Indian people who dominated (13th-16th cc.) the central Andes || a member of the royal dynasty of this people || the emperor of this people [Span. fr. Quechua=prince]

—The Inca Empire, centered on Cuzco, Peru, reached its greatest extent in the 15th c., from Ecuador to N. Chile. Despite the absence of the wheel and of a system of writing, it achieved a high level of civilization, with massive stone and adobe buildings and an extensive system of roads. The Incas showed skill in terracing, irrigation and mining and produced fine textiles, metalwork and pottery. They were governed by an absolute monarchy, supported by a ritualized, hierarchic religion. The Inca Empire was weakened by civil war (1525-32) between Huascar and Atahualpa, and the latter was overthrown (1533) by the invading Spaniards under Pizarro. There were sporadic Inca revolts against Spanish rule until the 19th c.

in·cal·cu·la·bil·i·ty (inkælkjuləbíliti:) *n.* the quality or state of being incalculable

in·cal·cu·la·ble (inkælkjuləb'l) *adj.* not able to be reckoned || unpredictable || (*loosely*) very great, *incalculable risks* **in·cál·cu·la·bly** *adv.*

in·can·desce (inkandés) *pres. part.* **in·can·desc·ing** *past* and *past part.* **in·can·desced** *v.i.* to be or become incandescent || *v.t.* to make incandescent [fr. L. *incandescere*, to become white]

in·can·des·cence (inkəndés'ns) *n.* the quality or state of being incandescent

in·can·des·cent (inkəndés'nt) *adj.* (of bodies heated to a high temperature) emitting a white or bright red light || having the property of emitting white or bright red light when heated to a high temperature || of or pertaining to light emitted by a body at a high temperature [fr. L. *incandescens* (*incandescentis*)]

incandescent lamp a lamp consisting of a glass bulb evacuated, or filled with an inert gas, and containing a (usually) tungsten filament heated to incandescence by an electric current

in·can·ta·tion (inkəntéiʃən) *n.* a series of words or syllables, chanted or uttered in order to cast a magic spell || a chanting or uttering of such words || a magic spell [F.]

in·cap (ínkæp) *n.* **1.** (*mil.*) a chemical agent that incapacitates the enemy **2.** an incapacitant

in·ca·pa·bil·i·ty (inkeipəbíliti:) *n.* the quality or state of being incapable

in·ca·pa·ble (inkéipəb'l) *adj.* not capable, *incapable of hard work* || incompetent || (*law*) having no legal standing or qualification **in·cá·pa·bly** *adv.* [fr. M. L. *incapabilis*]

in·ca·pac·i·tant (inkəpǽsət'nt) *n.* a thing that incapacitates a person, esp. a chemical. *also* incapacitator

in·ca·pac·i·tate (inkəpǽsiteit) *pres. part.* **in·ca·pac·i·tat·ing** *past* and *past part.* **in·ca·pac·i·tat·ed** *v.t.* to make incapable, *incapacitated by illness* || to disqualify **in·ca·pac·i·tá·tion** *n.* [INCAPACITY]

in·ca·pac·i·ty (inkəpǽsiti:) *n.* the state or quality of being incapable [fr. M. L. *incapacitas*, F. *incapacité*]

in·car·cer·ate (inkársəreit) *pres. part.* **in·car·cer·at·ing** *past* and *past part.* **in·car·cer·at·ed** *v.t.* to imprison **in·car·cer·á·tion** *n.* [L. *incarcerare* (*incarceratus*)]

in·car·na·dine (inkárnədain, inkárnədi:n) **1.** *adj.* having the pinkish color of flesh || having the color of blood **2.** *v.t. pres. part.* **in·car·na·din·ing** *past* and *past part.* **in·car·na·dined** (*rhet.*) to color incarnadine, esp. red **3.** *n.* an incarnadine color [F. *incarnadin*, *incarnadine* fr. Ital.]

in·car·nate (inkárnit) *adj.* embodied, esp. in human flesh, *the incarnate God, he is greed incarnate* **2.** (inkárneit) *pres. part.* **in·car·nat·ing** *past* and *past part.* **in·car·nat·ed** *v.t.* to embody, esp. in human form || to give material form to || to be the embodiment of [fr. L. *incarnatus*, made flesh]

in·car·na·tion (inkarnéiʃən) *n.* an incarnating or being incarnated || an embodiment, *he is the incarnation of patience* **the In·car·na·tion** the union of God and man in the person of Christ [F.]

incase *ENCASE

in·cau·tion (inkɔ́ʃən) *n.* lack of caution

in·cau·tious (inkɔ́ʃəs) *adj.* lacking caution

in·cen·der·jell (inséndərdʒel) *n.* (*mil.*) flamethrower or firebomb fuel, made of napalm

in·cen·di·a·rism (inséndiəriʒəm) *n.* a malicious setting of fire to property (cf. ARSON) || the arousing of rebellion, conflict etc. by speech or action

in·cen·di·a·ry (inséndi:eri) **1.** *adj.* pertaining to the malicious burning of property || (of certain chemicals, bombs etc.) causing fires to start || arousing or tending to arouse rebellion, conflict etc. **2.** *pl.* **in·cen·di·a·ries** *n.* someone who is incendiary || an incendiary substance, bomb etc. [fr. L. *incendiarius* fr. *incendium*, fire]

in·cen·dive (inséndiv) *adj.* of an incendiary

in·cense (ínsens) **1.** *n.* a mixture of gums, spices etc. which when burned emit perfumed vapor, used in religious ceremonies etc. **2.** *v. pres. part.* **in·cens·ing** *past* and *past part.* **in·censed** *v.t.* to make fragrant with incense || to burn incense for (a god, a dead spirit etc.) || *v.i.* to burn incense, esp. in offering [M.E. *ansens*, *encenz* fr. O.F.]

in·cense (inséns) *pres. part.* **in·cens·ing** *past* and *past part.* **in·censed** *v.t.* to make angry [O.F. *incenser*, to set on fire]

in·cen·tive (inséntiv) *adj.* inciting to action, *incentive schemes to secure higher production* [fr. L. *incentivus* fr. *incinere*, to set the tune]

incentive *n.* something that serves as a stimulus to action by appealing to self-interest [fr. L. *incentivum*]

in·cept (insépt) *v.t.* (*biol.*) to take in (food etc.), ingest [fr. L. *incipere* (*inceptus*), to begin]

in·cep·tion (insépʃən) *n.* a beginning, originating [fr. L. *inceptio* (*inceptionis*)]

in·cep·tive (inséptiv) **1.** *adj.* beginning, initial ‖ (*gram.*) of a verbal aspect which denotes the beginning of an action **2.** *n.* (*gram.*) an inceptive word or phrase [F. *inceptif*]

in·cer·ti·tude (insé:rtitu:d, insé:rtitju:d) *n.* uncertainty [F.]

in·ces·san·cy (insés'nsi:) *n.* the state or quality of being incessant

in·ces·sant (insés'nt) *adj.* never ceasing ‖ continuous [F.]

in·cest (ínsest) *n.* sexual intercourse between persons so closely related that marriage between them is forbidden by law [fr. L. *incestum* fr. *incestus* adj., unchaste]

in·ces·tu·ous (insésʃu:əs) *adj.* of or having the nature of incest ‖ guilty of incest [fr. L. *incestuosus*]

inch (intʃ) **1.** *n.* a unit of length equal to the twelfth part of a foot (2.54 cm.)‖ a small amount, *not an inch of room* ‖ a unit of pressure equal to that of a vertical column of mercury one inch in height **every inch** thoroughly, in every respect, *every inch a lady* **within an inch of** nearly to the point of, *within an inch of succeeding* **2.** *v.t.* and *i.* to move very gradually (as though an inch at a time) [O.E. *ynce*]

in·cho·ate (inkóuit, ínkoueit) *adj.* in its first stage of development, just begun ‖ not fully formed, *inchoate plans* **in·cho·a·tive** (ínkoueitiv) **1.** *adj.* (*gram.*) inceptive **2.** *n.* (*gram.*) an inceptive verb [fr. L. *inchoare* (*inchoatus*), to begin]

In·chon (íntʃɒn) (*Korean* Chemulpho, *Jap.* Jinsen) an ice-free port (pop. 1,083,906) on the Yellow Sea coast of South Korea. Opened to foreign trade in 1883, it expanded under Japanese exploitation (1894–1905)

inch·worm (íntʃwə:rm) *n.* a looper

in·ci·dence (ínsidəns) *n.* the rate or extent to which something occurs, *the increasing incidence of road accidents* the fact of occurring, *a single incidence of malaria* ‖ (*phys.*) the arrival of radiation or of a moving body at a surface (*ANGLE OF INCIDENCE) [F.]

in·ci·dent (ínsidənt) **1.** *n.* an event seen as part of a whole situation, occurring by chance, not by design ‖ an episode ‖ a limited occurrence of trouble, *a frontier incident* ‖ (*law*) a privilege etc. dependent upon something else **2.** *adj.* of that which falls upon a surface etc., *incident light* ‖ (*law*) dependent upon something else ‖ (with 'to') arising or liable to arise in the course of, *risks incident to a profession*

in·ci·den·tal (insidént'l) **1.** *adj.* occurring by chance ‖ of secondary importance ‖ arising out of something else, *incidental expenses involved in attending a meeting* ‖ (with 'to') likely to arise from, *the worries incidental to motherhood* **2.** *n.* something incidental ‖ (*pl.*) casual expenses **in·ci·dén·tal·ly** *adv.* used to introduce a remark made parenthetically, *incidentally, she found the book you asked for* ‖ in a way not primarily intended [F.]

incidental music music composed to accompany the action of a play etc.

in·cin·er·ate (insínəreit) *pres. part.* **in·cin·er·at·ing** *past* and *past part.* **in·cin·er·at·ed** *v.t.* and *i.* to burn to ashes **in·cin·er·á·tion** *n.* **in·cín·er·a·tor** *n.* a device constructed for burning refuse etc. in [fr. M.L. *incinerare* (*incineratus*)]

In·cin·fi·dén·cia Mi·nei·ra (i:nkɒnfi:dá:sjami:néirɑ) a conspiracy (1789) in Brazil against the Portuguese power. It marks the beginning of national independence

in·cip·i·ence (insípi:əns) *n.* the quality or state of being incipient ‖ a beginning **in·cip·i·en·cy** *pl.* **in·cip·i·en·cies** *n.*

in·cip·i·ent (insípi:ənt) *adj.* beginning, at an early stage, *incipient paralysis* [fr. L. *incipiens* (*incipientis*) fr. *incipere*, to begin]

in·cise (insáiz) *pres. part.* **in·cis·ing** *past* and *past part.* **in·cised** *v.t.* to make a cut in ‖ to carve or engrave a pattern, inscription etc. into ‖ to carve or engrave (a pattern, inscription etc.) [F. *inciser*]

in·ci·sion (insíʒən) *n.* an incising ‖ a cut made by incising ‖ the quality of being incisive [F.]

in·ci·sive (insáisiv) *adj.* keen and penetrating, *incisive comments* [fr. M.L. *incisivus*, cutting]

in·ci·sor (insáizər) *n.* a tooth adapted for cutting ‖ one of the front teeth between the canines in either jaw **in·ci·so·ry** *adj.* (of teeth) adapted for cutting [M.L. and Mod. L.=cutter]

in·ci·ta·tion (insaitéiʃən) *n.* an inciting or being incited [F.]

in·cite (insáit) *pres. part.* **in·cit·ing** *past* and *past part.* **in·cit·ed** *v.t.* to stir (someone) to action ‖ to cause by encouraging, *to incite rebellion* **in·cite·ment** *n.* an inciting ‖ something that incites [F. *inciter*]

in·ci·vil·i·ty (insivíliti:) *pl.* **in·ci·vil·i·ties** *n.* rudeness ‖ an instance of rudeness [fr. F. *incivilité*]

in·clear·ing (ínklịəriŋ) *n.* (*Br.*, *collect.*) the checks received by a bank through the clearing-house

in·clem·en·cy (inklémənsi:) *pl.* **in·clem·en·cies** *n.* the state or quality of being inclement ‖ an instance of this [fr. L. *inclementia*]

in·cle·ment (inklémənt) *adj.* (of weather or climate) severe, rough, stormy ‖ (*rhet.*) harsh, merciless [fr. L. *inclemens* (*inclementis*)]

in·cli·na·tion (inklinéiʃən) *n.* a mental propensity ‖ liking, *it was against her inclination to vote* ‖ a physical tendency, *an inclination to stoutness* ‖ an inclining or being inclined from the vertical or horizontal ‖ an incline ‖ the angle of approach of one line or plane to another ‖ dip (angle between the direction of the earth's magnetic field and the horizontal) [fr. F. *inclination*]

in·cline 1. (inkláin) *v. pres. part.* **in·clin·ing** *past* and *past part.* **in·clined** *v.i.* to deviate from the vertical or horizontal, to slant or slope ‖ to tend, have an inclination, *to incline toward someone's view* ‖ *v.t.* to cause to deviate from the vertical or horizontal ‖ to bow or bend, *to incline one's head* ‖ to dispose, *to be inclined to agree with someone* **2.** (ínklain) *n.* an inclined plane, a slope **in·clined** *adj.* mentally disposed ‖ at an angle, sloping, slanting [M.E. *encline* fr. O.F.]

inclined plane a plane surface at an oblique angle to the plane of the horizon

in·cli·nom·e·ter (inklinómitər) *n.* an instrument that measures the angle of inclination of an aircraft to the horizontal ‖ a dip needle [fr. L. *inclinare*, to incline +METER]

inclose *ENCLOSE

inclosure *ENCLOSURE

in·clude (inklú:d) *pres. part.* **in·clud·ing** *past* and *past part.* **in·clud·ed** *v.t.* to contain as part of a whole **in·clúd·ed** *adj.* comprised or contained ‖ (*bot.*, of stamens and pistils) not protruding beyond the corolla, not exserted [fr. L. *includere*, to close in]

in·clu·sion (inklú:ʒən) *n.* an including or being included ‖ (*geol.*) a gaseous, liquid or solid foreign body enclosed by a mineral [fr. L. *inclusio* (*inclusionis*)]

inclusion body an intracellular particle characterizing certain virus diseases

in·clu·sive (inklú:siv) *adj.* including everything, comprehensive, *an inclusive list* ‖ including the specified limits, *pages 10-15 inclusive* ‖ (with 'of') taking account of, *the price, inclusive of transport, is $100* [fr. M.L. *inclusivus*]

in·cog·ni·to (inkógnitou, ìnkɒgní:tou) **1.** *adj.* being under an assumed name or character **2.** *adv.* with an assumed name or character, *to travel incognito* **3.** *pl.* **in·cog·ni·tos** *n.* a person who is incognito ‖ the assumed identity of a person who is incognito [Ital.]

in·cog·ni·zance (inkógniz'ns) *n.* the quality of being incognizant ‖ lack of knowledge, awareness or recognition

in·cog·ni·zant (inkógniz'nt) *adj.* (with 'of') unaware

in·co·her·ence (ìnkouhíərəns) *n.* the quality or state of being incoherent ‖ something incoherent **in·co·hér·en·cy** *pl.* **in·co·her·en·cies** *n.*

in·co·her·ent (ìnkouhíərənt) *adj.* (of ideas, language, speech etc.) not arranged in any logical order, disjointed and unintelligible ‖ unable to speak clearly and with continuity

in·com·bus·ti·bil·i·ty (ìnkəmbʌstəbíliti:) *n.* the quality or state of being incombustible

in·com·bus·ti·ble (ìnkəmbʌstəb'l) **1.** *adj.* not combustible **2.** *n.* something that is incombustible **in·com·bús·ti·bly** *adv.*

in·come (ínkʌm) *n.* whatever is received as gain, e.g. wages or salary, receipts from business, dividends from investments etc. [M.E. fr. O.E. *in*, in+ *cuman*, to come]

in·com·er (ínkʌmər) *n.* an immigrant ‖ a successor as tenant

incomes policy (*economics*) program designed to control prices by limiting rises in income (wages, rents, etc.) to no more than increases in output

income tax a tax levied on the annual income of a person, business etc.

in·com·ing (ínkʌmiŋ) **1.** *adj.* coming in or about to come in ‖ taking the place formerly held by someone else, *incoming tenants* **2.** *n.* a coming in ‖ (*pl.*) gains received, revenue

in·com·men·su·ra·bil·i·ty (ìnkəmenʃərəbíliti:, ìnkəmensərəbíliti:) *n.* the state or quality of being incommensurable

in·com·men·su·ra·ble (ìnkəménʃərəb'l, ìnkəménsərəb'l) **1.** *adj.* having no common measure or basis of comparison, *quarts and acres are incommensurable* ‖ (*math.*) having no common integral divisor except 1, *3 and 4 are incommensurable* ‖ incommensurate **2.** *n.* a quantity which is incommensurable with another **in·com·mén·su·ra·bly** *adv.* [fr. M.L. *incommensurabilis*]

in·com·men·su·rate (ìnkəménʃərit, ìnkəménsərit) *adj.* not commensurate ‖ not in proper proportion, *his reward is incommensurate with his effort*

in·com·mode (ìnkəmóud) *pres. part.* **in·com·mod·ing** *past* and *past part.* **in·com·mod·ed** *v.t.* to inconvenience ‖ to cause discomfort or annoyance to, bother [F. *incommoder*]

in·com·mo·di·ous (ìnkəmóudi:əs) *adj.* not roomy enough

in·com·mu·ni·ca·bil·i·ty (ìnkəmju:nikəbíliti:) *n.* the state or quality of being incommunicable

in·com·mu·ni·ca·ble (ìnkəmjú:nikəb'l) *adj.* not subject to or capable of being communicated or told **in·com·mú·ni·ca·bly** *adv.*

in·com·mu·ni·cá·do (ìnkəmju:nikádou) *adj.* deprived of or having no means of communication with others ‖ in solitary confinement [Span. *incomunicado*]

in·com·mu·ni·ca·tive (ìnkəmjú:nikeitiv, ìnkəmjú:nikətiv) *adj.* uncommunicative

in·com·mut·a·ble (ìnkəmjú:təb'l) *adj.* not subject to or capable of being changed ‖ not capable of being exchanged **in·com·mút·a·bly** *adv.* [fr. L. *incommutabilis*]

in·com·pact (inkəmpǽkt) *adj.* not compact

in·com·pa·ra·bil·i·ty (inkɒmpərəbíliti:) *n.* the state or quality of being incomparable

in·com·pa·ra·ble (inkómpərəb'l) *adj.* of things that cannot be compared ‖ of a thing or quality so superior that no other can be compared with it **in·cóm·pa·ra·bly** *adv.* [F.]

in·com·pat·i·bil·i·ty (inkəmpǽtəbíliti:) *n.* the state or quality of being incompatible

in·com·pat·i·ble (inkəmpǽtəb'l) **1.** *adj.* not compatible ‖ (of benefices) not able to be filled by the same person at the same time ‖ (*med.*, of drugs etc.) not able to be mixed together without undesirable results **2.** *n.* (*pl.*) things that are not compatible **in·com·pát·i·bly** *adv.* [fr. M.L. *incompatibilis*, (of benefices) not compatible]

in·com·pe·tence (inkómpitəns) *n.* the state or quality of being incompetent [F. *in compétence*]

in·com·pe·ten·cy (inkómpitənsi:) *pl.* **in·com·pe·ten·cies** *n.* incompetence ‖ (*pl.*) instances of incompetence [INCOMPETENCE or INCOMPETENT]

in·com·pe·tent (inkómpitənt) **1.** *adj.* not competent **2.** *n.* a person who is incompetent [F. *incompétent*]

in·com·plete (inkəmplí:t) *adj.* not complete [fr. L. *incompletus*]

in·com·pre·hen·si·bil·i·ty (inkɒmprihensəbíliti:) *n.* the state or quality of being incomprehensible

in·com·pre·hen·si·ble (inkɒmprihénsəb'l) *adj.* that cannot be understood **in·com·pre·hén·si·bly** *adv.* [fr. L. *incomprehensibilis*]

in·com·pre·hen·sion (inkɒmprihénʃən) *n.* failure to understand

in·com·pres·si·bil·i·ty (ìnkəmpresəbíliti:) *n.* the state or quality of being incompressible

in·com·pres·si·ble (ìnkəmpresáb'l) *adj.* not compressible ‖ (*loosely*) of that which can only be slightly compressed (e.g. a liquid)

in·com·put·a·ble (inkəmpjú:təb'l) *adj.* not able to be computed

in·con·ceiv·a·bil·i·ty (inkənsí:vəbíliti:) *n.* the state or quality of being inconceivable

in·con·ceiv·a·ble (inkənsí:vəb'l) *adj.* not mentally conceivable, not imaginable ‖ not believable **in·con·céiv·a·bly** *adv.*

in·con·clu·sive (ìnkənklú:siv) *adj.* failing to lead to or result in a conclusion, *an inconclusive argument*

CONCISE PRONUNCIATION KEY: **(a)** æ, c*a*t; ɑ, c*ar*; ɔ f*aw*n; ei, sn*a*ke. **(e)** e, h*e*n; i:, sh*ee*p; iə, d*ee*r; ɛə, b*ea*r. **(i)** i, f*i*sh; ai, t*i*ger; ə:, b*ir*d. **(o)** o, *o*x; au, c*ow*; ou, g*oa*t; u, p*oo*r; ɔi, r*oy*al. **(u)** ʌ, d*u*ck; u, b*u*ll; u:, g*oo*se; ə, b*a*cillus; ju:, c*u*be. x, lo*ch*; θ, *th*ink; ð, bo*th*er; z, *Z*en; ʒ, cor*s*age; dʒ, sava*g*e; ŋ, ora*ng*utang; j, *y*ak; ʃ, *fi*sh; tʃ, fe*tch*; 'l, rabb*le*; 'n, redd*en*. Complete pronunciation key appears inside front cover.

in·con·den·sa·bil·i·ty (inkəndensəbíliti:) *n.* the quality of being incondensable

in·con·den·sa·ble (inkəndénsəb'l) *adj.* not able to be condensed

in·con·gru·ence (inkóŋgru:əns) *n.* the quality or state of being incongruent

in·con·gru·ent (inkóŋgru:ənt) *adj.* incongruous ‖ (*geom.*) not congruent [fr. L. *incongruens (incongruentis)*]

in·con·gru·i·ty (inkɒŋgrú:iti:) *pl.* **in·con·gru·i·ties** *n.* the quality of being incongruous ‖ something incongruous [fr. M.L. *incongruitas*]

in·con·gru·ous (inkóŋgru:əs) *adj.* not in harmony or agreement, *his profession of belief and his actions are incongruous* ‖ incompatible with the context or surroundings [fr. L. *incongruus*]

in·con·se·quence (inkónsikwəns) *n.* lack of logical sequence or of relevance ‖ an instance of this [fr. L. *inconsequentia*]

in·con·se·quent (inkónsikwənt) *adj.* not derived logically from a premise, illogical ‖ irrelevant ‖ unimportant [fr. L. *inconsequens (inconsequentis)*]

in·con·se·quen·tial (inkɒnsikwénʃəl) *adj.* of no importance or significance ‖ irrelevant ‖ not worthy of being taken seriously

in·con·sid·er·a·ble (inkənsídərəb'l) *adj.* very small, *an inconsiderable amount* ‖ notworthy of consideration, trivial **in·con·sid·er·a·bly** *adv.* [F. *inconsidérable*]

in·con·sid·er·ate (inkənsídərit) *adj.* lacking, or showing a lack of, regard for the feelings or well-being of someone else [fr. L. *inconsideratus*]

in·con·sist·en·cy (inkənsístənsi:) *pl.* **in·con·sist·en·cies** *n.* the state or quality of being inconsistent ‖ an instance of this

in·con·sist·ent (inkənsístənt) *adj.* self-contradictory, *an inconsistent account* ‖ (with 'with') in contradiction, not in harmony, *his actions are inconsistent with his principles* ‖ (of behavior) changing for no apparent reason ‖ (of a person) showing such behavior

in·con·sol·a·bil·i·ty (inkənsoulə bíliti:) *n.* the quality of being inconsolable

in·con·sol·a·ble (inkənsóulə b'l) *adj.* too grieved to be consoled **in·con·sól·a·bly** *adv.* [fr. L. *inconsolabilis*]

in·con·so·nant (inkónsənənt) *adj.* not consonant, not in harmony, not in keeping

in·con·spic·u·ous (inkənspíkju:əs) *adj.* not attracting attention, hardly noticeable [fr. L.L. *inconspicuus*]

in·con·stan·cy (inkónstənsi:) *pl.* **in·con·stan·cies** *n.* the quality or state of being inconstant ‖ an instance of this [fr. L. *inconstantia*]

in·con·stant (inkónstənt) *adj.* not constant, changeable ‖ fickle [F.]

in·con·test·a·bil·i·ty (inkɒntestəbíliti:) *n.* the quality or state of being incontestable

in·con·test·a·ble (inkɒntéstəb'l) *adj.* of that which cannot be doubted, denied or disputed **in·con·tést·a·bly** *adv.* [F.]

in·con·ti·nence (inkóntinəns) *n.* the quality or state of being incontinent [F. or fr. L. *incontinentia*]

in·con·ti·nent (inkóntinənt) *adj.* lacking self-restraint, esp. sexually ‖ unable to control the evacuation of the bladder or bowels [F. or fr. L. *incontinens (incontinentis)*]

in·con·tro·vert·i·bil·i·ty (inkɒntrəvə:rtəbíliti:) *n.* the quality of being incontrovertible

in·con·tro·vert·i·ble (inkɒntrəvə:rtəb'l) *adj.* not subject to denial or doubt **in·con·tro·vért·i·bly** *adv.*

in·con·ven·ience (inkənví:njəns) **1.** *n.* something which causes difficulty or annoyance esp. by interfering with one's plans or routine ‖ the difficulty or annoyance thus caused **2.** *v.t. pres. part.* **in·con·ven·ienc·ing** *past and past part.* **in·con·ven·ienced** to cause to suffer inconvenience [O.F.]

in·con·ven·ient (inkənví:njənt) *adj.* not convenient [F. *inconvénient*]

in·con·vert·i·bil·i·ty (inkənvə:rtəbíliti:) *n.* the quality or state of being inconvertible

in·con·vert·i·ble (inkənvə́:rtəb'l) *adj.* not convertible or exchangeable, esp. of currency that cannot be exchanged for foreign currency, or of paper money that cannot be converted into specie **in·con·vért·i·bly** *adv.*

in·co·or·di·nate (inkouɔ́:rd'nit) *adj.* lacking coordination **in·co·or·di·na·tion** (inkouɔːrd'néiʃən) *n.* lack of coordination, esp. of muscular coordination

in·cor·po·ra·ble (inkɔ́:rpərəb'l) *adj.* capable of being incorporated [fr. L. *incorporare*]

in·cor·po·rate 1. (inkɔ́:rpəreit) *v. pres. part.* **in·cor·po·rat·ing** *past and past part.* **in·cor·po·rat·ed** *v.t.* to unite into a whole ‖ (with 'in' or 'into') to include, *incorporate these items in your list* ‖ to form into a legal corporation ‖ to receive into a legal corporation ‖ *v.i.* to form a legal corporation ‖ to become combined or united **2.** (inkɔ́:rpərit) *adj.* formed or united in a whole ‖ formed into a corporation [fr. L.L. *incorporare (incorporatus)*]

in·cor·po·ra·tion (inkɔːrpəréiʃən) *n.* an incorporating or being incorporated [fr. L.L. *incorporatio (incorporationis)*]

in·cor·po·ra·tive (inkɔ́:rpəreitiv, inkɔ́:rpərətiv) *adj.* incorporating, tending to incorporate

in·cor·po·re·al (inkɔːrpóːri:əl, inkɔːrpóuri:əl) *adj.* not composed of matter ‖ (*law*, e.g. of patents) having no material or tangible quality, but deriving from property having physical existence [fr. L. *incorporeus*]

in·cor·po·re·i·ty (inkɔːrpərí:iti:) *pl.* **in·cor·po·re·i·ties** *n.* the quality or state of being incorporeal ‖ something incorporeal [fr. M.L. *incorporeitas*]

in·cor·rect (inkərékt) *adj.* not true, in error, *an incorrect answer* ‖ containing inaccuracies, *fluent but incorrect Arabic* ‖ not conforming to accepted standards, improper, *incorrect behavior* [fr. L. *incorrectus*]

in·cor·ri·gi·bil·i·ty (inkɒridʒəbíliti:, inkɒridʒəbíliti:) *n.* the state or quality of being incorrigible

in·cor·ri·gi·ble (inkɔ́ridʒəb'l, inkɒridʒəb'l) *adj.* (of a person, bad habit etc.) not capable of being corrected, esp. bad beyond hope of reform **in·cór·ri·gi·bly** *adv.* [F.]

in·cor·rupt·i·bil·i·ty (inkərʌptəbíliti:) *n.* the quality or state of being incorruptible

in·cor·rupt·i·ble (inkərʌ́ptəb'l) *adj.* impossible to corrupt morally, esp. by bribery ‖ not subject to physical decay or deterioration **in·cor·rúpt·i·bly** *adv.* [F.]

in·cras·sate (inkrǽsit, inkrǽseit) *adj.* (*biol.*) thickened, becoming thicker, swollen in form **in·crás·sat·ed** *adj.* **in·cras·sá·tion** *n.* a thickening [fr. L. *incrassatus*]

in·crease 1. (inkrí:s) *v. pres. part.* **in·creas·ing** *past and past part.* **in·creased** *v.i.* to become greater in size, amount, number, value, degree etc. ‖ *v.t.* to make greater in size, amount, number, value, degree etc. **2.** (ínkri:s) *n.* a growth in size, amount, number, value, degree etc. ‖ the amount by which something grows, *a 50% increase* ‖ something produced by growth **on the increase** growing, increasing **in·créas·ing·ly** *adv.* to a continually increasing degree [M.E. *incresse* fr. A.F.]

in·cred·i·bil·i·ty (inkredəbíliti:) *n.* the quality or state of being incredible

in·cred·i·ble (inkrédəb'l) *adj.* impossible to believe ‖ so remarkable as to be hard to believe or to believe possible **in·créd·i·bly** *adv.* [fr. L. *incredibilis*]

in·cre·du·li·ty (inkrədú:liti:, inkrədjú:liti:) *n.* the quality or state of being incredulous [F. *incrédulité*]

in·cred·u·lous (inkrédʒuləs) *adj.* not believing, skeptical ‖ showing disbelief, *an incredulous look* [fr. L. *incredulus*]

in·cre·ment (ínkrəmənt) *n.* an increase or growth, esp. in profits, salary etc. ‖ the amount by which something increases ‖ (*math.*) any finite change (increase or decrease) in the value of a variable, or of its dependent function **in·cre·men·tal** (inkrəmént'l) *adj.* [fr. L. *incrementum*]

in·cre·tion (inkrí:ʃən) *n.* (*physiol.*) secretion (e.g. of hormones) into the tissues or circulatory system, as opposed to secretion of waste for elimination ‖ a product of such secretion, e.g. a hormone [fr. IN- (in) + SECRETION]

in·crim·i·nate (inkrímineit) *pres. part.* **in·crim·i·nat·ing** *past and past part.* **in·crim·i·nat·ed** *v.t.* to involve in a charge of crime, *his evidence incriminated the local doctor* **in·crim·i·na·to·ry** (inkríminətɔːri, inkríminətɔuri:) *adj.* [fr. M.L. *incriminare (incriminatus)*]

incrust *ENCRUST

in·crus·ta·tion (inkrʌstéiʃən) *n.* a hard crust or coating ‖ a facing of marble etc. on a building [fr. L.L. *incrustatio (incrustationis)*]

in·cu·bate (ínkjubeit, íŋkjubeit) *pres. part.* **in·cu·bat·ing** *past and past part.* **in·cu·bat·ed** *v.t.* (of a bird) to keep (eggs) warm until they hatch, by sitting on them ‖ to keep (eggs, embryos etc.) in favorable conditions for hatching or developing, esp. in an incubator ‖ *v.i.* (of a bird) to brood ‖ (of eggs, embryos etc.) to develop in favorable

conditions, esp. in an incubator ‖ (of disease germs) to be in the period of incubation [fr. L. *incubare (incubatus)* to lie on]

in·cu·ba·tion (inkjubéiʃən, iŋkjubéiʃən) *n.* an incubating or being incubated ‖ the time between infection and the outbreak of disease [fr. L. *incubatio (incubationis)*, a lying on]

in·cu·ba·tive (ínkjubeitiv, íŋkjubeitiv) *adj.* of or relating to incubation

in·cu·ba·tor (ínkjubeitər, íŋkjubeitər) *n.* an apparatus for keeping eggs warm until they hatch ‖ an apparatus for surrounding premature babies with a controlled environment ‖ an apparatus for developing bacteria [L.]

in·cu·ba·to·ry (ínkjubətɔːri:, íŋkjubətɔuri:) *adj.* incubative

in·cu·bus (ínkjubəs, íŋkjubəs) *pl.* **in·cu·bi** (ínkjubai), **in·cu·bus·es** *n.* an evil spirit said to descend on people while they sleep and to have sexual intercourse with women (cf. SUCCUBUS) ‖ a person or thing that weighs overpoweringly on one [L.L. = nightmare]

incudes *pl.* of INCUS

in·cul·cate (inkʌ́lkeit, ínkʌlkeit) *pres. part.* **in·cul·cat·ing** *past and past part.* **in·cul·cat·ed** *v.t.* to teach (something), impress upon the mind, by constant repetition and emphasis **in·cul·cá·tion** *n.* **in·cúl·ca·tor** *n.* [fr. L. *inculcare (inculcatus)*, to stamp on]

in·cul·pate (inkʌ́lpeit, ínkʌlpeit) *pres. part.* **in·cul·pat·ing** *past and past part.* **in·cul·pat·ed** *v.t.* to involve in guilt ‖ to throw blame on **in·cul·pa·to·ry** (inkʌ́lpətɔːri:, inkʌ́lpətɔuri:) *adj.* implying guilt [fr. M.L. *inculpare (inculpatus)*]

in·cum·ben·cy (inkʌ́mbənsi:) *pl.* **in·cum·ben·cies** *n.* the quality or state of being incumbent ‖ the office and duties of an incumbent ‖ the period of office held ‖ an obligation, moral duty

in·cum·bent (inkʌ́mbənt) *adj.* (with 'on', 'upon') resting as an obligation or duty, *it is incumbent on you to be there* ‖ (*biol.*) lying or pressing (upon something) [fr. L. *incumbere*, to lie on]

incumbent *n.* the holder of an ecclesiastical benefice ‖ the holder of any office [fr. M.L. *incumbere*, to possess]

in·cu·na·ble (inkjú:nəb'l) *n.* a book printed before 1501 **in·cu·nab·u·la** (inkjunǽbjulə) *pl. n.* these collectively **in·cu·náb·u·lar** *adj.* [fr. L. *incunabula* fr. *cunae*, cradle]

in·cur (inkə́:r) *pres. part.* **in·cur·ring** *past and past part.* **in·curred** *v.t.* to lay oneself open to, bring upon oneself, *to incur blame* ‖ to meet with (esp. something undesirable), *to incur injury* [fr. L. *incurrere*, to run into or toward]

in·cur·a·bil·i·ty (inkjuərəbíliti:) *n.* the state or quality of being incurable

in·cur·a·ble (inkjúərəb'l) *adj.* incapable of being cured ‖ incapable of being corrected **in·cúr·a·bly** *adv.* [O.F.]

in·cu·ri·ous (inkjúəri:əs) *adj.* lacking the desire to know [fr. L. *incuriosus*]

in·cur·rence (inkə́:rəns, inkʌ́rəns) *n.* an incurring or being incurred [fr. *incurrent*, flowing in fr. L. *incurrens (incurrentis)* fr. *incurrere*, to run into]

in·cur·sion (inkə́:rʒən, inkə́:rʃən) *n.* an intrusion ‖ a sudden invasion, raid [fr. L. *incursio (incursionis)*, a running into]

in·cur·sive (inkə́:rsiv) *adj.* tending to make incursions, aggressive [fr. L. *incurrere (incursus)*, to run into]

in·cur·vate 1. (inkə́:rveit, ínkə:rveit) *v.t. pres. part.* **in·cur·vat·ing** *past and past part.* **in·cur·vat·ed** *v.t.* to cause to curve inward **2.** (inkə́:rvit, ínkə:rveit) *adj.* curved inward, incurved [fr. L. *incurvare (incurvatus)*, to bend]

in·curve (inkə́:rv) *pres. part.* **in·curv·ing** *past and past part.* **in·curved** *v.t.* and *i.* to curve inwards [fr. L. *incurvare*, to bend]

in·cus (íŋkəs) *pl.* **in·cu·des** (iŋkjú:di:z) *n.* the middle bone of three small bones in the ear [L. = anvil]

in·cuse (inkjú:z, inkjú:s) **1.** *adj.* (of the impression on a coin etc.) stamped or hammered in **2.** *n.* an impression stamped on a coin or medal etc. **in·cúsed** *adj.* [fr. L. *incudere (incusus)*, to work on the anvil]

Ind. Indiana ‖ India ‖ Indian

in·debt·ed (indétid) *adj.* owing money ‖ owing gratitude [M.E. *endetted* after O.F. *endetté*]

in·de·cen·cy (indí:'nsi:) *pl.* **in·de·cen·cies** *n.* the quality or state of being indecent ‖ an instance of this [fr. L. *indecentia*, unseemliness]

in·de·cent (indí:s'nt) *adj.* morally offensive, *indecent language* ‖ lacking modesty, *indecent dress* ‖ indecorous [F. *indécent*]

indecent assault (*law*) a sexual assault committed by a man on a woman which does not amount to rape

indecent exposure intentional showing of the genitals in circumstances in which this offends against accepted standards of behavior

in·cid·u·ous (indisídʒu:əs) *adj.* evergreen

in·de·ci·pher·a·bil·i·ty (indisaifərəbíliti:) *n.* the quality or state of being indecipherable

in·de·ci·pher·a·ble (ïndisáifərəb'l) *adj.* not able to be deciphered

in·de·ci·sion (ïndisíʒən) *n.* the state or quality of being indecisive [F. *indécision*]

in·de·ci·sive (ïndisáisiv) *adj.* not decisive, indefinite, *an indecisive answer* ‖ hesitant, irresolute

in·de·clin·a·ble (ïndikláinəb'l) *adj.* (*gram.*) not declinable, having no inflections [F. *indéclinable*]

in·dec·o·rous (indékərəs) *adj.* not decorous ‖ unseemly, in bad taste ‖ mildly obscene [fr. L. *indecorus*]

in·de·co·rum (ïndikɔ́rəm, ïndikóurəm) *n.* lack of decorum ‖ impropriety ‖ an indecorous action [L., *adj.*]

in·deed (indí:d) **1.** *adv.* admittedly, in fact, certainly, *it is indeed true but that is no excuse* **2.** *interj.* an expression denoting surprise, disbelief etc.

indef. indefinite

in·de·fat·i·ga·bil·i·ty (indifætigəbíliti:) *n.* the state or quality of being indefatigable

in·de·fat·i·ga·ble (indifǽtigəb'l) *adj.* impossible to tire out **in·de·fát·i·ga·bly** *adv.* [F. *indéfatigable*]

in·de·fea·si·bil·i·ty (ïndifi:zəbíliti:) *n.* the quality or state of being indefeasible

in·de·fea·si·ble (ïndifí:zəb'l) *adj.* that cannot be annulled, removed or forfeited, *an indefeasible right* **in·de·féa·si·bly** *adv.*

in·de·fect·i·bil·i·ty (ïndifektəbíliti:) *n.* the quality of being indefectible

in·de·fect·i·ble (indiféktəb'l) *adj.* unfailing, not subject to decay ‖ without faults [fr. IN- (not)+ obs. *defectible*, subject to defect or decay]

in·de·fen·si·bil·i·ty (ïndifensəbíliti:) *n.* the state or quality of being indefensible

in·de·fen·si·ble (ïndifénsəb'l) *adj.* not possible to justify or condone ‖ not possible to defend against armed attack **in·de·fén·si·bly** *adv.*

in·de·fin·a·ble (indifáinəb'l) *adj.* not possible to define or describe **in·de·fín·a·bly** *adv.*

in·def·i·nite (indéfinit) *adj.* not clearly stated, vague, *indefinite plans* ‖ not limited, *an indefinite period* ‖ (*gram.*, of adjectives, pronouns etc.) not specifying or limiting [fr. L. *indefinitus*]

indefinite article (*gram.*) the article ('a' or 'an') not specifying or limiting the noun it is used with

in·de·his·cence (ïndihísˈns) *n.* (*bot.*) the quality or state of being indehiscent

in·de·his·cent (ïndihísˈnt) *adj.* (*bot.*, of certain fruits) not splitting at maturity, not opening to release seeds or spores

in·del·i·bil·i·ty (indeləbíliti:) *n.* the quality or state of being indelible

in·del·i·ble (indéləb'l) *adj.* not possible to rub out or delete ‖ that cannot be eradicated from the mind, *indelible memories* ‖ making a mark that cannot be erased, *an indelible pencil* **in·dél·i·bly** *adv.* [fr. L. *indelebilis*]

in·del·i·ca·cy (indélikəsi:) *pl.* **in·del·i·ca·cies** *n.* the quality of being indelicate ‖ an indelicate remark or action

in·del·i·cate (indélikit) *adj.* coarse, mildly indecent ‖ showing tactlessness or insensitivity

in·dem·ni·fi·ca·tion (indemnifikéiʃən) *n.* an indemnifying or being indemnified ‖ a payment which indemnifies

in·dem·ni·fy (indémnifai) *pres. part.* **in·dem·ni·fy·ing** *past* and *past part.* **in·dem·ni·fied** *v.t.* to secure against harm or loss ‖ to compensate for loss or injury [fr. L. *indemnis*, unhurt]

in·dem·ni·ty (indémniti:) *pl.* **in·dem·ni·ties** *n.* insurance or protection against loss or injury ‖ legal exemption from a penalty incurred ‖ compensation for a loss or injury sustained ‖ the money paid to a victorious enemy by a defeated country [F. *indemnité*]

in·de·mon·stra·ble (indimónstrəb'l, idémənstrəb'l) *adj.* not provable

in·dent 1. (indént) *v.t.* to notch, make jagged ‖ to set in (written matter or type) from a margin ‖ (*law*) to cut or divide (a document) along an irregular line, so that the validity of each part

may be proved by its correspondence with the other ‖ (*law*) to draw up (a document) in two or more identical copies ‖ (*Br.*) to draw up an order for (goods) ‖ (*Br.*) to requisition goods from ‖ *v.i.* to set written or printed matter in from a margin ‖ to form a notch or jagged edge ‖ (*Br.*) to write out an official order for goods **2.** (índent) *n.* an indentation ‖ an indenture ‖ (*Br.*) an official order for goods or supplies [M.E. *endent* fr. O.F.]

in·dent 1. (indént) *v.t.* to impress (a mark, pattern etc.) in something ‖ to make a dent in **2.** (índent) *n.* an indentation (notch)

in·den·ta·tion (indentéiʃən) *n.* a notch, jagged cut ‖ a deep recess in a coastline ‖ a line of type or written matter set in from the margin ‖ the space left by this setting in

in·den·tion (indénʃən) *n.* an indentation in writing or printing

in·den·ture (indéntʃər) **1.** *n.* a written contract of agreement, originally separated into two halves with notched edges, the validity of each part being proved by its correspondence with the other ‖ (usually *pl.*) a contract binding one person to work for another for a prescribed length of time ‖ an official certificate, list, inventory etc. **2.** *v.t. pres. part.* **in·den·tur·ing** *past* and *past part.* **in·den·tured** to bind by indentures [M.E. *endenture* fr. O.F.]

in·de·pend·ence (indipéndəns) *n.* the quality or state of being independent

Independence Day *FOURTH OF JULY

in·de·pend·en·cy (indipéndənsi:) *pl.* **in·de·pend·en·cies** *n.* an autonomous state, a territory not controlled or dominated by another power **In·de·pend·en·cy** the Congregationalist principle that the local congregation or church is an autonomous body free from ecclesiastical control [INDEPENDENT]

in·de·pend·ent (indipéndənt) *adj.* free from the authority, control or influence of others, self-governing ‖ causally unconnected, *these factors are independent of each other* ‖ self-supporting, not dependent on others for one's living ‖ not having to work for one's living ‖ not committed to an organized political party, *the independent vote* ‖ (*gram.*, of a clause) not subordinate ‖ (*math.*, of a variable) not depending on another for its value **2.** *n.* an independent person or thing, esp. a person who acts and votes without being committed to a party **In·de·pend·ent** a Congregationalist ‖ (*hist.*) a Brownist

Independent Labour Party (*Br.*, *abbr.* I.L.P.) a working-class political party founded (1893) by Keir Hardie. It allied itself (1900) with the trade unions to found the Labour party

in-depth (índepθ) *adj.* beyond the superficial; comprehensive, e.g., *an in-depth study*

in·de·scrib·a·bil·i·ty (ïndiskraibəbíliti:) *n.* the state or quality of being indescribable

in·de·scrib·a·ble (ïndiskráibəb'l) *adj.* ‖ not possible to describe ‖ surpassing description, *indescribable beauty* **in·de·scrib·a·bly** *adv.*

in·de·struct·i·bil·i·ty (ïndistrʌktəbíliti:) *n.* the state or quality of being indestructible

in·de·struct·i·ble (ïndistrʌ́ktəb'l) *adj.* impossible to destroy **in·de·strúct·i·bly** *adv.*

in·de·ter·mi·na·ble (inditə́:rminəb'l) *adj.* impossible to ascertain or define, *an indeterminable amount* ‖ not possible to decide [fr. L.L. *indeterminabilis*]

in·de·ter·mi·nate (inditə́:rminit) *adj.* indefinite, undefined ‖ not fixed ‖ vague ‖ (*math.*) of a problem having an indefinite number of solutions ‖ (*bot.*) racemose ‖ (*bot.*) having floral leaves which do not overlap in the bud **in·de·ter·mi·na·tion** (inditərminéiʃən) *n.* the state or quality of being indeterminate ‖ lack of determination [L. *indeterminatus*]

in·de·ter·min·ism (inditə́:rminizəm) *n.* (*philos.*) the doctrine that the will is to some extent free and not entirely determined **in·de·tér·min·ist** *n.* and *adj.* **in·de·ter·min·is·tic** *adj.*

in·dex (índeks) **1.** *pl.* **in·dex·es**, **in·di·ces** (índisi:z) *n.* the forefinger ‖ a pointer on a dial or measuring instrument ‖ something that indicates, a sign, *the number of new cars is an index of prosperity* ‖ an alphabetical list of names, subjects, titles etc., giving page numbers where reference is made, and generally placed at the back of a book ‖ (*printing*) (*math.*, *pl.* indices) a symbol showing the power or root of a given quantity ‖ a numerical ratio deduced from observations and used as an indicator of a process or condition, *cost-of-living-index* **In·dex** the Index Librorum Prohibitorum **2.** *v.t.* to make an index for (a book etc.) ‖ to include an index ‖

to move (a machine tool or work held in a machine tool) so that a particular operation is repeated at set distances [L.]

in·dex·a·tion or **indexing** (indekséiʃən) *n.* (*economics*) **1.** system of creating a parity between two economic forces, e.g., wages and cost of living **2.** automatic widening of a category, e.g., of income tax brackets to offset inflation. —**index system** *n.* application of indexation

index crime one of the seven types of crime tabulated in the Uniform Crime Reports compiled by the Federal Bureau of Investigation

In·dex Ex·pur·ga·to·ri·us (índeksekspə:rgətóri:əs, índekspə:rgətóuri:əs) *INDEX LIBRORUM PROHIBITORUM

index finger the forefinger

In·dex Li·bro·rum Pro·hib·i·to·rum (índekslaibrórəmprouhibítòrəm, índekslaibróurəmprouhibítóurəm) (*hist.*) a list of books regarded as endangering faith or morals which Roman Catholics were forbidden by Church authority to read in whole or in part without permission. It included the Index Expurgatorius of books forbidden until they had been revised or had omissions made in them. It was suppressed in 1966

index number (*econ.*) a number used to indicate percentage of change in the level of production etc. at one time, in comparison with the level (usually given as 100) at a chosen base time

index of consumer sentiment (*economics*) index based on a quarterly survey conducted by the University of Michigan in a nationwide sample of approximately 2,000 families, to determine whether families are currently better or worse off financially than a year before

index of refraction the refractive index

In·di·a (índi:ə) a subcontinent (area 1,586,979 sq. miles) of S. Asia, a vast triangle whose base is the Himalayas and whose apex is Cape Comorin in the Indian Ocean, 2,000 miles south. Political units: Bangladesh, the republic of India, Pakistan, Bhutan and Nepal ‖ the republic of India.

—Four main strains may be distinguished among the Indian peoples: the Dravidian, the Vedda, the Aryan (or Indo-Afghan) and the Mongoloid. The first two are regarded as aboriginal and are found in greatest concentration in S. India and the Deccan. The last two are thought to be invaders: the Aryans (Caucasians) are found purest in Pakistan and N. India, the Mongoloid esp. in the Himalayas and Assam

India a republic (area 1,261,597 sq. miles, pop. 683,997,512) and member of the British Commonwealth in S. Asia: Capital: New Delhi. Largest cities: Calcutta, Bombay, Madras. Union territories: the Andaman, Nicobar, Laccadive, Minicoy and Amindivi Islands. People: *INDIA (subcontinent). Official languages: Hindi (Devanagari script) and English. 46% of the population speak Hindi, Urdu or Punjabi. Main linguistic minorities: 10% Telugu, 8% Tamil, 8% Marathi, 8% Bengali, 5% Gujarati, 4.5% Kannada, 3% Oriya, 3% Malayalam, 1% Assamese, also Kashmiri and Sanskrit. Religion: 84% Hindu, 10% Moslem. Minorities: Christians, Sikhs (esp. in the Punjab), Jains (esp. in Gujarat and Maharashtra), Animists (esp. in the extreme east), Buddhists, Parsees, and a very few Jews. The land is 50% arable, 18% forest, 14% pasture and grazing and 8% irrigated. Parts of the north extend into the Himalayas. Highest peak: Nanda Devi, 25,645 ft, in Himachal Pradesh. Great river plains cover most of the rest of N. India: the Punjab plains, the valleys of the Ganges, Jumna and Gogra, and the Ganges delta. In the extreme northeast (Assam) are the Shillong plateau (to 6,000 ft) and the Brahmaputra valley. In the northwest, between R. Sutlej and the Rann of Kutch, is the Thar Desert (irrigated around northern Rajasthan and Haryana). Peninsular India (south of the Vindhya Mtns, 1,500–4,000 ft) is a vast tableland (the Deccan) of low craggy hills and sluggish rivers. It contains the mountains of central India (Aravalli in the west, Chota Nagpur in the east), and rises along the coasts in the Western and Eastern Ghats to 8,640 ft in the S. Western Ghats, or Nilgiri Hills. The climate is controlled by the northeast monsoons (Oct.–Mar.) and the southwest monsoons (Apr.–Sept.). Seasons: cold, except in the south (Nov.–Feb.), hot (Mar.–May), rainy (June–Oct.). Average temperatures (F.): (Jan.) 32° in the Himalayas, 50°–55° in Kashmir,

---

CONCISE PRONUNCIATION KEY: (a) æ, c*a*t; ɑ, c*ar*; ɔ f*aw*n; ei, sn*a*ke. (e) e, h*e*n; i:, sh*ee*p; iə, d*ee*r; ɛə, b*ear*. (i) i, f*i*sh; ai, t*i*ger; ə:, b*i*rd. (o) o, *o*x; au, c*ow*; ou, g*oa*t; u, p*oo*r; ɔi, r*oy*al. (u) ʌ, d*u*ck; u, b*u*ll; u:, g*oo*se; ə, b*a*cillus; ju:, c*u*be. x, lo*ch*; θ, *th*ink; ð, bo*th*er; z, *Z*en; ʒ, cor*s*age; dʒ, sa*v*age; ŋ, ora*ng*uta*ng*; j, *y*ak; ʃ, *f*ish; tʃ, fe*tch*; 'l, rabb*le*; 'n, redd*en*. Complete pronunciation key appears inside front cover.

80° in the south, (May) 80° in the northeast, 85° along the west coast and Ganges delta, 90° in the south, east and north, 95° in the center. Rainfall: 426 ins on the Shillong plateau, 75–150 ins along the Malabar coast, the lower slopes of the Himalayas and the lower Brahmaputra, over 60 ins along the Himalayas and lower Ganges, 50 ins in Madras, 45 ins in Visakhapatnam, over 30 ins in the river valleys of N. India, 15–30 ins along the S. Coromandel coast, in the Punjab, in Delhi, Agra and the interior of S. India, under 10 ins in the Thar. Livestock: cattle, water buffaloes, goats, sheep, poultry, horses. Crops: cereals, rice, sugarcane, jute, cotton, peanuts, rape and mustard, tobacco, spices, vegetables, fruit, tea, coffee, rubber, opium, wool. Woods: teak, sal, deodar. Minerals: coal, manganese ore, petroleum (Assam), iron ore, mica, copper, ilmenite, gypsum, bauxite, chromite, marble, sandstone, granite. Industries: cotton, jute and silk textiles, engineering, iron and steel, sugar, chemicals, pottery, shipbuilding, hydroelectricity. Exports: tea, jute, cotton, leather, iron ore, peanuts, manganese ore, mica, coffee, sugar. Imports: machinery, wheat, cotton, oil, vehicles, chemicals, rice, metals. Main ports: Bombay, Calcutta, Madras, Cochin, Visakhapatnam. There are 62 universities, the three oldest being Calcutta, Bombay and Madras. Monetary unit: Indian rupee (100 paise). HISTORY. The earliest known Indian civilization is that of the Indus valley (c. third millennium B.C.), centered on Mohenjo-Daro and Harappa. The Aryans invaded the Punjab (c. 1500 B.C.) and spread through N. India to Bengal (c. 800 B.C.), displacing the Dravidian inhabitants. The Aryan religion, based on the Vedas, became incorporated in Brahmanism (c. 1000 B.C.), Jainism and Buddhism (6th c. B. C.). Alexander the Great invaded the Punjab (327 B.C.), but the Greeks were driven out by Chandragupta, the founder of the Maurya Empire (325–184 B.C.). Hinduism was the state religion until the reign (c. 273 B.C.–c. 232 B.C.) of Asoka, who replaced it by Buddhism. On his death, the Maurya Empire, which now included most of the subcontinent, began to disintegrate. N. India was invaded and ruled by the Greeks (2nd c. B.C.), and the Parthians (1st c. B.C.–1st c. A.D.). The Gupta dynasty (c. 320–c. 544) created a new empire in N. India, but failed to gain control of the south. Hindu art and culture reached their zenith in this period. The Hun invasion (6th c.) and the internecine warfare of the Rajputs weakened N. India in the face of invasions from the northwest by Turks and Persians (1001–26) under Mahmud of Ghazni. The Delhi sultanate (1206–1526) conquered most of the Hindu states except Kashmir, but was weakened when Timur captured Delhi (1398). It was replaced in the north by separate Moslem kingdoms, which were subdued (1526) by Babur, the founder of the Mogul Empire (1526–1707). During the reign (1556–1605) of Akbar, Mogul power was extended to most of northern and central India and the administration of the empire was reformed. Mogul architecture reached its height under the rule (1627–58) of Shah Jahan, but the empire began to disintegrate after the reign (1658–1707) of Aurangzeb.

European interest in India began with Vasco da Gama's arrival (1498) at Calicut. The British East India Company established trading posts at Surat (1612), Bombay (1661) and Calcutta (1690), driving off Portuguese and Dutch opposition. With the decline of the Mogul empire, and the emergence of the Marathas, the British and French tried to extend their influence over the native states (18th c.). The ensuing Anglo-French conflict (1746–63) resulted in the expulsion of the French by the military victories of Clive. The British raj was extended by Warren Hastings, and by 1850 covered the whole of India. After the Indian Mutiny (1857), the control of India passed to the British Crown (1858), and Queen Victoria became empress of India (1877). Indian desire for self-government led to the formation of the Indian National Congress (1885) and the Moslem League (1906). After the 1st world war, the Government of India Act (1919) failed to transfer real power to elected officials. Gandhi led a policy of passive resistance to British rule. Provincial legislatures were set up by the Government of India Act (1935), but the rift between Hindus and Moslems continued to widen. A mission (1942) led by Sir Stafford Cripps failed to unify Indian

leaders on a formula for a transfer of power, and at the end of the 2nd world war a policy of partition was agreed on. On Aug. 15, 1947, the country was partitioned to form the two new states of India and Pakistan. The princely states (more than 500 in number) which had political agreements with British India, were allowed to join either India or Pakistan. The partition was marked by great bloodshed and there was a huge refugee problem. Hyderabad, the largest of the princely states, joined India (1949) but Kashmir, having borders with both India and Pakistan, presented a problem. In the end the maharaja opted to join India, but Pakistan contested the decision and a bitter dispute followed, leading to U.N. intervention. Kashmir was formally admitted to the Indian Union (1957), but parts of its western mountainous regions continued to be controlled by Pakistan.

Under the constitution of the Republic of India (Jan. 26, 1950), India is a union of states, each with its own governor and legislative assembly. The Congress party under Nehru created (1949–56) a strong central government. By 1956, the former French territories had been incorporated in the republic. The Portuguese possession of Goa was invaded (1961) and annexed (1962). Overpopulation and frontier disputes with China on the northwest and northeast borders have strained India's economy. The long-standing dispute with Pakistan over Kashmir broke briefly into open war (1965). Shortly after signing an agreement at Tashkent with Pakistan to restore normal relations between the two countries, Shastri, the prime minister, died, and was succeeded by Indira Gandhi in 1966. Her first 11 years in office saw many improvements in agriculture, irrigation, and power production; sources of natural gas and oil were discovered; and many industries were nationalized. In 1974, India entered the nuclear age with the explosion of its first nuclear device. India helped establish Bangladesh as an independent state in 1971, and in 1975 Sikkim became an Indian state. Economic and social problems continued, however, and mounting political opposition along with a rash of strikes and riots persuaded Gandhi to declare a state of emergency in 1975, during which time many political opponents were jailed and constitutional rights suspended. In March 1977 the emergency was lifted, and after elections were held Gandhi resigned in favor of an opposition coalition. This coalition did not hold together, however, and Gandhi returned to office in a caretaker government; she was reelected in 1980. Sikh opposition forces became violently active in the early 1980s. The government attempted in June 1984 to put down a violent Sikh separatist movement in Amritsar, and in October Gandhi was assassinated by Sikh members of her security guard. She was succeeded as prime minister by her son Rajiv Gandhi, and his party won an overwhelming victory in the December 1984 elections. Regional settlements in the Punjab and Assam were negotiated in 1985

India ink (*Am.=Br.* Indian ink) a black pigment, consisting of lampblack mixed with a binder, used in painting, lettering etc. || the liquid ink made from this pigment

In·di·an (índi:ən) **1.** *n.* a citizen of the republic of India || one of the original inhabitants of America || any of the American Indian languages **2.** *adj.* of or pertaining to the subcontinent or the republic of India || of or pertaining to the citizens of the republic of India, or to their culture etc. || of or pertaining to the original inhabitants of America, their languages, culture etc. (*LATIN AMERICAN INDIANS, *NORTH AMERICAN INDIANS)

In·di·an·a (índi:ǽnə) (*abbr.* Ind.) a state (area 36,291 sq. miles, pop, 5,479,000) on midwestern plains of the U.S.A. Capital: Indianapolis. Agriculture (80% is farmed): corn and other cereals, tomatoes, soybeans, pigs. Resources: coal, building limestone, oil. Industries: iron and steel, motor vehicles, aircraft and rail equipment, oil refining, machinery. Chief universities: Indiana University (1824) at Bloomington, Purdue (1869) at Lafayette and Notre Dame (1842) at South Bend. Indiana was settled (18th c.) by French fur traders, was ceded (1763) to Britain, and with the Revolution passed (1779) under the control of the U.S.A., of which it became (1816) the 19th state

Indian Affairs, Bureau of (BIA), U.S. federal agency that handles Indian matters such as education, mineral and water rights, land leasing, social services, law enforcement and job training on Indian reservations. Originally a part of the War Department from 1824, it became part of the Department of the Interior in 1849 and is directed by the department's assistant secretary of Indian affairs

In·di·an·ap·o·lis (índi:ənǽpəlis) the capital (pop. 700,807, with agglom. 698,000) of Indiana, center of the corn belt: agricultural trade, meat packing, metallurgy, pharmaceuticals

Indian club a bottle-shaped wood or metal club, used in exercises to strengthen the muscles

Indian corn *CORN (maize)

Indian Desert *THAR

Indian file single file [after the American Indian way of moving along trails]

Indian giver (*pop.*) a person who gives a present and then asks for it back

Indian hemp *Apocynum cannabinum*, fam. *Apocynaceae*, a North American dogbane from which a fiber for cordage was formerly made || hemp || sunn hemp

Indian ink (*Br.*) India ink

in·di·a·nis·mo (i:ndjɑní:smɔ) *n.* a cultural movement in Latin America, esp. (and originally) in Mexico, which draws national pride from native folklore and the native race. In Mexico it owes much to Emiliano Zapata and to the mural painters Diego Rivera, José Clemente Orozco, and David Alfaro Siqueiros [Span.]

Indian meal cornmeal

Indian millet durra

Indian Mutiny a rebellion (1857–8) of the Bengal Sepoys against British rule in India. It was largely caused by Hindu opposition to British attempts to impose social reforms. The revolt spread quickly through central India, causing much bloodshed, and was repressed with great severity. It resulted in the Government of India Act (1858), by which the rule of India passed from the East India Company to the Crown

Indian National Congress a political organization founded in 1885 in India to promote constitutional progress. Under Gandhi and Nehru it campaigned for independence after the 1st world war. After 1947 the Congress party remained dominant in India

In·di·an·ness (índi:ənnjs) *n.* the quality of being Indian (Native American or Eastern)

Indian Ocean the ocean (area incl. seas, gulfs and Antarctic waters, 29,000,000 sq. miles) between Africa, Asia, and Australia. Length (Pakistan-Antarctica): 6,000 miles. Width (South Africa to Australia): 6,500 miles. The Great Indian Ridge (the Maldive Is and Mauritius are summits) running to Antarctica divides it into an eastern valley, relatively unaccidented, and a western valley broken by smaller ridges culminating in many islands. Average valley depth: 2,700 fathoms. Deeps reach 4,100 fathoms (Sundas trench). The monsoons, changing direction with the seasons, reverse its currents: Oct.–Apr. generally north, May–Sept. south and west

Indians, North American *NORTH AMERICAN INDIANS

Indian summer a period of warm, dry weather in late autumn, esp. in North America

Indian Territory country set aside under the Indian Intercourse Act (1834) for Indians || the eastern part of present Oklahoma, where Indians were gradually forced to settle

India paper a very thin, soft but strong paper originally made in China and Japan, used for making prints of engravings || a thin, tough printing paper, used esp. for Bibles, prayer books etc.

india rubber natural rubber || a rubber eraser

Indic *INDIC LANGUAGES

indic. indicative

in·di·can (índikən) *n.* a natural glucoside found in plants of genus *Indigofera*, the decomposition of which makes indigo dye || a normal constituent of urine which yields indigo upon oxidation [fr. L. *indicum*, indigo]

in·di·cate (índikeit) *pres. part.* **in·di·cat·ing** *past* and *past part.* **in·di·cat·ed** *v.t.* to direct attention to || to point out, show, *a signpost indicates the road* || to denote the probability of, *his symptoms indicate mumps* || to state in brief, *indicate what you think about this* [fr. L. *indicare (indicatus)*, to make known]

in·di·ca·tion (índikéiʃən) *n.* something that indicates || an indicating or being indicated [F.]

in·dic·a·tive (indíkətiv) 1. *adj.* showing, giving an indication, *his expression was indicative of his resentment* ‖ (*gram.*) of the mood that expresses an action definitely, as distinct from stating a possible action, thought or desire (cf. IMPERATIVE, cf. SUBJUNCTIVE) 2. *n.* (*gram.*) the indicative mood ‖ (*gram.*) a verb in this mood [fr. F. *indicatif*]

in·di·ca·tor (índikeitər) *n.* something which points out or gives information, e.g. an instrument giving readings on a machine, or a board in a station showing train arrivals and departures ‖ (*chem.*) a substance (e.g. litmus) which shows by its color or change in color that a particular concentration of hydrogen or hydroxyl ions is present [L.L.]

indices *alt. pl.* of INDEX

In·dic languages (índik) a branch of the Indo-European language family incl. Pali, the Prakrit languages, Sanskrit, Hindi, Urdu and others of India, Sri Lanka and Pakistan

in·dict (indáit) *v.t.* (esp. of a grand jury) to accuse formally of an offense **in·dict·a·ble** *adj.* liable to be indicted ‖ (of an action) making the doer liable for indictment [M.E. *enditen* fr. A.F.]

in·dict·ment (indáitmənt) *n.* an indicting or being indicted ‖ (*law*) a formal written statement accusing a person or persons of a crime [A.F. *enditement, endictement*]

Indies *EAST INDIES, *WEST INDIES

in·dif·fer·ence (indífərəns, indífrəns) *n.* lack of interest or feeling, *he heard the news with complete indifference* ‖ unimportance, *a matter of complete indifference* [fr. L. *indifferentia*]

indifference curve (*econ.*) a curve indicating all possible comparative quantities of goods or services in equal demand by, or of equal use to, a consumer

in·dif·fer·ent (indífərənt, indífrənt) *adj.* not interested, *indifferent to classical music* ‖ having no preference, impartial ‖ affording no grounds for preference, *what colors are chosen is indifferent to him* ‖ rather poor, mediocre ‖ (*chem., elec.*) showing no response, neutral [F. or fr. L. *indifferens* (*indifferentis*)]

in·dif·fer·ent·ism (indífərəntizəm, indífrəntizəm) *n.* an adopted attitude of indifference, esp. toward religion ‖ the belief that differences in religious forms are unimportant **in·dif·fer·ent·ist** *n.*

in·di·gence (índidʒəns) *n.* the quality or state of being indigent [F.]

in·dig·e·nous (indídʒənəs) *adj.* born, growing or originating in the locality, not imported ‖ of or relating to natives, *indigenous customs* ‖ (with 'to') innate, inborn [fr. L.L. *indigenus*]

in·di·gent (índidʒənt) *adj.* needy, poor [F.]

in·di·gest·i·bil·i·ty (indidʒestəbíliti:) *n.* the quality of being indigestible

in·di·gest·i·ble (indidʒéstəb'l) *adj.* not easy to digest ‖ not possible to digest ‖ not easy to absorb mentally, *an indigestible mass of statistics* [fr. L. *indigestibilis*]

in·di·ges·tion (indidʒéstʃən) *n.* difficulty in digesting food ‖ pain caused by difficulty in digesting food [F.]

in·dig·nant (indígnənt) *adj.* angered by unwarranted accusation, injustice, meanness etc. ‖ showing such anger, *indignant looks* [fr. L. *indignari* (*indignatus*), to regard as unworthy]

in·dig·na·tion (indignéiʃən) *n.* anger aroused by injustice, unkindness, unwarranted accusation, meanness etc. [F. *indigenous customes* ‖ (with 'to') innate, inborn [fr. L.L. *indigenus*]

in·dig·ni·ty (indígniti:) *pl.* **in·dig·ni·ties** *n.* treatment that makes one feel humiliated ‖ an insult or outrage ‖ the quality of being humiliating [fr. L. *indignitas*]

in·di·go (índigou) 1. *pl.* **in·di·gos, in·di·goes** *n.* a blue dye obtained from plants esp. of genus *Indigofera*, fam. *Papilionaceae*, now generally made synthetically ‖ the color of this dye ‖ any of several indigo-yielding plants, esp. a member of *Indigofera* 2. *adj.* of the color of indigo [fr. L. *indicum*]

indigo bird the indigo bunting

indigo bunting *Passerina cyanea*, a North American finch. The male has the head and upper parts bright indigo

in·di·goid (índigoid) *adj.* (of a dye, pigment etc.) having coloring properties similar to those of indigo

in·di·rect (indirékt) *adj.* not following the shortest route from one point to another, roundabout, *an indirect path* ‖ not going straight to the point, oblique ‖ dishonest, not straightforward, *indirect business dealings* ‖ not immediate, *an indirect cause* [F. or fr. L. *indirectus*]

indirect discourse (*Am.*=*Br.* indirect speech, *gram.*) a construction used in relating what a person has said without quoting him, e.g. 'he said that he would come' to express 'he said: "I will come"'

in·di·rec·tion (indirékʃən, indairékʃən) *n.* guile, lack of straightforwardness ‖ roundabout methods ‖ aimlessness [fr. INDIRECT, after DIRECTION]

indirect lighting lighting installed so as to be reflected from a ceiling or other surface diffusely, the source of the light being hidden

indirect object (*gram.*) the word or words designating the person (e.g. 'me' in 'give me your gun') or thing (e.g. 'room' in 'give the room a cleaning') to whom or to which something is given, or the person or thing for whom or for which something is done (cf. DIRECT OBJECT)

indirect speech (*Br.*) indirect discourse

indirect tax a tax levied on someone other than the person on whom its burden falls in the long run, e.g. a tax on goods which is ultimately paid, in the form of a price increase, by the consumer

in·dis·cern·i·ble (indisə́:rnəb'l) *adj.* not discernible, not capable of being seen **in·dis·cern·i·bly** *adv.*

in·dis·ci·pline (indísəplin) *n.* lack of discipline

in·dis·creet (indiskrít) *adj.* lacking or showing a lack of prudence, good judgment or tact [prob. F. *indiscret*]

in·dis·crete (indiskrít) *adj.* not divided into separate parts [fr. L. *indiscretus*]

in·dis·cre·tion (indiskréʃən) *n.* lack of prudence, tact etc. ‖ an indiscreet speech or action [F.]

in·dis·crim·i·nate (indiskríminit) *adj.* having or showing a lack of discernment, failing to make proper distinctions, *indiscriminate praise* ‖ making no distinctions, random, *indiscriminate slaughter*

in·dis·pen·sa·bil·i·ty (indispensəbíliti:) *n.* the quality or state of being indispensable

in·dis·pen·sa·ble (indispénsəb'l) *adj.* absolutely necessary, impossible to do without **in·dis·pén·sa·bly** *adv.* [fr. M.L. *indispensabilis*]

in·dis·pose (indispóuz) *pres. part.* **in·dis·pos·ing** *past* and *past part.* **in·dis·posed** *v.t.* to upset somewhat the state of mind or health of, *a cold indisposed him for the day* **in·dis·pósed** *adj.* slightly unwell ‖ unwilling, averse

in·dis·po·si·tion (indispəzíʃən) *n.* a slight illness, esp. one that does not last long ‖ a disinclination

in·dis·put·a·bil·i·ty (indispju:təbíliti:) *n.* the state or quality of being indisputable

in·dis·put·a·ble (indispju:təb'l) *adj.* unquestionable, incontestable, *an indisputable truth* **in·dis·pút·a·bly** *adv.* [fr. L.L. *indisputabilis*]

in·dis·sol·u·bil·i·ty (indispoljubíliti:) *n.* the state or quality of being indissoluble

in·dis·sol·u·ble (indispóljub'l) *adj.* lasting, indestructible, *indissoluble friendship* ‖ not possible to dissolve or break up **in·dis·sól·u·bly** *adv.* [fr. L. *indissolubilis*]

in·dis·tinct (indistínkt) *adj.* difficult to see or hear for want of clarity ‖ confused, vague, *indistinct recollections* [fr. L. *indistinctus*]

in·dis·tinc·tive (indistínktiv) *adj.* not distinctive, having nothing to distinguish it from others

in·dis·tin·guish·a·ble (indistíngwiʃəb'l) *adj.* not distinguishable, not capable of being differentiated, *the copy was indistinguishable from the original* ‖ impossible to discern, *the car number was indistinguishable from where he was* **in·dis·tín·guish·a·bly** *adv.*

in·dite (indáit) *pres. part.* **in·dit·ing** *past* and *past part.* **in·dit·ed** *v.t.* (*rhet.*) to write down (a poem, speech etc.) [M.E. *enditen* fr. O.F.]

in·di·um (índiəm) *n.* a metallic element (symbol In, at. no. 49, at. mass 114.82), used as an electroplated coating on bearing metals and as a constituent of dental alloys [fr. L. *indicum*, indigo]

in·di·vid·u·al (individʒu:əl) 1. *adj.* existing as a complete and separate entity ‖ of, relating to, used by or intended for only one person or thing ‖ distinctive, strikingly different from others, *an individual style of dress* 2. *n.* one person, animal, organism etc. as distinguished from a class, group etc. ‖ a person, *a strange individual* [fr. M.L. *individualis*]

in·di·vid·u·al·ism (individʒu:əlizəm) *n.* the assertion of individual characteristics, *his individualism contrasts with the conformity of his sons* ‖ self-assertion in disregard of others ‖

(*philos.*) the doctrine that only individual things (and not universals) are real ‖ a social or ethical doctrine stressing the importance of the individual rather than that of the group ‖ the doctrine that private economic enterprise should not be restricted by government or social regulation [F. *individualisme*]

in·di·vid·u·al·ist (individʒu:əlist) *n.* someone who shows or asserts individuality in speech, actions or thoughts ‖ an advocate of individualism as a philosophical, social or ethical doctrine

in·di·vid·u·al·is·tic *adj.* **in·di·vid·u·al·is·ti·cal·ly** *adv.* [INDIVIDUAL]

in·di·vid·u·al·i·ty (individʒu:æliti:) *n.* the quality or characteristics that make one person or thing different from others ‖ the quality or state of being individual

in·di·vid·u·al·i·za·tion (individʒu:əlizéiʃən) *n.* an individualizing or being individualized

in·di·vid·u·al·ize (individʒu:əlaiz) *pres. part.* **in·di·vid·u·al·iz·ing** *past* and *past part.* **in·di·vid·u·al·ized** *v.t.* to give an individual character to ‖ to specify, particularize, *individualize each item*

in·di·vid·u·al·ly (individʒu:əli:) *adv.* one by one, separately ‖ in a personal way, *all three paint quite individually*

in·di·vid·u·ate (individʒu:eit) *pres. part.* **in·di·vid·u·at·ing** *past* and *past part.* **in·di·vid·u·at·ed** *v.t.* to distinguish from others in the same group ‖ to make into an individual entity [fr. M.L. *individuare* (*individuatus*), to make individual]

in·di·vid·u·a·tion (individʒu:éiʃən) *n.* an individuating or being individuated [fr. M.L. *individuatio* (*individuationis*)]

in·di·vis·i·bil·i·ty (indivizəbíliti:) *n.* the state or quality of being indivisible

in·di·vis·i·ble (indivízəb'l) *adj.* impossible to divide into parts ‖ (*math.*) impossible to divide without leaving a remainder **in·di·vís·i·bly** *adv.* [fr. L.L. *indivisibilis*]

In·do-Ar·y·an (indouéəri:ən, indouéərjən) 1. *n.* a member of one of the peoples of India speaking an IndoEuropean language 2. *adj.* of or relating to these peoples ‖ of or relating to one of the Indo-European languages spoken in India

In·do·chi·na (indoutʃáinə) (*geog.*) the peninsula of S.E. Asia between the Bay of Bengal, the South China Sea and the Malacca Strait. It comprises Burma, Thailand, Laos, Cambodia, Vietnam and Malaya ‖ (*hist.*) the former colonial possessions of France in this region, comprising Vietnam, Cambodia and Laos (*FRENCH INDOCHINA)

In·do·chi·nese (indoutʃaini:z, indoutʃaini:s) 1. *adj.* of or pertaining to Indochina ‖ of or pertaining to one of the races or languages of Indochina 2. *n.* an inhabitant of Indochina ‖ any one of the languages of Indochina

in·doc·ile (indós'l, *Br.* indóusail) *adj.* unruly, difficult to control, train or teach **in·do·cil·i·ty** (indousíliti:, indousíliti:) *n.* [F. or fr. L. *indocilis*]

in·doc·tri·nate (indóktrineit) *pres. part.* **in·doc·tri·nat·ing** *past* and *past part.* **in·doc·tri·nat·ed** *v.t.* to instill certain ideas or beliefs into, esp. so as to cause to embrace an ideology ‖ to teach rudiments to **in·doc·tri·ná·tion** *n.* [fr. M.L. *in-* + *doctrinare* (*doctrinatus*), to instruct]

in·do·cy·a·nine green [$C_{43}H_{47}N_2O_6S_2$] (indousáiəni:n) (*pharm.*) green dye used to diagnose heart and liver function

In·do-Eu·ro·pe·an (indoujuərəpí:ən) 1. *adj.* of or relating to a family of languages incl. most of those spoken in Europe and many of S.W. Asia and India. The main branches of the IndoEuropean family are Albanian, Armenian, Baltic, Celtic, Germanic, Greek, Indic, Iranian, Italic, Slavic, Tocharian and, in some classifications, Hittite 2. *n.* the Indo-European family of languages ‖ the hypothetical prehistoric language regarded as the parent of the IndoEuropean languages and reconstructed by modern scholars

In·do-Ger·man·ic (indoudʒə:rmǽnik) *adj.* and *n.* Indo-European

In·do-I·ra·ni·an (indouiréini:ən) 1. *adj.* Of or pertaining to a subfamily of the Indo-European language family, comprising the Indic and Iranian branches 2. *n.* the hypothetical prehistoric language from which the Indic and Iranian languages are descended ‖ a member of a people originally speaking an Indo-Iranian language

in·dole (indoul) *n.* a white crystalline azole, C_8H_7N, found in coal tar etc. and as a product of protein decomposition in the intestines, (and obtained artificially from indigo. It has an unpleasant smell but is used in perfumes [ult. fr. L. *indicum*, indigo + *oleum*, oil]

in·do·lence (índ'ləns) *n.* the state or quality of being indolent [F. or fr. L. *indolentia*, freedom from pain]

in·do·lent (índ'lənt) *adj.* disliking exertion, lazy ‖ (*med.*) causing little or no pain ‖ (*med.*) slow to heal ‖ (*med.*) spreading slowly [fr. L.L. *indolens* (*indolentis*), feeling no pain]

in·do·meth·a·cin [C$_{19}$H$_{16}$ClNO$_4$] (ìndoumèθə-sən) *n.* (*pharm.*) pain-relieving drug used in treating arthritis; marketed as Indocin

in·dom·i·ta·ble (indómitəb'l) *adj.* unconquerable, not to be subdued **in·dóm·i·ta·bly** *adv.* [fr. L.L. *indomitabilis*]

In·do·ne·sia (indəní:ʒə) a republic (area 736,469 sq. miles, pop. 162,200,000) in the Malay Archipelago, S.E. Asia, comprising the Sundas (except parts of Borneo and Timor), the Moluccas, and W. New Guinea, in all over 3,000 islands. Capital: Djakarta. People: Malays of many ethnic groups, with Papuan, Melanesian and Negrito (esp. in the Lesser Sundas), Chinese, Indian and Arab (esp. on the coasts) admixture, 2% Chinese, Arab and Indian minorities. Language: Indonesian languages (30 languages, 250 dialects), Papuan (in New Guinea and adjacent islands). Official language: Indonesian. Religion: mainly Moslem, with Protestant (2%), Roman Catholic (1%), Buddhist (1%), Hindu (esp. in Bali, Taoist and Confucianist minorities. 60% of the land is forest. The largely volcanic ridge which forms the backbone of the islands rises to 12,467 ft (Kerintji) in Sumatra, 12,060 ft (Semeroe) in Java, and 12,224 ft (Rindjani) in Lombok. Average temperatures (F.): 82° in Djakarta, higher in Borneo, lower in Sulawesi. Rainfall: Padang 180 ins, Palembang, Java and Sulawesi 100 ins. Rainy season in Java: Dec.–Feb. Livestock: cattle, sheep, goats, water buffaloes. Agricultural products: rice, corn, cassava, sweet potatoes, soybeans, sugar, tea, coffee, palm oil and kernels, peanuts, copra, rubber. Woods: esp. teak (E. and W. central Java). Minerals: tin (Bangka, Belitung), oil (E. Sumatra, E. Java, E. Borneo), bauxite (Riouw Archipelago), coal, manganese, salt (Madura), copper, diamonds (S. Borneo). Manufactures and industries: textiles, shipbuilding, paper, matches, tires, wood products, engineering, glass, chemicals, cement, fishing, hats, batik cloth, printing, metal working, jewelry, bricks, tiles. Exports: rubber, petroleum, tin, copra, palm oil and kernels, tea, coffee, tobacco, kapok, pepper, quinine. Imports: rice, flour, cotton goods, machinery, oil, vehicles, paper, yarns and thread. There are 20 universities. Monetary unit: rupiah (100 sen). HISTORY. Buddhist and Hindu empires from India grew up in Indonesia (7th–13th cc.), but by the 16th c. Islam had become the main religion and the empires had disintegrated. The Portuguese captured Malacca (1511) and began to set up trading posts, but were challenged by the arrival of the Dutch (1596) and the English (1600). The Dutch East India Company emerged triumphant (1623) and became the chief power in the area, its territories being taken over (1798) by the Dutch government and given the name of Dutch East Indies. The islands were occupied (1811–15) by the British. A nationalistic movement grew in the 20th c., esp. during the Japanese occupation (1942–5), after which Indonesia was proclaimed a republic (Aug. 17, 1945) under Sukarno. Active Dutch opposition continued until 1947, and the United States of Indonesia were officially recognized (1949). Indonesia again became a republic (1950) in union with the Netherlands. This union was abrogated (1956) and Indonesia's debt to the Netherlands repudiated. An army revolt (1957–61) was put down, and the constitution was altered (1960) to give the president very wide powers. The Netherlands ceded West Irian to Indonesia (1963). Indonesia carried out guerrilla attacks on Malaysia (1963–6). It was the first country ever to leave the U.N. (1965), but rejoined (1966). Sukarno was forced (1967) to give up his powers. Gen. Suharto became became president (1968–   ). A series of 5-year plans, largely funded by foreign aid, aimed at developing agriculture and industry

In·do·ne·sian (indəní:ʒən) **1.** *adj.* of or pertaining to Indonesia, its inhabitants, languages etc. ‖ of or relating to a group of languages forming

the largest division of the Austronesian language family, spoken in the Malay Peninsula and Malay Archipelago, and in parts of Thailand, Formosa and Madagascar. The most important Indonesian language is Malay **2.** *n.* a native or inhabitant of Indonesia ‖ the national language of the Republic of Indonesia, a dialect of Malay

in·door (índɔr, índour) *adj.* situated, used, or done inside a house or building rather than outside, *indoor games*

in·doors (índɔrz, indóurz) *adv.* inside a building, *it's warmer indoors* ‖ into a building, *let's go indoors*

In·dore (índɔr) a city (pop. 395,000) in Madhya Pradesh, India, in the valley of R. Narbada: cotton mills

indorse *ENDORSE

In·dra (índrə) Vedic god of rain and thunder

in·draft, in·draught (índræft, índraft) *n.* an inward flow or current of water, air etc.

in·drawn (índrɔn) *adj.* (of breath etc.) drawn in ‖ tending to introspection

In·dre (ɛ́dr) a department (area 2,664 sq. miles, pop. 247,000) of central France (*BERRY, *MANCHE, *ORLÉANAIS, *TOURAINE). Chief town: Châteauroux

In·dre-et-Loire (ɛ́dreilwær) a department (area 2,377 sq. miles, pop. 438,000) of N.W. France (*TOURAINE, *ANJOU). Chief town: Tours

in·dri (índri) *n. Indris brevicaudatus*, the largest of the Madagascar lemurs, about 2 ft long, with a short tail and black and white markings [F. fr. Malagasy *indry!*, look! (exclamation mistaken for the name of the animal)]

in·du·bi·ta·ble (indú:bitəb'l, indjú:bitəb'l) *adj.* that cannot be doubted, unquestionable **in·dú·bi·ta·bly** *adv.* [F. or fr. L. *indubitabilis*]

in·duce (indú:s, indjú:s) *pres. part.* **in·duc·ing** *past* and *past part.* **in·duced** *v.t.* to persuade ‖ to give rise to, cause ‖ to infer, draw (a conclusion) by induction ‖ to produce (an electric current or magnetism) by induction **in·dúce·ment** *n.* an inducing or being induced ‖ something that persuades or motivates **in·dúc·i·ble** *adj.* [fr. L. *inducere*, to lead in or toward]

in·duc·er (indú:sər) *n.* (*genetics*) a substance used to inactivate a genetic suppressor and to activate a structural gene

in·duct (indÁkt) *v.t.* to install formally in office ‖ to install (a clergyman) in his benefice ‖ to bring in as a member, initiate ‖ to bring into the armed forces under a draft law **in·dúct·ance** *n.* the property of an electrical circuit by which an electromotive force is generated by a change in the current either in the circuit itself (self-inductance) or in a neighboring circuit (mutual inductance). This property depends upon the dimensions and spatial arrangements of the circuits, and is measured in henrys **in·duc·tée** *n.* someone inducted into the armed forces [fr. L. *inducere* (*inductus*)]

in·duc·tile (indÁktəl, *Br.* indÁktail) *adj.* not ductile **in·duc·til·i·ty** (indÁktíliti) *n.*

in·duc·tion (indÁkʃən) *n.* (*logic*) the drawing of a general conclusion from a number of known facts ‖ a general conclusion arrived at in this way ‖ an inducing or bringing about ‖ the formal act of placing a clergyman in his benefice ‖ initiation into an office or society ‖ the formalities by which someone is made a member of the armed forces under a draft law (*math.*) a method by which the general validity of a mathematical statement or theorem may be inferred from a demonstration of its validity for a specific case, by showing e.g. that if it is true for a specific value of the variable (n) then it must also be true for the succeeding value (n + 1) etc. ‖ (*phys.*) the production of magnetism or electromotive force or the separation of charge in a body (e.g. a conductor or magnetic substance) by a neighboring body, not in contact with it, bearing a charge or magnetism, or by a changing magnetic flux (*ELECTROMAGNETIC INDUCTION, *ELECTROSTATIC INDUCTION, *INDUCTANCE, *MAGNETIC INDUCTION) [F.]

induction coil a device for obtaining interrupted high-voltage direct current. It consists of a primary input coil, a vibrator which stops the flow of current periodically, and a secondary coil, of more windings than the primary, in which a high voltage is induced. The induction coil is used to produce electrical discharge, e.g. for the spark plugs in internal-combustion engines

induction period an initial period in some chemical processes (esp. free radical reactions) during which the rate of reaction is very slow. It

may be attributed to a variety of causes, e.g. the presence of inhibitors or the dependence of the process upon minimum concentrations of intermediates which must be produced first

in·duc·tive (indÁktiv) *adj.* (*logic*) based on, or pertaining to, induction ‖ (*elec.*) pertaining to electrical or magnetic induction ‖ (*physiol.*) tending to bring about a change [fr. L. *inductivus*]

in·duc·tor (indÁktər) *n.* someone who inducts ‖ any part of an apparatus for electrical induction ‖ a substance which can bring about a particular development in embryonic or other hitherto undifferentiated tissue ‖ a substance which increases the rate of chemical change and is used up during the reaction (cf. CATALYST) [L.=one who introduces]

in·dulge (indÁldʒ) *pres. part.* **in·dulg·ing** *past* and *past part.* **in·dulged** *v.t.* to treat with excessive kindness and affection, pamper ‖ to comply with, humor (a caprice etc.) ‖ to give way to, *to indulge one's anger* ‖ *v.i.* to allow oneself a gratification ‖ (with 'in') to treat oneself to [fr. L. *indulgere*, to be courteous to]

in·dul·gence (indÁldʒəns) **1.** *n.* an indulging or being indulged ‖ self-indulgence ‖ a gratification, habit etc. that is indulged in ‖ an extension of time for payment of a bill or note, granted as a favor ‖ (*Roman Catholicism*) remission of, or exemption from, purgatorial punishment for sins **2.** *v.t. pres. part.* **in·dul·genc·ing** *past* and *past part.* **in·dul·genced** (*Roman Catholicism*) to attach an indulgence to the saying of (a prayer) or handling of (an object) **in·dúl·genced** *adj.* (*Roman Catholicism*, of a prayer, object etc.) procuring an indulgence for the sayer, handler etc. [F. or fr. L. *indulgentia*]

Indulgence, Declaration of (*Eng. hist.*) a proclamation of religious liberties, esp. those issued (1672 and 1687) by Charles II and James II for the benefit of Roman Catholics and Protestant dissenters

in·dul·gent (indÁldʒənt) *adj.* having or showing indulgence [fr. L. *indulgens* (*indulgentis*)]

in·dult (indÁlt) *n.* (*Rom. Catholicism*) special permission, granted by the pope, for something not normally sanctioned [F. or fr. L. *indultum* fr. *indulgere* (*indultus*)]

in·du·men·tum (indumén təm, indjumén təm) *pl.* **in·du·men·ta** (indumén tə, indjumén tə) *n.* a hairy covering on a leaf or insect ‖ a bird's plumage [L. = a covering]

in·du·pli·cate (indú:plikit, indjú:plikit) *adj.* (in vernation) having leaves in a bud bent or rolled without overlapping ‖ (in aestivation) having the edges of the calyx or corolla folded inward

in·du·rate (indureit, índjureit) *pres. part.* **in·du·rat·ing** *past* and *past part.* **in·du·rat·ed** *v.t.* and *i.* to harden physically or morally [fr. L. *indurare* (*induratus*)]

in·du·ra·tion (induréiʃən, indjuréiʃən) *n.* an indurating or becoming indurated ‖ something indurated, a hardened formation [F. or fr. M.L. *induratio* (*indurationis*)]

in·du·ra·tive (indureitiv, índjureitiv) *adj.* of, relating to or causing induration

In·dus (índəs) a river (1,900 miles long, draining 372,000 sq. miles) which flows from S.W. Tibet through Kashmir and West Pakistan to a delta on the Arabian Sea. It is navigable for small steamers as far as Hyderabad. Principal dams: Sukkur (storage), Kotri, near Hyderabad (storage and hydroelectricity). With its five tributaries (the Jhelum, Chenab, Ravi, Beas and Sutlej) it is one of the world's major river systems, supporting 50 million people. The development of the Indus Basin with the opening of Mangla dam (in Pakistan, 1967) and the construction of Tarbela dam (on the Indus, 1974)

Indus civilization *MOHENJO-DARO

in·du·si·al (indú:ziəl, indjú:zi:əl) *adj.* of, pertaining to or being an indusium

in·du·si·um (indú:zi:əm, indjú:zi:əm) *pl.* **in·du·si·a** (indú:zi:ə, indjú:zi:ə) *n.* (*biol.*) a covering membrane, esp. an amnion ‖ an outgrowth of the leaf covering the sorus of a fern [L.=tunic]

in·dus·tri·al (indÁstri:əl) **1.** *adj.* of, connected with or characterized by industry, *an industrial nation* **2.** *n.* (*pl.*) stocks, bonds or other securities of industrial companies [fr. L. *industria* and F. *industriel*]

industrial alcohol ethyl alcohol, often mixed with water, and usually with some other substance to denature it, for use in industry

industrial arts the techniques and processes used in industry as a subject of study in schools

CONCISE PRONUNCIATION KEY: **(a)** æ, c*a*t; ɑ, c*a*r; ɔ f*aw*n; ei, sn*a*ke. **(e)** e, h*e*n; i:, sh*ee*p; iə, d*ee*r; ɛə, b*ea*r. **(i)** i, f*i*sh; ai, t*i*ger; ə:, b*i*rd. **(o)** o, *o*x; au, c*ow*; ou, g*oa*t; u, p*oo*r; ɔi, r*oy*al. **(u)** ʌ, d*u*ck; u, b*u*ll; u:, g*oo*se; ə, b*a*cillus; ju:, c*u*be. x, lo*ch*; θ, *th*ink; ð, bo*th*er; z, *Z*en; ʒ, corsa*g*e; dʒ, sava*g*e; ŋ, orangута*ng*; j, *y*ak; ʃ, *f*ish; tʃ, fet*ch*; 'l, rabb*le*; 'n, redd*en*. Complete pronunciation key appears inside front cover.

in·dus·tri·al·ism (indʌstri:əlizəm) *n.* a social system making industry the principal activity of a society **in·dús·tri·al·ist** *n.* an owner, director or manager of a large-scale industry

in·dus·tri·al·i·za·tion (indʌstri:əlizéiʃən) *n.* an industrializing or being industrialized

in·dus·tri·al·ize (indʌstri:əlaiz) *pres. part.* **in·dus·tri·al·iz·ing** *past* and *past part.* **in·dus·tri·al·ized** *v.t.* to make industrial in character ‖ to organize as an industry ‖ *v.i.* to become industrial in character

industrial revenue bond (*securities*) bond issue usually for an income-producing project, which pays interest only if earned, sometimes municipally sponsored and tax-exempt

Industrial Revolution the mechanization of industry and the consequent changes in social and economic organization, esp. in Britain (late 18th and early 19th cc.). The change from domestic industry to the factory system began in the textile industry, which was transformed by such inventions as Kay's flying shuttle (1733), Hargreaves's spinning jenny (1764), Arkwright's water frame (1769), Compton's mule (1779) and Cartwright's power loom (1785). Newcomen's steam engine (1705), perfected (1765) by Watt, provided a power supply. Ironmaking was improved when Darby used coke to smelt ore (c. 1709), and when Huntsman's crucible process (c. 1750) and Cort's puddling furnace (1784) came into use. Large-scale steel production became possible with Bessemer's converter (1856) and the Siemens-Martin open-hearth process (1866). Communications were improved by the canals of Bridgewater and Brindley, the roads of Telford and Macadam, the locomotives of Stephenson, and the railroad engineering of Brunel. The 18th-c. improvements in agricultural method, led by Tull, Townshend and Bakewell, freed rural labor for industry and increased the productivity of the land. The rapid growth of towns, mostly near coalfields, gave rise to bad working and housing conditions, which inspired Luddite riots, trade unionism and Chartism. Economic thought was transformed by the laissez-faire theories of Adam Smith, Ricardo and Malthus. After 1830 similar industrial revolutions took place in France and Belgium, followed by Germany (after 1850), the U.S.A. (after 1860), Japan (after 1870) and Russia (after 1900). India and China are undergoing industrial revolutions now

industrial school a school teaching industrial arts

Industrial Workers of the World a revolutionary labor organization (*abbr.* I.W.W.: its members were known as 'Wobblies') founded (1905) in Chicago, Ill., to provide industrial unionism for unskilled workers. Its goal, to create a world-wide working-class movement which could take control of the world's means of production and abolish the wage system, was to be achieved through such action as sabotage and strikes. It became the first U.S. labor organization to be placed (1949) on the federal government's subversive list

in·dus·tri·ous (indʌstri:əs) *adj.* hardworking [fr. L.L. *industriosus* or F. *industrieux*]

in·dus·try (índəstri:) *pl.* **in·dus·tries** *n.* the section of an economy concerned with manufacturing ‖ a specific type of manufacturing, business etc., *the steel industry* ‖ any of various large-scale money-making activities, *the tourist industry* ‖ diligence, application [F. *industrie* or fr. L. *industria*, diligence]

in·dwell (indwél) *pres. part.* **in·dwell·ing** *past* and *past part.* **in·dwelt** (indwélt) *v.i.* to reside as an inner force ‖ *v.t.* to reside within as an inner force

In·dy (dɛ̃di:), Vincent d' (Paul Marie Théodore, 1851–1931), French composer. He wrote symphonies, chamber music and operas, and was an influential teacher

I·ne (áinə, íne) (*d.* c. 726), king of Wessex (688–c. 726). He issued (c. 693) an early code of laws

-ine *suffix* of or pertaining to, made of, like, as in 'hyacinthine' [fr. L. *-īnus*, *-inus* fr. Gk]

in·e·bri·ate (iní:bri:eit) *v.t. pres. part.* **in·e·bri·at·ing** *past* and *past part.* **in·e·bri·at·ed** to intoxicate ‖ to exhilarate emotionally **2.** (iní:bri:it) *adj.* (*rhet.*) drunk **3.** (iní:bri:it) *n.* a habitual drunkard **in·é·bri·at·ed** *adj.* **in·e·bri·á·tion** *n.* [fr. L. *inebriare* (*inebriatus*)]

in·e·bri·e·ty (inibráiiti:) *n.* (*rhet.*) drunkenness ‖ (*rhet.*) the habit of getting drunk [IN-(*in*)+*ebriety*, drunkenness]

in·ed·i·bil·i·ty (inedəbíliti:) *n.* the quality or state of being inedible

in·ed·i·ble (inédəb'l) *adj.* not fit to be eaten ‖ not at all pleasant to eat

in·ed·it·ed (inéditid) *adj.* unpublished

in·ef·fa·bil·i·ty (inefəbíliti:) *n.* the quality or state of being ineffable

in·ef·fa·ble (inéfəb'l) *adj.* incapable of being expressed or adequately described, *ineffable beauty* ‖ that must not be spoken, *God's ineffable name* **in·ef·fa·bly** *adv.* [F.]

in·ef·face·a·ble (iniféisəb'l) *adj.* not possible to wipe out, *an ineffaceable disgrace* **in·ef·fáce·a·bly** *adv.*

in·ef·fec·tive (iniféktiv) *adj.* not producing the desired effect ‖ (of a person) incompetent, ineffectual

in·ef·fec·tu·al (iniféktʃu:əl) *adj.* not effectual

in·ef·fi·ca·cious (inefikéiʃəs) *adj.* not capable of producing the desired result

in·ef·fi·ca·cy (inéfikəsi:) *n.* the quality or state of being inefficacious [fr. L.L. *inefficacia*]

in·ef·fi·cien·cy (inifíʃənsi:) *pl.* **in·ef·fi·cien·cies** *n.* the quality or state of being inefficient ‖ an instance of this

in·ef·fi·cient (inifíʃənt) *adj.* not efficient

in·e·las·tic (inilæstik) *adj.* not elastic ‖ not adaptable, *an inelastic arrangement* ‖ (*econ.*, of supply and demand) not easily conditioned by or responsive to fluctuations or changing conditions **in·e·las·tic·i·ty** (inilæstísiti:) *n.*

in·el·e·gance (inéligəns) *n.* the quality of being inelegant **in·el·e·gan·cy** (inéligənsi:) *pl.* **in·el·e·gan·cies** *n.* something inelegant

in·el·e·gant (inéligənt) *adj.* lacking in grace, polish etc. ‖ lacking in qualities required by good taste [F. *inélégant*]

in·el·i·gi·bil·i·ty (inelidʒəbíliti:) *n.* the quality of being ineligible

in·el·i·gi·ble (inélidʒəb'l) **1.** *adj.* not eligible **2.** *n.* someone not eligible

in·e·luc·ta·bil·i·ty (inilʌktəbíliti:) *n.* the state or quality of being ineluctable

in·e·luc·ta·ble (inilʌktəb'l) *adj.* impossible to escape from or to avoid, *ineluctable necessity* **in·e·lúc·ta·bly** *adv.* [fr. L. *ineluctabilis*]

in·ept (inépt) *adj.* out of place, not apt ‖ incompetent ‖ silly, foolish, *inept remarks* [fr. L. *ineptus*]

in·ept·i·tude (inéptitu:d, inéptitju:d) *n.* the quality or state of being inept ‖ something inept [fr. L. *ineptitudo*]

in·e·qual·i·ty (inikwóliti:) *pl.* **in·e·qual·i·ties** *n.* lack of equality ‖ an instance of this, with respect to size, social status income, amount, value, quality etc. ‖ lack of regularity, unevenness ‖ a variation from the usual movement of a star, planet etc. ‖ the amount of such variation ‖ (*math.*) the fact or statement that two quantities are not equal, using the signs < ('is less than'),> ('is greater than'), ≠ ('is not equal to') [O.F. *inéqualité*]

in·eq·ui·ta·ble (inékwitəb'l) *adj.* unjust, unfair

in·eq·ui·ty (inékwiti:) *pl.* **in·eq·ui·ties** *n.* unfairness, injustice ‖ an instance of this

in·e·rad·i·ca·ble (inirǽdikəb'l) *adj.* that cannot be undone, forgotten etc., *ineradicable damage* **in·e·rád·i·ca·bly** *adv.*

in·er·ra·ble (inérəb'l, iné:rəb'l) *adj.* incapable of making a mistake **in·ér·ra·bly** *adv.* [fr. L. *inerrabilis*]

in·ert (iná:rt) *adj.* incapable of moving, acting, or resisting an opposing force, *inert matter* ‖ devoid of mental energy, making no imaginative effort, hard to get to move or act ‖ (*chem.*) unreactive with other substances [fr. L. *iners* (*inertis*), unskilled, inactive]

inert gas any of several unreactive gaseous elements belonging to group O of the periodic table (e.g. helium, neon, krypton, argon), compounds of which have only recently been prepared (e.g. esp. with fluorine and oxygen) ‖ any unreactive gas, esp. one (e.g. nitrogen) that does not support combustion or burn

in·er·tia (iná:rʃə) *n.* the property of matter that causes its velocity to be constant in the absence of external forces (*LAW OF MOTION) ‖ the quality or state of being inert **in·ér·tial** *adj.* [L.+inactivity]

inertial guidance the control of the trajectory of a missile or aircraft by means of self-contained instruments that are actuated by changes in the velocity of the missile or aircraft

inertial mass mass as determined by impact experiments and according to the law of conservation of momentum

inertial system a nonaccelerated frame of reference, being one in which Newtonian mechanics is valid

inertia selling (*Br.*) technique of sending unsolicited merchandise followed by a bill

in·es·cap·a·ble (iniskéipəb'l) *adj.* impossible to escape or avoid, *inescapable conclusions*

in·es·sen·tial (inisénʃəl) **1.** *adj.* not essential **2.** *n.* something that is not essential

in·es·ti·ma·ble (inéstəməb'l) *adj.* too great to be assessed, *inestimable kindness* **in·és·ti·ma·bly** *adv.* [F.]

in·ev·i·ta·bil·i·ty (inevitəbíliti:) *n.* the quality or state of being inevitable

in·ev·i·ta·ble (inévitəb'l) *adj.* unavoidable ‖ certain to happen **in·év·i·ta·bly** *adv.* [fr. L. *inevitabilis*]

in·ex·act (inigzǽkt) *adj.* not exact, inaccurate ‖ (of a person) tending to be inaccurate

in·ex·act·i·tude (inigzǽktitu:d, inigzǽktitju:d) *n.* the quality of being inexact ‖ an instance of this

in·ex·cus·a·bil·i·ty (iniskskju:zəbíliti:) *n.* the quality of being inexcusable

in·ex·cus·a·ble (iniskskjú:zəb'l) *adj.* impossible to excuse or justify, *inexcusable rudeness* **in·ex·cús·a·bly** *adv.* [fr. L. *inexcusabilis*]

in·ex·haust·i·bil·i·ty (inigzɔ:stəbíliti:) *n.* the state or quality of being inexhaustible

in·ex·haust·i·ble (inigzɔ́:stəb'l) *adj.* impossible to use up **in·ex·háust·i·bly** *adv.*

in·ex·o·ra·bil·i·ty (ineksərəbíliti:) *n.* the quality of being inexorable

in·ex·o·ra·ble (inéksərəb'l) *adj.* impossible to move or influence by entreating **in·éx·o·ra·bly** *adv.* [fr. L. *inexorabilis*]

in·ex·pe·di·en·cy (inikspí:di:ənsi:) *n.* the quality or state of being inexpedient

in·ex·pe·di·ent (inikspí:di:ənt) *adj.* not expedient

in·ex·pen·sive (inikspénsiv) *adj.* not expensive

in·ex·pe·ri·ence (inikspíəri:əns) *n.* lack of experience of a practical nature ‖ lack of the skill resulting from experience [F.]

in·ex·pe·ri·enced (inikspíəri:ənst) *adj.* lacking practical experience ‖ lacking the skill resulting from experience

in·ex·pert (inékspə:rt, inikspé:rt) *adj.* lacking or showing a lack of skill [O.F.]

in·ex·pi·a·ble (inékspi:əb'l) *adj.* that cannot be atoned for **in·éx·pi·a·bly** *adv.* [fr. L. *inexpiabilis*]

in·ex·pli·ca·bil·i·ty (ineksplikəbíliti:, inikspli·kəbíliti:) *n.* the quality of being inexplicable

in·ex·pli·ca·ble (inéksplikəb'l, iníksplikəb'l) *adj.* not capable of being explained **in·éx·pli·ca·bly** *adv.* [F.]

in·ex·plic·it (iniksplísit) *adj.* not explicit

in·ex·pres·si·bil·i·ty (inikspresəbíliti:) *n.* the quality of being inexpressible

in·ex·pres·si·ble (iniksprésəb'l) *adj.* not capable of being put into words **in·ex·prés·si·bly** *adv.*

in·ex·pres·sive (iniksprésiv) *adj.* devoid of expression, *an inexpressive face* ‖ failing to communicate meaning, *inexpressive gestures*

in·ex·pug·na·ble (inikspʌ́gnəb'l, inikspjú:nəb'l) *adj.* (*rhet.*) unconquerable **in·ex·púg·na·bly** *adv.* [F.]

in·ex·ten·si·ble (iniksténsəb'l) *adj.* not capable of being extended

in ex·ten·so (iniksténsou) *adv.* at length, in detail, not in summary fashion [L.]

in·ex·tin·guish·a·ble (inikstíngwiʃəb'l) *adj.* that cannot be extinguished **in·ex·tin·guish·a·bly** *adv.*

in ex·tre·mis (inikstrí:mis, inekstrémi:s) at the point of death [L.=in extremity]

in·ex·tri·ca·bil·i·ty (inekstrikəbíliti:, inikstrikə·bíliti:) *n.* the quality or state of being inextricable

in·ex·tri·ca·ble (inékstrikəb'l, iníkstrikəb'l) *adj.* from which one cannot extricate oneself, *an inextricable maze* ‖ not capable of being solved, *an inextricable dilemma* ‖ that cannot be untied or unraveled **in·éx·tri·ca·bly** *adv.* [fr. L. *inextricabilis*]

in·fal·li·bil·i·ty (infæləbíliti:) *n.* the quality or state of being infallible (*PAPAL INFALLIBILITY)

in·fal·li·ble (infǽləb'l) *adj.* incapable of error ‖ never failing, *an infallible cure* ‖ (of the pope) incapable of error when speaking ex cathedra on questions of faith and morals **in·fál·li·bly** *adv.* [fr. M.L. *infallibilis*]

in·fa·mous (ínfəməs) *adj.* of foul reputation, *an infamous tyrant* ‖ arousing horror, deserving to be detested, *the infamous practice of torturing prisoners* [fr. M. L. *infamous*]

in·fa·my (ínfəmi:) *pl.* **in·fa·mies** *n.* the quality of being infamous ‖ an infamous action ‖ public disgrace of a criminal convicted of an infamous crime [F. *infamie*]

in·fan·cy (ínfənsi:) *pl.* **in·fan·cies** *n.* the state or period of being an infant [fr. L. *infantia*, inability to speak]

in·fant (ínfənt) **1.** *n.* a very young child, esp. one not yet able to walk or talk ‖ (*law*) a person not yet legally independent, a minor ‖ (*Br.*) a pupil aged 5-7 **2.** *adj.* on or pertaining to infants or being in infancy [O.F. *enfant*]

in·fan·ta (infǽntə) *n.* the daughter of a king of Spain or of Portugal ‖ the wife of an infante **in·fan·te** (infǽnti:, infǽntei) *n.* a son other than the eldest son of the king of Spain or of Portugal [Span. and Port.]

in·fan·ti·cide (infǽntisaid) *n.* the killing of an infant ‖ a person who kills an infant [F.]

in·fan·tile (ínfəntail, ínfəntail) *adj.* of or pertaining to infants, *infantile diseases* ‖ not appropriate in an adult, childish [fr. L.L. *infantilis*]

infantile paralysis poliomyelitis

in·fan·ti·lism (ínfəntəlizəm, infǽntəlizəm) *n.* the persistence of childish characteristics into later life. Physical infantilism may result from endocrine disease or malfunction such as the failure of the thyroid or pituitary gland to develop (cf. REGRESSION)

in·fan·try (ínfəntri:) *pl.* **in·fan·tries** *n.* a branch of an army consisting of soldiers trained to fight on foot [F. *infanterie*]

in·fan·try·man (ínfəntri:mən) *pl.* **in·fan·try·men** (ínfəntri:mən) *n.* a soldier in an infantry regiment

infant school (*Br.*) a school for very young children, usually under the age of seven

in·farct (ínfɑrkt) *n.* (*med.*) a clearly limited area of mortified tissue and hemorrhage in an organ, caused by obstruction of the local arteries [fr. M.L. or Mod. L. *infarctus* fr. *infarcire*, to stuff]

in·fat·u·ate (infǽtʃueit) *pres. part.* **in·fat·u·at·ing** *past* and *past part.* **in·fat·u·at·ed** *v.t.* to inspire with a foolish and excessive passion **in·fat·u·à·tion** *n.* [fr. L. *infatuare* (*infatuatus*), to make a fool of]

in·fau·na (ínfɔnə) *n.* benthic animal life, esp. at the soft portion of the ocean bottom. *Cf* EPIFAUNA

in·fect (infékt) *v.t.* to transfer a disease or a disease-causing agent to (an individual or an organ) ‖ (of a pathogenic organism) to invade or attack (an individual or organ) ‖ to contaminate with pathogens, *to infect a water supply* ‖ to affect (another) with one's own emotion, belief etc. [fr. L. *inficere* (*infectus*), to taint]

in·fec·tion (infékʃən) *n.* an infecting or being infected ‖ a disease etc. produced by infecting ‖ something which infects [F.]

in·fec·tious (infékʃəs) *adj.* able to cause infection ‖ caused by infection ‖ easily communicated, *infectious laughter*

infectious mononucleosis a mild, infectious, febrile disease characterized by headache, weakness, and enlargement of the lymph glands

in·fec·tive (inféktiv) *adj.* causing infection [fr. L. *infectivus*]

in·fe·lic·i·tous (infəlísitəs) *adj.* not suitable to the circumstances, ill-chosen, *an infelicitous speech*

in·fe·lic·i·ty (infəlísiti:) *pl.* **in·fe·lic·i·ties** *n.* unsuitability of expression or behavior ‖ something infelicitous (*old-fash.*) misfortune [fr. L. *infelicitas*]

in·fer (infə́r) *pres. part.* **in·fer·ring** *past* and *past part.* **in·ferred** *v.t.* to arrive at by reasoning, deduce ‖ (*loosely*) to guess ‖ to hint, imply **in·fér·a·ble**, **in·fér·i·ble** *adj.* [fr. L. *inferre*, to bring in]

in·fer·ence (ínfərəns) *n.* an inferring ‖ something inferred **in·fer·en·tial** (infərénʃəl) *adj.* [fr. M. L. *inferentia*]

inferible *INFERABLE

in·fe·ri·or (infíəri:ər) **1.** *adj.* of poor quality, *an inferior product* ‖ (with 'to') of poorer quality, *this product is inferior to that one* ‖ of low or lower rank, status etc., *an inferior officer* ‖ (*astron.*) nearer the sun than is the earth, *Mercury and Venus are inferior planets* ‖ (*bot.*) growing or arising below another part or organ ‖ (*anat.*) situated below a like part or organ or below the normal position ‖ (*printing*) placed below the line of type, e.g. '2' in 'H₂O' **2.** *n.* a person of lower rank or capacity or thing that is inferior ‖ (*printing*) a character placed below the line of type **in·fe·ri·or·i·ty** (infḭəri:ɔ́riti:, infḭəri:ɔ́riti:)

pl. **in·fe·ri·or·i·ties** *n.* [L., comp. of *inferus*, low]

inferiority complex a neurotic condition resulting from subconscious belief in one's inferiority to others, leading to timidity or else overcompensated by aggressive behavior

in·fer·nal (infə́rn'l) *adj.* of hell or the underworld ‖ (*pop.*) as unbearable as hell, fiendish, *an infernal row* ‖ (*pop.*) tiresome, irritating, *an infernal nuisance* [F.]

infernal machine a concealed device incorporating an explosive, and meant to cause damage or kill

in·fer·no (infə́rnou) *n.* any hellish place or state of horror or destruction [Ital.]

in·fer·tile (infə́rt'l, *Br.* infə́rtail) *adj.* not fertile, barren **in·fer·til·i·ty** (infə:rtíliti:) *n.* [F.]

in·fest (infést) *v.t.* to overrun or swarm about in, in large numbers, so as to be dangerous or unpleasant, *infested with mice* [F. *infester* or fr. L. *infestare*]

in·fes·ta·tion (infestéiʃən) *n.* an infesting or being infested [fr. L.L. *infestatio* (*infestationis*)]

in·fi·del (infid'l) **1.** *n.* (*hist.*) a person professing a religious faith other than that of the speaker ‖ (*loosely*) someone having no religious faith, an atheist **2.** *adj.* pertaining to an infidel [O.F. *infidèle*]

in·fi·del·i·ty (infidéliti:) *pl.* **in·fi·del·i·ties** *n.* failure in loyalty ‖ an instance of this ‖ adultery ‖ lack of exactness in copying ‖ an instance of this ‖ lack of religious belief [fr. L. *infidelitas*]

in·field (ínfi:ld) *n.* (*baseball*) the square area on a playing field enclosed by the three bases and home plate ‖ (*baseball*) the fielders in this area ‖ (*cricket*) the part of the ground near the wicket ‖ (*cricket*) the fielders positioned there ‖ farmland near the farmhouse

in·field·er (ínfi:ldər) *n.* (*baseball* and *cricket*) a fielder in the infield

in·fight·ing (ínfaitiŋ) *n.* fighting or boxing close to one's opponent, not at arm's length ‖ fighting that is not openly acknowledged as such ‖ fighting without rules

in·fil·trate (ínfiltreit, infíltreit) **1.** *v. pres. part.* **in·fil·trat·ing** *past* and *past part.* **in·fil·trat·ed** (*mil.*) to penetrate in small numbers at various points into enemy territory ‖ to work unobtrusively and in small numbers into an organization etc. so as to form a threat to its integrity ‖ to permeate or pass through a substance, by or as if by filtering ‖ *v.t.* to permeate by or as if by filtration, *to infiltrate enemy lines* ‖ to cause to do this, *to infiltrate troops behind enemy lines* **2.** *n.* something that infiltrates, esp. a substance that passes into body tissues and forms an unhealthy accumulation **in·fil·trà·tion** *n.*

in fi·ne (ínfáini:) in short [fr. L. *finis*, end]

in·fi·nite (ínfinit) **1.** *adj.* absolutely without limits, endless ‖ too great to be measured on any imaginable scale, *God's infinite mercy* ‖ (*loosely*) very great ‖ (*gram.*, of a verb form) not limited by person, number or mood ‖ (*math.*) of a value or series the limit of which cannot be defined or expressed **2.** *n.* something infinite [fr. L. *infinitus*, unbounded]

in·fin·i·tes·i·mal (infinitésəməl) *adj.* too small to be measured ‖ (*math.*) of a process which deals with variables too small to be measured [fr. Mod. L. *infinitesimus*]

infinitesimal calculus differential calculus ‖ integral calculus

in·fin·i·tive (infínitiv) **1.** *adj.* of an uninflected verb form conveying simply the idea of the action of the verb without limitation of person, number or mood, and used with 'to' or with an auxiliary verb: e.g. 'come' in the sentences 'try to come' and 'you may come' **2.** *n.* such a verb form [fr. L. *infinitivus*]

in·fin·i·tude (infínitju:d, infínitju:d) *n.* the quality of being infinite ‖ an unlimited number, quality or extent, *the infinitude of space*

in·fin·i·ty (infíniti:) *pl.* **in·fin·i·ties** *n.* the quality of being infinite ‖ that which is infinite ‖ (*loosely*) an indefinitely large amount or number ‖ (*phys.*) a distance so great that rays of light which originate from a point at that distance can be considered parallel ‖ (*math.*, symbol ∞) an infinite quantity that may be positive or negative [F. *infinité*]

in·firm (infə́rm) *adj.* physically weak (esp. through age) ‖ morally weak, *infirm of purpose* [fr. L. *infirmus*]

in·fir·ma·ry (infə́rməri:) *pl.* **in·fir·ma·ries** *n.* a place where the sick are cared for in a school or other institution ‖ (in names of institutions) a hospital [fr. M. L. *infirmaria*]

in·fir·ma·to·ry (infə́rmətɔri:) *adj.* of denigration tending to make infirm or insubstantial

in·fir·mi·ty (infə́rmiti:) *pl.* **in·fir·mi·ties** *n.* the quality or state of being infirm ‖ an instance of this ‖ a defect in character, flaw [fr. L. *infirmitas*, weakness]

in·fi·tah (infítɑ) *n.* Egypt's open-door policy of a modified free market economy designed to attract foreign investments; adopted in 1974

in·fix 1. (infíks) *v.t.* to instill, *to infix an impression on the mind* ‖ (*gram.*) to insert (a formative element) into a word **2.** (ínfiks) *n.* (*gram.*) a formative element placed within a word (cf. PREFIX, cf. SUFFIX) [fr. L. *infigere* (*infixus*), to fix into]

in·flame (infléim) *pres. part.* **in·flam·ing** *past* and *past part.* **in·flamed** *v.t.* to excite passion in, arouse, esp. to anger ‖ to redden with or as if with flames ‖ (*med.*) to cause inflammation in [M.E. *enflamme* fr. O.F.]

in·flam·ma·bil·i·ty (inflæməbíliti:) *n.* the state or quality of being inflammable

in·flam·ma·ble (inflǽməb'l) *adj.* easily set on fire ‖ easily excited or angered ‖ liable to degenerate into violence, *an inflammable situation* **in·flám·ma·bly** *adv.* [INFLAME]

in·flam·ma·tion (infləméiʃən) *n.* the response of body tissue to infection or to many kinds of injury, characterized by an increase of blood flow to the injured part, with heat, redness, pain, swelling and, occasionally, loss of function ‖ the state of being inflamed ‖ the stirring up of passion, esp. anger [fr. L. *inflammatio* (*inflammationis*), a setting on fire]

in·flam·ma·to·ry (inflǽmətɔri:, inflǽmətouri:) *adj.* tending to arouse destructive passions, *inflammatory propaganda* ‖ causing or accompanying a bodily inflammation [fr. L. *inflammare* (*inflammatus*), to set on fire]

in·flat·a·ble (infléitəb'l) *adj.* capable of being inflated

inflatable structures hollow plastic structures capable of sustaining themselves when inflated, used for indoor tennis courts, warehousing, and temporary exhibitions

in·flate (infléit) *pres. part.* **in·flat·ing** *past* and *past part.* **in·flat·ed** *v.t.* to cause to swell out with air or gas ‖ to cause to swell with pride, vanity etc. ‖ (*econ.*) to raise (prices) artificially ‖ (*econ.*) to increase the volume of (currency) so that a rise in prices follows **in·flát·ed** *adj.* puffed out with air or gas ‖ (of language) bombastic ‖ elated with excessive pride, vanity etc. ‖ (of currency) increased abnormally in volume ‖ (of prices) raised artificially [fr. L. *inflare* (*inflatus*), to blow]

in·fla·tion (infléiʃən) *n.* an inflating or being inflated ‖ a general rise in prices brought about by an increase in the ratio of currency and credit to the goods available. Moderate, controlled (e.g. by credit squeeze) inflation is normal and helps to maintain full employment, but uncontrolled inflation leads to a boom and a slump ‖ (*econ.*) a sharp increase in the amount of paper money put into circulation **in·flá·tion·ar·y** *adj.* [fr. L. *inflatio* (*inflationis*)]

inflationary spiral a continuing price rise resulting from the tendency of wage increases to put up costs and of cost increases to lead to demands for higher wages

in·flect (inflékt) *v.t.* (*gram.*) to treat (word forms) with inflection ‖ to modulate (the voice) ‖ (*bot.*) to bend (part of a plant) inward or toward the main axis ‖ *v.i.* (*gram.*) to be characterized by inflection [fr. L. *inflectere*, to bend in]

in·flec·tion, *Br.* also **in·flex·ion** (inflékʃən) *n.* a turning or bending, *inflection of light* ‖ a change in tone or pitch of voice ‖ (*gram.*) a change of word forms and endings to indicate change of case, tense etc. ‖ (*gram.*) the use of inflected forms ‖ (*gram.*) an inflectional element, e.g. a suffix ‖ (*math.*) the change of a curve or arc from convex to concave or conversely **in·fléc·tion·al**, *Br.* also **in·fléx·ion·al** *adj.* [fr. L. *inflexio* (*inflexionis*)]

in·flec·tive (infléktiv) *adj.* (*gram.*) produced by or using inflection

in·flexed (inflékst) *adj.* (*biol.*) bent inward or downward, toward the axis, *inflexed petals* [fr. L. *inflexus*]

in·flex·i·bil·i·ty (infleksəbíliti:) *n.* the quality or state of being inflexible

in·flex·i·ble (infléksəb'l) *adj.* not capable of being bent, *an inflexible rod* ‖ unchangeable, *inflexible determination* ‖ incapable of change, rigid, unadaptable **in·fléx·i·bly** *adv.* [fr. L. *inflexibilis*]

inflexion *INFLECTION

CONCISE PRONUNCIATION KEY: (a) æ, cat; ɑ, car; ɔ fawn; ei, snake. (e) e, hen; i:, sheep; iə, deer; ɛə, bear. (i) i, fish; ai, tiger; ə:, bird. (o) o, ox; au, cow; ou, goat; u, poor; ɔi, royal. (u) ʌ, duck; u, bull; u:, goose; ə, bacillus; ju:, cube. x, loch; θ, think; δ, bother; z, Zen; ʒ, corsage; dʒ, savage; ŋ, orangutang; j, yak; ʃ, fish; tʃ, fetch; 'l, rabble; 'n, redden. Complete pronunciation key appears inside front cover.

in·flict (inflíkt) v.t. to cause or give (wounds, pain etc.) by or as if by striking ‖ to impose (a penalty etc.) [fr. L. *infligere (inflictus)*]

in·flic·tion (inflíkʃən) n. the act of inflicting ‖ that which is inflicted [fr. L.L. *inflictio (inflictionis)*]

in·flic·tive (inflíktiv) adj. tending to inflict

in·flight (infláit) adj. of something carried, provided, or done aboard a plane while traveling, e.g., *in-flight luggage, in-flight movies*

in·flo·res·cence (inflorés'ns, inflourés'ns) n. the way in which flowers are arranged or develop on an axis ‖ a flower cluster on a plant ‖ a flowering [Mod. L. *inflorescentia*] .

in·flow (inflou) n. a flowing in ‖ that which flows in

in·flu·ence (ínflu:əns) 1. n. a person's indirect power over men, events or things, e.g. through wisdom, wealth, force of character etc., and not as the exercise of physical force or formal authority ‖ a comparable power in a thing, *the moon's influence on the tides* ‖ a person or thing having such power ‖ such power used to sway authority, *he got the job by influence* (elec.) induction **to have influence at court** (Br.) to be able to sway people in authority 2. v.t. pres. part. **in·flu·enc·ing** past and past part. **in·fluenced** to have or exert influence on ‖ (slang) to spike (a drink); to add alcoholic liquor [F.=emanation from the stars]

in·flu·en·tial (influ:énʃəl) adj. possessing or exerting influence [fr. M.L. *influentia*, influence]

in·flu·en·za (influ:énzə) n. an acute, infectious respiratory disease, spreading very easily, caused by any of several viruses and characterized by fever, head and limb pains and prostration [Ital.=influence (of the stars)]

in·flux (ínflʌks) n. a flowing in (of a liquid, gas etc.) ‖ the place where a river joins another body of water ‖ the mouth of a river ‖ a flowing in of people or things, *an influx of visitors* [F. or fr. L.L. *influxus*]

in·fold (infóuld) v.t. to enfold

in·form (infórm) v.t. to communicate information to ‖ to be the principle that gives form or character to, *love of nature informs all his work* ‖ v.i. to give information ‖ (with 'against') to denounce someone, supply information leading to an accusation [M.E. *enforme* fr. O.F.]

in·for·mal (infórməl) adj. free of conventional forms or restrictions, *informal conversations between heads of state* ‖ suitable for relaxed, casual, ordinary circumstances **in·for·mál·i·ty** pl. **in·for·mal·i·ties** n. the quality or state of being informal ‖ an informal action

in·form·ant (infórmənt) n. someone who communicates information [fr. L. *informans (informantis)*]

in·for·mat·ics or **information science** (ìnfərmǽtiks) n. science of obtaining and transmitting information. —**information scientist** n.

in·for·ma·tion (ìnfərméiʃən) n. the communication of news, knowledge etc. a fact or facts told or communicated ‖ data fed to a machine ‖ the giving of secrets to the police in return for pay or advantage ‖ an item thus given ‖ knowledge obtained by search, study etc. ‖ (law) a complaint or accusation communicated to a magistrate ‖ (law) a formal accusation by the public prosecutor, often substituted for indictment **in·for·má·tion·al** adj. [M.E. *enformacion* fr. O.F.]

information desk (Am.=Br. inquiry office) a place in a railroad station etc. where information is available

in·form·a·tive (infórmətiv) adj. giving information, instructive [fr. L. *informare (informatus)*, to inform]

in·formed (infórmd) adj. instructed ‖ cultivated, *an informed mind*

informed consent (med.) consent obtained from a patient for the performance of a specific medical, surgical, or research procedure after the procedure and risks involved have been fully explained in nontechnical terms and understood

in·form·er (infórmər) n. someone who informs, esp. someone who sells information to the police etc.

in·for·mer·cial (ìnfərmé:rʃəl) n. cable television commercial, sometimes called "minidocumentary without a product"

in·fo·tain·ment (infətéinmənt) (broadcasting, slang) program containing information plus entertainment

infra- prefix below [L.]

in·frac·tion (infrǽkʃən) n. a violation of law, regulations etc. [fr. L. *infractio (infractionis)*]

in·fra dig (infrədig) adj. (esp. Br.) beneath one's dignity [short for L. *infra dignitatem*, beneath dignity]

INFRAL (computer acronym) for information retrieval automatic language, a computer programming language to provide bibliographies from indexes adapting COBOL and ALGOL, designed by National Biomedical Research Foundation

in·fra·lap·sar·i·an (infrəlæpséəri:ən) 1. n. a believer in the Calvinist doctrine that the election of some men to salvation followed and was a consequence of man's fall (cf. SUPRALAPSARIAN) 2. adj. of or relating to this doctrine or to one believing in it **in·fra·lap·sár·i·an·ism** n. [fr. L. *infra*, under+*lapsus*, fall]

in·fran·gi·bil·i·ty (infrænd3ibíliti:) n. the quality or state of being infrangible

in·fran·gi·ble (infrǽnd3əb'l) adj. not to be violated, an infrangible law ‖ not capable of being broken or separated into parts

in·fra·red (infrəréd) 1. adj. producing, relating to, or produced by infrared radiation 2. n. such radiation [fr. L. *infra*, below+RED]

infrared camera a camera with detectors that respond to infrared energy radiated by any heat

infrared film film carrying an emulsion especially sensitive to the near infrared portion of the electromagnetic spectrum

infrared maser or **iraser** (optics) an optical maser that utilizes the frequency of infrared for pumping, emitting radiation at millimeter wavelengths

infrared radiation (abbr. IR radiation) electromagnetic waves of length greater than visible light but less than microwaves (between 7.6 x 10^{-5} cm. and 0.1 cm.). Infrared radiation is perceived as heat and is produced by or causes changes in the vibrational and translational motions of atoms and molecules. It is employed in some cooking devices, for therapeutic heat treatments, and for photography in fog or darkness

infrared radiometer instrument for measuring electromagnetic radiant energy and acoustic energy used in spacecraft

in·fra·sound (infrəsáund) n. extremely low-frequency sound waves, esp. produced during a storm, by "soundless" dog whistles

in·fra·struc·ture (ínfrəstrʌktʃər) n. the whole system of bases, services, training establishments etc. required for the use of troops in military operations ‖ the basic framework of any organization [fr. L. *infra*, below+STRUCTURE]

in·fre·quen·cy (infrí:kwənsi:) n. the quality of being infrequent

in·fre·quent (infrí:kwənt) adj. happening rarely [fr. L. *infrequens (infrequentis)*]

in·fringe (infrínd3) pres. part. **in·fring·ing** past and past part. **in·fringed** v.t. to fail to conform with, violate, *to infringe copyright regulations* ‖ v.i. to encroach, *to infringe on someone's rights* **in·fringe·ment** n. [fr. L. *infringere (infractus)*, to break]

in·fun·dib·u·lum (infʌndíbjuləm) pl. **in·fun·dib·u·la** (infʌndíbjulə) n. (anat.) any of several funnel-shaped parts, esp. the stalk connecting the pituitary gland with the brain **in·fun·dib·u·lar** adj. [L.=a funnel]

in·fu·ri·ate (infjúəri:eit) pres. part. **in·fu·ri·at·ing** past and past part. **in·fu·ri·at·ed** v.t. to fill with fury, enrage [fr. M.L. *infuriare (infuriatus)*]

in·fuse (infjú:z) pres. part. **in·fus·ing** past and past part. **in·fused** v.t. to inspire, *to infuse people with enthusiasm* ‖ to instill, *to infuse enthusiasm into people* ‖ to soak (tea leaves etc.) in liquid that has boiled, so as to extract the flavor v.i. to be soaked thus [fr. L. *infundere (infusus)*, to pour in]

in·fu·si·bil·i·ty (infju:zəbíliti:) n. inability to be fused

in·fu·si·ble (infjú:zəb'l) adj. not capable of being fused

in·fu·sion (infjú:3ən) n. an infusing or being infused ‖ a liquid resulting from infusing, e.g. tea ‖ something blended or mixed in [F. or fr. L. *infusio (infusionis)*]

in·fu·so·ri·an (infju:só:ri:ən, infju:sóuri:ən) n. a member of *Infusoria*, a group of protozoans frequently developed in infusions of decaying organic matter and stagnant water [fr. Mod. L. *Infusoria*]

-ing suffix in nouns formed esp. from verbs, expressing the action of the verb, as in 'singing is

a hard profession' [O.E. *-ung*, *-ing*, of Gmc origin]

-ing suffix used to form the present participle of verb [fr. O.E. *-ende* fr. L. *-ent-*]

-ing suffix in nouns to express 'of a certain kind', as in 'gelding' [O.E., of Gmc origin]

In·ga·ví (i:ŋgaví:) a plain in W. Bolivia, site of a battle (1841) in which José Ballivián routed the Peruvians under Agustín Gamarra and assured the independence of Bolivia

in·gem·i·nate (ind3émineit) pres. part. **in·gem·i·nat·ing** past and past part. **in·gem·i·nat·ed** v.t. (rhet.) to repeat, esp. in order to emphasize [fr. L. *ingeminare (ingeminatus)*]

in·gen·ious (ind3í:njəs) adj. clever in inventing or contriving, *an ingenious liar* ‖ cleverly invented, contrived, *an ingenious solution* [F. *ingénieux* or fr. L. *ingeniosus*]

in·gé·nue, in·ge·nue (ɛ̃3ɛny: ɛ̃3ɑnju: ɛ̃3einy) n. a naïve, unsophisticated girl ‖ (theater) the role of such a character ‖ an actress who plays such a role [F., fem. of *ingénu* adj., ingenuous]

in·ge·nu·i·ty (ind3ənjú:iti:, ind3ənú:iti:) n. cleverness in contriving or inventing [fr. L. *ingenuitas*, ingenuousness]

in·gen·u·ous (ind3énju:əs) adj. innocent, naive ‖ frank, candid [fr. L. *ingenuus*, freeborn, frank]

in·gest (ind3ést) v.t. to take (food) into the digestive system [fr. L. *ingerere (ingestus)*, to put in]

in·ges·ta (ind3éstə) pl. n. materials taken into the body via the digestive tract [L., neuter pl. of *ingestus* fr. *ingerere*, to carry into]

in·ges·tion (ind3éstʃən) n. an ingesting or being ingested [fr. L.L. *ingestio (ingestionis)*]

in·ges·tive (ind3éstiv) adj. of or relating to ingestion

in·gle·nook (íŋg'lnuk) n. a chimney corner [origin unknown]

in·glo·ri·ous (inglóri:əs, inglóuri:əs) adj. shameful, disgraceful, *an inglorious defeat* ‖ (rhet.) without fame or distinction, *an inglorious career* [fr. L. *ingloriosus*, humble]

in·goal (íngoul) n. (rugby) either of two areas, each extending not more than 25 yds, behind each goal line

in·got (íŋgət) n. a lump of metal, esp. of gold, silver or steel, cast in convenient form (usually oblong) for transport and storage [M.E., origin unknown]

ingrain *ENGRAIN

ingrain carpet a reversible carpet made of wool dyed in the raw state

in·grained (ingréind, íngreind) adj. thoroughly imbued, *an ingrained habit* ‖ inveterate, thorough, *an ingrained pessimist* [past part. of INGRAIN or IN adv.+ *grained*, past part. of GRAIN]

in·grate (íngreit) n. (rhet.) someone who shows ingratitude [fr. L. *ingratus*]

in·gra·ti·ate (ingréiʃi:eit) pres. part. **in·gra·ti·at·ing** past and past part. **in·gra·ti·at·ed** v.t. to get (oneself) into the good graces of another, esp. by guile, *he ingratiated himself with the boss by flattery* [perh. fr. Ital. *ingratiare*, to bring into favor]

in·grat·i·tude (ingrǽtitu:d, ingrǽtitju:d) n. lack of gratitude ‖ an instance of this [F.]

in·gre·di·ent (ingrí:di:ənt) n. an element in a mixture, constituent, *the ingredients of a cake* [fr. L. *ingrediens (ingredientis)*]

In·gres (ɛ̃gr), Jean Auguste Dominique (1780–1867), French painter. A superb draftsman, noted for the academic perfection and refined sensuality of his nudes, he also painted portraits and historical scenes

in·gress (íngres) n. the right or ability to go in, *he was given ingress to the special session* ‖ (rhet.) a going in [fr. L. *ingressus*]

in·grow·ing (íngrouiŋ) adj. growing inward, esp. (of a nail) growing into the flesh

in·grown (íngroun) adj. grown inward, esp. (of a finger or toe nail) having the tip embedded in the flesh ‖ innate

in·gui·nal (íngwin'l) adj. of, relating to or located in the region of the groin [fr. L. *inguinalis* fr. *inguen (inguinis)*, groin]

in·gur·gi·tate (ingé:rd3iteit) pres. part. **in·gur·gi·tat·ing** past and past part. **in·gur·gi·tat·ed** v.t. to swallow greedily or in large quantities **in·gur·gi·tá·tion** n. [fr. L. *ingurgitare (ingurgitatus)*, to pour in]

in·hab·it (inhǽbit) v.t. to live in [M.E. *enhabit* fr. O.F.]

in·hab·it·a·ble (inhǽbitəb'l) adj. capable of being inhabited or fit to be inhabited

in·hab·it·an·cy (inhǽbitənsi:) *pl.* **in·hab·it·an·cies** *n.* an inhabiting or being inhabited ‖ a residing for a period in order to acquire legal rights as an inhabitant

in·hab·it·ant (inhǽbitənt) *n.* a permanent resident in a place [A.F. and O.F.]

in·ha·bi·ta·tion (inhæbitéiʃən) *n.* an inhabiting or being inhabited [fr. L.L. *inhabitatio* (*inhabitationis*)]

in·hal·ant (inhéilənt) **1.** *adj.* used in inhaling **2.** *n.* something inhaled, esp. a medicine [fr. L. *inhalans* (*inhalantis*), breathing in]

in·ha·la·tion (inhəléiʃən) *n.* the act or an instance of inhaling [fr. L. *inhalare* (*inhalatus*)]

in·hale (inhéil) *pres. part.* **in·hal·ing** *past* and *past part.* **in·haled** *v.t.* to breathe (something) in, *city dwellers inhale foul air* ‖ to take (tobacco smoke) into the lungs before blowing it out ‖ *v.i.* to breathe in (opp. EXHALE) **in·hál·er** *n.* an apparatus which facilitates the inhalation of medicines ‖ someone who inhales [fr. L. *inhalare*, to breathe upon]

in·har·mo·ni·ous (inhɑrmóuni:əs) *adj.* lacking harmony, discordant ‖ jarring

in·haul (ínhɔl) *n.* (*naut.*) a rope etc. for hauling in **in·hául·er** *n.*

in·here (inhíər) *pres. part.* **in·her·ing** *past* and *past part.* **in·hered** *v.i.* to be inherent [fr. L. *inhaerere*, to stick in]

in·her·ence (inhíərəns, inhérəns) *n.* an inhering or being inherent ‖ (*philos.*) the relation of an attribute to a substance or subject **in·hér·en·cy** *n.* [fr. M.L. *inhaerentia*]

in·her·ent (inhíərənt, inhérənt) *adj.* existing in someone or something as a permanent characteristic or quality [fr. L. *inhaerens* (*inhaerentis*)]

in·her·it (inhérit) *v.t.* to receive by legacy ‖ to receive by heredity ‖ to receive (something previously in another's possession) as if by legacy, *he inherited his brother's clothes* ‖ *v.i.* to come into an inheritance [M.E. *enherite*, to make heir, fr. O.F.]

in·her·it·a·bil·i·ty (inheritəbíliti:) *n.* the quality of being inheritable

in·her·it·a·ble (inhéritəb'l) *adj.* capable of being inherited ‖ (*law*) being qualified to inherit [A.F. *enheritable*, *inheritable*, able to be made heir]

in·her·it·ance (inhéritəns) *n.* the act of inheriting ‖ something inherited [A.F. *enheritance*]

inheritance tax (*Am.=Br.* death duty) a tax on the estate of a dead person, sometimes determined strictly by the size of the estate, sometimes by the degree of consanguinity of the inheritors, or other factors. Inheritance taxes may be legally avoided under some governments, e.g. by making outright gifts to close kin a specified length of time before death

in·her·i·tor (inhéritər) *n.* someone who inherits, an heir

in·her·i·tress (inhéritris) *n.* a female inheritor

in·hib·it (inhíbit) *v.t.* to hold in check, restrain (a natural impulse) either consciously or unconsciously ‖ to obstruct, suppress, *these early experiences inhibited his adult development* ‖ (*eccles.*) to prohibit (a clergyman) from performing clerical duties [fr. L. *inhibere* (*inhibitus*)]

in·hi·bi·tion (inhibíʃən) *n.* an inhibiting or being inhibited ‖ one of the conscious or unconscious mechanisms whereby unacceptable impulses (sexual, aggressive etc.) are subdued or repressed [O.F. *inibicion*, *inhibition*]

in·hib·i·tor (inhíbitər) *n.* a person or thing causing inhibition ‖ (*chem.*) any substance restraining a chemical reaction ‖ a substance that restrains the activity of another (e.g. of an enzyme)

in·hib·i·to·ry (inhíbitɔ:ri:, inhíbitouri:) *adj.* of, pertaining to or causing inhibition [fr. M.L. *inhibitorius*]

in·hos·pi·ta·ble (inhóspitəb'l, inhɑspítəb'l) *adj.* not offering hospitality ‖ (of a place or region) not affording sustenance, barren **in·hós·pi·ta·bly** *adv.* [O.F.]

in·hos·pi·tal·i·ty (inhɒispitǽliti:) *n.* lack of hospitality [fr. L. *inhospitalitas*]

in·house (ínháus) *adj.* of service agencies maintained as part of the client company, e.g., *in-house lawyer, advertising agency, etc.*

in·hu·man (inhjú:mən) *adj.* lacking, or showing a lack of, the qualities of mercy etc. considered proper to human beings, *inhuman cruelty* ‖ machinelike, lacking or showing a lack of human warmth ‖ not belonging to or suggestive of the human race, *an inhuman howl* [fr. L. *inhumanus*]

in·hu·mane (inhju:méin) *adj.* lacking normal kindness

in·hu·man·i·ty (inhju:mǽniti:) *pl.* **in·hu·man·i·ties** *n.* the quality or state of being inhuman ‖ (esp. *pl.*) an inhuman or cruel act [F. *inhumanité* or fr. L, *inhumanitas*]

in·hu·ma·tion (inhju:méiʃən) *n.* an inhuming or being inhumed

in·hume (inhjú:m) *pres. part.* **in·hum·ing** *past* and *past part.* **in·humed** *v.t.* to bury [fr. L. *inhumare*]

in·im·i·cal (inímik'l) *adj.* hostile ‖ harmful, unfavorable, *a policy inimical to the national interest* [fr. L.L. *inimicalis*]

in·im·i·ta·bil·i·ty (inimitəbíliti:) *n.* the quality or state of being inimitable

in·im·i·ta·ble (inímitəb'l) *adj.* not capable of being imitated, esp. too good to be successfully imitated **in·ím·i·ta·bly** *adv.* [fr. L. *inimitabilis*]

I·ning (í:níŋ) *KULDJA

I·ni·ni (i:ni:ní:) a river, and the vast hinterland administrative division, of French Guiana

in·i·on (íni:ən) *n.* the projection of the skull at the back of the head [Gk=nape of the neck]

in·iq·ui·tous (iníkwitəs) *adj.* characterized by iniquity

in·iq·ui·ty (iníkwiti:) *pl.* **in·iq·ui·ties** *n.* great wickedness or injustice ‖ an instance of this [O.F. *iniquité*]

in·i·tial (iníʃəl) **1.** *adj.* of or occurring at the very beginning ‖ designating the first letter or syllable of a word **2.** *n.* (esp. *pl.*) the first letter of a personal name, *W.S. are the initials of William Shakespeare* ‖ a large decorative letter used esp. at the beginning of a chapter in a book **3.** *v.t. pres. part.* **in·i·tial·ing**, esp. *Br.* **in·i·tial·ling** *past* and *past part.* **in·i·tialed**, esp. *Br.* **in·i·tialled** to sign or mark with an initial or initials [fr. L. *initialis*]

in·i·tial·ism (iníʃəlizəm) *n.* the formation of acronyms from the first letter of titles, e.g., UNICEF

in·i·tial·ize (iníʃəlaiz) *v.* **1.** to count from a beginning **2.** (*computer*) to set up a starting condition; to set the counter or other factors at specified values. **—initialization** *n.*

initial teaching alphabet a 44-symbol alphabet for teaching beginning English reading

in·i·ti·ate 1. (iníʃi:eit) *v.t. pres. part.* **in·i·ti·at·ing** *past* and *past part.* **in·i·ti·at·ed** to cause to begin, *to initiate an investigation* ‖ to instruct in the fundamentals of a subject ‖ to introduce ceremonially into a society etc. **2.** (iníʃi:it) *adj.* having been initiated **3.** (iníʃi:it) *n.* someone who has been initiated [fr. L. *initiare* (*initiatus*), to begin]

in·i·ti·a·tion (iniʃi:éiʃən) *n.* an initiating or being initiated ‖ the rite of introduction into a society etc. [fr. L. *initiatio* (*initiationis*), a beginning]

in·i·ti·a·tive (iníʃi:ətiv) *n.* personal capacity for thinking up and initiating action ‖ an inception that shows this quality ‖ the power or right to introduce a policy or a measure ‖ the right of voters to initiate legislation **on one's own initiative** acting on one's own idea without prompting **to take the initiative** to be the first to act [F.]

initiative *adj.* of or pertaining to initiation ‖ initiating [fr. L. *initiare* (*initiatus*)]

in·i·ti·a·tor (iníʃi:eitər) *n.* a person who or thing that initiates [L.L.]

in·i·ti·a·to·ry (iníʃi:ətɔ:ri:, iníʃi:ətɔuri:) *adj.* introductory ‖ pertaining to initiation ‖ initiating [fr. L. *initiare* (*initiatus*)]

in·ject (indʒékt) *v.t.* to force (a fluid) into a body esp. by means of a hypodermic syringe, *to inject a vaccine* ‖ to force a fluid into (a cavity, tissue etc.) ‖ to administer an injection to ‖ to introduce (a new or different quality) into a person or a thing, *to inject enthusiasm into a squad* [fr. L. *injicere* (*injectus*), to throw]

in·jec·tion (indʒékʃən) *n.* the act of injecting ‖ the introduction of a substance, esp. a drug, into the body esp. by means of a hypodermic syringe ‖ a substance, esp. a drug in solution, that is injected ‖ process of sending a satellite into orbit [fr. L. *injectio* (*injectionis*)]

injection laser a semiconductor laser utilizing injection of electrons and carriers for excitation

in·jec·tor (indʒéktər) *n.* a person who or thing that injects ‖ a device for feeding water into a steam boiler

injector razor shaving device with removable single-edge blades inserted by a blade dispenser

in·ju·di·cious (indʒu:díʃəs) *adj.* lacking or showing a lack of good judgment

in·junc·tion (indʒʌ́ŋkʃən) *n.* an authoritative command, *parental injunctions* ‖ (*law*) a written order from a court forbidding or requiring some action [fr. L.L. *injunctio* (*injunctionis*)]

in·jure (índʒər) *pres. part.* **in·jur·ing** *past* and *past part.* **in·jured** *v.t.* to inflict a wound, fracture or other physical hurt upon ‖ to cause intangible detriment or hurt to, *to injure a reputation, to injure someone's feelings* [INJURY]

in·ju·ri·ous (indʒúəri:əs) *adj.* causing or likely to cause injury ‖ (of language) offensive, insulting, likely to damage a reputation [F. *injurieux*]

in·ju·ry (índʒəri:) *pl.* **in·ju·ries** *n.* physical impairment resulting from violence or accident ‖ unjust or offensive treatment, *suffering from a sense of injury* ‖ an instance of physical or moral hurt ‖ (*law*) an actionable wrong [fr. L. *injuria*, a wrong]

in·jus·tice (indʒʌ́stis) *n.* violation of justice, unfairness ‖ an instance of this **to do an injustice to someone** to judge someone unfairly [F.]

ink (iŋk) **1.** *n.* a colored fluid used for writing or printing ‖ (*zool.*) a black liquid ejected by cephalopods to screen escape **2.** *v.t.* to cover or mark with ink [M.E. *enke* fr. O.F.]

Ink·er·man, Battle of (íŋkərmən) a French and British victory (1854) over the Russians during the Crimean War

ink·horn (íŋkhɔrn) *n.* (*hist.*) a small portable ink container, esp. of horn

ink·i·ness (íŋki:nis) the quality or state of being inky

ink-jet printer (íŋkdʒet) (*typography*) device that ejects ink particles from nozzles to form printed material, utilizing electrostatic acceleration

ink·ling (íŋkliŋ) *n.* the slightest notion, *I haven't an inkling of what you mean* ‖ a faint suggestion, intimation [fr. older *inkle* v., to hint]

ink·stand (íŋkstænd) *n.* a holder for ink bottles ‖ an inkwell

ink·well (íŋkwel) *n.* a container for writing ink, e.g. one fitted into a hole in a school desk

ink·y (íŋki:) *comp.* **ink·i·er** *superl.* **ink·i·est** *adj.* very dark or black ‖ covered or marked with ink

inlaid *past* and *past part,* of INLAY

in·land (ínlənd) **1.** *n.* the interior of a country, away from the coast **2.** *adj.* away from the coast toward the interior of a country ‖ (esp. *Br.*) internal, domestic, *inland trade* **3.** *adv.* in or toward the interior of a country

inland revenue (*Br.*) internal revenue

Inland Sea (*Jap.* Seto Naikai) a narrow body of water (240 miles long) lying between the islands of Honshu, Kyushu and Shikoku, Japan. It contains some 300 small islands, is bordered by mountains, and is extremely beautiful

in-law (ínlɔ) *n.* (*pop.*, usually *pl.*) a relative by marriage

in·lay (ínlei) **1.** *v.t. pres. part.* **in·lay·ing** *past* and *past part.* **in·laid** (ínleid) to set (a material or pattern) into another material or object by cutting a design out of its surface and filling the space with a different material, *to inlay mother-of-pearl into ebony* ‖ to decorate (a material or object) in this way, *to inlay a walnut table with ivory* ‖ to set (an illustration) into a thicker sheet of paper which serves as both mount and protection **2.** *n.* the process of inlaying ‖ a design made by inlaying ‖ the material used in inlaying ‖ (*dentistry*) a filling of metal etc. cemented into a cavity

in·let (ínlit) *n.* a narrow arm of the sea or of a river ‖ a passage between islands into a lagoon ‖ an opening, entrance

in·li·er (ínlaiər) *n.* (*geol.*) an outcrop of rock surrounded by rock of later formation [fr. IN- (in) + *lier*, something that reclines]

in-line (ínláin) *adj.* of something with units arranged in a straight line, e.g., in-line printing

in·ly·ing (ínlaiiŋ) *adj.* inland, situated toward the interior

In·man (ínmən), Henry (1801–46), U.S. landscape and portrait painter. His sitters included William Wordsworth, President Martin Van Buren, and Chief Justice John Marshall

INMARSAT (ínmɑrsæt) (*acronym*) for international maritime satellite, a commercial marine satellite communication and navigation system of U.S. Maritime Administration. *Cf* MARISAT

in·mate (ínmeit) *n.* a person living in an institution, esp. in a mental hospital ‖ one of several occupants of a dwelling

in me·mo·ri·am (inməmɔ́ri:əm, inməmɔ́uri:əm) *adv.* in memory of [L.]

CONCISE PRONUNCIATION KEY: **(a)** æ, c*a*t; ɑ, c*a*r; ɔ f*aw*n; ei, sn*a*ke. **(e)** e, h*e*n; i:, sh*ee*p; iə, d*ee*r; ɛə, b*ea*r. **(i)** i, f*i*sh; ai, t*i*ger; ə:, b*i*rd. **(o)** o, *o*x; au, c*ow*; ou, g*oa*t; u, p*oo*r; ɔi, r*oy*al. **(u)** ʌ, d*u*ck; u, b*u*ll; u:, g*oo*se; ə, b*a*cillus; ju:, c*u*be. x, lo*ch*; θ, *th*ink; ð, bo*th*er; z, *Z*en; ʒ, corsa*g*e; dʒ, sava*g*e; ŋ, orangutan*g*; j, *y*ak; ʃ, *fi*sh; tʃ, fe*tch*; 'l, rabb*le*; 'n, redd*en*. Complete pronunciation key appears inside front cover.

in·most (ínmoust) *adj.* farthest within, *the inmost room* ‖ most private or secret, *inmost thoughts* [O.E. *innemest*]

Inn (in) an Alpine river (320 miles long) flowing northeast from Switzerland through the Engadine Valley, W. Austria and S.E. Germany, to the Danube at Passau (Bavaria)

inn (in) *n.* (*hist.*) a hotel ‖ (*hist.*, now used in names) a tavern [O.E. *inn*, dwelling]

in·nards (ínərdz) *pl. n.* (pop.) viscera, entrails [altered fr. INWARDS]

in·nate (inéit) *adj.* belonging to a person's nature ‖ inherent in a thing ‖ (*philos.*) originating in the mind itself, i.e. not acquired from direct experience, *innate ideas* [fr. L.L. *innatus*]

in·nate·ness hypothesis (inéitnəs) (*linguistics*) view, esp. in generative grammar, that at least some grammatical competence is innate

in·ner (ínər) **1.** *adj.* located within, contained near the center, *the inner rooms of a house* ‖ of the mind or spirit, *the inner life* ‖ near a center of vitality or influence, *the inner circle of the government* ‖ not obvious, hidden, *the inner meaning* **2.** *n.* the ring on a target next to the bull's eye ‖ a shot that hits this [O.E. *innera, innra, innre*]

inner circle group close to the center of activity and/or decision making

inner city the central, most densely occupied portion of an urban center *also* central city Cf OUTER CITY

inner ear *EAR

Inner Light (in Quaker doctrine) the presence of God in the human soul as a spiritual and moral guide

Inner Mongolia *MONGOLIA, INNER

in·ner·most (ínərmoust) *adj.* inmost

inner space 1. hydrospace (which see) **2.** the subconscious, esp. under the influence of LSD **3.** suggestion of depth in an abstract painting

Inner Temple *INNS OF COURT

inner tube an inflatable rubber tube inside the outer covering of a tire

in·ner·vate (ínəːrveit) *pres. part.* **in·ner·vat·ing** *past* and *past part.* **in·ner·vat·ed** *v.t.* (*physiol.*) to provide (a part of the body) with nerves ‖ to stimulate (a nerve or organ) to activity **in·ner·vá·tion** *n.* an innervating or being innervated ‖ the distribution of nerves to or in a part of the body [fr. IN-(in)+L. *nervus*, nerve]

In·ness (ínis), George (1825–94), U.S. Romantic landscape painter, known for his idyllic canvases, including 'Peace and Plenty' (1865). He became a convert (from 1875) to nature mysticism, and such paintings as 'Autumn Oaks' (1875) are marked by greater freedom in form and an effusion of color

In·nig·keit (ínigkait) *n.* (*German; often italics*) warm sincerity, esp. of music

in·ning (íniŋ) *n.* (*baseball*) the period in which each team has a turn at bat **in·nings** *pl.* **in·nings** *n.* (*cricket*) a team's or batsman's batting period [O.E. *innung*]

inn·keep·er (ínki:pər) *n.* (*hist.*) the proprietor of an inn

in·no·cence (ínəs'ns) *n.* the quality or state of being innocent [F.]

in·no·cent (ínəs'nt) **1.** *adj.* free from guilt, *innocent of a crime* ‖ knowing nothing of evil, free from sin ‖ naive, simple-minded ‖ harmless, *an innocent occupation* ‖ (*med.*) benign ‖ (*rhet.*) devoid, *floors innocent of carpets* **2.** *n.* an innocent person [O.F.]

In·no·cent I (ínəs'nt), St (*d.* 417), pope (401–17). Feast: July 28

Innocent II (*d.* 1143), pope (1130–43). After a dispute, his election was recognized at the instance of St Bernard of Clairvaux. He condemned the teachings of Abelard

Innocent III (c. 1160–1216), pope (1198–1216). His belief that the spiritual power should dominate the temporal brought him into conflict with many sovereigns: notably King John of England and Otto IV, whom he excommunicated in 1208 and 1210 respectively. He launched (1202) the 4th Crusade, and sent an army (1209) against the Albigenses. He convened the fourth Lateran Council (1215)

Innocent IV (c. 1190–1254), pope (1243–54). He resumed the policies of Innocent III, waging war on Frederick II and his sons

Innocent X (1574–1655), pope (1644–55). He condemned Jansenism

Innocent XI (1611–89), pope (1676–89). An ascetic and a reformer, he quarreled with Louis XIV over the right to appoint bishops (*GALLICANISM)

Innocent XII (1615–1700), pope (1691–1700). He ended the quarrel with Louis XIV over Gallicanism

Innocents, Massacre of the the mass slaughter of the children of Bethlehem, ordered by Herod the Great, with the intention of killing the infant Jesus (Matthew ii, 16). Their martyrdom is commemorated on Holy Innocents' Day, Dec. 28

in·noc·u·ous (inókju:əs) *adj.* not actively harmful, *an innocuous drug* ‖ calculated to give no offense, *an innocuous speech* ‖ lacking in force, *pleasant but innocuous watercolors* [fr. L. *innocuus*]

in·nom·i·nate (inóminit) *adj.* not named [fr. L.L. *innominatus*]

innominate bone the hipbone

in·no·vate (ínouveit) *pres. part.* **in·no·vat·ing** *past* and *past part.* **in·no·vat·ed** *v.i.* to make changes, introduce new practices etc. [fr. L. *innovare* (*innovatus*), to renew]

in·no·va·tion (inouvéiʃən) *n.* the act of innovating ‖ something newly introduced [fr. L. *innovatio* (*innovationis*)]

in·no·va·tor (ínouveitər) *n.* someone who innovates **in·no·va·to·ry** (ínouvətɔːri:, ínouvətouri:) *adj.*

Inns·bruck (ínsbruk) the capital (pop. 115,197) of the Tirol, Austria, in a valley of the E. Alps on the Inn, a historic communications center (at the foot of the Brenner Pass) and a resort: university (1677)

Inns of Court four sets of buildings in London—Lincoln's Inn, Gray's Inn, the Inner Temple and the Middle Temple—belonging to the four legal societies which qualify persons to practice at the bar ‖ the four societies themselves, which are descended from medieval law schools

in·nu·en·do (inju:éndou) *pl.* **in·nu·en·does** *n.* an oblique referring or insinuating ‖ an instance of such hinting, always critical and usually malicious ‖ (*law*, in an action for libel or slander) that part of the complaint which interprets the expressions alleged to be libelous or slanderous [L.=by nodding at, intimating]

in·nu·mer·a·ble (inú:mərəb'l, injú:mərəb'l) *adj.* too many to be counted ‖ very many **in·nú·mer·a·bly** *adv.* [fr. L. *innumerabilis*]

in·oc·u·la·ble (inókjuləb'l) *adj.* capable of being infected by inoculation ‖ capable of being communicated by inoculation

in·oc·u·late (inókjuleit) *pres. part.* **in·oc·u·lat·ing** *past* and *past part.* **in·oc·u·lat·ed** *v.t.* to introduce a disease into (an organism) by transmitting the agent which causes it, e.g. when a vaccine is introduced into an organism to protect against subsequent infection ‖ to introduce (a disease) into an organism in this way (*IMMUNITY) ‖ to introduce microorganisms etc. into (soil etc.) ‖ to introduce particular ideas into (a person's mind) so as to imbue him with them [fr. L. *inoculare* (*inoculatus*), to engraft]

in·oc·u·la·tion (inɔkjuléiʃən) *n.* the act of inoculating ‖ an instance of this ‖ mental preparation or conditioning [fr. L. *inoculatio* (*inoculationis*), a grafting]

in·oc·u·la·tive (inókjuleitiv, inókjulətiv) *adj.* of or pertaining to inoculation

in·oc·u·la·tor (inókjuleitər) *n.* a person who or thing that inoculates

in·oc·u·lum (inókjuləm) *n.* the material (microorganisms etc.) used in inoculation ‖ bacteria placed in compost to start biological action [Mod. L.]

in·o·dor·ous (inóudərəs) *adj.* without odor [fr. L. *inodorus*]

in·of·fen·sive (inəfénsiv) *adj.* not causing offense ‖ harmless

in·of·fi·cious (inəfíʃəs) *adj.* (*law*) contrary to moral duty, *an inofficious testament* [fr. L. *inofficiosus*]

I·nö·nü (inəːný), Ismet (1884–1973), Turkish statesman. He was president of Turkey (1938–50) and prime minister (1923–4, 1925–37 and 1961–5)

in·op·er·a·ble (inópərəb'l) *adj.* (*surg.*) not able to be treated by operation [prob. fr. F. *inopérable*]

in·op·er·a·tive (inópərətiv, inópəreitiv) *adj.* (esp. of laws, rules etc.) having no effect, not in operation

in·op·por·tune (inɔpərtú:n, inɔpərtjú:n) *adj.* not opportune, esp. happening at a wrong or inconvenient time [fr. L.L. *inopportunus*, unfitting]

in·or·di·nate (inórd'nit) *adj.* not within reasonable bounds, *inordinate pride* ‖ (of emotion) not

rightly directed [fr. L. *inordinatus*, disordered]

in·or·gan·ic (inɔrgǽnik) *adj.* (*chem.*) of or relating to elements and compounds not regarded as organic ‖ not composed of plant or animal material ‖ not arising from natural processes, artificial, *inorganic world languages* **in·or·gán·i·cal·ly** *adv.*

inorganic chemistry the branch of chemistry concerned with chemical elements and their compounds, other than the compounds of carbon (cf. ORGANIC CHEMISTRY), but including the simpler compounds of carbon, e.g. carbon dioxide, hydrogen cyanide

in·os·cu·late (inóskjuleit) *pres. part.* **in·os·cu·lat·ing** *past* and *past part.* **in·os·cu·lat·ed** *v.i.* and *t.* to unite, esp. by contact or by the joining of openings (e.g. in anastomosis) **in·os·cu·lá·tion** *n.* [fr. IN- (into)+L. *osculare*, to provide with a mouth or opening]

in·pa·tient (ínpeiʃənt) *n.* a person who is lodged, fed and treated in a hospital (opp. OUTPATIENT)

in·phase (ínfeiz) *adj.* (*elec.*) of the same phase

in·put (ínput) *n.* something put in, esp. power or energy supplied to a machine or storage system ‖ effort put into any project ‖ (*computer*) data fed into a computer

input measure a measure of the quality of services based on the number, type, and quality of resources used in the production of the services

in·put-out·put tables (ínputáutput) (*economics*) the amount of output that goes to each industry as raw materials or semifinished products and amounts that go to final markets

input system (*computer*) the portion of a computer (or other device) that accepts data. — **input system. —input unit**

in·quest (ínkwest) *n.* a judicial or official inquiry esp. before a jury, usually to inquire into the cause of death where this is not certified by a doctor or where the possibility of crime cannot be ruled out ‖ the jury engaged in such an inquiry ‖ the result of the inquiry ‖ a minute and semi-accusing investigation [M.E. *enqueste* fr. O.F.]

in·qui·e·tude (inkwáiitu:d, inkwáiitju:d) *n.* (*rhet.*) disquietude [F. *inquiétude* or fr. L.L. *inquietudo*]

in·qui·line (ínkwəlain, ínkwəlin) *n.* (*zool.*) any animal which lives in the burrow, nest etc. of an animal of another species [fr. L. *inquilinus*, a tenant]

in·quire, en·quire (inkwáiər) *pres. part.* **in·quir·ing, en·quir·ing** *past* and *past part.* **in·quired, en·quired** *v.t.* to seek (information) by asking, *to inquire a person's name* ‖ *v.i.* to ask questions, *he inquired about her progress* ‖ (with 'after') to ask about the health or welfare of ‖ (with 'for') to seek to get by asking, *to inquire for a book* ‖ (with 'for') to ask to see (a person) ‖ (with 'into') to investigate [M.E. *enquere, enqueren* fr. O.F.]

in·quir·y, en·quir·y (inkwáiəri:, ínkwəri:, énkwəri:) *pl.* **in·quir·ies, en·quir·ies** *n.* the act of inquiring ‖ a question ‖ an investigation [older *enquery* fr. *enquere* v., to inquire]

inquiry agent (*Br.*) a private detective

inquiry office (*Br.*) information desk

in·qui·si·tion (inkwizíʃən) *n.* an investigation by close interrogation, esp. one which disregards the feelings of the person subjected to it ‖ (*law*, in certain contexts) a judicial inquiry the **Inquisition** a court of the Roman Catholic Church originally set up (c. 1233) to inquire into the heresy of the Albigenses. It became notorious for its use of torture and secret denunciation. The medieval Inquisition was changed (1542) into a Church department, the Congregation of the Holy Office, to deal with questions of faith, morals, heresy and censorship. This was reformed and renamed the Sacred Congregation for the Doctrine of the Faith (1965). The Spanish Inquisition was a separate body, established (1478) by the Spanish monarchy as a political instrument under Torquemada. It was abolished in 1820 **in·qui·si·tion·al** *adj.* [O.F.]

in·quis·i·tive (inkwízitiv) *adj.* wanting to ferret out the private concerns of other people ‖ asking a lot of questions [O.F. *inquisitif*]

in·quis·i·tor (inkwízitər) *n.* a person officially appointed to investigate ‖ a cruel, severe questioner ‖ a member of the Spanish Inquisition [O.F. *inquisiteur*]

in·quis·i·to·ri·al (inkwizitóːri:əl, inkwizitóuri:əl) *adj.* pertaining to an inquisition ‖ having power to conduct inquisitions ‖ characterized by offensive, browbeating questioning, *an inquisitorial manner* ‖ (*law*) having to do with a system of criminal procedure in which the judge is also prosecutor, or with one which is secret, and under which the person accused must answer questioning [fr. M.L. *inquisitorius*]

in re (*law, commerce* etc.) re

in·road (ínroud) *n.* (usually *pl.*) a heavy encroachment, *inroads on one's time* ‖ a raid, *inroads into enemy territory*

in·rush (ínrʌʃ) *n.* a rushing in, influx, *an inrush of visitors*

ins. inches ‖ inspector ‖ insurance ‖ insulation ‖ insulated

In Sa·lah (insaláh) (*Arab.* 'Ayn-Sālih) a town (pop. 17,000) and oasis in the Algerian Sahara in an area producing natural gas

in·sal·i·vate (insǽliveit) *pres. part.* **in·sal·i·vat·ing** *past and past part.* **in·sal·i·vat·ed** *v.t.* to mix (food) with saliva when chewing **in·sal·i·vá·tion** *n.*

in·sa·lu·bri·ous (insəlú:briːəs) *adj.* (*rhet.*) unhealthy for mind or body **in·sa·lu·bri·ty** (insəlú:britiː) *n.* [fr. L. *insalubris*]

in·sane (inséin) *adj.* afflicted with a mental illness severe enough to make one incapable of leading a normal life ‖ showing such affliction, *insane delusions* ‖ (*loosely*) highly reckless or foolish [fr. L. *insanus*]

insane asylum a mental hospital

in·san·i·tar·y (insǽniteriː) *adj.* so dirty as to be conducive to disease

in·san·i·ty (insǽnitiː) *pl.* **in·san·i·ties** *n.* the state of being insane ‖ (*law*) such a lack of mental health as to exempt a person from legal responsibility ‖ (*loosely*) a foolish act [fr. L. *insanitas*]

in·sa·tia·bil·i·ty (inseiʃəbíliti:, inseiʃiːəbíliti:) *n.* the quality or state of being insatiable

in·sa·tia·ble (inséiʃəb'l, inséiʃiːəb'l) *adj.* incapable of being satisfied ‖ continually craving **in·sá·tia·bly** *adv.* [O.F. *insaciable* or fr. L. *insatiabilis*]

in·sa·ti·ate (inséiʃiːit) *adj.* never satisfied [fr. L. *insatiatus*]

in-school program (ínsku:l) noncurriculum activity carried on in an educational institution

in·scribe (inskráib) *pres. part.* **in·scrib·ing** *past and past part.* **in·scribed** *v.t.* to write in (a book) or cut in (stone or metal) ‖ to write or engrave (words or symbols) on a surface ‖ to add (a name) to a list, *he inscribed them as new donors* ‖ to impress ineffaceably (on the mind or memory) ‖ to dedicate (a book etc.) informally ‖ (*geom.*) to draw (a figure) within another of different shape so that they touch at certain points on their boundaries ‖ (*Br., finance*) to issue (a loan) as shares with registered shareholders [fr. L. *inscribere*]

in·scrip·tion (inskrípʃən) *n.* an inscribed text ‖ the art of inscribing ‖ an informal dedication, e.g. in a book ‖ (*Br.*) the inscribing of securities ‖ (*Br., pl.*) inscribed securities **in·scrip·tion·al** *adj.* [fr. L. *inscriptio (inscriptionis)*]

in·scrip·tive (inskríptiv) *adj.* of, relating to or being an inscription [fr. L. *inscribere (inscriptus)*]

in·scru·ta·bil·i·ty (inskru:təbíliti:) *n.* the quality or state of being inscrutable

in·scru·ta·ble (inskrú:təb'l) *adj.* of such a kind that the meaning or intention cannot be perceived **in·scrú·ta·bly** *adv.* [fr. L.L. *inscrutabilis*]

in·sect (ínsekt) *n.* a member of the class *Insecta*, phylum *Arthropoda*, with external skeleton and jointed legs. The body is divided in three sections: the head, thorax and abdomen. Most have wings and three pairs of thoracic limbs. Respiration is by tracheae. The head is generally well defined and bears one pair of antennae, three pairs of mouthparts and one pair of eyes. The largest group of all living creatures, insects are mainly adapted to life on land but some live in an aquatic or semiaquatic environment. More than 1,000,000 species are known ‖ any creature (the spider, tick, mite etc.) resembling an insect [fr. L. (*animal*) *insectum*, a notched animal]

in·sec·tar·i·um (insektéəri:əm) *pl.* **in·sec·tar·i·a** *n.* a place for keeping and breeding insects under observation [fr. L. *insecta*, insects]

in·sec·ti·cide (inséktisaid) *n.* any chemical preparation used for killing insect pests [fr. L. *insectum*, insect+*caedere*, to kill]

in·sec·ti·vore (inséktivɔr, inséktivour) *n.* a member of *Insectivora*, an order of small, insect-eating, usually nocturnal mammals incl. moles,

shrews, hedgehogs etc. [Mod. F. fr. L. *insectivorus*, insect-eating]

in·sec·tiv·o·rous (insektívərəs) *adj.* feeding chiefly on insects ‖ (of some plants, e.g. the sundew and Venus's flytrap) capturing and digesting insects [fr. Mod. L. *insectivorus*]

in·se·cure (insikjúər) *adj.* not safe, liable to collapse, give way etc. ‖ [fr. M.L. *insecurus*]

in·se·cu·ri·ty (insikjúəriti:) *pl.* **in·se·cu·ri·ties** *n.* the state or quality of being insecure ‖ something insecure [fr. M.L. *insecuritas*]

in·sem·i·nate (insémineit) *pres. part.* **in·sem·i·nat·ing** *past and past part.* **in·sem·i·nat·ed** *v.t.* to introduce seed into, esp. by sexual intercourse or by artificially injected semen ‖ to plant (ideas) in someone's mind **in·sem·i·ná·tion** *n.* [fr. L. *inseminare (inseminatus)*, to sow in]

in·sen·sate (insénseit) *adj.* inhumane, brutal ‖ without sense perception ‖ lacking moral or emotional perception, insensitive ‖ foolish, *insensate risks* [fr. L.L. *insensatus*, having no sensation]

in·sen·si·bil·i·ty (insensəbíliti:) *n.* the quality or state of being insensible [fr. L.L. *insensibilitas*]

in·sen·si·ble (insénsəb'l) *adj.* indifferent, *insensible to sorrow* ‖ not aware, *insensible of the risk* ‖ not feeling, *insensible to cold* ‖ unconscious, *he lay there insensible* ‖ so slight or gradual as not to be noticeable, *by insensible degrees* **in·sén·si·bly** *adv.* [fr. L. *insensibilis*]

in·sen·si·tive (insénsitiv) *adj.* not mentally or emotionally sensitive ‖ not physically sensitive

in·sen·tient (insénʃənt) *adj.* without power of perception or sensation

in·sep·a·ra·bil·i·ty (inseparabíliti:) *n.* the quality or state of being inseparable

in·sep·a·ra·ble (insépərəb'l) *adj.* incapable of being separated ‖ (of people) utterly devoted in friendship ‖ (*gram.*, of a prefix) added at the beginning of a word but not a word in itself (e.g. 'mis', 'un' etc.) **in·sép·a·ra·bly** *adv.* [fr. L. *inseparabilis*]

in·sert 1. (insɔ́:rt) *v.t.* to put inside, *to insert a key in a lock* ‖ to add as an integral part, *to insert a clause in a contract* **2.** (ínsə:rt) *n.* something inserted ‖ an extra page set within a newspaper, magazine or book **in·sért·ed** *adj.* (*biol.*, esp. of the parts of a flower) attached to or growing out of something naturally [fr. L. *inserere (insertus)*, to join]

in·ser·tion (insɔ́:rʃən) *n.* an inserting or being inserted ‖ something inserted ‖ one inclusion of a newspaper announcement or advertisement ‖ (*biol.*) the point where a plant or body part grows out of another ‖ a band of lace, embroidery etc. made to be inserted into other materials [fr. L. *insertio (insertionis)*]

in-ser·vice training (insɔ́:rvəs) training courses offered to employees by the employer, esp. in government service

in·ses·so·ri·al (insesɔ́ri:əl, insesóuri:əl) *adj.* (of birds) perching ‖ (of birds' feet) adapted for perching [fr. Mod. L. *Insessores*, ult. fr. L. *insidere*, to sit in]

in·set (ínset) *n.* a small picture, map, diagram etc. included within a larger one but separated off from it ‖ an extra page set within a newspaper, magazine or book ‖ a piece of cloth set into a dress etc.

in·set (inét) *pres. part.* **in·set·ting** *past* and *past part.* **in·set** *v.t.* to put in, insert ‖ (*printing, past and past part.* **in·set·ted**) to impose (pages) for binding with a single central stitching, by wrapping signatures around a central signature instead of collating them in sequence

in·shore (inʃɔ́r, ínʃour) **1.** *adj.* near the shore, *inshore fishing* ‖ moving towards the shore, *an inshore breeze* **2.** *adv.* to or towards the shore, *to drift inshore* **inshore of** nearer to the shore than

in·side (ínsáid) **1.** *n.* the inner portion or side of something ‖ the side of a path, sidewalk etc. furthest from the road ‖ (*pl., pop.*) the stomach and intestines, *a pain in one's insides* **the inside of the week** (*Br.*) the working days, Monday to Friday inclusive **2.** *adj.* situated in the inner portion or on the inner surface ‖ of or relating to knowledge etc. that is not generally available, *inside information* **3.** *adv.* in or into the inner part of something, *stay inside till the rain stops* **inside of** (*pop.*) before the end of (a given amount of time) ‖ (*pop.*) in the inner part of, *put this box inside of that one* **4.** *prep.* at or toward the inner side or portion of, *stay inside the gates*

inside job (*pop.*) a crime committed by or with the assistance of someone employed or trusted by the victim

inside out *adv.* having the inner surface where the outer surface normally is **to know (something) inside out** to have a very thorough knowledge of (something) **to turn inside out** to be able to have the inner surface where the outer surface normally is **to turn (something) inside out** to reverse the places of the inner and outer surfaces of (something) ‖ to search (a house, closet etc.) very thoroughly

Inside Passage a protected waterway (950 miles long) along the Canadian–S. Alaskan coast beginning at Puget Sound, separated from the Pacific by Vancouver I., the Queen Charlotte Is, and the Alexander Archipelago

in·sid·er (insáidər) *n.* a member of a group, organization etc. who, because of his position, has special information, rights, privileges etc.

in·sid·i·ous (insídi:əs) *adj.* working or acting maliciously with subtlety and stealth ‖ acting gradually and imperceptibly, *an insidious illness* [fr. L. *insidiosus*, cunning]

in·sight (ínsait) *n.* the imaginative power to see into and understand immediately (a person, situation etc.) ‖ an item of knowledge gained through this power, *this gave us fresh insights into the difficulties to be faced*

in·sig·ni·a (insígni:ə) *pl. n.* symbols of authority or importance ‖ emblems used as distinguishing marks or signs [L., pl. of *insigne*, a badge of office]

in·sig·nif·i·cance (insignífikəns) *n.* the quality or state of being insignificant

in·sig·nif·i·cant (insignífikənt) *adj.* having no importance ‖ meaningless, *an insignificant remark* ‖ small, *an insignificant cottage* ‖ personally unimpressive or lacking social standing

in·sin·cere (insinsíər) *adj.* not sincere **in·sin·cer·i·ty** (insinséritiː) *pl.* **in·sin·cer·i·ties** *n.* the quality or state of being insincere ‖ something insincere [fr. L. *insincerus*, not genuine]

in·sin·u·ate (insínjuːeit) *pres. part.* **in·sin·u·at·ing** *past and past part.* **in·sin·u·at·ed** *v.t.* to suggest or hint indirectly, imply slyly, esp. maliciously **to insinuate oneself** to make one's way gradually by stealth and cleverness, *to insinuate oneself into someone's favor* [fr. L. *insinuare (insinuatus)*, to curve]

in·sin·u·a·tion (insinjuːéiʃən) *n.* the act of insinuating ‖ an oblique, esp. malicious suggestion [fr. L. *insinuatio (insinuationis)*, a winding]

in·sin·u·a·tor (insínjuːeitər) *n.* someone who insinuates [L.]

in·sip·id (insípid) *adj.* (of food) tasteless ‖ (of people or things) vapid, uninteresting **in·si·píd·i·ty** *pl.* **in·si·pid·i·ties** *n.* the quality or state of being insipid ‖ an insipid remark etc. [fr. L.L. *insipidus*]

in·sist (insíst) *v.t.* to assert emphatically, *he insists that it was so* ‖ to demand peremptorily, *he insists that you apologize* ‖ *v.i.* to repeat a request, assertion etc. with persistence, *if you insist you will only make him angry* ‖ (with 'on' or 'upon') to make a specified demand authoritatively, *to insist on punctuality* ‖ to assert a specified intention, *he insists on driving her home* **in·síst·ence** *n.* the state or quality of being insistent ‖ the act of insisting **in·síst·en·cy** *n.* [fr. L. *insistere*, to stand on]

in·sist·ent (insístənt) *adj.* compelling attention, *the insistent beat of a drum* ‖ persistent, *insistent requests for payment* **in·síst·ent·ly** *adv.* [fr. L. *insistens (insistentis)* fr. *insistere*, to stand on]

in si·tu (insáitu:, insáitjuː, insítuː) *adv.* on the spot, at the original site [L.]

in·so·bri·e·ty (insəbráiiti:) *n.* lack of sobriety or restraint

in·so·far (insoufár) *adv.* (with 'as') to the extent that, *insofar as he was able*

in·so·late (ínsəleit) *pres. part.* **in·so·lat·ing** *past and past part.* **in·so·lat·ed** *v.t.* to expose to the sun's rays, e.g. for bleaching, curing etc. [fr. L. *insolare (insolatus)*]

in·so·la·tion (insəléiʃən) *n.* exposure (for ripening, drying etc.) to the sun's rays ‖ sunstroke ‖ (*meteor.*) solar radiation as received e.g. by the earth ‖ (*meteor.*) the rate of delivery of all direct solar energy on a given area [fr. L. *insolatio (insolationis)*]

in·sole (ínsoul) *n.* the inside sole of a shoe ‖ an additional inside sole, for warmth, fit, protection etc.

in·so·lence (ínsələns) *n.* the quality of being insolent ‖ an instance of this [fr. L. *insolentia*]

in·so·lent (ínsələnt) *adj.* rudely disrespectful [fr. L. *insolens* (*insolentis*), unaccustomed]

in·sol·u·bil·i·ty (insɒljubíliti:) *n.* the quality or state of being insoluble [fr. L. *insolubilis*]

in·sol·u·ble (insɒljub'l) *adj.* (*chem.*) not soluble, or soluble only slightly or with difficulty ‖ unable to be solved, *an insoluble mystery* **in·sól·u·bly** *adv.* [fr. L. *insolubilis*]

in·sol·ven·cy (insɒlvənsi:) *n.* the fact or condition of being insolvent

in·sol·vent (insɒlvənt) **1.** *adj.* unable to pay one's debts ‖ (of an estate etc.) not sufficient to pay all debts ‖ relating to insolvency or insolvents, *insolvent laws* **2.** *n.* someone who cannot pay his debts

in·som·ni·a (insómni:ə) *n.* persistent inability to sleep **in·som·ni·ac** (insómni:æk) *n.* a person suffering from this inability [L.]

in·so·much (insoumʌtʃ) *adv.* (with 'as' or 'that') to the extent or degree

in·sou·ci·ance (insú:si:əns) *n.* carefree indifference. e.g. for what other people will think about one's behavior [F.]

in·sou·ci·ant (insú:si:ənt) *adj.* showing insouciance [F.]

in·spect (inspékt) *v.t.* to examine formally, e.g. for completeness or quality ‖ to pass in review ceremonially ‖ to look closely at, scrutinize [fr. L. *inspicere* (*inspectus*)]

in·spec·tion (inspékʃən) *n.* the process of inspecting ‖ an instance of this [F.]

in·spec·tor (inspéktər) *n.* someone officially appointed to make inspections and report to an authority ‖ a police officer ranking below a superintendent **in·spéc·to·ral** *adj.* **in·spec·tor·ate** (inspéktərit) *n.* the office of an inspector ‖ a staff of inspectors ‖ a district under an inspector **in·spec·to·ri·al** (ìnspektóri:əl, ìnspektóuri:əl) *adj.* of or pertaining to an inspector or inspectors [L.]

in·spi·ra·tion (inspəréiʃən) *n.* (*theol.*) divine influence, seen as the working of the Holy Spirit in the human soul ‖ the creative impulse of an artist, often seen as a supernatural prompting ‖ a person who or thing that inspires ‖ an inspired idea ‖ a breathing in, inhaling **in·spi·rá·tion·al** *adj.* [O.F.]

in·spir·a·to·ry (inspáiərətɔri:, inspáiərətouri:) *adj.* (*physiol.*) having to do with breathing in, *inspiratory muscles* [fr. L. *inspirare* (*inspiratus*), to breathe into]

in·spire (inspáiər) *pres. part.* **in·spir·ing** *past and past part.* **in·spired** *v.t.* to move by divine influence ‖ to fill with creative power ‖ to stimulate, *to inspire confidence* ‖ to affect, *to inspire someone with disgust* ‖ to suggest, be the motivating but unnamed power behind, *the article was inspired by a member of the government* ‖ to inhale (air etc.) [O.F. *enspirer, inspirer,* to breathe into]

in·spir·it (inspírit) *v.t.* to put courage or enthusiasm into

in·spis·sate (inspíseit, ínspiseit) *pres. part.* **in·spis·sat·ing** *past and past part.* **in·spis·sat·ed** *v.t. and i.* to thicken, condense [fr. L.L. *inspissare* (*inspissatus*)]

in·sta·bil·i·ty (instəbíliti:) *pl.* **in·sta·bil·i·ties** *n.* lack of physical, moral or emotional stability ‖ an instance of this [F. *instabilité*]

in·stall (instɔ́l) *v.t.* to place (a person) ceremonially in a position of power or dignity, *to install a bishop* ‖ to set in position for use, *to install electricity* ‖ to settle, establish in some place or state [fr. M.L. *installare*]

in·stal·la·tion (instəléiʃən) *n.* an installing or being installed ‖ an apparatus set in position for use, *a lighting installation* ‖ a military establishment, incl. the base and all its equipment [fr. M.L. *installatio* (*installationis*)]

in·stall·ment, in·stal·ment (instɔ́lmənt) *n.* one of the parts of a serial ‖ part of the sum paid at regular intervals over an extended period, *the sum was paid in monthly installments of $50* [fr. earlier *estall* fr. O.F. *estaler,* to fix]

in·stall·ment, instal·ment *n.* an installing or being installed

in·stall·ment plan (*Am.=Br.* hire-purchase) a system under which a buyer obtains the immediate use of something by agreeing with the seller to pay for it by installments over a specified period of time

in·stance (ínstəns) **1.** *n.* an example, illustration **at the instance of** (*rhet.*) at the request of **for instance** as an illustration **in the first instance** initially, at the first stage **2.** *v.t. pres. part.* **in·stanc·ing** *past and past part.* **in·stanced** to cite as example ‖ to illustrate by citing an example [F.=urgency]

in·stan·cy (ínstənsi:) *n.* urgency, insistence [fr. L. *instantia*]

in·stant (ínstənt) **1.** *adj.* urgent, *a matter of instant importance* ‖ immediate, *instant disapproval* ‖ (*commerce, abbr.* inst.) of the current month, *the 9th inst.* ‖ (of coffee, soup etc.) in soluble form, ready to be prepared by adding a liquid **2.** *n.* a short space of time, *he returned in an instant* ‖ a particular moment, *come here this instant* [F.]

in·stan·ta·ne·ous (instəntéini:əs) *adj.* happening in an instant, *death was instantaneous* ‖ done immediately, *an instantaneous reaction* [fr. L. *instans* (*instantis*)]

instant interest interest on a deposit credited or paid in advance at the time the deposit is made

instant lotteries lotteries in which a player learns immediately if he or she has won

in·stant·ly (ínstəntli:) *adv.* at once, without the least delay

in·star (instár) *n.* (*zool.*) an arthropod, at a specified stage between successive molts ‖ (*zool.*) such a stage [Mod. L. fr. L.=a form, shape]

in·stead (instéd) *adv.* as an alternative **instead of** in place of, rather than

in·step (ínstep) *n.* the arching area of the middle of the human foot, esp. the upper surface of this area ‖ the part of a shoe or stocking covering this area ‖ the part of the hind leg of a horse between hock and pastern joint

in·sti·gate (ínstigeit) *pres. part.* **in·sti·gat·ing** *past and past part.* **in·sti·gat·ed** *v.t.* to bring about by inciting, *to instigate a rebellion* ‖ to incite (someone) [fr. L. *instigare* (*instigatus*)]

in·sti·ga·tion (instigéiʃən) *n.* an instigating or being instigated ‖ something that instigates, a stimulus [fr. L. *instigatio* (*instigationis*)]

in·sti·ga·tor (ínstigeitər) *n.* someone who instigates

in·still, in·stil (instíl) *pres. part.* **in·still·ing, in·stil·ling** *past and past part.* **in·stilled** *v.t.* to cause someone to absorb (ideas, feelings etc.) gradually ‖ to put in drop by drop [fr. L. *instillare,* to put in by drops]

in·stil·la·tion (instəléiʃən) *n.* the act of instilling ‖ something instilled [fr. L. *instillatio* (*instillationis*)]

in·stinct 1. (ínstiŋkt) *n.* a specific, complex pattern of responses by an organism, supposedly inherited, which is quite independent of any thought processes: the instinct that attracts moths to bright-colored flowers for food may also attract them to a candle flame at night and destroy them ‖ (*pop.*) the ability to form a judgment without using the reasoning process, *he can tell a good picture by instinct* ‖ (*pop.*) any drive or impulse **2.** (instíŋkt) *adj.* (*rhet.*, with 'with') deeply imbued **in·stínc·tive, in·stinc·tual** *adjs* [fr. L. *instinguere* (*instinctus*), to incite]

In·sti·tut de France (ɛ̃sti:tydəfrɑ̃s) a French cultural institution founded in 1795, today comprising five academies: l'académie française (*FRENCH ACADEMY), l'académie des inscriptions et belles-lettres, l'académie des sciences, l'académie des beaux-arts and l'académie des sciences morales et politiques

in·sti·tute (ínstitu:t, ínstitju:t) *n.* an institution for study or research ‖ an institution devoted to some specific welfare purpose ‖ (*Br.*) an institution offering social and educational activities for adults, *the village institute* ‖ a building or offices for any of these purposes ‖ (*pl.*) a collection or summary of principles, esp. in law ‖ a short course of instruction or a seminar [fr. L. *institutum,* purpose, plan]

institute *pres. part.* **in·sti·tut·ing** *past and past part.* **in·sti·tut·ed** *v.t.* to set up, found, *to institute an annual poetry festival* ‖ to take the initial steps that will cause (something) to come into being, *to institute an inquiry* ‖ to invest (a clergyman) with a spiritual charge [fr. L. *instituere* (*institutus*)]

Institute for Advanced Study a research center in Princeton, New Jersey, founded in 1930 for postdoctorate scholars, esp. mathematicians and historians. It shares facilities with Princeton University but is a distinct organization

in·sti·tu·tion (institú:ʃən, institjú:ʃən) *n.* an organization whose purpose is to further public welfare, learning etc. ‖ the building or group of buildings used by such an establishment ‖ the act of instituting something ‖ the investing of a clergyman with his spiritual charge ‖ an established law or custom ‖ (*pop.*) a person who is a familiar sight in a locality ‖ (*pl.*) a collection of rules or laws **in·sti·tú·tion·al** *adj.* pertaining to

an institution or institutions ‖ having organized institutions, *institutional religion* [O.F.]

institutional advertising (*Am.=Br.* prestige advertising) publicity intended not to increase short-term sales but to establish a reputation for excellence with a view to long-term sales increase

in·sti·tu·tion·al·ism (institú:ʃənlizəm, ìnstitjú:ʃən'lizəm) *n.* belief in the usefulness or authority of established institutions (e.g. in religion) ‖ the characteristic rigidity, standardization etc. apt to pervade a public or private institution or to affect the outlook of its officials

in·sti·tu·tion·al·ize (institú:ʃən'laiz, ìnstitjú:ʃən'laiz) *pres. part.* **in·sti·tu·tion·al·iz·ing** *past and past part.* **in·sti·tu·tion·al·ized** *v.t.* to make institutional in character

In·sti·tu·to Na·cio·nal de Re·for·ma A·gra·ria (i:nsti:tú:tɒnɑsjɒnál de refɔ́rmaɑgrárjɑ) (*abbr.* INRA) a revolutionary instrument of agrarian reform which Fidel Castro formed in Cuba during his struggle against Batista. In the first years of the revolution it served as the real government of Cuba, with authority over the ministries

in·struct (instrʌ́kt) *v.t.* to teach (a person) ‖ to command, order, esp. formally, *to instruct one's lawyer to make an inquiry* ‖ to advise, inform, *the judge instructed the jury about procedure* [fr. L. *instruere* (*instructus*), to pile up]

in·struc·tion (instrʌ́kʃən) *n.* the act of instructing ‖ knowledge imparted by instructing ‖ (*pl.*) a direction for procedure, *the instructions are on the bottle* ‖ (*pl.*) a set of orders or an order, *he had distinct instructions to be at the house* ‖ (*computer*) a code that sets in motion an operation in a program **in·strúc·tion·al** *adj.* [O.F.]

in·struc·tive (instrʌ́ktiv) *adj.* serving to instruct, *instructive criticisms* [fr. L. *instruere* (*instructus*), to pile up]

in·struc·tor (instrʌ́ktər) *n.* someone who instructs, a teacher ‖ a college or university teacher ranking next below an assistant professor **in·strúc·tor·ship** *n.* **in·strúc·tress** *n.* a female instructor [L.]

in·stru·ment (ínstrəmənt) **1.** *n.* any object used for making, doing, achieving or promoting something, an implement, *surgical instruments* ‖ a means, *language is an instrument for communication* ‖ a person made use of by another ‖ a device for producing music ‖ (*law*) a deed, bond or other document embodying a right or obligation **2.** *v.t.* to equip with instruments ‖ to orchestrate (a score) [F.]

in·stru·men·tal (instrəmént'l) *adj.* serving as an instrument, helping to bring something about ‖ (*mus.*) written for or performed on instruments or an instrument, not vocal ‖ of, relating to or involving mechanical instruments, *instrumental navigation* ‖ (*gram.*) of or designating a case denoting the means in an action **in·stru·mén·tal·ism** *n.* the theory in pragmatism that the veracity of ideas is determined by their utility **in·stru·mén·tal·ist** *n.* a performer on a musical instrument **in·stru·men·tál·i·ty** *n.* the quality or state of being instrumental ‖ agency or means [F.]

instrumental conditioning (*behavioral psych.*) a procedure that provides rewards to reinforce a desired spontaneous response. *also* operant conditioning

in·stru·men·ta·tion (instrəməntéiʃən) *n.* (*mus.*) the arrangement of a composition for particular instruments ‖ the use or installation of mechanical instruments ‖ the branch of science concerned with the development and use of instruments [F.]

instrument flying navigation of an aircraft completely by data obtained from the instruments inside it

instrument landing system (*abbr.* I.L.S.) a system for guiding aircraft safely to the ground by radio beams

in·sub·or·di·nate (insəbɔ́rd'nit) *adj.* not submitting to authority, rebellious

in·sub·or·di·na·tion (insəbɔrd'néiʃən) *n.* the quality or state of being insubordinate

in·sub·stan·tial (insəbstænʃəl) *adj.* not firm or solid, weak, *insubstantial arguments* ‖ unreal, imaginary, *insubstantial fears* **in·sub·stan·ti·al·i·ty** (insəbstænʃi:æliti:) *n.* fr. L.L. and M.L. *insubstantialis,* not real]

in·suf·fer·a·ble (insʌ́fərəb'l) *adj.* very hard to endure, *insufferable agonies* ‖ not to be tolerated, *insufferable rudeness* **in·súf·fer·a·bly** *adv.* [fr. IN- (not)+ obs. *sufferable,* tolerable]

in·suf·fi·cien·cy (insəfíʃənsi:) *pl.* **in·suf·fi·cien·**

cies *n.* the quality or state of being insufficient || an instance of this, *to be aware of one's own insufficiencies* || (*med.*) failure of an organ or tissue (esp. a muscle or heart valve) to perform its normal function [fr. L.L. *insufficientia*]

in·suf·fi·cient (insəfíʃənt) *adj.* not sufficient [O.F. or fr. L. *insufficiens* (*insufficientis*)]

in·suf·flate (insʌfleit, ínsəfleit) *pres. part.* **in·suf·flat·ing** *past and past part.* **in·suf·flat·ed** *v.t.* to blow or breathe on or into || (*med.*) to blow into an opening in the body [fr. L. *insufflare* (*insufflatus*), to blow into]

in·suf·fla·tion (insəfléiʃən) *n.* an insufflating or being insufflated || (*eccles.*) a breathing upon a person or the water at baptism, to symbolize divine inspiration and the expelling of evil spirits [fr. L. *insufflatio* (*insufflationis*)]

in·suf·fla·tor (insəfleitər) *n.* a device for insufflating

in·su·lar (ínsulər, ínsjulər) *adj.* of, inhabiting, situated on or forming an island || narrow-minded, having or showing local prejudices, *an insular attitude* || (*med.*) of certain islands of cells or tissue **in·su·lar·i·ty** (insulǽriti:, insjulǽriti:) *n.* [fr. L. *insularis*]

Insular Cases U.S. judicial cases following the Spanish-American War, to decide whether the inhabitants of U.S. colonies had the same rights as U.S. citizens. The U.S. Supreme Court declared (1901) that such inhabitants enjoy the protection of the Constitution only when they are specifically granted such rights by Congress

in·su·late (ínsuleit, ínsjuleit) *pres. part.* **in·su·lat·ing** *past and past part.* **in·su·lat·ed** *v.t.* (*phys.*) to prevent (a conductor) from receiving or emitting energy in the form of heat, electricity etc., usually by surrounding it with a non-conductor || to place in an isolated situation, to segregate **in·su·la·tion** *n.* an insulating or being insulated || material used to insulate **in·su·la·tor** *n.* a material or device that serves to insulate [fr. L. *insula*, island]

in·su·lin (ínsulin, ínsjulin) *n.* a hormone, produced by the islets of Langerhans, that maintains the level of sugar in the blood. The synthetic material is used in the treatment of diabetes mellitus [fr. L. *insula*, island]

insulin pump (*med.*) device that functions as an artificial pancreas to deliver insulin into bloodstream in steady amounts

in·sult (ínsʌlt) *n.* a remark or act showing contempt and calculated to offend someone in his dignity [F.]

in·sult (insʌlt) *v.t.* to abuse in speech or action in such a way as to show contempt [fr. L. *insultare*, to leap upon]

in·su·per·a·bil·i·ty (insu:pərəbíliti:) *n.* the quality or state of being insuperable

in·su·per·a·ble (insú:pərəb'l) *adj.* (usually of abstractions) that cannot be overcome or passed over, *an insuperable barrier to friendship* **in·su·per·a·bly** *adv.* [fr. L. *insuperabilis*]

in·sup·por·ta·ble (insəpórtəb'l) *adj.* not bearable, unendurable || not justifiable or provable, *insupportable allegations* **in·sup·pór·ta·bly** *adv.* [F. or fr. eccles. L. *insupportabilis*]

in·sur·a·bil·i·ty (inʃuərəbíliti:) *n.* the quality or state of being insurable

in·sur·a·ble (inʃúərəb'l) *adj.* capable of being insured

in·sur·ance (inʃúərəns) *n.* the practice by which an individual secures financial compensation for a specified loss or damage resulting from risk of any sort, by contract with a company to which he pays regular premiums || the profession of drawing up such contracts || the contract drawn up || the protection afforded by this || the premium demanded for such protection || the sum for which something is insured [fr. O.F. *enseurance*]

insurance policy the contract drawn up between an individual and an insurance company

in·sur·ant (inʃúərənt) *n.* someone to whom an insurance policy is issued [INSURE]

in·sure (inʃúər) *pres. part.* **in·sur·ing** *past and past part.* **in·sured** *v.t.* to take out insurance for, *to insure one's property against theft* || to issue an insurance policy for, *the company insured his property for $10,000* || to ensure || *v.i.* (often with 'against') to make provision || to contract for or take out insurance **in·súr·er** *n.* a person or company issuing an insurance policy [alt. of ENSURE]

in·sur·gence (insə́:rdʒəns) *n.* an insurrection **in·sur·gen·cy** (insə́:rdʒənsi:) *n.* the state or quality of being insurgent

in·sur·gent (insə́:rdʒənt) **1.** *n.* a rebel against a lawful government or civil authority || a member of a political party who rebels against the party line **2.** *adj.* rebelling against a lawful government or civil authority || rebelling against a political party line [fr. L. *insurgens* (*insurgentis*), rising up]

in·sur·mount·a·ble (insərmáuntəb'l) *adj.* not capable of being overcome, *insurmountable difficulties* **in·sur·móunt·a·bly** *adv.*

in·sur·rec·tion (insərékʃən) *n.* organized opposition to authority || a revolt **in·sur·réc·tion·al** *adj.* **in·sur·réc·tion·ar·y 1.** *adj.* of, involving or producing insurrection **2.** *pl.* **in·sur·rec·tion·ar·ies** *n.* someone who takes part in an insurrection **in·sur·réc·tion·ist** *n.* [F.]

in·sus·cep·ti·bil·i·ty (insəseptəbíliti:) *n.* the quality or state of being insusceptible

in·sus·cep·ti·ble (insəséptəb'l) *adj.* not susceptible

in·swing·er (ínswiŋər) *n.* (*cricket*) a ball swerving in flight from the bowler's hand from off to leg

int. interest || international || interval

in·tact (intǽkt) *adj.* left in its complete state, undamaged [fr. L. *intactus*]

in·tag·lio (intáljou, intǽljou) *n.* an engraved design in stone, esp. one cut into a hollow below the plane surface, giving a relief image when pressed into wax etc. || a seal or gem engraved in this way (cf. CAMEO) || the technique of engraving designs in this way || (*printing*) a process in which the design, etched or engraved into the surface of the plates, provides ink-retaining hollows from which the impression is taken [Ital.]

in·take (ínteik) *n.* the place where a liquid or gas is taken into a pipe etc. || a taking in, *an intake of breath* || a quantity or amount taken in || (*mining*) an air shaft || (*Br., mil.*) a batch of recruits

in·tan·gi·bil·i·ty (intændʒəbíliti:) *n.* the quality of state of being intangible

in·tan·gi·ble (intǽndʒəb'l) **1.** *adj.* not tangible || not readily defined, vague, *intangible fears* **2.** *n.* something that is not tangible **in·tán·gi·bly** *adv.* [fr. M.L. *intangibilis*]

in·tar·si·a (intársi:ə) *n.* a decoration consisting of pieces of wood inlaid as a mosaic in a wood background || the art of making this decoration [G. fr. Ital. *intarsio*]

in·te·ger (íntidʒər) *n.* (*math.*) a whole number || an entity [L.=whole]

in·te·gra·ble (íntigrəb'l) *adj.* (*math.*) capable of being integrated [fr. L. *integrare*, to make whole]

in·te·gral (íntigrəl) **1.** *adj.* necessary to complete an entity, essentially part of some whole, *English is an integral part of his studies* || forming a single unit with something else, *the handle is integral with the shaft* || whole and complete || (*math.*) related to an integer || (*math.*) concerned with integration **2.** *n.* the integral whole || (*math.*) the result of the process of mathematical integration **in·te·gral·i·ty** (intigrǽliti:) *n.* [fr. L.L. *integralis*, pertaining to a whole]

integral calculus a branch of mathematical analysis that deals with the techniques of finding expressions for and of evaluating the integrals of functions, esp. for the calculation of areas, lengths over curves, volumes, moments etc., and with the solution of simple differential equations

integral domain (*math.*) a ring in which the order of entries is not material, where the product of the nonzero elements is never zero. *also* entire ring

in·te·gral·is·mo (i:ntegrali:smɔ) *n.* the fascist movement in Brazil

in·te·grand (íntigrænd) *n.* (*math.*) an expression to be integrated [fr. L. *integrandus* fr. *integrare*, to make whole]

in·te·grant (íntigrənt) **1.** *adj.* integral **2.** *n.* a component part [fr. L. *integrans* (*integrantis*)]

in·te·grate (íntigreit) *pres. part.* **in·te·grat·ing** *past and past part.* **in·te·grat·ed** *v.t.* to make complete by adding parts || to absorb into an existing whole, *immigrants are quickly integrated into the community* || (*math.*) to calculate the integral of || (*math.*) to perform the process of integration upon || to end the racial segregation of, give full, equal membership in a group or in society to || *v.i.* to become racially integrated [fr. L. *integrare* (*integratus*)]

integrated battlefield (*mil.*) war area involving nuclear, chemical, and conventional weapons

integrated circuit (*electr.*) an electronic circuit consisting of a series of interconnected amplifying devices, transistors, resistors, capacitors in gates, etc., etched or imprinted on a plaque or chip of semiconductor material so as to carry a computer message. *abbr.* IC. —**integrated circuitry** *n.*

in·te·gra·tion (intigréiʃən) *n.* an integrating or being integrated || (*math.*, symbol ∫ or Σ) a process of summing infinitesimals, esp. between stated limits || the coordination of personality and environment || (*psychol.*) the organizing of psychological reactions, perceptions etc. into a balanced, whole personality || the unification of educational systems previously segregated by race || the giving of full civil or membership rights to those deprived of them on racial grounds **in·te·grá·tion·ist** *n.* someone in favor of integration [fr. L. *integratio* (*integrationis*), a renewing, restoring]

in·te·gra·tor (íntigreitər) *n.* a person who or thing that integrates || a device for performing integrations mechanically [L.]

in·teg·ri·ty (intégriti:) *n.* moral soundness, probity || wholeness, completeness, *to perform a work in its integrity* || the quality or state of being unimpaired [fr. L. *integritas*, wholeness]

in·teg·ro·dif·fer·en·tial (intægroudifərénʃəl) *n.* (*math.*) containing both integrals of a function in area measurement and differentials or rate of change measurements, of a function

in·teg·u·ment (intégjumənt) *n.* an outer covering, esp. (*biol.*) a coating structure or layer, e.g. skin, shell or rind **in·teg·u·men·ta·ry** (integjuméntəri:) *adj.* [fr. L. *integumentum*, covering]

in·tel·lect (íntəlekt) *n.* the faculty of knowing, as distinct from feeling or willing || mental power, intelligence || a person of superior reasoning power [fr. L. *intellegere* (*intellectus*), to understand]

in·tel·lec·tion (intəlékʃən) *n.* the act or process of using the intellect || a thought or idea produced by using the intellect [fr. L.L. and M.L. *intellectio* (*intellectionis*)]

in·tel·lec·tive (intəléktiv) *adj.* relating to or involving the intellect [fr. L.L. *intellectivus*]

in·tel·lec·tu·al (intəléktʃuːəl) **1.** *adj.* relating to, using or performed by the intellect || (of a person) concerned with the activities of the intellect **2.** *n.* a person who is concerned with the activities of the intellect **in·tel·léc·tu·al·ism** *n.* (*philos.*) a doctrine discovering the principle of reality in reason alone || (*philos.*) the doctrine that knowledge is derived from reason alone || preoccupation with the process of thought at the expense of its aims [fr. L. *intellectualis*]

in·tel·lec·tu·al·i·ty (intələktʃuːǽliti:) *n.* the quality or state of being intellectual [fr. L.L. *intellectualitas*]

in·tel·lec·tu·al·ize (intəléktʃuːəlaiz) *pres. part.* **in·tel·lec·tu·al·iz·ing** *past and past part.* **in·tel·lec·tu·al·ized** *v.t.* to make intellectual in character, treat as an object of purely intellectual interest, esp. by neglecting emotional factors || *v.i.* to reason, esp. leaving practical considerations aside

in·tel·li·gence (intélidʒəns) *n.* the ability to perceive logical relationships and use one's knowledge to solve problems and respond appropriately to novel situations || news, information || the obtaining of secret information, esp. for military purposes || (*computer*) capability of performing some functions usu. associated with human reasoning, etc. || an organization for the obtaining of such information [F.]

intelligence amplifier any aid to solving problems, e.g., slide rule, computer, mathematical rules

intelligence quotient (*abbr.* I.Q.) a number supposed to denote a person's intelligence, obtained by dividing his mental age by his chronological age and multiplying the result by 100: a person of average intelligence would thus have an I.Q. of 100

intelligence test any of various standardized tests designed to measure the capacity of a person to take in information, solve problems etc.

in·tel·li·gent (intélidʒənt) *adj.* having or showing a high degree of intelligence || endowed with intelligence, capable of reasoning [fr. L. *intelligens* (*intelligentis*), understanding]

intelligent printer (*computer*) output device using laser light beams to transform digital data into printed characters and graphics, eliminating impact printers. *Cf* LASER-BEAM PRINTER

in·tel·li·gent·si·a (intelidʒéntsi:ə) n. (collect.) the class in a society comprising the well-educated and esp. intellectual persons, as distinguished from manual workers [Russ. intelligentsiya fr. L. intelligentia, intelligence]

in·tel·li·gi·bil·i·ty (intelidʒəbíliti:) n. the quality or state of being intelligible

in·tel·li·gi·ble (intélidʒəb'l) adj. that can be understood, an intelligible explanation || (philos.) that can be perceived by the intellect **in·tél·li·gi·bly** adv. [fr. L. intelligibilis]

In·tel·post (íntelpoust) n. proposed U.S. international electronic postal service

In·tel·sat (íntelsæt) n. **1.** (acronym) for International Telecommunications Satellite, a consortium of 70 nations cooperating in communications by satellite **2.** the satellites

in·tem·per·ance (intémpərəns) n. lack of moderation, esp. habitual excessive indulgence in alcohol [F. intempérance]

in·tem·per·ate (intémpərit) adj. not temperate [fr. L. intemperatus]

in·tend (inténd) v.t. to have as intention, he intends to leave tomorrow || to have in mind a specified purpose, a destination for, he intended the gift as a mark of appreciation [M.E. entende fr. F., ult. fr. L. intendere, to stretch out]

in·tend·ance (inténdəns) n. the function of an intendant [F.]

in·tend·an·cy (inténdənsi:) pl. **in·tend·an·cies** n. the position or function of an intendant [INTENDANT]

in·tend·ant (inténdənt) n. a man in charge of a public department in some countries || (esp. hist.) the controller of a large household || (F. hist.) the king's representative in a province, charged with the inspection of various public services in the 17th and 18th cc. [F.]

in·tend·ed (inténdid) **1.** adj. planned || deliberate, an intended snub **2.** n. (pop.) one's fiancé or fiancée

in·tend·ment (inténdmənt) n. (law) the true legal meaning [F. entendement, understanding]

in·tense (inténs) adj. very great, extreme, intense heat, intense concentration || (of a color) very deep or concentrated || (of a person) fervently earnest [F.]

in·ten·si·fi·ca·tion (intensifikéiʃən) n. an intensifying or being intensified

in·ten·si·fy (inténsifai) pres. part. **in·ten·si·fy·ing** past and past part. **in·ten·si·fied** v.t. to render (a quality, emotion etc.) more intense || (photog.) to increase the sharpness of (the image) by chemical action || v.i. (of a quality, emotion etc.) to become more intense [fr. L. intensus, stretched]

in·ten·sion (inténʃən) n. (logic) the sum of the attributes contained in a concept or implied by a term **in·tén·sion·al** adj. [fr. L. intensio (intensionis), a stretching forth]

in·ten·si·ty (inténsiti:) pl. **in·ten·si·ties** n. the quality or state of being intense || (phys.) the magnitude of force or energy per unit area, charge or mass, used as a measure of the activity or effect of physical agencies, e.g. electric-field intensity, luminous-flux intensity, sound intensity etc.

in·ten·sive (inténsiv) **1.** adj. concentrated, an intensive study of the classics || (agric.) of a system of farming aimed at raising yield per unit area || (gram.) of a word giving force or emphasis to another, e.g. 'himself' in the sentence 'he did it himself' **2.** n. (gram.) an intensive word, prefix etc. [F. intensif]

intensive care unit (med.) a specialized nursing unit within a hospital where seriously ill patients receive constant nursing care and electronically monitored observation. abbr. **ICU.** — **intensive-care** adj.

in·tent (intént) adj. (with 'on' or 'upon') having a firm intention, intent on doing good || (with 'on' or 'upon') having one's attention concentrated, intent on one's studies || intense, searching, an intent look [fr. L. intendere (intentus), to stretch, strain]

intent n. intention, with good intent, with intent to steal **to all intents and purposes** virtually, practically [M.E. entente fr. O.F.]

in·ten·tion (inténʃən) n. that which one is resolved to do, purpose || meaning, significance, what is the intention behind this question? || (logic) a concept || (eccles.) the will to apply the benefits of prayers or a mass to a particular person or object || (eccles.) the person or object for whom the prayers or mass are meant || (med.) the process or manner in which a wound heals (*FIRST INTENTION, *SECOND INTENTION) [O.F. entention]

in·ten·tion·al (inténʃən'l) adj. done on purpose || of or relating to a logical concept [fr. M.L. intentionalis, of or pertaining to intention]

in·ten·tioned (inténʃənd) adj. having or showing an intention of a specified nature, well-intentioned remarks

in·ter (intó:r) pres. part. **in·ter·ring** past and past part. **in·terred** v.t. to put (a dead body) in the ground or in a tomb [O.F. enterrer]

inter- (íntər) prefix between, within || reciprocal || occurring, played, carried on etc. between || involving two or more [L. inter prep. and adv., between, among]

in·ter·act (intərǽkt) v.i. to act upon each other, wages and prices interact ceaselessly **in·ter·ac·tion** (intərǽkʃən) n. **in·ter·ác·tive** adj.

Inter-American Conference, Tenth a conference held (1954) in Caracas, with all members represented except Costa Rica. John Foster Dulles, U.S. Secretary of State, who had called the meeting on behalf of United Fruit, sponsored an anti-Communist resolution, which was adopted by a vote of 17 to 1 (Guatemala opposing, Mexico and Argentina abstaining). A successful coup by Col. Castillo Armas was at once engineered in Guatemala

Inter-American Development Bank (abbr. IDB), a U.S. government agency established (1959) to assist Latin-American republics to develop their human and natural resources. The bank was originally capitalized at $1 billion, of which $450 million was contributed by the U.S.A. It approved its first loan in 1961

Inter-American Economic and Social Council a meeting of the Organization of American States which adopted (1961) the Charter of Punta del Este

Inter-American Treaty of Reciprocal Assistance (Rio Treaty), a treaty signed (1947) in Rio de Janeiro which declared that an armed attack by any state (American as well as non-American) against any American state would be considered an attack against all the American states

in·ter·breed (intərbrí:d) pres. part. **in·ter·breed·ing** past and past part. **in·ter·bred** (intərbréd) v.t. to crossbreed (plants or animals of different varieties) || v.i. (of plants or animals of different varieties) to undergo crossbreeding

in·ter·ca·lar·y (intó:rkələri:, intərkǽləri:) adj. (of a day or month) intercalated || (of a year) having an intercalated day, month etc. || interpolated [fr. L. intercalarius]

in·ter·ca·late (intó:rkəleit) pres. part. **in·ter·ca·lat·ing** part and past part. **in·ter·ca·lat·ed** v.t. to insert (a day or month) in a calendar, in order to make the calendar year correspond to the solar year || to interpolate || (geol.) to interpose between rock strata [fr. L. intercalare (intercalatus)]

in·ter·ca·la·tion (intə:rkəléiʃən) n. an intercalating or being intercalated || something intercalated [fr. L. intercalatio (intercalationis)]

in·ter·cede (intərsí:d) pres. part. **in·ter·ced·ing** past and past part. **in·ter·ced·ed** v.i. to intervene on behalf of another || to intervene so as to attempt reconciliation [fr. L. intercedere]

in·ter·cel·lu·lar (intərséljulər) adj. placed between or among cells

in·ter·cept (intərsépt) **1.** v.t. to seize (something) before it can reach its destination, to intercept enemy messages || (math.) to bound (part of a line, curve etc.) between two points **2.** n. (math.) a part of a line, curve etc. bounded in this way **in·ter·cep·tion** (intərsépʃən) n. **in·ter·cép·tive** adj. **in·ter·cép·tor** n. someone who or something that intercepts || a fighting plane with strong climbing power used in defense [fr. L. intercipere (interceptus), to interrupt]

in·ter·ces·sion (intərséʃən) n. the act of interceding || a prayer or petition on another's behalf [fr. L. intercessio (intercessionis)]

in·ter·ces·sor (intərsésər) n. a person who intercedes for another **in·ter·cés·so·ry** adj. [L.]

in·ter·change (íntərtʃeindʒ) n. a substitution for one another of two things or two sets of things, interchange of the front and rear tires evens wear || mutual exchange, an interchange of letters || a junction on separate levels of two or more highways, allowing vehicles to change from one to another without lines of traffic crossing [O.F. entrechange, a change]

in·ter·change (intərtʃéindʒ) pres. part. **in·ter·**

changing past and past part. **in·ter·changed** v.t. to substitute (two things or sets of things) for each other, to interchange front and rear tires || to exchange, to interchange ideas || v.i. (of two things or sets of things) to change places [O.F. entrechangier, to change]

in·ter·change·a·bil·i·ty (intərtʃeindʒəbíliti:) n. the quality or state of being interchangeable

in·ter·change·a·ble (intərtʃéindʒəb'l) adj. (of two or more things) capable of being mutually substituted **in·ter·chánge·a·bly** adv. [O.F. entrechangeable]

in·ter·col·le·giate (intərkəlí:dʒit, intərkəlí:dʒi:it) adj. participated in or supported by two or more colleges or universities, an intercollegiate orchestra

in·ter·com (íntərkom) n. (pop.) a two-way communication system in an office, aircraft, ship etc. [shortened fr. intercommunication system]

in·ter·com·mu·ni·cate (intərkəmjú:nikeit) pres. part. **in·ter·com·mu·ni·cat·ing** past and past part. **in·ter·com·mu·ni·cat·ed** v.i. (of two or more things) to communicate **in·ter·com·mu·ni·cá·tion** n.

in·ter·com·mun·ion (intərkəmjú:njən) n. communion between Churches or denominations officially recognizing one another

in·ter·com·mu·ni·ty (intərkəmjú:niti:) n. the quality of being common to various bodies || a sharing in common

in·ter·con·nect (intərkənékt) v.t. to connect (two or more things) || v.i. (of two or more things) to be connected

in·ter·con·nec·tion Br. also **in·ter·con·nex·ion** (intərkənékʃən) n. an interconnecting or being interconnected

in·ter·con·ti·nen·tal (intərkontinént'l) adj. between or among continents

in·ter·cos·tal (intərkóstəl, intərkóstəl) adj. (anat.) between the ribs || (bot.) between the veins or nerves of a leaf [fr. Mod. L. intercostalis]

in·ter·course (íntərkɔrs, íntərkours) n. reciprocal social or commercial dealings between individuals, groups or nations || sexual union between two people [O.F. entrecours, exchange]

in·ter·cur·rent (intərkó·rənt, intərkʌ́rənt) adj. occurring during the course of some process || (of a disease) occurring during the course of another disease and affecting it

in·ter·date (intərdéit) v. to have social contact with a person of another religion

in·ter·de·nom·i·na·tion·al (intərdinɔminéiʃən'l) adj. common to or involving two or more religious denominations

in·ter·den·tal (intərdént'l) adj. (phon.) articulated by placing the tip of the tongue between the front teeth

in·ter·de·pend (intərdipénd) v.i. to depend upon one another

in·ter·de·pend·ence (intərdipéndəns) n. dependence of two or more things on each other **in·ter·de·pénd·en·cy** n.

in·ter·de·pen·dent (intərdipéndənt) adj. dependent upon each other

in·ter·dict 1. (íntərdikt) n. (Roman Catholicism) a barring of a person or group from the sacraments, Church services and Christian burial || a decree that prohibits **2.** (intərdíkt) v.t. to place an interdict on [M.E. entredit fr. O.F.]

in·ter·dic·tion (intərdíkʃən) n. an interdicting or being interdicted [fr. L. interdictio (interdictionis)]

in·ter·dic·to·ry (intərdíktəri:) adj. relating to or having the nature of an interdict [fr. L.L. interdictorius]

in·ter·est (íntərist, íntrist) **1.** n. curiosity about, or intellectual or emotional involvement in something || something on which these feelings are fixed, music is his main interest || the power to arouse these feelings, local color added interest to the novel || concern for one's own advantage or profit, to act out of interest || advantage, profit, it is to your interest to work hard || importance, consequence, a matter of interest to the community || a legal or financial stake, right or title to a thing, she holds a 60% interest in the firm || a premium paid for the use of capital, 6½% interest (*COMPOUND INTEREST, *SIMPLE INTEREST) || the money so paid || a group having a common concern in industry etc., the shipping interest (*VESTED INTEREST) **in the interest of** for the sake of, in the interest of humanity **2.** v.t. to arouse the attention or curiosity of || to cause to participate, esp. financially, try to interest a bank in the plan || to involve the welfare of, affect **in·ter·est·ed** *adj.* feeling or showing attention or curiosity ‖ having a share or concern in something and esp. likely to be prejudiced for this reason, *he is an interested party and cannot serve on the jury* ‖ motivated by a concern for one's own welfare or gain **ín·ter·est·ing** *adj.* [fr. older *interess* fr. A.F.]

interest group groups organized to promote legislation or political action or to change public opinion. *also* lobby, pressure group

in·ter·face (íntərfeis) *n.* a surface forming the common boundary of two bodies or two spaces ‖ the boundary between phases in a heterogeneous system, e.g. the surface formed between a liquid and a solid or between two immiscible liquids ‖ (*jargon*) a device that bridges different systems, people, ideas, technologies, etc. ‖ point at which two elements of a system join ‖ the method of integrating these two elements **in·ter·fa·cial** (intərféiʃəl) *adj.*

in·ter·fac·ing (intərfeisiŋ) *n.* (*sewing*) a stiffening cloth sewn between the facing and the outside of a garment to help collars etc. to keep their form

in·ter·fere (intərfíər) *pres. part.* **in·ter·fer·ing** *past* and *past part.* **in·ter·fered** *v.i.* (with 'with') to conflict in such a way as to hinder something, *the pillar interferes with the view* ‖ to take an active but unwelcome part in someone else's activity ‖ (of a horse) to strike the opposite fetlock with a hoof ‖ (*phys.*, in wave motion) to superimpose an opposite displacement of a medium ‖ (*patent law*) to claim priority for an invention ‖ (*football*) to clear the way for the ball carrier by blocking players of the opposing team ‖ (*football*) to obstruct illegally an attempt by a player to receive a pass **in·ter·fér·ence** *n.* the act of interfering ‖ (*games*) obstruction, e.g. (*football*) the obstruction of opposing tacklers to protect the ball carrier ‖ (*football*) the illegal blocking of the receiving of the pass ‖ (*radio*) a confusion of sounds preventing good reception ‖ (*radio*) that which produces such a confusion ‖ a wave phenomenon that results from the mutual effect of two or more waves passing through a given region at the same time, producing reinforcement at some points and neutralization at other points. The displacement at any point of intersection of two or more waves is given by the principle of superposition. Interference is observed in sound waves (*BEAT) and light waves (*NEWTON'S RINGS), and is used in analytical optical instruments for the measurement of small linear displacements and other effects (*INTERFEROMETER) **to run interference for** (*football*) to clear the way for (the ball carrier) by obstructing opposing tacklers **in·ter·fe·ren·tial** (intərfərénʃəl) *adj.* [O.F. *s'entreférir*, to strike each other]

in·ter·fer·om·e·ter (intərfərómitər) *n.* an optical instrument that allows two beams of light derived from a single source (and thus of the same frequency and in phase at identical distances from the source) to traverse paths whose difference in length determines the nature of the interference pattern obtained when the beams are allowed to interfere. The wavelength of light can be measured if the path length difference is known, and vice versa

interferometer homing (*mil.*) a missile-guidance system depending on echoes received by antenna precisely spaced within a few wave lengths

in·ter·fer·on (intərfíərən) *n.* (*biochem.*) antibody protein sensitive to foreign nucleic acid, produced in cells of some mammals as a deterrent to replication of viruses and bacteria, esp. those created by gene-splicing techniques in other organisms

in·ter·fold (intərfóuld) *v.t.* to fold (paper sheets) so that one folds around a fold of the next one

in·ter·fuse (intərfjú:z) *pres. part.* **in·ter·fus·ing** *past* and *past part.* **in·ter·fused** *v.t.* to mix intimately (one thing with another) ‖ to pervade ‖ *v.i.* to intermingle, blend **in·ter·fu·sion** (intərfjú:ʒən) *n.* [fr. L. *interfundere* (*interfusus*), to pour between]

in·ter·im (íntərim) 1. *n.* an interval between two actions **in the interim** meanwhile 2. *adj.* provisional, temporary, *an interim decision* [L. *adv.*=meanwhile]

in·te·ri·or (intíəri:ər) 1. *adj.* of, relating to or placed at the inner part of something ‖ having to do with the domestic affairs of a country, *interior markets* ‖ in or towards the part of a country away from the coast or frontier ‖ having to do with the mind or soul ‖ having to do with the essential nature of something, *the interior*

meaning *of the play* 2. *n.* the inner part of something ‖ a picture or a stage or movie set showing the inside of a house or other building ‖ the part of a country away from the coast or frontier ‖ the inner character or nature of someone or something **the Interior** (in administrative titles) the domestic affairs of a country [L., comp. of *inter*, within]

interior angle (*math.*) the angle inside a polygon between adjacent sides ‖ (*math.*) the angle made by a transversal inside either of a pair of straight lines which it intersects

interior monologue a literary device in which a character's thoughts, memories etc. are presented as a continuous flow emerging from the subconscious into the conscious. It is employed in stream-of-consciousness writing

Interior, U.S. Department of, federal cabinet-level department that oversees conservation and fish and wildlife programs, manages the national parks system and mineral mining and administers Indian and territorial affairs. Founded in 1849, its departments include the National Park Service, the Bureau of Mines, the U.S. Fish and Wildlife Service and the Bureau of Indian Affairs

interj. interjection

in·ter·ja·cent (intərdʒéis'nt) *adj.* occurring or situated between or among others [fr. L. *interjacens* (*interjacentis*)]

in·ter·ject (intərdʒékt) *v.t.* to interpose (a remark or question) abruptly in a conversation etc. [fr. L. *interjicere* (*interjectus*), to throw in]

in·ter·jec·tion (intərdʒékʃən) *n.* (*gram.*) an exclamation expressing emotion, not forming part of a sentence: it may be a word or phrase or an inarticulate cry (e.g. 'ouch!') ‖ an interjected remark ‖ the act of interjecting **in·ter·jéc·tion·al, in·ter·jec·to·ry** (intərdʒéktəri) *adjs.* [F.]

in·ter·lace (intərléis) *pres. part.* **in·ter·lac·ing** *past* and *past part.* **in·ter·laced** *v.t.* to cross (things) over and under as if by weaving, *to interlace one's fingers* ‖ to vary by mixing in other things, *to interlace a talk with demonstrations* ‖ (*computer*) to arrange data of a sequence among data of other sequences in storage, retaining the identity of each; designed to reduce access time ‖ *v.i.* to be combined as if by weaving **in·ter·láce·ment** *n.* [M.E. *entrelace* fr. F.]

In·ter·la·ken (íntərlɑkən,intərlúkən) a resort (pop. 4,735) on the Aare between Lakes Thun and Brienz in Bern, Switzerland

in·ter·lard (intərlárd) *v.t.* to intersperse (speech or writing) with foreign or extraneous words etc. [F. *entrelarder*, to mix with layers of fat]

in·ter·leaf (íntərli:f) *pl.* **in·ter·leaves** (íntərli:vz) *n.* a blank leaf bound between the printed leaves in a book for writing notes on or a sheet of thin paper inserted to protect a color plate

in·ter·leave (intərlí:v) *pres. part.* **in·ter·leav·ing** *past* and *past part.* **in·ter·leaved** *v.t.* to insert an interleaf or interleaves between pages of (a book)

in·ter·line (intərláin) *pres. part.* **in·ter·lin·ing** *past* and *past part.* **in·ter·lined** *v.t.* to write or print something between the lines of (a book etc.) [M.E. fr. M.L. *interlineare*]

in·ter·line (intərláin) *pres. part.* **in·ter·lin·ing** *past* and *past part.* **in·ter·lined** *v.t.* to put a second lining between the ordinary lining and the outer material of (a garment)

in·ter·lin·e·ar (intərlíni:ər) *adj.* (of written or printed matter) inserted between the lines of a text ‖ containing written or printed words between the lines ‖ having different versions on different lines, *an interlinear Bible* [fr. M.L. *interlinearis*]

in·ter·lin·e·a·tion (intərlini:éiʃən) *n.* the act of interlining a text ‖ a written or printed insertion between lines [fr. M.L. *interlineare* (*interlineatus*)]

in·ter·lin·ing (íntərlainiŋ) *n.* a lining between the ordinary lining and the outer material of a garment

in·ter·lock (intərlók) 1. *v.t.* to engage locking parts of (two things) so that they are held rigidly together ‖ to arrange (the parts of a mechanical system) so that they cannot move independently of each other ‖ *v.i.* to be connected in this way 2. *adj.* knitted with interlocking stitches

in·ter·lock·ing (intərlókiŋ) *adj.* of a system for borrowing of power resources among power utilities to meet emergencies

in·ter·lo·cu·tion (intərloukjú:ʃən) *n.* (*rhet.*) conversation, dialogue [fr. L. *interlocutio* (*interlocutionis*)]

in·ter·loc·u·tor (intərlókjutər) *n.* (*rhet.*) a person who takes part in a dialogue or conversation ‖ a person who acts as leader of a minstrel show, putting questions from his place in the middle of the line to the end man [fr. L. *interloqui* (*interlocutus*), to converse]

in·ter·loc·u·to·ry (intərlókjutəri, intərlókjutouri:) *adj.* (*rhet.*) conversational ‖ interjected, *interlocutory oaths* ‖ (*law*) pronounced and arising during legal procedure, not final, *an interlocutory decree* [INTERLOCUTION]

in·ter·lope (intərlóup) *pres. part.* **in·ter·lop·ing** *past* and *past part.* **in·ter·loped** *v.i.* to meddle in the affairs of others ‖ (*hist.*) to interfere illegally in the trading of others **in·ter·lop·er** *n.* someone who interlopes ‖ someone who intrudes on the property of another [fr. INTER-+*lope*, dial. alt. of LEAP]

in·ter·lude (íntərlu:d) *n.* a period of time between two actions ‖ a dramatic or musical performance to fill an interval [fr. M.L. *interludium*]

in·ter·mar·riage (intərmǽridʒ) *n.* marriage between members of different social, racial, religious or tribal groups ‖ marriage between close relations

in·ter·mar·ry (intərmǽri:) *pres. part.* **in·ter·mar·ry·ing** *past* and *past part.* **in·ter·mar·ried** *v.i.* (of members of different social, racial, religious or tribal groups) to marry ‖ (of closely related people) to marry

in·ter·me·di·a (intərmí:di:ə) *n.* 1. art forms involving various arts and sciences, e.g., films, dance, sculpture, and electronics, in one project 2. cinema combined with live entertainment.— **intermedia** *adj. Cf* MIXED MEDIA, MULTIMEDIA

in·ter·me·di·ar·y (intərmí:di:ɛri) 1. *adj.* being between two things, events etc. ‖ of, pertaining to or involving mediation 2. *pl.* **in·ter·me·di·ar·ies** *n.* someone who or something that mediates [fr. L. *intermedium*]

in·ter·me·di·ate (intərmí:di:it) 1. *adj.* being between two things, events, extremes etc. 2. *n.* someone through whom two other parties communicate ‖ something between others in a series ‖ of a motor vehicle, in size between compact and standard [fr. M.L. *intermediatus*]

in·ter·me·di·ate (intərmí:di:eit) *pres. part.* **in·ter·me·di·at·ing** *past* and *past part.* **in·ter·me·di·at·ed** *v.i.* to act as an intermediary **in·ter·me·di·á·tion, in·ter·mé·di·a·tor** *ns*

intermediate boson (*particle phys.*) hypothetical particle, either positively or negatively charged, on which there is no restriction on the number of particles that exist simultaneously in the same state. *also* intermediate vector boson, W particle

in·ter·ment (intá:rmənt) *n.* a burial

in·ter·mez·zo (intərmétsou, intərmédzou) *pl.* **in·ter·mez·zi** (intərmétsi:, intərmédzi:), **in·ter·mez·zos** *n.* a short musical or dramatic piece interpolated in the middle or between the acts of an opera or play ‖ (*mus.*) a short movement between major sections, e.g. of a symphony ‖ (*mus.*) a short concert piece ‖ an episode [Ital.]

in·ter·mi·na·ble (intá:rminəb'l) *adj.* seemingly endless, tediously long, *an interminable lecture* **in·tér·mi·na·bly** *adv.* [F. or fr. L.L. *interminabilis*]

in·ter·min·gle (intərmíŋg'l) *pres. part.* **in·ter·min·gling**, *past* and *past part.* **in·ter·min·gled** *v.t.* to mix (two things) together ‖ to mix (one thing) with other things ‖ *v.i.* to become mixed together

in·ter·mis·sion (intərmíʃən) *n.* (*Am.*=*Br.* interval) an interval between acts of a play or parts of any performance ‖ an interval coming between periods of activity [fr. L. *intermissio* (*intermissionis*)]

in·ter·mit (intərmít) *pres. part.* **in·ter·mit·ting** *past* and *past part.* **in·ter·mit·ted** *v.t.* to cease for a while or from time to time ‖ *v.i.* to stop for a while or from time to time [fr. L. *intermittere*]

in·ter·mit·tence (intərmít'ns) *n.* the quality or state of being intermittent ‖ a ceasing from time to time ‖ an occurring from time to time **in·ter·mít·ten·cy** *pl.* **in·ter·mit·ten·cies** *n.* [F.]

in·ter·mit·tent (intərmít'nt) *adj.* stopping from time to time ‖ occurring at intervals [fr. L. *intermittens* (*intermittentis*)]

intermittent current an electric current that flows and halts intermittently without reversing

in·ter·mix (intərmíks) *v.t.* and *i.*, to mix together, intermingle **in·ter·mix·ture** (intərmíkstʃər) *n.* [fr. older *intermixt*, *adj.* fr. L. *intermiscere* (*intermixtus*), to mix together]

CONCISE PRONUNCIATION KEY: (**a**) æ, c*a*t; ɑ, c*a*r; ɔ f*aw*n; ei, sn*a*ke. (**e**) e, h*e*n; i., sh*ee*p; iə, d*ee*r; ɛə, b*ea*r. (**i**) i, f*i*sh; ai, t*i*ger; ə:, b*i*rd. (**o**) o, *o*x; au, c*ow*; ou, g*oa*t; u, p*oo*r; ɔi, r*oy*al. (**u**) ʌ, d*u*ck; u, b*u*ll; u:, g*oo*se; ə, b*a*cillus; ju:, c*u*be. x, lo*ch*; θ, *th*ink; ð, bo*th*er; z, *Z*en; ʒ, corsa*g*e; dʒ, sava*g*e; ŋ, oranguta*ng*; j, *y*ak; ʃ, *fish*; tʃ, fe*tch*; 'l, rabb*le*; 'n, redd*en*. Complete pronunciation key appears inside front cover.

in·ter·mod·al (intərmóud'l) *adj.* of freight carried by more than one type of carrier to a single destination, e.g., train and truck

in·tern (íntə:rn) **1.** *n.* (also **ín·terne**) a newly qualified doctor serving in a hospital to complete his training **2.** *v.i.* (of a newly qualified doctor) to serve in a hospital to complete one's training ‖ *v.t.* (intə́:rn) to detain (someone, esp. an alien or a prisoner of war) within prescribed boundaries [F. *interne*, internal]

in·ter·nal (intə́:rn'l) *adj.* of or on the inside ‖ inside the body, *internal injuries* ‖ involving the mind, soul, conscience etc. ‖ pertaining to the domestic affairs of a country ‖ pertaining to the essential nature of a thing, intrinsic [fr. M.L. *internalis*]

internal angle an interior angle

internal-combustion engine a heat engine in which the combustion takes place within the engine itself, usually in a cylinder rather than externally in a furnace etc.

internal evidence evidence furnished by the thing under consideration without confirmation from some outside source

internal medicine the branch of medicine that concentrates on the diagnosis and nonsurgical treatment of disease

internal pollution ingestion of harmful synthetic substances

internal revenue (*Am.=Br.* inland revenue) government income from taxation within a country

Internal Security Act of 1950 a U.S. Congressional act which enabled the president to declare an 'internal security emergency' and authorized the attorney general to round up and detain persons believed to be engaged in acts of espionage or sabotage

in·ter·na·tion·al (intərnǽʃən'l) **1.** *adj.* common to, involving or used by two or more nations ‖ known or operating in more than one country, *an international thief* **2.** *n.* (Br.) a player in an official game or match against another country

In·ter·na·tion·al (hist.) any of several worldwide socialist or communist organizations. The 1st International, known as the International Workingmen's Association, was founded (1864) by Marx, and was weakened (1872) by a dispute between Marx and Bakunin, and was dissolved (1876). The 2nd International was formed (1889), but failed in its attempt to prevent war (1914). Efforts to revive it in the 1920s were ineffectual. The 3rd International, the Comintern, was set up by Russia (1919) and dissolved (1943). It was succeeded by the Cominform (1947-56). The 4th International was set up (1937) by Trotsky, in opposition to the Comintern

International Atomic Energy Agency (abbr. I.A.E.A.) an agency of the U.N., set up in 1957 to promote the peaceful uses of atomic energy

international atomic time any of several standardized systems of horology based on atomic resonance, e.g., standard cesium-133 transition. *abbr.* IAT

International Bank for Reconstruction and Development *WORLD BANK

International Brigade (hist.) a military unit, formed of foreign antifascist volunteers, which fought on the side of the republicans in the Spanish Civil War (1936–9)

International Business Machines (abbr. IBM), the world's largest manufacturers of computers. It was originally the Computing-Tabulating-Recording Company, founded (1914) by Thomas John Watson (1874–1956) and renamed (1924)

international candle a unit of luminous intensity equal to that of 5 sq.mm. of platinum at its melting point (1773.5℃.)

International Civil Aviation Organization (abbr. I.C.A.O.) an agency of the U.N., set up in 1947 to promote safety and cooperation in international air transport

International Conference of American States, First a conference held (1889–90) in Washington, D.C. on the initiative of James G. Blaine, U.S. secretary of state. It gave birth to the International Bureau of American Republics, later renamed the Pan-American Union

International Conference of American States, Sixth a conference held (1928) in Havana, at which the U.S. delegation proposed a reform of the Pan-American Union. The motion, that the Union should not exercise political functions, was rejected

International Conference of American States, Seventh a conference held (1933) in Montevideo in which the U.S.A. accepted the doctrine of nonintervention with qualifications

International Conference of American States, Eighth a conference held (1938) in Lima which declared that any attack by a non-American state against any American state would be regarded as an attack against all of them (Declaration of Lima)

International Conference of American States, Ninth a conference held (1948) in Bogotá. The name Union of American Republics was changed to Organization of American States (O.A.S.). The Bogotá Charter established the organizational guidelines for the O.A.S.: International Conferences were renamed Inter-American Conferences; the central and permanent organ of the O.A.S., the Pan-American Union, retained its name and became the general secretariat. Its supervisory board, the former Governing Board of the Pan-American Union, became known as the Council of the Organization. Three permanent organs of this council were established: Inter-American Council of Jurists, Inter-American Economic and Social Council, Inter-American Cultural Council. Meetings of foreign affairs ministers were to be called upon the request and with the consent of member states

International Court of Justice the main judicial organ of the U.N., organized in 1945 to replace the earlier World Court set up in 1922 by the League of Nations. The court, which consists of 15 judges and sits at The Hague, exists to settle international legal disputes. Any breach of its decisions may be referred to the U.N. Security Council

International Criminal Police Commission *INTERPOL

international date line an imaginary line between the poles, running along the 180th meridian except where this would cause local complications, conventionally marking the place where each calendar day begins. A traveler changes the date one day forward on crossing the line from east to west and one day backward on crossing it from west to east

In·ter·na·tion·ale (intərnæʃonǽl, ēternæsjonæl) a revolutionary song used by many socialist and communist parties

International Finance Corporation (abbr. I.F.C.) an agency of the U.N., set up in 1956 to stimulate private investment in less-developed countries. It is affiliated with the World Bank

International Fund for Agricultural Development specialized United Nations lending agency created in June 1976 to help developing countries increase food production. *abbr.* IFAD

International Geophysical Year a period (July 1, 1957–Dec. 31, 1958) when intensified and coordinated programs of geophysical and astronomical research were conducted by 70 countries

international Gothic a style of painting in late 14th-c. France, Burgundy, Italy, Germany and Bohemia, characterized by a new realism in the treatment of detail, while retaining the austerity of earlier Gothic art. Its exponents include the Limbourg brothers in Burgundy and Gentile da Fabriano in Italy

International Harvester Company a U.S. farm machinery enterprise formed in 1902. It introduced (1918) the rear power takeoff, providing power for the operation of mounted and drawn implements directly by the tractor engine, which was universally accepted

in·ter·na·tion·al·ism (intərnǽʃən'lizəm) *n.* a belief in friendly cooperation between nations for mutual benefit ‖ the quality or state of being international

in·ter·na·tion·al·ist (intərnǽʃən'list) *n.* a believer in the principle of internationalism ‖ a specialist in international law

in·ter·na·tion·al·i·za·tion (intərnæʃən'lizéiʃən) *n.* an internationalizing or being internationalized

in·ter·na·tion·al·ize (intərnǽʃən'laiz) *pres. part.* **in·ter·na·tion·al·iz·ing** *past* and *past part.* **in·ter·na·tion·al·ized** *v.t.* to make international in character ‖ to bring (a territory) under the combined control of several nations

International Labor Organization (abbr. I.L.O.) an agency, founded in 1919 and affiliated with the U.N. in 1946, to improve labor and living conditions and to promote economic and social stability. Nobel peace prize (1969)

international law the body of unenforceable but widely accepted rules that govern relations between states, incl. laws of neutrality and of war

International Monetary Fund (abbr. IMF) a specialized agency affiliated with the U.N., designed to stabilize international monetary exchange rates. Its articles of agreement were signed at Bretton Woods, N.H., in 1944 and the fund began operations in 1947

International Phonetic Alphabet (abbr. I.P.A.) a universal system of letters and symbols (used in this book in a modified form) representing speech sounds

International Red Cross an organization for the prevention and alleviation of human suffering, founded in Geneva (1864) by Dunant. It was initially set up to aid prisoners, the sick and the wounded in wartime, but after the 1st world war it extended its work to disaster relief and public health. It now works through national Red Cross societies

International Refugee Organization (abbr. I.R.O.) an agency of the U.N. (1948–51) which undertook the care and repatriation of displaced persons and resettled more than a million refugees

international style the predominant style of 20th-c. architecture. Developed by Oud, Gropius, Le Corbusier and Mies van der Rohe, it achieved universality by 1950. Its adherents stress simplicity, purity of line, functional planning, undisguised use of modern materials (e.g. steel and concrete), exploration of dynamic spatial relationships, and cooperation in realms of scientific, cultural and aesthetic development.

International System of Units international standard for seven measurement units, established in 1960 for quantities of length, time, mass, electric current, temperature, luminosity intensity, and substance. *also* Système International d'Unités. *abbr.* SI

International Telecommunication Union (abbr. I.T.U.) an agency founded in 1865 and affiliated to the U.N. in 1957. It promotes cooperation for the improvement and use of telegraph, television and radio services

interne *INTERN

in·ter·ne·cine (intərní:sain, intərnési:n) *adj.* destructive to all parties involved, *internecine war* ‖ of fighting within a group [fr. L. *internecinus* fr. *internecium*, slaughter]

in·tern·ee (intə:rní:) *n.* an interned person, esp. in wartime

in·tern·ist (ínta:rnist, intə́:rnist) *n.* a specialist in internal medicine

in·tern·ment (intə́:rnmənt) *n.* an interning or being interned

in·ter·nod·al (intərnóud'l) *adj.* (biol.) between two nodes ‖ (biol.) of, relating to or forming an internode

in·ter·node (íntərnoud) *n.* (biol.) a section between two nodes

in·tern·ship (intə́:rnʃip) *n.* the position of an intern in a hospital ‖ the period of serving as an intern

in·ter·nun·ci·o (intərnʎnʃi:ou, intərnʎnsi:ou) *n.* a papal envoy ranking below a nuncio, sent to courts where no nuncio is accredited or while there is no nuncio there [fr. Ital. *internunzio*]

in·ter·o·cep·tive (intərouséptiv) *adj.* (physiol.) capable of receiving stimuli from within the organism, used in receiving these, or concerned with receiving these, e.g. through the viscera (cf. EXTEROCEPTIVE, cf. PROPRIOCEPTIVE) [INTERIOR + RECEPTIVE]

in·ter·o·cep·tor (intərouséptər) *n.* (physiol.) a receptor capable of receiving stimuli from within the organism [Mod. L.]

in·ter·op·er·a·ble (intərópərəb'l) *adj.* capable of operating compatibly individually or together

in·ter·pel·late (intə́:rpəleit) *pres. part.* **in·ter·pel·lat·ing** *past* and *past part.* **in·ter·pel·lat·ed** *v.t.* (in some legislative bodies) to demand an explanation and defense of a decision or policy from (a minister) [fr. L. *interpellare* (*interpellatus*), to interrupt in speaking]

in·ter·pel·la·tion (intə:rpəléiʃən) *n.* the act of interpellating [fr. L. *interpellatio* (*interpellationis*), an interrupting]

in·ter·pen·e·trate (intərpénitreit) *pres. part.* **in·ter·pen·e·trat·ing** *past* and *past part.* **in·ter·pen·e·trat·ed** *v.t.* to penetrate (something) thoroughly ‖ *v.i.* to penetrate each other ‖ to penetrate thoroughly

in·ter·pen·e·tra·tion (intərpenitréiʃən) *n.* an interpenetrating or being interpenetrated

in·ter·pen·e·tra·tive (ĭntərpénĭtreĭtiv) *adj.* interpenetrating

in·ter·plan·e·tar·y (ĭntərplǽnĭteri:) *adj.* situated between the planets

in·ter·play 1. (ĭntərplei) *n.* an acting upon each other with reciprocal effect **2.** (ĭntərpléi) *v.i.* to act upon each other

in·ter·plead (ĭntərplí:d) *v.i.* (*law*) to go on trial with each other to settle a point on which the action of a third party depends **in·ter·pléad·er** *n.* (*law*) a proceeding in which a party of whom two or more adverse parties make the same claim, and who does not claim the item in controversy for himself, compels those parties to litigate among themselves and so relieves himself of the possible suits that they might bring against him [fr. A.F. *enterpleder*]

In·ter·pol (íntərpoul, íntərpɔl) the International Criminal Police Commission, which has its headquarters at Paris. It provides liaison between member nations in searching for international criminals

in·ter·po·late (intə́:rpəleit) *pres. part.* **in·ter·po·lat·ing** *past* and *past part.* **in·ter·po·lat·ed** *v.t.* to put (new words, passages etc.) into a text ǁ to alter or corrupt (a text) by such additions ǁ to enter with (a remark) into a conversation between others ǁ (*math.*) to insert (intermediate values or terms) in a given series ǁ *v.i.* to introduce new words or passages in a text or a remark into a conversation [fr. L. *interpolare* (*interpolatus*), to polish up]

in·ter·po·la·tion (intə:rpəléiʃən) *n.* an interpolating or being interpolated ǁ something interpolated [F. or fr. L. *interpolatio* (*interpolationis*), a polishing]

in·ter·pos·al (ĭntərpóuz'l) *n.* the act of interposing

in·ter·pose (ĭntərpóuz) *pres. part.* **in·ter·pos·ing** *past* and *past part.* **in·ter·posed** *v.t.* to introduce (a remark etc.) into a conversation ǁ to introduce (something) so that it intervenes, *he interposed his own wishes between me and my choice of career* ǁ to introduce as an insertion, *to interpose an additional clause* ǁ *v.i.* to interrupt ǁ to intervene [F. *interposer*]

in·ter·po·si·tion (ĭntərpəzíʃən) *n.* an interposing or being interposed ǁ something interposed ǁ the doctrine that a state of the U.S.A. may oppose any Federal action which seems to that state to encroach on its sovereignty [F.]

in·ter·pret (intə́:rprit) *v.t.* to explain the meaning of (a work of art, dream etc.) ǁ to attribute a specified meaning to, *he interpreted their laughter as an insult* ǁ to express one's conception of (a role, musical work etc.) by performing it ǁ *v.i.* to act as a linguistic interpreter [F. *interpréter* or fr. L. *interpretari*]

in·ter·pre·ta·tion (intə:rpritéiʃən) *n.* an interpreting or being interpreted ǁ an explanation produced by interpreting ǁ the essential meaning of something, *what is the interpretation of this poem?* ǁ the act of translating a speech orally from one language into another ǁ an instance of this [F. *interprétation* or fr. L. *interpretatio* (*interpretationis*)]

in·ter·pre·ta·tive (intə́:rpriteitiv) *adj.* explanatory ǁ relating to interpretation [fr. L. *interpretari* (*interpretatus*), to interpret]

in·ter·pret·er (intə́:rpritər) *n.* someone who interprets, esp. someone who translates a foreign language orally, e.g. in a conversation carried on in different languages ǁ (*computer*) a program that converts the instructions in a source program into a machine language and then executes it ǁ a punch-card machine that will imprint information indicated by the holes punched [M.E. *interpretour* fr. O.F.]

in·ter·pre·tive (intə́:rpritiv) *adj.* interpretative

in·ter·ra·bang or **in·ter·bang** (íntérəbæŋ) *n.* a punctuation mark simultaneously expressing questioning and astonishment

in·ter·ra·cial (ĭntərréiʃəl) *adj.* of, relating to, involving or belonging to members of two or more races

in·ter·reg·num (ĭntərrégnəm) *pl.* **in·ter·reg·nums**, **in·ter·reg·na** (ĭntərrégnə) *n.* a period during which there is no ruler in office ǁ a period when administrative or governmental functions are suspended [L. fr. *inter*, between + *regnum*, reign]

in·ter·re·lat·ed (ĭntərriléitid) *adj.* having a close connection, related to each other

in·ter·re·la·tion (ĭntərriléiʃən) *n.* a mutual relationship **in·ter·re·lá·tion·ship** *n.*

in·ter·ro·gate (intérəgeit) *pres. part.* **in·ter·ro·gat·ing** *past* and *past part.* **in·ter·ro·gat·ed** *v.t.* to ask questions of, esp. formally ǁ (*computer*) to

send a machine-coded instruction requiring a response ǁ *v.i.* to make an interrogation [fr. L. *interrogare* (*interrogatus*)]

in·ter·ro·ga·tion (intərəgéiʃən) *n.* the act of interrogating ǁ an instance of this ǁ a question [F. or fr. L. *interrogatio* (*interrogationis*)]

in·ter·ro·ga·tive (intərógətiv) **1.** *adj.* having the form of or expressing a question, *an interrogative look* ǁ (*gram.*) designating a word, phrase etc. used in asking a question **2.** *n.* (*gram.*) a word expressing a question [fr. L.L. *interrogativus*]

in·ter·ro·ga·tor (intérəgeitər) *n.* someone who interrogates [L.L.]

in·ter·rog·a·to·ry (intərógətɔri:, intərógətouri:) **1.** *adj.* indicating a question, *an interrogatory tone of voice* ǁ having to do with questioning **2.** *n. pl.* **in·ter·rog·a·to·ries** (*law*) a formal question put in a court of law to be answered in writing by an accused person or a witness [fr. L.L. *interrogatorius*]

in·ter·rupt (intərápt) *v.t.* to stop abruptly but briefly (a discussion, a person who is speaking etc.) esp. by starting to speak oneself ǁ to obstruct (a view etc.) ǁ to make a break in the continuity of, *the remark interrupted his flow of thought* ǁ (*computer*) a signal to delay operations while another program is interspersed ǁ *v.i.* to interfere in some action ǁ to cause a discussion, person speaking etc. to cease abruptly, esp. by entering in with a remark etc. **in·ter·rúpt·er, in·ter·rúp·tor** *n.* someone who or something that interrupts, esp. (*elec.*) a device used to open and close a circuit [fr. L. *interrumpere* (*interruptus*), to break apart, break off]

in·ter·rup·tion (intərápʃən) *n.* an interrupting or being interrupted ǁ something that interrupts ǁ the time during which something is interrupted [fr. L. *interruptio* (*interruptionis*)]

interruptor *INTERRUPTER

in·ter·scho·las·tic (intərskəlǽstik) *adj.* between, or among, schools

in·ter·sect (intərsékt) *v.t.* to divide by passing through or across, *a river intersects the property* ǁ *v.i.* to meet and cross each other, *the lines intersect at X* [fr. L. *intersecare* (*intersectus*), to cut between, cut off]

in·ter·sec·tion (intərsékʃən) *n.* the act of intersecting ǁ the point at which lines cut across each other (or the line at which planes do so) ǁ a place where two roads cross each other **in·ter·séc·tion·al** *adj.* [fr. L. *intersectio* (*intersectionis*)]

in·ter·sex (íntərseks) *n.* an organism with sexual characteristics intermediate between those of the typical male and typical female of its species

intersex *UNISEX

in·ter·sex·u·al (intərséksʃu:əl) *adj.* (*biol.*) pertaining to an intersex ǁ existing between the sexes

in·ter·space 1. (íntərspeis) *n.* an intervening space **2.** (intərspéis) *v.t. pres. part.* **in·ter·spac·ing** *past* and *past part.* **in·ter·spaced** to put or occupy a space between

in·ter·sperse (intərspé:rs) *pres. part.* **in·ter·spers·ing** *past* and *past part.* **in·ter·spersed** *v.t.* to put here and there among other things ǁ to diversify, *to intersperse a lecture with anecdotes* **in·ter·sper·sion** (intərspé:rʃən) *n.* [fr. L. *interspergere* (*interspersus*)]

in·ter·state (intərstéit) *adj.* common to, involving or taking place between two or more states

Interstate Commerce Act a U.S. Congressional act (1887) which provided for the regulation of railroads in interstate commerce and prohibited pooling and discriminatory rates and rebates

Interstate Commerce Commission a U.S. government agency for regulating the practices and rates of carriers operating interstate services

in·ter·stel·lar (intərstélər) *adj.* among or between the stars

in·ter·stice (intá:rstis) *pl.* **in·ter·stic·es** (intá:rstisiz, intá:rstisi:z) *n.* a small space between two things **in·ter·sti·tial** (intərstíʃəl) *adj.* [fr. L. *interstitium*]

in·ter·stock (íntərstɒk) *n.* (*botany*) in grafting, an additional piece inserted between stock and scion, usually to induce dwarfing or to aid the union

in·ter·strat·i·fy (intərstrǽtifai) *pres. part.* **in·ter·strat·i·fy·ing** *past* and *past part.* **in·ter·strat·i·fied** *v.t.* to insert (one layer, stratum or body) between others ǁ *v.i.* to lie between other layers, strata or bodies

in·ter·trib·al (intərtráib'l) *adj.* common to or involving two or more tribes

in·ter·trop·i·cal (intərtrópik'l) *adj.* located or occurring between or within the tropics

in·ter·twine (intərtwáin) *pres. part.* **in·ter·twin·ing** *past* and *past part.* **in·ter·twined** *v.t.* to interlace (two or more things) ǁ to interlace (one thing) with another ǁ *v.i.* to become interlaced

in·ter·ur·ban (intərá:rbən) *adj.* (of public transportation etc.) traveling between or connecting cities

in·ter·val (íntərvəl) *n.* a period of time between two actions or events ǁ a space between two points ǁ (*Br.*) an intermission (interval between acts of a play) ǁ (*mus.*) the difference of pitch between two tones **at intervals** here and there ǁ now and then [M.E. *enterval, intervalle* fr. L. *intervallum*, space between ramparts]

in·ter·vale (íntərveil) *n.* an area of low-lying land, esp. between hills or along a river [M.E. var. of INTERVAL]

in·ter·vene (intərví:n) *pres. part.* **in·ter·ven·ing** *past* and *past part.* **in·ter·vened** *v.i.* to happen unexpectedly esp. so as to modify or prevent some event etc. ǁ to happen between points of time, events etc., *the intervening days seemed years* ǁ (*law*) to impose oneself as a third party to a lawsuit so as to protect one's own interests [fr. L. *intervenire*]

in·ter·ven·ient (intərví:njənt) *adj.* intervening [fr. L. *interveniens* (*intervenientis*)]

in·ter·ven·tion (intərvénʃən) *n.* the act of intervening ǁ interference in the affairs of others, e.g. by one state in the affairs of another [fr. L.L. *interventio* (*interventionis*)]

in·ter·view (íntərvju:) **1.** *n.* a meeting of persons face to face esp. for formal discussion ǁ a formal meeting between an applicant (e.g. for a job) and the person who is to examine his qualifications ǁ a meeting between a press, radio or television reporter and a person who is to be the subject of an article, program etc. ǁ the published article or program resulting from this meeting **2.** *v.t.* to meet with (someone) to examine his qualifications or to get information etc. from him [F. *entrevue*]

in·ter·weave (intərwí:v) *pres. part.* **in·ter·weav·ing** *past* **in·ter·wove** (intərwóuv) *past part.* **in·ter·wo·ven** (intərwóuvən) *v.t.* to weave together ǁ to mingle (two or more things), each retaining its identity, *the voice and piano parts are closely interwoven* ǁ *v.i.* to become woven together ǁ to mingle while retaining identity

in·ter·wind (intərwáind) *pres. part.* **in·ter·wind·ing** *past* and *past part.* **in·ter·wound** (intərwáund) *v.t. and i.* to wind together

interwove *past* of INTERWEAVE

interwoven *past part.* of INTERWEAVE

in·tes·ta·cy (intéstəsi:) *n.* (*law*) the quality or state of being intestate or having died intestate

in·tes·tate (intéstit) **1.** *adj.* not having made any valid will ǁ not bequeathed in a will, *an intestate estate* **2.** *n.* a person who dies without having made a valid will [fr. O.F. *intestat*]

in·tes·ti·nal (intéstin'l) *adj.* relating to or in the intestines [fr. M.L. or Mod. L. *intestinalis*]

intestinal fortitude (*pop.*) courage and stamina

in·tes·tine (intéstin) *n.* (usually *pl.*) the portion of the alimentary canal in vertebrates between the stomach and the anus. It consists of two major divisions: the anterior portion or small intestine and the posterior portion or large intestine ǁ the entire alimentary canal of many invertebrates when roughly straight and tubular [fr. L. *intestinum*]

in the dark (*mil.*) in military air intercept, a code meaning "not visible on my scope"

in·ti·ma·cy (íntəməsi:) *pl.* **in·ti·ma·cies** *n.* the quality or state of being intimate ǁ an intimate act ǁ (a euphemism for) illicit sexual intercourse

in·ti·mate 1. (íntəmit) *adj.* being on familiar, esp. affectionate, personal terms, *intimate friends* ǁ relating to or showing such an acquaintance, *intimate glances* ǁ very private and personal, *an intimate affair* ǁ warmly personal, *an intimate style of painting* ǁ resulting from close study, *an intimate knowledge of old country customs* ǁ having illicit sexual relations ǁ of or pertaining to the essential nature of something, *the intimate workings of the mind* **2.** (íntəmit) *n.* a familiar friend **3.** (íntəmeit) *v.t. pres. part.* **in·ti·mat·ing** *past* and *past part.* **in·ti·mat·ed** to hint, give someone to understand (something) ǁ (*old-fash.*) to announce, disclose

CONCISE PRONUNCIATION KEY: **(a)** æ, c*a*t; ɑ, c*a*r; ɔ, f*aw*n; ei, sn*a*ke. **(e)** e, h*e*n; i:, sh*ee*p; iə, d*ee*r; ɛə, b*ea*r. **(i)** i, f*i*sh; ai, t*i*ger; ə:, b*i*rd. **(o)** o, *o*x; au, c*ow*; ou, g*oa*t; u, p*oo*r; ɔi, r*oy*al. **(u)** ʌ, d*u*ck; u, b*u*ll; u:, g*oo*se; ə, b*a*cillus; ju:, c*u*be. x, lo*ch*; θ, *th*ink; ð, bo*th*er; z, *Z*en; ʒ, corsa*g*e; dʒ, sava*g*e; ŋ, orangutan*g*; j, *y*ak; ʃ, *fi*sh; tʃ, fe*tch*; 'l, ra*bb*le; 'n, re*dd*en. Complete pronunciation key appears inside front cover.

in·ti·ma·tion (intəméiʃən) *n.* something that gives an insight or inkling, *intimations of joys to come* ‖ the act of intimating [F.]

in·tim·i·date (intímideit) *pres. part.* **in·tim·i·dat·ing** *past* and *past part.* **in·tim·i·dat·ed** *v.t.* to frighten, esp. to influence by threats, *to intimidate a witness* **in·tim·i·dá·tion, in·tím·i·da·tor** *ns* [fr. M.L. *intimidare (intimidatus)*]

in·tinc·tion (intíŋkʃən) *n.* (*eccles.*) a dipping of the bread into the wine during Communion so as to administer both together [fr. L.L. *intinctio (intinctionis)*]

in·to (íntu:) *prep.* from the outside to the inside of ‖ toward the middle of (a period of time), *to talk far into the night* ‖ up against, *his car ran into a tree* ‖ acquiring the substance, form or condition of, *driven into a frenzy* ‖ (*math.*) expressing division, *3 into 27 is 9* [O.E.]

in·tol·er·a·bil·i·ty (intɔlərəbíliti:) *n.* the quality or state of being intolerable

in·tol·er·a·ble (intɔ́lərəb'l) *adj.* that cannot be tolerated **in·tól·er·a·bly** *adv.* [fr. L. *intolerabilis*]

Intolerable Acts (*hist.*) the name given to five laws passed (1774) by the British parliament to reestablish order in the American colonies after the Boston Tea Party (1773). They did much to unite the Thirteen Colonies before the Revolutionary War

in·tol·er·ance (intɔ́lərəns) *n.* the quality or state of being intolerant [fr. L. *intolerantia*]

in·tol·er·ant (intɔ́lərənt) *adj.* not tolerating beliefs etc. that differ from one's own ‖ unfriendly or hostile towards persons of another racial or religious group ‖ (with 'of') unwilling to put up with something specified, *intolerant of stupidity* ‖ (with 'of') unable to endure something specified, *intolerant of great heat* [fr. L. *intolerans (intolerantis)*]

in·to·nate (íntouneit) *pres. part.* **in·to·nat·ing** *past* and *past part.* **in·to·nat·ed** *v.t.* to intone **in·to·ná·tion** *n.* the modulation of the voice ‖ (*eccles.*) the act of intoning ‖ (*eccles.*) the opening phrase of a Gregorian chant, sung by the priest ‖ the producing of musical sounds, with regard to accuracy of pitch **in·tone** (intóun) *pres. part.* **in·ton·ing** *past* and *past part.* **in·toned** *v.t.* to chant, *to intone prayers* ‖ to sing the opening phrase of (a plainsong melody etc.) ‖ *v.i.* to utter a droning or monotonous singing sound [fr. M.L. *intonare (intonatus)*, to intone]

in to·to (intóutou) *adv.* as a whole, completely, altogether [L.=on the whole]

in·tox·i·cant (intɔ́ksikənt) **1.** *adj.* intoxicating **2.** *n.* something that intoxicates, esp. an alcoholic drink [fr. M.L. *intoxicans (intoxicantis)*]

in·tox·i·cate (intɔ́ksikeit) *pres. part.* **in·tox·i·cat·ing** *past* and *past part.* **in·tox·i·cat·ed** *v.t.* (of an alcoholic drink, drug etc.) to cause to lose physical or mental control ‖ to exhilarate ‖ (*med.*) to poison **in·tox·i·cá·tion** *n.* [fr. M.L. *intoxicare (intoxicatus)*, to poison, drug]

intra- (íntrə) *prefix* on the inside, within [fr. L. *intra*]

Intracoastal Waterway, U.S. water route along the Atlantic coast from Boston to Key West, Florida, and along the Gulf of Mexico's coast from Apalachee Bay, Florida, to Brownsville, Texas, for 3,000 miles (4,800 km.). It is used for both commercial shipping and recreation and is maintained by the Army Corps of Engineers

in·trac·ta·bil·i·ty (intræktəbíliti:) *n.* the quality or state of being intractable

in·trac·ta·ble (intræktəb'l) *adj.* not docile, not easily led or persuaded ‖ (of things) unmanageable, difficult to deal with **in·trác·ta·bly** *adv.* [fr. L. *intractabilis*]

in·tra·day (intrədéi) *adj.* occurring during a single day

in·tra·dos (intréidɔs, íntrədɔs) *n.* (*archit.*) the inner curve of an arch or vault (cf. EXTRADOS) [F. fr. L. *intra*, within+F. *dos*, back]

in·tra·gres·sant (intrəgrésənt) *n.* (*genetics*) gene of one species transferred to another by hybridization

in·tra·mu·ral (intrəmjúərəl) *adj.* occurring within the limits of specific (esp. academic) groups, *intramural athletics* ‖ (*biol.*) within the substance of the wall of an organ or cell [fr. INTRA-+L. *murus*, wall]

in·tra·mus·cu·lar (intrəmʌ́skjulər) *adj.* within or injected into a muscle

in·tran·si·gence (intrénsidʒəns) *n.* the quality or state of being intransigent **in·trán·si·gen·cy** *n.*

in·tran·si·gent (intrénsidʒənt) **1.** *adj.* refusing to compromise, immovably adhering to a position or point of view **2.** *n.* a person who refuses to change his opinion or point of view [F. *intransigeant* fr. Span. *los intransigentes*, extreme republicans of 1873-4]

in·tran·si·tive (intrénsitiv) **1.** *adj.* (*gram.*, of verbs) not governing a direct object **2.** *n.* (*gram.*) an intransitive verb (cf. TRANSITIVE) [fr. L. *intransitivus*, not passing over]

in·tra·op·er·a·tive (intrəɔ́pərətiv) *adj.* (*med.*) occurring during the surgical operation

in·tra·per·son·al (intrəpə:rsən'l) *adj.* occurring within a person's mind

in·tra·pop·u·la·tion (intrəpɔpjuléiʃən) *adj.* occurring within the population

in·tra·state (intrəstéit) *adj.* within a state

in·tra·u·ter·ine device or **intrauterine contraceptive device** (intrəjú:tərən) (*med.*) plastic or steel coil or loop, etc., placed within the uterus to prevent conception. *abbr.* **IUD** or **IUCD.** Cf LIPPES LOOP

in·tra·vas·cu·lar (intrəvǽskjələr) *adj.* occurring within the arterial system. **—intravascularly** *adv.*

in·tra·ve·hic·u·lar (intrəvi:híkjulər) *adj.* inside the vehicle

in·tra·ve·nous (intrəví:nəs) *adj.* in or into a vein, *intravenous feeding* [fr. INTRA-+L. *vena*, vein]

in·trep·id (intrépid) *adj.* fearlessly facing up to danger, risk or hardship **in·tre·pid·i·ty** (intrepíditi:) *n.* [fr. L. *intrepidus*]

in·tri·ca·cy (íntrikəsi:) *pl.* **in·tri·ca·cies** *n.* the quality or state of being intricate ‖ an intricate part or detail

in·tri·cate (íntrikit) *adj.* having a complicated organization, with many parts or aspects difficult to follow or grasp [fr. L. *intricare (intricatus)*, to entangle, perplex]

in·tri·gant, in·tri·guant (íntri:gənt) *n.* someone who engages in intrigue **in·tri·gante, in·tri·guante** (íntri:gænt) *n.* a woman who does this [F. *intriguant*]

in·trigue (intrí:g, íntri:g) *n.* secret plotting, scheming to secure an advantage or hurt an adversary ‖ a plot ‖ (*old-fash.*) a secret and illicit love affair [F. fr. Ital.]

in·trigue (intrí:g) *pres. part.* **in·tri·guing** *past* and *past part.* **in·trigued** *v.i.* to use intrigue, plot secretly ‖ *v.t.* to arouse the interest or curiosity of [F. *intriguer* fr. Ital.]

in·trin·sic (intrínsik) *adj.* inherent, essential, *the book has no intrinsic merit, the brooch has no intrinsic value* ‖ (*anat.*, esp. of certain muscles) contained completely within an organ or part (cf. EXTRINSIC) **in·trín·si·cal·ly** *adv.* [F. *intrinsèque*]

intrinsic energy (*phys.*) the energy possessed by a body which would all be released if it expanded adiabatically to a state of infinite dispersion ‖ (*chem.*) the energy possessed by a substance which can be emitted in the form of heat when the substance undergoes chemical change

intrinsic tracer (*chem.*) a natural isotope used for tracing through physical processing

intro. introduction

intro- (íntrou) *prefix* to the inside [L. *adv.*]

introd. introduction

in·tro·duce (intrədú:s, intrədjú:s) *pres. part.* **in·tro·duc·ing** *past* and *past part.* **in·tro·duced** *v.t.* to make someone acquainted with (a person) formally ‖ to make (two persons) formally acquainted with each other ‖ to bring into use or practice, *to introduce a new fashion* ‖ to add as a feature, *to introduce thieves' slang into a novel* ‖ to bring into conversation etc. as a topic ‖ to begin, *to introduce a speech with an anecdote* ‖ to lead (someone) to discover a specified subject, author etc., *to introduce someone to atonal music* ‖ to offer (something new) for sale, *to introduce a new toothpaste* ‖ to insert, *to introduce a tube into a patient's windpipe* ‖ to bring (a bill etc.) before a legislative body for discussion [fr. L. *introducere*]

in·tro·duc·tion (intrədʌ́kʃən) *n.* something that introduces a subject, action etc. ‖ an explanatory or commenting section of a book, preceding the text proper and often by someone other than the book's author ‖ the opening section of a musical composition ‖ an introducing or being introduced ‖ something introduced, *the entertainment tax was an unwelcome introduction* [F.]

in·tro·duc·tive (intrədʌ́ktiv) *adj.* introductory [fr. L. *introducere (introductus)*]

in·tro·duc·to·ry (intrədʌ́ktəri:) *adj.* serving as an introduction, preliminary [fr. L.L. *introductorius*]

in·troit (íntroit) *n.* (*Anglican Communion*) a psalm or hymn sung or played at the beginning of the communion service **In·troit** the first part of the proper of the Mass, usually a psalm verse and an antiphon followed by the Gloria Patri [F. *introit*]

in·tro·jec·tion (intrədʒékʃən) *n.* (*psychol.*) the process by which the images of external objects are transformed into elements in the life of the unconscious [fr. INTRO-+PROJECTION]

in·tro·mis·sion (intrəmíʃən) *n.* an inserting, esp. (*biol.*) of the penis in the vagina, or the keeping of it there ‖ the time during which it is kept there [fr. L. *intromittere (intromissus)*, to send in, or fr. F.]

in·tro·mit (intrəmít) *pres. part.* **in·tro·mit·ting** *past* and *past part.* **in·tro·mit·ted** *v.t.* to put in, insert [fr. L. *intromittere*, to send in]

in·tro·mit·tent (intrəmít'nt) *adj.* (*biol.*) adapted for intromission [fr. L. *intromittens (intromittentis)*]

in·trorse (intrɔ́rs) *adj.* (*bot.*, esp. of an anther) turned inward or towards the plant's center (cf. EXTRORSE) [fr. L. *introrsus*, turned inward]

in·tro·spect (intrəspékt) *v.i.* to examine one's own thoughts and feelings **in·tro·spéc·tion** *n.* **in·tro·spéc·tive** *adj.* [fr. L. *introspicere (introspectus)*, to look into]

in·tro·ver·sion (intrəvə́:rʒən, intrəvə́:rʃən) *n.* an introverting or being introverted ‖ (*psychol.*) an inclination or tendency toward introspection (opp. EXTROVERSION) **in·tro·vér·sive** *adj.* [fr. Mod. L. *introversio (introversionis)*]

in·tro·vert (íntrəvə:rt) **1.** *v.t.* to direct (one's mind, thoughts) upon oneself ‖ (*zool.*) to draw (an organ) into its sheath or base **2.** *n.* (*psychol.*) someone who is more interested in himself and his own mental or emotional processes than in outside events etc. (cf. EXTROVERT) ‖ (*zool.*) an organ that is or can be drawn into its sheath or base **in·tro·vér·tive** *adj.* [fr. INTRO-+L. *vertere*, to turn]

in·trude (intrú:d) *pres. part.* **in·trud·ing** *past* and *past part.* **in·trud·ed** *v.t.* to thrust or force (something) in an unwelcome way, *to intrude one's opinions upon someone* ‖ (*geol.*) to force (molten rock) between other rock strata ‖ *v.i.* to enter, break in in an unwelcome way [fr. L. *intrudere*]

In·trud·er (intrú:dər) *n.* (*mil.*) U.S. twin turbojet engine, dual crew, all-weather aircraft (KA-6), with an integrated attack navigation computer system to locate pinpoint targets while at low altitude and capable of carrying 2,000 lbs of nuclear and/or conventional ordnance and advanced air-to-ground missile systems; designed to operate from aircraft carriers; made by Grumman

in·tru·sion (intrú:ʒən) *n.* the act of intruding ‖ an instance of this ‖ (*law*) wrongful entry upon someone else's property or seizure of his goods ‖ (*geol.*) a portion of intruded rock [O.F.]

in·tru·sive (intrú:siv) *adj.* intruding or apt to intrude ‖ (*geol.*, of rock) forced into another rock stratum while molten ‖ (*geol.*) formed of such rock (cf. EFFUSIVE) [fr. L. *intrudere (intrusus)*, to thrust in]

in·tu·bate (íntubeit, íntjubeit) *pres. part.* **in·tu·bat·ing** *past* and *past part.* **in·tu·bat·ed** *v.t.* to insert a tube into (a hollow organ, e.g. the trachea) to keep it open **in·tu·bá·tion** *n.* [fr. IN-(in)+L. *tuba*, tube]

in·tu·it (intú:it, intjú:it) *v.t.* and *i.* to know or learn by intuition [fr. L. *intueri (intuitus)*, to instruct]

in·tu·i·tion (intu:íʃən, intju:íʃən) *n.* (*philos.*) a perception or view ‖ immediate apprehension of truth, or supposed truth, in the absence of conscious rational processes **in·tu·í·tion·al** *adj.* [F.]

in·tu·i·tion·al·ism (intu:íʃən'lizəm, intju:íʃən'lizəm) *n.* intuitionism

in·tu·i·tion·ism (intu:íʃənizəm, intju:íʃənizəm) *n.* (*philos.*) the doctrine that perceived objects are intuitively recognized as real ‖ (*philos.*) the doctrine that truth, ethical principles etc. are intuitively apprehended

in·tu·i·tive (intú:itiv, intjú:itiv) *adj.* having, perceived by, or relating to intuition [fr. M.L. *intuitivus*]

in·tu·i·tiv·ism (intú:itivizəm, intjú:itivizəm) *n.* the belief that ethical truths are known intuitively

in·tu·mesce (intumés, intjumés) *pres. part.* **in--**

tu·mesc·ing *past* and *past part.* **in·tu·mesced** *v.i.* to swell up, expand, bubble up etc., esp. as a result of heat [fr. L. *intumescere*]

in·tu·mes·cence (ĭntumés'ns, ĭntjumés'ns) *n.* the act of intumescing ‖ (*biol.*) a swollen part, e.g. a tumor [F.]

in·tu·mes·cent (ĭntumés'nt, ĭntjumés'nt) *adj.* showing intumescence [fr. L. *intumescens* (*intumescentis*)]

in·tus·sus·cept (ĭntəssəsépt) *v.t.* to cause (an intestine) to enter a neighboring portion of intestine, resulting in blockage [fr. L. *intus*, within + *suscipere* (*susceptus*), to take up]

in·tus·sus·cep·tion (ĭntəssəsépʃən) *n.* an intussuscepting or being intussuscepted ‖ a taking in of food etc. and converting of it into tissue [fr. L. *intus*, within + *susceptio* (*susceptionis*), a taking up]

in·unc·tion (ĭnáŋkʃən) *n.* an anointing, esp. for medicinal purposes [fr. L. *nunctio* (*inunctionis*)]

in·un·date (ínʌndeit) *pres. part.* **in·un·dat·ing** *past* and *past part.* **in·un·dat·ed** *v.t.* to flood ‖ to overwhelm, *inundated with bills* [fr. L. *inundare* (*inundatus*)]

in·un·da·tion (ĭnʌndéiʃən) *n.* an inundating or being inundated ‖ a flood [fr. L. *inundatio* (*inundationis*)]

in·ur·bane (ĭnəːrbéin) *adj.* lacking urbanity, not refined in manner [fr. L. *inurbanus*]

in·ur·ban·i·ty (ĭnəːrbǽniti:) *n.* the quality or state of being inurbane

in·ure (ĭnúər, ĭnjúər) *pres. part.* **in·ur·ing** *past* and *past part.* **in·ured** *v.t.* to accustom (to something unpleasant), cause by habituation to be less sensitive ‖ *v.i.* (*law*) to come into operation, take effect **in·úre·ment** *n.* [fr. IN- + obs. *ure*, custom, practice]

in·urn (ĭnə́ːrn) *v.t.* to put (ashes) into a funeral urn

in·u·tile (ĭnjúːtil) *adj.* not for practical use [F.]

in·u·til·i·ty (ĭnjuːtíliti:) *n.* the quality or state of being inutile [F. *inutilité*]

in vac·u·o (ĭnvǽkju:ou) *adv.* in a vacuum ‖ without being related to practical application, relevant facts etc., *the theory was propounded in vacuo* [L. = in an empty space]

in·vade (ĭnvéid) *pres. part.* **in·vad·ing** *past* and *past part.* **in·vad·ed** *v.t.* to enter (a country, region etc.) esp. by armed force ‖ to crowd into as if taking possession of *tourists invade Paris during the summer* ‖ to encroach on ‖ to intrude upon, *to invade someone's privacy* ‖ *v.i.* to make an invasion [fr. L. *invadere*]

in·vag·i·nate (ĭnvǽdʒineit) *pres. part.* **in·vag·i·nat·ing** *past* and *past part.* **in·vag·i·nat·ed** *v.t.* to put into a sheath ‖ to fold inward, causing an outer surface to become an inner surface ‖ *v.i.* to become sheathed or infolded [fr. L. *in*, in + *vagina*, sheath]

in·val·id (ĭnvǽlid) *adj.* not valid, having no legal force, *an invalid contract* [fr. L. *invalidus*]

in·va·lid (ínvəlid, *Br.* ínvəli:d) **1.** *adj.* ill, esp. chronically ill or disabled ‖ suitable for a sick person, *an invalid diet* **2.** *n.* an invalid person **3.** *v.t.* to make ill, disable ‖ (with 'out of') to remove, release from esp. military service as an invalid [fr. L. *invalidus*]

in·val·i·date (ĭnvǽlideit) *pres. part.* **in·val·i·dat·ing** *past* and *past part.* **in·val·i·dat·ed** *v.t.* to make invalid, deprive of efficacy **in·val·i·dá·tion** *n.*

in·va·lid·ism (ínvəlidizəm, *Br.* ínvəli:dizəm) *n.* the quality or state of being an invalid

in·val·u·a·ble (ĭnvǽlju:əb'l) *adj.* having a value too great to be measured ‖ (*loosely*) very valuable **in·vál·u·a·bly** *adv.*

in·var (ĭnvaːr) *n.* a nickel-iron alloy containing about 36% nickel, which has a negligible coefficient of linear expansion and is used in the manufacture of precision instruments [shortened fr. INVARIABLE]

in·var·i·a·bil·i·ty (ĭnvɛ́əri:əbíliti:) *n.* the quality or state of being invariable

in·var·i·a·ble (ĭnvɛ́əri:əb'l) **1.** *adj.* never changing, constant **2.** *n.* something constant **in·vár·i·a·bly** *adv.* [fr. IN- (not) + VARIABLE or fr. F.]

in·var·i·ant (ĭnvɛ́əri:ənt) **1.** *adj.* not varying **2.** *n.* (*math.*) a quantity invariable under certain conditions, esp. during a transformation from one set of coordinates to another

in·va·sion (ĭnvéiʒən) *n.* an invading or being invaded ‖ (*med.*, of a disease) the onset [F.]

in·va·sive (ĭnvéisiv) *adj.* of, pertaining to, or having the nature of, invasion ‖ tending to invade [F. *invasif*]

in·vec·tive (ĭnvéktiv) *n.* violently abusive language ‖ a violent verbal attack [F. *invectif*]

in·veigh (ĭnvéi) *v.i.* (with 'against') to speak angrily and bitterly, rail, *to inveigh against bureaucracy* [fr. L. *invehi*, to attack (pass. of *invehere*, to carry into)]

in·vei·gle (ĭnvéig'l, ĭnvíːg'l) *pres. part.* **in·vei·gling** *past* and *past part.* **in·vei·gled** *v.t.* to cajole, wheedle by deceptive means ‖ to get by cajolery, *he inveigled a subscription out of them* **in·véi·gle·ment** *n.* [earlier *envegle* ult. fr. F. *aveugler*, to blind]

in·vent (ĭnvént) *v.t.* to devise, originate (a new device, method etc.), *Morse invented the telegraph* ‖ to think up, *to invent a story* [fr. L. *invenire* (*inventus*), to come upon]

in·ven·tion (ĭnvénʃən) *n.* the act of inventing ‖ something invented ‖ the ability to think things up, ingenuity ‖ (*mus.*) a short keyboard composition in esp. two-part counterpoint, esp. as composed by Bach [O.F. *invencion*, *envention*]

in·ven·tive (ĭnvéntiv) *adj.* of, relating to or showing a talent for invention [O.F. *inventif*]

in·ven·tor (ĭnvéntər) *n.* someone who invents, esp. the originator of a new device, method etc. [L.]

in·ven·to·ry (ínvəntɔːri:, ínvəntouri:) **1.** *pl.* **in·ven·to·ries** *n.* an itemized list, esp. of property ‖ the making of such a list ‖ (*commerce*) stocktaking **2.** *v.t. pres. part.* **in·ven·to·ry·ing** *past* and *past part.* **in·ven·to·ried** to make an inventory of [fr. M.L. *inventorium*]

In·ver·car·gill (ĭnvərkáːrgil) a seaport (pop. 49,900) in South Island, New Zealand: sawmills, meat-packing

In·ver·ness (ĭnvərnés) a county (area 4,211 sq. miles, pop. 82,000) in N. Scotland, including most of the Hebrides ‖ its county town (pop. 36,600), a port on Moray Firth

in·verse (ĭnvə́ːrs, ínvəːrs) **1.** *adj.* inverted in position or relation, reversed ‖ (*math.*) of a relationship between variables in which one variable increases in proportion as the other decreases **2.** *n.* a direct opposite [fr. L. *invertere* (*inversus*), to turn inwards]

inverse-square law (*phys.*) the law which states that the variation of a quantity (e.g. illumination) with respect to the distance from the source is proportional to the reciprocal of the square of the distance

in·ver·sion (ĭnvə́ːrʒən, ĭnvə́ːrʃən) *n.* an inverting or being inverted ‖ something inverted ‖ (*gram.*) a reversal of the usual order of the words in a sentence ‖ (*math.*) the interchanging of numerator and denominator ‖ (*phon.*) the turning backward and upward of the tip of the tongue ‖ (*chem.*) the conversion of a dextrorotatory substance into a levorotatory one or vice versa ‖ (*mus.*) a position of a chord with a note other than its root in the base ‖ (*mus.*) the repeating of a melody with its intervals inverted ‖ (*mus.*) the interchanging of upper and lower melodies in counterpoint ‖ (*meteor.*) an unusual condition in a layer of air in which the warmest portion is closest to the earth, near the surface ‖ (*meteor.*) similar departure from normal air-temperature layering for other reasons ‖ (*phys.*) condition of a surface layer of a semiconductor opposite of the bulk of material, usu. by electrical application ‖ (*communications*) process of speech scrambling by use of a higher frequency beat mixed with a fixed audio frequency ‖ homosexuality [fr. L. *inversio* (*inversionis*)]

in·vert 1. (ĭnvə́ːrt) *v.t.* to turn upside down ‖ to reverse the order or position of ‖ (*mus.*) to change the relative position of the notes of (a chord, interval or phrase) ‖ (*chem.*) to cause to undergo inversion ‖ *v.i.* (*chem.*) to undergo inversion **2.** (ínvəːrt) *n.* a homosexual [fr. L. *invertere*, to turn in]

in·vert·ase (ĭnvə́ːrteis, ínvəːrteiz) *n.* an enzyme present in many plants and in animal intestines which is able to invert sucrose [INVERT *v.*]

in·ver·te·brate (ĭnvə́ːrtəbrit, ĭnvə́ːrtəbreit) **1.** *adj.* having no backbone **2.** *n.* an animal having no internal skeleton or backbone, e.g. a protozoan, coelenterate, worm, arthropod or echinoderm [fr. Mod. L. *invertebratus*]

inverted comma (*printing*) an upside-down comma at the top of the line (') ‖ (*Br.*, *pl.*) quotation marks

inverted mordent (*mus.*) a pralltriller

invert sugar a mixture of glucose and levulose produced by the inversion of sucrose and often occurring naturally in fruits

in·vest (ĭnvést) *v.t.* to put (money) to a use expected to yield a profit or income ‖ to confer the insignia of office or rank upon ‖ to envelop,

wrap up as if in a cloak, *invested with an air of mystery* ‖ to besiege ‖ *v.i.* to make an investment [fr. L. *investire*, to clothe]

in·ves·ti·gate (ĭnvéstigeit) *pres. part.* **in·ves·ti·gat·ing** *past* and *past part.* **in·ves·ti·gat·ed** *v.t.* to seek information about by searching into or examining ‖ *v.i.* to make an investigation [fr. L. *investigare* (*investigatus*), to trace out]

in·ves·ti·ga·tion (ĭnvestigéiʃən) *n.* an examination for the purpose of discovering information about something ‖ the process of investigating [F.]

in·ves·ti·ga·tion·al new drug (ĭnvestigéiʃən'l) a drug not yet approved by the FDA for marketing to the general public, available solely for experimental purposes intended to determine its safety and effectiveness. *abbr.* IND

in·ves·ti·ga·tor (ĭnvéstigeitər) *n.* someone who investigates

in·ves·ti·tive (ĭnvéstitiv) *adj.* (*law*) relating to the vesting of a right etc. [fr. L. *invesiire* (*investitus*), to clothe]

in·ves·ti·ture (ĭnvéstitʃər) *n.* the act or ceremony of investing someone with an honor or office [fr. M.L. *investitura* fr. *investire*, to clothe]

Investiture Controversy the struggle (1075–1122) between the papacy and secular rulers for the right to elect and install bishops. It began (1075) when Pope Gregory VII forbade Henry IV of Germany to conduct lay investitures, and was settled in compromise by the Concordat of Worms (1122) between Henry V and Calixtus II. In England, the controversy took the form of a long quarrel between Henry I and Anselm, which also ended in compromise (1107)

in·vest·ment (ĭnvéstmənt) *n.* the act of investing, esp. of money ‖ something invested, esp. money ‖ something in which money is invested, *a new tractor would be a good investment* ‖ the outer covering of an animal ‖ (*zool.*) the outer layer of an organ

investment bank a bank specializing in the purchase and sale of securities and the raising of capital funds

in·ves·tor (ĭnvéstər) *n.* someone who invests

in·vet·er·a·cy (ĭnvétərəsi:) *n.* the quality or state of being inveterate

in·vet·er·ate (ĭnvétərit) *adj.* deep-rooted, firmly established, *an inveterate dislike* ‖ confirmed in some habit, *an inveterate liar* [fr. L. *inveterare* (*inveteratus*), to make old]

in·vid·i·ous (ĭnvídi:əs) *adj.* causing envy or ill-feeling, esp. by unfair discrimination, *an invidious appointment* [fr. L. *invidiosus*]

in·vig·i·late (ĭnvídʒəleit) *pres. part.* **in·vig·i·lat·ing** *past* and *past part.* **in·vig·i·lat·ed** *v.i.* (*Br.*) to proctor **in·vig·i·la·tor** *n.* [fr. L. *invigilare* (*invigilatus*), to watch]

in·vig·o·rate (ĭnvígəreit) *pres. part.* **in·vig·o·rat·ing** *past* and *past part.* **in·vig·o·rat·ed** *v.t.* to fill with vigor, enliven **in·vig·o·rá·tion** *n.* [ult. fr. L. *in*, in + *vigor*, vigor]

in·vin·ci·bil·i·ty (ĭnvinsəbíliti:) *n.* the state or quality of being invincible

in·vin·ci·ble (ĭnvínsəb'l) *adj.* that cannot be conquered or overcome **in·vín·ci·bly** *adv.* [F.]

in·vi·o·la·bil·i·ty (ĭnvaiələbíliti:) *n.* the quality or state of being inviolable

in·vi·o·la·ble (ĭnváiələb'l) *adj.* that cannot be violated ‖ that must not be violated **in·ví·o·la·bly** *adv.* [fr. L. *inviolabilis* or fr. F.]

in·vi·o·la·cy (ĭnváiələsi:) *n.* the state or quality of being inviolate

in·vi·o·late (ĭnváiəlit) *adj.* not violated [fr. L. *inviolatus*]

in·vis·i·bil·i·ty (ĭnvizəbíliti:) *n.* the quality or state of being invisible

in·vis·i·ble (ĭnvízəb'l) *adj.* that cannot be seen because of its nature, *the invisible soul* ‖ that cannot be seen because it is concealed, very small etc., *microbes are invisible to the naked eye* ‖ (*commerce*, e.g. of goodwill) not accountable in regular statements

invisible ink any of several kinds of ink which do not become visible on paper until specially treated

invisible supply (*statistics*) **1.** uncounted stocks of a commodity in the hands of wholesalers, manufacturers, and producers that cannot be identified accurately **2.** stocks outside commercial channels but theoretically available to the market

in·vis·i·bly (ĭnvízəbli:) *adv.* in such a way as to be invisible

in·vi·ta·tion (ĭnvitéiʃən) *n.* the act of inviting ‖ something that invites, *his sneer was an invita-*

CONCISE PRONUNCIATION KEY: **(a)** æ, *cat*; ɑ, *car*; ɔ *fawn*; ei, *snake*. **(e)** e, *hen*; i:, *sheep*; iə, *deer*; ɛə, *bear*. **(i)** i, *fish*; ai, *tiger*; əː, *bird*. **(o)** o, *ox*; au, *cow*; ou, *goat*; u, *poor*; ɔi, *royal*. **(u)** ʌ, *duck*; u, *bull*; uː, *goose*; ə, *bacillus*; juː, *cube*. x, *loch*; θ, *think*; ð, *bother*; z, *Zen*; ʒ, *corsage*; dʒ, *savage*; ŋ, *orangutang*; j, *yak*; ʃ, *fish*; tʃ, *fetch*; 'l, *rabble*; 'n, *redden*. Complete pronunciation key appears inside front cover.

tion to a fight || the message used in inviting [fr. L. *invitatio* (*invitationis*)]

in·vite (inváit) *pres. part.* **in·vit·ing** *past* and *past part.* **in·vit·ed** *v.t.* to ask (someone) hospitably to come somewhere or to do or participate in something || to ask for, *your suggestions are invited* || to request (someone to do something), *he invited volunteers to step forward* || to tend to bring about unintentionally, *to invite trouble* **in·vit·ing** *adj.* tempting, attractive, *an inviting fireside* [F. *inviter*]

in vi·tro fertilization (inví:trou) (*med.*) fertilization of an egg outside the body

in·vo·ca·tion (invəkéiʃən) *n.* the act of invoking God, the Muses etc. for aid, inspiration etc. || a prayer, incantation etc. used in invoking [O.F.]

in·voc·a·to·ry (invɔ́kətɔri:, invɔ́kətɔri:) *adj.* of, involving or used in invocation [fr. L. *invocare* (*invocatus*), to invoke]

in·voice (ínvɔis) 1. *n.* an itemized list of goods dispatched or delivered to a buyer, with prices and charges 2. *v.t. pres. part.* **in·voic·ing** *past* and *past part.* **in·voiced** to make an invoice of (goods) [prob. fr. older *invoyes*, pl. of *invoy* fr. 16th-c. F. *envoy* fr. *envoyer*, to send]

in·voke (invóuk) *pres. part.* **in·vok·ing** *past* and *past part.* **in·voked** *v.t.* to appeal to (God, a deity etc.) in prayer etc. || to ask for in supplication || to refer to for support etc., *he invoked his special powers to justify the action* [F. *invoquer*]

in·vo·lu·cel (invɔ́ljusel) *n.* (*bot.*) a secondary involucre, e.g. at the base of a secondary umbel [fr. Mod. L. *involucellum*, dim. of *involucrum*, a case]

in·vo·lu·cre (ínvɔlu:kər) *n.* (*bot.*) a calyxlike structure formed of bracts around or just below the base of a usually condensed inflorescence, e.g. in composite plants || (*anat.*) an envelope or membranous covering [F.]

in·vo·lu·crum (invɔlú:krəm) *pl.* **in·vo·lu·cra** (invɔlú:krə) *n.* an involucre [L. fr. *involvere*, to envelop]

in·vol·un·tar·i·ly (invɔ́ləntərili:, invɔ̀ləntéərili:) *adv.* in an involuntary manner

in·vol·un·tar·i·ness (invɔ́ləntəri:nis) *n.* the quality or state of being involuntary

in·vol·un·tar·y (invɔ́ləntəri:) *adj.* not intended, *an involuntary giving of offense* || (*physiol.*) of reactions which are not controlled by the will, e.g. the movements of the esophagus in swallowing [fr. L. *in voluntarius*]

in·vo·lute (ínvɔlu:t) 1. *adj.* (*bot.*, of leaves) having edges rolled inward at each side || (*zool.*, of shells) closely coiled 2. *n.* (*geom.*) a curve traced by the end of a thread as it is unwound from or wound upon another curve (cf. EVOLUTE) **ín·vo·lut·ed** *adj.* complicated, intricate [fr. L. *involvere* (*involutus*), to roll inward]

in·vo·lu·tion (invɔlú:ʃən) *n.* a curling inward || a part that curls inward || an entanglement, complication || (*math.*) the raising of a quantity to any power || (*biol.*) degeneration of an organ etc. || (*med.*) the shrinking of an organ etc. to its normal size after enlargement || (*biol.*) the onset of old age, marked in women by the menopause, and in both sexes by declining vigor [fr. L. *involutio* (*involutionis*)]

in·volve (invɔ́lv) *pres. part.* **in·volv·ing** *past* and *past part.* **in·volved** *v.t.* to include, concern, *this problem involves us all* || to entail, *the job involves little work* **in·vólved** *adj.* complicated **in·vólve·ment** *n.* [fr. L. *involvere*, to enfold]

in·vul·ner·a·bil·i·ty (invʌ̀lnərəbíliti:) *n.* the quality or state of being invulnerable

in·vul·ner·a·ble (invʌ́lnərəb'l) *adj.* not susceptible to injury, damage etc. || able to resist any attack **in·vul·ner·a·bly** *adv.* [fr. L. *invulnerabilis*]

in·ward (ínwərd) 1. *adj.* directed toward the inside, *an inward slope* || relating to the mind or soul, *inward peace* 2. *adv.* toward the inside || into the mind or soul, *to turn one's thoughts inward* [O.E. *innanweard*, *inneweard*, *inweard*]

in·ward·ly (ínwərdli:) *adv.* internally || in mind or spirit || so as not to be audible, *to groan inwardly* [O.E. *inweardlice*]

in·ward·ness (ínwərdnis) *n.* the inner nature of something || spirituality

in·wards (ínwərdz) *adv.* inward

in·weave (ínwí:v) *pres. part.* **in·weav·ing** *past* **in·wove** (ínwóuv) *past part.* **in·wo·ven** (ínwóuvən) *v.t.* to weave (one thing) into another || to weave (two or more things) together || to add another material etc. to (something) by or as if by weaving

in·wrought (ínrɔ́t) *adj.* (of a pattern) woven or worked into a fabric etc. || (of a fabric) decorated with a pattern woven or worked in

I·o (áiou) (*Gk mythol.*) a princess of Argos, whom Zeus changed into a heifer. Hera tormented her with a gadfly and drove her to Egypt, where she changed back into a woman

I/O (*computer abbr.*) for input/output

Io·an·ni·na (jɔánjinɑ) a town (pop. 40,130) in N.W. Greece on Lake Ioannina, the agricultural center of Epirus: textiles, gold and silver work

i·o·date (áiədeit) 1. *n.* any salt of iodic acid 2. *v.t. pres. part.* **i·o·dat·ing** *past* and *past part.* **i·o·dat·ed** to treat with iodine [IODIC]

i·od·ic (aiɔ́dik) *adj.* of, pertaining to or containing iodine [fr. F. *iodique* fr. *iode*, iodine]

iodic acid an acid, HIO_3, formed by the oxidation of iodine

i·o·dide (áiədaid) *n.* a binary compound of iodine with usually a more electropositive element or radical [fr. F. *iode*, iodine]

i·o·dine (áiədain, *Br.*, *chem.* also áiədi:n) *n.* a nonmetalic element (symbol I, at. no. 53, at. mass 126.904), a solid at ordinary temperature, subliming to give a violet vapor when heated. It is obtained from sodium iodate, $NaIO_3$, which occurs in Chile saltpeter, and from some seaweeds etc. It is essential to the healthy functioning of the thyroid gland (*GOITER) || (*pop.*) tincture of iodine, used as an antiseptic [fr. F. *iode* fr. Gk *iōdēs*, violet-colored]

i·o·dism (áiədizəm) *n.* (*med.*) a morbid condition caused by excessive use of or sensitivity to iodine or its compounds [fr. F. *iode*, iodine]

i·o·dize (áiədaiz) *pres. part.* **i·o·diz·ing** *past* and *past part.* **i·o·dized** *v.t.* to add iodine or an iodine compound to [fr. Mod. L. *iodum*, iodine]

iodochlorhydroxyquin *CLIOQUINOL

i·od·o·form (aiɔ́dəfɔrm) *n.* a yellow, crystalline substance, CHI_3, used as an antiseptic [fr. F. *iode*, iodine+FORMYL]

i·o·do·quin·ol (aioudoukwínɔl) *n.* (*pharm.*) $[C_9H_5I_2NO]$ antiprotozoan agent used to treat amebic dysentery (formerly called diihydroxyquin), marketed as Diodoquin, Ioquin, Moebiquin, and Yodoxin

i·on (áiɔn, áiən) *n.* (*chem.*) an atom or group of atoms which has either an excess or a deficiency of electrons and is thus electrically charged. An ion may be formed in a gas or in a solution and is capable of carrying current through either [Gk *ion*, pres. part. of *ienai*, to go]

-ion *suffix* indicating an act or state, as in 'induction', 'confusion' [fr. F.-*ion*, L. -*io* (-*ionis*)]

I·o·na (aióunə) a small island of the Inner Hebrides, where St Columba founded a monastery (563). It was a missionary center of Celtic Christianity

Ionesco, (i:ounéskou) Eugene (u-zhen) (1912–), French playwright, born in Rumania. His 'antiplays' join farce with tragedy and dreams with the bizarre and grotesque. He wrote 'The Lesson' (1951), 'Exit the King' (1960), 'A Stroll in the Air' (1963), 'Hunger and Thirst' (1964), 'La Vase' (1971) and 'Man With Bags' (1977)

ion etching method of eroding glass, metals, tissue, etc., by bombardment with high-energy ions to reveal structural features

ion exchange a reversible chemical process that results in the interchange of one type of ion in a solution for those of a similar charge present on an insoluble solid (*ION-EXCHANGE RESIN) over which the solution is passed. The process is widely used for the softening of hard water and for the removal of undesirable substances from some industrial chemicals

ion-exchange resin any of various synthetic or naturally occurring polymeric materials that contain either acidic groups for exchanging cations or basic groups for exchanging anions and that are used in various ion-exchange processes. Most such resins may be reactivated after use by contact with a renewing solution

I·o·ni·a (aióuni:ə) an ancient district on the west coast of Asia Minor which included many Aegean islands. It was settled (c. 1000 B.C.) by Greeks from Attica. Twelve rich cities arose. Ionian schools of philosophy, art, poetry and literature flourished and influenced the later development of Athenian culture. The cities fell to Cyrus the Great of Persia (c. 547 B.C.), revolted (c. 500 B.C.) and were conquered by Alexander the Great (334 B.C.). They became

part of the Roman province of Asia. Under Turkish conquest (11th c.) they declined

I·o·ni·an (aióuni:ən) 1. *adj.* of Ionia || (*hist.*) of a people who settled in Ionia and eastern Greece 2. *n.* a native of Ionia, esp. an Ionian Greek [fr. L. *Ionius* fr. Gk]

Ionian Islands a mountainous group of islands (area 751 sq. miles, pop. 184,443) in the Ionian Sea. Corfu, Paxos, Leukas, Ithaca, Cephalonia and Zante are off the west coast of Greece. Cerigo is off the southern tip of Greece. Olives, vines, currants and citrus fruits are grown in the densely populated plains. The islands were under Venetian rule from the 15th c. to 1797. They were disputed between France and Britain (1797–1815) and were in British possession from 1815, until handed over to Greece in 1864

Ionian mode (*mus.*) an authentic mode introduced in the 16th c., represented by the white piano keys ascending from C

Ionian Sea that part of the Mediterranean between Greece and S.E. Italy

I·on·ic (aiɔ́nik) 1. *adj.* of Ionia or the Ionians || (*archit.*) of or like one of the classical orders of architecture characterized by the spiral volutes of the capitals and by columns 9 times their diameter in height **i·on·ic** (*classical poetry*) consisting of ionics 2. *n.* a dialect of the ancient Greek language of which Attic was a development **ionic** (*classical poetry*) a foot of two long and two short syllables (major ionic) or two short and two long syllables (minor ionic), used e.g. by Alcman, Alcaeus and Sappho || (*pl.*) a meter of ionic feet [fr. L. *Ionicus* fr. Gk]

ionic *adj.* pertaining to ions [ION]

ionic bond an electrovalent bond

i·on·ic·i·ty (aiɔnísiti:) *n.* capacity for ionization

ion implanatation (*electr.*) technique for electronically implanting impurities in silicon chips in the making of semiconductors, by directing a beam of ions onto the chips

i·on·i·za·tion (aiənizéiʃən) *n.* an ionizing or being ionized

ionization potential the smallest potential difference that will separate an electron from a neutral atom in the gas phase, given as the product of the charge on the electron and the potential difference in volts (cf. ELECTRON AFFINITY)

i·o·nize (áiənaiz) *pres. part.* **i·o·niz·ing** *past* and *past part.* **i·o·nized** *v.t.* to convert into ions (e.g. by addition to an ionizing solvent or by means of high-energy radiation) || *v.i.* to be converted wholly or partly into ions [ION]

i·on·ized layer (áiənaizd) (*meteor.*) strata of atmosphere, e.g., E layer, that may reflect radio waves from the earth

i·on·o·mer (aiɔ́nəmər) (*chem.*) tough transparent plastic product produced by ionic bonding

i·on·o·sonde (aiɔ́nəspnd) *n.* (*meteor.*) a device for measuring height of ionized layers above the earth by the reflection line of short waves

i·on·o·sphere (aiɔ́nəsfiər) *n.* the portion of the atmosphere between about 31 miles and 250 miles from the surface of the earth containing gases that have been ionized by ultraviolet rays and X rays from the sun. The resulting charged particles are found concentrated in different regions of the ionosphere (*D REGION, E REGION, *F REGION) and refract radio waves back toward the earth's surface. This permits transmission of radio messages around the world. The degree of ionization and height above the earth for each region depends upon time of day, season and solar cycle

ion propulsion or **ionic propulsion** movement caused by rearward expulsion of ionized particles. —**ion rocket** *n.*

ionspheric wave *SKY WAVE. —**isogrivation** *n.*

i·ont·o·phor·e·sis (aiɔntəfɔri:sis) *n.* (*med.*) introduction of water-soluble chemicals into the skin using a galvanic machine

I·os (áiɔs) a small island (pop. 2,000) in the Cyclades, Greece

i·o·ta (aióutə) *n.* the ninth letter (I, ι=i) of the Greek alphabet || a very small amount, jot, *not one iota of truth* [Gk]

IOU (áióujú:) a note acknowledging a debt, bearing these letters, the amount owed and the signature of the debtor [I OWE YOU]

I·o·wa (áiəwə) (*abbr.* Ia.) a state (area 56,290 sq. miles, pop. 2,905,000) on the midwestern plains of the U.S.A. Capital: Des Moines. Agriculture: corn (leading state producer with Illinois), oats and other cereals, fodder crops, hogs (first state producer), poultry, beef and dairy cattle. Resources: building materials, some coal. Indus-

---

CONCISE PRONUNCIATION KEY: **(a)** æ, c**a**t; ɑ, c**a**r; ɔ f**a**wn; ei, sn**a**ke. **(e)** e, h**e**n; i:, sh**ee**p; iə, d**ee**r; εə, b**ea**r. **(i)** i, f**i**sh; ai, t**i**ger; ə:, b**i**rd. **(o)** o, **o**x; au, c**ow**; ou, g**oa**t; u, p**oo**r; ɔi, r**oy**al. **(u)** ʌ, d**u**ck; u, b**u**ll; u:, g**oo**se; ə, b**a**cillus; ju:, c**u**be. x, lo**ch**; θ, **th**ink; ð, bo**th**er; z, **Z**en; ʒ, corsa**g**e; dʒ, sava**g**e; ŋ, orangutan**g**; j, **y**ak; ʃ, **fish**; tʃ, fe**tch**; 'l, rabb**le**; 'n, redd**en**. Complete pronunciation key appears inside front cover.

tries: food processing, machinery. State university (1847) at Iowa City. Iowa was explored by the French (late 17th c.), ceded to Spain (1762) and returned to France (1800). As part of the Louisiana Purchase (1803), it passed to the U.S.A., of which it became (1846) the 29th state

ip·e·cac (ípikæk) n. the ipecacuanha plant or a medicinal preparation made from its rhizome and roots

ip·e·cac·u·an·ha (ipikækju:ǽnə) n. *Cephaelis ipecacuanha*, fam. *Rubiaceae*, a creeping plant of tropical South America ‖ a preparation made from its dried rhizome and roots, used in medicine as an emetic etc. [Port. fr. Tupi-Guarani]

Iph·i·ge·ni·a (ifidʒináiə, ifidʒini:ə) (Gk mythol.) the daughter of Agamemnon and Clytemnestra. She was rescued by Artemis from being sacrificed in Aulis by Agamemnon and was taken to Tauris, where she became a priestess. Having recognized her brother Orestes, brought to her for sacrifice, she escaped with him

I·poh (í:pou) a town (pop. 300,727) in Perak, Malaysia: tin mines

ip·o·moe·a (ipəmí:ə, aipəmí:ə) n. a member of *Ipomoea*, fam. *Convolvulaceae*, a large genus of tropical and temperate climbing plants incl. the morning glories and the sweet potato [Mod. L. fr. Gk *ips* (*ipos*), worm + *homoios*, like]

ip·so fac·to (ípsoufǽktou) adv. by that very fact [L.]

Ip·swich (ípswitʃ) the county town (pop. 115,000) of Suffolk, England, a county borough, river port and produce market

I.Q. (áikjú:) *INTELLIGENCE QUOTIENT

Iq·bal (ikbál) Sir Mohammed (1875–1938), Indian poet. He wrote philosophic and reflective poetry in Urdu and in Persian

I·qui·que (i:kí:kə) a port (pop.63,600) in N. Chile on the Pacific, exporting nitrates and iodine: oil refineries

I·qui·tos (i:kí:təs) a port and trading center (pop. 110,242) in N.E. Peru on the Amazon, 2,300 miles from the Atlantic, but reached by oceangoing vessels. Exports: cotton, lumber, rubber, nuts, coffee

Ir (chem.) iridium

ir- (ir) prefix form of IN- before r

I.R.A. *IRISH REPUBLICAN ARMY

IRA (acronym) for Individual Retirement Account, federal-government-approved plan for employees not covered by an employer, into which limited contributions are tax-deductible

I·ran (irán, irǽn) (Persia) an Islamic republic (area 267,000 sq. miles, pop. 40,476,000) of W. Asia. Capital: Tehran. People and language: Persian, with Kurd, Baluchi, Arab, Turkish and other minorities. Religion: Moslem (90% Shi'ite, 5% Sunnite, 3% Sufi), with Christian, Bahai, Jewish and Parsee minorities. 10% of the land is cultivated and 15% is pasture. There are mountains on all sides of the central desert plateau (4,000 ft), the highest being the Zagros (several peaks over 14,000 ft), which occupy, with their foothills, most of the western half of the country. The chief fertile region and most of the forests lie in the Caspian coastal strip, north of the Elburz Mtns (Demavend, 18,600 ft). The wide Persian Gulf coastal plain is fertile only in the northwest, around the Karun River. North of this region lie the country's chief oil fields. The southeast is a rocky wilderness. Average temperatures (F.) in Jan. and July: Tehran 36° and 88°, Isfahan 39° and 81°, Shiraz 42° and 78°. Rainfall: Caspian coast and the northwest 20–50 ins, central plateau under 15 ins, Ahwaz 7 ins, Meshed 1 in. Livestock: sheep, goats, cattle, donkeys, horses, camels. Agricultural products: wool, cotton, silk, fruit, nuts, cereals, vegetables, sugar beets, rice, tobacco, gum, lumber, oilseeds. Minerals: oil, coal, iron ore, copper, lead, chromite, zinc, salt, turquoises. Industries: oil refining (Abadan, Kermanshah), carpets, textiles, foodstuffs, metalwork, cement, fishing. Exports: oil and petroleum products, raw cotton, carpets, fruit, wool, hides and skins, silk, opium, tobacco. Imports: machinery, iron and steel, sugar, chemicals, vehicles, tires, tea. Universities: Shiraz, Tehran, Tabriz, Rezayeh, Isfahan, Meshed, Ahwaz. Monetary unit: rial (100 dinars). HISTORY. The country was occupied (1941–6) by Britain and the U.S.S.R. Reza Shah Pahlavi was forced to abdicate (1941) in favor of his son, Mohammed Reza Pahlavi, who obliged the U.S.S.R. to evacuate Azerbaijan (1946). Mossadegh national-

ized all foreign interests in the oil industry (1951), and a British blockade caused serious economic difficulties until a new agreement was signed (1954) after Mossadegh's arrest. Iran joined the Baghdad Pact (1955). Muhammed Reza Shah Pahlavi in 1963 put into effect a wide-ranging program of reforms affecting land distribution, the status of women, and industrialization. The resulting social dislocation and corruption caused a split with the clergy and in the late 1970's street rioting prompted the shah to evoke military rule (1978). Opposition gradually centered around exiled Islamic fundamentalist Ayatollah Ruhollah Khomeini, who returned to Iran in Feb. 1979, soon after the shah had lifted military rule and left the country. Khomeini immediately began to reverse the Westernization movement. On Feb. 12, Iran was proclaimed an Islamic republic; a constitution approved at the end of the year called for an elected president, a unicameral parliament, and a council of guardians (religious leaders). Supreme authority was vested in a *faqih* (supreme religious guide) and Khomeini accepted that position for life. Various opposing forces were gradually eliminated, and strict Islamic codes of behavior and dress were imposed on all Iranians. A long international crisis began in Nov. 1979 when the U.S. embassy in Tehran was seized by militant students; the hostages were released in Jan. 1981. In Sept. 1980 a border dispute with Iraq evolved into war that still continues (For early history *PERSIA)

I·ra·ni·an (iréini:ən) 1. adj. of or relating to Iran, its people or its language 2. n. a native of Iran ‖ the modern Persian language [fr. Pers. *īrān*, Persia]

Iranian languages a branch of the Indo-European language family, incl. Old and Modern Persian, Avestan, Kurdish, Pushtu, Baluchi, Ossetic etc.

I·raq (irák, irǽk) a republic (area 169,240 sq. miles, pop. 9,440,000) of W. Asia. Capital: Baghdad. People and language: mainly Arab, 13% Kurdish, small Turkish and Persian minorities. Religion: mainly Moslem (Sunnite in the north, Shi'ite in the south) with Christian and Yezidi minorities. The land is 12% arable, with intensive irrigation. Except for the mountains of Kurdistan (cut by four tributaries of the Tigris in the northeast, bordering Iran, it is a plain. The fertile center (ancient Mesopotamia) is watered by the Tigris and Euphrates, which join above Basra to form the Shatt-el-Arab. This flows through a marshy delta to the short Persian Gulf coast. Average temperatures (F.) in the plains: (Jan.) 60° (35° at night), (Jul.) 110° (75°-80° at night). The mountains have snow in winter. Rainfall: 30-40 ins in the mountains, 16 ins at Mosul, 10 ins east of the Tigris, 6 ins at Baghdad and west of the Euphrates. Livestock: sheep, goats, donkeys, horses, mules, camels. Agricultural products: wheat and barley in winter, rice in summer, dates (80% of world production), wool, cotton, corn, millet, sesame, tobacco (Kurdistan). Chief industry: oil refining. Other industries: textiles, bricks, cement, milling, tanning. Exports: oil, cereals, dates, rice, wool, cotton, hides and skins. Imports: iron and steel, tea, textiles, sugar, vehicles, lumber, paper, machinery. Port: Basra. University: Baghdad (1958). Universities at Mosul and Basra were chartered by the Iraqi government early in 1967. Monetary unit: Iraqi dinar (1,000 fils). HISTORY. Iraq, coextensive with ancient Mesopotamia, saw the rise of Sumerian civilization (4th millennium B.C.), and of the empires of Babylonia, Assyria and Chaldea. It was conquered (5th c. B.C.) by the Achaemenids, by Alexander the Great (333 B.C.) and by the Seleucids (312 B.C.). After struggles between the Parthians, the Romans and the Sassanids, it fell (633–9 A.D.) to the Arabs. As the center of the Abbasid caliphate (750–1258), Baghdad became renowned for mathematics, astronomy, geography, medicine and philosophy, but was overthrown (1258) by the Mongols under Hulagu. Iraq fell (16th c.) to the Turks, and was part of the Ottoman Empire (1639–1918). It was occupied by the British during the 1st world war and became (1920) a British mandated territory, with Faisal I as king (1921–33). The country became independent (1932) but was again occupied by the British (1941–5) after a pro-Nazi coup d'etat (1941). Iraq joined the Arab League (1945) and was a member (1955–9) of the Baghdad Pact. Faisal II was assassinated in a coup d'etat (1958) led by Kas-

sem, and a republic was established. Kassem was overthrown and killed in another coup d'etat (1963). The new government under his successor, Col. Aref, sought closer links with the United Arab Republic. Col. Aref was killed (1966) accidentally and was succeeded by his brother who was overthrown by an army coup d'etat (July 1968) and succeeded by Gen. Hassan El Bakr as president of the republic. The conflict with the Kurds ended (1970). Saddam Hussein succeeded El-Bakr in 1979. A long-standing border dispute with Iran erupted in 1980 into war, which still continues. Iraq receives Soviet military aid but resumed diplomatic relations with the U.S. in 1984

I·ra·qi (iráki:, irǽki) 1. n. a native of Iraq ‖ the Arabic dialect spoken in Iraq 2. adj. of Iraq, its people, language or culture [Arab. *'irāqīy*]

I·ra·qi·an (iráki:ən, irǽki:ən) n. and adj. Iraqi

i·ras·ci·bil·i·ty (irǽsəbíliti:) n. the quality or state of being irascible

i·ras·ci·ble (irǽsəb'l) adj. quick-tempered **i·ras·ci·bly** adv. [F.]

ir·a·ser (əréizər) (acronym) for infrared maser

i·rate (airéit) adj. angry or showing anger [fr. L. *iratus*]

I·ra·zú (i:rəsú:) the largest volcano (11,200 ft, still active) in Costa Rica, in the central part of the state

Ire. Ireland

ire (áiər) n. (rhet.) anger **íre·ful** adj. [O.F. *ire*, *yre*]

Ire·land (áiərlənd) an island (area 31,840 sq. miles) of the British Isles, to the west of Great Britain, divided into the Irish Republic and Northern Ireland. HISTORY. Settled by Celts (c. 500 B.C.), Ireland became divided into the rival kingdoms of Meath, Ulster, Leinster, Munster and Connacht. Christianity was introduced (432) by St Patrick, and Ireland became a leading cultural center of Europe (6th–9th cc.). Norse invasions (795–1014) were halted (1014) by Brian Boru, but Ireland was still split in warring kingdoms when the English invasion began (1170) under Pembroke. The invaders soon mingled with the Irish and by the early 15th c. only the Pale remained under direct English rule. Henry VII attempted to bring Ireland under English jurisdiction by means of Poynings' Law (1495). Opposition to English rule increased when the Penal Laws attempted to impose Protestantism, and the political struggle became merged in conflict between Catholics and Protestants. Rebellions in the reign of Elizabeth I were put down brutally, and Protestant Scots were settled in Ulster. Another rebellion (1641–52) was put down by Cromwell with great loss of life, and was followed by a thorough Protestant settlement. The Irish supported James II in his unsuccessful attempt to retain the throne and were defeated by William III at the Boyne (1690). Absentee landlordism worsened the already bad economic conditions. Grattan and the Irish volunteer army obtained an independent parliament (1782). Continued Irish unrest and Wolfe Tone's rebellion (1798) led to the Act of Union (1800) and Irish representation in the British Parliament. O'Connell's agitation resulted in the granting of Catholic Emancipation (1829). The potato famine (1845–9) decimated the population and caused mass emigration. The Fenians forced Gladstone to disestablish the Irish Church (1869) and to pass the Irish Land Act (1870), giving security of tenure to Irish tenants. The campaign of Parnell and Davitt led to the Irish Land Act (1881), which guaranteed fair rents, and to unsuccessful attempts to pass Home Rule bills (1886 and 1893). With civil war imminent in Ireland, a Home Rule Act was passed (1914) despite Conservative opposition, but its application was delayed until after the lst world war. The Easter rebellion (1916) was put down, but guerrilla warfare ensued. The brutality of the Black and Tans caused widespread hostility to the English, and Sinn Fein won an electoral victory (1918). The Home Rule Act (1920) incorporated the northeast in the United Kingdom of Great Britain and Northern Ireland. The negotiations of Griffith and Collins incorporated the rest of Ireland in the Irish Free State (1921), with dominion status. For subsequent history *NORTHERN IRELAND, *IRISH REPUBLIC)

I·re·nae·us (airiní:əs), St (c. 130–c. 202), Greek Father, bishop of Lyon. He wrote 'Against the Heresies', a spirited attack on Gnosticism. Feast: June 28

CONCISE PRONUNCIATION KEY: **(a)** æ, c*a*t; ɑ, c*a*r; ɔ f*aw*n; ei, sn*a*ke. **(e)** e, h*e*n; i:, sh*ee*p; iə, d*ee*r; ɛə, b*ea*r. **(i)** i, f*i*sh; ai, t*i*ger; ə:, b*i*rd. **(o)** o, *o*x; au, c*ow*; ou, g*oa*t; u, p*oo*r; ɔi, r*oy*al. **(u)** ʌ, d*u*ck; u, b*u*ll; u:, g*oo*se; ə, b*a*cillus; ju:, c*u*be. x, lo*ch*; θ, *th*ink; ð, bo*th*er; z, *Z*en; ʒ, corsa*g*e. dʒ, sava*g*e; ŋ, orangutan*g*; j, *y*ak; ʃ, *fi*sh; tʃ, fe*tch*; 'l, rabb*le*; 'n, redd*en*. Complete pronunciation key appears inside front cover.

i·ren·ic (airénik, airí:nik) *adj.* (esp. *theol.*) pacific, conciliatory **i·rén·i·cal** *adj.* **i·rén·ics** *n.* (*theol.*) irenic theology, concerned with promoting unity among Christian Churches [fr. Gk *eirēnikos* fr. *eirēnē*, peace]

Ire·ton (áiərtən), Henry (1611–51), English parliamentarian general in the Civil War. He was one of the judges of Charles I

I·ri·an Jaya (í:ri:ɒnbærǽt) (or Irian Barat or West Irian) a province (area 160,618 sq. miles, pop. 1,173,875) of Indonesia, occupying the western half of New Guinea and adjacent islands. Capital: Djajapura (formerly Sukarnapura). Lingua franca: Malay. Exports: petroleum (from the northwestern peninsula), coconut oil, kapok, cocoa and coffee (grown on coastal plantations), copra, nutmeg, crocodile skins. Formerly Netherlands New Guinea, the territory became part of Indonesia in 1963 and by plebiscite (1969) chose to remain so. During the 2nd world war it was invaded (1942) by Japanese forces but was recovered (1943–4) by an Allied air, sea, and jungle attack

irides alt. *pl.* of IRIS

ir·i·des·cence (iridés'ns) *n.* the quality or state of being iridescent || a play of changing colors, e.g. on a soap bubble

ir·i·des·cent (iridés'nt) *adj.* having shifting rainbowlike colors [fr. L. *iris* (*iridis*), rainbow]

i·rid·i·um (irídi:əm, airídi:əm) *n.* a metallic element (symbol Ir, at. no. 77, at. mass 192.2) resembling platinum. It is hard and chemically resistant, and is used in alloys and in scientific instruments and for tipping pen points etc. [fr. L. *iris* (*iridis*), rainbow]

I·ris (áiris) (*Gk mythol.*) the goddess of the rainbow, daughter of Electra and sister of the Harpies

i·ris (áiris) *pl.* **i·ris·es, ir·i·des** (íridi:z, áiridi:z) *n.* the broad colored muscular ring surrounding the pupil of the eye || (*pl.* also **i·ris**) a member of *Iris*, fam. *Iridaceae*, a genus of perennial plants with rhizomes or bulbs. About 180 species are found throughout temperate regions of the northern hemisphere. They are cultivated for their flowers || a kind of iridescent rock crystal [Gk *iris* (*iridos*), rainbow]

iris diaphragm an adjustable diaphragm of thin overlapping plates for controlling the admission of light to the lens of a camera etc.

I·rish (áiriʃ) **1.** *adj.* of or relating to Ireland, its people or its language **2.** *n.* the Celtic language spoken by about 400,000 people in Ireland. Irish is recorded in 8th-c. manuscripts and some inscriptions are earlier **the Irish** the people of Ireland [older *I'risc* fr. O.E. *I'ras*, the inhabitants of Ireland]

Irish Free State a former name (1921–37) of the Irish Republic

I·rish·ism (áiriʃizəm) *n.* a characteristically Irish expression or custom

I·rish·man (áiriʃmən) *pl.* **I·rish·men** (áiriʃmən) *n.* a man of Irish birth or nationality

Irish moss carrageen

Irish Republic (*Ir.* Eire) a republic (area 26,600 sq. miles, pop. 3,440,400) in N.W. Europe. Capital: Dublin. It occupies four-fifths of Ireland. Languages: English and Irish (Erse). Religion: 94% Roman Catholic, 5% Protestant. The land is 65% arable and pasture, 30% grazing and 2% forest. The central limestone plain (average elevation 250 ft) is hilly except where peat bogs have accumulated (the largest being the Bog of Allen, where the peat is 20 ft deep). The plain is drained by the Boyne, Shannon and Erne, and is surrounded by broken mountain masses, except for the lowland stretch east of Dublin, which is free of bogs. The mountains are highest in the southwest (Carrantuohill in Macgillicuddy's Reeks, 3,414 ft). The western peninsulas of Donegal, Mayo, Connemara and Kerry contain granite ridges and bog-covered schists. Average temperatures (F.): (Jan.) 45° in the west, 42° in the east, (Jul.) 60° in the southwest, 57° in the northwest. Rainfall: over 80 ins in Donegal, Connemara and Kerry, 40–100 ins in the uplands, under 30 ins along the coast north of Dublin. Livestock: cattle, sheep, poultry, horses, hogs. Crops: cereals, root vegetables, flax, hay. Exports: live animals, meat and poultry, dairy products, fish (esp. herring, mackerel), beer and whiskey, textiles (esp. linen, tweed). Domestic industries: tobacco, food and fodder processing, vehicle assembly, clothing. Imports: machinery, tobacco, fodder, petroleum, chemicals, coal, wheat and corn, iron and steel, fruit, paper. Chief ports: Dublin, Cork, Waterford, Limerick. Universities: Trin-

ity College, Dublin, and a National University incorporating colleges in Dublin, Galway, and Cork. Monetary unit: Irish pound (100 pence). HISTORY. The Irish Free State was established in 1921. (For previous history *IRELAND.*) De Valera refused to accept the treaty signed by Collins and Griffith, and civil war broke out (1922–3). De Valera's party, Fianna Fail, gained a parliamentary majority (1932) and a new constitution was introduced (1937), renaming the country Eire. Eire remained neutral in the 2nd world war. It became completely independent (1948), and the Irish Republic was proclaimed (Apr. 18, 1949). De Valera became prime minister (1951) and president (1959). The Irish Republic joined the U.N. (1955). Entry into the E.E.C. was fully negotiated (1972). Garrett Fitzgerald served as prime minister June 1981–March 1982, and Dec. 1982–), leading a Fine Gael-Labour party coalition. In 1985 he negotiated an agreement with Britain giving the Irish government a consultive role regarding Northern Ireland

Irish Republican Army (*abbr.* I.R.A.) an Irish nationalist revolutionary movement formed during the 1st world war and outlawed in 1939. It carried out raids on Northern Ireland (1950s) with the aim of ending the partition of Ireland, and was active in Northern Ireland (1968–72) in the clash between Protestants and Catholics. During the 1980's the Social Democratic and Labor party (SDLP) seemed to lose support to the IRA and the Provisional Sinn Fein, its political branch

Irish Republican Brotherhood *FENIAN

Irish Sea the part of the Atlantic between Ireland and England

Irish setter a member of a breed of large, lean, reddish-brown setters

Irish stew stewed meat with carrots, potatoes, onions etc. in a thick gravy

Irish terrier a medium-sized terrier of a breed with wiry, reddish hair

Irish whiskey whiskey made in Ireland, esp. from barley

Irish wolfhound a very large, tall wolfhound of a breed with a wiry coat

I·rish·wom·an (áiriʃwụmən) *pl.* **I·rish·wom·en** (áiriʃwịmən) *n.* a woman of Irish birth or nationality

irk (ə:rk) *v.t.* to irritate, annoy **irk·some** (ə́:rksəm) *adj.* [M.E. *irken*]

Ir·kutsk (irkú:tsk) a town (pop. 550,000) in the R.S.F.S.R., U.S.S.R., in S.E. Siberia on the Angara and on the Trans-Siberian railroad: mining (gold, coal, salt), livestock, lumber, furs

I.R.O. *INTERNATIONAL REFUGEE ORGANIZATION

i·ron (áiərn) **1.** *n.* a widely occurring and widely used metallic element (symbol Fe, at. no. 26, at. mass 55.847) that is heavy, malleable, ductile, magnetic, and silver gray in color. It rusts readily in moist air. It is chemically active and is usually divalent or trivalent, forming ferrous and ferric compounds respectively (*CAST IRON, *PIG IRON, *STEEL, *WROUGHT IRON) || an implement, formerly of iron but now usually of stainless steel, used hot to press garments etc. || a branding iron || (*golf*) a club with an iron or steel head used for lofting the ball || (*naut., pl.*) chains, *the prisoner was put in irons* || the hard, unyielding quality of iron, *a man of iron* || a preparation containing iron, used to combat anemia etc. **to have other** (or **many**) **irons in the fire** to have other (or many) projects in hand **to strike while the iron is hot** to act at exactly the right moment, without delay **2.** *v.t.* to press with an iron || to cover or furnish with iron **to iron out** to remove (a difficulty etc.) [O.E. *īren, īsern, īsen*]

I·ron Age (áiərn) the period of human culture following the Bronze Age and characterized by the smelting and use of iron. It began among the Hittites c. 1400 B.C., and reached S. Europe c. 1000 B.C. It reached N. Europe later, and may be divided into the Hallstatt and La Tène cultures

i·ron·bark (áiərnbɑrk) *n.* any of several Australian eucalyptus trees having very hard, gray bark

i·ron·bound (áiərnbaụnd) *adj.* bound with iron || (*rhet.*, of a coast) bordered by rocks || unyielding, inflexible

Iron Chancellor *BISMARCK

i·ron·clad (áiərnklæd) **1.** *adj.* protected with iron plates || (e.g. of contracts or agreements) hard to break, not readily changed **2.** *n.* (*hist.*) a wooden ship armored with iron plates

Iron Cross a German military decoration instituted (1813) by Frederick William III of Prussia

Iron Curtain the ideological barrier separating the U.S.S.R. and the Communist countries of E. Europe from the West [popularized (1946) by Churchill]

Iron Duke *WELLINGTON, 1st Duke of

Iron Gate (*G.* Eisernes Tor) a gorge of the Danube on the Yugoslav-Rumanian border between the S. Carpathians and the N. Balkans

iron gray, iron grey 1. *adj.* of the gray color of cast iron when its surface is freshly broken **2.** *n.* this color [O.E. *īsengræg*]

i·ron·ic (airónik) *adj.* of, using, or said with irony **i·rón·i·cal** *adj.* [fr. L.L. *ironicus* fr. Gk]

ironing board a padded board on which clothes etc. are ironed

iron hand harshly rigorous rule

i·ro·nist (áirənist) *n.* someone who uses irony esp. for literary effect [fr. Gk *eirōn*, dissembler]

iron lung a large metal device enclosing a patient except for his head, used for administering artificial respiration, esp. when the chest muscles have been paralyzed in poliomyelitis

Iron Mask, the Man in the (*d.* 1703), a mysterious prisoner of state imprisoned (1698–1703) in the Bastille. His identity was kept a close secret, and he has been variously identified as a half brother or illegitimate son of Louis XIV or as various English, French or Italian nobles

i·ron·mas·ter (áiərnmæstər, áiərnmɒstər) *n.* a manufacturer of iron

iron mold, iron mould a stain or mark made by ink, rust etc. on cloth

i·ron·mon·ger (áiərnmʌŋgər, áiərnmɒŋgər) *n.* (*Br.*) a hardware dealer **i·ron·mon·ger·y** *pl.* **i·ron·mon·ger·ies** *n.* (*Br.*) hardware || (*Br.*) a hardware store || (*Br.*) the business of a hardware dealer [fr. IRON + *monger*, a dealer]

iron mould *IRON MOLD

iron rations (esp. *Br.*) a personal supply of food for use in emergency, esp. for a soldier

I·ron·sides (áiərnsaịdz) Oliver Cromwell's cavalry in the English Civil War

i·ron·stone (áiərnstoụn) *n.* any of several iron ores containing silica impurities || a white stoneware

i·ron·ware (áiərnwₑɑr) *n.* articles made of iron, esp. household utensils

i·ron·wood (áiərnwụd) *n.* any of various trees or shrubs yielding very hard and heavy wood, e.g. lignum vitae, quebracho, ebony || the wood of any of these trees

i·ron·work (áiərnwə:rk) *n.* (*collect.*) articles made of iron **i·ron·work·er** *n.* someone who makes articles of iron || someone employed at an ironworks **i·ron·works** *n.* an iron foundry

i·ro·ny (áiərni:) *pl.* **i·ro·nies** *n.* a manner of speaking or writing in which the meaning literally expressed is the opposite of the meaning intended and which aims at ridicule, humor or sarcasm || the quality of an event or situation which is the opposite of what is promised, expected etc., and which therefore seems to mock one's expectations || a literary technique in which characters and situations are treated in such a way as to show the incongruities between appearance and reality, intention and achievement etc., the writer's personal view being unmistakably implied though not always openly stated (*DRAMATIC IRONY, *SOCRATIC IRONY) [fr. L. *ironia* fr. Gk *eirōneia*, simulated ignorance]

I·ro·quoi·an (irəkwóiən) **1.** *adj.* of or relating to one of the main linguistic families of North American Indians || of or relating to the Iroquois **2.** *n.* the Iroquoian language family

Ir·o·quois (írəkwɔi) *n.* a member of a confederacy of North American Indian tribes founded (c. 1570) to eliminate incessant intertribal warfare and cannibalism. It included the Mohawk, Oneida, Onondaga, Cayuga and Seneca and, later, the Tuscarora and others. They occupied the region between Virginia and Ontario (16th–18th cc.). They were allied with the British, first against the French and later against the American revolutionaries. Their descendants live mostly in southern Canada

Iroquois (*mil.*) a light single rotor helicopter (UH-1) utilized for cargo/personnel transport and attack helicopter support. Some Iroquois are armed with machine guns and light air-to-ground rockets

ir·ra·di·ance (iréidi:əns) *n.* the quality or state of being irradiant || something emitted by or as if by irradiation

ir·ra·di·ant (iréidi:ənt) *adj.* radiating light [fr. L. *irradians* (*irradiantis*)]

ir·ra·di·ate (iréidi:eit) *pres. part.* **ir·ra·di·at·ing** *past* and *past part.* **ir·ra·di·at·ed** *v.t.* to treat by exposure to infrared, ultraviolet, X rays or other rays || to shine on, light up || to give out, radiate, *his whole being irradiated happiness* || to make suddenly intensely clear [fr. L. *irradiare* (*irradiatus*), to illumine]

ir·ra·di·a·tion (ireidi:éiʃən) *n.* treatment by exposure to radiation (e.g. heat, X rays, radioactive emanations) || the emission of radiation as heat, light etc. || the apparent increase in brightness of a white or light-colored object when seen against a dark background || the quantity of radiation falling on a given region, expressed e.g. in watts/sq. in. [F.=an irradiating]

ir·ra·tion·al (iræʃən'l) **1.** *adj.* not rational, unreasonable || without reasoning power || (*math.*) not commensurable with a finite number **2.** *n.* (*math.*) an irrational number [fr. L. *irrationalis*]

Ir·ra·wad·dy (irəwódi;,irəwódi) Burma's main river and traffic route. It flows 1,350 miles from near the Tibetan border through the Mandalay plain and a vast delta to the Bay of Bengal. It is navigable for 900 miles

ir·re·claim·a·bil·i·ty (irikleiməbiliti:) *n.* the quality or state of being irreclaimable

ir·re·claim·a·ble (irikléiməb'l) *adj.* incapable of being reclaimed **ir·re·claim·a·bly** *adv.*

ir·rec·on·cil·a·bil·i·ty (irekənsailəbíliti:) *n.* the quality or state of being irreconcilable

ir·rec·on·cil·a·ble (irékənsailəb'l, irekənsáiləb'l) **1.** *adj.* incapable of being placated or won over, *irreconcilable enemies* || incompatible, inconsistent, *irreconcilable stories* **2.** *n.* a person who is irreconcilable, esp. one who opposes compromise as a matter of principle || (*pl.*) ideas, beliefs etc. that cannot be brought into agreement **ir·rec·on·cil·a·bly** *adv.*

ir·re·cov·er·a·ble (irikʌvərəb'l) *adj.* that cannot be recovered, *irrecoverable debts* || that cannot be made right, *irrecoverable mistakes* **ir·re·cóv·er·a·bly** *adv.*

ir·re·cu·sa·ble (irikjú:zəb'l) *adj.* that cannot be rejected or refused, *irrecusable evidence* **ir·re·cú·sa·bly** *adv.* [F. *irrécusable* or fr. L.L. *irrecusabilis*]

ir·re·deem·a·ble (iridí:məb'l) *adj.* that cannot be reclaimed or reformed || (of paper money) not capable of being exchanged for coin || (of a government loan or annuity) not redeemable **ir·re·déem·a·bly** *adv.*

ir·re·den·tist (iridéntist) *n.* someone who advocates the incorporation within his own country of other areas having linguistic or ethnic connections **Ir·re·den·tist** (*Ital. hist.*) someone who advocated the annexation by Italy of Italian-speaking areas still occupied by Austria after the Seven Weeks' War (1866) **ir·re·dén·tism** *n.* [fr. Ital. *irredentista* after *Italia irredenta*, unredeemed Italy]

ir·re·duc·i·ble (iridjú:səb'l, iridjú:səb'l) *adj.* that cannot be reduced or made smaller, *an irreducible price* || unable to be expressed in simpler terms **ir·re·dúc·i·bly** *adv.*

ir·ref·ra·ga·bil·i·ty (irefrəgəbíliti:) *n.* the quality or state of being irrefragable

ir·ref·ra·ga·ble (iréfrəgəb'l) *adj.* (of an argument) that cannot be refuted || (of a person) that cannot be contradicted **ir·réf·ra·ga·bly** *adv.* [fr. L.L. *irrefragabilis*]

ir·re·fran·gi·ble (irifrǽndʒəb'l) *adj.* inviolable, that cannot be broken || (*optics*) not capable of being refracted

ir·ref·u·ta·bil·i·ty (irefjutəbíliti:, irifju:təbíliti:) *n.* the quality or state of being irrefutable

ir·ref·u·ta·ble (iréfjutəb'l, irifjú:təb'l) *adj.* that cannot be refuted **ir·réf·u·ta·bly** *adv.* [fr. L. *irrefutabilis*]

ir·reg·u·lar (irégjulər) **1.** *adj.* not following an even pattern or sequence of occurrence, activity etc., *irregular attendance* || asymmetrical, *irregular teeth* || not in accordance with normal practice, *an irregular request* || (*gram.*) not inflected or declined in the usual manner, *an irregular verb* || (*mil.*, of a soldier) not belonging to the standing army of a country || (*bot.*, of the parts of a plant) not uniform in shape etc. **2.** *n.* (*pl.*) irregular troops [M.E. *irreguler* fr. O.F.]

irregular forces (*mil.*) armed individuals or groups not members of the regular armed forces; police, or other internal security forces

ir·reg·u·lar·i·ty (iregjulǽriti:) *pl.* **ir·reg·u·lar·i·ties** *n.* the quality or state of being irregular || something irregular [F. *irrégularité*]

ir·rel·a·tive (irélətiv) *adj.* unrelated || not relative, absolute

ir·rel·e·vance (irélɘvəns) *n.* the quality or state of being irrelevant || something irrelevant **ir·rél·e·van·cy** *pl.* **ir·rel·e·van·cies** *n.*

ir·rel·e·vant (irélɘvənt) *adj.* not applicable, not related to whatever is being considered, discussed etc.

ir·re·li·gion (irilídʒən) *n.* lack of religion || hostility toward religion [fr. L. *irreligio* (*irreligionis*)]

ir·re·li·gious (irilídʒəs) *adj.* hostile or showing hostility toward religion || without religion [fr. L. *irreligiosus*]

ir·re·me·di·a·ble (irimí:di:əb'l) *adj.* that cannot be remedied or corrected **ir·re·mé·di·a·bly** *adv.* [fr. L. *irremediabilis*]

ir·re·mis·si·ble (irimísəb'l) *adj.* unpardonable || (of an obligation etc.) inescapable **ir·re·mis·si·bly** *adv.* [F. *irrémissible*]

ir·re·mov·a·bil·i·ty (irimu:vəbíliti:) *n.* the quality or state of being irremovable

ir·re·mov·a·ble (irimú:vəb'l) *adj.* fixed, not removable **ir·re·móv·a·bly** *adv.*

ir·rep·a·ra·bil·i·ty (irepərəbíliti:) *n.* the quality or state of being irreparable

ir·rep·a·ra·ble (irépərəb'l) *adj.* that cannot be repaired, remedied, retrieved etc., *an irreparable loss* **ir·rép·a·ra·bly** *adv.* [F. *irréparable*]

ir·re·place·a·ble (iripléisəb'l) *adj.* for whom or for which there is no substitute, that cannot be replaced if broken, lost etc.

ir·re·pres·si·bil·i·ty (iripresəbíliti:) *n.* the quality or state of being irrepressible

ir·re·pres·si·ble (iriprésəb'l) *adj.* that cannot be controlled or repressed, *irrepressible laughter* **ir·re·prés·si·bly** *adv.*

ir·re·proach·a·bil·i·ty (iriprəutʃəbíliti:) *n.* the quality or state of being irreproachable

ir·re·proach·a·ble (iripróutʃəb'l) *adj.* not subject to reproach, showing no faults or flaws **ir·re·próach·a·bly** *adv.* [F. *irréprochable*]

ir·re·sist·i·bil·i·ty (irizistəbíliti:) *n.* the quality or state of being irresistible

ir·re·sist·i·ble (irizístəb'l) *adj.* too powerful, tempting, charming etc. to be resisted **ir·re·sist·i·bly** *adv.* [fr. L.L. *irrisistibilis*]

ir·res·o·lute (irézəlu:t) *adj.* hesitant, undecided || habitually lacking firmness of purpose [fr. L. *irresolutus*]

ir·res·o·lu·tion (irezəlú:ʃən) *n.* the quality or state of being irresolute

ir·re·solv·a·ble (irizólvəb'l) *adj.* (of a problem) not able to be solved || that cannot be broken down into components

ir·re·spec·tive (irispéktiv) *adv.* (only in the phrase) **irrespective of** without regard to, *he went to the rescue irrespective of the danger*

ir·re·spon·si·bil·i·ty (irisponsəbíliti:) *n.* the quality or state of being irresponsible

ir·re·spon·si·ble (irispónsəb'l) *adj.* having or showing no sense of responsibility || not legally responsible for one's actions **ir·re·spón·si·bly** *adv.*

ir·re·spon·sive (irispónsiv) *adj.* not responsive

ir·re·ten·tive (iriténtiv) *adj.* not retentive

ir·re·triev·a·bil·i·ty (iritri:vəbíliti:) *n.* the state or quality of being irretrievable

ir·re·triev·a·ble (iritrí:vəb'l) *adj.* that cannot be retrieved, regained, made good etc. **ir·re·triev·a·bly** *adv.*

ir·rev·er·ence (irévərəns) *n.* the quality or state of being irreverent || an irreverent action, remark etc. [fr. L. *irreverentia*]

ir·rev·er·ent (irévərənt) *adj.* lacking reverence || lacking respect [fr. L. *irreverens* (*irreverentis*)]

ir·re·vers·i·bil·i·ty (irivə:rsəbíliti:) *n.* the quality or state of being irreversible

ir·re·vers·i·ble (irivə́:rsəb'l) *adj.* not reversible **ir·re·vérs·i·bly** *adv.*

ir·rev·o·ca·bil·i·ty (irevəkəbíliti:) *n.* the quality or state of being irrevocable

ir·rev·o·ca·ble (irévəkəb'l) *adj.* that cannot be revoked or altered **ir·rév·o·ca·bly** *adv.* [fr. L. *irrevocabilis*]

ir·ri·ga·ble (irigəb'l) *adj.* capable of being irrigated [fr. L. *irrigare*, to water]

ir·ri·gate (irigeit) *pres. part.* **ir·ri·gat·ing** *past* and *past part.* **ir·ri·gat·ed** *v.t.* to provide (land) with water by building artificial channels, flooding, spraying etc. || (*med.*) to wash (a wound etc.) with a constant flow of liquid [fr. L. *irrigare* (*irrigatus*)]

ir·ri·ga·tion (irigéiʃən) *n.* the artificial increase of water supply to assist the growing of crops || (*med.*) washing with a flow of water for cleans-

ing and disinfecting **ir·ri·ga·tion·al** *adj.* [fr. L. *irrigatio* (*irrigationis*)]

ir·ri·ga·tive (irigeitiv) *adj.* of, relating to or used in irrigation

ir·ri·ga·tor (irigeitər) *n.* someone who or something which irrigates [L.L.]

ir·ri·ta·bil·i·ty (iritəbíliti:) *n.* the quality or state of being irritable [fr. L. *irritabilitas*]

ir·ri·ta·ble (íritəb'l) *adj.* easily annoyed, apt to become impatient or exasperated || (of a part of the body) oversensitive, apt to become sore, inflamed etc. || (*physiol.*, of nerves etc.) very sensitive to stimuli **ir·ri·ta·bly** *adv.* [fr. L. *irritabilis*]

ir·ri·tan·cy (íritənsi:) *n.* the quality or state of being irritating

ir·ri·tant (íritənt) **1.** *adj.* causing esp. physical irritation **2.** *n.* something that irritates [fr. L. *irritans* (*irritantis*)]

ir·ri·tate (íriteit) *pres. part.* **ir·ri·tat·ing** *past* and *past part.* **ir·ri·tat·ed** *v.t.* to cause to be impatiently angry, annoy || to make sore or uncomfortable, *the soap irritates his skin* || (*physiol.*) to stimulate (an organ, muscle etc.) [fr. L. *irritare* (*irritatus*), to incite]

ir·ri·ta·tion (iritéiʃən) *n.* an irritating or being irritated || something that irritates [fr. L. *irritatio* (*irritationis*)]

ir·rupt (irápt) *v.i.* to break in suddenly, burst in violently [fr. L. *irrumpere* (*irruptus*)]

ir·rup·tion (irápʃən) *n.* a sudden bursting in [fr. L. *irruptio* (*irruptionis*)]

ir·rup·tive (iráptiv) *adj.* irrupting or tending to cause irruption

ir·tron (ə́:rtrɑn) *n.* region in galaxy that emits large amounts of infrared radiation

Ir·tysh (írtiʃ) a river (2,750 miles long, incl. headstream) rising in Sinkiang Uighur, E. China, and flowing north across Kazakhstan and S.W. Siberia, U.S.S.R., to the Ob

Irving (ə́:rviŋ), Sir Henry (John Henry Brodribb, 1838–1905), British actor. As actor-manager of the Lyceum theater in London (1878–99), he was most famous for his Shakespearian roles

Irving, Washington (1783–1859), American novelist and essayist. 'The Sketch Book of Geoffrey Crayon, Gent.' (1819–20) includes the short stories 'The Legend of Sleepy Hollow' and 'Rip van Winkle'

is (iz) 3rd pers. sing. pres. tense of BE

is. island, isle

Isa *ISE

I·saac (áizək) one of the Hebrew patriarchs, son of Abraham and Sarah, father of Esau and Jacob

Isaac I Comnenus (c. 1005–61), Byzantine emperor (1057–9), founder of the Comnenus dynasty

Isaac II Angelus (d. 1204), Byzantine emperor (1185–95 and 1203–4). Deposed and blinded (1195) by his brother, he was restored (1203) by the 4th Crusade

I·saacs (áizəks), Jorge (1837–95), Colombian poet and novelist. His 'María' (1867), depicting life in the Cordilleras of his native Cauca valley, is one of the most famous Latin-American novels

Is·a·bel·la (izəbélə) (c. 1292–1358), queen of England, consort of Edward II, daughter of Philippe IV of France. She plotted successfully with Roger Mortimer to depose and murder her husband (1327)

Isabella I (1451–1504), queen of Castile (1474–1504). Her marriage (1469) to the future Ferdinand V united Castile and Aragon and helped to found Spanish unity

Isabella II (1830–1904), queen of Spain (1833–68), daughter of Ferdinand VII. Her reactionary reign ended with her deposition

i·sa·gog·ic (aisəgódʒik) *adj.* introductory **i·sa·góg·ics** *n.* the study of the literary history of the Bible as a preliminary to exegesis [fr. L. *isagogicus*, introductory fr. Gk]

I·sa·iah (aizéiə, esp. *Br.* aizáiə) (late 8th c. B.C.) a Major Prophet of the Old Testament || the book of the Old Testament attributed to him, considered by many scholars to be the work of at least three authors. Chapters i-xxxv are metrical prophecies, several of them messianic, directed chiefly against Syria and Assyria. Chapters xxxvi-xxxix form a section of prophetic prose narrative, and Chapters xl-lxvi are metrical prophecies on the theme of redemption. Many passages of the book (viii-xii, xl-xlii and liii) are taken by Christians to refer directly to Christ

is·al·lo·bar (aisæləbar, áisæləbar) *n.* (*meteor.*) a line on a chart connecting all the places experiencing the same changes in atmospheric pressure within a given period [fr. Gk *isos*, equal+*allos*, other+*baros*, weight]

ISBN *abbr.* for International Standard Book Number

is·che·mi·a or **is·chae·mi·a** (iskí:mi:ə) *n.* (*med.*) blood deficiency in part of a body —**ischaemic** *adj.*

Is·chia (íski:ə, í:skjɑ) an Italian island (area 18 sq. miles, pop. 14,389) in the Tyrrhenian Sea outside the Bay of Naples, a health resort: mineral springs, wine

is·chi·ad·ic (iski:ǽdik) *adj.* ischiatic [fr. L. *ischiadicus*, relating to a pain in the hip fr. Gk]

is·chi·at·ic (iski:ǽtik) *adj.* of or relating to the ischium [fr. M.L. *ischiaticus*, relating to a pain in the hip, altered fr. *ischiadicus*]

is·chi·um (íski:əm) *pl.* **is·chi·a** (íski:ə) *n.* one of the three sections of the hipbone, located dorsally and below the ilium [L. fr. Gk *ischion*, hip joint]

-ise *-IZE

I·se, I·sa (í:sə) the sacred city (pop. 106,435) of Shintoism, in S. Honshu, Japan. Shrines (Inner Shrine, dedicated to the Sun Goddess, 3rd c. A.D. and Outer Shrine, dedicated to the Goddess of Farms, Crops, Food and Sericulture, 5th c. A.D.) University

I·se·beau of Bavaria (i:zæbou) (1371–1435), French queen, consort of Charles VI. She was several times regent (1392–1422) during the insanity of her husband, and was mainly responsible for the Treaty of Troyes

I·sère (i:zer) a department (area 3,178 sq. miles, pop. 860,400) in S.E. France (*DAUPHINÉ). Chief town: Grenoble

I·seult (isú:lt, izú:lt) *TRISTAN

Is·fa·han (isfəhán) (Esfahan) a city (pop. 671,825) of Iran, center of a region growing wheat, rice, cotton and tobacco, and traditional center of the textile industry. It was the capital of Persia (11th c. and 1590–1722). Mosques

-ish *suffix* indicating nationality, as in 'Scottish' ‖ like, as in 'waspish' ‖ tending to, as in 'bookish' ‖ (of time or age) approximately, as in 'sixish', 'sixtyish' ‖ somewhat, as in 'yellowish' [of Gmc origin, cognate with Gk *-iskos*, dim. suffix]

Ish·ma·el (íʃmeiəl, íʃmi:əl) father of the Arab peoples (Ishmaelites), progenitor of 12 Beduin tribes of the Arabian desert. He was the son of Abraham by his Egyptian bondswoman Hagar (Genesis xvi, 1–16), He was thus not a true Israelite, and for Jews and Christians his name became synonymous with an outcast

Ish·ma·el·ite (íʃmeiəlait, íʃmi:əlait) *n.* a descendant of Ishmael ‖ an outcast

Ish·tar (íʃtər) the Babylonian and Assyrian goddess of fertility and love, identified with Aphrodite, Venus or Astarte

Is·i·dore of Seville (ízidər, ízidour), St (c. 560–636), Spanish scholar and prelate. His encyclopedic work 'Etymologiae' did much to transmit classical learning to the Middle Ages. Feast: Apr. 4

i·sin·glass (áizinglæs, áizinglɑs, áizinglæs, áizinglɑs) *n.* a white, sticky semitransparent substance obtained from the air bladders of certain fish, esp. sturgeon, and containing about 90% gelatin, used in making jellies, glue etc., for clarifying alcoholic beverages and for preserving eggs ‖ mica, esp. in thin sheets [etym. doubtful]

I·sis (áisis) an Egyptian nature goddess, sister and wife of Osiris. Her cult spread (3rd c. B.C.) to Greece and Rome, and she became widely worshiped in the Greco-Roman world

Isis the name of the R. Thames from its source to just below Oxford

Is·ken·de·run (i:skəndərú:n) (formerly Alexandretta) a seaport and naval base (pop. 23,000) on the Mediterranean coast of Turkey

Is·lam (íslem, íslam, islám) *n.* a religious and social system based on the teachings of Mohammed as preserved in the Koran and the Sunna. Mohammed was convinced of the falsity of traditional Arab idolatry. This had been centered on Mecca, particularly in the worship of gods represented by sacred stones in the Kaaba. Mohammed's earliest preaching stressed four points: the sole sovereignty of Allah, the sinfulness of idolatry, the certainty of resurrection with the rewards of heaven and the punishments of hell, and his own divine vocation as prophet of this new revelation. This was inevitably rejected by the Meccans, but to Mohammed's surprise it was also rejected by the Jews and Christians of the neighboring city of Medina where he settled in 622 (the year 1 of the

Moslem calendar). As a result Mohammed accused the Jews of misinterpreting the Old Testament, of turning the universalistic religion of Abraham into an exclusive nationalistic system, and of rejecting the virgin-born prophet Jesus who had already been sent by Allah to show the Jews where they had gone wrong. He accused the Christians of a reversion from monotheism (he was referring to the doctrine of the Trinity), of blasphemy against Allah by saying that his prophet Jesus had been defeated in the humiliation of crucifixion, and of idolatry (icon-worship). All these teachings were opposed to the will of Allah, which was now fully revealed to his chosen prophet, Mohammed.

Mohammed found sufficient support among his fellow Arabs of Medina to enable him eventually to coerce the Meccans into accepting his leadership over the whole area. Even at Medina it had become clear that Islam involved the whole conduct of the community, its government and its social patterns as well as its worship. The success of Islam in the joint community of Mecca, Medina and the neighboring tribes led to a tremendous expansion which necessarily took political and military form. Almost within a century of Mohammed's death (632) all the Middle Eastern countries (formerly Christian, Jewish or Parsee), N.W. India, the N. African seaboard and Spain were incorporated into Islam. Further advance into Europe was stopped at Poitiers (732). At first the system was ruled by the caliphs, but gradually independent kingdoms within Islam came into existence, to some extent encouraged by Shi'ite and Sufi sectarianism. Islam withstood the Crusades (1096-1291), and conquered India (11th c.), Malaya (12th c.), Indonesia (13th c.), Turkey and Constantinople (1453) and the Balkans. It was expelled from Spain (1492), but threatened W. Europe at the siege of Vienna (1529). Its influence was extended by the Ottoman empire. There are now about 400 million Moslems (compared with 250 million in 1907). They predominate in N. Africa, Pakistan, Turkey, Iran, Jordan, Arabia, Iraq, Afghanistan and Indonesia (over 90%), the Sudan (70%) and Syria (60%). In Malaya they form 50% of the population and in Albania and Lebanon over 30%. Large minorities exist in India, China, Africa south of the Sahara, U.S.S.R. and the Balkans [Arab=surrender]

Is·lam·a·bad (islamabád) the capital (pop. 277,318) of Pakistan on the Potwar Plateau near Rawalpindi

Is·lam·ic (islǽmik, islámik, izlǽmik, izlámik) *adj.* of or relating to Islam **Is·lám·ics** *n.* the study of the principles and history of Islam **Is·lam·ism** (íslamizam, izlámizam) *n.* **Is·lam·ist** *n.* **Is·lam·ite** (íslamait, izlámait) *n.* and *adj.*

is·land (áilənd) **1.** *n.* a piece of land, smaller than a continent, entirely surrounded by water ‖ anything isolated like an island ‖ (*physiol.*) a group of cells differentiated from the surrounding tissue ‖ (*naut.*) the superstructure of a ship **2.** *v.t.* to cause to be or to resemble an island ‖ to isolate ‖ to cause to be dotted with or as if with islands **is·land·er** *n.* someone who lives or was born on an island [O.E. *īgland, īland*]

island of Langerhans islet of Langerhans

island universe any galaxy other than the Milky Way

isle (ail) *n.* (*rhet.*) an island esp. a small one [M.E. *ile* fr. O.F.]

Isle of Ely *ELY, ISLE OF

Isles du Vent (i:ldyvã) *WINDWARD ISLANDS (French Polynesia)

Isles Sous le Vent (i:lsu:ləvã) *LEEWARD ISLANDS (French Polynesia)

is·let (áilit) *n.* a small island [F. *islette*]

islet of Lang·er·hans (lǽŋgərhænz, lúŋərhɑnts) one of the groups of cells in the pancreas which produce insulin (*ENDOCRINE GLAND) [after Paul *Langerhans* (d. 1888), G. physician]

ism (izəm) *n.* a distinctive doctrine, practice or school (often used contemptuously) [F. *-isme* fr. L. fr. Gk]

-ism *suffix* expressing action, as in 'hooliganism', state, as in 'pauperism', doctrine, as in 'Freudianism', characteristic, as in 'heroism' etc.

Is·ma·il I (ismaí:l) (c. 1487–1524), shah of Persia (1502–24), founder of the Safavid dynasty. He established the first national government in Persia since the Arab conquest, made Shi'ism the state religion and conquered the Uzbeks (1510)

Is·ma·'i·li (ismaí:li:) *n.* a member of a sect of the Shi'ite Moslems living in Syria, Iran, Afghanistan and esp. India, about 20 million in all. The head (imam) is the Aga Khan [fr. *Isma'il* (d. 760), son of the sixth imam. The sect claims him as the rightful seventh imam]

Is·ma·i·li·a (ismai:lí:ɑ) a town (pop. 146,000) in Egypt, midpoint station of the Suez Canal. It has rail connections with Cairo, Suez and Port Said

Ismail Pasha (1830–95), viceroy (1863–6) then khedive (1866–79) of Egypt. He drove his country to bankruptcy by his modernizing reforms, had to accept Anglo-French financial control (1876), and was forced to abdicate (1879). The Suez Canal was completed (1869) during his reign

isn't (íz'nt) *contr.* of IS NOT

iso- (áisou) *prefix* equal [fr. Gk *isos*]

i·so·bar (áisobɑr) *n.* (*meteor.*) a line on a chart or map connecting places having the same barometric pressure at a given time ‖ (*chem.*) one of two or more elements with the same atomic mass but different atomic number (cf. ISOTOPE)

i·so·bár·ic *adj.* [fr. Gk *isobarēs*, of equal weight]

i·so·bu·tane (aisoubjú:tein) *n.* liquid vaporized in geothermal units utilizing naturally moderate (140–300°F) heated water

i·so·bu·tyl·ene (aisəbjú:t'li:n) *n.* a gaseous hydrocarbon, $(CH_3)_2C=CH_2$, used esp. in making butyl rubber

i·so·cen·tre (áisousentər) *n.* the point on a photograph intersected by the bisector of the angle between the plumbline and the photograph perpendicular

i·so·cheim (áisəkaim) *n.* (*meteor.*) a line on a map or chart connecting places having the same mean winter temperature **i·so·chéi·mal** *adj.* [fr. Gk *isos*, equal+*cheima*, winter weather]

i·so·chor, i·so·chore (áisəkɔr, áisəkour) *n.* (*phys.*) a line showing how pressure varies with temperature under conditions of constant volume [fr. ISO-+Gk *chōros*, place]

i·so·chro·mat·ic (aisoukrəmǽtik) *adj.* of the same color or tint ‖ orthochromatic

i·soch·ro·nal (aisókrən'l) *adj.* of equal duration ‖ keeping the same time ‖ recurring at equal intervals **i·soch·ro·nism** *n.* the quality or state of being isochronal ‖ (of a pendulum) the property of having a uniform period of vibration for different arcs of swing **i·sóch·ro·nous** *adj.* [fr. Mod. L. *isochronus* fr. Gk]

i·so·chrons (áisəkrɒnz) *n.* (*cartography*) concentric lines that join distances from a central port of equal travel times

i·so·cli·nal (aisəkláin'l) **1.** *adj.* (*geol.*) of strata which have the same angle of dip ‖ pertaining to a line on a map joining places of equal magnetic inclination ‖ of, relating to or being an isocline **2.** *n.* an isoclinal line **i·so·cline** *n.* (*geol.*) an anticline or syncline in which the two sides of rock bed have the same dip **i·so·clin·ic** (aisəklinik) *adj.* [fr. ISO-+Gk *kleinein*, to lean]

i·soc·ra·cy (aisókrəsi:) *pl.* **i·soc·ra·cies** *n.* a government or system of government in which everyone has equal political power [fr. Gk *isokratia*, equality of power or social rights]

I·soc·ra·tes (aisókrəti:z) (436–338 B.C.), Athenian orator. He mostly wrote orations for others to deliver, and was a great teacher of rhetoric. He advocated Greek unity against Persia, but failed to appreciate the dangerous growth of Macedonian power

i·so·cyc·lic (aisousíklik, aisousáiklik) *adj.* of an organic compound containing one or more rings made up of atoms of the same element (cf. HETEROCYCLIC)

i·so·di·a·met·ric (aisoudaiəmétrik) *adj.* (esp. *bot.*, of rounded or polyhedral cells) having equal dimension in all directions ‖ having equal diameters

i·so·dy·nam·ic (aisoudainǽmik) *adj.* having or relating to equal force, esp. equal magnetic intensity [fr. Gk *isodunamos*]

isodynamic line a line on a map joining places where the horizontal component of the earth's magnetic field is the same

i·so·e·lec·tric (aisouiléktrik) *adj.* (*phys.*) having the same electric potential

i·so·en·zyme or **i·so·zyme** (aisouénzaim) *n.* (*biochem.*) functionally similar enzymes chemically and electrophonetically different —**isoenzymatic** *adj.* —**esonzymatic** *adj.*

i·so·gam·ete (aisougǽmi:t, aisougəmí:t) *n.* (*biol.*) one of a pair of conjugating gametes having no sexual differentiation (cf. HETEROGA-METE)

i·sog·a·mous (aisógamǝs) *adj.* (*biol.*) characterized or reproducing by the uniting of isogametes (cf. HETEROGAMOUS) **i·sóg·a·my** *n.* [fr. ISO-+Gk *gamos*, marriage]

i·so·ge·o·therm (aisoudʒi:θθǝrm) *n.* (*geol.*) an imaginary line joining places under the earth's surface having the same mean temperature **i·so·ge·o·thér·mal**, **i·so·ge·o·thér·mic** *adjs.* [fr. ISO-+Gk *gē*, earth+*thermē*, heat]

i·so·gloss (áisǝglɔs, áisǝglɒs) *n.* a line on a map separating regions according to linguistic differences of pronunciation, vocabulary, syntax [fr. ISO-+Gk *glōssa*, tongue]

i·sog·o·nal (aisógǝn'l) *adj.* having equal angles **i·so·gon·ic** (aisǝgónik) **1.** *adj.* isogonal **2.** *n.* an isogonic line [fr. ISO-+Gk *gōnia*, angle]

isogonic line a line on a map joining places on the earth's surface where the magnetic declination is the same

i·so·griv (áisougriv) *n.* (*cartography*) a line on a map that joins points of equal angular difference between grid north and magnetic north *Cf* GRIVATION

i·so·hy·et (aisouháiǝt) *n.* (*cartography*) line on a map marking areas of equal rainfall

i·so·late (áisǝleit) *pres. part.* **i·so·lat·ing** *past* and *past part.* **i·so·lat·ed** *v.t.* to place apart and alone ‖ to place (a patient with a contagious disease) apart from others to prevent the spread of the disease ‖ (*chem.*) to obtain (a substance) from one of its compounds ‖ (*elec.*) to insulate ‖ (*bacteriol.*) to grow a pure culture of (a bacterium) **i·so·lat·ing** *adj.* of or relating to a language characterized by the use of a single word to represent a single idea, syntactical relations resting on the order of joining up the words and the use of particles (cf. AGGLUTINATE, cf. INFLECTION) [back-formation fr. *isolated* adj. fr. F. *isolé* or fr. F. *isoler*]

isolated camera (*electr.*) **1.** camera fixed on one area or person in an event, especially a sporting event, used for instant replay **2.** the technique utilizing the camera for replay

i·so·la·tion (aisǝléiʃǝn) *n.* an isolating or being isolated **i·so·la·tion·ism** (aisǝléiʃǝnizǝm) *n.* the policy of avoiding alliances and undertakings with other countries, as practiced by Britain in the late 19th c. and the U.S.A. throughout the 19th c. [F.]

I·sol·de (izɔ́ldǝ, isóuldǝ) *TRISTAN

i·so·lettes (aisǝléts) *n.* (*med.*) environmentally controlled plastic containers for premature infants

i·so·mer (áisǝmǝr) *n.* a compound, ion or radical isomeric with one or more others ‖ a nuclide isomeric with one or more others **i·so·mer·ic** (aisǝmérik) *adj.* exhibiting isomerism **i·som·er·ism** (aisómǝrizǝm) *n.* the phenomenon exhibited by two or more compounds, ions or radicals which contain identical numbers and kinds of atoms but which are constituted in different ways. Isomers have identical molecules but different structural formulas (*STEREOISOMERISM, *STRUCTURAL ISOMERISM) ‖ the phenomenon exhibited by two or more nuclides having identical mass number and atomic number but different rates of nuclear decay ‖ the condition of having an equal number of different parts **i·sóm·er·ous** *adj.* exhibiting isomerism (opp. HETEROMEROUS) [fr. Gk *isomerēs*, sharing equally]

i·som·er·ize (aisómǝraiz) *pres. part.* **i·som·er·iz·ing** *past* and *past part.* **i·som·er·ized** *v.t.* to cause to be converted from one isomeric form to another ‖ *v.i.* to be converted from one isomeric form to another (e.g. by chemical or physical means)

i·so·met·ric (aisométrik) *adj.* having the same measure or dimensions **i·so·mét·ric·al** *adj.* [fr. Gk *isometria*, equal measure]

isometric exercise an exercise for developing muscle tone by pressing, pulling etc. against resistance

isometric line (*phys.*) a line showing changes of pressure or temperature under conditions of constant volume

isometric projection (*engin.*) a drawing in which the three axes of the object drawn are shown as equally inclined to the surface of the drawing, so that dimensions can be read to scale

i·so·morph (áisǝmɔrʃ) *n.* either of two things which have the same shape because their compositions are analogous **i·so·mór·phic** *adj.* **i·so·mór·phism** *n.* (*crystall.*) similarity of shape or structure, usually due to similarity of compo-

sition ‖ (*biol.*) apparent similarity of individuals of different race or species **i·so·mór·phous** *adj.* [fr. ISO-+Gk *morphē*, shape]

i·so·mor·phic (aisǝmórfik) *adj.* (*math.*) of one-to-one correspondence **—isomorphism** *n.*

i·so·oc·tane (aisouóktein) *n.* (*chem.*) a branched chain octane or a combination of such octanes, e.g. the inflammable liquid hydrocarbon $(CH_3)_2CHCH_2C(CH_3)_3$ used in determining the octane number of fuels [fr. *iso-*, having a branched chain of carbon atoms+OCTANE]

i·so·phyl·lous (aisǝfílǝs) *adj.* (*bot.*) bearing foliage of the same shape on one plant or plant part [fr. ISO-+Gk *phullon*, leaf]

i·so·pleth (áisǝpleθ) *n.* (esp. *meteor.*) a graph showing the frequency of any phenomenon as a function of two variables ‖ (*math.*) a straight line on a graph joining corresponding values of the variables when one of the variables has a constant value [fr. ISO-+Gk *plēthos*, number, quantity]

i·so·pod (áisǝpod) *n.* a member of *Isopoda*, an order of crustaceans incl. freshwater, saltwater and some terrestrial forms (e.g. wood lice) **i·sop·o·dan** (aisópǝdǝn), **i·sóp·o·dous** *adjs* [fr. ISO-+Gk *pous* (*podos*), foot]

i·so·prene (áisǝpri:n) *n.* the compound $CH_2=C(CH_3)CH=CH_2$, used in the manufacture of synthetic rubber. Many natural products (e.g. rubber, terpenes, vitamin A) have structures that may be considered as being composed of many branching isoprene chains linked together in various ways [etym. doubtful]

i·sop·ter (aisóptǝr) *n.* a termite **i·sóp·ter·an**, **i·sóp·ter·ous** *adjs* [fr. ISO-+Gk *pteron*, wing]

i·so·quants (áisǝkwɒnts) *n.* (*economics*) a graphic contour of various production possibilities under different conditions where the object of the production is to reach the highest output

i·sos·ce·les (aisósǝli:z) *adj.* (of a triangle) having two sides equal [L.L. fr. Gk *isoskelēs*, equallegged]

i·so·seis·mal (aisousáizmǝl) **1.** *adj.* of, experiencing or indicating equal intensity of earthquake shock **2.** *n.* a line on a map connecting points of equal intensity of earthquake shock **i·so·séis·mic** *adj.* [fr. ISO-+Gk *seismos*, earthquake]

i·so·spin (áisǝspin) *n.* (*nuclear phys.*) quantity number without physical meaning, representing the difference between neutrons and protons with different charges but behaving in the same way. *also* isobaric spin, isotopic spin

i·sos·ta·sy (aisóstǝsi) *n.* (*geol.*) the condition of relative equilibrium of the earth's crust, presumed to be maintained by the adjustment in density of underlying rock in response to changes in pressure [fr. ISO-+Gk *stasis*, a standing still]

i·so·stat·ic (aisoustǽtik) *adj.* under equal pressure from every side ‖ in hydrostatic equilibrium ‖ of, relating to or characterized by isostasy

i·sos·ter·ism (aisóstǝrizǝm) *n.* the existence of molecules with different atoms but the same total number of electrons in the same arrangement (e.g. CO_2 and N_2O) [fr. ISO-+Gk *stereos*, solid]

i·so·ten·i·scope (aisǝténǝskoup) *n.* (*chem.*) U-shape tube to measure the pressure at which a liquid and its vapor are at an equilibrium at a given temperature, i.e., the boiling point of a liquid excluding the atmosphere factor

i·so·there (áisǝθiǝr) *n.* a line on a map or chart connecting places with the same mean summer temperature [F. *isothère* fr. Gk *isos*, equal+*theros*, summer]

i·so·therm (áisǝθǝrm) *n.* a line on a map joining places having the same mean temperature or the same temperature at one time ‖ a line on a chart showing changes in pressure or volume at constant temperature **i·so·thér·mal 1.** *adj.* having the same temperature ‖ without a change in temperature ‖ relating to or showing changes in pressure or volume at constant temperature **2.** *n.* an isotherm [F. *isotherme* fr. Gk *isos*, equal+*thermē*, heat]

i·so·ton·ic (aisǝtónik) *adj.* (*physiol.*, of muscles) having equal tension ‖ (*chem.*) having equal osmotic pressures **i·so·tón·ic·i·ty** (aisǝtɒnisiti) *n.* [fr. ISO-+Gk *tonos*, tension]

i·so·ton·ics (aisǝtóniks) *n.* weight-training with barbells and other objects. *also* isotonic exercise

i·so·tope (áisǝtoup) *n.* (*chem.*) one of two or more forms of an element that are distinguished by small integral differences in atomic mass and

usually slight differences in physical and chemical properties (those depending on mass) but that have the same atomic number. Isotopes of an element are indicated by specifying the mass number in conjunction with the name or symbol for the element (e.g. carbon 14 or ^{14}C) **i·so·top·ic** (aisǝtópik) *adj.* [fr. ISO-+Gk *topos*, place]

i·so·tron (áisǝtron) *n.* (*phys.*) device for separating isotopes according to their mass

i·so·trop·ic (aisǝtrópik) *adj.* (*phys.*) having the same values for properties measured along axes in any direction (cf. ANISOTROPIC) ‖ (*biol.*) not having predetermined axes **i·sot·ro·pous** (aisótrǝpǝs) *adj.* **i·sót·ro·py** *n.* [fr. ISO-+Gk *tropos*, a turning]

Is·ra·el (ízreiǝl, ízri:ǝl) a republic (area 7,993 sq. miles, pop. 4,085,000) in W. Asia. Capital: Jerusalem. Largest town: Tel Aviv. Official languages: Hebrew and Arabic. Religion: 89% Jewish, 8% Moslem, 2% Christian, 1% Druze. Except for hills (highest point 3,963 ft) in the north, center and around Jerusalem, it is a plain. The north (Galilee) and center are fertile, esp. along the upper Jordan valley and the Mediterranean coast. The south is desert (*NEGEV). Average temperature (F.): Tel Aviv 55°–80°, Jerusalem 45°–75°, Dead Sea 58°–88°, with a summer mean of 100° in parts of the Jordan valley. Rainfall: Galilee 36 ins, Jerusalem 16 ins, Jordan valley 5 ins, S. Negev nil. Livestock: poultry, cattle, sheep, goats. Agricultural products: fruits and vines, bananas, olives and tobacco, cereals and vegetables. Mineral resources: potash, bromine and salt (Dead Sea), phosphate and oil. Manufactures and industries: chemicals, metal products, textiles, tires, diamonds, paper, plastics, leather goods, glass, pottery, precision instruments, foodstuffs, electrical goods, cement. Exports: citrus fruit, fruit juices, textiles, wine, candies, diamonds, chemicals, vehicles, tires. Imports: machinery, vehicles, precious metals, cereals, oil, chemicals, wood. Ports: Ashdod, Haifa, Eilat. Universities: Jerusalem, Tel Aviv, Ramat Gan. Monetary unit: Israeli pound (100 agorot). HISTORY. (For history up to 1948 *PALESTINE.) Israel declared itself an independent republic (May 14, 1948), on the day that the British mandate over Palestine ended, and a government was formed with Weizmann as president and Ben Gurion as prime minister (1948). The country was invaded by the Arab League, and the U.N. imposed a cease-fire (1948). An armistice was concluded (1949) between Israel and her Arab neighbors, but border incidents continued throughout the 1950s. Israel passed a law (1950) giving every Jew the right to immigrate to Israel, and the population doubled between 1948 and 1959. After clashes in the Gaza Strip (1955–6), Egypt refused Israeli ships the right of passage through the Suez Canal (1956). Israel, with British and French support, invaded Sinai and the Gaza Strip, but was forced by the U.N. to withdraw (1957). Israel received (1952–65) reparations from Germany for Nazi attempts to exterminate the Jews during the 2nd world war. The plan to divert the waters of the River Jordan in order to irrigate the Negev caused further incidents with Syria and Jordan (1960s). Arab countermeasures to divert the headwaters of the Jordan, and frontier raids into Israel and the Israeli counterraids, were further threats to peace. A third Israeli-Arab war broke out on June 5, 1967. After one week of fighting on three fronts (Sinai, Jordan and Syria) Israel extended its frontiers to control by force of arms the west bank of the Jordan, the east bank of the Suez Canal and the Sinai peninsula, and annexed the Jordanian part of Jerusalem. In the Yom Kippur War (1973) Israel defended itself against a surprise Arab attack. A right-wing government under prime minister Menachem Begin took power in 1977 and signed a peace treaty with Egypt in 1979. However, in 1980 Begin proclaimed all of Jerusalem as Israel's capital city, and Israel continued to settle the West Bank. Israel invaded Lebanon in 1982 to rout PLO guerrillas there. In September 1984 a Labor-Likud coalition, led by prime minister Peres, took office and began withdrawing Israeli troops from Lebanon. In 1985 Peres made peace overtures to Jordan

Israel (Bible) Jacob ‖ the 12 Hebrew tribes descended from Jacob's sons Reuben, Simeon, Judah, Zebulun, Issachar, Dan, Gad, Asher, Naphtali, and Benjamin, and from Joseph's sons Ephraim and Manasseh. A 13th tribe, that of Levi, was granted no land ‖ (*hist.*) an ancient

CONCISE PRONUNCIATION KEY: (**a**) æ, c*a*t; ɑ, c*a*r; ɔ f*aw*n; ei, sn*a*ke. (**e**) e, h*e*n; i:, sh*ee*p; iǝ, d*ee*r; ɛǝ, b*ea*r. (**i**) i, f*i*sh; ai, t*i*ger; ǝ:, b*i*rd. (**o**) o, *o*x; au, c*ow*; ou, g*oa*t; u, p*oo*r; ɔi, r*oy*al. (**u**) ʌ, d*u*ck; u, b*u*ll; u:, g*oo*se; ǝ, b*a*cillus; ju:, c*u*be. x, lo*ch*; θ, *th*ink; ð, bo*th*er; z, *Z*en; ʒ, cor*s*age; dʒ, sava*g*e; ŋ, orangutan*g*; j, *y*ak; ʃ, *fi*sh; tʃ, fe*tch*; 'l, rabb*le*; 'n, redd*en*. Complete pronunciation key appears inside front cover.

kingdom established by 10 Hebrew tribes in the north of Palestine (c. 932–c. 722 B.C.) ‖ the Jews

Is·rae·li (izréili:) **1.** *adj.* of or relating to the modern state of Israel **2.** *n.* a native or inhabitant of the modern state of Israel

Is·ra·el·ite (ízreiəlait, ízri:əlait) *n.* a Jew ‖ a member of one of the 12 tribes of Israel ‖ (*hist.*) an inhabitant of the ancient kingdom of Israel

Is·sa·char (ísəkər, ísəkər), Hebrew patriarch, son of Jacob ‖ the Israelite tribe of which he was the ancestor

Is·sei (í:sei) *pl.* **Is·sei, Is·seis** *n.* a Japanese immigrant to America, esp. to the U.S.A. (cf. KIBEI, cf. NISEI, cf. SANSEI) [Jap.=first generation]

is·su·a·ble (íʃu:əb'l) *adj.* capable of issuing or being issued ‖ capable of being legally presented as an issue

is·su·ance (íʃu:əns) *n.* the act of issuing

is·su·ant (íʃu:ənt) *adj.* (*heraldry*) coming forth from the bottom of a chief or rising from some other bearing or from the base of an escutcheon

is·sue (íʃu:) **1.** *n.* a flowing, going or passing out ‖ a place or means of going or flowing out, outlet ‖ a publishing or giving out ‖ something published or given out ‖ an outcome, result, *no one knows what the final issue will be* ‖ a question, point etc. under dispute or discussion, *a matter of concern* ‖ (*med.*) a discharge of blood etc. ‖ (*med.*) an incision made to induce such a discharge ‖ (*law*) offspring **at issue** in disagreement ‖ in dispute to **bring** (or **put**) **to an issue** to cause to reach the point where a decision can and must be made **to join issue** to take a conflicting view **to take issue** to disagree **2.** *v. pres. part.* **is·su·ing** *past* and *past part.* **is·sued** *v.i.* to come or flow forth ‖ to be derived, result ‖ (*law*) to be descended ‖ to be put into circulation ‖ *v.t.* to publish or give out ‖ to put into circulation, *to issue a new coinage* [O.F. *issue, eissue*]

Is·sus, Battle of (ísəs) the victory (333 B.C.) of Alexander the Great over Darius III of Persia

Is·syk Kul (sikkə́:l) a lake (area 2,400 sq. miles) in N.E. Kirghizstan, U.S.S.R., 5,280 ft up in the Ala-Tau Mtns but ice-free even in winter

-ist *suffix* denoting someone who does, makes, plays, sells etc. the thing indicated, as in 'harpist', 'tobacconist', or who has a specialized sphere of interest, as in 'biologist', or who adheres to a school or doctrine, as in 'syndicalist', or who has some special character trait, as in 'masochist'

Is·tan·bul (ístænbul, ístænbu:l) a Turkish city (pop. 2,772,708) on the Bosporus where it joins the Sea of Marmara, incl. historic Constantinople and Galata-Pera (the old foreign quarter) on the European side and Scutari on the Asian. Industries: textiles, tobacco, shipbuilding. It is Turkey's chief entry port and financial center. The Ottoman era (1453–1923) gave it its architectural character (narrow streets, low buildings and many mosques). Byzantine monuments: St Sophia (523–36), now a national museum, and the wall of Constantinople (5th c.). There are large foreign minorities (esp. Greek, Armenian, Jewish). University (1900)

isth·mi·an (ísmi:ən, *Br.* also ísθmi:ən) *adj.* of or pertaining to an isthmus

Isthmian games (*Gk hist.*) games in honor of Poseidon celebrated biennially at the Isthmus of Corinth

isth·mus (ísməs, *Br.* also ísθməs) *n.* a narrow strip of land joining two larger tracts ‖ (*anat.*) a narrow structure connecting two larger parts [L. fr. Gk *isthmos*, neck]

is·tle (ístli:) *n.* a fiber obtained from any of several tropical American plants, e.g. from *Bromelia sylvestris* and plants of genus *Agave*, used for basketry, cordage etc. [corrup. of Mex. *ixtli*]

Is·tri·a (ístri:ə) a peninsula (area 1,545 sq. miles) at the head of the Adriatic, part of Yugoslavia except for Trieste. It was ruled by Austria (1815–1920) and Italy (1920–47), and ceded to Yugoslavia by treaty (1947)

it (it) **1.** *pron.*, 3rd person sing., nominative and objective cases an inanimate object, infant, animal, group or collection, unidentified person, idea, situation etc. already mentioned or under examination, *what is it?*, *he saw the house the day before it burned*, *he saw it, they argued about it for hours* ‖ the subject of an impersonal verb, expressing a state or condition, *it is raining, it is 7 o'clock, it makes her happy* ‖ the

anticipatory subject or object of a verb whose actual subject, object or complement is another word, phrase or clause, *it is my sister whom you are looking for, he thought it wrong to take life* ‖ the indefinite object after verbs which usually have no object, *to rough it, to go it alone* **2.** *n.* (*children's games*) the player whose turn it is to chase or hunt for the other players [O.E. *hit*]

It. Italian

Ital. Italian, Italy

ital. italic

I·tal·ian (itǽljən) **1.** *adj.* of or relating to Italy, its people or its language **2.** *n.* a native or inhabitant of Italy ‖ the Romance language of Italy [fr. L. *Italianus*]

I·tal·ian·ate (itǽljənit, itǽljəneit) *adj.* having an Italian form or character [fr. Ital. *Italianato*]

Italian East Africa a former Italian colony (1936–41) comprising Eritrea, Ethiopia and Italian Somaliland

I·tal·ian·ism (itǽljənizəm) *n.* a characteristically Italian expression, custom, quality etc. ‖ interest in or fondness for Italy or Italian customs etc.

I·tal·ian·ize (itǽljənaiz) *pres. part.* **I·tal·ian·iz·ing** *past* and *past part.* **I·tal·ian·ized** *v.t.* to make Italian in character, outlook etc. ‖ *v.i.* to become Italian in character, outlook etc. [F. *italianiser*]

Italian Somaliland *SOMALIA

Italian Wars the struggle (1494–1559) between France and Spain for control of Italy. In the first part (up to 1515), Charles VIII, Louis XII and François I of France fought Aragon and the papacy for control of Naples and Milan, while the Italian towns changed sides to suit their own interests. François I renewed the war (1521) against the Emperor Charles V, but France was forced to abandon her claims to Italy in the Treaty of Cateau-Cambrésis (1559)

I·tal·ic (itǽlik) **1.** *adj.* of or relating to ancient Italy, usually excluding Rome ‖ designating the branch of Indo-European languages incl. Latin, ancient Italian languages, and the Romance languages descended from Latin **i·tal·ic** of, relating to or printed in a type slanting to the upper right, introduced (c. 1501) by Aldus Manutius and now used esp. for stress, to set off a word or phrase from its context etc. Italics are used in this book esp. to distinguish the examples and to mark the parts of speech **2.** *n.* the Italic languages collectively **i·tal·ics** *pl. n.* italic letters [fr. L. *Italicus* fr. Gk]

i·tal·i·cize (itǽlisaiz) *pres. part.* **i·tal·i·ciz·ing** *past* and *past part.* **i·tal·i·cized** *v.t.* to print in italics ‖ to underline (printer's copy) to indicate that it should be set in italics ‖ *v.i.* to use italics

It·a·ly (ít'li:) a republic (area incl. Sicily and Sardinia 116,280 sq. miles, pop. 53,656,000) in S. Europe. Capital: Rome. Language: Italian with a small German minority in Trentino-Alto Adige. Religion: Roman Catholic (official), with 100,000 Protestants, 50,000 Jews. The land is 50% arable, 20% pasture and grazing, 18% forest (mainly beech, chestnut, oak). The Alps (Monte Rosa, 15,217 ft, Gran Paradiso, 13,324 ft) cross the north in an arc from the Riviera to Yugoslavia, broken by large lakes (Como, Maggiore, Garda) and river valleys. They drop to the N. Italian plain (Po valley), which widens to the lagoon region of the Po delta. The Apennines (few peaks over 5,000 ft), which form the backbone of peninsular Italy, are broken by river valleys (notably those of the Arno and Tiber) and plateaus. They are highest in the east (9,560 ft in the Gran Sasso massif, Abruzzi e Molise). The only large plains are those of Campania (west) and Apulia (east). Average temperatures (F.) in Jan. and Jul.: Alps under 30° and 45°, Milan 34° and 75°, Rome 50° and 77°, Calabria 64° and 80°. Rainfall: W. Alps 60 ins, E. Alps over 80 ins, E. Po valley, Tuscany and Latium 20 ins, Apulia, S. Sicily and Sardinia under 20 ins. Livestock: sheep, cattle, goats, hogs, horses, donkeys, mules. Crops: wheat, rice, other cereals, citrus and other fruit, olives, vines, nuts, root vegetables, market produce, hemp, tobacco. Minerals: sulfur, mercury, pyrites, iron ore, manganese, lead and zinc, bauxite, coal, oil. Manufactures and industries: textiles (cotton, silk, wool and man-made fibers), engineering, clothing, chemicals, wood products, iron and steel, vehicles, aluminum, food processing, wine, pottery, glass, oil refining, electricity, ships, tourism. Exports:

textiles, fruit, vegetables, wine, vehicles, chemicals, footwear. Imports: crude oil, coal, corn, machinery, coffee, meat, rubber, metals, wood. Ports: Genoa, Venice, Naples, Trieste. There are 28 universities, the oldest being Bologna (1200), Padua (1222) and Naples (1224). Monetary unit: lira (100 centesimi). HISTORY. Prehistoric Italy was inhabited by Ligurian and Illyrian peoples. The Etruscans settled in the north, and the Greeks colonized the south (8th c. B.C.). The Gauls penetrated central Italy (5th c. B.C.) but by the mid-4th c. B.C. the peninsula was dominated by Rome. By 272 B.C. the Romans had united Italy, and by 146 B.C. had colonized the Mediterranean and conquered Greece. The Roman Empire replaced (31 B.C.) the republic, began to decline economically (2nd c. A.D.) and was divided (395) into the Byzantine Empire and the Western Roman Empire. The latter fell (476) to Odoacer, who was himself conquered (493) by the Ostrogoths. Justinian I retook (552) Italy for the Byzantine Empire, but had to cede the north (568) to the Lombards, who gained power while the empire was weakened by iconoclasm (8th c.). Pépin II, king of the Franks, intervened (754) in favor of the papacy, and his son Charlemagne defeated the Lombards and took the titles of king of Lombardy (774) and Emperor (800). Saracen invasions of the south and Sicily (9th c.) and the collapse (843) of the Frankish empire led to a period of confusion which ended (962) when Otto I united the crowns of Germany and Italy in the Holy Roman Empire. The Normans conquered (11th c.) Apulia, Calabria and Sicily. The Investiture Controversy (1075–1122) alienated Emperors and popes, and semi-independent city-states arose in northern and central Italy. Frederick I's attempt to restore imperial power was defeated (1176) by the Lombard League, and he made peace with the papacy (1177), the city-states (1183) and the Normans (1186). The Italian cities took sides in the struggle between Guelphs and Ghibellines, which further weakened the empire and allowed Innocent III to reassert papal power (1198–1216). The papacy waned, however, during the captivity (1309–77) at Avignon. The house of Anjou gained power (1266) in Sicily, but was expelled in the revolt of the Sicilian Vespers (1282) and was replaced by the house of Aragon. Sporadic fighting reduced the multiplicity of small states to five main ones by the end of the 15th c.: the duchy of Milan, the republics of Florence and Venice, the Papal States and the kingdom of Naples. Economically prosperous under such families as the Visconti of Milan and the Medici of Florence, the states fostered the arts and played a leading part in the Renaissance. The ruinous Italian Wars began (1494) with a French invasion under Charles VIII, but the Spaniards gained control when the emperor Charles V was crowned (1530) king of Italy. France abandoned to Spain her pretensions in Italy by the treaty of Cateau-Cambrésis (1559). Spain and the Counter-Reformation dominated Italy until the War of the Spanish Succession (1701–14), after which Austria gained Milan and Naples (1713) and Sicily (1720). Sardinia gained Savoy (1720) and, after the War of the Austrian Succession (1740–8), part of Milan. Tuscany passed to the Hapsburgs and Sicily to the Spanish Bourbons (1734). Napoleon invaded northern Italy (1796), set up the Cisalpine Republic (1797) and proclaimed himself king of Italy (1804), extending French control over the whole peninsula by 1810. The Congress of Vienna (1815) restored Sardinia to the house of Savoy, and the rest of Italy to Austrian influence. The reactionary policies of Metternich led to the formation of secret societies such as the Carbonari, and a movement for independence, the Risorgimento. After the failure of revolutions in Naples (1820) and Piedmont (1821), Mazzini founded (1831) the 'Young Italy' movement with a united republic as its aim. Revolutions were widespread in 1848, but the republic established in Rome by Mazzini and Garibaldi was quickly overthrown by a French army. Charles Albert of Sardinia declared war on Austria (1848) but was heavily defeated at Novara (1849). His son Victor Emmanuel II chose as prime minister Cavour, who obtained the support of Napoleon III in another war (1859) against Austria. Victories at Magenta and Solferino (1859) gave Lombardy to Sardinia. Tuscany, Modena, Parma, Bologna and the Romagna voted (1860)

CONCISE PRONUNCIATION KEY: **(a)** æ, c*a*t; ɑ, c*ar*; ɔ f*aw*n; ei, sn*a*ke. **(e)** e, h*e*n; i:, sh*ee*p; iə, d*eer*; ɛə, b*ear*. **(i)** i, f*i*sh; ai, t*i*ger; ə:, b*ir*d. **(o)** o, *o*x; au, c*ow*; ou, g*oa*t; u, p*oor*; ɔi, r*oy*al. **(u)** ʌ, d*u*ck; u, b*u*ll; u:, g*oo*se; ə, b*a*cillus; ju:, c*u*be. x, lo*ch*; θ, *th*ink; ð, bo*th*er; z, *Z*en; ʒ, corsa*ge*; dʒ, sava*ge*; ŋ, orangutan*g*; j, *y*ak; ʃ, *f*ish; tʃ, fe*tch*; 'l, rabb*le*; 'n, redde*n*. Complete pronunciation key appears inside front cover.

to join Sardinia. Garibaldi led (1860) an expedition to Sicily, which also joined Sardinia, together with Naples. Victor Emmanuel II was proclaimed (Mar. 17, 1861) king of Italy. Venice was acquired after the Seven Weeks' War (1866) and Rome during the Franco Prussian War (1870–1). Rome became the capital of Italy (1871), but the papacy refused to recognize the loss of its temporal power until 1929, when it was given sovereignty over Vatican City. The French occupation (1881) of Tunisia led Italy to join Germany and Austria in the Triple Alliance (1882). Italian colonization, which began (1882–90) in Eritrea and Italian Somaliland, was stopped (1896) by the Ethiopians. Italy entered (1915) the 1st world war on the side of the Allies, and gained (1919) Trentino-Alto Adige. Rijeka was seized (1919) and annexed (1924). The Fascists marched on Rome (1922), formed a government under Mussolini, and organized (1926) a totalitarian state. Italy conquered Ethiopia (1935–6). The Rome-Berlin Axis was formed (1936) with Nazi Germany, and Italy intervened (1936) on behalf of Franco in the Spanish Civil War. Mussolini seized (1939) Albania, and entered (1940) the 2nd world war on the side of Germany. Heavy defeats and social unrest brought about Mussolini's fall (1943). His successor, Badoglio, made peace with the Allies and declared war on Germany (1943). After the liberation (1945), the monarchy was replaced (1946) by a republic. By the peace treaty (1947), Italy lost Istria to Yugoslavia, and her African colonies became independent. Italy retained the trusteeship for Italian Somaliland until 1960. Italy received American aid under the Marshall Plan (1947), and joined NATO (1949) and the E.E.C. (1958). The dispute with Yugoslavia over Trieste was settled (1954), and the economy largely restored. The Christian Democrats, the leading party since the war, have been increasingly challenged by a growing Communist party, which won ⅓ of the votes in the 1970s and had a strong local following. Led by Enrico Berlinguer, the Communists espoused Euro-Communism which advocates independence of the Soviets. Labor unrest, government scandals, and extremists' terror tactics disrupted Italy's politics. Coalition governments, consisting of Christian Democrats, Socialists, and Republicans, continued to lead until 1981 when Spadolini, a Republican, became prime minister, to be succeeded in 1983 by Socialist Craxi, who resigned in 1985 but later returned to office

I·ta·ma·ra·ti (itamaratí:) the Brazilian Ministry of Foreign Affairs [after the palace which it occupied in Rio de Janeiro]

itch (itʃ) *n.* an irritation or tickle in the skin ‖ a restless longing, *an itch to travel* **the itch** scabies [O.E. *gicce*]

itch *v.i.* to feel an irritating or tickling sensation ‖ to have a restless longing [fr. O. E. *giccan*]

itch·i·ness (ítʃi:nis) *n.* the quality or state of being itchy

itch mite any of several parasitic mites which burrow into the skin of men and animals, causing itch, esp. *Sarcoptes scabiei*, which causes scabies

itch·y (ítʃi:) *comp.* **itch·i·er** *superl.* **itch·i·est** *adj.* feeling or causing an itch

-ite *suffix* an adherent of a person or party, as in 'Jacksonite' ‖ a mineral, chemical compound etc., as in 'sulfite' ‖ a part of the body, as in 'somite' ‖ a commercial product, as in 'vulcanite'

i·tem (áitəm) **1.** *adv.* likewise (used only when introducing a new article in a list etc.) **2.** *n.* a single article, unit, feature or particular in a list, account, series, collection etc. ‖ a piece of news **i·tem·ize** (áitəmaiz) *pres. part.* **i·tem·iz·ing** *past* and *past part.* **i·tem·ized** *v.t.* to set down and specify the items of, *to itemize a bill* [L. adv.=in the same way]

I·té·nez (i:ténes) *GUAPORÉ

it·er·ate (ítəreit) *pres. part.* **it·er·at·ing** *past* and *past part.* **it·er·at·ed** *v.t.* to say again, repeat [fr. L. *iterare* (*iteratus*), to do again]

it·er·a·tion (itəréiʃən) *n.* an iterating or being iterated ‖ an instance of this ‖ something iterated ‖ (*computer*) technique for calculating by repeating a series of operations until the desired solution is achieved [fr. L. *iteratio* (*iterationis*)]

it·er·a·tive (ítəreitiv, ítərətiv) *adj.* repetitious ‖ (*gram.*) frequentative [fr. F. *itératif*]

Ith·a·ca (íθəkə) a Greek island (area 36 sq. miles, pop. 4,150) of the Ionian group, the kingdom of Odysseus

ith·y·phal·lic (iθəfǽlik) **1.** *adj.* relating to the phallus carried in Bacchic festivals ‖ in the meter (— ∪ — ∪ —) of the Bacchic hymns ‖ (*art*, of figures in pictures or statues) having an erect penis **2.** *n.* a poem in the meter of the Bacchic hymns [fr. L. *ithyphallicus* fr. Gk fr. *ithus*, erect+*phallos*, phallus]

i·tin·er·a·cy (aitinərəsi:,itinərəsi:) *pl.* **i·tin·er·a·cies** *n.* itinerancy [fr. L.L. *itinerari* (*itineratus*), to travel]

i·tin·er·an·cy (aitínərənsi:, itínərənsi:) *pl.* **i·tin·er·an·cies** *n.* the quality or state of being itinerant ‖ a duty, ministry etc. that involves traveling from place to place ‖ a group of persons engaged in such a duty etc.

i·tin·er·ant (aitínərənt, itínərənt) *adj.* traveling from place to place ‖ (esp. of a judge or a Methodist minister) traveling on circuit ‖ involving travel from place to place [fr. L.L. and M.L. *itinerans* (*itinerantis*)]

i·tin·er·ar·y (aitínəreri:, itínəreri:) *pl.* **i·tin·er·ar·ies** *n.* a route taken or planned ‖ a record or account of a journey ‖ a guidebook [fr. L.L. *itinerarium*]

i·tin·er·ate (aitínəreit, itínəreit) *pres. part.* **i·tin·er·at·ing** *past* and *past part.* **i·tin·er·at·ed** *v.i.* (esp. of a judge or a Methodist minister) to travel from place to place **i·tin·er·a·tion** *n.* [fr. L.L. *itinerari* (*itineratus*)]

-itis *suffix* denoting inflammation, as in 'tracheitis' [Sk -*itis*]

it'll (ít'l) *contr.* of IT WILL, IT SHALL

I·to (í:tou), Hirobumi (1841–1909), Japanese statesman, prime minister (1885–8, 1892–6, 1898 and 1900–1). He was largely responsible for the modernization of Japan on Western lines, and drafted the constitution of 1889

its (its) *possessive adj.* of, pertaining to or belonging to it, *he dropped the pitcher and broke its spout* ‖ experienced, made or done by it

it's (its) *contr.* of IT IS ‖ *contr.* of IT HAS, *it's been a terrible day*

it·self (itsélf) *pron.* refl. form of IT, *the dog has hurt itself* ‖ emphatic form of IT, *the horse itself knows the way* **by itself** unaided, *the doll sits up by itself* ‖ in isolation, alone, *the house stands by itself* **in itself** considered for itself alone, intrinsically, *the talk was all right in itself but it went on too long*

I.T.U. *INTERNATIONAL TELECOMMUNICATION UNION

I·tur·bi·de (i:tú:rbi:ðe), Agustín de (1783–1824), Mexican revolutionary, emperor of Mexico (1822–3). He led the Mexican revolt against Spanish rule (1821), and proclaimed an empire (1822), but was forced into exile (1823). He was shot on his return to Mexico

ITV (*abbr.*) for instructional television

-ity *suffix* indicating state or quality, as in 'modernity' [M.E. -*ite* fr. F. -*ite*, L. -*itas* (-*itatis*)]

It·zá (i:tsá) *pl.* **It·zá, It·zás** *n.* a Mexican Indian group of Mayas of Yucatán and Petén (Guatemala). Before the Spanish conquest their capital was Chichén-Itzá. They were probably responsible for introducing into Yucatán the worship of Toltec gods including Quetzalcoatl ‖ a member of this group ‖ a dialect spoken by them [Span., of Amerind origin]

IUCD (*abbr.*) for intrauterine contraceptive device

IUD (*acronym*) for intrauterine device

I·van I (áivən) (c. 1304–41), prince of Vladimir and grand duke of Moscow (1328–40). He greatly increased the size of the grand duchy of Moscow, strengthened its finances, and made Moscow his ecclesiastical capital

Ivan III Va·sil·ie·vich (vəsíljəvitʃ) 'the Great' (1440–1505), grand duke of Moscow (1462–1505). He consolidated the grand duchy of Moscow by conquest and legal reforms, and established autocratic government

Ivan IV Vasilievich 'the Terrible' (1530–84), grand duke of Moscow (1533–84) who took (1547) the title of czar of Russia. His ruthless persecution of the boyars, his destruction of the free cities (Novgorod, 1570) and his conquest of Kazan (1552), Astrakhan (1554) and Siberia created a unified Russian state. He killed his own son (1551) in rage

Ivan VI (1740–64), czar of Russia (1740–1). As an infant he was overthrown by the Empress Elizabeth, and murdered after 22 years of imprisonment

I·va·no·vo (ivǽnəvə) a city (pop. 470,000) of the R.S.F.S.R., U.S.S.R., 145 miles northeast of Moscow. Industries: textiles, engineering, food

I've (aiv) *contr.* of I HAVE

-ive *suffix* denoting tendency, function etc., as in 'selective' [partly fr. L. -*ivus*, partly F. -*if*, -*ive*]

Ives (aivz), Charles Edward (1874–1954), American composer. He experimented with polytonality, multiple rhythms and other techniques in advance of his time. His works include five symphonies and 'Three Places in New England' for orchestra, as well as choral and chamber music and songs

Ives, Frederick Eugene (1856–1937), U.S. inventor who contributed to the technique of photoengraving. His inventions include the 'halftone' process (1878), which he developed (1885–6) for commercial production

i·vied (áivi:d) *adj.* covered with ivy

I·vig·tut (í:vigtu:t) a Danish settlement (pop. 200) 175 miles northwest of Cape Farewell on the southwest coast of Greenland. Its quarries include one of the world's largest cryolite mines

i·vo·ry (áivəri:, áivri:) *pl.* **i·vo·ries** *n.* the hard creamy-white dentine forming the tusks of the elephant, and the canine teeth of the hippopotamus, narwhal and walrus ‖ the dentine of any teeth ‖ the color of ivory ‖ (*pl.*) things made of ivory, esp. (*pop.*) piano keys, teeth, dice [O.F. *yvoire*]

ivory black a black pigment made from calcined ivory or from bone black

Ivory Coast a republic (area 124,510 sq. miles, pop. 8,890,000) in W. Africa. Capital: Abidjan. People: mainly Agni and Baulé (allied to the Ashanti), Kru, Mandingo and Senufo. Language: French, Kwa languages, Mandingo and others. Religion: 65% local religions, 23% Moslem, 10% Christian. Behind the surf beaches and coastal lagoons lies an alluvial plain 40 miles wide. Inland a plateau rises over 1,000 ft, giving way in the west to the Nimba Mtns (5,000 ft). In the north the predominant rain forest gives way to savanna. Mean temperature: 70°. Rainfall: mainly 80–100 ins, less in the far north. Livestock: cattle, sheep, goats. Agricultural products: coffee, cocoa, yams, manioc, bananas, cereals incl. rice, palm oil, peanuts, shea butter, cotton, pineapples. Minerals: diamonds, gold, manganese. Manufactures: palm oil, fruit juice, weaving, pottery. Exports: coffee, cocoa, bananas, tropical hardwoods. Imports: textiles, metals, cement, wine, fuels and oil. Ports: Abidjan, Sassandra, Tabou. Monetary unit: franc CFA. HISTORY. This part of the Guinea coast saw the development of Sudanic kingdoms (13th c.). The Portuguese established settlements to trade in ivory and slaves (16th c.), but were replaced (19th c.) by the French, who established a protectorate over the coastal region (1842). The Ivory Coast became a French colony (1893) and part of French West Africa (1895). It became a member of the French Union (1946) and an autonomous republic within the French Community (1958). It gained complete independence (Aug. 7, 1960) outside the French Community and joined the U.N. (1960). It rejoined the Community. Felix Houphouët-Boigny has been president since independence

ivory nut the seed of *Phytelephas macrocarpa*, a South American palm which has a very hard endosperm (*VEGETABLE IVORY) used for making buttons etc.

ivory tower an image connoting a state of withdrawal from the practical issues of life in society into a world of purely intellectual concerns

i·vy (áivi:) *pl.* **i·vies** *n. Hedera helix*, fam. *Araliaceae*, an evergreen woody climbing or creeping plant, native to temperate regions of Europe and Asia, often grown as ornament on walls etc. ‖ any of various similar climbing plants (*POISON IVY) [O.E. *ifig*]

Ivy League a group of long-established distinguished colleges of the eastern U.S.A., comprising Harvard, Yale, Princeton, Cornell, Columbia, Dartmouth, Brown, and the University of Pennsylvania

I·wo (í:wou) a town (pop. 214,000) in W. Nigeria, 25 miles northeast of Ibadan

I·wo Ji·ma (í:woudʒi:ma) the largest (area c. 8 sq. miles) and most important of the Volcano Is in the W. Pacific. During the 2nd world war it served as a Japanese air base. A U.S. marine

CONCISE PRONUNCIATION KEY: **(a)** æ, c*a*t; ɑ, c*a*r; ɔ f*a*wn; ei, sn*a*ke. **(e)** e, h*e*n; i:, sh*ee*p; iə, d*ee*r; ɛə, b*ea*r. **(i)** i, f*i*sh; ai, t*i*ger; ə:, b*i*rd. **(o)** o, *o*x; au, c*ow*; ou, g*oa*t; u, p*oo*r; ɔi, r*oy*al. **(u)** ʌ, d*u*ck; u, b*u*ll; u:, g*oo*se; ə, b*a*cillus; ju:, c*u*be. x, lo*ch*; θ, *th*ink; ð, bo*th*er; z, *Z*en; ʒ, cor*s*age; dʒ, sava*g*e; ŋ, oranguta*ng*; j, *y*ak; ʃ, *fi*sh; tʃ, fe*tch*; 'l, rabb*le*; 'n, redd*en*. Complete pronunciation key appears inside front cover.

landing (1945) gained the island for the Allies

ix·i·a (íksi:ə) *n.* a member of *Ixia*, fam. *Iridaceae*, a genus of bulbous South African plants, having racemes of brightly colored flowers [L. fr. Gk]

Ix·i·on (iksáiən) (*Gk mythol.*) king of Thessaly, father of the Centaurs. As punishment for his attempted seduction of Hera, he was tied to a fiery wheel revolving forever

Ixtaccihuatl *IZTACCIHUATL

ix·tle (íkstli:, ístli:) *n.* istle

Ix·tlil·xo·chitl II (iʃtlilʃóutʃit'l) (c. 1500–50), Aztec chief of Texcoco who joined forces with Hernán Cortés in the capture of Tenochtitlán at the beginning of the Spanish conquest

-ize, -ise *suffix* indicating to act on, subject to, or affect in the way indicated, as in 'hypnotize', 'christianize', or to become as indicated, as in 'crystallize' or to do something indicated, as in 'fraternize'

I·zhevsk (iʒéfsk) the capital (pop. 574,000) of the Udmurt A.S.S.R., U.S.S.R.: mechanical engineering

Iz·mir (ismíər) (Smyrna) an ancient city (pop. 955,000) of Turkey, its chief port in Asia Minor, at the head of the Gulf of Smyrna, Anatolia: figs, raisins, tobacco, carpets, silk

Iz·tac·ci·huatl, Ix·tac·ci·huatl (istɑksí:wɑt'l) an extinct volcano (17,342 ft) with three summits, southeast of Mexico City, Mexico

CONCISE PRONUNCIATION KEY: **(a)** æ, c*a*t; ɑ, c*a*r; ɔ f*aw*n; ei, sn*a*ke. **(e)** e, h*e*n; i:, sh*ee*p; iə, d*ee*r; ɛə, b*ea*r. **(i)** i, f*i*sh; ai, t*i*ger; ə:, b*i*rd. **(o)** o, *o*x; au, c*ow*; ou, g*oa*t; u, p*oo*r; ɔi, r*oy*al. **(u)** ʌ, d*u*ck; u, b*u*ll; u:, g*oo*se; ə, b*a*cill*u*s; ju:, c*u*be. x, lo*ch*; θ, *th*ink; ð, bo*th*er; z, *Z*en; ʒ, corsa*g*e; dʒ, sava*ge*; ŋ, oranguta*ng*; j, *y*ak; ʃ, fi*sh*; tʃ, fe*tch*; 'l, rabb*le*; 'n, redd*en*. Complete pronunciation key appears inside front cover.

	EARLY NORTH SEMITIC	PHOENICIAN	EARLY HEBREW	EARLY GREEK	CLASSICAL GREEK	ETRUSCAN		EARLY LATIN	CLASSICAL LATIN
						Early	Classical		
J	₹	٦	٦	⟨	ᛁ	ᛁ	ᛁ	ᛁ	ᛁ

CURSIVE MAJUSCULE (ROMAN)	CURSIVE MINUSCULE (ROMAN)	ANGLO-IRISH MAJUSCULE	CAROLINE MINUSCULE	VENETIAN MINUSCULE (ITALIC)	N. ITALIAN MINUSCULE (ROMAN)
ı	ı	ı	ı	*i*	ı

A. C. SYLVESTER, CAMBRIDGE, ENGLAND

Development of the letter J, beginning with the early North Semitic letter. Evolution of both the majuscule, or capital, letter J and the minuscule, or lowercase, letter j are shown.

J, j (dʒei) the tenth letter of the English alphabet

jab (dʒæb) **1.** *v.t. pres. part.* **jab·bing** *past* and *past part.* **jabbed** to penetrate suddenly with a pointed object, *he jabbed his finger with a needle* ‖ to thrust, *he jabbed a needle into his finger* ‖ to poke sharply, *he jabbed me with his elbow* ‖ to give a short straight blow with the fist to ‖ *v.i.* (with 'at') to make short thrusts **2.** *n.* a quick poke or stab [etym. doubtful]

Jab·al·pur (dʒʌb'lpúər) (Jubbulpore) a city (pop. 426,224) of central Madhya Pradesh, India: oil mills, textiles. University (1957)

jab·ber (dʒæbər) *v.i.* to talk rapidly without making the meaning clear ‖ to make unintelligible sounds resembling speech ‖ *v.t.* to say in a confused manner, *he jabbered some nonsense* **2.** *n.* this kind of speech or noise [imit.]

jab·i·ru (dʒæbəru:) *n. Jabiru mycteria*, fam. *Ciconiidae*, a large wading bird of tropical America [Tupi-Guarani]

jab·o·ran·di (dʒæbərǽndi) *n.* the dried leaflets of a South American shrub, *Pilocarpus jaborandi*, fam. *Rutaceae*, containing alkaloids incl. pilocarpine ‖ the dried leaves of *P. microphyllus* or the root of *Piper jaboranai*, fam. *Piperaceae*, a Brazilian plant, both yielding pilocarpine [Tupi-Guarani]

ja·bot (ʒæbóu, *Br.* ʒǽbou) *n.* a ruffled or pleated frill, of lace or cloth, worn down the front of a woman's blouse or bodice ‖ (esp. *hist.*) a similar frill at the front of a man's shirt [F.]

jac·a·mar (dʒǽkəmɑr) *n.* any of several moderately small birds (5-12 ins) of fam. *Galbulidae*, inhabiting tropical forests from southern Mexico to southern Brazil [F., fr. Tupi *jacamáciri*]

jac·a·na (dʒǽkənə) *n.* a member of *Jacanidae*, a fam. of tropical wading birds having long, straight toes enabling them to walk over floating aquatic plants [fr. Port. *jacana* fr. Tupi-Guarani]

jac·a·ran·da (dʒǽkərændə) *n.* a Brazilian tree of fam. *Bignoniaceae* which yields hardwood ‖ any of several leguminous trees of South America and the West Indies which produce fragrant woods and showy flowers [Tupi-Guarani]

ja·cinth (dʒéisinθ, dʒǽsinθ) *n.* (*mineral.*) a hyacinth [M.E. *iacynt, iacinct* fr. O.F.]

jack (dʒæk) **1.** *n.* a device for raising an automobile or other heavy load, e.g. by a screw or lever system or by a hydraulic system ‖ (*naut.*) an iron bar at the masthead which supports a royal mast ‖ (*naut.*) a small flag flown usually from the bow to show nationality, or as a signal ‖ a playing card depicting a soldier or servant, ranking in value just below a queen ‖ the male of various animals ‖ the white ball in a game of bowls ‖ a jackstone ‖ (*Am., pl.* =*Br.* dibs) a children's game in which the player picks up small objects while bouncing a ball **2.** *v.t.* (with 'up') to lift with a jack ‖ (with 'up') to raise or increase, *the price of steel was jacked up* [a nickname for John]

jack *n. Artocarpus heterophyllus*, fam. *Moraceae*, an East Indian tree with large edible fruit similar to the breadfruit ‖ this fruit [Port. *jaca* fr. Malay]

jack *n.* (in the phrase) **every man jack** every-one

jack·al (dʒækl) *n.* any of various wild dogs, esp. *Canis aureus*, fam. *Canidae*, native to S.E. Europe, N. Africa and S. Asia. They are gregarious and nocturnal [corrup. of Turk. *chakál* fr. Pers. *shagál*]

jack·a·napes (dʒǽkəneips) *n.* a conceited, impertinent young man or boy [etym. doubtful]

jack·ass (dʒǽkæs) *n.* the male ass ‖ a stupid person

jack·boot (dʒǽkbu:t) *n.* (esp. *hist.*) a heavy leather boot extending above the knee worn in the 17th and 18th cc. ‖ (*mil.*) a knee-high leather boot worn e.g. by Nazi troops ‖ military pressure, bullying

jack·daw (dʒǽkdɔ) *n. Corvus monedula*, fam. *Corvidae*, a black and gray bird of Europe and Asia that can be tamed and taught to talk

jack·et (dʒǽkit) **1.** *n.* a short coat, worn as part of a suit or with nonmatching trousers or skirt ‖ a detachable paper cover of a book ‖ an outer tube or other casing through which cold water, steam etc. can be passed to maintain the inner vessel at a desired temperature (e.g. in a condenser used in distillation) or used for protection or thermal insulation of the inner vessel (e.g. of a boiler) ‖ the metal casing of a projectile ‖ the skin of a cooked potato **2.** *v.t.* to surround with a jacket [O.F. *jaquet, jacquet*]

Jack Frost an imaginary man responsible for laying frost

jack·fruit (dʒǽkfru:t) *n.* the jack (East Indian tree) ‖ its fruit

jack·ham·mer (dʒǽkhæmər) *n.* a rock drill worked by compressed air. It is held by the person using it in his hands

jack-in-of·fice (dʒǽkinɔfis, dʒǽkinɒfis) *pl.* **jacks-in-of·fice** *n.* a pretentious, self-important man in a position of authority

jack-in-the-box (dʒǽkinðəbɒks) *pl.* **jack-in-the-box·es** *n.* a child's toy consisting of a figure which springs from a box when the lid is lifted

Jack-in-the-Green (dʒǽkinðəgri:n) *pl.* **Jack-in-the-Greens, Jacks-in-the-Green** *n.* (*Eng. hist.*) a boy dressed as a chimney sweep, enclosed in a leaf-covered wicker frame in May Day sports. He is a favorite figure in medieval carvings and stained glass

Jack Ketch (ketʃ) (*Br.*) the hangman [after John (commonly called Jack) *Ketch* (d. 1686), English executioner]

jack·knife (dʒǽknaif) *pl.* **jack·knives** (dʒǽknaivz) *n.* a large pocketknife ‖ a dive in which the diver keeps his legs straight and touches his feet before straightening out to enter the water **2.** *v.i. pres. part.* **jack·knif·ing** *past* and *past part.* **jack·knifed** to perform a jackknife dive

jack-of-all-trades (dʒǽkəvɔltréidz) *pl.* **jacks-of-all-trades** *n.* a person able to do many kinds of practical work

jack-o'-lan·tern (dʒǽkələntərn) *n.* a hollowed out pumpkin with a cutout face illuminated from inside with a candle ‖ the will-o'-the-wisp

jack pine *Pinus Banksiana*, a pine of northern North America

jack plane a medium-size plane used in the first stages of planing wood

jack·pot (dʒǽkpɒt) *n.* (*gambling*, esp. *poker*) the accumulated kitty **to hit the jackpot** (*pop.*) to win all that there is to win ‖ (*pop.*) to be suddenly very successful

jack·rab·bit (dʒǽkræbit) *n.* a member of *Lepus*, fam. *Leporidae*, a genus of large hares of western North America with long ears and long hind legs

Jack·son (dʒǽksən), Andrew (1767–1845), seventh president (1829–37) of the U.S.A., a Democrat. During the War of 1812 he defeated (1814) the Creek Indians at Horseshoe Bend (for which he was promoted to general) and (1815) the British at the Battle of New Orleans. His concept of democracy led him to oppose monopolies and the privileged class, and to advocate increased popular participation in government and greater opportunities for the farmer, artisan, and small businessman. By his support of a protective tariff favoring the industrial East, he antagonized his Southern vice-president, John Calhoun, who resigned (1832). A champion of strong federal government, he nevertheless vetoed (1832) the bill to recharter the national bank, establishing the 'pet bank' system of chosen state banks. His administration was marked by the development of the spoils system of patronage, exemplified by his 'Kitchen Cabinet' of favorite advisors

Jackson, Jesse Louis (1941–), U.S. black leader, active in the civil rights movement. A Baptist minister, he was responsible for organizing and directing Operation Breadbasket in Chicago (1966–77). He also established People United to Save Humanity (PUSH) in 1971 and was a candidate for the Democratic presidential nomination in 1984

CONCISE PRONUNCIATION KEY: (a) æ, cat; ɑ, car; ɔ fawn; ei, snake. **(e)** e, hen; i:, sheep; iə, deer; εə, bear. **(i)** i, fish; ai, tiger; ə:, bird. **(o)** o, ox; au, cow; ou, goat; u, poor; ɔi, royal. **(u)** ʌ, duck; u, bull; u:, goose; ə, bacillus; ju:, cube. x, loch; θ, think; δ, bother; z, Zen; ʒ, corsage; dʒ, savage; ŋ, orangutang; j, yak; ʃ, fish; tʃ, fetch; 'l, rabble; 'n, redden. Complete pronunciation key appears inside front cover.

Jackson, Michael Joe (1958–), U.S. singer and dancer, noted for his frail look and high voice, who began his career in the 1960s as part of the Jackson Five, a singing group, with his brothers. He embarked on his career as a soloist with the album 'Off the Wall' (1978) and broke all sales records with 'Thriller' (1982). He and his brothers reunited for their 1984 'Victory' tour

Jackson, Robert Houghwout (1892–1954), U.S. associate justice of the Supreme Court (1941–54). He served as U.S. solicitor general (1938–40) and attorney general (1940–1) before being appointed to the Court by Pres. Franklin D. Roosevelt. He defended civil rights and advocated judicial restraint. He was U.S. chief counsel at the Nazi war crimes trials in Nuremberg in 1945–6. He wrote 'The Case Against the Nazi War Criminals' (1945) and 'The Supreme Court in the American System of Government' (1955)

Jackson, Sheldon (1834–1909), U.S. Presbyterian missionary. He founded (1859–83) over 100 churches throughout the Rocky Mtns states. He introduced (1892) the domesticated Siberian reindeer into Alaska, where it provided an important food resource. He helped to lay (1885–1908) the foundations for Alaska's admission into the Union

Jackson, Thomas Jonathan 'Stonewall' (1824–63), American Confederate general during the Civil War, famous for his command at the 1st Battle of Bull Run (1861)

Jackson the capital (pop. 202,895) of Mississippi: cotton, lumber, textiles, natural gas

Jack·so·ni·an (djæksóuni:ən) 1. *adj.* of or pertaining to Andrew Jackson, or his ideas 2. *n.* a follower of Andrew Jackson

Jack·son·ville (dʒǽksənvil) a port (pop. 556,370) of central Florida, on the St Johns River near the Atlantic, shipping lumber, naval supplies and produce

jack staff the flagstaff from which a jack is flown

jack·stay (dʒǽkstei) *n.* (*naut.*) a rope or rod running along the yard to which a sail is made fast ‖ (*naut.*) a rope or rod running up and down a mast for the yard to travel on

jack·stone (dʒǽkstoun) *n.* a small metal object or stone used in jacks ‖ (*pl.*) jacks

jack·straw (dʒǽkstrɔ) *n.* a straw or similar object used in the game of jackstraws ‖ (*pl.*) a game played by throwing a bundle of straws or similar objects into a heap and then trying to draw them away singly without moving any other straw

Jack-tar (dʒǽktár) *n.* a sailor [from the time when one of his duties was to caulk the seams between the wooden planks]

jack-up (dʒǽkʌp) *n.* 1. type of offshore drilling rig from which legs are lowered to the sea bed 2. *v.* (*colloq.*) to increase

Ja·cob (dʒéikəb) Hebrew patriarch, surnamed Israel, son of Isaac, younger twin brother of Esau. His sons and grandsons were the founders of the tribes of Israel

Jac·o·be·an (dʒækəbí:ən) *adj.* of or relating to the era or reign (1603–25) of James I of England ‖ of or relating to the English Renaissance style of architecture, furniture or decoration of the early 17th c.

Ja·co·bi (dʒəkóubi:), Abraham (1830–1919), German-U.S. physician. He became (1860) the first professor of children's diseases in the U.S.A., at New York Medical College, and established (1862) in New York City the first special clinic in the U.S.A. for such diseases

Jacobi, Karl Gustav Jacob (1804–51), German mathematician, noted for his investigations into elliptic functions and determinants

Jac·o·bin (dʒǽkəbin) *n.* (*F. hist.*) a French Dominican friar ‖ (*F. hist.*) a member of a political club of the French Revolution, founded (May 1789) among the deputies at Versailles, and taking its name from the former monastery in Paris where it met from Oct. 1789. Led by Robespierre, the club became increasingly radical, overthrew the Girondists (1793) and instituted the Terror. It was closed after the coup d'etat of Thermidor (1794) **Jac·o·bin·ic** *adj.* **Jác·o·bin·ism** *n.*

Jac·o·bite (dʒǽkəbait) *n.* (*Br. hist.*) a supporter of the Stuart claim to the throne after the Glorious Revolution (1688-9). After the death (1701) in exile of James II, the Jacobites supported the claims of his son, James Francis Edward Stuart, and then of the latter's sons, Charles Edward Stuart and Cardinal Henry Stuart. The Jacobites were strongest in Ireland, where a rebellion was defeated at the Boyne (1690). Scotland then became the center of the cause, and Jacobite risings were crushed in 1708, 1715, 1719 and 1745. The cause then declined as a political force. Jacobite sympathies remained as an inspiration for ballads and literature

Jacobite Church a Monophysite sect of Syria, Iraq and India founded in the 6th c. It is regarded as heretical by the Roman Catholic and Greek Orthodox Churches

Ja·cob·sen (jákɔpsən), Arne (1902–71), Danish architect, influenced by Le Corbusier and Mies van der Rohe. The pure functional simplicity of his buildings is tempered with elegance of proportion and fineness of detail, notably in Rødovre Town Hall (1955) and the Scandinavian Airlines System Building (1959) in Copenhagen. He also designed furniture, silverware and fabrics

Jacob's ladder (*naut.*) a hanging ladder of rope or chain with rungs of wood or iron ‖ (*bot.*) *Polemonium caeruleum*, a European perennial with bright blue or white flowers, or any of several related plants [after the patriarch Jacob's vision (Genesis xxviii, 12) of a ladder from earth to heaven]

Ja·co·bus de Vo·ra·gi·ne (dʒəkóubəsdeivɔrǽdʒinei) (c. 1230–98), Italian hagiographer (*GOLDEN LEGEND)

Jac·quard loom (dʒǽkɑrd) a loom fitted with a device for weaving figured fabrics [after Joseph-Marie *Jacquard* (1752-1834), F. inventor]

Jac·que·rie (ʒækri:) (*F. hist.*) a revolt (1358) of peasants in N. France against the feudal nobility. It was provoked by the ravages of wandering soldiers after the Battle of Poitiers. It was ruthlessly put down

jac·ta·tion (dʒæktéiʃən) *n.* a boast ‖ (*med.*) jactitation [fr. L. *jactatio* (*jactationis*)]

jac·ti·ta·tion (dʒæktitéiʃən) *n.* (*med.*) excessive bodily restlessness or twitching ‖ (*law*) a false claim or statement which is injurious to another [fr. M.L. *jactitatio* (*jactitationis*), a false declaration]

jade (dʒeid) *n.* a hard stone that is either jadeite or nephrite, used in jewelry, ornaments etc. [F. fr. Span. (*piedra de) ijada*, colic (stone)]

jad·ed (dʒéidid) *adj.* dulled by satiety ‖ tired

jade·ite (dʒéidait) *n.* a silicate of sodium and aluminum, usually green or white, a highly prized form of jade

Ja·dot·ville (ʒædouvi:l) *LIKASI

jae·ger (jéigər) *n.* a predatory bird of fam. *Stercorariidae* inhabiting northern seas (*SKUA) [G. = hunter]

Ja·én (hɑén) a province (area 5,203 sq. miles, pop. 736,000) of S. Spain ‖ its capital (pop. 78,156) (*ANDALUSIA)

Jaf·fa (dʒǽfə) (ancient Joppa) a former port of Israel, now part of Tel Aviv. Largely peopled by Arabs, it was captured (1948) by Israel and united (1949) with Tel Aviv, despite a U.N. decision that Jaffa should be an Arab port. Ashdod replaced Tel Aviv-Jaffa as a port (1965)

Jaff·na (dʒǽfnə) a port (pop. 62,500) of Sri Lanka, on Jaffna Peninsula, handling cotton, tobacco, lumber

jag (dʒæg) 1. *n.* an irregular, sharp-edged projection 2. *v.t. pres. part.* **jag·ging** past and past part. **jagged** to cut or fashion such a projection in [imit.]

jag *n.* (*pop.*) a spree, esp. a drinking bout [origin unknown]

Jag·an (dʒǽgən), Cheddi (1918–) Guyanan statesman, first prime minister of British Guiana (1961–4)

Jag·an·nath (dʒʌ́gənət) *PURI, *JUGGERNAUT

Jag·a·tai (dʒægətái) (d. 1242), Mongol conqueror, son of Genghis Khan. He ruled the region of Turkestan (1227–9)

Ja·gel·lo (jəgélou) *JAGIELLO

jag·ged (dʒǽgid) *adj.* having sharp projections

jag·ger·y (dʒǽgəri:) *n.* a palm sugar made in India [Hindi *jagrī*]

jag·gy (dʒǽgi:) *comp.* **jag·gi·er** *superl.* **jag·gi·est** *adj.* having many jags

Ja·giel·lo (jəgjélou) (or Jagello) a dynasty which ruled Poland and Lithuania (1386–1572), Hungary (1440–4, and 1490–1526) and Bohemia (1471–1526)

jag·uar (dʒǽgwɑr) *pl.* **jag·uars, jag·uar** *n. Felis onca*, fam. *Felidae*, a large carnivore found in the American tropics, having brownish-yellow fur with dark spots each encircled with a dark ring [Tupi-Guarani *yaguara, jaguara*]

Jahan *SHAH JAHAN

Ja·han·gir, Je·han·gir (dʒihángiər) (1569–1627), Mogul emperor (1605–27), son of Akbar. His rule degenerated into a corrupt tyranny, while government was left largely to his Persian wife

Jahveh, Jahweh *YAHWEH

jai a·lai (háilai) *pl.* **jai a·lais** *n.* a game of Basque origin involving two or four players who use wicker baskets attached to the wrist to catch and fling a small hard ball against the wall of a long court of varying dimensions [Span. fr. Basque *jai*, festival + *alai*, merry]

jail (dʒeil) 1. *n.* a civil prison 2. *v.t.* to put in prison [M.E. *gayole, gaille, gaile* fr. O.N.F., M.E. *jaiole, jayle, jaile* fr. O.F.]

jail·bird (dʒéilbə:rd) *n.* someone who is, or who is often, in jail

jail·break (dʒéilbreik) *n.* an escape from prison

jail·er, jail·or (dʒéilər) *n.* someone in charge of a jail or its inmates

jail·house (dʒéilhaus) *pl.* **jail·hous·es** (dʒéilhouziz) *n.* a jail

Jain (dʒain, dʒein) 1. *n.* someone who professes Jainism 2. *adj.* of Jainism or its adherents [Hindi *jaina* fr. Skr., of or relating to a Buddha or saint]

Jain·ism (dʒáinizəm, dʒéinizəm) *n.* a religion of India having about 1,600,000 adherents. It originated (6th c. B.C.), like Buddhism, in reaction to Hinduism. Its major prophet and founder is Vardhamana, also called Mahavira and Jina, said to have lived in the 6th c. B.C. Jains believe strongly in ahimsa or nonviolence to any living and therefore eternal creature. All believers strive to attain Nirvana. A monk may achieve this goal through 12 years of asceticism. A layman must pass through nine transmigrations determined by karma. Their deity is a collection of equal souls who have reached this state of perfection. The Jain temples are one of the glories of India

Jain·ist (dʒáinist, dʒéinist) *n.* and *adj.* Jain

Jai·pur (dʒaipúər) the capital (pop. 966,677) of Rajasthan, India, and of the former principality of Jaipur. Manufactures: textiles, glass, enamel, jewelry. Palace (18th c.)

Jakarta *DJAKARTA

Ja·lal-ud-Din Ru·mi (dʒəlʌ́lədí:nrúmi:) (1207–73), Persian poet and mystic

jal·ap (dʒǽləp) *n.* a purgative drug obtained from the tuberous roots of *Exogonium purga*, fam. *Convolvulaceae*, a Mexican plant ‖ this plant or any of various related plants that yield this drug [fr. *Jalapa*, a town in Mexico]

jal·ap·in (dʒǽləpin) *n.* a resinous glucoside found in jalap

Ja·lis·co (hɑlí:skɔ) a Pacific coast state (area 30,941 sq. miles, pop. 4,293,549) of Mexico. The Sierra Madre divides it into a heavily forested coastal plain and a high plateau region (average elevation 5,000 ft). Colima (13,110 ft) and Nevado de Colima (14,219 ft) in the south are active volcanoes. Largest lake: Chapala, a popular resort and fishing area. Capital: Guadalajara. Agricultural and forest products: corn, wheat, beans, sugarcane, cotton, rice, indigo, tobacco, rubber, palm oil. Stock raising is important. Minerals: silver, gold, cinnabar and others

ja·lop·y (dʒəlópi:) *pl.* **ja·lop·ies** *n.* (*pop.*) an old, dilapidated model, esp. an automobile [origin unknown]

jal·ou·sie (dʒǽləsi:, *Br.* ʒǽlu:zi) *n.* a shutter or blind consisting of horizontal, often adjustable, overlapping slats inclined at an angle to the vertical [F.]

jam (dʒæm) *n.* a sweet thick mixture made by simmering fruit with sugar at the boiling point [perh. fr. JAM v.t., to bruise]

jam 1. *v. pres. part.* **jam·ming** past and past part. **jammed** *v.t.* to force (a body) to enter a confined or small space, *he jammed four apples in his pocket* ‖ to bruise by crushing between two solid objects, *to jam one's finger in a car door* ‖ (with 'against' or 'down') to force or push, *he jammed the bookcase against the door* ‖ to block or impede the movement by or by crowding etc., *the parade jammed traffic all over town* ‖ to force or wedge (a movable part of a machine) ‖ (*radio*) to interfere with (reception) by superimposing signals on the transmitting wavelength ‖ *v.i.* to become immovably fixed or wedged ‖ to crowd tightly together **to jam on the brakes** to apply the brakes of a vehicle suddenly and forcefully 2. *n.* the result of jamming, *a traffic jam* ‖ (*pop.*) a difficult or unpleasant situation ‖

CONCISE PRONUNCIATION KEY: (**a**) æ, c*a*t; ɑ, c*a*r; ɔ f*a*wn; ei, sn*a*ke. (**e**) e, h*e*n; i:, sh*ee*p; iə, d*ee*r; ɛə, b*ea*r. (**i**) i, f*i*sh; ai, t*i*ger; ə:, b*i*rd. (**o**) o, *o*x; au, c*ow*; ou, g*oa*t; u, p*oo*r; ɔi, r*oy*al. (**u**) ʌ, d*u*ck; u, b*u*ll; u:, g*oo*se; ə, b*a*cillus; ju:, c*u*be. x, lo*ch*; θ, *th*ink; ð, bo*th*er; z, *Z*en; ʒ, cor*s*age; dʒ, sava*ge*; ŋ, oranguta*ng*; j, *y*ak; ʃ, *f*ish; tʃ, fe*tch*; 'l, rabb*le*; 'n, redd*en*. Complete pronunciation key appears inside front cover.

(*roller skating*) in a derby, a round designed to score points by a member of the team who spurts to pass members of the opposing team [imit.]

Ja·mai·ca (dʒəméikə) an island (area 4,411 sq. miles, pop. 2,222,000) and independent state in the West Indies, in the Greater Antilles group (*ANTILLES). Capital: Kingston. People: mainly of African origin and Mulatto. Language: English. Religion: mainly Animist, 15% Protestant, 7% Roman Catholic. The land consists of a limestone plateau in the center and west, and the Blue Mtns, rising to 7,400 ft in the east. Average temperatures (F.): 78° along the coast, 73° at 1,000–3,000 ft, 60° at 5,500 ft. Rainfall: over 100 ins in the mountains, over 60 ins in the north and east, 44 ins in Kingston. The whole island is subject to hurricanes, and the south to drought. Livestock: cattle, goats, hogs, horses. Minerals: bauxite (lst world producer), gypsum. Industries: alumina, rum, cigars, cement, oil and sugar refining, tourism. Exports: sugar, bananas, bauxite, alumina, rum, fruit, pimento. Domestic crops: coffee, cocoa, corn, coconuts, tobacco, ginger. Imports: meat, fish, dairy products, wheat flour, vehicles, building materials, textiles, fuel. Ports: Kingston, Montego Bay (northwest coast). University of the West Indies at Mona (1962). Monetary unit: Jamaican pound (20 shillings). HISTORY. The island was discovered (1494) by Columbus, and was ruled (1509–1655) by the Spaniards, who virtually exterminated the Arawaks, the original inhabitants. African slaves were imported. The British captured Jamaica (1655), colonized it, and made it a center of the American slave trade (18th c.) until the abolition of slavery (1833) by the British in the West Indies. It was made a British Crown Colony (1866), attained a measure of self-government (1944), and under premier (1959–62) Norman Manley, the first prime minister (1962–7) Sir Alexander Bustamante, it became (Aug. 6, 1962) an independent state within the Commonwealth. However, Manley's pledge (1958) to the Federation of the West Indies was opposed by Bustamante, and when the cause of secession was upheld (1961) in a general referendum the Federation, bereft of its key member, was doomed. Jamaica achieved full independence in 1962, and Bustamante became the first prime minister. Michael Manley succeeded him in 1972, and a trade deficit brought Jamaica close to bankruptcy by 1980. Political discontent forced new elections in which the Conservative Labor party leader, Edward Seaga was elected prime minister

jamb (dʒæm) *n.* one of the vertical sides of a doorframe, windowframe, fireplace etc. ‖ (*armor*) a jambeau [F. *jambe*, leg]

jam·beau (dʒǽmbou) *n.* (*armor*) a piece of armor for the leg below the knee [fr. F. *jambe*, leg]

jam·bo·ree (dʒæmbərí:) *n.* an international scouts' camp ‖ (*pop.*) a festive gathering ‖ (*pop.*) a spree [origin unknown]

James (dʒeimz) the brother or cousin of Jesus. He became the head of the Church at Jerusalem (Acts xv). Josephus records his martyrdom by stoning

James, St, 'the Greater', one of the 12 Apostles, son of Zebedee and brother of St John. He was martyred (44 A.D.) by Herod Agrippa I. He is the patron saint of Spain. Feast: July 25

James, St, 'the Less', one of the 12 Apostles, son of Alphaeus. Feast: May 1

James I (1566–1625), king of England and Ireland (1603–25) and (as James VI, 1567–1625) of Scotland, son of Mary Queen of Scots. Succeeding to the throne of Scotland on the forced abdication (1567) of his mother, he was under the power of regents until 1583. He made little protest at the execution (1587) of his mother, and he succeeded to the English throne on the death (1603) of Elizabeth I. He rapidly lost all popularity by his hostility to Puritanism at the Hampton Court conference (1604), his sale of titles and monopolies, his subservience to Spain, his domination by favorites such as Buckingham, and personal morals that shocked contemporaries. Disappointed Catholics formed the unsuccessful Gunpowder Plot (1605) to blow up king and parliament. James's stubborn insistence on the divine right of kings clashed with a growing spirit of independence in the Commons, and he left a legacy of constitutional conflict to his son Charles I. The Authorized

Version of the Bible was published (1611) during his reign

James·i·an, James·e·an (dʒéimzi:ən) *adj.* of, referring to, or like Henry James as a writer ‖ of or relating to the ideas of William James

James II (1633–1701), king of England, of Ireland and (as James VII) of Scotland (1685–8), son of Charles I. Unpopular on account of his Roman Catholic sympathies, he succeeded to the throne on the death (1685) of his brother Charles II. The ruthless suppression of Monmouth's rebellion (1685), and James's attempts to appoint Catholics to office and to raise a standing army, aroused widespread alarm. Tories joined with Whigs in inviting William of Orange, James's son-in-law, to invade (1688). In the face of the Glorious Revolution, James fled to France, leaving parliament to accept William III and Mary II as joint sovereigns. A Jacobite attempt to restore him to the throne failed at the Boyne (1690)

James I (1394–1437), king of Scotland (1424–37), son of Robert III. His throne was usurped while he was a prisoner in England (1406–24)

James II (1430–60), king of Scotland (1437–60), son of James I. He was killed while invading England during the Wars of the Roses

James III (1451–88), king of Scotland (1460–88), son of James II. His attempts to reduce the power of the nobility led to rebellions, in the course of which he was defeated and killed

James IV (1473–1513), king of Scotland (1488–1513), son of James III. He restored order, made peace with England (1499), and married (1502) Margaret Tudor. He was killed at Flodden Field in a disastrous attempt to invade England

James V (1512–42), king of Scotland (1513–42), son of James IV. His attempt (1542) to make war on Henry VIII of England ended in his defeat and death

James VI king of Scotland *JAMES I of England

James VII king of Scotland *JAMES II of England

James I 'the Conqueror' (1208–76), king of Aragon (1213–76). He captured the Balearic Is (1229–35) and Valencia (1238) from the Moors

James II (c. 1260–1327), king of Aragon (1291–1327) and of Sicily (1286–95)

James, Henry (1843–1916), novelist and short-story writer. American by birth, he became a naturalized British subject in 1915. His works reveal a brilliant exploration and judgment of human behavior. James had other characteristic concerns: with the artist as supreme representative of 'fine' consciousness, with the American investigating (as a puritan innocent) the more subtle but possibly corrupt fabric of European life, and, technically, with the dramatic effect of using a narrator whose consciousness colors the story he is telling and who is himself meant to be judged by the reader (a technique used in 'The Turn of the Screw', 1898). The great middle-period novels, esp. 'Portrait of a Lady' (1881), 'The Awkward Age' (1899) and 'The Bostonians' (1886), render with strength and delicacy the problems of right conduct seen as an aesthetic ideal. The reader is given only the most delicate of hints, and the business of assessment becomes as strenuous as in real life. Other novels include 'The Wings of the Dove' (1902), 'The Ambassadors' (1903) and 'The Golden Bowl' (1904). James's prefaces to his own novels are important critical pieces

James, Jesse Woodson (1847–82), U.S. outlaw. He led (from 1867) the notorious 'James band' of bank and train robbers. He was gunned down by two members of his gang, who betrayed him for the $10,000 reward posted

James, William (1842–1910), American philosopher and psychologist, brother of Henry James. He was one of the founders of pragmatism, and is also known for his work in analytical psychology. His works include 'Principles of Psychology' (1890), 'The Will to Believe' (1897) and 'Varieties of Religious Experience' (1902)

James a river (340 miles long) of central Virginia, flowing east through a broad estuary into the Chesapeake Bay. It is navigable beyond Richmond

James Bay the southern extension of the Hudson Bay (c. 280 miles long, 150 miles wide) between N.E. Ontario and W. Quebec provinces, Canada

James Edward prince of Wales *STUART, JAMES FRANCIS EDWARD

James, Epistle of the 20th book of the New Testament, of uncertain authorship and date. It emphasizes the necessity of works as an expression of faith

Jame·son (dʒéims'n), Sir Leander Starr (1853–1917), British statesman in South Africa. As associate of Cecil Rhodes, he led the Jameson Raid. After imprisonment in Britain, he returned to South Africa and was prime minister of Cape Colony (1904–8)

Jameson Raid an armed attack (1895–6) from Bechuanaland to the Transvaal, led by L.S. Jameson with the aim of helping the Uitlanders to overthrow Kruger's government. The failure of the raid caused Rhodes to resign as prime minister of Cape Colony. It also caused a worsening of Anglo-Boer relations which helped to bring on the Boer War

James·town (dʒéimztaun) the first permanent English settlement in America (founded May 13, 1607, capital of Virginia until 1698), near Norfolk, now in Colonial National Historical Park

Ja·mi (dʒámi:) (Nur-ud-din Abd-ur-Rahman ibn Ahmad, 1414–92), Persian poet and Sufi mystic

Jammes (ʒæm), Francis (1868–1938) French poet and novelist. His works, concerned with humble provincial life and reflecting his Catholic faith, include 'les Géorgiques chrétiennes' (1911–12)

Jam·mu (dʒámu:) **and Kashmir** *KASHMIR

jam-pack (dʒæmpǽk) *v.t.* to cram (something) with a great many things

jams (dʒæmz) *n.* **1.** a form of short pajamas with a drawstring **2.** baggy knee-length swim trunks with drawstring worn by men

jam session (*pop.*) informal improvisation by a group of jazz instrumentalists, chiefly for their own enjoyment

Jam·shed·pur (dʒámʃedpúr) a city (pop. 356,783, with agglom. 283,000) in S. Bihar, India: iron and steel works

Ja·ná·ček (jánatʃek) Leoš (1854–1928) Czech composer. His style was determined by native folk music and by his effort to link music to the natural rhythms and inflections of speech. His works include 'Diary of One Who Vanished' (1916), a song cycle, and the operas 'Jenufa' (1904), 'The Makropulos Affair' (1923–24) and 'The Cunning Little Vixen' (1921–23). He also wrote two deeply personal string quartets, the startlingly modern and disconcerting 'Sinfonietta' (1926), and piano music

Jane Crow (dʒein) prejudice against women

Jane Sey·mour (dʒéinsí:mɔr, dʒéinsí:mour) (c. 1509–37), 3rd wife of Henry VIII of England. She died soon after giving birth to the future Edward VI

jan·gle (dʒǽŋg'l) **1.** *n.* an unpleasant combination of clanging or ringing sounds **2.** *v. pres. part.* **jan·gling** *past and past part.* **jan·gled** *v.i.* to produce this sound ‖ *v.t.* to make (something) produce this sound [O.F. *jangler*]

Janissary *JANIZARY

jan·i·tor (dʒǽnitər) *n.* a caretaker of a building, set of offices etc. ‖ a doorkeeper **ján·i·tress** *n.* a woman janitor

Jan·i·zar·y, Jan·is·sar·y (dʒǽnisəri) *n.* (*hist.*) a member of an elite force of Turkish infantry (c. 1330-1826), originally recruited from Christian youths who had been seized to form a bodyguard for the sultan ‖ a Turkish soldier [fr. Turk. *yenitsheri*, new soldiers]

Jan May·en (jænmáiən) an island (144 sq. miles) between Svalbard and Iceland in the Arctic Ocean annexed by Norway (1929): weather station

Jan·sen (dʒǽnsən), Cornelis (1585–1638), Dutch Roman Catholic theologian who, with Duvergier de Hauranne, advocated a closer interpretation of the principles of St Augustine, as maintained by Baius. Jansen emphasized the Augustinian tenets of predestination and the necessity of divine grace for conversion. The 'Augustinus', his study of St Augustine's works published in 1640, was condemned by papal bulls (1643, 1653)

Jan·sen·ism (dʒǽnsənizəm) *n.* a theological doctrine stemming from the writings of Jansen which took root esp. in France. His ideas were defended by Duvergier de Hauranne, Pascal and other scholars of Port Royal against the Jesuits and in spite of papal bulls condemning the 'Augustinus'. The Jansenists were persecuted by Louis XIV, who destroyed the convent of Port Royal (1712). Jansenism was condemned by papal bulls (1656, 1713). The power of Jansenism was broken, although it continued as a tendency within the French Church until the Revolution

Jan·sen·ist (dʒænsʼnist) 1. *n.* an adherent of Jansenism 2. *adj.* of or relating to Jansenism

jan·thi·na (dʒænθinə) *n.* a gregarious, oceanic, gastropodous mollusk, with violet-colored shell. When irritated it pours out violet secretions for concealment, like the ink of the cuttlefish [L. fr. Gk *ianthinos*, violet-colored]

Jan·u·ar·ius (dʒænju:ɛ́ari:əs), St (*d. c.* 305), Christian martyr of the Diocletian persecution. He is the patron saint of Naples. Feast: Sept. 19

Jan·u·ar·y (dʒænju:ɛ̣ri) *n.* (*abbr.* Jan.) the 1st month of the year, having 31 days [M.E. *Ieniuer* fr. O.N.F. fr. L. *Januarius* (*mensis*), the month of JANUS]

Ja·nus (dʒéinəs) the most ancient of the Roman gods, represented by a doublefaced head to signify his knowledge of the present and future. He was god of the doorway and protector of all entrances

Jan·us-faced (dʒéinəsfeist) *adj.* deceitful ‖ having two clearly distinguished aspects [after JANUS, Roman god of the doorway]

Janus technique (dʒéinəs) a method used by aircraft for measuring ground speed, utilizing the Doppler signal by radiating microwave signals forward and backward, subtracting the echo time of the aft beam from the fore beam

Ja·pan (dʒəpǽn) (*Jap.* Nippon) an empire (area 144,000 sq. miles, pop. 118,529,000) in E. Asia. Capital: Tokyo. Religion: mainly Shintoist and Buddhist, 2% new cults, small Christian minority. Japan consists of four main islands: (north-south) Hokkaido, Honshu (the largest and most populous), Shikoku and Kyushu, with hundreds of smaller ones, not all inhabited, off the coasts. The land is 16% arable, 3% pasture and 61% forest. It is 75% mountainous and largely volcanic. Highest mountains: Hida range, central Honshu (*FUJIYAMA). Hundreds of short swift rivers flow from the mountains, forming narrow interior basins. The coastal plains. usually narrow, are widest north of Tokyo (Kanto Plain), around Nagoya and Osaka on Honshu and on N.W. Kyushu and N.E. Hokkaido. Earthquakes and, in the east, autumn typhoons, are frequent. Average temperatures (F.): (Jan.) 14° in Asahigawa (Hokkaido), 37° in Tokyo, 45° in S. Kyushu, (Aug.) 69° in Sapporo (Hokkaido), 77° in Tokyo, 81° in Osaka. Rainfall: under 40 ins in E. Hokkaido, 40–60 ins in W. Hokkaido, N.E. Honshu and the Inland Sea, over 80 ins in central Honshu, S. Shikoku and S. Kyushu, 60–80 ins elsewhere. There is relatively little livestock (except in Hokkaido, where dairying is important). Agricultural products: rice (the major crop) and other cereals, soybeans, sugar beets, fruit, sweet potatoes, tea, tobacco, flax, pyrethrum. Japan's fisheries (including whaling) are the most valuable in the world. Resources: coal, copper, lead, manganese, iron ore, zinc, tungsten, magnesium, barite, cadmium, gold, silver, oil, timber, hydroelectricity. Exports: iron and steel, fabrics, electric and electronic machinery, ships (world leader), light manufactures, fish. Other industries: chemicals, paper, forestry, aluminum, watchmaking, glass, pottery, optical goods, plastics. Imports: fuel oil, raw cotton, machinery, raw wool, iron ore, wheat and flour, coal, crude rubber, sugar. Ports: Yokohama, Osaka, Kobe. There are 75 state universities, the oldest being Tokyo (1877). Monetary unit: yen. HISTORY. According to Shinto belief, the first Japanese emperor, Jimmu (c. 660 B.C.), was a descendant of the sun-goddess. Japan was influenced by Chinese culture through contact with Korea (1st–4th cc.), and adopted Chinese script (400) and Buddhism (c. 552). This gave rise to the Taikwa (Great Reform) edict which changed Japan's social, political and economic life. A centralized government was established at Nara (710) and moved to Kyoto (784). During the Heian period (784–1184) a Japanese culture developed, but civil war broke out between rival clans (10th–12th cc.). Yoritomo (c. 1147–99), the first of the shoguns, founded a feudal system and during the Kamakura period (1185–1333) bushido evolved. Kublai Khan's invasions (1274, 1281) were repelled, but they impoverished Japan. By the 15th c. warfare among the clans was continuous, yet the arts flourished and Japan traded widely with the

Asian mainland. The first Europeans to arrive (1542) were the Portuguese. St Francis Xavier introduced Christianity (1549). Feudal lords and powerful Buddhist sects increased the struggle for power (16th c.) but three men, Nobunaga, Hideyoshi and Ieyasu, united Japan and restored order. Through fear of foreign influence the autocratic Tokugawa shogunate (1603–1867) had, by 1640, expelled all foreigners, stopped foreign trade, forbidden travel and abolished Christianity. Japan's isolation was broken by the arrival (1853) of an American expedition under Perry. The Meiji era began with the accession (1867) of the Emperor Mutsuhito, who restored supreme power to the imperial line and ended the domination (12th–mid-19th cc.) of the shoguns. Feudalism was abolished (1871), a parliament (Diet) was established, a constitution was adopted (1889) and Japan began to industrialize along Western lines. After the first Sino-Japanese War (1894–5) Japan acquired Taiwan. Victory in the Russo-Japanese War (1904–5) increased Japan's prestige, and the annexation of Korea (1910) expanded her empire. The 1st world war enabled Japan to acquire the German-leased territory of Shantung, and secure a mandate over the former German islands in the Pacific. It also increased her markets. Japan attacked Manchuria (1931) and started the 2nd Sino-Japanese War, during which Peking was attacked (1937). Japan aligned herself with Germany and Italy (1940), invaded Indochina (1940) and made a surprise attack on the U.S. naval base at Pearl Harbor (Dec. 7, 1941). During the 2nd world war Japan conquered the Philippines, the Dutch East Indies, Malaya, Singapore, Burma, Thailand and Indochina, as well as many Pacific island groups. Allied victories (end of 1942) and U.S. atomic bombs dropped on Hiroshima and Nagasaki led to Japan's surrender (Aug. 14, 1945, signed Sept. 2, 1945). Japan was occupied (1945–51) by the Allies under Gen. Douglas MacArthur. A new democratic constitution (1946) deprived the Emperor Hirohito of his executive powers and abolished the dogma of his divinity. A peace treaty (1951) between Japan and 48 countries established her sovereignty (1952). Intensive postwar American aid (until 1952) and U.S. military expenditure in Japan during the Korean War (1950–3) largely contributed to the recovery of Japan's economy. She is now the most industrialized nation in Asia. The liberal-democratic party has held power since 1952. Nakasone Yasuhiro became leader of the party and prime minister in 1982

ja·pan (dʒəpǽn) 1. *n.* a hard black varnish, originally from Japan ‖ work varnished with this substance and ornamented in the Japanese style 2. *v.t. pres. part.* **ja·pan·ning** *past* and *past part.* **ja· panned** to varnish and ornament in this way [after JAPAN fr. Chin. *jihpun*, sunrise]

Jap·a·nese (dʒæpəni:z, dʒæpəni:s) 1. *adj.* of Japan, its people, culture, language 2. *pl.* **Jap·a·nese** *n.* a native or inhabitant of Japan ‖ the language of Japan

Japanese beetle a small green and brown beetle, *Popillia japonica,* fam. *Scarabaeidae,* feeding on leaves and fruits when adult, on grass roots in the grub phase. Introduced from Japan, it is a serious pest in America

Japanese ivy *Parthenocissus tricuspidata,* fam. *Vitaceae,* a creeper native to China and Japan. It has three-lobed leaves and climbs by tendrils ending in suction disks

Japanese language the language spoken by about 90 million inhabitants of Japan. Two systems of writing are used concurrently. The *kanji* or *honji* ideographic characters are borrowed from Chinese, and are used to express the chief meaningful words (i.e. substantives and the root meaning of verbs and adjectives). Along with these are the two sets of *kana* symbols, which are phonetic. The *hiragana* are used to represent the items which have grammatical function. The *katakana* are used to transcribe foreign words. The *katakana* are also used in official documents, advertisements etc. The Japanese language shows a relationship to Korean

Japanese quince *Chaenomeles lagenaria,* fam. *Rosaceae,* a shrub native to China bearing ornamental scarlet blossoms

Japan, Sea of an arm (area c. 400,000 sq. miles) of the Pacific, between Japan and the

Asian mainland, part of the world's most important fishing area

jape (dʒeip) 1. *v.i. pres. part.* **jap·ing** *past* and *past part.* **japed** (*old-fash.*) to joke, jest 2. *n.* (*old-fash.*) a jest, joke [origin unknown]

Jap·lish (dʒǽpliʃ) *n.* English infiltrated into Japanese as spoken by Japanese *Cf* FRINGLISH, HINGLISH, SPANGLISH

ja·pon·i·ca (dʒəpɔ́nikə) *n.* the Japanese quince [Mod. L.]

Ja·pu·rá (ʒəpurá) a river (c. 1,300 miles long) rising in S.W. Colombia (where it is called the Caquetá) and flowing into the Amazon in Brazil

jar (dʒɑr) *n.* a container of earthenware, glass or stone, usually without a handle, and cylindrical in shape, with a short wide neck (or none) and wide mouth ‖ the quantity contained in a jar, *a jar of jam* [F. *jarre* fr. Arab. *jarrah,* an earthenware water container]

jar *n.* (only in the phrase) **on the jar** (of a door) partly opened, ajar [O.E. *cyrr,* a turn]

jar 1. *v.t. pres. part.* **jar·ring** *past* and *past part.* **jarred** to make an impact on (a body) which causes it to vibrate irregularly ‖ to make a discordant sound by impact on (the eardrum) ‖ to stimulate (someone) in such a way as to cause unpleasant nervous responses ‖ *v.i.* to vibrate in an irregular way ‖ (of colors, shapes, styles etc., or of a sound, or of opinions or interests) to be discordant ‖ (with 'on' or 'upon') to have an unpleasant effect on the sympathies, *his manner jars on them* 2. *n.* a discordant sound or an irregular vibration resulting from an impact or stimulus [prob. imit.]

jar·di·niere, jar·di·nière (dʒɑrd'niɛ́r, esp. *Br.* pɑrdinʒɛ́ar) *n.* an ornamental stand for plant pots ‖ a large ornamental receptacle for a potted plant ‖ several vegetables cubed and cooked, together or separately, as a garnish for meat [F.]

jar·gon (dʒɑ́rgən) *n.* the vocabulary of a specialized field, esp. when it is unnecessarily obscure to the uninitiated [O.F.=chattering (of birds)]

jargon *n.* a translucent or smoky variety of zircon found in Ceylon [F. fr. Ital. *giargone,* zircon]

jar·goon (dʒɑrgú:n) *n.* jargon (zircon)

jar·rah (dʒɛ́rə) *n. Eucalyptus marginata,* fam. *Myrtaceae,* a tree of W. Australia, yielding very hard wood [fr. *Jerryhl,* native name]

Jar·row (dʒǽrou) an industrial town (pop. 29,000) in Durham, England. Nearby is the monastery founded (682) by Benedict Biscop, at which Bede spent most of his life

Jar·ry (ʒæri:), Alfred (1873–1907), French writer. His farce 'Ubu Roi' (1896) satirizes the bourgeoisie

Jaruzelski (jɑru:ʃélski:), Wojciech (1923–), Polish prime minister (1981–5) and president (1985–). He was part of the Polish army organized in the Soviet Union during World War II and by 1973 had been promoted through the ranks to general in Communist Poland. He was defense minister (1968–81) before becoming prime minister. He was responsible for suppressing the Solidarity labor movement

jas·mine, jas·min (dʒǽsmin, dʒǽzmin) *n.* a member of *Jasminum,* fam. *Oleaceae,* a genus of climbing or erect shrubs of warm and temperate climates, having very fragrant yellow or white flowers. *J. officinale* is used in the manufacture of perfume [Arab. *yásmin* fr. Pers.]

Ja·son (dʒéis'n) (*Gk mythol.*) a prince who led the Argonauts to win the Golden Fleece with the aid of Medea

jas·per (dʒǽspər) *n.* an opaque variety of reddish, brown, green or yellow quartz, used as an ornamental stone [M.E. *iaspre* fr. O.F. fr. L. fr. Gk]

Jas·pers (jáspərs), Karl (1883–1969), German philosopher. His philosophy has been termed transcendent existentialism. He believed that man achieves authentic existence by taking individual responsibility in his concrete historical situation, in his community and in communication with other men. Each man's life is a venture. His works include 'Man in the Modern Age' (1933) and 'The Perennial Scope of Philosophy' (1949)

Jas·sy *IASI

Jat (jat) *n.* a member of an IndoEuropean people of the Punjab and Uttar Pradesh, India [Hindi]

Ja·ta·ka (dʒátədə) one of the collected tales relating the various incarnations of Buddha previous to Gautama Buddha

jaun·dice (dʒɔ́ndis) **1.** *n.* a yellowish coloring of the skin, whites of the eyes and various body tissues and body fluids. It results from excessive bile in the bloodstream due to damage to or malfunction of the liver or bile ducts **2.** *pres. part.* **jaun·dic·ing** *past and past part.* **jaun·diced** ‖ *v.t.* to cause (someone) to become hostile or embittered **jáun·diced** *adj.* afflicted with jaundice ‖ hostile, embittered, *to see a matter with a jaundiced eye* [F. *jaunice* fr. *jaune*, yellow]

jaunt (dʒɔnt) **1.** *n.* a short journey made purely for pleasure **2.** *v.i.* to make such a journey [origin unknown]

jaun·ti·ly (dʒɔ́ntili:) *adv.* in a jaunty manner

jaun·ti·ness (dʒɔ́nti:nis) *n.* the state or quality of being jaunty

jaunting car an Irish, two-wheeled, horse-drawn, open vehicle, with two seats over the wheels set back-to-back and a place for the driver to sit

jaun·ty (dʒɔ́nti:) *comp.* **jaun·ti·er** *superl.* **jaun·ti·est** *adj.* gay and perky, spirited [older form *jantee* or *janty* fr. F. *gentil*, noble, gentle]

Jau·rés (ʒoures) Jean (1859–1914), French socialist leader and historian. A brilliant orator, he championed the cause of Dreyfus. In the newspaper 'l'Humanité', which he founded (1904), he campaigned against extreme nationalism. His efforts to avert war led to his assassination by a nationalist fanatic on the eve of the 1st world war

Ja·va (dʒávə) an island (area 50,390 sq. miles, pop., with Madura, 91,269,528) of Indonesia, across the Java Sea from Borneo. Capital: Djakarta. Other centers: Surabaya, Surakarta (Solo), Jogjakarta. Java is a region of high volcanic mountains (Semeroe, 12,060 ft), with good harbors. It is the political, economic and cultural center of the country. Products: rubber, coffee, tea, tobacco, teak, coal, petroleum. HISTORY. The island was colonized (1st–7th cc.) by Hindus, who established kingdoms covering much of Indonesia (8th–13th cc.). As the Hindu states declined, Islam gained ground, and a Moslem state was established (16th c.). The Portuguese arrived (1511) and were superseded after 1596 by the Dutch. Except for British occupation (1811–15), Java remained in Dutch possession until the 2nd world war. After Japanese occupation (1942–5), Java became part of Indonesia

Java man *PITHECANTHROPUS

Ja·va·nese (dʒɑvəni:z, dʒɑvəni:s) **1.** *pl.* **Ja·va·nese** *n.* a native or inhabitant of Java ‖ the language of Java **2.** *adj.* pertaining to Java, its people, language or culture

Java Sea the part (area about 120,000 sq. miles) of the Pacific between Borneo, Sumatra, Java and Sulawesi, adjoining the Flores Sea

Java Sea, Battle of a naval engagement (Feb. 1942) in the 2nd world war in which Japanese warships defeated U.S. naval forces

jave·lin (dʒǽvlin, dʒǽvəlin) *n.* a lightweight spear, thrown by hand, esp. (*hist.*) as a weapon of war or for hunting ‖ (*sports*) an adaptation of this, with a shaft not less than 260 cm. (about 8½ ft), thrown for distance as a field event [F. *javeline*]

jaw (dʒɔ) **1.** *n.* either of two bony or cartilaginous structures of vertebrates forming part of the mouth. Both are fleshy or sheathed in horn and bear teeth or horny plates (*MAXILLA, *MANDIBLE) ‖ (*pl.*) these structures and the attached muscles and nerves which make it possible to open and close the mouth ‖ a similar structure in invertebrates ‖ (*pl.*) the parts of a tool between which things are gripped or crushed, *the jaws of a vise* ‖ (*pl.*) the narrow entrance into a ravine etc. ‖ (*pl., rhet.*) a place of danger, *the jaws of death* **2.** *v.i.* to talk at great length, esp. in reproach ‖ to chat [M.E. *jaw, jawe* orig. *jow, jowe*]

jaw·bone (dʒɔ́boun) *n.* either of the jaws, esp. the mandible

jawboning an attempt to achieve an objective by talking, including urging, warning, threatening —**jawbone** *v.*

jaw·break·er (dʒɔ́breikər) *n.* (*pop.*) a word which is difficult to pronounce ‖ (*pop.*) a candy of a kind that can not be crunched

Jay (dʒei), John (1745–1829), American statesman, president of the Continental Congress (1778–9), foreign secretary (1784–9) and chief justice (1789–95). He negotiated (1794) the treaty known as 'Jay's Treaty' between the U.S.A. and Britain

jay *n. Garrulus glandarius*, fam. *Corvidae*, a common European bird having light brown plumage, a black and white crest and blue and black barred wing coverts. It has a grating voice, and often robs the nests of other birds ‖ any of several related birds, e.g. the blue jay [O.F.]

Ja·ya·de·va (dʒaijədéivə) (c. 1200), Sanskrit poet and author of 'Gitagovinda', a poem celebrating the loves of Krishna

Jayawardene (jʒeiəwárdənə), Junius Richard (1906–), Sri Lankan president (1978–). After serving in various government posts, he became prime minister when his United National party came into power in 1977. That position became president under a new constitution in 1978. Although Sri Lanka's economy improved under his rule, conflict with the Tamil minority remained a serious problem

Jay's Treaty an Anglo-U.S. commercial treaty negotiated by Lord Grenville, the British foreign minister, and John Jay, President Washington's special envoy, and signed in London on Nov. 19, 1794. The treaty, which provided for the evacuation of British forts in the northwestern U.S.A., compensation for Britain's spoliations against American shipping, American payment of pre-Revolutionary debts to British merchants, and the establishment of committees to determine Anglo-U.S. North American boundaries, was denounced by Republicans as pro-British and by France as a violation of Franco-U.S. commercial practices. Although the treaty involved the U.S.A. in an undeclared naval war (1798–1800) with France, it preserved peace with Great Britain, and became the prototype of modern international arbitration

jay·walk (dʒéiwɔk) *v.i.* to cross a street carelessly without regard for the traffic or pedestrian regulations

jazz (dʒæz) **1.** *n.* syncopated music played over strong dance rhythm ‖ dance music derived from this ‖ a dance to this music **2.** *v.t.* to play or dance jazz ‖ *v.t.* to transform or arrange (music) into jazz ‖ (with 'up') (*pop.*) to make more lively **jázz·y** *comp.* **jazz·i·er** *superl.* **jazz·i·est** *adj.* resembling jazz ‖ (*pop.*) excessively vivid or ostentatious [Creole]

jazz·o·theque (dʒǽzətɛk) *n.* a restaurant that offers recorded jazz music for dancing

jazz poetry poetry designed to be read accompanied by jazz music, popular in the 1960s in U.S. and Britain

jazz-rock (dʒǽzrɔk) *n.* mixture of jazz and rock 'n' roll music

J car Chevrolet Corp. four-cylinder compact motor vehicle with high gasoline mileage; produced in 1981

J-curve (*economics*) the expected shape of a graph of a nation's balance of payment following currency devaluation

jeal·ous (dʒéləs) *adj.* racked by jealousy ‖ manifesting jealousy, *a jealous fit* ‖ valuing highly and guarding, *to be jealous of one's good name* [M.E. fr. O.F. fr. M.L. *zelosus* fr. Gk *zēlos*, zeal]

jeal·ous·y (dʒéləsi:) *pl.* **jeal·ous·ies** *n.* a state of fear, suspicion or envy caused by a real or imagined threat or challenge to one's possessive instincts. It may be provoked by rivalry, esp. in sexual love, by competition or by desires for the qualities or possessions of another ‖ a zealous desire to preserve an existing situation or relationship [O.F. *gelosie, jalousie*]

Jean (ʒã) (1921–), grand duke of Luxembourg (1964–)

Jean 'the Fearless' (1371–1419), duke of Burgundy (1404–19), son of Philippe the Bold. His savage rivalry with Louis duc d'Orléans weakened France during the Hundred Years' War, and allowed Henry V of England to conquer much of France

Jean I (1316), king of France (1316), posthumous son of Louis X. He lived only a few days

Jean II 'the Good' (1319–64), king of France (1350–64), son of Philippe VI. He was defeated by the Black Prince at Poitiers (1356) and was held captive in England (1357–60). He was released on condition of paying a ransom and giving hostages, but returned to England (1364) when one of the hostages, his son, escaped

Jean-Bap·tiste de la Salle (ʒãbæpti:stdələsæl), St (1651–1719), French priest and educationist. He pioneered the establishment of free primary schools for the poor, and founded (1682) the Order of the Brothers of the Christian Schools, a lay order devoted to Christian education, now widely distributed in Europe and the U.S.A. He is the patron saint of teachers. Feast: May 15

Jean de Meung, Jean de Meun (ʒãdəmœ̃) (Jean Clopinel, c. 1250–c. 1305), French poet, author of the second part of the 'Roman de la rose' (c. 1275–80) (*LORRIS)

Jeanne d'Arc (ʒændrk) *JOAN OF ARC

Jean-Paul (ʒãpɔl) (Johann Paul Friedrich Richter, 1763–1825), German romantic novelist. Among his works are 'Hesperus' (1795), 'Titan' (1800–3) and 'Flegeljahre' (1804–5)

Jeans (dʒi:nz), Sir James Hopwood (1877–1946), English physicist and astronomer who researched into the dynamic theory of gases and its applications to the structure and evolution of the stars. He was also a popular-science writer

jeans (dʒi:nz) *pl. n.* pants made from a heavy durable cotton cloth in a twill weave [M.E. *Gene, Jene,* for Genoa, Italy]

Jed·da (dʒídə) a port (pop. 561,104) on the Red Sea in Hejaz, Saudi Arabia, the chief port for Mecca

jeep (dʒi:p) *n.* (esp. *mil.*) a small, strong motor vehicle with four-wheel drive [fr. *G.P.=general purposes*]

jeer (dʒiər) **1.** *v.i.* to speak in mockery or derision ‖ (with 'at') to scoff or laugh with contempt, *to jeer at an idea* ‖ *v.t.* to pour scorn on **2.** *n.* the act of jeering ‖ a jeering remark or noise [origin unknown]

jeers (dʒiərz) *pl. n.* (naut.) the rigging for hoisting and lowering the lower yards [origin unknown]

Jef·fers (dʒéfərz), (John) Robinson (1887–1962), U.S. poet. Much of his poetry, notably 'Tamar and Other Poems' (1924), has a Pacific coast setting and reveals the disillusionment of the period after the 1st world war

Jef·fer·son (dʒéfərs'n), Thomas (1743–1826), third president (1801–9) of the U.S.A. A scholarly lawyer, he led vigorous attacks against British colonial policy, served as a member of the Continental Congress (1775–6), and drafted the Declaration of Independence (1776). He established (1783–4) the U.S. coinage on the decimal system, with the dollar as the basic unit. He prepared the original draft of the Northwest Ordinance of 1787. As minister to France (1785–9) he sympathized with the cause of the French Revolution. As secretary of state (1790–3) under President George Washington, he strongly opposed Alexander Hamilton's financial policy and became leader of the anti-federalists, a group which evolved into the modern Democratic party. As vice-president (1796–1800) of the U.S.A., he drafted the Kentucky Resolutions, the first states' rights interpretation of the Constitution. As president (the first to be inaugurated in Washington, D.C.), he believed in strong federal involvement in foreign affairs but a lesser concern in the affairs of state and local governments. He pushed through the Louisiana Purchase (1803) and organized the Louis and Clark expedition (1803–6). He upheld the Nonimportation Act (1806) and the Embargo Act (1807). In later life he excelled as an architect

Jefferson City the capital (pop. 33,619) of Missouri

Jef·fer·so·ni·an (dʒéfərsóuni:ən) **1.** *adj.* of or pertaining to Thomas Jefferson or his policies **2.** *n.* a follower of Thomas Jefferson

Jef·frey (dʒéfri:), Francis, Lord Jeffrey (1773–1850), Scottish literary critic and judge. As editor of the 'Edinburgh Review' (1802–29), he wrote severe articles esp. on the works of Wordsworth, Keats and Byron

Jef·freys (dʒéfri:z), George, 1st Baron Jeffreys of Wem (1648–89), English judge. In the 'bloody assize' of 1685 he pronounced savage sentences on those involved in Monmouth's rebellion

jehad *JIHAD

Jehan *SHAH JAHAN

Jehengir *JAHANGIR

Je·hol (dʒəhɔ́l) *CHENGTEH

Je·ho·vah (dʒihóuvə) *n.* an Old Testament name for God used by Christians [fr. Heb., an incorrect transliteration of *Jahveh* or *Yahweh*]

Jehovah's Witness a member of the Christian sect of Jehovah's Witnesses founded (1872) in Pennsylvania by Charles T. Russell and now having about 645,000 members in the world. They accept a literal interpretation of the Bible and stress the imminent coming of a terrestrial,

---

CONCISE PRONUNCIATION KEY: **(a)** æ, c*a*t; ɑ, c*a*r; ɔ f*aw*n; ei, sn*a*ke. **(e)** e, h*e*n; i:, sh*ee*p; iə, d*ee*r; ɛə, b*ea*r. **(i)** i, f*i*sh; ai, t*i*ger; ə:, b*ir*d. **(o)** o, *o*x; au, c*ow*; ou, g*oa*t; u, p*oo*r; ɔi, r*oy*al. **(u)** ʌ, d*u*ck; u, b*u*ll; u:, g*oo*se; ə, *a*bacus; ju:, c*u*be. x, lo*ch*; θ, *th*ink; ð, bo*th*er; z, *Z*en; ʒ, cor*s*age; dʒ, sava*ge*; ŋ, orangutan*g*; j, *y*ak; ʃ, *fi*sh; tʃ, fe*tch*; 'l, rabb*le*; 'n, redd*en*. Complete pronunciation key appears inside front cover.

theocratic kingdom, into which only the Witnesses will pass

Je·hu (dʒíːhjuː) (d. c. 820 B.C.), king of Israel (c. 846–c. 820 B.C.). Elisha, who anointed him king, dominated Israel during his reign

je·june (dʒidʒúːn) adj. (rhet.) lacking substance or nourishment ‖ (of a speech or writing) lacking interest or substance ‖ juvenile, immature [fr. L. jejunus, fasting]

je·ju·num (dʒidʒúːnəm) pl. **je·ju·na** (dʒidʒúːnə) n. the middle portion of the small intestine, between the duodenum and the ileum [fr. L. jejunus, fasting (because of a former belief that the jejunum was empty after death)]

Je·kyll-and-Hyde (dʒékələnháid) 1. n. a person having two conflicting personalities, one good and the other evil 2. adj. (of a character or existence) characterized by a good-and-evil dichotomy [after the chief character in 'The Strange Case of Dr Jekyll and Mr Hyde' (1886) by Robert Louis Stevenson]

Je·la·čič od Bu·zi·ma (jélatʃitʃodbúzimə), Count Josip (1801–59), Croatian soldier and administrator. He led the unsuccessful attempt to free Croatia from Hungarian rule (1848)

jell (dʒel) v.i. to assume the consistency of a jelly ‖ (of ideas, plans etc.) to take shape ‖ v.t. to cause to become jelly ‖ (of ideas, plans etc.) to cause to take shape [JELLY]

Jel·li·coe (dʒélikou), John Rushworth, 1st Earl Jellicoe (1859–1935), British admiral. He commanded the British navy during the 1st world war, and kept the German fleet off the high seas from 1916 to the end of the war by his action at the Battle of Jutland

jel·lied (dʒéliːd) adj. given the consistency of a jelly ‖ containing or coated with jelly [JELLY]

jel·ly (dʒéli) 1. pl. **jel·lies** n. a semitransparent, soft food preparation, having an elastic consistency due to the presence of gelatin or other gelatinous substances, used e.g. as a garnish or preservative for meats, or with the addition of fruit juices as a dessert ‖ a food prepared by boiling fruit containing pectin with sugar and allowing the juice to cool ‖ any substance resembling this in consistency 2. v. pres. part. **jel·ly·ing** past and past part. **jel·lied** v.i. to become jelly ‖ v.t. to make into jelly [M.E. gelé fr. F. gelée, frost]

jel·ly·bean (dʒéliːbiːn) n. a sugarcoated, bean-shaped candy with a chewy center

jelly bomb (mil.) an incendiary device containing jellied gasoline

jel·ly·fish (dʒéliːfiʃ) n. any of several marine coelenterates that are the sexually reproducing form of hydrozoans and scyphozoans which exhibit alternation of generations. They are free-swimming, consisting essentially of a contractile umbrella fringed with stinging filaments ‖ (pop.) someone lacking in self-reliance and firmness of will

jelly roll a thin layer of sponge cake covered with jelly and rolled up

Je·mappes, Battle of (ʒəmǽp), a battle (Nov. 6, 1792) of the French Revolutionary Wars, in which the French defeat of the Austrians opened the way for the conquest of Belgium

jem·my (dʒémi) pl. **jem·mies** n. (Br.) a jimmy [dim. of James]

Je·na (jéinə) an old town (pop. 102,538) on the Saale in Thuringia, E. Germany. Manufactures: glass, optical instruments. University (1558), observatory

Jena, Battle of a battle (1806) in which Napoleon decisively defeated a Prussian army during the Napoleonic Wars

Jen·ghiz Khan (dʒéŋɡiskán) Genghis Khan

Jen·kins' Ear, War of (dʒéŋkinz) a war (1739–41) between Britain and Spain, arising out of an incident (1731) in which a British mariner, Robert Jenkins, claimed that his ear had been cut off by Spanish coast guards. The war merged into the War of the Austrian Succession

Jen·ner (dʒénər), Edward (1749–1823), English physician who discovered that inoculation with cowpox vaccine creates immunity to smallpox

jen·ny (dʒéni) pl. **jen·nies** n. the female of various animals, esp. the ass ‖ the spinning jenny [a nickname for Jane or Janet]

jeop·ard·ize (dʒépərdaiz) pres. part. **jeop·ard·iz·ing** past and past part. **jeop·ard·ized** v.t. to put in jeopardy

jeop·ard·y (dʒépərdi) n. the state of being exposed to danger ‖ (law) the state of being liable to conviction [M.E. iuparti, fr. O.F. iu parti, an

evenly divided game (chess term) in which either contestant can lose]

Jeph·thah (dʒéfθə) (12th c. B.C.), Judge of Israel. He sacrificed his daughter because of a rash vow to kill the first living being to meet him on his return from victory over the Ammonite invaders

je·quir·i·ty (dʒikwíriti) pl. **je·quir·i·ties** n. Abrus precatorius, fam. Fabaceae, a tropical twining shrub whose hard red and black seeds are used as beads and weights. The roots provide a licorice substitute ‖ these seeds [fr. F. fr. Tupi Guarani]

Je·qui·ti·nho·nha (ʒəkiːtiːnjónjə) a river (c. 500 miles long) in E. Brazil, flowing into the Atlantic

jer·bo·a (dʒərbóuə) n. any of various members of fam. Dipodidae, small nocturnal, leaping rodents living in the deserts and plains of N. Africa, Asia and E. Europe. They are 6-8 ins long with a tufted tail longer than the body, and look like miniature kangaroos [Mod. L. fr. Arab.]

jer·e·mi·ad (dʒerimáiəd) n. a long, doleful expression of anger and sorrow about wrongs or evil deeds [after the lamentations of Jeremiah in the Bible]

Jer·e·mi·ah (dʒerimáiə) (late 7th and early 6th cc. B.C.) a Major Prophet of the Old Testament. He lived at the time of the collapse of Assyria and the fall of Jerusalem. He urged moral reform. His emphasis on an individual relationship between God and man marked a transition from the idea of an exclusive, national relationship between God and the Jews. His vision of the new covenant had great influence on New Testament teaching ‖ the book of the Old Testament relating his life and prophecies

Je·rez de la Fron·te·ra (héreθðelä frɔntérä) (formerly Xeres) an agricultural trading town (pop. 128,000) in Cádiz, S.W. Spain, headquarters of the sherry trade

Jer·i·cho (dʒérikou) a town (pop. 8,000) of Jordan near the Dead Sea. Ancient Jericho was the first town which the Israelites saw when they entered the Promised Land. God told Joshua to march all the people around its walls for seven days, carrying the Ark of the Covenant in great pomp, with the priests sounding trumpets. On the seventh day Joshua told the people to shout, and the walls tumbled (Joshua vi)

jerk (dʒɔːrk) 1. n. a sudden, abrupt movement or change of motion ‖ an involuntary muscular spasm due to reflex action 2. v.t. to move (a body) by applying a short, sudden force ‖ to throw or bowl (a ball) without following through ‖ to utter in short, abrupt phrases ‖ v.i. to move with sudden stops and starts ‖ to make a sudden, short movement ‖ to throw or bowl a ball without following through [prob. imit.]

jerk v.t. to cure (meat, esp. beef) by drying long thin strips of it in the sun [corrup. of Am.-Span. charquear]

jerk·i·ly (dʒɔ́ːrkili) adv. in a jerky manner

jer·kin (dʒɔ́ːrkin) n. (hist.) a man's short, snug, sleeveless and collarless jacket worn in the 16th and 17th cc. ‖ a sleeveless jacket worn by men or women [origin unknown]

jerk·i·ness (dʒɔ́ːrkinis) n. the state or quality of being jerky

jerk·wa·ter (dʒɔ́ːrkwɔtər, dʒɔ́ːrkwɒtər) adj. (pop.) small, insignificant, a jerkwater town [after the trains which took on water in remote places]

jerk·y (dʒɔ́ːrki) comp. **jerk·i·er** superl. **jerk·i·est** adj. moving in jerks ‖ characterized by jerks

jer·o·bo·am (dʒerəbóuəm) n. a wine bottle several times the normal size

Je·ro·bo·am I (dʒerəbóuəm) (d. c. 910 B.C.), first king of the northern kingdom of Israel (c. 923–c. 910 B.C.). His revolt against Rehoboam led to the separation of Israel from Judah

Jeroboam II (d. c. 749 B.C.), king of Israel (c. 789–c. 749 B.C.)

Je·rome (dʒəróum), St (Eusebius Hieronymus, c. 347–420), Father of the Church. He was one of the greatest scholars and apologists of the early Church. His Latin translation of the Bible largely forms the Vulgate

Jerome of Prague (c. 1370–1416), Bohemian religious reformer. Influenced by Wyclif, he attempted to defend Hus at the Council of Constance, and was burned as a heretic

jer·ri·can, jer·ry can (dʒéri·kæn) n. a portable rectangular gasoline container [fr. jerry, a nickname for a German soldier during the 1st world war]

jer·ry (dʒéri) pl. **jer·ries** n. (Br.) a chamber pot [origin unknown]

jer·ry-build·er (dʒéri·bildər) n. a person who builds buildings of inferior construction with poor materials [origin unknown]

jer·ry-build·ing (dʒéri·bildiŋ) n. the construction of jerry-built buildings ‖ (pl.) jerry-built buildings

jer·ry-built (dʒéri·bilt) adj. badly built of poor materials

jerry can *JERRICAN

jerrymander *GERRYMANDER

Jer·sey (dʒɔ́ːrzi) the southernmost and largest island (area 45 sq. miles, pop. 76,050) of the Channel Is. Capital: St Helier. Official language: French

jersey n. a machine-knitted cloth of wool, cotton, silk etc. ‖ an article of clothing for the upper body, knitted of wool or cotton, with long or short sleeves **Jer·sey** a cow of a breed first raised on Jersey I. and noted for the high butterfat content of its milk [after the island JERSEY]

Jersey City a port (pop. 223,532) of New Jersey, on New York Harbor: meat-packing, chemicals, petroleum

Je·ru·sa·lem (dʒərúːsələm) the holy city of Jews and Christians, sacred also to Moslems. It had been divided between Jordan (the old city, pop. 424,400) and Israel (the new city, pop. 468,200) until Israel annexed the Jordanian part after the third Israeli-Arab War (June 1967). It is at 2,500 ft above sea level, 35 miles from the Mediterranean. It originated in the 2nd millennium B.C., and was chosen by David as the capital of the Hebrews. When Solomon built the Temple (10th c. B.C.) it became a Jewish spiritual center. It fell to the Babylonians (586 B.C.), was rebuilt under Ezra, and was captured by the Greeks (332 B.C.) and the Romans (63 B.C.). The Temple was destroyed (70 A.D.), and Jerusalem was rebuilt by the Romans as a pagan city (132). It became Christian (325), but it fell to the Moslems (638). It was captured (1099) by the Crusaders and was made the capital of the Latin Kingdom of Jerusalem. It was recaptured (1187) by the Moslems. Jerusalem was taken (1917) by British forces, and was the center of the British mandate of Palestine (1920–48). After much fighting, the Arabs gained the old city, while the Jews held the new city (1949), and the division continued until the unification of 1967

Jerusalem artichoke *ARTICHOKE

jess (dʒes) 1. n. also **jesse** (dʒes) (falconry) either of the short leather straps or silk ribbons tied around the legs of a trained hawk. The leash is attached to them by a ring 2. v.t. to put jesses on (a hawk) [M.E. ges fr. O.F. get, throw]

jes·sa·mine (dʒésəmin) n. jasmine

Jes·se (dʒési) father of David, and thus traditionally the first ancestor of Jesus

jesse *JESS

Jes·sel·ton (dʒésəltən) *KOTA KINABALU

Jesse window a window which depicts a genealogical tree showing the descent of Christ from Jesse

jest (dʒest) 1. n. a word or deed designed to evoke laughter ‖ a taunting remark or action ‖ an object which excites both laughter and contempt 2. v.i. to speak frivolously or jokingly ‖ to speak tauntingly **jest·er** n. a person who jests ‖ (hist.) a professional buffoon employed by a king or nobleman as a member of his household [O.F. geste, jeste fr. L. gesta, deeds]

Jes·u·it (dʒéʒuːit, dʒéʒjuːit) 1. n. a member of the Society of Jesus 2. adj. of or relating to the Society of Jesus or its members **Jes·u·it·ic, Jes·u·it·i·cal** adjs. characteristic of a Jesuit ‖ (pejorative) cunning and hypocritical

Je·sus (dʒíːzəs) (c. 6 B.C.–30 A.D.) a Jewish religious leader whom Christians worship as the Son of God and Savior of Mankind, the Christ. His life, teaching, death and resurrection are described in the Gospels of the New Testament, while the Epistles supply other details. Jesus was the son of Mary, wife of Joseph, a carpenter of Nazareth, and they were in Bethlehem at the time of the birth because a census was being taken. According to the gospel Mary was his only human parent (*VIRGIN BIRTH). The exact date of birth is unknown, but was probably between 8 and 4 B.C. (The Christian reckoning which dates the birth as 1 A.D. is based on a miscalculation of Dionysius Exiguus.) As a Jew, Jesus was circumcised, brought up in the knowledge of the Law, and confirmed. Other details of his youth and early manhood are unknown. He was baptized (c. 27) by his cousin, John the Baptist, who was preaching in the valley of the Jordan, and he then retired to the wilderness in readiness for his mission. He began preaching in Galilee, working miracles of exorcism and healing, teaching by parables, and attracting a growing number of disciples. His message was the coming of the Kingdom of God and his mission was to prepare men for it. His Sermon on the Mount transformed the application of the Mosaic Law. After a three-year ministry, in which he won the hostility of the Pharisees and scribes, he entered Jerusalem for the Passover. Here he drove the money-changers out of the Temple, and priests persuaded Judas Iscariot, one of his disciples, to betray him. Jesus ate the Last Supper with the disciples and went to pray in the garden of Gethsemane where he was arrested. He was taken before the high priest, and then turned over to the Romans, the occupying power, as a blasphemer and disturber of the peace. Pontius Pilate, the Roman governor, found no reason to condemn him and would have released him, but yielded to the will of the mob and ordered him to be crucified. The sentence was carried out at Calvary, outside Jerusalem. His body was removed to a tomb, from which he rose three days later. After the Resurrection Jesus appeared several times to his disciples, and, 40 days later, ascended into heaven.

Jesus had portrayed God as a self-giving father of mankind, in contrast to Jehovah, the 'jealous God' of the Old Testament (and in contrast to the gods and goddesses of pagan Rome), and this revolution in religious thought was to become a continuing process through the Holy Spirit working in the Church (*CHRISTIANITY)

Jesus and Mary, Congregation of *CEUDIST

Jesus freak a participant in an antidrug culture youth movement devoted to fundamentalist religion, communal living, and street preaching

Jesus movement or **Jesus revolution** (*evangelical*) movement among lay Protestants to spread New Testament teachings independently of established dominations —**Jesus shop** *n*. store carrying religious appurtenances

Jesus, Society of an order of Roman Catholic priests founded (1540) by St Ignatius Loyola. It was organized to support the papacy and orthodox Catholic faith against heresy, and for foreign missions. Its constitution was military and autocratic, and it was subject only to the pope. Its representation and decisive influence at the Council of Trent (1545–63) are a tribute to Jesuit scholarship, as also are men such as Robert Bellarmine and Francisco de Suárez. By the end of the 16th c. the Jesuit system of education, based on the principles of humanism, was established. Today the order has schools and universities in all parts of the world. Francis Xavier was the order's first great missionary, working in Asia (1541–52). The order was itself expelled (18th c.) by European countries which feared its influential power. The Society was suppressed (1773) by Clement XIV and restored (1814) under Pius VII. The spiritual and intellectual training of Jesuits is rigorous and long. Ignatius's 'Spiritual Exercises' remain the basis of their religious life. The Society is the largest religious order and the largest foreign missionary organization in the world

jet (dʒet) **1.** *n*. a stream of vapor, gas or liquid coming out fast from a narrow orifice ‖ the narrow pipe or orifice which controls such a stream ‖ an airplane having a jet engine ‖ a jet engine **2.** *v. pres. part.* **jet·ting** *past* and *past part.* **jet·ted** *v.i.* to issue as a jet ‖ *v.i.* to emit a jet of [F. *jeter*, to throw]

jet *n*. (*mineral.*) a very hard and very black form of natural carbon with high luster, used for ornamental purposes [O. F. *jaiet* fr. L. fr. Gk]

jet avator (*aerospace*) device designed to direct the exhaust of a rocket to effect change in direction of the craft

jet belt or **jet flying belt** device powered by a small jet motor for lifting an individual up to 25 ft in the air and horizontally for a short distance

jet-black (dʒetblæk) *adj.* intensely black

jet-boat (dʒetbout) *n*. boat propelled by a jet engine

jet-borne (dʒetbɔrn) *adj.* carried by a jet aircraft

jet deflexion (*aerospace*) system of propulsion designed to create a downward thrust to assist take-off

jet engine a motor deriving propulsive power from jets of fuel combustion products and heated air that are discharged rearward with great velocity, to give forward motion

jet·foil (dʒetfɔil) *n*. a jet-propelled air-cushion seagoing vehicle, e.g., the ferry between Brighton and Dieppe *Cf* AIR-CUSHION VEHICLE, HOVERCRAFT

jet-hop (dʒethɒp) *n*. a short trip by jet aircraft

jet lag fatigue, irritability, and other mental and physical symptoms resulting from travel through several time zones *also* jet fatigue, jet syndrome

jet-pro·pelled (dʒetprəpéld) *adj.* driven by jet propulsion

jet propulsion reaction propulsion in which the propulsion unit obtains oxygen from the air as distinguished from rocket propulsion in which the unit carries its own oxygen-producing material —**jet-propulsion** *adj.* of a gasoline or other fuel turbine jet unit that discharges hot gas through a tail pipe and a nozzle, affording a thrust that propels the aircraft *Cf* ROCKET PROPULSION

jet·sam (dʒetsəm) *n*. the cargo, gear etc. thrown overboard from a ship in distress to lighten the load. It sinks or is washed ashore (cf. FLOTSAM) [older form *jetson* fr. O.F. *getaison*, act of throwing]

jet set the happy few socially prominent internationally [from much flying about in pursuit of pleasure)

Jet Star (*mil.*) a small, fast, support-type transport aircraft (C-140) powered by four turbojet engines podded two on each side of the fuselage

jet stream a narrow current of high-velocity westerly winds, close to the tropopause

jet·ti·son (dʒetis'n) **1.** *n*. the act of throwing cargo, gear etc. overboard to lighten the load of a ship in distress **2.** *v.t.* to throw overboard as jetsam ‖ to discard (part of any load) which has become an encumbrance [A.F. *getteson*, O. F. *getaison*]

jet·ty (dʒeti:) *pl.* **jet·ties** *n*. a structure built out into the water of a sea, lake or river to shelter a harbor or to break waves or currents ‖ a small landing wharf [M.E. *getey, gettey* fr. O.F. *getee, jetee*, a throwing]

Jev·ons (dʒévənz), William Stanley (1835–82), British economist and logician. In 'The Theory of Political Economy' (1871) he formulated the theory of marginal utility, and demonstrated the mathematical relationship between value and utility

Jew (dʒu:) *n*. a member of the worldwide Semitic group who claim descent from Abraham and whose religion is Judaism ‖ a descendant of Jacob, an Israelite ‖ a member of the Hebrew tribe of Judah ‖ (*hist.*) an inhabitant of the ancient kingdom of Judah [M.E. *gyu, giu* etc. fr. O.F. *giu, gyu, giue* fr. L. fr. Gk fr. Heb.]

—The Old Testament traces the origin of the Jews to Abraham, who emigrated (early 2nd millennium B.C.) from Mesopotamia to Canaan. His descendants, the 12 tribes of Israel, settled in N. Egypt (c. 16th c. B.C.), where they became a persecuted slave race. Moses led them out of Egypt (14th or 13th cc. B.C.) and through the wilderness of Sinai for 40 years, during which the Jewish monotheistic religion became an ethical religion. The Jews entered Canaan (c. 12th c. B.C.) and, after fighting many wars with local tribes, became settled on both sides of the Jordan (c. 1000 B.C.). Ruled at first by Judges, they set up a monarchy under Saul (c. 1040- c. 1012 B.C.) to meet the threat of the Philistines. In the reigns of David (c. 1012- c. 972 B.C.) and Solomon (c. 972-c. 932 B.C.) Jerusalem became the spiritual and political capital of the Jews. Under Rehoboam, the kingdom split (c. 932 B.C.) into Israel in the north and Judah in the south. The former fell (c. 722 B.C.) to the Assyrians under Sargon II. The latter was conquered (586 B.C.) by the Babylonians under Nebuchadnezzar II, and its inhabitants carried off into the Babylonian Captivity (586-538 B.C.). The conquest (539 B.C.) of Babylonia by Cyrus II was followed by the return of the exiles and the rebuilding (516 B.C.) of the Temple. Under the prophets, the Jewish religion incorporated belief in immortality, and Jewish law was codified in the Torah. Conquered (333 B.C.) by Alexander the Great, the Jews resisted Hellenism, revolted (c. 168-142 B.C.) under the Maccabees, and gained

a measure of political independence (142-63 B.C.). Palestine was conquered (63 B.C.) by the Romans under Pompey, but a puppet Jewish dynasty was maintained, including Herod (37-4 B.C.). A national revolt (66 A.D.) against Roman rule was put down with great severity, and the Temple destroyed (70). A further revolt (135) was followed by the expulsion of the Jews from Palestine. Despite this dispersion, the Jews maintained their language and religion. The Talmud was compiled (6th c.) in Babylonia, where until the 11th c. there was an important Jewish minority. Jewish culture attained a golden age in Spain (9th-12th cc.), and the Jews came to dominate international trade as they could practice usury, which was officially forbidden to Christians. Jews were expelled from England (1290), France (1306) and, after persecution during the Inquisition, from Spain (1492) and Portugal (1497). They resettled in Poland, parts of Italy, Holland (from the late 16th c.) and England (after 1656). Greater toleration began with the Revolutionary War (1775-83) and the French Revolution (1789-99), and full legal emancipation was achieved in France (1791), Denmark (1849), Britain (1858), Austria-Hungary (1867), Italy (1870), Germany (1870), Switzerland (1871) and the U.S.S.R. (1917). Anti-Semitism remained strong, and about 6,000,000 Jews were exterminated by the Nazi régime. Zionism was founded (1897), and a Jewish national homeland was created (1948) in Israel. There are about 12,000,000 Jews (3,500,000 in Europe, 5,000,000 in the U.S.A., 800,000 in Canada and 1,900,000 in Israel)

Jew·el (dʒúːəl), John (1522–71), English prelate, bishop of Salisbury (1560–71). His 'Apologia ecclesiae Anglicanae,' (1562) was a definitive statement of the Elizabethan Church settlement, and led to much controversy with the Roman Catholic Church

jewel *n*. a precious stone prized for its beauty and rarity, e.g. an emerald or ruby ‖ an ornament of gold, platinum, silver or other costly metal set with precious stones ‖ a pivot bearing made of precious stone, esp. a ruby, in a watch ‖ a person, often one socially inferior, whose qualities one is praising **jéw·eled, jéw·elled** *adj.* set with jewels [M.E. *iuel, iuwele, iuall* fr. A.F.]

jew·el·er, jew·el·ler (dʒúːələr) *n*. someone who trades in or makes jewelry [A.F. *jueler*]

jewelers' rouge, jewellers' rouge colcothar of the finest quality

jew·el·ry, esp. *Br.* **jew·el·ler·y** (dʒúːəlri:) *n*. (*collect.*) personal ornaments made of precious or base metals, and precious or imitation stones [O.F. *iuelerye*]

Jew·ess (dʒúːis) *n*. a female Jew

Jew·ish (dʒúːiʃ) *adj.* of, belonging to or characteristic of the Jews

Jewish calendar a calendar, reckoned from the year 3761 B.C., based on lunar cycles of 19 years. It is used in calculating Jewish history, Jewish holidays etc. The months of the Jewish calendar are:

1. Tishri (30 days, sometimes called Ethanim, beginning at the first new moon after the autumn equinox)
2. Cheshvan (29 or 30 days, sometimes called Marcheshvan or Bul)
3. Kislev (29 or 30 days)
4. Tebet (29 days)
5. Shebat (30 days)
6. Adar (29-30 days)
7. Nisan (30 days, sometimes called Abib)
8. Iyar (29 days, sometimes called Zif)
9. Sivan (30 days)
10. Tammuz (29 days)
11. Ab (30 days)
12. Elul (29 days)

The month Veadar (29 days, sometimes called Adar Sheni) is added seven times every 19 years between the months of Adar and Nisan

Jew·ry (dʒúːri:, dʒúːəri:) *n*. the Jewish people ‖ (*hist.*) a district populated by Jews ‖ (*hist.*) Judaea [A.F. *juerie*, O.F. *juierie*]

Jew's harp, jew's harp a musical instrument about 3 ins long consisting of a metal frame holding a thin metal strip. The frame is held in the mouth, which serves as a sound box, and the metal strip is made to twang with the forefinger, the note emitted being made to vary by altering the shape of the mouth

Jez·e·bel (dʒézəb'l, dʒézəbel) (*d.* c. 846 B.C.), Phoenician princess, wife of King Ahab of Is-

CONCISE PRONUNCIATION KEY: **(a)** æ, c*a*t; ɑ, c*a*r; ɔ f*aw*n; ei, sn*a*ke. **(e)** e, h*e*n; i:, sh*ee*p; iə, d*ee*r; ɛə, b*ea*r. **(i)** i, f*i*sh; ai, t*i*ger; ə:, b*i*rd. **(o)** o, *o*x; au, c*ow*; ou, g*oa*t; u, p*oo*r; ɔi, r*oy*al. **(u)** ʌ, d*u*ck; u, b*u*ll; u:, g*oo*se; ə, b*a*cillus; ju:, c*u*be. x, lo*ch*; θ, *th*ink; ð, bo*th*er; z, *Z*en; ʒ, corsa*g*e. dʒ, sava*g*e; ŋ, oranguta*ng*; j, *y*ak; ʃ, *fi*sh; tʃ, fe*tch*; 'l, rabb*le*; 'n, redd*en*. Complete pronunciation key appears inside front cover.

rael. Her idolatry and wickedness have made her name a symbol of feminine depravity

Jhan·si (dʒánsi:) a city (pop. 173,292) in Uttar Pradesh, India, a rail center

Jhe·lum (dʒéiləm) a tributary (500 miles long, navigable most of its length) of the Indus, flowing from the Himalayas through the Vale of Kashmir, then south, as the Kashmir-Pakistan frontier, into the Punjab, West Pakistan

jib, gib, *Br.* also **jibb** (dʒib) *pres. part.* **jib·bing, gib·bing** *past* and *past part.* **jibbed, gibbed** *v.i.* (of a horse) to move sideways and refuse to move forward ‖ (of a person) to show unwillingness or refuse to go ahead in some way, *to jib at a task* [etym. doubtful]

jib *n.* (*naut.*) a triangular sail stretching from the masthead to the bowsprit or from the foretopmast head to the jibboom ‖ the long arm of a crane ‖ the boom of a derrick [origin unknown]

jib, jibb, *Br.* also **gibb** *pres. part.* **jib·bing,** *Br.* also **gib·bing** *past* and *past part.* **jibbed,** *Br.* also **gibbed** *v.t.* (*naut.*) to cause (a sail or yard) to shift from one side of a vessel to the other ‖ *v.i.* (*naut.* of a sail, yard or boom) to jibe [etym. doubtful]

jib·bah, jib·ba (dʒíbə) *n.* a jubbah [Egypt.]

jibber *GIBBER

jib·boom (dʒíbbú:m) *n.* (*naut.*) a wooden spar attached to the end of the bowsprit

jibe, gibe (dʒaib) *pres. part.* **jib·ing, gib·ing** *past* and *past part.* **jibed, gibed** *v.i.* to agree, be in accordance, *her version of what happened doesn't jibe with his* [origin unknown]

jibe *GIBE (jeer)

jibe, gybe (dʒaib) *pres. part.* **jib·ing, gyb·ing** *past* and *past part.* **jibed, gybed** *v.i.* (*naut.*, of a fore-and-aft sail or its boom) to swing from one side of the boat to the other ‖ to change course with this result ‖ *v.t.* to cause to jibe [Du. *gijben* perh. infl. by JIB]

Jibuti *DJIBOUTI

Jidda *JEDDA

jif·fy (dʒífi:) *n.* (*pop.*) an instant [origin unknown]

Jiffy bag trade name for padded bag used for shipping, esp. books; manufactured by Jiffy Mfg. Co.

jig (dʒig) **1.** *n.* a rapid, gay, springy dance ‖ the music for such a dance ‖ a gigue ‖ (*engin.*) a device which maintains the proper positional relationship between a material and the machine that is working on it ‖ (*mineral.*) a device for jigging ore **2.** *v. pres. part.* **jig·ging** *past* and *past part.* **jigged** *v.t.* to dance as a jig ‖ to move (something) up and down in rapid succession ‖ to separate the denser minerals from (crushed ore) by shaking it up and down in water in a large perforated container ‖ (*engin.*) to use a jig on ‖ *v.i.* to dance a jig ‖ to move with rapid up-and-down motions **jig·ger** *n.* a person or thing that jigs ‖ (*mineral.*) a jig ‖ (*naut.*) a small sail stepped to a jiggermast ‖ (*naut.*) a small vessel carrying such a sail ‖ a jiggermast ‖ (*naut.*) a light tackle ‖ (*pottery*) a lathe carrying a revolving mold, for shaping clay with a profile ‖ (*golf*) an iron with a narrow, fairly well-lofted face, used for approaches ‖ (*billiards*) a support for a cue ‖ a small container (1½ fl. oz.) used to measure whiskey or other spirits ‖ the quantity held by such a container [origin unknown]

jigger *n.* a chigoe ‖ a harvest bug [corrup. of CHIGOE]

jig·ger·mast (dʒígərməst, dʒígərmæst, dʒígərmɑst) *n.* a mast stepped in the stern of a jigger, yawl or other small vessel

jig·gle (dʒíg'l) *pres. part.* **jig·gling** *past* and *past part.* **jig·gled** *v.i.* to move in quick little successive motions ‖ *v.t.* to cause (something) to move with quick little successive motions [dim. or freq. of JIG]

jig·saw (dʒígsɔ) *n.* a mechanical saw with a vertical blade used to cut along irregular or curved lines ‖ a jigsaw puzzle [JIG v.]

jigsaw puzzle a picture mounted on wood or cardboard cut into many irregular pieces, to be reassembled as a pastime

ji·had, je·had (dʒihɑ́d) *n.* a holy war fought by Moslems against unbelievers [Arab.]

jilt (dʒilt) *v.t.* to break with (a lover who does not want to end the relationship) in a callously light-hearted way [origin unknown]

Jiménez (hi:méineθ), Juan Ramon (1881–1958), Spanish poet, winner of the Nobel Prize for literature (1956). His works include 'Violet Souls' (1900), 'Platero and I' (1914–7), "All Seasons in One' (1946) and 'Animal of the Depths' (1949)

Jiménez de Cisneros *CISNEROS

Ji·mé·nez de Que·sa·da (hi:méneθðekesáða) Gonzalo (c. 1499–1579), Spanish conquistador. He led (1536–8) an expedition through N. and central Colombia in search of El Dorado, conquered (1537) the Chibcha, and founded (1538) Bogotá. He was made (1550) marshal of New Granada

Jim·mu (dʒímu:) the legendary first emperor of Japan, a descendant of the sun-goddess. He is supposed to have conquered the country (c. 660 B.C.) and to have ruled until 585 B.C.

jim·my (dʒími:) **1.** *pl.* **jim·mies** *n.* a thick bar of iron with one end flattened as a chisel edge, used by burglars for forcing doors or windows ‖ **2.** *v.t. pres. part.* **jim·my·ing** *past* and *past part.* **jim·mied** to pry open esp. with a jimmy

jim·son·weed (dʒíms'nwi:d) *n. Datura stramonium,* fam. *Solanaceae,* a tall, very poisonous annual weed of tropical origin, now found in various parts of the world. It has evil-smelling foliage and bears showy white or violet flowers [after *Jamestown,* Va]

Jin·a (dʒína) *JAINISM

jin·gle (dʒíŋg'l) **1.** *v. pres. part.* **jin·gling** *past* and *past part.* **jin·gled** *v.t.* to cause (something) to produce a jingle ‖ *v.i.* to make a jingle **2.** *n.* a pleasing sound composed of a number of high-pitched percussion notes in continuous but unrhythmical combination ‖ something which produces a jingle ‖ a catchy succession of words that ring against one another due to alliteration, rhyme etc. **jin·gly** *adj.* [imit.]

jin·go·ism (dʒíŋgouizəm) *n.* advocacy of an aggressively nationalist foreign policy **jin·go·ist** *n.* **jin·go·is·tic** *adj.* [after the exclamatory refrain 'by jingo' in a popular British song of 1878]

jinks (dʒiŋks) *pl. n.* high jinks

jinn (dʒin) *n.* (*Moslem demonology*) a spirit which inhabits the earth. It can assume different forms and wields supernatural power ‖ (*collect., Moslem demonology*) these spirits as a class [Arab. *jinni,* pl. *jinn,* a spirit]

Jin·nah (dʒína), Mohammed Ali (1876–1948), Pakistani statesman. He led the Moslem League's struggle (1934–47) to establish the independent state of Pakistan, of which he became the first governor-general (1947–8)

jin·rik·i·sha, jin·rick·sha (dʒinríkʃə, dʒinríkʃɔ) *n.* a light, small, two-wheeled Oriental vehicle, chiefly for passenger use, drawn by one man [Jap. *jin,* man+*riki,* power+*sha,* vehicle]

Jin·sen (dʒi:nsén) *INCHON

jinx (dʒiŋks) **1.** *n.* (*pop.*) a person or thing bringing bad luck ‖ (*pop.*) an evil spell **2.** *v.t.* (*pop.*) to cause (someone) bad luck ‖ (*pop.*) to put a jinx on (someone) [etym, doubtful]

ji·pi·ja·pa (hi:pi:hápə) *n. Carludovica palmata,* fam. *Cyclanthaceae,* a palmlike plant of Central and South America whose leaves are used for making panama hats

jit·ter (dʒítər) **1.** *v.i.* to tremble with anxiety **2.** *n.* (*esp. pl.*) a fit of acute anxiety **jít·ter·y** *adj.* [imit.]

jit·ter·bug (dʒítərbʌg) **1.** *n.* a lively dance based on standardized steps and patterns often accompanied by acrobatics (splits, somersaults etc.) and danced to swing and esp. boogie-woogie. It originated in the U.S.A. in the 1920s, was esp. popular in the 1940s, and was spread internationally by U.S. armed forces during the 2nd world war ‖ a person who dances this ‖ (*hist.*) someone devoted to jazz **2.** *v.i. pres. part.* **jit·ter·bug·ging** *past* and *past part.* **jit·ter·bugged** to dance the jitterbug

Ji·va·ro (hí:vɑrɔ) *pl.* **Ji·va·ro, Ji·va·ros** *n.* a group of South American Indians inhabiting the lower E. Andean slopes in E. Ecuador and Peru, formerly headhunters known for their head-shrinking practices. Families live in community houses, subsisting on wild fruits, hunting and fishing (using blowguns and poisoned darts), and pottery-making and clothweaving. In the 1960s they numbered about 20,000 ‖ a member of this group ‖ the language of this group **Ji·va·ró·an** *adj.* [Span. *Jíbaro,* of Amerind origin]

jive (dʒaiv) *adj.* (*slang*) phony

Jo·a·chim (dʒóuəkim), St (1st c. B.C.), traditionally the father of the Virgin Mary. Feast: Aug. 16

Joachim of Flo·ris (flóris) (c. 1130–1202), Italian mystic. His 'Expositio ın Apocalypsim' was a mystical interpretation of history, and had great influence in the 13th and 14th cc.

Joan of Arc (dʒóuən·ɑ́rk), St (*F.* Jeanne d'Arc, 1412–31), French national heroine, the Maid of

Orléans, a peasant girl of Domrémy in N.E. France. She heard saints' voices urging her to help the dauphin, Charles VII, to regain the throne from the English, who were at that time victorious in the Hundred Years' War. She convinced Charles of her mission, and led a large army to raise the siege of Orléans (1429). She had Charles crowned at Reims (1429), but was captured by the Burgundians (1430), who sold her to the English. Joan was tried for heresy and sorcery by an ecclesiastical court at Rouen, was condemned, and burned at the stake. Her condemnation was annulled (1456) and she was canonized (1920). Feast: May 30

Jo·áo Pes·so·a (ʒaupesóa) (or Paraíba) a city (pop. 287,607) in E. Brazil. It exports cotton, sugar and minerals

Job (dʒoub) **1.** a book of the Old Testament, variously dated 7th–4th cc. B.C. It is written in a dramatic form and relates the story of Job, a Jewish patriarch, who endured great sufferings but kept his faith in God

job (dʒɔb) **1.** *n.* a specific piece of work, esp. done for pay ‖ an occupation as a steady source of livelihood, *to be out of a job* ‖ (*pop.*) a difficult task, *he found it a job to make both ends meet* ‖ (*Br., pop.*) a set of circumstances, *it is a good job he was at home when you called* ‖ (*pop.*) a robbery or burglary etc. ‖ a public office turned to private advantage **to make a good job of something** to do something well **2.** *v.t. pres. part.* **job·bing** *past* and *past part.* **jobbed** to pass (specific pieces of work) to others for an agreed price, *he jobbed a good deal of the work to smaller firms* ‖ to buy and sell (goods) as a middleman ‖ to buy and sell (stocks and shares) ‖ to hire (someone) for a specific job or period ‖ to turn (a matter) to personal and corrupt gain ‖ (*esp. Br.*) to arrange a benefit for (someone) by use of influence amounting to dishonesty, *he jobbed his son into the position* ‖ *v.i.* to do various pieces of work, from time to time, for pay ‖ to turn public office to private advantage **to job off** to sell (surplus or superseded goods) cheaply in bulk **jób·ber** *n.* a stockjobber ‖ a middleman ‖ a corrupt public servant **jób·ber·y** *n.* the act of jobbing by a public servant [origin unknown]

job action production inhibition by employees to enforce demands on an employer, usu. short of a strike, e.g., slowdown, sick calls

jobbing gardener (*Br.*) a gardener working part-time for more than one employer, and paid by the hour

jobbing printer (*Br.*) a job printer

Job Corps, U.S. federal agency that provides job training for disadvantaged youth. It involves ½ to 2 years of training for youths from 16 to 21 years old in more than 100 centers in the U.S. and Puerto Rico. Under the Department of Labor, the agency was begun in 1964 as a result of the Economic Opportunity Act, part of Pres. Lyndon B. Johnson's 'War on Poverty'

job enrichment (*business*) practice of providing opportunity for greater on-the-job challenge and personal activities to relieve boredom and alienation in work, esp. for repetitive and mechanistic tasks

job·hold·er (dʒɔbhouldər) *n.* someone with a regular job

job hopper one who changes jobs frequently, usu. to obtain a higher salary —**job hop** *v.* — **job hopping** *n.*

job lot a collection of miscellaneous articles, usually of small value, offered for sale as a single lot ‖ an inferior set (of goods, objects etc.) ‖ (of paper) an amount less than a standard saleable quantity

job printer (*Am.*=*Br.* jobbing printer) a printer of billheads, handbills, tickets etc. (not books or newspapers)

Job's comforter a supposed friend whose apparent sympathy makes matters worse [after JOB the patriarch]

Jo·cas·ta (dʒoukǽstə) *OEDIPUS

jock (dʒɔk) *n.* (*colloq.*) an athlete

jock·ey (dʒɔ́ki:) **1.** *n.* a professional rider in horse racing **2.** *v.t.* to edge (a person, thing, situation) by tact in the direction one wishes to impose ‖ to ride (a horse) as jockey ‖ *v.i.* to work one's way into a better position by deft handling of a person, thing or situation [dim. of *Jock,* Scot. for Jack]

jock·strap (dʒɔ́kstræp) *n.* a protective support for the genitals worn by male athletes etc. [fr. slang *jock,* penis fr. earlier *jockam* (origin unknown)+STRAP]

jo·cose (dʒoukóus) *adj.* given to joking, full of jokes **jo·cos·i·ty** (dʒoukɒsiti:) *n.* [fr. L. *jocosus*]

CONCISE PRONUNCIATION KEY: **(a)** æ, c*a*t; ɑ, c*a*r; ɔ f*aw*n; ei, sn*a*ke. **(e)** e, h*e*n; i:, sh*ee*p; iə, d*ee*r; ɛə, b*ea*r. **(i)** i, f*i*sh; ai, t*i*ger; ə:, b*i*rd. **(o)** o, *o*x; au, c*ow*; ou, g*oa*t; u, p*oo*r; ɔi, r*oy*al. **(u)** ʌ, d*u*ck; u, b*u*ll; u:, g*oo*se; ə, b*a*cillus; ju:, c*u*be. x, lo*ch*; θ, *th*ink; ð, bo*th*er; z, *Z*en; ʒ, cor*s*age; dʒ, sava*g*e; ŋ, orangutan*g*; j, *y*ak; ʃ, *f*ish; tʃ, fe*tch*; 'l, rabb*le*; 'n, redd*en*. Complete pronunciation key appears inside front cover.

joc·u·lar (dʒɒkjulər) *adj.* joking or given to joking **joc·u·lar·i·ty** (dʒɒkjulæriti:) *n.* [fr. L. *jocularis*]

joc·und (dʒɒkənd, dʒóukənd) *adj.* (*rhet.*) likely to inspire joyfulness ‖ cheerful **joc·ún·di·ty** *n.* [O.F. *jocond, jocund*]

Jo·delle (ʒoudel), Étienne (1532–73), French dramatist, a member of the Pléiade. His 'Cléopâtre Captive' (1552) was the first French classical tragedy imitated from the ancients

Jodh·pur (dʒódpur) a city (pop. 317,612) in Rajasthan, India, capital of the former principality of Jodhpur. It is a commercial center and wheat market

jodh·purs (dʒɒdpuərz) *pl. n.* pants for horseback riding, fitting tightly from the knee to the ankle, worn with a low boot [after JODHPUR]

Jo·do (dʒóudou) *BUDDHISM

Jod·rell Bank (dʒɒdrəl) an experimental research station in radio astronomy in Cheshire, England

Jo·el (dʒóuəl) a Minor Prophet of the Old Testament ‖ the book of the Old Testament bearing his name. It contains apocalyptic visions and foretells an outpouring of the Holy Spirit

Joffre (ʒɔfr), Joseph Jacques Césaire (1852–1931), French marshal. He commanded the French army (1914–16) and was largely responsible for the victory of the Marne (1914)

jog (dʒɒg) **1.** *v. pres. part.* **jog·ging** *past* and *past part.* **jogged** *v.t.* to give (something) a slight push, *to jog someone's elbow* ‖ to cause (something) to move or become active, *to jog someone's memory* ‖ *v.i.* to move as if forced to do so by a series of pushes, *to jog up and down on a horse* ‖ (with 'on' or 'along') to move along at a regular pace without hurrying ‖ to exercise using such a pace **2.** *n.* a slight push ‖ a slow pace or movement [prob. imit.]

jog *n.* a part that sticks out or recedes from the general line or surface of something, e.g. of a building [fr. JAG, irregular projection and fr. JOGGLE *n.*]

jogging (*sports*) slow running

jog·gle (dʒɒg'l) *pres. part.* **jog·gling** *past* and *past part.* **jog·gled** *v.t.* to move or shake (something) by a series of slight pushes or jerks ‖ *v.i.* to move or shake slightly [perh. fr. JOG]

joggle 1. *n.* a joint in stone or other material consisting of tight-fitting notches and projections to prevent one part from slipping ‖ such a notch or projection **2.** *v.t. pres. part.* **jog·gling** *past* and *past part.* **jog·gled** to join in this way [etym. doubtful]

Jog·ja·kar·ta (dʒougjəkártə) a town (pop. 342,267) in S. Java, Indonesia, noted for arts and handicrafts. University

jog·trot (dʒɒgtrɒt) **1.** *n.* a slow, monotonous, slightly jolting trot ‖ a slow, dull or leisurely progressing **2.** *v.t. pres. part.* **jog·trot·ting** *past* and *past part.* **jog·trot·ted** to move at a jogtrot **jóg·trot** *adj.* and *adv.*

Jo·han·nes·burg (dʒouhǽnisbə:rg) the largest city (pop. 1,726,073) in South Africa in the Transvaal, at 5,737 ft. It is the industrial center of the world's biggest gold-mining district (*WITWATERSRAND) and a livestock and produce market. University of Witwatersrand (1922)

John (dʒɒn), St (*d.* c. 100), an early disciple of Christ, one of the 12 Apostles, brother of St James the Greater. The fourth Gospel, the three Epistles of John, and Revelation have been attributed to him. Symbol: a young man. Feast: Dec. 27

John Bull a personification of England or the English people insofar as stolidity and determination mark the national character [after a character personifying England in 'The History of *John Bull*' (1712) by John Arbuthnot (1667–1735), English physician and man of letters]

John Doe a popular term for the average U.S. citizen ‖ (*law*) a name used to designate a party to legal proceedings whose identity is not known, or a fictitious personage

John Dory *DORY (fish)

john·ny·cake, jon·ny·cake (dʒɒni:keik) *n.* a bread made from cornmeal ‖ (*Austral.*) a (wheat) bread baked as small cakes on the ashes, or fried

John·ny-come-late·ly (dʒɒni:kʌmléitli:) *n.* a latecomer, esp. someone who was slow to recognize the success of some venture and begins to participate later than most of the other participants

John·son·ese (dʒɒnsəní:z, dʒɒnsəní:s) *n.* the language of Dr Samuel Johnson, marked by balanced locutions and full of words of Latin derivation

John·so·ni·an (dʒɒnsóuni:ən) *adj.* of, or in the manner of, Samuel Johnson, esp. with reference to his use of words of Latin derivation

John VIII (*d.* 882), pope (872–82). An opponent of St Ignatius of Constantinople, he tried unsuccessfully to settle the differences between the Greek and Latin Churches. He was forced (877) to pay tribute to the Saracens to keep them from entering Rome

John XII (c. 937–64), pope (955–64). Previously the ally of Otto I, he turned against him and was deposed (963). John returned (963), excommunicated Otto and was murdered

John XXII (1244–1334), pope (1316–34). His pontificate was disturbed by a long struggle with Louis IV the Bavarian, in which John's claim to extensive temporal power was opposed by Marsiglio of Padua and William of Occam

John XXIII (1881–1963), pope (1958–63). An energetic reformer, he summoned the 2nd Vatican Council

John XXIII (c. 1370–1419), antipope (1410–15). Elected during the Great Schism, he was deposed by the Council of Constance

John I Tzi·mis·ces (tsimísi:z) (c.925–76), Byzantine emperor (969–76). He usurped the throne, and drove the Russians out of E. Bulgaria and the Arabs out of Syria

John II Comnenus (1088–1143), Byzantine emperor (1118–43). A just and mild ruler, he campaigned against the Magyars and Serbs and challenged the Normans in Sicily

John V Pa·lae·ol·o·gus (peili:óləgəs) (1332–91), Byzantine emperor (1341–76 and 1379–91). His throne was usurped until 1355 by John VI. He lost Serbia to the Ottoman Turks

John VI Can·ta·cu·zene (kæntəku:zí:n) (c. 1292–1383), Byzantine emperor (1341–55). He usurped the throne of John V, and allowed the Ottoman Turks to penetrate into Europe

John VIII Palaeologus (1390–1448). Byzantine emperor (1425–48). He agreed (1439) to the union of the Eastern and Western Churches, in a vain attempt to get help against the Turks

John 'Lackland' (1167–1216), king of England (1199–1216), son of Henry II. Having attempted unsuccessfully to usurp the throne during the captivity of his brother Richard I, he succeeded on Richard's death (1199). A revolt in Brittany involved him in war in France and the loss (1203–5) of Normandy, Anjou, Brittany, Maine and Touraine, confirmed by a crushing defeat at Bouvines (1214). His refusal to accept Langton as archbishop of Canterbury (1207) brought England under interdict (1208) and ended with John's submission to the papacy (1213). The barony, alienated by the failure of royal policy and by the financial exactions of this and preceding reigns, forced John to agree to the terms of Magna Carta (1215). His attempts to evade the agreement brought war with the barons, during which John died

John I 'the Great' (Port. João) (c. 1357–1433), king of Portugal (1385–1433). He won independence for Portugal in a great victory over Castile (1385). His reign marked the beginning of Portuguese expansion in Africa

John II 'the Perfect' (1455–95), king of Portugal (1481–95). He encouraged exploration, and signed (1494) the Treaty of Tordesillas with Spain

John III 'the Pious' (1502–57), king of Portugal (1521–57). He introduced (1531) the Inquisition into Portugal. With the founding at Bahia of the first Portuguese colony in America, the Portuguese empire was at its greatest extent, but economic decline began in Portugal itself

John IV 'the Fortunate' (c. 1604–56), king of Portugal (1640–56), the first king of the house of Bragança. He succeeded to the throne after a successful revolution against Spanish rule (1640), precipitating a war with Spain (1640–68)

John V 'the Magnanimous' (1689–1750), king of Portugal (1706–50). A patron of the arts and sciences, he squandered the royal resources

John VI 'the Clement' (1767–1826), regent (1792–1816) and king (1816–26) of Portugal. French invasion (1807) forced him to flee to Brazil, where he stayed until 1821. Brazil became independent (1822) under his son Pedro I

John I (1350–95), king of Aragon (1387–95). He was a brilliant patron of learning

John II (1397–1479), king of Aragon and Sicily (1458–79) and of Navarre (1425–79). He put down (1472) a rising in Catalonia, and passed

on a strong inheritance to his son, who ruled as Ferdinand V of Castile

John kings of France *JEAN

John 'the Fearless' *JEAN 'the Fearless'

John (1296–1346), king of Bohemia (1310–46), son of Emperor Henry VII. He became blind in 1340, and died fighting at Crécy

John I Za·po·lya (zápɔlja) (1487–1540), king of Hungary (1526–40). Succeeding to the throne after the Battle of Mohacs (1526), he was involved in a struggle with the future Emperor Ferdinand I until 1538

John III So·bie·ski (sɒbjéski:) (1624–96), king of Poland (1674–96). He raised the siege of Vienna (1683), and turned back the Turkish invasion of Europe

John, Don, of Austria (c. 1545–78), Spanish general and admiral, son of Emperor Charles V. He defeated the Turks at Lepanto (1571)

John, Augustus Edwin (1878–1962), English portrait painter and etcher

John Baptist de la Salle, St *JEAN BAPTISTE DE LA SALLE

John Birch Society (dʒɒnbá:rtʃ) a U.S. anti-Communist political organization founded (1958) by Robert H. W. Welch, Jr. It is named after an Army Air Corps intelligence captain killed by Communist Chinese in 1945. It organizes study groups to analyze Communist strategy, and resistance cells to be activated in the event of a Communist takeover

John Bos·co (bóskou), St (1815–88), Italian priest. He founded (c. 1851) the Society of St Francis of Sales (*SALESIAN). Feast: Jan. 31

John Chrys·os·tom (krísəstəm), St (c. 347–407), patriarch of Constantinople (398–404), one of the Greek Fathers. He wrote a treatise on the priesthood and many biblical commentaries, and was famous for his eloquence. Feast: Jan. 27

John de Baliol *BALIOL, JOHN DE

John, Epistles of the 23rd, 24th and 25th books of the New Testament, attributed to St John and thought to have been written in the late 1st c.

John Eudes (ə:d), St (1601–80), French priest. He founded (1643) the Congregation of Jesus and Mary (*EUDIST). Feast: Aug. 19

John Fisher, St *FISHER, ST JOHN

John George I (1585–1656), elector of Saxony (1611–56). He concluded the Treaty of Prague (1635) with Ferdinand II, but his participation in the Thirty Years' War ruined Saxony

John, Gospel according to St the fourth Gospel of the New Testament, attributed to St John, probably written in the late 1st c. A.D. It relates the ministry, passion and resurrection of Christ, and contains a metaphysical interpretation of Christ as the incarnate Word of God

John Henry the legendary hero of a popular American ballad. In a contest with a steam drill, he smashes more rock than the machine but dies 'with his hammer in his hand'. He symbolizes man's futile struggle against the machine, and the black man's battle with the white man

John of Damascus, St (c. 675–749), Syrian monk and Greek Father. His most notable work, 'The Fount of Wisdom', includes a systematization of early theology and defense of Eastern dogma. Feast: Mar. 27

John of Gaunt (gɔnt) (1340–99), duke of Lancaster, son of Edward III. The virtual ruler of England in the last years of his father's reign, he continued to dominate the administration during much of the minority of his nephew, Richard II. Distrusted by the court and by the Church, he spent much time trying to conquer Castile, without success

John of Lancaster (1389–1435), duke of Bedford, son of Henry IV of England. On the death (1422) of his brother, Henry V, he became protector of England and regent of France for Henry VI. His attempt to strengthen the English administration in France failed with the rise of Joan of Arc

John of Leyden (John Buckholdt, c. 1502–36), Dutch Anabaptist leader. He overthrew the civil and religious authorities at Münster (1534) and established a theocracy, with himself as king of the new Zion. The town was recaptured by the prince bishop (1535) and he and his followers were tortured and executed

John of Salisbury (c. 1115–80), English scholar and bishop of Chartres (1176–80). He was a friend and supporter of Thomas à Becket. His 'Policraticus' (1159) is a treatise on the

CONCISE PRONUNCIATION KEY: **(a)** æ, c*a*t; ɑ, c*a*r; ɔ f*aw*n; ei, sn*a*ke. **(e)** e, h*e*n; i:, sh*ee*p; iə, d*ee*r; ɛə, b*ea*r. **(i)** i, f*i*sh; ai, t*i*ger; ə:, b*i*rd. **(o)** o, *o*x; au, c*ow*; ou, g*oa*t; u, p*oo*r; ɔi, r*oy*al. **(u)** ʌ, d*u*ck; u, b*u*ll; u:, g*oo*se; ə, *a*bacillus; ju:, c*u*be. x, lo*ch*; θ, *th*ink; δ, *b*other; z, *Z*en; ʒ, corsa*g*e; dʒ, sava*g*e; ŋ, orangutan*g*; j, *y*ak; ʃ, *f*ish; tʃ, fe*tch*; 'l, rabb*le*; 'n, redd*en*. Complete pronunciation key appears inside front cover.

relationship of Church and State in government

John of the Cross, St (Juan de Yepes, 1542–91, San Juan de la Cruz), Spanish Carmelite monk and poet, who founded the discalced Carmelites. His mystical verse gives expression to the supreme type of one kind of Christian experience. Feast: Nov. 24

John O'Groats (ougróuts) a spot on the coast of Scotland commonly taken as the northernmost point of Great Britain, where a Dutchman, John de Groot, built a house in the 16th c.

John Paul I (dʒɒnpɔl) (1912–78), born Albino Luciani, pope for 34 days from August 26 to September 28, 1978. He was patriarch of Venice from 1970 before being elevated to pope upon the death of Pope Paul VI

John Paul II (1920–   ), born Karol Josef Woltyla in Wadowice, Poland, pope (1978–   ). He was bishop of Krakow, Poland, from 1964 and became a cardinal in 1967. He succeeded John Paul I as pope in 1978. The first non-Italian pope in over 450 years, he was a staunch advocate of conservatism regarding doctrine and discipline and tried to bring together the different factions in the Church as a result of Vatican II. He traveled extensively and was the target of assassination attempts (1981, 1982)

Johns (dʒɒnz), Jasper (1930–   ), U.S. painter, associated with the abstract expressionist school of painting. He used imagery, painted everyday objects, and incorporated 'found' objects in his works. His most well-known works include 'Target with Four Faces' (1955), 'Flag on a Foreign Field' (1957) and a bronze sculpture 'Painted Bronze' (1964)

Johns Hopkins University a private university in Baltimore, Maryland, opened in 1876, named after its founder (1794–1873), a financier. It is esp. noted for its medical school

John·son (dʒɒnsən), Andrew (1808–75), 17th president (1865–9) of the U.S.A., following the assassination of President Abraham Lincoln. A Southern Democrat and Unionist, he pursued a Reconstruction program which was based on the theory that the southern states had never seceded from the Union. Since he denied equal civil rights to blacks and rejected the disqualification from office of Confederate leaders, he was denounced by the radical Republicans. After Congress passed the Tenure of Office Act (1867), he was impeached and narrowly escaped being removed from office for his dismissal of his secretary of war Edwin Stanton. His administration was notable for the purchase (1867) of Alaska, esp. in order to prevent Russian encroachment southward

Johnson, Hiram Warren (1866–1945), governor (1910–17) of California. He ended the dominance of the Southern Pacific Railroad in California politics and set the state in the forefront of progressive reform

Johnson, Lyndon Baines (1908–73), 36th president of the U.S.A. (1963–9), following the assassination of President John Kennedy. A Democrat, he is esp. noted for the 'War on Poverty' at home, a large-scale federal government program aimed at eradicating poverty, and for the Civil Rights Acts of 1964 and 1965. During his administration, the U.S.A. sent massive military support to South Vietnam and intervened (1965) in the Dominican Republic. Popular discontent with his political manner and his foreign policy, esp. in Vietnam, made itself felt. He decided (1968) not to run for reelection to a second term

Johnson, Reverdy (1796–1876), U.S. lawyer, senator, and diplomat who appeared in a number of famous Supreme Court cases including the Dred Scott decision (1857)

Johnson, Samuel (1709–84), English poet, critic, essayist, moralist and lexicographer. His poetry (e.g. 'London', 1738 and 'The Vanity of Human Wishes', 1749) continued the central 18th-c. tradition of moral satire made more weighty. His essays in 'The Rambler' (1750–2) and in 'The Idler' (1758–60) continued the tradition of Addison's 'Spectator', forming the opinions and molding the manners of a serious urban audience. His 'Dictionary' was the first systematic study of the English tongue, and tended to stabilize educated usage. 'Rasselas' (1759) was a classic in the tradition of the moral fable in an exotic setting. His 'Lives of the Poets' (1779–81), a history of English poetry since Cowley, expressed a coherent view of the kinds of poetry, and influenced public taste until the 1830s. His edition of Shakespeare com-

bined positive textual advance with appreciative criticism. His periodical writing, his journals and his recorded conversation (*BOSWELL) all show a powerful intellect with a grasp of history, a strong conservative bent in politics, a deep and troubled religious sense, a persistent melancholia, and (in spite of his contentiousness and incisiveness) a deep humility and kindness

Johnson, William (1771–1834), U.S. jurist, associate justice (1804–34) of the U.S. Supreme Court who established the Court's traditional right of dissent. He introduced the practice by which one member of the Court delivers the majority opinion, while the other members may record their separate opinions

Johnson Act of 1934 a U.S. Congressional act which forbade loans to any country in default of its war debt to the U.S.A.

Johns·ton (dʒɒnstən), Albert Sidney (1803–62), Confederate general in the Civil War who, despite bitter criticism over his defeats, notably Nashville, retained the confidence of President Jefferson Davis

Johnston, Joseph Eggleston (1807–91), Confederate general in the Civil War. He is credited with the victory at Bull Run. His sound strategy was overruled by Jefferson Davis at Vicksburg and during the advance toward Atlanta

John the Baptist, St (d. c. 30), Jewish prophet, son of St Elizabeth and St Zacharias (Luke i, 13–45), and cousin of Jesus. He preached (c. 28) a mission of national repentance in preparation for the imminent coming of the Messiah. He baptized those who came to him, including Jesus, in the Jordan. Herod Antipas had him beheaded at the insistence of Salome and Herodias. Feasts: June 24 (birth), Aug. 29 (death)

Jo·hore, Jo·hor (dʒouhɔ́r, dʒouhóur) a state (area 7,330 sq. miles, pop. 1,601,504) of Malaysia in S. Malaya. Capital: Johore Bahru (pop. 75,000). Ruled from the 14th c. by the sultan of Malacca and his representatives, Johore entered treaty relations with Britain (1885) and joined the Federation of Malaya (1948)

joie de vivre (ʒwadəví:vrə) high spirits just from joy at being alive [F., lit.=joy of living]

join (dʒɔin) 1. *v.t.* to bring (things or persons) together to make a single unit, *to join hands, to join in matrimony* ‖ to bring (two things) together so that they communicate, *the rivers are joined by a canal* ‖ to fasten (one thing to another), *join the skirt to the bodice by a band* ‖ to be contiguous with,' *the U.S.A. joins Canada along an immense frontier* ‖ to become a member of (an organization or group) ‖ to enter into the company of (another person or persons), *will you join us for dinner?* ‖ *v.i.* to become united ‖ to be contiguous ‖ to become a member of an organization or group **to join in** to take part in, *to join in a discussion* **to join up** to enlist in the armed forces 2. *n.* the act of joining ‖ a point, line or surface of contact, *the joins can hardly be seen* [O.F. *joindre* (*joign-*)]

join·der (dʒɔindər) *n.* (esp. *law*) the act of joining, e.g. as plaintiffs or defendants [F. *joindre*]

join·er (dʒɔinər) *n.* a person who makes the wooden fittings for a structure (cf. CARPENTER) **join·er·y** *n.* (*collect.*) articles made by a joiner ‖ the craft of constructing such articles

joint (dʒɔint) 1. *n.* the place where two or more things or parts of things are joined together ‖ the structure, mechanism or material effecting such a joining together. It may allow movement of the joined parts or maintain them in a rigid position ‖ (*anat.*) a place where two or more bones come together, together with cartilage, fluid etc. in the case of movable joints ‖ (*bot.*) the articulation point on a stem from which a leaf arises ‖ (*geol.*) a line of fissure in rock, not causing dislocation ‖ one of the portions into which a butcher divides a carcass, esp. for roasting, or this as roasted and served at the table ‖ (*pop.*) any establishment, esp. a low-class place of entertainment **out of joint** (of a bone) no longer having its head in the socket 2. *v.t.* to fit (something) together by means of a joint ‖ to divide (a carcass) into joints ‖ to plane and prepare (planks of wood) so that they may be fitted together ‖ to point (masonry) [O.F. *joint* and *jointe*]

joint *adj.* owned, made or done in common with one or more persons, groups, governments etc. [F.]

Joint Chiefs of Staff a committee (*abbr.* JCS) comprising the chief military advisors to the

U.S. President, the Secretary of Defense and the National Security Council. It was created (1942) to assist the president in directing U.S. forces in the 2nd world war. After the war it was given statutory recognition and a full-time staff, comprising the army chief of staff, the air force chief of staff, the chief of naval operations, and a chairman. A fifth seat is reserved for the commandant of the Marine Corps, whenever his attendance is required

joint committee a government committee with members from both houses of a bicameral legislature

joint·er (dʒɔintər) *n.* (*masonry*) a tool used in pointing ‖ (*woodwork*) a long plane used to shape the edges of planks to be jointed together

joint resolution a resolution passed by both houses of a bicameral legislature, eligible in due process to become a law

joint·ress (dʒɔintris) *n.* a woman holding a jointure

joint stock stock or capital owned by a number of people in a common fund

joint-stock company a firm whose capital is held as joint stock by a number of shareholders, who may independently sell or dispose of their shares

joint stool a stool made of parts pegged together by mortise and tenon joints

joint tenancy (*law*) a tenure held by two or more joint tenants. At the death of one tenant, the title passes to the surviving joint tenant or tenants and so on to the last surviving tenant

join·ture (dʒɔintʃər) 1. *n.* (*law, hist.*) an estate settled upon a married woman by her husband for her use after his death 2. *v.t. pres. part.* **join·tur·ing** past and past part. **join·tured** to settle a jointure on [F.]

joint·worm (dʒɔintwə:rm) *n.,* the larva of any of several flies of the genus *Harmolita,* fam. *Eurytomidae,* found in the U.S.A. They pierce the stems of grain, causing swellings at the puncture

Join·ville (ʒwĕvi:l), Jean de (c. 1224–1317), French soldier and chronicler. He accompanied Louis IX on the 7th Crusade (1248–54). His memoirs (1305–9) form a lavish biography of Louis IX, a valuable source for the history of the times and a fine example of early French prose

joist (dʒɔist) *n.* one of a number of parallel wood or steel beams which support floorboards or ceiling laths etc. [M.E. *giste, gyste* fr. O.F.]

jo·jo·ba (həhóubə) *n.* a peanut-sized desert bean from which an extract is used as a source for cosmetics and hair-care preparations

joke (dʒouk) 1. *n.* an action, saying, event or circumstance which causes or is intended to cause amusement or laughter ‖ something to be treated lightly, as not important, and with humor ‖ a person who is laughed at because he is ridiculous 2. *v.t. pres. part.* **jok·ing** past and past part. **joked** to make jokes **jók·er** *n.* someone who makes jokes ‖ (*cards*) a 53rd card, usually depicting a jester, used only in certain games, as either wild or having the highest value ‖ an apparently unimportant clause inserted in a political bill to make it inoperative or ambiguous ‖ an unsuspected clause, phrase or word in a contract etc. radically changing its character **jók·ing·ly** *adv.* [perh. fr. L. *jocus*]

Jo·liot-Cu·rie (ʒɔljoukyri:), Jean-Frédéric (1900–58), and Irène (1897–1956). French physicists, husband and wife, who shared (1935) a Nobel prize for their discovery of induced radioactivity

Jol·li·et, Jo·li·et (dʒɒli:ét, dʒɒuli:ét, ʒɔlje), Louis (1645–1700), French explorer who, with Father Jacques Marquette, discovered (1673) the Mississippi River

jol·li·fi·ca·tion (dʒɒlifikéiʃən) *n.* (*pop.*) a party or celebration

jol·li·fy (dʒɒlifai) *pres. part.* **jol·li·fy·ing** past and past part. **jol·li·fied** *v.i.* (*pop.*) to make merry

jol·li·ness (dʒɒli:nis) *n.* the state or quality of being jolly

jol·li·ty (dʒɒliti) *pl.* **jol·li·ties** *n.* jolliness ‖ (*Br.*) gregarious festivity [M.E. *jolivete, jolite* fr. O.F.]

jol·ly (dʒɒli) 1. *comp.* **jol·li·er** *superl.* **jol·li·est** *adj.* full of good humor and fun, *a jolly fellow* ‖ (*Br., pop.*) slightly drunk 2. *adv.* (*Br., pop.*) very, *a jolly good fellow* 3. *v.t. pres. part.* **jol·ly·ing** past and past part. **jol·lied** to chaff or joke with (someone) good-humoredly, esp. as a method of persuasion, *try and jolly him into doing it* [M.E. *jolif, joly* fr. O.F.]

jolly boat (*naut.*) a ship's small boat used for general jobs

Jolly Roger (*hist.*) a pirate flag depicting a white skull and crossbones on a black field

Jo·lo (hóulou) *SULU ARCHIPELAGO

jolt (dʒoult) 1. *v.t.* to cause (something) to move or shake by a sudden jerk ‖ *v.i.* to move with jolts 2. *n.* a rough jerk ‖ a sudden shock to one's feelings [etym. doubtful]

jon *JUN

Jo·nah (dʒóunə) a Minor Prophet (8th c. B.C.) of the Old Testament ‖ the book of the Old Testament of which he is the hero. The book tells the allegorical story of how Jonah, shirking his task of preaching to Nineveh, was swallowed by a whale and cast up alive on dry land three days later

Jones (dʒounz), Inigo (1573–1651), English architect and theatrical designer. His buildings are notable for their restrained strength and beauty of proportion. They include the Banqueting Hall of Whitehall Palace, London (1619–22) and the Queen's House at Greenwich (1617–35, now a part of the National Maritime Museum). He designed settings for numerous court masques, and introduced the use of the proscenium arch and movable scenery in England

Jones, James (1921–77), U.S. writer, whose novel 'From Here to Eternity' (1951; film, 1953) formed the first in a trilogy of war novels. 'The Thin Red Line' (1962; film, 1964) and 'Whistle' (1978) completed the trilogy. Other works include 'Some Came Running' (1957; film, 1958), 'Go to the Widow-Maker' (1967) and 'A Touch of Danger' (1973)

Jones, John Luther (Casey) (1864–1900), U.S. railroad engineer. His death in a collision with a freight train (he gave his life to save the passengers and crew) has been celebrated in a ballad originally composed by Wallace Saunders, a black roundhouse worker, and since revamped in many versions

Jones, John Paul (1747–92), American naval hero during the Revolutionary War. He served (1788–9) as rear admiral in the Russian navy

Jones, LeRoi *BARAKA, IMAMU AMIRI

Jones, Rufus Matthew (1863–1948), U.S. Quaker philosopher. He published over 50 books, mainly on mysticism and Quaker history

Jones Act of 1917 a U.S. Congressional act which made Puerto Rico an organized territory of the U.S.A. and made Puerto Ricans U.S. citizens, albeit withholding certain rights provided under the U.S. Constitution

Jones·town (dʒóunztaun) *n.* suicidal catastrophe, from the mass suicide at Jonestown, Guyana in 1978

jon·gleur (ʒɔ̃glə:r) *n.* (*hist.*) a wandering medieval minstrel [F.]

Jön·kö·ping (jə́:ntʃə:piŋ) a town (pop. 50,000) at the south end of Lake Vättern, Sweden: matches, paper

jonnycake *JOHNNYCAKE

jon·quil (dʒɔ́ŋkwil) *n. Narcissus jonquilla*, fam. *Amaryllidaceae*, a bulbous plant grown for its yellow or white flowers, characterized by a short corona ‖ these flowers [fr. Mod. L. *jonquilla* fr. L. *juncus*, rush]

Jon·son (dʒɔ́nsən), Ben (1572–1637), English dramatist and poet. He is the principal creator of the comedy of humors in English, e.g. 'Every Man in his Humour' (1601), 'Volpone: or the Foxe' (1607), 'The Alchemist' (1612) and 'Bartholomew Fayre' (1631). His characters are drawn from every class, though he mainly satirizes contemporary London middle-class life. The comedies are broad yet subtle, and severe without wanton cruelty, for they are based on a firm set of traditional moral values. His two tragedies, 'Sejanus His Fall' (1605) and 'Catiline His Conspiracy' (1611), are in classical style, for Jonson considered himself as a reviver of these literary modes. He also wrote beautifully constructed lyrics. He wrote many court masques for James I, often collaborating with Inigo Jones

Joplin (dʒɔ́plən), Scott (1868–1917), U.S. black composer, responsible for the major development of ragtime music. The son of slaves, he studied classical music and was an itinerant pianist in his younger years. His rag compositions for the piano include 'Maple Leaf Rag' (1899) and the music featured in the movie 'The Sting' (1973). He also wrote the opera 'Tree-

monisha' (1911) and was awarded, posthumously, the Pulitzer Prize in music (1976)

Jop·pa (dʒɔ́pə) * JAFFA

Jor·daens (jɔ́rdɑns), Jakob (1593–1678), Flemish painter whose work is marked by warm and cheerful coloring. An assistant to Rubens, he later became the most popular representative of Flemish baroque naturalism

Jor·dan (dʒɔ́rd'n), David Starr (1851–1931), U.S. philosopher. He was first president (1891–1913) of Stanford University. He opposed imperialism and advocated world federalism. He was chief director of the World Peace Foundation

Jordan a river (200 miles long) flowing south from the Anti-Lebanon Mtns through Israel and Jordan to the Dead Sea. It is not navigable and is mostly below sea level. St John baptized in its waters. Israel began diverting water from Lake Tiberias to irrigate the Negev (1964), and an Arab counterplan to divert the headwaters of the Jordan into Jordanian territory was made. The question of the diversion of the Jordan has been a continuing cause of border incidents between Israel and its Arab neighbors

Jordan a kingdom (area 36,715 sq. miles, pop. 2,794,000) in W. Asia. Capital: Amman. People: Arab (mostly Bedouin in the east) with a small Circassian minority. 30% of the population are refugees from Palestine. Language: Arabic. Religion: 80% Sunnite Moslem, 8% Christian (mainly Greek Orthodox). 80% of the land is desert. All, except the fertile Jordan river valley in the northwest, and the Dead Sea and the dry valley which continue it (*GREAT RIFT VALLEY), is over 1,500 ft. West of the Jordan, in former Palestine, is a range of eroded hills. The eastern (desert) plateau, rising sharply from the Great Rift Valley, culminates in isolated massifs (e.g. Gebel Ajlun, 3,800 ft) in the north and a broad highland (highest point Esh Shara, 5,240 ft) in the center. Average temperatures (F.) for Jan. and Jul.: Jerusalem 46° and 75°, Amman 46° and 92°, Jericho 55° and 88°. Rainfall (chiefly Nov.–Apr.): 35 ins on Gebel Ajlun, 12 ins at Amman, under 4 ins in the south and east. Livestock: goats, sheep, cattle, camels. Crops: cereals incl. wheat, pulses, sesame, tobacco, grapes, olives, dates. The Dead Sea is rich in potash, bromine, magnesium chloride and sodium chloride, largely unexploited. Manufactures: foodstuffs, soap, cigarettes, matches, cement. Exports: cereals, fruit, vegetables, phosphates, hides, wool. Imports: petroleum products, textiles, sugar, machinery, iron and steel, motor vehicles. Aqaba is the only seaport. University (1962). Monetary unit: Jordan dinar (1000 fils). HISTORY. Known in biblical times as Gilead, Moab and Edom, Jordan became part of the empires of the Nabataeans (4th c. B.C.–1st c. A.D.), the Seleucids (2nd c. B.C.), the Romans (2nd c. A.D.), the Byzantines (4th–6th cc.), the Moslem Umayyads (661–750), the Abbasids (750–1258) and the Mamelukes (1250–1516). Under the Ottoman Turks (1516–1918) it was administered as a province of Syria. Under the name of Transjordan it became (1922) a League of Nations mandate under British control, with Abdullah as emir. It finally gained independence (Mar. 22, 1946). Arab Palestine was occupied (1949) and incorporated (1950) within the Hashemite Kingdom of Jordan. Hussein became king (1952) and received British and American aid in maintaining his regime against subversive attempts by the United Arab Republic. The harnessing of the Jordan waters caused conflict between Jordan and Israel. Following the third Israeli-Arab war (1967) Israel occupied Jordan's territories west of the Jordan, and annexed the Jordanian part of Jerusalem. Fighting broke out (Sept. 1970) between the royal forces and Palestinian guerrillas. In 1974, at the Arab Summit Conference, Hussein conceded the West Bank as an independent Palestinian state, and Jordan joined other Arab states in condemning the 1979 Israeli-Egyptian treaty regarding control of the West Bank. The impasse over the West Bank continued into the late 1980s. Jordan was also unable to resolve the problems with the PLO, which sought to represent Palestinians in Jordan.

Jordan almond an almond exported from Málaga, Spain and used in confectionery ‖ (*Am.* = *Br.* sugar almond) a candy consisting of an almond with a hard coating of sugar

Jordan curve theorem (*math. topology*) given two two-dimensional spaces *X* and *Y*, a function that maps a loop in *X* to a loop in *Y* also maps points inside the loop in *X*

Jos (dʒɔs) a tin-mining center (pop. 112,912) and capital of Benue Plateau State, Nigeria

Jo·seph (dʒóuzif, dʒóusif) Hebrew patriarch, the favorite son of Jacob and Rachel. Sold into slavery by his jealous brothers, he became governor of Egypt. He forgave his brothers and obtained the pharaoh's permission for the Israelites to settle in Goshen (Genesis xxxvii, xxxixxli)

Joseph, St (*d.* early 1st c.), the husband of Mary the mother of Jesus Christ. He was a carpenter by trade. He led Mary and the infant Jesus to safety from Herod's persecution. He is not mentioned in the Gospels after Jesus was 12. Feast: Mar. 19

Joseph I (1678–1711), Holy Roman Emperor (1705–11), king of Hungary (1687–1711), son of Leopold I. He continued the war of the Spanish Succession against France, in an attempt to put his brother, the future Emperor Charles VI, on the Spanish throne

Joseph II (1741–90), Holy Roman Emperor and archduke of Austria (1765–90), son of Francis I. After the death (1780) of his mother, Maria Theresa, with whom he had ruled jointly, he began a series of sweeping reforms of trade, law, education and taxes. He founded hospitals, and he granted freedom of worship. This benevolent despotism caused serious unrest and later had to be renounced

Joseph I (1714–77), king of Portugal (1750–77), son of John V. His reign was dominated by the marquês de Pombal

Joseph, Chief (c1840–1904), Nez Percé Indian chief during the Nez Percé War (1877) and leader of the Nez Percé retreat from Oregon to Montana (over 1,000 miles; 1,600 km) in an attempt to reach the Canadian border. Friends of the government, the Nez Percé exchanged their lands for a large reservation area in Oregon and Idaho, but balked when the U.S. took back part of the Oregon land where gold was discovered in 1863. Joseph led his people against a much larger U.S. army and defeated them in several battles before retreating north, only to be captured 30 miles (48 km) from Canada

Joseph, Père (François Le Clerc du Tremblay, 1577–1638), French monk and statesman. As secretary and adviser to Richelieu he became known as the 'Grey Eminence'

Jo·sé·phine (ʒouzeifí:n) (Marie-Josèphe Rose Tascher de La Pagerie, 1763–1814), empress of the French (1804–9). The widow of the vicomte de Beauharnais, she married (1796) Napoleon I, but the marriage was annulled (1809)

Joseph of Ar·i·ma·thae·a (æriməθí:ə) St (1st c.), a disciple of Jesus and member of the Sanhedrin. On the evening of the Crucifixion, he persuaded Pontius Pilate to let him and Nicodemus take down Christ's body from the cross for burial. According to legend, he brought the Holy Grail to Britain. Feast: Mar. 17

Jo·seph·son junction (dʒóuzəfsən) (*electr.*) device that emits microwave radiation, consisting of two superconductors joined with an intervening gap, to which driving voltage is applied

Jo·se·phus (dʒousí:fəs), Flavius (37–c. 100), Jewish soldier and historian. He wrote 'The Jewish War' (c. 75) and 'The Antiquities of the Jews' (93)

josh (dʒɔʃ) *v.t.* (*pop.*) to tease (someone) without malice ‖ (*pop.*) to exchange jokes with (someone) ‖ *v.i.* (*pop.*) to joke [origin unknown]

Josh·u·a (dʒɔ́ʃuːə) an Israelite leader who, as the successor of Moses, led his people into Canaan ‖ the book of the Old Testament which relates this conquest and the division of the land among the 12 tribes of Israel

Jo·si·ah (dʒousáiə) (*d.* c. 609 B.C.), king of Judah (c. 641–c. 609 B.C.). During his reign the book of the Law (probably Deuteronomy) was discovered in the Temple. He led a religious reform movement, suppressing idolatry and centering religious activity in Jerusalem

Jo·squin des Prés (ʒɔskɛ̃deiprei) (c. 1450–1521), Flemish composer. He wrote motets and masses and other church music of transcendent spirituality, and was one of the creators of polyphonic song

joss (dʒɔs) *n.* a Chinese idol [perh. corrup. of Port. *deos*, god]

joss house a Chinese temple for idol worship

CONCISE PRONUNCIATION KEY: **(a)** æ, c*a*t; ɑ, c*a*r; ɔ f*aw*n; ei, sn*a*ke. **(e)** e, h*e*n; i:, sh*ee*p; iə, d*ee*r; ɛə, b*ea*r. **(i)** i, f*i*sh; ai, t*i*ger; ə:, b*i*rd. **(o)** o, *o*x; au, c*ow*; ou, g*oa*t; u, p*oo*r; ɔi, r*oy*al. **(u)** ʌ, d*u*ck; u, b*u*ll; u:, g*oo*se; ə, bacill*u*s; ju:, c*u*be. x, lo*ch*; θ, *th*ink; δ, bo*th*er; z, *Z*en; ʒ, cor*s*age; dʒ, sa*v*ag*e*; ŋ, oranguta*ng*; j, *y*ak; ʃ, fi*sh*; tʃ, fe*tch*; 'l, rabb*le*; 'n, redd*en*. Complete pronunciation key appears inside front cover.

joss stick a small stick of incense burned in a joss house or at an altar of a shrine room or place of worship

jos·tle (dʒɒsˈl) 1. *n.* a jostling or being jostled 2. *v. pres. part.* **jos·tling** *past* and *past part.* **jos·tled** *v.t.* to push and shove against (someone) ‖ to struggle with (someone) ‖ *v.i.* to push and shove ‖ to struggle with someone for something [alt. of *justle* fr. M.E. *joust, just*]

jot (dʒɒt) 1. *n.* (in negative or quasinegative constructions) a very small amount, *hardly a jot of evidence* 2. *v.t. pres. part.* **jot·ting** *past* and *past part.* **jot·ted** (with 'down') to make a quick written note **jót·ting** *n.* a brief note or memorandum [fr. L. *iota* fr. Gk *iōta*, the letter i, the smallest letter of the alphabet]

Jo·tun·hei·men (jóutunheimən) Norway's highest mountain region in the south center (Galdhöpiggen 8,097 ft, Glittertind 8,048 ft). Glaciers

jou·al (ʒúːəl) *n.* a French-Canadian patois

Jou·bert (ʒuːber), Barthélemy Catherine (1769–99), French general. He distinguished himself in Napoleon's Italian campaign (1796–7)

Joule (dʒuːl, dʒaul), James Prescott (1818–89), English physicist. His many discoveries in electricity and thermodynamics include the determination of the mechanical equivalent of heat and the Joule-Thompson effect

joule *n.* (*phys.*) the unit of work and energy in the mks system, equal to the work done by a force of 1 newton acting through a distance of 1 meter and equivalent to 10^7 ergs [after J. P. JOULE]

Joule effect the conversion of mechanical, electrical or magnetic energy into heat

Joule-Thompson effect (*phys.*) the change in temperature that accompanies the adiabatic expansion of a gas through a porous plug from a higher to a lower pressure. The effect demonstrates the existence of intermolecular forces in gases (cf. KINETIC THEORY)

jounce (dʒauns) 1. *v. pres. part.* **jounc·ing** *past* and *past part.* **jounced** *v.t.* and *i.* to jolt and bump very roughly 2. *n.* a very rough jolt [etym. doubtful]

jour·nal (dʒɜːrnˈl) *n.* a record of events, personal experiences and thoughts etc., kept day by day ‖ a daily record of business transactions ‖ (in double-entry bookkeeping) the book in which transactions are first noted with accompanying information as to debiting and crediting particular accounts ‖ a newspaper or magazine published at regular intervals ‖ the account of the proceedings of e.g. a learned society ‖ (*naut.*) a logbook ‖ (*engin.*) the part of a rotating shaft, axle etc. which turns in a bearing [O.F. *jurnal, jornal, journal,* daily]

journal box (*engin.*) the metal casing for the journal of a shaft and its bearings

jour·nal·ese (dʒəːrnˈlíːz, dʒəːrnˈlíːs) *n.* loose, slangy, cliché-ridden, insensitive writing

jour·nal·ism (dʒɜːrnˈlizəm) *n.* the profession of collecting news for, writing for, editing or managing a newspaper or other periodical ‖ journalistic writing [fr. F. *journalisme*]

jour·nal·ist (dʒɜːrnˈlist) *n.* a professional writer for or editor of a newspaper or other periodical **jour·nal·is·tic** *adj.* of journalists or journalism, esp. of journalese

jour·nal·ize (dʒɜːrnˈlaiz) *pres. part.* **jour·nal·iz·ing** *past* and *past part.* **jour·nal·ized** *v.t.* (*bookkeeping*) to enter in a journal

jour·ney (dʒɜːrniː) 1. *pl.* **jour·neys** 1. a movement over a considerable distance from one place to another, esp. by land or air (cf. VOYAGE) ‖ a distance as defined by the time taken to cover it, *a day's journey* 2. *v.i.* to make a journey [O.F. *jornee, journee,* day, day's travel, day's work]

jour·ney·man (dʒɜːrniːmən) *pl.* **jour·ney·men** (dʒɜːrniːmən) *n.* a craftsman who has completed his training and works for an employer ‖ someone who is competent but not exceptional in his work

jour·ney·work (dʒɜːrniːwəːrk) *n.* the work done by a journeyman

joust (dʒaust) 1. *n.* (*hist.*) a combat in the lists, esp. for sport between two knights in armor or men-at-arms, mounted on horseback and armed with lances 2. *v.i.* (*hist.*) to fight a joust [O.F. *juster, joster, jouster*]

Jove (dʒouv) *JUPITER (Rom. mythol.)

jo·vi·al (dʒóuviːəl) *adj.* good-humored and full of jokes or conviviality **jo·vi·al·i·ty** *n.* [F.]

JOVIAL (*computer acronym*) for Jules Own Version of International Algebraic Language, a computer programming language designed by System Development Corporation

Jow·ett (dʒáuit), Benjamin (1817–93), English classical scholar, and educator. He made many translations from the Greek, the most notable being 'Plato's Dialogues' (1871). He was master of Balliol College, Oxford, from 1870

jowl (dʒaul) *n.* the chin and neck, when heavy with sagging flesh ‖ the dewlap of a cow etc. ‖ the wattle of a turkey etc. [M.E. *cholle, choll, chol*]

jowl *n.* a jawbone, esp. the lower jaw ‖ a cheek [alt. of M.E. *chavel, chauel, chawl* fr. O.E. *ceafl*]

joy (dʒɔi) *n.* intense happiness or great delight ‖ that which gives rise to this emotion, or on which the emotion centers ‖ the outward expression of the emotion [O.F. *joie, joye*]

Joyce (dʒɔis), James (1882–1941), Irish writer. He lived after 1904 on the Continent, but centered his whole literary work on Ireland, esp. on Dublin. In his first novel, 'A Portrait of the Artist as a Young Man' (1916), he introduced the stream-of-consciousness technique (which he was to perfect in 'Ulysses'). The novel traces the evolution of its hero, Stephen Dedalus, from infancy to young manhood, centering in his renunciation of the Catholic faith and exploring those aspects in him that reveal the unique perceptiveness, sensitivity and detachment of the artist. The short stories 'Dubliners' (1914) had already described lower-middle-class Dublin existence and made subtle use of symbols to give depth and universality to their themes. 'Ulysses' (1922) was Joyce's masterpiece. Written into the peregrinations of its hero, Leopold Bloom, are such archetypal themes as the Odyssey, the biblical Exodus, and the Hamlet legend. The book is an enormous sequence of bravura passages: stream-of-consciousness, interior monologues, elaborate parody, phantasmagoria, bare narrative. In his last book, 'Finnegans Wake' (1939), Joyce used the freedom granted by the dream-world setting in an attempt to tap the unconscious racial memory, exploiting the innate suggestiveness of words in language liberated from confinements of convention and syntax. Other works include the play 'Exiles' (1918), 'Pomes Penyeach' (1927), 'Collected Poems' (1936) and various critical writings. The fusion of realism and symbolism characterizes his literary achievement, and Joyce's innovations in language and style have profoundly influenced 20th-c. writing

joy·ful (dʒɔ́ifəl) *adj.* filled with, causing or showing joy

joy·ous (dʒɔ́iəs) *adj.* full of joy ‖ expressing joy [A.F.]

joy·ride (dʒɔ́iraid) *n.* (*pop.*) a ride in a car for pleasure, esp. when unauthorized

J.P. Justice of the Peace

j particle a neutral meson with mass of 0.3095 megaelectron volts, spin quantum of 1 with lifetime of 10–20, discovered by Burton Richter and Samuel C. C. Ting *also* psi particle

Jr., jr. Junior, junior

j-stroke (dʒéistrouk) *n.* (*canoeing*) backward and outward paddle movement continuing outward used to counter draft and correct trim; made by Stern Paddler

Juan Carlos I, King of Spain (1938–), son of Don Juan of Bourbon and grandson of King Alphonso XIII. In 1962 he married Princess Sophia of Greece and in 1969 the Spanish Cortes approved his designation by General Franco as king to succeed the dictator on his death or retirement. Juan Carlos acceded to the throne on Nov. 22, 1975, following Franco's death. He brought Spain from dictatorship to parliamentary government and was instrumental in thwarting a threatened military takeover in 1981

Juan de Fu·ca Strait (wɒndəfjúːkə) a strait (100 miles long, 11–17 miles wide) between Vancouver I., Canada and N.W. Washington

Juan Fer·nán·dez (hwánfernándeθ) a group of three Pacific islands (land area 70 sq. miles) belonging to Chile

Juá·rez (hwáreθ), Benito Pablo (1806–72), Mexican statesman. As minister of justice (1855–8), he instituted many reforms, breaking the power of the Church and the army. Becoming provisional president (1858–61), he led the liberal factions to victory in a civil war against the conservatives. As president (1861–72), he resisted the imperialistic designs of Napoleon III and his puppet, Maximilian

Ju·ba (dʒúːbə) a river flowing 1,000 miles from central Ethiopia across S.W. Somalia into the Indian Ocean

Ju·bail (dʒuːbáil) *BYBLOS

jub·bah, jub·ba (dʒúbə, dʒúbə) *n.* a long, loose coat worn by Moslems and Parsees [Arab.]

Jubbulpore *JABALPUR

ju·bi·lance (dʒúːbələns) *n.* the state of being jubilant

ju·bi·lant (dʒúːbələnt) *adj.* rejoicing, esp. in celebration of success or victory [fr. L. *jubilans* (*jubilantis*) fr. *jubilare,* to shout for joy]

ju·bi·late (dʒúːbəleit) *pres. part.* **ju·bi·lat·ing** *past* and *past part.* **ju·bi·lat·ed** *v.i.* to be jubilant [fr. L. *jubilare* (*jubilatus*), to shout for joy]

ju·bi·la·tion (dʒuːbəléifən) *n.* a jubilating ‖ an instance of this [fr. L. *jubilatio* (*jubilationis*) fr. *jubilare,* to shout for joy]

ju·bi·lee (dʒúːbəli:, dʒúːbəli:) *n.* a 50th anniversary ‖ an anniversary other than the 50th, *silver jubilee* (25th), *diamond jubilee* (60th) ‖ a celebration of such anniversaries ‖ (*Jewish hist.*) a festival held at 50-year intervals to celebrate the deliverance from Egypt ‖ (*Roman Catholicism*) a year of special indulgence [F. *jubilé* fr. L.L. fr. Gk fr. Heb.]

Jú·car (húːkar) a river (300 miles long) flowing from Cuenca, E. Spain, to the Mediterranean below Valencia

Judaea *JUDEA

Ju·dae·o-, Judeo- (dʒuːdíːou, dʒuːdéiou) *prefix* Jewish [fr. L. *judaeus,* Jewish]

Ju·dah (dʒúːdə) Hebrew patriarch, son of Jacob ‖ the Israelite tribe of which he was the ancestor ‖ (*hist.*) the ancient kingdom established by this tribe in the south of Palestine (c. 932–586 B.C.)

Ju·da·ic (dʒuːdéiik) *adj.* of or relating to the Jews, their traditions and culture ‖ of or relating to Judaism **Ju·dá·i·cal** *adj.* [fr. L. *Judaicus* fr. Gk]

Ju·da·ism (dʒúːdi:izəm, dʒuːdéiizəm) *n.* the religion of the Jews ‖ the Jews at large [fr. L. *Judaismus* fr. Gk]

—Judaism as a religion is a belief in one, universal God as creator, conceived of as personal. It interprets history as God's covenanted choice of the Jews to be the vehicle of his revelation and ultimate rule. The basis of this revelation was made on Mount Sinai when the Ten Commandments were delivered to Moses, in the context of the teaching of the Pentateuch. This law has, over the centuries, been codified and made applicable to all situations in life. Judaism looks for a messianic age when God's rule will be made actual in the world. It assumed its modern form after the return of the Jews from the Babylonian Captivity (586-538 B.C.). After the destruction of the Temple (70 A.D.), religious life became centered on the synagogue and the home, while the priesthood was replaced by the rabbi. Judaism has been sustained by the hopes that the Jews would return to the Promised Land of Canaan and that a Messiah would arise to rule Israel and the world. Modern Judaism has become divided into orthodox, conservative, and reformed groups

Ju·da·ize (dʒuːdi:aiz, dʒúːdeiaiz) *pres. part.* **Ju·da·iz·ing** *past* and *past part.* **Ju·da·ized** *v.t.* to make Jewish ‖ to imbue with the ideas or practices of Judaism ‖ *v.i.* to hold the belief and follow the rites of Judaism

Ju·das (dʒúːdəs), St *JUDE

ju·das (dʒúːdəs) *n.* a peephole in a door

Judas Is·car·i·ot (iskǽriət) one of the 12 Apostles. He betrayed Christ to the Jewish high priests for 30 pieces of silver

Judas Maccabaeus *MACCABAEUS, JUDAS

Judas tree *Cercis siliquastrum,* fam. *Leguminosae,* an ornamental tree, native to S. Europe and Asia, bearing purple blossoms in early spring [fr. the belief that *Judas* Iscariot hanged himself from such a tree]

judas window a judas

Jude (dʒuːd), St (1st c.), one of the 12 Apostles, also known as Thaddaeus. Feast: Oct. 28

Ju·de·a, Ju·dae·a (dʒuːdíːə) the Greco-Roman name for southern Palestine

Jude, Epistle of the 26th book of the New Testament, of uncertain authorship (late 1st c.). It is a warning against heresy

Ju·de·o- *JUDAEO

judge (dʒʌdʒ) *pres. part.* **judg·ing** *past* and *past part.* **judged** *v.t.* to hear (a case) and pronounce sentence upon (a person) ‖ to hear (a case) and apply the law to (a question) ‖ to examine and determine the relative merits of (exhibits, contestants etc.) ‖ to consider to be, *he judged it* prudent to wait ‖ (*Jewish hist.*) to govern (people, a province etc.) ‖ to estimate, *to judge a distance* v.i. to arrive at an opinion ‖ to act as a judge [O.F. *jugier*]

judge *n.* a civil law officer of the highest rank, who tries cases in a court of law ‖ a courtesy title for any of several law officers who may try cases in lower courts ‖ any person appointed to settle a dispute, or to decide the relative merits of competitors (exhibitors, athletes etc.) ‖ a person qualified by knowledge and experience to assess quality, *a good judge of horses* **Judge** (*Jewish hist.*) a chief civil and military ruler of the Hebrews between Joshua's death and the establishment of a monarchy under Saul [M.E. *juge* fr. O.F.]

judge advocate *pl.* **judge advocates** a staff officer who is legal adviser to a commander ‖ the officer who prosecutes in a court martial

Judge Advocate General a major general in the Army or Air Force who is the senior legal officer

judgement *JUDGMENT

Judg·es (dʒʌdʒiz) a book of the Old Testament which relates the history of the Hebrews under the rule of the Judges, from the death of Joshua to the birth of Samuel

judge·ship (dʒʌdʒʃip) *n.* the office or term of office of a judge

judg·ment, judge·ment *n.* the process of judging in law ‖ the pronouncement of a decision, *to give judgment* ‖ a legal decision or sentence ‖ an opinion ‖ the ability to weigh matters prudently, *a man of sound judgment* ‖ the process of assessing, *an error of judgment* ‖ (*pop.*) a blow of fate thought of by onlookers as a just retribution [F. *jugement*]

judgment debt (*law*) a debt which must be paid by the order of a court

ju·di·ca·to·ry (dʒuːdikətɔːri, dʒuːdikətʊəri) *n.* the judiciary ‖ a court of law [fr. M. L. *judicatorium*, court of law, fr. *judicare* (*judicatus*) to judge]

ju·di·ca·ture (dʒuːdikeitʃər) *n.* the administration of justice in general ‖ the office, acts or power of a judge ‖ a body of judges ‖ a law court [fr. M.L. *judicatura* fr. L. *judicare* (*judicatus*), to judge]

ju·di·cial (dʒuːdiʃəl) *adj.* of the administration of justice or of acts, places, persons or powers associated with it ‖ of the use of the power and process of critical judgment, *a judicial turn of mind* [fr. L. *judicialis*]

judicial murder a sentence of death pronounced in due course of law but nevertheless considered to be unjust

judicial review the constitutional doctrine that the judiciary, and ultimately the Supreme Court, is granted the power to determine whether or not a law passed by Congress or an act executed by the President is in accordance with the Constitution. If the courts decide adversely, the law or act is declared invalid

judicial separation a legal separation

ju·di·ci·ar·y (dʒuːdiʃieri, dʒuːdiʃəri) *pl.* **ju·di·ci·ar·ies** *n.* the apparatus of law and its administrators ‖ the judicial branch of government [fr. L. *judiciarius*]

ju·di·cious (dʒuːdiʃəs) *adj.* (of acts etc.) governed by or arising from sound judgment ‖ (of persons) using sound judgment [fr. F. *judicieux* (*judicieuse*)]

Ju·dith (dʒuːdiθ) a Jewish heroine in the war against Babylon, who killed the enemy general Holofernes. She is the subject of a book included in the Roman Catholic canon but in the Apocrypha in the King James Bible

ju·do (dʒuːdou) *n.* a modern form of jujitsu [Jap.]

ju·do·ist (dʒuːdouist) *n.* Judo enthusiast — **judoman** *n.* Judo participant

Jud·son (dʒʌdsən), Adoniram (1788–1850), U.S. Baptist missionary (from 1813) to Burma. He produced (1826) a Burmese-English dictionary, still regarded as standard, and (1834) a Burmese Bible

Judson, Edward Zane Carroll (pen name, Ned Buntline, 1823–86), U.S. adventurer and author who created the sensational latter-19th-c. dime novel starring dare-devilish heroes, e.g. 'Red Ralph the Ranger' (1870)

Ju·dy (dʒuːdi) *PUNCH AND JUDY

judy (*mil.*) in air intercept, a code meaning *I have contact and am taking over the intercept*

jug (dʒʌg) *n.* a vessel for holding and pouring liquids, (*Am.*) never with a lip (cf. PITCHER), (*Br.*) usually with a lip [origin unknown]

jug band a musical team that uses jugs, washboards, cans, etc., for instruments

Ju·gend·stil (juːgəntʃtiːl) *ART NOUVEAU

jug·ger·naut (dʒʌgərnɔt) *n.* an irresistible destructive force [Hindi *Jagannath*, lord of the world, a title for Krishna. Votaries were said to cast themselves under the wheels of the massive cart on which his image was dragged in procession at Puri, India]

jug·gle (dʒʌgˈl) **1.** *v. pres. part.* **jug·gling** *past and past part.* **jug·gled** v.i. to perform tricks of dexterity, esp. to throw several objects into the air one after another, catching them and throwing them again, repeatedly and rhythmically without a pause ‖ (with 'with') to make complex, confusing play, *to juggle with ideas* v.t. to perform tricks of dexterity with (objects) by juggling ‖ to alter (facts or figures) with the intention of deceiving **2.** *n.* an act of juggling ‖ a fraud [fr. O.F. *jogler, jugler*]

jug·gler (dʒʌglər) *n.* someone who juggles, esp. professionally [O.F. *joglere, juglere, jouglere*]

Jugoslav etc. *YUGOSLAV etc.

jug·u·lar (dʒʌgjulər) **1.** *adj.* (*anat.*) of or located in the neck or throat ‖ (*zool.*, of a fish) having fins beneath and in front of the pectoral fins ‖ (*zool.*, of fins) so located **2.** *n.* a jugular vein ‖ a vulnerable point [fr. Mod. L. *jugularis* fr. L. *jugulum*, collarbone]

jugular vein, internal a vein, running through the neck, which collects blood from the internal areas of the skull and the external areas of the face

jugular vein, external a small vein which collects blood from the external areas of the skull and the internal areas of the face

Ju·gur·tha (dʒugɑːrθə) (c. 154–105 B.C.), king of Numidia. After many campaigns against the Romans (112–106 B.C.), he was defeated (106 B.C.) by Marius and brought captive to Rome

juice (dʒuːs) *n.* the fluid contained in or extracted from fruits and vegetables ‖ a fluid in or extracted from the animal body, *digestive juices, beef juice* ‖ (*pop.*) gasoline, electricity etc. [F. *jus*]

juic·i·ness (dʒuːsiːnis) *n.* the state or quality of being juicy

juic·y (dʒuːsi) *comp.* **juic·i·er** *superl.* **juic·i·est** *adj.* rich in juice ‖ (*pop.*) profitable, *juicy rewards* ‖ (*pop.*) sexy, racy, *juicy stories*

Juil·li·ard (dʒuːliːɑrd), Augustus D. (1836–1919), U.S. banker and industrialist. He bequeathed his fortune to promote musical education and operatic production in the U.S.A. The Juilliard School of Music was opened (1924) in New York City

ju·ji·tsu, ju·ju·tsu (dʒuːdʒitsuː) *n.* a Japanese method of self-defense by which one attempts to disable an opponent with the minimum of personal risk and physical exertion, turning the opponent's strength to one's own advantage by upsetting his balance [Jap. = soft art]

ju·ju (dʒuːdʒuː) *n.* a W. African fetish to which supernatural powers are attributed ‖ the magic associated with such a fetish [native name]

ju·jube (dʒuːdʒuːb) *n.* an edible drupe, the fruit of a member of *Ziziphus*, fam. *Rhamnaceae* ‖ a plant, found in warm climates, yielding this fruit ‖ a candy made of gelatin or gum arabic and flavored with jujube or a similar flavor [F. *jujube* fr. M.L. fr. Gk]

jujutsu *JUJITSU

juke·box (dʒuːkbɒks) *n.* a coin-operated record player [fr. Gullah (dialect of an Afro-American group inhabiting the seacoast and islands of South Carolina, Georgia and a small part of N.E. Florida) *juke, joog*, wicked, disorderly]

ju·lep (dʒuːlip) *n.* a cool drink flavored with syrup, sugar or herbs ‖ a similar drink used medicinally as a vehicle ‖ a mint julep [F. fr. Arab. fr. Pers. *gulāb*, rose water]

Ju·lian (dʒuːljən) 'the Apostate' (Flavius Claudius Julianus, c. 331–63), Roman emperor (361–3). Educated as a Christian, he reverted to paganism and tried to make the Roman Empire pagan again

Ju·li·an·a (dʒuːliːænə) (1909–), queen of the Netherlands (1948–). She succeeded on the abdication of her mother, Queen Wilhelmina, and in turn abdicated in favor of her eldest daughter Beatrice on April 30, 1980

Julian calendar the solar calendar introduced (46 B.C.) by Julius Caesar. It was based on the ancient Egyptian calendar. It established the length of the year as 365 days and 6 hours with a 366-day year occurring every fourth year (*GREGORIAN CALENDAR). The year was also divided into 12 months having 30, 31 or 28 days

Ju·li·a·ne·haab (juːliɑːnəhɔp) the largest Danish settlement (pop. 3,500), near the southern end of Greenland

Ju·lie (dʒuːliː) *n.* (*mil.*) submarine detection system utilizing a Jezebel sonobuoy that picks up and broadcasts the echo of a detonated underwater charge, providing information on range and bearing

ju·li·enne (dʒuːliːén) *n.* a clear soup strained from meat broth, with shreds of onion, carrot etc. added [F.]

Jul·ius I (dʒuːljəs), St (d. 352), pope (337–52). He attempted to deal with the Arian heresy. Feast: Apr. 12

Julius II (1443–1513), pope (1503–13). He restored the Papal States to the papacy by suppressing Venice (1509) and driving France from Italy (1511) with the aid of the Holy League. He helped to make Rome an artistic and intellectual center of the Renaissance, esp. through his patronage of Bramante, Raphael, who painted his portrait, and Michelangelo. He began the building of St Peter's at Rome

Julius III (1487–1555), pope (1550–5). He took a prominent part in the Council of Trent

Julius Caesar *CAESAR

Jul·lun·dar (dʒʌləndər) a town (pop. 296,106) in the Punjab, N.W. India. It is a railroad and agriculture center, and has flour and silk mills

Ju·ly (dʒuːlái, dʒəlái) *n.* the seventh month of the year, having 31 days [M.E. *Jule* fr. O.F. fr. L. *Julius*, after Julius Caesar]

July Monarchy *LOUIS-PHILIPPE

jum·ble (dʒʌmbˈl) **1.** *n.* a disorderly or confused group of things, persons etc. **2.** *v.t. pres. part.* **jum·bling** *past and past part.* **jum·bled** (with 'up' or 'together') to mix (things) in a jumble [imit.]

jumble sale (*Br.*) a rummage sale

jum·bo (dʒʌmbou) **1.** *n.* (*pop.*) someone or something conspicuously larger than the norm **2.** *adj.* very large, *jumbo jet* [an elephant in the Barnum circus fr. Swahili *jumbe*, chief]

jumbo cut (*cinema*) in motion picture production, an abrupt change from one scene to another with no transition, usu. due to decisions in editing *Cf* JUMP CUT

jumbo jet a high-capacity jet airliner able to carry 500 passengers and 200 tons of freight, e.g., Boeing 747

Jum·na (dʒʌmnə) the chief tributary (860 miles long) of the Ganges, rising in the Himalayas, N. India. The junction at Allahabad is a sacred bathing place

jump (dʒʌmp) **1.** *v.i.* to rise momentarily into the air, esp. by springing with the aid of leg and foot muscles ‖ to leap from one place to another ‖ to make a sudden involuntary movement, esp. when startled ‖ to shift quickly from one state, topic etc. to another ‖ (of prices, wages etc.) to rise quickly ‖ (*computer*) to depart from a normal sequence to another ‖ (*checkers* etc.) to move a man over an opponent's man, thereby capturing it ‖ to deviate from an expected course, order etc. *v.t.* to pass over (something) by jumping ‖ to cause to jump ‖ to pass over, evade or ignore (something) ‖ to make (prices, wages etc.) rise quickly ‖ (*checkers* etc.) to capture (an opponent's man) by jumping it ‖ (*pop.*) to attack (someone) esp. with malicious intent ‖ (*mining*) to drill (rock etc.) with a jumper **to jump a bid** (at a sale or in playing bridge) to make a bid that raises the bidding by more than one point **to jump a claim** to seize a mining right etc. to which somebody else has a previous right **to jump ahead** to move rapidly in front, passing others on the way **to jump a queue** (*Br.*) to go ahead of others, disregarding their rights of position **to jump at** to accept at once, without hesitation, *to jump at a chance* **to jump a train** (*pop.*) to board a moving train to avoid paying the fare **to jump down someone's throat** to reprimand someone with sudden vehemence **to jump into** to enter suddenly, rashly or enthusiastically into (a situation, undertaking etc.) **to jump on** to reprimand (someone) abruptly and severely **to jump rope** (*Am.*=*Br.* skip) to jump repeatedly for fun or for exercise over a rope made to pass rapidly over the head and under the feet **to jump ship** (of a sailor etc.) to leave the ship while legally obliged to remain **to jump the gun** (*pop.*) to start too soon **to jump the track** (or *Br.*, the rails) (of a train etc.) to leave the rails suddenly **to jump to conclusions** to make an unjustified assumption **to jump up** to get up quickly, e.g. out of a chair ‖ to rise rapidly by steep increases

CONCISE PRONUNCIATION KEY: (**a**) æ, c**a**t; ɑ, c**ar**; ɔ, f**aw**n; ei, sn**a**ke. (**e**) e, h**e**n; i:, sh**ee**p; iə, d**ee**r; ɛə, b**ear**. (**i**) i, f**i**sh; ai, t**i**ger; əː, b**ir**d. (**o**) o, **o**x; au, c**ow**; ou, g**oa**t; u, p**oor**; ɔi, r**oy**al. (**u**) ʌ, d**u**ck; u, b**u**ll; uː, g**oo**se; ə, b**a**cillus; juː, c**u**be. x, lo**ch**; θ, **th**ink; ð, bo**th**er; z, **Z**en; ʒ, cor**s**age; dʒ, sava**g**e; ŋ, oranguta**n**g; j, **y**ak; ʃ, **fi**sh; tʃ, **fe**tch; 'l, rabb**le**; 'n, redd**en**. Complete pronunciation key appears inside front cover.

2. *n.* the act of jumping ‖ a sudden startled movement ‖ a sudden rise, *prices went up with a jump* ‖ something to be jumped over, *steeplechase jumps* ‖ a distance jumped ‖ a gap in an otherwise continuous process, e.g. in an argument, or a train of thought etc. ‖ (*checkers* etc.) a move by which a capture is made **to be one jump ahead** to be in advance of rivals by virtue of smartness or cleverness [perh. imit.]

jump bid (*bridge*) a bid of more than is needed to overcall the bid just made

jump cut (*cinema*) the removal of portions of a sequence to speed up or stop an action —**jump-cut** *v.*

jump·er (dʒʌmpər) *n.* a loose jacket worn by workmen, sailors etc. ‖ a sleeveless, one-piece dress worn over a blouse ‖ (*Br*) a knitted pullover usually with sleeves, worn by women and children [perh. fr. obsolete *jump*, a short coat, fr. F. obsolete *juppe* fr. *jupe*, a skirt]

jumper *n.* someone or something that jumps, esp. a horse trained to jump obstacles in show riding ‖ (*elec.*) a short length of wire used to mend a break in or cut off part of a circuit ‖ (*mining*) a drill for drilling rock ‖ (*Br., pop.*) a ticket inspector who boards a public service vehicle (bus etc.)

jumpers *SPONGES

jump·i·ly (dʒʌmpili:) *adv.* in a jumpy manner

jump·i·ness (dʒʌmpi:nis) *n.* the state or quality of being jumpy

jumping bean a seed of any of several members of *Sebastiania* and *Sapium*, fam. *Euphorbiaceae*, genera of Mexican shrubs. A moth larva inside the seed causes it to jump about

jumping deer *Cariacus macrotis*, fam. *Cervidae*, a deer having a black tail and usually long ears, found west of the Mississippi in the U.S.A.

jumping jack a flat toy figure that has jointed limbs. It performs a jerky dance by the operation of a string or sliding stick ‖ (*calisthenics*) traditional exercise of jumping with legs together to legs apart, raising arms overhead at the same time

jump-off (dʒʌmpɔf, dʒʌmpɒf) *n.* the time a race begins or a military attack is launched

jump rope (*Am.=Br.* skipping rope) a rope used for jumping rope (*JUMP)

jump seat a folding seat e.g. between the front and rear seats of an automobile ‖ the small rear seat behind the driver's seat in a sports car

jump suit a uniform worn by paratroopers for making a parachute jump ‖ a garment consisting of shirt top and pants all in one piece

jump·y (dʒʌmpi:) *comp.* **jump·i·er** *superl.* **jump·i·est** *adj.* marked by jumps ‖ proceeding in jumps ‖ in a nervous or apprehensive state

jun (dʒʌn) *n.* a unit of currency of North Korea ‖ a coin of the value of one jun [Korean]

jun·co (dʒʌŋkou) *n.* any North American finch of genus *Junco* [Span.= rush]

junc·tion (dʒʌŋkʃən) *n.* the place where two or more things join, *a railroad junction* ‖ a joining or being joined [fr. L. *junctio* (*junctionis*) fr. *jungere*, to join]

junc·ture (dʒʌŋktʃər) *n.* a joining or being joined ‖ (esp. *anat.*) a place of joining or structure effecting a joining ‖ a point in time as determined by certain events and circumstances ‖ (*linguistics*) the transition between speech sounds which marks a phonological boundary (of a word, sentence etc.) [fr. L. *junctura* fr. *jungere*, to join]

June (dʒu:n) *n.* the sixth month of the year, having 30 days [M.E. fr. F. *juin*]

Ju·neau (dʒú:nou) the capital (pop. 19,483) of Alaska, on the Inside Passage, a port with an ice-free harbor: gold, salmon, fur-farming, timber

June beetle a June bug

June·ber·ry (dʒú:nberi:) *pl.* **June·ber·ries** *n.* a member of *Amelanchier*, fam. *Rosaceae*, a genus of North American shrubs or trees bearing white flowers and edible red or purple fruit ‖ this fruit

June bug any of various members of the genera *Phyllophaga*, *Polyphylla* and *Cotinis*, fam. *Scarabaeidae*, genera of North American beetles. They feed on plant leaves and first appear in June ‖ a member of the genus *Phyllopertha*, fam. *Scarabaeidae*, a genus of similar European beetles

Jung (juŋ), Carl Gustav (1875–1961), Swiss psychologist. In 1912 he founded the school of analytical psychology. His system resembles Freud's in many respects, but replaces Freud's sexual emphasis with other factors: in particu-

lar, the collective (or racial) unconscious and its archetypes such as the hero and the mother goddess. His writings include 'The Psychology of the Unconscious' (1916)

Jung·frau (júŋfrau) a peak (13,668 ft) in the Bernese Alps, Switzerland

jun·gle (dʒʌŋg'l) *n.* an area of land overgrown with tangled shrubs, vines, trees, roots and tall vegetation, found in the Tropics ‖ this dense growth ‖ an intermingled number of things difficult to analyze or sort out, *a jungle of administrative regulations* [Hindi *jangal*, waste ground]

Jungle gym a structure of vertical and horizontal bars for children to climb and play on [Trademark]

Ju·nín (hu:ní:n) a village in central Peru, site of the first battle (Aug. 6, 1824) for Peruvian independence, in which Simón Bolívar defeated the Spaniards. The date is celebrated as the birthday of the republic of Bolivia

jun·ior (dʒú:njər) **1.** (*abbr.* **jr**) *adj.* younger, used esp. to distinguish son from father when both have the same name, *John Brown junior* ‖ lower in status, *junior partner* ‖ less advanced, *a junior school* ‖ more recently appointed, *a junior committee member* ‖ later in date, *their foundation is junior to ours by six years* ‖ of or relating to the third year of studies in a high school or college **2.** *n.* a younger person or person of lower status ‖ a high school or college student in the third year of studies [L. *juvenior* comp. of *juvenis*, young]

Junior Achievement a U.S.-Canadian educational organization founded (1926) by Horace A. Moses of Massachusetts. It provides teenagers with an opportunity to gain business experience by organizing and operating their own small businesses, guided by volunteer advisors from business and industry

junior college a school covering the first two years of college work

junior high school a school, including the seventh, eighth and ninth grades, which follows elementary school and precedes senior high school

jun·ior·i·ty (dʒu:njóriti:, dʒu:njóriti:) *n.* the condition or quality of being junior

junior school (*Br.*) a school for children 7-11

ju·ni·per (dʒú:nəpər) *n.* a member of *Juniperus*, fam. *Cupressaceae*, a genus of evergreen shrubs and trees widely distributed over the northern hemisphere, esp. those species having low or trailing branches. They have needle shaped, whorled leaves, and berries whose oil is used to flavor gin and some liqueurs. The wood is used in cabinetmaking and for pencils [fr. L. *juniperus*]

Jun·ius, Letters of (dʒú:njəs) a series of political essays published 1769–72, attacking George III and his ministers in scathing terms. The identity of the author was a closely guarded secret, but he has been variously identified as Sir Philip Francis (1740–1818), or the 2nd earl of Shelburne, or his secretary Laughlin Macleane (1727–77)

junk (dʒʌŋk) *n.* (*naut.*) a sailing vessel used in the Orient, esp. China and Java. It has a flat bottom, high poop and overhanging stern, and carries lugsails [Javanese *djong*]

junk 1. *n.* (*collect.*) objects having neither value nor further use for their owner ‖ (*pop.*) rubbish ‖ (*naut.*) lengths of old rope or cable used in making mats, swabs, oakum etc. ‖ (*naut.*) hard salted meat **2.** *v.t.* to sell or give up (something) as junk [origin unknown]

Jun·ker (júŋkər) *n.* (*hist.*) a member of the landed gentry in eastern Germany, esp. in Prussia [fr. M. Du. *jonckher*, young lord] —The Junkers, a class noted for their militarism, kept their great estates intact in E. Prussia until the 19th c. They dominated Prussia, and later Germany, until 1918, by their control of the higher ranks of the army and the civil service. Bismarck, Hindenburg and Hitler all came to power with their support

jun·ket (dʒʌŋkit) **1.** *n.* a food prepared from milk set with rennet, with sugar and flavoring added ‖ an excursion, outing ‖ a pleasure trip made at public expense and ostensibly as an official duty **2.** *v.i.* to go on a junket ‖ (*old-fash.*) to feast [etym, doubtful]

junk food foods with limited nutritional value used principally as snacks

junk·ie (dʒʌŋki:) *n.* (*pop.*) a drug addict, esp. a heroin addict [fr. slang *junk*, narcotics]

junk sculpture art forms created from miscellaneous manufactured products, usu. discarded items —**junk sculptor** *n.*

junk·yard (dʒʌŋkjord) *n.* a yard where a person who sells junk accumulates his stock

Ju·no (dʒú:nou) (*Rom. mythol.*) the goddess of women and childbirth and, as wife of Jupiter, queen of the gods. She was identified with the Greek Hera

Ju·no·esque (dʒu:nouésk) *adj.* having a stately beauty

jun·ta (húntə, dʒʌntə) *n.* (*hist.*) a legislative or administrative council in Spain, Italy or South America ‖ a junto [Span. and Port. *junta* fr. L. *jungere*, to join]

jun·to (dʒʌntou) *pl.* **jun·tos** *n.* a political or other group of persons united by a common purpose [corrup. of JUNTA]

Ju·pi·ter (dʒú:pitər) (*Rom. mythol.*) the god of the sky and the king of the gods, identified with the Greek Zeus ‖ the fifth planet from the sun (mean orbital diameter=4.835 x 10^8 miles) and the largest planet in the solar system (mass approx. 1.87 x 10^{24} tons, 318 times more massive than the Earth) with a mean diameter of 88,000 miles (it is noticeably elliptical). Jupiter revolves around the sun with a sidereal period of 11.862 earth-years and rotates with a period of approx. 9 hrs 55 mins. Its equator is hardly inclined to the plane of its orbit, so that there is little seasonal variation. Telescopic examination shows Jupiter as a yellow disk with several more or less permanent belts parallel to the equator that are generally reddish-brown in color. There are also a number of special features of unexplained origin which appear to be atmospheric in nature. The atmosphere is thought to consist of compressed or condensed gases, e.g. hydrogen, methane and ammonia at about −140°C. Jupiter has at least 16 satellites. The planet was observed by Voyager spacecraft I and II in 1979

Ju·ra (jyrǣ) a department (area 1,951 sq. miles, pop. 234,000) in E. France (*FRANCHE-COMTÉ). Chief town: Lons-le-Saunier

Jura a range of rugged, wooded mountains in E. France and W. Switzerland, curving around the northwest edge of the Swiss plateau. Highest peak: Crêt de la Neige, 5,650 ft. Occupations: dairy farming, forestry, light industries

ju·ral (dʒúrəl) *adj.* of or relating to the law ‖ of or relating to rights and obligations [fr. L. *jus* (*juris*), right, law]

Ju·ras·sic (dʒurǣsik) *adj.* of the middle period or system of the Mesozoic era (*GEOLOGICAL TIME) the Jurassic period or system of rocks [after the JURA mountains]

ju·rid·ic (dʒurídik) *adj.* juridical **ju·rid·i·cal** *adj.* of the administration of justice, courts of justice, or jurisprudence [fr. L. *juridicus*]

ju·ri·met·rics (dʒurəmétriks) *n.* application of social science and a scientific approach to study of jurisprudence —**jurimetrician** *n.* or **jurimetricist**

ju·ris·con·sult (dʒúəriskənsʌlt) *n.* someone learned in law, esp. civil and international [fr. L. *jurisconsultus*]

ju·ris·dic·tion (dʒuərisdikʃən) *n.* the legal power to administer and enforce the law ‖ the exercising of this power ‖ the region within which this power is valid or in which a person has authority ‖ authority **ju·ris·dic·tion·al** *adj.* [O.F. *jurediction* fr. L.]

ju·ris·pru·dence (dʒuərisprú:d'ns) *n.* the science or philosophy of law ‖ a legal system or body of laws **ju·ris·pru·dén·tial** *adj.* [fr. L. *jurisprudentia*]

ju·ris·pru·dent (dʒuərisprú:d'nt) *adj.* skilled in jurisprudence [F.]

ju·rist (dʒúərist) *n.* a lawyer or judge ‖ a scholar of jurisprudence, esp. one who writes on this subject ‖ (*Br.*) a law student **ju·ris·tic, ju·ris·ti·cal** *adjs.* of or relating to a jurist ‖ legal ‖ instituted by law [F. *juriste*]

ju·ror (dʒúərər) *n.* a member of a jury ‖ someone who has sworn an oath [A.F. *jurour*, O. F. *jureor*]

Ju·rue·na (hu:rwéna) *TAPAJOS

ju·ry (dʒúəri:) *pl.* **ju·ries** *n.* a body of (usually 12) responsible, impartial citizens summoned to hear evidence in a court of law and bound under oath to give an honest answer based on this evidence to questions put before them ‖ a body of persons appointed to judge a contest etc. [A.F. *juree, jure*, O.F. *jurée*, oath, legal inquiry]

jury box the usually enclosed part of the courtroom where the jury sits during a trial

---

CONCISE PRONUNCIATION KEY: **(a)** æ, cat; ɑ, car; ɔ fawn; ei, snake. **(e)** e, hen; i:, sheep; iə, deer; ɛə, bear. **(i)** i, fish; ai, tiger; əː, bird. **(o)** o, ox; au, cow; ou, goat; u, poor; ɔi, royal. **(u)** ʌ, duck; u, bull; u:, goose; ə, bacillus; ju:, cube. x, loch; θ, think; ð, bother; z, Zen; ʒ, corsage; dʒ, savage; ŋ, orangutang; j, yak; ʃ, fish; tʃ, fetch; 'l, rabble; 'n, redden. Complete pronunciation key appears inside front cover.

ju·ry·man (dʒúəriːmən) pl. **ju·ry·men** (dʒúəriːmən) n. a juror

ju·ry·mast (dʒúəriːmæst, dʒuəriːmɑst) n. (Br., naut.) a temporary mast, erected in place of one damaged or carried away by storm [origin unknown]

jury of matrons (Br.) a jury, comprised of married women who have borne children, impaneled where pregnancy is pleaded in stay of execution

jus·sive (dʒʌ́siv) 1. adj. (gram.) expressing a command 2. n. (gram.) a jussive word, form etc. [fr. L. jubere (jussus), to command]

just (dʒʌst) 1. adj. appropriate in kind and degree in the generally accepted body of ethical law, a just sentence ‖ obeying the currently accepted ethical laws, a just man ‖ legally valid, a just title to ownership ‖ deserved, merited, a just reward ‖ well founded, a just fear ‖ accurate, a just assessment 2. adv. exactly, precisely, it is just as you said, just 9 o'clock ‖ very recently, their engagement has just been announced ‖ by a very narrow margin, he just missed the train ‖ directly, the house is just across the road ‖ only, just one left ‖ no more than, he is just a private ‖ (pop.) very, your policemen are just wonderful, he sounded just furious ‖ (pop., as an intensive) won't you, just listen to this! just help me to clear the table **just about** very nearly, I lost it just about here, I have just about had enough **just in case** as a precaution in the unlikely event that, hide just in case he asks to see you **just now** at this time, I am busy just now ‖ a short time ago, I saw him just now **just then** exactly at that time or moment **just the same** nevertheless [F. juste or fr. L. justus]

jus·tice (dʒʌ́stis) n. behavior to oneself or to another which is strictly in accord with currently accepted ethical law or as decreed by legal authority ‖ rectitude of the soul enlivened by grace (*CARDINAL VIRTUES) ‖ the process of law, to be brought to justice ‖ a person appointed to administer the law as judge or magistrate **Justice** a title for a judge, Mr Justice Brown **in justice to** in order to be fair to **to do oneself justice** to make one's real abilities apparent **to do justice to** to behave with justice towards ‖ (pop.) to act in such a way as to show full appreciation of the worth or importance of, to do justice to an occasion [O.F. justise, justice fr. L.]

justice of the peace (Am., abbr. J.P.) an elected (sometimes an appointed) law officer with jurisdiction in the lowest state courts. He may also have certain administrative duties, e.g. holding inquests and performing marriage services ‖ (Br., abbr. J.P.) a magistrate whose main duty is to preside at a magistrates' court. J.P.s are usually unpaid and without a professional legal qualification. (They are advised by salaried clerks.) They also have administrative duties, esp. the granting of licenses

Justice, U.S. Department of, federal agency, headed by the attorney general, that enforces federal laws, handles all legal matters for the government and advises the president and executive department heads on legal matters. An assistant attorney general heads each of the six divisions: Antitrust, Civil, Criminal, Civil Rights, Land and Natural Resources and Tax. Established in 1870, the department also includes the Federal Bureau of Investigation (FBI), the Federal Bureau of Prisons, the Immi-

gration and Naturalization Service and the Drug Enforcement Administration

jus·ti·ci·a·ble (dʒʌstíʃiːəbˈl) adj. (of a person or a dispute) liable to be tried in a court of law [A.F. and O.F.]

jus·ti·ci·a·lis·mo (huːstjiːsiːɑlíːsmɔ) n. the political philosophy of Juan Perón, which claimed to be a third position equidistant from capitalism and Communism

jus·ti·ci·ar (dʒʌstíʃiːər) 1. n. (Eng. hist.) the chief political and judicial officer of the realm (11th-13th cc.) 2. adj. of or relating to the judicature [fr. M.L. justitiarius]

jus·ti·ci·a·ry (dʒʌstíʃiːeri:, dʒʌstíʃəri:) pl. **jus·ti·ci·ar·ies** n. a justiciar ‖ an administrator of justice [fr. M.L. justitiaria or justiciaria]

jus·ti·fi·a·bil·i·ty (dʒʌstifaiəbíliti:) n. the quality or state of being justifiable

jus·ti·fi·a·ble (dʒʌstifáiəbˈl, dʒʌstifaiəbˈl) adj. able to be justified [F.]

justifiable homicide homicide committed in self-defense, during the performance of duty or to prevent a heinous crime

jus·ti·fi·a·bly (dʒʌstifaiəbli:, dʒʌstifaiəbli:) adv. in a justifiable way

jus·ti·fi·ca·tion (dʒʌstifikéiʃən) n. a justifying or being justified ‖ that which justifies ‖ (printing) the arranging of a line of type so that it evenly fills the measure [fr. L.L. justificatio (justificationis)]

jus·tif·i·ca·to·ry (dʒʌstífikətɔri:, dʒʌstifikátəuri:) adj. tending to justify [fr. L.L. justificare (justificatus)]

jus·ti·fy (dʒʌ́stifai) pres. part. **jus·ti·fy·ing** past and past part. **jus·ti·fied** v.t. to show or prove (something or someone) to be just or right, nothing can justify such conduct, it would be difficult to justify him ‖ (theol.) to declare to be free from the penalty of sin ‖ (printing) to make (lines of type) equal in length by adjusting the spaces between the words ‖ v.i. (printing) to form a true line, capable of being set evenly to the measure [F. justifier fr. L. justificare]

Jus·tin (dʒʌ́stin) (2nd or 3rd c. A.D.), Latin historian, author of a summary of the no longer extant 'Historiae Philippicae' of Pompeius Trogus

Jus·tin·i·an I (dʒʌstíniːən) (483–565), Byzantine emperor (527–65). His generals Belisarius and Narses defeated (523 and 529) the Persians, captured N. Africa from the Vandals (533), and overthrew the Ostrogoths in Italy (552-5). The legal codification he commissioned resulted in the 'Corpus juris civilis', which became the principal source for Roman law. He rebuilt the church of St Sophia at Constantinople

Justin Martyr, St (c. 100–c. 165), Samarian Christian apologist and martyr. A platonist philosopher who was converted to Christianity, he became an outstanding apologist. His works include 'Apology of the Christian Religion' (c. 155) and 'Dialogue with Trypho the Jew' (c. 160). Feast: Apr. 14

just·ly (dʒʌ́stli:) adv. with justice ‖ with accuracy ‖ deservedly

Jus·to (húːstɔ), Águstin Pedro (1876–1943), Argentine president (1932–8). Under his semi-dictatorship the economy was controlled by price-fixing etc. He authorized the Roca-Runciman treaties (1933, 1936) with Great Britain, which gave British capital and exports favored treatment in Argentina in return for a guaran-

teed market in Great Britain for Argentina's meat exports

jut (dʒʌt) 1. v. pres. part. **jut·ting** past and past part. **jut·ted** v.i. to protrude from, stick out ‖ v.t. to cause (something) to protrude 2. n. a projection [var. of JET V.]

Jute (dʒuːt) n. a member of a Germanic tribe, probably from the mouth of the Rhine, who settled (5th c.) in England in Kent, Hampshire and the Isle of Wight [fr. M.L. Jutae, Juti pl., akin to O.N. Jōtar]

jute n. a fiber made from the bark of Corchorus olitorius or C. capsularis, fam. Tiliaceae, plants native to tropical Asia and cultivated esp. in E. Bengal and East Pakistan. It is widely used for cotton baling and sacking, cordage and paper ‖ these plants [fr. Bengali jhōto, jhuto]

Jut·land (dʒʌ́tlənd) (Dan. Jylland) a peninsula of N. Europe comprising the mainland of Denmark (Jylland) and Schleswig-Holstein, Germany

Jutland, Battle of the main naval engagement (May 31, 1916) of the 1st world war, fought about 60 miles west of Jutland. The German fleet won a tactical success over the British fleet under Jellicoe, but did not put out to sea for the rest of the war

Ju·ve·nal (dʒuːvənˈl) (c. 60–c. 140), Roman poet and satirist. His 16 verse satires denounce the political and social conditions of imperial Rome

ju·ve·nile (dʒuːvənail, dʒuːvənˈl, dʒuːvənil) 1. adj. relating to youth or young people ‖ meant for young people, juvenile fiction ‖ immature, juvenile behavior 2. n. a child or young person ‖ (publishing, librarianship) a book meant for young people ‖ an actor who plays the role of a young man, or such a role [fr. L. juvenilis]

juvenile court (law) a court concerned with cases involving young persons under a certain age, which varies in different areas of jurisdiction. It relies heavily on rehabilitation and preventive techniques

juvenile hormone (entomology) insect secretion regulating metamorphosis and growth that can be made synthetically; used to destroy by disrupting insect life cycles

juvenile lead an actor who plays the most important role for a young person in a play, or such a role

ju·ve·nil·i·a (dʒuːvəníliːə) pl. n. works produced during the youth of an author or artist [L.]

ju·ve·nil·i·ty (dʒuːvəníliti:) n. the state or quality of being juvenile [fr. L. juvenilitas]

ju·ve·nil·i·za·tion (dʒuːvənəlizéiʃən) n. prolonging immaturity —**juvenilize** v.

Ju·ven·tas (dʒuːvéntæs) (Rom. mythol.) the goddess of youth, identified with the Greek Hebe

jux·ta·pose (dʒʌkstəpóuz) pres. part. **jux·ta·pos·ing** past and past part. **jux·ta·posed** v.t. to place (things, facts etc.) side by side [F.]

jux·ta·po·si·tion (dʒʌkstəpəzíʃən) n. a juxtaposing or being juxtaposed [F.]

J visa a special visa category authorized by the U.S. Information and Educational Exchange (Smith-Mundt) Act of 1948. Individuals with J visas may be admitted to U.S. for the purpose of pursuing a full-time program of study but must be absent from the U.S. for two years after their studies have ended before they may reenter as an immigrant

Jyl·land (jǽlɑn) the Danish mainland (area 11,411 sq. miles) (*DENMARK)

	EARLY NORTH SEMITIC	PHOENICIAN	EARLY HEBREW (GEZER)	EARLY GREEK	CLASSICAL GREEK	ETRUSCAN		EARLY LATIN	CLASSICAL LATIN
						Early	Classical		
K	↓	ㅋ	⅄	ㅓ	K	K	K	ㅓ	K

		VENETIAN MINUSCULE (ITALIC)	MODERN (LOWER CASE)
		k	k

A. C. SYLVESTER, CAMBRIDGE, ENGLAND

Development of the letter K, beginning with the early North Semitic letter. Evolution of both the majuscule, or capital, letter K and the minuscule, or lowercase, letter k are shown.

K, k (kei) the 11th letter of the English alphabet

K (*Chem*) potassium ‖ Kelvin (temperature scale)

K2 (keitú:) (or Dapsang, formerly Mt Godwin Austen) the second highest mountain in the world (28,250 ft), in the Karakoram Range, N. Kashmir

Kaa·ba, Caa·ba (kúbə) the sanctuary at Mecca enclosing the Black Stone, which is the most sacred object of Islam. This is the principal place of pilgrimage for Moslems, and the point to which they turn in prayer [fr. Arab. *ka'bah*, square building]

Kaap·stad (kúpstət) *CAPE TOWN

Kab·ar·di·no-Bai·kar·i·an A.S.S.R. (kæbərdí:-noubɔlkǽri:ən) an autonomous republic (area 4,825 sq. miles, pop. 688,000) of the U.S.S.R., on the north slopes of the Caucasus. Capital: Nalchik

Kabinda *CABINDA

Ka·bu·ki (kabú:ki:, kəbú:ki:) the popular Japanese drama, incorporating song and dance, and performed solely by men. It originated in the 17th c. as an offshoot of Nō drama and is characterized by exaggerated, highly stylized acting, elaborate scenery and heavy makeup [Jap.]

Ka·bul (kúbul) the capital (pop. 1,036,407) of Afghanistan, on the Kabul River, a tributary of the Indus. It commands strategic mountain passes into Pakistan (*KHYBER PASS). Industry: wool

Kab·we (kúbwe) (formerly Broken Hill) a town (pop. 147,000) in Zambia: a mining center for zinc, vanadium and lead

Ka·byle (kəbáil) *n.* a member of a chiefly agricultural Berber people, inhabiting a mountainous region of N.E. Algeria ‖ their Hamitic language

Ka·chin (kətʃín) a mountainous state (area 16,000 sq. miles, pop. 500,000) of N. Burma, partly inhabited by the Kachins, a tribal people who practice dry-rice farming and speak Kachin, a Tibeto-Burmese language. Capital: Myitkyina

Ká·dár (kúdar), János (1912–), Hungarian statesman, Communist prime minister of Hungary (1956–8 and 1961–5), First Secretary of the Communist party from 1957

kadi *CADI

Ka·du·na (kədú:nə) the capital (pop. 202,000) of North Central State, Nigeria, on the Kaduna River. It is a rail and trade center (cotton, sorghum and ginger). Industries: cotton milling, furniture, pottery

Kaf·fir, Kaf·ir (kǽfər) *n.* a member of a group of Bantu-speaking peoples of South Africa ‖ their language ‖ (*Br.*, *pl.*) South African mining shares

kaffir corn, kafir corn any of several sorghums, with relatively juicy stalks, grown in dry regions for grain and fodder [Arab. *kāfir*, infidel+CORN]

Kafir *KAFFIR

Ka·fir (kǽfər) *n.* a member of a tribe living in part of the Hindu Kush, N.E. Afghanistan

Kaf·ka (kúfka), Franz (1883–1924), Czech writer, living in Prague, writing in German. In his lifetime he published an extract from his journal, and a few short stories (collected 1919). His fame rests chiefly on the novels 'The Trial' and 'The Castle', published (in 1925 and 1926 respectively) in disregard of his express wishes. Keenly aware of man's anguish, isolation, perplexity and frustration, specifically in the setting of the mechanized, bureaucratized modern world, he derived myths from his insights. Kafka's situations and incidents are utterly fantastic, but he makes the reader believe in them by his wealth of concrete detail and the unsmiling matter-of-factness of his style, modeled in part on the police reports of his day

Kaf·ka·esque (kɒfkəésk) *adj.* sordidly unreal, esp. of government activities, from the work of the Czech writer Frank Kafka

Kaftan *CAFTAN

Ka·fu·e (kəfú:i:) a river (600 miles long) of central Zambia, a tributary of the Zambezi

Ka·ga·wa (kúgawá), Toyohiko (1888–1960), Japanese Christian social reformer and evangelist. He organized peasant cooperatives and dealt with labor problems after the 1923 earthquake

Ka·ge·ra (kagéərə) *WHITE NILE

Ka·go·shi·ma (kúgoʃí:ma) a port (pop. 505,000) at the head of Kagoshima Bay, S. Kyushu, Japan: textiles, glassware, bamboo goods, Satsuma porcelain

Kai·e·teur Falls (kaiətúər) a waterfall (740 ft high, c. 350 ft wide) in central Guyana on the Potaro River

Kai·feng (káifŋ̩) the capital (pop. 700,000) of Honan, China, on the Hwang Ho. As Pienchieng, it was capital of China (960–1126), and contains temples and palaces of the Sung dynasty

kail *KALE

kai·nite (kúinait, kéinait) (*chem.*) *n.* KMg (SO₄)Cl·3H₂O, a salt, hydrous chlorosulfate of magnesium and potassium, used as a source of potassium salts and as a fertilizer [fr. Gk *kainos*, new]

Kair·ouan (kerwã) a Moslem holy city (pop. 54,000), with beautiful mosques, in N.E. Tunisia: carpets, leather goods. It was famous as a center of Moslem learning from the 9th c. to the early 11th c.

Kai·ser (káizər), Georg (1878–1945), German expressionist dramatist. His plays include 'The Jewish Widow' (1911), 'The Burgher of Calais' (1914), 'From Morn to Midnight' (1916), 'Gas I and II' (1918–20), 'The Fire in the Opera House' (1919)

Kai·ser (káizər) *n.* (*hist.*) the emperor of Austria (1804–1918) ‖ (*hist.*) the emperor of Germany (1871–1918) ‖ (*hist.*) the head of the Holy Roman Empire [G. fr. L. *Caesar*]

Ka·jar, Qa·jar (kɑdʒár) a dynasty which ruled Persia (1794–1925)

ka·ka (kúkə) *n. Nestor meridionalis*, an olivebrown New Zealand parrot marked with red and gray markings, often kept as a pet [Maori]

ka·ka·po (kɒkəpóu) *pl.* **ka·ka·pos** *n. Strigops habroptilus*, a green and brown New Zealand parrot rapidly becoming extinct. It is nocturnal, has little power of flight, and lives in holes or burrows in the ground [Maori]

ka·ke·mo·no (kúkemɔ́nɔ, kɒkəmóunou) *pl.* **ka·ke·mo·no, ka·ke·mo·nos** *n.* a Japanese painting or inscription on silk or paper. Mounted on a roller, it may be hung on the wall [Jap. *kake*-, to hang+*mono*, thing]

Ka·ki·na·da (kɒkinúdə) (Cocanada) a seaport (pop. 75,000) of E. Andhra, India, exporting tobacco

ka·la-a·zar (kɒlaɑzár, kɒlɑǽzər) *n.* a chronic infectious disease occurring chiefly in the Tropics and marked by irregular fever and enlargement of the spleen and liver. It is caused by a parasite transmitted by the bite of infected sand flies [fr. Hindi *kālā*, black+Pers. *āzār*, disease]

Ka·la·ha·ri (kɒlahári:) a semidesert highland region (area 200,000 sq. miles) of South Africa, mainly in Botswana, sparsely inhabited by Bushmen and Hottentots

ka·lash·ni·kov (kɒláʃnikəv) *n.* (*mil.*) a Soviet submachine gun

kale, kail (keil) *n. Brassica oleracea acephala*, fam. *Cruciferae*, a variety of leafy nonheading cabbage [var. of COLE]

ka·lei·do·scope (kəláidəskɒup) *n.* a tubular viewing device containing two plane mirrors set at an angle of 60° to one another and multiple fragments of colored glass or paper etc. These produce symmetrical patterns, which shift when the instrument is rotated ‖ something which is continually changing **ka·lei·do·scop·ic** (kəláidəskɒpik) *adj.* [fr. Gk *kalos*, beautiful+*eidos*, form+*-scope*, allowing to view]

Ka·le·mi·e (kɒléimjei) * ALBERTVILLE

kalends *CALENDS

CONCISE PRONUNCIATION KEY: (a) æ, c*a*t; ɑ, c*a*r; ɔ, f*aw*n; ei, sn*a*ke. **(e)** e, h*e*n; i:, sh*ee*p; iə, d*ee*r; ɛə, b*ea*r. **(i)** i, f*i*sh; ai, t*i*ger; ə:, b*i*rd. **(o)** o, *o*x; au, c*ow*; ou, g*oa*t; u, p*oo*r; ɔi, r*oy*al. **(u)** ʌ, d*u*ck; u, b*u*ll; u:, g*oo*se; ə, b*a*cillus; ju:, c*u*be. x, lo*ch*; θ, *th*ink; ð, bo*th*er; z, *Z*en; ʒ, cor*s*age; dʒ, sava*g*e; ŋ, orangutan*g*; j, *y*ak; ʃ, *f*ish; tʃ, fet*ch*; 'l, rabb*le*; 'n, redd*en*. Complete pronunciation key appears inside front cover.

Kal·gan (kálgán) *CHANGCHIAKOW

Kal·goor·lie (kælgúərli:) a gold-mining center (pop. with its suburb, Boulder, 20,500) in Western Australia

Ka·li·da·sa (kɑlidásə) (prob. 1st c.), Indian poet and dramatist who wrote in Sanskrit. His work includes three verse dramas, 'Sakuntala', 'Vikramorvasiya' and 'Malavikagnimitra', two epics, 'Raghuvamsa' and 'Kumara-sambhava', and some shorter lyrics

Ka·li·man·tan (kɑli:mántan) the part (area 208,298 sq. miles) of Borneo belonging to Indonesia, formerly belonging to the Netherlands. Chief towns: Pontianak, Bandjarmasin

ka·lim·ba (kəlímbə) *n.* musical instrument consisting of an 8-in hollow piece of wood with metal strips inserted lengthwise; made to vibrate with thumbs

Ka·li·nin (kɑlí:nin), Mikhail Ivanovich (1875–1946), Russian statesman. An early follower of Lenin, he helped to organize the 1917 revolution. He was chairman of the Central Excutive Committee (1919–38) and of the Supreme Soviet (1938–46) of the U.S.S.R.

Kalinin a city (pop. 412,000) of the R.S.F.S.R., U.S.S.R., on the Volga: engineering, textiles

Ka·li·nin·grad (kɑlí:ningrɑd) a port (pop. 355,000) of the U.S.S.R. (before 1945 Königsberg, E. Prussia). It is the center of an enclave of the R.S.F.S.R. in Lithuania, near the Baltic: shipbuilding, mechanical engineering, pulp and paper milling, food processing

kal·lid·in [$C_{50}H_{73}N_{15}O_{11}$] (kǽlədən) *n.* (*physiol.*) a compound containing 9 or 10 amino acids derived from a plasma alpha globulin kallidinogen, which reduces blood pressure, increases capillary permeability, relaxes certain smooth blood muscles, and produces edema. *syn* bradykinin

kal·lik·re·in (kælikrí:in) *n.* (*physiol.*) an enzyme in saliva, urine, pancreatic juices, and blood plasma that releases kallidin from alpha globulin *Cf* KALLIDIN

Kal·man filter (kǽlmən) (*acoustics*) **1.** technique for computer evaluation of various sensors in inertial navigation systems **2.** system used to reduce random noise

Kal·mar, Union of (kálmɑr) the union (1397) of the crowns of Denmark, Sweden and Norway. Sweden revolted (1523) under Gustavus I against Danish rule, but Denmark and Norway remained united until 1814

Kal·muck (kǽlmʌk) *n.* a member of a Buddhist nomadic Mongolian people inhabiting Kalmyk A.S.S.R. || their Mongolian language

Kal·myk A.S.S.R. (kǽlmik) an autonomous republic (area 29,400 sq. miies, pop. 301,000) of the R.S.F.S.R., U.S.S.R., in the steppe around the Volga delta. Capital: Elista (formerly Stepnoi, pop. 22,000)

Ka·ma (kámə) a river (1,260 miles long) of western U.S.S.R., flowing from the Urals to the Volga near Kazan, a major shipping route (port: Perm) and source of power

Ka·ma (kámə) the Hindu god of erotic love

ka·ma·graph (kǽməgræf) *n.* special printing press that faithfully duplicates up to 250 copies of a painting, including raised brush strokes, destroying the original in the process. It was developed by André Cocard —**kamagraphy** *n.* the process

Ka·ma·ku·ra (kámakú:rɑ) a town (pop. 168,609) in central Honshu, Japan. It has 80 shrines, and a famous 42-ft-high Buddha (1252)

Ka·ma·kur·i (kɑmə́lkúri) *adj.* of the period A.D. 1170–1350 when Zen Buddhist art styles were introduced to Japan

Kam·a·ran (kǽmərən) an island (area 22 sq. miles, pop. 2,000) in the southern Red Sea off the Yemen coast, a dependency of the People's Democratic Republic of Yemen

Ka·ma·su·tra (kɑmɑsú:trə) a Sanskrit treatise (4th–7th cc.) on rules of love

Kam·chat·ka (kɑmtʃátkɑ) a peninsula (750 miles long) of N.E. Siberia, U.S.S.R., between the Sea of Okhotsk and the Bering Sea. Two active volcanic ranges (highest peak 15,661 ft) and a central valley run north-south. Products: coal, peat, petroleum, fish, furs, lumber. Chief town: Petropavlovsk-Kamchatski

ka·mi (kámi:) *n.* a sacred power, esp. one of the Shinto deities [Jap.=god]

ka·mi·ka·ze (kɑməkázi:) *n.* a member of the Japanese air force during the 2nd world war who deliberately crashed his bomb-laden plane into targets, usually ships || the plane in such an attack [Jap. fr. *kami*, god+*kaze*, wind]

Kam·pa·la (kɑmpálɑ) the capital (pop. 458,423) of Uganda, in Buganda. Makerere College (1939) of the University of East Africa (1963)

Kampf·pan·zer Leonard (kámpfpanzər) (*mil.*) tank of German Federal Republic, with 105-mm guns and speed of 65 km/hr

Kampuchea *CAMBODIA

Kam·pu·che·a (kɑmpu:tʃéiə) *n.* Southeast Asian nation, formerly Cambodia —**Kampuchean** *adj.*

ka·nak·a (kənǽkə, kǽnəkə) *n.* a South Sea Islander || a native of Hawaii [Hawaiian=man]

kan·a·my·cin (kænəmáisən) *n.* [$C_{18}H_{36}N_4O_{11}$] (*pharm.*) broad-spectrum antibiotic; marketed as Kantrex

Ka·nan·ga (kənáŋgə) (formerly Luluabourg) a town (pop. 141,000) on R. Lulua, an affluent of the Kasai River, in S. central Zaïre. It is the center of a cotton-growing district

Ka·na·rese (kɑnɑrí:z, kɑnɑrí:s) **1.** *n.* a member of a people of Mysore, S. India **2.** *adj.* of these people

Ka·na·za·wa (kánɑzáwɑ) a port (pop. 418,000) of Honshu, Japan: textiles (silk), handicrafts

Kan·chen·jun·ga (kɑntʃəndʒúŋgə) a mountain (28,146 ft) of the Himalayas between India and Nepal, considered the third highest in the world

Kan·chi·pu·ram (kɑntʃí:pərəm) (Conjeeveram), a Hindu sacred city (pop. 110,657) in N.E. Madras, India: textiles

Kan·da·har (kʌndɑhár) a city (pop. 191,000) of S.E. Afghanistan, an old commercial center, and the main outlet for trade with India

Kan·din·sky (kændínski:), Wassily (1866–1944), Russian painter, naturalized German (1928), then French (1939). In Fauve and expressionist experimentation he pursued a line of abstraction culminating in 1910 with the first purely abstract, nonobjective works. In these he painted free, spontaneous forms using color and line alone for their expressive power. By 1921 he was painting more calculated compositions of geometric forms. He wrote 'Concerning the Spiritual in Art' (1912). With Marc he originated the Blaue Reiter movement (1911). From 1922 to 1933 he taught at the Bauhaus. His work strongly influenced abstract expressionism

Kand·la (kándla) a fast-developing port on the west coast of India in Gujarat, handling esp. grain, cloth and lumber. It is a rail terminus and airport. Saltworks

Kan·dy (kændí:, kándi:) a town (pop. 85,000) of central Sri Lanka, the former capital (1592–1815): Buddhist shrines

Kane (kein), Elisha Kent (1820–57), U.S. arctic explorer. His expedition (1853–5) to northwest Greenland reached the highest northern latitude (80° 35') attained at that time

Ka·nem (kánəm) an ancient Sudanic state (10th–19th cc.) north of Lake Chad

kan·ga·roo (kæŋgərú:) *pl.* **kan·ga·roos, kan·ga·roo** *n.* a member of *Macropodidae*, a family of herbivorous, marsupial mammals of Australia and the nearby islands. They have large powerful hind legs and move by leaping. They have a long, tapering tail and short forelimbs. Kangaroo flesh is edible and the skin is used in making shoes and gloves [perh. native word]

Kangaroo (*mil.*) U.S.S.R. air-to-surface missile (SS-3)

kangaroo court an unauthorized court, or self-appointed group sitting as a court, usually mocking or ignoring legal procedure and justice

kangaroo rat a small rodent of fam. *Heteromyidae* of western North America, esp. of genus *Dipodomys*, with long hind legs adapted for jumping

K'ang-Hsi (kánʃi:) (1654–1722), Chinese emperor (c. 1661–1722) of the Manchu dynasty. His conquest of Formosa and Mongolia enlarged the frontiers of China, and the country prospered under his rule. He was a patron of literature and art

Kan Kan (kúkɑ) a rail terminus (pop. 29,000) in eastern Guinea: rice, brickworks, sawmills

Kan·na·da (kánədə, kǽnədə) *n.* the language spoken by the Kanarese

Ka·no (kánou) the capital (pop. 700,000, mostly Moslems) of Kano State, Nigeria, a center for trans-Saharan trade. Exports: peanuts, cattle, hides. It was the capital of a Hausa kingdom (16th c.)

Ka·no·nen·jagd·pan·zer (kɑnounenjágdpanstər) *n.* (*mil.*) armored artillery weapon of German Federal Republic (KJPZ 4-5) carrying 90-mm gun

Kan·pur (kánpur) (Cawnpore) a city (pop. 1,154,388) in Uttar Pradesh, India, on the Ganges: wool, leather, textiles

Kan·sas (kǽnzəs) (*abbr.* Kan.) a state (area 82,264 sq. miles, pop. 2,408,000) on the midwestern plains of the U.S.A. Capital: Topeka. Chief cities: Wichita, Kansas City. Agriculture: wheat, fodder crops, beef cattle. Resources: oil and natural gas, coal, lead, zinc. Industries: food processing, transport equipment, oil refining. State university (1865) at Lawrence. As part of the Louisiana Purchase (1803), Kansas passed to the U.S.A., of which it became (1861) the 34th state

Kansas City two cities, one (pop. 448,159) in Missouri, the other (pop. 161,807) in Kansas. They face each other across the Kansas River where it joins the Missouri, and together form a port and railroad junction, a livestock-trade and meat-packing center

Kansas-Nebraska Act (*Am. hist.*) a law (May 30, 1854) which provided that settlers in the newly created territories of Kansas and Nebraska should decide whether to have slavery or not. It nullified the Missouri Compromise and greatly increased the tensions which led to the Civil War

Kan·su (kǽnsú:) a province (pop. 12,650,000) of N. central China which includes the Ningsia-Hui autonomous region. Capital: Lanchow

Kant (kænt, kɑnt), Immanuel (1724–1804), German philosopher, founder of critical idealism. His most famous work, 'Critique of Pure Reason' (1781), is an inquiry into the limits of knowledge. According to Kant, the ultimate nature of reality (of the 'things in themselves') remains forever inaccessible to the human mind. What we can know is phenomena. The mind impresses its forms of sensibility (space and time) on the original data of the senses and orders them according to the categories of thought (causality, substance etc.). In his 'Critique of Practical Reason' (1788) he finds a new foundation for ethics and religion in the categorical imperative. 'The Critique of Judgment' (1790) establishes a bridge between his theoretical and moral philosophy through the ideas of beauty and formal development

Kant·i·an (kǽnti:ən) **1.** *adj.* of or relating to Kant or his philosophy || deriving from Kant **2.** *n.* a follower of Kant

kan·zu (kǽnzu:) *n.* a long white garment worn by some Africans, e.g. the Swahili [Swahili]

Kao·hsiung (gáuʃjún) a port and industrial center (pop. 1,250,000) of S.W. Taiwan: oil refineries

Ka·o·lack (kúɔlæk, káulæk) a town (pop. 47,000), port and rail terminus in W. Senegal, on the Saloum River, exporting peanuts

Kao·lan (káulán) *LANCHOW

kao·liang (káuljún) *n.* any of a group of grain sorghums of E. Asia, esp. China and Manchuria, grown for food. The stalks are used for thatching etc. [Chin. fr. *kao*, tall+*liang*, grain]

ka·o·lin, ka·o·line (kéiəlin) *n.* a fine, usually white clay of which kaolinite is the main constituent. It is used in the making of porcelain, in medicine, as a filler (e.g. in papermaking) etc. [F. fr. Chin. *kao-ling*, a hill in Kiangsi province]

ka·o·lin·ite (kéiəlinait) *n.* $Al_2Si_2O_5(OH)_4$, a finely crystalline form of hydrated aluminum silicate, formed mainly by the weathering of feldspar [KAOLIN]

ka·on (kéiɑn) *n.* (*nuclear phys.*) term for four nuclear particles with a mass of 497.8 MEV (million electronvolts), a lifetime of 10^{-10} seconds, distinguished as K, $K_s°$, and $K_L°$, weight 960 times greater than electrons *also* K-meson —**kaonic** or **K-mesic** *adj. Cf* MUON, PION

Ka·pell·meis·ter (kɑpélmaistər) *n.* (*hist.*) the musical director of the chapel of a pope or prince || (*hist.*) the resident conductor of a patrician's orchestra [G.]

Kap·lan (kǽplən), Mordecai Menahem (1881–1983), U.S. religious leader. He founded the Reconstructionist movement in Judaism, dating from the publication of his 'Judaism as a Civilization' (1934). He established (1916) the first U.S. synagogue center in New York and (1922) the Society for the Advancement of Judaism

ka·pok (kéipɔk, kǽpək) *n.* the surface fibers from the seed pods of the ceiba. The hollow, buoyant, resilient, waterproof fibers are used as

CONCISE PRONUNCIATION KEY: **(a)** æ, c*a*t; ɑ, c*a*r; ɔ f*aw*n; ei, sn*a*ke. **(e)** e, h*e*n; i:, sh*ee*p; iə, d*ee*r; ɛə, b*ea*r. **(i)** i, f*i*sh; ai, t*i*ger; ə:, b*i*rd. **(o)** o, *o*x; au, c*ow*; ou, g*oa*t; u, p*oo*r; ɔi, r*oy*al. **(u)** ʌ, d*u*ck; u, b*u*ll; u:, g*oo*se; ə, b*a*cillus; ju:, c*u*be. x, lo*ch*; θ, *th*ink; ð, bo*th*er; z, *Z*en; ʒ, corsa*g*e. dʒ, sava*g*e; ŋ, orangutan*g*; j, *y*ak; ʃ, *f*ish; tʃ, fe*tch*; 'l, ra*bb*le; 'n, red*en*. Complete pronunciation key appears inside front cover.

insulation, and for stuffing cushions, mattresses etc. The oil from the seeds is used in soapmaking [Malay *kāpok*]

kapok tree the silk-cotton tree

Kap·o·si's sarcoma (kəpóusi:z) (*med.*) rare form of cancer found in homosexual men over age 50; characterized by violet spots or lumps on the body

kap·pa (kǽpə) *n.* the tenth letter (K, χ=k) of the Greek alphabet

Kap·ton foil (kǽptən) protective shield that shuts out sun's thermal energy but permits radio waves to pass through; developed by Hughes Aircraft Co.

Ka·ra Bo·gaz Gol (kɑrábɔgázgʌ́l) a gulf (area 7,000 sq. miles) of the Caspian Sea, Turkmenistan, U.S.S.R.: sulfates, sodium chloride and other salts

Ka·ra·chi (kərátʃi:) the chief town and port (pop. 5,103,000) of Pakistan, the former capital (1947–60), northwest of the Indus delta in Sind. Industries: food processing, handicrafts, wool milling. University (1951)

Ka·ra·fu·to (kárəfu:tɔ) *SAKHALIN

Ka·ra·gan·da (kɑrəgəndá) a city (pop. 583,000) of Kazakhstan, U.S.S.R.: coal, tungsten

Kar·a·george (kǽrədʒɔ́rdʒ) (George Petrović, c. 1752–1817), Serbian revolutionary leader. He led the successful Serbian revolt against Turkish rule (1804) and seized power (1808–13), founding the Karageorgević dynasty

Kar·a·geor·ge·vić (kǽrədʒɔ́rdʒəvitʃ) a Serbian dynasty founded by Karageorge which ruled Serbia (1842–58 and 1903–18) and Yugoslavia (1918–45)

Kar·a·ite (kɛ́əraait) *n.* a member of a Jewish religious sect founded in the 8th c. by a Syrian Jew, Anan ben David. It rejected the Talmud and incorporated Christian and Moslem elements. Its adherents were mainly influential in the Crimea and Lithuania, but are now largely dispersed **Kar·a·ism** (kɛ́ərəizəm), **Kar·a·it·ism** (kɛ́ərɑaitizəm) *ns* [fr. Heb. *q'rāim,* those who base their religious belief solely on scripture]

Ka·ra·Kal·pak A.S.S.R. (kərəkəlpák, kʊrəkəlpák) an autonomous republic (area 79,631 sq. miles, pop. 544,000) of Uzbekistan, U.S.S.R., on the Aral Sea. Capital: Nukus (pop. 39,000)

Ka·ra·ko·ram (kʊrəkɔ́rəm, kʊrəkóurəm) a mountain range (300 miles long) of N. Kashmir extending into Tibet, having 60 peaks over 22,000 ft (*K2) and great glaciers. It is crossed by several high passes, notably the Karakoru (18,290 ft)

Ka·ra·ko·rum (kʊrəkɔ́rəm, kʊrəkóurəm) the ruined ancient capital of the Mongol Empire (1234–1409), near Ulan Bator, Outer Mongolia

Kar·a·kul (kǽrək'l) *n.* a breed of brown-haired sheep from Bukhara ‖ the black, tightly curled skin of a newborn lamb of this breed, yielding valuable fur (*ASTRAKHAN, *PERSIAN LAMB) [after *Kara Kul,* a lake in Tadzhikistan, U.S.S.R.]

Ka·ra-Kum (kɑrəkú:m) a desert (area 120,000 sq. miles) in Turkmenistan, U.S.S.R., west of the Amu Darya. Irrigation canal

kar·at, *esp. Br.* **car·at** (kǽrət) *n.* a measure of the purity of gold. Pure gold is 24 karat, 18-karat gold has six parts of alloy

ka·ra·te (kərɑti:) *n.* a Japanese system of unarmed self-defense, by body blows with the hands, knees, feet etc.

Ka·re·li·an (kərí:liən, kərí:ljən) **1.** *adj.* of or relating to the Karelian A.S.S.R., or its people, or their language **2.** *n.* a native or inhabitant of the Karelian A.S.S.R. ‖ the Finno-Ugric language spoken by the Karelian people

Karelian A.S.S.R. an autonomous republic (area 69,720 sq. miles, pop. 768,000) of the R.S.F.S.R., U.S.S.R., on the E. Scandinavian peninsula, bordering Finland. It is a land of lakes, forests and granite. People: 25% Karelians and Finns, the rest Russians. Capital: Petrozavodsk

Karelian Isthmus a strip of land, about 65 miles wide, between Lake Ladoga and the Gulf of Finland. Finland ceded it to the U.S.S.R. (1940), recaptured it (1941) but again surrendered it to the U.S.S.R. (1947)

Karen a partly mountainous state (pop. 400,000) of S.E. Burma, extending south into Tenasserim. Capital: Papun

Ka·ren (kərén) *n.* a member of any of several chiefly agricultural tribes inhabiting eastern and southern Burma ‖ any of several related languages spoken by these people

Ka·ren·ni (kəréni:) *KAYAH

Ka·ri·ba Dam (korí:bɑ) one of the world's biggest hydroelectric dams, on the Zambesi (Kariba Gorge) between Zambia and Zimbabwe, supplying power to both countries

Ka·ri·kal (kʊrikál) a part (area 52 sq. miles, pop. 76,000) of Pondicherry, India on the Coromandel coast, a French enclave until 1962

kar·i·te (kǽriti:) *n. Butyrospermum parkii,* fam. *Sapotaceae,* a tropical African tree whose seeds yield shea butter [F. *karité*]

karite butter shea butter

Karl Franz Josef (kɑrl) emperor of Austria *CHARLES I

Kar·li (kɑ́rli:) a Village near Poona in Bombay province, India: Buddhist temple-cave (1st c. B.C.)

Karl-Marx-Stadt (kɑ́rlmɑ́rksʃtát) (formerly Chemnitz) a district (area 2,320 sq. miles, pop. 2,095,000) of East Germany in former Saxony ‖ its center (pop. 320,000), a great metal-working and machinery and textile-manufacturing town

Kar·lo·vy Va·ry (kɑ́rlɔviári) *KARLSBAD

Kar·lo·witz, Treaty of (kɑ́rlɔvits) a peace treaty signed (1699) between the Ottoman Empire, Venice, Poland, Russia and the Emperor Leopold I, who gained Hungary, Croatia and Slovenia

Karls·bad (kɑ́rlsbɑt, kɑ́rlzbæd) (*Czech.* Karlovy Vary) a spa (pop. 61,000) in N.W. Bohemia, Czechoslovakia, celebrated for its hot springs

Karlsbad Decrees repressive measures (1819) designed by Metternich to exterminate liberalism in Germany by censoring the press, strictly controlling the universities, and supressing secret societies. They were provoked by the murder of von Kotzebue by a demented student

Karls·ruh·e (kɑ́rlzru:ə) a city (pop. 274,000) near the Rhine in N.W. Baden-Württemberg, West Germany, a commercial and industrial center: perfume, beer, hardware, machinery, radio and electrical equipment

kar·ma (kɑ́rmə) *n.* (*Buddhism* and *Hinduism*) the power, resulting from an individual's volitional acts, which determines his cycle of reincarnations before he attains release from this world ‖ (*Buddhism* and *Hinduism*) the sum total of the acts done in one stage of a person's existence, which determine his destiny in the next stage ‖ (*Jainism*) a form of matter which can contaminate a soul and postpone its attaining Nirvana **kár·mic** *adj.* [Skr.]

Kar·nak (kɑ́rnæk) *THEBES (Egypt)

Kar·na·li (kɑrnáli:) *GOGRA

Ka·ro·lyi (kɑ́rɔlji), Count Mihály (1875–1955), Hungarian statesman. He was prime minister of Hungary (1918) and provisional president of the republic (1919) until superseded by Kun

Kar·roo, Ka·roo (kɑrú:) *pl.* **Kar·roos, Ka·roos** *n.* any of several arid tablelands in southern Africa, esp. Great Karroo and Little Karroo, between Cape Town and Port Elizabeth, and North Karroo, in N. Cape Province, south of the Kalahari Desert [Hottentot]

karst (kɑrst) *n.* a barren limestone region characterized by fissures, caves and underground channels [G.]

Ka·run (kɑrú:n) a navigable river flowing 528 miles from W. Iran into the Shatt-el-Arab on the Iraqi border

kar·y·o·ki·ne·sis (kæri:oukiní:sis, kæri:oukiní:sis) *n.* the series of changes in the nucleus of a cell in mitosis ‖ mitosis [fr. Gk *karnon,* nut, kernel+*kinēsis,* motion]

kar·y·o·plasm (kǽri:əplæzəm) *n.* nucleoplasm [fr. Gk *karnon,* nut, kernel+*plasma,* something molded or formed]

Ka·sai (kɑsái) a river (1,338 miles) flowing east from central Angola, then north to form the border, and through southwestern Zaïre to the Congo River (R. Zaïre)

Kas·a·vu·bu (kæsəvú:bu:, kɑsɑvú:bu:), Joseph (1910–69), Zaïran statesman, first president (1960–5) of the (then) Democratic Republic of the Congo. He called in U.N. forces when civil war broke out after independence (1960)

Kash·gar (kɑ́fgɑ́r) (*Chin.* Shufu) a trading center (pop. 100,000) in Sinkiang, China, at the west edge of the Tarim basin

Kash·mir (kǽfmiər, kæʃmíər) a disputed region (area 86,024 sq. miles, pop. 7,700,000) of central Asia, north of India. Chief city: Srinagar. Language: Kashmiri. People: *INDIA (subcontinent). Religion: 67% Moslem, 30% Hindu, with Sikh, Buddhist and other minorities. The N. Himalayas run through the center separated from the Karakorams, in the southeast, by the upper Indus valley. Southwest of the Himala-

yas the Jhelum forms the deep Vale of Kashmir (80 miles long, 20 miles wide, elevation 4,000–6,000 ft), the only large arable section (cereals, fruit, vegetables). Industries: forestry, handicrafts, textiles. The south and east (called Jammu and Kashmir) are administered by India, while the north and west (Azad Kashmir) are occupied and claimed by Pakistan. A part of the northwest of Ladakh, in the northeast, is occupied and claimed by China. The region was under Hindu rule until the 14th c., when it fell to the Moslems, who ruled until 1819. It became a Sikh kingdom (1819) and came under British rule (1846). After the partition of India (1947), fighting broke out between India and Pakistan, and the U.N. imposed a cease-fire (1949), pending a plebiscite which has never been held. India officially annexed Kashmir (1957), but Pakistan continued to occupy the north and west. China began to occupy Ladakh in the early 1950s. India and Pakistan were briefly at war over Kashmir (1965). In 1972 the Indian and Pakistan sections of Kashmir were divided by a 'line of control'

Kash·mir·i (kæʃmíari) *n.* a native or inhabitant of Kashmir ‖ the Indic language of Kashmir

KA-6 *INTRUDER

Kassel * CASSEL

Kas·sem (kɑssí:m, kɑ́si:m), Abdul Karim (1914–63), Iraqi general and politician. He overthrew the monarchy (1958), established a republic, and became prime minister (1958–63). He was killed when his régime was overthrown

Kas·site (kǽsait) a member of a dynasty which ruled Babylonia (c. 1750–c. 1200 B.C.)

kat·a·bat·ic (kætəbǽtik) *adj.* of the downward flow of air, esp. cold air [fr. Gk *katabainein,* to go down]

kat·a·bol·ic, cat·a·bol·ic (kætəbólik) *adj.* related to or characterized by katabolism

ka·tab·o·lism, cat·ab·o·lism (kətǽbəlizəm) *n.* destructive metabolism in which complex compounds are converted into simpler ones with the release of energy (opp. ANABOLISM) [fr. Gk *katabolē,* a throwing down]

Ka·tan·ga (kətángə, kətǽngə) a region (renamed Shaba) of southeastern Zaïre, containing great deposits of copper, gold, radium and uranium, and by far the richest area in the country. A former province, it seceded (1960), was reintegrated (1963), and was divided up administratively

Katar *QATAR

kath·a·rom·e·ter (kæθərómitər) *n.* an apparatus used for the analysis of gas mixtures by measuring their thermal conductivity [fr. Gk *katharos,* pure+METER]

katharsis *CATHARSIS

Kath·er·i·na Ge·bel (kæθərí:nədʒéb'l) the highest moutain (8,662 ft) of Egypt, in S. central Sinai, site of a monastery since 250

Katherine *CATHERINE

Ka·thi·a·war (kʊti:əwár) a peninsula (area 23,242 sq. miles) of Gujarat, N.W. India, growing millet and cotton

Kat·kov (kútkɔf), Mikhail Nikiforovich (1818–87), Russian journalist. As unofficial personal adviser to Alexander III he influenced Russian policy

Kat·man·du (kɑtmɑndú:) the capital (pop. 393,494) of Nepal, in the Bishanmati River valley of the Himalayas, near the Indian frontier: administrative, business and religious center

Ka·to·wi·ce (kʊtɔví:tse) (before 1922 G. Kattowitz, 1953–6 Stalinogród) an industrial center (pop. 348,900) of S. Poland (Upper Silesia): coal and zinc mines, metal and chemical industries

Kat·si·na (kǽtsinə) a walled town (pop. 112,230) in N. Nigeria, capital (17th and 18th cc.) of the kingdom of Bornu: trade in cotton, cattle, peanuts

kat·su·ra tree (kǽtsərə) *Cercidiphyllum japonicum,* a Japanese tree grown in the U.S.A.

Kat·te·gat (kǽtəgæt) the strait (150 miles long) between Jutland and Sweden, connected to the North Sea by the Skagerrak (with which it forms a bent arm) and with the Baltic by passages known as the Great Belt, Little Belt and Øresund

Kat·to·witz (kútouvíts) *KATOWICE

ka·ty·did, ca·ty·did (kéiti:did) *n.* a member of those species of fam. *Tettigoniidae* of large, green, arboreal American grasshoppers whose males make a strident sound with their fore wings [imit.]

CONCISE PRONUNCIATION KEY: **(a)** æ, c*a*t; ɑ, c*a*r; ɔ f*aw*n; ei, sn*a*ke. **(e)** e, h*e*n; i:, sh*ee*p; iə, d*ee*r; ɛə, b*ea*r. **(i)** i, f*i*sh; ai, t*i*ger; ə:, b*i*rd. **(o)** o, *o*x; au, c*ow*; ou, g*oa*t; u, p*oo*r; ɔi, r*oy*al. **(u)** ʌ, d*u*ck; u, b*u*ll; u:, g*oo*se; ə, bacill*u*s; ju:, c*u*be. x, lo*ch*; θ, *th*ink; δ, bo*th*er; z, *Z*en; ʒ, corsa*g*e; dʒ, sava*g*e; ŋ, oranguta*ng*; j, *y*ak; ʃ, *f*ish; tʃ, *f*etch; 'l, rabb*le*; 'n, red*den.* Complete pronunciation key appears inside front cover.

Ka·tyn (kətín) n. woods near Smolensk where bodies of 5,000 Polish officers were found; part of a group of 15,000 alleged to have been killed by the Soviet Army in 1943

Ka·tyu·sha (kətúʃə) n. (mil.) U.S.S.R. multiple-barrelled rocket launcher

Katz v. U.S.A. (kæts) a landmark decision (1967) of the U.S. Supreme Court which held that wiretapping was covered by the Fourth Amendment's prohibition against unreasonable searches and seizures, and that police must obtain wiretap warrants before using eavesdrop devices

Kauff·mann (káufmən), Angelica (1741–1807), Swiss painter of portraits and decorative panels, esp. of historical subjects. She lived in London (1766–81)

Kaufman (kófmən), George S. (1889–1961), U.S. playwright and director. Drama critic for 'The New York Times' from 1917 to 1930, he wrote 'Dulcy' (1921), 'To the Ladies' (1922) and 'The Butter and Egg Man' (1925) with Marc Connelly. He collaborated with Edna Ferber on 'The Royal Family' (1927), 'Dinner at Eight' (1932) and 'Stage Door' (1936), among others, and with Moss Hart on 'Once in a Lifetime' (1930), 'You Can't Take It with You' (1936; Pulitzer Prize) and 'The Man Who Came to Dinner' (1939)

Kau·nas (káunəs) (formerly Kovno) a city (pop. 383,000) of Lithuania, U.S.S.R., on the Niemen, formerly the capital (1918–40) of independent Lithuania. Industries: machines, textiles, chemicals. University (1922)

Ka·un·da (kaú:ndə), Kenneth David (1924–), Zambian statesman. He was the first prime minister of Northern Rhodesia (1964) and led his country to independence as Zambia, becoming its first president (1964–). He made Zambia a one-party state (1972) in an effort to reduce tribal factionalism

Kau·nitz-Riet·berg (káunitsrí:tberk), Wenzel Anton, Prince von (1711–94), Austrian statesman. He represented Austria in negotiating the Treaty of Aix-la-Chapelle (1748), and secured a French alliance while ambassador to France (1750-3). For nearly 40 years he dominated Austrian politics and European diplomacy, furthering Hapsburg interests at the expense of Prussia

kau·ri (káuri:) pl. **kau·ris** n. a member of Agathis, a genus of evergreen trees, esp. A. australis, fam. Pinaceae, a tall New Zealand timber tree ‖ the wood of this tree ‖ the resin obtained from this tree, used for varnishes [Maori]

ka·va, ca·va (kávə) n. Piper methysticum, fam. Piperaceae, an Australasian pepper shrub ‖ an intoxicating drink made from its crushed roots [Polynesian]

Ka·val·la (kavála) (ancient Neapolis) a walled seaport (pop. 56,260) of E. Macedonia, Greece: tobacco

Ka·ve·ri (kávəri:) * CAUVERY

Ka·wa·sa·ki (káwɑsáki:) a city (pop. 1,055,345) in Honshu, Japan, on Tokyo Bay, a great industrial center and dockyard: textiles, steel, shipbuilding

Ka·wa·sak·i disease (kɑwɑsáki:) (med.) an untreatable lymph-node syndrome formerly called Mu Coocutaneas, which causes heart attacks in children under 5 yrs; first reported in Japan in 1970

Kay (kei), John (1704–c. 1778), British inventor of the flying shuttle (1733) and of a power loom for narrow goods (1745), advances in textile manufacturing which influenced the course of the Industrial Revolution

Ka·yah (káijə) a mountainous state (area 4,500 sq. miles, pop. 85,000) of S.E. Burma, formed (1947) from three feudal states (Karenni), inhabited by Karen tribes. Capital: Loikaw

kay·ak (káiæk) n. an Eskimo canoe made of sealskins stretched taut over a light wooden frame, completely closed in around the paddler ‖ a similar canvas-covered canoe [Eskimo]

Kayes (keiz) a port (pop. 30,000) in Mali on the Senegal River, a produce and livestock market: kapok ginning, tanning

kay·o (kéióu) **1.** n. (pop.) a knockout in boxing **2.** v.t. to knock (someone) out in boxing [fr. K.O., abbr. for knockout]

Kay·se·ri (kaiserí:) a district and town (pop. 281,320) of central Turkey. As Caesarea Mazaca it was the chief city of ancient Cappadocia

Ka·zakh·stan (kɑzakstán) a constituent republic (area 1,048,070 sq. miles, pop. 14,685,000) of the U.S.S.R., in central Asia. Capital: Alma-Ata. The Kirghiz Steppe lies in the center, and the rest is generally dry. Agriculture: livestock (esp. sheep), wheat in the north, cotton, fruit, vines, tobacco, and rubber under irrigation in the south. Resources: coal, tungsten, oil, copper, lead and zinc (about half the Russian reserves of these last three). Industries: metallurgical, chemical, heavy engineering. Part of Turkestan, Kazakhstan became a Soviet Republic in 1920 and a constituent republic in 1936

Ka·zak, Ka·zakh (kəzák) n. an Islamic, Turkic people of central Asia ‖ a member of this people ‖ their Turkic language

Ka·zan (kazánj) the capital (pop. 1,011,000) of Tatar A.S.S.R., U.S.S.R., and formerly of a Tatar khanate conquered (1552) by Ivan IV. Long a Russian outpost in the east, it is a commercial and industrial center. University (1804)

Kazantzakis (kazandzáki:s), Nikos (1883–1957), Greek writer and poet, who attempted to find similarities in the different world views from Marx to Buddha to Christ. His epic poem 'The Odyssey: A Modern Sequel' (1938) continues Homer's story. His novels include 'Zorba the Greek' (1946; film, 1965), 'The Last Temptation of Christ' (1955) and 'God's Pauper: Saint Francis of Assisi' (1956)

Kazvin *QAZVIN

k bar short form of kilobar, unit of pressure equal to 100 megapascals abbr. kb

kc. kilocycle

KC-97 *STRATOFREIGHTER

KC-10 adaptation of DC-10 for refueling, tanker, and cargo missions; with capacity of 85 tons; made by McDonnell-Douglas

K-day (mil.) the basic date for the introduction of a convoy system on any particular convoy lane Cf D-DAY

ke·a (kéiə, kí:ə) n. Nestor notabilis, a large, dull-green parrot of New Zealand, by nature insectivorous, but liable to attack sheep to eat their kidney fat [Maori, imit.]

Kean (ki:n), Edmund (1787–1833), English actor, esp. famous in Shakespearean roles

Kearny (kárni:), Stephen Watts (1794–1848), U.S. military leader, officer in the War of 1812 and Mexican War and governor of California (1847). After the War of 1812, he served in various frontier posts. He commanded the Army of the West in the Mexican War (1846–7) and achieved victories in New Mexico and California. Named governor of California for about 4 months, he went on to Mexico to govern Veracruz and Mexico City

Keats (ki:ts), John (1795–1821), English poet. His early work was lush and unequal, but 'Endymion' (1818) shows his growing powers. The famous 1820 volume contained the great 'Odes' ('Ode to a Nightingale', 'Ode on a Grecian Urn', 'Ode to Psyche', 'To Autumn', 'Ode on Melancholy'), 'The Eve of St Agnes', 'Lamia' and 'Hyperion'. He died of tuberculosis at 25. His letters are among the finest in the language and reveal the growth of his poetic genius. The main characteristic of his poetry is sensual apprehension—diffuse, hectic and undisciplined at first, but later more and more concrete and organized: so that the celebration of the immediate and evanescent is turned into lasting art

Ke·ble (kí:b'l), John (1792–1866), British churchman and poet. His sermon (1833) on 'National Apostasy' is considered to have begun the Oxford movement. His religious verse includes 'The Christian Year' (1827)

Keb·ne·kai·se (kɛbnəkáisə) the highest peak (6,963 ft) of the Kjölen Mtns, in N. Sweden

Kecs·ke·mét (kétʃkemeit) a town (pop. 93,000) of the Hungarian plain, near Budapest, economic center of an agricultural region

Ke·dah (kéidə) a state (area 3,660 sq. miles, pop. 1,102,200) of Malaysia in N.W. Malaya. Capital: Alor Star. It was ruled by Siam until 1909, when sovereignty was transferred to Britain. It joined the Federation of Malaya (1948)

kedge (kedʒ) **1.** v. pres. part. **kedg·ing** past and past part. **kedged** v.t. to move (a ship) by a light cable attached to a light anchor some distance away ‖ v.i. (of a ship) to move in this way **2.** n. a light anchor used in kedging a ship [etym. doubtful]

kedge anchor a kedge

ked·ger·ee (kédʒəri:) n. a dish of rice, fish, eggs etc. ‖ an Indian stew of rice, pulse, onions etc. [Hindi khichri, Skr. k'rsara]

keel (ki:l) **1.** n. the curved base of the framework of a ship, extending from bow to stern ‖ a similar structure in an airship ‖ (biol.) a carina, e.g. in birds, flowers and grasses **to be on an even keel** (of a ship) to have no list ‖ (of a person) to be well balanced **2.** v.t. to turn (a ship) so that its keel is uppermost ‖ v.i. (of a ship) to roll over **to keel over** to capsize [prob. O.N. kjölr]

keel n. a flat-bottomed vessel, or barge, used esp. for carrying coal ‖ the load of coal it carries [M. Du. kiel, ship]

keel·boat (kí:lbout) n. a shallow freight boat formerly used on the Mississippi, usually towed or poled or rowed, but having a keel to permit sailing

Kee·ler (kí:lər), James Edward (1857–1900), U.S. astronomer. He discovered (1891) that the rings of Saturn revolve around the planet like a multitude of small independent satellites and (1898) that the spiral form is dominant among the nongaseous nebulae now known as external galaxies. He established the reflecting telescope as the best instrument for photographing faint celestial objects

keel·haul (kí:lhɔl) v.t. (hist.) to haul (a person) under the keel of a ship as a punishment [fr. Du. kielhalen]

keel·son, kel·son (kéls'n) n. the longitudinal structure in a wooden ship by which a ship's floor timbers are fastened to the keel ‖ a comparable structure or set of iron plates in an iron ship [L.G. kielswin]

keen (ki:n) adj. (of a cutting edge) sharp ‖ (fig.) cutting or piercing, a keen wind ‖ (of a sensual stimulus) strong, keen scent ‖ (of the mind or the senses) acute, keen sight ‖ (of a mental process) acute, incisive, keen wit ‖ (of feelings) intense, a keen desire ‖ enthusiastic, a keen golfer ‖ (Br., of prices) low, very competitive **to be keen on** to like (someone or something) very much [O.E. cēne, wise]

keen n. an often high-pitched wailing made by the Irish in mourning the dead [fr. Ir. caoine]

keen v.i. to utter a mourning keen ‖ v.t. to mourn with a keen [ult. fr. Ir. caoinim, I wail]

keep (ki:p) **1.** v. pres. part. **keep·ing** past and past part. **kept** (kept) v.t. to continue to have in one's hands, mind, a place etc. ‖ to refrain from destroying, continue to have in one's possession ‖ to continue to have under one's control, to keep one's temper ‖ to be responsible for providing with the necessities of life, a large family to keep ‖ to own and manage, to keep a shop ‖ to carry in stock for sale, this shop doesn't keep what we want ‖ to fulfill (a promise etc.) ‖ to maintain (a written record), to keep the account books ‖ to employ in personal service, to keep a maid ‖ to maintain, to keep a car in good condition ‖ to raise (livestock) ‖ to observe or celebrate, to keep the sabbath ‖ to maintain (someone, something) in a certain condition, position etc., to keep (someone) waiting, to keep (something) dry ‖ to hold under arrest, to keep in prison ‖ to prevent, bad weather kept them from going ‖ to refrain from disclosing, to keep a secret ‖ to regulate one's conduct or habits in accordance with, to keep late hours ‖ v.i. to continue, to stay, if you keep on this road you'll arrive at the village ‖ to remain in good condition, not be spoiled, over a period of time, this wine doesn't keep **to keep at** to continue to work on ‖ to nag **to keep away** to prevent (someone or something) from coming closer ‖ to remain at a distance **to keep away from** to avoid **to keep back** to force back, the police kept the crowd back ‖ to refrain from revealing, he kept back some of the facts **to keep from** to prevent from ‖ to prevent oneself from ‖ to force to remain apart from ‖ to refrain from disclosing (something) to (someone) **to keep going** to persevere with an action, although ill and exhausted, he kept going ‖ to continue to live, the whiskey helped him to keep going ‖ to enable (someone) to continue, live etc. ‖ to act so that (something) does not fail, stop etc. **to keep in** to hide (feelings, emotions etc.) ‖ (Br.) to stay indoors ‖ to force (someone) to stay indoors, after school, as punishment **to keep in mind** to remember constantly **to keep in touch with** to maintain contact with **to keep in with** to be careful to remain on good terms with **to keep it up** to maintain one's effort **to keep off** to stay clear of ‖ to prevent from approaching **to keep on** to continue to wear (garments etc.) ‖ to continue persistently, to keep on trying **to keep on at** (Br.) to nag **to keep to** to adhere to ‖ to remain in (the house etc.) **to keep to oneself** to avoid other people, esp. to avoid taking others into one's confidence **to keep to the right** (**left**) to stay on the right-hand (left-hand) side of the road, path etc. **to keep track of** to continue informing oneself about **to keep up** to sustain, *keep up your spirits* ‖ to continue, *the rain kept up all day* ‖ to prevent from going to bed ‖ to maintain (a property) ‖ to maintain in the air **to keep up appearances** to make it appear that one is in a better material or moral position than is the case **to keep up with** to continue to be equal with, *he has difficulty keeping up with the rest of the class* **to keep up with the Joneses** to attempt to have as high a standard of living as one's neighbors **to keep well** to continue to have good health **2.** *n.* (*hist.*) a strong tower within the walls of a fortress ‖ food and other items needed for maintenance, *he hardly earns his keep* **for keeps** not intended to be given back, *it's yours for keeps* ‖ permanently, *he has come back for keeps* **keep·er** *n.* someone, esp. a gamekeeper, who keeps, manages, guards etc. ‖ a bar of soft iron joining the opposite poles of a magnet to prevent loss of magnetism ‖ a contrivance for maintaining something in position, e.g. a latch ‖ something, e.g. an apple, which retains its quality for a long time **keep·ing** *n.* care, charge, *to have in one's keeping* ‖ the action of one who keeps **in** (**out of**) **keeping** (**with**) in (out of) harmony (with), *his behavior is not in keeping with his profession* [late O.E. *cēpan*]

keep·er (kí:pər) *n.* (*football*) a play in which the quarterback keeps the ball and runs with it
keep·sake (kí:pseik) *n.* something kept as a reminder of the giver or of an occasion
Kees·hond (kéishond) *pl.* **Kees·hon·den** (kéishond'n) *n.* a dog of a breed of medium build having a thick coat of long hair, somewhat resembling the chow [Du.]
Kee·wa·tin (ki:wéit'n) a district (area incl. water: 228,160 sq. miles) in the S.E. Northwest Territories, Canada, incl. the east section of Canada northwest of the Hudson Bay and the islands in the Hudson Bay and James Bay. It is administered from Ottawa
keg (keg) *n.* a small cask or barrel holding (*Am.*) less than 30 gals or (*Br.*) less than 10 gals [corrup. of older *cag*]
Kei·tel (káit'l), Wilhelm (1882–1946), German field marshal. Chief of the German general staff (1938–45) and a close adviser of Hitler, he signed Germany's unconditional surrender at the end of the 2nd world war. He was condemned at the Nuremberg war crimes trial and hanged
Kek·ko·nen (kékɔnen), Urho Kaleva (1900–), Finnish statesman, prime minister (1950–3 and 1954–6) and president (1956–81) of Finland
Ke·ku·lé formula (kéikələi) *STRUCTURAL FORMULA
Ke·ku·lé von Stra·do·nitz (kéikəleifənʃtrádounits), Friedrich August (1829–96), German chemist who discovered the ring structure of benzene and other organic compounds and the tetravalency of carbon
Ke·lan·tan (kəlʌntán) a state (area 5,750 sq. miles, pop. 877,575) of Malaysia in N.E. Malaya. Capital: Kota Bharu. It was ruled (19th c.) by Siam. It passed (1909) to Britain. It joined the Federation of Malaya (1948)
Kel·ler (kélər), Gottfried (1819–90), Swiss author, who wrote in German. His works include an autobiographical novel 'Der grüne Heinrich' (1855, revised 1879) and collections of short stories
Keller, Helen Adams (1880–1968), American woman who overcame the handicap of her blindness and deafness and raised funds by her books and lectures for the training of the blind and other charitable causes
Kel·logg (kélɒg, kélɔg), Frank Billings (1856–1937), American statesman. As U.S. secretary of state (1925–9), he negotiated the Kellogg-Briand Pact. Nobel peace prize (1929)
Kellogg-Briand pact an agreement banning war signed (Aug. 27, 1928) by Kellogg and Briand, representing the U.S.A. and France respectively, and ultimately ratified by more than 60 countries. With no means of enforcement, it remained a dead letter in the face of Nazi aggression of the 1930s
Kells, The Book of (kelz) an 8th-c. illuminated Latin manuscript of the Gospels at Trinity College, Dublin. It is one of the finest examples of Celtic illumination
Kel·ly (kéli:), Ellsworth (1923–), American painter and sculptor. The apparently clear and

simple forms of his paintings, painted on a huge scale in flat color, reveal themselves as complex and compelling
Kelly, Howard Atwood (1858–1943), U.S. gynecologist and surgeon. He pioneered in the use of radium for the treatment of cancer and in the use of cocaine for local anesthesia. He invented a number of diagnostic tools and made innovations in operative technique
keloid *CHELOID
kelp (kelp) *n.* any of various large brown seaweeds esp. of order *Laminariales* or *Fucales* ‖ the ash resulting from burning kelp, formerly used widely in the production of iodine and alkali [M.E. *culp*, origin unknown]
kelson *KEELSON
Kelt (kelt) *n.* a Celt
kelt (kelt) *n.* a salmon or sea trout after spawning [origin unknown]
Kelt (kelt) *n.* (*mil.*) U.S.S.R. air-to-surface rocket weighing 400 lbs, with a 120-mi range, homing and radar direction
Kel·tic (kéltik) *adj.* and *n.* Celtic
Kel·vin (kélvin), William Thomson, 1st Baron Kelvin of Largs (1824–1907), British physicist. He did work in thermodynamics and also made contributions to electricity and magnetism. His inventions include the mirror galvanometer and the quadrant electrometer. He proposed the Kelvin scale of temperature
Kelvin scale a temperature scale, having a degree equal to the centigrade degree but having a zero of temperature defined by the extrapolation of the ideal gas law to zero volume. The freezing point of water on it is 273.16°
Ke·mal (kemál) *ATATÜRK
Ke·me·ro·vo (kémərʌvʌ) a city (pop. 486,000) of the Kuznetsk Basin, R.S.F.S.R., U.S.S.R., a railroad center: coal mining, chemical industries
Kempe (kemp), Margery (c. 1373–c. 1430), English religious writer, author of 'The Book of Margery Kempe', relating her pilgrimages and mystic experiences
Kempis, Thomas à *THOMAS À KEMPIS
ken (ken) *n.* (with 'within' or 'beyond') the range of one's knowledge [fr. older *ken v.*, to make known]
ke·naf (kənæf) *n. Hibiscus cannabinus*, a fiber plant native to the East Indies, widely cultivated ‖ its fiber, used for canvas and cordage [Pers.]
Ke·nai Peninsula (kí:nai), a peninsula (c. 160 miles long, 130 miles wide) of S. Alaska, extending from Anchorage into the Gulf of Alaska
Ken·dall (kénd'l), Edward Calvin (1886–1972), U.S. biochemist who (with Philip S. Hench) isolated cortisone for clinical treatment of rheumatoid arthritis, earning (with Tadeusz Reichstein of Switzerland) the 1950 Nobel prize in physiology and medicine
Kennedy, Edward Moore ("Teddy") (kénidi:), (1932–), U.S. political leader, Democratic senator from Massachusetts (1962–), younger brother of John Fitzgerald Kennedy and Robert F. Kennedy. Despite a back injury (1964) and the controversy surrounding an accident (1969) on Chappaquiddick Island, Mass., in which he drove off a bridge and a woman passenger was drowned, he remained influential in the Senate and in national politics. Considered a liberal, he ran for the Democratic presidential nomination in 1980, but lost to Jimmy Carter
Ken·ne·dy (kénidi:), John Fitzgerald (1917–63), 35th president (1961–3) of the U.S.A., a Democrat. He was the youngest man and the first Roman Catholic ever to be elected president. He published (1956) 'Profiles in Courage', sketches of U.S. political leaders who ignored public opinion to follow their own consciences. As president he introduced his New Frontier program. His tacit encouragement of the unsuccessful Bay of Pigs invasion (1961) of Cuba by anti-Castro forces received general censure, but he was acclaimed for forcing the Soviet Union to withdraw (1962) its missiles from Cuba. He expanded aid to anti-Communist forces in Vietnam, and negotiated with the Soviet Union a limited ban on nuclear testing. He established the Peace Corps and initiated Alliance for Progress. His administration was marked by Civil Rights demonstrations and the first U.S. manned space flights. He was assassinated by Lee Harvey Oswald
Kennedy, Joseph Patrick (1888–1969), U.S. financier. He made a fortune in the motion-

picture industry and in real estate. He was appointed (1937) ambassador to Great Britain by Franklin Roosevelt and served until 1940. He was the father of John Fitzgerald and Robert Francis
Kennedy, Robert Francis (1925–68), U.S. attorney general (1961–4) under Presidents John Kennedy and Lyndon Johnson. He championed civil rights and antitrust, antiracketeering litigation. In the race for the Democratic presidential nomination, he was assassinated by Sirhan Sirhan, a Jordanian immigrant, in Los Angeles
Kennedy Round the negotiations between certain countries (esp. the U.S.A., the European Economic Community, Great Britain, Switzerland, the Scandinavian countries, Yugoslavia, Czechoslovakia and Poland) under the General Agreement on Tariffs and Trade which secured (July 1967) a multilateral reduction of customs tariffs, with implementation of the various programs for completion by Jan. 1, 1972. The name derives from President J. F. Kennedy's authorization (June 1962) by the U.S. Congress to reduce the U.S. tariff if other developed countries agreed to do the same
ken·nel (kén'l) **1.** *n.* (*pl.*) a place where dogs are kept, bred, trained etc. ‖ (*Br.*) a doghouse **2.** *v.t. pres. part.* **ken·nel·ing**, esp. Br. **ken·nel·ling** *past* and *past part.* **ken·neled**, esp. Br. **ken·nelled** to keep or put (a dog) in a kennel [prob. fr. O.N.F.]
Ken·nel (kén'l) *n.* (*mil.*) U.S.S.R. air-to-surface turbojet missile (AS-1), with 100-mi range and both beam-riding and radar direction
Ken·nel·ly (kén'li:), Arthur Edwin (1861–1939), American electrical engineer who predicted the existence of the ionosphere and who also made important contributions to the mathematical methods used in electrical engineering (*HEAVISIDE, *KENNELLY-HEAVISIDE LAYER, *IONOSPHERE)
Kennelly-Heaviside layer the ionosphere, esp. its E. region
Ken·neth I (kéniθ) (*d.* c. 858), king of Scotland (c. 841–58). His victory (c. 841) over the Picts made him the traditional founder of the kingdom of Scotland
ke·no·sis (kinóusis) *n.* (*theol.*) Christ's voluntary giving up of attributes of divinity in taking human flesh and suffering crucifixion **ke·not·ic** (kinótik) *adj.* [Gk *kenōsis*, an emptying]
Ken·sett (kénsit), John Frederick (1816–72), U.S. painter known for his landscapes of New York and New England
Kent (kent), James (1763–1847), U.S. jurist. His written opinions, as compiled in 'Commentaries on American Law' (1826–30), which adopted Roman law principles where the common-law system was deficient, strongly influenced Anglo-American legal development
Kent, Rockwell (1882–1971), U.S. artist, known for his strikingly realistic paintings, notably 'The Trapper' and 'Maine Winter', and for his dramatic illustrations
Kent a county (area 1,525 sq. miles, pop. 1,463,055) in S.E. England. County town: Maidstone. University at Canterbury (1964) ‖ (*hist.*) a kingdom of AngloSaxon England, settled (5th c.) by the Jutes. It was the dominant kingdom (late 6th c.) under Ethelbert and was the center of Augustine's mission
Ken·tish (kéntiʃ) *adj.* of Kent, England, or its inhabitants [O.E. *Centisc* ult. fr. L. *Cantia*, Kent]
kent·ledge (kéntledʒ) *n.* bars of pig iron used as permanent ballast [fr. F. *quintelage*]
Ken·tuck·y (kəntʌki:) (*abbr.* Ky.) a state (area 40,395 sq. miles, pop. 3,667,000) in east central U.S.A. Capital: Frankfort. Chief city: Louisville. The east is in the Appalachians and the remainder is largely undulating lowland. Agriculture: tobacco, corn and fodder crops, horse breeding, cattle and dairy products. Resources: coal, oil and natural gas, fluorspar, clays. Industries: food processing, machinery, chemicals, metal products, tobacco products. State university (1865) at Lexington. Kentucky was settled in the 18th c., and became (1792) the 15th state
Ken·ya (kí:njə, kénjə) a state (area 224,960 sq. miles, pop. 17,142,000) in E. Africa. Capital: Nairobi. People and language: Bantu (70%, incl. Kikuyu, Kamba, Luhya, Nyika and others), Nilotic (Luo), Nilo-Hamitic (Masai, Nandi, Kipsigi, Suk, Turkana) and Hamitic (Somali, Galla) groups, with 2% Indians and Pakistanis, 1% English and a small Arabic minority. Lan-

CONCISE PRONUNCIATION KEY: (**a**) æ, c*a*t; ɑ, c*a*r; ɑ ɔ f*aw*n; ei, sn*a*ke. (**e**) e, h*e*n; i:, sh*ee*p; iə, d*ee*r; ɛə, b*ea*r. (**i**) i, f*i*sh; ai, t*i*ger; əː, b*i*rd. (**o**) o, *o*x; au, c*ow*; ou, g*oa*t; u, p*oo*r; ɔi, r*oy*al. (**u**) ʌ, d*u*ck; u, b*u*ll; uː, g*oo*se; ə, b*a*cillus; juː, c*u*be. x, lo*ch*; θ, *th*ink; ð, bo*th*er; z, *Z*en; ʒ, corsa*g*e; dʒ, sava*g*e; ŋ, oranguta*ng*; j, *y*ak; ʃ, *fi*sh; tʃ, fet*ch*; 'l, rabb*le*; 'n, redd*en*. Complete pronunciation key appears inside front cover.

guages: Swahili, English, Arabic, Kenyan languages. Religion: mainly local African religions, 12% Christian, with Moslem and Hindu minorities. The fertile coastal strip (Temborai) gives way to the Nyika country (all N. Kenya and the southeast), a region of scrubland pasture (1,000–5,000 ft) with a cultivated belt along River Tana. The Great Rift Valley (30–40 miles wide) runs north-south between the highlands (5,000–10,000 ft) of the center and southeast, which culminate in the Mt Elgon massif (14,178 ft) on the Uganda border, and the Mt Kenya massif (17,040 ft) and Aberdare Mtns (13,000 ft) in the center. Average temperatures (F.): Mombasa 76°–82°, Nairobi 56°–79°. Rainfall: Mombasa 48 ins, Nairobi 32 ins, highlands 40–100 ins, elsewhere under 15 ins. Livestock: cattle, hogs, sheep, goats. Agricultural products: coffee, cereals, sisal, tea, pyrethrum, sugar, coconuts, cashew nuts, cotton, peanuts, sesame, potatoes, beans, wattle, dairy products, hides and skins, lumber. Minerals: sodium carbonate, copper, salt, gold, diatomite, mullite. Manufactures: limestone products, cement, flour, leather, footwear, wattle extract. Exports: coffee, sisal fiber, tea, petroleum products, pyrethrum, meat, hides and skins, sodium carbonate. Imports: machinery, fuel oils and gasoline, metal goods, cotton fabrics, vehicles, paper, chemicals, iron and steel. Port: Mombasa (at Kilindini, 2 miles away). University College of the University of East Africa at Nairobi (1956). Monetary unit: shilling (100 cents). HISTORY. The coastal region was settled (7th c.) by Arab and Persian traders, and controlled (16th and 17th cc.) by the Portuguese. By 1740 Arabs had expelled the latter. A British trading company gained control (1888). The area became a British protectorate (1895), and then became the Crown Colony of Kenya (1920). Increasing nationalism led to the Mau Mau uprising (1952–9). Kenya became independent (Dec. 12, 1963) under the leadership of Kenyatta, and became (Dec. 12, 1964) a republic within the British Commonwealth. Kenyatta remained president until his death (1978) and was succeeded by Daniel arap Moi. Land reforms undertaken in 1963 had failed by the early 1980's, and the pressure of a growing populace on agriculture led to an attempted coup (1982)

Kenya, Mt an extinct volcano (17,040 ft) in central Kenya, just south of the equator

Ken·ya·pith·e·cus (kenjəpíθəkəs) *n.* a humanoid ape said to have lived 14–20 million years ago discovered near Lake Victoria c. 1962 by Louis S. B. Leakey

Ken·yat·ta (kenjátə), Jomo (c. 1893–1978), Kikuyu nationalist leader and Kenya statesman. Imprisoned (1953–9) as a leader of the Mau Mau rebellion, he was elected president (1961) of the Kenya African National Union (K.A.N.U.). He became independent Kenya's first prime minister (1963) and president of the republic of Kenya (1964)

Ke·ogh Act plan (kí:ou) a plan, available since 1963, under the Self-employed Individual's Tax Retirement Act (Keogh Act), which permits a self-employed individual to establish and to make tax-deductible contributions to a formal retirement plan, called an IRA account

Ke·phal·li·ni·a (kefuli:ní:ə) *CEPHALONIA

ke·pi (kéipi:, képi:) *pl.* **ke·pis** *n.* a circular flat-topped hat with a horizontal peak worn by some French officers, policemen, officials etc. [F. *képi* fr. G. Swiss *käppi* dim. of *kappe*, cap]

Kep·ler (képlər), Johannes (1571–1630), German astronomer and mathematician. He worked with Tycho Brahe and formulated three laws of planetary motion (*KEPLERS LAWS). These form the basis for all modern planetary astronomy, and led Newton to his discovery of the law of gravitation. Kepler published his findings in 'Astronomia nova' (1609) and 'De harmonice mundi' (1619)

Kepler's laws three laws of planetary motion established by Kepler which state that: **1.** every planet has an elliptical orbit with the center of the sun as one focus **2.** the radius vector of a planet moves over equal areas of the ellipse in equal intervals of time **3.** the ratio of the square of a planetary year to the cube of its mean distance from the sun is identical for all planets

Ke·pone (kí:poun) *n.* (*chem.*) a pesticide ingredient suspected of being carcinogenic; alleged to have caused serious neurological damage in workers who helped in its production

kept *past* and *past part.* of KEEP

Ker·ak (kéruk, kerák) (or El Kerak, *ancient* Kir Moab, called Krak by the Crusaders) a town (pop. 4,000) of S. central Jordan. It was the citadel of Moab. Frankish castle (1136)

Ke·ra·la (kéirələ) a state (area 15,003 sq. miles, pop. 23,483,000) in S.W. India bordering the Arabian Sea. There is a fertile plain along the coast rising inland to the Western Ghats. Agriculture, forestry and mining

ker·a·tin (kérətin) *n.* a fibrous protein forming the basis of epidermal structures, e.g. horn, hair, nails etc. [fr. Gk *keras* (*keratos*), horn]

ker·a·tose (kérətous) *adj.* (of certain sponges) having a horny skeleton [fr. Gk *keras* (*keratos*), horn]

kerb (kə:rb) *n.* *CURB (edging bordering a street pavement) [var. of CURB]

kerbstone *CURBSTONE

Kerch (kertʃ), a seaport and industrial center (pop. 159,000) of the E. Crimea, Ukraine, U.S.S.R.

ker·chief (kə́:rtʃif) *n.* a cloth, usually folded to a triangular shape, worn by a woman over her head [M.E. *curchef, kerchef* fr. O.F.]

Kerch Strait a shallow strait (25 miles long, and at its narrowest 2 miles wide) connecting the Sea of Azov and the Black Sea

Ke·ren·ski (kərénski:), Aleksandr Feodorovich (1881–1970), Russian revolutionary leader, naturalized American. A prominent member of the duma (1912–17), he was briefly premier (July–Nov. 1917) but was overthrown by the Bolsheviks and fled (Nov. 1917)

kerf (kə:rf) *n.* a notch, slit or groove made by an ax or saw [O.E. *cyrf*]

Ker·gue·len (kə́:rgələn) an archipelago comprising some 300 islands (land area 1,400 sq. miles) in the S. Indian Ocean, part of the French Southern and Antarctic Territories: research stations, seal-oil plant

Ker·mad·ec Islands (kərmǽdək) a group of islands (area 13 sq. miles) in the S. Pacific, 600 miles northeast of New Zealand, of which they are a dependency

Ker·man (kərmán) a city (pop. 140,309) of S.E. Iran, at 6,000 ft, noted for its rugs, shawls and brasswork. Mosque (11th c.)

Ker·man·shah (kərmánʃá) a communications center (pop. 290,861) of W. Iran: rug weaving, food processing, petroleum refining. It is the historic capital of the region of the same name

ker·mes (kə́:rmi:z) *pl.* **ker·mes** *n.* the dried bodies of the pregnant female of *Kermes*, fam. *Kermesidae*, a genus of scale found on the kermes oak from which a red dye is made ‖ this dye ‖ the kermes oak [fr. F. *kermès* fr. Arab. and Pers. *qirmiz*]

kermes oak *Quercus coccinea*, fam. *Fagaceae*, a small Mediterranean evergreen on which the kermes insect is found

kern (kə:rn) *n.* (*printing*) part of a letter (e.g. the tail of 'y' or head of 'f') which projects beyond the body of the metal type [F. *carne*, projecting angle]

ker·nel (kə́:rn'l) *n.* the soft, usually edible, innermost part of a seed ‖ the whole grain of a cereal ‖ the center, or essential part, of an argument etc. ‖ (*math.*) a known function *K* of two variables that appears in an integral equation. It may have any of the following properties: (1) symmetric: $K(x,z)=KL(z,x)$; (2) Hermitian: $K(x,z)=K*(z,x)$, where * indicates complex conjugate; (3) singular: $K(x,z)$ has a discontinuity [O.E. *cyrnel* dim. of *corn*, grain]

kernel sentence (*grammar*) a basic sentence containing noun, verb, and adjective phrase or noun phrase

ker·o·sene, ker·o·sine (kérəsi:n, kǽrəsi:n, kérəsi:n, kærəsí:n) *n.* (*Am.*=*Br.* paraffin oil) any of various mixtures of similar hydrocarbons which are liquid to semisolid and are used as fuels and solvents [fr. Gk *kēros*, wax]

Ker·ou·ac (kéru:æk), Jack (1922–69), American writer whose novel 'On the Road' (1957) and other writings depicted the beat generation

Kerr cell (kar, kə:r) (*phys.*) a cell for obtaining birefringence by establishing a high potential difference between metal electrodes sealed into a glass cell containing pure nitrobenzene [after John *Kerr* (1824-1907), Scottish physicist]

Ker·ry (kéri:) the western county (area 1,815 sq. miles, pop. 122,770) of Munster province, Irish Republic. County seat: Tralee

Ker·ry (kéri:) *n.* (*mil.*) U.S.S.R. air-to-surface missile (AS-7) for Fencer aircraft

Kerry Blue Terrier a terrier of a large Irish breed with a soft, short, blue-gray coat [after KERRY, Ireland]

Kes·sels·dorf, Battle of (késəlzdɔrf) a Prussian victory (Dec. 14, 1745) over Austria and Saxony in the War of the Austrian Succession

Kes·te·ven, the Parts of (kestí:vən) an administrative county (area 724 sq. miles. pop. 547,560) of Lincolnshire, England. Administrative center: Sleaford

kes·trel (késtrəl) *n.* *Falco tinnunculus*, fam. *Falconidae*, a small European falcon which hovers in midair against the wind, watching for prey [etym. doubtful]

ketch (ketʃ) *n.* a two-masted sailing vessel, rigged fore and aft, the mizzenmast being stepped further forward than in a yawl [fr. older *cache* perh. fr. CATCH]

ketch·up, cat·sup (kétʃəp, kǽtʃəp) *n.* a sauce prepared from tomatoes, spices etc. [prob. fr. Chin. *kôechiap* or *kêtsiap*, tomato sauce]

ke·to·glu·tar·ic acid (ki:touglu:túrik) (*biochem.*) a salt or acid produced in the metabolism of proteins or carbohydrates

ke·tone (kí:toun) *n.* (*chem.*) one of a series of organic compounds of the general formula R-CO-R, in which the carbonyl group is united with two monovalent hydrocarbon radicals [G. *keton*, a modification of acetone]

ke·to·sis (kitóusis) *n.* the presence of an excess of ketones, esp. acetone, in the system (due to diabetes etc.) [Mod. L. *ket-* fr. KETONE+-*osis*, increase]

Kett (ket), Robert (*d.* 1549), English rebel. He led a revolt (1549) against enclosures and stormed Norwich, but was defeated and executed

ket·tle (két'l) *n.* a teakettle ‖ a large metal cooking utensil **a pretty** (or **fine**) **kettle of fish** a state of affairs involving confusion, embarrassment etc. [O.E. *cetel* prob. fr. L. *catillus*]

ket·tle·drum (két'ldrʌm) *n.* (*mus.*) a large drum having a hemispherical brass or copper shell and a parchment drumhead

kev·el (kévəl) *n.* (*naut.*) a belaying cleat or peg, usually in pairs [O.N.F. *keville*, F. *cheville*, pin, peg]

Kevlar (kévlər) *n.* trade name for DuPont bullet-deflecting fabric used for protective vests

Ke·wee·naw·an (ki:wi:nɔ́ən) *adj.* of or relating to a division of the Proterozoic [after *Keeweenan* Peninsula, a peninsula of N.W. Michigan extending into L. Superior]

Key (ki:), Francis Scott (1779–1843), American lawyer. He wrote the words of the U.S. national anthem 'The Star Spangled Banner' (1814). officially adopted in 1931

key (ki:) *n.* a reef or low island, esp. a coral island off S. Florida [fr. Span. *cayo*, shoal]

key 1. *pl.* **keys** *n.* an instrument for locking and unlocking a lock ‖ an instrument used to wind up a spring, e.g. in a clock ‖ a pin, wedge etc. of metal or wood driven into component parts of a machine, joint etc. to fasten or tighten them ‖ a slotted instrument for opening e.g. a can of sardines ‖ a device which fastens together and finishes off something, e.g. a keystone ‖ (*building*) the first coat of plaster which is applied to the laths, forming a rigid base for an outer coat, or any roughening process on a surface to which plaster etc. is to be applied ‖ (*fig.*) something which affords or prohibits entrance, possession etc., *the key to the Mediterranean* ‖ something which enables someone to explain, solve or decipher a problem, dilemma, code etc. ‖ (*biol.*) a table listing the chief characteristics of groups etc. to facilitate the identification of a specimen ‖ (*mus.*) a series or system of notes, related in frequency to that of a particular note, *the key of B minor* ‖ (*mus.*) the lever which opens or closes a hole in some wind instruments (e.g. oboe) or which actuates a hammer or plectrum in a keyboard instrument ‖ the disk which actuates a printing lever, e.g. in a typewriter, Linotype machine etc. ‖ (*elec.*) a switch or plug which opens or cuts a circuit ‖ a tone or style of writing or expression, *in a plaintive key* ‖ (*pl.*) the ecclesiastical authority vested in the pope as the successor to St. Peter **2.** *adj.* of critical importance, *a key industry* [O.E. *cāeg* and *cǣge*, ult. origin unknown]

key *v.t. pres. part.* **key·ing** *past* and *past part.* **keyed** to furnish with a key or keys ‖ to attune, *key your remarks to the mood of the audience* ‖ to roughen or pit (a surface) to help it to hold applied plaster etc. **to key up** to make nervously tense [M.E. *keige, keigen, keie, keien* fr. *keige*, key n.]

key·board (ki:bɔrd, kí:bourd) **1.** *n.* the keys of a piano, organ, typewriter etc. **2.** *v.t.* (*printing*) to set (copy) by using a composing machine with a keyboard ‖ (*computer*) to use the keyboard to record data

key club a private club established to provide liquor and/or entertainment, esp. to avoid curfew or licensing

key·er (kí:ər) *n.* (*electr.*) device that increases or decreases a transmitter's amplitude or frequency according to the material to be sent

key·hole (kí:houl) *n.* the small hole through which a key is inserted into a lock

Keynes (keinz), John Maynard, 1st Baron Keynes of Tilton (1883–1946), British economist and financial expert. His 'General Theory of Employment, Interest and Money' (1936) gave a new analysis of the trade cycle, stressing changes in investment (i.e. buying of capital goods) as the key to changes in total demand. As measures of economic control, he advocated interest-rate changes, public works to ensure full employment, and income redistribution such that the purchasing power of consumers should grow proportionally with the development of the means of production. As leader of the British delegation to the Bretton Woods Conference (1944), he played a major role in the formation of the International Monetary Fund and the World Bank

key·note (kí:nout) *n.* the tone to which the other tones of a musical key are related by their frequencies ‖ the basic idea or principle informing a speech, policy etc.

key punch the keyboard machine that cuts the holes in punched cards **key-punch** *v.t.* to cut holes in with a key punch

key·set (kí:set) *n.* a keyboard

key signature (*mus.*) one or more sharps or flats placed after the clef on the staff to indicate the key

key·stone (kí:stoun) *n.* (*archit.*) the central stone in an arch, bearing the lateral and vertical stresses and binding the structure of the arch together

key·stroke (kí:strouk) *n.* the action of striking a keyboard symbol

Key West city of Florida on the continental limits of the U.S.A., a winter resort (pop. 24,382) on an island in the Florida Keys: fisheries, cigar making, tourism

K·fir (kə́fiər) *n.* (*mil.*) Israeli fighter plane (Hebrew: Lion Cub) with speed of Mach 2.2, carrying 30-mm cannon, seven hardpoints for missiles, infrared homing for air-to-air missiles

KH-11 (*mil.*) U.S.S.R. spy satellite

Kha·ba·rovsk (xəbárʌfsk) the capital (pop. 545,000) of Khabarovsk territory in N.E. Siberia, U.S.S.R., a railroad center: oil refining, engineering industries

Kha·cha·tu·ri·an (kətʃətúəriːən, xɑtʃɑturjɑ́n), Aram Ilich (1903–   ), Russian composer and conductor. His work combines folk melodies with the declamation typical of much modern Russian music

Khair·pur (káirpur) a region (former princely state) of W. central Pakistan, bordering the Thar ‖ its capital (pop. 18,000)

khak·i (kǽki, káki) *pl.* **khak·is** *n.* a light yellowish-brown color ‖ the cloth of this color, esp. as used for the uniforms of soldiers [Urdu *khākī* fr. *khāk*, dust]

Kha·li·fa (kəlí:fə) the title assumed by Abdullah et Taaisha (c. 1846–99), Sudanese Moslem leader. Succeeding the Mahdi (1885), he established his capital at Omdurman, where he was heavily defeated (1898) by an Anglo-Egyptian army under Kitchener

Kha·ma (kámə), Sir Seretse (1921–80), Botswana statesman, chief of the Bamangwato. His marriage to a white woman in 1948 led to his exile (1950–6). He was the first prime minister (1965–6) of Bechuanaland, which he led to independence as Botswana in 1966

kham·sin (kǽmsin, kæmsí:n) *n.* a hot, sand-laden Egyptian wind from the Sahara blowing usually in spring for about 50 days (cf. SIROCCO) [Arab. fr. *khamsín*, fifty]

Khan, Ayub Mohammed *AYUB KHAN

khan (kɑn, kæn) *n.* a caravanserai [Arab. *khān*, inn]

khan *n.* (*hist.*) the title of Chinese emperors of the Middle Ages who also ruled Tatar, Turkish and Mongol tribes ‖ a title of nobility, or a local ruler or official in Pakistan, Afghanistan, Iran and the like ‖ the office or authority of a khan [Turki *khān*, lord]

Kha·rag·pur (kárəgpur) a town (pop. 148,000) in W. Bengal, N.E. India, a technical research center

Khar·kov (kárkɒf, xárkəf) the largest industrial center (pop. 1,464,000) of the Ukraine, U.S.S.R., supplied with coal and steel from the Donbas: heavy engineering, chemical industries

Khar·toum (kɑrtú:m) the capital (pop. 400,000) of the Sudan, a port on the Blue Nile near its junction with the White Nile. It was the scene of Gordon's unsuccessful stand against the Mahdi (1885), and was recaptured by Kitchener (1898)

Kha·zar (kəzár) *n.* a member of an ancient Tatar people who established an empire in S.E. Russia (7th–early 11th cc.)

khe·dive (kədí:v) *n.* (*hist.*) the title conferred on the viceroys of Egypt (1867–1914) by the sultan of Turkey [F. *khédive* fr. Turk.]

Khing·an Mtns (ʃiŋán) two mountain ranges of N.E. China, north and west of the Manchurian plain, which is separated from the Amur valley by the Lesser Khingan (*Chin.* Hsiao-hsing-an, highest point 3,600 ft) and from the Gobi Desert by the Great Khingan (*Chin.* Ta-hsing-an, 4,000–8,000 ft)

Khmer (kmer) *n.* a member of an ancient race of Cambodia. The Khmer kingdom, with its capital at Angkor Thom, reached a high level of culture (9th and 10th cc.) before falling (1430) to the Thais ‖ a language of the Mon-Khmer family

Khmer Republic *CAMBODIA

Khmer Rouge armed group supporting forces of United National Cambodian front, sponsored by North Vietnam and China during 1974–1975

Khoi·san (kɔ́isən) *n.* a family of African languages including Bushman and Hottentot ‖ a member of an African people speaking a Khoisan language

Khomeini (koumeiní:), Ayatollah Ruhollah (1901–   ), Iranian leader of Shiite Moslems and head of Iran (1979–   ). He led the anti-Shah movement from exile from 1963 and took over in 1979, when the Shah had left Iran, declaring himself leader for life. He supported the militant students who took hostages at the U.S. embassy (1979–81), the war with Iraq (1980–   ) and opposed freedom of speech and Western customs

Khos·ru I (xɒsrú:) (d. 579), king of Persia (531–79), who extended his rule to Bactria (560), the Yemen (570) and parts of Armenia and Caucasia. He reformed the tax system and encouraged the arts

Kho·tan (xóután) (*Chin.* Hotien) an oasis town (pop. 134,000) in S.W. Sinkiang, China: silk weaving, carpets

khoums (ku:mz) *n.* unit of currency in Mauritania, equal to 1/5 ougiya

Khrush·chev (krúʃtʃɒf, xruʃtʃɒ́f), Nikita Sergeyevich (1894–1971), Russian statesman, premier of the Soviet Union (1958–64), first secretary of the Soviet Communist party (1953–64). He rose rapidly to power after Stalin's death (1953), ousting possible rivals and reversing Stalinist policy until the Hungarian revolt (1956). His administration saw the growth of the U.S.S.R.'s industrial and agricultural strength, and outstanding developments in space research. A skilled diplomat, he traveled widely, but his insistence on peaceful coexistence led to a breach (1963) with the Chinese Communist party and contributed to his downfall (1964)

Khu·fu (kú:fu) (or Cheops) Egyptian king (c. 2590–c. 2568 B.C.) of the 4th dynasty, the builder of the largest of the pyramids at Giza

khur·ta (kú:rta) *n.* East Indian garment consisting of long, loose-fitting collarless shirt

Khy·ber Pass (káibər) a narrow 28-mile mountain pass (summit 3,370 ft) connecting Kabul, Afghanistan with Peshawar, Pakistan. It was the scene of bitter fighting (1838–42 and 1878–80) between the British and the Afghans

kHz (*abbr.*) for kiloherz

Kiang·ling (dʒjáŋlíŋ) (formerly Kingchow) a walled town (pop. 300,000) in Hupei, E. China, on the Yangtze. It was the capital of the Chou kingdom (8th–5th cc. B.C.)

Kiang·si (dʒjáɴsí:) a province (area 77,281 sq. miles, pop. 32,290,000) of S.E. China. Capital: Nanchang

Kiang·su (dʒjánsú:) a province (pop. 58,930,000) of central E. China on the mouth of the Yangtze. Capital: Nanking. Chief city: Shanghai

Kiang·tu (dʒjántú:) (or Yangchow) a town (pop. 127,000) in N. Kiangsu, China, on the Grand Canal, with engineering and food-processing industries. Its walls and palaces date back to the 6th c., when it was one of the three capitals of the Sui dynasty

Kiao·chow (dʒjáudʒóu) a territory (200 sq. miles) on the S.E. Shantung peninsula, E. China, leased to Germany (1898) for 99 years, taken by Japan (1914), and restored to China (1922). Chief town: Tsingtao

kib·butz (kibúts) *pl.* **kib·but·zim** (kibutsí:m) *n.* a collective farm or settlement in Israel characterized by cooperative ownership and communal organization [fr. Mod. Heb. *qibbūs* fr. Heb., a gathering]

Ki·bei (kí:béi) *pl.* **Ki·bei, Ki·beis** *n.* a native American citizen born of immigrant Japanese parents and educated mostly in Japan (cf. NISEI, cf. ISSEI, cf. SANSEI) [Jap.]

Kib·lah (kíblə) *n.* the direction of the Kaaba, towards which Moslems turn in prayer [Arab. *qiblah*]

kick (kik) *n.* the indented base of a glass bottle [origin unknown]

kick 1. *v.t.* to hit (something) with the foot voluntarily or involuntarily ‖ to move (something) by hitting it with the foot ‖ (*football, soccer*) to score (a goal or point) by propelling the ball thus ‖ *v.i.* to strike out with the foot ‖ (of a firearm) to recoil when fired ‖ (*pop.*) to protest or complain, *he kicked when asked to work another hour* **to be alive and kicking** (*pop.*) to be well and strong **to kick around** to treat roughly ‖ to lead a wandering life without roots **to kick oneself** to heap reproaches upon oneself **to kick one's heels** (*Br.*) to wait about in forced idleness **to kick off** to begin a game of soccer by kicking the ball ‖ (*pop.*) to begin an activity, discussion etc. **to kick up** to cause (a fuss, row etc.) **2.** *n.* the act of kicking or an instance of this ‖ a jolt from a firearm recoil ‖ (*soccer* etc.) an opportunity to kick ‖ (*soccer* etc.) a person with respect to his ability to kick the ball ‖ (*soccer* etc.) power in kicking ‖ (*pop.*) a pleasant stimulus or thrill of pleasure [M.E. *kike, kyke*]

kick·back (kíkbæk) *n.* a percentage of the sale price given secretly to the middleman or the purchaser by the seller ‖ a money exaction made by someone in a position to give or withhold favors

kick·er (kíkər) *n.* (*colloq.*) the offsetting factor generally not evident

Kicking Horse Pass a mountain pass in the Canadian Rockies, on the boundary between Alberta and S.E. British Columbia

kick·off (kíkɒf, kíkɒf) *n.* the act of beginning something, e.g. a football game

kick out (*surfing*) action of pressing the rear of a surfboard to turn it so as to surmount a wave

kick·stand (kíkstænd) *n.* a swivel rod prop for a stationary motorcycle or bicycle

kick starter a motorcycle starter consisting of a foot-operated lever

kick·y (kíki) *adj.* (*colloq.*) of something stimulating a thrill or kick —**kick** *n.* thrill, e.g., *Get a kick out of it*

kid (kid) *pres. part.* **kid·ding** *past* and *past part.* **kid·ded** *v.t.* (*pop.*) to deceive ‖ (*pop.*) to tease (someone) good-naturedly ‖ *v.i.* (*pop.*) to tease someone or something good-naturedly ‖ (*pop.*) to joke, esp. to say something without really meaning it [perh. fr. KID n.]

kid 1. *n.* a young goat, esp. less than one year old ‖ kidskin ‖ the young of various other animals, e.g. an antelope ‖ (*pop.*) a child **2.** *v.i. pres. part.* **kid·ding** *past* and *past part.* **kid·ded** (of goats) to give birth **3.** *adj.* made of kidskin ‖ (*pop.*) younger, *a kid brother* [M.E. *kide, kede, kid* prob. fr. O.N. *kith*]

Kidd (kid), William (c. 1645–1701), Scottish pirate. Despite a commission from the English government to loot French ships, he was tried for piracy and murder, and hanged. He became famous in legend as 'Captain Kidd'

Kid·der·min·ster (kídərminstər) *n.* an ingrain carpet [after *Kidderminster*, Worcestershire, England, where it was originally made]

kid·dle (kíd'l) *n.* a dam or weir in a river, or a set of stakes in the sea, equipped with nets for catching fish [A.F. *kidel, kydel*, O.F. *quidel*]

kid gloves gloves made of kidskin **to handle with kid gloves** to treat with great caution or tact

kid·nap (kídnæp) *pres. part.* **kid·nap·ping,**
kid·nap·ing *past and past part.* **kid·napped,**
kid·naped *v.t.* to take away and hold (a person)
by force [KID, child+obs. *nap*, to snatch, seize]
kid·ney (kídni:) *pl.* **kid·neys** *n.* one of a pair of
abdominal organs (*ABDOMEN) in all verte-
brates. They filter impurities from the blood
and excrete them as urine. They also help to
maintain the acidity and other important
chemical characteristics of the blood at a constant level. Failure of kidney function leads to
an accumulation of impurities and other disorders of the blood (*UREMIA). Kidney diseases
include nephritis, infection, kidney stones and
tumors || (*rhet.*) kind, sort [origin unknown]
kidney bean the seed of any bean plant developed from *Phaseolus vulgaris,* fam. *Papiliona-
ceae* || any dark red kidneyshaped bean || (esp.
Br.) the scarlet runner
kidney machine (*med.*) device for kidney dialysis, for removal of toxic substances
kidney stone a small mineral deposit which
crystallizes out of the urine usually as a result
of infection or malnutrition
kid·skin (kídskin) *n.* the skin of young goats
used as leather
Kiel (ki:l) the capital (pop. 256,500) of Schleswig-Holstein, West Germany, a port on the
Baltic. Industries: fishing, shipbuilding, engineering. University (1665). It is connected by
the North Sea by the Kiel canal (built 1887–95,
enlarged 1909–14), which cuts across Schleswig-Holstein to the Elbe estuary (61 miles)
Kiel·ce (kjéltse) a city (pop. 184,000) in S. central Poland: metal, chemical and marble industries
kier (kiər) *n.* a large vat in which textiles are
bleached etc. [etym. doubtful]
Kier·ke·gaard (kíərkəgard, kíərkəgɔr), Sören
Aaby (1813–55), Danish philosopher. His philosophy is rooted in the individual as subject.
He examined the philosophical principles of
Christianity as the religion of the individual
soul. He wrote of man's struggle for freedom,
and his dread, anguish and loneliness in the
face of this freedom. He is generally regarded as
a leading precursor of existentialism. Among
his works are 'Either/Or' (1843) and 'Concept of
Dread' (1844)
kie·sel·guhr, kie·sel·gur (kí:zəlguər) *n.* porous
or loose diatomite [G.]
Ki·ev (kí:jəf) the capital (pop. 2,355,000) of the
Ukraine, U.S.S.R., a port on the Dnieper River,
and a commercial, industrial and transport center. Founded in the 9th c., it was the capital of a
Varangian state from 988 until its decline in
the 12th c., and was the ecclesiastical capital
(1051–1240) of the Russian Orthodox Church.
It was destroyed by the Mongols (1240). Byzantine cathedral (St Sophia, 11th c.), monastery
(1108)
kif·i (kífi:) *n.* in North Africa, an opiate
Ki·ga·li (ki:gáli:) the capital (pop. 117,749) and
airport of Rwanda, in the central plateau
Ki·ku·chi lines (kəkú:tʃi:) (*electr.*) diffraction
pattern created when electron beams pass
through a crystalline solid; used to examine the
structure of the crystal
Ki·ku·yu (kikú:ju:) *n.* a member of a chiefly ag-
ricultural Bantu tribe in Kenya || the Bantu
language of these people
Kil·dare (kildéər) a southeastern county (area
654 sq. miles, pop. 104,122) of Leinster province, Irish Republic. County seat: Naas
kil·der·kin (kíldərkin) *n.* a small cask [corrup.
of M. Du. *kinderkin*]
Kil·i·man·ja·ro (kiləmənʤárou) the highest
mountain in Africa. It comprises two snow-covered peaks, Kibo (19,317 ft) and Mawenzi
(16,900 ft). It is in N.E. Tanzania near the
Kenya border
Kil·ken·ny (kilkéni:) a southeastern county
(area 796 sq. miles, pop. 70,806) of Leinster
province, Irish Republic. County seat: Kilkenny
kill (kil) **1.** *v.t.* to cause life to cease in || to
deprive of further existence or effectiveness,
this has killed my hopes || to defeat or veto (leg-
islation) || (*pop.*) to cut off power in (an engine,
machine etc.) || (*pop.*) to cause (someone) to be
overcome with laughter, admiration etc. ||
(*racket games*) to play (a ball) so that one's oppo-
nent can make no effective stroke || (*Br.,* soccer)
to stop (the ball) dead in play || *v.i.* to destroy
life, *to kill for money* **dressed to kill** showily
overdressed || dressed to make a stunning im-
pression **to kill time** to occupy oneself with
some activity in order to pass time **2.** *n.* the act

of killing || the animal or animals killed, *a good
kill* [origin unknown]
Kil·lar·ney (kilárni:) a town (pop. 7,678) in
Kerry, Munster province, Irish Republic, near
the lakes of Killarney, a tourist center
Killarney *adj.* (*geol.*) of a North American
mountain-making episode during the late Proterozoic period [after the *Killarney* Mtns in
Ontario, Canada]
kill·er (kílər) *n.* someone who has killed or is
likely to kill || something (e.g. illness, poison)
likely or certain to kill
killer whale *Orcinus orca,* fam. *Delphinidae,* a
large, fierce whale that preys on seals, large
fish etc.
kil·lick (kílik) *n.* a heavy stone or small anchor
used to moor a fishing boat [origin unknown]
kill·ing (kíliŋ) **1.** *n.* the act of someone or some-
thing that kills or an instance of this || (*pop.*) a
sudden success or stroke of luck, esp. as a result
of financial speculation **2.** *adj.* able to kill ||
(*pop.*) exhausting, *a killing pace* || (*pop.*) irre-
sistibly funny
kill·joy (kílʤɔi) *n.* someone who spoils the fun or
happiness of another
kil·lock (kílək) *n.* a killick
kill probability (*mil.*) a measure of the probability of destroying a target
kill ratio (*mil.*) proportion of casualties to total
number involved or to adversary casualties *also*
kill rate Cf BODY COUNT
Kil·mer (kílmər), (Alfred) Joyce (1886–1918),
U.S. poet, best known for his poem 'Trees'
(1913)
kiln (kil, kiln) *n.* a chamber of brick etc., with a
fire, used to burn, bake or dry [O.E. *cylene* fr. L.
culina, kitchen]
kiln-dry (kíldrai, kílndrai) *pres. part.*
kiln-dry·ing *past and past part.* **kiln-dried** *v.t.*
to dry in a kiln
kil·o (kílou, kí:lou) *pl.* **kil·os** *n.* *KILOGRAM
kilo- (kilou) *prefix* a thousand [F. fr. Gk *chil-
ioi*]
ki·lo·bar (kíləbɑr) *n.* unit of 1,000 bars of pressure *also* k bar *abbr.* **kb**
kil·o·baud (kíləbɔd) *n.* (*computer*) transmission
rate unit of 1,000 bits of data per second *abbr.* **k
Bd**
kil·o·bit (kíləbit) *n.* (*computer*) unit of 1,000 bits
of information Cf GIGABIT, MEGABIT, TERABIT
kil·o·cal·o·rie (kíləkæləri:) *n.* a kilogram calorie
kil·o·cy·cle (kíləsaik'l) *n.* (*abbr.* kc.) a unit of
frequency equal to 1,000 cycles per second
kil·o·gram, kil·o·gramme (kíləgræm) *n.* (*abbr.*
kg. or shortened to kilo) the standard metric
unit of mass, defined as the mass of a standard
piece of platinum-iridium alloy preserved in
Paris (=2.2046 lb.)
kilogram calorie 1,000 calories, the heat required to raise the temperature of 1 kilogram of
water 1°C
kilogramme *KILOGRAM
kil·o·hertz (kí:ləhə:rts) *n.* (*abbr.* kHz) a radio-
frequency unit equal to 1000 cycles per second
kil·o·li·ter, *Br.* **kil·o·li·tre** (kíləli:tər) *n.* (*abbr.*
kl.) 1,000 liters
kil·o·me·ter, *Br.* **kil·o·me·tre** (kíləmí:tər,
kilómitər) *n.* (*abbr.* km.) 1,000 meters
kil·o·oer·sted (kílouə:rstəd) *n.* 1,000 oersted, a
unit of electrical intensity
kilorad *KRAD
kil·o·ton (kíltəʌn) *n.* one thousand tons || an ex-
plosive force equal to that of 1000 tons of TNT
kiloton weapon (*mil.*) a nuclear weapon, the
yield of which is measured in terms of thousands of tons of trinitrotoluene explosive equivalents, producing yields from 1 to 999 kilotons
Cf NOMINAL WEAPON, SUBKILOTON WEAPON
kil·o·volt (kíləvoult) *n.* (*abbr.* kv.) a unit of electromotive force equal to 1,000 volts
kil·o·watt (kíləwɒt) *n.* (*abbr.* kw.) a unit of
power equal to 1,000 watts
kil·o·watt-hour (kíləwɒtáuər) *n.* a unit of work,
being the work done in one hour at the rate of
1,000 watts
kilt (kilt) *n.* a heavily pleated knee-length tartan skirt worn esp. by the Highlanders of
Scotland [fr. older *kilt* v., to pleat vertically,
prob. fr. Scand.]
kil·ter (kíltər) *n.* (in phrase) **out of kilter** not in
order, not in good condition [origin unknown]
Ki·lung (kí:lúŋ) (also Chilung, formerly Kirun),
the principal port (pop. 145,000) of Formosa, on
the north coast

Kil·wa (kílwɑ) a port (pop. 3,000) of S. Tanzania.
On an island in its bay are ruins of the capital of
the ancient Zenj Empire, founded c. 975
Kim·ber·ley (kímbərli:) a town (pop. 144,923) in
Cape Province, South Africa, a great diamond
center
Kim·mel (kíməl), Husband Edward (1882–
1969), U.S. admiral who was commander in
chief of the U.S. Pacific fleet at Pearl Harbor,
Hawaii, at the time of the Japanese air attack
(1941). He was retired (1942) when a board of
inquiry found him guilty of 'dereliction of duty',
but a Congressional Investigating Committee
quashed (1946) the charge, finding him guilty
only of errors in judgment
ki·mo·no (kəmóunə, kəmóunou) *pl.* **ki·mo·nos**
n. a long, loose Japanese robe, having a sash
and wide sleeves, worn by men or women || a
dressing gown in imitation of this [Jap.]
kin (kin) *n.* (*old-fash., collect.*) ancestral family ||
(*old-fash.* except in anthropology, *collect.*) relatives [O.E. *cynn,* family, clan]
kinaesthesia *KINESTHESIA
kinaesthesis *KINESTHESIS
kinaesthetic *KINESTHETIC
ki·nase (káineis, kíneis) *n.* a chemical substance which activates a diastase [KINETIC+
-*ase,* enzyme]
Kin·car·dine (kinkárdin) a former county (area
382 sq. miles) in E. Scotland. County town:
Stonehaven
kind (kaind) *n.* a group or division of persons or
things having one or more characteristics,
qualities, interests etc. in common **in kind** in
goods, not money || in a similar way, *to reply to
insults in kind* **nothing of the kind** (*emphatic*)
quite different **of a kind** belonging to the same
group || of a poor or bad variety within a group,
coffee of a kind **something of the kind** something similar [O.E. *gecynd*]
kind *adj.* sympathetic, helpful, friendly ||
thoughtful and gentle, *kind to animals* || well-
disposed, *kind to his servants* || showing such
qualities, *kind words* || pleasant or beneficial in
action, *a kind climate* [O.E. *gecynde*]
kin·der·gar·ten (kíndərgart'n, kíndərgard'n) *n.*
a school or class in which very young children
are encouraged to develop their skills and social
behavior by games, exercises, handicrafts etc.
(*FRÖBEL) [G.=a garden for children]
kind-heart·ed (káindhártid) *adj.* having a kind
nature
Kin·di (kíndi:) *AL-KINDI
kin·dle (kínd'l) *pres. part.* **kin·dling** *past and
past part.* **kin·dled** *v.t.* to cause (a fire) to begin
to burn || (*rhet.*) to cause (an emotion) to be felt
or intensified, *the speech kindled their anger* ||
v.i. to begin to burn (*rhet.,* of emotions) to begin
to be excited [perh. fr. O.N. *kynda*]
kind·li·ness (káindli:nis) *n.* the quality of being
kindly or an instance of this
kin·dling (kíndliŋ) *n.* the act of lighting a fire or
an instance of this || dry twigs, pieces of wood
etc. used to start a fire
kind·ly (káindli:) *comp.* **kind·li·er** *superl.*
kind·li·est *adj.* having or showing a mild, kind
nature [O.E. *gecyndelīc* fr. *gecynde,* kind]
kindly *adv.* in a kind way, *he treated her kindly*
|| please, *kindly come this way* **to take some-
thing kindly** to consider something to be
meant as kind, *take it kindly if I make some criticisms* **to take kindly to** to like, *he took kindly
to the idea* [O.E. *gecyndelīce* fr. *gecynde,* kind]
kind·ness (káindnis) *n.* the quality of being
kind or an instance of this **to do (someone) a
kindness** to render (someone) a small service
kin·dred (kíndrid) **1.** *n.* (*old-fash., collect.*) kin
2. *adj.* having kinship, *kindred tribes* || having a
common origin, *kindred languages* || being in
many ways similar, *kindred spirits* [M.E. fr.
KIN+-*reden* fr. O.E. *rǣden,* condition]
kine *archaic pl.* of COW
kin·e·mat·ic (kinəmætik) *adj.* of motion considered apart from its cause **kin·e·mát·ics** *n.* a
branch of dynamics dealing with motion in time
and space but disregarding mass and force [fr.
Gk *kinēma* (*kinēmatos*) fr. *kinein,* to move]
kin·e·scope (kíniskoup) *n.* a type of cathode-ray
tube with a luminescent screen on which im-
ages are produced, used in television etc. || a
moving picture made from kinescope images
[trademark fr. Gk *kinein,* to move+*skopein,* to
watch]
ki·ne·sis (kiní:sis, kainí:sis) *n.* physical move-
ment || (*biol.*) nonspecific movement in response
to a stimulus (*TAXIS, *TROPISM) [Mod. L. fr. Gk
kinēsis, motion]

CONCISE PRONUNCIATION KEY: **(a)** æ, *cat;* ɑ, *car;* ɔ *fawn;* ei, *snake.* **(e)** e, *hen;* i:, *sheep;* iə, *deer;* ɛə, *bear.* **(i)** i, *fish;* ai, *tiger;* ə:, *bird.*
(o) o, *ox;* au, *cow;* ou, *goat;* u, *poor;* ɔi, *royal.* **(u)** ʌ, *duck;* u, *bull;* u:, *goose;* ə, *bacillus;* ju:, *cube.* x, *loch;* θ, *think;* δ, *bother;* z, *Zen;* ʒ, *corsage;*
dʒ, *savage;* ŋ, *orangutang;* j, *yak;* ʃ, *fish;* tʃ, *fetch;* 'l, *rabble;* 'n, *redden.* Complete pronunciation key appears inside front cover.

kin·es·the·sia, kin·aes·the·sia (kɪnisθíːʒə) *n.* kinesthesis

kin·es·the·sis, kin·aes·the·sis (kɪnisθíːsis) *n.* the sensation of movement, tension etc. in various body parts received by the nerve ends in the muscles, tendons and joints **kin·es·thet·ic, kin·aes·thet·ic** (kɪnisθétik) *adj.* [fr. Gk *kinein,* to move + *aisthēsis,* sensation]

kin·e·the·od·o·lite (kɪneθíːɒdoulait) *n.* (*mil.*) camera for tracking missiles or aircraft, made up of a camera and odometer; used at airports

ki·net·ic (kinétik, kainétik) *adj.* of or relating to motion || producing motion [fr. Gk *kinētikos,* moving]

kinetic art an art form in which portions of the structure move, deriving energy from imbalances, the motion of viewer, etc., e.g., works of Alexander Calder —**kinetic artist** *n.* —**kinet·icism** *n.* —**kineticist** *n. Cf* MOBILES, STABILES

kinetic energy (*phys.*) the energy of a moving mass associated with its speed and equal to half the product of the mass and the square of the velocity

ki·net·ics (kinétiks, kainétiks) *n.* the branch of physics that deals with the relation of force and changes of motion || a branch of physical chemistry that deals with the rates and paths of chemical reactions, *reaction kinetics*

kinetic theory (*phys.*) a theory that derives the properties of fluids (esp. gases) from first principles with the aid of certain simplifying assumptions. It is supposed that fluids are composed of a vast number of very small particles (so small that at ordinary pressures the actual volume of the particles is negligible compared with the volume that they occupy) and that these particles exert no forces on each other except when in contact (i.e. during a collision). It is further assumed that the particles of a fluid are in a state of continuous motion at high speeds in random directions, and that collisions between particles and with the confining walls take place in very great numbers and in such a manner that the overall kinetic energy of the system is conserved. By application of the laws of physics and certain statistical principles it is shown that the observed pressure of a gas is related to the kinetic energy of its particles, which in turn is a function of its temperature. The kinetic theory provides simple explanations for the physical behavior of gases, leads directly to the ideal gas law, and has helped in the understanding of the general properties of fluids

ki·ne·tin [$C_{10}H_9N_5O$] (káinətən) *n.* plant hormone that stimulates cell division in plants, synthetically derived from yeast

ki·ne·to·some (kənétəsoum) *n.* (*cytol.*) **1.** a specialized part of a cell that stimulates growth of cilia or flagella **2.** (*biol.*) a staining granule at the ends of hairlike cells of some plants or animals *syn.* basal body

kin·folk (kínfouk) *n.* (*old-fash., collect.*) kinsfolk

King (kɪŋ), Clarence (1842–1901), U.S. geologist and a founding-director of the U.S. geological survey. He served as chief of the U.S. geological exploration of the 40th parallel. His 'Systematic Geology' (1878) led to a systematic survey of the U.S.A.

King, Ernest Joseph (1878–1956), U.S. admiral, who served (1941–5) as commander in chief of U.S. naval operations, directing the return of U.S. naval forces into Japanese-held waters

King, Martin Luther, Jr (1929–68), Afro-American clergyman, founder of the Southern Christian Leadership Conference, and a leader of the nonviolent movement for racial equality in the U.S.A. His nation-wide campaign, including civil rights marches and boycotts, spurred a Supreme Court ruling (1957) that racial segregation in public transportation was unlawful, the Civil Rights Act (1964), and the Voting Rights Act (1965). The 1963 March on Washington, at which he delivered his 'I Have a Dream' speech, was followed in 1964 by the awarding of the Nobel peace prize. He was assassinated (1968) by James Earl Ray while preparing to lead a march by striking sanitation workers in Memphis, Tenn. In 1983 his birthday (Jan. 15) was designated a national holiday

King, Rufus (1755–1827), U.S. statesman. A delegate (1784–7) to the Continental Congress, he helped to draft the Ordinance of 1787 and was largely responsible for the exclusion of slavery from the Northwest Territory. A Ham-

iltonian, he became (1789) one of New York's first two U.S. Senators

King, William Lyon Mackenzie (1874–1950), Canadian Liberal statesman, prime minister (1921–30 and 1935–48). He was an expert on industrial relations, and gave Canada strong leadership during the 2nd world war

King, William Rufus Devane (1786–1853), U.S. diplomat and senator from Alabama (1819–44, 1848–53). As minister (1844–6) to France, he presented to the French government the case against any foreign intervention aimed at preventing the annexation of Texas to the U.S.A. He was elected U.S. vice-president with President Franklin Pierce, but died before he could take up the position

king (kɪŋ) *n.* a male monarch || a magnate || the chief person or thing of its kind or class, *the lion is the king of beasts* || (*cards*) a card representing a king, intermediate in value between queen and ace || (*chess*) the piece in whose defense the game is played || (*checkers*) a crowned piece, which can be moved diagonally in any direction [O.E. *cyning*]

king·bird (kíŋbəːrd) *n.* any of several American insect-eating birds of fam. *Tyrannidae,* including the eastern kingbird (*Tyrannus tyrannus*) inhabiting esp. eastern North America, the gray kingbird (*T. dominicensis dominicensis*) inhabiting Georgia and the West Indies, and the Arkansas kingbird (*T. verticalis*) inhabiting the western U.S.A.

king·bolt (kíŋboult) *n.* a vertical bolt fastening the body of a car or railroad coach to the forward axle

King·chow (gíŋdʒóu) * KIANGLING

king cobra *Naja hannah,* fam. *Elapidae,* a poisonous hooded snake, up to 12 ft in length, of India and eastward to the Philippines

king crab a member of *Xiphosura,* class *Merostomata,* an order of large marine arthropods found off the eastern coast of North America and off eastern Asia, esp. the horseshoe crab. King crabs have a strong chitinous U-shaped shell with a long spear at the hind end, 12 pairs of ventral appendages, two dorsal compound eyes and two simple eyes

king·dom (kíŋdəm) *n.* the territory over which a king or queen has authority || a state, area etc. having a monarchal form of government || one of the three most comprehensive groups used to classify nature, *the animal, plant and mineral kingdoms* **kingdom come** (*pop.*) the next world [O.E. *cyningdōm*]

King·fish (kíŋfiʃ) *n.* (*mil.*) U.S.S.R. air-to-surface missile (SS-6) for Soviet interceptor jets Tu-16 and Tu-26 with a 20-km range and speed of Mach 3.0

king·fish·er (kíŋfiʃər) *n.* a member of *Alcedinidae,* a family of river and lake birds having a large, usually crested head, a dagger-shaped bill, brilliant plumage and small bodies

King George's War the American aspect (1745–8) of the War of the Austrian Succession. A British expedition captured Louisburg, Nova Scotia, from the French but the Treaty of Aix-la-Chapelle (1745) returned the town to the French (1748). The war embittered relations between French and British settlers

King James Bible (*Am.=Br.* Authorized Version) the English translation of the Old and New Testaments made by command of King James I and appointed to be read in churches, first published in 1611 (*BIBLE)

King·lake (kíŋleik), Alexander William (1808–91), British writer. He wrote 'Eōthen' (1844), an amusing account of a journey in the Middle East, and 'The Invasion of the Crimea' (1863–87)

king·ly (kíŋli) *comp.* **king·li·er** *superl.* **king·li·est** *adj.* of, like or suitable in a king

king·mak·er (kíŋmeikər) *n.* someone who pulls the strings of power to put another into public office

king of arms (*Br.*) an officer of arms of the highest rank

King Philip's War one of the bloodiest 17th-c. wars between the American colonists of New England and the Indians (1675–6). Several colonial townships were annihilated, but the war ended in the complete defeat of the Indians. Their leader, King Philip, was chief of the Wampanoag Indians (of Algonquian linguistic stock)

king·pin (kíŋpin) *n.* (*bowling*) the central or number 5 pin || (*pop.*) the chief person in an undertaking || a kingbolt

king post (*archit.*) the vertical post in a roof, connecting the ridge to the tie beam

Kings (kɪŋz) two books of the Old Testament relating the history of the Hebrews from the death of David to the Babylonian destruction of Judah

King's English (esp. *Br.*) correct English as to grammar and pronunciation

king's evil (*hist.*) scrofula [fr. the belief that it could be cured by the touch of the king]

king·ship (kíŋʃip) *n.* the state or office of a king

king-size (kíŋsaiz) *adj.* (of a cigarette) longer than the size of most brands || larger than usual

king-sized (kíŋsaizd) *adj.* king-size

Kings·ley (kíŋzliː), Charles (1819–75), English clergyman and writer. He wrote novels, e.g. 'Alton Locke' (1850), historical novels, e.g. 'Westward Ho!' (1855), and the children's story 'The Water Babies' (1863)

Kingsley, Mary Henrietta (1862–1900), English writer, whose travels and ethnological observations were recorded in 'Travels in West Africa' (1897) and 'West African Studies' (1899)

King's (Queen's) Bench (*Br. hist.*) a court of law formerly presided over by the sovereign of England. It became (1875) one of the divisions of the Supreme Court of Judicature

King's (Queen's) Counsel (*abbr.* K.C., Q.C., *Br.*) a group of eminent barristers selected on the nomination of the lord chancellor in England, or of the lord president of the court of session in Scotland, to serve as counsel to the Crown || a member of this group

King's (Queen's) Proctor an English official of the probate, divorce and admiralty divisions of the Supreme Court of Judicature who may intervene in proceedings if collusion is suspected

king's (queen's) shilling (*Br., hist.*) a shilling which, if accepted by a man from a recruiting sergeant, bound him legally (prior to 1879) as an enlisted soldier

Kings·ton (kíŋstən, kíŋstən) the capital (pop. 700,000) and chief port of Jamaica, founded in 1693, on a landlocked harbor. Industries: food processing, tanning, tourism

Kingston a city (pop. 52,616) on the northeast shore of Lake Ontario, Canada, near the head of the St Lawrence River. It is a transshipment point for the Welland Ship Canal. It was the former capital of Canada (1841–4). Queens University (1841), Royal Military College (1876)

Kings·town (kíŋstən) *DUN LAOGHAIRE

King-teh-chen (gíŋdʌdʒén) *FOWLIANG

King William's War the American aspect (1689–97) of the War of the Grand Alliance, fought by England and her American colonies against the French and the Indians. It was ended by the Treaty of Ryswick (1697), but the peace was soon broken by Queen Anne's War

kink (kɪŋk) *n.* a sharp twist or loop in a wire, rope, hair etc. || a sudden, slight deviation interrupting a straight line || a sharp muscle pain in e.g. the back or a leg || (*pop.*) an odd trait of character or mental quirk [prob. Du. *kink, twist*]

kink *v.i.* to form a kink || *v.t.* to cause (something) to form a kink [prob. fr. Du. *kinken*]

kin·ka·jou (kíŋkədʒuː) *n. Cercoleptes caudivolvulus,* fam. *Procyonidae,* an omnivorous, arboreal, nocturnal mammal about 3 ft in length found in Central and South America. It has yellowish fur and a long prehensile tail [fr. F. *quincajou,* of Algonquian origin]

kink·y (kíŋki) *comp.* **kink·i·er** *superl.* **kink·i·est** *adj.* (esp. of hair) having kinks || (*colloq.*) of peculiar tastes in sexual satisfaction; by extension, in other areas

kinky boot (*Br.*) knee-length woman's boot

ki·no (kíːnou) *n.* any of various dark black or red gums or juices obtained from several Indian and Australian trees, used in tanning and medicine [prob. W. African]

ki·no·plasm (kíːnouplæzəm) *n.* very active specialized protoplasm responsible for the formation of mobile cell structures, e.g. cilia and filaments (opp. TROPHOPLASM) [fr. Gk *kinēma,* motion + *plasm,* formative material, ult. fr. Mod. L. *plasma,* the fluid part of the blood]

Kin·ross (kinrós, kinrós) a former county (area 82 sq. miles) in E. central Scotland. County town: Kinross

Kin·sey (kínzi:), Alfred Charles (1894–1956), U.S. zoologist. His studies of the sexual life of

CONCISE PRONUNCIATION KEY: **(a)** æ, c*a*t; ɑ, c*a*r; ɔ f*aw*n; ei, sn*a*ke. **(e)** e, h*e*n; iː, sh*ee*p; iə, d*ee*r; ɛə, b*ea*r. **(i)** i, f*i*sh; ai, t*i*ger; əː, b*i*rd. **(o)** o, *o*x; au, c*ow*; ou, g*oa*t; u, p*oo*r; ɔi, r*oy*al. **(u)** ʌ, d*u*ck; u, b*u*ll; uː, g*oo*se; ə, b*a*cillus; juː, c*u*be. x, lo*ch*; θ, *th*ink; ð, bo*th*er; z, *Z*en; ʒ, cor*s*age; dʒ, sava*g*e; ŋ, orangutan*g*; j, *y*ak; ʃ, *fi*sh; tʃ, fet*ch*; ˈl, rabb*le*; ˈn, redd*en*. Complete pronunciation key appears inside front cover.

human beings led him to found (1947) the Institute for Sex Research at Indiana University. His 'Sexual Behavior in the Human Male' (1948) and 'Sexual Behavior in the Human Female' (1953), were both based on 18,500 personal interviews

kins·folk (kínzfouk) *n.* (*old-fash.*, *collect.*) relatives, including those by marriage

Kin·sha·sa (kínʃɑsɑ) (formerly Leopoldville) the capital (pop. 1,990,717) of Zaïre, 250 miles inland from Matadi on the Congo River (River Zaïre). With its neighboring port, it is an industrial and commercial center: textiles, chemicals, engineering, food processing. Roman Catholic University (1954)

kin·ship (kínʃip) *n.* the condition of being related ‖ the condition of being similar

kinship system (*anthrop.*) a social system of various forms governing the reciprocal obligations between members of a culture who are held to be related

ki·osk (kí:ɒsk, káiɒsk) *n.* a small outdoor structure, e.g. a newsstand or bandstand [fr. F. *kiosque* fr. Turk. *kiūshk*, pavilion]

Ki·o·wa (káiəwə) *pl.* **Ki·o·wa, Ki·o·was** *n.* an American Indian people of the southern Great Plains. In the late 1800s they were forced to share a reservation in S.W. Oklahoma with the Comanche and numbered about 2,000 ‖ a member of this people ‖ their language

kip (kip) *n.* the standard monetary unit of Laos ‖ a coin or note of this value [Siamese]

kip *n.* the undressed hide of a young animal, esp. a calf, used in making leather ‖ a bundle of such hides [origin unknown]

Kip·ling (kíplin), Rudyard (1865–1936), English author. His early writings were based on the life of the English, civilian and military, in India, where he worked on a newspaper. On his return to England (1889) he became a successful author of poems, short stories and novels, following the publication of 'Plain Tales from the Hills' (1888). His other prose works include 'The Jungle Book' (1894), 'Second Jungle Book' (1895), 'Stalky and Co.' (1899), 'Kim' (1901), and 'Just So Stories' (1902). His interest was in the world of men: of men using their power and skill, e.g. as represented by the self-sacrificing administrator upholding civilization and toiling to extend it. He was a great story-teller and his style at its best is intensely vivid and concrete. His collected poems include 'Barrack-Room Ballads' (1892) and 'Recessional and other poems' (1899)

kip·per (kípər) **1.** *n.* a herring or salmon split open, cleaned, salted and smoked **2.** *v.t.* to cure (a fish) in this way [etym. doubtful]

Kipper (*mil.*) U.S.S.R. air-to-surface turbojet missile (AS-2), with 130-mi range, beam riding and radar direction

Kipp generator (kip) (*chem.*) a glass apparatus for producing a gas at room temperature by the action of a liquid on a solid and delivering it in controlled amounts [after Petrus Jacobus *Kipp* (1808-64), Du. chemist]

Kir·by (kə́:rbi:), William (1817–1906), Canadian novelist. His 'The Golden Dog' (1877) is a historical romance depicting life in Quebec under the French regime

Kirch·hoff (kí:rxhəf), Gustav Robert (1824–87), German physicist. With Bunsen he developed the spectroscope and explained the Fraunhofer lines. This led to his discovery with Bunsen (1861) of cesium and rubidium. He also formulated Kirchhoff's laws

Kirchhoff's law a law in physics stating that the algebraic sum of the currents in any branches of a circuit that meet at a point is zero ‖ a law in physics stating that the algebraic sum of the electromotive forces in the branches of any closed loop of an electrical network is equal to the algebraic sum of the current-resistance products in the branches of that loop [after G. R. *Kirchhoff*]

Kir·ghiz (kirgí:z) *pl.* **Kir·ghiz, Kir·ghiz·es** *n.* a member of a Mongolian people of the Central Asian steppes ‖ their Turkic language

Kir·ghi·zia (kirgí:ʒə) a constituent republic (area 76,460 sq. miles, pop. 3,723,000) of the U.S.S.R. in central Asia. Capital: Frunze (formerly Pishpek). It is entirely mountainous. Agriculture: livestock breeding and (in the valleys) sugar beets, corn, cotton, wheat, vegetables, fruit. Resources: some coal. Industries: agricultural processing, textiles. Part of Turkestan, Kirghizia has been under Russian rule

since 1876. It became an autonomous republic (1926) and a constituent republic (1936)

Kiribati, Republic of, formerly part of the Gilbert and Ellice Islands (area 275 sq. miles, pop. 61,000) spread over 2,000,000 sq. miles of the Central Pacific. Capital: Tarawa (pop. 20,148). People: about 83% Micronesian, 14% Polynesian, 3% Chinese and European. There are 33 islands, including the Gilberts (including Banaba or Ocean Island), 8 of the Line Islands and 8 of the Phoenix Islands. Average day temperatures (F.): 80°–90°. Rainfall: 40 ins near the equator, 100 ins in the N. Products: phosphates, copra, coconuts, fish, handicrafts (*TUVALU, *LINE ISLANDS, *PHOENIX ISLANDS). History: The islands were first visited (1765) by the British. The Gilbert and Ellice Is. became a British protectorate (1892) and a colony (1915). They suffered during the Japanese occupation (1942-3). The American forces largely regained them after a fierce battle at Tarawa (1943) and established bases there until the end of the war. In 1975, the independent nation of Tuvalu was formed from the Ellice Islands, and Kiribati was granted independence in 1979

Kir·i·li·an photography (kəríli:ən) U.S.S.R.-invented filming technique that reveals body transpiration in the form of coronal emanations, sometimes used to warn of impending illness

Kir·in (kí:rín) a province (area 72,000 sq. miles, pop. 13,400,000) of N.E. China, north of the Korean border. Capital: Changchun ‖ *YUNGKI

kir·in (kirin) *n.* unicornlike animal of Japanese mythology

kirk (kə:rk) *n.* (*Scot.*) a church **the Kirk** the Church of Scotland, as distinguished from the Episcopal Church of Scotland [var. of CHURCH]

Kirk·cud·bright (kərkú:bri:) a former county (area 899 sq. miles) in S.W. Scotland. County town: Kirkcudbright

Kir·kuk (kirkú:k) a town (pop. 207,852) in N.E. Iraq, center of a great oil field, with pipelines to Lebanon and Syria

Kir Mo·ab (kə:rmóuæb) *KERAK

Ki·rov (kí:rʌf) a city (pop. 404,000) of the E. European R.S.F.S.R., U.S.S.R., an industrial center (textiles, agricultural machinery) and railroad junction. As Vyatka, it was capital of a republic annexed (1482) to Moscow by Ivan III

Ki·ro·vo·grad (kı̇:rʌvʌgrát) a city (pop. 246,000) of the central Ukraine, U.S.S.R.: agricultural trade, engineering

kirsch (kiərʃ) *n.* an alcoholic liquor distilled from cherries [fr. G. *kirsche*, cherry]

Ki·run (kí:rú:n) *KILUNG

Ki·ru·na (kí:rynɑ) a mining center (pop. 30,534) of N. Sweden (Lapland): rich high-grade iron deposits

kirund native language of Burundi, a derivative of Bantu

Ki·san·ga·ni (kizɑ́ngɑni:) (formerly Stanleyville) a port and commercial center (pop. 339,210) in northeastern Zaïre, on the upper Congo (River Zaïre)

Kish (kiʃ) an ancient Sumerian city of Mesopotamia, which established an empire covering much of S.W. Asia (3rd millennium B.C.)

Ki·shi·nev (kiʃinjɔ́f) the capital (pop. 559,000) of Moldavia, U.S.S.R., center of a tobacco and vine-growing region

kis·met (kízmit, kísmit) *n.* fate as a predetermining power ‖ one's fate [Turk. fr. Arab.]

kiss (kis) *n.* an instance of kissing ‖ any of several kinds of small, highly sweetened candy or meringue [M.E. fr. *kissen*, to kiss]

kiss *v.t.* to press or touch with the lips as an expression of passion, affection or respect ‖ (*billiards*, of a ball) to hit (another ball) with a light, glancing impact ‖ *v.i.* to join lips ‖ (*billiards*) to hit another ball or (of two balls) to come together with a light impact [O.E. *cyssan*]

Kis·si (kísi:) *pl.* **Kis·si, Kis·sis** *n.* a member of a W. African people living in Guinea, Liberia and Sierra Leone ‖ their language

kissing disease (*colloq.*) infectious mononucleosis

Kissinger (kísəndʒər), Henry Alfred (1923–), U.S. statesman, born in Germany, secretary of state (1973–7). After serving in World War II, he taught at Harvard University (1954–69), consulted on foreign policy for Presidents Kennedy and Johnson and directed the National Security Council until 1975. As secretary of state under Presidents Nixon and Ford, he established stronger ties with the Soviet Union

and reopened relations with China; he negotiated cease-fire arrangements in the Arab-Israeli War of 1973 and in Vietnam for which he shared the 1973 Nobel Peace Prize; and he was instrumental in the signing of SALT I. He headed the commission to study U.S. policy in Central America (1983) and wrote his memoirs in 'White House Years' (1979) and 'Years of Upheaval' (1982)

kissing gate (*Br.*) a gate swung between U-shaped or V-shaped enclosures, keeping cattle in and permitting one person to pass through at a time

kiss of death an association, relationship etc. that will lead inevitably to catastrophe, though superficially innocuous

Kist·na (kístnə) (Krishna) a holy river in the Deccan, India, flowing 800 miles from the Western Ghats across Hyderabad into the Bay of Bengal, dammed for irrigation and hydroelectric power

Ki·su·mu (ki:sú:mu:) a port (pop. 149,000) on the eastern side of Lake Victoria, W. Kenya

Ki·swa·hi·li (kíswahí:li:) *n.* Swahili

kit (kit) **1.** *n.* a collection of tools, accessories and supplies necessary for a particular profession, act or service and usually contained in a bag, box etc. ‖ (esp. *Br.*) a soldier's equipment exclusive of arms ‖ (esp. *Br.*) clothes suitable for a particular occasion or activity **2.** *v.t. pres. part.* **kit·ting** *past* and *past part.* **kit·ted** (esp. *Br.*, with 'out' or 'up') to supply with regulation equipment [prob. fr. M. Du. *kitte*, a wooden vessel]

Ki·ta-Kyu·shu (kı̇:tɑkjú:ʃu:) a port (pop. 1,065,084) of Japan, in N. Kyushu. It is a big industrial conurbation (iron and steel metallurgy) and also important as a fishing port

kit and caboodle (*pop.*, in phrase) **the whole kit and caboodle** the whole lot (of things or people), *he got rid of the whole kit and caboodle*

kit bag (*Br.*) a soldier's duffel bag

kitch·en (kítʃən) *n.* the part of a house, restaurant etc. where food is prepared [O.E. *cycene* fr. L.]

Kitchen (*mil.*) U.S.S.R. air-to-surface solid-fuel missile (SS-4) weighing 660 lbs, with a 500-mi range

kitchen cabinet a kitchen cupboard fitted with drawers, shelves etc. ‖ an unofficial group of advisers to whom a head of government pays more attention than he does to his official advisers

Kitch·e·ner (kítʃənər), Horatio Herbert, 1st Earl Kitchener of Khartoum (1850–1916), British field marshal. After his unsuccessful attempt to relieve Gordon at Khartoum (1885), he became governor-general of the E. Sudan (1886–8). As head of the Egyptian army (1892–8), he drove the Mahdists out of the Sudan, crushing them at Omdurman (1898). He was commander in chief of British forces (1900–2) in the Boer War and also in India (1902–9). As war minister (1914–16) he mobilized the British army in the 1st world war. He was drowned on a voyage to Russia

kitch·en·ette (kítʃənét) *n.* a small room or alcove equipped as a kitchen

kitchen garden a garden where esp. household vegetables are grown

kitchen midden a collection of bones, shells and other refuse, marking the site of a prehistoric dwelling [trans. of Dan. *kjökkenmödding* or *kökkenmödding*]

kitchen police *K.P.

kitchen sink drama pejorative term for English plays about the working class, popular in the 1950s

kite (kait) *n.* a member of *Accipitridae*, a family of small hawks having a forked tail, long wings and a buoyant flight, esp. *Milvus milvus*, a European species. They prey on rabbits, reptiles and small birds ‖ a light, usually wooden, typically diamond-shaped framework covered with paper or material and flown on the wind at the end of a long string ‖ (*pl.*) the highest and topmost sails of a ship, used only in very light winds ‖ (*commerce*) a check, bill or other document having no solid backing but used to raise money or sustain credit ‖ a trial balloon ‖ (*mil.*) in naval mine warfare, a device that, when towed, submerges and places mines at a predetermined level without sideways displacement ‖ airborne radar reflector dropped from a craft to deceive the enemy [O.E. *cȳta*]

CONCISE PRONUNCIATION KEY: **(a)** æ, c*a*t; ɑ, c*a*r; ɔ f*aw*n; ei, sn*a*ke. **(e)** e, h*e*n; i:, sh*ee*p; iə, d*ee*r; ɛə, b*ea*r. **(i)** i, f*i*sh; ai, t*i*ger; ə:, b*i*rd. **(o)** o, *o*x; au, c*ow*; ou, g*oa*t; u, p*oo*r; ɔi, r*oy*al. **(u)** ʌ, d*u*ck; u, b*u*ll; u:, g*oo*se; ə, b*a*cillus; ju:, c*u*be. x, lo*ch*; θ, *th*ink; ð, bo*th*er; z, *Z*en; ʒ, cor*s*age; dʒ, sava*g*e; ŋ, oranguta*ng*; j, *y*ak; ʃ, *f*ish; tʃ, fet*ch*; 'l, rabb*le*; 'n, red*den*. Complete pronunciation key appears inside front cover.

kite·mark (káitmɑrk) *n.* certification of standard of performance by British Standards Institution

kith (kiθ) *n.* (only in phrase) **kith and kin** friends and relatives ‖ relatives [O.E. *cȳthth, cȳth,* knowledge, one's country]

kit home prefabricated parts of a house ready to be assembled

kiting 1. (*med.*) practice of increasing the quantity of a drug ordered by a prescription. **2.** (*banking*) practice of depositing checks in various, usually distant banks, to keep balances available or to cover checks with uncollected amounts

kitsch (kitʃ) *n.* professionally produced art in bad taste —**kitschy** *adj.*

kit·ten (kít'n) **1.** *n.* a young cat, esp. a domesticated cat **2.** *v.i.* to bring forth kittens **kít·ten·ish** *adj.* playful and winning [ME. *kitoun* prob. fr. A.F.]

kit·ti·wake (kíti:weik) *n.* a member of *Rissa,* fam. *Laridae,* a family of gulls, esp. *R. tridactyla* of the N. Atlantic, having a rudimentary hind toe [imit.]

kit·ty (kíti:) *pl.* **kit·ties** *n.* (*card games*) a pool into which each player puts a stake ‖ (*card games*) the cards left over after a deal ‖ a pool or fund of money or goods [origin unknown]

kitty *pl.* **kitties** *n.* (*pop.*) cat, kitten [fr *kit,* short for KITTEN]

Kiu·chuan (kjú:dʒwán) (formerly Suchow) a town (pop. 247,000) in N.W. Kansu, China, the center of an agricultural region

Ki·vu (ki:vu:) a lake (length 65 miles, area 1,025 sq. miles) between Zaïre and Rwanda, in the Great Rift Valley

Ki·wa·nis International (kiwánis) a U.S.-canadian organization of business and professional men, founded (1915) in Detroit, Mich. Its clubs are concerned with public affairs, ethical standards of business, agricultural programs etc.

ki·wi (kí:wi:) *pl.* **ki·wis** *n.* an apteryx ‖ Chinese gooseberry, an egg-size fruit with sweet green pulp, native to New Zealand ‖ a native of New Zealand [Maori]

Ki·zil Ir·mak (kizíliɔrmák) a river of Turkey, rising east of Sivas and flowing 715 miles to the Black Sea

Kjö·len (tʃɔ́:lən) (*Swed.* Kölen) a mountain chain along the Norwegian Swedish frontier above Trondheim (*KEBNEKAISE)

Kla·gen·furt (klágənfurt) the capital (pop. 86,221) of Carinthia, S. Austria, with metal and chemical industries. Cathedral (16th c.)

Klai·pe·da (kláipeda) (formerly Memel) a port (pop. 181,000) of Lithuania, U.S.S.R., on the Baltic at the mouth of the Niemen: chemical, textile and wood pulp industries

klax·on (klǽks'n) *n.* a powerful, electrically operated horn, esp. (*Br.*) on a motor vehicle [fr. a former trademark]

Klé·ber (kleiber), Jean-Baptiste (1753–1800), French general. He remained in command of the French army in Egypt (1799–1800) when Napoleon returned to France

Klee (klei), Paul (1879–1940), Swiss painter. He analyzed the elements and process of composition, and formulated what might be called a pictorial dialectic, demonstrating the power of lines, colors and forms to evoke sensations of weight, tension, movement etc. Combining this knowledge with acute perception of human nature, he painted abstract works, discovering in forms and lines the suggestion of a face, figure or object, which he imbued with humorous significance, often whimsical, at times satiric. He was active in the Blaue Reiter and taught at the Bauhaus (1921–31). His lectures were published in 'The Thinking Eye' ('Das bildnerische Denken', 1956)

Kleen·ex (klí:neks) *n.* a disposable paper tissue, esp. one used as a handkerchief [Trademark]

Klein (klain), Melanie (1882–1960), Austrian psychoanalyst. She studied children's fantasies

Kleist (klaist), Heinrich von (1777–1811), German romantic poet, dramatist and short-story writer. His works include 'Der zerbrochene Krug' (1803) and 'Der Prinz von Homburg' (written by 1810, published 1821)

klep·toc·ra·cy (kleptókrəsi:) *n.* government by thieves

klep·to·ma·ni·a (kleptəméini:ə, kleptəméinjə) *n.* a compulsive, neurotic desire to steal, esp. when not motivated by any desire or need for economic gain **klep·to·má·ni·ac** *n.* [fr. Gk *kleptēs,* thief+MANIA]

Klimt (kli:mt), Gustav (1862–1918), Austrian painter and illustrator, cofounder of the art nouveau Vienna Secession movement. His paintings emphasized the primal forces and the sensual. His works include 3 murals ('Philosophy,' 1900; 'Medicine,' 1901; 'Jurisprudence,' 1902), 'Judith' (1901), 'Beethoven frieze' (1902), 'Hope I' (1903) and 'The Kiss' (1907–8). He also did many book illustrations

Kline (klain), Franz (1910–62), American painter, an adherent of abstract expressionism. His works are usually composed of strong black strokes on a white ground

Kline·fel·ter's syndrome (kláinfeltərz) (*med.*) hypogonadism, the absence of testicular secretion, etc., due to presence of two X and one Y chromosomes; named for H. F. Klinefelter, Jr., U.S. physician, in 1912

Kling·er (klíŋər), Friedrich Maximilian von (1752–1831), German writer. His drama 'Sturm und Drang' (1776) gave its name to the Sturm und Drang movement

klip·spring·er (klípspriŋər) *n. Oreotragus oreotragus,* fam. *Bovidae,* a small mountain antelope of S. and E. Africa [Afrik. fr. *klip,* rock+*springer,* springer]

Klon·dike, the (klóndaik) a region (almost 8,000 sq. miles) of the Yukon, Canada, on the Alaskan frontier, scene of a gold rush (1897–8)

Klop·stock (klɔ́pʃtɔk), Friedrich Gottlieb (1724–1803), German poet. His best-known work is 'Der Messias' (1745–73), an epic in 20 cantos

kludge (klʌdʒ) *n.* **1.** (*slang*) a ridiculous assortment of unmatched and unworkable parts **2.** (*computer*) term of endearment for a pet computer, esp. one with undesirable characteristics

klutz (klʌts) *n.* a clumsy person —**klutzy** *adj.*

Klys·tron (klístrɔn, kláistrən) *n.*(*phys.*) an electron tube which separates electrons of different velocities by deviating their paths in an electromagnetic field, thus enabling an ultrahigh-frequency current to be isolated [Trademark]

km. kilometer, kilometers

K-mesic *KAON

K-meson *KAON

knack (næk) *n.* a special deftness learned by practice, *a knack for remembering names* [etym. doubtful]

knack·er (nǽkər) *n.* (*Br.*) a dealer in old ships, cars etc. due to be junked ‖ (*Br.*) someone who buys and slaughters old horses for dog food and various products of the carcass [origin unknown]

knap (næp) *pres. part.* **knap·ping** *past* and *past part.* **knapped** *v.t.* to cleave and shape (flints or stones) [imit.]

Knapp (næp), Seaman Asahel (1833–1911), U.S. agriculturalist and educator. He created (1904) the farm demonstration method, by which a specialist would initiate a farmer into improved techniques on the farmer's own farm

knap·sack (nǽpsæk) *n.* a canvas bag, used to carry supplies, worn strapped to the back [L.G.]

knar (nɑr) *n.* a knot in wood ‖ a barkcovered protuberance on the trunk or root of a tree [M.E. *knarre,* a rough rock]

knave (neiv) *n.* (*old-fash.*) a cheat, a rogue ‖ (*cards*) a jack **knav·er·y** (néivəri:) *pl.* **knav·er·ies** *n.* the practice of low cunning ‖ an instance of this **knáv·ish** *adj.* [O.E. *cnafa,* a youth]

knead (ni:d) *v.t.* to work (dough, clay) into a homogeneous mass with the hands ‖ to massage (a muscle or limb) as if working dough [O.E. *cnedan*]

knee (ni:) **1.** *n.* the knee joint in man ‖ the area surrounding this joint ‖ the corresponding joint in an animal ‖ something resembling a bent knee, e.g. a piece of wood or iron used to connect upright beams ‖ the part of a garment that covers the knee **to bring (someone) to his knees** to cause (someone) to submit **to go on one's knees** to beg humbly of **2.** *v.t.* to strike (someone) with the knee [O.E. *cnēo, cnēow*]

knee breeches breeches, esp. of silk

knee·cap (ní:kæp) *n.* a heart-shaped sesamoid bone located in front of and protecting the knee joint

knee capping shooting at the knees to cripple, a technique used by Italian terrorists

knee-deep (ní:di:p) *adj.* reaching up to the knees ‖ immersed up to the knees ‖ deeply involved (in debt, work etc.)

knee-hole desk (ní:houl) a flat-topped desk with a space for one's legs between its two tiers of drawers

knee jerk an upward kick occurring by reflex action when the tendon below the kneecap is tapped

knee joint the joint in man between the femur and the tibia ‖ a toggle joint

kneel (ni:l) *pres. part.* **kneel·ing** *past* and *past part.* **knelt** (nelt), **kneeled** *v.i.* to rest or fall on one or both knees [O.E. *cnēowlian*]

knee-pan (ní:pæn) *n.* the kneecap

knell (nel) **1.** *n.* the sonorous, doleful sound of a single bell tolled as a token of mourning ‖ (*rhet.*) a warning of death or disaster **2.** *v.i.* to toll a bell ‖ *v.t.* to summon by a bell or as if by a bell [O.E. *cnyll*]

Knell·er (nélər), Sir Godfrey (1646–1723), English portrait painter of German birth. He painted hundreds of works, the best of which are full of insight and done with great freedom and vivacity. He was official court painter from 1680

knelt *alt. past* and *past part.* of KNEEL

Knes·set (knéset) *n.* the parliament of Israel [Heb., *lit.*=gathering]

knew *past* of KNOW

knick·er·bock·ers (níkərbɒkərz) *pl. n.* (*old-fash.*) knickers [after Diedrich *Knickerbocker,* the imaginary author of Washington Irving's 'History of New York' (1809)]

knick·ers (níkərz) *pl. n.* loose-fitting trousers gathered in just below the knees ‖ (*Br.*) girl's or women's panties or drawers [shortening of KNICKERBOCKERS]

knick-knack (níknæk) *n.* any trivial small ornamental article [redupl. of *knack,* a toy]

knife (naif) **1.** *pl.* **knives** (naivz) *n.* a hand tool, culinary utensil or weapon used for cutting, consisting of a blade (usually steel) fixed to a handle and having one edge sharp ‖ a cutting edge in a machine **to get** (or **have**) **one's knife into someone** to have taken a strong dislike to someone and use every opportunity to attack him in one way or another **2.** *v.t. pres. part.* **knif·ing** *past* and *past part.* **knifed** to cut or stab with a knife ‖ to use sly methods on in order to defeat, harm or betray [O.E. *cnīf*]

knife-edge (náifedʒ) *n.* something compared to the sharp edge of a knife blade, e.g. an edge of rock or ice or a situation involving a dangerous or delicate choice ‖ a sharp-edged, wedge-shaped, steel fulcrum

knife rest a glass, china or metal rest to put a knife down on at the table

knight (nait) **1.** *n.* a man given the rank of knighthood by the British monarch in recognition of merit, esp. in public service. He has the title 'Sir', his wife having the title 'Lady'. His rank is next below that of a baronet, and is not hereditary ‖ (*hist.*) a man of noble birth who, having served as page and squire, was given an honorable military rank (*KNIGHTHOOD) ‖ (*hist.*) a military attendant on a lord or his lady ‖ (*chess*) a piece shaped like a horse's head. Its move comprises one lateral and two vertical or two lateral and one vertical squares and it can move over an occupied square **2.** *v.t.* to make a knight of [O.E. *cniht, cneoht,* boy, youth]

knight bachelor *pl.* **knights bachelors, knights bachelor** (*hist.*) a young knight serving under the standard of another and belonging to no particular order ‖ a member of the lowest rank of knighthood

knight-er·rant (náitérənt) *pl.* **knights-errant** *n.* (*hist.*) a mounted knight who traveled in search of chivalrous adventures

knight·hood (náithud) *n.* the rank of a knight ‖ (*hist.*) the profession of a knight [O.E. *cnihthād*]

—Knighthood was established as a military profession both in England and in continental Europe by the 10th c. By the 11th c. it had become a feudal institution, associated with the holding of land. In return for lands held from his overlord, each knight was supposed to render 40 days' military service per year, although this might be varied or commuted as scutage. By the time of the Crusades, a religious element was added, and the accolade was often preceded by vigil before the altar. The knightly code embodied courage, piety, honor, loyalty and respect for womanhood. Since knighthood remained non-hereditary, while land was handed down on a hereditary basis, there grew up a body of landless knights, who often banded together in military orders. The chief of these were the Knights Hospitalers and the Knights

Templars. The excesses of the latter began to bring knighthood into disrepute, and as cavalry declined in importance in warfare, knighthood became obsolete. By the 16th c. it was becoming a civil rather than a military honor (*CHIVALRY)

Knight Hospitaler, a member of the Order of the Hospital of St John of Jerusalem, a military and religious order founded (11th c.) to care for poor or sick pilgrims in Jerusalem, and recognized (1113) by the papacy. The Hospitalers took an active part in the Crusades, but were driven from Palestine (1291). They conquered Rhodes (1310), becoming known as the Knights of Rhodes. Their wealth and power increased, but they lost Rhodes to the Turks (1522). The Emperor Charles V gave them the sovereignty of Malta (1530), after which they were generally known as the Knights of Malta. They continued to fight the Turks during the 16th c. and remained in control of the island until 1798, when they were deposed by Napoleon and took refuge in Russia. The order was reconstituted (1879) by the papacy as a charitable organization for the care of the sick and wounded. The emblem of the order is a white Maltese cross on a black ground

knight·ly (náitli:) *adj.* (*hist.*) appropriate to a knight

Knight of Columbus a member of an American fraternal benefit society of Roman Catholic men, founded 1882

Knight of Malta *KNIGHT HOSPITALER

Knight of St John of Jerusalem *KNIGHT HOSPITALER

Knights of Labor a U.S. labor organization founded (1869) by Philadelphia tailors. Internationally respected under the leadership of Terence Powderly, it aimed through educational means to gain an 8-hour working day, to abolish child and convict labor, and to eliminate private banks. Unsuccessful strikes, the Haymarket Square Riot, excessive centralization of authority, and the emergence of the American Federation of Labor detracted from its prestige and led to its dissolution by 1900

Knight Templar *pl.* **Knights Templars** a member of the Order of the Poor Knights of Christ, a military and religious order founded in 1118 for the protection of pilgrims to the Holy Land. As a result of their military prowess, and of the attraction of their organization for men of noble birth and wealth, the Knights Templars became a powerful influence in the affairs of Europe. At the instigation of King Philippe IV of France the order was suppressed in 1312 by Pope Clement V

knit (nit) **1.** *v. pres. part.* **knit·ting** *past* and *past part.* **knit·ted, knit** *v.t.* to fashion (a garment, fabric etc.) by working yarn of wool, silk etc. on knitting needles or specialized machines in a succession of interlocking stitches ‖ to work (yarn) in this way ‖ to cause to join as if grown together or interwoven, *the treaty knit the economies of the two nations together* ‖ *v.i.* to practice knitting ‖ (esp. of a broken bone) to unite **to knit one's brows** to draw the eyebrows together in a frown **2.** *n.* a stitch in knitting in which the yarn is held behind the work and the right needle is inserted into a stitch behind the left needle, to form a new stitch (cf. PURL) **knit·ting** *n.* the act of someone who knits, or the process of a machine which knits ‖ work being knitted [O.E. *cnyttan*, to tie in a knot]

knitting needle one of two or more thin, long rods pointed at one or both ends, used in knitting by hand

knives *pl.* of KNIFE

knob (nɒb) *n.* a rounded, protuberant part of an object ‖ a rounded handle, e.g. of a door ‖ a rounded hill ‖ (*Br.*) a small lump of something, e.g. of coal or sugar [M.E.]

knob·ble (nɒb'l) *n.* a small knob **knób·bly** *adj.* [dim. of KNOB]

knob·by (nɒbi:) *comp.* **knob·bi·er** *superl.* **knob·bi·est** *adj.* having knobs ‖ like a knob

knob·ker·rie (nɒbkeri:) *n.* a short club with a thick, knobbed end [Afrik. *knopkirie*]

knock (nɒk) **1.** *v.t.* to make a sudden impact on ‖ (esp. with 'down', 'in', 'off', 'onto' etc.) to cause to move or fall by a sudden impact ‖ (with 'down') to demolish (a building etc.) ‖ to cause to come together with a sudden impact ‖ to cause by making a sudden impact on, *the car knocked a hole in the fence* ‖ (*pop.*) to find fault with ‖ *v.i.* to rap on a door with the knuckles or a knocker ‖ to come together with a sudden impact ‖ (of an internal-combustion engine) to make a rapping

sound due to faulty combustion ‖ (*pop.*) to find fault **to knock around** (or **about**) to subject to rough treatment ‖ to lead a roving life, *he has knocked about all over Europe* **to knock down** to sell (something) to the highest bidder at an auction ‖ to persuade (a seller) to reduce his price ‖ to reduce (a price) **to knock off** to do (a piece of work) esp. quickly and shoddily ‖ to cease (work) ‖ to deduct from, *he knocked a dollar off the price* ‖ to cease work **to knock on** (*rugby*) to hit the ball with the hand or arm toward the opponent's goal **to knock out** to empty by knocking, *to knock out a pipe* ‖ to render unconscious ‖ (*boxing*) to make incapable of getting up during the count ‖ to do (something) hastily ‖ (*pop.*) to exhaust, make weary **to knock together** to construct in a rough and ready way **to knock up** (*pop.*) to make (a woman) pregnant ‖ (*Br.*) to awaken ‖ (*Br.*) to make ill or exhausted ‖ (*cricket*) to score (runs) **2.** *n.* the impact or sound made by knocking ‖ a piece of bad luck or misfortune [O.E. *cnocian*]

knock·a·bout (nɒkəbaut) **1.** *adj.* (of clothing) suitable for rough work or play ‖ (of a play, film etc.) funny in a wildly farcical way, often involving slapstick or burlesque **2.** *n.* a sloop with a mainsail and jib, but no bowsprit ‖ knock about comedy

knock·down (nɒkdaun) *adj.* of a blow which knocks down ‖ of a price which has been knocked down to the lowest possible level ‖ of a large object so constructed that it may be taken apart for transportation

knock·er (nɒkər) *n.* a hinged, hammerlike attachment on a metal base fastened to a door, used in rapping for admittance ‖ (*Br.*) door-to-door salesman

knock-kneed (nɒkni:d) *adj.* having the legs curved inwards

knock-off (nɒkɔf) *n.* cheap, illicit reproduction of fine originals, esp. in fashion

knock·out (nɒkaut) *n.* (*abbr.* K.O.) a blow in boxing which makes a boxer unable to get up before he is counted out ‖ the act of delivering such a blow or an instance of this ‖ someone or something superlatively attractive ‖ (*Br.*) a sale at which articles are resold by auction after having been bought in on behalf of the operating group at a rigged price by cutting out competition ‖ (*Br.*) the act of doing this or an instance of this

knock-up (nɒkʌp) *n.* (*sports*) practice with bat or racket and ball just prior to a game

knoll (noul) *n.* a small rounded hill [O.E. *cnoll*, hilltop]

knop (nɒp) *n.* a decorative knob, esp. on glassware [M.E., etym. doubtful]

Knos·sos (nɒsəs) (Cnossus) the capital of Minos, Crete. Excavations begun in 1900, under Sir Arthur Evans, revealed its palace and the surrounding city (c. 2000 B.C.) as having been the center of a flourishing Minoan civilization

knot (nɒt) **1.** *n.* a place in a thread, string etc. where the thread passes through a loop in its own length and is pulled tight ‖ a place where two or more threads, strings etc. are joined by passing each of them through loops in the other and pulling tight ‖ a tangle of threads, strings etc. drawn tight ‖ an ornamental boss of ribbon, silver cord etc., e.g. a shoulder knot ‖ a lump, protrusion etc. in animal tissue or bone, esp. a constriction in a muscle ‖ a protrusion of growing plant tissues, e.g. in a grass stem, or where a branch grows from a tree trunk (or the hard cross section of this in a plank) ‖ a cluster of persons or things ‖ a difficulty, a problem hard to solve ‖ (*naut.*) a portion, marked off by knots, of a line attached to a log, formerly used to measure a ship's speed ‖ (*naut.*) a unit of speed, being 1 nautical mile per hour **2.** *v. pres. part.* **knot·ting** *past* and *past part.* **knot·ted** *v.t.* to tie in or with a knot ‖ to cause to form a knot ‖ *v.i.* to become tied in knots [O.E. *cnotta*]

knot *n.* a member of *Calidris*, a genus of sandpipers that migrate to temperate climates in winter and breed in the Arctic [origin unknown]

knot·grass (nɒtgræs, nɒtgrɑs) *n. Polygonum aviculare*, fam. *Polygonaceae*, a creeping weed with a jointed stem and small white, pink or green flowers

knot·hole (nɒthoul) *n.* a hole in a plank or log where a knot has fallen out

knot·ti·ness (nɒti:nis) *n.* the quality of being knotty

knot·ty (nɒti:) *comp.* **knot·ti·er** *superl.* **knot·ti·est** *adj.* having knots ‖ (of a problem etc.) hard to solve

knout (naut) **1.** *n.* a whip of leather strips with a short wooden handle, formerly used to flog criminals in Russia **2.** *v.t.* to flog with a knout [fr. F. spelling of Russ. *knut*]

know (nou) **1.** *v. pres. part.* **know·ing** *past* **knew** (nu:, nju:) *past part.* **known** (noun) *v.t.* to apprehend with the conscious mind, *to know truth from falsehood* ‖ to be acquainted with by experience, *do you know Athens?*, *to know hunger* ‖ to recognize, *he would know her if he saw her again* ‖ to have acquired skill in, *she knows how to swim* ‖ to be able to imagine, *we don't know how she manages* ‖ to be informed about, be in possession of the facts about, *do you know how old he is?* ‖ to have committed to memory, *to know one's lines in a play* ‖ to realize, *he doesn't know what is good for him* ‖ to be irrationally convinced of, *I always knew it would turn out badly* ‖ *v.i.* to possess knowledge, understanding or awareness of something ‖ to be certain of or convinced about something **to be known as** to be widely reputed to be, *he is known as a fair judge* **to know better than to** to be prudent or disciplined enough not to, *you should know better than to play with knives* **to know of** to be aware of **to know one's own mind** to be firm in one's opinions, wishes or decisions **to make oneself known** to introduce oneself **2.** *n.* (only in) **in the know** having inside information or sharing a secret [O.E. *cnāwan*]

know-all (nouɔl) *n.* and *adj.* know-it-all

know-how (nouhau) *n.* (*pop.*) thorough knowledge of the theory and esp. practice of a process, procedure etc.

know·ing (nouiŋ) *adj.* of a gesture or of behavior which suggests that a person has penetrated a secret or knows more than he admits or knows more than you do ‖ shrewd, *a knowing fellow* **know·ing·ly** *adv.* in a knowing manner ‖ deliberately

know-it-all (nouitɔl) **1.** *n.* someone who thinks he has not much to learn from other people **2.** *adj.* of or pertaining to a knowall

knowl·edge (nɒlidʒ) *n.* the state of knowing, cognition ‖ understanding, *intuitive knowledge* ‖ that which is known, *to apply one's knowledge* **to one's knowledge** so far as one knows **knowl·edge·a·ble** (nɒlidʒəb'l) *adj.* knowing a great deal, well-informed, *he is very knowledgeable about Sumerian art* [M.E. *knaulage*, *knowleche* fr. KNOW + obscure -*leche*]

known *past part.* of KNOW

Know-Noth·ing (nounʌθiŋ) *n.* (*Am. hist.*) a member of an American political party which flourished 1854–9, opposing immigration, esp. of Roman Catholics, and supporting slavery [after 'I know nothing', the reply given by the party's members to inquisitive questions]

Knox (nɒks), Henry (1750–1806), American general in the Revolutionary War. He founded (1779) a forerunner of the U.S. Military Academy at West Point. He was appointed (1789) the first U.S. secretary of war. He was a founder of the Society of the Cincinnati

Knox, John (c. 1505–72), Scottish religious leader, founder of Scottish Presbyterianism. Trained as a Roman Catholic priest, he was converted to Protestantism (c. 1545) by Wishart. As chaplain (1551–3) to Edward VI, he helped to draw up the 1552 Book of Common Prayer. In exile on the Continent (1553–9), he conferred with Calvin, and published his 'First Blast of the Trumpet Against the Monstrous Regiment of Women' (1558), a protest against the rule of Mary I in England and Mary of Guise in Scotland. After civil war (1559–60) had established Protestantism in Scotland, Knox played an important part in framing the 'Confession of Faith' (1560), which repudiated papal authority and forbade the Mass, but his 'Book of Discipline' (1560), in which he planned a rigid Calvinism, was rejected (1561) by the nobles

Knox, Philander Chase (1853–1921), U.S. politician. He served (1901–4) as attorney general under President William McKinley, and set new control on big business. He was secretary of state (1909–13) under President William Taft, extending U.S. interests in Latin America and the Near and Far East. His latter pursuit was criticized as 'dollar diplomacy'

Knox·ville (nɒksvil) a commercial and industrial center (pop. 175,030) of Tennessee, on the Tennessee River, headquarters of the Tennessee Valley Authority. State university

knuck·le (nʌk'l) **1.** *n.* a joint in the finger, esp. one at the base of each finger ‖ a bony knob

CONCISE PRONUNCIATION KEY: **(a)** æ, c*a*t; ɑ, c*a*r; ɔ f*aw*n; ei, sn*a*ke. **(e)** e, h*e*n; i:, sh*ee*p; iə, d*ee*r; εə, b*ea*r. **(i)** i, f*i*sh; ai, t*ig*er; ə:, b*ir*d. **(o)** o, *o*x; au, c*ow*; ou, g*oa*t; u, p*oo*r; ɔi, r*oy*al. **(u)** ʌ, d*u*ck; u, b*u*ll; u:, g*oo*se; ə, b*a*cillus; ju:, c*u*be. x, lo*ch*; θ, *th*ink; δ, bo*th*er; z, *Z*en; ʒ, cor*s*age; dʒ, sava*g*e; ŋ, oranguta*ng*; j, *y*ak; ʃ, *f*ish; tʃ, fe*tch*; 'l, rabb*le*; 'n, redd*en*. Complete pronunciation key appears inside front cover.

formed at each finger joint when the hand is clenched ‖ the middle joint of the tarsus of an animal ‖ a piece of meat comprising this joint and the surrounding flesh, *a knuckle of pork* ‖ a joint in a structure which has the shape of a knuckle or functions like one, e.g. the parts of a hinge containing the rotating pin **to be near the knuckle** to verge on indecency **2.** *v. pres. part.* **knuck·ling** *past* and *past part.* **knuck·led** *v.t.* to hit or rub with the knuckles ‖ *v.i.* **to knuckle down** to discipline oneself into beginning work **to knuckle under** to submit [M.E. *knokel*]

knuck·le·bone (nʌk'lbọun) *n.* a bone of a knuckle joint ‖ an animal bone with a rounded knob at the joint end

knuck·le·dust·er (nʌk'ldʌstər) *n.* brass knuckles

knuck·le·walk (nʌk'lwɔk) *v.* to walk with knuckles touching the ground, as some simians do

knur (nə:r) *n.* a hard excrescence, e.g. in a tree trunk [M.E. *knorre, knurre*]

knurl (nə:rl) *n.* a knot or knobby projection ‖ a bead or ridge raised as an ornament on a metal surface, or provided to afford a better grip

K.O. (kéɪou) **1.** *abbr.* (*boxing*) knockout **2.** *pl.* **K.O.'s** *n.* (*boxing*) knockout **3.** *pres. part.* **KO'ing** *past* and *past part.* **KO'd** *v.t.* (*boxing*) to knock out

ko·a (kóuə) *n. Acacia koa,* fam. *Papilionaceae,* a Hawaiian tree, the fine-grained wood of which is used in cabinetmaking ‖ this wood [native name]

ko·a·la (kouálə) *n. Phascolarctus cinereus,* fam. *Phlangeridae,* a sturdy marsupial of E. Australia, about 2 ft long, with thick gray fur, sometimes called a bear. Its claws are adapted for climbing trees, and it lives chiefly in the eucalyptus, feeding on its buds and shoots [native name]

Ko·be (kóubi:) a port (pop. 1,394,388) of Honshu, Japan, at the east end of the Inland Sea, serving Osaka, with shipbuilding, textile and chemical industries. University

Koblenz *COBLENZ

ko·bo (kóubou) *pl. kobo n.* unit of Nigerian currency, equal to ¹⁄₁₀₀ naira

Koch (kɔx), Robert (1843–1910), German bacteriologist who established the bacterial origin of anthrax (1876), typhoid (1880), tuberculosis (1882) and cholera (1883). He contributed to the understanding and control of these and other diseases esp. by preventive inoculations. Nobel prize (1905)

Ko·cha·now·ski (kɔxɑnɔ́fski:), Jan (1530–84), Polish poet, author of lyrics and satires, and of the elegiac 'Laments' (1580). He also wrote a Polish version of the Psalms of David

Ko·chi (kóutʃi:) a fishing port and agricultural center (pop. 224,000) in S. Shikoku, Japan

Ko·dak (kóudæk) *n.* a small hand camera [Trademark]

Ko·dá·ly (kódai), Zoltán (1882–1967), Hungarian composer and conductor, whose works, often based on native music, include 'Háry János' (1926), an opera, and 'Psalmus Hungaricus' (1923), for chorus and orchestra

Ko·di·ak (kóudi:æk) the largest island (area 3,465 sq. miles) of Alaska, south of the Aleutian Peninsula: salmon, furs

Kodiak bear *Ursus middendorffi,* fam. *Ursidae,* the very large brown bear of Alaska, sometimes weighing over 1,400 lbs

Ko·dok (kóudok) *FASHODA

ko·el (kóuəl) *n.* any of several members of *Eudynamys,* a genus of cuckoos found in India, New Guinea and Australia [Hindi *kóil* fr. Skr.]

Koestler (késtlər), Arthur (1905–83), British writer, born in Hungary, who wrote on psychology and disillusionment with Communism. A member of the German Communist party (1931–8), he emigrated to Britain and became a citizen in 1945. His novels include 'Darkness at Noon' (1940), 'The Sleepwalkers' (1959), 'The Act of Creation' (1964), 'The Thirteenth Tribe' (1976), 'Janus' (1978), 'Bricks to Babel' (1980) and 'Kaleidoscope' (1981). He committed suicide in 1983

ko·gai (kougái) (Japanese; usu. italics) environmental pollution

kohl (koul) *n.* a finely powdered antimony used esp. in the East by women to darken the rims of the eyelids [Arab.]

Köh·ler (ké:lər), Wolfgang (1887–1967), German-U.S. psychologist who discovered many new aspects of the Gestalt theory, of figural

aftereffects, and of electrical processes in the brain

kohl·ra·bi (koulrábi:, kóulrɑbi:) *pl.* **kohl·ra·bies** *n.* any of various cabbages with an edible turniplike stem, cultivated as a vegetable or cattle fodder [G. fr. Ital.]

ko·jah (kóudʒa) *n.* long-haired mutant mink with soft, thick pelt

Ko·kand (kʌkánt) a trade and industrial center (pop. 155,000) of Uzbekistan, U.S.S.R., in the Ferghana Valley

Ko·kiu (gɔ́dʒióu) China's chief tin-mining center (pop. 160,000), in S. Yunnan

Ko·ko Nor (kóukóunɔ́r) *TSING HAI

Ko·kosch·ka (koukɔ́ʃkɑ), Oskar (1886–1980), German expressionist painter. His portraits and landscapes combine traditional representational elements (which predominate) with expressionist tendencies to distort elements

Ko·ku·ra (kókurá) a port in N. Kyushu, Japan, part of the KitaKyushu conurbation

ko·la nut, co·la nut (kóulə) the fruit of the kola tree chewed as a mild stimulant and used as a tonic, a digestive, and in the manufacture of soft drinks [W. African]

Ko·la Peninsula (kɔ́lə) the northeast arm (5,000 sq. miles) of the Scandinavian peninsula, between the Barents Sea and the White Sea, part of the R.S.F.S.R., U.S.S.R., peopled by Lapps and Russians. The north is tundra, the south forest. Minerals: nickel, cobalt, copper. Chief town: Murmansk

Ko·lar Gold Fields (koulár) a town (pop. 160,000) in E. Mysore, center of India's gold-mining industry

kola tree, cola tree a member of *Cola,* fam. *Sterculiaceae,* a genus of tropical trees from which kola nuts are obtained, esp. *C. nitida* [W. African]

Kol·chak (kʌltʃák), Aleksandr Vasilyevich (1874–1920), Russian admiral and counter-revolutionary. He carried off a coup d'état (1918) in Siberia, and was recognized as ruler of Russia by the Allies. He was betrayed to the Bolsheviks (1920) and shot

Kö·len (ké:lən) *KJÖLEN

Kol·ha·pur (kóulhɑpú:r) a city (pop. 259,050) in Maharashtra, India: agricultural trade

ko·lin·sky (kɑlínski:) *pl.* **ko·lin·skies** *n.* any of various Asiatic minks, esp. *Mustela sibirica,* fam. *Mustelidae* ‖ their fur [Russ. after *Kola,* district in N.W. Russia]

kol·khoz (kʌlxɔ́z) *n.* a collective farm in the U.S.S.R. [Russ. *kollektivnoe,* collective+*khozaistvo,* farm]

Koll·witz (kɔ́lvits), Käthe (1867–1945), German lithographer, known esp. for compassionate studies of the poor

Köln (kə:ln) *COLOGNE

Ko·ly·ma (kɑlimá) a river of N.E. Siberia, U.S.S.R., flowing 1,600 miles northeast from the Khabarovsk territory to the Arctic Ocean, navigable for 1,000 miles. Its upper course crosses a large goldfield

Ko·mi A.S.S.R. (kɔ́mji) an autonomous republic (area 162,000 sq. miles, pop. 1,147,000) of the R.S.F.S.R., U.S.S.R., in the N.W. Urals, inhabited by the Komi, a Finnish people. Capital: Syktyvkar (pop. 180,000)

Komintern *COMINTERN

Kom·so·molsk (kʌmsəmólsk) a city (pop. 274,000) of E. Siberia, U.S.S.R., on the Amur, founded (1932) by young Communist volunteers: steelworks, oil refineries, shipyards

Konia *KONYA

Kö·nig·grätz, Battle of (ké:nixgrɛts) *SADOWA, BATTLE OF

Kö·nigs·berg (ké:nixsbərk) *KALININGRAD

Kö·nigs·hüt·te (ké:nixshytə) *CHORZÓW

Ko·no·ye (kɔ́njé), Prince Fumimaro (1891–1945), Japanese statesman, prime minister of Japan (1937–9 and 1940–1). He committed suicide before he could be tried as a war criminal

Kon·stanz (kɔ́nstɑnts) *CONSTANCE

Kon·ya, Kon·ia (kɔ́nja) (ancient Iconium) a walled city (pop. 246,727) of central Turkey, an agricultural market

kook (ku:k) *n.* (*colloq.*) an eccentric —**kookily** *adv.* —**kookiness** *n.* —**kooky** *adj.*

kook·a·bur·ra (kukəbá:rə) *n. Dacelo gigas,* fam. *Alcedinidae,* a large Australian kingfisher having a raucous laughlike call [native name]

Koo·ning (dəku:niŋ), Willem de (1904–), American painter born in Holland, an originator of abstract expressionism

kopeck *COPECK

kop·je (kópi:) *n.* a small hill in South Africa [Du., dim. of *kop,* head]

kor·a (kóurə) *n.* musical instrument with 21 strings, native to West Africa

Ko·ran (kɔrán, kourán, kɔræn, kouræn) *n.* the holy scripture of Islam, claimed to be a direct transmission of the word of God revealed to Mohammed. It consists of 114 suras, poetic utterances of varying lengths. The definitive version was prepared under the third caliphate (c. 650-6). Its provisions govern all the transactions of Moslem daily life and local law as well as Moslem worship. It has been translated from the Arabic into many languages **Ko·ran·ic** (kɔrǽnik, kourǽnik) *adj.* [Arab. *qurān, qorān,* recitation]

Kor·do·fan (kɔrdoufán) a province (area 146,929 sq. miles, pop. 2,052,000) of the central Sudan: gum arabic, cotton, cattle

Ko·re·a (kɔri:ə, kourí:ə) a peninsula in N.E. Asia, extending south from Manchuria between the Sea of Japan and the Yellow Sea, and divided into the Republic of Korea (South Korea) and the Democratic People's Republic of Korea (North Korea). HISTORY. China founded a colony in the north of Korea (12th c. B.C.) and extended her influence over the whole country (7th c. B.C.). Korea was invaded by Mongol forces (1231–60). Buddhism was replaced (early 15th c.) by Confucianism as the official creed. Invasions from Japan were repelled (1592, 1597). Manchu invasions (1627, 1636) brought Korea under Chinese control for three centuries Korea's isolation ended with the opening of ports to Japanese trade (1876). As a result of the 1st Sino-Japanese War (1894–5), Korea became independent (1895). After the Russo-Japanese War, Korea became a Japanese protectorate (1905) and was officially annexed (1910). During the 2nd world war, the U.S.A., China and Britain promised Korea independence (1943) at the end of the war. After the surrender of Japan, Korea was divided at the 38th parallel into two zones of occupation (1945). The U.S.S.R. controlled the north, where industry and trade were concentrated, and the U.S.A. controlled the agricultural south. Elections were held (1948) in the south, a democratic constitution was promulgated and the Republic of Korea, with Syngman Rhee as its first president, was proclaimed (July 17, 1948). In the north, a people's republic, the Democratic People's Republic of Korea was proclaimed (Sept. 9, 1948). Innumerable incidents culminated in the Korean War (1950–3). (For subsequent history *KOREA, DEMOCRATIC PEOPLE'S REPUBLIC OF, *KOREA, REPUBLIC OF)

Korea, Democratic People's Republic of (North Korea) a republic (area 46,814 sq. miles, pop. 19,630,000) in N.E. Asia. Capital: Pyongyang. Language: Korean. Religions: Buddhism, Confucianism, Shamanism, Tonghak. The land is 18% arable and 80% forest (largely coniferous). Rugged mountains, rising to 9,003 ft (Mt Paektu), cover the north-central area. They lead into a chain which extends down the eastern coast into South Korea. In the west are fertile lowlands watered by large, navigable rivers (Chon-ghon, Taedong). Average temperatures (F.): Pyongyang (Jan.) 18°, (July) 72° (winters are much colder in the interior and east). Rainfall varies from 20 ins along the Yalu River (Manhurian border) to 60 ins in the south. Livestock: cattle, hogs, sheep, goats, rabbits and poultry. Over 40% of cultivated land is under irrigation. Agricultural products: cereals (esp. rice and corn, vegetables, flax, hemp, tobacco, meat, milk, fruit, silk, eggs. Minerals: iron ore, tungsten, coal, lead, gold and silver. Industries: iron and steel, chemicals (esp. fertilizers), building materials, ships, hydroelectricity (Yalu River), tractors, textiles, consumer goods, oil refining, fishing. Imports: agricultural products, machinery, fuels, textiles. Leading seaports: Chungjin, Heungnam. University: Kim Il Sung (1946), in Pyongyang. Monetary unit: North Korean won (100 jun). HISTORY. After the Korean War (for previous history *KOREA) North Korea was absorbed in the Soviet defense and economic system, and attempts were made to develop industry. During the 1960's North Korea tried to dissociate itself from the dispute between China and the U.S.S.R.; it declared its political independence in 1966. Neither China nor the U.S.S.R. intervened during the 'Pueblo' incident (1968), which brought about increased tension. Allegations of North Korean involvement in the

CONCISE PRONUNCIATION KEY: **(a)** æ, c*a*t; ɑ, c*a*r; ɔ f*aw*n; ei, sn*a*ke. **(e)** e, h*e*n; i:, sh*ee*p; iə, d*ee*r; ɛə, b*ea*r. **(i)** i, f*i*sh; ai, t*i*ger; ə:, b*i*rd. **(o)** o, *o*x; au, c*ow*; ou, g*oa*t; u, p*oo*r; ɔi, r*oy*al. **(u)** ʌ, d*u*ck; u, b*u*ll; u:, g*oo*se; ə, b*a*cillus; ju:, c*u*be. x, lo*ch*; θ, *th*ink; ð, bo*th*er; z, *Z*en; ʒ, corsa*ge*; dʒ, sava*ge*; ŋ, ora*ng*utang; j, *y*ak; ʃ, *f*ish; tʃ, fe*tch*; 'l, rabb*le*; 'n, redd*en*. Complete pronunciation key appears inside front cover.

assassination of several key South Korean officials in Burma (1983) strained relations with South Korea, but subsequent talks on trade and other issues eased tensions somewhat

Ko·re·a·gate (kərí:əgeit) n. series of scandals involving bribe and favor-taking by U.S. Congressmen from Tong Sun Park, Korean businessman, and other South Korean agents

Ko·re·an (kərí:ən, kourí:ən) 1. n. a native or inhabitant of Korea || the language of these people 2. adj. of Korea || of the Koreans or their language

Korea, Republic of (South Korea) a republic (area 38,452 sq. miles, pop. 41,999,000) in N.E. Asia. Capital: Seoul. Religion: Confucianism, Shamanism and Buddhism, with Christian and Tonghak minorities. Language: Korean. The land is 21% arable and 57% forest (deciduous and tropical). Mountains, less rugged than in the north, run down the east coast (to 5,160 ft) and into the south center (to 6,280 ft), divided in the southeast by the basin of the Naktong River (navigable for 200 miles). The west consists of cultivated plains, watered by wide rivers (Han, Kum, Yongsan) which cross the country from the east. There are over 3,000 offshore islands, the largest being Cheju (area 710 sq. miles, pop. 255,000) off the south coast. Average temperatures (F.) in Jan. and July: Seoul 20° and 74°, the south 35° and 77°. Rainfall: 50–60 ins (increasing southwards). Livestock: cattle, hogs, poultry. Agricultural products: rice, cereals, soybeans, tobacco, cotton, fruit. Fisheries, including whaling, are important. Mineral resources: tungsten (2nd world producer), graphite, iron ore, copper, kaolin, gold, silver, lead. Manufactures and industries: textiles, cement, foodstuffs, machinery and metals, cotton, footwear, tires, paper, electricity, matches, ships, pottery. Exports: graphite, tungsten, iron ores, raw silk, fish and fish products, seaweed, cotton sheeting. Imports: foodstuffs, chemicals (esp. fertilizers), cloth, machinery, fuels and oil. Ports: Pusan, Mokpo, Inchon, Masan. There are 15 universities. Monetary unit: South Korean hwan (100 won). HISTORY (for previous history *KOREA). Aid from the U.S.A. and the U.N. enabled South Korea to rebuild its economy after the Korean War, but overpopulation, a low level of industrialization, shortage of natural resources and the maintenance of a large standing army present critical problems. Rhee's government was forced to resign (1960) and a military junta took power (1961) led by Gen. Park Chung Hee, who was elected president in 1963. Resentment against Park's increasing powers led to the imposition of military rule (1972) and in 1975 all political opposition was banned. Park was fatally shot (1979), and Prime Minister Choi Kyu Hah was subsequently elected president. An uprising in Kwangju, sparked by protests against the reimposition of martial law (1980), was suppressed by the army, and soon after, a military committee led by Chun Doo Hwan took power. Chun became president (1981) under the terms of a new constitution. The shooting down of a Korean Air line passenger plane (1983) that had strayed into Soviet air space caused international tension. In 1985 an opposition party led by Kim Dae Jung won an impressive number of seats in the assembly, a major setback for Chun and his ruling party

Korean War the war (June 25, 1950–July 27, 1953) between North Korea, supported by Chinese Communist forces, and South Korea, supported by the U.N., whose forces came very largely from the U.S.A. The North Koreans invaded South Korea, and rapidly drove U.N. forces under MacArthur back to a small area around Pusan (Aug. 1950). MacArthur launched (Sept. 1950) a counteroffensive with a surprise landing at Inchon, a hundred miles behind the fighting front. U.N. forces recaptured (Sept. 1950) Seoul, drove the invaders back north of the 38th parallel, and advanced through North Korea, capturing Pyongyang, until they reached (Nov. 1950) the Manchurian frontier. But on Nov. 26, 1951, a quarter of a million Chinese troops crossed the frontier and threw back the U.N. forces with heavy losses. In this second phase of the war, the Chinese recovered all North Korea, recaptured Seoul, and carried the war even farther southward. When MacArthur complained openly against the restrictions under which President Truman required him to make war, and even issued a personal demand to the Chinese to surrender,

Truman replaced him with Gen. Matthew Ridgway. U.N. forces again recaptured Seoul and by spring of 1951 the contending armies were facing each other along a line close to the 38th parallel. Negotiations for a truce began (July 1951) and agreement was reached (1953) for division of the country on the basis of approximately the final battle line, which actually gave South Korea more territory than it had held before hostilities. Total U.N. casualties numbered 118,515 dead, of which 33,729 were U.S., and 264,581 wounded, of which 103,284 were U.S.

Korn·berg (kórnbərg), Arthur (1918–), U.S. physician and biochemist. He shared with Severo Ochoa the 1959 Nobel prize for medicine for his work on the synthesis of nucleic acids. He discovered an enzyme ensuring the synthesis of deoxyribonucleic acid

ko·ru·na (kórunə) pl. **ko·run** (kórun), **ko·ru·ny** (kóruni), **ko·ru·nas** (kórunəs) n. the basic monetary unit of Czechoslovakia || a coin worth one koruna [Czech=crown]

Korzyb·ski (kərzípski:), Alfred Habdank Skarbek (1879–1950), Polish-U.S. scientist and philosopher, who founded general semantics. He wrote 'Science and Sanity: an Introduction to Non-Aristotelian Systems and General Semantics' (1933)

Kos, Cos (kɒs, kɔs) an island (area 111 sq. miles, pop. 17,939) in the Dodecanese

Kos·ci·us·ko (kɔʃtʃúʃkɔ, kɒsi:ʌskou), Tadeusz Andrzej Bonawentura (1746–1817), Polish general and patriot. He served with distinction in the American army in the Revolutionary War, returned to Poland (1784), and led an unsuccessful revolt against Russia (1794)

Kos·ci·us·ko, Mt (kɒsi:ʌskou) the highest mountain (7,316 ft) of Australia, in the Australian Alps, New South Wales

ko·sher (kóuʃər) adj. (of food) conforming to the requirements of the Jewish dietary laws || (of shops, restaurants etc.) selling, preparing or serving such food || (pop.) genuine, legitimate [Heb. kāshēr, fit, proper]

Ko·ši·ce (kóʃitse) the chief trade center (pop. 191,000) of E. Slovakia, Czechoslovakia. Gothic cathedral (14th c.)

Ko·so·vo-Me·to·hi·ja (kósɔvɔmetóhi:ja) an autonomous province (area 4,200 sq. miles, pop. 886,000, largely Albanian) in S.W. Serbia, Yugoslavia. Capital: Pristina. Products: cereals, tobacco, fruit, cattle and sheep

Ko·so·vo Po·lje, Battle of (kósɔvɔpólje) a battle (1389) in which the Turks defeated a combined army of Serbs, Albanians, Bosnians, Montenegrins and Bulgarians, breaking the power of Serbia and Bulgaria, and subjecting them to the Ottoman Empire

Kos·suth (kɔʃu:t), Lajos (1802–94), Hungarian statesman. He was a main leader of the Hungarian revolution of 1848, and headed the revolutionary government. He was forced into exile (1849) when Russian and Austrian troops crushed the revolution

Ko·sy·gin (kʌsí:gín), Alexei Nikolayevich (1904–80), Russian statesman, premier of the Soviet Union (1964–80)

Ko·ta·ba·ru (kóutəbáru:) *SUKARNAPURA

Ko·ta Bha·ru (kóutəbáru:) the capital (pop. 170,559) of Kelantan, Malaysia, a sea and river port near the Thai border

Ko·ta Kin·a·ba·lu (kóutəkinəbəlú:) (formerly Jesselton) the capital (pop. 22,000) of Sabah, Malaysia, on the coast of N.E. Borneo, exporting rubber

Kottbus *COTTBUS

Kot·ze·bue (kótsəbu:) August Friedrich Ferdinand von (1761–1819), German dramatist whose work includes 'Menschenhass und Reue' (1789). His murder by a demented German student provoked the Karlsbad Decrees

kou·miss, ku·miss (kú:mis) n. an alcoholic drink made by fermenting mare's or camel's milk [F. koumis fr. Tatar kumiz]

Kou·rou (ku:ru:) a town (pop. 5,000) in French Guiana, 26 miles north of Cayenne. It was selected (1967) as the site of a $102-million French space center.

Kov·no (kóvnʌ) *KAUNAS

Ko·weit (kouwéit) *KUWAIT

Kow·loon (káulú:n) *HONG KONG

kow·tow (káutáu, kóutáu) v.i. to kneel, touching the ground with the forehead, as a token of homage or deep respect among the Chinese || to humble oneself in a servile way [Chin. k'o-t'ou fr. k'o, knock + t'ou, head]

Ko·zhi·kode (kóuʒikóud) (Calicut) the chief port (pop. 160,000) on the Malabar Coast, Madras, India. It was the first Indian port reached by da Gama (1498). Products: textiles, coffee, cocoa, spices

K.P. (kéipí:) (mil.) enlisted men detailed for work in army kitchens || this work [abbr. of kitchen police]

K particle *KAON

Kra (krɑ) the isthmus of Thailand connecting the Malay Peninsula and the Asian mainland

kraal (krɑl) n. a S. African village, or group of huts, enclosed by a palisade || an enclosure for cattle or sheep in S. Africa [Afrik.]

krad (kræd) n. unit of gamma-ray radiation from K-radiation, equal to 1,000 rads (each of 100 ergs) syn. kilorad

Krafft-E·bing (kráftéibiŋ), Baron Richard von (1840–1902), German neurologist and pioneer in psychiatry. His most famous work is 'Psychopathia Sexualis' (1886, Eng. trans. 1892)

kraft (kræft, krɑft) n. strong brown paper made from sulfate wood pulp, and used for wrapping, paper bags and as a dielectric [G.=strength]

krait (krait) n. any of several members of Bungarus, a genus of deadly poisonous snakes of S.E. Asia [Hindi karait]

Krak (krɑk) *KERAK

Kra·ka·tan (krɑkatán) *KRAKATOA

Kra·ka·to·a (krɑkətóuə) (Krakatan) a small volcanic island between Sumatra and Java, Indonesia, almost destroyed in an eruption (1883)

Kra·ków (krǽkau, krákuf) a city (pop. 706,100) on the Upper Vistula, S. Poland, a great trade center, with machinery, food and chemical industries. It was the capital (14th–17th cc.). Gothic cathedral (14th c.). University (1364)

Kras·no·dar (krɑsnədár) a city (pop. 595,000) of the southwest R.S.F.S.R., U.S.S.R., an industrial center of Caucasia: oil refining, engineering, textiles

Kras·no·yarsk (krɑsnəjársk) a city (pop. 845,000) of central Siberia, U.S.S.R., on the Yenisei: oil refineries, engineering, synthetic rubber, hydroelectricity

kra·ter (kréitər) n. (hist.) a large vase for mixing wine and water used by the ancient Greeks and Romans [Gk]

K ration an emergency food ration developed in the 2nd world war for U.S. armed forces [K for Ancel Keys (1904–), U.S. physiologist]

KREEP (kri:p) n. moon rock with high content of potassium, phosphorous, and rare minerals, dated 4.5 billion yrs old Cf FERROPSEUDOBROOKITE

Kre·feld (kréifelt) a town (pop. 224,100) of North Rhine-Westphalia, West Germany, on the lower Rhine: textiles

Kre·mer (kréimər) *MERCATOR

krem·lin (krémlin) n. a fortress or citadel of a Russian city **Krem·lin** the citadel (founded in the 12th c.) of Moscow and seat of the Russian government. It contains the former Imperial Palace, three cathedrals (15th–17th cc.) and many official buildings **the Kremlin** the Russian government [F. fr. Russ. kreml, citadel fr. Tatar]

Krem·lin·ol·o·gist (krémlənálədʒəst) n. an expert on the workings and the thinking of Soviet internal and external politics —**Kremlinological** adj. —**Kremlinology** n.

krim·mer, crim·mer (krímər) n. a tightly curled gray fur made from the skins of young lambs in the Crimea [fr. Russ. Krim, Crimea]

kris, creese (kri:s) pl. **kris·es, crees·es** n. a wavy-bladed dagger used by Malays [Malay]

Krish·na (kríʃnə) (Hindu religion) the eighth avatar of Vishnu. He is widely worshipped as a god

Krishna (river) *KISTNA

Krishna Men·on (ménən), Vengalil Krishnan (1896–1974), Indian statesman. He became Indian high commissioner in London (1947–52), and minister of defense (1957–62) after playing a leading part in the Indian independence movement

Kris·ti·an·i·a (krjstiáni:ɑ, krjstʃi:ǽni:ə) *OSLO

Kris·tian·sand (krístʃənsænd, krjstjansán) a port (pop. 60,700) of S. Norway, on the Skagerrak

Kri·voi Rog (krivóirók) a city (pop. 650,000) of the Ukraine, U.S.S.R., on the east edge of the Donets Basin: iron and coal mines

kro·na (krú:nɑ) pl. **kro·nor** (krú:nur) n. the standard monetary unit of Sweden (= 100 öre) || a coin worth one of this value [Swed.=crown]

kro·na (krú:na) *pl.* **kro·nur** (krú:nyr) *n.* the standard monetary unit of Iceland ‖ a note of this value [Icelandic=crown]

kro·ne (krú:nə) *pl.* **kro·ner** (krú:nər) *n.* the standard monetary unit of Denmark and of Norway (=100 öre) ‖ a coin or note representing one krone [Dan.=crown]

Kro·nos (króunɒs) Cronus

Kron·stadt (krʌnʃtát) a fortified naval port (pop. 175,264) on the small island of Kotlin in the Gulf of Finland, 32 miles west of Leningrad, U.S.S.R. It was founded (1703) by Peter I

Kro·pot·kin (krʌpótkin), Prince Pyotr Alekseyevich (1842–1921), Russian social philosopher and anarchist. In 'Mutual Aid' (1902) he expressed his belief in the fundamental goodness of living creatures. Other works are 'The Great French Revolution' (1909) and 'Ethics' (1924)

Kru *C.R.U

Kru·ger (krú:gər), Stephanus Johannes Paulus (1825–1904), also known as 'Paul Kruger' and 'Oom Paul', Boer statesman. As president of the Transvaal (1883–1900), he steadfastly opposed Cecil Rhodes and British expansion in South Africa. His refusal to enfranchise the Uitlanders provoked the Jameson Raid (1895) and led to the Boer War (1899–1902)

Kruger National park the world's largest game preserve (area over 8,400 sq. miles) in the Transvaal, South Africa, founded (1898) by Kruger

Kru·gers·dorp (krú:gərzdɔrp) a mining center (pop. 102,940) in the Transvaal, South Africa: gold, manganese

kruller *CRULLER

Krupp (krʌp, krup) a family of German industrialists whose factories in Essen played a large part in the growth of German militarism from Bismarck to Hitler, as well as in the postwar economic recovery of West Germany

Kry·lov (krilóf), Ivan Andreevich (1769–1844), Russian author, most famous for his fables

kryp·ton (krípton) *n.* an inert, colorless, gaseous element (symbol Kr, at. no. 36, at. mass 83.80), forming 1 part in 1 million parts by volume of the atmosphere. It is separated during the production of oxygen from liquid air and is used in fluorescent and incandescent lamps [fr. Gk *krupton*, hidden]

kshat·ri·ya (kʃǽtri:ə) *n.* a Hindu of the second of the four chief castes, comprising warriors and rulers (*BRAHMIN, *SUDRA, *VAISYA) [Skr. fr. *ksha-tra*, rule]

Kua·la Lum·pur (kwáləlumpúər) the capital (pop. 937,875) of Malaysia and a commercial center: tin, rubber. University (1962). It was designated a separate federal territory (1974)

Ku·bi·tschek (kú:bitʃek), Juscelino de Oliveira (1902–), Brazilian statesman and president (1956–61). He gave new impetus to the economy and transferred (1960) the capital to Brasília, which he had built to develop the interior

Ku·blai Khan (kú:blaikán) (c. 1216–94), Mongol emperor (1260–94), grandson of Genghis Khan. By 1279 he had completed his family's conquest of China and established his capital at Cambaluc (modern Peking). He also added Korea and Burma to his empire, which extended from the Black Sea to the China Sea. He encouraged Chinese culture and he invited Christian missionaries, although Buddhism was the established religion. His attempt to invade Cochin-China (1278) and Japan (1274–81) failed. He founded the Yuan dynasty (1279–1368)

Ku·ching (kú:tʃiŋ) the capital (pop. 120,000) and port of Sarawak: rice and sago mills

Ku·chuk Kai·na·rji, Treaty of (ku:tʃú:kkainárji) a treaty (1774) between Russia and Turkey, giving Russia part of the Crimea, and placing Moldavia and Walachia under Turkish suzerainty. Orthodox Christians in the Ottoman Empire were placed under Russian protection. The treaty ended the Russo-Turkish War (1768–74) and was one of the origins of the Eastern Question

ku·dos (kúdos, kjú:dɒs, kú:dous, kjú:dous) *n.* praise, credit [Gk=glory]

Kufic *CUFIC

Kui·by·shev (kújbiʃəf) (formerly Samara) a city (pop. 1,244,000) of the R.S.F.S.R., U.S.S.R., on the Volga: engineering, paper, oil refining

Ku Klux Klan (kú:klʌksklæn, kjú:klʌksklæn) an American secret society, founded c. 1866 to maintain white supremacy and to oppose the rule of carpetbaggers in the South after the Civil War. Its increasing violence brought it into disrepute, and it was declared illegal (1871) ‖ a terrorist nationalist secret society, founded (1915) in the U.S.A. Anti-black, anti-Jew, anti-Catholic and anti-foreigner, it won many followers in the 1920s.

kuk·ri (kúkri:) *n.* a short, curved knife used by Gurkhas [Hindi]

Ku·kul·cán (ku:ku:lkán) the Mayan deity identified with the Toltec-Aztec Quetzalcóatl, and honored in the great pyramid at Chichén Itzá

ku·lak (kulák, kú:lɒk) *n.* a member of a well-to-do class of Russian peasants who were enabled to become landowners by the agrarian reforms (1906) of Stolypin. The kulaks opposed collectivization after the Bolshevik revolution and were liquidated (1929) as a class by Stalin [Russ.]

Kul·dja (kúldʒá) (*Chin.* Ining) a town (pop. 108,000) in N.W. Sinkiang, China, the trade center of a fruit-growing district

Kul·tur·kampf (kultú:rkɑmpf) *n.* Bismarck's struggle (1872-9) against the Catholic clergy, involving the expulsion of the Jesuits from Germany (1872) and the severance of relations between Prussia and the Holy See [G. *kultur*, culture + *kampf*, battle]

Ku·ma·mo·to (kú:mɑmɔ́tɔ) a commercial city (pop. 526,000) of W. Kyushu, Japan, a Buddhist pilgrimage place. Castle (16th c.)

Ku·ma·si (kumási) the capital (pop. 351,629) of Ashanti, Ghana, a trade (cocoa, livestock) and communications center. It was capital of the Ashanti kingdom (17th–19th cc.). University (1961)

Kum·ba·ko·nam (kụ:mbəkóunəm) a town (pop. 112,000) in Madras, India, on the Cauvery delta: silk weaving, brasswork. Brahman temples

kumiss *KOUMISS

küm·mel (kýmǝl) *n.* a colorless liqueur flavored with caraway seeds [G.]

kum·quat, cum·quat (kʌ́mkwɒt) *n.* a member of *Fortunella*, fam. *Rutaceae*, a genus of Asiatic citrus trees ‖ a fruit of any of these trees [dial. Chin. fr. *Chin chii*, golden orange]

kumrl (kʌ́mǝrl) *n.* the above-ground bed of a fox

Kun (kun), Béla (1886–1937), Hungarian communist leader. He overthrew the régime of Karolyi, and became (1919) president of Hungary, which he reorganized on communist lines. He was forced into exile four months later

kun·da·li·ni (kụndəlí:ni:) *n.* (*yoga*) life force believed to be at the base of the spine, which when aroused, triggers intelligence and spiritual insight

kung fu (kǝŋfú:) *n.* an oriental self-defense technique

Kung·ka Shan (kúŋkɑʃán) *MINYA KONKA

Kun·lun (kúnlún) a mountain system (1,000 miles long) of Central Asia, often over 20,000 ft (Ulagh Muztagh, 25,340 ft, is China's highest peak). It forms the northern frontier of Tibet, dropping to the Tarim basin and Gobi Desert, and extends east into China

Kun·ming (kúnmíŋ) (formerly Yunnanfu) the capital (pop. 1,990,603) of Yunnan, S.W. China, on the Burma Road, connected by air with India and by rail with North Vietnam: copper foundries, hydroelectric plants. University

kunz·ite (kúntsait) *n.* (*mineral.*) a lilac-colored, crystalline variety of spodumene, used as a gem [after G. F. *Kunz* (1856–1932), U.S. gem expert]

Kuo·min·tang (kwóumịntæŋ, gwómíndáŋ) a Chinese political party (lit. 'the nationalist people's party') founded (1911) by Sun Yat-sen, with the aim of founding a modern state through nationalism, democracy and socialism. Under Chiang Kai-shek it ruled China (1926–49). It withdrew to Taiwan after military defeat by the Communists

Ku·ra (kurá) (ancient Cyrus) a river (825 miles long, navigable for 300 miles) of Caucasia, rising in N.E. Turkey and flowing through Georgia and Azerbaijan, U.S.S.R., into the Caspian: hydroelectricity (Tbilisi)

kur·cha·to·vi·um (kərtʃǝtóuvi:ǝm) *n.* Soviet name for element 104, Rutherfordium, created by bombarding plutonium 242 with neon 22; named for I. V. Kurchatov, Russian physicist

Kurd (kə:rd, ku:rd) 1. *n.* a native of Kurdistan ‖ the Indo-European language of the Kurds 2. *adj.* of the Kurds or of Kurdistan **Kúrd·ish** 1. *adj.* of the Kurds or their language 2. *n.* the Kurdish language

—The Kurds are a Sunni Moslem people of farmers (grain, cotton, tobacco, fruit), herders (horses, oxen, sheep, goats) and rugmakers. Nationalist rebellions have been frequent

Kur·di·stan (kə:rdistæn, ku:rdistán) a mountainous region (pop. 2,500,000) in the adjoining parts of Turkey, Iraq and Iran, inhabited by the Kurds. Kurdish autonomy in Iraq was recognized (1970) by the Iraqi government

Ku·re (kú:ré) a port (pop. 235,000) and naval base in S.W. Honshu, Japan, on Hiroshima Bay: shipyards

Ku·ri·a Mu·ri·a Islands (kúǝri:əmúǝri:ǝ) a group of five barren islands (area 28 sq. miles, pop. 78) 20–40 miles off the coast of Oman

Ku·rile Islands (kúǝril, kurí:l) a group of 32 volcanic islands (total area 6,159 sq. miles, pop. 6,000) stretching 730 miles between the Kamchatka peninsula, U.S.S.R., and Hokkaido, Japan. The Yalta Conference granted them to the U.S.S.R.

Kursk (kursk) a town (pop. 390,000) in the W. central R.S.F.R., U.S.S.R., center of a rich agricultural region: engineering, textiles

ku·ru (kúru:) *n.* (*med.*) viral degenerative central nervous system disease, native to the Fore tribes in New Guinea, said to have been acquired through ritual cannibalism. It is characterized by trembling, spasticity, and progressive dementia

ku·rus (kurú:ʃ) *pl.* **ku·rus** *n.* a Turkish monetary unit equal to one hundredth of a Turkish pound ‖ a coin of this value [Turk.]

ku·sam (kú:sæm) *n. Schleichera oleosa*, fam. *Sapindaceae*, a tree of S.E. Asia yielding a hard, red wood and seeds from which macassar oil is obtained [origin unknown]

Kusch (kuʃ), Polykarp (1911–), U.S. physicist. He shared with Willis Eugene Lamb, Jr the 1955 Nobel prize in physics for work in precise measurement of electromagnetic properties of the electron

Kus·ko·kwim (kʌ́skoukwim) a river (c. 550 miles long) rising in the Alaska Range and flowing southwest to Kuskokwim Bay, an inlet of the Bering Sea

Kutch (kʌtʃ) a former state of India, now part of Gujarat (*RANN OF KUTCH)

Ku·tu·zov (kutú:zəf), Mikhail Ilarionovich (1745–1813), Russian field marshal. Succeeding Barclay de Tolly as commander in chief of the Russian army (1812), he was heavily defeated at Borodino (1812), and continued Barclay de Tolly's policy of retreat. He harried Napoleon's army brilliantly on the retreat from Moscow, winning a decisive victory at the Beresina (1812)

Ku·wait, Ku·weit (kuwéit, kuwáit) a state (area 5,800 sq. miles, pop. 1,562,200) on the northwest coast of the Persian Gulf. Capital: Kuwait (pop. 60,400). The neutral zone (pop. wholly nomadic) in the southeast is administered jointly by Kuwait and Saudi Arabia. Language: Arabic. Religion: Moslem. The country is mainly desert, with subsistence farming (dates, cereals, vegetables). Average temperature (F.): 75°. The economy is based on oil. Main oil field: Burgan. Refinery: Mina al Ahmadi. Other industries: dhow building, bricks, concrete. Exports: oil. Imports: food, clothing, vehicles, machinery. University (1966). Monetary unit: dinar (1,000 fils). HISTORY. The town of Kuwait, founded (17th c.) by Arabs, became a British base (1793). The territory was under British protection (1899–1961), after which Kuwait's full independence was recognized. When Iraq claimed the area (1961), British troops intervened, and were replaced by forces of the Arab League (1961). Iraq dropped its claim (1963). Some Palestinian and Iranian migrants were expelled in the mid-1980's after terrorist acts by Shiite Muslim extremists. Persian Gulf shipping was disrupted during the 1980's by the Iran-Iraq war

Kuz·bas (kú:zbɑs) *KUZNETSK BASIN.

Kuz·nets (kúznets), Simon (1901–85), Russian-U.S. economist awarded the 1971 Nobel prize for economics 'for his empirically founded interpretation of economic growth from the mid-19th c.' He introduced the term 'gross national product'

Kuz·netsk Basin (kuznjétsk) (Kuzbas), an industrial region of the R.S.F.S.R., in W. Siberia. It is the richest coal basin (area 10,000 sq. miles) of the U.S.S.R., with iron ore deposits. Industries: iron and steel and other metal products, coke, chemicals. It is developing rapidly. Chief center: Novokuznetsk

---

CONCISE PRONUNCIATION KEY: (a) æ, c*a*t; ɑ, c*a*r; ɔ f*aw*n; ei, sn*a*ke. (e) e, h*e*n; i:, sh*ee*p; iǝ, d*ee*r; ɛǝ, b*ea*r. (i) i, f*i*sh; ai, t*i*ger; ǝ:, b*i*rd. (o) o, *o*x; au, c*ow*; ou, g*oa*t; u, p*oo*r; ɔi, r*oy*al. (u) ʌ, d*u*ck; u, b*u*ll; u:, g*oo*se; ǝ, b*a*cillus; ju:, c*u*be. x, lo*ch*; θ, *th*ink; ð, *b*o*th*er; z, *Z*en; ʒ, cor*s*age; dʒ, sa*v*age; ŋ, ora*ng*utan*g*; j, *y*ak; ʃ, *f*ish; tʃ, fe*tch*; 'l, rabb*le*; 'n, redd*en*. Complete pronunciation key appears inside front cover.

K value (*envir.*) erosion rate per unit of erosion index in a cultivated continuous fallow soil

kvass (kvɑs) *pl.* **kvass·es** *n.* a beer made in E. Europe from a mixture of rye, barley and other cereals [Russ. *kvas*]

kvetch (kəvétʃ) (Yiddish) *n.* one who complains continuously —**kvetch** *v.*

kwa (kwɑ) *n.* a group of W. African languages spoken from Liberia to Nigeria along the coast and in the immediate hinterland. It includes the Akan languages, Agni, Yoruba, Ibo, Edo and Nupe

kwa·cha (kwátʃə) *n.* the monetary unit of Zambia, divided into 100 ngwee ‖ a coin of the value of one kwacha ‖ unit of currency in Malawi, equal to 100 tambola

Kwa·ja·lein (kwódʒəlin) (Kwajalong) a coral atoll in the Marshall Is of the central Pacific, site of a battle (1944) in the 2nd world war in which U.S. Marines defeated the Japanese defenders

Kwa·N·de·be·le (kwáendəbi:li:) *n.* Black African state in Transvaal under self-rule, est. April 1981

Kwang·chow (gwándʒóu) (formerly Canton) the capital (pop. 1,840,000) of Kwangtung province, S. China, an industrial and trading center. For centuries it was the country's chief port. University (1924). The city was held by the Japanese (1938–45)

Kwang·ju (gwándʒú:) a town and rail center (pop. 315,000) in S. Korea: textiles, brewing, rice milling

Kwang·si-Chuang (gwáṇsí:dʒwáṇ) a region (area 85,173 sq. miles, pop. 24,000,000), autonomous since 1957, in S. central China. Capital: Nanning

Kwang·tung (gwándúṇ) a province (area 83,918 sq. miles, pop. 41,000,000) of S.E. China. Capital: Kwangchow

Kwan·tung (gwándúṇ) (formerly Kwantung Leased Territory) the tip (area 1,444 sq. miles) of the Liaotung peninsula, S. Manchuria, China, containing Dairen and Port Arthur. It was leased to Russia (1898), transferred to Japan (1905) and controlled by the U.S.S.R. (1945–52)

kwan·za (kwánzə) *n.* unit of currency in Angola, equal to 100 lwei

kwash·i·or·kor (kwæʃi:órkɔr, kwɑʃi:órkɔr) *n.* acute malnutrition of children and infants chiefly in tropical Africa, caused by deficiency of protein and manifested by retarded growth and changes in the hair, skin and internal organs [native name in Ghana]

Kwei·chow (gwéidʒóu) a province (area 69,278 sq miles, pop. 17,400,000) in the interior of S. central China. Capital: Kweiyang

Kwei·chu (gwéidʒú:) * KWEIYANG

Kwei·lin (gwéilin) a commercial center (pop. 145,000) in N. Kwangsi-Chuang, China: cotton mills

Kwei·sui (gwéiswéi) *HUHEHOT

Kwei·yang (gwéijáṇ) (Kweichu) the capital (pop. 504,000) of Kweichow, S.W. China, on the Burma Road: light industries

KWIC (kwik) *n.* (*computer acronym*) for key word in context, a computer-oriented form of indexing based on key words or titles transformed to avoid ambiguity, designed by IBM

KWOC (kwɑk) *n.* (*computer acronym*) for key word out of context, an alphabetical index based on key words followed by text created by a computer

kyat (kjɑt, ki:át) *n.* the basic monetary unit of Burma (=100 pyas) ‖ a coin of the value of one kyat [Burmese]

Kyd (kid), Thomas (1558–94), English dramatist. His 'The Spanish Tragedy' (1586) was the prototype of the Elizabethan revenge tragedy

ky·mo·graph (káiməgræf, káiməgrɑf) *n.* an instrument for recording pressure changes, e.g. of blood pressure or sound waves ‖ an instrument for recording on X-ray film the movement of an internal organ (e.g. the heart) [fr. Gk *kuma*, wave+ *graphos*, written]

Kyo·ga (kjóugə) a lake (area c. 1,000 sq. miles) in central Uganda

Kyo·to (kjótɔ, ki:óutou) a city (pop. 1,464,964) and the ancient capital (794–1868) of Japan, in S. Honshu. Long famous for its artisans, it is now part of the Kobe-Osaka industrial complex. It is a center of Buddhism and has a famous 59-ft statue of Buddha. There are several universities

ky·pho·sis (kaifóusis) *n.* abnormal backward curvature of the spine resulting in a hump (cf. LORDOSIS, *SCOLIOSIS) **ky·phot·ic** (kaifótik) *adj.* [Mod. L. fr. Gk fr. *kuphos*, humpbacked]

Kyr·i·e e·le·i·son (kíri:ęięléiis'n) a phrase used in the liturgy of the Mass in the Orthodox Eastern and Roman Catholic Churches ‖ the translation of this used in the Anglican liturgy ‖ a musical setting for any of these [L.L. fr. Gk *kurie eleēson*, Lord have mercy]

Ky·the·ra (kí:θi:rɑ) *CYTHERA

kyu·do (ki:u:dou) *n.* Japanese archery technique designed to develop concentration and coordination

Kyu·shu (kjú:ʃu:) the southernmost and most densely populated island (area 16,250 sq. miles, pop. 13,600,200) of Japan's four main islands. Chief town: Nagasaki. Main industries: agriculture, mining, manufacturing (*JAPAN)

Ky·zyl-Kum (kizílkum) a desert (area 116,000 sq. miles) in Uzbekistan and Kazakhstan, U.S.S.R., between the Syr-Darya and the Amu-Darya: agriculture (under irrigation), Karakul sheep. Afforestation is in progress

---

CONCISE PRONUNCIATION KEY: **(a)** æ, c*a*t; ɑ, c*a*r; ɔ, f*aw*n; ei, sn*a*ke. **(e)** e, h*e*n; i:, sh*ee*p; iə, d*ee*r; ɛə, b*ea*r. **(i)** i, f*i*sh; ai, t*i*ger; ə:, b*i*rd. **(o)** o, *o*x; au, c*ow*; ou, g*oa*t; u, p*oo*r; ɔi, r*oy*al. **(u)** ʌ, d*u*ck; u, b*u*ll; u:, g*oo*se; ə, b*a*cillus; ju:, c*u*be. x, lo*ch*; θ, *th*ink; δ, *b*o*th*er; z, *Z*en; ʒ, cor*s*age; dʒ, *s*avage; ŋ, ora*n*gutang; j, *y*ak; ʃ, *f*ish; tʃ, fe*tch*; 'l, rabb*le*; 'n, redde*n*. Complete pronunciation key appears inside front cover.

EARLY NORTH SEMITIC	PHOENICIAN	EARLY HEBREW	EARLY GREEK	CLASSICAL GREEK	ETRUSCAN		CLASSICAL LATIN
					Early	Classical	
L	⌐	⌐	⌐	∧	⌄	⌄	L

CURSIVE MAJUSCULE (ROMAN)		ANGLO-IRISH MAJUSCULE	CAROLINE MINUSCULE	VENETIAN MINUSCULE (ITALIC)	N. ITALIAN MINUSCULE (ROMAN)
⌐		⌐	l	(	l

A. C. SYLVESTER, CAMBRIDGE, ENGLAND

Development of the letter L, beginning with the early North Semitic letter. Evolution of both the majuscule, or capital, letter L and the minuscule, or lowercase, letter l are shown.

L, l (el) the 12th letter of the English alphabet ‖ the symbol (L) for 50 in Roman numerals

L. Latin

l. line ‖ length

La. Louisiana

la, *Br.* also **lah** (lɑ) *n.* (*mus.*) the note A in the fixed-do system of solmization ‖ the sixth note in any diatonic scale in movable-do solmization

La (*chem.*) lanthanum

Laaland *LOLLAND

lab (læb) *n.* a laboratory

La·ba·die (læbædi:), Jean de (1610–74), French religious reformer. A Catholic priest, he became a Protestant and, influenced by Calvin, founded (c. 1668) the Labadists, a religious community in Amsterdam holding children and goods in common. The Labadists had died out by the mid-18th c.

Lab·a·dist (læbædist) *n.* a member of the religious sect founded by Jean de Labadie

La·ban (lábən), Rudolf von (1879–1958), Austrian choreographer and teacher. He founded (1911) the Central European School of dancing, at Munich. His very influential ideas are at the source of modern expressionist dancing. The system of dance notation which he proposed (1928), called 'Labanotation' since 1953, is used in the U.S.A. and the U.S.S.R.

La·ban notation (léibæn) system of recording choreography, esp. ballet, created by Rudolf von Laban

lab·a·rum (læbərəm) *n.* (*hist.*) the imperial standard adopted by Constantine the Great when he became a Christian, having a golden wreath and the chi-rho [L.]

lab·da·num (læbdənəm) *n.* ladanum [medical L. fr. L. *ladanum*]

La·bé (læbei), Louise (1524–66), French woman poet, author of love poems (1555). She was known as 'la Belle Cordière'

La·be (lúbə) *ELBE

lab·e·fac·tion (læbəfækʃən) *n.* (*rhet.*) a shaking or weakening, overthrow, downfall [fr. L. *labefacere*), to cause to shake]

la·bel (léib'l) **1.** *n.* a piece of paper, card, metal etc. to be attached to an article with the name, ownership, destination, description etc. of the article inscribed on it ‖ short name or phrase applied to a person to indicate broadly allegiance, persuasion etc., *political labels* ‖ (*archit.*) a dripstone **2.** *v.t. pres. part.* **la·bel·ing,** esp. *Br.* **la·bel·ling** *past* and *past part.* **la·beled,** esp. *Br.* **la·belled** *v.t.* to attach a label to ‖ (*pop.*) to classify [O.F.=a ribbon]

la·bel·lum (ləbéləm) *pl.* **la·bel·la** (ləbélə) *n.* (*bot.*) the lower petal, morphologically posterior, of an orchid ‖ (*zool.*) a small lobe beneath the labrum or labial palp in insects ‖ (*zool.*) a

proboscis lobe in two-winged flies [L. dim. of *labrum,* lip]

la·bi·al (léibi:əl) **1.** *adj.* of the lips or labia ‖ serving as or resembling a lip ‖ (*phon.*, e.g. 'p' and 'b') requiring particular use of the lips ‖ (*mus.*, e.g. of a flute and some organ pipes) producing sound by the movement of air across a lip or liplike edge **2.** *n.* (*phon.*) a labial sound **la·bi·al·i·zá·tion** *n.* **lá·bi·al·ize** *pres. part.* **la·bi·al·iz·ing** *past* and *past part.* **la·bi·al·ized** *v.t.* to utter as or change to a labial sound [fr. M. L. *labialis* fr. L. *labium,* lip]

la·bi·ate 1. (léibi:it, léibi:eit) *adj.* (*bot.*) having the corolla so divided that one part overlaps the other ‖ having labia **2.** (léibi:eit) *n.* a member of *Labiatae,* order *Polemoniales,* a family of aromatic plants and shrubs with four-lobed ovaries, e.g. sage, thyme [fr. Mod. L. *labiatus* fr. L. *labium,* lip]

La·biche (læbi:ʃ), Eugène Marin (1815–88), French playwright. His farcical comedies include 'le Chapeau de paille d'Italie' (1851) and 'le Voyage de M. Perrichon' (1860)

la·bile (léibil, léibail) *adj.* liable to undergo physical or chemical change ‖ unstable [fr. L. *labilis,* apt to slip]

la·bi·o·den·tal (leibi:oudént'l) **1.** *adj.* (*phon.*, e.g. of 'f' and 'v') made with lip and teeth **2.** *n.* (*phon.*) a labiodental sound [fr. L. *labium,* lip+DENTAL]

la·bi·o·na·sal (leibi:ounéiz'l) **1.** *adj.* (*phon.*, e.g. of 'm') made with the lips and the nasal passage **2.** *n.* (*phon.*) a labionasal sound [fr. L. *labium,* lip+NASAL]

la·bi·o·ve·lar (leibi:ouví:lər) **1.** *adj.* (*phon.*, e.g. of 'w') made with the lips rounded and the back of the tongue near or touching the velum **2.** *n.* (*phon.*) a labiovelar sound [fr. L. *labium,* lip+VELAR]

la·bi·um (léibi:əm) *pl.* **la·bi·a** (léibi:ə) *n.* a lip or liplike part ‖ (*anat.*) a liplike fold of the vulva ‖ (*zool.*, in insects) the underlip, formed by the partial fusion of the second maxillae ‖ (*bot.*) the lower lip of a labiate corolla [L.=lip]

la·bor, *Br.* **la·bour** (léibər) *n.* prolonged hard work ‖ a task demanding great effort ‖ the muscular uterine contractions preceding childbirth ‖ the period of time that these contractions last ‖ (*econ.*) work as a production factor ‖ those who work in contrast to those who own or manage ‖ workers as an economic or political force [O.F. *labor, labour*]

labor, *Br.* **labour** *v.i.* to work hard ‖ to make slow, painful progress ‖ (of a ship) to pitch and roll in heavy seas ‖ (with 'under') to suffer from, be impeded by, *to labor under a misapprehension* ‖ *v.t.* to express in unnecessary detail and at length, *to labor a point* [F. *labourer*]

Labor, American Federation of *AMERICAN FEDERATION OF LABOR AND CONGRESS OF INDUSTRIAL ORGANIZATIONS

lab·o·ra·to·ry (læbrətɔri:, læbrətouri:, *Br.* ləbɔ́rətəri) *pl.* **lab·o·ra·to·ries** *n.* (often shortened to 'lab') a place equipped and used for experimental study, research, analysis, testing or (usually small-scale) preparation, in any branch of science [fr. M.L. *laboratorium*]

labor certification certification by the U.S. Department of Labor that an alien seeking to immigrate to the U.S. provides a needed skill. It is required before a permanent visa is issued

Labor Day, *Br.* **Labour Day** a day set apart as a legal or bank holiday in honor of the workers, e.g. May 1 in many countries, the first Monday in September in the U.S.A. and Canada

la·bored, *Br.* **la·boured** (léibərd) *adj.* done, or seeming to be done, with difficulty

la·bor·er, *Br.* **la·bour·er** (léibərər) *n.* a wage earner who does unskilled work [LABOR]

la·bor·in·ten·sive (léibərinténsiv) *adj.* (*economics*) **1.** of production that requires a high proportion of labor **2.** of method of production that substitutes high labor input for capital investment **3.** of areas where such policies prevail *ant.* capital-intensive

la·bo·ri·ous (ləbɔ́ri:əs, ləbóuri:əs) *adj.* involving prolonged, hard work ‖ hardworking ‖ labored [fr. F. *laborieux* or fr. L. *laboriosus*]

la·bor·ite, *Br.* **la·bour·ite** (léibərait) *n.* a member of a group backing the interests of labor

labor of love, *Br.* **labour of love** a task undertaken purely for the pleasure or satisfaction of doing it

labor relations, *Br.* **labour relations** relations between management and workers

la·bor·sav·ing, *Br.* **la·bour·sav·ing** (léibərseivin) *adj.* (of a process or equipment) reducing the labor required for an operation

labor shed (*economics*) the area from which labor supply is drawn

labor theory of value, *Br.* **labour theory of value** the Marxist theory that the value of a product is derived from the labor required to produce it

labor union the organization in any industry of the workers (membership being in some cases compulsory) for collective bargaining with the employers over terms of employment and conditions of work

Labor, U.S. Department of, federal agency founded in 1913 to safeguard the U.S. worker's welfare and working conditions. It oversees and regulates federal laws that involve pay, hours, conditions, insurance, compensation and discrimination. The Employment and Training Administration aids states with public employment services and training programs. The

CONCISE PRONUNCIATION KEY: **(a)** æ, *cat;* ɑ, *car;* ɔ *fawn;* ei, *snake.* **(e)** e, *hen;* i:, *sheep;* iə, *deer;* ɛə, *bear.* **(i)** i, *fish;* ai, *tiger;* əː, *bird.* **(o)** o, *ox;* au, *cow;* ou, *goat;* u, *poor;* ɔi, *royal.* **(u)** ʌ, *duck;* u, *bull;* uː, *goose;* ə, *bacillus;* juː, *cube.* x, *loch;* θ, *think;* ð, *bother;* z, *Zen;* ʒ, *corsage;* dʒ, *savage;* ŋ, ora*ng*utang; j, *yak;* ʃ, *fish;* tʃ, *fetch;* 'l, *rabble;* 'n, *redden.* Complete pronunciation key appears inside front cover.

Labor-Management Services Administration regulates and checks on labor unions and private pension plans. The Employment Standards Administration administers compensation laws. The Occupational Safety and Health Administration handles workers' health and safety and the Bureau of Labor Statistics compiles records

labour *LABOR

Labour 1. *n.* the Labour party 2. *adj.* of or belonging to the Labour party

laboured *LABORED

labourer *LABORER

labour exchange (*Br.*) an employment exchange

labourite *LABORITE

La·bour·ite *n.* a member of the British Labour party

Labour party a socialist party in Great Britain founded (1900) by the trade unions and the Independent Labour party. It participated (1915–18) in the war coalition government, became the main opposition party (1922), and formed minority governments (1924 and 1929–31) under MacDonald. The Labour party again took part in a war coalition (1940–5). It formed its first majority government (1945–51) under Attlee, nationalized many basic industries, and instituted the welfare state. It returned to power (1964–70) under Wilson and again from 1974 to 1979

labour relations *LABOR RELATIONS

laboursaving *LABORSAVING

labour theory of value *LABOR THEORY OF VALUE

Lab·ra·dor (lǽbrədɔr) a region (113,000 sq. miles, pop. 33,052) on the east coast of Canada, forming part of Newfoundland province. It is part of the Canadian Shield. The northern tundra gives place to coniferous forest in the south. Resources: iron ore, timber, hydroelectricity. Industries: iron mining, trapping, fishing

Labrador retriever a retriever of a breed having a heavy build and a short, thick black coat

la·bret (léibrit) *n.* an ornament of stone, wood or shell inserted in the lip, e.g. in New Guinea [fr. L. *labrum,* lip]

la·brum (léibrəm) *n.* a lip, or liplike part ‖ (*zool.*) the anterior lip of certain arthropods ‖ (*zool.*) the outer margin of univalve gastropod shells [L.=lip]

La Bru·yère (lǽbryjer), Jean de (1645–96), French moralist, famous for his 'Caractères' (1688–96). They are acute analyses of how various kinds of men reveal their real qualities. The view of man is firmly classical, the mood often, satirical, sometimes disenchanted

La·bu·an (ləbú:ən) an island (35 sq. miles) off N.W. Borneo, forming part of Sabah

la·bur·num (ləbə́:rnəm) *n.* a member of *Laburnum,* fam. *Papilionaceae,* a genus of small trees native to Europe and W. Asia with hanging racemes of yellow flowers and poisonous seeds [L.]

lab·y·rinth (lǽbərinθ) *n.* a confusion of winding passages through which it is extremely difficult to find one's way ‖ a maze of paths bordered by high hedges in a park etc. ‖ a tortuous arrangement, *the labyrinth of legal procedure* ‖ (*anat.*) the inner ear **lab·y·rin·thine** *adj.* [L. fr. Gk *laburinthos*]

lac (læk) *n.* a resinous substance exuded by lac insects, found as an incrustation on banyan and fig trees, and used in making shellac and lacquer [fr. Hind. *lākh*]

lac *LAKH

Lac·ca·dive, Min·i·coy and A·min·di·vi Islands (lǽkədaiv, mínikɔi, ʌmindí:ví:) a group of 14 small islands (area 10 sq. miles, pop. 40,237) in the Indian Ocean, administered by India since 1956. Renamed Lakshadweep in 1973. People: Moplas (mixed Hindu and Arab). Language: Malayalam, Mahl (akin to old Sinhalese) on Minicoy. Products: coconuts, fish

lac·co·lite (lǽkəlait) *n.* laccolith

lac·co·lith (lǽkəliθ) *n.* (*geol.*) a mass of volcanic or igneous rock intruded between strata and forcing the overlying strata upwards to form domes [fr. Gk *lakkos,* cistern + *lithos,* stone]

lace (leis) 1. *n.* a patterned fabric of open texture, worked in silk, linen or cotton thread ‖ a braid of gold or silver for trimming uniforms ‖ a cord or thin strip of leather, passed through eyelets and used to draw together the opposite edges of a shoe, tent flap etc. [M.E. *las* fr. O.F.]

lace *pres. part.* **lac·ing** *past* and *past part.* **laced** *v.t.* to draw together using a lace ‖ to pass (a lace) through eyelets etc. ‖ to attach ornamental lace to ‖ to add liquor to (coffee etc.) ‖ to compress the waist of (a person) by pulling tight the laces of a corset etc. ‖ (*pop.*) to lash, beat ‖ to streak or mark as if with braid ‖ *v.i.* to be fastened by a lace **to lace into** to attack (someone) physically or verbally or rebuke (someone) vehemently [fr. O.F. *lacier*]

Lac·e·dae·mon (læsidí:mən) (*Gk hist.*) Sparta

Lac·e·dae·mo·ni·an (læsidimóuni:ən) (*Gk hist.*) 1. *adj.* Spartan 2. *n.* a Spartan

lac·er·ate (lǽsəreit)*pres. part.* **lac·er·at·ing** *past* and *past part.* **lac·er·at·ed** *v.t.* to rend (the flesh) with a tearing movement ‖ to affect with painful emotions **lác·er·at·ed** *adj.* mangled, torn ‖ (*biol.*) having edges deeply and irregularly incised **lac·er·á·tion** *n.* [fr. L. *lacerare (laceratus)*]

lac·er·til·i·an (læsərtíli:ən) 1. *adj.* of a lizard 2. *n.* a lizard [fr. Mod. L. *Lacertilia,* the suborder of lizards]

la·cer·tine (ləsə́:rti:n) *adj.* lizardlike ‖ having markings resembling those of lizards [fr. *lacerta,* lizard]

lace·wing (léiswiŋ) *n.* any of several neuropterons, esp. of the genera *Chrysopa* and *Hemerobius,* having delicate, iridescent wings

lace·work (léiswə:rk) *n.* a lacy decoration, esp. in architecture

La·chaise (læʃez), Gaston (1882–1935), U.S. sculptor. His works include decora tions, notably for New York's International Building at Rockefeller Center, and single figures, notably his monumental 'Standing Woman' (Museum of Modern Art, New York)

lach·es (lǽtʃis) *n.* (*law*) neglect in carrying out a legal duty ‖ (*law*) undue delay in claiming privilege or asserting a right ‖ (*rhet.*) culpable negligence [M.E. *lacchesse, lachesse* fr. O.F.]

Lach·e·sis (lǽtʃisis) *FATES

Lach·lan (lǽklən) a tributary (800 miles long) of the Murrumbidgee, flowing east from the Great Dividing Range through central New South Wales, Australia

lach·ry·mal, lac·ri·mal (lǽkrəməl) *adj.* of or pertaining to tears ‖ of the ducts, glands etc. concerned in the production of tears [fr. M.L. *lacrimalis, lachrymalis*]

lachrymal vase (*Rom. hist.*) a small funeral vessel for perfume or ointment, popularly supposed to be a receptacle for the tears of the bereaved

lachrymator *LACRIMATOR

lachrymatory *LACRIMATORY

lach·ry·mose (lǽkrəmous) *adj.* (*rhet.*) tearful ‖ causing tears, mournful [fr. L. *lacrimosus*]

la·ci·ness (léisi:nis) *n.* the quality of being lacy

lac·ing (léisiŋ) *n.* laces used for fastening ‖ ornamental trimming, esp. on a uniform ‖ a small addition of alcoholic liquor, e.g. brandy, to coffee or some other drink, or to food ‖ (*pop.*) a beating, lashing ‖ the act of someone who laces [M.E.]

la·cin·i·ate (ləsíni:it, ləsíni:eit) *adj.* (*biol.*) deeply and irregularly cut, jagged, e.g. of a leaf or petal fringe **la·cín·i·at·ed** *adj.* [fr. L. *lacinia,* a flap]

lac insect *Laccifer lacca,* fam. *Lacciferidae,* a homopterous insect of S.E. Asia which produces lac

lack (læk) 1. *n.* want, need, the fact or state of not having something or enough of something ‖ that which is missing or needed 2. *v.t.* to be wanting in, *to lack money, to lack ability* ‖ *v.i.* to be wanting, *humor is lacking in his speeches* [M.E. *lac*]

lack·a·dai·si·cal (lækədéizik'l) *adj.* (of a person or attitude) lacking in proper carefulness, seriousness, energy etc. [fr. obs. interj. *lackaday,* alas the day, and originally applied to people fond of saying this]

lack·ey (lǽki) *pl.* **lack·eys** *n.* (*hist.*) a liveried manservant ‖ a servile and obsequious person [fr. F. *laquais*]

lack·ing (lǽkiŋ) *prep.* short of, without, *a kettle lacking a lid*

lack·lus·ter, *Br.* **lack·lus·tre** (lǽklʌstər) *adj.* lacking in vitality or brilliance

La·clos (læklou), Pierre Choderlos de (1741–1803), French artillery officer and writer, famous for his only novel, 'les Liaisons dangereuses' (1782), written in letter form and savagely depicting the corrupt morals of the time

la·combe or **La combe** (ləkóum) *n.* swine type that produces a white bacon; named for an experimental station in Alberta, Canada

La Con·da·mine (lækɔ̃dæmi:n), Charles Marie de (1701–74), French mathematician, geographer and traveler. He took part (1735) in Peru in the measurement of one degree of the meridian at the equator. He went on to make the first scientific exploration of the Amazon

La·co·ni·a, La·ko·ni·a (ləkóuni:ə) a mountainous, pastoral region of Greece in the S.E. Peloponnesus. In ancient times, its chief city-state was Sparta

la·con·ic (ləkónik) *adj.* using terse, unemotional language **la·cón·i·cal·ly** *adv.* **la·con·i·cism** (ləkónisizəm) *n.* unemotional brevity of speech or an instance of this [fr. Gk *Lakōnikos* fr. *Lakōn,* Spartan]

lac operon (lǽc ópərɔn) *n.* (*genetics*) genetic unit, isolated in 1969, that controls metabolism of milk sugar in bacteria —**lac** *adj.*

La·cor·daire (lækɔrder), Jean-Baptiste Henri (1802–61), French preacher and theologian. He preached a brilliant series of sermons in favor of liberalism (1830s and 40s), but went into exile under Napoleon III

La Co·ru·ña (lakɔrú:nja) (*Eng.* Co-runna) a province (area 3,051 sq. miles, pop. 1,083,415) of Galicia, N.W. Spain ‖ its capital (pop. 383,925), a port and military and naval station. The Spanish Armada was assembled in its harbor (1588), and the port was sacked (1598) by Drake. It was the scene of the Battle of Corunna (1809)

lac·quer (lǽkər) 1. *n.* a hard, glossy varnish, derived from shellac, colored, and applied to wood and to some metals for decoration or protection ‖ (*commerce*) any hard gloss paint ‖ ware coated with lacquer and often inlaid with metal, ivory etc. ‖ a liquid coating containing a cellulose derivative used as a protective film or finish in industrial processes ‖ a hair spray ‖ a natural varnish, esp. the sap of the Japanese varnish tree 2. *v.t.* to coat with lacquer [fr. obs. F. *lacre,* sealing wax]

lacrimal *LACHRYMAL

lac·ri·ma·tor, lach·ry·ma·tor (lǽkrəmeitər) *n.* any substance that produces tears, e.g. tear gas [fr. L. *lacrima,* tear]

lac·ri·ma·to·ry, lach·ry·ma·to·ry (lǽkrəmətɔri:, lǽkrəmətouri:) 1. *adj.* pertaining to, or causing, the flow of tears 2. *pl.* **lac·ri·ma·to·ries, lach·ry·ma·to·ries** *n.* a lachrymal vase [ult. fr. L. *lacrimare,* to shed tears]

la·crosse (ləkrɔ́s, ləkrós) *n.* a field game of North American Indian origin, played between two teams of (*Am.*) 10 players or (*Br.*) 12 players, each having a curved stick (crosse) fitted with a shallow net, used to throw, catch and carry the small, hard, rubber ball. The object is to throw the ball into the opponents' goal [F. *la,* the + *crosse,* hooked stick]

lac·tase (lǽkteis) *n.* (*biochem.*) an enzyme which hydrolyzes lactose [fr. L. *lac (lactis),* milk + DIASTASE]

lac·tate (lǽkteit) *n.* a salt or ester of lactic acid [LACTIC]

lactate *v.i. pres. part.* **lac·tat·ing** *past* and *past part.* **lac·tat·ed** to secrete milk [fr. L. *lactare (lactatus)*]

lac·ta·tion (læktéiʃən) *n.* the secreting and giving of milk by the mammary glands ‖ the period of milk production [fr. L. *lactare (lactatus),* to suckle]

lac·te·al (lǽkti:əl) 1. *adj.* of, like or producing milk ‖ conveying or containing a milky fluid, e.g. chyle ‖ of the lacteals 2. *n.* one of the lymphatic vessels which convey chyle from the intestine to the thoracic duct [fr. L. *lacteus,* milky]

lac·tes·cence (læktés'ns) *n.* the quality of being milky ‖ (*bot.*) the flow of milklike sap [LACTESCENT]

lac·tes·cent (læktés'nt) *adj.* becoming milky ‖ giving a milky fluid ‖ secreting mllk [fr. L. *lactescens (lactescentis)* fr. *lactescere,* to turn into milk]

lac·tic (lǽktik) *adj.* of or pertaining to milk ‖ pertaining to the production of lactic acid [fr. L. *lac (lactis),* milk]

lactic acid a hygroscopic acid, $C_3H_6O_3$, found in sour milk etc., where it is formed by bacterial fermentation as a racemic mixture of its optically active dextrorotatory and levorotatory isomers. It is used in the food and plastics industries, in tanning and in medicine

lac·tif·er·ous (læktífərəs) adj. yielding or conveying milk or a milky fluid [fr. L. lactifer fr. lac (lactis), milk+ferre, to bear]

lac·to·ba·cil·lus (læktoubəsíləs) pl. **lac·to·ba·cil·li** (læktoubəsílai) n. a member of Lactobacillus, fam. Lactobacillaceae, a genus of bacteria which produce lactic acid in the fermentation of carbohydrates, esp. in milk [fr. L. lac (lactis), milk+BACILLUS]

lac·tom·e·ter (læktómitər) n. an instrument for determining the specific gravity of milk [fr. L. lac (lactis), milk+METER]

lac·tose (læktous) n. a slightly sweet dextrorotatory sugar, $C_{12}H_{22}O_{11}$, present in milk. On hydrolysis it gives glucose and galactose. On fermentation it gives lactic acid [fr. L. lac (lactis), milk]

la·cu·na (ləkjú:nə) pl. **la·cu·nae** (ləkjú:ni:), **la·cu·nas** n. an empty space or missing portion in something which is otherwise continuous ‖ a minute cavity in a bone, containing bone cells ‖ (biol.) a space or cavity in or among cells **la·cu·nal, la·cu·nar, la·cu·na·ry** adjs [L.=hole]

la·cus·trine (ləkástrin, ləkástrain) adj. of or living in lakes ‖ of prehistoric lake dwellings [fr. L. lacus, lake]

la·cy (léisi:) comp. **la·ci·er** superl. **la·ci·est** adj. of or resembling lace

lad (læd) n. a boy or youth ‖ (Br.) a youth who works in a racing stable, riding the horse for which he is responsible at exercise etc. ‖ (Br., pop.) someone who chases the girls [M.E. ladde, origin unknown]

La·dakh (lədák) a mountainous area of N.E. Kashmir, on the Indian-Tibetan border, partly occupied and claimed by China since the early 1950s

lad·a·num (lædnəm) n. a soft, dark, odorous resin obtained from leaves and twigs of various Mediterranean rockroses, and used in perfumery [L. fr. Gk]

LADAR (léidər) n. (acronym) laser detection and ranging, a radar system in which radar substitutes for microwaves used for space tracking and exploration

lad·der (lædər) 1. n. a portable device consisting usually of two long wood or metal uprights or two ropes joined at short intervals by crosspieces (rungs) which serve as footrests, for climbing up and down ‖ any means of personal step-by-step advancement ‖ (Br.) a run in a stocking 2. v.i. (Br., of a stocking) to run ‖ v.t. (Br.) to cause (a stocking) to run [O.E. hlǣder]

lad·der·back (lædərbæk) adj. (of a chair) having a back composed of two upright posts joined by transverse slats

ladder polymer (chem.) polymer constructed of two linked molecular chains resembling a ladder; resistant to high temperature

ladder truck a fire engine on which an extension ladder is mounted

lad·die (lædi:) n. (esp. Scots dialect) a young boy

lade (leid) pres. part. **lad·ing** past **lad·ed** past part. **lad·en** (léid'n) v.t. to put goods on board (a ship) or to take (goods) on board **lád·en** adj. loaded, branches laden with apples ‖ (rhet.) heavily burdened, laden with grief [O.E. hladan, to load]

la·di·da (ládi:dá) adj. affected, snobbish [imitating the vowels prominent in affected English upper-class pronunciation]

La·din (lədí:n) n. Rhaeto-Romanic as spoken in Trentino-Alto Adige [Rhaeto-Romanic fr. L. Latinus, Latin]

Lad·is·las (lædisləs, lǽdislas) *LADISLAUS

Ladislaus II (1456–1516), king of Bohemia (1471–1516) and, as Uladislaus II, of Hungary (1490–1516). A member of the Jagiello family, he was elected to the Bohemian throne, but his rule was contested until 1490 by Matthias Corvinus of Hungary

Lad·is·laus I (lædisləs) (or Ladislas, Hung. László), St (c. 1040–95), king of Hungary (1077–95). He supported the claims of the papacy over the Holy Roman Empire, and annexed Slavonia, Croatia and Transylvania. Feast: June 27

Ladislaus IV (1262–90), king of Hungary (1272–90). His introduction of the customs of the Cumans, his mother's people, was unpopular, and his reign degenerated into anarchy

Ladislaus II (Polish Wladyslaw) (c. 1350–1434) king of Poland (1386–1434), grand duke of Lithuania (1377–86), founder of the Jagiello dynasty. He introduced Christianity into Lith-

uania, which he united with Poland. He defeated the Teutonic Knights at Tannenberg

Ladislaus III (1424–44), king of Poland (1434–44) and, as Uladislaus I, of Hungary (1440–4). With Hunyadi as his chief commander, he made war on the Turks (1443) and was killed in battle

la·dle (léid'l) 1. n. a spoon with a long handle and a large, cuplike bowl, used for transferring soup, stew etc. from one receptacle to another ‖ a similarly shaped instrument for transferring molten metal 2. v.t. pres. part. **la·dling** past and past part. **la·dled** (often with 'out') to transfer with a ladle ‖ to distribute freely, to ladle out compliments [O.E. hlǣdel]

La·do·ga (ládəgə) the largest lake (area 7,100 sq. miles) in Europe, in the R.S.F.S.R. (mainly in the Karelian A.S.S.R.), U.S.S.R., near Leningrad, frozen in winter. With Lake Onega, to which it is connected by river, it forms part of the Baltic-White Sea waterway. The River Neva links it to the Gulf of Finland. Fisheries

la·dy (léidi:) pl. **la·dies** n. a woman of the wealthy, leisured class ‖ any woman who behaves with the dignity and social grace ascribed to women of this class ‖ (in polite and conventional usage) a woman ‖ used as a courtesy title, lady mayoress **La·dy** a British title of rank for the wife of a knight, baronet or man given the courtesy title of Lord, and for the daughter of an earl, marquess or duke. It is also used as a form of address or reference for a marchioness, countess, viscountess or baroness [O.E. hlǣfdīge]

la·dy·bird (léidi:bə:rd) n. a ladybug

la·dy·bug (léidi:bʌg) n. a member of Coccinellidae, a family of small coleopteron insects having round backs that are often spotted and brightly colored. They feed chiefly on aphids and plant lice [=bird of Our Lady]

Lady chapel a chapel dedicated to the Virgin Mary in a cathedral or church

Lady Day the feast of the Annunciation ‖ (Br.) a quarter day, Mar. 25

la·dy·fin·ger (léidi:fiŋgər) n. a little sponge cake roughly in the shape of a finger

la·dy·in·wait·ing (léidi:inwéitiŋ) pl. **la·dies·in·wait·ing** n. a lady appointed to attend upon a queen or a princess

la·dy·kill·er (léidi:kilər) n. (old-fash.) a man who is irresistible to women, or who has this reputation

la·dy·like (léidi:laik) adj. with the dignity, courtesy and quiet reserve of a lady ‖ suitable for a lady ‖ effeminate

La·dy·ship (léidi:ʃip) n. (preceded by 'your' or 'her') a title used by servants etc. in addressing or speaking of a Lady

lady's maid a maid who cares for a lady's clothes, and assists her in dressing, etc.

La·dy·smith (léidi:smiθ) a town (pop. 16,000), in Natal, South Africa, in which British troops were besieged (Nov. 2, 1899–Feb. 28, 1900) by Transvaal forces during the Boer War

lady's slipper any of various North American orchids, esp. of the genus Cypripedium, having an underlip shaped like a slipper

La·e·trile (léiətril) n. (pharm.) trademark for a substance derived from the chemical amygdalin, found naturally in the pits of apricots, peaches, and bitter almonds. In the U.S., Laetrile is on the American Cancer Society's Unproven Methods List, elsewhere it is used as a treatment for cancer

laevorotatory *LEVOROTATORY

laevulose *LEVULOSE

La Farge (ləfár3) John (1835–1910), U.S. painter and author. He is best known for his mural in the church of the Ascension, New York City, and, as the inventor of opalescent glass, for his contributions to the art of stained glass

La·fa·yette, La Fa·yette (læfæjet) Marie-Joseph, marquis de (1757–1834), French general and statesman. He helped the revolutionists in America (1777–82) and commanded the National Guard in two French revolutions (1789–92, 1830) as a liberal monarchist

La Fayette, Lafayette, Marie-Madeleine, comtesse de (1634–93), French novelist, famous for her 'la Princesse de Clèves' (1678), the first French psychological novel

Laf·fite, La·fitte (ləfí:t) Jean (1780–c. 1825), U.S. privateer, smuggler, and patriot. Holding (1810–14) a privateer commission from the republic of Cartagena (present Colombia), he preyed on Spanish commerce. During the War of 1812 he gave important aid to General An-

drew Jackson in the battle of New Orleans (1815), winning in return a U.S. pardon. Continuing (1817) his privateering, he was forced (1821) by the U.S. government to flee in his ship, and was never heard from again

La Fol·lette (ləfólit), Robert Marion (1855–1927), U.S. politician, governor (1900–06) of Wisconsin and senator (1906–25) from Wisconsin. He campaigned (1924) for the U.S. presidency on the Progressive party ticket, winning about 5 million votes

La Fon·taine (ləfɔ̃ten), Jean de (1621–95), French poet. His 'Fables' (1668–94) are his masterpiece. Most of the stories derive from Aesop or Phaedrus, but in his manner of telling them he expressed a complete view of life, satirizing the failures of men and of society. The style of the 'Fables' is supple and varied. The general tone is one of colloquial simplicity, interspersed with rhetorical cadences used for purposes of irony, and by moments of quiet, tender lyricism. The overall effect is one of artful naturalness. La Fontaine also wrote 'Contes' (1665–74)

La·Fon·taine (ləfɔ̃ten), Sir Louis Hippolyte (1807–64), Canadian judge and joint leader in the LaFontaine-Baldwin ministry ('the great ministry' 1848–51), which established responsible government in Canada. His considerable legislation included the Rebellion Losses bill which precipitated the Montreal riots of 1849

La·forgue (læfɔrg), Jules (1860–87), French Symbolist poet, whose works include 'les Complaintes' (1885) and 'l'Imitation de Notre-Dame la Lune' (1886). His enormous influence on 20th-c. poets, esp. Eliot, lies in his original technique: extreme allusiveness, the telescoping of the logic of his imagery to give startling transitions and transpositions, the use of images from modern life, and a deprecating irony

LAFTA *LATIN AMERICA FREE TRADE AREA

lag (læg) 1. v.i. pres. part. **lag·ging** past and past part. **lagged** to go slowly ‖ (with 'behind') to fail to keep up with others ‖ (billiards) to string 2. n. the act of lagging or an instance of this ‖ the distance or time between one thing, event etc. and another ‖ (phys.) the time lapse between a cause and its effect [prob. fr. Scand.]

lag 1. n. a covering to reduce heat loss 2. v.t. pres. part. **lag·ging** past and past part. **lagged** to cover (a pipe, boiler etc.) with nonconducting material in order to reduce heat loss [prob. O.N. lögg, barrel rim]

lag·an (lægən) n. (law) goods jettisoned at sea but attached to a buoy so that they may be found again [O.F. lagan, laguen, lagand prob. fr. Scand.]

La·gash (léigæʃ) (or Shirpurla) an ancient Sumerian city which flourished in the 3rd and 2nd millennia B.C.

Lageos (lági:ous) n. satellite equipped with quartz reflector on its outer surfaces that emits laser beams that compute reflection time in order to measure earth's crust and to detect movement of tectonic plates

la·ger (lágər) n. a light beer fermented for a longer period at a lower temperature than most beers [fr. G. lager-bier, beer brewed for storing]

lag·gard (lægərd) 1. adj. lagging 2. n. a person who is slow, lazy or slack in his duty [LAG]

lag·ging (lægiŋ) n. a lag ‖ the materials used in making lags

lagging indicators (economics) economic statistical indices that tend to follow the changes in business conditions, e.g., unit labor costs, inventories

la·gniappe, la·gnappe (lænjæp, lænjæp) n. a small gift presented to a customer by a storekeeper ‖ a gratuity or unexpected gift [Louisiana F. fr. Am. Span. la ñapa, the addition, var. of yapa fr. Quechna]

lag·o·morph (lægəmɔrf) n. a member of Lagomorpha, an order of gnawing mammals including the hare, rabbit and pika. They are similar to rodents but are characterized by two pairs of double incisors in the upper jaw **lag·o·mór·phic, lag·o·mór·phous** adjs [fr. Gk lagós, hare+morphē, form]

la·goon (ləgú:n) n. a shallow stretch of water partly or completely separated from the sea by a strip of sand or an atoll ‖ a shallow freshwater lake incompletely or narrowly separated from a larger lake or river [F. lagune or fr. Span. or Ital. laguna]

La·gos (léigɒs) the capital (pop. 4,800,000) of Lagos State, Nigeria, a port and rail terminus on a lagoon off the Gulf of Guinea. University

(1962). A slave market (16th–19th cc.), Lagos was ceded to Britain (1861) and used as a base for the suppression of the slave trade

La·gos Doctrine (léigəs) statements by President Jimmy Carter, March–April 1978, committing U.S. support to racial equality, one-person one-vote in Africa, national independence, and other civil-libertarian issues

La·grange (lægrɑ̃ʒ), Joseph-Louis, comte de (1736–1813), French mathematician. His principal work was in pure mathematics, including differential equations and the calculus of variations and in mechanics ('Mécanique analytique', 1788). He presided over the committee which introduced the metric system (1793)

La Guai·ra (lɑgwáirə) a seaport and the most important commercial town (pop. c. 20,344) in Venezuela, eight miles north of Caracas. It has a good harbor, dry dock, and shipbuilding plant

La Guar·di·a (lɑgwɑ́rdiːə), Fiorello Henry (1882–1947), American public official. As mayor of New York (1933–45), he promoted town-planning and slum-clearance projects. He helped to frame the Norris-LaGuardia Act (1932), protecting the rights of striking workers and banning yellow-dog contracts

lah *LA

La·hore (ləhɔ́r, ləhóur) the largest city (pop. 2,165,372) of Pakistan. Industries: textiles, pottery, carpets, food processing, engineering, chemicals, steel, films, nuclear research. A Mogul capital (16th–17th cc.), Lahore was annexed (1849) by the British and made the capital of the Punjab until 1947, when it became part of Pakistan. Mogul fort and palace, mosques of Aurangzeb (17th c.) and Wazir Khan (1634). University (1882)

Lai·bach (láibax) *LJUBLJANA

Laibach, Congress of a conference held (1821) in Ljubljana (now in Yugoslavia) by Russia, Austria, Prussia and Britain. Britain's refusal to agree to intervention in the revolt in Naples marked a breach with the other powers

la·ic (léiik) 1. *adj.* lay 2. *n.* a layman **lá·i·cal** *adj.* [fr. L.L. *laicus* fr. Gk *laos*, the people]

la·i·cize (léiisaiz) *pres. part.* **la·i·ciz·ing** *past* and *past part.* **la·i·cized** *v.t.* to divest (a school, office etc.) of its clerical character or monopoly [LAIC]

laid *past* and *past part.* of LAY

laid-back (léidbæk) *adj.* (*slang*) 1. relaxed 2. providing the image of relaxation *ant.* uptight

laid paper paper watermarked with parallel lines by the wires of the screen in the process of manufacture (cf. WOVE PAPER)

lain *past part.* of LIE (to have the body in a horizontal position)

lair (lɛər) *n.* a place in which a wild animal rests and feeds its young ‖ a hiding place of outlaws [O.E. *leger*, a lying place, bed]

laird (lɛərd) *n.* a Scottish landowner [Scot. var. of LORD]

lais·sez-faire, lais·ser-faire (lẹseiféər) *n.* the philosophy or practice of avoiding planning, esp. (*econ.*) the doctrine of avoiding government controls in economic affairs. The doctrine, which was a reaction against mercantilism, was popularized by the physiocrats (18th c.), found its classical expression in Adam Smith's 'Wealth of Nations' (1776), and was dominant in the 19th c. [F.=let act, i.e. let things alone]

la·i·ty (léiiti:) *n.* laymen [LAY *adj.*]

La·ius (léiəs) *OEDIPUS

lak (læk) *n.* the standard monetary unit of Albania, consisting of 100 quintars ‖ a coin worth this [Albanian]

lake (leik) *n.* a large expanse of water surrounded by land or by land and a manmade retainer, e.g. a dam. It may be fed by rivers, springs or local precipitation [M.E. *lac* fr. O.F.]

lake *n.* a deep red insoluble dye precipitated from lac or cochineal ‖ any similar dye [var. of LAC]

Lake District a beautiful mountainous area of N.W. England. Its largest lakes are Windermere, Ullswater, Derwentwater and Coniston Water. It was the home of the Lake poets (Wordsworth, Coleridge, Southey)

lake dweller someone inhabiting a lake dwelling

lake dwelling a primitive habitation built on a platform supported by piles in a marsh or in the shallows of a lake. Remains of such dwellings dating from the Neolithic, Bronze and Iron Ages have been found in Swiss and Italian lakes and others (*CRANNOG) in Scotland and

Ireland. Lake dwellings are still used in parts of tropical America, Africa, New Guinea etc.

Lake of the Woods a lake (c. 65 miles long, 10–60 miles wide) in N. Minnesota, extending into E. Manitoba and W. Ontario, Canada. It empties into Lake Winnipeg

Lake poets *LAKE DISTRICT

lake·scape (léikskeip) *n.* 1. all or part of a lake 2. its surface islands, shoreline features and scenery that can be viewed from a point on, or along, the lake

lake trout *Salvelinus namaycush*, a large freshwater food fish found in Canadian lakes and in the northern U.S.A.

lakh, lac (lɑk) *n.* (in India) 100,000, esp. as a quantity of rupees [Hindustani]

la·ko·da (lɑkóudə) *n.* a suedelike sham sealskin

Lakonia *LACONIA

Laksh·mi (lɑ́kʃmi:) (*Hindu mythol.*) the wife of Vishnu, goddess of beauty and prosperity

La·lande (lælɑ̃d), Joseph-Jérôme Lefrançois de (1732–1807), French astronomer. He made observations on the parallax of the moon. His works include 'Traité d'astronomie' (1764) and 'Bibliographie astronomique' (1803)

Lal·lans (lælənz) *n.* the lowland Scots dialect, esp. as cultivated by modern Scottish writers (e.g. Hugh Macdiarmid) as a medium of literary expression [Scot. var. of LOWLAND]

lal·la·tion (læléiʃən) *n.* lambdacism [fr. L. *lallare*, to sing a lullaby]

la·ma (lɑ́mə) *n.* a Lamaistic priest or monk **La·ma·ism** (lɑ́məizəm) *n.* a form of Buddhism found in Tibet, Bhutan, Sikkim, Mongolia, Nepal and parts of Siberia, N. India and S.W. China. Derived from Mahayana Buddhism, and combining the erotic mysticism of Tantrism with the Animist cult of Shamanism, it was established in Tibet (c. 750). In 1641 the Mongols set up the Dalai Lama to rule Tibet from Lhasa, while in the Tashi Lumpo monastery near Shigatse the Panchen Lama became the spiritual head of Lamaism. The lamas claim succession by direct divine reincarnation, the Dalai from Bodhisattva Avalokiteshvara, ancestor of the Tibetans, and the Panchen from Amitabha, the Buddha of light. Lamaism is a religion of magical formulas, prayer wheels, and incantations to the accompaniment of horns and drums. The 14th Dalai Lama was exiled to India in 1959, and in the 1960s Lamaism lost its hold on Tibet **La·ma·ist** *n.* **La·ma·is·tic** *adj.* [fr. Tibetan *blama*]

La·mar (ləmɑ́r), Lucius Quintus Cincinnatus (1825–93), U.S. statesman, best known for his efforts in the Senate to reconcile the North and South after the Civil War, and for his service as associate justice of the U.S. supreme court

La·marck (læmǽrk), Jean-Baptiste de Monet, chevalier de (1744–1829), French naturalist. His theory that characteristics acquired during the lifetime of an organism could be inherited, propounded as a basis for evolution, was developed in 'Histoire naturelle des animaux sans vertèbres' (1815–22)

La·marck·ism (ləmɑ́rkizəm) *n.* (*biol.*) the evolutionary theory that characteristics acquired by plants and animals as a result of environmental changes may be inherited

La Mar·mo·ra (lɑmɑ́rmɔrə), Alfonso Ferrero, marchese di (1804–78), Italian statesman and general, prime minister of Sardinia (1859 and 1865–6). He thoroughly reorganized the Sardinian army, and led the Sardinian contingent in the Crimean War

La·mar·tine (læmærti:n), Alphonse de (1790–1869), French poet, man of letters and statesman. The early 'Méditations poétiques' (1820), lyrical and darkly melancholy in the Byronic manner (e.g. 'le Lac'), show Lamartine as the first of the great French Romantics, at least in sentiment and attitude. His later volumes were less successful and he wrote little poetry after 1839. He was briefly head of the provisional government after the 1848 revolution

la·ma·ser·y (lɑ́məseri) *n.* *pl.* **la·ma·ser·ies** *n.* a monastery of lamas [F. *lamaserie*]

La·maze method (ləmɑ́z) technique of natural childbirth attained through psychoprophylaxis and without anesthetics —**Lamaze** *adj.*

Lamb (læm), Charles (1775–1834), English essayist and critic. His 'Specimens of English Dramatic Poets' (1808) was influential in reviving interest in Shakespeare and his contemporaries. As 'Elia', he wrote (1820–5) for the 'London Magazine' a series of gently whimsical

essays (collected 1822, 1833) which started a whole tradition of English essay writing

Lamb, Willis Eugene, Jr. (1913–), U.S. physicist who shared with Polykarp Kusch the 1955 Nobel prize for physics for measurement experiments with atomic hydrogen

lamb 1. *n.* a young sheep ‖ the flesh of this as food ‖ a meek, mild, innocent, or particularly lovable person ‖ lambskin 2. *v.i.* (of a ewe) to give birth ‖ *v.t.* to give birth to (a lamb) [O.E.]

lam·baste (læmbéist) *pres. part.* **lam·bast·ing** *past* and *past part.* **lam·bast·ed** *v.t.* to give a hard whipping to ‖ to scold [perh. *lam* (slang), to whip + BASTE]

lamb·da (læmdə) *n.* the 11th letter (λ, λ=1) of the Greek alphabet

lamb·da·cism (læmdəsizəm) *n.* a poor articulation of 'l' ‖ the replacing of 'l' by another sound ‖ the replacing of a sound by 'l' [fr. L.L. *lambdacismus* fr. Gk]

lambda particle (*particle phys.*) elementary unstable baryon particle with no charge and a mass of 1115.5 MeV and a lifetime of 2.5 × 10^{-10}, decaying into a nucleon and a pion

lamb·doid (læmdoid) *adj.* having the shape of a lambda ‖ of the lambdoid suture **lamb·doi·dal** *adj.* [F. *lambdoíde* fr. Mod. L. fr. Gk]

lambdoid suture (*anat.*) the suture between the occipital bone and the two parietal bones of the skull

lam·ben·cy (læmbənsi) *pl.* **lam·ben·cies** *n.* the quality of being lambent ‖ something which is lambent

lam·bent (læmbənt) *adj.* (of light or flame) moving about on a surface, seeming to touch it gently ‖ softly glowing ‖ light and sparkling (esp. of humor) [fr. L. *lambens* (*lambentis*) fr. *lambere*, to lick]

lam·bert (læmbərt) *n.* (*phys.*) the cgs unit of brightness, equal to that of a perfectly diffusing surface when it reflects or emits 1 lumen per sq. cm. [after J. H. *Lambert* (1728-77), G. physicist]

Lam·beth Conference (læmbiθ) a convocation of the bishops of the Anglican Communion, held every ten years in England at Lambeth Palace, London, the residence of the archbishop of Canterbury

lamb·kin (læmkin) *n.* a small, very young lamb ‖ a term of affection for a child [dim. of LAMB]

Lamb of God Christ [from the sacrificial Paschal lamb of the Jews, after e.g. John i, 29]

lam·bre·kin (læmbərkin, læmbrəkin) *n.* (*hist.*) a covering of cloth etc. worn on a helmet as a protection from the sun, rain etc. ‖ a piece of ornamental drapery hanging from a shelf etc. [F.]

lamb·skin (læmskin) *n.* the dressed skin of a lamb used as leather ‖ this skin with the wool left on it

Lamb·ton (læmtən), John George *DURHAM, 1st earl of

lame (leim) *n.* a lamina, esp. of metal ‖ (*pl.*) the overlapping plates used in the flexible elements of armor [F.]

lame 1. *adj.* unable to walk, run etc. normally because of a defect of, or injury to, a foot or leg ‖ (of a leg or foot) having such an injury or defect ‖ stiff and sore, *a lame back* ‖ having no force or effectiveness, *a lame excuse* ‖ (of meter) faltering 2. *v.t. pres. part.* **lam·ing** *past* and *past part.* **lamed** to make lame [O.E. *lama*]

la·mé (læméi) *n.* a fabric woven from metal thread, usually gold or silver, mixed with silk or other fiber [F.]

lame duck an ineffectual person ‖ (*stock exchange*) someone who is unable to fulfill his financial obligations ‖ (*pop.*) an elected officer or group that has lost a bid for reelection but continues to hold office until the term expires

la·mel·la (ləmélə) *pl.* **la·mel·lae** (ləméli:), **la·mel·las** *n.* a thin plate or layer, esp. of bone or tissue ‖ the gill of an agaric fungus **la·mél·lar, la·mel·late** (ləméleit, ləmélit), **la·mél·lat·ed** *adjs* [L., dim. of *lamina*, plate]

la·mel·li·branch (ləméləbræŋk) *n.* a member of *Lamellibranchia*, a class of bivalve mollusks including clams, oysters and mussels [fr. L. *lamella*, a thin plate + Gk *branchia*, a gill]

la·mel·li·corn (ləmélikɔrn) 1. *adj.* (of certain beetles) having antennae joints expanded into flattened plates ‖ (of antennae) having such flattened joints 2. *n.* a lamellicorn beetle [fr. Mod. L. *lamellicornnis* fr. L. *lamella*, thin plate + *cornu*, horn]

la·mel·li·ros·tral (ləmélirɔ́strəl, ləmeliróstrəl) *adj.* (e.g. of ducks, geese, swans, flamingos) having a beak with lamellae for straining out mud and water from food [fr. Mod. L. *lamellirostris* fr. LAMELLA+L. *rostrum*, beak]

la·mel·lose (ləmélous) *adj.* composed of lamellae

La·men·nais (læmne), Félicité Robert de (1782–1854), French religious and political writer. He entered orders (1816) and began as an apologist of theocratic principles, then moved via Catholic liberalism to become an apostle of revolutionary doctrines. He was condemned by the pope (1832). His 'Paroles d'un croyant' appeared in 1834

la·ment (ləmént) *v.t.* to mourn for ǁ to show or feel regret for ǁ *v.i.* to mourn ǁ to show or feel regret [fr. L. *lamentari* fr. *lamentum*, a lament]

lament *n.* an expression of mourning or grieving ǁ such mourning or grieving in a literary or musical form [fr. L. *lamentum*]

lam·en·ta·ble (læməntəb'l, ləméntəb'l) *adj.* giving cause for adverse comment ǁ giving cause for lament **lám·en·ta·bly** *adv.* [fr. F., or fr. L. *lamentabilis*]

lam·en·ta·tion (læməntéiʃən) *n.* the act of lamenting or an instance of this [fr. F., or fr. L. *lamentatio (lamentationis)*]

Lam·en·ta·tions (læməntéiʃənz) a book of the Old Testament which laments in five poems the destruction of Jerusalem (586 B.C.). It was formerly attributed to Jeremiah but is now considered to date from the mid-6th c. B.C.

La·mi·a (léimi:ə) (*Gk mythol.*) a grief-maddened woman who took revenge for the deaths of her own children, killed by Hera, by killing the children of others

La·mi·a (lɑmí:ɑ) an agricultural center (pop. 27,000) in E. central Greece: tobacco, cereals, olives

la·mi·a (léimi:ə) *n.* (*later classical mythol.*) a fabulous monster, half woman and half serpent, who sucked the blood of her lovers [L.]

lam·i·na (læminə) *pl.* **lam·i·nae** (læmini:), **lam·i·nas** *n.* any thin plate or scale (e.g. of bone or metal) ǁ (*bot.*) the blade of a leaf or petal (cf. PETIOLE) **lám·i·nar** *adj.* [L.=a plate]

laminar flow smooth, although not necessarily uniform, flow in which adjoining levels do not mix

lam·i·nar·i·a (læminéəri:ə) *n.* a member of *Laminaria*, fam. *Laminariaceae*, a genus of brown marine kelps from which algin may be extracted [Mod. L.]

lam·i·nate (læmineit) *pres. part.* **lam·i·nat·ing** *past* and *past part.* **lam·i·nat·ed** *v.t.* to make or split into thin plates or layers ǁ to make (plywood, plastic etc.) by uniting layer upon layer ǁ *v.i.* to split into laminae [LAMINA]

lam·i·nate (læminit) *adj.* having or composed of a lamina or laminae [fr. Mod. L. *laminatus*]

lam·i·na·tion (læminéiʃən) *n.* a laminating or being laminated ǁ (*geol.*) the occurrence of minor layers of stratified sedimentary rock [LAMINA]

laminography *TOMOGRAPHY

lam·i·nose (læminous) *adj.* laminate [LAMINA]

Lam·mas (læməs) *n.* (*Eng. hist.*), Aug. 1, a former harvest festival [O.E. *hlāfmæsse*, loaf mass]

lam·mer·gei·er, lam·mer·gey·er (læmərgaiər) *n. Gypaëtus barbatus aureus*, a very large bird of prey, inhabiting high mountain ranges in S. Europe, Asia and N. Africa [G. *lämmergeier* fr. *lämmer*, lambs+*geier*, vulture]

lamp (læmp) *n.* a device for giving off light without being consumed itself, e.g. an oil lamp ǁ a similar device for giving off invisible radiation, e.g. an infrared lamp [F. *lampe* fr. L. fr. Gk]

lamp·black (læmpblæk) *n.* a fine black soot, obtained by the incomplete combustion of certain carbonaceous materials. It is used as a pigment, e.g. in printer's ink

lamp·light (læmplait) *n.* the light given out by a lamp **lámp·light·er** *n.* (esp. *hist.*) a person paid to light lamps, esp. streetlights

Lamp·man (læmpmən), Archibald (1861–99), Canadian nature poet. His descriptive, reflective poems, notably 'Morning on the Lièvre', 'Heat', and 'In November', were inspired by the countryside of Ottawa and Quebec

lam·poon (læmpú:n) **1.** *n.* a piece of satirical verse or other writing designed to ridicule or discredit someone **2.** *v.t.* to attack (someone) in this way [F. *lampon*, drinking song]

lamp·post (læmppoust) *n.* a tall post on which an outdoor lamp is mounted, esp. a lamp used for lighting a street

lam·prey (læmpri) *n.* a member of *Hyperoartia*, an order of marine or freshwater vertebrates,

found in North American, Eurasian and subarctic waters. It is an eel-like fish with tooth-studded mouth used as a sucker when it preys upon other fish. It is the most primitive extant vertebrate [M.E. fr. O.F. *lampreie*]

lamp·shade (læmpʃeid) *n.* an opaque or semiopaque shade for softening the glare or directing the light of a lamp

LANAC (lænæk) *n.* (*acronym*) laminar air navigation anticollision, a radio navigation system for aircraft based on ground communication

Lan·ark (lænərk) a former county (area 879 sq. miles) of S. central Scotland. Its administrative center was Glasgow ǁ its county town (pop. 8,000), a former residence of Scottish kings

la·nate (léineit) *adj.* (esp. of certain leaves) covered with short, soft woolly hairs [fr. L. *lanatus*, woolly]

Lan·ca·shire (læŋkəʃiər) (*abbr.* Lancs.) a county (area 1,875 sq. miles, pop. 1,372,118) of N.W. England. County town: Lancaster

Lan·cas·ter (læŋkəstər) an English royal dynasty (1399–1461), whose reigning members were Henry IV, Henry V and Henry VI. Their claim to the throne, based on their descent from John of Gaunt, was contested by the house of York (*ROSES, WARS OF THE)

Lancaster, John of Gaunt, duke of *JOHN OF GAUNT

Lancaster, John of *JOHN OF LANCASTER

Lancaster, Joseph (1778–1838), British educator. He founded free elementary schools in Britain and the U.S.A., based on a system in which older pupils were responsible for supervising and teaching younger ones

Lancaster the county town (pop. 49,000) of Lancashire, England. Manufactures: linoleum, agricultural machinery, textiles. University (1964)

Lan·cas·tri·an (læŋkæstri:ən) **1.** *adj.* of Lancashire **2.** *n.* a native of Lancashire ǁ (*hist.*) a member or adherent of the house of Lancaster in the Wars of the Roses

lance (læns, lɑns) *n.* (*hist.*) a mounted soldier's weapon consisting of a long shaft with a pointed steel end ǁ a similar weapon for killing a harpooned whale, spearing fish etc. ǁ a lancet (instrument) ǁ a launce [F.]

lance *pres. part.* **lanc·ing** *past* and *past part.* **lanced** *v.t.* to pierce with a lance ǁ to pierce or cut with a lancet [O.F. *lancier*]

Lance (*mil.*) a mobile, storable, liquid propellant, surface-to-surface guided missile, with nuclear and nonnuclear capability, designed to support an Army corps with long-range fires

lance corporal (*U.S. Marines*) an enlisted man ranking above a private first class and below a corporal ǁ (*Br. mil.*) a noncommissioned officer ranking immediately below a corporal [after older *lancepesade* fr. Ital. *lancia spezzata*, broken lance, i.e. army veteran]

lance·let (lénslit, lónslit) *n.* a small (up to 4 ins) marine animal of genus *Branchiostoma* and related genera that burrows in the sand in shallow waters of warm seas [LANCE]

Lan·ce·lot du Lac (lɑsloudyælæk), Sir Lanncelot of the Lake, one of the knights in the Arthurian legend, loved by Guinevere

lan·ce·o·late (lénsi:əlit, lénsi:əleit) *adj.* narrowing to a point at each end or at the tip [fr. L. *lanceolatus* fr. *lanceola*, dim. of *lancea*, lance]

lanc·er (lénsər, lónsər) *n.* a soldier of a cavalry regiment (orig. armed with a lance) ǁ (*pl.*) a set of quadrilles, popular in the late 19th and early 20th cc. ǁ the music for these [F. *lancier*]

lance snake the fer-de-lance

lan·cet (lénsit, lónsit) *n.* a sharp-pointed, two-edged surgical instrument ǁ (*archit.*) a lancet arch or window [fr. O.F. or F. *lancette*, dim. of LANCE]

lancet arch (*archit.*) an acutely pointed arch

lancet window (*archit.*) a high, narrow window topped with a lancet arch

lance·wood (lénswud, lónswud) *n.* the tough, elastic wood of *Oxandra lanceolata*, fam. *Annonaceae*, and other trees of South America, used for fishing rods, billiard cues etc. ǁ a member of the species *O. lanceolata*

Lan·chow (lɑ́nd̥ʒóu) (Kaolan) capital (pop. 699,000) of Kansu, N.W. China, on the Hwang-ho, a road and rail junction on trade routes to Central Asia: food processing, chemical, textile and oil industries. University

land (lænd) **1.** *n.* the solid surface of the earth where it is not covered with water ǁ a particular area of this, distinguished from other areas by political, geographical, economic or other considerations, *the land of the Visigoths, a land of*

plenty, *forest land* ǁ such an area in relation to its owner, *their land goes up to that wood* ǁ the soil, esp. in relation to its quality or use, *heavy land, building land* ǁ the surface between the grooves of the rifling in guns **the land** the country, esp. agricultural areas, as distinct from the city **to see how the land lies** to find out the true state of affairs, esp. secretly or unobtrusively, in order to assess a situation **2.** *v.i.* to step onto land from a ship ǁ to arrive, *to land at one's destination* ǁ (of an aircraft) to come to rest on the ground or on water ǁ (of a boat) to come into port or ashore ǁ to reach the ground after jumping, falling etc., *to land awkwardly* ǁ *v.t.* to put on shore from a ship ǁ to bring (an aircraft) to land ǁ to bring (someone) to his destination ǁ to deliver (a blow) ǁ to bring (a fish) to shore ǁ to obtain to one's benefit, *to land a good job* ǁ to place or find (oneself) in a particular state or situation, *to land oneself in trouble* **to land on one's feet** to be fortunate or successful ǁ to emerge safely from an awkward situation **to land up** to find oneself in the end in some specified place or situation after a journey or incident, end up, wind up [O.E.]

land agent (*Br.*) the manager of an estate ǁ an agent acting for the sale of public or private land

land arm mode (*mil.*) a mode of operation in which automatic sequence is used to engage and disengage appropriate modes of an aircraft automatic flight control system in order to execute the various flight phases necessary for completing an automatic approach and landing

lan·dau (lǽndɔ, lǽndau) *n.* (*hist.*) a four-wheeled passenger carriage with a folding hood ǁ a closed automobile with a folding roof over the rear seat **lan·dau·let, lan·dau·lette** (lǽndɔlét) *n.* (*hist.*) a small landau carriage ǁ an automobile having an open driver's seat and a folding roof over the rear seat [after *Landau*, Bavaria, Germany]

land bank a bank which issues currency in exchange for mortgages on land or other transactions in real property

land breeze a breeze blowing off the land toward the sea

land crab any of various crabs, esp. of fam. *Gecarinidae*, that are found in warm climates and live on land but breed in the sea

land·ed (lǽndid) *adj.* owning land, *a landed proprietor* ǁ consisting of land, *landed property* [LAND *n.*]

land·er (lǽndər) *n.* (*astronautics*) space satellite vehicle for landing on the moon or other celestial body *Cf* SOFTLANDING

Landes (lɑ̃d) a region of sand dunes and pine forests behind the coast of S.W. France. Tourism, fishing, oysters ǁ a department (area 3,604 sq. miles, pop. 277,000) of S.W. France (*GUYENNE, *GASCONY). Chief town: Mont-de-Marsan

land·fall (lǽndfɔl) *n.* (*naut., aeron.*) the sighting of land after a voyage ǁ (*naut., aeron.*) the arrival on this land

land freeze prohibition on sale of land, usu. by a government agency

land·grab·ber (lǽndgræbər) *n.* someone who seizes land illegally, esp. in Ireland after the eviction of a tenant farmer

land-grant (lǽndgrænt, lǽndgrɑnt) *adj.* (of a railroad etc.) built on land given by the federal government ǁ (of a college or university) built on property originally given by the federal government or receiving federal aid on the stipulation that practical courses be offered, esp. in agriculture and the mechanical arts

Land-grant Colleges and Universities U.S. educational institutions established on public lands by the Morrill Act

land·grave (lǽndgreiv) *n.* (*hist.*) a German count having a certain territorial jurisdiction ǁ (*hist.*) the title of certain German princes [Middle High G. *lantgrâve*]

land·gra·vi·ate (lǽndgréivi:it) *n.* the office, jurisdiction or authority of a landgrave [fr. M.L. *landgraviatus*]

land·gra·vine (lǽndgrəvi:n) *n.* (*hist.*) the wife of a landgrave ǁ (*hist.*) a female holder of a landgraviate [fr. G. *landgräfin* or Du. *landgravin*]

land·hold·er (lǽndhoulder) *n.* a person who owns or rents land

land·ing (lǽndiŋ) *n.* a disembarking or being disembarked ǁ a bringing or coming to land or to shore ǁ an alighting of an aircraft ǁ a place where goods or persons are landed or taken aboard ‖ a level place at the top of a flight of stairs or between two flights of stairs

landing craft an amphibious vehicle used to land invading troops and armored equipment

landing gear the structure that takes the shock when an aircraft is brought down onto land or water and that supports the aircraft's weight

landing net an angler's bag-shaped net for gathering a hooked fish out of the water

landing stage a pier or platform for embarking and disembarking goods and passengers

landing strip a runway kept in a fit state for aircraft to use but not having airport facilities

land·la·dy (lǽndleidi:) pl. **land·la·dies** n. a woman who runs a boarding house or an inn, or takes in lodgers ‖ a woman who leases property to others

land·locked (lǽndlɒkt) adj. (of water) almost or completely surrounded by land ‖ (of fish, e.g. some salmon) prevented from leaving fresh water for the sea, or not doing so ‖ (of a country) without a seacoast

land·lord (lǽndlɔrd) n. a man who leases property to another ‖ the owner of a boardinghouse or inn **lánd·lord·ism** n. the system under which land is worked by tenants or landlords

land·lub·ber (lǽndlʌbər) n. (naut.) someone who has no knowledge of the sea or ships [LAND+lubber, a lout]

land·mark (lǽndmɑrk) n. a prominent feature on land, esp. one which acts as a guide in following a route or marking a boundary ‖ any monument of historic etc. interest ‖ an event which is of special significance in a process or period of change

land·mass (lǽndmæs) n. a very large area of land as opposed to an ocean

land mine (mil.) an explosive mine concealed on or in the ground ‖ a large mine dropped by parachute over the land to cause extensive surface damage

land office a government office for transactions and business relating to public lands

land-office business (pop.) a thriving business

Land of Promise *PROMISED LAND

Lan·don (lǽndən), Alfred Mossman (1887–), U.S. progressive governor of Kansas and, as the only Republican gubernatorial incumbent winner in 1934, Republican candidate (1936) for the U.S. presidency. Carrying only Maine and Vermont, he obtained the lowest number of electoral votes (eight) on record in the 20th c.

Lan·dor (lǽndɔr, lǽndər), Walter Savage (1775–1864), English poet and prose writer, best known for his 'Imaginary Conversations' (1824–8, 1829, 1846)

Land Ordinance of 1785 a U.S. Congressional ordinance which provided a geographical system for the disposition of the ungranted lands of the West. It provided for survey before settlement, for division of the land into rectilinear blocks (640 acres each), and for the reservation of one section in each township for public purposes

land·own·er (lǽndounər) n. a person who owns land

land-poor (lǽndpuər) adj. poor as a result of owning much unremunerative land

land power a nation with a large and powerful army ‖ military strength on land

land rail the corncrake

land reclamation the improvement or creation of land, esp. for cultivation, by irrigation, dikes, drainage etc.

land retirement *SOIL BANK

land·scape (lǽndskeip) 1. n. a painting or photograph of a piece of inland scenery ‖ such a piece of scenery 2. v. pres. part. **land·scap·ing** past and past part. **land·scaped** v.t. to beautify (land, property etc.) by modifying or enhancing the natural scenery ‖ v.i. to engage in landscape gardening or landscape architecture [Du. landschap]

landscape architect an expert in landscape architecture

landscape architecture the planning, modifying and arranging of a large piece of land with an eye to scenic beauty, esp. with reference to the siting of roads, buildings etc.

landscape gardener an expert in landscape gardening

landscape gardening the planning and planting of gardens and grounds, esp. so as to produce picturesque and harmonious effects

Land·seer (lǽndsiər), Sir Edwin Henry

73), English painter. His animal pictures (for which he is best known) are brilliant but sentimental

Land's End (lǽndzénd) the southwestern tip of England, in Cornwall. Its granite cliffs rise to 100 ft

land·slide (lǽndslaid) n. the slipping down from a hillside or cliff of masses of earth and rock ‖ this rock and earth ‖ an overwhelming majority of votes cast for one political party or one politician ‖ an overwhelming electoral victory

land·slip (lǽndslip) n. (Br.) a landslide (the slipping down of rock and earth and the rock etc. itself)

lands·man (lántsmən) pl. **lands·leit** (lántslait) n. a Jew from the same town or region as oneself, esp. an Eastern European Jew [Yiddish]

land-to-land (lǽndtəlǽnd) adj. (mil.) of a missile sent from the ground to a target on the ground also ground-to-ground

land·ward (lǽndwərd) 1. adj. located towards the land 2. adv. towards the land **lánd·wards** adv.

land yacht a sail-powered beach vehicle, usu. with three wheels also sand yacht

Lane (lein), Franklin Knight (1864–1921), U.S. lawyer. He was secretary of the interior (1913–20) under President Woodrow Wilson. As a cabinet member he promoted Indian welfare, land reclamation, and the construction (1924) of a railroad between Seward and Fairbanks, Alaska

lane (lein) n. a narrow country road, esp. one edged with hedges or fences ‖ a narrow street or alley, esp. one edged with walls or buildings ‖ a prescribed channel for sea or air traffic ‖ one of a series of parallel marked sections of road ‖ one of a series of similar marked strips on a running track ‖ a passage left between rows of persons ‖ a channel of water in an ice field ‖ a wooden bowling alley [O.E. lane, lone]

Lan·franc (lǽnfræŋk) (c. 1005–89), Norman ecclesiastic, archbishop of Canterbury (1070–89). He carried out William I's policy of replacing English bishops by Normans and helped to reorganize and reform the English Church. He attended to its finances, established ecclesiastical courts, and made the archbishopric of York subject to Canterbury

Lang (læŋ), Cosmo Gordon, 1st Baron Lang of Lambeth (1864–1945), British prelate, friend and adviser of George V. As archbishop of Canterbury (1928–42), he played a part in the abdication of Edward VIII

lang. language

Lang·e·land (lǽŋələn) a small island (area 110 sq. miles, pop. 20,000) of Denmark. Chief town: Rudkøbing

Langerhans * ISLET OF LANGERHANS

Lang·land (lǽŋlənd), William (c. 1332–c. 1400), English poet, author of 'The Vision of Piers the Plowman', a vast allegorical poem. Presented as a series of dreams, it is a powerfully realistic and satirical picture of 14th-c. England as well as a great religious poem, exploring the nature of the good Christian life in the individual and society. The poem exists in three versions, representing successive revisions by the author (c. 1362, c. 1377, 1390). The style is homely, vigorous and direct. The verse is unrhymed, stressed and highly alliterative, representing a continuation of the Anglo-Saxon poetic tradition in contrast to the continental tradition exemplified by Chaucer

Lang·ley (lǽŋli:), Samuel Pierpont (1834–1906), U.S. astronomer and physicist. He invented the bolometer, an instrument which enabled him to measure the intensity of solar radiation at various wave lengths. A pioneer aviationist, he devised (1896) a steam-driven pilotless airplane

Lang·muir (lǽŋmjuər), Irving (1881–1957), U.S. physical chemist who won the 1932 Nobel prize in chemistry for work in surface chemistry. He devised techniques to transform supercooled clouds into ice crystals by seeding clouds with silver iodide. His research led to new technology, such as vacuum tubes for use in television sets, the gas-filled tungsten lamp, and atomic hydrogen welding

Lang·muir probe (lǽŋmju:r) (plasma phys.) a device used to measure temperature and density of plasma by calculations from an electrical discharge

lan·gous·tine (læŋəstíːn) n. a small lobster ‖ a prawn

Lang·ton (lǽŋtən), Stephen (c. 1150–1228), English cardinal, archbishop of Canterbury

(1207–28). King John's refusal to recognize his appointment (1207) was the immediate cause of the dispute with the papacy and the placing of England under an interdict (1208). After his recognition (1213) Langton played an important part in the baronial opposition and contributed to the drawing up of Magna Carta

lan·guage (lǽŋgwidʒ) n. the organized system of speech used by human beings as a means of communication among themselves ‖ any such differentiated system as used by a section of the human race, the English language ‖ such a system enriched by words and phrases used by persons having special knowledge, scientific language ‖ such a system adapted to a special purpose, the language of diplomacy ‖ a manner of expressing oneself, strong language ‖ any other organized system of communication, e.g. by symbols, mathematical language, or gestures, deaf-and-dumb language ‖ any apparently organized system of communication, the language of animals ‖ literary style, use of words [F. langage]

—Languages are in a constant process of change, in sound, in form and in meaning, so long as they are spoken. The evolution of language is generally from complex forms to simpler and more freely combinable elements: thus French has fewer inflections than Latin, and Latin fewer than Sanskrit. English is structurally one of the simplest.

The origin of language is not known. Theories that language derives from echoic imitation, sound symbolism, instinctive cries, releases of breath accompanying exertion, or oral 'gestures' originally corresponding to bodily movement, account for only a small part of the known phenomena of language.

Languages are analyzed into families, of which the most studied is Indo-European. Other large families include Hamitic, Semitic, Finno-Ugric and Sino-Tibetan. The exact groupings vary, and many languages remain unclassified: some do not appear to be susceptible of classification, e.g. many American Indian languages. The languages most spoken at the present day are (in order) Chinese, English, Hindustani, Russian, Spanish, German, Japanese, French, Malay and Bengali. Of these, English is nearest to being an international language [*LINGUISTICS]

language laboratory a workshop for language study equipped with audiovisual aids

Langue·doc (lãgdɔk) a former province of France bordering the Mediterranean, including the S.E. Massif Central and a basin curving around it from the Garonne to the Rhône. It includes parts of Haute-Garonne and Tarn-et-Garonne in the Garonne valley, Tarn, Lozère, Haute-Loire and Ardèche in the Massif Central, and Aude, Hérault and Gard between the mountains and the coast. Industries: cattle raising and forestry in the mountains, agriculture (cereals, fruit, vegetables, wines) in the basin, tourism. Chief towns: Toulouse (the historic capital and modern industrial center), Montpellier, Nîmes, Narbonne. The region, formed around the countship of Toulouse, was named after its language (*LANGUE D'OC). After the Albigenses had been crushed, Languedoc was annexed by France (1271)

langue d'oc (lãgdɔk) n. a group of dialects spoken in France, south of a line running between Poitiers and Grenoble, during the Middle Ages and surviving esp. in Provençal. The oldest extant texts belong to the 10th c. Langue d'oc flourished as a literary language during the 12th and 13th cc. (*TROUBADOUR) and was revived (late 19th c.) by Mistral and others [F.=language of oc (fr. the use of oc for 'yes')]

langue d'oïl (lãgdɔil, lãgdɔi:l) a group of dialects spoken in the Middle Ages in central and N. France, from which modern French is descended (cf. LANGUE D'OC) [F.=language of oïl (fr. the use of oïl for 'yes')]

lan·guid (lǽŋgwid) adj. without vitality ‖ without interest, indifferent ‖ lacking in activity, sluggish [F. languide or fr. L. languidus]

lan·guish (lǽŋgwiʃ) v.i. to become languid ‖ to live under dispiriting conditions, to languish in prison ‖ to pine ‖ to assume a languid expression in an effort to win sympathy or affection ‖ to wane, his interest languished [F. languir (languiss-)]

lan·guor (lǽŋgər) n. a state of languishing or being languid **lan·guor·ous** (lǽŋgərəs) adj. [O. F. fr. L. languere, to languish]

lan·gur (lʌngúər) n. a member of *Presbytis*, fam. *Colobidae*, a genus of slender, long-tailed Asiatic monkeys with a chin tuft [Hindi]

laniard *LANYARD

lan·i·ar·y (læni:eri:) 1. adj. (of teeth) adapted for tearing 2. pl. **lan·i·ar·ies** n. a canine tooth [fr. L. *laniarius*, relating to a butcher]

La·nier (ləníər), Sidney (1842–81), U.S. poet and musician. His poems reflect his upbringing in the traditional old South and his struggle to adjust to the new industrialism and value structure of the post-Civil War era. 'Corn' (1874) treats of agricultural conditions in the South, and 'The Symphony' (1875) depicts industrial conditions in the North

lank (læŋk) adj. extremely slim ‖ (of plants) inordinately long and slender ‖ (of hair) long, straight and lifeless-looking [O.E. *hlanc*, loose]

lank·i·ness (læŋki:nis) n. the state or quality of being lanky

lank·y (læŋki:) comp. **lank·i·er** superl. **lank·i·est** adj. (of a person) tall, thin and ungainly ‖ (of limbs) longer and thinner than is graceful [LANK]

lan·ner (lænər) n. *Falco biarmicus feldeggii*, a falcon of S. Europe, esp. the female, used in falconry ‖ a related falcon, esp. the female, of N. Africa and S. Asia **lan·ner·et** (lænəret) n. a male lanner [fr. F. *lanier*]

lan·o·lin (lænˈlin) n. a waxy substance obtained from wool grease, readily absorbed by the skin and used in ointments and cosmetics [fr. L. *lana*, wool+*oleum*, oil]

lan·o·line (lænˈliːn) n. lanolin

Lans·bur·y (lænzbəri:), George (1859–1940), British politician, leader of the Labour party (1931–5). He resigned because his pacifism was unacceptable to his party

Lans·downe (lænzdaun), Henry Charles Keith Petty-Fitzmaurice, 5th marquess of (1845–1927), British statesman. He was governor-general of Canada (1883–8), viceroy of India (1888–93) and secretary for war (1895–1900). As Conservative foreign secretary (1900–5), he formed alliances with Japan (1902) and France (1904). In 1917 he published in a newspaper a letter which made unauthorized proposals for a compromise peace with the Germans, in an effort to hasten the end of the 1st world war

lan·sign (lænsən) n. (semantics) symbolic word, character, or sound that represents an idea or thing

Lan·sing (lænsiŋ), Robert (1864–1928), U.S. international lawyer. As secretary of state (1915–20) under President Woodrow Wilson, he urged Wilson to enter the 1st world war, sought peace with Mexico, and promoted Pan-American solidarity. He negotiated the Lansing-Ishii agreement with Japan, which declared continuance of the 'open door' policy. He also negotiated the purchase of the Danish West Indies

Lansing the capital (pop. 130,414) of Michigan: chemical and engineering industries, esp. cars

lans·que·net (lˈænskənet, lánskənet) n. (hist.) a mercenary foot soldier, armed with a pike or lance, in continental, esp. German, armies (15th–18th cc.) ‖ a card game of German origin [F. fr. G.]

lan·tern (læntərn) n. a portable case with transparent sides containing a source of light and protecting this from wind and rain ‖ a glass structure in a roof or in the upper part of a dome, admitting light ‖ the chamber of a lighthouse containing the light ‖ a magic lantern [fr. F. *lanterne*]

lantern fly any of several tropical insects, esp. members of genera *Lanternaria* and *Fulgora*, fam. *Fulgoridae*, having a hollow anterior prolongation of the head

lantern jaw an underhung jaw ‖ (pl.) long, bony jaws **lan·tern-jawed** (læntərnʤɔd) adj. having lantern jaws or a lantern jaw

lantern pinion a gear pinion consisting of two parallel disks connected at their peripheries by a series of bars and used in horology

lantern wheel a lantern pinion

lan·tha·nide (lænθənaid) n. a rare earth element, symbol Ln [fr. M.L. *lanthanum*]

lanthanide series a series of 15 elements within the first very long period of the periodic table, beginning with lanthanum (at. no. 57) and ending with lutetium (at. no. 71). They often occur together naturally. Many form colored, usually tripositive ions which are strongly paramagnetic

lan·tha·num (lænθənəm) n. a chemical element (symbol La, at. no. 57, at. mass 138.91), one of

the rare-earth metals [fr. Gk *lanthanein*, to lie hidden]

Lan·ti·an or **Lan·ti·en man** (lænti:ən) remains of an extinct primitive man found in Shensi, China, in 1964, dated c. 500,000 B.C.

la·nu·gi·nous (lənú:dʒinəs, lənju:dʒínəs) adj. covered with down ‖ downy [fr. L. *lanuginosus*]

la·nu·go (lənú:gou, lənjú:gou) n. soft, downy hair ‖ the downy covering on a fetus [L. fr. *lana*, wool]

lan·yard, lan·iard (lænjərd) n. (naut.) a short cord or rope used for fastening ‖ a cord worn around the neck and holding a knife, whistle etc. ‖ (hist.) a cord with a hook attached used to fire a cannon [fr. F. *lanière*, strap, cord]

Lao (lau) 1. pl. **Lao, Laos** n. a member of a Thai people living in Laos and N.E. Thailand ‖ the Thai language of these people 2. adj. of these people

La·oc·o·ön (leiɒ́koun) (Gk mythol.) a Trojan priest of Apollo, who protested during the Trojan War against bringing the wooden horse into Troy. This offended the god, and Laocoön was killed with his two sons by two sea serpents. The Vatican statue (1st c. B.C.) showing the struggle with the serpents gave rise to Lessing's essay on the proper subject of painting and poetry

La·od·i·ce·a (leiɒdisí:ə, leiəudisi:ɔ́) *LATAKIA

Laoigh·is (léiiʃ, li:ʃ) (Eng. Leix, formerly Queen's) an inland county (area 664 sq. miles, pop. 51,169) of Leinster province, Irish Republic. County seat: Port Laoighise (formerly Maryborough)

La·os (láous, léins, laus) a kingdom (area 88,780 sq. miles, pop. 3,901,000) in S.E. Asia. Administrative capital: Vientiane. Royal capital: Luang Prabang. People: 60% Lao with other Thai groups, various groups of Indonesian and Chinese origin, small Chinese and Vietnamese minorities. Official languages: Lao and French. Religion: Theravada Buddhism, with Animist and Christian minorities. Apart from the Mekong Valley (southwest) and the Plaine des Jarres (1,000 ft) around Luang Prabang, Laos is wooded and mountainous. It is highest in the northern central region (Phon Bia, 8,591 ft). Three quarters of the population live along the Mekong Valley. The climate is tropical with monsoons May–Oct. Rainfall: 50–80 ins. In the valley the temperature ranges from 50° to 100° F. Above 3,000 ft the climate is temperate. Livestock: cattle, water buffalo, hogs, elephants, poultry, horses. Crops: rice, corn, tobacco, citrus fruits, tea, coffee, potatoes, opium. Forest products: teak, benzoin, stick lac, cardomom, cinchona, ramie. Minerals: tin, iron ore. Industries: silk, pottery, leather goods, silverwork, lumber, rice milling, electricity, cigarettes, matches, soap. Exports: wood, tin, coffee, wood products. Imports: foodstuffs, machinery, metals, chemicals. The River Mekong is the principal highway. Monetary unit: kip. HISTORY. A province of the Khmer Empire (9th–13th cc.), Laos formed (14th c.) an independent kingdom which suffered invasions from Burma and Annam (17th and 18th cc.) and was conquered (1827) by the Thais. Laos became (1893 and 1904) part of French Indochina, and, after the Japanese occupation (1940–5), gained independence (1949) within the French Union. The country was unified after the Indochinese war (1946–54) and declared a neutral state, but civil war broke out (1960). This ended by a conference (1962) at Geneva, Switzerland, which established a coalition government of three princes representing right-wing, neutralist and Communist forces. Fighting between government and Communist troops was renewed (1963) and the latter received strong North Vietnamese reinforcements (esp. in 1969). North Vietnam used the so-called 'Ho Chi Minh trail' to transport troops and material through Laos to South Vietnam, and U.S. bombardments were frequent and intense. After the fall of South Vietnam and Cambodia (Kampuchea) in 1975, the Communist-backed Pathet Lao took control of Laos, and the monarchy was abolished that same year. Ties with Vietnam and the Soviet bloc were strengthened after Vietnam invaded Cambodia (1979), and Laos became increasingly economically dependent on Vietnam

La·o·tian (leióuʃən, láuʃən) 1. n. a Lao 2. adj. Lao

Lao-tzu, Lao-tse (láudzú) (c. 604–c. 531 B.C.), Chinese philosopher. He is the traditional

founder of Taoism, whose precepts are contained in his 'Tao Tê Ching' dictated before he left China for the west

lap (læp) n. the crook of the body between waist and knees of someone sitting down, taken as a snug resting place for a child, pet etc., or as a place to set something down conveniently **in the lap of luxury** having all the material comforts that one could desire **in the lap of the gods** as fate will determine [O.E. *lappa*, *læppa*, a flap]

lap (mil.) in naval mine warfare, the section of strip of an area assigned to a single sweeper or formation of sweepers for a run through the area

lap 1. v. pres. part. **lap·ping** past and past part. **lapped** v.t. to drink (liquid) by taking it up with the tongue ‖ (of water) to come repeatedly against (something) with a soft slapping sound ‖ v.i. to drink liquid by taking it up with the tongue ‖ to make a soft slapping sound **to lap up** to absorb or accept eagerly and quickly 2. n. an instance or the sound of lapping ‖ the amount drunk in a lap [O.E. *lapian*]

lap 1. v. pres. part. **lap·ping** past and past part. **lapped** v.i. (with 'about', 'around', 'in') to wrap ‖ (with 'over') to fold, to lap ‖ to cause to overlap ‖ to overlap ‖ to make a circuit of (a racecourse) ‖ to outdistance (a racing opponent) by one or more laps ‖ v.i. to cover partially ‖ to cover and extend beyond ‖ to make a circuit of a racecourse 2. n. a section that overlaps ‖ an amount of overlap ‖ a circuit of a racecourse ‖ a section or phase of a whole, *the last lap of the trip* [M.E. *lappe* prob. from LAP n., a fold]

lap 1. n. a rotating disk used to polish gems or metal surface 2. v.t. pres. part. **lap·ping** past and past part. **lapped** to polish with this [perh. fr. LAP n., overlap]

lap·a·ro·scope (læpərəskoup) n. (med.) an illuminated optical instrument for examining internal organs, piercing the body wall —**laparoscopy** n. surgery using the laparoscope

lap·a·rot·o·my (læpərɒ́təmi:) pl. **lap·a·rot·o·mies** n. a surgical incision in the abdominal wall to investigate suspected disease within the abdomen [fr. Gk *lapara*, flank+*-tomia*, cutting]

La Paz (ləpás) the administrative capital (pop. 881,404) of Bolivia (*SUCRE), on the northwestern plateau at 11,910 ft, commercial center of the country and seat of government. It was founded (1548) by the Spanish. Industries: tanning, brewing, distilling, light manufactures. Cathedral (19th–20th cc.). University

lap-belt (læpbelt) n. a motor vehicle seat belt

lap-dog (læpdɒg, læpdɒg) n. a small pet dog

la·pel (ləpél) n. the part of the front of a coat or dress folded back along the neckline [LAP n., (obs.) a fold]

lap·i·dar·y (læpíderi:) 1. pl. **lap·i·dar·ies** n. someone who cuts, polishes or engraves gems 2. adj. pertaining to precious stones ‖ engraved on stone ‖ (of literary style) tersely elegant and pithy [fr. L. *lapidarius* n. and adj.]

lap·i·des·cent (læpidésənt) adj. like stone, esp. of a stone monument

lap·is laz·u·li (læpislæzuli:, læpislæzjulai) n. (mineral.) a semiprecious stone of a fine deep blue color, essentially a sodium aluminum silicate containing some sulfur ‖ a bright blue pigment made from it ‖ its color [fr. L. *lapis*, stone+*lazulum* (*lazuli*), azure]

lap joint a joint in which one of the joined pieces laps over the other

La·place (ləplæs), Pierre Simon, marquis de (1749–1827), French physicist and astronomer. He demonstrated the stability of the solar system and its consistence with Newton's laws, and he attributed the origin of this system to condensation from a nebula. He also reconciled Newton's experimental and theoretical values for the velocity of sound by showing that the propagation of sound is an adiabatic process. With Lavoisier he made the first determination of the coefficient of expansion of a metal rod, and initiated the study of thermochemistry

Laplace equation the second order partial differential equation

$$\frac{\delta^2 u}{\delta x^2} + \frac{\delta^2 u}{\delta y^2} + \frac{\delta^2 u}{\delta z^2} = 0$$

(also written $\nabla^2 u = 0$)

where x, y, and z are independent variables and u is a function of them

La·plac·i·an (ləplǽsi:ən, ləpléiʃən) n. the differential operator ∇^2 that gives the left-hand side of the Laplace equation [after Pierre Simon LAPLACE]

Lap·land (læplænd) a region of Europe mostly above the Arctic Circle, comprising parts of Sweden, Norway, Finland and Russia (Kola Peninsula). Much of it is barren mountains or highland, but water power, iron ore and timber resources are considerable

Lap·land·er (læplændər) n. a Lapp

La Pla·ta (ləplátə) a city (pop. 408,300) of Argentina, on the Río de la Plata: meat packing, tanning, flour milling. National university (1897). Port: Ensenada

La·pointe (læpwět), Ernest (1876–1941), Canadian statesman. He negotiated (1923) with the U.S.A. a treaty—the first signed by a Canadian alone and with full powers from the Crown—concerning fisheries in the Pacific

Lapp (læp) n. a member of a Mongoloid people inhabiting Lapland, who are chiefly reindeer-herding nomads ‖ any of the Finno-Ugric languages spoken by these people [Swed.]

lap·pet (læpit) n. a fold or flap on a cap or other garment ‖ (hist.) a streamer hanging from a lady's headdress [fr. older lap fr. O.E. lappa]

lap robe (Am.=Br. travelling rug) a small blanket or fur tucked around the legs of a passenger in an automobile, on a boat etc.

lapse (læps) 1. n. a passing away, the lapse of time ‖ a slip or minor mistake, a lapse of memory ‖ a failure or miscarriage through some fault, a lapse of justice ‖ a falling away, a lapse from grace ‖ a falling into disuse, the lapse of a custom ‖ the invalidation of some right through failure to exercise it or lack of attention 2. v.i. pres. part. **laps·ing** past and past part. **lapsed** to cease to be, the custom has lapsed ‖ to become void through lack of attention, his right to the property has lapsed ‖ to slip or fall back, to lapse into one's native tongue ‖ to slip from virtue or right conduct, to lapse into bad habits ‖ (of time) to pass [fr. L. lapsus, slip]

LAPSE n. (med. acronym) long-term ambulatory physiological surveillance equipment, device for reporting on vital signs in a patient, used in hospital intensive care units

lapsed funds (economics) in the federal budget, unobligated budget authority that by law has ceased to be available for obligation because of the expiration of the period for which it was available

lapse rate the rate of change of a meteorological element with altitude, esp. the rate of decrease of temperature

lap·strake (læpstreik) 1. adj. (of a boat) clinker-built 2. n. a clinker-built boat [LAP n., overlap+STRAKE]

lap·streak (læpstri:k) n. and adj. lapstrake [LAP n., overlap+STREAK]

lap track (mil.) the center line of a lap; ideally, the track to be followed by the sweep or detecting gear

lap turn (mil.) the maneuver a minesweeper carries out during the period between the completion of one run and the commencement of the run immediately following

lap width (mil.) the swept path of the ship or ship formation divided by the percentage coverage being swept to

lap·wing (læpwiŋ) n. Vanellus vanellus, fam. Charadriidae, a green-crested, shrill-voiced plover of temperate regions of Europe, Asia and N. Africa, having mainly black and white markings and broad rounded wings. It is gregarious [O.E. hléapwince]

Lar·a·mide (lærəmaid) adj. (geol.) of a North American mountain-making episode of the early Cenozoic era [fr. the Laramie Mtns in Wyoming and Colorado]

lar·board (lárbord) adj. and n. (naut., old-fash.) port (left side of a ship etc.) [M.E. ladeborde, laddeborde fr. ladde-, lathe perh. fr. LADE+O.E. bord, ship's side]

lar·ce·nous (lársənəs) adj. of or pertaining to larceny ‖ guilty of larceny

lar·ce·ny (lársəni:) pl. **lar·ce·nies** n. (law) the illegal taking and removal of another's personal property without his knowledge or consent and with the express intention of depriving the owner of such property [prob. fr. A.F. larcin]

larch (lartʃ) n. a member of Larix, fam. Pinaceae, a genus of coniferous trees of the northern hemisphere having deciduous leaves and durable wood. The bark is a source of tannin ‖ the wood of such a tree [fr. G. lärche]

lard (lard) n. the rendered fat of pigs, esp. the abdominal fat, used in cooking [O.F. lard, bacon]

lard v.t. to flavor and make more fatty by inserting bacon or pork strips before cooking ‖ to cover with lard ‖ to flavor or enrich (speech or writing) by using flowery phrases, foreign words etc. [fr. F. larder]

lar·da·ceous (lardéiʃəs) adj. of or resembling lard

lar·der (lárdər) n. a cool room in which meat and other foods are stored until ready for use, or the foods themselves [O.F. lardier]

lar·es (léəri:z) pl. n. (Rom. mythol.) divinities of agriculture or spirits of ancestors, originally worshipped at crossroads and later regarded as household gods with the penates [L.]

large (lardʒ) 1. adj. extensive in area or scope ‖ of greater size, capacity or number than average for its kind, a large wart, large debts ‖ broad, a large view in the matter ‖ (naut., of a wind) favorable 2. adv. (naut.) with the wind aft of the beam, sailing large **at large** free, the escaped prisoner is still at large ‖ in general, society at large condemns political trials ‖ with vagueness and at length, he talked at large about his misfortunes **-at-large** (used postpositively) representing or selected by a whole body or area rather than any part, a congressman-at-large [F.]

large calorie a kilogram calorie

large intestine the posterior division of the vertebrate intestine, divided into the cecum, colon and rectum, serving esp. to extract moisture from the undigested remnants of food and to store them until they may be expelled as feces

large·ly (lárdʒli:) adv. in large measure, mostly, the rumor was largely true

large-scale (lárdʒskéil) adj. extensive, having great scope ‖ made to a large scale

large-scale integration (computer) densely packed (10,000 per sq in) digital storage and logic elements on a semiconductor chip. abbr LSI

large ship a ship over 450 ft in length

lar·gess, lar·gesse (lardʒés, lárdʒis) n. the giving of bounty by a superior to an inferior ‖ (rhet.) the bounty given ‖ generosity on a big scale [O.F.]

lar·ghet·to (largétou) 1. adv. and adj. (mus.) in rather slow time 2. n. (mus.) a larghetto movement or piece [Ital.]

lar·go (lárgou) 1. adv. and adj. (mus.) in very slow time, solemn and dignified 2. n. (mus.) a largo movement or piece [Ital.= broad]

lar·i·at (læri:ət) n. a lasso ‖ a long rope or leather line used with or without a noose for tethering a grazing animal [Span. la reata]

La·ris·sa, La·ri·sa (lərísə, larí:sa) a town (pop. 72,760) of Thessaly, Greece: agricultural trade, sugar industry

lark (lark) n. any of several songbirds of fam. Alaudidae, native to Europe, Asia and N. Africa, and having a long hind claw, esp. the skylark ‖ any of various unrelated ground birds, e.g. a meadowlark [O.E. lœwerce, láferce]

lark 1. n. (pop.) something done for fun or mild adventure, often with gently mischievous intent 2. v.i. (with 'around' or 'about') to play around [perh. fr. LARK (the bird)]

lark·spur (lárkspə:r) n. a member of genus Delphinium, fam. Ranunculaceae, esp. a cultivated, annual species having a spur-shaped calyx (cf. DELPHINIUM)

Lar·mor precession (lármor) (phys.) the precession of a particle possessing a magnetic moment [after Sir Joseph Larmor (1857–1942), British physicist]

La Roche·fou·cauld (læroʃfu:kou), François, duc de (1613–80), French moralist. His fame rests on 'Réflexions ou sentences et maximes morales' (1664). In these acute, elegant, pithy aphorisms, taking as their subject the heart and passions of man, he insists that self-interest dominates men's actions, even those which appear to be altruistic

La Ro·chelle (lærɔʃel) a major fishing port (pop. 75,367) in Charente-Maritime, W. France, formerly capital of Aunis. It was the chief stronghold (1554–1628) of the Huguenots. City hall (16th c.), fortifications (14th, 15th and 17th cc.)

La·rousse (læru:s), Pierre Athanase (1817–75), French grammarian and encyclopedist. He founded (1852) the publishing house which bears his name and began (1866) the compilation of his 'Grand Dictionnaire universel du XIXe siècle' (published 1876)

Lar·re·ta (larréta), Enrique Rodríguez (1875–1961), Argentinian novelist. His 'La gloria de don Ramiro' (1908) depicts the age of Philip II

Larreta Declaration a note prepared (1945) by Uruguay's foreign minister, Eduardo Rodríguez Larreta, which justified occasional multilateral intervention in Latin America. It was denounced by every other Latin American republic but was endorsed by the United States. It was legally recognized by, and incorporated into, the Inter-American Treaty of Reciprocal Assistance (Rio Treaty)

Lars Por·se·na (lárzpɔrsənə) legendary king of Clusium, a powerful city of Etruria. He besieged Rome in order to reinstate Tarquinius Priscus, but his first attack was fought off by Horatius Cocles

lar·va (lárvə) pl. **lar·vae** (lárvi:), **lar·vas** n. the free-living, immature state in many insects (e.g. butterflies) and certain animals (e.g. frogs) that is basically unlike the adult form, usually passing after a period of growth and minor changes to the pupa and thence to the adult (*METAMORPHOSIS) **lár·val** adj. [L.=ghost]

lar·yn·ga·phone (ləríŋəfoun) n. microphone device for amplifying laryngal sounds when placed at the speaker's throat, avoiding background noise

la·ryn·ge·al (ləríndʒi:əl, lærindʒí:əl) adj. of or pertaining to the larynx [fr. Mod. L. laryngeus]

larynges alt. pl. of LARYNX

lar·yn·gi·tis (lærindʒáitis) n. inflammation of the larynx [Mod. L. fr. larynx (laryngis), larynx+-itis, inflammation]

lar·yn·gol·o·gy (læriŋgólədʒi:) n. (med.) the study and treatment of the larynx and associated nasal passages [fr. Mod. L. larynx (laryngis), larynx+Gk logos, word]

la·ryn·go·scope (ləríŋgəskoup) n. an instrument used to examine the larynx [fr. Mod. L. larynx (laryngis), larynx+Gk skopein, to observe]

lar·ynx (læriŋks) pl. **la·ryn·ges** (ləríndʒi:z), **lar·ynx·es** n. an organ of the respiratory tract of air-breathing vertebrates situated above the windpipe. It consists of an elaborate arrangement of cartilage and muscles and, in man and various mammals, contains a pair of vocal cords which vibrate to produce voice sounds [Mod. L.]

La Salle (læsæl), René Robert Cavelier de (1643–87), French explorer and trader in North America. He emigrated to Montreal (1666) and from there explored regions drained by the Illinois and Mississippi Rivers, and founded Louisiana (1682)

La Salle, St Jean-Baptiste de *JEAN-BAPTISTE DE LA SALLE

las·car (læskər) n. an East Indian seaman [Urdu lashkar, army or shortening of lashkarī adj., military]

Las Ca·sas (laskásas), Bartolomé de (1474–1566). Spanish missionary and historian. His 'Historia de las Indias (published 1875–6) is a valuable source for early Spanish colonization in America

Las Cases (læskáz), Emmanuel, comte de (1766–1842), French historian, author of 'Mémorial de Sainte-Hélène' (1822–3), a record of Napoleon's life and conversations in exile

Las·caux (læskou) a cave in S.W. France with fine Magdalenian animal paintings; closed to the public to preserve the paintings

las·civ·i·ous (ləsívi:əs) adj. marked by or expressing sexual lust ‖ stimulating sexual lust [fr. L.L. lasciviosus]

lase (leiz) pres. part. **las·ing** past and past part. **lased** v.i. to function as a laser [back-formation fr. LASER]

La Selle (læsél) a mountain group in S.E. Haiti, Hispaniola Is, West Indies. Highest peak: La Selle (8,793 ft)

la·ser (léizer) n. a maser operating at optical frequencies to produce a high-energy monochromatic beam of light or infrared radiation [Light Amplification by Stimulated Emission of Radiation]

laser altimeter device that measures altitude by utilizing the time of the reflection of light from the surface

laser anemometer wind-velocity measuring device that utilizes two laser beams at right angles that respond to the physical law that light changes velocity when passing through a moving transparent medium

laser-beam printer (léizərbiːm) low-power laser beam that, when applied to a dry powder, produces an image on a photoconductive drum on a dye-coated ribbon in contact with paper *Cf* INTELLIGENT PRINTER

laser camera a night-photography camera utilizing the scanning of two almost invisible and undetectable beams, one sending the light, the other picking up the reflection

laser ceilometer device for measuring cloud ceiling by computing the time for a beam to reach a cloud and be reflected back

laser communication optical device in which the laser beam is modulated for voice, picture, or data transmission. It is used primarily between earth and airspace

laser designator (*mil.*) a device emitting a beam of laser energy used to mark a specific place or object

laser drill laser beam using a ruby that creates intense heat in highly concentrated point (0.0001 in) for use in precision working extremely hard materials, esp. gems *Cf* LASER SCRIBER

laser flash tube pumping device using xenon for high-intensity laser flashes

laser fusion experimental process designed to heat a pellet of deuterium and tritium to the required 100 million degrees Centigrade necessary for a fusion reaction *also* laser beam

laser guidance unit device incorporating a laser seeker to locate target and provide guidance commands to the control system of a missile, projectile, or bomb —**laser-guided bomb** *n.*

laser interferometer laser device for measuring very small distances

laser intrusion detector device that sends a very thin invisible beam across a distance (as large as an airfield) which, when broken, alerts of an intrusion

laser jamming a countermeasure device that directs energy to a hostile receiver to confuse radar, tracking, interference, range-finding, etc.

laser memory (*computer*) memory device utilizing extremely small surface to record data

laser photocoagulator (*med.*) device for sending laser beams through the eye for retina therapy

laser radar or **ladar** device for using the reflection of laser beams for long-distance radar

laser radiation detector photo device for detecting illumination by virtually invisible radar beams, used for protection of vulnerable targets

laser rangefinder device for measuring short target distances by measuring the elapsed time for echoes of pulses to return

laser recorder device that reproduces a radio or video signal on film or paper

la·ser·scope (léizərskoup) *n.* device for scanning and imaging through fog, providing a three-dimensional image; used on the sea or underwater for navigation within harbors

laser scriber device for making thin slices of diamonds, silicon, gallium, arsenide, etc., by vaporizing grooves in the material *Cf* LASER DRILL

laser seisometer device for detecting seismic strains on the earth's surface by measuring the round-trip time of a beam sent to two points

laser target designating system (*mil.*) a system used to direct (aim or point) laser energy at a target, consisting of the laser designator or laser target marker with its display and control components necessary to fix on the target and direct the beam of laser energy on to it

laser threshold the minimum energy necessary to start a lasing action

laser welding the use of a laser beam to provide heat for spot welding, used for precision welds

lash (læʃ) **1.** *n.* a stroke with a whip ‖ the striking part of a whip ‖ a whip ‖ a movement or stroke like that of a whip ‖ an eyelash **2.** *v.t.* to strike with a whip or similar instrument ‖ to drive on as if with a whip, *he lashed his audience into a rage* ‖ to beat against, *waves lashed the rocks* ‖ to make (something) move like the lashing of a whip, *the lion lashed its tail* ‖ to attack violently with words ‖ *v.i.* to move like the stroke of a whip ‖ to make a stroke with a whip **to lash out** ‖ to make sudden violent attacking movements with the limbs, *the horse lashed out with its hoofs* ‖ to speak angrily and with vehemence [origin unknown]

lash *v.t.* (esp. *naut.*) to fasten or bind with a rope etc. **lásh·ing** *n.* (esp. *naut.*) a rope, wire etc. so used [etym. doubtful]

LASH or **lash** *n.* (*acronym*) lighter aboard ship, a freight transportation system in which center loaded barges are placed inside the hull of large freighters —**lash** *adj.*

lash·ings (læʃiŋz) *pl. n.* (*Br.*, *pop.*, only in the phrase) **lashings of** lots of [LASH v., to strike]

Lash·kar (lʌʃkər) *GWALIOR

las·ing (léiziŋ) *n.* the creation of laser beams by exciting electrons into high energy *Cf.* LASE

Las Pal·mas (lʌspálmʌs) a province (area 1,279 sq. miles, pop. 756,353) of Spain, in the Canary Is ‖ its capital (pop. 366,454) on the northwest coast of Gran Canaria, a tourist resort. Cathedral of Santa Ana (1497)

L-as·par·agi·nase (élæspærǽdʒʌneis) *n.* an enzyme that breaks down a phipiological form of asparagine, obtained esp. from bacteria, used in treatment of leukemia

La Spe·zia (lʌspétsjʌ) a port (pop. 120,717) on the coast of Liguria, Italy's chief naval base: shipbuilding, oil refining, engineering

lass (læs) *n.* (*rhet.* or esp. *Scot.*) a girl or young woman [M.E. *lasce, lasse*]

Las·sa fever (lǽsʌ) (*med.*) a contagious, usu. fatal, viral disease identified in Lassa, Nigeria, in 1970, believed to be transmitted by mice

Las·salle (lʌsál), Ferdinand (1825–64), German socialist writer. Although influenced by Marx, he advocated state action rather than revolution. He founded (1863) a workers' political party which later became the Social Democratic party

las·sie (lǽsiː) *n.* (esp. *Scot.*) a young girl [dim. of LASS]

las·si·tude (lǽsituːd, lǽsitjuːd) *n.* weariness of spirit [F.]

Las·so (lǽsou), Orlando di (Roland de Lassus, c. 1530–94), Flemish composer. His vast output of polyphonic music included madrigals, songs, motets and masses

las·so (lǽsou) **1.** *pl.* **las·sos, las·soes** *n.* a long leather thong or rope with a running noose, used esp. by Argentine gauchos and North American cowboys for catching cattle or horses **2.** *v.t.* to catch with a lasso [Span. *lazo*]

last (læst, lɑːst) *n.* one of several units of weight or capacity, varying in amount for different localities and commodities (grain, herring etc.) [O.E. *hlœst*]

last *n.* a wood or iron form shaped like the human foot used in shoemaking **to stick to one's last** to attend to one's own business ‖ to restrict oneself to one's proper field of activity [O.E. *lœste*]

last *v.i.* to go on existing for a period of time, *his illness lasted a month* ‖ to continue without being used up, *these apples will last through the winter* ‖ to exist in good condition for a period of time, *made to last* ‖ *v.t.* to go on meeting the need of (someone), *this coat will last me for years* ‖ (with 'out') to arrive at the end of (a period of time or whatever occupies it), *we shall never last out the party without some more whiskey* [O.E. *lœstan*, to follow, carry out]

last **1.** *adj.* most distant from an observer, *the last house on the road* or most distant from a goal or winning position, *the last man in a race* ‖ nearest to the present time, *the last figures are still not final* or to some other named time, *the last meeting he attended before he was ill* or occurring after all other similar events have occurred, *it will be the last house to be built on this road* ‖ which will not, or cannot, be followed by any other person or thing of the same kind, *her last hope, the last survivor* ‖ being the least likely, *the last person one would suspect* **last but not least** final in order of mention but not least important **the last** (or **latest**) **thing** the newest fashion **2.** *n.* someone or something which comes or is last ‖ the just-mentioned person or thing ‖ the end, *he will never hear the last of it* ‖ (*rhet.*) death, *true to the last* ‖ (*rhet.*) the final performance of a specific action, *to breathe one's last* **at last** in the end, finally **at long last** finally after much delay **3.** *adv.* finally, last, *we visited Naples* ‖ most recently, *I saw him last in Paris* [O.E. *latost, latest*]

Las·tex (lǽsteks) *n.* trademark for latex strands wound with a variety of textile yarns; manufactured by Uniroyal, Inc.

last hurrah the final effort, from the title of a 1956 book by Edwin O'Connor

last·ing (lǽstiŋ, lɑːstiŋ) **1.** *adj.* existing for a long period of time, *a lasting peace* **2.** *n.* a durable, closely woven fabric used for the top part of shoes, for covering buttons etc. [LAST v.]

Last Judgment, Last Judgement the judgment at the end of the world, when God will determine the fates of all men

last·ly (lǽstliː, lɑːstliː) *adv.* in the last place ‖ in conclusion

last quarter the phase of the moon, a week after full moon, when half of its disk is illuminated by the sun

Last Supper the supper of Christ and his disciples on the eve of Christ's betrayal. The Christian sacrament of the Eucharist or Holy Communion recalls this meal

Las Ve·gas (lʌsvéigʌs) a gambling resort (pop. 164,674) in the desert of Nevada

Las Vi·llas (lʌzvíːjʌs) a central province (area 8,264 sq. miles, pop. 1,235,000) of Cuba. Capital: Santa Clara. Agriculture: sugarcane, tobacco, coffee, rice, corn. Industries: alcohol distilleries, tanneries, tobacco factories, chemical plants

Lász·ló (láslou) kings of Hungary *LADISLAUS

lat. latitude

Lat·a·ki·a, Lat·ta·ki·a (lætʌkíːʌ) a port (pop. 196,791) in N.W. Syria on the site of the Roman city of Laodicea. Industry: tobacco

latch (lætʃ) **1.** *n.* a fastening for a door or gate consisting of a pivoted bar which falls into, or can be lifted out of, a catch ‖ any similar door or window fastening ‖ a spring lock which fastens a door that can be opened without a key from one side only **on the latch** (of a door) shut but not locked **2.** *v.t.* to fasten by means of a latch [M.E. *lacche*, fr. O.E. *lœccan*, to catch]

latch·key (lætʃkiː) *pl.* **latch·keys** *n.* a key which releases a spring lock

latchkey child child who returns from school while parents are at work

latch·string (lætʃstriŋ) *n.* a piece of string connected to a latch and passed through a hole in the door so that the latch can be raised from the outside

late (leit) *adj.* coming or happening after the usual, expected or proper time, *a late arrival* ‖ continuing longer than usual, expected or proper, *a late meeting* ‖ at or near the end of a period of time, piece of work, series etc., *late Middle English* ‖ belonging to a recent or relatively recent time in the past, *the latest models* ‖ recently in existence but now over, *during the late war* ‖ recently resigned ‖ recently dead ‖ ripening or blooming after earlier varieties [O.E. *lœt*]

late *adv.* after the usual, expected or proper time ‖ at or to a time far on in a period of time, *it survived late into the Middle Ages* ‖ recently, *as late as last week* **of late** recently **late in the day** too late to be of any help or to be taken seriously [O.E. *late* fr. *lœt*, late adj.]

late-bloom·er (leitblúːmər) *n.* one that matures later than normally —**late-blooming** *adj.*

la·teen (lʌtíːn) **1.** *adj.* of or having a lateen sail **2.** *n.* a lateen sail [F. *latine* for *voile latine*, Latin sail]

lateen sail a triangular sail common to many Mediterranean boats, esp. of N. Africa

Late Greek the Greek language after the classical period, esp. the written language from c. 200 A.D. to c. 600

Late Latin the Latin language after the classical period, esp. in writings of the western Roman Empire from c. 200 to c. 600

late·ly (léitliː) *adv.* recently, in recent times

la·ten·cy (léitnsiː) *n.* the quality or state of being latent

La Tène (læten) *adj.* of a late Iron Age culture in Europe (c. 450 B.C.–1st c. A.D.), characterized by Celtic hilltop forts, the making of enamel ornaments and the spread of agriculture [after *La Tène*, archaeological site on the Lake of Neuchâtel, Switzerland]

la·tent (léitnt) *adj.* hidden, dormant, but capable of being developed ‖ present but not seen until some change occurs [fr. L. *latens* (*latentis*) fr. *latere*, to lie hidden]

latent heat (*phys.*) the thermal energy required to effect any isothermal chemical or physical change ‖ the thermal energy released in such a change

latent root (*math.*) values contained in a differential or integral equation that has solutions satisfying given boundary conditions only for certain values and a parameter *also* eigenvalue

lat·er·al (lætʌrʌl) **1.** *adj.* of, to or from the side ‖ (*anat.*) located to one side of the central axis of the body ‖ (*bot.*) located on one side of a plant organ or to one side of the central axis of the plant, branch etc. ‖ (of a family branch) de-

CONCISE PRONUNCIATION KEY: (**a**) æ, c*a*t; ɑ, c*a*r; ɔ f*aw*n; ei, sn*a*ke. (**e**) e, h*e*n; iː, sh*ee*p; iə, d*ee*r; ɛə, b*ea*r. (**i**) i, f*i*sh; ai, t*i*ger; əː, b*i*rd. (**o**) o, *o*x; au, c*ow*; ou, g*oa*t; u, p*oo*r; ɔi, r*oy*al. (**u**) ʌ, d*u*ck; u, b*u*ll; uː, g*oo*se; ə, b*a*cillus; juː, c*u*be. x, lo*ch*; θ, *th*ink; ð, bo*th*er; z, *Z*en; ʒ, cor*s*age; dʒ, sa*v*age; ŋ, ora*n*gutang; j, *y*ak; ʃ, *f*ish; tʃ, fe*tch*; 'l, rabb*le*; 'n, redd*en*. Complete pronunciation key appears inside front cover.

scended from a brother or sister of someone in the direct line || (*phon.*) pronounced with the breath passing along either side or both sides of the tongue **2.** *n.* something or a part of something located at the side, e.g. a lateral branch || (*phon.*) a lateral sound [fr. L. *lateralis*]

lateral line a longitudinal line running along each side of the body of most fishes, marking the position of sensory cells

lateral recording a disk recorded with a side-to-side motion of the stylus —**lateral recording** *n.*

lateral thinking problem-solving technique involving the by-passing of disconcerting details, obstacles, or changing approach, sometimes reformulating the problem, said to be characteristic of divergers. The term was coined by Edward de Pono, 1970

lateral ventricle the internal cavity of each hemisphere of the cerebrum

Lat·er·an (lǽtərən) the site in Rome, Italy, on the Caelian Hill, where the church of St John Lateran is located. Its basilica is the cathedral church of Rome. Its palace was the official residence of the popes until 1309

Lateran Council any of five ecumenical councils of the Roman Catholic Church held (1123, 1139, 1179, 1215 and 1512–17) in the church of St John Lateran. The fourth council (1215), under Innocent III, confirmed both the spiritual and temporal power of the papacy

Lateran Treaty the agreement concluded (1929) between Italy and the papacy, by which the Vatican City was recognized as a sovereign state. It ended the estrangement between the papacy and the kingdom of Italy which had lasted since the Italian occupation of Rome (1870)

lat·er·ite (lǽtərait) *n.* a clay containing aluminum and iron oxides [fr. L. *later*, brick]

lat·er·i·za·tion (lætərəzéiʃən) *n.* (*geol.*) a destructive process due to erosion, stimulated particularly when vegetation is removed —**laterize** *v.*

la·tex (léiteks) *pl.* **lat·i·ces** (lǽtisi:z), **la·tex·es** (lǽteksi:z) *n.* a milky, usually whitish fluid obtained from various trees and plants, e.g. rubber plants, euphorbias etc. It is the raw material of rubber, chicle and other products || any of several similar synthetic products, used e.g. as binders in paint [L.=liquid]

lath (læθ, lɑ́θ) **1.** *pl.* **laths** (læθs, lɑθs, læðz, lɑðz) *n.* a long, thin, narrow strip of wood, used esp. nailed to joists as a foundation for plaster or for supporting slates **2.** *v.t.* to provide with laths [O.E. *lætt*]

lathe (leið) **1.** *n.* a machine used to shape or cut wood, metal etc., which holds the material fast in rapid rotation against the cutting component **2.** *v.t. pres. part.* **lath·ing** *past* and *past part.* **lathed** to shape or cut on a lathe [perh. fr. LATH, etym. doubtful]

lath·er (lǽðər) **1.** *n.* the foamy froth produced when soap (or other detergent) is agitated in water || foamy froth from excessive sweat, esp. on a horse **2.** *v.i.* to form lather, or become covered with it || *v.t.* to cover with lather **lath·er·y** *adj.* [O.E. *léathor*, washing soda]

lath·ing (lǽθiŋ, lɑ́θiŋ) *n.* the act or process of constructing with laths || laths collectively

lath·y·rism (lǽθərizəm) *n.* (*med.*) a human and animal, esp. horse, disease symptomized by tremors, cramps, and deformity, caused by the eating of peas or meal containing a certain variety of chick peas *also* lupinosis —**latherytic** *adj.*

latices alt. *pl.* of *LATEX

la·tic·i·fer (leitísəfər) *n.* (*bot.*) a plant cell containing latex

lat·i·cif·er·ous (lætisífərəs) *adj.* conveying, having or secreting latex [fr. L. *latex* (*laticis*), latex+-*ferous*, bearing]

la·ti·fun·dio (lɒti:fú:ndjo) *n.* (*hist.*) a large landed property in Latin America cultivated by peons (first Indians, then mestizos) for the Spanish Crown [Span. fr. L. *latifundium*, piece of landed property]

lat·i·fun·dism (lætifʌ́ndizəm) *n.* the holding of land in large estates —**latifundist** *n.* the owner

Lat·i·mer (lǽtəmər), Hugh (c. 1485–1555), English bishop. His sermons are an eloquent attack on the social and ecclesiastical abuses of his age. A zealous Protestant, he refused to forsake his beliefs after the accession of Mary I and was burned at the stake

lat·i·me·ri·a (lætəmíri:ə) *n.* a member of *Latimeria*, fam. *Latimeridae*, a genus of coelacanth

fishes having two dorsal fins. First discovered in 1939, it was previously known only in fossil forms of the Devonian to Cretaceous periods [Mod. L. after Marjorie Courtenay-*Latimer* (1907–   ), South African museum director]

Lat·in (lǽt'n) **1.** *adj.* of ancient Latium or its inhabitants || relating to or written in the Latin language || of the branch of the Roman Catholic Church which uses the Latin rite || of persons, countries etc. whose native or official language is a Romance language **2.** *n.* a native or inhabitant of ancient Latium || the Latin language || a person whose mother tongue is a Romance language [fr. L. *Latinus*]

Latin America the countries of North America (excepting French-speaking parts of Canada), South America and Central America where French, Spanish and Portuguese are spoken

Latin America Free Trade Area (LAFTA), an organization created (1960) by the Montevideo Pact, signed by Argentina, Brazil, Chile, Mexico, Paraguay, Peru and Uruguay, and later by Bolivia, Colombia, Ecuador and Venezuela

Latin-American 1. *adj.* of or relating to Latin America **2.** *n.* a native or inhabitant of Latin America

Latin American Free Trade Association an organization set up in 1961 to promote economic cooperation. In 1980 it was renamed the Latin American Integration Association. Its members are Argentina, Bolivia, Brazil, Chile, Colombia, Ecuador, Mexico, Paraguay, Peru, Uruguay and Venezuela

Latin American Indians the indigenous peoples inhabiting present Latin America. Like the North American Indians, they are of the Mongoloid stock that reached the Western Hemisphere, presumably via the Bering Strait, in a series of migrations which began about 25,000 years ago and which reached the tip of South America about 4,000 years ago. At the time of discovery by the white man, the Latin American Indians numbered at least 15 million, perhaps far more. Population was densest in Mesoamerica and the Central Andes, where intensive agriculture was practiced and where highly developed civilizations flourished (*MAYA, *INCA). Population was sparsest in the marginal regions (Chaco, Patagonia, forests of Brazil), where society was nomadic. This demographic pattern still prevails. The Topi Indians of Brazil remained among the most primitive. During the colonization process the population was decimated, as a result of disease and forced labor. Since colonization the Indians have been exploited as agricultural and industrial laborers. The proportion of Indians to total population is now highest (40–50%) in Ecuador, Bolivia, Peru and Guatemala.

Cultural groups are distinguished regionally. They consist of the Greater Southwest (the Pima-Pueblo of the South-western U.S.A. and N. Mexico), Mesoamerica (Nahua-Maya), the Circumcaribbean (i.e. the Antilles and surrounding mainland areas), Central Andean (Incas), Tropical Forests and Southern Andean, and Marginal Regions, inhabited by scattered tribes. Some 1,700 separate languages have been classified. Various governments have implemented programs to provide education and higher living standards and to integrate the Indians into national life

Latin American Integration Association *LATIN AMERICAN FREE TRADE ASSOCIATION

Latin cross a cross consisting of a long upright bar crossed near the top by a shorter transverse bar

Latin Empire of Constantinople a feudal state (1204–61) set up in the S. Balkans by the leaders of the 4th Crusade after they had captured Constantinople and deposed the Byzantine emperor. It was ended when the Greeks recaptured Constantinople (1261)

La·ti·ni (lɒti:ni:), Brunetto (c. 1220–c. 1294), Florentine scholar, author of the encyclopedic work 'Li Livres dou trésor' (c. 1265) in langue d'oïl

Lat·in·ism (lǽt'nizəm) *n.* a word or stylistic construction imitating a Latin model

Lat·in·ist (lǽt'nist) *n.* a specialist in Latin

La·tin·i·ty (lətíniti:) *n.* the quality of the Latin language || the use of Latin [fr. L. *latinitas*]

Lat·in·ize (lǽt'naiz) *pres. part.* **Lat·in·iz·ing** *past* and *past part.* **Lat·in·ized** *v.t.* to give a Latin form to (a word or phrase) || to adapt to the usage of the Latin peoples or the Latin Church || *v.i.* to use Latin words and idioms in a non-Latin language [fr. L. *latinizare*]

Latin Kingdom of Jerusalem a feudal state (1099–1187) set up in Syria and Palestine by the leaders of the 1st Crusade, with Godfrey de Bouillon as its first ruler. It was revived at Acre (1191) by the 3rd Crusade, but fell (1291) to the Saracens

Latin language the language of ancient Latium and ancient Rome. Latin is an Italic language of the Indo-European family and is itself the basis of the Romance languages. The earliest known record of Latin, an inscription on a brooch, dates from c. 600 B.C. The language reached its highest development and expression in Classical Latin. With the rise of the Roman Empire, Latin spread over the whole of the known world, and remained the dominant international language of the Church, government and education until the 16th c. Latin remains the official language of the Holy See (*OLD LATIN, *CLASSICAL LATIN, *LATE LATIN, *MEDIEVAL LATIN, *MODERN LATIN)

Latin Quarter a part of Paris on the left bank of the Seine, the historic student quarter, still containing the city's chief educational institutions

Latin rite liturgical forms of Christian worship using Latin. The term is used esp. to designate the Roman Catholic Church in the West

Latin rock a mixture of Latin music, rock 'n' roll, and jazz

La·ti·nus (lətáinəs) a legendary king of ancient Latium whose daughter Lavinia married Aeneas

lat·i·tude (lǽtitu:d, lǽtitju:d) *n.* the angular distance of a place on the earth's surface from the equator as measured in degrees, minutes and seconds, the equator being latitude 0°, the poles latitude 90° N. or S. (cf. LONGITUDE) || the possibility of acting as one pleases, esp. the permitted extent of departure from some line of conduct or set of conventions, *school rules allow the individual little latitude* || (*astron.*) the angular distance of a heavenly body from the ecliptic || (esp. *pl.*) a region in relation to average distance from the equator, *the temperate latitudes* **lat·i·tú·di·nal** *adj.* [fr. L. *latitudo* (*latitudinis*), breadth]

lat·i·tu·di·nar·i·an (lætitu:d'néəri:ən, lætitju:d'néəri:ən) **1.** *adj.* permitting others or oneself to depart widely from fixed lines of conduct or belief **2.** *n.* such a person **Lat·i·tu·di·nar·i·an** (*Anglican Church*) someone who favors wide differences of doctrine and ritual within the Church. The term was specially applied, in an opprobrious sense, in the 17th c., to the Cambridge Platonists and others whose broadmindedness took precedence over Anglican dogma. They paved the way for 18th-c. rationalism and tolerance **lat·i·tu·di·nár·i·an·ism** *n.* [fr. L. *latitudo* (*latitudinis*), breadth]

La·ti·um (léiʃi:əm) (*hist.*) the ancient territory of central Italy inhabited by the Latins from the 10th c. B.C. until dominated by Rome (4th c. B.C.) || (*Ital.* Lazio) a region (area 6,636 sq. miles, pop. 4,958,500) including Rome. The Campagna di Roma and the Pontine Marshes lie between volcanic hills to the north and south. Products: fodder, cereals, fruit, olives, wine

La Tour (lætu:r), Georges de (c. 1593–1652), French painter. His scenes are mostly religious, and their arrested movement conveys quiet intensity. The colors are sober, though warm. In the later work forms are greatly simplified: the combination of strong simplified light, almost abstract form, absence of movement, but intense emotion, conveys a mystical abstraction supervening on a moment of drama

La Tour, Maurice Quentin de (1704–88), French pastelist. His work shows lively observation of humanity

La Trappe (lætræp) *TRAPPIST

La Tré·mo·ille (lætreimoui:l), Louis de, prince de Talmont (1460–1525), French soldier. He led Charles VIII's invasion of Brittany (1488), and was Louis XII's commander in the Italian Wars

la·tri·a (lətráiə) *n.* (*Roman Catholicism*) worship offered to God alone (*DULIA, *HYPERDULIA) [L.L. fr. Gk *latreia*, service]

la·trine (lətrí:n) *n.* a toilet in an army camp, factory etc. [F.]

Lattakia *LATAKIA

lat·ten (lǽt'n) *n.* an alloy of or similar to brass, used esp. in the Middle Ages for church furnishings [O.F. *laton*, *laiton*]

lat·ter (lǽtər) **1.** *adj.* of the second of two, *the latter half of the week* || of the second-mentioned of two, *we know both the 1805 and the 1850 ver-*

CONCISE PRONUNCIATION KEY: **(a)** æ, c*a*t;   ɑ, c*a*r;   ɔ f*aw*n;   ei, sn*a*ke.   **(e)** e, h*e*n;   i:, sh*ee*p;   iə, d*ee*r;   ɛə, b*ea*r.   **(i)** i, f*i*sh;   ai, t*i*ger;   ə:, b*i*rd. **(o)** o, *o*x;   au, c*ow*;   ou, g*oa*t;   u, p*oo*r;   ɔi, r*oy*al.   **(u)** ʌ, d*u*ck;   u, b*u*ll;   u:, g*oo*se;   ə, *a*bacillus;   ju:, c*u*be.   x, lo*ch*;   θ, *th*ink;   ð, *b*o*th*er;   z, *Z*en;   ʒ, cor*s*age; dʒ, sava*g*e;   ŋ, ora*n*gutang;   j, *y*ak;   ʃ, *fi*sh;   tʃ, *f*e*tch*;   'l, rab*ble*;   'n, red*den*.   Complete pronunciation key appears inside front cover.

sion but prefer the latter one **2.** *pron.* the latter person or thing [O.E. *lætra,* later]
lat·ter-day (lǽtərdei) *adj.* of very recent or present time
Latter-Day Saint a Mormon
lat·ter·ly (lǽtərli:) *adv.* (*old-fash.*) recently, of late
lat·tice (lǽtis) **1.** *n.* a framework or structure of wooden or metal laths crossing one another at regular intervals, leaving spaces between them and used, e.g. as a screen or ornamental feature ‖ something resembling the crisscross pattern of this ‖ (*phys.*) a geometrical arrangement of points over an area or in space, e.g. of fissionable material in a nuclear reactor ‖ (*cartography*) a network of intersecting positional lines printed on a map or chart from which a fix may be obtained **2.** *v.t. pres. part.* **lat·tic·ing** *past* and *past part.* **lat·ticed** to furnish with a lattice ‖ to make a lattice of [O.F. and F. *lattis*]
lattice girder a girder constructed of two flanges connected by iron latticework
lattice window a window of small glass panes set in a lattice of lead strips
lat·tice·work (lǽtiswə:rk) *n.* a lattice ‖ (*collect.*) lattices
Lat·vi·a (lǽtvi:ə) a constituent republic (area 25,590 sq. miles, pop. 2,521,000) of the U.S.S.R. in N.E. Europe, on the Baltic. Capital: Riga. It is low-lying, heavily forested, and predominantly industrial. Crops: cereals, flax. Livestock: meat and dairy cattle. Resources: timber. Industries: steel, rolled metal, machinery, paper, textiles, mineral fertilizers. It developed as a trading center and was conquered by the Teutonic knights (13th c.), Poland (1561–81), Sweden (1621) and Russia (1710–95). It became an independent republic (1918) and a constituent republic (1940)
Lat·vi·an (lǽtvi:ən) **1.** *adj.* of or relating to Latvia, its people, language etc. **2.** *n.* a native or inhabitant of Latvia ‖ the Baltic language spoken in Latvia
Lau·bach (láubæk), Frank (1885–1970), U.S. missionary. His 'each one teach one' educational technique helped 100 million people in Asia, Africa, and South America to learn to read
Laud (lɔd), William (1573–1645), English prelate, archbishop of Canterbury (1633–45). As the principal religious adviser of Charles I, he persecuted the Puritans and tried to enforce High Church ritual throughout England and Scotland. He was impeached (1640) by the Long Parliament, and executed (1645)
laud (lɔd) *v.t.* (*rhet.*) to praise [fr. L. *laudare*]
laud *n.* (*rhet.*) praise or a hymn of praise [O.F. *laude*]
laud·a·bil·i·ty (lɔdəbíliti:) *n.* the quality of being laudable
laud·a·ble (lɔ́dəb'l) *adj.* worthy of praise **laud·a·bly** *adv.* [fr. L. *laudabilis*]
lau·da·num (lɔ́dnəm, lɔ́dnəm) *n.* a preparation of opium, esp. its solution in alcohol [Mod. L. fr. *ladanum*]
laud·a·to·ry (lɔ́dətɔri:, lɔ́dətɔuri:) *adj.* praising, complimentary, *a laudatory speech* [fr. L. *laudatorius*]
Lau·der·dale (lɔ́dərdeil), John Maitland, duke of (1616–82), Scottish statesman. He won the confidence of Charles II during the Civil War, and became a member of the Cabal
Lauds (lɔdz) *n.,* construed as *sing.* or *pl.* (*eccles.*) the second of the canonical services (or, with matins, the first), sung at dawn in monastic houses
Laue (láuə), Max von (1879–1960), German physicist. He demonstrated the wave nature of X rays and studied their diffraction by crystals. Nobel prize (1914)
Laue pattern a photograph produced by X rays diffracted by a thin crystal plate, from which the crystal parameters may be determined (*X-RAY DIFFRACTION) [after Max Von *Laue*]
laugh (læf, lɑf) **1.** *v.i.* to express amusement, mirth, contempt, fear etc. by inarticulate, explosive sounds which result from the forcing out of air from the lungs, usually accompanied by convulsive muscular movements, esp. of the face ‖ to experience these emotions, esp. silently or inwardly ‖ *v.t.* to utter with a laugh or as if with a laugh ‖ to cause (someone) to do something by playfully mocking him **to laugh at** to burst into laughter because of ‖ to express contempt for **to laugh away** to cause (fears, doubts etc.) to vanish by treating them with ridicule **to laugh in someone's face** to treat someone with mocking defiance to his face **to laugh**

(something) off to seek to get out of (criticism, a difficult situation etc.) by making a joke of it **to laugh out of** (or **on**) **the other** (or **wrong**) **side of one's mouth** to weep **to laugh** (**someone**) **out of court** to make (someone) appear so ridiculous that he ceases to command attention **to laugh over** (**something**) to laugh at (something) while thinking of it **to laugh up** (or **in**) **one's sleeve** to be secretly pleased with oneself because one has been more clever than a rival **2.** *n.* an instance of laughing ‖ (*pop.*) a joke, cause of amusement **good for a laugh** likely to produce a laugh but not much else **to raise a laugh** to cause laughter **láugh·a·ble** *adj.* such as to cause amusement or contempt **láugh·a·bly** *adv.* [O.E. *hlehhan, hliehhan*]
laugh·ing (lǽfiŋ, láfiŋ) *adj.* that laughs ‖ causing amusement, esp. in the phrase **no** (or **not a**) **laughing matter** something likely to have serious consequences
laughing gas nitrous oxide
laughing jackass the kookaburra
laugh·ing·stock (lǽfiŋstɒk, láfiŋstɒk) *n.* an object of ridicule
laugh-line (lǽflain) *n.* **1.** a facial wrinkle around the eyes formed by habitual smiling **2.** a one-line joke
laugh·ter (lǽftər, láftər) *n.* the act of laughing ‖ the sound accompanying this [O.E. *hleahtor*]
laugh track a recording of audience laughter, sometimes dubbed into audience-participation programs *also* canned laughter
launce, lance (læns, lɑns) *n.* the sand eel [perh. fr. F. *lance,* a lance]
Laun·ce·lot of the Lake, Sir (lǽnsələt, lǽnsəlɒt, lánsələt) *LANCELOT DU LAC
Laun·ces·ton (lɔ́nsestən) a port (pop. 63,386) of N.E. Tasmania, Australia, trading in minerals, fruit and wool
launch (lɔntʃ) **1.** *v.t.* to cause (esp. a newly built ship) to move from land into water ‖ to cause (a glider) to become airborne ‖ to plan and cause to become operative, *to launch a new enterprise* ‖ to cause (something) to be propelled up or forward, *to launch a rocket* **to launch forth** to begin something long or tedious, *to launch forth into an explanation* **to launch out** to begin some large or hazardous undertaking, e.g. one requiring a large financial outlay **2.** *n.* the act of launching a ship, missile etc. [O.N.F. *lancher*]
launch *n.* a fast, small, power-driven boat, used on rivers or for short sea trips [fr. Span. *lancha,* pinnace perh. fr. Malay]
launching pad (*rocketry*) the platform from which a rocket is launched; by extension, any springboard, esp. political
launch pad (*rocketry*) a launch pad
launch vehicle (*astronautics*) the rocket propulsion device for a spacecraft
launch window (*astronautics*) the period when weather and position of moon and planets are auspicious for the launching of a spacecraft
laun·der (lɔ́ndər) **1.** *n.* (*mining*) an orewashing trough **2.** *v.t.* to wash (clothes etc.) ‖ to wash and iron ‖ *v.i.* to do laundry ‖ (of clothes etc.) to bear laundering ‖ to legitimatize illegally obtained funds by processing through a third party business [fr. older *lavender* fr. O.F. *lavandier,* someone who washes]
laun·der·ette (lɔndərét, lɔ́ndəret) *n.* a laundromat [fr. *Launderette,* a trademark]
laun·dress (lɔ́ndris) *n.* a woman whose job is laundering clothes [LAUNDER]
laun·dro·mat (lɔ́ndrəmæt) *n.* premises where customers can use washing machines and usually dryers for a fee [fr. *Laundromat,* a trademark]
laun·dry (lɔ́ndri:) *pl.* **laun·dries** *n.* a place in a home, apartment house etc. equipped for laundering clothes etc. ‖ a commercial establishment equipped and staffed to launder clothes etc. ‖ a batch of clothes etc. to be laundered [M.E. *lavendry* fr. F.]
laundry list a long list of anything, esp. things to do
laur·a·sia (lɔréiʒə) *n.* a hypothetical supercontinent comprising Asia, North America, and Europe during the Cenozoic era (60 million yrs ago) *Cf* GONDWANA
lau·re·ate (lɔ́ri:it) **1.** *adj.* (*rhet.*) wreathed or crowned with laurel as a symbol of honor or excellence ‖ consisting of laurel **2.** *n.* a poet laureate **láu·re·ate·ship** *n.* [fr. L. *laureatus*]
lau·rel (lɔ́rəl, lɒ́rəl) *n.* a member of genus *Laurus,* fam. Lauraceae, esp. *L. nobilis,* a tree of S. Europe whose glossy green foliage was used to make a crown or wreath of honor in ancient Greece and Rome ‖ any of various evergreen

trees or shrubs resembling the European laurel, e.g. the spurge laurel **to look to one's laurels** to make the effort needed to retain some threatened distinction **to rest on one's laurels** to be content with past achievement and make no more effort [O. F. *laurier, lorier*]
Lau·rens (lɔrɑ̃s), Henri (1885–1954), French cubist sculptor. He created abstract works, the curved lines and massive forms of which derive from the female figure
Lau·rens (lɔ́rəns), Henry (1724–92), U.S. Revolutionary War statesman who was president (1777–8) of the Philadelphia continental congress. He attempted (1780) to negotiate for Congress a loan of $10 million from Holland but was captured with incriminating evidence by the British, and this led to war between Great Britain and the United Provinces. He served (1782) as an American commissioner to Great Britain, signing the preliminary Anglo-American peace treaty
Lau·ren·tian (lɔrénʃən) *adj.* (*geol.*) of a North American mountain-making episode during the early Archeozoic era [after ST LAWRENCE River]
Laurentian Highlands (Laurentian Mtns) a range between the St Lawrence River and Hudson Bay in S. Quebec province, Canada. Highest point: Mont Tremblant (3,150 ft)
Laurentian Plateau the Canadian Shield
Lau·ri·er (lɔ́ri:ei), Sir Wilfrid (1841–1919), Canadian Liberal statesman. As prime minister of Canada (1896–1911), he promoted a sense of Canadian unity and strengthened imperial relations
lau·rus·tine (lɔ́rəstain, lɔ́rəsti:n) *n.* laurustinus
lau·rus·ti·nus (lɔrəstáinəs, lɔrəsti:nəs) *n. Viburnum tinus,* fam. Caprifoliaceae, an evergreen winter-flowering shrub native to Mediterranean regions [Mod. L.]
Lau·sanne (louzán) the capital (pop. 132,800) of Vaud, Switzerland, on the north shore of the Lake of Geneva. Industries: chocolate, precision instruments, furniture, publishing, tourism. Cathedral (mainly 19th c.), university
Lausanne, Treaty of the final settlement (1923) between the Allies and Turkey after the 1st world war. Its major provisions were Turkey's surrender of her claims to non-Turkish regions of the Ottoman Empire and the demilitarization of the Bosporus and the Dardanelles
Lau·ta·ro (lautárou) (c. 1535–57), chief of the Araucano Indians. He defeated and executed (1554) Valdivia at Tucapel. He was himself defeated and put to death by Francisco de Villagra (c. 1512–63)
Lau·ta·ro (lautárɔ) a secret society formed (1812) in Buenos Aires to fight for American independence
Lau·tré·a·mont (loutreiæmɔ̃), comte de (Isidore Ducasse, 1846–70), French poet, best known for the 'Chants de Maldoror' (1868), in strange lyrical prose, and 'Poésies' (1870). He is regarded as a precursor of surrealism
la·va (lávə) *n.* molten rock which issues from a volcano or volcanic vent in the liquid state ‖ any of the solid materials obtained when this is cooled [Ital. fr. *lavare,* to wash, fr. its similarity to floodwater]
la·va·bo (ləvéibou, ləvábou) *n.* (*eccles.*) the ritual washing of the celebrant's hands before the Eucharist ‖ the towel or basin used in this ritual [L.=will wash (the first word of Psalm xxvi, 6)]
La·val (lævæl), Pierre (1883–1945), French politician. He was prime minister (1931–2, 1934–6) and was the virtual head (1942–4) of the Vichy government. He was executed for collaboration
lav·a·liere (lævəlíər) *n.* a pendant worn on a chain around the neck [F. *Lavallière* after Louise de La Vallière, a mistress of Louis XIV]
La·va·lle·ja (lɑvəjéha), Juan Antonio (1784–1853), Uruguayan general, leader of the expedition of the Thirty Three which freed (1825) the Banda Oriental from Brazilian domination
Laval University the principal university (Roman Catholic, 1852) of French Canada, at Quebec
lav·a·to·ry (lǽvətɔri:, lǽvətɔuri:) *pl.* **lav·a·to·ries** *n.* a room with a toilet and a washbasin ‖ a room with a washbasin ‖ (esp. *Br.*) a toilet [fr. L. *lavatorium,* a place for washing]

lave (leiv) *pres. part.* **lav·ing** *past* and *past part.* **laved** *v.i.* (*rhet.*) to wash or flow against [O.E. *lafian*, to pour, fr. L. *lavare*, to wash]

lav·en·der (lǽvəndər) *n. Lavandula officinalis*, fam. *Labiatae*, a small European shrub, native to the S. Alps. It has small gray-green leaves with sweetly scented pale mauve flowers from which an essential oil, used in perfumery, is obtained ‖ the color of these flowers ‖ the dried flowers and stalks of the plant used in sachets etc. [A.F. *lavendre*]

la·ver (léivər) *n.* any of various purplish marine algae, esp. edible species of genus *Porphyra* [L.=a water plant]

la·ver·bread (léivərbred) *n.* a loaf of dried seaweed prepared in some areas of Britain as a gourmet food

Lavie (lɑviː) *n.* (*mil.*) 1980 version of Israeli Kfir aircraft

lav·ish (lǽviʃ) **1.** *adj.* given or provided with great generosity and abundance ‖ giving or providing in this way **2.** *v.t.* to bestow with large generosity [fr. older *lavish* n., profusion fr. O.F. *lavache, lavasse*, a downpour]

La·voi·sier (lǽvwæzjei), Antoine-Laurent (1743–94), French chemist, one of the founders of modern chemistry. He refuted the phlogiston theory by his work on combustion and, independently of Priestley, he identified (1777) and named oxygen. He also demonstrated the indestructibility of matter

Law (lɔ), Andrew Bonar (1858–1923), Canadian-born British Conservative statesman. He was chancellor of the exchequer (1916–19) and lord privy seal (1919–22) under Lloyd George, whom he succeeded as prime minister (1922–3)

Law, John (1671–1729), Scottish financier, controller-general of finances in France (1720). He was authorized by Philippe, duc d'Orléans, to found (1716) the first bank in France and a company to colonize Louisiana (1717). Excessive issue of notes and speculation were followed by a crash in which Law and thousands of investors were ruined (1720)

Law, William (1686–1761), English clergyman. His 'Serious Call to a Devout and Holy Life' (1728) contributed greatly to the evangelical revival

law (lɔ) *n.* a custom or practice recognized as binding by a community, esp. as a result of having been so decreed by the governing authority ‖ the whole body of such customs or practices, *the law of the land* ‖ obedience to such customs or practices, *to maintain law and order* ‖ such customs or practices considered as a branch of knowledge ‖ the profession of interpreting and enforcing such customs or practices ‖ an aspect of such customs or practices, *civil law*, or a body of customs or practices applicable to a specific group, community etc., *military law* ‖ the principles of common law, as distinguished from equity ‖ a relationship between cause and effect, or a statement of what occurs in nature, as found by observation and experiment to be true, *the law of gravitation, the law of supply and demand* ‖ (in a discipline or moral code) a practice accepted as correct, a rule **the Law** the precepts contained in the Pentateuch **to be a law unto oneself** to act according to one's own code of conduct, without regard for the opinions of others **to go to law** to seek the protection of the law, esp. in a court action in support of some claim **to lay down the law** to be pompously authoritative and dogmatic **to take the law into one's own hands** to act, esp. to punish, outside the sanction of the law [O.E. *lagu* fr. O.N.]

law-a·bid·ing (lɔ́əbaidiŋ) *adj.* obedient to the law

law and order a political slogan for programs to curb violence and crime, often viewed as antiblack —**law-and-order** *adj.*

law·break·er (lɔ́breikər) *n.* someone who acts contrary to the law **láw·break·ing** *n.* and *adj.*

law·court (lɔ́kɔrt, lɔ́kourt) *n.* a judicial courtroom ‖ the persons assembled there to administer justice ‖ all those present in the courtroom

law·ful (lɔ́fəl) *adj.* allowed by law ‖ legitimate, *a lawful ruler* ‖ valid, enforceable by law, *a lawful contract*

law·giv·er (lɔ́givər) *n.* (*rhet.*) someone who makes or promulgates laws, esp. a code of laws

law·less (lɔ́lis) *adj.* having no regard for laws ‖ without law, *a lawless region* ‖ illegal ‖ disorderly

law lord (*Br.*) a member of the House of Lords who because of his legal knowledge and experience is appointed to participate when the Lords are carrying out their judicial functions

law·mak·er (lɔ́meikər) *n.* someone who makes or enacts laws, a legislator **láw·mak·ing** *n.* and *adj.*

Law·man (lɔ́mæn) *LAYAMON

law merchant (*hist.*) a body of customary law, international in scope, which formerly regulated dealings between merchants ‖ (*Br.*) commercial law

lawn (lɔn) *n.* a fine, lightweight linen or cotton fabric [after *Laon*, a French town]

lawn *n.* a stretch of grass-covered land kept closely cut [O.F. *launde*, a wooded ground fr. O. Celt.]

lawn bowling (*Am.*=*Br.* bowls) an ancient outdoor pastime played on a green 38–42 yds square, individual games being played on a rink 18–21 ft wide within the green. Each player has four bowls, unevenly weighted, or biased. He bowls these underarm at the jack, a small white ball, at the opposite end of the rink. The object is to touch the jack with a bowl, or get as close as possible

lawn mower a machine, operated by power or by hand, for trimming a lawn

lawn tennis a game for two opposing players or two pairs of opponents played on a grass or hard-surface court 78 ft long and 27 ft wide for singles or 36 ft wide for doubles. The court is divided by a net, 3 ft high at the center, over which the players hit the white, felt-covered rubber ball with a racket strung with gut or nylon. A match consists of the best of three sets (women) or five (men)

law of contradiction (*logic*) a law stating that a thing cannot at the same time be and not be of a specified kind or quality

law officer a public official appointed to interpret and administer the law, esp. (*Br.*) the legal advisers (the attorney general and solicitor general) of the government

law of gravitation a statement in physics formulated by Newton: the force of attraction between any two masses in the universe is directly proportional to the product of the masses and inversely proportional to the square of the distance between their centers of mass

law of mass action an empirical law stating that the rate of a chemical reaction is proportional to the molecular concentrations of the reacting substances

Law of Moses the Mosaic Law

law of motion one of three statements in classical physics. The first, which is due to Galileo and is called the principle of inertia or Newton's first law, states that the velocity of a body is a constant in the absence of external forces. The second, which is due to Newton and is called Newton's second law or Newton's law of motion, states the definition of force. The third, which is also due to Newton, states that when two bodies interact the force exerted by the first on the second is equal in magnitude and opposite in direction to the force exerted by the second on the first

law of parsimony principle in logic that the simplest theory is preferred to explanations involving additional factors *also* Occam's razor

law of reflection an empirical law in optics stating that when a light ray is reflected at a plane surface the angle of incidence is equal to the angle of reflection, and that the reflected ray lies in the plane of the incident ray and the normal to the surface at the point of reflection (*GEOMETRICAL OPTICS)

law of refraction an empirical law in optics stating that when a ray of light is refracted at the interface of two isotropic media the ratio of the sine of the angle of incidence to the sine of the angle of refraction is equal to the refractive index (*SNELL'S LAW) and the refracted ray lies in the plane determined by the incident ray and the normal to the surface at the point of incidence (*GEOMETRICAL OPTICS)

law of thermodynamics one of three laws in physics. The first states the principle of the conservation of mass-energy. The second specifies that any real process may occur spontaneously only with an increase in the entropy of the system. Thus the first law only establishes the conditions that must obtain if a process does occur; the second law establishes the conditions that must be met before a process is possible. The third law states that the entropy of a per-

fectly crystalline substance is zero at the zero of absolute temperature

Law of the Sea Conferences international agreement made in Geneva in 1958 and 1960 defining base lines for contiguous zones, innocent passage, recovery of food and resources from the seabed, and conservation of sea life

Lawrence, St (*d.* 258), Roman deacon. According to legend he was martyred on a gridiron. Feast: Aug. 10

Law·rence (lɔ́rəns, lɔ́rəns), David Herbert (1885–1930), English novelist. essayist and poet. His novels include 'Sons and Lovers' (1913), 'The Rainbow' (1915), 'Women in Love' (1920) and 'Lady Chatterley's Lover' (1928). Lawrence was chiefly concerned with the nature that lies below the fixed ego of describable characteristics and moral preoccupations, esp. as revealed in the immediate flow of sympathy or antipathy between two persons before it is rationalized, repressed or distorted by shame, fear or convention. His view of the sex relationship springs from this central vision. He strove to show the relationship as deep and true, never as trivial, merely sensual or cerebral. For Lawrence 20th-c. society, esp. industrial England, was a corrosive and falsifier of human relations. His short stories are less dogmatic. His poems (collected edition 1964), essays, travel books and letters alone would have made the reputation of a lesser man

Lawrence, Ernest Orlando (1901–58), American physicist. He invented the cyclotron. Nobel prize (1939)

Lawrence, Sir Thomas (1769–1830), English portrait painter

Lawrence, Thomas Edward (1888–1935), British scholar and soldier. He gained fame as 'Lawrence of Arabia' for his leading part in the Arab revolt against the Turks (1916–18) in Hejaz and Palestine. His adventures are described in his 'The Seven Pillars of Wisdom' (1926). After Britain refused Arab demands (1919), he tried to withdraw into obscurity (1922)

Lawrence a city (pop. 52,738) in eastern Kansas founded (1854) by New England antislavery radicals who were sent to outvote proslavery settlers. It became a symbol of the free-state movement. It is the site of the University of Kansas (founded 1866)

Lawrence tube *CHROMOTRON

law·ren·ci·um (lɔrénsiːəm, lɔrénsiəm) *n.* a radioactive element (symbol Lw, at. no. 103, mass of isotope of longest known half-life 257) which disintegrates into mendelevium [after E.O. *Lawrence* (1901–58), American physicist]

Laws of the Indies a code of Spanish laws compiled (1681) for the government of the New World

law·suit (lɔ́suːt) *n.* a claim brought for judgment before a lawcourt

law·yer (lɔ́jər, lɔ́iər) *n.* someone qualified to practice law, as an attorney, advocate etc.

lax (læks) *adj.* free from tension, slack, *a lax rein* ‖ not strict, *lax morals* ‖ careless, negligent, *lax in his duties* ‖ (*phon.*, of vowels) pronounced with relaxed tongue and associated muscles ‖ (of the bowels) loose [fr. L. *laxus*]

lax·a·tive (lǽksətiv) **1.** *adj.* loosening the bowels and relieving constipation **2.** *n.* a laxative medicine [F.]

lax·i·ty (lǽksiti:) *n.* the quality or condition of being lax [F. *laxité*]

lay (lei) **1.** *v. pres. part.* **lay·ing** *past* and *past part.* **laid** (leid) *v.t.* to place in a more or less horizontal position on a more or less horizontal surface with a minimum of impact ‖ to do this ceremonially, *to lay a wreath* ‖ to apply (paint, plaster etc.) to ‖ to place in position, *to lay the foundations* ‖ to place (something abstract), *to lay great importance on cleanliness* ‖ to bring forth (an egg) ‖ to beat down flat, *the storm laid the oats* ‖ to stake as a bet or wager ‖ to present, put forth (a claim etc.) ‖ to prepare (a fire) for lighting ‖ to get (the table) ready for a meal ‖ to make even, smooth down (nap etc.) ‖ to cover, *the floor was laid with carpet* ‖ to set (a field gun) on target ‖ to set (a trap) ‖ to devise (a plan) ‖ to impose as a penalty etc., *to lay an embargo* ‖ to cause to subside, *the storm laid the dust* ‖ to ascribe a setting to, *the story is laid in Tahiti* ‖ to impute (blame, responsibility etc.) ‖ *v.i.* to bring forth eggs ‖ (esp. *naut.*) to be in a specified position, *the ship lay at anchor* **to be able to lay one's hand (or hands) on** to be able to find at once (what one is looking for) **to lay an ax** (*Br.* axe) **to** to begin to chop down **to lay aside** to

CONCISE PRONUNCIATION KEY: **(a)** æ, c*a*t; ɑ, c*a*r; ɔ f*aw*n; ei, sn*a*ke. **(e)** e, h*e*n; iː, sh*ee*p; iə, d*ee*r; ɛə, b*ea*r. **(i)** i, f*i*sh; ai, t*i*ger; əː, b*i*rd. **(o)** o, *o*x; au, c*ow*; ou, g*oa*t; u, p*oo*r; ɔi, r*oy*al. **(u)** ʌ, d*u*ck; u, b*u*ll; uː, g*oo*se; ə, b*a*cillus; juː, c*u*be. x, lo*ch*; θ, *th*ink; ð, bo*th*er; z, *Z*en; ʒ, corsa*g*e; dʒ, sava*g*e; ŋ, ora*ng*utang; j, *y*ak; ʃ, *fi*sh; tʃ, fe*tch*; ˈl, rabb*le*; ˈn, redd*en*. Complete pronunciation key appears inside front cover.

place to one side esp. as of no immediate use or importance ‖ to save (money etc.) for later use **to lay away** (or **by**) to place in store ‖ to accumulate (money) as savings **to lay bare** (*rhet.*) to uncover **to lay before** to present to for discussion, consideration etc. **to lay down** to surrender (arms) ‖ to sacrifice (one's life) ‖ to begin to construct, *the ship was laid down six years ago* ‖ to state authoritatively, *to lay down a principle* ‖ to place (a bet) ‖ to store away (wine) **to lay eyes on** to see **to lay hands on** to seize **to lay hold of** to grasp **to lay in** to obtain and store **to lay into** to attack fiercely **to lay it on** to flatter extravagantly ‖ to charge excessively ‖ to boast outrageously **to lay low** (*pop.*) to knock (someone) down ‖ (of a disease) to cause (someone) to be sick or physically weakened **to lay off** to discharge from employment, esp. temporarily ‖ to stop the operation of (a factory etc.) ‖ (*pop.*) to refrain from (some activity) ‖ (of a bookmaker) to place (part of a bet) with another bookmaker so as to reduce the risk ‖ (*naut.*) to steer (a boat) away from ‖ to stop work **to lay on** (*Br.*) to connect (gas, water, electricity etc.) ‖ (*pop.*) to make arrangements for the provision of, *to lay on entertainment and food* ‖ to deliver blows **to lay oneself out** to exert oneself, go to some special trouble (in order to do something) **to lay on the line** to put up (money) in full ‖ to make (an offer, statement) without reservations or conditions **to lay open** to cut, or in some other way act, so as to expose, *he laid open the wound, the victory laid open the road to Rome* **to lay out** to arrange or dispose in an orderly way ‖ to spend (money) in a planned way ‖ to prepare (a corpse) for burial ‖ (*pop.*) to render (someone) unconscious **to lay over** to stop for a usually short period during a journey **to lay to** (*naut.*) to check the motion of (a ship) by heading her into the wind ‖ (*naut.*, of a ship) to lie to **to lay up** to put (a ship, automobile etc.) out of commission until wanted for future use ‖ to cause to remain in bed through illness **2.** *n.* the manner, position or direction in which something lies ‖ an animal's lie **the lay of the land** the main aspects of a situation as one discerns it [O.E. *lecgan*]

lay *n.* a short narrative poem intended to be sung, esp. one of a primitive heroic nature [O.F. *lai*]

lay *adj.* of a layman or laymen [fr. older F. *lai*]

lay *past* of LIE (to have the body in a horizontal position)

Lay·a·mon (láiəmən) (also Lawman) English poet and priest (c. 1200). He was author of the 'Brut', a chronicle of Britain. It is the first extant English treatment of King Arthur and marks the transition from alliterative to rhymed verse

lay brother a man who lives in a monastery, under vows and wearing the habit, but employed only in manual or domestic work

lay-by (léibai) *n.* a stretch of a canal or river where boats can moor or pass ‖ a railroad siding ‖ (*Br.*) a widening of the road, or a short loop, where vehicles can pull in out of the line of traffic and halt ‖ (*agriculture*) the last operation in producing a field crop

lay clerk a choirman in an Anglican cathedral who leads the responses ‖ a parish clerk

lay day one of a certain number of days allowed by a charter party for the loading or unloading of cargo ‖ a day in which a vessel is delayed in port

lay·er (léiər) **1.** *n.* one thickness, coating etc. of one or more substances lying upon or under one or more other substances ‖ a laying hen ‖ the member of a gun crew who lays the gun ‖ a machine that twists rope ‖ a shoot or branch of a plant which is set into the ground to take root while still attached to the parent plant (from which it is later severed) ‖ a plant propagated in this way **2.** *v.t.* to root (a plant) from a layer ‖ *v.i.* to form in layers, strata etc. ‖ (of a plant) to form a layer or layers [LAY v.]

layer depth (*mil.*) the depth from the surface of the sea to the point above the first major negative thermocline at which sound velocity is maximum

layer tint *HYPSOMETRIC TINTING

lay·ette (leiét) *n.* the outfit of clothing, furniture, linen etc. for a newborn child [F.]

lay figure a jointed model of the human body, used by artists esp. for arranging drapery [fr. older *lay-man* ult. fr. Du. *led*, limb+*man*, man]

lay·man (léimən) *pl.* **lay·men** (léimən) *n.* a person who is not a priest or cleric ‖ a person without recognized status or expert knowledge, in contrast to a professional man

lay·off (léiɔf, léiɒf) *n.* the act of laying off an employee ‖ a period of withdrawal from some activity, *the boxer had no wind after his long layoff*

lay of the land *LAY

lay·out (léiaut) *n.* the act of arranging or disposing something in an orderly fashion ‖ the way in which things are placed in relation to one another, esp. print and illustration for typographical display ‖ a plan or mockup for such display

lay·o·ver (léiouvər) *n.* a stop or stay in a place during a journey

lay reader a person licensed to conduct certain religious services though not a priest or minister of religion

lay·shaft (léiʃæft, léiʃɑft) *n.* a mechanism to transmit power from a main drive, esp. a shaft in a gear box to transmit motion between sets of gears

lay sister a woman who lives in a convent, under vows and wearing the habit, but employed only in manual or domestic work

laz·a·ret (læzərét) *n.* a lazaretto [F.]

laz·a·ret·to (læzərétou) *pl.* **laz·a·ret·tos** *n.* a hospital for persons with contagious diseases, esp. lepers ‖ a ship or building set apart for quarantine purposes ‖ a place between decks in merchant ships where provisions are kept [Ital. *lazareto*]

Laz·a·rist (læzərist) *n.* a Roman Catholic priest or lay brother of the Congregation of the Priests of the Mission founded (1625) by St Vincent de Paul

Laz·a·rus (læzərəs) the friend whom Jesus brought back to life after he had been buried four days (John xi) ‖ a poor leper whose story is told in the parable of the wicked rich man (Luke xvi, 19–25)

Lazarus, Emma (1849–87), U.S. poet. She composed 'The New Colossus' (*LIBERTY, STATUE OF)

laze (leiz) **1.** *v. pres. part.* **laz·ing** *past* and *past part.* **lazed** *v.i.* to act lazily, to idle ‖ *v.t.* (with 'away') to pass (time) without doing any work **2.** *n.* the act of lazing or an instance of this [LAZY]

laz·i·ly (léizili:) *adv.* in a lazy manner

laz·i·ness (léizi:nis) *n.* the quality or state of being lazy

La·zio (lútsjɔ) *LATIUM

la·zy (léizi:) *comp.* **la·zi·er** *superl.* **la·zi·est** *adj.* with little will to work, idle ‖ characterized by or inducing lack of exertion, *a long, lazy day* ‖ slow-moving, *a lazy stream* [formerly *laysy* perh. fr. LAY v.]

la·zy·bones (léizi:bounz) *n.* (*pop.*) a lazy person

Lazy Dog (*mil.*) an antipersonnel bomb that explodes in midair scattering steel pellets

lazy eye (*med.*) poor vision of structurally sound eyes, usu. resulting from poor nutrition *also* amblyopia

lazy Su·san (léizi:sú:zən) a revolving tray used on a table for serving food

lb. pound

L-band (élbænd) *n.* range of 390–1,550 MHz in ultra-high radio frequency used in satellite communication *Cf* S-BAND

lbf (*phys. abbr.*) for pound force, a measure of thrust that equals the acceleration from gravity on one pound of mass

l.c. lowercase

LC_{50} standard measure of toxicity of median lethal concentration, i.e., how much is required to kill half of the experimental organisms

LDC (*abbr.*) for less developed country (which see)

L-do·pa [$C_9H_{11}NO_4$] (éldóupə) *n.* (*pharm.*) an amino acid that stimulates the formation of dopamine in the brain, used to relieve symptoms of Parkinson's disease; marketed as Dopar, Larodopa, or Levodopa *also* L-Dihydroxyphenylalanine *Cf* DOPAMINE

L-driv·er (éldréivər) *n.* (Br.) a learner driver

Lea (li:), Homer (1876–1912), U.S. military analyst. His experiences in China and Japan, including his service as chief of staff under Sun Yat-sen, are described in 'The Valor of Ignorance' (1909). In this book he warned of Japanese military ambitions, and accurately predicted a U.S.-Japanese war in which Hawaii would be Japan's key objective

lea (li:) *n.* (*rhet.*) an expanse of grass-land, a meadow [O.E. *léa*, *léah*, open ground]

lea *n.* a varying measure of textile yarn, usually 120 yds for cotton and silk and 300 yds for linen [perh. fr. F. *lier*, to tie]

leach 1. *v.t.* to cause (water etc.) to percolate through something ‖ to remove soluble matter from (ashes etc.) by percolation ‖ to wash away (soluble matter) ‖ *v.i.* to pass out by the action of percolating water **2.** *n.* a sieve used in leaching ‖ the act of leaching or an instance of this [prob. O.E. *leccan*, to water]

leach·ate (lí:tʃeit) *n.* (*envir.*) materials that pollute water as it seeps through solid waste

leach·ing (lí:tʃiŋ) *n.* (*envir.*) process by which nutrient chemicals or contaminants are dissolved and carried away by water or moved into a lower layer of soil

Lea·cock (lí:kɒk), Stephen Butler (1869–1944), Canadian humorist, author of whimsical, satirical stories and essays including 'Literary Lapses' (1910)

lead (li:d) **1.** *v. pres. part.* **lead·ing** *past* and *past part.* **led** (led) *v.t.* to show (someone) the way to go by accompanying him ‖ to force (someone) to go with oneself ‖ (of a road etc.) to take (someone) to a place ‖ to hold and take (someone or something) to a place, *he led the horse into the ring* ‖ to show (someone) the way to go by markings, indications etc., *these discoveries led him to the solution of the mystery* ‖ to cause (water etc.) to go in a specific direction ‖ to persuade to do or believe something ‖ to cause to do or believe something ‖ to direct, supervise the actions, policies, workings of (a company, nation, military force etc.) ‖ to conduct (an orchestra, chorus etc.) ‖ (*Br.*) to be the principal violinist of (an orchestra) ‖ to be the player of (a band or chamber orchestra) who conducts ‖ to be moving at the head of (a procession, race etc.) ‖ to hold first place in, *to lead the world in literacy* ‖ to cause to follow one's example, *to lead into evil ways* ‖ (*cards*) to play as the first card of a hand ‖ to go through, pass, live (life etc.) ‖ to cause someone to go through, pass, live (a particular sort of life), *she led him a miserable existence* ‖ (*shooting*) to aim in front of (a moving object), *to lead a partridge* ‖ *v.i.* to be at the head of a group in motion ‖ to show the way, *the lights led to the river* ‖ to be a way, channel etc. ‖ (of a road etc.) to go in a certain direction ‖ to bring about a specified result ‖ to hold the directorial or foremost position ‖ (*cards*) to make the first play ‖ (*boxing*) to begin a series of blows, *to lead with the left* ‖ (*Br., law*) to conduct a case as principal counsel, *to lead for the prosecution* **to lead off** to begin **to lead on** to entice (someone of the opposite sex) ‖ to cause (someone) to go further in some action than his prudence or moral sense would otherwise have allowed **to lead up to** to prepare the way for, e.g. in conversation or in a plot **2.** *n.* a showing of the way ‖ a clue as to direction ‖ the principal or guiding part in a group action ‖ the foremost or front position ‖ the state of being in this position ‖ the distance, time etc. by which one is in front of others, *a lead of 10 yards* ‖ leadership, *he didn't give the lead they looked for* ‖ example, *they all followed his lead* ‖ (*cards*) the act or opportunity of playing first ‖ (*cards*) the card so played ‖ (*acting*) the most important role ‖ (*acting*) someone who plays such a role ‖ an artificial waterway, esp. one going to a mill ‖ a leash for an animal ‖ a wire along which current is conveyed to or from a piece of electrical apparatus ‖ (*boxing*) the first blow of a series of attacking blows ‖ (*journalism*) the most important news article in a newspaper ‖ (*journalism*) the opening paragraph or paragraphs of a news story containing the essential facts ‖ an open channel in an ice field ‖ (*mining*) a lode ‖ (*mining*) a stratum of gold-bearing gravel in an old riverbed ‖ (*naut.*) the course of a rope [O.E. *lædan*]

lead (led) **1.** *n.* a soft, very dense, malleable and ductile, divalent or tetravalent metallic element (symbol Pb, at. no. 82, at. mass 207.19). It is bright bluish white in color, but readily tarnishes to a dull gray. Its chief ore is galena. Lead is used (often in the form of its alloys) in pipework (e.g. in plumbing), protective coverings or linings, type metal, solder, and as a shield against radioactivity. Some of its chemical compounds are used as pigments ‖ (*printing*) a thin strip of metal inserted between lines of type ‖ (*pl.*, *glazing*) thin strips of lead between which small panes of glass are held ‖ (*pl.*, *Br.*) the flat parts of a roof that can be walked on **2.**

v.t. to cover or frame with lead ‖ (*printing*) to separate (lines of type) with leads [O.E. *lēad*]

lead acetate the white, poisonous, very soluble lead salt (CH₃COO)₂Pb·3H₂O, used as a mordant

lead arsenate the poisonous white crystalline salt Pb₃(AsO₄)₂, used as an insecticide

lead carbonate the poisonous white lead salt PbCO₃, occurring naturally as cerussite ‖ the poisonous basic salt 2PbCO₃·Pb(OH)₂, known also as white lead

lead dioxide *LEAD OXIDE

lead·en (léd'n) *adj.* made of lead ‖ of a dull gray color, *a leaden sky* ‖ very heavy, hard to lift, *a leaden weight* ‖ oppressive, *a leaden silence* ‖ sluggish, lacking animation, *a leaden pace* [O.E. *lēaden*]

lead·er (lí:dər) *n.* someone who acts as a guide ‖ a directing head or chief e.g. of a political party ‖ someone who or something that leads a body of moving troops, animals etc. ‖ someone or something that holds first place ‖ a conductor of a musical group, esp. of one in which he also performs ‖ (*Br.*) a counsel who leads in a case ‖ (*Br.*) a King's (Queen's) Counsel ‖ (*Br.*) a counsel having seniority within a circuit ‖ (*Br.*) a concertmaster ‖ (*bot.*) a shoot growing from the apex of a stem or branch ‖ (*pl., printing*) a series of dots to lead the eye horizontally along a line (e.g. in tabular display) ‖ (*Br.*) an editorial ‖ (*commerce*) a loss leader ‖ a pipe for conducting water ‖ the front horse in a harnessed team ‖ (*fishing*) a length of gut to which the hook is attached **lead·er·ship** *n.* the position of a leader ‖ the quality displayed by a leader ‖ the act of leading or an instance of this [LEAD v.]

lead-free (lédfri:) *adj.* of nonleaded gasoline

lead-in (lí:din) *n.* a wire conducting impulses from an aerial to a radio set ‖ something that introduces, e.g. an announcer's introduction of a broadcaster

lead·ing (lí:diŋ) 1. *adj.* coming first, e.g. in a procession, *the leading float*; prominent, influential, *a leading critic* 2. *n.* the act of someone or something that leads

lead·ing (lédiŋ) *n.* (*printing*) lead (thin strip of metal) or the spacing between lines achieved by such leads

leading article the most important story in a magazine or other periodical ‖ (*Br.*) an editorial ‖ (*Br.*) a loss leader

leading case (*law*) a case which is taken as a precedent in deciding subsequent cases

leading edge (*aeron.*) the foremost edge of an airfoil (cf. TRAILING EDGE)

leading indicators (*economics*) economic time series each of which usu. reaches business cycle peak and trough ahead of general economic activity; e.g., average weekly overtime hours in manufacturing, average workweek of production workers

leading lady an actress playing the female lead in a play, film etc.

leading man an actor playing the male lead in a play, film etc.

leading note (*mus.*) a leading tone

leading question a question so phrased that it is hard to avoid giving the answer the questioner hopes for

leading tone (*mus.*) a subtonic

lead line (led) a sounding line

lead monoxide *LEAD OXIDE

lead-off (lí:dɔf, lí:dɒf) *n.* a beginning ‖ (*sports*) a player who leads off **lead-off** *adj.* of someone who or something that leads off, *a lead-off batter*

lead oxide (led) lead monoxide, PbO, a yellow to brown compound used in the manufacture of lead storage battery plates, glass, glazes, glazes, paints etc., known also as litharge and massicot ‖ lead dioxide, PbO₂, a brown compound used as an oxidizing agent and in lead storage batteries ‖ the orange-red tetroxide Pb₃O₄, used in corrosion-resistant paints, as an oxidizing agent, and in glass manufacture. It is known as red lead or minium

lead poisoning chronic poisoning caused by the introduction of lead or lead salts into the body

lead screw (lí:d) a screw that moves the saddle of a lathe when it is cutting screw threads

leads·man (lédzmən) *pl.* **leads·men** (lédzmən) *n.* (*naut.*) a person who uses a sounding line to make soundings

lead sulfide (led) the black insoluble compound PbS, occurring naturally as galena

lead wool lead in a fibrous state, used for sealing joints in lead pipes

leaf (li:f) 1. *pl.* **leaves** (li:vz) *n.* a thin expanded outgrowth of a plant stem or a twig, usually green and consisting essentially of a broad blade and a stalk. Leaves present a surface at which transpiration (*STOMA), respiration and the absorption of light needed for the photosynthesis of food can occur. Typically the leaf blade has an internal structure consisting of a vascular skeleton embedded in photosynthetic and supporting tissue and sheathed by an epidermis (*MESOPHYLL) ‖ a single sheet of folded paper, consisting in a book of two pages back to back ‖ metal rolled or hammered into a thin sheet, *gold leaf* ‖ a small sheet of this ‖ the movable section of a table top which can be added or removed, or one which can be raised on hinges to extend the surface area ‖ a similar hinged section in a folding shutter or door etc. ‖ leaves of tea, tobacco etc. as an item of commerce ‖ (*pop.*) a petal, esp. of a rose **in leaf** with the leaves spread open **to take a leaf out of someone's book** to follow someone's example **to turn over a new leaf** to make a fresh start in an attempt to improve one's behavior 2. *v.i.* to produce leaves ‖ (with 'through') to turn over the pages of (a book etc.) quickly and glance at the contents [O.E. *lēaf*]

leaf·age (lí:fidʒ) *n.* foliage

leaf·hop·per (lí:fhɒpər) *n.* a member of *Cicadellidae*, a family of hopping insects which suck the juice of plant leaves

leaf·i·ness (lí:fi:nis) *n.* the quality of being leafy

leaf insect any of various members of *Phylliidae*, a family of orthopterous insects, chiefly of the East Indies, having green wings and legs, resembling the leaves among which they live

leaf·let (lí:flit) *n.* a small printed sheet of paper, single or folded but not stitched, distributed free and usually containing advertising, propaganda etc. ‖ an individual unit of a compound leaf ‖ a small or immature leaf

leaf mold, *Br.* **leaf mould** fully decayed leaves rich in nitrogenous plant food used as fertilizer

leaf peekers tourists who visit areas during season when leaves are changing color

leaf spring a suspension spring composed of a number of separate thin metal plates fastened together

leaf·stalk (lí:fstɔk) *n.* a petiole

leaf·y (lí:fi:) *comp.* **leaf·i·er** *superl.* **leaf·i·est** *adj.* full of leaves ‖ like a leaf

league (li:g) 1. *n.* an association of persons, cities etc. formed to assist one another in some way, *the Hanseatic League* ‖ an association of football, baseball or other athletic clubs agreeing to play against one another under agreed rules **the League** (F. or *Ital. hist.*) the Holy League ‖ (*G. hist.*) the Catholic League ‖ the League of Nations **in league with** in alliance with (usually implying that no good will come of the alliance) 2. *v.i.* and *t. pres. part.* **lea·guing** *past* and *past part.* **leagued** to unite in a league [F. *ligue* fr. Ital. *liga*]

league *n.* (*hist.*) a measure of distance, usually about three miles [M.E. *leuge, leuke, lege* etc. fr. L.L., perh. of Celt. origin]

League of Nations an international organization (1920–46) set up after the 1st world war to promote international cooperation and to achieve international peace and security. It had 49 original members and 13 other states joined later. Although President Wilson was one of the chief architects of the organization, the U.S.A. refused to join. The League lacked means to enforce its decisions and was unable to prevent the 2nd world war. It was dissolved in 1946 and was succeeded by the U.N.

League of Three Emperors the Dreikaiserbund

League of Women Voters of the United States a nonpartisan feminine organization founded in 1920 'to promote political responsibility through informed and active participation of citizens in government'. It supports the principle of international cooperation

Lea·hy (léihi:), William Daniel (1875–1959), U.S. admiral and chief of naval operations (1937–9). He filled the newly created position of chief of staff to Presidents Franklin Roosevelt and Harry Truman

leak (li:k) *n.* a small hole, crack etc. in a wall, container etc. through which e.g. fluid or light escapes or penetrates ‖ (*elec.*) a point in a conductor where current escapes ‖ (*elec.*) this loss of current ‖ the act of leaking ‖ that which leaks or is leaked **to spring a leak** to develop a hole etc.

through which a fluid or light escapes or penetrates [perh. O.N. *leke*]

leak *v.i.* (e.g. of a fluid or light, with 'in' or 'out') to pass through a small hole or crack in a retaining or excluding wall, container etc. ‖ to have a small hole or crack through which something (e.g. usually retained or excluded fluid or light) can pass ‖ (of secret or restricted information) to become known to people not intended to have the information *v.t.* to allow (e.g. fluid or light) to leak ‖ to allow (secret or restricted information) to leak **léak·age** *n.* the act of leaking or an instance of this ‖ something which has leaked or the amount leaked ‖ (*commerce*) an allowance for loss due to leaking, e.g. of liquids in transit [O.N. *leka,* to drip]

Leakey (lí:ki:) **Family,** British anthropologists, Louis S. B. (1903–72), his wife Mary (1913–) and their son Richard (1944–). Louis and Mary excavated fossil sites at Olduvai Gorge, Tanzania, where they discovered human fossils dating back 1.75 million years, including *Australopithecus boisei, Homo habilis* and *Homo erectus.* They also documented the history of the Stone Age. Richard's excavations were mainly in S. Ethiopia; he documented fossils 3 million years old

leak·i·ness (lí:ki:nis) *n.* the state or quality of being leaky

leak·y (lí:ki:) *comp.* **leak·i·er** *superl.* **leak·i·est** *adj.* allowing fluids etc. to leak in or out

lean (li:n) 1. *v. pres. part.* **lean·ing** *past* and *past part.* **leaned,** *Br.* also **leant** (lent) *v.i.* to be or stand not quite upright ‖ to place the body, or part of the body, in such a position ‖ (with 'on', 'upon') to depend for support or encouragement ‖ to incline in opinion or feeling, *to lean towards communism* ‖ *v.t.* to cause to lean ‖ to place for support, *he leaned his elbows on the table* **to lean over backward** to spare no effort in trying (to do something) 2. *n.* the act of leaning or an instance of this [O.E. *hlinian, hleonian*]

lean 1. *adj.* having little fat, *lean meat* ‖ (of a person or animal) thin but not excessively so ‖ having or producing little of value, *lean years* 2. *n.* that part of meat which has little fat [O.E. *hlǣne*]

Le·an·der (li:ǽndər) *HERO

lean·ing (lí:niŋ) *n.* tendency, inclination [LEAN v.]

leant *alt. past* and *past part.* of LEAN

lean-to (lí:ntu:) *n.* a shed or other small outbuilding with a sloping roof, the upper end of which rests against the wall of another building

leap (li:p) *n.* the act of leaping ‖ the distance leaped ‖ something to be leaped ‖ an abrupt change **a leap in the dark** an act of which one cannot assess the difficulties or consequences and which one decides by faith or instinct, not reason, to perform **by leaps and bounds** very fast, *profits have gone up by leaps and bounds* [O.E. *hlyp*]

leap *pres. part.* **leap·ing** *past* and *past part.* **leaped, leapt** (lept) *v.i.* to project the body through the air from one place to another with a sudden movement by the muscular effort of the legs or feet, esp. with more force than is usually suggested by 'jump' ‖ to rise quickly as if with a leap ‖ *v.t.* to pass over by leaping ‖ to cause to leap [O.E. *hlēapan*]

leap·frog (lí:pfrɔg, lí:pfrɒg) 1. *n.* a game in which the participants in turn vault with legs astride over the others' bent backs 2. *v. pres. part.* **leap·frog·ging** *past* and *past part.* **leap·frogged** *v.i.* to play this game, or vault thus ‖ *v.t.* to vault over in this manner ‖ (*mil.*) to advance (forces) by dividing them into two portions, each in turn being halted, usually to provide protection, while the other advances

leapt *alt. past* and *past part.* of LEAP

leap year a year having Feb. 29 as an additional day, making 366 in all, occurring in the Gregorian calendar whenever the year's date is divisible by 4 with the exception of those divisible by 100 but not by 400. This device accommodates the calendar to the difference between the calendar day and the solar day ‖ an intercalary year in any calendar

Lear (liər), Edward (1812–88), English humorist and painter. He wrote and illustrated 'A Book of Nonsense' (1846, 1861, 1863) and 'Nonsense Songs' (1871, 1872, 1877)

learn (lərn) *pres. part.* **learn·ing** *past* and *past part.* **learned, learnt** (lərnt) *v.t.* to acquire knowledge of or skill in by study, instruction, practice or experience ‖ to commit to memory ‖ to come to know or be aware of ‖ *v.i.* to acquire

CONCISE PRONUNCIATION KEY: **(a)** æ, c*a*t; ɑ, c*a*r; ɔ f*aw*n; ei, sn*a*ke. **(e)** e, h*e*n; i:, sh*ee*p; iə, d*ee*r; ɛə, b*ea*r. **(i)** i, f*i*sh; ai, t*i*ger; ə:, b*i*rd. **(o)** o, *o*x; au, c*ow*; ou, g*oa*t; u, p*oo*r; ɔi, r*oy*al. **(u)** ʌ, d*u*ck; u, b*u*ll; u:, g*oo*se; ə, b*a*cill*u*s; ju:, c*u*be. x, lo*ch*; θ, *th*ink; ð, bo*th*er; z, *Z*en; ʒ, cor*s*age. dʒ, sava*g*e; ŋ, ora*n*guta*n*g; j, *y*ak; ʃ, *f*ish; tʃ, fe*tch*; 'l, rabb*le*; 'n, redd*en*. Complete pronunciation key appears inside front cover.

knowledge or skill ‖ (with 'of') to become aware, be told **learn·ed** (lə:rnid) *adj.* having a great deal of knowledge ‖ (*Br.*) used as a conventional form of address or reference in a court of law or parliament for a lawyer, *my learned friend* ‖ characterized by or demanding profound knowledge, *a learned speech* **léarn·er** *n.* **léarn·ing** *n.* a large and well organized body of usually nonscientific ideas, acquired and retained by long and great effort, *a man of great learning* ‖ the mental process itself ‖ the acquisition of skills or mental attitudes [O.E. *leornian*]

learning curve (*psych.*) a graphic display of the relationship of learning and performance

learnt alt. *past* and *past part.* of LEARN

LEASAT (lí:sæt) *n.* U.S. Navy space shuttle, launched in 1983

lease (li:s) *n.* a legal contract between lessor and lessee putting land or property of the former at the disposal of the latter usually for a stated period, for a stipulated rent, and under other specified conditions ‖ the document itself ‖ the period stated **to get** (or **take, have**) **a new lease on** (or **of**) **life** to survive a dangerous or difficult period and renew one's energy, drive, optimism etc. [A.F. *les*]

lease *n.* (*weaving*) the system of controlling and separating the warp threads using a lease rod ‖ (*weaving*) one or more cords for raising certain warp threads in weaving a pattern

lease *pres. part.* **leas·ing** *past* and *past part.* **leased** *v.t.* to put (land, buildings etc.) at the disposal of a lessee under a lease ‖ to take (property, buildings etc.) into one's own use under a lease [A.F. *lesser*]

lease·hold (lí:should) **1.** *adj.* (of property) held under a lease **2.** *n.* the legal right of holding property as stated in a lease ‖ property held under a lease **léase·hold·er** *n.* a person who holds property as lessee [fr. LEASE *n.* after 'freehold']

lease-lend (lí:slénd) *n.* the original name for lend-lease

lease rod (*weaving*) one of two rods used to separate and control warp threads

leash (li:ʃ) **1.** *n.* a strap, cord or chain fastened to the collar of an animal or jess of a hawk for control ‖ a set of three hounds, hares etc. **to strain at the leash** to be intensely eager to act but prevented from doing so **2.** *v.t.* to put a leash on [O.F. *lesse, laisse*]

least (li:st) **1.** *adj.* (*superl.* of LITTLE) smallest in size, amount, quality, importance etc. **the least** (usually after a negative) smallest, slightest, *not the least suspicion* **2.** *n.* the smallest amount, *it was the least he could do* **at least** as the bare minimum to satisfy legitimate expectations, even if any wider statement could be disputed, *at least you should say thank you* **at the least** at a minimum estimate, *it will cost twice as much at the least* **not in the least** not in the slightest degree **least of all** with the smallest justification, *none of us can afford to criticize, you least of all* **3.** *adv.* in the smallest degree [O.E. *lǣst, lǣsest*]

least common denominator the lowest common denominator

least common multiple the lowest common multiple

least·ways (lí:stwẹiz) *adv.* (*dialect*) leastwise

least·wise (lí:stwẹiz) *adv.* (*pop.*) at least, at any rate

leath·er (léðər) **1.** *n.* the skin of an animal, cleaned and made flexible and durable by tanning, and used for shoes, luggage, harness etc. ‖ something made of this, e.g. a stirrup leather ‖ a piece of chamois leather used for polishing **2.** *adj.* pertaining to, or made of, leather [O.E. *lether*]

leath·er·back (léðərbæk) *n. Dermochelys coriacea,* fam. *Dermochelidae,* a gigantic soft-shelled marine turtle (up to 9 ft in length and 1,000 lbs in weight), found in warm waters, esp. of the Atlantic

Leath·er·ette (leðərét) *n.* imitation leather made from paper, cloth or plastic and used for travel bags, bookbinding etc. [Trademark]

leath·er·jack·et (léðərdʒækit) *n.* (*Br.*) the grub of the crane fly

leath·ern (léðərn) *adj.* (*old-fash.*) made of leather ‖ leathery [O.E. *letheren*]

leath·er·neck (léðərnẹk) *n.* a U.S. marine [after the leather collar lining of the original Marine uniform]

leath·er·wood (léðərwụd) *n. Dirca palustris,* fam. *Thymelaeaceae,* a North American shrub having a tough bark and small yellow flowers

leath·er·y (léðəri:) *adj.* like leather in consistency or appearance ‖ tough

leave (li:v) *n.* permission, esp. to be absent from (esp. *mil.*) duty or from a place of duty ‖ the period of such absence, *seven days' leave* **on leave** absent from duty with permission **to take leave of** to say goodbye to **to take leave of one's senses** to behave so foolishly as to seem temporarily insane **to take one's leave** to say goodbye and go [O.E. *léaf*]

leave 1. *v. pres. part.* **leav·ing** *past* and *past part.* **left** (left) *v.i.* to depart, go away ‖ to cease to reside in a certain place, attend school, serve an employer etc. ‖ *v.t.* to allow to remain by oversight, *he left his hat on the train* ‖ to deposit before going off, *to leave a tip* ‖ to cause to remain as a consequence, sign etc., *the wound left a scar* ‖ to be survived by, *he leaves a wife and three children* ‖ to produce as a remainder, *4 from 6 leaves 2* ‖ to let remain, *his interpretation leaves room for argument* ‖ to bequeath, *he left her all his money* ‖ to omit to eat, *don't leave any of your dinner* ‖ to put off dealing with, *he'll leave those letters till tomorrow* ‖ to cause or allow (someone or something) to continue in a certain way, condition, activity etc., *we left him painting the gate, they left the gate open* ‖ to allow to do or continue to do something without interference, *we left him to paint the gate* ‖ to cause or allow (something) to become the concern, property or responsibility of someone else, *she left the job for you* ‖ to cause or allow (someone) to assume a concern, responsibility etc., *we left him in charge* ‖ to deposit for transmission or collection, *she left a message for him* ‖ to situate (a place) with respect to one's own position after going past, through or around it, *we left the town on our right* ‖ to go away from, out of etc., *to leave the room, the train left the track* ‖ to cease to reside in (a certain place), attend (school) or serve (an employer) etc. ‖ to abandon, *he left his wife* **to be left with** to continue to have (a feeling, idea, responsibility etc.) after, or as a result of, a previous event, *she was left with a feeling of relief, he was left with the child to look after* **to leave alone** to stop interfering with or not interfere with **to leave behind** to go away without ‖ to cause or allow to remain as a consequence or sign, *he left behind nothing but happy memories* **to leave go** (*pop.,* often with 'of', considered substandard) to let go, cease to hold, *you must not leave go of my hand* **to leave off** to cease, *leave off work* ‖ to stop wearing (a garment) **to leave out** to omit ‖ to put (something) where it will be available, *he left the key out for you* **to leave over** (*Br.*) to postpone dealing with, *leave the matter over until tomorrow* **to leave to chance** to allow chance to settle a matter **2.** *n.* (*billiards*) the position of the balls as one's opponent leaves them [O.E. *lǣfan*]

leave *pres. part.* **leav·ing** *past* and *past part.* **leaved** *v.i.* to put out leaves

leav·en (lévən) **1.** *n.* a substance added to dough which, by fermentation, produces carbon dioxide gas and thus makes the dough rise and become porous ‖ some already fermenting dough used to spread the process through a larger amount ‖ something mixed in which induces a general change for the better, *the whole school benefits from its leaven of brighter children* **2.** *v.t.* to cause (dough) to ferment by adding leaven ‖ to cause a general change for the better in, esp. to make as though light and airy [F. *levain*]

leave of absence permission to be absent from duty or from a place of duty ‖ the period of such leave

leav·er (lí:vər) *n.* (*mil.*) an independent merchant ship that breaks off from the main convoy

leave-tak·ing (lí:vteikiŋ) *n.* a saying goodbye

leav·ings (lí:viŋz) *pl. n.* things left over as no longer wanted [LEAVE v.]

Lea·vis (lí:vis) Frank Raymond (1895–1978), English critic and editor. His books on English literature, and on the place of culture and education in modern life, include 'The Great Tradition' (1948). He edited the critical journal 'Scrutiny' (1932–53)

Leb·a·nese (lẹbəní:z, lẹbəní:s) **1.** *adj.* of or pertaining to Lebanon or its people **2.** *n.* a native of Lebanon

Leb·a·non (lébənən) a republic (area 3,400 sq. miles, pop. 2,601,000) on the east shore of the Mediterranean, in W. Asia. Capital: Beirut. 8% of the population are Arab refugees from Palestine. Language: Arabic (some French and

English). Religion: 54% Christian (mainly Maronite), 43% Moslem. 26% of the land is cultivated. 50% lies over 3,000 ft. Between the Lebanon Mtns in the center, running the length of the country, and the Anti-Lebanon Mtns along the Syrian frontier lie the fertile valleys of the Litani and Orontes Rivers. Highest point: Al-Qurnat al-Sawdā (11,024 ft) in the Lebanon Mtns. Average temperatures (F.): on the coast 55° (Jan.) and 81° (Aug.). Rainfall: 35 ins on the plains, 60 ins in the mountains. Livestock: goats, sheep, cattle, donkeys. Crops: oranges, apples, grapes, olives, wheat, potatoes, bananas, tobacco, cotton, mulberries. Minerals: iron ore. Industries: textiles, foodstuffs, light machinery, oil refining (Tripoli and Saida, termini of pipelines from Iraq and Saudi Arabia), chemicals, tourism, cement, furniture, printing. Exports: fruit, vegetables. Imports: precious stones and metals, animals, machinery, cereals, vehicles. Ports: Beirut, Tripoli. There are four universities in Beirut, the oldest being the American (1866) and the French (1875). Monetary unit: Lebanese pound (100 piastres). HISTORY. A major center of Phoenician civilization, Lebanon was conquered by the Persians (538 B.C.), by Alexander the Great (333 B.C.), and by the Romans (64 B.C.), and became part of the Byzantine Empire. Overrun by the Arabs (634–40), it came under the Ottoman Empire (1516). It became autonomous (1861) after a massacre of Christians (1860) had incited the European powers to intervene. With Syria, Lebanon became a French mandate (1920) and a republic (1926). In the 2nd world war, it was controlled by the Vichy government until occupied by the British and Free French (1941). It became independent (1944) and joined the Arab League and the U.N. (1945). Civil war in 1958 was ended when U.S. Marines landed in Beirut, but dissension continued between Moslems and Christian factions. Tensions were exacerbated by the activities of the Palestine Liberation Organization (PLO), which launched guerrilla raids against Israel from inside Lebanon. Civil war broke out again in 1975 and Syria intervened on behalf of the Moslems. An Israeli invasion of southern Lebanon (1978) ended when a U.N. peacekeeping force was sent to the area, but Israeli forces invaded again (1982), occupied Beirut and forced the evacuation of PLO headquarters from Beirut. A multinational peacekeeping force was called in by Pres. Amin Gemayel, who signed an agreement with Israel (1983) providing for a continuing Israeli role in southern Lebanon. Syria, however, rejected this accord. Fighting continued between Lebanon's militias, which included rival Palestinian groups, and terrorist bomb attacks were conducted on the multinational force, including U.S. Marines headquartered at Beirut airport. The multinational force was withdrawn in 1984. Gemayel then repudiated the Lebanese-Israeli security agreement and installed a new pro-Syrian cabinet, but the cabinet resigned (1985) and the government remained unstable. Israel removed most of its troops from Lebanon, but conflicting Israeli-Syrian interests and other external pressures continue to compound Lebanon's internal problems

Lebanon Mtns *LEBANON

leb·ku·chen (lébku:k'n) *n.* a cake of citron, almonds, brown sugar, lemon rind and juice, nutmeg, cloves, and cinnamon with honey

Le·blanc (ləblã), Nicolas (1742–1806), French chemist who invented a process for manufacturing sodium carbonate from common salt, now replaced by the Solvay process

Le Brun (ləbrœ̃), Charles (1619–90), French painter, responsible for the principal decorations at Versailles

LeCarré (ləkaréi), John (1931–), British writer, born David Cornwell, who writes, mainly, espionage thrillers gleaned from his service with the British Foreign Service (1961–4). His novels include 'The Spy Who Came in from the Cold' (1963; film, 1966), 'The Looking Glass War' (1965), 'Tinker, Tailor, Soldier, Spy' (1974), 'The Honourable Schoolboy' (1977), 'Smiley's People' (1980), 'The Little Drummer Girl' (1983) and 'A Perfect Spy' (1986)

lech (letʃ) *v.* to lust; to be a lecher —**lech** *n.* one who leches

Le Cha·te·lier's principle (ləʃætəljei) (*phys., chem.*) the statement that when a system in equilibrium is subjected to a stress it tends to a new equilibrium that opposes the effect of the

CONCISE PRONUNCIATION KEY: **(a)** æ, c**a**t; ɑ, c**a**r; ɔ f**aw**n; ei, sn**a**ke. **(e)** e, h**e**n; i:, sh**ee**p; iə, d**ee**r; ɛə, b**ea**r. **(i)** i, f**i**sh; ai, t**i**ger; ə:, b**i**rd. **(o)** o, **o**x; au, c**ow**; ou, g**oa**t; u, p**oo**r; ɔi, r**oy**al. **(u)** ʌ, d**u**ck; u, b**u**ll; u:, g**oo**se; ə, b**a**cill**u**s; ju:, c**u**be. x, lo**ch**; θ, **th**ink; ð, **b**o**th**er; z, **Z**en; ʒ, corsa**g**e; dʒ, sava**g**e; ŋ, ora**ng**utang; j, **y**ak; ʃ, **f**i**sh**; tʃ, fe**tch**; 'l, rabb**le**; 'n, red**den**. Complete pronunciation key appears inside front cover.

stress [after Henry-Louis *Le Châtelier* (1850-1936), F. chemist]

lech·er (létʃər) *n.* a man given to lechery [O.F. *lecheor, lecheur, lechur*]

lech·er·ous (létʃərəs) *adj.* given to, characterized by or encouraging lechery [O.F. *lecheros*]

lech·er·y (létʃəri:) *n.* gross indulgence in carnal pleasure [O.F. *lecherie, licherie*]

lec·i·thin (lésəθin) *n.* (*biochem.*) a fatty substance containing nitrogen and phosphorus, occurring in the cellular tissues of living things [fr. Gk *lekithos*, yolk of an egg]

Le·clair (ləkler), Jean-Marie (1697–1764), French composer whose works include operas, ballets and concerti for violin and flute

Le·clan·ché cell (ləklūʃei) a primary cell with a carbon anode, a zinc cathode and an ammonium chloride electrolyte. The common dry battery is an adaptation of this [after Georges *Leclanché* (1839-82), F. chemist]

Le·comp·ton Constitution (ləkómptən) a pro-slavery constitution (1857) of the territory of Kansas, opposed by the Free State party but supported by President James Buchanan. Senator Stephen Douglas initiated a referendum in Kansas which rejected (1858) the constitution. Kansas was admitted (1861) as a free state

Le·conte de Lisle (ləkɔ̄tdəli:l), Charles Marie René (1818–94), French Parnassian poet. A frigid splendor characterizes his primarily visual, though highsounding, art, and he drew on exotic sources of inspiration. His principal volumes were 'Poèmes antiques' (1852) and 'Poèmes barbares' (1862)

Le Cor·bu·sier (ləkɔrbysjei) (Charles Edouard Jeanneret-Gris, 1887–1965), French architect, town planner and painter, of Swiss birth. He built vast communal buildings (e.g. at Marseilles, France, 1946–52), and functional cities (e.g. Chandigarh, India, 1954), mostly using steel and raw concrete. After 1945 his work had tremendous influence (*INTERNATIONAL STYLE)

lec·tern (léktərn) *n.* a raised desk in a church on which the Bible is placed for reading the Scriptures aloud ‖ a similar desk for supporting music in the choir ‖ a stand with a sloping top for holding a reader's or lecturer's book, papers etc. [M.E. *lettrum* ult. fr. L.L. *lectrum*]

lec·tin (léktin) *n.* a plant substance that acts as an antibody in animals, used esp. in human blood agglutinization

lec·tion (lékʃən) *n.* a reading of Scripture as part of a church service ‖ a variant in the text of a specific edition, copy etc. [O.F. *lectiun*]

lec·tion·ar·y (lékʃəneri:) *pl.* **lec·tion·ar·ies** *n.* a book containing a selection of passages from the Scriptures to be read at church services [fr. eccles. L. *lectionarium*]

lec·tor (léktər, léktɔr) *n.* (*Roman Catholicism*) a member of the third-ranking minor order whose duty is to read the Scripture lessons in church ‖ a title held by some lecturers in some universities [L.]

lec·ture (léktʃər) 1. *n.* a prepared disquisition made to an audience, class, etc., designed to instruct or explain at some length ‖ a long and tedious reprimand 2. *v. pres. part.* **lec·tur·ing** *past* and *past part.* **lec·tured** *v.i.* to deliver a lecture or series of lectures ‖ *v.t.* to instruct by giving a lecture ‖ to reprimand (someone) tediously and at length **léc·tur·er** *n.* someone who professionally instructs by giving lectures **léc·ture·ship** *n.* the official position held by a professional lecturer in a college or university [fr. L. *lectura*]

led *past* and *past part.* of LEAD

LED (*electr. abbr.*) for light-emitting diode, an electronic-readout solid-state lamp used in digital clocks, etc.

Le·da (lí:də) (*Gk mythol.*) the wife of a king of Sparta. She was loved by Zeus, who came to her in the form of a swan. She was the mother of Castor, Pollux, Helen and Clytemnestra

Le·der·berg (léidərbə:rg), Joshua (1925–), U.S. geneticist. He shared (with E. L. Tatum and G. W. Beadle) the 1958 Nobel prize in physiology and medicine for discoveries in bacterial heredity, including the demonstration that sexual reproduction occurs in bacteria

ledge (ledʒ) *n.* a narrow horizontal projection in a vertical or steep surface ‖ a ridge of rock, esp. under water ‖ (*mining*) a stratum of rock rich in ore [M.E. *legge* prob. fr. *leggen*, to lay]

ledg·er (lédʒər) *n.* (*bookkeeping*) a large book in which are recorded the credits and debits of commercial transactions ‖ a flat gravestone ‖ (*building*) a horizontal scaffold pole parallel to the wall [prob. fr. M.E. *leggen*, to lay]

ledger line (*mus.*) a short horizontal line extending the stave above or below

Lee (li:), Arthur (1740–92), U.S. diplomat during the Revolutionary War who sought recognition of the Continental Congress and aid for it from European nations. With Benjamin Franklin and Silas Deane he signed (1778) an alliance treaty with France

Lee, Charles (1731–82), American general, British-born, in the Revolutionary War

Lee, Fitzhugh (1835–1905), Confederate general in the Civil War and U.S. cavalry general in the Spanish-American War. He was consul general (1896–9) in Havana, Cuba

Lee, Henry (1756–1818), American general in the Revolutionary War. He was known as 'Light-Horse Harry'. He was the father of Robert E. Lee

Lee, Richard Henry (1732–94), U.S. Whig statesman during the Revolutionary period. He introduced the second continental congress resolutions for declaring independence, for forming foreign alliances, and for preparing a plan of confederation, which led to the drafting of the Declaration of Independence

Lee, Robert Edward (1807–70), American commander in chief of the Confederate army in the American Civil War (1861–5). His military genius and character won him the admiration of both North and South

lee 1. *n.* the sheltered side, opposite to that against which the wind blows ‖ shelter, *in the lee of the jetty* 2. *adj.* of, pertaining to or located on the sheltered side [O.E. *hlēo*, shelter]

lee board a plank or metal sheet lowered into the water on the lee side of a flat-bottomed vessel to prevent its drifting in that direction

leech (li:tʃ) *n.* a member of *Hirudinea*, a class of segmented, chiefly aquatic, suctorial annelids, which cling hard to the skin of an animal while sucking blood and relinquish their hold when fully distended ‖ a human parasite [O.E. *lœce*]

leech *n.* a vertical edge of a square sail ‖ the after edge of a fore-and-aft sail [prob. rel. to O.N. *lik*, Du. *lijk*]

Leeds (li:dz) an industrial city (pop. 716,000) and county borough of Yorkshire, England: metallurgy (esp. iron and steel), textiles, engineering, tanning. Roman Catholic cathedral (20th c.). University (1904)

leek (li:k) *n. Allium porrum*, fam. *Liliaceae*, an edible vegetable, native to S. Asia, allied to the onion but having a long slender cylindrical bulb [O.E. *lēac*]

Lee Kuan Yew (lí:kwánjú:) (1923–), Singapore statesman, prime minister since independence (1959). He has encouraged foreign investment (Japanese, European) and industrial development

leer (liər) 1. *v.t.* to cast a knowing sidelong look that travesties a smile, and may indicate lust, malicious triumph or stupidity 2. *n.* such a look [etym. doubtful]

leer *LEHR

leer·y (líəri:) *adj.* suspicious, wary [perh. fr. archaic *leer* adj., looking with a leer]

lees (li:z) *pl. n.* the sediment on the bottom of a cask of wine, a cup of coffee etc. [M.E. *lie* (sing.) fr. O.F. perh. of Celt. origin]

leet (li:t) *n.* (*Eng. hist.*) a court of record for petty crimes, usually held annually by the steward of a manor, lordship or hundred ‖ the jurisdiction of such a court [M.E. fr. A.F. *lete* perh. fr. O.E. *lǣth*]

Leeu·war·den (léivɑrd'n) the capital (pop. 84,367) of Friesland, Netherlands: butter, cheese

Leeu·wen·hoek (léivənhu:k), Anton van (1632–1723), Dutch microscopist and biologist. He developed accurate small lenses and microscopes. He discovered protozoa, spermatozoa, microbes and blood corpuscles. He also studied yeasts and the circulation of the blood

lee·ward (lí:wərd, *naut.* lú:ərd) 1. *n.* the lee direction (opp. WINDWARD) 2. *adj.* of this direction or side 3. *adv.* in the lee direction

Leeward and Windward Islands *LEEWARD ISLANDS, *WINDWARD ISLANDS

Leeward Islands the name of two island groups, one in the West Indies, the other (Isles Sous-le-Vent) in French Polynesia (*SOCIETY ISLANDS). The West Indian group are the northernmost of the Lesser Antilles (*ANTILLES)

lee·way (lí:wei) *n.* (*naut.*) the drift of a vessel to the leeward of her proper course ‖ (*aeron.*) the angle of drift of an aircraft due to crosswind ‖ margin of freedom of action ‖ a margin of time, money etc.

Le·fè·vre d'E·ta·ples (ləfevrdeitæpl), Jacques (c. 1450–1537), French theologian. A precursor of the Reformation, he translated the Bible into French (1523–30)

left (left) 1. *adj.* of or on the side of the body where the heart is situated, or on this side of a person's vertical axis of symmetry ‖ on or to this side as perceived by an observer ‖ (of a river bank) on this side of an observer facing downstream **Left** of, belonging to or associated with the Left 2. *adv.* in or to a left direction or side 3. *n.* the left side or direction ‖ (*boxing*) the left hand or a blow with this hand ‖ (*marching, dancing* etc.) the left foot **the Left** that section of a political party, system of political parties, organization, group etc. which differs most from traditional authority or opinion and which in legislative bodies is seated traditionally to the left of the presiding officer [O.E.=weak, left]

left *past* and *past part.* of LEAVE

left field (*baseball*) the left part of the outfield, viewed from the plate ‖ the position of the player defending this

left-field (léftfi:ld) *adj.* away from the center of the action

left-hand (léfthænd) *adj.* on or to the left side ‖ (of a screw or thing to be used by a left-handed person) left-handed

left-hand·ed (léfthǽndid) 1. *adj.* using the left hand more efficiently than the right hand ‖ (of a screw) having a counterclockwise thread ‖ adapted for use by someone who habitually uses his left hand, *a left-handed golf club* ‖ having a concealed, secondary and opposite meaning, *a left-handed compliment* ‖ (of a rope) left-laid 2. *adv.* with the left hand

Left·ist (léftist) 1. *n.* someone who belongs to the Left or tends to hold the views of the Left 2. *adj.* of, associated with or belonging to the Left

left-laid (léftleid) *adj.* (of a rope) having strands twisted to the left of the person viewing them lengthwise

left-luggage office (*Br.*) a checkroom (storeroom at a railroad station etc.)

left-o·ver (léftouvər) 1. *n.* an unused remainder, esp. food not eaten but kept for another meal 2. *adj.* remaining

left wing the section of a political party, government, group etc. holding the most left or radical views **léft-wing** *adj.* **léft-wing·er** *n.*

leg (leg) 1. *n.* one of the limbs supporting a human or animal body and used in moving it from place to place ‖ this portion of an animal (or part of it) as food, *a leg of lamb* ‖ a support for an object raised above the ground ‖ the part of a garment which covers a human leg ‖ one section of a V-shaped instrument, e.g. a pair of compasses ‖ (*math.*) a side of a triangle other than the base or hypotenuse ‖ one section or stage of a journey, a relay race etc. ‖ one of several games or events going to make up a competition, *the first leg of the trophy* ‖ (*naut.*) the course run by a sailing vessel on a single tack ‖ (*cricket*) the field to the left and rear of a right-handed batsman **not to have a leg to stand on** to lack any rational support **on one's last legs** at the end of one's endurance **on its last legs** hardly stable or useful any longer **to find one's legs** to recover one's ability to stand and walk (after illness or at sea) **to give (someone) a leg up** to help (someone) to climb up **to pull (someone's) leg** to make a fool of (someone) by making him believe what is not true **to set (someone) on his legs** to make (someone) physically well again, or reestablish (someone) in favorable circumstances **to stand on one's own legs** (*Br.*) to be independent **to stretch one's legs** to walk about, esp. after prolonged sitting 2. *v.i. pres. part.* **leg·ging** *past* and *past part.* **legged** (with 'it') to walk in a hurry or run [O.N. *leggr*, limb, leg]

leg·a·cy (légəsi:) *pl.* **leg·a·cies** *n.* money or property bequeathed in a will ‖ something resulting from and left behind by an action, event or person, *a legacy of hatred* [O.F. *legacie*, legateship]

le·gal (lí:g'l) *adj.* of or pertaining to law ‖ in agreement with, or as prescribed by, the law ‖ valid in law as distinct from equity ‖ (*theol.*) of or pertaining to the Law [fr. L. *legalis*]

legal age the age at which a person assumes complete legal rights and responsibilities by law

legal aid free counsel by a lawyer granted to a person who cannot pay legal fees in a court case

---

CONCISE PRONUNCIATION KEY: (**a**) æ, cat; ɑ, car; ɔ fawn; ei, snake. (**e**) e, hen; i:, sheep; iə, deer; ɛə, bear. (**i**) i, fish; ai, tiger; ə:, bird. (**o**) o, ox; au, cow; ou, goat; u, poor; ɔi, royal. (**u**) ʌ, duck; u, bull; u:, goose; ə, bacillus; ju:, cube. x, loch; θ, think; ð, bother; z, Zen; ʒ, corsage; dʒ, savage; ŋ, orangutang; j, yak; ʃ, fish; tʃ, fetch; 'l, rabble; 'n, redden. Complete pronunciation key appears inside front cover.

legal fiction an assumption conventionally allowed in law

legal holiday a day fixed by law as one on which no official business shall be done

le·gal·ism (líːgˈlizəm) *n.* close attention to, and precise obedience to, the stated requirements of the law, without regard to their intention (i.e. attention to the letter rather than to the spirit of the law) ‖ (*theol.*) the doctrine of strict adherence to the Law **Le·gal·ism** *n.* a political and philosophical doctrine of China (4th–3rd cc. B.C.) supporting government based on fixed legislation **lé·gal·ist** *n.* someone who practices legalism. **Le·gal·ist** *n.* someone who supported Legalism **le·gal·is·tic** *adj.* preoccupied with petty restrictions and red tape

le·gal·i·ty (liːgǽliti) *pl.* **le·gal·i·ties** *n.* accordance with the law ‖ (*theol.*) legalism ‖ (*pl.*) the requirements and procedure of the law, *the adoption was slowed down by legalities* [fr. F. *légalité*]

le·gal·ize (líːgˈlaiz) *pres. part.* **le·gal-iz·ing** *past* and *past part.* **le·gal·ized** *v.t.* to make legal

legal positivism concept of law as commands of authority without regard to moral considerations. The term was coined by N.L.A. Hart, *The Concept of Law* (1961) *Cf* LEGAL REALISM

legal realism approach to law as the interpretation of courts as to an individual's rights, without regard to moral considerations *Cf* LEGAL POSITIVISM

legal reserve the reserve of coin, bullion or other immediately available assets which a bank or insurance company is required by law to maintain to meet claims by depositors

legal separation a condition whereby a man and his wife live apart under a court arrangement but cannot remarry

legal tender currency which a tradesman or other creditor is bound by law to accept as payment

legal weight the weight of goods and their inner wrapping, excluding that of the container

leg·ate (légit) *n.* (*Roman Catholicism*) an ecclesiastic appointed by the pope to represent him and vested with his authority in temporal matters ‖ (*Rom. hist.*) a lieutenant attached to a general, or deputy attached to a provincial governor ‖ (*Rom. hist.*) a provincial governor of the Roman Empire [O.F. *legat*]

leg·ate (ligéit) *pres. part.* **le·gat·ing** *past* and *past part.* **le·gat·ed** *v.t.* (*law*) to bequeath **leg·a·tee** (legətíː) *n.* (*law*) someone to whom a legacy is due, or who receives a legacy [fr. L. *legare* (*legatus*), to bequeath]

leg·ate·ship (légitʃip) *n.* the office and authority of a legate

leg·a·tine (légətain, légətin) *adj.* of or pertaining to a legate

leg·a·tion (ligéiʃən) *n.* the official residence and office of a diplomatic representative of lower status than an ambassador (cf. EMBASSY) ‖ the representative and his staff ‖ a diplomatic mission ‖ legateship [fr. L. *legatio* (*legationis*)]

le·ga·to (ləgátou) **1.** *adj.* (*mus.*) connected, without breaks between the notes **2.** *adv.* smoothly and continuously (cf. STACCATO) [Ital.]

le·ga·tor (ligéitər, légətɔːr) *n.* someone who bequeaths ‖ a testator **leg·a·to·ri·al** (legətɔ́ːriəl, legətóuriːəl) *adj.* [L.]

leg before wicket (*abbr.* l.b.w.) (*cricket*) the stopping by the batsman's leg of a ball which would otherwise, in the umpire's opinion, have hit his wicket

leg bye (*cricket*) a run scored for a ball that has passed the wicket keeper after touching the batsman's body

leg·end (lédʒənd) *n.* a story, handed down from the past, which lacks accurate historical evidence but has been, and may still be, popularly accepted as true ‖ such stories ‖ (*hist.*) a story of the life of a saint ‖ (*hist.*) a collection of such stories ‖ an inscription, esp. on a coin or medal ‖ an explanation or comment beneath a photograph or cartoon, e.g. in a newspaper ‖ a key to a map etc. **leg·end·ar·y** (lédʒənderiː) *adj.* told of in legends [F. *légende* fr. M.L. *legenda*, what is read]

Le Gen·dre (ləʒádr), Adrien-Marie (1752–1833), French mathematician. He made important contributions to the theory of numbers and the theory of elliptic functions

Lé·ger (leiʒei), Fernand (1881–1955), French painter, who from 1910 took part in the cubist movement. He painted still lifes, figures and scenes typical of contemporary life, in a personal style marked by largeness of scale and

strong frank color laid on in unbroken areas. In evolving this he was inspired by the beauty of machines, with their basic geometric shapes and their complex but harmonious organization

leg·er·de·main (ledʒərdəméin) *n.* deception of the eye by quickness of the hand, esp. in conjuring [F. *léger de main*, light of hand]

legged (legd, légid) *adj.* (in combination) having legs of a specified number or type, *a scroll-legged table*

leg·gings (légiŋz) *pl. n.* a sturdy, protective outer covering for the legs, of various materials and lengths

leg·gy (légiː) *adj.* having long legs, esp. in comparison with the size of the body

Leg·horn (léghɔrn) *LIVORNO

leg·horn (léghɔrn) *n.* a straw of bearded wheat, cut while green, bleached and woven into hats ‖ such a hat **Leg·horn** (léghɔrn, légərn) a small hardy breed of domestic chicken [fr. straw orig. imported from *Leghorn*]

leg·i·bil·i·ty (ledʒəbíliː) *n.* the quality of being legible

leg·i·ble (lédʒəbˈl) *adj.* (of handwriting, inscriptions etc.) able to be read **lég·i·bly** *adv.* [fr. L.L. *legibilis*]

le·gion (líːdʒən) *n.* (*Rom. hist.*) a division of the Roman army, of 3,000–6,000 foot soldiers, often with additional cavalry, divided into 10 cohorts. During the republic it was commanded by a military tribune, and under the empire by a legionary legate ‖ a great number, *legions of ants* [O.F.]

le·gion·ar·y (líːdʒəneriː) **1.** *adj.* of, belonging to or constituting a legion **2.** *pl.* **le·gion·ar·ies** *n.* a soldier of the legion [fr. L. *legionarius*]

le·gion·naire (liːdʒənéər) *n.* a member of a legion, e.g. the foreign legion

Legionnaire's disease (*med.*) a form of pneumonia affecting the kidneys, liver, intestines, and nerves. It was first recognized at a 1976 convention of the American Legion in Philadelphia, Pa.

Legion of Honor, *Br.* **Legion of Honour** the French *Légion d'honneur*, an order of distinction for civil or military service instituted by Napoleon in 1802, comprising five classes

leg·is·late (lédʒisleit) *pres. part.* **leg·is·lat·ing** *past* and *past part.* **leg·is·lat·ed** *v.i.* to make laws ‖ *v.t.* to effect or cause to become by making laws [after LEGISLATION and LEGISLATOR]

leg·is·la·tion (ledʒisléiʃən) *n.* the process of legislating ‖ a law or body of laws enacted ‖ a law, bill etc. under consideration by a legislative body [fr. L.L. *legis latio* (*legis lationis*) fr. *lex* (*legis*), law+*latio*, proposing]

leg·is·la·tive (lédʒisleitiv) **1.** *adj.* empowered to legislate ‖ of or effected by legislation ‖ of a legislature **2.** *n.* a legislature [after LEGISLATION and LEGISLATOR]

leg·is·la·tor (lédʒisleitər) *n.* someone who makes laws, esp. a member of a legislative body [L.]

leg·is·la·ture (lédʒisleitʃər) *n.* the body empowered to make, amend or repeal laws for a nation or unit of a nation. In democratic countries, it usually consists of two chambers, one or both elected by popular suffrage [after LEGISLATOR]

le·git·i·ma·cy (lidʒítəməsiː) *n.* the quality or state of being legitimate

le·git·i·mate 1. (lidʒítimit) *adj.* born of a legally recognized marriage ‖ in accord with the provisions of law, *a legitimate claim* ‖ in accord with accepted rules and procedures, *legitimate expenses* ‖ in accord with rules of hereditary right, *legitimate king* ‖ in accord with the laws of logic, admissible, *a legitimate argument* ‖ (of drama or the theater) excluding farce, revue, musical comedy etc. ‖ (of a play) of a category excluding farce, revue, musical comedy etc. **2.** (lidʒítimeit) *v.t. pres. part.* **le·git·i·mat·ing** *past* and *past part.* **le·git·i·mat·ed** *v.t.* to make legitimate ‖ to establish as legitimately born ‖ to justify **le·git·i·ma·tize** (lidʒitimitaiz) *pres. part.* **le·git·i·ma·tiz·ing** *past* and *past part.* **le·git·i·ma·tized** *v.t.* to legitimate [fr. M.L. *legitimare* (*legitimatus*), to declare legal]

le·git·i·mism (ldʒítəmjzəm) *n.* the political view advocating the return of a deposed dynasty whose claim is based on direct descent [fr. F. *légitimisme*]

le·git·i·mist (lidʒítimist) *n.* someone advocating legitimism **Le·git·i·mist** (*F. hist.*) a supporter of the senior branch of the Bourbons in their claim to the French throne [fr. F. *légitimiste*]

le·git·i·mize (lidʒítəmaiz) *pres. part.* **le·git·i·miz·ing** *past* and *past part.* **le·git·i·mized** *v.t.* to make legitimate [fr. L. *legitimus* adj.]

leg-of-mut·ton (legəvmʌt'n) *adj.* (of sleeves) shaped something like a leg of mutton

leg·pull (légpul) *n.* (esp. *Br.*, *pop.*) an attempted or successful act of making a fool of someone

Le·gui·a y Sal·ce·do (legíːaisalsédo), Augusto Bernardino (1863–1932), Peruvian president (1908–12) who regained (1919) the presidency by a coup d'état. The harshness of his regime resulted in the creation of the reformist APRA party. In 1930 he was overthrown and imprisoned for malfeasance in office

le·gume (légjuːm) *n.* a dry dehiscent one-celled fruit, which splits along the suture of the single carpel, a pod (e.g. pea, bean) ‖ a plant having such fruits ‖ an edible seed of such a plant [F. *légume*]

le·gu·mi·nous (ləgjúːmənəs) *adj.* of, like or belonging to legumes [fr. L. *legumen* (*leguminis*), legume]

Le·har (léihar), Franz (1870–1948), Hungarian composer of operettas, including 'The Merry Widow' (1905)

Le Ha·vre (ləævr) a port (pop. 198,700, with agglom. 255,000) of Seine-Maritime, France, at the mouth of the Seine, handling most of the traffic with North America: shipbuilding, mechanical engineering, petroleum products, food processing

lehr, leer (liər) *n.* an annealing furnace for glass [G.=model, pattern]

lei (lei) *n.* a circlet of flowers, leaves etc. [Hawaiian]

Leib·niz (láibnits, láipnits), Baron Gottfried Wilhelm von (1646–1716), German philosopher and mathematician. In line with his philosophical optimism (the belief that nature is fundamentally harmonious and good), he supposed the world to be formed from self-existent substances (monads), themselves in mutual harmony and animated by a force emanating ultimately from the divine will. Leibniz developed the theory of calculus (1675–6) simultaneously with Newton

Leices·ter (léstər), Robert Dudley, earl of (c. 1532–88), English courtier, a favorite of Elizabeth I. He was appointed to command the army at the time of the Spanish Armada (1588)

Leicester the county town (pop. 280,324) of Leicestershire, England, a county borough. Industries: hosiery, shoes, engineering. University (1957)

Leices·ter·shire (léstərʃiər) (*abbr.* Leics.) a county (area 832 sq. miles, pop. 842,577) in central England. County town: Leicester

Leiden *LEYDEN

Lei·dy (láidiː), Joseph (1823–91), U.S. anatomist and parasitologist. His pioneer research on U.S. fossil deposits laid the foundation of American paleontology. His 'Researches into the Comparative Anatomy of the Liver' (1848) was the first thorough study of the liver. His 'A Flora and Fauna Within Living Animals' (1853) was the first important study of the alimentary canal's parasites. His discovery of *Trichina spiralis* in pork led to the prevention of trichinosis in man, and his studies on protozoa made him a U.S. authority

Leif Ericson *ERICSON

Lein·ster (lénstər) the southeast province (area 7,580 sq. miles, pop. 1,498,140) of the Irish Republic, comprising counties Carlow, Dublin, Kilkenny, Laoighis, Longford, Louth, Meath, Offaly, Westmeath, Wexford, Wicklow ‖ (*hist.*) an ancient kingdom of E. Ireland

Leip·zig (láipsig) an industrial and commercial city (pop. 564,600) in Saxony, East Germany, known esp. for publishing and printing. Other industries: metals, machinery, textiles, optical and musical instruments. Its fairs (now industrial) have been famous since the 14th c. and it was a music center in the 18th and 19th cc. The 2nd world war destroyed many old buildings. University (1409) ‖ the district (area 1,091 sq. miles, pop. 1,510,000) which includes it

Leipzig, Battle of the Battle of the Nations

Leis·ler (láislər), Jacob (1640–91), American political agitator. After the Glorious Revolution he seized (1689) the government of the colony of New York and assumed the title of lieutenant governor, and summoned (1690) the first American intercolonial congress. Refusing to relinquish his command to an appointee of the Crown, he was convicted (1691) of treason and hanged

leis·ter (líːstər) **1.** *n.* a fishing spear with three or more prongs **2.** *v.t.* to spear (fish) with this [fr. O.N. *liöster*]

lei·sure (líːʒər, léʒər) **1.** *n.* time when one is free from the need to do any work **at leisure** not working or busy ‖ without hurrying **at one's leisure** when convenient and without any compulsion to hurry **2.** *adj.* free from work, *leisure time* ‖ leisured **léi·sured** *adj.* having plenty of leisure, *the leisured classes* [M.E. *leiser* fr. O. F. *leisir*]

lei·sure·li·ness (líːʒərliːnis, léʒərliːnis) *n.* the state or quality of being leisurely

lei·sure·ly (líːʒərliː, léʒərliː) **1.** *adj.* unhurried **2.** *adv.* in an unhurried manner

leisure suit an informal man's suit including jacket and matching trousers, usu. of denim

Leith (liːθ) the port of Edinburgh, Scotland: shipbuilding

leit·mo·tiv, leit·mo·tif (láitmoutiːf) *n.* a recurrent musical phrase or short theme associated with a person, situation or idea, used esp. by Wagner [G.=leading motive]

Lei·trim (líːtrim) an inland county (area 589 sq. miles, pop. 28,360) of Connacht, Irish Republic. County seat: Carrick-on-Shannon

Leix *LAOIGHIS

lek (lek) *n.* the standard monetary unit of Albania, consisting of 100 quintars ‖ a coin worth this [Albanian]

lek·var (lékvɑr) *n.* a prune jam used as filling in Hungarian pastry

Le·land, Ley·land (líːlənd), John (c. 1506–52), English antiquary. He described his tour around England in search of antiquities (1536–42) in notes later edited as 'The Itinerary of John Leland the Antiquary' (1710), one of the earliest topographical accounts of England

Le·ly (líːliː), Sir Peter (1618–80), English painter, born in Germany. Succeeding Van Dyck in royal favor, he painted Charles I, Cromwell, Charles II and the aristocrats and beauties of the Cavalier courts

LEM (*astronautics abbr.*) for lunar excursion module

Lé·man, Lac (líːmən) *GENEVA, LAKE OF

Le Mans (ləmɑ̃) a city (pop. 145,976) of Sarthe, N.W. France, the old capital of Maine. It is the site of an annual automobile race. Industries: automobiles, agricultural machinery, textiles, food. Cathedral (12th and 13th cc.)

Le·may (ləméi), Curtis Emerson (1906–), U.S. air force general. In the 2nd world war he developed advanced bomber tactics. He served (1961–5) as chief of staff of the U.S. air force and was (1968) the vice-presidential nominee under George Wallace

Lem·berg (lémbəɾg, lémberx) *LVOV

lem·ma (lémə) *pl.* **lem·mas, lem·ma·ta** (lémətə) *n.* (*bot.*) the lower bract enclosing the flower in grasses [Gk=husk fr. *lepein*, to peel]

lemma *pl.* **lem·mas, lem·ma·ta** (lémətə) *n.* (*math.*) a subsidiary theorem, proved in order to be used in proving the main theorem ‖ (*logic*) a subsidiary proposition, esp. drawn from another body of thought ‖ a brief heading to a scholarly annotation ‖ a headword in a glossary [Gk *lèmma*, something assumed]

lem·ming (lémin) *n.* a member of *Lemmus* or *Dicrostonyx*, fam. *Muridae*, genera of small (4–5 ins) rodents inhabiting mainly Scandinavia, Siberia and northern North America. A European species, *L. lemmus*, is very prolific, and periodically hordes migrate towards (and often into) the sea, moving chiefly at night and destroying all vegetation [Norw.]

Lem·nos (lémnɒs) a hilly, fertile Greek island (area 184 sq. miles, pop. 17,789) in the N. Aegean

lem·on (lémən) *n. Citrus limon*, fam. *Rutaceae*, a tree, probably native to S.E. Asia, that is widely cultivated in Mediterranean countries and the southern U.S.A. ‖ its yellow oval fruit, having a thick rind and terminal nipple, the acid juice of which is used as a drink and in flavoring while the rind is a source of pectin and an essential oil ‖ the color of the ripe fruit [fr. F. *limon*]

lem·on·ade (ləmənéid) *n.* a drink made by mixing lemon juice and sugar with water ‖ a commercially made, lemon-flavored soft drink [fr. F. *limonade*]

lemon curd a preparation of lemon, sugar, butter and eggs, used as a filling in tarts and cakes

Lemon law provision in some laws requiring manufacturer to provide a full refund on purchases of over $5 where repair cannot be made within a reasonable period of use

lemon sole *Sole lascaris*, fam. *Soleidae*, a European flatfish

lemon squeezer (*Br.*) a reamer (device for extracting juice)

Le Moyne (ləmwæn), Jean Baptiste *BIENVILLE

Le Moyne d'I·ber·ville (ləmwændiːberviːl), Pierre (1661–1706), French sailor and explorer. He founded (1699) the colony of Louisiana and was appointed (1704) its first governor

lem·pi·ra (lempíərə) *n.* the basic monetary unit of Honduras, consisting of 100 centavos ‖ a note or coin worth this [after *Lempira* (1497–1537), an Indian chief of Honduras]

le·mur (líːmər) *n.* a member of *Lemuroidea*, a superfamily of nocturnal tree-dwelling mammals, allied to the monkey but having long snouts and bushy tails. They are found chiefly in the island of Madagascar **lem·u·rine** (lémjuriːn, lémjurain), **lém·u·roid** *adjs* [fr. L. *lemures*, night spirits]

Le·na (ljéinə) a river in Siberia, U.S.S.R., navigable for 2,000 of its 3,000 miles. It rises near Lake Baikal and ends in a wide delta on the Arctic Ocean

Le Nain (lənɛ̃) Louis (1593–1648), Antoine (1588–1648), and Mathieu (1607–77), French painters, brothers. No initials appear on their works, which include genre painting as well as religious and mythological subjects, and ascriptions are therefore doubtful

Le·nau (léinau), Nikolaus (Nikolaus Franz Niembsch Edler von Strehlenau, 1802–50), Hungarian lyric poet, who wrote mostly in German. His long dramatic poems include 'Faust' (1836) and 'Savonarola' (1837)

lend (lend) *pres. part.* **lend·ing** *past* and *past part.* **lent** (lent) *v.t.* to place in the temporary possession of another (for his use, enjoyment etc.) with the expectation of resuming possession later ‖ to loan (money) at interest ‖ to let out (books) for a fee ‖ to transfer (someone) to another job or service temporarily ‖ (*fig.*) to furnish, supply, *to lend dignity to a scene* ‖ *v.i.* to make a loan or loans **to lend a hand** to assist **to lend itself to** to be serviceable or well suited for, *this poem lends itself to declamation* **to lend oneself to** to allow oneself to participate in, *he would not lend himself to anything dishonorable* [O.E. *lǣnan*]

lending library a library where books are lent out, sometimes for a fee

lend-lease (léndliːs) *n.* (*hist.*) the arrangement announced (1941) by F. D. Roosevelt, in which the U.S.A. undertook to supply weapons and equipment to countries fighting the Axis. In return, the U.S.A. obtained the right to use certain Allied bases. The total U.S. contribution amounted to more than $50,000,000,000 before the scheme ended in 1945. Some countries made partial repayments in cash, others by goods and services

length (leŋθ, leŋkθ) *n.* linear extent in space from end to end measured in certain arbitrary units, *the length of a football field* ‖ the longer of the two linear dimensions of a surface or plane or the longest of the three linear dimensions of a solid ‖ extent in time from beginning to end ‖ a piece of something longer than it is wide, *two lengths of glass tubing* ‖ the length of a horse, boat etc., used as a unit in stating the distance between competitors in a race, *to win by two lengths* ‖ the quantity of a vowel or syllable ‖ (*cricket*) the distance from the bowler's wicket at which the ball pitches **at length** at last, after a long time ‖ in detail, taking a long time, *to explain at length* **full length, at full length** with the body stretched out **to go to any length** (or **lengths**) to set no limits to what one is prepared to do **to go to great length** (or **lengths**) to set hardly any limits on what one is prepared to do **to go to the length of** to go so far as to, *she wouldn't go to the length of actually calling him a liar* **to keep at arm's length** to avoid too intimate a contact with [O.E. *lengthu*]

length·en (léŋθən, léŋkθən) *v.i.* to become longer ‖ *v.t.* to cause (something) to become longer

length·i·ly (léŋθiliː, léŋkθiliː) *adv.* in a lengthy manner

length·i·ness (léŋθiːnis, léŋkθiːnis) *n.* the quality or state of being lengthy

length of stay the length of an inpatient's stay in a hospital or other health facility, a measure of use of health facilities, reported as an average number of days spent in a facility per admission or discharge. *abbr.* **LOS**

length·ways (léŋθweiz, léŋkθweiz) *adv.* lengthwise

length·wise (léŋθwaiz, léŋkθwaiz) **1.** *adv.* in the direction of the length **2.** *adj.* of, being or going in the direction of the length

length·y (léŋθiː, léŋkθiː) *comp.* **length·i·er** *superl.* **length·i·est** *adj.* unusually or excessively long, *a lengthy journey, a lengthy speech*

le·ni·ence (líːniːəns, líːnjəns) *n.* the quality of being lenient or an instance of this

le·ni·en·cy (líːniːənsiː, líːnjənsiː) *n.* lenience

le·ni·ent (líːniːənt, líːnjənt) *adj.* tolerant, disinclined to punish severely ‖ (of punishment, sentences etc.) mild, not as severe as the fault might justify [fr. L. *leniens* (*lenientis*) fr. *lenire*, to soften]

Len·in (lénin) (Vladimir Ilyich Ulyanov, 1870–1924), Russian Marxist revolutionary and writer. Of middle-class background, he studied law and, influenced by the works of Marx, became a revolutionary. In exile in Siberia (1897–1900) he wrote 'The Development of Capitalism in Russia' (1899), foreseeing a bourgeois revolution in Russia as the first step to the dictatorship of the proletariat. He became the leader of the left wing of the Social Democrats, known after 1903 as the Bolsheviks. After long quarrels with the Mensheviks and long periods abroad, he returned to Russia (1917) after the outbreak of the Russian Revolution. He overthrew Kerensky's government (Nov. 1917) and became head of the new government and virtual dictator (1917–24). After civil war (1918–21), Lenin stamped out opposition to the new regime, but was forced to modify his economic policy as a temporary concession to capitalism. Many of his ideas, esp. on the role of the party and the technique of revolution, have become accepted extensions of Marxism. His other published works include 'Imperialism, the Highest Stage of Capitalism' (1916) and 'The State and Revolution' (1917)

Lenin the second highest (23,386 ft) mountain of the U.S.S.R., in the Trans Alai, on the Tadzhikistan-Kirghizia border

Len·in·grad (léningræd) the second largest city and largest seaport (pop. 4,073,000) of the U.S.S.R., at the head of the Gulf of Finland, on the Neva delta. It was the capital of Russia (1713–1918) and is of great architectural and cultural importance. It is also a large industrial center: mechanical and electrical engineering (turbines), shipbuilding, chemicals, textiles, lumber and food processing. University (1819). Founded by Peter the Great as St Petersburg in 1703, it was renamed Petrograd in 1914. It was the center of the Russian Revolution of 1917. It was named Leningrad in 1924

le·nis (líːnis, léinis), **1.** *adj.* (*phon.*, of a consonant) pronounced with weak articulation **2.** *pl.* **le·nes** (líːniːz, léiniːz) *n.* (*phon.*) such a consonant [L.=soft]

len·i·tive (lénitiv) **1.** *adj.* soothing, relieving pain **2.** *n.* a palliative [fr. M.L. *lenitivus*]

len·i·ty (lénitiː) *n.* the quality or state of being lenient

Le Nôtre (lənoutr), André (1613–1700), French landscape gardener. He designed spacious formal gardens, e.g. at Versailles (1661) and the Tuileries, in Paris, making much use of light and water effects

lens (lenz) *pl.* **lens·es** *n.* a piece of glass, or other transparent refracting substance, with two opposite regular surfaces, of which at least one is curved, used in optical systems (a camera, a magnifying glass etc.) to converge or diverge light rays to form an image ‖ a combination of simple optical lenses ‖ a device used to focus or direct radiation other than light (e.g. a beam of electrons in an electron microscope) ‖ a transparent, almost spherical body behind the pupil of the eye, focusing light on to the retina ‖ a facet of a compound eye [fr. L. *lens* (*lentis*), lentil (fr. the shape)]

lens (*geol.*) deposit bound by curved converging surfaces in the shape of a convex lens

Lens, Battle of (lens) the last major battle (Aug. 20, 1648) of the Thirty Years' War. The French army, under Condé, defeated the Spanish army

Lent (lent) *n.* (in Roman Catholic and some other Western Christian Churches) the period of fasting and penitence during the 40 weekdays between Ash Wednesday and Easter Eve, recalling Christ's 40 days in the wilderness ‖ (in

Orthodox Eastern Churches) a longer period of similar character [O.E. *lencten*, spring]

lent *past* and *past part.* of LEND

Lent·en (léntən) *adj.* of, pertaining to, or used during, Lent [O.E. *lencten*, spring Lent]

len·ti·cel (léntisel) *n.* (*bot.*) a ventilating pore in the stems of woody plants [fr. Mod. L. *lenticella*]

len·tic·u·lar (lentíkjulər) *adj.* having both surfaces convex ‖ of or pertaining to a lens [fr. L.L. *lenticularis*]

len·til (léntil) *n. Lens esculenta*, fam. *Papilionaceae*, a small annual plant, widely cultivated in Europe and Asia, bearing short two-seeded pods. The seeds are eaten as a vegetable or made into a flour ‖ one of these seeds [F. *lentille*]

len·to (léntou) **1.** *adj.* (*mus.*) slow **2.** *adv.* (*mus.*) slowly [Ital.]

len·toid (léntɔid) *adj.* having the shape of a double convex lens [fr. L. *lens* (*lentis*), lentil]

l'en·voi (lénvɔi, lɑ̃vwœ) *ENVOY, ENVOI

Lenz (lents), Heinrich Friedrich Emil (1804–65), German physicist. He formulated Lenz's law (1834) on the direction of induced currents, and observed the relation between resistance and temperature

Lenz's law the law stating that when there is relative motion between a circuit and a magnetic field, the magnetic field due to the induced electric current opposes the motion [after H. F. E. *Lenz*]

Leo I (lí:ou), 'the Great' (c. 400–74), Byzantine emperor (457–74). A naval expedition which he sent against the Vandals in Africa was disastrously defeated (468)

Leo III 'the Isaurian' (c. 680–740), Byzantine emperor (717–40). He drove back the Arabs (717–18), and undertook legal, administrative and military reforms. His attack on image worship began the Iconoclast movement

Le·o I St, 'the Great' (c. 400–61), pope (440–61). He helped to establish the supremacy of the Roman see, and he persuaded Attila to retire from Rome (452). Feast: Roman Catholic Church, Apr. 11, Orthodox Church, Feb. 18

Leo III, St (*d.* 816), pope (795–816). He crowned Charlemagne (800). Feast: June 12

Leo IX, St (1002–54), pope (1049–54). He enforced clerical discipline, and was at war with the Normans in S. Italy. The separation of Eastern and Western Churches began during his pontificate. Feast: Apr. 19

Leo X (Giovanni de' Medici, 1475–1521), pope (1513–21). He was a munificent patron of Renaissance art, science and letters. He failed to appreciate the importance of the beginnings of the Reformation

Leo XIII (1810–1903), pope (1878–1903). In his encyclical letters, notably 'Rerum novarum' (1891), he reinvigorated Catholic teaching on social matters and urged the special need for Catholic action among the working class

Leo a northern constellation ‖ the fifth sign of the zodiac, represented as a lion [L.=lion]

Le·ón (leión), Luis de (1527–91), Spanish ecclesiastic and lyric poet. His odes (published 1631) treat spiritual subjects in a classical manner

León a city (pop. 557,000) of central Mexico at 5,600 ft. Crafts: leather, gold, and silver work. Industries: textiles, cement

León the second largest city (pop. 61,649) of Nicaragua, in the northwest. Spanish cathedral (18th c.). National university (1813)

León a region of N.W. Spain on the central tableland, forming León, Zamora and Salamanca provinces, and the western parts of Valladolid and Palencia. Products: coal, ores and lumber in the north (Cantabrian Mtns, in León and Palencia), cereals, cattle, vines. Historic capital: León. The kingdom of León was united with Asturias (10th c.) and with Castile (1037). It was independent (1065–72 and 1157–1230) but was finally united to Castile (1230)

León a province (area 5,936 sq. miles, pop. 1,141,700) of Spain, the northern part of historic León ‖ its capital (pop. 105,235), founded by the Romans. Gothic cathedral (13th–14th cc.)

Le·o·nar·do da Vin·ci (lị:ənárdoudəvínʃi:, leiənárdoudəvíntʃi:) (1452–1519), Italian painter of the Florentine school, and universal genius: sculptor, painter, military engineer, musician etc. His paintings include 'The Virgin of the Rocks' (of which the 1483–6 version is in Paris and that of c. 1493 in London), 'La Gioconda' or ('Mona Lisa', c. 1503), and 'The Last Supper' (c. 1495–8). In his mastery of light and

shadow he summed up and solved the predominant artistic problem of the 15th c., transfiguring the subject by a diffused light that creates a new, more poetic, more subtly suggestive reality. In his portrayal of individual personality, and in the compact, unified organization of his pictures, he ushered in the art of the High Renaissance. His drawings mingle scientific precision with intense imaginative power. His writings are copious and often of great literary quality. His notebooks reveal the immense range and power of his intellect. He studied anatomy, he thought of armored tanks and a flying machine, he worked out a complete cosmology, he concerned himself with the mechanism of the gun. He lives not only in his masterpieces, the man himself exerts a perennial hold on the mind and imagination

Le·on·ca·val·lo (lẹɔnkɑválla), Ruggiero (1858–1919), Italian composer, best known for his opera 'I Pagliacci' (1892)

le·o·ne (li:óuni) *pl.* **le·o·nes** (li:óuni:z) *n.* the principal unit of currency of Sierra Leone ‖ a note of the value of one leone

Le·o·ni (leóni:), Raúl (1905–), Venezuelan lawyer, politician, and president (1964–9)

Le·o·nid (lí:ənəd) *pl.* **Leonids** or **Leonides** (li:ónidi:z) *n.* (*astron.*) a comet visible in mid-November in area surrounding constellation Leo

Le·on·i·das (li:ónidəs) (*d.* 480 B.C.), king of Sparta (c. 490–480 B.C.). At the head of 300 Spartans and 700 Thespians he fought to the death against the Persians at Thermopylae

le·o·nine (lí:ənain) *adj.* of or like a lion, *a leonine appearance* [fr. L. *leoninus*]

leop·ard (lépərd) *n. Felis pardus*, fam. *Felidae*, a large, fierce, carnivorous mammal native to Africa and S. Asia, usually having a fawn to reddish-buff coat marked with irregular black spots ‖ any of various similar felines, e.g. the snow leopard, the cheetah ‖ the fur of a leopard ‖ (*heraldry*) a lion passant guardant [O.F. fr. L.L. fr. Gk *leopardos* fr. *leōn*, lion+*pardos*, pard (older name for leopard)]

Le·o·par·di (lị:əpárdi:, lẹɔpárdi:), Count Giacomo (1798–1837), Italian lyric poet, author of 'I Canti' (1824–35) and of works in prose and letters. A passionate melancholy informs the poems, which have universal Romantic themes, and which are supremely musical, noble in sentiment, at once clear and dense in expression, and formally of classical perfection

Le·o·pold I (lí:əpould) (1640–1705), Holy Roman Emperor (1658–1705), king of Hungary (1655–1705) and of Bohemia (1656–1705), son of Ferdinand III. Most of his reign was spent in conflict with Louis XIV of France in the 3rd Dutch War (1672–8 and again 1682–4). He joined (1689) the Grand Alliance against France, concluded the Treaty of Ryswick (1697), but resumed (1701) the struggle with Louis XIV in the War of the Spanish Succession

Leopold II (1747–92), Holy Roman Emperor (1790–2), king of Bohemia and Hungary (1790–2), son of Francis I. In support of his sister Marie-Antoinette he issued the Declaration of Pillnitz (1791), and made a military alliance with Prussia (1792)

Leopold I (1790–1865), king of the Belgians (1831–65). His rule helped to stabilize the new state of Belgium

Leopold II (1835–1909), king of the Belgians (1865–1909), son of Leopold I. His policies made Belgium an industrial and colonial power. He acquired personal control (1885) over the Congo Free State which later (1908) became a Belgian colony

Leopold III (1901–83), king of the Belgians (1934–51), son of Albert I. His unconditional surrender (1940) to Nazi Germany led to accusations of treason and to his enforced abdication (1951) in favor of his son Baudouin

Le·o·pold·ville (lí:əpouldvil) *KINSHASA

le·o·tard (lí:ətard) *n.* a skintight garment for the torso worn e.g. by dancers and acrobats [after Jules *Léotard*, 19th-c. F. aerial gymnast]

Le·pan·to, Battle of (lipǽntou) a decisive sea battle (1571) off Greece, in which Spain, Venice and the Vatican, under the command of Don John of Austria, broke Ottoman seapower

Lep·cha (léptʃə) *pl.* **Lep·cha, Lep·chas** *n.* a Mongoloid people of Sikkim ‖ a member of this people ‖ their Tibeto-Burman language

lep·er (lépər) *n.* a person suffering from leprosy ‖ (*rhet.*) a social outcast [M.E. *lepre*, leprosy fr. O.F. fr. L. fr. Gk]

lep·i·dop·ter·an (lẹpidɔ́ptərən) **1.** *n.* a member of *Lepidoptera*, an order of insects including moths and butterflies, having four wings covered with minute scales, often brightly colored. The order comprises more than 100,000 species, almost universally distributed. They undergo a complete metamorphosis, being hatched from eggs as caterpillars and passing though an inert chrysalis stage before emerging as full-grown winged insects **2.** *adj.* pertaining to lepidopterans **lep·i·dóp·ter·ist** *n.* a specialist in lepidopterans **lep·i·dóp·ter·on** *n.* **lep·i·dóp·ter·ous** *adj.* [fr. Mod. L. *Lepidoptera* fr. Gk *lepis* (*lepidos*), a scale+*pteron*, wing]

lep·i·do·si·ren (lẹpidousáirən) *n.* a member of *Lepidosiren* or *Protopterus*, fam. *Lepidosirenidae*, genera of South Ameridan dipnoans [fr. Gk *lepis* (*lepidos*), scale+SIREN]

Lep·i·dus (lépidəs), Marcus Aemilius (*d.* 13 B.C.), Roman statesman. He formed (43 B.C.) the 2nd Triumvirate with Mark Antony and Octavian, but was ousted by them (36 B.C.)

lep·re·chaun (léprikɔn, léprikon) *n.* (*Ir. mythol.*) a small mischievous male sprite [fr. O. Ir. *luchorpan* fr. *lu*, little+*corp*, body]

lep·ro·sy (léprəsi) *n.* a chronic infective disease due to the leprosy bacillus *Mycobacterium leprae*. It chiefly affects the skin, causing discolored patches, nodules and ulcers, and the nerves, causing loss of sensory perception and partial paralysis in the limbs, and sometimes deformity of the digits **lép·rous** *adj.* [O.F. *leprosie*]

lep·ton (léptən) *n.* (*phys.*) one of a group of four known fundamental particles, including the electron, muon and two neutrinos, which have small or zero rest mass, spin quantum number $\frac{1}{2}$, and which (except for the muon) are stable particles [Mod. L. fr. Gk *leptos*, husked+*-on*, fundamental particle]

lep·to·quark (léptəkwɔrk) *n.* (*particle phys.*) hypothetical particle of matter conceived by Dr. Andrei Dmitrevich Sakharov

Ler·do de Te·ja·da (lérðɔðetehɑ́ða), Sebastian (1825–89), president of Mexico (1872–7). Opposed by the Roman Catholic Church for his anticlerical position, by the progressives for the halfheartedness of his reform program, and by local leaders for his centralization of government, he was overthrown in an insurrection led by Porfirio Díaz

Lé·ri·da (léri:ða) a province (area (4,690 sq. miles, pop. 355,451) in Catalonia, N.E. Spain ‖ its capital (pop. 109,573), ancient Ilerda

Ler·ma (lérma), Francisco Gómez de Sandoval y Rojas, duque de (c. 1552–1625), Spanish statesman. As prime minister and favorite of Philip III (1598– 1618), he led a corrupt administration and amassed a fortune

Lerma River *SANTIAGO

Ler·mon·tov (lérmʌntʌf), Mikhail Yuriyevich (1814–41), Russian novelist and poet, best known for his novel 'A Hero of our Times' (1840)

Ler·na (lá:rnə) a marsh and stream in ancient Argolis where Hercules killed the many-headed hydra (*HERACLES)

Le·ros (lí:ros) an island (area 21 sq. miles, pop. 7,050) of the Dodecanese

Le·sage (ləsæʒ), Alain-René (1668–1747), French novelist, author of the picaresque novel 'Gil Blas de Santillane' (1715–35)

Lesage, Jean (1912–), French-Canadian politician, leader (1958) of Quebec's Liberal party, premier of Quebec (1960–6). He advanced the cause of French-Canadian nationalism and strove to win for Quebec the maximum possible autonomy within Canada

Les·bi·an (lézbi:ən) **1.** *adj.* pertaining to Lesbos ‖ relating to homosexuality in women **2.** *n.* a woman homosexual **Lés·bi·an·ism** *n.* [fr. L. *Lesbius* after LESBOS, where Sappho was born]

Les·bos (lézbɒs) (Gk Lesvos, formerly Mytilene) a mountainous Greek island (area 676 sq. miles, pop. 140,000) off the coast of Turkey: olive oil, cereals, citrus fruit. Capital: Mytilene (pop. 23,426), a port: tourism

lese maj·es·ty (li:zmǽdʒisti:) *n.* (*law*) an offense against the dignity of the sovereign power or its representative, esp. treason [fr. F. *lèse-majesté*]

le·sion (lí:ʒən) *n.* a change in the structure of a tissue or an organ due to injury or disease, usually resulting in impairment of normal function ‖ an injury [F. *lésion*]

Les·lie (lésli:, *Br.* lézli), Sir John (1766–1832), Scottish physicist. He invented the differential thermometer

---

Le·so·tho (lesóutou) (formerly Basutoland) a state (area 11,716 sq. miles, pop. 1,407,000) in Africa, an enclave in the Republic of South Africa. Capital: Maseru. Bantu languages are spoken. The land (5,000–11,000 ft) is 12% arable and supports sheep, goats and cattle. Rainfall: 30 ins. Temperature: 10°–95°F. Crops: corn, wheat, sorghum, vegetables. Exports: labor (60,000 workers per year to South Africa), wool, mohair. Imports: blankets, clothing, plows, household goods. University (1964). Currency: South African rand. HISTORY. By 1800 the aboriginals had been driven out by various tribes, which then united under Moshesh, a Basuto king. After a series of wars (1835–67) between the Basuto and the Boers, the territory came under British protection (1868) as Basutoland. The country was a British High Commission Territory after 1884. Constitutional reforms were introduced in 1960, elections were held (1965) and, as Lesotho, the country became an independent state within the Commonwealth (Oct. 4, 1966). It joined the U.N. (1966). Chief Jonathan, the prime minister, suspended (Jan. 1970) the constitution. The king went into exile for 8 months and on return swore to preserve the monarchy and keep it out of politics, but Prime Minister Jonathan declared a state of emergency, suspended the constitution and took away all the king's political authority. Lesotho became a limited monarchy

less (les) alt. *comp.* of LITTLE, cf. LESSER ‖ **1.** *adj.* smaller in size, degree, extent etc., *the less time it takes the better* ‖ not so much, *he has less strength than I have* ‖ lower in rank, *nobody less than a bishop will do for the wedding* **in less than no time** very quickly **no less than** as much as, *he paid no less than $10,000 for it* ‖ as many as, *no less than three people have offered to buy it* **nothing less** (with 'than') used to emphasize a following noun or adjective, *it was nothing less than criminal* **something** (or **somewhat**) **less than** far from being, *the remark was something less than polite* **2.** *prep.* made smaller by, *ten seven is three* **3.** *adv.* in or to a smaller degree or extent, *my head aches less now* **4.** *n.* the smaller in amount, size, degree, number, importance, *of the two evils it is the less* [O.E. *lœssa* adj., *lœs* adv.]

-less *suffix*, without, free from, lacking, as in, 'luckless' [fr. O.E. *léas*, devoid (of), free (from)]

LESS (*acronym*) least-cost estimating and scheduling system, management system designed by International Business Machines Corporation

less developed country a nation without significant economic growth, very low per capita income, and low literacy rate; so classified by the United Nations in 1971. *abbr.* **LDC**

les·see (lesí:) *n.* someone who is granted a lease [A.F.]

less·en (lés'n) *v.t.* to cause to become less ‖ *v.i.* to become less

Les·seps (leseps), Ferdinand Marie, vicomte de (1805–94), French engineer. He built the Suez Canal (1854–69). His later project (1876) for a Canal across the Isthmus of Panama ended in failure and financial scandal

less·er (lésər) alt. *comp.* of LITTLE, cf. less ‖ *adj.* smaller in size, amount, quality, importance etc., *choose the lesser of two risks* [LESS]

Lesser Antilles *ANTILLES

Les·sing (lésiŋ), Gotthold Ephraim (1729–81), German dramatist and critic, whose dramatic works include 'Minna von Barnhelm' (1767) and 'Nathan der Weise' (1778–9). His 'Laokoon' (1766) is a classic of modern aesthetics

les·son (lés'n) *n.* that which is taught to a pupil by a teacher, esp. during a given period of time ‖ this period of time ‖ something to be learned ‖ (*pl.*) a series of sessions of instruction, *lessons in Spanish* ‖ one unit in a series of sessions of instruction ‖ something, usually unpleasant, which serves as a warning or example, *his punishment has been a lesson to him* ‖ (*eccles.*) a part of the Bible read aloud in a service [fr. O.F. *lecon*]

les·sor (lésɔr, lesɔ́r) *n.* someone who grants a lease [A.F.]

lest (lest) *conj.* (relating an act to its negative result) in order that... not, *they kept quiet lest they should wake him* ‖ (relating a feeling of fear, anxiety etc. to an undesired but possible event) that, *he was anxious lest they might have missed the train* [O.E. *thy̆ lœs the*, by which the less]

Lesz·czyn·ski (leʃtʃínski:) a Polish noble family, whose most famous members were Stanislaus I and his daughter Marie Leszczynska

let (let) **1.** *v. pres. part.* **let·ting** past and past part. **let** *v.t.* to permit to ‖ (esp. *Br.*, often with 'out') to put (property, house, land etc.) at the temporary disposal of someone in return for rent ‖ (often with 'out') to portion out (work) ‖ (often with 'out') to assign (a contract) ‖ used as an auxiliary in the imperative 1st and 3rd persons in commands, *let x be the unknown quantity* or permissions, *let him do his worst* or exhortations, *let us try to work a little harder* ‖ *v.i.* (esp. *Br.*, often with 'out') to be rented or leased **let alone** without mentioning, *he can hardly pay the fees, let alone the extras* **to let alone, let be** to leave undisturbed **to let blood** to cause to bleed **to let down** to lower ‖ to cause (someone) disappointment by failing to do what was expected ‖ to lengthen (a skirt, hem etc.) **to let (someone) down gently** to soften the blow of a reproof, humiliation or disappointment by administering it mildly to (someone) **to let fall** to drop ‖ to mention as if by accident, *to let fall a hint in conversation* ‖ (*math.*) to drop (a perpendicular) **to let fly** to shoot or hurl ‖ to become violent in action or speech, *he let fly against what he considered to be an injustice* **to let go** to cease to hold on to ‖ to set free or allow to leave ‖ (*naut.*) to drop anchor **to let in** to insert into a surface ‖ to open the door to, admit **to let in for** to involve in, *to let oneself in for a lot of work* **to let in on** to make (someone) party to (a secret etc.) **to let into** to insert into a surface ‖ to admit, *to let (someone) into the secret* **to let (someone) know** to inform (someone) **to let loose** to free from restraint, release ‖ to speak harshly to, *he let loose at her* **to let off** to discharge (a firearm etc.) ‖ to set free without punishment or with a light punishment ‖ to release from the obligation of **to let on** to reveal a secret ‖ to pretend, *he let on that he was a police inspector* **to let oneself go** to throw off restraints **to let out** to set at large after confinement ‖ to make (a garment) larger or (a seam) smaller ‖ to reveal by accident **to let slip** to fail to take advantage of ‖ to reveal by accident **to let up** to relax one's efforts ‖ to become less, *the gale began to let up* **to let well enough** (*Br.* **well**) **alone** to refrain from interfering with things that are satisfactory **2.** *n.* (*Br.*) a letting for hire or rent, *to make a good let* [O.E. *lǣtan*]

let *n.* (*law*, only in) **without let or hindrance** without impediment ‖ (*lawn tennis, rackets* etc.) an obstruction of the ball, esp. contact with the top of the tennis net, necessitating a replay [fr. archaic *let* v., to hinder]

-let *suffix* added to nouns to express smallness or minor importance [fr. O.F. *-et, -ete*]

let·down (létdaun) *n.* a disappointment, esp. of confident expectations, or total failure to do what was relied on ‖ a relaxation or lowering of standards ‖ a drop in amount or volume

le·thal (lí:θəl) *adj.* causing or able to cause death [fr. L. *letalis, lethalis* fr. *letum, lethum*, death]

le·thar·gic (ləθárdʒik) *adj.* of, marked by or causing lethargy **le·thár·gi·cal·ly** *adv.* [fr. L. *lethargicus* fr. Gk]

leth·ar·gy (léθərdʒi:) *n.* the state of lacking energy and interest [fr. L. *lethargia* fr. Gk]

Le·the (lí:θi:) (*Gk mythol.*) a river in Hades, the water of which, when drunk, produced forgetfulness **Lé·the·an** *adj.* [L. fr. Gk *lēthē*, forgetfulness]

let's (lets) contr. of LET US in exhortations

Lett (let) *n.* a member of a people, closely related to the Lithuanians, living chiefly in Latvia

let·ter (létər) **1.** *n.* one of the printed or written symbols of an alphabet, used in representing speech sounds ‖ a written, printed or typed personal communication ‖ (often *pl.*) a document, written statement etc. constituting the authority for a particular action, status, privilege etc., *letter of advice, letters of marque* ‖ a printing type ‖ (*printing*) a font of type ‖ the stated terms and these only, *the letter of the law* ‖ (*pl.*) literature ‖ (*pl.*) scholarly study or knowledge, esp. of literature **to the letter** precisely and completely, *to obey instructions to the letter* **2.** *v.t.* to inscribe with letters ‖ to impress (letters) on a book cover or page [O.F. *lettre*]

letter bomb device contained in a letter that explodes when the letter is opened

letter box (esp. *Br.*) mail box

let·ter·card (létərkard) *n.* a card on which a letter may be written, and then folded once and sealed by its gummed edges, for mailing

let·tered (létərd) *adj.* marked with letters ‖ (*rhet.*) cultured ‖ (*rhet.*) learned, esp. in literature

let·ter·form (létərfɔrm) *n.* **1.** a lined sheet for guiding handwriting on letters **2.** the format or design of a letter

let·ter·head (létərhed) *n.* the heading (address etc.) printed at the top of writing paper ‖ (*commerce*) a piece of paper so printed

let·ter·ing (létəriŋ) *n.* the act of marking with letters ‖ such letters, esp. in regard to style or quality, as used in calligraphy

letter of advice a letter notifying the drawee of a bill of exchange that the bill has been issued

letter of credence (*internat. law*) a document accrediting a diplomat to a foreign power

letter of credit a letter addressed by a banker to an agent authorizing the agent to give credit, within stated limits, to the bearer named in the letter ‖ a letter from a banker to a client authorizing him to claim credit from the banker's agent

let·ter·per·fect (létərpə́:rfikt) *adj.* (of something memorized) perfect to the last detail ‖ (of a person) having completely memorized a text etc.

let·ter·press (létərpres) *n.* a method of direct printing from a raised, inked printing surface, as distinct from one using photographic negatives, jelly etc. ‖ (esp. *Br.*) the printed text of a publication as distinct from the illustrations in it

let·ter·set (létərset) *n.* a type of offset reproduction in which the image is taken from a letterpress plate

letters of administration a legal document authorizing a person to administer the estate of a deceased person

letters of marque (*hist.*) a state document authorizing a private citizen to seek reprisals against a foreign country or its citizens, esp. as a privateer [F. fr. Prov. *marca*, reprisal]

letters patent (*law*) a document issued by a government authorizing a person to exercise a right or privilege

letter stock (*securities*) corporate stock in a public corporation issued without SEC registration, usu. given for service or in a special transaction and subject to special restrictions in sale, releasable only by special letter from the SEC

Let·tic (létik) *adj.* Lettish

Let·tish (létiʃ) **1.** *adj.* of the Letts or the Latvians ‖ of the Latvian language **2.** *n.* the Latvian language

let·tre de ca·chet (letrdəkæʃei) *n.* (*F. hist.*) a private document issued (1560–1790) by the king, usually to command an arbitrary imprisonment or exile

let·tuce (létəs) *n.* a member of *Lactuca*, fam. *Compositae*, esp. *L. sativa*, a crisp-leaved, annual plant, widely cultivated in temperate regions and usually eaten raw in salads [M.E. *letuse*]

let·up (létʌp) *n.* a lessening of intensity or effort, respite

leu (leu) *pl.* **lei** (lei) *n.* the basic monetary unit of Rumania, consisting of 100 bani ‖ a coin or note of the value of one leu [Rumanian=lion]

leucaemia *LEUKEMIA

leucemia *LEUKEMIA

Leu·cip·pus of Miletus (lu:sípəs) (5th c. B.C.), Greek philosopher, originator of the atomist theory of matter

leu·co (lú:kou) *adj.* (*chem.*) white ‖ (*chem.*) colorless [fr. Gk *leukos*, white]

leucocyte *LEUKOCYTE

leucorrhoea *LEUKORRHEA

leu·co·tome (lú:kətoum) *n.* a narrow rotating blade used in lobotomies [fr. Gk *leukos*, white+*tomē*, cutting]

leu·cot·o·my (lu:kɔ́təmi:) *pl.* **leu·cot·o·mies** *n.* a lobotomy [fr. Gk *leukos*, white+*tomē*, cutting]

Leuc·tra, Battle of (lú:ktrə) a battle (371 B.C.) in which the Thebans under Epaminondas defeated the Spartans and gained power in central Greece

leu·ke·mi·a, leu·ce·mi·a, leu·kae·mi·a, leu·cae·mi·a (lu:kí:mi:ə) *n.* (*med.*) an acute or chronic disease of unknown origin which affects the leukocytes in the tissues, their number greatly increasing, sometimes without an equal increase in the leukocytes of the bloodstream [Mod. L. fr. Gk *leukos*, white+*haima*, blood]

CONCISE PRONUNCIATION KEY: **(a)** æ, cat; ɑ, car; ɔ fawn; ei, snake. **(e)** e, hen; i:, sheep; iə, deer; ɛə, bear. **(i)** i, fish; ai, tiger; ə:, bird. **(o)** o, ox; au, cow; ou, goat; u, poor; ɔi, royal. **(u)** ʌ, duck; u, bull; u:, goose; ə, bacillus; ju:, cube. x, loch; θ, think; ð, bother; z, Zen; ʒ, corsage; dʒ, savage; ŋ, orangutang; j, yak; ʃ, fish; tʃ, fetch; 'l, rabble; 'n, redden. Complete pronunciation key appears inside front cover.

leu·ko·cyte, leu·co·cyte (lú:kəsait) *n.* any of several types of microscopic, white, amorphous, nucleated cells occurring in the blood and in tissues, esp. in areas of inflammation or infection, and playing an important role in the body's defense against infection (*PHAGOCYTOSIS) [fr. Gk *leukos*, white + *kutos*, receptacle]

leu·ko·dys·tro·phy or **leu·co·dys·tro·phy** (lu:koudístrəfi:) *n.* (*med.*) degeneration of the white matter of the brain

leu·ko·pher·e·sis (lu:kofərí:sis) *n.* (*med.*) the removal of leukocytes from the blood for the purpose of donation, with the other blood portion returned to the donor

leu·kor·rhe·a, leu·cor·rhoe·a (lu:kərí:ə) *n.* (*med.*) a viscid white vaginal discharge [Mod. L. fr. Gk *leukos*, white + *rhoia*, flow]

Leut·ze (lɔ́itsə), Emanuel (1816–68), U.S. historical painter. His best-known work is 'Washington Crossing the Delaware'. His 'Westward the Course of Empire Takes its Way' (1860) decorates a stairway in the Capitol, Washington, D.C.

Leu·ven (lɔ́:ven) *LOUVAIN

lev (lef) *pl.* **lev·a** (léva) *n.* the standard monetary unit of Bulgaria ‖ a coin of this value [Bulgarian = lion]

lev·al·lor·phan (levalɔ́rfən) *n.* (*pharm.*) a morphine-antagonist drug related to morphine; marketed as Lorfan

Le·vant (livǽnt) the land around the eastern Mediterranean, esp. Syria and Lebanon [F. *levant* fr. *lever*, to rise (of the sun)]

le·vant·er (livǽntər) *n.* a strong easterly wind in the Mediterranean [LEVANT]

Le·van·tine (livǽntin, livǽntain, lévəntain) **1.** *adj.* of the Levant **2.** *n.* a native or inhabitant of the Levant, esp, one descended from European stock

le·va·tor (livéitər) *pl.* **lev·a·to·res** (levətɔ́ri:z, levətóuri:z) *n.* a muscle that raises some part of the body [L.L. fr. *levare*, to raise]

Le Vau (ləvou), Louis (1612–70), French architect, whose many works include the central part of the Palace of Versailles (1661–70)

lev·ee (lévi:) *n.* (*Br.*) a reception of men visitors held in the early afternoon by a monarch or his representative ‖ (*hist.*) a reception held by a monarch in the morning, on rising from bed [F. *levé* fr. *lever*, to raise]

levee *n.* an embankment built to prevent a river from overflowing ‖ a landing place from a river ‖ an embankment built to enclose an area of land to be flooded [F. *levée* fr. *lever*, to raise]

lev·el (lévəl) **1.** *n.* an instrument, esp. a spirit level, for testing whether something is horizontal ‖ a horizontal line, plane or surface ‖ a surveyor's level ‖ a piece of country which is horizontal or relatively so ‖ a horizontal condition ‖ the equilibrium of a fluid surface at a single altitude, *water seeks its own level* ‖ a position in a scale of importance, *the wage increase applies at all levels in the industry* ‖ a degree of attainment, *the general level of the class is high* ‖ a relative position in respect to some norm in a scale of estimating, *prices at inflated levels* ‖ the magnitude of any physical quantity, *a high hemoglobin level* ‖ (*mining*) a horizontal passage in a mine **on the level** (*pop.*) honest, truthful, *this information is on the level* ‖ (*pop.*) honestly, truthfully, *he told me on the level* **to find one's own level** to find a position (in a society) that corresponds with one's status and abilities **to take a level** to measure the difference in height between two points instrumentally **2.** *adj.* horizontal, having no part higher than another ‖ (of two or more persons, things etc., sometimes with 'with') being on the same level, *the children are level in their linguistic ability* ‖ (of two or more persons or things moving in the same direction, sometimes with 'with') being neither behind nor in front ‖ unchanging in magnitude, *a level temperature* ‖ unflustered, *a level head* ‖ not betraying emotion, *level tones* ‖ steady and direct, *a level look* ‖ (*phys.*) equipotential **3.** *v. pres. part.* **lev·el·ing**, esp. *Br.* **lev·el·ling** *past* and *past part.* **lev·eled**, esp. *Br.* **lev·elled** *v.t.* to make level, *the site must be leveled before it is built upon* ‖ to make level with the ground, *the buildings were leveled by the earthquake* ‖ to aim, direct, *to level a gun, to level an accusation* ‖ (*surveying*) to measure relative heights above a chosen level in (a piece of land) ‖ *v.i.* to become level **to level off** to make level, smooth ‖ (of aircraft) to come into a horizontal flying position, e.g. preparatory to landing [O.F. *livel*]

level crossing (*Br.*) a grade crossing

lev·el·er, esp. *Br.* **lev·el·ler** (lévələr) *n.* someone or something which brings things or people to the same level, *death is the great leveler* **Lev·el·ler** (*Eng. hist.*) a member of an extreme republican faction (1647–9) led by John Liburne, advocating total religious and social equality. It was suppressed by Cromwell in 1649

lev·el·head·ed (lévəlhédid) *adj.* showing balanced judgment and good sense

lev·el·ing rod, esp. *Br.* **lev·el·ling rod** (*surveying*) a rod used to measure the vertical distance between a point on the earth and the sight line of a surveyor's level

leveling staff, esp. *Br.* **levelling staff** (*surveying*) a leveling rod

leveller *LEVELER

levelling rod *LEVELING ROD

levelling staff *LEVELING STAFF

lev·er (lévər, lí:vər) **1.** *n.* a rigid bar turning about a fixed point, the fulcrum, used to modify or transmit a force or motion applied at a second point so that it acts at a third point ‖ anything which brings influence to bear **2.** *v.t.* to move with or as if with a lever ‖ *v.i.* to use a lever **lev·er·age** *n.* the action or effect of a lever ‖ the way in which influence is brought to bear [O.F. *leveour* fr. *lever*, to raise]

lev·er·et (lévərit) *n.* a young hare, esp. one in its first year [fr. O.F. *levrete* dim. of *levre*, hare]

Le Ver·rier (ləverjei), Urbain (1811–77), French astronomer. By studying the orbital aberrations of Uranus, he correctly calculated the existence, position and orbit of Neptune (*GALLE)

Le·vesque (ləvek), René (1922–   ), Canadian politician and leader of the Parti Québécois, which advocates for Quebec political independence from English-speaking Canada and economic reform in a partial common market with the rest of Canada. In 1985, Levesque resigned as party leader

Le·vi (lí:vai) Hebrew patriarch, son of Jacob and ancestor of the Levites

lev·i·a·ble (lévi:əb'l) *adj.* that may be levied or levied upon

le·vi·a·than (livái̯əθən) *n.* (*Bible*) a sea monster ‖ (*rhet.*) anything huge, esp. a whale or ship [L. fr. Heb. *livyāthān*]

lev·i·gate (lévigeit) *pres. part.* **lev·i·gat·ing** *past* and *past part.* **lev·i·gat·ed** *v.t.* to grind into a fine powder while in a moist state ‖ to separate (fine powder) from a coarse material by suspension in liquid [fr. L. *levigare* (*levigatus*), to make smooth]

Lev·ing·ston (lévinstən), Roberto Marcelo (1920–   ), Argentinian general, military intelligence expert, and president of the Republic (1970–71), following the removal of President Juan Carlos Ongania. His successor was Gen. Lanusse

Lev·in·son (lévinsən), Salmon Oliver (1865–1941), U.S. lawyer. He created (1918) the outlawry of war movement in the U.S.A., which advocated that changes in government brought about by violence were to be declared illegal by nation-states. This movement led to the enactment of the Kellog-Briand pact

lev·i·rate (lévirit, lí:vərit) *n.* the marriage of a dead man's brother or next of kin with his wife. Historically such marriage was sometimes an established custom, e.g. among the Hebrews **lev·i·rat·ic** (levərǽtik, li:vərǽtik), **lev·i·rát·i·cal** *adjs* [fr. L. *levir*, brother-in-law]

Lé·vi-Strauss (leívi:straus), Claude (1908–   ), French ethnologist. He advocates structuralism in ethnological interpretation and in the analysis of myths

lev·i·tate (léviteit) *pres. part.* **lev·i·tat·ing** *past* and *past part.* **lev·i·tat·ed** *v.i.* to rise or float in the air as if weightless ‖ *v.t.* to cause to rise or float in the air **lev·i·tá·tion** *n.* [fr. L. *levis*, light, after 'gravitate']

Le·vite (lí:vait) *n.* a member of the Israelite tribe descended from Levi. The Levites were allocated no land, but became the priests, or assistants of the priests, in the Temple [fr. L. *levita*, *levites* fr. Gk fr. Heb.]

Le·vit·i·cal (livítik'l) *adj.* of the Levites ‖ of the book Leviticus [fr. L.L. *leviticus*]

Le·vit·i·cus (livítikəs) the third book of the Old Testament, which contains Hebrew religious and social laws

lev·i·ty (léviti) *pl.* **lev·i·ties** *n.* lighthearted and frivolous behavior, esp. when not appropriate to the circumstances ‖ an instance of such behavior [fr. O.F. *levité*]

levodopa *L-DOPA

le·vo·ro·ta·to·ry, esp. *Br.* **lae·vo·ro·ta·to·ry** (li:vouroutətɔ́ri:, li:vouróutətouri:) *adj.* (usually of a substance which rotates the plane of linearly polarized light) rotating to the left or counterclockwise (*OPTICAL ROTATION, cf. DEXTROROTATORY) [fr. L. *laevus*, left + ROTATORY]

le·vo·thy·rox·ine [$C_{15}H_{11}I_4NO_4$] (levouθairóks-i:n) *n.* (*pharm.*) an active hormone of the thyroid gland; marketed as Synthroid

lev·u·lose, esp. *Br.* **laev·u·lose** (lévjulous) *n.* the levorotatory isomer of fructose [fr. L. *laevus*, left]

lev·y (lévi:) **1.** *pl.* **lev·ies** *n.* the imposition by a state or organization of a tax, duty, fine etc. ‖ the amount demanded, esp. per head ‖ (*rhet.*) the calling up of men for military service or the men called up ‖ (*law*) the seizure of property in accordance with a legal claim or judgment **2.** *v. pres. part.* **lev·y·ing** *past* and *past part.* **lev·ied** *v.t.* to impose (a tax, fine etc.) ‖ (*rhet.*) to call up (men) for military service ‖ (*rhet.*) to begin, make or carry on (war) ‖ (*law*) to seize (property) in accordance with a legal claim or judgment ‖ *v.i.* (*law*) to make a levy [F. *levée* fr. *lever*, to raise]

lewd (lu:d) *adj.* offending modesty, indecent ‖ lascivious [O.E. *lǽwede*, of obscure etymology]

Lew·es, Battle of (lú:is) a battle (1264) in which Simon de Montfort defeated and captured Henry III during the Barons' War

Lew·is (lú:is), Clive Staples (1898–1963), British author, noted for his 'The Allegory of Love' (1936), a study of medieval allegory and courtly love, and for his religious and children's books

Lewis, Isaac Newton (1858–1931), U.S. colonel and inventor of artillery devices. He is best known for his Lewis machine gun (1911), adopted by many countries in the 1st world war

Lewis, John Llewellyn (1880–1969), U.S. labor leader, president (1920–60) of the United Mine Workers of America. He headed (1935) the Committee of Industrial Organizations and became (1938) the first president of the Congress of Industrial Organizations

Lewis, Matthew Gregory (1775–1818), English author. His works include 'Ambrosio, or the Monk' (1795), an early horror novel

Lewis, Meriwether (1774–1809), American explorer. With William Clark (1770–1838), he led an expedition (1804–6) up the Missouri, over the Rockies, to the Pacific coast of America, opening up vast new territories

Lewis, Sinclair (1885–1951), American novelist. His books include 'Main Street' (1920) and 'Babbitt' (1922), in which he satirizes American small-town citizens. He won the Nobel prize for literature (1930)

Lewis, Wyndham (1884–1957), English painter and novelist. He first worked as a painter (*VORTICISM), but later became a trenchant critic, writing from a strongly independent right-wing point of view. His works include 'Time and Western Man' (1928), 'The Childermass' (1928) and 'The Apes of God' (1930)

Lewis (or Lewis with Harris), the northernmost and largest island (area 770 sq. miles, pop. 28,000) of the Outer Hebrides, N.W. Scotland. Chief town:. Stornoway

lew·is (lú:is) *n.* a device for gripping and hoisting heavy blocks of stone. It consists of a dovetail tenon expanded into a dovetail mortise [origin unknown]

lew·is·ite (lú:isait) *n.* dichloro-2-chlorovinyl-arsine, the oily liquid $C_2H_2AsCl_3$. Its vapor is potentially a blistering, lethal war gas [after W. L. Lewis (1878–1943), U.S. chemist]

lex·i·cal (léksik'l) *adj.* having to do with the words of a language or their meaning as defined in a dictionary (as opposed to their structural meaning) ‖ of or pertaining to a lexicon or lexicography [fr. Gk *lexikos*]

lex·i·cog·ra·pher (leksikógrəfər) *n.* someone who compiles or writes a dictionary **lex·i·co·graph·i·cal** (leksikəgrǽfik'l) *adj.* **lex·i·cóg·ra·phy** *n.* the process of compiling or writing a dictionary [fr. Gk *lexikographos*]

lex·i·co·log·i·cal (leksikəlódʒik'l) *adj.* of lexicology

lex·i·col·o·gist (leksikólədʒist) *n.* a specialist in lexicology

lex·i·col·o·gy (lĕksikólədʒi:) *n.* the science of the derivation and meaning of words

lex·i·con (léksikən, léksikon) *n.* a dictionary, esp. of ancient Greek, Hebrew, Syriac or Arabic ‖ the special vocabulary of a group, an individual, an occupational field etc., or the vocabulary of a language [Mod. L. fr. Gk *lexikon* fr. *lexis*, word]

lex·i·co·sta·tis·tics (léksəkoustətístiks) *n.* (*linguistics*) computation of the sharing of basic words among different languages (cognates) as a means of measuring separation of languages *Cf* GLOTTOCHRONOLOGY

Lex·ing·ton (léksiŋtən) a horsebreeding center and tobacco market (pop. 204,165) of central Kentucky: state university

Lexington and Concord, Battles of the opening engagements (Apr. 19, 1775) of the Revolutionary War (1775–83). Lexington is 10 miles northwest of Boston, Mass. Concord lies west of Lexington on River Concord

lex·is (léksəs) *pl.* **lexes** all the words of a language

lex·i·scope (léksiskoup) *n.* (*med.*) device that permits extraction of more information from X-rays, permitting reduced radiation exposures

ley (lei) *n.* land temporarily under grass [var. of LEA]

Ley·den (láid'n) (*Du.* Leiden) a town (pop. 103,457) of South Holland, Netherlands, near the coast. Industries: textiles (since the 15th c.), printing and publishing (since the 16th c.), metallurgy, food processing. University (1575)

Leyden jar an electrostatic capacitor of historical interest, consisting of a glass jar with inner and outer metal foil linings [invented at *Leyden* in 1745]

Leyden, John of *JOHN OF LEYDEN

Leyland *LELAND

Ley·te (léiti) an island (area 2,785 sq. miles, pop. 1,007,000) of the central Philippines (Visayas), off which the Americans defeated (Oct. 1944) the Japanese in a decisive sea battle of the 2nd world war. Part of the Japanese fleet was destroyed

LGBS (*mil. acronym*) for laser-guided bomb system manufactured by Texas Instruments

LGM-30 *MINUTEMAN

LGM-25C *TITAN II

LGP (*abbr.*) for liquified petroleum gas

Lha·sa (lásə) the capital (pop. 120,000) of Tibet at 11,380 ft. Founded in the 7th c., it was the spiritual center of Lamaism and the residence, long closed to Europeans, of the Dalai Lamas (17th c.–1950)

Lhote (lout), André (1885–1962), French cubist painter. He was also an influential teacher and writer

Li (*chem.*) lithium

li·a·bil·i·ty (laiəbíliti:) *pl.* **li·a·bil·i·ties** *n.* the quality or condition of being liable ‖ that which one is liable for ‖ (*pl.*) debts

li·a·ble (láiəb'l) *adj.* (with 'for') legally bound or responsible, *they are liable for his debts* ‖ (with 'to') subject to a tax, law, penalty etc., *liable to arrest* ‖ (with 'to') having a tendency, apt, *he is liable to catch cold* ‖ (with 'to') likely [etym. doubtful]

li·aise (li:éiz) *pres. part.* **li·ais·ing** *past* and *past part.* **li·aised** *v.i.* (*mil.*) to maintain liaison

li·ai·son (li:éizɔ, li:eizɔ̃) *n.* (*rhet.*) a love affair outside marriage ‖ (*mil.*, li:éizən) the establishment of harmonious cooperation between separate units of an armed force ‖ the continuation of the sound of a usually silent final consonant to the next word where this begins with a vowel or mute *h*, e.g. in French [F.]

li·a·na (li:ánə) *n.* a luxuriant woody or herbaceous climbing plant having its roots in the ground, found in tropical or semitropical forests [F. *liane* perh. fr. *lier*, to bind]

li·ane (li:án) *n.* a liana

Liao·ning (ljáuníŋ) a province (area 50,000 sq. miles, pop. 33,000,000) in S. Manchuria, China, a great industrial region. Capital: Shenyang

Liao·yang (ljáujáŋ) an industrial town (pop. 150,000) in E. Liaoning, N.E. China: textiles

Lia·quat A·li Khan (lják'táli:kán) (1895–1951), Pakistani statesman, first prime minister of Pakistan (1947–51). He was assassinated

li·ar (láiər) *n.* someone who tells a lie or habitually tells lies [O.E. *léogere*]

Li·ard (lí:ɑrd) a river (c. 550 miles long) rising in mountains in the S.E. Yukon, Canada, flowing east across British Columbia, and turning northwest into the Mackenzie River. The Alaska Highway follows it in N. British Columbia

li·as (láiəs) *n.* a blue limestone **the Li·as** the lower division of the Jurassic **li·as·sic, Li·as·sic** (laiǽsik) *adjs* [O.F. *liois*]

lib or **Lib** (lib) *adj.* (*colloq.*) of women's liberation; often meant disparagingly

li·ba·tion (laibéiʃən) *n.* the act of pouring wine or oil upon the ground as a sacrifice to a god ‖ the wine or oil so sacrificed [fr. L. *libatio* (*libationis*)]

Lib·by (líbi:), Willard Frank (1908–80), U.S. chemist who earned the 1960 Nobel prize in chemistry for his radiocarbon dating technique (*CARBON)

li·bel (láib'l) **1.** *n.* (*law*) a published statement, photograph etc. which without due cause has the result, or is intended to have the result, of bringing its subject into disrepute (cf. SLANDER) ‖ the act of publishing such a statement etc. ‖ (*pop.*) any false and insulting statement ‖ (with 'on') something that brings undeserved discredit, *this book is a libel on the American people* ‖ (*admiralty law, Br.* also *civil* and *eccles. law*) a plaintiff's written statement of his case and of the redress sought **2.** *v.t. pres. part.* **li·bel·ing**, esp. *Br.* **li·bel·ling** *past* and *past part.* **li·beled**, esp. *Br.* **li·belled** to publish a libel about ‖ (*pop.*) to insult, make false and malicious statements about ‖ (*law*) to bring suit against by filing a libel **li·bel·ous**, esp. *Br.* **li·bel·lous** *adj.* [O.F. *libel*, a little book]

Li·ber (láibər) (*Rom. mythol.*) the god of creativeness, later identified with Dionysus and Bacchus

lib·er·al (líbərəl, líbrəl) **1.** *adj.* giving freely, giving more than is necessary or usual ‖ generously large, more in quantity than is necessary or usual, *a liberal reward* ‖ involving a general enlarging of the mind beyond the merely professional or technical, *a liberal education* ‖ not subject to the common prejudices or conventions, *a liberal mind* ‖ admitting more than is directly expressed, not sticking to the letter, *a liberal interpretation of the rules* ‖ (*politics*) favorable to individual liberty, social reform and the removal of economic restraints (*LIBERALISM) ‖ admitting a free interpretation of religious doctrine and of its application to ritual and conduct, *a liberal Jew* **Lib·er·al** of or belonging to the Liberal party **2.** *n.* (*politics*) a person who holds liberal views **Liberal** a member or supporter of the Liberal party [O.F.]

liberal arts (*hist.*) the seven branches of medieval education (*TRIVIUM, *QUADRIVIUM) ‖ the humanities

lib·er·al·ism (líbərəlizəm, líbrəlizəm) *n.* the quality or state of being liberal ‖ a body of social, political, religious or economic doctrines or attitudes which are liberal

Lib·er·al·ism the policies of the Liberal party —As a political philosophy, liberalism was first apparent in Europe in the early 19th c. Since then it has taken varying forms at different times and in different places, but has always been characterized by progressive rather than conservative attitudes. Liberalism is critical of institutions, whether political or religious, which tend to restrict individual liberty, and places its faith in man's goodness and rationality. This has often expressed itself in demands for freedom of expression, equality of opportunity and universal education. But liberalism is distinguished from radicalism by its insistence on gradual, rather than violent, reform. Economic liberalism has its roots in the laissez-faire doctrines of Adam Smith, Malthus and Ricardo. As it developed in the 19th c., it was essentially a phenomenon of the commercial and industrial classes, favoring free trade and the fixing of wages and prices by competition, and opposing state intervention. In the late 19th c. liberalism was adapted in Britain to favor a limited amount of state intervention in order to provide welfare services and social security, though remaining an essentially individualist doctrine, in contrast to socialism

lib·er·al·i·ty (líbərǽliti:) *pl.* **lib·er·al·i·ties** *n.* the quality or state of being liberal ‖ an instance of liberal giving [O.F. *liberalité*]

lib·er·al·ize (líbərəlaiz, líbrəlaiz) *pres.part.* **lib·er·al·iz·ing** *past* and *past part.* **lib·er·al·ized** *v.t.* to make liberal ‖ *v.i.* to become liberal

Liberal party a British political party. The name Liberal was first adopted officially by the Whigs in 1868, although it had been used unofficially since the 1830s to describe reforming Whigs. The party became associated with free trade after the adhesion of the Peelites. one of whom, Gladstone, led the Liberals (1868–94) in

a program of political, social and educational reform. The party was split (1886) when the Liberal Unionists seceded, and was again divided over the Boer War, but was reorganized (1906) by Campbell-Bannerman. It was weakened by differences between Asquith and Lloyd George, and was replaced after 1922 by the Labour party as the effective force committed to reform

Liberal Republican (*Am. hist.*) a member of a political party formed (1872) by Republicans who were dissatisfied with Grant's administration

Liberal Unionist a member of a former British political group which seceded (1886) from the Liberal party in opposition to that party's policy of Irish Home Rule. Led by Joseph Chamberlain, the Liberal Unionists merged (late 19th c.) with the Conservative party

lib·er·ate (líbəreit) *pres. part.* **lib·er·at·ing** *past* and *past part.* **lib·er·at·ed** *v.t.* to set free, release ‖ (*chem.*) to free (e.g. a gas) from combination ‖ to change the status or ownership of, e.g., a nation, a piece of property [fr. L. *liberare* (*liberatus*)]

lib·er·a·tion (líbəréiʃən) *n.* a liberating or being liberated [fr. L. *liberatio* (*liberationis*)]

lib·er·a·tor (líbəreitər) *n.* someone who liberates, esp. someone who sets people free from political oppression

Li·be·ri·a (laibíəri:ə) a republic (area 43,000 sq. miles, pop. 2,160,000) of W. Africa. Capital: Monrovia. People: Mandingo and other African groups, small Americo-Liberian minority. Languages: English and African languages. Religion: local African religions, with Christian (mainly Protestant) and Moslem minorities. 60% of the land is tropical forest. The coastal plain rises abruptly to a plateau (1,500 ft) near the Guinea border. In the northwest the grasslands of the plateau give way to mountains (4,000 ft). Several navigable rivers cross from the plateau to the Gulf of Guinea. Average temperatures (F.): 76° (Aug.) and 85° (Mar.). Rainfall: 160–180 ins. Livestock: cattle. Agricultural products: rice, cassava, eddoes, sweet potatoes, coffee, sugarcane, cocoa, bananas, lumber, piassava fiber, palm kernels and oil, rubber. Mineral resources: diamonds, gold, iron ore. Manufactures: bricks, tiles, soap. Exports: iron ore, rubber, diamonds, palm kernels. Imports: machinery, food, chemicals, tobacco, fuels, cotton goods. Ports: Monrovia, Lower Buchanan. The merchant navy, consisting largely of foreign ships, has the fourth highest tonnage in the world. University: Monrovia. Monetary unit: U.S. dollar (100 cents). HISTORY. The Portuguese visited the coast in the 15th c., and were followed by French, Dutch and English traders. The present state of Liberia grew out of a settlement of freed Afro-American slaves (1822). It was proclaimed a republic (1847) and has kept close economic links with the U.S.A. Political power is almost wholly in the hands of the Americo-Liberians. Liberia became a member of the U.N. (1945). A coup in 1980 left Liberian foreign policies toward the U.S.A. and foreign business unchanged, but economic expectations were aroused that Liberia's new leaders could not meet. President Doe remained in power after 1985 elections but vote fraud was alleged. He survived a coup attempt later that year

Li·be·ri·an (laibíəri:ən) **1.** *adj.* of or relating to Liberia, its people etc. **2.** *n.* a native or inhabitant of Liberia

Li·ber·man·ism (lí:bərmənizm) *n.* advocacy of incentives and less centralized planning in the socialist economic system of U.S.S.R.; named for Yevsei Grigorevich Liberman

lib·er·tar·i·an (líbərtéəri:ən) **1.** *n.* someone who accepts the doctrine of free will ‖ an advocate of liberty, esp. in individual thought and action **2.** *adj.* of or pertaining to a libertarian [LIBERTY]

lib·er·tine (líbərti:n) **1.** *n.* (*rhet.*) a man who is dissolute in his sexual conduct ‖ (*hist.*) a freethinker **2.** *adj.* of or pertaining to a libertine [fr. L. *libertinus*, freedman]

lib·er·ty (líbərti:) *pl.* **lib·er·ties** *n.* the condition of being free to choose, esp. as between ways of acting or living, with an implication of wisdom and voluntary restraint (cf. LICENSE) ‖ the right to do as one pleases ‖ the condition of being free from physical confinement or captivity ‖ (*navy*) a short period of leave ‖ (*philos.*) free will at liberty free, *the escaped prisoner is still at liberty* ‖ (*pop.*) unemployed, not busy ‖ authorized, possessing the right, *I am not at liberty to tell* *you* **to take the liberty** (polite usage) to presume, *may I take the liberty of parking my car in your drive?* **to take liberties** to go beyond the bounds of what is proper [F. *liberté*]

Liberty Bell the bell in Independence Hall, Philadelphia, rung to proclaim (July 8, 1776) the signing of the Declaration of Independence

liberty boat a boat carrying sailors with leave to go ashore

Liberty Loan Act a U.S. Congressional act (1917) which permitted the U.S. government to borrow funds directly from the public. Five loans were floated in succession, bringing in over $20 billion

Liberty Loans four loans floated (1917–18) by the U.S. government during the 1st world war, together with a fifth, the Victory Loan, floated (1919) after the Armistice. From all the loans the department of the treasury received $21,435,370,600

Liberty party (*Am. hist.*) a political party formed (1840) in the U.S.A. to oppose slavery. It merged (1848) with other groups in the Free-Soil party

Liberty, Statue of a statue (151 ft high, with pedestal c. 305 ft high) in New York Harbor. Sculpted by Frédéric Auguste Bartholdi, it was presented (1886) by the people of France to commemorate the birth of the U.S.A. and the continuing friendships of the peoples of the French and American democracies. The statue was completely refurbished for centennial celebrations in 1986. The pedestal is inscribed with part of the sonnet 'The New Colossus' by Emma Lazarus:

> Give me your tired, your poor,
> Your huddled masses yearning
>   to breathe free,
> The wretched refuse of your
>   teeming shore,
> Send these, the homeless,
>   tempest-tost, to me:
> I lift my lamp beside the
>   golden door

li·bid·i·nal (libíd'n'l) *adj.* of or pertaining to the libido

li·bid·i·nous (libíd'nəs) *adj.* lustful ‖ libidinal [fr. L. *libidinosus*]

li·bi·do (libí:dou, libáidou) *n.* (*psychol.*) the vital impulse or energy motivating human behavior ‖ the sexual urge [L.= lust]

LIBOR (láibɔr) (*banking acronym*) for London interbank offered rate, the interest rate at which major London banks lend money to one another

Li·bra (láibrə, lí:brə) a southern constellation ‖ the seventh sign of the zodiac, represented as a balance [L. = a pound, a balance]

li·brar·i·an (laibréəriən) *n.* a person in charge of a library ‖ a member of a staff of library workers **li·brár·i·an·ship** *n.* (*Br.*) library science ‖ the office of a librarian [fr. L. *librarius* adj., having to do with books]

li·brar·y (láibreri:, láibrəri:) *pl.* **li·brar·ies** *n.* a room or building housing a collection of books, usually arranged according to some plan ‖ such a collection of books ‖ a number of books on related topics issued by a publisher, or a number of books similar in format [F. *librairie*, bookshop]

Library of Congress the national library of the U.S.A. in Washington, D.C., founded in 1800. It receives copies of all books copyrighted in the U.S.A.

library science (*Am.=Br.* librarianship) the principles of library maintenance and administration, including bibliography, cataloging etc.

li·brate (láibreit) *pres. part.* **li·brat·ing** *past* and *past part.* **li·brat·ed** *v.i.* to swing to and fro like a balance [fr. L. *librare* (*libratus*)]

li·bra·tion (laibréiʃən) *n.* (*astron.*) oscillation, esp. a real or apparent irregular movement of the moon, a planet etc. [fr. L. *libratio* (*librationis*)]

li·bra·to·ry (láibrətɔri:, láibrətouri:) *adj.* oscillatory [fr. L. *librare* (*libratus*), to balance]

li·bret·tist (librétist) *n.* the author of a libretto

li·bret·to (librétou) *pl.* **li·bret·tos, li·bret·ti** (librét:i:) *n.* the words of an opera, oratorio etc. ‖ a book in which these are printed [Ital.]

Li·bre·ville (lí:brəvi:l) the capital (pop. 251,400) of Gabon, a port on the Gabon estuary

Lib·ri·um (líbri:əm) *n.* trade name of the tranquilizer drug chlordiazepoxide

Lib·y·a (líbi:ə) a republic (area 679,358 sq. miles, pop. approx. 3,425,000, nearly one third

nomadic) in N. Africa. Capital: Tripoli. Largest towns: Tripoli, Benghazi. People: mainly Arabs and Arabic-speaking Berbers, with Tibbu, Tuareg, Italian (3%), Greek and other minorities. Official language: Arabic. Religion: Moslem (official), 3% Roman Catholic, small Jewish minority. The land lies mostly in the Sahara, but 14% (large oases near the coast and in the Fezzan) is arable and 4% pasture. The north and east are mainly a low plain, the south and west a plateau (1,000–3,000 ft) bordering the Tibesti Mtns of Chad. Average temperatures (F.): Jan. 50°, Jul. 70° in the northern tips of Tripolitania and Cyrenaica, 80° elsewhere. Annual rainfall: 15 ins in northernmost Tripolitania and Cyrenaica, 5–10 ins elsewhere near the coast, under 5 ins in the interior. Livestock: sheep, goats, camels. Agricultural products: dates, olives, oranges, peanuts, potatoes, tobacco, henna, tomatoes, barley, wheat, grapes, mulberries, figs, castor seed, almonds. Minerals: petroleum. Industries: petroleum refining, sponge and tuna fishing, dyeing, weaving, olive oil, bricks, salt, leather, esparto, carpets, footwear, clothing. Exports: petroleum, peanuts, hides and skins, camels, castor seeds, sponges, olive oil, livestock, esparto. Imports: drilling machines, iron, vehicles, wheat flour, clothing. Ports: Tripoli, Benghazi, Port Brega. University: faculties at Benghazi and Tripoli. Monetary unit: Libyan pound (100 piastres). HISTORY. Colonized by the Phoenicians (2nd millennium B.C.) and the Greeks (7th c. B.C.), Libya was ruled (323–264 B.C.) by the Ptolemies and made a Roman colony (96 B.C.). The Arabs conquered it (7th c.) and it was part of the Ottoman Empire from the 16th c. until it became an Italian colony (1912). It was the scene of much fighting (1942–3) in the 2nd world war. Italy renounced its claims (1947). On the recommendation of the U.N., Libya was declared independent (Dec. 24, 1951). It joined the Arab League (1953) and the U.N. (1955). The king was deposed (Sept. 1, 1969) by a military coup d'état, and the republic was proclaimed. Libya became (1971) a member of the Union of Arab Republics, with Egypt and Syria. Col. Muammar al Qaddafi, who led Libya's revolution, tried to transform Libya into an egalitarian, Islamic, socialist state of the masses. He resigned as secretary-general of the General People's Congress (1979) and held no formal office thereafter, but remained the country's leader. At different times he tried unsuccessfully to merge Libya with Egypt, Syria, Sudan, Tunisia, Chad and Morocco. An enemy of Israel, he also involved Libya in conflicts with the U.S.A., France and Great Britain. Libyan troops went to Uganda in 1979 in support of Pres. Idi Amin and to Chad during a civil war there in the early 1980's. Libya's suspected involvement in terrorist activities that resulted in the deaths of U.S. citizens led to the U.S. bombing of Libya in 1986

Lib·y·an (líbi:ən) **1.** *adj.* of Libya, its inhabitants etc. **2.** *n.* a native or inhabitant of Libya

Libyan Desert the part of the E. Sahara (rising to 6,000 ft) stretching from central Libya and the Tibesti Mtns on the Chad border to the Nile

lice *pl.* of LOUSE

li·cense, li·cence (láis'ns) **1.** *n.* a right formally granted in writing by an authority (who also has the power to withhold it), e.g. to drive a vehicle, marry, conduct certain businesses, possess a firearm etc. ‖ the official certificate of this right ‖ the generally recognized right of an artist, writer etc. to depart from strict adherence to rules or truth in his work, *poetic license* ‖ a degree of freedom, *he was allowed some license in interpreting the instructions* ‖ behavior in which liberty is abused or used in a socially undesirable way (cf. LIBERTY) ‖ licentious behavior ‖ a certificate of competence awarded by some European universities **2.** *v.t. pres. part.* **li·cens·ing, li·cenc·ing** *past* and *past part.* **li·censed, li·cenced** to grant a license to (someone) or for (**something**) **li·cen·see** (laisənsí:) *n.* someone to whom a license is granted **li·cens·er** *n.* someone who grants a license [F. *licence*]

li·cen·ti·ate (laisénʃi:it) *n.* someone holding a university license or a similar certificate from a college [fr. M.L. *licentiare* (*licentiatus*)]

li·cen·tious (laisénʃəs) *adj.* (of a person, book, play etc.) disregarding the laws of morality, esp. in sexual matters [fr. M.L. *licentiosus*]

lichee *LITCHI

li·chen (láikən) *Br.* also litʃen) *n.* a member of *Lichenes*, a group of plants composed of a fungus whose mycelium forms a matrix in which are distributed algae living in a symbiotic relation with the fungus. Lichens are found as un-differentiated branching plants on rocks and tree trunks, which are broken down by the saprophytic fungus of the lichen [L. fr. Gk *leichēn*]

li·chen·om·e·try (laikənómətri:) *n.* (*biol.*) determination of age of lichens and area in which they are growing by measurement of their diameter —**lichenometric** *adj.*

Lich·field (lítʃfi:ld) a city (pop. 14,000) of Staffordshire, England, on the Trent, with a three-spired cathedral (13th c.)

lich-gate *LYCH-GATE

lic·it (lísit) *adj.* permitted by law [fr. L. *licere* (*licitus*), to be permitted]

lick (lik) **1.** *v.t.* to draw the tongue over ‖ (of waves, fire, flames etc.) to play lightly over the surface of ‖ (*pop.*) to beat soundly in a competition ‖(*pop.*) to get the better of ‖ (*pop.*) to thrash, *beat* **to lick clean** to make clean by licking **to lick one's chops** (or **lips**) to feel eager anticipation **to lick into shape** to impose correct form on, *he'll get licked into shape at his new school* **to lick off** to take off by licking **to lick someone's shoes** (or **boots**) to be servile towards someone **to lick up** to swallow by licking **2.** *n.* the act of licking or an instance of this ‖ the amount taken up by the tongue in such a lick ‖ a quick light coating, e.g. of paint‖ (*pop.*) a great speed, *he ran at a tremendous lick* ‖ a salt lick [O.E. *liccian*]

lick·e·ty-split (líkiti:splít) *adv.* (*pop.*) at great speed

lick·ing (líkiŋ) *n.* (*pop.*) a thrashing, beating ‖ (*pop.*) a severe defeat in a competition

lick·spit·tle (líkspit'l) *n.* (*rhet.*) an abject flatterer

lic·o·rice, liq·uo·rice (líkəriʃ) *n.* a black extract made from the dried root of *Glycyrrhiza glabra*, fam. *Papilionaceae*, used as a demulcent and expectorant, in confectionery, and for flavoring tobacco‖ this plant or its root [M.E. *likorys* fr. A. F. fr. L. fr. Gk]

lic·tor (líktər, líktɔr) *n.* (*Rom. hist.*) a civil officer who attended a chief magistrate, bearing the fasces and clearing a way through the crowd for the magistrate to pass [L.]

lid (lid) *n.* a cover closing the top of a receptacle, fitting inside or outside its walls ‖ an eyelid ‖ an operculum in mosses ‖ the upper part of a pyxidium ‖ (*slang*) one ounce of marijuana [O.E. *hlid*]

li·dar (léidɑr) *n.* (*acronym*) laser infrared radar, a meterological device that utilizes a ruby laser infrared pulse for measuring conditions in the atmosphere

Li·di·ce (lídisi:, lí:ditʃei) a mining village in Bohemia, west of Prague, Czechoslovakia. On June 10, 1942 Nazi troops razed it to the ground, killed all the men and many of the women and deported all the children, as a reprisal for the assassination of Hitler's deputy in Bohemia and Moravia

Lie (li:), Trygve Halvdan (1896–1969), Norwegian statesman, secretary-general of the United Nations (1946–53)

lie (lai) **1.** *v.i. pres. part.* **ly·ing** (láiiŋ) *past* **lay** (lei) *past part.* **lain** (lein) to have the body more or less horizontal upon a surface ‖ (usually with 'down') to assume such a position ‖ to be in the grave ‖ to be or remain in a specified state, *to lie in ambush* ‖ to be situated in a specified place, *the town lies near the river* ‖ to be placed, *you know where your interest lies* ‖ to be for a period of time in some more or less horizontal position upon, or in some relation to, a surface, *the book lay on the table, a pall of smoke lies over the town* ‖ to be spread out to the view, *the town lay before us* ‖ (of ships) to float at anchor ‖ to press, weigh heavily e.g. on the consciousness or conscience ‖ to rest, remain, *the decision lies with you* ‖ (*law*) to stay undisturbed, *we'll let the matter lie* ‖ (*law*) to be admissible **to lie down under something** to accept something (esp. an insult or injustice) without protest or action **to lie in** (*old-fash.*) to be confined due to childbirth ‖ (*Br.*) to stay late in bed **to lie off** (*naut.*, of a vessel) to be at a certain distance from shore or another ship **to lie over** to be held for attention at a later date **to lie to** (*naut.*, of a vessel) almost to cease to move by sailing close-hauled **to lie up** (of vessels, motor vehicles etc.) to stay unused ‖ to stay in bed or at rest during an illness **to take lying down** to accept without protest **2.** *n.* the manner, position or direction in which something lies ‖ the place where a wild animal sleeps **the lie of the land** (esp. *Br.*) **the lay of the land** (*LAY) [O.E. *licgan*]

lie *pres. part.* **ly·ing** (lóiiŋ) *past and past part.* **lied** *v.i.* to tell a lie ‖ to deceive by making a false impression, *the camera never lies* ‖ *v.t.* to get (one's way) by lying [O.E. *lēogan*]

lie *n.* an intentionally false statement or impression ‖ something thought of as like this, *their whole relationship is a lie* **to give the lie to** to show to be false [O.E. *lyge*]

Lie algebra (*math.*) a system that groups independent quantities and applies algebraic operations to their relationships —**lie group** *n.*

Lie·ber (líːbər), Francis (1800–72), U.S. political philosopher, whose Civil War code of military regulations, 'Instruction for the Government of the Armies of the United States in the Field' (1863), was embodied into international law in the Hague conventions of 1899 and 1907

Lie·big (líːbig), Justus, Baron von (1803–73), German chemist. He made fundamental contributions to organic and agricultural chemistry. He introduced the concept of radicals, proposed a theory for acids, formulated the carbon and nitrogen cycles in nature and established the quantitative analysis of organic carbon and hydrogen. He discovered chloroform, isolated titanium, and devised a condenser and a method for silvering mirrors

Liech·ten·stein (líxtənʃtain) a principality (area 62 sq. miles, pop. 26,200) in central Europe between Austria and Switzerland. Capital: Vaduz (pop. 3,400). Language: German. Religion: Roman Catholic. The land is 25% arable, 28% pasture and 28% forest. It contains the western end of the Tirolean Alps (8,432 ft in the southeast) and a strip along the Rhine in the north. Chief products: cattle, wine, fruit, lumber, stamps, leather. Monetary unit: Swiss franc (100 centimes). Liechtenstein was created a principality (1719) within the Holy Roman Empire. It was part of the Confederation of the Rhine (1806–13) and of the German Confederation (1815–66), after which it was under Austrian influence until 1918. Liechtenstein formed a customs union (1923) with Switzerland. Prince Hans Adam was crowned in 1984, and women won the right to vote that same year

lied (liːt) *pl.* **lie·der** (líːdər) *n.* a vocal melody, composed together with a piano accompaniment as a setting for a German lyric text, of a type most highly developed in the 19th c., largely as a product of the German Romantic movement. Text, vocal melody and accompaniment are of virtually equal importance in the total effect of the composition. Schubert, Schumann, Brahms and Hugo Wolf were among the greatest lieder composers, drawing on the poems of Goethe, Schiller, Heine etc. in intensely expressive works [G.=song]

lie detector a device which registers the physical changes in the body (e.g. respiration, blood pressure) of someone under questioning. The record is interpreted as a guide to the person's veracity

lie-down or **lie-in** (léidaun) *n.* a protest demonstration by obstructing operations or traffic by lying or sitting in the area

Liège (ljeː) (*Flem.* Luik) a province (area 1,525 sq. miles, pop. 1,019,000) of E. Belgium in the Meuse valley and the Ardennes Mtns: coal mines ‖ its capital (pop. 207,496), Belgium's iron and steel center. Other industries: mechanical engineering, weapons, chemicals, glass. Cathedral (13th–16th cc.), university (1817), palace of the prince-bishops (16th c.). Liège is a river port connected with Antwerp by the Albert canal

liege (liːdʒ) **1.** *adj.* (*hist.*) entitled by right to feudal allegiance ‖ (*hist.*) bound under feudal law to serve another **2.** *n.* (*hist.*) a liege lord ‖ (*hist.*) a vassal [O.F. *lige*, *liege*]

liege·man (liːdʒmən) *pl.* **liege·men** (liːdʒmən) *n.* a feudal vassal or subject ‖ (*rhet.*) a faithful follower

lien (liːn, líːən) *n.* (*law*) the right to hold another's goods or property until a claim is met [F.]

li·erne (liːə́ːrn) *n.* (*archit.*, in Gothic vaulting) a crossrib between the main ribs [F.]

lieu (luː) *n.* (only in the phrases) **in lieu** instead **in lieu of** as a substitute for [F.]

lieu·ten·an·cy (luːténənsiː, *Br.* lefténənsiː) *pl.* **lieu·ten·an·cies** *n.* the office or position of a lieutenant

lieu·ten·ant (luːténənt, *Br.* lefténənt) *n.* someone acting for (i.e. holding the place of) a superior in rank ‖ (*navy*, *Am.* luːténənt, *Br.* ləténənt) an officer ranking immediately below a lieutenant commander ‖ (*U.S. mil.*) a first or second lieutenant ‖ (*Br.*, lefténənt) an army officer ranking below a captain and above a second lieutenant [F.]

lieutenant colonel an army officer ranking below a colonel and above a major ‖ an officer of the same rank in the U.S. air force or marine corps

lieutenant commander a naval officer ranking above a lieutenant and below a commander

lieutenant general an army officer ranking below a general and above a major general ‖ an officer of the same rank in the U.S. air force or marine corps

lieutenant governor a deputy governor ‖ (*Br.*) a provincial governor, responsible to a governor general

lieutenant junior grade a naval officer ranking immediately below a lieutenant

life (laif) *pl.* **lives** (laivz) *n.* the state of an organism characterized by certain processes or abilities that include metabolism, growth, reproduction and response ‖ the fact of being in this state, *is there any life left in him?* ‖ the period of time from birth to the present, *she has lived all her life in Dublin* ‖ the period of time from the present or another specified time to death, *she looks forward to a gay life, in prison for life* ‖ a person in terms of his life expectancy ‖ the period of this expectancy ‖ the period during which something may be expected to last, *these carpets have a long life* ‖ the aggregation of one's actions, thoughts, activities etc., *one's existence, a useful life* ‖ a specified period or aspect of one's existence, *his school life, his spiritual life* ‖ a way or manner of existence, *city life, the life of the natives* ‖ the presence and activities of animate, esp. human beings, *no sign of life* ‖ a human being, *to save a life* ‖ a group of specified animate creatures, *woodland life* ‖ the gay, animating presence, *he was the life of the party* ‖ a stimulating quality seeming to arise from inner energy, *the music is full of life* ‖ (*games*) a fresh start or another opportunity, *the batsman was given a life when the catch was dropped* **a matter of life and death** something that someone's life depends on ‖ a very critical matter **as big** (or **large**) **as life** (expressing surprise) in person, *but there he was as large as life* **for dear life** as if or because one's life depended on it, *he ran for dear life* **for the life of me** (used for emphasis) even if my life depended on it, *I cannot for the life of me understand why he did it* **from life** (*art*) from the living model **not on your life** certainly not **to bring to life** to cause to be lively **to come to life** to begin to be lively **to have the time of one's life** to enjoy oneself very much **to take life** to kill [O.E. *líf*]

life belt a life preserver of buoyant material worn about the waist

life-blood (láifblʌd) *n.* (*rhet.*) the blood ‖ something of vital importance to a group, organization etc., *confidence is the lifeblood of trade*

life-boat (láifbout) *n.* a land-based boat of special construction, able to negotiate stormy seas and equipped to save the lives of people shipwrecked ‖ a small emergency boat carried by a ship in perpetual readiness to put off passengers and crew if necessary

life buoy a buoyant float to which a person can cling for support in the water

life class an art class in which painters etc. work from the living model

life cycle the series of phases through which an organism passes from a specified early stage (e.g. conception, birth) to the identical stage in the succeeding generation

life expectancy the amount of time an individual or class of persons is expected to live, as calculated by actuaries

life-giv·ing (láifgivin) *adj.* giving or able to give energy or spiritual life

life-guard (láifgard) *n.* (*Am.*=*Br.* lifesaver) an expert swimmer employed to prevent or deal with swimming casualties at a swimming pool etc.

life history (*biol.*) the series of successive stages through which an organism passes from its first stage to its last

life insurance insurance under the terms of which a sum of money is paid to a beneficiary at the death of the person insured

life jacket a life preserver made like a sleeveless jacket

life·less (láiflis) *adj.* without life ‖ providing no stimulus, arousing no interest, *lifeless painting*

life·like (láiflaik) *adj.* looking like the original, *a lifelike portrait* ‖ like real life

life·line (láiflain) *n.* a rope used in saving or safeguarding life, e.g. one fired by a rocket to or from a vessel in distress so that a hawser can be made fast ‖ a rope attached to a diver's equipment for signaling and, if necessary, for raising him

life·long (láifloŋ, láifloŋ) *adj.* for the period of a lifetime

life peer (*Br.*) an ennobled person whose title is not passed on to his descendants **life peerage** *n.*

life preserver any of various devices used to buoy a person up in the water and prevent him from drowning

lif·er (láifər) *n.* (*pop.*) a prisoner serving a life sentence ‖ (*mil.*) a career soldier

life·sav·er (láifseivər) *n.* (*Br.*) a lifeguard

life science any of a group of sciences encompassing human activity, e.g., medicine, biology, psychology, sociology, anthropology, etc. —**life scientist** *n.*

life-size (láifsaiz) *adj.* (of a portrait, sculpture etc.) of the same size as the subject **life-sized** *adj.*

life style 1. (*psych.*) method of achieving feeling of adequacy and status used during growth as conceived by Austrian psychiatrist Alfred Adler **2.** the way in which an individual lives, e.g., as to dress, habits, friendships, values, etc.

life-style concept (léifsteil) marketing concept that recognizes that individual or family life-styles play an important role in consumption and spending patterns

life-sup·port system (léifsəport) an apparatus that provides basic elements, e.g., oxygen, water, food, temperature control, waste disposal, etc., to sustain life, e.g., in a space vehicle

life table a mortality table

life-time (láiftaim) *n.* the duration of the life of a person, thing, institution etc. ‖ (*pop.*) a very long time

lifetime reserve (*insurance*) in the Medicare hospital insurance program, a reserve of 60 days of inpatient hospital care available over an individual's lifetime that the individual may use after he or she has used the maximum 90 days allowed in a single benefit period

LIFO (léifou) *n.* (*acronym*) last-in-first-out policy in inventory accounting *Cf* FIFO

lift (lift) **1.** *v.t.* to raise to a higher position, hoist ‖ (*rhet.*) to direct up to God, *to lift up one's heart* ‖ to take from the ground, *to lift potatoes* ‖ (*pop.*) to steal ‖ to plagiarize (material) ‖ to remove, *to lift an embargo* ‖ to pay off (a mortgage etc.) ‖ *v.i.* to move upwards, disperse, *the fog lifted* **to lift one's hand against** to strike to **lift** (or **lift up**) **one's voice against** (*rhet.*) to protest against **2.** *n.* the act of lifting or an instance of this ‖ (*Br.*) an elevator (apparatus for raising or lowering) ‖ a mechanical hoist ‖ the load that is lifted ‖ the distance through which something is lifted or rises ‖ (*pop.*) an emotional bolstering up, *new clothes gave her the lift she needed* ‖ a free ride in a vehicle offered to someone to help him on his journey ‖ (*envir.*) compacted solid waste covered over in a sanitary landfill ‖ one of the layers of leather in the heel of a shoe ‖ (*aeron.*) the upward force exerted by air pressure against the undersurface of the wings of an aircraft, counteracting the force of gravity ‖ an airlift [O.N. *lypta*]

lift·er (líftər) *n.* comb with long prongs used to create an afro hairstyle

lift·ing body (líftiŋ) (*astronautics*) apparatus capable of traveling into and through space and returning

lift-off (líftof, líftof) *n.* the action of a rocket **leaving its** launch pad or of a helicopter etc. becoming airborne ‖ the moment this action occurs

lift pump a suction pump

lift valve a puppet valve

lig·a·ment (lígəmənt) *n.* (*anat.*) a short fibrous band which connects one bone with another or supports an organ ‖ any similar band of connective tissue **lig·a·men·tal** (ligəmént'l), **lig·a·men·ta·ry** (ligəméntəri), **lig·a·men·tous** (ligəméntəs) *adjs* [fr. L. *ligamentum*]

---

li·gase (láigeis) n. (biochem.) an enzyme that catalyzes the linking of two molecules, usu. involving a nucleoside triphosphate changed into diphosphate and monophosphate also synthetase

li·gate (láigeit) pres. part. **li·gat·ing** past and past part. **li·gat·ed** v.t. to ligature [fr. L. ligare (ligatus), to bind]

lig·a·ture (lígətfər, lígətfuər) 1. n. something used to bind or unite || (med.) a piece of nylon, wire etc. used as a surgical suture || the action of binding with such a suture || (printing) a character consisting of two or more letters joined by a stroke or tie || (mus.) a slur or tie joining notes together 2. v.t. pres. part. **lig·a·tur·ing** past and past part. **lig·a·tured** to bind with a ligature [fr. L. ligatura, a tie]

light (lait) n. the wave band of electromagnetic radiation between the wavelengths 3,800 angstrom units and 7,600 angstrom units, to which the retina of the eye is sensitive and which the brain interprets (*SPECTROSCOPY) || the portion of the electromagnetic spectrum including infrared, visible and ultraviolet radiation, e.g. ultraviolet light || the presence of this radiation (opp. DARKNESS) || a source of this radiation, shine your light on the keyhole || this radiation as related to its source, by the light of the moon || such radiation considered as being a person's own rightful source of illumination, don't stand in my light || a brightness, there was a light at the end of the tunnel || a vivacious or spirited look, the light in her eyes || mental illumination, power to explain things, the light of reason || someone who is a luminary, a light of the English court || the aspect in which something is seen, in a favorable light || (archit.) an aperture by which light is admitted to a building, esp. a division of a mullioned window or a glass pane in a greenhouse or frame || daylight || daytime || daylight with respect to a particular orientation, a north light || a flame or spark used to ignite something, or the thing providing this flame or spark, have you got a light for my cigarette?, put a light to the fire || (painting) a bright part of a picture, light and shade || (painting) the effect of light on objects or scenes as represented in a picture || a light used as a signal || (pl., theater) illuminated letters outside a theater **according to one's lights** according to one's principles **in the light of** as a result of taking into consideration, in the light of these changes we must revise our plan **to bring** (or **come**) **to light** to make (or become) known **to see the light** to be born, come into being, that lecture of his first saw the light 30 years ago || to come to understand || to have a spiritual revelation [O.E. lēoht]

light adj. of little weight, not heavy || having low specific gravity and small weight in relation to volume || having less than the correct weight || having less than the usual weight or amount || constructed of light parts or materials, a light wooden shed || having, because of its texture, small mass in relation to volume, light pastry || making a small impact, a light touch || made for small loads and quick movement, a light truck || lightly armed and speedy, light cavalry || quick-moving, nimble, light on her feet || not strenuous, easy to do, a light task || easily disturbed, a light sleeper || easy to bear, a light punishment || designed merely to amuse and give pleasure, light entertainment || lacking proper seriousness, frivolous, light conduct || dizzy, having a feeling of slight loss of stability || (of food) easy to digest, not very substantial || (of wine, ale etc.) having a relatively small alcoholic content || (games) deficient, to be one trick light || (of a building) not massive || (of soil) easily broken up, free of clay **to make light of** to appear to attach little importance to, he made light of his injury **to make light work of** to accomplish with ease || to defeat with ease **to travel light** to travel with little luggage with a **light heart** cheerfully [O.E. lēoht akin to G. leicht]

light adj. having considerable light, not dark, the room is light and airy || pale in color, light hair || (of a color) pale, a light blue hat [O.E. lēoht akin to G. licht]

light pres. part. **light·ing** past and past part. **lit** (lit), **light·ed** v.t. to cause to emit light or burn, to light a lamp, to light a fire || to show the way to by carrying a light, we will light you down the path || v.i. to become lit **to light up** to give light (or more light) to, the fire lit up the neighborhood || to become brighter, his countenance lit up || to start smoking one's pipe or cigarette [O.E. lihtan]

light pres. part. **light·ing** past and past part. **lit**, **light·ed** v.i. to come to rest, as a bird does from flight **to light on** (or **upon**) to discover by chance, he suddenly lit on the solution **to light into** (pop.) to attack vehemently [O.E. lihtan fr. O. Teut. type lihtjan]

light chain (biochem.) one of the four polypeptide compounds containing two or more linked amino acids that form antibodies Cf HEAVY CHAIN

light-day (láitdei) n. 1/365th of a light year, about 16 billion miles also light week, light month

light-emit·ting diode (láiti:mítin) 1. (electr.) a semiconductor that produces spontaneous and noncoherent visible or infrared wave lengths in electromagnetic radiation 2. (computer) output in a calculator that exhibits the result of a sequence. abbr. **LED**

light·en (láit'n) v.t. to make lighter, lighten the load || to reduce the load of, lighten a ship || to relieve, mitigate, lighten one's guilt feelings || to make more interesting or amusing, touches of humor lightened the lecture || v.i. to become lighter [LIGHT adj., not heavy]

lighten v.t. to make (a dark place) lighter || to make (a color etc.) lighter || v.t. to become brighter || (of lightning) to flash [LIGHT adj., not dark]

light·er (láitər) n. a device for lighting a cigarette etc. [LIGHT v., to cause to emit light]

lighter 1. n. a large, usually flat-bottomed, boat used to transport goods to or from a ship which cannot be docked or brought to a jetty etc. 2. v.t. to transport by lighter **light·er·age** n. this transporting or the cost of it **light·er·man** (láitərman) pl. **light·er·men** (láitərmen) n. someone employed on a lighter [Du. lichter or fr. older light v., to unload]

light·face (láitfeis) n. (printing) type characterized by thin lines

light-fin·gered (láitfingərd) adj. expert in stealing, esp. in picking pockets

light-head·ed (láithédid) adj. not quite in control of one's words or behavior, from delirium, drink, exhaustion etc. || frivolous, silly

light-heart·ed (láithártid) adj. free from cares or worries, cheerful

light heavyweight a professional boxer whose weight does not exceed 175 lbs || an amateur boxer whose weight does not exceed (Am.) 178 lbs or (Br.) 174 lbs

light horse (hist.) light cavalry

light·house (láithaus) pl. **light·hous·es** (láithauziz) n. a tall permanent structure, equipped with a usually revolving beacon light giving a signal to warn ships at night or in fog of the proximity of rocks, shore etc.

light·ly (láitli) adv. in a manner devoid of heaviness [O.E. lēohtlice fr. lēoht adj., light (not heavy)]

light meter an exposure meter

light middleweight an amateur boxer whose weight does not exceed 156 lbs

light-mind·ed (láitmáindid) adj. frivolous

light·ness (láitnis) n. the quality of an object that depends on its ability to reflect or transmit light (*COLOR) || degree of illumination [O.E. lihtnes fr. liht, lēoht adj., light (not dark)]

lightness n. the quality of being by no means heavy (opp. HEAVINESS)

light·ning (láitnin) 1. n. an electric discharge, e.g. a flash or a spark, between clouds or between a cloud and the earth 2. adj. as quick as lightning, a lightning move || of or pertaining to lightning [LIGHTEN, to give light to]

lightning arrester a device which protects electrical equipment from possible damage due to lightning or other momentary surges of high voltage

lightning bug a firefly

lightning conductor (Br.) a lightning rod

lightning rod (Am.=Br. lightning conductor) an earthed metal rod attached to a building to divert lightning from it or to reduce the likelihood of damage by lightning

light pen (computer) a hand-held instrument used for making changes in the information on a cathode ray display

lights (laits) pl. n. the lungs of slaughtered cattle, pigs or sheep [LIGHT adj., of little weight]

light·ship (láitfip) n. (naut.) a permanently anchored vessel furnished with a beacon and a siren for warning ships of sunken rocks, shoals etc.

light show 1. (entertainment) display of colored, often flashing, lights 2. display using flashing

colored lights, films, etc., that imitates the hallucinations produced by psychedelic drugs

lights-out (láitsáut) n. (mil.) a call or signal to turn out lights || an obligatory bedtime in boarding schools, camps etc.

light water (phys.) ordinary water, as distinguished from heavy water (which see)

light·weight (láitweit) 1. n. a professional boxer whose weight does not exceed 135 lbs || an amateur boxer whose weight does not exceed (Am.) 132 lbs or (Br.) 140 lbs 2. adj. of a lightweight || of less than usual weight, a lightweight coat

light welterweight an amateur boxer whose weight does not exceed 139 lbs

light whiskey type of whiskey with a lighter body and fewer flavor components

light-year (láitjər) n. an astronomical unit of distance: the distance traveled by light in one terrestrial year, i.e. 5.88 x 10^{12} miles

lign·al·oe (lainǽlou) n. aloes (the drug) || the fragrant wood of the East Indian tree Aquilaria agallocha, fam. Thymelaeaceae, burned as a perfume || the wood of a member of genus Bursera, fam. Burseraceae, esp. B. aloexylon, of Mexico [fr. L.L. lignum aloës, wood of aloe]

lig·ne·ous (lígni:əs) adj. of or similar to wood [fr. L. ligneus]

lig·nin (lígnin) n. a complex, polymeric substance which, with cellulose, causes the thickening and strengthening of plant cell walls and forms the bulk of the woody structure of plants [fr. L. lignum, wood]

lig·nite (lígnait) n. coal intermediate between peat and bituminous coal and containing much volatile matter [F.]

lig·no·caine (lígnəkein) [$C_{14}H_{22}N_2O$] or **li·do·caine** (Br.) (laidəkein) n. (pharm.) a local anesthetic; marketed as Xylocaine

lig·no·cel·lu·lose (lignouséljulous) n. any of several substances constituting the cell walls of woody stems and consisting of an intimate chemical association between lignin and cellulose [fr. L. lignum, wood + CELLULOSE]

lig·num vi·tae (lignəmváiti:) n. any of several guaiacum trees, esp. Guaiacum officinale, fam. Zygophyllaceae, a tropical American tree which produces a very heavy wood and a resin (*GUAIACUM) || the wood of this tree [L.=wood of life]

lig·u·la (lígjulə) pl. **lig·u·lae** (lígjuli:), **lig·u·las** n. a ligule || (zool.) a median structure between the labial palps of insects **lig·u·late** (lígjulit, lígjuleit) adj. having or forming a ligule || (bot. of a corolla in composite ray florets) strap-shaped [L. ligula, strap fr. lingua, tongue]

lig·ule (lígju:l) n. (bot.) a small flap of tissue or scale borne on a leaf or perianth segment near its base || (bot.) a ligulate corolla in composite ray florets || (zool.) a lobe on the parapodium of certain annelids [fr. L. ligula, strap]

Li·guo·ri (li:gwóri:), Alfonso Maria de' *ALPHONSUS LIGUORI

Li·gu·ri·a (ligjúəri:ə) a region (area 2,088 sq. miles, pop. 1,852,900) of N.W. Italy, consisting of the narrow coastal strip along the Gulf of Genoa. Capital: Genoa. Products: flowers, fruit, ships, chemicals, metallurgical products. Liguria was conquered (2nd c. B.C.) by the Romans, and was controlled by Genoa until it was annexed (1815) to Sardinia

lik·a·ble, like·a·ble (láikəb'l) adj. amiable, of a kind that elicits liking, a likable scoundrel [LIKE v.]

Li·ka·si (li:kǽsi:) (formerly Jadotville) a copper-mining town (pop. 146,394) in Katanga (Shaba), Zaïre

like (laik) 1. adj. identical, equal or almost equal, if you give $100 I'll give a like sum || faithful to the original, the portrait was pretty but not very like || resembling each other or one another in appearance or character, the brothers are very like **of like minds** of the same opinion **something like** (pop.) as it should be, or almost so 2. prep. characteristic of, it would be just like her to forget || indicative of, it looks like rain || to compare with, there's nothing like swimming for exercise || of the same nature as, to be compared with, what is she like? || in such a manner as, stop shouting like that || in the same way as, she waddles like a duck || identical or almost so, he looks like his father **to feel like** to be in the mood for 3. adv. (in the phrases) **as like as not, like as not, like enough,** probably 4. conj. (pop.) as, in the same way as, do it like he does || (pop.) similar to, it was like when you came home || 5. n. counterpart, equal, we'll never see her like again **and the like** and similar things, his pocket was filled with nails, marbles, string, *worms and the like* **the likes of me (you, him** etc.) people of the same rank, class etc. as me (you, him etc.), *such luxury isn't for the likes of me* [O.E. *gelīc*]

like 1. *v.t. pres. part.* **lik·ing** *past* and *past part.* **liked** to find pleasing, agreeable or attractive ‖ to be fond of ‖ (with infinitive) to make it a practice (to do something) from prudence, *I like to check his work as he's often inaccurate* ‖ to choose in a spirit of self-congratulation, *he likes to think he never makes mistakes* ‖ (in conditional constructions) to want to have, *he would like a cup of tea* ‖ (in conditional constructions) to wish, *he'd like to help* ‖ (with 'how') to feel about, *how do you like his new play?* **2.** *n.* (*pl.*) preferences, *we share the same likes and dislikes* [O.E. *līcian*]

-like *suffix* similar to, as in 'dreamlike' ‖ befitting, as in 'ladylike'

likeable *LIKABLE

like·li·hood (láikli:hud) *n.* probability

like·ly (láikli:) **1.** *adj. comp.* **like·li·er** *superl.* **like·li·est** probable ‖ plausible, credible, *a likely account* ‖ suitable, promising for a certain purpose, *a likely place for mushrooms* ‖ appearing capable, *a likely candidate* **likely to** probably going to, *it is likely to be wet* **2.** *adv.* (often with 'most' or 'very') probably, *she'll very likely cry when you go* **as likely as not, likely as not** quite possibly [O.N. *likligr*]

like-mind·ed (láikmáindid) *adj.* of the same opinion

lik·en (láikən) *v.t.* (with 'to', 'with') to represent as similar [LIKE adj.]

like·ness (láiknis) *n.* a similarity, resemblance ‖ a portrait, esp. with respect to its lifelike quality ‖ form, appearance, *in the likeness of a swan* [O.E. *līcnes*]

like·wise (láikwaiz) **1.** *adv.* similarly, in the same way **2.** *conj.* also, moreover [abbr. fr. *in like wise*, in a similar way]

lik·ing (láikiŋ) *n.* affection ‖ preference, taste **to one's liking** meeting with one's approval [O.E. *līcung*]

li·ku·ta (li:kú:ta) *pl.* **ma·ku·ta** (makú:ta) *n.* one hundredth of a zaïre ‖ a coin of this value

li·lac (láilək, láilæk) **1.** *n.* a member of *Syringa*, fam. *Oleaceae*, esp. *S. vulgaris*, a small deciduous tree native to Europe widely cultivated for its highly scented pinkish-mauve flowers, or a cultivated white variety ‖ flowers of these trees ‖ the pinkish-mauve color of *S. vulgaris* **2.** *adj.* of this color [F. prob. ult. fr. Pers. *lilak*, var. of *nilak* fr. *nil*, blue]

Lil·burne (lílbə:rn), John (c. 1614–57), English political leader. His pamphlets 'England's Birthright' (1645) and 'An Agreement of the People' (1648) advocated an extreme form of republican government and were the basis of the Levellers' program

lil·i·a·ceous (lili:éiʃəs) *adj.* of, pertaining to, or like a lily [fr. L. *liliaceus* fr. *lilium*, lily]

Lil·i·en·thal (líli:əntɑl), Otto (1848–96), German aeronautical engineer. He experimented in the production and piloting of gliders

Li·li·u·o·ka·la·ni (li:li:u:oukɑláni:), Lydia Kamekeha (1838–1917), queen (1891–3) of the Hawaiian Islands. For her disregard of the constitution of 1887, she was overthrown (1893) and a republic was proclaimed (1894). Her attempt (1895) to regain the throne led to the islands becoming (1898) a U.S. territory

Lille (li:l) an old textile center and commercial city (pop. 177,218) in N.E. France, near the Belgian frontier. University (1530)

Lil·lie (líli:), Frank Rattray (1870–1947), U.S. zoologist, best known for his research in embryology. He wrote 'The Development of the Chick' (1908, 3rd edn 1952). He was founding-president of the Woods Hole Oceanographic Institution in Massachusetts

lil·li·pu·tian (lilipjú:ʃən) *adj.* unusually and exceedingly small [fr. *Lilliput*, the island in Swift's 'Gulliver's Travels' where the people were only 6 ins tall]

Li·long·we (lilóŋwei) the capital of Malawi, in the S. central part of the country (pop. 102,400)

lilt (lilt) *n.* a gentle, pleasing, rising and falling rhythm in songs, voices, etc., *an Irish lilt* ‖ a gay melody with a lightly swinging rhythm ‖ a light swaying or sprightly movement, *a lilt in his step* **lilt·ing** *adj.* having or characterized by a lilt [M.E. *lulte*]

lil·y (líli:) *pl.* **lil·ies** *n.* a member of *Lilium*, fam. *Liliaceae*, a genus of bulbous, perennial plants, native to the northern hemisphere and cultivated for their showy flowers ‖ such a

flower ‖ any of various plants of the same family bearing flowers like those of genus *Lilium*, e.g. the day lily ‖ something compared to a lily in purity, delicacy, whiteness etc. ‖ (*heraldry*) the fleur-de-lis [O.E. *lilie* fr. L. fr. Gk]

lil·y-liv·ered (líli:lívərd) *adj.* (*rhet.*) cowardly

lily of the valley *Convallaria majalis*, fam. *Liliaceae*, a hardy perennial with underground creeping stem native to Europe and E. Asia and cultivated for its small, white, bell-shaped, scented flowers which are also distilled for perfume ‖ the dried rhizome and roots of this plant, yielding a cardiac stimulant and diuretic similar to digitalis

lily pad a floating leaf of the water lily

lil·y-white (líli:hwáit, líli:wáit) *adj.* (usually used ironically) unsoiled by work or dishonest dealings, *lily-white hands* ‖ pure, innocent

LIM (*abbr.*) for linear-induction motor, used in air-cushion vehicles

Li·ma (lí:mə) the capital (pop. 3,968,972) of Peru, founded by Pizarro (1535). It is eight miles inland from its port Callao, on the central coast. Industries: textiles, food processing, chemicals, engineering. Cathedral (1746), university (1551)

li·ma bean (láimə) any bean derived from *Phaseolus limensis*, fam. *Papilionaceae*, a tropical American species. They are bushy or tall-growing plants, cultivated for their edible greenish-white seeds ‖ one of these seeds

limb (lim) **1.** *n.* one of the projecting paired appendages (e.g. arm, leg, wing, fin, parapodium) of an animal body ‖ a large bough of a tree ‖ an arm of a cross ‖ a spur of a mountain ‖ either half of an archery bow **out on a limb** in a vulnerable position from which there is no going back ‖ (*Br.*) away from the center of activity **2.** *v.t.* to tear or cut away a limb of [O.E. *lim*]

limb *n.* the outer edge of the disk of the sun, moon, or other celestial body ‖ the graduated edge of a leveling rod, quadrant etc. ‖ (*bot.*) the broader spreading part of a petal, corolla or calyx, contrasted with the narrower basal part [fr. L. *limbus*, border]

lim·bate (límbeit) *adj.* (*biol.*) bordered, as when one color is surrounded by an edging of another [fr. L.L. *limbatus*]

Lim·be (límbei) *BLANTYRE-LIMBE

lim·ber (límbər) **1.** *n.* (*mil.*) the detachable ammunition chest of a tractor-drawn gun **2.** *v.t.* (*mil.*, usually with 'up') to attach (a limber and gun) to the towing tractor [etym. doubtful]

limber 1. *adj.* bending easily, flexible ‖ having a supple body **2.** *v.i.* (with 'up') to flex one's muscles and make one's limbs supple before some physical exertion ‖ *v.t.* (with 'up') to make supple [perh. fr. LIMB, body appendage]

lim·bers (límbərz) *pl. n.* (naut.) the gutters on each side of the inner keel which allow the water to drain into the well [etym. doubtful]

lim·bic (límbik) *adj.* (*physiol.*) of the circumferential portion of the brain

lim·bo (límbou) *n.* a dwelling place on the borders of hell to which some theologies consign souls who cannot go to heaven through no fault of their own, esp. the souls of unbaptized children or the souls of the righteous who died before Christ's coming ‖ a place or condition in which people or things lie neglected or forgotten ‖ West Indian dance involving bending backward under a gradually lowered horizontal bar. It is often performed in competition [fr. L. *in limbo*, on the border, fr. *limbus*, hem, border]

Lim·bourg (límbə:rk), Pol de (late 14th c.–early 15th c.), Flemish miniaturist, who with his two brothers was responsible for most of the illumination of 'les Très Riches Heures du Duc de Berry' (c. 1411–16)

Lim·bourg (lēbu:r) a province (area 929 sq. miles, pop. 639,000) in N.E. Belgium. Capital: Hasselt

Lim·burg (límbə:rg) the southernmost province (area 846 sq. miles, pop. 1,073,403) of the Netherlands. Capital: Maastricht

Lim·burg·er (límbə:rgər) *n.* a soft cheese of pungent odor and strong flavor [after LIMBOURG, Belgium]

lim·bus (límbəs) *n.* (*biol.*) a border distinctly marked by color or structure [L.= hem, border]

lim·dis (límdəs) *adj.* code word meaning available for "limited distribution of documents" (less than 100)

lime (laim) **1.** *n.* (*chem.*) a caustic and highly infusible solid consisting essentially of calcium oxide, obtained when calcium carbonate is

strongly heated. It is used in building, agriculture, metallurgy and for the treatment of sewage etc. ‖ birdlime **2.** *v.t. pres. part.* **lim·ing** *past* and *past part.* **limed** to spread lime over (a field etc.) ‖ to dress (hides), using lime and water ‖ to smear with birdlime [O.E *lim*]

lime *n.* *Tilia europa*, fam. *Tiliaceae*, a tree of northern temperate regions with fragrant whitish-yellow blossoms, ornamental heart-shaped leaves and white wood [prob. fr. earlier *line*, lind (older name for LINDEN)]

lime *n.* *Citrus aurantifolia*, fam. *Rutaceae*, a citrus tree native to the East Indies and cultivated in the U.S.A. and West Indies for its yellowish-green fruits, which are a source of ascorbic acid and yield a juice used in flavoring ‖ this fruit [F. fr. Span. fr. Arab.]

lime·burn·er (láimbə:rnər) *n.* someone who reduces limestone to lime in a limekiln

lime·kiln (láimkiln, láimkil) *n.* a kiln in which chalk or limestone is strongly heated to produce lime

lime·light (láimlait) *n.* an intense white light produced when lime is heated in an oxyhydrogen flame, formerly used in signaling and for stage lighting ‖ the flood of publicity accorded to a public figure

li·men (láimən) *n.* (*psychol.*) the threshold of consciousness, the limit below which a stimulus is not perceived [L.=threshold]

lime pit a pit containing lime and water in which hides are soaked to remove the hair ‖ a limestone quarry

Lim·er·ick (límərik), Thomas Dongan, 2nd Earl of (1634–1715), Colonial governor of New York (1682–8). He called the first representative assembly in New York, and he fostered a 'Charter of Liberties' and broad religious tolerance. Recognizing the strategic location of his state, he fixed the boundaries between New York and the contiguous colonies and later with Canada

Limerick an inland county (area 1,037 sq. miles, pop. 161,661) of Munster province, Irish Republic ‖ its county seat (pop. 60,736), the chief port on the west coast. Industries: food processing, textiles

lim·er·ick (límərik) *n.* a five-lined nonsense verse rhyming *aabba* popularized by Edward Lear. The first, second and fifth lines have three feet and the third and fourth lines have two feet [prob. fr. a chorus 'Will you come up to Limerick?']

lime·stone (láimstoun) *n.* a hard rock formed by the deposition of organic remains (e.g. seashells) that consists mainly of calcium carbonate

lime·wa·ter (láimwɒtər, láimwɒtər) *n.* an aqueous solution of calcium hydroxide

lim·ey (láimi:) *n.* (*pop.*) an Englishman, esp. an English sailor [fr. *lime juicer*, a British ship, so called because of the former compulsory use of lime juice to prevent scurvy]

li·mic·o·line (laimíkəlain) *adj.* (*zool.*, esp. of birds) living on the shore, e.g, plovers, snipes [fr. L. *limicola* fr. *limus*, mud +*colere*, to dwell]

lim·i·nal (límin'l) *adj.* (*psychol.*) of or pertaining to the limen [fr. L. *limen* (*liminis*), threshold]

lim·it (límit) **1.** *n.* (often *pl.*) the furthest extent, amount etc., *the limits of his knowledge* ‖ (often *pl.*) boundary, confines, *within the limits of the estate* ‖ a point which may not or cannot be passed, *speed limit* ‖ an established highest or lowest amount, quantity, size etc., *the limit is six players per game* ‖ (*math.*) either of two values between which an integral is to be evaluated ‖ (*math.*) the value or number to which a mathematical sequence, series or function tends as the independent variable approaches certain prescribed values (e.g. ±infinity) ‖ the limit ‖ someone or something that goes too far and cannot be endured **within limits** within moderation, to a moderate extent, *you can trust him within limits* **without limit** without restriction **2.** *v.t.* to restrict, *limit him to 5,000 words for his review* ‖ to serve as a limit to [fr. F. *limite*]

lim·i·ta·tion (limitéiʃən) *n.* a limiting or being limited ‖ something that limits ‖ a limit of capability, *he is a brilliant professor but has his limitations as an administrator* ‖ (*law*) the period fixed by statute of limitation after which a claimant cannot bring an action [fr. L. *limitatio* (*limitationis*)]

limited company (*Br.*, *abbr.* Limited or Ltd) a company in which the responsibility of a share-

CONCISE PRONUNCIATION KEY: **(a)** æ, c*a*t; ɑ, c*a*r; ɔ f*aw*n; ei, sn*a*ke. **(e)** e, h*e*n; i:, sh*ee*p; iə, d*ee*r; ɛə, b*ea*r. **(i)** i, f*i*sh; ai, t*i*ger; ə:, b*i*rd. **(o)** o, *o*x; au, c*ow*; ou, g*oa*t; u, p*oo*r; ɔi, r*oy*al. **(u)** ʌ, d*u*ck; u, b*u*ll; u:, g*oo*se; ə, b*a*cillus; ju:, c*u*be. x, lo*ch*; θ, *th*ink; ð, bo*th*er; z, *Z*en; ʒ, cor*s*age; dʒ, sa*v*age; ŋ, ora*ng*utan*g*; j, *y*ak; ʃ, *fi*sh; tʃ, fe*tch*; 'l, rab*ble*; 'n, red*den*. Complete pronunciation key appears inside front cover.

holder in case of debt is restricted according to the amount of his personal interest

limited edition an edition of a book, pamphlet etc. having a restricted, specified number of copies

limited-liability company a limited company

limited monarchy a monarchy whose powers are restricted by its constitution

limited war (*mil.*) armed conflict short of general war, exclusive of incident. Its objective is not the total defeat of the enemy

lim·it·ing (límitiŋ) *adj.* (*gram.*) of any of a class of words whose meaning restricts the word modified (e.g. 'two', 'that', 'several') ‖ confining, restrictive

limits to growth (*economics*) hypothesis that the interaction of inadequate food supply, contained population growth, dwindling natural resources, industrial growth, and increased pollution over a period of the next 60 years would lead to a planetary doomsday; reported to the Club of Rome, 1972

limn (lim) *v.t.* (*rhet.*) to paint ‖ (*rhet.*) to portray, e.g. in words **lim·ner** (límnər, límər) *n.* (*hist.*) an illuminator of medieval manuscripts ‖ (*rhet.*) a painter [fr. older *lumine* fr. O.F. *luminer*, to illuminate (manuscripts)]

lim·nol·o·gy (limnólədʒi:) *n.* the science of the biological and other phenomena of fresh water, esp. of ponds and lakes [fr. Gk *limnē*, marsh+*logos*, discourse]

lim·o (límou) *n.* short for limousine

Li·moges (li:móuʒ) a city (pop. 143,689) of Haute-Vienne, W. France, the old capital of Limousin, famous for its enamel industry, which was fully developed by the 13th c., and for its porcelain. Other industries: shoes, textiles, engineering, leather. Cathedral (13th–16th cc.). The center of the city is medieval

lim·o·nene (límani:n) *n.* a liquid terpene, $C_{10}H_{16}$, smelling like lemons and occurring in many essential oils [fr. F. *limon*, lemon]

li·mon·ite (láimənait) *n.* natural hydrated ferric oxide, of variable composition, usually rust-colored or yellow ocher [prob. fr. Gk *leimón*, meadow]

Li·mo·sin (li:mouzē) a famous French family of enamelers, from Limoges. Léonard (c. 1505–1577) is the most famous. He is said to have painted over 2,000 works

Li·mou·sin (li:mu:zē) a former province of France in the N.W. Massif Central, including Corrèze and parts of Creuse and Haute-Vienne, consisting largely of rocky plateaus, cut by deep gorges. Present-day industries: livestock (cattle and sheep) in the hills, crafts (tapestries, porcelain) and light manufactures in the main valley. Towns: Limoges (the historic capital) and Tulle. Limousin was the northernmost langue d'oc-speaking region. A Carolingian countship, partitioned in the 10th c., it passed to England with Aquitaine (1152), was disputed until 1374, when France secured it, and was annexed to the crown by Henri IV (1607)

lim·ou·sine (líməzi:n, liməzí:n) *n.* a car with a closed body and a partitioned seat for the driver ‖ a luxurious car [F.]

limousine liberal a wealthy liberal

limp (limp) **1.** *v.i.* to walk awkwardly or painfully because of some deformity or injury to one leg ‖ to move slowly or with difficulty, *the damaged ship limped into the harbor* ‖ (of verse) to have a halting rhythm **2.** *n.* a lame or crippled walk, *he walks with a limp* [etym. doubtful]

limp *adj.* floppy, not stiff or crisp ‖ (*bookbinding*) not stiffened with boards, *limp covers* ‖ lacking in energy, weak, feeble, *a limp handshake, limp with fatigue* [origin unknown]

limp·en (límpən) *v.* to become limp

lim·pet (límpit) *n.* a gastropod mollusk, with a conical shell, that clings tightly to rocks, esp. one of fam. *Acmaeidae* or *Patellidae*, widely distributed in tropical and temperate seas [O.E. *lempedu* fr. L. L. *lampreda*]

lim·pid (límpid) *adj.* (*rhet.*) clear, transparent, *limpid water, a limpid style* **lim·pid·i·ty** *n.* [fr. F. *limpide* or L. *limpidus*]

limp·kin (límpkin) *n. Aramus pictus*, fam. *Aramidae*, a long-billed, large wading bird inhabiting Florida, Central America and the West Indies [etym. doubtful]

Lim·po·po (limpóupou) a river (1,000 miles long) which forms the northern boundary of the Transvaal, South Africa, then flows across S. central Mozambique to the Indian Ocean

lim·y (láimi:) *comp.* **lim·i·er** *superl.* **lim·i·est** *adj.* like, made of, containing or covered with lime

LINAC (línæk) *n.* (*acronym*) linear accelerator, a straight-line particle accelerator used for increasing the energy of positive ions by action of alternating voltages, used for study of particles in cancer therapy *Cf* HILAC

lin·age, line·age (láinidʒ) *n.* the number of lines in printed or written matter ‖ payment to the writer according to the number of lines

li·nar (láinər) *n.* (*meteor*) point sources that emit energy at wavelengths characteristic of the spectral line of particular chemicals

linch·pin (líntʃpin) *n.* a pin passed through the end of an axle to keep the wheel on ‖ something essential on which everything else depends, *the linchpin of the prosecution's case* [older *linch*, linchpin+PIN]

Lin·coln (líŋkən), Abraham (1809–65), 16th president (1861–5) of the U.S.A., a Republican. Born in Kentucky and brought up in the backwoods of Indiana, he taught himself law, entered (1847) Congress, and campaigned against slavery, notably in the Lincoln-Douglas Debates (1858). His election as president, on an antislavery program, provoked the secession of the Southern states. He waged with vigor the ensuing Civil War (1861–5) to restore and preserve the Union. In 1863 he issued the Emancipation Proclamation and delivered the Gettysburg Address. He promised amnesty and moderation to the defeated South, but was assassinated by John Wilkes Booth, a Southern fanatic (*GETTYSBURG ADDRESS)

Lincoln the county town (pop. 71,900) of Lincolnshire, England, a county borough. Gothic cathedral (11th–13th cc.)

Lincoln the capital (pop. 171,932) of Nebraska, a rail center and grain and livestock market: food processing, oil refining, engineering. State university (1871)

Lincoln–Douglas Debates U.S. political debates held (1858) in Illinois, in which Abraham Lincoln, campaigning against the extension of slavery, and Stephen Douglas, advocating his Freeport Doctrine, vied for the Illinois senatorial seat. Douglas won the seat, but Lincoln won a national reputation from the debates

Lincoln Highway the first transcontinental highway in the U.S.A., extending (appox. 3,331 miles) through 13 states from New York City to San Francisco. It was dedicated (1913) as a memorial to Abraham Lincoln

Lincoln's Birthday the birthday (Feb. 12) of Abraham Lincoln, a legal holiday in many U.S. states

Lin·coln·shire (líŋkənʃiər) (*abbr.* Lincs.) a county (area 2,664 sq. miles, pop. 524,500) on the east coast of England. County town: Lincoln

Lincoln's Inn *INNS OF COURT

lin·co·my·cin [$C_{18}H_{34}N_2O_6S$] (liŋkəméis'n) *n.* (*pharm.*) antibiotic effective against gram-positive cocci; marketed as Lincocin

lin·dane [$C_6H_6Cl_6$] (líndein) *n.* (*chem.*) powerful insecticide, formerly called gamma benzene hexachloride, used as a parasiticide in treatment of scabies and pediculosis; marketed as Kwell

Lindbergh (línbə:rg), Anne Morrow (1906–   ), U.S. writer, wife of Charles A. Lindbergh. She worked with her husband in aviation and wrote about it in 'North to the Orient' (1935) and 'Listen! The Wind' (1938). Other works include 'Gift from the Sea' (1955), 'Bring Me a Unicorn' (1972), 'Hour of Gold, Hour of Lead' (1973), 'Locked Rooms and Open Doors' (1974) and 'War Within and Without' (1980)

Lind·bergh Charles Augustus (1902–74), U.S. aviator. He made the first solo flight of the Atlantic (1927), flying the 3,600 miles from New York to Paris in 33½ hours

lin·de·man glass (líndəmən) a glass made of materials having an atomic number less than oxygen (8), used for low-voltage tubes because it does not resist long-wavelength X-rays

lin·den (líndən) *n.* a member of *Tilia*, fam. *Tiliaceae*, e.g. the lime or the basswood ‖ the wood of such a tree [O.E. *linden* adj. fr. *lind*, linden]

Lin·dis·farne (líndisfarn) *HOLY ISLAND

Lind·say (líndzi), Sir David (1486–1555), Scottish poet, best known for his satirical morality play 'Ane Satyre of the thrie estaits' (1540) and the romance 'A Historie of squyer mildrum' (1594)

Lindsay, Vachel (1879–1931), U. S. poet. His works, which make use of jazz rhythms, include 'The Congo' (1914)

Lind·sey, the Parts of (líndzi:) an administrative county (area 1,520 sq. miles, pop. 547,560) of Lincolnshire. Administrative center: Lincoln

line (lain) **1.** *n.* (esp. *naut.*) a length of rope ‖ a length of cord, thread etc. with a hook, used with or without a rod for catching fish ‖ a clothesline ‖ a telephone wire or cable, or this route of communication ‖ a pipe or similar retainer through which liquids, gases etc. may be transported, e.g. a gas line ‖ a length of cord, wire etc. used in measuring and leveling, e.g. in laying building foundations ‖ a long thin stroke marked on a surface ‖ the way an artist uses such lines, *purity of line* ‖ something thought of as like a long thin stroke on a surface, e.g. a ridge of hills, band of color etc. ‖ (*games*) a mark showing the limits or various divisions of a field or court, *the goal line* ‖ the boundary or limit of an area, piece of property etc. ‖ an imaginary mark denoting the separation of one state, category, idea etc. from another, *the fine line between neurosis and psychosis* ‖ (*math.*) that which has length but not breadth ‖ (*geog.*) a meridian or parallel, *a line of latitude or longitude* ‖ (usually with 'the') the equator ‖ a curve on a map, graph etc. connecting points with a specified common property ‖ an outline, contour, *the spare line of his profile, the classic lines of the town hall* ‖ (*naut., pl.*) the outlines of a vessel seen in horizontal, vertical or oblique sections ‖ the style or cut of a garment ‖ a wrinkle or crease in the skin ‖ a row, *a line of trees* ‖ a row of written, typed or printed words ‖ a brief letter ‖ (*mus.*) one of the horizontal strokes of a staff ‖ a single row of words in a poem ‖ (*pl.*) the words of an actor's part, *to forget one's lines* ‖ (*Br., pop., pl.*) a marriage certificate ‖ (*Br., pl.*) a certain number of lines of verse, or repetitions of a sentence, to be written out as a school punishment ‖ (*football*) the players arranged in a row even with the ball or 1 ft from it at the start of a play ‖ (*football*) the line of scrimmage ‖ (*mil.*) a linked series of trenches and fortifications, *the front line* ‖ (*Br., mil., pl.*) a row of huts or tents, *troops must not leave their lines* ‖ (*mil.*) a row of men or companies ranged side by side (opp. COLUMN) ‖ (*mil., hist.*) the body of regular, numbered infantry regiments of an army ‖ (*hist.*) the body of fighting ships of a navy ‖ a regular series or service of ships, buses etc. between given places, or the company running it ‖ a number of things, persons or events which come one after another in time in a regular manner or series, *a long line of distinguished public servants, direct line of descent* ‖ (*rhet.*) lineage, family, *he comes of a good line* ‖ a direction, *line of advance, line of march, in the line of fire* ‖ route, *lines of communication* ‖ a single track of rail ‖ a rail route, or part of a rail system, *the suburban line* ‖ a course of conduct, direction of thought, or mode of procedure, *follow the party line* ‖ a branch of business or activity, *he's in the building line* ‖ the activity in which one feels oneself competent or happy, *oil painting isn't really my line* ‖ (*commerce*) a stock of a certain kind of goods, *a cheap line in ready-made suits* **all along the line** at every point **hard lines** (esp. *Br.*) bad luck **in line for** due for, in the running for, *in line for promotion* **line abreast** (of ships) side by side **line astern** (of ships) one behind another **on the lines of** like, modeled on **to be hung on the line** (*Br.*) to have a picture accepted for showing at the Royal Academy and hung at eye level **to be in (out of) line with** to agree (disagree) with **to bring into line** to make agree **to come into line** to fall into agreement or conformity **to draw the line at** to consider to be beyond the limit of what is acceptable, *he draws the line at using violence* **to drop a line** to write a brief letter or note **to fall into line with** to adjust oneself to the wishes of **to get a line on** to obtain information on **to give a line on** to reveal some of the ideas or the general drift of, *can you give me a line on the chairman's opinion?* **to have a line on** to form an idea about or have information about **to read between the lines** to understand what is being implied without its being made explicit **to toe the line** to touch a line or mark with the toes at the start of a race ‖ to obey the rules and regulations, conform ‖ **to toe the party line** to keep to the officially approved way of thinking **2.** *v. pres. part.* **lin·ing** *past* and *past part.* **lined** *v.t.* to mark or cover with lines ‖ to stand or be in a line along, *crowds lined the streets* ‖ to place or arrange in a line along, *a shore lined with villas*

‖ to set or arrange in a line ‖ (with 'up') to make arrangements about, *to line up support for a candidate* ‖ *v.i.* (with 'up') to form a line, *they lined up at the entrance* [partly O.E. *line* prob. fr. L. and partly F. *ligne*]

line *pres. part.* **lin·ing** *past* and *past part.* **lined** *v.t.* to provide with an inner layer ‖ to be such an inner layer for ‖ (*bookbinding*, often with 'up') to reinforce the back of (a book) with glue and muslin etc. **to line one's purse** (or **pocket**) to enrich oneself by dishonest or surreptitious methods, esp. by accepting bribes [fr. older *line*, flax fr. O.E. *lin*]

line·age (láinidʒ) *LINAGE

lin·e·age (líni:idʒ) *n.* (*rhet.*) a line of descent, ancestry, *a family of ancient lineage* [M.E. *lignage, linage* fr. O.F.]

lin·e·al (líni:əl) *adj.* in the direct line of descent ‖ of or in lines [F. *linéal*]

lin·e·a·ments (líni:əmənts) *pl. n.* facial features [F. *linéament*]

lin·e·ar (líni:ər) *adj.* of or in lines, *a linear pattern* ‖ (of a unit of measure) involving one dimension only ‖ able to be shown as a straight line on a graph ‖ (esp. *bot.*) long and narrow and of uniform width ‖ (*electronics*) responding in a manner directly proportional to the input or stimulus or being such a response ‖ (of a painting etc.) having well-defined lines and outlines ‖ (*psych.*) of the tendency to follow the sequence of a printed line ‖ (*math.*) of an equation where both sides are linear functions of the variables ‖ (*computer*) of a programming technique for solving a problem to maximize or minimize the ratio of various quantities in a mix for a best result [fr. L. *linearis*]

linear accelerator a device used to accelerate particles (esp. electrons) by allowing them to fall successively through small differences of potential. The fields involved are arranged in a line, sometimes with paths as long as 2 miles. The newest linear accelerators produce electrons of energies in the neighborhood of 10^{10}eV

Linear A, Linear B linear forms of writing used at Knossos on Crete and on the Greek mainland in the 2d millennium B.C.

linear algebra (*math.*) the branch of mathematics that studies linear relations between numbers

linear B a hieroglyphic script of late Minoan Crete (c. 1450-c. 1375 B.C.), deciphered (1953) as archaic Greek by Michael Ventris

linear equation (*math.*) an equation whose variables are of the first power only

lin·e·ar-in·duc·tion motor or **linear motor** (lini:ərindʌkʃən) a device that produces thrust without torque by using movement of the magnetic field *abbr.* **LIM**

linear integrated circuit (*electr.*) device for amplifying signals in an integrated circuit

linear measure a system of measuring length ‖ the unit of measurement used, e.g. foot, meter

linear perspective (*art*) perspective in which depicted sizes, distances and relative positions are made to appear to correspond to actual ones

linear tariff cut (*economics*) a reduction in all tariffs by the same percentage

lin·e·a·tion (lini:éiʃən) *n.* a marking with or arrangement in lines [fr. L. *lineatio* (*lineationis*)]

line block a linecut

line·breed·ing (láinbri:diŋ) *n.* the inbreeding of animals descended from an ancestor having some desirable characteristic which it is wished to strengthen and perpetuate

line·cut (láinkʌt) *n.* a metal plate processed photomechanically for printing from by letterpress, the metal other than the printing surface being etched away to a lower level. The printing surface consists of lines or solid areas not broken up by a screen into dots ‖ a print made from such a plate line drawing ‖ a drawing made with pen, pencil etc. and showing only solid lines or solid masses

line drive (*baseball*) a ball which is hit so that it flies in a straight line just above the ground

line engraving an engraving done by means of incised lines, or this process ‖ a plate so engraved ‖ a picture produced by this process (cf. ETCHING, cf. MEZZOTINT)

Line Islands a group of 11 coral islands (area 295 sq. miles) in the central Pacific. Eight of the islands are part of KIRIBATI. Palmyra and Jarvis Is and Kingman Reef are administered by the U.S.A.

line judge (*football*) linesman who keeps track of the official game time

line·man (láinmən) *pl.* **line·men** (láinmən) *n.* someone who installs and repairs telegraph and telephone wires or power lines ‖ someone who carries the line in surveying etc. ‖ (*football*) any player positioned in the line at the start of a play ‖ (*Br.*) a railroad linesman

lin·en (línən) **1.** *n.* cloth made from flax fiber, varying in coarseness from cambric to canvas ‖ yarn or thread made from flax ‖ (*collect.*) articles made of this cloth or formerly usually made of it, e.g. shirts, underclothes, sheets, towels, tablecloths **to wash one's dirty linen in public** to discuss matters which reflect badly on oneself or one's close associates in front of other people or in print **2.** *adj.* made of flax or linen [O.E. *línen,* made of flax]

lin·en-drap·er (línəndreipər) *n.* (*Br.,* old-fash.) a dealer in cloth

lin·en·fold (línənfould) *n.* a decoration carved or molded in the pattern of folds of linen

line of battle (*hist.*) the position of troops or ships arranged for fighting a battle

line of fire the imaginary line from gun to target

line of force a line that shows the direction of the force in a magnetic or electric field

line of least resistance the course of action which calls for the minimum effort or will cause least bother

line of vision an imaginary line from an observed object to the eye of the observer

line·o·late (líni:əleit) *adj.* (*biol.*) marked with very fine lines **lin·e·o·lat·ed** *adj.* [fr. L. *lineola* dim. of *linea,* line]

line-out (láinaut) *n.* (*rugby*) a play to restart the game after the ball has gone into touch. The forwards are drawn up in parallel lines at right angles to the touchline

line printer device that composes and prints in lines, e.g., from Linotype —**line print** *v.* —**line printing** *n.*

lin·er (láinər) *n.* a large passenger ship or airliner belonging to a regular line ‖ (*baseball*) a line drive [LINE n.]

liner *n.* someone who provides linings ‖ something used for lining, e.g. the removable metal sleeve inside a gun, or a glass container inside a silver saltcellar [LINE v. (to provide with an inner layer)]

line score (*baseball*) record of runs, hits, and errors made by each team in a game *Cf* BOX SCORE

lines·man (láinzmən) *pl.* **lines·men** (láinzmən) *n.* (*tennis* etc.) an assistant official who signals whether the ball crosses or touches the line, and where ‖ (*football*) an official who marks distances gained or lost and where the ball goes out of play, and who reports certain violations of the rules to the referee ‖ a telephone, telegraph or power-line lineman ‖ (*Br., rail.*) a trackman

line-up (láinʌp) *n.* a row of people made to assemble, esp. by the police, for identification of suspected criminals ‖ (*football, baseball*) a list of players and their respective playing positions ‖ an enumeration of people with a common purpose, *a lineup of the prospective condidates*

ling (liŋ) *n. Molva molva,* fam. *Gadidae,* a long slender codlike fish of N. Europe, used for food either salted or dried ‖ the North American burbot [M.E. *lenge, lienge, linge* prob. rel. to LONG *adj.*]

ling *n.* heather, esp. *Calluna vulgaris,* fam. *Ericaceae,* a common species native to N. and W. Europe [O.N. *lyng*]

-ling *suffix* used to form diminutives, as in 'duckling' ‖ used to denote one of a specified kind, as in 'nestling' [O.E. fr. Gmc]

lin·gam (líŋgəm) *n.* a phallic symbol in the Hindu worship of Siva [Skr.=symbol]

lin·ger (líŋgər) *v.i.* to dawdle ‖ to loiter ‖ to stay on because one is loath to go ‖ to dwell (upon a subject), *he lingered lovingly over the account of his exploits* ‖ to be slow in dying or in dying out, *the sound lingered in the air* ‖ *v.t.* (with 'out') to pass (time) slowly, often in suffering [O.E. *lengan,* to stay]

lin·ge·rie (lɒnʒəréi, lɛʒri:) *n.* (esp. *commerce*) women's underclothing [F.]

lin·go (líŋgou) *pl.* **lin·goes, lin·gos** *n.* (pop.) a foreign language, considered as being peculiar ‖ jargon ‖ an unusual vocabulary or a way of using words that is peculiar to an individual [perh. corrup. of LINGUA FRANCA]

lin·gua (líŋgwə) *pl.* **lin·guae** (líŋgwi:) *n.* (*zool.*) a tongue or tonguelike structure [L.=tongue]

lingua fran·ca (fræŋkə) *n.* any language, esp. a hybrid one, serving as a common language between different peoples ‖ a language composed of Italian, French, Greek, Spanish and Arabic, used in Mediterranean ports [Ital.=Frankish language]

lin·gual (líŋgwəl) *adj.* of, like or near the tongue ‖ (*phon.*) articulated esp. with the tongue, e.g. the 'l' sound ‖ linguistic [fr. M.L. *lingualis*]

lin·gui·form (líŋgwifɔrm) *adj.* (*biol.*) tongue-shaped [fr. LINGUA]

lin·guist (líŋgwist) *n.* someone who is proficient in several foreign languages ‖ someone who exhibits a facility in learning a foreign language ‖ a specialist in linguistics **lin·guis·tic** *adj.* of or relating to languages or linguistics

lin·guis·tics *n.* the scientific study of language or languages whether from a historical and comparative (*DIACHRONIC) or from a descriptive, structural (*SYNCHRONIC) point of view (cf. PHILOLOGY). Linguistics is concerned with the system of sounds of language, esp. sound change (*PHONOLOGY), its inflections and word formation (*MORPHOLOGY), its sentence structure (*SYNTAX) and its meaning change (*SEMANTICS), as well as minor features, e.g. spelling [fr. L. *lingua,* tongue]

lin·gu·late (líŋgjuleit) *adj.* (*biol.*) linguiform [fr. L. *lingulatus*]

Li·niers (li:njei, li:njérs), Jacques (Santiago) de (1753–1810), Franco-Spanish seaman, who participated in the recapture of Buenos Aires from the British. Appointed (1807) viceroy of the River Plate, he remained loyal to the monarchist cause. Taken prisoner by the patriots, he was executed in Córdoba

lin·i·ment (línəmənt) *n.* a liquid medicinal preparation for rubbing into the skin to relieve pain and muscular stiffness [fr. L. *linimentum* fr. *linire,* to smear]

lin·ing (láiniŋ) *n.* the material which lines an inner surface, e.g. of a garment ‖ (*bookbinding*) the material used to reinforce a book's spine ‖ a providing with a lining [LINE v. (to provide with an inner layer)]

link (liŋk) **1.** *n.* a ring or loop of a chain ‖ one of the divisions of a surveyor's chain (=7.92 ins) ‖ a sausage forming part of a chain ‖ a cuff link ‖ someone or something that joins other people or things, *the child was the only link between the estranged parents* ‖ (*mech.*) a joining part needed to transmit force or motion ‖ (*computer*) portion of a program or equipment that directs information from one part to another, e.g., data link **2.** *v.t.* (often with 'up') to join ‖ to entwine (arms) by looping one's arm around another's ‖ *v.i.* (often with 'up') to join up, form an association [prob. fr. O.N.]

link *n.* (*hist.*) a torch made of pitch and tow carried to light someone's way in the streets [perh. fr. LINK n. (a ring)]

link·age (líŋkidʒ) *n.* a linking or being linked ‖ (*biol.*) the tendency of closely spaced genes on a chromosome to be transmitted as a unit (whence the association of certain hereditary characteristics) ‖ an international political strategy relating two or more issues in negotiations, and then using them as tradeoffs or pressure points, much as in a "carrot and stick" technique ‖ (*systems analysis*) a recurrent sequence that produces a reaction in another sequence ‖ practice of linking congressional salaries to those of other federal officials ‖ (*chem.*) the way in which atoms or radicals are bonded in a molecule ‖ (*mech.*) a system of links or rods to transmit movement or power [LINK n.]

linked (liŋkt) *n.* (of genes) exhibiting linkage

link·ing verb a verb ('be', 'feel', 'seem' etc.) that connects a subject and predicate

link·man (líŋkmən) *pl.* **link·men** (líŋkmən) *n.* (*hist.*) a man whose job was to carry a link (torch)

Lin·kö·ping (líntʃəːpiŋ) a city (pop. 112,600) of E. Götaland, Sweden, manufacturing rolling stock, aircraft and linen. Cathedral (1230–1350)

links (liŋks) *pl. n.* a golf course [O.E. *hlinc,* rising ground]

links·land (líŋkslænd) *n.* dunes

Link trainer a ground device which can simulate airplane movement, used to train pilots [after E. A. *Link* (1904–), U.S. inventor]

link-up (líŋkʌp) *n.* a connection or contact ‖ a means of contact, communication or connection

Lin·lith·gow (linlíθgou) *WEST LOTHIAN

Lin·nae·an, Lin·ne·an (liníːən) *adj.* of or pertaining to the system of binomial nomenclature devised by Linnaeus

Lin·nae·us (liníːəs), Carolus (Carl Linné, 1707–78), Swedish botanist who devised the system of binomial classification which, though considerably altered, is still in use today. He first used specific names in 'Genera plantarum' (1737). His classification of plants into 24 classes, based on the number and arrangement of the stamens, has been entirely superseded. He also made a classification of the animal kingdom

lin·net (línit) *n. Carduelis cannabina*, fam. *Fringillidae*, a small songbird with brownish-gray or white plumage, native to Europe, N. Africa and central Asia [(O.F. *linette* fr. *lin*, flax (because it feeds on flax seeds))]

li·no·cut (láinəkʌt) *n.* a printing surface made by cutting a picture or design in relief on a piece of linoleum ‖ a print made from this [LINOLEUM+CUT]

lin·o·le·ic acid (lin'líːik) a liquid unsaturated fatty acid, $C_{17}H_{31}COOH$, considered essential in animal nutrition [fr. Gk *linon*, flax + OLEIC]

li·no·le·um (linóuliːəm) *n.* a floor covering made by coating canvas with oxidized linseed oil mixed with resins and fillers (e.g. cork) [fr. L. *linum*, flax + *oleum*, oil]

Li·no·tron (láinətrɒn) *n.* (*typography*) a cathode-ray photocomposition device that converts data from magnetic tapes to print at high speed

Lin Piao (línpjáu) (1908–71), Chinese Communist general and statesman, minister of defense (from 1959). He was designated (1969) successor to Mao Tse-tung but died mysteriously, reported to have been killed in a plane crash while fleeing to the USSR after trying to usurp power

lin·sang (línsæŋ) *n.* a member of *Prionodon*, a genus of mammals of the East Indies and Australia, related to the civet [Javanese]

lin·seed (línsiːd) *n.* the seed of flax, from which linseed oil is extracted. It is also used medicinally as a demulcent and emollient [O.E. *linsǣd* fr. *líne*, flax + *sǣd*, seed]

linseed cake cattle feed made from the residue after the oil has been expressed from linseed

linseed oil a drying oil obtained from linseed, used in making linoleum, paint, printing ink and for oiling woods

lin·stock (línstɒk) *n.* (*hist.*) a forked staff which held a lighted match used for firing a cannon [fr. Du. *lontstok* fr. *lont*, match + *stok*, stick]

lint (lint) *n.* a material used for dressing wounds and made by rubbing linen cloth on one side until it is soft and fluffy ‖ bits of loose thread, fluff etc., esp when these collect in dust on clothing etc. [M.E. *linnet* perh. fr. F. *linette*, linseed]

lin·tel (lint'l) *n.* the slab of stone or wood placed across the top of a doorway or window frame **lín·teled**, esp. *Br.* **lin·telled** *adj.* [O.F.=threshold]

lin·ter (líntər) *n.* a machine for removing fluff from ginned cottonseed ‖ (*pl.*) these short, soft, cotton fibers, used in making padding etc.

Lin·ton (líntən), Ralph (1893–1953), U.S. anthropologist and pioneer in cultural anthropology. His 'The Study of Man' (1936) is a synthesis of theories from anthropology, psychology, and sociology concerning the nature of human culture

lin·u·ron [$C_9H_{10}C_2Cl_2N_2$] (línjuːrən) *n.* (*chem.*) a herbicide used in vegetable patches

Linz (lints) a port and rail center (pop. 199,910) on the Danube in N. Austria: metal, chemical and engineering industries

li·on (láiən) *n. Felis leo*, fam. *Felidae*, a large carnivorous mammal, up to 12 ft in length and 600 lbs in weight, native to Africa and S. Asia. Lions are tawny in color, with a tufted tail and, in the male, a thick, full-flowing mane ‖ (*rhet.*) a man thought of as being like a lion because of his courage, leadership or strength ‖ a celebrity, esp. one thought of as a desirable and impressive guest **in the lion's mouth** in an acutely dangerous position **the lion's share** the largest share [A.F. *liun* fr. L. fr. Gk]

li·on·ess (láiənis) *n.* the female lion [O.F. *lionesse*, *lionnesse*, *leonesse*]

li·on·heart·ed (láiənhɑrtid) *adj.* (*rhet.*) brave as a lion

li·on·ize (láiənaiz) *pres. part.* **li·on·iz·ing** *past* and *past part.* **li·on·ized** *v.t.* to treat as a celebrity and make a great fuss over

lip (lip) **1.** *n.* one of the two fleshy, muscular, highly sensitive folds bordering the mouth,

lined on the outside by skin, and on the inside by the translucent membrane of the mouth ‖ (*biol.*) a lip-shaped structure ‖ the edge of a cavity, opening, vessel, wound etc. ‖ the rim of a vessel, esp. that part which juts out to form a pouring spout ‖ (*pop.*) impudent talk, answering back etc. **to hang on someone's lips** to listen to someone with complete attention **to keep a stiff upper lip** to endure without flinching, show fortitude **to lick** (or **smack**) **one's lips** to show eager anticipation **2.** *adj.* (*phon.*) labial [O.E. *lippa*]

Li·pa·ri Islands (líːpɑriː) seven volcanic Italian islands (area 46 sq. miles, pop. 16,037) off N. Sicily. Products: Malmsey wine, pumice. Stromboli and Vulcano are active volcanoes

lip·a·roid (lípərɔid) *adj.* fatlike ‖ fatty [fr. Gk *liparos*, shining]

li·pase (láipeis, líːpeis) *n.* (*biol.*) an enzyme that aids the hydrolysis or synthesis of fats [fr. Gk *lipos*, fat]

Lip·chitz, Lip·schitz (lípʃits), Jacques (1891–1973), American sculptor of the French school, born in Lithuania, living in America after 1940. His cubist works are derived from the human figure or from objects. In later work, this original cubist style became more abstract, with added power and expressiveness

lip·id (lípid) *n.* (*biochem.*) one of a very large group of organic compounds which includes fats, waxes, phosphatides etc. with carbohydrates and proteins they constitute the principal components of living cells [fr. Gk *lipos*, fat]

lip·ide (lípaid) *n.* a lipid

Lipizzaner *LIPPIZANER

Lip·mann (lípmən), Fritz Albert (1899–1986), U.S. biochemist who shared (with H. A. Krebs) the 1953 Nobel prize in medicine and physiology for the discovery of coenzyme A, a vital catalyst in cellular metabolism

lip microphone a microphone applied to the upper lip to eliminate surrounding noise

lip·oid (lípɔid) (*chem.*) **1.** *adj.* fatlike **2.** *n.* a fat or fatlike substance [fr. Gk *lipos*, fat]

li·po·ma (lipóumə) *pl.* **li·po·mas, li·po·ma·ta** (lipóumətə) *n.* (*med.*) a fatty tumor [Mod. L. fr. Gk *lipos*, fat]

lip·o·pol·y·sac·cha·ride (laípoupɑlisǽkəraid) *n.* (*biochem.*) a large molecule compounded of fats and sugar

lip·o·tro·pins (lɑipoutróupinz) *n.* (*biochem.*) pituitary hormones that dispose of fats —**lipo·tropic** *adj.* having an affinity for fats

Lippes loop (lípəs) an S-shape intrauterine contraceptive device, named for Jack Lippes, American physician

Lip·pi (líːppiː), Filippino (c. 1457–1504), Italian painter, son of Fra Filippo Lippi. His work, mainly altarpieces and frescoes, many of which survive in Rome and Florence, was entirely devotional

Lippi, Fra Filippo (c. 1406–69), Italian painter, father of Filippino Lippi. Under the patronage of the Medicis he painted brilliantly colored frescoes and altarpieces at Prato (1452–64) and Spoleto (1466–9)

Lip·pi·za·ner, Lip·iz·za·ner (lípitsɑnər) *n.* a member of a breed of horses raised at the Austrian Imperial Stud, famous for their feats of dressage [fr. G. fr. *Lippiza, Lipizza*, N.W. Yugoslavia, where the Imperial Stud was located]

Lipp·mann (líːpmæn), Gabriel (1845–1921), French physicist. He devised one of the earliest methods of color photography. Nobel prize in physics (1908)

Lipp·mann (lípmən), Walter (1899–1974), U.S. newspaper commentator. He contributed to Wilson's Fourteen Points and to the concept of the League of Nations. His writings on public affairs include 'Public Opinion' (1927) and 'The Good Society' (1937)

lip·read (lípriːd) *pres. part.* **lip·read·ing** *past* and *past part.* **lip·read** (lípred) *v.t.* to understand by lipreading ‖ *v.i.* to do lipreading

lip·read·er (líprːdər) *n.* someone who does lipreading

lip·read·ing (líprːdiŋ) *n.* a method of understanding speech by observing the movements of the speaker's lips. It may be learned by deaf people

LIPS (*computer acronym*) list processing, a programming language used for list processing, text manipulation, and artificial intelligence

Lipschitz *LIPCHITZ

lip service insincere expression of approval, agreement, adherence etc.

lip·stick (lípstik) *n.* a stick of cosmetic, usually in a retractable holder, for coloring the lips

lip·synch (lípsiŋk) *n.* a technique for prerecording songs or providing off-stage vocalizing so that the entertainer on stage need only make lip movements coinciding with the song he or she appears to be singing

li·quate (láikweit) *pres. part.* **li·quat·ing** *past* and *past part.* **li·quat·ed** *v.t.* (often with 'out') to separate (a solid mixture, esp. a metal) by liquation [fr. L. *liquare* (*liquatus*), to melt]

li·qua·tion (laikwéiʃən) *n.* the purification of a solid mixture by heating until one constituent melts and can be drained off [fr. L. *liquatio* (*liquationis*) fr. *liquare*, to melt]

liq·ue·fa·cient (likwiféiʃənt) *n.* something which liquefies a substance or aids in liquefaction [fr. L. *liquefaciens* (*liquefacientis*) fr. *liquefacere*, to make liquid]

liq·ue·fac·tion (likwəfǽkʃən) *n.* a liquefying or being liquefied

liq·ue·fi·a·ble (líkwifaiəb'l) *adj.* capable of being liquefied

liq·ue·fi·er (líkwifaiər) *n.* an apparatus in which gases are liquefied

liq·ue·fy (líkwifai) *v. pres. part.* **liq·ue·fy·ing** *past* and *past part.* **liq·ue·fied** *v.t.* to make liquid ‖ *v.i.* to become liquid [F. *liquéfier*]

li·ques·cent (likwés'nt) *adj.* becoming or liable to become liquid [fr. L. *liquescens* (*liquescentis*) fr. *liquescere*, to become liquid]

li·queur (likə́ːr, *Br.* esp. likjúə) *n.* a strongly flavored and highly fortified alcoholic liquor, e.g. chartreuse or benedictine ‖ a mixture of sugar and aged wine for inducing second fermentation in the making of champagne [F.]

liqueur brandy (*Br.*) a high-quality brandy for drinking as a liqueur

liq·uid (líkwid) **1.** *adj.* of or being a fluid substance which under the influence of small forces assumes a shape imposed by its container but does not expand indefinitely (cf. SOLID, cf. GAS, *KINETIC THEORY) ‖ transparent, clear, *the liquid air of a mountain meadow* ‖ (of sounds) flowing, musical, *the liquid notes of the thrush* ‖ (*phon.*, of a consonant) pronounced with the slightest contact of the tongue and mouth, e.g. 'l' and 'r' ‖ readily changeable for cash, *liquid assets* **2.** *n.* a liquid substance ‖ a liquid consonant [O.F. *liquide*]

liq·ui·date (líkwideit) *pres. part.* **liq·ui·dat·ing** *past* and *past part.* **liq·ui·dat·ed** *v.t.* to pay or settle (a debt) ‖ to wind up (a company or business) by realizing its assets, paying its debts and distributing the balance to the shareholders ‖ to clear up, put an end to ‖ to eradicate, exterminate (opponents, enemies etc.) ‖ to convert into cash ‖ *v.i.* to become liquidated **liq·ui·da·tion** *n.* a liquidating or being liquidated ‖ the condition of being liquidated **líq·ui·da·tor** *n.* someone appointed to supervise the liquidation of a company [fr. L.L. *liquidare* (*liquidatus*), to make liquid]

liquid crystal a liquid showing certain properties, e.g. birefringence, which are otherwise possessed only by crystals

liquid crystal displays (*electr.*) sheets of glass with sealed-in transparent liquid, used for viewing alphanumeric readouts for small electronic products, e.g., digital watches, calculators. abbr. LCD

liquid fire (*mil.*) an inflammable chemical mixture which can be shot in a stream, e.g. from a flamethrower

li·quid·i·ty (likwíditi) *n.* the quality or state of being liquid [fr. L. *liquiditas*]

liq·uid·ize (líkwidaiz) *pres. part.* **liq·uid·iz·ing** *past* and *past part.* **liq·uid·ized** *v.t.* to cause to be liquid

liquid laser (*optics*) a laser that utilizes rare earth ions dissolved in a dyed liquid as an active material, e.g., chelate, dye

liquid measure a unit or system of units for measuring liquids

liquid paraffin a mineral oil derived from petroleum and used as a laxative

liq·ui·dus (líkwidəs) *n.* a liquidus curve [L. = liquid]

liquidus curve a curve, usually expressing the temperature-composition relationship of a mixture between the melting points of its pure components, that indicates the temperatures above which only the liquid phase exists (cf. SOLIDUS)

liq·uor (líkər) *n.* drink (gin, whiskey etc.) of high alcoholic content ‖ any liquid or juice, e.g. the water in which something has been cooked ‖ (*pharm.*) a solution of a specified drug in water [O.F. *licur, licour, likeur*]

liquorice *LICORICE

li·ra (líərə, lí:ra) *pl.* **li·re** (lí:re), **li·ras** *n.* the standard monetary unit of Italy, consisting of 100 centesimi ‖ a coin or note of this value [Ital.]

lir·i·pipe (líri:paip) *n.* (*hist.*) the long tail of a hood, forming part of academic and clerical dress [etym. doubtful]

Lis·bo·a (li:ʒbôə), Antônio Francisco (1730–1814), Brazilian sculptor and architect, famous for his churches and his statues of the prophets (1800) in Congonhas do Campo. He was called 'O Aleijardinho' (little crippled one) because his hands were deformed by leprosy

Lis·bon (lízbən) (*Port.* Lisboa) the capital (pop. 812,385) of Portugal, a great port at the mouth of the Tagus. Industries: food processing, textiles, chemicals, machinery, shipbuilding. An earthquake (1755) destroyed half the city, afterwards rebuilt in magnificent style on a symmetrical plan by Pombal. The old quarter (Alfama) has Moorish and medieval buildings. University (1910)

isle (lail) *n.* a fine, tightly twisted cotton thread, used esp. for socks and gloves [fr. *Lille*, France, where it was originally made]

lisp (lisp) 1. *v.i.* to mispronounce 's' or 'z' as 'th' ‖ to speak with a lisp or as if with a lisp ‖ *v.t.* to utter with a lisp or as if with a lisp 2. *n.* a lisping pronunciation [fr. O.E. *wlisp, wlips* adj., lisping]

Lis·sa·jous (li:sæʒu:), Jules Antoine (1822–80), French physicist. He is known for his study of the result of combining simple periodic motions at right angles to one another. A Lissajous figure represents the path traced by a body moving under such conditions

lis·some, lis·som (lísəm) *adj.* lithe, slim and supple [contr. fr. old-fash. *lithesome*]

List (list), Friedrich (1789–1846), German economist. A protectionist, he was a leading advocate of the Zollverein

list *n.* (*Br.*) the selvage of cloth ‖ a strip of material, esp. a thin strip cut from the edge of a piece of wood ‖ (*pl., hist.*) the fences enclosing a tilting ground ‖ (*pl., hist.*) a tilting ground **to enter the lists** to become a participant in a contest [O.E. *liste*, border]

list 1. *n.* a number of names of persons or things having something in common, written out systematically one beneath or after another, *make a list of the jobs you want done* ‖ a catalog 2. *v.t.* to make a list of ‖ to put on a list ‖ to register (a security) on a stock exchange [F. *liste*]

list 1. *n.* (esp. of a ship) a lean to one side 2. *v.i.* (esp. of a ship) to lean to one side [origin unknown]

lis·ten (lís'n) *v.i.* to use one's ears consciously in order to hear, *he listened at the door but couldn't tell what they were saying* ‖ to pay attention to speech, music etc., *listen to me instead of gazing out of the window* ‖ to be influenced by, *you mustn't listen to his threats or his promises* **to listen in** to listen to someone else's conversation ‖ (*old-fash.*) to listen to a radio broadcast [Old Northumbrian *lysna*]

Lis·ter (lístər), Joseph, 1st Baron Lister of Lyme Regis (1827–1912), English surgeon. On the basis of Pasteur's research into fermentation, he introduced the principles of disinfection and antisepsis into surgery

list·er (lístər) *n.* a plow with a double moldboard [ult. fr. LIST (a strip)]

list·less (lístlis) *adj.* lacking energy ‖ spent in languor, *a listless afternoon* ‖ uninterested, indifferent, *listless spectators* [fr. older *list*, inclination]

list price the price of an article as shown in a catalog, advertisement etc.

Liszt (list), Franz (1811–86), Hungarian composer and pianist. As a composer he was prolific: he wrote symphonic program music (e.g. 'Dante', 1867 and 'Faust', 1857), 20 'Hungarian Rhapsodies', piano concertos, songs, and a vast number of piano pieces and piano transcriptions. One of the greatest virtuoso pianists, he evolved new techniques of playing, made harmonic innovations in composition and developed the Romantic idiom

lit alt. *past* and *past part.* of LIGHT (to cause to emit light) ‖ alt. *past* and *past part.* of LIGHT (to come to rest)

Li·ta·ni (li:táni:) a river (90 miles long) of Lebanon, rising, like the Orontes, near Baalbek but flowing south, then west to the Mediterranean north of Tyre

lit·a·ny (lít'ni:) *pl.* **lit·a·nies** *n.* a prayer of petition used in public worship, esp. processions, recited by the officiant with recurrent responses from the congregation [fr. M.L. *litania, letania* fr. Gk]

li·tchi, li·chee (lí:tʃi:) *n.* Litchichinensis, fam. *Sapindaceae*, a tree native to China but cultivated in India and the Philippines for its juicy, edible fruit ‖ this fruit, which has a hard seed and scaly outer shell [fr. Chin. *li-chi*]

lit·er·ar·ism (lítərerizəm) *n.* concern with literary or humanistic values vs. scientism

lit·crit (lítkrít) *n.* literary criticism

li·ter, li·tre (lí:tər) *n.* the metric unit of capacity, defined as the volume of 1 kg. of pure, air-free water at 4°C and 760 mm. of pressure (=1,000.028 c.c., 1,000 milliliters, and approx. 0.22 gallon or 1.76 pints) [F. *litre* fr. L. fr. Gk]

lit·er·a·cy (lítərəsi:) *n.* the condition or quality of being literate

lit·er·al (lítərəl) 1. *adj.* true in the usual sense of the words used, not metaphorical or exaggerated, *it is to be understood in a poetic, not a literal sense* ‖ (of a translation) following the original closely or even word for word ‖ prosaic, matter-of-fact, *a literal mind* ‖ of, relating to or expressed by a letter of the alphabet, *literal errors* 2. *n.* a literal misprint **lit·er·al·ism** *n.* a tendency to interpret words, statements etc. in their literal sense ‖ (in painting, writing etc.) realism **lit·er·al·ist** *n.* someone practicing literalism [O.F.]

lit·er·ar·i·ly (lítərerili:) *adv.* in a literary way or manner

lit·er·ar·i·ness (lítəreri:nis) *n.* the state or quality of being literary

lit·er·ar·y (lítəreri:) *adj.* of, being or about literature, *literary criticism* ‖ producing, well versed in or connected with literature, *a literary figure* ‖ characteristic of a written as distinct from a spoken style, *a literary turn of phrase* [fr. L. *litterarius*]

literary executor a person entrusted with a testator's literary property: copyrights, unpublished works etc.

lit·er·ate (lítərit) 1. *adj.* able to read and write 2. *n.* someone who can read and write [fr. L. *litteratus*]

lit·er·a·ture (lítərətʃər) *n.* written compositions in prose or verse, esp. of lasting quality and artistic merit ‖ writings produced in a certain country or during a certain period, *French literature, Romantic literature* ‖ (*rhet.*) the occupation or profession of writing or studying such works ‖ the realm of written composition, *he is famous in literature* ‖ books or treatises on a particular subject, *there is a mass of literature on the Greek theater* ‖ (*pop.*) any printed matter even if devoid of literary merit, e.g. travel folders [fr. L. *litteratura*]

lith·arge (líθardʒ) *n.* (*chem.*) fused yellow-orange lead monoxide, PbO [fr. O.F. *litarge* fr. L. fr. Gk]

lithe (laið) *adj.* slim, sinewy and supple ‖ indicating suppleness and agility, *the lithe movements of a panther* [O.E. *lithe*, gentle]

lith·i·a (líθi:ə) *n.* lithium oxide, Li₂O

li·thi·a·sis (liθáiəsis) *n.* (*med.*) the formation of gravel-like crystals in the body, esp. in the gall and urinary bladders [Mod. L. fr. Gk fr. *lithos*, stone]

lith·ic (líθik) *adj.* of or pertaining to stone [fr. Gk *lithos*, stone]

lithic *adj.* of or pertaining to lithium

lith·i·um (líθi:əm) *n.* an element of the alkali metal group (symbol Li, at. no. 3, at. mass 6.939). It is the lightest known metal and is used in alloys [fr. Gk *lithos*, stone]

lithium batteries lightweight electric batteries used in watches

lith·og·en·ous (liθódʒənəs) *adj.* originating from stone

lith·o·graph (líθəgræf, líθəgrɑf) 1. *v.t.* to print by the process of lithography 2. *n.* an impression or print so made **li·thog·ra·pher** (liθógrəfər) *n.* someone skilled in lithography [LITHOGRAPHY]

lith·o·graph·ic (liθəgræfik) *adj.* of, pertaining to or produced by lithography

li·thog·ra·phy (liθógrəfi:) *n.* the art or process of printing from a smooth surface (a prepared stone, aluminum or zinc) on which the image to be printed is ink-receptive, the rest being ink-repellent (*OFFSET) [fr. Gk *lithos*, stone +*graphos*, written]

lith·o·log·i·cal (liθəlódʒik'l) *adj.* of or relating to lithology

li·thol·o·gy (liθóládʒi:) *n.* the study of stones and rocks ‖ the nature of a rock or rock formation described in terms of its composition, color, texture and structure [fr. Gk *lithos*, stone+*logos*, word]

lith·o·marge (líθəmardʒ) *n.* a smooth, closely packed kaolin [fr. Mod. L. *lithomarga* fr. Gk *lithos*, stone+L. *marga*, marl]

lith·o·phyte (líθəfait) *n.* (*bot.*) a plant growing on rock or stone [fr. Gk *lithos*, stone+*phuton*, plant]

lith·o·pone (líθəpoun) *n.* a white pigment, consisting of a mixture of zinc sulfide and barium sulfate, used in the manufacture of linoleum, paint etc. [fr. Gk *lithos*, stone +*ponos*, work]

lith·o·print (líθəprint) *n.* a lithograph

lith·o·sphere (líθəsfiər) *n.* (*geol.*) the earth's solid exterior crust (cf. ATMOSPHERE, cf. HYDROSPHERE) [fr. Gk *lithos*, stone+SPHERE]

lith·o·spher·ic (liθəsfiərik) *adj.* (*geol.*) of the rocky crust of the earth

li·thot·o·my (liθótəmi:) *n.* (*med.*) a surgical operation to remove a stone from the bladder [fr. L.L. *lithotomia* fr. Gk fr. *lithos*, stone+*tomia*, a cutting]

li·thot·ri·ty (liθótriti:) *n.* (*med.*) the crushing of a stone in the bladder so that it can pass through the urethra [fr. Gk *lithos*, stone+*tripsis*, rubbing]

Lith·u·a·ni·a (liθu:éini:ə) a constituent republic (area 25,170 sq. miles, pop. 3,399,000) of the U.S.S.R. in N.E. Europe, on the Baltic. Capital: Vilnius. It is a low-lying region with many lakes. Agriculture: root crops, cereals, cattle. Resources: timber. Industries: heavy engineering, shipbuilding and building materials. Lithuania developed as an independent unit against the Teutonic Knights (13th c.), and its power grew until unification with Poland (1386). Acquired by Russia (1795), it became an independent republic (1919) and a constituent republic (1940)

Lith·u·a·ni·an (liθu:éini:ən) 1. *adj.* of or pertaining to Lithuania, its language or people 2. *n.* a native or inhabitant of Lithuania ‖ the Baltic language of Lithuania

lit·i·gant (lítigənt) 1. *adj.* engaged in a lawsuit 2. *n.* someone engaged in a lawsuit [F.]

lit·i·gate (lítigeit) *pres. part.* **lit·i·gat·ing** *past* and *past part.* **lit·i·gat·ed** *v.i.* to go to law, to carry on a lawsuit ‖ *v.t.* to contest at law **lit·i·gá·tion** [fr. L. *litigare* (*litigatus*)]

li·ti·gious (litídʒəs) *adj.* fond of engaging in lawsuits ‖ subject to dispute at law ‖ of or about lawsuits [fr. F. *litigieux*]

lit·mus (lítməs) *n.* a dye obtained from various lichens, esp. *Roccella tinctoria*, fam. *Roccellaceae*, turned red by acid and blue by alkali [fr. M. Du. *leecmos*]

litmus paper absorbent paper treated with litmus, used as an indicator for acids and alkalis

litmus test originally a paper used to test acidity and alkalinity; by extension, 'an acid test,' a definitive test —**litmusless** *adj.* neutral

li·top·tern (laitóptə:rn) *n.* a member of *Litopterna*, an extinct order of hoofed herbivorous mammals of the Paleocene to the Pleistocene epochs, confined to South America [fr. Gk *litos*, smooth+*pterna*, heel]

li·to·tes (laitóuti:z) *pl.* **li·to·tes** *n.* understatement in which an affirmation is expressed by the negative of its contrary, often used for emphasis or ironically, e.g. 'the loss was no laughing matter' ‖ an instance of this (cf. HYPERBOLE, cf. MEIOSIS) [Gk *litotes* fr. *litos*, plain, simple]

litre *LITER

lit·ter (lítər) 1. *n.* rubbish, e.g. scraps of paper, orange peel etc., lying about in disorder ‖ a state of disorder or untidiness ‖ the young brought forth at one birth by a multiparous animal, esp. a sow or bitch ‖ straw or other bedding provided for animals or as a protection for plants ‖ the top layer of leaves, twigs and other organic matter on a forest floor ‖ a stretcher ‖ (*hist.*) a couch with a curtained canopy for carrying a passenger 2. *v.t.* to be litter in (a place) ‖ to leave litter in (a place) ‖ to throw down as litter ‖ to bed down (an animal) with straw etc. ‖ to cover (a floor) with straw etc. ‖ *v.i.* (of an animal) to bring forth young [A.F. *litere*, O.F. *litiere*, bed]

litter bag a container, usu. of plastic, used for rubbish disposal —**litterbin** *n.*

lit·ter·bug (lítərbʌg) *n.* someone who drops litter on a street or in some other public area

---

CONCISE PRONUNCIATION KEY: **(a)** æ, c*a*t; ɑ, c*a*r; ɔ f*aw*n; ei, sn*a*ke. **(e)** e, h*e*n; i:, sh*ee*p; iə, d*ee*r; ɛə, b*ea*r. **(i)** i, f*i*sh; ai, t*i*ger; ə:, b*i*rd. **(o)** o, *o*x; au, c*ow*; ou, g*oa*t; u, p*oo*r; ɔi, r*oy*al. **(u)** ʌ, d*u*ck; u, b*u*ll; u:, g*oo*se; ə, b*a*cillus; ju:, c*u*be. x, lo*ch*; θ, *th*ink; ð, bo*th*er; z, *Z*en; ʒ, corsa*g*e; dʒ, sava*g*e; ŋ, ora*n*gutang; j, *y*ak; ʃ, *f*ish; tʃ, fe*tch*; 'l, rabb*le*; 'n, redd*en*. Complete pronunciation key appears inside front cover.

lit·tle (lít'l) **1.** *adj. comp.* **less** (les), **lesser** (lésər), **lit·tler** *superl.* **least** (li:st), **lit·tlest** small in size, amount, number, degree etc. ‖ (of children) young, *the little ones* ‖ used as a term of endearment, *bless your little soul* ‖ short, not having great height, *a little woman* ‖ (of distance or duration) short, brief, *a little way to the left, a little while* ‖ trivial, *little details* ‖ petty, mean, *little minds* ‖ guileful, *he knows your little game* ‖ operating on a small scale, *little businesses* **a little** some, even though small in amount, *give me a little time, show a little kindness* **2.** *adv. comp.* **less** *superl.* **least** not much, very slightly, *she read little and wrote less* ‖ (with 'to care', 'dream', 'guess', 'know', 'think' etc.) not at all, *little does he guess* **a little** somewhat, *a little flustered* ‖ sometimes, *he still sees her a little* ‖ for a short time or distance **3.** *n.* a small amount, *the little I possess, what little I could do* ‖ not much, *he did little to help* **a little** a short time, *stay for a little* ‖ a short distance, *go along the road a little* **in little** on a small scale **little by little** gradually **little or nothing** hardly anything **to make little of** to attach small importance to **to think little of** to have a low opinion of ‖ to have no hesitancy about [O.E. *lytel, lytel*]

Little Bear *URSA MINOR

Little Bighorn a river (approx. 90 miles long) of northern Wyoming and southern Montana, site in Montana of the Battle of Little Bighorn (*CRAZY HORSE)

Little Dipper *URSA MINOR

Little Entente a political, economic and military alliance formed (1920–1) by Czechoslovakia, Rumania and Yugoslavia against Germany, Austria, Hungary and Italy. It was weakened by the rise (1933) of Hitler, and collapsed (1938) when Germany invaded Czechoslovakia

little finger the fourth and smallest finger of the hand

little magazine a small, noncommercial magazine publishing esp. experimental writing and criticism

Little Rock the capital (pop. 158,461) of Arkansas, a commercial center with cottonseed-oil, lumber and electrical engineering industries, and bauxite mining nearby. It was one of the first Southern towns to begin implementing the Supreme Court's ruling on desegregation in schools, provoking demonstrations (1958)

Little Russian a Ukrainian ‖ the Ukrainian or Ruthenian languages ‖ a Ruthenian

little theater a small theater usually presenting experimental, noncommercial plays often with an amateur cast

little toe the smallest and outermost toe of the foot

Little Turtle (c. 1752–1812), American Indian chief of the Miami tribe, known for his military prowess and oratorical ability. He defeated (1791) federal troops on the Wabash River but then advocated peace, signing the Treaty of Greenville (1795). Under this the Indians ceded land in Ohio, Illinois, Indiana, and Michigan to the U.S.A.

lit·to·ral (lítərəl) **1.** *adj.* of, on or along the shore **2.** *n.* a coastal region, esp. the area of a shore between high and low tide levels [fr. L. *littoralis*]

Lit·tré (li:trei), Maximilien Paul Emile (1801–81), French lexicographer and philosopher, famous for his 'Dictionnaire de la langue française' (1863–73) and for his modified restatement of the doctrines of positivism (*COMTE)

li·tur·gi·cal (lité:rdʒik'l) *adj.* of or concerning liturgy **li·túr·gics** *pl. n.* the study of liturgies ‖ the branch of theology dealing with the forms of public worship [fr. L.L. *liturgicus* fr. Gk *leitourgikos*]

lit·ur·gist (lítərdʒist) *n.* an authority on liturgies ‖ a compiler of a liturgy

lit·ur·gy (lítərdʒi:) *pl.* **lit·ur·gies** *n.* the public rites and services of the Christian Church ‖ the Eucharist office in the Orthodox Eastern Church [fr. M.L. *liturgia* fr. Gk]

Liu Shao·chi (ljú:ʃáutʃí:) (1898–1969), Chinese Communist politician, president of the Chinese People's Republic (1959–68). He was dismissed (Nov. 1968) from all his positions. In 1980 he was posthumously rehabilitated

liv·a·ble, live·a·ble (lívəb'l) *adj.* good for living in, *a very livable house* ‖ able to be lived, worth living, *life is just not livable under such conditions* ‖ (esp. *Br.*, of a person, with 'with') easy to get along with

live (liv) *pres. part.* **liv·ing** *past* and *past part.* **lived** *v.i.* to have life as an animal or plant ‖ to continue in this state, *the longer we live the more we learn* ‖ (with 'on', 'upon') to subsist, maintain life, *they live on a handful of rice a day* ‖ (with 'on', 'upon', 'by') to obtain the means of life, *she lives by sewing* ‖ to flourish, remain in people's memory, *the names of these heroes will live forever* ‖ to conduct or pass one's life in a certain manner, *to live quietly, live like a pig* ‖ to realize fully the potentialities of life, *only in the mountains does she feel she's really living* ‖ to reside, dwell, *he lives next door* ‖ to survive dangers and terrors, *few lived to tell the tale* ‖ to spend the daytime, *we live in this room and sleep in that one* ‖ *v.t.* to pass, spend, *live a happy life* ‖ to enjoy or experience vicariously, *he lived every second of the film* ‖ to carry out in one's life the principles of, *to live one's religion* **to live and let live** to live as one wishes and allow others to do the same ‖ to be tolerant of others' views, weaknesses etc. **to live (something) down** to live so that people forget (a past failure or mistake in one's life) **to live for** to devote oneself wholly to **to live in** (esp. of servants) to live where one works **to live on** to continue alive **to live out** to spend the remainder of (one's days, life etc.) ‖ (esp. of servants and soldiers) to live away from one's work or duty **to live through** to survive, *no boat could live through this storm* **to live up to** to attain expected standards in ‖ to put (one's ideals) into practice ‖ (*Br.*) to spend the total amount of (one's income) **to live with** to live with (someone) as husband or wife outside marriage [O.E. *libban*]

live (laiv) *adj.* living, not dead ‖ existing, not fictional, *a real live cowboy* ‖ energetic, lively ‖ full of interest and importance, *a live topic for debate* ‖ glowing, *live coals* ‖ unexploded, *a live bomb* ‖ (of a broadcast) direct, not recorded ‖ carrying electric current, *a live wire* ‖ (of machinery) imparting or having motion ‖ (*printing*, of type) still in use or set up ready to be printed from ‖ (*printing*, of copy) not typeset or not proofread [fr. older *on life*, ALIVE]

liveable *LIVABLE

live-in (lívin) *adj.* **1.** of those who live where they work or fraternize e.g. a live-in maid, club member **2.** extension of sit-in (which see)

live-in friend a lover with whom one lives

live·li·hood (láivli:hud) *n.* means of subsistence [O.E. *liflād* fr. lif, life + lād, course, assimilated to obs. *livelihood*, liveliness]

live·li·ness (láivli:nis) *n.* the state or quality of being lively

live load (laiv) the stresses laid upon a structure in addition to its own weight (cf. DEAD LOAD)

live·long (lívlɒŋ, lívlɒŋ) *adj.* (*rhet.*, of day or night) whole, entire, complete (with connotations of delight or weariness) [*lief*, obs. adj., dear + LONG adj.]

live·ly (láivli:) *comp.* **live·li·er** *superl.* **live·li·est 1.** *adj.* brisk, vigorous, full of zest and spirit, *a lively mind* ‖ vivid, *a lively description* ‖ active, intense, *a lively sense of humor* ‖ brilliant, fresh, *lively colors* ‖ busy, exciting, dangerous, *demonstrators gave the police a lively time* ‖ riding buoyantly on the sea, *a lively boat* ‖ fast and quick to respond, *a lively little car* ‖ (*cricket*) causing the ball to come off quickly, *a lively wicket* **2.** *adv.* in a lively way [O.E. *liflic*, lifelike]

liv·en (láivən) *v.t.* (often with 'up') to enliven ‖ *v.i.* (often with 'up') to become brisker, brighter, more active

live oak any of several American evergreen oaks, esp. *Quercus virginiana*, fam. *Fagaceae*, of the southern U.S.A., which yields tough, durable wood

liv·er (lívər) *n.* a large, vascular, glandular organ of vertebrates that plays an important role in digestion (e.g. the production of bile), that converts carbohydrates to glycogen, which it then stores, and that elaborates many important substances (esp. of the blood). In man it is dark red, divided into five lobes, and located in the upper right portion of the abdominal cavity immediately below the diaphragm ‖ any of various large organs associated with the digestive tract of invertebrates ‖ the liver of an animal eaten as food [O.E. *lifer*]

liver *n.* a person who lives in a specified manner, *a clean liver, a loose liver*

liver fluke any of various parasitic flatworms (such as *Fasciola hepatica*, fam. *Fasciolidae*, the

liver fluke of sheep) that invade the liver of animals (*TREMATODE)

liv·er·ied (lívəri:d) *adj.* wearing livery

liv·er·ish (lívərif) *adj.* suffering from liver disorders ‖ out of sorts, ill-tempered

Liv·er·more (lívərmɔr, lívərmour), Mary Ashton (née Rice, 1820–1905), U.S. reformer. During the Civil War she fought for the abolition of slavery and for temperance and social reform, and later campaigned for women's suffrage, education, and remunerative employment

Liv·er·pool (lívərpu:l), Robert Banks Jenkinson, 2nd Earl of (1770–1828), British statesman, prime minister (1812–27). His Tory ministry enforced repressive legislation at the end of the Napoleonic Wars, but later introduced reforms, under the influence of Canning, Huskisson and Peel

Liverpool the second largest port (pop. 1,513,070) of England, a county borough in Lancashire on the Mersey estuary: shipbuilding, engineering, food processing, sugar refining. University (1903)

liv·er·wort (lívərwə:rt) *n.* any member of *Hepaticae* (*BRYOPHYTE), a class of primitive green land plants related to the mosses

liv·er·wurst (lívərwę:rst, lívərwurst) *n.* a smoked sausage made of liver and pork [part trans. of G. *Leberwurst* fr. Leber, liver + Wurst, sausage]

liv·er·y (lívəri:) *pl.* **liv·er·ies** *n.* the costume worn by the servants of some noble or rich household or court ‖ (*Br.*) the distinct costume or dress worn formerly by members of a livery company ‖ (*Br.*) the members of a livery company ‖ (*law*) the legal delivery of property, esp. (*Br.*) from a court of wards ‖ (*Br.*, *law*) a writ guaranteeing this delivery [A.F. *liveré*]

livery company (*Br.*) one of the London city companies, which were permitted to wear their own livery

liv·er·y·man (lívəri:mən) *pl.* **liv·er·y·men** (lívəri:mən) *n.* a keeper of a livery stable ‖ a man who works in a livery stable ‖ (*Br.*) a member of a livery company who is also a freeman of the City of London

livery stable a stable where horses are offered for hire, or where horses can be boarded

live·stock (láivstɒk) *n.* animals, esp. cattle, kept on a farm for breeding, dairy products, sale etc.

live wire a wire connected to a source of electric power ‖ (*pop.*) a person full of energy and initiative

Liv·i·a Dru·sil·la (lívi:ədru:síIə) (c. 56 B.C.–29 A.D.), Roman empress. As wife of Augustus, she became the first Roman empress (27 B.C.) and continued to wield power in the reign of Tiberius, her son by an earlier marriage

liv·id (lívid) *adj.* bluish-gray in color, like lead ‖ discolored as if by bruising ‖ (*pop.*) exceedingly angry **li·víd·i·ty** *n.* [fr. L. *lividus*]

liv·ing (lívin) **1.** *n.* the condition of having life ‖ the action of a being having life ‖ livelihood, *he earns his living by selling seeds* ‖ manner of conducting life, *high living* ‖ (*Br.*) a Church office to which certain benefits (e.g. a vicarage) and revenues are attached **2.** *adj.* endowed with life ‖ having continuing effect, *a living ideal* ‖ still spoken, *a living language* ‖ now existing, *the greatest living sculptor* ‖ lifelike, *a living likeness* ‖ natural, not moved or detached by man, *carved out of the living rock* ‖ of or pertaining to life, *living conditions* ‖ sufficient for life, *a living wage* **in living memory** capable of being remembered by people still alive, *the worst typhoon in living memory*

living room the room in a house where the family spends most of the day when at home, esp. as distinct from bedroom or kitchen

Liv·ing·ston (lívinstən), Edward (1764–1836), U.S. statesman. His 'Livingston Code' of criminal law and procedure has been widely consulted in Europe and America. As secretary of state (1831–3) under President Andrew Jackson, he prepared the Anti-Nullification Proclamation (1832)

Livingston, Robert R. (1746–1813), first chancellor of the state of New York (1777–1801), first secretary of foreign affairs (1781–9) under the Articles of Confederation, and U.S. minister to France (1801–3). He negotiated, with James Monroe, the Louisiana purchase. Having won (1798) a New York monopoly of steam navigation, he and Robert Fulton introduced (1807) their first successful steam vessel, the 'Clermont'

CONCISE PRONUNCIATION KEY: **(a)** æ, cat; ɑ, car; ɔ fawn; ei, snake. **(e)** e, hen; i:, sheep; iə, deer; ɛə, bear. **(i)** i, fish; ai, tiger; ə:, bird. **(o)** o, ox; au, cow; ou, goat; u, poor; ɔi, royal. **(u)** ʌ, duck; u, bull; u:, goose; ə, bacillus; ju:, cube. x, loch; θ, think; ð, bother; z, Zen; ʒ, corsage; dʒ, savage; ŋ, orangutang; j, yak; ʃ, fish; tʃ, fetch; 'l, rabble; 'n, redden. Complete pronunciation key appears inside front cover.

Liv·ing·stone (lívingstən), David (1813–73), Scottish missionary and explorer. Beginning his missionary career (1841) in what is now Botswana, he crossed the Kalahari Desert, reached the Zambezi (1851) and traveled west to Luanda (1853). He then crossed Africa from west to east, discovering Victoria Falls (1855) and reaching the mouth of the Zambezi (1856). He explored the basin of Lake Malawi (1857–64), Lake Bangweu'lu (1868) and the upper reaches of the Congo. Feared lost, he was found (1871) near Lake Tanganyika by Stanley. He devoted his life to the destruction of the slave trade in Africa. He wrote 'Missionary Travels' (1857) and 'The Zambezi and Its Tributaries' (1865)

Livingstone a town (pop. 80,000) in S. Zambia on the Zambezi River near Victoria Falls

living wage a wage that is above mere subsistence level but leaves nothing to spare for luxuries

living will a written request to have one's life terminated at any time when only artificial means can sustain it

live-out (lívaut) adj. of those who do not live where they work where living-in is customary Cf LIVE-IN

Li·vo·ni·a (livóuni:ə) a former Russian province (1783–1918) comprising parts of Latvia and Estonia

Li·vor·no (livórnou) (Eng. Leghorn) a port (pop. 177,700) on the coast of Tuscany, Italy, an important trade center. Industries: shipbuilding, oil refining, metallurgy

Liv·y (lívi:) (Titus Livius, 59 B.C.–17 A.D.), Roman historian. His 'History of Rome' (only 35 of the 142 books survive) lacks critical method but is remarkable for its patriotic tone and vivid style

lix·iv·i·ate (liksívi:eit) pres. part. **lix·iv·i·at·ing** past and past part. **lix·iv·i·at·ed** v.t. to separate (a substance) into its soluble and insoluble constituents by washing water through it **lix·iv·i·á·tion** n. [fr. L. lixivius, made into lye]

liz·ard (lízərd) n. a member of Lacertilia, order Squamata, a suborder of reptiles found chiefly in warm climates. They have a relatively long body and tail (varying in size from 2 ins to 10 ft), movable eyelids and a single temporal opening. Most species are quadrupeds though some, having become adapted to burrowing, are legless. Their scaly skin is shed periodically ‖ leather made from lizard skin [O.F. lesard]

Lju·blja·na (lju:bljá:nə) (G. Laibach) the capital (pop. 253,061) of Slovenia, N.W. Yugoslavia, an agricultural market with metal, engineering and textile industries. Cathedral (18th c.), university (1920)

lla·ma (lá:mə) pl. **lla·mas**, **lla·ma** n. any of several domesticated or wild South American ruminant mammals, fam. Camelidae, closely allied to the camel but smaller (about 4 ft high), humpless and woolly-coated, esp. Lama guanicoe glama, a domesticated South American guanaco used as a beast of burden ‖ cloth made from the wool of these animals [Span.]

Lla·ne·lli (θlæne:θli:) a port (pop. 30,000) of Carmarthenshire, S. Wales: metallurgical and chemical industries

Lla·no Es·ta·ca·do (lánouestəkádou, lǽnouestəkádou) (or Staked Plain) a vast, semiarid plateau (height 1,000–5,000 ft) in New Mexico and Texas. It contains important natural gas and oil fields

lla·nos (lánous) pl. n. tropical grasslands of the upper Orinoco basin in northern South America [Span.]

Llan·qui·hue, Lake (jankí:wei) a lake (c. 240 sq. miles) in S. central Chile, draining into the Pacific

Lle·ras Ca·mar·go (ljéraskəmárgou), Alberto (1906–), Colombian Liberal politician and president (1945–6, 1958–62). In the restoration of Colombian democracy after the dictatorship of Gustavo Rojas Pinilla, he served as first president under the Frente Nacional, an agreement between the Liberal and Conservative parties to alternate in power for a period of 16 years

Lleras Re·stre·po (restréipo), Carlos (1908–), Colombian economist, politician, and president of the Republic (1966–70). He inherited severe financial difficulties and political unrest fostered by Castro-type guerrillas. He diversified the economy, ending Colombia's dependence on coffee. He stressed economic cooperation, fathering (1969) the Andean Common Market agreement reached by Colombia, Bolivia, Chile, Ecuador and Peru

Llew·el·yn ap Gruf·fydd (θlu:élinæpgrífið) (d. 1282), Welsh prince, grandson of Llewelyn ap Iorwerth. His title was officially recognized (1267), but he refused to do homage to Edward I of England (1272), and was defeated (1277 and 1282) when the English annexed Wales

Llewelyn ap Ior·werth (i:órwə:rθ) (c. 1173–1240), Welsh prince. He joined the baronial revolt against King John of England, gained recognition of Welsh rights in Magna Carta (1215), and established his supremacy over other Welsh princes

Lloyd (lɔid), Christine Marie Evert (1954–), U.S. tennis player, noted for her two-handed backhand and calmness under pressure. She won Wimbledon (1974, 1976, 1981) and the U.S. (1975–8, 1980, 1982), French (1974–5, 1979–80, 1983, 1985), and Australian (1982, 1984) Opens

Lloyd George (lɔiddʒɔ́rdʒ), David, 1st Earl Lloyd George of Dwyfor (1863–1945), British statesman. As Liberal chancellor of the exchequer (1908–15), he introduced many social reforms, including old-age pensions (1908) and national insurance (1911). His budget of 1909, proposing a supertax and a tax on land values, was rejected by the Lords, and so precipitated the crisis which led to the Parliament Act (1911). He served in the cabinet during the 1st world war, and, as prime minister (1916–22) of a coalition government increasingly dominated by Conservatives, he brought the war effort to a victorious close, and attended the Paris Peace Conference (1919)

Lloyd's (lɔidz) a London society of underwriters dealing in insurance, esp. marine insurance. It grew from a coffeehouse founded by Edward Lloyd (1648–1712) in 1686. It operates on a world-wide basis, and has published (since 1734) Lloyd's list, a newspaper giving information daily about shipping

Lloyd's Register of Ships a register, published annually since 1766, of seagoing vessels classified according to their seaworthiness and cargo capacity

Llu·llai·lla·co (ju:jaijáko) a volcano (22,057 ft) in the Andes of N. Chile, near the Argentina boundary

LM (lem) n. (acronym) lunar excursion module or lunar module

LNG (abbr.) for liquified natural gas

lo (lou) interj. (rhet.) esp. in the phrase **lo and behold!** by a curious chance [fr. M.E. lō, exclamation of grief or surprise and fr. M.E. lo prob. fr. lōke, imper. of LOOK v.]

loach (loutʃ) n. a member of Cobitidae, a family of edible freshwater fish native to Europe and Asia [F. loche]

load (loud) 1. n. something which is supported by or carried in something, a full load of passengers, he carried a load of wood on his back ‖ the weight of a mass on its support ‖ the forces to which a support is subjected, the load on this beam is more than it will bear ‖ an amount usually carried or delivered of a specified material, often in a specified mode of conveyance, a truck load of gravel ‖ an amount that can be dealt with at one time by a machine, this washing machine takes a load of six pounds ‖ an amount of work expected to be done, continual drafts place a heavy load on the heating system ‖ (engin.) the resistance, apart from friction, offered to the working of an engine, the working load ‖ (elec.) the amount of electrical energy taken from a source at a given time, the new power station will share the load at peak hours ‖ the quantity of electrical power taken up by a machine, circuit etc. ‖ (pl., pop.) a large amount, loads of money ‖ something which is ceaselessly worrisome, painful etc., you've taken a load off my mind 2. v.t. (often with 'up') to put a load on or in ‖ to put as a load ‖to be a load or weight on ‖ to make heavier ‖ to treat with an adulterant, filler etc. ‖ to add a weight to (dice) so that they fall as one wants them to ‖ to add weight or importance to, he loaded his arguments with facts that could not be challenged ‖ to cause (one's chances) to be unfavorable, the odds were loaded against him ‖ to insert the charge, cartridge or shell in (a firearm or gun) ‖ to insert (film) in a camera ‖ (often with 'with') to burden ‖ (often with 'on') to place as a burden upon ‖ (often with 'with') to give (someone) a great deal of ‖ (insurance) to add a loading to ‖ v.i. (often with 'up') to take on a load ‖ to charge a firearm or put the ammunition into a gun [O.E. lād, way, journey, means of transport]

load displacement (naut.) the displacement of a fully loaded ship

load·er (lóudər) n. someone or something that loads ‖ (in compounds) a gun loaded in a specified way, a muzzle-loader

load factor the ratio of the average load to the maximum load

load·ing (lóudin) n. (insurance) an amount added to an insurance premium in special circumstances ‖ a filler or stuffing used by paper, rubber or cloth manufacturers etc.

load line (naut.) a Plimsoll line or other line indicating how high a boat is or may be loaded

load-shed·ding (lóudʃedin) n. cutback of electric power to prevent a blackout

loadstar *LODESTAR

loadstone *LODESTONE

loaf (louf) pl. **loaves** (louvz) n. a portion of bread baked in a separate, shaped piece ‖ meat or other food done up in a similar shaped piece ‖ a sugar loaf [O.E. hlāf]

loaf v.i. to waste time, be idle ‖ v.t. (usually with 'away') to pass (time) in idleness **lóaf·er** n. a lazy person [origin unknown]

loaf·er (lóufər) n. a type of leather walking shoe with a broad flat heel and uppers like moccasins [fr. Loafer, a trademark]

lo·a·i·a·sis (louəáiəsis) n. a W. African disease due to worm infestation of skin and eye tissue [Mod. L. fr. Loa loa, the worm that causes it]

loam (loum) n. a loose rich soil of clay and sand, with some organic matter ‖ a clay and sand mixture used in making bricks and molds ‖ any fertile soil **lóam·y** comp. **loam·i·er** superl. **loam·i·est** adj. [O.E. lām]

loan (loun) 1. n. something lent, usually money, on condition that it is returned, with or without interest ‖ a lending, permission to use, may we have the loan of your ladder? ‖ (hist.) a contribution from individuals or public bodies exacted by a government ‖ a loanword **on loan** under conditions of lending 2. v.t. to grant a loan of [O.N. lān]

loan-word (lóunwə:rd) n. a word adopted from a foreign language and freely used. Loanwords may be assimilated in form, spelling and pronunciation to the borrowing language (e.g. 'chief') or they may retain the foreign spelling and pronunciation (e.g. 'chef'). English relies heavily for its vocabulary on Latin, French, Greek and Scandinavian loanwords, in that order [after G. lehnwort]

loath, loth (louθ) adj. (rhet., used predicatively) unwilling, reluctant, he is loath to issue a summons **nothing loath** without any reluctance [O.E. lāth]

loathe (louð) pres. part. **loath·ing** past and past part. **loathed** v.t. to regard with disgust or abhorrence ‖ (pop.) to dislike strongly **lóath·ing** n. detestation, abhorrence **loath·some** (lóuðsəm) adj. exciting disgust, repulsive ‖ nauseating [O.E. lāthiun]

loaves pl. of LOAF

lob (lob) 1. v.t. pres. part. **lob·bing** past and past part. **lobbed** to toss or propel (e.g. a ball) without great force in a fairly high parabola ‖ (cricket) to bowl underhand ‖ (tennis) to hit (the ball) in a high parabola, usually to the back of the opponent's court 2. n. a ball tossed, bowled or hit in this manner [earlier lob, a slow, awkward person]

lo·bar (lóubər, lóubar) adj. of a lobe, esp. the lobes of the lungs, lobar pneumonia [fr. Mod. L. lobaris]

lo·bate (lóubeit) adj. (biol.) divided into lobes ‖ (biol.) lobe-shaped **lo·bá·tion** n. [fr. Mod. L. lobatus fr. lobus, lobe]

lob·by (lóbi:) 1. pl. **lob·bies** n. a corridor or room, esp. one from which the main rooms lead off, used as an entrance hall, vestibule, waiting room, anteroom etc. ‖ the part of a legislative building to which the public has access to meet with legislators ‖ (Br.) one of two corridors in which members of parliament vote ‖ a group of people trying to bring pressure to bear on legislators to pursue policies favorable to their interests 2. v. pres. part. **lob·by·ing** past and past part. **lob·bied** v.t. to try to influence (legislators) in favor of a certain policy by constantly seeking interviews, writing letters, bringing external pressures to bear etc. ‖ v.i. to influence legislators in this way **lób·by·ist** n. a person who lobbies [fr. M.L. lobium, lobia, gallery]

lob·by-fod·der (lóbi:fɒdər) n. a legislator or administrator susceptible to pressure from lobbyists

---

lobe (loub) *n.* the soft rounded lower end of the human ear ‖ any similarly shaped part of an organ, esp. of the brain or lungs ‖ a cotyledon **lobed** *adj.* having a lobe or lobes [fr. L.L. *lobus* fr. Gk]

lo·bel·ia (loubí:ljə) *n.* a member of *Lobelia,* fam. *Lobeliaceae,* a genus of herbaceous plants of wide distribution, characterized by a deeply split corolla and blue, red or white flowers ‖ the dried leaves of *L. inflata* of North America yielding poisonous alkaloids used in medicine as an antispasmodic and emetic [after Matthias de *Lobel* (1538-1616), Flemish botanist]

Lo·bi·to (loubí:tou) a port (pop. 59,528) in Angola, S.W. Africa, connected by rail with the copper-mining areas of the Democratic Republic of the Congo and Zambia

lob·lol·ly pine (lóblɔli:) *Pinus taeda,* fam. *Pinaceae,* a tall, bushy pine of central and southeastern U.S.A. with thick reddish-brown bark and spiny-tipped cones

lo·bot·o·mized (ləbótəmaizd) *adj.* metaphorically, of someone with no emotional response

lo·bot·o·my (ləbótəmi) *pl.* **lo·bot·o·mies** *n.* a surgical severance of nerve tracts of the brain, to relieve certain mental disorders [fr. LOBE+Gk *tomē,* a cutting]

lob·scouse (lóbskaus) *n.* (*hist.*) a sailor's stew consisting of meat, potatoes, hardtack etc. [origin unknown]

lob·ster (lóbstər) *pl.* **lob·sters, lob·ster** *n.* a member of *Homaridae,* a family of marine crustaceans, esp. *Homarus americanus* found off the Atlantic seaboard of North America, *H. vulgaris* found off the Atlantic coast of Europe and *H. capensis* of southern Africa. *Palinurus* species are found in Australia, New Zealand and other Pacific waters. They are edible decapods with large claws, a curved, fanlike tail used in swimming, and stalked compound eyes ‖ their flesh eaten as food [O.E. *lothustra* fr. L. *locusta,* locust, lobster]

lobster pot a trap for catching lobsters

lob·u·lar (lóbjulər) *adj.* of or like a lobule

lob·ule (lóbju:l) *n.* a small lobe or a subdivision of a lobe [fr. Mod. L. *lobulus* dim. of *lobus,* lobe]

lo·cal (lóuk'l) **1.** *adj.* of, relating to or restricted to a particular place or area, *the local telephone service, a local bylaw* ‖ narrow, restricted, parochial, *a local viewpoint* ‖ affecting or being in one part only, *a local infection* ‖ (of trains, buses etc.) stopping at every station ‖ (*math.*) of a locus **2.** *n.* someone who lives or works in a particular neighborhood or area ‖ a local train, bus etc. ‖ a postage stamp valid only in a limited area ‖ the local branch of a large organization, esp. of a trade union ‖ (*Br.*) the neighborhood pub or neighborhood moviehouse [F.]

local color, *Br.* **local colour** vividness and actuality in a novel, film etc. achieved by describing or photographing in detail scenes, customs etc. characteristic of the locale of the work

lo·cale (louk ́ l, louk ́ l) *n.* a place or location, esp. as the site of certain activities, a setting, *Marseille is the locale of the novel* [F. adj.=local]

local government the government of small districts, e.g. counties, cities, boroughs, towns, urban districts and rural districts, conducted in a democracy by representative bodies with paid expert administrators. These elected bodies of councilmen and aldermen can levy local taxes and receive, as well, grants from the central government. They can pass bylaws and, within the laws of the central or state governments, have much local responsibility and initiative in matters of education, town planning, housing, health, communications and police

lo·cal·ism (lóuk'lizəm) *n.* a local variant in pronunciation, idiom or custom ‖ absorption in local affairs

lo·cal·i·ty (loukǽliti) *pl.* **lo·cal·i·ties** *n.* a particular district or neighborhood ‖ the fact or state of being situated in time or space, *every object has locality* ‖ place with regard to the ability to find one's way around, *a poor sense of locality* [F. localité]

lo·cal·i·za·tion (lɔuk'lizéiʃən) *n.* a localizing or being localized

lo·cal·ize (lóuk'laiz) *pres. part.* **lo·cal·iz·ing** *past and past part.* **lo·cal·ized** *v.t.* to restrict to a specific area, *localized pain* ‖ to attach to local districts, *localized administration* ‖ to give local characteristics to

local option the privilege of local voting upon certain regulations, esp. concerning the sale of alcoholic beverages

local preacher a layman licensed to preach in a particular district

local time time expressed with reference to the meridian of a particular place, as distinct from standard time

Lo·car·no Pact (loukárnou) a series of treaties concluded (1925) by Britain, France, Germany, Italy, Belgium, Czechoslovakia and Poland. The boundaries of France, Belgium and Germany were guaranteed, and those countries agreed not to attack one another. Part of the Rhineland was to be demilitarized. The Locarno Pact was violated (1936) by Hitler

lo·cate (lóukeit, loukéit) *pres. part.* **lo·cat·ing** *past* and *past part.* **lo·cat·ed** *v.t.* to look for and discover ‖ to situate, set in position, *he located himself near the door* ‖ to define the limits of a claim to land or a mining right ‖ *v.i.* to take up residence or set up business [fr. L. *locare* (*locatus*), to rent out]

lo·ca·tion (loukéiʃən) *n.* a locating or being located ‖ a geographical situation, *the location of the factory is close to the railroad* ‖ a tract of land located, *a mining location* ‖ (*movies*) a site chosen outside the studio for purposes of filming [fr. L. *locatio* (*locationis*), a renting out]

loc·a·tive (lóukətiv) **1.** *adj.* (*gram.*) belonging to or being a grammatical case indicating place where **2.** *n.* (*gram.*) the locative case [fr. L. *locare* (*locatus*), to place, rent out]

loch (lɔk, lɔx) *n.* (*Scot.*) a lake ‖ (*Scot.*) an almost landlocked arm of the sea [Gael.]

loch·i·a (lóukətiv) *pl.* **loch·i·a** *n.* (*med.*) a discharge from the uterus and vagina following childbirth [Mod. L. fr. Gk]

loci *pl.* of LOCUS

lock (lɔk) *n.* a curl, tress or tuft of hair as it naturally grows and divides on the head ‖ (*pl., rhet.*) the hair of the head ‖ a tuft of wool, cotton or flax [O.E. *loc*]

lock 1. *n.* a fastening device for doors, lids, drawers etc., in which a bolt is secured and released by a mechanism operated usually by a key acting on moving components (wards), or by some other means, such as a combination ‖ a device for preventing movement in a wheel ‖ (*hist.*) a mechanism for exploding the charge of a gun ‖ any of several holds in wrestling which prevent the part held from moving ‖ (*wagering*) a game where the team selected cannot lose ‖ a part of a canal or river enclosed between gates, in which the level of the water can be controlled, thus providing access from one level reach of navigable water to another (cf. CANAL) ‖ the extent to which a vehicle's front wheels can be turned across the plane of the back wheels, *full lock is two complete turns of the steering wheel* ‖ an airlock. **lock, stock and barrel** completely, *he turned them out lock, stock and barrel* **under lock and key** put away very safely **2.** *v.t.* to fasten (a door etc.) with a lock ‖ to fasten by fitting parts together ‖ (*printing*) to fasten (type) in a chase by securing the quoins ‖ to move (a ship) by means of a lock or locks ‖ to join tightly, *they locked their fingers together* ‖ *v.i.* to become fastened with a lock ‖ to become fastened as if locked, *the parts of the puzzle lock together to form a cube* ‖ (of a ship) to pass by means of a lock or locks ‖ (of a vehicle) to allow the front wheels to turn across the plane of the back wheels ‖ (of wheels) to move in this way ‖ to become fixed, stop revolving, *the wheel locked when he braked and the car skidded* **to lock away** to keep in a locked container **to lock in** to prevent from leaving **to lock out** to prevent from entering ‖ to prevent (employees) from working (*LOCKOUT) **to lock up** to shut by fastening with locks, *lock up the house* ‖ to shut a house etc., *lock up before you leave* ‖ to put away in a container with a lock, *lock up the money* ‖ to imprison ‖ to invest so as to be difficult to lay hands on quickly, *his money is all locked up in longterm securities* [O.E. *loc*]

lock·age (lókidʒ) *n.* the passing of a vessel through a lock or an instance of this ‖ the toll exacted for using a lock ‖ the system of locks on a waterway ‖ the amount a boat rises or falls in a lock ‖ the volume of water transferred in the process of going through a lock

Locke (lɔk), John (1632–1704), English philosopher. In his 'Essay Concerning Human Understanding' (1690) he rejects 'innate' knowledge, basing knowledge on experience of the senses (*EMPIRICISM) and reflection by the mind, though allowing an intuitive knowledge of God's existence'. In 'Two Treatises of Civil Government' (1690) he defends the English revolution of 1688. Against Hobbes he upholds 'natural rights' (life, liberty, property etc.), and in opposition to the divine right of kings he bases state power on a social contract with a right to revolt. His ideas had a profound effect on 18th-c. thought (*HUME) and on revolutionary movements, esp. in France and North America

locked-in (lóktín) *adj.* committed to a position; being in a position where a change is not practical, e.g., of an investment position

locked-on (lóktón) *adj.* **1.** of condition fixed to follow automatically, e.g., radar to a fixed object being tracked **2.** condition permitting transfer from one undersea or space craft to another

lock·er (lókər) *n.* a small cupboard usually with a lock, allotted to an individual for storage, coats etc., e.g. in a factory or school ‖ a storeroom or compartment in a ship ‖ a storage compartment in a deep-freezing plant available for rent

lock·et (lókit) *n.* a small, usually precious metal case worn or hung around the neck, e.g. on a chain, often containing a portrait or lock of hair kept for sentimental reasons [fr. O.F. *locquet*]

Lock·heed C-130E (lókhi:d) Lockheed Model 382, a four-turboprop engine plane with two underwing full tanks, medium-range combat transport, 43,811-lb payload; known as Hercules

Lock·heed L 1011-400 230-passenger service plane, with a range of 3,680 mi

lock-in clause (lókin) a provision in a promissory note or bond that prevents prepayment

lock·jaw (lókdʒɔ) *n.* (*med.*) an early symptom of tetanus marked by muscular spasms of the jaws and inability to open them

lock·keep·er (lókki:pər) *n.* a person responsible for the working of a lock on a canal or river

lock·nut (lóknʌt) *n.* a nut locking another firmly into position ‖ a self-locking nut

lock on (*mil.*) continuous and automatic tracking of a target in one or more coordinates, e.g., range, bearing, elevation —**lock-on** *v.*

lock·out (lókaut) *n.* a refusal on an employer's part to admit workers except on his own stipulated conditions of employment

lock-out compartment in an underwater craft where pressure is sufficient to prevent entry of water

lock·smith (lóksmiθ) *n.* someone who makes and mends locks and keys

lock·step (lókstep) *n.* a method of marching in extremely close file ‖ a rigid arrangement

lock·stitch (lókstitʃ) *n.* a sewing machine stitch in which two threads are interwoven

lock·up (lókʌp) *n.* a locking up or being locked up ‖ (*pop.*) a prison building or cell, esp. of a local or temporary nature ‖ (*Br.*) a lock-up garage or store

lock-up garage (*Br.*) a garage which can be locked and which is not on the same site as the user's house or premises

lock-up shop (*Br.*) a shop without living quarters

lo·co (lóukou) **1.** *n.* locoweed ‖ loco disease **2.** *adj.* (*pop.*) crazy, insane [Span.=insane]

loco disease a disease of cattle, horses and sheep affecting the motor and nervous centers of the brain, caused by eating locoweed

lo·co·ism (lóukouizəm) *n.* loco disease

lo·co·mo·tion (loukəmóuʃən) *n.* the act or the power of moving from one place to another ‖ travel with respect to the method of moving [fr. L. *loco,* ablative of *locus,* place+*motio* (*motionis*), motion]

lo·co·mo·tive (loukəmóutiv) **1.** *n.* a self-propelled vehicle running on rails, used to haul railroad trains **2.** *adj.* having power of or used in locomotion, *locomotive organs* [fr. L. *loco,* ablative of *locus,* place+*motivus,* motive]

lo·co·mo·tor (loukəmóutər) *adj.* of or pertaining to locomotion [fr. L. *loco,* ablative of *locus,* place+*motor,* that which imparts motion]

locomotor ataxia tabes dorsalis

lo·co·mo·to·ry (loukəmóutəri:) *adj.* locomotor ‖ having locomotive power [fr. L. *loco,* ablative of *locus,* place+older *motory* adj., causing motion]

lo·co·weed (lóukouwi:d) *n.* a member of *Astragalus* or *Oxytropis,* fam. *Papilionaceae,* genera of poisonous plants found in western North America that can cause loco disease

Lo·cris (lóukris) an ancient region of central Greece

loc·u·lus (lókjuləs) *pl.* **loc·u·li** (lókjulai) *n.* (*biol.*) a small cavity, e.g. in an ovary or an anther [L., dim. of *locus,* a place]

CONCISE PRONUNCIATION KEY: **(a)** æ, cat; ɑ, car; ɔ fawn; ei, snake. **(e)** e, hen; i:, sheep; iə, deer; ɛə, bear. **(i)** i, fish; ai, tiger; ə:, bird. **(o)** o, ox; au, cow; ou, goat; u, poor; ɔi, royal. **(u)** ʌ, duck; u, bull; u:, goose; ə, bacillus; ju:, cube. x, loch; θ, think; ð, bother; z, Zen; ʒ, corsage; dʒ, savage; ŋ, orangutang; j, yak; ʃ, fish; tʃ, fetch; 'l, rabble; 'n, redden. Complete pronunciation key appears inside front cover.

lo·cum te·nens (lóukəmtí:nenz) n. (abbr. locum) a substitute acting for a doctor or clergyman over a period of time [M.L.= one holding (another's) place]

lo·cus (lóukəs) pl. **lo·ci** (lóusai) n. (math.) a system of points, lines or surfaces representing a given condition or law ‖ (genetics) the relative position of a gene on a chromosome ‖ (esp. legal contexts) the exact place of something [L.=place]

lo·cus clas·si·cus (lóukəsklǽsikəs) n. a well-known passage or work which illustrates some point or subject with perfect clarity and authority [L.]

lo·cus stan·di (lóukesstǽndai) n. the right to appear in court or be heard on any question [L.]

lo·cust (lóukəst) n. a member of Acrididae, a family of grasshoppers having short antennae, esp. those members which migrate in countless numbers, devouring all vegetation in their path ‖ a cicada ‖ a locust tree ‖ the wood of a locust tree [O.F. locuste or L. locusta, locust, lobster]

locust bean the pod of a carob tree

locust bird Pastor sturnus or P. roseus, fam. Sturnidae, a chiefly Asian locust-eating bird having mostly black plumage, with rose-colored back and abdomen

locust borer Megacyllene robiniae, a beetle whose larvae attack the locust tree

locust tree any of several trees of fam. Papilionaceae having hard wood, e.g. the carob and Robinia pseudoacacia, a tree of eastern North America

locust years metaphorically, a period of famine, years of privation

lo·cu·tion (loukjú:ʃən) n. a turn of speech, a word, phrase or idiom considered from a stylistic, point of view [fr. L. locutio (locutionis)]

Lod (lɔd) *LYDDA

lo·dar (lóudar) n. (mil.) a device that notes and records reception of loran signals

lode (loud) n. a deposit of ore as a vein in a rock

lode·star, load·star (lóudstar) n. a star that guides navigators, usually the polestar ‖ a guiding principle [fr. LODE, (obs.) way+STAR]

lode·stone, load·stone (lóudstoun) n. a naturally occurring magnetic iron ore (*MAGNETITE) ‖ a thing that exerts a very strong attraction over people or a person [fr. LODE, (obs.) way+STONE]

Lodge (lɔdʒ), Henry Cabot (1850–1924), U.S. statesman and author. A prominent Republican senator from Massachusetts (1893–1924), he became a leading critic of President Wilson's policies, attaching reservations to Wilson's proposals for a League of Nations treaty. He served as one of four U.S. delegates to the Washington conference on the limitation of armaments (1921)

lodge (lɔdʒ) n. a small house at the gates of the park or on the grounds of a large country house, usually occupied by an employee or leased to a tenant ‖ a house inhabited during the sporting season only, a hunting lodge ‖ a porter's office at the entrance to a college, factory etc. ‖ (Br.) the residence of the master of a Cambridge University college ‖ the meeting hall of a branch of a Masonic or similar body, or the members of the branch collectively ‖ the den of a beaver or otter ‖ an American Indian's tepee or wigwam ‖ the inhabitants of such a dwelling, thought of as a unit [M.E. loge, logge fr. O.F. loge, loige, arbor, hut]

lodge pres. part. **lodg·ing** past and past part. **lodged** v.i. to live in someone else's house, paying for accommodation ‖ to become fixed, come to a resting-place, a bullet lodged in his brain ‖ v.t. (old-fash.) to accommodate, she lodged them in her own home ‖ (old-fash.) to be a dwelling place for ‖ to cause to be held securely, lodge your foot in that cleft ‖ to place, deposit ‖ to put in a place for safety, a deposit was lodged with the solicitor ‖ to vest, power lodged in a junta ‖ to beat down (vegetation) ‖ to make formal statement of, to lodge an official complaint **lodg·er** n. someone who occupies a rented room in another person's house **lódg·ing** n. temporary accommodation in a lodging house etc., board and lodging ‖ a place providing this ‖ (pl.) a room or rooms to live in rented in someone else's house [O.F. logier]

Lodge Corollary a resolution (1912) of Senator Henry Cabot Lodge which extended the Monroe Doctrine to non-European nations, in response to a rumored attempt by Japanese interests to buy a fishing base in Lower California

lodgement *LODGMENT

lodging house (Br.) a rooming house

lodg·ment, lodge·ment (lɔ́dʒmənt) n. (mil.) a foothold in enemy positions, or the hasty defense thrown up to consolidate it ‖ (Br., law) a depositing of money or such a deposit ‖ the accumulation of a deposit, a lodgment of soot on a chimney ledge [F. logement]

Lódz (lɔdz) a textile and clothing center (pop. 798,000) in central Poland

Loeb (lə:b), Jacques (1859–1924), German-U.S. pioneer in experimental biology. He experimented on artificial parthenogenesis, the physiology of the brain, animal tropisms, regeneration, and duration of life. He later contributed to the theory of colloidal behavior

lo·ess, löss (lóues, les) pl. **lo·ess, löss·es** n. (geol.) a deposit of fine yellowish soil transported by the wind. Mixed with silt and humus it is very fertile. There are large deposits in Europe, Asia and North America [G. löss]

lo·far (lóufar) n. (mil.) a system for detecting patterns of underwater sounds for submarine surveillance

lo·fi (lóufei) n. inferior reproduction of sound — **lo·fi** adj.

Lo·fo·ten Islands (loufóut'n) a rugged mountainous Norwegian archipelago (area 1,560 sq. miles, pop. 56,066) above the Arctic Circle, with some of the world's richest cod fisheries

loft (lɔft, lɔft) 1. n. a room in the roof, an attic ‖ a room over a stable for hay ‖ the upper story of a warehouse or factory ‖ a pigeon house ‖ a gallery in a church or hall ‖ (golf) the backward slope in the head of a club ‖ (golf) a stroke which sends a ball in a high arc above the ground 2. v.t. (esp. golf) to hit in a high arc above the ground ‖ to send into space **loft·er** n. (golf) an iron club with a slanted face used to loft the ball [O.E. loft, sky, air fr. O.N.]

LOFT (acronym) low-frequency radio telescope

loft·i·ly (lɔ́ftili:, lɔ́ftili:) adv. in a lofty manner

loft·i·ness (lɔ́fti:nis, lɔ́fti:nis) n. the quality of being lofty

lofting iron a lofter

loft·y (lɔ́fti:, lɔ́fti:) comp. **loft·i·er** superl. **loft·i·est** adj. (rhet.) imposingly tall, towering, a lofty spire ‖ proud, haughty, lofty contempt ‖ sublime, elevated, lofty principles, lofty eloquence [LOFT]

log *LOGARITHM

log (lɔg, lɒg) 1. n. a long and heavy piece of the trunk or a branch of a tree, usually cut and trimmed but otherwise unshaped, and with the bark still on ‖ a shorter segment of similarly unshaped timber used for fuel ‖ (naut.) a device for gauging the speed of a ship, usually consisting of a float, thrown out at the stern, with a regularly knotted line attached to a reel on the ship ‖ a logbook or the record entered in it 2. v. pres. part. **log·ging** past and past part. **logged** v.t. to enter in a logbook ‖ to go (a specified distance) as entered in a logbook ‖ to have experience of flying or sailing for (a specified distance or amount of time), he has logged over 2,000 flying hours ‖ to enter (a seaman's name) in the logbook as having committed some offense ‖ to cut (trees) into logs ‖ to cut down the trees of (an area) ‖ v.i. to cut down trees into logs and transport them to a place of sale [M.E. logge]

log·air (lɔ́gɛər) n. (mil.) long-term contract airlift service within continental U.S. for the movement of cargo in support of the logistics systems of the military services Cf QUICK-TRANS

Lo·gan (lóugən), Sir William Edmond (1798–1875), Canadian geologist, known as the father of Precambrian geology. His maps were used in compiling the first geological map of Great Britain. As head (1843–69) of the Canadian Geological Survey, he mapped much of the geology of Canada, summarized in his 'The Geology of Canada' (1863)

Logan the highest mountain (19,850 ft) of Canada, in the S.W. Yukon

lo·gan·ber·ry (lóugənbɛri:) pl. **lo·gan·ber·ries** n. Rubus ursinus loganobaccus, fam. Rosaceae, a variety of biennial dewberry plant bearing a large, edible, dark red berry ‖ this fruit [after James L. Logan (1841–1928), U.S. horticulturist who developed it]

log·a·oe·dic (lɒgəi:dik, lɒgəi:dik) 1. adj. (of a poetic verse) consisting of both dactyls and trochees or iambs and anapests 2. n. a logaoedic verse [fr. L.L. logaoedicus fr. Gk fr. logos, word+aoid, song]

log·a·rithm (lɔ́gəriðəm, lɔ́gəriðəm) n.(abbr. log) the power to which a selected number b (the

base) must be raised in order to be equal to the number a under consideration: if $a = b^n$, n is the logarithm of a to a base b (written as $\log_b a$) **log·a·rith·mic** adj. **log·a·rith·mi·cal·ly** adv. [fr. Mod. L. logarithmus fr. Gk logos, ratio+arithmos, number]

log·book (lɔ́gbuk, lɒ́gbuk) n. a book containing a record of the progress of a ship and all events of the voyage, kept daily ‖ any similar record, e.g. of a plane's flight, the flying hours of a pilot, a traveler's journey, the mechanical history of an engine or its components etc.

loge (louʒ) n. a box in a theater or opera house [F.]

log·ger (lɔ́gər) n. someone who earns his living by logging

log·ger·head (lɔ́gərhed, lɒ́gərhed) n. an iron implement consisting of a long handle with a ball at the end, heated to melt tar, pitch etc. ‖ a post fixed in a whaling boat to turn the line around when it is running out too fast ‖ any of several members of fam. Cheloniidae, a family of large marine turtles, esp. Caretta caretta, a carnivorous species found in the Atlantic ‖ a snapping turtle **at loggerheads** involved in an argument in which both sides stubbornly refuse to give way [prob. fr. dial. logger n., log+HEAD]

log·gia (lɔ́dʒə, lɒ́dʒə) n. a roofed, usually outdoor gallery or arcade, attached on one side to a building and open on the opposite side [Ital.]

log·ging (lɔ́giŋ) n. the business of chopping down trees, cutting them into logs, and sending them to sawmills etc.

logia alt. pl. of LOGION

log·ic (lɔ́dʒik) n. the science of pure reasoning ‖ conformity with the principles of this science, rationality ‖ a sequence of reasoning ‖ a way of reasoning or arguing ‖ compelling power, the inevitability by which certain causes have certain results, logic of necessity, logic of events ‖ inherent guiding principles, the logic of art [F. logique fr. M.L. fr. Gk logikē, of reasoning] —Classical logic derives from the series of treatises of Aristotle known as the 'Organon' (or instrument of science). Concerned with sound thinking, it shows how conclusions can be validly derived from given principles (*DIALECTIC). From the Renaissance, because of its association with traditional metaphysics, logic was neglected until its method was identified with mathematical processes in George Boole's 'Mathematical Analysis of Logic' (1847). The further identification of mathematics and logic is embodied in the 'Principia Mathematica' of Whitehead and Russell (1910-13). (*SYMBOLIC LOGIC)

logic (computer) 1. an electronic operation simulating the logic as programmed, including various types of gates and on/off circuits used to solve problems 2. principles and applications of truth tables and factors in computers 3. the science that deals with the creation of the circuits

log·i·cal (lɔ́dʒik'l) adj. related to or employed in logic ‖ consistent with correct reasoning, a logical deduction ‖ capable of or skilled in logical argument, a logical mind ‖ inevitably following from the application of reason, he seems the logical choice for fullback **log·i·cal·i·ty** (lɒdʒikǽliti:) n. [M.L. logicalis fr. L. logical]

logical positivism a 20th-c. form of philosophical thought (*POSITIVISM) which stems from empiricism as modified by the modern non-Aristotelian system of logic. Its salient aim has been to create a comprehensive philosophy of science and, through emphasizing the fundamentally linguistic nature of philosophic problems, to destroy traditional metaphysics. Its chief exponent has been Ludwig Wittgenstein

logic element *FUNCTIONAL ELEMENT

logic gates (computer) solid-state semiconductor device that performs arithmetic/logic operations. It has two input lines so as to accept the "on" and "off" signal, and one output line

lo·gi·cian (loudʒíʃən) n. a specialist in logic [F. logicien]

log in v. to check in, e.g., for use of a computer

lo·gi·on (lóudʒi:ɒn, lɒ́gi:ɒn) pl. **lo·gi·a** (lóudʒi:ə, lɒ́gi:ə), **lo·gi·ons** n. a saying of Christ not to be found in the Gospels but recorded in some other writings [Gk=oracle]

lo·gis·tic (loudʒístik) adj. of or pertaining to logistics [fr. M.L. logisticus fr. Gk]

lo·gis·tics (loudʒístiks) n. the branch of military science concerned with troop movements and supplies ‖ symbolic logic [fr. F. logistique]

log·nor·mal (lɔgnɔ́rməl) *adj.* with symmetrical distribution of logarithms

log·o·gram (lɔ́gəgræm, lɔ́gəgræm) *n.* an arbitrary symbol (e.g. in shorthand) representing a complete word [fr. Gk *logos,* word+*gramma,* a letter]

lo·gom·a·chy (lougóməki:) *n.* contention over verbal points, or one which is all words and no sense [fr. Gk *logomachia* fr. *logos,* word+-*machia,* fighting]

lo·gos (lóugɒs, lógɒs) *n.* (*Gk philos.*) reason, regarded as the controlling principle of the universe **Lo·gos** (*Christian theology*) the word of God, identified with Christ in the Gospel according to St John [Gk=word, reason]

log·roll (lɔ́groul, lógroul) *v.t.* to procure the passage of (a bill) by logrolling ‖ *v.i.* to engage in political logrolling [back-formation fr. LOG-ROLLING]

log·roll·ing (lɔ́grouliŋ, lógrouliŋ) *n.* the act of propelling logs in the water with the feet ‖ a game for (usually) two people on a floating log, which is rotated with the feet. The winner stays on and the loser doesn't ‖ an arrangement by which legislators exchange votes or assistance so as to get their own particular projects carried out ‖ (*Br.*) mutual praising in literary publications of one another's books by authors to promote sales

Lo·gro·ño (lɔgrónjɔ) a province (area 1,946 sq. miles, pop. 253,295) in N. Spain (*OLD CASTILE) ‖ its capital (pop. 110,980)

log·wood (lɔ́gwʊd, lógwʊd) *n. Haematoxylon campechianum,* fam. *Caesalpinaceae,* a dark, gnarled tree growing in Central America and the Caribbean area ‖ its heartwood ‖ hematoxylin

lo·gy (lóugi:) *comp.* **lo·gi·er** *superl.* **lo·gi·est** *adj.* heavy and sluggish ‖ dull [etym. doubtful]

-logy *suffix* indicating 'study of', 'science of, as in 'Egyptology' ‖ used in nouns referring to writing or discourse, as in 'hagiology' [earlier -*logie* fr. F. fr. M.L. -*logia* fr. Gk, partly from *légein,* to speak and partly fr. *logos,* word, discourse]

loid (lɔid) *n.* a plastic strip used to open a spring lock without a key

loin (lɔin) *n.* the cut of meat taken from the hindquarters of an animal ‖ (esp. *pl.*) the area in a man or quadruped on either side of the spinal column between the hipbone and ribs [fr. O.F. *loigne, logne*]

loin-cloth (lɔ́inkləθ, lɔ́inkloθ) *pl.* **loin-cloths** (lɔ́inkləθs, lɔ́inkloθs, lɔ́inkləðz, lɔ́inkloðz) *n.* a garment worn by a man about his loins in hot countries, often the only garment he wears

Loire (lwær) a department (area 1,852 sq. miles, pop. 742,400) in S.E. central France (*LYONNAIS). Chief town: Saint-Étienne

Loire France's longest river (630 miles), rising in the Cévennes and flowing northwest to Orléans, then west to the Atlantic through a large estuary (below Nantes). Because of sudden extreme changes of volume it is liable to flood and has little traffic. The middle and lower valleys are famous for their châteaus

Loire-At·lan·tique (lwærætlɑ̃ti:k) a department (area 2,693 sq. miles, pop. 934,500) in N.W. France (*BRITTANY). Chief town: Nantes

Loire, Haute- *HAUTE-LOIRE

Loi·ret (lwære) a department (area 2,629 sq. miles, pop. 490,200) in N. central France (*ORLÉANAIS). Chief town: Orléans

Loir-et-Cher (lwæreifer) a department (area 2,478 sq. miles, pop. 283,700) in N. central France (*TOURAINE, ORLÉANAIS). Chief town: Blois

Loi·sy (lwæzi:), Alfred (1857–1940), founder of French Modernism. His free biblical exegesis under German influence led to his excommunication (1908)

loi·ter (lɔ́itər) *v.i.* to hang around, stay or wander about near some spot apparently aimlessly ‖ to be slow in the running of an errand, making of a journey etc., with stops for idling, gossip, play etc. ‖ *v.t.* (with 'away') to waste in idleness, *to loiter one's time away* [M. Du. *loteren,* to wag about]

loll (lɒl) *v.i.* to hang in a loosely relaxed, drooping way, *his head lolled drunkenly* ‖ (of the tongue) to hang out ‖ to stand or sit in a lazy, comfortable attitude ‖ *v.t.* to allow to dangle [etym. doubtful]

Lol·land (lɔ́læn) (*Dan.* Laaland) *DENMARK

Lol·lard (lɔ́lərd) *n.* (*hist.*) a member of a Dutch heretical sect (14th c.) ‖ a follower of Wyclif in England and Scotland (14th and 15th cc.). Lollards attacked the Church for its worldliness and corruption, denied transubstantiation, and held that the Bible, interpreted by the individual, provided the only rule necessary for holy life. Lollard teaching had a wide appeal, but was severely repressed in the 15th c., notably under Henry IV. It left a legacy of anticlericalism which may have influenced the course of the Reformation in England **Lól·lard·y, Lól·lard·ry** *ns* the practices and beliefs of the Lollards [fr. M. Du. *lollaert,* mumbler]

lol·li·pop, lol·ly·pop (lóli:pɒp) *n.* a piece of hard candy on a stick [origin unknown]

lol·lop (lóləp) *v.i.* (*pop.*) to move along with a bounding motion ‖ (*Br.*) to move with loose, lazy strides [LOLL]

lollypop *LOLLIPOP

Lo·ma·mi (loumámi:) a river (900 miles long) of the Democratic Republic of the Congo, rising in the south and joining the Congo River below Kisangani

Lo·mas de Za·mo·ra (lómasðesamɔra) a city (pop. 275,000) in E. Argentina, a suburb of Buenos Aires

Lo·ma Ti·na (lómatí:na) *TRUJILLO, MT

Lombard, Peter (c. 1110–60), Italian theologian. His 'Sententiarum libri quatuor', in which he systematized theological doctrines and the objections made to them, was a classical authority until the Reformation

Lom·bard (lómbərd, lómbard) **1.** *n.* (*hist.*) a member of a Teutonic people who conquered (568) northern Italy and established the kingdom of Lombardy, overthrown (774) by Charlemagne ‖ an inhabitant of Lombardy **2.** *adj.* of or pertaining to Lombards or Lombardy [F. fr. Ital. *lombardo* fr. L.L. *Langobardus, Longobardus*]

Lom·bar·dic (lɔmbárdik) *adj.* Lombard [fr. M.L. *lombardicus*]

Lombard League (*hist.*) a coalition of Italian towns formed (1167) to resist Emperor Frederick I's claim to rule them. It broke up after 1183, but was revived (1226–37) against Frederick II

Lom·bard·y (lómbərdi:) a region (area 9,188 sq. miles, pop. 8,894,236) of N. Italy, mainly north of the Po. The plain, with its intensive farming (corn, rice, and cattle) and many industrial cities (Milan, Brescia, Bergamo etc.), is one of Europe's most densely populated areas. Fruit and olives flourish in the belt between the plain and the Alps in the north, where cattle farming is important. HISTORY. After the fall (774) of the kingdom of the Lombards, Lombardy broke up into a number of independent duchies and city-states. The Lombards became famous (13th c.) as bankers and moneylenders throughout western Europe. The area was ruled by Spain (1535–1713) and Austria (1713–97). After Napoleonic rule (1797–1815), Lombardy was restored to Austria as part of Lombardy-Venetia but was captured (1859) by Sardinia, and joined (1861) the kingdom of Italy

Lombardy poplar *Populus nigra italica,* a fastigiate poplar with sharply ascending branches

Lom·bard·y-Ve·ne·tia (lómbərdi:vəní:ʃə) a kingdom formed of Lombardy and Veneto, the Italian provinces of the Austrian Empire, from 1815, with Milan as its capital. Lombardy was freed in 1859 and Venetia in 1866

Lom·bok (lɒmbók) a volcanic island (area 1,826 sq. miles, pop. 1,300,324) in the Lesser Sundas, Indonesia. Capital: Mataram (pop. 20,000)

Lo·mé (loumei) the capital (pop. 247,000) of the Republic of Togo, a port

lo·ment (lóument) *n.* (*bot.*) a long pod which is constricted between the seeds and bursts transversely into two or more one-seeded segments at maturity [fr. L. *lomentum,* bean meal]

lo·men·ta·ceous (louməntéiʃəs) *adj.* of or bearing loments [LOMENTUM]

lo·men·tum (louméntəm) *pl.* **lo·men·ta** (louméntə), **lo·men·tums** *n.* (*bot.*) a loment [L.=bean meal]

Lo·mond, Loch (lóumənd) a lake (23 miles long, 1–5 miles wide) in W. Scotland, near Glasgow: tourism

Lo·mo·no·sov (ləmʌnɔ́sʌf), Mikhail Vasilievich (1711–65), Russian poet and scientist. He wrote a grammar (1755) and a treatise on style which laid the foundation of modern literary Russian

lo·mus·tine [$C_9H_{16}ClN_3O_2$] (loumʌstí:n) *n.* (*pharm.*) anticancer drug used for postoperative treatment of brain tumors and in treating Hodgkin's disease; marketed as CeeNU

L-1011 (*mil.*) long-range transport plane made by Lockheed

London, Jack (lándən) (John Griffith) (1876–1916), U.S. writer of adventure. He wrote of his own fight to survive, from the Oakland, California, docks to the North Atlantic and the Klondike to an attempted sail around the world. His works include 'The Son of the Wolf' (1900), 'The Cruise of the Dazzler' (1902), 'The Call of the Wild' (1903), 'The Sea-Wolf' (1904), 'Tales of the Fish Patrol' (1905), 'White Fang' (1906), 'The Road' (1907), 'The Iron Heel' (1908) and 'Smoke Bellew' (1912)

London the capital of England and of Great Britain, the political center of the Commonwealth, and a major port, 40 miles from the mouth of River Thames. Administratively it consists of: **1.** the City of London (area 1 sq. mile, pop. 4,580), the original nucleus, retaining a medieval system of government of courts of aldermen and an elected lord mayor **2.** Greater London, made up of 12 Inner London boroughs (area 117 sq. miles, pop. 6,713,165, comprising Camden, Greenwich, Hackney, Hammersmith, Islington, Kensington and Chelsea, Lamberth, Lewisham, Southwark, Tower Hamlets, Wandsworth and the City of Westminster) and 20 Outer London boroughs (area 220 sq. miles, pop. 8,186,000, comprising Barnet, Brent, Ealing, Enfield, Haringey, Harrow, Hillingdon, Hounslow, Croydon, Kingston upon Thames, Merton, Richmond upon Thames, Sutton, Bexley, Bromley, Newham, Barking, Havering, Redbridge and Waltham Forest).

The City, on the north bank of the Thames, is one of the world's leading banking and financial centers. It contains Guildhall (1411–23) and St Paul's Cathedral (1675–1710). The Port of London lies to the east and its docks extend for 25 miles along the Thames. The Tower of London (11th c.) lies just east of the City. The West End includes Westminster, the area of central government administration, St James's Palace (1531–3), several parks, and fine examples of domestic architecture (esp. 18th–19th cc.). Industries (esp. in the East End and the suburbs): printing, publishing, electrical and mechanical engineering, chemicals, clothing, food processing, plastics. Some of London's cultural institutions are: University (1836), British Museum (1753), National Gallery (1838), Tate Gallery (1897), Covent Garden Opera House (1856–8) and Royal Festival Hall (1951).

—London flourished (1st–early 5th cc.) under the Romans as Londinium, a trading center and port. It flourished again from the 9th c. and received its first charter (1066) from William I. After the plague of 1665 and the fire of 1666, much of it was rebuilt under the direction of Wren. The Industrial Revolution (18th c.) and the advent of the railroads (mid-19th c.) accelerated its growth. Much was destroyed by air raids in the 2nd world war, and rebuilding has given parts of London a new vertical, geometrical aspect. It has been a multiracial city with large population groups from England's former colonies

London a city (pop. 254,280) of Ontario, Canada, south of Toronto, a market center with food and engineering industries. University (1878)

London Company a London corporation which was granted (1606) a charter by James I to locate colonies in America, founding (1607) the colony of Jamestown. Known after 1612 as the Virginia Company, it became a self-governing body and, with the arrival (1619) of Sir George Yeardly (c. 1587–1627) as governor of Virginia, it introduced representative government to America. It was dissolved (1624) by the Crown

Lon·don·der·ry (lándənderi:) a former county (area 814 sq. miles) in the extreme north of Northern Ireland ‖ its county town, a port and the second city of Northern Ireland

London, Treaty of an agreement (1604, ratified by the Treaty of Antwerp) in which England and the Netherlands claimed the right to land not yet discovered in the Americas. It thus repudiated the Treaty of Tordesillas ‖ an agreement signed (1827) by Britain, France and Russia establishing the kingdom of Greece ‖ an agreement signed (1839) by Britain, France, Prussia, Russia and Austria separating Belgium and the Netherlands and guaranteeing Belgian independence and neutrality ‖ a secret agreement between Italy, France,

Britain and Russia (1915), promising Italy the Trentino (the northeastern part of Trentino-Aldo Adige), Trieste and other territorial concessions in return for entering the 1st world war on the side of the Allies

London, University of the third oldest (1836) university in England, founded by Whig and Radical dissenters headed by the poet Thomas Campbell, to meet the demands of a growing middle class for higher education, esp. in chemistry and physics. Oxford and Cambridge paid small attention to these subjects, and in any case restricted their degrees to members of the Church of England. London, chartered in 1836, was the first English university to offer science degrees (1859) and to award degrees to women (1868). It has instituted a system of external examinations permitting students abroad to receive its degrees, and has encouraged the growth of university colleges both in Great Britain and overseas. There are fourteen colleges scattered throughout the city and 69 other colleges, schools and institutes of the university

lone (loun) *adj.* (*rhet.*) single, alone, not one of a pack or group || (*rhet.*) isolated **to play a lone hand** to act with complete independence **lóne-li-ness** *n.* the state or quality of being lonely || an instance of this **lóne-ly** *comp.* **lone-li-er** *superl.* **lone-li-est** *adj.* solitary and feeling miserable because of the lack of company || isolated, *a lonely spot on the moors* || unfrequented, *a lonely road* || (*rhet.*) completely without companions **lóne-some** *adj.* (of people) lonely and sad because of the lack of company || (of places etc.) unfrequented **by** (or **on**) **one's lonesome** by oneself, on one's own [shortened by aphesis fr. ALONE]

Long (lɔŋ, lɒŋ), Huey Pierce (1893–1935), U.S. politician, governor of Louisiana (1928–31) and U.S. senator (1931) until his assassination. A demagogue, he gained much popular support by his proposals for a radical egalitarian redistribution of wealth

long (lɔŋ, lɒŋ) **1.** *comp.* **long-er** (lɔ́ŋgər, lɒ́ŋgər) *superl.* **long-est** (lɔ́ŋgəst, lɒ́ŋgəst) *adj.* measuring a considerable or more than usual distance from one end to the other in space or duration || of specified length or duration, *planks ten feet long* || of or being the longer or longest in dimension, *the long side of the room* || seeming long, tedious, *we had to walk two long miles* || extending to relatively remote time, far back or forward, *a long memory, a long friendship* || containing many items in a series, *a long list* || (*phon.*, of a vowel or syllable) of relatively extended duration || (*prosody*, of a syllable) stressed || (esp. *classical prosody*, of a syllable) of relatively extended duration || (*finance*) holding goods in expectation of a rise in prices || (*pop.*, with 'on') equipped with a great deal of, *he is long on practical experience but short on theoretical knowledge* || (of betting odds) in which a bettor stands to win a large multiple of his stake || served in a tall glass, *a long drink* **in the long run** eventually, *you're bound to profit in the long run* **long in the tooth** (of a person or animal) aged **of long standing** with a lengthy history, *a quarrel of long standing* **2.** *n.* a long interval or period of time, *not for long, before long* || (esp. in classical prosody) a long syllable || (*finance*) someone who holds goods in expectation of a rising market **the long and the short of it** the result or total outcome, briefly stated [O.E. *lang, long*]

long *comp.* **long-er** (lɔ́ŋgər, lɒ́ŋgər) *superl.* **long-est** (lɔ́ŋgəst, lɒ́ŋgəst) *adv.* for a long time, *we have long been of that opinion* || by a long time, *long ago, long before he arrived* || throughout a specified period, *all night long* || (*comp.*, with 'no', 'any', 'much' etc.) after a specified or implied time, *we shall not wait any longer* **as** (or **so**) **long as** provided that, *you can come home late as long as you tell me in advance* **so long** (*pop.*) goodbye [O.E. *lange, longe*]

long *v.i.* to desire earnestly and intensely [O.E. *langian,* to lengthen]

long. longitude

long-and-short work (*archit.*) work in which quoins are arranged horizontally and vertically

Long Beach a resort and naval base (pop. 361,334) of S. California: oil wells and refineries, light industries

long-boat (lɔ́ŋbout, lɒ́ŋbout) *n.* (*hist.*) the largest boat carried aboard a sailing ship

long-bow (lɔ́ŋbou, lɒ́ŋbou) *n.* a medieval bow, made of yew or ash, up to 6 ft in length, and drawn by hand (cf. CROSSBOW)

long-cloth (lɔ́ŋklɔθ, lɔ́ŋklɔθ, lɒ́ŋklɒθ, lɒ́ŋklɒθ) *n.* a soft-finished bleached cotton cloth of fine quality

long distance telephone communication with a distant place || the service or operator providing this **long-distance** (lɔ́ŋdístəns, lɒ́ŋdístəns) *adj.* covering a relatively long distance, *a long-distance telephone call* || (esp. *Br.*, of weather reports) made a certain period in advance

long division arithmetical division in which the several stages are indicated in detail

long-drawn-out (lɔ́ŋdrɔ́náut, lɒ́ŋdrɔ́náut) *adj.* excessively prolonged, *long-drawn-out explanations*

longe, lunge (lʌndʒ) **1.** *n.* a long rope held by a trainer to guide and control a horse as it moves around him in a wide circle || a circular exercise ground for training horses **2.** *v.t. pres. part.* **longe-ing, lung-ing** to train or exercise (a horse) in this way [F. *longe,* halter]

lon-ge-ron (lɒ́ndʒərən) *n.* (*aeron.*) a long spar or girder built lengthwise into the fuselage [F.]

lon-gev-i-ty (lɒndʒéviti:) *n.* long life or unusually long life [fr. L. *longaevitas*]

Long-fel-low (lɔ́ŋfelou, lɒ́ŋfelou), Henry Wadsworth (1807–82), American poet, best known for his long narrative poems on historical subjects, esp. 'The Song of Hiawatha' (1855) and 'Evangeline' (1847)

Long-ford (lɔ́ŋfərd, lɒ́ŋfərd) a county (area 403 sq. miles, pop. 28,250) in Leinster, Irish Republic. County seat: Longford (pop. 4,000)

long-hand (lɔ́ŋhænd, lɒ́ŋhænd) *n.* handwriting as opposed to typescript or shorthand

long-head (lɔ́ŋhed, lɒ́ŋhed) *n.* a head with a low cephalic index || someone who is dolichocephalic

long hop (*cricket*) a short-pitched ball

long-house (lɔ́ŋhaus, lɒ́ŋhaus) *pl.* **long-hous-es** (lɔ́ŋhauziz, lɒ́ŋhauziz) *n.* the communal dwelling of certain peoples, e.g. Land Dyaks, Iroquois

long hundredweight the British hundredweight of 112 lbs

long-ing (lɔ́ŋiŋ, lɒ́ŋiŋ) *n.* intense desire for what is not immediately attainable, or an instance of this [O.E. *langung* fr. *langian,* to long]

Lon-gi-nus (lɒndʒáinəs), Dionysius Cassius (c. 213–73), Greek rhetorician and philosopher. The treatise 'Longinus on the Sublime' was incorrectly attributed to him

Long Island an island (118 miles long, 12–13 miles wide) of New York State, separated from the mainland by the East River and Long Island Sound, an arm (110 miles long) of the Atlantic. Part (Brooklyn and Queens) of New York City is on its western end. The rest (the part actually known as Long Island) serves the city as suburbs, has extensive manufacturing, and has numerous beach resorts

lon-gi-tude (lɔ́ndʒitu:d, lɒ́ndʒitju:d) *n.* the angular distance between the meridian passing through a given point on the earth's surface and the poles, and the standard meridian at Greenwich, England. It is measured in degrees east or west of Greenwich, which represents 0° longitude [fr. L. *longitudo,* length]

lon-gi-tu-di-nal (lɒndʒitú:d'n'l, lɒndʒitjú:d'n'l) *adj.* of longitude || lengthwise, *divided in longitudinal strips* [fr. L. *longitudo (longitudinis),* length]

longitudinal wave a wave (e.g. a sound wave) in which the particles of the medium oscillate in the direction of propagation of the wave

long jump (*Br., athletics*) the broad jump

long-leaf pine (lɔ́ŋli:f, lɒ́ŋli:f) *Pinus palustris,* fam. *Pinaceae,* a large pine of the southern U.S.A., an important source of wood and naval stores || its coarse-grained wood

long-lived (lɔ́ŋlívd, lɒ́ŋlívd) *adj.* having a long life

long off (*cricket*) a deep fielder behind the bowler on the off side || this fielding position

long on (*cricket*) a deep fielder behind the bowler on the on side || this fielding position

Long Parliament (*Eng. hist.*) the parliament (1640–53) called by Charles I. Led by Pym and Hampden, it brought about the execution of Strafford and Laud, abolished Star Chamber, and drew up the Grand Remonstrance (1641). The Civil War (1642–52) broke out, and parliament, divided on religious issues, was reduced by Pride's Purge (1648) to a Rump Parliament of Independent extremi ts. This parliament ordered Charles's execution (1649) and was itself

suppressed (1653) by Cromwell. The Long Parliament was not formally dissolved until 1660

long-play-ing (lɔ́ŋpléiiŋ, lɒ́ŋpléiiŋ) *adj.* (of a phonograph record) playing at a speed of 33 1/3 revolutions or less per minute

long primer an old size of type (10 point) between bourgeois and small pica

long-range (lɔ́ŋréindʒ, lɒ́ŋréindʒ) *adj.* of or effective over long distances, *long-range artillery* || covering a long period of time, *a long-range study of world population problems*

long-shore-man (lɔ́ŋfɔrmən, lɒ́ŋfɔrmən, lɔ́ŋfɔurmən, lɒ́ŋfɔurmən) *pl.* **long-shore-men** (lɔ́ŋfɔrmən, lɒ́ŋfɔrmən, lɔ́ŋfɔurmən, lɒ́ŋfɔurmən) *n.* a stevedore || (*Br.*) a man employed in shore fishing, esp. for shellfish

long shot a wager in which the chance of winning is slim but the reward great || a difficult or dangerous undertaking hardly likely to be successful, but if successful then very rewarding **not by a long shot** not at all, not by any manner of means

long-sight-ed (lɔ́ŋsáitid, lɒ́ŋsáitid) *adj.* hypermetropic

long-stand-ing (lɔ́ŋstǽndiŋ, lɒ́ŋstǽndiŋ) *adj.* that has long existed, *a long-standing pact*

long stop (*cricket*) an auxiliary fielder behind the wicketkeeper (not used in firstclass cricket) || this fielding pásition

Long-street (lɔ́ŋstri:t, lɒ́ŋstri:t), James (1821–1904), Confederate general in the Civil War

long-suf-fer-ing (lɔ́ŋsʌ́fəriŋ, lɒ́ŋsʌ́fəriŋ) *adj.* patient, not easily provoked

long suit (*cards*) the suit in which one holds the most cards || something at which a person excels

long-term (lɔ́ŋtə:rm, lɒ́ŋtə:rm) *adj.* acting over or involving a long period of time, *a long-term policy* || of assets held for a period sufficient to qualify for federal income tax long-term gains treatment

long-term care health and/or personal care services required by chronically ill, aged, disabled, or retarded persons, in an institution or at home, on a long-term basis

Long Term Defense Program (*mil.*) a long-range plan to coordinate the defense plans and weapons production of the members of the NATO alliance; devised at the 1977 NATO summit conference and unanimously approved at the 1978 NATO summit conference *abbr.* **LTDP**

long ton (*Br.*) a unit of weight, equal to 2,240 lbs or 20 cwt

lon-guette (lɒŋgét) *n.* women's dress or skirt reaching to midcalf

lon-gueur (lɒŋgə́:r) *n.* (usually *pl.*) a tedious or long-winded passage in a book, play etc. [F.]

Lon-gus (lɔ́ŋgəs) (3rd c.) Greek writer, author of the pastoral romance 'Daphnis and Chloë'

long vacation (*Br.*) the summer recess for universities and law courts

long-ways (lɔ́ŋweiz, lɒ́ŋweiz) *adv.* lengthwise

long-wind-ed (lɔ́ŋwíndid, lɒ́ŋwíndid) *adj.* unnecessarily prolonged, tedious, protracted

Lon Nol (lɒnnóul) (1913–　), Cambodian political leader, president (1972–5). He served as chief of general staff and minister of defense (1955–6), commander in chief (1960), deputy prime minister (1963) and prime minister (1966–7, 1969–72) before overthrowing Prince Sihanouk and becoming president of the newly-proclaimed Khmer Republic. However, civil war broke out in 1974 and by 1975 the Khmer Rouge had taken over the government and Lon Nol was exiled to Hawaii

Lönn-rot (lə́:nru:t), Elias (1802–84), Finnish scholar, who compiled the national epic, the 'Kalevala', by selecting and adapting collected popular ballads and legends

loo (lu:) *n.* a card game with money penalties || such a penalty or an instance of having to pay it [shortened fr. *lanterloo* fr. F. *lanturelu,* a nonsense refrain of a 17th-c. song]

loofah *LUFFA

look (luk) *v.i.* to use the faculty of sight, make an effort to see, *we looked but couldn't find it* || (esp. imperative) to pay attention, *look and see how clever she is* || to direct the eyes in a particular direction, *look at me* || to direct one's mental faculties in a particular direction, *look at the facts* || to appear, *he looks ill* || to be facing in a particular direction, *the window looks north* || to manifest surprise, wonder etc. by staring, gaping etc., *don't just stand there looking* || *v.t.* to direct one's eyes at, examine, regard intensely || to find out, come to know through seeing, *look what time the clock says* || to show by

CONCISE PRONUNCIATION KEY: **(a)** æ, c*a*t; ɑ, c*a*r; ɔ f*aw*n; ei, sn*a*ke. **(e)** e, h*e*n; i:, sh*ee*p; iə, d*ee*r; ɛə, b*ea*r. **(i)** i, f*i*sh; ai, t*i*ger; ə:, b*i*rd. **(o)** o, *o*x; au, c*ow*; ou, g*oa*t; u, p*oo*r; ɔi, r*oy*al. **(u)** ʌ, d*u*ck; u, b*u*ll; u:, g*oo*se; ə, b*a*cillus; ju:, c*u*be. x, lo*ch*; θ, *th*ink; ð, bo*th*er; z, *Z*en; ʒ, corsa*g*e. dʒ, sava*g*e; ŋ, ora*n*gutang; j, *y*ak; ʃ, fi*sh*; tʃ, fe*tch*; 'l, rabb*le*; 'n, redd*en*. Complete pronunciation key appears inside front cover.

one's expression, *he looks sadness itself* ‖ to have an appearance that befits or corresponds to, *the actor looked the role, she looks her age* ‖ (followed by an infinitive) to expect, anticipate, *he is looking to be promoted* **look here!** an expostulating or calling for attention, *look here! you can't do that!* **to look after** to take care of **to look ahead** to consider the future **to look alive** to be quick and alert **to look around** (or **about**) to examine one's surroundings ‖ to consider the situation, circumstances etc. before making plans **to look as if** (or **though**) to indicate a specified possibility, *it looks as if there will be a strike* **to look at** (in neg. sentences) to consider as a possible option, to take an interest in, *he wouldn't look at his lunch* **to look at (someone)** by the appearance of (someone), *you wouldn't guess she was 80 to look at her* **to look back** to look into the past ‖ (esp. in neg. sentences) to show unwillingness to persevere, *you can't look back at this stage of the work* ‖ (*Br.*) to come back, visit again, *I'll look back later* ‖ (in neg. sentences) to cease to prosper, *he never looked back after his first sale* **to look down on** (or **upon**) to consider inferior **to look for** to search for ‖ to hope for expectantly, *we're looking for big things from you* **to look forward to** to anticipate, esp. with pleasure **to look in** to stop for a brief visit **to look into** to inquire into **to look like** to resemble ‖ (*probability*) to promise or threaten, *it looks like a winner, it looks like rain* **to look on** to regard, *she looks on him with awe, he looks on her as a child* ‖ to be a spectator, *you work and we'll look on* **to look oneself** to look perfectly well **to look out** (often with 'for') to be on one's guard, *look out for snakes* ‖ (with 'for') to see if one can discover, *look out for George on the train* ‖ to have a view, *the house looks out on fields* ‖ (*Br.*) to find and select, *look out some old clothes for the rummage sale* **to look over** to inspect esp. briefly **to look sharp** to hurry up **to look through** to stare at without seeing or deliberately ignore, *he looked right through me* ‖ to examine or inspect briefly **to look to** to attend to, *look to your own shortcomings* ‖ (*rhet.*) to be careful of, *look to your manners* ‖ to rely on, *he looks to you for a bit of sense* **to look up** to show improvement, *things are looking up at last* **to look up to** to admire, respect **to look (something) up** to seek information about, *look it up in the dictionary* **to look (someone) up** to call on, visit, *you ought to look him up* **to look (someone or something) up and down** to inspect closely, esp. contemptuously **2.** *n.* a glance, a regard, *he gave her a withering look* ‖ appearance, *they aren't rich by the look of them* ‖ (*pl.*) personal, esp. facial, aspect, *she has her mother's looks* **to take a look at** to look at briefly ‖ to examine with a view to verification or correction [O.E. *lōcian*]

look·er-on (lúkərón, lúkərón) *pl.* **look·ers-on** *n.* a spectator

look-in (lúkin) *n.* a chance of participating or succeeding, *the runt of the litter didn't have a look-in at feeding time* ‖ a brief visit or a quick inspection ‖ (*football*) a fast pass to a player running diagonally toward the center of the field

look·ing (lúkin) *adj.* (only in combination) having a specified appearance, *good-looking*

looking glass a mirror ‖ glass used for mirrors

look·ing-glass (lúkinglæs) *adj.* of a reverse of the normal, e.g. a looking-glass world, solution, politics, or approach

look·out (lúkaut) *n.* the act of looking out, a keeping watch ‖ an observation post for this purpose, e.g. a crow's nest ‖ someone stationed to keep a watch ‖ (*Br.*) prospect, *if he fails, it will be a poor lookout for us* ‖ (*pop.*) concern (esp. with any attendant risk), *if he wants to make a fool of himself that's his lookout* **on the lookout** in a state of watchfulness

Lookout Mountain a mountain ridge in S.E. Tennessee (extending into Georgia and Alabama). A Union victory was won (1863) here, near Chattanooga

look-up table (lúkəp) compilation of reference data, frequently in tabulated form, to assist in locating specific information —**look-up** *n.* process of using such a table

loom (lu:m) **1.** *v.i.* to appear indistinctly, to come into sight, usually somewhat menacingly, e.g. through a mist, *suddenly the cliff loomed up through the fog* ‖ to figure as a future threat or ordeal, *the impending trial loomed large in his mind* **2.** *n.* the indistinct and somewhat menacing appearance of something seen e.g. through

mist or fog, *straining to catch the first loom of the headland* [origin unknown]

loom *n.* the shaft of an oar, or the part inboard from the oarlock [Scand.]

loom *n.* a loon [O.N. *lōmr*]

loom *n.* a frame or machine operated by hand or driven by power for weaving cloth [M.E. *lome* fr. O.E. *gelōma*, utensil]

loon (lu:n) *n.* a member of *Gaviformes*, an order of large, aquatic, diving birds native to northern climates ‖ a grebe [fr. LOOM]

loon *n.* someone extremely silly, esp. someone who has just done something extremely silly [earlier *lown*, *lowne*, etym. doubtful]

loon·y (lú:ni:) *comp.* **loon·i·er** *superl.* **loon·i·est** *adj.* (*pop.*) crazy ‖ (*pop.*) extremely silly or foolish [shortened fr. LUNATIC]

loop (lu:p) **1.** *n.* a closed figure with a curved outline and central aperture, as formed when a curve, string or wire etc. crosses itself ‖ anything of this shape, e.g. the running noose of a lasso ‖ a figure curving back on itself but not closed, *a loop in the road* ‖ a rail or telegraph line that breaks away from the main line and later rejoins it ‖ (*elec.*) a closed circuit ‖ (*med.*) (usu. preceded by 'the') Lippes loop ‖ (*phys.*) an antinode ‖ the figure performed in looping the loop **to knock** (or **throw**) **for a loop** to throw into a totally unexpected state of surprise, bewilderment or inactivity ‖ to cause to suffer a sudden reversal of fortune **2.** *v.t.* to form into a loop ‖ to fasten with a loop ‖ to enclose or encircle in or with a loop ‖ *v.i.* to move in a loop or loops ‖ to become or form a loop **to loop the loop** (*aeron.*) to travel around a complete loop in a vertical plane [M.E. *loupe*, etym. doubtful]

loop·er (lú:pər) *n.* any of several caterpillars, usually geometers, which progress by a series of looping and straightening movements

loop·hole (lú:phoul) *n.* a narrow vertical slit in a wall to admit light and air ‖ (*hist.*) a similar slit for firing missiles through ‖ a way of evading a situation, rule, law etc., *to discover a loophole in a contract*

loose (lu:s) **1.** *adj.* not fitting tightly ‖ not bound together, *loose papers* ‖ not fastened, not firmly fixed, *loose floorboards* ‖ made or allowed to hang freely, *loose draperies* ‖ unconfined, *there are loose dogs at the farm* ‖ not compact or tightly knit, *trample down the loose soil* ‖ (of build, limbs) long or tall and rather gangly ‖ slack, *loose reins* ‖ careless, vague, *bad punctuation is a sign of loose thinking* ‖ not exact, a *loose definition* ‖ free, not literal, *a loose translation* ‖ (*football*, of a game, play) in which the players do not use tight formations ‖ (*cricket*, of bowling, fielding etc.) not rigorous, sloppy ‖ lacking moral restraint, *loose morals, loose talk* ‖ not under strict control, *a loose tongue, loose bowels* ‖ not in a container, *loose change* **2.** *adv.* in a loose way **to break** (or **get**) **loose** to escape from confinement or control **to come** (or **work**) **loose** to become unfastened ‖ to cease to fit tightly **to cut loose** to free oneself from ties **to let** (or **set**) **loose** to release from confinement or control **3.** *n.* (*rugby*, with 'the') open play, as distinct from setpieces like scrummages and lineouts **on the loose** freed from control or restrictions **4.** *v. pres. part.* **loos·ing** *past* and *past part.* **loosed** *v.t.* to set free ‖ to unfasten, release, or *loose one's hold* ‖ to untie (a rope) or make (a boat) free of its moorings ‖ (with 'off') to fire (a gun, ammunition etc.) ‖ *v.i.* (with 'off') to fire a gun [M.E. *lōs*, fr. O.N.]

loose-box (lú:sbɒks) *n.* (*Br.*) a box stall

loose change petty items, unimportant things

loose cover (*Br.*) a slipcover

loose end something left hanging loose ‖ something still to be brought into conformity with the rest of an otherwise finished work **at loose ends** having nothing special to do, without occupation

loose-joint·ed (lú:sdʒɔ́intid) *adj.* moving with more than usual freedom of articulation

loose-leaf (lú:sli:f) *adj.* incorporating a device which enables sheets of paper to be removed or inserted at will, *a looseleaf album* ‖ (of paper etc.) for use in such a device

loos·en (lú:s'n) *v.t.* to make less tight ‖ to unfasten ‖ to make less restrained, *drink loosened his tongue* ‖ to make less firm, less fixed in place ‖ to make less tightly packed or arranged ‖ to relax (the bowels) ‖ to ease (a cough) ‖ to relax (regulations, discipline ‖ *v.i.* to become loose [fr. LOOSE adj.]

loose-strife (lú:strʌif) *n.* a member of *Lysimachia*, fam. *Primulaceae*, esp. *L. vulgaris*, having

racemes of yellow flowers ‖ a member of *Lythrum*, fam. *Lythraceae*, esp. *L. salicaria*, a marsh plant having long spikes of purple flowers

loot (lu:t) **1.** *n.* booty, plunder ‖ (*pop.*) goods stolen or come by illicitly **2.** *v.t.* to pillage (a place), esp. after a battle or some other calamity ‖ to carry off as booty ‖ *v.i.* to steal by pillaging [fr. Hind. *lūt*]

lop (lɒp) **1.** *v.t. pres. part.* **lop·ping** *past* and *past part.* **lopped** (often with 'off') to trim (branches) from a tree ‖ to trim (a tree) by cutting off branches ‖ (with 'off') to cut off, reduce as though by one swift blow, *taxes lop off nearly half his salary* **2.** *n.* the small branches and twigs of a tree that can't be sold to a lumber dealer [origin unknown]

lop *pres. part.* **lop·ping** *past* and *past part.* **lopped** *v.i.* to hang loosely, droop, e.g. of a spaniel's ears ‖ (of a rabbit) to go with short unhurried bounds [perh. imit.]

lop 1. *v.i. pres. part.* **lop·ping** *past* and *past part.* **lopped** (of water) to break in small choppy waves **2.** *n.* the breaking of such waves [imit.]

lope (loup) *v.i. pres. part.* **lop·ing** *past* and *past part.* **loped** (esp. of animals) to move at less than a run with a long effortless stride and the body well down to the ground [O.N. *hloupa*]

lope *n.* (esp. in animals) a loping stride [O.N. *hloup*]

lop-eared (lópiərd) *adj.* with ears flopping over

Lo·pe de Ve·ga (lɔ́pedevéga) (Lope Félix de Vega Carpio, 1562–1635), Spanish poet, dramatist and novelist. Approximaely 500 works are extant. He was the first great writer of the Spanish theater, establishing many forms which characterize its Golden Age. He divided his plays into three acts, ignored the unities of time and place and drew his characters from all classes. He used popular themes, esp. love and honor, and combined popular and classical meters. Like Shakespeare, he was a popular entertainer, an artist and a poet

lo·per·a·mide [$C_{29}H_{33}ClN_2O_2$] (loupéramaid) *n.* (*pharm.*) a synthetic antidiarrheal; marketed as Imodium

Ló·pez (lópeθ), Carlos Antonio (1790–1862), Paraguayan statesman, president of Paraguay (1844–62). Under his arbitrary rule, an army and navy were organized and economic conditions were improved

Ló·pez (lópes), Francisco Solano (c. 1827–70), Paraguayan dictator. He seized (1862) power after the death of his father, Carlos Antonio López. When Brazil intervened in Uruguay, he followed suit (1864), precipitating (1865) the War of the Triple Alliance, which ended in Paraguay's defeat by Brazil, Argentina, and Uruguay. He was responsible for the installation of South America's first telegraph system

López A·re·lla·no (areɦáno), Osvaldo (1921–), Honduran aviator, politician, chief of the military junta which deposed (1963) Ramón Villeda Morales, and constitutional president (1963–71, 1972–)

López Portillo y Pacheco (loupeθpourtí:jou), José (1920–), Mexican statesman, president (1976–82). He served as secretary of finances and public credit (1973–5) before being elected to the presidency. He bolstered the economy by oil production early in his term, but, by 1982, had to nationalize the banks and devalue the peso due to the fall in oil prices. He was succeeded by Miguel de la Madrid Hurtado

López Ve·lar·de (velárðe), Ramón (1888–1921), Mexican lawyer and poet. His 'La Sangre devota' (1916), 'Suave patria', and 'El son del corazón' (1932) combine the exotic with the yearning of the soul

López y Fuen·tes (i:fwéntes), Gregorio (1895–1966), Mexican writer. His novels 'Tierra' (1932), 'Mi general' (1934), and 'El indio' (1935) depict the Mexican Revolution from the point of view of the Indian

loph·o·branch (lófəbræŋk) **1.** *n.* a member of *Lophobranchii*, an order of teleost fishes having tufted gills, e.g. the sea horse, pipefish **2.** *adj.* of or relating to a lophobranch **loph·o·bran·chi·ate** (lofəbræŋki:it) *adj.* and *n.* [fr. Gk *lophos*, crest + *branchia*, gills]

lop·sid·ed (lópsaidid) *adj.* drooping at one side, *a lopsided smile* ‖ unevenly balanced

lo·qua·cious (loukwéiʃəs) *adj.* talkative [fr. L. *loquax*, *loquacis*)]

lo·quac·i·ty (loukwǽsiti:) *n.* the quality or habit of indulging in a great flow of talk [fr. F. *loquacité*]

CONCISE PRONUNCIATION KEY: **(a)** æ, c*a*t; ɑ, c*a*r; ɔ f*aw*n; ei, sn*a*ke. **(e)** e, h*e*n; i:, sh*ee*p; iə, d*ee*r; ɛə, b*ea*r. **(i)** i, f*i*sh; ai, t*i*ger; əː, b*i*rd. **(o)** o, *o*x; au, c*ow*; ou, g*oa*t; u, p*oo*r; ɔi, r*oy*al. **(u)** ʌ, d*u*ck; u, b*u*ll; u:, g*oo*se; ə, b*a*cill*u*s; ju:, c*u*be. x, lo*ch*; θ, *th*ink; ð, bo*th*er; z, *Z*en; ʒ, cor*s*age; dʒ, sa*v*age; ŋ, ora*n*gutang; j, *y*ak; ʃ, *f*ish; tʃ, fe*tch*; 'l, rabb*le*; 'n, redd*en*. Complete pronunciation key appears inside front cover.

lo·quat (lóukwæt) *n. Eriobotrya japonica*, fam. *Rosaceae*, an evergreen tree bearing small, reddish fruit, widely grown in tropical and subtropical climates ‖ this fruit [Chin. *luh kwat=rush* orange]

lo·ral (lɔ́rəl, lóurəl) *adj.* (*zool.*) of or situated at the lore [fr. L. *lorum*, strap]

lo·ran (lɔ́ræn, lóuræn) *n.* a system by which navigators receive the radio signals of two pairs of radio stations of known location and use them to locate a ship or aircraft [*Long Range Navigation*]

lor·a·ze·pam [$C_{15}H_{10}CI_2N_2O_2$] (lɔrázəpæm) *n.* (*pharm.*) a central nervous system tranquilizer, used to relieve anxiety and insomnia; marketed as Ativan

Lorca, Federico García *GARCÍA LORCA

lord (lɔrd) **1.** *n.* (*Br.*) a nobleman or person entitled to use 'Lord' before his name ‖ (*Br.*) the first word in certain official titles, *lord chief justice* ‖ (*Br.*) a member of certain boards exercising high state office ‖ (*hist.*) a master, ruler, sovereign ‖ (*hist.*) a feudal estate owner in relation to his tenants ‖ a business magnate, *the steel lords* **Lord** a British title of rank given as a courtesy title to the younger son of a duke or marquess. It is also used as a form of address or reference for a baron, marquess, earl or viscount or any holder of the courtesy title of Lord **the Lord** God ‖ Christ **our Lord** Christ **the Lords** (*Br.*) the House of Lords **to live like a lord** to live in great luxury **2.** *v.i.* (only in the phrase) **to lord it over** to be imperious or bossy towards [O.E. *hláford*]

lord chancellor *pl.* **lords chancellor, lord chancellors** a British officer of state who is Speaker of the House of Lords, head of the judiciary and keeper of the great seal

lord high steward (*Br.*) the official who manages coronations and presides over the trial of a peer

lord lieutenant *pl.* **lords lieutenant, lord lieutenants** the appointed representative of the Crown in an English county ‖ (*hist.*) the title of an English viceroy in Ireland up to 1922

lord·ling (lɔ́rdliŋ) *n.* a petty, unimportant lord

lord·ly (lɔ́rdli) *comp.* **lord·li·er** *superl.* **lord·li·est** *adj.* (*rhet.*) magnificent, of or befitting a lord ‖ haughty, lofty, *lordly contempt* [O.E. *hláfordlic*]

lord mayor (*Br.*, in certain large cities) the title for the mayor

lord of misrule (*Br. hist.*) a leader of Christmas revels

lor·do·sis (lɔrdóusis) *n.* abnormal forward curvature of the spine (cf. KYPHOSIS, *SCOLIOSIS)

lor·dot·ic (lɔrdótik) *adj.* (Mod. L. fr. Gk fr. *lordos*, bent backward]

lord president of the council a British cabinet minister who is nominally chairman of the privy council and who is usually available to assume special responsibilities

lord privy seal a British officer of state, nominally keeper of the privy seal and a member of the cabinet, often with special responsibilities

lord protector (*Eng. hist.*) the title adopted by Oliver Cromwell and Richard Cromwell as head of the Commonwealth (1653-8 and 1658-9 respectively)

Lord's day Sunday

lord·ship (lɔ́rdʃip) *n.* the rank or dignity of a noble lord ‖ (*hist.*) the lands or estate under a lord's jurisdiction ‖ (*rhet.*) power, authority **your** (or **his**) **lordship** a form of address (or reference) for peers (with the exception of dukes), bishops and judges

Lord's Prayer the prayer, beginning 'Our Father', which Jesus taught his disciples (Matthew vi, 9-13)

Lord's Supper the Eucharist

lore (lɔr, lour) *n.* the knowledge and stock of beliefs relating to a certain subject place, person etc. [O.E. *lár*]

lore *n.* (*zool.*) the space between a bird's bill and eye ‖ (*zool.*) the space between a snake's eye and nostril [fr. L. *lorum*, strap]

Lor·e·lei (lɔ́rəlai) a siren of German legend who sat on a rock in the Rhine and lured sailors to their death by her singing

Lo·rentz (lóurents), Hendrik Antoon (1853–1928), Dutch physicist. He made basic contributions to the electronic theory of matter. He explained the Zeeman effect and developed the principle that a moving body gets shorter in the direction of its motion (the Lorentz-Fitzgerald contraction). Nobel prize for physics, with Zeeman (1902)

Lorenz (lóurents), Konrad (1903–), Austrian ethnologist, cowinner of the Nobel prize for physiology or medicine (1973). He first described the imprinting process, the bonding of child to parent, and studied aggression in human behavior. He wrote 'King Solomon's Ring' (1949), 'Man Meets Dog' (1950), 'On Aggression' (1963) and 'Studies in Animal and Human Behavior' (1965)

Lo·ren·zet·ti (lɔrentsétti:), Ambrogio (*d.* 1348) and Pietro (c. 1280–c. 1348), Italian painters (brothers) of the Sienese school. The frescos and altarpieces of Pietro (e.g. at Assisi and Siena) are traditional in iconography and style and preoccupied with linear rhythms, and are powerfully expressive, with great beauty of color and a deep religious solemnity. Ambrogio is less traditional and more inventive, showing a Florentine interest in perspective and three-dimensional effects, and an entirely original interest in landscape and the detail of everyday life, e.g. in his frescos 'Good and Bad Government', at Siena

Lo·ren·zo Mo·na·co (lɔréntsomónako) (c. 1370–1425), Italian painter and miniaturist. His earliest devotional paintings are in the Sienese style, while his later works anticipate the international Gothic style

lor·gnette (lɔrnjét) *n.* a pair of eyeglasses or opera glasses with a long handle [F.]

lor·i·cate (lɔ́rikeit, lɔ́rikeit) *adj.* (*zool.*) covered with protective shell or scales [fr. L. *loricatus* fr. *lorica*, cuirass]

lo·ris (lɔ́ris, lóiris) *n. Loris gracilis*, fam. *Lorisidae*, a slender lemur of Ceylon and S. India ‖ *Bradicebus tardigradus*, fam. *Lorisidae*, a larger, slow-moving lemur of India and the East Indies [F.]

Lorrain, Claude *CLAUDE LORRAIN

Lor·raine (lɔren) a former province of E. France, between the Vosges massif and the Paris basin, comprising Meuse, Moselle, Meurthe-et-Moselle and Vosges departments. The mountains slope down in the northeast to a plateau containing salt and coal deposits. The western plain, broken by hills, has mixed farming, hop fields and brewing, and heavy industry based on great iron fields in Moselle. Chief towns: Nancy, Metz. Part of Lotharingia until the 10th c., it became a duchy of the Holy Roman Empire. France occupied parts of it from 1552 until 1766, when the whole was ceded to France. Moselle was part of the territory gained (1871) by Germany (*ALSACE-LORRAINE) and subsequently restored to France

Lorris, Guillaume de *GUILLAUME DE LORRIS

lor·ry (lɔ́ri:, lɔ́ri:) *pl.* **lor·ries** *n.* (*Br.*) a truck [etym. doubtful]

lo·ry (lɔ́ri:, lóuri:) *pl.* **lo·ries** *n.* any of several brightly colored parrots, chiefly of genera *Domicella, Trichoglossus, Chalcopsitta* and *Eos*, found esp. in New Guinea and Australia [Malay *lūri*]

LOS (*abbr.*) **1.** line of sight. **2.** (*football*) line of scrimmage

Lo·sa·da (lɔsáða), Diego de (*d.* 1569), Spanish conquistador, founder (1567) of Caracas

Los An·ge·les (lɔsǽndʒələs, lɔsǽndʒələs) the third largest city (area 454 sq. miles, pop. 3,022,247, with agglom. 7,477,657, increasing rapidly) of the U.S.A., an industrial center and port in S. California, in a great agricultural district and oil field. Main industries: motion pictures and television (*HOLLYWOOD), aeronautical, mechanical and electrical engineering. University of California (1919). In 1984, Los Angeles hosted the summer Olympics

lose (lu:z) *pres. part.* **los·ing** *past* and *past part.* **lost** (lɔst, lost) *v.t.* to become unable to find ‖ to cease to have, fail to keep, *to lose one's sense of proportion* ‖ to be deprived of, *to lose a leg* ‖ to be deprived of through death, *he has just lost his wife* ‖ to get rid of, *to lose weight* ‖ to waste, *he lost no time in telling us* ‖ to fail to win, *to lose a game* ‖ to miss, *he hates to lose a day in the sun* ‖ to fail to keep in sight ‖ to shake off (someone trailing) ‖ to fail to grasp or understand, *we lost the point of his argument* ‖ to fail to hear, *she lost most of the sermon* ‖ to cause the loss of, cost, *her rudeness lost her the job* ‖ (of a timepiece) to become slow by, *my watch is losing three minutes a day* ‖ to decrease in, *to lose speed* ‖ *v.i.* to fail to win, be defeated ‖ to suffer loss, be at a disadvantage, *you won't lose on the deal* **to lose ground** to fall back, give way, lose a lead or advantage **to lose interest** to cease to interest, *the film soon lost interest* ‖ to cease to be interested, *he lost interest in the project* **to lose**

oneself (esp. *Br.*) to go astray, get lost ‖ to become engrossed in **to lose sight of** to fail to keep in view **to lose track of** to cease to keep in touch with or be fully informed about **to lose out** (*pop.*) to be unsuccessful **los·er** (lú:zər) *n.* someone or something that loses ‖ (*bridge*) a card that will not take a trick ‖ (*tennis*) a stroke that does not win a point **to be a good** (**bad**) **loser** to accept defeat with good (bad) grace [O.E. *losian*]

löss *LOESS

loss (lɔs, los) *n.* a losing or an instance of this ‖ a person, thing or quantity that is lost ‖ the harm, trouble, sadness etc. caused by losing someone or something ‖ defeat, *this game is their first loss* ‖ (*pl.*) soldiers reported as having been killed, wounded or captured ‖ excess of cost over selling price, *to sell at a loss* or the amount of this ‖ the financial detriment suffered by an insured person as a result of damage to property, theft etc. ‖ energy wasted in a machine, circuit etc. e.g. through poor insulation or ventilation ‖ decrease in quality or degree, *loss in weight* [partly fr. O.E. *los*, rout, and partly back-formation fr. LOST]

loss leader (*commerce*) an article sold at a loss to arouse customer interest in other stock

lost (lɔst, lost) *past* and *past part.* of LOSE ‖ *adj.* in verbal senses, esp. unable to be found ‖ unable to find the way ‖ wasted, *many lost hours* ‖ missed, *a lost opportunity* ‖ not producing the desired effect, *sarcasm is lost on her* ‖ that one has failed to win ‖ ruined ‖ (of persons) killed ‖ bewildered ‖ helpless, *he's lost without his glasses* ‖ no longer practiced or known ‖ (*rhet.*) damned, *a lost soul* ‖ (*rhet.*) insensible, *lost to all sense of honor* ‖ engrossed, *lost in a book* **lost to the world** so engrossed in something as to be unaware of one's surroundings

lost cause a movement that no longer has any chance of success

lost tribes the 10 tribes of Israel which were taken captive (c. 722 B.C.) by Sargon II of Assyria, and which never returned to Palestine (II Kings xvii, 6)

Lot (lɔt) (*Bible*) the nephew of Abraham. Lot's wife was turned into a pillar of salt when she looked back during their flight from Sodom (Genesis xix)

Lot (lɔt) a department (area 2,017 sq. miles, pop. 150,700) in S. France (*GUYENNE). Chief town: Cahors (pop. 21,903)

Lot (lɔt) a northern tributary (300 miles long) of the Garonne in S.W. France, rising in the Cévennes

lot (lɔt) **1.** *n.* one of a number of portions into which a quantity or substance may be divided for allotment ‖ (*rhet.*) one's fate or destiny in life ‖ an article or set of articles offered as an item for sale at an auction ‖ a plot or area of land having established limits, *the house and the lot it stands on*, a *used-car lot* ‖ (*movies*) a studio and the surrounding land belonging to it ‖ a set of people or things **to draw lots** to decide by using some method of random choice, such as selecting a straw etc. from a bundle of straws of different length concealed in the hand, or by drawing names out of a hat etc. **a bad lot** (*pop.*) a person of bad character **a lot, lots** a large number or amount, *what a lot of rabbits!*, *you'll need lots of patience* **by lot** by drawing lots, *they chose the captain by lot* **the lot** the whole quantity or number, *we had a fine show of dahlias but frost ruined the lot* **to fall to someone's lot** to devolve on someone as a task to be done **to throw in one's lot with** to elect to share the fortunes of, join up with **2.** *adv.* **a lot** much, considerably, to a great extent, *a lot better* [O.E. *hlot*]

Lot-et-Ga·ronne (lɔteigærɔn) a department (area 2,078 sq. miles, pop. 292,600) in S.W. France (*GUYENNE, *GASCONY). Chief town: Agen (pop. 35,839)

loth *LOATH

Lo·thair I (louθéər) (795–855), Holy Roman Emperor (840–55), son of Emperor Louis I. His brothers Louis the German and Charles the Bald forced him to agree to the partition of the Carolingian Empire in the Treaty of Verdun (843)

Lothair II 'the Saxon' (c. 1070–1137), Holy Roman Emperor (1133–7) and German king (1125–37). His election to the German throne started the conflict between Guelphs and Ghibellines

Lo·tha·rin·gi·a (louθəríndʒi:ə) (*hist.*) a region of N. Europe, bounded by the Scheldt, the Meuse and the Rhine. It was the part of the Carolingian Empire assigned by the Treaty of Verdun (843) to Lothair I. It was divided (c. 959) into two duchies, the southern one of which became Lorraine

Lo·ti (lou'ti:), Pierre (Louis Marie Julien Viaud, 1850–1923), French novelist. His works include 'le Mariage de Loti' (1882) and 'Pêcheur d'Islande' (1886)

lo·tion (lóu'ʃən) n. a liquid medicinal or cosmetic preparation applied to the skin [fr. L. *loto* (*lotionis*), a washing]

lot·ter·y (lót'əri:) pl. **lot·ter·ies** n. a method of raising money by the sale of a large number of tickets and the subsequent chance selection of certain ones entitling the bearers of these to a prize [fr. Ital. *lotteria*]

lot·to (lót'ou) n. a form of bingo using slightly different numbered cards [F. fr. Ital. fr. Gmc]

lo·tus (lóu'təs) n. (*Gk mythol.*) a fruit which when eaten was said to cause a state of forgetfulness and languor (*LOTUS-EATER), or the tree bearing this fruit ‖ any of various trees believed to be the lotus tree of the ancients, e.g. *Ziziphus lotus*, fam. *Rhamnaceae*, a N. African tree, bearing an edible yellow drupe ‖ any of various water lilies, esp. of Egypt and India ‖ a representation of a water lily, found esp. in ancient Egyptian art ‖ a member of *Lotus*, fam. *Papilionaceae*, a genus of meadow flowers, e.g. bird's-foot trefoil [L. fr. Gk *lōtos*]

lo·tus-eat·er (lóu'təs;i:tər) n. a person thought of as passing his time in daydreaming and the enjoyment of pleasure, free of all responsibility [fr. Gk *Lōtophagoi*, a people who, in the 'Odyssey', ate the lotus fruit]

lotus position (*yoga*) sitting with arms on knees and legs folded, with the feet placed above calves or thighs

loud (laud) adj. producing a powerful stimulus on the ear ‖ clamoring, noisy ‖ showy, conspicuous, *loud colors* ‖ vulgar, unrefined, *loud manners* **to be loud in one's praises** to praise with emphasis and insistence [O.E. *hlūd*]

loud adv. in a loud manner [O.E. *hlūde*]

loud·en (láud'n) v.t. to intensify the sound of ‖ v.i. to become more intense in sound [fr. LOUD adj.]

loud-hail·er (láud'héilər) n. a bullhorn

loud-mouthed (láudmạuðd, láudmạuθt) adj. given to loud, boasting talk

loud·speak·er (láudspí:kər) n. a device that converts electrical impulses into sounds loud enough to be heard some distance away, as incorporated e.g. in a radio or in public-address systems

lough (lɔk, lɔx) n. (*Ir.*) a lake ‖ (*Ir.*) an arm of the sea [Gael. *loch*]

Lou·is (lú:is), Joe (Joseph Louis Barrow, 1914–81), U.S. boxer and heavyweight champion of the world (1937–49). He defended his title against more contenders than any other such champion had done

lou·is d'or (lú:i:dɔ́r) pl. **lou·is d'or** n. (*F. hist.*) a gold coin struck by Louis XIII (1640), used until 1793 ‖ (*F. hist.*) a napoleon [F.]

Louis I (lú:i:) (1786–1868), king of Bavaria (1825–48). His rule became reactionary after 1830, and he was deposed by the revolution of 1848. He made Munich a center of the arts

Louis II (1845–86), king of Bavaria (1864–86). He was a lavish patron of Wagner

Louis I, king of the Franks *LOUIS I, Holy Roman Emperor

Louis II (846–79), king of the Franks (877–9), son of Charles II

Louis III (c. 863–882), French king (879–82), son of Louis II. He divided the kingdom with his brother Carloman (*d.* 884), and defeated the invading Normans (881)

Louis IV (c. 921–54), French king (936–54), son of Charles III. He struggled vainly to control the great nobles, particularly Hugh the Great

Lou·is Qua·torze (lú:i:kætórz) of the classical styles of furniture, architecture, ornament etc. characteristic of the reign of Louis XIV of France

Lou·is Quinze (lú:i:kɛ̃z) of the styles of furniture, architecture, ornament etc. characteristic of the reign of Louis XV of France

Lou·is Seize (lú:i:séz) of the styles of furniture, architecture, ornament etc. characteristic of the reign of Louis XVI of France

Lou·is Treize (lú:i:tréz) of the styles of furniture, architecture, ornament etc. characteristic of the reign of Louis XIII

Louis V (c. 967–987), French king (986–7). He was the last Carolingian ruler of France and was succeeded by Hugh Capet

Louis VI (c. 1081–1137), king of France (1108–37), son of Philippe I. He asserted his rights as suzerain and rallied the great nobles to defeat (1124) the Emperor Henry V. His reign marks the beginning of effective royal power in France. He was almost continuously at war with Henry I of England. His chief minister was Suger

Louis VII (c. 1120–80), king of France (1137–80), son of Louis VI. He organized the disastrous 2nd Crusade (1147–9). He lost Aquitaine and large territories in S. France when Henry Plantagenet (later Henry II of England) married his divorced wife, Eleanor of Aquitaine (1152)

Louis VIII (1187–1226), king of France (1223–6), son of Philippe II. He unsuccessfully invaded England (1216–7), drove the English from Poitou (1224) and led a crusade against the Albigenses (1226)

Louis IX, Saint Louis (1214–70), king of France (1226–70), son of Louis VIII. He made a generous peace with the king of Aragon (1258) and with England (1259), extended royal authority and strengthened the central government. The administration of justice and the taxation system were developed and improved. The leader of the 7th and 8th Crusades, he was captured (1250) during the former (1248–54) and died at Tunis as he was setting out on the latter. Pious, ascetic and just, he was the embodiment of the medieval ideal of the Christian king. He gave France unprecedented prosperity and peace, and his fame was such that he often acted as arbiter in European affairs. He was canonized (1297). Feast: Aug. 25

Louis X (1289–1316), king of France (1314–16) and of Navarre (1305–16), son of Philippe IV. He ceded charters to the nobles of various provinces, defining their rights and privileges (1315)

Louis XI (1423–83), king of France (1461–83), son of Charles VII. He defeated (1477) a rebellion of nobles, led by Charles the Bold, duke of Burgundy. By 1483 he had united nearly all of France except Brittany, and had laid the basis for the absolute rule of later French kings

Louis XII (1462–1515), king of France (1498–1515), son of Charles, duc d'Orléans. He succeeded his cousin Charles VIII. He waged a series of fruitless Italian Wars (1499–1504, 1508–13) and was finally driven out (1513) by the Holy League. At home he improved the administration of justice and encouraged trade

Louis XIII (1601–43), king of France (1610–43), son of Henri IV. During the regency (1610–17) of his mother Marie de' Medici, the country was torn by civil strife. He left the conduct of state affairs to Luynes (1617–21), to Richelieu, whom he appointed chief minister (1624–42), and to Mazarin (1642–3)

Louis XIV 'the Great', 'le Roi Soleil' (1638–1715), king of France (1643–1715), son of Louis XIII. His mother, Anne of Austria, and her chief minister, Mazarin, acted as regents until 1661. The power of the Hapsburgs was checked by the Treaties of Westphalia (1648), and France was shaken by the Fronde (1648–53). After 1661, Louis established personal rule. In a series of wars—the War of Devolution (1667–8), the Dutch War (1672–8), the War of the Grand Alliance (1689–97) and the War of the Spanish Succession (1701–14)—France increased her territory, but was left financially exhausted. Louis's persecution of Protestants culminated in the revocation (1685) of the Edict of Nantes, which led to a mass flight of Huguenots from France and to the loss of Protestant alliances in Europe. His court, in the palace which he built at Versailles, was the most magnificent in Europe and the most civilizing. Louis was served by great men, esp. Colbert in financial affairs, Louvois in military matters and Vauban in fortifications. Under his patronage in the arts and literature France realized a classical ideal which has informed men's minds ever since

Louis XV (1710–74), king of France (1715–74), great-grandson of Louis XIV. Under the regency (1715–23) of Philippe, duc d'Orléans, and under the ministry (1726–43) of Fleury, trade prospered until the outbreak of the War of the Polish Succession (1733–5), from which France gained Lorraine. The War of the Austrian Succession (1740–8) brought no gains, and the Seven Years' War (1756–63) resulted in the loss of most of France's overseas possessions.

The king's policies were increasingly influenced by his mistresses, Mme de Pompadour and Mme du Barry. The financial strain of the wars and the excesses of the court alienated growing numbers of intellectuals (e.g. physiocrats and Encyclopedists)

Louis XVI (1754–93), king of France (1774–92), grandson of Louis XV. The efforts of his finance ministers, Turgot and Necker, were unable to save the French government from financial and political collapse. All attempts at reform were opposed by the privileged nobility and by a section of the court led by the queen, Marie Antoinette. French intervention (1778–83) in the Revolutionary War caused virtual bankruptcy and led to the summoning of the States General (1789) for the first time since 1614. The French Revolution broke out (1789) and the royal family soon became virtual prisoners of the Paris mob. Louis might still have survived as a constitutional monarch but for his indecision, his intrigues with foreign powers and his attempted flight (1791). He was deposed (1792), found guilty of treason, and guillotined

Louis XVIII (1755–1824), king of France (1814–15, 1815–24), brother of Louis XVI. Exiled (1791–1814) during the French Revolution, he was put on the throne by the allied victory over Napoleon, but was again forced to flee during the Hundred Days (1815). His government, at first in the hands of moderates, became increasingly reactionary as the ultra-royalists gained power

Louis II 'the German' (c. 804–76), king of the East Franks (817–43) and king of Germany (843–76), son of Emperor Louis I

Lou·is I 'the Pious' (778–840), Holy Roman Emperor and king of the Franks (814–40), son of Charlemagne. His attempts to preserve the unity of the empire failed because of the quarrels and rebellions of his four sons, and he was deposed

Louis II (c. 822–75), Holy Roman Emperor (855–75) and king of Italy (844–75), son of Lothair I

Louis IV 'the Bavarian' (c. 1287–1347), Holy Roman Emperor (1328–46) and German king (1328–46). In his long struggle for supremacy over the papacy, he was supported by William of Occam and Marsiglio of Padua

Louis I 'the Great' (1326–82), king of Hungary (1342–82) and of Poland (1370–82). He made war successfully on the Venetians, the Tatars, the Lithuanians and the Turks, and extended his rule to Serbia, Wallachia, Moldavia and Bulgaria. His campaigns brought Hungary into contact with the Italian Renaissance

Louis II (1506–26), king of Hungary and Bohemia (1516–26). The last of the Jagiello dynasty, he was defeated and killed by the Turks at Mohacs (1526)

Lou·i·si·an·a (lu:i:zi:ǽnə) (*abbr.* La.) a state (area 48,523 sq. miles, pop. 4,362,000) in the southern U.S.A. Capital: Baton Rouge. Chief city: New Orleans. It contains some hill country but is chiefly low-lying and includes the Mississippi delta. Agriculture: sugarcane (chief producer in continental U.S.A.), cotton, rice, sweet potatoes. Resources: oil, natural gas, sulfur, salt. Industries: oil refining, food processing, chemicals, pulp and paper, fisheries. Principal universities: Tulane (1834) at New Orleans, Louisiana State (1860) near Baton Rouge. Louisiana was a French colony (1699–1762), was ceded to Spain (1762), returned to France (1800) and was bought, as part of the Louisiana Purchase (1803), by the U.S.A., of which it became (1812) the 18th state

Louisiana Purchase a tract of land (828,000 sq. miles), comprising the western part of the Mississippi valley, bought by the U.S.A. from France in 1803 for $15,000,000. It now forms the states of Louisiana, Arkansas, Missouri, Iowa and Nebraska, and part of Oklahoma, Kansas, Colorado, Wyoming, Montana, North Dakota, South Dakota and Minnesota. The area had been opened up by France, ceded to Spain (1762) and returned to France (1800)

Louis Napoleon *NAPOLEON III

Lou·is-Phi·lippe (lú:i:fi:lí:p) (1773–1850), king of the French (1830–48), son of Louis Philippe Joseph, duc d'Orléans. In exile (1793–1815) during the French Revolution, he came to the throne when the reactionary rule of Charles X was overthrown by the revolution of July, 1830. Under this 'July Monarchy' the upper bourgeoisie prospered, but discontent grew when the

---

government failed to make liberal reforms and when the king's foreign policy ended in failure. The revolution of 1848 forced him to abdicate and to flee to England

Lou·is·ville (lúːiːvil) the largest city (pop. 298,451) of Kentucky, a tobacco market, with iron, tanning and furniture industries. University of Louisville (1846). The Kentucky Derby, the famous annual horse race, has been run at Louisville since 1875

lounge (laundʒ) **1.** *v. pres. part.* **loung·ing** *past* and *past part.* **lounged** *v.i.* to loll, sit or stand in a lazy manner ‖ to saunter idly ‖ *v.t.* (with 'away') to pass (time) in idleness or loafing **2.** *n.* (esp. *Br.*) the sitting room in a private house ‖ a room in a hotel, club etc. with easy chairs for relaxation ‖ a long sofa with a headrest at one end [etym. doubtful]

lounge suit (*Br.*) a man's suit for ordinary daytime wear

lour *LOWER

Lourdes (luːrd, luərdz) a town (pop. 17,870) in Hautes-Pyrénées, S.W. France. Its shrine to the Virgin is a great Roman Catholic pilgrimage place, esp. for the sick (*BERNADETTE). Cures worked here are accepted as miraculous only after strict investigation by ecclesiastical and medical authority

Lou·ren·ço Mar·ques *MAPUTO

lour·ing (láuriŋ, láuəriŋ) *adj.* lowering

louse (laus) *pl.* **lice** (lais) *n.* a member of *Anoplura* or *Mallophaga*, orders of small, wingless parasitic insects with mouthparts adapted for sucking or biting. They attack warm-blooded animals, esp. on the body or in the hair or feathers ‖ any of various small arthropods which are parasitic on plants or animals, e.g. plant lice ‖ (*pop., pl.* **louses**) a person for whom one feels contempt **lous·y** (láuziː) *comp.* **lous·i·er** *superl.* **lous·i·est** infested with lice ‖ (*pop.*) rotten, disgusting, bad in quality, *a lousy film* ‖ (*pop.*, with 'with') as if infested with lice, *the place was lousy with detectives* ‖ (*pop.*) excessively well supplied, *he's lousy with money* [O.E. *lūs*]

lout (laut) *n.* a rough, clumsy, stupid fellow [origin unknown]

Louth (lauð) a northeastern county (area 317 sq. miles, pop. 74,951) of Leinster, Irish Republic. County seat: Dundalk (pop. 20,000)

lout·ish (láutiʃ) *adj.* like or characteristic of a lout

Lou·vain (luːvɛ̃) (*Flem.* Leuven) a town (pop. 84,459) of Brabant, Belgium: a textile center in the 13th c., the seat since 1426 of a university noted as a Roman Catholic theological center. Flamboyant Gothic town hall (1445–63)

lou·ver, lou·vre (lúːvər) *n.* an arrangement of overlapping boards or slats with gaps between them so that air is admitted but rain excluded ‖ one of these boards or slats ‖ a slit like opening in the body of a car for ventilation or escape of engine heat **lóu·vered, lóu·vred** *adj.* [M.E. *luver, lover* fr. O.F. *lover*]

Louverture *TOUSSAINT LOUVERTURE

Lou·vois (luːvwæ), François Michel Le Tellier, marquis de (1641–91), French statesman. As Louis XIV's minister of war (1666–91), he carried out military reforms which made the French army the most powerful in Europe. He supported, and brutally enforced, the revocation (1685) of the Edict of Nantes, and helped to shape Louis XIV's aggressive foreign policy

Lou·vre (luːvr) the national museum and art gallery of France, in Paris. It was a former royal palace, the present building being begun by François I in 1546, successively enlarged, and converted to its present use after the French Revolution

louvre *LOUVER

lov·a·ble, love·a·ble (lávəb'l) *adj.* for whom people instinctively feel warm affection **lóv·a·bly, lóve·a·bly** *adv.*

lov·age (lávidʒ) *n.* any of several perennial herbs, fam. *Umbelliferae*, esp. *Levisticum officinale*, native to S. Europe, cultivated for use in flavoring and perfumery [M.E. *loveache* fr. O.F. *leveshe*]

lov·at (lávət) *n.* a bluish-green color, esp. in tweed [fr. *Lovat*, in Inverness, Scotland]

love (lav) *n.* a powerful emotion felt for another person manifesting itself in deep affection, devotion or sexual desire ‖ the object of this emotion ‖ God's regard for his creatures ‖ charity (the virtue) ‖ a great liking, fondness, *love of books* ‖ (*tennis, rackets* etc.) no score, nothing **for love or** (or **nor**) **money** (after a negative) by any means, *you couldn't get a ticket for love or money* **in love** feeling love, esp. sexual love

there's no love lost between them they heartily dislike each other **to fall in love** to experience the emotions of love, esp. suddenly and unexpectedly ‖ to be taken with a possessive liking, *she fell in love with the cottage at once* **to give one's love** to convey one's affectionate greetings **to make love** to show by one's actions one's feelings of sexual love, esp. to have sexual intercourse **to send one's love** to ask for one's affectionate greetings to be conveyed [O.E. *lufu*]

love *pres. part.* **lov·ing** *past* and *past part.* **loved** *v.t.* to feel the passion of love for ‖ to be fond of ‖ to delight in, enjoy, *she loves messing about in the garden* ‖ *v.i.* to be in love [O.E. *lufian*]

loveable *LOVABLE

love affair a romantic or sexual relationship between two people in love and not married to one another

love beads bead necklaces worn by hippies as a symbol of love for humankind and of peace

love·bird (lávbəːrd) *n.* any of several small parrots, esp. members of genera *Psittacula* of South America, *Loriculus* of Asia or *Agapornis* of Africa, that exhibit much affection for their mates. They are often kept as cage birds

love·bug (lávbʌg) *n.* (*entomology*) *Plecia nearotica*, small black bionid fly common in southwest U.S., noted for its obvious copulation

love child an illegitimate child

love-crossed (lávkrɒst) *adj.* disappointed in love

love feast the agape (meal) ‖ among certain denominations, a religious service in imitation of the early Christian agape

love-in (lávin) *n.* a gathering, often by hippies, to celebrate love or to express their mutual love

love-in-a-mist (lávinəmist) *n.* *Nigella damascena*, fam. *Ranunculaceae*, an annual European plant cultivated for its blue flowers surrounded by delicate bracts ‖ *Passiflora foetida*, fam. *Passifloraceae*, a West Indian passion flower with similar bracts

Lo·vei·ra-Chi·ri·no (lɔvéiraʧiːríːnɔ), Carlos (1882–1928), Cuban novelist, author of 'Los ciegos' and 'Juan Criollo'

Love·joy (lávdʒɔi), Elijah Parish (1802–37), U.S. abolitionist, killed by a mob while protecting his antislavery press. His death greatly strengthened the abolitionist movement

Love·lace (lávleis), Richard (1618–c. 1657), English Cavalier poet. His collections of lyrics were 'Lucasta: epodes, odes, sonnets, songs' (1649) and 'Lucasta: posthume poems' (1659)

love-lies-bleed·ing (lávlaizbliːdiŋ) *n.* a member of *Amaranthus*, fam. *Amaranthaceae*, esp. *A. caudatus*, a garden flower cultivated for its long drooping spike of purplish-red flowers

love·li·ness (lávliːnis) *n.* the state or quality of being lovely

Lov·ell (lával), Sir Bernard (1913–), British physicist, director of Jodrell Bank since 1951

love·lorn (lávlɔːrn) *adj.* (*rhet.*) forsaken by the person one loves ‖ (*rhet.*) pining, languishing with unhappy love

love·ly (lávliː) *comp.* **love·li·er** *superl.* **love·li·est** *adj.* beautiful, *a lovely girl, a lovely tree* ‖ delightful, pleasing, *we had a lovely time* [O.E. *luflic*]

love-mak·ing (lávmeikiŋ) *n.* courtship ‖ sexual intercourse [M.E. *love making*]

love match a marriage made for love (not for considerations of advantage, but not necessarily ruling out such advantage)

lov·er (lávər) *n.* a man in relation to his mistress ‖ a man in relation to some person (other than a mistress) whom he loves ‖ (*pl.*) two people in love with one another ‖ someone who greatly enjoys something specified, *a lover of good food*

love seat a small couch or double chair seating two persons

love·sick (lávsik) *adj.* (*rhet.*) languishing because obsessed by love

lov·ing (láviŋ) *adj.* devoted, affectionate ‖ expressing or feeling love

loving cup a large double-handled drinking cup passed around at a banquet for everyone to drink from in turn

lov·ing-kind·ness (láviŋkáindnis) *n.* (*rhet.*) tender, benevolent, merciful love

low (lou) **1.** *v.i.* (of a cow) to moo ‖ to make a noise like a moo **2.** *n.* the moo of a cow [O.E. *hlōwan*]

low 1. *adj* being at, or reaching to, a position at a relatively small distance above some plane of reference (e.g. the ground or sea level) ‖ (of lat-

itude) close to the equator ‖ coming or reaching far downward, *a low bow* ‖ at or near the bottom of some real or imagined scale of measurement, *low wages, low intelligence* ‖ at or near the bottom of some scale of moral or social values or ranking, *of low birth, the lower classes* ‖ mean, contemptible, *a low trick* ‖ obscene, *a low remark* ‖ depressed, *low spirits* ‖ weak, *the fever left him feeling low* ‖ small in number or amount, *the figures for diphtheria deaths remain low* ‖ depleted to the point of being nearly gone or exhausted, *our water supply is getting low* ‖ unfavorable, *a low opinion* ‖ little advanced in biological evolution, *a low form of life* ‖ (*phon.*, of a vowel) open ‖ quiet, soft, *a low whisper* ‖ (*mus.*, of a note etc.) produced by relatively few vibrations ‖ (of a gear) having the smallest ratio of wheel revolutions to engine revolutions **to lay low** (*rhet.*) to knock down, overthrow, *he laid his enemies low* ‖ to make helpless or bedridden, *he is laid low with flu* **to lie low** to stay hidden ‖ to avoid attracting attention while awaiting a change in events **2.** *adv.* in or to a low position, *the clouds hung low* ‖ in or to a mean or abject position, *he wouldn't sink as low as that* ‖ quietly, softly, *speak lower* deeply, in or to a low pitch, *she can't sing any lower* **3.** *n.* low gear ‖ (*meteor.*) an area of low barometric pressure ‖ low level, *membership has sunk to an all-time low* [O.N. *lāgr*]

low·ball (lóubɔːl) *n.* an unfair action, esp. a deceptive price designed to induce a customer to buy —**lowball** *v.*

low·born (lóubɔːrn) *adj.* of humble birth

low·boy (lóubɔi) *n.* a low table with drawers, used esp. as a dressing table

low·bred (lóubred) *adj.* of low breeding ‖ indicating low breeding, vulgar, *a lowbred remark*

low·brow (lóubrau) **1.** *n.* someone whose taste in entertainment, literature etc. is for the popular and nonintellectual (cf. HIGHBROW) **2.** *adj.* having or catering to such tastes

low camp a poorly selected, artistically mediocre bit of nostalgia —**low-camp** *adj.*

Low Church of the practices and principles of a Low Churchman

Low Churchman a member of that part of the Anglican Church which emphasizes the evangelical side of its teaching and minimizes the importance of Church ritual and the priestly office (cf. HIGH CHURCHMAN)

low comedy comedy based chiefly on physical action and broadly funny situations

Low Countries the collective name for Belgium, Luxembourg and the Netherlands

low-down (lóudaun) *adj.* (*pop.*) mean, contemptible

low·down *n.* (*pop.*) the real facts of a situation as known to someone with inside information

Low·ell (lóual), Abbott Lawrence (1856–1943), U.S. educator and Harvard University president (1909–33). His administration doubled student enrollment, trebled the faculty, increased endowments from $22 million to $130 million, and added new professional schools. He reorganized (1930) the undergraduate body into residential units modeled on those in English universities

Lowell, Amy (1874–1925), U.S. poet and critic, best known for her 'Patterns' and 'Lilacs'

Lowell, James Russell (1819–91), U.S. romantic poet and editor. His satirical works include 'Biglow Papers' (1848), political and social lampoons written in Yankee dialect. His literary criticism includes 'Fireside Travels' (1864), 'Among My Books' (1870) and 'My Study Windows' (1871). His 'The Letters of James Russell Lowell' (1893) and 'New Letters' (1932) are commentaries on public affairs and the literary activities of his generation

Lowell, Percival (1855–1916), U.S. astronomer who founded the Lowell Observatory at Flagstaff, Arizona. His 'Mars and Its Canals' (1906) postulated that the canals are strips of cultivated vegetation dependent upon irrigation. His research led to the discovery of Pluto (1930)

Lowell, Robert (1917–77), U.S. poet. His works, full of symbolism, include 'Lord Weary's Castle' (1946) and 'The Dolphin' (1973), both Pulitzer prize winners, and 'Day by Day' (1977), his final work

low·er (lóuər) **1.** *adj. comp.* of LOW ‖ (*biol.*) relatively little advanced in biological evolution **2.** *v.t.* to let down ‖ to reduce, *to lower prices* ‖ to make less loud, *to lower one's voice* ‖ (*mus.*) to depress in pitch ‖ to reduce the height of ‖ to bring down, degrade, *his arrogance lowered him in her estimation* ‖ *v.i.* to become lower ‖ to decrease ‖ (*naut.*) to lower a boat, *lower away!* **3.** *n.* a lower berth

Lower Austria (*G.* Niederösterreich) the largest province (area 7,402 sq. miles, pop. 1,400,000) of Austria, containing most of the Vienna basin. Capital: Krems (pop. 14,000)

Lower California (*Span.* Baja California) an arid peninsula (800 miles long, 30–145 miles wide) of W. Mexico, bordering California, separated from the mainland by the Gulf of California. It is divided between a northern state (Baja California, pop. 854,561, capital: Mexicali) and a southern federal territory (Baja California Sur, pop. 123,786) below the 28th parallel. A chain of mountains, rising to 10,000 ft, runs its length. Industries: mining (copper, zinc, gold, silver), tourism, fishing

Lower Canada (*hist.*) a province of Canada (1791–1840) which was predominantly French in population. It now constitutes the province of Quebec

lower, lour (láuər) **1.** *v.i.* to scowl, look sulky ‖ to look dark and threatening, *storm clouds lowered on the horizon* **2.** *n.* a scowl ‖ a gloomy, threatening appearance [M.E. *louren*]

low·er·case (lóuərkéis) **1.** *n.* (*printing*) letters etc., other than capitals **2.** *adj.* (*abbr.* l.c., of a letter) not capital, in its small form, e.g. a, b, c (cf. UPPERCASE)

lower class the class of people generally considered to rank below the middle class. The usual criteria are lack of secondary education and employment for wages, not salary **lów·er-cláss** *adj.*

lower deck the deck immediately above the hold ‖ (in four-decked ships) the second deck above the hold ‖ (*Br. navy*) the petty officers and men of a ship, as distinguished from the officers

lower house the popular and usually more representative house of a legislative assembly with two chambers, e.g. the House of Commons, the House of Representatives (cf. UPPER HOUSE)

low·er·ing (láuəriŋ, láuriŋ) *adj.* (of the sky, clouds) black and threatening ‖ (of someone's face, expression etc.) scowling, sullen

low·er·most (lóuərmoust) *adj.* lowest

Lower Saxony *SAXONY, LOWER

Lower Silurian the Ordovician

lowest common denominator the smallest quantity which is divisible, without remainder, by all the denominators of a number of fractions

lowest common multiple (*abbr.* L.C.M.) the smallest quantity divisible, without remainder, by specified smaller numbers. Thus 24 is the lowest common multiple of 2, 3, 4, 6, 8, 12

Lowes·toft (lóustɒft) a fishing port (pop. 55,231) in Suffolk, England. Lowestoft ware is noted 18th-c. fine bone china

Low German *GERMAN LANGUAGE

low-grade (lóugréid) *adj.* of inferior quality

Low·ie (lóui:), Robert Harry (1883–1957), U.S. cultural anthropologist, noted for his ethnographic study on the Crow Indians

low·land (lóulənd) **1.** *n.* relatively low and fairly level country **2.** *adj.* pertaining to such country **Low·land** pertaining to the Lowlands of Scotland **lów·land·er** *n.* a native of a lowland **Low·land·er** a native of the Lowlands of Scotland

Lowlands of Scotland that part of central Scotland around the Forth and Clyde valleys separating the Highlands from the southern uplands (*SCOTLAND)

Low Latin Late or Medieval Latin

low life the life of the lower classes as treated in literature, esp. in its more picturesquely sordid aspects

low·li·ness (lóuli:nis) *n.* the quality or state of being lowly

low·ly (lóuli:) **1.** *adj. comp.* **low·li·er** *superl.* **low·li·est** (*rhet.*) humble, modest, unpretentious, *a lowly cottage* ‖ far down in a scale or hierarchy, *lowly occupations* **2.** *adv.* in a lowly manner

Low Mass a Mass which is said, not sung. The celebrant is assisted by one acolyte (cf. HIGH MASS)

low option (*insurance*) the lower of two or more insurance benefits that can be chosen by a subscriber *Cf* HIGH OPTION

low-pitched (lóupítʃt) *adj.* (of sound) low in pitch, deep, not shrill ‖ (of a roof) having a gentle slope

low-pres·sure (lóupréʃər) *adj.* having, demanding or utilizing a relatively low pressure of steam, air, gas etc. ‖ relaxed, not aggressive, *a low-pressure sales campaign*

low profile inconspicuous, esp. for the purpose of avoiding publicity

low relief bas-relief

low rise a multifamily residential structure not exceeding two stories in height —**low-rise** *adj.* *Cf* HIGH RISE

low silhouette low profile

low-spir·it·ed (lóuspíritid) *adj.* depressed, dejected

Low Sunday the first Sunday after Easter

low-ten·sion (lóutenʃən) *adj.* having a low voltage ‖ made for use at low voltage

low-test (lóutést) *adj.* (of liquid fuels) having a high boiling point

low tide the tide at lowest ebb ‖ the level of the sea then ‖ the time of lowest ebb

low water low tide ‖ a low level of water in a lake or river **in low water** (*Br.*) short of money

lox *n.* (acronym) liquid oxygen, used as a cryogenic fuel at 183°C

lox·o·drom·ic (lɒksədrómik) *adj.* of or relating to rhumb lines or sailing on rhumb lines **lox·o·dróm·ics** *n.* the art of sailing on rhumb lines [fr. Gk *loxos*, oblique+*dromos*, course]

loy·al (lɔ́iəl) *adj.* faithful to any person to whom fidelity is owed ‖ faithful in allegiance to the government of one's country ‖ personally devoted to a sovereign or ruler ‖ displaying fidelity, *a loyal address* **lóy·al·ist** *n.* someone who is loyal, esp. someone who remains loyal in times of revolt ‖ (*Am. hist.*) someone who sided with the British during the Revolutionary War ‖ someone who supported the Union cause during the Civil War **Loy·al·ist** (*Br. hist.*) someone who rendered loyalty to the Stuarts ‖ (*Span. hist.*) someone who remained loyal to the elected republican government in opposition to Franco in the Spanish Civil War [F.]

loy·al·ty (lɔ́iəlti:) *pl.* **loy·al·ties** *n.* the quality or state of being loyal or an instance of this [O.F. *loialté*]

Loyalty Islands an archipelago (total area 815 sq. miles, pop. 11,000) consisting of three large islands (Maré, Lifou, Uvéa) and many small islands. They are part of New Caledonia: coconuts, copra, rubber, taro, fruit

Loyalty Oath (*Am. hist.*) a rigorous oath of allegiance to the U.S.A. required after the Civil War of those who had adhered to the Confederate cause, as a condition of reentry into public life. The Supreme Court repudiated certain of the Loyalty Oaths as unconstitutional bills of attainder

Loyola *IGNATIUS LOYOLA

loz·enge (lózindʒ) *n.* a four-sided figure having all sides equal and having two oblique and two obtuse angles, e.g. a rhombus, a diamond ‖ a small medicinal candy (originally lozenge-shaped) to be dissolved in the mouth ‖ a diamond-shaped windowpane ‖ (*heraldry*) a diamond-shaped bearing or device ‖ (*heraldry*) a diamond-shaped escutcheon, used esp. by spinsters and widows [O.F. *losenge*]

Lo·zère (louzér) a department (area 1,996 sq. miles, pop. 74,800) in S. France (*LANGUEDOC). Chief town: Mende (pop. 11,977)

LP (élpí:) **1.** *adj.* (of a phonograph record) long-playing **2.** *n.* a long-playing phonograph record

lpm (often capitalized) (*abbr.*) lines per minute

LPN (*abbr.*) licensed practical nurse

LRL (*abbr.*) lunar receiving laboratory, term-sealed building for reception of astronauts and lunar material from the moon

LRV (*abbr.*) lunar roving vehicle *Cf* LUNAR ROVER

LSD lysergic acid diethylamide, a crystalline compound $C_{15}H_{15}N_2CON(C_2H_5)_2$ which can produce hallucinations

Ltd. Limited

L-tryp·to·phan (éltríptəfæn) *n.* (*biochem.*) an amino acid that stimulates the production of serotonin, a hormone affecting sleep

Lu (*chem.*) lutetium

Lu·a·la·ba (lu:aláɒba) *CONGO (river)

Lu·an·da (lu:ǽndə) the capital (pop. 540,800) of Angola, a seaport, founded by the Portuguese (1575): oil refining

Luang Pra·bang (lwánprɑbán) the traditional royal capital (pop. 44,244) of Laos, a commercial center on the upper Mekong, with many Buddhist shrines (cf. VIENTIANE)

lub·ber (lʌ́bər) *n.* a clumsy sullen sailor [etym. doubtful]

Lub·bock (lʌ́bək) an industrial city (pop. 173,979) and railroad center in N.W. Texas: feed mills, meat-packing, dairying

Lü·beck (lýbek) a seaport (pop. 244,790) in Schleswig-Holstein, West Germany, connected to the Elbe by canal. Products: ships, ironwork, preserved foods, chemicals, organs. Some Gothic buildings (e.g. the Marienkirche, 13th c.) survived the 2nd world war. The first German town on the Baltic (1143), it was the leader of the Hanseatic League

Lübeck, Treaty of a treaty concluded May 22, 1629 between Emperor Ferdinand II and Christian IV of Denmark, ending the Danish period of the Thirty Years' War. Danish possessions were restored in return for a Danish pledge to abandon claims in Germany

Lu·blin (lú:bli:n) a Polish city (pop. 281,900) 100 miles southeast of Warsaw, with textile, food, drink and mechanical engineering industries. State university and Roman Catholic university. Cathedral (16th c.)

lu·bri·cant (lú:brikənt) **1.** *n.* a substance (e.g. grease, oil, soap) that when introduced between solid surfaces which move over one another reduces resistance to movement, heat production and wear (i.e. friction and its effects) by forming a fluid film between the surfaces **2.** *adj.* lubricating [fr. L. *lubricans* (*lubricantis*) fr. *lubricare*, to lubricate]

lu·bri·cate (lú:brikeit) *pres. part.* **lu·bri·cat·ing** *past* and *past part.* **lu·bri·cat·ed** *v.t.* to make smooth or slippery ‖ to diminish friction by applying a lubricant to **lu·bri·cá·tion, lú·bri·ca·tor** *ns* [fr. L. *lubricare* (*lubricatus*)]

lu·bric·i·ty (lu:brísiti:) *n.* lewdness ‖ smoothness, oiliness [fr. F. *lubricité* or L. *lubricitas*]

Lu·bum·ba·shi (lubúmbaʃi:) (formerly Elisabethville) the capital (pop. 401,600) of the province of South Katanga (South Shaba), Zaïre, and center of a rich copper-mining area

Lu·can (lú:kən) (Marcus Annaeus Lucanus, 39–65), Roman poet. His epic poem 'Pharsalia' describes the civil war between Caesar and Pompey

Lu·ca·ni·a (lu:kéini:ə) *BASILICATA

Lucas (lú:kəs), George (1944–), U.S. director, producer and screenwriter, noted esp. for 'Star Wars' (1977), 'The Empire Strikes Back' (1980) and 'Return of the Jedi' (1983). He also produced 'American Graffiti' (1973) and made 'Raiders of the Lost Ark' (1981) and its sequel, 'Indiana Jones and the Temple of Doom' (1984), with Steven Spielberg

Lu·cas van Ley·den (lú:kəsvænláid'n) (c. 1494–1533), Dutch painter and engraver. In his delicate and imaginative woodcuts and engravings he was very much influenced by Dürer. His paintings, which are lively in detail and brilliant in color, include everyday scenes as well as allegorical and religious works

Luc·ca (lú:kkɑ) a city (pop. 91,658) of Etruscan origin in N.W. Italy. Manufactures: olive oil, tobacco, textiles. Romanesque cathedral (11th c.), city walls (16th c.), 70 churches. An independent republic from the 12th c., it was annexed to Tuscany in 1847

Luce (lu:s), Clare Boothe (1903–), U.S. playwright and ambassador. Her plays include two American satires, 'The Women' (1936) and 'Kiss the Boys Goodbye' (1938), and the anti-Fascist 'Margin for Error' (1939). She served (1953–6) as ambassador to Italy

Luce, Henry Robinson (1898–1967), U.S. editor-publisher who founded (1923) the weekly news magazine 'Time', the monthly business magazine 'Fortune' (1930), the illustrated weekly 'Life' (1936), and the weekly 'Sports Illustrated' (1954)

Luce, Stephen Bleecker (1827–1917), U.S. naval officer who became (1884) founding-president of the Naval War College at Newport, R.I., an institution for training seamen for service in the Navy and the merchant marine

luce (lu:s) *n.* (*zool.*) a pike, esp. an adult one [O.F. *lus*]

lu·cen·cy (lú:s'nsi:) *n.* the state or quality of being lucent

lu·cent (lú:s'nt) *adj.* clear, translucent [fr. L. *lucens* (*lucentis*) fr. *lucere*, to shine]

lucern *LUCERNE (alfalfa)

Lu·cerne (lu:sə́:rn) (G. Luzern) a canton (area 575 sq. miles, pop. 290,000), largely German-speaking and Roman Catholic, of central Switzerland ‖ its capital (pop. 65,300) a medieval

CONCISE PRONUNCIATION KEY: (**a**) æ, c**a**t; ɑ, c**a**r; ɔ f**aw**n; ei, sn**a**ke. (**e**) e, h**e**n; i:, sh**ee**p; iə, d**ee**r; ɛə, b**ea**r. (**i**) i, f**i**sh; ai, t**i**ger; ə:, b**i**rd. (**o**) o, **o**x; au, c**ow**; ou, g**oa**t; u, p**oo**r; ɔi, r**oy**al. (**u**) ʌ, d**u**ck; u, b**u**ll; u:, g**oo**se; ə, b**a**cillus; ju:, c**u**be. x, lo**ch**; θ, **th**ink; δ, bo**th**er; z, **Z**en; ʒ, cor**s**age; dʒ, sava**g**e; ŋ, ora**n**gutang; j, **y**ak; ʃ, **fi**sh; tʃ, **fe**tch; 'l, rabb**le**; 'n, redd**en**. Complete pronunciation key appears inside front cover.

town and tourist center on the Lake of Lucerne, which is 24 miles long

lu·cerne, lu·cern (luːsə́ːrn) n. (Br.) alfalfa [fr. F. luzerne]

Lu·chow (lúːdʒóu) *HOFEI

Luchow *LUHSIEN

Lu·cian of Sa·mos·a·ta (lúːʃənəvsəmɔ́səta) (c. 115–c. 200), Greek writer, author of 'Dialogues of the Dead', the satirical novel 'True History' and many literary parodies

lu·cid (lúːsid) adj. clear, easily understood, a lucid argument ‖ sane, a lucid interval **lu·cíd·i·ty** n. [fr. L. lucidus, bright]

Lu·ci·fer (lúːsifər) n. (rhet.) the morning star ‖ a name given by the Church Fathers to Satan, in interpretation of Isaiah xiv, 12 [L. fr. lux (lucis), light + ferre, to bring]

lu·cif·er·ase (luːsífəreis) n. an enzyme which catalyzes the oxidation of luciferin [fr. LUCIFERIN]

lu·cif·er·in (luːsífərin) n. a pigment found in luminiferous organisms (e.g. fireflies) which gives out light in its oxidation by luciferase [fr. L. lucifer, light]

Lu·cil·i·us (luːsíliːəs), Gaius (c. 180–102 B.C.), Latin poet, founder of Roman satire

Lu·cite (lúːsait) n. a transparent acrylic resin or plastic produced in the U.S.A., essentially polymerized methyl methacrylate, used e.g. in aircraft (cf. PERSPEX) [trademark]

luck (lʌk) n. chance, it's a matter of luck whether we are successful ‖ good fortune, a stroke of luck ‖ success due to chance ‖ the tendency of a person to be persistently fortunate or unfortunate, it's just my luck to get caught in the rain **as luck would have it** fortunately ‖ unfortunately **for luck** to bring success or good fortune, he wore his mascot for luck ‖ as an unsolicited bonus or extra, here's a copy for luck **to be down on one's luck** to be going through a time of bad luck **to be in (out of) luck** to be fortunate (unfortunate), esp. in some specified set of circumstances **to try one's luck** to take a chance, esp. in gambling [L. G. luk, shortened fr. geluk]

luck·i·ly (lʌ́kili:) adv. in a lucky manner, fortunately

luck·i·ness (lʌ́ki:nis) n. the state or quality of being lucky

Luck·now (lʌ́knau) the capital (pop. 826,426) of Uttar Pradesh, India, in the Ganges valley, a commercial center with textile, chemical and engineering industries. University (1921). A British garrison was besieged there for five months (1857–8) during the Indian Mutiny

luck out v. (slang) to have events turn out fortunately

luck·y (lʌ́ki:) comp. **luck·i·er** superl. **luck·i·est** adj. having good luck, esp. habitually ‖ being more successful than one deserves or could expect, you were lucky to come in first ‖ bringing or supposed to bring good luck, a lucky charm ‖ successful due to chance, a lucky shot

lucky dip (Br.) a grab bag

lu·cra·tive (lúːkrətiv) adj. bringing in plenty of money, very profitable [fr. L. lucrativus]

lu·cre (lúːkər) n. (esp. in the phrase) **filthy lucre** money [fr. L. lucrum]

Lu·cre·tia (luːkríːʃə) a Roman who, according to legend, killed herself after being raped by a son of Tarquinius Superbus. The incident led to a popular rising against Tarquinius Superbus and his expulsion from Rome (510 B.C.)

Lu·cre·tius (luːkríːʃəs) (c. 99–55 B.C.), Roman philosopher and poet, author of the philosophical poem 'De rerum natura', in which he expounded the atomist theories of Epicurus, and which despite its didactic character is a work of lyrical beauty

lu·cu·brate (lúːkjubreit) pres.part. **lu·cu·brat·ing** past and past part. **lu·cu·brat·ed** v.i. (rhet.) to study or write laboriously [fr. L. lucubrare (lucubratus), to work by candlelight]

lu·cu·bra·tion (luːkjubréiʃən) n. (esp. pl., rhet.) an instance of laboriously excogitated speech or writing [fr. L. lucubratio (lucubrationis) fr. lucubrare, to work by candlelight]

Lu·cul·lus (luːkʌ́ləs), Lucius Licinius (c. 110–c. 56 B.C.), Roman general. He defeated (72 B.C.) Mithridates VI. He was famous for the marvelous food he served to his guests

Ludd·ite (lʌ́dait) n. (Eng. hist.) a member of those groups of workers who deliberately smashed machinery in the industrial centers of the East Midlands, Lancashire and Yorkshire (1811-16), believing it to be a cause of unemployment [after Ned Ludd, a late 18th-c. riot leader]

Lu·den·dorff (lúːd'ndɔrf), Erich (1865–1937), German general. He was Hindenburg's chief of staff in the 1st world war, and is thought to have been responsible for many of his victories. He became a Nazi (1923)

Lu·dhi·a·na (luːdiːáːnə) a town (pop. 397,850) in the eastern Punjab, India: textiles, metallurgy, engineering

lu·dic (lúːdik) adj. of play; playful

lu·di·crous (lúːdikrəs) adj. absurd, ridiculous, arousing mocking laughter [fr. L. ludicrus]

lu·do (lúːdou) n. (esp. Br.) a children's game for up to four players, played with dice and counters on a special board [L.=I play]

Lud·wig (lúːdvix) Holy Roman Emperors, kings of Germany and kings of Bohemia *LOUIS

Lud·wigs·ha·fen (luːdvíxsháːfən) a town (pop. 160,300) on the Rhine in Rhineland-Palatinate, West Germany: chemical industries

luff (lʌf) 1. n. (naut.) the side of a fore-and-aft sail nearest the mast or stay ‖ (Br.) the broadest part of a ship's bow, before the sides begin to curve in 2. v.i. (naut., often with 'up') to bring the head of a ship nearer the wind ‖ (naut., of a sail) to wrinkle along the luff because of being too close to the wind ‖ v.t. (naut., sometimes with 'up') to bring the head of (a ship) nearer the wind ‖ (naut.) to move (the helm) so as to sail nearer the wind ‖ (naut.) to cause (a sail) to wrinkle along the luff because of sailing too close to the wind ‖ (yachting) to get to windward of (another boat) [prob. F. lof, a steering oar or other contrivance]

luf·fa, loo·fah (lúːfə) n. a member of Luffa, fam. Cucurbitaceae, a genus of tropical climbing plants bearing a gourdlike fruit ‖ this fruit ‖ the fibrous skeleton of this fruit used as a sponge [Egypt. Arab. lufah]

lug (lʌg) n. a lugsail

lug n. something which sticks out like an ear, e.g. one of a pair of flat handles on a casserole ‖ (mech.) a projection on a casting to which a part (e.g. a bolt) may be fitted [perh. Scand.]

lug n. a lugworm

lug 1. v. pres.part. **lug·ging** past and past part. **lugged** v.t. to haul (something heavy) clumsily, with great expenditure of effort, half pulling and half carrying ‖ to introduce or bring in irrelevantly, to lug anecdotes into a discussion ‖ to bring or take (someone) along at great effort, she lugged the children to the circus ‖ v.i. to tug 2. n. an act of lugging [prob. Scand.]

Lu·ga·no (luːgáːnou) a resort (pop. 22,280) in Ticino, S. Switzerland, on Lake Lugano

Lu·gansk (luːgánsk) *VOROSHILOVGRAD

Lu·gard (luːgárd), Frederick Dealtry, 1st Baron Lugard of Abinger (1858–1945), British soldier and colonial administrator. As high commissioner he was responsible for the pacification of Nigeria (1900–6) and, as governor (1912–19), for the unification of Nigeria through indirect rule

luge (luːʒ) n. a small sled for one person [F.]

lug·gage (lʌ́gidʒ) n. suitcases, bags and trunks full of a traveler's belongings ‖ empty suitcases, trunks etc. [LUG v.]

lug·ger (lʌ́gər) n. (naut) a small fishing or coasting boat with one or more lugsails [perh. fr. LUGSAIL]

Lu·go (lúːgou) a province (area 3,814 sq. miles, pop. 399,185) of N.W. Spain (*GALICIA)

lug·sail (lʌ́gsəl, lʌ́gseil) n. (naut.) a four-cornered sail bent on a yard which is slung at a point two thirds of its length from the peak and hoisted and lowered with the sail [etym. doubtful]

lu·gu·bri·ous (luːgúːbriːəs, lugjúːbriːəs) adj. dismal, mournful [fr. L. lugubris]

lug·worm (lʌ́gwəːrm) n. a member of Arenicola, a genus of North American and European marine annelids that breathe through 13 pairs of tufted gills. They leave little coils of sand on the seashore, when burrowing after the tide has ebbed, and are used as bait [etym. doubtful]

Lu·hsien (lúːʃjən) (formerly Luchow) a town (pop. 289,000) in S.E. Szechwan, China, on the Yangtze: agricultural trade, iron, oil

Luik (lɔik) *LIÈGE

Lu·kács (lúːkɑtʃ), György (1885–1971), Hungarian philosopher, sociologist and critic. His philosophical development was from Kant to Hegel to Marx and Lenin, but he was never an orthodox adherent of Communist philosophy. He was best known for his work on aesthetics and the sociology of literature, and for his studies of literary genres (esp. drama and the novel). Among his most important works are 'History and Class Consciousness' (1923) and

'Studies in European Realism' (1946, trans. 1950)

Luke, Gospel according to St (luːk) the third Gospel of the New Testament, attributed to St Luke and probably written in the late 1st c. A.D. It recounts the birth, life and teaching of Christ

Luke, St an early Christian evangelist, regarded as the author of the third Gospel and of the Acts of the Apostles. Symbol: an ox. Feast: Oct. 18

luke·warm (lúːkwɔ́rm) adj. tepid, not very warm ‖ unenthusiastic, halfhearted [fr. obs. luke, tepid + WARM]

Lu·le·å (lúːleɔ) a port (pop. 66,834) of N. Sweden on the Gulf of Bothnia: iron smelting, wood pulping

Lull (luːl, luːj), Ramón (c. 1235–1315), Spanish philosopher and theologian, called the 'doctor illuminatus'. His principal work of scholastic philosophy is the 'Ars generalis sive magna'. As a mystic he is considered the forerunner of St Teresa

lull (lʌl) 1. v.t. to calm, soothe, e.g. by rocking or singing, to lull a child to sleep ‖ to quiet, esp. by guile, to lull suspicions with a plausible story ‖ v.i. to become less in intensity or strength 2. n. a temporary period of peace and quiet ‖ a temporary drop in activity, a lull in business [imit. of the sounds of a lullaby]

lull·a·by (lʌ́ləbai) pl. **lull·a·bies** n. a soothing song to put a baby to sleep [imit.]

Lul·ly (lyli:), Jean-Baptiste (1632–87), French composer of Italian origin. He composed ballets and incidental music for the comedies of Molière at the court of Louis XIV (1658–70). He wrote, with the librettist Philippe Quinault, the first French opera, 'Cadmus et Hermione' (1673), and followed it with 18 other operas, e.g. 'Alceste' (1674), 'Acis et Galatée' (1687)

Lu·lu·a·bourg (luːlúːəbuːr) *KANANGA

lum·ba·go (lʌmbéigou) n. a muscular pain in the lower part of the back [L. fr. lumbus, loin]

lum·bar (lʌ́mbər, lʌ́mbɑr) adj. of or in the region of the loins or the vertebrae lying between the sacrum and the thoracic vertebrae [fr. Mod. L. lumbaris]

lum·ber (lʌ́mbər) 1. n. wood suitable for, or prepared for, use in construction, esp. just felled and roughly sawn into logs and planks ‖ little-used pieces of furniture or junk, stored away and taking up room 2. v.t. to fell and saw timber into logs and remove it from (an area) ‖ (often with 'up') to fill up (a room or other place) with lumber, the yard was lumbered up with rusty, old machines ‖ v.i. to cut down trees and saw them into logs [prob. fr. LUMBER V. (to move clumsily), also formerly connected with older lumber, pawnbroker's shop]

lumber v.i. to move clumsily, heavily and noisily [etym. doubtful]

lum·ber·jack (lʌ́mbərdʒæk) n. someone who cuts timber and gets it ready for the sawmill or market

lum·ber·man (lʌ́mbərmən) pl. **lum·ber·men** (lʌ́mbərmən) n. someone employed in cutting down trees and preparing them for market, esp. as a manager

lumber room a room, esp. in a house, in which furniture, luggage etc. is stored

lum·ber·yard (lʌ́mbərjɑrd) n. an area where cut and sized lumber is kept for sale

lum·bri·cal (lʌ́mbrik'l) 1. n. one of the muscles used in flexing fingers or toes 2. adj. of or pertaining to a lumbrical [fr. Mod. L. lumbricalis fr. lumbricus, worm]

lum·bri·coid (lʌ́mbrikɔid) 1. adj. resembling an earthworm 2. n. such an animal [fr. Mod. L. (Ascaris) lumbricoides]

lu·men (lúːmən) pl. **lu·mi·na** (lúːmənə), **lu·mens** n. a unit of light measurement: the light emitted per unit solid angle by a uniform point source of one candela ‖ (anat.) the bore or cavity of a tubular part or organ ‖ the central cavity of a cell [L.=light]

Lu·mière (lymjer), Auguste (1862–1954), French biologist noted for his collaboration with his brother Louis in photographic research

Lumière, Louis (1864–1948), French chemist. He produced a working cinematograph (1895) and a system for color photography (1903)

lu·mi·nal art or **lu·mi·nist art** (lúːminəl) art form based on arrangement of lights or lighting

lu·mi·nar·y (lúːmineri) pl. **lu·mi·nar·ies** n. a body giving light, esp. the sun or moon ‖ a person of outstanding intellectual, spiritual or moral quality [fr. O.F. *luminarie*]

lu·mi·nes·cence (lu:minés'ns) *n.* the emission of electromagnetic radiation esp. in the visible region by a substance (e.g. a phosphor) during and/or following stimulation by any of various forms of energy except heat (*PHOSPHORESCENCE, * FLUORESCENCE, cf. INCANDESCENCE). In general the process involves the emission of radiation by an atomic electron, in falling from an excited energy state to which it has been brought by the absorption of energy. The latter may be derived from a chemical reaction (*BIOLUMINESCENCE), from electron bombardment or from subjection to electromagnetic radiation or to electric fields [LUMINESCENT]

lu·mi·nes·cent (lu:minés'nt) *adj.* of, relating to or exhibiting luminescence [fr. L. *lumen* (*luminis*), light]

lu·mi·nif·er·ous (lu:minífərəs) *adj.* producing, transmitting or giving off light [fr. L. *lumen* (*luminis*), *light*+*ferre*, to bring]

lu·mi·nos·i·ty (lu:minɒsiti) *pl.* **lu·mi·nos·i·ties** *n.* the state or quality of being luminous ‖ the amount of radiation emitted by a star or other heavenly body ‖ (*phys.*) the ratio of light to heat contained in radiant energy, used esp. in measurements of perception [LUMINOUS]

lu·mi·nous (lú:minəs) *adj.* emitting a steady, diffused light ‖ shining, bright, *a luminous landscape* ‖ lucid, enlightening and inspiring, *luminous prose* [fr. L. *luminosus*]

luminous flux the rate of transfer of radiant energy (usually in the visible region of the electromagnetic spectrum) across a given surface, usually measured in lumens

luminous intensity a quantity that measures the light-giving power of a source, usually expressed in candles

Lum·mer (lúmər) Otto (1860–1925), German physicist. He devised, with Eugen Brodhun (*b.* 1860), an accurate photometer. His work with Ernst Pringsheim (1859–1917) on black body radiation led to Planck's formulation of the quantum theory

lump (lʌmp) **1.** *n.* a firm irregular mass, *a lump of coal* ‖ (of sugar) a cube ‖ a large amount or quantity ‖ a dull, heavy awkward person, *a lump of a boy* ‖ a swelling, or other hard bump, such as is caused by a heavy blow **a lump in one's throat** a feeling of pressure in one's throat, caused by repressed emotion **in a lump** all at one time **in the lump** taking things as a whole **2.** *v.t.* to put together in a lump ‖ to treat alike without discrimination, *he lumped together all other religions as mere superstition* ‖ *v.i.* to move heavily ‖ to form into lumps [M.E. *lump*, origin unknown]

lump *v.t.* (*pop.*) to put up with, endure, *if you don't like it you can lump it* [etym. doubtful]

lump·er (lʌmpər) *n.* a workman who handles cargoes, e.g. a stevedore [LUMP v. (to move heavily)]

lump·i·ly (lʌmpili:) *adv.* so as to collect in lumps

lump·i·ness (lʌmpi:nis) *n.* the state or quality of being lumpy

lump·ish (lʌmpiʃ) *adj.* heavy and rather stupid-looking [LUMP n. (mass) and v.]

lump sugar sugar in small cubes

lump sum a sum of money given at one time, not in installments

lump·y (lʌmpi:) *comp.* **lump·i·er** *superl.* **lump·i·est** *adj.* full of or covered with lumps ‖ (of water) choppy [LUMP n. (mass)]

Lu·mum·ba (lumúmbə) Patrice (1925–61), Congolese statesman, first prime minister (1960) of the newly independent Democratic Republic of the Congo. He was arrested after a coup d'état (1960) and killed in Katanga (1961)

Lu·na (lú:nə) (*Rom. mythol.*) goddess of the moon, with whom Selene was identified

lu·na·base (lú:nəbeis) *adj.* (*astron.*) of the flat surface of the moon

lu·na·cy (lú:nəsi:) *n.* the state of being a lunatic ‖ (*law*) insanity ‖ (*loosely*) incredible foolishness [LUNATIC]

lu·na moth (lú:nə) *Actias luna*, fam. *Saturniidae*, a large North American moth with crescent-marked light-green wings, the hind pair ending in long tails

lu·na·naut or **lu·nar·naut** (lú:nənɔt) *n.* (*astronautics*) one who travels to the moon

lu·nar (lú:nər) *adj.* to do with the moon, *lunar crater* ‖ measured according to the phases of the moon, *a lunar month* ‖ similar to that of the moon, *a bleak, lunar landscape* ‖ crescent-

---

shaped ‖ of or pertaining to silver [fr. L. *lunaris*]

lunar cycle the Metonic cycle

lunar excursion or **lunar module** (*astronautics*) space vehicle used to carry astronauts from command module to the moon landing and back. *abbr.* LEM

lu·nar·ite (lú:nərait) *adj.* (*astron.*) of the upland moon surface

lunar month the period from one new moon to the next, averaging 29 days, 12 hours, 44 minutes, 2.8 seconds

lunar rover (*astronautics*) vehicle resembling a golf cart designed for manned travel on the moon's surface *also* moon car, moon crawler, moon rover *Cf* LUNOKHOD

lu·nar·scape (lú:nərskeip) *n.* view of the lunar surface *also* moonscape

lunar year a period of 12 lunar months

lu·nate (lú:neit) *adj.* (*biol.*) crescent-shaped [fr. L. *lunatus*]

lu·na·tic (lú:nətik) **1.** *adj.* mad, insane ‖ exceptionally foolish or irresponsible, *a lunatic plan of escape* ‖ wildly frivolous, *the show has a kind of lunatic gaiety* **2.** *n.* (*law*) a person who is insane ‖ a wildly foolish or eccentric person [fr. L.L. *lunaticus* fr. *luna*, moon]

lunatic fringe the eccentrics or extremists loosely associated with a political, social or artistic movement

lu·na·tion (lu:néiʃən) *n.* the lunar month [fr. M.L. *lunatio* (*lunationis*)]

lunch (lʌntʃ) **1.** *n.* the midday meal **2.** *v.i.* to eat lunch [perh. fr. LUMP n.]

lunch·eon (lʌntʃən) *n.* the midday meal, lunch, esp. this meal taken with ceremony [LUNCH]

lunch·eon·ette (lʌntʃənét) *n.* an eating place serving light lunches or sandwiches

lunch·room (lʌntʃru:m, lʌntʃrum) *n.* a restaurant where light meals are served, esp. lunches

Lund (lʌnd) a city (pop. 78,487) in southernmost Sweden. Romanesque cathedral (11th–12th cc.). University (1668)

Lun·dy (lʌndi:) Benjamin (1789–1839), U.S. philanthropist and abolitionist. He organized (1815) the antislavery 'Union Humane' society and a newspaper, the 'Genius of Universal Emancipation' (1821). He traveled extensively in search of a suitable location outside the U.S.A. to which emancipated slaves might be sent

lune (lu:n) *n.* (*geom.*) a figure formed on a plane by two intersecting arcs of circles or on a sphere by two great circles [F.=moon]

lune *n.* a hawk's leash [var. of older *loyn* fr. O.F. *loigne*]

lu·nette (lu:nét) *n.* (*archit.*) a semicircular panel in a dome or ceiling, esp. one occurring under an arch or vault, often decorated with a painting or mural ‖ any opening, oval or circular, admitting light into a vault or dome ‖ a fortification, larger than a redan, consisting of two faces forming a salient angle, and two flanks [F., dim. of *lune*, moon]

lung (lʌŋ) *n.* one of the pair of spongy saclike organs that oxygenate the blood in air-breathing vertebrates and remove carbon dioxide from it [O.E. *lungen*]

lung book (*zool.*) the respiratory organ of some arachnids, e.g. scorpions and spiders, formed like a purse with numerous compartments

lunge *LONGE

lunge (lʌndʒ) **1.** *n.* a sudden thrust, e.g. with a foil in fencing ‖ a sudden, forward plunging movement of the body **2.** *v. pres. part.* **lung·ing** *past* and *past part.* **lunged** *v.i.* to make a lunge ‖ to start off suddenly, *the car lunged forward* ‖ *v.t.* to cause to make a lunge [earlier *allonge* fr. F. *allonger*, to lengthen]

lung·fish (lʌŋfiʃ) *n.* a member of *Dipnoi* or *Cladistia*, orders of fish that breathe through a lunglike organ as well as gills

Lung·ki (lʌŋkí:) (Changchow) a commercial center (pop. 297,000) in Fukien, China, near Amoy

Lung·kiang (lʌŋdʒján) (Tsitsihar) a town in E. Heilungkiang, China, a market for agricultural products, hides

lung·worm (lʌŋwərm) *n.* any of various nematode worms that are parasitic in the lungs and air passages of mammals

lung·wort (lʌŋwərt) *n.* *Pulmonaria officinalis*, fam. *Boraginaceae*, a European perennial herb with white-spotted leaves like diseased lungs ‖ *Lobaria pulmonaria*, fam. *Stictaceae*, a lichen used in perfumery and tanning ‖ any of several

---

plants formerly considered effective in treating lung diseases

lu·ni·log·i·cal (lu:nəlódʒik'l) *adj.* of the study of the moon

lu·ni·sol·ar (lu:nisóulər) *adj.* pertaining to or involving the joint action of the sun and moon, *lunisolar tides* [fr. L. *luna*, moon+SOLAR]

lunisolar precession the principal component of the precession of the equinoxes, due to lunisolar action

lu·no·khod (lú:nəkɒd) *n.* (*astronautics*) unmanned Soviet vehicle for moon surface exploration, directed by radio signals from earth *Cf* LUNAR ROVER

lunula (*physiol.*) half-moon–shaped white area at base of the fingernail

lu·nu·late (lú:njuleit) *adj.* (*biol.*) with crescent-shaped markings ‖ (*biol.*) crescent-shaped [fr. L. *lunula*, dim. of *luna*, moon]

lu·nule (lú:nju:l) *n.* something shaped like a crescent, e.g. the half-moon at the base of the fingernail [F. fr. L. *lunula* dim. of *luna*, moon]

Lu·per·ca·li·a (lu:pərkéili:ə) an annual festival (Feb. 15) in ancient Rome in honor of Lupercus, the guardian of fields and flocks, to ensure the fertility of the crops, herds and people

lu·pine, lu·pin (lú:pin) *n.* a member of *Lupinus*, fam. *Papilionaceae*, a genus of perennial plants cultivated chiefly in Europe and North America for their vivid upright racemes [fr. L. *lupinus*, *lupinum*]

lu·pine (lú:pain) *adj.* of or resembling a wolf [fr. L. *lupinus*]

lu·pus (lú:pəs) *n.* any of various destructive skin diseases affecting chiefly the face and hands, esp. *Lupus vulgaris*, tuberculosis of the skin [L.=wolf]

Lur (luər) *pl.* **Lur, Lurs** *n.* a member of a largely nomadic Moslem people inhabiting the Zagros Mtns of Iran

Lur·çat (lyrsæ) Jean (1892–1966), French painter and designer of tapestries who was mainly responsible for the renewal of the art of tapestry in France in the 20th c.

lurch (lə:rtʃ) **1.** *n.* a sudden roll to one side, e.g. by a ship in heavy seas ‖ a sudden jolt or staggering movement ‖ a staggering gait **2.** *v.i.* to make a lurch ‖ to move with lurches, stagger [origin unknown]

lurch *n.* (only in the phrase) **to leave in the lurch** to desert, abandon (someone) in a difficult or awkward situation [F. *lourche*, a game like backgammon, or a defeat in it]

lure (luər) **1.** *n.* (*falconry*) a bunch of colored feathers containing the falcon's food which entices it back after a training flight ‖ some quality or thing that entices or attracts, *the lure of adventure* ‖ a device to attract animals, esp. fish, by guile **2.** *v.t. pres. part.* **lur·ing** *past* and *past part.* **lured** to entice, tempt with the promise of pleasure or gain ‖ (*falconry*) to attract (a hawk) with a lure [O.F. *leurre, loerre, loire*]

Lur·gi process (lə́:rgi:) the complete gasification of low-grade coal, leaving no coke residue

lu·rid (lúərid) *adj.* gaudy, sensational, *paperbacks in lurid covers* ‖ fascinatingly repulsive, *lurid details of the trial* ‖ reddish and menacing, *the flames cast a lurid light over the scene* ‖ ashen, pallid [fr. L. *luridus*, pale yellow]

lurk (lə:rk) *v.i.* to lie hidden waiting to attack ‖ to prowl or skulk around, esp. with some mischief in mind ‖ to be latent or hardly noticed, *a lurking suspicion* [etym. doubtful]

Lu·sa·ka (lu:sákə) the capital (pop. 152,000) of Zambia, on the railroad, center of a farming and mining region

lus·cious (lʌʃəs) *adj.* rich, full and delicious in flavor or smell ‖ affording other rich sensual delights, *the luscious feeling of cool water on a hot day* ‖ excessively rich or luxuriant, *his poems are marked by luscious imagery* ‖ (*pop.*) voluptuously attractive, *a luscious blonde* [perh. a form of DELICIOUS]

lush (lʌʃ) *adj.* growing thickly and richly, luxuriant, *lush vegetation* ‖ characterized by luxuriant vegetation, *lush meadows* ‖ luscious, *lush imagery* ‖ effusive, extravagant, *lush sentimentality* [etym. doubtful]

Lu·shun (lú:ʃun) (formerly Port Arthur) a port and naval base at the end of Liaotung peninsula, China, terminus of the S. Manchurian railroad. It was held by the Japanese (1894, 1905–45). With Talien it forms the agglomeration of Luta (pop. 1,508,000)

Lu·si·ta·ni·a (lu:sitéini:ə) a Roman province covering the west of the Iberian Peninsula

---

CONCISE PRONUNCIATION KEY: **(a)** æ, c*a*t; ɑ, c*a*r; ɔ, f*aw*n; ei, sn*a*ke. **(e)** e, h*e*n; i:, sh*ee*p; iə, d*ee*r; ɛə, b*ea*r. **(i)** i, f*i*sh; ai, t*i*ger; ə:, b*i*rd. **(o)** o, *o*x; au, c*ow*; ou, g*oa*t; u, p*oo*r; ɔi, r*oy*al. **(u)** ʌ, d*u*ck; u, b*u*ll; u:, g*oo*se; ə, b*a*cillus; ju:, c*u*be. x, lo*ch*; θ, *th*ink; ð, bo*th*er; z, *Z*en; ʒ, cor*s*age; dʒ, sava*g*e; ŋ, ora*n*guta*ng*; j, *y*ak; ʃ, *f*ish; tʃ, fe*tch*; 'l, rabb*le*; 'n, redd*en*. Complete pronunciation key appears inside front cover.

'Lusitania' a British liner sunk off Ireland (May 7, 1915) by a German submarine, with the loss of 1,198 lives. The sinking helped to bring the U.S.A. into the 1st world war

lust (lʌst) **1.** *n.* strong sexual desire without idealized or spiritualized feelings ‖ any passionate desire, *a lust for power* **2.** *v.i.* (*rhet.*, often with 'for') to have a passionate desire [O.E. *lust*, pleasure]

lus·ter, esp. *Br.* **lus·tre** (lʌ́stər) **1.** *n.* a surface sheen or gloss on a surface reflecting light ‖ the quality of having such a gloss ‖ radiance, brightness, *the luster of the stars* ‖ splendor, renown, distinction, *his achievements will add luster to his name* ‖ a glass pendant, or chandelier hung with them ‖ lusterware ‖ (esp. *Br.*) a kind of cotton and wool fabric with a glossy surface ‖ (*mineral.*) the appearance of the surface of a mineral with regard to its light-reflecting quality **2.** *v.t. pres. part.* **lus·ter·ing, lus·tring** *past* and *past part.* **lus·tered, lus·tred** to add luster to ‖ to give (pottery or cloth) a luster finish [F. *lustre*]

luster, esp. *Br.* **lustre** *n.* a lustrum (a five-year period)

lus·ter·ware, esp. *Br.*, **lus·tre·ware** (lʌ́stərwęɑr) *n.* earthenware pottery decorated by applying to the glaze metallic oxides which acquire extreme brilliancy when fired

lust·ful (lʌ́stfəl) *adj.* full of lust ‖ characterized by lust

lust·i·ly (lʌ́stili) *adv.* in a lusty way

lust·i·ness (lʌ́sti:nis) *n.* the state or quality of being lusty

lus·tral (lʌ́strəl) *adj.* of or used in lustration [fr. L. *lustralis*]

lus·trate (lʌ́streit) *pres. part.* **lus·trat·ing** *past* and *past part.* **lus·trat·ed** *v.t.* to purify by lustration [fr. L. *lustrare* (*lustratus*)]

lus·tra·tion (lʌstréiʃən) *n.* a purification ceremony, e.g. washing, performed before entering a holy place or before some important occasion [fr. L. *lustratio* (*lustrationis*)]

lustre *LUSTER

lustreware *LUSTERWARE

lus·trous (lʌ́strəs) *adj.* shining, having a luster

lus·trum (lʌ́strəm) *pl.* **lus·trums, lus·tra** (lʌ́strə) *n.* (*Rom. hist.*) a sacrificial purification rite carried out after each five-year census ‖ a period of five years [L.]

lust·y (lʌ́sti:) *comp.* **lust·i·er** *superl.* **lust·i·est** *adj.* vigorous, strong, sturdy, *the child's lusty crying* [LUST]

Lu·ta (lú:tɑ) *LUSHUN, *TALIEN

lu·tan·ist, lu·ten·ist (lú:tənist) *n.* someone who plays the lute

lute (lu:t) *n.* a substance used for plugging a joint, or sealing or coating a porous surface [O.F. *lut* or fr. L. *lutum*, mud]

lute *pres. part.* **lut·ing** *past* and *past part.* **lut·ed** *v.t.* to cover or seal with lute, esp. to join (two pieces of half-dry pottery) with wet clay [fr. L. *lutare* fr. *lutum*, mud]

lute *n.* a stringed musical instrument with a pear-shaped body (cf. GUITAR) and a fretted neck, played by plucking the strings with the fingers. Of Arabic or Persian origin, the lute was introduced (c. 8th c.) to Europe and was extensively used up to the 18th c. as a solo, accompanying and ensemble instrument **lute·nist** *LUTANIST [O.F. *lut* fr. Arab.]

lu·te·o·ly·sin (lu:ti:oulái̯sin) *n.* (*biochem.*) a chemical product of the endometrium that destroys corpus luteum; studied as a possible contraceptive

lu·te·ti·um (lu:tí:ʃi:əm) *n.* a trivalent rare earth (symbol Lu, at. no. 71, at. mass 174.97) [Mod. L. fr. *Lutetia*, Paris]

Lu·ther (lú:θər), Martin (1483–1546), German leader of the Reformation. He was the son of a Thuringian miner. He entered Erfurt University (1501) but by 1505 gave up the idea of becoming a lawyer, and entered the Augustinian monastery at Erfurt. In 1507, now a priest, he began a career as a theological teacher. At Wittenberg University (1508) he met and was influenced by Johann Staupitz (d. 1524, vicar general of the Augustinians in Germany), whom he later succeeded (1512) as professor of biblical theology. He developed (1512–13) the idea of justification by faith, and attacked (1517) Tetzel's sale of indulgences, by posting 95 theses on the church door at Wittenberg. These provoked a major controversy with Eck, who accused Luther of heresy. Luther's refusal to recant (1518), and his attack on papal authority, resulted in his excommunication

(1521). The Diet of Worms ordered his seizure (1521), but he was protected by the elector of Saxony in Wartburg Castle, where he began his German translation of the Bible (1521–2). His popularity was weakened by his opposition to the Peasants' War (1524–5). After lengthy controversies with Erasmus and the humanists on the one hand, and with Zwingli on the other, Luther sanctioned Melanchthon's Augsburg Confession (1530), which was to provide the basic creed of the Lutheran Church (*LUTHERANISM)

Lu·ther·an (lú:θərən) **1.** *adj.* of or relating to Martin Luther ‖ of the Protestant denomination founded by Luther, or its teachings **2.** *n.* a member of the Lutheran Church **Lú·ther·an·ism** *n.* a Protestant faith following the doctrines of Luther. It was formed between 1517 and 1580, and had its origin as an organization in the state Church of Saxony set up in 1526. After a series of disputes with the Calvinists and a protracted quarrel between strict and moderate Lutherans, the doctrine and orders of Lutheranism were defined by the Augsburg Confession (1530), two catechisms by Luther (1529) and the 'Book of Concord' (1580, containing all the principal statements of the Lutheran faith). From 1580 to 1680 its orthodoxy was consolidated on the bases provided by Melanchthon. In the 18th c. its orthodoxy was debilitated by the reaction of Pietism, at first in the form of enthusiasm (e.g. Count Zinzendorf's Moravians, 1722) and then by rationalism and liberalism. In 1817 the Prussian State forcibly united Lutherans and the Reformed Church. In the 20th c., under the influence of Karl Barth and the belated impact of Kierkegaard's critique of 19th-c. Lutheranism, there was a revival of orthodoxy, and in 1946 the two Churches united to form the Evangelical Church in Germany (E.K.D.). Where Lutheranism is the state Church its clergy are usually paid by the state. Historically its characteristic doctrines have been justification by faith and consubstantiation, while its order can be either episcopal (e.g. Sweden, Germany) or synodal (e.g. U.S.A., Holland). Lutheranism spread from Saxony to Silesia, East Prussia, Denmark and Norway, Sweden, Iceland, Rumania, the Baltic States, Hungary, Bohemia and the U.S.A. There are about 70 million Lutherans, over half of them in Germany. Lutheranism is predominant in Scandinavia, Iceland and East Germany. There are important minorities in the U.S.A. (8 million), Canada (663,000), Austria (400,000), Hungary (430,000), Czechoslovakia (485,000), Rumania (250,000), Latvian S.S.R. (600,000), Estonian S.S.R. (350,000), Lithuanian S.S.R. (215,000) and Brazil (500,000), and smaller ones in the Netherlands, Yugoslavia, Poland and France

Lu·thu·li (lutú:li:, lutjú:li:), Chief Albert John (1899–1967), South African politician, president (1952–60) of the African National Congress. He was an advocate of nonviolent resistance to apartheid. Nobel peace prize (1961)

Lu·ton (lú:t'n) a town (pop. 164,049) of Bedfordshire, England: straw hats, cars, light engineering

Lut·yens (lʌ́tjənz), Sir Edwin Landseer (1869–1944), English architect. He was the chief architect and city planner of New Delhi, India

Lü·tzen, Battle of (lýtsən) a battle (1632) in the Thirty Years' War in which Gustavus II of Sweden defeated the Austrian army under Wallenstein. Gustavus was killed in the battle ‖ a battle (1813) in which Napoleon defeated Russian and Prussian armies with heavy losses

lux (lʌks) *pl.* **lux, lux·es** *n.* an international unit of illumination equal to the direct illumination on a surface which is everywhere 1 meter from a uniform point source of 1 international candle. It is also equal to 1 lumen per square meter [L.=light]

lux·ate (lʌ́kseit) *pres. part.* **lux·at·ing** *past* and *past part.* **lux·at·ed** *v.t.* (*med.*) to dislocate (e.g. a joint) **lux·á·tion** *n.* [fr. L. *luxare* (*luxatus*)]

Lux·em·bourg (lyksɑ̃bu:r, *Eng.* lʌ́ksəmbə:rg) the capital (pop. 78,900) of Luxembourg. Industries: metallurgy, textiles, engineering, pottery. Palace (1580), cathedral (1613)

Luxembourg the southernmost province (area 1,705 sq. miles, pop. 219,000) of Belgium. Capital: Arlon (pop. 11,000)

Luxembourg, Lux·em·burg a Grand Duchy (area 999 sq. miles, pop. 400,000) in W. Europe. Capital: Luxembourg. Languages: French, Ger-

man and patois. Religion: 97% Roman Catholic, 1% Protestant, 1% Jewish. The land is 28% arable, 25% pasture and 33% forest. In the north the Oesling, part of the Ardennes, lies between 1,300 and 1,750 ft. In the south the Gutland, part of the Lorraine scarp, averages 900 ft. Climate: continental. Livestock: cattle, hogs, horses, poultry. Agricultural products: oats, potatoes, barley, roses, fruit and wine. Mineral resources: iron ore. Manufactures and industries: mining, iron and steel, metal founding, electricity, leather, shoes, rubber, brewing, distilling, slates, cement. Exports and imports are included in the trade returns for Belgium. Monetary unit: Luxembourg franc. HISTORY. One of the largest fiefs in the Holy Roman Empire, Luxembourg was made a duchy in 1354, and was under the rule of Burgundy (1443–1506), Spain (1506–1714), Austria (1714–95) and France (1795–1815). It was made a Grand Duchy by the Congress of Vienna (1815). The western part was incorporated into Belgium (1839) and the remainder was recognized (1867) as an independent neutral state. It was twice occupied by the Germans (1914–18, 1940–4) and joined Benelux (1944), NATO (1949), and the EEC (1958)

Lux·em·burg effect (lʌ́ksəmbə:rg) (*electr.*) interference between two radio signals due to the irregular character of the ionosphere through which radio waves pass

Lux·or (lʌ́ksɔr) *THEBES (Egypt)

lux·u·ri·ance (lʌgzúəri:əns, lʌkʃúəri:əns) *n.* the state or quality of being luxuriant

lux·u·ri·ant (lʌgzúəri:ənt, lʌkʃúəri:ənt) *adj.* abundant or exuberant in growth, *luxuriant vegetation* ‖ prolific, richly varied, *a luxuriant imagination* ‖ (of style) richly figurative, florid, *luxuriant prose* [fr. L. *luxurians* (*luxuriantis*) fr. *luxuriare*, to grow rank]

lux·u·ri·ate (lʌgzúəri:eit, lʌkʃúəri:eit) *pres. part.* **lux·u·ri·at·ing** *past* and *past part.* **lux·u·ri·at·ed** *v.i.* (often with 'in') to revel, enjoy consciously, *he luxuriated in his new found freedom* ‖ to grow or develop in profusion [fr. L. *luxuriare* (*luxuriatus*), to grow rank]

lux·u·ri·ous (lʌgzúəri:əs, lʌkʃúəri:əs) *adj.* opulent, sumptuous, richly comfortable, *a luxurious apartment* ‖ self-indulgent, extravagant, *a luxurious life* ‖ sensually delightful, *a luxurious sense of well-being* [fr. O. F. *luxurius*]

lux·u·ry (lʌ́kʃəri:, lʌ́gzəri:) *pl.* **lux·u·ries** *n.* habitual indulgence in expensive food, clothes, comforts etc., *a life of luxury* ‖ something enjoyable, relatively costly, but not indispensable, *smoking is his only luxury* ‖ something voluptuously enjoyed, *the luxury of a hot bath when one is tired* ‖ abundance of rich comforts, *lapped in luxury* [O.F. *luxurie*]

Lu·ynes (lyi:n), Charles d'Albert, duc de (1578–1621), French statesman, minister (1617–21) to Louis XIII

Lu·zern (lu:tsérn) *LUCERNE

Lu·zon (lu:zón) the largest island (area 40,420 sq. miles, pop. 22,598,000) of the Philippine Is. It is the most northerly of the main islands. A mountain range (150 miles long) runs along the northwest coast and another range (215 miles long) is parallel with the southeast coast, the rest of the island being broken by lower ridges. Highest point: Mt Mayon (7,943 ft), in the extreme southeast. The country's chief rice-growing region lies in a large south-central valley. Minerals: copper, gold, uranium, asbestos, chrome. Main town: Manila

LVN licensed vocational nurse (a practical nurse in California or Texas)

Lvov (lvəf) (*Polish* Lwów, *G.* Lemberg) a city (pop. 699,000) of the N. Ukraine, U.S.S.R. Industries: engineering, textiles, metallurgy, food processing. University (1784)

LVTE-1 *LANDING VEHICLE TRACKED ENGINEER

l·wei (ləwéi) *n.* unit of currency in Angola, equal to 1/100th kwanza

-ly *suffix* used to form adverbs from adjectives, as in 'sadly' ‖ (in time-unit nouns) every, as in 'monthly' [fr. O.E. *-lice* fr. O. Gmc *-liko-*]

-ly *suffix* like, characteristic of, as in 'womanly' [fr. O.F. *-lic, -lic*, O. Gmc. *-liko-*]

Ly·all·pur *FAISALABAD

Lyau·tey (ljoutei), Louis-Hubert Gonzalve (1854–1934), French soldier and colonial administrator, marshal of France. As resident general in Morocco (1912–25), he was very successful in developing the Moroccan economy and in the work of pacification

ly·can·thrope (láikənθroup) *n.* a person suffer-

---

ing from lycanthropy ‖ a werewolf **ly·can·throp·ic** (laikənθrópik) adj. [LYCANTHROPY]

ly·can·thro·py (laikǽnθrəpi:) n. magical transformation into a wolf ‖ a form of insanity in which the victim believes himself to be a wolf or similar beast [fr. Gk *lukanthropia* fr. *lukos*, wolf + *anthropos*, man]

ly·cée (li:sei) n. a state-maintained secondary school in France [F.]

Ly·ce·um (laisí:əm) the garden in Athens where Aristotle taught [L. fr. Gk *Lukeion* fr. *Lukeios*, epithet of Apollo, whose temple was next to the Lyceum]

lych-gate, lich-gate (lítʃgeit) n. a roofed gateway into a Christian burial ground. Traditionally, it provides a shelter while the first part of the burial service is read [fr. obs. *lich*, corpse + GATE]

lych·nis (líknis) n. a member of *Lychnis*, fam. *Caryophyllaceae*, a genus of perennial plants of the northern hemisphere, with red or white flowers, e.g. ragged robin [L. fr. Gk *luchnis*, a red flower]

Ly·ci·a (líʃi:ə) an ancient territory of southern Asia Minor. Its southern coast bordered the Mediterranean

ly·co·pod (láikəppd) n. any of various club mosses of the genus *Lycopodium*, fam. *Lycopodiaceae* (*LYCOPODIUM POWDER) [fr. Mod. L. *Lycopodium* fr. Gk *lukos*, wolf + *pous* (*podos*), foot]

ly·co·po·di·um powder (laikəpóudi:əm) a fine yellowish flammable powder consisting of the spores of a lycopod (esp. *Lycopodium clavatum*), used as a cosmetic and as a component of fireworks

ly·cop·sid (laikópsid) n. a member of *Lycopsida*, a subphylum of small green vascular plants including the club mosses and many large fossil forms, which were the dominant plant of the Carboniferous period and important as coal producers [fr. Mod. L. *Lycopsida* fr. L. *lycopsis*, a plant]

Ly·cur·gus (laikə́rgəs) (c. 9th c. B.C.), Spartan lawgiver. He is the traditional founder of the Spartan constitution and military system

Lycurgus (c. 396–c. 324 B.C.), Athenian orator and statesman. A political ally of Demosthenes, he administered the public revenue (338–326 B.C.) with great diligence and rectitude

Lyd·da (lídə) (Heb. Lod) a town (pop. 30,500) in central Israel, the traditional birthplace of St George

lydd·ite (lídait) n. a powerful explosive consisting mainly of picric acid [fr. *Lydd*, Kent, where it was first tested]

Lyd·gate (lídgeit), John (c. 1370–c. 1450), prolific English poet, and monk. He was a follower of Chaucer. His longer works include translations, e.g. 'The Hystorye, Sege and Dystruccion of Troye' (c. 1412–20) and 'The Falle of Princis' (c. 1430). Lydgate lacks Chaucer's broad humanity, his humor and his technical artistry. Lydgate's best work is in his 150 shorter religious and secular poems

Lyd·i·a (lídi:ə) an ancient kingdom of central Asia Minor. It prospered (7th c. B.C. to mid-6th c. B.C.), notably under Croesus, and had a magnificent capital at Sardis. It was probably the first state to issue coins (c. 625 B.C.) and to melt and work gold ore. It was conquered by the Persians (546 B.C.)

Lyd·i·an mode (lídi:ən) (mus.) a medieval authentic mode represented by the white piano keys ascending from F ‖ an ancient Greek mode represented by the white piano keys descending from C

lye (lai) n. an alkaline solution of mainly potassium carbonate originally made by leaching wood ashes and used e.g. in soapmaking ‖ any strong alkaline solution, esp. one used for washing [O.E. lēag]

lying pres. part. of LIE (to have the body in a horizontal position)

lying pres. part. of LIE (to tell a lie)

ly·ing-in (láiiŋin) n. (old-fash.) confinement for childbirth

Lyl·y (líli:), John (c. 1554–1606), English dramatist and novelist. His romantic comedies include 'Alexander, Campaspe and Diogenes' (1584) and 'Endymion' (1591). Euphuism takes its name from the hero of his two novels 'Euphues: the anatomy of wit' (1579, 1580)

Lym·nae·a (limní:ə) n. (biol.) a snail that carries a fluke (the trematode worm) that causes fascioliasis, a liver infection, in mammals

lymph (limf) n. a colorless, plasmalike fluid that bathes many of the tissues of vetebrates, is conducted from these tissues to the blood circulatory system, and serves to lubricate and cleanse them (*LYMPH GLAND, *LYMPHATIC) [fr. L. *lympha*, clear water]

lym·phan·gi·og·ra·phy or **lym·phog·raphy** (limfændʒi:ógrəfi:) n. (med.) radiographic recording of the lymphatic vessels and nodes after injection of radiopaque material. —**lymphangiogram** or **lymphogram** n. —**lymphangiographic** or **lymphographic** adj.

lym·phat·ic (limfǽtik) 1. adj. relating to, produced by or conveying lymph ‖ (of a person or his temperament) sluggish, flabby, languid 2. n. any of the fine-walled vessels draining most tissues and conducting lymph to the thoracic duct. The vessels range in size from capillary to veinlike ducts [fr. L. *lymphaticus*, mad, frenzied]

lymph gland one of a system of glands, located throughout the body in association with the lymph vessels, that serve to filter debris from the lymph and also to produce lymphocytes

lymph node a lymph gland

lym·pho·cyte (límfəsait) n. a leucocyte inhabiting both the blood and lymph, that is produced from lymphoid tissue and that is an active phagocyte [fr. LYMPH + Gk *kytos*, hollow vessel]

lym·phoid (límfoid) adj. of or resembling lymph ‖ of or resembling the tissue of lymph glands

lym·pho·pro·lif·er·a·tive (límfəprəlífəreitiv) adj. (med.) of the proliferation of lymphoid tissue, e.g., as in malignant lymphomas

Lynch (lintʃ), Benito (1885–1951), Argentinean writer. He introduced a modern phase of the gaucho novel with his 'Los caranchos de la Florida' (1916), and diverged from the gaucho genre with the simple and ironic 'El inglés de los gruesos' (1924)

lynch (lintʃ) v.t. (of a mob) to take the law into its own hands and kill (someone) in punishment for a real or presumed crime [after Col. Charles *Lynch* (*LYNCH LAW]

lynch law the summary trial and punishment of offenders by a self-constituted court outside due process of the law [prob. after Col. Charles *Lynch* (1736-96), American justice of the peace and farmer, who presided over such extrajudicial courts]

lynx (liŋks) pl. **lynx**, **lynx·es** n. a member of *Lynx*, fam. *Felidae*, a genus of wildcats native to the northern hemisphere, e.g. the bobcat. They are somewhat larger than a domestic cat, with relatively long, tufted ears and a short tail ‖ the fur of a lynx [L. fr. Gk]

Lynx (mil.) U.S. command and reconnaissance vehicle (M-114 A1), armed with machine guns

lynx-eyed (líŋksaid) adj. very keensighted

Ly·on (láiən), Mary (Mason) (1797–1849), U.S. pioneer woman educator. She founded (1835) Mt Holyoke Female Seminary in South Hadley, Mass., serving (from 1837) as its first principal

Lyon (ljɔ̃) (Eng. Lyons) the third largest city (pop. 462,841; agglom. 1,170,660) of France, a great commercial center at the confluence of the Rhône and Saône, in Rhône department. Industries: textiles (Europe's chief silk and rayon producer), engineering, chemical and pharmaceutical products. Gothic cathedral (12th–15th cc.). Town hall (17th c.). University (1808)

Lyon·nais (ljɔne) a former province of France in the E. Massif Central, comprising Rhône and Loire departments. Its mountains are cut by wide river valleys. Industries: mixed farming, wine (Beaujolais), coal mining, varied manufactures (at Lyon and Saint-Etienne). Lyonnais proper (most of modern Rhône), a countship from the 10th c., was attached to the crown in 1312, and the remaining territories by 1527

ly·on·naise (laiənéiz, ljɔnez) adj. (of potatoes) boiled, sliced and fried with onions [fr. F. *à la Lyonnaise*, in the manner of Lyons]

Ly·ons (láiənz), Joseph Aloysius (1879–1939), Australian prime minister (1932–9). He left the Labour party to form the coalition United Australia party (1931) and led Australia out of economic depression

Lyons *LYON

ly·o·phil·ic (laiəfilik) adj. (chem.) denoting strong affinity between the dispersed and continuous phases in a colloid [fr. Gk *luein*, to loosen + *philos*, loving]

ly·oph·i·li·za·tion (laiɒfələzéiʃən) n. the process of quick freezing, followed by dehydration in a high vacuum *also* freeze-drying —**lyophilizer** n. the device used; the person operating Cf CRYOGENICS

ly·o·pho·bic (laiəfóubik) adj. (chem.) denoting a lack of strong affinity between the dispersed and continuous phases in a colloid [fr. Gk *luein*, to loosen + *phobos*, fearing]

ly·press·in [$C_{46}H_{65}N_{13}O_{12}S_2$] (liprésin) n. (pharm.) antidiuretic and vasopressor hormone derived from the pituitary glands of pigs (sometimes made synthetically)

ly·rate (láirit, láireit) adj. (bot.) lyreshaped [fr. Mod. L. *lyratus* fr. *lyra*, lyre]

lyre (láiər) n. an ancient stringed musical instrument having two symmetrical, curved arms. The strings, plucked by a plectrum, run between the base and yoke joining the arms at the top. It was used by the ancient Greeks to accompany songs [F. *lyre* fr. L. fr. Gk]

lyre-bird (láiərbə:rd) n. a member of *Menura*, fam. *Menuridae*, a genus of Australian songbirds, esp. *M. novaehollandiae*, a species whose males have tail feathers of three kinds, in shape and arrangement resembling a lyre

lyr·ic (lírik) 1. adj. (of poetry) expressing the poet's intense personal emotions, usually in short poems divided into stanzas ‖ (of a poet) writing such poetry ‖ (of a singing voice) pure, light and free, not brilliant or deeply charged with emotion ‖ of or written to be accompanied by the lyre, *Greek lyric odes* ‖ meant to be sung set to music 2. n. a lyric poem ‖ (Am. pl., Br. also sing.) the words of a popular song [fr. F. *lyrique* or fr. L. *lyricus* fr. Gk]

lyr·i·cal (lírik'l) adj. (old-fash., of poetry) lyric ‖ written or expressed in language appropriate to lyric poetry ‖ (pop.) passionately enthusiastic, esp. in praising [fr. F. *lyrique* or fr. L. *lyricus* fr. Gk]

lyr·i·cism (lírisizəm) n. lyric quality or style ‖ great enthusiasm

lyr·i·cist (lírisist) n. someone who writes the words for popular songs

Ly·san·der (laisǽndər) (d. 395 B.C.), Spartan general and statesman. He destroyed the Athenian fleet at Aegospotami (405 B.C.) in the Peloponnesian War

Lys·i·as (lísi:æs) Greek orator (c. 458–c. 380 B.C.). His speeches, written in the everyday language of his time, are models of precision and simplicity

Ly·sim·a·chus (laisíməkəs) (c. 360–281 B.C.), Greek general. He succeeded to Thrace on the death (323 B.C.) of Alexander the Great, and became (286 B.C.) satrap of Macedonia

ly·sin (láisin) n. any of a class of substances that can produce lysis, esp. of red blood cells [LYSIS]

ly·sine (láisi:n, láisin) n. a basic amino acid, $H_2N(CH_2)_4CH(NH_2)COOH$, essential in human and animal nutrition [fr. Gk *lusis*, a loosening, dissolving]

Ly·sip·pus (laisípəs) (4th c. B.C.), Greek sculptor. His work, mainly in bronze, was famous for its grace

ly·sis (láisis) pl. **ly·ses** (láisi:z) n. (med.) the gradual lowering of a fever (cf. CRISIS) ‖ (med.) a process of disintegration or dissolving, e.g. of blood cells or bacteria [L. fr. Gk *lusis*, a loosening, dissolving]

ly·so·cline (láisəklain) n. layer of seawater (depth of about 4,000 m) at which certain chemicals dissolve

ly·sol (láisɒl) n. a brown liquid containing creosol, used as an antiseptic and disinfectant [fr. *Lysol*, a trademark]

ly·so·some (láisəsoum) n. (cytol.) specialized subcellular structure containing enzymes that digest certain chemicals —**lysosomal** adj.

ly·so·staph·in (laisəstǽfin) n. (biochem.) enzyme that destroys staphylococcal bacteria by attacking the cell wall

ly·stro·sau·rus (laistrósɔrəs) n. mammal-like reptile of Triassic period (200 million yrs ago), fossils of which have been found in South Africa, India, China, and Russia

lyt·ta (lítə) n. a cartilaginous or fibrous rod embedded longitudinally in the tongue of dogs and several other carnivores [L. fr. Gk = madness, rabies]

Lyt·tel·ton (lít'ltən) the port (pop. 3,000) of Christchurch, New Zealand

Lytton *BULWER-LYTTON

	EARLY NORTH SEMITIC	PHOENICIAN	EARLY HEBREW (GEZER)	EARLY GREEK	CLASSICAL GREEK	ETRUSCAN		EARLY LATIN	CLASSICAL LATIN
						Early	Classical		
M	٤	ᛘ	۶	ᛉ	ᛘ	ᛘ	ᛉ	ᛉ	M

CURSIVE MAJUSCULE (ROMAN)	CURSIVE MINUSCULE (ROMAN)	ANGLO-IRISH MAJUSCULE	CAROLINE MINUSCULE	VENETIAN MINUSCULE (ITALIC)	N. ITALIAN MINISCULE (ROMAN)
ᵚ	m	m	m	m	m

A. C. SYLVESTER, CAMBRIDGE, ENGLAND

Development of the letter M, beginning with the early North Semitic letter. Evolution of both the majuscule, or capital, letter M and the minuscule, or lowercase, letter m are shown.

M, m (em) the 13th letter of the English alphabet ‖ the symbol (**M**) for 1,000 in Roman numerals

ma (mɑ) n. mother [shortened fr. *mamma*]

ma'am (mæm,mɑm) n. a polite term of address to a woman ‖ (*Br.*) the term of address to the queen or a royal princess [shortened fr. MADAM]

Maas (mɑs) *MEUSE

Maas·tricht (mɑ́strixt) (formerly Maestricht) the capital (pop. 112,605) of Limburg, Netherlands, on the Meuse: light manufactures. Romanesque church

MABE (*abbr.*) master of agricultural business and economics

Ma·bil·lon (mæbi·jɔ́), Jean (1632–1707), French Benedictine scholar, author of 'Acta sanctorum ordinis S. Benedicti' (1668–1701) and of the treatise that founded the science of diplomatics, 'De re diplomatica' (1681)

Mab·i·no·gi·on (mæbinóudʒi:ən) a collection of Welsh legends, compiled in the 14th and 15th cc. It is one of the sources of the Arthurian legend

Ma·bu·se (məbú·zə) (Jan Gossaert, c. 1472–c. 1534), Flemish painter, one of the artists through whom Italian Renaissance art began to affect the art of N. Europe. His rather dry, static figures are set in elaborate classical architectural settings

mac, mack (mæk) n. (*Br., pop.*) a mackintosh

MAC (*abbr.*) Municipal Assistance Corporation, oversight agency established in June 1975 by banks and U.S. Congress to control New York City finances and to refinance indebtedness to prevent default and municipal bankruptcy

ma·ca·bre (məkɑbr, məkɑ́bər) *adj.* suggestive of the terrifying aspect of death [F. perh. fr. O.F. *Macabé*, Maccabaeus]

ma·ca·co (məkɑ́kou) n. any of several lemurs of Africa and Asia, esp. *Lemur macaco* [F. *mococo*, of unknown origin]

mac·ad·am (məkǽdəm) n. small broken stones which, having angular faces,fit closely together when pressed by a heavy roller and so constitute an even and durable road surface ‖ a road having such a surface **mac·ád·am·ize** *pres. part.* **mac·ad·am·iz·ing** *past* and *past part.* **mac·ad·am·ized** *v.t.* to construct (a road surface) of layers of macadam, generally using tar as a binding surface [after John Loudon *McAdam* (1756–1836), Scot. civil engineer]

Mc·A·doo (mækədu:), William Gibbs (1863–1941), U.S. lawyer and railroad executive. He served as secretary of the treasury (1913–18) under President Woodrow Wilson, directing the start of the Federal Reserve System, and as director-general (1917–19) of U.S. railroads during the period of government operation

Ma·cao (məkáu) (*Port.* Macau) a Portuguese territory (area 6 sq. miles, pop. 280,000) off S. China, in the Si-kiang delta. It comprises the city of Macao on the southern tip of Chung-shan (Macao) Peninsula, and two offshore islands. People: Chinese, small European minority. It is a transit and fishing port and a resort. The Portuguese settlement began in 1557 and was confirmed by treaty with China (1887). An appointed governor leads the government, which was granted internal autonomy in 1976

Ma·ca·pa·gal (mɑkɑpɑgál), Diosdado (1910–) Filipino statesman, president (1962–5) of the Philippines

ma·caque (məkák) n. any of several short-tailed monkeys of genus *Macaca*, found in Asia, the East Indies and N.W. Africa, esp. the rhesus monkey. In Europe the only macaque is the Barbary ape, *M. sylvana*, on Gibraltar [Fr. Port. *macaco*, monkey]

mac·a·ro·ni (mækəróuni:) *pl.* **mac·a·ro·nies** n. a pasta made of semolina, usually rolled into long thin tubes which are hard and brittle when dried, softening when boiled for eating ‖ (*hist.*) an 18th-c. English dandy affecting continental mannerisms [Ital. *macaroni*]

mac·a·ron·ic (mækərónik) *adj.* of writing, esp. burlesque verse, in which words of different origin (e.g. Latinized and modern words) are mixed together **mac·a·rón·ics** *pl. n.* verses of this kind [fr. Mod. L. *macaronicus*, like macaroni]

mac·a·roon (mækərú:n) n. a small sweet crisp cookie mainly made of egg whites, sugar and almond or coconut flavoring [F. *macaron* fr. Ital.]

Mac·Ar·thur (məkɑ́rθər), Douglas (1880–1964), American general. He commanded the American defense of the Philippines (1941–2), and defeated the Japanese in the Pacific (1944–5). He was commander (1950–1) of the U.N. forces in the Korean War, until recalled by Truman because of differing policies

Macassar *MAKASSAR

Macassar oil an oil made from seeds of the kusam, used mainly as a hairdressing ‖ any similar oil used as a hairdressing [fr. *Macassar*, var. of MAKASSAR]

Ma·cau (məkáu) *MACAO

Ma·cau·lay (məkɔ́li:), Thomas Babington, 1st Baron Macaulay of Rothley (1800–59), British historian, statesman and writer. His 'History of England from the Accession of James the Second' (1849–61) was written in a dramatic style, with strong Whig prejudice. He also wrote a collection of essays (1843) and a book of poems, 'Lays of Ancient Rome' (1842)

ma·caw (məkɔ́) n. any of several large, bright-feathered parrots of genus *Ara* and related genera, of Central and South America [Port. *macao*]

Mac·ca·bae·us (mækəbí:əs), Judas (d. 161 B.C.), Jewish patriot and leader of the revolt of the Maccabees. He was defeated and killed by the army of Demetrius I Soter

Mac·ca·be·an (mækəbí:ən) *adj.* pertaining to the Maccabees

Mac·ca·bee (mǽkəbi) n. a member of a Jewish family who led a revolt (c. 168-142 B.C.) against the Hellenizing policy of Antiochus IV and established themselves as rulers of Palestine (142–63 B.C.) ‖ a supporter of this revolt

Mac·ca·bees (mǽkəbi:z) two books dealing with Jewish history and theology (late 2nd c. B.C.), placed in the Apocrypha in the Authorized Version, but included in the Roman Catholic canon

Mc·Car·ran (məkɑ́rən), Patrick Anthony (1876–1954), U.S. politician. As U.S. Senator from Nevada, he sponsored two controversial acts, the McCarran-Wood Act and the McCarran-Walter Act, which were passed over President Harry Truman's vetoes. He strongly supported Senator Joseph McCarthy's anti-Communist campaign

McCarran-Walter Act (Immigration and Nationality Act), a U.S. Congressional act (1952) sponsored by U.S. Senator Patrick McCarran. It codified existing immigration legislation, tightened the laws governing the admission, exclusion, and deportation of dangerous aliens, retained immigration quotas by country of origin and made them applicable to Asiatic countries, and provided for selective immigration on the basis of skills

McCarran-Wood Act (Internal Security Act), a U.S. Congressional act (1950) sponsored by U.S. Senator Patrick McCarran. It required the registration of all Communists with the attorney general and made it unlawful for those with Communist affiliations to participate in defense or government work

Mc·Car·thy (məkɑ́rθi:), Eugene (1916–), U.S. public official. As U.S. senator from Minnesota, he campaigned unsuccessfully for the 1968 Democratic nomination for the U.S. presidency, advocating an end to U.S. participation in the war in Vietnam, and won impressive support esp. from college youth. He retired from the Senate (1971) and ran for president again (1976), this time as an independent. He lost this race also, as well as a bid to return to the Senate (1982)

McCarthy, Joseph Raymond (1909–57), American Republican senator. He led a campaign (1950–4) against alleged Communist infiltra-

CONCISE PRONUNCIATION KEY: (**a**) æ, c*a*t; ɑ, c*ar*; ɔ f*aw*n; ei, sn*a*ke. (**e**) e, h*e*n; i:, sh*ee*p; iə, d*eer*; ɛə, b*ear*. (**i**) i, f*i*sh; ai, t*i*ger; ə:, b*ir*d. (**o**) o, *o*x; au, c*ow*; ou, g*oa*t; u, p*oo*r; ɔi, r*oy*al. (**u**) ʌ, d*u*ck; u, b*u*ll; u:, g*oo*se; ə, b*a*cillus; ju:, c*u*be. x, lo*ch*; θ, *th*ink; ð, bo*th*er; z, *Z*en; ʒ, corsa*g*e; dʒ, sava*g*e; ŋ, ora*ng*utang; j, *y*ak; ʃ, *fi*sh; tʃ, fe*tch*; 'l, rabb*le*; 'n, redd*en*. Complete pronunciation key appears inside front cover.

tion in the U.S. administration. He was censured (1954) by the U.S. Senate

Mc·Car·thy·ism (məkárθi:izəm) *n.* paranoic fear of Communists leading to government oppression and persecution of all persons of other than extreme right-wing conviction and manifestation of complete disregard for civil and basic human rights of those often falsely accused; from Wisconsin Senator Joseph R. McCarthy

mac·chi·net·ta (mɒki:néta) *n.* (*It.*) a type of drip coffee maker

Mc·Clel·lan (məklélən), George Brinton (1826–85), American general. He was commander in chief (1861–2) of the Union forces in the Civil War

Mc·Clintock (məklíntɒk), Barbara (1902–) U.S. geneticist, winner of the Nobel Prize for physiology or medicine (1983). She conducted research at Carnegie Institution of Washington from 1941 and at Cold Spring Harbor Laboratories and discovered that genes move within chromosomes, thus facilitating the study of some diseases and of the hereditary process

Mc·Clure (məklúər), Sir Robert John le Mesurier (1807–73), British naval officer. He discovered the Northwest Passage (1850)

Mc·Cor·mick (məkórmik), Cyrus Hall (1809–84), American inventor. He invented the mechanical reaper (1831)

McCormick, Robert Rutherford (1880–1955), U.S. journalist. With his cousin Joseph Patterson he controlled (from 1910) the 'Chicago Tribune', espousing isolationism and right-wing extremism and building the largest circulation of any Midwestern newspaper. With Patterson he founded (1919) the 'New York Daily News' etc.

Mc·Coy, the real (məkɔ́i) the genuine thing, not an imitation or substitute [al. of Scot. *Mckay*, with reference to disputed headship of the clan]

Mc·Crack·en Group (məkrǽkən) international group of seven economists, headed by Paul McCracken, working with a group from the Organization for Economic Cooperation and Development (OECD), to study the prospects of long-term economic growth affecting developed countries in the 1970s

Mc·Cul·lers (məkʌ́lə:rz), Carson (1917–67), U.S. novelist, born in Columbus, Georgia. Her novels and short stories, concerned esp. with the spiritual solitude of the individual, include 'The Heart is a Lonely Hunter' (1940), 'Reflections in a Golden Eye' (1941), 'The Member of the Wedding' (1946), 'The Ballad of the Sad Cafe' (1951), 'The Clock Without Hands' (1961)

'Mc·Cul·loch v. Maryland' (məkʌ́lək) a decision (1819) of the U.S. Supreme Court under John Marshall, which determined that the government held not only the powers expressly conferred upon its legislative, executive, and judicial branches, but also whatever authority was 'appropriate' to put such powers into effect. Although the U.S. Constitution refers only to 'necessary and proper' authority, the court held to the Hamiltonian view of the Constitution that it 'implies' powers to the government and that, when the end and means are legitimate, an act of Congress cannot be held unconstitutional

Mc·Diar·mid (məkdə́:rmit), Hugh (Christopher Murray Grieve, 1892–1978), Scottish poet, prominent in the revival of Scottish literature in the 1920s

Mac·don·ald (məkdɒn'ld), Flora (c. 1721–90), Scottish Jacobite heroine. She helped Prince Charles Edward Stuart to escape (1746) to the Continent after Culloden

Mac·Don·ald (məkdɒ́n'ld), James Ramsay (1866–1937), British statesman. One of the founders of the Labour party, he was prime minister and foreign secretary of the first Labour government (1924). He was again prime minister (1929–35), but he lost Labour support by forming a coalition National government after 1931

MacDonald, John Sandfield (1812–72), Canadian Conservative statesman. As the premier (1867–71) of Ontario, he initiated, in close cooperation with the federal government, the organization of provincial education

Macdonald, Sir John Alexander (1815–91), Canadian Conservative statesman. He did much to establish the Confederation of Canada (1867), and was its first prime minister (1867–73 and 1878–91)

Mac·don·nell Ranges (mækdənél) a mountain range in Northern Territory, central Australia. Highest point: Mt Ziel (4,955 ft)

Mac·Dow·ell (məkdáuəl), Edward Alexander (1861–1908), U.S. composer. His works, essentially in the post romantic tradition, include the Woodland Sketches for piano (1896), the Second 'Indian' Suite for orchestra (1897), Sea Pieces (1898), and New England Idyls (1902)

Mc·Duf·fie (məkdʌ́fi:), George (1790–1851), U.S. politician and states' rights advocate. As a member (1821–34) of the House of Representatives, he strongly influenced the drafting of the 'Tariff of abominations' (1828), opposed protective tariffs, advocated the doctrine of nullification, and served as governor of South Carolina (1834–6) and in the U.S. Senate (1842–6)

mace (meis) *n.* (*hist.*) a club with a heavy, spiked metal head, used as a weapon for shattering armor, esp. helmets ‖ an ornamented staff of office, carried before certain officials (e.g. the Speaker of the House of Commons) ‖ the bearer of such a staff [O.F. *masse*, *mace*]

mace *n.* a spice made from the outer covering of the nutmeg kernel [M.E. *macis* fr. F.]

Mace 1. (*mil.*) Air Force surface-to-surface radar-guided low-level attack missile (MGM-13) containing a navigation system, with a range of 600 miles **2.** tradename of a temporarily incapacitating liquid nerve irritant in aerosol form that is sprayed into a person's face and causes irritation of eyes, dizziness, etc. It is often used as a personal defense weapon and by the police to disable rioters —**mace** *v.* to use mace

ma·cé·doine (mæseidwan) *n.* a dish of mixed, diced fruit or vegetables [F.]

Mac·e·don (mæsidən) an ancient kingdom in N.E. Greece, settled in the 3rd millennium B.C., which, under Philip II, rose to dominate Greece (4th c. B.C.). Under Alexander the Great, the Macedonians defeated the Persian Empire, and remained a great power until Macedon was annexed by Rome (146 B.C.)

Mac·e·do·ni·a (mæsidóuni:ə) a constituent republic (area 10,227 sq. miles, pop. 1,406,000) of Yugoslavia. It is largely mountainous and lies in the south between Albania, Greece and Bulgaria. Capital: Skoplje. Crops: cereals, fruit, tobacco, poppies. Mineral resources: chromium, lead, zinc

Macedonia a region of the Balkan peninsula, northwest of the Aegean, covering part of N. Greece, S. Yugoslavia and S.W. Bulgaria. It is almost entirely mountainous. Formerly Macedon, the region was incorporated in the Byzantine Empire (395) and passed to Bulgaria (9th c.) and Serbia (14th c.). It was under Turkish control from 1389 until the Balkan Wars (1912–13), after which it was divided among Greece, Serbia and Bulgaria

Ma·cei·ó (məseió) a cotton and sugar port (pop. 323,601) in N.E. Brazil: metallurgical and textile industries

Mc·Enroe (mǽkenrou), John Patrick (1959–) U.S. tennis player known for his serve, net game and quick temper on the court. He became a professional in 1978 and among many other championships won the U.S. Open (1979–1981, 1984) and the British Open at Wimbledon (1981, 1983–4)

mac·er·ate (mǽsəreit) *pres. part.* **mac·er·at·ing** *past* and *past part.* **mac·er·at·ed** *v.t.* to soften or separate (e.g. food in the digestive tract) by soaking ‖ to cause to waste away, esp. by fasting ‖ *v.i.* to become softened or separated by soaking ‖ to waste away, esp. by fasting **mac·er·a·tion** *n.* [fr. L. *macerare* (*maceratus*), to soften]

Mc·Gee (məgí:), Thomas D'Arcy (1825–68), Irish-Canadian politician and writer. As president (1862–3) of the council in the Reform Administration and minister of agriculture (1864–7), he greatly influenced the movement leading to Canadian federation. He was assassinated

Mc·Gil·li·vray (məgílivrei), Alexander (1759–93), Creek Indian chief. A British agent during the Revolutionary War, he maintained Creek loyalty to the Crown. He negotiated (1790) the Treaty of New York with President George Washington, in which the Creeks acknowledged U.S. sovereignty over part of their territory, acquired lands claimed by Georgia, and agreed to keep the peace. In the pay of the Spanish, he repudiated (1792) the treaty, and led Indian attacks against frontier settlements

Mc·Gill University (məgíl) a private university in Montreal, Canada, founded by the legacy of James McGill (1744–1813), a Montreal fur merchant and philanthropist, and opened in 1829. It includes Royal Victoria College for women. It has a renowned medical museum and library

Mac·gil·ly·cud·dy's Reeks (məgílikʌdi:zrí:ks) a mountain range in Kerry. S.W. Irish Republic. Highest point: Carrantuohill (3,414 ft)

Mc·Govern (məgʌ́vərn), George Stanley (1922–) U.S. politician, Democratic senator from South Dakota (1962–81). He was a U.S. representative (1957–61) in Congress and director of Food for Peace (1961–2) before being elected to the Senate. In 1972, he lost the presidential election to Richard M. Nixon. He made an unsuccessful bid for the 1984 Democratic presidential nomination

Mac·Greg·or (məgrégər), Robert *ROB ROY

Mach (mɑk, mæk) *n.* Mach number [after Ernst *Mach* (1838–1916), Austrian physicist]

Ma·cha·do de As·sis (məʃádudiasí:s), Joaquim Maria (1839–1908), Brazilian poet and author of the Parnassian school and author of realist and psychological novels, esp. 'Dom Casmurro' (1900)

Ma·cha·do y Mo·ra·les (matʃádɔi:mɔráles), Gerardo (1871–1939), Cuban general and 5th president of the Republic (1925–33) until his overthrow. He was one of Cuba's major dictators

Ma·cha·do y Ru·iz (matʃádɔi:rú:i:θ), Antonio (1875–1939), Spanish poet. His works include 'Soledades' (1903) and 'Nuevas Canciones' (1924)

Mach angle (*aeron.*) the angle between the axis of a moving projectile and the envelope of the waves produced. The sine of this angle equals the ratio of the velocity of the projectile to the velocity of sound

ma·chet·e (mətʃéti:, məʃéti:) *n.* a long heavy, broad-bladed knife used esp. in Central and South America and the West Indies as a tool and a weapon [Span.]

Mach hold mode (*mil.*) a control mode in a flight control system by which the desired flying speed of an aircraft is maintained automatically

Mach·i·a·vel·li (mæki:əvéli:), Niccoló (1469–1527), Florentine statesman, political theorist and writer. Alarmed by the anarchy of the Italian city-states, he advocated ('Il Principe', 1513) the establishment and maintenance of authority by any effective means. Evil acts of the ruler were justified by the evil acts of the ruled

Mach·i·a·vel·li·an (mæki:əvéli:ən) *adj.* of or relating to the political theories of Machiavelli ‖ characterized by cunning and duplicity **Mach·i·a·vél·li·an·ism** *n.*

ma·chic·o·late (mætʃíkəleit) *pres. part.* **ma·chic·o·lat·ing** *past* and *past part.* **ma·chic·o·lat·ed** *v.t.* to furnish with machicolations [back-formation fr. MACHICOLATION]

ma·chic·o·la·tion (mətʃikəléiʃən) *n.* (*hist.*) an aperture between the corbels of a projecting parapet through which missiles, boiling oil etc. could be hurled down on assailants ‖ a parapet so constructed [fr. M.L. *machicolare* (*machicolatus*), to furnish with such apertures]

mach·i·nate (mækineit) *pres. part.* **mach·i·nat·ing** *past* and *past part.* **mach·i·nat·ed** *v.i.* to form a plot or intrigue, esp. in order to work harm [fr. L. *machinari* (*machinatus*)]

mach·i·na·tion (mækinéiʃən) *n.* the act of machinating ‖ a plot, scheme

mach·i·na·tor (mækineitər) *n.* someone who machinates, an intriguer

ma·chine (məʃí:n) **1.** *n.* an apparatus, made of organized, interacting parts, which takes in some form of energy, modifies it, and delivers it in a more suitable form for a desired function ‖ a thing or system resembling such an apparatus in acting with regularity as a result of the interaction of its component parts ‖ a person who acts like such an apparatus, apparently without exercising his will, thought or imagination ‖ an organization whose members collaborate for some purpose, *a political machine* **2.** *v.t. pres. part.* **ma·chin·ing** *past* and *past part.* **ma·chined** to make or operate on by machinery [F.]

machine art any art form that is made up of mechanical or electronic devices *Cf* AUTODESTRUCTIVE ART, MACHINE SCULPTURE

machine gun a gun which automatically feeds ammunition into its breech, enabling rapid fire

CONCISE PRONUNCIATION KEY: (a) æ, *cat*; ɑ, *car*; ɔ *fawn*; ei, *snake*. **(e)** e, *hen*; i:, *sheep*; iə, *deer*; ɛə, *bear*. **(i)** i, *fish*; ai, *tiger*; ə:, *bird*. **(o)** o, *ox*; au, *cow*; ou, *goat*; u, *poor*; ɔi, *royal*. **(u)** ʌ, *duck*; u, *bull*; u:, *goose*; ə, *bacillus*; ju:, *cube*. x, *loch*; θ, *think*; ð, *bother*; z, *Zen*; ʒ, *corsage*; dʒ, *savage*; ŋ, ora*n*gutang; j, *y*ak; ʃ, *fish*; tʃ, *fetch*; 'l, rabb*le*; 'n, redd*en*. Complete pronunciation key appears inside front cover.

to be maintained **ma·chine-gun** *pres. part.* **ma·chine-gun·ning** *past* and *past part.* **ma·chine-gunned** *v.t.* to shoot at with a machine gun ‖ *v.i.* to fire a machine gun

machine language or **machine-oriented language** (*computer*) instruction code that can be used directly by a computer without translation *Cf* COMPILER LANGUAGE, COMPUTER LANGUAGE

ma·chine-made (məʃíːnméid) *adj.* made by machinery, not by hand

ma·chine-read·a·ble (məʃínríːdəb'l) *adj.* (*computer*) capable of being processed by a computer without change

ma·chin·er·y (məʃíːnəriː) *n.* (*collect.*) machines in general ‖ the assembled parts of a machine ‖ the organization of various processes so that a certain purpose may be fulfilled, *the machinery of the law*

machine sculpture sculpture incorporating mechanical or electronic devices *Cf* MACHINE ART

machine shop a workshop in which machines or machine parts are made and assembled

machine time the period during which a device is used, esp. in a business operation

machine tool a power-driven machine fitted with a tool or tools for gear and screw cutting, boring, planing, drilling etc.

machine translation (*computer*) instructions translated by a computer from one computer language to another *abbr.* **MT**

machine word a group of binary digits that a processing unit normally handles in making a transfer

ma·chin·ist (məʃíːnist) *n.* someone who makes, assembles, repairs or operates machines [fr. F. *machiniste* and MACHINE]

ma·chis·mo or **ma·cho** (matʃíːzmou) *n.* (*Sp.*) exaggerated masculinity; manly assurance —**macho** *adj.*

Mach no/yes (*mil.*) in air intercept, a code meaning 'I have reached maximum speed and am not/am closing in on my target'

Mach number (*aeron.*) the ratio of the speed of a moving object to the speed of sound in the medium through which it travels

Mach stem the shock front formed by the fusion of the direct and reflected shock fronts from an explosion, generally used with reference to a blast wave propagated in the air and reflected at the surface of the earth *also* **Mach front**

Mach trim compensator an automatic flight-control subsystem that provides pitch trim of an aircraft as a function of Mach number

Ma·chu Pic·chu (mátʃuːpíːktʃuː) an Inca citadel of white granite, mainly intact, occupying a narrow ridge (at 6,750 ft) in the Peruvian Andes 50 miles north of Cuzco

macintosh *MACKINTOSH

mack *MAC

Mack·ay (məkái), Clarence Hungerford (1874–1938), U.S. capitalist and philanthropist. As president of the Mackay system of telegraphs and cables, he directed the completion (1904) of the first trans-Pacific cable between the U.S.A. and the Far East. He became (1928) the first to combine radio, cables and telegraphs under one management. He donated more than $1.5 million to the University of Nevada

Mac·Kaye (məkái), (James Morrison) Steele (1842-94), U.S. playwright, actor, theater manager, and inventor. He founded the first school of dramatic expression, and originated 'harmonic gymnastics'. His inventions include overhead lighting (1874), the first moving 'double stage' (1879), and folding theater seats

Mac·ken·zie (məkénzi:), Sir Alexander (c. 1764–1820), Scottish explorer and trader in North America. He followed the river which now bears his name to its mouth (1789), and crossed the Rocky Mtns to reach the Pacific (1793)

Mackenzie, Alexander (1822–92), prime minister of Canada (1873–8). He headed the first Canadian Liberal administration

Mackenzie, William Lyon (1795–1861), Canadian journalist and insurgent leader. As leader of the unsuccessful Reform Party of Upper Canada, he attempted (1837) a rebellion to seize Toronto from British colonial rule. Escaping to the U.S.A., he set up a provisional government on Navy Is. in the Niagara River, but was imprisoned by U.S. authorities for violating neutrality laws. His actions eventually led to the British grant of responsible government in Canada (1848)

Mackenzie a district (area incl. water, 527,490 sq. miles) in the central and W. Northwest Ter-

ritories, Canada, incl. the land between the Yukon Territory and the Keewatin District and most of the Mackenzie River valley. It is administered from Ottawa. Resources: uranium

Mackenzie the second largest river system (2,514 miles long) of North America, between the Canadian Shield and the Rocky Mtns, W. Canada. It includes the Peace, the Finlay, the Slave, the Athabasca and other rivers flowing into Great Slave Lake, and the Mackenzie River proper (1,000 miles) flowing out of Great Slave Lake through the Northwest Territories to a delta on the Arctic Ocean

Mackenzie King *KING

Mackenzie Mtns a range in the E. Yukon Territory and W. Mackenzie District, Canada. Highest point: Mt Sir James McBrien (9,049 ft)

mack·er·el (mǽkrəl) *pl.* **mack·er·el, mack·er·els** *n.* a fish of the suborder *Scombroidea,* esp. *Scomber scombrus,* an important food fish of the North Atlantic with a silver belly and a green back usually marked with dark bars [O.F. *makerel,* origin unknown]

mackerel sky a sky with rows of cirrocumulus clouds resembling the patterns on a mackerel's back

Mack·i·nac, Straits of (mǽkinɔ, mǽkinæk) straits (c. 4 miles wide at the narrowest point) in N. Michigan, separating the Upper and Lower Michigan peninsulas and connecting Lake Huron and Lake Michigan

mack·i·naw (mǽkinɔ) *n.* (*Am. hist.*) a heavy woolen blanket originally distributed by the U.S. government to North American Indians ‖ (*Am.*) a short, double-breasted, belted coat of thick wool napped and felted [after *Mackinaw* City, Mich.]

Mc·Kin·ley (məkínliː), William (1843–1901), 25th president (1897–1901) of the U.S.A., a Republican. He won the presidency by championing the gold standard and a high tariff policy. His administration was notable for the Spanish-American War (1898–9), after which the U.S.A. emerged as a world power. An advocate of expansionism, he acquired the Philippines, annexed Hawaii, took virtual control of Cuba, and pursued the Open Door policy in China. He was assassinated in Buffalo, N.Y., by Leon Czolgosz, an anarchist

McKinley a mountain (20,300 ft) in S. central Alaska (Alaska Range), the highest point in North America

McKinley Tariff Act a U.S. Congressional Act (1890) sponsored by William McKinley, then representative from Ohio. It called for highly protective tariffs. Its unpopularity helped to defeat the Republicans in the 1892 presidential elections

Mack·in·tosh (mǽkintɔʃ), Charles Rennie (1868–1928), Scottish architect who worked in the art nouveau style in Great Britain and produced works foreshadowing functionalism

mack·in·tosh, mac·in·tosh (mǽkintɔʃ) *n.* (esp. *Br.*) a raincoat [after Charles *Macintosh* (1766–1843), Scottish chemist]

mack·le, *Br.* also **mac·le** (mǽk'l) **1.** *n.* (*printing*) a blurred ink impression, causing printed letters to appear double **2.** *v.t.* and *i. pres. part.* **mack·ling,** *Br.* also **mac·ling** *past* and *past part.* **mack·led,** *Br.* also **mac·led** (*printing*) to blur [fr. F. *macule*]

Mc·Lane (məkléin), Louis (1786–1857), U.S. congressman (1817–27), secretary of the treasury (1831–3), secretary of state (1833–4), and diplomat under Andrew Jackson's administration. As U.S. minister to England (1829–31), he negotiated an agreement which reopened trade between the U.S.A. and the British West Indies. He was sent (1845) by President James Polk on a special mission to England to negotiate an Anglo-U.S. settlement of the Oregon boundary dispute

ma·cle (mǽk'l) *n.* (*crystall.*) a twinned crystal ‖ (*mineral.*) a dark spot in certain minerals [F.]

Mc·Lean (məkléin), John (1785–1861), U.S. politician and jurist. He served (1823–9) as postmaster general under Presidents Monroe and John Adams, and (1829–61) as associate justice of the Supreme Court, filing his dissenting opinion in the Dred Scott case

Mac·Leish (məklíːʃ), Archibald (1892–1982), American poet and playwright. His works include 'Conquistador' (1932), 'Collected Poems, 1917–52' (1952) and the play 'J.B.' (1958)

Mac·leod (məkláud), John James Rickard (1876–1935), Scottish physiologist. With Ban-

ting, he isolated insulin. They shared the Nobel Prize in medicine (1923)

Mc·Lu·han (məklúːən), Herbert Marshall (1911–80), Canadian sociologist. He holds that the chief technology of communication in a society has a determining effect on everything important in that society, even the thought processes of individuals. His many published works including 'Understanding Media' (1964) and 'The Medium is the Message' (1967)

Mac·Ma·hon (mǽkmæɔ), Edme Patrice Maurice, Comte de, duc de Magenta (1808–93), French monarchist statesman, marshal of France, president of France (1873–9)

Mc·Ma·hon (məkmáən), William (1908–), Australian statesman, prime minister (1971–2)

Mc·Mil·lan (məkmílən), Edwin Mattison (1907–), U.S. physicist, co-winner with Glenn Seaborg of the 1951 Nobel Prize in chemistry, for research on the chemistry of the transuranium elements, and co-discoverer with Philip H. Abelson of neptunium and plutonium (1940)

Mac·mil·lan (məkmílən), Maurice Harold (1894–), British Conservative statesman. As prime minister (1957–63), he did much to restore the popularity of the Conservative party after the Suez crisis (1956). In 1984 he took the hereditary title Earl of Stockton

Mc·Na·ma·ra (mæknəmærə), Robert Strange (1916–), U.S. political leader and business executive. He became (1960) the first president of the Ford Motor Company to be selected from outside the Ford family. He served (1961–8) as U.S. secretary of defense under Presidents John Kennedy and Lyndon Johnson and then assumed direction of the World Bank (1968–81)

Mc·Naugh·ton (məknɔ́t'n), Andrew George Latta (1887–1966), Canadian general, commander of the Canadian army in Great Britain during the 2nd world war

Mac·Neice (məkníːs), Louis (1907–63), British poet. He is best known for his 'Autumn Journal' (1939), and for his translation (1936) of the 'Agamemnon' of Aeschylus

Ma·con (méikən), Nathaniel (1758–1837), U.S. political leader and outspoken defender of states' rights and slavery. A partisan Jeffersonian Republican, he served (1801–7) as speaker of the house. Appointed (1809) chairman of the house foreign relations committee, he strove to prevent the enactment of 'Macon's Bill No. 2', which virtually ended the U.S. embargo of British and French trade

'Macon's Bill No. 2' a U.S. Congressional bill (1810), paradoxically named after Nathaniel Macon, who was not its author and who opposed it. It restored commerce with all nations (*EMBARGO ACT OF 1807) but threatened to revert to nonintercourse with Great Britain or France if either reversed its commercial policies

Mc·Pherson (məkfɔ́ːrs'n), Aimee Semple (1890–1944) U.S. evangelist, born in Canada, founder of the Church of the Foursquare Gospel (1927). She conducted revival campaigns with her first husband Robert Semple and, after his death (1910), remarried and carried on the revivals. She opened Angelus Temple (1923), established a college and radio station and, eventually, her church based on the 'foursquare movement'—Jesus Christ as savior, baptizer, healer and coming king. Despite scandal, she continued to preach and lead her church until her death

Mac·Pher·son (məkfɔ́ːrs'n), James (1763–96), Scottish poet. He published his own verse as a translation of the work of Ossian, the legendary 3rd-c. Gaelic poet, creating a Romantic international vogue for early Irish heroic themes

Mac·quar·ie Islands (məkwóriː) an archipelago in the S. Pacific, politically part of Tasmania, Australia, 850 miles off the southeast coast. It comprises Macquarie Is. (89 sq. miles) and adjacent islets. Meteorological stations

mac·ra·me, mac·ra·mé (mǽkrəmei) *n.* a lace or trimming made of knotted cord or thread [perh. fr. Turk. *maqrama,* handkerchief fr. Arab.]

Ma·cri·nus (məkráinəs), Marcus Opellius (164–218), Roman emperor (217–18). An army officer, he murdered his predecessor, Caracalla

macro- combining form meaning 'large,' e.g., *macrochange, macrocontract, macroenergy, macrofluidics, macrolevel, macrophallic, macroplan, macroscale, macrostrategy, macroworld Cf* MAXI-, MEGA-, META-, MICRO-, MINI-

mac·ro·bi·ot·ics (mækroubaióᵗiks) *n.* a Zen-influenced food cult that holds that foods are yin (feminine) and/or yang (masculine), and that a vegetarian diet is in balance and in harmony with the cosmos; originated by George Osawa

mac·ro·ce·phal·lic (mækrousəfælik) *adj.* having an abnormally large head || (of a head) abnormally large (cf. MICROCEPHALIC) **mac·ro·ceph·a·lous** (mækrouséfələs) *adj.* **mac·ro·céph·a·ly** *n.* [fr. Gk *makrokephalos* fr. *makros, large+kephalē,* head]

mac·ro·cosm (mækrəkɒzəm) *n.* the universe as contrasted with a microcosm **mac·ro·cós·mic** *adj.* [fr. F. *macrocosme* fr. M.L. fr. Gk]

mac·ro·cyte (mækrəsait) *n.* an abnormally large red blood corpuscle occurring in some types of anemia [fr. Gk *makros,* large+*kutos,* cell]

mac·ro·e·co·nom·ics (mækrouekənómiks) *n.* (*economics*) income theory based on the balance of demand (consumer, business, government) with supply of goods, stimulated by encouragement of private expenditure and government deficit spending, conceived in 1935 by English economist John Maynard Keynes *Cf* MICROECONOMICS

mac·ro·gam·ete (mækrougǽmi:t) *n.* the larger of two conjugating gametes, usually regarded as female (cf. MICROGAMETE) [fr. Gk *makros,* large+GAMETE]

mac·ro·glob·u·lin (mækrouglóbjələn) *n.* (*biochem.*) an immunoglobulin in the blood serum comprising 5% to 10% of the serum antibodies *also* Gamma-M globulin —**macroglobulin·e·mia** (*med.*) disorder of too much Gamma-M in the blood

mac·ro·in·struc·tion (mækrouinstrʌkʃən) *n.* or **mac·ro** (mækrou) (*computer*) a coded instruction that commands a sequence of operations *Cf* MICROINSTRUCTION

mac·ro·lide antibiotic (mækroulaid) (*biochem.*) class of large ring-shape streptomycin antibiotics from a fungus

mac·ro·mol·e·cule (mækroumɒlikju:l) *n.* a molecule of extremely high molecular mass, often the result of polymerization, e.g. one of a protein, cellulose or many types of synthetic plastic [fr. Gk *makros,* large+MOLECULE]

mac·ron (mækrɒn, méikrɒn) *n.* a mark (-) placed over a long vowel or a long or stressed syllable [Gk neut. of *makros,* large]

mac·ro·or·gan·ism (mækrouórgənizəm) *n.* an organism visible to the naked eye *ant.* microorganism

mac·ro·scop·ic (mækrəskópik) *adj.* visible to the unaided eye (cf. MICROSCOPIC) [fr. Gk *makros,* large+*skopos,* observer]

mac·ro·son·ics (mækrousóniks) *n.* (*acoustics*) the science of sound at large amplitudes beyond the validity of linear approximations, e.g., in ultrasonics for clearing, drilling

mac·ro·spore (mækrəspɔr, mækrəspour) *n.* a megaspore **mac·ro·spór·ic** *adj.* [fr. Gk *makros,* large+SPORE]

ma·cru·ral (məkrúrəl) *adj.* of, relating to or belonging to *Macrura,* a suborder of decapod crustaceans incl. lobsters and shrimps **ma·crú·ran** *adj.* and *n.* **ma·crú·rous** *adj.* macrural || long-tailed [fr. Mod. L. *Macrura* fr. Gk *makros,* great, long+*oura,* tail]

mac·u·la (mækjulə) *pl.* **mac·u·lae** (mækjuli:), **mac·u·las** *n.* a spot in a crystal caused by the presence of other minerals || a dark spot on the sun or moon || a stain or spot on the skin || (*anat.*) any of various structures forming a spot differentiated from surrounding tissue [L.=stain]

macula lu·te·a (lú:ti:ə) *n.* the yellow spot of the retina [Mod. L.]

mac·u·lar (mækjulər) *adj.* of or pertaining to a spot or spots || marked with a spot or spots

mac·u·late (mækjulit, mækjuleit) *adj.* marked with spots or blotches **mac·u·lat·ed** (mækjuleitid) *adj.* **mac·u·lá·tion** *n.* a spot, macula [fr. L. *maculare (maculatus),* to spot or stain]

MACV (*mil. acronym*) Military Assistance Command, Vietnam, U.S. military command in Vietnam

mad (mæd) *comp.* **mad·der** *superl.* **mad·dest** *adj.* insane || showing insanity, *mad ravings* (*pop.*) utterly foolish, irrational || (*pop.*) rash || (*pop.,* often with 'at') angry || (*pop.,* with 'about' or 'on') wildly enthusiastic about some specified thing, person etc., *mad about ballet* || (of a dog) rabid **like mad** with great enthusiasm || frantically, *working like mad* [O.E. *gemædd*]

MAD (*mil. acronym*) mutual assured destruction, e.g., in case of nuclear attack

Mad·a·gas·car (mædəgæskər) (formerly Malagasy Republic) a socialist republic (area 229,975 sq. miles, pop. 9,389,000) occupying Madagascar and adjacent islets. Capital: Tananarive. People: Malagasy (of Malay and Melanesian origin, with African admixture), small French, Comorian, Indian, Chinese and Arab minorities. Languages: Malagasy, French. Religion: Animist with Roman Catholic, Protestant and Moslem minorities. The Central Plateau (2,500–4,500 ft) covers two thirds of the island. Three major massifs stand out: Andringitra in the south, Ankaratra (8,674 ft) in the center, and the Tsaratanana (9,450 ft) in the north. The eastern coastal strip (30 miles wide), characterized by eroded hills and dunes, contains lagoons linked by the Canal des Pangalanes. The west is a region of plains and low plateaus (60–120 miles wide). Most of the island is tropical grassland, though in the southwest semi-desert conditions prevail. Average temperatures (F.): Tananarive (4,060 ft) 65°, Tamatave 75°, Majunga 80°. Rainfall: Tananarive 53 ins, Majunga 65 ins, Tamatave 118 ins. The economic structure is based on large plantations. Livestock: cattle, goats, sheep, pigs. Minerals: mica, graphite, phosphates, quartz, ilmenite, zircon, beryl, columbite, gold, coal, uranium. Industries: textiles, metalworking, light manufactures, meat preserving, cement, foodstuffs, rum. Exports: coffee, vanilla, sugar, rice, tobacco, cloves, raffia, peanuts, perfumes, meat, minerals. Crops: manioc, corn, sweet potatoes, coconuts, sisal, fruit, cotton, vegetables. Imports: vehicles, metals, textiles, chemicals, cement, fuel, foodstuffs, electrical appliances, machinery, clothing. Chief ports: Tamatave, Diégo Suarez, Majunga. University: Tananarive (1961). Monetary unit: franc CFA. HISTORY. Populated by Melanesians, Malays and Africans, and known to the Arabs since the 12th c., Madagascar was visited (16th c.) by Portuguese, French and English navigators. French colonization began (18th c.), but clashed (early 19th c.) with native rulers. After a war (1883–5), the entire island became a French protectorate (1895) and a colony (1896). It was occupied (1942–3) by the British. The French gave Madagascar limited representative government (1946), and put down a nationalist revolt (1947). As the Malagasy Republic, the island became an autonomous republic within the French Community (1958) and gained full independence (June 25, 1960) within the Community. It became a one-party socialist republic in 1975

mad·am (mædəm) *n.* (*pl.* **mes·dames,** meidǽm) a polite title used in addressing a woman || (*pl.* **mad·ams**) a woman in charge of a brothel [O.E. *ma dame,* my lady]

madame (mædəm, mədǽm, medǽm) *pl.* **mes·dames** (meidǽm, meidǽm) a courtesy title for a married Frenchwoman (the equivalent of 'Mrs') || a courtesy title for a married woman who is neither American nor English [F.]

mad·cap (mædkæp) **1.** *n.* someone given to capricious behavior conspicuously lacking prudence **2.** *adj.* (of a person or action) foolishly impulsive

mad·den (mæd'n) *v.t.* to make mad

mad·der (mædər) *n.* a usually red dye, originally made from the root of any of several Old World plants of genus *Rubia,* fam. *Rubiaceae,* esp. *R. tinctorum* || any of the plants from which this dye is obtained || the root of any of these plants [O.E. *mædere*]

made *past* and *past part.* of MAKE || *adj.* constructed in a specified way, a strongly *made swing* || certain to achieve success, esp. material success, *he'll be a made man* || not natural, *made fur* **made for** destined or as though destined for, *the role was made for him*

Ma·dei·ra (mədíərə) a mountainous, subtropical Portuguese island (area 280 sq. miles, pop. 265,000) in the Atlantic about 360 miles west of Morocco. Capital: Funchal. Highest point: Pico Ruivo (6,056 ft). Products: Madeira wine, sugar, fruit, fish, wicker furniture, embroidery. Madeira was settled (early 15th c.) by the Portuguese. It was occupied by the British (1801, 1807–14)

Madeira the main tributary (900 miles long, navigable for 800 miles) of the Amazon, in N.W. Brazil

Ma·dei·ra (mədíərə) *n.* a fortified wine produced on the island of Madeira

mad·e·moi·selle (mædəmzél, mædmwəzél) *n.* a courtesy title for an unmarried French girl or woman (the equivalent of 'Miss') || a courtesy title for an unmarried girl or woman who is neither American nor English

Ma·de·ro (mɑðéro), Francisco Indalecio (1873–1913), Mexican statesman, leader of the revolutionary movement which overthrew (1911) Porfirio Díaz. He was president of the Republic (1911–13). He and his vice-president Pino Suárez were assassinated (1913) by followers of Victoriano Huerta

made-to-or·der (méidtuːɔ́rdər) *adj.* made to individual requirements (cf. READY-MADE)

made-up (méidʌp) *adj.* based on imaginary things or events, not on facts || wearing makeup

mad·house (mædhaus) *pl.* **mad·hous·es** (mædhauziz) *n.* (*pop.*) a mental hospital || (*pop.*) a scene of uproar or confusion

Ma·dhya Pra·desh (mʌ́djəprədéiʃ) (until 1950 Central Provinces and Berar) a state (area 171,217 sq. miles, pop. 51,230,000) of central India, comprising three upland areas separated by plains. Capital: Bhopal. Crops: cereals, cotton, tobacco. Industries: forestry, mining (coal, manganese, iron), paper, steel, cottage industries (textiles, leatherwork)

Mad·i·son (mædis'n), Dolley Payne (1768–1849) U.S. first lady, wife of Pres. James Madison. She was White House hostess for widower Pres. Thomas Jefferson before her husband came into office (1809–17). When the British attacked Washington, D.C. in 1814, she was responsible for saving important papers and valuables

Madison (mædis'n), James (1751–1836), fourth president (1809–17) of the U.S.A., a Democratic Republican. He was a member of the Continental Congress (1780–3, 1787–8), and greatly influenced the form of the U.S. Constitution (1789). He vigorously sought support for the Constitution and contributed to the Federalist Papers. He served (1801–9) as secretary of state under President Thomas Jefferson. Under his administration, the provocations of the 'war hawks' largely precipitated the War of 1812. He witnessed the burning (1814) of the White House by the British

Madison the capital (pop. 170,616) of Wisconsin. Industries: food processing, engineering, chemicals. University of Wisconsin (1849)

mad·man (mædmæn, mædmən) *pl.* **mad·men** (mædmen, mædmən) *n.* a man who is insane or acts as if he were

ma·don·na (mədónə) *n.* a statue or picture of the Virgin Mary [Ital.=my lady]

Ma·dras *TAMIL NADU

ma·dras (mædrəs, mədrʌs, mædrəs) *n.* a fine fabric, esp. of cotton, originally made in Madras, India || a light, open fabric, esp. of cotton, with heavy woolen designs, used for curtains

mad·re·pore (mædrəpɔr, mædrəpour) *n.* any of several tropical corals of order *Madreporaria,* forming the chief constituent of coral reefs. They are usually colonial, and always have an ectodermal calcareous skeleton **mad·re·pór·ite** *n.* (*zool.*) the perforated plate at the distal end of the stone canal in echinoderms [fr. Mod. L. *Madrepora* or F. *madrépore*]

Ma·drid (mədríd) the capital (pop. 3,274,000) and commercial center of Spain. Industries: engineering, light manufacturing. Few monuments date from before the 18th c. The Prado (1785), the national museum, contains one of the greatest painting collections in Europe. University (founded at Alcalá de Henares in 1508, moved to Madrid in 1836). A Moorish fortress (10th c.), Madrid was captured (1083) by Castile, and became (1561) the capital of Spain || the province (area 3,084 sq. miles, pop. 3,860,000) of which it is the capital (*NEW CASTILE)

Madrid, Treaty of an agreement (1670) between England and Spain to revoke all letters of marque and to abstain from pillage. Spain also recognized England's possessions in the West Indies, including Jamaica

mad·ri·gal (mædrig'l) *n.* (*mus.*) a contrapuntal secular composition for several voices, either unaccompanied or with instrumental doubling or replacing of one or more parts. The madrigal was widely current in 16th-c. and 17th-c. Europe as a revival of a 14th-c. Italian form || a short medieval poem, usually a love poem, suitable for being set to music [fr. Ital. *madrigale*]

ma·dro·ña laurel (mədróunjə) *ARBUTUS

Mad·u·ra (mædurə, mədjúərə) an island (area 1,770 sq. miles, pop. 2,500,000) off N.E. Java, Indonesia, heavily populated: agriculture,

CONCISE PRONUNCIATION KEY: **(a)** æ, c*a*t; ɑ, c*a*r; ɔ f*aw*n; ei, sn*a*ke. **(e)** e, h*e*n; i:, sh*ee*p; iə, d*ee*r; ɛə, b*ea*r. **(i)** i, f*i*sh; ai, t*ig*er; əː, b*ir*d. **(o)** o, *o*x; au, c*ow*; ou, g*oa*t; u, p*oo*r; ɔi, r*oy*al. **(u)** ʌ, d*u*ck; u, b*u*ll; uː, g*oo*se; ə, b*a*cillus; juː, c*u*be. x, lo*ch*; θ, *th*ink; δ, bo*th*er; z, *Z*en; ʒ, cor*s*age; dʒ, sa*v*age; ŋ, ora*ng*utang; j, *y*ak; ʃ, *fi*sh; tʃ, fe*tch*; 'l, rabb*le*; 'n, redd*en*. Complete pronunciation key appears inside front cover.

fishing, cattle raising, salt mining. Chief town: Pamekasan

Mad·u·rai (mædjurai) (formerly Madura) a town (pop. 549,114) of Madras, India: textiles, brasswork, woodcarving, agricultural machinery. Brahmanic temple (16th–17th cc.)

Mad·u·rese (mædəri:z, mædəri:s) pl. **Mad·u·rese** n. a member of an Indonesian people of Madura ‖ the Austronesian language of this people

mad·wom·an (mædwumən) pl. **mad·wom·en** (mædwimən) n. a woman who is insane or acts as if she were

Mae·ba·shi (mæbáʃi:) a town (pop. 199,000) in central Honshu, Japan: silk

Mae·ce·nas (mi:síːnəs) n. a lavish patron of literature or art [after Gaius Cilnius *Maecenas* (c. 69 B.C.–8 B.C.), friend and adviser of the emperor Augustus and patron of Horace and Virgil]

mael·strom (méilstrəm) n. a large and dangerous whirlpool ‖ (rhet.) a turbulent situation [after the *Maelstrom*, a whirlpool off the west coast of Norway]

mae·nad (mí:næd) n. (hist.) a bacchante **mae·nád·ic** adj. [fr. L. *Maenas* (*Maenadis*) fr. Gk]

ma·es·to·so (mæstóuzou) 1. adj. (mus.) stately and in moderate tempo 2. adv. (mus.) in a stately manner and in moderate tempo [Ital.=majestic]

Maestricht * MAASTRICHT

maes·tro (máistrou, mɑéstrɔ) pl. **maes·tros**, **ma·es·tri** (mɑéstri:) n. a great musical conductor, composer or teacher ‖ a master in any art [Ital.=master]

Mae·ter·linck (méitərliŋk, meterlɛ̃k), Comte Maurice (1864–1949), Belgian poet, dramatist and essayist. His works include the plays 'Pelléas and Mélisande' (1892) and 'The Blue Bird' (1908), and the essay 'The Life of the Bee' (1901)

Mae West (méiwést) an inflatable life jacket used by airmen [after *Mae West* (1892–1980), U.S. film actress]

Maf·e·king (mǽfəkiŋ) a town (pop. 27,728) of Cape Province, South Africa, where a British force under Baden-Powell was besieged (1899–1900) during the Boer War for seven months and successfully relieved

Maf·fei galaxy (astron.) one of two celestial galaxies nearest earth

Ma·fi·a, Maf·fi·a (mɑ́fi:ə) n. a network of secret societies imposing its own justice instead of the official administration in Sicily (19th and 20th cc.) ‖ a worldwide criminal organization ‖ by extension, any clique or exclusive ethnic or nonethnic group with power in a special field, e.g., Irish mafia, musical mafia [Ital. (Sicilian dial.)=swagger, bluster]

Ma·ga·dan (məgədán) a seaport (pop. 62,000) on the northern shore of the Sea of Okhotsk, E. Siberia, U.S.S.R.

Ma·ga·dhi (mɑ́gədi) n. one of the Prakrit languages of India

Ma·ga·lhães (məgəljéi:s) *MAGELLAN

ma·ga·zine (mægəzí:n) n. a paperback periodical publication of writings by different authors, often illustrated and with advertisements ‖ a storage place for arms, ammunition and explosives ‖ a receptacle for cartridges which are to be fed into the breech of a rifle, machine gun etc., or for films or plates to be fed into some cameras [F. *magasin* fr. Arab.]

Mag·da·len (mǽgdələn) (or Magdalene) Mary of Magdala (Luke viii, 2), the disciple of Christ identified with the 'sinner' of Luke vii, 37. She is traditionally represented as a penitent prostitute

Mag·da·le·na (mægdəlí:nə, mɑgðɑléna) a river (1,060 miles long) of Colombia, flowing north from the E. Andes to the Caribbean

Mag·da·le·ne (mægdəlí:ni) *MAGDALEN

Mag·da·le·ni·an (mægdəlí:ni:ən) adj. of the last Paleolithic epoch, associated with Cro-Magnon man and characterized by bone and ivory carving and by the perfection of cave art [after *La Madeleine* in S.W. France]

Magdalen Islands an island group comprising nine main islands and many islets (area 102 sq. miles, pop. 14,130) in the Gulf of St Lawrence, Canada. Most of the inhabitants are Acadians

Mag·de·burg (mǽgdəbəːrg) a port (pop. 283,548) on the Elbe in East Germany. Industries: metallurgy, chemicals, textiles, mechanical engineering. Gothic cathedral (13th c.). Magdeburg was the site of a bloody siege led by Tilly during the Thirty Years' War (1631) resulting in a victory for the Catholic League ‖

the district (area 2,986 sq. miles, pop. 1,373,000) including it (*SAXONYANHALT)

Magdeburg hemispheres *GUERICKE

Ma·gel·lan (mədʒélən), Ferdinand (Port. Fernão de Magalhães, c. 1489–1521), Portuguese navigator. Sailing with five ships from Spain (Sept. 20, 1519), he reached the coast of South America and navigated (1520) the strait which now bears his name. He crossed the Pacific to the Philippines, where he was killed by natives. One of his ships, commanded by del Cano, returned to Spain (Sept. 6, 1522), and so was the first to circumnavigate the globe

Magellan, Strait of a strait (370 miles long, 2½–15 miles wide) between the tip of South America and Tierra del Fuego, linking the Atlantic and the Pacific

ma·gen·ta (mədʒéntə) 1. n. a brilliant, bluish-red aniline dye, $C_{20}H_{22}N_3OCl$, prepared from aniline and toluidine ‖ the color of this dye 2. adj. having this color [after *Magenta*, Italy]

Ma·gen·ta, Battle of (mədʒéntə) a French and Sardinian victory (1859) over Austrian forces in northern Italy

Mag·gio·re (maddʒɔ́re) a lake (area 81 sq. miles) formed by River Ticino at the southern edge of the Alps, in southern Switzerland and N. Italy

mag·got (mǽgət) n. an insect larva, e.g. that of the housefly, without appendages or distinct head **mag·got·y** adj. [M.E. etym. doubtful]

Ma·ghreb (mágrib) the Arabic name for extreme N.W. Africa, incl. Morocco, Algeria, Tunisia and sometimes Libya

magi pl. of MAGUS

mag·ic (mǽdʒik) n. the art which claims to control and manipulate the secret forces of nature by occult and ritualistic methods ‖ the practice of this art ‖ any mysterious power or phenomenon which defies analysis or explanation ‖ the art or practice of producing illusions etc. by sleight of hand [fr. O.F. *magique*]

magic adj. of, relating to, used in or produced by magic ‖ having an effect like one produced by magic **mag·i·cal** adj. [F. *magique*]

magic acid (chem.) acid formed by antimony pentafluoride dissolved in fluorosulphonic acid that readily loses an ion to an alkali

ma·gi·cian (mədʒíʃən) n. a person who practices magic [F. *magicien*]

magic lantern an early form of projector, throwing an enlarged image of a transparency on a white screen

Magic Marker trade name for device with felt tip and quick drying ink, used in package marking, drawing, etc.

magic number 1. the marginal number that assures winning in a series of games 2. (phys.) a number indicating stability in a proton or neutron count

Magic Phones trade name for Japanese electronic device that deactivates mechanism recording incoming calls, enabling caller to avoid any charge

magic square a square containing numbers so arranged that when added along any row, column or diagonal they have the same sum

magilp *MEGILP

Ma·gi·not line (mǽʒinou) a series of French fortifications built (1927–36) along France's eastern frontier from Switzerland to Belgium. Thought to be impregnable, it was turned by the Germans when they invaded France (1940) through Belgium [after André *Maginot* (1877–1932), war minister]

mag·is·te·ri·al (mædʒistíəri:əl) adj. of or relating to a magistrate or his office ‖ authoritative, made or done with masterly skill [fr. M.L. *magisterialis*]

mag·is·tra·cy (mǽdʒistrəsi:) pl. **mag·is·tra·cies** n. the office, acts, authority etc. of a magistrate ‖ a group of magistrates ‖ the district under a magistrate

mag·is·trate (mǽdʒistreit, mǽdʒistrit) n. an inferior judicial officer, esp. a civil justice of the peace ‖ (broadly) a civil legislative or executive officer [fr. L. *magistratus* fr. *magister*, master]

magistrates' court (Br.) a local court with criminal jurisdiction, dealing with lesser offenses and presided over by a magistrate or magistrates. It passes more serious crimes to the quarter sessions. It also has jurisdiction over various local civil and administrative matters

mag·is·tra·ture (mǽdʒistreitʃər, mǽdʒistrətʃuər) n. the general body or system of magistrates and their functions ‖ the term of office of a magistrate [F.]

mag·is·trel (mǽdʒistrəl) adj. (pharm., of a prescription) specially prepared, not included in a pharmacopoeia (cf. OFFICINAL) [F. or fr. L. *magistralis*, of a master]

mag·lev (mǽglev) n. a flying train using magnetic force to levitate an entire train achieving 300 mph, raised by on-board magnets chilled with liquid helium to a superconducting state

mag·ma (mǽgmə) n. a thin paste consisting of a crude mixture of mineral or organic matter ‖ (geol.) the viscous molten matter beneath the earth's solid crust, forming igneous rocks when it cools and crystallizes ‖ (pharm.) a suspension of a precipitated substance in a liquid **mag·mat·ic** (mægmǽtik) adj. [L. fr. Gk *magma* fr. *massein*, to knead]

Mag·na Car·ta, Mag·na Char·ta (mǽgnəkɑ́rtə) a feudal charter of liberties issued (1215) at Runnymede by King John under the coercion of the barons and a group of churchmen under Langton. The charter attempted to protect the rights of the barony against encroachment by the royal prerogative. The barons, angry at royal attempts to increase feudal dues, raised an armed rebellion and forced John to accede to the charter. He repudiated it immediately afterwards, but it was reissued (1216 and 1217) by Henry III and regularly confirmed by later kings. Its interpretation as the touchstone of English liberty dates from the 17th c., when parliamentarians tried to read into it the principles of trial by jury and of no taxation without representation

Mag·na Grae·ci·a (mǽgnəgrí:ʃi:ə) the Greek colonies in S. Italy (8th–4th cc. B.C.)

mag·na·nim·i·ty (mægnənímiti:) pl. **mag·na·nim·i·ties** n. the quality of being magnanimous ‖ a magnanimous action [F. *magnanimité*]

mag·nan·i·mous (mægnǽnim008, adj. generously and benevolently overlooking faults, not subject to resentment, envy etc. [fr. L. *magnanimus*]

mag·nate (mǽgneit, mǽgnit) n. a person of great prominence and wealth, esp. someone important in big business or industry, a cotton magnate [fr. L. L. *magnas* (*magnatis*) fr. *magnus*, great]

mag·ne·sia (mægní:ʒə, mægní:ʃə) n. a white low-melting solid oxide of magnesium (MgO), that occurs naturally or is obtained by calcining the carbonates of magnesium. It is used in the manufacture of refractories, in medicine as a mild laxative and antacid, and in the manufacture of fertilizer and chemicals **mag·né·sian** adj. [fr. M.L. *magnesia* fr. Gk *Magnesia lithos*, the Magnesian stone, after *Magnesia* in Thessaly]

mag·ne·site (mǽgnisait) n. magnesium carbonate, $MgCO_3$, a mineral usually occurring in white masses and used in the manufacture of refractories, chemicals and fertilizers [F. *magnésite*]

mag·ne·sium (mægní:ʒəm, mægní:zi:əm) n. a light divalent silvery metallic element (symbol Mg, at. no. 12, at. wt. 24.312) that occurs in nature in combination only(esp. as the carbonates magnesite and dolomite and as the chloride carnallite) in sea water, plants and animals (e.g. in chlorophyll and animal bones). It is obtained chiefly by electrolysis of its fused salts (often the chlorides). It is used structurally, alloyed with aluminum, e.g. in aircraft, and in many other ways (*EPSOM SALTS, *MILK OF MAGNESIA) [MAGNESIA]

magnesium carbonate $MgCO_3$, a white powder used in the manufacture of inks, dentifrice, cosmetics and many other products

magnesium hydroxide $Mg(OH)_2$, a white powder used as an antacid and as a laxative

magnesium sulfate $MgSO_4$, a white crystalline compound used in medicine and in textile processing, matches, explosives etc.

mag·net (mǽgnit) n. a piece of steel, iron, cobalt, nickel or alloy exhibiting ferromagnetism ‖ the magnetized needle of a compass ‖ the soft-iron core and surrounding coil of an electromagnet ‖ something or someone exerting a powerful attraction [O.F. *magnete* fr. L. fr. Gk]

mag·net·ic (mægnétik) adj. of or relating to a magnet or to magnetism ‖ taking the north magnetic pole as reference ‖ (esp. of a ferromagnetic substance) magnetized or capable of being magnetized ‖ strongly attractive, a magnetic personality **mag·nét·i·cal·ly** adv. [fr. Mod. L. *magneticus*]

magnetic amplifier a device consisting of one or more ferromagnetic cores with windings arranged in such a way as to allow modulations of an amplified amplitude of an alternating current flowing in one winding by a direct or low-frequency alternating current flowing in another winding

magnetic bottle (*nuclear phys.*) the magnetic field that confines plasma in a thermonuclear reaction

magnetic bubble (*computer*) a small mobile region of magnetism on which great amounts of data may be stored magnetically, designed to replace the computer chip

magnetic card a plastic card containing a magnetized strip, usu. for identification; used as credit cards, bank machine cards, commuter tickets, keys for electronic locks

magnetic compass a compass consisting of a suspended or pivoted magnetic needle that responds to the earth's magnetic field, lining up with the magnetic poles (cf. GYROCOMPASS)

magnetic core (*computer*) a ferrous coil of doughnut-shaped units used as a storage system *also* **core**

magnetic declination *DECLINATION (compass angle)

magnetic disk (*computer*) a coated disk used to record data for storage *Cf* DISC

mag·net·ic·en·ceph·a·lo·gram (mægnętikenséfəlŏgræm) *n.* (*med.*) a chart of the brain's magnetic field *abbr.* **MEG**

magnetic equator *ACLINIC LINE

magnetic field a region of space, surrounding a moving charge (e.g. in a conductor) or a magnetic pole, in which a moving charge or magnetic pole experiences a force. This force is over and above the purely electrostatic ones associated with charged particles at rest. A magnetic field exerts a force on a charged particle only if it is in motion, and charged particles produce magnetic fields only when they are in motion

magnetic flux the product of the area of a surface and the average normal component of the magnetic intensity over that surface, usually expressed in maxwells or webers

magnetic flux density magnetic induction

magnetic inclination dip (angle between the direction of the earth's magnetic field and the horizontal)

magnetic induction the magnetic flux passing through unit area of a magnetic field perpendicular to the direction of the magnetic force

$$\left(\text{mks unit} = \frac{\text{Weber}}{\text{m}^2} \right)$$

‖ the induction of magnetism in a body in a magnetic field or in the flux established by a magnetomotive force

magnetic intensity a vector quantity associated with any point in a magnetic field giving the force that would act on a unit north magnetic pole placed at that point in a vacuum

magnetic meridian any line, approximating a great circle, passing through the north and south magnetic poles. A magnetic compass needle aligns itself along this

magnetic mine a submarine mine triggered by the magnetic attraction of a metal vessel ‖ a mine that responds to the magnetic field of a target

magnetic minehunting (*mil.*) the process of using magnetic detectors to determine the presence of mines or minelike objects

magnetic moment a vector quantity whose vector product with the intensity of the surrounding magnetic field gives the torque on a magnet, a current-bearing conductor or a magnetic dipole

magnetic north the direction towards which the north-seeking pole of a compass needle points, i.e. the direction of the magnetic meridian at any point on the earths surface (cf. NORTH POLE)

magnetic nuclear resonance magnetic resonance (which see)

magnetic permeability (symbol [μ]) the ratio of the density of magnetic flux in a body to the strength of the magnetic field which induces it. The absolute permeability of free space, in the electromagnetic system of units, is unity. The permeability of a substance relative to free space is given by the ratio of magnetic flux density in the material to that in a vacuum when both are produced by the same field. The relative permeability for ferromagnetic substances is usually much larger than unity, that for paramagnetic substances close to but greater than unity and that for diamagnetic substances less than unity but greater than zero

magnetic pole a pole of a magnet ‖ one of the two regions on the earth's surface, not identical with the geographical poles, at which the dip is 90°

magnetic recorder an electronic apparatus that converts sound (speech, music etc.) into electrical signals and then into variations in the magnetization of a wire or tape of magnetic material. The sound may be reproduced by passing the tape through a system functioning in an inverse sense. The recording on the tape is permanent if not intentionally or accidentally erased. A similar system has been devised for operation with a television camera, recording television pictures as magnetic information which may be used later to reproduce the images (*VIDEO TAPE)

magnetic resonance (*phys.*) the phenomenon in which spin systems absorb energy when certain spin frequencies are synchronized with alternating magnetic frequencies *syn.* spin resonance

mag·net·ics (mægnétiks) *n.* the science of magnetism

magnetic storm a marked amount of natural disturbance in the earth's magnetic field. Magnetic storms seem to be related to solar activity, although detailed correlations have not been found (*SUNSPOT CYCLE)

magnetic susceptibility the ratio of the magnetization (i.e. magnetic moment per unit volume) in a substance to the corresponding magnetizing force (cf. MAGNETIC PERMEABILITY)

magnetic variation declination (compass angle)

mag·net·ism (mægnitizəm) *n.* a group of physical phenomena associated with the interaction of a magnetic field with matter. The field arises either from the movement of electrical charges in conductors or, in the case of natural and artificial permanent magnets, from a property of the magnetic substance (the presence of magnetic poles). All substances experience some force in a magnetic field, the direction and magnitude of the force serving to distinguish between three types of magnetic effect: diamagnetism, paramagnetism and ferromagnetism (*MAGNETIC PERMEABILITY) ‖ the study of the behavior and effects of magnetic fields ‖ (*fig.*) the ability to attract by personal charm

mag·net·ite (mægnitait) *n.* a black iron spinel (FeOFe₂O₃) that is an important iron ore and is sometimes naturally magnetic [fr. G. *magnetit*]

mag·net·i·za·tion (mægnitizéiʃən) *n.* a magnetizing or being magnetized ‖ intensity of magnetic force measured by magnetic moment per unit volume

mag·net·ize (mægnitaiz) *pres. part.* **mag·net·iz·ing** *past* and *past part.* **mag·net·ized** *v.t.* to make (something) magnetic ‖ to exert an irresistible influence upon [MAGNET]

mag·ne·to (mægni:tou) *n.* a small dynamo fitted with a spark coil, used to generate current for the ignition in an internal-combustion engine [fr. Gk *magnēs* (*magnētos*), magnet]

mag·ne·to·car·di·o·graph (mægni:toukɔ́rdi:ougræf) *n.* (*med.*) device used to record cardiac action in the magnetic field around the heart — **magnetocardiogram** *n.* the tracing

mag·ne·to·chem·is·try (mægni:toukémistri:) *n.* the study of the effects of magnetism on chemical change

mag·ne·to·gas·dy·nam·ics (mægni:tougæsdainǽmiks) *n.* (*phys.*) study of interaction between plasma movement and magnetic fields *also* **magnetohydrodynamics**

mag·ne·to·hy·dro·dy·nam·ics (mægni:touhaidroudainǽmiks) *n.* the branch of physics that studies the behavior of plasmas in the presence of electric and magnetic fields

mag·ne·tom·i·ter (mægnitómitər) *n.* an instrument used for comparing the strengths of magnetic fields and magnetic moments

mag·ne·to·mo·tive force (mægni:toumóutiv) a force that is the cause of magnetic flux being given by the integral along the line or circuit of the intensity of the magnetic field

mag·ne·to·op·tics (mægni:touóptiks) *n.* the science of the effect of a magnetic field on the behavior of light, esp. its polarization (*FARADAY EFFECT)

mag·ne·to·pause (mægni:təpɔz) *n.* outer boundary of earth's magnetic field (c. 40,000 mi.) where interplanetary magnetic field begins

mag·ne·to·plas·ma·dy·nam·ic (mægni:touplæz-

mədainǽmik) *adj.* of the use of ionized gas in a magnetic field to produce electric current — **magnetoplasmadynamics** *n.*

mag·ne·to·sphere (mægni:təsfjər) *n.* the region of the magnetic field surrounding a celestial body —**magnetospheric** *adj.*

mag·ne·to·stric·tion (mægni:toustrík∫ən) *n.* the change in the dimensions of a ferromagnetic body when placed in a magnetic field or when magnetized by the application of a suitable stress

mag·ne·to·tel·lur·ic (mægni:toutəlúərik) *adj.* of the earth's magnetic areas

magnet program program designed to attract white students to a predominantly black school

mag·ne·tron (mægnitrɒn) *n.* any of several types of vacuum diode in which the electrons coming from the cathode follow a path which varies periodically in curvature (i.e. the electrons are alternately accelerated and decelerated), due to the interaction of a radiofrequency electric field and a constant magnetic field. The velocity-modulated anode current is fed to the oscillatory circuit generating the radiofrequency field, thus maintaining and amplifying the oscillations in the oscillatory circuit. The tube is used to generate power in the microwave region, esp. for use in radar [MAGNET+ELECTRON]

mag·ni·cide (mægnəsaid) *n.* murder of someone of importance

Mag·nif·i·cat (mægnífikæt) *n.* the utterance of the Virgin Mary to Elizabeth (Luke i, 46–55, *VISITATION, THE) ‖ a musical setting of this used in certain church services [L. *Magnificat anima mea Dominum*, my soul doth magnify the Lord]

mag·ni·fi·ca·tion (mægnifikéiʃən) *n.* (*phys.*) the act or process of apparently changing the dimensions of an object by optical methods, often measured by the ratio of the apparent linear dimensions to the corresponding actual ones, or the ratio of the angle subtended at the eye by the magnified image to the angle subtended there by the object ‖ the ability to be apparently changed in this way ‖ (*rhet.*) a celebrating with praise [fr. L. *magnificatio* (*magnificationis*)]

mag·nif·i·cence (mægnífis'ns) *n.* the quality of being magnificent ‖ an instance of this[F.]

mag·nif·i·cent (mægnífis'nt) *adj.* so splendid, lavish, beautiful etc. as to arouse admiration and wonder [O.F.]

mag·ni·fi·er (mægnifaiər) *n.* a magnifying glass

mag·ni·fy (mægnifai) *pres. part.* **mag·ni·fy·ing** *past* and *past part.* **mag·ni·fied** *v.t.* to make (something) appear larger or more important than it is, *he is inclined to magnify the difficulties* ‖ (*phys.*) to make (an object) look larger by substituting for it an image which subtends a wider angle at the eye ‖ (*rhet.*) to celebrate with praise, laud ‖ *v.i.* to increase or be able to increase the size of the appearance of an object [fr. L. *magnificare*]

magnifying glass a lens (e.g. a plano-convex lens of short focal length) producing a magnified visual image

magnifying power (esp. of visual instruments) magnification

mag·nil·o·quence (mægníləkwəns) *n.* the quality of being magniloquent

mag·nil·o·quent (mægníləkwənt) *adj.* (of language) richly ornamented with extravagant adjectives or phrases, highflown [fr. L. *magniloquus*]

mag·nis·tor (mægnístər) *n.* (*electr.*) any device that utilizes the effect of a magnetic field on injection plasma, esp. in a semiconductor

magnitizdat *SAMIZDAT

Mag·ni·to·gorsk (mægnjitɒgórsk) a city (pop. 406,000) of the R.S.F.S.R., U.S.S.R. at the southeastern end of the Urals: iron and steel, rubber, chemicals, metallurgy

mag·ni·tude (mægnitu:d, mægnitju:d) *n.* size ‖ largeness in size or number ‖ importance ‖ (*astron.*) a number designating the relative brightness of a star on a scale where a star of magnitude +1.00 is exactly 2.512 times brighter than a star of magnitude 2.00 and 6.25 times brighter than a star of magnitude 3.00 etc. The range of brightness has been extended photographically to about 24 magnitudes (a factor of 10¹⁴ in brightness) ‖ (*math.*) a number denoting the relative measure of a quantity [fr. L. *magnitudo*]

mag·nol·ia (mægnóuljə) *n.* a member of *Magnolia*, fam. *Magnoliaceae*, a genus of trees and shrubs native to Asia and North America, having large alternate leaves and large terminal white, pink or yellowish waxy flowers [Mod. L. after Pierre *Magnol* (1638–1715), F. botanist]

mag·non (mǽgnən) *n.* (*nuclear phys.*) 1. a quasiparticle created to describe the deviation of a nuclear spin in a magnetic field 2. a measure of the amount of spin wave energy in an elementary particle *syn.* quantized spin wave

mag·nox (mǽgnɒks) *n.* British nuclear reactor utilizing natural uranium enclosed in magnesium alloy cans for fuel

mag·num (mǽgnəm) *n.* a bottle for wine or liquor, holding two quarts ‖ the amount held by such a bottle [L. neut. sing. of *magnus* adj., great]

magnum opus *n.* the best achievement of an artist ‖ a great work of art [L.=great work]

mag·nus hitch (mǽgnəs) a knot used to hitch a line to a spar etc. [etym. doubtful]

Ma·goon (məgú:n), Charles Edward (1861–1920), U.S. administrator. After preparing (1904) laws for the Panama Canal Zone, he became (1905) its first governor and minister to Panama. Serving (1906–9) as provisional governor of Cuba, he reorganized Cuban affairs and returned (1909) the government to the people under the leadership of José Miguel Gómez

mag·pie (mǽgpai) *n.* a member of *Pica*, a genus of birds of the crow family, usually having black and white plumage and a long tail, living in Asia, Europe, N. Africa and North America. They are known for their thievery and loud chatter ‖ a chatterbox [fr. *Mag*, dim. of Margaret+PIE (magpie)]

Mag·say·say (magsáisai), Ramón (1907–57), Philippine soldier and political leader who, as secretary of defense and third president (1953–7), defeated the communist-led Hukbalahap (Huk) movement after the 2nd world war

mag·uey (mǽgwei) *n.* any plant belonging to the genera *Agave* and *Furcraea*, esp. the century plant [Span. fr. Haitian]

ma·gus (méigəs) *pl.* **ma·gi** (méidʒai) *n.* (*hist.*) a member of the priestly caste of ancient Persia, a Zoroastrian priest **Má·gus** one of the three wise men (Matthew ii) who brought gifts and paid homage to the infant Jesus at Bethlehem (*EPIPHANY) [L.]

Mag·yar (mǽgjɑr) 1. *n.* a member of the originally Ural-Altaic people who settled in Hungary in the 9th c. ‖ the Hungarian language 2. *adj.* of or pertaining to the people of Hungary, or to their language

Ma·ha·ba·li·pu·ram (məhúbəli:púərəm) (or Mamallapuram), a group of 7th-c. Hindu carved monuments near Madras in S. India, sometimes called 'The Seven Pagodas'

Ma·ha·bha·ra·ta (məhǽbúrətə) one of the two great Sanskrit poems of Hinduism (*RAMAYANA). Its 100,000 couplets tell of the struggles between rival factions of the Bharata clan, incorporating a large amount of legend, history and philosophy (*BHAGAVAD-GITA). A variety of writers appear to have added to the poem between 500 B.C. and 500 A.D.

Ma·hal·la el Ku·bra (məhǽləelkú:brə) a town (pop. 293,000) in the Nile delta, Egypt: cotton, textiles

Ma·han (məhǽn), Alfred Thayer (1840–1914), U.S. naval officer and historian. His 'The Influence of Sea Power upon History, 1660–1783' (1890) and 'The Influence of Sea Power upon the French Revolution and Empire, 1793–1812' (1892) maintained that control of the sea was the decisive factor in warfare

Ma·ha·na·di (məhánədi:) a river flowing 550 miles from S.E. Madhya Pradesh, India, to the Bay of Bengal, used for extensive irrigation

ma·ha·ra·ja, ma·ha·ra·jah (mɑhərɑ́dʒə) *n.* a Hindu prince ranking above a raja, esp. a ruler of one of certain native states of India [Hindi]

ma·ha·ra·nee, ma·ha·ra·ni (mɑhərɑ́ni:) *n.* the wife of a maharaja ‖ a Hindu princess, ranking above a ranee, ruling one of certain Indian states [Hindi]

Ma·ha·rash·tra (məhárɑ́ʃtrə) a state (area 118,717 sq. miles, pop. 57,430,000) on the northwest coast of India. Capital: Bombay. Products: cotton, sugar, millet, textiles

Ma·ha·rash·tri (məhárɑ́ʃtri:) *n.* one of the Prakrit languages of India

ma·ha·ri·shi (məhárəʃi:) *n.* 1. a Hindu religious teacher 2. (capitalized) a guru title

ma·hat·ma (məhátmə) *n.* (in India, and among theosophists) a wise and holy man ‖ (*Buddhism*) one of a class of Indian and Tibetan sages

thought to possess preternatural powers [fr. Skr. *mahátman*, great-souled]

Ma·ha·vi·ra (mɑhəví:rə) *JAINISM

Ma·ha·ya·na Buddhism (mɑhəjánə) *BUDDHISM

Mah·di (mádi:) *n.* the messiah looked for by Moslems ‖ the title assumed by Mohammed Ahmed (1848–85), Sudanese Moslem leader. He led a revolt (1881) against Egyptian rule of the Sudan and he besieged Gordon in Khartoum (1885) ‖ (*hist.*) a title assumed by several Moslem claimants to messiahship **Máh·dist** *n.* [Arab. *mahdiy*, the inspired one]

Ma·hé (mɑhéi) a port (area 23 sq. miles) of Pondicherry on the Malabar Coast, India. It was formerly a French settlement

Ma·he (mɑéi) *SEYCHELLES

Ma·hi·can (mɑhí:kən) *pl.* **Ma·hi·can, Ma·hi·cans** *n.* an Indian people of the upper Hudson River valley and surrounding region ‖ a member of this people ‖ an Algonquian language spoken by this people [Mahican lit.=wolf]

mah·jongg, mah jong (mɑdʒɔŋ, mɑ́ʒɔŋ) *n.* a game of Chinese origin played with 144 little tiles [Chin.=sparrows]

Mah·ler (múlər), Gustav (1860–1911), Austrian composer and conductor. His music, influenced by Bruckner and Wagner, includes nine symphonies (and an uncompleted tenth) of great length, for huge orchestras, often with vocal parts. He also wrote 'The Song of the Earth' (1908), a symphonic song cycle, and over 40 songs

mahlstick *MAULSTICK

Mah·mud of Ghaz·ni (mɑmú:dəvgázni:) (c. 971–c. 1031), Moslem sultan (999–c. 1031) of the Afghan kingdom of Ghazni, which he extended into India (1001–26) and Persia (1029)

ma·hog·a·ny (məhógəni:) *pl.* **ma·hog·a·nies** 1. the wood of any of several trees of fam. *Meliaceae*, esp. the reddish brown wood of the West Indian *Swietonia mahogani*, which takes a high polish and is widely used in cabinetmaking ‖ the color of the wood ‖ a tree producing this wood 2. *adj.* of, pertaining to or made of mahogany ‖ of the dark-reddish-brown color of mahogany [origin unknown]

Ma·hom·et (məhómit) *MOHAMMED

Ma·hom·e·tan (məhómitən) *n.* and *adj.* Mohammedan, Moslem

ma·hout (məháut) *n.* the keeper and driver of a trained elephant [Hindi *mahāut, mahāwat*]

Mahratta *MARATHA

Mahratti *MARATHI

Mai·a (máiə) (*Gk. mythol.*) the daughter of Atlas and mother of Hermes. She was the eldest of the Pleiades

maid (meid) *n.* a female domestic servant ‖ (*rhet.*) a girl ‖ (*rhet.*) a virgin [shortened fr. MAIDEN]

maid·en (méid'n) 1. *n.* (*rhet.*) a girl ‖ (*rhet.*) a virgin ‖ (*cricket*) a maiden over 2. *adj.* (*rhet.*) ‖ (*rhet.*) unmarried ‖ being the first of its kind, *a ship's maiden voyage* ‖ of a horse that has not won a race ‖ of a race open only to such horses [O.E. *mægden*]

Maiden (*mil.*) NATO name for Su-11, U.S.S.R. turbojet fighter adapted from Su-9; operational since 1969

maid·en·hair (méid'nhɛ̞r) *n.* a member of *Adiantum*, a genus of ferns having delicate fronds, esp. *A. capillus-veneris*

maidenhair tree the ginkgo

maid·en·head (méid'nhɛd) *n.* the hymen

maid·en·hood (méid'nhud) *n.* the state of being a maiden ‖ the time of being a maiden

maid·en·ly (méid'nli:) *adj.* of, like or appropriate to a maiden

maiden name a woman's family name before she married

maiden over (*cricket*) an over in which no runs are scored

maid of all work someone or something made to do a wide variety of tasks

maid of honor, *Br.* **maid of honour** an unmarried lady in attendance on a queen or princess ‖ a bride's chief (unmarried) wedding attendant (cf. MATRON OF HONOR)

maid·ser·vant (méidsɛ:rvənt) *n.* (*hist.*) a female servant

Mai·du·gu·ri (maidú:gəri:) a town (pop. 189,000) of North Eastern State, Nigeria: peanuts, hides and skins

ma·ieu·tic (meijú:tik) *adj.* of the method of questioning by which Socrates brought a person to consciousness of latent knowledge [Gk *maieutikos* fr. *maieusthai* fr. *maia*, midwife]

mai·gre (méigər) *adj.* (of a day) prescribed for fasting ‖ (of food) not containing flesh or its juices, and thus suitable for a fast day [F.=lean]

Mai·kop (máikɒp) a city (pop. 128,000) of the R.S.F.S.R., U.S.S.R., in N.W. Caucasia. It is the center of a rich oil-bearing district

mail (meil) *collect. n.* (*hist.*) armor composed of interlocking rings or chains or of overlapping plates ‖ (*zool.*) a hard protective covering, e.g. of a lobster [F. *maille*, mesh]

mail 1. *n.* the public organization dealing with the collection and delivery of correspondence and other postal matter ‖ the letters and parcels sent by this organization 2. *v.t.* to send by this organization [M.E. *male*, a bag fr. O.F. fr. Gmc]

mail·bag (méilbæg) *n.* a sack for shipment or delivery of mail

mail·box (méilbɒks) *n.* a box, provided by the public organization dealing with the mail, into which people drop their letters for dispatch ‖ a box into which letters etc. delivered to an address are placed

mail cover examination of, and notation of information from, the unopened mail of a person under surveillance

Mai·ler (méilər), Norman (1923–   ), U.S. novelist, best known for his 'The Naked and the Dead' (1948), which presents a horrifying account of modern warfare. 'The Armies of the Night' (1968) won the Pulitzer Prize and the National Book Award. 'The Executioner's Song' (1979), a novel about a real-life murderer's execution; 'Ancient Evenings' (1983), a novel set in ancient Egypt; and 'Tough Guys Don't Dance' (1985), a murder mystery, exemplify his versatility

Mail·gram (méilgræm) *n.* trademark of Western Union Co. for service in which a message is wired to the post office nearest to the addressee and then specially delivered by the postman

Mail·lart (máijɑr), Robert (1872–1940), Swiss engineer, distinguished for his bridges in reinforced concrete and his invention (1910) of a unified construction element of a beamless floor and flare-topped columns

Mail·lol (máijɔl), Aristide (1861–1944), French sculptor. His favorite theme was the female nude, simplified, robust, sensual and monumental

mail·man (méilmæn) *pl.* **mail·men** (méilmɛn) *n.* a man employed to collect and deliver mail

mail order an order, sent by mail, for goods to be delivered by mail **mail-or·der** *adj.*

maim (meim) *v.t.* to deprive of the full or partial use of a limb or limbs by inflicting an injury [M.E. *maynhe, mayn* fr. O.F.]

Mai·mon·i·des (maimónidi:z) (Rabbi Moses ben Maimon, 1135–1204), Spanish-Jewish physician, theologian and philosopher. He sought to reconcile biblical and Rabbinic teaching with philosophy, esp. with Aristotelianism. His most important philosophical treatise was 'Guide of the Perplexed'

Main (main) a river (300 miles long, navigable for about 200 miles) in West Germany. It rises near the Czechoslovakian frontier and flows west to join the Rhine opposite Mainz

main (mein) 1. *n.* a principal pipe system, duct etc. for drainage, gas, water etc. ‖ (*rhet.*) the high sea **in the main** for the most part, in most respects **with might and main** with all one's strength 2. *adj.* most important, chief, principal ‖ (*naut.*) of or connected with the mainsail or mainmast **by main force** by exerting the utmost strength **the main chance** whatever is most in one's own interest [O. E. *mægen*, force]

main brace (*naut.*) a brace attached to the main yard (*SPLICE)

main clause (*gram.*) a clause in a complex sentence which may stand syntactically by itself as a complete sentence (cf. SUBORDINATE CLAUSE)

Maine (men) a former province of N.W. France, forming most of Mayenne department in the Armorican Massif (cattle, sheep, hog breeding) and Sarthe, sloping down to the Paris basin (mixed farming, livestock). The southwest is pine forest. Historic capital: Le Mans. A countship (10th c.), it was attached to Anjou (1126) and was ruled by England until 1203. It was annexed by the French crown (1481)

Maine (mein) (*abbr.* **Me.**) a state (area 33,215 sq. miles, pop. 1,133,000 on the extreme northeastern coast of the U.S.A. Capital: Augusta. It is largely hilly, with the White Mtns lying in

CONCISE PRONUNCIATION KEY: (**a**) æ, c**a**t; ɑ, c**a**r; ɔ f**a**wn; ei, sn**a**ke. (**e**) e, h**e**n; i:, sh**ee**p; iə, d**ee**r; ɛə, b**ea**r. (**i**) i, f**i**sh; ai, t**i**ger; ə:, b**i**rd. (**o**) o, **o**x; au, c**ow**; ou, g**oa**t; u, p**oo**r; ɔi, r**oy**al. (**u**) ʌ, d**u**ck; u, b**u**ll; u:, g**oo**se; ə, b**a**cillus; ju:, c**u**be. x, lo**ch**; θ, **th**ink; ð, bo**th**er; z, **Z**en; ʒ, cor**s**age; dʒ, sava**ge**; ŋ, ora**ng**utang; j, **y**ak; ʃ, **fi**sh; tʃ, fe**tch**; 'l, ra**bble**; 'n, red**den**. Complete pronunciation key appears inside front cover.

the west. Agriculture: potatoes, poultry and eggs, dairy products, apples. Fisheries. Resources: timber, building materials, feldspar, mica. Industries: pulp and paper, shoes, food processing, shipbuilding. State university (1865) at Orono. Maine was visited (1498) by Cabot, and colonized (17th and 18th cc.) by the English. It became (1820) the 23rd state of the U.S.A.

Maine de Bi·ran (mendəbi:rã) (Marie François Pierre Gonthier de Biran, 1766–1824), French philosopher. He stressed the importance of the will in the development of thought. Opposed to Condillac and other 18th-c. materialists, he had a profound influence on Victor Cousin

Maine-et-Loire (meneilwær) a department (area 2,811 sq. miles, pop. 629,800) in W. France (*ANJOU). Chief town: Angers

'Maine', U.S.S. (mein) a battleship sunk (1898) following a mysterious explosion in Havana harbor. An enraged U.S. public, spurred on esp. by the Hearst press, blamed the Spanish. The catchword, 'Remember the Maine' was a factor leading to the Spanish-American War

main·frame (méinfreim) n. (computer) the central processing unit containing the control unit and the circuits Cf INPUT UNIT, OUTPUT UNIT, STORAGE

main·land (méinlənd, méinlænd) n. a continuous land mass as compared with an island

main·line (méinláin) v. to inject a drug directly into a vein for greater effect

main·ly (méinli:) adv. chiefly, principally, the lecture consisted mainly of platitudes

main·mast (méinmæst, méinmɒst, méinməst) n. the principal mast of a vessel

main road an important through road, esp. (Br.) one maintained by the local authority

main·sail (méinseil, méinsəl) n. a sail bent to the main yard of a square-rigged vessel ‖ a sail set to the after part of a mainmast in a fore-and-aft rig

main·sheet (méinʃi:t) n. (naut.) a line that controls and secures the mainsail

main·spring (méinspriŋ) n. the chief spring in a clockwork mechanism ‖ the principal activating power or motive, ambition is the mainspring of his activity

main·stay (méinstei) n. (naut.) a stay from the maintop to the foot of the foremast ‖ a principal support

main·stream (méinstri:m) n. the dominant trend in thought, culture, fashion etc.

main·street (méinstri:t) v. to campaign for political office by personally visiting small communities

main·tain (meintéin) v.t. to cause to remain unaltered or unimpaired ‖ to declare to be true, valid etc. ‖ to defend the truth, validity etc. of ‖ to preserve against attack ‖ to provide for the needs of, to maintain a large household [M.E. maintene, mainteine fr. F.]

main·te·nance (méintənəns) n. a maintaining or being maintained ‖ the provisions, money etc. needed for subsistence ‖ (law) intervention by a third party who has no clear interest in a suit [F.]

maintenance of membership a provision in some union contracts whereby an employee who belongs to the union or joins it during the time set by the contract must remain in good standing with the union or be discharged

Main·te·non (mẽtanɔ̃), Françoise d'Aubigné, marquise de (1635–1719), mistress and later second wife of Louis XIV. Her influence on royal policy, notably as regards the revocation of the Edict of Nantes, is debatable

main·top (méintɒp) n. (naut.) a small platform above the head of the lower mainmast

main yard (naut.) the yard on which the mainsail is extended

Mainz (maints) a city (pop. 183,900) of Roman foundation on the middle Rhine, West Germany, opposite the mouth of the Main, capital of the Rhineland-Palatinate. It is a center of industry, of river and rail communications, and of the Rhine wine trade. Romanesque cathedral. University (1477)

Mai·po (máipɔ), a river and llano of Chile, and the site (south of Santiago) of the battle (1818) in which San Martín defeated the Royalist forces of Osorio and declared the independence of Chile (Apr. 5, 1818)

mai·son·ette (meizənét) n. (Br.) a duplex [F. maisonnette, a small house]

Mais·tre (mestr), Joseph, comte de (1753–1821), French writer, the most effective of the neo-Catholic anti-Revolution writers. He urged

a limited and Catholic monarchy. His works include 'Du pape' (1819) and 'les Soirées de Saint-Pétersbourg' (1821)

Maistre, Xavier, comte de (1763–1852), French writer, brother of Joseph, author of 'Voyage autour de ma chambre' (1795) and 'la Jeune Sibérienne' (1825)

mai tai (máitái) n. an alcoholic drink with a rum base, curaçao, orgeat, and fruit juices, served with ice and a cherry or pineapple garnish; said to be from the South Pacific

Mait·land (méitlənd), Frederic William (1850–1906), British legal historian. His works include 'The History of English Law before the Time of Edward I' (with Sir Frederick Pollock, 1895) and 'Domesday Book and Beyond' (1897)

Maitland, John *LAUDERDALE

mai·tre d'hô·tel (metrdoutel) pl. **maî·tres d'hô·tel** (metrdoutel) n. a headwaiter ‖ the butler or steward of a large household [F.]

maize (meiz) n. corn (Zea mays) [Span. maiz, of Cuban origin]

ma·jes·tic (mədʒéstik) adj. having majesty **ma·jés·ti·cal** adj.

maj·es·ty (mædʒisti) pl. **maj·es·ties** n. royal stateliness, splendor etc. ‖ sovereign power ‖ (religious art) a representation of God, Christ, the Virgin Mary or the persons of the Trinity, enthroned in glory **Maj·es·ty** (with second or third person possessive pronoun) the title used in addressing or referring to a king, queen or emperor [F. majesté]

ma·jol·i·ca (mədʒɒlikə) n. a tin-glazed Italian Renaissance earthenware, decorated over the white ground with bright metallic oxides ‖ a modern reproduction of it [Ital. majolica prob. after Majolica, 14th-c. var. of MAJORCA]

ma·jor (méidʒər) **1.** adj. greater in importance, size etc. than something else, the major part ‖ of great magnitude or importance ‖ (law) of full legal age ‖ (mus., of a scale) having semitones between the third and fourth and between the seventh and eighth notes, the distance between all other consecutive notes being a tone ‖ (mus., of a key) based on such a scale ‖ (mus., of a chord) built of the first, third and fifth notes of such a scale ‖ (mus., of an interval) being between the tonic and the second, third, sixth or seventh degrees of such a scale ‖ of or designating an academic subject studied more extensively and intensively than others **2.** n. (law) a person of full legal age ‖ a major subject of study **3.** v.i. (with 'in') to study a specified major subject [L., comp. of magnus, great]

major n. an army officer ranking below a lieutenant colonel and above a captain ‖ an officer of the same rank in the U.S. air force or marine corps [F.]

majorana particle or **majorana neutrino** (méidʒɔrɑnə) (njuːtríːnou) n. (particle phys.) an elementary particle equivalent to an antineutrino, in which double beta decay results in emission and absorption of a neutrino, with zero mass in accordance with the Dirac equation

major axis (math.) the axis of an ellipse, passing through its foci

Ma·jor·ca (mədʒɔ́rkə) *BALEARIC ISLANDS

ma·jor·do·mo (méidʒərdóumou) n. the chief steward in an Italian or Spanish noble household ‖ (rhet.) a butler or steward [fr. Span. mayordomo]

ma·jor·ette (meidʒərét) n. a drum majorette

major general an officer in the U.S. army, air force or marine corps ranking below a lieutenant general and above a brigadier general ‖ (Br.) an army officer ranking below a lieutenant general and above a brigadier

ma·jor·i·tar·i·an (mədʒɔrətéəriːən) n. a member of the so-called silent majority

ma·jor·i·ty (mədʒɔ́riti:, mədʒɒ́riti:) pl. **ma·jor·i·ties** n. the greater number or part, esp. more than half the total number ‖ the amount by which a greater part exceeds a smaller, he won by a large majority ‖ (mil.) the rank of major ‖ (law) full legal age [F. majorité]

major league either of two U.S. professional baseball leagues of highest quality and status, the American League and the National League ‖ any of several similar U.S. athletic leagues, esp. in ice hockey and basketball

major medical insurance (insurance) health policy providing substantial reimbursement for medical and hospital expenses beyond the limitations of ordinary health insurance policies

major orders (Roman Catholicism) the three ministerial orders: priesthood, diaconate, sub-

diaconate ‖ (Anglican Church) the three ministerial orders of episcopate, priesthood, diaconate

major planet one of the nine largest primary planets (in order of distance out from the sun): Mercury, Venus, Earth, Mars, Jupiter, Saturn, Uranus, Neptune and Pluto

major premise, major premiss (logic) a statement of a general rule forming the first proposition of a syllogism

Major Prophets *PROPHET

major suit (bridge) hearts or spades, which score higher than clubs or diamonds (cf. MINOR SUIT)

major surgery or **major operation** (med.) surgical procedure involving potential danger to the patient or requiring a general anesthesia or special skill Cf MINOR SURGERY

major term (logic) the term which is the predicate of the conclusion of a syllogism

Ma·jun·ga (mədʒʌ́ŋgə) a port (pop. 34,000) of N.W. Madagascar

ma·jus·cule (mædʒəskjuːl) **1.** n. a large form of a letter of the alphabet, a capital or uncial such as was used on manuscripts before minuscule writing came into use ‖ a letter in this form **2.** adj. written in majuscules (cf. MINUSCULE) [F.]

Ma·kar·i·os III (məkɑ́riːɒs) (1913–77), Greek Cypriot statesman, archbishop of the Orthodox Church. He led the Cypriot struggle for independence, and was the first president of Cyprus (1960–77)

Ma·kas·sar, Ma·cas·sar (məkǽsər) the capital (pop. 434,766) of Sulawesi, Indonesia, a port. University (1956)

Makassar Strait the channel (450 miles long, average width 155 miles) between Borneo and Sulawesi, connecting the Celebes and Java Seas

make (meik) **1.** v. pres. part. **mak·ing** past and past part. **made** (meid) v.t. to bring (something) into being, cause to exist ‖ to use (something already in being) in order to bring something else into being, she made the material into a dress ‖ to contrive by imaginative effort, to make a design ‖ to arrive at (a choice, decision, conclusion) after thought ‖ to cause to occur, to make a noise ‖ to cause to acquire some specified quality, a fire will make the room more comfortable ‖ to cause to become something specified, make him your president ‖ (with 'of') to cause (someone or something) to become or seem (something), to make a mess of a job, she made a fool of him ‖ to cause to acquire a specified mental or emotional state, to make someone sad ‖ to compel ‖ to cause to perform a specified action, to make a clock work ‖ to perform, to make a journey ‖ to utter (a remark, a statement) ‖ to deliver (a speech) ‖ to amass, build up by accumulating, to make a collection of seashells ‖ to arrange, to make the bed ‖ to establish, frame, to make a set of rules ‖ (law) to draw up (e.g. a contract) ‖ to reckon as being, what do you make the total? ‖ to add up to, be the equivalent of, 2 pints make 1 quart ‖ to constitute, will you make a fourth for bridge? ‖ to turn out to be, have the qualities needed for, he will make a good lawyer ‖ to assure the success of, that performance will make him ‖ to go a distance of, to make 50 miles in a day ‖ (often with 'it') to succeed in arriving at (a desired goal), you can make it if you hurry, will they make the finals? ‖ to gain (money etc.), to make a profit on a deal ‖ to earn (money etc.), he makes $80 a week ‖ to close (an electric circuit) ‖ to achieve, to make a high score ‖ (cards) to win (a trick) ‖ (cards) to shuffle ‖ (cards) to name (a bid) ‖ v.i. (with infin.) to start, he made to go ‖ (with 'for', 'toward' etc.) to go in a specified direction, to make toward the door ‖ (with 'for') to lead to a specified result, it makes for harmony ‖ (with an adjective) to cause oneself to become as specified, to make sure ‖ (of the tide, water in a ship etc.) to rise, increase in depth **to make a break** with to cease to have relations with **to make as if** to pretend, he made as if he hadn't heard **to make believe** to pretend **to make do with** to manage with (what is available) **to make much of** to cherish or be particularly attentive to **to make off** to run away **to make off with** to steal **to make or break, to make or mar,** to have a decisive effect on for good or bad **to make out** to understand ‖ to manage to see (something) with difficulty ‖ to decipher ‖ to suggest as true, pretend, he made out that he had not done it ‖ to draw up (a bill, total etc.) ‖ (pop.) to succeed, get along satisfactorily ‖ (pop.) to neck **to make over** to transfer ownership of, to make over property to someone

to make shift to do one's best under adverse conditions **to make time** to advance at a specified rate of progress, *the train made good time* **to make up** to invent (a story) ‖ to put an end to (a quarrel) by being reconciled ‖ to mix the ingredients of (a prescription) ‖ to arrange the typographical elements of (a page) as an entity ‖ to take the action needed to eliminate (a deficiency), *to make up lost time by extra work* ‖ to apply cosmetics to ‖ to repeat (an academic course) which one has failed, or take (an examination) from which one has been absent ‖ (*Br.*) to pave ‖ to end a quarrel by becoming reconciled ‖ to apply cosmetics to ‖ (*theater*) to put on cosmetics, costume etc. for a role ‖ (with 'for') to compensate for ‖ to seek the favor of (someone), esp. by flattery **2.** *n.* provenance of manufacture, *he knows all the makes of French cars* ‖ style or quality of making, *she liked the cloth but not the make of the coat* ‖ (*elec.*) the closing of a circuit ‖ (*cards*) a turn at shuffling ‖ (*bridge*) the declaration of trumps ‖ quality of personality, *the job is too small for someone of his make* **on the make** aggressively seeking financial or social advantage [O.E. *macian*]
make and break a control which completes and breaks an electrical circuit
make-be·lieve (méikbilị:v) **1.** *n.* a pretending, e.g. in children's play ‖ a willful deceiving **2.** *adj.* pretended, involving make-believe
make it *v.* (*colloq.*) **1.** to achieve success in business **2.** to have sexual intercourse
Ma·kem·ie (məkémi:, məkéimi:), Francis (c. 1658–1708), U.S. clergyman. He was the founder (1706) in Philadelphia of U.S. Presbyterianism
make out or **make it** *v.* (*slang or colloq.*) to perform sexual intercourse on a date
mak·er (méikər) *n.* someone who makes, usually in compounds indicating the thing made, *brickmaker, shoemaker* ‖ (*law*) someone who signs a promissory note **Mak·er** God
make·read·y (méikrεdi:) *n.* (*printing*) the final preparing of type or a plate for printing, so as to adjust the spread of pressure on the machine to ensure even impression ‖ (*printing*) the material used
make·shift (méikʃift) **1.** *n.* something used temporarily as a substitute **2.** *adj.* serving as, or resembling, a makeshift
make·up (méikʌp) *n.* the way in which the parts of something are put together ‖ cosmetics ‖ the art of applying cosmetics ‖ (*printing*) the arrangement of various elements (text, titles, illustrations etc.) of printed matter on a page ‖ (*pop.*) a special examination taken to make up for one missed through illness etc.
make waves *v.* (*slang or colloq.*) to upset the normal course of activities
make·weight (méikwεit) *n.* something added to a scale to complete a required weight ‖ a person or thing added only to fill out a gap etc. rather than on grounds of intrinsic worth
Ma·ke·yev·ka (məkéijefkə) a city (pop. 442,000) of the Ukraine, U.S.S.R., in the Donbas: iron and steel
Ma·khach·ka·la (mʌxətʃkəlá) (formerly Petrovsk) the capital (pop. 269,000) of the Daghestan A.S.S.R., U.S.S.R., a port on the Caspian: fishing, fish canning, oil refining
mak·ing (méikiŋ) *n.* the action of someone who makes, *a mistake of his making* ‖ the process by which something is made ‖ (*pl.*) essential qualities, *he has the makings of a leader* ‖ a means or process by which success is achieved, *military service was the making of him* ‖ (*pl.*) earnings [pres. part. of MAKE]
Ma·kin Island (mákin, méikin) one of the Gilbert Is, and the site of an engagement (1943) in the 2nd world war. It was the first Japanese-held island to be recaptured by the Allies in the central Pacific
Mak·kah (mækə) *MECCA
makuta *LIKUTA
mal- (mæl) *prefix* badly, wrong ‖ bad [fr. F. *mal* adv. fr. L. *male*, ill, bad]
Mal·a·bar Coast (mæləbɑr) the coast on the west of India from the southern tip of Mysore to Cape Comorin at the southern tip
Malabo (formerly Santa Isabel) the capital (pop. 37,237) of Equatorial Guinea, a port on Fernando Poo exporting cacao and coffee
Ma·lac·ca (məlækə) a state (area 640 sq. miles, pop. 453,153) of Malaysia in S.W. Malaya. Capital: Malacca (pop. 88,073). It was founded (end of the 14th c.) by a fugitive Sumatran prince. It was conquered by the Portuguese (1511) and

the Dutch (1641). It was ceded (1824) to Britain and joined the Federation of Malaya (1948)
Malacca cane the cut, dried and polished stem of *Calamus rotang*, an Asiatic palm, used esp. for walking sticks [after *Malacca*, in Malaya]
Malacca Strait a sea passage (500 miles long) between the southern end of the Malay Peninsula and Sumatra, connecting the Indian Ocean and the South China Sea
Mal·a·chi (mæləkai) a Minor Prophet (c. 5th c. B.C.) of the Old Testament ‖ the Old Testament book bearing his name. It rebukes the priests and people of Israel for their neglect of religion
mal·a·chite (mæləkait) *n.* a bright green basic copper carbonate, $Cu_2CO_3 (OH)_2$, occurring as a mineral, used polished for making decorative objects [O. F. *melochite*]
mal·a·col·o·gy (mæləkólədʒi:) *n.* the branch of zoology that deals with mollusks [F. *malacologie*]
mal·a·cos·tra·can (mæləkóstrəkən) *n.* a member of *Malacostraca*, a subclass of crustaceans including amphipods, isopods and decapods [fr. Gk *malakostraka* fr. *malakos*, soft+*ostrakon*, shell]
mal·ad·just·ed (mælədʒʌstid) *adj.* (of a person) psychologically unable to adjust his behavior to the conditions of his social environment
mal·ad·just·ment (mælədʒʌstmənt) *n.* the quality or state of being maladjusted ‖ an instance of this
mal·ad·min·is·tra·tion (mælədmịnistréiʃən) *n.* inefficient or corrupt administration
mal·a·droit (mælədróit) *adj.* lacking in tact ‖ physically clumsy [F.]
mal·a·dy (mælədi:) *pl.* **mal·a·dies** *n.* a physical, mental or moral disorder [F. *maladie*, illness]
Má·la·ga (mæləgə) a province (area 2,812 sq. miles, pop. 1,036,261) of Andalusia, S. Spain ‖ its capital (pop. 405,500), a flourishing port: chemical and textile industries, paper mills. Málaga was founded (c. 1100 B.C.) by the Phoenicians. It has Moorish fortifications (14th c.). Cathedral (16th–18th cc.)
Mal·a·ga (mæləgə) *n.* a sweet, dark, fortified wine made in the region of Málaga
Mal·a·gas·y (mæləgǽsi:) **1.** *adj.* of or relating to the Malagasy Republic, its people, language etc. **2.** *pl.* **Mal·a·gas·y, Mal·a·gas·ies** *n.* a native or inhabitant of Madagascar or the Malagasy Republic ‖ the Austronesian language spoken by the Malagasy people
Malagasy Republic *MADAGASCAR
ma·laise (mæléiz) *n.* a feeling of general discomfort, of being below one's normal standard of health ‖ a feeling of being emotionally ill at ease or apprehensive [F.]
Ma·lan (məlæn), Daniel François (1874–1959), South African Nationalist statesman, prime minister (1948–54). He was a firm advocate of apartheid
Ma·lang (məlæŋ) a town (pop. 422,428) in E. Java, Indonesia, an agricultural center for coffee, tea, tobacco and sugarcane. Industries: engineering, textiles. University (1961)
mal·a·prop·ism (mæləprɒpizəm) *n.* a ludicrous misuse of a word [after Mrs *Malaprop* in Sheridan's 'The Rivals']
mal·ap·ro·pos (mælæprəpóu) **1.** *adv.* at an unsuitable time, or in an inappropriate manner **2.** *adj.* inopportune [F. *mal à propos*, inopportune]
Mä·lar (málər) (or Mälaren) a lake (area 440 sq. miles) in S.E. central Sweden, at whose mouth Stockholm lies
ma·lar (méilər) **1.** *adj.* (*anat.*) of or pertaining to the cheek or the cheekbone **2.** *n.* (*anat.*) the cheekbone [fr. Mod. L. *malaris* fr. L. *mala*, cheek]
ma·lar·i·a (məléəri:ə) *n.* an infectious, chiefly tropical disease characterized by periodic chills and fever, splenic enlargement and anemia. It is caused by parasitic protozoa of the genus *Plasmodium*, transmitted by the bite of the anopheles mosquito. It may recur many years later without reinfection even after treatment **ma·lár·i·al, ma·lár·i·ous** *adjs* [Ital. *mal'aria*, contr. of *mala aria*, bad air]
Ma·la·tes·ta (mɑlɑtésta) an Italian family which ruled Rimini (13th–15th cc.). Its most famous member was Sigismondo Pandolfo Malatesta (1417–68), soldier and patron of the arts
Ma·la·wi (məláwi:) (formerly Nyasaland) a republic (area 45,747 sq. miles, pop. 6,829,000) in central Africa. Capital: Lilongwe (pop. 120,000). People: Bantuspeaking peoples

(Chewa, Nyanja, Yao, Tumbuka, Lomwe and Sena), small Asian and European minorities. Languages: English (official) and Chichewa. Religion: mainly local African, 65% nominal Christian, 16% Moslem. The land is approx. one-third cultivated and 19% forest (teak, cedar, mahogany). Except for the valley (1,500 ft) formed by Lake Malawi (along the eastern border) and the Shire River, which drains it southward, it consists of elevated plateaus (averaging 5,000–7,000 ft), the highest being the Nyika Plateau (8,000 ft) in the west center, and the Mlanje Massif (9,848 ft) in the southeast. The climate is temperate above 3,000 ft. The Shire Valley has a maximum average temperature of 115°F. (Oct. and Nov.). Rainfall: 35 ins in the lowlands, 50 ins in the highlands. Livestock: goats, cattle, pigs. Minerals: coal, bauxite. Industries: tobacco, rope and string, soap, hydroelectricity. Exports: tea, tobacco, corn, cotton, peanuts, tung oil, labor (to Zimbabwe). Domestic crops: cereals, vegetables. Imports: cotton textiles, machinery, vehicles, clothing, gasoline. University of Malawi (1965), at Zomba. Monetary unit: pound (20 shillings). HISTORY. The country was visited by Portuguese explorers (17th and 18th cc.). Warfare broke out (early 19th c.) between the Yao and the Ngoni, who had invaded from the northeast and south respectively. Livingstone explored Lake Malawi (1859) and Christian missions were established to combat tribal warfare and slave trading. British forces prevented the Portuguese from annexing the south of the country (1889), suppressed Arab slave traders (1887–99) and pacified the Yao and the Ngoni. A British protectorate was established (1891), taking the name of Nyasaland (1907). It formed part of the Central African Federation (1953–63), until increasing African opposition led to its dissolution. Nyasaland became self-governing (1963) under Dr Banda as its first prime minister. As Malawi, it became an independent state within the Commonwealth (July 6, 1964), and a republic within the Commonwealth (July 6, 1966). Banda became president (1966) and was declared president-for-life (1971). He also became head of the cabinet and holder of several cabinet posts
Malawi a lake in central Africa, formerly Lake Nyasa, part of the southward extension of the Great Rift Valley. It lies about 1,500 ft above sea level and is 350 miles long by about 25 miles broad. It drains southward through the Shire River into the Zambezi. It was explored by Livingstone (1859)
Ma·lay (məléi, méilei) **1.** *n.* a member of a people inhabiting the Malay Peninsula and Malay Archipelago ‖ the language of this people **2.** *adj.* of, or related to the Malays or their language (*MALAY LANGUAGE)
Malay Malayalam
Ma·lay·a (məléiə) a state (itself a federation of 11 states, total area 50,700 sq. miles) occupying most of the Malay Peninsula and forming part of Malaysia
Ma·lay·a·lam (mæləjáləm) *n.* the language of the peoples of the Malabar Coast of India, a Dravidian dialect akin to Tamil
Ma·lay·a·li (mæləjáli:) *pl.* **Mal·a·ya·lis, Mal·a·ya·lim** (mæləjálim) *n.* an inhabitant of the Malabar Coast of India, speaking Malayalam
Ma·lay·an (məléiən) **1.** *adj.* Malay **2.** *n.* a citizen of Malaya
Malay Archipelago a group of islands, largely mountainous, between S.E. Asia and N. Australia, incl. the Philippines, the Sundas and Moluccas (Indonesia), and New Guinea
Malay language the most important of the Indonesian languages, serving as a lingua franca. The earliest surviving Malay manuscripts (c. 1600) are in an alphabet of S. Indian origin. Malay has been written for centuries in an augmented Arabic alphabet, but both the Dutch and the British have transcribed the Arabic symbols into the Roman alphabet. Malay has many loanwords from a great variety of languages. The Malays have a great store of folk tales, told by generations of wandering storytellers
Ma·lay·o·Pol·y·ne·sian (məléiouppliní:ʒən) **1.** *adj.* Austronesian ‖ of or relating to the Malay people of Polynesia **2.** *n.* a member of the Malay people of Polynesia
Malay Peninsula a peninsula (area 70,000 sq. miles), the southernmost extremity of Asia, extending south from the Isthmus of Kra between

CONCISE PRONUNCIATION KEY: **(a)** æ, c*a*t; ɑ, c*a*r; ɔ f*a*wn; ei, sn*a*ke. **(e)** e, h*e*n; i:, sh*ee*p; iə, d*ee*r; εə, b*ea*r. **(i)** i, f*i*sh; ai, t*i*ger; ə:, b*i*rd. **(o)** o, *o*x; au, c*ow*; ou, g*oa*t; u, p*oo*r; ɔi, r*oy*al. **(u)** ʌ, d*u*ck; u, b*u*ll; u:, g*oo*se; ə, b*a*cillus; ju:, c*u*be. x, lo*ch*; θ, *th*ink; δ, *b*o*th*er; z, *Z*en; ʒ, corsa*g*e; dʒ, sava*g*e; ŋ, ora*ng*utang; j, *y*ak; ʃ, *fi*sh; tʃ, fe*tch*; 'l, rabb*le*; 'n, redd*en*. Complete pronunciation key appears inside front cover.

the Indian Ocean and the S. China Sea comprising S. Thailand and the whole of Malaya

Ma·lay·sia (məléiʒə, məléifə) a nation (area 127,315 sq. miles, pop. 15,300,000) in southeast Asia, including the 11 states of Malaya, Sarawak and Sabah. Capital: Kuala Lumpur. People: 50% Malay, 35% Chinese, 10% Indians, 5% non-Malay indigenous tribal peoples. National language: Bahasa Malaysia. Monetary unit: Ringgit. Religion: 55% Moslem, 30% Buddhist, 3% Christian, with Confucianist, Taoist, Hindu and Sikh minorities. Malaysia consists of two parts, separated by more than 400 miles of the China Sea: the southern tip of the Malay Peninsula, south of Thailand, and the northern portion of the island of Borneo (Sabah and Sarawak). The Central Range runs two thirds of the way down the peninsula, rising to 7,161 ft (Gunong Korbu). The shorter Western Range rises to 6,105 ft (Bintang) in the north. East of the Central Range and north of the Pahang River the Trengganu Highlands rise to 7,186 ft (Gunong Tahan). The main plains are the Pahang Basin, Johore, the northeast lowlands, and the western coastlands. Sarawak is mostly coastal plain. Sabah's narrow coastal plain gradually gives way to mountains that divide Malaysia from Indonesia. Average temperatures (F.): 68–79° in the mountains (under 60° at night), 80°–95° in the plains and along the coasts (over 70° at night). Rainfall: average 100–120 ins, Kelantan 120 ins, Kuala Lumpur 95 ins, Perak 100 ins. Rainy seasons: northeast monsoons (heavy in the east) Nov.–Mar., southwest monsoons June–Sept. Livestock: oxen, water buffalo, goats, hogs. Agricultural products: rice (northwest and southwest), palm oil and kernels, copra, coconuts, pineapples, bananas, cacao. Exports: rubber (40% of world production), tin (40% of world production), iron ore, palm and coconut oil, bananas. Other products: bauxite, ilmenite, gold, columbite, wolfram, scheelite, rubber goods, lumber, cement, bricks, soap, tobacco, fish. Imports: food, manufactured goods, machinery, chemicals, fuels and oil. Ports: Penang, Port Swettenham. University: Kuala Lumpur (1959). HISTORY. The Malay Peninsula was settled by migrants from central Asia (5th millennium B.C.) and from Indonesia (3rd millennium B.C.). It fell under the commerical and cultural influence of Hindu India (2nd c. A.D.). It was dominated (9th–14th cc.) by a Buddhist state centered on Sumatra. Most of the region was converted to Islam by the 15th c. The Portuguese captured Malacca (1511), but were in turn expelled by the Dutch (1641). Britain acquired Penang (1786), Singapore (1819), and Malacca (1824). Britain began (1874) to form treaties with the local rulers, establishing Perak, Selangor, Negri Sembilan and Pahang as the Federated Malay States (1895) and Perlis, Kelantan, Trengganu and Kedah as the Unfederated Malay States (1909), joined by Johore (1914). Rubber, introduced in 1877, became a dominant crop, and the production of tin was mechanized. After the Japanese occupation (1941–5), the former Straits Settlements colony was dissolved, and a union of Malaya replaced the Federated and Unfederated Malay States (1946). The union was in turn replaced by the Federation of Malaya (1948), but the country was troubled by communist guerrilla raids. Self-government was achieved (1955). Malaya became an independent member of the Commonwealth (Aug. 31, 1957) and became part of Malaysia (Sept. 16, 1963). Sinapore seceded (1965). Prime Minister Tunku Abdul Rahman (1963–9) resigned during Malay–Chinese riots and was succeeded by Tun Abdul Razak (1970–6), who died in office. Hussein Onn, the deputy prime minister, took over. His term was marked by further Chinese-Malay tensions (1978, 1980) and by Communist insurgency from 1975. Mahathir bin Mohamad became prime minister (1981)

Ma·lay·sian (məléiʒən, məléifən) **1.** adj. of or relating to Malaysia **2.** n. an inhabitant of Malaysia

Mal·colm III (mǽlkəm) (d. 1093), king of Scotland (1057–93). He was at war with England (1077–80). He did much to consolidate the kingdom of Scotland

Malcolm X (eks) (Malcolm Little, 1925–65), U.S. black leader who was assassinated in Harlem, N.Y.C., apparently by political rivals. He had been second in command of the Black Muslims until 1964, when he broke with the group to form his own Black Nationalist Movement

mal·con·tent (mǽlkəntent) n. someone who is discontented, esp. with the government, and ready to make trouble [O.F.]

Mal·dive Islands (mɔ́ldaiv, mǽldaiv) a republic (area 115 sq. miles, pop. 155,000) in the Indian Ocean 400 miles southwest of Sri Lanka. Capital: Malé (pop. 29,600). Of the 2,000 coral islands, 220 are inhabited. People: of Sinhalese origin. Language: a dialect of Sinhalese. Religion: Moslem. Crops: coconuts, millet, fruit. Industry: fishing. Monetary unit: Maldivian rupee. HISTORY. The islands were under British protection (1887–1965), but are now fully independent. Britain is guaranteed the use of an air base until 1986

Mal·div·i·an (mɔldíviən, mældíviən) adj. of or relating to the Maldive Islands

mal du siè·cle (mɔldəsjékl) n. (Fr.) disquietude, pessimism, melancholy, lack of confidence in the future

male (meil) **1.** adj. of the sex in animals or plants that fertilizes in order to reproduce (symbol ♂) ‖ (bot.) pertaining to any reproductive structure that contains elements for fertilizing female elements ‖ of, pertaining to or characteristic of men, a male audience ‖ manly ‖ (engin.) of or being a part designed to fit into another part, a male screw ‖ (of a gem) having hardness, depth or brilliance **2.** n. a male person, animal or plant [M.E. masle fr. O.F.]

Male·branche (mælbrãf), Nicolas de (1638–1715), French philosopher. He developed the doctrine of occasionalism. His outstanding work is 'Recherche de la vérité' (1674–8)

male chauvinism exaggerated masculine pride and conviction that men are superior to women, that women should be socially and/or politically subservient to men —**male chauvinist** n. Cf SEXISM

mal·e·dic·tion (mælidíkfən) n. a curse called down upon someone [fr. L. maledictio (maledictionis)]

mal·e·fac·tion (mæləfǽkfən) n. an evil deed, crime [fr. L. malefactio (malefactionis)]

mal·e·fac·tor (mǽləfæktər) n. someone who does evil, esp. someone who commits a crime [L. fr. malefacere, to do ill]

male fern Dryopteris filix-mas, a European and North American fern. An oleoresin used for expelling tapeworms is obtained from its rhizome and fronds

ma·lef·ic (məléfik) adj. (esp. astrology) causing evil or harm [fr. L. maleficus]

ma·lef·i·cent (məléfis'nt) adj. doing evil or harm ‖ having the nature of a crime [fr. L. maleficens (maleficentis)]

ma·le·ic acid (məlí:ik) a crystalline unsaturated dicarboxylic acid, HOOCCH=CHCOOH, used in making polyester resins [fr. F. maléique]

Mal·en·kov (maljénkʌf), Georgi Maximilianovich (1903–), Russian statesman, premier of the U.S.S.R. (1953–5). He was banished to Siberia (1957) after taking part in an attempt to depose Khrushchev, and was expelled from the Communist party (1964)

male pill (med.) a contraceptive drug designed to make male sperm sterile

male screw a screw (cylindrical or conical pin with its surface cut in a spiral groove) fitting into a female screw, nut etc.

Ma·le·vich (məléivitf), Kasimir (1878–1935), Russian painter and sculptor whose geometric abstractions culminated in a white square on a white ground in 'White on White' (1919)

ma·lev·o·lence (məlévələns) n. the quality of being malevolent [O.F. malivolence, malevolence]

ma·lev·o·lent (məlévələnt) adj. having or showing a desire to do harm [O.F. malivolent]

mal·fea·sance (mælfí:'ns) n. (law) the committing of illegal acts by a public official ‖ (law) an instance of this **mal·fea·sant** adj. and n. [fr. O. F. malfaisance, wrongdoing]

mal·for·ma·tion (mælfɔrméifən) n. the quality of being malformed ‖ something malformed **mal·formed** adj. abnormal in structure, badly made

mal·func·tion (mælfʌ́ŋkfən) **1.** v.i. (esp. used in the pres. part.) to function improperly **2.** n. malfunctioning ‖ an instance of this

Mal·herbe (mælerb), François de (1555–1628), French poet and critic. He showed the way to classical correctness, moderation, purity of diction and regularity of meter

Ma·li (máli:) (formerly French Sudan) a republic (area 478,767 sq. miles, pop. 7,160,000) in W. Africa. Capital: Bamako. People: 28% Bam-

bara, 10% Fulani, with smaller Sarakole, Songhai, Malinke, Tuareg, Dogon, Senufo, Moorish and Toucouleur groups. Principal languages: French, Sudanic dialects. Religion: 53% Moslem, 45% local African, very small Christian minorities. The land is a flat plain (750–1,200 ft), except for the Adrar des Iforas massif (2,000–2,500 ft) in the northeast, and the Bandiagara plateau in the loop of the Niger. The north is desert (merging with the Sahara), the center (the 'Sahel') is arid grazing land, the south (near the Niger) is savanna. Average temperatures (F.): Timbuktu 71° (Jan.) and 95° (May). Rainfall: under 8 ins in the desert, 9 ins in Timbuktu, 8–25 ins in the Sahel, 25–65 ins in the south. Livestock: cattle, sheep, goats, donkeys, camels. Crops: cereals, peanuts, cotton, manioc, almonds, kapok, gum, dates, yams, sisal. Irrigation is provided by the Sansanding Barrage on the Niger. River fishing is important. Mineral resources: salt. Industries: tanning, weaving, carpets, foodstuffs. Exports: peanuts, dried fish, animals, cotton, hides and skins, karite butter, gum. Imports: textiles, foodstuffs, machinery, vehicles, gasoline, building material, sugar. Monetary unit: franc. HISTORY. The ancient Sudanic state of Ghana (4th–13th cc.) covered much of the area, followed by the Moslem state of Mali (13th–15th cc.) and the Songhai Empire (15th–16th cc.). The French conquered the country (1880–95) and integrated it into French West Africa as the French Sudan. The regions of Niger and Upper Volta were detached from it (1911 and 1919) to form separate territories. It became an autonomous republic within the French Community (1958), and was briefly united (1959–60) with Senegal in the Mali Federation. The French Sudan became fully independent (Sept. 22, 1960) as the Republic of Mali, and joined the U.N. (1960). A successful army coup d'état was mounted (Nov. 20, 1968) and a military regime was established. It has promised a return to civilian political life

ma·li·bu board (mǽləbu:) n. (surfing) lightweight plastic board, 9 to 10 ft. long, with a convex bottom, round front, and square back; named for Malibu Beach, California

mal·ic (mǽlik) adj. (chem.) of action involving catalysis of malic acid, (e.g., found in apples) to pyruvic acid and carbon dioxide, e.g., malic enzyme

mal·ic acid (mǽlik, méilik) $C_4H_6O_5$, a colorless crystalline acid having three isomers, the most common one occurring in unripe apples and other fruits [F. malique fr. L. malum, apple]

ma·lice (mǽlis) n. the will to do harm to another [F.]

malice aforethought (law) the premeditated desire to harm in someone who has committed a crime, esp. murder

ma·li·cious (məlífəs) adj. having or showing malice [O.F. malicius]

ma·lign (məláin) adj. having an evil effect, doing harm, a malign influence ‖ (med.) malignant [O.F. maligne, malin]

malign v.t. to make false or misleading statements about (someone) so as to injure him [O.F. malignier, maliner, to plot]

ma·lig·nan·cy (məlígnənsi:) pl. **ma·lig·nan·cies** n. the quality or state of being malignant ‖ an instance of this ‖ (med.) a malignant tumor

ma·lig·nant (məlígnənt) adj. feeling, showing or acting with extreme ill will ‖ (med., of a disease) tending to be fatal without treatment ‖ (med., of a tumor) tending to metastasize and lead to death [fr. L.L. malignans (malignantis)]

ma·lig·ni·ty (məlígniti:) n. the quality or state of being malignant [O.F. malignité]

Ma·lin·che (mælí:ntfe) (d. c. 1530), Mexican Indian, daughter of a cacique, and interpreter and concubine of Hernán Cortés, who called her Doña Marina. Although her name has become a synonym for one who fraternizes with the enemy, her services as an interpreter probably saved the Indians from worse atrocities which might have been committed through ignorance

Ma·lines (mæli:n) (Flem. Mechelen) a Belgian city (pop. 77,377) on the Dyle River between Antwerp and Brussels, the seat of the primate of Belgium (*MERCIER): railway workshops, lace, carpets, furniture. Cathedral (13th–15th cc.), Town Hall (1311–26)

ma·lin·ger (məlíŋgər) v.i. to pretend to be ill, or exaggerate a real illness, in order to avoid one's work or responsibility [perh. fr. F. *malingre*, sickly]

Ma·lin·ke (məlíŋkei) *pl.* **Ma·lin·ke, Ma·lin·kes** *n.* a member of a Mandingo people of W. Africa ‖ the language of this people

Ma·li·nov·sky (mælinɔ́vski:), Rodion Yakovlevich (1898–1967), Russian marshal. He commanded the defense of Stalingrad (1942), and was Soviet minister of defense (1957–67)

mall (mɔl) *n.* a usually public, treelined walk [after the *Mall*, a London thoroughfare]

mall *MAUL

mal·lard (mǽlərd) *pl.* **mal·lard, mal·lards** *n.* *Anas platyrhynchos*, the common wild duck. The name applies to both sexes [O.F. *malart, mallart*, wild drake]

Mal·lar·mé (mælɑrmei), Stéphane (1842–98), French poet. Perhaps the only pure symbolist poet, Mallarmé sought in poetry to imitate the action of music: to have a very precise effect on the reader's mind not by making direct statements but by creating a web of interrelated suggestions and overtones, using related metaphors as a musician might use related themes. The ordinary syntax of logical statement is not abandoned, but curiously inverted or interrupted. Punctuation is sometimes abandoned, because it tends to limit the possibilities of meaning. The reader has to submit and resubmit his attention until the poem 'works'. In this subtlety and indirection Mallarmé is the father of modern poetry

mal·le·a·bil·i·ty (mæli:əbíliti:) *n.* the quality or state of being malleable

mal·le·a·ble (mǽli:əb'l) *adj.* (esp. of a metal) able to have its shape changed permanently through the applying of stress, e.g. by hammering ‖ (of a person's character) easily affected or formed by external influences [O.F.]

mal·lee (mǽli:) *n.* any of several Australian dwarf eucalypti of arid regions, esp. *Eucalyptus dumosa* and *E. oleosa* ‖ the dense thicket they form [native Austral.]

mal·le·o·lar (məlí:ələr) *adj.* of or relating to a malleolus

mal·le·o·lus (məlí:ələs) *pl.* **mal·le·o·li** (məlí:əlai) *n.* one of the two rounded bony projections on either side of the ankle [L. dim. of *malleus*, a hammer]

mal·let (mǽlit) *n.* a hammer, usually of wood, used to strike a wooden object (chisel handle, tent peg etc.) without the risk of splitting it ‖ (*croquet, polo*) a longhandled hammer used to strike the ball [F. *maillet*, wooden hammer]

mal·le·us (mǽli:əs) *pl.* **mal·le·i** (mǽli:ai) *n.* the outermost of the three bones in the middle ear of mammals [L.=hammer]

Ma·llor·ca (məjórkə, mɑljórkɑ) *BALEARIC ISLANDS

mal·low (mǽlou) *n.* a European wild plant of fam. *Malvaceae*, order *Malvales*, esp. *Malva sylvestris*, which has hairy stems and leaves and pink or mauve flowers, and *M. rotundiflora*, the dwarf mallow, which has rounded leaves and blue flowers [O.E. *mealuwe* fr. L. *malva*]

malm (mom) *n.* a soft, friable, chalky rock ‖ marl ‖ a mixture of clay and chalk used in brickmaking [O.E. *mealm*, sand]

Malm·ö (mɑ́lmə) Sweden's third largest city (pop. 230,380), a port and industrial center: shipbuilding, textiles, shoemaking, cement, engineering

Malm·sey (mɑ́mzi) *n.* a sweet, originally Greek wine now made throughout the Mediterranean (*MALVASIA) [fr. M.L. *malmasia*, corrup. of Gk *Monembasia*, a town in Greece]

mal·nu·tri·tion (mælnu:tríʃən, mælnju:tríʃən) *n.* poor nutrition caused by an inadequate or unbalanced diet, or by defective assimilation or utilization of nutrients (*DIET)

mal·o·dor·ous (mælóudərəs) *adj.* having a foul smell

mal·o·lac·tic (mæloulǽktik) *adj.* (*chem.*) of bacterial action resulting in conversion of malic acid to lactic acid, e.g., in winemaking

ma·lo·nic acid (məlóunik, məlónik) a crystalline dicarboxylic acid, CH₂(COOH)₂, used in organic syntheses [F. *malonique*]

Mal·o·ry (mǽləri:), Sir Thomas (d. 1471), English author. His 'Le Morte D'Arthur', one of the first books printed by Caxton (1485), was a prose collection of Arthurian tales translated from the French

Mal·pigh·i·an body (mælpígi:ən) (*anat.*) one of several small masses of blood vessels occurring in the kidney ‖ any nodule of lymphatic tissue in the spleen [after Marcello *Malpighi* (1628–94), Ital. physiologist]

Malpighian corpuscle a Malpighian body

Malpighian tube one of the tubular outgrowths of the alimentary canal of most insects and of some other arthropods. They function mainly as excretory organs

Mal·pla·quet, Battle of (mǽlplæke) a costly victory (1709) of an Allied army under Marlborough and Eugène over a French army. It was the last and greatest pitched battle of the war of the Spanish Succession

mal·po·si·tion (mælpəzíʃən) *n.* (*med.*) faulty position, esp. of the fetus in the uterus

mal·prac·tice (mælprǽktis) *n.* (*law*) the improper treatment of a patient by a doctor ‖ (*law*) illegal action taken in one's own interest by a person in a position of trust

mal·prax·is (mælprǽksis) *n.* malpractice

Mal·raux (mælrou), André (1901–76), French writer and statesman, minister of cultural affairs (1959–69). His novels include 'la Condition Humaine' (1933), about uprisings (1925–7) in Shanghai, and 'l'Espoir' (1937), which deals with the Spanish Civil War. His 'les Voix du silence' (1951) is a study of the psychological basis of art

malt (mɔlt) **1.** *n.* grain, esp. barley, allowed to germinate in water and then heated and dried, used in brewing and distilling **2.** *v.t.* to convert (grain) into malt ‖ to prepare with malt ‖ *v.i.* to become malt [O.E. *mealt*]

Mal·ta (mɔ́ltə) an independent state (area 122 sq. miles, pop. 366,000) within the Commonwealth, comprised of the islands of Malta (95 sq. miles), Gozo (26 sq. miles) and Comino (1 sq. mile) in the Mediterranean, 60 miles south of Sicily. Capital: Valletta. Languages: English, Maltese. Religion: Roman Catholic. Malta is a treeless, limestone island rising to 758 ft. Average temperatures (F.): (Jan.) 58°, (Jul.) 80°. Rainfall: 20 ins. Livestock: goats, sheep, cattle, pigs. Crops: cereals, potatoes, vegetables, tomatoes, flowers, grapes, fruit. Industries: fishing, shipyards, building, light manufactures, tourism. Exports: textiles, potatoes, gloves, wine, flowers. Imports: metals, vehicles, foodstuffs, machinery, electrical goods, fuels. Malta is an important naval base and port. University (1769). Monetary unit: Maltese pound. HISTORY. The island was ruled successively by the Phoenicians, the Greeks and the Romans. According to tradition, it was converted to Christianity c. 60 by St Paul. Malta was captured (870) by the Saracens, who were expelled (1090) by the Norman rulers of Sicily. It passed under the rule of Aragon (1283) and was given (1530) as the fief to the Knights Hospitalers by the Emperor Charles V. The Knights repelled a Turkish siege (1565) and developed the island as a fortified outpost of Christendom and as a trade center. It was captured by the French (1798) and the British (1800), and officially annexed by Britain (1814). A strategic British naval base, Malta withstood heavy German and Italian bombardments in the 2nd world war, and the island was awarded (1942) the George Cross for its heroism. It was given internal self-government (1947) and became a fully independent member of the Commonwealth (Sept. 21, 1964). By 1979 all British forces had withdrawn. Because of overpopulation and unemployment, Malta began a program of sponsored emigration. It is an associate member of the E.E.C. Conflicts arose between the ruling Labour party and the opposition Nationalists and the Roman Catholic Church in the 1980s

Malta fever undulant fever

Malta, Knight of *KNIGHT HOSPITALER

malt·ase (mɔ́lteis) *n.* an enzyme occurring in plants and animals, which accelerates the hydrolysis of maltose into glucose [MALT]

malted milk a preparation of dried milk and malted cereals ‖ a drink made from this mixed with milk, ice cream and flavoring

Mal·tese (mɔltí:z, mɔltí:s) **1.** *adj.* of, pertaining to or characteristic of Malta, its people, language etc. **2.** *pl.* **Mal·tese** *n.* a native of Malta ‖ the Semitic language of the Maltese, a form of Arabic with a large admixture of Italian

Maltese cross a cross consisting of four equal arms widening from a common junction towards their free ends which are indented by a V

Mal·thus (mǽlθəs), Thomas Robert (1766–1834), British economist. In his 'Essay on the Principle of Population' (1798), he argued that, because population increases by a geometrical ratio while means of subsistence increase by an

arithmetical ratio, poverty and suffering are unavoidable

Mal·thu·si·an (mælθú:zi:ən) *adj.* of or pertaining to Malthus or his doctrines

malt·ose (mɔ́ltous) *n.* a hard, soluble, crystalline sugar, C₁₂H₂₂O₁₁, formed in brewing and distilling and as an intermediate product in metabolism [F.]

mal·treat (mæltrí:t) *v.t.* to treat abusively **mal·tréat·ment** *n.* [F. *maltraiter*]

malt·ster (mɔ́ltstər) *n.* someone whose trade is to make or sell malt

malt sugar maltose

Ma·lu·ku (mɑlɔ́:kə) *MOLUCCAS

Ma·lus (mǽlys), Etienne-Louis (1775–1812), French physicist who discovered the polarization of refracted and reflected light

mal·va·sia (mælvɑzí:ə) *n.* a variety of grape from which Malmsey is made [Ital. *Malvasia*, corrup. of Gk *Monembasia*, town in Greece]

mal·ver·sa·tion (mælvərséiʃən) *n.* (*law*) corrupt behavior by someone in a position of trust [F.]

mama *MAMMA (mother)

Ma·mal·la·pu·ram (məmələpú:rəm) *MAHABALLIPURAM

mam·ba (mómbə) *n.* any of several members of *bendraspis*, a genus of very poisonous African snakes, esp. *D. angusticeps* [Zulu *im-amba*]

mam·bo (mámbou) *n.* a Latin American ballroom dance in 4/4 syncopated time [musicians' slang fr. Span.]

Mam·e·luke (mǽməlu:k) *n.* (*hist.*) a member of a Moslem sultanate, virtual rulers of Egypt (1250–1517). They were defeated by Napoleon in the Battle of the Pyramids (1798), and destroyed by Mohammed Ali (1811). The Mamelukes were originally a mounted military force, recruited from Circassian or Turkish slaves convened to Islam, brought up in the courts of Moslem rulers or caliphs [F. *Mameluk* fr. Arab. *mamlūk*, slave]

ma·mil·la, mam·mil·la (mæmílə) *pl.* **ma·mil·lae, mum·mil·lae** (mæmíli:) *n.* (*anat.*) a nipple ‖ (*biol.*) any protuberance or organ resembling a nipple [L. *mamilla* dim. of *mamma*, breast]

mam·il·lar·y, mam·mil·lar·y (mǽməleri:) *adj.* of or relating to the breasts ‖ shaped like a breast [fr. L. *mamillaris*]

mam·ma, ma·ma (mámə, məmá) *n.* (a child's word for) mother

mam·ma (mǽmə) *pl.* **mam·mae** (mǽmi:) *n.* (*anat.*) the female glandular organ which secretes milk, characteristic of mammals [L.]

mam·mal (mǽməl) *n.* a member of *Mammalia*, the highest class of vertebrates, including man. The many distinguishing characteristics include warm blood, hair more or less covering the body, mammary glands to nourish the young, a diaphragm used in respiration and a four-chambered heart with a circuit to the lungs separate from the systemic circulation **ma·ma·li·an** (məméili:ən) *adj.* [fr. Mod. L. *Mammalia* fr. L.L. *mammalis* adj. fr. *mamma*, breast]

mam·mal·o·gy (mæmǽlədʒi:) *n.* the branch of zoology concerned with the study of mammals [fr. Mod. L. *Mammalia*+Gk *logos*, word]

mam·ma·ry (mǽməri:) *adj.* of, relating to or affecting the mammae

mam·mee (mæmí:) *n. Mammea americana*, fam. *Guttiferoe*, a tropical American tree cultivated for its edible, pulpy fruit ‖ the fruit of this tree ‖ the sapodilla [Span. *mamey* fr. Haitian]

mam·mif·er·ous (mæmífərəs) *adj.* having breasts ‖ mammalian [fr. L. *mamma*, breast]

mam·mi·form (mǽmifɔrm) *adj.* having the shape of a breast [fr. L. *mamma*, breast]

mammilla *MAMILLA

mammillary *MAMILLARY

mam·mo·graph (mǽməgræf) or **mam·mo·gram** (mǽməgræm) *n.* (*med.*) breast X-ray, used to detect breast cancer, sometimes taken after an injection of a contrast medium, capable of exposing very small growths —**mammogram** *n.* X-ray picture —**mammography** *n.* process

Mam·mon (mǽmən) *n.* a personification of wealth as an evil god or influence [M.E. fr. L.L. *mamona, mammona* fr. Gk fr. Aram. *māmŏn, māmŏnā*, wealth]

mam·mo·plas·ty (mǽməplæsti:) *n.* (*med.*) plastic surgery of the breast, sometimes involving silicone-rubber injection

mam·moth (mǽmə) **1.** *n.* any of several extinct elephants, distinguished by great size, long hair and long curved tusks, esp. *Mammuthus primigenius*, the woolly mammoth, found preserved in ice in Siberia ‖ something of very great size **2.** *adj.* of very great size [Russ. *mammot*, origin unknown]

Ma·mo·ré (mɑmɔréi) a river (600 miles) flowing north from central Bolivia into Brazil, a headstream of the Madeira

man (mæn) *pl.* **men** (men) *n. Homo sapiens,* a member of a race of erect, biped mammals, with a highly developed brain, having the powers of articulate speech, abstract reasoning and imagination ‖ the human race in general ‖ an adult human male ‖ a person having the fortitude etc. regarded as proper in an adult human male ‖ a husband (only in 'man and wife') ‖ a male employee, esp. a valet ‖ (*chess* etc.) one of the pieces used in playing **as one man** in unison, unanimously **man for man** comparing individuals in one group with those in another, *man for man the teams were evenly matched* **to a man** (in apposition) every individual without exception, *they volunteered to a man* [O.E. *man, mann, mon, monn*]

man *pres. part.* **man·ning** *past* and *past part.* **manned** *v.t.* to supply (a post, vessel, field gun etc.) with the man or men needed ‖ to take one's operational position at (a gun, helm etc.) [O.E. *mannian*]

ma·na (mɑ́nə) *n.* an immaterial power believed by many primitive peoples to be inherent in certain privileged persons and things [Polynesian]

man·a·bout-town (mǽnəḅauttáun) *pl.* **men·a·bout-town** (ménəḅauttáun) *n.* a man who leads a fashionable social life

man·a·cle (mǽnək'l) **1.** *n.* (usually *pl.*) a steel clasp, heavy chain or handcuff used to bind a person's wrists close together *v.t. pres. part.* **man·a·cling** *past* and *past part.* **man·a·cled** to fasten manacles on (someone) ‖ to restrict the freedom of action of (someone) as if by manacles [M.E. *manicle* fr. O.F.]

man·age (mǽnidʒ) *v. pres. part.* **man·ag·ing** *past* and *past part.* **man·aged** *v.t.* to exercise control over, *to manage a shop* ‖ to handle, manipulate, *to manage a rifle* ‖ to influence (someone) so that he does as one wishes ‖ to use economically and with forethought, *to manage one's resources* ‖ (often with infin.) to succeed in accomplishing or handling, but with difficulty, *she managed to persuade him, can you manage another?* ‖ *v.i.* to be able to cope with a situation, *can you manage on your own?* ‖ to contrive to make one's budget suffice **man·age·a·bíl·i·ty** *n.* **mán·age·a·ble** *adj.* **mán·age·a·bly** *adv.* [fr. Ital. *maneggiare,* to handle]

man·age·ment (mǽnidʒmənt) *n.* a managing or being managed ‖ (of a business or other collective enterprise) the body of those in positions of administrative authority

management information system (*business*) a systems approach to the study of information needed by management, made possible by use of computers, utilizing creation of models involving the entire environment as well as internal information

man·ag·er (mǽnidʒər) *n.* someone who manages a company, department, institution etc. ‖ someone who manages household or other affairs in a specified way, *his wife is a good manager* ‖ (*law*) someone appointed to administer an estate in chancery etc. ‖ someone who administers the business affairs of an artistic, athletic or other enterprise ‖ someone who looks after the financial interests of an entertainer, athlete etc. **man·ag·er·ess** (mǽnidʒəris, *Br.* mænidʒərés) *n.* a female manager **man·a·ge·ri·al** (mǽnidʒíəri:əl) *adj.*

man·a·ge·ri·al·ist (mǽnədʒíəri:əlist) *n.* one who believes that government, business, etc., should be run by professional managers, e.g., city managers

Ma·na·gua (mənɑ́gwə) the capital (pop. 552,900) of Nicaragua, on Lake Managua (area 386 sq. miles) in the west central volcanic region. It is largely modern, rebuilt twice: once after the 1931 earthquake and fire and again after the devastating 1972 earthquake that caused 10,000 casualties. Industries: food processing, building materials. University (1961)

man·a·kin (mǽnəkin) *n.* any of several members of *Pipridae,* a family of small, gaily colored tropical American birds [var. of MANIKIN]

man amplifier a device attached to the body that enables the person to perform superhuman feats of strength or withstand the application of great pressure

Manaos *MANAUS

Ma·nas·sas 1st and 2nd Battle of (mənǽsəs), the 1st and 2nd Battles of Bull Run

Ma·nas·seh (mənǽsə) Hebrew patriarch, son of Joseph ‖ the Israelite tribe of which he was the ancestor

man-at-arms (mǽnətɑ́rmz) *pl.* **men-at-arms** (ménətɑ́rmz) *n.* (*hist.*) a heavily armed, esp. mounted, soldier

man·a·tee (mǽnətí:) *n.* any of several members of *Trichechus,* order *Sirenia,* a genus of herbivorous swimming mammals up to 12 ft long, of the rivers and coasts of tropical America, the West Indies, and W. Africa, esp. *T. manatus,* which has been widely hunted for food and for its blubber [Span. *manati* fr. Carib]

Ma·naus, Ma·naos (mənáus) a port (pop. 462,800) of N.W. Brazil, on the Rio Negro near its junction with the Amazon, accessible to ocean steamers. It was the center of a rubber boom (early 20th c.)

man·ca·la (mɑnkɑ́lə) *n.* basic ancient boardgame, played with 8 to 12 cups holding seeds; played in many parts of the world

Manche (mɑ̃ʃ) a department (area 2,475 sq. miles, pop. 451,700) in N.W. France (*NORMANDY). Chief town: Saint-Lô

Man·ches·ter (mǽntʃistər) an industrial and commercial center (pop. 449,168), a county borough in Lancashire, England, connected with the Mersey estuary and the sea by the Manchester Ship Canal (35½ miles long, opened 1894). Products: machinery, aircraft, cotton textiles, clothing, paper, foodstuffs, chemicals. University (1880)

Man·ches·ter (mǽntʃestər) a manufacturing and industrial city (pop. 90,936) in S. New Hampshire, the largest city in the state: cotton and woolen goods, cigars, shoes

Manchester school (mǽntʃistər) a group of British political economists (19th c.), led by Cobden and Bright, advocating free trade and laissez-faire

man·chi·neel (mǽntʃiní:l) *n. Hippomane mancinella,* fam. *Euphorbiaceae,* a tropical American tree with poisonous latex and apple-shaped, acrid fruit ‖ its wood, used in cabinetmaking [F. *mancenille* fr. Span. *manzanilla* dim. of *manzana,* apple]

Man·chu (mæntʃú:) **1.** *adj.* of or relating to Manchuria, its people, language etc. **2.** *pl.* **Man·chu, Man·chus** *n.* (*hist.*) a member of a Mongolian people from Manchuria which conquered China (17th c.) and established the Manchu, or Ch'ing, dynasty (1644–1912) ‖ the Tungusic language spoken by the Manchus

Man·chu·kuo (mæntʃú:kwóu) *MANCHURIA

Man·chu·ri·a (mæntʃúəri:ə) a historical region (approx. 585,000 sq. miles) of N.E. China, now comprising Heilungkiang, Kirin and Liaoning provinces and part of the Inner Mongolian Autonomous Region. Settled by nomadic tribes and by the Chinese (c. 1000 B.C.), it became part of the Chinese empire (3rd c. B.C.). Manchurian tribes dominated China (10th–14th cc. and, under the Manchu dynasty, 1644–1912). Russia forced China (1858–60) to cede parts of Manchuria, which was disputed (1895–1905) between Russia and Japan. It was occupied (1932–45) by Japan as the puppet kingdom of Manchukuo, but reverted (1945) to China

man·ci·ple (mǽnsəp'l) *n.* a steward who provisions a college, a monastery, one of the Inns of Court etc. [O.F. *manciple, mancipe*]

Man·co Ca·pac I (mɑ́ŋkoukápɑk) 12th-c. legendary founder of the Inca empire, of its capital at Cuzco, and of the Inca dynasty

Manco Capac II (d. c. 1544), the last Inca sovereign, murdered by the Spaniards

Man·dae·an (mændí:ən) *n.* a member of an ancient Gnostic sect surviving in S. Iraq ‖ the Aramaic language used in Mandaean writings [fr. Mandaean *mandayyā* trans. of Gk *gnōstikoi,* Gnostics]

Man·da·lay (mænd'léi) the chief city (pop. 417,266) of Upper Burma, a port on the Irrawaddy. Industries: silk weaving, gold, silver and jade work, wood carving. It is the center of Burmese Buddhism and contains a famous monastery and many pagodas. University (1957)

man·da·mus (mændéiməs) *n.* (*law*) a writ issued by the Kings' (Queen's) Bench Division of the British High Court of Justice, requiring that a specified public duty shall be done ‖ (*law*) a writ made by a higher court to a lower one or to a corporation or an individual, requiring that a specified thing be done [L.=we command]

Man·dan (mǽndæn) *pl.* **Man·dan, Man·dans** *n.* a sedentary Plains Indian people who inhabited (18th c.) south central North Dakota. When

visited (1804) by Lewis and Clark they numbered about 1,250. They were placed (1870) on the Fort Berthold Reservation, North Dakota ‖ a member of this people ‖ their language

man·da·rin (mǽndərin) *n.* a Mandarin orange ‖ the strong orange-red color of this fruit [fr. F. *mandarine*]

man·darin *n.* (*hist.*) a Chinese public official ‖ a person with literary influence, often an elder and a reactionary **Mandarin** the official standard Chinese dialect [Port. *mandarim* fr. Malay *mantri,* minister of state fr. Hindi]

mandarin duck *Aix galericulata,* a brightly feathered, crested duck native to China

man·da·rine (mǽndərí:n) *n.* a mandarin orange [F.]

mandarin orange *Citrus reticulata,* a small Chinese orange tree which bears small, sweet oranges with very loose skins ‖ the fruit of this tree (cf. TANGERINE)

man·da·tar·y (mǽndətɛri) *pl.* **man·da·tar·ies** *n.* a nation to which a mandate is given [fr. L. *mandatarius*]

man·date (mǽndeit) **1.** *n.* an instruction, or authorization given or conferred ‖ instructions concerning policy, assumed to be given by constituents to a legislative body or its members ‖ (*law*) an order by a court or legal officer to an inferior court or officer ‖ (*Br., law*) a contract to deliver goods in bail ‖ (*hist.*) a commission given to a state by the League of Nations to administer, as trustee, a specified territory ‖ a mandated territory **2.** *v.t. pres. part.* **man·dat·ing** *past* and *past part.* **man·dat·ed** to assign (a territory) as a mandate, *New Guinea was mandated to Australia* [fr. L. *mandatum,* a command]

man·da·to·ry (mǽndətɔri:, mǽndətɔuri:) **1.** *adj.* of, relating to or having the force of a mandate **2.** **man·da·to·ries** *n.* a mandatary [fr. L.L. *mandatorius*]

Man·de (mǽndei) *pl.* **Man·de, Man·des** *n.* a member of the Mandingo people ‖ a group of W. African languages including Malinke, Susu etc.

Man·de·ville, Sir John (mǽndəvil) (14th c.), the presumed author of 'The Voiage and Travaile of Sir John Mandeville' (c. 1357–71), a book of travels and adventures, originally in French, which purports to be an account of the author's travels between 1322 and 1357 across three parts of the world. It is largely a compilation of the works and travels of others

man·di·ble (mǽndəb'l) *n.* (*anat.*) the lower jaw, formed either of a single bone or of fused bones ‖ (*zool.*) either part of the beak of a bird ‖ (*zool.*) either of the pair of outermost mouth appendages in an arthropod, often forming biting jaws **man·dib·u·lar** (mændíbjulər) *adj.* [fr. L.L. *mandibula*]

Man·din·go (mændíŋgou) *pl.* **Man·din·gos, Man·din·goes** *n.* a member of a people of W. Africa, esp. of Mali, Senegal and the Ivory Coast ‖ the Sudanic language spoken by this people

man·do·lin, man·do·line (mǽnd'lin, mǽnd'lín) *n.* a musical instrument of the lute family, having paired metal strings mounted on a deep, round-backed body and played with a plectrum [fr. F. *mandoline* fr. Ital.]

man·drag·o·ra (mændrǽgərə) *n.* mandrake [L.L. fr. Gk]

man·drake (mǽndreik) *n. Mandragora officinarum,* fam. *Solanaceae,* a plant of Mediterranean regions ‖ its forked root, used for its narcotic and emetic effects [M.E. *mandragge* fr. L. fr. Gk]

man·drel (mǽndrəl) *n.* the axis (e.g. of a lathe) inserted in a work being turned or machined, to hold it while it revolves ‖ a cylindrical rod around which other metal is forged or shaped [origin unknown]

man·dril (mǽndril) *n.* a mandrel

man·drill (mǽndril) *n. Mandrillus mormon,* a large, ferocious baboon of W. Africa. It has red buttock callosities and, in the male, cheek protuberances striped with brilliant red and blue [MAN+older *drill,* a kind of **baboon** prob. fr. native name]

mane (mein) *n.* the long hair growing on the top or sides of the neck of some animals, e.g. of the horse or lion [O.E. *manu*]

man-eat·er (mǽni:tər) *n.* an animal that eats human flesh, e.g. a lion, tiger or crocodile ‖ *Carcharodon carcharias,* a large tropical shark

man·eb [C₄H₆MnN₂S₄] (mǽneb) *n.* (*organic chem.*) a fungicide, irritating to skin, eyes, nose, throat

---

ma·nège, ma·nege (mænéʒ, mænéiʒ) n. a riding academy ‖ the training of horses ‖ the exercises used in training horses [F.]

Ma·nes (méini:z, máneis) pl. n. (Rom. Antiq.) the souls of the dead, venerated as divinities **ma·nes** n. the soul of a dead person as an object of reverence [L.]

Ma·net (mænéi, F. mæne), Édouard (1832–83), French painter. After 1870 he was associated with the Impressionists and came to use the lighter colors and free handling of Impressionism, and shared their interest in natural light as opposed to studio light. His earlier work is characterized by broad, fluid brushwork, an interest in direct, natural treatment of character in the tradition of Velazquez and Goya, and a remarkably predominant use of black, with strong, unmodulated dark-light contrasts e.g. in 'le Déjeuner sur l'herbe' (1863) and 'Olympia' (1865)

ma·neu·ver, esp. Br. **ma·nœu·vre** (mənú:vər) n. a tactical movement of military troops, naval vessels etc. ‖ (usually pl.) training exercises involving such movement ‖ a cleverly thought-out or dextrous movement, action or plan [F. manœuvre]

maneuver, esp. Br. **manœuvre** pres. part. **ma·neu·ver·ing** past and past part. **ma·neu·vered**, esp. Br. **ma·nœu·vred** v.t. to cause (troops etc.) to perform maneuvers ‖ to move, manage or guide cleverly and dextrously ‖ to cause by clever contriving, they maneuvered his resignation ‖ (with 'into' or 'out of') to cause to acquire or lose a specified condition, position etc., they maneuvered him out of office ‖ v.i. to engage in a maneuver or maneuvers **ma·neu·ver·a·bil·i·ty**, esp. Br. **ma·nœv·ra·bil·i·ty** n. **ma·néu·ver·a·ble**, esp. Br. **ma·nóeuv·ra·ble** adj. [fr. F. manœuvrer]

Man·fred (mǽnfrid) (c. 1232–66), king of Sicily (1258–66), son of Emperor Frederick II. He struggled against the papacy for control of Italy, and was killed fighting an army led by Charles of Anjou

Man Friday a reliable and efficient male employee who performs a wide range of tasks and is regarded as indispensable [after Friday, native servant in Defoe's novel 'Robinson Crusoe' (1719)]

man·ful (mǽnfəl) adj. manly (brave and resolute)

man·ga·bey (mǽŋgəbei) n. a longtailed monkey of the genus Cercocebus, native to tropical Africa [fr. Mangabey, region of Madagascar]

Man·ga·lore (mǽŋgəlór) n. a port (pop. 165,174) of Mysore, India, on the Malabar coast: food processing, textiles, tiles

man·ga·nate (mǽŋgənit, mǽŋgəneit) n. any of several groups of salts containing manganese in the anion, e.g. a salt of manganic acid

man·ga·nese (mǽŋgəni:s, mǽŋgəni:z) n. a grayish-white, polyvalent metallic element (symbol Mn, at. no. 25, at. mass 54.93) that is usually hard and brittle, occurring in nature usually as an oxide, carbonate or silicate. Because of its high reactivity, it is found in a large variety of compounds. It is chiefly used in the form of ferromanganese in steelmaking [F. manganèse fr. Ital.]

manganese dioxide MnO_2, a dark brown or gray-black insoluble compound used as an oxidizing agent and a catalyst

man·gan·ic (mæŋgǽnik) adj. of, relating to, or derived from manganese, esp. of compounds in which it is trivalent

manganic acid H_2MnO_4, an acid known only in solution and by its salts

Manganin (mǽŋgənin) trade name for an alloy of copper (84%), manganese (15%), and nickel (4%) with a low temperature coefficient of resistance (38 × 10^{-8} ohmmeters), used in making precision resistors

man·ga·nite (mǽŋgənait) n. MnO(OH), an ore of manganese ‖ any of a series of unstable salts resulting from the reaction of manganese dioxide with a base

man·ga·nous (mǽŋgənəs) adj. of, relating to, or derived from manganese, esp. of compounds in which it is bivalent

mange (meindʒ) n. any of several contagious skin diseases of domestic animals and sometimes man, caused by parasitic mites, and marked esp. by hair loss [M.E. manjewe fr. O.F.]

man·gel-wur·zel (mǽŋg'lwə́:rz'l) n. a variety of beet ‖ its root, used for feeding cattle etc. [G. fr. mangold, beet+wurzel, root]

man·ger (méindʒər) n. a trough from which horses and cattle feed in their stalls [F. mangeoire]

man·gi·ly (méindʒili:) adv. in a mangy manner

man·gi·ness (méindʒi:nis) n. the state or quality of being mangy

Man·gla (mʌ́ŋglə) the site of a great Indian dam on the Jhelum (*INDUS)

man·gle (mǽŋg'l) pres. part. **man·gling** past and past part. **man·gled** v.t. to hack or cut or crush with or as if with repeated blows ‖ to ruin by bad interpretation, pronunciation etc. [fr. A.E. mangler, mahangler]

mangle 1. n. a machine having heated rollers between which damp linen is pressed smooth ‖ (Br.) a heavy, old-fashioned wringer 2. v.t. pres. part. **man·gling** past and past part. **man·gled** to press in a mangle [Du. mangel fr. mangelen, to mangle]

man·go (mǽŋgou) pl. **man·goes, man·gos** n. Mangifera indica, fam. Anacardiaceae, a large Indian tree cultivated widely for its fruit ‖ the fruit of this tree, a large, juicy drupe with aromatic pulp, eaten ripe or used green in jam, pickles etc. [Port. manga fr. Malay fr. Tamil]

man·gold (mǽŋgəld) n. a mangel-wurzel

man·gold-wur·zel (mǽŋgəldwə́:rz'l) n. a mangel-wurzel

man·go·nel (mǽŋgənel) n. (hist.) a medieval military machine for hurling large stones etc. [O.F. dim. of L.L. mangona, mangonum fr. Gk]

man·go·steen (mǽŋgəsti:n) n. Garcinia mangostana, fam. Guttiferae, a small East Indian tree ‖ its sweet purplish fruit [Malay mangustan]

man·grove (mǽŋgrouv) n. a member of Rhizophora, fam. Rhizophoraceae, a genus of tropical trees or shrubs growing in swampy ground. Its many prop roots bind the mud, gradually building land [obscure, but synonymous with Port. mangue or Span. mangle. The spelling was influenced by 'grove']

mangrove swamp the association of tropical trees and shrubs at the mouth of rivers and along coasts, over which the tide flows daily, leaving the mud bare at low water

man·gy (méindʒi:) comp. **man·gi·er** superl. **man·gi·est** adj. infected with mange ‖ of or relating to mange ‖ shabby, poorly kept-up

man·han·dle (mǽnhænd'l) pres. part. **man·han·dling** past and past part. **man·han·dled** v.t. to handle roughly, beat up, the police began manhandling the demonstrators ‖ to move by manual force, without the use of a machine

Man·hat·tan (mænhǽtən) a borough (pop. 1,428,285) of New York City, consisting of Manhattan Is. (12.5 miles long, 2.5 miles wide), the financial, commercial and cultural center of the city, and adjacent islets

Manhattan Project a U.S. program initiated at the advent of 2nd world war to produce the atomic bomb. It was headed first by Vannevar Bush and then by Gen. Leslie Groves and was conducted at Oak Ridge, Tennessee, although it was named for the Manhattan Engineer District of the U.S. Army Corps of Engineers. Research was conducted at various universities under Arthur Compton of the University of Chicago; J. Robert Oppenheimer directed the weapons laboratory at Los Alamos, New Mexico. In 1945 the first atomic bomb was tested at Alamogordo, New Mexico

man·hole (mǽnhoul) n. a hole in a floor, street etc. allowing access to a sewer, pipe etc.

man·hood (mǽnhud) n. the state or period of being an adult male ‖ manly qualities of courage and fortitude ‖ (rhet.) men collectively, England's manhood

man-hour (mǽnauər) n. the amount of work done by one man in one hour, as a statistical unit of measurement of labor cost in production

Ma·ni (mǽni:) *MANICHAEISM

ma·ni·a (méini:ə) n. a form of mental disorder marked by great elation and violent action (*MANIC-DEPRESSIVE PSYCHOSIS) ‖ (pop.) an irrational and prolonged desire or enthusiasm, a mania for gambling ‖ used as a suffix in compounds denoting specific kinds of mental disorder, e.g. kleptomania [L. fr. Gk mania, madness]

ma·ni·ac (méini:æk) 1. adj. of, relating to or typical of mania ‖ affected with mania 2. n. a person affected with mania **ma·ni·a·cal** (mənáiək'l) adj. [fr. L. L. maniacus, affected with mania]

man·ic (mǽnik) adj. (psychol.) affected with mania ‖ pertaining to or resembling mania [fr. Gk manikos]

man·ic-de·pres·sive psychosis (mǽnikdiprésiv) a mental illness commonly characterized by self-disparagement and melancholia alternating with self-assertiveness and unreasonable elation

Man·i·chae·an, Man·i·che·an (mænikí:ən) 1. adj. of or relating to Manichaeism 2. n. an adherent of Manichaeism

Man·i·chae·ism (mæniki:izəm) n. the religion founded by Mani (c. 216–c. 276), a Persian who held that the universe is dually controlled by opposing powers of good and evil, which had become intermingled in the present age, but at a future time would be separated and return to their own realms. Mani's followers were to aid this separation by leading an ascetic life. The religion spread widely in Asia and around the Mediterranean, but died out in the West by the 6th c., although it was a major religion in the East until the 14th c. It influenced several early Christian heresies

ma·ni·cot·ti (mænikóti:) pl. manicotti (It.) a dish of stuffed tubular pasta shells, usu. filled with ricotta cheese and sometimes beef, mushrooms, bread crumbs, onions. It is often covered with a tomato sauce

man·i·cure (mǽnikjuər) 1. n. a beauty treatment for the hands, esp. the nails 2. v.t. pres. part. **man·i·cur·ing** past and past part. **man·i·cured** to give a manicure to (the hands) ‖ to give a manicure to the hands of (a person) **mán·i·cur·ist** n. a person who gives manicures [F. fr. manus hand]

man·i·fest (mǽnifest) n. a detailed list of a ship's cargo, submitted to Customs officers [F. manifeste]

manifest v.t. to show plainly, make manifest ‖ to list in a ship's manifest [fr. F. manifester or L. manifestare]

manifest adj. immediately evident to sense perception or to the mind [fr. L. manifestus, touched with the hand]

man·i·fes·ta·tion (mænifestéiʃən) n. a manifesting or being manifested ‖ a public demonstration, esp. by a political group ‖ something that makes manifest the presence or existence of something else, his present was a manifestation of his goodwill ‖ a form or phenomenon by which a spirit makes itself manifest [fr. L. L. manifestatio (manifestationis)]

Manifest Destiny (Am. hist.) a term implying divine sanction for U.S. territorial expansion. It was coined in an 1845 issue of the 'United States magazine and Democratic Review', edited by John L. O'Sullivan

man·i·fes·to (mæniféstou) pl. **man·i·fes·tos, man·i·fes·toes** n. a public statement of opinions or intentions, esp. on behalf of an organized and authoritative body of persons [Ital.]

man·i·fold (mǽnifould) 1. adj. having many different parts, applications, forms etc. ‖ (of things, qualities etc.) numerous and varied, manifold difficulties 2. n. a copy made by manifolding ‖ (engin.) a pipe with several lateral outlets for connecting it with other pipes 3. v.t. to make a number of carbon copies of (a letter etc.) [O.E. manigfeald]

man·i·kin, man·ni·kin (mǽnikin) n. a tiny man ‖ an anatomical model of the human body with detachable parts for revealing structures ‖ a mannequin (dummy) [Du. manneken dim. of man, man]

Ma·ni·la (mənílə) the capital, chief port and commercial center (pop. 5,900,000) of the Philippines on Manila Bay, S.W. Luzon, one of Asia's best harbors. Industries: textiles, light manufactures. Chief universities: University of the Philippines (1908), Santo Tomás (1611)

Manila, Ma·nil·la n. Manila hemp ‖ Manila paper ‖ a cigar or cheroot made of Philippine tobacco

Manila Bay a landlocked inlet and natural harbor of the South China Sea in the Philippine Is. It was the site of an engagement (1898) in which U.S. Admiral George Dewey destroyed the Spanish fleet at the beginning of the Spanish-American War

Manila hemp, Manilla hemp a tough, pliable fiber used for cordage, esp. marine ropes, obtained from leafstalks of Musa textitis, fam. Musaceae, a Philippine plant ‖ this plant

Manila paper, Manilla paper a strong, light brown or buff paper, originally made from Manila hemp

Manilla *MANILA

---

man in the street the hypothetical average member of the community

man·i·oc (mǽni:ɒk, méini:ɒk) n. cassava [of Tupi origin]

man·i·ple (mǽnəp'l) n. a strip of material worn over the left arm by a priest celebrating Mass ‖ (hist.) a unit of the Roman army, comprising 60 or 120 men [O.F. maniple]

ma·nip·u·late (mənípjuleit) pres. part. **ma·nip·u·lating** past and past part. **ma·nip·u·lat·ed** v.t. to handle, esp. with skill, to manipulate the controls of a machine ‖ to deal with mentally, to manipulate one's arguments ‖ to cause by clever maneuvering to act as one wishes ‖ to make dishonest changes in (e.g. election results) so as to suit one's purpose ‖ (commerce) to influence (a market) by cunningly calculated trading etc. [backformation fr. MANIPULATION]

ma·nip·u·la·tion (mənipjuléiʃən) n. a manipulating or being manipulated ‖ an instance of this [F.]

ma·nip·u·la·tor (mənípjuleitər) n. someone who or something that manipulates [MANIPULATE]

Man·i·pur (mǽnəpuər) a Union Territory (area 8,628 sq. miles, pop. 1,433,691) of N.E. India, a high plateau surrounded by mountains. Capital: Imphal. Products: rice, fruit, bamboo, teak

Man, Isle of an island (area 227 sq. miles, pop. 48,000) in the Irish Sea, forming a division of Great Britain, administered under its own ancient laws. Capital: Douglas. Industries: farming, sheep raising, fishing, lead and zinc mining, tourism. The Manx language barely survives. The island was ruled by Norway (c. 600–1266) and Scotland (1266–90), after which it was disputed between England and Scotland until 1346, when it passed to England, coming into the possession of the English crown (1399)

ma·ni·to (mǽnitou) pl. **ma·ni·tos, man·i·to** n. manitou **man·i·tou, man·i·tu** (mǽnitu:) pl. **man·i·tous, man·i·tou, man·i·tus, man·i·tu** n. the name given by the Algonquian Indians to a pervading spirit or deity having supernatural powers (good or evil) over the vital forces of nature [Algonquian]

Man·i·to·ba (mǽnətóubə) a province (area 251,000 sq. miles, pop. 1,051,500 of central Canada. It is divided between the Canadian Shield and the prairies. Capital: Winnipeg. Agriculture: cereals (esp. wheat), vegetables, cattle. Resources: furs, nickel, copper, zinc, gold, silver, oil, timber, hydroelectric power. Industries: food processing, iron and steel, rolling stock, clothing, printing, publishing. The Hudson's Bay Company controlled early settlements (1811–70). Canada bought the company's rights (1869) and made Manitoba a province (1870)

Manitoba, Lake a lake (area 1,817 sq. miles) in S. Manitoba province, Canada, draining into Lake Winnipeg

Ma·ni·za·les (mɒni:sáles) a city and coffee center (pop. 246,036) in the Andes of W. central Colombia

man·kind (mǽnkaind) n. the human race ‖ men as contrasted with women

Man·ley (mǽnli:), Norman (1893–1969), Jamaican statesman. He founded (1938) the People's National Party. As chief minister (1955–9) and premier (1959–62) of Jamaica, he led his country to independence

man·like (mǽnlaik) adj. having the qualities proper to a man ‖ resembling a man

man·li·ness (mǽnli:nis) n. the state or quality of being manly

man·ly (mǽnli:) comp. **man·li·er** superl. **man·li·est** adj. having qualities regarded as proper in a man, e.g. courage ‖ befitting a man, manly sports

man-made (mǽnmeid) adj. made by man, artificial, not natural

Mann (mæn, mɒn), Heinrich (1871–1950), German writer, brother of Thomas Mann. His works include the grotesque novels 'The Blue Angel' (1905) and 'The Goddesses' (1902–3)

Mann, Horace (1796–1859), U.S. educator. As secretary (1837–49) of the newly created Massachusetts board of education, he successfully campaigned for teacher-training institutions, better schoolhouses and teaching equipment, and higher salaries for teachers

Mann, Thomas (1875–1955), German writer. Many of his books are concerned with the problem of the talented man who does not fit in, either because he does not accept society's values or because his talent is linked with disease

or corruption. Mann's works include the short story 'Death in Venice' (1913) and the novels 'Buddenbrooks' (1901), 'The Magic Mountain' (1924) and 'Doctor Faustus' (1947)

man·na (mǽnə) n. (Bible) food miraculously supplied to the Israelites in the wilderness (Exodus xvi, 14–36) ‖ any food for the mind or spirit that is felt as something miraculously given ‖ a dried sweet exudation from certain European ash trees, used as a laxative [O.E. fr. L.L. fr. Gk fr. Heb.]

manned orbiting laboratory a manned research satellite abbr. **MOL** Cf SKYLAB

man·ne·quin (mǽnikin) n. a model (person who demonstrates clothes) ‖ a dummy figure used by dressmakers, tailors or artists [var. of MANIKIN]

man·ner (mǽnər) n. a way of doing something ‖ (pl.) social behavior with respect to standards, it is bad manners to interrupt ‖ (pl.) correct social behavior, he has no manners ‖ (pl.) human behavior as manifested in society, a comedy of manners **all manner of** all kinds of **by any (no) manner of means** by any (no) means **to the manner born** accustomed by birth and upbringing to know how to behave in given circumstances **mán·nered** adj. (usually in combination) having manners of a given kind, well-mannered ‖ having mannerisms, a mannered style of writing [A. F. manere]

Man·ner·heim (mǽnərhaim), Baron Carl Gustav Emil (1867–1951), Finnish marshal and statesman. He was regent (1918–19) of Finland and planned the Mannerheim line, a 65-mile system of defenses along Finland's Russian border (1930s). He was head of the armed forces (1939–40 and 1941–4) and was president of Finland (1944–6)

man·ner·ism (mǽnərizəm) n. an affected gesture, habit, manner of speaking etc. ‖ adherence to a personal artistic or literary style marked by affectation **Man·ner·ism** a 16th-c. style of painting and architecture, chiefly Italian, broadly characterized by distorted, elongated, unquiet human figures and harsh color, used to intensify the emotional impact. Michelangelo, Tintoretto, El Greco all produced Mannerist masterpieces **mán·ner·ist, Mán·ner·ist** adjs

man·ner·li·ness (mǽnərli:nis) n. the quality of being mannerly

man·ner·ly (mǽnərli:) adj. having or showing good manners

Mann·heim (mǽnhaim) a port and industrial center (pop. 309,059) in Baden, West Germany, at the confluence of the Rhine and the Neckar: metallurgy, machinery, cars, textiles, chemical products, food

mannikin *MANIKIN

Man·ning (mǽniŋ), Henry Edward (1808–92), English churchman. After being a member of the Oxford movement, he was received into the Roman Catholic Church (1851). As archbishop of Westminster (1865–92) he began the building of Westminster Cathedral, and was made cardinal (1875)

man·nish (mǽniʃ) adj. inappropriately like a man, a mannish woman ‖ inappropriately characteristic of a man, she has a mannish stride

man·ni·tol (mǽnitɒl) n. $C_6H_8(OH)_6$, a white crystalline alcohol used in kidney-function diagnoses [fr. mannite, mannitol fr. MANNA]

man·nose (mǽnous) n. $C_6H_{12}O_6$, a sugar obtained by oxidizing mannitol [MANNITOL]

manoeuvre *MANEUVER

man of letters an author of serious literary works

man of straw a person who has authority in appearance only, usually used as a shield for someone else or as a cover for doubtfully honest transactions ‖ an imaginary person invented to put forward a point of view which can easily be countered

man of the world a man who has practical social wisdom as a result of wide experience

man-of-war (mǽnəvwɔ́r) pl. **men-of-war** (mén·əvwɔ́r) n. a warship

ma·nom·e·ter (mənɒmitər) n. an instrument for measuring gaseous or vapor pressure [fr. F. manomètre fr. Gk manos, thin+metron, measure]

man-on-man (mǽnɒnmæn) adj. (sports) in competitive team sports, of the defense strategy of assigning one defensive person for one offensive player —**man-on-man** adv.

man·or (mǽnər) n. (hist.) a medieval landed estate held by a lord under the feudal system and worked by serfs or tenant farmers as a largely self-sufficient economic unit, chiefly in W. Eu-

rope. The tenants rendered dues in kind, money or services in return for their land, and the lord enjoyed certain rights over both land and tenants, e.g. the right to hold a court ‖ (Am. hist.) land occupied for a long term or in perpetuity by tenants who paid a perpetual fixed rent to the landowner **ma·no·ri·al** (mənɔ́ri:əl, mənóuri:əl) adj. [O.F. manoir, habitation]

man-o'-war bird (mǽnəwɔ́r) a frigate bird

man·pow·er (mǽnpauər) n. the persons available for some purpose, regarded as one of the resources of a nation, industry etc.

man-rate (mǽnreit) v. (astronautics) to certify a passenger-carrying space vehicle as safe for flight

man·sard (mǽnsərd) n. a roof divided into a steep lower part and a less steep upper part on all four sides ‖ the story under such a roof [after N. F. Mansart]

Man·sart (mɑ́sær), Nicolas François (1598–1666), French architect. His buildings include the façade of the Hôtel Carnavalet in Paris, part of Blois Château etc.

Mansart (Jules Hardouin-Mansart, 1646–1708), French architect. He designed many famous French buildings, incl. much of the palace at Versailles

manse (mæns) n. the house of a Presbyterian minister [fr. M.L. mansus, mansum, mansa, dwelling]

man·serv·ant (mǽnsə:rvənt) pl. **men·serv·ants** (ménsə:rvənts) n. a male domestic employee

Mans·feld (mɑ́nsfelt), Peter Ernst von (1580–1626), German soldier. He commanded the Protestant forces in the early part of the Thirty Years' War

Mans·field (mǽnzfi:ld), Katherine (Kathleen Mansfield Beauchamp, 1888–1923), British short-story writer, born in New Zealand. Her works include 'Bliss' (1920) and 'The Garden Party' (1922)

Mansfield, Mt the highest point (4,393 ft) in the Green Mtns, N. Vermont, part of the Appalachian system

man·sion (mǽnʃən) n. a very large, imposing house [O.F.]

man·slaugh·ter (mǽnslɔtər) n. (law) the unlawful killing of a human being without malicious intent

man space (mil.) the space and weight factor used to determine the combat capacity of vehicles, craft, and transport aircraft, based on the requirements of one person with individual equipment

man·sue·tude (mǽnswitu:d, mǽnswitju:d) n. (rhet.) gentleness ‖ submissiveness [fr. L. mansuetudo]

Man·sû·ra (mænsúərə) a town (pop. 258,000) of the Nile delta, Egypt, near Damietta: cotton trade and weaving, tanning

Man·te·gna (mɑnténjə), Andrea (1431–1506), Italian painter. His art is characterized by solidly modeled human figures against backgrounds which resemble theatrical sets, and by a highly dramatic use of perspective, esp. of foreshortening. His extant works include the 'Martyrdom of St Christopher' from a fresco cycle in Padua (c. 1459), and the paintings 'St Sebastian' (c. 1460) and 'The Dead Christ' (1506)

man·tel (mǽnt'l) n. an ornamental structure above and around a fireplace [var. of MANTLE]

man·tel·et (mǽnt'lit, mǽntlit) n. (hist.) a movable shelter used to shield besiegers in attack ‖ a short cape [O.F. mantelet dim. of mantel, coat]

man·tel·piece (mǽnt'lpi:s) n. a mantel

man·tel·shelf (mǽnt'lʃelf) pl. **man·tel·shelves** (mǽnt'lʃelvz) n. a shelf above a fireplace, usually part of the mantelpiece

man·tel·tree (mǽnt'ltri:) n. a beam or stone forming the lintel of a fireplace and supporting the masonry above

man·tic (mǽntik) adj. pertaining to or having the power of divination [fr. Gk mantikos]

man·til·la (mæntílə) n. a woman's scarf, often of lace, worn over the head and shoulders, esp. in Spain and S. America [Span., dim. of manta, cloak]

Man·ti·ne·a, Battle of (mæntiní:ə) the battle (362 B.C.) in which Epaminondas was killed while leading the Thebans to victory over the Spartans

man·tis (mǽntis) pl. **man·tis·es, man·tes** (mǽnti:z) n. an orthopterous carnivorous insect belonging to Mantis or a related genus of fam. Manteidae, having a slender body and long prothorax (*PRAYING MANTIS) [Mod. L. fr. Gk *mantis*, prophet]

man·tis·sa (mæntísə) *n.* (*math.*) the decimal part of a logarithm [L.=makeweight]

man·tle (mænt'l) **1.** *n.* a loose outer garment or sleeveless cloak ‖ anything that covers or conceals, *the mantle of secrecy* ‖ (*metall.*) a blast furnace's outer wall and casing, above the hearth ‖ (*zool.*) the fold of the body wall of mollusks, enclosing the viscera, lining the shell and containing shell-forming glands ‖ the back, scapulars and wings of a bird when these are of one color which differs from the rest of the plumage ‖ a small hood of net material coated with any of certain substances which, when heated by a gas flame, emit bright light **2.** *v. pres. part.* **man·tling** *past* and *past part.* **man·tled** *v.t.* to cover with or as if with a mantle ‖ *v.i.* (of liquids) to become coated with scum etc. ‖ (*falconry*, of a hawk) to spread each wing in succession over the corresponding outstretched leg [O.E. *mentel* and O.F. *mantel* ult. fr. L. *mantellum*, cloak]

man·tle·rock (mænt'lrɒk) *n.* the layer of residual rock fragments and soil covering solid rock

mant·let (mæntlit) *n.* a mantelet

man·tling (mæntliŋ) *n.* (*heraldry*) the ornamental drapery or scroll often shown around an achievement ‖ the mantle of a bird [MANTLE v.]

Man·tu·a (mæntʃuːə) an ancient city (pop. 65,926) of S.E. Lombardy, Italy: ducal palace (13th–17th cc.), cathedral (14th c.)

man·u·al (mænjuːəl) **1.** *adj.* relating to, done with or operated by the hands **2.** *n.* a book containing information set out briefly ‖ a hand-played keyboard on an organ or harpsichord [fr. L. *manualis* fr. *manus*, hand]

manual alphabet a deaf-and-dumb alphabet

manual training courses in the manual arts offered to school students and, in special classes, to adults

Man·u·el I Comnenus (mænjuːəl) (c. 1120–80), Byzantine emperor (1143–80), son of John II. He sided with the papacy against the Emperor Frederick I with the aim of uniting the Western and Eastern Empires, but was crushingly defeated by the Turks (1176)

Manuel II Palaeologus (c. 1348–1425), Byzantine emperor (1391–1425), son of John V. He appealed unsuccessfully to the West for aid against the Turks, who besieged Constantinople several times during his reign

Manuel I (1469–1521), king of Portugal (1495–1521). His reign saw the maritime and commercial expansion of Portugal after the discoveries of da Gama, Cabral and other navigators

Manuel II (1889–1932), last king of Portugal (1908–10). He was dethroned by revolution and fled to Britain (1910)

man·u·fac·ture (mænjufǽktʃər) **1.** *n.* the making of things on a large scale, by hand or machine or both, esp. with division of labor ‖ something made in this way **2.** *v.t. pres. part.* **man·u·fac·tur·ing** *past* and *past part.* **man·u·fac·tured** to make (goods) in this way ‖ to make up, fabricate (evidence, an excuse etc.) **man·u·fac·tur·er** *n.* [F.]

man·u·mis·sion (mænjumíʃən) *n.* a formal freeing or being freed from slavery [F.]

man·u·mit (mænjumít) *pres. part.* **man·u·mit·ting** *past* and *past part.* **man·u·mit·ted** *v.t.* to free from slavery [fr. L. *manumittere*]

ma·nure (mənúər, mənjúər) **1.** *v.t. pres. part.* **ma·nur·ing** *past* and *past part.* **ma·nured** to add dung, compost or chemicals to (soil) in order to fertilize it **2.** *n.* matter, esp. dung, added to soil for fertilizing [A.F. *maynoverer*, to work with the hands]

ma·nus (méinəs) *pl.* **ma·nus** *n.* (*anat.*) the human wrist and hand ‖ (*zool.*) the corresponding part of other vertebrates [L.=hand]

man·u·script (mænjuskript) **1.** *n.* (*abbr.* MS, *pl.* MSS) a document or book written by hand ‖ an author's written or typewritten copy of his work, as opposed to the printed copies made from it **2.** *adj.* written by hand [fr. M.L. *manuscriptus* fr. L. *manu*, by hand+*scribere* (*scriptus*), to write]

Manutius, Aldus *ALDUS MANUTIUS

Manx (mæŋks) **1.** *adj.* of or relating to the Isle of Man, its people, language etc. **2.** *n.* the Celtic language of the Isle of Man, now almost extinct

Manx cat a breed of domestic cat having no visible tail but having rudimentary tail vertebrae

Manx·man (mæŋksmən) *pl.* **Manx·men** (mæŋksmən) *n.* a native or inhabitant of the Isle of Man

man·y (méni) **1.** *adj. comp.* **more** (mɔr, mour) *superl.* **most** (moust) consisting of a large but indefinite number, *he has been there many times* ‖ (*rhet.*, before 'a' or 'an') being one of a large but indefinite number of things, people etc., *he has been there many a time* **as many** the same number of, *he has been there as many times as you have* **to be one too many for** to outdo or defeat **2.** *n.* (followed by 'of') a large, indefinite number (of people, things etc.), *many of the guests came late* **a good** (*great*) **many** a quite (very) large number **the many** the majority of people **3.** *pron.* a large, indefinite number of people or things [O.E. *manig*, *mœnig*, *monig*]

man·y·plies (méni:plaiz) *n.* the omasum [MANY+plies, pl. of PLY, a fold]

man·y·sid·ed (méni:sáidid) *adj.* having many sides ‖ having many interests or skills

Man·zo·ni (mæntsóuni), Alessandro (1785–1873), Italian novelist and poet. The revised version (1840) of his Romantic novel 'I Promessi Sposi' (1827) strongly influenced the establishment of Tuscan as the Italian literary language

MAO (*chem. abbr.*) monoamine oxidase

Mao flu *ASIAN FLU

MAOI (*chem. abbr.*) monoamine oxidase inhibitor

Mao·ism (máuizəm) *n.* philosophy and application of Marxism-Leninism with an accent on egalitarianism, developed by Chinese Communist leader Mao Zedong —**Maoist** *adj.* —**Maoize** *v.* to convert to Maoism *GANG OF FOUR, MAO TSE-TUNG

Mao·ri (máuri:) **1.** *pl.* **Mao·ri, Mao·ris** *n.* a member of the aboriginal Polynesian race of New Zealand ‖ their Austronesian language **2.** *adj.* of or relating to the Maori or their language

Mao Tse-tung (máutsetúŋ, máudzədúŋ) (1893–1976), Chinese statesman. One of the founders of the Chinese Communist party (1921), he organized peasant and industrial unions (1921–6) and, after the Communists had split from the Kuomintang (1927), set up communes in Hunan. He led the march of the Red Army from Kiangsi to Yenan (1934–5), advocated national unity in the 2nd Sino-Japanese war (1937–45) and expelled the Kuomintang forces from the mainland (1949). He was chairman of the People's Republic of China (1949–58) and remained the effective ruler of China as chairman of the Communist party of China (from 1943). He was also a poet and political theorist. In 1966 he launched the Cultural Revolution. He survived an assassination plot (1971). In 1972 he was host to U.S. President Nixon, hoping that closer ties with the U.S. would lessen the influence on China of the U.S.S.R.

map (mæp) **1.** *n.* a representation in scale, usually on a flat surface, of part or the whole of the earth's surface, showing physical, political or other features ‖ a similar representation of part of the heavens **2.** *v.t. pres. part.* **map·ping** *past* and *past part.* **mapped** to represent on a map ‖ (often with 'out') to establish the main features of (a plan, project etc.) **to put on the map** to make well known **to wipe off the map** to destroy completely (a city etc.) [fr. M.L. *mappa mundi*, map of the world, fr. L. *mappa*, napkin]

ma·ple (méip'l) *n.* a member of *Acer*, fam. *Aceraceae*, a large genus of hardwood trees and shrubs, largely of the north temperate zone ‖ their hard, lightcolored, close-grained wood, used for furniture etc. ‖ the flavor of maple sap (*SUGAR MAPLE) [O.E. *mapeltrēow*, maple tree]

maple sugar sugar obtained from maple syrup

maple syrup a syrup consisting of the concentrated sap of the sugar maple

map projection *PROJECTION

'Mapp v. Ohio' (mæp) a landmark case (1961) of U.S. jurisprudence, in which the Supreme Court declared that evidence seized in an illegal search may not be introduced at a person's trial

Maputo (məpúːtou) (formerly Lourenço Marques) the capital (pop. 383,775) of Mozambique, a seaport and a rail terminus. Industries: iron working, textiles, food processing, brewing

ma·quis (mækiː) *n.* the copse association of the Mediterranean coasts, consisting esp. of myrtles, heaths, arbutus, rose laurel, ilex and cork

oak. It is particularly fine in Corsica ‖ the French Resistance organization (1943-5) which made guerrilla war on the German army of occupation in the 2nd world war ‖ a local unit of members of the French Resistance [F. fr. Corsican Ital. *macchia*, thicket]

mar (mɑr) *pres. part.* **mar·ring** *past* and *past part.* **marred** *v.t.* to lessen the perfection of [O.E. *merren*, to hinder]

mar·a·bou (mærəbuː) *n.* a stork belonging to genus *Leptoptilos*, esp. *L. crumeniferus* of W. Africa and the adjutant bird ‖ the downy feathers from under the tail and wings of one of these birds, used for trimming hats and dresses [F. *marabout* fr. Arab. *murabit*, hermit]

mar·a·bout (mærəbuː, mærəbuːt) *n.* a Moslem hermit or holy man, esp. in N. and W. Africa ‖ his shrine or tomb [fr. Arab. *murabit*]

ma·ra·ca (məráːkə) *n.* a dried gourd containing pebbles, usually one of a pair used as a musical percussion instrument [Port. *maracá* prob. fr. Tupi]

Mar·a·cai·bo (mærəkáibou) a lake (area 6,300 sq. miles) in N.W. Venezuela, surrounded by rich oil fields ‖ the second largest city (pop. 900,000) of Venezuela, chief port for its petroleum industry, on the channel linking Lake Maracaibo with the Gulf of Venezuela, an arm of the Caribbean

Ma·ra·cay (mɑrəkái) a city (pop. 301,000) in a coffee and cacao producing region in N. Venezuela, 70 miles southwest of Caracas

MarAd (mɑrǽd) (*acronym*) U.S. Maritime Administration

mar·ag·ing steel (mɑréidʒiŋ) a strong age-hardened, low-carbon steel alloy of 6–7% nickel, cobalt, molybdenum, titanium, columbium, and aluminum, utilizing rapid cooling to repress the chemical change of dissolved carbon or other chemicals

Ma·ra·jó (mɑrɑʒɔ́) an island (area 14,000 sq. miles) in the Amazon delta, N.E. Brazil: cattle raising

Ma·ra·ñón (mɑrɑnjɔ́n) a river (c. 1,000 miles long) rising in the Andes in W. central Peru. It joins the Ucayali to form, largely, the Amazon

ma·ras·ca (mərǽskə) *n. Prunus cerasus marasca*, a small, black, bitter Dalmatian cherry from which maraschino is made [Ital.]

mar·a·schi·no (mærəskíːnou, mærəʃíːnou) *n.* a liqueur distilled from the marasca [Ital. fr. *marasca*]

maraschino cherry a cherry preserved in maraschino

ma·ras·mic (mərǽzmik) *adj.* of or pertaining to marasmus

ma·ras·mus (mərǽzməs) *n.* (*med.*) a wasting away of the body, esp. in infants, caused by malnutrition [Mod. L. fr. Gk]

Ma·rat (mærǽ), Jean-Paul (1743–93), French revolutionist. He founded (1789) an extreme radical newspaper and was elected (1792) to the Convention, where he helped to overthrow the Girondists. His inflammatory articles helped to incite the September massacres. He was stabbed to death by Charlotte Corday

Ma·ra·tha, Mah·rat·ta (mərúːtə) *n.* a member of a people of W. central India. The Marathas founded an empire (1674) in central India under Sivaji, after the fall of the Mogul empire. It degenerated to a confederacy of warring states, subdued (1818) by the British

Ma·ra·thi, Mah·rat·ti (mərúːti) *n.* the Indic language of the Marathas, widely spoken in Maharashtra

mar·a·thon (mærəθɒn, mærəθən) *n.* a long-distance race, esp. one run over 26 miles 385 yards in the Olympic Games ‖ any contest testing endurance over a long period, *a dance marathon* [after the exploit of a Greek messenger who ran the 25 miles to Athens to carry news of the victory at *Marathon*]

Mar·a·thon, Battle of (mærəθɒn, mærəθən) a Greek victory (490 B.C.), led by Miltiades, over the Persians during the Persian Wars

marathon group encounter (*psych.*) a form of psychotherapy utilizing an intensive interactive group experience in an extended session designed to lead to personal insight

ma·raud (mərɔ́d) *v.i.* to roam about making raids and pillaging ‖ *v.t.* (esp. *pass.*) to raid, *marauded areas* [F. *marauder* fr. *maraud*, vagabond]

Mar·beck, Mer·becke (mɑrbek), John (c. 1510–c. 1585), English composer. His 'Boke of

Common Praier noted' (1550) provided the first musical setting of the Anglican services

mar·ble (márbl) **1.** *n.* naturally occurring calcium carbonate which has been crystallized from limestone under heat and pressure, forming a hard rock capable of taking a high polish and often veined or mottled by the presence of other crystallized minerals ‖ a piece of sculpture made of this material ‖ a small ball made of something resembling this material, used as a toy ‖ (*pl.*) a game played with these small balls **2.** *v.t. pres. part.* **mar·bling** *past* and *past part.* **mar·bled** to treat (something) so as to give it the mottled or veined appearance of marble **3.** *adj.* of, pertaining to, or like marble [M.E. *marbre, marble* fr. F.]

mar·ble·ize (márblaiz) *pres. part.* **mar·ble·iz·ing** *past* and *past part.* **mar·ble·ized** *v.t.* to marble

mar·bling (márblin) *n.* the act or process of making or being made to look like marble, esp. with respect to color ‖ a marbled appearance ‖ the alternating of layers of fat and lean in some meat

Mar·burg (márbuərk) a town (pop. 47,500) in Hesse, West Germany, with a noted castle (13th–15th cc.), church (13th c.) and university (1527)

Marburg virus *GREEN MONKEY DISEASE

'Mar·bu·ry v. Madison' (márbəri:) a decision (1803) of the U.S. Supreme Court under John Marshall. William Marbury, who had been commissioned justice of the peace by President John Adams in one of his 'midnight appointments', was denied the post by the incoming administration of President Thomas Jefferson (secretary of state: James Madison). The court held that, although Marbury was entitled to the commission, the statute which he invoked was unconstitutional because it gave the Supreme Court an authority which was implicitly denied to it by the U.S. Constitution (Article 3). It was the first decision by the Supreme Court authorizing all courts to review the constitutionality of legislation

Marc (mark), Franz (1880–1916), German painter, an originator of the Blaue Reiter. He painted animals in rhythmic, richly colored compositions

marc (mark) *n.* the residue of compressed grapes or certain other fruits ‖ a brandy made from this residue [F.]

mar·ca·site (márkəsait) *n.* a white, orthorhombic form of iron pyrites, used ornamentally ‖ a piece of jewelry made from this [fr. M.L. *marcasita*]

Mar·cel·lus (marséləs), Marcus Claudius (c. 268–208 B.C.), Roman commander in the 2nd Punic War. He captured Syracuse (212 B.C.) after a two-year siege

mar·ces·cence (marsés'ns) *n.* the condition of being marcescent

mar·ces·cent (marsés'nt) *adj.* (*bot.*, of a plant part) withering without detaching itself from the plant [fr. L. *marcescens* (*marcescentis*), withering]

March (martʃ) *n.* (*abbr.* Mar.) the 3rd month of the year, having 31 days [M.E. *march* fr. A.F. and O.F.]

march (martʃ) *n.* the act of marching ‖ a steady regular gait used in marching ‖ a distance covered by marching ‖ steady progress, *the march of time* ‖ a piece of music to accompany marching **on the march** marching **to steal a march on** to gain an advantage over by clever action [F. *marche*]

march *n.* (*hist.*) a border between countries ‖ (*hist.*) the land near this border ‖ (*hist.*) a territory ‖ (*pl., hist.*) the border territory between England and Wales or between England and Scotland [F. *marche* fr. Gmc]

march *v.i.* to walk with an even, firm stride, esp. (*mil.*) in step with a body of troops ‖ to advance at an even rate of speed, *time marches on* ‖ *v.t.* (esp. *mil.*) to cause to proceed with an even, firm stride, *he marched his troops out of town* ‖ to cause to go, using force, *they marched him off to prison* [F. *marcher*]

Mar·chand (mærʃɑ̃), Jean-Baptiste (1863–1934), French general and explorer. He led an expedition (1897–8) across Africa from the Congo to the White Nile and occupied Fashoda (1898), but withdrew after a prolonged diplomatic crisis with Britain

Marche (mærʃ) a former province of France in the N.W. Massif Central, including Creuse department and parts of Haute-Vienne, Indre and Charente. Historic capital: Guéret. Industries:

agriculture (wheat, fodder crops), cattle breeding. Originally a march of Aquitaine, it passed to the Bourbons (15th c.) and was confiscated (1527) by the crown

March·es, the (mártʃiz) (*Ital.* Le Marche) a region (area 3,744 sq. miles, pop. 1,397,000) of E. central Italy between the Apennines and the Adriatic, largely agricultural (vegetables, cereals, silk, sheep and hog raising). Other industries: forestry and wood products, fishing. Capital: Ancona

marching orders (*Br.*) walking papers, dismissal

mar·chion·ese (mártʃənis) *n.* the wife or widow of an English marquis ‖ a lady having in her own right the rank equivalent to that of a marquis [fr. M.L. *marchionissa*]

Mar Chi·qui·ta (martʃi:kí:ta) a lake (45 miles long) in N. central Argentina

march·land (mártʃlænd, mártʃlənd) *n.* a region near or on a frontier

march·pane (mártʃpein) *n.* marzipan [origin unknown]

march·past (mártʃpæst, mártʃpɑst) *pl.* **march·pasts** *n.* a ceremonial march of troops in formation, esp. in review

Mar·ci·on (mársi:ɒn, mársi:ɒn) (early 2nd c.), Christian philosopher of Asia Minor. He taught that the good, merciful God revealed by Christ and the stern Creator of the Old Testament were two distinct beings, the Creator being inferior. He held that Christ did not really live in the flesh, but was a manifestation of the Father

Mar·co·ni (markóuni:), Guglielmo (1874–1937), Italian physicist. He developed wireless telegraphy, transmitting across the Atlantic (1901). Nobel Prize (1909)

Marco Polo *POLO, MARCO

Mar·cos (márkɔs), Ferdinand (1919–), Filipino statesman, president (1966–84) of the Philippines. He imposed martial law (1972–81) to counter student unrest, Communist terrorism, and a Moslem separatist movement. He amended the constitution giving him the right to rule by decree and became increasingly authoritarian. His involvement in arranging the assassination of opposition leader Benigno Aquino (1983) and blatant fraud in the 1985 presidential election led to massive public demonstrations against him and he was forced to flee the country (1986)

Mar·cus Au·re·li·us (márkəsɔrí:li:əs) (Marcus Annius Verus, 121–180), Roman emperor (161–180), adopted son of Antoninus Pius. A distinguished Stoic philosopher, he recorded his view of life in his 'Meditations'. He introduced many social reforms and founded charitable institutions, but persecuted Christians violently. He defended the empire successfully against the Germanic tribes on the Danube

Mar·cu·se (markú:zə), Herbert (1898–1979), German-U.S. philosopher and educator, professor of philosophy at the University of California at San Diego from 1965. In such works as 'One-Dimensional Man' (1965) he attempted to adapt the principles of Marxist revolution and Freudian psychology to contemporary conditions. He was widely admired by leftist youth throughout the world

Mar·cy (mársi:), William Learned (1786–1857), U.S. statesman and Democratic politician. He was a member of the Albany Regency and, after withdrawing his support of Martin Van Buren, led the Hunkers. As secretary of state (1853–7) under President Franklin Pierce, he negotiated the Gadsden Purchase, the 'Black Warrior' affair with Spain, and problems with Nicaragua

Marcy, Mt the highest peak (5,344 ft) in the Adirondack Mtns, in N.E. New York State

Mar del Pla·ta (marðelplátə) a seaside resort (pop. 302,282) in E. Argentina

Mar·di Gras (márdi:grɑ, márdi:grá) Shrove Tuesday, as celebrated in many Catholic communities, notably in Nice, Rio de Janeiro and in New Orleans, with masquerades and dancing [F.=fat Tuesday]

Mar·duk (márduk) the chief god of Babylon from the 19th c. B.C.

mare (mɛər) *n.* a female horse (cf. FILLY) ‖ the female of any equine animal [O.E. *mere*]

Mar·ek's disease (márəks) (*med.*) a cancer of lymph glands in poultry caused by a virus

Ma·ren·go, Battle of (məréŋgou) a decisive battle in N. Italy (June 14, 1800) in which a French army under Napoleon crushed the Austrian army during the French Revolutionary Wars

mare's nest *pl.* **mare's nests, mares' nests** something sought for, that looks full of promise and turns out to be useless or a hoax

mare's tail *pl.* **mare's tails, mares' tails** *Hippuris vulgaris,* fam. *Haloragaceae,* an aquatic plant with long stalks and shoots covered with fine leaves ‖ a cirrus cloud in long streaks

Mar·fan syndrome or **Mar·fan's syndrome** (marfán) (*med.*) an inherited disease of the connective tissue characterized by elongated bones and chest defects; named for Antonin B. J. Marfan, French pediatrician

Mar·ga·ret (márgərit, márgrit), St (c. 1045–93), queen of Scotland (c. 1067–93), wife of Malcolm III and granddaughter of Edmund Ironside. Her ecclesiastical reforms resolved differences between the English and Scottish Churches. Feast: June 10 (Scotland Nov. 16)

Margaret (1353–1412), queen and effective ruler of Denmark and Norway (c. 1387–1412) and of Sweden (1389–1412). She united the three kingdoms by the Union of Kalmar (1397) under her nephew Eric of Pomerania

Margaret of Angoulême (*F.* Marguerite d'Angoulême), (1492–1549) queen of Navarre (1527–49). Her court was a brilliant literary circle. She wrote the 'Heptameron', a collection of tales on the model of Boccaccio's 'Decameron'. She gave protection to Protestants

Margaret of Anjou (1430–82), queen consort of Henry VI of England. Her husband's attacks of insanity after 1453 left her as the effective ruler. She was the leader of the Lancastrian cause in the Wars of the Roses until decisively defeated at Tewkesbury (1471)

Margaret of Austria (1480–1530), daughter of the Emperor Maximilian I. As regent of the Netherlands (1507–15 and 1518–30), she played an important part in forming the League of Cambrai (1508) and in the Treaty of Cambrai (1529)

Margaret of Navarre (*F.* Marguerite de Navarre) Margaret of Angoulême

Margaret of Valois (*F.* Marguerite de Valois) (1553–1615), daughter of Henri II. As consort (1572–99) of Henri IV, she was queen of France and Navarre. Her marriage was annulled. She was the author of poems and memoirs

Margaret Tudor (1489–1541), queen consort of James IV of Scotland and daughter of Henry VII of England. It was as her great-grandson that James VI of Scotland claimed the English throne as James I (1603)

mar·ga·rine (márdʒərin, márdʒəri:n, márgəri:n) *n.* a substitute for butter prepared from milk and certain edible purified animal or vegetable fats, with added vitamins etc. [F.]

Mar·ga·ri·ta (margarí:tə) an island and chief port of the Venezuelan state of Nueva Esparta (area c. 444 sq. miles, pop. 26,000) in the Caribbean Sea. It was discovered (1498) by Columbus

mar·gay (márgei) *n. Felis tigrina,* a small, spotted cat of Central and South America [F. fr. Port. fr. Tupi]

Marg·graf (márkgraf), Andreas Sigismund (1709–82), German chemist. He discovered the sugar content of sugar beets (1747) and the alumina content of clay, and isolated zinc from calamine

Mar·ghe·ri·ta, Mt (margerí:tə) *RUWENZORI

mar·gin (márdʒin) **1.** *n.* an outer limiting edge ‖ a narrow area adjacent to the border of something ‖ the space between written or printed matter and an edge of the paper, esp. at the left or right of the text ‖ an extra supply of something forming a reserve in case of need ‖ a limit beyond which something ceases to exist or to be possible or tolerable, *behavior beyond the margin of decency* ‖ (*commerce*) the difference between net sales and costs, out of which expenses and profits come ‖ (*econ.*) the least profit at which a transaction is economically sound ‖ (*psychol.*) the borderline between consciousness and unconscious processes ‖ (*stock exchange*) cash or collateral paid to a broker as security ‖ (*stock exchange*) a speculation in which the broker shares ‖ (*stock exchange*) a buyer's equity if his account is closed at the market price **2.** *v.t.* (*stock exchange*) to deposit a margin upon (stock) [fr. L. *margo* (*marginis*)]

mar·gin·al (márdʒin'l) *adj.* of or written in the margin of a page ‖ close to the limit of acceptability, *a marginal profit* ‖ at or close to an edge [fr. Mod. L. *marginalis*]

mar·gi·na·li·a (mardʒinéili:ə) *pl. n.* notes written or printed in the margin of a book or page ‖ a published collection of such notes [L.]

---

mar·gin·al·ize (márdʒɪnəlaiz) v. to cause to live on the margins of society by excluding from participation in any group effort

marginal utility (*econ.*) the added utility resulting from the addition of one unit of production

mar·grave (márgreiv) n. (*hist.*) a German hereditary title of nobility, originally the title of a military governor of a border province [M. Du. *markgrave*]

mar·gra·vi·ate (mɑrgréivi:it) n. (*hist.*) the territory ruled by a margrave [perh. fr. M.L. *margraviatus*]

mar·gra·vine (márgrəvi:n) n. (*hist.*) the wife of a margrave [Du. *markgravin*]

Mar·gre·the II (margréite) (1940–), queen of Denmark (1972–), daughter of King Frederick IX

mar·gue·rite (mɑrgərí:t) n. *Bellis perennis*, the English daisy ‖ any of several single-flowered chrysanthemums, esp. *Chrysanthemum frutescens* of the Canary Is [F.]

Marguerite d'Angoulême *MARGARET OF ANGOULÊME

Marguerite de Navarre *MARGARET OF ANGOULÊME

Marguerite de Valois *MARGARET OF VALOIS

Ma·ri·a I (mərí:ə) (1734–1816), queen of Portugal (1777–1816), daughter of Joseph I. She ruled jointly until 1786 with her husband and uncle Pedro III. She became insane (1788), her son the future John VI ruling as regent (1792–1816)

Maria II 'da Gloria' (1819–53), queen of Portugal (1826–53). Her father, Pedro IV, abdicated the Portuguese throne in her favor, but her uncle Miguel deposed her (1828) and she was restored only after a civil war (1832–3)

Mar·i·an (méəri:ən) adj. of or pertaining to the Virgin Mary ‖ (*hist.*) of or pertaining to Mary I of England

Mar·i·an·a Islands (mɛəri:ǽnə, mæri:ɑ́nə) a chain of 15 islands in the N. Pacific, discovered by Magellan (1521), the chief being Guam, Saipan, Rota and Tinian. Except for Guam, they form a part (area 246 sq. miles, pop. 16,862) of the U.S. Trust Territory of the Pacific set up in 1947

Ma·ri·a·na·o (mɑrjɑnɑ́ɔ) a suburb (pop. 236,000) of Havana, Cuba, a seaside resort

Ma·ri·anne (mǽrjæn) the French Republic, e.g. as personified on coins etc. [F. after a republican society of the 1850s]

Ma·ri·án·ské Láz·ně (márijɑnskelázɲe) *MARIENBAD

Ma·ri A.S.S.R. (mári) an autonomous republic (area 8,994 sq. miles, pop. 771,000) of the E. European R.S.F.S.R., U.S.S.R. Capital: Yoshkar Ola (pop. 88,000). People: Finnish

Ma·ri·a The·re·sa (mərí:ətəri:sə, mərái̯ətəri:zə) (*G.* Maria Theresia) (1717–80), archduchess of Austria, queen of Hungary and Bohemia (1740–80), empress of the Holy Roman Empire, daughter of Charles VI. She succeeded by virtue of the Pragmatic Sanction (1713), and claimed the throne of the Holy Roman Empire for her husband, the future Francis I. She obtained this after the War of the Austrian Succession (1740–8), in which she lost Silesia to Prussia. Her attempts to regain Silesia caused the Seven Years' War (1756–63). She received Galicia in the first partition of Poland (1722). On the death of Francis I (1765) she named her son Emperor as Joseph II, but ruled jointly with him until her death

Maria Theresa dollar an Austrian silver dollar, dated 1780, used as currency in the Middle East. It is the basic monetary unit of Muscat and Oman

Ma·ri·bor (mɑ́ribɔr) a town (pop. 97,167) of Slovenia, Yugoslavia, on the Drava in a fruit and wine region. Cathedral (12th c.)

mar·i·cul·ture (mǽrikəltʃər) n. sea farming, i.e., cultivation of plants and animals in a controlled saltwater environment —**mariculturist** n.

Ma·rie An·toi·nette (mæri:ɑ̀twænet, məri:ɑ̀ntwɑnét) (1755–93), queen of France (1774–92), wife of Louis XVI and daughter of Francis I and Maria Theresa of Austria. She became hated as the center of a reactionary clique at the French court. After the outbreak of the French Revolution, she intrigued with the Austrian court for foreign intervention to crush the revolution. She was imprisoned with her husband (1792) and, after his execution, was tried for treason and guillotined

Ma·rie Byrd Land (mərí:) the sector of Antarctica between 100°W. and 150°W. south of 73°S., claimed by the U.S.A.

Ma·rie de' Med·i·ci (məri:dəmédítʃi:) (1573–1642), queen of France, wife of Henri IV. After Henri IV's assassination (1610), she became regent for her son Louis XIII, abandoning France's anti-Hapsburg policy in favor of an alliance with Spain. She was forced into exile (1617), was reconciled with Louis (1622), and was again forced into exile (1630) by Richelieu

Ma·rie Ga·lante (mæri:gælɑ̀t) *GUADELOUPE

Ma·rie Lesz·czyn·ska (mæri:leʃtʃínska) (1703–68), queen consort of Louis XV of France, daughter of Stanislaus I of Poland. Her marriage (1725) involved France in the war of the Polish Succession

Ma·rie-Louise (mæri:lwi:z) (1791–1847), empress of the French (1810–15), duchess of Parma, Piacenza and Guastalla (1816–47), daughter of Emperor Francis II and second wife of Napoleon I

Ma·ri·en·bad (mərí:ənbɑt) (*Czech.* Mariánské Lázně) a spa (pop. 13,402) in N.W. Bohemia, Czechoslovakia

Ma·ri·ette (mærjet), Auguste-Edouard (1821–81), French Egyptologist. He excavated (1851) the temple of Serapis at Memphis

mar·i·gold (mǽrigould) n. *Calendula officinalis*, an annual composite garden plant with yellow or orange flowers, native to Europe ‖ any of several plants bearing yellow or orange flowers (*AFRICAN MARIGOLD, *FRENCH MARIGOLD, *MARSH MARIGOLD) [MARY, the Virgin+obs. *gold*, marigold]

mar·i·jua·na (mærəwɑ́nə, mærəhwɑ́nə) n. the dried leaves and top of *Cannabis sativa*, the common hemp, often smoked as a narcotic [Span.]

ma·rim·ba (mərímbə) n. a musical instrument of African origin, resembling a xylophone [Bantu *marimba*, *malimba*]

Ma·rin (mærin), John (1870–1953), American watercolorist. His landscapes, while suggesting aspects of abstract expressionism, remain closely representational of their subjects

ma·ri·na (mərí:nə) n. a boat basin that rents moorings and provides other services for small craft [Ital. and Span.]

mar·i·nade (mærinéid) **1.** n. a combination of wine or vinegar with oil, herbs and spices, in which meat or fish is sometimes steeped **2.** v.t. pres. part. **mar·i·nad·ing** past and past part. **mar·i·nad·ed** to marinate [F. fr. Span.]

mar·i·nate (mærineit) pres. part. **mar·i·nat·ing** past and past part. **mar·i·nat·ed** v.t. to season by steeping in a marinade [fr. MARINADE]

ma·rine (mərí:n) **1.** adj. of, relating to, found in or produced by the sea ‖ of or relating to shipping or navigation **2.** n. a member of a class of soldiers specially trained in combined operations with the navy ‖ seagoing ships collectively, the *merchant marine* [F. *marin*, *marine*]

mar·i·ner (mærinər) n. a sailor ‖ (esp. *law*) someone employed on a seagoing ship [A.F.]

mariner's compass a navigational compass consisting of a pair or pairs of magnets attached to a compass card, pivoted, usually in a liquid, and mounted on gimbals in a binnacle

marine science the sciences of the oceans, including oceanography, marine biology, etc.

Ma·ri·ni (mərí:ni), Marino (1901–80), Italian sculptor. He is known esp. for his horses and riders, intensely dramatic and expressive in their refined simplicity of form

Mar·i·ol·a·try (mɛəri:ɔ́lətri:) n. worship of the Virgin Mary with the kind of worship that should be given to God alone (*MARY, THE VIRGIN) [fr. Gk *Maria*, Mary+*latreia*, worship]

Mar·i·on (mæri:ən, méəri:ən), Francis (c. 1732–95), American patriot and guerrilla leader during the Revolutionary War. Having organized (1780) a cavalry troop, the chief colonial force in South Carolina, he broke British lines of communication, captured scouting parties, and intimidated the Loyalists. He retired to the swamps when his force was outnumbered, and became known as the 'Swamp Fox' for his virtuosity in guerrilla warfare

mar·i·on·ette (mæri:ənét) n. a puppet moved by strings [F. *marionnette* fr. *Marion* dim. of *Marie*, proper name]

Ma·ri·otte (mærjɔt), Edme (c. 1620–84), French physicist who independently discovered (1676) Boyle's Law. He also discovered the blind spot of the eye

MARISAT (mǽrisæt) n. (*acronym*) maritime satellite, a ship-to-shore communication satellite orbiting at a fixed point above the earth

Mar·ist (méərist) n. a member of the Society of Mary, a Roman Catholic order founded in France c. 1816. The order devotes itself to education and missionary work, esp. in the W. Pacific

Ma·ri·tain (mæri:tɛ̃), Jacques (1882–1973), French neo-Thomist Catholic philosopher. In 'Trois Réformateurs' (1925), he attacked the doctrines of Luther, Descartes and Rousseau

mar·i·tal (mærit'l) adj. of or relating to marriage or married life [fr. L. *maritalis* fr. *maritus*, husband]

mar·i·time (mæritaim) adj. of, connected with, or bordering on the sea [fr. L. *maritimus*]

maritime climate the climate of an area in which extremes of temperature are moderated by the influence of the sea, so that summers are comparatively cool and winters relatively mild

Maritime Provinces the Canadian provinces of Nova Scotia, New Brunswick and Prince Edward Island

Ma·rit·sa (mərí:tsə) (*Turk.* Meriç, *Gk.* Evros) a river (272 miles long) rising in the Rhodope Mtns, S.W. Bulgaria, and flowing into the Aegean, forming the border between Greece and Turkey

Ma·ri·u·pol (mæri:ú:pɔl) *ZHDANOV

Mar·i·us (méəri:əs), Gaius (c. 155–86 B.C.), Roman general. Victorious over Jugurtha (106 B.C.) and over the Teutons (102 B.C.), he became the political rival of Sulla. As the leader of the popular party, he opposed (88–86 B.C.) Sulla in the first of the great civil wars at Rome

Ma·ri·vaux (mæri:vou), Pierre Carlet de Chamblain de (1688–1763), French dramatist and novelist. His plays, witty examinations of the growth of love and its relationship with moral worth, include 'le Jeu de l'amour et du hasard' (1730) and 'les Fausses Confidences' (1737). His novels include 'la Vie de Marianne, (1731–41) and 'le Paysan parvenu' (1735)

mar·jo·ram (márdʒərəm) n. any of several aromatic plants used in cookery, belonging to the genera *Origanum* and *Majorana*, fam. *Labiatae*, esp. *O. vulgare*, wild marjoram, and *M. hortensis*, sweet marjoram [O.F. *majorane*]

Mark (mɑrk), St (1st c.), an early Christian evangelist, traditionally the author of the Gospel according to St Mark. Symbol: a winged lion. Feast: Apr. 25 (*MARK, GOSPEL ACCORDING TO ST)

mark (mɑrk) n. a spot, stain, scratch etc. breaking the uniform appearance of a solid surface, *the tires left marks on the road* ‖ something that indicates the presence of something else, *his business shows all the marks of success* ‖ any distinguishing characteristic ‖ an object whose position is known, used as a fixed reference point or guide ‖ a letter, numeral etc. put on something to indicate quality, provenance, ownership etc. ‖ an impression or influence, *he leaves his mark on everyone he teaches* ‖ a letter or numeral used by a teacher to indicate his assessment of the quality of a piece of work ‖ something aimed at, *he hit the mark nine times* ‖ a cross or other symbol used as a substitute for a signature by a person who cannot write ‖ the line from which a runner starts in a race ‖ (*boxing*) the pit of the stomach ‖ (*bowls*) the jack ‖ (*rugby*) the dent made by a player's heel when he makes a fair catch. He may kick from it without interference ‖ (*vet.*) a hollow on a horse's incisor, by which its age can be estimated **a man of mark** a man of importance **below** (or **not up to**) **the mark** unsatisfactory **beside the mark** irrelevant **quick (slow) off the mark** quick (slow) in making a start **to make one's mark** to achieve recognition of some personal quality or attainment ‖ (of someone who cannot write) to put a cross etc. instead of one's signature on a document [O.E. *mearc*, boundary, sign]

mark v.t. to make a mark on ‖ to disfigure, *badly marked by smallpox* ‖ to be a distinguishing trait of ‖ to indicate, *his silence marked his anger* ‖ to assess the merit of (a piece of work) by a letter, numeral etc. ‖ to show the position of, *mark the place with a cross* ‖ (*Br.*, *games*) to watch and keep close to (an opponent) in order to hinder his actions ‖ to heed, pay attention to **to mark down** (**up**) to lower (raise) the price of **to mark off** to indicate the extent or limit of, he marked off six feet on the plank **to mark out** to indicate the shape or plan of **to mark time**

(*mil.*) to move the feet in marching rhythm without going forward ‖ to maintain a routine without making any progress, or be kept busy in some way which postpones the chance one seeks to progress [O.E. *mearcian*]

mark *n.* a deutsche mark ‖ a coin representing this value [late O.E. *marc*, a unit of weight]

Mark Antony *ANTONY

mark·down (márkdaun) *n.* a price reduction ‖ the amount by which a price is lowered

marked (markt) *adj.* bearing a mark or marks ‖ noticeable, *marked ability* **a marked man** a man wanted by his enemies ‖ a man destined for fame or promotion **mark·ed·ly** (márkidli:) *adv.*

mark·er (márkər) *n.* someone who marks ‖ a device for marking ‖ (*genetics*) a genetic element identifiable in a person who carries it

mar·ket (márkit) **1.** *n.* a place where many sellers display and sell their goods ‖ the demand for a commodity, *how big is the market for this product?* ‖ a region or outlet for successful trading ‖ the body of persons concerned with buying and selling a particular class of goods, *the beef market* ‖ the class of persons to whom a particular commodity can readily be sold, *teenagers are the chief market for blue jeans* ‖ dealings in stocks or goods, *the market was active yesterday* **in the market for** looking for a chance to buy **into (or on) the market** offered to the public for sale **2.** *v.t.* to sell (goods) in a market ‖ *v.i.* to go shopping for provisions ‖ to see to the business of selling goods **mar·ket·a·bíl·i·ty** *n.* **már·ket·a·ble** *adj.* able to attract a buyer if offered for sale [O.E. fr. O.N.F.]

market garden a land area on which vegetables are grown for market

market order (*stock exchange*) any order to buy or sell commodities, stocks etc. at the market price

mar·ket·place (márkitpleis) *n.* an open area in a town used as a market ‖ (*rhet.*) the world of commerce ‖ the area of life in which ideas, values etc. are examined and treated as competitive

market price the price at which a commodity can be bought or sold in a market

market research the gathering of information about consumers' likes and dislikes of certain goods and services

market town (*Br.*) a town having the legal right to hold a public market on fixed days

market value the value a commodity would have if it were to be offered for public sale

Mark, Gospel according to St the second Gospel of the New Testament, traditionally attributed to St Mark, and probably written c. 68 A.D. It recounts Christ's ministry and his Passion and Resurrection (*MARK)

mark·ing (márkiŋ) *n.* the making of a mark ‖ the awarding of a mark ‖ a mark ‖ the arrangement of marks on an object, *a fur with beautiful marking*

marking panel *PANEL CODE

mark·ka (márkka) *pl.* **mark·kaa** (márkka), **mark·kas** *n.* the main monetary unit of Finland, consisting of 100 pennia [Fin.]

mark mark (*mil.*) command from ground controller for aircraft to release bombs

Mar·kov chain (márkɔf) (*statistics*) the aspect of probability theory that analyzes discrete states in which transition is a fixed probability not affected by the past history of the system; named for Andrei A. Markov, Russian mathematician —**Markov process** *n.* a continuing process based on the chain

mark sensing a system for marking a card or paper (esp. a multiple-choice questionnaire) with an ordinary graphite or special pencil so that the marks can be read by a computer

marks·man (márksmən) *pl.* **marks·men** (márksmən) *n.* a person who shoots at a target with a gun, rifle etc., esp. one who shoots well, *he's no marksman* (*U.S. Army*) the lowest proficiency rating in shooting ‖ a soldier with this rating (cf. SHARPSHOOTER, cf. EXPERT) **marks·man·ship** *n.* skill in shooting

mark·up (márkʌp) *n.* an increase in the price of a thing ‖ the amount of this increase ‖ the amount added to the cost of an article in establishing a selling price that will cover overhead and produce a net profit

marl (marl) **1.** *n.* a crumbly soil composed chiefly of clay with a high percentage of calcareous matter, used for fertilizer and in making bricks ‖ any other soft, loose soil **2.** *v.t.* to supply (land) with marl [O.F. *marle*]

marl *v.t.* to secure with a marline, making a hitch at every turn [Du. and L.G. *marlen*]

Marl·bor·ough (mólbərə, márlbə:rou, márlbʌrou), John Churchill, 1st duke of (1650–1722), English soldier and statesman. He played a prominent part in suppressing Monmouth's rebellion (1685) and was raised to the peerage by James II. The king's religious policy caused him to defect to William III when the latter invaded England (1688). Disgraced (1692–8) for his Jacobite sympathies, he returned to favor under Anne, to whom his wife Sarah (1660–1744) was attendant. His brilliant command of English forces in the War of the Spanish Succession (1701–14) and his victories at Blenheim (1704), Ramillies (1706), Oudenarde (1708) and Malplaquet (1709) brought him high honor. Political changes at court led to his fall from favor (1711)

Marl·bor·ough (márlbərə, márlbə:rou, márlbʌrou) a region (area 4,220 sq. miles, pop. 29,000) of N.E. South Island, New Zealand: sheep farming, mining (coal, gold copper). Center: Blenheim

mar·lin (márlin) *n.* a member of *Makaira*, fam. *Istiophoridae*, a genus of big-game sea fish [MARLINSPIKE]

mar·line (márlin) *n.* a two-stranded rope, usually tarred, used for lashing [Du. *marlijn*]

mar·line·spike, mar·lin·spike (márlinspaik) *n.* a pointed iron tool used to separate strands of rope or wire when splicing [prob. fr. older *marling spike* fr. pres. part. of MARL V.+SPIKE]

mar·lite (márlait) *n.* a hard variety of marl resistant to the action of air

Mar·lowe (márlou), Christopher (1564–93), English dramatist and poet. In his 'Tamburlaine the Great' (1590), 'The Tragicall History of Doctor Faustus' (1604), 'The Rich Jew of Malta' (1633) and 'Edward II' (1594), he virtually founded Elizabethan tragedy, and made blank verse its medium

mar·ma·lade (márməleid) *n.* a preserve made by boiling shredded oranges, or other citrus fruits, with sugar [F. *marmelade* fr. Port. fr. L. fr. Gk]

Mar·ma·ra, Sea of (mármərə) (ancient Propontis) an inland sea (area 4,250 sq. miles) dividing European (or Balkan) Turkey from Asian Turkey (Asia Minor), connected to the Aegean by the Dardanelles and to the Black Sea by the Bosporus

mar·ma·rize (márməraiz) *pres. part.* **mar·ma·riz·ing** *past* and *past part.* **mar·ma·rized** *v.t.* to convert (limestone) into marble [MARMAROSIS]

mar·ma·ro·sis (mərməróusis) *n.* the converting of limestone into marble [fr. Gk *marmaros*, marble]

Marmes man (marms) fossil of Mongoloid men believed to have lived in Washington State 11,000 yrs ago; discovered in 1965

Már·mol (mármɔl), José (1818–71), Argentinian romantic writer and political rebel. His works include 'Canto del pelegrino' (verse), the play 'El poeta y El conquistador', and the novel 'Amalia', which describes Buenos Aires at the time of the tyrant Rosas

Mar·mo·ra, Sea of (mármərə) the Sea of Marmara

mar·mo·re·al (marmóri:əl, marmóuri:əl) *adj.* made of or resembling marble [fr. L. *marmoreus*]

mar·mo·set (márməzet) *n.* any of several very small, agile South and Central American monkeys of fam. *Callithricidae*, having long, nonprehensile tails and thick soft fur [O.F. *marmouset*, grotesque image]

mar·mot (mármət) *n.* a member of *Marmota*, a genus of thick-bodied, shortlegged rodents with coarse fur and small ears, related to the squirrel. They live gregariously in burrows and hibernate in winter. Various species are found in N. America (*WOODCHUCK), central and N. Europe and central and N. Asia [fr. F. *marmotte*]

Marne a department (area 3,167 sq. miles, pop. 530,400) in N.E. France (*CHAMPAGNE). Chief town: Châlons-sur-Marne

Marne (marn) a river (325 miles long) rising in Champagne, N.E. France, and flowing into the Seine just above Paris. It was the scene of two important battles of the 1st world war. In the 1st (Sept. 5–10, 1914) the Allies halted the German drive toward Paris. In the 2nd (July 18–Aug. 6, 1918) the Allies checked the last German offensive of the war

Marne-Haute *HAUTE-MARNE

mar·o·cain (mærəkein) *n.* a ribbed crepe of silk or rayon with other yarns resembling crepe de Chine, but coarser [F. *marocain* fr. *Maroc*, Morocco]

Mar·o·ni (məróuni:) a river (c. 420 miles long) of South America which forms the boundary between Surinam and French Guiana and empties into the Atlantic

Mar·o·nite (mærənait) *n.* a member of an Eastern Christian sect founded in the 7th c., in communion with the Roman Catholic Church since the 12th c. Maronites are chiefly found in Lebanon, their head is the patriarch of Antioch, elected by the bishops and approved by the pope. Worship is in Syriac or Arabic, and married men are accepted for the priesthood. The Maronites were much persecuted and were notably the victims of a massacre by the Druses (1860)

Ma·roon (mərú:n) *n.* (*Am. hist.*) a fugitive slave living in the West Indies ‖ a free black descended from such fugitive slaves [fr. Am. Span. Cimarrón, wild (of runaway animals, later of slaves)]

ma·roon *v.t.* to land (someone) on a desolate shore and leave him to his fate [F. *marron* perh. fr. Span. *cimarrón*, wild]

ma·roon (mərú:n) **1.** *n.* a dark brownish-red color ‖ a device for firing gunpowder, esp. as a warning signal **2.** *adj.* of the color maroon [F. *marron*, chestnut]

Ma·rot (mærou), Clément (1496–1544), French poet, notable for the elegant lightness, wit and unaffected grace of his style. His works include the 'Epîtres', 'Elégies', 'Epigrammes' and the translation of 30 Psalms (1541)

Mar·prel·ate (marprélit), Martin, the pseudonym of the unidentified author or authors of a number of vituperative Puritan pamphlets (1588–9), satirizing the prelacy of the Church of England. An early example of prose satire, the Marprelate tracts show the bitterness underlying the Elizabethan Church settlement

Marquand (márkwənd), John Phillips (1893–1960) U.S. writer who wrote about Boston's upper class society. He also wrote about espionage and adventure and invented Mr. Moto, a Japanese detective. 'The Late George Apley' (1937) brought him a Pulitzer Prize. Other works include 'H.M. Pulham Esquire' (1941), 'So Little Time' (1943), 'Repent in Haste' (1945), 'Point of No Return' (1949) and 'Sincerely, Willis Wayde' (1958)

marque (mark) *LETTERS OF MARQUE

mar·quee (markí:) *n.* a large tent set up for outdoor receptions, garden parties etc. ‖ a permanent rooflike projection over the entrance to a theater, moviehouse etc. [fr. F. *marquise*, misunderstood as a plural]

Mar·que·sas Islands (markéisəs, markéizəs) (F. Iles Marquises) an archipelago (land area 376 sq. miles, pop. 5,592) comprising 13 mountainous islands, of volcanic origin, in French Polynesia. Main islands: Nukuhiva, Hivaoa. Religion: mainly Roman Catholic. Main export: copra

mar·quess (márkwis) *n.* (*Br.*) a marquis [MARQUIS]

mar·que·try, mar·que·te·rie (márkitri:) *pl.* **mar·que·tries, mar·que·te·ries** *n.* the process of inlaying wood with strips of other wood, ivory etc. in a decorative pattern, used in furniture etc. ‖ furniture etc. inlaid with such decoration [F. *marqueterie*]

Mar·quette (mærket), Jacques (1637–75), French Jesuit missionary and explorer in North America. With Louis Jolliet he discovered (1673) the Mississippi River

mar·quis (márkwis, markí:) *n.* a European and English title of nobility ranking below duke and above earl or count ‖ the holder of this title [O.F. *marchis*]

mar·quise (markí:z) *n.* (in non-English orders of nobility) the wife of a marquis ‖ a ring set with a pointed oval gem or cluster of gems ‖ a gem cut in a pointed oval shape [F.]

Mar·ra·kesh, Mar·ra·kech (mærəkéʃ) a town (pop. 332,700) of S.W. central Morocco in the High Atlas foothills, a railroad and caravan route terminus, consisting of a modern and a medieval city (palace, mosques): food processing, carpets, textiles, leatherwork

mar·ram (mærəm) *n. Ammophila arenaria*, a thin-bladed European grass which roots deeply in sand and is grown to bind dunes [O.N. *maralmr* fr. *marr*, sea+*halmr*,straw]

mar·riage (mæridʒ) *n.* the institution under which a man and a woman become legally united on a permanent basis ‖ the act of entering into this institution ‖ the wedding ceremony ‖ the entering into the married state as a religious rite ‖ an intimate linking together, *a true marriage of minds* ‖ (*cards*) the declaration of king and queen of the same suit, esp. in pinochle or bezique **mar·riage·a·bíl·i·ty** *n.* **már·riage·a·ble** *adj.* fit for marriage [M.E. *mariage* fr. F.]

marriage of convenience a marriage made for social or financial benefit

mar·ried (mǽri:d) *adj.* joined in marriage, *a married couple* ‖ of or pertaining to marriage, *married life* [past part. of MARRY]

married failure (*mil.*) in naval mine warfare, a moored mine lying on the seabed that has failed to release from its sinker owing to defective mechanism

mar·ron gla·cé (mǽrəngl&æsei, mærɔ̃glæsei) *pl.* **mar·rons gla·cés** *n.* a chestnut preserved in syrup and glazed with sugar [F.]

mar·row (mǽrou) *n.* a soft tissue filling up the cavities in most bones, where many cells of the blood are manufactured ‖ the pith of certain plants ‖ the essential part of something ‖ (*Br.*) a vegetable marrow [O.E. *mearg, mearh*]

mar·row·bone (mǽroubəun) *n.* a bone containing marrow, used in cooking

mar·row·fat (mǽroufæt) *n.* a pea with large, rich, wrinkly seeds

mar·ry (mǽri:) *pres. part.* **mar·ry·ing** *past* and *past part.* **mar·ried** *v.t.* to join (two people) in marriage ‖ to take in marriage, *she married him last month* ‖ to give in marriage, *he married his daughter to a stockbroker* ‖ to join closely or match (two things, e.g. two materials, two colors) ‖ *v.i.* to enter into marriage **to marry into** to become part of (a family) by marriage **to marry (someone) off** to give (someone) in marriage so as to cease to be responsible for (her) [F. *marier*]

Mar·ry·at (mǽri:ət), Frederick (1792–1848), English naval captain and writer of adventure stories, mostly for boys, e.g. 'Mr. Midshipman Easy' (1836) and 'The Children of the New Forest' (1847)

Mars (mɑrz) (*Rom. mythol.*) the god of war, identified with the Greek Ares ‖ the fourth planet from the sun (mean orbital diameter = 1.415 x 108 miles) of mass about 1/10 that of the Earth (6.34 x 10^{20} tons) and diameter approx. 4,225 miles. Mars revolves about the sun with a sidereal period of 687 Earth-days and rotates once in 24 hrs 37 mins. Diurnal and seasonal changes closely resemble those on the Earth, but its night temperatures are thought to be very low. Its daytime temperatures, esp. in the equatorial region, are comparable to those on the Earth. Since 1965 satellites have studied and photographed Mars. The surface is pitted with craters, like the Moon's. The 'canals' that can be observed with a telescope are optical illusions. The atmosphere is very rarefied (1/150th of the Earth's atmospheric pressure) and is composed of 97% carbon dioxide, a little carbon monoxide, oxygen and traces of water. Mars has two small satellites, Phobos and Deimos

Mars, Jean Price (*b.* 1876), Haitian black writer who, in the 1920s, was among the first to urge blacks to accept their African heritage and to use it as a cultural resource

MARS (*mil. acronym*) military affiliate radio system, a worldwide amateur radio operating network that serves as an emergency or auxiliary system for the military

Mar·sa·la (mɑrsálə) *n.* a sweet wine made at Marsala, Sicily

Mars·den (mɑ́rzdən), Samuel (1765–1838), British missionary in New Zealand. He established (1814) the first Christian mission among the Maoris

Mar·seil·laise (mærseijez) the French national anthem, composed by Rouget de Lisle and introduced (1792) to Paris by soldiers from Marseille

Mar·seille (mærseij) (*Eng.* Marseilles) the second largest city (pop. 907,854, with agglom. 1,004,536) of France, in Bouches-du-Rhône department, a great Mediterranean port and trading town (esp. with Africa), founded (c. 600 B.C.) as a Greek colony. Industries: shipbuilding, oil refining, chemicals. The medieval town, around the old port, was largely destroyed in the 2nd world war. University (1409)

Marsh, Othniel Charles (1831–99), U.S. paleontologist and first professor of paleontology at Yale University. During expeditions in

the western U.S.A., he discovered bones of Cretaceous toothed birds, swimming and flying reptiles, and the fossil ancestors of the horse

marsh (mɑrʃ) *n.* a tract of low-lying land, usually wet or periodically wet [O.E. *mersc, merisc*]

Mar·shal, (mɑ́rʃəl), William *PEMBROKE, 1st earl of

mar·shal (mɑ́rʃəl) **1.** *n.* (*Br.*) the highest rank of officer in the R.A.F., ranking above an air chief marshal ‖ a military commander of the highest rank in certain armies ‖ someone who regulates ceremonies and directs processions ‖ (*Br.*) an official who accompanies a High Court judge ‖ a U.S. civil officer responsible in a judicial district for the processes of the law ‖ (*hist.*) a medieval officer of state, usually commanding the armed forces *EARL MARSHAL **2.** *v.t. pres. part.* **mar·shal·ing**, esp. *Br.* **mar·shal·ling** *past* and *past part.* **mar·shaled**, esp. *Br.* **mar·shalled** to arrange in correct order, *to marshal a procession* ‖ (*heraldry*) to place in order (e.g. the coats in a shield) [O. F. *mareschal, marescal* fr. Gmc]

marshaling yard, esp. *Br.* **marshalling yard** a railroad yard where cars are sorted and made up into trains

Mar·shall (mɑ́rʃəl), Alfred (1842–1924), British economist. In 'Principles of Economics' (1890), for years a standard text, he set out to reconcile classical and modern theories of cost and value

Marshall, George Catlett (1880–1959), American general and statesman. He was U.S. chief of staff (1939–45), secretary of state (1947–9) and secretary of defense (1950–1). He proposed (1947) the Marshall Plan. Nobel Peace Prize (1953)

Marshall, John (1755–1835), American lawyer, chief justice of the U.S.A. (1801–35). A Federalist, he did much to decide the interpretation of the U.S. Constitution, and by the wisdom of his decisions made the Supreme Court a powerful institution

Marshall, Thomas Riley (1854–1925) U.S. statesman, vice president (1913–21). He served as governor of Indiana (1909–13) before becoming vice president under Pres. Woodrow Wilson

Marshall, Thurgood (1908–) U.S. lawyer and the first black associate justice of the Supreme Court. As a practicing lawyer he specialized in civil rights and argued many times before the Supreme Court. He was chief of legal defense for the National Association for the Advancement of Colored People (NAACP) (1940–65) before being appointed solicitor general of the U.S.A. (1965–7). He was nominated to the Supreme Court by Pres. Lyndon B. Johnson. Generally a liberal, he advocated ending racial discrimination and expanding voting and defendants' rights. He dissented in *Williams v. Florida* (1969) and *San Antonio Independent School District v. Rodriguez* (1973) and wrote the majority opinion in *Benton v. Maryland* (1969), *Dunn v. Blumstein* (1972) and *Hodel v. Indiana* (1981)

Marshall Islands a group of 34 atolls (area 160 sq. miles, pop. 27,096) in the W. Pacific Ocean, part of the U.S. Trust Territory of the Pacific

Marshall Plan the name popularly given to the European Recovery Program, an arrangement proposed (1947) by G. C. Marshall, under which the U.S.A. supplied material and financial aid to Europe after the 2nd world war. The plan came into force in 1948, was administered by the O.E.E.C. and was completed in 1952

marsh gas a clear, odorless, inflammable gas formed largely of methane, produced by vegetation when it decomposes ‖ methane

marsh·land (mɑ́rʃlænd) *n.* marshy terrain [O.E. *merscland*]

marsh·mal·low (mɑ́rʃmelou, mɑ́rʃmælou) *n. Althaea officinalis*, fam. *Malvaceae*, a perennial plant growing in marshes, the root of which yields abundant mucilage formerly used in medicine and confectionery ‖ a soft white confection made from glucose, sugar, albumen and gelatin [O.E. *merscmealwe*]

marsh marigold a plant of genus *Caltha*, fam. *Ranunculaceae*, esp. *C. palustris*, which grows in swamps and has bright yellow flowers

marsh·y (mɑ́rʃi:) *comp.* **marsh·i·er** *superl.* **marsh·i·est** *adj.* of, relating to, consisting of or found in a marsh

Mar·si·glio of Padua (mɑrsíːljo) (Marsilio da Padova, c. 1275–c. 1343), Italian scholar and

political theorist. In his 'Defensor pacis' (1324), he claimed that the ruler expressed the popular will as the delegate of the people, and that in temporal matters the Church should be subject to the State. The book was written to support the Emperor Louis IV in his dispute with John XXII and was a major contribution to medieval political thought

Mar·sok·hod (mɑrsókɔd) *n.* (*astronautics*) Soviet-designed unmanned vehicle for exploration of Mars, used in 1970 *Cf* LUNOKHOD, PLANETOKHOD

Mars·ton (mɑ́rstən), John (c. 1576–1634), English dramatist and satirist. His plays include 'Antonio and Mellida' (1602), 'Antonio's Revenge' (1602) and 'The Malcontent' (1604)

Marston Moor, Battle of a battle (July 2, 1644) near York during the English Civil War. It gave Cromwell control of the north of England

mar·su·pi·al (mɑrsúːpi:əl) **1.** *n.* a member of *Marsupialia*, the lowest order of mammals incl. the kangaroo, opossum etc. The female usually has no placenta, and bears imperfectly developed young, nourished and carried by the mother, until fully developed, in an external abdominal pouch **2.** *adj.* of, relating to or being a marsupial [fr. Mod. L. *marsupialis* fr. L. *marsupium*, pouch]

mar·su·pi·um (mɑrsúːpi:əm) *pl.* **mar·su·pi·a** (mɑrsúːpi:ə) *n.* the fold of skin forming a pouch on the abdomen of the female marsupial, enclosing the mammary glands ‖ a similar structure for carrying eggs or young in a fish, crustacean etc. [L. fr. Gk]

mart (mɑrt) *n.* a trading center [Du. *markt*, a fair]

Martel, Charles *CHARLES MARTEL

mar·tel·lo tower (mɑrtélou) one of the small circular forts built on the British coast during the Napoleonic Wars against a possible French invasion [corrup. of Cape *Mortella*, Corsica, where a similar fort was captured with difficulty by the British in 1794]

mar·ten (mɑ́rtin, mɑ́rt'n) *n.* a member of *Martes*, fam. *Mustelidae*, a genus of carnivorous mammals, related to weasels. Martens are widely distributed in northern lands and greatly valued for their fur ‖ the fur of these animals [M.E. *martren* fr. O.F. *martrine* fr. Gmc]

Mar·tha's Vineyard (mɑ́rθəz) an island (20 miles long, 10 miles wide) and summer resort 5 miles south of Cape Cod, across Vineyard Sound between the Elizabeth Is. and Nantucket Is., off S.E. Massachusetts

Mar·tí (mɑrtí:), José (1853–95), Cuban writer and patriot, and hero of Cuban independence. After a long period of exile, during which he founded (1892) in New York the Cuban Revolutionary party, he landed with a force at Playitas but was killed in action at Dos Ríos. In poetry he was one of the founders of modernism. His works include, in verse, 'Ismaelillo', 'Versos libros', and 'Versos sencillos', the novel 'Amistad funesta', and various essays

Mar·tial (mɑ́rʃəl) (Marcus Valerius Martialis, c. 40–c. 104), Latin poet, born in Spain, author of 12 or more books of 'Epigrams'

mar·tial (mɑ́rʃəl) *adj.* of, relating to, suited to or suggestive of war [F. *martial* fr. L. *martialis*, of Mars, god of war]

martial art any of several Oriental techniques of self-defense, e.g., karate, judo, tai-chi

martial law a code of law enforced in emergency by the military arm of a government as a protection from internal disturbance or external attack and superseding the civil law for the time of its enforcement ‖ the law enforced by the military authority of an invading or occupying power, affecting persons and property in the invaded or occupied territory

Mar·tian (mɑ́rʃən) **1.** *adj.* of, relating to or characteristic of the planet Mars or of its hypothetical inhabitants **2.** *n.* a hypothetical inhabitant of Mars [fr. L. *Martius*]

Mar·tin (mɑ́rtin, mɑ́rt'n), St (c. 316–c. 397), bishop of Tours (371–c. 397). He founded several of the earliest monasteries in France and spread Christianity in the west of the country. Feast: Nov. 11

mar·tin (mɑ́rtin, mɑ́rt'n) *n.* any of several swallows, esp. the house martin [F. *Martin* fr. L. *Martinus*, man's name]

Martin I, St (*d.* 655), pope (649–55). He convoked the first Lateran Council to condemn Monothelitism. Feast: Nov. 12

CONCISE PRONUNCIATION KEY: (a) æ, c*a*t; ɑ, c*a*r; ɔ f*aw*n; ei, sn*a*ke. **(e)** e, h*e*n; i:, sh*ee*p; iə, d*ee*r; ɛə, b*ea*r. **(i)** i, f*i*sh; ai, t*i*ger; ə:, b*i*rd. **(o)** o, *o*x; au, c*ow*; ou, g*oa*t; u, p*oo*r; ɔi, r*oy*al. **(u)** ʌ, d*u*ck; u, b*u*ll; u:, g*oo*se; ə, b*a*cillus; ju:, c*u*be. x, lo*ch*; θ, *th*ink; ð, bo*th*er; z, *Z*en; ʒ, corsa*g*e; dʒ, sava*g*e; ŋ, ora*ng*utang; j, *y*ak; ʃ, *fi*sh; tʃ, fe*tch*; 'l, rabb*le*; 'n, redd*en*. Complete pronunciation key appears inside front cover.

Martin IV (c. 1210–85), pope (1281–5). He supported Charles I of Naples and Sicily, and opposed the house of Aragon in Sicily after the Sicilian Vespers

Martin V (1368–1431), pope (1417–31). His election marked the end of the Great Schism. He reestablished the papacy in Rome and restored its authority

Martin, Glenn Luther (1886–1955), U.S. pioneer airplane inventor and manufacturer. Martin bombers and flying boats were in worldwide use during the 2nd world war

Mar·tin du Gard (mærtɛ̃dygær), Roger (1881–1958), French writer. He is best known for his series of novels 'les Thibault' (8 vols., 1922–40)

Mar·tin·eau (mártinou), Harriet (1802–76), British writer on socioeconomic subjects ('Society in America,' 1837) and author of popular children's books ('The Playfellow', 1841)

Martineau, James (1805–1900), British Unitarian philosopher, brother of Harriet Martineau. In 'Types of Ethical Theory' (1885) he argued that morality is not the product of custom but its maker and that the power of moral judgment is the basis of moral life. In 'A Study of Religion' (1888) he set Darwinian evolution within a theistic philosophy

mar·ti·net (mɑrt'nét) n. a strict disciplinarian [after Jean *Martinet* (d. 1672), F. army officer]

Mar·tí·nez Cam·pos (mɑrtí:neθkámpɔs), Arsenio (1831–1900), Spanish general. He suppressed (1878) an uprising in Cuba, negotiating the Peace of Zanjón. Appointed captain-general of Cuba, he failed to contain the uprising of 1895 and was replaced by Weyler

mar·tin·gale (mártiŋgeil) n. a strap connecting a horse's girth to the noseband, bit or reins, to prevent the horse from tossing its head back ‖ (naut.) the lower stay for a jibboom ‖ a system of doubling the stakes after each loss in gambling [F., origin unknown]

Mar·ti·ni (mɑrtí:ni:), Simone (c. 1284–1344), Sienese painter. His work, marked by strong linear rhythms, includes the 'Annunciation' (1333) painted in collaboration with Lippo Memmi, now in the Uffizi, and the 'Virgin in Majesty' fresco (1315) in the Palazzo Pubblico at Siena

mar·ti·ni (mɑrtí:ni:) n. a cocktail made usually with gin and dry vermouth

Mar·ti·nique (mɑrt'ní:k) a mountainous, volcanic island (area 427 sq. miles, pop. 308,169) of the Windward group, West Indies, forming an overseas department of France. Chief town and port: Fort-de-France. People: mainly Mulatto, with African and Creole minorities. Mean annual temperature (F.): 80°. Rainfall: 87 ins. Highest point: 4,800 ft. Products: sugar, rum, bananas, pineapples, cocoa. Martinique was discovered (c. 1502) by Columbus and was colonized by the French after 1635. It became an overseas department of France in 1946

Mar·tin·mas (mártinməs), (abbr. M.) the feast of St Martin (Nov. 11) [ST MARTIN + MASS]

Mar·ti·nů (mártinu:), Bohuslav (1890–1959), Czech composer. His many works include operas, symphonies and chamber music in a markedly individual style

mart·let (mártlit) n. (heraldry) a mythical bird with no feet, borne as a charge [F. martelet]

mar·tyr (mártər) 1. n. someone who suffers death rather than renounce his faith ‖ someone who suffers greatly for some cause or principle **to be a martyr to** to suffer continually from, a martyr to hayfever **to make a martyr of oneself** to seek esteem by making it clear that one is doing a good deed at considerable self-sacrifice 2. v.t. to put to death for refusing to renounce the faith ‖ to inflict great suffering upon [O.E. fr. L. fr. Gk]

mar·tyr·dom (mártərdəm) n. the death or putting to death of a martyr ‖ great suffering [O.E. martyrdōm]

mar·tyr·ize (mártəraiz) pres. part. **mar·tyr·iz·ing** past and past part. **mar·tyr·ized** v.t. to martyr [fr. M.L. martyrizare]

mar·tyr·ol·o·gy (mɑrtərólədʒi:) pl. **mar·tyr·ol·o·gies** n. a history or list of Christian martyrs [fr. M.L. martyrologium fr. Gk]

mar·tyr·y (mártəri) pl. **mar·tyr·ies** n. a shrine, chapel etc. built in honor of a martyr [fr. M.L. martyrium fr. Gk]

mar·vel (márvəl) n. something that causes astonishment and admiration [O.F. merveille]

marvel pres. part. **mar·veling**, esp. Br. **mar-**

vel·ling past and past part. **mar·veled**, esp. Br. **mar·velled** v.i. to be filled with wonder or astonishment, I marvel at his patience ‖ v.t. to be filled with wonder or astonishment at, I marvel that he is so patient [O.F. merveillier]

Mar·vell (márvəl), Andrew (1621–78), English poet. A Puritan, he survived the Restoration and wrote satire on the new era. His poetry, which combines ingenious thought, delicate observation and elegant music, provoked what has become one of the standard definitions of 17th-c. poetical wit: 'a tough reasonableness beneath the slight lyric grace' (Eliot)

mar·vel-of-Pe·ru (márvələvpərú:) n. (bot.) the four-o'clock

mar·vel·ous, esp. Br. **mar·vel·lous** (márvələs) adj. causing one to marvel ‖ (pop.) very fine, excellent, a marvelous opportunity ‖ of or pertaining to the supernatural [O.F merveiltos]

Marx (mɑrks), Karl (1818–83), German economist and social philosopher. After studying law and philosophy, and editing a liberal newspaper in Germany, he went to Paris (1843). With Engels, his friend and collaborator, he published the 'Communist Manifesto' (1848), in which international socialism was publicly proclaimed for the first time. He participated in revolutionary movements in Germany (1848–9), was expelled, and went to London (1850), where he spent the rest of his life studying economics and working to further the cause of socialism. He founded (1864) the 1st International and published (1867) the first volume of 'Das Kapital.' The second and third volumes were published (1885–94) by Engels. In this book, Marx expounded his view of history, economics and social change (*MARXISM)

Marx Brothers a U.S. family of comedians, Chico (Leonard) (1887–1961), Harpo (Adolph) (1888–1964), Groucho (Julius) (1890–1977), Gummo (Milton) (1892–1977) and Zeppo (Herbert) (1901–1979). Among the many films in which they appeared were 'Animal Crackers' (1930), 'Monkey Business' (1931), 'Duck Soup' (1933) and 'A Night at the Opera' (1935). Groucho later had a successful television career

Marx·i·an (márksi:ən) 1. adj. of, relating to or supporting Marxism 2. n. a Marxist

Marx·ism (márksizəm) n. the political, economic and social system advocated by Marx and Engels and their followers. Its philosophical bases are dialectical materialism and historical materialism. It sees capitalist society in terms of the exploitation of the proletariat by the bourgeoisie (*LABOR THEORY OF VALUE, *SURPLUS VALUE). It holds that communism, the political aspect of the system, will be achieved when the class struggle results in the overthrow of capitalism by the dictatorship of the proletariat and when a classless society has emerged from the withering away of the State

Marx·ist (márksist) 1. n. someone who professes Marxism 2. adj. of, relating to or characteristic of Marx or Marxism

Ma·ry I (méəri:) ('Mary Tudor' or 'Bloody Mary', 1516–58), queen of England (1553–8), daughter of Henry VIII and Catherine of Aragon. Brought up a Roman Catholic and excluded from court after her mother's divorce (1533), she succeeded to the throne (1553) after the death of her half brother Edward VI and the usurpation of Lady Jane Grey. Her marriage (1554) to Philip II of Spain, and the consequent Spanish alliance, provoked rebellion in England. The restoration of Catholicism (1554) was followed by a religious persecution (1555–8) in the course of which nearly 300 Protestants were put to death, among them Ridley, Latimer and Cranmer. England was drawn into a war between France and Spain (1557) and lost Calais (1558), the last English possession in France

Mary II (1662–94), queen of England, Scotland and Ireland (1689–94), daughter of James II. A Protestant, she married (1677) William of Orange, with whom she was proclaimed joint sovereign of England (1689) after the Glorious Revolution (1688), her husband taking the title of William III

Mary Gregory style of 19th-century glassware with enameled figures of children

Mar·y·land (mérələnd) (abbr. **Md.**) a state (area 10,577 sq. miles, pop. 4,265,000) on the middle Atlantic coast of the U.S.A. Capital: Annapolis. Chief city: Baltimore. The lowlands surrounding the Chesapeake Bay give way in the west to a part of the Appalachians. Agriculture: dairy products, poultry, vegetables (esp. tomatoes),

corn, tobacco. Resources: coal, building materials. Industries: steel, metal products, transport equipment, shipbuilding, chemicals, food processing, fishing. Chief universities: Johns Hopkins (1876) and University of Maryland (1807) at College Park. Maryland was colonized by the English (17th c.) and named after Queen Henrietta Maria. One of the Thirteen Colonies, it became the 7th State of the U.S.A.

Maryland's Act Concerning Religion *TOLERATION ACT OF 1649

Mary Magdalene *MAGDALEN

Mary of Guise (1515–60), queen consort of James V of Scotland, regent of Scotland (1554–60) for her daughter Mary Queen of Scots. She unsuccessfully called in French troops when Knox led a Protestant rebellion (1559–60) against her policy of uniting France and Scotland

Mary Queen of Scots (Mary Stuart, 1542–87), queen of Scotland (1542–67) and, as the consort of François II, queen of France (1559–60), daughter of James V and Mary of Guise. An ardent Catholic, she returned (1561) to Scotland after the deaths of her husband and her mother, to face the newly established Protestantism and the disaffected nobility. She married (1565) her cousin Lord Darnley, who, after murdering Mary's secretary Rizzio (1566), was himself murdered (1567), apparently with Mary's connivance. Her marriage (1567) to Bothwell, widely suspected of being Darnley's murderer, provoked a rebellion in which she was forced to abdicate (1567) in favor of her son, James VI of Scotland. Fleeing to England, whose throne she claimed by virtue of her descent from Margaret Tudor, she was imprisoned (1568) by Elizabeth I. After 19 years in prison, she was implicated in the Babington plot (1586) and executed for treason (1587)

Mary, Society of *MARIST

Mary Stuart *MARY QUEEN OF SCOTS

Mary, the Virgin the mother of Jesus and according to the Gospel his only human parent (*VIRGIN BIRTH). She was the wife of St Joseph, and, according to tradition, the daughter of St Joachim and St Anne. As the Mother of God she is venerated in the Roman Catholic Church with hyperdulia. Feast days in the Western Church: Immaculate Conception (Dec. 8), Nativity (Sept. 8), Annunciation (Mar. 25), Visitation (July 2), Purification (Feb. 2), Assumption (Aug. 15). Marian devotions include the Rosary and the Angelus

Mary Tudor *MARY I

Mary Washington College *VIRGINIA, UNIVERSITY OF

mar·zi·pan (márzəpæn) n. a confection of ground almonds, sugar and white of egg [G.]

Ma·sac·cio (məsáttʃo) (Tommaso di ser Giovanni di Mone, 1401–c. 1428), Italian painter, of crucial importance in the history of Renaissance painting. Working in heroic style, he virtually introduced tonal and linear perspective. His vigorous, fully modeled figures are set in a dramatic relationship to their imposing surroundings. Masaccio's chief surviving work is the fresco series (not all by him) in the Brancacci chapel of Sta Maria del Carmine, Florence

Ma·sai (məsái) pl. **Ma·sai, Ma·sais** n. a member of an African nomadic people inhabiting part of Kenya and Tanganyika ‖ a Nilotic language of this people

Ma·sa·ryk (mǽsərik), Jan Garrigue (1886–1948), Czech statesman, son of T. G. Masaryk. He was foreign minister in the Czech government-in-exile during the 2nd world war, and in the postwar Czech government until his alleged suicide a few weeks after the Communists gained control

Masaryk, Tomàš Garrigue (1850–1937), Czech statesman and philosopher. A liberal, he favored national independence for the peoples of Austria-Hungary, and gained international support for his view in Britain (1914–17), Russia (1917) and the U.S.A. (1918). With Allied backing, he became the first president of Czechoslovakia (1918–35)

Mas·ba·te (məsbátei) a mountainous island (area 1,262 sq. miles, pop. 230,000) of the central Philippines (Visayas): mining (copper, gold, manganese), cattle breeding

Mas·ca·gni (məskánji:), Pietro (1863–1945), Italian composer, best known for the one-act opera 'Cavalleria Rusticana' (1890)

---

mas·car·a (mæskǽrə, Br. mæskǽrə) n. a cosmetic for darkening esp. the eyelashes [after *Mascara*, town in Algeria]

mas·cle (mǽsk'l, mǽsk'l) n. (*heraldry*) a charge in the form of a lozenge with a lozenge-shaped opening [O.F.]

mas·con (mǽskɒn) n. (*astron.*) high concentrations of mass below the maria (seas of the moon) that tend to distort the direction of the moon's gravitational force *also* **mass concentrations**

mas·cot (mǽskət, mǽskɒt) n. an object, animal or person whose presence is supposed to bring good luck [F. *mascotte*]

mas·cu·line (mǽskjulin, Br. mǽskjulin) **1.** adj. of the male sex || relating to or characteristic of men || mannish || (*gram.*) designating or belonging to the gender of words referring to things male or originally regarded as male **2.** n. (*gram.*) the masculine gender || a word having this gender [F. *masculin*]

masculine caesura a caesura immediately following a long or stressed syllable

masculine ending the ending of a line with a stressed syllable

masculine rhyme a rhyme of only one stressed syllable, e.g. 'delay, today'

mas·cu·lin·ist (mǽskjulənist) n. one in favor of special male privileges *syn.* male chauvinist

mas·cu·lin·i·ty (mæskjulíniti:) n. the quality or state of being masculine

mase (meiz) v. to create or amplify microwaves *Cf* LASE

Mase·field (méisfi:ld), John Edward (1878–1967), English poet, critic and novelist. He was poet laureate (1930–67)

ma·ser (méizər) n. any of a class of amplifiers and oscillators that convert the internal energy of a molecular or atomic system into microwave energy by the interaction of electromagnetic radiation with the system. In this way waves with precisely determined frequencies may be obtained. A maser operating at optical frequencies is known as a laser or optical maser [Microwave Amplification by Stimulated Emission of Radiation]

Mas·e·ru (mǽzəru:) the capital (pop. 45,000) of Lesotho

mash (mæʃ) **1.** n. a mixture of things crushed together into a pulp, usually with liquid added || a dry or moistened mixture of ground grain used as poultry and livestock feed || (*brewing*) a mixture of crushed grain or malt with hot water to form wort **2.** v.t. to cause to become a mash, by grinding, crushing etc. || (*brewing*) to mix (grain, malt etc.) with hot water to form wort [O.E. *mǽsc-, mǽx-*]

Mash·am (mǽsəm, mǽʃəm), Mrs (after 1712, Lady) Abigail (d. 1734), favorite of Queen Anne of England. She became bedchamber woman to the queen (1704) and her influence secured the dominance of the Tories Harley and Bolingbroke

mash·ie, mash·y (mǽʃi:) pl. **mash·ies** n. (*golf*) an iron with a deep blade set well back, used for medium distances [origin unknown]

mashie niblick (*golf*) an iron with the blade sloping more than a mashie but less than a niblick

mashy *MASHIE

mask (mæsk, mɑsk) **1.** n. any of several coverings for the face, worn as a disguise, as protection, or to filter air breathed in or out || (*fig.*) a disguise or method of concealment, *under a mask of friendship* || a likeness, esp. a cast of a face || a hollow model of a head, worn by ancient Greek and Roman actors or by participants in a carnival procession || a respirator, esp. one through which an anesthetic is inhaled || (*electr.*) the design of an integrated circuit || (*archit.*) a reproduction of a face as an ornament or gargoyle || the head of a fox, dog, cat etc. || (*photog.*) a screen used to modify the size or shape of an image || (*printing*) an opaque screen used to cover part of a plate **2.** v.t. to cover with a mask || (*fig.*) to conceal with some disguise, to *mask one's feelings* || (*photog.*) to modify the shape or size of (an image) using a mask [F. *masque*]

masked ball a ball at which the participants wear masks

Mas·ke·lyne (mǽskəlin), Nevil (1732–1811), English astronomer. He determined the mean density of the earth (1774). He was astronomer royal (1765–1811)

mask·er (mǽskər, mɑ́skər) n. someone who wears a mask in a masquerade

masking tape an adhesive tape for covering surfaces not to be painted

---

mas·o·chism (mǽsəkizəm, mǽzəkizəm) n. (*psychol.*) a condition in which the subject delights in being hurt or humiliated, esp. as a form of sexual perversion (cf. SADISM) **más·o·chist** n.

mas·o·chis·tic adj. [after L. Von Sacher*Masoch* (1836–95), Austrian novelist who described it]

Ma·so·li·no (mɑsɒlí:nɔ) (Tommaso di Cristoforo Fini, 1383–c. 1447), Florentine early Renaissance painter. He was influenced by his pupil Masaccio: they both worked on the frescos in the Brancacci chapel in Florence

Ma·son (méis'n), George (1725–92), U.S. statesman. At the Virginia constitutional convention (1776) he drafted the declaration of the rights of man, which influenced Thomas Jefferson's draft of the Declaration of Independence. A member of the Philadelphia Constitutional Convention of 1787, he opposed ratification of the federal constitution, but advocated the drafting of the Bill of Rights

Mason, John (1586–1635), English colonial administrator. He received (1629) from the Crown an area between the Merrimack and the Piscataqua Rivers, which he named New Hampshire

Mason, John Young (1799–1859), U.S. political leader and diplomat. He joined with James Buchanan, U.S. minister to Great Britain, and Pierre Soulé, U.S. minister to Spain, in drawing up the Ostend Manifesto

ma·son (méis'n) n. a craftsman who builds with stone, brick etc. **Ma·son·ic** (məsɒ́nik) adj. of or related to the Free and Accepted Masons [O. F. *masson, maçon*]

Ma·son-Dix·on line (méis'ndíksən) the boundary line between Pennsylvania and Maryland. Pennsylvania and Virginia agreed (1779) to extend the line westward, and the western boundary of Pennsylvania was fixed. Before the Civil War, it was part of the boundary between the free and the slave states [after Charles *Mason* and Jeremiah *Dixon*, Eng. astronomers who surveyed the boundary (1763–7)]

ma·son·ry (méis'nri:) n. that which is built by a mason || the mason's craft **Ma·son·ry** Freemasonry [F. *maçonnerie*]

Ma·so·rah, Mas·so·ra (məsɔ́rə, mə- sɔ́urə) n. a collection of marginal notes and criticism on the text of the Hebrew Bible, compiled mainly in Aramaic (6th-10th cc.) [ult. fr. Heb. *masoreth*, bond (of the covenant)]

Mas·o·rete, Mas·so·rete (mǽsəri:t) n. one of the biblical scholars who compiled the Masorah || a scholar learned in the Masorah **Mas·o·ret·ic, Mas·so·ret·ic** (mæsərétik) adj. [misapplication of Heb. *masōreth*]

Mas·o·rite (mǽsərait) n. a Masorete

masque (mæsk, mɑsk) n. (*hist.*) a semi-dramatic amateur performance popular in 16th-c. and 17th-c. England, combining verse, music, mime and spectacle || (*hist.*) a masked ball [var. of MASK]

mas·quer·ade (mæskəréid) **1.** n. a ball at which masks are worn || a false show for pretense or concealment of the truth **2.** v.i. pres. part. **mas·quer·ad·ing** past and past part. **mas·quer·ad·ed** to wear a disguise || to put on a false outward show **mas·quer·ád·er** n. [fr. Span. *mascarada* fr. *mascara*, mask]

Mass (mæs, mɑs) n. the celebration of the Eucharist in the Roman Catholic and some Anglican Churches || music written for this celebration [O.E. *mæsse* fr. L.]

mass (mæs) n. (*phys.*) a property of matter that (with length and time) constitutes one of the fundamental, undefined quantities upon which all physical measurements are based, and which is intuitively associated with the amount of matter a body contains || an aggregation of a quantity of matter, *the pond became a solid mass of ice* || (*loosely*) a large amount or number, *masses of money* || massiveness || an expanse, esp. of color or shade in a painting (the larger part or number, *the mass of men share this belief* **in the mass** generally, *they are good citizens in the mass* **the masses** the ordinary working people in a community, as opposed to the privileged [F. *masse* fr. L. prob. fr. Gk]

mass v.i. and t. to gather together into a mass [F. *masser*]

MASS (*computer acronym*) multiple access sequential selection, a system for large-scale data storage, utilizing magnetic tape and discs to increase data storage capacity and reduce access time

Mas·sa·chu·setts (mæsətʃúːsits) (*abbr.* **Mass.**) a state (area 8,257 sq. miles, pop. 5,781,000) on the northeast coast of the U.S.A. Capital: Bos-

---

ton. It is largely hilly, even in the coastal lowlands, becoming mountainous in the west. Agriculture: poultry and dairy products, flowers, cranberries. Resources: building materials. Industries: textiles and clothing, leather goods, machinery, electrical equipment, fishing. Chief universities: Harvard (1636), Brandeis (1948) at Waltham, University of Massachusetts (1863) at Amherst, Boston University (1839). Massachusetts was the scene of the Pilgrims' landing (1620), and it developed (17th c.) as a Puritan colony. One of the Thirteen Colonies, it became (1788) the 6th state of the U.S.A.

Massachusetts Bay an inlet (c. 50 miles long, 25 miles wide) of the Atlantic Ocean, extending along the east coast of Massachusetts to Cape Cod. Boston is at its west end

Massachusetts Institute of Technology (*abbr.* **M.I.T.**) a leading private technical and scientific university of the U.S.A., in Cambridge, Mass. It was chartered in 1861, opened in 1865

mas·sa·cre (mǽsəkər) n. a ruthless, indiscriminate killing of many people or animals [F., origin unknown]

massacre pres. part. **mas·sa·cring** past and past part. **mas·sa·cred** v.t. to kill (many people or animals) ruthlessly and indiscriminately [F. *massacrer*]

Massacre of St Bartholomew *BARTHOLOMEW, MASSACRE OF ST

Massacre of the Innocents *INNOCENTS, MASSACRE OF THE

mas·sage (məsáʒ, esp. Br. mǽsɑ3) **1.** n. treatment of the muscles etc. by rubbing or kneading **2.** v.t. pres. part. **mas·sag·ing** past and past part. **mas·saged** to apply this treatment to [F.]

Mas·sa·soit (mǽsəsɔit) (c. 1580–1661), chief of the Wampanoag Indians of Massachusetts. Meeting with Governor John Carver, he signed (1621) a peace treaty which remained inviolate for 54 years

Mas·sa·wa (məsáwə) the chief port (pop. 19,820) of Ethiopia, in Eritrea: pearl trade

masscult *MASS CULTURE

mass culture 1. tastes in the arts and entertainment popular with a large segment of the population, contrasted with "high culture" *also* popular culture *Cf* ADMASS, POP ART **2.** any of the arts disseminated via mass media *syn.* masscult n., adj.

mass defect the difference between the isotopic mass and the isotopic mass number of an atom

mas·sé (mæséi) n. (*billiards*) a stroke made with an almost vertical cue on the side of the ball, to pass it around another ball [F.]

Mas·sé·na (mæseinæ), André, prince d'Essling (1758–1817), French marshal. He won brilliant victories in Italy (1796–7) in the French Revolutionary Wars

mass-energy equation the equation for the interconversion of mass and energy $E=mc^2$, where E is the energy in joules, m is the mass in kg and c is the speed of light in meters/sec.

Mas·se·net (mæsonéi, mǽsne), Jules Emile Frédéric (1842–1912), French composer, best known for the operas 'Manon' (1884) and 'Thaïs' (1894)

mas·se·ter (mæsítər) n. either of two muscles which control the lower jaw and aid in mastication [Mod. L. fr. Gk *masētēr*, a chewer]

mas·seur (mæsó:r) n. a man who professionally gives massage **mas·seuse** (mæsó:z) n. a female masseur [F.]

Mas·sey (mǽsi:), Vincent (1887–1967), Canadian statesman. He was the first Canadian to be governor-general of Canada (1952–9)

mas·si·cot (mǽsikɒt) n. unfused yellow lead monoxide, PbO, that occurs naturally [F., origin unknown]

mas·sif (mǽsi:f) n. an elevated mass, usually mountainous, with a number of peaks rising from it || a large portion of the earth's crust which has shifted as a block without internal folding, faulting etc. [F.]

Mas·sif Cen·tral (mæsi:fsátræl) a mountainous plateau (averaging 2,600 ft) covering most of S. central France (36,000 sq. miles). Summit: Puy de Sancy (6,188 ft). Resources: hydroelectricity, coal. Livestock breeding and subsistence farming are the main occupations, but there are industrial centers (Clermont-Ferrand, Alès)

Massine (mɑsí:n), Leonid (1895–1979) Russian choreographer and dancer, creator of innovative and comic ballets, born Leonid Myassine. As part of the Ballets Russes de Serge Diaghi-

---

CONCISE PRONUNCIATION KEY: **(a)** æ, c*a*t; ɑ, c*a*r; ɔ f*aw*n; ei, sn*a*ke. **(e)** e, h*e*n; i:, sh*ee*p; iə, d*ee*r; ɛə, b*ea*r. **(i)** i, f*i*sh; ai, t*i*ger; **(o)** o, *o*x; au, c*ow*; ou, g*oa*t; u, p*oo*r; ɔi, r*oy*al. **(u)** ʌ, d*u*ck; u, b*u*ll; u:, g*oo*se; ə, b*a*cillus; ju:, c*u*be. x, lo*ch*; θ, *th*ink; ð, bo*th*er; z, *Z*en; ʒ, corsage; dʒ, savage; ŋ, ora*ng*utan; j, *y*ak; ʃ, *f*ish; tʃ, fe*tch*; 'l, rabb*le*; 'n, redd*en*. Complete pronunciation key appears inside front cover.

lev he choreographed 'Parade' (1917), 'The Three-Cornered Hat' (1919) and 'The Fantastic Toyshop' (1919). He also choreographed with the Colonel W. de Basil's Company (1933–8) and the Ballets Russes de Monte Carlo (1938–41)

Mas·sin·ger (mǽsindʒər), Philip (1583–c. 1640), English dramatist, best known for his 'A New Way to pay Old Debts' (1633)

mas·sive (mǽsiv) adj. huge and weighty ‖ large in degree, quality etc., a massive price increase ‖ (of gold or silver articles) composed throughout of the metal (not plated or hollow) ‖ (geol.) having no regular form and, often, no crystalline structure [fr. F. massif]

mass·less (mǽsləs) adj. (nuclear phys.) with a mass of zero

mass marketing (business) a program designed to sell a particular product to all consumers in a geographic area (e.g., Eastern seaboard states, continental U.S.) through the use of one marketing program and one marketing system

mass media the means of communication (radio, newspapers etc.) aimed at the widest possible audience

mass meeting a large gathering of people in connection with some matter of public interest

mass number an integer representing the number of nucleons in a nuclide, expressing the mass of an isotope on the 1962 atomic mass scale (cf. ATOMIC MASS)

mass observation (esp. Br.) the study and recording of the actions, customs, habits etc. of ordinary people, used in market research, journalism, political campaigning etc.

Mas·son (mæsɔ̃), André (1896–), French painter, an originator of surrealism. He developed automatism as a painting method, producing abstract compositions of ambiguous forms and rich color. He influenced abstract expressionism

Massora *MASORAH
Massorete *MASORETE

mass-pro·duce (mǽsprədúːs, mǽsprədjúːs) pres. part. **mass-pro·duc·ing** past and past part. **mass-pro·duced** v.t. to manufacture (goods) by mass production **máss-pro·dúced** adj.

mass production production of one article or type of goods in large numbers by a standardized mechanical process

mass spectrograph a mass spectrometer equipped with a device for photographing the mass spectrum formed

mass spectrometer an apparatus used or separating a stream of charged particles (ions) based on the variation of the trajectory of a charged particle in magnetic and electric fields and its charge-to-mass ratio. The mass spectrometer is used to identify isotopes and determine their relative abundance, and in the analysis of complex organic and inorganic mixtures (*MASS SPECTROGRAPH)

mass spectrum a spectrum obtained by means of a mass spectrometer or a mass spectrograph representing the composition of the ion beam ordered according to the relative abundance of ions of e.g. increasing charge-to-mass ratio

mass termination assembly a method of connecting an electrical wire harness to a terminal, used in stereo sets, washing machines, television sets, etc.

mass transit means (e.g., subways) for transporting large numbers of people on prearranged routes on prescribed schedules

Mas·sys (mɑsáis), Quentin (or Quentin Matsys, c. 1465–1530), Flemish painter. Besides his religious paintings ('St Anne triptych', 'The Burial of Christ'), he painted portraits against landscape backgrounds, scholars ('Erasmus') in the study, and genre subjects ('The Banker and his Wife'). He remained in the 15th-c. tradition, while discreetly introducing new Italian ideas learned esp. from Leonardo and Raphael

mast (mæst, most) 1. n. a long pole of wood or metal set up on a ship's keel or deck to carry sails or other rigging ‖ an upright pole or other structure for carrying radio aerials etc. ‖ any upright pole, e.g. the pole in some cranes ‖ (U.S. Navy and Marine Corps) an officers' session for hearing complaints and imposing discipline **to sail before the mast** to serve as a common sailor (from the practice of quartering sailors in the forecastle) 2. v.t. to put a mast or masts on [O.E. mœst]

mast n. the nuts of beech, oaks, chestnut etc., found in the forest, esp. as food for wild boar, etc. [O.E. mæste, mæst]

mas·ta·ba (mǽstəbə) n. an ancient Egyptian tomb with a flat roof and sloping sides [Arab. mastaba, bench]

mas·ter (mǽstər, mɑ́stər) 1. n. a man in control or authority ‖ someone who gets the better of a rival, at last he had met his master ‖ a spiritual leader or guide ‖ someone regarded as great in his field, who serves as inspiration to later generations, the masters of French literature ‖ a person of consummate skill, in an art, technique etc., a master of the clarinet ‖ an employer, as contrasted with 'man', 'servant', 'apprentice' ‖ a skilled workman qualified to work on his own, a master printer ‖ the captain of a merchant ship ‖ a person with a degree between a bachelor's and a doctor's ‖ (esp. Br.) a male teacher in a school ‖ a person in authority over a hunt ‖ the owner of a pet animal ‖ the owner of a slave ‖ (used esp. by servants) the male head of a household ‖ (Scot. peerage) the eldest son of a peer, or the heir presumptive to a peerage ‖ the head of a college, guild, masonic lodge etc. ‖ a matrix from which duplicates (e.g. phonograph records) can be made **Mas·ter** a courtesy title for a boy, in the place of Mister 2. v.t. to gain control over, overcome, to master one's fear ‖ to become completely skilled in, to master a language 3. adj. largest, most important, master bedroom ‖ clearly outstanding in some profession, occupation etc., a master planner ‖ controlling the operation of a number of individually controlled devices, master switch ‖ being one's own boss in a trade, master plumber [O.F. maistre and O.E. mægester fr. L.]

mas·ter-at-arms (mǽstərətɑ́rmz, mɑ́stərətɑ́rmz) pl. **mas·ters-at-arms** n. a petty officer in charge of discipline, prisoners etc. on a man-of-war

mas·ter·ful (mǽstərfəl, mɑ́stərfəl) adj. domineering, wanting to dictate to others ‖ having or showing the qualities appropriate to a master, e.g. the ability to command

mas·ter-hand (mǽstərhænd, mɑ́stərhænd) n. an expert ‖ expert ability

master key a key that opens many locks, each of which is normally opened by an individual key

mas·ter·li·ness (mǽstərliːnis, mɑ́stərliːnis) n. the state or quality of being masterly

mas·ter·ly (mǽstərliː, mɑ́stərliː) adj. showing consummate skill

master mariner the captain of a merchant ship ‖ any seaman officially qualified to command a merchant ship

master mason a skilled mason **Master Mason** a fully qualified Freemason

mas·ter·mind (mǽstərmaind, mɑ́stərmaind) 1. n. the intellect behind some impressive piece of planning, organization etc. ‖ a person of outstanding intellect 2. v.t. to be the mastermind of (a plot etc.)

master of ceremonies (abbr. M.C.) someone who introduces the items, performers etc. at an entertainment ‖ someone who organizes and looks after details at a dance or other formal occasion

mas·ter·piece (mǽstərpiːs, mɑ́stərpiːs) n. a work of art etc. made with consummate skill ‖ an individual's best piece of creative work

Mas·ters (mǽstərz, mɑ́stərz), Edgar Lee (1869–1950), U.S. poet and novelist. His 'Spoon River Anthology' (1915), free-verse epitaphs in monologue form spoken from the grave by former inhabitants of a fictitious village in Illinois, is the first work in American literature dealing with the 'revolt from the village' theme

master sergeant (U.S. Army and Marine Corps) a noncommissioned officer ranking next below a sergeant major ‖ (U.S. Air Force) a noncommissioned officer ranking next above a technical sergeant

mas·ter·ship (mǽstərʃip, mɑ́stərʃip) n. the office of master in a school etc.

mas·ter-slave manipulator (mǽstərsléiv) a device with mechanical hands used to handle radioactive materials while operator is protected by a shield

mas·ter·stroke (mǽstərstrouk, mɑ́stərstrouk) n. an exceedingly clever tactical move

mas·ter·work (mǽstərwəːrk, mɑ́stərwəːrk) n. a masterpiece

mas·ter·y (mǽstəriː, mɑ́stəriː) n. command, control ‖ thorough knowledge or skill in a specified field [O.F. maistrie]

mast·head (mǽsthɛd, mɑ́sthɛd) 1. n. the highest part of a ship's mast, esp. of the lower mast ‖ the sailor stationed near here as a lookout ‖ the part of a newspaper, magazine etc. giving the names of the owner, editors and staff, as well as subscription rates etc. 2. v.t. to send (a sailor) to stand at the masthead as punishment ‖ to hoist (a flag etc.) to the masthead

mas·tic (mǽstik) n. a resin or gum exuding from Pistacia lentiscus, a small S. European evergreen tree. It is used in making high-grade varnish ‖ the tree itself ‖ any of several pasty substances used as cements [F. fr. L.L. fr. Gk]

mas·ti·cate (mǽstikeit) pres. part. **mas·ti·cat·ing** past and past part. **mas·ti·cat·ed** v.t. to chew ‖ to grind (rubber etc.) to a pulp ‖ v.i. to chew food etc. **mas·ti·cá·tion, más·ti·ca·tor** ns [fr. L.L. masticare (masticatus)]

mas·ti·ca·to·ry (mǽstikətɔːri:, mǽstikətouri:) 1. adj. (zool.) adapted for chewing 2. pl. **mas·ti·ca·to·ries** n. a medicinal substance to be chewed to increase secretion of saliva [fr. Mod. L. masticatorius fr. masticare, to chew]

mas·tiff (mǽstif) n. a member of a breed of big, powerful, short-haired dogs with drooping ears and hanging lips, used formerly as fighting dogs, now as watchdogs [after O.F. mastin]

mas·ti·goph·o·ran (mæstəgɔ́fərən) adj. (zool.) any of a class (Mastigophora) of flagellated protozoans that may be parasitic but are seldom found within cells

mas·ti·tis (mæstáitis) n. inflammation of the breast or mammary gland [Mod. L. fr. Gk mastos, breast]

mas·to·don (mǽstədɒn) n. any of several extinct mammals of fam. Mammutidae related to modern elephants, but differing from them esp. in the shape of their molar teeth [Mod. L. fr. Gk mastos, breast+odous (odontos), tooth]

mas·toid (mǽstɔid) 1. adj. shaped like a breast or nipple ‖ of or designating the nipplelike process of the temporal bone behind the ear 2. n. this process [fr. Mod. L. mastoides, breast-shaped]

mas·toid·i·tis (mæstɔidáitis) n. inflammation of the mastoid

mas·tur·bate (mǽstərbeit) pres. part. **mas·tur·bat·ing** past and past part. **mas·tur·bat·ed** v.i. to produce orgasm in oneself by manipulation of the genitals, erotic fantasies etc., exclusive of sexual intercourse ‖ v.t. to produce orgasm in (someone) by manipulation of the genitals **mas·tur·bá·tion** n. [fr. L. masturbari (masturbatus)]

Ma·su·di (məsuːdiː) (Arab. Abu-al-Hasan 'Ali al-Mas'udi, d. c. 956), Arab historian and geographer. He wrote a history of the universe based on material gathered in Africa and Asia

Ma·su·li·pat·nam (mʌsəlipʌ́tnəm) a port (pop. 60,000) in Andhra Pradesh, India, on River Kistna, Bay of Bengal: cotton and rice

ma·su·ri·um (məzúəri:əm) n. the former name of technetium [after Masuria, a region in N.E. Poland]

mat (mæt) 1. n. a piece of coarse material used as a floor covering ‖ a small decorative piece of cloth, woven straw, cork etc. on which vases, ornaments, hot dishes etc. may be set ‖ any tangled or twisted mass, a mat of hair ‖ a thick floor covering used to cushion falls in gymnastics ‖ (naut.) a thick web of rope yarn used to protect rigging from friction 2. v. pres. part. **mat·ting** past and past part. **mat·ted** v.t. to cover with mats or matting ‖ to tangle (hair etc.) ‖ v.i. to become tangled [O.E. matt, meatt, meatte fr. L.L.]

mat, matt, matte pres. part. **mat·ting, matt·ing** past and past part. **mat·ted, matt·ed** v.t. to render dull (gilding, metal etc.) ‖ to frost (glass) [F. mater]

mat, matt, matte 1. n. a mount (for pictures) ‖ the dull finish of unburnished gold, e.g. in painting or gilding ‖ (metalwork) a dull, roughened or frosted groundwork ‖ (printing) a matrix 2. adj. without luster or shine [F. mat]

MAT (abbr.) masters of arts in teaching

Mat·a·be·le·land (mætəbíːliːlænd) an agricultural and mining region (area 70,118 sq. miles) of W. Zimbabwe. Chief town: Bulawayo

Ma·ta·di (mətáːdiː) the chief port (pop. 162,396) of Zaïre, at the head of the Congo River (Zaïre) estuary

ma·ta·dor (mǽtədɔːr) n. (bullfighting) the man whose role is to kill the bull with his sword ‖ (cards) one of the principal cards in quadrille, ombre etc. [Span.]

CONCISE PRONUNCIATION KEY: **(a)** æ, cat; ɑ, car; ɔ fawn; ei, snake. **(e)** e, hen; i:, sheep; iə, deer; ɛə, bear. **(i)** i, fish; ai, tiger; əː, bird. **(o)** o, ox; au, cow; ou, goat; u, poor; ɔi, royal. **(u)** ʌ, duck; u, bull; uː, goose; ə, bacillus; juː, cube. x, loch; θ, think; ð, bother; z, Zen; ʒ, corsage; dʒ, savage; ŋ, orangutang; j, yak; ʃ, fish; tʃ, fetch; 'l, rabble; 'n, redden. Complete pronunciation key appears inside front cover.

Mata Hari (mátɑhári:) (1876–1917), Dutch exotic dancer and spy, b. Margaretha Geertruida Zelle, who spied for the Germans during 1st world war. She was captured and, after a trial, was executed by the French, but questions about her actual guilt remain

Ma·ta·mo·ros (mɑtɑmɔ́rɔs), Mariano (1770–1814), Mexican priest and patriot. In the struggle for Mexican independence he served as the lieutenant of Morelos. He was captured at the defeat of Puruarán and executed in Valladolid

Matamoros a commercial center and border port (pop. 186,480) in the Mexican state of Tamaulipas, 28 miles from the mouth of the Rio Grande, on its south bank opposite Brownsville, Texas

Ma·tan·zas (mɑtánsɑs) the smallest populated province (area 3,259 sq. miles, pop. 463,000) in W. central Cuba. Capital: Matanzas. Chief crop: sugarcane. Manufactures: rope, shoes, fertilizers, matches

Matanzas a city (pop. 64,000) and municipality (pop. 83,000) of W. central Cuba. It is the capital of its province, and has a fine harbor: sugar exportation

match (mætʃ) 1. *n.* someone who or something that can be opposed to or compete with another on an equal footing ‖ one of two persons or things exactly alike ‖ a person or thing harmonizing well with another ‖ a pair of persons or things with regard to the way in which they harmonize with each other, *those colors are a poor match* ‖ a person with regard to his or her suitability as a husband or wife ‖ a marriage ‖ a game or contest between two teams or persons 2. *v.t.* to bring into competition, *to match one's wits against another's* ‖ to equal, *nobody can match him in ping pong* ‖ to be in harmony with, *her skirt doesn't match her blouse* ‖ to be the exact counterpart of ‖ to find an exact counterpart for ‖ to cause (two people or things) to be in harmony ‖ to toss (coins) in gambling or as a way of deciding something contested ‖ to toss coins with (a person) to decide something, *I'll match you to see who goes first* ‖ *v.i.* to have the same color, shape etc. as what is taken for comparison ‖ to harmonize with something ‖ (of two things) to be exactly the same with respect to color, shape etc. [O.E. *gamœcca, gemecca*, a mate]

match *n.* a small, thin piece of wood (sometimes of plastic), covered at one end with material of low ignition point which will burn when heated by the friction of striking it on a rough surface [O. F. *mesche, meiche*, wick]

match·board (mætʃbɔrd, mætʃbourd) *n.* a board with a rabbeted edge or with a tongue in one edge and a groove in the other, for fitting into similar boards. Matchboards are used for ceilings, floors etc.

match·book (mætʃbʊk) *n.* a slim cardboard container in which rows of cardboard safety matches are fastened

match·box (mætʃbɒks) *n.* a small box, with a prepared striking surface, in which matches are packed

match·et (mætʃit) *n.* a machete

matching funds 1. monies raised in proportion to the amount of grant, usu. as a prerequisite for the grant 2. the grant that is to be so matched

match·less (mætʃlis) *adj.* impossible to equal in excellence etc.

match·lock (mætʃlɒk) *n.* (*hist.*) a slow-burning cord for lowering into the breech of a musket so as to fire the charge ‖ (*hist.*) a musket with such a lock

match·mak·er (mætʃmeikər) *n.* someone who delights or engages in arranging marriages for others **match·mak·ing** *n.* and *adj.*

match play (*golf*) a form of the game in which the scoring is by number of holes won, not by number of strokes (cf. MEDAL PLAY)

match point (*sports*) the last point needed to win a match

match·wood (mætʃwʊd) *n.* wood suitable for matches **to make matchwood of** (*Br.*) to smash to pieces ‖ (*Br.*) to defeat crushingly

mate (meit) 1. *v.t.* checkmate 2. *v.t. pres. part.* **mat·ing** *past* and *past part.* **mat·ed** to checkmate [M.E. *mat* fr. O.F. *eshec mat*, checkmate]

mate 1. *n.* the male or female of a couple ‖ one of a pair of objects ‖ (in compounds) a companion, *classmate* ‖ (*Br., pop.*) a fellow worker ‖ a partner in marriage ‖ a deck officer on a merchant ship who ranks below the captain and carries

out his orders ‖ (*U.S. Navy*) an assistant to a warrant officer, ranking as a petty officer ‖ any assistant, *plumber's mate* 2. *v. pres. part.* **mat·ing** *past* and *past part.* **mat·ed** *v.t.* to pair (birds, animals) for breeding ‖ *v.i.* (of birds, animals) to copulate [perh. fr. M.L.G. or M. Du.]

ma·té (mætéi) *n.* a tealike drink containing caffeine, made from the dried leaves of *Ilex paraguayensis*, a South American holly ‖ this holly [Span. *mate* fr. Quechua *mati*, calabash]

ma·te·ri·al (mɑtíɑri:əl) 1. *adj.* of or consisting of matter ‖ (of behavior, ideas) worldly, not spiritual ‖ connected or concerned with bodily comfort, *material needs* ‖ substantially important, *a side plot not material to the main story* ‖ (*law*) important for the determination of a cause or for the outcome of a case 2. *n.* the stuff from which a thing is made ‖ cloth ‖ data constituting the basis of a more finished composition, *the material for a historical novel* ‖ (*pl.*) necessary tools, equipment etc., *writing materials* [fr. L.L. *materialis*]

ma·te·ri·al·ism (mɑtíɑri:əlizəm) *n.* (*philos.*) the theory that matter is the basic reality of the universe, hence that everything is material or can be shown to derive ultimately from matter. Materialism probably emerged in the 4th c. B.C. with Democritus' atomist theory. It has been the basic premise of many philosophical systems (cf. PRAGMATISM, cf. POSITIVISM, cf. MARXISM) [fr. Mod. L. *materialismus*]

ma·te·ri·al·ist (mɑtíɑri:əlist) *n.* someone who values material things more than spiritual ones ‖ someone who holds the philosophical beliefs of materialism **ma·te·ri·al·is·tic** *adj.* **ma·te·ri·al·is·ti·cal·ly** *adv.* [fr. Mod. L. *materialista*]

ma·te·ri·al·i·ty (mɑtíɑri:æliti:) *n.* the quality or state of being material ‖ matter [fr. Mod. L. *materialitas*]

ma·te·ri·al·i·za·tion (mɑtíɑri:əlizéiʃən) *n.* a materializing or being materialized ‖ an apparition of a spirit

ma·te·ri·al·ize (mɑtíɑri:əlaiz) *pres. part.* **ma·te·ri·al·iz·ing** *past* and *past part.* **ma·te·ri·al·ized** *v.t.* to give material characteristics or form to ‖ to cause (a spirit) to appear ‖ *v.i.* to become tangible, *his grandiose scheme never materialized* ‖ (of spirits) to appear in bodily form

ma·te·ri·al·ly (mɑtíɑri:əli:) *adv.* to a considerable degree, substantially ‖ with regard to matter or material things ‖ of matter as distinguished from form

materials science study of the properties of materials

ma·te·ri·a med·i·ca (mɑtíɑri:əmédikə) *n.* substances used in preparing medicines ‖ the science of the source, nature and properties of these substances [M.L.]

ma·té·ri·el, ma·te·ri·el (mɑtíɑri:él) *n.* the equipment and supplies used in a business or in the armed forces (cf. PERSONNEL)

ma·ter·nal (mɑtɔ́:rn'l) *adj.* of or pertaining to a mother ‖ motherly ‖ related through the mother, *a maternal uncle* [fr. F. *maternel*]

ma·ter·ni·ty (mɑtɔ́:rniti:) 1. *n.* the state of being a mother ‖ motherliness 2. *adj.* of or pertaining to the time when a woman is pregnant or has just had a baby, or to pregnancy or childbirth, *maternity ward* [fr. F. *maternité*]

maternity clothes clothes for pregnant women

mat·e·y (méiti:) *adj.* (*Br., pop.*) friendly and companionable

math (mæθ) *n.* (*pop.*) mathematics

math·e·mat·i·cal (mæθəmætik'l) *adj.* of, pertaining to or using mathematics, *a mathematical calculation* ‖ used in mathematics, *a mathematical table* ‖ very precise, *mathematical accuracy* [fr. L. *mathematicus*]

mathematical biology science utilizing mathematical models of biological phenomena for research

mathematical linguistics (*linguistics*) study of the mathematical properties of language, applying statistical and algebraic concepts

mathematical logic symbolic logic

math·e·ma·ti·cian (mæθəmətiʃən) *n.* a specialist in mathematics [F. *mathématicien*]

math·e·mat·ics (mæθəmætiks) *n.* the science of expressing and studying the relationships between quantities and magnitudes as represented by numbers and symbols [pl. of obs. *mathematic n.* fr. Gk]

Math·er (mæðər, mæθər), Cotton (1663–1728), New England Puritan Congregational minister and author, the son of Increase Mather. A powerful voice in New England affairs, he led the

revolt against the rule of Sir Edmund Andros. His 'Memorable Provinces Relating to Witchcraft and Possessions' (1689) helped to promote the Salem witch trials. He contributed, however, to the founding of Yale University and to making New England a cultural capital

Mather, Increase (1639–1723), American Congregational minister, author, and statesman. After Charles II had rescinded the original Massachusetts charter, under which the colonists were entitled to elect their own governor, Mather secured its partial restoration. He served (1685–1701) as president of Harvard University and published his 'Cases of Conscience' (1693) concerning the Salem witch trials

maths (mæθs) *n.* (*Br., pop.*) mathematics

Ma·thu·ra (mátura) (Muttra) a Hindu pilgrimage center (pop. 132,028) in N. Uttar Pradesh, India, on the Jumna, traditional birthplace of Krishna

Ma·til·da (mɑtíldə) (1046–1115), countess of Tuscany. She supported Pope Gregory VII in his struggle with the Emperor Henry IV. The lands which she bequeathed to the papacy were long disputed between the Empire and the Holy See

Matilda (1102–67), queen of England (1141) and, by her marriage (1114) to Henry V, empress of the Holy Roman Empire. After her husband's death (1125), her father Henry I made her heiress to the English throne (1126) and she married (c. 1128) Geoffrey Plantagenet, count of Anjou. On her father's death (1135), the English throne was usurped by her cousin Stephen. Mathilda invaded England (1139) and dethroned Stephen (1141), but was overthrown six months later. The war ended (1153) when her son Henry (later Henry II) was recognized as heir to the throne

mat·in·al (mætin'l, mæt'n'l) *adj.* of or occurring in the early morning [F.]

mat·i·nee, mat·i·née (mæt·néi) *n.* an afternoon performance at a moviehouse or theater [F. *matinée*, morning]

matinee idol, matinée idol an actor who has a special appeal for women because of his looks and charm

Mat·ins, *Br.* also **Mat·tins** (mætinz, mæt'nz) *pl. n.* (Roman Catholicism) the first of the canonical hours in the breviary, followed by lauds ‖ (Anglican Communion) the service of Morning Prayer [fr. F. *matines*]

Ma·tisse (mæti:s), Henri (1869–1954), French painter and sculptor, leader of the Fauves. His works have a luxuriance and gaiety arising from a free, bold and inventive use of pure color. They are highly decorative, with strong patterns which have affinities with the natural but stylized forms used in Middle Eastern decoration. He was also a master draftsman

Ma·to Gros·so (mátugrɔ́su) the thinly populated savanna plateau region (approx. 485,000 sq. miles) of W. central Brazil: cattle raising

mat·rass, mat·trass (mætrɑs) *n.* a long, rounded glass container, used in distilling etc. [F. *matras*]

ma·tri·arch (méitri:ɑrk) *n.* a woman who rules a group, esp. a mother having authority over her immediate family or over a larger family group ‖ a venerable old woman **ma·tri·ar·chal** *adj.* of or like a matriarch ‖ based on or pertaining to a matriarchy **má·tri·ar·chate** *n.* a community etc. ruled by a matriarch **má·tri·ar·chy** *pl.* **ma·tri·ar·chies** *n.* a form of social organization in which descent is traced through the mothers ‖ government by women ‖ a matriarchate [fr. L. *matr-* fr. *mater*, mother, after 'patriarch']

matrices alt. *pl.* of MATRIX

mat·ri·cid·al (mætrisáid'l, meitrisáid'l) *adj.* of or pertaining to matricide

mat·ri·cide (mætrisaid, méitrisaid) *n.* the murder of a mother by her child [fr. L. *matricidium* fr. *mater*, mother+*caedere*, to kill]

matricide *n.* a person who kills his mother [fr. L. *matricida* fr. *mater*, mother+*caedere*, to kill]

ma·tric·u·late (mɑtríkjuleit) *pres. part.* **ma·tric·u·lat·ing** *past* and *past part.* **ma·tric·u·lat·ed** *v.t.* to enroll in a university or college ‖ *v.i.* to be enrolled as a member of a university or college **ma·tric·u·lá·tion** *n.* [fr. M.L. *matriculare* (*matriculatus*) fr. L. L. *matricula*, a register]

mat·ri·fo·cal (mætrəfóuk'l) and **mat·ri·cen·tred** (mætrəsentərd) *adj.* (anthropology) of a social group, e.g., a tribe, centered on the mother figure

mat·ri·lin·e·al (mætrəlíni:əl, meitrəlíni:əl) *adj.* tracing descent or kinship through the mother [fr. L. *mater*, mother+LINEAL]

mat·ri·lo·cal (mætrəlóuk'l, meitrəlóuk'l) *adj.* of or pertaining to residence at the habitation of the wife's family or tribe [fr. L. *mater*, mother+LOCAL]

mat·ri·mo·ni·al (mætrəmóuni:əl) *adj.* pertaining to marriage or married life [F.]

mat·ri·mo·ny (mætrəmouni:) *pl.* **mat·ri·mo·nies** *n.* the state of being married ‖ marriage as a Christian sacrament ‖ (*cards*) the declaration of king and queen as trumps in some games [O.F. *matremoine*]

ma·trix (méitriks, mætriks) *pl.* **mat·ri·ces** (méitrisi:z, mætrisi:z), **ma·trix·es** *n.* a mold in which type or other matter in relief is shaped or cast ‖ a place within which something is formed and developed ‖ any natural material, e.g. rock, in which gems, fossils, metals etc. are found ‖ the impression left in a rock when a fossil etc. has been removed ‖ an array of mathematical elements subject to certain algebraic laws and used notably to express the conditions in which a system of linear equations has a solution ‖ (*biol.*) the substance between the cells of connective tissue ‖ (*bot.*) a body upon which lichen or fungus grows ‖ (*anat.*) the part beneath the body and root of a nail ‖ (*computer*) a table of variables ‖ an arrangement of circuit elements to perform particular functions [L.=womb]

matrix algebra (*math.*) a form of algebra dealing with addition and multiplication of matrices

matrix isolation (*chem.*) a technique for isolating molecules in an inert solid (matrix) for study

matrix mechanics a branch of quantum mechanics that treats the coordinates and momenta associated e.g. with the electrons in an atom as matrices rather than quantities having definite values, and that gives essentially the same results as wave mechanics

ma·tron (méitrən) *n.* a married woman or a widow, usually having children and no longer young ‖ a person who superintends the domestic affairs of a public institution, e.g. a prison or hospital ‖ (*Br.*) a woman in a boarding school who fills a maternal role in looking after the children's welfare ‖ (*Br.*) a woman superintendent of nurses in a hospital ‖ a female attendant or guard in a women's prison or in some other public institution **má·tron·li·ness** *n.* **má·tron·ly** *adj.* [F. *matrone*]

matron of honor, *Br.* **matron of honour** a married woman acting as a bride's chief attendant (cf. MAID OF HONOR, cf. BRIDESMAID)

Ma·tsu·ya·ma (matsujama) a port (pop. 407,969) of Shikoku, Japan, on the Inland Sea: textiles, paper products

matt, matte *MAT

matte (mæt) *n.* (*metall.*) an impure mixture of sulfides obtained during the smelting of sulfide ores of metals [F.]

mat·ted (mætid) *adj.* (of hair) in a tangled, sticky-looking mess ‖ clogged with undergrowth or covered with dense growth ‖ made from, or covered with, mats

mat·ter (mætər) **1.** *n.* that which any physical thing is composed of ‖ (*phys.*) that which occupies space and possesses inertia ‖ a substance serving a specified purpose, *coloring matter* ‖ content as distinct from form, *subject matter* ‖ importance, *it is of no matter* ‖ a circumstance, issue, topic etc., *a matter requiring attention*, *business matters* ‖ trouble, difficulty, *what's the matter?* ‖ (*law*) the facts as opposed to principles ‖ pus ‖ type set up or impressions from this **for that matter** as far as that is concerned **in the matter of** as regards **2.** *v.i.* to be of importance ‖ to suppurate [M.E. *materie, matere, matiere* fr. O. F.]

Mat·ter·horn (mætərhɔrn) (*F.* le Cervin, *Ital.* il Cervino) a famous peak (14,780 ft) in the Pennine Alps, on the Swiss-Italian frontier

matter of course something expected as natural or logical in the course of events **mát·ter-of-cóurse** *adj.*

matter of fact a fact, as distinct from a supposition **mát·ter-of-fáct** *adj.* practical and down-to-earth ‖ unimaginative, merely truthful, *a matter-of-fact account of the adventure*

Mat·thew (mǽθju:), St (*d.* c. 70), one of the 12 Apostles, traditionally the author of the Gospel according to St Matthew. Symbol: a winged man. Feast: Sept. 21 (Orthodox Church Nov. 16)

Matthew, Gospel according to St the first Gospel of the New Testament, traditionally attributed to St Matthew and thought to have been written in the late 1st c. It contains five of Christ's discourses, inc. the Sermon on the Mount

Matthew Paris *PARIS, Matthew

Mat·thi·as (məθáiəs), St (*d.* 61 or 64), the Apostle chosen by lot to fill the place of Judas Iscariot (Acts i, 21-6). Feast: Feb. 24

Matthias (1557–1619), Holy Roman Emperor (1612–19), king of Bohemia (1611–17) and of Hungary (1608–18), son of Maximilian II. He succeeded his incompetent brother Rudolf II, but failed in his policy of uniting the Protestant Union and the Catholic League. The Thirty Years' War broke out (1618) during his reign

Matthias Cor·vi·nus (kɔrváinəs) (c. 1440–90), king of Hungary (1458–90) and Bohemia (1478–90), son of János Hunyadi. He fought the Turks and captured Vienna (1485), which he made his capital. He extended his power over much of central Europe, and was a patron of learning and science

mat·ting (mætiŋ) *n.* a dull surface or finish in gilding, glassmaking etc. ‖ the production of this surface ‖ a border for a picture

matting *n.* woven material, esp. of hemp, grass, bast etc., used for floor covering etc.

Mattins *MATINS

mat·tock (mætək) *n.* a tool shaped like a pick, the head having usually one end pointed and the other flat with a sharp edge. It is used for loosening soil, digging up and cutting roots etc. [O.E. *mattuc, meottuc*]

Mat·tos (mátɔs), Gregório de (1633–96), Brazilian poet. He wrote of the corruption of the Church, the venality of government officials, and the injustices of the social system under Portuguese rule

mattress *MATRASS

mat·tress (mætris) *n.* a flat case of some strong fabric, e.g. canvas, stuffed with hair, feathers, sponge rubber etc., put on a bedstead or serving as a bed ‖ a mat of brushwood or poles used in dikes, dams etc. to prevent erosion [O. F. *materas*]

mat·u·rate (mætʃureit) *pres. part.* **mat·u·rat·ing** *past* and *past part.* **mat·u·rat·ed** *v.i.* to mature ‖ *v.t.* to cause to ripen [fr. L. *maturare* (*maturatus*)]

mat·u·ra·tion (mætʃuréiʃən) *n.* the full development of adult characteristics, e.g. the development of adult organs or tissues, the development of emotional maturity etc. ‖ the entire process leading to the production of haploid gametes from diploid spermatogonia or oogonia, involving usually two meiotic divisions and including the structural and physiological changes preparing the gametes for fertilization (*MEIOSIS) [F.]

maturation division meiosis

ma·ture (mətúər, mətjúər, mətʃúər) *adj.* having reached a state of full natural development, *a mature person* ‖ ripe ‖ of or relating to the time when development is complete, *his mature years* ‖ (of decisions etc.) involving or arrived at after prolonged and careful thought ‖ (of a bond etc.) due ‖ (*geol.*, of a river etc.) having reached a state of maximum development [fr. L. *maturus*, ripe]

mature *pres. part.* **ma·tur·ing** *past* and *past part.* **ma·tured** *v.t.* to cause to become mature ‖ *v.i.* to become mature [fr. obs. F. *maturer* and MATURE adj.]

ma·tu·ri·ty (mətúəriti:, mətjúəriti:, mətʃúəriti:) *n.* the quality or state of being mature ‖ (of bonds etc.) a becoming due [fr. F. *maturité* or L. *maturitas*]

ma·tu·ti·nal (mətú:t'n'l, mətjú:t'n'l) *adj.* of or occurring in the morning [fr. L. *matutinalis*]

mat·zo, mat·zoh (mútzə) *pl.* **mat·zoth** (mátsout), **mat·zos** *n.* an unleavened bread eaten by Jews at Passover [Yiddish *matse* fr. Heb. *massāh*]

maud·lin (mɔ́dlin) *adj.* weakly and tearfully sentimental, esp. when drunk [O.F. *Madelaine*, Magdalen, often depicted as weeping]

Maugham (mɔm), William Somerset (1874–1965), English novelist, playwright and writer of short stories in a sophisticated, satirical style. His novels include 'Of Human Bondage' (1915), 'Cakes and Ale' (1930), and 'The Razor's Edge' (1944)

Mau·i (máui:) the second largest island (area 728 sq. miles, pop. 70,847) of the Hawaiian group

maul (mɔl) **1.** *n.* (also **mall**) any of several kinds of heavy hammer, usually wooden, for driving in stakes, wedges etc. **2.** *v.t.* (also **mall**) to attack savagely and injure, *the lion mauled its trainer* ‖ to treat roughly, *the child mauled his kitten* ‖ to attack with violent criticism ‖ to split (wood) with a maul and wedge [fr. F. *maid*]

maul·stick, mahl·stick (mɔ́lstik) *n.* a light stick with a padded head, used by painters to support and steady the brush hand [fr. Du. *maalstok* fr. *malen*, to paint+*stok*, stick]

Mau Mau (máumau) a secret society in Kenya, drawn chiefly from the Kikuyu, which aimed at driving European settlers out of Kenya. Its terrorist rebellion (1952–9) against the Kenya government was put down by British troops, and its supposed leader, Kenyatta, imprisoned (1953–9)

Mau·na Ke·a (máunəkéiə) an extinct volcano in N. central Hawaii Is., Hawaii. It rises 32,000 ft from its base on the ocean floor (13,784 ft above sea level)

Mau·na Lo·a (máunəlóuə) a double-cratered, active volcano (13,680 ft) on central Hawaii Is., Hawaii

maund (mɔnd) *n.* any of several units of weight in India and W. Asia [Hindi and Pers. *man*]

maun·der (mɔ́ndər) *v.i.* to talk ramblingly, with no obvious purpose ‖ to move or act aimlessly and slowly [etym. doubtful]

maun·dy money (mɔ́ndi:) specially minted coins given to the poor by a royal personage in a Maundy Thursday ceremony, esp. in Westminster Abbey [O.F. *mandé*, commandment, from Jesus's words after washing his disciples' feet, 'a new commandment I give you, that ye love one another' (John xiii, 34)]

Maundy Thursday the Thursday before Easter

Mau·pas·sant (moupæsã), Guy de (1850–93), French writer. He was a master of the short-story form, writing in a naturalistic, terse style. His stories include 'Boule de suif' (1880), 'Mademoiselle Fifi' (1882) etc. Among his novels are 'Une vie' (1883) and 'Bel Ami' (1885)

Mau·riac (mourjæk), François (1885–1970), French writer. His novels are usually set in the Bordeaux country and often depict violent conflicts between religious beliefs and passion, or between the individual and the family. They include 'Génitrix' (1924), 'le Désert de l'amour' (1925), 'Thérèse Desqueyroux' (1927), 'le Noeud de vipères' (1932)

Mau·rice (mɔ́ris, mɔ́ris) (1521–53), duke (1541–7) and elector (1547–53) of Saxony. Although a Protestant, he allied himself with Charles V in the Schmalkaldic War (1546–7), but subsequently turned against Charles and signed the Treaty of Passau (1552) with the future Emperor Ferdinand I

Maurice of Nassau (1567–1625), prince of Orange (1618–25), stadtholder of the Netherlands (1584–1625), son of William the Silent. He fought successfully (1590–1609) against Spanish rule. He ordered the execution (1619) of his former ally Barneveldt, to whom much of the commercial prosperity of his reign was due

Mau·ri·ta·ni·a (mɔritéini:ə) an Islamic republic (area 397,955 sq. miles, pop. 1,731,000) in N.W. Africa. Capital: Nouakchott. People: 84% Moors (Arabs and Berbers, mostly nomadic herdsmen with Toucouleur, Sarakolle and Fulani minorities, mainly farmers, in the far south). Languages: Arabic, Berber dialects, French, Hamitic and Sudanese dialects. State religion: Islam. Social organization is largely tribal. Most of the country is in the Sahara, with a less arid region, the Sahel (gum arabic, dates) in the south, and a fertile strip (cereals, peanuts, sweet potatoes) along the River Senegal. Inland plateaus rise to 3,000 ft in the north. Average temperatures: (Jan.) 70°F., (July) 80°F. Rainfall: under 5 ins in the Sahara, 10–20 ins in the south. Livestock: sheep, goats, camels. Resources: iron (rich deposits in the northwest near Fort Gouraud), copper, salt, fish. Exports: minerals, gum, meat, fish products. Imports: sugar, rice, tea, flour, manufactured goods. Railroad: Fort Gouraud–Port Etienne (1963). Monetary unit: CFA franc. HISTORY. Inhabited by Berbers since the 4th c., the area was invaded by Beduins (12th c.). It was recognized as within the French sphere of influence (1817), made a protectorate (1903) and attached to French West Africa (1904). It became a colony (1920), an autonomous republic within the French Community (1958) and fully indepen-

---

CONCISE PRONUNCIATION KEY: **(a)** æ, cat; ɑ, car; ɔ fawn; ei, snake. **(e)** e, hen; i:, sheep; iə, deer; ɛə, bear. **(i)** i, fish; ai, tiger; ə:, bird. **(o)** o, ox; au, cow; ou, goat; u, poor; ɔi, royal. **(u)** ʌ, duck; u, bull; u:, goose; ə, bacillus; ju:, cube. x, loch; θ, think; ð, bother; z, Zen; ʒ, corsage; dʒ, savage; ŋ, orangutang; j, yak; ʃ, fish; tʃ, fetch; 'l, rabble; 'n, redden. Complete pronunciation key appears inside front cover.

dent (Nov. 28, 1960). A war with the Algerian-backed Polisario Front guerrillas of the Spanish Sahara (now Western Sahara) after Mauritania annexed one-third of that former colony (1976) led to a severe economic crisis and the overthrow of the government (1978). Mauritania relinquished its claim (1979), signed a treaty of friendship with Algeria and Tunisia (1983) and formally recognized the Polisario government (1984). It then moved to improve relations with Morocco and Libya while reaffirming its support for the Polisario

Mau·ri·tius (mɔrí∫əs) an island state (area 720 sq. miles, pop. 1,018,000) in the Indian Ocean, 500 miles east of the Malagasy Republic. It is a member of the U.N. and of the Commonwealth. Capital: Port Louis. The country includes Rodrigues Is. and the Lesser Dependencies (Agalega and Cargados Carajos, total area 11 sq. miles, pop. 10,000). People: 65% of Indian origin, with Chinese, European, Malagasy, African, Sinhalese and Malay minorities. Languages: English (official), French, Creole, Chinese, Hindi, Arabic, Urdu, Tamil. Religion: largely Hindu and Roman Catholic, with Moslem and Buddhist minorities. The volcanic central plateau, steep in the west, rises to 2,711 ft and contains inland plains at 1,200 ft. Average temperatures (F.): Port Louis 74°, 67° in the mountains. Rainfall: 30–50 ins at sea level, 200 ins high up. Agricultural and forestry products: sugar, tea, timber. Industries: sugar refining, aloe and jute fiber, sacks, foodstuffs. Exports: sugar (98% of exports). Imports: manufactures, foodstuffs. Monetary unit: Mauritius rupee (100 cents). HISTORY. The island was visited by Arabs and Malays in the Middle Ages and by the Portuguese (1507). It was named after Maurice of Nassau by the Dutch (1598), who settled it intermittently (1683–1710). It was claimed (1715) by the French, and captured (1810) by the British. Indians immigrated in large numbers to work on the sugar plantations after slavery was abolished in the British Empire (1834). Universal adult suffrage was introduced (1958), and successive constitutional changes (1961 and 1964) prepared the island for independence (Mar. 12, 1968). Since then it has claimed the British Indian Ocean Territory, which it administered until 1965

Mau·rois (mourwæ), André (Emile Herzog, 1885–1967), French writer. He is best known for his popular biographies of Shelley, Disraeli, Byron, Dickens etc.

Mau·ry (mɔ́ri:, mɔ́ri:), Matthew Fontaine (1806–73), American hydrographer. He made wind and current charts of the Atlantic, Pacific and Indian Oceans. His 'Physical Geography of the Sea' (1855) was the first textbook of modern oceanography

Mau·ry·a (máuri:ə) an Indian dynasty (325–184 B.C.), founded by Chandragupta. It extended its power over most of India and Afghanistan

mau·so·le·um (mɔsəli:əm, mɔzəli:əm) pl. **mau·so·le·ums, mau·so·le·a** (mɔsəli:ə, mɔzəli:ə) n. a large and elaborate tomb, or a building housing tombs [L. fr. Gk mausōleiom fr. MAUSOLUS]

Mau·so·lus (mɔsóuləs) (d. c. 353 B.C.), satrap of Caria (c. 377–c. 353 B.C.). His monumental tomb at Halicarnassus was one of the Seven Wonders of the World. It was destroyed by an earthquake in the Middle Ages

mauve (mouv) 1. n. a pale purple dye obtained from crude aniline, the first to be prepared synthetically ‖ the color of this dye 2. adj. having this color [F.]

ma·ven or **ma·vin** or **may·vin** (méivən) n. (colloq.) (Hebrew) an expert

mav·er·ick (mǽvərik) n. (pop.) a person who refuses to conform and acts independently ‖ a member of a political party who will not toe the party line ‖ an unbranded animal on the range, esp. a motherless calf [after Samuel Augustus Maverick (1803–70), a Texas owner of unbranded cattle]

Maverick (mil.) an air-to-surface missile (AGM-65) designed for use against stationary or moving small, hard targets (e.g., tanks, armored vehicles, field fortifications), of 500-lb. weight, made in various versions inc. scene magnification, laser seeker to home on an illuminated object and imaging infrared seeker; produced in 1972 by Hughes Aircraft

maw (mɔ) n. the abomasum of a ruminant ‖ the crop of a granivorous bird [O. E. maga, stomach]

mawk·ish (mɔ́ki∫) adj. weakly or cloyingly sentimental [fr. older mawk, maggot fr. O.N. mathkr, worm]

Max·en·tius (mæksén∫əs), Marcus Aurelius Valerius (c. 280–312), Roman emperor (306–12), son of Maximian. He seized power helped by the Praetorians and reconquered N. Africa, but was defeated (312) by Constantine I

max·i (mǽksi) n. woman's skirt or coat extending to the ankle also maxicoat; maxiskirt Cf MICRO-, MIDI-, MINI

maxi- combining form meaning "very large" e.g., maxidress, maxiskirt Cf MACRO-, MEGA-, META-, MICRO-, MINI-

maxicoat *MAXI

max·il·la (mæksilə) pl. **max·il·lae** (mæksíli:), **max·il·las** n. either of the parts of the upper jaw behind the premaxilla ‖ the upper jaw ‖ an appendage of most arthropods, posterior to the mandible, modified in various ways according to function **max·il·lar·y** (mæksiləri:, mæksələri:) 1. adj. of, pertaining to, or in the region of the maxilla 2. n. pl. **max·il·lar·ies** (anat.) the maxilla [L.=jaw]

Max·im (mæksim), Hiram Percy (1869–1936), U.S. inventor, son of Sir Hiram Maxim. He devised the Maxim silencer (1908) for explosive weapons

Maxim, Sir Hiram Stevens (1840–1916), British inventor, of U.S. origin. He is best known for his Maxim machine gun (1884)

Maxim, Hudson (1853–1927), U.S. inventor, brother of Sir Hiram Maxim. He invented a high explosive (Maximite), smokeless powders, and a self-combustive compound to propel torpedoes

max·im (mæksim) n. a succinct general truth, moral reflection or rule of conduct [F. maxime]

max·i·mal (mæksəməl) adj. to the greatest possible degree ‖ pertaining to or being a maximum [MAXIMUM]

Max·im·i·an (mæksími:ən) (Marcus Aurelius Valerius Maximianus, d. 310), Roman emperor (286–305 and 306–8), associate of Diocletian

Max·i·mil·ian (mæksəmíljən) (1832–67), emperor of Mexico (1864–7), archduke of Austria, brother of Franz Joseph. After Napoleon III's ill-advised invasion of Mexico, he accepted the imperial throne, but was kept in power only by French troops. When these were withdrawn, he was captured and shot by the troops of Juárez, who rapidly reconquered the country

Maximilian I (1459–1519), Holy Roman Emperor (1493–1519), king of Germany (1486–1519), son of Frederick III. His dynastic marriages involved him in a series of wars with France, the Swiss Confederation and Venice. His consequent financial difficulties started the dependency of emperors on loans from the Fugger family. Maximilian was a patron of Dürer and other artists, and his reign saw the beginnings of the Reformation

Maximilian II (1527–76), Holy Roman Emperor (1562–76), king of Bohemia and Germany (1564–76), and of Hungary (1563–76), son of Ferdinand I

Maximilian I (1573–1651), Duke of Bavaria (1597–1651) and elector palatine (1623–51). He formed the Catholic League (1609) and played an important part in the Thirty Years' War, defeating the Elector Frederick V at the White Mountain (1620)

max·i·min (mæksəmin) n. (logic) the maximum of a group of minima Cf MINIMAX

Max·i·min I (mæksəmin) (Gaius Julius Verus Maximinus, 173–238), Roman emperor (253–8). A Thracian peasant, he was the first Roman emperor to have come from the ranks of the army

Maximin II (Gaius Galerius Valerius Maximinus, d. 314), Roman emperor (308–14)

max·i·mize (mæksəmaiz) pres. part. **max·i·miz·ing** past and past part. **max·i·mized** v.t. to magnify to the greatest possible degree ‖ to make the most of [fr. L. maximus, greatest]

max·i·mum (mæksəməm) 1. pl. **max·i·mums, max·i·ma** (mæksəmə) n. the greatest possible amount, number or degree ‖ the greatest amount, number or degree actually reached 2. adj. greatest in amount, number or degree, at maximum speed ‖ relating to, marking or setting a maximum [L. neut. superl. of magnus, great]

maximum likelihood method (statistics) technique providing a likelihood distribution probability so great that an estimate of the random variables is produced

maximum permissible exposure (med.) the total radiation exposure to which an average person may be exposed without harm

Max·i·mus (mæksəməs), Magnus Clemens (d. 388), Roman emperor (383–8). He proclaimed himself emperor in Britain and overthrew Gratian in Gaul (383), but was defeated and killed by Theodosius I

maxiskirt *MAXI

Max·well (mǽkswəl, mǽkswẹl), James Clerk (1831–79), Scottish physicist, distinguished for his contributions to the electromagnetic theory of light and the kinetic theory of gases

max·well (mǽkswəl, mǽkswẹl) n. the cgs electromagnetic unit (symbol M) of magnetic flux, equal to the flux through 1 sq. c. of a magnetic field in the air having an induction of 1 gauss [after James C. Maxwell]

Maxwell-Boltzmann distribution a fundamental statistical equation in both classical and quantum statistical mechanics that gives the distribution of a physical variable (e.g. velocity, position) over the particles of a gas in equilibrium at constant temperature. The relation implies as a direct consequence the equipartition of energy, and is the basic equation of the kinetic theory of gases

May (mei), Sir Thomas Erskine, 1st Baron Farnborough (1815–86), British constitutional jurist. His 'Practical Treatise on the Law, Privileges, Proceedings, and Usage of Parliament' (1844) is the standard guide to parliamentary procedure in Britain and many other countries

May n. the fifth month of the year, having 31 days **may** the blossoming branches of the hawthorn ‖ the hawthorn [M.E. mai fr. O.F.]

may infin. and parts. lacking. neg. **may not, mayn't** 3rd pers. sing. **may** past **might** (mait) (or, by suppletion, 'was', were able to') auxiliary v. to be permitted to, you may go now ‖ expressing possibility, you may be right ‖ used in clauses expressing result, purpose, concession or condition, he complains so that he may have sympathy ‖ used to express a wish, hope, prayer, may they both be happy [O.E. mœg, magon, meahte]

Ma·ya (májə) n. a member of an Indian people inhabiting the Yucatán peninsula, S. Mexico, Guatemala and part of Honduras ‖ their language, spoken by about 300,000 **Má·yan** adj. and n. [Span.]
—The origins of the Mayan civilization have been traced back to before 1000 B.C. It flourished (4th–8th cc.), declined (9th c.), and revived (10th c.) under Toltec influence, before being conquered by the Spanish (16th c.). The Mayas left stone temples built on pyramids and adorned with sculpture. They excelled in painting and pottery, developed a system of hieroglyphic writing, and elaborated a mathematical system which enabled them to devise a very accurate calendar. They were organized in city-states (each ruled by a hierarchic aristocracy and priesthood) which at various times formed confederacies. They worshipped a pantheon of deities

ma·ya (májə) n. (Hindu philos.) illusion [Skr. máyā]

Ma·ya·kov·sky (mɑjəkɔ́fski:), Vladimir Vladimirovich (1893–1930), Russian poet and playwright. He glorified the revolution, in verse remarkable for its verbal invention, wordplay etc.

may·ap·ple (méiæp'l) n. Podophyllum peltatum, fam. Berberidaceae, a North American plant with a poisonous rhizome, which yields the drug podophyllin. It sends up yearly two peltate leaves and a single large white flower ‖ its edible eggshaped yellow fruit

may·be (méibi:) adv. perhaps, possibly but not certainly [M.E. for it may be]

May Day the first day of May, celebrated in the U.S.S.R., France and other European countries and the Philippines as an international workers' festival. Spring festival customs of great antiquity survive in some places

May·day (méidei) n. an international distress call in radio telephoning [fr. F. m'aider, help me]

Ma·yenne (mæjen) a department (area 1,986 sq. miles, pop. 261,800) in N.W. France (*MAINE, *ANJOU). Chief town: Laval

May·er (máiər), Julius Robert von (1814–78), German physicist. He calculated the mechanical equivalent of heat (1842)

may·flow·er (méiflaυər) n. any of several plants blooming in May or in early spring, esp. the trailing arbutus, and any of several anemones

May·flow·er the ship in which the Pilgrims sailed (1620)

Mayflower Compact an agreement drawn up (1620) by the passengers aboard the 'Mayflower', designed to unify the colonists by providing a temporary government based on the will of the majority. It was the basis of the original Plymouth government and all succeeding government of the colony

may·fly (méiflai) *pl.* **may·flies** *n.* a lacy-winged, aquatic imago insect of the order *Plectoptera* having a short (1–2 days) adult life and a lengthy (up to 2 years) nymph stage

may·hem (méihem) *n.* (*law*) the malicious, permanent maiming or mutilating of a person, rendering him partly or wholly defenseless [A.F. *mahem, mahaym*]

May·o (méiou) a family of U.S. physicians who founded what became the Mayo Clinic at Rochester, Minn. The chief contributors were William James Mayo (1861–1939), who specialized in stomach surgery, and his brother Charles Horace Mayo (1865–1939), who specialized in goiter surgery and neurosurgery

Mayo, Henry Thomas (1856–1937), U.S. admiral and commander in chief of the U.S. fleet during the 1st world war. Following the Tampico incident (1914), he led the expedition to Veracruz

Mayo a western county (area 2,084 sq. miles, pop. 109,525) of the Irish Republic. County seat: Castlebar (*CONNACHT)

may·on·naise (meiənéiz) *n.* a thick creamy dressing of egg yolks beaten with oil, vinegar and seasoning, usually served as a garnish for cold fish, salads etc. [F., origin unknown]

may·or (méiər, meər) *n.* the head of a municipal corporation of a city, town etc. **máy·or·al** *adj.* [M.E. *mair, mer* fr. F. *maire*]

may·or·al·ty (méiərəlti:, méərəlti:) *pl.* **may·or·al·ties** *n.* the office, or term of office, of a mayor [fr. O.F. *mairalté*]

may·or·ess (méiəris, méəris) *n.* the mayor's wife, or his official hostess ‖ a female mayor

mayor of the palace (*hist.*) the chief minister of the Frankish kings. Under the later Merovingians the mayors of the palace increased their power, until they usurped the throne (751) and founded the Carolingian dynasty

may·pole (méipoul) *n.* a tall pole decorated with flowers, streamers etc. around which people dance on May Day

Maz·a·rin (mǽzərin, mæzærë) Jules (Giulio Mazarini, 1602–61), Italian-born French cardinal and statesman. Sent as papal nuncio to Paris (1634–6), he was made cardinal (1641) on the recommendation of Richelieu and Louis XIII. He became (1642) Richelieu's successor as chief minister, thanks to his influence over Anne of Austria, the regent for her son, the young Louis XIV. He obtained favorable terms at Westphalia (1648), but his fiscal policy provoked the Fronde (1648–53). He acquired land from Spain in the Treaty of the Pyrenees (1659) and arranged the marriage (1660) of Louis XIV and the Infanta. He created a powerful central administration, but he weakened the royal finances

Ma·za·tlán (mɑsɑtlán) Mexico's chief Pacific port (pop. 161,600) and rail center: fishing, tourism

Maz·da·ism (mǽzdəizəm) *n.* Zoroastrianism [fr. Avestan *mazda*, the good principle in Pers. theology]

maze (meiz) *n.* a contrived ornamental, complex layout of paths, often hedged ‖ something intricately complicated or confusing [fr. older *maze* v., to bewilder fr. AMAZE]

Ma·zep·pa (məzépə), Ivan Stepanovich (c. 1644–1709), Cossack hetman in the Ukraine (1687–1709). At first an ally of Peter I of Russia, he made an alliance with Charles XII of Sweden and fled to Turkey after the Russians decisively defeated the Swedes (1709)

ma·zer (méizər) *n.* a large hardwood drinking bowl usually mounted with silver [fr. O.F. *masere*, maplewood fr. Gmc]

ma·zur·ka (məzə́rkə) *n.* a lively Polish dance in triple time ‖ the music for this dance [Polish = a woman of the Polish province of Mazovia]

ma·zy (méizi:) *comp.* **ma·zi·er** *superl.* **ma·zi·est** *adj.* like a maze

Maz·zi·ni (mɑtsíːni:), Giuseppe (1805–72), Italian patriot and revolutionist. He founded (1831) Young Italy, a secret society with the aim of making Italy a united independent republic. From exile, he organized a series of

unsuccessful revolts in Italy, and helped to establish a short-lived republic in Rome (1849). His reliance on secret revolutionary methods proved less effective in uniting Italy than the more practical policies of Cavour

Mba·bane ('mbabán) the capital (pop. 38,636) of Swaziland, on the High Veld

Mban·da·ka ('mbǽndəkə) (formerly Coquilhatville) a port (pop. 52,000) in Zaïre, on the Congo River (Zaïre). It was founded (1883) by Stanley as Equator

mbi·ra (embíərə) *n.* African musical instrument that consists of a gourd, a wooden box, and strips of wood or metal that are plucked with the thumb and/or fingers

MBO (*abbr.*) management by objective, a managerial technique designed for planning, achieving, and evaluating business or project goals

mbo·ra (embórə) *n.* African musical instrument made of hollow wood with lengthwise metal strips that are vibrated with the thumbs

Mc *names beginning thus are listed at 'Mac'*

M.C. *MASTER OF CEREMONIES

MCS (*abbr.*) master of computer science

Md. Maryland

M.D. doctor of medicine

M-day (émdei) *n.* (*mil.*) the day on which mobilization is to begin *Cf* D-DAY, K-DAY.

Me. Maine

me (mi:) *pron., objective case of 'I'*, take me with you, give it to me [O.E. *me, mē*]

me *n.* (*Br., mus.*) mi

mea·con·ing (míːkəniŋ) *n.* (*mil.*) a system of receiving radio-beacon signals and rebroadcasting them on the same frequency in order to confuse navigation and cause inaccurate bearings to be obtained *Cf* BEACON

Mead (mi:d), Margaret (1901–78), U.S. anthropologist, best known for her research into child rearing, personality, and culture in primitive societies, chiefly among the peoples of Oceania

mead (mi:d) *n.* an alcoholic drink of fermented honey, water, malt etc. [O.E. *meodu*]

Meade (mi:d), George Gordon (1815–72), Union general in the Civil War. He won the battle of Gettysburg (1863)

mead·ow (médou) *n.* a piece of grassland, esp. one used for hay ‖ a piece of low-lying grassland along a body of water [M.E. *medwe, medewe* fr. O.E. *mǣdwe*, oblique case of *mǣd*, meadow]

mead·ow·lark (médoulɑrk) *n.* any of several North American brownish members of *Sturnella*, fam. *Icteridae*, a genus of passerine birds with yellow breast and buff and black markings

meadow saffron *COLCHICUM

mead·ow·sweet (médouswiːt) *n.* any of several plants of genus *Filipendula*, fam. *Rosaceae*, esp. F. *ulmaria*, with white, sweet-smelling flowers and pinnate leaves, found in damp meadows ‖ any of several plants of genus *Spiraea*, fam. *Rosaceae*

mea·ger, esp. *Br.* **mea·gre** (míːgər) *adj.* low in quantity or quality, *meager rewards, a meager supper* [M.E. *megre* fr. O.F.]

meal (mi:l) *n.* the edible part of coarsely ground grain ‖ any similarly ground substance [O.E. *melo*]

meal *n.* food eaten alone or in company to satisfy hunger or at a set hour as part of daily routine ‖ the time or occasion of taking this food [O.E. *mǣl*, measure, fixed time, meal]

meal·ie (míːli:) *n.* (*South Africa, esp. pl.*) corn ‖ (*South Africa*) an ear of corn [Afrik. *milje* fr. Port. *milho*, millet, corn]

meal·i·ness (míːlinis) *n.* the state or quality of being mealy

meals on wheels semipublic service that delivers hot meals to the homebound

meal·time (míːltaim) *n.* the routine time at which one takes a meal

meal·worm (míːlwəːrm) *n.* the larva of certain beetles of fam. *Tenebrionidae*. Mealworms live on (and pollute) flour and meal

meal·y (míːli:) *comp.* **meal·i·er** *superl.* **meal·i·est** *adj.* powdery and dry, like meal, *a mealy potato* ‖ of or containing meal ‖ (of complexion) sallow, unhealthy looking ‖ covered with meal or powder ‖ (of an animal) spotted with a second color ‖ mealymouthed

meal·y·mouthed (míːliːmauɖð, míːliːmauθt) *adj.* not frank or forthright in speech, esp. avoiding unpalatable truths or epithets liable to offend

mean (mi:n) **1.** *adj.* midway between two extremes in number, quantity, degree, kind, value etc. ‖ having the value which is most fre-

quent, *mean rainfall, mean temperature* **2.** *n.* something occupying a mean position with regard to number, quantity, degree, kind, value etc. ‖ (*math.* an average ‖ (*math.*) the second or third term of a proposition ‖ the middle term of a syllogism [O.F. *men, meen, moien* etc.]

mean *adj.* stingy ‖ small-minded, petty ‖ unkind or positively spiteful ‖ bad-tempered ‖ of poor quality, esp. shabby or squalid, *a row of mean, dingy houses* **no mean** a very good, *he is no mean trumpeter* [O.E. *gemǣne*, possessed in common]

mean *pres. part.* **mean·ing** *past* and *past part.* **meant** (ment) *v.t.* to intend, *she didn't mean to hurt you, the remark was meant to offend him* ‖ to denote, *what does this word mean?, the accident means more expense* ‖ to intend to signify, *what does he mean by that remark?* ‖ *v.i.* to have a specified degree of importance, *his garden meant a lot to him* **to mean well** to be well intentioned [O.E. *mǣnan*]

mean calorie 1/100 of the quantity of heat required to raise the temperature of 1 gram of water from 0°C. to 100°C. It differs slightly from the calorie because of small temperature variations in the specific heat of water

me·an·der (mi:ǽndər) **1.** *n.* a winding of a stream or river ‖ (often *pl.*) a rambling stroll ‖ an ornamental linear pattern, e.g. in ancient Greek design **2.** *v.i.* (of a stream) to follow a winding course ‖ to wander aimlessly [L. *meander* fr. Gk *Maiandros*, a river in Phrygia]

mean distance the arithmetic mean of the greatest and smallest distances of a planet's orbit from the sun, equal to half the major axis of the orbit

mean·ing (míːniŋ) **1.** *n.* that which is intended or meant **2.** *adj.* expressive, conveying emotion etc., *a meaning look* ‖ (in compounds) having intentions of a specified kind, *well-meaning efforts* **mean·ing·ful, mean·ing·less** *adjs.*

mean·ness (míːnnis) *n.* the state or quality of being mean ‖ a mean act

means (mi:nz) *pl. n.* that which enables some purpose to be fulfilled ‖ the method used to achieve a purpose ‖ material resources (income etc.) **by all means** certainly **by any means** possibly, *could you by any means lend me some money?* **by means of** by making use of **by no means** certainly not, in no way, *he is by no means stupid* **to live beyond (within) one's means** to spend more (less) than one's income [MEAN n.]

mean solar day the period of time between successive returns of the mean sun to the meridian, containing 86,400 mean solar seconds

mean solar hour 3,600 mean solar seconds

mean solar minute 60 mean solar seconds

mean solar second the standard unit of time in the cgs system of units, equal to 1/86,400 of a mean solar day

means test an examination of a person's financial position to determine whether or not to make him a grant from public funds

mean sun a fictitious body which moves along the celestial equator at a constant rate equal to the average rate of the actual sun. It is used to define the mean solar day

meant *past* and *past part.* of MEAN

mean·time (míːntaim) **1.** *adv.* during the intervening time ‖ during the same time as something else is or was going on **2.** *n.* (only in) the **meantime** the intervening time ‖ the same time as something else is or was going on

mean·tone temperament (míːntoun) (*mus., hist.*) a system of tuning in which the intervals between semitones of a fixed-pitch instrument are adjusted to give as nearly natural tuning as possible for the key of C major (cf. EQUAL TEMPERAMENT)

mean·while (míːnhwail, míːnwail) **1.** *adv.* meantime **2.** *n.* (only in) **the meanwhile** the meantime

Mea·ny (míːni:), George (1894–1980), U.S. labor leader, president (1955–79) of the AFL-CIO. He attempted to rid the organization of its corrupt and racket-infested affiliates

mea·sles (míːz'lz) *n.* a contagious disease caused by a virus and common in children. It is characterized by catarrh, fever and skin eruption ‖ German measles ‖ a disease of cattle and swine caused by the larvae of certain tapeworms [M.E. *maseles* pl. fr. Gmc]

mea·sly (míːzli:) *comp.* **mea·sli·er** *superl.* **mea·sli·est** *adj.* (*pop.*) of very little value, size etc., *a measly gift* ‖ infected with measles [MEASLES]

meas·ur·a·bil·i·ty (meʒərəbíliti:) *n.* the state or quality of being measurable

meas·ur·a·ble (méʒərəb'l) adj. that can be measured **méas·ur·a·bly** adv. [M.E. fr. F. mesurable]

meas·ure (méʒər) n. the magnitude of something as determined by measuring ‖ an instrument used to determine magnitude ‖ a unit of length, volume etc. as a standard for measuring ‖ a system of units used in measuring, metric measure ‖ amount, extent or degree, to achieve a measure of success ‖ a criterion for determining quality, degree etc., a test providing a measure of ability ‖ an appropriate amount or portion, give him his measure of praise ‖ a limit, joy without measure ‖ an act designed to achieve a purpose, measures to ensure victory ‖ a legislation bill or statute ‖ (printing) the width of a page or column of type ‖ (mus.) a bar ‖ rhythm in verse or music ‖ (pl., geol.) stratified minerals, coal measures **for good measure** as an addition, he threw in a bunch of parsley for good measure **in a measure** to some extent **made to measure** (of clothes) made according to the measurements of the individual **to take measures** to do things (so as to achieve some purpose) **to take the measure of** to judge the nature of (a person, situation etc.) [F. mesure]

measure pres. part. **meas·ur·ing** past and past part. **meas·ured** v.t. to determine the magnitude, extent, degree etc. of in terms of some standard ‖ to judge the quality or nature of in terms of some standard ‖ (with 'against') to bring into comparison (with) ‖ to serve to determine the magnitude, extent, degree etc. of, a thermometer measures temperature ‖ v.i. to have a specified magnitude, extent, quantity etc., the property measured 30 acres ‖ to be able to be measured **to measure off** to mark the end of (a measured length) **to measure one's length** (pop.) to fall flat on the ground involuntarily **to measure out** to measure (a specified length) ‖ to give, distribute or allot by measuring **to measure up to** to reach the standard of, to measure up to expectations **méas·ured** adj. accurately determined and serving as a standard, a measured mile ‖ steady and deliberate, a measured tread ‖ (of speech etc.) carefully thought out, calculated **méas·ure·less** adj. of boundless size or extent ‖ vast **méas·ure·ment** n. a measuring or being measured ‖ the magnitude, length, degree etc. of something in terms of a selected unit [F. mesurer]

measuring worm a looper

meat (mi:t) n. the flesh of animals (usually excepting fish and poultry) used for food ‖ the edible part of an animal, the meat of a lobster ‖ (fig.) the substance or essence of something, the meat of the essay is in the last two sections [O.E. mete]

meat-and-po·ta·toes (mí:tənpətéitouz) n. basic food, by extension, basics

meat fly any of several flies, e.g. the bluebottle, whose maggots feed on flesh

Meath (mi:ð) an eastern county (area 903 sq. miles, pop. 71,729) of Leinster, Irish Republic. County seat: Trim ‖ (hist.) an ancient kingdom of E. Ireland

meat·i·ness (mí:ti:nis) n. the quality of being meaty

meat-pack·ing (mí:tpækiŋ) n. the wholesale meat trade, including slaughtering, processing and distribution

meat safe (Br.) a safe (provisions closet)

me·a·tus (mi:éitəs) pl. **me·a·tus·es, me·a·tus** (anat.) a passage or channel in the body, esp. the opening of the nose, ear etc. [L.=a passage]

meat·y (mí:ti) comp. **meat·i·er** superl. **meat·i·est** adj. of, like or consisting of meat ‖ (fig.) full of substance, stimulating thought, a meaty book

mec·a·myl·a·mine [$C_{11}H_{21}NH$] (mèkəmíləmi:n) n. (pharm.) a drug used to blockade ganglions and reduce high blood pressure; marketed as Inversine

Mec·ca (mékə) (Arab. Makkah) the chief holy city (pop. 367,000) of Islam, capital of the Hejaz, Saudi Arabia, in a valley surrounded by hills, 50 miles from the Red Sea (Jedda). Its economy depends upon pilgrims. The birthplace of Mohammed, it was always part of the Arab Moslem empires until its capture by the Ottoman Turks (1517). It was the center of the independent Hejaz (1916–24), until captured by ibn Saud. University

mecca n. any place regarded by a group of people as a center of attraction or a goal, a mecca for tourists [after MECCA]

Mec·can·o (məkǽnou, məkánou) n. a construction toy consisting of many metal components from which engineering models can be built [trademark]

me·chan·ic (məkǽnik) n. a workman skilled in making, using or repairing machinery [fr. L. mechanicus adj., pertaining to machines, fr. Gk]

me·chan·i·cal (məkǽnik'l) adj. pertaining to or involving machines ‖ operated or produced by a machine ‖ made or done as if by machinery and therefore lacking spontaneity or interest ‖ of or pertaining to the subject matter of mechanics [fr. L.L. mechanicus fr. Gk]

mechanical advantage the ratio of the working force derived from a simple machine to the force applied to the machine, giving a measure of the aid offered by the use of a machine in transmitting force

mechanical bank a toy bank usually in the form of an animal or comic figure, in which a coin placed in position is automatically deposited by a lever, e.g., a hunter shoots a penny into a bear's mouth. It was popular in the 19th century

mechanical drawing drawing done with instruments, e.g. to prepare a blueprint

mechanical equivalent of heat the value of a unit of mechanical work in terms of the heat that it generates, being 4.185 joules-calorie

me·chan·i·cal·ly (məkǽnikli:) adv. in a mechanical way

mechanical translation (computer) automatic computer translation of text from one language to another

me·chan·ics (məkǽniks) n. a branch of physics (*KINEMATICS) that deals with energy and force in their relation to material bodies (*QUANTUM MECHANICS, *DYNAMICS, *STATICS, *STATISTICAL MECHANICS) ‖ the application of mechanics to the operation and design of machines ‖ the mechanism or way of operating of a machine or process, the mechanics of advertising [MECHANIC]

mech·a·nism (mékənizəm) n. a structure of interacting parts working mechanically ‖ any system, process etc. composed of parts which, working together, resemble the workings of a machine ‖ a machine-like device, system, process etc. by means of which some result is achieved, a defense mechanism ‖ (philos.) the theory that the workings of the universe can be explained by physics and chemistry (cf. VITALISM) **méch·a·nist** n. someone who believes in the mechanistic theory of the universe **mech·a·nís·tic** adj. [fr. Mod. L. mechanismus fr. Gk mēchanē, machine]

mech·a·ni·za·tion (mèkənizéiʃən) n. a mechanizing or being mechanized

mech·a·nize (mékənaiz) pres. part. **mech·a·niz·ing** past and past part. **mech·a·nized** v.t. to make mechanical ‖ to operate by machinery ‖ to introduce the use of machines in (an industry etc.) ‖ to equip (an army etc.) with tanks, armored motor vehicles etc.

me·chan·o·re·cep·tor (mèkənouriséptər) n. a body organ sensitive to mechanical stimuli, e.g., intestines **—mechanoreception** n. **—mechanoreceptive** adj.

Me·che·len (méxələn) *MALINES

Mechitarist *MEKHITARIST

Mech·lin lace (méklin) a fine bobbin lace with floral motifs, originally made in Malines, Belgium [fr. Mechlin, Eng. name for Malines]

Meck·len·burg (méklənbə:rg) a former state of East Germany on the northern plain, an irregular wooded plateau, dotted with hundreds of lakes, between the lower Elbe and Oder, divided since 1952 into Rostock, Schwerin and Neubrandenburg districts. Crops: rye, oats, potatoes, sugar beet. Industries: mechanical engineering, fishing (in the Baltic). Main towns: Rostock, Stralsund (ports), Schwerin. The region was colonized by Germans (12th c.) and the native (Wend) princes were made dukes of the Holy Roman Empire (1348). It was divided after the Thirty Years' War into two duchies which supported Prussia against Austria, but joined the German Empire (1871). They were recombined in 1934

Mecklenburg Declaration of Independence a controversial declaration supposedly proclaimed by the citizens of Mecklenburg Co. at Charlotte, N.C., on May 20, 1775. It is known, at least, that these citizens adopted (May 31, 1775) strong anti-British resolutions which declared all Crown officials, civil and military,

suspended from their offices, thus implying independence without actually declaring it

mec·lo·fen·an·ate (mekloufénəneit) n. nonsteroidal, anti-inflammatory analgesic, marketed as Meclomen

med·al (méd'l) n. a small, flat piece of metal, cast with an inscription or design, that commemorates an event or is awarded in recognition for distinguished service, for an achievement etc. ‖ such a piece of metal bearing a religious image [F. médaille fr. Ital.]

med·al·ist, med·al·list (méd'list) n. someone who has won a medal ‖ an engraver of medals

me·dal·lic (mədǽlik) adj. relating to or depicted on a medal

me·dal·lion (mədǽljən) n. a large medal ‖ something shaped like this, e.g. a decorative tablet, panel or carpet design ‖ a license to operate a taxicab [F. médaillon fr. Ital.]

medallist *MEDALIST

medal play (golf) a form of the game in which the scoring is by number of strokes, not number of holes (cf. MATCH PLAY)

Me·dan (medán) the chief town (pop. 635,562) of N. Sumatra, Indonesia, center of a rubber and tobacco-growing region

med·dle (méd'l) pres. part. **med·dling** past and past part. **med·dled** v.i. (with 'in' or 'with') to concern or busy oneself impudently or interferingly, don't meddle in my affairs **méd·dle·some** adj. given to meddling [O.F. medler, mesdler]

Mede (mi:d) n. an inhabitant of ancient Media [fr. L. Medus fr. Gk]

Me·de·a (mídí:ə) (Gk mythol.) a famous sorceress, daughter of Aeetes, king of Colchis. She accompanied Jason, helping him with magic arts to win the Golden Fleece. When Jason deserted her she killed the children she had borne him

Me·del·lín (medejí:n) the chief industrial center (pop. 1,506,661) of Colombia, 150 miles northwest of Bogotá, in a coffee-growing region. Industries: textiles, engineering, metallurgy, chemicals. There are two universities

med·e·vac (médəvæk) n. (mil.) military medical helicopter, esp. for evacuating wounded from the battlefield

Med·ex (médeks) n. program to develop physicians' assistants, designed for former military medical corpsmen with independent duty experience

med·fly (médflai) n. short form for Mediterranean fruit fly

Me·di·a (mí:di:ə) an ancient country in N.W. Iran, which flourished mid-7th c. –6th c. B.C., conquered Assyria and destroyed Nineveh (612 B.C.) and was defeated (mid-6th c. B.C.) by the Persians under Cyrus II

me·di·a (mí:di:ə) pl. **me·di·ae** (mí:di:i:) n. (anat.) the middle membrane of a blood or lymph vessel [L. fem. of medius, middle]

media alt. pl. of MEDIUM

mediaeval *MEDIEVAL

me·di·al (mí:di:əl) 1. adj. situated in the middle ‖ of or being an average or mean ‖ (phon., of a sound or letter) situated within a word 2. n. a medial letter [fr. L.L. medialis]

me·di·an (mí:di:ən) 1. adj. designating a plane dividing a body or part into symmetrical halves ‖ situated in this plane ‖ of or pertaining to a median 2. n. something situated in the middle ‖ (geom.) a line joining a vertex of a triangle to the middle of the opposite side ‖ (math.) a quantity situated in a series so as to have as many quantities below it as above, the median of 3, 6, 8, 14 and 15 is 8 ‖ a median artery, vein, nerve etc. [fr. L. medianus]

me·di·ant (mí:di:ənt) n. (mus.) the third degree of a scale, midway between tonic and dominant [fr. Ital. mediante]

me·di·as·ti·num (mi:di:əstáinəm) pl. **me·di·as·ti·na** (mi:di:əstáinə) n. a membranous middle septum, esp. between the lungs ‖ the space between the pleural sacs, containing the heart and other chest viscera except the lungs [Mod. L. fr. M.L. mediastinus, in the middle]

me·di·ate 1. (mí:di:eit) v. pres. part. **me·di·at·ing** past and past part. **me·di·ated** v.t. to bring about (a settlement) by reconciling conflicting parties ‖ to settle (a dispute etc.) by reconciling conflicting parties ‖ to act as agent in conveying, communicating etc. ‖ v.i. to intervene in order to bring about a reconciliation 2. (mí:di:it) adj. acting indirectly, through some agency [fr. L.L. mediare (mediatus), to halve, to be in the middle]

me·di·a·tion (mi:di:éiʃən) n. a mediating or being mediated [O.F. mediacion]

me·di·a·tor (mí:di:eitər) *n.* someone who mediates **me·di·a·to·ri·al** (mi:di:ətóri:əl, mi:di:ətóuri:əl), **mé·di·a·to·ry** *adjs* [F. *médiateur*]

med·ic (médik) *n.* (*pop.*) a physician or surgeon, or a student or military corpsman doing medical work

med·ic, med·ick (médik) *n.* a member of *Medicago*, fam. *Papilionaceae*, a genus of Old World plants with cloverlike flowers, used as forage, including alfalfa [fr. L. *medica* fr. Gk *Mēdikē* (*poa*), (grass) of Media]

med·i·ca·ble (médikəb'i) *adj.* able to be effectively treated by medicine [fr. L. *medicabilis*]

Med·i·caid (médikeid) *n.* government-administered program in U.S. to provide medical services to the poor; financed jointly by federal and state governments *Cf* MEDI-CAL, MEDICARE

Medicaid mill a medical clinic depending substantially on low-income and poor patients whose bills are paid by Medicaid funds

med·i·cal (médik'l) 1. *adj.* of, concerned with or relating to the practice of medicine (often as contrasted with surgery etc.) 2. *n.* (*pop.*) a medical examination required by authority [F. *médical*]

Med·i·Cal (médikæl) *n.* California's Medicaid program

medical audit a detailed evaluation of selected medical records by qualified professional staff. Medical audits are used in some hospitals, group practices, and private practices for evaluating professional performance by comparing it with accepted criteria and current professional judgment

Medical College Admissions Test a nationally standardized test generally required or strongly recommended by most medical schools in the U.S. as part of their admission process *abbr.* **MCAT**

medical indigency (*social service*) the condition of having insufficient income to pay for adequate medical care without depriving oneself or dependents of essentials of living — **medical indigent** *n.*

medical jurisprudence the science that deals with the application of medical knowledge to legal problems

medically needy (*social service*) in the Medicaid program, persons with sufficient income and resources to pay for basic living expenses (i.e., those not on welfare; the so-called working poor) but not sufficient to pay for their medical care

medically underserved area (*social service*) a geographic location, i.e., an urban or rural area, with insufficient health resources to meet the medical needs of the population

med·ic·a·ment (mədikəmənt, médikəmənt) *n.* a medicine [F. *médicament*]

Med·i·care, med·i·care (médikeər) *n.* a U.S. government insurance program that provides medical care for old people [MEDICAL CARE]

med·i·cate (médikeit) *pres. part.* **med·i·cat·ing** *past* and *past part.* **med·i·cat·ed** *v.t.* to saturate with a medical preparation, *a medicated skin cream* **med·i·ca·tion** *n.* the act of medicating ‖ a substance used in medicating **med·i·ca·tive** (médikeitiv, médikətiv) *adj.* [fr. L. *medicare* (*medicatus*)]

med·i·chair (méditʃeər) *n.* (*med.*) an electrode-equipped chair used to monitor physiological activity of a patient

Med·i·ci (méditʃi:) a family which played an illustrious part (14th–17th cc.) in the political and cultural history of Florence and Tuscany, first as wool merchants and bankers, later as dukes or princes (1434–1737)

Medici, Catherine de' *CATHERINE DE'MEDICI

Medici, Cosimo de' (1389–1464), Italian banker and prince. A great patron of the arts, he made Florence a center of the Renaissance

Mé·di·ci (médi:si:), Emílio Garrastazú (1907–), Brazilian general and president (1969–74) of the military junta which took power in 1964. He introduced (1970) a 'revolutionary state', a constitutional order that preserves the appearance of an elected congress but reserves practically unlimited powers for the president to use at his discretion

Medici, Giovanni de *LEO X

Medici, Giulio de' *CLEMENT VII

Medici, Lorenzo de', 'the Magnificent' (1449–92), ruler of Florence (1469–92). An astute politician, a poet and scholar, and a patron of the arts and of learning, he was one of the leading figures of the Italian Renaissance, and made

Florence one of the richest and most powerful city–states in Europe

Medici, Marie de' *MARIE DE'MEDICI

me·di·ci·nal (medísin'l) *adj.* relating to medicine, esp. having healing properties **me·dic·i·nal·ly** *adv.* [fr. L. *medicinalis*]

med·i·cine (médisin, *Br.* esp. médsin) *n.* any preparation or substance used in the treatment of disease ‖ the science of the prevention and cure of disease and of health preservation ‖ the branch of this science dealing with curative substances rather than with surgery, obstetrics etc. ‖ the medical profession **to take one's medicine** to submit stoically to punishment etc. that one deserves [fr. O.F. *medecine*]

medicine ball a heavy stuffed leather ball thrown and caught for exercise

medicine man a doctor-magician of undeveloped societies, esp. among North American Indians

medick *MEDIC

Med·i·cred·it (médikredət) *n.* one of several proposed national health insurance plans designed to encourage the voluntary purchase of qualified private health insurance policies by granting tax credits against personal income taxes in order to finance, in part or in whole, the premium cost of such plans

med·i·e·val, med·i·ae·val (medi:í:vəl, mi:di:í:vəl) *adj.* of, relating to or characteristic of the Middle Ages **med·i·é·val·ism, med·i·áe·val·ism** *n.* the characteristic spirit, institutions, arts etc. of the Middle Ages ‖ the conscious imitation or adoption of these ‖ a custom etc. surviving from or suggestive of the Middle Ages **med·i·é·val·ist, med·i·áe·val·ist** *n.* [fr. Mod. L. *medium aevum*, middle age]

Medieval Latin the literary and liturgical Latin used throughout medieval Europe (7th–15th cc.)

Med·i·gap policy (médigæp) (*insurance*) a health insurance policy designed to supplement Medicare

Me·dill (mədíl), Joseph (1823–99), U.S. journalist, chief editor (from 1874) of the 'Chicago Tribune'. He greatly influenced the formation of the Republican party and advocated the emancipation and arming of slaves

Me·di·na (medí:na), José Toribio (1852–1930), Chilean author and Hispanic-American bibliographer. His many works include 'Historiadores de Chile' (33 vols, 1888–1902), the 'Biblioteca hispano-americana' (7 vols, 1897–1907), and 'La Araucana' (5 folio vols, 1910–18)

Me·di·na (medí:na) (*Arab.* Al-Madina) the second holy city (pop. 198,000) of Islam, in a date-growing oasis 210 miles north of Mecca. It was Mohammed's capital after his flight from Mecca (622). The mosque (15th c.) contains the tombs of Mohammed, Fatima and the first two caliphs. University

Me·di·na An·ga·ri·ta (medi:nɑɑngari:ta), Isaías (1897–1953), Venezuelan general and president (1941–5). He enacted Venezuela's first democratic reforms, with the first petroleum laws, but was overthrown by a coalition of leftist Rómulo Betancourt and rightist military elements

me·di·o·cre (mi:di:óukər) *adj.* neither good nor bad, without distinction ‖ of distinctly poor quality [F. *médiocre*]

me·di·oc·ri·ty (mi:di:ɔkriti:) *pl.* **me·di·oc·ri·ties** *n.* the state or quality of being mediocre ‖ a mediocre person [F. *médiocrité*]

me·di·og·ra·phy (mi:di:ógrəfi:) *n.* a compilation of materials in all media on a subject, e.g., films, posters, books, etc.

med·i·tate (méditeit) *pres. part.* **med·i·tat·ing** *past* and *past part.* **med·i·tat·ed** *v.i.* (with 'on' or 'upon') to reflect deeply ‖ to spend time in the spiritual exercise of thinking about some religious theme ‖ *v.t.* to contemplate, esp. as a plan, *to meditate revenge* [fr. L. *meditari* (*meditatus*)]

med·i·ta·tion (méditéiʃən) *n.* deep, serious thought ‖ reflection on a religious subject as a spiritual exercise [F. *méditation* or fr. L. *meditatio* (*meditationis*)]

med·i·ta·tive (méditeitiv) *adj.* of, pertaining to or given to meditation

med·i·ter·ra·ne·an (méditəréini:ən) *adj.* surrounded by land **Med·i·ter·ra·ne·an** 1. *adj.* pertaining to the Mediterranean Sea, the region around it, or to the inhabitants of this region 2. *n.* the Mediterranean Sea [fr. L. *mediterraneus* fr. *medius*, middle+*terra*, land]

Mediterranean climate *SUBTROPICAL CLIMATE

Mediterranean fever undulant fever

Mediterranean Sea a large sea (area 1,145,000 sq. miles) enclosed by Europe, Asia Minor, Lebanon, Syria, Israel and Africa, connected to the Atlantic by the Strait of Gibraltar and to the Black Sea by the Bosporus and the Dardanelles. It includes the Tyrrhenian, Adriatic, Ionian and Aegean Seas. An important trading area since ancient times, it was a valuable trade route to the East until the discovery (1498) of a route around the Cape of Good Hope. Its importance revived with the opening (1869) of the Suez Canal

me·di·um (mí:di:əm) 1. *pl.* **me·di·ums, me·di·a** *n.* a means, *money is a medium of exchange* ‖ a middle quality or degree ‖ something through which a force is transmitted, *ether is the hypothetical medium for light waves* ‖ the material that an artist works with, *watercolor is his medium* ‖ a liquid in which a dry pigment can be suspended ‖ the substance making up the natural habitat of an organism ‖ (pl., **media**) *MASS MEDIA ‖ environment ‖ (*biol., pl.* **me·di·a**) the substance in which displayed or preserved specimens are put ‖ (*biol., pl.* **me·di·a**) a substance in which a culture can be grown ‖ (*spiritualism, pl.* **me·di·ums**) a person credited with special powers for communicating between the living and the dead ‖ a size of paper between demy and royal, commonly 23 x 18 ins ‖ *MASS MEDIA 2. *adj.* of that which is a mean with regard to quality, degree, size, distance etc. ‖ average, *medium height* [L., neut. of *medius*, middle]

med·lar (médlər) *n. Mespilus germanica*, fam. *Rosaceae*, a small tree native to S. Europe and S.W. Asia, cultivated for its brownish fruit, which is made into preserves or eaten when partly decayed ‖ a fruit of this tree [O.F. *medler*]

med·ley (médli:) *pl.* **med·leys** *n.* a confused mixture, *a medley of voices* ‖ a miscellaneous musical or literary collection [O.F. *medlee*]

medley race a swimming race in which a different type of stroke must be used for each length of the pool ‖ a relay race in which each contestant runs a different distance

Mé·doc (meidɔk) *n.* a wine from the region of Médoc, near Bordeaux, France

me·dul·la (mədΛlə) *pl.* **me·dul·las, me·dul·lae** (mədΛli:) *n.* (*anat.*) the central part of an organ, e.g. the kidney ‖ the marrow of bone ‖ the medulla oblongata ‖ the sheath of some nerve fibers [L.=marrow]

me·dul·la ob·lon·ga·ta (mədΛləpblɔngátə, mə-dΛləpblɔngátə) *pl.* **me·dul·la ob·lon·ga·tas, me·dul·lae ob·lon·ga·tae** (mədΛli:pblɔngáti:, mədΛli:pblɔngáti:) *n.* that part of the brainstem (*BRAIN) continuous posteriorly with the spinal cord. It contains centers controlling many involuntary vital functions, e.g. cardiovascular activities and respiration [L.=oblong medulla]

med·ul·lar·y (méd'ļeri:, médзəļeri:, mədΛləri:) *adj.* of or relating to the medulla oblongata or a medulla of any organ or tissue of the body ‖ of or relating to the pith of a plant [fr. L.L. *medularis*]

medullary ray (*bot.*) a vascular ray

Me·du·sa (mədú:sə, mədjú:sə) (*Gk mythol.*) one of the three Gorgons. She was killed by Perseus, who looked at her reflection, not directly at her

me·du·sa (mədú:sə, mədjú:sə) *pl.* **me·du·sae** (mədú:si:, mədjú:si:) *n.* a jellyfish [L. fr. Gk *medousa*, guardian]

Medusa (*med.*) a form of white eosinophil blood cell with many tentacles; discovered by Dr. Jacob S. Hanker in 1980

Med·way (médwei) a river flowing 70 miles through Sussex and Kent, England, to the Thames estuary

meed (mi:d) *n.* (*rhet.*) recompense [O.E. *mēd*]

meek (mi:k) *adj.* humbly submissive ‖ too mild, lacking spirit [M.E. *meoc* fr. O.N. *miukr*]

meer·kat (míərkæt) *n.* any of several mammals related to the mongoose, esp. *Cynictis penicillata* of S. Africa ‖ the suricate [Du.=a kind of monkey]

meer·schaum (míərʃəm, míərʃɔm) *n.* hydrated magnesium silicate, a soft white claylike mineral found mostly in Asia Minor ‖ a tobacco pipe with a bowl made of this [G.=sea foam]

Mee·rut (míərət) a communications center (pop. 270,993) of N.W. Uttar Pradesh, India: food processing, steel

meet (mi:t) **1.** v. *pres. part.* **meet·ing** *past* and *past part.* **met** (met) *v.t.* to come face-to-face with, *to meet someone in the street* ‖ to be present at the arrival of, *to meet a plane* ‖ to make the acquaintance of, be introduced to ‖ to keep an appointment with ‖ to satisfy (a demand, need etc.) ‖ to fight with, play against, *he will meet him in the semifinals* ‖ to face up to (criticism, trouble etc.) ‖ to pay, *the committee met all his expenses* ‖ to come into the company of ‖ to come into contact with, *this lane meets the main road a mile from here* ‖ to deal with, *to meet a problem* ‖ *v.i.* to come face-to-face or into one another's company ‖ to be united, *the rivers meet below the city* ‖ to become acquainted, *we met yesterday* ‖ to come together to contend, *the finalists meet tomorrow* ‖ to assemble, *the group met in the lobby* ‖ (with 'with') to encounter, *his book met with success* ‖ (with 'with') to confer **to meet (someone) halfway** to offer (someone) a generous compromise **to meet up with** to meet unexpectedly **2.** *n.* a gathering of hounds and huntsmen for a hunt ‖ (*Am.=Br.* meeting) a gathering for a sporting event **méet·ing** *n.* a coming together of people or things ‖ a gathering of people, esp. for business purposes, *a committee meeting* ‖ the people so assembled ‖ a Nonconformist assembly for worship ‖ (*Br.*) a meet (sporting event) [O.E. *metan*]
meet *adj.* (*rhet.*) proper, right, fitting [M.E. *mēte* prob. fr. O.E. *gemēte*, fitting]
meet·ing·house (mí:tiŋhaus) *pl.* **meet·ing·hous·es** (mí:tiŋhauziz) *n.* a building for worship by Friends
me·fen·a·mic acid [C₁₅H₁₅NO₂] (mefenámik) (*pharm.*) a fever-reducing, pain-relieving, anti-inflammatory drug; marketed as Ponstel
mega- (mégə) *prefix* great ‖ (with units of measurement etc.) multiplied by a million [Gk *mega-* fr. *megas,* great]
meg·a·bit (mégəbit) *n.* (*computer*) one million bits (of information)
meg·a·bucks (mégəbʌks) *n.* (*slang*) a huge sum of money
meg·a·ce·phal·ic (megəsəfælik) *adj.* having a head of larger than average size (cf. MACROCEPHALIC) **meg·a·ceph·a·lous** (megəséfələs) *adj.* **meg·a·céph·a·ly** *n.*
meg·a·cy·cle (mégəsaik'l) *n.* a unit of frequency equal to 1 million cycles per second
meg·a·death (mégədeθ) *n.* (*mil.*) one million deaths—used in relation to nuclear warfare
meg·a·gam·ete (megəgæmi:t, megəgəmi:t) *n.* a macrogamete
meg·a·hertz (mégəheərts) *n.* (*abbr.* MHz, *phys.*) a radio-frequency unit equal to one million cycles per second
meg·a·jet (mégədʒet) *n.* a larger and faster jet aircraft than now available
meg·a·lith (mégəliθ) *n.* a huge stone, usually unhewn, used in prehistoric monuments and construction [MEGALITHIC]
meg·a·lith·ic (megəlí[o]ik) *adj.* built with megaliths ‖ of or designating a people building with megaliths, or their culture [fr. MEGA-+Gk *lithos,* stone]
meg·a·lo·blast (mégəloublæst) *n.* an erythroblast ‖ a large, nucleated red blood cell occurring in pernicious anemia [fr. Gk *megalo,* great+*-blast,* germ]
meg·a·lo·ce·phal·ic (megəlousəfælik) *adj.* megacephalic **meg·a·lo·ceph·a·lous** (megəlouséfələs) *adj.* **meg·a·lo·céph·a·ly** *n.* [fr. Gk *megas,* large+CEPHALIC]
meg·a·lo·ma·ni·a (megəloumáini:ə) *n.* delusions of grandeur as a form of insanity ‖ a passion for doing things on a very large scale **meg·a·lo·má·ni·ac** *n.* and *adj.* [Mod. L. fr. Gk *megalo,* great+MANIA]
meg·a·lo·saur (mégələsɔr) *n.* a member of *Megalosaurus,* fam. *Megalosauridae,* a genus of huge carnivorous dinosaurs of the Mesozoic [fr. Gk *megalo-,* great+*sauros,* lizard]
meg·a·ma·chine (megəməʃi:n) *n.* a government system that acts in terms of the multitude rather than in consideration of individuals, coined by Lewis Mumford
meg·a·phone (mégəfoun) *n.* a trumpet-shaped instrument used to magnify or direct the voice [fr. MEGA-+Gk *phone,* voice]
meg·a·pod (mégəpɒd) *n.* a megapode
meg·a·pode (mégəpoud) *n.* a member of *Megapodiidae,* a family of large-footed gallinaceous birds found mainly in Australia and islands nearby. Their eggs are hatched in decomposing organic debris [fr. Mod. L. *Megapodius* fr. Gk *megas,* large+*pous* (*podos*), foot]

Meg·a·ra (mégərə) a town (pop. 17,260) in Greece, on the Isthmus of Corinth: wine, flour, bauxite. It was an important city-state from the 8th c. B.C., with Sicilian and Black Sea colonies
meg·a·rad (mégəræd) *n.* one million rads of absorbed radiation
Me·gar·i·an (məgéəri:ən) **1.** *adj.* of or relating to Megara **2.** *n.* a native or inhabitant of Megara ‖ a philosopher of the Megarian school
Megarian school an ancient Greek (4th c. B.C.) group of philosophers in Megara, chiefly known for their sophistic quibbling
meg·a·spore (mégəspɔr, mégəspour) *n.* the larger type of spore produced by heterosporous plants, giving rise to the female gametophyte (cf. MICROSPORE) **meg·a·spór·ic** *adj*
me·gass, me·gasse (məgǽs) *n.* bagasse [origin unknown]
meg·a·struc·ture (mégəstrʌktʃər) *n.* a huge building
meg·a·there (mégəθər) *n.* a member of *Megatherium,* fam. *Megatheriidae,* an extinct genus of huge, herbivorous, sloth-like animals of the American Pliocene and Pleistocene [Mod. L. *Megatherium* after Gk *mega thērion,* great beast]
meg·a·ton (mégətʌn) *n.* an explosive power equal to that of a million tons of TNT
meg·a·unit (mégəju:nət) *n.* one million units
meg·a·vi·ta·min (megəváitəmən) *n.* (*med.*) huge amounts or doses of vitamins, sometimes used to treat mental or emotional illness. The term was coined by Dr. Abraham Hoffer and Humphrey Osmond
meg·a·watt (mégəwɒt) *n.* a unit of power equal to one million watts
Me·gid·do (məgídou) an ancient fortified town (now ruins) in N. Israel. It occupied a key strategic position between Egypt and Mesopotamia
me·gil·läh (məgílə) *n.* (*Hebrew*) a scroll relating the story of Esther and Haman, read aloud at the celebration of Purim
megillah *n.* (*slang*) (Yiddish, from the Hebrew *megillāh*) a long, detailed story; the complete story or details
me·gilp, ma·gilp (məgílp) *n.* a vehicle for oil colors, usually made of linseed oil and mastic varnish [origin unknown]
meg·ohm (mégoum) *n.* a unit of resistance equal to one million ohms [MEGA- OHM]
me·grim (mí:grim) *n.* (*old-fash.*) migraine ‖ (esp. *pl.,* in horses, cattle etc.) staggers **the megrims** (*pop., old-fash.*) low spirits [F. *migraine*]
Me·he·met A·li (mihémitalí:), Mohammed Ali
Mehta (meíta), Zubin (1936–), Indian symphony conductor. After studying in Vienna, he began directing the Montreal Symphony in 1960 and the Los Angeles Philharmonic in 1962. He debuted at the Metropolitan Opera in 1965, directed the Israel Philharmonic in 1969 and became director of the New York Philharmonic in 1978
Meigh·en (mí:ən), Arthur (1874–1960), Canadian statesman, Conservative leader, and prime minister (1921–2, 1926). He framed the closure rule, which permitted for the first time the limiting of debate in the House of Commons. He largely influenced the statute (1917) introducing conscription and altering the franchise. He drafted enactments nationalizing all major Canadian railroads except the Canadian Pacific
M-80s (eméiti:z) *n.* (*mil.*) powerful, dangerous detonating fireworks introduced in 1979
Mei·ji (meidʒi:) the name ('enlightened peace') by which the Emperor Mutsuhito of Japan was known during his reign
Meil·hac (meijæk), Henri (1831–97), French playwright. Alone or in collaboration with Halévy, he wrote the librettos for several Offenbach operettas
mei·o·sis (maióusis) *n.* rhetorical understatement in order to give emphasis (cf. LITOTES, cf. HYPERBOLE) ‖ (*biol.*) the process of nuclear division leading to the production of haploid cells (e.g. gametes) containing only one of the pair of homologous chromosomes derived from the parents. It is usually accomplished in two stages: the first includes synapsis and subsequent replication of the doubled chromosomes, giving daughter cells with a haploid number of doubled chromosomes, and the second involves the splitting without prior replication of the doubled chromosomes (*PROPHASE, *METAPHASE, *ANAPHASE, *TELOPHASE, cf. MITOSIS) **mei·ot·ic**

(maiótik) *adj.* pertaining to meiosis [Gk fr. *meioun,* to lessen]
Meir (máiər, méii:r), Golda (1908–78), Israeli stateswoman, prime minister (1969–74)
Meis·sen (máis'n) a town (pop. 43,920) on the Elbe in former Saxony, E. Germany, renowned since 1710 for its porcelain. Castle (15th c.), Gothic cathedral (13th–15th cc.)
meis·ter·sing·er (máistərsiŋər) *n.* a member of any of several German guilds of the 14th–16th cc. (formed esp. of artisans) devoted to poetry and music [G.=master singer]
Meit·ner (máitnər), Lise (1878–1968), Austrian physicist, who discovered protoactinium (with Hahn) and studied the fission of uranium
Mekh·i·tar·ist, Mech·i·tar·ist (mekitúrist) *n.* a member of an order of Benedictine monks of the Armenian rite, settled principally at Venice since 1717 [after Peter *Mekhitar* (1670–1749), Armenian religious reformer]
Mek·nès (meknés) an agricultural center (pop. 248,000) of N.W. Morocco. Industries: woolen textiles, carpet weaving, food processing. Gates (17th–18th cc.). Meknès was the capital of a sultanate (late 17th–early 18th cc.)
Me·kong (mí:kɒŋ) a river (2,600 miles long, navigable for 340) rising in Tibet. It flows through Yunnan, China, and separates Burma from Laos and then Thailand from Laos. It crosses the Cambodian plain, and divides to form a delta in Vietnam. The delta is a great rice-growing area
mel·an·cho·li·a (melənkóuli:ə) *n.* a form of mental disorder characterized by extreme dejection [L.L.=melancholy]
mel·an·chol·ic (melənkɒlik) *adj.* having a tendency towards melancholy ‖ producing melancholy [fr. L.L. *melancholicus* fr. Gk]
mel·an·chol·y (melənkɒli:) **1.** *n.* depression, low spirits ‖ sad thoughtfulness ‖ (*hist.*) one of the four humors **2.** *adj.* sad, depressed ‖ expressing sadness, *a melancholy smile* ‖ causing sadness, *a melancholy view* [O.F. *melancolie, melencolie* fr. L. ult. fr. Gk *melas* (*melanos*), black+*cholē,* bile]
Me·lanch·thon (melǽŋθɒn) (Philipp Schwarzerd, 1497–1560), German humanist and theological reformer. He became the great champion and systematizer of the doctrines of Luther. His 'Loci communes' (1521) was the first ordered presentation of Reformation doctrine. He was mainly responsible for the Augsburg Confession (1530). He founded public schools and reorganized the university system in Germany
Mel·a·ne·sia (meləní:ʒə) the southwestern division of Oceania, including New Caledonia and the Bismarck, Solomon, New Hebrides, Fiji and smaller archipelagoes. New Guinea is sometimes included on racial grounds
Mel·a·ne·sian (meləní:ʒən) **1.** *adj.* pertaining to Melanesia or its people ‖ designating the group of Austronesian languages of the natives of Melanesia **2.** *n.* a native of Melanesia
mé·lange, me·lange (meiláʒ) *n.* a heterogeneous mixture [F.]
me·la·ni·an (məléini:ən) *adj.* having very dark skin, hair or eyes [fr. F. *mélanien*]
me·lan·ic (məlǽnik) *adj.* of, characterized by or affected by melanism or melanosis [fr. Gk *melas* (*melanos*), black]
mel·a·nin (mélənin) *n.* a dark brown or black pigment, found in men and animals, that makes the hair and skin dark [fr. Gk *melas* (*melanos*), black]
mel·a·nism (mélənizəm) *n.* abnormal development of black pigment in the skin of a mammal or plumage of a bird ‖ the characteristic of having very dark hair, skin or eyes [fr. Gk *melas* (*melanos*), black]
mel·a·nite (mélənait) *n.* a black variety of garnet [fr. Gk *melas* (*melanos*), black]
mel·a·no·blast (mélənoublæst) *n.* a cell producing melanin [fr. Gk *melas* (*melanos*), black+*blastos,* bud]
mel·a·noch·ro·i (melənókrouai) *pl. n.* Caucasians having dark hair and pale skin **mel·a·noch·roid** (melənókroid) *adj.* [Mod. L. fr. Gk *melas* (*melanos*), black+*ochros,* pale]
mel·a·no·sis (melənóusis) *n.* the abnormal development of melanin in body tissues **mel·a·not·ic** (melənótik) *adj.* [Mod. L. ult. fr. Gk *melanousthai,* to become black]
mel·a·to·nin (melətóunən) *n.* **1.** [C₁₃H₁₆O₂N₂] (*biochem.*) a pineal gland secretion that inhibits the cycle of sexual desire and physical

CONCISE PRONUNCIATION KEY: **(a)** æ, c*a*t; ɑ, c*a*r; ɔ f*aw*n; ei, sn*a*ke. **(e)** e, h*e*n; i:, sh*ee*p; iə, d*ee*r; ɛə, b*ea*r. **(i)** i, f*i*sh; ai, t*i*ger; ə:, b*i*rd. **(o)** o, *o*x; au, c*ow*; ou, g*oa*t; u, p*oo*r; ɔi, r*oy*al. **(u)** ʌ, d*u*ck; u, b*u*ll; u:, g*oo*se; ə, b*a*cillus; ju:, c*u*be. x, lo*ch*; θ, *th*ink; ð, bo*th*er; z, *Z*en; ʒ, cor*s*age; dʒ, sava*g*e; ŋ, ora*ng*utang; j, *y*ak; ʃ, *fi*sh; tʃ, fet*ch*; 'l, ra*bble*; 'n, re*dden*. Complete pronunciation key appears inside front cover.

changes in sexual organs, esp. in women 2. a salve used for lightening skin color

Mel·bourne (mélbərn), William Lamb, 2nd Viscount (1779–1848), British Whig statesman. As prime minister (1834, 1835–41), he was the leading adviser to the young Queen Victoria

Melbourne the capital (area 714 sq. miles, pop. 2,694,100) of Victoria, Australia and the country's second largest city, a seaport and trading center (wool, livestock). Industries: engineering, food processing, textiles. University (1853)

Mel·chite, Mel·kite (mélkait) n. (hist.) a Christian of Egypt or Syria who accepted the decrees against Nestorians and Monophysites of the Council of Chalcedon (451) ‖ a Uniate Eastern Christian following the Byzantine rite and using primarily Arabic in the liturgy [fr. L. Melchita, royalists ult. fr. Syrian malkå, king]

Mel·chiz·e·dek (melkízidek) priest-king of Salem. He blessed Abraham upon his return from battle and served him bread and wine (Genesis xiv, 18–20), and is taken as an archetype of the priesthood of Christ

meld (meld) 1. v.t. to declare (a card or cards) for scoring ‖ v.i. to declare a card or combination of cards for scoring 2. n. a melding ‖ the cards declared ‖ the score made by melding [prob. fr. G. melden, to announce]

Mel·e·a·ger (meli:éigər) (Gk. mythol.) a hero who, with his uncles, killed the boar that Artemis had sent to ravage the country. He then killed his uncles in a quarrel over its head and hide, and his mother caused his death by throwing into the fire a log of which it had been foretold that when it was burned, Meleager would die

me·lee, mê·lée (méilei, mélei) n. a confused struggle involving a group or groups [F. mélée]

Mel·ga·re·jo (melgaréhɔ), Mariano (1820–72), Bolivian general and dictator (1864–71). He dispossessed the Indians of their lands. He yielded territory to Brazil which was vital for Bolivia's access to the sea. He was assassinated after being deposed by revolution

Me·liès (meljes), Georges (1861–1938), French pioneer of the movies. He made about 4,000 films before 1914, the first being 'Une partie de cartes' (1896)

Me·lil·la (melí:lja) a seaport (pop. 57,000) on the E. Moroccan coast, a Spanish enclave and free port

mel·io·rate (mí:ljəreit) pres. part. **mel·io·rat·ing** past and past part. **mel·io·rat·ed** v.t. and i. (rhet.) to improve **mel·io·rá·tion** n. [fr. L.L. meliorare (melioratus)]

mel·io·rism (mí:ljərizəm) n. (philos.) the theory that the state of the world (being neither good nor evil) can be improved by human endeavor **mél·io·rist** n. [fr. L. melior, better]

me·lis·ma (məlízmə) pl. **me·lis·ma·ta** (məlízmətə) n. a group of notes sung to one syllable in plainsong [Gk=melody]

Melkite *MELCHITE

Me·lla (méja), Ramón Matías (1816–64), Dominican general and patriot, who (with Juan Pablo Duarte and Francisco del Rosario Sánchez) proclaimed (1844) Dominican independence

mel·lif·er·ous (məlífərəs) adj. yielding or producing honey [fr. L. mellifer fr. mel (mellis), honey+-fer, bearing]

mel·lif·lu·ous (məlíflu:əs) adj. (of a voice or words) sweet to listen to [fr. L. mellifluus fr. mel(mellis), honey+fluere, to flow]

Mel·lon (mélən), Andrew William (1855–1937), American financier and philanthropist, U.S. secretary of the treasury (1921–32)

mel·lo·tron (mélətran) n. a computer-programmed electronic musical instrument

mel·low (mélou) 1. adj. (of sound, color etc.) full and rich, not harsh ‖ (of mood) warmly human, genial ‖ (of a person) having the kindly understanding and sympathy that comes from age and experience ‖ (of wine) well-matured, smooth, free of acidity ‖ (of fruit) soft, ripe and sweet ‖ very mildly, benignly drunk 2. v.t. to make mellow ‖ v.i. to become mellow [M.E. melwe, melowe prob. fr. O.E. melo, meal]

mel·o·dern (mélədə:rn) n. (electr.) a receiver of all types of electromagnetic radiation received as vertical pips on a cathode ray screen, used for monitoring and countermeasures

me·lod·ic (məlódik) adj. of, pertaining to or containing melody **me·lód·i·cal·ly** adv. [fr. F. mélodique]

me·lod·i·ca (melóudikə) n. a harmonica-like wind instrument with a piano keyboard

melodic minor scale (mus.) a minor scale which, when ascending, has semitones between the second and third and between the seventh and eighth steps, the other intervals being whole tones. In descent, the seventh and sixth steps are both flattened, so that it becomes the same as the natural minor

me·lo·di·ous (məlóudi:əs) adj. (of sound) pleasing to the ear, esp. through being melodic [O.F. melodieus]

mel·o·dra·ma (mélədramə, mélədræmə) n. a play with a sensational plot and violent emotional appeal ‖ sensational events or dramatic, exaggerated behavior **mel·o·dra·mat·ic** (melədrəmǽtik) adj. **mel·o·dra·mát·i·cal·ly** adv. [fr. older melodrame fr. F. mélodrame fr. Gk melos, music+F. drame, drama]

mel·o·dy (mélədi) pl. **mel·o·dies** n. (mus.) a succession of single notes of different pitch so arranged in relation to each other as to be a recognizable entity ‖ (mus.) the principal part in a piece of harmonized music (cf. HARMONY) ‖ sweet, pleasing music [O.F. melodie fr. L.L. fr. Gk melōdia fr. melos, song+aeidein, to sing]

mel·on (mélən) n. the edible fruit of either the muskmelon or the watermelon ‖ either of these plants [F.]

Me·los (mélɒs) *MILOS

Mel·pom·e·ne (melpóməni:) (Gk mythol.) the Muse of tragedy

melt (melt) 1. v. pres. part. **melt·ing** past and past part. **melt·ed**, (rhet. and adjectival) **mol·ten** (móultən) v.i. (of something solid) to become liquefied by the action of heat ‖ to dissolve ‖ (fig.) to become soft as if by dissolving, his heart melted with pity ‖ (with 'into', of an image, sound etc.) to blend (with another) ‖ v.t. to cause to become liquid, by heating ‖ to dissolve ‖ (fig.) to soften as if by dissolving, his pleading melted her ‖ (with 'down') to cause (metal objects) to be reduced to liquefied metal, by heating 2. n. something molten ‖ an amount of some substance melted in one operation [O.E. meltan v.i. and meltan, mieltan v.t.]

melt·down (méltdaun) n. (nuclear phys.) the melting of the protective cases surrounding a nuclear reactor, resulting in release of radiation

melting point the temperature at which a solid melts under normal pressure

melting pot a container in which objects are melted ‖ the condition of being under consideration or reorganization, our plans are still in the melting pot ‖ a country or society in which peoples of many races and cultures mingle to form a whole

mel·ton (méltən) n. a heavy woolen cloth with a short nap and a smooth finish, used for overcoats [after Melton Mowbray in Leicestershire, England, where the cloth was first made]

Mel·ville (mélvil), George Wallace (1841–1912), U.S. arctic explorer and naval engineer. Accompanying George Delong on the ill-fated polar expedition (1879) of the 'Jeannette', he led a search party which recovered the bodies and records of the crew. As engineer in chief (1887–1903) of the U.S. navy, he introduced improvements, including the triple screw

Melville, Herman (1819–91), American writer. The novel 'Moby Dick' (1851), his epic masterpiece, tells of the allegorical disastrous hunt at sea for a white whale. His other works include the novels 'Typee' (1846) and 'Omoo' (1847), the posthumous short novel 'Billy Budd, Foretopman' (1924), short stories and poetry

Melville Peninsula a peninsula (250 miles long, 70–135 miles wide) between the Foxe Basin and the Gulf of Boothia in the Northwest Territories, Canada

mem·ber (mémbər) n. a person who belongs to a group or organization ‖ a part of the body, esp. a limb ‖ a distinct part of a whole, esp. of a building, a sentence, a mathematical equation etc. ‖ (Br.) a member of parliament [M.E. membre fr. F. fr. L. membrum, limb]

member of parliament (abbr. M.P.) an elected representative in the British parliament

mem·ber·ship (mémbərʃip) n. the state of being a member ‖ the total number of members, a membership of 200

mem·brane (mémbrein) n. a very thin, strong, pliable tissue which covers, lines or connects parts of an animal or vegetable body ‖ a piece of parchment forming part of a roll [fr. L. membrana]

membrane bone a bone originating in membranous tissue, not as cartilage

mem·bra·nous (mémbrənəs) adj. of, characterized by the forming of, or like a membrane [fr. F. membraneux]

Me·mel (méiməl) *KLAIPEDA

me·men·to (məméntou) pl. **me·men·toes, me·men·tos** n. an object kept as a reminder of a person, event etc., mementoes of vanished civilizations [L., imper. of meminisse, to remember]

me·men·to mo·ri (məméntoumɔ́rai, məméntoumɔ́urai) pl. **me·men·to mo·ri** n. something, e.g. a death's head, that serves as a reminder of death [L.=remember that you must die]

Mem·ling (mémliŋ), Hans (or Hans Memlinc, c. 1433–94), Flemish painter of portraits and of sacred works including 'The Mystic Marriage of St Catherine' (1479) and 'Adoration of the Magi' (1479)

Mem·non (mémnɒn) (Gk mythol.) a king of Ethiopia who helped Priam in the Trojan War and was killed by Achilles ‖ a huge statue of Amenhotep III at Thebes, Egypt, said to have emitted musical sounds at daybreak

mem·o (mémou) pl. **mem·os** n. a memorandum

mem·oir (mémwar) n. a history or record of events written by someone who has special knowledge of them, usually through personal experience ‖ an essay on a specialized subject by an expert ‖ (usually pl.) an autobiography, esp. about the writer's part in public life ‖ a biography, normally of a person known to the writer [F. mémoire masc. fr. mémoire fem., memory]

mem·o·ra·bil·i·a (memərəbíli:ə) pl. n. memorable things or events [L., neut. pl. of memorabilis adj., memorable]

mem·o·ra·ble (mémərəb'l) adj. outstanding, worthy of being remembered **mém·o·ra·bly** adv. [fr. L. memorabilis]

mem·o·ran·dum (memərǽndəm) pl. **mem·o·ran·dums, mem·o·ran·da** (memərǽndə) n. a brief record of an event or analysis of a situation, made for one's own future reference or to inform others, and sometimes embodying an instruction or recommendation ‖ an informal letter, usually unsigned, used e.g. in interoffice communication ‖ (diplomacy) an informal written statement or inquiry ‖ (law) a short document recording the terms of an agreement [L.=it should be remembered fr. memorare, to remember]

me·mo·ri·al (məmɔ́ri:əl, məmɔ́uri:əl) 1. adj. commemorative, a memorial tablet 2. n. a monument commemorating a person or event ‖ a statement of facts prepared as the basis of a petition ‖ an informal state paper, or memorandum ‖ (pl.) a historical account [O.F.]

Memorial Day a national holiday of the U.S.A., originally commemorating those who died in the Civil War but observed now as a day of remembrance for all Americans killed on active service (May 30 in most states, Apr. 26, May 10 or June 3 in the South)

me·mo·ri·al·ize (məmɔ́ri:əlaiz, məmɔ́uri:əlaiz) pres. part. **me·mo·ri·al·iz·ing** past and past part. **me·mo·ri·al·ized** v.t. to commemorate ‖ to petition with a memorial

mem·o·rize (méməraiz) pres. part. **mem·o·riz·ing** past and past part. **mem·o·rized** v.t. to commit to memory

mem·o·ry (méməri) pl. **mem·o·ries** n. the faculty by which sense impressions and information are retained consciously or unconsciously in the mind and subsequently recalled ‖ a person's capacity to remember ‖ a mental image or impression of a past event, something learned etc., happy memories of childhood ‖ the total store of mentally retained impressions and knowledge, to draw from memory ‖ the length of time over which recollection extends, not within memory ‖ the posthumous reputation of a person in memory of as an affectionate or respectful record of [O.F. memorie, memoire]

memory bank (computer) a computer data storage

memory cell or **memory** (computer) a computer memory storage element for one bit of data

memory drum (computer) computer data storage, usu. on magnetic tape or cylinder

memory switch (computer) switching device that can be set on or off by a change of voltage

mem·o·ry-trace (méməri:treis) n. (psych.) 1. an intentionally forgotten or repressed experience that may unconsciously affect subsequent behavior 2. a chemical change in the brain that results from the use of the brain

Mem·phis (mémfis) an ancient town of N. Egypt. It was the capital of Egypt (c. 3100–c. 2100 B.C.)

Memphis the largest city (pop. 646,356) in Tennessee, on the Mississippi River, a cotton and lumber market. Industries: wood and cottonseed products, automobiles, chemicals, drugs

men pl. of MAN

men·ace (ménis) n. a threat ‖ anything that constitutes a threat, *under the menace of atomic war* [M.E. *manasce, manace* fr. O.F. ult. fr. L. *minari* v., to threaten]

menace pres. part. **men·ac·ing** past and post part. **men·aced** v.t. and i. to threaten [F. *menacer*]

mé·nage (meináʒ) n. a household [O.F. *manaige, menaige,* the members of a household]

me·nag·er·ie (mənǽdʒəri:) n. a collection of animals exhibited in cages ‖ the place where the animals are kept or exhibited [F. *ménagerie*]

Men·ai Strait (ménai) a channel which separates the Isle of Anglesey from the mainland of Caernarvon, Wales. It is 14 miles long and ½ to 2 miles wide, and is crossed by two bridges

Me·nan·der (minǽndər) (c. 342–c. 291 B.C.), Greek comic dramatist. Only one complete play ('The Dyskolos') survives, with many fragments of others. Menander painted his characters boldly. His well-constructed plots generally dealt with thwarted love

men·a·zon [C₆H₈N₅O₂PS₂] (ménəzon) n. (chem.) an organophosphate insecticide used against aphids, sometimes as antiparisitic for animals

Men·ci·us (ménʃi:əs) (Meng-tse, c. 372–c. 289 B.C.), Chinese philosopher. He taught and developed the humanist principles of Confucianism

Menck·en (méŋkən), Henry Louis (H.L.) (1880–1956), U.S. writer and controversial critic of American life. His 'Prejudices' (6 vols, 1919–27), a collection of essays and reviews, satirizes organized religion, business and middle-class values. A linguistic scholar, he published 'The American Language' (1919)

mend (mend) 1. v.t. to repair (cloth, china etc.) ‖ to repair (a hole, tear, break etc.) ‖ to cause to become better, *to mend one's ways* ‖ (Br.) to add fuel to (a fire) ‖ v.i. to improve, esp. to recover from an illness 2. n. a mended place, e.g. a patched hole, a glued break in china etc. **on the mend** improving, esp. in health after illness [AMEND]

men·da·cious (mendéiʃəs) adj. untruthful [fr. L. *mendax (mendacis)*]

men·dac·i·ty (mendǽsiti:) pl. **men·dac·i·ties** n. the quality or state of being mendacious ‖ an instance of this [fr. L.L. *mendacitas*]

Men·de (méndi:) pl. **Men·de, Men·des** n. a people of Sierra Leone and Liberia, allied to the Mandingo ‖ a member of this people ‖ their Mande language

Men·del (méndˀl), Gregor Johann (1822–84), Austrian monk and botanist. He experimented on the hybridization of green peas. Some of the results were published (1866, 1869), but their importance in the study of heredity was not appreciated until they were rediscovered in 1900 (*MENDEL'S LAWS, *GENETICS)

men·de·le·vi·um (mendəli:vi:əm) n. a radioactive element, artificially produced, symbol Md or MV, at. no. 101, mass of isotope of longest known half-life 256 [Mod. L., after MENDELEYEV]

Men·de·le·yev (mendəléiəf), Dmitri Ivanovich (1834–1907), Russian chemist. He constructed (1879) the periodic table of atomic weights for chemical elements

Men·de·li·an (mendí:li:ən) adj. of or according to Mendel's laws or discoveries

Men·del·ism (méndˀlizəm) n. the principles governing inheritance of characters in plants and animals worked out by Mendel, and their operation. The principles have been extended and modified by subsequent investigation (*MENDEL'S LAWS)

Mendel's laws three principles in genetics, which have been shown since Mendel enumerated them to be subject to many specific exceptions: (1) during the formation of the gamete (*MEIOSIS), paired genetic units representing alternate characteristics (e.g. curly hair or straight hair) separate, individual gametes receiving only one element of the pair (2) the process in which corresponding genetic units unite during the formation of the zygote is governed by chance. The distribution for a given character in the offspring represents the proba-

bility of appearance of that character (3) one of the pair of genetic units combining in the zygote is dominant and the other recessive. Characters do not appear as a mixture of qualities of each unit but are inherited on an all-or-none basis

Men·del·sohn (méndəls'n), Erich (1887–1953), English architect, born in Germany. Through the imaginative use of modern materials and technology, he achieved a near-sculptural effect in his buildings

Men·dels·sohn (méndəls'n, méndəlzoun), Felix (Jacob Ludwig Felix Mendelssohn-Bartholdy, 1809–47), German composer. His best works have a fresh tonal color and inventive use of melody which give them a gracefully youthful quality. His many works include the incidental music to Shakespeare's 'A Midsummer Night's Dream', five symphonies, the E minor violin concerto, several overtures, 'Elijah' and other oratorios, chamber music and piano solos etc.

Mendelssohn, Moses (1729–86), German philosopher who helped to break down anti-Jewish prejudices and to modernize Judaism. His principal works are 'Phaedon' (1767) and 'Jerusalem' (1783)

Men·des France (mɛ̃desfrɑ̃s), Pierre (1907–82), French statesman. As prime minister of France (1954–5), he concluded the war in Indochina and he granted independence to Tunisia

men·di·can·cy (méndikənsi:) n. the practice of begging ‖ the state of being a beggar

men·di·cant (méndikənt) 1. adj. begging, used esp. of some orders of friars whose rule requires them to live by begging, no property being allowed 2. n. (rhet.) a beggar ‖ a friar of a mendicant order [fr. L. *mendicans (mendicantis)* fr. *mendicare,* to beg]

men·dic·i·ty (mendisiti:) n. mendicancy [F. *mendicité*]

Men·do·ci·no, Cape (mendəsí:nou) a promontory of N.W. California, the westernmost point of the state

Men·do·za (mendósa), Gonzalo de (d. 1558), Spanish conquistador and cofounder (with Juan de Salazar y Espinoza, b. 1508) of Asunción (1537). He was appointed (1556) governor of the territory of Río de la Plata

Mendoza, Pedro de (c. 1487–1537), Spanish conquistador, first adelantado (governor) of Río de la Plata, and founder of Buenos Aires (1536)

Mendoza a city (pop. 118,568) in W. Argentina, center of a wine-producing area. It was greatly damaged by an earthquake and fire (1861)

Men·e·la·us (men'léiəs) legendary king of Sparta, son of Atreus, brother of Agamemnon. He was the husband of Helen

Men·e·lik II (mén'lik) (1844–1913), emperor of Ethiopia (1889–1913). His defeat of the Italians (1896) assured Ethiopia's independence and consolidated its power

Me·nén·dez de A·vi·lés (menéndeθðeavi:lés), Pedro (1519–74), Spanish soldier and sailor. He served as governor of Cuba and *adelantado* of Florida, where he founded (1565) St Augustine

Me·nes (mí:ni:z) (c. 3110 B.C.), first king of the 1st dynasty of Egypt. According to Herodotus, he founded Memphis and united Upper and Lower Egypt

men·folk (ménfouk) pl. n. men, esp. the men of a family or tribe

Meng-tse *MENCIUS

Meng-tsz, Meng-tzu (mʌ́ndzʌ) a city (pop. 200,000) of S.E. Yunnan, China: tin mining, metallurgy

men·ha·den (menhéid'n) pl. **men·ha·den, men·ha·dens** n. *Brevoortia tyrannus,* fam. *Clupeidae,* a fish found in great abundance along the Atlantic coast of North America. It is used as manure, and produces a valuable oil [Am. Ind. *munnawhateaûg*]

men·hir (ménhiər) n. a tall, oblong, roughly cut stone, standing on its end, either alone or as part of a group in prehistoric monuments. They are found esp. in Brittany, France [Breton fr. *men,* stone + *hir,* long]

me·ni·al (mí:ni:əl, mí:njəl) 1. adj. (of work) servile, lowly 2. n. (rhet.) a domestic servant ‖ (rhet.) a servile person [A.F. *meignal, menial,* pertaining to a household]

Meniere's Disease (mənjéirz) an ear disorder whose symptoms include dizziness, vertigo, ringing and hearing loss due to excess inner ear fluid (engolymph). Symptoms can last from a few hours to a few days and can recur

me·nin·ge·al (məníndʒi:əl) adj. pertaining to the meninges [fr. Mod. L. *meningeus* fr. *meninx (meninges),* meningeal membrane]

meninges *MENINX

men·in·gi·tis (məníndʒáitis) n. inflammation of the meninges (esp. the pia mater and arachnoid), often caused by a microorganism (e.g. the tubercule bacillus, the meningococcus or pneumococcus) [Mod. L. ult. fr. Gk *mēninx (mēningos),* membrane]

me·nin·go·coc·cus (məniŋgoukɔ́kəs) pl. **me·nin·go·coc·ci** (məniŋgoukɔ́ksai) n. *Neisseria meningitidis,* a bacterium which causes cerebrospinal meningitis

me·ninx (mí:niŋks) pl. **me·nin·ges** (məníndʒi:z) n. any one of the three membranes, dura mater, pia mater and arachnoid, which surround and protect the brain and spinal cord [Mod. L. fr. Gk *mēninx,* membrane]

me·nis·cus (mənískəs) pl. **me·nis·ci** (mənísai), **me·nis·cus·es** n. (math.) a crescent-shaped figure ‖ a concavo-convex or convexo-concave lens ‖ the upper surface of a liquid in a tube, concave when the liquid wets the walls of the tube and convex when it does not [Mod. L. fr. Gk *mēniskos,* crescent]

Men·non·ite (ménənait) n. a member of a Protestant sect in the Netherlands, Germany and America. The Mennonites, who developed out of the Anabaptist movement, refuse military service, public office and oath-taking, and seek holiness by discipline [after *Menno* Simons (c. 1496-1561), Du. religious reformer]

me·nol·o·gy (mi:nɔ́lədʒi:) pl. **me·nol·o·gies** n. a calendar with notes on the lives of the saints and martyrs, esp. one used in the Greek Orthodox Church [fr. Mod. L. *menologium* fr. L. Gk *mēnologion* fr. Gk *mēn,* month + *logos,* word]

Me·nom·i·ni, Me·nom·i·nee (mənɔ́mini:) pl. **Me·nom·i·ni, Me·nom·i·ni·s, Me·nom·i·nee, Me·nom·i·nees** n. an American Indian people centered (17th-20th cc.) in Wisconsin and Michigan. They intermarried considerably with French settlers. They lived under federal control on a reservation in N. central Wisconsin from 1554 to 1961, when it was made a county of Wisconsin. In the 1960s they numbered about 3,700 ‖ a member of this people ‖ their Algonquian language

Menon, Krishna *KRISHNA MENON

men·o·pause (ménəpɔz) n. the time when the menstrual cycle ceases, either abruptly or gradually, usually between the ages of 40 and 50 [fr. *meno-* fr. Gk *mēn (mēnos),* month + *pauein,* to stop]

me·nor·ah (mənɔ́ra, mənɔ́urə) n. the Jewish eight-branched candlestick, with a shammash, lit nightly on the feast of Hanukkah [Heb.]

Me·nor·ca (mənɔ́rkə) *BALEARIC ISLANDS

men·or·rha·gi·a (menəréidʒi:ə) n. excessive menstrual bleeding [Mod. L. fr. Gk *mēn (mēnos),* month + *-rhagia,* excess flow]

Me·not·ti (menɔ́tti:), Gian-Carlo (1911–), Italian–American composer, now living in Scotland. He is best known for his operas, which include 'The Medium' (1946) 'The Consul' (1950) and 'Amahl and the Night Visitors' (1951), the first opera specifically composed for American television

men·ses (ménsi:z) pl. n. the discharge of the mucous lining of the womb occurring in the menstrual cycle [L. pl. of *mensis,* month]

Men·she·vik (ménʃəvik) n. (hist.) a member of the moderate minority faction of the Russian Social Democratic party which split (1903) from the Bolsheviks and was absorbed or liquidated after 1918 by the Russian Communist party

Men·shi·kov (ménʃikɔf), Prince Aleksandr Danilovich (1672–1729), Russian field marshal and statesman. Companion and adviser of Peter the Great, he was virtual ruler of Russia (1725–7)

Men's Liberation movement designed to change traditional role behavior of men in the social structure *also* **Men's Lib** (often used disparagingly)

men·stru·al (ménstru:əl) adj. of or pertaining to the menses [F. *menstruel*]

menstrual cycle the cycle of changes in the reproductive organs of women and female higher anthropoids. It culminates in uterine bleeding about every 28 days. These changes have the function of preparing the womb for pregnancy, should the ovum become fertilized at about the middle of the cycle. Menstruation commonly starts between the ages of 12 and 15 and continues till between 40 and 50 (*MENOPAUSE)

menstrual synchrony phenomenon of women who are close friends or who live together tending to have menstrual cycles at the same time

men·stru·ate (ménstru:eit) *pres. part.* **men·stru·at·ing** *past* and *past part.* **men·stru·at·ed** *v.i.* to discharge the menses **men·stru·a·tion** *n.* [fr. L. *menstruare* (*menstruatus*)]

men·stru·um (ménstru:əm) *pl.* **men·stru·ums, men·stru·a** (ménstru:ə) *n.* a liquid which can dissolve or hold in suspension a solid [L. neuter of *menstruus* adj., monthly, fr. the alchemistic analogy with menstrual flow]

men·sur·a·bil·i·ty (menʃərəbíliti:) *n.* the quality or state of being mensurable

men·sur·a·ble (ménʃərəb'l) *adj.* measurable [F.]

men·su·ral (ménʃərəl) *adj.* pertaining to measuring [fr. M.L. *mensuralis*]

men·su·ra·tion (menʃəréiʃən) *n.* the branch of applied mathematics concerned with measuring lengths, areas and volumes ‖ the act or process of measuring [fr. L.L. *mensuratio* (*mensurationis*) fr. *mensurare*, to measure]

-ment *suffix* denoting an action or the result of the action, as in 'internment', or a means

men·tal (mént'l) *adj.* of or pertaining to the mind ‖ done by or taking place in the mind, *mental arithmetic, mental torment* ‖ intended for the care of the insane, a *mental hospital* ‖ (*Br., pop.*) mentally ill [F.]

mental *adj.* (*anat.*) pertaining to the chin [F. fr. L. *mentum*, chin]

mental age an assessment of a person's intelligence in terms of an age scale for normal performance

mental deficiency a level of mental development low enough to prevent a child from obtaining benefit from an ordinary school education, or an adult from maintaining himself except in a protected environment (*IDIOT, *IMBECILE, *MORON)

men·tal·i·ty (mentæliti:) *pl.* **men·tal·i·ties** *n.* the manner of thinking, esp. the attitude toward life, society etc., of an individual or group, *a typically Southern mentality* ‖ intellectual capacity

men·thol (ménθɔl) *n.* a white crystalline substance, $C_{10}H_{19}OH$, with a strong smell of peppermint, obtained from oil of peppermint and used to relieve pain, itching and nasal congestion **men·tho·lat·ed** (ménθəleitid) *adj.* containing menthol ‖ treated with menthol [G. fr. L. *mentha*, mint]

men·tion (ménʃən) *n.* a mentioning or being mentioned ‖ an instance of this **to make mention of** to mention [F. fr. L. *mentio* (*mentionis*) fr. *mens*, mind]

mention *v.t.* to refer to, esp. casually ‖ to cite the name of (a person) as official recognition of merit **don't mention it** thanks (or apologies) are unnecessary **not to mention** without taking into consideration, *the dampness is unpleasant, not to mention the cold* [F. *mentionner*]

Men·tor (méntər, méntɔr) (*Gk mythol.*) the friend of Odysseus and tutor of his son Telemachus

men·tor (méntər, méntɔr) *n.* an experienced and trusted friend and adviser [after MENTOR (friend of Odysseus)]

men·u (ménju:) *n.* a restaurant's list of the dishes available ‖ a list of the dishes served at a formal meal ‖ the dishes served [F.]

Men·zies (ménzi:z) Sir Robert Gordon (1894–1978), Australian Liberal statesman, prime minister of Australia (1939–41, 1949–66)

me·ow, mi·aow (mi:áu) **1.** *n.* the cry of a cat **2.** *v.i.* (of a cat) to make its cry [imit.]

Meph·is·to·phe·le·an, Meph·is·to·phe·li·an (mefistəfi:li:ən) *adj.* having the diabolical qualities or appearance of Mephistopheles

Meph·i·stoph·e·les (mefistófili:z) the devil in the Faust legend [G., etym. doubtful]

me·phit·ic (məfítik) *adj.* bad-smelling ‖ noxious or poisonous [fr. MEPHITIS]

me·phi·tis (məfáitis) *n.* a poisonous or bad-smelling exhalation of gas from the earth, e.g. from decaying organic substances [L.]

mer·can·tile (mə́:rkəntail, mə́:rkəntil) *adj.* pertaining to or engaged in trade or commerce **mér·can·til·ism** *n.* trade and commerce ‖ the theory (16th-17th c.) that a country's strength and prosperity depended on the amassing of bullion reserves. This was to be achieved by developing production for export, limiting imports and prohibiting the export of bullion **mér·can·til·ist** *n.* [F. fr. Ital.]

mer·cap·tan (mərkǽptən) *n.* any of several volatile and bad-smelling compounds resembling alcohols, but with sulfur in the place of the oxygen. Their general formula is RSH [G. fr. L. *mer-* curium *captans*, catching mercury]

Mer·ca·tor (məːrkéitər), Gerardus (Gerhard Kremer, 1512–94), Flemish geographer and mathematician. He devised (1569) the method of map projection based upon straight lines of longitude and latitude intersecting at right angles, and published a world atlas (1594)

Mer·ce·da·rio (merseðúrjo) a peak (22,210 ft) in W. Argentina, near the Chilean border

mer·ce·nar·i·ness (mə́:rsəneri:nis) *n.* the state or quality of being mercenary

mer·ce·nar·y (mə́:rsəneri:) **1.** *adj.* inspired merely by a desire for gain **2.** *pl.* **mer·ce·nar·ies** *n.* a hired soldier serving a country other than his own [fr. L. *mercenarius* fr. *merces*, reward]

mer·cer (mə́:rsər) *n.* (*Br.*) a dealer in textiles, esp. fine fabrics [F. *mercier*]

mer·cer·ize (mə́:rsəraiz) *pres. part.* **mer·cer·iz·ing** *past* and *past part.* **mer·cer·ized** *v.t.* to treat (cotton thread or fabric) with caustic alkali to strengthen it and make it slightly glossy [after John *Mercer* (1791-1866), Eng. inventor of the process]

mer·cer·y (mə́:rsɔri:) *n.* (*Br.*) textiles sold by a mercer [F. *mercerie*]

mer·chan·dise 1. (mə́:rtʃəndaiz, mə́:rtʃəndais) *n.* (*collect.*) goods bought and sold in commerce **2.** (mə́:rtʃəndaiz) *v. pres. part.* **mer·chan·dis·ing** *past* and *past part.* **mer·chan·dised** *v.t.* to promote the sale of (goods) ‖ *v.i.* to practice the buying and selling of goods [F. *marchandise*]

mer·chant (mə́:rtʃənt) **1.** *n.* a person who directs large-scale trade, esp. with a foreign country ‖ a retailer **2.** *adj.* of or pertaining to a merchant or to trade ‖ of or pertaining to the merchant marine [O.F. *marchand*]

merchant bank a bank combining the functions of acceptance house and in- vestment bank

merchant guild *GUILD

mer·chant·man (mə́:rtʃəntmən) *pl.* **mer·chant·men** (mə́:rtʃəntmən) *n.* a ship used for commerce

merchant marine (*Am.=Br.* merchant navy) the ships of a nation used in commerce ‖ their officers or crew

merchant navy (*Br.*) merchant marine

Mer·ci·a (mə́:rʃi:ə) an Anglo-Saxon kingdom in central England, founded c. 500. It rose to dominance (7th c.) under Penda and its power was strengthened (8th c.) by Offa, but it was absorbed (9th c.) by the Danelaw and Wessex

Mer·cier (mersjei), Désiré Joseph (1851–1926), Belgian cardinal and philosopher. He was the effective leader of Belgium during the German occupation in the 1st world war. He worked for Christian unity (esp. the ecumenical conference known as the Malines Conversations, 1921–3)

Mercier Honoré (1840–94), Canadian politician, an opponent of confederation and champion of French-Canadian interests. As premier (1887–91) of Quebec he passed the Jesuit Estates act, which compensated the Society of Jesus for property confiscated by the Crown in the early 19th c.

mer·ci·ful (mə́:rsifəl) *adj.* showing or feeling mercy

mer·ci·less (mə́:rsilis) *adj.* showing no mercy

mer·cu·ri·al (mərkjúəri:əl) **1.** *adj.* having the qualities associated with the god Mercury, esp. quick-wittedness, eloquence, changeability ‖ pertaining to or containing mercury **2.** *n* a drug containing mercury **mer·cú·ri·al·ism** *n.* (*med.*) mercury poisoning [F *mercuriel, mercurial*]

mer·cu·ric (mərkjúərik) *adj.* of compounds of divalent mercury

mercuric chloride the poisonous corrosive salt $HgCl_2$

mercuric sulfide the compound HgS occurring naturally in red (*CINNABAR) and black forms and also produced synthetically

Mer·cu·ro·chrome (mərkjúərəkroum) *n.* a red dye $[C_{20}H_8Br_2HgNa_2O_6]$ used in solution as an antiseptic [trademark]

mer·cu·rous (mərkjúərəs, mə́:rkjərəs) *adj.* of compounds of monovalent mercury

mercurous chloride the salt Hg_2Cl_2, used as a purgative

Mer·cu·ry (mə́:rkjəri:) (*Rom. mythol.*) the god of commerce, thieves and eloquence, and messenger of the gods, identified with the Greek Hermes ‖ the first planet from the sun (average diameter of orbit=36,002,000 miles) and the smallest major planet (3,000 miles in diameter,

mass ¹⁄₂₉ that of the earth, i.e. 3.21×10^{20} tons) of the solar system. It revolves about the sun with a period (sidereal) of 88 days, has no known satellites and appears to rotate once every 59 earth-days. Its surface, unprotected by an atmosphere, is at a very high temperature when subjected to the rays of the sun and a very low temperature elsewhere

mer·cu·ry (mə́:rkjəri:) *n.* a silverwhite, poisonous, metallic element (symbol Hg, at. no. 80, at. mass 200.59), liquid above $-35.85°C$ and boiling at 356.9°C under normal pressure. Mercury is used in thermometers and other scientific instruments, and in dentistry, pharmacy etc. [after MERCURY (the Roman god)]

mercury arc an electrical discharge through mercury vapor giving bluish light rich in ultra-violet radiation and used for various purposes, e.g. in rectifiers, fluorescent lamps and mercury vapor lamps

mercury barometer a barometer consisting of a long vertical tube, sealed at the top end, and with its bottom open end immersed in a vessel of mercury. The vertical height of the column of mercury which the atmosphere will support is taken as a measure of atmospheric pressure

mercury fulminate the explosive compound $Hg(ONC)_2$, used as a detonator

mercury-vapor lamp, *Br.* **mercury-vapour lamp** an electric lamp incorporating a mercury arc. It is widely used for street illumination and for maintaining a sterile atmosphere in hospital operating rooms

mer·cy (mə́:rsi:) *pl.* **mer·cies** *n.* compassionate rather than severe behavior towards someone in one's power ‖ a thing to be thankful for, *it's a mercy that the doctor arrived in time* **at the mercy of** completely in the power of (something or someone potentially harmful or adverse) [M.E. *merci* fr. F.]

mercy killing euthanasia

mere (miər) *adj.* being no more or better than, *mere foolishness, a mere versifier* [fr. L. *merus*, pure, unmixed]

mere *n.* (*Br.*) a large pond or lake [O.E.]

Mer·e·dith (méridiθ), George (1828–1909), English novelist and poet. He wrote mannered, satirical novels of the upper classes, with complex psychological studies. His novels include 'Beauchamp's Career' (1876), 'The Egoist' (1879) and 'Diana of the Crossways' (1885). His poetry includes the long narrative sequence 'Modern Love' (1862)

mere·ly (míərli:) *adv.* in no way more than as specified, *merely pretentious, merely a formality*

mer·e·tri·cious (meritríʃəs) *adj.* superficially and spuriously attractive [fr. L. *meretricius* fr. *meretrix* (*meretricis*), a prostitute]

Me·rezh·kov·ski (mereʃkɔ́fski:), Dmitri Sergeyevich (1865–1941), Russian novelist and critic who tried to reconcile the spiritual values of Christianity and paganism. His best-known novels are 'Julian the Apostate' (also translated as 'The Death of the Gods'), 'Peter and Alexis' and 'December 14th'

mer·gan·ser (mərgǽnsər) *n.* a member of *Mergus*, a genus of fish-eating ducks of great diving power, having a long narrow serrated bill hooked at the tip [Mod. L. fr. L. *mergus*, diving bird+*anser*, goose]

merge (mə:rdʒ) *pres. part.* **merg·ing** *past* and *post port.* **merged** *v.t.* to unite or blend (two or more things), *to merge two firms* ‖ *v.i.* to become united or blended, *the two firms have merged*

mérg·er *n.* the combination of two companies or businesses e.g. by the major company's issuing stock in replacement of most of the stock of the smaller company [fr. L. *mergere*, to dip]

Mer·gen·thal·er (mə́:rgəntŏlər), Ottmar (1854–99), U.S. inventor of the Linotype machine (1886), which, by speeding the printing process of composition and reducing its cost, furthered the expansion of publishing industries and so led to an increase in literacy

Me·ric (meri:tʃ) *MARITSA

Mé·ri·da (mériðə) the chief town (pop. 269,582) of Yucatán, Mexico, center of a henequen-growing district. Port: Progreso. It has many 16th-c. Spanish buildings, including a cathedral

Mérida a town (pop. 40,059) in Badajoz, S.W. Spain. It was the capital of Roman Lusitania. Roman remains: temples, aqueduct, circus, theater, bridge, amphitheater etc.

me·rid·i·an (mərídi:ən) **1.** *adj.* pertaining to noon, esp. to the position of the sun at noon ‖ (*rhet.*) at the highest point of success or greatness **2.** *n.* a great circle of the celestial sphere,

CONCISE PRONUNCIATION KEY: **(a)** æ, *cat*; ɑ, *car*; ɔ *fawn*; ei, *snake*. **(e)** e, *hen*; i:, *sheep*; iə, *deer*; ɛə, *bear*. **(i)** i, *fish*; ai, *tiger*; ə:, *bird*. **(o)** o, *ox*; au, *cow*; ou, *goat*; u, *poor*; ɔi, *royal*. **(u)** ʌ, *duck*; u, *bull*; u:, *goose*; ə, *bacillus*; ju:, *cube*. x, *loch*; θ, *think*; ð, *bother*; z, *Zen*; ʒ, *corsage*; dʒ, *savage*; ŋ, *orangutang*; j, *yak*; ʃ, *fish*; tʃ, *fetch*; 'l, *rabble*; 'n, *redden*. Complete pronunciation key appears inside front cover.

passing through its poles and the zenith of a given point ‖ a great circle on the surface of the earth, passing through the poles and a given place ‖ (archaic) the highest apparent elevation of the sun or a star ‖ a curve formed by the intersection of a surface of revolution and a plane through the axis of revolution ‖ (rhet.) the highest point of success or greatness [O.F. meridien or fr. L. meridianus fr. meridies, noon]

me·rid·ic (mərídik) adj. (biol.) composed of some defined and some undefined (except water) constituents *HOLIDIC, OLIGIDIC

me·rid·i·o·nal (mərídiːənˈl) 1. adj. of, pertaining to or characteristic of the people of S. Europe, esp. S. France ‖ of or pertaining to a meridian 2. n. a native of S. Europe, esp. S. France [F.]

Mé·ri·mée (meiri:mei), Prosper (1803–70), French novelist and essayist. He is best known for his short novels, including 'Colomba' (1840) and 'Carmen' (1845)

me·ringue (mərǽŋ) n. a light, fluffy baked mixture of sugar and beaten egg whites used as topping on cakes etc. ‖ a small cake made of this [F.]

me·ri·no (mərí:nou) pl. **me·ri·nos** n. a sheep of a Spanish breed having very fine white wool ‖ a soft fabric, originally made of this wool, now made of a wool and cotton mixture ‖ a fine woolen yarn, used esp. in making underwear [Span.]

Mer·i·on·eth·shire (meri:ónəθˌʃiər) a county (area 660 sq. miles, pop. 39,000) in W. Wales. County town: Dolgellau

mer·i·stem (méristəm) n. a growing plant tissue found segregated in specific regions of a plant (e.g. at the apex of the stem). It consists of small, roughly equal-sized cells capable of indefinite reduplication and giving rise eventually to the various tissues and organs (*CAMBIUM) [fr. Gk meristos, divided]

mer·it (mérit) n. excellence, the quality of deserving praise ‖ the intrinsic goodness or badness of something or someone ‖ spiritual credit ‖ (pl., esp. law) the intrinsic rights and wrongs of a case [O.F. merite]

merit v.t. to be worthy of, to merit praise, merit punishment [F. mériter]

mer·i·toc·ra·cy (meritókrəsi:) n. government by, or educational and/or social-status advancement of, the most intelligent or talented members of a society —**meritocrat** n. —**meritocratic** adj.

mer·i·to·ri·ous (meritó:riːəs, meritóuri:əs) adj. deserving praise or reward [fr. L. meritorius]

Mer·leau-Pon·ty (merloupɔ̃ti:), Maurice (1908–61), French philosopher. He was an existentialist until 1953, when he broke with Sartre. From then on he devoted himself to phenomenological analyses. He is the author of 'Sens et Non-Sens' (1948)

Mer·lin (mə́:rlin) (5th c.), a prophet and magician of Celtic tradition. He appears in the Arthurian legend

mer·lin (mə́:rlin) n. Falco aesalon, a small European falcon [A.F. merilun fr. O.F. esmerillon perh. fr. Gmc]

mer·lon (mə́:rlən) n. the high, solid part between two embrasures of a crenellated parapet [F. fr. Ital. merlone]

mer·maid (mə́:rmeid) n. a mythical sea creature with the tail of a fish and the head, arms and trunk of a woman [MERE (lake)+MAID]

mer·man (mə́:rmæn) pl. **mer·men** (mə́:rmen) n. a mythical sea creature with the tail of a fish and the head, arms and trunk of a man [MERE (lake)+MAN after MERMAID]

mer·o·blas·tic (merəblǽstik) adj. relating to ova that undergo only partial cleavage in development (cf. HOLOBLASTIC) [fr. Gk meros, part+blastos, germ]

merocode *MICROPROGRAMMING

mer·o·mic·tic (merəmíktik) adj. (envir.) with incomplete circulation, esp. of a lake

mer·o·my·o·sin (merəmáiəsən) n. (biochem.) one of two (one light, one heavy) myosins derived from the breaking down of protein structure by proteolysis

Mer·o·vin·gi·an (merəvíndʒi:ən) 1. n. one of the second dynasty of Frankish kings (448-751) 2. adj. pertaining to these kings [fr. F. Mérovingien ult. fr. Meroveus, the traditional founder of the dynasty]
—The Merovingian kingdom was expanded (late 5th c.) by Clovis to cover most of Gaul and S.W. Germany, but was divided (6th c.) between the warring kingdoms of Neustria and Austrasia. Dagobert I restored unity, but after his death (639) power passed to the mayors of the

palace, who deposed the last of the Merovingians (751), and ruled as the Carolingians

Mer·rill (mérəl), Frank Dow (1903–55), U.S. general. During the 2nd world war he organized and led 'Merrill's Marauders', an American volunteer group, specially trained in jungle warfare, which recaptured (1944) N. Burma from the Japanese

mer·ri·ly (mérili:) adv. in a merry way

'Mer·ri·mack' (mérəmæk) *MONITOR' AND 'MERRIMACK'

mer·ri·ment (mérimənt) n. laughter and gaiety

Mer·ritt (mérit), Wesley (1834–1910), U.S. general. As commander in chief (1898) of U.S. forces in the Philippines, he cooperated with Admiral George Dewey in the capture of Manila

mer·ry (méri:) comp. **mer·ri·er** superl. **mer·ri·est** adj. gay, cheerful and happy ‖ showing these qualities, a merry laugh **to make merry** (old-fash.) to be gay and festive [O.E. myrige]

Mer·ry-An·drew (méri:ǽndru:) n. a buffoon [MERRY+Andrew (proper name)]

mer·ry-go-round (méri:gouraund) n. a machine in a fair or amusement park, with a circular, revolving platform, colored canopy and models of horses etc. as seats on which children ride around to music ‖ a revolving device on which children ride in a playground

mer·ry·mak·er (méri:meikər) n. someone taking part in merrymaking

mer·ry·mak·ing (méri:meikiŋ) n. festivity, conviviality

mer·ry·thought (méri:θɔt) n. (Br., old-fash.) the wishbone

Mer·sey (mə́:rzi:) a river (70 miles long), flowing between Lancashire and Cheshire, England, into the Irish Sea. Its 16-mile estuary, navigable for ocean vessels, is linked to Manchester by ship canal. Ports: Liverpool, Birkenhead

me·sa (méisə) n. a high, steep-sided rock plateau, esp. in the southwest U.S.A. [Span.]

mé·sal·liance (meizæljás, meizáliəns) n. a marriage with someone socially inferior [F.]

Mes·bic (mézbik) n. (acronym) Minority Enterprise Small Business Investment Company, a corporation chartered for financing minority-owned business with U.S. federal guarantees

mes·cal (meskǽl) n. Lophophora Williamsii, a small cactus of Mexico and the southwest U.S.A., yielding mescaline ‖ a Mexican liquor distilled from several species of agave [Span. mezcal fr. Nahuatl mexcalli]

mescal button one of the dried tops of the mescal cactus

mes·ca·line (méskəli:n) n. a powerful drug made from mescal buttons. It has narcotic properties and causes hallucinations and convulsions

mesdames *MADAM, *MADAME

me·sem·bry·an·the·mum (mizembri:ǽnθəməm) n. a member of Mesembryanthemum, fam. Aicoaceae, a genus of S. African plants with fleshy leaves and commonly with pink or white flowers [Mod. L. fr. Gk mesēmbria, midday+anthenon, flower]

mes·en·ce·phal·ic (mezensəfǽlik) adj. of or pertaining to the midbrain [MESENCEPHALON]

mes·en·ceph·a·lon (mezenséfələn) n. the midbrain [Mod. L. fr. Gk mesos, middle+enkephalon, encephalon]

mes·en·chyme (mézenkaim) n. connective tissue of the mesoderm, giving rise to bone, tissues, cartilage, blood lymphatics etc. [Mod. L. fr. Gk mesos, middle+enchuma, infusion]

mes·en·ter·ic (mezentérik) adj. of the mesentery

mes·en·ter·i·tis (mezentəráitis) n. inflammation of the mesentery

mes·en·ter·y (mézenteri:) pl. **mes·en·ter·ies** (-i:z) n. the membrane covering the intestines and connecting them with the back of the abdominal cavity [fr. M. L. mesenterium fr. Gk mesos, middle+enteron, intestine]

mesh (meʃ) 1. n. one of the open spaces between the strands of a net ‖ (pl.) the strands of a net ‖ (pl.) something which captures and holds fast, the meshes of the law ‖ a network or net **in mesh** (of gears) engaged 2. v.t. to cause to become interlocked ‖ v.i. (of cogwheels etc.) to become interlocked [related to O.E. max, net and O.N. moskve]

Me·shed (meʃéd) an ancient trading center (pop. 670,180), and holy city for Shi'ite Moslems

in N.E. Iran. Manufactures: cotton, woolen and leather goods, carpets

mesh·work (méʃwə:rk) n. meshes, network

me·si·al (mí:zi:əl) adj. of, in or along the median vertical plane dividing an animal into equal right and left halves [fr. Gk mesos, middle]

me·sit·y·lene (misít'li:n) n. a colorless aromatic hydrocarbon, $C_6H_3(CH_3)_3$, found in coal tar and petroleum or synthesized from acetone [fr. mesityl, the hypothetical radical of acetone fr. Gk mesitēs, a mediator]

mes·mer·ic (mezmérik) adj. of or pertaining to mesmerism **mes·mer·i·cal·ly** adv.

mes·mer·ism (mézmərizəm) n. hypnotism ‖ the state of being hypnotized ‖ the theory of the uses of hypnotism **més·mer·ist** n. **més·mer·ize** pres. part. **mes·mer·iz·ing** past and past part. **mes·mer·ized** v.t. to induce the state of being hypnotized in (someone) [after F.A. Mesmer (1734-1815), Austrian physician who used the method]

mesne (mi:n) adj. (law) middle, intermediate, esp. with respect to time [F.]

mesne lord (hist.) someone holding land of a superior, and in turn acting as lord to his own tenants

Mes·o·a·mer·i·ca (mezouəmérikə, mesouəmérikə) (esp. archaeol.) Central America

mes·o·blast (mézəblæst, mésəblæst) n. (embry.) the mesoderm or middle germ layer of an embryo **mes·o·blás·tic** adj. [fr. Gk mesos, middle+blastos, germ]

mes·o·carp (mézəkarp, mésəkarp) n. (bot.) the middle layer of a pericarp when it is differentiated into three layers [fr. Gk mesos, middle+karpos, fruit]

mes·o·ce·phal·ic (mezousəfǽlik, mesousəfǽlik) adj. mesencephalic [fr. Gk mesos, middle+kephalē, head]

mes·o·derm (mézədə:rm, mésədə:rm) n. (embry.) the middle germ layer of a three-layered embryo. It is the source of bone, muscle and connective tissue in the adult **mes·o·dér·mal** adj. [fr. Gk mesos, middle+derma, skin]

mes·o·gas·tri·um (mezougǽstri:əm, mesougǽstri:əm) pl. **mes·o·gas·tri·a** (mezougǽstri:ə, mesougǽstri:ə) n. a mesentery connecting the stomach with the dorsal abdominal wall in an embryo ‖ the middle abdominal region [Mod. L. fr. Gk mesos, middle+gastēr, stomach]

Mes·o·lith·ic (mezəlíθik, mesəlíθik) adj. of the third period of the Stone Age, intermediate between the Paleolithic and the Neolithic. The Mesolithic period is characterized by the development of the bow and arrow and of pottery, and lasted (in Europe) c. 8000–c. 6000 B.C. [fr. Gk mesos, middle+lithos, stone]

mes·o·morph (mézəmɔrf, mésəmɔrf) n. a mesomorphic body or individual ‖ a mesophyte **mes·o·mór·phic** adj. (biol.) having the physique associated with a predominance in bodily development of organs and tissues derived from the mesodermal layer of the embryo (e.g. blood, bones, muscles, connective tissue), of an average or athletic type of body build (cf. ECTOMORPHIC, cf. ENDOMORPHIC) ‖ (esp. of crystalline substances) relating to or characterized by an intermediate physical state **mes·o·mór·phism**, **més·o·mor·phy** ns [fr. Gk mesos, middle+morphe, form]

me·son (mí:zɒn, mézɒn) n. one of a group of five known fundamental particles of intermediate rest mass, spin quantum number 0 and variable net charge. Some mesons are thought to be involved in the interaction of nucleons (*QUANTUM THEORY OF FIELDS) [Gk neuter of mesos, middle]

meson factory (particle phys.) device to accelerate particles, producing beams of mesons for the probing of atomic nuclei

mes·o·pause (mézəpɔz, mésəpɔz) n. the uppermost boundary of the mesosphere, occurring between 48 and 55 miles. It is the level at which a temperature minimum occurs

mes·o·pe·lag·ic (mezəpəlǽdʒik) adj. of ocean depths from 600 to 3,000 ft.

mes·o·phyll (mézəfil, mésəfil) n. the internal photosynthetic and supporting tissue of a leaf blade, through which branch the vascular system and accessory skeletal structures (*PALISADE PARENCHYMA, *SPONGY PARENCHYMA) [fr, Gk mesos, middle+phullon, leaf]

mes·o·phyte (mézəfait, mésəfait) n. a plant growing in medium moisture conditions **mes·o·phyt·ic** (mezəfítik, mesəfítik) adj. [fr. Gk mesos, middle+phuton, plant]

Mes·o·po·ta·mi·a (mẹsəpətéimi:ə) a region of S.W. Asia between the Tigris and Euphrates Rivers, now largely coextensive with Iraq

mes·o·scale analysis (mézəskeil) (envir.) the total pollution of an area from all sources

mes·o·scaph or **mes·o·scaphe** (mézəskæf) n. undersea exploration submarine at medium depths

mes·o·some (mézəsoum) n. (biochem.) the structure of a cell that causes the formation of new cell walls at each division

mes·o·sphere (mézəsfjər, mésəsfjər) n. the division of the earth's atmosphere extending from the stratopause to about 55 miles. In this region the temperature first increases rapidly with altitude and then decreases, the inversion occurring at about 30 miles above the earth's surface (*MESOPAUSE)

mes·o·the·li·o·ma (mezəθi:li:óumə) n. (med.) cancer on surface of lung and abdominal cavities

mes·o·the·li·um mẹzəθi:li:əm, mẹsəθi:li:əm) pl. **mes·o·the·li·a** (mẹzəθi:li:ə, mẹsəθi:li:ə) n. any epithelium of mesodermal origin (*MESODERM) [Mod. L. fr. Gk mesos, MIDDLE+EPITHELIUM]

mes·o·tho·rax (mẹzouθóræks, mẹsouθóræks, mẹzouθóuræks, mẹsouθóuræks), pl. **mes·o·tho·rax·es, mes·o·tho·ra·ces** (mẹzouθórəsi:z, mẹsouθórəsi:z, mẹzouθóurəsi:z, mẹsouθóurəsi:z) n. the middle segment of the thorax of an insect [fr. Gk mesos, middle+THORAX]

mes·o·tron (mézətrɒn, mósətron) n. a meson [Mod. L. fr. Gk mesos, middle+ELECTRON]

Mes·o·zo·ic (mẹzəzóuik, mẹsəzóuik) adj. (geol.) of the era between the Paleozoic and Cenozoic, characterized by reptiles, e.g. the dinosaurs, and by evergreen trees (*GEOLOGICAL TIME) the **Mesozoic** this era [fr. Gk mesos, middle+zoon, animal]

mes·quite, mes·quit (meskí:t) n. a plant of genus Prosopis, fam. Papilionaceae, esp. P. juliflora, a S.W. North American tree which yields a gum resembling gum arabic. Its sugary pods are used as food and fodder [Span. mezquite fr. Nahuatl mizquitl]

mess (mes) 1. n. a state of untidiness or disorder || an unpleasant, troubling, awkward situation or condition, his rash behavior got him into a mess || (mil.) a number of men or women, usually of the same rank, who have meals together || the place where they eat || the meals they eat together 2. v.t. to make a mess of || v.i. to take meals in a mess **to mess around** to amuse oneself without any clear program, he loves messing around in boats || (with 'with') to handle something inexpertly, stop messing around with that gun [fr. O.F. mes, portion of food]

mes·sage (mésidʒ) n. a written or spoken communication from one person to another || an inspired revelation, the message of an angel || ethical or spiritual teaching, a film with a message for modern youth || an official communication, a presidential message [F.]

Mes·sa·ger (mesæʒei), André Charles Prosper (1853–1929), French composer, esp. of comic operas

message switching center *DATA SWITCHING CENTER

mes·sage v. (substandard) to send a message to, e.g., messaging Moscow

Mes·sa·li·na (mẹsəláinə), Valeria (c. 25–48), Roman empress, wife of Claudius I, notorious for her debauchery

mes·sen·ger (mésəndʒər) n. a person who carries a message || a person employed by a firm to do errands || a courier [M.E. messager fr. F.]

messenger RNA (genetics) a form of RNA carrying genetic information from the nuclear DNA to the ribosome where the indicated protein is created also **MERNA** Cf TRANSFER DNA, TRANSFER RNA

Mes·se·ni·a (mẹsí:ni:ə) a fertile region in the S.W. Peloponnesus, Greece. The Messenians were subdued by the Spartans (8th–5th cc. B.C.) and made their helots. Epaminondas liberated them in 369 B.C.

Mes·si·aen (mesi:ā), Olivier (1908–), French composer. His music is marked by great rhythmical complexity and wide range of tone-color. He has been greatly influenced by Hindu music. He has written church music, songs, organ music and piano music as well as many works for the orchestra and has been a very influential teacher

Mes·si·ah (məsáiə) n. the leader and deliverer of the Jews, whose coming was prophesied in the Old Testament || (Christianity) Christ **mes·si·**

ah any leader and liberator of any oppressed people [M.E. Messie fr. F. fr. L. Messias fr. Gk fr. Aram. m'shihā, the anointed one]

Mes·si·an·ic (mẹsi:ǽnik) adj. pertaining to the Messiah **mes·si·an·ic** adj. pertaining to or characteristic of a messiah [fr. Mod. L. Messianicus]

mes·si·ly (mésili:) adv. in a messy manner

Mes·si·na (mesí:nə) a port (pop. 254,715) of N.E. Sicily, founded by the Greeks (c. 700 B.C.) on the Straits of Messina (20 miles long, 2–10 miles wide), which separate the island from mainland Italy. Industries: food processing, olive oil, shipbuilding, fishing. University (1549). In 1908 an earthquake destroyed the (now rebuilt) city, killing many thousands

mess·i·ness (mési:nis) n. the quality or state of being messy

mess kit a kit of cooking and eating utensils carried by soldiers or campers

mess·mate (mésmeit) n. someone who shares one's mess in the armed forces

Messrs (mésərz) pl. n. used as the plural of Mr, e.g. in a formal list or before the name of a professional or business firm, Messrs J. Jackson and Co. [F. messieurs, gentlemen]

mes·suage (méswidʒ) n. (law) a dwelling house, with its outbuildings and land [A.F.]

mes·sy (mési:) comp. **mess·i·er** superl. **mess·i·est** adj. untidy or disordered || (of a task, situation etc.) disagreeably confused, awkward and troublesome

mes·ti·zo (mestí:zou) pl. **mes·ti·zos, mes·ti·zoes** n. a person of mixed parentage, esp. one of Spanish or Portuguese and American Indian descent [Span. mestizo and Port. mestico]

mes·tra·nol [$C_{21}H_{26}O_2$] (méstrənɒl) n. (chem.) synthetic estrogen used in oral contraceptives

Meš·tro·vić (méʒtrəvitʃ), Ivan (1883–1962), Yugoslav sculptor, naturalized American. His works include portraits and religious and legendary figures

met past and past part. of MEET

Me·ta (métə) a river (c. 685 miles long) rising in W. central Colombia, flowing to form a part of the Colombia-Venezuelan boundary, and emptying into the Orinoco River

meta- combining form meaning "beyond the usual," used principally in technical terminology, e.g., metaculture, metagalaxy, metaprogram, metavolcanic Cf MACRO-, MAXI-, MEGA-, MICRO-, MINI-

met·a·bol·ic (mẹtəbólik) adj. of, involving, characterized by, or caused by metabolism [fr. Gk metabolikos, changeable]

me·tab·o·lism (mətǽbəlizəm) n. the sum total of the chemical processes of living organisms, which result in growth, the production of energy and the maintenance of the vital functions, and in which the waste products of these processes are rendered harmless (*ANABOLISM, *KATABOLISM) **me·táb·o·lite** n. a substance produced in metabolism || a substance essential to a metabolic change **me·táb·o·lize** pres. part. **me·tab·o·liz·ing** past and past part. **me·tab·o·lized** v.t. and i. to change by metabolism [fr. Gk metabolē, change]

met·a·car·pal (mẹtəkárp'l) 1. adj. of or pertaining to the metacarpus 2. n. a metacarpal bone

met·a·car·pus (mẹtəkárpəs) n. the part of the hand, esp. the bones, between the wrist and the fingers || the corresponding part in animals [Mod. L. fr. Gk metakarpion]

met·a·cen·tric (mẹtəséntrik) adj. (cytol.) of the condition in which the spindle attachment of the chromosome controlling cell division is near the middle

me·tage (mí:tidʒ) n. the official measuring of weights amd loads in transport || the charge made for doing this [METE V.]

met·a·gen·e·sis (mẹtədʒénisis) n. alternation of sexual and asexual generations **met·a·ge·net·ic** (mẹtədʒənétik) adj. [Mod. L. fr. Gk meta, through+genesis, origin]

met·a·his·to·ry (mẹtəhístəri:) n. the philosophy of history designed (1) to develop laws of historical development, or (2) to analyze history critically —**metahistorian** n.

met·al (mét'l) 1. n. an element, the structure of whose atoms is such that these readily lose electrons to form positively charged ions. Metals usually have luster and a high specific gravity, and are malleable, ductile and good conductors of heat and electricity || a compound or alloy of such an element (*PERIODIC TABLE) || (Br.) broken stone for surfacing roads etc. || (Br., pl.) the rails of a railroad || molten glass || (heraldry) either of the tinctures argent || (printing) type

metal 2. v.t. pres. part. **met·al·ing**, esp. Br. **met·al·ling** past and past part. **met·aled**, esp. Br. **met·alled** to supply or cover with metal || (Br.) to mend(a road) with metal (broken stone) [O.F. metal, metail fr. L. fr. Gk metallon, mine]

me·tal·lic (mətǽlik) adj. made of, like or having the properties of a metal **me·tál·li·cal·ly** adv. [fr. L. metallicus]

met·al·lid·ing (mét'laidən) n. (metallurgy) process of creating alloys on outer layers of a metal substance by diffusing one metal to the surface of another through high-temperature electrolysis, for the purpose of strengthening the surface of the metal —**metallide** v.

met·al·lif·er·ous (mẹt'lífərəs) adj. containing, producing or yielding metal [fr. L. metallifer]

met·al·li·za·tion, met·al·i·za·tion (mẹt'lizéiʃən) n. the process of metallizing

met·al·lize, met·al·ize (mét'laiz) pres. part. **met·al·liz·ing, met·al·iz·ing** past and past part. **met·al·lized, met·al·ized** v.t. to make metallic || to coat or impregnate with metal

met·al·log·ra·phy (mẹt'lógrəfi:) n. the study of the structure and properties of metals and alloys [fr. Mod. L. metallographia fr. Gk]

met·al·loid (mét'loid) 1. adj. resembling a metal || of, relating to or designating a metalloid 2. n. an element (e.g. arsenic, tellurium) having certain properties intermediate between those characteristic of metals and those characteristic of nonmetals (*SEMICONDUCTOR) || a nonmetal which can be combined with a metal to form an alloy

met·al·lur·gic (mẹt'lɔ́:rdʒik) adj. metallurgical **met·al·lúr·gi·cal** adj. of or pertaining to metallurgy

met·al·lur·gist (mét'lɔ:rdʒist, esp. Br. mitǽlə:rdʒist) n. a specialist in metallurgy

met·al·lur·gy (mét'lɔ:rdʒi:, esp. Br. mitǽlə:rdʒi:) n. the science of extracting metals from their ores, of freeing them from impurities (*REFINING), of studying their physical and chemical suitability for particulal uses etc. [fr. Mod. L. metallurgia fr. Gk]

metal point wheel a metal daisy-wheel print element used in word processors

met·al·work (mét'lwə:rk) n. the craft of working metal || things made out of metal **mét·al·work·er** n. **mét·al·work·ing**

met·a·mer (métəmər) n. (chem.) an isomeric compound having the same percentage composition and molecular weight as another, but different chemical properties

met·a·mere (métəmiər) n. (zool.) one of the body segments of an animal showing metamerism, e.g. the caterpillar, earthworm etc.

met·a·mer·ic (mẹtəmérik) adj. (biol. and chem.) showing metamerism

met·am·er·ism (mətǽmərizəm) n. (chem.) isomerism || (biol.) the condition of a body divided into more or less similar segments [fr. Gk meta, with+meros, part]

met·a·mor·phic (mẹtəmórfik) adj. causing or resulting from metamorphosis [fr. Gk meta, changed in+morphē, shape after METAMORPHOSIS]

metamorphic rock igneous rock or sedimentary rock which underwent a complete transformation in character and appearance due to heat, pressure or the action of wind and water

met·a·mor·phism (mẹtəmórfizəm) n. metamorphosis || (geol.) transformation in the character of igneous or sedimentary rock, resulting in more compact metamorphic rock [METAMORPHIC]

met·a·mor·phose (mẹtəmórfouz, mẹtəmórfous) pres. part. **met·a·mor·phos·ing** past and past part. **met·a·mor·phosed** v.t. to change into a different physical form || to change the appearance or character of || v.i. to undergo metamorphosis [F. métamorphoser]

met·a·mor·pho·sis (mẹtəmórfəsis) pl. **met·a·mor·pho·ses** (mẹtəmórfəsi:z) n. a marked change of form and structure undergone by an animal from embryo to adult stage, e.g. in insects, amphibians, echinoderms etc. || a transformation of one structure into another, e.g. stamens into petals || a striking change of appearance, character, form etc. [L. fr. Gk metamorphōsis, transformation]

met·a·phase (métəfeiz) n. the second stage in mitosis and meiosis in which the doubled chromosomes line up on an equatorial plane between the poles of the spindle and begin to separate (*PROPHASE, *ANAPHASE, *TELOPHASE) [fr. Gk meta, later+PHASE]

met·a·phor (métəfər, métəfər) n. a figure of speech in which a name or quality is attributed to something to which it is not literally applicable, e.g. 'an icy glance', 'nerves of steel' (cf. SIMILE) **met·a·phor·ic** (mĕtəfórik, mĕtəfórik), **met·a·phór·i·cal** adjs [F. métaphore fr. L. fr. Gk]

met·a·phys·i·cal (mĕtəfízik'l) **1.** adj. of or pertaining to a school of 17th-c. English poets, including Donne, Herbert, Vaughan, Crashaw, who blended emotion with intellectual ingenuity, and made much use of the conceit **2.** n. a poet of this school

met·a·phy·si·cian (mĕtəfizíʃən) n. a person schooled in metaphysics [F. métaphysicien]

me·ta·phys·ics (mĕtəfíziks) n. the branch of philosophy dealing with the first principles of things. It includes ontology and cosmology [older metaphysic fr. M.L. metaphysica fr. Gk ta metaphusika, (the books of Aristotle) after the 'Physics']

met·a·plasm (métəplæzəm) n. (biol.) lifeless material derived from protoplasm **met·a·plás·mic** adj. [fr. Gk meta, after+PROTOPLASM]

met·a·psy·chol·o·gy (mĕtəsaikólədʒi:) n. the study of the philosophical aspects of psychology and of its role in the physical universe [fr. Gk meta, with+PSYCHOLOGY]

met·a·ram·in·ol [$C_9H_{13}NO_2$] (metəræminəl) n. (pharm.) sympathomimetic drug used to shrink mucosa; marketed as Aramine or Pressonel

met·a·so·ma·tism (mĕtəsóumətizəm) n. metasomatosis [fr. Gk meta, changed by+Gk sōma, body]

met·a·so·ma·to·sis (mĕtəsoumətóusis) n. (geol.) an extension of the process of metamorphism, in which the chemical composition of rocks undergoes partial change [Mod. L. fr. Gk meta, changed in+sōma, body]

met·a·sta·ble (métəstéib'l) adj. (phys., chem., e.g. of a supercooled liquid) precariously stable [fr. Gk meta, after+STABLE]

Me·ta·sta·sio (metəstázjɔ), (Pietro Trapassi, 1698–1782), Italian poet and author of many librettos

me·tas·ta·sis (mətǽstəsis) pl. **me·tas·ta·ses** (mətǽstəsi:z) n. the spreading of disease from one part of the body to another, e.g. in cancer ‖ an instance of this **me·tás·ta·size** pres. part. **met·a·siz·ing** past and past part. **met·a·sta·sized** v.i. to spread by metastasis [L.L. fr. Gk=transition]

met·a·tar·sal (mĕtətárs'l) adj. of or pertaining to the metatarsus

met·a·tar·sus (mĕtətársəs) pl. **met·a·tar·si** (mĕtətársai) n. the part of the human foot, esp. the bones, between the ankle and toes ‖ the corresponding part in animals [Mod. L. fr. Gk meta, behind+tarsos, flat of the foot]

me·tath·e·sis (mətǽθisis) pl. **me·tath·e·ses** (mətǽθisi:z) n. (gram.) the interchange of position between sounds in a word ‖ (chem.) double decomposition **met·a·thet·i·cal** (mĕtəθétik'l) adj. [fr. L.L. Gk=transposition]

met·a·tho·rax (mĕtəθóræks, metəθóuræks) pl. **met·a·tho·rax·es, met·a·tho·ra·ces** (mĕtəθórəsi:z, metəθóurəsi:z) n. the rear segment of the thorax of an insect [Mod. L. fr. Gk meta, behind+THORAX]

Me·tau·rus (mitɔ́rəs) a river of central Italy, scene of Rome's decisive victory (207 B.C.) over Hasdrubal in the 2nd Punic War

Me·tax·as (mitǽksəs), Ioannis (1871–1941), Greek general. He was dictator of Greece (1936–41) and defeated (1940) the Italians in their invasion of Greece

met·a·zo·an (mĕtəzóuən) **1.** n. any member of the order Metazoa, which includes all animal organisms of more than one cell, except usually sponges (Parazoa) **2.** adj. pertaining to the order Metazoa or to a metazoan **met·a·zó·ic** adj. [fr. Gk meta, later+zōon, animal]

mete (mi:t) pres. part. **met·ing** past and past part. **met·ed** v.t. (with 'out') to distribute, apportion, deal out, to mete out punishment [O.E. metan, to measure]

Me·tel·lus (mətéləs), Lucius Caecilius (d. c. 221 B.C.), Roman consul (251 B.C.). He defeated the Carthaginian attack on Sicily in the 1st Punic War

Metellus Mac·e·don·i·cus (mæsidónikəs), Quintus Caecilius (d. 115 B.C.), Roman praetor (148 B.C.). He conquered Macedonia (146 B.C.)

Metellus Nu·mid·i·cus (nu:mídikəs, nju:mídikəs), Quintus Caecilius (d. c. 91 B.C.), Roman consul (109 B.C.) and commander in the war against Jugurtha

Metellus Scip·i·o (sípi:ou), Quintus Caecilius (d. 46 B.C.), Roman consul (52 B.C.). An ally of Pompey, he fought unsuccessfully against Julius Caesar

met·em·psy·cho·sis (mĕtempsikóusis, mĕtemsikóusis) pl. **met·em·psy·cho·ses** (mĕtempsikóusi:z, mĕtemsikóusi:z) n. transmigration of souls ‖ an instance of this [L.L. fr. Gk metempsuchōsis]

me·te·or (mí:ti:ər) n. a solid body from outer space, which glows with the heat generated by friction as it enters the earth's atmosphere [fr. Mod. L. meteorum fr. Gk meteōra pl., astronomical phenomena]

me·te·or·ic (mi:ti:órik, mi:ti:órik) adj. of or pertaining to meteors ‖ brilliant and rapid, a meteoric rise to fame ‖ of, relating to or originating in the earth's atmosphere **me·te·ór·i·cal·ly** adv. [fr. M.L. meteoricus, of the high atmosphere, and fr. METEOR]

me·te·or·ite (mí:ti:ərait) n. a meteor which reaches the surface of the earth in solid form, either in one piece or in fragments

me·te·or·oid (mí:ti:ərɔid) n. a meteor, whether within or outside the earth's atmosphere

me·te·or·oi·dal (mi:ti:ərɔid'l) adj. of a meteoroid

me·te·or·o·log·ic (mi:ti:ərəlódʒik) adj. meteorological **me·te·or·o·lóg·i·cal** of or pertaining to meteorology

me·te·or·ol·o·gist (mi:ti:ərólədʒist) n. a specialist in meteorology [fr. Gk meteōrologos]

me·te·or·ol·o·gy (mi:ti:ərólədʒi:) n. the study of conditions in the earth's atmosphere, esp. for making weather forecasts ‖ the general weather conditions of a region [fr. Gk meteōrologia fr. meteōra, atmospheric phenomena+logos, word]

me·te·o·sat (mí:ti:əsæt) n. meteorological satellite made by Aerospatiale of France and launched by Cosmos (consortium of France, Italy, and Germany) in 1977, as part of GARP (worldwide Global Atmospheric Research Program)

me·te·pa [$C_9H_{18}N_3OP$] (méti:pə) n. (chem.) an insect sterilizing agent

me·ter (mí:tər) **1.** n. an instrument for measuring and recording the amount of flow of something (e.g. gas) or the amount of duration of use of something **2.** v.t. to measure with a meter ‖ (esp. Am.) to stamp (mail) with a postage meter [prob. fr. METE]

me·ter, esp. Br. **me·tre** (mí:tər) n. (abbr. m.) the fundamental unit of length in the metric system, defined as the length measured in vacuo of 1,650,763.73 wavelengths of the light emitted by krypton (isotope 86) in the transition $2P_{10}$-$^5D_5$. (This definition, officially adopted by the International Conference on Weights and Measures in 1960, did not change the length of the meter, but only the standard by which it is defined.) 1m.=about 39.37 ins [fr. F. mètre fr. Gk metron, measure]

meter, esp. Br. **metre** n. the rhythmic recurrence of patterns within a line of poetry or in lines of poetry, based e.g. on stress or on number of syllables or on a combination of these or on number of feet ‖ musical rhythm [O.E. meter fr. L. metrum fr. Gk metron, measure]

meter candle *LUX

meter-kilogram-second system, Br. **metre-kilogram-second system** (abbr. mks) a metric system of units based on the meter, kilogram and second as the units of length, mass and time

meter maid attendant who oversees meter parking, issuing summonses for violations of parking violations

methadone (méθədoun) a synthetic narcotic used to relieve pain and to detoxify drug addicts. First used in Germany during the 2nd world war as a substitute for morphine, it reduces chronic pain. Because its properties and effects imitate heroin, it has become a popular treatment for gradual heroin withdrawal

meth·am·phet·a·mine [$C_{10}H_{15}N$] (mĕθæmfétəmi:n) n. (pharm.) a central nervous system stimulant similar to amphetamine, used in treating narcolepsy, Parkinson's disease, alcoholism, depression, and obesity, with many side effects; marketed under many trade names also desoxyphedrine, methylamphetamine

meth·ane (méθein) n. an odorless, colorless, inflammable hydrocarbon, CH_4, which forms explosive mixtures with air. It results from the decay of organic matter (*MARSH GAS) and is found in natural gas and in coal mines (*FIRE-

DAMP). It is an important constituent of coal gas. It is the first of the alkanes [METHYL]

methane sulfomate [CH_3SO_3H] (chem.) a salt or ester of methane sulfonic acid also mesylate

me·than·o·gens (meθǽnədʒenz) n. (biol.) methane-producing organisms believed to have evolved more than 3.5 billion years ago also archaebacteria

meth·a·nol (méθənol) n. methyl alcohol, a colorless poisonous liquid, CH_3 OH, originally obtained from wood, and now made synthetically. It is used as a solvent, in denaturing ethyl alcohol, and in the manufacture of formaldehyde etc. [METHANE]

meth·a·pyr·i·lene [$C_{14}H_{19}N_3S$] (meθəpírili:n) n. (pharm.) antihistamine ingredient in many sleeping pills banned by U.S. Food and Drug Administration in 1979 as cancer-causing in animals also thenylpyramine

me·tha·qua·lone [$C_{16}H_{14}N_2O$] (meθákwəloun) n. (pharm.) non-barbituate sedative and hypnotic used as a tranquilizer; marketed as Quaalude, Sopor, and Parest

meth·i·cil·lin [$C_{17}H_{20}N_2O_6S$] (meθəsílən) n. (pharm.) synthetic penicillin, used esp. against penicillin-resistant staphylococci; marketed as Celbenin and Staphcillin

meth·od (méθəd) n. a way of doing something ‖ a procedure for doing something ‖ orderliness in doing, planning etc., to lack method ‖ an orderly arrangement or system **me·thod·i·cal** (məθódik'l) adj. [fr. L. fr. Gk methodos fr. meta, after+hodos, way]

method or **method acting** school of acting based in identifying with the feelings of the character portrayed, so that the actor "becomes" the character; devised by Russian actor Konstantin Stanislavski

Meth·od·ism (méθədizəm) n. the tenets and organization of several Protestant denominations which sprang from the revival within the Church of England led by John and Charles Wesley from 1729. Theologically, Methodism is Arminian in sympathy. Its organization depends on lay preachers, on the weekly meeting, and on the annual conference which is its supreme authority. It spread rapidly after 1739 in England and North America and was formally separated from the Church of England (1791). It has about 13½ million members, about two thirds being in the U.S.A.

Meth·od·ist (méθədist) **1.** n. an adherent of Methodism **2.** adj. pertaining or belonging to Methodism

Methodius, St *CYRIL AND METHODIUS

meth·od·ize (méθədaiz) pres. part. **meth·od·iz·ing** past and past part. **meth·od·ized** v.t. to make orderly, classify or systematize

meth·od·ol·o·gy (meθədólədʒi:) pl. **meth·od·ol·o·gies** n. a branch of philosophy dealing with the science of method or procedure ‖ a system of methods and rules applied in a science **meth·od·o·log·i·cal** (meθəd'lódʒik'l) adj. [fr. Mod. L. methodologia or F. méthodologie]

me·thol·y·flu·rane [$C_3N_4Cl_2F_2O$] (meθblifijú:rein) n. (pharm.) a nonexplosive general anesthetic; marketed as Penthrane

meth·o·trex·ate [$C_{20}H_{22}N_8O_5$] (meθətrékseit) n. (pharm.) toxic drug used to combat folic acid in treatment of psoriasis and leukemia also amethropterin

Meth·u·en Treaty (méθju:ən) a commercial agreement (1703) between Portugal and England, by which England conceded a preferential tariff on Portuguese wines and Portugal allowed the import of English woolens. It was an economic link between the two countries until 1835 and helped to popularize the drinking of port in England. The agreement was negotiated by John Methuen (c. 1650–1706), British ambassador to Portugal

Me·thu·se·lah (məθú:zələ, məθjú:zələ) Hebrew patriarch, Noah's grandfather, who lived 969 years (Genesis v, 27). He is taken as the standard of phenomenal longevity

meth·yl (méθəl) n. the organic alkyl radical CH_3, of methanol etc. [F. méthyle, G. methyl ult. fr. Gk methu, wine+hule, wood]

methyl acetate a volatile, combustible, fragrant ester, CH_3COOCH_3, used chiefly as a solvent

methyl alcohol methanol

meth·yl·a·pro·pine bromide [$C_{17}H_{23}NO_3$-CH_3Br] (meθələpróupi:n) n. (pharm.) dosage form of atropine that depresses the nervous system; marketed as Metropine also atropine methylbromide

---

meth·yl·ase (méθəleis) n. (chem.) a catalytic enzyme that helps introduce methyl into a compound —**methalate** v.

meth·yl·ate (méθəleit) pres. part. **meth·yl·at·ing** past and past part. **meth·yl·at·ed** v.t. to add methanol to

methylated spirit ethyl alcohol denatured with methanol

meth·yl·do·pa [$C_{10}H_{13}NO_4$] (meθəldóupə) n. (pharm.) drug used to reduce high blood pressure; marketed as Aldomet

meth·yl·ene (méθəli:n) n. a bivalent hydrocarbon radical, CH_2 found only in compounds [fr. F. méthylène]

methylene blue a soluble, intensely blue dye, used in medicine and as a biological stain

meth·yl·mer·cu·ry [CH_3HgCN] (meθəlmé:rkjə ri:) n. (chem.) highly toxic fungicide and pesticide used to treat seeds also nitrile, methylmercury cyanide

meth·yl·par·a·thi·on [$C_8H_{10}NO_5PS$] (meθəlpɛərəθáiən) n. (chem.) highly toxic synthetic organophosphate insecticide used to combat boll weevils, rice bugs, cutworms, and leafhoppers

meth·yl·phen·i·date [$C_{14}H_{19}NO_2$] (meθəlfénədeit) n. (pharm.) a central nervous system stimulant used to increase alertness and relieve depression; marketed as Ritalin

meth·yl·pred·ni·so·lone [$C_{22}H_{30}O_5$] (meθəlprednísəloun) n. (pharm.) an anti-inflammatory hormone; marketed as Medrol

meth·y·ser·gide [$C_{21}H_{27}N_3O_2$] (meθəsé:rdʒaid) n. (pharm.) drug used to relieve vascular headaches; marketed as Sansert

me·tic·u·lous (mətíkjuləs) adj. paying or showing scrupulous attention to detail [fr. L. meticulosus fr. metus, fear]

mé·tier (méitjei) n. one's profession or vocation or proper work [F.]

mé·tis, Br. **me·tis** (meití:s) n. someone of mixed racial ancestry, esp. part French and part American Indian [F. métis]

met·o·clo·pra·mide [$C_{14}H_{22}ClN_2O_2$] (metəklóuprəmaid) n. relaxant for upper GI tract, used to facilitate diagnostic procedures, marketed as Reglan

Me·tol (mí:tɔl) n. a weak reducing agent, used as a developer of photographic film [G., trademark]

Me·ton·ic cycle (mətónik) a period of 19 years covering all the phases of the moon, after which the new moons occur again on the same cycle of dates [fr. Mod. L. Metonicus after Meton (5th c. B.C) Athenian astronomer]

met·o·nym (métənim) n. a word used in metonymy [fr. assumed Gk metónymia]

met·o·nym·i·cal (metənímik'l) adj. of, characterized by or using metonymy

me·ton·y·my (mətónəmi) n. a figure of speech characterized by the use of the name of one thing in place of the name of something that it symbolizes, e.g. 'crown' for 'king' [fr. L.L. metonymia fr. Gk metōnumia, change of name]

"me-too" drug (mí:tú:) a drug that is identical, similar, or closely related to a drug produced for which a new drug application has been approved, the sale of which is permitted under the same approval procedure

met·o·pe (métəpi:, métoup) n. (archit.) the rectangular space between two triglyphs of a Doric frieze [fr. L. metopa fr. Gk metopē fr. meta, between+opai, holes]

me·top·ic (mətópik) adj. (anat.) pertaining to the forehead [fr. Gk metōpon, forehead]

metre *METER

met·ric (métrik) adj. pertaining to the meter (unit of length) [fr. F. métrique]

met·ri·cal (métrik'l) adj. pertaining to or composed in meter ‖ pertaining to measurement [fr. L.L. metricus fr. Gk metrikos, relating to measurement, relating to poetic meter]

met·ri·cate (métrəkeit) or **met·ri·fi·cate** (mətrífəkeit) v. (Br.) to adopt the metric system — **metrification** n. conversion to the metric system —**metrify** v.

metric centner a unit of weight equaling 100 kg. or 220.46 lbs (cf. HUNDREDWEIGHT)

metric system a decimal system of measurement of length (incl. area and volume) and mass (incl. weight). The unit of mass is the kilogram, the unit of length is the meter, and occasionally a distinction is made between volume, measured in units based upon the cubic meter, and capacity, based upon the liter

metric ton a metric mass unit equal to 1,000 kg. (=2,204.6 lbs)

met·ro (métrou) n. 1. metropolitan regional government, including suburbs 2. Washington, D.C. subway—**metro** adj.

Met·ro·lin·er (métroulainər) n. Amtrak express train, esp. from Boston to Washington, D.C.

met·ro·log·i·cal (metrəlódʒik'l) adj. of or relating to metrology

me·trol·o·gy (mətrólədʒi:) pl. **me·trol·o·gies** n. the science of weights and measures ‖ a system of weights and measures [fr. Gk metron, measure+logos, word]

me·tro·ni·da·zole [$C_6H_9N_3O_3$] (metrənáidəzoul) n. (pharm.) drug effective against Trichomonas vaginalis and Entameba histolytica; marketed as Flagyl

met·ro·nome (métrənoum) n. a clockwork device with a moving, audible indicator, which can be regulated to different speeds, used esp. to mark musical time **met·ro·nom·ic** (metrənómik) adj. [fr. Gk metron, measure+nomos, law]

met·ro·nym·ic (metrənímik) 1. adj. (of a name) derived from the name of a mother or of a female ancestor 2. n. a metronymic name [fr. Gk mētrōnumikos fr. mētēr, mother+onuma, onoma, name]

me·trop·o·lis (mətrópəlis) n. the chief city of a country or region ‖ any busy center of commerce etc. ‖ the see of a metropolitan bishop [L. fr. Gk mētropolis fr. mētēr, mother+polis, city]

met·ro·pol·i·tan (metrəpólitən) 1. adj. of, pertaining to or characteristic of a metropolis ‖ pertaining to a metropolitan 2. n. (Orthodox Eastern Church) a head of an ecclesiastical province, ranking between archbishop and patriarch ‖ (Western Church) an archbishop [fr. L.L. metropolitanus fr. Gk]

Metropolitan Museum of Art *NEW YORK

Metropolitan Opera Company an operatic organization in New York, originally private. Its first production (1833) was Gounod's 'Faust'. It became (1940) the publicly sponsored Metropolitan Opera Association, Inc.

me·trop·o·lol [$C_{15}H_{25}NO_3$] (metrópələl) n. (pharm.) beta-blocking agent used to reduce high blood pressure; marketed as Lopressor

me·tror·rha·gi·a (mi:trəréidʒiːə) n. bleeding from the womb occurring between menstrual periods [Mod. L. fr. Gk mētra, uterus+-rhagia, a breaking forth]

Met·ter·nich (métərnix), Clemens Werzel Lothar, Prince von (1773–1859), Austrian statesman. He was Austrian ambassador in Paris (1806–9), then minister of foreign affairs (1809–48). He is credited with arranging the marriage between Napoleon and Marie-Louise of Austria (1810). He helped to form the Quadruple Alliance against Napoleon (1814), and dominated the Congress of Vienna (1815). His attempts to repress liberalism (*KARLSBAD DECREES) dominated Europe until his fall from power (1848)

Met·they (metei), André (1871–1920), French potter. Rouault, Bonnard, Derain, Vlaminck and Redon all decorated pots made by him

met·tle (mét'l) n. (rhet.) spirit, courage or fortitude **on one's mettle** determined to do one's best in response to some challenge **met·tle·some** adj. (esp. of a horse) spirited [var. of METAL]

me·tyr·a·pone [$C_{14}H_{14}N_2O$] (metéərəpoun) n. (pharm.) drug used to diagnose pituitary function by blocking creation of steroids; marketed as Metopirdone

Metz (mets) a port (pop. 117,199) of Moselle department, France, on the Moselle. Industries: metallurgy, engineering, food processing, brewing. Cathedral (13th–16th cc.)

Meung, Jean de *JEAN DE MEUNG

Meurthe-et-Mo·selle (mə:rtɛimɔzel) a department (area 2,036 sq. miles, pop. 722,600) in N.E. France (*LORRAINE). Chief town: Nancy

Meuse (mə:z) a department (area 2,408 sq. miles, pop. 203,900) in N.E. France (*CHAMPAGNE, *LORRAINE). Chief town: Bar-le-Duc

Meuse (Du. and Flem. Maas) a navigable river (575 miles long) rising in N. France, flowing through E. Belgium and the Netherlands, then curving west to the Rhine delta (North Sea). Chief port: Liège

MEV, MeV, mev (MEV) million electron-volts

mew (mju:) 1. v.i. (of a cat or gull) to utter its cry 2. n. the sound made by a cat or a gull [imit.]

mew 1. v.t. to put (a hawk) in a cage ‖ v.i. (of a hawk) to molt 2. n. a cage for hawks and falcons, esp. while they are molting [F. muer, to molt]

mew n. a sea mew [O.E. mæw]

mewl, mule (mju:l) pres. part. **mewl·ing, muling** past and past part. **mewled, muled** v.i. to whimper or cry ‖ (of a cat or gull) to mew [imit.]

mews (mju:z) n. (orig. pl. now construed as sing., esp. Br.) stables built around an open yard or in a row, with living accommodation above [MEW (a hawk's cage), from the Royal Mews, London, where royal hawks were mewed]

Mex. Mexico

Mex·ca·la (meskála) *BALSAS, RÍO DE LAS

Mex·i·cal·i (meksikǽli; mehi:káli:) a border town (pop. 349,493) of N.W. Mexico, center of a rich agricultural district (cotton, vines, citrus fruit)

Mex·i·can (méksikən) 1. adj. of or pertaining to Mexico, its inhabitants, culture etc. 2. n. a native or inhabitant of Mexico ‖ the Nahuatl language ‖ the Spanish language as spoken in Mexico

Mexican hairless a small dog of a breed found in Mexico, with practically no hair

Mexican Plateau *ANAHUAC

Mexican War a war (1846–8) between the U.S.A. and Mexico, caused mainly by the American annexation of Texas (1845). The U.S.A. won after two years of hard fighting. The war was ended by the Treaty of Guadalupe Hidalgo (1848)

Mex·i·co (méksikou) a federal republic (area 763,944 sq. miles, pop. 67,382,581) of North America. Capital: Mexico City. People: 60% mestizo, 30% Indian (esp. Aztec, Mixtec and Maya), 10% European, small African and Chinese minorities. Languages: Spanish and 31 Indian language groups. Religion: 95% Roman Catholic, 3% Protestant, small Jewish and Animist minorities. Half the land is over 3,000 ft. The entire central section is a plateau (the Anahuac, 3,600 ft at the northern border, 8,000 ft in the south), surrounded on three sides by mountains: the Eastern, Western, and Southern Sierra Madre. The plateau, desert in the north, contains lakes, swamps, and large basins (incl. the Valley of Mexico, 7,400 ft, around Mexico City) in the center and is covered with tropical forest in the south. A belt of volcanoes (Citlaltepetl, 18,843 ft) crosses it near the center. Southeast of the plateau, across the Isthmus of Tehuantepec, are the Chiapas Highlands, rising to over 9,000 ft, largely jungle. Lower California is also mountainous. The only lowland regions, except for river valleys, are narrow coastal plains, the Sonora desert in the far northwest, and Yucatán peninsula (jungle). Average temperatures (F.): below 3,000 ft, 70°–80°, 3,000–6,000 ft, 55°–75°, above 6,000 ft, 54°–65°. Rainfall: 44 ins along the coasts, 24 ins on the plateau, 100 ins near the southern Gulf coast (Chiapas and Yucatán), 5 ins in the Sonora desert. About 25% of the land is potentially arable but only about 14% is farmed, owing to lack of irrigation (40% of cultivated land is irrigated). Chief occupation: subsistence agriculture. Crops: corn, wheat, sugarcane, coffee, cotton, vegetables, rice, beans, oranges, sisal, alfalfa, sesame, guayule. Livestock: cattle, goats, hogs, poultry, sheep, horses, donkeys, mules. Forest products: lumber, chicle, pitch, resins, turpentine, gums. Mineral resources: silver (20% of world production), copper, lead, zinc, manganese, sulfur, oil and natural gas (a leading world producer), iron ore, coal, gold, antimony, graphite, bismuth, mercury, arsenic, cadmium, tin, tungsten. Manufactures and industries: iron and steel, oil refining, textiles, rubber, foodstuffs, chemicals, plastics, agricultural machinery, tourism, fishing, cigars, paper, glass. Exports: silver, cotton, coffee, cattle, sugar, shrimps, sulfur, oil, lead, zinc, copper, tomatoes. Imports: vehicles, machinery, chemicals, oil, iron and steel, rubber, newsprint, wool, corn. Chief ports: Veracruz, Tampico. There are 26 universities, the oldest being Mexico City (1552). Monetary unit: peso (100 centavos). HISTORY. Mexico saw the growth of several Indian civilizations, including the Maya, the Toltec and the Aztec. It was conquered (1519–25) by the Spaniards under Cortés, and became one of the richest Spanish colonies. Hidalgo y Costilla began (1810) the revolt against Spanish rule, which culminated in the short-lived empire (1822–3) of Iturbide, and the republic proclaimed (1823) by Santa Anna. The U.S.A. annexed Texas (1845) and, after the Mexican War (1846–8), California and New Mexico. Santa Anna was overthrown (1855), and liberal reforms were instituted under the influence of Juárez, but civil war broke out between conservatives and liberals (1858–61). The French intervened, and attempted to impose an empire (1864–7) under Maximilian, after which Juárez regained control. Some economic progress was made under the presidency of Diaz, but he was overthrown (1911) and a period of civil struggle and political instability followed. A more liberal constitution was introduced (1917), and was followed by social reforms. Under Lázaro Cárdenas (1934–40), Mexico nationalized (1938) all foreign-owned oil fields. In 1942, following the sinking of Mexican tankers, Mexico declared war on the Axis. After the 2nd world war, agriculture, industry and communications were all greatly improved, as befitted a nation whose population increased over 130% between 1920 and 1960. The official government revolutionary party (PRI) maintained popular support. Ruiz Cortines (president 1952–8) introduced (1954) women's suffrage. López Mateos (president 1958–64) and Díaz Ordaz (president 1964–70) concentrated on land reform. Luis Echeverria Álvarez (president 1970–6) had a term marked by economic instability and political unrest. He was followed by José López Portillo (1976–82) whose term saw economic growth and prosperity due to the exploitation of newly-discovered oil reserves. By 1982, however, when Miguel de la Madrid Hurtado became president, the decline in oil prices had left the country near economic collapse. Austerity measures and restructuring of Mexico's foreign debt brought some relief, but the economy was further strained by severe earthquakes (1985) that devastated the capital and killed thousands. Income from tourism immediately declined, adding to Mexico's economic woes. The problem of illegal immigrants entering the U.S. seeking employment strained Mexico-U.S. relations

México a small interior state (area 8,286 sq. miles, pop. 7,545,692) on the central plateau of Mexico, surrounding Mexico City on the north, east, and west. Its height (8,000 ft above sea level) provides a mild climate and sustains a heavy population (229 persons per sq. mile). Capital: Toluca (pop. 77,000). Agriculture (cereals, maguey, coffee, sugarcane, fruits), manufacturing and mining are the economic mainstays

Mexico City (*Span.* México) the capital (pop. 9,373,353) of Mexico and of the Federal District, near the south end of thc central plateau at 7,415 ft. Industries: textiles, metallurgy, vehicle assembly, tourism. Seaport: Veracruz. The center of the city is a great square, the Zócalo, surrounded by Spanish public buildings (incl. the cathedral, 1573–1791). There are famous modern buildings with murals by Orozco, Rivera, Sigueiros and others. University (1551). Before the Spanish conquest (1521) under Cortés, this was the Aztec capital, Tenochtitlán. The Olympic Games were hosted in 1968 and in 1985 an earthquake caused extensive damage and thousands of deaths.

Mexico, Gulf of a gulf (716,000 sq. miles) bordered by the southeast U.S.A. and E. Mexico, joining the Atlantic north of Cuba and the Caribbean south of it

Mexico, University of the oldest university in North America, founded (1553) as the Royal and Pontifical University of Mexico. It was interrupted during the 19th c. and reopened in 1910, as the National Autonomous University of Mexico (UNAM)

Mey·er (máiər), Adolf (1866–1950), U.S. psychiatrist who revolutionized methods for mental health treatment, creating and directing (1910–41) the Henry Phipps psychiatric clinic at Johns Hopkins University

Meyer, Conrad Ferdinand (1825–98), Swiss poet and author of short historical novels, including 'Das Amulett' (1873) and 'Der Heilige' (1880)

Mey·er·beer (máiərbçer, máiərbjər), Giacomo (Jakob Liebmann Beer, 1791–1864), German composer. Many of his operas, e.g. 'Robert le diable' (1831), 'les Huguenots' (1836) and 'le Prophète' (1849), were produced in Paris

me·zu·zah, me·zu·za (məzúzə, məzú:zə) *pl.* **me·zu·zoth** (məzúzout, məzú:zout), **me·zu·zahs, me·zu·zas** n. (*Judaism*) a piece of parchment inscribed on one side with a name of God (Shaddai) and on the other side with lines from Deuteronomy (vi, 4-9 and xi, 13-21). It is rolled in a scroll, placed in a case, and fastened to the

doorposts of Jewish homes [Heb. *mezūzāh*, doorpost]

mez·za·nine (mézəni:n, mezəni:n) n. a low-ceilinged extra story between two main ones, usually just above the ground floor ‖ the first balcony in some theaters or the first few rows of it [F. fr. Ital. *mezzanino* dim. of *mezzano*, middle]

mez·zo for·te (métsoufɔ́rti:, médzoufɔ́rti:) adv. (*mus.*) moderately loud [Ital.]

mez·zo pia·no (métsoupjánou, médzoupjánou) adv. (*mus.*) moderately soft [Ital.]

mez·zo-re·lie·vo, mez·zo ri·lie·vo (métsouriljévou, médzouriljévou) n. (*art*) relief in which figures project from the flat background to about half of what would be their natural volume [Ital. *mezzo*, half+*rilievo*, relief]

mez·zo-so·pra·no (métsousəprǽnou, métsousəpránou, médzousəprǽnou, médzousəpránou)n. a woman's singing voice, between the soprano and contralto in register ‖ a singer with such a voice [Ital. fr. *mezzo*, half+*soprano*, soprano]

mez·zo·tint (métsoutjnt, médzoutjnt) **1.** n. a method of engraving on copper or steel, in which the whole plate is roughened and parts are then scraped smooth or left rough to obtain light or dark surfaces ‖ a print made by this method **2.** v.t. to engrave (a subject) by this method [fr. Ital. *mezzotinto* fr. *mezzo*, half+*tinto*, tint]

M-4 *BISON

M4 1E2 *REDEYE

mg. milligram

mgd (*abbr.*) million gallons per day, unit of measurement of water flow

MGM-51 *SHILLELAGH

MGM-13 *MACE

MGM-29A *SERGEANT

MGR-1 *HONEST JOHN

mh (*abbr.*) millihenry

MHG. Middle High German

mho (mou) n. (*elec.*) a unit of conductance equal to the reciprocal of the ohm [OHM spelled backward]

MHz (*abbr.*) megahertz

mhom·e·ter (móumi:tər) n. (*electr.*) a gauge of conductance in mhos used in instruments. The current SI unit is the siemans

mi, *Br.* also **me** (mi:) n. (*mus.*) the note E in the fixed-do system of solmization ‖ the third note of any diatonic scale in movable-do solmization

mi. mile

MIA (*mil. abbr.*) missing in action

Mi·am·i (maiǽmi:) the largest city (pop. 346,931) in Florida, on the southeast coast, a popular resort, and a financial center

Mi·am·i (maiǽmi:) *pl.* **Mi·am·i, Mi·am·is** n. an Indian people of North America, first encountered (17th c.) in the Great Lakes area. In the 1960s about 150 inhabited California and Oklahoma ‖ a member of this people ‖ a dialect of the Illinois language

miaow *MEOW

mi·as·ma (mi:ǽzmə) *pl.* **mi·as·mas, mi·as·ma·ta** (mi:ǽzmətə) n. a poisonous gas or vapor ‖ a cold, damp mist rising from the ground, once thought to cause malaria **mi·ás·mal, mi·as·mat·ic** (mɑiæzmǽtik), **mi·ás·mic** adjs [Mod. L. fr. Gk *miasma*, pollution]

mi·aul (mi:ául) v.i. (of a cat) to wail [fr. F. *miauler*, imit.]

mi·ca (máikə) n. any of several transparent silicates which can be split into very thin, pliable sheets. Mica is used as an electrical insulator and as a heat resistant substitute for glass in stove doors etc. **mi·cá·ceous** adj. [L.=crumb]

Mi·cah (máikə) a Minor Prophet (8th c. B.C.) of the Old Testament. He prophesied the destruction of Jerusalem as a punishment for the sins of Israel and Judah ‖ the book of the Old Testament containing his prophecies

mice *pl.* of MOUSE

mi·celle (misél) n. (*chem.* and *biol.*) a unit composed of complex molecules, in colloids, which can alter in size without a chemical change [Mod. L. *micella* fr. *mica*, a grain, crumb]

Mich. Michigan

Mi·chael (máik'l) an archangel of Jewish and Christian tradition. To Christians he is St Michael. Feast: Sept. 29

Michael (1596–1645), czar of Russia (1613–45), founder of the Romanov dynasty. Elected czar, he built up an autocratic government, ending the troubles following the death of Boris Godunov

Michael (1921–), last king of Rumania (1927–30, 1940–7). He formed an alliance with

the Allies (1944), but abdicated under Communist pressure (1947)

Mi·chae·lis constant (maikéiləs) a measure of enzyme reaction in concentration of moles per liter; named for Leonor Michaelis, American biochemist *abbr.* **Km**

Mich·ael·mas (mík'lməs) n. the feast of St Michael (Sept. 29), a quarter day in England

Michaelmas daisy any of several wild asters native to North America

Michaelmas term the term of the British High Court of Justice beginning soon after Michaelmas ‖ the first term of the academic year in British universities, beginning in late September or early October

Michael VIII Pa·lae·ol·o·gus (peili:ɒlagəs) (1224–82), Byzantine emperor (1261–82). The first of the Palaeologus dynasty, he usurped the throne and fought Naples, where he instigated the Sicilian Vespers (1282)

Mi·chel·an·ge·lo (maik'lǽndʒəlou, *Ital.* mi:kelándʒelɔ) (Michelangelo Buonarotti, 1475–1564), Florentine painter, sculptor, architect and poet. He is a towering figure of the Renaissance, and he far transcends it: his vision of man in his beauty and nobility and in his spiritual energy and despairing anguish is of all time. Michelangelo was brought up in Florence, and there became imbued with Neoplatonism. But he left the city after the death of his patron Lorenzo de' Medici and carved his first great works in Rome: notably the 'Pietà' of St Peter's (c. 1500) which at once made him famous. He went back to Florence for four years, and in this period carved the colossal 'David'. He also worked on the cartoon (now lost) for a huge fresco for the Council Hall. It contained hundreds of figures of horsemen and bathing soldiers, and in this work and the 'David' and others of the period he was seen to be using the nude figure only, in its infinite variety of gestures and movements, to convey a complete statement, as the ancients had done. In 1505 Pope Julius II recalled him to Rome, and commissioned him to execute his tomb. The project in various forms, initially grandiose but ultimately much reduced in scope, was to occupy his mind for 40 years. The 'Moses' in S. Pietro in Vincoli, Rome, dating from 1513–16 (just after the death of Julius) was an element of this project, and it is one of his greatest works. Julius II also commissioned him (1508) to paint the ceiling of the Sistine Chapel (his private chapel): the almost superhuman task was finished by 1512. Its subject, from Genesis, is God's creation of the world and of man, the Fall, and man's continuance in sin. Shortly following this and the carving of the 'Moses', Michelangelo worked on the Medici Chapel in Florence, containing the tombs of Lorenzo and Giuliano de' Medici. Their idealized portraits are grouped with reclining figures of 'Day' and 'Night', 'Evening' and 'Dawn'. In all he worked on the chapel over 14 years (1520–34), as architect as well as sculptor, then left it for pupils to finish. In these years he also built the Biblioteca Medicea-Laurenziana in Florence. In 1534 he settled in Rome, and painted the 'Last Judgment' fresco in the Sistine Chapel behind the high altar, 25 years after the painting of the ceiling. The huge work, full of swirling figures and terrible images of despair, was finished in 1541. He also worked on the designs for the remodeled St Peter's, wrote poems, and sculpted three Pietàs. They belong to the last, intensely devout years of his life: images of the reconciling love of the crucified Christ, most sublimely realized in the 'Rondanini Pietà' now in Milan

Mi·che·let (mi:ʃle), Jules (1798–1874), French liberal historian. His 'Histoire de France' (1833–67) and his 'Histoire de la révolution française' (1847–53) are vividly written in the grand manner

Mi·che·loz·zo (mi:kelɔ́ttsɔ) (Michelozzo di Bartolommeo, 1396–1472), Italian architect and sculptor. He assisted Ghiberti and collaborated with Donatello. His independent works include the library of San Giorgio Maggiore at Venice (c. 1433) and the Palazzo Riccardi for the Medicis at Florence (c. 1444)

Mi·chel·son (máik'lsən), Albert Abraham (1852–1931), American physicist. In the classical Michelson-Morley experiment with Edward W. Morley he determined the velocity of light. Their findings contributed to Einstein's theory of relativity. Nobel Prize (1907)

CONCISE PRONUNCIATION KEY: **(a)** æ, c**a**t; ɑ, c**a**r; ɔ f**a**wn; ei, sn**a**ke. **(e)** e, h**e**n; i:, sh**ee**p; iə, d**ee**r; ɛə, b**ea**r. **(i)** i, f**i**sh; ai, t**i**ger; ə:, b**i**rd. **(o)** o, **o**x; au, c**ow**; ou, g**oa**t; u, p**oo**r; ɔi, r**oy**al. **(u)** ʌ, d**u**ck; u, b**u**ll; u:, g**oo**se; ə, b**a**cillus; ju:, c**u**be. x, lo**ch**; θ, **th**ink; ð, bo**th**er; z, **Z**en; ʒ, cor**s**age. dʒ, sava**g**e; ŋ, ora**n**g-uta**ng**; j, **y**ak; ʃ, **f**ish; tʃ, fe**tch**; 'l, rabb**le**; 'n, redd**en**. Complete pronunciation key appears inside front cover.

Mich·e·ner (míʃənər), James Albert (1907–), U.S. author. His short stories, 'Tales of the South Pacific' (1947), were adapted to musical comedy and cinema ('South Pacific'). His best-sellers include 'Sayonara' (1954) and 'Hawaii' (1959), 'Centennial' (1974), 'Chesapeake' (1978), 'The Covenant' (1980), 'Space' (1982), 'Poland' (1983), and 'Texas' (1985)

Michener, Roland (1900–), governor-general of Canada (1967–73)

Mich·i·gan (míʃigən) the third largest lake (area 22,400 sq. miles) of the Great Lakes of North America, the only one wholly in the U.S.A., south of Lake Superior. Chief ports: Chicago, Milwaukee (*ST LAWRENCE SEAWAY)

Michigan (abbr. **Mich.**) a state (area 58,216 sq. miles, pop. 9,109,000) of the N. central U.S.A. Capital: Lansing. Chief city: Detroit. It is formed by two generally low-lying peninsulas in the midst of the Great Lakes, and is mainly industrial. Agriculture: dairy and beef cattle, corn and cereals, fruit, poultry. Resources: timber, iron ore, salt, limestone (cement), copper, some oil. Industries: motor vehicles (Detroit is a world center), cement, machinery, metal and food processing, chemicals. State universities at Ann Arbor (1817) and East Lansing (1855). Michigan was explored by the French (17th c.) and was ceded to Britain (1763). It passed (1783) to the U.S.A., of which it became (1837) the 26th state

Michigan, University of one of the largest U.S. educational institutions and one of the oldest state universities. Founded (1817) in Detroit, it was moved (1837) to Ann Arbor

Mi·cho·a·cán (miːtʃɔəkán) a central agricultural and mining state (area 23,113 sq. miles, pop. 3,030,300) of Mexico, bisected by mountains running from the high central Mexican plateau. Highest peak: Tancitaro (12,605 ft). Capital: Morelia. Economy: forest products, tropical crops, cereals, gold, silver, lead, cinnabar, copper, coal, oil and sulfur. Extensive irrigation is necessary

Mick·ey Mouse (míki:máus) n. (slang.) **1.** a trivial thing. —**Mickey Mouse** adj. e.g., Mickey Mouse courses at a university **2.** v. (cinema) to synchronize background music with animated cartoon action

Mic·kie·wicz (mitskjévitʃ), Adam (1798–1855), Polish poet. His 'Ballads and Romances' (1822) initiated the Polish romantic movement

Mic·mac (míkmæk) n. a member of a tribe of Algonquian Indians inhabiting part of E. Canada and Newfoundland

MICR (computer abbr.) magnetic ink character recognition

micro- (máikrou) prefix (esp. in scientific terms) small, minute || (elec.) a millionth of, as in 'microfarad' [fr. Gk mikro- fr. mikros, small]

micro- adj. of women's garments, shorter than mini

mi·cro·a·nal·y·sis (máikrouənælisis) n. (chem.) the analysis of very small quantities of materials

mi·crobe (máikroub) n. a microorganism, esp. one which causes disease **mi·cró·bi·al, mi·cró·bic** adjs [F. fr. Gk mikros, small+bios, life]

mi·cro·beam (máikroubiːm) n. radiation concentrated on a microscopic specimen

mi·cro·bi·cide (máikróubisaid) n. a substance that kills microbes [MICROBE+L. caedere, to kill]

mi·cro·bi·ol·o·gy (máikroubaióladʒi:) n. the branch of biology concerned with microorganisms

mi·cro·bod·y (máikroubɑdi:) n. (biochem.) a group of particles smaller than a cell, containing enzymes, esp. D-amino acid oxidase and other oxidases, found in some cells also peroxisome

mi·cro·cap·sule (máikroukæpsəl) n. a very small soluble capsule containing a compound released when the capsule is broken or dissolved —**microencapsulate** v. to enclose in a microcapsule —**microencapsulation** n.

mi·cro·ce·phal·ic (máikrousəfælik) adj. having an abnormally small head || (of a head) abnormally small (cf. MACROCEPHALIC) **mi·cro·ceph·a·lous** (máikrouséfələs) adj. **mi·cro·céph·a·ly** n. [fr. Gk mikros, small+kephalē, head]

mi·cro·chem·is·try (máikroukémistri:) n. chemistry dealing with minute quantities, esp. in analysis

mi·cro·chip (máikroutʃip) n. (computer) computer circuit on a chip of less than ½ in. in diameter and as small as 1 mm, created by photographic reduction Cf CHIP

mi·cro·cir·cuit·ry (máikrousə:rkətri:) n. (electr.) miniaturized circuitry structures, usu. produced photographically on silicon chips as small as one millimeter, used in computers, space equipment, and similar devices also **microelectronic circuitry, microminiature circuitry** —**microcircuit** n.

mi·cro·cir·cu·la·tion (máikrousə:rkjəléiʃən) n. (med.) blood circulating through the capillaries

mi·cro·cli·mate (máikrouklàimət) n. (meteor.) temperature, humidity, etc., within a particular vicinity due to its topography, drainage, etc.

mi·cro·cli·ma·tol·o·gy (máikrouklàimətóladʒi:) n. the study of climate in a small area where weather conditions otherwise similar to the surrounding conditions are affected by soil, altitude, exposure etc.

mi·cro·cline (máikrəklain) n. a silicate of potassium and aluminum, resembling orthoclase [fr. G. mikroklin fr. Gk mikros, small+klinein, to incline]

mi·cro·coc·cus (máikrəkókəs) pl. **mi·cro·coc·ci** (máikrəkóksai) n. a member of Microccus, fam. Micrococcaceae, a genus of heterotrophic, globular bacteria that reproduce by fission, are usually aerobic, and include pathogenic, toxin-producing forms [fr. Mod. L. Micrococcus fr. Gk mikros, small+COCCUS]

mi·cro·com·pu·ter or **micro** (máikroukəmpjú:tər) n. (computer) a complete tiny computer processor digital device with a single integrated-circuit chip with a capacity smaller than that of a minicomputer Cf MINICOMPUTER

mi·cro·cor·neal lens (máikroukórni:əl) a type of contact lens covering part of the cornea Cf HAPTIC LENS

mi·cro·cosm (máikrəkɒzəm) n. (philos.) the universe in miniature || anything regarded as being the universe in miniature (cf. MACROCOSM) **mi·cro·cós·mic** adj. [fr. F. microcosme fr. M.L. fr. late Gk mikros kosmos, small cosmos]

microcosmic salt sodium ammonium hydrogen phosphate, $Na·NH_4·HPO_4·4H_2O$. When heated, it forms a transparent phosphate bead used in analysis

mi·cro·crack (máikroukræk) n. a microscopic crack usu. in a material, e.g., in glass, steel

mi·cro·crys·tal·line (máikroukrístəlin) adj. having crystals visible only through a microscope

mi·cro·cul·ture (máikroukʌltʒər) n. **1.** (biol.) a culture of microorganisms **2.** (social science) the culture of an isolated group of people with limited experience —**microcultural** adj.

mi·cro·cyte (máikrəsait) n. an abnormally small red blood corpuscle found in some types of anemia [MICRO-+-cyte fr. Gk kutos, cell]

mi·cro·dot (máikroudɑt) n. the photographic reproduction of a document reduced to the size of a dot

mi·cro·e·col·o·gy (máikrouikóladʒi:) n. the ecology of very small areas —**microecological** adj.

mi·cro·e·co·nom·ics (máikrouekənómiks) n. the study of economics dealing with individual decision units and their effect on prices, supply, demand, resources, and the free market Cf MACROECONOMICS

mi·cro·e·lec·trode (máikrouiléktroud) n. a small electrode, e.g., one inserted into living tissue for research purposes

mi·cro·e·lec·tron·ics (máikrouiléktróniks) n. the study of miniaturization of electronic components —**microelectronic** adj. —**microelectronically** adv. Cf MICROCHIP

mi·cro·far·ad (máikroufǽrad) n. (elec.) a unit of capacitance equal to 10^{-6} farad

mi·cro·fiche (máikroufiʃ) n. a document substantially reduced (to 8 mm or smaller), usu. filed with other microfiches on a card for long-term storage

microfiche reader device for enlarging any projecting microfiche images

mi·cro·film (máikrəfilm) **1.** n. a very small photographic film, convenient for storage and transportation, used esp. for photographing documents etc. **2.** v.t. to reproduce on microfilm

mi·cro·flash (máikrouflæʃ) n. a short-duration high-intensity light used in making photographs

mi·cro·form (máikrəfɔrm) n. **1.** material reduced substantially (e.g., to 35-mm film) to microfilm or microfiche for storage **2.** the process of reproduction Cf MICROIMAGE, MICROFICHE, MICROFILM

mi·cro·gam·ete (máikrougǽmi:t, máikrougámi:t) n. the smaller of two conjugating gametes, usually regarded as male (cf. MACROGAMETE)

mi·cro·gauss (máikrougaus) n. (electr.) one millionth of a gauss (of magnetic flux density or magnetic induction)

mi·cro·graph (máikrəgræf, máikrəgrɑf) n. a drawing of an object as seen through a microscope || an instrument for minute writing or engraving || (phys.) an instrument for recording small movements by magnifying them on a diaphragm **mi·cro·graph·ic** (máikrəgrǽfik) adj.

mi·cro·graph·ics (máikrəgrǽfiks) n. production of art or documents greatly reduced in size, esp. in microform or microfiche, for the purpose of saving space

mi·crog·ra·phy (maikrógrafi:) n. the description or examination of microscopic objects || the art of executing minute writing [MICRO-+Gk graphos, written]

mi·cro·groove (máikrəgruːv) n. the very fine groove on a long-playing record

mi·cro·im·age (máikrouímidʒ) n. the original document for reproduction on microform or microfiche

mi·cro·in·struc·tion (máikrouinstrákʃən) n. (computer) an instruction for a single operation Cf MACROINSTRUCTION

mi·cro·lens (máikrələnz) n. lens for photographing microscopic objects

mi·cro·ma·chine (máikrouməʃi:n) n. (electrical eng.) a miniature electrical device designed to simulate a full-scale machine —**micromachining** v.

mi·cro·me·te·or·ite (máikroumi:ti:ərait) n. a very small meteorite that can penetrate the earth's atmosphere without disintegrating

mi·cro·me·te·or·oid (máikroumí:ti:ərɔid) n. (astron.) a meteorite the size of a grain of sand also **micrometeorite**

mi·crom·e·ter (maikrómitər) n. an instrument fitted with scale and vernier for measuring very small objects and distances [fr. F. micromètre]

mi·cro·mi·cron (máikroumáikrɒn) n. one millionth of a micron

mi·cro·min·i·a·tur·iz·a·tion (máikroumini:ətʃurəzéiʃən) n. production of very small models of equipment —**microminiature** n. the product —**microminiaturize** v. to make smaller than miniature

mi·cro·mod·ule (máikroumódʒu:l) n. a module made smaller than ordinary miniatures

mi·cro·mor·phol·o·gy (máikrəmorfóladʒi:) n. study of microstructure, e.g., of soils —**micromorphologic** adj. —**micromorphological** adj. —**micromorphologically** adv. —**micromorphology** n. the structure studied

mi·cron (máikrɒn) n. (phys.) a millionth of a meter, symbol μ (=10,000 angstrom units) [fr. Gk mikron neut. of mikros, small]

Mi·cro·ne·sia (máikrəní:ʒə, máikrəní:ʃə) the northwestern division of Oceania, comprising some 2,250 small islands and atolls: the Mariana, Gilbert, Marshall and Caroline groups, with Wake Is., Ocean Is., and smaller single islands. Micronesians, in physical type predominately Asiatic, are considered to be of mixed Melanesian, Polynesian and Malay stock (*U.S. TRUST TERRITORY OF THE PACIFIC)

Mi·cro·ne·sian (máikrəní:ʒən, máikrəní:ʃən) **1.** adj. of or pertaining to Micronesia **2.** n. a native of Micronesia || any of the Austronesian languages spoken there

mi·cron·ics (maikróniks) n. **1.** microcomputer technology **2.** miniaturized electronics

mi·cro·or·gan·ism (máikrouórgənizəm) n. any organism of microscopic or submicroscopic size, e.g. a bacterium, protozoan, virus etc.

mi·cro·phone (máikrəfoun) n. an instrument for amplifying or transmitting sound. It uses the energy of sound waves to modify electric currents which, after transmission by wire or radio, can be reconverted into sound waves **mi·cro·phon·ic** (máikrəfónik) adj. [fr. MICRO-+Gk phōnē, sound]

mi·cro·pho·to·graph (máikroufóutəgræf, máikroufóutəgrɑf) n. a very small photograph which normally is magnified to make details clear

mi·cro·pop·u·la·tion (máikroupɑpjəléiʃən) n. **1.** the organisms of a selected small area **2.** microorganisms in a sample (of soil, tissue, air, etc.) for study

mi·cro·probe (máikrəprɒub) n. **1.** device used to examine a microscopic area by measuring the emissions spectrum created by radiation **2.** device used for analyzing the chemical composition of materials by using an electron beam (laser) with optical apparatus

mi·cro·pro·ces·sing unit (maikrouprɒsesiŋ) (*computer*) the processing unit, input/output, buffer, and circuits of a microcomputer *abbr.* **MPU**

mi·cro·pro·ces·sor (maikrouprɒsesər) *n.* the arithmetic-logical operational part (processing unit) of a microcomputer, usu. consisting of one or a few integrated circuit chips, sometimes with a memory unit *abbr.* **MP**

mi·cro·pro·gram·ming (maikrəprɒugræmiŋ) *n.* (*computer*) method of operation using elementary instructions (microinstructions) in sequence (microprogram) already stored in the unit, thus permitting a buildup of machine instructions from the basics built into the computer hardware. The code used is a merocode

mi·cro·pro·pul·sion (maikrəprəpʌlʃən) *n.* small oscillations of the earth's magnetic field

mi·cro·pub·lish·ing (maikroupʌbliʃiŋ) *n.* production of documents or graphics on microfiche or other microforms —**micropublication** *n.* —**micropublish** *v.* —**micropublisher** *n.*

mi·cro·py·lar (maikrəpailər) *adj.* of or pertaining to a micropyle

mi·cro·pyle (maikrəpail) *n.* (*biol.*) a specialized region on the surface of many eggs through which the spermatozoon enters ‖ a minute aperture in some spores through which protoplasts escape ‖ a minute aperture in the coating of an ovule of a seed plant through which the pollen tube enters the embryo sac (*FERTILIZATION) [F. fr. Gk *mikros*, small + *pulē*, gate]

mi·cro·scope (maikrəskoup) *n.* an optical instrument used to examine minute objects by giving an enlarged, well resolved image of them. A compound microscope usually consists of an objective and an eyepiece mounted in a tube with a variable apparatus for directing and concentrating light on the object. Microscopes are usually classified by the type or origin of the radiation employed for image formation, e.g. the ultraviolet microscope, polarizing microscope etc. (cf. ELECTRON MICROSCOPE) [fr. Mod. L. *microscopium* fr. Gk *mikros*, small + *skopein*, to watch]

mi·cro·scop·ic (maikrəskɒpik) *adj.* too small to be visible to the naked eye ‖ very small ‖ of, pertaining to or involving the use of a microscope **mi·cro·scop·i·cal** *adj.* **mi·cro·scóp·i·cal·ly** *adv.* [fr. Mod. L. *microscopicus*]

mi·cros·co·pist (maikrɒskəpist) *n.* a specialist in the use of microscopes

mi·cros·co·py (maikrɒskəpi) *n.* the study of objects by means of a microscope

mi·cro·sec·ond (maikrəsekənd) *n.* a unit of time equal to one millionth of a second

mi·cro·seism (maikrəsaizəm) *n.* a very slight earth tremor [fr. MICRO- + Gk *seismos*, earthquake]

mi·cro·sleep (maikrəsli:p) *n.* momentary blackouts in lieu of sleep

mi·cro·slide (maikrəslaid) *n.* a slide used in microscopic work

mi·cro·some (maikrəsoum) *n.* a granule of protoplasm, esp. a minute particle in cytoplasm, a center for enzyme localization [MICRO- + Gk *sōma*, body]

mi·cro·spore (maikrəspɔr, maikrəspour) *n.* the smaller type of spore produced by heterosporous plants, giving rise to the male gametophyte (cf. MEGASPORE) **mi·cro·spor·ic** (maikrəspɔrik, maikrəspɒrik), **mi·cro·spor·ous** (maikrəspɔrəs, maikrəspóurəs, maikróspərəs) *adjs*

mi·cro·sur·ger·y (maikrousə́:rdʒəri:) *n.* (*med.*) surgery utilizing large magnification (with a microscope) of the area affected

mi·cro·tag·gants (maikroutægənts) *n.* minute color-coded particles incorporated into liquids, plastics, explosives, feed, etc., to make them identifiable

mi·cro·teach·ing (maikrouti:tʃiŋ) *n.* technique for teacher-training in which a short class is presented to a small group (5 to 10 students), evaluated by all concerned, reconstructed, presented to another group, and reevaluated, esp. using video tapings

mi·cro·tek·tite (maikroutéktait) *n.* (*geol.*) fine grains of tektite found in ocean sediment

mi·cro·tome (maikrətoum) *n.* an instrument for cutting thin sections of organic matter for microscopic examination **mi·crot·o·my** (maikrɒtəmi:) *n.* [fr. MICRO- + Gk *-tomos*, cutting]

mi·cro·tone (maikrətoun) *n.* (*music*) a tone smaller than a semitone, utilizing a scale of 24

or 36 chromatic notes, e.g., as in Chinese, Indian, Greek music

mi·cro·tron (maikrətrɒn) *n.* (*nuclear phys.*) an accelerator combining elements of the cyclotron and the linear accelerator with a circular path in which the energy of electrons may be increased to several million electron volts

mi·cro·tu·bule (maikroutú:bju:l) *n.* a minuscule cylindrical structure extant in many body cells

mi·cro·vas·cu·lar (maikrouvǽskjələr) *adj.* (*physiol.*) of capillaries

mi·cro·vi·sion (maikrouvíʒən) *n.* a system for blind landing of aircraft that permits the pilot to see the runway and his relative position on a screen

mi·cro·wave (maikrouweiv) *n.* an electromagnetic wave of wavelength less than 10 m. in the radio-frequency range, esp. one between 1 m. and 1 cm. (i.e. between 30 and 300 megacycles). Microwaves may be transmitted over distances of 50–80 km. (30–50 miles) by means of microwave relay stations, and are used as carrier waves in telephone, telegraph and television transmission as well as in radar and radio astronomy (*SPECTROSCOPY)

microwave communication the sending of messages by the use of directed microwave beams over a series of relays less than 80 km apart

microwave oven an oven that utilizes electromagnetic energy below the microwave spectrum for rapid food preparation, e.g., cooking, thawing, dehydration

microwave relay station a structure used in line-of-sight microwave transmission consisting of a receiving antenna, an amplifier and a microwave transmitter usually placed at the top of a tower. Television, telegraph and telephone communication are transmitted over large distances by means of a series of such stations

microwave spectrum the emission or absorption spectrum of a substance in the microwave band. Microwaves cause changes in the quantized rotational energy levels of molecules possessing dipole moments, and these spectra, when analyzed, give information as to the symmetry, dimensions and dipole moments of the molecule being studied

mic·tu·rate (miktʃureit) *pres. part.* **mic·tu·rat·ing** *past* and *past part.* **mic·tu·rat·ed** *v.i.* to urinate **mic·tu·ri·tion** (miktʃuríʃən) *n.* the act of urinating [fr. L. *micturire*]

mid (mid) *adj.* (only in compounds) in the middle of, *midmorning* ‖ (*phon.*, of certain vowels) pronounced with the tongue in a position between high and low [O.E. *midd*]

mid·air (mídɛər) *n.* the air thought of as a region well above the ground, *gazing into midair*

Mi·das (maidəs) legendary king of Phrygia. Dionysus granted his wish that everything he touched should turn to gold. When even his daughter and his food became gold he rid himself of this power by bathing in the river Pactolus. As judge of a musical contest he preferred Pan to Apollo and for punishment were given ass's ears

mid·brain (mídbrein) *n.* the middle division of the developing embryonic vertebrate brain ‖ that part of the adult vertebrate brain derived from the embryonic midbrain and consisting of the brainstem in the middle of the brain. Control of eyeball movement is one of its functions

mid·cen·tral (midséntrəl) *adj.* (*phon.*, of a vowel) articulated with the tongue arched centrally, in a position between its highest and lowest point

mid·cult (mídkʌlt) *n.* the conventional culture of the middle class

mid·day (mídei) *n.* the middle of the day, when the sun appears to be directly overhead [O.E. *middæg*]

Mid·del·burg (mídlbə:rg) the chief town (pop. 23,000) of Zeeland, Netherlands, on Walcheren Is.: Town Hall (15th–16th cc.). Metallurgy, textile and food industries

mid·den (mídn) *n.* (*archaeol.*) a kitchen midden [M.E. *midding* prob. fr. O.N.]

mid·dle (mídl) **1.** *adj.* central, *the middle rung of a ladder* ‖ intermediate ‖ medium or average in size, quality, status etc. ‖ (*gram.*) of or designating a verbal voice in ancient Greek expressing reflexive or reciprocal actions or intransitive conditions **Mid·dle** designating a language at a stage in its development intermediate be-

tween 'Old' and 'Modern' **2.** *n.* a place or moment or thing occupying a middle position, *the middle of the week* ‖ (*pop.*) the waist [O.E. *middel*]

middle age the period of life from about 40 to 65 **míd·dle-áged** *adj.*

Middle Ages the period of European history from the fall of the Roman Empire (476) to the late 15th c.

Middle America a geographical term for the area covered by Mexico, Central America, and the Caribbean islands as far east as Trinidad

Middle America the middle-income, politically middle-of-the-road segment of the U.S. population, chiefly in the Midwest —**Middle American** *n.* Cf SILENT MAJORITY

Middle Atlantic States New York, New Jersey and Pennsylvania

middle C (*mus.*) the note C tuned to a frequency of 261.62, found at approximately the middle of the piano keyboard

middle class the class of people including those in professional and commercial occupations. Other usual criteria are: relatively median income, secondary or higher education, and the holding of generally conformist views **míd·dle-cláss** *adj.*

middle distance the part of a picture or view between the background and foreground

middle ear the part of the ear between the external ear and the inner ear

Middle East the region of S.W. Asia and N.E. Africa stretching from Turkey through Iran, Iraq and Arabia to the Sudan and the countries bordering the E. Mediterranean **Middle Eastern** *adj.*

Middle English *ENGLISH LANGUAGE

Middle High German High German as it was spoken from c. 1100 to c. 1500

mid·dle·man (mídlmæn) *pl.* **mid·dle·men** (mídlmen) *n.* anyone engaged in trade who buys goods from the producer and sells them to the retailer or consumer

mid·dle·most (mídlmoust) *adj.* midmost

middle of the road a policy etc. which avoids extremes **míd·dle-of-the-róad** *adj.*

Mid·dles·brough (mídlzbrə) a port (pop. 149,770) and county borough in Yorkshire, England on the Tees estuary. Industries: engineering, shipbuilding

Mid·dle·sex (mídlseks) a former county of S.E. England

Middle Temple *INNS OF COURT

middle term (*logic*) the term in a syllogism which is common to both premises, and from which a conclusion is drawn

Mid·dle·ton (mídltən), Thomas (c. 1580–1627), English dramatist. His early plays, e.g. 'A Chaste Maid in Cheapside' (c. 1612), were concerned with London low life. 'A Game at Chesse' (1625) is a political allegory. 'Women Beware Women' (printed 1657) is a tragedy

middle watch (*naut.*) the watch between midnight and 4 a.m.

mid·dle·weight (mídlweit) *n.* a professional boxer whose weight does not exceed 160 lbs ‖ an amateur boxer whose weight does not exceed (*Am.*) 165 lbs or (*Br.*) 160 lbs

Middle West the area of the U.S.A. between the Rocky Mountains and the Alleghenies, north of the Ohio River and the southern borders of Kansas and Missouri **Middle Western** *adj.* **Middle Westerner** *n.*

mid·dling (mídliŋ) **1.** *adj.* of medium size or quality **2.** *n.* (*pl.*) coarse ground wheat for use as animal feed ‖ pork or bacon from between the shoulder and the ham [MID or MIDDLE]

mid·dy (mídi:) *pl.* **mid·dies** *n.* (*pop.*) a midshipman ‖ a loose, hip-length woman's or child's blouse with a broad collar like a sailor's [MIDSHIPMAN]

middy blouse a middy

midge (midʒ) *n.* any of many small gnatlike insects, esp. a member of fam. *Chironomidae*, *Ceratopogonidae* or *Cecidomyiidae* [O.E. *mycg*]

midg·et (mídʒit) **1.** *n.* a very small person, esp. one normally proportioned (cf. DWARF) ‖ anything much smaller than others of its kind **2.** *adj.* very small [dim. of MIDGE]

Mi·di (mi:di:) *n.* the south of France [F.]

mid·i (mídi:) *n.* a woman's dress, skirt, or coat reaching to midcalf *also* longuette Cf MAXI, MICRO-, MINI

Mid·i·an·ite (mídi:ənait) *n.* (*Bible*) a member of a nomadic Arabian tribe which fought the Israelites [fr. Heb. *Midhyān*, name of a son of Abraham]

CONCISE PRONUNCIATION KEY: (**a**) æ, c*a*t; ɑ, c*a*r; ɔ f*aw*n; ei, sn*a*ke. (**e**) e, h*e*n; i:, sh*ee*p; iə, d*ee*r; ɛə, b*ea*r. (**i**) i, f*i*sh; ai, t*i*ger; ə:, b*i*rd. (**o**) o, *o*x; au, c*ow*; ou, g*oa*t; u, p*oo*r; ɔi, r*oy*al. (**u**) ʌ, d*u*ck; u, b*u*ll; u:, g*oo*se; ə, ba*c*illus; ju:, c*u*be. x, lo*ch*; θ, *th*ink; ð, *b*o*th*er; z, *Z*en; ʒ, cor*s*age; dʒ, sa*v*age; ŋ, ora*n*gutang; j, *y*ak; ʃ, *fi*sh; tʃ, fe*tch*; ʼl, rabb*le*; ʼn, redd*en*. Complete pronunciation key appears inside front cover.

mid·i·ron (mídai̯ərn) n. (golf) an iron with little loft used for medium-distance fairway shots

mid·land (mídlənd) 1. n. the central region of a country **the Mid·lands** the central counties of England 2. adj. of or pertaining to a midland **Mid·land** of or pertaining to the Midlands

Mid·lo·thi·an (midlóuði:ən) a former county of S.E. Scotland. County town was Edinburgh

mid·most (mídmoust) adj. exactly in the middle

mid·night (mídnai̯t) 1. n. 12 o'clock at night 2. adj. of or happening at this time **to burn the midnight oil** to work late into the night [O.E. midniht]

midnight sun the sun when shining at midnight in the Arctic or Antarctic summer

mid off (cricket) a fielding position on the batsman's right front, near the bowler ‖ the fielder at this position

mid on (cricket) a fielding position on the batsman's left front, near the bowler ‖ the fielder in this position

Mid·rash (mídraʃ) pl. **Mid·ra·shim** (midraʃíːm) n. an ancient rabbinical commentary on a biblical text. The earliest collections of Midrashim come from the 2nd c. B.C. but their content is older [Heb.+explanation]

mid·rib (mídrib) n. the central vein of a leaf

mid·riff (mídrif) n. the part of the body including the lower ribs and the top of the abdominal cavity [O.E. midhrif]

mid·ship (mídʃip) adj. pertaining to the middle part of a boat or ship

mid·ship·man (mídʃipmən) pl. **mid·ship·men** (mídʃipmən) n. a student training for the rank of ensign in the U.S.Navy ‖ (hist.) a junior officer of the British Royal Navy, ranking between cadet and sublieutenant

mid·ships (mídʃips) adv. amidships

midst (midst) n. (only in phrases) **in our midst** among us **in the midst of** in the middle of ‖ in the course of [prob. fr. M.E. middes, the middle and middest adj., most central]

mid·stream (mídstriːm) n. the middle of a stream **to change horses in midstream** to change one's policies in the middle of some enterprise

mid·sum·mer (mídsʌmər) n. the middle of the summer ‖ the period of the summer solstice (around June 22) in the northern hemisphere

Midsummer Day the feast of St John the Baptist (June 24), a quarter day in England

mid·term (mídtəːrm) n. the middle of a school term, term of office etc. ‖ (pop.) an academic examination at the middle of a term

Mid·way (mídwei̯) a coral atoll (area 28 sq. miles, pop. 2,100) comprising two small islands, in the Pacific 1,300 miles northwest of Honolulu. Discovered (1859) and annexed (1867) by the U.S.A., they are a U.S. air and naval base. They were the scene of a decisive sea and air battle (June 4–6, 1942) in which U.S. forces severely defeated a Japanese fleet

mid·way 1. (mídwei̯) n. the part of an exhibition, fair etc. where sideshows and amusements are located 2. (mídwéi̯) adv. halfway [O.E. midweg]

mid·week (mídwiːk) n. the middle of the week **mid·week·ly** adj. happening, appearing etc. in the middle of every week

Mid·west (mídwést) n. the Middle West **Mid·wést·ern** adj. **Mid·wést·ern·er** n.

Mid-Western Nigeria a former region (area 14,614 sq. miles, pop. 2,533,000) of Nigeria on the west side of the lower Niger. Capital: Benin (*NIGERIA)

mid·wife (mídwai̯f) pl. **mid·wives** (mídwai̯vz) n. a woman who assists in the delivery of babies **mid·wife·ry** (mídwai̯fəri:, mídwifri:) n. obstetrics [M.E. midwyf fr. O.E. mid, with+wíf, wife, woman]

mid·win·ter (mídwíntər) n. the middle of winter

mid·year (mídji̯ər) 1. n. the middle of the year ‖ (pl., pop.) examinations in the middle of the academic year 2. adj. of or pertaining to this part of the year or these examinations

mien (miːn) n. (rhet.) bearing, demeanor or appearance as signs an observer can interpret [prob. shortened fr. obs. demean, mien fr. DEMEAN v.]

Mies van der Ro·he (míːsvǽndərou, míːsvǽndərróu̯ə), Ludwig (1886–1969), American architect born in Germany. Influenced by Behrens and by the De Stijl movement, he directed the Bauhaus (1930–3) and led the emergence of the international style. His buildings were among the first to use revealed structural ele-

ments and facades composed of glass sheets enclosed in metal frames. His works include the Seagram building (New York, 1958, with Philip Johnson)

miff (mif) v.t. (pop.) to offend [fr. older miff n., a petty quarrel, perh. imit.]

MI-5 (Br.) the section of Military Intelligence concerned with the security of the State

might (mai̯t) n. strength, power **with might and main** (rhet.) with one's utmost force [O.E. miht]

might past of MAY ‖ used as an auxiliary verb to express a degree of possibility less than that expressed by 'may', and (esp. Br.) to request permission

might·i·ly (mái̯tili:) adv. (rhet.) with great might ‖ (pop.) extremely [MIGHTY]

might·i·ness (mái̯tiːnis) n. (rhet.) the quality of being mighty

might·n't (mái̯t'nt) contr. of MIGHT NOT

might·y (mái̯ti:) 1. comp. **might·i·er** superl. **might·i·est** adj. (rhet.) large and strong, esp. in physique ‖ (rhet.) great and powerful 2. adv. (pop.) very, mighty fine [O.E. mihtig]

Migne (miːnj), Jacques-Paul (1800–75), French priest. His 'Patrologia Latina' and 'Patrologia Graeca' are great collections of the works of the Church Fathers

mi·gnon·ette (minjənét) n. a plant of the genus Reseda, fam. Resedaceae, native to W. Asia and the Mediterranean, esp. the cultivated species, R. odorata, with small greenish flowers and a sweet scent [F. mignonnette, dim. of mignon, dainty]

mi·graine (mái̯grein) n. a severe, periodically recurring headache, usually on one side of the head, often accompanied by nausea, vertigo etc. [F. fr. L. hemicrania fr. Gk hēmikrania fr. hēmi, half+kranion, skull]

mi·grant (mái̯grənt) 1. adj. making a periodical migration 2. n. an animal, esp. a bird, that migrates ‖ a person who migrates [fr. L. migrans (migrantis)]

mi·grate (mái̯greit) pres. part. **mi·grat·ing** past and post part. **mi·grat·ed** v.i. (of certain birds, fishes etc.) to change habitat, esp. at certain seasons ‖ (of people) to leave one country or region to settle or work for a period in another ‖ (of a plant) to extend its habitat into a new area ‖ (chem., of an atom or group of atoms) to move from one position in a molecule to another ‖ (chem., of an ion) to move from one electrode to another under the influence of electromotive force [fr. L. migrare (migratus)]

mi·gra·tion (mai̯gréi̯ʃən) n. the act or process of migrating ‖ an instance of this ‖ a group of migrating animals, persons etc. [fr. L. migratio (migrationis)]

mi·gra·tor (mái̯greitər) n. someone who or something that migrates

mi·gra·to·ry (mái̯grətɔri:, mái̯grətou̯ri:) adj. given to migrating ‖ relating to migration ‖ roving or wandering [fr. L. migrare (migratus)]

MiG-25 or **MIG-25** (mígtwenti:fái̯v) n. (mil.) (NATO name, Foxbat) U.S.S.R. twin-engine jet missile-launching plane, with speed of Mach 2.8, ceiling of 80,000 ft., capable of carrying 4,400 lbs. It is said to be the most potent weapon in U.S.S.R. arsenal

MiG-21 or **MIG-21 MF** (mígtwenti:wʌ́n) n. (mil.) U.S.S.R. fighter plane with speed of Mach 2.1, ceiling above 3,000 ft., two infrared homing missiles, two rocket packs, and 57-mm rockets

MiG-27 or **MIG-27** (mígtwenti:sévən) n. (mil.) U.S.S.R. single-engine jet fighter plane with six-barrel Gatling gun, laser range-finder, five pylons for carrying external missiles or equipment

MiG-23 or **MIG-23** (mígtwenti:θriː) n. (mil.) U.S.S.R. single-engine jet fighter plane with approximate speed of Mach 1, with twin-barrel Gatling gun, with two pylons for fighter equipment

Mi·guel (migél) (1802–66), Portuguese prince, son of John VI. Regent (1826–8) for Maria II, he usurped the throne (1828) and instituted a reactionary regime. Liberal uprisings and foreign intervention forced him to abdicate (1834)

mi·ka·do (mikádou̯) n. a title (used esp. by non-Japanese) of the emperor of Japan [Jap. mi, exalted+kado, gate, door]

mike (mai̯k) n. (pop.) a microphone

mil (mil) n. a unit of measurement, used esp. for the diameter of wire, equivalent to 1/1000 in. or 0.0254 mm. [short for L. millesimum, thousandth]

milage *MILEAGE

Mi·lan (milǽn) (Ital. Milano) the second largest city (pop. 1,580,810) of Italy, on the Lombardy plain, a great communications and trading center. Industries: textiles (esp. silk and manmade fibers), automobile, aircraft and mechanical engineering, leather, rubber, oil refineries, printing, publishing, banking. Gothic cathedral (begun 1386), La Scala opera house (1778), Biblioteca Ambrosiana (1609). University (1924). HISTORY. Dating back to pre-Roman times, Milan developed under its archbishops after the collapse of the Lombards' dominion (774), became virtually free of Imperial rule (1183), and extended its power over Lombardy under the Visconti. It became a duchy (1395), and was a center of the Renaissance under the Sforza. It was later attached to the crowns of Spain (1535–1713) and Austria (1713–96 and 1815–59). It was incorporated into Italy in 1861

Mil·an·ese (miləníːz, miləníːs) 1. adj. of or pertaining to Milan, its people, customs etc. 2. n. pl. **Mil·an·ese** a native or inhabitant of Milan **the Milanese** the lands of the former duchy of Milan

milch (miltʃ) adj. (of domestic animals) giving milk and kept for this, a milch cow [M.E. mielch, milche fr. O.E.]

mild (mai̯ld) adj. gentle and moderate, not severe or extreme, mild punishment ‖ (of weather) fairly warm and windless ‖ (of food etc.) not having a strong taste ‖ (of a disease) not acute ‖ (of ale or beer) not strongly flavored with hops (cf. BITTER) ‖ (of steel) tough and easily worked, with little carbon [O.E. milde]

mil·dew (míldu:, míldju:) 1. n. a whitish, fuzzy growth produced on the surface of various forms of organic matter and living plants by certain fungi ‖ a fungus causing this growth 2. v.t. to affect with mildew ‖ v.i. to become covered with mildew **míl·dew·y** adj. [O.E. mildēaw, meledēaw, honeydew]

mile (mai̯l) n. a unit of linear measurement equaling 1,760 yds (1,609.35 m.) ‖ a nautical mile **míle·age, míl·age** n. a number of miles traveled ‖ the distance in miles from one place to another ‖ an allowance for traveling expenses at a given rate per mile ‖ a fixed expense per mile, e.g. for railroad transportation [O.E. míl fr. L. milia (passuum) a thousand (paces)]

mile·post (mái̯lpoust) n. a post marking the distance in miles from some place

mil·er (mái̯lər) n. a man or a horse specializing in races of one mile

Mi·le·sian (milíː3ən, mailíː3ən) 1. adj. of or relating to ancient Miletus, its inhabitants etc. 2. n. a native or inhabitant of ancient Miletus or a member of the school of philosophy there

mile·stone (mái̯lstoun) n. a stone by the roadside showing the distance in miles from nearby important towns ‖ an event of significance in the history of a nation, person etc.

Mi·le·tus (milíːtəs) an ancient Ionian maritime city of Asia Minor. It prospered as a colonizing state (8th–6th cc. B.C.) and had a notable school of philosophy (6th c. B.C.). It was conquered by the Lydians (late 6th c. B.C.), by the Persians (494–479 B.C.), by Alexander the Great (334 B.C.) and by the Romans

mil·foil (mílfɔil) n. the yarrow [O.F.]

Mi·lhaud (mi:jou̯), Darius (1892–1974), French composer, a member of 'Les Six'. His works, in which he experimented esp. with polytonality, included operas, symphonies, concertos, ballets, string quartets, songs etc.

mil·i·ar·i·a (mili:éəri:ə) n. prickly heat [Mod. L. fr. L. fem. of miliarius adj., of millet]

mil·i·ar·y (míli:eri:) adj. (med.) resembling a millet seed or seeds in size or formation [fr. L. miliarius fr. milium, millet]

miliary fever an epidemic disease marked by fever, excessive sweating and small, red, miliary vesicles

miliary tuberculosis tuberculosis in which the infection is carried in the blood stream, forming minute tubercles in various parts of the body

mi·lieu (milːjéː) n. environment [F.]

mil·i·tan·cy (mílitənsi:) n. the quality or state of being militant

mil·i·tant (mílitənt) 1. adj. engaged in fighting ‖ aggressive in support of a cause, a militant free trader 2. n. a militant person [F.]

mil·i·tar·i·a (militéəri:ə) n. collectible military souvenirs

mil·i·tar·i·ly (militéərili:, míliterili:) adv. in a military manner ‖ from a military point of view

mil·i·ta·rism (mílitərizəm) n. the policy of constantly building up armaments and the armed forces or of threatening armed aggression ‖ the tendency in a society to encourage an excessively military spirit [F. *militarisme*]

mil·i·ta·rist (mílitərist) 1. *n.* a person who encourages militarism 2. *adj.* characterized by or imbued with militarism **mil·i·ta·ris·tic** *adj.* **mil·i·ta·ris·ti·cal·ly** *adv.* [MILITARY]

mil·i·ta·rize (mílitəraiz) *pres. part.* **mil·i·ta·riz·ing** *past and past part.* **mil·i·ta·rized** to build up the military strength of, make military ‖ to imbue with military spirit

mil·i·tar·y (mílitəri:) *adj.* of, pertaining to or involving the armed forces or warfare **the military** the army [fr. F. *militaire*]

military currency currency prepared by a military power and declared by a military commander to be legal tender for use in areas occupied by a military force

military government a government established in conquered territory by the conquering power, whose laws adopt or replace the formerly prevailing civil law

mil·i·tar·y-in·dus·tri·al complex (mílitəri:indΛstri:əl) the military and military-supported industry, in general viewed as a cohesive political force. The term was coined by President Dwight D. Eisenhower

military law law governing the armed forces (cf. MARTIAL LAW)

military police a corps of soldiers acting as police for the army

mil·i·tate (míliteit) *pres. part.* **mil·i·tat·ing** *past and past part.* **mil·i·tat·ed** *v.i.* (of evidence, circumstances etc.) to have weight, *the findings militate against his theory* [fr. L. *militare* (*militatus*), to serve as a soldier]

mil·i·tia (milíʃə) *n.* a reserve body of citizens enrolled for military duties, called upon only in an emergency ‖ (*Br. hist.*) a reserve force of men conscripted within a county, under the command of the lord lieutenant, esp. such a corps formed after the Militia Act of 1757 ‖ these forces ‖ all able-bodied male citizens between 18 and 45 who are not already members of the regular armed forces and who are declared by authority subject to a call to military service **mil·i·tia·man** (milíʃəmən) *pl.* **mil·i·tia·men** (milíʃəmən) *n.* a member of the militia [L.=military service]

Milk (milk) a river (625 miles long) rising in N.W. Montana, flowing across the Canadian border, continuing eastward along S. Alberta province, reentering Montana and flowing eastward into the Missouri River

milk (milk) *n.* a white or yellowish liquid consisting of small fat globules suspended in a watery solution, secreted by the mammary glands for the nutrition of the newborn. It contains all the nutrient substances (proteins and enzymes, fats, sugars, minerals and vitamins) necessary for growth, but is deficient in iron ‖ such a secretion drawn from a cow, goat etc. for use as human food ‖ a liquid resembling this secretion, e.g. coconut juice or latex **to cry over spilled** (or **spilt**) **milk** to regret or fuss about something that cannot be remedied [O.E. *meolc, milc*]

milk *v.t.* to draw or press milk from (a cow, goat etc.) ‖ to extract (milk) from an animal ‖ to extract (money etc.) to one's advantage from someone or something, esp. over a period of time ‖ to exploit (someone), esp. to extract money from ‖ to draw the sap from (a plant) ‖ to draw the venom from (a snake) ‖ *v.i.* to yield milk ‖ to draw milk [O.E. *milcian*]

milk-and-wa·ter (mílkənwótər, mílkənwótər) *adj.* insipid

milk·er (mílkər) *n.* a person who milks ‖ a machine for milking cows ‖ a cow etc. that gives milk

milk fever any of several mild infectious fevers occurring in women immediately after childbirth ‖ a similar disease, often paralytic, affecting cows after calving

milk-float (mílkflout) *n.* (*Br.*) a milkman's cart or truck

milk·i·ness (mílki:nis) *n.* the quality or state of being milky

milk leg a swelling of the legs sometimes occurring in women after childbirth

milk·maid (mílkmeid) *n.* (*old-fash.*) a dairymaid

milk·man (mílkmæn) *pl.* **milk·men** (mílkmen) *n.* a man on a milk round who sells or delivers milk

milk of magnesia a suspension of magnesium hydroxide, Mg(OH)$_2$, in water, used as a mild

alkali in reducing stomach acidity and as a laxative

milk shake a cold drink of milk, flavoring, and often ice cream, beaten until frothy

milk·shed (mílkʃed) *n.* a dairy farm area supplying milk for a city

milk snake *Lampropeltis triangulum*, a common harmless North American snake which feeds on rodents though popularly supposed to drink milk

milk·sop (mílksɒp) *n.* a man or boy who lacks proper spirit

milk sugar lactose

milk tooth one of the small temporary teeth in young mammals

milk·weed (mílkwi:d) *n.* any of several plants yielding a milky latex or juice

milk·wort (mílkwərt, mílkwort) *n.* any of several plants of genus *Polygala*, fam. *Polygalaceae*, esp. *P. vulgaris*, a small European perennial formerly believed to increase lactation

milk·y (mílki:) *comp.* **milk·i·er** *superl.* **milk·i·est** *adj.* of, like or containing milk ‖ (of a liquid) cloudy, whitish in color

Milky Way the spiral galaxy of which our solar system is a part. It contains billions of stars, nebulae etc. At night its central plane appears to an observer on the earth as an irregular band of faint light forming a complete circle on the celestial sphere

Mill (mil), James (1773–1836), British historian, philosopher and economist. In his 'Elements of Political Economy' (1821) and his 'Analysis of the Phenomena of the Human Mind' (1829), he continued the work of Bentham and Hume. He also wrote a 'History of India' (1817)

Mill, John Stuart (1806–73), British economist and philosopher, son of James Mill. He was a leader of the Utilitarian movement and a renowned exponent of individual liberty, the rights of the minority and the need for a public conscience. His essay 'On Liberty' (1859) is a celebrated document of political economy. Other works are 'A System of Logic' (1843), 'The Principles of Political Economy' (1848), 'Utilitarianism' (1861), 'Autobiography' (1873)

mill (mil) 1. *n.* a building containing machinery which grinds grain into flour ‖ a machine that grinds grain ‖ a small hand-operated machine for grinding some solid substance, e.g. coffee beans or pepper ‖ a building containing machinery used in some kinds of manufacture, *cotton mill* ‖ one of the machines used in such manufacture **to be put** (or **go**) **through the mill** to undergo some grueling experience 2. *v.t.* to grind (grain, beans etc.) ‖ to work (something) in a mill ‖ to full (cloth) ‖ to cut grooves across the rim edge of (a coin) ‖ *v.i.* (with 'around') (of a crowd, herd etc.) to move about in a confused mass [O.E. *mylen* fr. L.L. *molinum, molina*]

mill *n.* a U.S. monetary unit equal to one tenth of a cent, used as a money of account [short for L. *millesimus*, thousandth]

Mil·lais (miléi), Sir John Everett (1829–96), British painter. He helped to form the Pre-Raphaelite Brotherhood

Mil·lay (miléi), Edna St Vincent (1892–1950), American poet, one of the most popular poets of the 1920s

mill·board (mílbɔrd, mílbourd) *n.* a thick pasteboard used for making book covers [alt. of *milled board*]

mill·dam (míldæm) *n.* a dam made across a stream to build up a sufficient supply of water to turn a mill wheel ‖ a millpond

mil·le·fio·ri (milifjóri:) *n.* an ornamental glass made from sections of fused glass rods of varying sizes and colors. Embedded in clear glass, it is used esp. for floral-patterned paperweights etc. [Ital. fr. *mille*, thousand+*fiori*, flowers]

mil·le·nar·i·an (mɪlənéəri:ən) 1. *adj.* of, pertaining to or believing in the millennium (Christ's reign on earth) 2. *n.* a person who believes in the millennium **mil·le·nar·y** (mílənɛri:, milénəri) 1. *adj.* pertaining to the millennium ‖ consisting of or pertaining to a thousand (esp. years) 2. *pl.* **mil·le·nar·ies** *n.* a period of 1,000 years ‖ a millenarian ‖ a 1,000th anniversary [fr. L. *millenarius*, containing a thousand]

mil·len·ni·al (miléni:əl) *adj.* of or relating to a millennium ‖ of or relating to the millennium foretold in the Bible

mil·len·ni·um (miléni:əm) *pl.* **mil·len·ni·ums**, **mil·len·ni·a** (miléni:ə) *n.* a period of 1,000 years ‖ a 1,000th anniversary ‖ the reign of Christ on

earth, foretold in Rev. xx, 1–5 [Mod. L. fr. L. *mille*, thousand+*annus*, year]

millepede *MILLIPEDE

mil·le·pore (míləpor, míləpour) *n.* a member of *Milleporina*, order *Milleporina*, a genus of stony corals forming with madrepores the chief constituent of coral reefs [fr. Mod. L. *millepora* fr. *mille*, thousand+*porus*, passage]

Mil·ler (mílər), Arthur (1915–), American dramatist. His plays include 'Death of a Salesman' (1949), 'A View from the Bridge' (1955), 'After the Fall' (1964), and 'The Creation of the World and Other Business' (1972). He also won praise for his screenplay for the film 'The Misfits' (1961)

Miller, Henry (1891–1980), American author, best known for his novels 'Tropic of Cancer' (1934) and 'Tropic of Capricorn' (1938)

Miller, William (1782–1849), U.S. religious revivalist. He founded Millerism, a movement which sought to revive belief in the physical and imminent second coming of Christ. After two mispredictions (1843, 1844) of the date of the second coming, the movement (50,000–100,000 believers) slowly dissolved

mill·er (mílər) *n.* someone who owns or directs work at a mill, esp. a flour mill ‖ any of several white or white-powdered insects, e.g. the cockchafer [perh. fr. M.E. *myll, myln*, mill]

mil·ler·ite (mílərait) *n.* nickel sulfide, NiS, usually occurring in yellow crystals [after W. H. *Miller* (1801–80), Eng. mineralogist]

mill·er's-thumb (mílərzθΛm) *n.* *Cottus gobio*, a small freshwater fish of Europe and North America ‖ any of various spiny-finned sculpins of North America

mil·les·i·mal (milésəməl) *adj.* thousandth ‖ pertaining to a thousandth [fr. L. *millesimus*, thousand]

Mil·let (mi:le), Jean-François (1815–75), French painter, an outstanding member of the Barbizon school. He is best known for his pictures of peasants at work, esp. 'The Angelus' (1859) and 'The Gleaners' (1857)

mil·let (mílit) *n.* any of several smallgrained cereal grasses, esp. *Panicium miliaceum*, whose grain is widely used in Europe and Asia for human food and for birdseed, and is grown for cattlefood and hay in the U.S.A. and Canada ‖ the grain of any of these cereals [F.]

millet grass a grass of the genus *Milium*, esp. *M. effusum*, a tall woodland grass of North America

milli- (mili) *prefix* (esp. in terms of the metric system) one thousandth

mil·liard (míljərd, míljard) *n.* *NUMBER TABLE [F.]

mil·li·bar (míləbar) *n.* (*phys.*) a unit of atmospheric pressure equal to 1,000 dynes per sq. cm. or about 1/32 in. of mercury

mil·lième (miljém) *n.* a monetary unit of Tunisia, one thousandth of a dinar or a coin of this value ‖ a monetary unit of Egypt and Libya, one thousandth of a pound, or a coin of this value [F.]

mil·li·gram, *Br.* also **mi·li·gramme** (míligræm) *n.* a thousandth of a gram

mil·li·hen·ry (míləhenri:) *n.* (*electr.*) unit of inductance, one thousandth of a henry *abbr.* **mh**

mil·li·hertz (míləhə:rts) *n.* unit of frequency, one thousandth of a hertz *abbr.* **MHz**

Mil·li·kan (mílikən), Robert Andrews (1868–1953), American physicist. He studied cosmic rays, X rays, and the free expansion of gases. He isolated the electron and measured its electric charge. Nobel Prize (1923)

mil·li·li·ter, esp. *Br.* **mil·li·li·tre** (míləli:tər) *n.* (*phys.*) one thousandth of a liter

mil·li·me·ter, esp. *Br.* **mil·li·me·tre** (míləmi:tər) *n.* (*abbr.* mm.) one thousandth of a meter

millimeter wave detection system (*mil.*) an antenna-computer guidance system in antitank missiles

mil·li·mi·cron (míləmaikron) *n.* one thousandth of a micron (symbol *mμ*)

mil·li·ner (mílinər) *n.* someone who makes, trims or sells women's hats and headdresses **mil·li·ner·y** (mílinɛri:) *pl.* **mil·li·ner·ies** *n.* the hats and headdresses made or sold by a milliner ‖ a milliner's work or business [fr. *Milaner*, a trader in fancy goods from *Milan*, Italy]

milling cutter a rotary cutter for shaping metal, used in a milling machine

milling machine a machine tool for shaping metal

mil·lion (míljən) 1. *n.* a thousand thousands (*NUMBER TABLE) ‖ the cardinal number representing this (1,000,000, M) **millions of** a very large, indefinite number of 2. *adj.* being a thousand times a thousand [F. fr. Ital. *millione*]

mil·lion·aire (miljənéər) *n.* a person whose possessions are worth a million or more dollars, pounds, francs etc. [F. *millionnaire*]

mil·lionth (míljənθ) 1. *adj.* being number 1,000,000 in a series (*NUMBER TABLE) ‖ being one of the 1,000,000 equal parts of anything 2. *n.* the person or thing next after the 999,999th ‖ one of 1,000,000 equal parts of anything (1/1,000,000)

mil·li·pede, mil·le·pede (míləpi:d) *n.* any of several members of *Diplopoda*, a class of arthropods having a body divided in many segments, with two pairs of legs on most of the segments [fr. L. *millepeda*, woodlouse fr. L. *mille*, thousand+*pes* (*pedis*), foot]

mill·pond (mílpɒnd) *n.* the pond formed by a milldam

mill·race (mílreis) *n.* the strong current of water through the sluice of a milldam, which drives the mill wheel ‖ the channel in which this current runs

Mills (milz), Clark (1810–83), U.S. sculptor whose bronze statue of Andrew Jackson, the first U.S. equestrian work, was placed (1853) in Lafayette Square across from the White House. He designed (1860) an equestrian statue of George Washington commissioned by Congress. He made (1863) a bronze casting, placed on the Capitol dome, of Thomas Crawford's huge statue representing Freedom or Armed Liberty

mill·stone (mílstoun) *n.* one of two large circular channeled slabs of stone, between which grain is ground, the grain being fed into a hole in the middle of the upper one **a millstone around one's neck** some burden (e.g. a moral obligation) that prevents all freedom of action or self-fulfillment

millstone grit a hard, coarse siliceous rock used for making millstones, found just beneath coal measures

mill·stream (mílstri:m) *n.* the water running through a millrace

mill wheel a broad wheel fitted with flanges, which is driven by the millstream and works a mill's machinery

mill·wright (mílrait) *n.* a person who builds mills or mill machinery

Milne (miln), Alan Alexander (1882–1956) British writer, known for his children's stories, esp. his tales about Christopher Robin. He wrote 'Winnie-the-Pooh' (1926) and 'The House at Pooh Corner' (1928). His books of verse include 'When We Were Very Young' (1924) and 'Now We are Six' (1926). He also wrote dramas, including 'Mr. Pim Passes' (1920)

Mil·ner (milnər), Alfred, 1st Viscount Milner (1854–1925), British statesman and colonial administrator. He was high commissioner for South Africa (1897–1905). He could not prevent the outbreak of the Boer War, but was responsible afterwards for much administrative reconstruction in the Transvaal and the Orange River Colony

Mi·lo (máilou) (late 6th c. B.C.), Greek athlete of Croton, six times victor in wrestling in both the Olympic and Pythian games

Milo, Titus Annius Papianus (c. 95–48 B.C.), Roman tribune (57 B.C.). He was accused of murder, and was defended in the 'Pro Milone' (52 B.C.), a speech that Cicero did not dare deliver as written

Mi·los (mí:los) (Melos) a Greek island (area 71 sq. miles, pop. 6,000) in the Cyclades. Chief town: Plaka. Exports: pumice, gypsum. The sculpture known as the Venus de Milo (now in the Louvre) was discovered here (1820)

Mi·loš O·bre·no·vić (mí:lɔʃoubrénəvitʃ) (1780–1860), prince of Serbia (1817–39 and 1858–60). A herdsman, he assassinated Karageorge and was proclaimed prince (1817), founding the Obrenović dynasty

milque·toast (mílktoust) *n.* a timid man easily dominated, esp. by his wife or his boss [after Caspar *Milquetoast*, comic-strip character invented by H.T. Webster (1885–1952), U.S. cartoonist, after *milk toast*, invalid food of buttered toast in warm milk]

milt (milt) 1. *n.* the reproductive glands of a male fish when filled with secretion prior to breeding ‖ the secretion itself 2. *v.i.* to impregnate the roe of a female fish with milt **mílt·er** *n.*

a male fish at the spawning season [O.E. *milte*, spleen]

Mil·ti·a·des (miltáiədi:z) (c. 540–c. 489 B.C.), Athenian general who won the decisive victory over the Persians at Marathon (490 B.C.)

Mil·ton (míltən), John (1608–74), English poet. His best-known early works are the odes 'L'Allegro' and 'Il Penseroso', the masque 'Comus' and the pastoral elegy 'Lycidas', all written before 1638. He was in Italy 1638–9 and returned to find England on the verge of the Civil War. From 1640 to c. 1647 he was engaged in the pamphleteering which produced the 'Areopagitica' (1644), a passionate appeal for greater freedom of the press. Under Cromwell he held the government post of secretary for foreign tongues (1649) and was even more fully occupied with polemics until the Restoration (1660). During this period he went blind. By 1658 he had begun his epic masterpiece on the Fall, 'Paradise Lost', conceived in his youth and written in poetry of magnificent plenitude 'to justify the ways of God to men'. He probably completed it by 1665. It was followed by 'Paradise Regained' (1671) and by the biblical tragedy 'Samson Agonistes' (1671). In England and throughout Europe these works and his exquisite minor poetry had an influence which grew throughout the 18th c., and which was at its greatest in the 19th c.

Mil·wau·kee (milwɔki:) the largest city (pop. 636,212) in Wisconsin, a port on Lake Michigan: meat packing, brewing, engineering, metallurgy

mime (maim) 1. *n.* a form of entertainment in which story and emotion are conveyed by gesture only, without words, but often with music and decor ‖ an entertainment of this kind ‖ an actor in this kind of entertainment ‖ (*hist.*) a Greek or Roman satirical or farcical comedy with mimicry and dancing 2. *v. pres. part.* **mim·ing** *past* and *past part.* **mimed** *v.t.* to act (a story etc.) in mime ‖ to mimic ‖ *v.i.* to enact a story without words [fr. L. *mimus* fr. Gk]

mim·e·o (mími:ou) *n.* the document product of a mimeograph machine

mim·e·o·graph (mími:əgræf, mími:əgrɑf) 1. *n.* a machine for making many copies of a document written or typed on a stencil ‖ a copy made on such a machine 2. *v.t.* to copy with a mimeograph ‖ to make (copies) on a mimeograph [fr. Gk *mimeomai*, I imitate+*graphos*, written]

mi·me·sis (mimí:sis, maimí:sis) *n.* (*biol.*) mimicry ‖ the representation of nature in artistic creation [Gk=imitation]

mi·met·ic (mimétik, maimétik) *adj.* (*biol.*) exhibiting mimicry ‖ pertaining to mime ‖ apt to mimic or imitate [fr. Gk *mimētikos*]

MIM-14 *NIKE HERCULES

mim·ic (mímik) 1. *adj.* copying or imitating something, *mimic warfare* 2. *n.* someone who imitates others, often satirically ‖ (*biol.*) something which exhibits mimicry 3. *v.t. pres. part.* **mim·ick·ing** *past* and *past part.* **mim·icked** to imitate, esp. in order to ridicule ‖ (*biol.*) to exhibit mimicry of **mím·ic·ry** *pl.* **mim·ic·ries** *n.* the act of mimicking ‖ an instance of this ‖ (*biol.*) the superficial resemblance that an organism may show to some other animate or inanimate structure, and which serves as a means of concealment [fr. L. *mimicus* fr. Gk]

mi·mo·sa (mimóusə, mimóuzə) *n.* a member of *Mimosa*, fam. *Papilionaceae*, a genus of trees, shrubs and low-growing plants of tropical and warm regions, incl. *M. pudica*, the sensitive plant ‖ a plant of the related genus *Acacia* [Mod. L. prob. fr. *mimus*, mime]

MIM-23 *HAWK

MIM-72 *CHAPARRAL

min. minimum ‖ minute (time)

mina *MYNA

mi·na·cious (minéifəs) *adj.* (*rhet.*) threatening [fr. L. *minax* (*minacis*)]

Mi·nae·an (mini:ən) 1. *adj.* of or relating to a people who developed a prosperous kingdom (c. 1200 B.C.–c. 650 B.C.) in S.W. Arabia on the route followed by caravans transporting incense and spices from the Indian Ocean to the Mediterranean 2. *n.* one of these people

Mi·na el Mo·zo (mí:nælmóθo), Francisco Javier (1789–1817), Spanish adventurer and a leader in the struggle for Mexican independence. He was executed by the Spaniards

Min·a·ma·ta disease (mìnimɑtə) (*med.*) poisoning due to organic mercuric compounds in fish polluted by industrial waste, causing lesions in the central nervous system, esp. in Japan in 1950s

min·a·ret (mìnərét, mínəret) *n.* a tall slender tower of a mosque, having one or more balconies, from which Moslems are summoned to prayer [Arab. *manārah, manārat*]

Mi·nas de Ri·o·tin·to (mí:nɑzðerí:ɔtí:nto) *RIO TINTO

min·a·to·ry (mínətɔri:, mínətɔuri:) *adj.* menacing [fr. L.L. *minatorius*]

mi·naud·ière (mìnɔdjéər) *n.* (Fr.) woman's cosmetics carrying case, usu. of metal, sometimes jewelled

mince (mins) 1. *v. pres. part.* **minc·ing** *past* and *past part.* **minced** *v.t.* to cut up (meat etc.) into very small pieces ‖ to utter (words etc.) with affected refinement ‖ *v.i.* to walk with short steps and an affected swaying motion ‖ to talk or behave with affected elegance **not to mince matters** (or **one's words**) to speak bluntly 2. *n.* mincemeat ‖ minced meat [M.E. *mynce, mynsh* fr. O.F.]

mince·meat (mínsmi:t) *n.* a chopped mixture of apples, dried fruits etc., often with suet, used as a filling in pies **to make mincemeat of** to give a thorough beating to ‖ to destroy (an argument etc.)

minc·ing (mínsiŋ) *adj.* (of someone's gait, or his steps) affectedly dainty so as to draw attention ‖ behaving or talking with excessively affected refinement

mind (maind) 1. *n.* the seat of consciousness, thought, feeling and will ‖ the intellect ‖ opinion, *they were of the same mind* ‖ desire, purpose, *he had no mind to put up with any nonsense* ‖ sanity, *to lose one's mind* ‖ a person viewed as an intellect, *Freud was a seminal mind* ‖ mentality, *the liberal mind* ‖ (*philos.*) consciousness as an element in reality (contrasted with matter) **on one's mind** occupying one's thoughts, esp. as a source of worry **to bear in mind** to continue to remember **to be in one's right mind** to be sane **to be of one mind** (of two or more people) to be in complete agreement **to be of two minds** to be undecided **to be out of one's mind** to be insane **to bring to mind** to be a reminder of **to call to mind** to be a reminder of ‖ to recall **to have a good mind to** to feel inclined to **to have half a mind to** to feel somewhat inclined to **to have in mind** to intend ‖ to be thinking of **to keep in mind** to continue to remember **to keep one's mind on** to pay attention to **to make up one's mind** to decide **to my mind** in my opinion **to put** (someone) **in mind of** to remind (someone) of **to put** (something) **from** (or **out of**) **one's mind** to force oneself to forget (something) **to set one's mind on** to be determined to do or have **to speak one's mind** to say what one thinks **to take** (someone's) **mind off** to distract (someone's) attention from, help (him) to stop worrying about 2. *v.t.* to have charge of, take care of ‖ to look out for, be careful of, *mind the step* ‖ to object to (often in polite questions or commands), *would you mind closing the door?* ‖ to concern oneself with, *mind your own business* ‖ to pay attention to, heed, *mind what I say!* ‖ to obey ‖ to worry about, *you mustn't mind the discomfort* ‖ *v.i.* to worry, *don't mind about the gossip* ‖ to have an objection, *if nobody minds I'll open the window* ‖ to be attentive, *now mind! you must hurry home* ‖ to be obedient **never mind** do not worry [M.E. *mynd* fr. O.E. *gemynd*, memory]

Min·da·na·o (mìndənáou) the second largest island (area 36,537 sq. miles, pop. 10,894,000) of the Philippines, the southernmost of the main islands. There are several peaks over 5,000 ft (Mt Apo, 9,540 ft). The country's chief hemp-growing region is around Davao, the largest town

mind-bog·gling (máindbɒgliŋ) *adj.* astounding; too complex for a person to comprehend fully

mind·ed (máindid) *adj.* disposed, inclined, *she can create trouble if she is minded to do so* ‖ (in compounds) having a specific type of mind, *weak-minded*

mind-ex·pand·ing (máindikspændiŋ) *adj.* of the effect of a hallucinogenic drug

mind·ful (máindfəl) *adj.* (with 'of') giving thought or heed to ‖ (with 'of') remembering gratefully, *mindful of her past kindness*

mind·less (máindlis) *adj.* having no mind ‖ (with 'of') careless, heedless, *mindless of the danger*

Min·do·ro (mindɔ́rou, mindóurou) an island (area 3,759 sq. miles, pop. 472,396) of the Philippines, off S. Luzon: coal mines

mind reader someone who is skilled at mind reading

mind reading the sensing or perceiving of another's thoughts or intentions by intuition alone

mind's eye the interior vision which forms a mental image of a remembered or imagined scene

mine (main) *possessive pron.* that or those belonging to me, *the fault is mine, friends of mine, that must be your coat because mine is torn* [O.E. *mīn*]

mine *n.* an excavation in the earth from which minerals are extracted ‖ this excavation with its accompanying buildings, shafts etc. ‖ a deposit of ore etc. ‖ a rich source, *a mine of information* ‖ (*mil.*) an explosive charge in a container, placed on or under the earth or in the sea, or dropped from the air. Mines exist in great variety (antipersonnel, antitank etc.), activated in a variety of ways according to their kind (acoustic, magnetic etc.) ‖ (*mil.*) a tunnel dug to bury an explosive under an enemy installation [F.]

mine *pres. part.* **min·ing** *past* and *past part.* **mined** *v.i.* to dig a mine ‖ to put explosive mines on or under the earth or in the water ‖ *v.t.* to dig below the surface of (the earth) ‖ to dig (ores etc.) from the earth ‖ (*mil.*) to lay a mine beneath ‖ (*mil.*) to dig a mine beneath ‖ to destroy by mining [fr. F. *miner*]

mine·field (máinfi:ld) *n.* an area on land or in the sea where mines have been laid

mine·lay·er (máinleiǝr) *n.* a ship used to lay underwater mines

min·er (máinǝr) *n.* a man who works in a mine ‖ a soldier who lays mines [M.E. *mynur, minour* fr. O.F.]

min·er·al (mínǝrǝl) **l.** *n.* any of various naturally occurring substances (e.g. ores, petroleum, natural gas, sand, clay, coal) of more or less homogeneous composition obtained from the earth for man's use ‖ (*chem.*) a solid, homogeneous crystalline chemical element or compound, formed by natural processes and usually extracted from the earth ‖ (*loosely*) any inorganic substance **2.** *adj.* of, containing or consisting of minerals ‖ (*loosely*) inorganic **min·er·al·ize** *pres. part.* **min·er·al·iz·ing** *past* and *past part.* **min·er·al·ized** *v.t.* to convert into a mineral ‖ to convert (a metal) into an ore ‖ to impregnate with a mineral [M.L. *minerale* neut. of *mineralis*, mineral]

mineral jelly a substance resembling petroleum jelly, derived from petroleum and used as a stabilizer in explosives

min·er·al·og·i·cal (mìnǝrǝlódʒikˈl) *adj.* of or pertaining to mineralogy

min·er·al·o·gist (mìnǝrǽlǝdʒist, mìnǝrólǝdʒist) *n.* a specialist in mineralogy

min·er·al·o·gy (mìnǝrǽlǝdʒi:, mìnǝrólǝdʒi:) *n.* the science of minerals [fr. MINERAL+Gk *logos*, word]

mineral oil any oil of mineral origin, esp. petroleum

mineral water water containing mineral salts or gases, esp. with medicinal value ‖ (*pl., Br.*) aerated soft drinks

mineral wool fiber spun from molten slag and used for insulating and filtering

Mi·ner·va (miné:rvǝ) (*Rom. mythol.*) goddess of wisdom, the arts, sciences and handicrafts. Her cult was introduced to Rome by the Etruscans and she became identified with the Greek Athene

min·e·stro·ne (mìnistróuni:) *n.* a thick vegetable soup made with dried beans, vermicelli etc. [Ital.]

mine·sweep·er (máinswi:pǝr) *n.* a ship used to clear away sea mines

minever *MINIVER

Ming (miŋ) a Chinese dynasty (1368–1644). It overthrew the Mongols, but power gradually fell to the corrupt imperial eunuchs. Chinese culture and art flourished, notably porcelain, painting, architecture and sculpture. Encyclopedias were compiled and a public works campaign was initiated. Despite the dynasty's isolationist policy, trading contacts were established with Europe

min·gle (míŋgˈl) *pres. part.* **min·gling** *past* and *past part.* **min·gled** *v.t.* to mix, blend ‖ to bring together, *to mingle guests* ‖ *v.i.* to become part of a mixture, combination, group etc., *their voices mingled in song, to mingle with the crowd* [M.E. *mengel* fr. O.E. *mengan*, to mix]

min·gy (míndʒi:) *comp.* **min·gi·er** *superl.* **min·gi·est** *adj.* (*Br., pop.*) mean, stingy [perh. fr. MEAN+STINGY]

Min·ho (mínhóu) *MIÑO

Min·how (mínhóu) *FOOCHOW

mini- combining form meaning "small," esp. of something that is usu. large, long, or important, e.g., *miniboom, minicrisis, minicruise, minimovie, minipark, minirecession, minishorts, minisuit.* Cf MACRO-, MAXI-, MEGA-, META-, MICRO-

min·i (míni) *n.* a short woman's skirt, usu. worn 2 to 4 inches above the knee *also* **miniskirt** Cf MAXI, MICRO-, MIDI

min·i·ate (míni:eit) *pres. part.* **min·i·at·ing** *past* and *past part.* **min·i·at·ed** *v.t.* to paint with vermilion ‖ to illuminate (a manuscript) esp. with red letters [fr. L. *miniare (miniatus)*, to color with red lead]

min·i·a·ture (míni:ǝtʃǝr, mínitʃǝr) **1.** *n.* a very small painting in illuminated manuscripts ‖ a small painting on vellum, ivory etc. ‖ the art of painting miniatures ‖ a small model **in miniature** on a small scale **2.** *adj.* on a small scale, *miniature golf* **mín·i·a·tur·ist** *n.* an artist specializing in miniatures [fr. Ital. *miniatura* fr. M.L.]

miniaturization (*electr.*) the construction of smaller technical (esp. electronic) systems by using smaller components in order to save weight and space

min·i·a·tur·ize (míni:ǝtʃǝraiz, mínǝtʃǝraiz) *v.t.* to construct (e.g. electronic equipment) so as to occupy a smaller space than would be usual, thus reducing weight as well as volume

min·i·bike (mínibaik) *n.* small one-passenger motorcycle with a low body and high handlebars

min·i·bridge (mínibridʒ) *n.* a system of pricing and handling container shipments at a single rate when sent by two carriers, e.g., rail and ship

min·i·bus (mínibǝs) *n.* small bus seating 6–12 passengers, esp. one by Volkswagen

min·i·cam (mínikæm) *n.* portable TV camera

min·i·car (mínikɑr) *n.* a car that is smaller than a compact *also* subcompact

min·i·cell (mínisel) *n.* (*genetics*) a small bacterial cell capable of transferring extrachromosomal particles (DNA) to normal cells

min·i·com·put·er (mínikǝmpjú:tǝr) *n.* (*computer*) a complete desktop digital computer processor device with a minimum capacity of 4,096 bytes and a limit of 8–16 bit words Cf MICROCOMPUTER

Minicoy *LACCADIVE, MINICOY and AMINDIVI ISLANDS

mi·ni·fun·di·o (minifú:ndjo) *n.* a very small farm in Latin America ‖ (*hist.*) a tiny plot of land cultivated by the Spanish settlers for their personal use, in return for military service (cf. LATIFUNDIO) [Span.]

min·im (mínim) *n.* (*Am.*) a unit of fluid measure equal to 1/60 fluid dram (=.003759 cu. in.) ‖ (*Br.*) a unit of fluid measure equal to 1/60 fluid dram (=.003612 cu. in., about 1 drop) ‖ a downstroke in writing ‖ (*Br., mus.*) a half note [fr. L. *minimus* adj., smallest]

min·i·mal (mínǝmǝl) *adj.* pertaining to the least or smallest possible, *minimal requirements* ‖ very small, *a minimal charge*

min·i·mal·ism (mínǝmǝlizǝm) *n.* abstract art form (esp. sculpture) that eliminates illusion and embellishment and emphasizes structure (usu. simple geometric shapes) and color field; coined by critic Barbara Rose of work by Larry Bell, Donald Judd, Robert Morris *also* minimal art, *reductivism, rejectivism* **—minimalist, minimal artist** *n.*

min·i·max (mínimæks) *n.* (*statistics*) the minimum in a group of maxima Cf MAXIMUM

minimax theorem (*math.*) **1.** game-theory principle that the optimal strategy of a party in a conflict should be to work to minimize maximum losses and to maximize minimal winnings **2.** game-theory precept that the lowest maximum loss should equal the highest minimum gain *also* minimal theorem

min·i·mi (mínimi:) *n.* (*mil. acronym*) minimitrailleuse, Belgian 5.56 caliber machine gun, weight 24.5 lbs., capable of firing 1,100 rounds per min.

min·i·mize (mínǝmaiz) *pres. part.* **min·i·miz·ing** *past* and *past part.* **min·i·mized** *v.t.* to reduce to the smallest possible degree or amount, *to minimize formalities* ‖ to estimate at the smallest possible degree or amount, *he minimized the inconvenience out of politeness* ‖ to underestimate, *don't minimize the risks* [fr. L. *minimus*, smallest]

min·i·mum (mínǝmǝm) **1.** *pl.* **min·i·ma** (mínǝmǝ), **min·i·mums** *n.* the least possible amount,

number or degree, *keep expenses to a minimum* ‖ the lowest amount, number or degree actually reached, *a temperature minimum* **2.** *adj.* least in amount, number or degree [L. neut. of *minimus*, smallest]

minimum residual radioactivity weapon (*mil.*) a nuclear weapon designed to have optimum reduction of unwanted effects from fallout, rainout, and burst-site radioactivity, e.g., the neutron bomb

minimum wage a wage fixed legally or by contract as the lowest allowed for a given type of work ‖ a living wage

min·ing (máiniŋ) *n.* the act or process of extracting coal, ore etc. from a mine or mines ‖ the industry based on this ‖ the laying of explosive mines

min·ion (mínjǝn) *n.* a servile follower ‖ (*printing*) a type size (about 7 point) between nonpareil and brevier **min·ion·étte** *n.* (*printing, Am.=Br.* emerald) a size of type, slightly larger than 6 point [F. *mignon*, favorite]

min·i·pig (mínipig) *n.* (*zool.*) a small pig bred esp. to be used in medical research

min·i·pill (mínipil) *n.* (*med.*) oral contraceptive with minimum progesterone and no estrogen

min·i·print·er (miniprintǝr) *n.* (*computer*) an output device without a keyboard, capable of printing alphanumeric data on paper at a speed of less than 120 characters per second

min·i·se·ries (mínisiǝri:z) *n.* television drama or documentary presented in segments over two or more days, but not presented as a continuing program

min·i·ski (míniski:) *n.* (*sports*) a short ski, usu. used by learners and for ski-bobbing

miniskirt *MINI

min·i·state (mínisteit) *n.* a very small independent nation, such as Monaco *also* microstate

min·is·ter (mínistǝr) *n.* a person in charge of some high office of state, esp. one responsible for the administration of an autonomous public service department, *minister of health* ‖ a diplomat ranking below an ambassador ‖ a person authorized to conduct worship, administer sacraments etc. in a Christian church, esp. (*Am.*) any Protestant clergyman, (*Br.*) a Nonconformist clergyman ‖ (*rhet.*) an agent, *a minister of the divine wrath* [O.F. *ministre*, servant]

minister *v.i.* to give aid or service, *to minister to a person's needs* ‖ to serve as a minister of religion, *to minister to a congregation*

min·is·te·ri·al (mìnistíǝri:ǝl) *adj.* of or pertaining to a minister [fr. F. *ministériel*]

minister of religion (*Br.*) any Protestant clergyman

minister without portfolio a member of a government free of departmental responsibility

min·is·trant (mínistrǝnt) **1.** *adj.* (*rhet.*) ministering **2.** *n.* (*eccles.*) someone ministering [fr. L. *ministrans (ministrantis)*]

min·is·tra·tion (mìnistréiʃǝn) *n.* the action of ministering to someone's needs ‖ (esp. *pl.*) an instance of this ‖ the act of ministering in religious matters [fr. L. *ministratio (ministrationis)*]

min·is·try (mínistri:) *pl.* **min·is·tries** *n.* (in some countries) a ministerial department of a government, *ministry of labor* ‖ a governing body of ministers ‖ its tenure of office ‖ (in some countries) the building occupied by a ministerial department ‖ the office and duties of a minister of religion ‖ the period during which a minister serves a congregation [late M.E. *ministerie* fr. L. *ministerium*, a ministering]

min·i·sub (mínisʌb) *n.* a one- or two-person submarine used for underwater research

min·i·track radio (mínitræk) (*electr.*) a radio receiver capable of tracking satellites or aircraft, equipped with telemeter-type signal transmitter

min·i·tri·al (mínitraiǝl) *n.* out-of-court hearings with set rules presented to a neutral expert. Minitrials are designed to save on court costs in settling minor disagreements

min·i·um (míni:ǝm) *n.* the tetroxide Pb_4O_3 (*LEAD OXIDE) [L.=cinnabar]

min·i·ver, min·e·ver (mínivǝr) *n.* (*hist.*) a type of fine white fur, esp. the winter fur of the ermine used in ceremonial dress [fr. F. *menu vair*, little vair]

mink (miŋk) *pl.* **mink, minks** *n.* the highly valued pelt or fur of one of several small semiaquatic carnivorous mammals of genus *Mustela*, fam. *Mustelidae*, closely related to and resembling the weasel and the ferret ‖ one of these animals. Mink are found in temperate and cool regions of Asia, North America and

CONCISE PRONUNCIATION KEY: **(a)** æ, c*a*t; ɑ, c*a*r; ɔ f*aw*n; ei, sn*a*ke. **(e)** e, h*e*n; i:, sh*ee*p; iǝ, d*ee*r; ɛǝ, b*ea*r. **(i)** i, f*i*sh; ai, t*i*ger; ǝ:, b*i*rd. **(o)** o, *o*x; au, c*ow*; ou, g*oa*t; u, p*oo*r; ɔi, r*oy*al. **(u)** ʌ, d*u*ck; u, b*u*ll; u:, g*oo*se; ǝ, b*a*cillus; ju:, c*u*be. x, lo*ch*; θ, *th*ink; ð, bo*th*er; z, *Z*en; ʒ, cor*s*age; dʒ, sava*g*e; ŋ, ora*n*gutang; j, *y*ak; ʃ, *fi*sh; tʃ, fe*tch*; 'l, rabb*le*; 'n, redd*en*. Complete pronunciation key appears inside front cover.

Europe. Breeding has produced many pastel shades from the original chestnut brown ‖ a coat etc. made of the fur [related to Swed. *mänk, menk*]

Minn. Minnesota

Min·ne·ap·o·lis (miniːǽpəlis) the largest city (pop. 370,951) in Minnesota, head port of the Mississippi River. Industries: flour milling, dairy food processing, precision instruments. University of Minnesota

min·ne·sing·er (mínisiŋər) *n.* one of a group of medieval, chiefly aristocratic German poets (c. 1150–c. 1350) who, like the troubadours, composed and sang songs esp. on the subjects of love and beauty (*WALTHER VON DER VOGELWEIDE) [G. fr. *minne*, love+*singer*, singer]

Min·ne·so·ta (minisóutə) (*abbr.* **Minn.**) a state (area 84,068 sq. miles, pop. 4,133,000) in the N. central U.S.A. Capital: St Paul. Chief city: Minneapolis. It is formed by glaciated lowlands with uplands in the east. Though it is primarily an industrial state, agriculture is important: beef and dairy cattle, hogs, poultry, cereals. Resources: iron ore (over half U.S. output). Industries: food processing, farm machinery, iron mining, flour milling, metal products, printing and publishing. State university (1869) at Minneapolis. Minnesota was explored by the French (17th c.). Part of it was ceded (1763) to Britain and passed (1783) to the U.S.A. The rest was included in the Louisiana Purchase (1803). It became (1858) the 32nd state of the U.S.A.

Minnesota, University of one of the largest U.S. institutions of higher education. It was established in 1851 and began instruction in 1869

min·now (mínou) *pl.* **min·nows, min·now** *n.* *Phoxinus phoxinus*, fam. *Cyprinidae*, a small freshwater fish about 3 ins long, allied to the carp, native to the northern hemisphere and the East Indies, used as fishing bait ‖ (*loosely*) any of several very small fish [prob. rel. to (postulated) O.E. *mynwe*]

Mi·ño (míːnjɔ) (*Port.* Minho) a river (171 miles long) rising in N. Lugo, Spain (Galicia) and flowing south to the Atlantic, forming the northwest Spanish-Portuguese border

Mi·no·an (minóuən) *adj.* (*archaeol.*) belonging to the culture which flourished (c. 3000–c. 1400 B.C.) on Crete, named after the legendary King Minos of Crete. Excavations at Knossos, begun in 1900 by Sir Arthur Evans, revealed a palace (c. 2000 B.C.) of complex plan, and the remains of a prosperous civilization remarkable for its naturalistic art and sculpture. Tablets bearing linear syllabic script were discovered (*LINEAR B)

mi·nor (máinər) **1.** *adj.* less in importance, size etc. than something else ‖ not having reached the full legal age ‖ (*mus.*, of a scale) having a semitone between the second and third and usually between the fifth and sixth notes (*HARMONIC MINOR SCALE, *MELODIC MINOR SCALE, *NATURAL MINOR SCALE) ‖ (*mus.*, of a key) based on such a scale ‖ (*mus.*, of a chord) built of the first, third and fifth notes of such a scale ‖ (*mus.*, of an interval) smaller by a semitone than a corresponding major interval, *a minor sixth* ‖ of or designating an academic subject constituting a secondary specialization **2.** *n.* (*law*) a person under full legal age ‖ a minor subject of study **3.** *v.i.* (with 'in') to study a specified minor subject [L.=less]

Mi·nor·ca (minɔ́rkə) *BALEARIC ISLANDS

minor canon a canon regularly employed in cathedral services without being a member of the chapter

minor control *PHOTOGRAMMETRIC CONTROL

Mi·nor·ite (máinərait) *n.* a Franciscan friar

mi·nor·i·ty (mainɔ́riti:, mainóriti:, minɔ́riti:, minóriti:) *pl.* **mi·nor·i·ties** *n.* the smaller number, less than half of a total, *voters against the motion were in the minority* ‖ a group distinguished by its religious, political, racial or other characteristics from a larger group or society of which it forms a part ‖ the state or period of being under legal age [fr. F. *minorité*]

minor league one of the U.S. leagues of professional athletic clubs other than the major leagues, esp. a baseball league other than the two major leagues **mí·nor-léague** *adj.*

minor mode (*mus.*) the arrangement of tones and semitones constituting the minor scale

minor orders (*Roman Catholicism*) the orders of acolyte, exorcist, lector and doorkeeper

minor planet an asteroid

minor premise, minor premiss (*logic*) the premise in a syllogism that contains the minor term

Minor Prophets *PROPHET

minor suit (*bridge*) diamonds or clubs (cf. MAJOR SUIT)

minor surgery or **minor operation** (*med.*) a surgical procedure that normally is not hazardous to the patient, e.g., repair of lacerations, treatment of fractures, and biopsy *Cf* MAJOR SURGERY

minor term (*logic*) the subject of the conclusion of a syllogism

Min·os (máinos) (*Gk mythol.*) king of Crete, son of Zeus and Europa and husband of Pasiphae. He became one of the judges of the underworld (*MINOTAUR)

Mi·not (máinət), George Richards (1885–1950), U.S. physician and cowinner (with William Murphy and George Whipple) of the 1934 Nobel prize in medicine for research on liver therapy in pernicious anemia

Min·o·taur (mínətɔr) (*Gk mythol.*) a monster, part man and part bull, offspring of Pasiphae, wife of Minos. It was confined in the labyrinth of Crete, and finally killed by Theseus

mi·nox·i·dil (minɔ́ksidil) *n.* (*pharm.*) antihypertensive marketed as Loniten

Minsk (minsk) the capital (pop. 1,276,000) of Byelorussia, U.S.S.R., an industrial center: mechanical and radio engineering, food processing, textiles. University (1921). Under German occupation (1941–4) it was virtually destroyed and its Jewish community (40% of the prewar population) exterminated. The city has been rebuilt

min·ster (mínstər) *n.* (*Br.*) any of certain large churches or cathedrals, esp. one that is or was originally part of a monastery [O.E. *mynster*, monastery]

min·strel (mínstrəl) *n.* (*hist.*) a medieval musician who sang, recited, and accompanied himself on an instrument ‖ a member of a band of public entertainers, usually in blackface, who sing songs and tell jokes. Modern minstrel shows originated in the U.S.A. (early 19th c.) [O. F. *menestral*]

min·strel·sy (mínstrəlsi:) *pl.* **min·strel·sies** *n.* a minstrel's occupation ‖ a minstrel group ‖ minstrel poetry or songs [O. F. *menestralsie*]

mint (mint) *n.* any of various aromatic plants of fam. *Labiatae*, esp. a member of genus *Mentha*, native to Europe, Asia and Australia and widely cultivated for use as flavoring [O.E. *minte*]

mint 1. *n.* a place where official coins are made ‖ (often with 'of money') a vast sum **2.** *adj.* not marred or soiled, as if new, *in mint condition* **3.** *v.t.* to coin (money) ‖ to convert (metal) into money ‖ to invent, fabricate (images, phrases etc.) **mínt·age** *n.* the act or process of minting money ‖ money coined in a mint, esp. in a particular mint at a particular time ‖ a fee paid to a mint for coining [O.E. *mynet*, coin]

mint julep an alcoholic drink of bourbon or brandy, sugar, crushed ice and mint leaves, served in a tall glass

Min·to (míntou), Gilbert John Elliot-Murray-Kynynmound, 4th Earl of (1845–1914), British statesman. Together with Morley, he carried out administrative reforms (1909) while viceroy of India (1905–10), increasing Indian representation in the legislative councils

min·u·end (mínju:end) *n.* (*math.*) the number from which another (the subtrahend) is to be subtracted [fr. L. *minuendus*, gerundive of *minuere*, to diminish]

min·u·et (minju:ét) *n.* (*hist.*) a courtly dance in triple rhythm ‖ the music for this ‖ a piece of music in this style, often forming the third movement in a classical sonata, quartet etc. [fr. F. *menuet*]

mi·nus (máinəs) **1.** *prep.* reduced by, *10 minus 3 is 7* ‖ (*pop.*) deficient in, lacking, *he emerged minus his hat* **2.** *adj.* indicating subtraction, *the minus sign* ‖ negative, *a minus number* ‖ (used postpositively) somewhat less than, *a C minus mark* **3.** *n.* a minus sign ‖ a minus quantity [L. neut. of *minor* adj., less]

mi·nus·cule (mínəskju:l) **1.** *n.* any of several ancient and medieval kinds of cursive writing, using small forms of letters ‖ a single letter or a manuscript in this writing **2.** *adj.* very small ‖ written in minuscules (cf. MAJUSCULE) [F.]

minus sign (*math.*) the symbol (−) used to indicate subtraction

min·ute (mínət) **1.** *n.* a unit of time equal to a sixtieth of an hour ‖ an undefined short time,

please wait a minute ‖ a precise point in time, *at that minute he fell* ‖ the distance which can be traveled in a minute, *the house is 10 minutes away* ‖ a unit of angular measure (symbol ´) equal to a sixtieth of a degree ‖ a written record of a decision etc. made at a meeting ‖ a short written communication giving an instruction, making a recommendation or presenting an analysis **2.** *v.t. pres. part.* **min·ut·ing** past and past part. **min·ut·ed** to make a minute or minutes of [F.]

mi·nute (mainuː́t, mainjúːt) *adj.* tiny ‖ of small importance, trivial, *a very minute point* ‖ precise and detailed, *a minute account of the battle* [fr. L. *minuere* (*minutus*), to lessen]

minute gun a cannon fired every minute as a sign of mourning or as a distress signal

minute hand the long hand of a watch or clock marking the minutes as it moves on an hourly circuit

min·ute·man (mínətmæn) *pl.* **min·ute·men** (mínətmen) *n.* (*Am. hist.*) an armed civilian prepared to fight at a minute's notice, just prior to and during the Revolutionary War (1775–83)

Minuteman 3 (*mil.*) U.S. intercontinental 37-ton mobile missile, with three warheads. It carries 170 kilotons of explosives to within 240 yds. of target

mi·nu·ti·ae (minúːʃiːi:, minjúːʃiːi:) *pl. n.* finest points of detail, *the minutiae of committee procedure* [L. pl. of *minutia*, smallness]

minx (miŋks) *n.* a girl who uses her attractions to get what she wants, often by flirting [origin unknown]

Min·ya Kon·ka (mínjəkóŋkə) (*Chin.* Kungka Shan) a mountain (24,900 ft) of W. Szechwan, China, at the end of the Tibetan plateau

Mi·o·cene (máiəsi:n) *adj.* of the epoch or series of the Tertiary between the Pliocene and the Oligocene (*GEOLOGICAL TIME) **the Miocene** the Miocene epoch or series of rocks [fr. Gk *meiōn*, less+*kainos*, recent]

mi·o·sis, my·o·sis (maióusis) *pl.* **mi·o·ses, my·o·ses** (maióusi:z) *n.* abnormal contraction of the pupil of the eye **mi·ot·ic, my·ot·ic** (maiótik) *adj.* [fr. Gk *muein*, to close]

Mi·ra·beau (mírəbou), Honoré-Gabriel Riqueti, Comte de (1749–91), French revolutionist and statesman. He was elected to the States General (1789) as a deputy for the third estate. His oratory quickly made him a leader of the French Revolution, but he tried constantly to create a constitutional monarchy, and from May 1790 was in the pay of the court

mi·ra·cid·i·um (mairəsídi:əm) *pl.* **mi·ra·cid·i·a** (mairəsídi:ə) *n.* the ciliate embryo, the first stage in the life history of a trematode [Mod. L. fr. Gk *meirax* (*meirakos*), girl, boy]

mir·a·cle (mírək'l) *n.* a supernatural event regarded as due to divine action, e.g. one of the acts worked by Christ which revealed his divinity ‖ an extremely remarkable achievement or event, e.g. an unexpected piece of luck, *it was a miracle he wasn't hurt* ‖ a miracle play [O.F. fr. L. *miraculum* fr. *mirari*, to wonder]

miracle fruit (*Synsepalum dulcificum*) **1.** a berry that leaves a sweet aftertaste in food ingested after it, i.e., causes sour foods to taste sweet **2.** the shrub

miracle play a medieval religious play on a biblical story or an episode in the life of a saint. Miracle plays were performed in or near a church. Extraneous and often ribald material was gradually introduced and they were eventually banished from church premises. The plays represent an important stage in the history of the drama in Europe

miracle rice (*agriculture*) a hybrid rice that produces two to three times normal harvest

mi·rac·u·lous (mirǽkjuləs) *adj.* of, like, involving, or having the nature of a miracle ‖ reputed to work miracles, *a miraculous image* [fr. F. *miraculeux*]

mi·rage (mirá:ʒ) *n.* an optical phenomenon in which remote objects are seen inverted, as if mirrored in water, or suspended in midair. Mirages are caused by an unusual distribution of density in the atmosphere, and are often seen in deserts or over hot pavements ‖ something illusory, *the offer proved to be only a mirage* [F.]

Mi·ra·món (mirəmón), Miguel (1832–67), Mexican general and president (1859–60). Fighting against Juárez, he was defeated (1860) at San Miguel de Calpulalpan. With the Emperor Maximilian and General Tomás Mejía (1820–67) he was executed at Querétaro

---

CONCISE PRONUNCIATION KEY: **(a)** æ, cat; ɑ, car; ɔ fawn; ei, snake. **(e)** e, hen; iː, sheep; iə, deer; ɛə, bear. **(i)** i, fish; ai, tiger; əː, bird. **(o)** o, ox; au, cow; ou, goat; u, poor; ɔi, royal. **(u)** ʌ, duck; u, bull; uː, goose; ə, bacillus; juː, cube. x, loch; θ, think; ð, bother; z, Zen; ʒ, corsage; dʒ, savage; ŋ, orangutang; j, yak; ʃ, fish; tʃ, fetch; 'l, rabble; 'n, redden. Complete pronunciation key appears inside front cover.

MIRAN (míræn) (*mil. acronym*) missile ranging, a missile-tracking system utilizing microwave emissions, a missile beacon, and slave stations to measure velocity and range

Mi·ran·da (mi:rándə), Francisco de (1750–1816), Venezuelan revolutionary. He took part in the Venezuelan revolution of 1810–12, and was briefly dictator (1812)

'Miranda v. Arizona' (mírændə) a landmark decision (1966) of U.S. jurisprudence, in which the Supreme Court (by a 5–4 vote) reaffirmed a suspect's constitutional rights under the Fifth Amendment. Before interrogation the suspect must be warned by the police of his right to remain silent and that anything he says may be used in evidence against him. He has a right to consult a lawyer and have him present during the questioning; and if he cannot afford a lawyer, the state must provide one. The suspect also has the right to discontinue answering questions at any time during the process. If the suspect is not advised of his rights beforehand, any confession taken from him will be inadmissible at his trial. The decision was an attempt to end police methods of forcing confessions from people unaware of their constitutional rights

mire (máiər) 1. *n.* an area of swampy land ‖ deep soft mud 2. *v.t. pres. part.* **mir·ing** *past* and *past part.* **mired** to cause to be stuck fast in mire ‖ to spatter with mud [O.N. *mýrr*, swamp]

Mi·rim, Lake (mi:rí:) a lake (108 miles long) on the east border of Uruguay, separating Uruguay from the southern tip of Brazil

mir·i·ness (máiəri:nis) *n.* the quality or state of being miry

mirk *MURK

mirkily *MURKILY

mirkiness *MURKINESS

mirky *MURKY

Mi·ró (mi:róu), Joan (1893–1983), Spanish surrealist painter. He translated natural forms into simple abstract symbols, set in flat areas of pure color, which create a pervading sense of gaiety and warmth

mir·ror (mírər) 1. *n.* a polished surface, esp. of glass backed with silver or mercury, which reflects light, and on which images can therefore be seen ‖ any smooth or polished object whose surface reflects light and images ‖ a true portrayal or representation, *his novel is a mirror of the times* 2. *v.t.* to reflect in or as if in a mirror [M.E. *mirour* fr. O.F.]

mirror image the image of something, having its parts reversed by or as if by the reflecting action of a mirror

mirth (mə:rθ) *n.* merriment characterized esp. by laughter of the kind that greets ridiculous situations, jokes etc. **mírth·ful, mírth·less** *adjs* [O.E. *myrigth*]

MIRV (mə:rv) (*acronym*) multiple independently targeted reentry vehicle, a long-range missile with multiple warheads (from 2 to 20) each of which may be targeted separately. In U.S., it is capable of being fired from Polaris (underwater), Poseidon, Trident, or Minuteman *Cf* MRV

mir·y (máiəri:) *comp.* **mir·i·er** *superl.* **mir·i·est** *adj.* having the characteristics of or pertaining to mire or a mire ‖ bespattered with mud

Mir·za A·li Mo·ham·med (míərzaáli:mouhǽmid) *BAB

Mir·za Ho·sain A·li (míərzahu:sáinǽli:) *BAHA' ULLAH

Mir·za·pur (míərzapuər) a holy town (pop. 100,000) in Uttar Pradesh, India, on the Ganges near Varanasi (Benares). Products: shellac, cotton thread, carpets, brass. Temples, mosques

mis- (mis) *prefix* (in combination with verbs) badly or incorrectly ‖ (in combination with nouns) bad, incorrect, wrong [fr. O.E. fr. Gmc]

mis·ad·ven·ture (misədvéntʃər) *n.* an unlucky accident **death by misadventure** accidental death, i.e. not involving crime or negligence [M.E. fr. O.F. *mesaventure*]

mis·ad·vise (misədváiz) *pres. part.* **mis·ad·vis·ing** *past* and *past part.* **mis·ad·vised** *v.t.* to advise wrongly

mis·al·li·ance (misəláiəns) *n.* marriage between two people not well suited to each other, esp. a mésalliance

mis·an·thrope (mízənθroup, mísənθroup) *n.* a person who hates or distrusts all mankind **mis·an·throp·ic** (mizənθrópik, misənθrópik) *adj.* **mis·an·thróp·i·cal·ly** *adv.* **mis·an·thro·pist** (mizǽnθrəpist, misǽnθrəpist), **mis·án·thro·py** *ns* [fr. Gk *misanthrōpos* fr. *misein*, to hate+*anthrōpos*, man]

mis·ap·pli·ca·tion (misæplikéiʃən) *n.* a misapplying or being misapplied

mis·ap·ply (misəplái) *pres. part.* **mis·ap·ply·ing** *past* and *past part.* **mis·ap·plied** *v.t.* to use badly or mistakenly, *to misapply one's efforts* ‖ to use (money, funds etc.) dishonestly or without proper authorization

mis·ap·pre·hend (misæprihénd) *v.t.* to misunderstand **mis·ap·pre·hen·sion** (misæprihénʃən) *n.*

mis·ap·pro·pri·ate (misəpróupri:eit) *pres. part.* **mis·ap·pro·pri·at·ing** *past* and *past part.* **mis·ap·pro·pri·at·ed** *v.t.* to embezzle (funds) ‖ to apply (funds) without proper authorization **mis·ap·pro·pri·á·tion** *n.*

mis·be·come (misbikʌ́m) *pres. part.* **mis·be·com·ing** *past* **mis·be·came** (misbikéim) *past part.* **mis·be·come** *v.t.* to be appropriate for, *it misbecomes him to criticize*

mis·be·got·ten (misbigót'n) *adj.* badly conceived, *misbegotten schemes* ‖ (*rhet.*) illegitimate

mis·be·have (misbihéiv) *pres. part.* **mis·be·hav·ing** *past* and *past part.* **mis·be·haved** *v.i.* to behave badly ‖ *v. refl.* to behave (oneself) badly **mis·be·ha·vior,** esp. *Br.* **mis·be·ha·viour** (misbihéivjər) *n.*

mis·be·lief (misbilí:f) *n.* wrong belief, esp. in religion ‖ a wrong opinion, esp. in religion

mis·be·liev·er (misbilí:vər) *n.* someone who holds a wrong or heretical belief

mis·cal·cu·late (miskǽlkjuleit) *pres. part.* **mis·cal·cu·lat·ing** *past* and *past part.* **mis·cal·cu·lat·ed** *v.t.* and *i.* to calculate wrongly **mis·cal·cu·lá·tion** *n.*

mis·call (miskɔ́l) *v.t.* to call by a wrong name

mis·car·riage (miskǽridʒ) *n.* the expulsion of a human fetus from the womb before it is viable ‖ an instance of this ‖ mismanagement ‖ an instance of this, *a miscarriage of justice* ‖ failure of a letter, package etc. to reach its destination

mis·car·ry (miskǽri:) *pres. part.* **mis·car·ry·ing** *past* and *past part.* **mis·car·ried** *v.i.* (of a plan etc.) to go wrong ‖ to undergo a miscarriage of a fetus ‖ (of a letter etc.) to fail to reach its destination

mis·cast (miskǽst, miskást) *pres. part.* **mis·cast·ing** *past* and *past part.* **mis·cast** *v.t.* to give (an actor) an unsuitable part in a play ‖ to choose unsuitable actors for (a play) ‖ (*Br.*) to add up (figures) wrongly

mis·ce·ge·na·tion (misidʒinéiʃən, misedʒinéiʃən) *n.* interbreeding or marriage between members of different races [fr. L. *miscere*, to mix+*genus*, race]

mis·cel·la·ne·a (misəléini:ə) *pl. n.* a collection of miscellaneous writings ‖ odds and ends [L. neut. pl. of *miscellaneus*, miscellaneous]

mis·cel·la·ne·ous (misəléini:əs) *adj.* formed or consisting of things of several kinds [fr. L. *miscellaneus* fr. *miscellus*, mixed]

mis·cel·la·ny (mísəleini:, *Br.* miséləni) *pl.* **mis·cel·la·nies** *n.* a miscellaneous mixture ‖ a book containing miscellaneous literary pieces [prob. fr. F. *miscellanée*]

mis·chance (mistʃǽns, mistʃáns) *n.* bad luck ‖ an instance of this [O.F. *mescheance*]

mis·chief (místʃif) *n.* annoying but not seriously harmful behavior, esp. by children ‖ playful teasing ‖ harm **to make mischief between** to cause dissension between (people or groups) [O.F. *meschief, meschef,* misfortune]

mis·chie·vous (místʃivəs) *adj.* inclined toward or characterized by playful annoyance or teasing [A. F. *meschevous,* disastrous]

misch metal (miʃ) (*metallurgy*) an alloy of cerium, lanthanum, and didymium, used in some cathode glow tubes and in some steel and aluminum alloys

mis·ci·bil·i·ty (misəbíliti:) *n.* the quality or state of being miscible

mis·ci·ble (mísəb'l) *adj.* (esp. of liquids) capable of being mixed, esp. in any ratio [fr. L. *miscere,* to mix]

mis·code (miskóud) *v.* to provide an incorrect element in a genetic code

mis·col·or, *Br.* **mis·col·our** (miskʌ́lər) *v.t.* to misrepresent ‖ to give a wrong color to

mis·con·ceive (miskənsí:v) *pres. part.* **mis·con·ceiv·ing** *past* and *past part.* **mis·con·ceived** *v.t.* to misunderstand, interpret mistakenly

mis·con·cep·tion (miskənsépʃən) *n.* the act of misconceiving ‖ an instance of this

mis·con·duct 1. (miskóndəkt, miskɔ́ndʌkt) *n.* bad management ‖ behavior improper according to some code 2. (miskəndʌ́kt) *v.t.* to mismanage ‖ to conduct (oneself) improperly

mis·con·struc·tion (miskənstrʌ́kʃən) *n.* an incorrect interpretation

mis·con·strue (miskənstrú:) *pres. part.* **mis·con·stru·ing** *past* and *past part.* **mis·con·strued** *v.t.* to interpret mistakenly

mis·count 1. (miskáunt) *v.t.* to count incorrectly ‖ *v.i.* to make a wrong count 2. (mískaunt) *n.* an incorrect count, *a miscount of votes*

mis·cre·ant (mískri:ənt) 1. *adj.* (*rhet.*) evil 2. *n.* (*rhet.*) a criminal or villain [O.F. *mescreant,* unbelieving, heretical]

mis·cue (miskjú:) 1. *n.* (*billiards*) a bad shot caused by the cue tip's slipping off the ball 2. *v.i. pres. part.* **mis·cu·ing** *past* and *past part.* **mis·cued** (*billiards*) to make a miscue ‖ (*theater*) to miss one's cue or answer the wrong one

mis·date (misdéit) *pres. part.* **mis·dat·ing** *past* and *past part.* **mis·dat·ed** *v.t.* to put a wrong date on (a document etc.) ‖ to assign a wrong date to (an event etc.)

mis·deal (misdí:l) 1. *n.* (*cards*) a mistake made in dealing 2. *v.t.* and *i.* (*cards*) to deal incorrectly

mis·deed (misdí:d) *n.* an evil or criminal action [O.E. *misdǽd*]

mis·de·mean·ant (misdimí:nənt) *n.* (*law*) a person guilty of a misdemeanor [fr. older *misdemean,* to misconduct (oneself)]

mis·de·mean·or, *Br.* **mis·de·mean·our** (misdimí:nər) *n.* (*law*) an offense technically less than a felony, not punishable by death or long imprisonment ‖ a misdeed

mis·di·rect (misdirékt) *v.t.* to give wrong instructions to, esp. about a route ‖ to put a wrong address on (a letter etc.) ‖ (of a judge) to give incorrect instructions to (a jury) ‖ to aim (something) badly, *he misdirected his punch* **mis·di·réc·tion** *n.*

mis·do·ing (misdú:iŋ) *n.* (esp. *pl.*) a misdeed

mi·ser (máizər) *n.* an avaricious person, esp. one who lives in discomfort or squalor in order to hoard his wealth [L. adj.=wretched]

mis·er·a·ble (mízərəb'l) *adj.* extremely unhappy or uncomfortable ‖ causing misery, *a miserable cold* ‖ characterized by wretched discomfort and squalor, *a miserable hovel* ‖ extremely inadequate, poor or worthless, *a miserable piece of writing* **mís·er·a·bly** *adv.* [F. *misérable*]

Mis·e·re·re (mizəréəri:) *n.* the 51st Psalm (50th in the Douai Bible) beginning 'Have mercy upon me, O God' ‖ a musical setting of this [L. imper. sing. of *miserere,* to have mercy]

mis·er·i·cord, mis·er·i·corde (mízərikɔrd, mizérikɔrd) *n.* (*hist.*) a projecting shelf beneath a hinged choir stall, on which a person standing up could support himself when the seat was tipped up ‖ (*hist.*) a dining room in a monastery in which certain relaxations from fasting were permitted ‖ (*hist.*) a dagger used to give the death wound to an injured knight [O.F. fr. L. *misericordia,* compassion]

mi·ser·li·ness (máizərli:nis) *n.* the quality or state of being miserly

mi·ser·ly (máizərli:) *adj.* characteristic of or relating to a miser

mis·er·y (mízəri:) *pl.* **mis·er·ies** *n.* extreme wretchedness due to poverty, squalor etc. ‖ extreme unhappiness or suffering ‖ a cause of these states ‖ (*pop.*) a doleful, depressing person [O.F. *miserie*]

misery index a gauge of economic discomfort, the rate of inflation plus rate of unemployment

mis·es·ti·mate (miséstəmeit) 1. *v.t. pres. part.* **mis·es·ti·mat·ing** *past* and *past part.* **mis·es·ti·mat·ed** to estimate wrongly 2. (miséstəmit) *n.* a wrong estimate

mis·fea·sance (misfí:z'ns) *n.* (*law*) the illegal or improper performance of an action in itself lawful ‖ (*law*) an instance of this **mis·féa·sor** *n.* [O.F. *mesfaisance,* a transgression]

mis·fire (misfáiər) 1. *v.i. pres. part.* **mis·fir·ing** *past* and *past part.* **mis·fired** (of a gun or explosive charge) to fail to go off ‖ (of an internal-combustion engine) to fail to ignite properly or at the right time ‖ (of a plan, joke etc.) to fail to have the effect intended 2. *n.* a misfiring

mis·fit (mísfit) *n.* a person who is unable to adjust himself to society ‖ (mísfít) a garment etc. that does not fit

mis·for·tune (misfɔ́rtʃən) *n.* mischance, bad luck ‖ an instance of this

mis·give (misgív) *pres. part.* **mis·giv·ing** *past* **mis·gave** (misgéiv) *past part.* **mis·giv·en** (misgívən) *v.t.* (old-fash.) to fill with fear, doubt or foreboding, *his mind misgave him* **mis·giv·ing** *n.* distrust, apprehension, or anticipation of failure ‖ (esp. *pl.*) an instance of these feelings

---

mis·gov·ern (misgávərn) *v.t.* to govern badly **mis·góv·ern·ment** *n.*

mis·guid·ance (misgáid'ns) *n.* a misguiding

mis·guide (misgáid) *pres. part.* **mis·guid·ing** *past* and *past part.* **mis·guid·ed** *v.t.* to misdirect **mis·guid·ed** *adj.* mistaken because of false ideas, poor advice etc.

mis·han·dle (mishǽnd'l) *pres. part.* **mis·han·dling** *past* and *past part.* **mis·han·dled** *v.t.* to handle in a rough manner ‖ to deal badly or unwisely with (a situation etc.)

mis·hap (míshæp) *n.* an unlucky accident

mis·hear (mishíər) *pres. part.* **mis·hear·ing** *past* and *past part.* **mis·heard** (mishé:rd) *v.t.* to hear incorrectly

mis·hit 1. (míshit) *n.* a faulty stroke in a ball game, esp. in cricket 2. *v.t.* (mishít) *pres. part.* **mis·hit·ting** *past* and *past part.* **mis·hit** to hit (a ball) badly

mish·mash (míʃmaʃ) *n.* a hodgepodge

Mish·nah, Mish·na (míʃnə) *pl.* **Mish·na·yoth** (míʃnɑjóut) *n.* a compilation of the oral tradition of the Jewish Law, made probably by Judah ha-Nasi (135–c. 220). It is written in Hebrew, and forms the first part of the Talmud ‖ a paragraph of this compilation ‖ the teachings of a rabbi **Mish·na·ic** (miʃnéiik) *adj.* [Heb.=repetition, instruction]

mis·in·form (misinfórm) *v.t.* to give wrong or misleading information to **mis·in·for·ma·tion** (misinfərméiʃən) *n.*

mis·in·ter·pret (misinté:rprit) *v.t.* to interpret wrongly **mis·in·ter·pre·ta·tion** *n.*

mis·join·der (misdʒóindər) *n.* (*law*) the joining in a court action of parties or causes which do not properly belong to that action

mis·judge (misdʒÁdʒ) *pres. part.* **mis·judg·ing** *past* and *past part.* **mis·judged** *v.t.* to judge wrongly, *to misjudge a distance* ‖ to judge unfairly, *you misjudge him if you think he would bear malice* **mis·júdg·ment, mis·júdge·ment** *n.*

Mis·kolc (míʃkɔlts) a market and industrial town (pop. 211,200) in N.E. Hungary: engineering, chemicals, iron and steel, food processing. Technical university

mis·lay (misléi) *pres. part.* **mis·lay·ing** *past* and *past part.* **mis·laid** (misléid) *v.t.* to lose (something) temporarily by forgetting where one has put it

mis·lead (mislí:d) *pres. part.* **mis·lead·ing** *past* and *past part.* **mis·led** (misléd) *v.t.* to deceive by causing to infer something not actually true ‖ to lead in a wrong direction **mis·léad·ing** *adj.* [O. E. *mislǣdan*]

mis·man·age (mismǽnidʒ) *pres. part.* **mis·man·ag·ing** *past* and *past part.* **mis·man·aged** *v.t.* to manage incompetently or dishonestly **mis·mán·age·ment** *n.*

mis·match (mismǽtʃ) 1. *v.t.* to match incorrectly or inappropriately 2. *n.* an example of bad matching

mis·mate (misméit) *pres. part.* **mis·mat·ing** *past* and *past part.* **mis·mat·ed** *v.t.* and *i.* to mate inappropriately

mis·name (misnéim) *pres. part.* **mis·nam·ing** *past* and *past part.* **mis·named** *v.t.* to call by the wrong name

mis·no·mer (misnóumər) *n.* a wrong name or designation ‖ (*law*) the using of a wrong name or title, esp. in a document [A.F. and O.F. *mesnommer*, to misname]

mi·sog·a·mist (misógəmist) *n.* a person who hates marriage

mi·sog·a·my (misógəmi) *n.* hatred of marriage [fr. Gk *misein*, to hate+*gamos*, marriage]

mi·sog·y·nist (misódʒinist) *n.* a man who hates women **mi·sóg·y·nous** *adj.* **mi·sóg·y·ny** *n.* [fr. Gk *misein*, to hate+*gunē*, woman]

mis·o·ri·ent (misóuri:ent) *v.* 1. to fail in adjusting or in helping others adjust to facts or to a situation 2. to direct a person incorrectly — **misorientation** *n.*

mis·place (mispléis) *pres. part.* **mis·plac·ing** *past* and *past part.* **mis·placed** *v.t.* to put in the wrong place ‖ to bestow (affection, trust etc.) on a wrong object ‖ to mislay **mis·pláce·ment** *n.*

mis·play 1. (mispléi) *v.t.* (*sports*) to play wrongly or badly 2. (míspléi) *n.* an instance of misplaying

mis·plead·ing (misplí:diŋ) *n.* (*law*) an error in pleading

mis·print 1. (misprínt) *v.t.* to print inaccurately 2. (míspr̩int) *n.* a mistake in printing

mis·pri·sion (mispríʒən) *n.* (*law*) misconduct or neglect of duty, esp. by a public official ‖ (*law*) concealment of knowledge of a felony or of trea-

son by a person other than the culprit [A.F. *mesprisioun*]

mis·pro·nounce (misprənáuns) *pres. part.* **mis·pro·nounc·ing** *past* and *past part.* **mis·pro·nounced** *v.t.* and *i.* to pronounce incorrectly **mis·pro·nun·ci·a·tion** (misprənÁnsi:éiʃən) *n.* the act of mispronouncing ‖ an instance of this

mis·quo·ta·tion (miskwoutéiʃən) *n.* the act of misquoting ‖ an instance of this

mis·quote (miskwáut) *pres. part.* **mis·quot·ing** *past* and *past part.* **mis·quot·ed** *v.t.* and *i.* to quote incorrectly

mis·read (misrí:d) *pres. part.* **mis·read·ing** *past* and *past part.* **mis·read** (misréd) *v.t.* to read incorrectly ‖ to interpret incorrectly

mis·re·mem·ber (misrimémbər) *v.t.* to remember incorrectly

mis·rep·re·sent (misreprizént) *v.t.* to give a false impression or account of, either deliberately or unintentionally **mis·rep·re·sen·ta·tion** *n.* a false impression or account ‖ the act of misrepresenting

mis·rule (misrú:l) 1. *n.* bad or inadequate government 2. *v.t. pres. part.* **mis·rul·ing** *past* and *past part.* **mis·ruled** to rule (a country) badly **Miss.** Mississippi

Miss (mis) *pl.* **Miss·es** *n.* (followed by the name) the title of an unmarried woman or girl ‖ (not followed by the name) sometimes used as the title of address to an (esp. unknown) unmarried woman, *may I help you, Miss?* [shortened fr. MISTRESS]

miss (mis) 1. *v.t.* to fail to hit, reach, meet or make contact with, *to miss the target, to miss one's train* ‖ to allow (an opportunity etc.) to pass by ‖ to fail to perceive, *to miss the point* ‖ to notice the loss or absence of ‖ to regret the loss or absence of ‖ to escape, avoid, *he just missed going to jail* ‖ to fail or be unable to attend, *she missed her lesson* ‖ to omit, *the pianist missed a bar* ‖ *v.i.* (of engines) to fail to fire ‖ to fail to hit something aimed at **to miss stays** (*naut.*) to fail to go about from one course to another **to miss the boat** to fail to take advantage of an opportunity 2. *n.* a failure to hit or catch **to give (something) a miss** (*Br.*) to omit or avoid (something) [O.E. *missan*]

mis·sal (mís'l) *n.* (*Roman Catholicism*) a book containing everything said or sung at Mass for the entire year [fr. eccles. L. *missale* neut. of *missalis* adj., pertaining to the Mass]

missel thrush *MISTLE THRUSH

mis·sense mutation or **missense** (míssens) (*genetics*) a mutation in which codons that normally cause the inclusion of one amino acid cause a different amino acid to be included in the genetic code *Cf* NONSENSE MUTATION

mis·shap·en (misʃéipən) *adj.* deformed [M.E. fr. MIS-+*shapen*, shaped]

mis·sile (mís'l, *Br.* esp. mísail) 1. *n.* a weapon or object that is thrown or fired or designed for this 2. *adj.* suitable for throwing or being discharged at a distant target [fr. L. *missilis*]

missile decoy (*mil.*) an unarmed vehicle launched to attract enemy fire, confuse radar, and divert from penetration by enemy weapons systems

mis·sile·man (mísəlmən) *pl.* **mis·sile·men** (mísəlmən) *n.* someone concerned with the designing, building, operating or launching of missiles

miss·ing (mísiŋ) *adj.* lost or absent

missing link a hypothetical organism intermediate between two known types, esp. between the apes and man

mis·sion (míʃən) *n.* a group of people sent esp. abroad by a Church or other religious organization to make conversions ‖ the area of this group's operations ‖ the buildings acting as its center ‖ a group of people working temporarily in a parish to invigorate its religious life ‖ a set of services and sermons designed for the work of this group ‖ an isolated district served by the clergy from a neighboring church ‖ a body doing religious and charitable work in a particular section of society, *a seamen's mission* ‖ the building where such work is centered ‖ a body of representatives sent abroad for special diplomatic discussions etc. ‖ the work they are sent to do ‖ any task, esp. of a diplomatic nature, that one is sent to do ‖ a permanent diplomatic delegation abroad ‖ an aim in life, arising from a conviction or sense of calling ‖ an assigned combat operation, e.g. by aircraft [fr. L. *missio* (*missionis*), a sending]

mis·sion·ar·y (míʃəneri) 1. *n. pl.* **mis·sion·ar·ies** a person who undertakes the work of a religious mission 2. *adj.* of or pertaining to a religious mission ‖ characteristic of or perform-

ing the work of a missionary [fr. Mod. L. *missionarius* adj.]

missionary position (*colloq.*) in sexual intercourse, the position in which the female lies on her back and the male is on top facing her

mis·sion·er (míʃənər) *n.* a missionary, esp. one conducting a home parish mission

Mis·sis·sip·pi (misisípi) (*abbr.* **Miss.**) a state (area 47,716 sq. miles, pop. 2,551,000) in the S.E. central U.S.A. Capital: Jackson. It is mostly fertile plain, with uplands in the east. Agriculture: cotton, tung-oil seeds, cattle, poultry, corn. Resources: oil and natural gas, timber. Industries: pulp, paper, wood products, agricultural processing, clothing and textiles. State university (1844) at Oxford. Mississippi was a French colony (1699–1763), and passed to Britain (1763) and to the U.S.A. (1783). It became (1817) the 20th state of the U.S.A.

Mississippi the chief river system (providing 14,000 miles of waterway) of North America, draining the basin of the Middle Western U.S.A. between the Appalachians and the Rocky Mtns. Measured from the source of its chief headstream, the Missouri, it is 3,710 miles long. The Mississippi River proper rises in N. Minnesota and flows south, forming borders of nine states, for 2,350 miles, receiving the Missouri at St Louis and the Ohio (main eastern stream) at Cairo, Illinois, to a great delta on the Gulf of Mexico. Other ports: Minneapolis, Memphis, New Orleans

Mis·sis·sip·pi·an (misisípi:ən) 1. *adj.* of or relating to the state of Mississippi or the Mississippi River ‖ of or relating to the people of the state ‖ (*geol.*) of the period or system in North America corresponding to the earlier Carboniferous (*GEOLOGICAL TIME) the Mississippian the Mississippian period or system of rocks 2. *n.* a native or inhabitant of Mississippi

mis·sive (mísiv) *n.* a formal or official letter, esp. from someone in authority [fr. F. *missive* adj. or L. *missivus* adj., (a letter) sent or to be sent]

Mis·sour·i (mizúəri:) (*abbr.* **Mo.**) a state (area 69,686 sq. miles, pop. 4,951,000) in the central U.S.A. Capital: Jefferson City. Chief city: St Louis. The south is covered with forested hills, and the north is mainly plain. Agriculture: corn, soybeans, beef and dairy cattle, hogs. Resources: lead, coal, building materials. Industries: transport equipment, food processing, metal refining. Chief universities: University of Missouri (1839) at Columbia, Washington University (1857) at St Louis. Missouri was explored by the French (late 17th c.), was ceded to Spain (1762), and was returned to France (1800). As part of the Louisiana Purchase (1803) it was bought by the U.S.A., of which it became (1821) the 24th state

Missouri the chief headstream (2,315 miles long) of the Mississippi River system, rising in the Rocky Mtns in Montana, and flowing through North Dakota, South Dakota (forming the Iowa border) and Missouri to join the Mississippi at St Louis. Chief port: Kansas City

Missouri Compromise (*Am. hist.*) a group of measures passed (1820–1), admitting Missouri to the Union as a slave state and Maine as a free state and dividing the rest of the Louisiana Purchase into a slave area in the South and a free area in the North

mis·spell (misspél) *pres. part.* **mis·spell·ing** *past* and *past part.* **mis·spelled, mis·spelt** (misspélt) *v.t.* to spell incorrectly **mis·spéll·ing** *n.* an instance of incorrect spelling

mis·spend (misspénd) *pres. part.* **mis·spend·ing** *past* and *past part.* **mis·spent** (misspént) *v.t.* to spend wastefully

mis·state (misstéit) *pres. part.* **mis·stat·ing** *past* and *past part.* **mis·stat·ed** *v.t.* to state incorrectly **mis·státe·ment** *n.*

mis·step (misstép) *n.* a step taken in a wrong or clumsy way ‖ an error or blunder

mist (mist) *n.* a mass of minute particles of water, suspended in the atmosphere or precipitated in particles finer than raindrops ‖ (*Br., meteor.*) an atmosphere in which visibility is between 1,100 and 2,200 yds ‖ a film or haze before the eyes causing dimness of vision, *a mist of tears* ‖ a thin film of moisture on the surface of something [O.E.]

mist *v.i.* to become misty ‖ *v.t.* to make misty [O.E. *mistian*]

mis·tak·a·ble (mistéikəb'l) *adj.* that may be mistaken or misunderstood

mis·take (mistéik) 1. *v.t. pres. part.* **mis·tak·ing** *past* **mis·took** (mistúk) *past part.* **mis·tak·en**

(mistéikən) to misunderstand ‖ to form an incorrect estimate of, have a wrong opinion of ‖ to think wrongly that (someone or something) is another specified person or thing, *she mistook him for the professor* **there is no mistaking (something)** no one can fail to recognize (something), *there is no mistaking his sincerity* **2.** *n.* a misunderstanding ‖ an instance of incorrectness or of wrong opinion or judgment, *spelling mistakes, it was a mistake to think he could pass that examination* **and no mistake** (as an intensive) without doubt, certainly, *the plot is complicated and no mistake!* **mis·ták·en** *adj.* (of persons) committing an error in opinion or judgment ‖ involving error in judgment or behavior [O.N. *mistaka,* to take by mistake]

Mis·ter (místər) *n.* (*abbr.* Mr.) a courtesy title for any male adult not styled 'Sir', 'Dr' etc. ‖ a form of address to the holder of any of certain offices, *Mr. Chairman* **mister** (*pop.,* esp. used by beggars and children) sir [var. of MASTER]

Mis·ti (mí:sti:) a volcano (19,166 ft) in the Andes of S.W. Peru near Arequipa

mist·i·ly (místili:) *adv.* in a misty way

mis·time (mistáim) *pres. part.* **mis·tim·ing** *past and past part.* **mis·timed** *v.t.* to time (something) badly or incorrectly [O.E. *mistīmian*]

mist·i·ness (místi:nis) *n.* the quality or state of being misty

mis·tle thrush, mis·sel thrush (mísəlθrʌʃ) *Turdus viscivorus,* a large European thrush which eats mistletoe berries [O.E. *mistel,* basil, mistletoe]

mis·tle·toe (mís'ltou) *n. Viscum album,* fam. *Loranthaceae,* a Eurasian evergreen semiparasitic shrub growing on esp. deciduous trees, e.g. the apple. It has profuse dichotomous branching, thick, simple leaves, usually dioecious flowers, and bears a white viscous berry. At Christmas it is often hung in some Western countries from the ceiling, and it is traditional for any girl standing under it to be kissed ‖ any of several other plants of fam. *Loranthaceae* having similar characteristics, esp. any member of *Phoradendron,* a genus of American plants [O.E. *misteltān*]

mistook *past* of MISTAKE

Mis·tral (mi:stræl), Frédéric (1830–1914), French poet who worked to restore the Provençal language

Mis·tral (mi:strál), Gabriela (Lucila Godoy Alcayaga, 1889–1957), Chilean poetess

mis·tral (místrál, místrəl) *n.* a powerful, cold, dry northerly wind in the Mediterranean provinces of France [F.]

Mis·tram (místræm) *n.* (*mil.*) a system for measuring the trajectory of a missile, designed by General Electric Company

mis·trans·late (mistrænsléit, mistrænzléit) *pres. part.* **mis·trans·lat·ing** *past and past part.* **mis·trans·lat·ed** *v.t.* to translate wrongly **mis·trans·lá·tion** *n.*

mis·treat (mistrí:t) *v.t.* to treat wrongly or badly, abuse

mis·tress (místris) *n.* a woman in relation to a man not her husband with whom she frequently has sexual relations ‖ a woman in relation to her servants or pets ‖ (*Br.*) a woman schoolteacher ‖ a woman who is in control, *mistress of the situation* [O.F. *maistresse*]

mis·tri·al (mistráiəl) *n.* (*law*) a trial declared void because of an error in proceedings ‖ a trial in which the jury cannot agree upon a verdict

mis·trust (mistrást) **1.** *v.t.* to regard with suspicion ‖ to feel no confidence in, *he mistrusts his own capacities* **2.** *n.* suspicion ‖ lack of confidence **mis·trúst·ful** *adj.*

mist·y (místi:) *comp.* **mist·i·er** *superl.* **mist·i·est** *adj.* covered in mist ‖ characterized by mist, *a misty autumn day* ‖ blurred, indistinct, *a misty outline* [O.E. *mistig*]

mis·un·der·stand (misʌndərstǽnd) *pres. part.* **mis·un·der·stand·ing** *past and past part.* **mis·un·der·stood** *v.t.* to interpret incorrectly **mis·un·der·stánd·ing** *n.* a misinterpretation ‖ a quarrel or disagreement **mis·un·der·stóod** *adj.* wrongly interpreted ‖ not getting proper sympathy or appreciation

mis·us·age (misjú:sidʒ) *n.* incorrect usage, e.g. of words

mis·use 1. (misjú:s) *n.* improper or incorrect use **2.** (misjú:z) *v.t. pres. part.* **mis·us·ing** *past and past part.* **mis·used** to use improperly or incorrectly ‖ to treat wrongly or abusively

mis·us·er (misjú:zər) *n.* (*law*) the misuse of a privilege, benefit etc. [O.F. *mesuser*]

M.I.T. *MASSACHUSETTS INSTITUTE OF TECHNOLOGY

MIT (*securities abbr.*) market-if-touched or board order, an order that becomes a market order when a particular price is reached. A sell MIT is placed above the market; a buy MIT is placed below the market

mi·ta (míta) *n.* forced, unpaid labor that the Indians were compelled to perform for the colonists in Latin America [Span.]

Mitch·ell (mítʃəl), Margaret (1900–49), U.S. novelist, known for her 'Gone with the Wind' (1936), which depicted the Civil War and Reconstruction era from the southern point of view. It became the largest selling novel in the history of U.S. publishing

Mitchell, Wesley Clair (1874–1948), U.S. economist and pioneer in the quantitative study of economic behavior. He became the leading authority on business cycles

Mitchell, William ('Billy') (1879–1936), U.S. military officer and pioneer in military aviation. The outstanding U.S. combat air commander of the 1st world war, he foresaw the value of strategic bombing and mass airborne operations, the eclipse of the battleship by the airplane, and the strategic importance of Alaska and the polar areas. An outspoken critic of the military hierarchy, he was convicted (1925) by court-martial of insubordination, and resigned (1926) from the service

Mitchell, Mount the highest peak (6,684 ft) in the Appalachian Mtns. It is in the Black Mtns range in W. North Carolina, and is the highest point east of the Mississippi River

mite (mait) *n.* any of several widely distributed, minute, sometimes microscopic arachnids of order *Acarina,* closely related to and resembling ticks, though much smaller. They occur as parasites of vertebrates, insects and plants, causing various diseases, and are found as pests in stored food. They also occur in harmless free-living aquatic and terrestrial forms [O.E. *mite*]

mite *n.* (*hist.*) a coin of very small value ‖ a very small thing, quantity, contribution etc. [M. Du. *mite*]

mi·ter, esp. *Br.* **mi·tre** (máitər) *n.* a tall ornamented liturgical headdress worn by bishops and some abbots as a symbol of office [fr. F. *mitre* fr. L. fr. Gk *mitra,* belt, turban]

miter, esp. *Br.* **mitre 1.** *n.* (*carpentry*) a miter joint ‖ (*carpentry*) either of the surfaces that come together in a miter joint **2.** *v.t. pres. part.* **mi·ter·ing,** esp. *Br.* **mi·tring** *past and past part.* **mi·tered,** esp. *Br.* **mi·tred** to fit together in a miter joint ‖ to shape the ends of (two pieces of wood) for joining them in a miter joint [perh. fr. MITER, headdress]

miter box, esp. *Br.* **mitre box** (*carpentry*) a device for guiding the saw in constructing miter joints

miter joint, esp. *Br.* **mitre joint** (*carpentry*) an angled joint in which the line of junction bisects the angle

Mith·ra·ic (miθréiik) *adj.* of Mithras or Mithraism

Mith·ra·ism (míθreiizəm) *n.* the cult of Mithras. The religion spread from Persia through the Roman Empire from 68 B.C., esp. among merchants and in the army. It became a serious rival to Christianity (2nd and 3rd cc.) but declined in the 4th c. It was a personal faith, emphasizing the conflict of good and evil, and the reward of virtue and punishment of wickedness in the afterlife

Mith·ras (míθræs) the ancient Persian god of light and the sun, usually represented in the act of sacrificing a bull (* MITHRAISM)

Mith·ri·da·tes VI (miθrideíti:z) 'the Great' (c. 131–63 B.C.), king of Pontus (c. 115–63 B.C.). His expansionist policy in Asia Minor involved him in a series of wars with Rome (88–63 B.C.). His attempt to invade Greece was defeated (85 B.C.) by Sulla and he was expelled from Bithynia (72 B.C.) by Lucullus. Decisively defeated (66 B.C.) by Pompey, he committed suicide

mit·i·ga·ble (mítigəb'l) *adj.* capable of being mitigated [fr. L. *mitigare,* to mollify]

mit·i·gate (mítigeit) *pres. part.* **mit·i·gat·ing** *past and past part.* **mit·i·gat·ed** *v.t.* to make less severe, alleviate, *to mitigate grief* ‖ (*fig.*) to cause to put something in a less harsh light, *mitigating circumstances* **mit·i·gá·tion** *n.* **mit·i·ga·tive** (mítigeitiv) *adj.* **mít·i·ga·tor** *n.* **mit·i·ga·to·ry** (mítigətɔ:ri, mítigətouri:) *adj.* [fr. L. *mitigare* (*mitigatus*), to mollify]

Mi·tla (mí:tla) the sacred city of the Zapotecas, near Oaxaca, S. Mexico

mi·to·chon·dri·on (maitəkóndri:ən) *pl.* **mi·to·chon·dri·a** (maitəkóndri:ə) *n.* (*cytol.*) a specialized membrane structure within a cell that provides energy for a cell by addition of substances acted upon by enzymes

mi·to·gen (máitədʒen) *n.* a drug that promotes mitosis —**mitogenic** *adj.* —**mitogenicity** *n.*

mi·to·my·cin [C₁₅H₁₈N₄O₅] (maitəmáis'n) *n.* (*pharm.*) compound of antibiotics used in the treatment of cancer; marketed as Mutamycin

mi·to·sis (maitóusis, mitóusis) *n.* the process of cell division in which a sequence of nuclear changes, resulting in the production of daughter cells each having exactly the same chromosome complement as the parent, precedes cytoplasmic division (*PROPHASE, *METAPHASE, *ANAPHASE, *TELOPHASE, cf. MEIOSIS, cf. AMITOSIS) **mi·tot·ic** (maitótik, mitótik) *adj.* [Mod. L. fr. Gk *mitos,* thread]

mi·tral (máitrəl) *adj.* like a miter ‖ of or concerning the mitral valve [F.]

mitral valve the valve enabling blood to pass from the left auricle to the left ventricle, but not back again, in the heart of a higher vertebrate

Mi·tre (mí:tre) Bartolomé (1821–1906), Argentinian soldier and statesman. He was president (1862–8) of Argentina and successfully led the armies of Argentina, Brazil and Uruguay against Paraguay (1865–70)

mitre *MITER

Mitsch·er (mítʃər), Marc Andrew (1887–1947), U.S. admiral and commander of the aircraft-carrier force, Task Force 58, in the Pacific during the 2nd world war. He directed air action in the Battle of Midway, the Solomon Is campaign, the Battle of the Philippines, the Battle of Leyte Gulf, and in the capture of Iwo Jima and Okinawa

Mitsch·er·lick (mítʃərlix), Eilhard (1794–1863), German chemist. He discovered isomorphism (1819), observed the dimorphic character of sulfur, and was a pioneer in the study of catalysis

mitsvah *MITZVAH

mitt (mit) *n.* a glove which leaves the fingers and thumb bare ‖ (*baseball*) a padded glove used to catch the ball ‖ a mitten [MITTEN]

mit·ten (mít'n) *n.* a glove which has a single section for the four fingers and a separate division for the thumb ‖ a glove which leaves thumb and fingers bare [F. *mitaine*]

Mitterand (mí:təra), François (1916–), French statesman, president (1981–). A Socialist, he was a member of the National Assembly (1946–) and served as minister of state (1952–3), interior (1954–5) and justice (1956–7). In 1965 he became president of the Federation of the Democratic and Socialist Left and leader of the Socialist party in 1971. As president he leaned toward nationalization of banks and industries, increased welfare and government decentralization. Budget cuts due to inflation and recession caused a drop in popularity in the mid-1980s

mit·ti·mus (mítəməs) *n.* (*law*) a warrant committing a person to prison [L.=we send]

MI-24 helicopters (*mil.*) U.S.S.R. flying tanks

mitz·vah, mits·vah (mítsvə) *pl.* **mitz·voth, mits·voth** (mitsvóut), **mitz·vahs, mits·vahs** *n.* (*Judaism*) a biblical or rabbinical commandment ‖ (*Judaism*) an action in keeping with such a commandment, esp. an act of charity [Heb. *miswāh*]

mix (miks) **1.** *v.t.* to combine, *to mix business with pleasure* ‖ to bring together into a single uniform mass, *to mix ingredients* ‖ to prepare by putting ingredients together, *to mix a drink* ‖ to cause to associate, *her party mixed old and young together* ‖ to crossbreed ‖ *v.i.* to become mixed ‖ to be capable of being mixed ‖ to get along with others socially **to mix up** to mix thoroughly, *mix up the ingredients* ‖ (with 'with') to mistake for another, *people often mix him up with his brother* ‖ (with 'in') to involve, *don't mix him up in your intrigues* ‖ to cause mental confusion in **2.** *n.* a mixture ‖ a commercial preparation of various ingredients, *a cake mix* **mixed** *adj.* blended ‖ made up of different sorts, types, or qualities, *mixed feelings of sadness and pleasure* ‖ consisting of or including persons of both sexes, *mixed bathing* ‖ for or including people of different races, religions etc. ‖ (*bot.*) combining racemose and cymose formations ‖ (*phon.,* of vowels) central [fr. older *mixt* adj. fr. F. *mixte,* mixed]

mixed bag a miscellany in which some things are of good quality, some not

CONCISE PRONUNCIATION KEY: **(a)** æ, c*a*t; ɑ, c*ar*; ɔ f*aw*n; ei, sn*a*ke. **(e)** e, h*e*n; i:, sh*ee*p; iə, d*eer*; ɛə, b*ear*. **(i)** i, f*i*sh; ai, t*i*ger; ə:, b*ir*d. **(o)** o, *o*x; au, c*ow*; ou, g*oa*t; u, p*oo*r; ɔi, r*oy*al. **(u)** ʌ, d*u*ck; u, b*u*ll; u:, g*oo*se; ə, b*a*cill*u*s; ju:, c*u*be. x, lo*ch*; θ, *th*ink; ð, bo*th*er; z, *Z*en; ʒ, cor*s*age; dʒ, sava*g*e; ŋ, ora*n*gutang; j, *y*ak; ʃ, *fi*sh; tʃ, fe*tch*; 'l, rabb*le*; 'n, redd*en.* Complete pronunciation key appears inside front cover.

mixed doubles (*tennis*) a series of games in which a man and woman play against another man and woman

mixed economy (*economics*) an economic system with private capitalism, state ownership, cooperatives, e.g., Israel, Sweden

mixed farming the growing of crops etc. and the keeping of livestock on the same farm

mixed media the use of several types of communication devices in the same presentation, e.g., film, photographs, tapes, sculpture, slides, etc. —**mixed-media** adj. Cf INTERMEDIA, MULTIMEDIA

mixed metaphor a metaphor bringing together incongruous metaphors in one sentence

mixed number a number consisting of a whole number and a fraction

mixed-up (míkstʌp) adj. confused, esp. (*pop.*) emotionally

mix·er (míksər) n. a person with regard to his (specified) ability to mix socially ‖ a kitchen apparatus for beating or mixing foods ‖ an apparatus or person controlling sound volume from different sources in broadcasting

Mi·xe-Zo·que (mí:heisóukei) n. (Zoquean), a S. Mexican language stock comprising Mixe in E. Oaxaca, Zoque mainly in N.W. Chiapas, and Popoluca in E. central Veracruz. In the 1960s there were about 34,600 Mixe, 7,700 Zoque and 2,100 Popoluca

Mix·o·lyd·i·an mode (mɪksəlídi:ən) (*mus.*) a medieval authentic mode represented by the white piano keys ascending from G ‖ (*mus.*) the ancient Greek mode represented by the white piano keys descending from B [Gk *mixo-ludios*, half-Lydian]

Mix·tec (mí:stek) n. a member of an Indian people of S.W. Mexico, thought to have developed an advanced culture on the highlands of Mexico before the 7th c.

Mix·te·ca (mi:stéka) pl. **Mix·te·ca, Mix·te·cas** n. a Mexican people inhabiting the region of Oaxaca, Guerrero and Puebla. Towards the 10th c. the Mixtecas overcame the Zapotecas and introduced a brilliant culture, shown in the remnants of Monte Alban and Mitla. The Mixtec-Zapoteco language is spoken today by about 450,000 ‖ a member of this people

mix·ture (míkstʃər) n. a mixing or being mixed ‖ something made by mixing ‖ a yarn made of threads of different colors ‖ a fabric made from such yarn ‖ a heterogeneous collection ‖ an explosive charge of fuel and air in an internal-combustion engine ‖ (*chem.*) a substance made up of two or more components not in fixed proportion and which are held to retain their separate identities however thoroughly mingled (cf. COMPLEX, cf. COMPOUND) [fr. L. *mixtura*]

mix-up (míksʌp) n. a state of confusion ‖ an instance of this

Mi·ya·za·ki (mi:jazɑki:) an agricultural center and port (pop. 141,000) of S.E. Kyushu, Japan: Miyazaki-jingu Shinto shrine

miz·zen, miz·en (míz'n) n. (*naut.*) the lowest of the fore-and-aft sails of a ship ‖ a mizzenmast [F. *misaine*]

miz·zen·mast, (*Br.* esp.) **miz·en·mast** (míz'n·mæst, míz'nmæst, míz'nmɑst) n. the aftermost mast of a three-masted ship

miz·zle (míz'l) pres. part. **miz·zling** past and past part. **miz·zled** v.i. (*impers.*) to rain very finely [rel. to Du. dial. *miezelen*]

mks *METER-KILOGRAM-SECOND SYSTEM

MLD (*med. abbr.*) median lethal dose

MMPI (*psych. abbr.*) Minnesota Multiphasic Personality Inventory, psychological test of personality qualities involving 550 items, including validating scales

mne·mon·ic (ni:mɒnik, nimónik) 1. adj. meant to help the memory 2. n. an aid (e.g. a rhyme) to prompt the memory **mne·món·ics** n. the science or art of improving the memory ‖ a technique or system used to train the memory [fr. Gk *mnemonikos* fr. *mnasthai*, to remember]

Mne·mos·y·ne (ni:mózini:) (*Gk mythol.*) the goddess of memory and mother of the Muses

Mo. Missouri

mo. month

mo·a (móuə) n. any of several extinct flightless, ratite birds of New Zealand, belonging to fam. *Dinornithidae* and ranging from turkey-size to about 12 ft tall [Maori]

Mo·ab (móuæb) (*hist.*) an ancient region of Jordan, east of the Dead Sea, which flourished (9th–6th cc. B.C.), following a successful revolt against Israel (c. 850 B.C.) ‖ (or Kir Moab) its citadel (*KERAK)

moan (moun) 1. n. a low, long sound expressing pain or grief ‖ a sound resembling this, *the moan of the wind* 2. v.t. to say with a moan ‖ to lament about, bewail ‖ v.i. to utter a moan ‖ (of the wind etc.) to make a sound like a moan ‖ to complain or lament [M.E. *mone* prob. rel. to O.E. *mœnan*, to complain]

Moa·si·a (mí:ʃi:ə) (*hist.*) a province of the Roman Empire, extending north of Thrace and Macedonia to the Danube and the Black Sea

moat (mout) n. a deep, wide trench dug around a fortification, town etc. to prevent invasion, usually filled with water **móat·ed** adj. surrounded by a moat [M.E. *mote, mot* fr. O. F.]

mob (mɒb) 1. n. a large, esp. rough and disorderly crowd ‖ a gang of criminals **the mob** (used contemptuously) the lower classes of society 2. v. pres. part. **mob·bing** past and past part. **mobbed** v.t. to crowd around and inconvenience or molest ‖ to crowd into, *the streets were mobbed* ‖ v.i. to form a mob [older *mobile* fr. L. *mobile* (*vulgus*), excitable (crowd)]

mob·cap (mɒbkæp) n. (*hist.*) a woman's indoor cap with frills and a chin fastening, worn in the 18th and 19th cc. [fr. older *mob*, woman's cap]

Mo·bile (móubi:l) a port (pop. 178,157) of S.W. Alabama on Mobile Bay: shipbuilding, textiles, pulp and paper

mo·bile (móub'l, *Br.* esp. móubail) 1. adj. capable of moving or being moved ‖ moving or moved with ease ‖ extremely fluid ‖ (of facial expression or features) showing changes of feeling 2. n. a sculpture consisting of an arrangement of carefully balanced and suspended articulated forms kept constantly moving in various planes by air currents [F. fr. L. *mobilis*]

mobile missiles (*mil.*) proposed ICBM system (MX) of nuclear missiles that are constantly moved (on tracks) so as to avoid providing a knowable target

mo·bil·i·ty (moubíliti:) n. the state or quality of being mobile [F. *mobilité*]

mo·bi·li·za·tion (moubəlizéiʃən) n. a mobilizing or being mobilized [F. *mobilisation*]

mo·bi·lize (móubəlaiz) pres. part. **mo·bi·liz·ing** past and past part. **mo·bi·lized** v.t. (*mil.*) to assemble (troops) in readiness for active service ‖ v.i. (*mil.*) to be assembled in readiness for active service [fr. F. *mobiliser*]

Mö·bi·us strip or **Möbius band** (móbi:əs) (*topology*) the surface of a strip of paper twisted once, with ends glued, presenting a single edge

MOBS (mɒbz) n. (*mil. acronym*) multiple orbit bombardment system, weapons system utilizing warhead-carrying satellites

mob·ster (mɒbstər) n. (*pop.*) a member of a criminal gang

Mobutu Sese Seko (moubú:tu:séiseiseíkou) (1930–) Zairian president (1967–), born Joseph Désiré. Under Patrice Lumumba he was secretary of state for national defense, but overthrew Lumumba in 1960 and served as army commander in chief (1961–5) under Joseph Kasavubu. After overthrowing Kasavubu (1966) he became prime minister in 1966 and president in 1967

Mo·çam·bi·que (mousəmbí:kə) *MOZAMBIQUE

mo·camp (móukæmp) n. grounds providing facilities for trailers and campers, e.g., water, toilets, showers, etc.

moc·ca·sin (mɒkəsin) n. a soft heelless shoe of deerskin, worn by North American Indians ‖ a shoe resembling this ‖ a North American poisonous snake of genus *Agkistrodon*, esp. the water moccasin [of Algonquian origin]

moccasin flower the lady's slipper

mo·cha (móukə) n. a superior type of coffee grown in Arabia ‖ any coffee of superior quality ‖ a flavoring made with coffee or with chocolate and coffee [after *Mocha*, a seaport in S.W. Arabia]

mock (mɒk) 1. v.t. to ridicule ‖ to imitate, esp. in order to ridicule ‖ to thwart as if in ridicule, *the riots mocked their efforts at reconciliation* ‖ to disappoint, esp. so as to make (someone or something) seem ridiculous, *mocked by false expectations* ‖ v.i. (esp. with 'at') to express ridicule 2. adj. false, sham, *a mock battle* 3. n. (in the phrase) **to make a mock of** to ridicule [M.E. *mokken, mocque* fr. O. F. *mocquer*]

mock·er·y (mɒkəri:) pl. **mock·er·ies** n. derision, ridicule ‖ an object of mocking, *to make a mockery of someone's efforts* ‖ a travesty, *his replies were a mockery of the truth* [F. *moquerie*]

mock-he·ro·ic (mɒkhiróuik) adj. burlesquing heroic action, character etc.

mock·ing·bird (mɒkiŋbə:rd) n. *Mimus polyglottos,* fam. *Mimidae,* a bird of southern North America, Central America, and the West Indies which imitates the cries and notes of other birds

mock orange syringa

mock turtle soup a soup of calf's head etc., made to resemble the flavor of green turtle soup

mock-up (mɒkʌp) n. a dummy, built to scale, of an engine etc. ‖ anything designed to show the effect of a projected work (e.g. a book, a theater design etc.)

mod (mɒd) adj. boldly modern and unconventional, esp. of clothes, extended to music of the 1960s and early 1970s

mod·al (móud'l) adj. (*philos.*) relating to mode and not to substance ‖ (*logic*) expressing or indicating provisions as to the mode of application or effect, *a modal will* ‖ (*mus.*) written in one of the medieval modes ‖ (*gram.*) of or denoting verbal mood [fr. M.L. *modalis*]

modal auxiliary an auxiliary verb ('may', 'should' etc.) whose function is to determine the mood of a main verb

mo·dal·i·ty (moudǽliti:) pl. **mo·dal·i·ties** n. the quality or state of being modal ‖ (*logic*) the qualification of a proposition according to which it asserts or denies the possibility, impossibility, contingency or necessity of its content ‖ mode or method [fr. M.L. *modalitas*]

mode (moud) n. a way or manner of doing, being etc., *mode of address* ‖ a fashion (esp. style of clothes) ‖ any of various standing waves of which an oscillatory system is capable ‖ any of various simple vibrations that combine to give the overall vibration of an oscillating body or system (e.g. the normal modes of vibration of a molecule) ‖ (*mus.*) a way of ordering the notes in an octave according to the intervals between notes, esp. as used in the Middle Ages. Medieval modes took their names, but not their usage, from those of ancient Greece (*DORIAN MODE, *LYDIAN MODE, *MIXOLYDIAN MODE, *PHRYGIAN MODE) ‖ (*statistics*) the value of the variable occurring most often in a series of data ‖ (*philos.*) a form or aspect of an underlying substance ‖ (*gram.*) mood **the mode** common prevailing style or fashion in behavior, speech etc. [fr. L. *modus,* measure and F. *mode,* fashion]

mod·el (mód'l) 1. n. a three-dimensional representation, usually in miniature, of a thing to be constructed, sculptured etc., or of an object etc. that already exists ‖ a design intended for mass production ‖ something made to such a design ‖ a person or thing considered as an object for imitation ‖ a person who poses for an artist or photographer ‖ a person who demonstrates clothes by wearing them in front of customers ‖ (*economics*) a mathematical representation of the facts, factors, and inferences of an entity or situation, e.g., model of the economic condition when certain factors are added 2. adj. serving as or suitable to be a model 3. v. pres. part. **mod·el·ling,** esp. *Br.* **mod·el·ing** past and past part. **mod·eled, mod·elled** v.t. to make a model (representation) of ‖ to work (clay or other plastic material) ‖ to form in imitation of a model ‖ to wear (clothes) in demonstrations to customers ‖ (*art*) to give the effect of relief to ‖ v.i. to make a model or models, *to model in wax* ‖ to serve for modeling, *this clay models well* ‖ to pose as model for an artist or photographer ‖ to act as a mannequin [O.F. *modelle* fr. Ital.]

mode-locked (móudlɒkt) adj. of a laser that produces short pulses of light

Model Parliament (*Eng. hist.*) the parliament (1295) of Edward I, regarded by 19th-c. historians as a model for later parliamentary development, but now considered less significant

mo·dem (móudəm) n. (*computer acronym*) modulator-demodulator, a device that changes the form of data so that they can be transmitted by another medium, e.g., computerized data changed to electronic pulses for telephone transmission, then reconverted to computer-compatible data

Mo·de·na (mɔdéna) a city (pop. 180,526) of Etruscan origin in Emilia-Romagna, Italy, a former capital of the house of Este. Industries: engineering, shoes, food processing. Romanesque cathedral (1099–1184), palace (1643), Este library

mod·er·ate (mɒdərit) 1. adj. between extremes in size, quality, degree etc. ‖ avoiding excess in behavior etc., reasonable, *moderate in his requests* ‖ not very great or good, limited, *moderate skill* ‖ not severe or violent, *a moderate* climate ‖ (of political measures or views) not extremist ‖ (of a person) holding nonextremist political views **2.** *n.* a politically moderate person **3.** (módəreit) *v. pres. part.* **mod·er·at·ing** *past* and *past part.* **mod·er·at·ed** *v.t.* to make less extreme, violent, severe etc., *to moderate one's anger* ‖ to preside over (a meeting etc.) ‖ *v.i.* to become less extreme, violent, severe etc., *the wind is moderating* ‖ to preside over a meeting etc. [fr. L. *moderari (moderatus)*]

mod·er·a·tion (mɒdəréiʃən) *n.* the quality or state of being moderate ‖ the act of moderating **Mod·er·a·tions** (shortened to 'Mods') the first public examination at Oxford University for the B.A. degree in certain faculties **in moderation** without excess [F. *modération*]

mod·e·ra·to (mɒdərátou) *adj.* and *adv.* (*mus.*) with moderate speed [Ital.]

mod·er·a·tor (mɒdəreitər) *n.* a mediator ‖ someone who presides at a meeting, e.g. the presiding officer of various Protestant Church assemblies ‖ (*Br.*) an officer presiding over certain examinations at Cambridge and Oxford ‖ (*phys.*) a substance (e.g. graphite or deuterium) used to slow down the emissions of neutrons in a nuclear reactor

mod·ern (módərn) **1.** *adj.* of the present day, not ancient ‖ up-to-date, *the most modern styles* **2.** *n.* a person holding progressive opinions in conflict with earlier ideas ‖ (*printing*) a type with heavy strokes and straight hairline serifs [fr. L.L. *modernus*]

Modern Dance a form of free expressionist dance stemming from Isadora Duncan. Its style is not founded on the Classical ballet, it has its own vocabulary, and its own technique for developing the use of the whole body to convey emotion and ideas (*LABAN, *GRAHAM)

Modern English *ENGLISH LANGUAGE

Modern Greats (*Br.*) the school of politics, philosophy and economics at Oxford University

mod·ern·ism (módərnizəm) *n.* a term or expression that is modern ‖ mental acceptance of modern values **Mod·ern·ism** (*theol.*) a movement dating from the late 19th c. which aimed broadly at harmonizing traditional beliefs with modern scientific and philosophical thought. It had both Catholic and liberal Protestant exponents and was esp. strong in France, Britain, Italy and Germany. Pope Pius X condemned it (1907). In the Anglican Church Modernism continued to be influential for another generation **mód·ern·ist, Mód·ern·ist** *n.* and *adj.* **mod·ern·is·tic** *adj.* superficially avantgarde **mod·ern·is·ti·cal·ly** *adv.*

mo·dern·i·ty (mɒdə́:rniti:) *n.* the state or quality of being modern

mod·ern·i·za·tion (mɒdərnizéiʃən) *n.* a modernizing or being modernized ‖ an instance of this

mod·ern·ize (módərnaiz) *pres. part.* **mod·ern·iz·ing** *past* and *past part.* **mod·ern·ized** *v.t.* to change, in order to bring into harmony with modern taste and standards [fr. F. *moderniser*]

modern languages currently spoken languages, esp. of Europe, as a branch of academic study

Modern Latin Latin as it has been used since c. 1600, chiefly in scientific terminology

modern style *ART NOUVEAU

mod·est (módist) *adj.* aware of one's limitations, not vain or conceited ‖ avoiding pretension or display ‖ limited but not negligible, *a modest success* ‖ restrained and reasonable, *a modest request* ‖ shunning indecency **mód·es·ty** *n.* the quality of being modest [fr. F. *modeste*]

modesty panel a board so placed as to conceal the legs of a person seated behind a desk

mod·i·cum (módikəm) *n.* a small amount [L. neut. of *modicus*, moderate]

mod·i·fi·a·ble (módifaiəb'l) *adj.* capable of being modified

mod·i·fi·ca·tion (mɒdifikéiʃən) *n.* a modifying or being modified ‖ a partial change produced by modifying [F. or fr. L. *modificatio (modificationis)*]

mod·i·fi·er (módifaiər) *n.* someone who or something that modifies

mod·i·fy (módifai) *pres. part.* **mod·i·fy·ing** *past* and *past part.* **mod·i·fied** *v.t.* to change to some extent but not completely ‖ to make less extreme ‖ (*gram.*) to limit or qualify the general meaning of (a word, phrase, etc.) ‖ (*phon.*) to change the sound of (a vowel) by umlaut [F. *modifier*]

Mo·di·glia·ni (mɒdi:ljáni:), Amadeo (1884–1920), Italian painter. His style was in part derived from African sculpture. His portraits and nudes are distinguished by their elongation of form and purity of line

mo·dil·lion (moudíljən) *n.* (*archit.*) an ornamental bracket below the cornice of Corinthian and Composite pillars [fr. Ital. *modiglione*]

mod·ish (móudiʃ) *adj.* in the current mode or fashion (often used contemptuously)

mo·diste (moudí:st) *n.* a dressmaker or milliner [F.]

Mo·doc (móudɒk) *pl.* **Mo·doc, Mo·docs** *n.* a North American Indian people formerly of California and Oregon. The refusal (1870) of a band of Modocs to reside on a reservation brought about the Modoc War of 1872–3, which ended in their surrender and removal from their retreat to Oklahoma ‖ a member of this people ‖ their language

Mods (mɒdz) *n.* *MODERATIONS

mod·u·lar (módʒulər, módjulər) *adj.* of, relating to or based upon a module or a modulus [fr. Mod. L. *modularis*]

mod·u·late (módʒuleit, módjuleit) *pres. part.* **mod·u·lat·ing** *past* and *past part.* **mod·u·lat·ed** *v.t.* to regulate by a standard measure, esp. to vary the pitch of (a voice or other sound) ‖ (*radio*) to change intermittently the frequency, amplitude etc. of (a wave) ‖ *v.i.* (*mus.*) to lead out of one key into another in the course of a composition, the change itself forming an integral part of the composition ‖ (*radio*) to change intermittently the frequency, amplitude etc. of a wave [fr. L. *modulari (modulatus)*, to measure, modulate]

mod·u·la·tion (mɒdʒuléiʃən, mɒdjuléiʃən) *n.* a modulating or being modulated ‖ a variation produced by modulating [F. or fr. L. *modulatio (modulationis)*]

mod·u·la·tor (módʒuleitər, módjuleitər), *n.* someone who or something that modulates [L.]

mod·ule (módʒu:l, módju:l) *n.* a unit used as a standard of measurement, esp. (*archit.*) the size of a certain part of a structure used to determine the proportions of the rest ‖ (*rocketry*) a spacecraft unit that is self-contained and has a limited task or set of tasks to perform ‖ (*electronics*) an independent unit containing electronic components, esp. one that can be incorporated in a computer system ‖ (*math.*) a subset of a group that is being added ‖ (*architecture*) radius of the lower end of a column [F. or fr. L. *modulus*]

mod·u·lus (módʒuləs, módjuləs) *pl.* **mod·u·li** (módʒulai, módjulai) *n.* a constant that expresses the extent to which a given property is possessed by a substance or body ‖ the absolute value of a complex number ‖ an integer that divides without remainder the difference between two other integers [Mod. L.=small measure]

modulus of elasticity the constant value of the ratio between stress and strain in the range of elastic behavior of a body (*HOOKE'S LAW, *YOUNG s MODULUS)

modulus of rigidity (*phys.*) the ratio between the stress applied to a rigid body and the change of shape (measured by the angle of shear) which it produces

mo·dus o·pe·ran·di (móudusↄuperándi, móudəsↄpərǽndai) *n.* a manner of working or operating [L.]

modus vi·ven·di (móudusvivéndi:, móudəsvivéndai) *n.* an agreement establishing a temporary compromise between two groups in conflict [L.]

mo·fette, mof·fette (moufét) *n.* (*geol.*) an emanation of carbon dioxide and other gases from a fissure in the earth in areas of nearly extinct volcanic activity ‖ such a fissure in the earth's crust [F. fr. Ital.]

Mof·fatt (mófət), James (1870–1944), Scottish biblical scholar who translated the New Testament (1901) and the Old Testament (1924) into colloquial English

Mo·ga·di·scio (mɔgadí:ʃↄ) the capital (pop. 400,000) and chief port of Somalia

Mo·gol·lon (mougəjóun, mʌgɑjóun) *adj.* of or relating to an ancient Indian culture of the southwestern U.S.A. which developed from 300 B.C. to A.D. 1250 in parts of Arizona and New Mexico

Mo·gul (móug'l) *n.* a Mongolian, esp. a follower of Babur, who conquered India and founded an empire there (1526). Under Akbar, his grandson, the empire included N. and central India and most of Afghanistan, but it declined under Aurangzeb (1618–1712). The last emperor was deposed by the British (1857) **mo·gul** someone with conspicuous power and influence in a certain business or some clearly defined sphere, *a movie mogul* [Pers. and Arab. *mugul*]

mo·gul (móug'l) *n.* (*sports*) a bump, small hill, or mount on a ski run

Mo·hacs, Battle of (móuhɑtʃ) a Turkish victory (1526) over the Hungarians which led to the Turkish conquest of Hungary

mo·hair (móuhɛər) *n.* the hair of the Angora goat ‖ a fabric made wholly or partly from this ‖ a fabric of mixed cotton and wool resembling this fabric [fr. earlier *mocayare* ult. fr. Arab. *mukhayyar*]

Mo·ham·med (mouhǽmid) (*Turk.* Mahomet) (c. 570–632), the founder of Islam. He was born in Mecca, where he lived as a merchant, married Khadija, a rich widow, and had a daughter, Fatima. At the age of 40 he had a vision and began to preach as a prophet, exhorting the people to repentance, prayer, belief in the one god Allah, and alms-giving. In 622 to escape assassination he fled to Medina, where he set up a theocratic state. In 630 he conquered Mecca. He died in Medina (632), having established his authority throughout S.W. Arabia

Mohammad II (c. 1430–81), Ottoman sultan of Turkey (1451–81). His capture of Constantinople (1453) marked the end of the Byzantine Empire. He conquered much of the Balkans, until checked by Hunyadi and by Scanderbeg

Mohammed Ah·med (ámed) *MAHDI

Mohammed A·li (áli:) (1769–1849), Albanian-born viceroy of Egypt (1805–48). After seizing power (1805), he conquered Arabia (1811–18), the Sudan (1820–2) and, with his son Ibrahim Pasha, Syria (1832). The European powers forced him to withdraw to Egypt (1840), where his rule was made hereditary. His reforms began the modernization of Egypt

Mo·ham·med·an (mouhǽmidən) **1.** *n.* a Moslem, follower of Mohammed, the founder of Islam **2.** *adj.* pertaining to the religion or institutions founded by Mohammed (*ISLAM) **Mo·hám·med·an·ism** *n.* the religion founded by Mohammed

Mohammed Reza Pahlavi *PAHLAVI, MOHAMMED REZA

Mo·ha·ve (mouhávi:) *pl.* **Mo·ha·ve, Mo·ha·ves** *n.* an Indian people of the Colorado River valley in California, Arizona and Nevada ‖ a member of this people ‖ the language spoken by this people [Mohave *hamakhave*, three mountains, fr. the peaks near Needles, California regarded by the Mohave as the center of their territory]

Mo·hawk (móuhↄk) *pl.* **Mo·hawk, Mo·hawks** *n.* the easternmost people of the Iroquois confederacy, occupying villages near Schenectady, N.Y. They were feared by neighboring peoples for their prowess in warfare. During the French and Indian War, when the Mohawk espoused the British cause, a number defected to Canada to serve the cause of France. In the 1960s they numbered about 5,000. They are noted for their craftsmanship in steel ‖ the language of this people

Mo·he·gan (mouhí:gən) *pl.* **Mo·he·gan, Mo·he·gans** *n.* an Indian people of Southeastern Connecticut ‖ a member of this people

Mo·hen·jo·Da·ro (mouhéndʒoudárou) the site in Sind, India, of the ancient Indus civilization (c. third millennium B.C.), noted for its highly developed textiles and pottery

Mo·hi·can (mouhí:kən) *MAHICAN

Moh·ism (móuizəm) *n.* an egalitarian philosophical doctrine of China (5th–3rd cc. B.C.) advocating love and respect for all mankind **Móh·ist** *n.* an advocate of Mohism [after *Mo-ti* (5th c. B.C.), its founder]

Mohs' scale (mouz) a scale of hardness for minerals, in which 1 represents the hardness of talc, and 15 is the hardness of diamond (10 on the original scale) [after Friedrich *Mohs* (1773–1839), G. mineralogist]

Moi (mei), Daniel arap (1924–　), Kenyan president (1978–　). He served as vice president from 1967 until he succeeded Pres. Jomo Kenyatta upon his death. He was reelected twice

moi·e·ty (mↄíiti:) *pl.* **moi·e·ties** *n.* (esp. *law*) a half ‖ (*rhet.*) a part [M.E. *moite, moitie* fr. O.F. *moité, moitié*]

moil (mↄil) **1.** *v.i.* (*rhet.*) to drudge **2.** *n.* (*rhet.*) drudgery [O.F. *moillier*, to moisten]

moire (mwɑr) *n.* a watered fabric, esp. silk [F. fr. Eng. *mohair*]

CONCISE PRONUNCIATION KEY: **(a)** æ, c*a*t;　ɑ, c*ar*;　ↄ f*aw*n;　ei, sn*a*ke.　**(e)** e, h*e*n;　i:, sh*ee*p;　iə, d*ee*r;　ɛə, b*ear*.　**(i)** i, f*i*sh;　ai, t*i*ger;　ə:, b*ir*d. **(o)** o, *o*x;　au, c*ow*;　ou, g*oa*t;　u, p*oor*;　ↄi, r*oy*al.　**(u)** ʌ, d*u*ck;　u, b*u*ll;　u:, g*oo*se;　ə, b*a*cillus;　ju:, c*u*be.　x, lo*ch*;　θ, *th*ink;　ð, *b*other;　z, *Z*en;　ʒ, cor*s*age. dʒ, sava*g*e;　ŋ, ora*n*gutang;　j, *y*ak;　ʃ, *f*ish;　tʃ, fe*tch*;　'l, rabb*le*;　'n, redd*en*.　Complete pronunciation key appears inside front cover.

moi·ré (mwɑréi) 1. *adj.* having a wavy, watered appearance like moire 2. *n.* a wavy pattern, like that on watered silk ‖ moire [F.]

Mois·san (mwæsɑ̃), Ferdinand Frédéric Henri (1852–1907), French chemist. He isolated fluorine (1886) and invented the electric furnace (1892). Nobel prize (1906)

moist (mɔist) *adj.* slightly wet ‖ (of a climate) humid, having frequent rain **mois·ten** (mɔ́is'n) *v.t.* to make moist ‖ *v.i.* to become moist [O.F. moiste]

mois·ture (mɔ́istʃər) *n.* the diffused or condensed liquid, esp. water, which makes a gas or solid slightly damp [O.F. moistour]

Mo·ja·ve (mouhávi:) *MOHAVE

Mo·ji (moudʒi:) a port (pop. 1,065,000) of N. Kyushu, Japan, part of the Kita-Kyushu conurbation

mol (chem.) *MOLE

mo·lar (móulər) 1. *n.* one of the posterior teeth in mammals, adapted for grinding 2. *adj.* (of a tooth) adapted for grinding [fr. L. molaris, grinding]

molar *adj.* of a solution containing 1 mole of solute per liter of solution **mo·lar·i·ty** (moulǽriti:) *n.* molar concentration

mo·las·ses (məlǽsiz) *n.* (Am.=Br. treacle) the uncrystallized syrup produced in the process of refining sugar [pl. of older molasse fr. Port. melaço]

mold, esp. Br. **mould** (mould) 1. *n.* a hollow container into which fluid or plastic material is put and allowed to harden, so that the material takes on the container's interior shape ‖ the shape created in this way ‖ a pudding etc. shaped in such a container ‖ type, *a man of heroic mold* ‖ (archit.) a molding or group of moldings 2. *v.t.* to make, form into a certain shape ‖ to form by pouring into a mold ‖ to fit the contours of, *a dress that molds the figure* ‖ to form according to some pattern, *he molded his character on his father's* ‖ to modify the shape or character of, *the climate molded his character* ‖ to decorate with moldings ‖ *v.i.* to become covered with mold [M.E. mold, molde prob. fr. O.F. modle]

mold, esp. Br. **mould** *n.* humus ‖ topsoil of cultivated land [O.E. molde]

mold, esp. Br. **mould** *n.* a woolly or fluffy growth produced by various fungi on food, leather, clothes etc. that have been left in warm and moist air ‖ a fungus (e.g. a mucor) that produces mold [perh. fr. obs. mould adj., moldy fr. obs. moulen v., to grow or make moldy fr. Gmc]

Mol·dau (móldau) (Czech. Vltava) a tributary (267 miles long) of the Elbe in Bohemia, Czechoslovakia

Mol·da·vi·a (mɒldéivi:ə) a constituent republic (area 13,000 sq. miles, pop. 3,968,000) of the U.S.S.R. in S.E. Europe, bordering Rumania. Capital: Kishinev. It is a hilly plain, largely agricultural. Products: grapes (one third of Soviet vineyards), corn, root crops, sunflower seeds. Industries: wine, tobacco, food processing. It occupies most of former Bessarabia, and became a constituent republic in 1940

Moldavia the eastern region of Rumania. The west is occupied by the E. Carpathians (oil, rock salt). The east is a plain bounded by the Prut (wheat, corn). It united with Walachia to form Rumania (1859)

mold·board, esp. Br. **mould·board** (móuldbɔrd, móuldbɔurd) *n.* an iron plate attached to a plowshare, which turns over the earth ‖ the blade of a bulldozer or snowplow

mold·er, esp. Br. **mould·er** (móuldər) *v.i.* to crumble to dust, decay through age, *moldering ruins* [MOLD, humus]

mold·ing, esp. Br. **mould·ing** (móuldiŋ) *n.* anything formed by, in or as if in a mold, esp. (archit.) decorative work in stone, plaster etc. in a continuous band on the cornice of a building, outlining panels, on ceilings of rooms etc. ‖ an ornamental edging for a picture frame [MOLD v.]

mold·y, esp. Br. **mould·y** (móuldi:) comp. **mold·i·er**, esp. Br. **mould·i·er** superl. **mold·i·est**, esp. Br. **mould·i·est** adj. covered with mold ‖ (pop.) antiquated, *moldy ideas* ‖ (pop.) wretched, miserable, *a moldy job*

moldy fig (slang) an old-fashioned person, esp. one devoted to traditional jazz

mole (moul) *n.* any of several small burrowing insectivorous mammals, mostly of fam. Talpidae, with broad forefeet, small eyes and dark velvety fur. Moles are native to temperate regions of Europe, Asia and North America [M.E. mulle, molle, etym. doubtful]

mole *n.* a congenital mark or small permanent protuberance on the skin, often with hair roots [O.E. mál]

mole *n.* a wall of masonry constructed in the sea to form a breakwater ‖ a harbor formed by such a wall [F. môle]

mole *n.* (med.) an abnormal fleshy mass generated in the uterus [fr. F. môle fr. L. mola]

mole, mol *n.* (chem.) the amount of a substance having a mass numerically equal to its molecular mass but measured on a scale other than the atomic mass scale, esp. on the metric scale, and which, in the case of a gas, occupies about 22.4 liters at 1 atmosphere pressure and 0°C. [G. mol fr. molekül, molecule]

mole *n.* an intelligence agent who remains inactive for a long period of time, awaiting a particular order or event to become active

mo·lec·u·lar (məlékjulər) *adj.* pertaining to, involving or consisting of molecules [fr. Mod. L. molecula dim. of L. moles, mass]

molecular astronomy the study of chemical molecules in interstellar space

molecular biology the science of programming the genetic system and the creation of biological chemicals in living organism, e.g., in human insulin, human growth hormone, and interferon *Cf* GENE-SPLICING, RECOMBINANT DNA

molecular concentration molarity

molecular formula a chemical formula specifying the number of atoms of each element present in a given molecule (cf. STRUCTURAL FORMULA)

molecular fossil organic material extracted from rock, oldest of known fossils

molecular genetics the study of human evolution based on the theory of nucleotide base sequences

molecular mass the mass of a molecule on the atomic mass scale, usually taken as the sum of the atomic masses

molecular spectrum an emission spectrum arising from electronic, rotational and vibrational quantum transitions within molecules, usually consisting of broad bands which under high resolution are seen to consist of groups of fine lines. Each of these represents the interaction of vibrational and rotational transitions, the bands represent a blurred manifestation of the electronic transitions

molecular weight molecular mass

mol·e·cule (mɒ́likju:l) *n.* the smallest amount of a chemical element or compound which can exist while retaining the characteristic properties of the substance ‖ a little bit, a fragment [F. molécule]

mole·hill (móulhil) *n.* a small mound of soft earth thrown up by a mole burrowing underground **to make a mountain out of a molehill** to exaggerate absurdly the gravity of a trivial difficulty or mishap

mole rat any of several rodents that look or behave like moles, esp. a member of fam. Spalacidae, found in the E. Mediterranean

mole·skin (móulskin) *n.* the soft, dark gray fur of a mole ‖ a strong, twilled cotton fabric used for work clothes ‖ (pl.) trousers made of this fabric

mo·lest (məlést) *v.t.* to meddle with (someone) in such a way as to harm or annoy him [O. F. molester fr. L. molestare, to trouble, annoy]

mo·les·ta·tion (moulestéiʃən) *n.* a molesting or being molested [O.F.]

Mo·lière (mɔljer), (Jean-Baptiste Poquelin, 1622–73), French dramatist. After touring the French provinces (1645–58) as director of a small company of actors, he won the favor of Louis XIV and settled in Paris, where he began his series of great comedies with 'les Précieuses ridicules' (1659). His later successes include 'l'Ecole des femmes' (1662), 'le Tartuffe' (1664), 'le Misanthrope' (1666), 'le Médecin malgré lui' (1666), 'l'Avare' (1668), 'le Bourgeois gentilhomme' (1670), 'les Femmes savantes' (1672) and 'le Malade imaginaire' (1673). Molière satirized departures from the norm of rational social behavior. This satire is limited in some plays to the ridiculing of stock eccentricities (avarice, hypochondria etc.), but in his greatest plays he satirizes the subtler, deeper forms of obsession, e.g. religious bigotry, jealous love or assertive egoism, which blind man to the excesses of his behavior (*CLASSICISM)

Mo·li·na (mɒlí:nɑ), Luis de (1535–1600), Spanish theologian. Molinism, the system expounded in his 'Concordia liberi arbitrii cum gratiae donis' (1589), was a doctrine of grace safeguarding human free will and the doctrine of predestination

Molina, Tirso de *TIRSO DE MOLINA

mo·lin·done hydrochloride [$C_{16}H_{24}N_2O_2$] (moulíndoun) (n. pharm.) tranquilizer causing reduction of spontaneous locomotion and aggressiveness; marketed as Moban

Mo·li·nism (móulinizəm) *MOLINA

Mo·li·nos (mɒlí:nɔs), Miguel de (1628–96), Spanish priest. His 'Spiritual Guide' (1675) was the classic expression of quietism. He was condemned by the Inquisition (1687)

moll (mol) *n.* a gangster's girl [prob. fr. Moll, nickname for MARY

mol·li·fi·ca·tion (mɒlifikéiʃən) *n.* a mollifying or being mollified

mol·li·fy (mɒ́lifai) pres. part. **mol·li·fy·ing** past and past part. **mol·li·fied** *v.t.* to lessen the anger of ‖ to soften the effect of [fr. F. mollifier]

mol·lusc *MOLLUSK

mol·lus·coid (məlʌ́skɔid) 1. *n.* (in some classifications) a member of Molluscoidea, a phylum of invertebrate animals having some of the characterists of a mollusk 2. *adj.* resembling a mollusk or a molluscoid [fr. Mod. L. mollusca, mollusk]

mol·lusk, mol·lusc (mɒ́ləsk) *n.* a member of Mollusca, a phylum of unsegmented, coelomate, generally shelled and bilaterally symmetrical invertebrates possessing a muscular foot which is variously modified for digging, swimming or creeping. Mollusks include snails, mussels etc. [fr. F. mollusque]

Moll·witz, Battle of (mɒ́lvits) a battle (1711) in which a Prussian army under Frederick II defeated the Austrians during the war of the Austrian Succession. It demonstrated the superiority of infantry over cavalry

mol·ly·cod·dle (mɒ́li:kɒd'l) 1. *n.* a healthy person who likes to be pampered or treated as an invalid or an infant 2. *v.t. pres. part.* **mol·ly·cod·dling** past and past part. **mol·ly·cod·dled** to treat (someone) in this way [Molly, dim. of Mary (proper name)+CODDLE]

Mol·ly Ma·guires (mɒ́li:məgwáiərz) a secret organization of Irish-Americans formed (mid 1800s) in Pennsylvania to combat the inhumanity of the mineowners by sabotage and murder. After a private detective named McParlan infiltrated the group, befriended its leader, and turned in three of its chief members to be hanged, it was dissolved

Molly Pitcher, (mɒ́li:pítʃər) (1754–1832) American Revolutionary War heroine, born Mary Ludwig Hays. With her soldier husband (McCauley) at the Battle of Monmouth (1778), she carried pitchers of water onto the battlefield

Mo·loch (móulɒk, mɒ́lək) a Canaanite fire god to whom children were sacrificed

mo·loch (móulɒk) *n.* a member of Moloch, fam. Agamidae, a genus of spiny Australian lizards, esp. M. horridus ‖ (rhet.) something regarded as demanding a dreadful sacrifice [MOLOCH]

Mo·lo·tov (mɒ́lətɔf), Vyacheslav Mikhailovich (1890–), Russian statesman. A leader of the 1917 revolution, he was premier (1930–41) and foreign minister (1939–49, 1953–6) of the U.S.S.R. After breaking with Nikita Khrushchev (1957) he lost favor and became ambassador to Mongolia (1957–60) and representative to the International Atomic Energy Agency in Vienna (1960–1). He was expelled from the Communist party (1962)

Molotov *PERM

Molotov cocktail a crude hand grenade consisting of a bottle full of inflammable liquid and a wick

molt, esp. Br. **moult** (moult) 1. *v.i.* (of an animal) to shed feathers, fur, skin etc., which are later replaced by new growth ‖ *v.t.* to shed (feathers etc.) in this way 2. *n.* the act or process of molting, *in molt* ‖ the feathers, fur etc. that have been molted [M.E. mouten fr. O.E. fr. L. mutare, to change]

mol·ten (móultən) *adj.* melted, esp. by extremely high heat [alt. past part. of MELT]

molting hormone (biochem.) an insect hormone that stimulates growth of cuticle in preparation for molting and transformation *also* ecdysone or ecdyson *Cf* BRAIN HORMONE

Molt·ke (mɒ́ltkə), Helmuth Karl Bernhard, Count von (1800–91), Prussian soldier, head of the general staff of the Prussian army (1857–88). His reorganization of the army was largely responsible for Prussia's victories over Denmark (1864), Austria (1866) and France (1870–1)

mol·to (móltou) *adv.* (*mus.*) much, very [Ital.]

Mo·luc·cas (mɔlú:kəz) (formerly Spice Is) the section (land area 32,000 sq. miles, pop. 1,251,192) of the Malay Archipelago between Sulawesi and New Guinea, constituting a province (Maluku) of Indonesia. Capital: Ambon. Principal island: Halmahera. Religion: mainly Moslem. Volcanic and mountainous, the Moluccas produce spices, copra, rice, sago and lumber. They were contested between Portuguese, Spanish and Dutch traders (16th–17th cc.) for the monopoly of the spice trade, and were controlled by the Dutch (1814–1942) and the Japanese (1942–5). They became part of Indonesia (1949)

mo·lyb·de·nite (məlíbdənait) *n.* the mineral molybdenum disulfide, MoS₂. It has the laminated appearance of graphite and is the chief ore of molybdenum [fr. L. *molybdaena* ult. fr. Gk *molubdos*, lead]

mo·lyb·de·num (məlíbdənəm) *n.* a hard white metallic element (symbol Mo, at. no. 42, at. mass 95.94), which forms hard steel alloys **mo·lyb·dic** *adj.* relating to molybdenum in one of its higher valences **mo·lyb·dous** *adj.* relating to molybdenum in one of its lower valences [Mod. L. altered fr. L. *molybdaena*, lead]

mom (mɔm) *n.* (*pop.*) mother

mom-and-pop (mɔm'nɔp) *adj.* (*colloq.*) of a small family-owned retail business

Mom·ba·sa (mɔmbásə) the main port (pop. 350,000) of Kenya, terminus of the Kenya and Uganda railroad. Industries: oil refining, engineering, coffee, brewing. It was an Arab port from the 8th c.

mo·ment (móumənt) *n.* a small, indefinite period of time, *wait a moment* ‖ a particular time, *this is not the moment to discuss it* ‖ importance, *an event of great moment* ‖ (*phys.*) the tendency to produce motion around an axis or point (*MOMENT OF INERTIA) [fr. L. *momentum*]

mo·men·tar·i·ly (mouməntéərili) *adv.* for a moment

mo·men·tar·i·ness (móumənteri:nis) *n.* the quality or state of being momentary

mo·men·tar·y (móumənteri) *adj.* lasting only for a moment [fr. L. *momentarius*]

mo·ment·ly (móuməntli:) *adv.* from moment to moment, *momently increasing* ‖ for a moment, *he paused momently, then fell*

moment of a force a torque

moment of inertia (*phys.*) a quantity, analogous to mass for linear motion, defined as the ratio of a torque to the angular acceleration of the rotation it produces, both quantities being measured with respect to the same axis of rotation. The moment of inertia is equal to the sum of the products of the mass elements of a non-continuous rigid body and the squares of the perpendicular distances of each element to the axis of rotation

moment of truth a critical moment when a basic challenge must be met, esp. in an ongoing crisis

mo·men·tous (mouméntəs) *adj.* having great importance, *a momentous occasion*

mo·men·tum (mouméntəm) *pl.* **mo·men·ta** (mouméntə), **mo·men·tums** *n.* a measure of the quantity of motion, defined as the product of the mass and the velocity of a body, and determining the length of time during which constant force must act on a moving body to bring it to rest. Momentum is a vector quantity parallel to the velocity vector ‖ (*loosely*) the force built up by a moving body [L.]

Momm·sen (mɔ́mzen), Theodor (1817–1903), German historian. His 'History of Rome' (1854–6) and his studies of Latin inscriptions opened up the study of Roman history

mom·my (mɔ́mi:) *pl.* **mom·mies** *n.* (a child's word for) mother

Mon. Monday

mon·a·chal, mon·a·cal (mɔ́nək'l) *adj.* monastic [fr. L.L. *monachalis*]

mon·a·chism (mɔ́nəkizəm) *n.* monasticism [fr. L. *monachus*, monk]

Mon·a·co (mɔ́nəko, mɔnǽkɔ) a principality (area 6 sq. miles, pop. 26,000) of Europe on the Mediterranean, forming an enclave in Alpes-Maritimes, France. People: mainly French and Italian (12% Monegasque). Language: French. Monaco consists of Monaco Ville, a port and industrial section containing the palace, public buildings and oceanographic museum (1910), and of Monte Carlo, the residential and resort area (casino). Industries: tourism, chemicals,

food processing, precision instruments. Monetary unit: French franc. Monaco was given to a Genoese family (10th c.) and became a principality in the 16th c. It came under the protection of Spain (1524–1641) and France (1641–1793), and was annexed by France (1793–1815). It placed itself voluntarily under French protection (1861)

mon·ad (mónæd, móunæd) *n.* a minute organism or organic unit ‖ (*philos.*, in Leibniz's theory) a primary element of being [fr. L. *monas* (*monadis*), unit, fr. Gk]

mon·a·del·phous (mɔnədélfəs) *adj.* (*bot.*, e.g. of mallow) having the stamens united into one bundle by fusion of the filaments ‖ (*bot.*, of stamens) united in this way [fr. Gk *monos*, one+*adelphos*, brother]

mo·nad·ic (mənǽdik) *adj.* (of a plant) consisting of monads **mo·nád·i·cal** *adj.*

mon·ad·ism (mɔ́nædizəm, móunædizəm) *n.* Leibniz's theory that the world is made up of monads

Mon·a·ghan (mɔ́nəhən) an inland county (area 499 sq. miles, pop. 46,242) of Ulster province, Irish Republic ‖ its county seat (pop. 4,700)

mo·nan·drous (mənǽndrəs) *adj.* (of a plant) having flowers with only one stamen ‖ (of a flower) having only one stamen ‖ having only one male mate at a time ‖ relating to or characterized by monandry [fr. Gk *monandros*, having one husband]

mo·nan·dry (mənǽndri:) *n.* the social custom by which a woman has only one husband at a time (cf. POLYANDRY) ‖ (*bot.*, of a plant or flower) the state of being monandrous [fr. Gk *monos*, one+*anēr* (*andros*), male]

mon·arch (mɔ́nərk) *n.* a person ruling, usually by hereditary right and for his lifetime, over a kingdom or people, and invested with either absolute or constitutional power ‖ (*rhet.*) the chief person or thing of its kind or class ‖ *Danaus plexippus*, fam. *Danaidae*, a large orange and black American butterfly **mo·nar·chal** (mənárk'l) *adj.* [fr. L. *monarcha* fr. Gk]

mo·nar·chic (mənárkik) *adj.* of, relating to or having the characteristics of a monarchy or monarch **mo·nár·chi·cal** *adj.* [F. *monarchique*]

mon·ar·chism (mɔ́nərkizəm) *n.* the monarchical system of government ‖ belief in monarchical principles of government **món·ar·chist** *n.* [F. *monarchisme*]

mon·ar·chy (mɔ́nərki:) *pl.* **mon·ar·chies** *n.* a state ruled by a monarch ‖ rule by a monarch [F. *monarchie* fr. L. fr. Gk]

mon·as·ter·y (mɔ́nəsteri:) *pl.* **mon·as·ter·ies** *n.* the group of buildings housing a community of monks [fr. L.L. *monasterium* fr. Gk]

mo·nas·tic (mənǽstik) **1.** *adj.* pertaining to monks or to a monastery. The main Christian monastic orders are the Benedictines, Cistercians, Carthusians, Augustinians, Dominicans, Franciscans and the Carmelites **2.** *n.* a member of a monastic order **mo·nás·ti·cism** *n.* [fr. M.L. *monasticus* fr. Gk]

mon·a·tom·ic (mɔnətómik) *adj.* having one atom in the molecule ‖ univalent ‖ having one replaceable radical or atom [MONO-+ATOM]

mon·ax·i·al (mɔnǽksi:əl) *adj.* (*bot.*) having flowers that grow on the primary axis [fr. MONO-+L. *axis*, axis]

mon·a·zite (mɔ́nəzait) *n.* a phosphate mineral containing compounds of cerium, thorium and other rare-earth metals, found in sand and gravel deposits [G. *monazit* fr. Gk *monazein*, to live alone (fr. the fact that it is found in isolated crystals)]

Mon·ca·da (mɔnkáðа), José María (1867–1945), Nicaraguan writer, general, Liberal party leader and president (1929–33), after civil disturbances following the overthrow of Emiliano Chamorro had led to U.S. intervention

Mon·ce·ni·sio (mɔntʃeníːsjɔ) *MONT CENIS

Mön·chen-Glad·bach (má:nxənglátbαx) (formerly München-Gladbach) a town (pop. 258,000) in North RhineWestphalia, West Germany, near Düsseldorf: textiles, engineering

Monck, George *MONK

Mond (mɔnd, mount), Ludwig (1839–1909), British chemist of German origin. He invented the nickel carbonyl process (*MOND PROCESS) and developed industrial production of alkali

Mondale (mɔ́ndeil), Walter Frederick 'Fritz' (1928–   ), U.S. politician, lawyer, vice-president (1977–81). A protégé of Minnesota Democrat Hubert H. Humphrey, he was state

attorney general (1960–4), finished serving Humphrey's U.S. Senate term (1965–6) and was elected to the Senate on his own (1966, 1972). He was a very active vice-president, acting as Pres. Jimmy Carter's representative abroad and advisor at home. He and Carter were defeated in 1980; Mondale's 1984 presidential campaign, with the first woman vice-presidential candidate, Geraldine Ferraro, was unsuccessful

Mon·day (mʌ́ndi:, mʌ́ndei) *n.* the second day in the week [O.E. *mōnandæg*, moon's day]

Mond process a process used in the metallurgy of nickel, in which nickel carbonyl Ni(CO)₄ is formed and subsequently decomposed to deposit pure nickel, regenerating carbon monoxide

Mon·dri·an (mɔ́dri:ɑ̃), Piet (Pieter Mondriaan, 1872–1944), Dutch painter. Seeking a pure, universal art form, free from personal expression, he painted nonobjective works composed exclusively of horizontal and vertical lines and flat areas of primary colors, black and white. His theories (neoplasticism) have had a far-reaching influence in art, architecture and decoration (*STIJL, DE)

monecious *MONOECIOUS

Mon·e·gasque (mɔnəgǽsk) **1.** *adj.* of or relating to Monaco, its people, customs etc. **2.** *n.* a native or inhabitant of Monaco [F. *monégasque*]

Mo·nel metal, Mo·nell metal (mounél) an acid-resisting alloy of nickel (60–70%), copper (25–35%), iron, manganese, carbon and silicon, used in chemical engineering [after Ambrose *Monell* (*d.* 1921), U.S. manufacturer]

Mo·net (mɔneí), Claude (1840–1926), French painter. He was one of the founders of Impressionism, and with Renoir developed the technique of broken-color painting in which dabs of color laid side by side become blended by the eye of the viewer. He painted directly in the open air, often painting the same scene at different hours of the day for the varying effects of light. Light and subject merge almost completely in his last series of paintings ('Water Lilies'), and approach pure abstraction

mon·e·tar·i·ly (mɔnitéərili:, mʌnitéərili:, móniterili:, mʌ́niterili:) *adv.* with regard to money

mon·e·tar·ism (mónitərʌzəm) *n.* (*economics*) the theory or policy of regulating the economy, esp. with regard to inflation, by increasing or decreasing the amount and velocity of money in circulation —**monetrist** *n.*

mon·e·tar·y (móniteri:, mʌ́niteri:) *adj.* pertaining to money, esp. to coinage [fr. L. *monetarius*, of a mint]

monetary policy (*economics*) government action that has a direct impact on the amount of money in circulation Cf MONEY IN CIRCULATION

M-113AI *n.* (*mil.*) U.S. full-tracked personnel carrier with 107-cm mortar

mon·e·ti·za·tion (mɔnitizéiʃən, mʌnitizéiʃən) *n.* a monetizing or being monetized

mon·e·tize (mónitaiz, mʌ́nitaiz) *pres. part.* **mon·e·tiz·ing** *past* and *past part.* **mon·e·tized** *v.t.* to give a fixed value to (a metal or alloy used in coinage) ‖ to coin (a metal) [fr. L. *moneta*, mint, money]

mon·ey (mʌ́ni:) *pl.* **mon·eys, mon·ies** *n.* anything that serves as a medium of exchange for goods and services, in the form of tokens which have a value established by a commonly recognized authority, e.g. the government of a country, or by custom. The tokens are usually minted metal pieces (coinage), or promises to pay, recorded on paper (bank notes etc.) but may be whatever is locally accepted (beads, shells, cattle etc.) ‖ personal wealth, *his money is all in hotels* ‖ (*pl.*, esp. *law*) sums of money **money for jam** (*Br.*, *pop.*) duck soup **to coin money** to acquire wealth quickly **to get one's money's worth** to obtain full value for what one has expended in effort, money or time **to marry money** to marry a rich person **to pay money down** to pay cash at the time of purchase [O.F. *moneie*]

money box a box for small savings

Money Card trademark of bank card that permits bills to be charged directly to a checking account

money changer a person whose trade is to exchange money in one currency for that in another ‖ a device for dispensing small change

mon·eyed, mon·ied (mʌ́ni:d) *adj.* rich

mon·ey·grub·ber (mʌ́ni:grʌbər) *n.* a person who attaches far too much importance to acquiring money

CONCISE PRONUNCIATION KEY: (a) æ, c*a*t; ɑ, c*a*r; ɔ f*aw*n; ei, sn*a*ke. (e) e, h*e*n; i:, sh*ee*p; iə, d*ee*r; ɛə, b*ea*r. (i) i, f*i*sh; ai, t*i*ger; ə:, b*i*rd. (o) ɔ, *o*x; au, c*ow*; ou, g*oa*t; u, p*oo*r; ɔi, r*oy*al. (u) ʌ, d*u*ck; u, b*u*ll; u:, g*oo*se; ə, b*a*cillus; ju:, c*u*be. x, lo*ch*; θ, *th*ink; ð, bo*th*er; z, *Z*en; ʒ, cor*s*age; dʒ, sava*g*e; ŋ, ora*ng*utang; j, *y*ak; ʃ, *f*ish; tʃ, fe*tch*; 'l, rabb*le*; 'n, redd*en*. Complete pronunciation key appears inside front cover.

money in circulation (*economics*) U.S. total amount of metallic and paper money, current account deposits, Treasury currency and coin, Federal Reserve notes and demand deposits in the hands of banks and individuals—regarded by monetarists as a basic factor in the regulation of the economy —**M1A** money in the hands of the public and balances in interest-bearing checking accounts —**M1** money in circulation plus private demand deposits —**M2** M1, plus bank time and savings deposits other than large certificates of deposit —**M3** M2, plus deposits at mutual savings banks, savings and loan associations, and credit unions —**M4** M2, plus large negotiable certificates of deposit —**M5** M3, plus large negotiable certificates of deposit

mon·ey·lend·er (mʌ́ni:lendər) *n.* a person who professionally lends money at interest

money market the banks and financial institutions whose activities determine cost of capital and the relative value of currencies, government scrip etc.

money of account a monetary denomination not necessarily represented by coinage but used for convenience in keeping accounts, e.g. the British guinea and the U.S. mill

money order an order issued by a post office, in return for payment, instructing another post office to pay a sum of money to the person named in the order

mon·ey-spin·ner (mʌ́ni:spinər) *n.* (*Br.*) an enterprise or property which is very profitable ‖ (*Br.*, *pop.*) a small garden spider supposed to be a sign of financial luck if it crawls on one

mon·ey·wort (mʌ́ni:wəːt, mʌ́ni:wɔːrt) *n. Lysimachia nummularia*, fam. *Primulaceae*, a perennial trailing plant of European origin with round, glossy leaves and small yellow flowers in the axils of the leaves

Monge (mɔ̃ːʒ), Gaspard (1746–1818), French mathematician. He expounded the principles of descriptive geometry and of the theory of curvature

Mongkut (mɔ́ŋku:t), King of Siam (1804–68), Siamese ruler known for his modernization programs and establishment of closer ties with the West. A Buddhist monk, he succeeded his brother to the throne in 1851 and introduced Western studies and ways of government and economy to Siam. The king in 'The King and I' is based on Mongkut. He was also known as Rama IV

mon·go (mɔ́ŋgou) *pl.* **mon·go** *n.* a Mongolian monetary unit equal to one hundredth of a tughrik ‖ a coin of this value

Mon·gol (mɔ́ŋg'l, mɔ́ŋgol) 1. *n.* a member of the Mongolian people ‖ a native of Mongolia, of Inner Mongolia, or of the Mongolian People's Republic ‖ any of the Mongolian languages 2. *adj.* Mongolian —Under the leadership of Genghis Khan, Kublai Khan, Timur and Babur, the Mongols created a vast empire extending into China, India and central Europe (12th–16th cc.). They were driven from China (1368) by the Mings, and from Russia (1480) by Ivan III. They were converted to Lamaism in the 16th c.

Mon·go·li·a (mɔŋgóuli:ə) a region of central Asia, divided into Inner Mongolia and the Mongolian People's Republic. After Mongolia was conquered (1206) by Genghis Khan, it became the center of the vast empire of the Mongols. Outer Mongolia became (1921) the Mongolian People's Republic, and Inner Mongolia was incorporated in China (1949)

Mongolia, Inner an autonomous region (area 454,600 sq. miles, pop. 18,770,000) of N. China, adjoining the Mongolian People's Republic. Capital: Huhehot. The Gobi Desert is in the north. The Great Wall of China runs along the southern border. The region came under Chinese influence in the late 19th c., and became an autonomous region of China (1949)

Mon·go·li·an (mɔŋgóuli:ən) 1. *adj.* of or pertaining to the predominantly yellow-skinned race, one of the three main divisions of mankind, including most of the Asian peoples, Eskimos, North American Indians etc. (*MONGOL, cf. CAUCASIAN, cf. NEGRO) ‖ of or pertaining to Mongolia, its people etc. ‖ designating any of a group of Altaic languages, esp. the language of the Mongols ‖ afflicted with Mongolism 2. *n.* a member of the Mongolian race ‖ a native of Mongolia ‖ any of the Mongolian languages ‖ a person with Mongolism

Mongolian People's Republic (formerly Outer Mongolia) a republic (area 604,095 sq. miles, pop. 1,809,000) in Central Asia. Capital:

Ulan Bator. People: mainly Mongol, 4% Kazakhs, small minorities of Buriats, Russians and Chinese. Language: Mongolian (written since 1946 in Cyrillic characters). Religion: Buddhist Lamaism, Shamanism. The land is mainly grazing and pasture with 10% forest. It is largely a plateau (3,000 ft) with several interior drainage basins (notably the Gobi Desert in the south). Chief mountain ranges: Altai Mtns in the west (Tabun Bogdo, 15,266 ft), Sayan Mtns in the north (Munku Sardik, 11,453 ft) and Khangai Mtns in the center (Otgon Tanger, 12,295 ft). In the northwest there is an extensive lake district. Average temperatures (F.): Ulan Bator −15° (Jan.) and 64° (July), northern lake district −22° (Jan.) and 50° (July), Gobi Desert 5° (Jan.) and 77° (July). Rainfall: 10–20 ins in the north and west, 10 ins in Ulan Bator, under 10 ins in the south and east. Livestock: sheep, goats, horses, camels, cattle, esp. yaks. Agricultural products: cereals. Minerals: coal, iron ore, gold, tungsten, uranium, oil. Manufactures: textiles, machinery, electricity, bricks, footwear, processed foodstuffs, wood products, carpets. Exports: cattle, horses, wool, hides, meat, butter. Imports: machinery, flour, petroleum, metal goods, cotton goods, tea. University (1942). Monetary unit: tughrik (100 mongo). HISTORY. Under Chinese rule since the late 17th c., Outer Mongolia revolted (1921), and became the Mongolian People's Republic, in close relationship with the U.S.S.R. It joined the U.N. (1961)

Mon·gol·ic (mɔŋgólik) 1. *adj.* of or relating to the Mongolian race, people or language 2. *n.* the Mongolian group of languages

Mon·gol·ism (mɔ́ŋg'lizəm) *n.* a variety of congenital idiocy of unknown cause, so called because those afflicted have broad heads and slanting eyes

Mon·gol·oid (mɔ́ŋg'lɔid) 1. *adj.* of or pertaining to or having the characteristics of the Mongolian people ‖ of, relating to or afflicted with Mongolism 2. *n.* a member of the Mongolian race ‖ someone afflicted with Mongolism

mon·goose (mɔ́ŋgu:s) *pl.* **mon·goos·es** *n.* any of several small, agile, carnivorous mammals of genus *Herpestes*, fam. *Viverridae*, and related genera, native to Asia and Africa, esp. *H. nyula* of India, which kills and feeds on rodents and snakes [*Lemur mongoz*, a lemur of Madagascar [Marathi *mangūs*]

Mongoose code name for CIA project to overthrow Cuban premier Fidel Castro, of which the failed Bay of Pigs invasion (April 17, 1961) was a part

mon·grel (mʌ́ŋgrəl, mɔ́ŋgrəl) 1. *n.* something (esp. a dog) of mixed breed 2. *adj.* (esp. of a dog) of mixed breed [M.E. *mengrell* prob. fr. O.E. *mengan*, to mix]

monied *MONEYED

mon·i·ker, mon·ick·er, *Br.* esp. **mon·ni·ker** (mɔ́nikər) *n.* (*pop.*, *old-fash.*) one's name ‖ (*Br.*) an identification mark used by a tramp [origin unknown]

mo·nil·i·form (mounílifɔrm) *adj.* (*biol.*, e.g. of a root) constricted at regular intervals, giving the appearance of a string of beads [F. *moniliforme* or fr. Mod. L. *moniliformis* fr. L. *monile*, necklace]

mon·ism (mɔ́nizəm, móunizəm) *n.* the view, common to various philosophical systems, which reduces all reality to a single principle or substance (cf. DUALISM, cf. PLURALISM) **món·ist** *n.* **mo·nis·tic** (mənístik), **mo·nís·ti·cal** *adjs* [fr. Mod. L. *monismus* fr. Gk *monos*, single]

mo·ni·tion (mouníʃən) *n.* (*rhet.*) a warning ‖ (*law*) a summons or citation to appear and answer ‖ a formal letter from a bishop or ecclesiastical court, warning a clergyman to abstain from a specified offense [O.F. or fr. L. *monitio* (*monitionis*), instruction]

mon·i·tor (mɔ́nitər) 1. *n.* a pupil appointed to assist in keeping discipline etc. ‖ a person who or an instrument that monitors a broadcast or telephone communication ‖ any of several large tropical lizards of genus *Varanus*, fam. *Varanidae*, related to the iguana, supposed to give warning of nearby crocodiles ‖ (*hist.*) a warship of shallow draft, carrying heavy guns, dating from 1862 ‖ (*computer*) diagnostic program used to respond to questions about a computer program so as to warn of faults or failings ‖ any other device for a similar purpose on other systems 2. *v.t.* to check (broadcasts) for their information and significance ‖ to check (radio, television or telephonic communication) for quality of transmission ‖ (*phys.*) to test (materi-

als) for radioactivity **mon·i·to·ri·al** (mɒnitóːri:əl, mɒnitóuri:l) *adj.* **món·i·tor·ship** *n.* [L.=someone who warns]

'Monitor' and 'Merrimac', two U.S. ironclad vessels, the first to be used in naval warfare. During the Civil War they engaged in a duel at the Battle of Hampton Roads which resulted in a draw

mon·i·to·ry (mɔ́nitɔri:, mɔ́nitouri:) *adj.* being or giving a warning [fr. L. *monitorius*]

Monk, Monck (mʌŋk), George (1608–70), 1st duke of Albemarle, English general and naval commander. After serving in the English Civil War first on the side of the royalists and then on the side of parliament, he marched with an army on London (1660). The Rump Parliament was persuaded to dissolve itself, and a new assembly summoned which, by Monk's diplomacy, invited Charles II to the throne

monk (mʌŋk) *n.* a member of a religious community of men, bound by vows of obedience to the rules of the order [O. E. *munuc* fr. L. fr. Gk *monachos* adj., single, solitary]

mon·key (mʌ́ŋki:) 1. *pl.* **mon·keys** *n.* any of certain Old World or New World primates, generally smaller than the anthropoid apes, often arboreal and usually having prehensile hands and feet. New World monkeys comprise the families *Cebidae* (e.g. the spider monkeys) and *Callithricidae* (the marmosets). They have a broad, flat nose with nostrils far apart, usually prehensile tail, and are largely arboreal. Old World monkeys, which belong to fam. *Cercopithecidae*, have a foreshortened face, and nostrils directed downwards. They usually have naked callosities on the buttocks and a nonprehensile tail. Many are terrestrial. While superficially resembling the New World monkeys, they are more closely related to the anthropoid apes and man ‖ the fur of any of these animals ‖ (*loosely*) any of the primates except man, the lemurs and the tarsiers ‖ a playful, mischievous child ‖ (*mach.*) a weight used for driving something by falling on it, e.g. a drop hammer 2. *v.i.* (with 'with', 'around with') to tamper ‖ (with 'around') to act mischievously or playfully [etym. doubtful]

monkey bread the fruit of the baobab

monkey business (*pop.*) underhand dealings ‖ (*pop.*) mischief

monkey engine (*Br.*) a pile driver

monkey hang (*gymnastics*) swinging maneuver from bar or rings, with legs up and over back, between arms, under bar, ending with a one-arm hang

monkey jacket a short dress jacket without tails

mon·key-nut (mʌ́ŋki:nʌt) *n.* (esp. *Br.*) the peanut

monkey puzzle *Araucaria araucana*, fam. *Pinaceae*, a tall coniferous Chilean evergreen tree with whorled branches, stiff leaves arranged spirally, and edible seeds. It is often cultivated as an ornamental tree

mon·key-shines (mʌ́ŋki:ʃainz) *pl. n.* (*pop.*) playful, mischievous tricks

monkey wrench a wrench with an adjustable jaw

Mon-Khmer (móunkmér) *n.* a family of languages of S.E. Asia ‖ a group of languages within this family

monk·ish (mʌ́ŋkiʃ) *adj.* (*pejorative*) characteristic of or pertaining to monks

monk shoe a shoe with the vamp unbroken by a toe cap, fastened by a strap over the instep buckling at the side

monks·hood (mʌ́ŋkshud) *n. Aconitum napellus*, fam. *Ranunculaceae*, a highly poisonous plant cultivated for its showy white or blue flowers

Mon·mouth (mɔ́nməθ), James Scott, duke of (1649–85), English pretender. An illegitimate son of Charles II, he raised a Protestant rebellion in the west of England on the accession (1685) of James II. He was defeated at Sedgemoor and executed

Monmouth, Battle of a Revolutionary War engagement fought (1778) near the village of Monmouth Courthouse (now Freehold, N.J.). The patriots, choosing the location to cut off a British retreat, attacked the British but without warning called a retreat. Forces under George Washington rushed to the scene, thereby rescuing the patriots from rout

Mon·mouth·shire (mɔ́nməθʃiər) (*abbr.* Mon.) a county (area 546 sq. miles, pop. 465,000) of W. England, for most purposes considered part of

Wales. County town: Monmouth. Administrative center: Newport

monniker *MONIKER

mono- (mónou) *prefix* alone, single [fr. Gk *monos*, alone, single, only]

mon·o·a·mine (mɒnouəmíːn) *n.* (biochem.) an amino with a single amino acid, esp. serotonin [$C_{10}H_{12}N_2O$], that is functionally significant as a neurotransmitter —**mon·o·am·in·er·gic** (mɒnouæmənóːrdʒik) *adj.* involving monoamines

monoamine oxidase a naturally occurring enzyme that detoxifies amino compounds in ingested foodstuffs by oxidation *abbr.* **MAO**

mon·o·ba·sic (mɒnoubéisik) *adj.* of or designating an acid which ionizes to provide only one hydrogen ion from its molecule

mon·o·carp (mónəkɑrp *n.* a monocarpic plant [MONOCARPIC]

mon·o·car·pel·lar·y (mɒnoukɑ́rpələri:) *adj.* (bot.) having or consisting of only one carpel

mon·o·car·pic (mɒnoukɑ́rpik) *adj.* (of a plant) dying after bearing fruit once **mon·o·cár·pous** *adj.* having only one ovary developed from the gynoecium ‖ monocarpic [fr. Mod. L. *monocarpus*, monocarpellary fr. Gk *monos*, single+*karpos*, fruit]

mon·o·cha·si·um (mɒnoukéiʒi:əm, mɒnoukéipəm) *pl.* **mon·o·cha·si·a** (mɒnoukéiʒi:ə, mɒnoukéiʒə) *n.* (bot.) a cymose inflorescence with the main axis producing only one branch [Mod. L. fr. Gk *monos*, single+*chasis*, division]

mon·o·chord (mónəkɔrd) *n.* a device consisting of a wire under tension, mounted on a resonance box, for demonstrating and determining the mathematical relations between musical tones [F. *monocorde* fr. M.L. *monochordos* fr. Gk]

mon·o·chro·mat·ic (mɒnəkroumǽtik) *adj.* (phys.) of light of one wavelength only ‖ (loosely) consisting of one color ‖ of or pertaining to a monochrome [fr. Gk *monos*, single+*chrōmatikos*, chromatic]

mon·o·chrome (mónəkroum) *n.* a painting or drawing in only one color ‖ the process by which such a representation is made **mon·o·chró·mic**, **mon·o·chró·mi·cal** *adjs* [fr. Gk *monochrōmos*]

mon·o·cle (mónək'l) *n.* an optical lens for one eye, held in position by muscular contraction [F. fr. L.L.]

mon·o·cli·nal (mɒnoukláin'l) **1.** *adj.* (geol., of a stratum or rock layer) having a single consistent direction ‖ (geol., of strata or rock layers) dipping continuously in the same direction ‖ (geol., of a fold or structure) having strata etc. that dip continuously in the same direction **2.** *n.* a monocline **món·o·cline** *n.* (geol.) a monoclinal fold or structure **mon·o·clin·ic** (mɒnouklínik) *adj.* (of a crystal) having one oblique axial intersection [fr. Gk *monos*, single+*klinein*, to bend]

mon·o·cli·nous (mɒnoukláinəs) *adj.* (bot.) hermaphrodite [fr. F. *monocline* or Mod. L. *monoclinus* fr. Gk *monos*, single+*klinē*, bed]

mon·o·cot·y·le·don (mɒnoukɒt'líːd'n) *n.* a plant with a single cotyledon ‖ an angiosperm of the subclass *Monocotyledoneae* including plants whose embryo possesses only one cotyledon (e.g. grasses), having stems with no annual rings (e.g. palms) and that are generally herbaceous in habit **mon·o·cot·y·lé·don·ous** *adj.* [fr. Mod. L. fr. Gk *monos*, single+*kotulēdon*, cotyledon]

mon·o·crys·tal (mɒnəkríst'l) *n.* (chem.) a threadlike filament of synthetic crystal — **monocrystalline** *adj.*

mo·noc·u·lar (mɒnókjulər) *adj.* involving or affecting only one eye ‖ adapted to the use of one eye, e.g. most camera viewfinders [fr. L.L. *monoculus* fr. Gk *monos*, single+L. *oculus*, eye]

mon·o·cul·ture (mónəkʌltʃər) *n.* cultivation of one kind of crop exclusively

mon·o·cy·clic (mɒnousáiklik, mɒnousíklik) *adj.* (biol.) consisting of one ring or whorl ‖ (chem.) of an organic compound composed of one ring e.g. a benzene ring [fr. MONO+Gk *kuklos*, wheel]

mon·o·dac·tyl·ous (mɒnoudǽktələs) *adj.* having only one claw or digit [fr. MONO+Gk *daktulos*, finger]

mo·nod·ic (mɒnódik) *adj.* of or having the characteristics of monody **mo·nód·i·cal** *adj.* [fr. Gk *monōdikos*]

mon·o·dist (mónədist) *n.* someone who composes or sings a monody [MONODY]

mon·o·dy (mónədi) *pl.* **mon·o·dies** *n.* (Gk drama) an ode or dirge sung by one actor ‖ a poem lamenting someone's death ‖ (mus.) a style of composition in which a single voice carries the melody, the other parts serving as accompaniment (cf. POLYPHONY) ‖ (mus.) a composition (e.g. one of the 17th–c. Italian operas) in this style [fr. L. *monodia* fr. Gk]

mo·noe·cious, **mo·ne·cious** (mɒní:ʃəs) *adj.* (bot., e.g. of the oak) having both male and female flowers on the same plant ‖ (biol.) hermaphrodite [fr. Mod. L. *Monoecia*, a former bot. class fr. Gk *monos*, single+*oikos*, house]

mo·nog·a·mist (mɒnógəmist) *n.* someone who practices or believes in monogamy [fr. Gk *monogamos* adj., marrying only once]

mo·nog·a·mous (mɒnógəməs) *adj.* practicing or believing in monogamy ‖ characterized by monogamy, *a monogamous society*

mo·nog·a·my (mɒnógəmi:) *n.* marriage to only one husband or wife at a time ‖ (zool.) the condition or habit of having only one mate [fr. F. *monogamie*]

mon·o·gen·e·sis (mɒnoudʒénisis) *n.* the theory of the development of all organisms from a single cell or organism ‖ asexual reproduction ‖ monogenism **mon·o·ge·net·ic** (mɒnoudʒənétik) *adj.* [Mod. L.]

mon·o·gen·ic (mɒnədʒénik) *adj.* monogenetic [fr. Gk *monos*, single+*genos*, kind, origin]

mo·nog·e·nism (mɒnódʒənizəm) *n.* the theory that all the races of man are descended from a single pair or from a common type of progenitor **mo·nóg·e·ny** *n.* [fr. Gk *monos*, single+*genos*, origin]

mon·o·gram (mónəgræm) *n.* a character composed of two or more interwoven letters, esp. a person's initials **mon·o·gram·mat·ic** (mɒnougrəmǽtik) *adj.* [fr. L.L. *monogramma* fr. Gk *monos*, single+*gramma*, letter]

mon·o·graph (mónəgræf, mónəgrɑf) *n.* a treatise about a single subject or aspect of a subject **mo·nog·ra·pher** (mɒnógrəfər) *n.* **mon·o·graph·ic** (mɒnəgrǽfik) *adj.* **mon·o·gráph·i·cal·ly** *adv.* [MONO+Gk *-graphos*, written]

mo·nog·y·nous (mɒnódʒinəs) *adj.* practicing monogyny [fr. Gk *monos*, single+*gunē*, woman]

mo·nog·y·ny (mɒnódʒini:) *n.* the practice or state of having only one wife at a time [fr. MONO+Gk *gunē*, woman]

mon·o·hull (mónəhʌl) *n.* a sailing vessel with one hull *Cf* MULTIHULL

mon·o·ki·ni (mɒnəkíːni:) *n.* **1.** a bikini with top and bottom joined by a band **2.** a topless bathing suit for women

mo·nol·a·try (mɒnólətri:) *n.* the worship of only one god, while admitting the existence of other gods [fr. MONO+Gk *latreia*, worship]

mon·o·lith (món'liθ) *n.* a very large single block of stone, often one erected as a monument ‖ a large block of concrete etc. used in the construction of a dam or building **mon·o·líth·ic** *adj.* massive, solid [F. *monolithe* fr. Gk *monolithos* adj., made of one stone]

monolithic *adj.* (electr.) produced on a chip of a single crystal of semiconductor *Cf* INTEGRATED CIRCUIT

monolog *MONOLOGUE

mon·o·log·ic (mɒn'lódʒik) *adj.* of or pertaining to a monologue **mon·o·lóg·i·cal** *adj.*

mo·nol·o·gist (mɒnóləd3ist) *n.* a monologuist **mo·nól·o·gize** *pres. part.* **mo·nol·o·giz·ing** *past* and *past part.* **mo·nol·o·gized** *v.i.* to utter a monologue [fr. Gk *monologos* adj., speaking alone]

mon·o·logue, **mon·o·log** (món'lɔg, món'log) *n.* a long speech by one person ‖ a dramatic speech by one actor ‖ a writing in the form of a soliloquy [F. *monologue* fr. Gk *monologos*, speaking alone]

mon·o·ma·ni·a (mɒnouméini:ə) *n.* an obsessive interest in one thing to the exclusion of all others ‖ a form of mental illness characterized by irrationality on only one subject **mon·o·má·ni·ac** *n.* **mon·o·ma·ni·a·cal** (mɒnoumənáiək'l) *adj.* [Mod. L. fr. Gk *monos*, single+*mania*, mania]

mon·o·mer (mónəmər) *n.* the repeating structural unit of which a polymer is composed ‖ a substance composed of small molecules which under the proper conditions may unite to form a polymer [fr. MONO+Gk *meros*, part]

mon·o·me·tal·lic (mɒnoumətǽlik) *adj.* of, involving or using a single metal as the monetary standard ‖ of or consisting of one metal **mon·o·met·al·lism** (mɒnoumét'lizəm), **mon·o·mét·al·list** *ns*

mo·no·mi·al (mənóumi:əl) **1.** *n.* (math.) an expression consisting of one term only **2.** *adj.* (math.) of such an expression [MONO+BINOMIAL]

mon·o·mo·lec·u·lar (mɒnoumələkjulər) *adj.* of or designating a layer one molecule thick ‖ of or consisting of a single molecule

mon·o·mor·phic (mɒnoumórfik) *adj.* (of a taxonomic group) showing the same form in all its members ‖ (biol.) keeping the same form throughout its development [fr. Gk *monos*, single+*morphē*, form] .

Mo·non·ga·he·la (mɒnɒŋgəhíːlə) a river (128 miles long) rising in West Virginia and flowing north to Pittsburgh, Pennsylvania, where it joins the Ohio River

mon·o·nu·clear (mɒnounú:kli:ər) or **mono·nu·cle·ar** (mɒnounú:kliət) *adj.* having one nucleus

mon·o·nu·cle·o·sis (mɒnounu:kli:óusis, mɒnounju:kli:óusis) *n.* *INFECTIOUS MONONUCLEOSIS [Mod. L.]

mon·o·pet·al·ous (mɒnoupét'ləs) *adj.* (bot.) having one petal only ‖ (bot.) gamopetalous

mon·o·phon·ic (mɒnəfónik) *adj.* (mus.) consisting of a single, unaccompanied melodic line ‖ (mus.) consisting of a melodic line for solo voice, with a simple accompaniment ‖ of sound reproduction using a single channel to transmit the sounds (cf. STEREOPHONIC)

mo·noph·o·ny (mɒnófəni:) *n.* music that consists of a single, unaccompanied melodic line [MONO+Gk *phōnē*, sound, voice]

mon·oph·thong (mónəfθɒŋ, mónəfθɒŋ) *n.* a single, simple vowel sound (cf. DIPHTHONG) **mon·oph·thong·al** (mɒnəfθɒŋg'l, mɒnəfθɒŋg'l) *adj.* [fr. Gk *monophthongos* adj., having a single sound]

mon·o·phy·let·ic (mɒnoufailétik) *adj.* derived from a single common ancestral form ‖ belonging to a single stock [fr. MONO+Gk *phuletikos*, of a phylum]

mon·o·phyl·lous (mɒnoufíləs) *adj.* (bot., of a calyx) consisting of only one leaf ‖ (bot.) unifoliate [fr. MONO+Gk *phullon*, leaf]

Mo·noph·y·site (mənófisait) *n.* a person holding the belief that there is only one nature, the divine, in the person of Christ. The doctrine was propounded by Eutyches and condemned by the Council of Chalcedon (451). It is held by the Coptic, Syrian, Jacobite and Armenian Churches **Mon·o·phy·sit·ic** (mɒnoufisítik) *adj.* **Mo·noph·y·sit·ism** (mənófisaitizəm) *n.* [fr. eccl. L. *Monophysita* fr. Gk *monos*, single+*phusis*, nature]

mon·o·plane (mónəplein) *n.* an airplane with only one supporting surface

mon·o·ple·gi·a (mɒnouplí:dʒi:ə) *n.* paralysis of one limb or group of muscles **mon·o·plé·gic** *adj.* [fr. MONO+Gk *plēgē*, stroke]

mon·o·ploid (mónəplɔid) *adj.* (cytol.) having the characteristic number of chromosomes of a species (haploid) in a series of organisms with twice the number of chromosomes (polyploid)

mon·o·po·di·al (mɒnoupóudi:əl) *adj.* of, designating or characterized by a monopodium

mon·o·po·di·um (mɒnoupóudi:əm) *pl.* **mon·o·po·di·a** (mɒnoupóudi:ə) *n.* (bot.) the single main or primary axis of a plant or tree, from which all the main lateral branches grow (as in pines) [Mod. L. fr. Gk *monos*, single+*pous* (*podos*), foot]

mon·o·pole (mɒnəpoul) *n.* **1.** (electr.) a radio antenna with a single vertical element **2.** (particle phys.) a hypothetical particle with a single magnetic charge

mo·nop·o·list (mənópəlist) *n.* a person who has a monopoly or who favors monopoly **mo·nop·o·lís·tic** *adj.*

mo·nop·o·li·za·tion (mənɒpəlizéiʃən) *n.* a monopolizing or being monopolized

mo·nop·o·lize (mənópəlaiz) *pres. part.* **mo·nop·o·liz·ing** *past* and *past part.* **mo·nop·o·lized** *v.t.* to make a monopoly of ‖ to assume exclusive control or use of, *to monopolize a conversation*

mo·nop·o·ly (mənópəli:) *pl.* **mo·nop·o·lies** *n.* exclusive control of the supply of a product or service in a particular market ‖ an exclusive privilege to engage in a particular business or provide a particular service, granted by a ruler, state etc. ‖ a commodity under exclusive control ‖ a company having exclusive control [fr. L.L. *monopolium* fr. Gk]

mo·nop·ter·al (mounóptərəl) *adj.* of or relating to a monopteron

mo·nop·te·ron (mounóptərɒn) *n.* a classical circular building in which the roof is supported

CONCISE PRONUNCIATION KEY: **(a)** æ, c*a*t; ɑ, c*ar*; ɔ f*aw*n; ei, sn*a*ke. **(e)** e, h*e*n; iː, sh*ee*p; iə, d*ee*r; ɛə, b*ea*r. **(i)** i, f*i*sh; ai, t*i*ger; əː, b*i*rd. **(o)** o, *o*x; au, c*ow*; ou, g*oa*t; u, p*oo*r; ɔi, r*oy*al. **(u)** ʌ, d*u*ck; u, b*u*ll; uː, g*oo*se; ə, b*a*cillus; juː, c*u*be. x, lo*ch*; θ, *th*ink; ð, bo*th*er; z, *Z*en; ʒ, cor*s*age; dʒ, sava*ge*; ŋ, ora*ng*utang; j, *y*ak; ʃ, *fi*sh; tʃ, fe*tch*; 'l, rabb*le*; 'n, redd*en*. Complete pronunciation key appears inside front cover.

not by a wall but by a single ring of columns [L.L. fr. Gk *monopteros*, having one wing]

mon·o·rail (mónourẹil) *n.* a railway consisting of a single rail on which the wheels run ‖ this rail

mon·o·sac·cha·ride (mɒnousǽkəraid) *n.* a simple sugar, one of a class of carbohydrates containing one or more hydroxyl groups, a carbonyl group and a ring or chain of three or more carbon atoms

mon·o·sep·al·ous (mɒnousépələs) *adj.* (*bot.*) having only one sepal ‖ (*bot.*) gamosepalous

mon·o·sex·u·al (mɒnousékʃuːəl) *adj.* **1.** intended for persons of one sex *ant* unisexual **2.** having sexual orientation toward one sex *ant* bisexual —**monosexuality** *n.*

mon·o·some (mɒnəsoum) *n.* (*genetics*) an unpaired X chromosome *Cf* AUTOSOME

mon·o·sper·mous (mɒnouspɔ́:rməs) *adj.* (*bot.*) having only one seed [fr. MONO-+Gk *sperma*, seed]

mon·o·stich (mɒ́nəstik) *n.* a single metrical line ‖ a poem one line long [fr. L.L. *monostichum* fr. Gk fr. *monos*, single+*stichos*, line]

mo·nos·tro·phe (mənóstrəfi:, mɒ́nəstrouf) *n.* a poem whose stanzas all have the same metrical form ‖ a poem one stanza long [fr. Gk *monostrophos*]

mon·o·stroph·ic (mɒnoustrófik) *adj.* of, designating or having the nature of a monostrophe [fr. Gk *monostrophikos*]

mon·o·syl·lab·ic (mɒnousilǽbik) *adj.* (of a word) consisting of only one syllable ‖ (of speech) consisting of monosyllables ‖ (of a person) speaking in monosyllables **mon·o·syl·láb·i·cal·ly** *adv.* [fr. M.L. *monosyllabicus* fr. L.L. fr. Gk]

mon·o·syl·la·ble (mɒ́nəsiləb'l) *n.* a word of one syllable [fr. L.L. *monŏsyllabus*]

mon·o·sym·met·ric (mɒnousimétrik) *adj.* (*crystall.*) monoclinic ‖ (*biol.*) zygomorphic **mon·o·sym·mét·ri·cal** *adj.*

mon·o·tech·nic (mɒnoutéknik) *adj.* of a specialist in one field

mon·o·the·ism (mɒ́nəθi:izəm) *n.* belief in only one God (cf. POLYTHEISM) **món·o·the·ist** *n.*

mon·o·the·is·tic, mon·o·the·ís·ti·cal *adjs* [fr. Gk *monos*, single+*theos*, god]

Mo·noth·e·lite (mənóθəlait) *n.* an adherent of the heretical doctrine that Christ had one will but two natures. The doctrine was adopted (622) by the Byzantine Emperor Heraclius, but died out after it was condemned (680) at Constantinople **Mo·nóth·e·lit·ism** *n.* [fr. M.L. *monothelita* fr. late Gk *Monothelētēs* fr. Gk *monos*, single+*thelēin*, to will]

mon·o·tone (mɒ́nətoun) *n.* a succession of sounds of the same pitch ‖ a single tone without variation in pitch ‖ speech of unvarying pitch and stress [fr. Mod. L. *monotonus* adj., monotonous fr. Gk *monos*, single+*tonos*, tone]

mon·o·to·nic·i·ty (mɒnətounísiti:) *n.* (*electr.*) an analog-to-digital converter in a situation where increased input voltage results in increased output

mo·not·o·nous (mənót'nəs) *adj.* tediously repetitious, lacking variety, *monotonous work* ‖ characterized by a monotone [fr. Gk *monotonos*]

mo·not·o·ny (mənót'ni:) *n.* tedious lack of variety ‖ sameness of tone or pitch [fr. Gk *monotonia*]

mon·o·treme (mɒ́nətri:m) *n.* a member of *Monotremata*, subclass *Prototheria*, the one living order of primitive egg-laying mammals. They are native to the Australian region and include the echidna and duckbill [fr. Mod. L. fr. Gk *monos*, single+*trēma* (*trēmata*), perforation]

mon·o·trich·ic (mɒnətríkik) *adj.* monotrichous

mo·not·ri·chous (mənótrikəs) *adj.* (*biol.*, of bacteria) having a single flagellum at one pole [fr. MONO-+Gk *thrix* (*trichos*), hair]

mon·o·type (mɒ́nətaip) *n.* (*biol.*) a single type which constitutes a species or a genus ‖ a print on paper taken from a painting on glass or metal

Monotype *n.* (*printing*) a method of keyboarding and casting type by single letters in justified lines ‖ (*printing*) a machine which sets type in this way (cf. LINOTYPE) [trademark]

mon·o·un·sat·u·rate (mɒnouənsǽtʃərit) *n.* an oil or fat that has a single hydrogen atom in its carbon chain. It appears in most vegetable, seed oils, and fish oils —**monounsaturated** *adv. Cf* POLYUNSATURATE

mon·o·va·lent (mɒnouvéilənt) *adj.* (*chem.*) having a valence of one (cf. UNIVALENT) ‖ (*bacteriol.*)

having antibodies for one strain of bacteria only [MONO-+L. *valens* (*valentis*) fr. *valere*, to be worth]

mon·ox·ide (mɒnóksaid, mənóksaid) *n.* an oxide having only one atom of oxygen in each molecule, e.g. CO, carbon monoxide

Mon·roe (mənróu), Harriet (1860–1936), U.S. editor, critic, and poet who founded (1912) 'Poetry: a Magazine of Verse'. The first such anthology in U.S. literary history, it encouraged new and established poets and helped to finance them

Monroe, James (1758–1831), fifth president (1817–25) of the U.S.A., a Democratic Republican. Appointed (1802) special envoy to France by President Thomas Jefferson, he negotiated (1803) the Louisiana Purchase. He served (1811–17) as secretary of state and (1814–15) as secretary of war under President James Madison. His administration was notable for the enactment of the Missouri Compromise and the enunciation of the Monroe Doctrine

Monroe, Marilyn (1926–62), U.S. actress known for her blond looks and sex goddess roles, born Norma Jean Baker. She starred in 'Gentlemen Prefer Blondes' (1953), 'How to Marry a Millionaire' (1953), 'The Seven Year Itch' (1955), 'Bus Stop' (1956), 'Some Like It Hot' (1959) and 'The Misfits' (1961). Despite success, she became increasingly unhappy and died of an overdose of sleeping pills. Her second and third husbands were Joe DiMaggio and Arthur Miller respectively. Her life is recounted in 'After the Fall' (Arthur Miller, 1964) and 'Marilyn' (Norman Mailer, 1973) and in the play 'The Goddess' (Paddy Chayevsky, 1958)

Monroe Doctrine the declaration, drawn up by John Quincy Adams and enunciated (1823) by Monroe, that the Americas were not to be considered as a field for European colonization and that the U.S.A. would view with displeasure any European attempt to intervene in the political affairs of American countries. It dominated American diplomacy for the next century, and came, in the late 19th c., to be associated with the assertion of U.S. hegemony in Latin America

Mon·ro·vi·a (mənróuviːə) a port, the capital and largest city (pop. 171,880) of Liberia. It was founded (1822) by the American Colonization Society, during the administration of U.S. President James Monroe (for whom it is named), as a haven for freed slaves. The inhabitants are chiefly descended from former slave immigrants from the U.S.A. and the British West Indies. It is the seat of the University of Liberia

Mons (mɔ̃s) the capital (pop. 93,332) of Hainaut, Belgium. It is a canal port in the coal belt. Chapel (12th c.), town hall (15th c.). On Aug. 23, 1914 the retreat of the British Expeditionary Force began here after a battle against the German armies

Mon·sieur (məsjə:) *pl.* **Mes·sieurs** (meisjə:) *n.* the French equivalent of 'Mr', used as a courtesy title for a man and (without the surname) as a term of address to a man

Mon·si·gnor (mɒnsí:njər) *pl.* **Mon·si·gno·ri** (mɒnsi:njɔ́ri:), **Mon·si·gnors** *n.* (*abbr.* Msgr) a title given to certain dignitaries of the Roman Catholic Church ‖ a person with such a title [Ital. *Monsignore*]

mon·soon (mɒnsú:n) *n.* a wind system in which there is an almost complete reversal of prevailing direction from season to season, the primary cause being the difference in temperature over land and sea. It is esp. prominent in S.E. Asia ‖ the rainy summer season (Apr.–Sept.) in S.E. Asia [early Mod. Du. *monssoen* fr. Port. *monção* perh. fr. Arab. *mausim*, season]

mon·ster (mɒ́nstər) **1.** *n.* a deformed animal or plant ‖ an imaginary beast, usually compounded of incongruous parts e.g. centaur, sphinx etc. ‖ a person who is horrifyingly cruel, brutal, selfish etc. ‖ something of extraordinarily great size **2.** *adj.* of very great size [O.F. *monstre*]

mon·strance (mɒ́nstrəns) *n.* (*Roman Catholicism*) a vessel of gold or silver in which the consecrated Host is exposed to the congregation for veneration [O.F.]

mon·stre sa·cré (mɒ́nstrə sakréi) *n.* (*Fr.*: "sacred monster"; usu. italics) **1.** an eccentric celebrity whose quirks are accepted by the public **2.** a greater performer

mon·stros·i·ty (mɒnstrósiti:) *pl.* **mon·stros·i·ties** *n.* something monstrous ‖ the quality or

state of being monstrous [fr. L.L. *monstrositas*]

mon·strous (mɒ́nstrəs) *adj.* having or showing the qualities of a monster [O.F. *monstreux*]

Mont. Montana

mon·tage (mɒntáʒ) *n.* (*photog.*) the making of a single picture from several others or pieces of others ‖ a picture formed in this way ‖ (*radio* etc.) the creating of a single composite effect by using music, sound effects, snatches of dialogue etc. in quick succession ‖ the effect so produced ‖ (*movies*) a medley of shots built up into a single unified effect by cutting, dissolving etc. ‖ the technique or process involved in this [F.]

Mon·ta·gnard (mɒutanjár) *n.* (a member of an) aboriginal South Vietnamese highland people

Mon·ta·gu (mɒ́ntagju:), Charles, 1st earl of Halifax *HALIFAX

Montagu, Lady Mary Wortley (1689–1762), English writer known for her 'Letters from the East' (1717–18) written from Constantinople, where her husband was ambassador

Mon·taigne (mɒtenj, mɒntéin), Michel Eyquem de (1533–92), French moralist. He began his 'Essais' in 1571, and continued to add to them all his life. The essays provide the first attempt at a complete self-portrait in European literature, and reveal their author as a humane, tolerant man, questioning, a little skeptical, seeking wisdom from a wide range of sources

Mon·tal·vo (mɒntálvɔ), Juan (1832–89), Ecuadorian writer and tireless opponent of the Ecuadorian tyrant Gabriel García Moreno. Like Sarmiento, he presented the struggle as that between civilization and barbarism. His works include 'Catilinarias' and 'Capítulos que se le olvidaron a Cervantes'. The latter is a satire which presents his enemies as the enemies of Don Quixote

Mon·tan·a (mɒntǽnə) (*abbr.* Mont.) a state (area 147,138 sq. miles, pop. 801,000) in the northwest U.S.A., divided between the Rocky Mtns and the Great Plains. Capital: Helena. Agriculture: wheat, barley, sugar beets, fodder crops (largely irrigated), cattle, sheep. Resources: copper, gold, silver, lead, manganese, oil, timber. Industries: lumber products, smelting and refining, food processing. State university (1893) at Missoula, Bozeman and Butte. Most of Montana was included in the Louisiana Purchase (1803), but few settlers arrived before gold was discovered (1862). It became (1889) the 41st state of the U.S.A.

mon·tane (mɒntein) *adj.* of or pertaining to mountain regions, esp. of the vegetation growing in high land below the tree line [fr. L. *montanus*]

Mon·tan·ism (mɒ́ntənizəm) *n.* a heretical sect of Christianity. It originated (c. 150–72) in Phrygia with Montanus, who claimed a continuing revelatory gift of the Holy Spirit and prophesied the imminent return of Christ. Tertullian encouraged its asceticism and acceptance of martyrdom. The sect lost its importance in the West by the 3rd c. but continued in Asia Minor until suppressed by Justinian (mid-6th c.) **Món·tan·ist** *adj.* [after *Montanus* (2nd c.), its founder]

mon·tan wax (mɒ́ntæn) a bituminous wax extracted from some lignites and peats, used in polishes, carbon paper etc. [fr. S.. *montanus*, of a mountain]

Mont aux Sources (mɔ̃tousu:rs) the summit (10,761 ft) of the Drakensberg Mtns in N. Lesotho

Mont Blanc (mɔ̃blá) a massif in the Savoy Alps on the frontiers of France, Italy and Switzerland. Summit: 15,781 ft

Mont·calm (mɔ̃kælm, mɒntkám), Louis, Marquis de (1712–59), French general. He defended Canada against the British in the French and Indian War and was killed on the Heights of Abraham

Mont Ce·nis (mɔ̃seni:) (*Ital.* Moncenisio) a pass (6,831 ft) in the Graian Alps, between France and Italy, on the Lyon–Turin main road. The Mont Cenis railroad tunnel is 16 miles southwest

Mon·te·a·gu·do (mɒnteagu:ðɔ), Bernardo (1785–1825), Argentinian writer and independence leader who accompanied San Martín to Lima. His 'Escritos políticos' analyze the political organization of Hispanic America

Mon·te Al·ban (mɒnteálban) center of the Mixtec-Zapoteca civilization, near Oaxaca, S.W. Mexico, whose temples and pyramids still stand

Monte Car·lo (mónti:kárlou) *MONACO

CONCISE PRONUNCIATION KEY: **(a)** æ, c*a*t; ɑ, c*a*r; ɔ f*aw*n; ei, sn*a*ke. **(e)** e, h*e*n; i:, sh*ee*p; iə, d*ee*r; εə, b*ea*r. **(i)** i, f*i*sh; ai, t*i*ger; ə:, b*i*rd. **(o)** o, *o*x; au, c*ow*; ou, g*oa*t; u, p*oo*r; ɔi, r*oy*al. **(u)** ʌ, d*u*ck; u, b*u*ll; u:, g*oo*se; ə, b*a*cillus; ju:, c*u*be. x, lo*ch*; θ, *th*ink; ð, bo*th*er; z, *Z*en; ʒ, corsa*g*e; dʒ, sava*g*e; ŋ, ora*ng*utang; j, *y*ak; ʃ, *fi*sh; tʃ, fe*tch*; 'l, rabb*le*; 'n, redd*en*. Complete pronunciation key appears inside front cover.

Mon·te Car·lo Method (mɒnti:kárlou) (*math.*) a system of random statistical sampling used to obtain approximations of the probability of solving certain problems by trial and error or of the solution itself —**Monte Carlo** *adj.*

Monte Cas·si·no (mɒntekɑssí:nɔ) a monastery of S. Latium, Italy, founded (c. 529) by St Benedict of Nursia. It became a great center of learning. Destroyed (1944) by Allied bombing, it has been rebuilt

mon·teith (mɒntí:θ) *n.* a punch bowl, usually of silver and with a scalloped rim [perh. after the inventor]

Mon·te·ne·grin (mɒntəní:grin) 1. *adj.* of or relating to Montenegro, its people etc. 2. *n.* a native or inhabitant of Montenegro

Mon·te·ne·gro (mɒntəní:grou) a republic (area 5,343 sq. miles, pop. 565,000) of S.W. Yugoslavia, north of Albania. Capital: Titograd. It is an inaccessible karst mountain region with fertile depressions. Crops: corn, vines, tobacco, olives, figs. Livestock: sheep, hogs, goats. Industry: fishing (Lake Scutari). Montenegro remained independent after the Turkish conquest of Serbia (1389), and was never completely subdued by the Turks. It became (1918) part of the kingdom later called Yugoslavia

Mon·te·rey (mɒntəréi) a fishing port (pop. 27,558) of central California

Mon·ter·rey (mɒnterréi) an industrial and commercial center (pop. 2,463,500) of N.E. Mexico: metallurgy (iron and steel), building materials, food processing. University (1933)

Mon·tes·quieu (mɔ́teskjə:, mɒ́nteskju:), Charles Louis de Secondat, Baron de la Brède et de (1689–1755), French writer. His 'Lettres persanes' (1721) satirized contemporary social and political institutions in France. His greatest work, 'Esprit des lois' (1748), dealing with the nature of the state and the science of law, had much influence on later political thinking

Mon·tes·so·ri system (mɒntisóri:) a method of teaching children, 3–6 years old, based upon individual activity, free expression, individual attention, and an early introduction to writing and drawing [after Maria *Montessori* (1870–1952), Ital. educator and physician]

Mon·te·ver·di (mɒntevérdi:), Claudio (1567–1643), Italian composer. He virtually established the form of Italian opera with 'Orfeo' (1607), 'The Return of Ulysses' (1641), and 'The Coronation of Poppaea' (1642) etc. He also wrote madrigals, masses, cantatas etc. He was an innovator, using new harmonies and bringing a new dramatic power to vocal music, as well as to his orchestration

Mon·te·vi·de·o (mɒntəvidéiou) the capital, chief port and cultural center (pop. 1,229,748) of Uruguay, on the Río de la Plata estuary, a base for South Atlantic fishing. Industries: meat packing, food processing, leather. University (1833)

Montevideo Pact a commercial agreement (1960) creating the Latin America Free Trade Area (LAFTA). It was signed by Argentina, Brazil, Chile, Mexico, Paraguay, Peru and Uruguay, and later by Bolivia, Colombia, Ecuador and Venezuela

Mon·te·zu·ma (ɪɑpntizú:mə) (c. 1466–1520), Aztec emperor (c. 1502–20). He was killed during the Spanish conquest of Mexico under Cortés

Mon·te·zu·ma's revenge (mɒntəzú:məz) (*colloq.*) diarrhea and nausea commonly contracted by tourists in Mexico

Mont·fort (mɒ́ntfərt), Simon de (c. 1208–65), earl of Leicester, leader of the baronial revolt against Henry III, his brother-in-law. Discontented with Henry's misrule, he helped to draw up the Previsions of Oxford (1248) and, with the outbreak of the Barons' War (1264–6), captured the king at Lewes (1264). To strengthen his government he summoned a parliament (1265) representing both shires and boroughs but, deserted by some of the barons, he was defeated and killed at Evesham (1265)

Mont·gol·fier (mɔ̃golfjei), Jacques Etienne (1745–99), French inventor. With his brother, Joseph Michel (1740–1810), he devised and used the hot-air balloon

Mont·gom·er·y (məntgʌ́məri:), Bernard Law, 1st Viscount Montgomery of Alamein (1887–1976), British field marshal. He defeated a German army under Rommel at Alamein (1942), commanded the British army in Sicily and Italy (1943), and was military commander of the Allied invasion of Normandy (1944). He was chief of the imperial general staff (1946–9) and

helped to organize (1951–8) the defense system of NATO

Montgomery, Richard (1738–75), American Revolutionary general who led (1775) the invasion of Quebec, capturing Montreal. He died in the assault on Quebec

Mont·gom·er·y (mɒntgʌ́məri:) the capital (pop. 178,157) of Alabama, a market for cotton, livestock and lumber, with chemical industries. It became (1861) the first capital of the Confederacy and was the site of the inauguration of Jefferson Davis. The boycott (1956) by the black population of the city buses, forcing their desegregation, opened the militant U.S. civil rights movement

Mont·gom·er·y·shire (məntgʌ́məri:ʃiər) (*abbr.* Mont.) a county (area 797 sq. miles, pop. 44,000) of E. Wales. County town: Welshpool

month (mʌnθ) *n.* one of 12 periods into which the year is divided in the Gregorian calendar, varying between 28 and 31 days ‖ one of the periods of comparable length in any other calendar ‖ the period of rotation of the moon around the earth, approx. 29.5 days ‖ (*loosely*) a period of 4 weeks [O.E. *mōnath*]

Mon·ther·lant (mɔ̃terlɑ̃), Henry Millon de (1896–1972), French writer, famous as a stylist. His novels include 'les Célibataires' (1934) and 'les Jeunes Filles' (1936–9). His plays include 'la Reine morte' (1942), 'le Maître de Santiago' (1948), 'Port-Royal' (1954) and 'le Cardinal d'Espagne' (1960)

month·ly (mʌ́nθli:) 1. *adj.* lasting a month, *the moon's monthly rotation* ‖ occurring once each month, *a monthly payment* 2. *pl.* **month·lies** *n.* a periodical published once a month ‖ (*pl., pop.*) the menses 3. *adv.* once a month

Mon·ti·cel·lo (mntitʃélou, mɒntisélou) the estate, incl. the mansion which he designed, of Thomas Jefferson, near Charlottesville, Virginia

mon·ti·cule (mɒ́ntikju:l) *n.* a small hill, esp. a small volcanic cone [F. fr. L.L. *monticulus*]

Mont·pel·ier (mɒntpí:ljər) the capital (pop. 8,241) of Vermont

Mont·pel·lier (mɔ̃peljei) a city (pop. 195,603) in Hérault, S. France. Industries: engineering, textiles, food processing, wine. Gothic cathedral (14th c.), many Renaissance buildings. University (1289)

Mont·re·al (mɒntri:ɔ́l, mɔ̃reiæl) the largest city (pop. 980,354) and chief port of Canada, on Montreal Is. in the St Lawrence, S. Quebec. Language: two-thirds French, one-third English. The old French town (1642) is now the financial district. Industries: rolling stock, engineering, food processing, oil refining. Greatly modernized in the 1960s and 1970s, the city hosted the 1976 summer Olympic Games. Universities: McGill (chartered 1821), Montreal (1878)

Mon·treux (mɒtrə:) a resort (pop. 20,421) at the east end of the Lake of Geneva, Vaud, Switzerland

Mont·rose (mɒntróuz), James Graham, 5th earl of (1612–50), Scottish soldier. He led the Scottish royalists in the English Civil War

Mont-St-Mi·chel (mɔsɛ̃mi:ʃel) a walled village (pop. 270) in Manche department, France, surmounted by a towering abbey-fortress (founded 966, present buildings 12th–16th cc.) on a high rock in the bay between Normandy and Brittany. At low tide it is on the shore, but rising tides quickly surround it with water. A causeway (1875) connects it to the mainland

Mont·ser·rat (mɒntseræt) one of the Leeward Is, West Indies, a British colony (area 38 sq. miles, pop. 12,162). Capital and port: Plymouth (pop. 2,000). Colonized by Britain (17th and 18th cc.), the island was federated to the Leeward Is (1871–1956) and became a separate colony (1960)

Montt (mɔnt), Manuel (1809–80), Chilean statesman, president of the Republic (1851–61). He engaged Andrés Bello to draft the Código Civil (1855), which codified Chilean laws

mon·u·ment (mɒ́njumənt) *n.* something, typically a statue on a plinth or column, erected in memory of a person or event ‖ any structure etc. which acquires a memorial value with the passing of time ‖ a literary or scientific work of lasting value, *a monument of learning* (*law*) a natural or artificial landmark used to mark a boundary [fr. L. *monumentum, monimentum* fr. *monere,* to remind]

mon·u·men·tal (mɒnjumént'l) *adj.* of, like or serving as a monumen ‖ (*loosely*) very great,

monumental stupidity ‖ very large, massive [fr. L.L. *monumentalis*]

mon·u·ron [$C_9H_{11}C1N_2O$] (mɒnjərɒn) *n.* (*chem.*) a persistent herbicide used to destroy broad-leaved plants

mon·zo·nite (mɒ́nzənait) *n.* a granular igneous rock composed of augite, biotite, orthoclase and plagioclase [F. after Mt *Monzoni* in the Tyrol]

moo (mu:) 1. *n.* the characteristic deep vocal sound made by a cow 2. *v.i.* to make this sound [imit.]

mooch (mu:tʃ) *v.i.* (*pop.*) to wander about idly and aimlessly ‖ (*pop.*) to sponge [perh. ult. fr. O.F. *muchier,* to skulk]

mood (mu:d) *n.* (*gram.*) an aspect of a verb indicating whether the speaker regards the denoted action as a fact, a probability or possibility, a command etc. ‖ (*logic*) the nature of the connection between antecedent and consequent ‖ (*logic*) the form of a syllogism [var. of MODE]

mood *n.* an emotional state, *a happy mood* ‖ (*loosely*) a fit of bad temper [O.E. *mōd,* feeling]

mood drug drug that affects the state of the mind, e.g., sedatives and stimulants

mood·i·ly (mú:dili:) *adv.* in a moody manner

mood·i·ness (mú:di:nis) *n.* the state or quality of being moody

Moo·dy (mú:di:), Dwight Lyman (1837–99), U.S. evangelist whose tours (from 1870) throughout the U.S.A. and Great Britain, during which he preached God's love and mercy rather than retribution and hell-fire, drew massive and enthusiastic audiences. He founded several religious schools and institutes for children

Moody, William Vaughn (1869–1910), U.S. poet and dramatist, best known for his prose play 'The Great Divide' (produced on stage as 'A Sabine Woman', 1906)

mood·y (mú:di:) *comp.* **mood·i·er** *superl.* **mood·i·est** *adj.* characterized by gloomy moods or by sudden changes of mood ‖ gloomy, depressed [O.E. *mōdig* brave, spirited]

Moog synthesizer (mu:g) (*music*) an electronic keyboard musical instrument with a wide range

moon (mu:n) 1. *n.* the only natural satellite of the earth, being responsible (with the sun) for its tidal action ‖ any planetary satellite ‖ the earth's natural satellite as a source of light, *there is a moon tonight* ‖ (*rhet.*) a month **once in a blue moon** hardly ever, only at very long intervals 2. *v.i.* (often with 'around', 'about', 'over') to behave in a dreamy abstracted manner ‖ *v.t.* (with 'away') to spend (time) mooning [O.E. *mōna*]

—The earth's moon is a solid, almost spherical body 2,162 miles in diameter, of mass 7.2×10^{19} tons (or 0.0123 times the mass of the earth). It revolves in a slightly elliptical orbit about the earth (mean orbital diameter=238,857 miles), with a sidereal period of 27 days 7 hours 43.2 mins. Since its period of rotation is identical with its period of revolution it always keeps the same face toward the earth. The resulting changes in its aspect when viewed from the earth are called the phases of the moon. The visible surface of the moon presents strongly contrasting physical relief, including mountain ranges (one rises 30,000 ft above the surrounding plain) and walled craters of widely varying size and broad flat plains, called 'seas'. The moon lacks an atmosphere because the gravitational field at its surface (1/6 that of the earth at its surface) is insufficient to retain gases at the temperatures prevailing. The U.S.S.R. landed the first probe on the moon (Feb. 1966) and the U.S.A. landed (July 1969) the first men on the moon, and brought them back

moon·beam (mú:nbi̯:m) *n.* a beam of light from the moon

moon·blind (mú:nblaind) *adj.* afflicted with moon blindness

moon blindness a disease of horses characterized by recurrent inflammation of the eyes and eventual blindness

moon car *LUNAR ROVER

moon·craft (mú:nkræft) or **moon·ship** (mú:nʃip) *n.* a spacecraft for reaching the moon

moon crawler *LUNAR ROVER

Moo·ney (mú:ni:), James (1861–1921), U.S. ethnologist. He was the foremost authority of his time on the early history of the Indian peoples north of Mexico. He is known for his 'Aboriginal Population of America North of Mexico' (1928)

CONCISE PRONUNCIATION KEY: (a) æ, c*a*t; ɑ, c*a*r; ɔ f*aw*n; ei, sn*a*ke. (e) e, h*e*n; i:, sh*ee*p; iə, d*ee*r; ɛə, b*ea*r. (i) i, f*i*sh; ai, t*i*ger; ə:, b*i*rd. (o) o, *o*x; au, c*ow*; ou, g*oa*t; u, p*oo*r; ɔi, r*oy*al. (u) ʌ, d*u*ck; u, b*u*ll; u:, g*oo*se; ə, b*a*cill*u*s; ju:, c*u*be. x, lo*ch*; θ, *th*ink; ð, *th*is; z, Z*e*n; ʒ, cor*sa*ge; dʒ, sa*v*age; ŋ, ora*ng*uta*ng*; j, *y*ak; ʃ, *f*ish; tʃ, fe*tch*; 'l, rabb*le*; 'n, redd*en*. Complete pronunciation key appears inside front cover.

moon-faced (múːnfeist) *adj.* having a very round face

moon fall a landing on the moon

moon-flow-er (múːnflạuər) *n. Calonyction aculeatum,* a night-blooming morning glory of tropical America ‖ (*Br.*) *Chrysanthemum leucanthemum,* the oxeye daisy

Moon-ie (múːni) *n.* a member of the Unification Church headed by Sun-Myung Moon

moon-ing (múːniŋ) *n.* (*slang*) exposure of the buttocks in public

moon-light (múːnlạit) **1.** *n.* light received by reflection from the moon **2.** *v.i.* (*pop.*) to engage in moonlighting

moonlight flit (*Br., pop.*) a departure with one's possessions by night, without paying the rent due

moonlighting working at a job in addition to one's regular one **—moonlight** *v.* **—moonlighter** *n.*

moon-lit (múːnlịt) *adj.* illuminated by moonlight

moon-port (múːnpɔrt) *n.* **1.** earth station for a mooncraft **2.** launching area for mooncraft

moon-rise (múːnrạiz) *n.* the rising of the moon above the horizon ‖ the time of the moon's rising

moon rock rock or rocks brought to earth from the moon *Cf* FERROPSEUDOBROOKITE, KREEP

moon rover *LUNAR ROVER

moon-shine (múːnʃạin) *n.* nonsense, something imagined but not true ‖ (*pop.*) alcohol, esp. smuggled or illegally distilled whiskey ‖ (*rare*) moonlight **móon-shin-er** *n.* (*pop.*) someone who illegally distills or smuggles whiskey

moon-shot (múːnʃɔt) *n.* or **moon shoot** the launching of a spacecraft to the moon

moon-stone (múːnstọun) *n.* a translucent semiprecious pearly form of feldspar used as a gem

moon-struck (múːnstrʌk) *adj.* sentimental, fanciful ‖ (*rhet.*) mentally deranged

moon-walk (múːnwɔk) *n.* **1.** the first exploratory walk on the moon (made by Apollo 11 commander Neil A. Armstrong at 10:56 P.M. EDT, July 20, 1969; followed a few moments later by Colonel Edwin E. Aldrin, Jr.) **2.** any exploratory walk on the moon **—moonwalker** *n.*

moon-y (múːni) *comp.* **moon-i-er** *superl.* **moon-i-est** *adj.* mooning, dreamy and sentimental

moor (muər) *n.* (*esp. Br.*) a tract of open uncultivated ground, usually grown over with heather and coarse grasses and having a poor, acid, peaty soil ‖ (*esp. Br.*) a tract of such land preserved for game shooting [O.E. *mōr*]

moor *v.t.* to secure (a vessel, airship etc.) to the land or buoys by means of ropes, chains etc. ‖ *v.i.* to secure a vessel etc. by ropes etc. ‖ (of a vessel etc.) to be secured in this way **móor-age** *n.* a mooring or being moored ‖ a place for mooring ‖ a charge for mooring [M.E. *more* prob. Fr. Gmc]

Moor (muər) *n.* a native of Morocco of mixed Arabic and Berber origin ‖ (*hist.*) a Moslem settled in N. Africa, esp. one of those who invaded Spain in the 8th c. and were driven out in the 15th c., or a descendant of these people [F. *More, Maure* fr. L. fr. Gk]

moor-cock (múərkɔk) *n.* the male red grouse

Moore (muər), George (1852–1933), Irish novelist, noted for his mannered style. His books include 'Esther Waters' (1894), 'The Brook Kerith' (1916) and 'Héloïse and Abélard' (1921)

Moore, George Edward (1873–1958), English philosopher, author of 'Principia Ethica' (1903) and 'Philosophical Studies' (1922)

Moore, Henry (1898–1978), English sculptor. He was principally a carver, and mostly in stone. He believed in truth to material: he released from the block of stone the simple, often monumental, form which seems to him implicit in its shape, size and texture. Holes pierced right through the block are a feature of his work, giving a direct sense of the relationship of all the surface planes. His human forms constantly suggest larger forms, e.g. hills and cliffs: the shapes of the earth itself

Moore, Marianne (1857–1972), American poet. Highly polished, learned, witty, her verses seem to spring at her from unexpected sources: news or sporting events, an advertisement, a fable

Moore, Sir John (1761–1809), British general. He commanded (1808–9) the British army in the Peninsular War, but was fatally wounded during the evacuation of Corunna

Moore, Thomas (1779–1852), Irish poet. Many of his poems (e.g. 'Believe me if all those endearing young charms') were set to music

moor-fowl (múərfạul) *n.* the red grouse

moor-hen (múərhẹn) *n. Gallinula chloropus.* fam. *Rallidae,* a stout blackish bird with white tail coverts, about the size of a small domestic chicken, living in ponds and rivers of Europe ‖ the female of the red grouse

moor-ing (múəriŋ) *n.* (usually *pl.*) the cables, ropes etc. by which a vessel is moored ‖ the place where a vessel is moored

Moor-ish (múəriʃ) *adj.* of the Moors, esp. of their architecture

moor-land (múərlənd, múərlænd) *n.* (*Br.*) moors

moose (muːs) *pl.* **moose** *n. Alces americana,* a North American deer closely related to the European elk, having enormous branched antlers. Moose are found in the forests of Canada and the northern U.S.A., and weigh up to 1,000 lbs, reaching 7 ft in height at the shoulders [of Algonquian origin]

Moose Jaw a city and railroad center (pop. 33,941) in S. Saskatchewan, Canada: grain elevators, stockyards, lignite and clay deposits, flax growing. Saskatchewan Presbyterian College (1882)

moot (muːt) *v.t.* to put up (an idea etc.) for discussion ‖ (*Br., impers., pass.*) to rumor, suggest, say, *it was mooted that he would be the next ambassador* [O.E. *mōtian*]

moot 1. *n.* (*Eng. hist.*) an early medieval administrative assembly of a village, town etc. ‖ (*law*) a discussion of fictitious cases arranged for practice among law students **2.** *adj.* open to argument, uncertain, *a moot point* ‖ (*law*) no longer a matter of practical importance requiring a decision, *a moot issue* [M.E. *mot, imot* fr. O. E. *mōt, gemōt,* meeting]

mop (mɔp) **1.** *n.* an implement for washing or polishing floors etc., made of a bundle of rags or coarse yarn fastened to a stick ‖ something resembling this, e.g. thick, unruly hair **2.** *v.t. pres. part.* **mop-ping** *past* and *past part.* **mopped** to wipe clean with a mop ‖ to wipe moisture from, *to mop one's brow* ‖ (with 'up') to remove (moisture etc.) with or as if with a mop, *to mop up the last resistance* ‖ *v.i.* (with 'up') to clean a floor etc. with a mop ‖ (*mil.,* with 'up') to destroy the last elements of resistance in an area and complete the occupation of it [15th-c. *mappe* perh. fr. L. *mappa,* napkin]

mope (moup) **1.** *v. pres. part.* **mop-ing** *past* and *past part.* **moped** *v.i.* to be listless and gloomy ‖ *v.t.* (with 'away') to spend (time) being listless and gloomy **2.** *n.* (*esp. pl.*) a fit of low spirits **móp-ish** *adj.* [origin unknown]

mo-ped (móupẹd) *n.* a two-wheeled vehicle with motor or pedal option

mop-pet (mópit) *n.* a young child [fr. late M.E. *mop, mopp,* baby, rag doll+-ET]

mo-quette (moukét) *n.* a material with a velvety pile, made of wool or mohair on a cotton or jute base, used for upholstery and carpeting [F.]

MOR middle of the road

Mo-rad-a-bad (murádəbad) a railroad center and agricultural market (pop. 258,590) in Uttar Pradesh, India, 93 miles east of Delhi: cotton thread, brassware. Great Mosque (1631)

mo-raine (məréin) *n.* (*geol.*) the debris of rocks, gravel etc. left by a melting glacier ‖ the area so covered [F.]

mor-al (mórəl, mórəl) **1.** *adj.* concerned with right and wrong and the distinctions between them, *a moral problem* ‖ virtuous, good, *a moral man* ‖ capable of right or wrong action, *man is a moral being* ‖ serving to teach right action, *a moral tale* ‖ dependent upon moral law, *a moral obligation* ‖ (of a certainty) admitting of no reasonable doubt although not demonstrable ‖ relating to the mind or will, *moral support* **2.** *n.* the moral teaching contained in a fable, story, experience etc. ‖ (*pl.*) moral habits, esp. in sexual matters ‖ (*pl.*) principles of conduct [fr. L. *moralis*]

mo-rale (mɔræl) *n.* psychological state with regard to dependability, confidence, strength of purpose etc. [F.]

mor-al-ism (mórəlizəm, mórəlizəm) *n.* an attitude stressing the importance of moral considerations ‖ moralizing ‖ an instance of this ‖ morality as distinguished from religion

mor-al-ist (mórəlist, mórəlist) *n.* a person who moralizes ‖ a teacher of morals ‖ a student of or writer on human behavior **mor-al-ís-tic** *adj.*

mo-ral-i-ty (mɔræliti:) *pl.* **mo-ral-i-ties** *n.* ethics ‖ upright conduct ‖ conduct or attitude judged from the moral standpoint ‖ a morality play [F. *moralité*]

morality play a medieval allegorical play, esp. of 15th-c. and 16th-c. England and France, teaching moral lessons and typically with characters representing virtues and vices, though there are many types. The greatest English morality play, 'Everyman' (c. 1530), allegorizes man's journey through life (cf. MIRACLE PLAY)

mor-al-i-za-tion (mɔrəlizéiʃən, mɔrəlizéiʃən) *n.* the act of moralizing ‖ an instance of this

mor-al-ize (mórəlaiz, mórəlaiz) *pres. part.* **mor-al-iz-ing** *past* and *past part.* **mor-al-ized** *v.i.* to talk or write, esp. boringly or at length, on moral themes etc. ‖ *v.t.* to draw a moral from [F. *moraliser*]

moral law conduct standard among good men and independent of legal or religious prohibitions etc.

mor-al-ly (mórəli:, mórəli:) *adv.* with respect to moral conduct, standards etc. ‖ virtually, *morally certain of the outcome* ‖ with respect to the mind, *he is exhausted morally and physically*

Moral Majority U.S. movement established (1979) by the Rev. Jerry Falwell in Lynchburg, Va. Appealing mainly to fundamental Protestants, the movement's platform includes opposition to abortion, pornography, homosexuality, the Equal Rights Amendment, biological evolution and decreased military spending. This New Right movement was considered a factor in the 1980 elections when several liberal senators and incumbent President Jimmy Carter were defeated

moral philosophy that part of philosophy concerned with principles of behavior

Moral Re-Armament an evangelical religious cult founded at Oxford by Frank Buchman in 1921, formerly also known as the Oxford Group Movement and sometimes as Buchmanism (*BUCHMAN)

moral science moral philosophy

moral sense the power of distinguishing between right and wrong

moral support help by other than practical means, e.g. sympathy and encouragement

moral victory a technical defeat or indecisive outcome which is nevertheless open to interpretation as a victory because of some support or confirmation etc. that it brings to the vanquished

mo-rass (məræs) *n.* (*rhet.*) a marsh, swamp [Du. *moeras* fr. O.F.]

mor-a-to-ri-um (mɔrətóri:əm, mɔrətóuri:əm, mɔrətóri:əm, mɔrətóuri:əm) *pl.* **mor-a-to-ri-ums, mor-a-to-ri-a** (mɔrətóri:ə, mɔrətóuri:ə, mɔrətóri:ə, mɔrətóuri:ə) *n.* a legally authorized period of delay before debts have to be paid ‖ the authorization for this **mor-a-to-ry** (mórətɔri:, mórətɔuri:, mórətɔri:, mórətɔuri:) *adj.* of, pertaining to or granting a moratorium [Mod. L. neut. of L.L. *moratorius* fr. *morari,* to delay]

Mo-ra-vi-a (məréivi:ə, *Ital.* mɔrávja), Alberto (Alberto Pincherle, 1907–), Italian author of novels (incl. 'La Romena', 1947 and 'La Ciociara', 1957) and short stories (incl. 'Racconti romani', 1954). The spiritual apathy of modern man is the theme underlying the pictures of a certain bourgeois Roman society. Among his novels are 'Time of Discretion' (1979) and '1934' (1982)

Mo-ra-vi-a (məréivi:ə) the central region of Czechoslovakia, separated from Bohemia by the Bohemian-Moravian highlands and from Slovakia by the W. Carpathians. The center is a rich river basin (cereals, root vegetables). Main resource: coal. Industries: textiles, iron and steel, mechanical engineering. Historic capital: Brno. Moravia was occupied by Celts (c. 500 B.C.), Germanic tribes (2nd–6th cc.) and Slavs (9th c.). It was subject to Bohemia (1029–1197), passed to the Hapsburgs (1526) and became part of Czechoslovakia (1918)

Mo-ra-vi-an (məréivi:ən) **1.** *adj.* of or pertaining to Moravia or Moravians **2.** *n.* a native or inhabitant of Moravia ‖ a member of a Hussite Protestant sect reconstituted (1722) from a sect founded in Bohemia in 1467 ‖ the group of dialects spoken by Moravians, closely related to Czech and Slovak

Mo-ra-vi-a-Si-le-sia (məréivi:əsilíː3ə, məréivi:əsilíːʃə) a former province (1918–49) of Czechoslovakia, consisting of Moravia plus Czech (formerly Austrian) Silesia

Mo-rav-ská-Os-tra-va (mórafskaóstrava) *OSTRAVA

CONCISE PRONUNCIATION KEY: **(a)** æ, c*a*t; ɑ, c*a*r; ɔ f*aw*n; ei, sn*a*ke. **(e)** e, h*e*n; iː, sh*ee*p; iə, d*ee*r; ɛə, b*ea*r. **(i)** i, f*i*sh; ai, t*i*ger; əː, b*i*rd. **(o)** o, *o*x; au, c*ow*; ou, g*oa*t; u, p*oo*r; ɔi, r*oy*al. **(u)** ʌ, d*u*ck; u, b*u*ll; uː, g*oo*se; ə, b*a*cillus; juː, c*u*be. x, lo*ch*; θ, *th*ink; ð, bo*th*er; z, *Z*en; 3, corsa*g*e; dʒ, sava*g*e; ŋ, ora*ng*utan; j, *y*ak; ʃ, *fi*sh; tʃ, fe*tch*; 'l, rabb*le*; 'n, redd*en.* Complete pronunciation key appears inside front cover.

Mor·ay (mɔ́ːri:, mʌ́ri:) (formerly Elgin) a county (area 476 sq. miles, pop. 49,000) in N.E. Scotland. County town: Elgin

Moray Firth, the the northernmost of the two great inlets on the east coast of Scotland (*FORTH), esp. the head of this inlet, separating Ross and Cromarty county (to the north) from Nairn and Moray

Mo·ra·zán (mɔrəsán), Francisco (1792–1844), Honduran general, and promotor of Central American union. He served as chief of state of Honduras (1827–8), of the Central American Federation (1830–40), of El Salvador (1839–40), and of Costa Rica (1842), where he was assassinated

mor·bid (mɔ́rbid) adj. (of ideas etc.) not natural or healthy, unwholesome || (of a person) given to unwholesome (esp. gruesome) thoughts or feelings || gruesome, morbid details || relating to disease, a morbid growth **mor·bid·i·ty** n. the quality or state of being morbid || the incidence of disease in a given district [fr. L. morbidus, distressed]

mor·bif·ic (mɔrbífik) adj. causing disease [fr. F. morbifique or Mod. L. morbificus]

Mor·bi·han (mɔrbiːã́) a department (area 2,738 sq. miles, pop. 536,600) in N.W. France (*BRITTANY). Chief town: Vannes

mor·da·cious (mɔrdéiʃəs) adj. (rhet.) caustic, a mordacious speech [fr. L. mordax (mordacis), biting]

mor·dac·i·ty (mɔrdǽsiti:) n. the quality of being mordacious [fr. F. mordacité fr. L.]

mor·dan·cy (mɔ́rdnsi:) n. the quality of being mordant

mor·dant (mɔ́rd'nt) 1. adj. (of speech, wit etc.) incisive and caustic || (of acids) corrosive || serving to fix colors in dyeing 2. n. a corroding substance, esp. one used in etching || a substance which serves to fix color in dyeing, by combining with the dye to form an insoluble compound || a substance used to cause gold leaf or paint to adhere 3. v.t. to treat with a mordant [F., pres. part. of mordre, to bite]

mor·dent (mɔ́rdənt) n. (mus.) an ornament (·) placed directly above or below a written note, the note indicated being rapidly alternated in playing with the note below it (cf. PRALLTRILLER) [G. or fr. Ital. mordente]

Mor·do·vi·an A.S.S.R. (mɔrdóuvi:en) an autonomous republic (area 10,100 sq. miles, pop. 984,000) of the R.S.F.S.R., U.S.S.R., on the middle Volga. Capital: Saransk (pop. 91,000). People: over 50% Russian, with Mordovian (Finnish) and Tatar minorities

More (mɔr), Henry (1614–87), English philosopher, one of the Cambridge Platonists

More, Sir Thomas (1478–1535), English statesman and humanist scholar, canonized (1935) as St Thomas More (feast: July 6). A friend of Colet, Erasmus, and other Renaissance humanists, More succeeded (1529) Wolsey as lord chancellor to Henry VIII. He resigned (1532) after refusing to agree to the king's divorce from Catherine of Aragon. When he refused to conform to the Act of Supremacy, he was imprisoned (1534), found guilty of treason, and beheaded. His 'Utopia' (1516), written in Latin, contains his views of the ideal non-Christian state: a republic of philosophers

more (mɔr, mour) superl. **most** (moust) 1. adj. (comp. of MANY, MUCH) greater in quantity, amount, number or degree || additional, further, have some more wine 2. n. something additional or further || (construed as pl.) a greater number, many failed but more succeeded || a greater quantity or portion, some of his writing is good but more is trash 3. adv. (often as a comparative with many adjectives and most adverbs) to a greater degree or extent, you must attend more to business, more attractive, more easily || in addition, further, again, try once more **more and more** in a continually increasing degree || an increasing number or quantity **more or less** rather, to some undefined extent || virtually **no more** to no greater degree, not at all more, he could no more do it than I could || (rhet.) no longer, until his voice was heard no more || (rhet.) never again, he will walk with us no more || (rhet.) no longer in existence, the old cottage is no more [O.E. māra adj. and mā adv.]

Mo·re·a (mɔrí:ə) *PELOPONNESUS

mo·reen (məri:n) n. a coarse woolen or woolen and cotton fabric, often embossed or watered [perh. fr. MOIRE]

mo·rel (mərél) n. any of several edible fungi of genus Morchella, fam. Helvellaceae, esp. M. esculenta [F. morille]

morel n. any of various nightshades, csp. Solanum nigruni, the black nightshade [O.F. morele]

Mo·re·lia (mɔréiljə) (Valladolid, 1541–1828) an agricultural market (pop. 230,400) of central Mexico, 125 miles northwest of Mexico City: textiles, shawls, hats, tobacco. Spanish cathedral (16th c.), aqueduct (18th c.)

mo·rel·lo (mərélou) n. a cultivated dark-colored sour cherry used for jam [etym. doubtful]

Mo·re·los (morélos) an inland agricultural state (area 1,908 sq. miles, pop. 866,000) of Mexico, on the southern slope of the Mexican plateau. Scattered mountain ranges form many valleys. Capital: Cuernavaca (pop. 37,000). Agricultural products: sugar, rice, corn, coffee, wheat, fruit and vegetables

Mo·re·los y Pa·vón (mɔrélosi:pavón), José María (1765–1815), Mexican priest and patriot. A leader in the Mexican struggle for independence, he convoked (1813) the first national congress at Chilpancingo. He was defeated by Iturbide at Valladolid and Puruarán (Michoacán), taken prisoner, and executed

more·o·ver (mɔróuvər, mouróuvər) adv. further, besides, in addition to what has been said

mo·res (mɔ́reiz, mɔ́ri:z, mɔ́ureiz, mɔ́uri:z) pl. n. customs, esp. the fixed or traditional customs of a society, often acquiring the force of law [L.]

Mo·resque (mərésk) adj. (art, archit.) Moorish in style [F.]

Morgan (mɔ́rgən), Sir Henry (c. 1635–88), Welsh buccaneer. He was commissioned by the English to carry out raids on Spanish colonies in the Caribbean. He was made governor of Jamaica (1674)

Morgan, John Pierpont (1837–1913), U.S. financier who organized (1895) J. P. Morgan and Company, which became one of the world's most powerful banking houses. By 1902 he controlled about 5,000 miles of U.S. railroads. He is accredited with allaying the panic of 1907 and preserving the solvency of major banks and corporations

Morgan, John Pierpont, Jr. (1867–1943), successor to his father as head (1913–43) of J. P. Morgan and Company. He served during the 1st world war as purchasing agent for the British and French governments for several billion dollars' worth of supplies, and financed a large part of the Allied credit requirements in the U.S.A. by floating $1.5 billion in Allied bonds. Handling (1919–33) more than $6 billion in securities, the Morgan house was separated (1933) by the Securities Act into separate investment banking and commercial banking activities

Morgan, Thomas Hunt (1866–1945), American biologist. His experiments on Drosophila melanogaster, a fruit fly, established the chromosome theory of heredity. Nobel Prize for medicine (1933)

mor·ga·nat·ic (mɔrgənǽtik) adj. of or designating a form of marriage between a man of high rank, e.g. of the European nobility or royalty, and a woman of lower rank, in which the wife does not acquire her husband's rank and the offspring do not inherit the titles or possessions of the father || designating the wife in such a marriage **mor·ga·nát·i·cal·ly** adv. [fr. Mod. L. morgonaticus fr. M. L. (matrimonium ad) morganaticam fr. O.H.G. morgangeba, morning gift, a gift from the husband to the wife on the morning after marriage, the morganatic wife's only claim on her husband's possessions]

mor·gan·ite (mɔ́rgənait) n. a rose-colored variety of beryl [after J. P. MORGAN]

Morgan le Fay (ləféi) King Arthur's sister, in the Arthurian legend. She was a pupil of Merlin

Mor·gen·thau (mɔ́rgənθɔ), Henry, Jr. (1891–1967), U.S. secretary of the treasury (1934–45) under President Franklin Roosevelt. He spent about $370 billion, three times as much as his 50 predecessors combined, to finance the New Deal program and the 2nd world war

morgue (mɔrg) n. a place where dead bodies are laid out for identification || a place where photographs, clippings, back numbers etc. are kept for reference by a newspaper or magazine || such a collection [F.]

mor·i·bund (mɔ́rəbʌnd, mɔ́rəbʌnd) adj. near death || about to collapse, a moribund civilization [fr. L. moribundus]

Mo·ri·llo (mɔri:ljɔ), Pablo (1778–1837), Spanish general. From 1815 he led the brutal suppression in New Granada of the patriotic forces. He was defeated (1819) by Bolívar at Boyacá

mo·ri·on (mɔ́ri:ən, moúri:ən) n. (hist., 16th–17th cc.) a high-crested open helmet without beaver or visor, of Spanish origin [F. morion, Span. morrión or Ital. morione]

Mo·ris·co (mərískou) n. any of the Moors nominally converted to Christianity after the Christian reconquest of Spain (late 15th c.). The Moriscos were persecuted by the Inquisition. They rebelled (1500–2 and 1568–71), and were expelled from Spain (1609) [Span.]

Mor·ley (mɔ́rli:), Edward Williams (1838–1923), American chemist. He collaborated with Michelson on the determination of the velocity of light

Morley, John, Viscount Morley of Blackburn (1838–1923), British liberal statesman and biographer. As secretary of state for India (1905–10) he worked with Minto in carrying out administrative reforms. His biographies include 'Rousseau' (1873), 'Oliver Cromwell' (1900) and 'Gladstone' (1903)

Morley, Thomas (c. 1557–1603), English composer, one of the greatest Elizabethan writers of madrigals and part-songs

Mor·mon (mɔ́rmən) n. a member of the Church of Jesus Christ of Latter-day Saints, founded (1830) in New York State by Joseph Smith. His authority rested on the revelation to him of 'The Book of Mormon', an alleged preColumbian work giving the history of American peoples of Hebrew origin from the Diaspora to 600 A.D. After Smith's death, Brigham Young became leader and transferred the movement to Salt Lake City, Utah (1847), where a prosperous community was established. When the practice of polygamy was stopped, Utah was incorporated (1896) into the Union as the 45th state. Mormons believe that 'The Book of Mormon' is of equal inspiration with the Bible **Mór·mon·ism** n.

morn (mɔrn) n. (rhet.) morning [M.E. morne, morwen fr. O. E. morgen]

morn·ing (mɔ́rniŋ) 1. n. the early part of the day between midnight or dawn and noon || dawn || the first or early part, the morning of civilization 2. adj. relating to or occurring in the morning [M.E. morweninge fr. morwen, morn]

morn·ing-af·ter pill (mɔrniŋǽftər) oral contraceptive pill for women, effective if taken after sexual intercourse; usually DES (diethylstilbestrol)

morning glory pl. **morning glories** any of several climbing plants of genus lpomoèa, fam. Convolvulaceae, and related genera. They have bright cone-shaped flowers and alternate leaves

Morning Prayer the service used in the Church of England in the morning

morning sickness early-morning nausea and vomiting, a frequent symptom of pregnancy in the early months

morning star any of the planets Venus, Jupiter, Mars, Mercury, Saturn, when they rise before the sun, esp. Venus

morning watch (naut.) the watch from 4–8 a.m.

Mo·roc·can (mərókən) 1. adj. of or relating to Morocco, its people, customs etc. 2. n. a native or inhabitant of Morocco

Mo·roc·co (mərókou) a kingdom (area 171,305 sq. miles, pop. 21,666,000) in N.W. Africa. Capital: Rabat. Largest town: Casablanca. People: Arabs and Berbers, 3% European. Language: Arabic, Berber dialects, French and Spanish. Religion: Moslem (official, mainly Sunnite), 3% Roman Catholic, 1% Jewish. Three chains of the Atlas Mtns cross the country from northeast to southwest: the Middle Atlas, rising to 10,794 ft, the High Atlas to 13,665 ft (Mt Toubkal), and the Anti-Atlas to 10,840 ft. Along the Mediterranean from Tangier to Melilla are the coastal massifs (Er Rif in the center rising to 7,400 ft), part of the Maritime Atlas. To the west are plains and plateaus containing the bulk of the population. South and east of the Anti-Atlas is the Sahara. Average winter and summer temperatures (F.): Rabat 45° and 81°, Marrakesh 40° and 101°, Essaouira (west coast) 62° and 72°. Rainfall: Tangier 38 ins, Rabat 22 ins, Marrakesh 10 ins, Bou Denib (Sahara) 4 ins. The land is 25% arable and nearly 10% forest (mainly evergreen in the Atlas, gum trees and cork near the coasts, date palms in the desert). Crops: cereals, olives, dates, vegetables, grapes, citrus fruit. Livestock: sheep, goats, cattle, donkeys, mules, camels. Exports:

CONCISE PRONUNCIATION KEY: **(a)** æ, cat; ɑ, car; ɔ fawn; ei, snake. **(e)** e, hen; i:, sheep; iə, deer; ɛə, bear. **(i)** i, fish; ai, tiger; əː, bird. **(o)** o, ox; au, cow; ou, goat; u, poor; ɔi, royal. **(u)** ʌ, duck; u, bull; u:, goose; ə, bacillus; ju:, cube. x, loch; θ, think; ð, bother; z, Zen; ʒ, corsage; dʒ, savage; ŋ, orangutang; j, yak; ʃ, fish; tʃ, fetch; 'l, rabble; 'n, redden. Complete pronunciation key appears inside front cover.

phosphates (2nd world producer), cereals, manganese, molybdenum, cobalt, citrus fruit, lead, vegetables, cork, fish (sardines, mackerel, tunny), iron ore, handicraft products (esp. leather). Domestic industries: hydroelectricity, food processing, cement, textiles, light manufactures. Other minerals: coal, silver, zinc, petroleum. Main imports: sugar, petroleum, vehicles, other machinery, steel. Ports: Casablanca, Tangier, Safi. Universities at Rabat and Fez. Monetary unit: dirham (100 francs). HISTORY. The area was ruled by the Carthaginians and the Romans, and was invaded by Berber tribes (late 5th c.) and by Arabs (late 7th c.). The latter brought Islam, and built up a powerful Moorish empire in the Iberian Peninsula (8th–late 15th cc.). Morocco became a feudal state under a series of Moslem dynasties, including the Almoravides and the Almohades. Piracy was a main source of income (14th–19th cc.). Rivalry for control of Morocco provoked diplomatic crises between France and Germany (early 20th c.) until the country became a French protectorate (1912), with three small areas held by Spain. A Berber revolt in the Rif, led by Abd-el-Krim, was crushed (1920–6). After the 2nd world war, the growth of a nationalist movement led to riots and terrorist attacks, in the course of which the sultan was exiled (1953) and restored (1955) by the French. Morocco gained independence (1956), joined the U.N. (1956) and became a constitutional monarchy (1957). After a state of emergency had been declared, King Hassan II took over the administration (1965). When Mauritania renounced its claim to Western Sahara (1979), Morocco annexed the entire area and encouraged Moroccan settlement there. In 1986, King Hassan caused turmoil in the Arab world by meeting openly with Israel's leader

mo·roc·co (mərókou) n. high-grade leather, first made in Morocco, of goatskin tanned with sumac and used for bookbinding, handbags etc.

mo·ron (mɔ́ron, móurɒn) n. a mentally deficient person whose mental age in adulthood is about 8–12 years (cf. IDIOT, cf. IMBECILE) **mo·rón·ic** adj. [Gk *mōron*, neut. of *mōros*, foolish]

mo·rose (məróus) adj. glum, sour-tempered and unsocial [fr. L. *morosus*, peevish]

morph (mɔrf) n. (biol.) 1. an animal or plant different from genetic expectations *syn.* mutant, sport 2. a highly inbred population of a species with distinguishing characteristics

mor·pheme (mɔ́rfi:m) n. (linguistics, formerly) an element of language indicating a grammatical relationship, e.g. affix, preposition, conjunction etc., or intonation, accentuation etc. ‖ (linguistics) a unit containing no smaller meaningful parts, whether a free form (word) or a bound form (part of a word, e.g. '-s' to indicate plural, '-ness' making an abstract noun) [fr. F. *morphème* fr. Gk *morphē*, form]

Mor·phe·us (mɔ́rfi:əs, mɔ́rfju:s) (Gk mythol.) the god of dreams

mor·phi·a (mɔ́rfi:ə) n. morphine [Mod. L. fr. MORPHEUS]

mor·phine (mɔ́rfi:n) n. the principal alkaloid of opium, a bitter white crystalline base, $C_{17}H_{19}O_3N$, a habit-forming narcotic widely used for the relief of pain and as a sedative **mór·phin·ism** n. a diseased condition resulting from addiction to morphine ‖ addiction to morphine [G. *morphin* fr. MORPHEUS]

mor·pho·gen·e·sis (mɔrfoudʒénisis) n. (biol.) the origin and development of organs or parts of organisms [Mod. L. fr. Gk *morphē*, form+*genesis*, origin]

mor·pho·log·i·cal (mɔrfəlódʒik'i) adj. of or pertaining to morphology

mor·phol·o·gist (mɔrfólədʒist) n. a specialist in morphology

mor·phol·o·gy (mɔrfólədʒi:) pl. **mor·phol·o·gies** n. the branch of biology concerned with the form and structure of organisms ‖ (biol.) the collective features of form and structure of an organism or its parts ‖ (geol.) the external structure of rocks in relation to form or topographic features produced by erosion ‖ the branch of linguistics dealing with word formation, inflectional forms etc. [fr. Gk *morphe*, form+*logos*, word]

mor·pho·sis (mɔrfóusis) pl. **mor·pho·ses** (mɔrfóusi:z) n. (biol.) the mode of development of an organism or of one of its parts [Mod. L. fr. Gk *morphōsis*, a shaping]

Mor·rill (mɔ́rəl, mɒ́rəl), Justin Smith (1810–98), U.S. Congressional leader, serving

67) in the House and (1867–98) in the Senate. He sponsored the Morrill Act

Morrill Act a U.S. Congressional act (1862), sponsored by Representative Justin Morrill, which set the precedent of national aid to education. It provided grants of land to state colleges to teach subjects related to agriculture and the mechanical arts without excluding the general sciences and humanities. It provided for training in military science

Mor·ris (mɔ́ris, mɒ́ris), Gouverneur (1752–1816), U.S. statesman and diplomat. As chairman (1778) of the committee to negotiate peace with Great Britain, he declared that the recognition of independence must precede any negotiations for peace. As assistant (1781–5) to the superintendent of finance, he proposed the decimal coinage system and the dollar and cent as monetary units, which later became standard in the U.S.A. As a member of the Constitutional Convention of 1787, he secured veto power for the executive branch and composed the final form of the Constitution

Morris, Robert (1734–1806), U.S. merchant and banker who served (1776–8) as the financier of the Revolutionary War. As superintendent of finance (1781–4) under the Articles of Confederation, he secured the funds, by borrowing from the French, requisitioning from the states, and advancing from his personal fortune, that enabled George Washington to transport his army from N.Y. to Yorktown, thereby forcing the surrender (1781) of Lord Cornwallis. He established (1781) in Philadelphia the Bank of North America, later chartered by the state of Pennsylvania

Morris, William (1834–96), English poet, Pre-Raphaelite painter and designer. Believing that machine production was eliminating the craftsman and degrading the worker, he sought to produce by hand household objects which would bring back the beauty of craftsmanship into everyday life and testify to the dignity of handwork. He set up his own firm (1861), which produced wallpapers, furniture, stained glass and textiles. He also established the Kelmscott Press (1891), which produced many finely printed books

Morris, William Richard, 1st Viscount Nuffield *NUFFIELD

mor·ris (mɔ́ris, mɒ́ris) n. a dance performed in medieval Britain, and later on festival occasions, by men in fancy costumes with bells, rattles etc., often illustrating a legend, e.g. that of Robin Hood [fr. older *morys*, var. of MOORISH]

Morris Jes·up, Cape (dʒésəp) the northernmost point of Greenland and of known land in the entire Arctic Region

Mor·row (mɔ́rou, mɒ́rou), Dwight Whitney (1873–1931), U.S. lawyer, financier and statesman. As chairman (1925) of President Calvin Coolidge's aircraft board, he formulated a national military and civil aviation policy. As ambassador to Mexico (1927–30), he strengthened the Good Neighbor policy by settling oil debts and claims, and by helping to restore harmony between Church and State during the regime of Mexican President P. E. Calles

mor·row (mɔ́rou, mɒ́rou) n. (rhet.) the next day [M.E. *morwe, moru* shortened fr. *morwen*, morning]

Morse (mɔrs), Samuel Finley Breese (1791–1872), U.S. artist and inventor. He created (1838) the Morse Code, a sonic alphabet composed of dots (shorts) and dashes (longs), and built (1843) the first telegraph line in the U.S.A., from Baltimore to Washington

Morse code the telegraphic code invented by Morse, in which letters are represented telegraphically by dots and dashes (short and long sounds)

mor·sel (mɔ́rs,l) n. a small bite or mouthful of food ‖ a small piece, esp. a choice one, *a morsel of news* [O.F.]

mort (mɔrt) n. (hunting) a note blown on the horn when a deer is killed [F.]

mor·tal (mɔ́rt'l) 1. adj. inevitably subject to death, *man is mortal* ‖ fatal, *a mortal accident* ‖ ending only with death, *mortal combat* ‖ implacable, *a mortal enemy* ‖ (of pain, fear etc.) extreme ‖ relating to or accompanying death, *mortal agony* ‖ (Roman Catholicism, of a sin) entailing spiritual death (cf. VENIAL) ‖ (pop.) tedious, *he spoke for two mortal hours* ‖ (pop.) very great, *in a mortal hurry* 2. n. a human being [O.F. *mortel* or fr. L. *mortalis*]

mor·tal·i·ty (mɔrtǽliti) pl. **mor·tal·i·ties** n. the quality or state of being mortal ‖ the human race ‖ death on a large scale, e.g. through war ‖ the number of deaths in a given period or place ‖ the death rate [fr. F. *mortalité*]

mortality table a statistical table showing life expectancy at various ages

mor·tal·ly (mɔ́rt'li:) adv. in a mortal way, *mortally wounded* ‖ intensely, *mortally afraid*

mor·tar (mɔ́rtər) 1. n. a bowl made of strong material, in which substances are pounded and ground to powder with a pestle ‖ a short cannon used to fire shells at high trajectories ‖ a mixture of lime (or cement), sand and water, used for binding stones, bricks etc. in construction 2. v.t. to bind (bricks etc.) with mortar ‖ to bombard with mortar shells [O.E. *mortere* and F. *mortier*]

mor·tar·board (mɔ́rtərbɔrd, mɔ́rtərbourd) n. a board used by plasterers, bricklayers etc. for holding mortar ‖ an academic cap with a flat, square top

mort·gage (mɔ́rgidʒ) 1. n. a conditional conveyance of land, a house etc. as security for a loan. The property remains in the possession of the borrower but may be claimed by the lender if the loan and interest are not paid according to the agreed terms ‖ the documents making this agreement ‖ the state of property thus conveyed 2. v.t. pres. part. **mort·gag·ing** past and past part. **mort·gaged** to make over, grant (a house, land etc.) as security for debt by means of a mortgage ‖ to make (something) liable to future claims, *he mortgaged his independence by taking that job* **mort·ga·gee** (mɔrgidʒi:) n. a creditor who receives a mortgage **mort·ga·gor, mort·gag·er** (mɔ́rgidʒər) n. the debtor who gives his property in a mortgage [O.F.=dead pledge]

mortice *MORTISE

mor·ti·cian (mɔrtíʃən) n. an undertaker [fr. L. *mors (mortis)*, death]

mor·ti·fi·ca·tion (mɔrtifikéiʃən) n. a mortifying or being mortified ‖ a source of humiliation [F. or fr. eccles. L. *mortificatio (mortificationis)*]

mor·ti·fy (mɔ́rtifai) pres. part. **mor·ti·fy·ing** past and past part. **mor·ti·fied** v.t. to subdue (passions, bodily desires etc.) by discipline, *to mortify the flesh* ‖ to hurt or wound the feelings of, humiliate ‖ v.i. (med.) to become gangrenous [F. *mortifier*]

Mor·ti·mer (mɔ́rtəmər), Roger de (c. 1287–1330), 1st earl of March, English nobleman who deposed and murdered Edward II (1327), replacing him with Edward III. He became the virtual ruler of England until he was tried by Parliament and executed

mortise, mor·tice (mɔ́rtis) 1. n. a hole cut in material to take the end of another part, esp. a hole in a piece of wood designed to receive the shaped end (tenon) of another piece 2. v.t. pres. part. **mor·tis·ing, mor·tic·ing** past and past part. **mor·tised, mor·ticed** to join, fasten securely, esp. by mortise and tenon ‖ to cut a mortise in [F. *mortaise*]

mort·main (mɔ́rtmein) n. (law) possession or tenure of land etc. by ecclesiastical corporations, or by any corporation deemed to be perpetual ‖ (law) the condition of such property [A.F. *morte mayn*, O.F. *mortemain* fr. M.L. *mortua manus*, lit. dead hand]

Morton (mɔ́rt'n), Levi Parsons (1824–1920), U.S. vice-president (1889–93) and businessman. A banker, he founded Levi P. Morton and Company (from 1869 Morton, Bliss and Company), a firm that helped finance the Civil War. He was a U.S. representative (1879–81) and minister to France (1881–5) before serving as vice-president under Pres. Benjamin Harrison. He was later governor of New York (1895–7)

Morton (mɔ́rt'n), Oliver (Hazard) Perry (Throck) (1823–77), U.S. political leader and Civil War governor of Indiana (1861–71). Confronted with pro-Confederate elements in a northern border state, he succeeded in aligning Indiana with the Union cause

Morton, William Thomas Green (1819–68), U.S. dental surgeon who, conducting (1846) the first public demonstration on the use of ether, revealed its value to the medical world

mor·tu·ar·y (mɔ́rtʃuːeri:) 1. adj. of or relating to burial of the dead or to death, *a mortuary urn* 2. pl. **mor·tu·ar·ies** n. a place where dead bodies are kept before burial or cremation [fr. L. *mortuarius* adj., of the dead]

mor·u·la (mɔ́rulə) pl. **mor·u·lae** (mɔ́ruli:) n. (embryol.) a solid, spherical mass of blastomeres resulting from ovum cleavage which may give rise to the blastula and is distinguished from it by the absence of a cavity **mór·u·lar** adj. [Mod. L. dim. of L. morum, mulberry]

MOS (electr. abbr.) metal oxide semiconductor used in computer circuits

Mo·sa·ic (mouzéiik) adj. of or pertaining to Moses or his writings [fr. Mod. L. Mosaicus]

mo·sa·ic (mouzéiik) **1.** n. a form of surface decoration made by inlaying small pieces of colored glass, stone etc. ‖ a picture or design so made ‖ a number of aerial photographs placed together to form one continuous view of an area ‖ (bot.) mosaic disease ‖ (television) the photosensitive element in the electrode of the camera, consisting of many minute particles **2.** adj. of or relating to mosaic ‖ resembling mosaic in pattern or structure ‖ (of a plant) afflicted by mosaic disease [F. mosaïque fr. M.L. mosaicus, musaicus fr. Gk. mouseios, of the Muses]

mosaic disease (bot.) any of several virus diseases of certain flowering plants (e.g. tobacco, corn), characterized by pale mottled patches on the foliage

mosaic gold a yellow pigment, essentially stannic sulfide (SnS₂) ‖ ormolu

mo·sa·i·cist (mouzéiisist) n. someone who makes mosaics

Mosaic Law the Hebrew Law contained in the Pentateuch

mosaic society a state subdivided into many ethnic, religious, or racial entities

mos·cha·tel (mɒskətél) n. Adoxa moschatellina, fam. Adoxaceae, a small herbaceous plant of temperate zones with greenish blossoms and a musky scent [F. moscatelle fr. Ital.]

Mos·cow (mɒskou, mɒskau) (Russ. Moskva) the capital (pop. 7,831,000) of the U.S.S.R. and of the R.S.F.S.R., on the central Russian plain. The center is the Kremlin (the medieval citadel, now the seat of the government), between the Moskva River and Red Square (the chief public meeting place, containing Lenin's tomb, with the 16th-c. cathedral of St Basil at one side). Much of the old city (rebuilt, still largely in wood, after the 1812 fire) has been replaced with modern buildings. Industries (15% of Soviet production): heavy and precision engineering, textiles, chemicals, food processing. Moscow is the country's chief communications center (rail, air, and river) and cultural center. University (1775), Academy of Sciences, Moscow Art Theater (1898), Bolshoi Theater (opera, ballet), many museums. HISTORY. Already inhabited by the mid-11th c., Moscow became the capital of the grand duchy of Moscow, and a thriving commercial center (14th c.). It grew in importance as the capital of Russia until 1713, when Peter the Great transferred the capital to St Petersburg. Moscow was largely destroyed by fire when occupied by the French (1812), but was again made the capital in 1918

Mo·sel (móuz'l) *MOSELLE (river)

Mose·ley (móuzli), Henry Gwyn-Jeffreys (1887–1915), English physicist who discovered the relationship between the X-ray spectrum of an element and its atomic number, giving a physical meaning to the periodic classification of the elements

Mo·selle (mouzel) a department (area 2,405 sq. miles, pop. 1,006,400) of N.E. France (*LORRAINE). Chief town: Metz

Moselle (G. Mosel) a river (320 miles long, navigable for most of its length) flowing from the Vosges through Lorraine, E. France, through Luxembourg and then through the Rhineland, West Germany, to the Rhine at Coblenz. Canals join it to the Meuse and the Seine

Moselle (mouzél) n. a dry white wine made in the valley of the Moselle

Mo·ses (móuziz) (14th or 13th cc. B.C.), Israelite leader, prophet and legislator, one of the greatest figures in the Old Testament. He led the Israelites out of slavery in Egypt, for 40 years through the desert toward Canaan, but he died before they reached it. The Pentateuch describes how the Ten Commandments were promulgated through him, and the making of the criminal and liturgical laws of the Israelites

Moses, Grandma (Anna Mary Moses, 1860–1961), U.S. painter who, at the age of 78, began creating original farm scenes and landscapes

mo·sey (móuzi) v.i. (pop.) to move in a leisurely, sauntering way [origin unknown]

Mos·kva (mɒskva) *MOSCOW

Mos·lem (mɒzləm, mɒsləm) **1.** n. a believer in the religion of Islam **2.** adj. of or relating to the religion of Islam or its adherents [Arab. muslim, true believer fr. aslama, to surrender (to God)]

Moslem calendar a calendar reckoned from the year 622 A.D.(the year of the Hegira), based on lunar cycles of 30 years, of which 19 years contain 354 days and 11 intercalary years 355 days. The months of the Moslem calendar are:
1. Muharram (ancient Abib, 30 days)
2. Safar (29 days)
3. Rabi I (30 days)
4. Rabi II (29 days)
5. Jumada I (30 days)
6. Jumada II (29 days)
7. Rajab (30 days)
8. Sha'ban (29 days)
9. Ramadan (30 days)
10. Shawwal (29 days)
11. Dhu'l-Qu'dah (30 days)
12. Dhu'l-Hijja (29 days, 30 days in intercalary years)

Mos·lem·ism (mɒzləmizəm, mɒsləmizəm) n. (obs.) the religion of Islam

Moslem League an organization founded (1906) to maintain the rights of Moslems in India. Under the leadership of Jinnah it strove (1934–47) for an autonomous Moslem state and became the dominant party in Pakistan after the partition of India (1947)

mosque (mɒsk) n. a Moslem place of worship [fr. F. mosquée fr. Ital. fr. Span. fr. Arab. masjid]

mos·qui·to (məski:tou) pl. **mos·qui·toes, mos·qui·tos** n. any of many two winged flies of fam. Culicidae, distributed throughout the world, having a narrow abdomen, rigid proboscis and their wings fringed with scales. The female has a needlelike mouthpart for puncturing the skin of animals and man in order to suck the blood. The bite of the female mosquito causes an itchy, often painful swelling and may sometimes transmit serious diseases, e.g. malaria and yellow fever. The eggs are laid on the surface of stagnant water [Span. and Port., dim. of mosca, fly]

mosquito net a net hung around a bed, over a window etc., to keep out mosquitoes

moss (mɒs, mɔs) n. any member of Musci (*BRYOPHYTE), a class of primitive, green land plants in which the gametophyte developing from a protonema is differentiated into a simple vascular stem, rhizoid and leaves. The sporophyte develops from and is supported by the gametophyte, which is the conspicuous generation. Mosses are distributed throughout the world, growing on rock, trees and damp ground ‖ such plants collectively ‖ any of several mosslike plants (*CLUB Moss) [O.E. mos, bog]

Mos·sa·degh (mɒsadég), Mohammed (1882–1967), Iranian politician. As prime minister of Iran (1951–3), he nationalized British oil interests (1951) but was deposed and imprisoned (1953–6)

Möss·bau·er effect (mɔ́sbauər) (nuclear phys.) emission and absorption of radiation by nuclei without loss of energy; after German physicist Rudolf L. Mössbauer

moss-grown (mɔ́sgroun, mɔ́sgrɔun) adj. overgrown with moss ‖ antiquated

Mos·si (mɒ́si:) n. a people of Upper Volta. They founded a great kingdom (12th c. —early 16th c.) ‖ a member of this people ‖ the language they (and other peoples of Upper Volta) speak

moss·i·ness (mɒ́si:nis, mɔ́si:nis) n. the quality or state of being mossy

mos·so (móusou) adj. (mus.) animated [Ital.]

moss rose a garden variety of the cabbage rose, having a mosslike growth on the calyx and flower stalk

moss-troop·er (mɒ́strupər, mɔ́strupər) n. (hist.) a Royalist freebooter in the border country between England and Scotland in the 17th c.

moss·y (mɒ́si:, mɔ́si:) comp. **moss·i·er** superl. **moss·i·est** adj. covered with or abounding in moss or a mosslike growth ‖ like moss

most (moust) **1.** adj. (superl. of MUCH, MANY) greatest in number, quantity, amount, extent or degree **for the most part** in the greater number of instances ‖ as regards the major portion **2.** n. the greatest quantity, amount, extent or degree, most of the country is forest land ‖ (construed as pl.) the greatest number, the majority, most were in agreement **to make the most of** to use to the best advantage **3.** adv. (often as a superlative with many adjectives and most adverbs) to the greatest degree or extent, which do you like most?, the most interesting play, most quickly ‖ to a great degree, very, they had a most amusing time [O.E. mæst, mãst]

-most suffix indicating a superlative

most-favored-nation clause a common clause in trade treaties whereby any tariff reduction etc. granted to a second country can be extended to others. Its aim is to exclude preferences for a particular country

Most Honourable (Br.) the title of a marquis

most·ly (móustli) adv. in most cases, chiefly ‖ usually, he mostly spends weekends at home

Mo·sul (mousú:l) an ancient trading town (pop. 293,079) of N. Iraq, across the Tigris from the ruins of Nineveh: oil fields

mote (mout) n. a small particle, e.g. of dust floating in the air [O.E. mot]

mo·tel (moutél) a roadside hotel for motorists [MOTORIST + HOTEL]

mo·tet (moutét) n. (mus.) a polyphonic choral setting, usually unaccompanied, of a sacred Latin text not fixed in the liturgy, esp. as composed in the 13th–16th cc. [F.]

moth (mɒθ, mɔθ) pl. **moths** (mɒðz, mɔðz, mɔðz, mɒðz) n. any of several lepidopterous insects (division Heterocera) distinguished from butterflies by their tapering antennae and nocturnal habits ‖ (loosely) an insect whose larvae feed on fabrics, e.g. the carpet beetle [O.E. mohthe, moththe]

moth-ball (mɒθbɔl, mɔ́θbɔl) n. a small ball of naphthalene or camphor kept in clothing to prevent moths from getting into it

moth-eat·en (mɒ́θi:t'n, mɔ́θi:t'n) adj. (of cloth or clothing) partly eaten by moths ‖ decayed or dilapidated

moth·er (mʌ́ðər) **1.** n. a female parent, esp. a woman in relation to her child ‖ (rhet.) something regarded as a source, Greece, mother of democracy ‖ a woman in a position of authority like that of a mother, a mother superior **2.** adj. of, relating to or being a mother **3.** v.t. to take care of as a mother does, she likes to mother her boarders [O. E. mōdor]

mother n. a ropy mucilaginous substance produced by certain bacteria on the surface of vinegar during fermentation [prob. fr. MOTHER (parent)]

mother board (computer) board containing integrated circuits

Mother Car·ey's chicken (kéəri:z) any of several petrels, esp. the storm petrel

mother country a country in relation to its colonies, dependencies etc. ‖ the country of one's ancestors or of one's birth

moth·er·craft (mʌ́ðərkræft, mʌ́ðərkrɑft) n. the skills involved in looking after children

moth·er·hood (mʌ́ðərhud) n. the state of being a mother ‖ (rhet.) mothers as a class, the nation's motherhood

moth·er-in-law (mʌ́ðərinlɔ) pl. **moth·ers-in-law** n. a husband's or wife's mother

moth·er·land (mʌ́ðərlænd) n. a mother country

moth·er·li·ness (mʌ́ðərli:nis) n. the quality of being motherly

moth·er·ly (mʌ́ðərli:) adj. of or characteristic of a mother, motherly feelings ‖ having the qualities suitable in a mother, e.g. tenderness and affectionate solicitude [O.E. mōdorlic]

moth·er-of-pearl (mʌ́ðərəvpə́:rl) **1.** n. the hard pearly, iridescent internal layer of certain shells, e.g. oysters or abalones, used in making buttons, furniture inlays etc. **2.** adj. of, made of, or resembling mother-of-pearl

mother of vinegar mother (ropy mucilaginous substance)

mother's boy a youth or man lacking self-reliance and masculine ways and interests through being subjected to an overpossessive mother

Mother's Day a day set aside for honoring one's mother, usually the second Sunday in May

mother superior pl. **mother superiors, mothers superior** a nun who is the head of a convent

mother tongue one's native language

Moth·er·well (mʌ́ðərwəl, mʌ́ðərwel), Robert (1915–), U.S. painter and writer, and a leader of abstract expressionism

mother wit (old-fash.) common sense, native intelligence or wit

mo·tif (moutí:f) n. a feature or theme, esp. one dominant or recurring in a work of art, music or drama [F.]

mo·tile (móut'l, Br. móutail) adj. (biol.) showing, or capable of, spontaneous movement **mo·til·i·ty** (moutíliti) n. [fr. L. movere (motus), to move]

---

mo·tion (móuʃən) 1. *n.* the act or process of passing through space or changing position, *the motion of the planets around the sun* || an act or instance of moving the body or part of the body, *all her motions are clumsy* || a formal proposal made in an assembly, subsequently discussed and voted upon || (*law*) an application to a judge or court for a decision, ruling, order etc. || (*mus.*) change of pitch in one melody, or in two melodies with relation to each other || an evacuation of the bowels || (*often pl.*) the matter evacuated **in motion** moving **to go through the motions of** to perform the superficial gestures of (some action) often insincerely or perfunctorily 2. *v.t.* to direct by sign or gesture, *he motioned them to a seat* || *v.i.* to make a meaningful gesture, *he motioned with his head* **mó·tion·less** *adj.* perfectly still [F.]

motion picture a movie, esp. with a sound track

mo·ti·vate (móutiveit) *pres. part.* **mo·ti·vat·ing** *past and past part.* **mo·ti·vat·ed** *v.t.* to be the motive of, *kindness motivated the action* || to supply a motive to, *he hasn't satisfactorily motivated the hero's change of loyalties* || to make a course of study interesting to (a pupil) **mo·ti·vá·tion** *n.*

mo·tive (móutiv) 1. *n.* the sense of need, desire, fear etc. that prompts an individual to act || a motif 2. *v.t. pres. part.* **mo·tiv·ing** *past and past part.* **mo·tived** to motivate [F. *motif*]

motive *adj.* relating to movement || causing movement [fr. O.F. *motif* or M.L. *motivus*]

motive power power used to move or impel, esp. some form of mechanical energy (steam, electricity etc.) used to drive machinery

mo·tiv·i·ty (moutíviti:) *n.* the power of moving or of initiating motion

mot juste (mouʒyst) *n.* the exactly appropriate word or phrase [F.]

mot·ley (mótli:) 1. *adj.* miscellaneous, varied in character, type etc., *a motley crowd* || (esp. *hist.*, of a jester's clothes) parti-colored 2. *n.* (*hist.*) the professional dress of a jester, in two colors || an incongruous mixture, e.g. of colors [etym. doubtful]

mo·to·cross (móutoukrɔs) *n.* (*sports*) motorcycle race on a fixed course over a difficult terrain

Mo·to·li·ní·a (mɔtɔti:ní:ɑ), Toribio de (c. 1490–1569), Spanish Franciscan monk and historian, author of 'Historia de los indios de la Nueva España'. His missionary work in New Spain was marked by untiring zeal

mo·tor (móutər) 1. *n.* that which imparts motion, esp. a machine supplying motive power || an internal-combustion engine, oil or gasoline-driven || (*old-fash.*) an automobile || a rotating machine (e.g. a generator) transforming electrical into mechanical energy or sometimes vice versa || (*Br., pl.*) securities issued by companies manufacturing automobiles etc. 2. *adj.* of any form of movement, *motor activity* || of, pertaining to, or operated by a motor || (*physiol.*, of nerves) transmitting impulses from the central nervous system or a ganglion to a muscle causing movement 3. *v.i.* to travel by automobile [L.]

motor bicycle (*Br.*) a motorcycle

mo·tor·bike (móutərbaik) *n.* a motorcycle || a bicycle propelled by a motor

mo·tor·boat (móutərbout) *n.* a boat driven by an internal-combustion engine or electric motor

mo·tor·cade (móutərkeid) *n.* a procession or parade of automobiles [MOTORCAR+CALVALCADE]

mo·tor·car (móutərkɑr) *n.* (esp. *Br.*) an automobile

mo·tor·cy·cle (móutərsaik'l) 1. *n.* a two-wheeled, gasoline-driven vehicle larger and heavier than a bicycle, which carries its driver and may also carry one passenger on a pillion, and may sometimes have a sidecar 2. *v.i. pres. part.* **mo·tor·cy·cling** *past and past part.* **mo·tor·cy·cled** to drive a motorcycle **mó·tor·cy·clist** *n.*

motor home mobile dwelling built on a truck or bus chassis

motor hotel or **motor inn** an urban motel, usu. multistoried, esp. with free parking space

mo·tor·ist (móutərist) *n.* a person who drives an automobile, esp. regularly

mo·tor·i·za·tion (moutərizéiʃən) *n.* a motorizing or being motorized

mo·tor·ize (móutəraiz) *pres. part.* **mo·tor·iz·ing** *past and past part.* **mo·tor·ized** *v.t.* to equip with a motor or motors || to equip with motor-driven vehicles

mo·tor·man (móutərmən) *pl.* **mo·tor·men** (móutərmen) *n.* the driver of a train or other public motor-driven vehicle

motor scooter a scooter (motor vehicle)

motor torpedo boat a high-speed motorboat, 60–100 ft long, equipped with torpedo tubes, antiaircraft guns etc.

motor truck a truck (strong, four-wheeled vehicle)

mo·tor·way (móutərwei) *n.* (*Br.*) a wide divided road with several lanes and limited access, and which is carried over other main roads at a different level for high-speed through traffic

Mott, John Raleigh (1865–1955), U.S. evangelist who shared (with Emily Balch) the 1946 Nobel Prize for peace, for his work with international church and missionary movements

Mott, Lucretia (née Coffin, 1793–1880), U.S. pioneer in the suffragette movement. With Elizabeth Cady Stanton she convoked (1848) the Women's Rights Convention at Seneca Falls, N.Y.

mot·tle (mót'l) 1. *n.* a colored spot or blotch, esp. one of many on a surface || a blotchy surface appearance 2. *v.t. pres. part.* **mot·tling** *past and past part.* **mot·tled** to mark with blotches **mót·tled** *adj.* [prob. back-formation fr. MOTLEY]

mot·to (mótou) *pl.* **mot·toes, mot·tos** *n.* a short pithy sentence or phrase inscribed on a coat of arms etc. || a sentence or phrase used as a watchword, maxim or guiding principle || a passage prefixed to a chapter heading of a book or to the book itself [Ital.=saying]

moue (mu:) *n.* a grimace or pout [F.]

mou·flon, mouf·lon (mú:flɔn) *n. Ovis musimon*, a wild mountain sheep of Corsica and Sardinia. The male has large curved horns || any wild sheep with large horns [F. *mouflon* fr. Ital. dial.]

mouil·lé (mu:jei) *adj.* (*phon.*, of a consonant) palatalized [F.=moistened]

mou·jik, mu·zhik (mú:ʒik) *n.* (*hist.*) a Russian peasant [Russ.=peasant]

mou·lage (mu:lɑ́ʒ) *n.* the making of plaster molds, e.g. of footprints, esp. for use in criminology || a mold made for this use || a mold of a defect, used as a guide in surgery or therapy [F.=molding]

mould *MOLD

mouldboard *MOLDBOARD

moulder *MOLDER

moulding *MOLDING

mouldy *MOLDY

mou·lin (mu:lɛ̃) *n.* an almost vertical shaft in a glacier, formed by the dripping of surface water through a crack in the ice [F.=mill]

Mou·lins, the Master of (mu:lɛ̃) the name given to the painter of the 15th-c. triptych in Moulins cathedral, central France. Other works have been attributed to him on stylistic evidence

Moul·mein (mu:lméin, móuləmjain) a port (pop. 171,800) of Tenasserim, S. Burma, at the mouth of the Salween

moult *MOLT

mound (maund) *n.* an orb surmounting a crown or forming part of royal insignia [F. *monde,* the world]

mound 1. *n.* a bank of earth, esp. an artificial one, e.g. heaped on a grave or (*hist.*) for defensive purposes || a heap, *a mound of stones* || (*baseball*) a slight rise in the ground where the pitcher stands when pitching 2. *v.t.* to heap up into a mound || to enclose or fortify with mounds or ramparts [etym. doubtful]

Mound Builder a member of the prehistoric or pre-Columbian North American Indian tribes who built burial mounds, temple mounds and earthworks in the Mississippi Valley and near the Great Lakes

mount (maunt) *n.* (*abbr.* Mt) a mountain (used esp. before a mountain's name) || a high hill || (*palmistry*) one of the fleshy areas on the palm of the hand [O.E. *munt* fr. L.]

mount 1. *v.i.* to ascend || to get up on to something, *he mounted and rode away* || to increase in quantity, number, degree etc., *mounting debts* || *v.t.* to climb, *to mount a hill* || to place oneself in riding position on (a horse, bicycle etc.) || to provide with a horse, *he was well mounted by his host* || to equip with horses, *mounted police* || to help (someone) to get on a horse etc. || to put (something) high up, *to mount a statue on its pedestal* || to put in a fixed position, *to mount guns* || (of a vessel) to carry (guns) in position for use || to put (a picture etc.) inside a raised border, or against a contrasting

ground (of paper or material etc.) whose margins serve as a border || to prepare or set up for view, *to mount an exhibition* || to fix or prepare for microscopic examination, *to mount a slide* || to fit into a setting (of gold, silver etc.), *to mount a jewel* || to put (a play, opera etc.) on the stage || (of a male animal) to copulate with **to mount an offensive** (*mil.*) to prepare and make an attack 2. *n.* the act of mounting || something mounted, esp. a horse || a gun carriage for a cannon etc. || a ground or raised border used in mounting a drawing etc. || a glass slide on which microscopic specimens are mounted || a transparent hinge, card etc. for mounting postage stamps in an album || a setting of precious metal for jewels [O.F. *monter*]

Moun·tain (máuntən) (*F. hist.*) the extreme left wing of the Convention during the French Revolution, so called from the raised seats its members occupied. It chiefly comprised the Jacobins, the Cordeliers and the followers of Hébert

moun·tain (máuntən) *n.* a conspicuously elevated, steep part of the earth's surface, esp. one rising to more than 1,000 ft above the surrounding land || a high land mass containing a number of such projections || a great quantity, *a mountain of debts* [O. F. *montaigne*]
—There are three main types of mountain: volcanic mountains, mountains caused by bending of the earth's crust, and mountains caused by erosion. Volcanic mountains are formed by the ejection of lava and ash from volcanoes, are symmetrical in shape, and tend to occur as isolated peaks. Bending of the earth's crust may cause a fracturing of the rocks producing fault mountains such as the Sierra Nevada of California, or it may produce buckling as well as fracturing, causing the rocks to fall into ridges and furrows like a washboard. The Himalayas, Alps, Andes and Appalachians are examples of such folded mountains. Mountains are caused by erosion when weathering wears away the softer rocks and leaves the more resistant ones standing, e.g. the Catskills of New York

mountain ash any of several trees of genus *Sorbus*, fam. *Rosaceae*, esp. the rowan of Europe and Asia, and the American mountain ash, *S. americana*

moun·tain·eer (mauntəníər) 1. *n.* a person skilled in mountain climbing 2. *v.i.* to climb mountains

mountain goat *Oreamnos montanus,* a white long-haired mammal with slender black horns, resembling a goat, found in the mountains of N.W. North America

mountain laurel *Kalmia latifolia,* a North American evergreen shrub having glossy leaves and pink or white flower clusters

mountain lion a cougar

moun·tain·ous (máuntənəs) *adj.* containing mountains || huge [F. *montagneux*]

mountain sheep any of several wild sheep of mountain regions, esp. the bighorn

mountain sickness nausea, dizziness etc. caused by the rarefied air at high altitudes

moun·tain·side (máuntənsaid) *n.* the side of a mountain

Mountain standard time (*abbr.* M.S.T.) Mountain time

Mountain time (*abbr.* M.T.) one of the seven standard time divisions of the U.S.A. and Canada, seven hours behind Greenwich time and two hours behind Eastern standard time

moun·tain·top (máuntəntɒp) *n.* the top of a mountain

Mount·bat·ten (mauntbǽt'n), Louis Francis Albert Victor Nicholas, 1st Earl Mountbatten of Burma (1900–79), British statesman and admiral. He was supreme Allied commander in S.E. Asia (1943–6). As viceroy (1947) and governor-general (1947–8) of India he saw the dominions of India and Pakistan established. He was first sea lord (1955–9) and chief of the U.K. defense staff (1959–65). He was assassinated by a terrorist bomb set by the Irish Republican Army

Mount De·sert Island (dézərt) a mountainous, wooded island and summer resort off S.E. Maine (bridged to the mainland). It contains Cadillac Mt (1,532 ft), the highest point on the eastern seaboard. Champlain visited and named the island (1604)

moun·te·bank (máuntəbæŋk) *n.* a man who uses showmanship to exploit public credulity unscrupulously || (*hist.*) an itinerant seller of quack medicines who mounted a bench or platform and collected an audience by showman-

CONCISE PRONUNCIATION KEY: **(a)** æ, c*a*t; ɑ, c*a*r; ɔ f*aw*n; ei, sn*a*ke. **(e)** e, h*e*n; i:, sh*ee*p; iə, d*ee*r; ɛə, b*ea*r. **(i)** i, f*i*sh; ai, t*i*ger; ə:, b*i*rd. **(o)** o, *o*x; au, c*ow*; ou, g*oa*t; u, p*oo*r; ɔi, r*oy*al. **(u)** ʌ, d*u*ck; u, b*u*ll; u:, g*oo*se; ə, b*a*cillus; ju:, c*u*be. x, lo*ch*; θ, *th*ink; ð, bo*th*er; z, *Z*en; ʒ, corsa*g*e; dʒ, sava*g*e; ŋ, ora*n*gutang; j, *y*ak; ʃ, *fi*sh; tʃ, fe*tch*; 'l, rabb*le*; 'n, redd*en*. Complete pronunciation key appears inside front cover.

ship etc. [Ital. *montambanco, montimbanco* fr. *monta in banco,* mount on a bench]

Mount Hol·yoke College (hóuljouk, hóuli:ouk) a U.S. educational institution for women founded (1836) by Mary Lyon at South Hadley, Mass., as Mount Holyoke Female Seminary. In 1893 it was rechartered and renamed

Mountie *MOUNTY

mount·ing (máuntiŋ) *n.* a support or setting for a jewel, picture etc.

Mount McKinley National Park a U.S. nature reserve (area 3,030 sq. miles) in S. central Alaska, established (1917) by Congress

Mount Rainier National Park a U.S. nature reserve (area 100 sq. miles) in the Cascade Range of Washington

Mount Rushmore National Memorial a sculpture of the heads of George Washington, Thomas Jefferson, Abraham Lincoln, and Theodore Roosevelt, carved (1927–41) by Gutzon Borglum on the northeast side of Mt Rushmore in the living rock. Each head is about 60 ft high. The portraits represent the founding, expansion, preservation, and unification of the U.S.A.

Mount Ver·non (vá:rnən) the home and burial place of George Washington in N.E. Virginia on the Potomac, near Washington, D.C.

Mount·y, Mount·ie (máunti:) *pl.* **Mount·ies** *n.* (*pop.*) a member of the Royal Canadian Mounted Police

mourn (mɔrn) *v.i.* to express or feel grief esp. because of a death, *to mourn for a friend* ‖ to show customary tokens of grief for a given period after someone's death, e.g. to wear mourning ‖ *v.t.* to express or feel grief for (a dead person, someone's death etc.) [O.E. *murnan*]

Mourne, Mountains of (mɔrn) a range in S.E. Co. Down, Northern Ireland: Slieve Donard, 2,796 ft

mourn·er (mɔ́rnər) *n.* a person who mourns ‖ a person attending a funeral

mourn·ful (mɔ́rnfəl) *adj.* feeling or showing sadness, *a mournful expression* ‖ doleful, causing sadness, *a mournful tune*

mourn·ing (mɔ́rniŋ) *n.* grieving, lamentation ‖ the customary period during which a dead person is mourned ‖ the special clothes or tokens worn by a mourner

mourning dove *Zenaidura macrura Corolinensis,* a small wild dove of the U.S.A. with a mournful cry

mouse (maus) **1.** *pl.* **mice** (mais) *n.* any of a large number of rodents resembling rats but smaller, with hairless tails, esp. one of the smaller members of genus *Mus,* fam. *Muridae,* e.g. *M. musculus,* the house mouse, a common pest found in most parts of the world ‖ a timid or retiring person **2.** *v.i. pres. part.* **mous·ing** *past* and *past part.* **moused** (esp. of a cat) to hunt and catch mice **móus·er** *n.* an animal, esp. a cat, that is particularly good at catching mice [O.E. *mūs*]

mouse·trap (máustræp) *n.* a device for catching mice

mousey *MOUSY

mous·sa·ka (mu̞:səká) *n.* dish of ground lamb or beef and sliced eggplant, popular in Greece and Turkey

mousse (mu:s) *n.* a frothy frozen dessert of flavored whipped cream or a substitute of thin cream, egg white, gelatin etc. [F.]

mous·tache, mus·tache (məstáʃ, məstáʃ, mʌ́stæʃ) *n.* the hair on the upper lip, esp. of a man ‖ (*zool.*) bristles or hair around an animal's mouth [F. fr. Ital. fr. Gk]

Mous·te·ri·an, Mous·tie·ri·an (mu:stíəri:ən) *adj.* of a middle Paleolithic epoch characterized by the use of flake tools, and associated with Neanderthal man [after *Le Moustier* cave in S.W. France]

mous·y, mous·ey (máusi) *comp.* **mous·i·er** *superl.* **mous·i·est** *adj.* of, like or pertaining to a mouse. a *mousy smell* ‖ mouse-colored, *mousy hair* ‖ (of a person) lacking personality or drive

mouth 1. (mauθ)*pl.* **mouths** (mauðz) *n.* a cavity in the head containing the teeth for mastication, and the tongue, palate etc. for voice production, and bounded by the lips ‖ the external opening of the lips as a facial feature ‖ the opening in an animal's body through which food is taken in, regarded as the beginning of the alimentary canal ‖ a person viewed as something to be fed ‖ the mouth as the source of speech, *this sounds strange in your mouth* ‖ a horse's mouth with respect to its responsiveness to the

pressure of the bit, *a hard mouth* ‖ the part of a river where it empties into the sea **down in the mouth** depressed, dejected **to keep one's mouth shut** to say nothing, remain silent **to put words into someone's mouth** to represent someone as having said something he did not say ‖ to tell someone what to say **to take the words out of someone's mouth** to say just what someone else was about to say **2.** *v.* (mauð) *v.t.* to say, esp. in an affected manner ‖ to shape (words) with the lips without saying them ‖ to train (a horse) to the bit ‖ *v.i.* to speak in an affected manner ‖ to make a grimace **móuth·ful** *n.* the amount of food etc. that will go into the mouth easily **to say a mouthful** (*pop.*) to say something strikingly apt or true [O.E. *mūth*]

mouth organ a harmonica

mouth·part (máuθpɑrt) *n.* (*zool.*) a structure in the region of the mouth (e.g. of an insect)

mouth·piece (máuθpi:s) *n.* the part of a wind instrument to which the player's lips are applied ‖ something placed at the mouth. e.g. part of a horse's bit passing between the teeth ‖ the part of a tobacco pipe which is placed in the mouth ‖ the part of a telephone into which one speaks ‖ a spokesman, e.g. a person or newspaper delivering the opinion of others

mov·a·bil·i·ty, move·a·bil·i·ty (mu̞:vəbíliti:) *n.* the state or quality of being movable

mov·a·ble, move·a·ble (mú:vəbl) **1.** *adj.* capable of being moved ‖ (of property) that can be moved from a house, personal ‖ (of a religious feast) changing its date from year to year **2.** *n.* an article, esp. of furniture, that can be moved from a house (cf. FIXTURE) [O.F. *Br movable*]

move (mu:v) **1.** *v. pres. part.* **mov·ing** *past* and *past part.* **moved** *v.t.* to change the location or position of, *to move a table* ‖ to cause to become active, stir, *to move water around with a stick* ‖ to arouse the feelings (esp. of pity, sympathy etc.) of, *his account moved her deeply* ‖ to influence, impel, prompt, *her advice moved him to action* ‖ to cause (the bowels) to eject feces ‖ to propose formally in an assembly, *to move a vote of thanks* ‖ *v.i.* to be made active, stir, *a few leaves moved in the wind* ‖ to change location or position ‖ (with 'for') to make an appeal, application etc. in a law court, *the plaintiff moved for a rehearing* ‖ to be active, spend one's time, *he moves in literary circles* ‖ to change one's residence ‖ (often with 'on') to depart or start to depart ‖ to make progress, *the work moves slowly* ‖ (*chess. checkers* etc.) to change the position of a piece as part of the game ‖ to take action, *we must move at once in this matter* ‖ (of the bowels) to eject feces **as the spirit moves one** when one feels inclined **to move out (in)** to remove one's belongings from (take them into) a residence **to move up** to advance, e.g. when standing in line **2.** *n.* a calculated maneuver made to gain some advantage ‖ (*chess, checkers* etc.) the moving of a piece, or the turn of a player to move ‖ a change of place or residence, *we plan a move in the spring* **on the move** moving from place to place ‖ progressing ‖ departing **to get a move on** (*pop.*) to hurry up **to make a move** to stir, *don't make a move or I'll shoot* ‖ to go to a different place ‖ to take action [M.E. fr. A.F. *mover,* O.F. *movoir*]

moveability *MOVABILITY

moveable *MOVABLE

move·ment (mú:vmənt) *n.* the act or process of moving ‖ an instance of this ‖ an impulse, *he felt a movement of pity for them* ‖ the development of the action in a prose work ‖ the rhythmic quality of a poem ‖ the illusion of motion in a painting, sculpture etc. ‖ the moving parts of a mechanism (esp. of clockwork) ‖ (*mus.*) a usually self-contained structural division of a symphony, sonata etc. ‖ (*mus.*) the character of a composition with regard to rhythm and tempo ‖ a series of acts and events planned towards a definite end by a body of people, *the civil rights movement* ‖ a tactical moving of troops as part of a military or naval maneuver ‖ an emptying of the bowels ‖ the matter thus emptied ‖ (*commerce*) a change or trend in the price of some commodity or stock [O.F.]

mov·er (mú:vər) *n.* a person who or thing that moves, esp. a person who moves a formal proposal ‖ someone who professionally moves people's belongings from one residence to another

mo·vie (mú:vi:) *n.* (*Am.=Br.* film) a sequence of pictures projected on a screen from a developed and prepared film, esp. with an accompanying sound track ‖ a theater where such pictures are shown regularly to the public **the movies** such

entertainment in general ‖ this entertainment as a branch of industry ‖ a particular example of such entertainment, *let's go to the movies tonight* [MOVING PICTURES]

movie camera (*Am.=Br.* cinecamera) a camera for making movies, usually amateur, and using narrower film (16 or 8 mm.) than is used in the movie industry

mov·ie·go·er (mú:vi:gouər) *n.* (*Am.=Br.* cinemagoer) a person who goes frequently to the movies

movie house a building where movies are shown

mov·ing (mú:viŋ) *adj.* changing place, posture etc., *moving parts* ‖ causing movement or action, a *moving belt* ‖ affecting the feelings, esp. feelings of tenderness, pity, sympathy etc.

moving picture a movie (sequence of pictures)

moving staircase an escalator

mow (mou) *past part.* **mowed, mown** (moun) *v.t.* to cut (grass etc.) with a scythe. sickle, lawn mower etc. ‖ (with 'down') to cause to fall in great numbers, *mowed down by machine-gun fire* ‖ *v.i.* to cut grass etc. [O.E. *māwan*]

mow (mau) *n.* a stack of hay, grain etc., esp. in a barn ‖ the place in a barn where hay etc. is stored [O.E. *mūga,* heap]

mox·a (mɒ́ksə) *n.* (*med.*) a Japanese wormwood used medically as a cauterizing agent

mox·i·bus·tion (mɒksəbʌ́stʃən) *n.* therapeutic technique of applying heat by slowly burning moxa sticks held near diseased areas or acupuncture pressure points

Mo·zam·bique (mouzəmbí:k) a country (area 302,250 sq. miles, pop. 13,413,000) on the S.E. African coast. Capital: Maputo. People and language: mainly Bantu with small Portuguese and Asian minorities. Official language: Portuguese. The land is divided between wide coastal plains and grassy or wooded interior highlands (2,000–8,000 ft), from which several rivers (esp. the Limpopo and the Zambezi) flow east across the country. The northern savanna is one of Africa's chief big-game regions. Average yearly temperatures (F.): 71°–78° along the coasts, higher in river valleys. Rainfall: 30 ins in the south, 56 ins in the north. Chief occupations: subsistence agriculture (millet, manioc, sweet potatoes), sugar growing on plantations with conscripted labor. Exports: sugar, corn, raw and spun cotton, cashew nuts, copra, sisal, minerals (beryl, bauxite), labor to South African mines. Livestock: oxen, goats. Chief ports: Maputo, Quelimang, Sofala, Pemba. Mozambique was under Arab influence when it was captured by the Portuguese (early 16th c.) and became a center of the slave trade until 1878. An insurrection developed (1964) against the Portuguese and Mozambique achieved its independence (1975). It became a base for guerrilla forces from Rhodesia (now Zimbabwe) and South Africa until a 1979 cease-fire with Rhodesia (1979) and a nonaggression pact with South Africa (1984) were signed

Moz·ar·ab (mouzǽrəb) *n.* (*hist.*) a medieval Spanish Christian under allegiance to a Moorish king but allowed to follow his own religion **Moz·ár·a·bic** *adj.* [Span. *Mozarabic* fr. Arab. *musta'rib,* would-be Arab]

Mo·zart (móutsart), Wolfgang Amadeus (1756–91), Austrian composer. He showed a phenomenal, perhaps unique, musical precocity, beginning to compose at about the age of five. In his short life he produced a vast output, but remained poor, although his genius was acknowledged. Mozart assimilated a great variety of musical influences and mastered all the musical forms of his time. In spite of the great ease and speed with which he composed, his music shows a continuous growth in expressive power: the purity and grace which characterize his style, and constitute its immediate appeal, do not preclude emotional intensity and depth. Mozart's works include 41 numbered symphonies, of which the last three (all written in 1788) are esp. outstanding, a clarinet concerto (1791), concertos for piano, violin, French horn etc., string quartets, sonatas, serenades, divertimenti and many other orchestral and chamber works, the 'Requiem' (1791), finished after his death by Süssmayr, a pupil, other Masses and religious music, songs, and many operas, incl. 'The Abduction from the Seraglio' (1782), 'The Marriage of Figaro' (1786), 'Don Giovanni' (1787), 'Così fan tutte' (1790) and 'The Magic Flute' (1791)

CONCISE PRONUNCIATION KEY: **(a)** æ, c*a*t; ɑ, c*a*r; ɔ f*aw*n; ei, sn*a*ke. **(e)** e, h*e*n; i:, sh*ee*p; iə, d*ee*r; ɛə, b*ea*r. **(i)** i, f*i*sh; ai, t*i*ger; ə:, b*i*rd. **(o)** o, *o*x; au, c*ow*; ou, g*oa*t; u, p*oo*r; ɔi, r*oy*al. **(u)** ʌ, d*u*ck; u, b*u*ll; u:, g*oo*se; ə, b*a*cillus; ju:, c*u*be. x, lo*ch*; θ, *th*ink; ð, *b*o*th*er; z, *Z*en; ʒ, corsa*g*e; dʒ, sava*g*e; ŋ, ora*n*gutang; j, *y*ak; ʃ, *f*ish; tʃ, fe*tch*; 'l, rabb*le*; 'n, redd*en*. Complete pronunciation key appears inside front cover.

moz·zet·ta, mo·zet·ta (mouzétə) n. a short cape with an ornamental hood worn over a rochet by Roman Catholic Church dignitaries [Ital. *miozzetta*]

M.P. a member of the military police || (Br.) a member of Parliament

MPG (*acronym*) miles per gallon (esp. of gasoline, used in a motor vehicle)

mph, m·p·h. miles per hour

MPU (*electr. acronym*) microprocessing unit

Mr *MISTER, *MESSRS

mri·dan·ga (mridóŋgə) or **mri·dan·gam** (mridóŋgəm) n. (*music*) a two-headed, conical drum of India

MRNA (*abbr.*) messenger RNA

Mrs (misiz) n. a courtesy title for any married woman not styled 'Lady', 'Dr' etc., used before her name or her husband's, *Mrs Anthony Waterer* [abbr. of MISTRESS]

MRV (*mil. acronym*) multiple reentry vehicle, a long-range missile with multiple warheads that travel in the stratosphere and reenter the atmosphere individually. *Cf* MIRV

MSI (*electr. abbr.*) medium-scale integration, the creation of multiple units of integrated circuit on one chip of silicon. *Cf* LSI

M60 (emsíksti:) n. (*mil.*) British main battle tank with 105-mm, 0.51-caliber, and 0.5 anti-aircraft guns

ms., MS. *pl.* **mss., MSS.** manuscript

Ms (miz) n. a courtesy title for a woman, whether she is married or not

MSR (*mil. abbr.*) missile site radar, used at antiballistic missile sites

M.S.T. Mountain standard time

MSW (*abbr.*) 1. master of social welfare 2. master of social work

mt, Mt mountain, Mount

mu (mju:, mu:) n. the 12th letter (M, μ=m) of the Greek alphabet

much (mʌtʃ) *comp.* **more** (mɔr) *superl.* **most** (moust) 1. *adj.* (used esp. after an adverb, e.g. 'not', 'too', 'very') great in quantity, extent or degree, *not much rain* || very great, very good. *she is not much to look at* 2. n. a great quantity, extent or degree, *much of the land was flooded* || something great, important, admirable (used esp. in negative constructions), *his efforts didn't amount to much* 3. *adv.* to a great extent or degree, *he feels much better now, she doesn't like him very much* || almost, *the two look much the same* **much as** no matter to what extent or degree, however much, *we cannot come, much as we would like to* [M.E. *muche, moche, meche, miche*]

much·ness (mʌtʃnis) n. (in the phrase) **much of a muchness** average, leaving little to choose, *the candidates were all much of a muchness*

mu·cic acid (mjú:sik) a white crystalline diacid (CHOH)₄—(CO₂H)₂ obtained by the oxidation of gums, lactose etc. [F. *mucique*]

mu·ci·lage (mjú:səlidʒ) n. a sticky gelatinous substance found in seaweeds and in certain other plants || a solution of gum etc. prepared as an adhesive **mu·ci·lag·i·nous** (mju:səlǽdʒinəs) *adj.* sticky || containing or producing mucilage [F.]

mu·cin (mjú:sin) n. (*biochem.*) one of a series of mucoproteins originating from mucous membranes **mú·ci·nous** *adj.* [F. *mucine*]

muck (mʌk) 1. n. moist farmyard manure || dark, moist, fertile soil containing decomposing organic matter || dirt, filth || mud || (*pop.*) an untidy state, confusion, *in a muck* 2. *v.t.* to manure, *to muck a field* || (*pop.*) to make dirty, *to muck one's clothes* || (esp. *Br., pop.*) to bungle, spoil, *that's mucked his chances* **to muck about** (*Br., pop.*) to fool around || to interfere (with something) **to muck in** (*Br., pop.*) to join in on a casual, equal footing **to muck out** (*Br.*) to clean out (a stable, cowshed etc.) [M.E. *muk*, prob. fr. Scand.]

muck·rake (mʌ́kreik) *pres. part.* **muck·rak·ing** *past* and *past part.* **muck·raked** *v.i.* to make special efforts to uncover and to expose corruption in public affairs || to spread sensational or unsavory facts or rumors under the guise of exposing corruption

Muckrakers (mʌ́kreikərz) the name applied to those writers in the U.S.A in the early 20th century who exposed corruption through their writings. Muckrakers included Ray Stannard Baker, who wrote of racial discrimination in 'Following the Color Line' (1908); David Graham Phillips, who exposed child labor in 'The Treason and the Senate' (1906); Ida Tarbell; Thomas Lawson, who wrote of stock fraud in

'Frenzied Finance' (1905) and Charles Edward Russell, who fought social dislocation. The term was used by Theodore Roosevelt in 1906

muck·y (mʌ́ki:) *comp.* **muck·i·er** *superl.* **muck·i·est** *adj.* dirty || muddy

mu·coid (mjú:kɔid) n. (*biochem.*) any of a group of glycoproteins resembling mucus, occurring in the vitreous humor and cornea of the eye, in certain tissues, in cysts etc. [MUCUS]

mu·co·pro·tein (mju:koupróuti:n) n. a mucoid [fr. MUCUS+PROTEIN]

mu·cor (mjú:kɔr) n. a phycomycete of the genus *Mucor*, incl. many common molds, e.g. those which occur on bread, jam etc. [L. fr. *mucere*, to be moldy]

mu·co·sa (mju:kóusə) *pl.* **mu·co·sae** (mju:kóusi:), **mu·co·sa, mu·co·sas** n. (*anat.*) a mucous membrane [Mod. L.]

mu·cos·i·ty (mju:kósiti:) n. the state or quality of being mucous

mu·cous (mjú:kəs) *adj.* of, covered with or like mucus || containing or secreting mucus [fr. L. *mucosus*]

mucous membrane a moist membrane containing mucous glands, lining cavities and passages of the body, e.g. the respiratory, alimentary and genitourinary tracts

mu·cro (mjú:krou) *pl.* **mu·cro·nes** (mju:króuni:z) n. (*biol.*) a terminal point or process projecting sharply, esp. at the end of a leaf [Mod. L. fr. L.=sharp point]

mu·cro·nate (mjú:krəneit) *adj.* (*biol.*) ending abruptly in a sharp point **mú·cro·nat·ed** *adj.* [fr. L. *mucronatus*]

mu·cus (mjú:kəs) n. a slippery, slimy substance secreted by mucous glands covering and lubricating the inner surfaces of the respiratory, alimentary and genitourinary tracts etc. || a secretion resembling this in certain animals, e.g. snails [L. *mucus*, mucus of the nose]

mud (mʌd) n. a sticky mixture of water and earth or dust || malicious abuse to **fling** (or **sling, throw**) **mud at** to talk scandal about [M.E. *mode, mudde* prob. fr. L.G.]

mud bath a bath in mud for relief of rheumatism etc.

mud·di·ly (mʌ́dili:) *adv.* in a muddy manner

mud·di·ness (mʌ́di:nis) n. the state or quality of being muddy

mud·dle (mʌd'l) 1. *v. pres. part.* **mud·dling** *past* and *past part.* **mud·dled** *v.t.* to mix (things) in a confused manner, *his papers are terribly muddled* || to make (speech, words) unclear, *to muddle one's lines* || to bewilder, esp. with alcohol, *two drinks muddle him* || to make a mess of, bungle || *v.i.* (with 'about', 'away', 'on' etc.) to act in a confused, disorganized or bungling way 2. n. a state of disorder or messiness || a state of mental confusion [MUD]

mud·dle·head·ed (mʌ́d'lhedid) *adj.* given to mental confusion or bungling

mud·dy (mʌ́di:) 1. *adj.* *comp.* **mud·di·er** *superl.* **mud·di·est** covered with mud, *muddy shoes* || abounding in mud, *a muddy lane* || like mud in color or texture, *a muddy skin* || thick with sediment, *muddy coffee* || confused, muddled, *muddy ideas* || (of light) dull, murky, *a muddy sky* || (of color) lacking brightness or clarity 2. *v.t. pres. part.* **mud·dy·ing** *past* and *past part.* **mud·died** to make muddy || *v.i.* to become muddy

mud·fish (mʌ́dfiʃ) *pl.* **mud·fish, mud·fish·es** n. any of several fishes living in muddy water, burrowing in mud etc., e.g. the loach

mud flat an area of muddy ground covered by water at high tide

mud·guard (mʌ́dgɑrd) n. (Br.) a fender (metal cover over the wheel of a vehicle)

mud·lark (mʌ́dlɑrk) n. a child who grubs around looking for useful things in the mud of riverbanks, esp. of the Thames, in England || an urchin (mischievous young boy)

mud·pack (mʌ́dpæk) n. a cosmetic preparation for the face, consisting of fuller's earth and astringents

mud puppy *pl.* **mud puppies** any of several large gilled, aquatic, American salamanders, e.g. the axolotl, the hellbender, or any member of genus *Necturus*, fam. *Proteidae*, that live in underwater mud

mud·skip·per (mʌ́dskipər) n. any of several small gobies of genera *Periophthalmus* and *Boleophthalmus* of Asia and Polynesia, which have specially modified pectoral fins enabling them to leave the water

mud·sling·ing (mʌ́dsliŋiŋ) n. personal abuse, offensive remarks etc., e.g. as features of a political campaign

mu·ez·zin (mu:ézin, mju:ézin) n. a Moslem crier who calls out the hours of prayer from a minaret [Arab. *mu'adhdhin* fr. *adhana*, to proclaim]

muff (mʌf) n. a covering of fur etc. for protecting the hands from cold, shaped like a tube with open ends into which the hands are put [prob. Du. *mof* fr. F. *moufle*]

muff 1. *v.t.* (*cricket, baseball* etc.) to miss (a catch) || to bungle || *v.i.* to miss a catch in a game || to bungle something 2. n. (*cricket, baseball* etc.) a fumbled and dropped catch || a bungling performance || a bungler, esp. in games [origin unknown]

muf·fin (mʌ́fin) n. a quick bread made of batter containing egg, baked in a cup-shaped mold and eaten hot with butter || (Br.) an English muffin [origin unknown]

muf·fle (mʌ́fəl) n. a compartment or protective barrier in a kiln or furnace for firing substances which must be protected from flame [F. *moufle*, thick glove]

muffle n. the end of the muzzle in ruminants and certain other mammals [F. *mufle*, origin unknown]

muffle *pres. part.* **muf·fling** *past* and *past part.* **muf·fled** *v.t.* to cover up (the head, throat etc.) for protection against cold, esp. by wrapping oneself in a scarf etc. || to wrap or pad (a drum, oars etc.) to deaden sound || to deaden (sound) by wrapping, padding etc. || to restrict the diffusion of (criticism etc.) **múf·fler** n. a scarf for protecting the throat from cold || a device to deaden or muffle noise, esp. the felt pad of a piano hammer or (*Am.=Br.* silencer) a baffle in the exhaust pipe of an engine [O.F. *emmoufler*]

muf·ti (mʌ́fti:) n. an official expounder of Moslem law || civilian dress worn by someone who normally wears a military uniform || plain clothes as distinct from any uniform [Arab. fr. *aftā*, to decide a point of law]

mug (mʌg) 1. n. a drinking vessel, generally cylindrical in shape, with a handle || the amount it holds || (*pop.*) the face or mouth, *an ugly mug* || (Br., *pop.*) a dupe 2. *v. pres. part.* **mug·ging** *past* and *past part.* **mugged** *v.i.* (*pop.*) to grimace || *v.t.* to put a stranglehold on (someone) from behind or strike (him) or otherwise assault (him) in order to commit robbery **to mug up** (Br., *pop.*) to make an effort to find out and learn, *to mug up facts for a speech* || (Br., *pop.*) to study (a subject) by cramming **múg·ger** n. someone who assaults a person in order to rob him [origin unknown]

Mugabe (mu:gábei), Robert Gabriel (1924–) prime minister of Zimbabwe (1980–) and co-founder (1963) and president of the Zimbabwe African National Union (ZANU). Opposed to the white government of Rhodesia, he was imprisoned (1964–74), and when released he directed anti-Rhodesian guerrilla troops from bases in Mozambique. When black majority rule was agreed upon (1979), he was named leader of the newly named country in 1980

mug·gi·ness (mʌ́gi:nis) n. the state or quality of being muggy

mug·gins (mʌ́ginz) *pl.* **mug·gins** n. (esp. Br., *pop.*) a fool, simpleton [perh. fr. surname *Muggins*]

mug·gy (mʌ́gi:) *comp.* **mug·gi·er** *superl.* **mug·gi·est** *adj.* (of weather, climate etc.) warm and damp, oppressive [fr. older *mug*, to drizzle prob. fr. Scand.]

mug·wump (mʌ́gwʌmp) n. someone who is neutral or undecided, esp. in politics **Mug·wump** (*Am. hist.*) a Republican who voted for Cleveland, the Democratic nominee, instead of for the Republican candidate (James G. Blaine) in the presidential election of 1884 [Algonquian *mugquomp, mugwomp, chief*]

Mu·ham·med (muhǽmid) Mohammed

Mu·ham·med·an (muhǽmidən) n. and adj. Mohammedan

muis·hond (máishɔnt) n. either of two southern African weasels having white stripes on a black body. Both animals emit a foul odor if attacked (*SNAKE MUISHOND, *STRIPED MUISHOND) [Afrik. fr. Du. fr. M.Du. *muushont* fr. *muus*, mouse +*hont*, dog]

Mu·ja·hed·een (muʒáhedi:n) n. political group belonging to the national liberation movement of Iran; founded in 1961 to overthrow Shah Mohammed Pahlavi and later in opposition to Ayatollah Khomeini

Muk·den (mú:kdén) *SHENYANG

mu·lat·to (məlǽtou, mju:lǽtou) *pl.* **mul·at·toes, mu·lat·tos** n. the first-generation offspring of a European and a black [Span. *mulato*]

CONCISE PRONUNCIATION KEY: **(a)** æ, c*a*t; ɑ, c*a*r; ɔ f*aw*n; ei, sn*a*ke. **(e)** e, h*e*n; i:, sh*ee*p; iə, d*ee*r; ɛə, b*ea*r. **(i)** i, f*i*sh; ai, t*i*ger; ə:, b*i*rd. **(o)** o, *o*x; au, c*ow*; ou, g*oa*t; u, p*oo*r; ɔi, r*oy*al. **(u)** ʌ, d*u*ck; u, b*u*ll; u:, g*oo*se; ju:, c*u*be. x, lo*ch*; θ, *th*ink; ð, bo*th*er; z, *Z*en; ʒ, cor*s*age; dʒ, sava*ge*; ŋ, ora*ng*utang; j, *y*ak; ʃ, *fi*sh; tʃ, fe*tch*; 'l, rabb*le*; 'n, redd*en*. Complete pronunciation key appears inside front cover.

mul·ber·ry (mʎlbəri:, mʎlbəri:) *pl.* **mul·ber·ries** *n.* any of several members of *Morus*, fam *Moraceae*, a worldwide genus of trees cultivated for their delicious multiple fruit. The leaves of some species are used for feeding silkworms ‖ the fruit of any of these trees ‖ a rich, dark purple color [M.E. *mulberie, murberie* prob. fr. M.H.G. *mûlbere* fr. L. *morum*, mulberry]

mulch (mʎltʃ, mʎlʃ) **1.** *n.* a layer of wet straw, leaves, grass mowings, compost etc. spread over the roots of plants or trees to conserve moisture, protect from frost etc. **2.** *v.t.* to apply mulch to [rel. to G. dial. *molsch* adj., soft, decaying]

mulct (mʎlkt) *v.t.* to punish by means of a fine ‖ to get hold of the money of (someone) by swindling or extortion [fr. L. *mulctare, multare*]

mulct *n.* a fine ‖ a penalty ‖ a compulsory payment [fr. L. *mulcta, multa*]

Muldoon (mʎldú:n), Robert David (1921–), New Zealand prime minister (1975–84). He was a member of Parliament from 1960 and minister of finance (1967–72) before becoming prime minister

mule (mju:l) *n.* a slipper made without a back [F.]

mule *n.* a usually sterile hybrid produced by crossing a male ass and a mare, used as a pack animal. The mule unites the size and power of the horse with the perseverance and surefootedness of the ass (cf. HINNY) ‖ a stubborn or obstinate person, esp. when also stupid ‖ a sterile plant hybrid ‖ a sterile hybrid, esp. of a canary and some related bird ‖ a spinning machine which draws, twists and winds cotton, wool etc. [O.E. *mûl* fr. L. and fr. O.F. *mul, mule* fr. L.]

mule *MEWL

mule skinner (*pop.*) a muleteer

mu·le·teer (mju:lətíər) *n.* a driver of mules [F. *muletier*]

Mul·ha·cén (mu:laθén) a mountain (11,420 ft) of the Sierra Nevada, in Granada, the highest point in Spain

Mül·hau·sen (mýlhauz'n) *MULHOUSE

Mül·heim an der Ruhr (mýlhaimandɛrrú:r) an industrial town (pop. 179,900) in the Ruhr Valley, North Rhine-Westphalia, West Germany, between Duisburg and Essen

Mul·house (mʎlhaus) (G. Mülhausen), a town (pop. 114,000) of Haut-Rhin, E. France: textiles, machinery, potash. Town hall (16th c.)

mul·ish (mjú:liʃ) *adj.* obstinate, stubborn

mull (mʎl) *v.t.* (with 'over') to ponder, deliberate mentally over (some question or problem) [origin unknown]

mull *n.* a thin, soft muslin used esp. in bookbinding [fr. earlier *mulmull* fr. Hindi *malmal*]

mull *v.t.* to heat, sweeten, and flavor (wine, cider etc.) with spices [origin unknown]

mul·lah (mʎlə) *n.* a Moslem teacher of theology and sacred law [Pers., Turk. and Urdu *mullā* fr. Arab.]

mul·lein, mul·len (mʎlin) *n.* a member of *Verbascum*, fam. *Scrophulariaceae*, a genus of plants with woolly leaves and tall spiked yellow flowers, widely distributed in the northern hemisphere, esp. *V. thapsus* [A.F. *moleine*]

Mul·ler (mʎlər), Hermann Joseph (1890–1967), U.S. geneticist and winner of the 1946 Nobel Prize in medicine for his discovery that X rays greatly increase the rate of mutation of genes

mull·er (mʎlər) *n.* a device, such as a flat-surfaced stone, used to grind powders, pigments etc. against a slab [perh. fr. A. F.]

mul·let (mʎlit) *pl.* **mul·let, mul·lets** *n.* the gray mullet ‖ the red mullet [M.E. *molet, mulet* fr. O.F. *mulet*]

mul·li·ga·taw·ny (mʎligətɔ́:ni:) *n.* a highly seasoned East Indian curry soup [Tamil *milagutannir*, pepper water]

mul·lion (mʎljən) *n.* (*archit.*) a slender vertical bar separating the compartments or apertures in a screen or window (cf. TRANSOM) [prob. fr. O.F. *moinel, moynel, monial*]

mul·lite (mʎlait) *n.* a silicate of aluminum used as a refractory [after *Mull*, an island of the Hebrides]

Mulroney (mʎlru:ni:), Brian (1939–), Canadian statesman, prime minister (1984–). He was a businessman before he entered politics in 1976, when he failed to be elected leader of the Progressive Conservative party. In 1983 he assumed its leadership and became a member of the House of Commons and in 1984 succeeded incumbent Liberal John Turner as prime minister. Mulroney worked to stabilize the economy and for better relations between the provinces and federal government.

Mul·tan (mu:ltán) a walled city (pop. 730,000) of the Punjab, Pakistan, a communications center: textiles, pottery, chemicals, precision instruments, jewelry

multi- (mʎlti:, mʎltai) *prefix* having, containing or consisting of much or many ‖ many times, as in 'multimillionaire' [fr. L. *multus*, much, many]

mul·ti·ac·cess (mʎltiǽkses) *adj.* having multiple access, e.g., of computer time-sharing

mul·ti·cel·lu·lar (mʎlti:séljulər) *adj.* having many cells

mul·ti·col·ored, *Br.* **mul·ti·col·oured** (mʎlti:kʎlərd) *adj.* of many different colors

mul·ti·com·pa·ny (mʎltikʎmpəni:) *n.* an enterprise involving several companies in different industries *syn.* conglomerate

mul·ti·far·i·ous (mʎltifǽəri:əs) *adj.* having great variety or diversity [fr. L.L. *multifarius*]

mul·ti·fid (mʎltifid) *adj.* (*biol.*) cleft into many parts or lobes [fr. L. *multifidus*]

mul·ti·form (mʎltifɔrm) *adj.* having many forms, variously shaped **mul·ti·for·mi·ty** *n.* [fr. F. *multiforme* or L. *multiformis*]

mul·ti·germ (mʎltidʒə́:rm) *adj.* (*botany*) of a fruit capable of seeding several plants

mul·ti·hull (mʎltihʎl) *adj.* of a sailing vessel with more than one hull, usu. joined by a common deck *Cf* MONOHULL

mul·ti·lat·er·al (mʎlti:lǽtərəl) *adj.* involving the participation of more than two nations ‖ many-sided

mul·ti·lin·gual (mʎlti:lingwəl) *adj.* containing or expressed in several languages, *a multilingual text* ‖ capable of using several languages

mul·ti·me·di·a (mʎltimí:di:ə) *adj.* of a means of communication involving several media, e.g., film and sculpture, print matter, and voices *Cf* INTERMEDIA

mul·ti·mil·lion·aire (mʎlti:miljənéər) *n.* a person who possesses several million dollars, pounds etc.

mul·ti·na·tion·al corporation (mʎltinǽʃən'l) (*economics*) a business enterprise operating in several nations, esp. involved in world market

mul·ti·pack (mʎltipǽk) *n.* single package with two or more products

mul·tip·a·ra (mʎltipərə) *pl.* **mul·tip·a·rae** (mʎltípəri:) *n.* (*med.*) a woman who has borne more than one child [Mod. L. fr. *multiparus* adj., multiparous]

mul·tip·a·rous (mʎltípərəs) *adj.* (*zool.*) bearing several or more than one offspring at a birth ‖ (*med.*) of, pertaining to or being a multipara [fr. Mod. L. *multiparus*]

mul·ti·par·tite (mʎlti:pártait) *adj.* involving the participation of several nations, multilateral ‖ divided into many parts [fr. L. *multipartitus*, having many parts]

mul·ti·phase (mʎltifeiz) *adj.* (*elec.*) polyphase

mul·ti·pha·sic screening (mʎltiféizik) (*med.*) the use of a battery of screening tests in order to identify any of the several diseases being screened for in an apparently healthy population

mul·ti·ple (mʎltip'l) **1.** *adj.* having many parts, sections or components ‖ multifarious, manifold ‖ (*elec.*, of a circuit) having several parallel conductors ‖ (*elec.*) designating a group of terminals which make the circuit available at several points **2.** *n.* (*math.*) a quantity or number which contains another an exact number of times without a remainder, *21 is a multiple of 7* [F.]

mul·ti·ple-choice (mʎltip'ltʃɔ́is) *adj.* (of a question in a test) having several answers given from which the person tested must choose the correct one ‖ (of a test) containing such questions

multiple factors (*biol.*) genes having a joint or cumulative effect

multiple fruit (*bot.*) a collective fruit

multiple sclerosis a chronic, generally progressive disease in which the myelin of the central nervous system is replaced by sclerotic scars. Symptoms may include muscular weakness, tremors, defects of vision, sensation or speech, paralysis etc.

multiple shop (*Br.*) a chain store

mul·ti·plet (mʎltəplət) *n.* **1.** (*particle phys.*) a family of 8 to 10 nuclear particles with the same mass, hypercharge, and isotopic spin **2.** (*quantum mechanics*) closely spaced energy levels resulting from a weak splitting of an energy level, e.g., isoprin multiplets; also, related particles that can be split into a number of energy

levels **3.** (*phys.*) closely spaced lines in a spectrum composed of a group of related lines

mul·ti·plex (mʎltipleks) *adj.* (*elec.*) of a system capable of sending several simultaneous messages on one wave ‖ multiple [L.]

mul·ti·plex·or (mʎltəpleksər) *n.* (*communications*) device that can interleave data from two or more sources or distribute such interleaved data using a single channel —**multiplex** *v.* to use *Cf* MULTIPROGRAMMING

multiplexor channel (*computer*) a method for slow-speed data transmission between memory and the input-output devices, in which time is shared by many devices daisy-chained together

mul·ti·pli·a·ble (mʎltiplaiəb'l) *adj.* capable of being multiplied

mul·ti·plic·a·ble (mʎltiplikəb'l) *adj.* multipliable [fr. L. *multiplicabilis*]

mul·ti·pli·cand (mʎltiplikǽnd) *n.* (*math.*) the quantity or number to be multiplied by another [fr. L. *multiplicandus* fr. *multrplicare*, to multiply]

mul·ti·pli·ca·tion (mʎltiplikéiʃən) *n.* a multiplying or being multiplied ‖ (*math.*) the arithmetical process of multiplying numbers, which abbreviates the process of repeated addition [F.]

multiplication factor the reproduction factor

multiplication table an elementary arithmetical table giving the results of multiplication, usually from 1 times 1 to 12 times 12

mul·ti·pli·ca·tive (mʎltiplikeitiv, mʎltiplíkətiv) *adj.* capable of multiplying or tending to multiply [fr. M.L. *multiplicativus*]

mul·ti·plic·i·ty (mʎltiplísiti:) *n.* a great number ‖ the quality or state of being many or varied [fr. L. *multiplicitas*]

mul·ti·pli·er (mʎltiplaiər) *n.* someone who or something that multiplies ‖ (*math.*) the quantity or number by which the multiplicand is multiplied ‖ (*phys.*) an instrument for intensifying a force, electric current etc.

multiplier effect (*computer*) an output effect disproportionately larger than the input

mul·ti·ply (mʎltiplai) *pres. part.* **mul·ti·ply·ing** *past and past part.* **mul·ti·plied** *v.t.* (*math.*) to increase (a number or quantity) by adding the number or quantity to itself repeatedly in a single arithmetical step, *7 multiplied by 7 makes 49* ‖ to increase in number, quantity or intensity, *to multiply one's efforts* ‖ *v.i.* to increase in number or quantity ‖ to breed, *the species multiplies rapidly* [O.F. *multiplier*]

mul·ti·pro·cess·ing (mʎltəprósesiŋ) *n.* (*computer*) use of several processes to execute synchronized segments of a program —**multiprocessor** *n.* the unit

mul·ti·pro·gram·ming (mʎltəprógræmiŋ) *n.* (*computer*) interleaved execution of two or more programs sharing the time on a unit of equipment. *syn* multirunning *Cf* MULTIPLEXOR, PARALLEL PROCESSING

mul·ti·ra·cial·ism (mʎltəréiʃəlizəm) *n.* doctrine of equality of rights and opportunity among races in a social system

mul·ti·re·sist·ant (mʎltərizístənt) *adj.* (*med.*) of bacteria resistant to several antibiotics

multirunning *MULTIPROGRAMMING

mul·ti·source drug (mʎltəsɔurs) drug available for more than one manufacturer or distributor, often under different brand names, usu. subject to limits on reimbursement from insurers

mul·ti·spec·tral (mʎltəspéktrəl) *adj.* of photography having the ability to sense many spectra, e.g., infrared, microwaves, etc

mul·ti·tude (mʎltitu:d, mʎltitju:d) *n.* a great number, *a multitude of details* ‖ a crowd, a large gathering ‖ the quality or state of being numerous **the multitude** the common people [F. or fr. L. *multitudo*]

mul·ti·tu·di·nous (mʎltitú:d'nəs, mʎltitjú:d'nəs) *adj.* existing in great numbers [fr. L. *multitudo* (*multitudinis*)]

mul·ti·va·lent (mʎltivéiələnt) *adj.* (*chem.*) having more than one valence (cf. POLYVALENT) [fr. MULTI-+*valens* (*valentis*) fr. *valere*, to be strong]

mul·ti·ver·si·ty (mʎltəvə́:rsəti:) or **mul·ti·u·ni·ver·si·ty** (mʎltəju:nəvə́:rsəti:) *n.* a university with many campuses, each with many schools, each substantially autonomous. The term was coined by President Clark Kerr of the University of California at Berkeley *also* polyversity

mum (mʎm) **1.** *interj.* hush!, silence! **mum's the word** say nothing about it, keep it a secret **2.** *adj.* silent **3.** *v.i. pres. part.* **mum·ming** *past* and

CONCISE PRONUNCIATION KEY: **(a)** æ, c*a*t; ɑ, c*a*r; ɔ f*aw*n; ei, sn*a*ke. **(e)** e, h*e*n; i:, sh*ee*p; iə, d*ee*r; εə, b*ea*r. **(i)** i, f*i*sh; ai, t*i*ger; ə:, b*i*rd. **(o)** o, *o*x; au, c*ow*; ou, g*oa*t; u, p*oo*r; ɔi, r*oy*al. **(u)** ʌ, d*u*ck; u, b*u*ll; u:, g*oo*se; ə, *ba*cillus; ju:, c*u*be. x, lo*ch*; θ, *th*ink; ð, bo*th*er; z, *Z*en; ʒ, cor*s*age; dʒ, sa*v*age; ŋ, ora*n*gutang; j, *y*ak; ʃ, *f*ish; tʃ, fe*tch*; 'l, rabb*le*; 'n, redd*en*. Complete pronunciation key appears inside front cover.

past part. **mummed** to go from house to house for fun as one of a party of mummers, esp. at Christmas [imit.]

mum·ble (mʌmbˈl) **1.** *v. pres. part.* **mum·bling** *past* and *past part.* **mum·bled** *v.i.* to speak in a low indistinct way without proper articulation ‖ *v.t.* to utter inarticulately **2.** *n.* a low indistinct utterance or manner of speaking [M.E. *momele*]

mum·bo jum·bo (mʌmboudʒʌmbou) *n.* ritual given pointless importance in itself apart from the things signified ‖ unnecessarily complicated or meaningless language [*Mumbo Jumbo,* a supposed African idol or deity, perh. fr. Mandingo]

mu·me·son (múːmíːzɒn, múːmézɒn, mjúːmíː-zɒn, mjúːmézɒn) *n.* a muon

Mum·ford (mʌmfərd), Lewis (1895–1970), U.S. author and social philosopher. His works include the tetralogy comprising 'Technics and Civilization' (1934), 'The Culture of Cities' (1938), 'The Condition of Man' (1944), and 'The Conduct of Life' (1951)

mum·mer (mʌmər) *n.* a member of a group of actors who go from house to house acting in disguise, esp. at Christmas [O.F. *momeur*]

mum·mer·y (mʌməriː) *pl.* **mum·mer·ies** *n.* pointless and pretentious ceremonial ‖ an instance of this ‖ a performance by mummers [O.F. *mommerie,* F. *momerie,* mummers' performance]

mum·mi·fi·ca·tion (mʌmifikéiʃən) *n.* a mummifying or being mummified

mum·mi·fy (mʌmifai) *pres part.* **mum·mi·fy·ing** *past* and *past part.* **mum·mi·fied** *v.t.* to embalm and dry (a body) so as to preserve it ‖ to preserve, wrap up etc. like a mummy ‖ *v.i.* to shrivel up, dry [fr. F. *momifier*]

mum·my (mʌmiː) *pl.* **mum·mies** *n.* (esp *Br.,* a child's word for) mother

mummy *pl.* **mummies** *n.* a dead body embalmed for burial by the ancient Egyptians so as to be preserved from decay ‖ any dead body that has been naturally well preserved ‖ a rich brown bituminous pigment [F. *momie* fr. M.L. *mumia* fr. Arab.]

mummy case a case in the shape of the human body, decorated with symbols, in which ancient Egyptian mummies were placed for burial

mumps (mʌmps) *n.* an acute, contagious, virus disease, most common in children, marked by fever and swelling of the salivary glands of the neck and sometimes of the ovaries or testicles [pl. of obs. *mump,* a grimace]

Munch (muːŋk), Edvard (1863–1944), Norwegian expressionist painter and printmaker, esp. known for his woodcuts. His figure compositions often reveal themes of death, fear and anguish. Rhythmic background patterns intensify the feelings embodied in the sharply silhouetted, macabre figures

munch (mʌntʃ) *v.t.* and *i.* to chew with visible jaw movements and soft crunching sounds [prob. imit.]

Mun·chau·sen (mʌntʃauzˈn), Baron (Karl Friedrich Hieronymus von Münchhausen, 1720–97), German soldier and adventurer, whose fantastic tales of his experiences were the subject of a book in English by Rudolf Raspe (1785)

Mün·chen (mýnxən) *MUNICH

Mün·chen-Glad·bach (mýnxənglátbəx) *MÖN-CHEN-GLADBACH

mun·dane (mʌndéin, mʌndein) *adj.* ordinary, down-to-earth, matter-of-fact, esp. as contrasted with what is ideal [F. *mondain*]

mun·go (mʌ́ŋgou) *n.* woolen cloth made of secondhand material, poorer in quality than shoddy [origin unknown]

Mu·nich (mjúːnik) (G. München) the capital (pop. 1,288,200) of Bavaria, West Germany, just north of the Alps. Industries: brewing, heavy and precision engineering, publishing, clothing, food processing. Bavarian rulers of the 19th c. made it a cultural center, with famous museums (esp. the Glyptothek, 1816 and Alte Pinakothek, 1826), theaters etc. University (founded 1472, brought to Munich 1826). Many public buildings, badly damaged in the 2nd world war, have been restored, e.g. the Gothic cathedral (1468–88) and town hall (1470)

Munich Agreement a pact signed Sept. 29–30, 1938 by Neville Chamberlain, Hitler, Mussolini and Daladier, by which the Sudetenland was surrendered to Nazi Germany without Czech consent. This appeasement of Hitler encouraged further German aggression

mu·nic·i·pal (mjuːnísipˈl) *adj.* of, relating to or carried on by local self-government (esp. of a town, city etc.) [fr. L. *municipalis*]

municipal access channel cable television channel available for community use

municipal borough a borough in England or Wales with certain powers of self-government but included within an administrative county

mu·nic·i·pal·i·ty (mjuːnɪsəpǽliti:) *pl.* **mu·nic·i·pal·i·ties** *n.* a town, city or district having powers of local self-government ‖ the corporation or council which governs this [F. *municipalité*]

mu·nic·i·pal·i·za·tion (mjuːnɪsəpˈlizéiʃən) *n.* a municipalizing or being municipalized

mu·nic·i·pal·ize (mjuːnísəpˈlaiz) *pres. part.* **mu·nic·i·pal·iz·ing** *past* and *past part.* **mu·nic·i·pal·ized** *v.t.* to bring under municipal authority and control

mu·nif·i·cence (mjuːnífisˈns) *n.* the quality or state of being munificent ‖ an instance of this [F.]

mu·nif·i·cent (mjuːnífisˈnt) *adj.* lavish in giving ‖ characterized by generosity, *a munificent bequest* [fr. L. *munificens (munificentis)*]

mu·ni·ments (mjúːnəmənts) *pl. n.* (*law*) a document or documents kept as evidence of title or privilege [O.F.]

mu·ni·tion (mjuːníʃən) **1.** *n.* (*pl.*) military stores and equipment of all kinds, esp. ammunition and weapons **2.** *v.t.* to provide with munitions [F.]

Mu·ñoz Ma·rín (múːnjəsmaríːn), Luis (1898–1980), Puerto Rican politician and first elected governor (1948–60). He introduced (1952) a new constitution which defined Puerto Rico as an Associated Free State

Mun·ro (mənróu), H.H. *SAKI

Mun·ster (mʌ́nstər) the southernmost province (area 9,315 sq. miles, pop. 882,002) of the Irish Republic, comprising Clare, Cork, Kerry, Limerick, Tipperary and Waterford counties ‖ (*hist.*) an ancient kingdom of S. Ireland

Mün·ster (mýnstər) the historic capital (pop. 266,000) of Westphalia, in North Rhine-Westphalia, West Germany, center of an agricultural region. Industries: coal mining, brewing, food processing. Gothic cathedral (13th c.), town hall (14th c.). University (1780)

Mun·te·ni·a (mʌntíːniːə) the eastern part of Walachia

Muntz metal (mʌnts) an alloy of copper (60%) and zinc, harder than brass, used esp. for sheathing and bolts [after G. F. *Muntz* (1794–1857), Eng. metal manufacturer]

mu·on (mjúːɒn) *n.* (*phys.*) an unstable lepton of mass $105.66 + 10^6 eV$ and charge -1 found in cosmic rays [shortened fr. MU-MESON]

mu·on·i·um (muːóuniːəm) *n.* (*phys.*) an atom made up of an electron plus a positively charged mu-meson

Mu·rad I (murád) (c. 1326–89), Ottoman sultan (c. 1362–89). He extended the Ottoman Empire into Europe, making Adrianople his capital. He conquered Serbia at Kosovo Polje (1389), but was killed in the battle

mu·ral (mjúərəl) **1.** *adj.* of, relating to or like a wall ‖ on a wall, *mural paintings* **2.** *n.* a fresco or painting made directly on a wall [F.]

mu·ram·ic acid [$C_9H_{17}NO_7$] (*chem.*) a glucosamine joined to lactic acid that occurs in the walls of bacteria cells

Mu·ra·sa·ki Shi·ki·bu (muːrasaki:ʃi:ki:bu:) (Lady Murasaki) 11th-c. Japanese court writer, author of the romantic novel 'The Tale of Genji'

Mu·rat (myræ), Joachim (1767–1815), French marshal, king of Naples (1808–15). A brilliant cavalry commander, he helped Napoleon in the coup d'état of Brumaire (1799), and married (1800) Napoleon's sister. He was executed after Waterloo

Mur·chi·son Falls (mártʃisˈn) a series of falls and rapids (1,200 ft in 70 miles) in the Shire in Malawi

Mur·chi·son Falls a waterfall (118 ft) of the White Nile, just above Lake Albert in Uganda

Mur·cia (múːrθjə) a region of S.E. Spain, comprising the provinces of Murcia, bordering the Mediterranean and Albacete, inland. It slopes down from the dry central highland to an irrigated coastal plain. Crops: esparto, olives, wines, citrus fruit, dates. Industries: oil refining, some mining, food processing, textiles.

Chief towns: Murcia (the historic capital), Cartagena. It was annexed (1266) by Castile

Murcia a province (area 4,453 sq. miles, pop. 957,903) occupying the southern part of the region of Murcia, Spain ‖ its capital (pop. 178,700) on the coastal plain. Industries: textiles (esp. silk), food processing, gunpowder. The center is medieval. Cathedral (14th–18th c.), part Gothic, part baroque. University (1915)

mur·der (máːrdər) **1.** *n.* (*law*) the unlawful killing of a human being with malice aforethought (cf. MANSLAUGHTER) ‖ an instance of this ‖ (*law*) the unlawful killing of a person under certain circumstances, e.g. during the committing of a serious felony, or when accompanied by cruelty, torture etc. ‖ killing that is morally reprehensible and brutal, or an instance of this ‖ (*pop.*) circumstances of great danger or hardship, *it was murder driving over Easter weekend* **2.** *v.t.* to kill (a human being) unlawfully with malice aforethought ‖ to kill brutally, *the bombing murdered most of the civilian population* ‖ to spoil or ruin by bad performance or interpretation, *to murder a sonata* ‖ *v.i.* to commit murder [O.E. *morthor*]

mur·der·er (máːrdərər) *n.* a person guilty of murder **mur·der·ess** *n.* a woman guilty of murder [fr. MURDER V. and fr. A. F. *mordreour, murdreour*]

mur·der·ous (máːrdərəs) *adj.* relating to, like, involving, or having the nature of murder ‖ capable of or intending to commit murder

mu·rex (mjúəreks) *pl.* **mu·ri·ces** (mjúərisiːz), **mu·rex·es** *n.* a mollusk of fam. *Muricidae,* esp. a member of genus *Murex,* secreting Tyrian purple [L.]

Mur·frees·bor·o (máːrfriːzbəːrou, máːrfriːzbʌrou) *STONES RIVER, BATTLE OF

mu·ri·ate (mjúəriːeit) *n.* (*commerce*) chloride [F.]

mu·ri·at·ic acid (mjuəriːǽtik) (*commerce*) hydrochloric acid [fr. L. *muriaticus,* pickled in brine]

murices alt. *pl.* of MUREX

Mu·ri·llo (muːríːljo), Bartolomé Esteban (1617–82), Spanish painter. He painted religious subjects, and beggar boys and street urchins, and scenes of humble life. A certain hard naturalism is characteristic of the early work, but it passes into a style of warmth and feeling, later much sentimentalized

Murillo (muːríːjo), Pedro Domingo (d. 1809), Bolivian patriot who led (1809) a movement which ousted the Spanish authorities. He convoked an open Cabildo (meeting of representatives) which proclaimed Bolivian independence, but he was executed in a subsequent Spanish resurgence

murk, mirk (məːrk) *n.* (*rhet.*) thick darkness, intense gloom [O.E. *mirce*]

murk·i·ly, mirk·i·ly (máːrkiliː) *adv.* in a murky way or manner

murk·i·ness, mirk·i·ness (máːrkiːnis) *n.* the state or quality of being murky

murk·y, mirk·y (máːrkiː) *comp.* **murk·i·er, mirk·i·er** *superl.* **murk·i·est, mirk·i·est** *adj.* (of a place, atmosphere, etc.) thickly dark, intensely gloomy ‖ (of air etc.) heavy with mist, smoke etc.

Mur·mansk (murmánsk) the only perpetually ice-free port (pop. 381,000) of the northern U.S.S.R., in the N. Kola Peninsula (R.S.F.S.R.): fishing, shipyards

mur·mur (máːrmər) *v.i.* to utter a murmur ‖ *v.t.* to utter (words) in a soft, low, indistinct voice [F. *murmurer*]

murmur *n.* soft, low and indistinct speech ‖ a continuous low, soft sound (e.g. of water in a stream) ‖ a subdued grumble, a half-suppressed expression of complaint or objection ‖ (*med.*) an abnormal sound of the heart as detected by the stethoscope **múr·mur·ous** *adj.* [F. *murmure*]

Mu·ro·ran (muːrɔːran) a port (pop. 124,000) and naval base of N. Hokkaido, Japan: iron and steel

Mur·phy (máːrfiː), Frank (1890–1949) U.S. associate justice of the Supreme Court (1940–9). He was mayor of Detroit (1930–3), Philippines governor-general (1933–5) and high commissioner (1935–6), governor of Michigan (1937–9) and U.S. attorney general (1939–40) before being appointed to the Supreme Court by Pres. Franklin D. Roosevelt. A liberal, he advocated civil rights and championed minorities

Mur·phy's law (máːrfiːz) a satiric principle based on the theory that if anything can go wrong, it will; nothing is as easy as it looks; and everything takes longer than you think it will

mur·rain (mə́rin, mʌ́rin) *n.* any of several infectious diseases in cattle or plants [F. *morine*]

Mur·ray, Mor·ay (mə́ri:, mʌ́ri:), James Stuart, 1st earl of (c. 1531–70), regent of Scotland (1567–70), son of James V. A Protestant, he was partly responsible for the success of the Scottish Reformation. He made every effort to prolong the imprisonment of Mary Queen of Scots, his half sister

Murray the longest river (about 1,600 miles, partly navigable in the wet season) of Australia, rising near Mt Kosciusko and flowing west, as the New South Wales–Victoria border, to the Indian Ocean near Adelaide

mur·rhine glass (mə́rin, mʌ́rin) modern delicate glassware of fluorspar embedded with pieces of colored glass [fr. L. *murrinus, murrhinus* fr. *murra*, a valuable material used to make vases]

Mur·rum·bidg·ee (mə·rəmbí:dʒi:, mʌ́rəmbi:dʒi:) a river of New South Wales, Australia, flowing 980 miles from the Alps to the Murray: irrigation

Mu·sa, Geb·el (dʒéb'lmú:sə) *SINAI

mus·ca·del (mʌ́skədél) *n.* muscatel

mus·ca·dine (mʌ́skədin, mʌ́skədain) *n.* a variety of grape having the flavor or odor of musk, esp. *Vitis rotundifolia* of the southern U.S.A. [perh. fr. Prov. *muscat* (fem. *muscade*) adj., muscat]

mus·cat (mʌ́skæt) *n.* a muscadine grape [F. fr. Port.]

Mus·cat and O·man *OMAN

mus·ca·tel (mʌ́skətél) *n.* a strong sweet dessert wine made from muscat grapes ‖ a raisin made from the muscat grape [O.F. *muscadel, muscatel* fr. Prov.]

mus·cle (mʌ́s'l) **1.** *n.* a bundle of fibers (in human and animal bodies) which have the property of contracting and relaxing and which produce motion ‖ that part of the body or flesh which is composed of such fibers ‖ muscular strength **2.** *v.i. pres. part.* **mus·cling** *past* and *past part.* **mus·cled** (esp. in) **to muscle in** (*pop.*) to push one's way in (to some situation) without invitation, esp. so as to take advantage of someone else's efforts [F. or fr. L. *musculus*]

—There are two main varieties of muscle: voluntary and involuntary. Voluntary muscle is striated in appearance and may be contracted at will. It is usually attached at each end to different bones, which it brings closer together (e.g. in bending the arm) when it contracts. Involuntary muscle is smooth in appearance and may not be contracted at will. It is found chiefly in internal organs, such as the intestine wall and the heart, whose function is automatic

mus·cle-bound (mʌ́s'lbaund) *adj.* having some muscles stiff and enlarged, often because of excessive exercise

mus·co·va·do (mʌ́skəvádou) *n.* unrefined sugar, moist and dark, obtained from sugarcane juice by evaporation and the draining off of the molasses [Span. *mascabado* adj., (of sugar) of lowest quality, unrefined]

Mus·co·vite (mʌ́skəvait) **1.** *n.* a native or resident of the city or former duchy of Moscow ‖ (*hist.*) a Russian **2.** *adj.* of or relating to the city or former duchy of Moscow ‖ (*hist.*) Russian [fr. Mod L. *Muscovita* fr. *Muscovia*, Muscovy]

mus·co·vite (mʌ́skəvait) *n.* common mica [earlier *Muscovy* glass]

Mus·co·vy (mʌ́skəvi:) *n.* (*hist.*) the grand duchy of Moscow ‖ (*hist.*) Russia when the grand duchy was the dominant power (14th c.–1703)

Muscovy duck *Cairina moschata*, a tropical American duck, widely domesticated. It has a small crest, is glossy black, and is larger than a mallard

mus·cu·lar (mʌ́skjulər) *adj.* of or affecting the muscles ‖ having well-developed muscles **mus·cu·lár·i·ty** *n.* [fr. L. *musculus*, muscle]

muscular dystrophy a chronic hereditary disease marked by progressive wasting of muscles

mus·cu·la·ture (mʌ́skjulətʃər) *n.* the muscular system in a body or organ [F.]

Muse (mju:z) *n.* (*Gk mythol.*) one of the nine daughters of Zeus and Mnemosyne, divinities who preside over the arts and inspire mankind. In most attributions Clio is Muse of history, Calliope of epic poetry, Euterpe of music, Thalia of comedy, Melpomene of tragedy, Terpsich-

---

ore of the dance, Erato of love poetry, Polyhymnia of sacred song and Urania of astronomy [F. fr. L. *musa* fr. Gk *mousa*]

muse (mju:z) *n.* (*rhet.*) the source of a poet's or artist's inspiration [MUSE above]

muse *pres. part.* **mus·ing** *past* and *past part.* **mused** *v.i.* to meditate, think reflectively [F. *muser*]

mu·sette (mju:zét) *n.* (*mus.*) a kind of gavotte with a drone bass ‖ (*mus., hist.*) a small bagpipe played esp. in 17th-c. and 18th-c. France [F.]

mu·se·um (mju:zí:əm) *n.* a building used for the preservation and exhibition of objects illustrating human or natural history, esp. the arts or sciences [L. fr. Gk *mouseion*, temple of the Muses]

museum piece an absurdly antiquated person or thing ‖ an old object fine enough to be in a museum

mush (mʌʃ) *n.* any soft pulpy mass ‖ cornmeal boiled in water and eaten hot, as porridge, or when cold, cut in slices and fried ‖ (*pop.*) mawkish sentimentality [prob. var. of MASH]

mush 1. *n.* a journey across snow with a dogsled **2.** *interj.* a cry to encourage dog teams **3.** *v.i.* to travel across snow with a dogsled [perh. corrup. of F. *marche*, to go forward]

mush·i·ness (mʌ́ʃi:nis) *n.* the state or quality of being mushy

mush·room (mʌ́ʃru:m, mʌ́ʃrum) **1.** *n.* the exposed fleshy fruiting body of some fungi (e.g. most basidiomycetes) that consists of a stem which arises from an underground mycelium, and a pileus whose lower surface is the site of spore development. Mushrooms are widely distributed and have a wide range of shape, color and taste. Many are edible, some are poisonous **2.** *adj.* of or made from mushrooms ‖ like a mushroom in shape or in rapidity of growth and decay **3.** *v.i.* to grow with sudden rapidity ‖ to expand or spread out at the end so as to resemble a mushroom (e.g. of atomic explosions in the upper atmosphere) ‖ to pick mushrooms [F. *mousseron* perh. fr. *mousse*, moss]

mush·y (mʌ́ʃi:) *comp.* **mush·i·er** *superl.* **mush·i·est** *adj.* soft and pulpy, like mush ‖ (*pop.*) mawkishly sentimental

mu·sic (mjú:zik) *n.* the art of giving structural form and rhythmic pattern to combinations of sounds produced instrumentally or vocally ‖ instrumental or vocal sounds that have been combined in this way ‖ the written score of a composition of such sounds ‖ such scores collectively ‖ musical compositions collectively, *the music of Schubert* ‖ any series or combination of pleasant sounds, e.g. of wind in trees, songs of birds etc. ‖ the quality of being harmonious and pleasant to the ear, *the music of Keats' odes* **to face the music** to meet the consequences (esp. punishment) without shirking **to put** (or **set**) **to music** to compose music for the words of (a poem etc.) so that it can be sung [F. *musique* fr. L. *musica* fr. Gk *mousikē* (*technē*), art of the Muse]

mu·si·cal (mjú:zik'l) **1.** *adj.* of, relating to or having the nature of music, *a musical composition* ‖ talented or skilled in music, esp. as a performer or composer ‖ fond of music **2.** *n.* a musical comedy [F.]

musical box (*Br.*) a music box

musical comedy a type of light and often spectacular theatrical or film entertainment made up of songs, dialogue and dances, connected loosely by some sentimental or humorous plot

mu·si·cale (mju:zikǽl) *n.* a concert, generally at someone's home, as a form of social entertainment [F. (*soirée*) *musicale*, musical evening party]

musical glasses a glass harmonica

mu·si·cas·sette (mju:zikəsét) *n.* a cassette of tapes of musical recordings

music box (*Am.=Br.* musical box) a box with a clockwork apparatus for playing one or more tunes

music hall a theater specializing in entertainment by singers, dancers, comics, impersonators etc. ‖ this entertainment as a genre

mu·si·cian (mju:zíʃən) *n.* a person skilled in music, esp. a composer or performer [F. *musicien*]

music of the spheres a celestial harmony thought by the Pythagoreans to be produced by the vibrations of the spheres in which the planets moved

mu·si·col·o·gist (mju:zikóludʒist) *n.* a specialist in musicology

---

mu·si·col·o·gy (mju:zikóludʒi:) *n.* the study of music, its history, forms, methods etc. [fr. MUSIC+Gk *logos*, word]

musk (mʌsk) *n.* a reddish-brown substance with a pungent, lasting odor, secreted in a small sac under the skin near the reproductive organs of the male musk deer, used as a basis for perfumes ‖ the smell of this substance ‖ any of several strong-smelling substances obtained from the muskrat, musk-ox etc., used in preparing perfume ‖ *Mimulus moschatus*, fam. *Scrophulariaceae*, a perennial North American plant, the hairy leaves of which have a musky smell ‖ any of several other plants with a musklike smell [F. *musc* fr. L.L. *muscus* fr. Gk]

musk deer *Moschus moschiferus*, a small, sturdy deer of central Asia which secretes musk

musk duck *Biziura lobata*, an Australian duck which exudes a musky odor during the breeding season ‖ the muscovy duck

mus·keg (mʌ́skeg) *n.* a sphagnum bog of N. North America ‖ a thick deposit of partly decayed vegetable matter characteristic of wet northern regions [of Algonquian origin]

mus·kel·lunge (mʌ́skəlʌndʒ) *n.* *Esox masquinongy*, fam. *Esocidae*, a large pike of North America, prized as a game fish [of Algonquian origin]

mus·ket (mʌ́skit) *n.* (*hist.*) a portable infantry firearm (16th–19th cc.), the early models of which were ignited by a match and the later ones by a flintlock **mus·ket·éer** *n.* (*hist.*) a soldier armed with a musket [F. *mousquet* fr. Ital. *moschetto*, sparrow hawk]

mus·ket·ry (mʌ́skitri:) *n.* muskets, musketeers, or the art of handling muskets ‖ (*mil.*) the art and practice of rifle-shooting [fr. F. *mousquetterie*]

Muskhogean *MUSKOGEAN

musk·mel·on (mʌ́skmelən) *n.* *Cucumis melo*, fam. *Cucurbitaceae*, a usually musky-smelling, edible melon native to Asia and widely cultivated in warm, dry climates ‖ any of several distinct varieties of this species, e.g. the cantaloupe

Mus·ko·ge·an, Mus·kho·ge·an (mʌskougí:ən) *n.* a family of North American Indian languages, incl. Choctaw, Chickasaw, Creek, Seminole etc., now spoken chiefly in Oklahoma ‖ a member of one of the peoples speaking these languages

musk-ox (mʌ́skɒks) *pl.* **musk-ox·en** (mʌ́skɒksən) *n.* *Ovibos moschatus*, fam. *Bovidae*, a shaggy, long-haired mammal of Greenland and the Arctic regions of North America, with a musky odor

musk·rat (mʌ́skræt) *n.* *Fiber zibethica* (or *Ondatra zibethica*), fam. *Cricetidae*, a brown aquatic rodent of North America, about 12 ins long, with webbed hind feet and a hairless tail. It has a strong, musky odor. It burrows in banks of streams ‖ the valuable pelt or fur of this animal

musk rose *Rosa moschata*, a rose of the Mediterranean region whose flowers smell of musk

musk·wood (mʌ́skwud) *n.* *Oleatria argophylla*, a musk-scented tree of Australasia ‖ *Guarea trichilioides*, a musk-scented tree of tropical America ‖ the wood of either of these trees

musk·y (mʌ́ski:) *comp.* **musk·i·er** *superl.* **musk·i·est** *adj.* of, like or smelling of musk.

Mus·lim (mʌ́slim, mʌ́zlim) *n. and adj.* Moslem

mus·lin (mʌ́zlin) *n.* a woven cotton material ranging from light, soft and fine (used e.g. for dresses, curtains etc.) to coarse (used e.g. in bookbinding). It may be bleached or unbleached [F. *mousseline* fr. Ital. *mussolina* fr. *Mussolo*, the town of Mosul, Iraq]

mus·quash (mʌ́skwɒʃ) *n.* the muskrat ‖ (esp. *Br.*) the fur of the muskrat [fr. Algonquian]

muss (mʌs) **1.** *n.* (*pop.*) a mess, muddle **2.** *v.t.* (*pop.*) to disarrange, confuse, make a mess of [prob. var. of MESS]

mus·sel (mʌ́s'l) *n.* any of several bivalve marine or freshwater mollusks of the class *Lamellibranchia*, having dark, more or less oval shells. They are usually fixed to submerged rocks. Many genera are edible. The shell lining of certain freshwater forms is used in the manufacture of buttons [O.E. *muscle* fr. L.L.]

Mus·set (mysei), Alfred de (1810–57), French Romantic writer. His poems include 'les Nuits' (1835–7). His autobiographical novel 'la Confession d'un enfant du siècle' (1836) reveals attitudes and difficulties of his generation. His witty, delicate plays include the romantic

---

drama 'Lorenzaccio' (1834) and the comedy 'On ne badine pas avec l'amour' (1834)

Mus·so·li·ni (mųsəlí:ni:), Benito (1883–1945), Italian Fascist dictator. A schoolteacher and journalist, he became a leading member of the Socialist party, but was expelled (1914) when he urged support of the Allies in the 1st world war. He organized (1919) the Fascist party with a nationalist, syndicalist and anti-communist policy, based on force, supported by black-shirted military squads. He increased his influence by playing on economic discontent, organized a march on Rome (1922), and was appointed prime minister. As 'Il Duce', the leader, he established a totalitarian dictatorship, invaded Ethiopia (1935), intervened (1936) on behalf of Franco in the Spanish Civil War, and formed the Rome-Berlin Axis with Hitler (1936). He declared war on the Allies (1940) but military defeats led to his overthrow (1943). The Germans restored him as a puppet in N. Italy (1943–5) until he was captured by partisans and shot

Mus·sorg·sky (musórgski:), Modest (1839–81), Russian composer. He sought to follow common speech inflection in his vocal works, in which he excelled, achieving great dramatic power in his operas, notably 'Boris Godunov'. Among his song cycles are 'The Nursery' and 'Songs and Dances of Death'. His instrumental works include 'Pictures at an Exhibition' (1874) for piano, and the orchestral 'St John's Night on the Bare Mountain', revised and retitled by Rimsky-Korsakov

Mus·sul·man (mʌ́səlmən) 1. *n.* a Moslem 2. *adj.* Moslem [Pers. *musulmán* fr. Arab.]

mus·sy (mʌ́si:) *comp.* **mus·si·er** *superl.* **mus·si·est** *adj.* (*pop.*) messy

Mus·ta·fa Ke·mal (mustafákemál) *ATATÜRK

must, musth (mʌst) *n.* (of a male elephant or camel) a periodic state of violent frenzied sexual excitement **on** (or **in**) **must** in this state [Urdu *mast* adj., fr. *mast*, intoxicated]

must 1. invariable auxiliary *v.*, *infin.* and *parts* lacking, *neg.* **must not, mustn't** (with *infin.*) to be obliged or required or compelled to, *you must do your best* ‖ to be certain, probable or likely to, *you must be tired by now, the evidence shows that he must have done it* 2. *n.* (*pop.*) something that should be done, seen, read etc. without fail, *this film is a must* [O.E. *mōste*, past of *mōt*, may, be permitted to]

must *n.* mustiness ‖ mold [perh. fr. MUSTY]

must *n.* the juice of grapes before or during fermentation [fr. L. *mustum* neut. of *mustus*, fresh, new]

mustache *MOUSTACHE

mus·ta·chi·os (mʌstǽʃi:ouz) *pl. n.* a moustache, esp. a flamboyant one [fr. Span. *mostacho* and Ital. *mostaccio*]

mus·tang (mʌ́stæŋ) *n.* a small, tough, half-wild horse of the southwest U.S. plains [prob. fr. Span. *mestengo*, stray animal]

mustang grape *Vitis candicans,* a vine of the southwestern U.S.A. which bears small, reddish, pungent grapes ‖ one of these grapes

mus·tard (mʌ́stərd) *n.* any of certain plants of genus *Brassica,* fam. *Cruciferae* (formerly considered to be members of genus *Sinapis*), having linear beaked pods and yellow flowers. Some species are grown as a fodder crop and as green manure, as well as for the seeds ‖ the powdered seed of these plants, used in preparing a sharp-tasting yellow paste eaten as a condiment, or used as a counter-irritant in poultices and plasters ‖ the condiment made from the powdered seeds ‖ the color of the ground seed, a dark yellow [O.F. *mostarde, moustarde*]

mustard gas a poisonous oily liquid (CH$_2$·CH$_2$·Cl)$_2$S, sprayed from bursting shells in the form of fine droplets which burn and blister the skin and lungs, often fatally, used esp. in the 1st world war

mustard oil an oil made from mustard seeds, esp. one used in making soap

mustard plaster a plaster containing powdered mustard used as a counterirritant and rubefacient

mus·ter (mʌ́stər) *n.* the assembling of men (esp. troops) for inspection, roll call etc. ‖ a group of men so assembled **to pass muster** to be reckoned just good enough for the purpose required [O.F. *mostre, moustre,* a showing]

muster *v.t.* to assemble (troops) for inspection, roll call etc. ‖ to gather together, *they managed to muster a hundred signatures* ‖ (*fig.,* often with 'up') to collect, summon, *to muster up one's courage* ‖ (with 'out') to discharge from military

service ‖ *v.i.* to assemble or gather together [O.F. *mostrer, moustrer,* to show]

muster roll a list of the men in a ship's company or in a military unit

musth *MUST (state of excitement)

must·i·ness (mʌ́sti:nis) *n.* the state or quality of being musty

mustn't (mʌ́s'nt) *contr.* of MUST NOT

must·y (mʌ́sti:) *comp.* **must·i·er** *superl.* **must·i·est** *adj.* smelling or tasting moldy, stale, e.g. of things kept in a damp place and shut in ‖ old-fashioned, out-of-date [perh. rel. to MOIST]

mu·ta·bil·i·ty (mju:təbíliti:) *n.* the quality or state of being mutable

mu·ta·ble (mjú:təb'l) *adj.* liable to change or capable of being changed [fr. L. *mutabilis*]

mu·ta·gen (mjú:tədʒən) *n.* (*genetics*) any substance that causes changes in the genetic structure in subsequent generations —**mutagenicity** *n.* the capability —**mutagenic** *adj.* —**mutageneity** *n.* the process

mu·tant (mjú:t'nt) 1. *n.* (*biol.*) an individual organism with transmissible characteristics different from those of the parents, sufficient to form a new variety or even species 2. *adj.* undergoing or produced by mutation [fr. L. *mutans* (*mutantis*) fr. *mutare,* to change]

mu·tate (mjú:teit) *pres. part.* **mu·tat·ing** *past and past part.* **mu·tat·ed** *v.i.* to undergo mutation ‖ *v.t.* to cause mutation in [fr. L. *mutare* (*mutatus*), to change]

mu·ta·tion (mju:téiʃən) *n.* a changing or being changed ‖ (*biol.*) the hypothetical occurrence of new forms, arising through change in gene construction of the nucleus and differing sufficiently from the parent forms to constitute new varieties ‖ (*biol.*) the process by which such new forms arise ‖ (*biol.*) a mutant so produced ‖ (*linguistics*) umlaut ‖ (*linguistics*) the change, under certain conditions, of the initial consonant of a word ‖ (*mus.*) an organ stop which sounds a pitch equal to some harmonic (other than an octave) of the note played [F. *mutacion, mutation*]

mu·ta·tive (mjú:tətiv) *adj.* of, relating to or characterized by mutation [O.F. *mutatif*]

mute (mju:t) 1. *adj.* not speaking, not uttering a sound‖ permanently unable to utter meaningful speech, esp. as a result of being deaf from birth ‖ unable to make vocal sounds ‖ expressed by nonvocal means, *mute adoration* ‖ (*law*) refusing to plead, *to stand mute* ‖ (of a letter) not pronounced though written, e.g. the 'e' in 'late' ‖ (*phon.,* of a consonant) produced with momentary complete closure of the breath passage ‖ (*hunting,* of hounds) not giving tongue 2. *n.* a person who cannot speak, esp. a deaf-mute ‖ (*phon.*) a stop ‖ a clip clamped on the bridge of a stringed instrument to deaden the resonance of the strings ‖ a pad or cone-shaped piece of metal or other material inserted in the bell of a wind (esp. brass) instrument to deaden or distort the sound 3. *v.t. pres. part.* **mut·ing** *past and past part.* **mut·ed** to deaden or soften the sound of [M.E. *muet* fr. F.]

mu·ti·late (mjú:t'leit) *pres. part.* **mu·ti·lat·ing** *past and past part.* **mu·ti·lat·ed** *v.t.* to hack or tear off a limb or other important part of (a person or animal) ‖ to damage (something) seriously by destroying or removing some essential part of it [fr. L. *mutilare* (*mutilatus*)]

mu·ti·la·tion (mjú:t'léiʃən) *n.* a mutilating or being mutilated ‖ the resulting injury [fr. L. *mutilatio* (*mutilationis*)]

mu·ti·la·tor (mjú:t'lei̯tər) *n.* someone who mutilates

mu·ti·neer (mju:t'niər) *n.* someone guilty of mutiny [F. *mutinier*]

mu·ti·nous (mjú:t'nəs) *adj.* guilty of or inclined to mutiny ‖ rebellious, unruly [fr. earlier *mutine* fr. F. *mutin*]

mu·ti·ny (mjú:t'ni:) 1. *pl.* **mu·ti·nies** *n.* open revolt against lawful authority, esp. against naval or military authority 2. *v.i. pres. part.* **mu·ti·ny·ing** *past and past part.* **mu·ti·nied** to revolt against lawful authority, esp. naval or military authority [earlier *mutine* fr. F. *mutin*]

mu·tism (mjú:tizəm) *n.* inability or failure to speak, e.g. as a symptom of mental disease [fr. F. *mutisme*]

Mu·tsu·hi·to (mų:tsu:hí:tou) (1852–1912), emperor of Japan (1867–1912), known during his reign as Meiji. His reign marked the end of feudalism and isolation in Japan, and the start of the modernization of the country. Under the guidance of Ito, Japan began to industrialize,

and a western constitution was introduced (1889)

mutt (mʌt) *n.* (*pop.*) a mongrel dog [short for *muttonhead,* a stupid person]

mut·ter (mʌ́tər) 1. *v.i.* to speak in a low, indistinct voice with the lips nearly closed ‖ to murmur in annoyance or complaint ‖ *v.t.* to utter in a low, indistinct voice with the lips nearly closed 2. *n.* muttered sound or words [prob. imit.]

mut·ton (mʌ́t'n) *n.* the flesh of a full-grown sheep as food [M.E. *motoun, motom* fr. O.F.]

mut·ton·chops (mʌ́t'ntʃɒps) *pl. n.* side whiskers that are narrow near the ears and broad by the jaws

Mut·tra (mútrə) *MATHURA

mu·tu·al (mjú:tʃu:əl) *adj.* given to each other by each of two people, *mutual affection* ‖ (of two people) having the same relationship to each other, *mutual friends* ‖ done, shared or experienced in common by all members of a group, *mutual effort* [F. *mutuel*]

mutual fund a joint-stock company with no fixed capitalization, which invests in the stock of other companies

mutual insurance a form of insurance in which policyholders elect the company's officers and share its profits

mu·tu·al·ism (mjú:tʃu:əlizəm) *n.* the belief that mutual dependence is an essential underlying factor in the attainment of social well-being ‖ (*biol.*) symbiosis

mu·tu·al·i·ty (mjú:tʃu:æliti:) *n.* the quality or state of being mutual

mu·tule (mjú:tʃu:l) *n.* (*archit.*) a projecting block forming part of a Doric cornice [fr. F. fr. L. *mutulus,* modillion]

Mu·zak (mjú:zæk) *n.* trade name for piped-in recorded background music available in public places

muzhik *MOUJIK

muz·zi·ly (mʌ́zili:) *adv.* in a muzzy manner

muz·zi·ness (mʌ́zi:nis) *n.* the state or quality of being muzzy

muz·zle (mʌ́z'l) 1. *n.* the part of the head consisting of the projecting jaws and nose in certain animals, e.g. dogs, wolves and bears ‖ a cagelike contrivance of wires or straps put over this part of an animal (esp. a dog) to prevent it from biting or eating ‖ the mouth of a gun, where the bullet or shell comes out when fired 2. *v.t. pres. part.* **muz·zling** *past and post part.* **muz·zled** to put a muzzle on (an animal, esp. a dog) ‖ to prevent (criticism etc.) from being expressed [O. F. *musel, muzel, muisel*]

muzzle velocity the velocity with which a projectile leaves the gun

muz·zy (mʌ́zi:) *comp.* **muz·zi·er** *superl.* **muz·zi·est** *adj.* thickheaded and confused, esp. from liquor ‖ blurred, indistinct, *a muzzy outline* ‖ vague, showing mental confusion, *muzzy ideas* [perh. fr. obs. *mossy,* stupid]

MVP (*sports abbr.*) most valuable player

Mwan·za (mwanzə) a port (pop. 11,000) on southern Lake Victoria, Tanzania, terminus of the Dar-es-Salaam railroad

Mwe·ru (mwéiru:) a lake (area 1,700 sq. miles) between Zambia and the People's Republic of the Congo, at 3,000 ft

MX (*mil.*) U.S. land-based intercontinental, 86-ton missile with 10 warheads, carrying 300 kilotons with 8,000-mi range; 100-yd accuracy

my (mai) *possessive adj.* belonging to or relating to me ‖ (*prefixed,* in forms of address) connoting affection, familiarity, condescension etc., *my dear, my friend* ‖ used in interjections expressing surprise, shock, dismay etc. [M.E. *mī,* a shortened form of O.E. *mīn*]

my·al·gia (maiǽldʒə) *n.* pain in a muscle or in the muscles [Mod. L. fr. Gk *mus,* muscle+*algos,* pain]

my·ce·li·al (maisí:li:əl) *adj.* of or having the nature of mycelium **my·ce·li·an** *adj.*

my·ce·li·um (maisí:li:əm) *pl.* **my·ce·li·a** (maisí:li:ə) *n.* the network of entwined hyphae forming the typical vegetative structure of the thallus of fungi, varying considerably in size and manner of spreading [Mod. L. fr. Gk *mukēs,* mushroom+EPITHELIUM]

My·ce·nae (maisí:ni:) an ancient city of Argolis, Greece, seat of the kingdom of Agamemnon and center of the Mycenaean civilization. Principal remains: the royal palace, Lion Gate and Treasury of Atreus

My·ce·nae·an (maisəní:ən) *adj.* of the civilization which developed on the Greek mainland, influenced by Minoan Crete, and which reached its height c. 1400–1200 B.C.

my·ce·to·zo·an (maisị:təzóuən) *n.* (in former classifications) a myxomycophyte formerly regarded as a protozoan [fr. Mod. L. *Mycetozoa* fr. Gk *mukēs*, mushroom+*zōia*, animals]

my·co·bac·te·ri·um (máikoubæktíari:əm) *pl.* **my·co·bac·te·ri·a** (máikoubæktíəri:ə) *n.* a member of *Mycobacterium*, a genus of nonmotile, aerobic, gram-positive bacteria. M. *tuberculosis hominis* causes tuberculosis in man and M. *t. bovis* causes it in cattle and in man. *M. leprae* causes leprosy [Mod. L. fr. Gk *mukēs*, fungus+BACTERIUM]

my·col·o·gy (maikólədʒi:) *n.* that part of botany which deals with the study of fungi ‖ the fungal life of a region ‖ the life cycle of a fungus [fr. Gk *mukēs*, fungus+*logos*, word]

mycoplasma *PPLO

my·cor·rhi·za, my·co·rhi·za (maikəráizə) *n.* the association of fungal mycelium with roots of a higher plant, a partial symbiosis. The fungus takes on the function of root hairs which are lacking and forms a layer outside the root or within the outer tissues **my·cor·rhi·zal, my·co·rhi·zal, my·cor·rhi·zic, my·co·rhi·zic** *adjs* [Mod. L. fr. Gk *mukēs*, fungus+*rhiza*, root]

my·co·sis (maikóusis) *m.* (*med.*) any disease caused by fungi **my·cot·ic** (maikótik) *adj.* [fr. Gk *mukēs*, fungus]

my·co·tox·i·co·sis (maikoutoksikóusis) *n.* (*med.*) poisoning by a bacterial mold or fungus toxin, usu. from ingested food —**mycotoxic** *adj.* —**mycotoxin** *n.* Cf AFLATOXIN

my·dri·a·sis (midráiəsis) *n.* prolonged or excessive dilatation of the pupil of the eye **myd·ri·at·ic** (midri:ǽtik) **1.** *adj.* causing such dilatation **2.** *n.* a mydriatic agent, e.g. belladonna [L.L. fr. Gk]

my·e·lin, my·e·line (máiəlin) *n.* a white fatty substance forming the medullary sheath of certain nerve fibers [G. *myelin*, fr. Gk *muelos*, marrow]

my·e·li·tis (maiəláitis) *n.* an inflammation of the spinal cord or bone marrow [Mod. L. fr. Gk *muelos*, marrow]

my·e·lo·fi·bro·sis (maiəloufaibróusis) *n.* (*med.*) an increase in the fibrous connective tissue in the bone marrow, usu. caused by trauma — **myelofibrotic** *adj.*

my·e·loid (máiələid) *adj.* of or relating to the spinal cord ‖ of or relating to the bone marrow [fr. Gk *muelos*, marrow]

my·e·lo·pro·lif·er·a·tive syndrome (máiəloupralífərətiv) (*med.*) proliferation of one or more elements of the bone marrow

Myk·o·nos (míkənɔs) an island (area 35 sq. miles, pop. 4,000) in the Cyclades, Greece

My Lai (mí:lái) **incident** (1968) massacre of about 300 Vietnamese civilians by U.S. troops in a small village, My Lai, in Vietnam, that was known to be a rebel fortress. U.S. infantrymen, under Capt. Ernest Medinia and Lt. William Calley, Jr., expecting to encounter rebel forces, lashed out at all they encountered, killing women and children also. Some members of the infantry company were prosecuted by the U.S. Army, but only Calley was convicted (for the murder of 22 Vietnamese civilians)

My Lai (mí:lái) *n.* village in South Vietnam where the population was massacred by U.S. troops in 1968 on theory that area was a Vietcong base. The murders became a key issue in polarizing antiwar sentiment in U.S., *My Lai* is often used as an eponym or metaphorically

My·lar (máilɑr) *n.* (*chem.*) DuPont trade name for a polyester film plastic used for insulation, backing for magnet tape, balloons, etc. and as a polyester film used to cover a metallic yarn

my·na, my·nah, *Br.* esp. **mi·na** (máinə) *n.* any of several Asian starlings, esp. *Gracula religiosa*, often tamed and taught to imitate human speech, and *Acridotheres tristis*, an aggressive bird destructive to crops [Hindi *mainā*]

my·o·car·di·al (maiəkárdi:əl) *adj.* of or relating to the myocardium

my·o·car·di·um (maiəkárdi:əm) *pl.* **my·o·car·di·a** (maiəkárdi:ə) *n.* the middle muscular layer of the heart wall (cf. ENDOCARDIUM) [Mod. L. fr. Gk *mus* (*muos*), muscle+*kardiā*, heart]

my·o·e·lec·tric (maiouəléktrik) *adj.* (*physiol.*) of the use of electric power produced by muscles to move prosthetic devices —**myoelectrical** *adj.* —**myoelectrically** *adv.* —**myoelectricity** *n.*

my·o·gram (máiəgræm) *n.* a record of the force, speed etc. of muscular contractions [fr. Gk *mus* (*muos*), muscle+*gramma*, letter, piece of writing]

my·o·graph (máiəgræf, máiəgrɑf) *n.* an instrument for making a myogram [fr. Gk *mus* (*muos*), muscle+*graphos*, written]

my·ol·o·gy (maiólədʒi) *n.* the branch of anatomy dealing with muscles [fr. Mod. L. fr. Gk *mus* (*muos*), muscle+*logos*, word]

my·o·ma (maióumə) *pl.* **my·o·ma·ta** (maióumətə), **my·o·mas** *n.* a tumor consisting of muscular tissue **my·ó·ma·tous** *adj.* [Mod. L. fr. Gk *mus* (*muos*), muscle]

my·o·pi·a (maióupi:ə) *n.* the inability to see distant objects distinctly owing to a condition of the eye in which light from distant objects is brought to a focus before reaching the retina. This structural defect, which is common, is corrected by divergent spectacle lenses **my·op·ic** (maiópik) *adj.* relating to or affected by this condition [Mod. L. fr. Gk]

my·o·sin (máiəsin) *n.* a soluble protein present in contractile muscle fibers [fr. Gk *mus* (*muos*), muscle]

myosis *MIOSIS

my·o·so·tis (maiəsóutis) *n.* a member of *Myosotis*, a genus of plants with small blue, pink or white flowers, including the forget-me-not, growing in the temperate regions of both hemispheres [L. fr. Gk *muosōtis* fr. *mus* (*muos*), muscle+*ous* (*ōtos*), ear]

myotic *MIOTIC

my·o·tome (máiətoum) *n.* a muscular metamere of primitive vertebrates and segmented invertebrates [fr. Gk *mus* (*muos*), muscle+*tomē*, cutting]

Myrdal (méirdɑl), **Alva Reimer** (1902–86), Swedish sociologist, co-winner of the Nobel Peace Prize (1982), wife of Karl Gunnar Myrdal. She was Sweden's disarmament negotiator at the U.N. (1962–73) and a cabinet minister for disarmament and church affairs (1966–73). She wrote 'The Crisis in the Population Question' (1934) and 'The Game of Disarmament' (1978). She shared the Nobel Prize with Mexico's Alfonso García Robles

Myrdal, (**Karl**) **Gunnar** (1898–   ), Swedish sociologist and economist, co-winner of the Nobel Prize for economics (1974), husband of Alva Reimer Myrdal. Executive secretary of the UN's Economic Commission for Europe (1947–57) and Stockholm's Institute of International Studies' director, he shared the Nobel Prize with Friederich von Hayek for their money theories and economic and social relations analyses. He wrote 'An American Dilemma: The Negro Problem and Modern Democracy' (1944) and 'Challenge of World Poverty' (1970)

myr·i·ad (míri:əd) **1.** *n.* (usually *pl.* with 'of') a very large number, *myriads of insects* **2.** *adj.* countless, very many [fr. M.L. *myrias* (*myriadis*) fr. Gk *murias* (*muriados*) fr. *murioi*, ten thousand]

myr·i·a·pod, myr·i·o·pod (míri:əpɔd) *n.* a member of *Myriapoda* or *Myriopoda*, the lowest class of arthropodous animals, chiefly comprising *Chilopoda* (centipedes) and *Diplopoda* (millipedes) [fr. Mod. L. fr. Gk *murias*, many+*pous* (*podos*), foot]

myr·me·col·o·gy (mə:rmikólədʒi:) *n.* the scientific study of ants [fr. Gk *murmēx* (*murmēkos*), ant+*logos*, word]

myr·me·coph·i·lous (mə:rmikófələs) *adj.* (of certain insects) liking ants or helped by ants [fr. Gk *murmēx* (*murmēkos*), ant+*-philos*, loving]

Myr·mi·don (mə:rmidən) *n.* one of the Thessalian followers of Achilles at the siege of Troy

myr·mi·don (mə:rmidən) *n.* (*rhet.*) a loyal follower ‖ (*rhet.*) a subordinate who carries out orders unquestioningly and pitilessly [after MYRMIDON]

my·rob·a·lan (mairóbələn) *n.* the dried astringent fruit of any of several trees of the genus *Terminalia*, fam. *Combretaceae*, native to the East Indies. It contains tannin [F. *myrobolan* or L. *myrobalanum* fr. Gk]

My·ron (máirən) (5th c. B.C.), Greek sculptor. He worked chiefly in bronze, and his works, depicting action and expression, represent a breaking away from the formalism of the Archaic period

myrrh (mə:r) *n.* a gum resin with a sweet smell and a bitter taste, obtained from the bark of trees of genus *Commiphora*, fam. *Burseraceae*, in E. Africa and Arabia, and used in making perfumes, medicines, dentifrices and incense [O.E. *myrra* fr. L. *myrrha* fr. Gk fr. Semitic]

myr·tle (mə́:rt'l) *n.* a member of *Myrtus*, fam. *Myrtaceae*, a genus of fragrant evergreen plants native to W. Asia, long cultivated in Europe as ornamental trees, esp. *M. communis*, the Euro-

pean myrtle ‖ *Vinca minor*, a periwinkle [O.F. *mirtille*, *myrtille* fr. L.]

my·self (maisélf) *pron.* refl. form of 'I', *I knocked myself out* ‖ emphatic form of 'I', *I gave him the money myself* [M.E *meself*, *miself* fr. O.E. *me sylf*]

My·sore (maisór) a state, now called Karnataka, (area 74,210 sq. miles, pop. 33,600,000) of S. India on the Arabian Sea, divided between the Western Ghats (teak, ebony, cedar, bamboo, sandalwood) and an elevated plain in the east (rice, peanuts, cotton, fruit, tea, coffee). Capital: Bangalore. Minerals: gold (Kolar Gold Fields), manganese, iron ore, chromite. Industries: hydroelectricity, textiles, engineering, chemicals, food processing ‖ a commercial city (pop. 438,385) in the south, capital of the old landlocked state of Mysore. Industries: textiles (esp. silk), sandalwood oil, engineering. University (1916). Palace (1897)

mys·ta·gog·ic (mistəgódʒik) *adj.* of, relating to or characteristic of a mystagogue **mys·ta·góg·i·cal** *adj.*

mys·ta·gogue (místəgɔg, místəgɔg) *n.* someone who propounds a mystical doctrine, esp. (*hist.*) someone who initiated candidates into sacred mysteries (e.g. the Eleusinian mysteries) **mys·ta·go·gy** (místəgoudʒi:) *n.* [fr. L. *mystagogus* fr. Gk fr. *mustēs*, someone initiated into mysteries+*agōgis*, leading]

mys·te·ri·ous (mistíəri:əs) *adj.* of, relating to or characterized by mystery, suggestive of hidden secrets ‖ difficult or impossible to understand or interpret [fr. L. *mysterium*, mystery]

mys·te·ri·um (mistíri:əm) *n.* (*astron.*) hypothetical celestial body in the Milky Way that emits radio signals; possibly created by linking of hydrogen and oxygen with odd number of electrons, in a distinctive pattern

mys·ter·y (místəri:) *pl.* **mys·ter·ies** *n.* something that cannot be or has not been explained or understood, *he kept his activities a mystery* ‖ the quality or state of being incomprehensible or inexplicable, or of being kept a secret, *an air of mystery* ‖ a detective story ‖ (*pl.*) secret religious rites not revealed to the uninitiated, esp. those of ancient religions ‖ a religious tenet which rests on revelation and cannot be understood in terms of human reason ‖ a medieval religious drama based on a biblical theme [M.E. *misterye, mysterye* fr. A.F. fr. L. *muein*, to close (the lips or eyes)]

mys·tic (místik) **1.** *adj.* of or relating to mystics or mysticism ‖ of or relating to ancient religious mysteries ‖ having a hidden, secret, esoteric meaning, *a mystic formula* ‖ (*loosely*) mysterious, enigmatic **2.** *n.* a person who believes in mysticism, has mystical experiences or follows a mystical way of life **mýs·ti·cal** *adj.* of or relating to mysticism, spiritually true or real in a way which transcends man's reason, *the mystical union between Christ and his Church* **mys·ti·cism** (místisizəm) *n.* the doctrine or belief that direct spiritual apprehension of truth or union with God may be obtained through contemplation or insight in ways inaccessible to the senses or reason ‖ the experience of such direct apprehension of truth or union with God [O.F. *mystique* fr. L. *mysticus* fr. Gk *mustikos*, relating to secret rites]

mys·ti·fi·ca·tion (mistifikéiʃən) *n.* a mystifying or being mystified ‖ something that mystifies [fr. F.]

mys·ti·fy (místifai) *pres. part.* **mys·ti·fy·ing** *past* and *past part.* **mys·ti·fied** *v.t.* to puzzle, bewilder, baffle ‖ to make mysterious, surround with mystery [fr. F. *mystifier*]

mys·tique (misti:k) *n.* a quasi-mystical set of attitudes adopted towards some idea, person, art or skill, investing it with an esoteric significance [F. *mystique* adj., mystic]

myth (miθ) *n.* an old traditional story or legend, esp. one concerning fabulous or supernatural beings, giving expression to the early beliefs, aspirations and perceptions of a people and often serving to explain natural phenomena or the origins of a people etc. ‖ such stories collectively ‖ (*loosely*) any fictitious story or account or unfounded belief, *the myth of his superiority* ‖ (*loosely*) a person or thing with no real existence, *his rich uncle is a myth* [fr. Mod. L. *mythus* fr. Gk *muthos*]

myth·ic (míθik) *adj.* mythical **mýth·i·cal** *adj.* of, designating, relating to or existing in myth, *mythical gods* ‖ imaginary, nonexistent, *mythical wealth* **mýth·i·cize** *pres. part.* **mýth·i·cizing** *past* and *past part.* **myth·i·cized** *v.t.* to interpret as a myth ‖ to cause to become a myth [fr. L.L. *mythicus* fr. Gk]

myth·o·gen·ic (mɪθədʒénik) *adj.* of the formation of myths

myth·o·log·i·cal (mɪθəlódʒik'l) *adj.* of or pertaining to mythology [fr. L.L. *mythologicus* fr. Gk]

my·thol·o·gist (mɪθólədʒist) *n.* someone who makes a study of mythology ‖ someone who compiles myths or retells them [fr. L. *mythologus* fr. Gk]

my·thol·o·gize (mɪθólədʒaiz) *pres. part.* **my·thol·o·giz·ing** *past* and *past part.* **my·thol·o·gized** *v.i.* to classify, compare or write about myths ‖ to invent myths ‖ *v.t.* to mythicize

my·thol·o·gy (mɪθólədʒi:) *pl.* **my·thol·o·gies** *n.* a body of myths, esp. those relating to a people's gods and heroes and to their origins, or those

connected with a certain subject, *the mythology of plants* ‖ myths collectively ‖ the study of myths [F. *mythologie* or fr. L.L. *mythologia*]

myth·o·ma·ni·a (mɪθəméini:ə) *n.* an abnormal tendency to tell lies **myth·o·ma·ni·ac** (mɪθəméini:æk) *n.* and *adj.* [Mod. L. fr. Gk *muthos*, myth+MANIA]

myth·o·poe·ic (mɪθəpíːik) *adj.* myth-creating, *a mythopoeic people* [fr. Gk *muthopoios* fr. *muthos*, myth+*poiein*, to make]

Myt·i·le·ne (mɪt'líːniː) *LESBOS

myx·e·de·ma, myx·oe·de·ma (mɪksədíːmə) *n.* a disease caused by thyroid deficiency, marked by dryness and swelling of the skin and abnormal torpor [fr. Gk *muxa*, mucus+EDEMA]

myx·o·ma·to·sis (mɪksəmətóusis) *n.* a contagious, usually fatal virus infection of rabbits

[Mod. L. fr. *myxomata*, pl. of *myxoma*, a slimy, jellylike tumor fr. Gk]

myx·o·my·cete (mɪksoumaisíːt) *n.* a member of *Myxomycetes*, a subdivision of fungi in former classifications, now considered a separate phylum (*MYXOMYCOPHYTE) **myx·o·my·cé·tous** *adj.* [fr. Mod. L. *Myxomycetes* fr. Gk *muxa*, mucus+*mukēs*, mushroom]

Myx·o·my·ce·tes or **Mycetozoa** (mɪksoumeísiːtiːs) *n.* (*botany*) a group of simple organisms similar to fungi and protozoa, known as slime molds, that live on rotten wood and may be pathogenic to human beings

myx·o·my·co·phyte (mɪksoumáikəfait) *n.* a thallophyte of the phylum *Myxomycophyta*, comprising the slime molds [fr. Mod L. fr. Gk *muxa*, mucus+*mukēs*, mushroom+*phuton*, plant]

CONCISE PRONUNCIATION KEY: (a) æ, cat; ɑ, car; ɔ fawn; ei, snake. **(e)** e, hen; iː, sheep; iə, deer; ɛə, bear. **(i)** i, fish; ai, tiger; əː, bird. **(o)** o, ox; au, cow; ou, goat; u, poor; ɔi, royal. **(u)** ʌ, duck; u, bull; uː, goose; ə, bacillus; juː, cube. x, loch; θ, think; ð, bother; z, Zen; ʒ, corsage; dʒ, savage; ŋ, orangutang; j, yak; ʃ, fish; tʃ, fetch; 'l, rabble; 'n, redden. Complete pronunciation key appears inside front cover.

	EARLY NORTH SEMITIC	PHOENICIAN	EARLY HEBREW (GEZER)	EARLY GREEK	CLASSICAL GREEK	ETRUSCAN Early	ETRUSCAN Classical	EARLY LATIN	CLASSICAL LATIN
N	𐤍	𐤍	𐤍	Ν	Ν	Ν	Ν	Ν	N

	CURSIVE MAJUSCULE (ROMAN)	CURSIVE MINUSCULE (ROMAN)	ANGLO-IRISH MAJUSCULE	CAROLINE MINUSCULE	VENETIAN MINUSCULE (ITALIC)	N. ITALIAN MINUSCULE (ROMAN)
	ᴚ	n	Ꞑ	n	n	n

A. C. SYLVESTER, CAMBRIDGE, ENGLAND

Development of the letter N, beginning with the early North Semitic letter. Evolution of both the majuscule, or capital, letter N and the minuscule, or lowercase, letter n are shown.

N, n (en) the 14th letter of the English alphabet ‖ (*math.*) an indefinite number, *to the power of n, to the nth degree* ‖ (*printing*) an en

N, N. North, Northern

NAA (*abbr.*) of neutron activation analysis (which see)

N.A.A.C.P. *NATIONAL ASSOCIATION FOR THE ADVANCEMENT OF COLORED PEOPLE

nab (næb) *pres. part.* **nab·bing** past and *past part.* **nabbed** *v.t.* (*pop.*) to arrest ‖ (*pop.*) to get for oneself, by quick thinking or snatching [etym. doubtful]

Nab·a·tae·an (næbətíən) *n.* a member of an Arab people who established a kingdom (c. 312 B.C.–c. 106 A.D.) centered on Petra in Palestine

nab·la (næblə) *n.* a stringed musical instrument of the ancient Hebrews ‖ (*math.*) the symbol ∇, an inverted delta [Gk. of Semitic origin]

Nab·lus (næbləs) an agricultural center (pop. 444,233) of N. Jordan. As Shechem it was the capital of Samaria

na·bob (néibɒb) *n.* (*hist.*) a Moslem official under the Mogul emperors in India ‖ a very rich or distinguished person, esp. (*hist.*) a European returned from the East with a fortune [fr. Urdu *nawwāb*]

Na·bo·kov (nɑbókʌf, nábəkɔf), Vladimir (1899–1977), Russo-American novelist. He wrote 'Lolita' (1955), 'Pnin' (1957), 'Pale Fire' (1962), 'Ada' (1969), 'Transparent Things' (1972), and 'Harlequins' (1974)

Na·both (néibɒθ) an Israelite whose vineyard was seized by King Ahab after Naboth had refused to sell it and had been stoned to death on the orders of Jezebel, the king's wife (I Kings xxi)

Na·bu·co de A·rau·jo (nɑbú:kɔdearáuʒɔ), Joaquim Aurelio (1849–1910), Brazilian writer, abolitionist hero, and diplomat

na·celle (nəsél) *n.* an engine housing on an aircraft wing ‖ a housing under a dirigible for personnel or engines [F.]

Nach·ti·gal (náxtiɡɑl), Gustav (1834–85), German explorer. He explored the kingdom of Bornu and the region of Lake Chad (1869–74)

na·cre (néikər) *n.* mother-of-pearl **na·cre·ous** (néikri:əs) *adj.* [F.]

NAD (*biochem. abbr.*) of nicotinamide adinine dinucleotide, a coenzyme necessary for conversion of glucose to alcohol

Nader (néidər), Ralph (1934–), U.S. consumer advocate. He discovered and published information on consumer hazards beginning with auto safety ('Unsafe at Any Speed,' 1965). He founded study groups and organizations to research tax reform and health issues, develop citizen action groups, monitor the activities of Congress, lobby for new legislation, and finance legal action. He also advocated the creation of a federal office to represent consumer interests in regulatory hearings and decision-making

Na·der·ism (néidərizəm) *n.* Consumerism, after American reformer Ralph Nader

na·dir (néidiər, néidər) *n.* the lowest point, *the nadir of despair* ‖ the point of the celestial sphere diametrically opposite to the zenith [fr. Arab. *nadir* (as-samt), opposite to (the zenith)]

Na·dir Shah (nádiərʃá) (1688–1747), king of Persia (1736–47). He conquered Afghanistan (1738) and much of India (1739), and subdued the Russians and the Turks. His rule degenerated into a brutal tyranny

Nae·vi·us (ní:vi:əs), Gnaeus (c. 270–c. 200 B.C.), Roman poet and dramatist. Only fragments of his work survive. He took part in the 1st Punic War and evokes it in his epic 'Poenicum Bellum'

naevus *NEVUS

Na·fud, Ne·fud (nəfú:d), a red sandy desert in Saudi Arabia, north of the Great Sandy Desert

nag (næɡ) **1.** *v. pres. part.* **nag·ging** past and *past part.* **nagged** *v.t.* to scold or find fault with repeatedly ‖ *v.i.* to cause annoyance by scolding or repetition ‖ to cause persistent discomfort, *a nagging pain* **2.** *n.* a person who nags [prob. fr. Scand.]

nag *n.* an inferior or aged horse [etym. doubtful]

Na·ga (nágə) *n.* a member of one of a group of peoples of mixed origin and cultures inhabiting the Naga Hills ‖ a language of any of these peoples

Naga Hills a wooded range along the northern India-Burma border, between the Brahmaputra and Upper Chindwin valleys. Highest peak: Japvo (9,890 ft)

Na·ga·land (nágəlænd) a state (area 6,236 sq. miles, pop. 774,930) of N.E. India, in the Naga Hills: lumber, subsistence farming. Capital: Kohima. Formerly administered by Assam, it became an Indian state in 1963 after several years of fighting

na·ga·na (nəgánə) *n.* a fatal disease, carried by the tsetse fly, among horses and cattle in tropical Africa [fr. Zulu *u-nakane*]

Na·ga·sa·ki (nɒɡəsáki:, nægəsǽki) a seaport (pop. 450,246), coaling station and shipbuilding center of W. Kyushu, Japan. It was rebuilt after being almost totally destroyed (Aug. 9, 1945) by a U.S. atomic bomb during the 2nd world war

Na·go·ya (nagɔ́jə) an industrial center and port (pop. 2,108,400) of E. central Honshu, Japan: heavy engineering (cars, aircraft) and precision tools, porcelain, pottery. Buddhist and Shinto temples (11th c.). University (1949)

Nag·pur (nágpuər) a railroad center (pop. 1,219,461) of N.E. Maharashtra, India. Industries: cotton, textiles, metallurgy. University (1923)

Naguib *NEGUIB

Nagy (nɒdʒ), Imre (c. 1896–1958), Hungarian Communist statesman, prime minister of Hungary (1953–5 and 1956). He was executed by the Soviet police for siding with the Hungarian revolution of 1956

Na·ha (náhə) the chief port (pop. 304,550) of Okinawa, Ryukyu Is: textiles, pottery

Na·hal (náhal) *n.* Israeli army corps that establishes border agricultural settlements —**nahal** *n.* the settlement

Na·hua·tl (náwɑt'l) *n.* a group of peoples of southern Mexico and parts of Central America ‖ a member of this group ‖ the Uto-Aztecan language spoken by these peoples. About 700,000 use it **Na·hua·tlan** (náwɑtlən) *adj.*

Na·huel Hua·pí, Lake (nɑwélwɑpí:) a lake in the Andes Mtns (300 sq. miles, depth 1,000 ft in places) in S.W. Argentina, near the Chilean border

Na·hum (néihəm) a Minor Prophet (7th c. B.C.) of the Old Testament ‖ the book of the Old Testament containing his prophecies, including a description of the fall of Nineveh (which took place in 612 B.C.)

nai·ad (náiæd, néiæd) *pl.* **nai·ads, nai·a·des** (náiədi:z, néiədi:z) *n.* (*Gk and Rom. mythol.*) any of the nymphs who presided over springs and rivers [fr. L. *Naïas* (*Naïadis*) fr. Gk fr. *nan*, to flow]

na·if, na·ïf (nɑí:f) *adj.* naïve [F.]

nail (neil) *n.* the hard thin covering on the upper surface of the ends of the fingers or toes of men, monkeys etc. ‖ the claw of a bird or animal ‖ a thin, usually metal, spike, driven into an object (esp. wooden) to join it to another or to fix something to it **a nail in one's coffin** an experience etc. that is thought to shorten life, *the shock was another nail in his coffin* **hard as nails** hardhearted ‖ capable of bearing hardship **on the nail** (of payment) at once **to hit the nail on the head** to be or to find just the right words to describe or explain something accurately [O.E. *nægel*]

nail *v.t.* to fix with a nail ‖ to secure, *to nail a contract* ‖ to fix the attention of, *he nailed the audience with his accounts of the tortures* ‖ to prove (a lie) to be false ‖ (*pop.*) to catch, *to nail a thief* **to nail (a person) down** to obtain a definite promise or consent from (a person) **to nail one's colors to the mast** to declare fully and openly opinions to which one commits oneself [O.E. *næglan*]

CONCISE PRONUNCIATION KEY: **(a)** æ, c*a*t; ɑ, c*ar*; ɔ f*aw*n; ei, sn*a*ke. **(e)** e, h*e*n; i:, sh*ee*p; iə, d*ee*r; εə, b*ea*r. **(i)** i, f*i*sh; ai, t*i*ger; ə:, b*ir*d. **(o)** o, *o*x; au, c*ow*; ou, g*oa*t; u, p*oo*r; ɔi, r*oy*al. **(u)** ʌ, d*u*ck; u, b*u*ll; u:, g*oo*se; ə, b*a*cillus; ju:, c*u*be. x, lo*ch*; θ, *th*ink; ð, bo*th*er; z, *Z*en; ʒ, cor*s*age; dʒ, sava*g*e; ŋ, ora*n*gutang; j, *y*ak; ʃ, *f*ish; tʃ, fe*tch*; 'l, rabb*le*; 'n, redd*en*. Complete pronunciation key appears inside front cover.

nail polish (*Am.*=*Br.* nail varnish) a preparation, usually colored, used to give a glossy coating to fingernails or toenails

nail varnish *NAIL POLISH

nain·sook (néinsuk) *n.* a delicate cotton fabric used esp. in lingerie or infants' wear [fr. Hindi *nainsukh* fr. *nain*, eye+*sukh*, pleasure]

Nai·ra (náirə) *n.* currency unit in Nigeria, equal to 100 kobe (k)

Nairn (nɛərn) a former county of N.E. Scotland. In 1975 it became part of the Highland region

Nai·ro·bi (nairóubi:) the capital (pop. 827,800) of Kenya, in the central highlands (at 5,742 ft), a trade and communications center. Industries: meat packing, food processing, light manufactures. Royal College (1956) of the University of East Africa (1963)

Nai·smith (néismiθ), James (1861–1939), U.S. physical education director and inventor (1891) of the game of basketball

na·ive, na·ïve (naí:v) *adj.* lacking worldly experience or guile ‖ innocently direct but lacking mental power, *a naïve question* [F. fem. of *naïf*]

na·ive·té, na·ïve·té (naj:vtéi) *n.* simplicity, artlessness ‖ a naïve act etc. **na·ive·ty** (naí:vti:) *n.* [F.]

Nakasone Yasuhiro (nakasoúna jasuhírou) (1918–) Japanese statesman. He held various high government and Liberal-Democratic party posts during the 1960s and 1970s and became prime minister (1982–), stressing an active role for Japan in international affairs

na·ked (néikid) *adj.* without clothes, *we swam naked* ‖ (of parts of the body) uncovered, *a naked arm* ‖ without vegetation, leaves etc., *naked rock, naked trees* ‖ without decoration, *naked walls* ‖ undisguised, *the naked truth* ‖ (of a sword) out of its sheath ‖ without supplementary material, *a naked report* ‖ (*law*) lacking proven authority or evidence of validity, *a naked contract* **with the naked eye** without the aid of an optical instrument **ná·ked·ness** *n.* [fr. O.E. *nacod*]

Na·khi·che·van A.S.S.R. (nakitʃəván) an autonomous republic (area 2,120 sq. miles, pop. 231,000) of Azerbaijan, U.S.S.R., forming an enclave in Armenia on the Turkish and Iranian borders. Capital: Nakhichevan (pop. 21,000). The economy is based on agriculture (fruit, grapes, cotton, tobacco) and related industries

Na·khon Rat·si·ma (nakhɔnratsi:mə) (formerly Korat) a trade and communications center (pop. 114,000) in S. central Thailand: copper mines

Na·ku·ru (nakú:ru:) a town (pop. 66,000) in the Kenya Highlands, at 6,000 ft, on the Mombasa railroad

na·led [C₄H₇O₄PBr₂Cl₂] (néiled) *n.* (*chem.*) slightly toxic short-lived insecticide used against mosquitoes and in crop pest control

nal·i·dix·ic acid [C₁₂H₁₂N₂O₃] (neilədíksikǽsid) *n.* (*pharm.*) genitourinary antiseptic; marketed as NegGram

nal·ox·one [C₁₉H₂₁NO₄] (naelɒksoun) *n.* (*pharm.*) narcotic antagonist, esp. effective against morphine; marketed as Narcan

namable *NAMEABLE

Na·ma·qua·land (nəmákwəlænd) (or Namaland) a semiarid region (area about 100,000 sq. miles) in W. Namibia (Great Namaqualand), below Walvis Bay, and in N.W. Cape Province, South Africa (Little Namaqualand): cattle, sheep (esp. Karakul), wheat, diamonds, copper

nam·by-pam·by (næmbi:pǽmbi:) **1.** *adj.* weakly sentimental, lacking proper hardness, *a namby-pamby tale* **2.** *pl.* **nam·by-pam·bies** *n.* a boy or man lacking the physical and mental toughness properly expected of him [after the nickname of Ambrose Philips (c. 1675–1749), English poet who wrote sentimental pastorals]

name (neim) **1.** *n.* a word or words by which a person, place or thing is known ‖ a word or words by which an object of thought is known, *we give the name 'honor' to those qualities by which a good man wishes to be valued* ‖ a reputation, *this firm has a name for good workmanship* ‖ a noted person, *he is a great name in medicine* **by name** with individual mention, *he listed his pupils by name* ‖ by reputation but not by personal acquaintance, *they knew the lecturer by name* **in name, in name only** by mere designation but not in reality **in the name of** using the authority of, *I arrest you in the name of the law* ‖ with appeal to, *in the name of common sense* **to call (someone) names** to speak abusively to or of (someone) **to one's name** belonging to one, *she hadn't a penny to her name* **to put one's name down for** to apply for membership of (a club etc.) ‖ to have one's name put on a list as wishing to receive (publicity etc.) or take advantage of (an offer of some sort) **2.** *v.t. pres. part.* **nam·ing** *past* and *past part.* **named** to give a name to ‖ to identify by name, *the delinquent was named in court* ‖ to appoint, *he was named chancellor of the university* ‖ to specify, *name your weapon* ‖ (of the Speaker of the House of Commons) to mention (a member) by name as a reprimand **3.** *adj.* well-known, renowned, *a name brand* ‖ bearing, or intended for, a name, *name tag* **náme·a·ble, nám·a·ble** *adj.* [O.E. *nama*]

name day the feast day of the saint after whom a person is named

name-drop·ping (néimdrɒpiŋ) *n.* the practice of mentioning important people in conversation as one's friends, as a display of self-importance

name·less (néimlis) *adj.* not known by name, *a nameless hero* ‖ not mentioned by name, *a journalist who must be nameless gave me these facts* ‖ having no name ‖ too subtle or mysterious to name, *nameless wonders* ‖ too bad to name, *nameless crimes*

name·ly (néimli:) *adv.* that is to say, *England has two ancient universities, namely Oxford and Cambridge*

name of the game (often preceded by "the") the essential thing; the objective or essence of a project

name part (esp. *Br.*) a title role

name·plate (néimpleit) *n.* a plaque bearing the name of a person or firm

name·sake (néimseik) *n.* a person having the same name as another

Na·mib (námib) the desert coastal strip of Namibia, about 60 miles wide

Na·mib·i·a (nəmíbi:ə) (South West Africa) a territory (area 318,261 sq. miles, pop. 1,086,000) administered in effect as a part of South Africa. Capital: Windhoek. People: Bantu (Ovambo, Herero and Bergdamara), Hottentot (Nama), and Bushman, with 14% European and 5% Colored. Language: tribal languages, Afrikaans, German, English. Religion: mainly local African religions, 17% Lutheran, 9% Roman Catholic. The land is chiefly a plateau, averaging 3,500 ft and rising to 8,669 ft (Moltkeblick) near Windhoek. The Caprivi Strip (the territory's corridor to the Zambezi) and the far north are tropical forest, the north and center are savanna, giving way to semidesert (*KALAHARI) in the south and east. A 60-mile-wide coastal strip forms the Namib Desert, containing the isolated Brandberg Massif (8,481 ft). Average summer temperatures (F.): Windhoek 74°, Walvis Bay 60°. Inland below 6,000 ft there is intense summer heat. Rainfall: north and northeast over 20 ins, Windhoek highlands 12 ins, Namib Desert under 1 in. Livestock: cattle (north and center), sheep and goats (south). Industries: mining (diamonds, lead-copper-zinc and lead-vanadium concentrates, salt, copper, lime, cyanite, beryl, manganese), fishing, fish processing, ranching, subsistence farming. Exports: minerals, cattle, dairy products, fish, Karakul pelts. Chief port: Walvis Bay. HISTORY. The territory was annexed (1884) by Germany and was mandated by the League of Nations to South Africa (1920). South Africa virtually annexed it (1949), despite protests by the U.N. The U.N. terminated (1966) the mandate but South Africa described this as illegal, continued its administration, and prevented the U.N. administrative council from entering the area until 1967, when Namibia received its name. In 1973 the U.N. General Assembly recognized the South West Africa People's Organization (SWAPO) as the 'authentic representative of the Namibian people' and in 1978 called for withdrawal of South African troops. In 1976 Namibian whites and moderate blacks agreed on a constitution, but it was rejected by the U.N. Security Council and SWAPO. In Jan. 1983 South Africa again took direct control of Namibia and the question of independence became tied to Cuban troop withdrawal from Angola

Na·mur (næmyr) a French-speaking province (area 1,413 sq. miles, pop. 382,000) of S.W. Belgium: stone quarrying, kaolin, glass industry, tourism ‖ its capital (pop. 101,861) noted for cutlery and copper work. Citadel and cathedral (18th c.), baroque church (17th c.)

Na·nak (nánək) (1469–c. 1539), Indian religious leader, founder of Sikhism

Na·na Sa·hib (nánəsáhi:b) (Dandhu Panth, c. 1825–c. 1860), Indian leader of the Indian Mutiny (1857)

Nan·chang (nántʃán) the capital (pop. 508,000) of Kiangsi, S.E. China, at the tip of Poyang Hu on the Hangchow–Canton railroad: porcelain, textiles, engineering, chemical industries

Nan·cy (nási:) the main city (pop. 99,000, with agglom. 278,000) of Meurthe-et-Moselle, France, on the Rhine-Marne canal, old capital of Lorraine (12th–18th cc.). Industries: mechanical and electrical engineering, food processing, light manufacturing. Palace (16th c.), cathedral (18th c.). University (1768)

NAND or **NAND operator** (naend) *n.* (*computer*) a logical operator with the property that, if *P, Q,* and *R* are statements, the nand of *P, Q, R* is true if at least one statement is false, and false if all statements are true

Nan·ga Par·bat (nʌ́ŋgəpárbət) a peak (26,660 ft) in the Western Himalayas, Kashmir

nan·keen (næŋkí:n) *n.* a kind of buff-colored cotton cloth orginally imported from Nanking, China [after NANKING]

Nan·king (næŋkíŋ, nánkíŋ) the capital (pop. 2,130,000) of Kiangsu, E. China, the country's traditional literary center, on the Yangtze 170 miles east of Shanghai. Industries: silk and cotton textiles, mechanical and precision engineering, chemicals. University (1921). It was the capital of China (3rd–6th cc. and 1368–1421). The treaty ending the Opium War was signed here (1842). It was held (1853–64) by the Taiping rebels. It fell (1937) to the Japanese. The Kuomintang forces reoccupied it (1945–9). It contains the tombs of the first Ming emperor and of Sun Yat Sen

Nan·ling (nánlíŋ) a mountain range (rising to 6,000 ft) stretching from S.E. Kweichow to N. Kwangtung, China

nannie *NANNY

Nan·ning (náníŋ) (formerly Yungning) the capital (pop. 264,000) of Kwangsi-Chuang, S. China: an agricultural center linked by rail with North Vietnam

nan·ny, nan·nie (næni:) *pl.* **nan·nies** *n.* (esp. *Br.*) a child's nurse [fr. the name *Nan*, dim. of *Ann*]

nanny goat a female goat

nan·o (nænou) (*comb. form*) combining form meaning one billionth (10⁻⁹), e.g., nanoequivalent, nanometer, nanomole, nanovolt, nanowatt

nan·no·plank·ton or **nan·o·plank·ton** (nænouplǽŋktən) *n.* (*biol.*) microscopic plankton — **nannofossil** or **nanofossil** fossil of nannoplankton

nan·no·sur·ger·y (naenousə́:rdʒəri:) *n.* (*med.*) microsurgery conducted under an electron microscope; 10,000 times finer than microsurgery utilizing electron microscope and laser beams

Nan·sen (nánsən), Fridtjof (1861–1930), Norwegian scientist, polar explorer, politician and humanitarian. He crossed the Greenland ice sheet on skis (1888), explored the North Polar basin by letting his ship the 'Fram' drift in the pack ice, and reached 86° 14' N. by dog sled (1893–6). He was the League of Nations' chief organizer of relief for refugees and prisoners of war (1921–30). Nobel Peace Prize (1922)

Nan Shan (nánʃán) the northern range of the Kunjun Mtns, in Kansu and Tsinghai, central China, rising to 20,000 ft

Nantes (nắt) the chief town (pop. 256,693) of Loire-Atlantique, France, a port at the head of the Loire estuary. Industries: shipbuilding, food processing, metallurgy. Gothic cathedral (15th–19th cc.), castle (15th–18th cc.), 18th-c. houses

Nantes, Edict of an order promulgated (1598) by Henri IV of France, granting freedom of worship to French Protestants. Its revocation (1685) by Louis XIV caused many Huguenots to flee from France and weakened France diplomatically and economically

Nan·tuck·et (næntʌ́kit) an island (area 45 sq. miles, pop. 5,087) of Massachusetts, 25 miles off Cape Cod, with an excellent harbor. It was formerly (18th–19th cc.) a great whaling port, and is now a resort

Nantucket Sound a channel (c. 30 miles long, 25 miles wide) between the south coast of Cape Cod and Nantucket Is., S. E. Massachusetts, joining the Atlantic Ocean and Vineyard Sound

Nan·tung (nántúŋ) a town (pop. 260,000) on the Yangtze estuary, Kiangsu, E. China: cotton mills

nap (næp) **1.** *v.i. pres. part.* **nap·ping** *past* and *past part.* **napped** to sleep for a short time, esp. by day **to be caught napping** to be caught off guard **2.** *n.* a short sleep, esp. by day [O.E. *hnappian*]

nap 1. *n.* the soft, fuzzy surface on cloth or wool material (cf. PILE) **2.** *v.t. pres. part.* **nap·ping** *past* and *past part.* **napped** to raise such a surface on, by brushing, stroking etc. [M.E. *noppe*, prob. fr. Du.]

nap 1. *n.* (esp. *Br.*) napoleon (card game) ‖ napoleon (bid in this game) ‖ (*Br.*) a tip that a particular horse is almost certain to win a race **2.** *v.t. pres. part.* **nap·ping** *past* and *past part.* **napped** (*Br.*) to tip (a horse etc.) strongly [NAPOLEON]

na·palm (néipɑm) *n.* a fuel, made from jellied gasoline, used in incendiary bombs and flame-throwers ‖ a chemical thickener used in making this [fr. *naphthenic* and *palmitic* acids]

nape (neip) *n.* the back of the neck [M.E., etym. doubtful]

na·per·y (néipəri:) *n.* household linen, esp. table linen [M.E. fr. M.F. *naperie*]

Naph·ta·li (næftəlai) Hebrew patriarch, son of Jacob ‖ the Israelite tribe of which he was the ancestor

naph·tha (næfθə) *n.* any of several volatile mixtures of hydrocarbons obtained by distilling coal, tar, or petroleum and used as fuels, solvents and thinners for paint and varnish [L. fr. Gk]

naph·tha·lene (næfθəli:n) *n.* an aromatic binuclear crystalline hydrocarbon $C_{10}H_8$, occurring in coal tar and used in the manufacture of organic dyestuffs and as a fumigant (e.g. in mothballs) [NAPHTHA]

naph·thene (næfθi:n) *n.* any of a series of saturated cyclic paraffins of the general formula C_nH_{2n} that occur in petroleum and that yield aromatic hydrocarbons on dehydrogenation [NAPHTHA]

naph·thol (næfθɔl, næfθoul) *n.* either of two crystalline monohydroxy derivatives of naphthalene ($C_{10}H_7OH$), used as antiseptics and in making dyes ‖ any of several hydroxyl derivatives containing a naphthalene nucleus [NAPHTHA]

Na·pi·er (néipi:ər), Sir Charles James (1782–1853), British general. He served in the Peninsular War, and he led the British conquest of Sind (1841–3)

Napier, John (1550–1617), Scottish mathematician. He invented logarithms, and described their use in his 'Mirifici logarithmorum canonis descriptio' (1614). He also devised other methods of rapid calculation and introduced decimal notation

Napier the capital (pop. 42,900) of Hawke's Bay, North Island, New Zealand, a port

Napier's bones a set of graduated rods used for multiplication and division [after John *Napier*]

na·pi·form (néipi:fɔrm) *adj.* (*biol.*, of roots) having the shape of a turnip [fr. L. *napus*, turnip]

nap·kin (næpkin) *n.* a cloth used at meals for wiping the fingers and lips ‖ a sanitary towel ‖ (*Br.*) a diaper [M.E. perh. fr. F. *nappe*, tablecloth]

Na·ples (néipəlz) (*Ital.* Napoli) the third city (pop. 1,219,362) and second port of Italy, in Campania, built on hills rising around the Bay of Naples. Industries: tourism, food processing, shipbuilding, some metallurgy, oil refining and chemicals. The characteristic architecture is baroque. University (1224), National Museum. First a Greek colony, Naples became a favorite Roman resort, was conquered (6th c.) by the Byzantines, and became an autonomous duchy (763–1139). The Normans incorporated it (1140) in the Kingdom of the Two Sicilies, of which it was the capital (1282–1503)

Na·po (nápɔ) a river (c. 550 miles long) rising in the mountains of N. central Ecuador, flowing across the Peruvian border, and emptying into the Amazon

na·po·le·on (nəpóuli:ən) *n.* a former French gold coin worth 20 francs issued (1805) by Napoleon I and used during the 19th c. ‖ a card game in which each player has five cards and bids the number of tricks he expects to win. Payment is made to or by the highest bidder, according to his bid ‖ a bid of five tricks in this game, scoring double [after NAPOLEON]

Na·po·le·on I (nəpóuli:ən) (*F.* Napoléon Bonaparte, *Ital.* Napoleone Buonaparte, 1769–1821), emperor of the French (1804–15). A Corsican, born at Ajaccio, he was educated at military schools in France and entered the French army (1785). He welcomed the French Revolution, expressed Jacobin views, and distinguished himself at the siege of Toulon (1793). Briefly imprisoned after Thermidor, he was recalled by Barras, and successfully dispersed the Vendémiaire uprising (1795). He married (1796) Joséphine de Beauharnais. Napoleon's military genius was displayed in his command (1796–7) of the Italian campaign, in which he brilliantly defeated the Austrians and, on his own initiative, established the Cisalpine Republic and negotiated the Treaty of Campo-Formio (1797). He commanded (1798–9) an expedition to Egypt with the object of cutting England's route to India. He defeated the Mamelukes at the Battle of the Pyramids (1798), but was marooned in Egypt when Nelson destroyed the French fleet at the Battle of the Nile (1798). Napoleon escaped from Egypt (1799) and returned to France, where he overthrew the Directory in the coup d'état of Brumaire (1799). A member of the ensuing Consulate, he rapidly established a dictatorship with himself as first consul (1799–1804). Peace with Austria was established at Lunéville (1801) after further victories over Austria, at Marengo (1800) and Hohenlinden (1800), and the Peace of Amiens (1802) was signed with Britain. In France, Napoleon embarked on a thorough program of reform in which education and local government were reorganized, the currency stabilized and the Napoleonic Code established. A Concordat was negotiated with the papacy (1801). A plebiscite (1802) made Napoleon consul for life, and in 1804 he was proclaimed emperor of the French, crowning himself in the presence of the Pope. War with Europe was resumed in the Napoleonic Wars (1803–15), in which Napoleon gained a series of brilliant victories at Ulm (1805), Austerlitz (1805), Jena (1806), Friedland (1807) and Wagram (1809). Having failed at sea (Trafalgar, 1805), Napoleon tried to reduce Britain by an economic blockade, the Continental System. By 1808 he controlled the whole of continental Europe, which now included many puppet kingdoms ruled by members of the Bonaparte family. His first marriage was annulled, and he married (1810) Marie-Louise. He made their son king of Rome. The weakness of Napoleon's Empire was first shown in the Peninsular War (1808–14), and in his disastrous invasion of Russia (1812). After the retreat from Moscow, his depleted army was defeated (1813) at the Battle of the Nations. Napoleon abdicated (1814) and was exiled to Elba, but returned (1815), marched on Paris and tried to restore his empire during the Hundred Days. After his final defeat at Waterloo (1815), he was sent by the British to St Helena, where he was kept prisoner until his death. Napoleon, one of the greatest conquerors in history, displayed a genius for military tactics and civil administration. The legend which portrayed him as a champion of liberalism and nationalism grew in the 19th c., and helped his nephew, Napoleon III, to gain power in France. His remains were brought back to France (1840)

Na·po·le·on·ic (nəpouli:ónik) *adj.* of or relating to Napoleon I [NAPOLEON]

Napoleon II (1811–32), son of Napoleon I and Marie-Louise, known as the king of Rome (1811–14), prince of Parma (1814–18), duke of Reichstadt

Napoleon III (Louis Napoléon Bonaparte, 1808–73), emperor of the French (1852–70), son of Louis Bonaparte. In exile after 1815, he elaborated the Napoleonic legend in his book 'les Idées napoléoniennes' (1839). Having twice attempted unsuccessfully to raise military insurrection (1836, 1840), he returned to France after the revolution of 1848 and was elected president by a vast majority. A coup d'état (1851) and further plebiscites made him emperor (1852). His dictatorship, modified after 1859 by liberal reforms, brought prosperity. Banking, industry and agriculture were encouraged, and Paris was boldly replanned by Haussmann. Napoleon III intervened in Rome (1849) to restore the papacy, and the Crimean War (1854–6) increased French influence in Europe. He agreed with Cavour to intervene (1859) in Italy in return for Savoy and Nice, but withdrew when Italian unity threatened the Papal States. France acquired Cochinchina, and the Suez Canal was built. A French expedition to Mexico (1861–7) ended in disaster, and Napoleon III was lured by Bismarck into the Franco-Prussian War (1870–1), in which the regime collapsed. After a short imprisonment, he went into exile (1871) in England

Napoleonic Code the code of laws for France promulgated (1804) by Napoleon. It was based on Roman law, and follows the Corpus Juris Civilis in dividing civil law into personal status, property and the acquisition of property. It influenced most European countries except Britain, and, with amendments, is still in force in France

Napoleonic Wars the wars (1803–15) in which France under Napoleon I fought two coalitions of European powers. The Peace of Amiens having provided only a brief respite after the French Revolutionary Wars, Britain declared war on France (1803). Napoleon assembled a fleet at Boulogne to invade Britain, but the project collapsed when British naval supremacy was established at Trafalgar (1805). A coalition was formed against France (1805) by Britain, Austria, Russia and Sweden, but was crushed, Austria being defeated at Ulm (1805) and Austria and Russia at Austerlitz (1805). Prussia joined the coalition, and was beaten at Jena (1806). Russia's defeats at Eylau and Friedland (1807) were followed by the Treaty of Tilsit (1807). Napoleon defeated Sweden (1807). Austria tried to renew the war and was crushed at Wagram (1809). Napoleon now controlled nearly all the Continent: the Holy Roman Empire was dissolved (1806), and Germany was reorganized in the Confederation of the Rhine. The Helvetic Confederation and the Grand Duchy of Warsaw were bound to France by alliances. Napoleon appointed Jérôme Bonaparte king of Westphalia, Louis Bonaparte king of Holland, Joseph Bonaparte king of Spain, Eugène de Beauharnais king of Italy and Murat king of Naples. Britain alone remained, and Napoleon attempted to reduce it by an economic blockade, the Continental System, which proved impossible to enforce. The Peninsular War (1808–14) showed the weakness of Napoleon's Empire. Russia rejected the Continental System and was invaded (1812) by Napoleon, whose vast army reached Moscow but was much reduced by the Russian scorched-earth policy, and retreated under winter conditions which killed thousands more. A new coalition against France was formed (1813) by Prussia, Russia, Britain, Sweden and Austria and they were victorious at the Battle of the Nations (1813). The allies advanced on Paris, and Napoleon, having abdicated, was exiled to Elba. Louis XVIII took the French throne, and the Congress of Vienna assembled (1814) but rapidly dispersed (1815) when Napoleon returned to Paris. At the end of the Hundred Days he was finally defeated at Waterloo (1815). The Congress of Vienna resumed and worked out a European settlement

nappe (næp) *n.* a sheet of water falling from a weir ‖ (*geol.*) a recumbent anticline [F. *nappe*, tablecloth]

nap·py (næpi:) *pl.* **nap·pies** *n.* (*Br.*, *pop.*) a baby's diaper [NAPKIN]

Na·ra (nárə) a city (pop. 274,000) of S. Honshu, Japan, the country's first capital 710–84. Buddhist temple (7th c.)

Nar·ba·da (nərbádə) a river, sacred to Hindus, flowing 800 miles from central Madhya Pradesh, India, to the Arabian Sea

nar·ce·ine (nársi:i:n) *n.* a bitter crystalline alkaloid, $C_{23}H_{27}NO_8$, found in opium, sometimes used as a substitute for morphine [F. *narcéine* fr. Gk *narkē*, numbness]

nar·cis·sism (nársisizəm) *n.* a tendency to erotic self-love ‖ morbid or excessive self-admiration **nár·cis·sist** *n.* **nar·cis·sís·tic** *adj.* [after NARCISSUS (Gk mythol.)]

Nar·cis·sus (nərsísəs) (*Gk mythol.*) a beautiful youth who fell in love with his own reflection in water, died, and was turned into the flower that bears his name

nar·cis·sus (nərsísəs) *pl.* **nar·cis·si** (nərsísai), **nar·cis·sus·es** *n.* a member of *Narcissus*, fam. *Amaryllidaceae*, a genus of plants with white or yellow flowers growing from a bulb (*DAFFODIL, *JONQUIL) [L. fr. Gk *narkissos*]

nar·co·lep·sy (nárkəlepsi:) *n.* a disease marked by episodes of uncontrollable sleepiness **nar-**

co·lép·tic *adj.* [fr. Gk *narkē*, numbness + *lēpsia*, fit]

narc or nark (nαrk) *n.* (*slang*) an official investigator of narcotics violations *also* **narco**

nar·co·a·nal·y·sis (nαrkouənǽlisis) *n.* (*chem.*) procedure for reducing inhibitions used by administering scopolamine barbiturates and methedrine or other drugs to facilitate questioning and analysis

nar·co·sis (nαrkóusis) *n.* a state of unconsciousness induced by narcotics [Gk *narkōsis* fr. *narkoun*, to benumb]

nar·cot·ic (nαrkótik) **1.** *n.* a drug which dulls sensibility, relieves pain and induces sleepiness ‖ a drug subject to legal definitions as a narcotic regardless of its chemical features, e.g., LSD, marijuana **2.** *adj.* pertaining to or having the effects of narcotics **nar·co·tism** (nαrkətizəm) *n.* narcosis ‖ addiction to narcotics [fr. M.L. *narcoticus* or Gk *narkōtikos*, benumbing]

nard (nαrd) *n.* spikenard [O.F. *narde* fr. L. fr. Gk perh. ult. fr. Skr.]

nar·ghi·le, nar·gi·leh (nάrgili:) *n.* a hookah [fr. Pers. *nārgīleh* fr. *nārgil*, coconut, of which the bowl was originally made]

Na·ri·ño (nɑri:njɔ), Antonio (1765–1823), Colombian patriot and early fighter for Colombian independence. He was a leader of the revolution (1810) in Bogotá. As president of Cundinamarca he defeated (1811) the federal and royalist forces

nar·is (nǽris) *pl.* **nar·es** (nǽri:z) *n.* a nostril or nasal passage [L.]

nark (nαrk) *v.t.* (*Br., pop.*) to annoy, make cross [origin unknown]

Nar·ra·gan·sett (nærəgǽnsit) *pl.* **Nar·ra·gan·sett, Nar·ra·gan·setts** *n.* a member of an extinct Indian people of Rhode Island ‖ their Algonquian language [Algonquian = people of the small cape]

Narragansett Bay an inlet of the Atlantic running 30 miles north from S.E. Rhode Island

nar·rate (nǽreit, nærǽit) *pres. part.* **nar·rat·ing** *past and past part.* **nar·rat·ed** *v.t.* to tell or write (a story) ‖ to give an account of (events) ‖ *v.i.* to act as storyteller [fr. L. *narrare* (*narratus*)]

narrater *NARRATOR

nar·ra·tion (næréiʃən) *n.* the act or process of narrating ‖ an account or story ‖ speaking or writing that narrates [F. or fr. L. *narratio* (*narrationis*)]

nar·ra·tive (nǽrətiv) **1.** *n.* an orderly description of events, *a historical narrative* ‖ the act or art of narrating ‖ that part of a prose work which recounts events (as distinguished from conversation) **2.** *adj.* of, relating to or having the form of a narrative [fr. L. *narrativus*]

nar·ra·tor, nar·rat·er (nǽreitər) *n.* a person who narrates, esp. someone providing connecting explanations or descriptive passages in a theatrical performance

nar·row (nǽrou) **1.** *adj.* small in width ‖ restricted in scope, *a narrow definition* ‖ by a small margin, marginal, *a narrow majority* ‖ narrow-minded ‖ thorough, very precise, *a narrow questioning* ‖ (*stock exchange*) marked by little activity, *a narrow market* ‖ (*phon.*) tense, *a narrow vowel* **2.** *n.* (*esp. pl.*) a narrow passage in mountains or between two bodies of water **the Nar·rows** the strait between Staten Island and Long Island, New York ‖ the narrowest part of the Dardanelles **3.** *v.t.* to make narrower ‖ to fine down, limit further, *to narrow a definition* ‖ *v.i.* to become narrower [O.E. *nearu*]

narrow boat (*Br.*) a canal barge with a beam not exceeding 7 ft

narrow casting (*broadcasting*) creation of programs for broadcast to special interest audiences

narrow gauge, narrow gage (*rail.*) a gauge of less than 4 ft 8½ ins

narrow goods (*Br.*) ribbons, braid etc.

nar·row-mind·ed (nǽroumáindid) *adj.* lacking tolerance or breadth of ideas, esp. in views of conduct

Narrow Seas, the the English Channel and the Irish Sea

narrow shave a narrow escape

narrow squeak the extremely small margin by which one successfully negotiates an obstacle, overcomes a difficulty, or survives a danger

Nar·ses (nάrsi:z) (c. 478–c. 573), Byzantine general of Justinian I. He retook Italy for the Byzantine Empire by defeating the Ostrogoths (552–5), and was governor of Italy (554–67)

nar·thex (nάrθeks) *n.* a western portico in ancient churches ‖ a rectangular entry to the nave of a church [Gk *narthēx*, name of a plant]

Nar·vá·ez (nαrváeθ, nαrváes), Panfilo de (c. 1470–1528), Spanish conquistador. After participating in the conquest of Cuba he alienated Hernán Cortés, who defeated him at Cempoala (1520). He explored (1528) Florida and the Gulf Coast

Nar·vik (nάrvik) an ice-free port (pop. 19,500) and rail center of N. Norway, shipping iron ore from N. Sweden. An Allied expeditionary force captured it (May 1940) from the Germans in the 2nd world war after heavy fighting, but had to withdraw two weeks later

nar·whal, nar·wal (nάrwəl) *n. Monodon monoceros*, a cetaceous mammal found in northern seas, averaging 16 ft in length. The male's spirally grooved tusk (about 9 ft long) yields excellent ivory. Greenlanders obtain oil from narwhal blubber and use the gray spotted skin for leather [fr. Dan. or Swed. *narhval*]

nar·y (nέəri:) *adj.* (*pop.*) not any, never a [var. of *ne'er a*, contr. of *never a*]

NASA (nǽsə) (*acronym*) for National Aeronautics and Space Administration

na·sal (néiz'l) **1.** *adj.* of or pertaining to the nose ‖ (*phon.*) sounded with the velum lowered and often with the mouth passage wholly or partly closed so that the breath comes out of the nose ‖ characterized by such sounds, *a nasal voice* **2.** *n.* a sound so made [fr. Mod. L. *nasalis*]

nasal index the ratio of the breadth to the height of the nose, multiplied by 100

na·sal·i·ty (neizǽliti) *n.* the quality of being nasal

na·sal·i·za·tion (neiz'lizéiʃən) *n.* the act of making or becoming nasal

na·sal·ize (néiz'laiz) *pres. part.* **na·sal·iz·ing** *past and past part.* **na·sal·ized** *v.t.* to pronounce in a nasal manner ‖ *v.i.* to speak in a nasal manner

Nas·by (nǽzbi:), Petroleum V. (pen name of David Ross Locke, 1833–88), U.S. topical humorist and satirist of the Civil War period, a Unionist and Emancipationist. In his 'Nasby letters', which appeared (from 1861) in nationally circulated publications, he created the crude, ignorant character of Nasby who, arguing from the Southern extremist point of view, damned the Southern cause

nas·cen·cy (nǽsensi:) *n.* the condition of being nascent

nas·cent (nǽs'nt) *adj.* beginning to develop, *nascent talent* ‖ in the process of being born ‖ (*chem.*, of an atom or a molecule) at the moment of liberation or formation, when it is in a state of greater reactivity than normal (e.g. hydrogen atoms before they combine to form molecules) [fr. L. *nascens* (*nascentis*) fr. *nasci*, to be born]

NASDA Index (*securities*) listing of stocks offered for sale or purchase by National Association of Security Dealers of America not listed on a local exchange

nase·ber·ry (néizbəri:, néizberi:) *pl.* **nase·ber·ries** *n.* the sapodilla tree or its fruits [fr. Span. or Port. *néspera*, medlar]

Nase·by, Battle of (néizbi:) a decisive victory (June 14, 1645) of the parliamentarians under Fairfax and Cromwell over the royalists under Charles I and Prince Rupert during the English Civil War

Nash (næʃ), John (1752–1835), English architect and pioneer of town planning. He replanned several parts of London with fine terraces

Nash, Ogden (1902–71), U.S. humorous poet. His 20 volumes of verse include 'You Can't Get There from Here', 'I'm a Stranger Here Myself' and 'Bed Riddance'

Nash, Richard (1674–1762), English dandy, known as 'Beau Nash'. A leader of fashion and arbiter of manners, he did much to make Bath fashionable

Nashe (næʃ), Thomas (1567–1601), English writer and pamphleteer. He wrote one of the earliest English novels, 'The Unfortunate Traveller' (1594)

Nash·ville (nǽʃvil) the capital (pop. 455,651) of Tennessee, in the Tennessee River basin, an agricultural market. Industries: food and tobacco processing, music recording, mechanical engineering

Na·sik (nάsik) a Hindu holy city (pop. 170,091) in Maharashtra, India, on the Godavari, producing copper and brasswork and cotton textiles. Buddhist sculptured caves (1st–7th cc.)

na·si·on (néizi:ɒn) *n.* the point on the skull between the nose and the frontal bone [Mod. L.]

Nas·myth (néizmiθ), James (1808–90), Scottish engineer. He invented the steam hammer for forging (1839) and many other machine tools

Na·sr-ed-Din (nάsiəreddi:n) (1831–96), shah of Persia (1848–96). He introduced many European ideas into Persian administration and finance

Nas·sau (nǽsau) (*hist.*) a former duchy, now included in Hesse, West Germany. Its Dutch line of rulers took the title of prince of Orange, were stadtholders of the Netherlands, and included William the Silent, Maurice of Nassau, William II of Orange, and William III of Orange who became William III of England

Nas·sau (nǽsɔ) the capital (pop. 129,877), chief port and commercial and communications center of the Bahamas, on New Providence Is.: tourism

Nas·ser (nǽsər, nάsər), Gamal Abdel (1918–70), Egyptian army officer and statesman. He and Neguib led the military coup (1952) which overthrew Farouk. He was premier (1954–6) and president (1956–8) of Egypt, and president (1958–70) of the United Arab Republic. He was a champion of Pan-Arabism

Nast (nœst), Thomas (1840–1902), U.S. political cartoonist, best known for his attacks in Harper's Weekly on William 'Boss' Tweed and the corrupt Tammany Hall Democratic political machine in New York City in the early 1870s. He originated the use of the elephant as the Republican Party symbol and popularized its Democratic Party counterpart, the donkey. He also introduced the costume still used by artists for Santa Claus

na·stur·tium (næstɔ́:rʃəm) *n.* any member of *Tropaeolum*, fam. *Tropaeolaceae*, a genus of trailing plants native to South America, widely cultivated for their ornamental red or yellow flowers, esp. *T. majus* **Na·stur·tium** a genus of aquatic plants of fam. *Cruciferae*, including watercress [L.]

nas·ty (nǽsti:) *comp.* **nas·ti·er** *superl.* **nas·ti·est** *adj.* very unpleasant, repugnant, *a nasty taste* ‖ morally dirty, *a nasty mind* ‖ mean, vicious in a petty way, *nasty remarks* ‖ offensive, *a nasty temper* ‖ very bad, *a nasty storm* ‖ awkward to deal with, *a nasty problem* ‖ dangerous, *a nasty cut* [origin unknown]

Natal a port and communications center (pop. 350,000) of N.E. Brazil

Na·tal (nətǽl) a province (area 33,578 sq. miles, pop. 5,722,215) of South Africa, bordering the Indian Ocean. Capital: Pietermaritzburg. Chief city: Durban. It is formed by a coastal plain rising to highlands in the north and southwest. Products: sugarcane, citrus fruit, cereals, vegetables, cattle, livestock. Resources: coal, oil, some gold, timber. Industries: sugar refining, food processing, metallurgy, chemicals, motorvehicle assembly. The first European settlements were made by the British (1824) and Dutch (1837–40), who defeated the indigenous Zulus (1838). Britain annexed Natal to Cape Colony (1843). It became a separate colony (1856) and annexed Zululand (1897) and parts of the Transvaal (1903). It joined the Union of South Africa (1910)

na·tal (néit'l) *adj.* of or connected with birth [fr. L. *natalis*]

na·tal·i·ty (nətǽliti:, neitǽliti:) *n.* a birthrate [F. *natalité*]

na·ta·tion (nətéiʃən, *Am.* also neitéiʃən) *n.* (*rhet.*) the act or art of swimming [fr. L. *natatio* (*natationis*)]

na·ta·to·ri·al (neitətóri:əl, neitətóuri:əl) *adj.* natatory

na·ta·to·ry (néitətɔri:, néitətóuri:) *adj.* of, concerned with, or adapted for swimming [fr. L.L. *natatorius*]

Natch·ez (nǽtʃiz) *pl.* **Natch·ez** *n.* a member of an extinct American Indian tribe of the Muskogean linguistic group, formerly inhabiting the lower Mississippi region. They were conquered by the French (1730)

na·tes (néiti:z) *pl. n.* (*anat.*) the buttocks ‖ (*anat.*) the anterior pair of optic lobes in the brain

Na·than (néiθən) Hebrew prophet of the time of David and Solomon

Na·tion (néiʃən), Carry Amelia (née Moore, 1846–1911), U.S. temperance advocate. Alone, or sometimes accompanied by women singing hymns, she entered (1890s) saloons in Kansas, smashing the fixtures and stock with a hatchet

---

CONCISE PRONUNCIATION KEY: (a) æ, c*a*t; ɑ, c*a*r; ɔ f*aw*n; ei, sn*a*ke. **(e)** e, h*e*n; i:, sh*ee*p; iə, d*ee*r; εə, b*ea*r. **(i)** i, f*i*sh; ai, t*i*ger; ə:, b*i*rd. **(o)** o, *o*x; au, c*ow*; ou, g*oa*t; u, p*oo*r; ɔi, r*oy*al. **(u)** ʌ, d*u*ck; u, b*u*ll; u:, g*oo*se; ə, b*a*cillus; ju:, c*u*be. x, lo*ch*; θ, *th*ink; ð, bo*th*er; z, *Z*en; ʒ, corsa*g*e; dʒ, sava*g*e; ŋ, ora*ng*utan*g*; j, *y*ak; ʃ, *f*ish; tʃ, fe*tch*; 'l, rabb*le*; 'n, redd*en*. Complete pronunciation key appears inside front cover.

na·tion (néiʃən) *n.* a body of people recognized as an entity by virtue of their historical, linguistic or ethnic links ‖ a body of people united under a particular political organization, and usually occupying a defined territory ‖ a federation of American Indian tribes [F. fr. L. *natio* (*nationis*)]

na·tion·al (næʃən'l) **1.** *adj.* of or relating to a nation ‖ this in contrast with 'international' ‖ concerning the nation as a whole, nonlocal **2.** *n.* a member of a nation [F.]

National Aeronautics and Space Administration (NASA), the central civilian agency for direction of the U.S. space exploration program established (1958) by an act of Congress. Its activities are conducted by industry under contract and by its field establishments. Its staff includes over 15,000 scientists, engineers, technicians, and administrators. Its development program is divided into two main branches: launch vehicles and spacecraft. NASA's space shuttle program, developed in the 1970s and early 1980s, suffered a catastrophic accident in Jan. 1986 in which the shuttle 'Challenger' was completely destroyed and all 7 crew members died

National Archives and Records Service a U.S. organization which preserves, describes, and services federal records retained for their enduring value. It holds the nation's most important records dating from c. 1774, including the Declaration of Independence, the U.S. Constitution, and the Bill of Rights. Researchers have access to most of the records, some of which are available on microfilm

National Assembly the lower house of the French parliament ‖ (*F. hist.*) the title adopted by the third estate (June 17, 1789–Sept. 30, 1791) during the French Revolution

National Association for the Advancement of Colored People (*abbr.* N.A.A.C.P.) an American association, founded 1909, which aims at protecting and extending the rights of blacks in the U.S.A. by enforcement of civil rights legislation through court action

national bank a commercial bank chartered by and operated under the supervision of the federal government, and affiliated to the Federal Reserve System

National Convention *CONVENTION, THE NATIONAL

National Covenant (*Br. hist.*) an oath (1638), based on an earlier covenant of 1581, which aimed at uniting the Scots against the episcopal policy of Laud. Its adherents, the Covenanters, fought the Bishops' Wars, and struggled against the Stuarts' religious policy until 1688

national debt the amount of money owed by a national government, usually in the form of interest-bearing bonds issued to finance budget deficits, temporary emergencies (flood, fire, drought, famine, war) and public works. The management of the national debt, the issue price of securities, the determination of interest rates and maturity dates and the distribution and repayment of debt are all important in governmental monetary policy, stimulating investment and combating inflation

national disaster area an area that has been affected by major catastrophe as determined by the President of the U.S.

National Education Association (*abbr.* NEA), a U.S. organization for teachers of all grade levels in public and private schools, founded (1857) in Philadelphia, Pa., 'to elevate the character and advance the interest of the profession of teaching, and to promote the cause of popular education in the U.S.A.

National Endowment for the Arts U.S. program of federal grants to organizations and individuals in support of artistic and cultural production. *abbr* NEA

National Endowment for the Humanities U.S. program of federal grants to organizations in aid of the dissemination of knowledge: in language, literature, history, jurisprudence, philosophy, the practice of the arts, etc. *abbr* NEH

National Gallery, London *LONDON

National Geographic Society the world's largest scientific and educational society, founded (1888) in Washington, D.C., 'for the increase and diffusion of geographic knowledge'. It has supported Arctic and Antarctic expeditions, published first-hand accounts of explorers, launched (1930s) giant stratosphere balloons which attained the highest elevation

(13.71 miles) reached by man at that time, studied volcanic eruptions and earthquakes, helped bring national treasures (incl. the Carlsbad caverns and the California sequoias) into the U.S. park system, and excavated archaeological ruins. It publishes the monthly National Geographic Magazine and weekly bulletins to U.S. educators, librarians and students, and produces special programs for television

National Guard a state militia partly maintained by the U.S. government and held available for federal service ‖ (*F. hist.*) a bourgeois militia established in 1789

national income the net product of the goods and services consumed, plus the net change in capital stock, within a national economic unit, conceived in monetary terms. Its determination is important in establishing the origin, distribution and apportionment of income and in plotting economic development by its redistribution as investment and consumption

National Industrial Recovery Act a New Deal measure (1933) which created (1933) the National Recovery Administration (NRA). Its purpose was to relieve industrial unemployment by increasing wages and by eliminating unfair trade practices. Section 3 of Title 1, calling for the adoption by industry of fair competition codes to be approved by the president, was declared (1935) unconstitutional by the U.S. Supreme Court, which ruled that codification was solely a legislative function. Stripped of its most important provision, the NRA was dissolved (1936) by executive order

na·tion·al·ism (næʃən'lizəm) *n.* devotion to one's nation ‖ advocacy of national unity or independence

na·tion·al·ist (næʃən'list) **1.** *n.* a person who believes in or supports nationalism **Na·tion·al·ist** a member of a political group advocating national independence **2.** *adj.* of nationalism or nationalists **Na·tion·al·ist** of or relating to a Nationalist party **na·tion·al·is·tic** *adj.* **na·tion·al·is·ti·cal·ly** *adv.* [NATIONAL]

Nationalist China the Republic of China [after the ruling Chinese Nationalist Party, the Kuomintang]

na·tion·al·i·ty (næʃənæliti:) *pl* **na·tion·al·i·ties** *n.* membership of a nation ‖ existence as a nation ‖ a nation or ethnic group ‖ national character or quality [NATIONAL]

na·tion·al·i·za·tion (næʃən'lizéiʃən) *n.* a nationalizing or being nationalized

na·tion·al·ize (næʃən'laiz) *pres. part.* **na·tion·al·iz·ing** *past* and *past part.* **na·tion·al·ized** *v.t.* to put under national control or ownership ‖ to make national in character [NATIONAL]

National Labor Reform Party *NATIONAL LABOR UNION

National Labor Relations Act the Wagner Act

National Labor Relations Board (*abbr.* N.L.R.B.) a U.S. government agency, set up in 1935 and empowered under the Wagner and Taft-Hartley Acts to investigate labor controversies, to safeguard the rights of employees to bargain and organize, and to prevent unfair labor practices etc.

National Labor Union (*abbr.* NLU) a national organization of U.S. working men established (1866) in Baltimore. Its purpose was to prevent employers from using unscrupulous methods to check unionization. It acquired from Congress an 8-hour day for federally employed mechanics and laborers and the repeal (1868) of the Contract Labor Act (1864), which had permitted importation of European labor under contract. When reform unionists seized control of the NLU and it became the National Labor Reform Party, the trade unionists withdrew their membership. Beset by internal conflict, the party dissolved (1872)

National Liberation Front *VIETCONG

National Organization for Women (*abbr.* N.O.W.) U.S. women's civil rights organization, founded in 1966 with author Betty Friedan as its first president. Its purpose is to achieve 'full equality for women in truly equal partnership with men.' The world's largest such group, it comprises 800 local groups and 250,000 members. Its headquarters is in Washington, D.C.

national park an area of special historical or scenic value owned and administered for public enjoyment by a government or by an independent authority set up by a government

National Progressive Republican League a U.S. progressive Republican organization formed (1911) to seize control of the Republican

party from conservative Republicans. When the Republican Convention nominated (1912) William H. Taft for the presidency, the league became the Progressive party, popularly known as the Bull Moose party, and nominated Theodore Roosevelt as its candidate. Roosevelt lost the campaign, but the progressives, by splitting the Republican party, helped to elect the liberal Woodrow Wilson

national seashore federally maintained recreation area along a coast

National Security Council a U.S. top-secret council established in 1947 and composed of the president, vice-president, secretary of state, secretary of defense, and the director of the office of emergency preparedness. It advises the president on matters that require the coordination of domestic, foreign and military policies. Its operations and funds are not made known even to Congress

National Socialism *NATIONAL SOCIALIST GERMAN WORKERS' PARTY

National Socialist German Workers' Party a German political party (1918–45), reorganized (1920) and led by Hitler. Its ideology, National Socialism (Nazism or Naziism), was based on aggressive militarism, anti-Semitism, and the asserting of the racial superiority of the Aryans. The party increased its strength during the economic crisis of 1929–30, came to power (1933) under Hitler, and established a totalitarian regime which collapsed at the end of the 2nd world war

National Trust an organization founded (1895), and incorporated by act of Parliament (1907), for preserving historic buildings and monuments and places of natural beauty in Britain

na·tion·hood (néiʃənhud) *n.* the quality of being a nation

Nation of Islam *BLACK MUSLIMS

Nations, Battle of the a decisive victory (Oct. 16–19, 1813) of the Austrian, Russian and Prussian armies over Napoleon. The battle, fought near Leipzig, was a turning point in the Napoleonic Wars

na·tion·wide (néiʃənwáid) *adj.* extended or taking place throughout an entire nation

na·tive (néitiv) **1.** *n.* a person born in a given place, country etc., or whose parents are domiciled there at the time of his birth, *a native of Scotland* ‖ one of the original inhabitants of a country, esp. at the time of its discovery by Europeans, *Cook was murdered by hostile natives* ‖ an inhabitant as opposed to a visitor, *I'm not a native here* ‖ a plant or animal which originated in a district or area, i.e. was not imported or introduced **2.** *adj.* belonging to a person or thing by nature, inherent, *native intelligence* ‖ belonging to a person by birth, *native language* ‖ born in a particular place, country etc., *a native Norwegian* ‖ of or relating to the natives of a place ‖ (of plant or animal life) not introduced ‖ (of metals etc.) occurring in a pure state in nature, *native silver* [fr. L. *nativus*]

Native American (*adj.*) an American Indian — **Native-American** *adj.*

na·tive-born (néitivbɔ́rn) *adj.* born in the country or place specified, *a native-born Bostonian*

native state (*hist.*) an Indian state ruled by its own prince under British supervision

na·tiv·ism (néitivizəm) *n.* a policy of protecting and favoring the interests of the native inhabitants of a country as against those of immigrants ‖ (*philos.*) the doctrine of innate ideas

Na·tiv·i·ty (nətíviti:) *n.* the birth of Jesus Christ ‖ the festival commemorating this, Christmas ‖ the festival commemorating the birth of the Virgin Mary (Sept. 8) ‖ the festival commemorating the birth of John the Baptist (June 24) ‖ a work of art depicting Christ as a newborn baby **na·tiv·i·ty** *pl.* **na·tiv·i·ties** birth [F. *nativité*]

NATO (néitou) *NORTH ATLANTIC TREATY ORGANIZATION

na·tri·u·re·sis (neitri:jurísis) *n.* (*med.*) excessive excretion of sodium in the urine —**natriuretic** *adj.*

na·tron (néitrɒn) *n.* sodium carbonate occurring naturally as $Na_2CO_3 \cdot 10H_2O$ [F. and Span. fr. Arab. *natrūn* fr. Gk]

nat·ter (nǽtər) (*Br., pop.*) **1.** *v.i.* to talk trivially or chat at length **2.** *n.* (*Br., pop.*) a gossipy conversation

nat·ter·jack (nǽtərdʒæk) *n. Bufo calamita,* a European species of toad with a yellow stripe down the back and with short hind legs adapted for running [origin unknown]

CONCISE PRONUNCIATION KEY: (a) æ, cat; ɑ, car; ɔ fawn; ei, snake. (e) e, hen; i:, sheep; iə, deer; ɛə, bear. (i) i, fish; ai, tiger; ə:, bird. (o) o, ox; au, cow; ou, goat; u, poor; ɔi, royal. (u) ʌ, duck; u, bull; u:, goose; ə, bacillus; ju:, cube. x, loch; θ, think; ð, bother; z, Zen; ʒ, corsage; dʒ, savage; ŋ, orangutang; j, yak; ʃ, fish; tʃ, fetch; 'l, rabble; 'n, redden. Complete pronunciation key appears inside front cover.

nat·ti·ly (nǽtili:) *adv.* in a natty way

nat·ti·ness (nǽti:nis) *n.* the state or quality of being natty

nat·ty (nǽti:) *comp.* **nat·ti·er** *superl.* **nat·ti·est** *adj.* very neat and tidy ‖ jauntily smart [perh. fr. NEAT]

nat·u·ral (nǽtʃərəl, nǽtʃrəl) **1.** *adj.* pertaining to, existing in, or produced by nature, *natural rock formations* ‖ not supernatural, *a natural phenomenon* ‖ not artificial, *a natural blonde* ‖ pertaining to the study of nature, *natural classification* ‖ due to the operation of the ordinary course of nature, *natural death* ‖ in accordance with normal human nature, *it isn't natural to be without emotion* ‖ free from self-consciousness, at ease, *try to be natural before the microphone* ‖ of food containing no chemical additives ‖ illegitimate, *a natural child* ‖ unregenerate, *a natural man* ‖ (*mus.*, of a key or scale) having neither sharps nor flats ‖ (*mus.*, of a note) neither sharp nor flat ‖ (*chem.*) found in the crust of the earth **2.** *n.* (*pop.*) a person who takes naturally to an activity ‖ (*mus.*) a note which is not a sharp or a flat ‖ (*mus.*) the sign ♮, canceling a preceding sharp or flat ‖ a combination (of cards dealt etc.) which immediately wins the game ‖ a hair style using a person's natural hair type, esp. unstraightened hair on a black person [O.F.]

natural gas a combustible gas, issuing from the earth's crust through a natural or artificial opening, often associated with petroleum. It is used extensively as a fuel gas, and sometimes as a source of other chemicals

natural history the study of animal life, and sometimes also of plant life, usually in a popular manner ‖ (*hist.*) the systematic study of all natural objects: animal, vegetable and mineral

nat·u·ral·ism (nǽtʃərəlizəm, nǽtʃrəlizəm) *n.* a mode of thought (religious, moral or philosophical) glorifying nature and excluding supernatural and spiritual elements ‖ close adherence to nature in art or literature, esp. (in literature) the technique, chiefly associated with Zola, used to present a naturalistic philosophy, esp. by emphasizing the effect of heredity and environment on human nature and action

nat·u·ral·ist (nǽtʃərəlist, nǽtʃrəlist) *n.* a person who studies natural history ‖ a person who adheres to naturalism **nat·u·ral·is·tic** *adj.* **nat·u·ral·is·ti·cal·ly** *adv.* [fr. F. *naturaliste*]

nat·u·ral·i·za·tion (nætʃərəlizéiʃən, nætʃrəlizéiʃən) *n.* a naturalizing or being naturalized [NATURALIZE]

nat·u·ral·ize (nǽtʃərəlaiz) *pres. part.* **nat·u·ral·iz·ing** *past* and *past part.* **nat·u·ral·ized** *v.t.* to grant citizenship to (an immigrant) ‖ to introduce (a plant or an animal) into a new habitat where it flourishes ‖ to explain (phenomena) in terms of nature and exclude the supernatural ‖ to adopt (a word, custom etc.) from another language, culture etc. [fr. F. *naturaliser*]

natural justice justice based on innate human principles

natural law a law of cause and effect which always appears to be obeyed when changes occur in the physical world ‖ a body of law determined by an innate human sense of justice ‖ the laws obeyed by man's animal instincts as compared with moral law

nat·u·ral·ly (nǽtʃərəli:, nǽtʃrəli:) *adv.* in a natural or normal way ‖ as one would expect, of course ‖ by nature ‖ in accordance with the laws of nature [NATURAL]

natural minor scale (*mus.*) a minor scale having semitones between the second and third and between the fifth and sixth steps, the other intervals being whole tones

natural number (*math.*) a positive integer

natural philosopher (*hist.*) a person concerned with natural philosophy ‖ one of the ancient Greek philosophers concerned primarily with physical process, e.g. Anaximander

natural philosophy (*hist.*) natural science

natural religion a religion based on human reason, without divine revelation (cf. REVEALED RELIGION)

natural resources (of a country) what nature has provided and man can make use of, e.g. fertile soil, waterpower, minerals etc. ‖ (of a person) inborn capacities

natural science all science concerned with the physical world, including physics, biology and chemistry

natural selection a process occurring in nature which results in the survival of the fittest or elimination of individuals or groups, depending on adaptation to environment (*EVOLUTION)

natural theology a system of theology based on the study of nature and without divine revelation

na·ture (néitʃər) *ii.* the physical universe and the laws and forces which govern changes within it ‖ the essential character of something, *the nature of the argument* ‖ (of a substance) the permanent property or properties, *it is the nature of liquids to be fluid* ‖ (of persons) inborn character, disposition, *of a cheerful nature* ‖ a general character, *soup of a watery nature* ‖ sort, type, *other things of that nature* ‖ (of sexual relations) normality, *against nature* ‖ the condition of man prior to civilization **by nature** as a result of inherent quality or temperament **from nature** (of a painting etc.) done in the presence of the subject **in** (or **of**) **the nature of** equivalent to, virtually, *this trip is in the nature of work* (*STATE OF NATURE) [F.]

nature study the study of natural life and phenomena (plants, animals, weather etc.), esp. in a popular manner

nature trail a walkway in an undeveloped area suitable for the observation of unspoiled nature

naught (nɔt) *n.* (*rhet.*) nothing, nothingness ‖ (*math.*) a zero, nothing (*NUMBER TABLE) [O.E. *nāwiht*]

naugh·ti·ly (nɔ́tili:) *adv.* in a naughty way

naugh·ti·ness (nɔ́ti:nis) *n.* the state or quality of being naughty

naugh·ty (nɔ́ti:) *comp.* **naugh·ti·er** *superl.* **naugh·ti·est** *adj.* (esp. of children and their behavior) bad, disobedient ‖ mildly indecent, *a naughty story* [NAUGHT]

Nau·pli·a (nɔ́pli:ə) (*Gk* Navplion) the chief town (pop. 9,281) of Argolis, S. Greece, on the east coast of the Peloponnesus

nau·pli·us (nɔ́pli:əs) *pl.* **nau·pli·i** (nɔ́pli:ai) *n.* the earliest larval stage of entomostracan crustaceans and certain shrimps [L.=a kind of shellfish, fr. Gk]

Na·u·ru (naú:ru:) a coral island (area 8½ sq. miles, pop. 8,000) of Micronesia, administered by Australia as a U.N. trust territory up to Jan. 31, 1968 and since then an independent state: valuable phosphate deposits

nau·se·a (nɔ́ʒə, nɔ́ʃə, nɔ́zi:ə) *n.* a feeling of sickness with a desire to vomit ‖ strong disgust [L. fr. Gk *nausia*, seasickness]

nau·se·ate (nɔ́ʒi:eit, nɔ́ʃi:eit, nɔ́zi:eit) *pres. part.* **nau·se·at·ing** *past* and *past part.* **nau·se·at·ed** *v.t.* to cause a feeling of nausea in [fr. L. *nauseare* (*nauseatus*), to be seasick]

nau·seous (nɔ́ʃəs, nɔ́zi:əs) *adj.* causing nausea ‖ (*Am.*) nauseated

nautch (nɔtʃ) *n.* an entertainment in India by professional dancing girls [Hind. *nāch*]

nau·ti·cal (nɔ́tik'l) *adj.* of ships, seamen or navigation [fr. older *nautic* fr. F. *nautique*]

nautical mile one minute of a great circle of the earth, defined as (internationally) 1,852 meters (6,076.1033 ft) or (*Br.*) 6,080 ft

nau·ti·lus (nɔ́t'ləs) *pl.* **nau·ti·li** (nɔ́t'lai), **nau·ti·lus·es** *n.* a member of *Nautilus*, a genus of cephalopods with a coiled chambered shell, four gills and many short tentacles, found in shallow water, chiefly in the S. Pacific ‖ a paper nautilus [L. fr. Gk *nautilus*, sailor]

'Nautilus', U.S.S. the first atomic as well as the first steam submarine, launched in 1954 and named after Jules Verne's fictional prototype in his 'Twenty Thousand Leagues under the Sea'. It became (1958) the first vessel to make a transpolar crossing, pioneering the shortest known sea route between the Pacific Ocean and Europe

nav·a·glide (nǽviglaid) *n.* (*air traffic control*) an airport instrument approach system with capability of indicating distance, utilizing a single frequency

nav·a·globe (nǽvigloub) *n.* (*air traffic control*) long-distance navigation system for aircraft automatically indicating bearing, utilizing amplitude comparison of continuous-wave, low-frequency broadcasts

Nav·a·ho, Nav·a·jo (nǽvəhou, nɑ́vəhou) *pl.* **Nav·a·hos, Nav·a·jos, Nav·a·hoes, Nav·a·joes, Nav·a·ho, Nav·a·jo** *n.* a member of an Athapaskan people of Arizona, New Mexico and Utah ‖ this people ‖ their language

na·val (néivəl) *adj.* of, pertaining to or characteristic of a navy [fr. L. *navalis*]

Naval Limitation Treaty *WASHINGTON CONFERENCE

naval stores supplies for a navy excluding arms, esp. resinous substances (e.g. pitch, tar etc.)

na·var (néivɑr) *n.* (*air traffic control acronym*) for navigation and ranging, a navigation and traffic control system for aircraft

Nav·a·ri·no, Battle of (nævəríːnou) a naval battle (1827) off the Peloponnesus, Greece, in which a British, French and Russian fleet destroyed the Turkish and Egyptian fleets during the Greek War of Independence

Na·var·ra (nɑvɑ́rrɑ) a province (area 4,055 sq. miles, pop. 507,367) of Spain, between the ridge of the W. Pyrenees and the Ebro, the southern part of the old kingdom of Navarre. Capital: Pamplona

Na·varre (nəvǽr) a former kingdom of Europe, bordering the Bay of Biscay on both sides of the W. Pyrenees, now included in the French department of Pyrénées Atlantiques and the Spanish province of Navarra. Products: cereals, vines, root crops, cattle, lumber, hydroelectricity. Historic capital: Pamplona. The kingdom was established (824) by the Basques, and was attached (1076–1134) to Aragon. It then passed to various French powers. The part south of the Pyrenees was annexed (1515) to the Spanish Crown, leaving the northern part in French possession

nav·a·screen (nǽviskri:n) *n.* (*air traffic control*) an air traffic control system, utilizing information provided by radar, etc., displayed on a screen

nave (neiv) *n.* the central part of a church, extending from the main door to the choir or chancel [fr. L. *navis*, ship]

nave *n.* the central block or hub of a wheel, from which the spokes radiate [O. E. *nafu*]

na·vel (néivəl) *n.* a small hollow in the middle of the belly, marking the point of attachment of the umbilical cord [O.E. *nafela*]

navel orange a large, seedless orange with a navel-like formation at the top and a small, undeveloped, secondary fruit inside

nav·i·cert (nǽvisəːrt) *n.* a consular certificate confirming the manifest of a neutral ship, exempting her from search or seizure [NAVIGATION+CERTIFICATE]

na·vic·u·lar (nəvíkjulər) **1.** *adj.* (*anat.*, of a bone in the hand or foot) boat-shaped **2.** *n.* a navicular bone [fr. L.L. *navicularis*]

nav·i·ga·bil·i·ty (nævígəbíliti:) *n.* the state or quality of being navigable

nav·i·ga·ble (nǽvigəb'l) *adj.* (of rivers) allowing the passage of ships ‖ (of ships, balloons etc.) able to be steered or sailed [F.]

nav·i·gate (nǽvigeit) *pres. part.* **nav·i·gat·ing** *past* and *past part.* **nav·i·gat·ed** *v.t.* to direct the course of (a ship or aircraft) ‖ to travel by ship or aircraft across, over, up, down (a sea, river etc.) ‖ to direct (a path etc.), *to navigate one's way through difficult negotiations* ‖ *v.i.* to direct the course of a ship, aircraft or car [fr. L. *navigare* (*navigatus*)]

nav·i·ga·tion (nævigéiʃən) *n.* the act or practice of navigating ‖ the science by which geometry, astronomy, radar etc. are used to determine the position of a ship or aircraft and to direct its course ‖ maritime traffic, esp. the quantity of ships in passage, *navigation has increased in these waters* [fr. L. *navigatio* (*navigationis*)]

Navigation Act any of several laws passed (1651, and at subsequent dates in the 17th c.) by the English parliament to try to oust the Dutch from the carrying trade by the application of mercantilist principles. The acts required that the colonial trade should be limited to ships owned, commanded and mostly manned by Englishmen, that most commodities produced in the colonies should be sent only to England, and that all goods sent to the colonies should be shipped from English ports. American resentment at this limitation of trade was a cause of the Revolutionary War. The acts were repealed in 1849

nav·i·ga·tor (nǽvigeitər) *n.* a person who navigates or is skilled in navigation ‖ (*hist.*) a maritime explorer ‖ an automatic device for directing the course of an aircraft etc. [L.]

Nav·pli·on (nɑ́fpli:ɔn) *NAUPLIA

Navratilova (nævrətíilouvə), Martina (1954–) U.S. tennis player who defected from Czechoslovakia (1975) and became a U.S. citizen. Her career as a singles star began in 1978 and has produced 13 Grand Slam titles: 7 at Wimbledon (1978–9, 1982–6), 2 Australian (1981, 1983), 2 French (1982, 1984), and 2 U.S. Opens (1982–4). A dominant doubles player

---

from 1975, she won dozens of major titles, mostly with Pam Shriver; in 1983–5 they won 109 consecutive matches, a winning streak unique in tennis history. Navratilova's career earnings have made her the top money winner, man or woman, in tennis

NAVSTAR (*navigation acronym*) for navigation system using time and ranging, a worldwide system for locating aircraft and ships, utilizing 24 navigation satellites

nav·vy (nǽvi:) **1.** *pl.* **nav·vies** *n.* (*Br.*) an unskilled laborer usually doing heavy manual work, e.g. road-making **2.** *v.i.* (*Br.*) to work as a navvy [NAVIGATOR]

na·vy (néivi:) *pl.* **na·vies** *n.* a state's ships of war ‖ the organization and manpower of a state's force for war at sea ‖ navy blue [O.F. *navie*, fleet]

navy bean a small, white bean related to the kidney bean, dried for use as a food

navy blue a deep, dark blue [the color of the British naval uniform]

navy yard a naval shipyard

na·wab (nəwáb) *n.* a nabob ‖ a courtesy title, esp. for a Moslem prince [fr. Urdu *nawwāb*]

NAWAS (*acronym*) for national warning system for civil defense

Nax·a·lite (náksəlait) *n.* member of a Communist terrorist group in India, originally West Bengal —**Naxalism** *n.*

Nax·os (nǽksɔs) the largest island (area 171 sq. miles, pop. 14,201) of the Cyclades, Greece: wine, almonds, olive oil, emery

nay (nei) **1.** *adv.* (*rhet.*, for emphasis) and more than that, *I think, nay I firmly believe, that he is honest* ‖ (*archaic*) no **2.** *n.* a negative vote ‖ someone who votes against ‖ (*archaic*) a refusal or denial [M.E. fr. O.N. *nei*]

Na·ya·rit (nújari:t) a Pacific Coast state of Mexico with offshore islands (area 10,664 sq. miles, pop. 669,000). Mountains cut the land into deep gorges and valleys. Capital: Tepic (pop. 54,000). Main river: the Santiago. It is primarily an agricultural region (corn, tobacco, sugar, cotton, beans, coffee, woods and medicinal plants)

Naz·a·rene (nǽzəri:n) *n.* a native or inhabitant of Nazareth ‖ (in former Jewish or Moslem use) a Christian ‖ a member of an early Jewish-Christian sect **the Nazarene** Jesus Christ [fr. L. *Nazarenus* fr. Gk]

Naz·a·reth (nǽzəriθ) a town (pop. 36,700) of Israel, 18 miles southeast of Haifa. It was the home of Joseph and Mary, and the place where Jesus spent his youth

Naz·a·rite, Naz·i·rite (nǽzərait) *n.* a consecrated person among the ancient Hebrews, forbidden to drink wine, cut the hair or touch a corpse ‖ (*rare*) a Nazarene [fr. L. *Nazaraeus*]

naze (neiz) *n.* a promontory or headland [etym. doubtful]

Na·zi (nátsi:) **1.** *n.* (*hist.*) a member of the National Socialist German Workers' party ‖ (*hist.*) a supporter of Nazism **2.** *adj.* of or pertaining to this party **Ná·zism, Ná·zi·ism** *ns* **Ná·zi·fy** *pres. part.* **Na·zi·fy·ing** *past and past part.* **Na·zi·fied** *v.t.* to bring under Nazi domination [G. fr. *nationalsozialist*, national socialist]

Nazirite *NAZARITE

N.B. New Brunswick

n.b., N.B. note well [fr. L. *nota bene*]

N-bu·tyl·mer·cap·ti·on (N-bjutəlmə:rkǽpti:ɒn) *n.* (*chem.*) a petroleum liquid with skunklike odor, used as a protection against assault

N.C. North Carolina

NC (*computer abbr.*) of numeric control, control of machine tools by computer-directed mechanical devices

N.D. North Dakota

N. Dak. North Dakota

N'Djamena (formerly Fort Lamy) the capital (pop. 241,639) of Chad, on the Shari, a trade center in equatorial Africa

Ndo·la ('ndóulə) a town (pop. 323,000) of Zambia, on the Congo border, the rail center of the copper belt. It is the terminal of an oil pipeline from Dar es Salaam, Tanzania

NE, N.E. northeast

Neagh, Lough (lɔ́knéi, lɔ́knéi) a lake (area 153 sq. miles) of Northern Ireland, the largest in the British Isles

Ne·an·der·thal man (ni:ǽndərθɔl) a Paleolithic race of men associated with the Mousterian epoch and characterized by their stocky build, short massive neck, massive brow ridge, receding forehead and undeveloped chin [after the *Neanderthal* valley in W. Germany, where such a skeleton was found in 1856]

neap (ni:p) *n.* a neap tide [O.E. *nēpflōd*]

Ne·ap·o·lis (ni:ǽpəlis) *NAPLES

Ne·a·pol·i·tan (ni:əpólitən) **1.** *adj.* of or belonging to Naples **2.** *n.* a native or inhabitant of Naples [fr. L. *Neapolitanus*]

neap tide a tide at the first and third quarters of the moon, in which the high water is lower than at any other time [cf. SPRING TIDE]

near (niər) **1.** *adv.* at or within a short distance, *he lives near* ‖ (of times and seasons) not far off, *Christmas was drawing near* **near at hand** at a conveniently short distance ‖ not far off in future time **to come** (or sometimes **go**) **near to** to approach, be or do almost, *it came near to murder*, *she came near to killing him* **2.** *prep.* within a short distance of, *near the door* ‖ within a short time of, *near midnight* ‖ within a small amount or degree of, *near death* **3.** *adj.* not far distant in space, *a near neighbor* ‖ not far distant in time, *the near future* ‖ not far distant in relationship, *a near relative* ‖ not far removed in likeness or degree, *a near match* ‖ only just successful, narrow, *a near escape* ‖ (of a guess, estimate etc.) almost correct ‖ (of part of an animal) on its left ‖ (of an animal in harness flanked by another or others) on the left ‖ (of a part of a motor vehicle) on the nearside ‖ (esp. superl., of a route) direct **4.** *v.t.* to approach, *they were nearing the store* ‖ *v.i.* to come closer in time, *the examinations were nearing* [M.E. fr. O.N. *nœr*]

near·by 1. (níərbai) *adj.* near at hand, not far away **2.** (níərbái) *adv.* (*Br.* **near by**) not far away

Near East a term formerly used to denote the Balkan States and the area of the Ottoman Empire, now used as an alternative for the Middle East **Near East·ern** *adj.*

near-fall (níərfɔl) *n.* (*wrestling*) a fall in which both shoulders are held to the mat for between one and two seconds or within two inches of the mat for two seconds or more

near·ly (níərli:) *adv.* almost, *it is nearly midnight* ‖ closely, *nearly related* **not nearly** by no means, nothing like

near-miss (níərmís) *n.* an attempt or shot that is only just not successful ‖ (*mil.*) a shot, bomb burst etc. not on target but close enough to damage it

near point the point closest to the eye at which an object can be focused on the retina

near real time (*computer*) delay caused by automated processing and display between the occurrence of an event and reception of the data at some other location *Cf* REAL TIME

near·side (níərsaid) *n.* (*Br.*) the side (of a horse or motor vehicle) closest to the edge of the road (opp. OFFSIDE)

near·sight·ed (níərsaitid) *adj.* myopic

'Near v. Minnesota' (níər) a decision (1931) of the U.S. Supreme Court led by Chief Justice Charles Evans Hughes. It ruled against a state newspaper censorship law, and thus against the right of a state to limit freedom of the press

neat (ni:t) *adj.* clean and tidy, orderly, *a neat appearance* ‖ well made, well proportioned, *a neat figure* ‖ done with dexterity, *a neat job* ‖ usually doing orderly and careful work, *a neat worker* ‖ cleverly appropriate, *a neat reply* ‖ ingenious, *a neat device* ‖ (of drinks) undiluted, *neat whiskey* [fr. O.F. *neit, net*]

neat·lines (ní:tlainz) *n.* (*cartography*) the lines that bound the body of a map, usu. parallels and meridians *Cf* GRATICULE

neb (neb) *n.* a bird's beak ‖ a projecting tip [O.E. *nebb*]

NEB (*abbr.*) for the New English Bible

neb·bish (from the Yiddish) (nébiʃ) *n.* (*colloq.*) a meek, ineffectual person

Ne·bras·ka (nəbrǽskə) (*abbr.* Neb.) a Middle Western state (area 77,227 sq. miles, pop. 1,586,000). Capital: Lincoln. Chief city: Omaha. Agriculture: cereals, beef cattle, hogs. Resources: oil, building materials. Industries: food processing (esp. meat packing), some machinery. State university (1869) at Lincoln. Nebraska was explored (18th c.) by the French, ceded to Spain (1763), returned to France (1800) and, as part of the Louisiana Purchase (1803) bought by the U.S.A., of which it became (1867) the 37th state

Neb·u·chad·nez·zar II (nəbjukədnézər, nəbjukədnézər) (*d.* 562 B.C.), king of Babylonia (605–562 B.C.). He destroyed Jerusalem (586 B.C.), taking many Jews into captivity in Babylonia. He built the hanging gardens of Babylon.

The Babylonian Empire was at its height during his reign

neb·u·la (nébjulə) *pl.* **neb·u·lae** (néb-juli:) *n.* (*astron.*) a diffuse, cloudlike mass of usually luminous gas, glowing under the influence of radiation from nearby stars. Nebulae are found both within and outside the local galaxy. Occasionally they are not luminous, because of the lack of exciting radiation ‖ (*med.*) a clouded spot on the cornea **neb·u·lar** *adj.* [L.=mist]

nebular hypothesis the theory that the solar system was formed by the condensation of hot, gaseous nebulae

neb·u·los·i·ty (nebjulósiti:) *pl.* **neb·u·los·i·ties** *n.* the quality or condition of being nebulous ‖ a nebula [F. *nébulosité*]

neb·u·lous (nébjuləs) *adj.* vague, formless ‖ of or like a nebula [fr. L. *nebulosus*, cloudy]

nec·a·to·ri·a·sis (nekətɔ́ráiəsis) *n.* (*med.*) hookworm infection occurring in U.S., with the larvae entering through the area between the toes

nec·es·sar·i·an (nesisɛ́əri:ən) **1.** *n.* a necessitarian **2.** *adj.* necessitarian

nec·es·sar·i·ly (nesisɛ́rili:, nésisɛrili:) *adv.* as an inevitable consequence ‖ as a necessary result [NECESSARY]

nec·es·sary (nésisɛri:) **1.** *adj.* that is required, that must be, *is it necessary to keep the dog on a leash?* ‖ that cannot be done without, *oxygen is necessary for life* ‖ (*philos.*) unavoidable, in the nature of things, *a necessary consequence* **2.** **néc·es·sar·ies** *pl. n.* things that one cannot do without, essentials ‖ (*law*) things essential for the support of a dependent or of someone unable through mental deficiency or immaturity to see to his own affairs [fr. L. *necessarius*]

ne·ces·si·tar·i·an (nəsesitɛ́əri:ən) **1.** *n.* an advocate of necessitarianism **2.** *adj.* of or relating to necessitarianism **ne·ces·si·tár·i·an·ism** *n.* determinism [NECESSITY]

ne·ces·si·tate (nəsésiteit) *pres. part.* **ne·ces·si·tat·ing** *past and past part.* **ne·ces·si·tat·ed** *v.t.* to make necessary [fr. M. L. *necessitare* (*necessitatus*)]

ne·ces·si·tous (nəsésitəs) *adj.* (*rhet.*) needy, poor ‖ pressing unavoidable, *necessitous obligations* [fr. F. *nécessiteux*]

ne·ces·si·ty (nəsésiti:) *pl.* **ne·ces·si·ties** *n.* the state or quality of being necessary ‖ something that is necessary ‖ the state of being in need, esp. poverty **of necessity** necessarily **to bow to necessity** to recognize the inevitable and comply or conform **to make a virtue of necessity** to do something willingly that has to be done whether one likes it or not [F. *nécessité*]

neck (nek) **1.** *n.* that part of an animal which joins the head to the body, containing, in man, part of the spinal column, the windpipe, the gullet and important nerves and blood vessels ‖ the part of a garment that goes around the neck ‖ the narrowest part of an object, e.g. of a bottle ‖ a narrow stretch of land ‖ a strait ‖ (*archit.*) the lower part of a capital ‖ (*racing*) the approximate length of a horse's neck and head used as a distance in indicating a lead **neck and crop** bodily and unceremoniously, *to fling someone out neck and crop* **neck and neck** (in a competition, while it is in progress) virtually level, *they were galloping neck and neck* **neck or nothing** with willingness to risk everything **to break one's neck** (*pop.*) to go out of one's way, *he broke his neck to get her a job* **to get it in the neck** (*pop.*) to be reprimanded very severely **to risk one's neck** to put one's life in danger **2.** *v.i.* (*pop.*) to hug and kiss [O.E. *hnecca*]

Neck·ar (nékər) a river in Baden-Württemberg, West Germany, rising between the Black Forest and the Swabian Jura and flowing 247 miles north to the Rhine at Mannheim. It is navigable below Stuttgart

neck·band (nékbænd) *n.* that part of a shirt to which the collar is attached ‖ the edging of a garment at the neckline

Neck·er (nékər), Jacques (1732–1804), Swiss financier, director general of French finances (1776–81 and 1788–90). His attempts to reform the French finances failed in the face of opposition from the court. Having advised the summoning of the States General (1789), he proved too weak and indecisive to avert the French Revolution

neck·er·chief (nékərtʃif) *n.* a square of cloth worn around the neck [NECK+KERCHIEF]

neck·ing (nékin) *n.* (*archit.*) a small molding between the shaft and the capital of a column

CONCISE PRONUNCIATION KEY: (a) æ, c*a*t; ɑ, c*a*r; ɔ f*aw*n; ei, sn*a*ke. **(e)** e, h*e*n; i:, sh*ee*p; iə, d*ee*r; ɛə, b*ea*r. **(i)** i, f*i*sh; ai, t*i*ger; ə:, b*i*rd. **(o)** o, *o*x; au, c*ow*; ou, g*oa*t; u, p*oo*r; ɔi, r*oy*al. **(u)** ʌ, d*u*ck; u, b*u*ll; u:, g*oo*se; ə, b*a*cillus; ju:, c*u*be. x, lo*ch*; θ, *th*ink; ð, bo*th*er; z, *Z*en; ʒ, corsa*g*e. dʒ, sava*ge*; ŋ, ora*ng*utan; j, *y*ak; ʃ, *fi*sh; tʃ, fe*tch*; 'l, rab*ble*; 'n, red*den*. Complete pronunciation key appears inside front cover.

neck·lace (néklis) *n.* a string of beads or other small ornaments worn around the neck

neck·let (néklit) *n.* a close-fitting necklace

neck·line (néklain) *n.* the line formed by the neck of a garment

neck·tie (néktai) *n.* a tie (band of cloth)

neck·wear (nékwęǝr) *n.* (*commerce*) neckties, scarves and collars

nec·rol·o·gist (nǝkrólǝdʒist) *n.* a writer of obituaries

nec·rol·o·gy (nǝkrólǝdʒi:) *pl.* **nec·rol·o·gies** *n.* a list or register of the dead [fr. Gk *nekros*, dead body+*logos*, discourse]

nec·ro·man·cer (nékroumænsǝr) *n.* a person who practices necromancy

nec·ro·man·cy (nékroumænsi:) *n.* the art of foretelling the future or magically achieving some purpose by communication with the spirits of the dead ‖ black magic [fr. O.F. *nygromance* fr. L. fr. Gk]

nec·ro·man·tic (nekroumæntik) *adj.* of or relating to necromancy

nec·ro·phil·i·a (nękroufíli:ǝ) *n.* necrophily [Mod. L.]

ne·croph·i·ly (nǝkrófili:) *n.* an abnormal, usually erotic, fascination with corpses [ult. fr. NECROPHILIA]

ne·crop·o·lis (nǝkrópǝlis) *n.* a large cemetery, esp. one belonging to an ancient city [fr. Gk *nekropolis*]

nec·rop·sy (nékropsi:) *pl.* **nec·rop·sies** *n.* an autopsy [fr. Gk *nekropsi* fr. *nekros*, corpse+*opsis*, sight]

ne·crose (nǝkróus) *pres. past.* **ne·cros·ing** *past* and *past part.* **ne·crosed** *v.t.* to cause necrosis in ‖ *v.i.* to suffer necrosis

ne·cro·sis (nekróusis) *pl.* **ne·cro·ses** (nekróusi:z) *n.* the death of a piece of animal tissue from burning, loss of blood supply etc. or of plant tissue from cold, parasites etc. **ne·crot·ic** (nekrótik) *adj.* [Mod. L. fr. Gk *nekrōsis*]

ne·crot·o·my (nǝkrótǝmi:) *pl.* **ne·crot·o·mies** *n.* the surgical removal of a necrosed bone ‖ the dissection of corpses [fr. Gk *nekros*, dead body+*tomē*, cutting]

nec·tar (néktǝr) *n.* (*Gk and Rom. mythol.*) the drink of the gods ‖ a sweet substance secreted by the nectaries of plants and collected by bees to make honey [L. fr. Gk *nektar*]

nec·tar·e·ous (nektéǝri:ǝs) *adj.* nectarous

nec·tar·ine (nęktǝri:n) *n. Prunus persica nectarina*, fam. *Rosaceae*, a smooth-skinned variety of peach

nec·tar·ous (néktǝrǝs) *adj.* consisting of or resembling nectar

nec·ta·ry (néktǝri:) *pl.* **nec·ta·ries** *n.* a group of modified subepidermal cells secreting nectar in a flower [M.L. *nectarium*]

Ned·dy (nédi:) *n.* (*Br.*) nickname for National Economic Development Council of Great Britain

née, nee (nei) *adj.* (used in giving a married woman's maiden name) born with the family name of, *Mrs Brown née Smith* [F.]

need (ni:d) *n.* a condition necessitating supply or relief, *in need of reinforcements, in need of advice* ‖ a requirement for subsistence or for carrying out some function or activity, *a small income may satisfy one's needs* ‖ poverty, *she kept her need secret* ‖ obligation, *there is no need to write and thank him* **at need** as and when needed **if need be** if necessary, *if need be I'll lend you the money* **to have need of** to need [O.E. *nēd, nīed*]

need *v.i.* to be in want ‖ *v.t.* to be in need of, to require, *people need affection, the job needs to be done* ‖ verbal auxiliary (neg. **I** (etc.) **need not, needn't** interrog. **need I** (etc.)?, *3rd pers. sing.* **one need**) to be under a specified necessity or obligation, *he need not go, one need only consider the facts* [O.E. *nēodian*]

need·ful (ní:dfǝl) *adj.* (*old-fash.*) necessary, requisite

nee·dle (ní:d'l) **1.** *n.* a slender pointed piece of steel, bone etc. with an eye for carrying the thread, used in sewing, darning etc. ‖ a similar, larger instrument without an eye, used in knitting etc. ‖ a surgical instrument of similar shape, often with a hollow center, *a hypodermic needle* ‖ an object of similar shape, e.g. an obelisk ‖ a leaf of similar shape, e.g. of the pine ‖ the pointer of a compass or gauge ‖ a pointed tool used in engraving, etching etc. ‖ a phonograph stylus ‖ a short beam of wood used as a support in building **a needle in a haystack** something almost impossible to find **2.** *v.t. pres. part.* **nee·dling** *past* and *past part.* **nee·dled** (*pop.*) to tease or goad (someone) persistently ‖ (*build-*

ing) to support (a wall) with a needle beam [O.E. *nǣdl*]

needle coke a by-product of crude-oil production used for electrodes in electric arc furnaces for making steel; developed by Conoco

nee·dle·fish (ní:d'lfiʃ) *pl.* **nee·dle·fish, nee·dle·fish·es** *n.* any of the voracious elongated teleostean fishes of genus *Belone* and other related genera. They resemble, but are not related to, freshwater garfishes ‖ a pipefish

nee·dle·point (ní:d'lpɔint) **1.** *n.* a type of lace made on a paper or parchment pattern ‖ embroidery on canvas in cross-stitch, tent stitch etc. **2.** *adj.* of such lace or embroidery

need·less (ní:dlis) *adj.* unnecessary, *a needless waste* **needless to say** self-evidently, obviously

needle valve a valve in which the flow of liquid is controlled by the rise and fall of a thin pointed rod in a conical aperture

nee·dle·wom·an (ní:d'lwumǝn) *pl.* **nee·dle·wom·en** (ní:d'lwimǝn) *n.* a woman who does needlework

nee·dle·work (ní:d'lwǝːrk) *n.* embroidery, or any work done with a needle, esp. other than plain sewing, darning etc.

need·n't (ní:d'nt) *contr.* of NEED NOT

needs (ni:dz) *adv.* (*rhet.*, used before or after 'must') of necessity, *it must needs be done* or (*ironic*) with foolish perversity, *he must needs go and lose his passport* [O.E. *nēdes*]

need to know (*mil.*) a criterion used in security procedures that requires the custodians of classified information to establish, prior to disclosure, that the intended recipient must have access to the information in order to perform his or her official duties

need·y (ní:di:) *comp.* **need·i·er** *superl.* **need·i·est** *adj.* poverty-stricken

ne'er-do-well (néǝrdu:węl) **1.** *n.* a worthless person likely to get into trouble **2.** *adj.* of such a person [*ne'er*, contr. of NEVER]

ne·far·i·ous (niféǝri:ǝs) *adj.* (*rhet.*) wicked, iniquitous [fr. L. *nefarius*]

Nef·er·ti·ti (nefǝrtí:ti:) (14th c. B.C.), Egyptian queen of the 18th dynasty, wife of Amenhotep IV. Her portrait bust, found at Tell-el-Amarna, is a masterpiece of Egyptian art

Nefud *NAFUD

ne·gate (nigéit) *pres. part.* **ne·gat·ing** *past* and *past part.* **ne·gat·ed** *v.t.* to render null and void, as though nonexistent [fr. L. *negare (negatus)*]

ne·ga·tion (nigéiʃǝn) *n.* denial, contradiction ‖ something that is the absence or opposite of some positive quality, *his conduct is the negation of honesty* [F.]

neg·a·tive (négǝtiv) **1.** *adj.* having the effect of saying 'no', esp. to a question or request, *a negative reply* ‖ lacking in positive character, *a negative personality* ‖ not constructive, *negative criticism* ‖ not affirming the presence of something looked for, *the chemical test gave a negative reaction* ‖ (*math.*) of that which is measured by subtracting from zero on some scale of measurement, *minus ten is a negative quantity* ‖ opposite to a direction regarded as positive ‖ (*elec.*, of a charge) carried by electrons ‖ (*elec.* of an electrode (cathode)) of a cell or other electric device that is at the lower potential ‖ (*photog.*, of an image) in which the tones or colors of the subject are reversed ‖ (*physiol.*) relating to movement away from a stimulus, *negative phototaxis* ‖ (*logic*, of a statement) disagreeing with a premise or earlier statement **2.** *n.* a proposition which denies or contradicts ‖ a reply which has the effect of saying 'no' ‖ (*math.*) a quantity less than zero ‖ (*photog.*) a developed negative image, usually on a transparent base from which positive prints may be made ‖ (*elec.*) a negative plate or element in a voltaic cell **in the negative** with a negative reply, *she answered in the negative* ‖ with the effect of refusing or denying something, *her answer was in the negative* **3.** *v.t. pres. part.* **neg·a·tiv·ing** *past* and *past part.* **neg·a·tived** to reply 'no' to (a proposal) ‖ to contradict ‖ to prove false ‖ to neutralize [fr. F. *négatif* or fr. L.L. *negativus*]

negative feedback *FEEDBACK

negative growth (*economics*) 1977 proposal of the Club of Rome to limit economic growth in order to conserve natural resources on earth

negative income tax (*economics*) government payment to provide a minimum income *Cf* GUARANTEED ANNUAL INCOME

negative prescription (*Br., law*) limitation of the time within which a prescriptive title or right may be claimed

negative transfer (*behavioral psych.*) in learn-

ing, the carry-over of previous experience that impedes new responses

neg·a·tiv·ism (négǝtivizǝm) *n.* an attitude of resistance to other people's suggestions ‖ a negative philosophy (skepticism, agnosticism etc.)

neg·a·tiv·ist *n.* and *adj.*

neg·a·tiv·i·ty (negǝtíviti:) *n.* the quality or state of being negative

neg·a·to·ry (négǝtɔri:, négǝtɔuri:) *adj.* of the nature of negation

negentropy *ENTROPY

Neg·ev, Neg·eb (négev) the region of Israel south of Beersheba, formerly a desert. Irrigation schemes are making it increasingly productive (wheat, cotton, sugar beets, vegetables, fruit)

ne·glect (niglékt) **1.** *v.t.* to fail to perform (an act, duty etc.), esp. through carelessness ‖ to fail to attend to, to fail to care for, *the mother neglected her child* ‖ to fail to attend to, disregard, *many people neglect modern music* **2.** *n.* a neglecting ‖ negligence ‖ the state of being neglected **ne·glect·ful** *adj.* [fr. L. *neglegere* fr. *neg-*, not+*legere*, to pick up]

neg·li·gee, nég·li·gé (nęgliʒéi) *n.* a woman's light dressing gown, usually loose and flowing [F., past part. of *négliger*, to neglect]

neg·li·gence (néglidʒǝns) *n.* want of attention or care ‖ an instance of this **nég·li·gent** *adj.* [O. F.]

neg·li·gi·bil·i·ty (nęglidʒǝbíliti:) *n.* the quality or state of being negligible

neg·li·gi·ble (néglidʒǝb'l) *adj.* so small or unimportant that it may be neglected, disregarded or omitted [fr. L. *negligere*, to disregard]

ne·go·tia·bil·i·ty (nigouʃǝbíliti:, nigouʃi:ǝbíliti:) *n.* the state or quality of being negotiable

ne·go·tia·ble (nigóuʃǝb'l, nigóuʃi:ǝb'l) *adj.* which can be negotiated ‖ (*commerce*, of checks, bills of exchange, securities etc.) which can be transferred from one person to another, with or without endorsement

ne·go·ti·ate (nigóuʃi:eit) *pres. part.* **ne·go·ti·at·ing** *past* and *past part.* **ne·go·ti·at·ed** *v.i.* to discuss something in order to reach an agreement, confer ‖ *v.t.* to carry through (a transaction) by a process of discussion, *to negotiate the sale of an estate* ‖ to transfer or cash (a check, securities etc.) ‖ (*pop.*) to succeed in accomplishing, crossing, climbing etc. [fr. L. *negotiari* (*negotiatus*), to do business]

ne·go·ti·a·tion (nigouʃi:éiʃǝn) *n.* a negotiating ‖ (esp. *pl.*) discussion to bring about some result, esp. involving bargaining [fr. L. *negotiatio* (*negotiationis*)]

ne·go·ti·a·tor (nigóuʃi:eitǝr) *n.* a person who negotiates

Ne·gress (ní:gris) *n.* a female Negro [fr. F. *négresse*]

Ne·gret·ti (negrétti:) *PALMA VECCHIO

Ne·gril·lo (negrílou) *pl.* **Ne·gril·los, Ne·gril·loes** *n.* a member of an African Negroid people of small stature (e.g Bushmen, Pygmies) [Span., dim. of *negro*, a Negro]

Ne·gri Sem·bi·lan (nǝgrí:sǝmbi:lan) a state (area 2,565 sq. miles, pop. 563,955) of S.W. Malaysia. Capital: Seremban. Main port: Port Dickson. A confederation of largely independent states (18th c.), Negri Sembilan entered into treaties with Britain (1874–89) and joined the Federation of Malaya, later Malaysia (1948)

Ne·gri·to (nǝgrí:tou) *pl.* **Ne·gri·tos, Ne·gri·toes** *n.* a member of a Negroid people of small stature, inhabiting parts of S.E. Asia and Oceania [Span., dim. of *negro*, a Negro]

ne·gri·tude (négritu:d) *n.* **1.** the state and pride of being black **2.** pride in the cultural heritage of black people —**negritudinous** *adj.*

Ne·gro (ní:grou) **1.** *pl.* **Ne·groes** *n.* a member of the dark-skinned race, one of the three main anthropological divisions of mankind, living in Africa south of the Sahara (cf. CAUCASIAN, cf. MONGOLIAN) ‖ a descendant of this race in the U.S.A., the Caribbean etc. **2.** *adj.* of this race [Span. *negro*, black, a Negro]

Ne·groid (ní:grɔid) **1.** *adj.* like or related to the Negro race **2.** *n.* one of a people predominantly Negro but with some admixture [NEGRO]

ne·gro·ni (negróuni:) *n.* an alcoholic drink made of gin, sweet vermouth, and bitters

Ne·gro, Rí·o (ri:ɔnégrɔ) a river (c. 630 miles long) in S. central Argentina, flowing east into the Atlantic north of the Gulf of San Matías

Ne·gros (néigrous) an island (area 4,905 sq. miles, pop. 2,219,022) of the Visayas, central Philippines, producing esp. sugarcane. Highest point: Canalaon (8,087 ft)

CONCISE PRONUNCIATION KEY: **(a)** æ, c*a*t; ɑ, c*a*r; ɔ f*aw*n; ei, sn*a*ke. **(e)** e, h*e*n; i:, sh*ee*p; iǝ, d*ee*r; ɛǝ, b*ea*r. **(i)** i, f*i*sh; ai, t*i*ger; ǝ:, b*i*rd. **(o)** o, *o*x; au, c*ow*; ou, g*oa*t; u, p*oo*r; ɔi, r*oy*al. **(u)** ʌ, d*u*ck; u, b*u*ll; u:, g*oo*se; ǝ, b*a*cillus; ju:, c*u*be. x, lo*ch*; θ, *th*ink; δ, *b*o*th*er; z, *Z*en; ʒ, corsa*g*e; dʒ, sava*g*e; ŋ, ora*n*gutang; j, *y*ak; ʃ, *fi*sh; tʃ, *f*e*tch*; 'l, rabb*le*; 'n, redd*en*. Complete pronunciation key appears inside front cover.

Ne·gus (ní:gəs) *n.* a title of the sovereign of Ethiopia [Amharic]

ne·gus (ní:gəs) *n.* a drink of wine and hot water, sweetened, and often flavored with nutmeg or lemon juice [after Francis *Negus* (*d.* 1732), English soldier, its inventor]

Ne·he·mi·ah (nị:imáiə) a Jewish leader (5th c. B.C.) ‖ the book of the Old Testament which bears his name. It relates how Nehemiah led the Jews in rebuilding the walls of Jerusalem (c. 444 B.C.) and introduced religious reforms

Neh·ru (néiru:), Jawaharlal (1889–1964), Indian statesman. A Kashmiri Brahmin educated in England, he joined (1920) Gandhi's nationalist movement and was imprisoned eight times (1920–7) for leading resistance to British rule. He became president of the Indian National Congress (1929–30, 1936–7, 1946, 1951–4) and the first prime minister of the Union of India (1947–64). He maintained strict neutrality in foreign policy and fought the problems of poverty and overpopulation at home

Neh·ru jacket (neruə) *n.* men's high-collar, long-sleeved jacket, named for Indian prime minister Jawaharlal Nehru —**Nehru suit,** *n.* Nehru jacket with straight-legged trousers

neigh (nei) **1.** *v.i.* to make the cry of a horse **2.** *n.* this cry [O.E. *hnǽgan*]

neigh·bor, *Br.* **neigh·bour** (néibər) **1.** *n.* a person living next door or relatively close to another ‖ a person or thing situated near or relatively near to another, *the new building dwarfs its neighbors* **2.** *v.t.* to be situated near to, adjoin ‖ *v.i.* (with 'on' or 'upon') to abut [O.E. *nēahgebūr*]

neigh·bor·hood, *Br.* **neigh·bour·hood** (néibərhud) *n.* a district, *the houses in that neighborhood are expensive* ‖ the people in that district, *the whole neighborhood came* ‖ (*town planning*) an area of a town planned as a unit with its own shops, services and amenities **in the neighbor·hood of** close to (a place), approximately, *in the neighborhood of $1,000*

neigh·bor·ing, *Br.* **neigh·bour·ing** *adj.* situated in the neighborhood

neigh·bor·li·ness, *Br.* **neigh·bour·li·ness** (néibərli:nis) *n.* the quality or condition of being neighborly

neigh·bor·ly, *Br.* **neigh·bour·ly** (néibərli:) *adj.* friendly, sociable

neighbour *NEIGHBOR

neighbourhood *NEIGHBORHOOD

neighbouring *NEIGHBORING

neighbourliness *NEIGHBORLINESS

neighbourly *NEIGHBORLY

Neis·se (náisə) (*Pol.* Nysa) a tributary (140 miles long) of the Oder, rising in N. Czechoslovakia. It forms the lower Polish-East German border (*ODERNEISSE LINE)

nei·ther (ní:ðər, náiðər) **1.** *adj.* not either of two, *neither explanation is satisfactory* **2.** *pron.* not either of two (usually with a singular verb), *neither of the sisters has ever been abroad* **3.** *conj.* (negative correlative with 'not' to connect two or more alternatives), *his work was neither thorough nor rapid* ‖ nor yet, *he could not answer, and neither could his sister* **neither here nor there** irrelevant [M.E. *naither, neyther*]

Nejd (nedʒd) the eastern division (area 447,000 sq. miles, pop. 4,000,000) of Saudi Arabia. Capital: Riyadh. Products: petroleum, dates, cereals, coffee (oasis farms), pearls (Persian Gulf), hides, wool. Saudi Arabia has been built around it during the reign of Abdul Aziz ibn-Saud ‖ the whole central plateau of Arabia

Ne·kra·sov (njəkrásɔf), Nicolai Alekseyevich (1821–77), Russian poet and journalist. Passionate sympathy with the peasants and longing for the freeing of the serfs inform his best lyrics and longer poems

nek·ton (néktən) *n.* (*biol.*) organisms swimming actively in water, as opposed to drifting (cf. PLANKTON) [G. fr. Gk]

Nel·son (nélsən), Horatio, 1st Viscount Nelson (1758–1805), British admiral and national hero. He distinguished himself by his daring naval tactics during the French Revolutionary Wars (1792–1802), gaining brilliant victories at the Nile (1798) and Copenhagen (1801). He was killed at his greatest victory, Trafalgar (1805), having saved Britain from the threat of Napoleonic invasion

Nelson a region (area 6,910 sq. miles, pop. 66,000) in the mountainous northwest of South Island, New Zealand: fruit, hops, tobacco, dairy products ‖ its chief city and port (pop. 26,000): food processing

Nelson a partially navigable river (390 miles long: incl. its headstreams, about 1,660 miles long) of Manitoba, Canada, flowing northeast from Lake Winnipeg through several lakes into the Hudson Bay

nel·son (nélsən) *FULL NELSON, HALF NELSON

Ne·man (némən) the Niemen

Nemanja *STEVAN NEMANJA

nem·a·thel·minth (neməθélminθ) *n.* a worm of the *phylum Nemathelminthes*, with a cylindrical unsegmented body [fr. Gk *nēma* (*nēmatos*), thread+*helmins* (*helminthos*), worm]

Nematoda (*biol.*) a class of unisexual round worms

nem·a·tode (némətoud) **1.** *n.* a member of *Nematoda*, a phylum of unsegmented worms including the hookworm. They are found free-living in soil and water, and are parasites of most animals and plants **2.** *adj.* of or relating to these worms [fr. Gk *nēma* (*nēmatos*), thread]

Ne·me·a (ní:mi:ə, nimí:ə) a valley of Argolis, Greece, where Hercules choked the Nemean lion (*HERACLES) **Né·me·an** *adj.*

ne·mer·te·an (nimé:rti:ən) *n.* a marine worm of the class *Nemertea* (or other classification). Nemerteans are elongate and unsegmented and are often brightly colored [fr. Mod. L. fr. Gk *Nēmértes*, name of a sea nymph]

nem·e·sis (némisis) *pl.* **nem·e·ses** (némisi:z) *n.* retribution and punishment, esp. for evil on a vast scale ‖ an act of retributive justice [after *Nemesis*, the Greek goddess of justice and vengeance]

NEMO (*acronym*) not emanating from main office, a remote radio or television broadcast

Nen·ni·us (néni:əs) (late 8th c.), Welsh writer. His 'Historia Britonum' preserves ancient traditional accounts of Roman and Saxon England

neo- (ní:ou) *prefix* now, recent ‖ a later revival of ‖ recently discovered or developed ‖ (of hydrocarbons) recently classified [fr. Gk *neos*, new]

Ne·o·cene (ní:əsi:n) *adj.* of or relating to the later division of the Tertiary period or system, comprising the Miocene and the Pliocene epochs or series **the Neocene** this division of the Tertiary [NEO-+*cene* fr. Gk *kainos*, new]

ne·o·clas·sic (nị:ouklǽsik) *adj.* of or relating to the revival of classic style, esp. in art and literature ‖ of or relating to a school of postclassical economists led by Alfred Marshall **ne·o·clás·si·cal** *adj.* **ne·o·clás·si·cism, ne·o·clás·si·cist** *ns*

ne·o·co·lo·ni·al·ism (nị:oukəlóuni:əlizəm) *n.* economic domination, and consequent political power over, underdeveloped nations by former colonial powers —**neocolonial** *n., adj.* —**neo·colonialist** *n., adj.* *Cf* NEOIMPERIALISM

ne·o·Da·da (nị:oudádə) *n.* new Dadaism; anti-art art movement based on Dadaism but with greater attention paid to the object —**neo·Dadaism** *n.* —**neo-Dadaist** *n.*

ne·o·dym·i·um (nị:oudími:əm) *n.* a rare-earth element (symbol Nd, at. no. 60, at. mass 144.24) used for coloring glass violet [fr. NEO-+*didymium*, a mixture of rare-earth elements containing neodymium and formerly considered as an element]

neo-Firthian (*linguistics*) *FIRTHIAN

ne·o·gla·ci·a·tion (nị:ouglẹiʃi:éifən) *n.* (*geol.*) process of forming new glaciers —**neoglacial** *adj.*

ne·o·Goth·ic (nị:ougóθik) *adj.* of or relating to the revival of Gothic art and architecture in the 18th and 19th cc. in Europe and North America (*GOTHIC)

ne·o·im·pe·ri·al·ism (nị:ouimpíəri:əlizəm) *n.* revival of imperialism, esp. by the U.S., U.S.S.R., and China —**neoimperialist** *n., adj. Cf* NEOCOLONIALISM

ne·o·Im·pres·sion·ism (nị:ouimpréʃənizəm) *n.* pointillism

ne·o·Keynes·ian (nị:oukéinʒən) *adj.* (*economics*) of the revival of the policy of government-stimulation of the economy, esp. via increasing the money supply

ne·o·lith (ní:əliθ) *n.* a polished stone implement of the last period of the Stone Age **Ne·o·líth·ic** *adj.* of this period, following the Mesolithic, and characterized by the use of neoliths and ground tools of horn and bone. In this period, which lasted (in Europe and W. Asia) c. 6000–c. 3000 B.C., man learned to tame animals, to cultivate crops, to use the wheel and to weave [fr. NEO-+Gk *lithos*, stone]

neolithic revolution development of food economy in the Middle East 9,000–6,000 B.C., a prime step in civilizing process; coined by V. G. Childe, *The Neolithic Revolution* (1963)

ne·ol·o·gism (ni:ólədʒizəm) *n.* a new word or phrase ‖ a word or phrase used in a new meaning ‖ the use of such words or phrases **ne·ól·o·gist** *n.* **ne·ól·o·gize** *pres. part.* **ne·ol·o·giz·ing** *past* and *past part.* **ne·ol·o·gized** *v.i.* to make or use new words or invent new meanings for words [fr. F. *néologisme*]

ne·ol·o·gy (ni:ólədʒi:) *pl.* **ne·ol·o·gies** *n.* a neologism ‖ neologism [fr. F. *néologie*]

ne·on (ní:ɒn) *n.* an inert gaseous element (symbol Ne, at. no. 10, at. mass 20.183) found in the atmosphere and used at low pressure in a tube to convey an electronic discharge, which causes it to emit an intense orange-red light ‖ this light, esp. as used in illuminating advertisements [Gk, neut. of *neos*, new]

ne·o·na·tol·o·gy (nị:ouneitóladʒi:) *n.* (*med.*) study of the first 60 days of human infant's life

ne·o·phil·ia (nị:oufíli:ə) *n.* strong interest in new things —**neophiliac** *n.* the person affected —**neophilism** *n.* morbid or undue desire for the new *ant.* neophobia

ne·o·pho·bi·a (nị:oufóubi:ə) *n.* fear of new things or places *ant.* neophilia

ne·o·phyte (ní:əfait) *n.* a beginner, novice ‖ a new convert to a religion, esp. an early Christian ‖ (*Roman Catholicism*) a recently ordained priest or new member of a convent [fr. F. or fr. L.L. fr. Gk *neophytos*, newly planted]

ne·o·plasm (ní:əplæzəm) *n.* a new growth of excess tissue in plants and animals, either benign or malignant (cf. TUMOR) **ne·o·plas·tic** (nị:ouplǽstik) *adj.* [fr. NEO-+Gk *plasma*, formation]

ne·o·plas·tic (nị:ouplǽstik) *adj.* (*med.*) of a growth of abnormal tissue —**neoplastic** *n.* a tumor

ne·o·plas·ti·cism (nị:ouplǽstisiʒəm) *n.* the art theories of Piet Mondrian (*STIJL, DE)

Ne·o·pla·ton·ic (nị:ouplətónik) *adj.* of or relating to Neoplatonism

Ne·o·pla·to·nism (nị:oupléitənizəm) *n.* the revival and transformation of Platonic philosophy which flourished in various schools of the 3rd–6th cc. The movement was founded in Alexandria by Ammonius Saccas. Its leading exponents were Plotinus and Porphyry. Its ideas are a synthesis of Greek thought and of certain trends in Oriental mysticism. Its central doctrines are emanation, the belief that the human spirit can participate in the divine, and the belief in the transcendent One which is beyond all knowledge and all being ‖ these doctrines as adopted by medieval mystics and by humanists of the Italian Renaissance **Ne·o·plá·to·nist** *n.* and *adj.*

ne·o·prene (ní:əpri:n) *n.* a synthetic rubber polymer of composition $(CH_2 \cdot CH \cdot CCl \cdot CH_2)_n$, resistant to oil, sunlight, heat and oxidation

Ne·o·pro·pene (ni:ouróupi:n) *n.* (*chem.*) DuPont trademark for polychoropene, a rubber substitute used to cover cables

ne·o·Py·thag·o·re·an (nị:oupaiθægəri:ən) *n.* someone who held the doctrines of an Alexandrian school of philosophy (1st c. A.D.) which put a mystical interpretation on many Pythagorean ideas **ne·o·Py·thag·o·ré·an·ism** *n.*

ne·o·Scho·las·tic (nị:ouskəlǽstik) *adj.* of or relating to neo-Scholasticism

ne·o·Scho·las·ti·cism (nị:ouskəlǽstisiʒəm) *n.* neo-Thomism

ne·ot·e·ny (ni:ót'ni:) *n.* the retention of larval characters beyond the normal period ‖ the occurrence of adult characteristics in larvae ‖ process in evolution resulting in sexual maturity at an age corresponding to fetal stage of their ancestors, important in stimulating evolutionary change [fr. NEO-+Gk *teinein, n.* stretch]

ne·o·ter·ic area (nị:outérik) site containing important examples of man's modern culture, earmarked for future historic preservation, e.g., a momentous new building

ne·o·Tho·mism (nị:outóumizəm) to the intellectual renewal of Catholicism begun under Pope Leo XIII, based on the study of St Thomas Aquinas in the light of modern research and speculation **ne·o·Thó·mist** *adj.* and *n.*

Ne·pal (nipɔ́l) a kingdom (area 54,600 sq. miles, pop. 16,179,000) of Asia, lying along the central Himalayas. Capital: Katmandu. People: *INDIA (subcontinent). Language: Nepali (official), Hindi and Tibeto-Burman tribal languages, English. Religion: Hindu and Lamaist, 1% Moslem. The land (30% forest, 28% arable, 15%

CONCISE PRONUNCIATION KEY: **(a)** æ, c*a*t; ɑ, c*a*r; ɔ f*aw*n; ei, sn*a*ke. **(e)** e, h*e*n; i:, sh*ee*p; iə, d*ee*r; ɛə, b*ea*r. **(i)** i, f*i*sh; ai, t*i*ger; ə:, b*i*rd. **(o)** o, *o*x; au, c*ow*; ou, g*oa*t; u, p*oo*r; ɔi, r*oy*al. **(u)** ʌ, d*u*ck; u, b*u*ll; u:, g*oo*se; ə, b*a*cillus; ju:, c*u*be. x, lo*ch*; θ, *th*ink; ð, *b*other; z, *Z*en; ʒ, cor*s*age; dʒ, sa*v*age; ŋ, ora*ng*uta*ng*; j, *y*ak; ʃ, *f*ish; tʃ, fe*tch*; 'l, rabb*le*; 'n, red*den*. Complete pronunciation key appears inside front cover.

under permanent snow) slopes southward from the Himalaya crest (Tibetan border). Longitudinal river gorges separate the great massifs of the Himalayas, including Everest (29,028 ft), Kanchenjunga (28,146 ft), Dhaulagiri (26,795 ft) and Annapurna (26,502 ft). Below them are the Mahabharat Lekh (6,000–8,000 ft) and then the Siwalik Hills (2,000–3,500 ft) divided by many river valleys. The Terai, a swampy plain, lies along the Indian border. Seasons: rains (June–Oct.), cold (Oct.–Apr.), hot (Apr.–June). Average temperature (F.): Katmandu 52°–60°. The Terai is tropical, the mountains are arctic. Rainfall: 60–80 ins, but 100–150 ins in the eastern hills. Livestock: cattle, poultry, sheep, goats. Crops: cereals, potatoes, oil seeds, tobacco, jute, sugarcane, fruit, tea. Mineral resources: coal, copper, mica, graphite. Manufactures: jute, sugar, matches, glass, pottery, paper, cement, chemicals. Exports: agricultural products, jute, timber, medicinal herbs, hides and skins, cattle. Imports: textiles, cigarettes, salt, gasoline and fuels, sugar, machinery, footwear, paper, cement, iron and steel, tea. University: Tribhubana (1960). Monetary unit: Nepalese rupee (100 pice). HISTORY. Nepal was inhabited by Mongolian tribes until the 14th c., when Gurkhas and other Himalayan peoples migrated to the region, bringing Hinduism. It was divided into independent principalities (15th c.) and reunited (1769) under the Gurkhas, who invaded Tibet (1790) but were driven back by the Chinese (1791). After a border war with British India (1814–15) commercial relations were established with India. Nepal became a constitutional monarchy (1951) and joined the U.N. (1955). In 1959 the Hindu ruler, King Mahendra, dismissed the cabinet and parliament. The 1962 constitution provides for a non-party council government with a 140-member legislature. In 1980 King Birenda Bir Bikram Shah Dev called a referendum to modify the governmental system. The first direct parliamentary elections were held in 1981

Nep·a·lese (nepəlí:z) **1.** *n.* a native or inhabitant of Nepal ‖ Nepali **2.** *adj.* of or relating to Nepal or its people ‖ Nepali

Ne·pal·i (nipɔ́li:) **1.** *n.* the Indic language of Nepal ‖ a Nepalese **2.** *adj.* of or relating to Nepali ‖ Nepalese

ne·pen·the (nipénθi:) *n.* a drug thought by the ancient Greeks to relieve sorrow and pain [L. fr. Gk *nēpenthēs*, removing sorrow]

neph·a·nal·y·sis (nefənǽlisis) *n.* (*meteor.*) study of cloud formations as photographed by satellites

ne·phe·loid layer (nefəlɔid) (*envir.*) a level of turbid water found in some deep ocean waters near U.S. East Coast

ne·phel·o·me·ter (nefəlɔ́mitər) *n.* a device to observe, measure, and record light, esp. ultraviolet light, emitted by space objects

neph·ew (néfju:, *Br.* esp. névju:) *n.* a son of a person's brother or sister [O.F. *neveu*]

neph·o·lom·e·tar (nefəlɔ́mitər) *n.* a set of barium chloride standards used to estimate the turbidity of a liquid and the approximate number of bacteria in suspension in it ‖ an instrument transmitting and reflecting light, used for revealing the nature of suspensions in a liquid [fr. *nephelē*, a cloud+METER]

ne·phrid·i·um (nəfrídiəm) *pl.* **ne·phrid·i·a** (nəfrídiə) *n.* the usual excretory organ of invertebrates [Mod. L. fr. Gk *nephridion*, dim. of *nephros*, kidney]

neph·rite (néfrait) *n.* a silicate of calcium and magnesium forming a lesser quality of jade, formerly worn as a cure for kidney disease [G. *nephrit* fr. Gk *nephros*, kidney]

neph·rit·ic (nəfrítik) *adj.* related to the kidneys, renal ‖ of or relating to nephritis [fr. L.L. *nephriticus* fr. Gk]

ne·phri·tis (nəfráitis) *pl.* **ne·phrit·i·des** (nəfrítidi:z) *n.* inflammation of the kidney [fr. L.L. fr. Gk *nephros*, kidney]

Nep·i·gon (népigɒn) *NIPIGON

Nep·os (népous), Cornelius (c. 100–c. 25 B.C.), Roman author. He wrote a collection of biographies, 'De viris illustribus'

nep·o·tism (népətizəm) *n.* favoritism shown in the advancement of relatives, esp. by appointing them to offices for reasons other than personal worth **nep·o·tist** *n.* [fr. F. *népotisme* fr. Ital. *nepotismo* fr. *nepote*, nephew, because of favoritism shown by medieval prelates to their 'nephews' (often bastard sons)]

Nep·tune (néptu:n, néptju:n) (*Rom. mythol.*) the god of the sea, son of Saturn, brother of Jupiter and Pluto, identified with the Greek god Poseidon ‖ the eighth planet from the sun (mean orbital diameter=2.797 x 10⁹ miles). It is about 17 times more massive than the earth (mass=9.90 x 10²² tons, linear diameter =28,000 miles). It revolves about the sun with a sidereal period of 164.8 earth years and rotates on its axis with a period of 15.8 earth hours. Its atmosphere and physical condition resemble that of Jupiter, Saturn and Uranus. It has two known satellites, Triton and Nereid. Voyager 2 spacecraft is scheduled to reach Neptune in 1989

nep·tu·ni·um (neptú:ni:əm, neptjú:ni:əm) *n.* an unstable radioactive element (symbol Np, at. no. 93, weight of isotope of longest known half-life 237) artificially produced by uranium atoms in absorbing neutrons and changing to plutonium [Mod. L.]

nerd (nərd) *n.* (*slang*) a gauche, unsophisticated, or uncool person

Ne·re·id (nífəri:id) (*Gk mythol.*) a sea nymph, one of the 50 daughters of Nereus, the sea god

Neri *PHILIP NERI

Nernst (nernst), Walther Hermann (1864–1941), German physical chemist. He developed many aspects of the thermodynamics and physical chemistry of solutions and formulated the third law of thermodynamics. Nobel Prize (1920)

Nernst lamp or **Nernst glower** (nɛərnst) a zirconium oxide rod that becomes brilliantly incandescent when heated by an electric current in the air

Ne·ro (nífərou) (Nero Claudius Caesar, 37–68), Roman emperor (54–68), son of Agrippina. His rule began well under Seneca's guidance, but became increasingly despotic after he murdered Agrippina (59). He used the fire which destroyed much of Rome (64) as a pretext to persecute Christians. He executed many opponents after the discovery of a plot to depose him (65), and committed suicide when the governors of Gaul, Spain and Africa revolted against him

ner·o·li (nérəli:) *n.* an oil from the flowers of the Seville orange used in making liqueurs and perfumes (esp. eau de cologne) [fr. F. *néroli*, fr. the 17th-c. Italian princess of *Nerole*]

Ne·ru·da (nerú:ðə), Pablo (Ricardo Eliezer Neftalí Reyes y Basoalto, 1904–73), Chilean poet. His best-known collections of poems include 'Residencia en la tierra' (1933 and 1939) and 'Canto general' (1950). He received the Lenin Prize for Peace (1953) and the Nobel Prize for literature (1971)

Ner·va (nɔ́:rvə), Marcus Cocceius (c. 30–98), Roman emperor (96–8). Elected by the senate on the assassination of Domitian, he was noted for his liberal measures

ner·vate (nɔ́:rveit) *adj.* (*bot.*) of leaves having veins or nerves

ner·va·tion (nərvéiʃən) *n.* venation

nerve (nə:rv) **1.** *n.* any of the cordlike fibers or bundles of fibers of neural tissue that connect the nervous system with other organs of the body for the purpose of conducting nervous impulses to or away from these organs ‖ nervous fiber ‖ the vein of an insect wing ‖ the midrib or vein of a leaf ‖ courage, *climbing calls for strength and nerve* ‖ (*pop.*) impudence ‖ (*pl.*) emotional upset, resulting in fright, excitement or irritability **to get on one's nerves** to annoy one, *his cough gets on my nerves* **to have the nerve to do something** to be brave enough to do something ‖ (*pop.*) to be impudent enough to do something **to lose one's nerve** to lose self-confidence or courage **to strain every nerve** to make every possible effort **2.** *v.t. pres. part.* **nerv·ing** *past* and *past part.* **nerved** to invigorate or give courage to, *the brandy nerved him for one last effort* [fr. L. *nervus*]

nerve agent (*mil.*) a lethal agent causing paralysis by interfering with the transmission of nerve impulses

nerve cell one of the cells and its processes (*AXON, *DENDRITE) that constitute nervous tissue and that transmit and receive nervous impulses

nerve center, *Br.* **nerve centre** (*physiol.*) a group of interacting nerve cells controlling a specific sensory or motor activity ‖ the essential, or controlling, part of an organization, system, body etc.

nerve fiber, *Br.* **nerve fibre** an axon or dendrite together with its protective covering

Ner·vel (nervæl), Gérard de (Gérard Labrunie, 1808–55), French writer. His romantic poetry includes 'les Chimères' (1854). He translated Goethe's 'Faust' (1825) and wrote imaginative prose works, e.g. 'Sylvie' (1854) and 'Aurélia' (1855)

nerve·less (nɔ́:rvlis) *adj.* lacking in spirit or vigor ‖ (*bot.* and *entom.*) without nervures ‖ (*zool.*) without nerves

nerve-rack·ing, nerve-wrack·ing (nɔ́:rvrækiŋ) *adj.* causing strain to the nerves

Ner·vi (nérvi:), Pier Luigi (1891–1979), Italian architect and engineer. He made revolutionary technological innovations in architectural construction, esp. with reinforced concrete. His buildings include the Exhibition Hall, Turin (1948–9). He collaborated with Breuer and Bernard Zehrfuss in designing the UNESCO building, Paris (1953–8), and with Ponti in the Pirelli skyscraper, Milan (1955–9)

Ner·vo (nérvɔ), Amado (1870–1919), Mexican modernist poet noted for his metrical inovation and sensitivity, influenced by French symbolism. His works include 'Serenidad', 'Elevacíon', 'La amada inmóvil', 'Perlas negras', and 'Plenitud'

ner·vous (nɔ́:rvəs) *adj.* of or relating to the nerves or the nervous system ‖ originating in or affected by the nerves, *nervous energy* ‖ timid, apprehensive ‖ made up of nerves ‖ excitable, easily agitated ‖ selfconscious and without confidence, *she is nervous on the stage* [fr. L. *nervosus*]

nervous breakdown an attack of neurasthenia

nervous system the system in man and other vertebrates comprising the brain, the spinal cord, ganglia, and the motor and sensory nerves and their endings, that serves to produce muscular activity on the basis of stimuli received and interpreted by the brain (cf. CENTRAL NERVOUS SYSTEM, cf. AUTONOMIC NERVOUS SYSTEM)

ner·vure (nɔ́:rvjər) *n.* (*bot.*) a principal vein in a leaf ‖ (*zool.*) one of the riblike structures which support an insect's wing [F.]

nerv·y (nɔ́:rvi:) *comp.* **nerv·i·er** *superl.* **nerv·i·est** *adj.* (*pop.*) impudent, brazen ‖ (*esp. Br.*) irritable, nervous, on edge [NERVE]

nes·cience (néʃəns) *n.* (*rhet.*) ignorance [fr. L.L. *nescientia*]

nes·cient (néʃənt) *adj.* (*rhet.*) showing nescience [fr. L. *nesciens* fr. *nescire*, to be ignorant of]

-ness *suffix* denoting quality or state, as in 'fineness', 'singleness' [fr. O.E. *-nes, -nis, -nys*, orig. fr. *n.* of *n-* stems+suffix *-assus*]

Ness, Loch (lɔ́knés, lɔ́xnés) a lake (23 miles long) in Inverness, Scotland, forming part of the Caledonian Canal. Exceptionally deep (to 754 ft), it is alleged to contain a monster

Nes·sel·rode (nésəlroud), Karl Robert, Count (1780–1862), Russian statesman. He played a prominent part at the Congress of Vienna (1814–15). As foreign minister (1816–56) he was largely responsible for Russia's reactionary policy in Europe

nest (nest) **1.** *n.* the structure built or place chosen and prepared by a bird for holding its eggs during incubation and for rearing its young ‖ a place built or prepared by certain mammals (e.g. mice, moles, squirrels, rabbits) and by certain fish, reptiles, crustaceans and insects to rear their young in ‖ a brood or swarm ‖ a place of retreat, esp. snug and cozy ‖ a haunt of criminals etc., a den ‖ a collection of similar objects, esp. ones that fit into one another, *a nest of tables* ‖ a gun emplacement **2.** *v.t.* to place in protective packing ‖ *v.i.* to build and occupy a nest ‖ to bird's-nest ‖ (esp. of pieces of furniture) to stack compactly together [O.E.]

NEST (acronym) for Nuclear Energy Search Team, group in FBI responsible for control of nuclear crime

nest egg a real or imitation egg put in a hen's nest to induce her to continue laying there ‖ a sum of money kept in reserve

nes·tle (nés'l) *pres. part.* **nes·tling** *past* and *past part.* **nes·tled** *v.i.* to settle oneself down comfortably and snugly ‖ to press snugly (against), *she nestled against his shoulder* ‖ to lie protected, *the house nestles in the woods* ‖ *v.t.* to press snugly (the head etc.) ‖ to make snug, settle protectively, *she nestled the bird in her hand* [O.E. *nestlian*]

nest·ling (néstliŋ, nésliŋ) *n.* a bird too young to leave the nest [NEST]

Nes·tor (néstər) legendary wise old king of Pylos, the oldest prince to take part in the siege of Troy

Nes·to·ri·an (nestóri:ən, nestóuri:ən) *n.* a follower of Nestorius. Nestorians refused to accept the decision of the Council of Ephesus (431), withdrew to Persia, Mesopotamia and Arabia, and flourished until they were overrun by the Tatars (14th c.). A remnant survives in Kurdistan

Nestorian Church a Christian community of Iraq, Persia and the Malabar Coast. Its liturgy uses Syriac

Nes·to·ri·us (nestóri:əs, nestóuri:əs) (c. 380–c. 451), patriarch of Constantinople (428–31). He taught that there were two distinct persons in Christ, and was deposed for heresy by the Council of Ephesus (431)

net (net) **1.** *n.* an open-meshed fabric of cord, hair, nylon etc. ‖ a piece of such fabric used for catching fish, birds, insects or animals ‖ a piece of such fabric used for carrying, protecting, confining or dividing ‖ (*fig.*) a snare, trap ‖ a network ‖ (*cricket*) a netted enclosure for practice ‖ (*tennis* etc.) a ball which hits the net **2.** *v. pres. part.* **net·ting** *past and past part.* **net·ted** *v.t.* to catch or enclose with a net ‖ to make (an article) in network ‖ to mark or cover with a network pattern ‖ (*tennis* etc.) to drive (the ball) into the net ‖ *v.i.* to make nets or netting [O.E.]

net, *Br.* also **nett** (net) **1.** *adj.* clear of all charges and deductions, *a net profit* (opp. GROSS) ‖ clear of tare, *net weight* (opp. GROSS) **2.** *v.t. pres. part.* **net·ting, nett·ing** *past and pastpart.* **net·ted, nett·ed** to gain as a clear profit, *the firm netted $1,000 on the transaction* **3.** *n.* clear profit, net income, net amount, net weight etc. [F. *net*, clean, clear]

net·ball (nétbɔl) *n.* a game resembling basketball played by two teams of seven on a court usually 100x 50 ft. Goals are scored by throwing the ball, which resembles a soccer ball, so that it falls through a cylindrical net suspended from a ring several feet above the ground

net call sign a call sign that represents all stations within a network

net-chain-cell system (net tʃein sel) patterns of a clandestine organization, esp. for operational purposes. Net is a succession of echelons and specialists. Chain is a series of agents and informants who receive instructions from, and pass information to, a principal agent by cutouts and couriers. Cell is a grouping of personnel into relatively isolated and self-contained small units, each cell having contact with the rest of the organization only through an agent and a single member of the cell

neth·er (néðər) *adj.* (*rhet.*) lower, *the nether regions* [O.E. *neothera, nithera*]

Neth·er·land·er (néðərlændər) *n.* a native or inhabitant of the Netherlands [fr. Du. *Nederlander*]

Neth·er·lands (néðərləndz) a kingdom (mainland area 15,785 sq. miles, pop. 14,285,800) of W. Europe on the North Sea. Capitals: Amsterdam (official), The Hague (de facto). Overseas divisions: Surinam, Netherlands Antilles. Languages: Dutch and Frisian. Religion: 40% Roman Catholic, 37% Protestant, small Jewish and other minorities. The land is 29% arable, 38% pasture and 9% forest. Most of the west and of the region north of the Ijsselmere (in all, 40% of the country) is below sea level, protected by dunes and dikes. Much of the coast and of the former Zuider Zee is polder. The inland region is higher, rising to 300 ft in hills around the Rhine-Maas-Scheldt delta, and to over 1,000 ft in the southeastern plateau (Limburg). The east is largely peat and sandy heath. Average temperatures (F.): (Jan.) 30° in the northeast, 34° in the southwest, (Jul.) 68° in the northwest, 73° in the southeast. Rainfall: 22–32 ins. Livestock: cattle, pigs, poultry, sheep, horses. Agricultural products: cereals, vegetables, bulbs, potatoes, sugar beets, flax, colza, butter, cheese. Fisheries: chiefly herring, sole. Minerals: coal, oil, salt, natural gas, sandstone, china clay. Industries: metallurgy (esp. iron and steel), machinery, foodstuffs, chemicals, textiles, clothing, paper, pottery, glass, mining, leather, rubber, wood products, oil, shipbuilding, mechanical and electrical engineering, chocolate, cement, diamond cutting. Exports: machinery, fuels, pig iron, chemicals, dairy products, clothing, seeds, bulbs, meat and fish products, beer, cigars. Imports: machinery, food and tobacco, fuels, iron and steel, chemicals, textiles. Ports: Rotterdam, Amsterdam, Flushing, Hook of Holland, Schiedam, Dordrecht, Europoort. There are 6 universities, the oldest

being Leyden (1575) and Groningen (1614). Monetary unit: gulden (or guilder or florin), divided into 100 cents. HISTORY. Inhabited by Celts and Frisians, the lowlands of the Rhine were occupied by the Romans (1st c. B.C.), and taken by the Franks (5th–8th cc.). The area became part of Lotharingia (9th c.) and was divided into several fiefs of the Holy Roman Empire (11th c.). These were united under the dukes of Burgundy (15th c.), and passed to the Hapsburgs (1477) and to Philip II of Spain (1555). The Protestant and economically prosperous provinces of Holland and Zeeland rebelled against the rule of the duke of Alba (1568). William the Silent led the northern provinces to independence (1581), but in the south the struggle against Spain continued until the Peace of Westphalia (1648) recognized the Netherlands as an independent republic, known as the United Provinces. Under Maurice of Nassau, the Netherlands made rapid economic progress, building up a vast commercial empire in the East Indies, S. Africa and Brazil, and became a leading maritime power as well as a center of art and scholarship. The country was weakened by the Dutch Wars, the War of the Grand Alliance and the War of the Spanish Succession, and its economic power declined in the early 18th c. The French overran the Netherlands (1794–5), and established the Batavian Republic (1795–1806) and the Kingdom of Holland (1806–10). The Treaty of Paris (1814) reunited the Netherlands and Belgium, but the union was unsuccessful and collapsed in 1830. A liberal constitution was introduced (1848). During the reign (1890–1948) of Wilhelmina, the Netherlands remained neutral in the 1st world war and were occupied by the Germans (1940–5) during the 2nd world war. After the war, the Netherlands made a rapid economic recovery, and joined the U.N. (1945), Benelux (1947), NATO (1949) and the E.E.C. (1957). After a revolt (1945–9), Indonesia became independent (1949). Indonesia became independent (1949). A center-right coalition has ruled the Netherlands since 1977. Queen Juliana abdicated in 1980 in favor of her daughter Beatrix

Netherlands Antilles an overseas division (total area 382 sq. miles, pop. 256,000) of the Netherlands consisting of two island groups in the Lesser Antilles, West Indies: one (Curaçao and adjacent smaller islands) off N. Venezuela, the other (Southern St Martin and adjacent islets) in the Leeward Is. Capital and chief port: Willemstad, on Curaçao. The population (mainly African and mulatto, with a European minority) is largely concentrated on Curaçao. Official languages: Dutch in the southern group (where Spanish-based patois is mainly spoken) and English in the Leeward group. Annual rainfall: 40 ins in the southern group, 20 in the Leewards. Resources: phosphates (Curaçao), salt, aloes, tannin. Chief industry: oil refining (crude petroleum imported from Venezuela, amounting to 98% of exports) on Curaçao and Aruba. Most necessities are imported. Curaçao was discovered by the Spanish (1499), and was taken (1634) by the Dutch, who remained in control of the island except for 1807–14, when it was captured by the British

Netherlands East Indies the Dutch East Indies (*INDONESIA)

Netherlands Guinea *SURINAME

Netherlands New Guinea *IRIAN BARAT

neth·er·most (néðərmoust) *adj.* (*rhet.*) lowest, farthest down

net·su·ke (nétsuki:) *n.* a small ornament, usually of carved ivory or wood, used by the Japanese as a toggle to attach a purse etc. to the belt [Jap.]

nett *NET (adj. and v.)

net·ting (nétiŋ) *n.* the act or process of making nets ‖ the act or process of fishing with a net ‖ netted wire, thread or string ‖ a piece of such material [NET]

net·tle (nét'l) **1.** *n.* a plant of the genus *Urtica* or fam. *Urticaceae,* esp. the stinging nettle and the small nettle, with stinging hairs on the leaves. The young shoots are edible ‖ any of several unrelated plants, e.g. the dead nettle **2.** *v.t. pres. part.* **net·tling** *past and past part.* **net·tled** to irritate or provoke (someone) by small wounds to his pride [O.E. *netele*]

nettle rash hives

net·work (nétwɑ:rk) *n.* a fabric of crossed threads knotted at the intersections ‖ any set of interlinking lines resembling a net, *a network*

of roads ‖ an interconnected system, *a network of alliances* ‖ a chain of radio or television stations

network *v.* **1.** (British) to appear on a network **2.** to make connections among people or groups

Net·za·hual·có·yotl (netsɑwɑlkójɔt'l) (Famishing Coyote, 1409–72), Mexican poet, philosopher, astrologer, physician, historian, legislator, and king (1428–72) of Texcoco, which he delivered from tyranny. His poems are embodiments of Indian melancholy and stoicism

Neu·bran·den·burg (nɔibrándənburg) a walled town (pop. 31,000) of E. Mecklenburg, East Germany. Gothic church (14th c.) ‖ the district (area 4,322 sq. miles, pop. 645,000) including it

Neu·châ·tel (nə:ʃɑtel) a canton (area 309 sq. miles, pop. 158,368, mainly French-speaking and Protestant) of W. Switzerland, in the Jura ‖ its capital (pop. 34,428), on the Lake of Neuchâtel (area 84 sq. miles): 12th c. castle and church. University (founded as an academy in 1838, rechartered 1909)

Neu·mann (nɔimɑn), Johann Balthasar (1687–1753), German baroque architect. His best-known works are the church of Vierzehnheiligen in N. Bavaria and the Würzburg palace

Neumann, John (Janos) von (1903–57), U.S.-Hungarian scholar. His contributions, notably to mathematics and physical theory, include his theory of numbers as sets (1923), his 'Mathematical Foundations of Quantum Mechanics' (1926), and his invention of the theory of rings of operators (von Neumann algebras). A consultant for the U.S. Navy and Army during the 2nd world war, he helped to develop the atomic and hydrogen bomb

neume, neum (nu:m, nju:m) *n.* a symbol in medieval musical notation, used from the 7th c., for a syllable of vocal music, pitch being only relative ‖ a similar symbol in plainsong notation indicating pitch precisely [F. *neume* fr. M.L. fr. Gk *pneuma,* breath]

neu·ral (núərəl, njúərəl) *adj.* of or relating to the nerves or the nervous system [fr. Gk *neuron,* nerve]

neu·ral·gia (nurǽldʒə, njurǽldʒə) *n.* a severe intermittent pain in a nerve or nerves, usually without change in the nerve structure **neu·rál·gic** *adj.* [Mod. L. fr. Gk *neuron,* nerve+*algos,* pain]

neur·a·min·i·dase (nuəræmínideis) *n.* (*biochem.*) a bacterial enzyme, usu. found in intestinal or respiratory organs, that splits sialic acid from the polymer by breaking a neuraminic acid glycoside link

neu·ras·the·ni·a (nuərəsθí:ni:ə, njuərəsθí:ni:ə) *n.* a state of excessive fatigue and irritability, due to emotional conflict **neu·ras·then·ic** (nuərəsθénik, njuərəsθénik) *adj.* and *n.* [fr. Gk *neuron,* nerve+ASTHENIA]

neu·ris·tor (nuərístər) *n.* device that simulates a nerve fiber that will propagate signals to the brain

neu·rite (núərait, njúərait) *n.* an axon [fr. Gk *neuron,* nerve]

neu·ri·tis (nuráitis, njuráitis) *n.* a chronic condition of a nerve involving inflammation and degeneration, and causing pain and loss of nerve functions in the affected region [fr. Gk *neuron,* nerve]

neu·ro·ac·tive (nuərəǽktiv) *adj.* (*med.*) of a nerve stimulant

neu·ro·bi·ol·o·gy (nuərəbaiólədʒi:) *n.* study of the structure of the nervous system including its diseases —**neurobiological** *adj.* —**neurobiologically** *adv.* —**neurobiologist** *n.*

neu·ro·blast (nuərəblæst, njúərəblæst), *n.* an embryonic nerve cell [fr. Gk *neuron,* nerve+*blastos,* cell]

neu·ro·chem·i·cal (nuərəkémik'l) *n.* chemical that affects the nervous system —**neurochemist** *n.* —**neurochemistry** *n.*

neu·ro·chem·is·try (nuərəkémistri:) *n.* study of the chemistry of nerve tissue and the nervous system —**neurochemical** *adj.* —**neurochemically** *adv.* —**neurochemist** *n.*

neu·ro·coele (núərəsi:l, njúərəsi:l) *n.* the system of cavities in the interior of the central nervous system consisting of the spinal cord, central canal and the brain ventricles [fr. Gk *neuron,* nerve+*koilia,* cavity]

neu·ro·de·pres·sant (nuərədiprésənt) *n.* (*med.*) drug that depresses nervous system, e.g., atropine —**neurodepressive** *adj.*

neu·ro·en·do·cri·nol·o·gy (nuərəendoukrinóládʒi:) *n.* study of the effects of hormone

CONCISE PRONUNCIATION KEY: **(a)** æ, c*a*t; ɑ, c*ar*; ɔ f*aw*n; ei, sn*a*ke. **(e)** e, h*e*n; i:, sh*ee*p; iə, d*eer*; ɛə, b*ear*. **(i)** i, f*i*sh; ai, t*i*ger; ə:, b*ir*d. **(o)** o, *o*x; au, c*ow*; ou, g*oa*t; u, p*oor*; ɔi, r*oy*al. **(u)** ʌ, d*u*ck; u, b*u*ll; u:, g*oo*se; ə, b*a*cillus; ju:, c*u*be. x, lo*ch*; θ, *th*ink; ð, bo*th*er; z, *Z*en; ʒ, corsa*g*e; dʒ, sava*g*e; ŋ, ora*n*gutang; j, *y*ak; ʃ, *f*i*sh*; tʃ, fe*tch*; 'l, rabb*le*; 'n, redde*n*. Complete pronunciation key appears inside front cover.

secretions on the nervous system —**neuroen-docrine** adj. —**neuroendocrinological** adj. —**neuroendocrinologically** adv. —**neuren-docrinologist** n.

neu·rog·li·a (nurógli:ə, njurógli:ə) n. the supporting tissue of the nervous system [fr. Gk neuron, nerve+glia, glue]

neu·rog·li·o·cyte (nuərəgláiousait) n. (physiol.) cells in the fibrous tissue of brain and spinal cord —**neurogliama** n. a tumor —**neurogliosis** multiple tumors

neu·ro·hem·al organ (nuərəhí:məl) (physiol.) nerve organ that serves as a storage for secreted neurohormones

neu·ro·hy·po·phys·ial or **neu·ro·hy·po·phys-eal** (nuərəhi:poufízi:əl) adj. (physiol.) of the neural portion of the posterior pituitary and related hormonal secretions

neu·ro·kin·in (nuərəkínin) n. (biochem.) 1. a blood-vessel dilator that reduces blood pressure 2. a polypeptide protein believed to affect headaches

neu·ro·lep·tic (nuərəléptik) n. (med.) a tranquilizer used in treating mental illness, esp. psychosis —**neuroleptic** adj.

neu·ro·lep·to·an·al·ge·si·a or **neu·ro·lep·to·an-es·the·si·a** (nuərəleptouæn'ldʒi:ʒə) n. 1. (pharm.) a drug-induced semiconscious state induced by neuroleptic and analgesic drugs, usu. created to permit surgery —**neuroleptanalgesic** adj. 2. (med.) a state of semiconsciousness produced by a sedative or tranquilizing drug and a painkiller

neu·ro·log·i·cal (nuərəlódʒik'l, njuərəlódʒik'l) adj. of or relating to neurology

neu·rol·o·gist (nurólədʒist, njurólədʒist) n. a physician specializing in the diagnosis and treatment of diseases of the nervous system

neu·rol·o·gy (nurólədʒi:, njurólədʒi:) n. the branch of medicine dealing with all aspects of the nervous system [fr. Gk neuron, nerve+logos, discourse]

neu·ro·min·i·dase (nuərəmínideis) n. (biochem.) enzyme that attacks mucus, hypothesized as a base for a morning-after pill

neu·ron (núərɒn, njúərɒn) n. a nerve cell [Gk=nerve, sinew]

neu·rone (núəroun, njúəroun) n. a neuron

neu·ro·path (núərəpæθ, njúərəpæθ) n. a person subject to nervous disease **neu·ro·path·ic** adj.

neu·rop·a·thy (nurópəθi:, njurópəθi:) n. any of several diseases of the nervous system [fr. Gk neuron, nerve+pathein, to suffer]

neuropathy (med.) a disease of the peripheral nerves with no inflammation

neu·ro·phar·ma·col·o·gy (nuərəfɑrməkólədʒi:) n. study of drugs affecting the nervous system —**neuropharmacological** adj. —**neuropharmacologically** adv. —**neuropharmacologist** n.

neu·rop·ter·on (nuróptərən, njuróptərən) n. a member of Neuroptera, an order of flies with four membranous wings, chewing mouthparts and jointed antennae, incl. lacewings and the ant lion **neu·róp·ter·ous** adj. [fr. Gk neuron, nerve+pteron, wing]

neu·ro·sci·ence (nuərəsáiəns) n. of the study of the nervous system —**neuroscientist** n.

neu·ro·sen·so·ry (nuərəsénəri:) adj. of nerves that transmit impulses to a nerve center

neu·ro·sis (nuróusis, njuróusis) pl. **neu·ro·ses** (nuróusi:z, njuróusi:z) n. a nervous disorder not accompanied by structural change in the nervous system, and often with the symptoms of hysteria, anxiety, obsessions and compulsions

neu·rot·ic (nurótik, njurótik) 1. adj. of or relating to the nerves || of or affected by a neurosis 2. n. a person suffering from a neurosis **neu·rót·i·cism** n. [fr. Gk neuron, nerve]

neu·ro·trans·mit·ter (nuərətrænzmitər) n. (biol.) any chemical that carries impulses between nerve cells, reacting with a neighboring cell to produce a response, e.g., the hormone vasopressin

Neus·tri·a (núːstri:ə, njúːstri:ə) the western dominion of the Merovingian Franks, between the Loire and the Scheldt. It existed from the death of Clovis (511) until the early 8th c.

neu·ter (núːtər, njúːtər) 1. adj. (gram.) of the third gender, neither masculine nor feminine, which exists in some highly inflected languages || (gram., of verbs) neither active nor passive, intransitive || (bot., of flowers) sexless, without stamens or pistils || (biol.) sexually sterile or underdeveloped 2. n. (gram.) a word or form of neuter gender || the neuter gender || a castrated animal || a sexually underdeveloped female insect, e.g. the worker bee [F. neutre]

neu·ter·cane (núːtərkein) n. (meteor.) heavy frontal storm bordering on a hurricane in size and energy

Neu·tra (nɔ́itrə), Richard Joseph (1892–1970), Austrian-born American architect. He is known for his works in the international style

neu·tral (núːtrəl, njúːtrəl) 1. adj. assisting or siding with neither of two opposing sides in a war, dispute, controversy etc. || of, relating to or characteristic of a nation having declared a policy of neutrality || having no distinctive color or other quality, a neutral tone || (chem.) neither alkaline nor acid || (phys.) uncharged || (biol.) neuter || (phon., of a vowel) reduced in quality, esp. through lack of stress, so as to become a mid-central vowel (ə) 2. n. someone who, or something which, is neutral || (mech.) a disengaged position of gears [fr. L. neutralis fr. neuter, neither]

neu·tral·i·ty (nu:træliti:, nju:træliti:) n. the quality or state of being neutral || neutral status, e.g. of a seaport || (internat. law) the status of a State committed to a declared policy of nonparticipation in a war between other States || the status of any nation which remains neutral while hostilities between other nations are going on [NEUTRAL]

Neutrality Acts U.S. Congressional acts passed prior to U.S. entry into the 2nd world war. They reflected the nation's isolationism. The first act (1935) enabled the President to prohibit the exportation of arms to belligerents. By allowing the exportation of raw materials from which arms could be manufactured, it discriminated, unintentionally, in favor of industrial nations. The act was amended (1936–7) to prohibit financial aid to belligerents, which again served to favor the wealthier nations. A special act (1937) aimed specifically at the Spanish Civil War, forbade the exportation of war matériel to a nation in a state of civil war, thereby favoring the rebels who controlled the army at the expense of the Republican Loyalists

neu·tral·i·za·tion (nu:trəlizéiʃən, nju:trəlizéiʃən) n. a neutralizing or being neutralized || (chem.) the act or process of forming a salt from the reaction of an acid with a base

neu·tral·ize (núːtrəlaiz, njúːtrəlaiz) pres. part. **neu·tral·iz·ing** past and past part. **neu·tral·ized** v.t. to render ineffective by counterbalancing || (internat. law) to make (a country etc.) neutral || (chem.) to modify or destroy the peculiar properties of (a substance), e.g. to destroy the acidity of a substance by allowing it to react with a base || (phys.) to make electrically inert by combining equal positive and negative charges || to make (a color) neutral, setting it off against or blending it with its complementary [fr. F. neutraliser]

neutral point (phys., chem.) a condition of equilibrium between opposed forces or directions of change

neu·tri·no (nu:trí:nou, nju:trí:nou) n. (phys.) either of two leptons of 0 electric charge, 0 rest mass and right-handed orientation of spin emitted during radioactive beta decay and interacting very weakly with other particles (*QUANTUM THEORY OF FIELDS)

neu·tron (núːtrɒn, njúːtrɒn) n. a baryon of mass 939.5×10^6 eV (1.675×10^{-24} gm) and 0 electric charge which is a constituent of all atomic nuclei except that of the lightest hydrogen isotope. The neutron is thought to consist of a central core of positive charge surrounded by a shell of negative charge of equal magnitude (symbol n) [NEUTRAL+-on, fundamental particle]

neutron activation analysis (particle phys.) method of chemical analysis through bombardment of a specimen with neutrons abbr **NAA** Cf ACTIVATION ANALYSIS

neutron bomb (mil.) enhanced radiation weapon (which see)

neu·tron-in·duced activity (núːtrɒnindụːsd) (mil.) radioactivity induced in the ground or an object as a result of direct irradiation by neutrons, e.g., through use of enhanced radiation weapons

neutron radiography process of producing X-ray pictures through the use of a stream of neutrons

neutron shield personnel protection against neutron irradiation

neutron star (astron.) celestial body emitting x-rays, hypothetically conceived as nuclear particles from a collapsed star

neutron therapy (med.) medical treatment for cancer involving irradiation of the affected area with neutrons

Nev. Nevada

Ne·va (ní:və, njevá) a river (about 40 miles long) of the U.S.S.R., draining from Lakes Ladoga and Onega into the Gulf of Finland. Leningrad stands on its delta. Canals link it with the White Sea, the Volga and the Caspian Sea. It is usually frozen Nov.–Apr.

Ne·vad·a (nəvǽdə, nəvɑ́də) (abbr. Nev.) a western state (area 110,540 sq. miles, pop. 800,493) of the U.S.A. Capital: Carson City. Chief city: Las Vegas. It lies largely within the Great Basin, a desert plateau with isolated mountain ranges, salt lakes and shallow depressions. Agriculture: cattle and sheep ranching, fodder crops (dependent upon irrigation). Resources: copper, mercury, sand and gravel. Industries: smelting and refining of metals, tourism, esp. for gambling. State university (1874) at Reno. Nevada was explored (early 19th c.), and was ceded (1848) by Mexico to the U.S.A., of which it became (1864) the 36th state

né·vé (neivéi) n. granular snow and ice, formed from snow accumulated at the head of a glacier valley and eventually turning into a crystalline mass of ice as the glacier moves down [F. fr. Swiss dialect fr. L. nix (nivis), snow]

Nev·el·son (névəlsən), Louise (1900–), U.S. sculptress working in wood and terra cotta (*SCULPTURE)

nev·er (névər) adv. not at any time, not on any occasion || (rhet., in emphatic negation) not at all, never fear **never mind** it doesn't matter, don't worry **never a...** not a, never a care in the world [O.E. nǽfre]

nev·er·more (névərmɔ́r, névərmóur) adv. (rhet.) at no future time, nevermore to return

nev·er-nev·er land (névərnévər) an imaginary place or existence

never-never, the n. (Br., pop.) the installment plan

nev·er·the·less (nevərθəlés) adv. in spite of that, it's late, but it is still possible to get tickets nevertheless

Nev·ille (névəl), Richard, earl of Warwick *WARWICK

Ne·vis (ní:vis) an island (area 50 sq. miles, pop. 45,000) in the Leeward Is, part of the state of *ST KITTS-NEVIS

ne·vus, nae·vus (ní:vəs) pl. **ne·vi, nae·vi** (ní:vai) n. a pigmented area on the skin, usually congenital || a birthmark || a mole [L.]

new (nu:, nju:) 1. adj. made, discovered, known, heard or seen for the first time, a new house || recently made, produced or arrived, the new vintage || already in existence but discovered or known for the first time, that expression is new to me || replacing the former, a new teacher || different, she wears a new dress every day || poorly adapted through inexperience, he is still new to this work || freshly attempted, a new start || additional, further, a new installment || renewed, new strength || regenerated, the holiday made a new man of him || never before used, esp. not previously worn, new shoes || (with 'the') different from others of the same name or kind which have existed previously or for longer, the new Mrs Brown || (with 'the') having a specific modern change in character, the new criticism, the new journalism || having lately risen in social status, not in the established tradition, the new aristocracy || (of land) about to be cultivated for the first time || (of the moon) *NEW MOON **New** (of languages) in use since after the Middle Ages 2. adv. (in compounds) recently, as in 'new-mown' [O.E. niwe, néowe]

New Amsterdam the former name (1625–64) of New York City

New·ark (núːərk, njúːərk) the largest city (pop. 329,248) in New Jersey, a seaport, entrepôt and industrial center 10 miles southwest of New York City: electrical and mechanical engineering, metallurgy, food processing, textiles

New Bedford a seaport (pop. 98,478) in southern Massachusetts. It was famous in the mid-18th c. as one of the great whaling ports of the world

New·bolt (núːboult, njúːboult), Sir Henry John (1862–1938), British writer. He wrote patriotic poems in an imperialistic tone, e.g. 'Drake's Drum' (1914)

new-born (núːbɔrn, njúːbɔrn) adj. recently born || regenerated

New Britain the largest island (area 14,100 sq. miles, pop. 227,700) in the Bismarck Archipelago. Capital: Rabaul (pop. 12,000). Crescent-shaped, it is divided lengthwise by a volcanic range (summit: Father, 7,546 ft). Main exports: copra, cocoa. During the 2nd world war it served (1942–4) as a major Japanese naval base

New Bruns·wick (brʌnzwik) a province (area 28,354 sq. miles, pop. 710,500) on the Atlantic coastal lowlands of Canada. Capital: Fredericton. Chief city: St John. There are hilly uplands in the west. Agriculture: beef and dairy cattle, poultry, potatoes, fruit. Resources: timber, natural gas and oil, copper, lead, zinc, fish. Industries: pulp, paper and forest products, food processing (esp. fish). French settlements were established from 1604 but the area, as part of Acadia, was ceded to England (1713). It became a separate province (1784). It joined Canada (1867)

New Caledonia (F. Nouvelle Calédonie) an overseas territory (area 7,218 sq. miles, pop. 145,368, incl. French, Asian and Polynesian minorities) of France in the S.W. Pacific (Melanesia). Dependencies include the Loyalty group and several smaller islands. Capital: Nouméa. Mountainous and volcanic, the island is 6% arable, 9% forest. Exports: chrome, iron, nickel, copra, coffee, cotton. The island was discovered (1774) by Cook, was annexed by France (1853) and was used as a penal settlement until 1931. An outbreak of violence occurred in 1984 over the issue of independence, which resulted in new elections in 1985 for regional councils with control over most local affairs

New Castile (Span. Castilla la Nueva) the southern part of Castile forming the modern provinces of Madrid, Toledo, Ciudad Real, Cuenca and Guadalajara. Except for mountains in the north and east it is a treeless plain, largely pasture (cattle, sheep). Crops: cereals, beans, potatoes, vines. Main industry: mining (coal, mercury). Historic capital: Toledo

New Castile (Span. Nueva Castilla) the name given by the Spaniards to what was later Peru

New·cas·tle (nú:kæs'l, njú:kæs'l, nú:kɑs'l, njú:kɑs'l), Thomas Pelham Holles, 1st duke of (1693–1778), English statesman. As Whig prime minister (1754–60), he adopted a vacillating policy in the Seven Years' War. He was again in power 1757–62

Newcastle a coaling port (pop. with agglom. 251,132) of E. central New South Wales, Australia: iron and steel

Newcastle upon Tyne a port (pop. 192,454) and county borough, county town of Northumberland, England, 8 miles up the Tyne from the North Sea. It has shipped local coal since the 13th c. Industries: shipbuilding, iron and steel, chemicals. University (1963)

New·comb (nú:kəm, njú:kəm), Simon (1835–1909), U.S. astronomer. He introduced, jointly with A.M.W. Downing of the British Nautical Almanac office, a new set of the fundamental astronomical constants, and computed new tables of the planets which made it possible to calculate daily celestial positions with great accuracy

New·com·en (nu:kʌmən, nju:kʌmən), Thomas (1663–1729), English engineer. He invented a steam engine (1705) to raise water from mines

new·com·er (nú:kʌmər, njú:kʌmər) n. a recent arrival

New Deal (Am. hist.) the social and economic program implemented from 1933 to the 2nd world war under F.D. Roosevelt to combat the effects of the great depression of 1929. It used federal funds to strengthen the economy and relieve unemployment, chiefly through public works projects (e.g. Tennessee Valley Authority), relief to farmers and small businessmen, economic controls and labor reforms

New Delhi *DELHI

new drug a drug newly approved for public use by the Food and Drug Administration

new economics programs based on the Keynesian idea stabilizing an economy by government-controlled spending and taxation Cf NEO-KEYNESIAN

new·el (nú:əl, njú:əl) n. the central pillar of a winding staircase ‖ the top or bottom post of a handrail on a staircase [O. F. nouel, kernel, stone, newell]

newel post a newel

New England the northeasternmost region of the U.S.A. (comprising the states of Connecticut, Maine, Massachusetts, New Hampshire,

Rhode Island and Vermont), so named by John Smith when he explored it (1614)

New Eng·land·er a native or resident of New England

new·fan·gled (nú:fæŋg'ld, njú:fæŋg'ld) adj. (contemptuous) modern and inferior, newfangled ideas about farming [M.E. newefangel]

New Federalism decentralizing program of sharing federally administered functions and tax revenues with the states; advocated by President Richard M. Nixon —**New Federalist** n.

New Forest a woodland region (area 145 sq. miles) in S.W. Hampshire, England, between River Avon and the coast

New·found·land (nú:fəndlænd, njú:fəndlænd, nú:fəndlənd, njú:fəndlənd) an island (area 42,734 sq. miles, pop. 579,400, mostly of English and Irish origin) off E. Canada, at the mouth of the Gulf of St Lawrence. The land (35% forest) is largely an undulating plateau (over 1,000 ft, rising to 2,673 ft in the Long Range mountains), with a deeply indented coastline. Products: fish (esp. cod from the Grand Banks), pulp and paper, iron ore, copper, zinc, lead, fluorspar. 90% of the population lives along the coast. University: St John's (1925). Newfoundland was discovered (1497) by John Cabot, claimed (1583) for Elizabeth I by Sir Humphrey Gilbert and recognized (1713) as a British colony. Since 1949 it has (with Labrador) formed a province of Canada. Capital: St John's

Newfoundland n. a large dog of a breed of North American origin, with a dense, usually black, coat, noted for swimming power and intelligence

New·found·land·er (nú:fəndlændər, njú:fəndlændər, nú:fəndləndər, njú:fəndləndər, nju:fáundləndər, nu:fáundləndər) n. a native or inhabitant of Newfoundland

New France (hist.) the French territories of North America from the Mississippi to Hudson Bay, including Acadia and Louisiana (late 16th c.–18th c.). The colony was directed by trading companies until 1663, when it came under the direct control of Louis XIV and expanded greatly. As a result of the French and Indian War (1756–63), Louisiana was ceded to Spain (1762) and the rest of New France to Britain (1763)

New Frontier the foreign and domestic policy program launched by U.S. President John Kennedy. It provided for the expansion of the missile and space programs, the establishment of an Alliance for Progress in Latin America, and the creation of the Peace Corps. It called for domestic welfare measures and tax revisions to spur the economy, and, despite Southern Democratic resistance, a comprehensive civil rights program

New·gate (nú:git, njú:git) a former London prison (13th–19th cc.) which stood opposite the Old Bailey

New Granada the former name of Colombia

New Guinea an island (area 312,000 sq. miles, pop. 2,387,000) in the S.W. Pacific off N. Australia, divided into the Indonesian province of Irian Jaya (west) and Papua New Guinea (east). People and language: mainly Papuan, Negrito, and Melanesian, with Polynesian and Micronesian minorities. Religion: Animist, with small Christian (east and west) and Moslem (west) minorities. Social organization is largely tribal. A central mountain range runs northwest-southeast, with several snowcapped peaks over 15,000 ft (Mt Sukarno, 16,503 ft, in Irian Barat). The north, where rain forest alternates with savanna, is hilly. The south is a plain crossed by several large rivers (e.g. the Fly) and covered with jungle and mangrove swamp. Average temperatures (F.): 70°–90°, varying with altitude. Rainfall: 60 ins–100 ins in the south, 100–500 ins in the north and mountains. Main occupations: subsistence agriculture (sweet potatoes, taro, sago, sugarcane, fruit), fishing, pearl diving. HISTORY. The first Europeans to visit the island were Portuguese (1527). The west was annexed by the Dutch (1828–1963), the southeast by the British (1884–1905), and the northeast by the Germans (1884–1920). The two eastern parts came under Australian control, and were given a common administration (1949). The west (Irian Jaya) passed to Indonesia (1963)

New Guinea, Territory of *NORTHEAST NEW GUINEA

New Hampshire (abbr. N.H.) a state (area

9,304 sq. miles, pop. 951,000) of the U.S.A., in New England. Capital: Concord. The White Mtns lie in the north. Most of the remainder is hill country, with many lakes. Agriculture: poultry and dairy products, hay, vegetables, fruit. Resources: timber, granite. Industries: leather products, textiles, electrical products, machinery, pulp and paper. State university (1866) at Durham. One of the Thirteen Colonies, New Hampshire was settled by the English (17th c.) and became (1788) the 9th state of the U.S.A.

New Haven a seaport, entrepôt, and light manufacturing center (pop. 126,109) in Connecticut, on Long Island Sound, seat of Yale University

New Hebrides *VANUATU

New Ireland a mountainous island (area 3,800 sq. miles, pop. 65,705) in the Bismarck Archipelago. Chief town and port: Kavieng. The island has been under Australian mandate since 1921

New Jersey (abbr. N.J.) a state (area 8,204 sq. miles, pop. 7,468,000) on the mid-Atlantic coast of the U.S.A. Capital: Trenton. Chief city: Newark. The south is coastal plain, the north upland. Agriculture: poultry, dairy products, vegetables, fruit. Resources: building materials. Industries: metallurgy, oil refining, chemicals, paints and varnishes, motor vehicles and supplies, food processing. Chief universities: Princeton, Rutgers (1766) at New Brunswick. One of the Thirteen Colonies, New Jersey was colonized (early 17th c.) by the Dutch, and ceded (1664) to England. It became (1787) the 3rd state of the U.S.A.

New Jerusalem the celestial city, heaven (Revelation xxi, 2)

New Jerusalem, Church of the *SWEDENBORGIAN

New Latin Modern Latin

New Learning the study (15th-16th cc.) of the Bible and the Greek classics in the original. It influenced both the Renaissance and the Reformation

New Left 1. a disenchanted splinter of the Old Left, with utopian ideals and a predilection for direct action, as a reaction to disillusionment with Stalinism; typified by the Students for Democratic Society 2. antiestablishment movement advocating radical changes in international affairs, environmental controls, antipoverty programs, and drug-control legislation, popular in the 1960s —**New Leftist** n. Cf OLD LEFT, SDS

new·ly (nú:li:, njú:li:) adv. in a new way, music newly edited and arranged ‖ recently, a newly engaged couple

new·ly·wed (nú:li:wẹd, njú:li:wẹd) n. a person recently married

New·man (nú:mən, njú:mən), John (1801–90), British churchman, cardinal of the Roman Catholic Church. Ordained (1824) in the Anglican ministry, he took a leading part in the Oxford movement and wrote several of the 'Tracts for the Times' (1833–41). After his 'Tract 90' (1841) had provoked widespread Anglican protest, he was received into the Roman Catholic Church (1845) and appointed cardinal (1879). His works include 'An Essay on the Development of Christian Doctrine' (1845) and 'Apologia pro Vita Sua' (1864). He also wrote hymns, poetry, novels, histories and an important philosophical work, 'An Essay in Aid of a Grammar of Assent' (1870)

new mathematics modern approach to teaching mathematics resulting from new computer technology, with emphasis on axiomatic method including sets, Boolean algebra, equivalence relations, groups, and matrices also new math

New Mexico (abbr. N. Mex., New M., N.M.) a state (area 121,666 sq. miles, pop. 1,359,000) of the southwest U.S.A. Capital: Santa Fé. Chief city: Albuquerque. It is mainly semiarid mountain and plateau country, with high plains in the east. Agriculture: cattle and sheep, cotton, wheat, grain sorghums (one third of the arable is irrigated). Resources: uranium, oil, natural gas, potassium salt, copper, zinc. Industries: food processing, lumber, chemicals. State university (1889) at Albuquerque. New Mexico was explored (16th c.) by the Spanish. Most of it was ceded by Mexico (1848) and part was included in the Gadsden Purchase (1854). It became (1912) the 47th state of the U.S.A.

New Model army the English parliamentary army as it was reorganized in 1645 (*FAIRFAX)

new moon the phase or position of the moon when it is in conjunction with the sun ‖ the appearance of the moon as a thin crescent a few days after this

New Neth·er·land (néðərlənd) the former Dutch colony (1621–64) now comprising the states of New York and New Jersey

new novel (often initial capitals) an antinovel approach to fiction writing emphasizing psychological and physical detail, fresh aspects of reality, without, or with minimal characterizations, linear narrative, social or political content; exemplified by books of Alain Robbe-Grillet, Marguerite Duras, Nathalie Sarraute, and Michel Butor *also nouveau roman*

New Orleans the chief city (pop. 1,184,725) of Louisiana, and the country's second port for foreign trade, on the Mississippi 100 miles from its mouth. It is an entrepôt and rice and cotton market. Main industries: shipbuilding, sugar and oil refining, textiles, food processing, tourism. The town is built around the 'Vieux Carré', the old French quarter containing the cathedral of Saint-Louis

New Orleans, Battle of an engagement (1815) in the War of 1812 in New Orleans, La., in which U.S. troops under Andrew Jackson defeated the British force. The victory greatly advanced the political fortunes of Jackson

new penny unit of British decimal coinage after 1976

New Philosophers group of middle-class French intellectuals, disillusioned with traditional leftist politics, who attacked Marxism as an unworkable social doctrine; exemplified by Bernard-Henri Levy *also Nouveaux Philosophes*

New Politics program designed to substitute more voter participation for party power; advocated in the late 1960s by Senators Eugene J. McCarthy, Robert F. Kennedy, and George S. McGovern

new populism pejoratively "peanut populism," a style and system of communication with the public used by President Jimmy Carter

New·port (nú:pərt,   njú:pɔrt,   nú:pourt, njú:pourt) a port, naval base and fashionable resort (pop. 29,259) in Rhode Island, with many colonial buildings: yacht races, annual jazz festival

Newport a river port (pop. 105,374) in Monmouthshire, England, shipping local coal, iron and steel: engineering, chemicals, electrical appliances

Newport News a shipping port and import-export center (pop. 114,903) in S.E. Virginia. Manufactures: mattresses, metal fixtures, building accessories. Fisheries

New Providence the most populous island and resort of the Bahama group (area 58 sq. miles, pop. 81,000) between Andros Is. and Eleuthera Is. It contains Nassau, the capital and chief port of the Bahamas

New Right 1. political movement stressing nationalism and conservatism in government; opposing egalitarianism, calling for a meritocratic society; prominent in France in 1979 **2.** in U.S., a conservative Republican movement, esp. supporting Ronald Reagan presidency, increase in military spending, anti-Communism, and reduction in government-funded social programs

news (nu:z, nju:z) *n.* recent information, *have you any news of his whereabouts?* ‖ recent events, esp. as reported in newspapers, on the radio or on television [pl. of NEW after O.F. *noveles*]

news agency an organization which maintains a network of correspondents and sells its news reports to newspapers, periodicals and broadcasting companies

news·a·gent (nú:zeidʒənt, njú:zeidʒənt) *n.* a shopkeeper selling newspapers and periodicals

news·boy (nú:zbɔi, njú:zbɔi) *n.* a boy who sells or delivers newspapers

news·cast (nú:zkæst, njú:zkæst, nú:zkɑst, njú:zkɑst) *n.* a radio or television broadcast of the news **news·cast·er** *n.* someone who reports the news on radio or television [NEWS+BROADCAST]

New Siberian Islands (*Russ.* Novo Sibirskie Ostrova) a group of sparsely inhabited islands (area 11,000 sq. miles) in the Arctic Ocean, part of the Yakut A.S.S.R., U.S.S.R. Chief islands:

Kotelny Fadeevski, Novaya Sibir and the Lyakhov Is: fur, ivory

news·let·ter (nú:zlɛtər, njú:zlɛtər) *n.* a printed paper, usually issued periodically, containing information of interest to a particular profession, section of the community or pressure group

news·mak·er (nú:zmeikər) *n.* one who is newsworthy

news·man (nú:zmæn, njú:zmæn) *pl.* **news·men** (nú:zmɛn, njú:zmɛn) *n.* a newspaperman

New South Wales (*abbr.* N.S.W.) a state (area 309,433 sq. miles, pop. 5,126,217) in S. E. Australia. Capital: Sydney. A narrow coastal plain borders the Great Dividing Range. Vast central plains stretch to the Murray River basin. Agriculture: sheep, beef and dairy cattle, wheat and other cereals, potatoes, timber, citrus fruit, bananas. Resources: coal, silver, lead, zinc, some titanium, sulfur, copper and gold, hydroelectric power. Industries: agricultural processing, metal refining and products, iron and steel, chemicals, clothing, paper and printing. University of New South Wales (1958), University of Newcastle (1965), University of New England (1954)

New Spain the Spanish viceroyalty established (1535–1821) in Mexico

news·pa·per (nú:zpeipər, njú:zpeipər, nú:speipər, njú:speipər) *n.* a printed publication, usually published daily or weekly, which reports the latest news of current events and offers opinions on them ‖ an organization which produces such a publication

news·pa·per·man (nú:speipərmæn, njú:speipərmæn, nú:zpeipərmæn, njú:zpeipərmæn) *pl.* **news·pa·per·men** (nú:speipərmɛn, njú:speipərmɛn, nú:zpeipərmɛn, njú:zpeipərmɛn) *n.* a professional male journalist working on a newspaper

news·pa·per·wom·an (nú:speipərwumən, njú:speipərwumən, nú:zpeipərwumən, njú:zpeipərwumən) *pl.* **news·pa·per·wom·en** (nú:speipərwimən, njú:speipərwimən, nú:zpeipərwimən, njú:zpeipərwimən) *n.* a professional female journalist working on a newspaper

news·print (nú:zprint, njú:zprint) *n.* a cheap woodpulp paper used in newspaper production

news·reel (nú:zri:l, njú:zri:l) *n.* a film of current events

news·room (nú:zru:m, njú:zru:m, nú:zrum, njú:zrum) *n.* a room in a radio or television station from which the news is broadcast ‖ a room in a newspaper office where the news is edited

news·stand (nú:zstænd, njú:zstænd) *n.* a stall on a sidewalk or in a public building at which newspapers, magazines etc. are sold

New Style (in reckoning dates etc.) according to the Gregorian calendar

news·y (nú:zi:, njú:zi:) *comp.* **news·i·er** *superl.* **news·i·est** *adj.* (*pop.*) full of news

newt (nu:t, nju:t) *n.* a member of *Triturus*, a genus of small semiaquatic salamanders. They are air-breathing and oviparous and have a laterally compressed tail [for *ewt* (fr. *an ewt*) fr. O.E. *efete*]

New Territories *HONG KONG

New Testament the writings of the earliest disciples of Jesus, forming the second part of the Bible. The earliest of the 27 books are the letters written by Paul between 49 A.D. and 62 A.D. The four Gospels date from the late 1st c. and the remaining letters variously from 64 to 120 A.D.

New·ton (nú:t'n, njú:t'n), Sir Isaac (1642–1727), English mathematician, physicist, astronomer and philosopher, and the author of fundamental and seminal laws. He developed the theory of differential calculus at the same time as Leibniz. He discovered the dispersion of light into a colored spectrum by refraction through a prism, studied diffraction and interference of light, and invented the reflecting telescope. His work on light led to a corpuscular theory of its nature ('Opticks', 1704). He developed his inverse square law of gravitation in 'Philosophiae naturalis principia mathematica' (1678), applying it to planetary motion. The 'Principia' also elaborates on his laws of motion: (1) a body remains in its state of rest or uniform motion unless acted on by an external force, (2) change in motion is proportional to, and in the same direction as, the applied force, (3) to every action there is an equal and opposite reaction. In 1699 Newton became Master of the Mint

new·ton (nú:t'n, njú:t'n) *n.* a unit of force in the mks system defined as the force that would accelerate a mass of 1 kg. by 1 m. per sec. per sec. [after Sir Isaac *Newton*]

New·to·ni·an (nu:tóuni:ən, nju:tóuni:ən) **1.** *adj.* of Sir Isaac Newton or his theories, esp. of his theory of the universe as compared with the theory of relativity **2.** *n.* a follower of Newton

Newtonian telescope a reflecting telescope in which the image formed by the objective (a mirror) is diverted perpendicularly to the line of sight by a small plane mirror, and is viewed by an eyepiece at the side of the telescope tube

Newton's rings an interference phenomenon observed when a convex lens surface is placed in contact with a plane surface. A series of circular colored bands concentric with the point of contact is observed, because of the interference of the light waves reflected from the top and bottom of the air film between the two surfaces

New Town an administrative term designating any of several towns in Britain each planned as a complete unit to provide housing, employment and amenities for a population, restricted in total, scheduled under the New Towns Act (1946) with the aim of relieving overcrowding in London and other conurbations

new town 1. independent residential-industrial area created within 30 mi of a city (London, Paris) to relieve crowding of cities **2.** a satellite town or city, esp. British and French, planned near an urban center, esp. for housing urban workers

new wave 1. (*cinema*) art form using new photographic techniques to create abstract and symbolic images, often improvised, exemplified by films of Jean-Luc Godard and Alain Resnais in 1960s. *also nouvelle vague* **2.** (*music*) post-punk rock, involving bizarre clothing; popular in U.S. during 1980

New Wave culture *PUNK ROCK

New World the western hemisphere, esp. the American continents

new year the year approaching or just begun **New Year** the first days of a year

New Year's Day the first day of the calendar year (Jan. 1), celebrated as a legal holiday in many countries

New Year's Eve the evening before New Year's Day, given over to celebration

New York (*abbr.* N.Y.) an eastern state (area 49,576 sq. miles, pop. 17,659,000) of the U.S.A. Capital: Albany. Chief city: New York. It is an area of hill and mountain country, including the Adirondack Mtns. It is primarily industrial: clothing, printing and publishing, metal and food processing, machinery, electrical machinery, chemicals, transport equipment. Agriculture: dairy and poultry products, beef cattle, fruit, vegetables. Resources: building materials, salt, zinc, iron ore. Chief universities: Cornell, Columbia, University of Rochester (1848), New York University (1831) in New York City. One of the Thirteen Colonies, New York was settled (early 17th c.) by the Dutch and ceded (1664) to England. It became (1788) the 11th state of the U.S.A.

New York the chief city and port (pop. 7,086,096, with agglom. 16,601,620) of the U.S.A., at the mouth of the Hudson River in New York State. It consists of five boroughs: Brooklyn, Manhattan, the Bronx, Queens and Richmond, all except the Bronx being on islands. The waterways separating them are lined with docks. New York handles 35% of the country's international shipping and produces nearly a quarter of its total manufactures. Main industries: clothing, publishing, textiles, food processing, luxury goods. Heavy industry is concentrated nearby in New Jersey. Manhattan, the original site and still the center of the city, is the country's financial and commercial center. Major cultural institutions: Metropolitan Museum of Art (1870), Museum of Modern Art (1929), American Museum of Natural History (1869), Lincoln Center for the Performing Arts, Columbia and New York Universities. The skyline is dominated by skyscrapers, notably the Empire State Building and U.N. headquarters (1949–52). A settlement was established (early 17th c.) by the Dutch, and called New Amsterdam. The town was seized (1664) by the English and was renamed New York. It took a leading part in the Revolutionary War. The opening of the Erie Canal (1825) marked the beginning of its economic expansion

New Yorker a native or inhabitant of New York City or State

'New York Times Co. v. Sullivan' a landmark decision (1963) of the U.S. Supreme Court which ruled that a public official could not collect damages for even false criticism of his conduct, unless he proved that the statement was "made with 'actual malice'—that is, with knowledge that it was false, or with reckless disregard of whether it was or not". The decision thus raised the First Amendment right of free speech as a shield against state libel laws

'New York Times Co. v. U.S., and U.S. v. Washington Post Co.' a decision (1971) of the U.S. Supreme Court, following the first-ever attempt by the U.S. government to impose prior restraint on the press and thus prevent further publication of the Pentagon Papers. The court ruled (6-3) in favor of the press, conceding that prior restraint could be justified where the national interest might suffer irreparably, but denying that the government had established such a threat in this instance

New Zea·land (zí:lənd) an independent dominion (area 103,736 sq. miles, pop. 3,238,000) and member of the British Commonwealth, in the S. Pacific. Capital: Wellington. Largest town: Auckland. The country consists of North Island (area 44,281 sq. miles, pop. 1,820,000), South Island (area 58,093 sq. miles, pop. 771,000), Stewart Is. (670 sq. miles), the Chatham Is (372 sq. miles) and lesser islands (320 sq. miles). It also administers the Cook Is, Niue Is, Tokelau Is and Ross Dependency. People: 93% European, 7% Maori (nearly all in North Island). Languages: English and Maori. Religion: 65% Protestant, 12% Roman Catholic. The land is 48% pasture, 21% forest and 3% arable. The central mountain system running through North and South Islands is highest in the Southern Alps, South Island (Mt Cook, 12,349 ft), with glaciers, fiords, and pine forests in the west. S.W. South Island has large rain forests. Most of the fertile plains (the largest are the Canterbury Plains, South Island) and all the chief towns are on the east coasts, which are mountainous only in N. South Island (Kaikoura Range). Central North Island is a volcanic plateau (1,200–2,000 ft), with thermal springs, geysers etc., dominated by active cones (Ruapehu, 9,175 ft, Ngauruhoe, 7,515 ft) and inactive ones (Egmont, 8,260 ft). The surrounding area is barren but the coasts provide good pasture land. Hills continue to the northern tip. Average temperatures (F.): Auckland 51° (July) and 66° (Jan.), Wellington 47° and 61 °, Dunedin 39° and 59°. Rainfall: central South Island 13 ins, Auckland 45 ins, Dunedin 37 ins, Hokitika (W. South Island) 114 ins, Southern Alps 250 ins. Livestock: sheep, cattle, hogs. Agriculture (chief source of wealth): cereals (South Island), dairy produce (North Island), wool, meat. Resources: timber, coal, natural gas, iron, small deposits of other minerals, building materials, hydroelectricity. Industries: meat packing, dairy processing, vehicle assembly, wood and cork products, fertilizers, machinery, clothing, fruit and vegetable canning, electrical goods, textiles, leather, cardboard. Exports: wool, meat, butter, cheese, hides and skins, milk, casein, tallow, apples. Imports: machinery, vehicles, iron and steel, cotton goods, gasoline, paper, copper, oil and fuels, chemicals, rubber. Ports: Auckland, Wellington, Lyttelton, Dunedin. There are six universities. Monetary unit: New Zealand pound. HISTORY. New Zealand was settled by Maoris from Polynesia (probably c. 14th c.). It was visited (1642) by a Dutch expedition under Tasman, and was circumnavigated (1769) by a British expedition under Cook. Whaling stations and trading posts were established (late 18th c.), and a Christian mission was set up (1814). Britain began to colonize New Zealand (1840), drew up the Treaty of Waitangi (1840) with the Maori chiefs, and made the country a separate colony (1841). Responsible government was established (1856). Land disputes led to wars with the Maoris (1845–8 and 1860–72). The discovery of gold (1861) brought many new immigrants, and the introduction of refrigerated ships (1882) greatly increased the meat and dairy trade. Much advanced social legislation was introduced (1891–1914). New Zealand became a dominion (1907), fought in both world wars, formed the Anzus Pact with Australia and the U.S.A. (1951) and joined the South East

Asia Treaty Organization (1954). Manufacturing industry is being developed rapidly to reduce the dependence on agriculture. New Zealand's Territorial Sea and Exclusive Economic Zone Act (1978) extended its territorial fishing waters and boosted the fishing industry. Trade with Australia benefitted from a 1966 free-trade agreement. Queen Elizabeth II is recognized as queen and head of state; her representative is governor-general Sir David Stuart Beattie (1980–   ). David Lange took office as prime minister in 1984

New Zea·land·er (zí:ləndər) n. a native or inhabitant of New Zealand

next (nekst) **1.** adj. nearest in space, *the house next to ours* ‖ following in time without anything similar intervening, *the next train to London* ‖ ranking second, *next in importance* **next best** second best **next to** almost amounting to, *it was next to robbery* ‖ virtually, *next to impossible* **next to nothing** hardly anything **2.** adv. in the place, time or order immediately following, *next came the bishop* ‖ on the first occasion to come, *when we next see each other* **3.** prep. closest to, *on the shelf next the stove* [O.E. *nēahst*, next]

next-door (nékstdɔr, nékstdour) adj. in or at the next house, door etc., *their next-door neighbors* **next door** adv.

next of kin one's nearest relative or relatives, esp. (in some legal systems) as being entitled to inherit in the absence of a will

nex·us (néksəs) n. a tie, link, connection between members of a group ‖ a connected group or series [L. fr. *nectere* (*nexus*), to bind]

Ney (nei), Michel, duc d'Elchingen, prince de la Moskova (1769–1815), French marshal. Having served with great distinction in the Napoleonic Wars, he was made a peer by Louis XVIII. He deserted to Napoleon's cause during the Hundred Days and his execution for treason aroused widespread indignation in France

Nez Per·cé (nézpɔ́:rs, néipə:rséi) pl. **Nez Per·cés** n. a Shahaptian Indian of central Idaho, eastern Oregon and Wash. [F.=pierced nose]

Nfld. Newfoundland

N galaxy (astron.) a galaxy with a starlike nucleus

Ngo Dinh Diem (nóudí:ndjém) (1901–63), Vietnamese statesman, premier (1954–5) and president (1955–63) of South Vietnam. With U.S. military and economic aid, he introduced land reform and resisted guerrilla attacks from North Vietnam. His ultra-Catholic government was overthrown by a coup d'état in which he was killled

NGU (med. acronym) for nongonococcal urethritis

n-gul·trom (eŋultrəm) n. unit of paper currency in Bhutan Cf TIKCHUNG

Ngwane ('ŋwúnei) *SWAZILAND

ngwee ('ŋgwi:) n. one hundredth of a kwacha ‖ a coin of this value

N. H. New Hampshire

ni·a·cin (náiəsin) n. nicotinic acid [NICOTINIC ACID]

Ni·ag·a·ra (naiǽgrə) a river (36 miles long) between Lake Ontario and Lake Erie, separating Ontario, Canada, from New York State

Niagara Falls a waterfall in the Niagara, divided by an island into Horseshoe or Canadian Falls (2,600 ft wide, 162 ft high) and American Falls (1,000 ft wide, 167 ft high): tourism, hydroelectricity ‖ a resort (pop. 71,384) on the U.S. side of the Falls ‖ a resort (pop. 70,960) on the Canadian side

ni·al·a·mide [$C_{16}H_{18}N_4O_2$] (naiǽləmaid) n. (pharm.) a monoamine oxidase inhibitor sometimes used as an antidepressant; marketed as Niamid

Nia·mey (njámei) the capital (pop. 130,300) and airport of Niger, on the Upper Niger River

nib (nib) n. the metal point of a pen which transmits the ink to the paper ‖ a neb ‖ (pl.) crushed cacao beans [prob. var. of NEB]

nib·ble (nib'l) **1.** v. pres. part. **nib·bling** past and past part. **nib·bled** v.t. to take small, quick bites of, *mice have been nibbling the cheese* ‖v.i. (often with 'at' to take small, usually cautious, bites to show signs of interest(in a proposition etc.) **2.** n. the act of nibbling ‖ an instance of this ‖ a small bite [etym. doubtful]

Ni·be·lung·en·lied (ní:bəluŋənli:t) a Middle High German epic of unknown authorship (probably 12th c.). Its themes are faithfulness and revenge. Certain elements from it were used by Wagner in his cycle of musical dramas 'The Ring of the Nibelungen'

nib·lick (níblik) n. (golf) an iron with a deep, sharply slanting blade used for lofting shots, esp. out of hazards [etym. doubtful]

NIBMAR or **Nibma** (acronym) for 'no independence before majority African rule,' proposed as British policy toward African colonies in 1966

Ni·cae·a, Council of (naisí:ə) the first ecumenical council, convened (325) by Constantine I to condemn Arianism ‖ an ecumenical council (787) which attempted to suppress iconoclasm

Nic·a·ra·gua (nɪkərágwə) a republic (area 57,143 sq. miles, pop. 2,823,979) in Central America. Capital: Managua. People: 71% mestizo, 15% European, 9% African, 5% Indian. Language: Spanish. Religion: mainly Roman Catholic, 3% Protestant. 48% of the land is forest, 6% arable, 3% grazing. The center is a highland (5,000–7,000 ft). The east is a wide swampy coastal plain (Mosquito Coast), now being developed agriculturally. In the west a broad valley, containing Lakes Managua and Nicaragua, runs the length of the country, separated from the Pacific by a narrow chain of volcanic hills: 80% of the population lives in this valley. Communications are relatively undeveloped. One navigable river, the Escondido (150 miles long, incl. the headstream), flows from the central highlands to the Atlantic. Average temperatures (F.): lowlands 80°–86°, above 3,000 ft 70°–75°. Rainfall: (Mosquito Coast) 259 ins, central highlands 80 ins, volcanic slopes 65–75 ins, interior lowlands 50 ins. Livestock: cattle (in the west). Crops: cotton, rice, coffee, sugarcane, fruit, corn, sorghum, beans, sesame. Forest products: mahogany, cedar, rosewood. Minerals: gold, silver, copper. Industries: meat packing, dairy products, plywood, textiles, sugar refining, coffee, soap, cement, vegetable oils. Exports: cotton, coffee, gold, lumber, sugar, sesame. Imports: machinery, foodstuffs, chemicals, vehicles, iron and steel, textiles. Ports: Corinto (pop. 5,000) on the Pacific, Bluefields (pop. 17,000) on the Caribbean. Universities: León and Managua. Monetary unit: córdoba (100 centavos). HISTORY. The region was inhabited by Indian tribes when Columbus visited the coast (1502). The lowlands were explored by Spanish expeditions (1522 and 1524) and settlements were founded. These were joined (1570) to Guatemala. The British established a protectorate along the east coast (1687–1786). Nicaragua became independent of Spain (1821) and formed part of the Central American Federation (1823–38). Political unrest and confusion led to U.S. intervention (1912–25 and 1926–33). Nicaragua declared war on the Axis (1941) and joined the U.N. (1945). Gen. Anastasio Somoza (president 1937–56) was assassinated and was succeeded by his son Luis Somoza Debayle (president 1956–63). The Somoza family continued to govern the country through a close friend Rene Schick Gutiérrez (president 1963–6) and subsequently through another son of the former dictator, Anastasio Somoza Debayle (president 1967–79). After a bitter civil war Somoza was ousted and a 3-member FSLN junta ruled with a 51-member legislature. Somoza was assassinated in Paraguay in 1980. The new government experienced severe economic difficulties and developed increasingly close ties to Cuba. Nicaraguan-U.S. relations deteriorated following the former's involvement with leftist guerrillas in El Salvador in 1981; in 1983 the U.S. participated in military maneuvers with anti-Sandanista Nicaraguan guerrillas in Honduras. Support of these 'contras' became a U.S. political issue. Civil war continued and in 1985 the government imposed a state of emergency with suspension of civil rights

Nicaragua a lake (area 3,089 sq. miles) in S.W. Nicaragua. It contains freshwater sharks

Nic·a·ra·guan (nɪkərágwən) adj. of or relating to Nicaragua

Ni·ca·ra·o (ni:karáɔ) (16th c.), an Indian cacique of Central America who welcomed and aided the Spaniards. He gives his name to Nicaragua

Nice (ni:s) a port (pop. 344,481) of Alpes-Maritimes, S. France. Industries: metallurgy, textiles, food processing, flowers, tourism. Sardinia ceded it to France in 1860

nice (nais) adj. (used as a loose term of general approval) pleasant, kind, attractive, delightful, fine ‖ minutely subtle, evincing discrimination or fine judgment, *a nice distinction* ‖ delicate, precise, *a nice adjustment* ‖ sensitive, alert, *a nice ear for music* ‖ (ironical) unsatisfactory, *a nice mess we're in now* **nice and** (*pop.*, *intensive*) agreeably, *nice and warm* [O.F.=foolish, stupid fr. L. *nescius*, ignorant]

Ni·cene Creed (náisi:n) the Christian creed based mainly on the profession of faith formulated at the Council of Nicaea (325) and its elaboration at the Council of Constantinople (381). It is accepted by the Roman Catholic, Orthodox and several Protestant Churches

Ni·ceph·o·rus II Pho·cas (naiséfərəs fóukæs) (c. 913–69), Byzantine emperor (963–9). Having distinguished himself as a general under Constantine VII and Romanus II against the Arabs and the Saracens, he usurped the throne. He defeated the Arabs in Asia Minor, and the Bulgarians and Macedonians. He was murdered by John Tzimisces, who succeeded him as John I

ni·ce·ty (náisiti:) *pl.* **ni·ce·ties** *n.* delicacy and precision, *the job calls for nicety of judgment* ‖ the quality of requiring delicate treatment, *a problem of some nicety* ‖ (*pl.*) fine details, *the niceties of the question* **to a nicety** with exquisite accuracy, *adjusted to a nicety* [O.F. *niceté*, folly]

niche (nitʃ) **1.** *n.* a recess in a wall, esp. for a statue, vase etc. ‖ a place or position precisely suited to a person's talents, *he found his niche in administration* **2.** *v.t. pres. part.* **nich·ing** *past* and *past part.* **niched** to place in, or as if in, a niche [F.]

Nich·o·las (níkələs), St (4th c.), bishop of Myra in Lycia, patron saint of Russia and Greece, and of children, sailors, merchants and pawnbrokers. Feast: Dec. 6 (*SANTA CLAUS)

Nicholas I 'the Great', St (c. 800–67), pope (858–67), a wise and energetic administrator. Feast: Nov. 13

Nicholas II (c. 980–1061), pope (1059–61). He convened a Lateran Council (1059) to settle the rules governing papal elections

Nicholas V (1397–1455), pope (1447–55). A noted humanist scholar, he was one of the founders of the Vatican Library

Nicholas I (1796–1855), czar of Russia (1825–55), son of Paul I. A reactionary, he put down the Decembrist revolt (1825), strengthened the autocracy, suppressed religious toleration, and organized a system of secret police (1826). He crushed a rising in Poland (1830–1) and revolution in Hungary (1849). He was victorious in the Russo-Turkish War of 1828–9, but involved Russia in the Crimean War

Nicholas II (1868–1918), last czar of Russia (1894–1917), son of Alexander III. Under his weak rule, Russia was humiliated in the Russo-Japanese War (1904–5). After the revolution of 1905, he was persuaded to grant liberal reforms, including the establishment of a duma (1905), but then withdrew these concessions. His unpopularity, the subjection of his court to Rasputin, and Russian reverses in the 1st world war, led to his enforced abdication (1917). He and his family were shot by the Bolsheviks

Nicholas of Cu·sa (kjú:sa) (c. 1401–64), German mystical theologian and philosopher. He upheld the superiority of councils over popes in his 'De concordantia catholica' (1431–6) but later abandoned this view. His 'De docta ignorantia' (1440) was an attempt to apply mathematics to philosophy. He anticipated Copernicus in teaching that the earth was round and not the center of the universe

Nich·ol·son (níkəlsən), Ben (1894–1982), English painter. Influenced by cubism and by Mondrian, he painted abstract still lifes in which the subjects (vases, fruit, boats) become elegantly simplified formal symbols. He also created reliefs in refined geometric forms

Nichrome (*metallurgy*) trademark for an alloy of nickel, chromium, and often iron, produced by Driver-Harris Co

Ni·ci·as (níʃi:əs) (d. 413 B.C.), Athenian general and opponent of Cleon. He concluded the Peace of Nicias (421 B.C.) with Sparta, ending the first part of the Peloponnesian War

nick (nik) **1.** *n.* a notch serving as a guide, *put nicks in the trees to be felled* ‖ a shallow, usually unintentional, cut or chip, *he took a nick out of his finger* ‖ (*printing*) a notch on the shank of a piece of type **in the nick of time** just before it is too late **2.** *v.t.* to make a nick in, *the razor nicked his chin* ‖ to make a cut under (a horse's tail) so that it is carried higher [etym. doubtful]

nick·el (ník'l) **1.** *n.* a metallic element (symbol Ni, at. no. 28, at. mass 58.71) which is hard and rust-resisting and takes a fine polish. It is used as a protective and ornamental coating, deposited on other metals by electrolysis, and is alloyed with a number of other metals to form nickel steel, constantan etc. ‖ a five-cent coin in the U.S.A. and Canada **2.** *v.t. pres. part.* **nick·el·ing**, esp. *Br.* **nick·el·ling** *past* and *past part.* **nick·eled**, esp. *Br.* **nick·elled** to plate with nickel [abbr. fr. G. *kupfernickel*, the ore from which nickel was first obtained]

nick·el·o·de·on (nikəlóudi:ən) *n.* a jukebox ‖ (*hist.*) a movie house with an admission price of five cents [etym. doubtful]

nickel silver an alloy of nickel, copper and zinc, used in tableware and hospital equipment

Nicklaus (níklaus), Jack (1940–), U.S. golfer. Generally considered the best player in golf history, he has won more major championships (20) than any other player: the U.S. Amateur twice (1959, 1961); the Masters 6 times (1963, 1965, 1966, 1972, 1975, 1986); the PGA 5 times (1963, 1971, 1973, 1975, 1980); the U.S. Open 4 times (1962, 1967, 1972, 1980); and the British Open 3 times (1966, 1970, 1978). He is the all-time leading money winner on the professional tour.

nick·name (níkneim) **1.** *n.* a name by which a person is called familiarly, other than his real name. (It is commonly an altered form of the real name, e.g. 'Bill' for 'William', or descriptive, e.g. 'Shorty' for someone specially short) **2.** *v.t. pres. part.* **nick·nam·ing** *past* and *past part.* **nick·named** to dub with a nickname [fr. M.E. *an ekename*, a surname]

Nicobar Islands *ANDAMAN AND NICOBAR ISLANDS

Nic·o·de·mus (nikədí:məs) (1st c.), a Pharisee who helped Joseph of Arimathaea to bury the body of Jesus

Ni·co·let, Ni·col·let (níkəlei, *F.* ni:kɔlei), Jean (1598–1642), French-Canadian explorer. He was the first European to reach the Wisconsin area, landing (1634) at Green Bay

Nic·olls (níkəlz), Richard (1624–72), the first English governor of New York (1664–8), responsible for the smooth transition from Dutch to English rule

Nic·ol prism (ník'l) a compound calcite prism, used to obtain a single beam of plane-polarized light [after William *Nicol* (1768-1851), Scottish physicist]

Nic·o·si·a (nikousí:ə) the capital (pop. 117,000) of Cyprus, on the central plain. Industries: food processing, tobacco, textiles. Gothic cathedral (St Sophia, now a mosque), Venetian town walls (1567)

nic·o·tin·a·mide-ad·e·nine di·nu·cle·o·tide [C₂₁H₂₇N₇O₁₄P₂] (nicətínamaidǽdeni:n dainjəkli:outaid) (*biochem.*) coenzyme for many hydrogenase reactions important in metabolism as an oxidizing agent *also* nadide diphosphopyridine nucleotide *abbr.* **NAD**

nic·o·tin·a·mide-ad·e·nine di·nu·cle·o·tide phos·phate [C₂₁H₂₈N₇O₁₇P₃] (*biochem.*) a coenzyme for many other dehydrogenase reactions esp. for oxidation of glucose 6-phosphate in blood cells *also* triphosphopyridine *abbr.* **NADP**

nic·o·tine (níkəti:n) *n.* a very poisonous volatile alkaloid (C₁₀H₁₄N₂) which is the most active constituent of tobacco, from which it is obtained for use as an insecticide. It is responsible for the narcotic properties of tobacco [F. after Jacques *Nicot* (c. 1530-1600), French diplomat, who introduced tobacco into France (1560)]

nic·o·tin·ic acid (nikətínik) a crystalline heterocyclic acid, C₆H₅NO₂, one of the components of the vitamin B complex derived from the oxidation of nicotine. It is found in blood, yeast, bran etc. and is used in treating pellagra

Ni·co·ya (ni:kɔ́ja) (16th c.), an Indian cacique of Central America (now Nicaragua) at the time of the Spanish conquest

nic·tat·ing membrane (níkteitiŋ) a nictitating membrane

Nictheroy *NITEROI

nic·ti·tat·ing membrane (níktitʃeitiŋ) a thin membrane in reptiles, birds and many mammals, which assists in keeping the eye clean [fr. M.L. *nictitare* (*nictitatus*), to wink]

ni·dus (náidəs) *pl.* **ni·di** (náidai), **ni·dus·es** *n.* a nest or place in which insects, spiders etc. deposit eggs ‖ (*bot.*) a cavity for the development of spores ‖ (*biol.*) a breeding place in a living organism where disease germs develop [L.=nest]

Nid·wal·den (ní:tvɑldən) *UNTERWALDEN

Nie·buhr (ní:buər) Barthold Georg (1776–1831), German historian. His 'Roman History' (1811–32) is considered the first example of modern scientific historical writing

Niebuhr, Reinhold (1892–1971), U.S. Protestant theologian and social critic. His writings include 'Beyond Tragedy' (1937), 'The Nature and Destiny of Man' (1941–3), 'Faith and History' (1949)

niece (ni:s) *n.* a daughter of a person's brother or sister [F. *nièce*]

ni·el·lo (ni:élou) *pl.* **ni·el·li** (ni:éli:), **ni·el·los** *n.* a black metallic alloy used as filling for incised lines in silverwork etc. ‖ a piece of such work ‖ the technique it involves [Ital.]

Nie·men (ní:mən) (Neman) a navigable river (500 miles long) of the U.S.S.R., rising in Byelorussia and flowing through Lithuania to the Baltic

Nie·mey·er (ní:maier), Oscar (1907–), Brazilian architect. He has ingeniously adapted the international style to local conditions. He was architectural director for the planning of Brasília, and designed many of its buildings

Niepce (njeps), Joseph Nicéphore (1765–1833), French chemist. After experiments to develop a photographic process, he made the first photoengraving (1826). He later collaborated with Daguerre in developing the daguerreotype process

Nie·tzsche (ní:tʃe, ní:tʃi:), Friedrich Wilhelm (1844–1900), German philosopher, philologist and poet. Enthusiastic love of life was the ground of his philosophy. He did not produce a systematic doctrine, but by virtue of his insight into the existential situation of modern man, his perception of the cultural flattening of the industrial era, and his ideas on the breeding of a new aristocracy (cf. SUPERMAN), he was one of the major influences on 20th-c. thought. His most important works are collections of aphorisms, essays and prose poems, including 'The Birth of Tragedy' (1872), 'Thus Spake Zarathustra' (1883) and 'Beyond Good and Evil' (1886)

Niè·vre (njevr) a department (area 2,658 sq. miles, pop. 248,000) of central France (*NIVERNAIS, *ORLÉANAIS). Chief town: Nevers

nif·ty (nífti:) *comp.* **nif·ti·er** *superl.* **nif·ti·est** *adj.* (*pop.*) used as a term of admiring approval for a girl, sports car, chip shot etc., with the connotation of neatness, deftness, stylishness etc. [origin unknown]

Ni·ger (náidʒər) an inland republic (area 458,994 sq. miles, pop. 5,634,000) in W. Africa. Capital: Niamey. Main racial and linguistic groups: Hausa (52%), Fulani, Jerma and Songhai (Negroid groups), Tuareg. French is also used. Religion: 85% Moslem, 14% local African religions, small Christian minority. Except for the Aïr Massif in the north center, the land is a plateau (average height 1,000 ft), desert (the Sahara) in the north inhabited by the Tuaregs, semiarid grazing land (the Sahel) in the center inhabited by the Fulani, and savanna in the south with a cultivated strip along the River Niger and Nigerian border, containing most of the population. Average temperature (F.): 84°. Rainfall: 10–25 ins in the south, less in the north. Livestock: cattle, sheep, goats, donkeys, camels, horses. Crops: cereals, peanuts, beans, manioc, cotton. Resources: uranium, salt, natron, tin, gum arabic. Exports: peanuts, live animals, hides and skins, fish and turtles, cotton, dates, salt, gums. Imports: cotton fabrics, food, vehicles, machinery, oil, sugar. Monetary unit: CFA franc. HISTORY. The region formed part of the empire of Kanem (10th–19th cc.) and became a nexus for trade routes across the Sahara. European exploration began in the 19th c. The country was occupied (1900) by the French, and Niger became a French colony (1922). It became fully independent (Aug. 3, 1960). Niger suffered severely from a drought throughout the Sahel region, 1968–74. Niger's first president, Hamani Diori, was accused of mismanaging relief efforts and removed in 1974. Since then, a military and civilian council has ruled with Col. Seyni Kountché. Drought remained a problem in the early 1980s

Niger a river (2,600 miles long) of W. Africa, rising (as the Tembi) in the mountains of W. Guinea and flowing north, east and south, in an Arc through Mali, Niger and Nigeria, to its delta on the Gulf of Guinea. It is navigable for long stretches between rapids

Ni·ge·ri·a (naidʒíəri:ə) a republic (area 356,669 sq. miles, pop. 84,200,000) in tropical W. Africa and member of the British Commonwealth.

Capital: Lagos. Largest town: Ibadan. The federal structure in four regions: Northern, Western, Eastern, and Mid-Western Nigeria, together with the Federal Territory, Lagos was decreed (May 1966) no longer actual, and was replaced (Apr. 1968) by a federation of 12 states. Main ethnic groups: Hausa and Fulani (North), Ibo (East), Yoruba (West). Languages: English (official and commercial), Hausa, Ibo, Yoruba and over 200 other languages. Religion: 45% Moslem (dominant in the north), half the remainder Christian, the rest local African religions. The Niger and Benue Rivers, joining in central Nigeria, trisect the country. The northern third (desert in the far north and northeast) rises through savanna-covered hills to a central plateau (1,500–5,000 ft), largely agricultural. The eastern and western thirds have savanna in the center, giving way to rain forest. There is mangrove swamp along the Niger delta. There are mountains (3,000–7,000 ft) along the eastern frontier. Average temperatures (F.): 72°–87° near the coast, 66°–94° in the north. Rainfall: 60 ins in the north, 80 ins in the rain forest, 130 ins on the southeast coast. Rainy season: Apr.–Sept. in the north, Mar.–Nov. in the south. Livestock: cattle, sheep, goats. Main export crops: peanuts, cotton, palm oil and kernels, cocoa, cotton, rubber. Minerals: columbite (95% of world production), tin, coal, petroleum, gold. Manufactures and industries: oil extraction, meat packing, food processing, textiles, plywood, pottery, cement, margarine, soap, cigarettes. Exports: agricultural products, tin, hard and soft woods, hides and skins, columbite. Imports: machinery, cotton goods, bicycles, vehicles, fish, oil. Main ports: Lagos, Port Harcourt, Calabar. There are five universities, the oldest being Ibadan. Monetary unit: Nigerian pound. HISTORY. The kingdoms of Bornu, Benin and Hausa developed a high level of civilization and culture in the north and west of the country (10th–19th cc.). The Yoruba established themselves (c. 13th c.) in the southwest. Trade links were established between these kingdoms and the Mediterranean, and along the coast of W. Africa. The Portuguese explored the coast (late 15th c.) and developed the slave trade. The interior of the country was penetrated by British, French and German explorers (19th c.). Britain annexed Lagos (1861) in an attempt to stamp out slavery. A British protectorate was established over the lower Niger (1885), and a company was chartered (1886) to develop trade with the north. Britain created (1900) separate protectorates over Northern and Southern Nigeria, which were merged (1914) to form the colony of Nigeria. This was joined (1954) with the Southern Cameroons to form the Federation of Nigeria, which became an independent member of the Commonwealth (Oct. 1, 1960). The Southern Cameroons withdrew (Feb. 1961) and joined Cameroun, while the Northern Cameroons joined (June 1, 1961) Nigeria. Nigeria became a republic within the Commonwealth (Oct. 1, 1963). The prime minister, Sir Abubakar Tafawa Balewa, was killed (1966) in an army revolt which was put down by military leaders who then took power but who were overthrown six months later by an army mutiny. A massacre (1966) of the dominant Eastern group, the Ibos, led to the secession of the East from the federation as the Republic of Biafra (May 1967). Civil war followed. The midwestern region seceded (Sept. 1967), as the Republic of Benin but it was very quickly reintegrated and as the Mid-West State retained its former boundaries. The secession of Biafra was ended (Jan. 1970) by force of arms after 30 months of fighting. In 1975, Lt. Gen. Olusegun Obasanjo became head of state. The following year Abuja was chosen as the site of the new capital. In 1979 a new constitution took effect and elections brought a civilian government to power under President Shehu Shagari. He was overthrown in 1983, and Maj. Gen. Mohammed Buhari took power. A dramatic drop in oil prices led to economic crisis, and Buhari was overthrown in 1985 in an army coup

Ni·ge·ri·an (naidʒíəri:ən) **1.** n. a native or inhabitant of Nigeria **2.** adj. of or belonging to Nigeria

nig·gard (nígərd) n. a stingy person [etym. doubtful]

nig·gard·li·ness (nígərdli:nis) n. the quality or state of being niggardly

nig·gard·ly (nígərdli:) **1.** adj. stingy **2.** adv. in a stingy way

nig·ger (nígər) n. (offensive term of contempt) a Negro [older neger fr. F. nègre]

nigger in the woodpile something in a situation that is concealed or not straightforward, a lurking difficulty

nig·gle (níg'l) pres. part. **nig·gling** past and past part. **nig·gled** v.i. to pay excessive attention to unimportant details ‖ to criticize or raise difficulties in a petty, carping way **nig·gling** (níglin) adj. trifling, unimportant, niggling details ‖ too meticulous in conception and execution, niggling decoration [prob. fr. Scand.]

niggle n. a trifling problem

nigh (nai) adv, (archaic) near **nigh on** (archaic) almost, nigh on 40 years [O.E. nēah]

night (nait) n. the time during which the sun is below the horizon (opp. DAY) ‖ darkness, he went out into the night ‖ mental or moral darkness, the night of ignorance ‖ a period of affliction, the dark night of the soul ‖ a night or evening as a point of time ‖ an evening performance of a play etc., a first night ‖ a particular evening's program, ladies' night at the club **a night off** a night or evening taken off from work **a night out** a night or evening spent in entertainment outside the home **all night, all night long** throughout the night **at night** during the hours of darkness **by night** during the night as opposed to the day, it sleeps by day and hunts by night **night and day** continually **to have a good (bad) night** to sleep well (badly) **to make a night of it** to spend a night or evening in festivity [O.E. niht]

night bird *NIGHT OWL

night blindness nyctalopia

night-blooming cereus any of several cacti which bloom at night, esp. Selenicerus grandiflorus, a sprawling or climbing cactus with large white scented flowers native to America and the W. Indies

night·cap (náitkæp) n. a drink, esp. of liquor, taken at bedtime ‖ (old-fash.) a covering for the head, worn in bed

night cap (náitkæp) n. (mil.) night combat air patrol acronym **NCAP**

night·clothes (náitklouðz, náitklouz) pl. n. clothes worn in bed, e.g. pajamas

night·club (náitklʌb) n. a place of entertainment open at night serving drinks and sometimes food and usually having a floor show or dancing

night·dress (náitdres) n. a nightgown

night·fall (náitfɔl) n. the period just after sunset, dusk

night·glow (náitglou) n. airglow at night from atomic oxygen reactions in the atmosphere at 45–60 mi and ionic recombinations at 180 mi

night·gown (náitgaun) n. a loose (usually long) garment worn by women or children in bed

night·hawk (náithɔk) n. any of several goatsuckers of North America, esp. Chordeiles minor

nightie *NIGHTY

Night·in·gale (náitingeil), Florence (1820–1910), British nurse. Her work in organizing hospitals in the Crimea during the Crimean War pioneered modern nursing methods and did much to establish nursing as a respected profession. She established (1860) a training school and home for nurses

night·in·gale (náitingeil) n. any of several European thrushes, esp. Luscinia megarhyncha, noted for the song of the male, usually heard at night, in the breeding season [M.E. nihtingale fr. O.E. nihtegala fr. niht, night + galan, to sing]

night·jar (náitdʒɑr) n. Caprimulgus europaeus, a nocturnal insectivorous European goatsucker having buff and brown speckled plumage and noted for its harsh cry

night life activities going on in a town at night, esp. in places catering to pleasure, e.g. nightclubs ‖ the pursuit of such activities

night-light (náitlait) n. a small, dim, indoor light, often a wax candle, kept burning at night for children, invalids etc.

night-long (náitlɔŋ, náitlɒŋ) **1.** adj. lasting throughout the night **2.** adv. throughout the night

night·ly (náitli:) **1.** adj. happening every night or every evening **2.** adv. every night

night·mare (náitmeər) n. a terrifying dream ‖ a frightening experience or persistent fear, the car journey was a nightmare from beginning to end **night·mar·ish** adj. [M.E. fr. niht, night + mare, demon]

night owl (.Am.=Br. night bird) someone who prefers going to bed long after the conventional time

night piece a painting of a night scene

nights (naits) adv. (pop.) repeatedly or regularly at night

night school a school or other educational institution offering evening classes, esp. for adults

night·shade (náitʃeid) n. any plant of the genus Solanum, including henbane and belladonna [O.E. nihtscada]

night·shirt (náitʃərt) n. (old-fash.) a long garment worn in bed by boys or men

night-sight (náitsait) n. (mil.) sight on a weapon that makes possible vision in darkness

night soil human excrement collected at night in countries where the sanitary system requires it

night·stick (náitstik) n. a short thick stick used by policemen

night·time (náittaim) n. the period between dusk and dawn

night·view·er (náitvju:ər) n. surveillance device that makes possible vision in darkness

night-vi·sion binoculars (náitviʒən binókjulərz) n. small battery-powered television cameras containing small television picture tubes all in the format of wearable binoculars that are capable of vision in the dark

night vision telescope an electronically amplified telescope capable of night viewing without artificial illumination

night watch a person or persons acting as guard during the night ‖ the period in which this watch is kept

night watchman a watchman on duty at night ‖ in cricket, a player replacement sent in late in a game to defend the wicket

night·watch·man state (náitwɑtʃmən) a nation that devotes substantial legislation to protection of consumers and the public vis-à-vis vested commercial interests

nigh·ty, night·ie (náiti:) pl. **night·ies** n. (pop.) a nightgown

ni·gres·cence (naigrés'ns) n. the state or quality of being nigrescent ‖ the process of becoming black or dark

ni·gres·cent (naigrés'nt) adj. (of the skin, hair, eyes etc.) blackish [fr. L. nigrescere, to grow black]

nig·ri·tude (nígritu:d, nígritju:d) n. intense blackness [fr. L. nigritudo]

ni·hil·ism (náiəlizəm, náihilizəm, níhilizəm) n. an attitude rejecting all philosophical or ethical principles **Ni·hil·ism** (hist.) the doctrine or program of a 19th-c. and early 20th-c. Russian revolutionary group which rejected all forms of tradition and authoritarianism in politics, religion, morals and art **ni·hil·ist** n. a person advocating nihilism **ni·hil·is·tic** adj. [fr. L. nihil, nothing]

Nii·ga·ta (ni:gátə) the main port (pop. 458,000) of W. Honshu, Japan, at the mouth of the Shinano: oil refining, metallurgy, chemicals, textiles

Ni·jin·sky (nidʒínski:), Vaslav (1890–1950), Russian ballet dancer. His greatest successes were with Diaghlev's Russian Ballet in 'l'Après-midi d'un faune' and 'Spectre de la rose'

Nij·me·gen (náimeigən) a port (pop. 148,000) in Gelderland, Netherlands, on the Rhine: brewing, dairy products, machinery, shipbuilding

Nijmegen, Treaties of the treaties signed (1678–9) by the Netherlands, France, Spain, the Holy Roman Empire and Sweden at the end of the Dutch War of 1672–8. All land taken from the Netherlands was restored. France and Spain exchanged extensive territories

-nik (nik) (comb. form) (from the Yiddish) slang ending used to create words signifying "one of the group" or "devotee of," e.g., beatnik, peacenik, no-goodnik, computernik

Ni·ke (náiki:) (Gk mythol.) the goddess of victory, usually represented as a winged figure carrying a wreath and palm branch [Gk nikē, victory]

Ni·ke (náiki) n. (mil.) U.S. army surface-to-air guided missile, evolved through several stages (Nike-Ajax, Nike-Hercules, Nike-Zeus), weighing 2,200 lb, with an 80-mi range, now capable as an antimissile missile through phased-array radar

Nike Hercules an army air defense artillery surface-to-air guided missile system (MIM-14) providing nuclear or conventional air-defense

---

coverage against manned bombers and air-breathing missiles, with a capability of performing surface-to-surface missions

Ni·ko·la·yev (nìkɔlájəf) (Vernoleninsk) a port and naval base (pop. 447,000) of the Ukraine, U.S.S.R., on the estuary of the Southern Bug: shipbuilding, mechanical engineering

nil (nil) *n.* nothing ‖ (*esp. Br.*) a score of nothing [L.]

Nile (nail) (*Arab* El-Bahr, Bahr-en-Nil) a river of Africa, the world's longest, flowing from the equator to the Mediterranean, draining 1,293,000 sq. miles. The White Nile and the Blue Nile unite at Khartoum to form the great river which flows through Egypt. Its delta, beginning at Cairo, is 120 miles wide. Principal mouths: Rosetta (east of Alexandria), Damietta. The Nile is navigable in certain seasons as far as Lake Albert, except where cataracts or sudd make it impassable. It rises in April and floods in September. Egyptian agriculture formerly depended on the floods, but dams (e.g. Aswan) and barrages now control irrigation, besides providing hydroelectricity. Length from the source of the White Nile: 4,053 miles

Nile, Battle of the the British naval victory (1798) in which Nelson destroyed the French fleet, and thus isolated Napoleon and his army in Egypt

Nile green a pale yellowish-green color

nil·gai (nílgai) *pl.* **nil·gais, nil·gai** *n. Boselaphus tragocamelus,* a large bluish-gray antelope of India [Hindi fr. *nil,* blue+*gai,* cow]

Nil·gi·ri Hills (nílgiri:) a plateau (average height 6,500 ft) in Kerala and Madras, India. Highest point: Dodabetta, 8,670 ft

nil norm (*economics*) (*Br.*) minimum wage and maximum price standards set by the government on a scale providing maximum increases to underpaid workers or for increased productivity *also* zero norm

Ni·lo-Ham·ite (nàilouhǽmait) *n.* a member of a group of E. African cattle-raising peoples including the Masai

Ni·lot·ic (nailótik) **1.** *adj.* of or related to the Nile or the people of the Nile basin ‖ relating to the tall Negroid people living in the valley of the White Nile **2.** *n.* a group of languages spoken in the valley of the White Nile [fr. L. *Niloticus* fr. Gk]

nil·po·tent (nílpout'nt) *adj.* (*math.*) equalling zero when raised to a specified power

nim·ble (nímb'l) *adj.* light and quick in motion, agile, *nimble as a mountain goat* ‖ alert, quick-witted, *a nimble mind* **nim·bly** *adv.* [M.E. *nimmel* fr. O.E. *numol* fr. *niman,* to take]

nim·bo·stra·tus (nìmboustréitəs, nìmboustrǽtəs) *n.* a low gray cloud layer, bringing rain [fr. NIMBUS+ Mod. L. *stratus,* layer]

nim·bus (nímbəs) *pl.* **nim·bi** (nímbai), **nim·bus·es** *n.* (*art*) a halo ‖ a rain cloud extending over the entire sky [L.=cloud]

Nim·bus (nímbəs) *n.* (*aerospace*) one of NASA's closed-formation exploration satellites used for meteorology

Nimeiry, Muhammad Gaafar al- (niméiri:gəfár al) (1930–   ), Sudanese leader. As an army colonel he led the overthrow of the Muhammad Mahgoub government (1969), becoming prime minister later that year. He was president of Sudan (1971–85) until ousted in a coup led by Gen. Siwar al-Dahab. As president he ended a 17-year civil war in Sudan (1972) and supported the Egypt-Israel peace treaty of 1979 but was unable to solve the country's economic problems

Nîmes (ni:m) the chief town (pop. 132,000) of Gard, S. France. Industries: textiles, mechanical engineering. Arena and other Roman buildings

Nim·itz (nímits), Chester William (1885–1965), American admiral. He was commander in chief (1941–5) of the U.S. Pacific fleet in the 2nd world war

Nim·itz (nímits) *n.* (*mil.*) U.S. aircraft carrier

ni·mon·ic (nimónik) *adj.* (*metallurgy*) of a type of nickel-chromium alloy, with minute quantities of titanium, cobalt, aluminum, or carbon, that is highly resistant to heat and stress

Nim·rod (nímrod) the traditional founder of the Babylonian monarchy, and the archetype of a great hunter (Genesis x, 8–10)

nin·com·poop (nínkəmpu:p) *n.* a dolt, simpleton [origin unknown]

nine (nain) **1.** *adj.* being one more than eight (*NUMBER TABLE) **2.** *n.* three times three ‖ the cardinal number representing this (9, IX) ‖ nine

o'clock ‖ a playing card marked with nine symbols ‖ a team of nine members, esp. in baseball **dressed to** (or **up to) the nines** very elaborately dressed in an eye-catching way [O.E. *nigon*]

nine days' wonder something that arouses sensational interest for a while but is soon forgotten

nine·pin (náinpin) *n.* a bottle-shaped pin used in ninepins ‖ (*pl.,* construed as *sing.*) a game played by bowling at nine such pins set up in a pattern

Nine-Power Treaty an agreement reached (1922) at the Washington Conference (1921–2) by the U.S.A., Great Britain, France, Japan, Italy, Belgium, the Netherlands, Portugal, and China. The signatories undertook to respect China's territorial integrity, to help China maintain stable government, to promote the open-door policy in trade with China, and to refrain from seeking China's special favor

nine·teen (náintí:n) **1.** *adj.* being one more than 18 (*NUMBER TABLE) **2.** *n.* ten plus nine ‖ the cardinal number representing this (19, XIX) **to talk nineteen to the dozen** to talk continually [O.E. *nigontýne*]

1984 symbol of authoritarian, totalitarian, regimented future society, from *1984,* the novel by George Orwell *Cf* ORWELLIAN

nine·teenth (náintí:nθ) **1.** *adj.* being number 19 in a series (*NUMBER TABLE) ‖ being one of the 19 equal parts of anything **2.** *n.* the person or thing next after the 18th ‖ one of 19 equal parts of anything (1/19) ‖ the 19th day of a month [O.E. *nigontēotha*]

Nineteenth Amendment (1920) amendment to the U.S. Constitution that provides for equal voting rights for men and women. It states that the right of citizens to vote 'shall not be denied or abridged by the United States or by any State on account of sex.' This amendment came about as the result of a women's rights movement that began in the 1830s and was strongly reinforced by the participation of women in industry during World War I

nine·ti·eth (náintí:iθ) **1.** *adj.* being number 90 in a series (*NUMBER TABLE) ‖ being one of the 90 equal parts of anything **2.** *n.* the person or thing next after the 89th ‖ one of 90 equal parts of anything (1/90) [O.E.]

nine-to-fiver (náintu:fáivər) *n.* one who holds a regular job, esp. in an office

nine·ty (náinti:) **1.** *adj.* being ten more than 80 (*NUMBER TABLE) **2.** *pl.* **nine·ties** *n.* nine times ten ‖ the cardinal number representing this (90, XC) **the nineties** (of temperature, a person's age, a century etc.) the span 90-9 **the Nineties** the last decade of the 19th c. [O.E. *nigontíg*]

Nin·e·veh (nínəvə) an ancient city on the Tigris, the later capital of Assyria. It contained the palace and library of Ashurbanipal, and was destroyed (612 B.C.) by the Medes and Babylonians

Ninghsien (nínʃjén) *NINGPO

Ning·po (nínpou) (formerly Ninghsien), a fishing port (pop. 350,000) in Chekiang, E. China, enclosed by ancient walls: light manufactures

Ning·sia-Hui (nínʃjáhwí:) an autonomous region (area 30,000 sq. miles, pop. 3,000,000, mainly Mongols) in N.W. China. Capital: Yinchuan (formerly Ningsia, pop. 30,000)

Nin·i·an (níni:ən), St (c. 360–c. 432), British apostle of the Picts in Scotland. Feast: Sept. 16

nin·ny (níni:) *pl.* **nin·nies** *n.* a person who behaves stupidly [perh. for *an innocent*]

Ni·ño (ní:njɔ), Andrés (late 15th c. and early 16th c.), Spanish explorer of part of the Gulf of Panama and Nicaragua, and discoverer of the Gulf of Fonseca

Ni·ños Hé·ro·es (ní:njɔsérɔes) (*Span.*=child heroes), the Mexican cadets who defended (1847) heroically the castle of Chapultepec in Mexico City against a U.S. invading force

ninth (nainθ) **1.** *adj.* being number nine in a series (*NUMBER TABLE) ‖ being one of the nine equal parts of anything **2.** *n.* the person or thing next after the eighth ‖ one of nine equal parts of anything (1/9) ‖ the ninth day of a month **3.** *adv.* in the ninth place ‖ (followed by a superlative) except eight, *she is ninth biggest* [O.E. *nigotha*]

Ninth Amendment (1791) section of the Bill of Rights in the U.S. Constitution designed to protect certain inherent rights of the people not specified in the Constitution. This concern reflects a belief in inalienable natural human rights. It has been cited in various Supreme

Court decisions. (*Griswold v. Connecticut, Roe v. Wade, Doe v. Bolton*) as part of the basis of a constitutional right to privacy

Ni·o·be (náiəbi:) (*Gk mythol.*) queen of Thebes, daughter of Tantalus. Her numerous offspring were killed by Apollo and Artemis to punish Niobe for her boastfulness. She was turned into a stone figure of inconsolable grief

ni·o·bi·um (naióubi:əm) *n.* a rare steel-gray metallic element (symbol Nb, at. no. 41, at. mass 92.906) usually found in association with tantalum and used in alloys [Mod. L. fr. *Niobe*]

NIOS (*acronym*) for National Institute for Occupational Safety and Health *Cf* OSHA

nip (nip) *n.* a small measure or drink of liquor, *a nip of brandy* [etym. doubtful]

nip **1.** *v. pres. part.* **nip·ping** *past* and *past part.* **nipped** *v.t.* to pinch, squeeze sharply, *a crab nipped his toe* ‖ (with 'off') to pinch off, remove by pinching, *nip the side shoots off the tomato plants* ‖ (of frost) to damage (plants etc.) ‖ to benumb by cold, *nipped by the wind* ‖ *v.i.* (*esp. Br., pop.*) to move quickly, nimbly, *to nip on a bus* **to nip in the bud** to stop (something) before it has time to develop **2.** *n.* a sharp pinch or bite ‖ a mildly stinging coldness, *a nip in the air* [etym. doubtful]

ni·pa (ní:pə) *n.* a member of *Nipa,* a genus of creeping palms of E. Asia. Its sap is a source of sugar and its leaves are used for thatching ‖ an alcoholic drink made from its fermented sap [Span. fr. Malay *nipah*]

nip and tuck neck and neck

Nip·i·gon (nípigon) (or Nepigon) a lake (area 1,730 sq. miles) in S.W. Ontario province, Canada. Its outlet is the Nipigon River, flowing south to a bay in Lake Superior

nip·per (nípər) *n.* (*pl.*) small pincers for gripping or pulling, e.g. forceps, pliers etc. ‖ the claw of a crustacean ‖ the incisor tooth of a horse, esp. one of the middle four ‖ (*Br., pop.*) a young boy [NIP v.]

nip·ple (níp'l) *n.* a protuberance marking the opening of the mammary duct in mammals, e.g. of a woman's breast ‖ a teat on an infant's feeding bottle ‖ a protuberance shaped like this, e.g. on skin, metal, glass etc. ‖ a mechanical device for regulating the flow of a liquid [origin unknown]

Nip·pon (ni:pón) *JAPAN

Nip·pon·ese (nipəní:z, nipəní:s) *pl.* **Nip·pon·ese** *n.* and *adj.* Japanese

nip·py (nípi:) *comp.* **nip·pi·er** *superl.* **nip·pi·est** *adj.* chilly ‖ (*pop.,* of people) brisk ‖ (*pop.,* of motor vehicles) having good acceleration

Nir·va·na (nərvánə, nərvánə) *n.* (*Buddhism, Hinduism, Jainism*) a beatific spiritual condition attained by the extinction of desire, in which the individual is freed from karma ‖ (*Buddhism*) union with the supreme spirit [Skr. *nirvāna* fr. *nirvā,* to blow]

Nis, Nish (niʃ) a trade and communications center (pop. 127,654) in E. Serbia, Yugoslavia

ni·sei (ní:sei) *pl.* **ni·sei, ni·seis** *n.* a native American citizen born of immigrant Japanese parents and educated in the U.S.A. (cf. KIBEI, cf. ISSEI, cf. SANSEI) [Jap.=second generation]

Ni·shi·no·mi·ya (ni:ʃi:nəmí:ja) a city (pop. 410,000) on Osaka Bay, Honshu, Japan, producing saké, metals, machinery. Temples (7th c.)

ni·si (náisai) *adj.* (*law,* of a decree, order etc.) not final, effective unless cause to the contrary is shown before a fixed date (*DECREE NISI) [L.=unless]

ni·si pri·us (náisaipráiəs) *n.* (*law*) a trial of civil causes by assize judges [L.=unless before: words from the writ directing the sheriff to provide a jury on a certain day unless the judges come sooner]

nit (nit) *n.* an egg of a louse or other parasitic insect, esp. in human hair ‖ the insect when young ‖ unit of brightness equal to 1 candela per sq. meter, of cross section of perpendicular to the rays [O.E. *hnitu*]

NIT (*economics abbr.*) for negative income tax (which see)

ni·ter, esp. *Br.* **ni·tre** (náitər) *n.* potassium nitrate, esp. occurring naturally ‖ sodium nitrate, esp. in its natural form as caliche [F. fr. L. fr. Gk fr. Heb.]

Ni·te·rói, Nic·the·roy (nìtərɔ́i) a city (pop. 386,185) of Brazil, across Guanabara Bay from Rio de Janeiro: textiles, building materials, chemicals

Ni·tin·ol (naitinəl) *n.* (*metallurgy*) a nickel-titanium alloy capable of regaining its shape after heating, cooling, or crushing

nit·pick (nítpik) v. (colloq.) to criticize extremely minor details —**nit picker** n.

ni·trate (náitreit) **1.** n. a salt or ester of nitric acid ‖ potassium or sodium nitrate, esp. when used as fertilizer **2.** v.t. pres. part. **ni·trat·ing** past and past part. **ni·trat·ed** to treat or combine with nitric acid or a nitrate, esp. to convert into a nitro compound or a nitrate **ni·tra·tion** n. [NITER]

nitre *NITER

ni·tric (náitrik) adj. (of a compound) derived from nitrogen, esp. higher in valence than in the nitrous compounds [F. nitrique]

nitric acid a clear colorless fuming liquid (HNO_3) obtained by heating a mixture of sulfuric acid and sodium nitrate, and by catalytic oxidation of ammonia gas. It is used for dissolving certain metals, for etching and for the manufacture of nitrates, dyes and explosives

nitric oxide a colorless gas (NO) obtained by oxidation of nitrogen or ammonia. In contact with air it forms reddish-brown fumes of nitrogen peroxide, NO_2

ni·tri·fi·ca·tion (naitrifikéiʃən) n. the process of nitrifying, esp. the conversion of ammonium salts to nitrites and their further oxidation to nitrates by bacteria in the soil (*NITROBACTERIA)

ni·tri·fy (náitrifai) pres. part. **ni·tri·fy·ing** past and past part. **ni·tri·fied** v.t. to impregnate or combine with nitrogen or a nitrogen compound ‖ to convert by oxidation to nitrous acid, nitric acid or their salts [F. nitrifier]

ni·trile (náitril, náitrail) n. an organic compound of a class having the general formula RC≡N [fr. NITRE, var of NITER,+-ile fr. L. -ilis, -ilis, adj. suffix]

ni·trite (náitrait) n. a salt or ester of nitrous acid (HO_2N) [NITER]

ni·tro (náitrou) adj. (esp. of organic compounds) containing a radical (-NO_2) always linked through nitrogen

ni·tro·bac·te·ri·a (naitroubæktíəriːə) pl. n. soil bacteria causing nitrification [Mod. L.]

ni·tro·ben·zene (naitroubénziːn, naitroubenzíːn) n. a poisonous oil ($C_6H_5NO_2$), produced by the action of nitric acid on benzene and used in making explosives, perfumes, dyes etc.

ni·tro·cel·lu·lose (naitrouséljulous) n. cellulose nitrate

Ni·tro-Dur (naitroudur) n. (pharm.) trade name for nitroglycerine delivered through the skin by an applicator on a plastic strip

ni·tro·fu·ran·to·in (naitroufuræntouin) [$C_8H_4N_2O_2$] n. (pharm.) urinary antiseptic; marketed as Furadantin and Macrodantin

ni·tro·gen (náitrədʒən) n. a colorless, tasteless, gaseous element (symbol N, at. no. 7, at. mass 14.0067), the principal constituent of the atmosphere (78.1% by volume) and an essential constituent of living matter. Atmospheric nitrogen is the chief raw material for the manufacture of ammonia, nitric acid and nitrogenous fertilizers [F. nitrogène]

ni·tro·gen·ase (náitroudʒəneis) n. (pharm.) an enzyme that stimulates conversion of nitrogen to ammonia by bacteria

nitrogen cycle a cyclical series of natural processes by which nitrogen in the atmosphere is converted into soluble compounds (*NITROGEN FIXATION) mainly by the bacteria living in the nodules of leguminous plants, converted to amino acids and then plant proteins by plants growing in the enriched soil, transferred to animals when the plants are eaten, and finally returned to the atmosphere upon the decay of plant and animal matter

nitrogen fixation the industrial conversion of atmospheric nitrogen into compounds suitable for use, e.g. in fertilizers, explosives etc. ‖ the formation of nitrogenous compounds by the metabolic assimilation of atmospheric nitrogen by certain soil bacteria, e.g. those living symbiotically on the root nodules of various leguminous plants. When these bacteria die the fixed nitrogen is made available in the soil as plant food

ni·trog·e·nous (naitród3inəs) adj. of, relating to, or containing nitrogen

ni·tro·glyc·er·in, ni·tro·glyc·er·ine (naitrouglísərin) n. glyceryl trinitrate, $C_3H_5(NO_3)_3$, an unstable oily liquid obtained by nitration from glycerol. It explodes, esp. on percussion, and is used in making dynamite and other explosives and as a vasodilator in certain heart ailments

ni·tro·lo·tra·cet·ic acid (naitrouloutræsíːdik) (chem.) detergent ingredient with low carcinogenic properties abbr. **NTA**

ni·tro·sa·mines (naitróusamiːnz) n. carcinogenic nitrogen compounds derived from combining nitrites found in bacon and cured meats with secondary amines in the digestive process

ni·trous (náitrəs) adj. of, pertaining to or impregnated with niter ‖ (of a compound) containing nitrogen, esp. lower in valence than in the nitric compounds [fr. L. nitrosus]

nitrous oxide a colorless gas, N_2O, with a sweetish smell, used as an anesthetic. Its inhalation may lead to a state of exhilaration and laughter

nit·ty-grit·ty (níti:griti:) n. the basic issues; the essential, practical point —**nitty-gritty** adj.

nit·wit (nítwit) n. (pop.) an ignorant, stupid person [fr. G. dial. nit for nicht, not+WIT]

Ni·u·e (ni:úːei) an island territory (area 100 sq. miles, pop. 3,578) of New Zealand in the S. Pacific, 1,343 miles northeast of Auckland, discovered (1744) by Cook. Products: copra, bananas

Ni·ver·nais (ni:verne) a former province of France, in the S.E. Paris basin, forming most of Nièvre department, a region of low wooded hills and fertile valleys on the upper Loire: livestock, wine, metallurgy, engineering, chemicals. Historic capital: Nevers. A countship (9th–16th cc.), then a duchy, it was annexed by the French Crown in 1669

Nix·ie light (níkzi:lait) n. device that converts an electrical impulse into a visible number by activating a glow tube to provide a visual display in clocks, computer cash registers, etc. also Nixie tube

Nix·on (níksən), Richard Milhous (1913–), U.S. vice-president (1953–61) under Dwight D. Eisenhower and the 37th U.S. president (1969–74), a Republican. During his presidency U.S. military forces were withdrawn from Vietnam and U.S. relations with the People's Republic of China were considerably strengthened. At the beginning of his second term Nixon became embroiled in the Watergate scandal and resigned in the face of possible impeachment. His vice-president and successor, Gerald Ford, pardoned him for any crimes he may have committed. Nixon's writings include 'Six Crises' (1962), 'RN: The Memoirs of Richard Nixon' (1978), 'The Real War' (1980), and 'Leaders' (1982)

Nix·on Doc·trine (níksəndóktrin) n. presidential statement (1969) that Asian nations internally or externally threatened by Communism must rely on their own resources unless threatened militarily by a major power also Guam Doctrine

Ni·za·mi (nizáːmi:) (Nizām al-Din Ilyās ibn Yūsuf, c. 1140–c. 1202), Persian poet. His romantic epics include 'Haft Paikar' (1198) and 'Laili and Majnūn' (c. 1188)

Nizh·ni-Nov·go·rod (ní:ʒninóvgʌrʌd) *GORKI

Nizh·ni Ta·gil (ní:ʒnitagíːl) a mining center (pop. 404,000) of the R.S.F.S.R., U.S.S.R., in the central Urals: foundries, chemical industries

N. J. New Jersey

Nkru·mah ('nkrúːmə), Kwame (1909–72), Ghanaian statesman. He was the first prime minister of the Gold Coast (1952–7), which he led to independence as Ghana. He was prime minister of Ghana (1957–60) and president (1960–6). His rule was ended by a military coup (Feb. 1966)

NLF (abbr.) for National Liberation Front, civilian arm of South Vietnam Communists during war with U.S., 1965–1975

N.L.R.B. *NATIONAL LABOR RELATIONS BOARD

N. M. New Mexico

N. Mex. New Mexico

Nō (nou) n. the classical heroic drama of Japan which developed in the 14th c. from ancient religious dances with choric songs. It is characterized by highly formalized plots, stylized restrained acting, use of song and dance, wooden masks and elaborate costumes [Jap.=talent, ability]

no (nou) **1.** adv. used to express negation, refusal, denial etc. (opp. YES) ‖ (with a comparative adjective or adverb) not at all, not in any degree, no better than before ‖ (with 'or', to express a negative alternative) not, whether he likes it or no ‖ (expressing surprise or disbelief) surely not, 'She insulted me publicly.' 'No.!' **2.** pl. **noes, nos** n. the word 'no', he wouldn't take no for an answer ‖ (pl.) those who vote against a motion (opp. AYES) [O.E. nā fr. ne ā, nor ever]

no adj. not any, he has no money ‖ not a, quite other than a, he is no ger ius ‖ hardly any, it's no

distance ‖ (preceded by 'to be' and followed by a gerund) not any possibility of, there's no accounting for tastes [O.E. nān, nōn, none]

no., No. number

NOAA (acronym) for U.S. National Oceanic and Atmospheric Administration

No·ah (nóuə) Hebrew patriarch. On God's instruction he built the ark in which he, his family and representatives of all living creatures survived the Flood which God had ordained to destroy the rest of mankind for its wickedness (Genesis v, 28-x)

Noah's ark a child's model ark with its load of animals and Noah, his wife and their sons

No·ailles (nouaij), Anna de Brancovan, comtesse de (1876–1933), French poet. Her collections of poems include 'le Cœur innombrable' (1901), 'les Éblouissements' (1907) and 'les Vivants et les Morts' (1913)

no·as (nóuæz) n. ancient pink granite shrine carved from a single block, e.g., in Egypt

nob (nob) n. (Br., pop., old-fash.) a person of importance, wealth or rank [etym. doubtful]

nob n. (cribbage) the jack of the same suit as the card turned up in play [var. of KNOB]

no ball (cricket) a ball bowled contrary to the rules, counting one run if not scored off, and which cannot take a wicket **nó-ball** (cricket) v.t. to declare (a bowler) to have bowled a no ball

nob·ble (nób'l) pres. part. **nob·bling** past and past part. **nob·bled** v.t. (Br., pop.) to tamper with (a racehorse, greyhound etc.), esp. by drugging it, to prevent its winning a race ‖ (Br.) to catch [origin unknown]

No·bel (noubél), Alfred Bernhard (1833–96), Swedish chemist and engineer. With the fortune he made from his invention of dynamite (1866) and other explosives, he endowed five annual Nobel prizes, for outstanding contributions to physics, chemistry, physiology and medicine, literature, and peace. (See end of Part I)

no·bel·i·um (noubéli:əm) n. a radioactive element (symbol No, at. no. 102, weight of isotope of longest known half-life 253) produced artificially [after A. B. Nobel]

No·bi·le (nóbi:le), Umberto (1885–1978), Italian aeronautical engineer and Arctic explorer. With Amundsen, he piloted an airship over the North Pole (1926). He crashed on a polar flight (1928) and was rescued by aircraft. Amundsen died looking for him

no·bil·i·ar·y (noubíli:ɛri:) adj. of or pertaining to nobles or nobility [F. nobiliaire]

no·bil·i·ty (noubíliti) n. the quality or state of being noble ‖ a noble class, esp. (Br.) the peerage [fr. F. nobilité]

no·ble (nóub'l) **1.** adj. illustrious by rank or birth ‖ of high character, lofty ideals etc., noble sentiments ‖ magnanimous, generous, a noble gesture ‖ impressive, splendid, grand in appearance, a noble mansion ‖ having exceptional qualities, a noble horse ‖ (of metals) resistant to oxidation or corrosion **2.** n. a nobleman or noblewoman ‖ (hist.) any of several English or Scottish gold or silver coins [F.]

Noble Eight·fold Path (éitfould) the basis of the disciplines of Buddhism, as pronounced by the Buddha in his first sermon. The eight steps are not fully consecutive stages, but fall into three main groups: (1) right understanding (of Buddha's basic teaching) and right aspirations (toward benevolence and renunciation) (2) right speech (i.e. no lying or abuse), right conduct (i.e. no killing, no stealing, no overindulgence) and right means of livelihood (i.e. nothing tending to the use or encouragement of wrong speech or conduct) (3) right striving (toward the building up of good and the eradication of evil within oneself), right self-possession (involving self-knowledge and control of thought), and right contemplation (according to the traditional stages of meditation). This is also known as the Middle Path or the Buddhist way of life

noble gas an inert gas

no·ble·man (nóub'lmən) pl. **no·ble·men** (nóub'lmən) n. a man of noble rank, a peer

no·ble·wom·an (nóub'lwʋmən) pl. **no·ble·wom·en** (nóub'lwimən) n. a woman of noble rank, a peer

no·bly (nóubli:) adv. in a noble way ‖ of noble ancestry, nobly born

no·bod·y (nóubɒdi:, nóubʌdi:, nóubədi:) **1.** pron. not anybody, nobody came to the meeting **2.** pl. **no·bod·ies** a person of no importance, she married a mere nobody

No·bu·na·ga O·da (nɔbu:nɑgɑɔdɑ) (1534–82), Japanese general. He united central Japan (1559–68), deposed the shogun (1573) and, with his lieutenants Hideyoshi and Ieyasu, ruled in his place

No·che Tris·te (nótʃetrí:ste) the 'sad night' of June 30, 1520 when Hernán Cortés, defeated by the Mexicans, shed tears beneath a pine tree for the death of his comrades

nock (nɒk) **1.** n. a notch at either end of a bow for taking the string, or on the flight end of an arrow for receiving the bowstring **2.** v.t. to fit or set (the arrow) on the bowstring ‖ to make a notch in (a bow or arrow) [M.E. nocke]

no·con·tract (nóukɒntrækt) adj. code word meaning documents are to be distributed only within the Defense Department

noc·ti·lu·ca (nɒktəlú:kə) pl. **noc·ti·lu·cae** (nɒktəlú:si:), **noc·ti·lu·cas** n. any member of Noctiluca, a genus of marine flagellates, whose bioluminescence causes the phosphorescence of the sea [fr. L.=moon, lantern]

noc·tur·nal (nɒktə́:rn'l) adj. of or relating to the night ‖ happening at night ‖ (zool.) active mainly at night (cf. DIURNAL) [fr. L. L. nocturnalis]

noc·turne (nɒ́ktə:rn) n. a musical composition appropriate to, or evoking, night, usually pensive or dreamy, esp. for the piano ‖ a night piece [F.]

nod (nɒd) **1.** v. pres. part. **nod·ding** past and past part. **nod·ded** v.i. to bow the head forward quickly in greeting, agreement or command, to nod to an acquaintance ‖ to bow the head involuntarily because of sleepiness, he sat nodding over his work ‖ to sway lightly, the poppies nodded in the wind ‖ to make an error through momentary inattention ‖ v.t. to bow (the head) ‖ to indicate (assent, agreement etc.) by bowing the head **2.** n. a quick forward nodding movement of the head [etym. doubtful]

nod·al (nóud'l) adj. of, like or situated at a node or nodes

nodal point (phys.) either of two points on the axis of a lens system, so placed that an incident ray directed through one point produces a parallel emergent ray from the second point

nodding acquaintance a slight acquaintance

nod·dy (nɒ́di:) pl. **nod·dies** n. Anoüs stolidus, a blackish-brown tropical and subtropical tern [etym. doubtful]

node (noud) n. (bot.) a joint or knob on a stem from which leaves grow ‖ a knob on a root or branch ‖ (med.) a discrete mass of body tissue ‖ (med.) a small body protuberance, either normal or pathological ‖ (astron.) one of the two points in which the orbit of a planet intersects the ecliptic or where the orbit of a satellite intersects the plane of the orbit of its primary ‖ (phys.) a point of zero displacement in the path traversed by two or more wave trains, or in a vibrating string or air column ‖ (geom.) the point at which a looped curve cuts itself, which may be regarded as a point on either of the two loops intersecting, or such a point at which three or more loops intersect **nod·i·cal** adj. (astron.) of the nodes [fr. L. nodus, knot]

No·dier (nɔdjei), Charles (1780–1844), French writer. He is best known for his novel 'Trilby' (1822) and was influential in the Romantic movement

no·dose (nóudous) adj. having nodes, knots or swellings [fr. L. nodosus]

nod·u·lar (nɒ́dʒulər) adj. of, pertaining to or having nodules

nod·ule (nɒ́dʒu:l) n. a small rounded mass ‖ (bot.) a root nodule ‖ a small protuberance, e.g. a tumor or ganglion **nod·u·lose** (nɒ́dʒulous), **nod·u·lous** (nɒ́dʒuləs) adjs [fr. L. nodulus]

no·el, now·el (nouél) n. an exclamation of joy used in Christmas carols ‖ the Christmas season [fr. O.F. nouel]

no·e·sis (nouí:sis) n. (philos.) direct intellectual apprehension [Gk noēsis fr. noein, to perceive]

no·et·ic (nouétik) adj. of or relating to noesis [fr. Gk noētikos]

no-fault insurance (nóufɔ:ltinʃúərəns) n. legal provision in some states that motorists be reimbursed for medical expenses by their own insurance companies (sometimes with other provisions), no matter which party is at fault in an accident

no-fire line (nóufɑiərláin) n. (mil.) a line short of which artillery or ships do not fire except on request or approval of the supported commander, but beyond which they may fire at any time without danger to friendly troops

no·form (nóufɔrm) adj. code word for distribution of documents for no foreign dissemination

no-frills (nóufrílz) adj. (business) policy of minimum service as a cost-saving measure, esp. in retailing, by eliminating delivery, credit, and return privileges, etc., and dispensing with advertising

nog (nɒg) **1.** n. a wooden peg or block inserted in a wall as a hold for nails, screws etc. **2.** v.t. pres. part. **nog·ging** past and past part. **nogged** to secure with nogs ‖ to build with the use of nogging [origin unknown]

nog n. eggnog [origin unknown]

nog·gin (nɒ́gin) n. a small mug ‖ a liquid measure, usually 114 pints ‖ (pop.) someone's head, get that into your noggin ‖ [origin unknown]

nog·ging (nɒ́giŋ) n. brick masonry used to fill in the wooden frame of a building etc.

No·gu·chi (nogútʃi:), Isamu (1904–), U.S. sculptor. He made many innovations and is known esp. for his primitive figures showing mixed Oriental and Western influence

no-hit·ter (nóuhítər) n. (baseball) a game in which one team makes no hits

No·Ho (nóuhou) n. area in Manhattan north of Houston Street where factory buildings have been converted for living, esp. by artists

noil (nɔil) n. short hair or fiber esp. of wool combed from staple or waste silk [origin unknown]

noise (nɔiz) **1.** n. sound due to irregular vibration ‖ any sound which causes discomfort to the hearer ‖ (loosely) any sound, the noise of the wind in the trees ‖ a loud outcry, shouting, clamorous outbursts etc. ‖ irrelevant background sounds in a recording or film ‖ (electr.) radiation at several changing frequencies or amplitudes **2.** v.t. pres. part. **nois·ing** past and past part. **noised** (rhet.) with 'about', 'abroad') to spread by rumor ‖ to make noise; to bring a group's attention to a subject **noise·less** adj. silent [O.F., origin unknown]

noise jamming (mil.) a technique to produce clutter over enemy radar tracking screens

noise·mak·er (nɔ́izmeikər) n. a device for making noise, e.g. a horn or rattle used at celebrations etc.

noise pollution 1. excessive noise in the environment, typically from planes, autos, industry **2.** addition of sound to the environment beyond the natural sources; measured in intensity, duration, frequency, and frequency of occurrence

nois·i·ly (nɔ́izili:) adv. in a noisy way

nois·i·ness (nɔ́izi:nis) n. the quality of being noisy

noi·some (nɔ́isəm) adj. (rhet.) offensive to the smell, noisome fumes ‖ (rhet.) objectionable, disgusting, a noisome sight ‖ (rhet.) harmful, injurious, noisome living conditions [fr. obs. noy fr. ANNOY]

nois·y (nɔ́izi:) comp. **nois·i·er** superl. **nois·i·est** adj. making or usually making noise, a noisy car engine ‖ full of noise, a noisy street ‖ clamorous, a noisy crowd ‖ (of color, costume, style) violent, loud, a noisy check suit

no joy (mil.) in air intercept, a code meaning 'I have been unsuccessful' or 'I have no information'

Nol·de (nɔ́ldə), Emil (Emil Hansen, 1867–1956), German expressionist painter and printmaker. He painted landscapes, flowers, figure compositions and biblical scenes in rich combinations of brilliant and dark colors, thickly applied, revealing an intensely emotional, almost mystical, vision

nol·le pros·e·qui (nɒ́li:prɔ́sikwai) n. (law) an entry on a court record stating that the plaintiff or prosecutor will not continue with part or all of his suit or prosecution [L.=to be unwilling to pursue]

no-load (nóuloud) adj. (securities) of securities sold without a commission, i.e., sold at asset value without selling fees, e.g., mutual funds

no·mad (nóumæd) n. a member of a people, tribe etc. without a fixed location, wandering from place to place in search of pastureland for their flocks or herds, cultivable land or hunting grounds etc. ‖ a person who chooses to roam **no·mád·ic** adj. **nó·mad·ism** n. [fr. L. fr. Gk nomas (nomados)]

no-man's-land (nóumænzlænd) n. an unowned area, esp. an extraterritorial strip between facing frontiers ‖ a belt of debated ground between entrenched enemies

nom de plume (nɒmdəplú:m) pl. **nom de plumes** (nɒmdəplú:mz) n. a pen name [F.=pen name, probably coined in Britain]

Nome (noum) a city and commercial center of the Seward peninsula (pop. 2,301, principally Eskimos) in W. Alaska: mining (gold, tin). It was established as a result of the gold rush of 1896

no·men (nóumən) pl. **nom·i·na** (nɒ́minə) n. the second of the three names making up an ancient Roman name, e.g. 'Julius' in Gaius Julius Caesar (cf. AGNOMEN, cf. COGNOMEN, cf. PRAENOMEN) [L.]

no·men·cla·ture (nóumənkleitʃər, nouménklətʃər) n. the names used in a particular branch of knowledge, esp. names which classify things, the nomenclature of zoology ‖ systematic naming ‖ the names used within some category, e.g. village or street names [fr. L. nomenclatura]

nom·i·nal (nɒ́min'l) adj. existing only in name or form, not real or actual, a nominal ruler ‖ very small, hardly worth the name, a nominal fee ‖ of or consisting of a name or names, nominal versus essential distinctions ‖ normal; without unexpected deviation ‖ (of shares etc.) bearing the name of a person ‖ giving or listing names, a nominal roll ‖ (of an adjective or adverb used as a noun) substantival ‖ (of wages) measured in money rather than actual purchasing power (cf. REAL) [fr. L. nominalis]

nom·i·nal·ism (nɒ́min'lizəm) n. (philos.) the doctrine that there are no universal essences in reality and that abstract concepts are mere names. It was originated (11th c.) by Roscelin in opposition to realism, and was modified by Abelard to form conceptualism. It was revived (14th c.) by William of Occam and later influenced the development of empiricism **nóm·i·nal·ist** n. **nom·i·nal·is·tic** adj. [fr. F. nominalisme]

nominal value (commerce) the value as stated on a coin, note, bond etc.

nominal weapon (mil.) a nuclear weapon producing a yield of approximately 20 kilotons Cf KILOTON WEAPON, SUBKILOTON WEAPON

nom·i·nate (nɒ́mineit) pres. part. **nom·i·nat·ing** past and past part. **nom·i·nat·ed** v.t. to name as a candidate, he has been nominated for president ‖ to appoint to office [fr. L. nominare (nominatus)]

nom·i·na·tion (nɒmineíʃən) n. a nominating or being nominated ‖ the right of nominating ‖ an instance of nominating [O.F. nominacion]

nom·i·na·tive (nɒ́minətiv, nɒ́mnətiv) **1.** n. (gram.) the case of the subject of a verb, or of a word in agreement with it ‖ (gram.) a word in this case **2.** adj. (gram.) describing or pertaining to the nominative ‖ chosen or appointed by nomination (cf. ELECTIVE) [F. nominatif (nominative) or fr. L. nominativus]

nominative absolute a grammatically independent construction consisting of a noun or nominative pronoun and a predicate without a finite verb, used to modify the rest of the sentence, e.g. 'the key being lost, the box could not be opened'

nom·i·na·tor (nɒ́mineitər) n. a person who nominates

nom·i·nee (nɒminí:) n. a person nominated for a position or office [NOMINATE]

nom·o·gram (nɒ́məgræm) n. a graph designed to give general solutions to equations. One of the simplest types comprises three parallel lines graduated in such a way that a straight line joining two variables will give the corresponding value of a third [fr. Gk nomos, law+gramma, letter]

nom·o·graph (nɒ́məgræf) n. a graphic chart with three or more scales on which calculations may be made with a straight edge connecting known values to solve an equation

non- (nɒn) prefix not [L.]

non·ad·di·tive (nɒnǽditiv) adj. (math.) of a total not equal to the sum of the parts —**nonadditivity** n.

no·nage (nóunidʒ, nɒ́nidʒ) n. (law) the state of being under legal age ‖ (rhet.) immaturity [O.F.]

no·na·ge·nar·i·an (nɒunədʒənéəri:ən, nɒnədʒənéəri:ən) **1.** adj. 90 or over and less than 100 years old **2.** n. a person of this age [fr. L. nonagenarius]

non·ag·gres·sion (nɒnəgréʃən) **1.** n. abstention from aggression **2.** adj. of or pertaining to this, a nonaggression pact

non·a·gon (nɒ́nəgɒn) n. a plane polygon having nine sides and nine angles [fr. L. nonus, ninth, after HEXAGON]

non·al·co·hol·ic (nɒnælkəhɔ́lik, nɒnælkəhɒ́lik) adj. containing no alcohol

---

non·a·lign·ment (nɒnəláinmənt) *n.* the political attitude of a state, e.g., India, that does not associate or identify itself with the political ideology or objective espoused by another state, bloc of states, or international causes —**nonaligned state** a state that pursues a nonalignment policy

non·ap·pear·ance (nɒnəpíərəns) *n.* failure to appear, esp. in court

non·book (nɒnbúk) *n.* **1.** a bound volume containing organized material of no general value, e.g., a scrapbook, a souvenir journal **2.** pejorative term for a book with little content, usu. published to take advantage of a fad

nonce (nɒns) *n.* (only in the phrase) **for the nonce** for the time being [M.E. (*for tha)n anes*, (for) the once]

nonce word a word coined for a particular occasion and not accepted into general usage

non·cha·lance (nɒnʃəláns, nɒnʃəlns) *n.* the quality of being nonchalant

non·cha·lant (nɒnʃəlánt, nɒnʃələnt) *adj.* casual, *a nonchalant manner* ‖ off hand, without enthusiasm, *a nonchalant attitude* ‖ unperturbed, *nonchalant in the face of danger* [F.]

non·col·le·giate (nɒnkəlí:dʒit) *adj.* (of universities) not having colleges ‖ (of students) not belonging to a college

non·com·bat·ant (nɒnkɒmbətənt, nɒnkəmbǽt-'nt) **1.** *n.* a person in or attached to the armed forces whose duties do not include fighting ‖ a civilian **2.** *adj.* not involving combats ‖ of noncombatants

non·com·mis·sioned officer (nɒnkəmíʃənd) a subordinate officer in the armed forces, appointed from the ranks

non·com·mit·tal (nɒnkəmít'l) *adj.* not committing the speaker to either side in a dispute or to any particular attitude or course

non com·pos men·tis (nɒnkɒmpəs méntis) (*law*) not legally sane [L.]

non·con·duc·tor (nɒnkəndʌ́ktər) *n.* (*phys.*) a substance or object which does not readily conduct heat, electricity, sound etc.

non·con·form·ist (nɒnkənfɔ́rmist) **1.** *n.* a person who does not conform to the beliefs or ritual of an established Church ‖ a person who does not conform to rule or convention **Non·con·form·ist** (*Br.*) a member of a Protestant denomination dissenting from the Church of England. The first Nonconformists were the clergy, nearly 2,000 in number, who resigned their livings rather than accept the Act of Uniformity (1662). Nonconformists were granted official toleration (1689) and gained full religious and civil rights in the 19th c. The principal Nonconformist denominations are the Baptists, Congregationalists, Methodists, Presbyterians, Quakers and Unitarians **2.** *adj.* of or relating to a nonconformist **Non·con·form·ist** (*Br.*) of or relating to a Nonconformist

non·con·form·i·ty (nɒnkənfɔ́rmiti:) *n.* the beliefs or practices of nonconformists ‖ lack of correspondence between things, e.g. between words and actions **Non·con·form·i·ty** Protestant refusal to conform to the Church of England ‖ the body of Nonconformists

non·co·op·er·a·tion (nɒnkouɒpəréiʃən) *n.* failure or refusal to cooperate ‖ nonviolent civil disobedience, esp. (*hist.*) as advocated by Gandhi in India

non·dair·y (nɒndéəri) *adj.* containing nothing made of milk, e.g., coffee lightener (usu. to conform to Jewish dietary law of not mixing meat and milk in a meal)

non·de·script (nɒndiskrípt) **1.** *adj.* lacking distinctive characteristics ‖ not easily classified or described **2.** *n.* a nondescript person or thing [fr. NON·+L. *descriptus*, described]

non·de·struct·ive (nɒndistríktiv) *adj.* (*computer*) capable of being processed without destroying the parts —**nondestructively** *adv.*

non·dis·crim·i·na·tion (nɒndiskríminéiʃən) *n.* policy of not discriminating in service and treatment, esp. between blacks and whites, women and men, in jobs, housing, etc. —**nondiscriminatory** *adj.*

non·drink·er (nɒndríŋkər) *n.* one who does not drink alcoholic beverages —**nondrinking** *adj.*

none (nʌn) **1.** *pron.* not any, not one ‖ (*rhet.*) nobody, *none is guiltless* ‖ not any such thing or person, *if a hero is needed, he is none* ‖ no part, nothing, *he understood none of the lecture* **2.** *adv.* not at all, to no extent, by no amount, *he was none the wiser for his experience* [O.E. *nān* fr. *ne*, not+*ān*, one]

non·e·go (nɒní:gou) *n.* (*philos., psychol.*) the external world or its phenomena, as contrasted with the subject or ego

non·en·ti·ty (nɒnéntiti:) *pl.* **non·en·ti·ties** *n.* a person or thing of no importance or distinction ‖ nonexistence ‖ something existing only in the imagination

nones (nounz) *pl. n.* (in the ancient Roman calendar) the ninth day before the ides (both days included) ie., the 7th of March, May, July, October, and the 5th of all other months [fr. L. *nonae* fr. *nonus*, ninth]

nones *pl. n.* (*eccles.*) the daily office orig. said at the ninth hour (3 p.m.), now often earlier [pl. of *none*, the third quarter of the day, fr. F. or fr. L. *nona* fr. *nonus*, ninth]

non·es·sen·tial (nɒnisénʃəl) **1.** *adj.* not essential **2.** *n.* something not essential

none·such, non·such (nʌ́nsʌtʃ) *n.* a person or thing so excellent as to be without a rival

none·the·less, *Br*. none the less (nʌnðəlés) *adv.* nevertheless

non·e·vent (nɒnivént) *n.* a planned happening that results in nothing of significance

non·fea·sance (nɒnfí:z'ns) *n.* (*law*) failure to do something, esp. something that should have been done (cf. MALFEASANCE, MISFEASANCE) [fr. NON·+A.F. *fesance*, a doing]

non·fic·tion (nɒnfíkʃən) *n.* works of literature other than novels or short stories, esp. such works further distinguished from poetry and drama

non·gon·o·coc·cal urethritis (nɒngɒnəkók'l-juri:θráitis) *n.* (*med.*) sexually transmitted bacterial disease often complicated by pelvic inflammation, abdominal pains, sterility *also* nonspecific urethritis *abbr.* NGU

non·grad·ed (nɒngréidəd) *adj.* (*education*) of students or courses for which no rating is provided

no·nil·lion (nouníljən) *n.* *NUMBER TABLE [F. fr. L. *nonus*, ninth+MILLION]

nonimpact printer *LASER PRINTER

Nonintercourse Act of 1809 a U.S. Congressional act which, replacing the Embargo Act, reopened trade with all nations except Britain and France and agreed to resume trade with either of these belligerents if it ceased to violate the rights of neutrals. It was replaced by Macon's Bill No. 2

non·in·ter·ven·tion (nɒnintərvénʃən) *n.* a state or policy of not intervening, esp. in the internal affairs of other nations

non·join·der (nɒndʒóindər) *n.* (*law*) a failure to include a necessary party, plaintiff or defendant in a suit at law or in equity

non·ju·ror (nɒndʒúərər) *n.* (*Br. hist.*) any of more than 400 clergy who, on account of their Jacobite and High Church sympathies, refused to take the oath of allegiance to William III and Mary II after the revolution of 1688

non·lead·ed (nɒnlédəd) *adj.* of gasoline, containing no tetraethyl lead, an air pollutant *syn* lead-free, unleaded

non·met·al (nɒnmét'l) *n.* a chemical element that is neither a metal nor a metalloid (*PERIODIC TABLE)

non·nu·clear (nɒnnú:kli:ər) *adj.* of a nation without access to nuclear weapons

no·no (nóu nóu) *n.* an absolutely forbidden thing —**no-no** *adj.*

non·ob·jec·tive (nɒnɒbdʒéktiv) *adj.* of a work of art which does not represent recognizable objects or natural appearances

non·pa·reil (nɒnpərél) **1.** *n.* a person or thing of matchless excellence ‖ (*printing*) an old size of type, approx. 6-point ‖ (*pl., Am.=Br.* hundreds and thousands) very small pellets of colored sugar, used for decorating cakes **2.** *adj.* matchless [F.=unequaled]

non·par·ti·san (nɒnpártizən) **1.** *adj.* not involved in political party ties, *a nonpartisan issue* ‖ objective **2.** *n.* someone who is nonpartisan

non·per·sist·ent (nɒnpərsístənt) *adj.* (*envir.*) the quality of decomposing or losing effectiveness quickly, e.g., biodegradable

non·per·son (nɒnpə́:rs'n) *n.* a person whose existence is entirely ignored *Cf* UNPERSON

non·plus (nɒnplʌ́s) *pres. part.* **non·plus·ing**, esp. *Br*. **non·plus·sing** *past* and *past part.* **non·plused**, esp. *Br*. **non·plussed** *v.t.* to perplex completely, baffle [fr. L. *non plus*, not more]

non·point pollution (nɒnpóintpəlú:ʃən) pollution from unidentifiable sources

non·point source (nɒnpóintsɔ́rs) a contributing factor to water pollution that cannot be

traced to a specific spot, e.g., agricultural fertilizer runoff, sediment from construction

non·pro·duc·tive (nɒnprədʌ́ktiv) *adj.* not productive ‖ not directly concerned with production

non·prof·it (nɒnprɒ́fit) *adj.* not maintained or organized for profit

non·pro·lif·er·a·tion (nɒnproulífəréiʃən) *n.* program to halt expansion of nuclear weapon capability —**nonproliferation** *adj.*

non·quo·ta post (nɒnkwóutə poust) *n.* an international post open to all United Nations members and filled by an individual selected by a defined process from among nominees from all nations (vs. posts allocated on a national quota system)

non·rep·re·sen·ta·tion·al (nɒnreprizentéiʃən'l) *adj.* nonobjective

non·re·pro·duc·tive (nɒnri:prədʌ́ktiv) *adj.* not capable of reproducing

non·res·i·dent (nɒnrézidənt) **1.** *n.* a person staying in a district for only a short time ‖ a person not staying on the premises, *the hotel restaurant is open to residents and nonresidents* **2.** *adj.* not in residence, *nonresident members* ‖ living elsewhere (than on one's estate, in one's benefice etc.)

non·re·sis·tance (nɒnrizístəns) *n.* the pacifist doctrine of not meeting force by force

non·re·stric·tive clause (nɒnristríktiv) (*gram.*) a relative clause, usually set off by commas in English, which describes the antecedent without identifying it

non·sched·uled (nɒnskédʒu:ld, *Br*. nɒnʃédju:ld) *adj.* not working to a schedule ‖ not figuring on the schedule

non·sec·tar·i·an (nɒnsektéəri:ən) *adj.* not tied to any one religious denomination though not excluding any

non·sense (nɒnsens, nɒ́ns'ns) **1.** *n.* senseless or meaningless talk, language or ideas ‖ behavior that is foolish or not straightforward **2.** *interj.* I don't believe a word of it!

nonsense mutation or **nonsense** (*genetics*) mutation in which one of three codons that do not incorporate any amino acid results in the end of the polypeptide chain *Cf* MISSENSE MUTATION

nonsense verse humorous or whimsical verse often introducing invented meaningless words with an evocative sound

non·sen·si·cal (nɒnsénsik'l) *adj.* foolish, full of nonsense

non se·qui·tur (nɒnsékwitər) *pl.* **non-se·qui·turs** *n.* (*logic*) a conclusion that does not follow from the stated premise or premises [L.=it does not follow]

non·skid (nónskíd) *adj.* (of tires, road surfaces etc.) having a surface designed to prevent or limit skidding

nonspecific urethritis *NONGONOCOCCAL URETHRITIS

non·start·er (nɒnstártər) *n.* a contemplated project that was never begun

non·ster·oid or **non·ster·oid·al** (nɒnstéroid) *n.* (*biochem.*) not part of the group that includes sex hormones, bile acids, sterols, etc. —**nonsteroid** *adj.*

non·stick pan (nɒnstikpǽn) *n.* cooking utensil coated with Teflon or other solid lubricant that resists adhesion of fats

non·stop (nónstóp) *adj.* and *adv.* without a stop

nonsuch *NONESUCH

non·suit (nɒnsú:t) **1.** *n.* (*law*) a judgment against a plaintiff because of failure to make out a legal case etc. **2.** *v.t.* (*law*) to decide, judge or record that plaintiff has failed to establish a legal case or produce sufficient evidence [fr. O.F. *nonsute, nounsute*]

non·sup·port (nɒnsəpórt, nɒnsəpóurt) *n.* (*law*) failure to provide maintenance despite a court order

Non·tar·iff Barriers (nɒntǽrif báeri:ərz) practices other than the imposition of tariffs that tend to restrain international trade, e.g., internal taxation, antidumping or countervailing duties, customs fees, excessive documentation requirements, etc. *abbr.* NTBs

non trop·po (nɒntrópou) *adv.* (*mus.*) not excessively [Ital.]

non-U (nónju:) *adj.* not part of, or typical of, the upper classes

non·un·ion (nɒnjú:njən) *adj.* not belonging to a trade union ‖ not recognizing trade unions ‖ refusing to employ trade unionists

non·vec·tor (nɒnvéktər) *n.* (*biol.*) of nondisease-carrying animal, bird, or insect

CONCISE PRONUNCIATION KEY: **(a)** æ, c*a*t; ɑ, c*a*r; ɔ f*aw*n; ei, sn*a*ke. **(e)** e, h*e*n; i:, sh*ee*p; iə, d*ee*r; ɛə, b*ea*r. **(i)** i, f*i*sh; ai, t*i*ger; ə:, b*i*rd. **(o)** o, *o*x; au, c*ow*; ou, g*oa*t; u, p*oo*r; ɔi, r*oy*al. **(u)** ʌ, d*u*ck; u, b*u*ll; u:, g*oo*se; ə, b*a*cillus; ju:, c*u*be. x, lo*ch*; θ, *th*ink; ð, bo*th*er; z, *Z*en; ʒ, cor*s*age; dʒ, sava*g*e; ŋ, ora*ng*utang; j, *y*ak; ʃ, *f*ish; tʃ, fe*tch*; 'l, rabb*l*e; 'n, redde*n*. Complete pronunciation key appears inside front cover.

non·vi·o·lence (nɒnváiələns) *n.* the policy or practice of refusing to use violence, esp. as a way of meeting oppression

non·vo·caid (nɒnvóukeid) *n.* (*phonetics*) consonant sound except *y, w, r,* and *h also* contoid

noo·dle (nú:d'l) *n.* a strip of pasta, served in quantity e.g. with meat or in soup [G. *nudel*]

nook (nuk) *n.* a sheltered, hidden or quiet corner ‖ a recess in a room, esp. beside a fireplace [M.E. *noke, nok*]

noon (nu:n) *n.* 12 o'clock in the daytime [O.E. *nōn* fr. L. *nona* (*hora*), ninth (hour)]

noon·day (nú:ndei) *n.* (*rhet.*) midday

no one *pron.* nobody

noon·tide (nú:ntaid) *n.* the noon period [O.E. *nontid*]

noon·time (nú:ntaim) *n.* midday

Noord·bra·bant (nourtbrabánt) *NORTH BRABANT

noose (nu:s) **1.** *n.* a loop in a rope etc. with a running knot which draws tighter as the rope is pulled, e.g. in a snare, lasso or halter ‖ (*fig.*) a snare **2.** *v.t. pres. part.* **noos·ing** *past* and *past part.* **noosed** to entrap by a noose ‖ to arrange (cord) in a noose [etym. doubtful]

no·o·sphere (nú:sfjər) *n.* **1.** the biosphere after human alterations **2.** activities of human beings, esp. intellectual; conceived by French paleontologist Teilhard de Chardin

Noot·ka (nú:tkə, nútkə) *pl.* **Noot·ka, Noot·kas** *n.* a North American Indian people of the Wakashan linguistic stock, inhabiting the southwest coast of Vancouver Island, B.C. Their art was characterized by elaborate stylized carvings, esp. the totem pole. In 1778 James Cook estimated the population to be 7,500 ‖ a member of this people ‖ their language

no·pal (nóup'l) *n.* a member of *Nopalea,* a genus of cacti cultivated as a support for the cochineal insect ‖ the prickly pear [Span. fr. Mex. *nopalli,* cactus]

nor (nɔr) *conj.* used as a negative correlative with 'neither' to connect two or more alternatives, *he has neither brains nor brawn* ‖ (often with inversion of subject and verb) and not, *they don't know him, nor do they want to* [contr. of obs. *nother*]

NOR, NOR operator, or **NORgate** (nɔr) *n.* (*computer*) a logic circuit operator with the property that if *P, Q,* and *R* are statements, then the NOR is true if all the statements are false and false if at least one is true *Cf* AND, OR

NORAD (*mil.* acronym) for North American Defense Command, coordinator of continental defense network

Nor·bert (nórbərt), St (c. 1080–1134), German ecclesiastic. He founded the Premonstratensian order (1119). Feast: June 6

Nord (nɔr) a department (area 2,228 sq. miles, pop. 2,510,700) of N. France (*FLANDERS). Chief town: Lille

Nor·den·skjöld (nú:rdənʃə:ld), Baron Nils Adolf Erik (1832–1901), Swedish scientist and Arctic explorer. He was the first to navigate the Northeast Passage (1878–9)

Nor·dic (nórdik) **1.** *adj.* of or pertaining to the Germanic peoples of N. Europe (esp. Scandinavia), characterized by tall stature, fair hair and blue eyes ‖ (*skiing*) of jumping and cross-country events **2.** *n.* a person of this physical type [fr. F. *nordique*]

Nörd·ling·en, Battle of (nö:rtliŋin) a battle (1634) in which a Hapsburg army defeated a Swedish and German army during the Thirty Years' War ‖ a battle (1635) in which the French defeated a Hapsburg army during the Thirty Years' War

Nore (nɔr) a large sandbank in the center of the Thames estuary, marking the mouth of the river

nor·ep·i·neph·rine (nɔrepinéfri:n) *n.* a hormone produced by the medulla of the adrenal gland that stimulates constriction of the blood vessels and acts on the sympathetic nervous system (*ADRENALIN, *EPINEPHRINE)

nor·eth·in·drone [$C_{20}H_{26}O_2$] (noréθindroun) *n.* (*pharm.*) a progestational hormone used as an oral contraceptive; marketed as Norlutin

nor·e·thy·no·drel·mes·tra·nol [$C_{20}H_{26}O_2$] (norèθínoudrelméstrənəl) *n.* (*pharm.*) progestogen with estrogenic hormones added, used as an oral contraceptive; marketed as Enovid-E

Norfolk (nórfək), Thomas Howard, 2nd duke of (1443–1524). He commanded the English army at Flodden Field (1513) and was an influential adviser to Henry VIII

Norfolk, Thomas Howard, 3rd duke of (1543–1548). He put down the Pilgrimage of Grace (1536), but fell from royal favor when his niece, Catherine Howard, was executed (1542)

Norfolk a county (area 2,055 sq. miles, pop. 693,490) of E. England. County town: Norwich

Norfolk a port and naval base (pop. 266,979) of Virginia, at the mouth of the Chesapeake Bay: shipbuilding, textiles, vehicle assembly

Norfolk Island a territory (area 13 sq. miles, pop. 2,135 of Australia in the S. Pacific 950 miles northeast of Sydney, discovered by Cook (1774). Industries: whaling, lumber, fruit growing, tourism

Nor·folk jacket (nórfək) a loose-fitting, single-breasted shooting jacket with box pleats and belt

Nor·i·cum (nórikəm, nórikəm) (*hist.*) a province of the Roman Empire covering most of modern Austria

norm (nɔrm) *n.* an average, esp. one taken as a measure or standard of attainment, *production norms* ‖ that which is normal, *departures from the norm* [fr. L. *norma,* a carpenter's square, a rule]

nor·mal (nórməl) **1.** *adj.* conforming to a norm, standard, regular, *a normal temperature* ‖ (*psychol.*) conforming to the standard or average for a particular type or group ‖ (*loosely*) mentally or emotionally sound ‖ (*math.*) forming a right angle ‖ approximating a statistical norm or average ‖ (*chem.,* of a solution, *abbr.* N.) having a concentration of 1 gram equivalent of solute per liter of solution (cf. MOLAR) ‖ (*chem.* of a chain of carbon atoms in a hydrocarbon) straight, unbranched ‖ (*chem.,* of a salt) containing no ionizable hydrogen atoms or hydroxyl groups **2.** *n.* the usual or average state, level etc., *above the normal* ‖ (*math.*) a line drawn perpendicular to the tangent line at a point on a curve ‖ (*math.*) a plane perpendicular to the tangent plane to a surface at a point on the surface **nor·mal·cy** *n.* normality in the conditions governing human activity **nor·mal·i·ty** (normǽliti:) *n.* the state or quality of being normal [fr. L. *normalis* fr. *norma,* a rule]

nor·mal·i·za·tion (nɔrməlizéiʃən) *n.* the act or process of normalizing

nor·mal·ize (nórməlaiz) *pres. part.* **nor·mal·iz·ing** *past* and *past part.* **nor·mal·ized** *v.t.* to make normal

nor·mal·ly (nórməli:) *adv.* in a normal way ‖ in normal circumstances, under normal conditions

normal school a training school for elementary schoolteachers in some countries [after F. *école normale*]

Nor·man (nórmən) **1.** *adj.* pertaining to Normandy or the Normans ‖ of or relating to a variety of Romanesque architecture which originated (mid-10th c.) in Normandy and was used in England after the Norman Conquest **2.** *n.* a native of Normandy, esp. (*hist.*) one of the Northmen (*VIKING) who conquered Normandy (10th c.), or one of their Norman-French descendants. The Normans conquered England (1066) and parts of Italy (11th c.), and established (1130) the kingdom of Sicily [O.F. *Normans* pl. of *Normant* fr. Gmc *Northman*]

Nor·man-French (nórmənfréntʃ) *n.* the form of French spoken by the medieval Normans, and introduced by them into England

nor·ma·tive (nórmətiv) *adj.* of or relating to a norm ‖ establishing a norm [F. *normatif* (*normative*)]

Norman Conquest the conquest of England (1066) by William of Normandy (*WILLIAM I)

Nor·man·dy (nórməndi:) a former province of France on the English Channel, in the N.W. Paris basin, including Seine-Maritime, Calvados and Manche, and parts of Eure and Orne. The whole (but esp. Calvados) is a rich farming region: cheese and butter, meat, cereals, sugar beets, fruit, cider. Chief towns: Rouen (the old capital), Le Havre and Cherbourg (ports), and Caen. The region was raided (9th c.) by Vikings or Normans, from whom it takes its name. It was ceded (9th) by Charles III to Rollo. After one of his successors, William, conquered England (1066) it was intermittently in English possession until 1204, and was ravaged in the Hundred Years' War. Secured by France (1450), it remained semiautonomous. It was the scene of heavy fighting in the 2nd world war (June–Aug. 1944) when the Allies invaded

nor·mo·ther·mi·a (nɔrmouθə́:rmiə) *n.* (*physiol.*) normal body temperature **—normothermic** *adj.*

Nor·ris (nóris, nóris), (Benjamin) Frank(lin) (1870–1902), U.S. novelist of the naturalist school. Two parts of his projected trilogy, 'The Epic of the Wheat' were completed: 'The Octopus' (1901), depicting the brutal struggle between wheat farmers and railroad interests, and 'The Pit' (1903), dealing with unrestrained speculation on the Chicago grain market

Norris, George William (1861–1944), U.S. Congressman. As a nonpartisan senator (1912–43) from Nebraska, he drafted the 20th amendment to the constitution, abolishing the 'lame duck' sessions of Congress. He helped to establish the Tennessee Valley Authority. He also helped to draft an act restricting the use of injunctions in labor disputes, paving the way to a legal concept of labor-management relations

Nor·ris-La Guar·di·a Act (nórrislǝgwárdi:ǝ, nórrislǝgwárdi:ǝ) *LA GUARDIA

Norr·kö·ping (nórtʃǝ:piŋ) a port (pop. 118,064) of E. central Sweden: textiles, machinery, paper products, shipbuilding

Norr·land (nórlænd) *SWEDEN

Norse (nǝrs) **1.** *n.* the Scandinavian branch of the Germanic languages ‖ West Scandinavian, including Norwegian, Icelandic and Faroese **the Norse** the people of Scandinavia, esp. the Norwegians **2.** *adj.* of Norway or the Norwegians ‖ (*hist.*) pertaining to ancient Scandinavia or its language [prob. fr. Du. *noorsch,* Norwegian]

Norse·man (nórsmǝn) *pl.* **Norse·men** (nórsmǝn) *n.* (*hist.*) *VIKING

North (nɔrθ), Frederick, 2nd earl of Guilford and 8th Baron North (1732–92), British statesman. As chancellor of the exchequer (1767–70) and prime minister (1770–82) he was responsible for implementing George III's policy of taxing the colonies, and for organizing the British war effort in the Revolutionary War to which the policy led. He resigned after Cornwallis' surrender at Yorktown

North, Sir Thomas (c. 1535–c. 1602), English translator. His masterpiece was the version of Amyot's French translation of Plutarch's 'Lives of the Noble Grecians and Romans' (1579), on which Shakespeare drew freely

north (nɔrθ) **1.** *adv.* towards the north **2.** *n.* (usually with 'the') one of the four cardinal points of the compass (*abbr.* N., *COMPASS POINT, *MAGNETIC NORTH, *TRUE NORTH) ‖ the direction to the left of a person facing east **the North** the northern part of a country ‖ the states of the U.S.A. north of the Mason-Dixon line which fought for the Union in the Civil War **3.** *adj.* of, belonging to or situated towards the north ‖ facing north ‖ (of winds) blowing from the north [O.E.]

North America the third largest continent (area 9,400,000 sq. miles, pop. 325,400,000). Political units: Canada, Greenland, Mexico, St Pierre and Miquelon, the U.S.A., and those comprised in Central America and the West Indies (see separate articles)

North American 1. *adj.* of or pertaining to North America **2.** *n.* an inhabitant of this area

North American Indians the indigenous peoples of North America. In a series of migrations, the first of which took place about 25,000 years ago, they reached the western hemisphere presumably from Asia through the Bering Strait. Amerinds in general are classified by anthropologists as a single race, which explains their common physical characteristics, incl. Mongoloid features, coarse, straight black hair, dark eyes and a yellowish-brown to reddish-brown skin color. Prior to 1492, the population north of Mexico numbered about one to two million. They inhabited six major cultural areas (excluding the Arctic), i.e., Northwest Coast, Plains, Plateau, Eastern Woodlands, Northern, and Southwest. The struggle for domination in America between the Indian and white man, from the arrival (16th c.) of the Spanish and (17th c.) of the British and French to the formation of the U.S.A., could be said to have ended in 1890 when a U.S. cavalry force shot down about 200 men, women and children led by Sitting Bull, who had rebelled against their confinement to a reservation, in South Dakota. From the 1960s, U.S. Indians made a concerted effort to preserve their heritage and to exercise greater control over their affairs, previously dominated by the Bureau of Indian

Affairs (B.I.A.). In the 1980s, Indians were frequently successful in obtaining large settlements for lands taken illegally by the government

North·amp·ton (nɔrθæmptən) the county town (pop. 156,853) of Northamptonshire, England, a county borough. Manufactures: boots and shoes, leather, machinery, paint. Round church (12th c.)

North·amp·ton·shire (nɔrθæmptənʃiər) (abbr. Northants.) a county (area 914 sq. miles, pop. 527,532 excl. the Soke of Peterborough) of England in the S. Midlands. County town: Northampton

North Atlantic Drift the warm ocean current continuing the Gulf Stream across the N. Atlantic from Newfoundland to the Barents Sea. It has a considerable moderating influence on the climate of N.W. Europe

North Atlantic Treaty Organization (abbr. NATO) a mutual defensive alliance set up (Apr. 4, 1949) by Belgium, Canada, Denmark, France, Iceland, Italy, Luxembourg, the Netherlands, Norway, Portugal, the United Kingdom and the U.S.A. They pledged to unite their efforts for collective defense and to consider an armed attack on any member as an attack on all. This marked the first peacetime participation of the U.S.A. in a collective security arrangement outside the Americas. The chief policymaking body, the North Atlantic Council, meets at least once a week. The 1983 deployment of U.S. medium-range nuclear missiles in Europe caused controversy within the organization. Greece and Turkey joined in 1951, the Federal Republic of Germany in 1954 and Spain in 1982. Headquarters: Brussels

North Borneo *SABAH

North Brabant (Du. Noordbrabant) a province (area 1,965 sq. miles, pop. 1,543,000) in the S. Netherlands. Capital: s'Hertogenbosch (pop. 69,000). It was part of the medieval duchy of Brabant

north by east N. 11° 15′ E., one point east of due north (abbr. N. b. E., Br. esp. N. by E., *COMPASS POINT)

north by west N. 11° 15′ W., one point west of due north (abbr. N. b. W., Br. esp. N. by W., *COMPASS POINT)

North Cameroons the north section of the former British Cameroons, since 1961 part of Nigeria

North Car·o·li·na (kærəláinə) (abbr. N.C.) a state (area 52,712 sq. miles, pop. 6,019,000) on the S. Atlantic coast of the U.S.A. Capital: Raleigh. Chief city: Charlotte. The coastal region is flat, but there are ranges of the Appalachian Mtns in the west. Agriculture: tobacco, cotton, corn, hay, peanuts, poultry. Resources: timber, mica, feldspar. Manufactures: tobacco products, textiles, furniture, food products. State University (1789) at Chapel Hill. North Carolina, named after Charles I, was settled by the English (17th c.), and was one of the Thirteen Colonies. It became (1789) the 12th state of the U.S.A.

North·cliffe (nɔ́rθklif), Alfred Charles William Harmsworth, 1st Viscount (1865–1922), British newspaper proprietor. With his brother Harold Sidney Harmsworth, 1st Viscount Rothermere (1868–1940), he acquired a chain of newspapers, and founded the 'Daily Mail' (1896). Through this, the first cheap popular English newspaper, he influenced public opinion, esp. during the 1st world war

north·coun·try·man (nɔrθkʌ́ntri:mən) pl. **north·coun·try·men** (nɔrθkʌ́ntri:mən) n. (Br.) a native of N. England

North Dakota (abbr. N.D.) a state (area 70,775 sq. miles, pop. 670,000) on the fertile plains of N. central U.S.A. Capital: Bismarck. Agriculture (the chief occupation): wheat, barley, rye, linseed, cattle. Resources: oil, lignite, coal. Manufactures: agricultural products, oil products. State university (1883) at Grand Forks. The U.S.A. acquired part of the state in the Louisiana Purchase (1803) and the rest by treaty with Britain (1818). It became (1889) the 39th state of the U.S.A.

north·east (nɔrθíːst, nɔríːst) **1.** adv. towards the northeast **2.** n. (usually with 'the') the compass point or direction midway between north and east (abbr. N.E., *COMPASS POINT) **the Northeast** the northeastern part of a country **3.** adj. of, belonging to or situated towards the northeast ‖ (of winds) blowing from the northeast [O.E.]

northeast by east N. 56° 15′ E., one point east of due northeast (abbr. N.E. b. E., Br. esp. N.E. by E., *COMPASS POINT)

northeast by north N. 33° 45′ E., one point north of due northeast (abbr. N.E. b. N., Br. esp. N.E. by N., *COMPASS POINT)

north·east·er (nɔrθíːstər, nɔríːstər) n. a strong wind or gale from the northeast

north·east·er·ly (nɔrθíːstərli:, nɔríːstərli:) **1.** adj. and adv. in or towards the northeast ‖ (of winds) from that direction **2.** pl. **north·east·er·lies** n. a wind blowing from the northeast

north·east·ern (nɔrθíːstərn, nɔríːstərn) adj. situated, facing or moving towards the northeast ‖ of or relating to the northeast or the Northeast

Northeast New Guinea (or Territory of New Guinea) a former territory of Australia comprising N.E. New Guinea with the Bismarck Archipelago and the W. Solomon Is, part of Papua New Guinea

Northeast Passage a sea passage between the Atlantic and Pacific Oceans along the Arctic coasts of Europe and Asia. It was searched for unsuccessfully as a trade route to China by Willoughby and Chancellor (1553), Barents (1594–7) and Hudson (1607–9). It was first navigated (1878–9) by Nordenskjöld. Thanks to atom-powered icebreakers, it is a Russian sea lane serving N. Siberia

north·east·ward (nɔrθíːstwərd, nɔríːstwərd) adv. and adj. towards the northeast **north·east·wards** adv.

nor·ther·ly (nɔ́rðərli:) **1.** adj. and adv. in or towards the north ‖ (of winds) from the north **2.** pl. **nor·ther·lies** n. a wind blowing from the north [NORTH]

north·ern (nɔ́rðərn) adj. situated, facing or moving towards the north **Northern** of or relating to the North [O.E.]

North·ern·er (nɔ́rðərnər) n. a native or inhabitant of the North esp. of the Northern part of the U.S.A.

northern hemisphere the half of the earth north of the equator

Northern Ireland a country (area 5,462 sq. miles, pop. 1,537,000) occupying the northern fifth of Ireland. It is a division of the United Kingdom. Capital: Belfast. Language: English. Religion: 30% Presbyterian, 25% Church of England, 36% Roman Catholic. The mountains of the north are separated from the Mountains of Mourne in the south by the flax-producing Lough Neagh basin and the drumlin belt of N. Armagh. Only 2% of the land is forested. Average temperatures (F.): (Jan.) 41°, (July) 58°. Rainfall: 30–50 ins. Chief ports: Belfast, Londonderry. University of Belfast (1908). HISTORY. Northern Ireland officially became a part of the United Kingdom of Great Britain and Northern Ireland in 1920, with a separate parliament and limited self-government. (For previous history *IRELAND.) The Irish Republic refused to recognize it, and the Irish Republican Army carried out raids on property and communications in Northern Ireland (1950s). Relations between the two countries showed signs of improvement (1945). Fighting between Protestants and Catholics broke out (Dec. 1968) in Belfast and spread subsequently to other cities, causing a political crisis and bringing the country to the verge of civil war. The Northern Irish Parliament was suspended (March 1972). Whitehall assumed direct administration for a 12-month period, and tried to establish a legislature that allowed proportionate Roman Catholic representation. A Protestant extremist-organized general strike toppled the new government, and Britain resumed direct control, which it maintained into the 1980s. A 1985 agreement with Britain gave the Republic of Ireland a voice in the North's affairs in an attempt to establish peace

northern lights the aurora borealis

north·ern·most (nɔ́rðərnmoʊst) adj. furthest north

Northern Nigeria a former region (area 281,872 sq. miles) of Nigeria, comprising the northern four-fifths of the country. Capital: Kaduna

Northern Rhodesia *ZAMBIA

Northern Territory an administrative area (520,280 sq. miles, pop. 121,300) of N. central Australia. Capital: Darwin (pop. 20,000). The flat coastal plain is tropical, the interior tablelands are semiarid. Large areas are desert, particularly in the west. Main occupation: cat-

tle ranching. Minerals: gold, copper, uranium, some silver, tungsten, mica, manganese

Northern War a war (1700–21) in N. and E. Europe caused basically by the rivalry of Charles XII of Sweden and Peter I of Russia, esp. for control of the Baltic. Sweden defeated a coalition of Russia, Denmark and Saxony (1700–6), thanks to the bold military tactics of Charles XII, but was heavily defeated by Russia (1709). Turkey declared war on Russia (1710). In Poland and Scandinavia war continued from 1709 until Charles XII was killed (1718). Sweden lost Livonia and Karetia to Russia. The war marked the end of Sweden as a great power and the beginning of Russian interest in Europe

North Frisian Islands *FRISIAN ISLANDS

North German Confederation a political union of N. German states (1867–71) set up under Prussian domination after the Seven Weeks' War. The confederation was enlarged after the Franco-Prussian War to become the German Empire (1871)

North Holland *HOLLAND

north·ing (nɔ́rθiŋ) n. (naut.) a sailing towards the north ‖ (naut.) the distance thus sailed ‖ (cartography) northward from bottom to top reading of grid values on a map

North Island *NEW ZEALAND

North Korea *KOREA, DEMOCRATIC PEOPLE'S REPUBLIC OF

North Land *SEVERNAYA ZEMLYA

North·man (nɔ́rθmən) pl. **North·men** (nɔ́rθmən) n. (hist.) *VIKING

north-north-east (nɔrθnɔrθíːst, nɔrnɔríːst) **1.** adv. towards north-northeast **2.** n. N. 22° 30′ E., a compass point midway between north and northeast (abbr. N.N.E., *COMPASS POINT) **3.** adj. of or situated towards north-northeast ‖ (of winds) blowing from north-northeast

north-north-west (nɔrθnɔrθwést, nɔrnɔrwést) **1.** adv. towards north-northwest **2.** n. N. 22° 30′ W., a compass point midway between north and northwest (abbr. N.N.W., *COMPASS POINT) **3.** adj. of or situated towards north-northwest ‖ (of winds) blowing from north-northwest

North Ossetian A.S.S.R. an autonomous republic (area 3,100 sq. miles, pop. 601,000) in the R.S.F.S.R., U.S.S.R., on the northern slopes of the central Caucasus. Capital: Ordzhonikidze. People: Ossets and Russians

North Platte *PLATTE

North Pole the northern end of the earth's axis. The first man to reach it was Peary, in 1909 ‖ (astron.) the celestial zenith as viewed from the terrestrial pole ‖ the point in the earth's magnetic field from which lines of magnetic force radiate **north pole** the pole of a magnet that points toward the north when the magnet is allowed to rotate freely in the earth's magnetic field (cf. SOUTH POLE)

North Rhine–Westphalia (G. Nordrhein-Westfalen) the most industrialized and populous state (area 13,153 sq. miles, pop. 17,040,700) of West Germany, between the Weser and the Low Countries. It consists of the lower Rhineland, with the Ruhr, the northern edge of the Rhenish mountains, and the basin around Münster. The east is forest. Crops: cereals, potatoes, sugar beets. Chief industries: mining (coal, lignite, iron), mechanical engineering, textiles, glass, chemicals, tourism. Main towns: Bonn, Cologne, Düsseldorf (the capital), Duisburg, Dortmund. It was formed (1945) largely from the Prussian provinces of Rhine and Westphalia. Divided among numerous small powers until the Napoleonic conquest, the region was granted to Prussia in 1815

North Sea an arm (area 160,000 sq. miles) of the Atlantic lying between the British Isles, the Low Countries, Germany and Scandinavia. It is deepest off Norway. Shallows include the Dogger Bank. It is extremely rich in fish, and is the busiest shipping area in the world. Commercially exploitable quantities of natural gas were discovered under the sea bed (1965–6); their development esp. helped the economies of Norway and Britain

North Star the polestar

North·um·ber·land (nɔrθʌ́mbərlənd), John Dudley, duke of *WARWICK, John Dudley, earl of

Northumberland (abbr. Northumb.) the northernmost county (area 2,019 sq. miles, pop. 299,950) of England. County town: Newcastle upon Tyne

---

CONCISE PRONUNCIATION KEY: **(a)** æ, cat; ɑ, car; ɔ fawn; ei, snake. **(e)** e, hen; i:, sheep; iə, deer; ɛə, bear. **(i)** i, fish; ai, tiger; ə:, bird. **(o)** o, ox; au, cow; ou, goat; u, poor; ɔi, royal. **(u)** ʌ, duck; u, bull; u:, goose; ə, bacillus; ju:, cube. x, loch; θ, think; ð, bother; z, Zen; ʒ, corsage; dʒ, savage; ŋ, orangutang; j, yak; ʃ, fish; tʃ, fetch; 'l, rabble; 'n, redden. Complete pronunciation key appears inside front cover.

North·um·bri·a (nɔrθʎmbriːə) an Anglo-Saxon kingdom extending from the Forth to the Humber, formed (c. 605) by the union of two earlier kingdoms. It rose to dominance (early 7th c.) under Edwin, but soon declined. It was a center of learning (late 7th c.,) and was the home of Caedmon, Bede and Alcuin

North·um·bri·an (nɔrθʎmbriːən) n. the Old English dialect formerly spoken in Northumbria ‖ an inhabitant of Northumberland ‖ the modern dialect of this county

north·ward (nɔ́rθwərd, nɔ́rðərd) **1.** adv. and adj. towards the north **2.** n. the northward direction or part **north·wards** adv.

north·west (nɔrθwést, nɔrwést) **1.** adv. towards the northwest **2.** n. (usually with 'the') the compass point or direction midway between north and west (abbr. N.W., *COMPASS POINT) **the North·west** the northwestern part of a country **3.** adj. of, belonging to or situated towards the northwest ‖ (of winds) blowing from the northwest [O.E.]

northwest by north N. 33° 45′ W., one point north of due northwest (abbr. N.W. b. N., Br. esp. N.W. by N., *COMPASS POINT)

northwest by west N. 56° 15′ W., one point west of due northwest (abbr. N.W. b. W., Br. esp. N.W. by W., *COMPASS POINT)

North West Company an organization of fur-trading companies established in North America (1783) as rival to the Hudson's Bay Company, with which it was united (1821)

north·west·er (nɔrθwéstər, nɔrwéstər) n. a strong wind or gale from the northwest

north·west·er·ly (nɔrθwéstərli:, nɔrwéstərli:) **1.** adj. and adv. in or towards the northwest ‖ (of winds) from that direction **2.** pl. **north·west·er·lies** n. a wind blowing from the northwest

north·west·ern (nɔrθwéstərn, nɔrwéstərn) adj. situated, facing or moving towards the northwest ‖ of or relating to the northwest or the Northwest

North–West Frontier Province (hist.) a former province (1901–47) of British India on the border of Afghanistan, now part of Pakistan. For centuries the battleground of Pathans against Moguls, Sikhs and the British, it contains the Khyber and other vital passes

Northwest Ordinance (1787) one of the first declarations of the U.S. Congress. It outlined the methods, later accepted as custom, by which territories were organized and states admitted. It banned slavery in the Northwest Territory, encouraged free public education, and guaranteed religious freedom and trial by jury. It promised just and humane laws to preserve peace and friendship with the Indians

Northwest Passage a sea passage between the Atlantic and Pacific Oceans along the Arctic coast of North America. It was searched for unsuccessfully as an alternative route to Asia by Cabot (1497–8), Frobisher (1576–8), Davis (1585–7), Hudson (1609–11), and Baffin (1615–16). It was discovered (1850) by McClure, and was first navigated (1903–6) by Amundsen

Northwest Territories the part (area 1,304,903 sq. miles, pop. 49,000) of Canada lying north of the 60th parallel, including islands and excluding parts within Quebec, Newfoundland province, or the Yukon. Chief town: Yellowknife. The region is governed by a commissioner and council. It is largely treeless tundra, with long cold winters and short cool summers, Native Indians (south of the tree line) and Eskimos (north of it), together forming two-thirds of the population, live by hunting, fishing, and fur trapping. Minerals: gold, uranium, oil, pitchblende, nickel, iron. The territories, administered from 1670 by the Hudson's Bay Company, were transferred by the British government to Canada (1870)

Northwest Territory a tract of land (265,878 sq. miles) bounded by the Mississippi and Ohio Rivers and the Great Lakes, acquired (1783) by the U.S.A. after the Revolutionary War. It now forms the states of Ohio, Indiana, Illinois, Michigan, Wisconsin and part of Minnesota. The area was opened up (18th c.) by French trappers, and was ceded (1763) to Britain after the French and Indian War

north·west·ward (nɔrθwéstwərd, nɔrwéstwərd) adv. and adj. towards the northwest **north·west·wards** adv.

nor·trip·ty·line **hydrochloride** [C₁₉H₂₁N] (nərtríptiliːn hạidrouklɔ́raid) (pharm.) a psychic stimulant; marketed as Aventyl

Nor·way (nɔ́rwei) a kingdom (area 125,064 sq. miles, pop. 4,113,000) in N. W. Europe (Scandinavia). Capital: Oslo. Overseas territories: Svalbard, Jan Mayen Is., Queen Maud Land. People and language: Norwegian, small Lapp minority. Religion: Evangelical Lutheran (state Church), small Roman Catholic and other minorities. The land, almost entirely mountainous, is 74% unproductive, 23% forest, 3% cultivated and grazed. The coast is steep, fringed with islands (providing a protected sea passage) and deeply cut by fiords. The highest mountains are the Jotunheimen (Galdhopiggen, 8,100 ft) in the south center. Barren plateaus (Hardangervidda), lakes, and ice fields separate the mountain ranges. Average temperatures (F.): Bergen 35° (Jan.) and 57° (Jul.), Oslo 24° and 62°, Tromsö 25° and 52°, the Glomma valley (southeast, at 2,000 ft) 13° and 52°. Rainfall: extreme north 16 ins, coast 40–60 ins, Bergen 85 ins, Sogne fiord 100 ins. Livestock: cattle, sheep, poultry, hogs, goats, horses, reindeer. Agricultural products: cereals, potatoes, hay, dairy products. Fisheries: cod, herring, prawns, mackerel, salmon. Minerals: nickel, iron ore, copper, zinc, sulfur pyrites, titanium and molybdenum, silver, bismuth. Other resources: furs, hydroelectricity, timber, whales and seals. Exports: pulp and paper, metals, cod-liver oil, meat and dairy products, fish, whale and seal oils, fertilizers. Main industries: food processing, chemicals, textiles, machinery, clothing, wood. Main imports: machinery, vehicles, metals, fuel oil, textiles, cereals. Norway has the world's third largest merchant fleet. Ports: Oslo, Bergen, Stavanger, Trondheim, Narvik. Universities: Oslo (1811), Bergen (1946). Monetary unit: krone (100 öre). HISTORY. Norway was peopled by Germanic tribes early in the Christian era, and was united (late 9th c.) under Harald I. From Norway, the Vikings raided the shores of the North Sea and the Atlantic (8th–10th cc.) and Norwegian colonies were established. Christianity was introduced (11th c.). The Hanseatic League dominated Norwegian trade (12th c.). About half the population was killed by the Black Death (1349–50). Norway was united with Denmark and Sweden by the Union of Kalmar (1397) and remained little more than a Danish province until 1814, when it was united with Sweden. The 19th c. saw the growth of Norway's trade and shipping, and the spread of hostility toward Sweden. The union with Sweden was dissolved (1905) and Haakon VII was elected king of Norway. The country remained neutral in the 1st world war, developed its industries and became a leading maritime nation. Norway was occupied (1940–5) by the Germans, who established a puppet regime under Quisling, while the king and the cabinet set up a government-in-exile in London. Norway joined the U.N. (1945), NATO (1949) and the European Free Trade Association (1959). Entry into the E.E.C. was fully negotiated (1972) but a referendum rejected membership. Norway is part of the European Free Trade Association (EFTA). Offshore oil production in the North Sea began in 1975 although Norway's chief source of energy remains hydroelectric. In the late 1970s the reigning Labor party lost ground to the Conservatives, who in 1981 formed their first government in 53 years under prime minister Kåre Willoch

Nor·we·gian (nɔrwíːdʒən) **1.** n. a native of Norway ‖ the Germanic language of the Norwegians **2.** adj. pertaining to Norway, the Norwegians or their language [fr. M. L. Norvegia, Norway]

—The Norwegian language belongs to the Scandinavian branch of the Germanic languages along with Swedish and Danish. There are two official forms: Landsmål (or Nynorsk), based on Norwegian rural dialects, and Riksmål (or Bokmål), the traditional Danish-influenced language current since the Middle Ages

Nor·wich (nɔ́ridʒ, nɔ́ridʒ) the county town (pop. 119,000) of Norfolk, England, an agricultural market and county borough. Industry: shoes. Norman castle, cathedral (11th c.). University of East Anglia (1963)

Norwich School an English school of painting of the early 19th c., centered in Norwich. Its chief masters were Crome and Cotman

nose (nouz) **1.** n. the facial prominence above the mouth of man and other mammals, containing the nostrils and the nasal cavity, and serving as a respiratory and olfactory organ ‖ the corresponding part of the head of other animals ‖ a sense of smell, the dog has a very good nose ‖ an ability to detect what is hidden, a nose for scandal ‖ a forward or projecting part, the nose of an aircraft ‖ (racing) the approximate length of a horse's nose used as a distance in describing a result **on the nose** (pop.) exactly **to cut off one's nose to spite one's face** to do something hurtful to someone else knowing that it is also to one's own detriment **to follow one's nose** to go straight on ‖ to do as instinct suggests **to lead someone by the nose** to make someone foolishly do whatever one wants him to **to look down one's nose at** to show disdain for **to pay through the nose** to pay an exorbitant price **to poke** (or **stick**) **one's nose in** to interfere in (what is not one's proper business) **to put someone's nose out of joint** to make someone feel slighted **to speak through one's nose** to pronounce in a nasal manner **to thumb one's nose** to make a rude, derisive gesture by holding one's thumb to one's nose, with the fingers of the hand outstretched **to turn up one's nose at** to scorn **under someone's nose** immediately in front of someone **2.** v. pres. part. **nos·ing** past and past part. **nosed** v.t. (with 'out') to detect by or as if by smelling ‖ to work (one's way) forward, he nosed his way through the crowd ‖ to push with the nose, the horse nosed the stable door open ‖ v.i. **to nose about** (or **around**) to investigate, esp. inquisitively **to nose forward** (of a boat, motor vehicle etc.), to advance slowly and as if with great care **to nose into** to pry into, she is always nosing into their affairs [O.E. nosu]

nose bag a canvas bag containing fodder, slung over a horse's muzzle so that it can feed while in harness

nose·band (nóuzbænd) n. the part of a bridle which passes over the horse's nose and is attached to the cheek straps

nose·bleed (nóuzbliːd) n. epistaxis ‖ an attack of this

nose cone the cone-shaped section on the forward end of a rocket or guided missile, designed to withstand the heat generated by reentry

nose dive a sudden plunge of an aircraft towards the ground **nose-dive** (nóuzdaiv) pres. part. **nose-div·ing** past **nose-dived, nose-dove** (nóuzdouv) past part. **nose-dived** v.i. to plunge in this way

nose flute a flute blown with the nostrils (in Thailand, Fiji etc.)

nose·gay (nóuzgei) n. a posy, or small bunch of flowers

nose·piece (nóuzpiːs) n. (hist.) a piece of armor to protect the nose ‖ the lower end of a microscope ‖ a noseband

nose·rid·er (nóuzraidər) n. (surfing) one who performs stunts on the nose of the surfboard — **nose-ride** v.

nose ring a metal ring passed through the membrane between the nostrils of a pig to prevent it from rooting, or of a bull to enable it to be led ‖ an ornament worn though the nose by certain primitive peoples

nose wheelie skateboard riding when balanced toward the front wheels of the board

nosey *NOSY

nosey parker *NOSY PARKER

nosh (nɒʃ) n. between-meals goodies —**nosh** v. to partake in them —**nosher** n.

no-show (nóuʃou) n. one who makes a reservation and fails to keep it

nosh-up (nɒ́ʃʌp) n. (Br.) an elaborate meal (from the Yiddish)

nos·ing (nóuziŋ) n. the prominent edge of a molding ‖ the rounded edge of a step, projecting over the rise

no·sol·o·gy (nousɒ́lədʒiː) n. (med.) the classification of diseases [fr. Gk nosos, disease+logos, discourse]

nos·tal·gia (nɒstǽldʒə) n. a longing, usually sentimental, to experience again some real or imagined former pleasure **nos·tál·gic** adj. [Mod. L. fr. Gk nostos, a return home+algos, pain]

Nos·tra·da·mus (nɒstrədéiməs) (Michel de Nostredame, 1503–66), French physician and astrologer. He was the author of a popular book of rhymed prophecies, 'The Centuries' (1555)

nos·tril (nɒ́strəl) n. one of the external apertures of the nose [O.E. nosthyrl fr. nosu, nose+thȳrel, opening]

no-strings (noustriŋz) adj. without obligation

nos·trum (nɒ́strəm) n. a quack remedy [L. neut. of noster, ours]

nos·y, nos·ey (nóuzi:) comp. **nos·i·er** superl. **nos·i·est** adj. (pop.) offensively inquisitive [NOSE]

nosy park·er, nosey park·er (párkər) (pop.) an inquisitive busybody

not (nɒt) adv. (with auxiliary verbs and 'to be', often suffixed in the contracted form n't) used to express a negative, *they are not here, he wouldn't answer* ‖ (without a verb) used to introduce a clause, *not that it matters* ‖ used as an emphatic denial, *not him.!* ‖ (rhet.) used to emphasize the opposite, *not a few, not often* ‖ (with 'to say') used to introduce a stronger word or expression than one already used, *he is unkind, not to say cruel* ‖ (with 'to mention', 'to speak of') used to introduce a further, usually negative, consideration, *he rejected it for its costliness, not to mention its ugliness* **not a** not any, not one, *not a hope!, not a man among them* **not half** (Br.,pop.) very ‖ very much [M.E. unstressed form of NOUGHT]

NOT (nɒt) n. (computer) a logic operator or circuit in which if P is a statement, then the not of P is true if P is false, and false if P is true

no·ta·bil·i·ty (noutəbíliti:) pl. **no·ta·bil·i·ties** n. the quality of being notable ‖ a socially prominent person

no·ta·ble (nóutəb'l) 1. adj. worthy of note, *a notable achievement* 2. n. a prominent person, esp. of high social position **No·ta·ble** (F. hist.) a member of an assembly, largely aristocratic in composition, summoned by French kings for consultation in emergencies **nó·ta·bly** adv. in a notable way ‖ especially, particularly [F. fr. L. notabilis]

NOTAM (mil. acronym) for notice to airmen

notaphily *SYNGRAPH

no·tar·i·al (noutéəri:əl) adj. of or pertaining to a notary

no·ta·rize (nóutəraiz) pres. part. **no·ta·riz·ing** past and past part. **no·ta·rized** v.t. to validate (a legal document) as a notary

no·ta·ry (nóutəri:) pl. **no·ta·ries** n. (in some countries) a public officer appointed to administer oaths, draw up and attest documents etc. [fr. L. notarius, clerk]

notary public pl. **notaries public** a notary

no·ta·tion (noutéiʃən) n. the representation of numbers, quantities or other things by a set or scale of symbols ‖ a system of symbols used for this purpose, e.g. 0 to 9 in the decimal scale of notation ‖ (mus.) the system of writing down a piece of music by means of symbols ‖ (mus.) the symbols themselves [fr. L. notatio (notationis), a marking]

notch (nɒtʃ) 1. n. a V-shaped cut or indentation, esp. one made to record ‖ a narrow pass or gap between mountains 2. v.t. to cut notches in ‖ (often with 'up') to record (a score etc.) by or as if by notches [A.F. noche]

notch·back (nɒtʃbæk) n. a slant-roofed passenger car with a flat rear bumper Cf FASTBACK, HATCHBACK

note (nout) 1. n. (often pl.) a brief written record made to assist the memory ‖ a brief, informal, written communication ‖ a formal diplomatic communication, esp. one addressed personally, and usually in the first person ‖ a promissory note ‖ a bank note ‖ (mus.) a sound of definite pitch ‖ (mus.) a symbol denoting the pitch and duration of a musical sound ‖ (mus.) a key of a piano or similar instrument ‖ an indication of an underlying attitude or opinion, *there was a note of complacency in his remarks* ‖ distinction, eminence, *a person of note* **to compare notes** to exchange opinions and ideas about something **to strike a false note** to be unsuitable to the occasion ‖ to strike one as false **to strike the right note** to be, do or say what is exactly appropriate to the occasion **to take note** to pay attention ‖ (with 'of') to note mentally 2. v.t. pres. part. **not·ing** past and past part. **not·ed** to fix in the mind ‖ to pay special attention to ‖ (often with 'down') to make a written note of ‖ to take official notice of ‖ to call attention to, *the report noted a drop in sales* [O.F. fr. L. nota, a mark]

note·book (nóutbʊk) n. a book in which notes are written

note·case (nóutkeis) n. (Br.=Am. billfold) a wallet to keep paper money in

not·ed (nóutid) adj. eminent, well-known

note of hand a promissory note

note·pap·er (nóutpeipər) n. paper for letter-writing

note·wor·thy (nóutwə:rði:) adj. worthy of being noted, remarkable

noth·ing (nʌ́θiŋ) 1. n. no thing, not anything at all ‖ (loosely) not anything of importance or interest, *there's nothing on television tonight* ‖ (math.) naught, zero ‖ (pl.) trifling remarks, *sweet nothings* **for nothing** for no payment, *he let me have it for nothing* ‖ for no reward, *we took all that trouble for nothing* ‖ for no reason, *they quarreled for nothing* **but** no less than, *it is nothing but cheek on his part* ‖ only, *nothing but desert for miles* **nothing doing** no activity or success **nothing doing!** (pop.) no I won't! **there is nothing for it but** there is no alternative but **there is nothing in it** it is untrue ‖ (pop.) there is no profit to be gained from it **to come to nothing** to have no useful result **to have nothing to do with** to leave entirely alone, *have no dealings with* **to make nothing of** (something) to be unable to understand, *I made nothing of the lecture* ‖ to treat as unimportant, *he made nothing of his efforts* ‖ to make little or no use of, *he made nothing of the opportunity* **to make nothing of** (doing something) to treat (the doing of something) as no hardship, *she made nothing of running the whole house without help* **to say nothing of** not to mention, *it is a well-paid job, to say nothing of the short hours* **to think nothing of** not to hesitate to, to do readily, *she thinks nothing of walking 10 miles* 2. adv. not in any way, *the heat is nothing like yesterday* **nóth·ing·ness** n. the state of non-existence ‖ the absence of any thing whatsoever ‖ total insignificance, *a realization of one's own nothingness*

no·tice (nóutis) 1. n. mental awareness, attention, *it escaped his notice* ‖ a printed or written announcement displayed publicly or inserted in a newspaper etc., *a notice of forthcoming concerts* ‖ a review (of a book, exhibition etc.) in a newpaper etc. ‖ previous warning, *subject to change without notice* ‖ a warning that a contract is to terminate, *the firm gave him a month's notice* ‖ a warning that something must be done within a certain time, *the landlord gave him notice to leave* **at short notice** with very little advance warning, **on notice, under notice** in the condition of having been warned 2. v.t. pres. part. **no·tic·ing** past and past part. **no·ticed** to be or become aware of ‖ to write a notice of (a play etc.) **nó·tice·a·ble** adj. conspicuous ‖ capable of being noticed **nó·tice·a·bly** adv. [F.]

notice board (esp. Br.) a bulletin board

no·ti·fi·a·ble (nóutifaiəb'l) adj. (of diseases) that must be reported to the public health authorities

no·ti·fi·ca·tion (nóutifikéiʃən) n. a notifying or being notified ‖ a written or printed communication which formally gives notice

no·ti·fy (nóutifai) v.t. (Br.) to make (a fact) known to someone ‖ to inform (someone) of a fact [fr. F. notifier]

no·till·age or **no·till** (noutílidʒ) n. (agriculture) system of planting in a narrow trench with high use of weed-suppressant herbicides

no·tion (nóuʃən) n. a conception, idea, *his notion of a good novel is not hers* ‖ a general concept, *the notion of law* ‖ a theory or idea lacking precision or certainty, *the notion is not fully worked out in his mind* ‖ an understanding, *she had no notion what he meant* ‖ a whim or fancy, *his head was full of strange notions* ‖ (pl.) inexpensive small useful articles (hairpins, needles, thread, combs etc.) sold in a store [fr. L. notio (notionis) a concept]

no·tion·al (nóuʃən'l) adj. belonging to the realm of ideas, not of experience ‖ (of things) existing only in the mind [fr. M.L. notionalis]

no·to·chord (nóutəkɔrd) n. the dorsal unsegmented elastic rod of cells which forms a skeletal axis in chordates. It persists in the lowest vertebrates, but is transitory in the embryo of others, being replaced in the adult organisms by the vertebral column [fr. Gk nōton, back+chordē, cord]

no·to·ri·e·ty (noutəráiiti:) pl. **no·to·ri·e·ties** n. the quality or state of being notorious ‖ a notorious person [F. notoriété or fr. M.L. notorietas]

no·to·ri·ous (noutɔ́ri:əs, noutóuri:əs) adj. (pejorative) widely known, *a notorious criminal* ‖ widely known to someone's or something's discredit, *a place notorious for pickpockets* [fr. M.L. notorius, well-known]

not out (cricket, of a batsman, after an appeal to the umpire) not dismissed ‖ (cricket, of a batsman) with his innings uncompleted

No·tre Dame, Paris (nɒutrədám, nɒutrədéim) the cathedral (early Gothic, 1163–c. 1245) of Paris, France, on the Ile de la Cité

No·tre Dame, University of (nóutərdéim) a Roman Catholic U.S. educational institution founded (1842) at Notre Dame, Ind., by brothers of the Congregation of Holy Cross, a French religious community

no-trump (nóutrʌmp) 1. n. a bid or contract at bridge to play a hand with no suit as trumps 2. adj. being such a bid or contract

Not·ting·ham (nɒ́tiŋəm) the county town (pop. 282,900) of Nottinghamshire, England, on the Trent, a county borough. Main industries: bicycles, hosiery, lace, knitwear, textiles, coal mining, cigarettes. Castle (17th c.). Roman Catholic cathedral (1844, by Pugin). University (1948)

Not·ting·ham·shire (nɒ́tiŋəmʃiər) (abbr. Notts.) a county (area 844 sq. miles, pop. 974,100) in N. central England. County town: Nottingham

not·with·stand·ing (nɒtwiθstǽndiŋ) 1. prep. in spite of, *she believed him guilty, notwithstanding all the evidence* 2. adv. nevertheless, *notwithstanding, he believed it* 3. conj. although

Nouak·chott (nwɑkʃót) the capital (pop. 134,386) of Mauritania, near the coast

nou·gat (nú:gət, nú:gɑ) n. a confection of sugar, with almonds or other nuts or candied fruit or honey [F.]

nought (nɔt) n. (math.) a naught ‖ (rhet.) naught [O.E. nōwiht]

noughts-and-cross·es (nɔ́tsənkrɔ́siz) n. (Br.) tick-tack-toe

Nou·mé·a (nu:méiə) the capital and chief port (pop. 74,335) of New Caledonia, on the southwest coast: metallurgy

nou·men·on (nú:mənɒn) pl. **nou·me·na** (nú:mənə) n. (philos.) an object or pure thought not connected with sense perception [fr. Gk noou·menon, the thing perceived]

noun (naun) n. (gram.) a word used to name a person, place, thing, state or quality [A.F.]

nour·ish (nʌ́riʃ, nə́:riʃ) v.t. to supply or sustain with food ‖ to foster or keep alive in the mind, *to nourish a feeling of hatred* **nóur·ish·ment** n. food [fr. O.F. norir (noriss-)]

nous (naus, nu:s) n. (philos.) the mind, intellect ‖ (pop.) common sense [Gk]

nou·veau pauvre, pl. **nouveaux pauvres** (nu:vọupóuvr) n. (French) the newly poor ant nouveau riche

nouveau réalisme n. (Fr.) art form incorporating common objects and discards into an assemblage, as in works by Yves Klein, Jean Tingely, Daniel Spoerri, and Matial Roysse. The term was coined by French art critic Pierre Restany

nou·veau riche (nú:vourí:ʃ) pl. **nou·veaux riches** (nú:vourí:ʃ) n. someone newly rich who lacks social standing, culture etc. [F.]

nouveau roman *NEW NOVEL

nou·velle cuisine (nu:vəlkwizí:n) (Fr.) haute-cuisine cooking style without use of rich sauces or large quantities of butter and cream syn. cuisine minceur

Nov. November

no·va (nóuvə) n. a variable star which in a short period of time (e.g. several hours) may increase in apparent brightness by several magnitudes, often flaring up from a star invisible to the naked eye and eventually returning to this state. The cause of these explosive changes in luminosity is not known [L. fem. of novus, new]

no·va·chord (nóuvəkɔrd) n. an electronic pianolike instrument, with a range of six octaves, capable of a wide variety of tonal variation [fr. L. novus, new+CHORD]

no·vac·u·lite (nouvǽkjulait) n. a hard, fine-grained siliceous rock used to make whetstones [fr. L. novacula, a razor]

No·va·lis (nouvális) (Friedrich Leopold von Hardenberg, 1772–1801), German Romantic poet and novelist, author of the mystical 'Hymnen an die Nacht' (1800) and the unfinished novel 'Heinrich von Ofterdingen' (begun 1800)

No·va Lis·bo·a (nóvəli:ʒbóə) *HUAMBO

No·va·ra, Battle of (nəvárə) a battle fought (1849) in N. Italy in which Charles Albert of Sardinia was defeated by the Austrian army under Radetzky

No·va Sco·tia (nóuvəskóuʃə) a province (area 21,425 sq. miles, pop. 866,100) on the Atlantic coast of Canada, consisting of Nova Scotia and Cape Breton Is. Capital: Halifax. It is a plateau (average height 500 ft) with coastal lowlands by the Bay of Fundy and in the south of Cape Breton Is. Agriculture: dairying, poultry, fruit (esp. apples). Resources: fish, timber, coal, barite, gypsum, salt. Industries: oil refining, iron and steel, food processing, forestry products, shipbuilding. The area was first settled by the French (1605) as Acadia and changed hands several times between French and English until it was ceded to Britain (1713). It became a province of Canada (1867)

No·va·tion (nouvéiʃən) (d. c. 258), antipope (251–8). He founded a sect which merged (4th c.) with Donatism, but which persisted in N. Africa until the 6th c.

No·va·ya Zem·lya (nóvəjazemljá) a pair of islands (total area 36,000 sq. miles, pop. 100, Samoyed) in the Arctic Ocean directly north of the Urals, belonging to the R.S.F.S.R., U.S.S.R. Mainly elevated tundra, they are rich in game

nov·el (nóvəl) n. an imaginative prose narrative of some length, usually concerned with human experience and social behavior, and normally cast in the form of a connected story **the novel** this genre of literature [O.F. novelle]
—The form of the novel is very old: something similar was written in ancient Greece and Rome. In the Middle Ages poetry (e.g. Chaucer's 'Troilus and Criseyde'), collections of tales (Boccaccio's 'Decameron') and romances (the Arthurian legend) supplied the equivalent interest: humor, adventure, psychological penetration, storytelling. The novel proper emerged in the 16th c., initially as the picaresque novel, in which a lower-class hero has a series of adventures calling for resourcefulness, and in which the characteristics of certain broadly painted social classes are revealed (esp. in Spain, France and England). In 17th-c. France the novel took a great step forward with Mme de La Fayette's 'la Princesse de Cléves' (1678), in which the interest ceases to be in external events and focuses on motivation and mental conflict (i.e. it becomes moral). This deeper interest entered into English fiction with Richardson's 'Clarissa' (1747-8). The 19th c. was the great age of the European novel, in which the refinement of narrative and dramatic technique went hand in hand with a deeper interest in personality and behavior (or e.g. in Dickens and Zola), with the structure of society. In the greatest writers form and meaning are totally interdependent, e.g. in Kafka and Joyce

novel adj. new in one's experience and having an element of the unexpected ‖ new and ingenious [O.F.]

nov·el·ette (nɒvəlét) n. a short novel or long short story ‖ (Br.) a sentimental novel without literary pretension

nov·el·ist (nóvəlist) n. a person who writes novels

nov·el·ty (nóvəlti:) pl. **nov·el·ties** n. a novel thing or event ‖ the quality or state of being novel ‖ (commerce) a small manufactured article, esp. for personal or household adornment, usually without intrinsic value or merit [O.F. novelté]

No·vem·ber (nouvémbər) n. (abbr. Nov.) the 11th month of the year, having 30 days [L.=the ninth month of the Roman calendar, fr. novem, nine]

no·vem·de·cil·lion (nouvemdisíljən) n. *NUMBER TABLE [fr. L. novemdecim, nineteen+MILLION]

no·ve·na (nouví:nə) n. (Roman Catholic) a devotion with special prayers and services over nine days [M.L.]

Nov·go·rod (nóvɡʌrʌt) a rail center pop. 186,000), of the R.S.F.S.R., U.S.S.R., 100 miles southeast of Leningrad, once one of the most important cities in Russia. It was the capital of a principality (11th–15th cc.) and one of the chief centers of the Hanseatic League

nov·ice (nóvis) n. a beginner in some pursuit which demands skill ‖ (eccles.) a person received on probation into a religious order, prior to taking vows ‖ a person newly converted to Christianity [O.F.]

noviciate *NOVITIATE

No·vi Sad (nóvi:sád) the capital (pop. 170,800) of the Vojvodina, Yugoslavia, a port on the Danube: milling, distilling, electrical engineering

no·vi·ti·ate, no·vi·ci·ate (nouvíʃi:it, nouvíʃi:ʃeit) n. the state of being a novice ‖ a period of probation as a novice ‖ a place where novices are trained [fr. F. noviciat]

No·vo·caine (nóuvəkein) n. a synthetic alkaloid compound used as a local anesthetic [trademark, fr. L. novus, new+COCAINE]

No·vo·kuz·netsk (nɔvakuznétsk) (formerly Stalinsk) a city (pop. 555,100) of the R.S.F.S.R., U.S.S.R., in the Kuznetsk Basin: coal mining, iron and steel, metal alloys, heavy engineering, chemical and food industries

No·vo·si·birsk (nɔvʌsibí:rsk) (formerly Novonikolaevsk) the chief city (pop. 1,382,000, growing rapidly) of W. Siberia, R.S.F.S.R., U.S.S.R. on the Ob. It is the administrative center for the Kuznetsk Basin: metallurgy, mechanical engineering, textiles, food processing. It is on the Trans-Siberian Railroad

No·vo Si·bir·skie Os·tro·va (nɔvʌsibí:rski:jeʌstrʌvá) *NEW SIBERIAN ISLANDS

now (nau) **1.** adv. at the present time ‖ without delay, it is vital to act now ‖ used to introduce and emphasize a command, warning, reproof etc., now you listen to me! ‖ used to introduce or emphasize a further development or transition in a narrative, now, while this had been happening... ‖ (rhet., with following 'now') sometimes, the countryside swept past, now mountains, now plains ‖ at a certain time under consideration, the general now changed his tactics ‖ reckoning to the present moment, he has worked there a long time now **now and again, now and then** sometimes, occasionally **now now!** used to pacify, reprove etc. **now or never** used to affirm the necessity of grasping an opportunity which will not recur **2.** conj. (often with 'that') because, as, now that you have come you may as well stay **3.** n. (after 'by', 'for', 'from', 'up to', 'till', 'until' etc.) the present time [O.E. nū]

NOW (nau) **1.** for National Organization for Women **2.** (banking acronym) for negotiable order of withdrawal

NOW account (banking) interest-paying bank account using negotiable orders of withdrawal, a substitute for personal checking account, offered by some savings institutions

now·a·days (náuədeiz) **1.** adv. at the present time in history **2.** n. the present time, children of nowadays

no·way (nóuwei) adv. not in any way or degree, not at all

no·ways (nóuweiz) adv. noway

nowel *NOEL

Now Generation popular term for the young people of the 1960s and 1970s seeking instant gratification and solution to personal and world problems, with distinct ideas and fashions

no·where (nóuhwɛ̧ər, nóuwç̧ər) **1.** adv. not anywhere **nowhere near** at a considerable distance from, he lives nowhere near London ‖ not nearly, it was nowhere near as difficult as he expected **to get nowhere** (pop.) to make no progress towards being successful **2.** n. a state of not existing or seeming not to exist ‖ a place that does not exist

no·wise (nóuwaiz) adv. (rhet.) in no way, not at all

nox·ious (nókʃəs) adj. harmful, noxious gases ‖ corrupting, a noxious influence [fr. L. noxius]

noz·zle (nɒz'l) n. a projecting aperture at the end of a tube, pipe etc. serving as an outlet for a fluid etc. [dim. of NOSE]

NPT (abbr.) of nonproliferation treaty, an agreement to limit the availability of nuclear weapons

N. S. Nova Scotia

nsec (abbr.) for nanosecond, one billionth of a second

NSU (med. acronym) for nonspecific urethritis (which see)

Nsuk·ka ('nsú:kə) a town of E. Nigeria 30 miles north of Enugu. University (1960)

N. S. W. New South Wales

N. T. New Testament

NTA (organic chem.) nitrilotriacetic acid, a compound proposed for use to replace phosphates in detergents. It is considered a possible environmental hazard

nth (enθ) adj. being the last of a series **for the nth time** once again after countless times before **to the nth degree (or power)** to the uppermost limit

Nth country (mil.) the next addition to the group of powers possessing nuclear weapons, the next country of a series to acquire nuclear capabilities

N.T.P. (phys.) normal temperature and pressure, i.e. 0°C and a pressure which would

support a column of mercury 760 mm. high at 0°C at sea level in latitude 45°

nu (nju:, nu:) n. the thirteenth letter (N, v=n) of the Greek alphabet

nu·ance (nú:ɑns, njú:ɑns) n. a slight difference in color or in tone ‖ a slight difference in meaning, emotion etc. [F.]

nub (nʌb) n. a small lump ‖ a small knob of fibers dyed a different color and interspersed in the yarn or wool during spinning or weaving ‖ the crucial part of an argument, problem, story etc. [var. of KNOB]

Nu·ba (nú:bə) pl. **Nu·ba, Nu·bas** n. any of several Negroid peoples of the central Sudan ‖ a member of such a people ‖ any of several languages spoken by these peoples

nub·bin (nʌ́bin) n. a small or imperfect ear of corn ‖ an undeveloped or stunted fruit or vegetable [dim. of NUB]

nub·by (nʌ́bi) comp. **nub·bi·er** superl. **nub·bi·est** adj. (of yarn or wool) having nubs

Nu·bi·a (nú:bi:ə, njú:bi:ə) a region and ancient country of N. Africa extending along both sides of the Nile from Khartoum to Aswan. Modern Nubia includes the Nubian Desert

Nu·bi·an (nú:bi:ən, njú:bi:ən) **1.** n. one of the Negroid inhabitants of Nubia ‖ any of several languages spoken by them **2.** adj. of or relating to Nubia, the Nubians or a Nubian language

Nubian Desert the part of the Sahara elevation 1,200–9,000 ft) in the N.E. Sudan between the Nile and the Red Sea

nu·bile (nú:bail, njú:bail, nú:bil, njú:bil) adj. (of women) of an age or condition to marry **nu·bíl·i·ty** (nu:bíliti:, nju:bíliti:) n. [F. or fr. L. nubilis]

nu·cel·lar (nu:sélər, nju:sélər) adj. of or relating to a nucellus

nu·cel·lus (nu:séləs, nju:séləs) pl. **nu·cel·li** (nu:sélai, nju:sélai) n. (bot.) the central nutritive mass of cells in an ovule, containing the embryo sac [Mod. L.]

nu·cha (nú:kə, njú:kə) pl. **nu·chae** (nú:ki:, njú:ki:) n. (med.) the nape of the neck **nú·chal** adj. [M.L. fr. Arab.]

nu·cle·ar (nú:kli:ər, njú:kli:ər) adj. pertaining to a nucleus ‖ of or relating to atomic energy, nuclear weapons [NUCLEUS]

Nuclear Club the nations known to have nuclear weapons capability

nuclear column a hollow cylinder of water and spray thrown up from an underwater nuclear explosion through which the hot, high-pressure gases formed in the explosion are vented to the atmosphere Cf CAMOUFLET, CRATER

nuclear energy the energy available from the fission or fusion of atomic nuclei. This energy, which is enormously greater than that available from chemical or mechanical sources (the energy released by 1 pound of uranium during fission is equivalent to that derived from the combustion of 2½ million pounds of coal), results from the conversion of mass directly into energy (*PACKING FRACTION, *MASS-ENERGY EQUATION). This and the fact that uranium and thorium are among the more common elements in the earth's crust make nuclear energy a most important source of power

nuclear family family unit consisting of a husband, wife, and children Cf EXTENDED FAMILY

nuclear fission *FISSION

nuclear fusion *FUSION

nuclear isomer one of a group of nuclides exhibiting the same atomic and mass numbers but differing in energy content and half-life

nuclear magnetic resonance a phenomenon observed with certain atomic nuclei possessing a magnetic moment in the presence of an intense homogeneous external magnetic field in which they are capable of absorbing radiofrequency energy in changing from one quantized space orientation to another. This phenomenon forms the basis of a spectroscopic technique used esp. for determining the position and character of hydrogen nuclei in organic molecules

nuclear medicine use of isotopes and radiation detectors in diagnosis and therapy

nuclear nonproliferation a policy of stopping the spread of nuclear weapons to non-nuclear states

nuclear physics the branch of physics that deals with the structure, composition and transformations of the atomic nucleus, including the study of the fundamental particles

nuclear reactor *REACTOR (device in which a fission chain reaction is initiated)

CONCISE PRONUNCIATION KEY: **(a)** æ, cat; ɑ, car; ɔ fawn; ei, snake. **(e)** e, hen; i:, sheep; iə, deer; ɛə, bear. **(i)** i, fish; ai, tiger; ə:, bird. **(o)** o, ox; au, cow; ou, goat; u, poor; ɔi, royal. **(u)** ʌ, duck; u, bull; u:, goose; ə, bacillus; ju:, cube. x, loch; θ, think; ð, bother; z, Zen; ʒ, corsage; dʒ, savage; ŋ, orangutang; j, yak; ʃ, fish; tʃ, fetch; 'l, rabble; 'n, redden. Complete pronunciation key appears inside front cover.

Nuclear Regulatory Commission (*abbr.* N.R.C.) an independent U.S. government agency responsible for licensing and regulating civilian uses of nuclear materials. It replaced (1975) the Atomic Energy Commission under the provisions of the 1974 Energy Reorganization Act. Its major function is the use of nuclear energy to generate power. The NRC consists of five members appointed by the president. Its main offices are in Bethesda, Md, and there are five regional offices

nuclear safeguards a system of international safeguards devised by the International Atomic Energy Agency (IAEA) requiring countries to file regular reports on civilian nuclear activities and allow international inspectors to visit nuclear facilities. The 1968 Treaty on the Non-Proliferation of Nuclear Weapons (NPT) provides a framework within which the international safeguards are to operate

nuclear yield (*mil.*) the amount of energy released in the detonation of a nuclear weapon, measured in terms of kilotons or megatons of TNT required to produce the same amount of energy

nu·cle·ase (núːkliːeis, njúːkliːeis) *n.* (*biol.*) any of the enzymes which promote hydrolysis of nucleic acids [NUCLEUS]

nu·cle·ate 1. (núːkliːit, njúːkliːeit) *adj.* having a nucleus **2.** (núːkliːeit, njúːkliːeit) *v.i. pres. part.* **nu·cle·at·ing** *past* and *past part.* **nu·cle·at·ed** to form a nucleus [fr. L. *nucleare* (*nucleatus*), to become like a kernel]

nuclei *pl.* of NUCLEUS

nu·cle·ic acid (nuːklíːik, njuːklíːik, nuːkléiik, njuːkléiik) one of a group of complex polymeric acids found in all living cells, esp. in combination as nucleoproteins, and which on hydrolysis yield an organic base, a sugar and phosphoric acid. The molecules of sugar are condensed together with the molecules of phosphoric acid, forming long chains, while each molecule of sugar is bonded to either a purine or a pyrimidine molecule (the organic base), e.g. deoxyribonucleic acid

nu·cle·in (núːkliːin, njúːkliːin) *n.* any of several mixtures of nucleic acid and proteins rich in phosphorus, occurring in cell nuclei [NUCLEUS]

nu·cle·o·cap·sid (nuːkliːoukǽpsid) *n.* in a virus, the nucleic acid and protein surrounding it

nu·cle·o·gen·e·sis (nuːkliːoudʒénisis) *n.* (*nuclear phys.*) hypothesis regarding the creation of nuclei of atoms from fundamental plasma

nu·cle·o·lar (nuːklíːələr, njuːklíːələr) *adj.* of or forming a nucleolus

nu·cle·o·lus (nuːklíːələs, njuːklíːələs) *pl.* **nu·cle·o·li** (nuːklíːəlai, njuːklíːəlai) *n.* a rounded, predominantly protein mass occurring in the nucleus of many cells. Its precise function is uncertain [L. dim. of *nucleus*, kernel]

nu·cle·on (núːkliːɒn, njúːkliːɒn) *n.* (phys.) a neutron or a proton **nu·cle·on·ics** *n.* the study of nucleons or the nuclei of atoms || (*particle phys.*) a constituent particle of the atomic nucleus, applied to protons and neutrons, but intended to include any other particle found to exist in the nucleus || (*nuclear phys.*) a part of the atomic nucleus [NUCLEUS + on, fundamental particle]

nu·cle·one (núːklioun) *n.* (*biochem.*) the nuclear substance in a protoplast

nu·cle·o·phile (nuːklioufáil) *n.* (*nuclear phys.*) **1.** a substance attracted to the nuclei of atoms **2.** one highly interested in nuclear devices

nu·cle·o·phil·ic reagents (nuːklioufílik riːéidʒentz) *n.* any substance used to produce a characteristic reaction at centers of low electron density, to transfer electrons to other atoms or ions —**nucleophile** *n.*

nu·cle·o·plasm (núːkliːəplæzəm, njúːkliːəplæzəm) *n.* the protoplasm of the cell nucleus (cf. CYTOPLASM) **nu·cle·o·plas·mic** *adj.* [fr. NUCLEUS + Gk *plasma*, form]

nu·cle·o·pro·tein (nuːkliːoupróutiːn, njuːkliːoupróutiːn) *n.* one of a class of proteins in which the protein portion of the molecule is linked to a nucleic acid (the prosthetic group). Nucleoproteins are found as a constituent of cell nuclei, cytoplasm, genes and viruses, and play an essential role in the transmission of genetic characteristics from parent to offspring

nu·cle·o·side (núːkliːəsaid, njúːkliːəsaid) *n.* a crystalline hydrolysis product of nucleic acids that does not contain the phosphoric acid residue || (*biochem.*) a glycoside compound of pentose and purine or pyrimidine formed by removal of phosphate from a nucleotide (*NUCLEOTIDE) [NUCLEUS]

nu·cle·o·syn·the·sis (nuːkliːousínθisis) *n.* (*chem.*) process of creating chemical elements from the nuclei or protons of hydrogen

nu·cle·o·tide (núːkliːətaid, njúːkliːətaid) *n.* a compound formed by the partial hydrolysis of nucleic acids, being an ester of a nucleoside with phosphoric acid (*DEOXYRIBONUCLEIC ACID) || any compound of a group resembling those derived from nucleic acids by hydrolysis and including certain important biochemical products [fr. Mod. L. *nucleus*, nucleus]

nu·cle·us (núːkliːəs, njúːkliːəs) *pl.* **nu·cle·i** (núːkliːai, njúːkliːai) *n.* the central part of a whole, having its own identity, about which the rest of the whole gathers or grows || a center of activity, influence etc. || (*anat.*) a mass of gray matter or nerve cells in the central nervous system || (*astron.*) the brightest and densest part of the head of a comet, galaxy or other celestial body || (*biol.*) the inner spheroid protoplasmic mass of a cell, essential to the life of most cells and to the transmission of hereditary character. It is mainly composed of nucleoproteins || (*chem.*) a stable formation of atoms, e.g. the benzene ring || (*chem., phys.*) the positively charged dense mass at the center of an atom, having a complex structure consisting chiefly of protons and neutrons, and responsible for almost all the mass of the atom [L. = kernel]

nu·clide (núːklaid, njúːklaid) *n.* an atom identified by its nuclear constitution i.e. by its atomic number, mass number and energy content [NUCLEUS + -*ide*]

nude (nuːd, njuːd) **1.** *adj.* (of the body) naked || (of representations of the body) undraped || (*law*, of a contract etc.) not valid because lacking essential formalities **2.** *n.* an undraped figure in painting, sculpture etc. || such a figure in striptease etc. || (with 'the') the state of being nude [fr. L. *nudus*]

NUDET (*mil. acronym*) for nuclear detonation evaluation technique, a technique for detecting nuclear explosions

nudge (nʌdʒ) **1.** *v.t. pres. part.* **nudg·ing** *past* and *past part.* **nudged** to push gently, esp. with the elbow || to draw the attention of, or give a hint to(someone with, or as if with, such a push **2.** *n.* such push [etym. doubtful]

nu·di·branch (núːdəbræŋk, njúːdəbræŋk) *n.* a member of *Nudibranchia*, a suborder of marine mollusks without a shell and true gills, but often with branching external gills on the back [fr. F. *nudibranche*]

nud·ie (núːdiː) *n.* film or publication specializing in pictures of nudes —**nudie** *adj.*

nud·ism (núːdizəm, njúːdizəm) *n.* the belief in, and practice of, living naked, as being physically and psychologically beneficial

nud·ist 1. *n.* a person who accepts or practices nudism **2.** *adj.* of or pertaining to nudism or nudists [NUDE]

nu·di·ty (núːditiː, njúːditiː) *n.* the state or quality of being nude [F. *nudité* or fr. L. *nuditas* (*nuditatis*)]

nu·dome (núːdoum) *n.* (*nuclear phys.*) a device for short-range gamma-ray tracking, consisting of a dome-shape enclosure designed to receive radiation

Nu·er (núːər) *pl.* **Nu·er, Nu·ers** *n.* a Nilotic Negro people of Sudan and W. Ethiopia || a member of these people || their Nilotic language

Nue·vo La·re·do (nwévɔlaréðɔ) an important cattle and oil center (pop. 214,161 in Tamaulipas state, Mexico, on the Rio Grande River, opposite Laredo, Texas. A major highway (775 miles long) leading to Mexico City begins here

Nue·vo Le·ón (nwévɔleón) an industrial and agricultural state (area 24,925 sq. miles, pop. 2,463,298) of N. Mexico. There are forest-covered mountains in the southeast and subtropical valleys in the east (sugarcane cultivation), with desert (irrigation developments) in the north. Capital: Monterrey. Industries: ironworks, steelworks, smelting plants (the first heavy industry in Latin America) and textile enterprises. Agriculture: cotton, citrus, sugar, cereals and vegetables

Nuf·field (nʌ́fiːld), William Richard Morris, 1st Viscount (1877–1963), British automobile manufacturer and philanthropist. He gave money for the advancement of medicine and learning, endowing Nufield College at Oxford (1937) and the Nufield Foundation, a charitable trust (1943)

nu·ga·to·ry (núːgətɔriː, njúːgətɔriː, núːgətouriː, njúːgətouri) *adj.* of no importance or value || having no effect [fr. L. *nugatorius*]

nug·get (nʌ́git) *n.* a small lump of native precious metal, esp. gold [perh. dim. of dial. *nug*, lump]

nui·sance (núːsᵊns, njúːsᵊns) *n.* a person or thing causing annoyance or trouble, or preventing one from the full enjoyment of a pleasure (freedom, quiet etc.) || (*law*) an act or circumstance which causes annoyance or offense to another person or to the community at large [O.F.]

null (nʌl) *adj.* (*law*) having no force in law || of, relating to or amounting to zero [O.F. *nul* or fr. L. *nullus*, not any]

null and void completely invalid

nul·li·fi·ca·tion (nʌlifikéiʃən) *n.* a nullifying or being nullified || (*Am. hist.*) the doctrine, held by strong supporters of states' rights, that a state had the right to suspend a federal law within its own territory

nul·li·fy (nʌ́lifai) *pres. part.* **nul·li·fy·ing** *past* and *past part.* **nul·li·fied** *v.t.* to make null (esp. a contract etc.) [fr. L.L. *nullificare*]

nul·li·pa·ra (nʌlípərə) *n.* a woman who has never borne a child **nul·lip·a·rous** *adj.* [Mod. L. fr. *nullus*, none + *parere*, to bring forth]

nul·li·pore (nʌ́ləpɔr, nʌ́ləpour) *n.* any of several coralline algae which secrete lime [fr. L. *nullus*, no + PORE *n.*]

nul·li·ty (nʌ́litiː) *pl.* **nul·li·ties** *n.* (*law*) the state of being null or invalid || (*law*) something null [F. *nullité* or M.L. *nullitas*]

null set (*math.*) empty set in mathematics; a set with no members

Nu·man·ti·a (nuːmǽnʃiːə, njuːmǽnʃiːə) an ancient settlement in Spain, near the Douro. It was a center of Celtiberian resistance to the Romans until conquered (133 B.C.) by Scipio Aemilianus

Nu·ma Pom·pil·i·us (núːməpompíliːəs, njúːmə-pompíliːəs) legendary king of Rome, traditionally the founder of Roman ceremonial law and ritual

numb (nʌm) **1.** *adj.* lacking sensation, esp. as a result of exposure to cold || lacking the ability to feel any emotion, esp. as a result of shock, fatigue etc. || so possessed by a specified strong emotion as to be incapable of action, *numb with fear* || characterized by lack of sensation, *a numb feeling* **2.** *v.t.* to make numb [M.E. *nomyn* fr. older *nomen*, past part. of *nim*, to seize]

num·ber (nʌ́mbər) *n.* a word or symbol used to express how many or what place in a sequence, *one, two, three* etc. are cardinal numbers, and *first, second, third* etc. are ordinal numbers || a figure used to denote one thing in particular, *the number of the winning ticket* || a total || the property of being countable || an issue of a periodical, *the April number of this magazine* || an item (e.g. of singing or dancing) performed on

NUMBERS ABOVE ONE MILLION		
American	**British**	**Value**
billion	milliard	10^9
trillion	billion	10^{12}
quadrillion		10^{15}
quintillion	trillion	10^{18}
sextillion		10^{21}
septillion	quadrillion	10^{24}
octillion		10^{27}
nonillion	quintillion	10^{30}
decillion		10^{33}
undecillion	sextillion	10^{36}
duodecillion		10^{39}
tredecillion	septillion	10^{42}
quattuordecillion		10^{45}
quindecillion	octillion	10^{48}
sexdecillion		10^{51}
septendecillion	nonillion	10^{54}
octodecillion		10^{57}
novemdecillion	decillion	10^{60}
vigintillion		10^{63}
	undecillion	10^{66}
	duodecillion	10^{72}
	tredecillion	10^{78}
	quattuordecillion	10^{84}
	quindecillion	10^{90}
	sexdecillion	10^{96}
	septendecillion	10^{102}
	octodecillion	10^{108}
	novemdecillion	10^{114}
	vigintillion	10^{120}
centillion		10^{303}
	centillion	10^{600}

CONCISE PRONUNCIATION KEY: (**a**) æ, c*a*t; ɑ, c*a*r; ɔ f*aw*n; ei, sn*a*ke. (**e**) e, h*e*n; iː, sh*ee*p; iə, d*ee*r; ɛə, b*ea*r. (**i**) i, f*i*sh; ai, t*i*ger; əː, b*i*rd. (**o**) o, *o*x; au, c*ow*; ou, g*oa*t; u, p*oo*r; ɔi, r*o*yal. (**u**) ʌ, d*u*ck; u, b*u*ll; uː, g*oo*se; ə, b*a*cillus; juː, c*u*be. x, lo*ch*; θ, *th*ink; ð, bo*th*er; z, *Z*en; ʒ, corsa*g*e. dʒ, sava*g*e; ŋ, ora*ng*utang; j, *y*ak; ʃ, *fish*; tʃ, fe*tch*; 'l, rabb*le*; 'n, redd*en*. Complete pronunciation key appears inside front cover.

CARDINAL			ORDINAL
	Arabic symbol	Roman symbol	symbol
zero, naught, cipher	0		
one	1	I	first	1st
two	2	II	second	2nd, 2d
three	3	III	third	3rd, 3d
four	4	IV	fourth	4th
five	5	V	fifth	5th
six	6	VI	sixth	6th
seven	7	VII	seventh	7th
eight	8	VIII	eighth	8th
nine	9	IX	ninth	9th
ten	10	X	tenth	10th
eleven	11	XI	eleventh	11th
twelve	12	XII	twelfth	12th
thirteen	13	XIII	thirteenth	13th
fourteen	14	XIV	fourteenth	14th
fifteen	15	XV	fifteenth	15th
sixteen	16	XVI	sixteenth	16th
seventeen	17	XVII	seventeenth	17th
eighteen	18	XVIII	eighteenth	18th
nineteen	19	XIX	nineteenth	19th
twenty	20	XX	twentieth	20th
twenty-one	21	XXI	twenty-first	21st
twenty-two	22	XXII	twenty-second	22nd, 22d
thirty	30	XXX	thirtieth	30th
forty	40	XL	fortieth	40th
fifty	50	L	fiftieth	50th
sixty	60	LX	sixtieth	60th
seventy	70	LXX	seventieth	70th
eighty	80	LXXX	eightieth	80th
ninety	90	XC	ninetieth	90th
one hundred	100	C	one hundredth	100th
one hundred and one	101	CI	one hundred and first	101st
one hundred and twenty-four	124	CXXIV	one hundred and twenty-fourth	124th
two hundred	200	CC	two hundredth	200th
five hundred	500	D	five hundredth	500th
one thousand	1,000	M	one thousandth	1,000th
one thousand two hundred and twenty-five	1,225	MCCXXV	one thousand two hundred and twenty-fifth	1,225th
two thousand	2,000	MM	two thousandth	2,000th
one million	1,000,000	M̄	one millionth	1,000,000th

the stage, television etc. ‖ (*gram.*) a difference of form showing whether only one person or thing is meant, or more than one (cf. SINGULAR, cf. DUAL NUMBER, cf. PLURAL) ‖ such a form itself ‖ (pl.) arithmetic, *he is not good at numbers* ‖ a collection of persons, *she was not among their number* ‖ (pl.) a large collection of persons or things, *they came in great numbers* ‖ numerical superiority, *they won by sheer number* **the numbers** an illegal lottery in which betting depends on a selected multi-digit number turning up in some prearranged published context (e.g. stock market figures) **a number of** several, *they have a number of things to do* **beyond** (or **without**) **number** too many to be counted **number one** the first of a series‖ the best of many ‖ (pop.) one self, *he looks after number one* **one's number is up** (pop.) one is to die, through an ordeal etc. shortly **in number** in all, in total **times without number** too many times to be counted **to have some one's number** (pop.) to have penetrated someone's character or intentions [O.F. *nombre, numbre, numere*]

number *v.t.* to denote by a number, *he numbered the seats* ‖ to include within a collection, *he numbers them among his friends* ‖ to be equal to (a number), *the disciples numbered 12* ‖ *v.i.* (*mil.*, esp. with 'off') to call one's number at a roll call etc. **one's days are numbered** one has not much longer to live [O.F. *nombrer*]

num·ber·less (nʌ́mbərlis) *adj.* too many to be counted

number line (*math.*) an infinite line with points indicated by real numbers related to distance from zero

Num·bers (nʌ́mbərz) the fourth book of the Old Testament. It relates the Exodus from Mt Sinai as far as Moab

num·bers (nʌ́mbərz) *n.* an illegal lottery, usu. based on a published number, e.g., the day's clearinghouse total

numbers pool the numbers (lottery, *NUMBER)
numbers runner one who collects illegal bets in a numbers lottery

number theory a branch of mathematics that deals with the properties of the integers as distinguished from rational, real, or complex numbers. Most of the elementary theory relates to questions of divisibility and the distribution of prime numbers

numbskull *NUMSKULL

nu·men (nú:min, njú:min) *pl.* **nu·mi·na** (nú:minə, njú:minə) *n.* (originally in animistic religious belief, esp. in ancient Roman religion) a presiding or indwelling divine spirit [L.]

nu·mer·a·ble (nú:mərəb'l, njú:mərəb'l) *adj.* able to be counted [fr. L. *numerabilis*]

nu·mer·a·cy (nu:mérəsi:) *n.* literacy with numbers, e.g., the capacity to think in quantitative terms —**numerate** *adj.*

nu·mer·al (nú:mərəl, njú:mərəl) **1.** *n.* the symbol, or group of symbols, of a number (*ARABIC NUMERALS, *ROMAN NUMERALS) **2.** *adj.* pertaining to, having or denoting number, *a numeral adjective* [fr. L.L. *numeralis*, expressing a number]

nu·mer·ate (nú:məreit, njú:məreit) *pres. part.* **nu·mer·at·ing** *past* and *past part.* **nu·mer·at·ed** *v.t.* to enumerate

nu·mer·a·tion (nu:məréiʃən, nju:məréiʃən) *n.* a system or process of counting or numbering ‖ the reading of number symbols in words [fr. L. *numeratio* (*numerationis*)]

nu·mer·a·tor (nú:məreitər, njú:məreitər) *n.* (*math.*) that part of a fraction, written above the denominator and separated from it by a horizontal or oblique line, which denotes the number of parts, specified by the denominator, that are taken of the whole, e.g. 2 in 2/3 [L.L. fr. *numerare*, to number]

nu·mer·i·cal (nu:mérik'l, nju:mérik'l) *adj.* pertaining to or denoting number, *numerical quantity, numerical value* [fr. Mod. L. *numericus*]

numerical analysis science of approximate quantitative solutions to problems with parameters for margins of error

numerical control automating control of machine operations through the use of a programmed perforated or magnetic tape *abbr.* **NC** —**numerically controlled** *adj.*

numerical taxonomy (*biol.*) classification and evaluation of plants and animals into groups based on their affinities involving quantitative measurements

nu·mer·ol·o·gy (nu:mərólədʒi:, nju:mərólədʒi:) *n.* the study of the hidden, magical significance of numbers [fr. L. *numerus*, number+Gk *logos*, discourse]

nu·mer·ous (nú:mərəs, njú:mərəs) *adj.* of large number, composed of many, *a numerous family, numerous worries* [fr. L. *numerosus*]

Nu·mid·i·a (nu:mídi:ə, nju:mídi:ə) an ancient territory of N. Africa roughly covering modern Algeria. It was a Roman province (46 B.C.–5th c. A.D.)

nu·mi·nous (nú:minəs, njú:minəs) **1.** *n.* (with 'the') supernatural presence **2.** *adj.* relating to a numen ‖ filling one with a sensation of the divine presence [NUMEN]

nu·mis·mat·ic (nu:mizmætik, nju:mizmætik) *adj.* of or relating to the study of coins or currency **nu·mis·mat·ics, nu·mis·ma·tist** (nu:mízmətist, nju:mízmətist), **nu·mis·ma·tol·o·gy** (nu:mizmətólədʒi:, nju:mizmətólədʒi:) *n.* [fr. F. *numismatique*]

num·mu·lite (nʌ́mjulait) *n.* a fossilized shell of a member of *Nummulitidae*, a family of marine protozoans, forming Eocene and Oligocene strata **num·mu·lit·ic** (nʌmjulítik) *adj.* [fr. L. *nummulus*, dim. of *nummus*, coin]

num·skull, numb·skull (nʌ́mskʌl) *n.* a stupid person

nun (nʌn) *n.* a woman belonging to a religious order, esp. one under vows of poverty, chastity and obedience and living in a convent [O.E. *nunne* fr. L.]

nun buoy a buoy made of two cones with a common base [fr. obs. *nun*, spinning top]

Nunc Di·mit·tis (nʌŋkdimítis) *n.* a canticle used in certain church services, a musical setting of the Song of Simeon (Luke ii, 29-32) [L.=now lettest thou (thy servant) depart]

nun·cha·kus (nú:ntʃakuːs) *n. pl.* hardwood sticks usually 14 in long and 1¼ in in diameter connected by a cone; used by Japanese as self-defense weapons or by police for crowd control

nun·ci·a·ture (nʌ́nʃi:ətʃuər) *n.* the office or term of office of a nuncio [fr. Ital. *nunziatura*]

nun·ci·o (nʌ́nʃi:ou) *n.* an ambassador or representative of the pope to a government or court [Ital.]

nun·cu·pate (nʌ́ŋkjupeit) *v.t.* to state (a will) orally, instead of in writing **nun·cu·pá·tion** *n.* **nún·cu·pa·tive** *adj.* [fr. L. *nuncupare* (*nuncupatus*), to declare]

Nu·ñez (nú:njes), Rafael (1825–94), Colombian writer and statesman, president (1880–2, 1884–8). He converted Colombia from federalism to centralism, with a strong government based on the Catholic Church. His administration provoked (1899) the Thousand Days War

nun·na·tion (nʌnéiʃən) *n.* the addition of a final *n* in the declension of certain nouns (e.g. in Arabic) [fr. L. *nunnatio* (*nunnationis*) fr. Arab *nun*, *n.*]

nun·ner·y (nʌ́nəri:) *pl.* **nun·ner·ies** *n.* a communal residence of nuns [prob. fr. O.F. *nonnerie*]

Nu·pe (nú:pei, njú:pei) *pl.* **Nu·pe, Nu·pes** *n.* a people of central W. Nigeria ‖ a member of this people ‖ their language (*KWA)

nu·plex (nú:pleks) *n.* a complex of factories using nuclear power

nup·tial (nʌ́pʃəl) **1.** *adj.* pertaining to marriage **2.** *n.* (pl., rhet.) a wedding, marriage [F. or fr. L. *nuptialis*]

Nu·rem·berg (núərəmbə:rg, njúərəmbə:rg) (*G.* Nürnberg), the leading manufacturing town (pop. 492,400) of N. Bavaria, West Germany, with large mechanical and electrical engineering, motor vehicle, bicycle, metal, toy, pencil and other industries. It was an important medieval trading center and a center of the German Renaissance. It gave its name to the Nazi anti-Semitic laws (1935) and was the scene of the trial of major Nazi war criminals (1945–6)

Nu·rey·ev (nuréijef), Rudolf Hametovich (1938–) Soviet ballet dancer, living in the West since 1961. One of the most celebrated male dancers in ballet history, he appeared with bal-

CONCISE PRONUNCIATION KEY: (**a**) æ, c*a*t; ɑ, c*a*r; ɔ f*aw*n; ei, sn*a*ke. (**e**) e, h*e*n; i:, sh*ee*p; iə, d*ee*r; ɛə, b*ea*r. (**i**) i, f*i*sh; ai, t*i*ger; ə:, b*i*rd. (**o**) o, *o*x; au, c*ow*; ou, g*oa*t; u, p*oo*r; ɔi, r*oy*al. (**u**) ʌ, d*u*ck; u, b*u*ll; u:, g*oo*se; ə, b*a*cillus; ju:, c*u*be. x, lo*ch*; θ, *th*ink; ð, bo*th*er; z, *Z*en; ʒ, cor*s*age; dʒ, sava*g*e; ŋ, ora*ng*utang; j, *y*ak; ʃ, *fi*sh; tʃ, fe*tch*; 'l, rabb*le*; 'n, redd*en*. Complete pronunciation key appears inside front cover.

let companies in Great Britain, the United States, Europe and Australia after leaving the Kirov Ballet. He is perhaps best known for his performances with Margot Fonteyn in productions of Great Britain's Royal Ballet such as 'Giselle' (1962) and 'Marguerite and Armand' (1963). His own productions include 'Raymonda' (1964), 'Swan Lake' (1964), 'The Nutcracker' (1967), and 'The Tempest' (1982). He also danced in modern works and appeared in films. He became director of the Paris Opéra Ballet (1982)

nurse (nə:rs) *n.* a person, usually a woman, trained to care for the sick or the infirm under the direction of a doctor ‖ a woman employed to look after young children ‖ a dry nurse ‖ a wet nurse ‖ an individual member of a species (of ant, bee etc.) whose function is to protect or care for the young of the species ‖ a tree planted to protect others during their growth [M.E. *norice, nurice* fr. O.F.]

nurse *pres. part.* **nurs·ing** *past* and *past part.* **nursed** *v.t.* to take care of, be a nurse to (children, the sick, infirm etc.) ‖ to suckle (an infant) ‖ to hold protectively in the arms or lap ‖ to take special care of in order to promote growth or development, *to nurse one's delphiniums* ‖ to try to cure, esp. by taking care, *to nurse a cold* ‖ to take care of or consume slowly or sparingly in order to maintain a reserve, *to nurse one's strength* ‖ to keep (a feeling etc.) alive in one's mind, *to nurse a grudge* ‖ (*billiards*) to keep (balls) close together for a series of caroms ‖ (*Br.*) to try to win electoral support in (a constituency) by taking an active interest in its affairs over a long period before contesting an election ‖ (*racing*) to keep close to (another horse) to prevent it from breaking clear, or to (the rail) in order to retain the inside position ‖ *v.i.* to be a nurse ‖ (of a woman) to suckle a child ‖ (of a child) to feed at the breast [fr. older *nurish, nourish* fr. O.F.]

nurse anesthetist a registered nurse trained to work under supervision of an anesthesiologist or physician in administering anesthetic agents to patients before and after surgery and obstetrical and other procedures

nurseling *NURSLING

nurse·maid (nə:rsmeid) *n.* a girl or young woman employed to look after children

nurse midwife registered nurse who, by virtue of added knowledge and skill, has extended the lawful limits of his or her practice into the care of mothers and babies throughout the maternity cycle

nurse practitioner a specially trained nurse licensed to perform some functions usu. performed by physicians

nurs·er·y (nə:rsəri:) *pl.* **nurs·er·ies** *n.* a room set apart for children in a house ‖ (*Br.*) a day nursery ‖ a nursery school ‖ a place where young plants or trees are grown for subsequent transplanting ‖ a place where young animals, e.g. fish, are raised ‖ a place or set of circumstances in which people acquire a certain training, *a nursery for budding politicians* [prob. fr. O.F. *noricerie*]

nurs·er·y·man (nə:rsəri:mən) *pl.* **nurs·er·y·men** (nə:rsəri:mən) *n.* a man who owns or works in a nursery (place where young plants or trees are grown)

nursery rhyme a poem or jingle for children. Most English examples date from the 17th c.

nursery school a place suitably equipped and staffed where children below school age are cared for, play and begin their social training

nursing bottle a bottle to hold milk etc., with a nipple, for feeding babies

nursing home a home where special care is provided for old people or for convalescents ‖ (*Br.*) a small hospital, usually under private management

nursing technician an orderly in a hospital

nurs·ling, nurse·ling (nə:rsliŋ) *n.* a baby, esp. in relation to its nurse [NURSE v.]

nur·tur·ance (nə:rtʃərəns) *n.* food, care, attention, and affection —**nurturant** *adj.*

nur·ture (nə:rtʃər) **1.** *n.* (*rhet.*) food, or whatever nourishes figuratively ‖ (*rhet.*) up bringing, training, *tender nurture of sensitive minds* **2.** *v.t. pres. part.* **nur·tur·ing** *past* and *past part.* **nur·tured** to provide for (growing things, e.g. children, plants etc.) those conditions which are favorable to their healthy growth [O.F. *nourture, nurture*]

Nu·sa Teng·ga·ra (nú:zəteŋgárə, njú:zəteŋgárə) the Lesser Sundas (*SUNDA ISLANDS, *TIMOR)

nut (nʌt) **1.** *n.* a dry, dehiscent or indehiscent one-celled fruit or seed consisting of a fleshy kernel (often edible) enclosed in a hard or tough shell or pericarp ‖ the kernel itself ‖ a piece of metal, usually polygonal, whose central hole has a screw thread which engages on a screw or bolt, to hold one thing to another ‖ (*naut.*) a projection on the shank of an anchor ‖ (*mus.*, in stringed instruments) the ebony ledge at the end of the fingerboard over which the strings pass ‖ (*mus.*) the piece located at the lower end of a bow by means of which the hairs are tightened ‖ (*pl., Br.*) a small size of domestic coal, *kitchen nuts* ‖ (*pop.*) a person behaving in a crazy way **a hard nut to crack** a difficult problem to solve ‖ a difficult person to deal with in the way one would wish **2.** *v.i. pres. part.* **nut·ting** *past* and *past part.* **nut·ted** to gather edible nuts [O.E. *hnutu*]

nu·ta·tion (nu:téiʃən, nju:téiʃən) *n.* the act of nodding the head (esp. involuntarily) ‖ curvature or change of position in the organs of a growing plant ‖(*astron.*) a periodic change in the direction of the earth's axis due to the joint attractive forces of the sun and moon ‖ a small variation in the motion of precession of a spinning top or gyroscope [fr. L. *nutatio (nutationis)*, a nodding]

nut·crack·er (nʌtkrækər) *n.* (*Br. esp. pl.*) an instrument for cracking nutshells, typically consisting of two hinged arms between which the nut is held and compressed ‖ *Nucifraga caryocatactes,* fam. *Corvidae,* a dark brown European bird with white speckles

nut·gall (nʌtgɔl) *n.* a nut like gall formed on trees, esp. the oak

nut·hatch (nʌthætʃ) *n.* any of various members of *Sittidae,* a family of active birds that creep over the branches and trunks of trees, downwards as well as up, and that hammer away at nuts they have wedged into the bark [M.E. *nuthak,* altered fr. *notehache* fr. *note, nut*+*hache,* axe]

nut·let (nʌtlit) *n.* a little nut ‖ the stone of a drupe

nut·meat (nʌtmi:t) *n.* the edible part of a nut

nut·meg (nʌtmeg) *n.* a hard seed, used as a spice, obtained from *Myristica fragrans,* an evergreen tropical tree cultivated in the Moluccas and the West Indies (*MACE) ‖ the tree itself [partial trans. of A.F. *nois mugue*]

nut·pick (nʌtpik) *n.* a small instrument with a sharp point, used to extract the kernels of nuts

nu·tri·a (nú:tri:ə, njú:tri:ə) *n.* the fur of the coypu [Span.=otter]

nu·tri·ent (nú:tri:ənt, njú:tri:ənt) **1.** *n.* a substance serving as food, esp. for plants **2.** *adj.* nourishing [fr. L. *nutriens* fr. *nutrire,* to nourish]

nu·tri·ment (nú:trimənt, njú:trimənt) *n.* something which nourishes [fr. L. *nutrimentum* fr. *nutrire,* to nourish]

nu·tri·tion (nu:tríʃən, nju:tríʃən) *n.* a nourishing or being nourished, esp. the process of feeding. In animals this involves ingestion, digestion, absorption and assimilation (*DIET). Green plants require only inorganic substances

(water, carbon dioxide and mineral salts) from which to manufacture their food [fr. L. *nutritio (nutritionis)* fr. *nutrire,* to nourish]

nu·tri·tious (nu:tríʃəs, nju:tríʃəs) *adj.* nourishing [fr. L. *nutritius, nutricius* fr. *nutrix (nutricis)*, nurse]

nu·tri·tive (nú:tritiv, njú:tritiv) *adj.* of or relating to nutrition ‖ nourishing [F. *nutritif (nutritive)*]

nuts-and-bolts (nʌtsændbóults) *n.* practical operative details —**nuts-and-bolts** *adj.*

nut·shell (nʌtʃel) *n.* the hard shell of a nut **in a nutshell** succinctly

nut·ty (nʌti:) *comp.* **nut·ti·er** *superl.* **nut·ti·est** *adj.* tasting like nuts ‖ producing nuts ‖ silly

nux vom·i·ca (nʌksvómikə) *pl.* **nux vom·i·ca** *n.* the poisonous seed of *Strychnos nux-vomica,* an East Indian tree, which yields strychnine ‖ the tree itself [fr. M.L. *nux,* nut+*vomere,* to vomit]

nuz·zle (nʌz'l) *pres. part.* **nuz·zling** ‖ *past* and *past part.* **nuz·zled** *v.t.* to make pushing movements with the nose against, or into ‖ *v.i.* to thrust or press the nose against something or someone ‖ to snuggle or nestle [M.E. *nosel* fr. NOSE]

NVA (*mil. abbr.*) of North Vietnamese Army during the U.S. military involvement in Vietnam, 1965–1975

NW, N. W. Northwest

N. Y. New York State

Ny·a·sa (ni:æsə) the former name of Lake Malawi

Ny·a·sa·land (ni:æsəlænd) the former name of Malawi

N. Y. C. New York City

nyc·ta·lo·pi·a (niktəlóupi:ə) *n.* a defect of vision consisting of abnormally poor vision in dim lighting conditions [fr. Gk *nuktalōpia* fr. *nux (nuktos),* night+*alaos,* blind+*ōps,* eye]

nyc·ti·trop·ic (niktitrópik) *adj.* showing nyctitropism

nyc·tit·ro·pism (niktítrəpizəm) *n.* (*bot.*) a night turning movement responding to a stimulus from one direction only, or greatest from one direction [fr. Gk *nux (nuktos),* night+*tropos,* a turn]

Nye·re·re (njerére), Julius Kambarage (1921–), Tanzanian statesman. As president and founder (1954) of the Tanganyika African National Union he organized the movement for self-government and led Tanganyika to independence (1961). He was president of Tanganyika (1962–4), and then president of Tanzania (1964–85)

ny·lon (náilon) *n.* any of several polymeric, thermoplastic amides formed into strong elastic thread by forcing a melt through fine jets ‖ the fabric made from this thread ‖ (*pl.*) stockings made of this [coined word used formerly as a trademark]

nymph (nimf) *n.* (*Gk* and *Rom. mythol.*) one of the lesser goddesses, portrayed as beautiful girls, inhabiting fountains, trees, rivers, mountains ‖ an insect in the stage between larva and imago in a species displaying complete metamorphosis. Nymphs are generally immobile and are sometimes enclosed in a cocoon [F. *nymphe* fr. L. fr. Gk *numphē,* bride]

nym·pho·ma·ni·a (nimfəméini:ə) *n.* excessive sexual desire in a woman or female animal

nym·pho·ma·ni·ac (nimfəméini:æk) *n.* a woman with nymphomania [fr. Gk *numphē,* bride+*mania,* madness]

Ny·sa (nísə) *NEISSE

nys·tag·mic (nistǽgmik) *adj.* of or relating to nystagmus

nys·tag·mus (nistǽgməs) *n.* rapid involuntary oscillation of the eyeballs, usually the result of brain or ear disease [Mod. L. fr. Gk *nustagmos,* drowsiness]

N. Z. New Zealand

EARLY NORTH SEMITIC	PHOENICIAN	EARLY HEBREW (GEZER)	EARLY GREEK	CLASSICAL GREEK	ETRUSCAN	EARLY LATIN	CLASSICAL LATIN
O	O	O	O	O	Early O	O	O

CURSIVE MAJUSCULE (ROMAN)	CURSIVE MINUSCULE (ROMAN)	ANGLO-IRISH MAJUSCULE	CAROLINE MINUSCULE	VENETIAN MINUSCULE (ITALIC)	N. ITALIAN MINUSCULE (ROMAN)
O	ठ	O	O	O	O

A. C. SYLVESTER, CAMBRIDGE, ENGLAND

Development of the letter O, beginning with the early North Semitic letter. Evolution of both the majuscule, or capital, letter O and the minuscule, or lowercase, letter o are shown.

O, o (ou) the 15th letter of the English alphabet ‖ the sound of O used to denote zero, *point o five* (.05)

O *OH

oaf (ouf) *pl.* **oafs, oaves** (ouvz) *n.* a stupid lout **óaf·ish** *adj.* [older *auf*, akin to O.N. *álfr*, elf]

O·a·hu (ouáhu:) an island (area 589 sq. miles, pop. 762,565) of Hawaii, the location of Honolulu and of the naval base of Pearl Harbor

oak (ouk) *n.* a member of *Quercus* or *Lithocarpus*, fam. *Fagaceae*, genera of deciduous or evergreen trees and shrubs native to the northern hemisphere and including some 500 species. Oaks yield some tannin and hard, durable wood ‖ this wood, used esp. in shipbuilding and furniture [O.E. *āc*]

oak apple a hard, round, brown gall formed on the leaf bud of oaks by various gallflies

Oak-Apple Day (*Br.*) May 29, the anniversary of Charles II's restoration, commemorating his escape from Cromwellian troops (Sept. 6, 1651) by hiding in an oak tree

oak·en (óukən) *adj.* (*rhet.*) made of oak

oak gall an oak apple

Oak·land (óuklənd) a port (pop. 339,288) in California, on San Francisco Bay: metallurgy, fruit and vegetable canning, shipbuilding

Oak·ley (óukli:), Annie (Phoebe Anne Oakley Mozee, 1860–1926), U.S. markswoman. As a star in Buffalo Bill's Wild West show she made holes in playing cards with bullets, firing from a long way off

Oaks, The a British classic horse race (founded in 1779) for three-year-old fillies, run at Epsom on the Friday after the Derby

oa·kum (óukəm) *n.* loose fiber obtained by shredding old, usually tarred, hemp rope and used to caulk ship seams etc. [O.E. *ācumbe, ācuma* fr. *a-*, out+*camb*, comb]

OAO (*abbr.*) for Orbiting Astronomical Observatory, an unmanned satellite for astronomical research; designed by Westinghouse Corporation

oar (or, our) **1.** *n.* a long, usually flattened shaft with a flattened blade at one end, used as a lever in propelling a boat, the oarlock being the fulcrum ‖ an oarsman **to put** (or **shove, stich**) **one's oar in** to intrude, esp. in conversation with advice or an expression of opinion **to rest** (or **lie, lay**) **on one's oars** to sit back and do nothing after a period of activity, out of contentment with what has already been achieved **2.** *v.t.* and *i.* to row [O.E. *ār*]

oar·lock (órlok, óurlok) *n.* a device, usually U-shaped, fastened to the side or gunwale of a boat so as to hold the oar and provide leverage for its action

oars·man (órzmən, óurzmən) *pl.* **oars·men** (órzmən, óurzmən) *n.* a rower, esp. a proficient rower

O.A.S. *ORGANIZATION OF AMERICAN STATES

OASDHI (*acronym*) for Old Age, Survivors, Disability, and Health Insurance Programs, Social Security programs providing monthly benefits to retired and disabled workers and their dependents and to survivors of insured workers

o·a·sis (ouéisis) *pl.* **o·a·ses** (ouéisi:z) *n.* an area in a desert made fertile by the presence of water. It may consist of a clump of date palms around a small spring, which is typical of the Sahara, or, like the oases made by the Nile and Euphrates, it may support large agricultural populations ‖ a quiet, peaceful place in the midst of turbulent surroundings [L. fr. Gk *ōasis*, a fertile spot, perh. fr. Egyptian]

oast (oust) *n.* a kiln used to dry hops [O.E. *āst*]

oast·house (óusthaus) *pl.* **oast·hous·es** (óusthəuziz) *n.* an oast ‖ (*Br.*) a building containing an oast, drying floor etc., and fitted with a chimney vent which can rotate with the direction of the wind

oat (out) *n.* (usually *pl.*) a member of *Avena*, fam. *Graminae*, a genus of wild and cultivated grasses of temperate regions having a much-branched, panicle inflorescence, esp. *A. sativa* of moist, temperate regions. Oats are sown in spring and winter like wheat, and used as food for humans and animals ‖ (*pl.*) the crop or its yield **to feel one's oats** to feel important and powerful ‖ to feel frisky [O.E. *āte*]

oat·cake (óutkeik) *n.* a thin unleavened cake, made from oatmeal

oat·en (óut'n) *adj.* of, or made of, the grain or straw of oats ‖ of, or made of, oatmeal

Oates, Joyce Carol (1938–), U.S. writer and critic. A prolific writer in many genres, she produced novels, short stories and plays, often dramatizing the 'phenomenon of violence and its aftermath, in ways not unlike those of the Greek dramatists.' Her novels include the trilogy 'A Garden of Earthly Delights' (1967), 'Expensive People' (1968) and 'them' (1969); as well as 'Wonderland' (1971), 'Childwold' (1976), 'Unholy Loves' (1979) and 'A Bloodsmoor Romance' (1982). Short-story collections include 'Wheel of Love' (1970) and 'A Sentimental Education' (1981), and she has produced two volumes of criticism: 'New Heaven, New Earth' (1974) and 'Contraries' (1981)

Oates (outs), Lawrence Edward Grace (1880–1912), British explorer. On the return journey from the South Pole on Scott's last expedition (1910–13) Oates, crippled by frostbite and believing that his companions would have a better chance of getting back without him, walked out of the tent into a blizzard, to certain death

Oates, Titus (1649–1705), English conspirator. He fabricated the Popish Plot (1678), a supposed Catholic plot to overthrow Charles II. Oates's perjury caused an anti-Catholic panic, in the course of which 35 innocent people were executed

oath (ouθ) *pl.* **oaths** (ouðz, ouθs) *n.* the invoking of God or some sacred or revered person or thing as witness of the truth of a statement or the binding nature of a promise ‖ the statement or promise itself ‖ a prescribed form used in making such a statement or promise ‖ a profane use of a sacred name or phrase **to take an oath** to make the solemn undertaking constituted by an oath **under oath** obliged by oath to state the truth or keep a promise [O.E. *āth*]

oat·meal (óutmi:l) *n.* meal prepared by the coarse grinding of oats ‖ rolled oats, made by running hulled seed (groats) between rollers in a steam chamber, which softens the grain ‖ porridge prepared from such oats ‖ a grayish beige color

O.A.U. *ORGANIZATION OF AFRICAN UNITY

Oa·xa·ca (wəháka) a southern Pacific state (area 36,820 sq. miles, pop. 2,361,700), of Mexico, incl. most of the Isthmus of Tehuantepec. Capital: Oaxaca. Chief agricultural products: corn, wheat, coffee, sugar, tobacco, fibers and tropical fruits. Mining: gold, silver, uranium, diamonds, onyx, and other deposits. There are remains of stone buildings from Pre-Columbian times

Oaxaca (or Oaxaca de Juárez) the capital (pop. 122,800) of the state of Oaxaca in S. Mexico, on the central plateau, surrounded by mountains: woolen serapes, mining (gold, silver), agriculture (chiefly coffee)

Ob (ɔb) a river (2,500 miles long) rising in the Altai Mtns, Mongolian Republic, and flowing north across W. Siberia to the Arctic Ocean (Gulf of Ob). With the Irtysh and lesser tributaries, it drains 1,125,000 sq. miles and provides 17,000 miles of navigable waterway (frozen Nov.–May). Chief port: Novosibirsk

O·ba·di·ah (oubədáiə) a Minor Prophet (c. 5th c. B.C.) of the Old Testament ‖ the Old Testament book attributed to him. It foretells the punishment of Edom

ob·bli·ga·to (ɔbligátou) **1.** *adj.* (*mus.*, of an accompanying melody or the instrument playing it) having an essential role in the piece and therefore not to be omitted **2.** *pl.* **ob·bli·ga·tos, ob·bli·ga·ti** (ɔbligáti:) *n.* (*mus.*) an obbligato accompaniment (cf. AD LIBITUM) [Ital.=obligatory]

ob·du·ra·cy (ɔbdərəsi:, ɔbdjərəsi:) *n.* the quality or state of being obdurate

ob·du·rate (óbdərit, óbdjərit) *adj.* unyielding, in opinion or feeling, to influences seeking to effect a change [fr. L. *obdurare (obduratus),* to harden]

o·be·ah (óubi:ə) *n.* a form of sorcery practiced by some Africans and West Indians [W. African]

o·be·di·ence (oubí:di:əns) *n.* submission of one's own will to the will, expressed or otherwise, of another or to an impersonal embodiment of authority, *obedience to the State* ‖ an instance of acting in such a way as to display this submission ‖ (*eccles.*) jurisdiction, esp. the spiritual authority of the Roman Catholic Church over Catholics ‖ the sphere of such jurisdiction **in obedience to** according to the instructions or ruling of, *in obedience to the dictates of conscience* [F. *obédience*]

o·be·di·ent (oubí:di:ənt) *adj.* submitting one's will ‖ (*rhet.*) not resisting, *obedient to the wind's force* [O.F. *obédient*]

o·bei·sance (oubéisəns, oubí:səns) *n.* (*rhet.*) a movement of the body towards the ground, e.g. a curtsy, salaam etc., expressing very great respect for, or submission to, someone **to do** (or **make, pay**) **obeisance to** (*rhet.*) to perform an act of homage to [F. *obéissance, obedience*]

ob·e·lisk (óbəlisk) *n.* a vertical stone shaft, quadrangular in cross section and tapering to a pyramidal apex, usually worked in one piece ‖ (*printing*) a dagger ‖ an obelus [L. *obeliscus* fr. Gk]

ob·e·lize (óbəlaiz) *pres. part.* **ob·e·liz·ing** *past* and *past part.* **ob·e·lized** *v.t.* (*printing*) to mark with an obelus [fr. Gk *obelizein*]

ob·e·lus (óbələs) *pl.* **ob·e·li** (óbəlai) *n.* the mark − or [÷] inserted in ancient manuscripts to denote that a word or passage is of doubtful authenticity [L. fr. Gk *obelos,* a spit]

O·ber·am·mer·gau (oubərámərgau) a village (pop. 4,876) in Bavaria, West Germany, where a Passion play is acted by the villagers every ten years, fulfilling a vow made (1634) in gratitude for deliverance from plague

O·ber·hau·sen (óubərhauz'n) a town (pop. 229,300) of North Rhine–Westphalia, West Germany, in the Ruhr: metallurgy, metalwork, chemicals, coal mining

O·ber·lin College (óubərlin) an educational institution founded (1833) in Ohio. It pioneered coeducation and was the first college to admit blacks on an equal footing with whites

o·bese (oubí:s) *adj.* (of a person) very fat [fr. L. *obedere (obesus),* to eat away]

o·bes·i·ty (oubí:siti:) *n.* (*med.*) the state of being obese [fr. L. *obesitas*]

o·bey (oubéi) *v.t.* to be obedient to (a person, a principle etc.) ‖ (*phys., econ., chem.* etc.) to act in conformity with, *it obeys the law of gravitation* ‖ *v.i.* to be obedient [M.E. *obeien* fr. F.]

ob·fus·cate (óbfəskeit, obfáskeit) *pres. part.* **ob·fus·cat·ing** *past* and *past part.* **ob·fus·cat·ed** *v.t.* (*rhet.*) to confuse or bewilder ‖ to obscure, make hard to understand **ob·fus·cá·tion** *n.* [fr. L. *obfuscare (obfuscatus),* to darken]

o·bi (óubi) *n.* obeah

obi *n.* a long, wide sash, tied at the back, worn by Japanese women [Jap.]

O·bie (óubi:) *n.* annual prize in various categories for excellence in off-Broadway theatrical productions *Cf* OFF-BROADWAY

o·biq·ui·ty (obíwiti:) *n.* (*optics*) the characteristic in wide-angle or oblique photography that portrays the terrain and objects at such an angle and range that details necessary for interpretation are seriously masked or are on a very small scale, rendering interpretation difficult or impossible

o·bit (óubit, óbit) *n.* an obituary

o·bi·ter dic·tum (óbitərdíktəm) *pl.* **o·bi·ter dic·ta** (óbitərdíktə) *n.* (*law*) an incidental observation made by a judge, not material to his judgment and hence not binding ‖ an incidental observation, esp. of a pithy or memorable nature [L.=(something) said by the way]

o·bit·u·ar·ese (oubìtʃu:ərí:z) *n.* language and writing style of obituaries

o·bit·u·ar·y (oubítʃu:eri:) **1.** *adj.* relating to or recording the death of someone, *an obituary notice* **2.** *pl.* **o·bit·u·ar·ies** *n.* a notice announcing a person's death, or an article about someone who has just died, esp. in a newspaper or journal [M.L. *obituarius* fr. *obire,* to die]

ob·ject (óbdʒikt) *n.* a perceptible body or thing ‖ a thing or conception towards which the action of the thinking mind, considered as subject, is directed ‖ (*phys.*) a source of light waves, of which an image may be formed by reflection or refraction ‖ an aim or purpose ‖ a person or thing exciting attention or emotion, *why is he the object of such strong dislike?* ‖ (*gram.*) a noun, or noun equivalent, towards which the action of a transitive verb is directed, or that is governed by a preposition **price** (**money** etc.) **is no object** price (money etc.) need not be considered as a limiting factor [fr. M.L. *objectum,* a thing thrown before (the mind)]

ob·ject (əbdʒékt) *v.i.* (usually with 'to') to be opposed, have an aversion, *to object to someone's behavior* ‖ (with 'to') to express opposition, *no one objected to the decision when it was made* ‖ *v.t.* to present or put forth as an objection to a statement, proposal etc. [fr. L. *objicere (objectus),* to throw in the way]

ob·ject ball (óbdʒikt) *n.* (*billiards, pool*) the ball struck by the cue ‖ any ball that may be struck by the cue ball

ob·ject glass (óbdʒikt) (*optics*) an objective

ob·jec·ti·fy (obdʒéktəfai) *pres. part.* **ob·jec·ti·fy·ing** *past* and *past part.* **ob·jec·ti·fied** *v.t.* to identify (an idea) with an external object

ob·jec·tion (əbdʒékʃən) *n.* an act of objecting ‖ a feeling of opposition, dislike ‖ a reason for objecting or statement of such reasons **ob·jéc·tion·a·ble** *adj.* unpleasant, causing offense, *an objectionable manner* ‖ open to objection **ob·jéc·tion·a·bly** *adv.* [F.]

ob·jec·tive (əbdʒéktiv) **1.** *adj.* of or pertaining to an object ‖ having a real, substantial existence external to an observer ‖ pertaining to an external object or event quite independent of the observer's emotions or imagination ‖ unbiased, *to take an objective view* ‖ (*gram.*) of the case of an object governed by transitive verbs or prepositions **2.** *n.* an aim or goal ‖ (*mil.*) a place to be captured, destroyed etc. ‖ (*gram.*) the objective case ‖ something having an existence external to an observer ‖ (*optics*) the principal image-forming device in an optical instrument. In a microscope or refracting telescope it consists of a lens or a system of lenses forming an image of the object at the focal plane of the eyepiece [fr. M.L. *objectivus*]

objective correlative a set of objects, a situation, or a chain of events which an artist uses to evoke at once in the reader or beholder a particular emotion [coined by T. S. Eliot (1919)]

ob·jec·tiv·ism (əbdʒéktivizəm) *n.* the doctrine which gives precedence to knowledge of objects over knowledge of self **ob·jéc·tiv·ist** *n.* [OBJECTIVE]

ob·jec·tiv·i·ty (obdʒektíviti:) *n.* the state or quality of being objective

object language *TARGET LANGUAGE

ob·ject lesson (óbdʒikt) an outstanding example to be followed or to be taken as a warning

ob·jec·tor (əbdʒéktər) *n.* someone who objects

ob·jet trou·vé (obdʒéi truvéi) *n.* (*Fr.*) (often italics) "found object," a natural, nonartist-made object of aesthetic value

ob·jur·gate (óbdʒərgeit) *pres. part.* **ob·jur·gat·ing** *past* and *past part.* **ob·jur·gat·ed** *v.t.* (*rhet.*) to reprove strongly **ob·jur·gá·tion** *n.* **ob·jur·ga·to·ry** (obdʒə́:rgətɔri:, obdʒə́:rgətouri:) *adj.* [fr. L. *objurgare (objurgatus),* to scold]

ob·late (óbleit) *n.* (*Roman Catholicism*) a layman who attaches himself to a monastery, and makes his possessions over to it **Ob·late** (*Roman Catholicism*) a member of certain religious orders [fr. M.L. *oblatus* fr. L. *offerre,* to offer]

ob·late (óbleit, obléit) *adj.* (*geom.,* of a spheroid) flattened at the poles (opp. PROLATE) [fr. M.L. *oblatus*]

Ob·la·tion (oubléiʃən) *n.* the sacramental offering of the bread and wine to God in the Eucharist **ob·la·tion** the act of offering something in a sacred service ‖ such an offering ‖ any offering made to a church, esp. for charitable purposes **ob·lá·tion·al** *adj.* [O.F.]

ob·la·to·ry (óblatɔri:, óblatouri:) *adj.* of oblation or an oblation [fr. L. *offerre (oblatus),* to offer]

ob·li·gate 1. (óbligeit) *v.t. pres. part.* **ob·li·gat·ing** *past* and *past part.* **ob·li·gat·ed** to place (someone) under a moral or legal obligation ‖ to cause (someone) to be indebted by rendering him a service **2.** (óbligit, óbligeit) *adj.* (*biol.,* e.g. of certain parasites) restricted to a particular condition (cf. FACULTATIVE) [fr. L. *obligare (obligatus)*]

ob·li·ga·tion (obligéiʃən) *n.* an obligating or being obligated ‖ a binding legal agreement or a moral responsibility ‖ something which a person is bound to do or not do as a result of such an agreement or responsibility ‖ the restricting power inherent in such an agreement or responsibility [O.F.]

ob·lig·a·to·ry (əblígətɔri:, əblígətouri:) *adj.* which must be done, as required by civil or moral law ‖ required by authority, *attendance is not obligatory* ‖ of or being an obligation [fr. L.L. *obligatorius*]

o·blige (əbláidʒ) *pres. part.* **o·blig·ing** *past* and *past part.* **o·bliged** *v.t.* to cause (someone) by physical or moral means to do something ‖ to cause (someone) to be indebted by rendering him a service, favor etc. ‖ to render a service or favor to (*law*) to bind (someone) by contract or promise ‖ (*law,* of a contract etc.) to bind (someone) ‖ (with 'to') to be bound by feelings of indebtedness ‖ *v.i.* (*pop.*) to contribute entertainment, *the chorus obliged with an extra song* [O.F. *obliger*]

ob·li·gee (oblidʒí:) *n.* (*law*) a person to whom a bond is given [OBLIGE]

o·blig·ing (əbláidʒiŋ) *adj.* helpful and accommodating to others [OBLIGE]

ob·li·gor (obligór) *n.* (*law*) a person bound by a bond [OBLIGE]

o·blique (əblí:k) *adj.* (*geom.,* of a line or plane surface) having a direction which makes an angle less or greater than a right angle with a specified line or surface of reference ‖ (*geom.,* of a solid figure) having an axis not perpendicular to the plane of the base ‖ slanting, diverging ‖ (*anat.*) neither parallel nor vertical to the longer axis of the body or limb, *an oblique muscle* ‖ (*bot.,* of a leaf) having unequal sides ‖ indirect, implied but not specified, *an oblique reference* ‖ (*gram.*) of other cases than the nominative and vocative [fr. L. *obliquus*]

oblique angle any angle less or greater than a right angle

ob·liq·ui·ty (əblíkwiti:) *pl.* **ob·liq·ui·ties** *n.* departure from sound moral principle or behavior, or an instance of this ‖ the state of being oblique ‖ the extent of divergence from a straight direction [F. *obliquité*]

obliquity of the ecliptic the angle between the planes of the earth's equator and the ecliptic orbit

ob·lit·er·ate (əblítəreit) *pres. part.* **ob·lit·er·at·ing** *past* and *past part.* **ob·lit·er·at·ed** *v.t.* to remove all trace of, destroy ‖ to make illegible ‖ to blot out from memory, knowledge etc. **ob·lit·er·á·tion** *n.* [fr. L. *obliterare (obliteratus),* to blot out]

ob·liv·i·on (əblívi:ən) *n.* the state of being completely forgotten, *the custom has fallen into oblivion* ‖ utter forgetfulness, *he is in a state of oblivion about what led up to the accident* ‖ unconsciousness [O.F.]

ob·liv·i·ous (əblívi:əs) *adj.* totally unaware, *oblivious of danger* ‖ (*rhet.*) forgetful, neglectful, *oblivious of his responsibilities* [fr. L. *obliviosus*]

ob·long (óblɔŋ, óblɒŋ) **1.** *adj.* of a rectangular or oval figure or body with greater length than breadth or of greater breadth than height **2.** *n.* such a figure or body [fr. L. *oblongus,* relatively long]

ob·lo·quy (óbləkwi:) *n.* the state of being thought ill of, disgrace ‖ expressions of shameful or abusive condemnation [fr. L.L. *obloquium,* contradiction]

ob·nox·ious (əbnókʃəs) *adj.* unpleasant, offensive [fr. L. *obnoxiosus*]

o·boe (óubou) *n.* (*mus.*) a woodwind instrument with a long, thin double reed and a range of 2½ octaves up from B flat below middle C ‖ an organ stop producing a similar reedy quality **ó·bo·ist** *n.* someone who plays the oboe [Ital. fr. F.]

ob·ol (ób'l) *n.* an ancient Greek coin (one sixth of a drachma) ‖ an ancient Greek unit of weight (0.71 grams) [fr. L. *obolus*]

ob·o·lus (óbələs) *pl.* **ob·o·li** (óbəlai) *n.* an obol (coin) [L.]

O·bo·te (oubóutei), Milton (1924–), Uganda statesman, the first prime minister of independent Uganda (1962–6). He became president (1966) after a crisis had overthrown the Kabaka of Buganda as president. He was ousted by Idi Amin in 1971, but reelected president Dec. 1980 after Amin's overthrow. Obote was overthrown again in July 1985

ob·o·vate (obóuveit) *adj.* (*bot.,* of a leaf) having the narrow end attached to the stalk [fr. L. *ob-,* inversely+OVATE]

ob·o·void (obóuvɔid) *adj.* (*bot.*) eggshaped, with the broad end at the top, *an obovoid persimmon* [fr. L. *ob-,* inversely+OVOID]

O·bre·gón (obregón), Álvaro (1880–1928), Mexican general and president of the Republic (1920–4) who advanced the Revolution by implementing a program of political, social and economic reform. Reelected in 1928, he was assassinated before he could resume office

O·bre·no·vić (oubrénəvitʃ) a Serbian dynasty which ruled Serbia (1817–42 and 1858–1903), founded by Miloš Obrenović. Its members carried on a bitter feud with the Karageorgevic dynasty

Obrenović, Miloš *MILOŠ OBRENOVIĆ

ob·scene (əbsíːn) adj. of that which depraves, esp. of that which offends or wounds the imagination in sexual matters ‖ offensive, revolting [fr. F. obscène or L. obscenus]

ob·scen·i·ty (əbséniti:, əbsíːniti:) pl. **ob·scen·i·ties** n. the state or quality of being obscene ‖ (usually pl.) an instance of this, esp. an obscene utterance [fr. L. obscenitas or F. obscénité]

ob·scu·rant (əbskjúərənt) 1. n. an obscurantist 2. adj. obscurantist **ob·scu·rant·ism** (ɒbskjuəræntizem, əbskjúərəntiʒəm) n. the practices and beliefs of an obscurantist **ob·scu·rant·ist** 1. n. someone who opposes the development of new ideas 2. adj. of an obscurantist [fr. L. obscurans (obscurantis) fr. obscurare, to darken]

ob·scu·ra·tion (ɒbskjuréiʃən) n. an obscuring or being obscured [fr. L. obscuratio (obscurationis), fr. obscurare, to obscure]

ob·scure (əbskjúər) comp. **ob·scur·er** superl. **ob·scur·est** adj. dim, insufficiently lit ‖ difficult to see, e.g. through insufficient light or because partially covered by mist, fog etc. ‖ difficult to understand through insufficient information or abstruse expression etc. ‖ (of places) remote, out-of-the-way ‖ (of people) not attracting attention, not known to people at large ‖ indistinctly heard [O.F. obscur]

ob·scure pres. part. **ob·scur·ing** past and past part. **ob·scured** v.t. to make obscure ‖ to hide from view ‖ to dim the importance or glory of [fr. OBSCURE adj. or L. obscurare]

ob·scu·ri·ty (əbskjúəriti) pl. **ob·scu·ri·ties** n. the state or quality of being obscure ‖ something that is obscure [F. obscurité fr. L.]

ob·se·cra·tion (ɒbsikréiʃən) n. a supplication or entreaty, esp. in the form of a prayer [fr. L. obsecratio (obsecrationis) fr. obsecrare, to make sacred]

ob·se·quies (óbsikwi:z) pl. n. rites and ceremonies attaching to a funeral [A.F. obsequie fr. M.L. obsequiae]

ob·se·qui·ous (əbsíːkwi:əs) adj. (of behavior or attitude) so self-abasing as to lack a proper degree of personal dignity [fr. L. obsequiosus]

ob·serv·a·ble (əbzáːrvəb'l) adj. capable of being observed ‖ worthy of being observed

ob·serv·ance (əbzáːrvəns) n. the act of obeying a command, law, rule etc. ‖ the keeping of a custom, day of obligation etc. ‖ Lenten observance ‖ a ceremonial keeping, a nationwide observance of two minutes' silence ‖ (Roman Catholicism) a set of regulations for members of various religious orders ‖ (pl.) the ceremonies or rites performed in keeping a religious feast, custom etc. [F.]

ob·serv·an·cy (əbzáːrvənsi) n. the quality of being observant [fr. L. observantia]

ob·serv·ant (əbzáːrvənt) 1. adj. giving careful attention ‖ quick to observe ‖ strict in observance 2. n. **Ob·serv·ant** a member of the Franciscan friars observing the stricter rule of the order (cf. CONVENTUAL) [F.]

ob·ser·va·tion (ɒbzərvéiʃən) n. an observing or being observed ‖ the faculty of observing something observed or learned from observing ‖ an act of scientifically observing and recording e.g. a natural phenomenon, often using precision instruments ‖ a record so made ‖ an expression of an opinion **ob·ser·va·tion·al** adj. of or based on scientific observation [fr. L. observatio (observationis) fr. observare, to observe]

observation car a railroad lounge car with especially large windows to give passengers a good view of the scenery. It is usually the last car of the train

ob·serv·a·to·ry (əbzáːrvətɔ:ri, əbzáːrvətɔ:uri:) pl. **ob·serv·a·to·ries** n. a room or building sheltering instruments (telescopes, chronometers etc.) used by observers studying heavenly bodies ‖ a room or building for the study of other (e.g. meteorological) natural phenomena ‖ a structure which by its position commands an extensive view [fr. F. observatoire]

ob·serve (əbzáːrv) pres. part. **ob·serv·ing** past and past part. **ob·served** v.t. to look at with attention ‖ to comply with (a command, custom, law etc.) ‖ to celebrate ceremonially ‖ to watch or make a scientific measurement of with instruments, to observe an eclipse ‖ to perceive,

notice, come to know by seeing ‖ to comment ‖ v.i. to note attentively ‖ (with 'on' or 'upon') to comment ‖ to make observations with a precision instrument [F. observer]

ob·sess (əbsés) v.t. to occupy or engage the mind of (someone) to an inordinate degree, he is obsessed by the idea that war is imminent [fr. L. obsidere (obsessus), to besiege]

ob·ses·sion (əbséʃən) n. the state of being obsessed ‖ something or someone that obsesses **ob·ses·sion·al, ob·ses·sive** adjs of, being or causing an obsession [fr. L. obsessio (obsessionis) fr. obsidere, to obsess]

obsessive-compulsive neurosis a neurosis in which the sufferer feels compelled to think or do things which appear nonsensical and often alien to his personality. If a compulsion is resisted, the sufferer is unable to relax or sleep

ob·sid·i·an (əbsídi:ən) n. (mineral.) a dark colored, usually black, hard vitreous lava, resembling glass, used as a gemstone [fr. L. obsidianus for obsianus]

obsidian dating (geol.) the establishment of the age of an object by measurement of the rate of its surface hydration

ob·so·les·cence (ɒbsəlés'ns) n. the state of being virtually obsolete or the process of becoming obsolete ‖ (biol.) the process of becoming obsolescent or the state of being obsolescent [fr. L. obsolescens (obsolescentis) fr. obsolescere, to grow old]

ob·so·les·cent (ɒbsəlés'nt) adj. becoming obsolete ‖ (biol., of an organ, feature, characteristic, species etc.) slowly vanishing, vestigial [fr. L. obsolescens (obsolescentis) fr. obsolescere, to grow old]

ob·so·lete (óbsəli:t, ɒbsəli:t) adj. no longer in use, practice or favor, out-of-date ‖ (biol., of a plant or animal organ) rudimentary or vestigial as compared with corresponding organs in related species [fr. L. obsolescere (obsoletus), to grow old]

ob·sta·cle (óbstək'l) n. an obstruction, esp. one which prevents a forward movement or course of action, an obstacle to success [O.F.]

obstacle race a race in which runners must negotiate contrived obstacles

ob·stet·ric (ɒbstétrik) adj. (med.) pertaining to obstetrics **ob·stet·ri·cal** adj. [fr. Mod. L. obstetricus fr. obstetrix, midwife]

ob·ste·tri·cian (ɒbstitríʃən) n. a physician who specializes in obstetrics [fr. L. obstetricia, midwifery]

ob·stet·rics (ɒbstétriks) n. the branch of medical practice which is concerned with the care of mothers before, during and immediately after childbirth [OBSTETRIC]

ob·sti·na·cy (óbstinəsi) n. the quality or state of being obstinate [fr. M. L. obstinatia]

ob·sti·nate (óbstinit) adj. (of people) stubbornly adhering to an opinion or purpose ‖ (of people) stubbornly refusing to concede to reasonable arguments ‖ (of animals or things) stubbornly resisting attempts at controlling or manipulating, obstinate weeds ‖ (med.) stubbornly unresponsive to treatment, an obstinate case of malaria [fr. L. obstinare (obstinatus), to persist]

ob·strep·er·ous (əbstrépərəs) adj. noisily resisting control or defying commands [fr. L. obstreperus, noisy]

ob·struct (əbstrʌkt) v.t. to prevent or greatly impede (something) by placing an obstacle in its path ‖ to block from sight ‖ to close or practically close (a passage), a tumor obstructed the duodenum ‖ to hinder (a person or his action or purpose) by creating difficulty or opposition ‖ to practice obstruction, esp. in parliamentary or legislative procedure ‖ v.i. to hinder, impede [fr. L. obstruere (obstructus), to build against]

ob·struc·tion (əbstrʌkʃən) n. an obstructing or being obstructed ‖ something which obstructs ‖ prevention of legislative enactment by filibuster **ob·struc·tion·ism, ob·struc·tion·ist** ns [fr. L. obstructio (obstructionis) fr. obstruere, to build against]

ob·struc·tive (əbstrʌktiv) adj. of, being or producing an obstruction [fr. L. obstruere (obstructus), to build against]

ob·struc·tor (əbstrʌktər) n. someone or something that obstructs [fr. L. obstruere (obstructus), to build against]

ob·tain (əbtéin) v.t. to become the possessor of, secure for oneself or another ‖ v.i. (rhet.) to be usual, the custom still obtains in some districts **ob·tain·a·ble** adj. which can be obtained [M.E. obteine fr. F. fr. L.]

ob·tect·ed (ɒbtéktid) adj. (zool., of pupae) encased in a horny substance (holding the wings and legs to the body) ‖ (zool.) marked by such an encasing [fr. L. obtegere (obtectus), to cover up]

ob·trude (əbtrúːd) pres. part. **ob·trud·ing** past and past part. **ob·trud·ed** v.t. (with 'on' or 'upon') to force (someone or something) upon someone's attention, esp. unwarrantably [fr. L. obtrudere]

ob·tru·sion (əbtrúːʒən) n. an obtruding ‖ that which obtrudes [fr. L. obtrusio (obtrusionis) fr. obtrudere, to obtrude]

ob·tru·sive (əbtrúːsiv) adj. obtruding or tending to obtrude [fr. L. obtrudere (obtrusus), to obtrude]

ob·tu·rate (óbtəreit, ɒbtjəreit) pres. part. **ob·tu·rat·ing** past and past part. **ob·tu·rat·ed** v.t. to close (the breech of a gun) so as to prevent the escape of gas ‖ (esp. med., anat.) to close, obstruct (an aperture, passage etc.) [fr. L. obturare (obturatus), to stop up]

ob·tu·ra·tor (óbtəreitər, ɒbtjəreitər) n. (esp. med., anat.) something which obturates ‖ a device which obturates a gun [M.L.]

ob·tuse (əbtúːs, əbtjúːs) adj. (math.) of an angle greater than 90° but less than 180° ‖ not keenly perceptive or sensitive, an obtuse mind ‖ not acutely perceived, an obtuse pain ‖ (biol., of a plant or animal part) blunt-ended [fr. L. obtundere (obtusus), to blunt]

ob·verse (óbvəːrs, ɒbvɔ́ːrs) 1. adj. being a counterpart ‖ turned towards the spectator (opp. REVERSE) ‖ (biol.) having a base narrower than the apex 2. n. the principal surface of a coin, medal etc. (opp. REVERSE) ‖ the other side of a question or statement ‖ (logic) an inference made by denying the opposite of an affirmation [fr. L. obvertere (obversus), to turn towards]

ob·ver·sion (ɒbvɔ́ːrʒən, ɒbvɔ́ːrʃən) n. (logic) the act of inferring the obverse [fr. L. obversio (obversionis) fr. obvertere, to turn towards]

ob·vert (ɒbvɔ́ːrt) v.t. (logic) to make (an inference) by obversion [fr. L. obvertere]

ob·vi·ate (óbvi:eit) pres. part. **ob·vi·at·ing** past and past part. **ob·vi·at·ed** v.t. to remove, get rid of (a difficulty etc.) [fr. L. obviare (obviatus), to meet]

ob·vi·ous (óbvi:əs) adj. not requiring proof or demonstration, self-evident ‖ easily seen, attracting immediate attention ‖ (pop.) undesirably prominent [fr. L. obvius, in the way]

Ob·wal·den (óbvaldən) *UNTERWALDEN

OC (med. abbr.) for oral contraceptive

OCA (abbr.) for Office of Consumer Affairs (which see)

oc·a·ri·na (ɒkəríːnə) n. a small egg-shaped musical instrument, usually of metal or plastic, with finger holes, giving a mellow whistling tone [fr. Ital. oca, goose]

O'Ca·sey (oukéisi:), Sean (1884–1964), Irish playwright. His best-known plays, e.g. 'Juno and the Paycock' (1925) and 'The Plough and the Stars' (1926), are based on the life of the urban Irish working class, in the context of contemporary political events

Occam, William of *WILLIAM OCCAM

oc·ca·sion (əkéiʒən) 1. n. a set of circumstances associated with a point in time, we met on several occasions ‖ such a set of circumstances viewed as having special importance, it will be a great occasion or as being an opportunity or cause, an occasion for rejoicing on occasion from time to time, when the circumstances require to rise to the occasion to act with the degree of skill, generosity etc. required by the special circumstances in which someone is placed 2. v.t. to cause, directly or indirectly **oc·ca·sion·al** adj. occurring at irregular intervals of some length ‖ directly related to a special occasion, an occasional poem by the poet laureate ‖ designed for, and used, only on particular occasions, an occasional table [fr. L. occasio (occasionis) fr. occidere, to fall down]

oc·ca·sion·al·ism (əkéiʒən'lizəm) n. (philos.) the doctrine (e.g. as put forward by Malebranche) that mind and body are separate entities which interact only by the intervention of God **oc·ca·sion·al·ist** n. [OCCASIONAL]

oc·ca·sion·al·ly (əkéiʒən'li:) adv. at irregular intervals of some length [OCCASIONAL]

Oc·ci·den·tal (ɒksidént'l) 1. n. a member of a people living in the Occident 2. adj. of or relating to the Occident or an Occidental [F.]

Oc·ci·dent, the (óksidənt) n. (hist., politics, rhet.) originally Europe as opposed to Asia (the Orient); now extended to America and to other parts of the world peopled by those of European descent (opp. ORIENT) [F.]

oc·cip·i·tal (ɒksípit'l) *adj.* pertaining to the occiput [fr. L.L. or M.L. *occipitalis*] **oc·ci·put** (ɒ́ksəpʌt) *pl.* **oc·ci·puts, oc·cip·i·ta** (ɒksípitə) *n.* the back part of the skull of a vertebrate or insect [L.]

oc·clude (əklú:d) *pres. part.* **oc·clud·ing** *past and past part.* **oc·clud·ed** *v.t.* to close up (a passage) ‖ to keep (something) from passing through a passage ‖ (*chem.*) to adsorb and retain (esp. gases) ‖ (*meteorol.*) to cut off from contact with the surface of the earth, and force up by the convergence of a cold front on a warm one ‖ (*dentistry*) to cause (the counterpart tooth surfaces of the upper and lower jaw) to close against one another ‖ *v.i.* (*dentistry*, of the counterpart tooth surfaces of the upper and lower jaw) to close against one another ‖ (*meteorol.*) to become occluded [fr. L. *occludere*, to shut up]

oc·clu·sion (əklú:ʒən) *n.* an occluding or being occluded ‖ (*chem.*) the act or process by which some solid surfaces build up a local high concentration of the molecules of a gas or solute with which they are in contact (*ADSORPTION*) ‖ (*meteorol.*) a front, wind, storm etc. that has been occluded [fr. L. *occlusio* (*occlusionis*) fr. *occludere*, to shut up]

oc·cult (əkʌ́lt, ɒ́kʌlt) **1.** *adj.* beyond the range of normal perception ‖ secret, mysterious, esoteric ‖ dealing with magic, alchemy, astrology etc., *the occult sciences* **2.** *n.* (with 'the') that which is occult, the supernatural [fr. L. *occulere* (*occultus*), to cover over]

oc·cult (əkʌ́lt) *v.t.* (*astron.*) to obstruct the view of (a heavenly body) by passing between it and the observer on the earth ‖ *v.i.* (*astron.*) to become hidden from sight **oc·cul·tá·tion** *n.* (*astron.*) an occulting, esp. of a star or planet by the moon fr. L. *occultare*, to hide]

occulting light a light cut off at regular intervals, used e.g. as a lighthouse beacon or channel marker

oc·cult·ism (əkʌ́ltizəm) *n.* occult beliefs or practices [OCCULT *adj.*]

oc·cu·pan·cy (ɒ́kjupənsi) *pl.* **oc·cu·pan·cies** *n.* a taking or retaining possession by settling in or on something ‖ a residing or being resided in ‖ the act of becoming an occupant ‖ (*law*) the establishing of a right of ownership by taking possession of something which has no owner [OCCUPANT]

oc·cu·pant (ɒ́kjupənt) *n.* someone holding temporary or permanent rights of ownership or tenancy over a place or building which he occupies ‖ someone who occupies a particular space, position etc. ‖ (*law*) a person who has established his right by taking possession of ownerless land or property [fr. L. *occupans* (*occupantis*) fr. *occupare*, to occupy]

oc·cu·pa·tion (ɒkjupéiʃən) *n.* an occupying or being occupied, esp. by a military force ‖ a holding in one's possession, esp. as a resident or tenant ‖ an activity by which one earns one's living or fills one's time, or an instance of this **oc·cu·pá·tion·al** *adj.* arising from or pertaining to one's occupation or an occupation [F.]

Occupational Safety and Health Administration (*abbr.* O.S.H.A.) an agency of the U.S. Department of Labor established (1970) by Congress in the Occupational Safety and Health Act 'to assure so far as possible every working man and woman in the nation safe and healthful working conditions.' OSHA inspectors make frequent surprise inspections of workplaces to see that basic standards are adhered to; violators are fined. Regulations include standards on worker exposure to various toxic materials as well as job safety

occupational therapy (*med.*) a method of treatment employing prescribed mental or physical activities (e.g. rugmaking), used esp. in cases of mental illness

oc·cu·pi·er (ɒ́kjupaiər) *n.* (*Br.*) someone in possession of a house, shop, land etc.) as owner or tenant [OCCUPY]

oc·cu·py (ɒ́kjupai) *pres. part.* **oc·cu·py·ing** *past and past part.* **oc·cu·pied** *v.t.* to take, or have, possession of by settling in or on, esp. as resident or tenant ‖ to reside in ‖ to take or retain possession of by military force ‖ to fill (a space or period of time) ‖ (of someone) to fill (a position ‖ to keep (one's mind) busy ‖ to keep employed [fr. O.F. *occuper* fr. L.]

oc·cur (əkə́:r) *pres. part.* **oc·cur·ring** *past and past part.* **oc·curred** *v.i.* to happen, to be at a point in time or during a period of time, *it is not likely to occur this year* ‖ to be found at a place or

within a region, *these plants rarely occur in this country* ‖ (of an idea) to come into the conscious mind [fr. L. *occurrere*, to run toward]

oc·cur·rence (əkə́:rəns, əkʌ́rəns) *n.* the fact, act or process of occurring ‖ something which occurs [fr. older *occurrent* fr. F.]

o·cean (óuʃən) *n.* the part (seven tenths) of the earth's surface which consists of salt water ‖ one of its chief expanses, *the Atlantic Ocean* ‖ any great expanse, *an ocean of sand* [fr. F. *océan* fr. L. fr. Gk *ōkeanos*]

oceanaut *AQUANAUT

ocean engineer an engineer who deals with equipment and techniques for the study of the oceans —**ocean engineering** *n.*

O·ce·an·i·a (ouʃi:ǽni:ə, ouʃi:úni:ə) collective name for the islands of the South Seas. They are mainly volcanic or project as coral reefs. Unlike the Malay Archipelago, New Zealand or the Aleutians, they are not considered as belonging to the Asian, Australian or American continents. Oceania is divided into Micronesia, Melanesia and Polynesia

O·ce·an·i·an (ouʃi:ǽini:ən, ouʃi:úni:ən) **1.** *n.* a native of Oceania **2.** *adj.* pertaining to Oceania or its inhabitants

o·ce·an·ic (ouʃi:ǽnik) *adj.* of, relating to or found in the ocean **O·ce·an·ic** *adj.* Oceanian ‖ of the Austronesian language family [fr. M.L. or Mod. L. *oceanicus*]

o·ce·an·ics (ouʃi:ǽniks) *n.* scientific study of the life and products of oceans

O·ce·a·nid (ousí:ənid) *pl.* **O·ce·a·nids, O·ce·an·i·des** (ousi:ǽnidi:z) *n.* (Gk *mythol.*) one of the sea nymphs, daughters of Oceanus [fr. Gk *ōkeanis* (*ōkeanidos*)]

o·cea·nog·ra·pher (ouʃənɒ́grəfər) *n.* someone who specializes in oceanography

o·cea·no·graph·ic (ouʃənəgrǽfik) *adj.* of or relating to oceanography **o·cea·no·gráph·i·cal** *adj.*

o·cea·nog·ra·phy (ouʃənɒ́grəfi:) *n.* the science concerned with the study of the ocean. It includes distribution, biology, chemical composition, currents, the physiography of the ocean floor, and the nature of sea bottom deposits [fr. Gk *ōkeanos*, ocean+*graphos*, written]

o·cea·nol·o·gy (ouʃi:ænɒ́lədʒi:) *n.* the study of all aspects of the ocean and its environment, including plant and animal life —**oceanologic** or **oceanological** *adj.* —**oceanologically** *adv.* —**oceanologist** or **oceanographer** *n.*

O·ce·a·nus (ousí:ənəs) (*Gk mythol.*) one of the Titans, and a personification of the waters of the earth

o·cel·lar (ousélər) *adj.* pertaining to an ocellus [fr. L. *ocellus*, dim. of *oculus*, eye]

oc·el·lat·ed (ɒ́səleitid) *adj.* having ocelli ‖ like an eye [fr. L. *ocellus*, dim. of *oculus*, eye]

oc·cel·lus (ouséləs) *pl.* **o·cel·li** (ousélai) *n.* (*zool.*) a simple eye or eyespot found in many lower animals ‖ (*zool.*) one of the simple eyes forming a compound eye ‖ (*zool.*) an eyelike marking in certain insects, birds etc. [L. dim. of *oculus*, eye]

o·ce·lot (óusəlɒt,ósəlɒt) *n. Felis pardalis,* fam. *Felidae,* a wildcat (up to 3 ft in length), having gray or yellow fur with dark stripes and spots. It is native to S. North America and South America and inhabits forests, feeding on birds and rodents ‖ its pelt or fur [F. fr. Mex. *tlalocelotl* fr. *tlalli,* field+*ocelotl,* jaguar]

o·cher, o·chre (óukər) *n.* a yellow or red form of hydrated ferric oxide Fe₂O₃, occurring naturally and used as a pigment ‖ the color of yellow ocher [F. *ocre* fr. L. fr. Gk]

o·cher·ous (óukərəs) *adj.* of, like or containing ocher ‖ of the color ocher [fr. Mod. L. *ochreus*]

och·loc·ra·cy (ɒklɒ́krəsi:) *n.* rule by the mob **och·lo·crat** (ɒ́kləkræt) *n.* someone who advocates or participates in ochlocracy **och·lo·crát·ic** *adj.* [F. *ochlocratie* fr. Gk]

O·cho·a (ɔtʃɔ́ə), Severo (1905–), Spanish-U.S. physician and biochemist, co-winner (with Arthur Kornberg) of the 1959 Nobel prize in medicine, for discovering the enzyme system that led to the synthesis of compounds resembling naturally occurring ribonucleic acid (RNA)

o·chra·tox·in (ɒkrətɒ́ksin) *n.* (*chem.*) a poisonous substance produced by the plant fungus *Aspergillus ochraceus*

ochre *OCHER

ochrea *OCREA

o·chre·ous (óukərəs) *adj.* ocherous [fr. Mod. L. *ochreus*]

o·chrous (óukrəs) *adj.* ocherous [OCHER]

Ochs (ɒks), Adolph Simon (1858–1935), U.S. journalist who, as owner (from 1896) of the New York Times, made it one of the world's greatest newspapers. He introduced rotogravure printing of pictures, a book review supplement, and (1913) the New York Times Index, the only complete U.S. newspaper index

o'clock (əklɒ́k) *adv.* by the clock ‖ at a position in relation to a person or observer thought of as being at the center of a clockface with the numeral 12 directly ahead or above, *the target is at 2 o'clock from the church steeple* [contr. for 'of the clock']

O'Con·nell (oukón'l), Daniel (1775–1847), Irish national leader. A lawyer, he campaigned successfully for Catholic emancipation (1829), but his movement to repeal the Act of Union proved too moderate to be effective

O'Con·nor (oukɒ́nər), Feargus Edward (1794–1855), Irish radical politician, one of the leaders of Chartism

O'Connor, Sandra Day (1930–) U.S. Supreme Court justice, the first woman to be appointed. Before being named to the court by President Reagan (1981), she served as Arizona state senate Republican majority leader (1972–4) and as a judge on the Maricopa County (Ariz.) Superior Court (1974–9) and the Arizona Court of Appeals (1979–81). A conservative except in some defendants' rights cases such as *Tibbs v. Florida* (1982), upholding double jeopardy, and *Arizona v. Rumsey* (1984), concerning the death penalty, she also wrote the majority opinion in *Ford v. Equal Employment Opportunity Commission* (1982) and the dissenting opinion in *Akron v. Akron Center* (1983)

OCR (*computer abbr.*) for optical character recognition, a computer's capacity to read written material

oc·re·a, och·re·a (ɒ́kri:ə, óukri:ə) *pl.* **oc·re·ae, och·re·ae** (ɒ́kri:i:, óukri:i:) (*bot.*) a sheath formed around a stem by a stipule or the union of two stipules **óc·re·ate** *adj.* [L.=a legging]

Oct. October

oc·ta·chord (ɒ́ktəkɔrd) *n.* a musical instrument with eight strings ‖ a system of eight tones, e.g. on the diatonic scale [L.L. *octachordus* fr. Gk *oktō,* eight+*chordē,* chord]

oc·tad (ɒ́ktæd) *n.* a group of eight [fr. L. *octas* (*octadis*) fr. Gk]

oc·ta·gon (ɒ́ktəgɒn) *n.* (*geom.*) a plane figure having eight sides ‖ an object or building having eight sides [fr. L. *octagonos* fr. Gk]

oc·tag·o·nal (ɒktǽgən'l) *adj.* being an octagon [fr. Mod. L. *octogonalis*]

oc·ta·he·dral (ɒktəhí:drəl) *adj.* of or being an octahedron

oc·ta·he·drite (ɒktəhí:drait) *n.* (*mineral.*) anatase [fr. L.L. *octahedros* fr. Gk]

oc·ta·he·dron (ɒktəhí:drən) *pl.* **oc·ta·he·drons, oc·ta·he·dra** (ɒktəhí:drə) *n.* (*geom.*) a solid figure with eight plane faces, usually equilateral triangles [fr. Gk *octahedron,* eight-sided]

oc·tam·e·ter (ɒktǽmitər) **1.** *adj.* (of a line of poetry) containing eight measures or feet **2.** *n.* such a line [L. fr. Gk]

oc·tane (ɒ́ktein) *n.* (*chem.*) any of various isomeric liquid paraffin hydrocarbons having the formula C_8H_{18} ‖ octane number [fr. Gk *octō,* eight]

octane number (of a fuel) the percentage by volume of isooctane in a mixture of this and normal heptane which matches in knocking properties a fuel under test. Knocking decreases as the octane number increases

oc·tant (ɒ́ktənt) *n.* an eighth of the circumference of a circle ‖ the eighth part of a circle as bounded by this arc and two radii ‖ (*astron.*) one of the eight parts of space divided by three planes intersecting at right angles ‖ (*astron.*) the position of a heavenly body when it is 45° distant from a reference point ‖ (*naut.*) an instrument like a sextant, but having 45 degrees on the arc [fr. L.L. *octans* (*octantis*), a halfquadrant fr. *octo,* eight]

Oc·ta·teuch (ɒ́ktətu:k, ɒ́ktətju:k) *n.* the first eight books of the Old Testament [fr. L.L. *octateuchus* fr. Gk]

oc·tave (ɒ́ktiv,ɒ́kteiv) **1.** *n.* (*mus.*) the note having twice or one half the frequency of a given note, i.e. a note eight steps above or below a given note in the diatonic scale, inclusive of both notes ‖ (*mus.*) the interval between these outside notes ‖ (*mus.*) a combination of these notes ‖ an organ stop sounding a note eight steps above the note played ‖ (*poetry*) a stanza of eight lines, e.g. ottava rima ‖ the first eight lines of a sonnet ‖ (*fencing*) the eighth parrying position ‖ (ókteiv) the eighth day, including the festival itself, after a church festival ‖ (ókteiv) the week after the festival **2.** *adj.* consisting of eight parts or an octave ‖ (*mus.*) producing tones an octave higher, *an octavo stop* [F.]

octave coupler (*mus.*) a coupler attached to the keyboard of an organ, which connects each note with its octave

Oc·ta·vi·a (pktéiviːə) (c. 70–11 B.C.), sister of Augustus, wife of Mark Antony

Octavia (42–62), daughter of Claudius I and first wife of Nero, who put her to death

Oc·ta·vi·an (pktéiviːən) (Octavianus) the name of Augustus before he became emperor

oc·ta·vo (pktéivou, pktáːvou) (*abbr.* 8vo) *n.* the size of a book leaf formed by folding a sheet three times, giving eight leaves or 16 pages ‖ paper of this size ‖ a book having pages of this size [L. fr. *in octavo*, in an eighth]

oc·ten·ni·al (pkténiːəl) *adj.* occurring once in every eight years ‖ lasting for eight years [fr. L. *octennium*, a period of eight years fr. *octo*, eight+*annus*, year]

oc·tet, oc·tette (pktét) *n.* a musical composition written for eight players or singers ‖ a group of eight players or singers performing together ‖ a group of eight lines of verse [fr. L. *octo*, eight]

oc·til·lion (pktíljən) *n.* *NUMBER TABLE [F. fr. L. *octo*, eight+MILLION]

Oc·to·ber (pktóubər) *n.* (*abbr.* Oct.) the tenth month of the year, having 31 days [L. fr. *octo*, eight, originally the eighth month in the Roman calendar]

October Revolution (*hist.*) the Russian revolution of Nov. 7, 1917 (Oct. 25 in the Russian calendar) as a result of which the Bolsheviks seized power

Oc·to·brist (pktóubrist) *n.* (*Russ. hist.*) a member of a moderate political party supporting the constitutional reforms granted (Oct. 1905) by Nicholas 11 after the Russian revolution of 1905

oc·to·de·cil·lion (pktoudisíljən) *n.* * NUMBER TABLE [fr. L. *octodecim*, eighteen+MILLION]

oc·to·dec·i·mo (pktədésəmou) *n.* (*abbr.* 18mo) the size of a book leaf formed by folding a sheet to make 18 leaves or 36 pages, usually 4 ins x 6 1-2 ins ‖ paper of this size ‖ a book having pages of this size [fr. L. *in octodecimo*, in eighteenths]

oc·to·ge·nar·i·an (pktədʒənéːriːən) **1.** *n.* a person between 80 and 90 years old **2.** *adj.* of such a person or such an age [fr. L. *octogenarius*]

oc·to·nar·y (óktənɛri) **1.** *pl.* **oc·to·nar·ies** *n.* a group of eight ‖ a stanza of eight lines, esp. of Psalm 119, which has such stanzas for each letter of the Hebrew alphabet **2.** *adj.* of the number eight ‖ being eight in number ‖ going in groups of eight [fr. L. *octonarius*, containing eight]

oc·to·pod (óktəpɒd) **1.** *n.* any animal having eight limbs, esp. an octopus **2.** *adj.* having eight limbs ‖ of an octopod [fr. Gk *oktōpous* (*oktōpo-dos*), octopus]

oc·to·pus (óktəpəs) *pl.* **oc·to·pus·es, oc·to·pi** (óktəpai) *n.* a marine cephalopod mollusk of fam. *Octopodidae*. Octopuses have eight arms equipped with suckers, and a large head including highly developed eyes and a strong beak. Some species are edible, while others feed in commercially valuable lobster and crab regions ‖ something thought of as like an octopus, esp. a business organization having many branches and tending to get control of small local businesses [Mod. L. fr. Gk *oktōpous*, eight-footed]

oc·to·push (óktəpʊʃ) *n.* (*sports*) underwater hockey played with two six-person teams, with the puck being pushed along the bottom of a pool

oc·to·roon (pktərúːn) *n.* a person of one-eighth black ancestry and seven-eighths white [fr. L. *octo*, eight+QUADROON]

oc·to·syl·lab·ic (pktousilǽbik) **1.** *adj.* having eight syllables ‖ (of a poem) having lines with eight syllables each **2.** *n.* an octosyllabic line of poetry [fr. L. L. *octosyllabus*]

oc·to·syl·la·ble (óctəsiləb'l) **1.** *n.* a word of eight syllables ‖ an octosyllabic **2.** *adj.* octosyllabic [fr. L.L. *octosyllabus* fr. Gk]

oc·tu·ple (óktupʼl,óktjupʼl, pktúːpʼl, pktjúːpʼl) **1.** *adj.* eight times as much or as many **2.** *n.* the product of a number multiplied by eight **3.** *v.* *pres. part.* **oc·tu·pling** *past* and *past part.* **oc·tu·pled** *v.t.* to multiply by eight ‖ *v.i.* to increase by eight times as much [fr. L. *octuplus*]

oc·u·lar (ókjulər) **1.** *adj.* of, by, with or pertaining to the eye, *ocular defects* **2.** *n.* the eyepiece of

an optical instrument [fr. L. *ocularis* fr. *oculus*, eye]

oc·u·lar·ist (ókjulərist) *n.* (*Br.*) a maker of artificial eyes

oc·u·list (ókjulist) *n.* an ophthalmologist ‖ an optometrist [F. *oculiste*]

oc·u·lo·mo·ter (pkuloumóutər) *adj.* moving the eyeball ‖ involving movement of the eyeball, e.g. in certain diseases [fr. L. *oculus*, eye+MOTOR]

od (ɒd, oud) *n.* a hypothetical force pervading all nature and sometimes manifesting itself in supernatural phenomena [G., coined in 1850 by Baron Karl Ludwig von Reichenbach (1788–1869), G. chemist]

OD 1. (*abbr.*) for overdose of a drug **2.** one who has taken an overdose of a drug —**OD** *v.*

o·da·lisque, o·da·lisk (óud'lisk) *n.* a female slave or concubine in a harem, esp. in Turkey [F. fr. Turk. *ōdaliq*]

odd (ɒd) **1.** *adj.* of a number which is not a multiple of 2 (opp. EVEN) ‖ numbered, signified, known by such a number, *the odd pages* ‖ (placed after the noun) of a number or quantity which would only be accurate if an unspecified small addition were made, *200-odd people attended* ‖ of the one remaining after an odd number of persons or things have been grouped in two equal portions, *odd man out* ‖ of the one person or thing in excess of a fixed number, *odd man over* ‖ lacking a mate to make a pair, *an odd shoe* ‖ not serving to complete a set or series, *an odd volume* ‖ unusual, not fitting in to the accepted pattern, *his behavior was very odd* ‖ miscellaneous, random, *a few odd possessions remained* ‖ occasional, *at odd moments* ‖ out-of-the-way, *an odd corner of the world* **2.** *n.* (*golf*) a stroke in excess of the number played by an opponent ‖ (*Br.*, *golf*) a stroke which the weaker player is allowed to deduct at each hole from his score [O.N. *oddi*, triangle, odd number]

Odd Fellow a member of the Independent Order of Odd Fellows, a friendly society founded (18th c.) in England as a secret fraternity. Branches exist in the U.S.A. and in Europe

odd·i·ty (óditi) *pl.* **odd·i·ties** *n.* something which or someone who does not conform to the accepted standard of normality ‖ the quality of being odd

odd jobs miscellaneous small pieces of work for unskilled labor

odd·lot·ter (pdlótər) *n.* (*securities*) one who invests principally in odd lots (usu. fewer than 100 shares) of securities

odd·ment (ódmənt) *n.* something left over, a remnant etc., *an oddment of silk* ‖ something left over from a complete set, e.g. a book, a dish ‖ (*pl.*) odds and ends ‖ (*printing*) the pages of a book in excess of an even working of complete signatures

odds (ɒdz) *pl.* *n.* the measure or ratio of inequality, *the odds against him were 2 to 1* ‖ the chances of success or failure, *the odds are in his favor, they fought against great odds* ‖ probability, *the odds are that he will come* ‖ the advantage given by a bettor who appears to have the greater chance of winning a wager, *he'll give you 7 to 1 odds* ‖ the ratio supposed to exist between the chances of winning or losing a wager and which is used as a basis for reckoning bets ‖ material difference, *what odds does it make whether we go now or later?* **at odds with** in conflict with [ODD]

odds and ends fragments ‖ small, heterogeneous objects or items

odds-on (ódzón,ódzón) *adj.* (of a competitor) considered more likely to win than to lose ‖ fairly safe, *an odds-on chance*

ode (oud) *n.* a poem, usually of complex structure and exalted lyrical or rhapsodic mood, on some stated theme. Odes were originally written to be sung. The form (i.e., length of stanzas, meter etc.) varies considerably. In European literature the ode was most popular in the 16th to 19th cc., beginning as a conscious imitation of Greek and Roman models, esp. Pindar and Horace [F. fr. L.L. fr. Gk]

O·den·se (óuðənsə) the chief port, commercial and industrial center (pop. 168,200) of Fünen Is., Denmark: mechanical engineering, shipbuilding, textiles. Cathedral (13th c.)

O·der (óudər) (*Pol.* Odra) a navigable river (560 miles long) rising in Moravia, Czechoslovakia and flowing northwest through Silesia and Pomerania, Poland, forming part of the East German frontier, to the Baltic at Szczecin. Other ports: Wroclaw, Frankfurt an der Oder. It has an extensive canal system

Oder-Neisse line the boundary between Poland and East Germany, agreed at the Potsdam Conference (1945), and recognized (1970) 'de facto' by West Germany

O·des·sa (oudésə) a port, resort, and communications center (pop. 1,057,000) of the Ukraine, on the Black Sea. Industries: agricultural machinery, rolling stock, chemicals, food processing, light manufactures. University (1864)

O·dets (oudéts), Clifford (1906–63), American dramatist. His plays include 'Waiting for Lefty' (1935) and 'Golden Boy' (1937)

O·din (óudin) (*Norse mythol.*) the chief god. He was the god of war, of wisdom and of poetry and was associated with the Anglo-Saxon Wodan

o·di·ous (óudiːəs) *adj.* offensive, hateful [A.F.]

o·di·um (óudiːəm) *n.* hatred or condemnation by the community ‖ the state or quality of being subjected to such hatred ‖ the hatefulness of some act or stigma involved in some situation [L.=hatred]

O·do (óudou) *EUDES

O·do·a·cer (pudouéisər) (c. 434–93), chieftain of the Heruli, a Germanic tribe. He overthrew (476) the Western Roman Empire, and took the title 'king of Italy', though recognizing the authority of the Byzantine emperor Zeno. He was overthrown and murdered by Theodoric

o·dom·e·ter (oudómitər) *n.* an instrument used to measure distance traveled [fr. Gk *hodos*, way+*metron*, measure]

o·don·to·blast (oudóntəblæst) *n.* (*anat.*) a surface cell on the pulp of a tooth which produces dentine [fr. Gk *odous* (*odontos*), tooth+*blastos*, bud]

o·don·to·glos·sum (oudpntəglósəm) *n.* a member of *Odontoglossum*, fam. *Orchidaceae*, a genus of tropical American epiphytic orchids. They have highly colored flowers and many hybrids are cultivated [Mod. L. fr. Gk *odous* (*odontos*), tooth+*glossa*, tongue]

o·don·to·graph (oudóntəgræf, oudóntəgrɑf) *n.* an instrument used to mark off the outlines of gear teeth [fr. Gk *odous* (*odontos*), tooth+*graphos*, written]

o·don·toid (oudóntɔid) *adj.* (*anat.* and *zool.*) toothlike ‖ of the odontoid process [fr. Gk *odontoeidēs*]

odontoid process (*anat.*) a toothlike peg on the axis around which the atlas rotates. It was the central part of the atlas, which has become free and finally fused with the axis

o·don·to·log·i·cal (oudɒnt'lódʒik'l) *adj.* of or pertaining to odontology

o·don·tol·o·gist (oudɒntólədʒist) *n.* a specialist in odontology

o·don·tol·o·gy (oudɒntólədʒiː) *n.* the science which treats of the structure, growth and diseases of teeth [fr. Gk *odous* (*odontos*), tooth+*logos*, discourse]

o·don·toph·o·ral (oudɒntófərəl) *adj.* of or relating to an odontophore

o·don·to·phore (oudóntəfɔr, oudóntəfour) *n.* (*zool.*) a tooth-bearing organ in mollusks including the radula, cartilage and muscles **o·don·toph·o·rous** (oudɒntófərəs) *adj.* [fr. Gk *odontophoros,tooth*- bearing]

o·dor, *Br.* o·dour (óudər) *n.* something which stimulates the sense of smell ‖ the characteristic smell of something ‖ suggestion, *a faint odor of suspicion* [A. F. *odour*, O. F. *odor*]

o·dor·if·er·ous (oudərífərəs) *adj.* diffusing an odor, either pleasant or obnoxious [fr. L. *odorifer*]

odor of sanctity, *Br.* odour of sanctity a fragrance believed to emanate from the bodies of saints during life or immediately after death ‖ a reputation for holiness or goodness

o·dor·ous (óudərəs) *adj.* (*rhet.*) odoriferous [fr. L. *odor*, odor+ous]

odour *ODOR

O·dys·se·us (oudísjuːs, oudísiːəs) (*Gk mythol.*) son of Laertes, king of Ithaca, and hero of the Odyssey

Od·ys·sey (ódisiː) a Greek epic poem in 24 books, probably composed before 700 B.C., attributed to Homer. It recounts the adventures of Odysseus after the fall of Troy. He visits the land of the Cyclops and the island of Circe, consults Tiresias in Hades and eludes the Sirens but is shipwrecked, and escapes alone to the island of Calypso. After ten years' wandering he returns home to Ithaca and takes vengeance on the suitors of his wife, Penelope

od·ys·sey (ódisiː) *n.* (*rhet.*) a series of adventures and vicissitudes [after Homer's ODYSSEY]

O.E.C.D. *ORGANIZATION FOR ECONOMIC COOPER-ATION AND DEVELOPMENT

Oe·co·lam·pa·di·us (i:koulæmpéidi:əs), Johannes (Johann Hussgen, 1482–1531), German religious reformer. He defended Zwingli's views on the Eucharist against Luther at Marburg (1529)

oecology *ECOLOGY

oecumenic *ECUMENIC

oecumenicity *ECUMENICITY

oedema *EDEMA

Oed·i·pus (édəpəs, í:dəpəs) (*Gk mythol.*) the son of Laius, king of Thebes, and Jocasta. Because of the oracle that he would kill his father and marry his mother, he was left on a hillside, but was rescued and brought up as the son of the king of Corinth. Hearing the oracle, Oedipus left Corinth. While traveling he met and killed Laius, without recognizing him. After ridding Thebes of the Sphinx, he married Jocasta and became king, unwittingly fulfilling the oracle. Later realizing the truth of his birth, he stabbed out his eyes and went into exile with his daughter Antigone as guide. His story was used by Sophocles in 'Oedipus Rex' and 'Oedipus at Colonus'

Oedipus complex (*Freudian psychol.*, esp. of a male child) the psychological, esp. sexual, drives developing usually from the ages 3 to 6, associated with the child's attachment to the parent of the opposite sex, and resentment of the parent of the same sex, whom the child considers his rival (cf. ELECTRA COMPLEX)

O.E.E.C. *ORGANIZATION FOR EUROPEAN ECONOMIC COOPERATION

Oeh·len·schlä·ger (ɔ́:lənʃleigər), Adam Gottlob (1779–1850), Danish poet. Much influenced by Goethe and Schiller, he became Denmark's outstanding Romantic poet and playwright, reviving many old Scandinavian romances and sagas

oeil-de-boeuf (ə:jdəbə:f) *pl.* **oeils-de-boeuf** (ə:jdəbə:f) *n.* (*archit.*) a small circular or oval window used esp. in the 17th and 18th cc. [F.=eye of an ox]

oenology *ENOLOGY

OEO (*abbr.*) for Office of Economic Opportunity (which see)

Oer·sted (ɔ́:rsted), Hans Christian (1777–1851), Danish physicist and chemist. He was the founder of electromagnetism (1820) and also the first to isolate aluminum

oer·sted (ɔ́:rsted) *n.* a unit of magnetic intensity in the cgs electromagnetic system, defined as the intensity of the magnetic field in which a unit magnetic pole (in vacuo) experiences a force of 1 dyne in the field direction [after Hans Christian OERSTED]

oesophagus *ESOPHAGUS

oestrogen *ESTROGEN

oestrogenic *ESTROGENIC

oestrone *ESTRONE

oestrous *ESTROUS

oestrous cycle *ESTROUS CYCLE

oestruate *ESTRUATE

oestrum *ESTRUM

oestrus *ESTRUS

Oe·ta Mtns (í:tə) an eastward-pointing spur (summit: 7,062 ft) of the Pindus Mtns in Thessaly, Greece, above the pass of Thermopylae

of (ʌv, ɒv) *prep.* in a direction from, *south of the border* ‖ during, *the events of last year* ‖ expressing cause, *he died of grief, he is proud of his son* ‖ derived from, *of good family, the light of the sun* ‖ originating or coming from, *citizens of Paris* ‖ produced by, *the novels of Gorky* ‖ expressing deprivation, separation, *robbed of his livelihood, cured of his illness* ‖ constituted by, *a crowd of men, a roll of linen* ‖ made from, *a coat of wool* ‖ relating to, pertaining to, concerning, about, *news of the disaster, we think highly of him* ‖ having as a quality, *a man of distinction* ‖ with respect to, *slow of speech* ‖ for, *love of money* ‖ possessing, *a man of property* ‖ belonging to, *the property of a man* ‖ containing, *a basket of strawberries* ‖ designated as, specified as, *the city of London, a distance of 10 miles* ‖ indicating the object of an action implied by the preceding agent noun, *a reader of mysteries, a writer of ghost stories* ‖ (in telling time) before, *5 of 1* ‖ set aside for, *the hour of prayer* ‖ indicating the whole that includes the part denoted by the preceding word, *two is half of four, one of his sisters* ‖ indicating simple apposition, *a terror of a child* [O.E. unstressed form of *af, œf, away*]

OFE (*abbr.*) for Office of Federal Elections (which see)

off (ɔf, ɒf) **1.** *adv.* at a distance in time or space, *his visit is a long way off, the lake is 10 miles off* ‖ so as to be at a distance, *he ran off* ‖ so as to be separated in some way, *he took his coat off* ‖ so as to deviate from a course, *turn off into the lane* ‖ so as to be no longer in operation etc., *turn the light off* ‖ so as to be smaller, fewer etc., *the population is dying off* ‖ away from one's usual activity etc., *he took a year off* ‖ into a state of unconsciousness, *he dozed off* ‖ (*naut.*) away from shore ‖ (*naut.*) away from the wind ‖ (*theater*) offstage **off and on, on and off** from time to time, at frequent intervals **off with!** put off! remove! **2.** *prep.* at a distance from, *my house is off the main road* ‖ in a direction diverging from, *the street leads off the main road* ‖ not engaged in (a usual occupation) or attending to (a usual concern), *off work, off guard* ‖ from the substance of, *they lived off the garden* ‖ so as to be separated from in some way, *it fell off the table, off the point* ‖ not up to a usual standard etc. in, *off his game* ‖ (*pop.*) abstaining from, *she is off pastries* ‖ no longer pleasurably excited by, *she is off thrillers* ‖ (*naut.*) away from (shore) **3.** *adj.* far, further away, *the off side of the road* ‖ not on, attached, united, *her shoes are off* ‖ in error, *his answer is 30 points off* ‖ not functioning, *the light is off* ‖ canceled, *the match is off* ‖ just away, *the horses are off* ‖ less, fewer, *subscriptions are off this week* ‖ free of the obligations of one's usual activity, *she is always off on Saturday and Sunday* ‖ not up to standard, *an off day* ‖ (*esp. Br.*) become unfit for consumption, *the milk is off* ‖ remote, *an off chance* ‖ (of part of an animal) on its right ‖ (of an animal in harness flanked by another or others) on the right ‖ (*Br.*, of part of a motor vehicle) on the offside ‖ (*cricket*) of the side of the wicket or field opposite the side on which the batsman stands ‖ circumstanced, *well off* ‖ (*naut.*) toward the sea ‖ wrong, *his aim was badly off* ‖ (*pop.*) odd, eccentric **4.** *n.* the fact or condition of being off, *offs and ons* ‖ (*cricket*) the off side **5.** *interj.* go away **6.** *v.* (*slang*) to kill [var. of OF]

Of·fa (ɔ́fə) (d. 796), king of Mercia (757–96). His authority was recognized throughout England south of the Humber, enabling him to claim the title 'king of the English'. He constructed an earthwork, Offa's Dyke, between Mercia and Wales

of·fal (ɔ́fəl, ɒ́fəl) *n.* all parts of an animal which are removed from the carcass when it is dressed for food, e.g. entrails, heart, liver, kidneys, head, tail ‖ a by-product in any of various processes of milling, manufacturing etc. ‖ waste material, refuse [fr. OFF adv.+FALL n.]

Of·fa·ly (ɔ́fəli, ɒ́fəli) an inland county (area 771 sq. miles, pop. 51,829) in Leinster province, Irish Republic. County seat: Tullamore (pop. 6,000)

off-beat (ɔ́fbi:t, ɒ́fbi:t) **1.** *adj.* (*pop.*) of or having a style which departs from the ordinary or conventional **2.** *n.* (*mus.*) the unaccented beat in a measure

off-Broad·way (ɔ́fbrɔ́dwei) **1.** *adj.* of small (with fewer than 300 seats) New York City theaters usu. presenting plays out of the theatrical mainstream and/or located away from the midtown theater district **2.** *n.* the theaters as a group *Cf* OBIE

off-cam·er·a (ɔ́fkæmərə) *adj., adv.* not being photographed, esp. during a filming session *Cf* ON-CAMERA

off-col·or, *Br.* **off-col·our** (ɔ́fkʌ́lər, ɒ́fkʌ́lər) *adj.* not in normal health, *she is a bit off color today* ‖ not of the standard color ‖ below accepted standards of propriety, *an off color joke*

Of·fen·bach (ɔ́fənbæk), Jacques (real name uncertain, 1819–80), French composer of German origin. He wrote 102 light operas, incl. 'Orphée aux enfers' (1858), 'la Vie Parisienne' (1866) and 'les Contes d'Hoffman' (produced 1881)

Of·fen·bach (ɔ́fənbɑx) a town (pop. 111,200) of Hesse, West Germany, adjoining Frankfurt-am-Main: leather, chemical and machine industries

of·fence *OFFENSE

of·fend (əfénd) *v.t.* to affront, hurt the feelings of (someone) ‖ to arouse feelings of disgust in, *the last act will probably offend you* ‖ *v.i.* (often with 'against') to act contrary to law, moral principle etc., *this verdict offends against one's idea of justice* ‖ to cause resentment or disgust **of·fénd·er** *n.* [O.F. *offendre*]

of·fense, of·fence (əféns, ɔ́fens, ɒ́fens) *n.* an act against the law ‖ a sin ‖ the act of offending someone ‖ the state of being offended ‖ something which causes someone to be offended ‖ the act of attacking (cf. DEFENSE) ‖ (*sports*) a team in possession of the ball **to take offense** to consider oneself affronted ‖ to be scandalized [M.E. and O.F. *offens*, a cause of annoyance, and M.E. and F. *offense*, a hurt or wrong]

of·fen·sive (əfénsiv, ɔ́fensiv, ɒ́fensiv) **1.** *adj.* insulting, intended to give offense ‖ revolting to the senses, *an offensive smell* ‖ aggressive, ready or serving for attack, *offensive weapons* **2.** *n.* a large-scale attack, *to mount an offensive* ‖ an attitude of intended aggression, *on the offensive* [fr. M.L. *offensivus*]

of·fer (ɔ́fər, ɒ́fər) *n.* something offered for acceptance, rejection or consideration ‖ an expression of willingness to give or do something ‖ a sum named by a would be purchaser in bargaining **on offer** up for sale [F. *offre*]

offer *v.t.* to put forward for acceptance, rejection or consideration, *to offer an opinion* ‖ to hold out in the hand or present ‖ to present in order to meet a specific requirement, *students may offer physics as a subsidiary subject* ‖ (followed by an infinitive) to state one's inclination or preparedness (to do something), *to offer to drive* ‖ to make or give, *to offer resistance* ‖ to present to notice or view, *to offer a fine prospect* ‖ to present for sale, *to offer the whole set* ‖ to bid, propose as a price ‖ to afford, make available, *the north face offers the best ascent* ‖ (often with 'up') to present (a sacrifice or prayer) ‖ *v.i.* (esp. *Br.*) to present itself, *as soon as opportunity offers* ‖ to make an offering or sacrifice [F. *offrir* and O.E. *offrain* fr. L.]

of·fer·ing (ɔ́fəriŋ, ɒ́fəriŋ) *n.* the act of offering ‖ something offered, esp. a gift to propitiate or appease. *a peace offering* ‖ a contribution to a church to help support it or its various activities [O.E. *offrung*]

offering price (*securities*) the net value of the assets of an open-end mutual fund, plus or minus a load, at which shares are bought or sold by the fund

of·fer·to·ry (ɔ́fərtɔri, ɔ́fərtɔuri:, ɒ́fərtɔri, ɒ́fərtɔuri:) *pl.* **of·fer·to·ries** *n.* (*eccles.*) the part of the Mass or communion service when the gifts of bread and wine are offered to God ‖ an anthem sung by the choir during this part of the ritual ‖ the collection of money taken at a religious service [fr. M.L. *offertorium*, place to which offerings were brought]

off·hand (ɔ́fhænd, ɒ́fhænd) **1.** *adv.* without preparation or reference, *offhand would you say we are still three miles away?* **2.** *adj.* done without preparation or reference ‖ curt or casual to the point of rudeness **óff·hánd·ed** *adj.*

of·fice (ɔ́fis, ɒ́fis) *n.* a room or premises for administrative or clerical work, or for transacting business ‖ the personnel working in such an office ‖ a doctor's consulting room ‖ a position of authority in administration, *the office of chairman* ‖ the fact or state of holding a public position of authority, *men in office* ‖ (*Roman Catholicism*) the service of the breviary, or this with respect to a particular occasion ‖ (*Anglican Church*) morning or evening prayer ‖ any religious rite, *the office of the Mass* ‖ (*Br., pl.*) the service parts of a large house (e.g. kitchen, pantries) **Of·fice** (*Br.*) a government department, *the Home Office* ‖ an administrative division below a department, *the Public Records Office* [A.F. and O.F.]

office boy a boy employed in a business office as messenger and to do odd jobs

of·fice·hold·er (ɔ́fishoulder, ɒ́fishoulder) *n.* someone who holds a public office, whether by election or by appointment

Office of Consumer Affairs U.S. executive department office created in 1971 to advise the President of consumer interests *abbr.* **OCA**

Office of Economic Opportunity (*abbr.* OEO) a U.S. government agency authorized under the Economic Opportunity Act of 1964. It is the official name of the War on Poverty declared (1964) by President Lyndon Johnson

Office of Federal Elections a semiautonomous office in the General Accounting Office (GAO) to monitor campaign contributions *abbr.* **OFE**

Office of Management and Budget executive office created in 1970 to prepare the U.S. government budget for the President *abbr.* **OMB**

of·fi·cer (ɔ́fisər, ɒ́fisər) **1.** *n.* a person holding a public appointment, *a customs officer* ‖ a constable or policeman ‖ a person holding a position of responsibility and trust in a company, club etc., e.g. a president, secretary or treasurer ‖ a person holding a commission to command others in the army, navy, air force etc. or merchant

CONCISE PRONUNCIATION KEY: **(a)** æ, c*a*t; ɑ, c*a*r; ɔ f*aw*n; ei, sn*a*ke. **(e)** e, h*e*n; i:, sh*ee*p; iə, d*ee*r; ɛə, b*ea*r. **(i)** i, f*i*sh; ai, t*i*ger; ə:, b*i*rd. **(o)** o, *o*x; au, c*ow*; ou, g*oa*t; u, p*oo*r; ɔi, r*oy*al. **(u)** ʌ, d*u*ck; u, b*u*ll; u:, g*oo*se; ə, b*a*cillus; ju:, c*u*be. x, lo*ch*; θ, *th*ink; ð, bo*th*er; z, *Z*en; ʒ, corsa*g*e; dʒ, sava*g*e; ŋ, ora*ng*utan*g*; j, *y*ak; ʃ, *fi*sh; tʃ, fe*tch*; 'l, rabb*le*; 'n, redd*en*. Complete pronunciation key appears inside front cover.

marine 2. *v.t.* to command as officer ‖ to provide with officers [A.F. and O.F. *officier*]

officer of arms (*heraldry*) an officer with the duties of a herald or supervising heralds

officer of the day (*mil.*) an officer in charge of preserving order etc. on a particular day

office worker a clerical worker in administration

of·fi·cial (əfíʃəl) *n.* a person who holds a public office or is employed on authorized duties, *a bank official* ‖ an appointed judge of an ecclesiastical court [F. fr. L. *officialis*]

official *adj.* of or relating to an office or the administering of an office ‖ (of persons) holding an office ‖ vouched for by authority or an authority, *an official report* ‖ arbitrarily fixed for public celebration, *the queen's official birthday* ‖ deriving from the functions of an officer, *an official welcome* ‖ (*pharm.*) described by the pharmacopoeia **of·fi·cial·dom** *n.* [fr. L. *officialis*]

of·fi·cial·ese (əfíʃəlí:z) *n.* the stilted, long-winded, often obscure language characteristic of government forms and documents [OFFICIAL]

of·fi·ci·al·is, *pl* **-les** (ɒfíʃí:alis) *n.* in a Roman Catholic diocese, the judge of a matrimonial court

of·fi·ci·ant (əfíʃí:ənt) *n.* a priest or minister performing a religious service [fr. M. L. *officians* (*officiantis*) fr. *officiare*, to officiate]

of·fi·ci·ar·y (əfíʃí:ɛri:) *adj.* (of a title or rank) deriving from or connected with the holding of an office ‖ (of a person) holding such a title or rank [fr. M.L. *officiarius*]

of·fi·ci·ate (əfíʃí:eit) *pres. part.* **of·fi·ci·at·ing** *past* and *past part.* **of·fi·ci·at·ed** *v.i.* to perform a religious service ‖ to act in a position of formal responsibility e.g. chairman, umpire etc. [fr. M.L. *officiare* (*officiatus*)]

of·fic·i·nal (əfísin'l, ɒfisáin'l) *adj.* (*pharm.*) characterizing an approved medicine or drug stocked by dispensers (cf. MAGISTRAL) ‖ (of plants) used in medicine [fr. M.L. *officinalis*]

of·fi·cious (əfíʃəs) *adj.* too zealously exercising authority ‖ offering unwanted services or intruding with unsought advice ‖ (*diplomacy*) unofficial, *officious talks* [fr. L. *officiosus*, obliging]

of·fing (ɔ́fiŋ, ɒfiŋ) *n.* the part of the sea visible from shore, between anchoring ground and horizon ‖ a ship's position at a distance from the shore **in the offing** near, likely to appear or happen soon, *there is a storm in the offing* [OFF adv.]

off·ish (ɔ́fiʃ, ɒfiʃ) *adj.* aloof, distant in manner

off·is·land (ɔ́fáilənd) *n.* an island near the mainland **—off·islander** *n.* one not resident on an island

off·li·cense (ɔ́flais'ns, ɒflais'ns) *n.* (*Br.*) a license to sell alcoholic beverages for consumption off the premises ‖ (*Br.*) a shop, public house etc. having such a license

off·line (ɔ́fláin) *adj.* (*computer*) of a computer not part of, or under the control of, the central computer *Cf* ON-LINE

off-off-Broad·way (ɒfɔfbrɔ́dwei) *adj.* **1.** of very small, usu. experimental New York theater seating 200 persons or less **2.** *n.* the theaters as a group *abbr.* **OOB**

off-peak (ɔ́fpí:k, ɒfpí:k) *adj.* below the maximum, or referring to this condition, *use electricity at off-peak hours*

off·print (ɔ́fprint, ɒfprint) **1.** *n.* an extract from a larger publication (e.g. an article from a journal) printed and published separately **2.** *v.t.* to reprint (such an extract)

off-road vehicle (ɔ́fróudví:ik'l) *n.* motor vehicle capable of traveling over unprepared surfaces, e.g., for reaching remote areas *abbr.* **ORV**

off-scour·ings (ɔ́fskауəriŋz, ɒfskауəriŋz) *pl. n.* (esp. *fig.*) refuse, dregs, *the off-scourings of humanity*

off·set (ɔ́fset, ɒfset) **1.** *n.* a short lateral branch from a stem or root which is a source of propagation ‖ an offshoot (branch of a family) ‖ a spur from a range of hills ‖ a compensation or counterbalance ‖ (*archit.*) a sloping ledge in a wall made by narrowing the upper thickness ‖ (*elec.*) a conductor leading from a main ‖ (*surveying*) a short distance measured perpendicularly from the main line of measurement ‖ (*mech.*) a bend made in a pipe to circumvent an obstacle ‖ (*printing*) setoff ‖ a method of printing in which the impression is first transferred from a flat plate to a rubber-surfaced cylinder and thence to paper **2.** *v.t. pres. part.* **off·set·ting** *past* and

past part. **off·set** to balance (one thing) against another, to compensate for, *his winnings offset my losses* ‖ (*printing*) to set off, because the ink is not drying properly ‖ to make an offset in (a wall, pipe etc.) **3.** *adj.* of or printed by offset

offset lithography the offset printing method

off·shoot (ɔ́fʃu:t, ɒfʃu:t) *n.* a shoot, or branch from a main stem ‖ a subsidiary activity, by-product ‖ a collateral branch of a family etc.

off-shore (ɔ́fʃɔr, ɔ́fʃɔur, ɒfʃɔr, ɒfʃɔur) **1.** *adj.* moving away from the shore and towards the sea, *an offshore wind* ‖ located at a little distance from the shore, *offshore fisheries* **2.** *adv.* from the shore ‖ at a distance from the shore

off-shore funds (*securities*) investments made from outside the U.S., avoiding certain taxes and controls of the Securities and Exchange Commission

off·side (ɔ́fsáid, ɒfsáid) *n.* (*Br.*) the side (of a horse or motor vehicle) closest to the center of the road (opp. NEARSIDE) ‖ an instance of being off side

off side *adj.* (of a player in football, hockey etc.) in a position in relation to the ball and opposing players where the rules debar him from participation in the play

off·spring (ɔ́fspriŋ, ɒfspriŋ) *n.* a child or children, progeny

off·stage (ɔ́fstéidʒ, ɒfstéidʒ) **1.** *adv.* away from the stage, out of sight of the audience ‖ in private life, when not acting **2.** *adj.* done or existing offstage

off-the-books (ɔ́fðəbúks) *adj.* of payments, e.g., wages, of which no record is made by the payer. The receiver is thus able to avoid taxation if he or she so wishes

off-the-pig (ɔ́fðəpíg) *adj.* (*Br.*) off the rack, ready-to-wear

off-the-rack (ɔ́fðəræk) *adj.* of ready-to-wear clothing

off-the-re·cord (ɔ́fðərékərd, ɒfðərékərd) *adj.* not for publication, *an off-the-record statement*

off-track betting (ɔ́ftrækbétiŋ) *n.* wagering carried on away from the racetrack, usu. on a pari-mutuel basis

off-white (ɔ́fhwáit, ɔ́fwáit, ɒfhwáit, ɒfwáit) *adj.* not absolutely white, with a yellowish, ivory tinge

oft (ɔft, ɒft) *adv.* (*rhet.*, usually combined with a past or present participle) often, *an oft-told tale* [O.E.]

of·ten (ɔ́fən, ɒfən) *adv.* frequently, repeatedly at short intervals, *they often come to visit us* ‖ in a number of instances, *it is often the case* [extended fr. M.E. *ofte*]

ogam *OGHAM

O·ga·sa·wa·ra (ougasawára) *BONIN ISLANDS

Og·bo·mo·sho (ɒgbómouʃou) a commercial center (pop. 432,000) of W. Nigeria, 50 miles northeast of Ibadan

o·gee (óudʒi:) **1.** *n.* a molding showing an S-shape in cross-section **2.** *adj.* formed by an S-shaped curve or curves, *an ogee arch* [prob. fr. F. *ogive*]

og·ham, og·am (ɔ́gəm, ógəm) *n.* the script of the oldest known form of Goidelic. Some 300 inscriptions in the oghamic alphabet, probably dating from the 5th c. or earlier, have been discovered in the British Isles, mostly in S.W. Ireland. The letters are formed by strokes cut along or across a vertical line, e.g. on the edge of an upright stone ‖ an inscription in this script ‖ a character of this alphabet **óg·ham·ic, óg·am·ic** *adj.* [O. Ir. *ogam, ogum*, Mod. Ir. *ogham, ogam*]

o·gi·val (oudʒáivəl) *adj.* (*archit.*) of, relating to or like an ogive ‖ (*archit.*) characterized by the use of ogives

o·give (óudʒaiv) *n.* (*archit.*) a groin or rib of a Gothic vault crossing it diagonally ‖ a pointed arch ‖ (*statistics*) the curve in a chart representing cumulative frequency distribution [F.]

o·gle (óug'l) **1.** *v. pres. part.* **o·gling** *past* and *part.* **o·gled** *v.i.* to cast amorous glances ‖ *v.t.* to try to attract by giving enticing looks **2.** *n.* an amorous or provocative glance [prob. fr. Du. or L.G.]

O·gle·thorpe (óugəlθɔrp), James Edward (1696–1785), British general and philanthropist. Seeking a home for the poor and destitute, he secured (1732) a colonial charter and led (1733) the first settlers to Georgia, founding Savannah

OGO (abbr.) of orbiting geographical observatory, an unmanned satellite designed to gather physical data about the earth

O·gou·é (ougu:wei) a river (700 miles long, navigable for 250 miles) rising in the north of the

Republic of the Congo and flowing across Gabon to the Atlantic

OGPU (ógpu:) *n.* (*hist.*) the former name of the Soviet Russian secret police [initial letters of Russian title *Obedinennoe Gosudarstvennoe Politicheskoe Upravlenie*, United State Political Administration]

o·gre (óugər) *n.* a fairy-tale monster or giant who eats humans ‖ a hideous or cruel man **ó·gre·ish, o.grish** (óugriʃ) *adjs* [F.]

oh, O (ou) *interj.* an exclamation used to attract attention, or to express surprise, disapproval, admiration, fear or doubt

O'Har·a (ouhɛ́ərə, ouhǽrə), John Henry (1905–70), U.S. novelist and short story writer. His novels, notably 'Appointment in Samarra' (1934), 'Butterfield 8' (1935), 'Pal Joey' (1940), 'Ten North Frederick' (1955), and 'From the Terrace' (1958) focus on American suburban society, esp. the upper classes, with photographic realism

O'Hig·gins (ouhíginz), Bernardo (1776–1842), Chilean soldier and statesman. He was the natural son of the Spanish nobleman Ambrosio O'Higgins, marquis de Osorno, who became viceroy of Peru. With José San Martín, Bernardo liberated Chile from Spanish rule (1817) and was supreme director of the country (1817–23)

O·hi·o (ouháiou) (*abbr.* O.) a state (area 41,222 sq. miles, pop. 10,791,000) of the northeast central U.S.A., on Lake Erie. Capital: Columbus. Chief city: Cleveland. It is mainly low-lying, with hills in the east. Agriculture: beef and dairy cattle, hogs, poultry, sheep, cereals, vegetables. Resources: coal, some oil and natural gas, limestone and sandstone. Industries: iron and steel, chemicals, machine tools, electrical machinery and equipment, transport equipment, metal, rubber and clay products, food processing. Chief universities: Ohio State (1870) at Columbus, Ohio (1809) at Athens, Western Reserve (1826) at Cleveland. The French ceded Ohio to Britain (1763), and it became part of the Northwest Territory (1787). It became (1803) the 17th state of the U.S.A.

Ohio a river (981 miles long) flowing west from Pittsburgh, Pennsylvania (it marks the southern borders of Ohio, Indiana and E. Illinois) to the Mississippi at Cairo. Canalization (1929) has made its full length navigable

Ohm (oum), Georg Simon (1789–1854), German physicist. He investigated galvanic currents, discovered the distribution of emf in an electrical circuit, and established a definite relation between current, resistance and emf (*OHM'S LAW)

ohm (oum) *n.* the mks unit of electrical resistance, equal to the resistance in which a current of 1 ampere dissipates 1 watt of power or the resistance of a circuit in which a potential of 1 volt produces a current of 1 ampere ‖ a cgs unit of acoustic resistance, reactance or impedance [after Georg Simon OHM]

ohm·age (óumidʒ) *n.* electrical resistance stated in ohms

ohm-am·me·ter (óumǽmi:tər) *n.* an instrument (a combined ohmmeter and ammeter) for measuring both electrical resistance and current

ohm-me·ter (óummi:tər) *n.* an instrument (e.g. a Wheatstone bridge) for measuring electrical resistance, usually in ohms

Ohm's law an empirical statement in physics relating the current (I), potential difference (E) and resistance (R) in a conductor. For a conductor subject to constant current and potential difference the resistance is given by $R = \dfrac{E}{I}$

oil (ɔil) **1.** *n.* one of a large group of substances which are typically viscous liquids or easily liquefiable solids. They are insoluble in water, and may have animal, vegetable (sometimes called fatty oils), mineral or synthetic origin. Their uses vary, according to their type: thus essential oils (e.g. petroleum) are used as fuels and lubricants, and others are used for their medicinal or food value ‖ petroleum ‖ a toilet preparation, *hair oil* ‖ (*pl.*, *painting*) oil color, *to paint in oils* ‖ a painting worked in oil colors **to pour oil on the flames** to intensify the violence of a quarrel **to pour oil on troubled waters** to exert a soothing influence **2.** *v.t.* to lubricate with oil ‖ to treat with oil, e.g. so as to make flexible or watertight ‖ to convert into oil, e.g. by melting ‖ *v.i.* to become an oil, or become oily ‖ (*naut.*) to take oil aboard as fuel [M.E. *oli, olie, oile* fr. O.F.]

oil·berg (ɔ́ilbəːrg) n. a large oil-tanker (capacity, 200,000 tons)

oil·bird (ɔ́ilbəːrd) n. the guacharo

oil burner a burner which vaporizes or atomizes fuel oil, mixing it with air and igniting it so that a surface (e.g. the brick of a baker's oven) can be heated directly by the flame

oil cake fodder consisting of pressed seeds (e.g. linseed, cotton, soybean) from which the oil has been extracted

oil·can (ɔ́ilkæn) n. an oil container, esp. a lubricating can with a long slender spout

oil·cloth (ɔ́ilklɔθ, ɔ́ilklɔθ) pl. **oil·cloths** (ɔ́ilklɔθs, ɔ́ilklɔθs, ɔ́ilklɔðz, ɔ́ilklɔðz) n. cotton cloth treated with an oil-based finish to make it resistant to moisture. It is used for table or shelf covers, rainproof garments etc. ‖ a piece of this, or a garment of this

oil color, Br. **oil colour** pigment used in oil painting ‖ oil paint

oiled silk silk cloth treated with oil to make it waterproof

oilfield an area containing subterranean stocks of oil, esp. when this is being exploited

oil fingerprinting method of identifying an oil spill so its cause can be traced

oil·i·ly (ɔ́ilili:) adv. in an oily way, unctuously

oil·i·ness (ɔ́ili:nis) n. the state or quality of being oily

oil of vitriol concentrated sulfuric acid

oil paint paint mixed with drying oil, used esp. by artists for painting on prepared canvas or other surface

oil painting the art of painting in oil paints ‖ a picture painted in oil paints

oil palm Elaeis guineensis, fam. Palmae, a commercially valuable wild tree of W. Africa, which is also cultivated in the Congo, Indonesia, Malaysia, and South and Central America. The mesocarp of its fruit yields palm oil and the palm kernel a cruder oil

Oil Reserves Scandal ('Teapot Dome' scandal) a U.S. scandal involving high government officials in the Warren Harding administration. Albert B. Fall, secretary of the interior, persuaded President Harding to transfer the administration of the U.S. naval petroleum reserves from the secretary of the navy to Fall's department. In secret negotiations without competitive bidding, Fall issued leases which granted certain companies exclusive right to oil and gas at the Teapot Dome reserve, Wyo. and the Elk Hills and Buena Vista Hills reserves, Calif. A Congressional investigation and resolution (1924) revealed that Fall had received more than $200,000 in Liberty bonds from companies benefiting by the leases. The Supreme Court ruled the contracts fraudulent and in a criminal action Fall was convicted of bribery

oil·seed (ɔ́ilsiːd) n. any of various oil-producing seeds, e.g. castor bean, cotton-seed, linseed

oil·skin (ɔ́ilskin) n. a rough cloth treated with oil to make it waterproof ‖ a waterproof raincoat made of oilskin ‖ (pl.) jacket and trousers made of oilskin, worn by sailors, fishermen etc.

oil slick a film of oil floating on water

oil·stone (ɔ́ilstoun) n. a strip of stone impregnated with oil for use as a whetstone

oil·stove (ɔ́ilstouv) n. a heating or cooking stove using oil as fuel

oil well a well from which petroleum is extracted

oil·y (ɔ́ili:) comp. **oil·i·er** superl. **oil·i·est** adj. containing, saturated with, or covered with oil ‖ having the characteristics of oil ‖ (of human behavior) heavily ingratiating, using suave hypocrisy, an oily smile

oint·ment (ɔ́intmənt) n. an unguent used externally for healing or cleansing the skin, or for ritual anointing [M.E. oignement fr. O. F.]

Oise (wæz) a department (area 2,272 sq. miles, pop. 606,300) of north central France (*ILE DE FRANCE, *PICARDY). Chief town: Beauvais

O·je·da (ɔhéðá), Alonso de (c. 1466–c. 1515), Spanish conquistador. With Juan de La Cosa and Amerigo Vespucci he explored the coast of Venezuela. He discovered (1499) the island of Curaçao

O·jib·wa (oudʒíbwə, oudʒíbwei) pl. **O·jib·wa, O·jib·was** n. a (U.S.-Canadian) Indian group, first reported (1640) living in Michigan's upper peninsula. After driving out the Dakota Indians, they occupied N. Minnesota, and some settled along Lake Winnipeg. The Canadian members (Saulteurs) number about 20,000. The U.S. members, one of the largest remnants of the aboriginal population in the U.S.A., number about 30,000, 80% being of mixed blood.

The Ojibwa are celebrated in Longfellow's 'The Song of Hiawatha' (1855)

O·jos del Sa·la·do (ɔhɔsðelsɑláðɔ) a mountain (22,572 ft) in N.W. Argentina, near the Chilean border

OK, o·kay (oukéi, óukéi) **1.** adj. all right, agreed, that's OK with me **2.** v.t. pres. part. **OK'ing, o·kay·ing** past and past part. **OK'd, o·kayed** to approve, endorse **3.** pl. **OK's, o·kays** n. an endorsement or authorization [perh. fr. phrase 'oll korrect'=all correct, all right, or after the O.K. Club (1840), an American Democratic organization supporting President Van Buren for reelection, the name being derived from the initials of Old Kinderhook, New York, his birthplace]

o·ka·pi (oukápi:) n. Okapia Johnstoni, a herbivorous mammal related to the giraffe but smaller, with shorter neck and legs, found in the forests of the N.E. Democratic Republic of the Congo. The upper legs and hindquarters are striped black and white and the body is a rich reddish brown. It was discovered (1900) by Sir Harry Johnston (1858-1929), British explorer, and closely resembles fossil giraffes of the Miocene and Pliocene [native name]

okay *OK

O·ka·ya·ma (oukajámə) a port (pop. 546,000) of S.W. Honshu, Japan, on the Inland Sea: cotton textiles, porcelain

O·kee·cho·bee, Lake (ouki:tʃóubi:) the largest lake (c. 40 miles long, 24 miles wide) in southern U.S.A., at the northern edge of the Everglades in S. Florida

O'Keeffe (ouki:f), Georgia (1887–1986) U.S. painter known especially for her bold flower paintings and studies of animal bones. She had her first one-woman show (1917) at the 291 Gallery of the photographer Alfred Stieglitz, whom she married in 1924. Her flower paintings first appeared in the 1920s. In 1929 she visited New Mexico and made her home there from 1949. Her works during the period after her first visit reflected the atmosphere and scenery of the southwestern desert, most notably in the 'Pelvis Series' (1943). She was one of the outstanding American modernist painters throughout her long and prolific career

O·ke·ghem (ɔ́kəgəm), Johannes (or Ockeghem, c. 1430–c. 1495), Flemish composer and teacher. He wrote songs, Masses and motets (e.g. the Mass 'Missa cujusvis toni' and a motet for 36 voices). His use of counterpoint had a great influence on early church music

O·khotsk, Sea of (oukɔ́tsk) an inlet (area 582,000 sq. miles) of the Pacific on the coast of E. Siberia, U.S.S.R., nearly enclosed by the Kamchatka Peninsula, the Kurile Is, Hokkaido (Japan) and Sakhalin Is.

O·ki·na·wa (oukinɑ́wə, oukinɑ́uwə) the central island group of the Ryukyu archipelago ‖ the largest island (area 454 sq. miles, pop. 1,096,000) of this group, and of the Ryukyus. Capital and chief port: Naha. It was the site of the last great U.S. amphibious campaign (1945) of the 2nd world war. After the war it was placed under U.S. military authority and served as a strategic U.S. base in the Korean and Indochina Wars. The U.S.A. returned it to Japan in 1972, maintaining bases on the island

Okla. Oklahoma

O·kla·ho·ma (oukləhóumə) (abbr. Okla.) a state (area 69,919 sq. miles, pop. 3,177,000) in the S. central U.S.A. Capital: Oklahoma City. The west is chiefly plain country, and the east rugged upland. Agriculture: wheat, cotton, sorghums, beef cattle. Resources: oil, natural gas, coal. Industries: oil refining, food and metal processing, machinery. State university (1890) at Norman. The U.S.A. acquired most of Oklahoma as part of the Louisiana Purchase (1803). It was declared (1834) Indian territory, from which whites were barred for 55 years. It became (1907) the 46th state of the U.S.A.

Oklahoma City the capital (pop. 403,213) of Oklahoma, a communications center and air base, on one of the country's richest oil fields (struck in 1928): oil refining and related industries, cattle trade, farm machinery

O·ko·van·go (oukəvǽŋgou) a river (600 miles long) rising as the Cubango in the highlands of Angola and emptying into the Okovango basin, a vast marsh in N. Botswana

o·kra (óukrə) n. Hibiscus esculentus, fam. Malvaceae, a tall annual of W. African origin, cultivated in the West Indies and the southern

U.S.A. Its gummy pods are used in soups and stews, or served as a vegetable ‖ these pods ‖ gumbo (soup) [prob. W. African]

O·laf I (óulaf) (c. 969–1000), king of Norway (c. 995–1000). He began the conversion of the Norwegians to Christianity and attempted unsuccessfully to unify Scandinavia

Olaf II, St (c. 995–1030), patron saint and king (1015–28) of Norway. He continued the conversion of the Norwegians to Christianity, but was overthrown when Cnut invaded Norway (1028). Feast: July 29

O·land (ɔ́:lɑnd) the second largest island (area 519 sq. miles, pop. 20,361) of Sweden, just off the southeast coast. Chief town: Borgholm (pop. 3,000). Industries: mixed farming, lime and alum, cement, tourism

O·lav V (óulaf) (1903–), king of Norway (1957–), son of Haakon VII

old (ould) **1.** adj. advanced in years ‖ having a specified age or duration ‖ of or pertaining to advanced age or to persons advanced in years ‖ having characteristics or manners of an elderly person ‖ no longer new, old clothes ‖ stale, old bread ‖ experienced, an old salt ‖ inveterate, an old offender ‖ former, my old Latin teacher ‖ of, belonging to or done in the past, the old days ‖ antique, old silver ‖ of long standing, old friends ‖ familiar, accustomed, the same old faces ‖ out-of-date, an old timetable ‖ distinguishing an object from a similar one of a later date, the old year ‖ (often **Old**) distinguishing an earlier style, period, stage etc. from a later one, Old English ‖ the Old Testament ‖ (pop., often with 'good') used to convey either familiar regard or contempt, good old Joe, a dirty old man ‖ (pop.) used to intensify other adjectives, he'll eat any old thing **an old head on young shoulders** a young person with the wisdom of someone older and more experienced **2.** n. (only in the phrases) **the old** old people **of old** in the old days, from olden times ‖ (rhet.) from long experience, she knew his tricks of old [O.E. ald]

Old Bailey the Central Criminal Court of England, in London, so called because it stands in the ancient bailey of the city wall

old boy (Br.) a boy or man in relation to the school he attended

Old Castile (Span. Castilla la Vieja) the northern part of Castile, forming the provinces of Santander, Burgos, Longroño, Soria, Segovia and Ávila, and the eastern parts of Valladolid and Palencia. The Guadalquivir valley (cereals, vegetables, vines) forms the center. Segovia and Soria, in the south, have pine forests. The rest is largely cattle and sheep pasture. Industries: forestry (esp. resin extraction), food processing. Historic capital: Burgos

Old Catholic a member of a group of small national Churches in Europe and the U.S.A., which separated (some in the 18th c., but the majority c. 1870) from the Roman Catholic Church on questions of dogma, while retaining Catholic ritual. Old Catholics specifically reject papal infallibility and the Immaculate Conception. Since 1932 Old Catholics have been in full communion with the Church of England

Old Church Slavic Old Church Slavonic

Old Church Slavonic a South Slavic language, the oldest known form of Slavic. First documented in the 9th c., it continues as a liturgical language in some Slavic countries

old country a term used by immigrants in referring to the land of their birth

old·en (óuldən) adj. (only in the phrases) **in olden days, in olden times** belonging to a time long past [OLD]

Ol·den·bar·ne·veldt (ouldənbárnəvelt) *BARNEVELDT

Ol·den·burg (óuldənburx) a walled town (pop. 134,600) in Lower Saxony, West Germany. Industries: tobacco, light manufacturing. Palace (17th c.)

Old English *ENGLISH LANGUAGE

Old English sheep dog a sheep dog of a rough-haired, short-tailed breed

old face (Br., printing) old style

old-fash·ioned (ouldfǽʃənd) adj. of or belonging to former times, old-fashioned glasses ‖ out-of-date, old-fashioned ideas ‖ retaining the ideas, standards etc. of a past age

old fo·gy, old fo·gey (fóugi:) pl. **old fo·gies, old fo·geys** n. a bore with oldfashioned, ridiculously conservative ideas [perh. var. of FOGGY]

Old French *FRENCH

old girl (Br.) a girl or woman in relation to the school she attended

Old Glory a nickname for the U.S. flag

old gold n. a dull yellow color like tarnished gold

Old Guard (hist.) the imperial guard created by Napoleon I in 1804 **old guard** the unbending, conservative section of a community, group etc. [trans. F. *Vieille Garde*]

Old·ham (óuldəm) a county borough (pop. 95,467) in Lancashire, England: textiles (esp. cottons), textile machinery

old hand someone with long practice or experience in a particular activity, area etc.

Old High German High German as used c. 750–c. 1100

Old Icelandic the Icelandic language from c. 9th c. to the middle of the 16th c.

old·ies (óuldi:z) n. songs, records, films, etc., popular years ago

Old Iranian either of two languages used in Iran before the Christian era (*AVESTAN, *OLD PERSIAN)

Old Irish the Irish language before the 11th c.

old lag (Br.) a hardened criminal who has often been in prison

Old Latin Latin from c. 6th c. B.C. to c. 100 B.C.

Old Left traditional Marxist movement Cf LEFTIST

old-line (óuldláin) adj. having an established reputation, long experienced, *an old-line firm* ‖ conservative in outlook

Old Low German Low German as used prior to the 12th c.

old maid a middle-aged or elderly woman who has never married ‖ a prim, fussy person ‖ a card game in which the players match pairs

old man (pop.) one's father or husband **Old Man, the** (pop.) one's boss

old master a great painter of former times, esp. of the 16th and 17th cc. in Europe ‖ a painting by such an artist

old money wealth accumulated in previous generations

Old Norse the language of Norway and its colonies until the 14th c.

Old Persian an Old Iranian language known from cuneiform inscriptions (6th-5th cc. B.C.)

Old Pretender *STUART, James Francis Edward

old rose a deep soft grayish pink color

Old Saxon the West Germanic language used by the Saxons of N.W. Germany up to the 12th c.

old school a group of people who adhere to the ideas, methods or standards of a previous age

old school tie (Br.) a public school tie worn by past members of the school ‖ (esp. Br.) the attitude of conservatism and upper-class solidarity traditionally attributed to former members of such schools

old style (printing, Am.=Br. old face) a type style characterized by slanting ascender serifs and relatively little tone change between thick and thin strokes **Old Style** (abbr. O.S.) according to the Julian, not the Gregorian, calendar

Old Testament the first 39 books of the Bible, setting out the covenant of God with the Hebrews and the history of the Hebrews (*PENTATEUCH, *HAGIOGRAPHA, *APOCRYPHA)

old-time (óuldtáim) adj. of, belonging to or characteristic of former times

old-tim·er (óuldtáimər) n. someone who has been doing the same thing or been at the same place for a long time

old wives' tale a superstitious notion without any scientific foundation

Old World the eastern hemisphere, esp. the European continent **old-world** (óuldwə́:rld) adj. picturesquely old-fashioned

o·le·ag·i·nous (ouli:ǽdʒinəs) adj. oily, producing oil [fr. F. *oléagineux*]

o·le·an·der (ouli:ǽndər) n. *Nerium oleander*, fam. *Apocynaceae*, a poisonous evergreen shrub with beautiful red and white flowers, widely cultivated in warm countries [M.L., etym. doubtful]

o·le·an·do·my·cin [C₃₅H₆₁NO₁₂] (ouli:ændəmáisin) n. (pharm.) a basic antibiotic used to treat gram-positive organisms resistant to penicillin and other drugs

o·le·as·ter (ouli:ǽstər) n. a member of *Elaeagnus*, fam. *Elaeagnaceae*, esp. *E. angustifolia*, a large shrub or small tree native to Europe and Asia ‖ a wild olive tree [L. fr. *olea*, olive tree]

o·le·ate (óuli:eit) n. (chem.) a salt of oleic acid

o·lec·ra·non (oulékrənɒn, oulikréinɒn) n. (anat.) the bony protuberance on the upper end of the ulna [Gk *ōlekrānon* fr. *ōlenē*, elbow + *kranion*, the head]

o·le·fin, o·le·fine (óuləfin) n. (chem.) an open-chain hydrocarbon with at least one double bond, esp. of the general formula C_nH_{2n}

o·le·ic (óuli:ik, ouli:ik) adj. (chem.) of, obtained from or found in oil ‖ of oleic acid [fr. L. *oleum*, oil]

oleic acid a liquid unsaturated acid, $CH_3(CH_2)_7CH=CH(CH_2)_7COOH$, that occurs widely in plant and animal fats as glycerides and that is used chiefly in making soaps and detergents

o·le·in (óuli:in) n. (chem.) a glyceride of oleic acid ‖ the liquid part of a fat (cf. STEARINE) [F. *oléine*]

o·le·o (óuli:ou) n. margarine [shortened fr. OLEO-MARGARINE]

o·le·o·graph (óuli:ougræf, óuli:ougrɒf) n. a chromolithograph meant to resemble an oil painting

o·le·o·mar·ga·rine (ouli:oumárdʒərin, ouli:oumárdʒəri:n) n. margarine [fr. L. *oleum*, oil + MARGARINE]

o·le·o·phit·ic (ouli:oufítik) adj. having the capacity to attract oil to itself

o·le·o·res·in (ouli:ourézin) n. a mixture of an essential oil and resin found in a natural state or prepared for pharmaceutical purposes [fr. L. *oleum*, oil + RESIN]

O·lé·ron (ɔleirɔ́) an island (area 67 sq. miles, pop. 14,000) southwest of La Rochelle, France, part of Charente Maritime: fisheries (esp. oysters), tourism

ol·fac·tion (ɒlfǽkʃən) n. the sense of smell ‖ the act of smelling **ol·fac·tive** adj. [fr. L. *olfacere*, to smell]

ol·fac·to·ry (ɒlfǽktəri, ɒlfǽktri:) adj. of or relating to smelling or the sense of smell [fr. L. *olfactor* n. fr. *olfacere*, to smell]

olfactory lobe a pair of lobes of the vertebrate brain, projections of the cerebral hemispheres. The cranial nerves associated with the sense of smell arise from them

ol·fac·tron·ics (ɒlfæktrɒ́niks) n. science of odors and their detection, esp. with instruments — **olfactronic** adj. of the capability

Ol·ga (ɒ́lgə), St (d. 969), duchess of Kiev. She did much to spread Christianity in Kiev. Feast: July 11

o·lib·a·num (ɒlíbənəm, oulíbənəm) n. frankincense [M.L.]

ol·i·garch (ɒ́ligɑrk) n. a member of an oligarchy **ol·i·gár·chic, ol·i·gár·chi·cal** adjs **ol·i·gár·chi·cal·ly** adv. [fr. Gk *oligarchēs* fr. *oligos*, few + *archein*, to rule]

ol·i·gar·chy (ɒ́ligɑrki:) pl. **ol·i·gar·chies** n. a form of government in which power is in the hands of a few ‖ a state or country ruled in this way ‖ the governing members of an oligarchy [fr. Gk *oligarchia*]

oli·gid·ic (ɒligídik) adj. (chem.) composed of undefined (except water) constituents Cf HOLIDIC, MERIDIC

Ol·i·go·cene (óligousi:n) adj. (geol.) of the epoch or series of the Tertiary between the Miocene and the Eocene (*GEOLOGICAL TIME) **the Oligocene** the Oligocene epoch or series of rocks [fr. Gk *oligos*, little + *kainos*, new]

ol·i·go·chaete (óligouki:t) 1. n. a member of *Oligochaeta*, a class of hermaphrodite terrestial and freshwater annelids without parapodia 2. adj. of or relating to an oligochaete [fr. Mod. L. *Oligochaeta* fr. Gk *oligos*, few + *chaite*, mane, bristle]

ol·i·go·clase (óligoukleis) n. a mineral of the plagioclase group [fr. Gk *oligos*, little + *klasis*, fracture]

o·lig·o·mer (ɒlígoumər) n. (organic chem.) a short-chain polymer with 6.4 recurring monomer units ant. —**oligomeric** adj. Cf MONOMER

ol·i·go·mer·ic (ɒligoumárik) adj. (botany) made up of few parts —**oligomer** n. —**oligomeric** adj. —**oligomerization** adv.

ol·i·go·my·cin (ɒligoumáisin) n. (pharm.) a class of fungicidal antibiotics derived from actinomycete

ol·i·go·nu·cle·o·tide (ɒligonú:kli:ətaid) n. (organic chem.) a substance made up of few nucleotides

ol·i·gop·o·ly (ɒligɒ́pəli:) n. control of a market by a few producers, no one producer being dominant [fr. Gk *oligos*, few + *polein*, to sell]

ol·i·go·sac·cha·ride (ɒligousǽkəraid) n. (chem.) one of a class of carbohydrates containing a known small number of monosaccharide units, usually 2, 3 or 4, and of usually simple known structure [fr. Gk *oligos*, few + SACCHARIDE]

o·li·go·troph·ic (ɒligoutrɒ́fik) adj. of deep clear lakes with low nutrient supplies, with a high dissolved-oxygen level and containing little organic matter

o·lim (ouli:n) n. (Hebrew) Jews who immigrate to Israel Cf ALIYA

ol·i·va·ceous (ɒləvéiʃəs) adj. resembling an olive ‖ having the yellow-green color of an olive [Mod. L. *olivaceus*, F. *olivacé*]

O·li·va·res (ɔliváres), Gaspar de Guzmán, conde de (1587–1645), Spanish statesman. As the minister of Philip IV, he was the virtual ruler of Spain (1621–43)

ol·i·va·ry (ɒ́livəri:) adj. (anat.) of or pertaining to an olivary body, i.e. either of two olive-shaped prominences located on each of the anterior surfaces of the medulla oblongata [fr. L. *olivarius*]

o·live (ɒ́liv) 1. n. *Olea europaea*, fam. *Oleaceae*, a small evergreen tree, with silvery green leaves, native to the Mediterranean region and now also cultivated in North and South America and Australia ‖ its small, oval, edible fruit (a drupe), which yields olive oil. This fruit, yellowish-green when unripe and almost black when ripe, is also eaten as a relish or an appetizer ‖ the wood of this tree ‖ the yellow-green color of the unripe fruit ‖ any tree of the genus *Olea* 2. adj. of or pertaining to the olive tree or its fruit ‖ of the color olive ‖ (of a complexion) of a light brownish-yellow color [F.]

olive drab a deep olive-green color ‖ a woolen or cotton fabric of this color used esp. for military uniforms

olive oil a yellow oil pressed from olives and used as a salad dressing, in cooking, in medicine and in soap manufacture etc.

Ol·i·ver (ɒ́livər), Isaac (c. 1566–1617), English miniature painter, of French origin. He was probably a pupil of Hilliard

Olives, Mount of the highest point (2,737 ft) in the range of hills east of Jerusalem

Olivier (oulívjei), Lawrence Kerr, Baron Olivier of Brighton (1907–) English actor, considered one of the finest English actors of the 20th century. Best known for his portrayals of Hamlet (1937; film, 1948) and Richard III (1945; film, 1955), he also performed other Shakespearean roles on stage as well as on film and in television productions. Equally successful in modern roles, he appeared in 'The Entertainer' (1957; film, 1960), 'Rhinoceros' (1960) and 'Long Day's Journey into Night' (1972). He was director of the National Theatre of England (1963–73). Knighted in 1947, he was made a life peer in 1970. His autobiography was published in 1982

ol·i·vine (ɒlíví:n, ɒlivi:n) n. a form of chrysolite [fr. L. *oliva*, olive]

o·lla (ɒ́lə) n. a wide-mouthed pot used for cooking olla-podrida [Span. *olla*, stew]

o·lla-po·dri·da (ɒləpɒdrí:də, ɔljəpɒdrí:ðə) n. a mixed dish of highly seasoned meat and vegetables cooked in an olla [Span.=rotten pot]

olm (oulm) n. a proteus [G.]

Ol·mec (ɒ́lmek) pl. **Ol·mec, Ol·mecs** n. an Olmeca

Ol·me·ca (ɒlméikə) pl. **Ol·me·ca, Ol·me·cas** n. an ancient Mexican people who inhabited the present states of Veracruz, Tabasco, and Oaxaca. They attained (800-100 B.C.) a relatively high degree of civilization

Ol·me·do (ɒlméðɔ), José Joaquín (1780–1847), Ecuadorian patriot, neoclassical poet, and president (1820) of the governing junta of Guayaquil. In 'La victoria de Junín, canto a Bolívar', and 'Al general Flores, vencedor en Miñarica', he sings the glories of Bolívar, Sucre and San Martín, and postulates a Pan-Americanism 'from pole to pole'

Olm·sted (óumsted), Frederick Law (1822–1903), U.S. landscape architect who designed plans for the development of U.S parks and public grounds, notably for Central Park, New York

Ol·mütz, Treaty of (ɔ́lmyts) a treaty signed (Nov. 29, 1850) between Prussia, Austria and Russia. It restored the German Confederation and returned Schleswig-Holstein to Denmark

Ol·ney (óulni:), Richard (1835–1917), U.S. lawyer and cabinet member. As attorney general (1893–5) under President Grover Cleveland, he set a precedent during the Pullman railroad strike by ordering U.S. attorneys to obtain federal court injunctions to restrain acts of violence. As secretary of state (1895–7) under Cleveland, he informed (1895) the British government in his 'Olney Corollary' to the Monroe

Doctrine that U.S. intervention was permissible, and even desirable, to force a settlement of any dispute involving the Monroe Doctrine

O·lo·mouc (ɔ́lɔmouts) (*G.* Olmütz) a former capital (pop. 103,000) of Moravia, Czechoslovakia, on the Morava, producing sugar, beer, chocolate, metal goods. Cathedral (12th–13th cc.). University (1581–1855, reestablished 1946)

o·lo·ro·so (pləróusou) *n.* basic type of sherry from which amorosa and cream sherry are made

Ol·te·ni·a (plti:ni:ə) the western part of Walachia

O·lym·pi·a (oulímpiə) the capital (pop. 27,447) of Washington state: brewing

Olympia a principal sanctuary of the Olympian gods, and scene of the ancient Olympic Games, in the W. Peloponnesus, Greece. Chief remains: temples of Zeus and Hera and the 'Hermes' of Praxiteles

O·lym·pi·ad (Oulímpi:æd) *n.* the four-year period between one Olympian festival and the next, used by the ancient Greeks in reckoning time ‖ a celebration of the modern Olympic Games [*F. Olympiade* fr. *L.* fr. *Gk*]

O·lym·pi·an (Oulímpi:ən) **1.** *adj.* of or relating to Olympus ‖ majestic, lofty in manner **2.** *n.* one of the gods supposed by the ancient Greeks to dwell upon Olympus, esp. Zeus [fr. *L.L. Olympianus*, fr. *Gk Olympios*, of Olympus]

O·lym·pic (oulímpik) **1.** *adj.* of or relating to Olympia, Greece, or Mount Olympus ‖ of or relating to the Olympic Games **2.** *n.* (*pl.*) the Olympic Games [fr. *L. Olympicus* fr. *Gk*]

Olympic Games an international amateur athletic competition which takes place every fourth year in whatever country the International Olympic Committee decides. The name is derived from the national athletic festival held at Olympia (776 B.C.–394 A.D.) in honor of Zeus by the ancient Greeks. The games were revived in 1896, when eight countries took part. Today most countries are represented in summer competitions for men and women, which include track and field athletics, as well as swimming, shooting, boxing etc. and, in separate Winter Games, winter sports. Some classic events, e.g. the pentathlon, are preserved. The games are opened with a spectacular ceremony, in which the Olympic flame is lit by a torch carried from Athens by relays of runners

O·lym·pus (oulímpəs) (*Gk* Olympos) the ancient name of several mountains in Greece, still used for the summit (9,800 ft) of a chain separating W. Thessaly from Macedonia. It was the dwelling place of the gods in Greek mythology

o·mah (oúmɑ) *n.* reputed large, hairy humanoid creature in the Pacific Northwest *also* Big Foot, sasquatch

O·ma·ha (oúməhɑ, óuməhɔ) *n.* a member of a Siouan tribe of North American Indians in N.E. Nebraska

Omaha the largest city (pop. 596,614) of Nebraska, on the Missouri River, a rail center and market (livestock, grain): meat packing, cereals and flour, dairy processing, oil refining

Oman (oumǽn) a sultanate (area 83,614 sq. miles, pop. 1,009,000) in the eastern corner of Arabia. Capital: Muscat (pop. 50,000). Chief town: Matrah. People: Arabs, with small Indian, African, Baluchi and Persian minorities. Language: Arabic. Religion: Moslem. The sultanate includes the tip of the Musandam Peninsula, separated from the rest of the country by the Trucial States. The Hajar Mtns in the north, rising to 10,200 ft, separate the fertile coastal plain from the Great Sandy Desert. In the south the Qara Mtns give some shelter to the oases of Dhufar. Average temperatures (F.): Muscat 70° (Jan.) and 90° (Jul.), more temperate in the central Nazwah oasis. Rainfall 4–8 ins along the coast, more in the mountains. Livestock: cattle, camels. Crops: cereals, dates, limes, pomegranates. Industries: petroleum, metalworking, fishing, fish preserving. Exports: petroleum, dates, limes, fish. Imports: foodstuffs, vehicles, tobacco, cotton goods, cement. Monetary unit: Indian rupee along the coast, Maria Theresa dollar inland, also the Omani local copper and nickel coins (baizas). The coast was controlled by the Portuguese (1508–1659) and the Turks (1659–1741). A sultanate thereafter, it dominated parts of Iran and E. Africa (19th c.). A treaty of friendship was signed with Britain (1891). Ruled from 1932 to his overthrow in 1970 by Sultan Said bin Taimur, Oman embarked in 1970 upon a

modernization program under his son, Qaboos (*KURIA MURIA ISLANDS)

O·mar ib·n al Khat·tab (óumɑríbənælkætáb) (c. 581–644), second Moslem caliph (634–44) in succession to Abu Bekr. He conquered Syria, Persia and Egypt

O·mar Khay·yám (óumɑrkaiɑ́m) (Ghiáth uddin Abul Fath Omar ibn Ibrahím al-Khayyám, c. 1050–1123), Persian writer and astronomer. His contemporary reputation was in mathematics and astronomy. Edward FitzGerald's version (1859) of his 'Rubáiyát' gave him his reputation as a poet in the West

o·ma·sum (Ouméisəm) *pl.* **o·ma·sa** (ouméisə) *n.* the division between the reticulum and the abomasum in a ruminant's stomach [L.=bullock's tripe]

O·may·yad (oumájɑd) an Umayyad

om·ber, esp. *Br.* **om·bre** (ómbər) *n.* a card game popular in the 17th and 18th cc. ‖ the player who tries to win the pool in this game [Span. *hombre*, man]

om·buds·man (ómbudzmən) *pl.* **om·buds·men** (ómbudzmən) *n.* a person appointed by a legislative body to receive, investigate and report on complaints by private individuals against government officials [Swed.=commissioner]

Om·dur·man (ɔmdə:rmɑ́n) a trading center (pop. 299,401) in the Sudan, on the Nile opposite Khartoum. It was the scene of Kitchener's Anglo-Egyptian victory (1898) over the forces of the Khalifa

o·me·ga (oumí:gə, ouméigə) *n.* the twenty-fourth and last letter (Ω, ω=o) of the Greek alphabet ‖ (*particle phys.*) the heaviest hyperon elementary particle, negatively charged with a mass of 1,672 MEV and a lifetime of 1.1×10^{-10}, decaying into xi and a pion, detected in 1964 [Gk *ō mega*=large O]

Omega 7 tight-wing terrorist group of Cuban exiles in the U.S.

om·e·let, om·e·lette (ómlit,ómə́lit) *n.* eggs beaten lightly together and cooked in a frying pan, often with cheese, ham, herbs etc. [*F. omelette*]

o·men (oúmən) **1.** *n.* a phenomenon or occurrence interpreted as a sign of good or evil to come ‖ (*rhet.*) presage or foreboding, *a bird of ill omen* **2.** *v.t.* (*rhet.*) to portend [L.]

o·men·tal (oumént'l) *adj.* of or in the omentum

o·men·tum (ouméntəm) *pl.* **o·men·ta** (oumántə) *n.* (*anat.*) a fold of the peritoneum connecting the abdominal viscera [L.]

om·i·cron (ómikrɔn, *Br.* oumáikrən) *n.* the fifteenth letter (O, o=o) of the Greek alphabet [Gk *ō mikron*=small O]

o·mi·nous (óminəs) *adj.* threatening, foreboding [fr. *L. ominosus*]

o·mis·si·ble (oumísəb'l) *adj.* able to be omitted [fr. *L. omittere* (*omissus*), to omit]

o·mis·sion (oumíʃən) *n.* an omitting or being omitted ‖ something which is left undone or left out [fr. *L. omissio* (*omissionis*)]

o·mit (oumít) *pres. part.* **o·mit·ting** *past* and *past part.* **o·mit·ted** *v.t.* to leave out either deliberately or through forgetfulness or neglect ‖ to neglect or fail (to do something) [fr. *L. omittere*]

om·ni·bus (ómnəbəs) **1.** *pl.* **om·ni·bus·es** *n.* a book collecting together several different but related works, *a boys' omnibus of adventure stories* ‖ (*old-fash.*) a bus **2.** *adj.* relating to or containing several miscellaneous items, *an omnibus clause in a bill* [fr. *L.*=for all, dative pl. of *omnis*, all]

omnibus account (*securities*) an account carried by one futures commission merchant with another futures commission merchant in which the transactions of two or more persons are combined

om·ni·com·pe·tent (ɔmnikómpitənt) *adj.* having jurisdiction or legal capacity to act in all cases [fr. *L. omnis*, all+COMPETENT]

om·ni·fac·et·ed (ɔmnəfǽsitəd) *adj.* showing all points of view

om·ni·fo·cal (ɔmnəfóuk'l) *adj.* (*optics*) of a bifocal lens with gradual transition of corrections

om·nip·o·tence (ɔmnípətəns) *n.* the state or quality of being omnipotent [fr. *L.L. omnipotentia*]

om·nip·o·tent (ɔmnípətənt) **1.** *adj.* allpowerful, having unlimited authority **2.** *n.* **the Om·nip·o·tent** God [F.]

om·ni·pres·ence (ɔmnəprézəns) *n.* the state or quality of being omnipresent [fr. *M.L. omnipraesentia*]

om·ni·pres·ent (ɔmnəprézənt) *adj.* ubiquitous, present everywhere [fr. *M.L. omnipraesens* (*omnipraesentis*)]

om·nis·cience (ɔmníʃəns) *n.* infinite knowledge or wisdom [fr. *M.L. omniscientia*]

om·nis·cient (ɔmníʃənt) *adj.* all-knowing, infinitely wise [fr. *Mod. L. omnisciens* (*omniscientis*)]

om·ni·vore (ómnivɔr, ómnivour) *n.* an animal (e.g. a man, a pig) adapted to eat a wide variety of food, both animal and vegetable. Omnivores have a gut intermediate in length between that of the herbivore (long) and the carnivore (short) [fr. *Mod. L. Omnivora*, omnivorous animals]

om·ni·vor·ous (ɔmnívərəs) *adj.* feeding on animal and vegetable substances ‖ taking in everything, not selective, *an omnivorous reader* [fr. *L. omnivorous*]

Omsk (ɔmsk) a city (pop. 1,080,000) of W. Siberia, R.S.F.S.R., U.S.S.R., on the Irtysh River. It is on the Trans-Siberian Railroad. It is an agricultural market, with engineering, food processing, chemical and textile industries

O·mu·ta (óumu:tɑ) a town (pop. 206,000) in N.W. Kyushu, Japan: coal mines, zinc refinery, steel works, cotton spinning, chemicals

on (ɔn, ɒn) **1.** *prep.* supported or suspended by, *a bucket on a chain* ‖ occupying part of and supported by, *the lamp on the desk* ‖ covering and supported by, *the cloth on the table* ‖ attached to, *the mirror on the wall* ‖ located at, *a house on Madison Avenue*, *the stain on the ceiling* ‖ immediately beside, near by, *castles on the Rhine* ‖ at the time or occasion of, *on Dec. 31, on his third visit* ‖ concerning, about, *a book on magic* ‖ used to indicate membership, *on the advisory board* ‖ engaged in, *away on a business trip* ‖ in a condition or state of, *on fire, on parole* ‖ deriving from, yielded by, *profit on a book* ‖ in the direction of, *the sun beat down on our heads* ‖ due to the use of, *drunk on whiskey* ‖ by, with or through the means of, *we went on the bus* ‖ (*pop.*) at the expense of, *have a drink on me* ‖ having as a basis, *on whose authority?* ‖ expressing manner, *on the loose, on the sly* ‖ added to, *brick on brick* ‖ directed against, *vengeance on the offenders* ‖ about to overwhelm, *the wave was nearly on them* ‖ **on time** punctual ‖ **to have something on someone** to be in possession of damaging information about someone **2.** *adv.* expressing forward movement or progress in space, *to hurry on ahead* ‖ or in time, *they talked on late into the night* ‖ in a situation of covering or contacting, *put the lid on* ‖ by way of clothing, *what did she have on?* ‖ in function or activity, *put the light on* ‖ as a planned activity, *have we anything on tonight?* ‖ working, *he's on one Sunday in three* ‖ or performing, *she's on in the second act* ‖ **and so on** and more of the same sort ‖ **on and off** intermittently ‖ **on and on** relentlessly continuing, *the rain went on and on* ‖ **to look on** to be an observer taking no active part **3.** *adj.* functioning, in action, *the light is on* ‖ (*cricket*) to, from or in the side of the wicket where the batsman stands and the corresponding part of the field, *an on drive* **4.** *n.* (*cricket*) the on side [O.E. *an, on*]

on·a·ger (ónədʒər) *n.* a wild ass of central Asia sometimes classified as *Equus onager*, fam. *Equidae*, and sometimes as a variety ‖ a medieval machine used for catapulting heavy stones [L.]

o·nan·ism (óunənizəm) *n.* interrupted coition ‖ masturbation [after *Onan* (Genesis xxxviii, 9)]

on-cam·er·a (ɔnkǽmərə) *adj.* being photographed, esp. for video or motion pictures *Cf* OFF-CAMERA

once (wʌns) **l.** *adv.* on one occasion only, *she met him once* ‖ a single time, *once a day* ‖ at any time, ever, *if the news is once printed* ‖ formerly, at some time, *he must have been young once* ‖ by one degree of relationship, *a cousin once removed* ‖ **more than once** several times ‖ **not once** never ‖ **once and (or once) for all** finally ‖ **once in a while** occasionally ‖ **once or twice** occasionally, a few times **2.** *conj.* whenever, *once it goes, it goes well* ‖ if ever, *once he realized what was meant, he would be furious* ‖ as soon as, *once they arrive, we can leave* **3.** *n.* one time, *once is enough* ‖ **all at once** at one and the same time, *crying and laughing all at once* ‖ suddenly, *all at once he leaped to his feet* ‖ **at once** immediately, *come at once* ‖ simultaneously, *you can't do two things at once* ‖ both, *she is at once clever and modest* ‖ **for once** on this particular occasion, for a change, *he's behaving himself for once* ‖ **this once** just on this particular

CONCISE PRONUNCIATION KEY: (a) æ, c*a*t; ɑ, c*a*r; ɔ f*aw*n; ei, sn*a*ke. (e) e, h*e*n; i:, sh*ee*p; iə, d*ee*r; ɛə, b*ea*r. (i) i, f*i*sh; ai, t*i*ger; ə:, b*i*rd. (o) o, *o*x; au, c*ow*; ou, g*oa*t; u, p*oo*r; ɔi, r*oy*al. (u) ʌ, d*u*ck; u, b*u*ll; u:, g*oo*se; ə, b*a*cillus; ju:, c*u*be. x, lo*ch*; θ, *th*ink; δ, *b*other; z, *Z*en; ʒ, corsa*g*e; dʒ, sava*g*e; ŋ, ora*ng*utan*g*; j, *y*ak; ʃ, *f*ish; tʃ, fe*tch*; 'l, rabb*le*; 'n, redd*en*. Complete pronunciation key appears inside front cover.

occasion, *please do it this once* [M.E. *ānes, ones* fr. *ān, on,* one]

once-o·ver (wʌ́nsouvər) *n.* (*pop.*) a quick examination, *just give these notes the once-over for me* ‖ a hasty cleaning dusting etc.

on·co·gene (ɔ́nkouʒən) *n.* (*genetics*) a gene that produces tumors —**oncogenicity** *n.*

on·co·gen·e·sis (ɔnkoudʒénisis) *n.* the beginnings of a tumor —**oncogenicity** *n.* the ability to produce a tumor *Cf* CARCINOGENIC

on·com·ing (ɔ́nkʌmiŋ, ɒ́nkʌmiŋ) **1.** *adj.* approaching, *the oncoming traffic* **2.** *n.* the approaching, *the oncoming of winter*

on·do·scope (ɔ́ndouskoup) *n.* (*electr.*) device to detect high-frequency radiation utilizing the ionization of gas in a glow-discharge tube

one (wʌn) **l.** *adj.* being a single unit (*NUMBER TABLE) ‖ being a particular unit, creature or thing as compared with another or others ‖ so closely identified as to be virtually a single unit, *horse and rider were one* ‖ on an unspecified (occasion), *one evening they appeared unexpectedly* ‖ a certain (person), *one John Brown telephoned* **for one thing** for one reason, *for one thing it didn't suit her and for another it was too expensive* **one and the same** exactly the same **one or two** a few **taking one thing with another** on balance **the one** the only, *the one item they were all agreed on* ‖ the (person, thing etc.) above all others, *the one present she wanted* **to be all one (to me,** him etc.) to be a matter of indifference (to me, him etc.) **2.** *pron.* a certain person or thing, usually of a specified kind, *one of their friends* ‖ any person whatever, *one must rest sometimes* ‖ (*rhet.*) someone, *like one possessed* ‖ (esp. *Br., pop.*) a joker or teaser, *you are a one* ‖ (*pop.*) a blow, *he gave him one on the jaw* ‖ (*pop.*) a joke (at someone's expense), *that's one on you* **all in one** combined, *he is cook, gardener and chauffeur all in one* **for one** at least, *he, for one, won't let you down* **after another** one after another successively **one and all** everyone without exception **one by one** one at a time **3.** *n.* the lowest of the cardinal numbers, denoting unity and represented by the figure 1 or the letter I ‖ a single unit, being or thing as compared with another or others, *the one he prefers* ‖ a thing or being of a specified kind, *my shoes are wet, so could you find me some dry ones?* ‖ one o'clock ‖ a domino marked with a single spot **at one** in agreement **to be a one for** to like very much, *he's a one for the girls* [O.E. *ān*]

one another referring to each of several reciprocally, *they all admired one another*

one-for-one (wʌ́nfɔrwʌ́n) *adj.* one professional for each client, e.g., in a hospital, school, etc.

O·ne·ga (ʌnéga) a lake (area 3,765 sq. miles) in the R.S.F.S.R. (mainly in the Karelian A.S.S.R.), U.S.S.R., frozen in winter. With Lake Ladoga it forms part of the Baltic-White Sea waterway, and it is linked to the Volga system by canal. Fisheries

one-horse (wʌ́nhɔrs, wʌ́nhours) *adj.* drawn or worked by one horse ‖ (*pop.*) utterly provincial, *a one-horse town* ‖ (*pop.*) second-rate

O·nei·da (ounáidə) *pl.* **O·nei·da, O·nei·das** *n.* a member of a North American Iroquoian Indian people ‖ the language of this people [fr. Iroquois *Oneyóde'=* stand-rock]

O'Neill (ouníːl), Eugene Gladstone (1888–1953), American dramatist. His plays include 'Emperor Jones' (1920), 'Desire under the Elms' (1924), 'Strange Interlude' (1928), 'Mourning Becomes Electra' (1931) and 'The Iceman Cometh' (1946). Basically a realist, he was one of the first writers to incorporate the findings of psychology into drama. He experimented widely with dramatic forms and themes and with staging techniques, greatly expanding the scope of modern drama

O'Neill, Thomas P., Jr. 'Tip' (1912–) U.S. politician, Speaker of the House of Representatives (1977–87). A Massachusetts Democrat, he served in Congress from 1952 until his retirement in 1987. He was known throughout his long career for his skill in effecting behind-the-scenes compromise

o·nei·ric (ounáirik) *adj.* of or relating to dreams [fr. Gk *oneiros*, a dream]

one-lin·er (wʌnláinər) *n.* a very short bit of wit or repartee

one·ness (wʌ́nnis) *n.* singleness, the quality of being one ‖ unity, the quality of being at one, *the oneness of their tastes and interests* ‖ wholeness, *oneness of personality*

one-on-one (wʌ́nɒnwʌ́n) *adj.* of a competition that pits one person directly against another

on·er·ous (ɔ́nərəs, óunərəs) *adj.* burdensome, troublesome [O.F. *onereus*]

one's (wʌnz) **1.** *contr.* of ONE IS **2.** *possessive adj.* of, pertaining to or belonging to one, *one's love affairs are one's own business* ‖ experienced, done or made by one

one·self (wʌnsélf) *pron.* refl. form of ONE, one owes it to oneself ‖ emphatic form of ONE, one would not choose it oneself **by oneself** unaided ‖ alone, without a companion or companions **in oneself** at heart, basically

one shot a project to be produced only once — **one-shot** *adj.*

one-sid·ed (wʌ́nsáidid) *adj.* limited to one side, *a one-sided decision* ‖ partial, unfair, *one-sided arguments* ‖ having only one side

one-stop tour charter (wʌnstɔ́p) round-trip air flight, booked 15 days ahead (30 days for an overseas flight) requiring a minimum four-day stop *acronym* OTC

one·time (wʌ́ntaim) *adj.* former, *a onetime schoolteacher* ‖ occurring only once

one-time-pad (wʌ́ntaimpæd) *n.* (*cryptography*) a series of random numbers each to be used only once in deciphering a code

one-track (wʌ́ntræk) *adj.* obsessed by or dwelling boringly on one thing only, *a one-track mind*

one-up (wʌ́nʌp) *adj.* **1.** one point ahead, in one-upmanship **2.** the technique of getting a point ahead **one-up** *v.* to score on a point —**one-upman** *n.*

one-up·man·ship (wʌnʌ́pmənʃip) *n.* program or technique of coming out ahead in personal relationships by placing an antagonist at a psychological disadvantage; coined by Stephen Potter

one-way (wʌ́nwéi) *adj.* moving or allowing movement in one direction only ‖ functioning in one direction only, *a one-way radio*

on·go·ing (ɔ́ngouiŋ, ɒ́ngouiŋ) *adj.* that is actively going on ‖ growing or developing

on·ion (ʌ́njən) *n. Allium cepa*, fam. *Liliaceae*, a Middle Eastern plant widely cultivated for its sharp-tasting edible bulb, consisting of layers arranged concentrically ‖ this bulb, cooked or pickled or raw, served as food **to know one's onions** (esp. *Br.*) to have thorough knowledge of a particular field [F. *oignon*]

on·ion·skin (ʌ́njənskin) *n.* the papery, yellowish-brown outer covering of the onion bulb ‖ a kind of very thin paper, used esp. in typing carbon copies

O·nitsh·a (ounítʃə) a commercial and agricultural center (pop. 220,000) in E. Nigeria, on the Niger. Roman Catholic cathedral (1935), Anglican cathedral (1952)

on·li·cense (ɔ́nlais'ns, ɒ́nlais'ns) *n.* a license to sell alcoholic drinks for consumption on the premises

on-line (ɔ́nláin) *adj.* (*computer*) of a system in which the central processing unit controls the operation and peripheral devices, e.g., storage, output —**on-line** *adj.*

on·look·er (ɔ́nlukər, ɒ́nlukər) *n.* a passive spectator

on·ly (óunliː) *adj.* single, sole, *an only child* ‖ belonging to a unique class, *these are the only ripe apples* ‖ alone worthy of consideration, *she's the only girl for him* [O.E. *ānlic* fr. *ǣnlīc*, unique, excellent]

only 1. *adv.* solely, *are you cross only because of that?* ‖ merely, just, *he was only joking* ‖ as little as, *she left only five minutes ago* ‖ as the sole consequence, *it will only upset you* **if only** used to express a wish or regret, *if only she had kept quiet* **only just** by a very small margin, *he only just missed the train* ‖ very shortly before or just recently, *she had only just bought it* **only too** (**pleased, true** etc.) very (pleased, true etc.) **2.** *conj.* but, except that, *he'd like to go only he promised not to* [M.E. *onliche* fr. *onlich* adj., only]

on·o·mat·o·poe·ia (ɒnəmætəpíːə) *n.* word-formation by imitation of the sound made by what is represented ‖ the effect achieved by grouping words chosen in imitation of a sound described ‖ such a word or group of words, e.g. 'splash', 'cuckoo' **on·o·mat·o·po·e·ic** *adj.* **on·o·mat·o·po·e·i·cal·ly** *adv.* **on·o·mat·o·po·et·ic** (ɒnəmætəpouétik) *adj.* **on·o·mat·o·po·et·i·cal·ly** *adv.* [L. fr. Gk *onomatopoiia*, the making of words]

on·rush (ɔ́nrʌʃ, ɒ́nrʌʃ) *n.* a sudden rush onward or forward

on·set (ɔ́nset, ɒ́nset) *n.* an attack ‖ the beginning of something thought of as an attack, *the onset of old age*

on·shore (ɔ́nʃɔr, ɔ́nʃour, ɒ́nʃɔr, ɒ́nʃour) **1.** *adj.* located on or near the shore ‖ moving toward the shore **2.** *adv.* toward the shore ‖ onto the shore

on·slaught (ɔ́nslɔt, ɒ́nslɔt) *n.* a fierce attack [fr. early Du. *aenslag*]

On·tar·i·o (ɒntέəri:ou) the leading agricultural and industrial province (area 412,582 sq. miles, pop. 8,625,107) of Canada. Capital: Toronto. Other main cities: Ottawa (the federal capital), Hamilton. Settlement is concentrated in the fertile Great Lakes–St Lawrence lowland in the south. N. Ontario lies largely on the Canadian Shield. Agriculture: beef and dairy cattle, hogs, poultry, tobacco, fodder crops, fruit. Resources: timber, nickel (50% of world supply), copper, gold, uranium, iron ore, oil, hydroelectric power. Industries: iron and steel, chemicals, motor vehicles, electrical machinery, pulp and paper, food processing. The region was inhabited by Huron Indians when the first French (1615) and English (1671) settlements were made. As part of New France, it was ceded to England (1763). It became a province of the Canadian Confederation (1867)

Ontario the smallest, most easterly lake (area 7,540 sq. miles) of the Great Lakes of the U.S.A. and Canada between Ontario and New York State, linked to Lake Erie by the Niagara River. Chief ports: Toronto, Rochester (*ST LAWRENCE SEAWAY)

on-the-job training (ɒnðədʒɔ́btréiniŋ) *n.* learning while working

on·to, *Br.* **on to** (ɔ́ntuː,ɒ́ntuː) *prep.* to a position on or upon, *climb onto the next branch* ‖ on the trail or track of, *he's onto a good thing*

on·to·gen·e·sis (ɒntədʒénisis) *n.* ontogeny [fr. Gk *on* (*ontos*), being+GENESIS]

on·tog·e·ny (ɒntódʒəni:) *n.* the history of the development of an individual organism (cf. PHYLOGENY) [fr. Gk *on* (*ontos*), being+*genes*, born of]

on·to·log·i·cal (ɒntəlódʒik'l) *adj.* of or relating to ontology

on·tol·o·gy (ɒntóladʒiː) *n.* the branch of metaphysics concerned with the essence of things ‖ the study of being [fr. Gk *on* (*ontos*), being+*logos*, discourse]

o·nus (óunəs) *n.* responsibility, burden [L.]

on·ward (ɔ́nwərd, ɒ́nwərd) **1.** *adj.* advancing, directed forward **2.** *adv.* further forward, towards the front **ón·wards** *adv.* onward

on·yx (ɒ́niks, óuniks) *n.* a chalcedony with layers of different colors [L. fr Gk *onux*, nail, onyx]

OOB (*abbr.*) for off-off-Broadway (which see)

o·o·cyte (óuəsait) *n.* an immature female germ cell just prior to the first maturation division (called the primary oocyte) or the member (secondary oocyte) of the pair so formed destined to become the ovum following the second maturation division (*MEIOSIS, *OOGENESIS) [fr. Gk *ōon*, egg+*kutos*, a hollow, a cell]

oo·dles (úːd'lz) *pl. n.* an abundance, *oodles of money* [origin unknown]

o·o·gen·e·sis (ouədʒénisis) *n.* the entire process of formation and maturation of the ovum from oogonium to primary and secondary oocytes, to ootid, and finally to the ovum [fr. Gk *ōon*, egg+GENESIS]

o·o·go·ni·um (ouəgóuniːəm) *pl.* **o·o·go·ni·a** (ouəgóuniːə) *n.* a primitive female germ cell giving rise to an oocyte (*OOGENESIS) ‖ the female sexual organ of certain algae and fungi producing eggs which give rise on fertilization to oospores (cf. ANTHERIDIUM) [fr. Gk *ōon*, egg+*gonos*, begetter]

o·o·lite (óuəlait) *n.* (*geol.*) a rock, esp. limestone, composed of round grains **o·o·lit·ic** (ouəlítik) *adj.* [F. *ōlithe*, Mod. L. *oōlires* fr. Gk *ōon*, egg+*lithos*, stone]

o·o·log·i·cal (ouəlódʒik'l) *adj.* of or relating to oology

o·ol·o·gist (ouóladʒist) *n.* someone who specializes in oology ‖ someone who collects birds' eggs

o·ol·o·gy (ouóladʒiː) *n.* the study of eggs, esp. those of birds [fr. Gk *ōon* egg+*logos*, discourse]

oo·long (úːlɔŋ, úːlɒŋ) *TEA [Chin. *wulung* fr. *wu*, black+*lung*, dragon]

Oom Paul (uːmpóuul) *KRUGER

o·o·phyte (óuəfait) *n.* (*bot.*) the sexual generation in archegoniate plants such as liverworts, mosses, ferns (cf. GAMETOPHYTE, cf. SPOROPHYTE) **o·o·phyt·ic** (ouəfitik) *adj.* [fr. Gk *ōon*, egg+*phuton*, plant]

CONCISE PRONUNCIATION KEY: **(a)** æ, cat; ɑ, car; ɔ fawn; ei, snake. **(e)** e, hen; iː, sheep; iə, deer; εə, bear. **(i)** i, fish; ai, tiger; əː, bird.
(o) o, ox; au, cow; ou, goat; u, poor; ɔi, royal. **(u)** ʌ, duck; u, bull; uː, goose; ə, bacillus; juː, cube. x, loch; θ, think; ð, bother; z, Zen; ʒ, corsage;
dʒ, savage; ŋ, orangutang; j, yak; ʃ, fish; tʃ, fetch; 'l, rabble; 'n, redden. Complete pronunciation key appears inside front cover.

o·o·sperm (óuəspəːrm) n. (zool.) a fertilized ovum ‖ (bot.) an oospore [fr. Gk ōon, egg + sperma, seed]

o·o·sphere (óuəsfiər) n. (biol.) an unfertilized ovum ‖ a female gamete, esp. of lower plants [fr. Gk ōon, egg+sphaira, sphere]

o·o·spore (óuəspɔːr, óuəspour) n. a resting spore produced by the gametophyte generation that gives rise eventually to the sporophyte generation of a plant (cf. ZYGOSPORE) **o·o·spor·ic** (ouəspórik, ouəspórik), **o·os·por·ous** (ouóspərəs, ouəspóːrəs, ouəspóurəs) adjs [fr. Gk ōon, egg+sporos, seed]

Oost·en·de (oustɛ́ndə) *OSTEND

Oo·ta·ca·mund (úːtəkamʌnd) a resort (pop. 30,000) in S. Madras, India, in the Nilgiri Hills at over 7,000 ft

o·o·the·ca (ouəθíːkə) pl. **o·o·the·cae** (ouəθíːsiː) n. (biol.) a hard-walled egg case **o·o·thé·cal** adj. [fr. Gk ōon, egg +thēkē, a case]

o·o·tid (óuətid) n. an immature haploid egg cell before the cytoplasmic changes which prepare it for fertilization during the final stages of the second meiotic division (*OOGENESIS) [fr. Gk ōon, egg+-id, structure or body of a specific kind. after 'spermatid']

ooze (uːz) 1. n. an infusion of bark used in tanning leather ‖ an oozing or that which oozes 2. v. pres. part. **ooz·ing** past and past part. **oozed** v.i. to flow slowly and viscously, esp. through small bodily apertures ‖ (of substances) to exude moisture etc. ‖ (fig.) to escape or leak out gradually and imperceptibly, he felt his courage oozing away ‖ v.t. to exude (moisture etc.) [M.E. wosen fr. wōs, juice, sap]

ooze n. mud saturated with water, esp. in a riverbed ‖ a deposit of shells (e.g. of foraminifers, volcanic dust etc. deposited on the bed of a deep Ocean **óoz·y** comp. **ooz·i·er** superl. **ooz·i·est** adj. containing, consisting of or like ooze ‖ exuding moisture etc. [O.E. wāse]

op. opus

o·pac·i·ty (oupǽsiti) pl. **o·pac·i·ties** the quality or state of being opaque ‖ the degree of being opaque ‖ obscurity of meaning ‖ mental obtuseness [F. opacité]

o·pah (óupə) n. Lampris regius or L. luna, fam. Lamprididae, a brightly colored edible fish with scarlet fins, inhabiting warm and temperate oceans [W. African]

o·pal (óup'l) n. SiO₂·nH₂O, an amorphous form of hydrous silica cut and used as a gem. Opals vary widely in color, and are usually iridescent, due to their refracting and reflecting light [fr. L. opalus fr. Skr.]

o·pal·es·cence (oup'lés'ns) n. the state or quality of being opalescent

o·pal·es·cent (oup'lés'nt) adj. being milkily iridescent

opal glass a translucent but not transparent glass, used esp. in ornamentation

o·pal·ine 1. (óup'lain, óup'liːn) adj. like an opal, opalescent 2. (óupəliːn) n. a translucent milky glass

o·paque (oupéik) 1. adj. of a medium whose molecular aggregation is such that radiant energy (usually light) cannot pass through it but is transformed into molecular kinetic energy (cf. TRANSLUCENT, cf. TRANSPARENT) ‖ obscure ‖ obtuse, slow-witted ‖ (bot.) not shining, dull 2. n. (photog.) an opaque paint used for blocking out sections of a negative [fr. L. opacus, shaded]

op art (ópárt) abstract art, usu. painting, creating a visually disconcerting effect, usu. with geometric patterns and optical illusion utilizing perspective pull and color also optical art — **op artist** n.

OPDAR *OPTICAL RADAR

OPEC (acronym) for Organization of Petroleum Exporting Countries, a combine of nations that produce substantially all commercial petroleum

Op-Ed page (ópédpéidʒ) a page placed opposite the editorial page of a newspaper on which individual points of view are expressed

o·pen (óupən) adj. not shut, an open window ‖ admitting customers, visitors etc., the shops are open ‖ expanded, unfolded, outspread, these buds will be open soon, leave the book open at the right page ‖ free and unoccupied, not engaged, he keeps Saturday mornings open for his students ‖ allowing passage, unblocked, the road is open ‖ exposed, unfenced, unobstructed, open country ‖ not closed or covered, an open carriage, an open sore exposed, open to attack ‖ receptive, open to suggestions ‖ generous, munificent, she gave with an open hand ‖ vacant, is

the position still open? ‖ available, only one course is open to us ‖ not definite, decided or concluded, an open question ‖ for any time but for no specified time, an open invitation ‖ undisguised, unconcealed, he looked on with open curiosity ‖ frank, concealing nothing in the mind, he was quite open with me ‖ not restricted, an open scholarship ‖ widely spaced, open ranks ‖ loose-textured, an open weave ‖ (of the bowels) not constipated ‖ (phon., of a vowel) pronounced with the tongue lowered ‖ (phon., of a consonant) pronounced with the speech organs not in contact ‖ (phon., of a syllable) ending with a vowel ‖ (of water) free from ice or other water hazards ‖ (naut.) not foggy ‖ (mus., of a string) not depressed by the finger ‖ (mus. of an organ pipe) not stopped at the end ‖ not having or not enforcing rules and regulations concerning gambling, drinking places etc., an open town ‖ offering legal hunting or fishing, the open season for geese ‖ (printing) having wide spaces between characters, words or lines ‖ (of an account) not closed, still operative [O.E.]

open v.t. to make open, to open a door ‖ to unwrap, unfasten, to open a parcel ‖ to unfold, to open a newspaper ‖ to begin, start (something), esp. functioning on a regular basis, to open a bank account, to open a restaurant ‖ to declare formally open, to open a conference ‖ to unblock, to make clear or passable, the thaw opened the river ‖ to loosen, to spread out, to open ranks ‖ to free (bodily passages) of obstructions ‖ to enlighten ‖ to make more responsive or sympathetic ‖ to make an incision in, to cut into, to open a wound ‖ to make (a way, path etc.) by removing or pushing aside obstacles ‖ to start (a card game) by bidding or betting first ‖ (law) to revoke (a judgment, decree etc.) ‖ in order to cause a delay and allow the parties time to prosecute or oppose ‖ (naut.) to get a view of by going beyond some obstruction ‖ v.i. to become open ‖ to expand, unfold, flowers open quickly in the warm weather ‖ to break open, come apart, the seam opened ‖ to begin, the book opens with a quotation ‖ to be revealed, the scene opened before their eyes ‖ to become receptive to ideas, to become aware (often with 'on' or 'into') to give access, the house opens onto the moor ‖ (often with 'on' or 'into') to have an opening or outlet, the bedrooms open on the courtyard ‖ to begin to be presented to the public, e.g. in a particular series of presentations, 'Hamlet' opens on Saturday **to open fire** to begin shooting **to open one's heart** (or **mind**) **to** to confide one's feelings (or thoughts) to **to open out** to unfold completely ‖ to develop, become more confident or communicative ‖ (Br.) to accelerate (a motor vehicle) to near top speed **to open the door to** to offer opportunity for, a degree opens the door to better jobs **to open the ground** to break up the ground by plowing or digging **to open up** to prepare (a house) for habitation after it has been unoccupied for some time ‖ to make accessible, to develop, to open up a new country ‖ to lay open, to open up an oyster ‖ to become active, trade is opening up again ‖ to speak without reticence, talk freely and readily [O.E. openian]

open n. (with 'the') the open air ‖ (with 'the') open country ‖ (with 'the') open water, water well out from shore ‖ (with 'the') public knowledge, why drag his secrets into the open? **to come into the open** to come out of hiding or cover [fr. OPEN adj. and OPEN v.]

open admissions 1. a policy of admitting any high school graduate to an institution of higher learning 2. policy of admitting any qualified student resident in or outside a neighborhood into a public school also open enrollment

open air the out-of-doors **o·pen-air** (óupənéər) adj. found in, performed in, or characteristic of the open air

o·pen-and-shut (óupənənʃʌ́t) adj. (pop.) quite obvious, simple, an open-and-shut case of blackmail

o·pen·cast (óupənkæst, óupənkɑst) adj. (Br.) opencut

open chain (chem.) an arrangement of atoms in a chain not having the ends connected to form a ring

open cheque (Br.) a check which has not been crossed and is payable to the bearer

open circuit an electric circuit in which no current flows, because of a break in its continuity

open city (mil.) a city in a war zone which is not occupied by a military force nor protected by military defenses. When so declared, it is immune under international law from attack

open classroom educational method using an informal curriculum centered on the discussion and investigation of subjects, carried on by students under teacher guidance also open corridor

o·pen-cut (óupənkʌt) adj. of a mine with the mineral strata exposed by the complete removal of the overlying strata, or of mining by this process

o·pen-door (óupəndɔ́r, óupəndóur) adj. of a policy of maintaining trade and other relations on equal terms with all nations, without discrimination or exclusion

o·pen-end·ed (óupənéndəd) adj. without a closing time or quantity, e.g., open-ended mortgage, mutual fund, drinking hours, prison term

open enrollment *OPEN ADMISSION

o·pen·er (óupənər) n. someone or something that opens, esp. a gadget for opening cans ‖ the first game in a series e.g. in baseball or bridge tournaments ‖ (pl., poker) cards of a designated value (usually a pair of jacks or better) permitting a player to start the betting

o·pen-eyed (óupənáid) adj. fully aware of the true facts of a situation and what they involve ‖ goggling, open-eyed with amazement

o·pen-faced (óupənféist) adj. (of a person) looking guilelessly sincere ‖ (of a sandwich or pie) having no top covering

o·pen-field (óupənfíːld) adj. (hist.) of a method of agriculture employed in medieval Europe in which arable land was divided into unfenced strips. These were cultivated usually under crop rotation, the various strips being worked by different peasants.

o·pen-hand·ed (óupənhǽndid) adj. generous

o·pen-heart·ed (óupənhártid) adj. of a generous nature

o·pen-hearth (óupənhárθ) adj. (metall.) of a furnace on the hearth of which pig iron and steel scrap are heated together in producer gas ‖ of this process

o·pen-heart surgery (óupənhártsəːrdʒəri) (med.) surgery with the heart exposed, esp. when the heart is hooked up to artificial blood circulation apparatus

open house informal hospitality on rather a large scale given to guests who care to avail themselves of a general invitation, they keep open house on Sunday evenings ‖ an instance of such hospitality, the dean of students had an open house for the freshman class

open housing of a real estate rental or sales policy barring racial discrimination

o·pen·ing (óupəniŋ) 1. n. a making or becoming open or an instance of this ‖ an act of initiating or beginning something ‖ a gap, an aperture, an opening in the hedge ‖ a beginning, the opening of a speech ‖ a counsel's initial statement of his case in court ‖ (stock exchange) the start of trading for the day, a vacancy in any kind of employment, esp. one thought of as an opportunity ‖ the occasion or ceremony when an exhibition, production of a play etc. becomes available to the public ‖ (chess) a recognized series of moves at the beginning of a game ‖ a forest clearing 2. adj. first, introductory, opening remarks

open letter a letter addressed to a particular individual but intended for public reading

o·pen-loop (óupənlúːp) adj. (eng.) of a process that has no self-correcting mechanism, depending entirely on input also control system Cf CLOSED-LOOP

o·pen·ly (óupənli) adv. frankly ‖ without concealment, publicly

open marriage an arrangement between spouses permitting each to carry on his or her activities (including extramarital sexual relations)

o·pen-mind·ed (óupənmáindid) adj. unprejudiced, ready to consider any suggestions or ideas

o·pen-mouthed (óupənmáuðd, óupənmáuθt) adj. gaping in hunger, astonishment or wonder

o·pen-of·fice environment (óupənófisinváirənmənt) system of office arrangement with movable, shoulder-level partitions

open order a disposition of troops with wide intervals between the units of the formation ‖ an order, esp. one placed with a stockbroker, which remains effective until canceled or filled ‖ a demand for goods leaving the seller a considerable margin in choosing what he will provide for the customer

open plan (*architecture*) arrangement of areas in a home or office by screens, changeable walls, floor or ceiling levels, etc., instead of stationary walls, facilitating layout changes and heating; developed by Frank Lloyd Wright

open plan school arrangement of classrooms with little or no visual or acoustic separations, with teachers cooperating in arrangement of students and subject presentations *Cf* TEAM TEACHING

open primary a primary election which does not require that members of a political party vote for candidates of that party. They may elect candidates of any party

open secret something theoretically a secret but in fact generally known

open sentence (*math.*) **1.** a statement in which the meaning is determined when an omitted quantity, word, or phrase is inserted **2.** an equation containing unknown quantities

open sesame something that removes all obstacles [from the command which opened the door to the thieves' treasure cave in 'Ali Baba and the Forty Thieves']

o·pen-shelf (óupənʃélf) *adj.* of or pertaining to a library or supermarket system in which users themselves fetch what they want from the shelves

open shop a firm or factory employing men who are not union members as well as those who are (cf. CLOSED SHOP)

open shopism policy of maintaining a non-union business operation

open sight a rear sight on a gun having an open notch

Open University an autonomous, independent, degree-awarding English university (chartered June 1, 1969) working through radio and television courses, instruction by correspondence and tutorials at local centers

open university a university teaching plan by radio or television offering four-yr degrees without prerequisite entrance requirements; offered by Milton Keynes, B.B.C. broadcaster

open verdict a judicial finding in a preliminary investigation determining that a crime has been committed but not specifying the criminal nor specifying violent death without determining the cause

o·pen·work (óupənwəːrk) *n.* any work, e.g. needlework, ironwork etc., that shows openings through it

op·er·a (ópərə,óprə) *n.* a stage drama with orchestral accompaniment, in which music is the dominant element, the performers singing all or most of their lines ‖ the score or libretto for such a drama ‖ a company that performs such dramas, or a theater designed for the performances of these ‖ such drama as an art form (*COMIC OPERA, *GRAND OPERA) [Ital.]

opera *pl.* of OPUS

op·er·a·ble (ópərəb'l) *adj.* admitting of a surgical operation ‖ capable of being operated [fr. L. *operari*, to operate]

o·pé·ra co·mique (ɔpeiræ̀kɔmiːk) *n.* French opera with spoken dialogue, whether comic or not (cf. COMIC OPERA) [F. orig.=comic opera]

opera glasses a very small pair of binoculars for use in a theater or opera house

opera hat a collapsible top hat

opera house a theater for the performance of operas

op·er·and (ópərænd) *n.* (*computer*) **1.** the portion of computation instructions that indicates the base quantities or the name of the operation, the result, parameter, or location **2.** any item of information

op·er·ant conditioning (ópərəntkəndíʃəniŋ) (*behavioral psych.*) technique of behavioral conditioning through manipulation of the consequences of previous behavior, through reinforcement *Cf* SKINNERIAN

op·er·ate (ópəreit) *pres. part.* **op·er·at·ing** *past and past part.* **op·er·at·ed** *v.i.* to be in action, function ‖ to take effect, *is the drug operating yet?* ‖ to perform an operation, esp. a surgical one ‖ to carry out military movements ‖ (of a stockbroker) to buy and sell ‖ *v.t.* to put into action, cause to work, *to operate a machine* ‖ to bring about, cause, *time has operated a change in him* ‖ to manage, run, *to operate a savings scheme* [fr. L. *operari* (*operatus*), to work]

op·er·at·ic (ópərǽtik) *adj.* of, relating to, or resembling opera **op·er·at·i·cal·ly** *adv.*

operating room (*Am.=Br.* operating theatre) a room in which surgical operations are performed, sometimes before a class of medical students

operating system (*computer*) the instructions and procedures for operating a device

operating theatre (*Br.*) an operating room

op·er·a·tion (ópəréiʃən) *n.* the act of operating, or an instance of this ‖ the way in which a thing works, *the operation of the valves needs improving* ‖ (*pl.*) work, activity, *operations on the site begin tomorrow* ‖ an instance of the work done by a surgeon ‖ a financial transaction, esp. a complex speculative one ‖ one of the specific processes or actions in a sequence ‖ (*computer*) the action indicated by a single instruction ‖ a military action on a large scale ‖ (*math.*) the process of altering a number or quantity by addition, subtraction, multiplication, division etc. **in operation** functioning or in working condition **o·per·a·tion·al** *adj.* of or connected with an operation, esp. a military one ‖ (e.g. of an aircraft) fit for action [O.F.]

operational research (*Br.*) operations research

operation code (*computer*) the reference label for an instruction *also* op code

Operation Overlord the code name of the plan devised (1943) in England by Gen. Dwight Eisenhower and his allied colleagues for the invasion of the European continent from the west. The plan, put into operation on D-Day (June 6, 1944), achieved its objective

operations research (*Am.=Br.* operational research) the application of scientific (esp. statistical) methods to the study of complex industrial, governmental or military problems

op·er·a·tive (ópərətiv, óprətiv, ópəreitiv) **1.** *adj.* working, in operation, *that law is no longer operative* ‖ effective, *an operative dose* ‖ relating to a surgical operation, *operative treatment* ‖ having to do with physical or mechanical operations, *operative skills* **2.** *n.* a hand (workman), e.g. in a factory ‖ a private detective [F. *opératif, opérative* or fr. L.L. *operativus*, creative, formative]

op·er·a·tor (ópəreitər) *n.* someone who operates a machine or instrument, esp. a telephone switchboard ‖ someone habitually engaged in large financial dealings ‖ (*pop.*) a shrewd individual capable of evading legal restrictions ‖ someone who runs a farm, mine, business etc. ‖ (*math.*) a term or function indicating some operation to be performed

operator gene (*genetics*) the portion of an operon nearest the repression protein *also* operator

o·per·cu·lar (oupə́ːrkjulər) *adj.* (*biol.*) of, relating to or having the nature of an operculum [fr. L. *operculum*, operculum]

o·per·cu·late (oupə́ːrkjulit, oupə́ːrkjuleit) *adj.* (*biol.*) having an operculum [fr. L. *operculare* (*operculatus*), to furnish with a lid]

o·per·cu·lum (oupə́ːrkjələm) *pl.* **o·per·cu·la** (oupə́ːrkjulə), **o·per·cu·lums** *n.* the gill cover of a fish ‖ a lid or covering flap of a moss capsule ‖ a plate on the foot of a gastropod, which closes the shell when the foot is retracted ‖ a covering or lid to various openings in different organisms, cells of bees etc. [L. fr. *operire*, to cover]

op·er·et·ta (ópəréta) *n.* a short, light opera, usually with spoken dialogue ‖ the musical score for this [Ital.]

op·er·on (ópərɒn) *n.* (*genetics*) a genetic unit made up of two coordinates (cistrons on the chromosome) that carries the genetic code, causing the synthesis of a protein in a polypeptide chain through an operator, regulated by a receptor sequence and a repressor *Cf* CISTRON

oph·i·cleide (ófiklaid) *n.* a deep-toned brass wind instrument consisting of a long tube bent back on itself, having finger keys. In modern orchestras it is replaced by the tuba [F. *ophicléide* fr. Gk *ophis*, serpent+*kleis*, key]

o·phid·i·an (oufídiːən) *n.* a snake [fr. Mod. L. *Ophidia*, name of the suborder fr. Gk *ophis*, snake]

oph·ite (ófait, óufait) *n.* any of several mottled, often green kinds of rock or marble, e.g. serpentine **o·phit·ic** (ɒfítik, oufítik) *adj.* [fr. L. *ophites* fr. Gk]

oph·thal·mi·a (ɒfθǽlmiːə, ɒpθǽlmiːə) *n.* inflammation of the eyeball or of the conjunctiva [L.L. fr. Gk fr. *ophthalmos*, eye]

oph·thal·mic (ɒfθǽlmik, ɒpθǽlmik) *adj.* of the eye [fr. L. *ophthalmicus* fr. Gk]

ophthalmic optician (*Br.*) an optometrist

oph·thal·mi·tis (ɒfθǽlmáitis, ɒpθǽlmáitis) *n.* ophthalmia [Mod. L. fr. Gk *ophthalmos*, eye]

oph·thal·mo·log·ic (ɒfθælməlɒ́dʒik, ɒpθælməlɒ́dʒik) *adj.* of or pertaining to ophthalmology **oph·thal·mo·log·i·cal** *adj.*

oph·thal·mol·o·gist (ɒfθælmɒ́lədʒist, ɒpθælmɒ́lədʒist, ɒfθælmɒ́lədʒist, ɒpθælmɒ́lədʒist) *n.* a doctor who specializes in eye diseases and defects [OPHTHALMOLOGY]

oph·thal·mol·o·gy (ɒfθælmɒ́lədʒiː, ɒfθælmɒ́lədʒiː, ɒpθælmɒ́lədʒiː, ɒpθəlmɒ́lədʒiː) *n.* the study of the eye and its diseases [fr. Gk *ophthalmos*, eye+*logos*, discourse]

oph·thal·mo·scope (ɒfθǽlmæskθoup, ɒpθǽlmæskoup) *n.* (*med.*) an instrument fitted with a mirror and a light for examining the inside of the eye **oph·thal·mo·scop·ic** (ɒfθǽlməskɒ́pik, ɒpθǽlməskɒ́pik) *adj.* [fr. Gk *ophthalmos*, eye+*skopein*, to observe]

o·pi·ate (óupiːit, óupiːeit) **1.** *n.* a drug containing opium, used to induce sleep or deaden pain ‖ anything that soothes or quiets **2.** *adj.* containing opium ‖ having the effect of an opiate [fr. M.L. *opiatus* adj., containing opium]

o·pine (oupáin) *pres. part.* **o·pin·ing** *past and past part.* **o·pined** *v.t.* to express or hold as an opinion, *he opined that the country was going to the dogs* [fr. L. *opinari*]

o·pin·ion (əpínjən) *n.* a mental estimate ‖ a belief or conviction, based on what seems probable or true but not on demonstrable fact ‖ the collective views of a large number of people, esp. on some particular topic, *to offend local opinion* ‖ a formal expression by an expert of what he judges to be the case or the right course of action, *counsel's opinion* [F. fr. L. *opinio* (*opinionis*)]

o·pin·ion·at·ed (əpínjəneitid) *adj.* stubbornly affirming one's own opinions, esp. through complacency or arrogance [fr. obs. *opiniated* perh. fr. L. *opinio*, opinion]

o·pin·ion·a·tive (əpínjəneitiv) *adj.* opinionated

O·pitz (óupits), Martin (1597–1639), German poet and critic. His 'Buch von der Deutschen Poeterey' (1624) had great influence in reviving classical meters, rhymes and style

o·pi·um (óupiːəm) *n.* a habit-forming, narcotic drug consisting of dried latex extracted from unripe capsules of the opium poppy. It was formerly used medically to soothe pain but is now largely replaced by its derivatives (*CODEINE, *MORPHINE). It is much smoked or eaten for pleasure as an intoxicant, esp. in Asia [L. fr. Gk *opion*, poppy juice, opium]

opium poppy *Papaver somniferum*, a flowering plant native to Asia Minor, cultivated for opium since ancient times. Its seeds are used in bakery goods, and yield an oil used in food, in soap etc.

Opium War a war (1839–42) between Britain and China, caused by British attempts to compel China to import opium from British India and to end the restrictions imposed by China on foreign trade. At the end of the war, China ceded Hong Kong to Britain and opened five ports to British trade

O·pol·e (ɒpóle) a province (area 3,633 sq. miles, pop. 927,000) in S.W. Poland ‖ its capital (*G.* Oppeln until 1945, pop. 107,500), an old town on the Oder, with cement and textile industries

o·pop·an·ax (oupópənæks) *n.* a gum resin formerly used as an aperient, obtained from the roots of *Opopanax chironium*, fam. *Umbelliferae*, a plant native to S. Europe and Asia Minor ‖ this plant, and other plants of genus *Opopanax* ‖ a gum resin used in perfumery, obtained from the trees *Commiphora erythraea* and *C. kataf* of Africa [L. fr. Gk fr. *opos*, juice+*panax*, all-healing, name of a plant]

O·por·to (oupɔ́rtou) (*Port.* Porto) Portugal's second largest city and port (pop. 311,800), on the Douro near its mouth. It is the export center for port wine. Manufactures: textiles (wool, cotton, silk, linen), leather, pottery, luxury goods. Cathedral (12th–13th cc.). University (1911)

o·pos·sum (əpósəm) *pl.* **o·pos·sums, o·pos·sum** *n.* a member of *Didelphidae*, an American family of nocturnal, largely arboreal marsupial mammals native to the eastern U.S.A., about 15 ins in length not including the long, prehensile tail. When threatened with danger or caught, they pretend to be dead [fr. an Algonquian language=white beast]

Op·peln (ɒpeln) *OPOLE

Op·pen·heim·er (ópənhaimər), Robert (1904–67), American physicist. He was director of the Los Alamos Laboratory, New Mexico (1943–5), which produced the first atomic bomb. Oppenheimer became a focus of controversy because of his opposition to the H bomb and his contacts with Communists. He received the Fermi Award in 1963

op·po·nent (əpóunənt) *n.* a person who or group that opposes another in a fight, game, debate, contest etc. || someone who opposes some idea, practice etc., *an opponent of capital punishment* [fr. L. *opponens* (*opponentis*) fr. *opponere*, to oppose]

op·por·tune (ɒpərtú:n, ɒpərtjú:n) *adj.* suitable, well chosen, *this is an opportune moment to remind him* || timely, *an opportune legacy* **op·por·tún·ism** *n.* the practice of grasping at opportunities without regard for moral considerations || the practice of adjusting one's policy in the light of each new situation as it arises, not according to principle or a plan **op·por·tún·ist** 1. *n.* someone who practices opportunism 2. *adj.* characterized by opportunism **op·por·tu·nís·tic** *adj.* [F. *opportun, opportune,* timely]

op·por·tu·ni·ty (ɒpərtú:niti:, ɒpərtjú:niti:) *pl.* **op·por·tu·ni·ties** *n.* a set of circumstances providing a chance or possibility, *will you have an opportunity to see him?* || a stroke of good fortune which presents itself and can either be grasped or lost [F. *opportunité*]

opportunity cost (*economics*) the value that resources used in a particular way would have if used in the best possible or another specified way *Cf* COST-BENEFIT

op·pos·a·bil·i·ty (əpóuzəbíliti:) *n.* the quality or state of being opposable

op·pos·a·ble (əpóuzəb'l) *adj.* capable of being resisted or opposed || capable of being placed opposite something else, *man's thumb and forefinger are opposable*

op·pose (əpóuz) *pres. part.* **op·pos·ing** *past* and *past part.* **op·posed** *v.t.* to express disagreement with or dislike of, or make an effort to stop or prevent the activity, efficacy or success of, *to oppose a political candidate, to oppose a suggestion* || to cause (something or someone) to be or act against something or someone [F. *opposer*]

op·po·site (ɒ́pəzit, ɒ́pəsit) 1. *adj.* in such a condition as to be pointing, looking, going etc. directly toward or away from someone or something, *in opposite directions, he ran across to the opposite house* || opposed, *a member of the opposite faction* || utterly different, *his tastes are completely opposite to hers* || (*bot.*, of leaves) placed in pairs, one on either side of the stem || (*bot.,* of floral parts) so placed that one part is before the other 2. *n.* something opposite, *she says one thing but means the opposite* 3. *adv.* on opposite sides, in an opposite position or direction 4. *prep.* in an opposite direction to or across from, *the hotel is opposite the church* || in a leading theatrical role complementary to, *he has played opposite her in many productions* [F. fr. L. *opponere* (*oppositus*)]

opposite number someone who holds a post or position corresponding to one's own or someone else's in another organization, government etc.

op·po·si·tion (ɒpəzíʃən) *n.* disagreement, hostility or resistance || the political group or groups in a democracy opposing the party in power and working to take its place by constitutional methods || any group opposing authority, or those opposing some proposal etc. || the act of setting opposite, or the state of being placed opposite || an opposite position || (*astron.*) the position of a heavenly body when it is directly opposite another one, esp. the sun, as seen from the earth || an opposite, a contrast || (*logic*) a difference in quality and/or quantity between two propositions with the same subject and predicate **op·po·sí·tion·al** *adj.* [fr. L. *oppositio* (*oppositionis*)]

op·press (əprés) *v.t.* to treat with unjust harshness, esp. to rule over tyrannically || to cause to feel mentally or spiritually burdened or physically as though suffocating [O.F. *oppresser* fr. M.L. fr. L. *opprimere* (*oppressus*), to press against]

op·pres·sion (əpréʃən) *n.* an oppressing or being oppressed || something that oppresses [F.]

op·pres·sive (əprésiv) *adj.* burdensome, unjustly harsh, *oppressive measures* || heavy, overpowering, *an oppressive atmosphere* [fr. M.L. *oppressivus*]

op·pres·sor (əprésər) *n.* someone who oppresses [A.F. *oppressour* and F. *oppresseur*]

op·pro·bri·ous (əpróubri:əs) *adj.* (*of* speech) abusive || infamous, disgraceful [fr. O. F. *opprobrieux* or L.L. *opprobriosus*]

op·pro·bri·um (əpróubri:əm) *n.* disgrace resulting from shameful behavior [L. fr. *opprobrare,* to reproach]

op·pugn (əpjú:n) *v.t.* to cast doubt on, question [fr. L. *oppugnare,* to attack]

op·so·nin (ɒ́psənin) *n.* a constituent of blood serum which makes disease-causing bacteria more readily consumed during phagocytosis [fr. Gk *opsōnion,* provisions]

opt (ɒpt) *v.i.* to make a choice [fr. F. *opter*]

op·ta·tive (ɒ́ptətiv) 1. *adj.* (*gram.*) expressing a desire or wish 2. *n.* (*gram.*) the optative mood or the verbal form expressing it, e.g. in Greek [F. *optatif, optative*]

op·tic (ɒ́ptik) 1. *adj.* relating to the eye or to vision 2. *n.* an optical system or part of one (lens, mirror etc.) **óp·ti·cal** *adj.* optic || designed to aid sight || acting on or actuated by light || relating to the science of optics [F. *optique* fr. M.L. *opticus* fr. Gk]

optical activity the ability of some substances to rotate the plane of linearly polarized light

optical art *OP ART

optical astronomy direct viewing of celestial bodies concentrating on using spectographs and other instruments —**optical astronomer** *n.* —**X-ray astronomy** *n. Cf* RADIO ASTRONOMY

optical axis a line perpendicular to the front surface of the cornea and going through the center of the pupil of the eye || the axis of symmetry of a radially symmetrical optical system || an optic axis

optical center, *Br.* **optical centre** the point of intersection of all the rays of light passing through a lens that experience no net deviation. This point (which may lie within, without or upon the surface of the lens) and the principal foci define the axis of the lens || the apparent center of a bounded flat surface (e.g. a printed page), esp. when it differs from the geometrical center

optical character reader (*computer*) device that scans printed or written characters, identifies them by stored data, creates a machine-readable code, and feeds these data into a data processor *abbr.* **OCR —optical character recognition** *n.*

optical computer computer that has input from holography, lasers, or memory banks, used in very high-speed processing for fingerprint identification and sharpening of the image —**optical computing** *n.*

optical fiber a glass fiber that carries light, used in chromatography, microsurgery, and automatic titrations

optical isomerism stereoisomerism in which the isomers have different effects on polarized light, due to the presence of one or more centers of asymmetry in the molecules of the isomeric substances

optical maser (*optics*) a laser

optical memory (*computer*) a computer storage responding to a laser beam

optical profilometer (*med.*) device used to measure three-dimensional contours optically, used to provide relief maps of internal organs. It is used in surgery, esp. of the palate

optical radar (*mil.*) system utilizing laser beams for measuring elevation of a missile during firing *acronym* OPDAR

optical reader (*computer*) a device for converting characters or symbols into computer input

optical rotation the angle through which the plane of linearly polarized light is rotated when it traverses an optically active substance. It depends upon the nature of the substance, the length of the path through the substance, and the wavelength of the light

optical scanner (*computer*) photoelectric scanning device for converting characters or other images into signals acceptable by a digital computer *Cf* OPTICAL CHARACTER READER

optical system the portion of an optical instrument (e.g. telescope, spectrophotometer) that acts upon and transmits light. It consists of prisms, gratings, lenses, mirrors etc.

optic axis (in a birefringent medium) a direction in which birefringence does not occur || the optical axis of the eye

op·ti·cian (ɒptíʃən) *n.* a person who makes or sells optical instruments, esp. glasses to correct vision [fr. F. *opticien*]

op·tics (ɒ́ptiks) *n.* the science of the origin, nature and laws of light (*PHYSICAL OPTICS, *GEOMETRICAL OPTICS)

op·ti·mal (ɒ́ptəməl) *adj.* most favorable, best [OPTIMUM+-*al,* adjectival suffix]

optimal ignorance a concept that the explosion of information and information sources eventually increases awareness and available choices to a point of diminishing returns, to a point where decisions cannot be made on time

op·ti·mism (ɒ́ptəmizəm) *n.* the inclination to take a hopeful view, the tendency to think that all will be for the best (opp. PESSIMISM) || (*philos.*) the doctrine (as expounded by Leibniz) that this world is the best of all possible worlds **óp·ti·mist** *n.* **op·ti·mís·tic** *adj.* **op·ti·mís·ti·cal·ly** *adv.* [F. *optimisme*]

op·ti·mum (ɒ́ptəməm) 1. *pl.* **op·ti·mums, op·ti·ma** (ɒ́ptəmə) *n.* the most favorable or best quality, number etc. || (*biol.*) the most favorable condition (e.g. of moisture, temperature) in which an organism will flourish 2. *adj.* most favorable or best possible for a certain purpose, or under certain conditions, *the optimum profitability for a firm of that size* [L. neut. of *optimus,* best]

op·tion (ɒ́pʃən) *n.* a choosing || that which is chosen || freedom of choice, *he had no option in the matter* || (*commerce*) the right, usually purchased, of buying or selling something at a certain rate and in a certain time **óp·tion·al** *adj.* not compulsory || left to a person's discretion or choice [F.]

op·to·e·lec·tron·ics (ɒptouilektróniks) *n.* study of solid-state and other electronic devices dealing with light, including cathode-ray tubes, lasers, diodes, optical memories, solar cells etc. —**op·to·e·lec·tron·ic** *adj.*

op·tom·e·ter (ɒptómitər) *n.* an instrument for measuring the refractive power of the eye **op·tóm·e·trist** *n.* someone who specializes in optometry **op·tóm·e·try** *n.* the profession of examining people's eyes for faults in refraction and prescribing corrective lenses and exercises [fr. Gk *optos,* visible+*metron,* measure]

op·to·phone (ɒ́ptəfoun) *n.* device that reads and converts printed characters into sounds, used esp. by the blind

opt out *v.* (*colloq.*) to choose not to participate

op·u·lence (ɒ́pjuləns) *n.* great wealth, riches || profuse abundance [fr. L. *opulentia*]

op·u·lent (ɒ́pjulənt) *adj.* extremely rich || profuse, luxuriant, *opulent growth* [fr. L. *opulens* (*opulentis*) or *opulentus,* fr. *ops* (*opis*), power, wealth]

o·pun·ti·a (oupʌ́nʃi:ə, oupʌ́nʃə) *n.* a prickly pear cactus [Mod. L. *Opuntia,* name of genus fr. L. *Opuntia* (*herba*)]

o·pus (óupəs) *pl.* **o·pe·ra** (ɒ́pərə), **o·pus·es** *n.* (*abbr.* op.) a musical composition (used esp. with a number to show the chronological position of a single composition among a composer's works) [L.=work]

o·pus·cule (oupʌ́skju:l) *n.* a small or minor work of literature etc. [F.]

o·pus·cu·lum (oupʌ́skjuləm) *pl.* **o·pus·cu·la** (oupʌ́skjulə) *n.* an opuscule [L. dim. of *opus,* work]

or (ɔr) *n.* (*heraldry*) the tincture gold or yellow [F.]

or *conj.* introducing an alternative, *clean or dirty* || introducing all but the first of a series of alternatives, *the sea can be blue or green or gray* || introducing only the last of a series of alternatives, *a person may be tall, short or of medium height* || introducing something that explains or is a synonym for the preceding, *the egg should be hard-boiled, or cooked until the inside is firm* || indicating vagueness or uncertainty, *nine or ten people were there* [M.E. *other, or* fr. O.E. *oththe*]

-or *suffix* denoting the person or thing performing the action of the verb, as in 'generator' [M.E. *-or, -our,* ult. fr. L. *-or* or *-ātor, -ētor, -itor* or *-itor.*

OR, OR operator, *or* **ORgate** (ɔr) *n.* (*computer*) a logic or circuit having the property that if *P* and *Q* are statements, then *OR* is true only if at least one is true, false if both are false

or·a·cle (ɔ́rək'l, ɒ́rək'l) *n.* the place where the ancient Greeks and Romans went to ask the advice of their gods about the future || the reply to their questions, often ambiguous or difficult to understand || the medium through which a god reveals his purpose || a person regarded as an infallibly wise prophet, judge or adviser || the advice, judgment etc. given by such a person [M.E. fr. F. fr. L. *oraculum*]

o·rac·u·lar (ɔrǽkjulər, ourǽkjulər) *adj.* of, relating to or being an oracle || like an oracle, esp. in authority, obscurity or ambiguity [fr. L. *oraculum,* oracle]

or·a·cy (ɔ́rəsi:) *n.* ability to hear and speak, from "literacy." The term was coined by British surgeon Andrew Wilkinson

O·ra·dea Ma·re (ɔrɑ́djəmɑ́re) (*Hung.* Nagyrárad, *G.* Grosswardein) a city (pop. 178,407) of W. Rumania (Transylvania). Industries: cotton and silk textiles, metallurgy. Greek Orthodox and Roman Catholic cathedrals (18th c.)

o·ral (ɔ́rəl, óurəl) **1.** *adj.* using speech rather than writing, spoken, *an oral examination* ‖ of or relating to the mouth, *oral surgery* ‖ done or taken by the mouth, *an oral dose* ‖ (*phon.*) spoken through the mouth with the nasal passage closed **2.** *n.* an oral examination [fr. L. *os* (*oris*), mouth]

oral history a cohesive record of an individual life or of an event (usu. relevant as social history) assembled through systematic interviewing of the person or persons concerned

O·ran (ɔrɑn) a port (pop. 500,000) of W. Algeria, in a rich agricultural district. Industries: chemicals and plastics, metalwork, tobacco, wool, clothing

O·range (ɔrɑ́ʒ) a market town (pop. 26,468) of Vaucluse, S. France, north of Avignon. Its Roman remains include an amphitheater, triumphal arch and aqueduct

or·ange (ɔ́rindʒ, ɒ́rindʒ) **1.** *n.* the reddish-yellow, globose or nearly globose fruit (a large berry) of any of certain trees of genus *Citrus*, fam. *Rutaceae*, which are native to China and Indochina but widely cultivated in tropical and subtropical climates ‖ any evergreen tree of genus *Citrus* which bears oranges, esp. *C. sinensis*, the common or sweet orange, *C. aurantium*, the Seville (or sour or bitter) orange, and *C. reticulata*, the mandarin orange ‖ the color of the fruit, a reddish yellow **2.** *adj.* having the color orange [M.E. *orenge, orange* fr. O. F. fr. Arab. *nāranj*]

or·ange·ade (ɔrindʒéid, ɒrindʒéid) *n.* a drink made from sweetened orange juice with water added ‖ a carbonated soft drink resembling this

orange blossom the white sweet-smelling flowers of the orange tree, traditionally carried in bridal bouquets

Orange Bowl the postseason college football game in Miami, Fla.

Orange, Cape a cape on the north coast of Brazil, near the French Guiana border

orange-flower water a solution of the essential oil (neroli) of the Seville orange, used in perfumery and in cooking

orange forces (*mil.*) those forces used in an enemy role during military maneuvers

Orange Free State a central province (area 49,866 sq. miles, pop. 1,932,000) of South Africa. Capital: Bloemfontein. It consists largely of high, undulating plains. Agriculture: stock raising (cattle and sheep), cereals. Resources: gold, coal, oil. Industries: fertilizer, agricultural machinery, clothing, cement. HISTORY. The region was occupied by Bushmen, Bechuanas and Zulus when the first Dutch settlements were made (early 19th c.). Boer settlers arrived (1836) as a result of the Great Trek, and established a republic (1837). It was annexed by Britain (1848) but became independent (1854) as the Orange Free State. Disagreements between the Boer government and the British led to the Boer War, in which Britain annexed the Orange Free State (1900). It was incorporated in the Union of South Africa (1910)

Or·ange·man (ɔ́rindʒmən, ɒ́rindʒmən) *pl.* **Or·ange·men** (ɔ́rindʒmən, ɒ́rindʒmən) *n.* a member of a Protestant political organization founded (1795) to maintain Protestant ascendancy in Ireland. Branches of the organization, now devoted to upholding Protestantism generally, have been formed in many English-speaking countries [after William III of England, prince of *Orange*]

orange pekoe a black tea from India or Sri Lanka made from the small top leaves only

Orange River the chief river (1,300 miles long) of South Africa, rising in the Drakensberg range in Lesotho and flowing westward through Orange Free State and Cape Province to the Atlantic. Chief tributary: the Vaal. A sandbar near its mouth prevents navigation. The Orange River Project (begun 1962) has harnessed the river for irrigation and hydroelectricity

or·ang·e·ry (ɔ́rindʒəri:, ɒ́rindʒəri:, ɔ́rindʒri:, ɒ́rindʒri:) *pl.* **or·ang·e·ries** *n.* a building specially designed for growing oranges in cool climates, and for protecting trees and shrubs

against frost [F. *orangerie* fr. *oranger*, orange tree]

orange stick a small slender stick of orangewood designed for manicuring nails

or·ange·wood (ɔ́rindʒwud, ɒ́rindʒwud) *n.* the wood of the orange tree used esp. for carving

o·rang·u·tan (ɔrǽŋutaen, ourǽŋutæn) *n. Pongo pygmaeus*, a large heavy reddish-brown anthropoid ape found in Borneo and Sumatra. It is well developed for arboreal life. having long, powerful arms, with hooking hands. Adult males may exceed 4 ft in height and 160 lbs in weight [fr. Malay *orang utan*, man of the forest]

Or·a·sul Sta·lin (ɔ́rəʃulstǽlin) *BRASOV

o·rate (ɔréit, ouréit) *pres. part.* **o·rat·ing** *past* and *past part.* **o·rat·ed** *v.i.* to hold forth in a bombastic style [fr. L. *orare* (*oratus*), to pray, and back-formation fr. ORATION]

o·ra·tion (ɔréiʃən, ouréiʃən) *n.* a formal speech or discourse, esp. one given on a ceremonial occasion [fr. L. *oratio* (*orationis*)]

o·ra·tor (ɔ́rətɔr, ɒ́rətər) *n.* a person who speaks in public, esp. one distinguished by his eloquence [A.F. *oratour*]

Or·a·to·ri·an (ɔrətɔ́ri:ən, ɒrətóuri:ən, ɒrətɔ́ri:ən, ɒrətóuri:ən) *n.* a member of the Congregation of the Oratory

or·a·tor·i·cal (ɔrətɔ́rik'l, ɒrətɔ́ri'l) *adj.* of or relating to an orator or to oratory ‖ given to using oratory [fr. L. *orator, orator*]

or·a·to·ri·o (ɔrətɔ́ri:ou, ɒrətɔ́ri:ou, ɔrətóuri:ou, ɒrətóuri:ou) *n.* a dramatic musical composition, esp. on a religious theme, with arias, recitative and choruses and with orchestral accompaniment, performed as a concert, without action, costume or scenery [Ital., used originally of musical services at the Oratory of St Philip Neri in Rome]

or·a·to·ry (ɔ́rətɔri:, ɔ́rətɔuri:, ɒ́rətɔri:, ɒ́rətɔuri:) *pl.* **or·a·to·ries** *n.* a chapel or a private place of worship [fr. L. *oratorium*, place of prayer]

oratory *n.* the art of public speaking ‖ rhetorical speech or language [fr. L. *oratoria* (*ars*), (art) of speaking]

Oratory, Congregation of the the religious society founded in Rome by St Philip Neri in 1564. Its members are secular priests living in community without vows. They are devoted to preaching, confessing and catechizing

orb (ɔrb) **1.** *n.* a sphere ‖ a heavenly body, e.g. the sun, moon etc. ‖ a round ball surmounted by a cross, as part of judicial or royal regalia in Christian countries, symbolizing the domination by Christ of secular power **2.** *v.t.* to form into a circle or sphere ‖ *v.i.* to move in an orbit ‖ to form an orb. [fr. L. *orbis*, ring, circle]

or·bic·u·lar (ɔrbíkjulər) *adj.* spherical ‖ circular ‖ (*anat.*, e.g. of a muscle) surrounding, encircling ‖ (*bot.*, of a leaf) round or shield-shaped ‖ (of rocks) containing rounded bodies, e.g. minerals grouped concentrically [fr. F. *orbiculaire* or L. *orbicularis*]

or·bic·u·late (ɔrbíkjuleit, ɔrbíkjulit) *adj.* orbicular [fr. L. *orbiculatus*]

or·bit (ɔ́rbit) **1.** *n.* the closed path, usually elliptical, in which a planet moves around the sun, or a satellite around the parent body ‖ the path of a body (e.g. a particle) in a force field (cf. ORBITAL) ‖ a sphere of influence or region of activity, *such matters are outside my orbit* ‖ the bony socket of the eye ‖ (*zool.*) the border or ring around the eye of a bird **2.** *v.i.* to move in an orbit ‖ *v.t.* to revolve in an orbit around ‖ to cause to revolve in an orbit

or·bit·al (ɔ́rbit'l) **1.** *adj.* of, relating to or describing an orbit **2.** *n.* a subdivision of the energy levels of the electronic structure of an atom or molecule) in which the motion of a single electron is represented in terms of quantized state of angular momentum, that is described mathematically by a wave function [fr. F. *orbite* or L. *orbita*, path, orbit]

orbital index (*craniometry*) the ratio of the length of the orbit of the eye to its greatest height, multiplied by 100

orbital injection (*aerospace*) the process of providing a space vehicle with sufficient velocity to establish an orbit

orbital steering (*biochem.*) process by which atoms within enzymes are guided at precise angles to permit them to form new molecular compounds in a biochemical reaction

or·bit·er (ɔ́rbitər) *n.* (*aerospace*) term applied generically to a spacecraft sent as a probe into orbit around a planet or other celestial body, as contrasted to a probe sent as a surface landing vehicle, or lander

orc (ɔrk) *n.* a cetacean of the genus *Orcinus* (or *Orca*), esp. the killer whale ‖ a grampus [fr. *orque* fr. L. *orca*, kind of whale]

Or·ca·gna (ɔrkɑ́nja), Andrea di Cione (c. 1308–c. 1368), Italian painter, architect and sculptor. The tabernacle in Orsanmichele, Florence, is his chief sculptural work. The altarpiece in the Strozzi chapel of S. Maria Novella, Florence, is the only painting certainly by him

or·ce·in (ɔ́rsi:in) *n.* a purple nitrogenous dye, the chief ingredient of archil and cudbear, formed by the action of ammonia and oxygen on orcinol [ORCIN]

or·chard (ɔ́rtʃərd) *n.* a stretch of land with cultivated fruit trees ‖ the trees collectively [O.E. *ortgeard* prob. fr. L. *hortus*, garden+O.E. *geard*, fence, enclosure]

or·ches·tra (ɔ́rkistrə, ɔ́rkestrə) *n.* a large body of instrumental musicians who perform symphonies etc., or a smaller group of musicians who play dinner music or dance music ‖ the instruments of either of such a group ‖ the orchestra pit in a theater ‖ (*Am.=Br.* orchestra stalls) the section of seats on the main floor of a theater, esp. the section nearest the stage ‖ the main floor of a theater **or·ches·tral** (ɔrkéstrəl) *adj.* [L. fr. Gk *orchēstra*, space where the chorus danced fr. *orcheesthai*, to dance]

orchestra pit the pit of a theater, where the orchestra sits

or·ches·trate (ɔ́rkistreit) *pres. part.* **or·ches·trat·ing** *past* and *past part.* **or·ches·trat·ed** *v.t.* to arrange, score or compose (music) for performance by an orchestra ‖ *v.i.* to arrange etc. music in this way **or·ches·tra·tion** *n.*

or·chid (ɔ́rkid) *n.* a member of *Orchidaceae*, order *Orchidales*, a family of perennial monocotyledonous terrestrial plants, epiphytes or saprophytes. They are cosmopolitan, and very abundant in the Tropics. The flowers differ from the normal monocotyledonous type, being more varied and complicated, with specialized pollinia and a twisted ovary. Many are cultivated for the brilliance of the flowers ‖ (*pl.*) compliments, praise **or·chi·da·ceous** (ɔrkidéiʃəs) *adj.* of, like or being a member of *Orchidaceae* [fr. Mod. L. *Orchidaceae* fr. L. *orchis* (assumed *orchidis*) fr. Gk *orchis*, testicle (from the shape of the roots)]

or·chil (ɔ́rtʃil, ɔ́rkil) *n.* archil [O.F. *orchel, orcheil*]

or·chis (ɔ́rkis) *n.* an orchid, esp. a member of genus *Orchis* [L. fr. Gk *orchis*, testicle (from the shape of the roots)]

or·cin (ɔ́rsin) *n.* orcinol

or·ci·nol (ɔ́rsinɔl, ɔ́rsinoul) *n.* a colorless crystalline phenol, $C_6H_3CH_3(OH)_2$, obtained from some lichens, aloes and derivatives of toluene, used to manufacture dyes [fr. Mod. L. *orcina* fr. Ital. *orcello*, archil]

or·dain (ɔrdéin) *v.t.* to consecrate (someone) a Christian deacon, priest etc. ‖ to qualify (a man) as a rabbi ‖ to appoint, decree, establish [A.F. *ordeiner, ordeigner* and O. F. *ordener* fr. L. *ordinare*, to put in order]

or·deal (ɔrdíːl, ɔrdíːl, ɔrdíːəl) *n.* a severe or exacting experience that tests character or powers of endurance, *24 hours of motor racing is a heavy ordeal* ‖ (*hist.*) an ancient method of establishing guilt or innocence, esp. in medieval Europe, by making an accused person undergo some painful or difficult physical test and seeing if God sustained him [O.E. *ordāl, ordēl*]

or·der (ɔ́rdər) *n.* a sequence, arrangement, the way one thing follows another, *alphabetical order* ‖ the condition in which everything is controlled as it should be, is in its right place, performing its correct function etc., *to put one's affairs in order* ‖ the proper working of the law, *peaceful regularity of public life, the police restored order after the riots* ‖ the rules, laws and structures which constitute a society, *the social order* ‖ (*philos.*) the natural, moral or spiritual system governing things in the universe ‖ the procedure by which a meeting or other assembly is governed, *a point of order* ‖ conformity with this, *to call a speaker to order* ‖ an authoritative instruction, command ‖ (*commerce*) an instruction to a tradesman or manufacturer to supply goods ‖ the goods supplied ‖ something ordered, e.g. in a restaurant, *has the girl brought your order?* ‖ a pass authorizing admission, *an order to view a house* ‖ (*archit.*) one of the orders of architecture ‖ a military or monastic brotherhood under discipline ‖ a secret fraternity united by common interest or for social purposes, *the Masonic order* ‖ (*pl.*) a social class, *the lower orders* ‖ a sort or kind, thought of as part of a hierarchy, *sentiments of a noble order* ‖ a group of people distinguished by special award made e.g. by the sovereign, or the award itself, *the order of the Garter* ‖ (*theol.*) one of the nine ranks of angels (*ANGEL) ‖ (*pl., eccles.*) the office of an ordained man in the Christian Church, *in deacon's orders* ‖ (*pl., eccles.*) ordination, *to take holy orders* ‖ (*eccles.*) a prescribed form of service ‖ (*eccles.*) one of the grades in the Christian ministry (*MAJOR ORDERS, *MINOR ORDERS) ‖ (*biol.*), in plant and animal classification) a category of closely allied organisms between family and class ‖ (*pl., mil.*) commands issued by an officer in command or by the competent authority, *standing orders* ‖ (*mil.*) equipment for a given purpose, *full marching order* ‖ (*mil.*) the position of a rifle after the command 'order arms' ‖ (*law*) a decision by a court or judge, usually not a final judgment ‖ (*finance*) a written direction to pay money or surrender goods ‖ (*math.*) degree of complexity, *an equation of the first order* **in order** in sequence ‖ in good condition ‖ according to the rules, e.g. of a meeting etc. ‖ suitable, *a toast would be in order* **in order that** with the intention that, *he worked hard in order that he might leave earlier* **in order to** (+infin.) for the purpose of (+pres. part.) **in short order** with no delay, *do it in short order* **of the order of** about as many as or as large as **on order** (of goods) requested but not yet delivered **on the order of** similar to, roughly like in style **out of order** out of proper sequence ‖ not according to the rules ‖ not in working condition ‖ inappropriate **to order** according to the specific requirements of the buyer, *a suit made to order* [fr. O.F. *ordre* fr. L. *ordo*]

order *v.t.* to put in order, *to order one's affairs* to give authoritative instruction to (someone) to do something or for (something) to be done ‖ (of fate) to ordain ‖ to request (goods etc.) to be supplied ‖ to prescribe as a remedy, *the doctor ordered complete rest* **to order arms** (*mil.*) to bring the rifle to an upright position with its butt against one's right foot, and remain at attention [M.E. *ordren* fr. *ordre*, order]

Or·der·ic Vi·ta·lis (ɔ́rdərikvaitéilis) (1075–c. 1143), Norman chronicler. His 'Historia ecclesiastica' is a valuable source for the history of his times

order-in-coun·cil (ɔ́rdərinkáunsəl) *pl.* **orders-in-coun·cil** *n.* an order issued by the British sovereign on the advice of the privy council, or by the governor general of a Commonwealth country with the advice of a similar council. Such orders are usually issued to deal with an emergency (e.g. those of 1807 and 1809 in answer to the Continental System) or with matters still subject to Crown prerogative (e.g. the government of a colony)

or·der·li·ness (ɔ́rdərlinis) *n.* the quality or state of being orderly

or·der·ly (ɔ́rdərli:) **1.** *adj.* in good order, well arranged, *an orderly office* ‖ disciplined and peaceable, *an orderly crowd* ‖ (*mil.*) of, relating to or charged with the execution or sending out of orders **2.** *pl.* **or·der·lies** *n.* a soldier attendant on an officer to carry messages, orders, etc. ‖ an attendant in charge of cleaning etc. in a hospital, often in a military hospital

orderly market *DISORDERLY MARKET

Orderly Marketing Agreement formal trade agreement between the U.S.A. and a foreign country in which the latter voluntarily agrees to limit, for a specified period, its exports to the U.S.A. of a particular industrial commodity, as an alternative to the imposition of quotas or higher tariffs *abbr.* **OMA**

orderly officer (*Br., mil.*) the officer of the day

orderly room a room in a barracks used for administrative workers

orders of architecture the characteristic styles of classical architecture, esp. as applied to columns. The five orders are: Doric, Ionic, Corinthian, Tuscan and Composite. The variations occur principally in the capitals but also in the heights of the columns relative to their width

Or·di·nal (ɔ́rd'n'l) *n.* the service book used in Anglican ordinations ‖ a book of directions for Roman Catholic services for every day in the year [fr. M.L. *ordinale*]

or·di·nal (ɔ́rd'n'l) **1.** *adj.* (of a number) showing position or order in a series, e.g. second (cf. CARDINAL NUMBER) ‖ of or relating to an order of plants or animals **2.** *n.* an ordinal number [fr. L.L. *ordinalis*, denoting order in a series]

ordinal value (*statistics*) a numerical evaluation representing only rank in a comparison with others

or·di·nance (ɔ́rd'nəns) *n.* a decree or authoritative order, e.g. of a council or municipal government ‖ a religious ceremony or rite that is not a sacrament ‖ (*Br., hist.*) a piece of legislation issued by the sovereign by virtue of the royal prerogative without the approval of parliament [O. F. *ordenance, ordonance*]

or·di·nand (ɔ́rd'nænd) *n.* a candidate for ordination [fr. L. *ordinandus* fr. *ordinare*, to ordain]

or·di·nar·i·ly (ɔrd'néərili:, ɔ́rd'nérili:) *adv.* generally, in the usual course of events

or·di·nar·i·ness (ɔ́rd'neri:nis) *n.* the quality or state of being ordinary

or·di·nar·y (ɔ́rd'neri:) *pl.* **or·di·nar·ies** *n.* (*eccles.*) a Church official (e.g. an archbishop, or a bishop or his deputy) having ecclesiastical jurisdiction over his territory ‖ (*eccles.*) an order of service, esp. the parts of the Mass that remain the same from day to day ‖ (in certain states of the U.S.A.) a judge of a court of probate ‖ (*heraldry*) a charge of the simplest, commonest kind ‖ (*Am.=Br.* penny-farthing) an early type of bicycle, popular about the 1870s, with a very large front wheel and a much smaller back wheel **in ordinary** (in titles) in regular attendance or service, *physician in ordinary* **out of the ordinary** unusual, exceptional or remarkable, *the performance was nothing out of the ordinary* [fr. O.F. and A. F. *ordinarie* fr. M. L. *ordinarius* adj. and *ordinarium* n. and fr. ORDINARY adj.]

ordinary *adj.* usual, *the ordinary way of getting there is by ship* ‖ not exceptional or unusual, undistinguished, *he shows only an ordinary amount of skill* [fr. L. *ordinarius*, regular]

ordinary seaman a sailor in the American or British merchant marine or in the Royal Navy, ranking below an able-bodied seaman

ordinary shares (*Br.*) common stock

or·di·nate (ɔ́rdnit, ɔ́rd'nit, ɔ́rd'neit) *n.* (*math.*) the vertical or *y*-coordinate in a plane coordinate system [fr. L. *ordinatus*, ordered]

or·di·na·tion (ɔrd'néiʃən) *n.* an ordaining or being ordained, esp. into the Christian ministry [fr. L. *ordinatio (ordinationis)*]

ord·nance (ɔ́rdnəns) *n.* heavy guns, artillery ‖ military stores and materials (ammunition, small arms etc.) ‖ the branch of the U.S. army or the British War Office concerned with the supply of essential stores and the maintenance of arsenals and depots [var. of ORDINANCE]

ordnance datum (*Br.*) mean sea level as defined for the ordnance survey

ordnance survey the government survey of Great Britain and Northern Ireland, including the preparation of official maps

Or·do·vi·cian (ɔrdəvíʃən) *adj.* (*geol.*) of the period or system of the Paleozoic era between the Cambrian and the Silurian (*GEOLOGICAL TIME) **the Ordovician** the Ordovician period or system of rocks [fr. L. *Ordovices*, a Celtic tribe from Wales]

or·dure (ɔ́rdjuər, ɔ́rdʒər) *n.* excrement, dung [F.]

Or·dzho·ni·kid·ze (ɔrdʒɒnikí:dze) (formerly Dzaudzhikau) the capital (pop. 287,000) of the North Ossetian A.S.S.R., R.S.F.S.R., U.S.S.R. Industries: food processing, zinc metallurgy, chemicals

Ore. Oregon

ore (ɔr, ouər) *n.* a naturally occurring metallic compound from which the metal can be extracted [O.E. *ār*, brass and O.E. *ōra*, unwrought metal]

ö·re (ə́:rə) *pl.* **ö·re** *n.* either of two units of currency of Denmark and Norway equal to 1/100 of a krone ‖ a Swedish unit of currency equal to 1/100 of a krona ‖ a coin of the value of any of these [Dan. and Norw. *øre* and Swed. *öre* fr. L. *aureus*, a gold coin]

o·re·ad (ɔ́ri:æd, óuri:æd) *n.* (*Gk* and *Rom. mythol.*) a mountain nymph [fr. L. *Oreas (Oreadis)* fr. *Gk* fr. *oros*, mountain]

o·rec·tic (ouréktik, ɔréktik) *adj.* (*philos.*) relating to or characterized by desire or appetite [fr. *Gk orektikos* fr. *oregein*, to desire, grasp after]

ore dressing the separation of an ore from waste material and from other ores

Oreg. Oregon

o·reg·a·no (ɔrégənou, ərégənou) *n.* origanum [Span. *orégano*, wild marjoram]

O·re·gon (ɔ́rigən, ɔ́rigʌn, ɔ́rigon, óurigon) (*abbr.* Oreg., Ore.) a state (area 96,981 sq. miles, pop. 2,649,000) on the N. Pacific coast of the U.S.A.

Capital: Salem. Chief city: Portland. It is mountainous (wooded Cascade and coast ranges) in the west, with plateaus in the east. Agriculture: beef and dairy cattle, wheat, fruit (irrigation is needed in the east). Main resources: timber, nickel, fish, building materials. Industries: lumber and forest products, food processing, metallurgy. State university (1872) at Eugene. Oregon was jointly occupied (1818–46) by Britain and the U.S.A., and was ceded (1846) by Britain to the U.S.A., of which it became (1859) the 33rd state

Oregon Question (*Am. hist.*) a dispute (1840s) over the western part of the boundary, left undetermined by the Anglo-American boundary commission of 1818, between the U.S.A. and Canada. The dispute was settled (1846) by a treaty extending the boundary along the 49° parallel from the Rocky Mtns to the Pacific coast. This gave the present states of Oregon, Washington and Idaho to the U.S.A., while Britain obtained Vancouver Is.

Oregon Trail the 2,000-mile overland route from the Missouri to the Columbia which was followed by American pioneers (1840s) moving west to settle in the Oregon region

O·rel (ourél, ɔrél) an agricultural market (pop. 209,000) of the R.S.F.S.R., U.S.S.R., 200 miles south of Moscow: engineering industries

O·rel·la·na (ɔreljána, ɔrejána), Francisco de (c. 1470–1550), Spanish explorer who discovered (1542) the Amazon

O·ren·burg (ɔ́renburg, ɔ́rənbə:rg) (formerly Chkalov 1938–57) a city (pop. 482,000) of the central R.S.F.S.R., U.S.S.R., on the Ural River, center of a mining region: metallurgy, engineering, brewing, food processing

O·ren·se (ɔrénse) (*Rom.* Aurium) a province (area 2,694 sq. miles, pop. 411,339) of N.W. Spain (*GALICIA)

O·res·tes (ɔrésti:z, ourésti:z) son of Agamemnon and Clytemnestra. He killed his mother and her lover, Aegisthus, to avenge their murder of Agamemnon. He was pursued by the Erinyes but was acquitted by the Areopagus

Ö·re·sund (ə́:rasʌnd) the strait (3½–17 miles wide) separating Zealand Is., Denmark, from Sweden

Orff (ɔrf), Carl (1895–1982), German composer. Among his compositions are 'Carmina Burana' (1937), a scenic oratorio based on medieval secular poems, and the dramatic works 'Antigone' (1949) and 'Trionfo di Afrodite' (1955)

Or·ford (ɔ́rfərd), 1st earl of *WALPOLE, SIR ROBERT

orfray *ORPHREY

or·gan (ɔ́rgən) *n.* a musical wind instrument, in its modern forms the largest, most versatile, and most powerful of instruments. It sounds when compressed air is passed through its pipes from bellows (usually electrically powered). It is played by manuals (keyboards) and foot pedals, and is controlled by stops which make possible a wide variety of tone qualities ‖ any of several similar keyboard instruments without pipes, e.g. the reed organ and the electric organ ‖ any of certain simple wind instruments of a specified kind, e.g. a barrel organ ‖ a structure of an animal (e.g. lung, stomach) or of a plant (e.g. pistil, leaf) adapted for some specific and usually essential function, *the organs of digestion* ‖ a means or instrument of action, *parliament is the chief organ of government in England* ‖ a medium of communication of opinion or information, esp. a publication attached to some group, party etc. [fr. L. *organum* fr. *Gk organon*, instrument]

or·gan·dy, or·gan·die (ɔ́rgəndi:) *n.* a fine, thin, stiff, semitransparent muslin used esp. for clothing and curtains [F. *organdi*]

or·gan-grind·er (ɔ́rgəngraindər) *n.* a street musician who plays a barrel organ

or·gan·ic (ɔrgǽnik) *adj.* of or relating to an organ of the body ‖ (*med.*) affecting the structure of the organism or an organ, *an organic disease* (cf. FUNCTIONAL) ‖ (*biol.*) having the physical structure characteristic of living organisms ‖ (*chem.*) of or relating to the compounds of carbon (other than some of its simpler compounds) ‖ inherent, structural, *the organic characteristics of this society* ‖ organized, systematic, esp. having parts that work together in a way that recalls the complex interactions of bodily organs, *the novel is an organic whole* ‖ (*law*) pertaining to the fundamental and constitutional laws by which countries or states are governed **or·gan·i·cal·ly** adv. [fr. L. organicus fr. Gk organon, instrument]

Organic Act of 1902 a U.S. Congressional act of the Theodore Roosevelt administration, which provided a constitution, a judicial code, and a system of laws for the Philippines

organic chemistry the branch of chemistry concerned with the compounds of carbon but excluding its simpler compounds (e.g. carbon dioxide, hydrogen cyanide) (cf. INORGANIC CHEMISTRY)

or·gan·ism (órgənizəm) n. (biol.) a living being or entity adapted for living by means of organs separate in function but dependent on one another ‖ any living being or its material structure, the organism of the herring is being studied ‖ any complete whole which by the integration, interaction and mutual dependence of its parts is comparable to a living being [fr. ORGANIZE]

or·gan·ist (órgənist) n. a person who plays the organ

or·gan·iz·a·ble (órgənạizəb'l) adj. capable of being organized

Or·ga·ni·za·ción de los Es·ta·dos Cen·tro·a·me·ri·ca·nos (órgani:sasjóndelɔsestáðɔssentrɔameri:kános) (abbr. ODECA) an organization of Central American states created in 1951 to advance economic, cultural and social cooperation among its members, which include all the republics of Central America except Panama

or·gan·i·za·tion (órgənizéiʃən) n. an organizing or being organized ‖ the way in which something is organized ‖ an association or society of people working together to some end, e.g. a business firm or a political party **or·gan·i·zá·tion·al** adj. [fr. M.L. organizatio (organizationis)]

organization chart (management) graphic table of duties and responsibilities of officers and departments of an organization

Organization for Economic Cooperation and Development (abbr. O.E.C.D.) the organization which replaced (1961) the Organization for European Economic Cooperation. It encourages the economic growth of member countries, works for the expansion of world trade, and helps underdeveloped countries. Its 24 members are: Australia, Austria, Belgium, Canada, Denmark, Finland, France, Great Britain, Greece, Iceland, Irish Republic, Italy, Japan, Luxembourg, the Netherlands, New Zealand, Norway, Portugal, Spain, Sweden, Switzerland, Turkey, the U.S.A. and West Germany. Headquarters: Paris

Organization for European Economic Cooperation (abbr. O.E.E.C.) an organization set up (1948) by 16 European nations to coordinate their economic activities and to assist the administration of the Marshall Plan. It was replaced by the Organization for Economic Cooperation and Development (1961)

organization man managerial employee of a large enterprise who is dominated by corporate ideology, ethics, aspirations and social expectations. The term was coined by William H. Whyte, The Organization Man (1956)

Organization of African Unity (abbr. O.A.U.) a Pan-African movement founded 1963 and now comprising nearly all independent African states

Organization of American States (abbr. O.A.S.) a body set up (1948) to promote social, economic and technical cooperation among American states and to act as a regional agency of the U.N. It has 32 member states. Headquarters: Washington, D.C.

Organization of Central American States an economic, cultural and social union of Costa Rica, Guatemala, Honduras, Nicaragua and El Salvador, formed in 1951

Organization of Petroleum Exporting Countries (abbr. O.P.E.C.) cartel formed (1960) by Iran, Iraq, Kuwait, Saudi Arabia and Venezuela to counter price cuts by American and European oil companies. It was later joined by Qatar (1961), Indonesia and Libya (1962), Abu Dhabi (now part of the United Arab Emirates) (1967), Algeria (1969), Nigeria (1971), and Ecuador and Gabon (1973). Originally limited to preventing further cuts in oil prices, by 1970 it began to press for price increases; in the period 1974–8 prices quadrupled, and in 1979 there was a 100 percent increase. By 1981, however, conservation measures by consuming countries coupled with high production by Saudi Arabia led to an oil surplus in consuming countries and by 1983 there was a worldwide glut, leading to

a precipitous reduction in price. O.P.E.C. members officially reduced the production ceiling and cut the benchmark price per barrel, but disagreement among participating countries on both production quotas and price weakened O.P.E.C.'s position during the late 1980s

or·gan·ize (órgənaiz) pres. part. **or·gan·iz·ing** past and past part. **or·gan·ized** v.t. to give an orderly or organic structure to, arrange the parts of (something) so that it works as a whole, to organize an army ‖ to make arrangements for, prepare, to organize an expedition ‖ to unionize (workers or an industry) ‖ v.i. to become organic or systematized **ór·gan·iz·er** n. someone who or something that organizes ‖ (biol.) a substance that acts as an inductor in embryonic development [fr. M. L. organizare]

or·gan·iz·er (órgənạizər) n. (physiol.) a region in the primitive nervous system of all animals that imposes a pattern of responses during early stages of development

or·ga·no·gen·e·sis (órgənoudʒénisis, ɔrgænədʒénisis) n. (biol.) morphogenesis [fr. Gk organon, organ+GENESIS]

or·ga·nog·ra·phy (órgənógrəfi:) n. (biol.) the describing of the organs of animals or plants [fr. Gk organon, organ+graphos, written]

or·ga·no·ther·a·py (órgənouθérəpi:, ɔrgænəθérəpi:) n. the treatment of disease by the administration of extracts from animal organs [fr. Gk organon, organ+THERAPY]

or·gan·a (órgənəm) pl. **or·ga·na** (órgənə), **or·ga·nums** (órgənəms) n. (mus.) a medieval form of part writing in which the cantus firmus is paralleled exactly at a fourth, fifth or octave above or below ‖ (mus.) one of the parts accompanying the cantus firmus in this way [L. fr. Gk organon, instrument, organ]

or·gan·za (órgǽnzə) n. a fine dress fabric of silk, rayon etc. like organdy, but stiffer [prob. fr. Lorganza, a trademark]

or·gan·zine (órgənzi:n) n. a fine, strong silk thread in which the twist runs opposite to the strand, used for the warp in silk weaving [F. organsin fr. Ital.]

or·gasm (órgæzəm) n. the climax of excitement in sexual intercourse ‖ an instance of this **or·gás·tic** adj. [fr. Mod. L. orgasmus fr. Gk orgaein, to swell]

or·gi·as·tic (órdʒi:ǽstik) adj. of, like or having the nature of an orgy [fr. Gk orgiastikos fr. orgiazein, to celebrate orgies]

or·gy (órdʒi:) pl. **or·gies** n. a bout of debauchery ‖ a display of excessive indulgence, an orgy of self-pity ‖ (pl., Gk and Rom. hist.) secret ceremonial rites in honor of any of certain gods [earlier orgies pl. fr. F. orgies fr. L. fr. Gk orgia, secret rites]

O·ri·be (orí:be), Manuel (1792–1857), Uruguyan general. He founded the Blanco (or nationalist) party in opposition to Riviera. He was president (1835–8)

or·i·el (órí:əl, óuri:əl) n. a windowed part of a room projecting from a face of a building and often supported by a corbel or bracket ‖ the window of such a projection ‖ any projecting upper-story window [O.F. oriol, porch, passage]

or·i·ent (órí:ənt, óuri:ənt) **1.** n. a highquality pearl, or its special luster **the O·ri·ent** the countries lying east of Europe, esp. the Far East (opp. OCCIDENT) **2.** adj. (rhet.) lustrous, bright (used orig. of the finest kinds of precious stones and pearls, from the East) [F. fr. L. oriens (orientis), the east, rising sun]

or·i·ent (órí:ent, óuri:ent) v.t. to determine the position of (someone or something) with reference to the points of the compass ‖ to place with regard to points of the compass ‖ to adjust (someone or something) to the surroundings or a situation ‖ to turn or guide in a specified direction ‖ to cause to face eastward, esp. to build (a church) with its altar at the eastern end, or bury (a body) with the feet pointing east [F. orienter, to place facing east]

O·ri·en·tal (ɔri:ént'l, ouri:ént'l) **1.** adj. of, relating to, characteristic of or coming from the Orient **2.** n. a native or inhabitant of the Orient, esp. of the Far East [F.]

Oriental beetle the Asiatic beetle

Or·i·en·tal·ism (ɔri:ént'lizəm, ouri:ént'lizəm) n. a characteristically Oriental trait, practice etc. ‖ the study of Oriental civilization, languages etc. **Or·i·én·tal·ist** n. a specialist in Oriental civilization, languages etc.

Or·i·en·tal·ize (ɔri:ént'laiz, ouri:ént'laiz) pres. part. **Or·i·en·tal·iz·ing** past and past part. **Or·i·en·tal·ized** v.t. to make Oriental in character or

tastes ‖ v.i. to become Oriental in character or tastes

or·i·en·tate (órí:enteit, óuri:enteit) pres. part. **or·i·en·tat·ing** past and past part. **or·i·en·tat·ed** v.t. to orient [fr. F. orienter]

or·i·en·ta·tion (órí:entéiʃən, óuri:entéiʃən) n. an orienting or being oriented ‖ position with relation to the points of the compass‖ situation of a church on an east-west axis so that the altar is at the east end ‖ (chem.) the relative position of atoms or groups about a nucleus or existing configuration ‖ the ordering of chemical groups, molecules or crystals in a particular or desired sense [fr. ORIENT v. or ORIENTATE]

O·rien·te (orjénte) the easternmost and largest province (area 14,128 sq. miles, pop. 2,600,000) of Cuba. Capital: Santiago. Agriculture: chiefly sugarcane. Mining: manganese, chromite, nickel, iron ore

or·i·en·teer·ing (ɔri:entíəriŋ) n. outdoor sport developed in Scandinavia in which competing participants find their way from checkpoint to checkpoint in an unfamiliar area using a map and a compass

or·i·fice (órifis, órifis) n. a mouthlike opening, nasal orifice [F.]

or·i·flamme (óriflæm, óriflæm) n. (hist.) the ancient royal standard of France, a red silk banderole dedicated to St Denis, carried into battle by French kings (11th-15th cc.) ‖ a symbol or rallying point in a struggle, campaign etc. [fr. O.F. oriflambe fr. L. aurum, gold+flamma, flame]

o·ri·ga·mi (ɔrəgámi:) n. the art or process of folding paper into representational or decorative forms [Jap.]

o·rig·a·num (orígənəm, arígənəm) n. Origanum vulgare, wild marjoram, and any of several other fragrant aromatic plants of fam. Labiatae and fam. Verbenaceae, used in cooking for seasoning

Or·i·gen (óridʒen, óridʒən) (c. 185–c. 254), Christian theologian. He was head of the Catechetical school of Alexandria (203–31). He was a biblical critic and exegete and expounded the allegorical meanings of the Scriptures (e.g. in 'Hexapla'). His 'De principiis' set forth a comprehensive Christian philosophy, but it survives only in fragments. His 'Contra Celsum' is an outstanding apologetic

Or·i·gen·ism (óridʒənizəm, óridʒənizəm) n. the doctrines attributed to Origen, condemned by the Council of Constantinople (553) **Or·i·gen·ist** n.

or·i·gin (óridʒin, óridʒin) n. the point in time or space at which a thing first exists ‖ the first existence of something ‖ a source or cause, the origin of a dispute ‖ (esp. pl.) a person's parentage or ancestry, of humble origins ‖ (anat.) the point of attachment of a muscle that is most firmly fixed [F. origine fr. L. origo (originis), beginning, source]

o·rig·i·nal (əridʒin'l) **1.** adj. of, relating to or belonging to an origin or beginning, the original plans were changed ‖ firsthand, not copied or derivative, an original work by Cézanne ‖ inventive, creative, an original mind ‖ designating something from which a copy, translation, summary etc. has been made, let us look at the original passage **2.** n. a model or archetype that has been copied, translated etc., the original of this copy is in the Louvre ‖ (old-fash.) a person who is eccentric in behavior or character [F.]

o·rig·i·nal·i·ty (əridʒinǽliti:) n. the quality or state of being original, esp. creative or novel [fr. F. originalité]

orig·i·nal sin (Christian theol.) the sin into which all men are said to be born as a result of the Fall

o·rig·i·nate (əridʒineit) pres. part. **o·rig·i·nat·ing** past and past part. **o·rig·i·nat·ed** v.i. (with 'in', 'from', 'with') to have its source or beginning, their friendship originated in a chance meeting ‖ v.t. to cause to begin, be the source of, to originate a new dance step **o·rig·i·ná·tion** n. origin, an originating or being originated [etym. doubtful]

o·ri·na·sal (ɔri:néiz'l, ouri:iéiz'l) **1.** adj. sounded through both nose and mouth, e.g. of the French nasalized vowels in 'cinq', 'pain' etc. **2.** n. an orinasal sound [fr. L. os (oris), mouth+NASAL]

Or·i·no·co (ɔrinóukou, ourinóukou) the chief river of Venezuela. From its source in the Sierra Parima (on the Brazilian frontier) to the Atlantic Ocean it is about 1,500 miles long. An arm, the Casiquiare, links it with the Río Negro and the Amazon. It has the third largest river basin in South America, draining almost 380,000 sq. miles

o·ri·ole (ɔ́ri:oul, óuri:oul) *n.* a member of *Orioli-dae,* an Old World family of passerine birds of warm and tropical regions, esp. *Oriolus oriolus,* the golden oriole, the male of which is bright yellow with black wings and tail ‖ a member of *Icteridae,* a New World family of birds including the Baltimore Oriole [fr. M.L. and Mod. L. *oriolus* fr. L. *aureolus* adj., golden]

O·ri·on (oráiən, ouráiən) a constellation in the southern part of the zodiac, represented in charts as a hunter with belt and sword [L. fr. *Oríon,* a giant and hunter of Gk mythol.]

O·ri·on (oráiən) (*mil.*) four-engine, turboprop, all weather, long-range, land-based antisubmarine aircarft (P-3 and EP-3), capable of carrying a varied assortment of search radar, nuclear depth charges and homing torpedoes

o·ri·son (ɔ́riz'n,óriz'n) *n.* (*rhet.*) a prayer [O.F. *oreisun, orison*]

O·ris·sa (orísə, ourísə) a state (area 60,136 sq. miles, pop. 26,370,271) of India on the Bay of Bengal. Capital: Bhubaneswar. Products: rice, tobacco, jute, turmeric, sugarcane, iron, manganese, fish, lumber, textiles

O·ri·ya (orí:jə) *n.* one of the main Indic languages of India, spoken in Orissa, and closely related to Bengali

Or·i·za·ba (ɔri:sábə) *CITLALTEPETL

Ork·ney Islands (ɔ́rkni:) an archipelago (90 islands and islets, a third of them inhabited) forming a county (land area 376 sq. miles, pop. 18,900) of Scotland, off the northeast coast. Main islands: Pomona (or Mainland), Hoy. County town: Kirkwall, on Pomona. Products: oats, root vegetables, lobster, cod. herring. Livestock: sheep, cattle

Orlando (ourlǽndou) a city (pop. 128,291) in the U.S.A. in east central Florida about 100 mi (160km) northeast of Tampa; seat of Orange County. Industries: citrus groves, aerospace industries, tourism. Walt Disney World is 15 mi (24km) southwest

orle (ɔrl) *n.* (*heraldry*) a band, half the width of the bordure, following the outline of the shield but not touching the edge of it [F. fr. O.F. *urle, ourle*]

Or·lé·a·nais (ɔrleiænei) a former province of France around the middle Loire, in the Paris basin, comprising Loiret, Loir-et-Cher and Eure-et-Loire departments. It is an agricultural region: cereals (*BEAUCE), sugar beet, vegetables, fruit. It contains large forests. Main towns: Orléans (the historical capital), Chartres, Blois. There are light industries. Part of the royal domain from the 10th c., it was created a duchy-apanage (1344) and was united to the French crown (1498)

Or·le·an·ist (ɔrlí:ənist, ɔrli:ænist) *n.* a supporter of the Orléans family which claims the French throne by descent from Louis XIV's younger brother Philippe, duc d'Orléans (1640-1701)

Or·lé·ans (ɔrleiɑ̃) the name of four princely houses of France, younger branches of the houses of Valois and Bourbon

Orléans, Charles, duc d' (1391-1465), son of Louis, duc d'Orléans. He was captured at Agincourt (1415) and held prisoner in England until 1440. He was a poet and a patron of letters

Orléans, Louis, duc d' (1372-1402), brother of Charles VI of France. His struggle for the throne after 1392 weakened France in the Hundred Years' War and led to his murder. He was the founder of the house of Valois-Orléans

Orléans, Louis-Philippe-Joseph, duc d' (1747-93), 'Philippe Egalité', French revolutionist. He helped the Jacobins to power and voted for the execution of Louis XVI. He was himself guillotined

Orléans, Phillippe, duc d' (1640-1701), brother of Louis XIV. He was the founder of the house of Bourbon-Orléans

Orléans, Phillippe, duc d' (1674-1723), son of Philippe, duc d'Orléans. As regent of France (1715-23) during the minority of Louis XV, he reversed the policy of Louis XIV. His attempt to reform the finances on the advice of John Law ended in disaster

Orléans a city (pop. 106,246) of Loiret, France, on the Loire, historic capital of Orléanais. It is a rail center. Industries: engineering, textiles, food processing. Cathedral (13th-17th cc.). Joan of Arc forced the English to raise the siege of Orléans (1429)

Or·ley (ɔrlí:), Bernard van (c. 1492-1542), Flemish painter, strongly influenced by the

Italians, esp. by Raphael. He also executed cartoons for tapestries

Or·lon (ɔ́rlɒn) *n.* a synthetic fiber somewhat like nylon, used in clothing etc. fabric made of this [trademark]

or·lop (ɔ́rlɒp) *n.* the lowest deck of a ship, esp. of a warship [Du. *overloop,* a covering]

Or·lov (ʌrlɔ́f), Count Grigori Grigorievich (1734-83), Russian nobleman. A lover of Catherine II, he was a leader of the plot which brought her to the throne

Or·mazd, Or·muzd (ɔ́rməzd) in the Zoroastrian religion, the supreme deity and creator of the world, patron of good, opposed to Ahriman, patron of evil

or·mer (ɔ́rmər) *n.* a haliotis [dial. F. fr. F. *ormier,* contr. of *oreille-de-mer* or fr. L. *auris maris,* sea ear (fr. its shape)]

or·mo·lu (ɔ́rməlu:) *n.* an alloy of copper, zinc and tin, made to resemble gold, used esp. for furniture decoration [F. *or moulu,* ground gold]

Or·monde (ɔ́rmənd), James Butler, 12th earl and 1st duke of (1610-88), Irish statesman. As lord lieutenant of Ireland (1644-7, 1648-50, 1661-9 and 1677-84), he upheld the policies of Strafford and the Stuart monarchy

Ormuzd *ORMAZD

or·na·ment 1. (ɔ́rnəmənt) *n.* an object, detail etc. meant to add beauty to something to which it is attached or applied or of which it is a part ‖ such objects, details etc. collectively, *a stone window rich in ornament* ‖ (*mus.*) a grace note or group of them, e.g. a turn or trill ‖ (*rhet.*) a person who enhances or does credit to his society, milieu, profession etc. ‖ (*eccles.*) an accessory used in worship or church furnishing **2.** (ɔ́rnəment) *v.t.* to add or apply an ornament or ornaments to **or·na·men·tal** (ɔrnəmént'l) *adj.* **or·na·men·ta·tion** (ɔrnəmentéiʃən) *n.* an ornamenting or being ornamented ‖ ornaments collectively [O. F. *ournement, ornement*]

or·nate (ɔrnéit) *adj.* elaborately adorned, *an ornate ceiling* ‖ (of literary style) making use of elaborate rhetorical devices [fr. L. *ornare (ornatus),* to adorn]

Orne (ɔrn) a department (area 2,371 sq. miles, pop. 293,500) of N.W. France (*NORMANDY). Chief town: Alençon

or·ner·y (ɔ́rnəri:) *adj.* (*pop.*) inclined to be stubborn and not cooperative [altered fr. ORDINARY]

or·ni·tho·log·i·cal (ɔrnəθəlɔ́dʒik'l) *adj.* of or pertaining to ornithology

or·ni·thol·o·gist (ɔrnəθɔ́lədʒist) *n.* a specialist in ornithology

or·ni·thol·o·gy (ɔrnəθɔ́lədʒi:) *n.* the branch of zoology which deals with birds [fr. Mod. L. *ornithologia* fr. Gk *ornithologos,* dealing with birds fr. *ornis (ornithos),* bird + *logos,* discourse]

or·ni·tho·rhyn·chus (ɔrnəθəríŋkəs) *n.* the platypus [Mod. L. *Ornithorhynchus,* name of genus fr. Gk *ornis (ornithos),* bird + *rhunchos,* bill]

or·o·gen·e·sis (ɔroudʒénisis) *pl.* **or·o·gen·e·ses** (ɔroudʒénisi:z) *n.* an orogeny **or·og·e·ny** (ɔrɔ́dʒəni:, ourɔ́dʒəni:) *pl.* **or·og·e·nies** *n.* the process by which mountains are made, esp. by folding of the earth's crust ‖ a series of mountain-making movements allied in area and period [fr. Gk *oros,* mountain + GENESIS]

or·o·graph·ic (ɔrəgrǽfik, ourəgrǽfik) *adj.* of or pertaining to mountains or to orography **or·o·gráph·i·cal** *adj.*

o·rog·ra·phy (ɔrɔ́grəfi:, ourɔ́grəfi:) *n.* the physical geography of mountains [fr. Gk *oros,* mountain + *graphos,* written]

o·ro·ide (ɔ́rouaid, óurouaid) *n.* a gold-colored alloy, chiefly of copper and zinc or tin, used for making cheap jewelry [F. *or,* gold + Gk *eidos,* form]

O·ron·tes (orɔ́nti:z, ourɔ́nti:z) (*Arab.* Nahr el 'Asi) an unnavigable river (246 miles long) rising near Baalbek in central Lebanon and flowing north through W. Syria (where it is dammed for irrigation) and into Turkey, then southwest, passing Antioch, to the Mediterranean

O·ro·si·us (oróuʃi:əs), Paulus (early 5th c. A.D.), Spanish Christian theologian and historian, disciple of St Augustine. His history of the world, 'Adversus paganos historiarum libri VII', was translated into Anglo-Saxon by Alfred the Great and was popular in medieval Europe

o·ro·tund (ɔ́rətʌnd, óurətʌnd) *adj.* (of voice, utterance) full and ringing clear ‖ (of style, delivery etc.) bombastic, pompous [fr. L. *ore rotundo,* with a round mouth]

O·roz·co (orɔ́sko), José Clemente (1883-1949), Mexican painter, well known for his murals painted in the U.S.A. (1927-32) and in Mexico City

O·roz·co y Ber·ra (orɔ́skoi:bérrɑ), Manuel (1816-81), Mexican archaeologist and historian, whose 'Historia del México antiguo' made him the world's foremost authority on the civilization of Anáhuac

or·phan (ɔ́rfən) **1.** *n.* a child whose parents are dead ‖ a child one of whose parents is dead **2.** *adj.* designating an orphan, *an orphan child* **3.** *v.t.* to bereave (a child) of his parents by death, *children orphaned by the war* **or·phan·age** *n.* an institution for the care and education of orphans [fr. L.L. *orphanus* fr. Gk *orphanos,* bereaved, without parents]

Or·phe·us (ɔ́rfi:əs, ɔ́rfju:s) (*Gk* mythol.) Thracian hero and musician regarded as the founder of Orphism. He was able to charm trees and wild beasts with the music of his lyre. When his wife Eurydice died, Orpheus went to Hades and persuaded Pluto to let him bring her back, but he lost her when he broke the condition not to look at her during the return journey. He was killed and dismembered by the bacchantes

Or·phic (ɔ́rfik) *adj.* of Orpheus, esp. of the secret rites and mysteries associated with Orphism ‖ mysterious, esoteric in language **Or·phism** *n.* an ascetic cult of ancient Greece, stressing the transmigration of souls, moral and ritual purity and individual responsibility for guilt, and having mystical rites of initiation and purification [fr. Gk *Orphikos*]

or·phrey, or·fray (ɔ́rfri:) *pl.* **or·phreys, or·frays** *n.* a band, usually of rich embroidery, attached to an ecclesiastical vestment [M.E. *orfreis,* embroidery fr. O.F.]

or·pi·ment (ɔ́rpəmənt) *n.* arsenic trisulfide, As_2S_3, existing as a crystalline mineral or an amorphous yellow powder, used for dyeing [O.F. fr. L. *auripigmentum,* gold pigment]

or·pine, or·pin (ɔ́rpin) *n. Sedum telephium,* fam. *Crafsulaceae,* a plant native to Europe and N. Asia, now found in cool climates. It has succulent leaves and pinkish purple blossoms, formerly used as a healing agent [F. *orpin,* prob. fr. *orpiment,* orpiment (fr. the color of the flowers of a related plant)]

Or·ping·ton (ɔ́rpintən) *n.* a member of a breed of large, deep-chested, shortlegged poultry, commonly buff-colored [fr. *Orpington,* town in Kent, England]

Orr (ɔr), John Boyd *BOYD ORR

or·rer·y (ɔ́rəri:) *pl.* **or·rer·ies** *n.* a clockwork model to illustrate relative positions and movements of the planets in the solar system, invented c. 1700 by George Graham (1675-1751), and popular in the 18th c. [after Charles Boyle, 4th earl of Orrery (1676-1731), for whom one was made]

or·ris (ɔ́ris,óris) *n.* a plant of the genus *Iris,* esp. *I florentina* ‖ orrisroot [prob. alteration of IRIS]

or·ris·root (ɔ́risru:t, órisrut, órisru:t, órisrut) *n.* the fragrant rootstock of any of several European irises, esp. *Iris florentina,* smelling of violets and used in perfumery and medicine

Or·si·ni (orsí:ni:), Felice (1819-58), Italian revolutionary. His unsuccessful attempt (1858) to assassinate Napoleon III as a traitor to the Italian revolutionary cause was instrumental in obtaining French intervention in Italy

Or·te·ga y Gas·set (ɔrtéigai:gɑset), José (1883-1955), Spanish essayist and philosopher. His best known book in translation is 'The Revolt of the Masses' (1932), a critique of modern social and cultural developments

ortho- (ɔ́rθou) *prefix* straight or vertical ‖ correct or proper ‖ regular [fr. Gk *orthos,* straight]

or·tho·ce·phal·ic (ɔrθousəfǽlik) *adj.* having a skull with a height from 70 to 75% of the length **or·tho·ceph·a·lous** (ɔrθəséfələs) *adj.* [fr. ORTHO- + Gk *kephalē,* head]

or·tho·chro·mat·ic (ɔrθoukrəmǽtik) *adj.* (*photog.*) of a film which is sensitive to green as well as to blue and violet wavelengths and thus gives a more accurate tone representation than ordinary film ‖ (*photog.,* of a plate etc.) sensitive to all colors except red [fr. ORTHO- + Gk *chrōmatikos,* chromatic]

or·tho·clase (ɔ́rθəkleiz, ɔ́rθəkleis) *n.* potassium feldspar, $KAlSi_3O_8$, a monoclinic mineral found in granite and other rocks and having cleavage at right angles (cf. PLAGIOCLASE) **or·tho·clas·tic** (ɔrθəklǽstik) *adj.* (of crystals) cleaving in directions at right angles to each other ‖ of or pertaining to orthoclase [fr. ORTHO-+Gk *klasis*, breaking, cleavage]

or·tho·don·tia (ɔrθədɒ́nʃiːə, ɔrθədɒ́nʃə) *n.* orthodontics **or·tho·dón·tic** *adj.* of or pertaining to orthodontics **or·tho·dón·tics** *n.* the branch of dentistry concerned with the prevention and correction of displacement or overcrowding of the teeth **or·tho·dón·tist** *n.* [Mod. L. fr. Gk *orthos*, straight, correct+*odous (odontos)*, tooth]

or·tho·dox (ɔ́rθədɒks) *adj.* of, conforming to or holding the official, accepted or standard opinions, not heretical or independent, *orthodox Marxism* (cf. HETERODOX) ‖ standardized, conventional, *is there an orthodox way of cooking an omelet?* **Or·tho·dox** of or belonging to the Orthodox Eastern Church [fr. Gk *orthodoxos*, right in opinion]

Orthodox Eastern Church that part of the Christian Church centered on the patriarchate of Constantinople, which became separate from western Christendom in 1054, when it refused to accept the supremacy of the pope and was excommunicated by Pope Leo IX. This excommunication was annulled in 1965. The Orthodox Church comprises 16 autocephalous patriarchates. Four of them date from Apostolic times but they diminished in influence with the rise of Islam. They are Constantinople (310,000, created 381), Alexandria (90,000, created 537), Antioch (287,000, created 519) and Jerusalem (45,000, created 451). The largest Churches are the Russian (end of 10th c., autocephalous in 1448, and dominant since, though its numerical strength, perhaps 100 million, is uncertain), the Greek (7 million, autocephalous in 1833), the Rumanian (4th c., 14 million, autocephalous 1925), the Serbian (9th c., 7½ million, autonomous 1219 and fully autocephalous 1879) and the Bulgarian (9th c., 6 million, autocephalous 917). The others are the Georgian, Albanian, Finnish, Polish, Cypriot, Czechoslovak and Mt Sinai. Orthodox communities in W. Europe, Australia and North and South America belong to the patriarchate of Antioch or that of Jerusalem. There are over 150 million Orthodox in the world. Before its break with Rome the Orthodox Church suffered several schisms as a result of Nestorian and Monophysite heresies. These produced the Ethiopian Church (mid-4th c., 5 million), the Armenian Church (end of 5th c., 4 million), the Coptic Church (mid-5th c., 3,000,000) and several smaller schismatic bodies. The leading Orthodox patriarchates are represented on the World Council of Churches. Doctrinally the orthodox differ little from Rome, but they accept only the first seven ecumenical councils (until 787), and deny purgatory and the Immaculate Conception. Emphasis is placed on ritual, monasticism and mysticism, and the priesthood is not always celibate. Historically they are closely associated with eastern European nationalism.

orthodox sleep (*physiol.*) the portion of sleep without dreams or rapid eye movement, important for body-function renewal *Cf* PARADOXICAL SLEEP

or·tho·dox·y (ɔ́rθədɒksi) *pl.* **or·tho·dox·ies** *n.* the quality or state of being orthodox (cf. HETERODOXY) ‖ an orthodox opinion or practice [fr. Gk *orthodoxia*]

or·tho·ep·ic (ɔrθouépik) *adj.* of or pertaining to orthoepy **or·thó·e·pist** *n.* a specialist in orthoepy

or·tho·e·py (ɔ́rθouepi:, ɔrθóuəpi:) *n.* the correct pronunciation of the words of a language ‖ the study of this [fr. Gk *orthoepeia*, correctness of diction]

or·tho·fer·rite (ɔrθəférait) *n.* (*computer*) a wafer of rare earth and iron magnetized to have the capability to store and transmit information

or·tho·gen·e·sis (ɔrθədʒénisis) *n.* (*biol.*) evolution in a definite direction through variations which, irrespective of natural selection or external forces, gradually produce a new and distinct type **or·tho·ge·net·ic** (ɔrθoudʒənétik) *adj.* [Mod. L. fr. Gk *orthos*, straight+*genesis*, origin]

or·thog·nath·ic (ɔrθəgnǽθik) *adj.* orthognathous

or·thog·na·thism (ɔrθógnəθizəm) *n.* the quality or state of being orthognathous

or·thog·na·thous (ɔrθógnəθəs) *adj.* having straight jaws which do not project (cf. PROGNATHOUS) [fr. ORTHO-+Gk *gnathos*, jaw]

or·thog·o·nal (ɔrθɒ́gən'l) *adj.* right angled, rectangular [F. fr. L. fr. Gk *orthos*, right+*gōnia*, angle]

or·tho·graph·ic (ɔrθəgrǽfik) *adj.* of or relating to orthography ‖ correct in spelling ‖ (*geom.*) of or containing perpendicular lines or right angles ‖ of a kind of projection used in mapmaking and architecture, in which all the rays are parallel, the viewer being assumed to be at an infinite distance **or·tho·gráph·i·cal** *adj.* [fr. ORTHOGRAPHY and fr. ORTHO-+Gk *graphos*, written]

or·thog·ra·phy (ɔrθógrəfi) *pl.* **or·thog·ra·phies** *n.* correct spelling ‖ spelling rules ‖ spelling of any style or kind, *he uses an old-fashioned orthography* ‖ an orthographic projection [O.F. *ortografie* fr. L. *orthographia* fr. Gk]

or·tho·ker·a·tol·o·gy (ɔrθəkerətó'lədʒi:) *n.* (*med.*) technique for correcting astigmatism by gradually altering cornea shape utilizing periodic changes of contact lenses

or·tho·mo·lec·u·lar medicine (ɔrθəmɒlékjulərmédisin) a philosophy of medicine that holds that disease, esp. mental illness, is curable by restoring normal body chemistry

or·tho·mor·phic projection (ɔrθəmɔ́rfik·prədʒékʃən) (*cartography*) map projection in which the scale, although varying throughout the map, is the same in all directions at any point, so that very small areas are represented by correct shape and bearings

or·tho·pe·dic, or·tho·pae·dic (ɔrθəpíːdik) *adj.* of, relating to or used in orthopedics

or·tho·pe·dics, or·tho·pae·dics (ɔrθəpíːdiks) *n.* the prevention or curing of deformities of bones, joints, ligaments, muscles and tendons, esp. in children **or·tho·pé·dist, or·tho·páe·dist** *n.* [fr. F. *orthopédie* and Mod. L. *orthopaedia* fr. Gk *orthos*, correct+*paidion*, child and *paideia*, rearing of children]

or·tho·phos·phor·ic acid (ɔrθoufɒsfɔ́rik, ɔrθoufɒsfórik) phosphoric acid

or·tho·psy·chi·a·try (ɔrθəsikáiətri) *n.* prevention and treatment of abnormal behavior integrating psychiatry, psychology, pediatrics, social services and the schools to stimulate healthy emotional development

or·thop·ter·an (ɔrθóptərən) **1.** *n.* an orthopteron **2.** *adj.* belonging to the order *Orthoptera* [Mod. L. *Orthoptera*]

or·thop·ter·on (ɔrθóptərən, ɔrθóptərɒn) *n.* a member of *Orthoptera*, an order of insects including grasshoppers, crickets, mantises etc., usually having leathery fore wings and pleated hind wings. They have chewing mouthparts, and are mostly vegetarian. They are largely terrestrial, and undergo incomplete metamorphosis **or·thóp·ter·ous** *adj.* [Mod. L. sing. of *Orthoptera* fr. Gk *orthos*, straight+*pteron*, wing]

or·thop·tic (ɔrθóptik) *adj.* of or relating to orthoptics **or·thóp·tics** *n.* the treatment of defective vision by exercises of the eye muscles etc. [fr. ORTHO-+Gk *optikos*, of or relating to sight]

orthoptics (*med.*) technique of eye exercises designed to correct the visual axes of eyes not properly coordinated for binocular vision — **orthoptist** *n.*

or·tho·rhom·bic (ɔrθərɒ́mbik) *adj.* (of crystals) having three unequal axes of symmetry at right angles to each other

or·tho·scope (ɔ́rθəskoup) *n.* an instrument for viewing the retina of the eye, the refraction due to the cornea being compensated by a layer of water **or·tho·scop·ic** (ɔrθəskópik) *adj.* giving an image of correct proportions [fr. ORTHO-+Gk *skopein*, to examine]

or·thos·ti·chous (ɔrθóstikəs) *adj.* (e.g. of leaves) arranged in vertical ranks [ORTHOSTICHY]

or·thos·ti·chy (ɔrθóstiki:) *pl.* **or·thos·ti·chies** *n.* (*bot.*) a hypothetical line along a stem axis connecting a pair or row of leaves or flowers growing in a direct line ‖ an arrangement of leaves etc. along such a line [fr. ORTHO-+Gk *stichos*, row]

or·thot·ics (ɔrθótiks) *n.* **1.** (*med.*) branch of medicine dealing with the mechanical support of weak joints and muscles —**or·thot·ic** *adj.* —**or·thot·ist** *n.* **2.** (*podiatry*) insert worn in shoe to support the foot, esp. for sports

or·tho·trop·ic (ɔrθətrópik) *adj.* (*bot.*, of a root or stem) growing more or less vertically **or·thot·ro·pism** (ɔrθótrəpizəm) *n.* (*bot.*) the tendency to grow vertically ‖ (*bot.*) vertical growth **or·thot·ro·pous** (ɔrθótrəpəs) *adj.* (*bot.*, of an ovule) having the chalaza, hilum and micropyle in a

straight line [fr. Mod. L. *orthotropus* fr. Gk fr. *ortho-*, straight+*tropos*, turning, turned]

Or·tiz Ru·bio (ɔrtíːsrúːbjo), Pascual (1877–1963), Mexican engineer, statesman and president of the Republic (1930–2)

or·to·lan (ɔ́rt'lən) *n. Emberiza hortulana*, a European bunting, formerly often caught and fattened for eating ‖ the sora ‖ the bobolink [F. fr. Prov. *ortolan* or Ital. *ortolano*, gardener]

O·ru·ro (ɔrúːrɔ) a city (pop. 124,091) of W. Bolivia, at 12,160 ft, the center of a mining district: gold, silver, copper, tin

Or·vie·to (ɔrvjétɔ) an ancient town (pop. 23,220) of Umbria, Italy. Cathedral (1290–1319), with frescos by Fra Angelico and Signorelli

Or·well (ɔ́rwəl, ɔ́rwel), George (Eric Arthur Blair, 1903–50), English novelist and satirist. His best-known works include 'Animal Farm' (1945) and '1984' (1949), expressing his fears for the destruction of the liberty of the individual

Or·well·i·an (ɔrwéliːən) *adj.* of the world described in *1984*, a novel by George Orwell, of totalitarian superstates where citizens are under constant surveillance and language and thoughts are controlled

-ory *suffix* having the function or effect of, as in 'vomitory' [A.F. *-ori, -orie*, O.F. *-oir, -oire* fr. L. *-orius, -oria, -orium*]

-ory *suffix* denoting place or instrument, as in 'oratory' [O.N.F. and A.F. *-orie* fr. L. *-oria, -orium*]

or·yx (ɔ́riks, óuriks) *pl.* **or·yx·es, or·yx** *n.* a member of *Oryx*, a genus of large antelopes with long, straight horns, found in the desert regions of Africa and Arabia [L. fr. Gk *orux*, pickaxe, antelope]

or·zo (ɔ́rzou) *n.* pasta in the shape of rice

os (ous) *pl.* **o·sar** (óusar) *n.* an esker [Swed. *ås*, a ridge]

O·sa·ka (ousáka) the second largest city (pop. 2,623,124) in Japan, a port laced by canals, on Osaka Bay, W. central Honshu, and center of the industrial belt: textiles, shipbuilding, iron and steel, chemicals. University (1931)

o·sar *pl.* of os ‖ taken as *sing. n.* (*pl.* **o·sars**) an esker [Swed. *åsar*, pl. of *ås*, a ridge]

Os·born (ɒ́zbərn), Henry Fairfield (1857–1935), U.S. paleontologist. As president (from 1908) of the American Museum of Natural History, he developed it into an outstanding research center with the world's largest and most important collection of fossil vertebrates

Os·borne (ɒ́zbərn), Dorothy (1627–95), English letter writer. Her fame rests on the series of letters she wrote to her future husband, Sir William Temple

Os·can (ɒ́skən) *n.* a member of a people anciently inhabiting central Italy ‖ their Italic language

Os·car (ɒ́skər) *n.* one of the annual Academy Awards presented since 1927 by the U.S. Academy of Motion Picture Arts and Sciences, founded (1927) in Hollywood, Calif. Awards are made in about 25 categories, notably for the best film production and best acting

Oscar (*mil.*) NATO term for U.S.S.R. class of subcruiser carrying missiles with 60-mi range

Os·car I (ɒ́skər) (1799–1859), king of Sweden and Norway (1844–59), son of Bernadotte

Oscar II (1829–1907), king of Sweden (1872–1907) and of Norway (1872–1905), son of Oscar I. He rejected Norwegian demands for greater autonomy, and the two kingdoms divided (1905)

Osceola (asi:óulə) (1803–38) American Seminole Indian, a leader of the Florida Seminoles during the Seminole Wars. Lured under a flag of truce to St. Augustine, Fla., he and other chiefs were seized and imprisoned by the U.S. government (1837). He died in a cell at Ft. Moultrie in Charleston harbor, S.C.

os·cil·late (ɒ́səleit) *pres. part.* **os·cil·lat·ing** *past and past part.* **os·cil·lat·ed** *v.i.* (of a rigid body pivoted on an axle) to swing to and fro ‖ to vibrate ‖ to waver, vacillate, *his ideas oscillate a good deal* ‖ to vary in condition or degree, fluctuate, *the temperature oscillated wildly during that month* ‖ *v.t.* to cause to oscillate [fr. L. *oscillare (oscillatus)*, to swing]

oscillating mine (*mil.*) a hydrostatically controlled mine that maintains a preset depth below the surface independently of the rise and fall of the tide

os·cil·la·tion (ɒsəléiʃən) *n.* an oscillating ‖ fluctuation ‖ (*elec.*) a current fluctuation in a circuit from positive to negative or from maxima to

CONCISE PRONUNCIATION KEY: **(a)** æ, c*a*t; ɑ, c*a*r; ɔ f*aw*n; ei, sn*a*ke. **(e)** e, h*e*n; iː, sh*ee*p; iə, d*ee*r; ɛə, b*ea*r. **(i)** i, f*i*sh; ai, t*i*ger; əː, b*i*rd. **(o)** o, *o*x; au, c*ow*; ou, g*oa*t; u, p*oo*r; ɔi, r*oy*al. **(u)** ʌ, d*u*ck; u, b*u*ll; uː, g*oo*se; ə, b*a*cillus; juː, c*u*be. x, lo*ch*; θ, *th*ink; ð, bo*th*er; z, *Z*en; ʒ, corsa*g*e; dʒ, sava*g*e; ŋ, ora*ng*uta*ng*; j, *y*ak; ʃ, *fi*sh; tʃ, fe*tch*; 'l, rabb*le*; 'n, redd*en*. Complete pronunciation key appears inside front cover.

minima ‖ (*phys.*) a single swing of an oscillating body, e.g. of a pendulum from one extreme to another ‖ (*math.*) the variation between highest and lowest values of a function **ós·cil·la·tor** *n.* something which oscillates ‖ (*elec.*) a device for the production of oscillations ‖ a device for measuring rigidity by means of the vibrations of a loaded wire [fr. L. *oscillatio* (*oscillationis*)]

os·cil·la·to·ry (ósǝlǝtɔri, ósǝlǝtouri) *adj.* characterized or marked by oscillation [fr. L. *oscillare* (*oscillatus*), to swing]

os·cil·lo·gram (ǝsílǝgræm) *n.* a record made by an oscillograph or by an oscilloscope

os·cil·lo·graph (ǝsílǝgræf, ǝsílǝgraf) *n.* an instrument recording rapidly changing electrical quantities (e.g. voltage) usually indirectly by means of some sensitive element, e.g. a beam of cathode rays (cf. OSCILLOSCOPE) [fr. OSCILLATE+Gk *graphos*, written]

os·cil·lo·scope (ǝsílǝskoup) *n.* (*phys.*) an instrument in which a beam of electrons is directed through horizontal and vertical deflecting plates to which an electrical potential is applied, causing deflection of the electron beam. The electrons fall on a fluorescent screen and produce a temporary trace. The instrument is used to analyze rapidly changing electrical quantities (e.g. voltage) [fr. OSCILLATE+Gk *skopein*, to look at]

os·cine (ósain) *adj.* of or relating to *Oscines,* a suborder of passerine birds with a highly specialized vocal apparatus [fr. Mod. L. *Oscines,* L. pl. of *oscen* (*oscinis*), songbird]

os·cu·lant (óskjulǝnt) *adj.* (*biol.*) forming a link connecting two species, groups etc. [fr. L. *osculans* (*osculantis*) fr. *osculari,* to kiss]

os·cu·lar (óskjulǝr) *adj.* (*rhet.*) of the mouth ‖ (*rhet.*) of kissing ‖ (*biol.*) of an osculum [fr. L. *oscularis* fr. *osculum,* little mouth, kiss]

os·cu·late (óskjuleit) *pres. part.* **os·cu·lat·ing** *past* and *past part.* **os·cu·lat·ed** *v.t.* (*math.,* of a curve, surface etc.) to coincide in three or more points with ‖ *v.i.* (*biol.*) to have characters intermediate between two groups, genera, species etc. [fr. L. *osculari* (*osculatus*), to kiss]

os·cu·la·tion (ɒskjuléiʃǝn) *n.* (*rhet.*) the act of kissing ‖ (*math.,* of a curve, surface etc.) the fact of coinciding in three or more points [fr. L. *osculatio* (*osculationis*) fr. *osculari,* to kiss]

os·cu·lum (óskjulǝm) *pl.* **os·cu·la** (óskjǝlǝ) *n.* one of the orifices or openings of a sponge through which water leaves the body [L.=a little mouth]

OSHA (*acronym*) U.S. Occupational Safety and Health Administration *Cf* NIOSH

O·shog·bo (ouʃógbou) a town (pop. 282,000) of W. Nigeria, about 50 miles northeast of Ibadan: cacao processing

O·si·an·der (ouzi:ǽndǝr) Andreas (Andreas Hosemann, 1498–1552), German Lutheran theologian. He put forward a mystical interpretation of the doctrine of justification by faith which led to a breach with other Lutherans

o·sier (óuʒǝr) **1.** *n.* any of several varieties of willow, esp. *Salix viminalis,* with pliable twigs used for basketry etc. ‖ a willow rod so used **2.** *adj.* of or made of osier [F.]

O·si·ris (ousáiris) the ancient Egyptian god of the underworld and judge of the dead, brother and husband of Isis and father of Horus. He was also often associated with fertility and its sources, the Nile and the sun: he was revived by Isis after being killed by his brother Seth, symbolizing the yearly renewal of the natural world

Os·lo (ózlou, óslou) (called Kristiania, 1624–1924) the capital (pop. 454,872), chief port and industrial center of Norway, at the head of Oslo fiord, in the southeast. Industries: food processing, mechanical engineering, shipbuilding, textiles, paper. Fortress (1300), royal palace (19th c.), town hall (1931–50), university (1811), national theater, museums. Oslo was founded c. 1050, destroyed by fire (1624) and rebuilt

Os·man I (osmán) (1259–1326), Turkish leader. A vassal of the Seljuks, he proclaimed his independence and founded the Ottoman Empire (c. 1288)

Os·man·li (ozmǽnli) **1.** *adj.* Ottoman **2.** *n.* an Ottoman ‖ the Turkic language of Turkey [fr. Turk. *osmiǎnli,* of or belonging to OSMAN]

Os·me·ña (osménja) Sergio (1878–1961), Filipino statesman, president (1944–6). Leader of the government in exile after the death of Quezon, he returned to the Philippines with the U.S. invasion forces

os·mic (ózmik) *adj.* (*chem.*) of compounds of osmium esp. when quadrivalent

os·mi·um (ózmi:ǝm) *n.* (*chem.*) a hard grayish metallic polyvalent element (symbol Os, at. no. 76, at. mass 190.2) of the platinum group, used finely divided as a catalyst for gas reactions and in alloys with platinum and iridium [Mod. L. fr. Gk *osmē,* smell (from its pungent smell)]

os·mole (ózmoul) *n.* (*chem.*) unit of osmotic pressure equal to that of an ideal solution, with a concentration of 1 mole of solute per liter

os·mo·sis (ozmóusis, ɒsmóusis) *n.* the passage of a solvent, but not its solute, through a semipermeable membrane into a more concentrated solution, tending to equalize the concentrations on either side of the membrane **os·mot·ic** (ozmótik, ɒsmótik) *adj.* [fr. obs. *osmose,* osmosis]

osmotic shock (*biol.*) effect on a living system of a sudden change in osmotic pressure

os·mous (ózmous) *adj.* (*chem.*) of compounds of osmium, esp. when bivalent

os·mund (ózmǝnd, ósmǝnd) *n.* a member of *Osmunda,* fam. *Osmundaceae,* a genus of tall rhizomic ferns, esp. *O. regalis* [origin unknown]

Os·na·brück (óznǝbryk) an old city (pop. 160,200) in Lower Saxony, West Germany: iron and steel, mechanical engineering, textiles, paper. The cathedral was begun under Charlemagne

OSO (*abbr.*) Orbiting Solar Observatory, a NASA solar research satellite

os·prey (óspri:) *n. Pandion haliaetus,* fam. *Pandionidae,* a hawk of cosmopolitan distribution with a white underside and head, a brown body, long pointed wings and long deeply curved opposed pairs of claws on its talons. It feeds entirely on fish ‖ a feather trimming for hats made from egret plumes [prob. fr L. *ossifraga,* lit. bonebreaker]

Os·sa (ósǝ) a mountain (6,490 ft) of Thessaly, Greece, overlooking the Gulf of Salonika

os·se·in (ósi:in) *n.* the organic basis of bone tissue, believed identical with collagen and left when the mineral content is eliminated [fr. L. *osseus,* bony]

os·se·ous (ósi:ǝs) *adj.* composed of or resembling bone, *osseous structure* ‖ having a bony skeleton, *osseous and cartilaginous fibers* ‖ rich in fossilized bones, *osseous layers* [fr. L. *osseus,* bony]

Os·set (ósit) *n.* a member of an Aryan people, possibly of Persian origin, living in the central Caucasus, U.S.S.R. (North Ossetian A.S.S.R. and N. Georgia, U.S.S.R.) since the 10th c., and speaking Ossetic

Os·se·tian (osí:ʃǝn) **1.** *adj.* Ossetic **2.** *n.* an Osset

Os·set·ic (osétik) **1.** *adj.* of the Ossets **2.** *n.* the Iranian language of the Ossets

Os·si·an (ósi:ǝn, óʃǝn) legendary Gaelic bard of the 3rd c. (*MACPHERSON)

os·si·cle (ósik'l) *n.* (*anat., zool.*) any of several small bones, esp. one of those in the middle ear, or in the sclerotic of some birds and reptiles ‖ any of several calcareous bodies, esp. one in the gastric mill of crustaceans, or in an echinoderm's test [fr. L. *ossiculum,* little bone]

os·sif·ic (osífik) *adj.* bone-forming [fr. L. *os* (*ossis*), bone]

os·si·fi·ca·tion (ɒsifikéiʃǝn) *n.* the process of becoming bone or an instance of this process ‖ the changing of body tissue into an osseous substance [OSSIFY]

os·si·fy (ósifai) *pres. part.* **os·si·fy·ing** *past* and *past part.* **os·si·fied** *v.i.* to change into bone ‖ (of ideas, behavior etc.) to make or become hardened, set or rigid ‖ *v.t.* to cause to change into bone ‖ to cause (ideas, behavior etc.) to become hardened, set or rigid [fr. L. *os* (*ossis*), bone]

os·so buc·co (ósou bú:kou) *n.* dish of veal shanks braised with chopped parsley, tomatoes, carrots, celery, onion, lemon peel, olive oil, dry white wine and seasonings

os·su·ar·y (óʃuːǝri) *pl.* **os·su·ar·ies** *n.* a container, chamber etc. for the bones of the dead [fr. L.L. *ossuarium*]

Ostade *VAN OSTADE, Adriaen

Ostade *VAN OSTADE, Isaac

os·te·al (ósti:ǝl) *adj.* of, relating to, or like bone ‖ sounding like a bone when struck [fr. Gk *osteon,* bone]

Ost·end (ɒsténd) (*Flem.* Oostende) a port and resort (pop. 71,400) of W. Flanders, Belgium, on the North Sea: fisheries, oyster beds. The port handles goods and passenger traffic with England (coal imports, food products, exports)

Ostend Manifesto a secret dispatch sent (1854) to William L. Marcy, U.S. secretary of state

under President Pierce, by the U.S. ministers to Great Britain, France and Spain, recommending that the U.S.A. acquire Cuba from Spain. If Spain would not sell Cuba, ran the dispatch, 'then by every law, human and divine, (the U.S.A. should) be justified in wresting it from Spain if (it possessed) the power'. Public reaction when the report leaked out led Marcy to reject the proposal

os·ten·si·ble (ɒsténsǝb'l) *adj.* apparent, pretended, avowed, *ostensible motives* **os·tén·si·bly** *adv.* [F.]

os·ten·sive (ɒsténsiv) *adj.* (*logic*) directly demonstrative ‖ ostensible [L.L. *ostensivus* fr. L. *ostendere* (*ostensus*), to show]

os·ten·so·ry (ɒsténsǝri:) *pl.* **os·ten·so·ries** *n.* (Roman Catholicism) a monstrance [fr. M.L. *ostensorium*]

os·ten·ta·tion (ɒstentéiʃǝn) *n.* unnecessary show or display of wealth, luxury, skill, learning etc. **os·ten·tá·tious** *adj.* fond of display, showy ‖ intended to attract attention, *an ostentatious manner* [F.]

os·te·o·ar·thri·tis (ɒsti:ouɑrθráitis) *n.* a degenerative condition in older people, chiefly of the knee and hip joints [fr. Gk *osteon,* bone+*arthritis,* gout]

os·te·o·blast (ósti:ǝblæst) *n.* a bone-forming cell [fr. Gk *osteon,* bone+*blastos,* bud]

os·te·oc·la·sis (ɒsti:óklǝsis) *n.* (*surgery*) the operation of breaking a bone in order to correct a deformity etc. [Gk *osteon,* bone+*klasis,* fracture]

os·te·o·clast (ósti:ǝklæst) *n.* (*anat.*) a cell in developing bone concerned esp. with the breaking down of unnecessary bone parts ‖ (*surgery*) an instrument for breaking bones in osteoclasis [G. *osteoklast* fr. Gk *osteon,* bone+*klastos,* broken]

os·te·o·log·ic (ɒsti:ǝlódʒik) *adj.* of or relating to osteology **os·te·o·lóg·i·cal** *adj.*

os·te·ol·o·gist (ɒsti:ólǝdʒist) *n.* someone who specializes in osteology

os·te·ol·o·gy (ɒsti:ólǝdʒi:) *n.* the scientific study of bones and bony structure ‖ the bony structure of an organism or part of an organism [fr. Gk *osteon,* bone+*logos,* discourse]

os·te·o·ma (ɒsti:óumǝ) *pl.* **os·te·o·mas, os·te·o·ma·ta** (ɒsti:óumǝtǝ) *n.* (*med.*) a benign bony tumor **os·te·ó·ma·tous** *adj.* [fr. Gk *osteon,* bone]

os·te·o·my·e·li·tis (ɒsti:oumaiǝláitis) *n.* inflammation of bone marrow [fr. Gk *osteon,* bone+*muelos,* marrow]

os·te·o·path (ósti:ǝpæθ) *n.* someone who specializes in osteopathy

os·te·o·path·ic (ɒsti:ǝpǽθik) *adj.* of or relating to osteopathy

os·te·op·a·thist (ɒsti:ópǝθist) *n.* an osteopath

os·te·op·a·thy (ɒsti:ópǝθi:) *n.* a form of medical treatment purporting to cure a wide variety of diseases primarily by manipulation of the joints of the body. This is based on the assumption that disease is due chiefly to skeletal deformation and its effects on nerves, blood vessels etc. [fr. Gk *osteon,* bone+*pathos,* feeling]

os·te·o·phyte (ósti:ǝfait) *n.* (*med.*) a small bony outgrowth **os·te·o·phyt·ic** (ɒsti:ǝfítik) *adj.* [fr. Gk *osteon,* bone+*phuton,* growth]

os·te·o·plas·tic (ɒsti:ǝplǽstik) *adj.* of or relating to osteoplasty

os·te·o·plas·ty (ósti:ǝplæsti:) *n.* (*surgery*) bone repair, esp. reconstruction of damaged or missing parts [fr. Gk *osteon,* bone+*plastos,* molded]

osteoporosis (ɒsti:oupouróusis) condition characterized by decrease in bone mass with decreased density and enlargement of bone spaces producing porosity and fragility. Senile and postmenopausal, or primary, osteoporosis, the most common type, occurs only in elderly persons and postmenopausal women. Disuse, or secondary, osteoporosis involves bones immobilized by paralytic disease or traumatic fractures or that have been subjected to prolonged weightlessness during space flight. Exercise programs, calcium-enriched diet, and sometimes estrogen replacement, are used in prevention and treatment

os·te·ot·o·my (ɒsti:ótǝmi:) *pl.* **os·te·ot·o·mies** *n.* (*surgery*) an operation of cutting bone or removing pieces of bone [fr. Gk *osteon,* bone+*-tomia,* cutting]

Os·ti·a (ósti:ǝ) the port of ancient Rome, at the old mouth of the Tiber, now 3 miles from the sea and the modern bathing resort of Ostia Marina (or Lido di Roma). The Roman town (4th c. B.C.– 3rd c. A.D.) has been extensively excavated

---

CONCISE PRONUNCIATION KEY: **(a)** æ, c*a*t; ɑ, c*a*r; ɔ f*aw*n; ei, sn*a*ke. **(e)** e, h*e*n; i:, sh*ee*p; iǝ, d*ee*r; ɛǝ, b*ea*r. **(i)** i, f*i*sh; ai, t*i*ger; ǝ:, b*i*rd. **(o)** o, *o*x; au, c*ow*; ou, g*oa*t; u, p*oo*r; ɔi, r*oy*al. **(u)** ʌ, d*u*ck; u, b*u*ll; u:, g*oo*se; ǝ, b*a*cillus; ju:, c*u*be. x, lo*ch*; θ, *th*ink; ð, bo*th*er; z, *Z*en; ʒ, cor*s*age; dʒ, sa*v*age; ŋ, ora*ng*utang; j, *y*ak; ʃ, *f*ish; tʃ, fe*tch*; 'l, rabb*le*; 'n, redd*en*. Complete pronunciation key appears inside front cover.

os·ti·ole (ósti:oul) *n.* a small aperture or pore, e.g. the opening of a perithecium or of a stoma ‖ an inhalant aperture of a sponge [fr. L. *ostiolum*, dim. of *ostium*, door]

ost·ler (óslər) *n.* (*hist.*) a hostler

ost·mark (óstmark) *n.* unit of currency of East Germany, equal to 100 pfennig

Ost·pol·i·tik (ɒstpólitik) *n.* West Germany's policy toward Eastern Europe, esp. during 1969–74, that was a forerunner of détente

os·tra·cism (óstrəsizəm) *n.* an ostracizing or being ostracized

os·tra·cize (óstrəsaiz) *pres. part.* **os·tra·ciz·ing** *past* and *past part.* **os·tra·cized** *v.t.* to refrain deliberately and ostentatiously from having any sociable dealings at all with, esp. in order to punish by humiliating, *he was ostracized by the village after the inquest* ‖ (*Gk hist.*) to banish (someone considered dangerous to the state) for 5 or 10 years by popular vote. The votes were registered on potsherds [fr. Gk *ostrakizein* fr. *ostrakon*, a potsherd]

Os·tra·va (óstrava) (formerly Moravská-Ostrava) the chief town (pop. 323,459, of N. Moravia, on the Oder, center of Czechoslovakia's main coal-mining district: iron and steel, heavy engineering, machinery, chemicals

os·trich (óstritʃ, ɒstritʃ) *n. Struthio camelus,* fam. *Struthionidae,* a cursorial flightless bird inhabiting the sandy plains of Africa and formerly Arabia. It is the largest living bird, attaining a height of 6-8 ft and a weight of 300 lbs., and capable of running at 40 miles an hour. The males are black and white, the females and young have a brown head and neck. The legs are bare, but the bodies are well feathered. The wing and tail feathers are used for ornamental trimming, e.g. of hats. The adults are gregarious and polygamous [O.F. *ostruce, ostruche* fr. pop. L. *avistruthio* fr. *avis,* bird+L.L. *struthio* fr. Gk *strouthiōn,* ostrich]

Os·tro·goth (óstrəgɒθ) *n.* a member of the eastern division of the Goths. They invaded Italy (488) under their king, Theodoric, and founded a kingdom which was destroyed (552-5) by Justinian 1

Os·trov·sky (ʌstrófski), Alexander Nikolayevich (1823–86), Russian dramatist. His plays, e.g. 'The Storm' (1860), were remarkable for their liberal tendencies

Ost·wald (óstvalt), Wilhelm (1853–1932), German chemist. He was a pioneer in electrochemistry and catalysis, and formulated Ostwald's law stating that the dissociation of an electrolyte tends to completion with infinite dilution

Os·ty·ak (ósti:æk) *n.* a member of a Ugrian people living in W. Siberia ‖ their Ugric language

Os·wald (ózwɔld), St (c. 604–42), king of Northumbria (633–42). He received St Aidan from Iona, and gave him Holy Island as the center for the conversion of Northumbria. Feast: Aug. 5

Oswald St (c. 925–92), English prelate, bishop of Worcester (962–92) and archbishop of York (972–92). With St Dunstan, he was one of the leaders of the 10th-c. monastic revival in England. Feast: Feb. 28

Oswald, Lee Harvey (1939–63), the alleged assassin of President John F. Kennedy. Oswald was in turn shot and killed by Jack Ruby. The Warren Commission Report found that Oswald 'acting alone and without advice or assistance' was the assassin of President Kennedy. An avowed Marxist, Oswald had lived in the U.S.S.R. for a short time. He had a childhood background of emotional disturbance

Os·wie·cim (ɔʃvjǽtsim) *AUSCHWITZ

Os·wy (ózwi:) (d. 671), king of Northumbria (642–71). He summoned the Synod of Whitby (664)

O·ta·go (outágou) the southernmost province (area 25,530 sq. miles, pop. 279,000) of South Island, New Zealand: fruit, sheep, dairy produce, some gold. University at Dunedin (1869)

O·ta·ru (outáru:) a port (pop. 189,000) of W. central Hokkaido, Japan: fisheries

o·ta·ry (óutəri) *n.* a member of *Otariidae,* a family of chiefly Antarctic seals having small, well-developed ears [fr. Mod. L. *otaria*]

OTB (*abbr.*) off-track betting, esp. in New York

OTC drug over-the-counter drug (which see)

OTEC (*acronym*) ocean thermal energy conversion, plants for conversion to tap tropical seas for electric power

oth·er (ʌðər) **1.** *adj.* different, not the same, *your other hand, some other time* ‖ alternative, *he has no other place to go* ‖ further or additional, *give some other examples* ‖ remaining, *where are your other sons?* ‖ of very different kind, *his tastes are quite other than mine* ‖ former, *the youth of other days* **every other** alternate, *skip every other line* **on the other hand** used to introduce an argument or fact in contrast with a previous one **other things being equal** if the conditions were the same in everything but the point under discussion, *other things being equal I should prefer to live here: but it is damp* **the other day** recently, a few days ago **the other world** life after death **2.** *n.* or *pron.* other person or thing, *show me some others, keep this eye closed and open the other, others can do as they please* **among others** with others, *my life was there among others* **one after the other** in succession, *difficulties arose one after the other* **one from the other** apart, *it is hard to tell the twins one from the other* **someone or other** some unknown person, *someone or other has broken my pen* **some time or other** someday, *he hopes to go to Italy some time or other* **3.** *adv.* **other than** in any other way, *he did not examine it other than casually* ‖ besides, *is anyone other than yourself coming?* [O.E. *ōther*]

oth·er·wise (ʌðərwaiz) **1.** *adv.* in another or different way, *you could hardly think otherwise* ‖ or else, *do it now, otherwise you will forget* ‖ in other respects, apart from that, *he was careless, but not otherwise to be blamed* ‖ under other circumstances, *he can't stay for two years, otherwise we would appoint him* **2.** *adj.* in a different state, *he does not wish it otherwise* ‖ different, *if circumstances were otherwise* [O.E *onōthre wīsan*]

oth·er·world·li·ness (ʌðərwə́:rldli:nis) *n.* the quality or state of being otherworldly

oth·er·world·ly (ʌðərwə́:rldli:) *adj.* concerned with spiritual matters, often to the exclusion of the affairs of this world ‖ hopelessly unpractical often because absorbed in speculation etc.

Oth·man (ɔθmán) (c. 578–656), 3rd Moslem caliph (644–56), father-in-law of Mohammed

O·tho (óuθou) (Holy Roman Emperors, and king of Greece) *OTTO

Otho, Marcus Salvius (32–69), Roman emperor (69). He was defeated by Vitellius shortly after his proclamation by the Praetorians, and committed suicide

o·tic (ótik, óutik) *adj.* of or relating to the ear [fr. Gk *otikos* fr. *ous* (*ōtos*), ear]

o·ti·ose (óuʃi:ous, óuti:ous) *adj.* (*rhet.*) idle, lazy, *otiose delights* ‖ superfluous, *otiose remarks* [fr. L. *otiosus,* at leisure]

O·tis (óutis), Elisha Graves (1811–61), American inventor. His invention of an elevator with a safety device (1852) made the building of skyscrapers a practical possibility

Otis, James (1725–83), American revolutionary leader. He was an eloquent critic of British colonial policy before the Revolutionary War

o·ti·tis (outáitis) *n.* inflammation of the ear [Mod. L. fr. Gk *ous* (*ōtos*), ear]

o·to·cyst (óutəsist) *n.* an organ of balance in invertebrates consisting of a sac containing a fluid and otoliths ‖ an embryonic auditory vesicle in vertebrates [fr. Gk *ous* (*ōtos*), ear+*kustis,* bladder]

o·to·lar·yn·gol·o·gy (outoulæriŋgólədʒi:) *n.* otorhinolaryngology [fr. Gk *ous, ōtos,* ear+*larunx* (*larungos*), larynx+*logos,* discourse]

o·to·lith (óut'liθ) *n.* a granule of calcium carbonate in the inner ear of a vertebrate. Several are attached to nerve cells, and through gravity register the equilibrium of the animal. They are also present in the otocysts of invertebrates and in some fishes [fr. Gk *ous* (*ōtos*), ear+*lithos,* stone]

O·to·mí (outəmí:) *pl.* **O·to·mí, O·to·mís** *n.* one of the original peoples of Mexico, now living in the states of Querétaro and Guanajuato ‖ a member of this people ‖ their language, probably the first spoken in Mexico, now used by about 450,000

o·to·rhi·no·lar·yn·gol·o·gy (outourainoulæriŋgólədʒi:) *n.* the medical science treating of ear, nose and throat disorders [fr. Gk *ous* (*ōtos*), ear+*rhis* (*rhinos*), nose+*larunx* (*larungos*), larynx+*logos,* discourse]

o·to·tox·ic (outoutóksik) *adj.* (*med.*) adversity affecting the ears, esp. the nerves —**o·to·tox·ic·i·ty** *n.*

O·tran·to, Strait of (outrǽntou) a channel (about 47 miles wide) between Albania and the heel of Italy, joining the Adriatic and Ionian Seas

ot·ta·va ri·ma (outávərí:mə) *pl.* **ot·ta·va ri·mas** *n.* a verse stanza of eight ten-syllabled lines (eleven-syllabled in Italian) rhyming abababcc [Ital.=octave rhyme]

Ot·ta·wa (ótəwə) the capital (pop. 291,000, with agglom. 717,978) of Canada, on hills along the Ottawa River in W. Ontario. Industries: lumber, pulp and paper, publishing, light manufacturing. Neo-Gothic parliament buildings (1916), national museums, University of Ottawa (1866). The town was founded in 1827 and was made the capital in 1867

Ottawa River the chief tributary (696 miles long) of the St Lawrence, separating Ontario, Canada, from Quebec

ot·ter (ótər) *n.* a member of *Lutra,* fam. *Mustelidae,* a genus of carnivorous aquatic mammals (cf. SEA OTTER). The otter has a flattish head, short ears, webbed toes, elongated tail and is approximately 2-4 ft in length. It feeds chiefly on fish and is of virtually cosmopolitan distribution ‖ its dark brown fur [O.E. *otr, ottor, oter*]

ot·ter·hound (ótərhaund) *n.* a dog of a rare British breed used for hunting otters. It derives partly from the bloodhound

otter trawl (*mil.*) in mine warfare, a device that, when towed, displaces sideway by use of kites to a predetermined distance, thus clearing a wide path *Cf* OROPESA SWEEP

Otto cycle the sequence of actions in a four-stroke internal-combustion engine: suction, compression, expansion, exhaust. The cycle results in two revolutions of the crankshaft [after Nikolaus August *Otto* (1832-91), German pioneer of the internal-combustion engine]

Ot·to I (ótou) 'the Great' (912–73), Holy Roman Emperor (962–73) and German king (936–73), son of Henry I. The greatest military and political power of his time in Europe, he repelled invasions of Magyars (955) and Slavs, and united the crowns of Germany and Italy

Otto II (953–83), Holy Roman Emperor jointly (967–73) with his father Otto I, and then alone (973–83), German king (961–83). He tried unsuccessfully to drive the Greeks from S. Italy (982)

Otto III (980–1002), Holy Roman Emperor (996–1002), German king (983–1002), but under the regency of his mother (983–91) and his grandmother (991–5). He was the son of Otto II

Otto IV (c. 1182–1218), Holy Roman Emperor (1209–15), German king (1208–15), son of Henry 'the Lion'. Excommunicated (1210) by Innocent III, he was deposed by Frederick II

Otto I (1815–67), king of Greece (1832–62), son of Louis I of Bavaria. He was chosen by a conference of European powers at London (1832) to rule the new kingdom of Greece. He proved extremely unpopular, and was deposed (1862) by a military revolt

Ot·to·car II (ótəkar) (c. 1230–78), king of Bohemia (1253–78). He expanded his territories to include Carinthia, Styria and part of Slovenia as well as Austria, Bohemia and Moravia, but was defeated (1276–8) by Rudolf I of Germany

Ot·to·man (ótəmən) **1.** *adj.* of or pertaining to the Turks or the Ottoman Empire **2.** *n.* a Turk [F. fr. Arab. *Othman*]

ot·to·man (ótəmən) *n.* an upholstered or cushioned seat, stool or sofa without a back

Ottoman Empire a Moslem state founded (c. 1288) in Asia Minor by Osman I. It expanded throughout Asia Minor and into Thrace (1345). The Ottomans captured Adrianople (1361), won a great victory at Kosovo Polje (1389), and took Serbia and Bulgaria. They captured Constantinople (1453). The Ottoman Empire reached its height during the reign (1520–66) of Suleiman II, when its power extended through the Balkans and S. Russia, throughout Asia Minor and down the valleys of the Tigris and Euphrates to the Persian Gulf, and through N. Africa as far west as Algeria. Its rulers assumed the caliphate (1517). The Ottomans were defeated at Lepanto (1571) and failed in their attempts to capture Vienna (1529 and 1683). Russia's desire to take advantage of the weakness of the Ottoman Empire (17th–19th cc.) gave rise to the Russo-Turkish Wars and the Eastern Question. The empire was severely weakened (19th c.) by its tyrannical and corrupt system of government and its disastrous financial position. It was overthrown (1922) by Atatürk, and in 1924 the Ottoman caliphate was abolished (*TUR-KEY)

Ot·way (ótwei), Thomas (1652–85), English playwright and poet. His plays include two tragedies in blank verse, 'The Orphan' (1680) and 'Venice Preserv'd' (1682)

Oua·ga·dou·gou (wægədú:gu:) the capital (pop. 247,877) of Burkina Faso, a trading center and terminus of the railroad to Abidjan

Ou·ban·gui (u:bāgi:) *UBANGI

Oubangui-Chari *CENTRAL AFRICAN REPUBLIC

ou·bli·ette (u:bli:ét) n. an underground dungeon opening only at the top [F. fr. oublier, to forget]

ouch (autʃ) interj. used on feeling a twinge of pain or in response to a cutting remark

Oud (aut), Jacobus Johannes Pieter (1890–1963), Dutch architect. A participant in the De Stijl movement, he was among the first to design in the international style (*STIJL, DE)

Ou·de·narde, Battle of (ú:dənard) a victory (1708) of an allied army under Marlborough and Eugène over the French during the War of the Spanish Succession

Oudjda *OUJDA

ought (ɔt) (infin. and parts. lacking, used only as present) auxiliary v. expressing duty or obligation, we ought to tell them, it ought not to be allowed, he ought to have known better ‖ expressing necessity or expedience, the grass ought to be cut ‖ expressing desirability, you ought to have been with us yesterday ‖ expressing strong likelihood, he ought to win the race easily [O.E. āhte past of āgan, owe]

ought *AUGHT

oughtn't (ɔ́t'nt) contr. of OUGHT NOT

ou·gi·ya (u:gíjə) n. unit of currency in Mauritania, equal to 5 koum

oui·ja (wí:dʒə, wí:dʒi:) n. a board marked with the alphabet and various signs, fitted with a planchette, and used to obtain messages in spiritualist practice [F. oui, yes and G. ja, yes]

Ouj·da, Oudj·da (u:dʒdá) an industrial city (pop. 155,800) of N. Morocco near the Algerian frontier: lead and coal-mining center

Ou·lu (áulu:) (Swed. Uleåborg) a port (pop. 93,806) of Finland near the head of the Gulf of Bothnia processing and exporting lumber

ounce (auns) n. (abbr. oz.) a unit of weight equal to 1/16 of a pound avoirdupois (28.35 gms) or 1/12 of a pound troy (31.1 gms) ‖ a very little, not an ounce of sympathy [O.F. unce]

ounce n. Felis uncia, fam. Felidae, a large feline carnivore inhabiting the mountains of Asia [fr. O.F. once, lonce]

our (auər) possessive adj. of, pertaining to or belonging to us ‖ experienced, done or made by us ‖ (used formally, esp. by a sovereign, author or judge) my, this is a mistake in our opinion [O.E. ūre orig. genitive pl. of first pers. pron., 'of us', later inflected as adj.]

Our Lady a title of the Virgin Mary

ours (auərz) possessive pron. that or those belonging to us, ours is an ancient race, this land of ours [fr. O.E. possessive pron. ur, ure, our]

our·self (auərsélf, arsélf) pl. **our·selves** (auərsélvz, arsélvz) pron. refl. form of WE, we blame ourselves for the accident ‖ emphatic form of WE, we did it ourselves ‖ (sing., used formally esp. by a sovereign, an author or a judge) myself

-ous suffix full of, as in 'gracious' ‖ possessing the qualities of, as in 'bulbous' ‖ (chem., in contrast to -ic suffix indicating the lower of two possible valencies, as in 'ferrous oxide'

oust (aust) v.t. (law) to dispossess of property or an inheritance ‖ (law) to take away (a privilege, right etc.) ‖ to force or drive out, eject [A. F. ouster, to take away]

oust·er (áustər) n. (law) an illegal or wrongful dispossession from property or an inheritance [A.F.=to oust]

out (aut) 1. adv. away from a place, situation etc., he flew out to Australia ‖ on the outside, to lock someone out ‖ away from home, place of work etc., he has just gone out ‖ (naut.) away from land, fishing 15 miles out ‖ on strike, the workers have walked out ‖ not in office, his party is out ‖ outside, out-of-doors, come out for a walk ‖ into violent or sudden activity, a fire broke out, war broke out ‖ expressing disappearance, elimination or omission, the stains will wash out, cross a word out, leave a word out ‖ so as to be no longer functioning, burning etc., put out the light ‖ expressing finality, my shirt is worn out, tired out ‖ expressing projection, his chin jutted out ‖ into sight, the sun came out ‖ into or in circulation, his book has just come out ‖ in or

into public knowledge, the secret came out ‖ openly, without reticence, tell him right out ‖ expressing distribution, hand out the money ‖ expressing extension or prolongation, stretch out your arm ‖ away from the center, interior etc., spread out ‖ into or in bloom, leaf etc., crocuses come out early ‖ having a determined purpose, out to make money, out for success ‖ expressing discord, they fell out ‖ into or in disuse, long skirts have gone out ‖ expressing selection, pick out the winners ‖ in error, my guess was out by 200 points ‖ (Am.=B. down) in the condition of having lost money on a transaction ‖ (pop.) into or in a state of unconsciousness, he passed out ‖ (baseball) in a manner producing an out, to strike out ‖ (baseball, cricket etc.) with the turn at bat finished, how was he put out? **all out** with one's whole effort, he has gone all out to win the election **out and away** by far **out from under** (pop.) away from difficulty or danger 2. adj. (of sizes of clothing) irregular, esp. very large ‖ (baseball, of a player) failing to get on a base or complete a successful play ‖ (cricket, of a batsman, after an appeal to the umpire) dismissed ‖ outward or giving access outward, the out door 3. prep. forth from, jump out the window ‖ on the outside of, hang it out the window 4. n. (pop.) a way out, an excuse ‖ (baseball) a failure to get on a base or complete a successful play ‖ (printing) a word or words inadvertently omitted from copy 5. interj. get out! go away! 6. v.i. (rhet.) to be revealed, the truth will out [O.E. ūt]

out- prefix beyond ‖ in excess of ‖ excelling

out·a·chieve (áutətʃi:v) v. to accomplish more than another person or persons

out·age (áutidʒ) n. 1. monies not accounted for 2. failure of electric power

out-and-out (áut'náut) 1. adj. complete, thorough, an out-and-out liar 2. adv. completely, thoroughly, an out-and-out crazy plan

out·back (áutbæk) n. (Austral., with 'the') a district remote from the main population centers

out·bal·ance (autbǽləns) pres. part. **out·bal·anc·ing** past and past part. **out·bal·anced** v.t. to outweigh

out·bid (autbíd) pres. part. **out·bid·ding** past and past part. **out·bid** v.t. to offer a higher price than, esp. at an auction sale ‖ (cards) to bid more than

out·board (áutbɔrd, áutbourd) 1. adj. on or towards the outside of a ship, boat, aircraft etc. ‖ (of a boat) having an outboard motor 2. adv. to or towards the outside of a boat, ship or aircraft

outboard motor a small internal-combustion engine that can be attached to the stern of a small boat

out·bound (áutbáund) adj. (of a ship) traveling away from her home port or country

out·brave (autbréiv) pres. part. **out·brav·ing** past and past part. **out·braved** v.t. to face up to and overcome by endurance, to outbrave hostile criticism

out·break (áutbreik) n. a sudden, violent bursting out, the outbreak of war ‖ an epidemic or near epidemic, an outbreak of smallpox ‖ a revolt, an insurrection

out·breed (autbrí:d) pres. part. **out·breed·ing** past and past part. **out·bred** (autbréd) v.t. to mate (animals not closely related, selected for their qualities) so as to improve stock ‖ to get rid of (an undesirable characteristic) by selective breeding **out·breed·ing** n. voluntary marriage outside the tribe, clan or social group (cf. EXOGAMY) ‖ the policy or practice of outbreeding animals

out·build·ing (áutbildiŋ) n. a building separate from, but near to and serving, an adjacent house or building

out·burst (áutbərst) n. a violent emotional fit, an outburst of laughter ‖ an eruption, sudden outbursts of flame

out·cast (áutkæst, áutkɑst) 1. adj. cast out from home, friends etc. or by society, an outcast waif 2. n. someone who has been so treated

out·caste (áutkæst, áutkɑst) 1. n. a person without caste or one driven from his caste 2. adj. without caste

out·class (autklǽs, autklɑ́s) v.t. to surpass by so much as to seem to belong to a higher class

out·come (áutkʌm) n. a result or consequence

out·crop (áutkrɔp) 1. n. (geol.) an exposure of a rock stratum at ground level ‖ the rocks so exposed 2. v.i. pres. part. **out·crop·ping** past and past part. **out·cropped** to be exposed on the surface of the ground

out·cry (áutkrai) pl. **out·cries** n. a public expression of anger or disapproval

out·date (autdéit) pres. part. **out·dat·ing** past and past part. **out·dat·ed** v.t. to make out of date or obsolete

out·dis·tance (autdístəns) pres. part. **out·dis·tanc·ing** past and past part. **out·dis·tanced** v.t. to leave far behind in a race, competition etc.

out·do (autdú:) pres. part. **out·do·ing** past and past part. **did** (autdíd) past part. **out·done** (autdʌ́n) v.t. to do better than, surpass, he outdoes everyone in athletics **not to be outdone** refusing defeat or loss of advantage **to outdo oneself** to excel oneself

out·door (áutdɔr, áutdour) adj. done or used outside the house ‖ of, in or characteristic of the open air

out·doors (autdɔ́rz, autdóurz) 1. adv. out of the house, please clean your boots outdoors ‖ in the open air, he prefers to be outdoors 2. n. the out-of-doors

out·er (áutər) 1. adj. farther out or outside, outer space ‖ away from the center, outer edges ‖ of or pertaining to the outside, outer clothing ‖ objective, external, outer relativity (cf. INNER) 2. n. the outside ring of a target ‖ a shot striking in this ring

outer city the suburbs

Outer Mongolia *MONGOLIAN PEOPLE'S REPUBLIC

outer·most (áutərmoust) adj. furthest out from the inside or the center, outermost layers

Outer Space Treaty of 1960 international agreement for universal protection of all astronauts

out·face (autféis) pres. part. **out·fac·ing** past and past part. **out·faced** v.t. to stare down ‖ to resist by bravery, to outface an enemy or by effrontery, to outface one's judges

out·fall (áutfɔl) n. the vent of a drain ‖ the outlet of a river etc.

out·field (áutfi:ld) n. (baseball, cricket) the part of the field farthest from the batter or batsman or the players stationed there ‖ a field at some distance from its holder's farmhouse

out·field·er (áutfi:ldər) n. (cricket and baseball) someone who plays in the outfield

out·fit (áutfit) 1. n. articles or instruments required to equip or fit out, a plumber's outfit ‖ the act of equipping ‖ clothing etc. for a special purpose, a tropical outfit ‖ a collection of components, a model glider outfit ‖ (pop.) persons making up an organization, institution, regiment etc., the whole outfit was against him 2. v.t. pres. part. **out·fit·ting** past and past part. **out·fit·ed** to supply with an outfit, to outfit a child for school ‖ to furnish, supply **óut·fit·ter** n. (commerce) a retail dealer in readymade clothing, sports material etc.

out·flank (autflǽŋk) v.t. (mil.) to extend one's own flank beyond the flank of (the enemy) ‖ to circumvent the plans of (an opponent) and retain the advantage

out·flow (áutflou) n. a flowing out, the outflow of science graduates ‖ the amount of such a flowing out

out·gen·er·al (autdʒénərəl) pres. part. **out·gen·er·al·ing**, esp. Br. **out·gen·er·al·ling** past and past part. **out·gen·er·aled**, esp. Br. **out·gen·er·alled** v.t. to surpass in generalship, outmaneuver

out·go 1. (áutgou) pl. **out·goes** n. outflow ‖ expenditure (opp. INCOME) 2. (autgóu) pres. part. **out·go·ing** past **out·went** (autwént) past part. **out·gone** (autgɔ́n, autgón) v.t. to go one better than, with an advantage over

out·go·ing (áutgouiŋ) 1. adj. going out, the outgoing tide ‖ leaving, outgoing ships ‖ retiring, the outgoing government ‖ willing to be sociable 2. n. (pl.) outlay, expenditure, he has heavy outgoings on his new house

out·grow (autgróu) pres. part. **out·grow·ing** past **out·grew** (autgrú:) past part. **out·grown** (autgróun) v.t. to grow too big for, to outgrow one's shirts ‖ to grow away from, become too old for, to outgrow childish habits ‖ to grow faster than, he has outgrown his elder brother

out·growth (áutgrouθ) n. that which grows out from something, a woody outgrowth on a tree trunk ‖ a result, product or by-product

out·gun (autgʌ́n) v. (slang) to be or do better than someone else

out·haul (áuthɔl) n. (naut.) a line used for hauling out a sail along a spar

out·house (áuthaus) pl. **out·hous·es** (áuthauziz) n. a small outbuilding (shed, outdoor toilet etc.)

out·ing (áutiŋ) n. a pleasure trip or excursion, sometimes organized for a large number of people, *a family outing* ‖ a walk outdoors ‖ an athletic contest, *a successful first outing* [OUT v.]

out·land·ish (autlǽndiʃ) adj. bizarre-looking, *outlandish clothing* ‖ uncouth, *outlandish manners* ‖ very remote and without amenities, *an outlandish place* [O.E. *ūtlendisc* fr. *ūtland*, a foreign land]

out·last (autlǽst, autlást) v.t. to last longer than, outlive

out·law (áutlɔ) n. (*hist.*) a person deprived of the protection of the law [O.E. *ūtlaga*]

outlaw v.t. to place beyond or deprive of the benefit of the law ‖ to cause, esp. by the force of public opinion, to be no longer tolerated ‖ (*law*) to void the legal force of (an act, contract, claim etc.) [O.E. *ūtlagian, geūtlagian* fr. *ūtlaga*, an outlaw]

out·law·ry (áutlɔːri) n. (*hist.*) the process of outlawing ‖ the state of being outlawed [A. F. *utlagerie, utlarie*]

out·lay 1. (áutlei) n. expenditure, *crippling outlay on armaments* ‖ an instance of this, *an outlay of two months' wages* **2.** (autléi) v.t. pres. part. **out·lay·ing** past and past part. **out·laid** to expend (money)

out·let (áutlet, áutlit) n. an opening which provides a way to the outside, *the outlet of a water pipe, Poland's outlet to the sea* ‖ a means of channeling, *an outlet for one's energies* ‖ a stream flowing from a lake or larger stream etc. ‖ (*commerce*) a market for goods ‖ (*Am.=Br.* point) a pair of terminals in an electric wiring system at which current may be taken for use

out·li·er (áutlaiər) n. (*geol.*) a separate part of a rock formation detached from the principal part by erosion

out·line (áutlain) **1.** n. a line or lines bounding the outer limits of a figure, *the outline of a triangle* or a solid object seen as a plane figure, *the outline of a tree* ‖ the shape defined by such bounding lines, *fill in the outline in red* ‖ a sketch showing only the outer bounding lines ‖ a rough draft of a plan, scheme of work etc. ‖ a short summary, often in note form and omitting detail, *an outline of a syllabus* ‖ a compendious presentation of general features, *an outline of history* ‖ (*pl.*) general principles or chief elements of a subject, *the outlines of English common law* **in outline** drawn etc. so as to show only the outer bounding lines ‖ indicating only the most significant matters **2.** v.t. pres. part. **out·lin·ing** past and past part. **out·lined** to draw or mark the outline of ‖ to give the main points of, *to outline a plan*

out·live (autlív) pres. part. **out·liv·ing** past and past part. **out·lived** v.t. to live longer than, survive ‖ to live down, *to outlive a disgrace*

out·look (áutluk) n. a prospect or view, *the house has a pleasant outlook* ‖ a prospect for the future, *a bad outlook for employment* ‖ a way of looking at things, *a narrow outlook on life*

out·ly·ing (áutlaiiŋ) adj. lying away from the center, *outlying troops* ‖ remote, *outlying villages*

out·ma·neu·ver, out·ma·nœu·vre (autmənúːvər) pres. part. **out·ma·neu·ver·ing, out·ma·nœu·vring** past and past part. **out·ma·neu·vered, out·ma·nœu·vred** v.t. to win strategic advantage over by a tactical maneuver ‖ to put oneself by cleverness or smartness in a stronger position than

out·match (autmǽtʃ) v.t. to be more than a match for, outdo

out·mod·ed (autmóudid) adj. left behind by changes or developments, *outmoded practices* ‖ no longer widely accepted, *outmoded doctrines* ‖ not fashionable, *outmoded dress* [trans. of F. *démodé*]

out·most (áutmoust) adj. outermost [var. of older *utmost, utmost*]

out·num·ber (autnʌ́mbər) v.t. to be greater than in number

out of prep. from the inside of, *out of the house* ‖ from the total of, *10 out of 15* ‖ away from, *out of town* ‖ beyond the reach of, *out of sight* ‖ outside the state or condition of, *out of wedlock* ‖ from (a material etc.), *built out of stone, can you get a skirt out of it?* ‖ due to, *out of hatred* ‖ not having any more of, *out of breath* ‖ (of a foal) born of (a specified dam)

out-of-bounds (áutəvbáundz) adj. and adv. (sports) beyond the limits of the area within which play is legal ‖ beyond the limits of what is acceptable, e.g. as regards behavior

out-of-date (áutəvdéit) adj. old-fashioned, *out-of-date clothes* ‖ not current, defective in regard to the present situation, *an out-of-date guidebook*

out-of-door (áutəvdɔ́r, áutəvdóur) adj. outdoor

out-of-doors (áutəvdɔ́rz, áutəvdóurz) **1.** adj. out-of-door **2.** n. everywhere outside the house ‖ the countryside

out of doors adv. outdoors

out-of-pock·et (áutəvpɔ́kit) adj. (Br., of expenses) for which one will be reimbursed

out-of-the-way (áutəvðəwéi) adj. distant, isolated ‖ unusual ‖ (Br., pop., of price, esp. neg.) excessively high

out·pa·tient (áutpeiʃənt) n. a person who is treated, but not lodged and fed, in a hospital (opp. INPATIENT)

out·play (autpléi) v.t. to play a game better than (an opponent)

out·point (autpóint) v.t. to make more points in a game etc. than (an opponent) ‖ (*naut.*) to sail closer to the wind than (an opponent in a race etc.)

out·port (áutpɔrt, áutpourt) n. a port outside a town or other port

out·post (áutpoust) n. (*mil.*) a position held by a detachment in front of the main body of troops to prevent surprise action ‖ (*mil.*) the soldiers holding this position ‖ a military base established by agreement in another country ‖ a settlement on a frontier or in a remote area

out·pour·ing (áutpɔriŋ, áutpouriŋ) n. the act of pouring out ‖ something poured out

out·put (áutput) n. the total product of a factory, mill etc. ‖ the amount produced of a specified product ‖ the amount produced by an individual or by one machine ‖ the amount of energy delivered by a machine ‖ the creative work of an artist, *a large output of film music*

output system the portion of a computer or other device that provides data, e.g., paper, tape, cathode ray tube

out·rage (áutreidʒ) **1.** n. a violent attack, esp. on people's rights or feelings or property ‖ a flagrant offense against order or dignity or against principles ‖ a feeling of angry resentment provoked by great injustice or offense to one's dignity **to do outrage to** to outrage **2.** v.t. pres. part. **out·rag·ing** past and past part. **out·raged** to subject to an outrage ‖ to make furious or angrily resentful [O.F. *ultrage, oultrage, outrage*]

out·ra·geous (autréidʒəs) adj. constituting an outrage ‖ (pop.) extravagant, outré, *an outrageous fashion* [O.F. *outrageus, oultrageus*]

out·range (autréindʒ) pres. part. **out·rang·ing** past and past part. **out·ranged** v.t. to go beyond in range

out·rank (autrǽŋk) v.t. to have a higher rank or greater importance than

ou·tré (uːtréi) adj. (of dress, opinions etc.) exaggerated to the point of eccentricity ‖ (of behavior) mildly shocking [F.]

out·reach (áutriːtʃ) n. **1.** the area of activities beyond the normal **2.** the distant uninhabited areas, e.g., in Australia **3.** (*social service*) provision of services to those unable to seek them

out·ride (autráid) pres. part. **out·rid·ing** past **out·rode** (autróud) past part. **out·rid·den** (autrídn) v.t. to ride faster or better than ‖ to ride out (e.g. a storm)

out·rid·er (áutraidər) n. a person riding alongside or ahead of someone as protection or to clear the way

out·rig·ger (áutrigər) n. a projecting structure of wood etc., e.g. from a mast to extend a sail or from a building to support a hoisting tackle ‖ a projecting metal bracket bearing the oarlock of a sculling boat to give greater leverage ‖ a projecting floating device at one or both sides of some canoes, to prevent upsetting

out·right 1. (autráit, áutrait) adv. not by installments or degrees, once for all, *to destroy outright* ‖ openly, straightforwardly, *tell him outright* **2.** adj. (áutrait) thorough, downright, *outright denial* ‖ complete, *outright fraud*

out·ri·val (autráivəl) pres. part. **out·ri·val·ing**, esp. Br. **out·ri·val·ling** past and past part. **out·ri·valed**, esp. Br. **out·ri·valled** v.t. to do better than (a rival)

out·run (autrʌ́n) pres. part. **out·run·ning** past **out·ran** (autrǽn) past part. **out·run** v.t. to run faster than ‖ (*fig.*) to go beyond the limits of, *his ambition outran his talents*

out·sell (autsél) pres. part. **out·sell·ing** past and past part. **out·sold** (autsóuld) v.t. to sell more than ‖ (of a product) to exceed (another) in sales

out·set (áutset) n. the first stage, the beginning

out·shine (autʃáin) pres. part. **out·shin·ing** past and past part. **out·shone** (autʃóun), **out·shined** v.t. to shine brighter than ‖ to surpass, *she outshone all rivals*

out·shoot (autʃúːt) pres. part. **out·shoot·ing** past and past part. **out·shot** (autʃót) v.t. to surpass in shooting

out·side (áutsáid, áutsaid) **1.** n. the surface, exterior, outer parts ‖ the space or region situated beyond a boundary, or other limit ‖ external appearance ‖ superficial aspect **at the outside** (or **very outside**) at the most, *there were 20 people there at the outside* **2.** adj. on, of or nearer the outside ‖ of, pertaining to or being the outer side of a curve, circle etc., *the outside wheel* ‖ carried on out-of-doors, *outside activities* ‖ (Br., radio or television) originating away from the studio ‖ from a source other than some specified or understood group, *an outside opinion* ‖ involving an extreme limit, *an outside estimate* ‖ not connected with one's main work or preoccupation, *outside interests* ‖ (of a chance) just within the limit of possibility **3.** adv. on or to the outside ‖ out-of-doors **4.** prep. on or to the outer side of, *wait outside the office* ‖ beyond the limits of, *outside the town* ‖ apart from, other than, *no one knows outside the family*

out·sid·er (autsáidər) n. a person not included in some particular group, party, clique etc. ‖ (Br.) a person held unfit to mix in good society ‖ a competitor (horse, athlete etc.) believed to have only an outside chance in a race

out·size (áutsaiz) **1.** n. an unusually large size of clothing ‖ an article of clothing of such a size **2.** adj. uncommonly large

out·skirts (áutskərts) pl. n. outlying parts remote from the center

out·smart (autsmárt) v.t. to outwit

out·spo·ken (autspóukən) adj. said without fear of the consequences, *outspoken criticism* ‖ not conventionally or prudently reticent, *an outspoken book*

out·spread (áutspréd) **1.** pres. part. **out·spread·ing** past and past part. **out·spread** v.t. and (rhet.) to spread out **2.** adj. (rhet.) stretched or spread out

out·stand·ing (autstǽndiŋ) adj. conspicuous, standing out, *an outstanding feature of the landscape* ‖ remarkable, *an outstanding achievement* ‖ not yet settled or completed, *outstanding debts*

out·sta·tion (áutsteiʃən) n. an outlying station or settlement

out·stay (autstéi) v.t. to stay longer than ‖ to surpass in staying power **to outstay one's welcome** to stay longer than one's hosts wish

out·stretched (áutstretʃt) adj. stretched out, *to lie outstretched*

out·strip (autstríp) pres. part. **out·strip·ping** past and past part. **out·stripped** v.t. to go at a quicker rate than and leave behind [OUT+obs. strip, to outstrip]

out·vote (autvóut) pres. part. **out·vot·ing** past and past part. **out·vot·ed** v.t. to defeat by a majority of votes

out·ward (áutwərd) **1.** adj. moving or directed toward the outside ‖ exterior, *the outward appearance of the house* ‖ superficial, *an outward appearance of calm* **2.** adv. towards the outside and away from the inside [O.E. *ūtweard*]

out·ward-bound (áutwərdbáund) adj. (of a ship) traveling away from the home port

out·ward·ly (áutwərdli) adv. externally, *outwardly visible* ‖ on the surface, *outwardly calm*

out·wards (áutwərdz) adv. outward [O.E. *ūtweardes*]

Outward WATS a Bell System long-distance telephone service that provides for bulk-rated outgoing station-to-station calls within geographical service areas

out·wear (autwéər) pres. part. **out·wear·ing** past **out·wore** (autwór, autwour) past part. **out·worn** (autwórn, autwóurn) v.t. to last longer in use than, *this shirt will outwear three ordinary ones*

out·weigh (autwéi) v.t. to exceed in weight or importance

out·wit (autwít) pres. part. **out·wit·ting** past and past part. **out·wit·ted** v.t. to defeat by cleverness or cunning

out·work (áutwəːrk) n. a part of a defense system outside the principal fortifications ‖ work subcontracted by a business and done off the premises

---

out·worn (áutwórn, áutwóurn) *past part.* of OUTWEAR ‖ *adj.* worn out, deprived of force by excessive use, *outworn quotations* ‖ outlived, *outworn conventions*

OV (*acronym*) **o**rbiter **v**ehicle, a space vehicle designed to orbit a celestial body

ova *pl.* of OVUM

o·val (óuvəl) **1.** *adj.* having the form of an ellipse ‖ egg-shaped **2.** *n.* an oval figure or shape [Mod. L. *ovalis* fr. *ovum* egg]

O·van·do Can·dia (ɔvándɔkándjɑ), Alfredo (1918–), Bolivian general, leader of the junta which deposed (1969) Siles Salinas shortly after the death of Gen. Rene Barrientos, and president (1969–70)

o·var·i·an (ouvéəri:ən) *adj.* of or pertaining to an ovary or the ovaries [fr. Mod. L. *ovarium*, ovary]

o·var·i·ec·to·my (ouvɛəri:éktəmi) *pl.* **o·var·i·ec·to·mies** *n.* (*surgery*) the removal of one or both ovaries [fr. Mod. L. *ovarium*, ovary+Gk *tomē*, a cutting]

o·var·i·ot·o·my (ouvɛəri:ótəmi) *pl.* **o·var·i·ot·o·mies** *n.* (*surgery*) the incision of the ovary ‖ an ovariectomy [fr. Mod. L. *ovarium*, ovary+Gk *tomē*, cutting]

o·va·ry (óuvəri) *pl.* **o·va·ries** *n.* one of a pair of female reproductive organs that produce eggs and (in vertebrates) female sex hormones (*ESTROGEN). These hormones are responsible for the production of female sexual characteristics (e.g. growth of breasts, shape of hips, tone of voice) and for the maintenance of the process of periodic fertility which in primates is known as the menstrual cycle (*ENDOCRINE GLAND) ‖ (*bot.*) the hollow chamber in which ovules are borne in angiospermous plants [fr. Mod. L. *ovarium* fr. *ovum* egg]

o·vate (óuveit) *adj.* (*biol.*) egg-shaped ‖ (*bot.*) of leaves) shaped like the outline of an egg, with the broad end at the base [fr. L. *ovatus*]

o·va·tion (ouvéiʃən) *n.* an enthusiastic public welcome, esp. a spontaneous outburst of applause expressing this [fr. L. *ovatio* (*ovarionis*) fr. *ovare*, to rejoice]

ov·en (Ávən) *n.* an enclosed cavity of stone, brick, metal etc. for baking, roasting, heating or drying [O.E. *ofn, ofen*]

ov·en·bird (Ávənbə:rd) *n.* a member of *Furnarius*, fam. *Furnariidae*, a genus of passerine birds native to South America. Their globular, oven-shaped nests, largely of clay and mud, have a winding entrance and inner partition ‖ *Seiurus aurocapillus*, an American warbler

o·ver (óuvər) **1.** *prep.* above, *the umbrella over his head* ‖ spread on the surface of, *paper littered over the desk* ‖ so as to cover, *ink spilled over the book* ‖ so as to close, *stretched over the neck of the bottle* ‖ in excess of, *over a thousand books* ‖ while occupied with, *let's talk about it over a glass of beer* ‖ near, *he dozed over the fire* ‖ so as to dominate, influence, change the opinion of etc., *a mood has come over him* ‖ in authority with respect to, *he rules over two million people* ‖ in a relationship of superiority to, *he increased his lead over them* ‖ across or above and to the other side of, *it flew over the field* ‖ on the other side of, *he lives over the hill* ‖ along, *drive over the new route* ‖ by means of, *over the telephone* ‖ throughout, in every part of, *she traveled over the whole Commonwealth* ‖ during, *over several days* ‖ more than, *over 100 pounds* ‖ covered or submerged up to, *over his knees in water* ‖ up to and including, *you must stay over Tom's birthday* ‖ about, concerned, in regard to, *we quarreled over the color* ‖ in preference to, *he chose the cheaper model over the more expensive one* ‖ across and down from, *he fell over the edge* ‖ against and across the top of, *she stumbled over the mat* **2.** *adv.* across, *throw it over to me* ‖ across and down from an edge, height etc. ‖ expressing upward and outward motion from a container, *the milk boiled over* ‖ so as to turn the upper surface forward and down, *fold it over* ‖ from one side to the other, *to turn over, he has gone over to the other party* ‖ expressing movement away from the perpendicular, *to knock a chair over, to fall over* ‖ so as to cover or change the whole surface, *whitewash it over* ‖ across a space or distance, *over in Ireland* ‖ away from a specified place, *in the next house over* ‖ (*pop.*) to one's or someone's house, *come over tonight* ‖ more, *it weighs two pounds and over* ‖ until a later time, *hold the work over* ‖ at the end or finish, *holidays are over* ‖ from beginning to end, *read it over* ‖ with thorough, precise and concentrated effort or attention, *talk the case over* ‖ in repetition, *count it three times over* ‖

afresh, *do it over again* ‖ from one person to another, *hand over the keys* **3.** *adj.* in excess, *the total was five dollars over* ‖ (*Br.*) remaining, left, *is there any soup over?* **4.** *n.* (*mil.*) a shot that falls beyond the target ‖ (*Br.*, esp. *pl.*) something in excess ‖ (*cricket*) the number of balls (usually six or eight) allowed between two calls of 'over!' from the umpire and bowled from each wicket alternately ‖ (*cricket*) the play during this period [O.E. *ofer*]

over– *prefix* over (adj., prep., adv.)

o·ver·act (ouvəríkt) *v.t.* to act (a part) in an exaggerated way ‖ *v.i.* to perform or act in an exaggerated way

over again once more

over against as opposed to, in contradistinction to

o·ver·age (óuvəridʒ) *n.* (*commerce*) a surplus of goods

o·ver·age (óuvəréidʒ) *adj.* beyond a specified or usual age

o·ver·all (óuvərɔl) *n.* (*pl.*) loose trousers of durable material, with apron and shoulder straps, worn when doing heavy or dirty jobs ‖ (*Br.*) a coverall

overall *adj.* including everything, total, *the overall cost* ‖ from end to end, *overall length*

over and above in addition to, besides, *a sum over and above the original estimate*

over and over again and again, repeatedly

over and over again repeatedly

o·ver·arch (ouvərártʃ) *v.t.* to form an arch over ‖ *v.i.* to form an arch

o·ver·arm (óuvərɑrm) *adj.* (esp. *Br.*) done with the arm raised above the shoulder ‖ of a swimming stroke in which the arm is lifted out of the water over the shoulder

o·ver·awe (ouvərɔ́) *pres. part.* **o·ver·aw·ing** *past* and *past part.* **o·ver·awed** *v.t.* to bring under submission or cause to feel humble by the effect of one's presence or manner or by majesty, beauty etc.

o·ver·bal·ance (ouvərbæləns) *pres. part.* **o·ver·bal·anc·ing** *past* and *past part.* **o·ver·bal·anced** *v.t.* to cause to lose balance ‖ *v.i.* to lose one's or its balance

o·ver·bear (ouvərbéər) *pres. part.* **o·ver·bear·ing** *past* **o·ver·bore** (ouvərbɔ́r, ouvərbóur) *past part.* **o·ver·borne** (ouvərbɔ́rn, ouvərbóurn) *v.t.* to bear down by greater force, weight, determination etc. *v.i.* to bear excessively (e.g. of a fruit tree) **o·ver·béar·ing** *adj.* aggressively masterful

o·ver·bid 1. (ouvərbíd) *v. pres. part.* **o·ver·bid·ding** *past* and *past part.* **o·ver·bid** *v.t.* to bid more than (someone) ‖ to bid more than the value of (something) ‖ (*Am.*=*Br.* overcall) to bid more than the value of (a hand of cards) ‖ (*Br.*, *cards*) to overcall (a preceding bid or player) ‖ **2.** (óuvərbid) *n.* an instance of bidding more than someone or more then the value of something

o·ver·blown (ouvərblóun) *adj.* (of flowers) just past full bloom [fr. OVER-+obs. *blow*, to blossom]

overblown *adj.* blowzy ‖ (of style) pretentious, windy [fr. older *overblow*, to blow excessively]

o·ver·board (óuvərbɔrd, óuvərbourd) *adv.* over the side of a ship etc., *to fall overboard* **to go overboard** to go to extremes

o·ver·bold (óuvərbóuld) *adj.* excessively bold

o·ver·book (ouvərbúk) *v.* to accept reservations beyond capacity, esp. for hotel and transportation facilities

o·ver·build (ouvərbíld) *pres. part.* **o·ver·build·ing** *past* and *past part.* **o·ver·built** (ouvərbílt) *v.i.* to build in excess of needs, market capacity etc. ‖ *v.t.* to build more buildings than are needed in (an area)

o·ver·bur·den (ouvərbə́:rd'n) *v.t.* to load or burden to excess

o·ver·buy (ouvərbái) *pres. part.* **o·ver·buy·ing** *past* and *past part.* **o·ver·bought** (ouvərbɔ́t) *v.t.* to buy in quantities greater than the demand ‖ *v.i.* to buy to excess, esp. beyond one's means or needs

o·ver·call 1. (ouvərkɔ́l) *v.t.* (*cards*) to bid more than (the preceding bid or player) ‖ (*Br.*) to overbid (a hand of cards) **2.** (óuvərkɔl) *n.* (*Br.*, *cards*) a bid which is more than one's partner's bid ‖ (*cards*) a bid which is more than the preceding bid ‖ an overbid

o·ver·cap·i·tal·ize (ouvərkǽpit'laiz) *pres. part.* **o·ver·cap·i·tal·iz·ing** *past* and *past part.* **o·ver·cap·i·tal·ized** *v.t.* to fix or estimate the capital of (a company etc.) higher than the actual cost or market value ‖ *v.i.* to put an unnecessarily large amount of capital in a business enterprise

o·ver·cast 1. (ouvərkǽst, ouvərkást) *v.t. pres. part.* **o·ver·cast·ing** *past* and *past part.* **o·ver·cast** (*sewing*) to stitch (raw edges) to prevent unraveling **2.** (óuvərkǽst, óuvərkɑst) *adj.* cloudy, covered with clouds

o·ver·cen·tral·i·za·tion (ouvərsentrəlizéiʃən) *n.* excessive concentration of power or control at one point, usu. at headquarters

o·ver·charge 1. (ouvərtʃárdʒ) *v. pres. part.* **o·ver·charg·ing** *past* and *past part.* **o·ver·charged** *v.t.* to charge (someone) too high a price ‖ to charge (an amount) in excess of a specified price ‖ to load too highly with electricity, explosive etc., or as if with these, *to overcharge a story with emotion* ‖ *v.i.* to charge excessively **2.** (óuvərtʃɑrdz) *n.* an excessive charge

o·ver·choice (óuvərtʃɔis) *n.* availability of too many choices

o·ver·cloud (ouvərkláud) *v.t.* to cover over with clouds or shadows ‖ to be a worrying or saddening presence in, *fear of madness overclouded her last years*

o·ver·coat (óuvərkout) *n.* a warm coat worn over ordinary clothes in cold weather

o·ver·come (ouvərkÁm) *pres. part.* **o·ver·com·ing** *past* **o·ver·came** (ouvərkéim) *past part.* **o·ver·come** *v.t.* (*rhet.*) to conquer, *to overcome one's enemies* ‖ to get the better of, *sleep overcame him* ‖ to overpower or overwhelm (a person) physically, *he was overcome by the gas fumes* or emotionally, *she was overcome by fear* [O. E. *ofercuman*]

o·ver·con·fi·dent (ouvərkónfidənt) *adj.* more confident than is warranted

o·ver·con·tain (ouvərkəntéin) *v.* excessive restraint, e.g., of emotions

o·ver·crop (ouvərkrɔ́p) *pres. part.* **o·ver·crop·ping** *past* and *past part.* **o·ver·cropped** *v.t.* to exhaust the fertility of (a piece of land) by taking too many crops from it

o·ver·crowd (ouvərkráud) *v.t.* to crowd more people or things in (a given space) than there is room for or than is desirable or permitted

o·ver·cul·ture (ouvərkÁltʃər) *n.* the underlying culture of a society

o·ver·de·vel·op (ouvərdivéləp) *v.t.* to develop too much ‖ (*photog.*) to develop (a plate or film) for too long or at too high a temperature etc.

o·ver·do (ouvərdú) *pres. part.* **over·do·ing** *past* **o·ver·did** (ouvərdíd) *past. part.* **o·ver·done** (ouvərdÁn) *v.t.* to exaggerate, carry too far, *he rather overdid his gratitude* ‖ (esp. *past part.*) to cook too long **to overdo it** to overtax one's strength ‖ to make too great a display

o·ver·dose 1. (ouvərdóus) *v.t. pres. part.* **o·ver·dos·ing** *past* and *past part.* **o·ver·dosed** to give an excessive dose to **2.** (óuvərdous) *n.* an excessive dose

o·ver·draft (óuvərdræft, óuvərdrɑft) *n.* the overdrawing of a bank account ‖ the sum overdrawn ‖ (*Br.* esp. **o·ver·draught**) a draft passing over a fire in a furnace

overdraft checking account (*banking*) a checking account that permits drawing of checks in excess of credit balance up to a preset amount

o·ver·draw (ouvərdrɔ́) *pres. part.* **o·ver·draw·ing** *past* **o·ver·drew** (ouvərdrú) *past part.* **o·ver·drawn** (ouvərdrɔ́n) *v.t.* to write a bank check for more money than is in (one's account) ‖ to exaggerate, *the characters in the novel were heavily overdrawn* ‖ *v.i.* to overdraw a bank account

o·ver·dress (ouvərdrés) *v.t.* to dress (someone) too showily or too smartly ‖ *v.i.* to dress in this way

o·ver·drive 1. (óuvərdraiv) *n.* a system of very high gearing to save waste of a car's engine power at high speeds. An automatic transmission gear passes a higher speed to the propeller shaft than the speed maintained by the engine **2.** *v.t.* (ouvərdráiv) *pres. part.* **o·ver·driv·ing** *past* **o·ver·drove** (ouvərdróuv) *past part.* **o·ver·driv·en** (ouvərdrivən) *v.* to overwork

o·ver·dub (óuvərdÁb) *v.* (*acoustics*) to add instrumental portions or voices to a finished recording

o·ver·due (ouvərdú, ouvərdjú) *adj.* not paid by the time it was due, *an overdue bill* ‖ behind the scheduled time of arrival, *the plane is overdue* ‖ more than ready, *overdue for independence*

o·ver·eat (ouvərí:t) *pres. part.* **o·ver·eat·ing** *past* **o·ver·ate** (ouvəréit, *Br.* also ouvərét) *past part.* **o·ver·eat·en** (ouvərí:t'n) *v.i.* to eat to the point of satiety and then eat more

o·ver·ed·u·cate (ouvéredʒukeit) *v.* to train to an unneeded capacity

o·ver·em·pha·size (ouvərémfəsaiz) *pres. part.* **o·ver·em·pha·siz·ing** *past* and *past part.* **o·ver·em·pha·sized** *v.t.* to put undue emphasis on

o·ver·em·ploy·ment (ouvərimplóimənt) *n.* (*econ.*) the condition of having more jobs available than there is labor to fill them

o·ver·es·ti·mate 1. (ouvəréstəmeit) *v. pres. part.* **o·ver·es·ti·mat·ing** *past* and *past part.* **o·ver·es·ti·mat·ed** *v.t.* to put the value, amount etc. of (something) too high || *v.i.* to make too high an estimate 2. (óuvəréstəmit) *n.* an estimate that is too high

o·ver·ex·ploi·ta·tion (ouvəriksplɔitéiʃən) *n.* (*envir.*) to remove more of a natural resource than can be replaced

o·ver·ex·pose (ouvərikspóuz) *pres. part.* **o·ver·ex·pos·ing** *past* and *past part.* **o·ver·ex·posed** *v.t.* to expose excessively || (*photog.*) to expose (a film etc.) for longer than is desirable

o·ver·fire air (óuvərfaiərɛ́ər) air forced into the top of an incinerator to fan the flame

o·ver·flow (ouvərflóu) *v.t.* (of liquids) to flow over the brim of, *the river overflowed its banks* || to flood, *the river overflowed the surrounding countryside* || *v.i.* to flood, spill over || to be abundant, *their generosity overflows* [O.E. *oferflōwan*]

o·ver·flow (óuvərflou) *n.* a flowing over || something which flows over || an outlet or receptacle for excess fluids

o·ver·glaze 1. (ouvərgléiz, óuvərgleiz) *v.t. pres. part.* **o·ver·glaz·ing** *past* and *past part.* **o·ver·glazed** to glaze over, e.g. in painting, pottery etc. 2. (óuvərgleiz) *n.* a glaze applied over another glaze 3. *adj.* (óuvərgleiz) done on glaze, *overglaze painting*

o·ver·grown (óuvərgróun) *adj.* grown over with rank weeds etc., *an overgrown garden* || grown to an excessive size [past part. of older *overgrow*]

o·ver·growth (óuvərgrouθ) *n.* excessive growth || dense vegetation, esp. of weeds, *a rank overgrowth of nettles*

o·ver·hand (óuvərhænd) 1. *adj.* thrown or executed with the hand above shoulder level || sewn with stitches over two edges forming a seam 2. *adv.* in an overhand way 3. *n.* an overhand stroke or delivery an overhand seam 4. *v.t.* to sew with overhand stitches **ó·ver·hand·ed** *adj.* and *adv.* overhand

o·ver·hang (ouvərhǽŋ) *v. pres. part.* **o·ver·hang·ing** *past* and *past part.* **o·ver·hung** (ouvərhʌ́ŋ) *v.t.* to jut out over, *medieval houses overhung the street* || *v.i.* to project 2. (óuvərhæŋ) *n.* the part or amount that hangs over

o·ver·haul 1. (ouvərhɔ́l) *v.t.* to examine thoroughly and repair or correct defects in || (esp. *naut.*) to overtake || (*naut.*) to loosen (a rope) by hauling it through the block in the opposite direction to that in which it was hoisted || (*naut.*) to release the blocks of (a tackle) 2. (óuvərhɔl) *n.* a thorough examination followed by the necessary repairs, renovations etc.

o·ver·head (óuvərhed) 1. *adj.* located. working etc. above one's head || (of expenses) due to charges necessary to the carrying on of a business 2. *n.* (*collect.*) expenses which are a general charge to a business and cannot be allotted to a particular job or process (e.g. rent, light, depreciation, administration, insurance, as opposed to materials, wages etc.) || (*Br.*) an item of such expenditure 3. *adv.* (óuvərhéd) above one's head

o·ver·hear (ouvərhiər) *pres. part.* **o·ver·hear·ing** *past* and *past part.* **o·ver·heard** (ouvərhə́rd) *v.t.* to hear (conversation etc.) accidentally or by eavesdropping

o·ver·heat (ouvərhí:t) *v.i.* to become too hot || *v.t.* to cause to become too hot || to cause to become cross and excited

o·ver·hit (ouvərhít) *v.* (*sports*) to strike harder than necessary, e.g., a tennis ball

o·ver·housed (ouvərháuzd) *adj.* having excess or excessive housing accommodations

O·ver·ijs·sel (ouvəráis'l) *n.* a province (area 1,254 sq. miles, pop. 1,027,836) of the E. Netherlands. Capital: Zwolle

o·ver·in·dulge (ouvərindʌ́ldʒ) *pres. part.* **o·ver·in·dulg·ing** *past* and *past part.* **o·ver·in·dulged** *v.t.* to treat with inordinate indulgence || *v.i.* to indulge in something (esp. food and drink) to excess

o·ver·in·flat·ed (ouvərinfléitid) *adj.* excessively overstated

o·ver·in·ter·pre·ta·tion (ouvərintə:rpritéiʃən) *n.* interpreting beyond the meanings intended

o·ver·is·sue (ouvəríʃu:, *Br.* ouvərísju:) 1. *n.* an issue of notes, shares, bonds etc. in excess of the authorized amount or available capital 2. *v.t. pres. part.* **o·ver·is·su·ing** *past* and *past part.* **o·ver·is·sued** to issue in excess

o·ver·joyed (ouvərdʒóid) *adj.* exceedingly delighted [past part. of older *overjoy*]

o·ver·kill (ouvərkíl) 1. *n.* national capacity in nuclear armament over and above what would be needed to destroy an enemy || an instance of destruction using this capacity 2. *v.* to exert more force than necessary, e.g., having the effect of extirpating several times over

o·ver·lad·en (ouvərléid'n) *adj.* loaded or burdened too heavily

o·ver·land (óuvərlænd, óuvərlənd) 1. *adv.* by land rather than sea 2. *adj.* going or made entirely or partly by land

o·ver·lap 1. (ouvərlǽp) *v. pres. part.* **o·ver·lap·ping** *past* and *past part.* **o·ver·lapped** *v.t.* to cover partly || to cover and extend beyond || *v.i.* to coincide partly 2. *n.* (óuvərlæp) an instance or place of overlapping || the extent of overlapping || the part that overlaps

o·ver·lay 1. (ouvərléi) *v.t. pres. part.* **o·ver·lay·ing** *past* and *past part.* **o·ver·laid** (ouvərléid) to cover the surface of || (*printing*) to put an overlay on or get the overlay ready for 2. *n.* (óuvərlei) a covering || an ornamental covering of veneer etc. || (*printing*) a layer of material used to secure a sharp, even impression by correcting for difference of metal height etc. || a sheet of tracing paper laid over e.g. a cartographer's rough map, for corrections to be indicated, or one bearing matter to be taken in conjunction with other matter, e.g. a grid to be placed over an air photograph

o·ver·lie (ouvərlái) *pres. part.* **o·ver·ly·ing** *past* **o·ver·lay** (ouvərléi) *past part.* **o·ver·lain** (ouvərléin) *v.t.* to lie over or on [early M.E. *oferliggen*]

o·ver·load 1. (ouvərlóud) *v.t.* to load too heavily 2. (óuvərloud) *n.* a load, charge etc. which is excessive

o·ver·look (ouvərlúk) *v.t.* to look over from above, *our house overlooks the valley* || to decide not to punish, *to overlook someone's carelessness* || to fail to notice, *he overlooked several errors* **o·ver·look·er** *n.* an overseer

o·ver·lord (óuvərlɔrd) *n.* (*hist.*) a feudal superior from whom lords held land and to whom they owed service || an absolute ruler

o·ver·ly (óuvərli:) *adv.* excessively

o·ver·man (ouvərmǽn) *pres. part.* **o·ver·man·ning** *past* and *past part.* **o·ver·manned** *v.t.* to have or supply too many men for (a given purpose or place)

o·ver·man·tel (óuvərmænt'l) *n.* an ornamental structure, often with a mirror, over a mantel

o·ver·mark (ouvərmárk) *v.* to give higher grades than are warranted

o·ver·mas·ter·ing (ouvərmǽstəriŋ, óuvərmástəriŋ) *adj.* dominating, uncontrollable

o·ver·much (óuvərmʌ́tʃ) 1. *adv.* to any great degree, *he doesn't enjoy such occasions overmuch* 2. *adj.* too much, *there was overmuch drinking at the dinner*

o·ver·nice (óuvərnáis) *adj.* too scrupulous or particular

o·ver·night 1. (ouvərnáit) *adv.* during or for the night || during the night just past 2. (óuvərnait) *adj.* during the evening or night, *an overnight journey* || lasting or staying one night, *overnight guests* || used for a single night, *an overnight case* || happening etc. in the space of one night, *overnight success*

o·ver·nu·tri·tion (ouvərnu:tríʃən) *n.* overeating, overfeeding

o·ver·oc·cu·pied (ouvərókju:paid) *adj.* crowded

o·ver·pass 1. (óuvərpæs, óuvərpʌs) *n.* (*Am.*=*Br.* flyover) a raised crossing, e.g. of a road over a railroad 2. (ouvərpǽs, óuvərpʌs) *pres. part.* **o·ver·pass·ing** *past* **o·ver·passed**, **o·ver·past** *v.t.* to pass over, travel over, go beyond (e.g. an area) || to get through, surmount (e.g. a difficulty) || to go beyond, surpass in amount, value etc. || to overlook, omit

o·ver·per·form (ouvərpərfórm) *v.* exceeding the intention of directions

o·ver·per·suade (ouvərpərswéid) *pres. part.* **o·ver·per·suad·ing** *past* and *past part.* **o·ver·per·suad·ed** *v.t.* to persuade (someone) to come to one's own point of view even against his own inclinations or better judgment

o·ver·play (ouvərpléi) *v.t.* to overact (a part) || to make too much of, overstress || (*cards*) to play (a hand) too optimistically || (*golf*) to strike a ball beyond (the green)

o·ver·plus (óuvərplʌs) *n.* a surplus

o·ver·pow·er (ouvərpáuər) *v.t.* to overcome physically, *he overpowered the thief, the heat overpowered him* to supply with more power than is desirable or necessary

o·ver·pre·scribe (ouvərpriskráib) *v.* (*med.*) to prescribe more drugs than are required —**o·ver·pre·scrip·tion** *n.* the practice

o·ver·pres·sure (óuvərpreʃər) *n.* (*mil.*) 1. the pressure resulting from the blast wave of an explosion, positive when it exceeds atmospheric pressure and negative during the passage of the wave when resulting pressures are less than atmospheric pressure 2. the atmospheric pressure above normal expressed in lbs per sq in, creating a blast wave in a nuclear explosion

o·ver·print 1. (ouvərprínt) *v.t.* (*printing*) to print (matter) on top of something already printed || (*printing*) to print matter on top of (something already printed) || (*photog.*) to print too long or with excess of light || to print too many copies of || (*philately*) to make an overprint on (a stamp) 2. (óuvərprint) *n.* (*philately*) a word, device, figure etc. printed across the surface of a stamp to alter its value or use || a stamp bearing such a print || something printed over other printed matter

o·ver·prize (ouvərpráiz) *pres. part.* **o·ver·priz·ing** *past* and *past part.* **o·ver·prized** *v.t.* to value excessively

o·ver·pro·duce (ouvərprədú:s, ouvərprədjú:s) *pres. part.* **o·ver·pro·duc·ing** *past* and *past part.* **o·ver·pro·duced** *v.t.* to produce in excess of demand or predetermined goals **o·ver·pro·duc·tion** (ouvərprədʌ́kʃən) *n.*

o·ver·proof (óuvərprú:f) *adj.* having higher alcoholic content than proof spirit

o·ver·qual·i·fied (ouvərkwólifaid) *adj.* having background and/or abilities beyond those required for a situation, e.g., a job

o·ver·quan·ti·fi·ca·tion (ouvərkwɒntifikéiʃən) *n.* placing too much emphasis on the quantity involved in a process

o·ver·rate (ouvərréit) *pres. part.* **o·ver·rat·ing** *past* and *past part.* **o·ver·rat·ed** *v.t.* to value or prize too highly || (*Br.*) to rate (property) too highly

o·ver·reach (ouvərrí:tʃ) *v.t.* to defeat (oneself or one's purposes) by being too ambitious, too clever, too grasping etc. || *v.i.* (of a horse) to strike the forefoot with the hind hoof

o·ver·ride (ouvərráid) *pres. part.* **o·ver·rid·ing** *past* **o·ver·rode** (ouvərróud) *past part.* **o·ver·rid·den** (ouvərríd'n) *v.t.* to decide to disregard or to go against || to dominate, *fear overrode all other emotions* || to ride (a horse) beyond its strength || of a broken bone) to overlap (another) [O.E. *oferrīdan*, to ride across]

o·ver·ripe (ouvərráip) *adj.* too ripe

o·ver·rule (ouvərrú:l) *pres. part.* **o·ver·rul·ing** *past* and *past part.* **o·ver·ruled** *v.t.* to give a legal decision or ruling about something which goes against (the decision or ruling of a lower authority)

o·ver·run 1. (ouvərrʌ́n) *v.t. pres. part.* **o·ver·run·ning** *past* **o·ver·ran** (ouvərrǽn) *past part.* **o·ver·run** (esp. *mil.*) to attack and obtain complete mastery over by weight of numbers, *they overran the enemy positions* || to infest, *rats overran the house* || to extend or go beyond (in space or time) || (*printing*) to move (letters or words) from one line to another or (a line or lines) from one page to another, because of an addition or deletion 2. (óuvərrʌn) *n.* an overrunning || the amount of this || a clear area beyond a runway used in case of emergency in landing an aircraft

o·ver·sea 1. (óuvərsi:) *adv.* (*Br.*) overseas 2. (óuvərsi:) *adj.* (*Br.*) overseas

o·ver·seas 1. (ouvərsí:z) *adv.* beyond the sea 2. (óuvərsi:z) *adj.* of or pertaining to countries or people or things beyond the sea

o·ver·see (ouvərsí:) *pres. part.* **o·ver·see·ing** *past* **o·ver·saw** (ouvərsɔ́) *past part.* **o·ver·seen** (ouvərsí:n) *v.t.* to supervise, direct, *he oversees the export department* **o·ver·se·er** *n.* a person in charge of work, a foreman or supervisor [O.E. *ofersēon*]

o·ver·sell (ouvərsél) *pres. part.* **o·ver·sell·ing** *past* and *past part.* **o·ver·sold** (ouvərsóuld) *v.t.* (*commerce*) to sell more of (a commodity, stock etc.) than one can deliver or that can be bought with advantage || (*pop.*) to praise too highly, make excessive claims for || (*pop.*) to cause (someone) to expect something better than the reality

o·ver·sew (ouvərsóu) *pres. part.* **o·ver·sew·ing** *past* **o·ver·sewed** *past* and *past part.* **o·ver·sewed**,

over·sewn (óuvərsoun) *v.t.* to sew (a seam) or sew (two pieces of material) together with vertical stitches passing over the outside edge or edges ‖ to overcast

o·ver·sha·dow (ouvərʃǽdou) *v.t.* to cast a shade over ‖ to cause to seem to have less than full merit, because of detrimental comparisons, *he is overshadowed by his brilliant brother* [O.E. *ofersceadwian*]

o·ver·shoe (óuvərʃu:) *n.* a shoe or boot worn over a shoe for warmth or protection against wet

o·ver·shoot (ouvərʃú:t) *pres. part.* **o·ver·shoot·ing** *past* and *past part.* **o·ver·shot** (ouvərʃót) *v.t.* to shoot over or beyond (a mark), *the bullet overshot its target* ‖ to miss an objective because of aiming too far or for too much ‖ to pass beyond in error, *the plane overshot the airfield* **to overshoot the mark** to overdo something, go too far **to overshoot oneself** to attempt more than one can accomplish

o·ver·shot (óuvərʃot) *adj.* having the upper jaw or lip projecting over the lower one, e.g. in certain breeds of dog ‖ (of a wheel) turned by water flowing from above

o·ver·side 1. (óuvrsaid) *adv.* (of loading or unloading ships) over the side, i.e. into or from lighters, not directly onto a quay **2.** (óuvərsaid) *adj.* done over the side of a ship

o·ver·sight (óuvərsait) *n.* failure to notice something or an instance of this ‖ supervision, *he has general oversight of the works*

o·ver·sing (ouvərsíŋ) *v.* to sing with more effort than required

o·ver·size 1. (óuvərsáiz) *adj.* of a size larger than normal **2.** (óuvərsaiz) *n.* a size that is larger than normal

o·ver·skirt (óuvərskə:rt) *n.* an outer skirt worn over and often only partly concealing the skirt or trousers under it

o·ver·sleep (ouvərslí:p) *pres. part.* **o·ver·sleep·ing** *past* and *past part.* **o·ver·slept** (ouvərslépt) *v.i.* to sleep beyond the time for getting up ‖ *v.t.* (esp. *Br.*) to find (oneself) in the situation of having done this

o·ver·spend (ouvərspénd) *pres. part.* **o·ver·spend·ing** *past* and *past part.* **o·ver·spent** (ouvərspént) *v.t.* to spend more (money, energy) than is prudent ‖ *v.i.* to spend too freely

o·ver·spill (óuvərspil) *n.* a spilling over ‖ something that is spilled over, e.g. surplus population, *the new towns are meant to take the overspill from the capital*

o·ver·spread (ouvərspréd) *pres. part.* **o·ver·spread·ing** *past* and *past part.* **o·ver·spread** *v.t.* to spread over, cover the surface of [O.E. *ofersprǣdan*]

o·ver·sta·bil·i·ty (ouvərstəbíliti) *n.* resistance to change

o·ver·state (ouvərstéit) *pres. part.* **o·ver·stat·ing** *past* and *past part.* **o·ver·stat·ed** *v.t.* to express in stronger terms than the truth warrants **ó·ver·státe·ment** *n.*

o·ver·stay (ouvərstéi) *v.t.* to stay beyond (a specified period), *to overstay one's leave* ‖ to continue a transaction in (a market) past the point of maximum profitability

o·ver·steer·ing (ouvərstíəriŋ) *n.* the necessity of steering more sharply in order to keep a course

o·ver·step (ouvərstép) *pres. part.* **o·ver·step·ping** *past* and *past part.* **o·ver·stepped** *v.t.* to go beyond (what is prudent or acceptable), *to overstep the limits of good taste*

o·ver·stock 1. (ouvərstók) *v.t.* to lay in or carry too large a stock of **2.** (óuvərstok) *n.* too large a stock

o·ver·struc·tured (ouvərstrʌ́ktʃərd) *adj.* having too much planned detail

o·ver·strung (ouvərstrʌ́ŋ) *adj.* (of nerves) intensely strained ‖ (of a person) excessively sensitive ‖ (*Br., mus.,* of a piano) having the strings arranged at different levels crossing obliquely, giving greater length of string

o·ver·sub·scribe (óuvərsəbskráib) *pres. part.* **o·ver·sub·scrib·ing** *past* and *past part.* **o·ver·sub·scribed** *v.t.* to subscribe more than is offered for sale (e.g. bonds), or than the amount required (e.g. a loan)

o·ver·sup·ply (ouvərsəplái) **1.** *n.* an excess supply **2.** *v.t. pres. part.* **o·ver·sup·ply·ing** *past* and *past part.* **o·ver·sup·plied** to supply in excess

o·ver·swing (óuvərswiŋ) *n.* (*golf*) a swing with excessive force resulting in too much follow-through and loss of balance

o·vert (óuvə:rt, ouvé:rt) *adj.* unconcealed, public, *an overt attack on authority* [O.F. *overt* fr. *ovrir,* to open]

o·ver·take (ouvərtéik) *pres. part.* **over·tak·ing** *past* **over·took** (ouvərtúk) *past part.* **o·ver·tak·en** (ouvərtéikən) *v.t.* (*Br.*) to pass (another vehicle etc. going in the same direction as oneself) ‖ to catch up with, *he overtook me and we had a long talk* ‖ to happen to or come upon suddenly and usually disagreeably, *a storm overtook them two hours later* ‖ to catch up with and do better than (in competition), *exports have already overtaken last year's figure* ‖ *v.i.* (*Br.*) to pass a vehicle traveling in the same direction as oneself

o·ver·talk (ouvərtók) *n.* (*colloq.*) excessive talk

o·ver·tax (ouvərtǽks) *v.t.* to strain by making excessive demands on, *to overtax one's strength* ‖ to tax excessively

o·ver·tech·nol·o·gize (ouvərteknóladʒi:z) *v.* to rely excessively on technology (vs. human factors)

o·ver-the-coun·ter drug (ouvərðəkáuntərdrág) a drug sold directly to the public without prescription e.g., aspirin *also* OTC drug

o·ver-the-falls (ouvərðəfɔ́lz) *n.* (*surfing*) maneuver over the crest of a wave

over-the-ho·ri·zon radar (ouvərðəhəráiz'n réidɑr) (*mil.*) a radar device in which beams are reflected from ionosphere layers; used to detect ballistic missiles

o·ver·throw (ouvərθróu) *v.t. pres. part.* **o·ver·throw·ing** *past* **o·ver·threw** (ouvərθrú:) *past part.* **o·ver·thrown** (ouvərθróun) to cause to fall from power, *to overthrow a government* ‖ (*games*) to throw (a ball) beyond the point intended ‖ (*rhet.*) to upset, overturn, *he overthrew the idols in the temple* **2.** *n.* an overthrowing or being overthrown ‖ (*cricket*) a fielder's return throw not stopped at the wicket, thus allowing further runs ‖ (*baseball*) a throw which misses its intended receiver, resulting in an error

o·ver·time (ouvərtáim) **1.** *n.* extra time worked, beyond regular hours ‖ money paid for such work ‖ (*sports*) extra playing time beyond the usual fixed limits of the game when the score is a tie **2.** *adv.* beyond the usual hours ‖ (*sports*) beyond the usual playing time **3.** *adj.* for overtime, *overtime pay* **4.** (óuvərtáim) *v.t. pres. part.* **o·ver·tim·ing** *past* and *past part.* **o·ver·timed** to give more than the proper time to, *to overtime a photographic exposure*

o·ver·tone (óuvərtoun) *n.* (*mus.*) one of the tones above the fundamental tone in a harmonic series ‖ the color of light reflected, e.g. by a paint film ‖ an implication or suggestion evoked by language

o·ver·top (ouvərtóp) *pres. part.* **o·ver·top·ping** *past* and *past part.* **o·ver·topped** *v.t.* to rise above the top of ‖ to prevail over, go beyond in importance, quality of performance etc.

o·ver·train (ouvərtréin) *v.t.* to cause to lose condition by excessive training

o·ver·trick (óuvərtrik) *n.* (*cards*) a trick over the number of tricks bid or needed

o·ver·trump (ouvərtrʌ́mp) *v.t.* (*cards*) to play a higher trump than that of (another player) ‖ *v.i.* (*cards*) to play a higher trump than one already exposed

o·ver·ture (óuvərtʃuər, óuvərtʃər) *n.* a preliminary proposal or a formal offer intended to assess the state of mind of the person or group addressed ‖ (*mus.*) an orchestral piece preceding the rise of the curtain in an opera, musical comedy etc. [O.F.=opening]

o·ver·turn 1. (ouvərtə́:rn) *v.t.* to turn over, upset ‖ to overthrow (e.g. a government) ‖ *v.i.* to turn over, upset **2.** (óuvərtə̣:rn) *n.* an overturning or being overturned ‖ (*environ.*) the complete circulation or mixing of upper and lower waters of a lake when temperatures and densities are similar ‖ the period of the mixing

o·ver·val·ue (ouvərvǽlju:) *pres. part.* **o·ver·val·u·ing** *past* and *past part.* **o·ver·val·ued** *v.t.* to value too highly

o·ver·view (óuvərvju:) *n.* a general survey

o·ver·ween·ing (ouvərwí:niŋ) *adj.* arrogant, presumptuous, *overweening pride* [pres. part. of older *overween,* to be conceited]

o·ver·weight 1. (óuvərweit) *n.* weight over that usual or required, *the shopkeeper gave me overweight* ‖ bodily weight that is higher than is compatible with good health, *he suffers from overweight* **2.** (ouvərwéit) *adj.* beyond the allowed weights, *overweight luggage* ‖ suffering from bodily overweight **3.** (ouvərwéit) *v.t.* to emphasize to excess, *philosophers sometimes overweight their negativism* ‖ to overburden, *his prose was overweighted with metaphors*

o·ver·whelm (ouvərhwélm, ouvərwélm) *v.t.* to submerge suddenly by irresistible force, *the village was overwhelmed by a tidal wave* ‖ to overpower, the *defense was overwhelmed by superior numbers* ‖ to leave emotionally too moved for speech or expression, *his generosity overwhelmed us* [OVER+older *whelm,* to roll]

o·ver·wind (ouvərwáind) *pres. part.* **o·ver·wind·ing** *past* and *past part.* **o·ver·wound** (ouvərwáund) *v.t.* to wind (e.g. a watch spring) too much or too tightly ‖ (*elec.*) to wind (a magnet) so that magnetic saturation demands less current than usual

o·ver·work (ouvərwə́:rk) **1.** *v.t.* to work excessively ‖ to use too often, to *overwork an expression* ‖ to weary or exhaust with too much work ‖ *v.i.* to work too hard **2.** *n.* work in such quantity that mental or physical health is endangered or affected

o·ver·wrought (ouvərrɔ́t) *adj.* worked up, under great nervous tension, *an overwrought child* ‖ much too elaborate, *an overwrought style* [older past part. of OVERWORK]

O·vid (óvid) (Publius Ovidius Naso, 43 B.C.–c. 17 A.D.), Latin poet. His polished, witty poetry, written chiefly in elegiac couplets, treats mainly of three subjects: passion and desire ('Amores', 'Ars amatoria'), mythology ('Metamorphoses', 'Fasti') and the sorrows of exile ('Tristia')

o·vi·duct (óuvidʌkt) *n.* (*anat., zool.*) a tube carrying eggs (ova) from the ovary to the exterior and often possessing modified regions, e.g. the uterus or a region where shell is produced by specialized secretions [fr. M.L. or Mod. L. *oviductus*]

O·vie·do (ouvié:idou, *Span.* ɔvjéðɔ) a province (area 4,205 sq. miles, pop. 1,127,007) of N. Spain ‖ its capital (pop. 175,400), center of the region's coal and iron ore mining, with iron and steel, chemical, textile and food-processing industries. University (1604). It was the capital (9th–11th cc.) of Asturias

o·vi·form (óuvifɔrm) *adj.* ovoid [fr. L. *ovum,* egg+*forma,* form]

o·vine (óuvain) *adj.* of or related to sheep [fr. L. *ovinus*]

o·vip·a·rous (ouvípərəs) *adj.* (*zool.*) producing eggs which hatch outside the maternal body (cf. OVOVIVIPAROUS, cf. VIVIPAROUS) ‖ describing reproduction by such eggs **o·vi·par·i·ty** (ouvipǽriti) *n.* [fr. L. *oviparus* fr. *ovum,* egg+*parere,* to bring forth]

o·vi·pos·it (óuvəpɒzit, ouvəpɒ́zit) *v.i.* (*zool.,* esp. of insects) to lay eggs [fr. L. *ovum,* egg+*ponere* (*positus*), to place]

o·vi·pos·i·tor (óuvəpɒzitər, ouvəpɒ́zitər) *n.* a specialized organ of female insects for depositing eggs, often capable of piercing animals or plants to deposit eggs inside them ‖ a tubular extension of the genital orifice in fish [fr. L. *ovum,* egg+*positor,* a placer fr. *ponere,* to place]

ov·i·sac (óuvisæk) *n.* (*zool.*) an egg capsule or receptacle, e.g. a Graafian follicle [fr. L. *ovum,* egg+SAC]

o·void (óuvɔid) **1.** *adj.* egg-shaped **2.** *n.* an egg-shaped body or surface [fr. Mod. L. *ovoides* fr. *ovum* egg]

o·vo·lo (óuvəlou) *pl.* **o·vo·li** (óuvəlai) *n.* (*archit.*) a convex, rounded molding, a quarter circle (Roman) or quarter ellipse (Greek) in section [fr. older Ital. *ovolo,* dim. of *ovo* (*ovo, uovo,* egg]

o·vo·tes·tis (óuvoutéstis) *pl.* **o·vo·tes·tes** (ouvoutésti:z) *n.* a hermaphrodite reproductive and endocrine gland produced in some animals, e.g. frogs, and in certain gastropods (*OVARY, *TESTICLE) [Mod. L. fr. L. *ovum,* egg+*testis,* testicle]

o·vo·vi·vip·a·rous (ouvouvaivípərəs) *adj.* (*zool.,* of many insects, some snails, a few reptiles etc.) producing eggs with definite shells, which hatch within the maternal body (cf. OVIPAROUS cf. VIVIPAROUS) [fr. L. *ovum,* egg+VIVIPAROUS]

o·vu·lar (óuvjulər) *adj.* relating to an ovule [fr. Mod. L. *ovularis* fr. *ovulum,* ovule]

o·vu·late (óuvjuleit) *pres. part.* **o·vu·lat·ing** *past* and *past part.* **o·vu·lat·ed** *v.i.* to produce an egg or eggs, or to discharge them from the ovary [fr. Mod. L. *ovulum,* ovule]

o·vule (óuvju:l) *n.* the structure within the ovary in seed plants containing the embryo sac and egg. It develops into the seed after fertilization [F.]

o·vum (óuvəm) *pl.* **o·va** (óuva) *n.* (*biol.*) the usually nonmotile female haploid gamete ‖ a mature egg or egg cell, esp. of mammals, fish or insects [L.=egg]

CONCISE PRONUNCIATION KEY: **(a)** æ, c*a*t; ɑ, c*a*r; ɔ f*aw*n; ei, sn*a*ke. **(e)** e, h*e*n; i:, sh*ee*p; iə, d*ee*r; ɛə, b*ea*r. **(i)** i, f*i*sh; ai, t*i*ger; ə:, b*i*rd. **(o)** o, *o*x; au, c*ow*; ou, g*oa*t; u, p*oo*r; ɔi, r*oy*al. **(u)** ʌ, d*u*ck; u, b*u*ll; u:, g*oo*se; ə, b*a*cillus; ju:, c*u*be. x, lo*ch*; θ, *th*ink; ð, bo*th*er; z, *Z*en; ʒ, cor*s*age. dʒ, sa*v*age; ŋ, ora*ng*utan*g*; j, *y*ak; ʃ, *f*ish; tʃ, fet*ch*; 'l, ra*bbl*e; 'n, re*dd*en. Complete pronunciation key appears inside front cover.

owe (ou) *pres. part.* **ow·ing** *past* and *past part.* **owed** *v.t.* to have an obligation to pay or repay (money etc.) in return for money etc. that one has received ‖ to have or bear (a specified feeling) toward someone, *to owe someone gratitude* ‖ to be or feel obliged to render (something), *to owe allegiance to one's country* ‖ to have, enjoy etc. (something) as a result of the action, existence etc. of a specified person, cause etc., *she owes her life to the doctors* ‖ *v.i.* to be in debt, *he still owes for his piano* [O.E. *āgan*, to own]

O·wen (óuən), Robert (1771–1858), British social reformer and socialist. A successful cotton manufacturer, he acquired mills at New Lanark in Scotland (1799), which he ran on model lines, limiting working hours, providing good housing and education, and establishing one of the first cooperative stores. He campaigned for social legislation and was partly responsible for the Factory Act of 1819. He formed the Grand National Consolidated Trades Union (1843). In 'New View of Society' (1813) he expounded the view that character is formed by social environment, and he advocated the cooperative system

Owen Falls a waterfall near the exit of the Nile from Lake Victoria, Uganda. A large dam here converts the lake into a reservoir for Egypt and the Sudan, and produces hydroelectric power for Uganda and Kenya

Owens (óuəns), Jesse (1913–80), U.S. track star, best known for his outstanding performance in the 1936 Olympic Games in which he won four gold medals, placing first in the 100-m sprint, the 200-m sprint and the broad jump. He was also a member of the winning U.S. 400-m relay team. He also achieved the finest one-day performance in track history (May 25, 1935), when he equaled the 100-yd dash world record at 9.4 sec. and set a new world long-jump record of 26ft 8.25in (8.13m) that stood for 25 years. He also set records in the 220-yd dash (20.3 sec.) and the 220-yd low hurdles (22.6 sec.)

ow·ing (óuiŋ) *adj.* due to be paid, *a small sum is still owing* **owing to** as a result of, caused by, *delay owing to traffic jams* [OWE]

owl (aul) *n.* a member of *Strigidae*, a large cosmopolitan family of nocturnal birds of prey. They have flattened faces and forward-facing eyes, hooked bills and powerful claws, and their soft, fluffy plumage allows them to fly noiselessly ‖ a solemn-appearing person, usually stupid [O.E. *ūle*]

owl·et (áulit) *n. Athene noctua*, a small European owl ‖ a young owl

owl·ish (áuliʃ) *adj.* (of a person, or his appearance) having characteristics suggestive of those of an owl

own (oun) **1.** *adj.* (usually following a possessive adj.) belonging to oneself or itself (often used to denote exclusive or particular possession or agency), *he brought his own lunch, he did it by his own effort* **to be one's own man** to be independent of the control or influence of others **2.** *n.* that which belongs to one of one's own belonging to one, *to have no money of one's own* **on one's own** independent ‖ independently or without the help etc. of others, *can you finish on you own?* **to come into one's own** to get what rightly belongs to one (esp. recognition or prosperity) **to get one's own back** to get one's revenge, get even **to hold one's own** to maintain one's position or strength [O.E. *āgen*, past part. of *āgan*, to own]

own *v.t.* to have, possess, be the proprietor of, *he owns the house and land* ‖ to acknowledge, *would he own his authorship of it?* ‖ *v.i.* (with 'to') to make an admission, *he owned to a sense of shame* **to own up** (*pop.*) to confess, admit guilt ‖ (*pop.*, with 'to') to confess frankly that one has committed a crime etc. **ówn·er, ówn·er·ship** *ns* [O.E. *āgnian*, to seize, gain, win fr. *āgen*, own]

own-brand (óunbrænd) *adj.* of a product carrying a private brand name, esp. that of a retailer, in contrast with an advertised brand

own·er·oc·cu·pied (óunərókju:paid) *adj.* lived-in by the owner instead of by a rental tenant — **own·er·oc·cu·pa·tion** *n.* —**own·er·oc·cu·pee** *n.*

ox (ɒks) *pl.* **ox·en** (óksən) *n.* a member of genus *Bos*, fam. *Bovidae*, esp. the adult castrated male of *B. taurus* kept as a draft animal or raised as food ‖ any of several animals of *Bos* and related genera, e.g. the bison, buffalo, yak [O.E. *oxa*]

ox·a·cill·in sodium [C₃H₃NO] (ɒksəsílin) *n.* (*pharm.*) semisynthetic substitute for penicillin effective against penicillin-resistant staphyloc-

cic infections; marketed as Prostaphin and Resistopen

ox·a·late (óksəleit) *n.* a salt or ester of oxalic acid [F.]

ox·al·ic acid (ɒksǽlik) a poisonous acid, (COOH)₂, found in plants of genus *Oxalis* and other plants and also produced synthetically. It is used in dyeing, fabric printing, bleaching, in metal polishes etc. [fr. F. *oxalique* fr. L. *oxalis*, oxalis]

ox·a·lis (óksəlis, ɒksǽlis) *n.* a member of *Oxalis*, fam. *Oxalidaceae*, a genus of plants of warm and tropical regions including wood sorrel etc., having purple, pink or white flowers and leaves with an acid taste [L. fr. Gk fr. *oxus*, sour]

ox·az·e·pam [C₁₅H₁₁ClN₂O₂] (ɒkséizəpæm) *n.* (*pharm.*) tranquilizing drug; marketed as Serax

ox·bow (óksbou) *n.* a collar for an ox, consisting of a U-shaped wooden frame, the upper ends of which pass through the bar of the yoke ‖ a crescent-shaped bend in a river, or the land within this bend

Ox·bridge·an, -ian (ɒksbrídʒən) *adj.* showing the qualities of a graduate of Oxford or Cambridge universities

ox·cart (ókskɑrt) *n.* a cart drawn by an ox or oxen

oxen *pl.* of ox

Ox·en·stier·na (óksənʃernə), Count Axel Gustaffson (1583–1654), Swedish statesman. An extremely able diplomat, he wielded great influence in the Thirty Years' War as minister to Gustavus II and Christina

ox·eye daisy (óksai) *Chrysanthemum leucanthemum*, a perennial composite with a woody stock, long white ray florets and yellow disk florets. It is a common grassland plant in temperate regions ‖ the black-eyed Susan any member of *Heliopsis*, a genus of yellow-flowered perennial plants of North America

Ox·fam (*acronym*) **Ox**ford Committee for **Fam**ine Relief

Ox·ford (óksfərd) the county town (pop. 117,400) of Oxfordshire, England, a county borough, on the Thames (here called the Isis), seat of Oxford University. Industries: printing, automobile engineering, steel works. Christ Church cathedral (12th c.)

ox·ford (óksfərd) a walking shoe laced above the instep ‖ a kind of cloth, usually cotton, used for shirts etc. [OXFORD, England]

Oxford and Asquith, 1st earl of *ASQUITH

Oxford Group Movement *MORAL RE-ARMAMENT

Oxford movement a 19th-c. reforming movement, also known as Tractarianism or Puseyism, within the Church of England. Led by Keble, Newman and Pusey, it began (1833) at Oxford University. It aimed at reaffirming the unbroken connection of the Church of England with the early Church, and at restoring the High Church ideals of the 17th c. Its views were publicized in 'Tracts for the Times' (1833–41), culminating in Newman's 'Tract 90' (1841) which attempted to interpret the Thirty-nine Articles in keeping with Roman Catholic doctrine. Through Anglo-Catholicism the movement has had a continuing effect on Anglican teaching, worship and ceremonial

Oxford, Provisions of (*Eng. hist.*) a scheme of government drawn up (1258) by the great council under the leadership of Simon de Montfort. It aimed at reforming central and local government and the king's household by appointing a baronial council to govern the country. Henry III's repudiation of the scheme precipitated the Barons' War (1264–6)

Ox·ford·shire (óksfərdʃiər) (*abbr.* Oxon.) a county (area 749 sq. miles, pop. 541,800) in the S. Midlands of England. County town: Oxford

Oxford University a university in Oxford, England, consisting of 30 colleges. It was established as a center of learning c. 1167. University College was founded in 1249, Balliol in 1263 and Merton in 1264

ox·hide (ókshaid) *n.* leather made from the skin of an ox

ox·i·dase (óksideiz, óksideis) *n.* an enzyme causing oxidation of substrates by removal of hydrogen, which combines with oxygen [OXIDATION + DIASTASE]

ox·i·da·tion (ɒksidéiʃən) *n.* an oxidizing or being oxidized (cf. REDUCTION, *OXIDATION-REDUCTION) [fr. *oxidate*, to oxidize]

oxidation-reduction a chemical reaction (also called a redox reaction) in which one or more electrons are transferred from one ion, atom or

molecule to another. All such reactions involve an oxidizing agent, which is reduced during the course of the reaction, and a reducing agent, which is oxidized

oxidation-reduction potential the potential (also called the redox potential) at which oxidation occurs at the anode and reduction at the cathode in an electrochemical cell. This potential is referred to that of a standard hydrogen electrode (taken as zero)

oxidation state the degree of oxidation of an atom or ion, usually expressed by a positive or negative number representing the formal ionic charge on each atom in a compound or complex ion, 0 representing the elemental state (*VALENCE)

ox·ide (óksaid) *n.* a compound of oxygen with another element or with an organic radical **ox·i·dize** (óksidaiz) *pres. part.* **ox·i·diz·ing** *past* and *past part.* **ox·i·dized** *v.t.* to combine with oxygen ‖ to remove one or more electrons from (a compound, ion or radical), thus changing the oxidation state to a larger positive or smaller negative number ‖ to cover (metal etc.) with an oxide coating ‖ *v.i.* to undergo oxidation [F.]

oxide of iridium metal that changes color in response to an electrical impulse and retains change, used in creating digital displays in watches, etc., developed by Bell Laboratories

ox·im·e·ter (ɒksímitər) *n.* (*med.*) device for measuring the oxygen content of blood in a person by passing a beam of light through the earlobe

ox·lip (ókslip) *n. Primula elatior*, a primula found in Europe and W. Asia ‖ a hybrid between the primrose and cowslip [O.E. *oxanslyppe*, ox's dropping, oxlip]

Ox·on. (óksən) *adj.* of Oxford University, *M.A.* (*Oxon.*) [fr. L. *Oxoniensis*]

Ox·o·ni·an (ɒksóuni:ən) **1.** *adj.* of the university or city of Oxford **2.** *n.* a student or graduate of Oxford University ‖ a native or resident of Oxford [fr. *Oxoflia*, Latinized name of Oxford]

ox·o·trem·or·ine [C₁₂H₁₈N₂O] (ɒksətrémərin) *n.* (*pharm.*) tremor-producing drug used in testing antitremor drugs

ox·tail (óksteil) *n.* the skinned tail of an ox, used to make a soup or stew

Ox·us (óksəs) *AMU-DARYA

ox·y·a·cet·y·lene (ɒksi:əsét'li:n) *adj.* of, consisting of or using a mixture of oxygen and acetylene, esp. as burned in a blowtorch to provide a sufficiently high temperature for welding or cutting metals [OXYGEN + ACETYLENE]

ox·y·ac·id (ɒksi:ǽsid) *n.* (*chem.*) an oxygen-containing acid

ox·y·gen (óksidʒən) *n.* a colorless, tasteless, normally gaseous element (symbol O, at. no. 8, at. mass 15.9994) [F. *oxygène*]
—Oxygen forms about 1/5 of the earth's atmosphere, 8/9 by weight of water, and a considerable proportion by weight of organic matter and of many minerals. It is the most abundant element of the earth's atmosphere and crust, and is essential to animal and plant life. It combines readily with many other elements to form oxides, combustion and respiration both involving such combination. Pure oxygen is extracted from liquefied air. It is used in oxygen blowpipes and oxyhydrogen and oxyacetylene flames for cutting and welding. The use of large amounts of oxygen in steelmaking furnaces speeds the decarbonizing reaction and makes it possible to treat lower grades of ore. Chemical applications of oxygen include the manufacture of concentrated nitric acid from ammonia and the oxidation of hydrocarbons obtained from petroleum

ox·y·ge·nase (óksidʒəneis) *n.* (*biochem.*) enzyme that makes possible the use of oxygen from the atmosphere by an organic cell

ox·y·gen·ate (óksidʒəneit) *pres. part.* **ox·y·gen·at·ing** *past* and *past part.* **ox·y·gen·at·ed** *v.t.* to impregnate or treat with oxygen to fill (blood etc.) with oxygen by breathing **ox·y·gen·á·tion** *n.* [F. *oxygéner*]

oxygen-hydrogen welding a process of gas welding by burning a mixture of oxygen and hydrogen, producing very high temperatures

ox·y·gen·ize (óksidʒənaiz) *pres. part.* **ox·y·gen·iz·ing** *past* and *past part.* **ox·y·gen·ized** *v.t.* to oxygenate

oxygen tent a tentlike canopy, placed over a patient's bed, in which a steady flow of oxygen is supplied to the patient

ox·y·he·mo·glo·bin, ox·y·hae·mo·glo·bin (ɒksi:hí:məglóubin, ɒksihí:məgloubin, ɒksihéməglóubin, ɒksihémɘglɒubin) *n.* an unstable compound of hemoglobin and oxygen, formed in the blood when oxygen is breathed (as air) into the lungs [OXYGEN+HEMOGLOBIN]

oxyhemoglobin *n.* (*chem.*) hemoglobin with oxygen

ox·y·hy·dro·gen (ɒksiháidrɘdʒɘn) *adj.* of, relating to, or consisting of a mixture of hydrogen and oxygen [OXYGEN+HYDROGEN]

ox·y·mo·ron (ɒksimɔ́rɒn, ɒksimóurɒn) *n.* a figure of speech in which apparently contradictory terms are combined to produce an epigrammatic effect, e.g. 'cruel only to be kind' [Gk *oxumōron* fr. *oxus*, sharp+*mōros*, foolish]

Ox·y·rhyn·chus (ɒksiríŋkɘs) (*Arab.* Behnesa) the site of an ancient Egyptian town about 100 miles south of Cairo, a rich source of Greek, Latin, demotic Egyptian, Coptic and Hebrew papyri

ox·y·to·cic (ɒksitóusik) **1.** *adj.* (*med.*) serving to hasten the process of birth by stimulating contraction of uterine smooth muscle **2.** *n.* (*med.*) an oxytocic substance **ox·y·to·cin** *n.* a hormone from the posterior pituitary gland, stimulating contraction of the uterine smooth muscle [fr. Gk *oxutokion* fr. *oxus*, acute+*tokos*, childbirth]

ox·y·tone (óksitɒun) **1.** *adj.* (esp. in Greek) having an acute accent on the last syllable **2.** *n.* an oxytone word [fr. Gk *oxutonos* fr. *oxus*, acute+*tonos*, accent]

O·ya·pock (ɔjǽpɒk) (or Oyapak) a river (300 miles long) rising in the Tumac-Humac Mtns of French Guiana, flowing northeast to form the Brazil–French Guiana boundary, and emptying into the Atlantic

o·yer and ter·mi·ner (ɔ́iɘrɘntɑ́:rminɘr) *n.* (*Br. law*) a royal commission conferring power to hear and determine criminal cases (*Am. law*) any of certain superior courts with similar powers [A.F.-to hear and determine]

o·yez, o·yes (oujés, oujéz) *interj.* listen! (uttered usually three times by a public crier or court officer to command attention and silence before a proclamation is read) [O.F. *oiez, oyez,* imper. of *oir,* to hear]

O·yo (ɔ́jou) a trading center (pop. 75,000) of W. Nigeria, manufacturing cotton textiles

oys·ter (ɔ́istɘr) *n.* an edible marine bivalve lamellibranch mollusk of fam. *Ostreidae,* having a rough irregular shell and living free on the sea floor or attached to submerged rocks, usually in temperate or tropical coastal waters or estuaries ‖ any of several mollusks resembling this, e.g. a pearl oyster ‖ a choice morsel of meat contained in a hollow of the pelvic bone on each side of the back of a chicken ‖ a color between light gray and white [O.F. *oistre, uistre, huistre* fr. obs. Ital. *ostrea* fr. L. fr. Gk]

oyster bed a place on the ocean floor where oysters breed or are cultivated

oyster catcher a member of *Haematopus,* fam. *Haematopodidae,* a widely distributed genus of rather large wading shorebirds which feed on small mollusks and worms. They usually have black and white plumage, stout pink legs and a strong bill

oyster crab *Pinnotheres ostreum,* a crab the female of which lives as a commensal in the gill cavity of an oyster

oyster farm a tract of sea bottom where oysters are bred

O·zark Mountains (óuzɑrk) a plateau (area about 50,000 sq. miles, elevation 1,500–2,500 ft), broken by hills, in parts of Missouri, Arkansas, Oklahoma, Kansas and Illinois: farming, livestock raising, lead and zinc mines

o·zo·ce·rite (ɒuzɘsíɘrait) *n.* a waxlike mineral fossil resin consisting of a mixture of hydrocarbons. It is used in making candles etc. [G. *ozokerit* fr. Gk *ozein,* to smell+*kĕros,* wax]

o·zo·ke·rite (ɒuzɘkíɘrait) *n.* ozocerite

o·zone (óuzoun, ouzóun) *n.* an allotropic form of oxygen in which three atoms form one molecule (O_3). It has a pungent smell, is produced by a silent discharge of electricity, and is present in the air after a thunderstorm. It is used commercially for sterilizing water, bleaching, purifying air etc. **o·zon·ic** (ouzɒ́nik, ouzóunik) *adj.* **o·zo·nif·er·ous** (ouzounífɘrɘs) *adj.* **o·zon·ize** (óuzɒunaiz) *pres. part.* **o·zon·iz·ing** *past and past part.* **o·zon·ized** *v.t.* to convert into ozone ‖ to treat or combine with ozone **o·zon·iz·er** (óuzounai̯zɘr) *n.* an apparatus that converts oyxen into ozone by passing a silent electrical discharge through it [Fr. fr. Gk *ozein,* to smell]

CONCISE PRONUNCIATION KEY: (**a**) æ, c*a*t; ɑ, c*a*r; ɔ f*aw*n; ei, sn*a*ke. (**e**) e, h*e*n; i:, sh*ee*p; iɘ, d*ee*r; ɛɘ, b*ea*r. (**i**) i, f*i*sh; ai, t*i*ger; ɘ:, b*i*rd. (**o**) o, *o*x; au, c*ow*; ou, g*oa*t; u, p*oo*r; ɔi, r*oy*al. (**u**) ʌ, d*u*ck; u, b*u*ll; u:, g*oo*se; ɘ, b*a*cillus; ju:, c*u*be. x, lo*ch*; θ, *th*ink; ð, bo*th*er; z, *Z*en; ʒ, corsa*g*e; dʒ, sava*g*e; ŋ, ora*ng*utang; j, *y*ak; ʃ, *f*ish; tʃ, fe*tch*; 'l, rabb*le*; 'n, redd*en*. Complete pronunciation key appears inside front cover.

	EARLY NORTH SEMITIC	PHOENICIAN	EARLY HEBREW (GEZER)	EARLY GREEK	CLASSICAL GREEK	ETRUSCAN		EARLY LATIN	CLASSICAL LATIN
						Early	Classical		
P	)	ר	ר	ר	П	٩	٩	Ր	P

	CURSIVE MAJUSCULE (ROMAN)	CURSIVE MINUSCULE (ROMAN)	ANGLO-IRISH MAJUSCULE	CAROLINE MINUSCULE	VENETIAN MINUSCULE (ITALIC)	N. ITALIAN MINUSCULE (ROMAN)
	p	ʃ	P	p	ρ	p

A. C. SYLVESTER, CAMBRIDGE, ENGLAND

Development of the letter P, beginning with the early North Semitic letter. Evolution of both the majuscule, or capital, letter P and the minuscule, or lowercase, letter p are shown.

P, p (pi:) the 16th letter of the English alphabet **to mind one's P's and Q's** to be careful to avoid language or behavior that could offend
Pa. Pennsylvania
pa (*phys. abbr.*) pascal, SI unit of pressure equal to the force of 1 newton acting over 1 sq. meter area
pab·u·lum (pǽbjuləm) (*rhet.*) nourishment [L.]
pa·ca (púkə, pǽkə) *n.* a member of *Cuniculus*, fam. *Dasyproctidae*, a genus of Central and South American rodents about 2 ft long, esp. *C. paca*, which is valued as food [Port. and Span. fr. Tupi]
Pa·ca·rai·ma (pækəráimə) a mountain range extending west to east along a part of the Brazil-Venezuela boundary. Highest peak: Mt Roraima (9,210 ft)
pace (peis) **1.** *n.* rate of traveling or progressing ‖ manner of walking or running ‖ a step made in walking ‖ the distance covered by a single step in walking, often taken as 30 ins ‖ (*Rom. hist.*) a unit of measurement, the distance between successive impacts of the same heel (about 60 ins) ‖ any of the gaits of a horse ‖ a fast horse's gait in which just the feet on one side are lifted and set down, then the feet on the other **to go the pace** (*Br.*) to go very fast ‖ (*Br.*) to lead a gay, dissipated life **to keep pace with** to move or develop at the same speed as, *keep pace with the times* **to put (someone or an animal) through his** (or **its**) **paces** to test or rehearse the abilities of (someone or an animal) **2.** *v. pres. part.* **pac·ing** past and *past part.* **paced** *v.i.* to walk with regular steps ‖ *v.t.* (often with 'off', 'out') to measure by counting the paces needed to walk the length of, *he paced out the length of the garden* ‖ to establish or regulate the pace or speed of, *he paced the runner on his bicycle* [O.F. *pas*]
pa·ce (péisi) *prep.* subject to the consent of, with due respect to the opinion of, *my view, pace the last speaker, is that we should adjourn* [L., ablative of *pax*, peace]
pace car (*auto racing*) a lead car that paces the field for one lap
pace lap (*auto racing*) warm-up run before a race
pace·mak·er (péismeikər) *n.* a person who sets the pace, e.g. for a race ‖ (*med.*) a part of the body serving to establish and maintain a rhythmic activity ‖ (*med.*) a device for stimulating the heart to resume a steady beat, or to restore the rhythm of an arrested heart
pac·er (péisər) *n.* a horse with a pacing gait, used esp. in harness racing
Pa·che·co A·re·co (patʃékɔərékɔ), Jorge (1921–), Uruguayan journalist, politician and president (1967–72)

Pa·cho·mi·us (pəkóumi:əs), St (c. 292–c. 346), Egyptian ascetic. He founded the first Christian monastic community living a communal life under a rule (c. 318). Feast: May 14
pach·y·derm (pǽkidə:rm) *n.* (*zool.*) any of certain thick-skinned, hoofed mammals, esp. the rhinoceros and elephant **pach·y·der·ma·tous** *adj.* [F. *pachyderme* fr. Gk *pachus*, thick+*derma*, skin]
pach·y·o·ste·o·morph (pæki:ɔ́sti:oumɔrf) . *n.* (*paleontology*) a level on the evolutionary scale where bone structure is heavy
pach·y·tene (pǽkiti:n) *adj.* of that part of the prophase stage in meiosis during which homologous chromosomes are associated as bivalents [fr. F. *pachytène* fr. Gk *pachus*, thick+*tainia*, band]
pa·ci·far·in (pɑsifǽrin) *n.* (*biochem.*) a substance produced by bacteria that prevents certain diseases *also* enterobactin
pa·cif·ic (pəsífik) *adj.* peaceful, seeking, making or tending toward peace, *pacific policies* ‖ unaggressive in disposition **Pa·cif·ic** of the Pacific Ocean or the regions bordering it **pa·cíf·i·cal·ly** *adv.* [fr. L. *pacificus*]
pac·i·fi·ca·tion (pæsifikéiʃən) *n.* a pacifying or being pacified ‖ (*mil.*) countering guerrilla activity [F.]
pa·cif·i·ca·to·ry (pəsífikətɔri:, pəsífikətɔuri:) *adj.* tending to promote peace [fr. *pacificator*, someone who pacifies, fr. L.]
Pacific Doctrine statement of U.S. policy by President Gerald Ford, December 7, 1976, of the normalization of relations with China, strategic partnership with Japan, assertion of U.S. interest in Southeast Asia and the acknowledged existence of political conflicts
Pacific Ocean the largest ocean (area incl. seas, gulfs and Antarctic waters: 63,800,000 sq. miles, over a third of the earth's surface), separating America from Asia and Australia. Length (Bering Strait–Antarctica): 9,000 miles. Width from Panama to Malaya: 11,000 miles. Submarine plateaus project hundreds of archipelagoes and single islands in the W. Pacific, with smaller ridges in mid-ocean. Average valley depth: 2,800 fathoms. Characteristic deeps along the continents and archipelagoes go down to 6 miles (6,300 fathoms in the Marianas trench). With its coasts it constitutes a great volcanic zone
Pacific standard time (*abbr.* P.S.T.) Pacific time
Pacific time (*abbr.* P.T.) one of the four standard time divisions of the U.S.A. and Canada, eight hours behind Greenwich time and three hours behind Eastern standard time
Pacific, War of the a war (1879–84) between Chile and the alliance of Bolivia and Peru,

fought over possession of nitrate deposits in the Atacama region. It ended in the Treaty of Ancón (Ecuador) and the truce at Valparaíso (1884). A definitive treaty was signed in 1904
pac·i·fi·er (pǽsifaiər) *n.* someone who pacifies ‖ (*Am.*=*Br.* dummy) a rubber nipple for babies to suck
pac·i·fism (pǽsifizəm) *n.* the belief that war is morally wrong and, in the long run, ineffective, and that disputes should be settled by negotiation **pác·i·fist** *n.* a person who subscribes to this [PACIFIC]
pac·i·fy (pǽsifai) *pres. part.* **pac·i·fy·ing** *past* and *past part.* **pac·i·fied** *v.t.* to cause (someone) to be calm, satisfied or no longer angry ‖ to establish peace in (a country etc.) [F. *pacifier*]
pack (pæk) **1.** *n.* a bundle or parcel of things, esp. one carried on the shoulders or back ‖ a company of animals, esp. of wolves or hounds ‖ a company or gang of people ‖ a great quantity, *a pack of lies* ‖ a packet or container, *a pack of cigarettes* ‖ a complete set of playing cards ‖ (*industry*) the amount of food packed in one season ‖ (*rugby*) the forwards, esp. when together in a scrum ‖ an area of sea full of pack ice ‖ a piece of wet or dry cloth, applied hot or cold as a medical or cosmetic treatment ‖ a treatment in which such a cloth is applied **2.** *v.t.* (often with 'up') to put in a container with other things, esp. for carrying on a trip, *pack your toothbrush* ‖ (often with 'up') to fill (a container) with things, *to pack a suitcase* ‖ to fill tightly, cram, *a train packed with people* ‖ to make into a wrapped parcel, *to pack a lunch* ‖ to put into protective containers for marketing or shipping ‖ (with 'off') to send (someone) away, esp. summarily ‖ (*Br., pop.,* with 'up') to cease (an activity) ‖ *v.i.* to put things together for a trip ‖ to settle into a solid or compact mass ‖ to assemble, crowd together ‖ to be capable of being put in a container with other things, *this suit will pack without wrinkling* ‖ (*Br., pop.,* with 'up') to cease operating ‖ (with 'off') to leave hastily and unceremoniously **to send (someone) packing** to dismiss (someone) unceremoniously [M.E. *packe, pakke* prob. fr. M. Flem. *pac* or Du. or L.G. *pak*]
pack *v.t.* to select members of (a committee etc.) so as to secure an unfair advantage [origin unknown]
pack·age (pǽkidʒ) **1.** *n.* a parcel or wrapped bundle ‖ a box or wrapper in which something is packed **2.** *v.t. pres. part.* **pack·ag·ing** *past* and *past part.* **pack·aged** to make into a parcel, *packaged foods* [PACK, to put in a container]
package deal an all-or-nothing arrangement in which a related group of items or services is sold for a lump sum ‖ an agreement in which the approval and acceptance of one proposal is con-

tingent upon the approval and acceptance of another

package store a shop licenced to sell in sealed containers liquor which may not be drunk on the premises

pack animal an animal, e.g. a mule, used for carrying loads

Pack·ard (pǽkərd), James Ward (1863–1928), U.S. engineer and inventor. He and his brother founded (1890) the Packard Electric Company, for which he invented many methods and instruments to improve incandescent lighting. He built (1899) the first Packard automobile and founded (1899) what became the Packard Motor Car Company

pack drill (*mil.*) punishment of a soldier by making him drill while carrying all his gear

packed tower (*envir.*) a pollution-control device that forces dirty air through a tower packed with crushed rock or wood chips while liquid is sprayed over the packing material, causing pollutants to dissolve or chemically react with the liquid

pack·er (pǽkər) *n.* someone who packs, esp. who packs goods professionally for transport or storage ‖ a firm that packs goods for transport or storage

pack·et (pǽkit) *n.* a small package or parcel ‖ a packet boat [dim. of PACK n.]

packet boat a boat sailing a regular route, carrying passengers, mail and packages

pack·horse (pǽkhɔrs) *n.* a horse used for carrying loads

pack ice blocks of sea ice crushed up together in a nearly solid mass

pack·ing (pǽkiŋ) *n.* the process of assembling things in a container, or of filling a container with things ‖ material (sawdust etc.) used to stuff the spaces between wrapped goods to prevent damage ‖ material used to fill cracks and joints etc. ‖ (*med.*) material used to fill an open wound or cavity to allow drainage and prevent closing

packing case a wooden crate in which goods are shipped or stored

packing fraction the difference between the mass of a group of nucleons in an atomic nucleus and the sum of their individual masses divided by the number of nucleons

packing house an establishment where food, esp. meat, is processed and packed to be sold at wholesale

packing ring a piston ring

pack·man (pǽkmən) *pl.* **pack·men** (pǽkmən) *n.* (*old-fash.*) a peddler

pack rat *Neotoma cinerea,* fam. *Cricetidae,* a rodent of the western U.S., about 6 ins long, with a bushy tail. It has plump cheek pouches in which it carries food and things to be hoarded

pack·sad·dle (pǽksæd'l) *n.* a saddle for carrying a load instead of a rider

pack·thread (pǽkθred) *n.* strong thick thread used for sewing or for tying up packages

pack·train (pǽktrein) *n.* a procession of pack animals, esp. of mules

pact (pækt) *n.* an agreement between two persons, or a treaty between states [O.F. *pact,* *pacte*]

pad (pæd) 1. *n.* something soft, e.g. a flat cushion or thick mat, used as a shock absorber ‖ a piece of soft material used to fill or distend, *a shoulder pad* ‖ (*sports*) a protective guard worn on the front of the legs etc. ‖ a number of sheets of paper fastened together along one edge ‖ (*colloq.*) person's apartment or residence ‖ graft for a group ‖ a small absorbent cushion soaked in ink, for inking a rubber stamp ‖ the fleshy cushion forming the sole of the paw of a dog, cat etc. ‖ the paw of a fox, hare etc. ‖ an insect's pulvillus ‖ the floating leaf of certain water plants, esp. a lily pad ‖ the socket of a brace ‖ a tool handle into which different tools may be inserted 2. *v.t.* *pres. part.* **pad·ding** *past and past part.* **pad·ded** to fill or line with soft material ‖ to lengthen (a piece of writing, speech etc.) by adding superfluous material [origin unknown]

pad 1. *v.i.* *pres. part.* **pad·ding** *past and past part.* **pad·ded** to walk steadily and unhurriedly ‖ to walk with muffled steps 2. *n.* the dull sound of a footfall [rel. to PAD, cushion, and imit.]

Pa·dang (pádaŋ) a trading center (pop. 196,339) of W. Sumatra, Indonesia. Its port, Telukbayur, lies 4 miles south. University (1956)

padded cell a room in a mental hospital or prison having padded walls to prevent a violent occupant from injuring himself

pad·ding (pǽdiŋ) *n.* the act of someone who pads ‖ the material used to pad something ‖ (*mil.*) extraneous text added to a message for the purpose of concealing its beginning, ending, or length

pad·dle (pǽd'l) 1. *v.i.* *pres. part.* **pad·dling** *past and past part.* **pad·dled** to wade or play in shallow water ‖ to toddle 2. *n.* the act or a period of paddling [origin unknown]

paddle 1. *n.* a wooden pole with a broad blade at one end, used singly without an oarlock to propel and guide a canoe or other small craft ‖ the act or period of using this or of using an oar in this way ‖ any of several implements resembling a canoe paddle, for stirring, mixing, beating etc. ‖ one of the projecting boards of a paddle wheel ‖ a seal's flipper ‖ a table-tennis racket 2. *v.* *pres. part.* **pad·dling** *past and past part.* **pad·dled** *v.t.* to propel (a canoe etc.) by using a paddle ‖ to convey (someone) in a canoe etc. propelled by a paddle ‖ (*pop.*) to spank ‖ *v.i.* to propel a canoe etc. by a paddle ‖ to row gently ‖ (of a bird) to move in water as if by means of paddles **to paddle one's own canoe** to get along without depending on others [origin unknown]

paddle box a structure covering the upper portion of a paddle wheel

paddle steamer a steam vessel propelled by a paddle wheel on each side

paddle tennis *PLATFORM TENNIS

paddle wheel a wheel with long boards projecting at right angles from its circumference, used to propel a boat

pad·dock (pǽdək) *n.* a small grassy enclosed area in which a horse can graze and exercise ‖ a racecourse enclosure in which the horses are walked for inspection and are saddled and unsaddled [var. of *parrock,* small field fr. O.E. *pearroc, pearruc*]

pad·dy (pǽdi) *pl.* **pad·dies** *n.* rice before harvesting or before husking ‖ a wet field in which rice is grown [Malay *padi*]

paddy *n.* (*Br., pop.*) a fit of bad temper [Irish *Padraig,* Patrick (proper name)]

paddy wagon (*pop.*) a patrol wagon [prob. fr. *Paddy,* Irishman]

Paderewski (padəréfski:), Ignace Jan (1860–1941), Polish statesman, pianist and composer. After his U.S. debut as a pianist (1891) he became the most beloved pianist since Franz Liszt. He donated all of his concert receipts from 1914–8 to Polish war victims. He became Polish representative to Washington (1918–9) and prime minister of Poland (1919–20). He led the exiled Polish government during the German occupation of World War II (1940–1). Of his many musical compositions only the Minuet in G and Piano Concerto, op. 17 are still performed

pad·lock (pǽdlɒk) 1. *n.* a small, portable lock, with a curved bar hinged to it at one end. The bar can be slipped through a hasp and staple, chain links etc., the free end then being fastened in the lock 2. *v.t.* to fasten with a padlock [origin unknown]

pa·dre (pádrei, pádri:) *n.* (*armed services, pop.*) a chaplain [Span., Ital. and Port.=priest, father]

Pad·u·a (pǽdʒu:ə, pǽdju:ə) (*Ital.* Padova) a walled city (pop. 242,000) of Veneto, Italy, 22 miles west of Venice, an agricultural market. Industries: chemical and agricultural engineering and food processing. Principal monuments: Palazzo della Ragione (12th c.), Basilica of St Anthony (13th c.), cathedral (16th c.). University (1222)

pae·an (pí:ən) *n.* a choral song of praise, triumph or rejoicing ‖ (*rhet.*) any extravagant expression of praise, triumph etc. [L. fr. Gk *paian* a hymn to Apollo fr. *Paian, Paiōn,* a name for Apollo]

paederast * PEDERAST

paederasty *PEDERASTY

paediatric *PEDIATRIC

pae·do·gen·e·sis, pe·do·gen·e·sis (pi:doudʒéni·sis) *n.* (*zool.*) reproduction by animals sexually mature but in all other respects in a pre-adult or larval stage (e.g. in the axolotl and certain dipteran insects) [fr. Gk *pais* (*paidos*), *child+genesis,* origin]

pae·on (pí:ən) *n.* (*prosody*) a metrical foot of four syllables, one long (or stressed) and three short (or unstressed) in any order **pae·on·ic** (pi:ɒ́nik) *adj.* [L. fr. Gk *paiōn*]

Paes·tum (péstəm) (*Gk* Posidonia) an ancient city (now ruins) in S. Campania, Italy, near Salerno, founded by Greeks (c. 600 B.C.), with

well preserved ruins of Doric preclassical temples

Pá·ez (páes), José Antonio (1790–1873), Venezuelan soldier and comrade-in-arms of Bolívar. He was in command of the llanero cavalry. On the separation of Venezuela from Gran Colombia he served (1831–5) as first president of the Republic, resuming office from 1839 to 1843. After exile (1850–8), he returned as dictator (1861–3)

pa·gan (péigən) 1. *n.* a heathen, esp. one who worshipped the gods of ancient Greece and Rome 2. *adj.* pertaining to or characteristic of a pagan [fr. L. *paganus,* civilian, in contrast to the Christian *miles,* soldier (of Christ)]

Pa·ga·ni·ni (pægəní:ni:), Niccolò (1782–1840), Italian violinist. His almost legendary virtuosity is reflected in the difficulty of many of his compositions

pa·gan·ism (péigənizəm) *n.* the state of being pagan ‖ pagan beliefs and practices [fr. eccles. L. *paganismus*]

pa·gan·ize (péigənaiz) *v.t.* *pres. part.* **pa·gan·iz·ing** *past and past part.* **pa·gan·ized** to make pagan [F. *paganiser*]

Page (peidʒ), Walter Hines (1855–1918), U.S. journalist and diplomat. As editor of several U.S. journals, incl. (1896–9) the 'Atlantic Monthly', he campaigned for reforms in southern agriculture, education and industry. Appointed (1913) U.S. ambassador to Great Britain, he strongly supported the Allied cause at the onset of the 1st world war. This alienated President Woodrow Wilson, who was then anxious to maintain American neutrality

page (peidʒ) 1. *n.* one side of a piece of paper or leaf of a book ‖ (*loosely*) a leaf of a book ‖ (*computer*) a single sheet of data ‖ a fixed block or number of blocks of data or instructions 2. *v.t.* *pres. part.* **pag·ing** *past and past part.* **paged** to make up (printed matter) into pages ‖ to number the pages of (a manuscript or printed text) [F.]

page 1. *n.* a boy or young man employed as a personal attendant in a royal or noble household ‖ a boy employed in a hotel to carry messages or otherwise be of personal service to guests ‖ a boy attendant upon the bride at a wedding ‖ (*hist.*) a young man in attendance upon a knight while himself in training for knighthood ‖ a boy attendant in a legislative body, esp. Congress 2. *v.t.* *pres. part.* **pag·ing** *past and past part.* **paged** to attend as a page ‖ to summon (a person, e.g. in a hotel) by calling his name repeatedly [O.F.]

pag·eant (pǽdʒənt) *n.* a colorful spectacle, either on a fixed stage or site or taking the form of a procession of tableaux representing esp. historical events ‖ a sequence of things or events resembling such a spectacle ‖ pageantry **pag·eant·ry** *n.* pageants collectively ‖ spectacular, colorful display [M.E. *pagyn, padgin* etc., a movable stage, prob. fr. L.]

page proof (*printing*) a proof printed from type that has been made up into pages

pag·i·nal (pǽdʒi'l) *adj.* of or relating to a page of a book etc. [fr. L.L. *paginalis*]

pag·i·nate (pǽdʒineit) *pres. part.* **pag·i·nat·ing** *past and past part.* **pag·i·nat·ed** *v.t.* to divide (a printed text) into pages ‖ to number the pages of (a manuscript or printed text) **pag·i·na·tion** *n.* a paginating or being paginated ‖ the numbers etc. distinguishing the pages of a book etc. [fr. L. *pagina,* page]

paging system an organized service that contacts via radio signal the carrier of a portable battery-operated receiver, e.g., a sales representative or physician, alerting him or her to make a telephone call in order to receive a message

pa·go·da (pəgoudə) *n.* an elaborately decorated Far Eastern sacred building, usually a tower with many stories that taper toward the top, with an upwardcurling, projecting roof over each story [fr. Port. and Ital. *pagode,* prob. fr. Pers.]

Pa·go Pa·go (páŋgoupáŋgou) *SAMOA, AMERICAN

Pa·hang (pəháŋ) the longest river (288 miles, navigable for 250) of Malaysia, flowing south and east from the central mountains to the South China Sea ‖ the state (area 13,820 sq. miles, pop. 419,000) through which it flows. Capital: Kuantan (a port). It came under British control in 1888 and joined the Federation of Malaya (now Malaysia) in 1948

Pah·la·vi, Peh·la·vi (pálvi:), Mohammed Reza (1919–80), shah of Iran (1941–79). After dis-

CONCISE PRONUNCIATION KEY: (**a**) æ, c*a*t; ɑ, c*a*r; ɔ f*aw*n; ei, sn*a*ke. (**e**) e, h*e*n; i:, sh*ee*p; iə, d*ee*r; ɛə, b*ea*r. (**i**) i, f*i*sh; ai, t*i*ger; ə:, b*i*rd. (**o**) o, *o*x; au, c*ow*; ou, g*oa*t; u, p*oo*r; ɔi, r*oy*al. (**u**) ʌ, d*u*ck; u, b*u*ll; u:, g*oo*se; ə, b*a*cillus; ju:, c*u*be. x, lo*ch*; θ, *th*ink; ð, bo*th*er; z, *Z*en; ʒ, corsa*g*e; dʒ, sava*g*e; ŋ, ora*ng*utang; j, *y*ak; ʃ, *fi*sh; tʃ, fe*tch*; 'l, rabb*le*; 'n, redd*en*. Complete pronunciation key appears inside front cover.

missing Mossadegh (1953), he exercised more direct control of the government, and promoted social and economic reforms, social and economic reforms, launching the so-called White Revolution (1963). He sought to control social unrest through Savak, the secret police. From 1978 opposition to him centered around the Ayatollah Khomeini, and in 1979 the Shah was deposed. His admission to the U.S.A. for medical treatment caused Iranian militants to seize hostages at the U.S. embassy in Teheran. The Shah went to Panama, then to Egypt, where he died

Pahlavi, Pehlevi, Reza Shah (1877–1944), shah of Iran (1925–41). An army officer, he gained power by a coup d'état (1921) which overthrew the Kajar dynasty, and was proclaimed shah (1925). He did much to modernize Iran but, because of his pro-Axis tendencies, was forced by Britain and the U.S.S.R. to abdicate (1941) in favor of his son, Mohammed Reza Pahlavi

Pah·la·vi, Peh·le·vi (púlǝvi:) *n.* the Persian language (3rd-7th cc.)

pahlavi, pehlevi *n.* a Persian gold coin containing **7.32** gms of gold, not constituting part of monetary circulation

Pah·sien (báfjén) *CHUNGKING

paid (peid) *past* and *past part.* of PAY ‖ *adj.* receiving wages or salary ‖ involving no stoppage of regular wages or salary, *paid holidays* **to put paid to** (*Br.*) to put an end to, esp. to thwart (some plan)

pail (peil) *n.* an open container, esp. of metal, usually almost cylindrical and wider at the top than at the bottom, having an arched handle at the top and used esp. for carrying liquids ‖ a pailful [etym. doubtful]

pail·ful (péilful) *pl.* **pail·fuls** *n.* the amount a pail will hold

paillasse *PALLIASSE

pail·lette (pæljét) *n.* a small piece of metal or foil used in enamel painting ‖ a spangle for ornamenting dresses [F., dim. of *paille,* straw]

pain (pein) **1.** *n.* an unpleasant sensation caused by the stimulation of certain nerves, esp. as a result of injury or sickness ‖ a distressing emotion, *his refusal caused her pain* ‖ (*pl.*) specially concentrated effort, *take pains to be accurate* ‖ (*pl.*) the labor of childbirth **on** (or **upon** or **under**) **pain of** with the certainty of incurring (some punishment) unless a specified command or condition is fulfilled, *you must sign the confession on pain of death* **to take pains** to make a special, concentrated effort **2.** *v.t.* to inflict esp. mental pain upon [O.F. *peine*]

Paine (pein), Thomas (1737–1809), British political writer and radical pamphleteer. He emigrated to Pennsylvania (1774) and supported the American colonies against Britain in his pamphlet 'Common Sense' (1776) and in his series 'The Crisis' (1776–83). Returning to Britain (1787), he wrote 'The Rights of Man' (1791–2) in answer to Burke's criticism of the French Revolution. He fled to France (1792), became a French citizen, and took a prominent part in French politics. His defense of deism in 'The Age of Reason' (1794–5) roused a storm of protest. He returned to the U.S.A. in 1802

pain·ful (péinfǝl) *adj.* causing or characterized by pain ‖ requiring or showing laborious care or effort

pain·less (péinlis) *adj.* not causing pain ‖ not requiring trouble or hard work

pains·tak·ing (péinzteikiŋ) *adj.* showing or using great care and effort

paint (peint) **1.** *v.t.* to apply paint to (a surface) ‖ to create (a picture, design etc.) on a surface, using paint ‖ to represent in paint, *to paint a landscape* ‖ to make a vivid written or spoken description of ‖ to apply cosmetics to ‖ to apply medicine etc. to (a throat etc.) as if applying paint ‖ (with 'out') to efface by covering with paint ‖ *v.i.* to practice the art of creating pictures with paint **to paint the town red** to go out and celebrate on a grand scale **2.** *n.* a liquid or paste consisting of a suspension of a pigment in oil or water etc. When spread over a surface, it dries to form a hard, thin covering colored by the pigment ‖ a pigment mixed with a water-soluble gum so as to form a cake ‖ the hardened skin on a painted surface, *the paint on the door is scratched* ‖ (*pop.*) cosmetics [O.F. *peindre*]

paint·brush (péintbrʌʃ) *n.* a brush of bristle, hair or fiber for applying paint

painted lady *Vanessa cardui,* a common orange butterfly with black and white spots

painted printed circuit (*electr.*) an integrated circuit painted or printed with conductive paint

paint·er (péintǝr) *n.* a rope attached to the bow of a boat and used to tie it up to a stake or ring on shore or to a towing vessel [origin unknown]

painter *n.* an artist who paints pictures ‖ an artisan who applies paint to walls etc. as a profession [A.F. *peintour*]

paint·er·ly (péintǝrli:) *adj.* of a style of painting that emphasizes color, tone and texture rather than line

paint-in (péintin) *n.* a cooperative volunteer venture to paint what requires painting

paint·ing (péintiŋ) *n.* a picture produced by applying paint to a surface ‖ the act or art of making such pictures

pair (peǝr) **1.** *pl.* **pairs, pair** *n.* a set of two things of the same kind, *a pair of laces* ‖ a single unit made up of two corresponding parts, *a pair of pliers* ‖ a thing consisting of two complementary parts, *a pair of pajamas* ‖ two persons associated together, e.g. a husband and wife, two friends, partners or dancers ‖ two persons of opposing views in a legislative body etc. who agree mutually not to record their votes on some issue ‖ either of these persons, or their agreement ‖ two playing cards of the same denomination ‖ two horses in harness **2.** *v.t.* to join (two people or things) in a pair ‖ to divide or arrange into groups of two ‖ *v.i.* to form a pair ‖ (with 'with') to agree with (a member of opposite views) that neither will vote **to pair off** to divide (members of a group) into pairs ‖ to join (two people or things) in a pair ‖ (of two people or things in a larger group) to form a pair [F. *paire*]

pair bond (*anthropology*) a monogamous union —**pair-bonding** *n.*

paired-as·so·ci·ate learning (péǝrdǝsóuʃi:tlǝrniŋ) a system of learning of analogous units in pairs to speed recall, esp. in the study of languages

pair of binoculars binoculars

pair of scales a simple beam balance

pair of virginals a virginal

pair production the total and simultaneous transformation of a photon into an electron and a positron by interaction with the electric field of a nucleus

pai·sa (páisǝ) *pl.* **pai·se** (páisei) *n.* a monetary unit of India, one hundredth of a rupee ‖ a monetary unit of Pakistan, one hundredth of a rupee ‖ a coin worth 1 paisa [Hindi]

Pais·ley (péizli:) a town (pop. 94,025) in Renfrew, Scotland, adjoining Glasgow, a thread-spinning center since the early 18th-c. Abbey (15th c.)

pais·ley (péizli:) *adj.* of a soft woolen material printed usually in rich colors with an elaborate abstract pattern having a characteristic teardrop-shaped motif ‖ of this pattern ‖ designating a garment, esp. a shawl, of this material [PAISLEY, Scotland]

pa·ja·mas, *Br.* **py·jam·as** (pǝdʒáməz) *pl. n.* a loose-fitting sleeping garment consisting of jacket and trousers, the latter suspended by a cord or elastic around the waist ‖ loose silk or cotton trousers worn by men and women Moslems in Eastern countries [Hind. *pajama, paijama* fr. Pers. *pae,* foot, *leg+jamah,* clothing]

Pak·i·stan (pækistæn, pákistan) a republic in S. Asia, (area 310,404 sq. miles, pop. 84,580,000) Capital: Islamabad. Pakistan controls the northern and eastern portions (Azad Kashmir) of Kashmir. People: *INDIA (subcontinent). Languages: English, Urdu. Religion: Moslem (official). Pakistan is 19% cultivated and 3% forest. The Hindu Kush, Pamirs and E. Himalayas cross the far north. Highest peak: Tirich Mir (26,263 ft) in the Hindu Kush. The west (former Baluchistan and Northwest Frontier Province) is a partly desert plateau, mainly 1,500–6,000 ft, joining that of Afghanistan with mountain ranges running mainly north-south (*SALT RANGE, *SULAIMAN RANGE). River valleys lead to the great passes: the Khyber, Bolan and Gumal. The east (former Punjab and Sind) is a fertile alluvial plain (Indus, Jhelum, Chenab and Sutlej Rivers, *INDUS) with waste areas along the Indian frontier (*THAR). Average summer and winter temperatures (F.): Quetta (plateau) 78° and 40°, plains 87° and 62°. Rainfall: Quetta 10 ins, plains 20 ins, mountains 40 ins. Livestock: cattle, water buffaloes, poultry, sheep, goats, camels. Crops: cereals, cotton, sugarcane, rape, mustard, fruit, tobacco. Minerals and other resources: coal, chromite, gypsum, oil, natural gas, bauxite, sulfur, limestone, iron ore, salt. Manufactures and industries: textiles, cotton, jute, chemicals, steel, oil refining, carpets, newsprint, paper, cigarettes, tanning, embroidery, pottery, glass, aluminum, cement, jute milling, hydroelectricity. Exports: raw jute, jute manufactures, raw cotton, raw wool, fish, hides and skins, cotton textiles, wheat, rice. Imports: machinery, iron and steel, wheat, oil and fuels, rice, chemicals, metals, vehicles. Chief port: Karachi. There are three universities. Monetary unit: Pakistani rupee (divided into 100 paisa). HISTORY. Pakistan was formed (1947) from the predominantly Moslem parts of India, as a result of the campaign led by Jinnah and the Moslem League. The partition was followed by riots in which thousands were killed. Several million Hindu refugees fled to India, and as many Moslems migrated from India to Pakistan. The newly formed dominion was at war with India over the status of Kashmir (1947–9) until the U.N. imposed a cease-fire. Pakistan struggled against economic difficulties and food shortages. It joined the South East Asia Treaty Organization (1954) and the Central Treaty Organization (1955). It became a republic within the Commonwealth (1956) but its constitution was suspended (1958) after a military coup and Ayub Khan assumed the presidency. A new constitution (1962) provided for a presidential form of government. The longstanding dispute with India over Kashmir broke briefly into open war (1965). Anarchy spread (Mar. 1969) through wide areas esp. of E. Pakistan. Ayub Khan resigned as president in favor of Gen. Yahya Khan. In 1971 the army put down an insurrection by partisans claiming independence for the eastern region. The influx into India of millions of refugees contributed to the outbreak (Dec. 1971) of a new conflict between India and Pakistan. The defeat of the Pakistani army led to the proclamation of a republic under the name Bangladesh (Free Bengal) in the territory comprising E. Pakistan. Yahya Khan resigned and was succeeded by Ali Bhutto. Under a third constitution (1973) Bhutto became prime minister of Pakistan until the army seized control again (1977). Gen. Zia ul-Haq became president (1978), and Bhutto was arrested and hanged. In an Islamic revival, a new series of laws was passed (1979) based on Islamic tenets, and the Islamization was endorsed by referendum (1984). The constitution was amended (1985) to strengthen Zia's powers and allow him to appoint the prime minister. An influx of over 3,000,000 Afghan refugees burdened Pakistan's economy and strained its relations with the U.S.S.R.

Pak·i·stan·i (pækistǽni:, pǝkistúni:) **1.** *n.* a native or inhabitant of Pakistan **2.** *adj.* of or from Pakistan

pal (pæl) **1.** *n.* (*pop.*) a close friend, buddy **2.** *v.i. pres. part.* **pal·ling** *past* and *past part.* **palled** (*pop.,* with 'up') to become a pal or pals ‖ (*pop.,* with 'around') to be together as pals [Romany (Eng. use)=brother, buddy]

pal·ace (pǽlis) *n.* a large, often ornate residence of an emperor, king, pope etc. ‖ (esp. *Br.*) an archbishop's or bishop's residence ‖ a large mansion ‖ a large, often ornate place of public entertainment [O.F. *palais, paleis*]

pal·a·din (pǽlǝdin) *n.* (*hist.*) one of the 12 peers of Charlemagne's court ‖ (*rhet.*) a hero or champion [F. fr. Ital.]

palaeobotany *PALEOBOTANY

Palaeocene *PALEOCENE

palaeographer *PALEOGRAPHFR

palaeographic *PALEOGRAPHIC

palaeography *PALEOGRAPHY

palaeolith *PALEOLITH

Pa·lae·ol·o·gus (peili:ólǝgǝs) a dynasty which ruled the Byzantine Empire (1261–1453). It was founded by Michael VIII, and ended with Constantine XI

palaeontologic *PALEONTOLOGIC

palaeontologist *PALEONTOLOGIST

palaeontology *PALEONTOLOGY

Palaeozoic *PALEOZOIC

Pa·la·mas (palamás), Kostas (1859–1943), Greek nationalist poet. His chief works include 'Hymn to Athena' (1889), 'Twelve Books of the Gipsy' (1907), 'The King's Flute' (1910)

pal·an·quin, pal·an·keen (pælǝnkí:n) *n.* a covered litter or couch carried on poles by four or six bearers and used in parts of the Far East [Port. *palanquim* fr. E. Ind.]

CONCISE PRONUNCIATION KEY: (a) æ, c*a*t; ɑ, c*a*r; ɔ f*aw*n; ei, sn*a*ke. **(e)** e, h*e*n; i:, sh*ee*p; iǝ, d*ee*r; ɛǝ, b*ea*r. **(i)** i, f*i*sh; ai, t*i*ger; ǝ:, b*i*rd. **(o)** o, *o*x; au, c*ow*; ou, g*oa*t; u, p*oo*r; ɔi, r*oy*al. **(u)** ʌ, d*u*ck; u, b*u*ll; u:, g*oo*se; ǝ, b*a*cillus; ju:, c*u*be. x, lo*ch*; θ, *th*ink; ð, bo*th*er; z, *Z*en; ʒ, cor*s*age; dʒ, sava*g*e; ŋ, ora*ng*utang; j, *y*ak; ʃ, *f*ish; tʃ, fe*tch*; 'l, rabb*l*e; 'n, redd*en*. Complete pronunciation key appears inside front cover.

palatability

Pali

pal·at·a·bil·i·ty (pælətəbíliti:) *n.* the quality or state of being palatable

pal·at·a·ble (pǽlətəb'l) *adj.* pleasant to taste ‖ pleasant or acceptable to the mind, *even friendly criticism can be far from palatable* **pál·at·a·bly** *adv.* [PALATE]

pal·a·tal (pǽlət'l) **1.** *adj.* pertaining to the palate ‖ (*phon.*) of a sound made with the front of the tongue raised against the hard palate **2.** *n.* (*phon.*) a sound so made

pal·a·tal·i·za·tion (pælət'lizéifən) *n.* the quality or state of being palatalized ‖ an instance of this **pál·a·tal·ize** *pres. part.* **pal·a·tal·iz·ing** *past* and *past part.* **pal·a·tal·ized** *v.t.* (*phon.*) to produce (a sound) with the front of the tongue against or near the hard palate [F.]

pal·ate (pǽlit) *n.* the roof of the mouth, separating the mouth cavity from the nasal cavity ‖ the sense of taste, *pleasing to the palate* [fr. L. *palatum*]

pa·la·tial (pəléifəl) *adj.* having the size, magnificence etc. of a palace [fr. L. *palatium*, palace]

pa·lat·i·nate (pəlǽt'neit, pəlǽt'nit) *n.* (*hist.*) the land ruled by a count palatine **the Palatinate** (*hist.*) either of two regions of Germany which together composed (1356) an electorate of the Holy Roman Empire. Both were attached to Bavaria (late 18th c.). The Rhine Palatinate (on the middle Rhine) is now in Rhineland-Palatinate, the Upper Palatinate on the Czechoslovakian border, in Bavaria [PALATINE]

pal·a·tine (pǽlətain) **1.** *n.* (*hist.*) a medieval overlord having sovereign privileges within his domain **the Palatine** the Palatine ‖ one of the seven hills of Rome **2.** *adj.* (used postpositively) having royal privileges, e.g. (*Br.*) the counties of Chester, Durham and Lancaster ‖ (used postpositively) having the privileges of a palatine ‖ of or pertaining to a palatinate [F. *palatin, palatine* fr. L. *palatinus*, belonging to the imperial palace]

pal·a·tine *adj.* (*anat.*) palatal ‖ designating either of two bones that form the hard palate [F. *palatin, palatine* fr. L. *palatum*, palate]

pa·lav·er (pəlǽvər, pəlávər) **1.** *n.* a long-drawn-out conferring or bargaining, esp. in tribal custom ‖ (*pop.*) any wordy discussion ‖ flowery, ingratiating language **2.** *v.i.* to engage in palaver or a palaver [Port. *palavra*, a word]

Pa·la·wan (pəláwan) the western-most island (area 4,550 sq. miles, pop. 236,635) of the Philippines with a central mountain range rising to 6,839 ft: manganese mines

pa·laz·zo pants (pəlátsou) *n.* women's pants with very wide legs, esp. for pajamas

pale (peil) *n.* a length of wood driven into the ground, with a pointed upper end, used with others in a fence ‖ an enclosed district or territory ‖ (*heraldry*) a vertical stripe dividing the shield into two halves **the Pale** (*hist.*) an area of varying extent around Dublin, Ireland, under English rule (14th–16th cc.) ‖ (*hist.*) an area around Calais, France, under English control (1346–1558) **beyond the pale** socially unacceptable [F. *pal*]

pale *adj.* lacking intensity of color or of illumination, *pale moonlight* ‖ (of complexion) of a whitish color [O.F. *palle, pale*]

pale *pres. part.* **pal·ing** *past* and *past part.* **paled** *v.i.* to become pale ‖ to lose importance or quality, esp. by contrast, *her beauty pales, next to yours* ‖ *v.t.* to make pale [fr. O.F. *palir*, F. *pâlir*]

pa·le·a (péili:ə) *pl.* **pa·le·ae** (péili:i:) *n.* a small bract on the base of a floret of a composite flower ‖ the inner chaffy bract in the flower of a grass ‖ the scaly growth of the epidermis in a fern [L.=chaff]

pale·face (péilfeis) *n.* a white-skinned person (supposed American Indian name for a non-Indian)

Pa·lem·bang (pɑlembáŋ) the chief city (pop. 582,961) and trade center of S. Sumatra, Indonesia, a river port 56 miles from the South China Sea: metallurgy, shipbuilding. University (1960)

Pa·len·ci·a (pəlénsi:ə) a province (area 3,256 sq. miles, pop. 186,512) of N. Spain (*OLD CASTILE, *LEÓN)

Pa·len·que (pəlénke) a town in Chiapas, Mexico. It was an important center of Mayan civilization, discovered in 1773

pa·le·o·bot·a·ny, pa·lae·o·bot·a·ny (peili:oubót·'ni:, pæli:oubót'ni:) *n.* the botany of fossil plants and plant impressions [fr. Gk *palaios*, ancient+BOTANY]

Pa·le·o·cene, Pa·lae·o·cene (péili:əsi:n, pæli:ə-si:n) *adj.* (*geol.*) of the earliest epoch or

series of the Tertiary (*GEOLOGICAL TIME) **the Paleocene, the Palaeocene** the Paleocene epoch or series of rocks [fr. Gk *palaios*, ancient+*kainos*, new]

pa·le·o·e·col·o·gy (peili:ouikólədʒi:) *n.* study of the ecology of past geological eras based on the analysis of fossils

pa·le·og·ra·pher, pa·lae·og·ra·pher (peili:ógrəfər, pæli:ógrəfər) *n.* a specialist in paleography

pa·le·o·graph·ic, pa·lae·o·graph·ic (peili:ə-grǽfik, pæli:əgrǽfik) *adj.* pertaining to paleography

pa·le·og·ra·phy, pa·lae·og·ra·phy (peili:ógrəfi:, pæli:ógrəfi:) *n.* the science of deciphering ancient manuscripts or inscriptions [fr. Mod. L. *palaeographia* fr. Gk *palaios*, ancient+*graphos*, written]

pa·le·o·lith, pa·lae·o·lith (péili:əliθ, pæli:əliθ) *n.* an unpolished chipped stone implement of the second period of the Stone Age. **Pa·le·o·lith·ic, Pa·lae·o·líth·ic** *adj.* of the second period of the Stone Age, characterized by the use of paleoliths. The Paleolithic period, which succeeded the Eolithic and preceded the Mesolithic, began with man's first certain attempts to shape tools and ended (in Europe) c. 8000 B.C. It is divided into epochs of cultural development: Abbevillian, Acheulean, Mousterian, Aurignacian and Magdalenian [fr. Gk *palaios*, ancient+*lithos*, stone]

pa·le·on·to·log·ic, pa·lae·on·to·log·ic (péili:ɒntəlódʒik, pæli:ɒntəlódʒik) *adj.* pertaining to paleontology **pa·le·on·to·lóg·i·cal, pá·lae·on·to·lóg·i·cal** *adj.*

pa·le·on·tol·o·gist, pa·lae·on·tol·o·gist (peili:-əntólədʒist, pæli:əntólədʒist) *n.* a specialist in paleontology

pa·le·on·tol·o·gy, pa·lae·on·tol·o·gy peili:ən-tólədʒi:, pæli:əntólədʒi:) *n.* the branch of geology concerned with the study of the fossil remains of animal and plant life of past geological periods [fr. Gk *palaios*, ancient+*onta* pl. of *on*, being+*logos*, word]

Pa·le·o·si·ber·i·an (peili:ousaibíəri:ən) *n.* a Siberian aborigine of an indeterminable racial classification

Pa·le·o·zo·ic, Pa·lae·o·zo·ic (peili:əzóuik, pæli:-əzóuik) *adj.* of the era of geological history between the Mesozoic and the Precambrian, characterized by the development of invertebrates and the appearance of reptiles, amphibians and seed-bearing plants (*GEOLOGICAL TIME) **the Paleozoic, the Palaeozoic** this era [fr. Gk *palaios*, ancient+*zōē*, life]

Pa·ler·mo (pəlɛ́ərmou, pəlɛ́:rmou) the capital (pop. 673,200) and chief port of Sicily, Italy, in the northwest. Industries: shipbuilding, metallurgy, chemicals, food processing, wine, cork, tourism. Norman palace, Byzantine mosaics, churches and cathedral (11th–12th cc.), Renaissance and 18th-c. monuments. University (1779)

Pal·es·tine (pǽlistain) a region on the eastern shore of the Mediterranean, now included in Israel. It is the Holy Land for Jews (as the land promised them by God) and for Christians (as the birthplace and home of Jesus Christ), and is a place of pilgrimage for Moslems. Originally referred to in the Old Testament as Canaan, it developed a pastoral economy (4th millennium B.C.), and was conquered (c. 1468 B.C.) by Egypt. After several other invasions, Egypt regained control (c. 1300 B.C.), but Philistines settled on the coast, Aramaeans in N. Syria and Israelites in the hill country (c. 1300–1000 B.C.). In the face of the Philistine menace, the Israelite tribes united under Saul, David and Solomon (c. 1040–c. 932 B.C.), but split (c. 932 B.C.) into two kingdoms, Israel in the north and Judah in the south. The former fell (c. 722 B.C.) to the Assyrians under Sargon II, and the latter was conquered (586 B.C.) by the Babylonians under Nebuchadnezzar II. The whole area was conquered by Cyrus II of Persia (539 B.C.) and by Alexander the Great (333 B.C.). Attempts to impose Hellenism provoked the revolt of the Maccabees (c. 168–142 B.C.), after which the Jews obtained political independence (142–63 B.C.) until occupied by the Romans under Pompey. During the reign (37–4 B.C.) of the Roman puppet Herod, Christ was born in Bethlehem. Increasing Roman control provoked a Jewish revolt (66 A.D.), the destruction of the Temple (70 A.D.) and the expulsion of the Jews from Judaea. Palestine became a Roman province and, after 330, part of the Byzantine Empire. It fell to the Arabs (638), and despite the Crusades

(1096–1270) remained under Moslem influence, being conquered (1516) by the Ottoman Turks. It continued under their rule until 1918, despite a brief invasion (1799) by Napoleon and Egyptian occupation (1831–40) under Ibrahim Pasha. The growth of Zionism (1890s) led to Jewish colonization from Europe. Turkish rule was ended by the British invasion (1917–18) under Allenby, aided by Lawrence. The Balfour Declaration (1917) established Palestine as the site of a national home for the Jews, and aroused bitter Arab opposition. Palestine became a British mandate (1920), but hostilities soon broke out between the Jews and Arabs. Jewish immigration increased (1930s) as a result of persecution in Europe and, despite a British attempt to limit it (1939), continued to grow during the 2nd world war. The U.N. recommended partition between the Arabs and Jews, but both sides refused (1947). The British mandate ended (May 14, 1948), and the State of Israel was proclaimed. After war (1948–9) between Israel and some states of the Arab League, Israel greatly increased her territory, Jerusalem was divided, Jordan acquired part of Palestine west of the Jordan and the Gaza Strip was occupied by Egypt. After the lightning third Israeli-Arab war (June 1967) Israel occupied Jordanian Palestine west of the Jordan as well as the Gaza Strip, while Jerusalem was reunited. The UN General Assembly reaffirmed the Palestinians' right to self-determination and national sovereignty (1974), and Jordan renounced its claims by signing the Rabat resolution proclaiming the Palestine Liberation Organization (PLO) the sole legitimate representative of the Palestinian people. None of the programs or strategies offered or advocated has provided a solution to the problem of a homeland for the Palestinians and many still live in refugee camps

Palestine Liberation Organization (pǽlistainlibəréifənɔrgənizéifən) (*abbr.* PLO) an organization composed of several Palestinian groups attempting to 'liberate' Palestine from what they view as an illegitimate Israeli state. Formed (1964) to represent Palestinian Arabs, it considers itself their political and military arm. Its charter vests supreme policy-making authority in the Palestine National Council. It was proclaimed sole legitimate representative of the Palestinian people by the Arab states (1974) and was recognized by the U.N. General Assembly as the 'representative of the Palestinian people.' Yasir Arafat became PLO chairman in 1969, but since 1983 the organization has been divided into pro- and anti-Arafat factions, the latter largely backed by Syria. Expelled from Jordan (1971), PLO forces established themselves in Lebanon, whence they launched attacks on Israel. Driven from Beirut (1982) by the Israeli army, they scattered throughout the Arab world. In 1985, Arafat and Jordan's King Hussein announced that the PLO would accept a negotiated settlement of the Arab-Israeli dispute, but Israel continued to refuse to negotiate with the PLO and the violence escalated. The PLO continued to be linked to and take credit for numerous terrorist activities worldwide

Pa·le·stri·na (pælistrí:nə), Giovanni Pierluigi da (c. 1525–94), Italian composer. He is best known for his noble polyphonic sacred choral works, including the 'Missa Papae Marcelli' (Mass dedicated to Pope Marcellus), many motets, a 'Stabat Mater' etc.

pal·ette (pǽlit) *n.* a small board on which a painter mixes his colors ‖ the range of colors used by a particular artist or for a particular picture ‖ (*armor*) one of the rounded iron plates at the armpit [F. dim. of *pale*, thin board]

palette knife an artist's thin, flexible knife used for mixing colors, cleaning the palette, and often for applying the paint

Pa·ley (péili:), William (1743–1805), English theologian whose 'Principles of Moral and Political Philosophy' (1785) and 'View of the Evidences of Christianity' (1794) had great popular success. His latitudinarianism was also expressed in 'Natural Theology' (1802)

pal·frey (pólfri:) *pl.* **pal·freys** *n.* (*hist.*) a small saddle horse, esp. for a lady [O.F. *palefrei*]

Pa·li (páli:) *n.* the old Indic canonical language, in which the early Buddhist literature was written. Pali has died out in India but survives in Burma and Thailand as a religious and literary language [fr. Skr. *pāli-bhāsā*, language of the canonical texts]

CONCISE PRONUNCIATION KEY: **(a)** æ, c*a*t; ɑ, c*a*r; ɔ, f*aw*n; ei, sn*a*ke. **(e)** e, h*e*n; i:, sh*ee*p; iə, d*ee*r; ɛə, b*ea*r. **(i)** i, f*i*sh; ai, t*i*ger; ə:, b*i*rd. **(o)** o, *o*x; au, c*ow*; ou, g*oa*t; u, p*oo*r; ɔi, r*oy*al. **(u)** ʌ, d*u*ck; u, b*u*ll; u:, g*oo*se; ə, *ba*cillus; ju:, c*u*be. x, lo*ch*; θ, *th*ink; ð, bo*th*er; z, *Z*en; ʒ, cor*s*age; dʒ, sava*ge*; ŋ, ora*ng*utang; j, *y*ak; ʃ, *f*ish; tʃ, fe*tch*; 'l, rabb*le*; 'n, redd*en*. Complete pronunciation key appears inside front cover.

pal·i·mo·ny (pǽləmouni:) *n.* settlement payment awarded to a separated partner of an unmarried couple that has lived together in division of assets or for maintenance; from the Lee Marvin-Michele Triola case

pal·imp·sest (pǽlimpsest) *n.* a parchment or tablet which has been reused after previous writing has been erased ‖ a manuscript on such a parchment or tablet [fr. L. *palimpsestus* fr. Gk *palin,* again+*psestos* fr. *psēn,* to rub smooth]

pal·in·drome (pǽlindroum) *n.* a word, sentence etc. which reads the same backward and forward (e.g. 'Madam I'm Adam') [fr. Gk *palindromos,* running back again]

pal·ing (péiliŋ) *n.* a fence made of pales ‖ pales collectively

pal·in·gen·e·sis (pælindʒénisis) *n.* (*biol.*) recapitulation ‖ metempsychosis ‖ regeneration ‖ (*geol.*) re-formation of granitic magma by melting and recrystallization [fr. Gk *palin,* again+*genesis,* origin]

pal·i·node (pǽlinoud) *n.* a poem in which a previous poem, usually satirical, is retracted ‖ a recantation [fr. L. *palinodia* fr. Gk *palin,* again+*ōdē,* song]

pal·i·sade (pæliséid) **1.** *n.* a fence of wooden or iron pales ‖ (*mil. hist.*) a strong, sharply pointed wooden stake set with many others in a row, upright or oblique, as a defense work ‖ a fence made of such stakes **2.** *v.t. pres. part.* **pal·i·sad·ing** *past and past part.* **pal·i·sad·ed** to enclose or fortify with palisades [F. *palissade*]

palisade parenchyma a tissue of the mesophyll usually on the upper side of the leaf blade consisting of a regular array of thin-walled cylindrical cells with abundant chloroplasts (cf. SPONGY PARENCHYMA)

Pa·lis·sy (pæli:si:), Bernard (1510–c. 1589), French potter. His most striking achievement was with wares ornamented with colored subjects in high relief

pall (pɔl) *v.i.* to cease to be interesting or attractive [perh. fr. APPALL]

pall *n.* a large piece of cloth, draped over a coffin or tomb ‖ something that casts gloom over an area by covering it, *a pall of smoke* ‖ (*eccles.*) a linen-covered piece of cardboard used to cover the chalice ‖ (*eccles.*) a pallium ‖ (*heraldry*) a bearing representing the front half of a Church dignitary's pallium [O.E. *pæll,* a cloth fr. L.]

Pal·la·di·an (pəléidiːən) *adj.* (*archit.*) in or of the style of Andrea Palladio

pal·lad·ic (pəlǽdik, pəléidik) *adj.* of compounds of tetravalent palladium

Pal·la·dio (pallǽdjɔ), Andrea (Andrea di Pietro, 1508–80), Italian Renaissance architect. He was largely responsible for the revival of classical architecture, first in Italy, and then throughout Europe. His principal achievement was his series of great mansions which set the style for later building in Europe and the U.S.A. His 'I quattro libri dell'architettura' (1570) has been reprinted many times

pal·la·di·um (pəléidiːəm) *n.* a metallic element (symbol Pd, at. no. 46, at. mass 106.4) resembling and occurring with platinum, used as a catalyst and in some alloys **pal·la·dous** (pəléidəs) *adj.* of compounds of divalent palladium [Mod. L. after *Pallas,* name of an asteroid]

Pal·las (pǽləs) one of the names of the Greek goddess Athena

pall·bear·er (pɔ́lbɛərər) *n.* one of the little group of men who carry the coffin at a funeral or who are its closest attendants

pal·let (pǽlit) *n.* (*heraldry*) an ordinary resembling a pale but having half its width [dim. of PALE n.]

pallet *n.* a narrow, hard bed ‖ a mattress stuffed with straw [M.E. *pailet* fr. F. *paille,* straw]

pallet *n.* a potter's flat-bladed wooden tool used in shaping clay ‖ a small flat-bladed knife used to transfer gold leaf to the object being gilded ‖ (*mach.*) a click or pawl which engages with the teeth of a ratchet wheel to convert one kind of motion into another, esp. in a clock or watch ‖ a portable platform used to haul materials to be stored, transported etc. ‖ a valve regulating the airflow to an organ pipe [F. *palette,* dim. of *pale,* spade, blade]

pallet truck a mechanical hoist for transporting a pallet (platform)

pal·liasse, pail·lasse (pǽljæs) *n.* a thin hard mattress stuffed with straw [F. *paillasse*]

pal·li·ate (pǽlieit) *pres. part.* **pal·li·at·ing** *past and past part.* **pal·li·at·ed** *v.t.* to cause (an evil) to seem less than it is, or disguise the gravity of (a fault) with excuses etc. ‖ to relieve (pain or

disease) but not cure it [fr. L. *palliatus,* cloaked]

pal·li·a·tion (pæliéiʃən) *n.* a palliating or being palliated ‖ something that palliates [F.]

pal·li·a·tive (pǽliəitiv, pǽliətiv) **1.** *adj.* serving to palliate **2.** *n.* something that palliates [F. fem. of *palliatif,* serving to conceal or cloak]

pal·lid (pǽlid) *adj.* (e.g. of complexion) abnormally pale ‖ lacking brightness or warmth of color [fr. L. *pallidus*]

pal·li·um (pǽliːəm) *pl.* **pal·li·a** (pǽliːə), **pal·li·ums** *n.* (*eccles.*) a circular white woolen band with pendants of white wool at front and back, worn by high Church dignitaries ‖ (*zool.*) the mantle of a mollusk or of a bird ‖ (*anat.*) the cortex of the brain [L.]

pal·lor (pǽlər) *n.* unusual paleness of the skin [L.]

palm (pɑm) **1.** *n.* the inner part of the hand, between wrist and fingers ‖ the corresponding part of a glove ‖ a flat extension of an implement, e.g. the blade of a paddle ‖ (*naut.*) the fluke of an anchor ‖ the broad flat part of an antler **to have an itching palm** to have a greedy desire for money **to hold** (or **have**) **someone in the palm of one's hand** to have someone at one's mercy **2.** *v.t.* to conceal in the palm, esp. for the purpose of cheating, *to palm a card* **to palm something off** (often with 'on') to get rid of something by inducing someone to take it [M.E. *paume* fr. F.]

palm *n.* a member of *Palmae* (or *Palmaceae*), order *Palmales,* a family of monocotyledonous, largely tropical trees and shrubs, generally having a tall trunk with no branches and a crown of large leaves ‖ the leaf of one of these trees ‖ one of these leaves or a substitute carried on Palm Sunday ‖ (*rhet.*) victory or success, or a token symbolizing this [O.E. *palm, palma, palme* fr. L. *palma*]

Pal·ma (pǽlma), Ricardo (1833–1919), Peruvian writer, the author of 'Tradiciones peruanas' (1872–1910), a leading account of the colonial era. He is known as the creator of a new genre, the tradición (historical anecdote)

Pal·ma (pǽlma) (*Span.* Palma de Mallorca) the capital (pop. 319,620) of the Balearic Is, Spain, a port and resort on S.W. Majorca. Catalan Gothic cathedral (13th–14th cc.)

pal·mar (pǽlmər, pǽlmɑr) *adj.* (*anat.*) of or in the palm

palm·a·ro·ta·tion (pɑmaroutéiʃən) *n.* massage technique pressing whole hand firmly on flesh and moving circularly

pal·ma·ry (pǽlmər:, pǽlmɑri:) *adj.* (*rhet.*) worthy of the palm of victory [fr. L. *palmarius*]

Palmas *LAS PALMAS

pal·mate (pǽlmit, pǽlmeit, pǽlmit, pǽlmeit) *adj.* shaped like a hand spread open, esp. (*bot.,* of a leaf) divided into lobes arising from a common center ‖ (*zool.*) having the toes webbed, as in most aquatic birds **pal·mat·ed** *adj.* [fr. L. *palmatus*]

Pal·ma Vec·chio (pǽlmavékkjɔ) (Jacopo Negretti, c. 1480–1528), Venetian painter. He excelled as a colorist and is chiefly known for his religious paintings and landscape backgrounds

Pal·mer (pǽmər), Alexander Mitchell (1872–1936), U.S. Attorney General (1919–21) under President Wilson. Palmer ordered the mass arrests of alleged subversives that are known as the 'Palmer raids'

Palmer, Samuel (1805–81), English painter and engraver. He is best known for his visionary landscapes, which show the influence of William Blake

palm·er (pǽmər) *n.* (*hist.*) a pilgrim carrying a palm leaf in token of having visited the Holy Land ‖ (*hist.*) an itinerant begging monk [A.F. *palmer, paumer*]

Palmer Archipelago (formerly Antarctic Archipelago) an island group, part of the Falkland Islands Dependencies, between South America and the Antarctic

Palmer Peninsula the southern part of the Antarctic Peninsula

Palm·er·ston (pǽmərstən), Henry John Temple, 3rd Viscount (1784–1865), British statesman. He entered parliament as a Tory (1807), joined the Whigs (1829), and was foreign secretary (1830–41 and 1846–51) and prime minister (1855–8 and 1859–65). A conservative in domestic policy, he supported liberal movements abroad, notably in Belgium (1830–1), Spain, Portugal (1832–4) and Italy (1858–61), and opposed French and Russian expansion in the Eastern Question. He brought the Crimean

War to a close, and maintained British neutrality in the American Civil War. His impulsive and high-handed approach to diplomacy brought him into conflict with his colleagues and Queen Victoria, as well as with foreign powers

Palmerston North an agricultural center (pop. 46,000) of S. North Island, New Zealand. University (1963)

palm·er·worm (pámərwə:rm) *n.* any of several caterpillars, esp. the larva of the moth *Dichomeris ligulellas,* which is very destructive to fruit trees

palm·et·to (pælmétou) *pl.* **pal·met·tos, pal·met·toes** *n.* any of several fan palms, esp. the cabbage palmetto and *Chamerops humilis,* the Mediterranean dwarf fan palm [Span. *palmito,* dim. of *palma,* palm]

palm·ist (pámist) *n.* a person who practices palmistry

palm·is·try (pámistri:) *n.* the practice or profession of foretelling a person's future or reading his character by interpreting the crease lines in the palm and other aspects of his hand [M.E. fr. *paume, palme,* palm]

pal·mit·ic acid (pælmítik, palmítik) a waxy crystalline solid acid, $C_{15}H_{31}COOH$, contained in palm oil and in most vegetable and animal fats [fr. F. *palmitique*]

pal·mi·tin (pǽlmitin) *n.* a glyceride of palmitic acid occurring in palm oil and other fats [F. *palmitine*]

palm kernel the seed of a palm yielding palm oil

palm oil a very sticky fat extracted from the fruit or seed of certain palms. The oil is a source of vitamin A, and is used in making soaps and for margarine, cosmetics, lubricants etc.

palm reader security device requiring personal identification with an encoded plastic card and the placement of the hand in a reader that scans its shape and size

palm sugar a coarse brown sugar made from palm sap

Palm Sunday the Sunday before Easter. It commemorates Christ's triumphal entry into Jerusalem, when the crowd strewed palm leaves in his path

palm wine the fermented sap of various palms, a very popular drink, esp. in parts of Africa

palm·y (pámi:) *comp.* **palm·i·er** *superl.* **palm·i·est** *adj.* of or like a palm (tree), or having many palms ‖ flourishing, prosperous, *palmy days*

Pal·my·ra (pælmáirə) an ancient city of Syria which flourished (1st c. B.C.–3rd c. A.D.) as an oasis on the trade routes across the Syrian desert and as the center of an empire stretching from Asia Minor to Egypt. It was conquered (273) by the Romans under Aurelian. The ruins include the great temple of Baal

pal·my·ra (pælmáirə) *n. Borassus flabellifer,* a fan palm much cultivated in India and Ceylon. It is used for thatch, matting, umbrellas, hats etc. and for lumber. Its sap is rich in sugar [older *palmeira* fr. Port.]

Pal·o·mar, Mount (pǽləmar) the site, in S.W. California, of an observatory containing a 200-inch reflecting telescope (1948)

pal·o·mi·no (pæləmí:nou) *pl.* **pal·o·mi·nos** *n.* a horse of a light tan or golden color with a whitish mane and tail [Span. adj.=of or like a dove]

palp (pælp) *n.* a palpus [F. *palpe* fr. L.]

pal·pa·bil·i·ty (pælpəbíliti:) *n.* the quality or state of being palpable ‖ something palpable

pal·pa·ble (pǽlpəb'l) *adj.* tangible, perceptible to the touch ‖ easily perceptible to the mind, obvious, *a palpable falsehood* **pál·pa·bly** *adv.* [fr. L.L. *palpabilis* fr. *palpare,* to touch gently]

pal·pal (pǽlpəl) *adj.* of the nature of or serving as a palpus

pal·pate (pǽlpeit) *adj.* (*zool.*) having a palpus [fr. PALPUS]

palpate *pres. part.* **pal·pat·ing** *past and past part.* **pal·pat·ed** *v.t.* to examine by feeling, esp. in medical examination **pal·pá·tion** *n.* [fr. L. *palpare* (*palpatus*), to touch gently]

pal·pe·bral (pǽlpəbrəl) *adj.* of, pertaining to or located on or near the eyelid [fr. L. *palpebra,* eyelid]

pal·pi·tate (pǽlpiteit) *pres. part.* **pal·pi·tat·ing** *past and past part.* **pal·pi·tat·ed** *v.i.* to tremble ‖ (of the heart) to throb rapidly and strongly [fr. L. *palpitare* (*palpitatus*)]

pal·pi·ta·tion (pælpitéiʃən) *n.* an irregular and violent heartbeat resulting from malfunction or from physical or emotional stress ‖ a trembling [fr. L. *palpitatio* (*palpitationis*)]

CONCISE PRONUNCIATION KEY: **(a)** æ, c*a*t; ɑ, c*a*r; ɔ f*aw*n; ei, sn*a*ke. **(e)** e, h*e*n; i:, sh*ee*p; iə, d*ee*r; ɛə, b*ea*r. **(i)** i, f*i*sh; ai, t*i*ger; ə:, b*i*rd. **(o)** o, *o*x; au, c*ow*; ou, g*oa*t; u, p*oo*r; ɔi, r*oy*al. **(u)** ʌ, d*u*ck; u, b*u*ll; u:, g*oo*se; ə, bacill*u*s; ju:, c*u*be. x, lo*ch*; θ, *th*ink; ð, b*o*ther; z, *Z*en; ʒ, cor*s*age; dʒ, sa*v*age; ŋ, ora*n*gutang; j, *y*ak; ʃ, *f*ish; tʃ, fe*tch*; 'l, rabb*le*; 'n, redd*en*. Complete pronunciation key appears inside front cover.

pal·pus (pǽlpəs) *pl.* **pal·pi** (pǽlpai) *n.* the maxillary or labial feeler of an insect, usually occurring in pairs ‖ a sensory appendage of a crustacean, worm etc. [L.=a feeler]

pal·sied (pɔ́lzi:d) *adj.* affected with palsy

pal·sy (pɔ́lzi:) *pl.* **pal·sies** *n.* (not used technically) paralysis, sometimes with shaking tremors [M.E *palesie, parlesie* fr. O.F. *paralisie* fr. L. fr. Gk]

pal·tri·ness (pɔ́ltri:nis) *n.* the quality of being paltry

pal·try (pɔ́ltri:) *comp.* **pal·tri·er** *superl.* **pal·tri·est** *adj.* trivial, petty, *a paltry sum* ‖ mean, despicable, *a paltry trick* [origin unknown]

pa·lu·dal (pəlú:d'l, pǽljəd'l) *adj.* of or pertaining to marshes ‖ (*med.*) malarial **pal·u·dism** (pǽljədizəm) *n.* malaria [fr. L. *palus (paludis)*, marsh]

pal·y (péili:) *adj.* (*heraldry*) (of a shield) divided into four or more vertical strips differing alternately in tint [fr. F. *palé*]

Pa·mirs, the (pəmíərz) a plateau, largely at 12,000–13,000 ft, with several peaks over 20,000 ft (*COMMUNISM, MT) covering most of Tadzhikistan, U.S.S.R. and the borders of China, Kashmir, Pakistan and Afghanistan. It is the center from which the Himalayas, Karakoram, Kunlun, Tien Shan and Hindu Kush extend

Pam·li·co Sound (pǽmlikou) an inlet (80 miles long, 8–30 miles wide) between the E. North Carolina mainland and island strips off the coast. It joins Albemarle Sound on the north

pam·pas (pǽmpəs) *pl. n.* treeless plains in South America, south of the Amazon, esp. the cattle-raising grasslands of E. central Argentina [Span. *pampa* fr. Quechua=plain]

pampas grass *Cortaderia selloana*, a South American grass with whitish silky panicles carried on stalks up to 12 ft high

pam·per (pǽmpər) *v.t.* to overindulge (someone), coddle [prob. fr. L.G.]

pam·phlet (pǽmflit) *n.* a small printed publication sewn or stitched as a paper-covered booklet, comprising an essay or treatise of a controversial, topical nature ‖ a small printed publication, often just a folder, containing informative literature **pam·phlet·eer 1.** *n.* a person who writes controversial pamphlets **2.** *v.i.* to write such pamphlets [M.E. *Pamphilet, Panflet* fr. *Pamphilus*, title of a 12th-c. L. amatory poem]

Pam·plo·na (pæmplóunə) the capital (pop. 167,762) of Navarra, Spain, and historical capital of Navarre. Industries: textiles, paper, mechanical engineering. Gothic cathedral (14th–15th cc.), citadel (16th c.). Famous bullfight festival (July)

Pan (pæn) (*Gk mythol.*) the god of flocks and herds, represented as a man having the legs of a goat and often a goat's horns and ears

pan (pæn) **1.** *n.* any of a number of metal containers of different shapes, used in cooking and baking ‖ any shallow, open receptacle of metal, earthenware or plastic, used for any of a variety of domestic purposes ‖ any container like this in shape, e.g. a vessel in which gold etc. is separated from gravel by washing ‖ a vessel for heating or evaporating ‖ one of the receptacles in a beam balance etc. ‖ a salt pan ‖ a layer of hardpan ‖ a flat expanse of ice floating in the sea, smaller than an ice floe ‖ (*mil.*) in air intercept, a code meaning the calling station has an urgent message to transmit concerning the safety of a ship, aircraft, or other vehicle, or of a person on board or within sight **2.** *v. pres. part.* **pan·ning** *past* and *past part.* **panned** *v.t.* to wash (gravel or sand bearing gold etc.) in a pan to separate the valuable particles from the rest ‖ to separate (gold etc.) from gravel or sand in this way ‖ (*pop.*) to criticize harshly (a play, concert etc.) ‖ *v.i.* to search for gold etc. by washing gravel or sand in a pan ‖ (esp. with 'out') to yield gold etc. when washed in this way ‖ (with 'out') to turn out (in some specified way), *it panned out poorly for him* ‖ (with 'out') to turn out well, *the project didn't pan out* [O.E. *panne, ponne*]

pan *pres. part.* **pan·ning** *past* and *past part.* **panned** *v.i.* to move a cinema or television camera to get a panoramic effect or to follow a moving object ‖ (of the camera) to be moved in this way ‖ *v.t.* to move (the camera) in this way [PANORAMA]

pan *n.* the leaf of the betel palm ‖ a preparation of betel nut, chewed as a masticatory in the East Indies [Hind. *pān*, betel leaf]

pan- *prefix* all ‖ completely [Gk *pan*, neut. of *pas*, all]

PAN *n.* peroxyacetyl nitrate, a pollutant ingredient of smog created by the action of sunlight on hydrocarbons and nitrogen oxides in the air

pan·a·ce·a (pænəsí:ə) *n.* a cure for all ills, a universal remedy [L. fr. Gk *panakeia*]

pa·nache (pənǽʃ) *n.* a tuft of feathers, esp. on the headdress or helmet ‖ bravura, swagger [F. fr. Ital. *pennacchio* fr. *penna*, feather]

Pan-Af·ri·can·ism (pænǽfrikənizəm) *n.* any of several 20th-c. movements among African states (esp. the Organization of African Unity) to promote African cooperation and unity, and to eliminate colonialism and white supremacy from Africa

Pan·a·ma (pǽnəmə) a republic (area incl. former Canal Zone 29,754 sq. miles, pop. 1,921,700) occupying the Isthmus of Panama (the narrowest part of Central America) with many offshore islands. Capital: Panama City. People: Mestizo (72%), with African (West Indian), white and Indian minorities (incl. 62,000 tribal Indians). Languages: Spanish, Indian languages, English. Religion: 95% Roman Catholic, 5% Protestant. The land is 3% cultivated and 7% pasture. The Central American cordillera runs the length of the country, sloping from 11,410 ft (Chiquirí) near Costa Rica and 7,000 ft on the Colombian border to low hills (500–1,500 ft) in the center, where the Panama Canal crosses. The Caribbean slope and coastal plains are jungle-covered. Agriculture and population are concentrated on the drier Pacific side (forest and savanna). Average temperatures (F.): coasts 87°, interior 66°. Rainfall: Colón 128 ins, N. Pacific coast 6 ins, Panama City 69 ins. Livestock: cattle, hogs, poultry, horses. Agricultural products: bananas, rice, sugarcane, corn, cocoa, hemp, abaca, coffee, coconuts. Forest products: mahogany, dyewoods. Mineral resources: gold, salt. Manufactures and industries: sugar, beer and spirits, cement, clothing, oil refining. Exports: bananas, shrimps, sugar, cocoa, coffee. Imports: manufactures, machinery, vehicles, food, chemicals, petroleum products. Panama's large merchant fleet is mainly foreign-owned. Ports: Panama City, Colón. University: Panama City (1935). Monetary unit: balboa (100 cents). HISTORY. The region was inhabited by Indian tribes when it was visited (1501) by a Spanish expedition. The isthmus was crossed (1513) by Balboa and became a vital link in the treasure route from Peru to Spain. It became part of the viceroyalty of Peru (1542) and of New Granada (1740), and shared the history of Colombia until Nov.3, 1903 when, with the encouragement of the U.S.A., it seized its independence from Spain. Panama immediately gave the U.S.A. permission to construct, use and control the Panama Canal. The canal was completed (1914) and provides a main source of revenue for Panama. A series of revolts and coups d'état have characterized Panama since 1940. Arnulfo Arias was three times (1941, 1949, 1968) deposed by the National Guard. José Remón, elected in 1952, was assassinated in 1955. Ernesto della Guardia (president 1956–60), Robert F. Chiari (president 1960–4), and Marco Robles (president 1964–8) governed constitutionally. Friction grew with the U.S.A. over the status of the Canal Zone. There were riots and agitation (1958, 1959) to fly the Panama flag alongside the U.S. flag in the Zone and to obtain jurisdiction of the canal from the U.S.A. A U.S. Congressional resolution (1960) opposed Panama's demand to fly its flag, but President Eisenhower allowed it to be displayed at one place in the Zone. Presidents John F. Kennedy and Roberto Chiari agreed (1962) that the flag could be flown throughout the Zone. Further anti-American riots in 1964 led Panama to suspend diplomatic relations with the U.S.A. Relations with the U.S. were resumed that same year and conferences were held to revise the Treaty of 1903. After the third dismissal of Arias, Panama was governed by a military junta, initially headed by Col. José M. Pinilla and then by Gen. Omar Torrijos, who remained Panama's most powerful political figure until his death (1981). He directed the promulgation of a new constitution (1972), which was amended (1978) to provide for the election of a president by the National Assembly. In 1983 major reforms provided for the popular election of the president. Aristides Royo (president 1978–82) was succeeded by Nicolás Ardito Ber

letta (1984–5), who resigned and was succeeded by Vice-President Eric Arturo Delvalle

pan·a·ma (pǽnəmə) *n.* a hat of fine material plaited from the dried young leaves of the jipijapa ‖ a machine-made imitation of this

Panama, Bay of *PANAMA, GULF OF

Panama Canal a ship canal (51 miles long) crossing central Panama, connecting the Atlantic and the Pacific. Transit time: 7–8 hours (through 6 pairs of locks). A French attempt under de Lesseps to build a canal (1881–9) had collapsed in bankruptcy. The U.S.A. negotiated a treaty (1903) with Panama, under which the U.S.A. obtained the right to build a canal and to occupy and control the Panama Canal Zone (5 miles on either side of the canal) in return for a payment of $100 million and an annuity of $250,000, raised by 1955 to $1,930,000. The canal was opened to shipping (1914). The U.S.A. and Panama agreed (1965) that a new treaty should recognize Panama's sovereignty over the Canal Zone, to be integrated in Panama, but negotiations were not completed until 1978, when two treaties were ratified by the U.S. Senate guaranteeing the canal's neutrality after the year 2000 and stipulating U.S. supervision of the canal, with increasing Panamanian participation, until 2000. At that time Panama assumes legal control. A new 36-mile sea-level canal, ten miles west of the present one, able to handle double the amount of shipping and to take ships of 150,000 tons, is in preparation

Panama City (*Span.* Panamá) the capital (pop. 467,000) of Panama, near the Pacific terminus of the Panama Canal. It was founded by Spaniards (1519). Industries: food processing, brewing, light manufactures. Cathedral (1760), university (1935)

Panama, Congress of a meeting called (1826) by Simón Bolívar in the hope of achieving solidarity among the nations of America. The congress was attended only by Colombia, Peru, Mexico, and Central America. It was the first and last of its kind

Panama disease a fungus disease of the banana characterized by withering of the leaves and the dying-off of the shoots

Panama, Gulf of a large inlet of the Pacific on the south coast of Panama. Its inner part is called the Bay of Panama and is the site of Panama City

Panama, Isthmus of the link (420 miles long) between North and South America, separating the Atlantic and Pacific Oceans

Pan-A·mer·i·can (pænəmérikən) *adj.* of, involving or relating to all the nations of North, Central and South America or their people

Pan-American Conference, Second a conference held (1901) in Mexico City, at which nine delegations, incl. the U.S.A., agreed that all future disputes would be settled peacefully

Pan-American Conference, Third a conference held (1906) in Rio de Janeiro. It was marked by a serious lack of harmony and by Latin American resentment of President Theodore Roosevelt's 'big stick' Corollary

Pan-American Congress *INTERNATIONAL CONFERENCE OF AMERICAN STATES, FIRST

Pan-American Highway an international road system running from Fairbanks, Alaska to Buenos Aires, Argentina, with branches to all Central and South American countries

Pan-A·mer·i·can·ism (pænəmérikənizəm) *n.* the movement to promote social, economic and political cooperation among all the states of the Americas (*PAN-AMERICAN UNION)

Pan-American Union an international agency established (1890) by the first Pan-American Conference (1889–90) to promote inter-American cooperation. It offers technical and information services to all the American republics, serves as the repository for inter-American documents, and promotes economic, social, judicial, and cultural relations. It became (1948) the general secretariat for the Organization of American States. Pan-American Day (Apr. 14) celebrates the anniversary of its founding

Pan-Ar·a·bism (pænǽrəbizəm) *n.* a movement to promote the political unity of the Arab peoples. It arose (early 20th c.) as a reaction to the Turkish-sponsored Pan-Turanism movement, and developed also as a reaction to British Zionist policy in Palestine. It gave rise to the formation of the Arab League (1945) and to attempts to form a United Arab Republic

Pa·nay (pɑnái) an island (area 4,446 sq. miles,

CONCISE PRONUNCIATION KEY: (**a**) æ, c*a*t; ɑ, c*a*r; ɔ f*aw*n; ei, sn*a*ke. (**e**) e, h*e*n; i:, sh*ee*p; iə, d*ee*r; ɛə, b*ea*r. (**i**) i, f*i*sh; ai, t*i*ger; ə:, b*i*rd. (**o**) o, *o*x; au, c*ow*; ou, g*oa*t; u, p*oo*r; ɔi, r*oy*al. (**u**) ʌ, d*u*ck; u, b*u*ll; u:, g*oo*se; ə, bacill*u*s; ju:, c*u*be. x, lo*ch*; θ, *th*ink; ð, bo*th*er; z, *Z*en; ʒ, cor*s*age; dʒ, sava*g*e; ŋ, ora*ng*utan*g*; j, *y*ak; ʃ, *f*ish; tʃ, fe*tch*; 'l, rabb*le*; 'n, redd*en*. Complete pronunciation key appears inside front cover.

pop. 2,144,544) of the central Philippines (Visayas), producing esp. rice. Chief town: Iloilo

pan·cake (pǽnkeik) **1.** *n.* a thin, flat cake made of batter cooked on a griddle, or in a pan ‖ (*wrestling*) maneuver in which an arm lock is placed over one of the opponent's arms and an attempt is made to grasp forearm or waist to pull opponent and twist for a backward fall **2.** *v. pres. part.* **pan·cak·ing** *past* and *past part.* **pan·caked** *v.i.* (*aviation*) to drop or land almost vertically though with the aircraft horizontal ‖ *v.t.* to cause (an aircraft) to do this

Pancake Day (*Br.*) Shrove Tuesday, when traditionally pancakes are eaten

Pan·cha·tan·tra (púntʃətántrə) a collection of didactic fables in Sanskrit of the 3rd or 4th c., still popular in India

Pan·chen Lama (pǽntʃən) *LAMA

pan·chro·mat·ic (pǽnkroumǽtik) *adj.* (of a photographic film) sensitive to all the wavelengths of the visible spectrum ‖ (of a lens) transmitting the whole of the visible spectrum

Pan·cras (pǽŋkrəs), St (*d.* 304), Roman martyr. According to legend, he was a boy of 14 when he was martyred. Feast: May 12

pan·cre·as (pǽŋkriəs) *n.* a large gland that in man lies behind the stomach. It consists of two portions, one secreting digestive juices which pass into the duodenum, the other secreting insulin which passes into the bloodstream (*ISLET OF LANGERHANS*) **pan·cre·at·ic** (pæŋkriːǽtik) *adj.* [Mod. L. fr. Gk *pankreas*, sweetbread]

pan·cre·a·tin (pǽŋkriːətin) *n.* any of several enzymes found in pancreatic juices, or a mixture of these ‖ a preparation containing such a mixture obtained from an animal's pancreas, for aiding digestion [fr. Gk *pankreas* (*pankreatos*), sweetbread]

pan·da (pǽndə) *n.* either of two mammals of fam. *Procyonidae*, related to the raccoon. *Aluropoda melanoleuca*, the giant panda, is a black and white bearlike animal of Tibet and S. China. *Ailurus fulgens*, of the Himalayas, has long, reddish-brown fur marked with black and white, and closely resembles the raccoon [perh. Nepalese]

pan·dect (pǽndekt) *n.* a complete code of laws **the Pandects** a summary of Roman civil law (530–3), forming part of Justinian I's 'Corpus juris civilis' [F. *pandecte* fr. L. fr. Gk *pan*, all+*dechesthai*, to receive]

pan·dem·ic (pændémik) *adj.* (of a disease) affecting a whole country, or the whole world (cf. ENDEMIC) [fr. Gk *pandēmos*, universal]

pan·de·mo·ni·um (pændəmóuniːəm) *n.* a state of utter confusion and uproar [fr. *Pandaemonium*, name for the capital of Hell, coined by Milton fr. Gk *pan*, all+*daimōn*, demon]

pan·der (pǽndər) **1.** *v.i.* (with 'to') to give active encouragement (to someone or something that should not be encouraged) or provide gratification (for someone or something that should not be gratified) **2.** *n.* a procurer for prostitutes ‖ someone who encourages the vices or weaknesses of another [M.E. *Pandare* fr. L. *Pandarus* fr. Gk *Pandaros*, one of the leaders in the Trojan War. In medieval romances he is the go-between for Troilus and Cressida]

pan·dit (pʌ́ndit) *n.* a Hindu learned in religion, laws and science [Hindi]

Pan·do·ra (pændɔ́rə, pændóurə) (*Gk mythol.*) the first woman, sent to earth as a punishment for Prometheus's crime of stealing fire from the gods. Zeus gave her a box which, when opened, let loose all human misfortunes, but hope remained in the bottom to comfort mankind

pane (pein) *n.* a single sheet of glass in a window, greenhouse etc. ‖ a division of a window etc. containing such a sheet of glass in a frame ‖ a flat side or edge of a many-sided object [F. *pan*, a piece of cloth]

pan·e·gyr·ic (pænidʒírik) **1.** *n.* a speech or writing eulogizing someone or something **2.** *adj.* having the nature of a panegyric **pan·e·gýr·i·cal** *adj.* **pan·e·gýr·ist** *n.* [F. *panégyrique* fr. L. fr. Gk *panēgurikos*, fit for a public assembly]

pan·el (pǽnˈl) **1.** *n.* a flat, rectangular piece of wood etc. forming part of a wall, door etc. but distinguished from the rest by being recessed, framed etc. ‖ a vertical strip of material let into or partially attached to a dress, skirt etc. as a structural or decorative element ‖ a thin board sometimes used instead of a canvas in oil painting ‖ a picture or photograph of much greater height than width ‖ a board etc. in which the controls or instruments of a machine etc. are set

‖ the padded lining of a saddle ‖ a pad used as a saddle ‖ a group of persons, usually experts, required to judge or give an answer, *a panel of jurors* **2.** *v.t. pres. part.* **pan·el·ing**, esp. *Br.* **pan·el·ling** *past* and *past part.* **pan·eled**, esp. *Br.* **pan·elled** to furnish with panels ‖ (*law*) to empanel **pán·el·ing**, esp. *Br.* **pán·el·ling** *n.* panels of wood applied to a wall or ceiling **pán·el·ist** *n.* a member of a panel (group of persons) [O.F.+piece of cloth]

panel code (*mil.*) prearranged code designed for visual communications, usu. between friendly units by making use of marking panels *also* **marking panel**

pang (pæŋ) *n.* a brief, keen spasm of pain ‖ a sudden mental or emotional pain, *pangs of conscience* [etym. doubtful]

Pan·gae·a (pændʒíːə) *n.* (*geol.*) a hypothetical single continent of the Triassic period (200 million yrs. ago); coined by Alfred Wegener

pan·gen·e·sis (pændʒénisis) *n.* a theory of heredity proposed by Darwin, that each cell of the body throws off particles (gemmules) into the blood, which circulate, subdivide, and collect in the reproductive cells

Pan-Ger·man·ism (pændʒə́ːrmənizəm) *n.* a movement (late 19th–20th cc.) to promote the union of all German-speaking people under German rule. It gave rise to German expansionist policy before the 1st world war, and its aims were later taken up by the National Socialist German Workers party

pan·go·lin (pǽŋgoulin) *n.* any of several members of genus *Manis*, order *Pholidota*, or related genera of scaly mammals of Asia and Africa, which feed on ants and roll themselves into a ball when attacked [Malay *peng-gōling*, roller]

pan·gram (pǽŋgræm) *n.* a sentence that involves all the letters of the alphabet preferably with little duplication, *the quick brown fox jumps over the lazy dog* —**pan·gram·mat·ic** *adj.*

pan·han·dle (pǽnhændˈl) **1.** *n.* a narrow, protruding strip of land or political territory, esp. the northern part of Texas between Oklahoma and New Mexico **2.** *v. pres. part.* **pan·han·dling** *past* and *past part.* **pan·han·dled** *v.i.* (*pop.*) to beg, esp. on the street

Pan·hel·len·ic (pænhəlénik) *adj.* relating to or including all Greece or all Greeks

pan·ic (pǽnik) **1.** *n.* intense, contagious fear affecting a body of people ‖ an instance of this fear, e.g. a widespread hysterical anxiety over the prevailing financial situation, resulting in hasty sale or protection of securities etc. ‖ intense, irrational fear felt by an individual **2.** *v. pres. part.* **pan·ick·ing** *past* and *past part.* **pan·icked** *v.i.* to lose rational control of one's behavior out of sudden intense fear ‖ *v.t.* to affect with panic **3.** *adj.* of, relating to or showing panic, *panic haste* [F. *panique* adj. fr. Gk *panikos*, of the god Pan, who was believed to cause unreasoning terror]

panic grass a member of *Panicum* or related genera of grasses incl. millet [fr. L. *panicum*, a kind of millet]

pan·ick·y (pǽniki) *adj.* liable to panic ‖ beginning to feel panic

pan·ic-strick·en (pǽnikstrikən) *adj.* madly frightened, filled with panic

pan·i·cle (pǽnikˈl) *n.* (*bot.*) a compound raceme ‖ a loose, irregular flower cluster [fr. L. *panicula* dim. of *panus*, tuft]

pan·ic·ulate (pǽnikstrʌk) *adj.* panic-stricken

pan·ic·u·late (pəníkjulit) *adj.* arranged in panicles **pa·nic·u·lat·ed** (pəníkjuleitid) *adj.* [fr. Mod. L. *paniculatus* fr. *panicula*, panicle]

Pan-Is·lam (pænízləm) *n.* a movement (late 19th–early 20th cc.) to promote political unity among Moslem nations, led by Turkey before the 1st world war **Pán-Is·lám·ic** *adj.* **Pán-Is·lam·ism** *n.*

Panjabi *PUNJABI

pan·jan·drum (pændʒǽndrəm) *n.* a mock title for a person of great self-importance [coined in 1755 by Samuel Foote (1720–77), Eng. playwright and actor]

Panj·nad (pʌndʒnád) *SUTLEJ

Pank·hurst (pǽŋkhəːrst), Emmeline (1858–1928), British suffragette. With her daughters Christabel (1880–1958) and Sylvia (1882–1960), she founded a militant suffragette movement (1903)

Pan·kow (pǽnkau) a suburb of East Berlin, seat of the government of the German Democratic Republic

panne (pæn) *n.* a soft fabric with a long pile, similar to velvet [F.]

pan·nier (pǽniər) *n.* a large basket, esp. one of a pair slung over the back of a beast of burden ‖ a large basket with a lid ‖ one of two bags of canvas, plastic, leather etc. slung over the back wheel of a bicycle or motorcycle ‖ (*hist.*) a frame of whalebone or wire used to distend a skirt at the hips or a puffed arrangement of cloth over a skirt around the hips [F. *panier*]

pan·ni·kin (pǽnikin) *n.* (*Br.*) a small metal drinking cup ‖ (*Br.*) the amount it contains [PAN, container]

Pa·no·an (púnouən) *n.* a major family of South American Indian languages. The best known of the Panoan-speaking peoples live in E. Peru, with related tribes extending into W. Brazil

pan·o·plied (pǽnəpliːd) *adj.* (*hist.*) wearing a complete suit of armor ‖ (*rhet.*) magnificently clothed or decked [PANOPLY]

pan·o·ply (pǽnəpliː) *pl.* **pan·o·plies** *n.* (*hist.*) a complete suit of armor ‖ rich ceremonial dress ‖ (*rhet.*) splendid display [fr. Gk *panoplia*, the full armor of a hoplite]

pan·o·ram·a (pænərǽmə, pænərámə) *n.* a wide uninterrupted view over a scene ‖ a picture, unrolled so as to give the impression of such a wide, continuous view ‖ a comprehensive survey of a series of events, *a panorama of Elizabethan history* **pan·o·rám·ic** *adj.* **pan·o·rám·i·cal·ly** *adv.* [fr. PAN-+Gk *horama*, view]

pan·pipe (pǽnpaip) *n.* (often *pl.*) a primitive musical instrument consisting of several small reed pipes of graduated length fixed side by side, played by blowing into the mouthpieces [PAN, Gk deity]

Pan-Slav·ism (pænslávizəm) *n.* a movement (19th and early 20th cc.) to promote the independence of Slav peoples, and their cultural and political unity. It began with a congress in Prague (1848) and was strongly supported by Russia to further her expansion in the Balkans. This gave rise to the Russo-Turkish War of 1877–8, but the alliance of Slav states collapsed in the 2nd Balkan War (1913). Pan-Slavism also represented a threat to Austria-Hungary, whose determination to crush Serbia in 1914 occasioned the 1st world war

pan·sy (pǽnzi) *pl.* **pan·sies** *n. Viola tricolor*, fam. *Violaceae*, a wild or cultivated plant with richly and variously colored flowers ‖ (*pop.*) an effeminate or homosexual man [older *pensee*, *pensy* fr. F. *pensée*, thought]

pant (pænt) **1.** *v.i.* to breathe quickly and in spasms, esp. after exertion, exposure to heat etc. ‖ (*rhet.* with 'for', 'after') to yearn ‖ (of the heart) to throb rapidly ‖ *v.t.* to utter gaspingly **2.** *n.* one of a series of spasms in labored breathing ‖ one of a series of throbs or gasps made by escaping steam [perh. shortened fr. O.F. *pantoisier*, *pantiser*]

pan·ta·lets, pan·ta·lettes (pænt'léts) *pl. n.* (*hist.*) long loose drawers, frilled at the bottom, worn by women and girls 1830–50 [dim. of PANTALOON]

pan·ta·loon (pænt'lúːn) *n.* (*pl., hist.*) tight trousers fastened with buttons below the calf or with straps under the shoe [after *Pantaloon*, a Venetian character in commedia dell'arte, usually depicted as a thin old man, wearing tight breeches continued below the knees as stockings, and who survives today as the butt of a clown in pantomime]

pant·dress (pǽntdres) *n.* woman's garment with a divided skirt resembling slacks

pan·tech·ni·con (pæntéknikən) *n.* (*Br.*) a very large moving van [fr. PAN-+Gk *technikon* adj., belonging to the arts]

Pan·tel·le·ri·a (pʌntɛlleríːə) a volcanic Italian island (area 32 sq. miles, pop. 8,327) in the Mediterranean, halfway between Tunisia and Sicily (with which it is administered). Chief town: Pantelleria. Products: wine, sponges, fish

pan·the·ism (pǽnθiːizəm) *n.* the belief or theory that God and the universe are identical. Among its best-known proponents are the Roman Stoics and Spinoza **pán·the·ist** *n.* **pan·the·is·tic** *adj.* [fr. PAN-+Gk *theos*, God]

pan·the·on (pǽnθiːɒn, pænθíːən) *n.* all the gods of a people, *the Hindu pantheon* ‖ a building where the famous dead of a nation are buried or memorialized ‖ a temple dedicated to all the gods **the Pantheon** a temple of this type built in Rome (c. 27 B.C.) and reconstructed in its present round, domed form c. 125 A.D. [L. fr. Gk fr. *pan*, all+*theios*, of or sacred to a god]

pan·ther (pǽnθər) *n.* a leopard, esp. a large

CONCISE PRONUNCIATION KEY: **(a)** æ, c*a*t; ɑ, c*a*r; ɔ f*aw*n; ei, sn*a*ke. **(e)** e, h*e*n; iː, sh*ee*p; iə, d*ee*r; εə, b*ea*r. **(i)** i, f*i*sh; ai, t*i*ger; əː, b*i*rd. **(o)** o, *o*x; au, c*ow*; ou, g*oa*t; u, p*oo*r; ɔi, r*oy*al. **(u)** ʌ, d*u*ck; u, b*u*ll; uː, g*oo*se; ə, b*a*cillus; juː, c*u*be. x, lo*ch*; θ, *th*ink; ð, *b*o*th*er; z, *Z*en; ʒ, cor*s*age; dʒ, sava*g*e; ŋ, orangutan*g*; j, *y*ak; ʃ, *fish*; tʃ, fe*tch*; 'l, rabb*le*; 'n, redd*en*. Complete pronunciation key appears inside front cover.

fierce one or a black one ‖ a cougar ‖ a jaguar [M.E. *pantere* fr. O.F. fr. L. fr. Gk]

pant·ie, pant·y (pǽnti:) *pl.* **pant·ies** *n.* (esp. *pl.*) underpants for a woman or a child

pan·tile (pǽntail) *n.* a roofing tile having a cross section shaped like an S with one curve larger than the other, designed to overlap the next tile [PAN, container+TILE]

pan·ti·soc·ra·cy (pæntisókrəsi:) *n.* (*hist.*) a classless, utopian society in which all are equal and all rule [coined by Coleridge (1794) fr. Gk *pant-*, all+*isokratia*, equal rule]

pan·to·graph (pǽntəgræf, pǽntəgrɑf) *n.* an instrument for copying a drawing on any chosen scale, consisting of an assembly of hinged rods arranged as a parallelogram, the whole being able to rotate around a fixed point ‖ (*elec.*) a device at the end of a trolley pole used to collect current [fr. Gk *pant-*, all+*-graphos*, written]

pan·to·mime (pǽntəmaim) **1.** *n.* a form of entertainment in which story and emotion are conveyed by gesture only, without words, but often with music and decor ‖ an English theatrical entertainment, usually at Christmastime, based on a traditional fairy tale but including topical comedy, clowns, and song and dance ‖ dumb show **2.** *v. pres. part.* **pan·to·mim·ing** *past* and *past part.* **pan·to·mimed** *v.t.* to represent by pantomime ‖ *v.i.* to express oneself by pantomime [fr. L. *pantomimus*, an actor in dumb show fr. Gk fr. *pant-*, all+*mimos*, mimic]

pan·to·mim·ic (pæntəmímik) *adj.* of, relating to or having the nature of pantomime [fr. L. *pantomimicus*]

pan·try (pǽntri:) *pl.* **pan·tries** *n.* a larder ‖ a room where the silver, glass etc. under the care of a butler are kept [A.F. *panetrie*, O.F. *paneterie*, bread room]

pants (pænts) *pl. n.* trousers ‖ (esp. *Br.*) short underpants [abbr. of PANTALOONS]

pant·suit (pǽntsu:t) *n.* a woman's garment of pants and blouse and/or jacket of same fabric *Cf* PANTDRESS

pan·tu·ran·i·an·ism (pæntu:rǽni:ænizəm) *n.* extremist political ideology in Greece with a restored Ottoman Empire as its ultimate goal

Pan-Tu·ran·ism (pǽntúrənizəm, pǽnjúrənizəm) *n.* an early 20th-c. movement aimed at uniting all peoples sharing a common Turkish heritage [PAN+*Turán*, ancient region of central Asia beyond the Oxus, north of Iran]

panty *PANTIE

pan·ty·hose or **pan·ti·hose** (pǽnti:houz) *n.* woman's garment consisting of panties and stockings as a single unit, originally conceived for women wearing miniskirts

Pa·o·li (paoli:), Pasquale (1725–1807), Corsican patriot. He was elected president (1755) by the Corsicans in their struggle against Genoese rule, but was forced to submit after Genoa sold the island to France (1768). He went into exile in Britain (1769–90) and persuaded the British government to intervene in Corsica (1794–6)

Pao·ting (bóudíŋ) (or Tsingyuan) an agricultural trading center (pop. 265,000) of central Hopei, China

Pao·tow (bóudóu) a steelmaking center (pop. 650,000) of Inner Mongolia, China, on the Hwang-ho

pap (pæp) *n.* soft, mashed or semi-liquid food for babies or invalids ‖ political patronage ‖ vapid literature etc. with no intellectual content [perh. fr. L.G. and G. *pappe*, Du. *pap*]

pa·pa (púpə, pəpá) *n.* (a child's word for) father [F. fr. Ital. fr. L.]

pa·pa·cy (péipəsi:) *pl.* **pa·pa·cies** *n.* the office of the pope ‖ a pope's term of office ‖ the organization of the Roman Catholic Church [fr. M.L. *papatia* fr. *papa*, pope]

Pa·pa·go (púpəgou) *pl.* **Pa·pa·go, Pa·pa·gos** *n.* a Uto-Aztecan American Indian people, whose development was strongly influenced (1687–1767) by Jesuit missionaries and (after 1767) by Franciscan missionaries. They supported (19th c.) the U.S. government against the Apache Indians. They number about 11,000, settled on three reservations in S. Arizona and scattered throughout N.W. Sonora, Mexico

pa·pa·in (pəpéiin, pəpáiin) *n.* a protein-hydrolyzing enzyme occurring in the milky juice of the green papaya, used to aid digestion and for tenderizing meat [PAPAYA]

pa·pal (péipəl) *adj.* of the pope, his office, jurisdiction, acts etc. [F. or fr. eccles. L. *papalis*]

papal cross a cross with three cross-bars of graduated length, the longest and lowest being at or near the middle of the vertical shaft

papal infallibility (*Roman Catholicism*) the doctrine (defined in 1870) that the pope when speaking ex cathedra on questions of faith and morals will be incapable of error

Papal States (*hist.*) a region of central Italy ruled (754–1870) by the popes. Originally given (754) to the papacy by Pépin III, the states were not under effective papal rule until the 16th c. They were invaded (1796–1814) by the French, but restored (1815) to the papacy. The liberal reforms of Pius IX were withdrawn after the revolution of 1848. Most of the region was joined (1861) to the new kingdom of Italy, but Rome was defended by the French until 1870, when it, too, was seized. The papacy refused to recognize its loss of temporal power until the Lateran Treaty (1929) gave it sovereignty over the Vatican

pa·pa·raz·zo, *pl.* **-i** (púpɑrɑtsou) *n.* an aggressive free-lance, celebrity-chasing photographer

pa·pav·er·in (pəpǽvərin, pəpéivərin) *n.* papaverine

pa·pav·er·ine (pəpǽvəri:n, pəpéivəri:n) *n.* an alkaloid, $C_{20}H_{21}O_4N$, a constituent of opium, also made synthetically from vanillin. It is used to control spasms and for local anesthesia [fr. L. *papaver*, poppy]

pa·paw, paw·paw (pópɔ, pəpó) *n.* the papaya ‖ any of several trees and shrubs of genus *Asimina*, fam. *Annonaceae*, esp. *A. triloba* of North America, which has an oblong yellow edible fruit ‖ this fruit [older *papaya*, *papay* fr. Span. and Port. fr. Carib.]

pa·pa·ya (pəpájə) *n. Carica papaya*, fam. *Caricaceae*, a Malaysian tree with a large yellow fruit like a honeydew melon, eaten fresh, cooked or preserved. It also grows in India and the West Indies, and is found well into central Africa [Span. fr. Carib.]

Pa·pe·e·te (pupi:éitei) the capital (pop. 25,342) of French Polynesia, a port and airport of W. Tahiti

Pa·pen (púpən), Franz von (1879–1969), German politician, chancellor of Germany (1932). He did much to bring Hitler to power, and helped to prepare the Nazi annexation of Austria (1938)

pa·per (péipər) **1.** *n.* a substance consisting of a felted thin sheet of compactly interlaced fibers of cellulose etc. obtained from wood, rags, straw etc. and used for writing, printing or drawing on, wrapping parcels, covering the walls of a room etc. ‖ a piece of this substance ‖ an essay, esp. on a scholarly subject ‖ an official document ‖ a set of examination questions or a student's written answers ‖ an essay which a student is required to write ‖ a newspaper ‖ (*pl.*) documents carried to prove identity, nationality etc. ‖ money (banknotes, bills etc.) in the form of written promises to pay ‖ a card, folder etc. containing or holding some item, *a paper of pins* ‖ (*pl.*) the collective letters, writings, documents etc. belonging or pertaining to a person **on paper** in writing ‖ hypothetically, in theory **2.** *adj.* made of paper ‖ hypothetical, not having any real substance, *paper promises* **3.** *v.t.* to cover (a wall etc.) with paper ‖ to distribute complimentary tickets to insure a substantial audience for a performance [A.F. and fr. O.F. *papier* fr. L. *papyrus* fr. Gk]
—Paper is prepared in a mill by reducing wood fiber, straw, grasses, rags etc. to a pulp by an alkali, extracting lignin and other noncellulose matter, bleaching (usually with chlorine or a hypochlorite), washing, adding a filler to give a smooth surface, rolling and drying. This process of manufacture originated in China 2,000 years ago. The qualities of the product range widely as to thickness (measured by the weight per area), surface etc.

pa·per·back (péipərbæk) *n.* a book bound in paper

paper chase the game of hare and hounds

paper factor (*chem.*) a natural terpene in the balsam fir tree, first discovered in newsprint, that is an effective insecticide affecting insect metamorphosis

paper gold (*economics*) special drawing rights for settlement of international accounts, through the International Monetary Fund *also* SDR

pa·per·hang·er (péipərhæŋər) *n.* a person who decorates rooms with wallpaper as a profession

paper knife a dull-bladed knife of wood, ivory etc. for opening letters, slitting the pages of untrimmed books etc.

paper money printed documents (e.g. dollar bills) issued by a government through banks and serving as currency

paper mulberry *Broussonetia papyrifera*, fam. *Moraceae*, an Asiatic tree used in making tapa, and grown as a shade tree in Europe and America

paper nautilus *Argonauta argos*, a dibranchiate cephalopod, the female of which produces a thin, non-chambered fragile shell in which the eggs are carried

paper tape (*computer*) a strip or roll of paper of varying widths from ¾ to 1 inch, on which punched holes carry data for computer input

pa·per-train (péipərtrein) *v.* to train a dog to defecate indoors on paper

pa·per·weight (péipərweit) *n.* a small, heavy object used to prevent papers from being scattered or blown away

paper work work such as filling in forms, keeping records, making out accounts etc.

pa·per·y (péipəri:) *adj.* having a consistency, or the flimsiness or thinness, of paper

Pa·phos (péifɔs) the ancient Greek center, in S.W. Cyprus, of the cult of Aphrodite, said to be where she set foot after emerging from the waves. Modern Paphos (pop. 7,000) is 10 miles distant

pa·pier col·lé (pɑpi:éar cɔlléi) *n.* (*Fr.*) art technique utilizing glue, paper, paint, crayon and other media *syn* collage

pa·pier-mâ·ché, pa·per-mâ·ché (péipərməʃéi) *n.* a light, tough material made of paper pulp mixed with a liquid adhesive, shaped or molded, and allowed to dry [F.=chewed paper]

pa·pil·i·o·na·ceous (pəpíli:ənéiʃəs) *adj.* (*bot.*, of certain flowers, e.g. the sweet pea) shaped like a butterfly ‖ of, relating or belonging to *Papilionaceae*, order *Rosales*, a large family of plants whose fruits are legumes [fr. L. *papilionaceus* fr. *papilio* (*papilionis*), butterfly]

pa·pil·la (pəpílə) *pl.* **pa·pil·lae** (pəpíli:) *n.* a small protuberance on a part of the body, e.g. the nipple, or on a plant ‖ a process extending into and nourishing the root of a growing tooth, hair or feather **pa·píl·lar·y, pa·píl·late** (pəpílit) *adjs* [L.=nipple]

pap·il·lo·ma (pæpəlóumə) *pl.* **pap·il·lo·ma·ta** (pæpəlóumətə), **pap·il·lo·mas** *n.* (*med.*) a benign tumor (e.g. a wart) of skin or mucous membrane [Mod. L. fr. *papilla*, nipple]

pap·il·lon (pæpəlon) *n.* a dog of a toy spaniel breed with large, open, erect ears and a fine silky coat (red, ruby, chestnut, puce, black-and-white, dark yellow or white with markings of these colors) with long fringes [F.=butterfly]

pap·il·lose (pæpilous) *adj.* papillate

Pa·pin (pæpɛ̃), Denis (1647–c. 1712), French physicist and pioneer in the development of the steam engine. He invented the autoclave, in which, under pressure, the boiling point of water was raised

Pa·pi·neau (pæpi:nou), Louis Joseph (1786–1871), Canadian politician and leader of the French-Canadian cause prior to the Rebellion of 1837. As speaker (1815–37) of the Legislative Assembly of Lower Canada, he inspired the Ninety-Two Resolutions, expressing French-Canadian grievances, passed (1834) by the Assembly

pa·pist (péipist) *n.* an advocate of papal supremacy ‖ (used in a hostile sense) a Roman Catholic **pa·pis·tic** (pəpístik), **pa·pís·ti·cal** *adjs* **pa·pist·ry** (péipistri:) *n.* [F. *papiste* or fr. 16th-c. L. *papista*]

pa·poose (pæpú:s, pəpú:s) *n.* a North American Indian baby [Algonquian]

pap·o·va·vi·rus (pæpóuvəvairəs) *n.* (*med.*) deoxyribonucleic acid viral group believed to cause warts and neoplasms, esp. in animals

pap·pus (pæpəs) *pl.* **pap·pi** (pæpai) *n.* (*bot.*) a downy or feathery tuft in place of a calyx, used in the fruit dispersal of e.g. composite plants (e.g. the thistle, dandelion) [Mod. L. fr. Gk *pappos*, old man]

pap·py (pæpi:) *comp.* **pap·pi·er** *superl.* **pap·pi·est** *adj.* soft and mushy like pap ‖ consisting of pap

pap·ri·ka (pæprí:kə, pæprikə) *n.* a mildly pungent, red spice ground from the dried ripe fruit of sweet pepper ‖ the fruit itself [Hung.]

Pap smear or **Papanicolaou smear** diagnostic test to detect uterine or cervical cancer, named for U.S. scientist George N. Papanicolaou

Pap·u·a (pæpju:ə) a former territory of Australia consisting of S.E. New Guinea with the

CONCISE PRONUNCIATION KEY: (**a**) æ, *cat*; ɑ, *car*; ɔ *fawn*; ei, *snake*. (**e**) e, *hen*; i:, *sheep*; iə, *deer*; ɛə, *bear*. (**i**) i, *fish*; ai, *tiger*; ə:, *bird*. (**o**) o, *ox*; au, *cow*; ou, *goat*; u, *poor*; ɔi, *royal*. (**u**) ʌ, *duck*; u, *bull*; u:, *goose*; ə, *bacillus*; ju:, *cube*. x, *loch*; θ, *think*; ð, *bother*; z, *Zen*; ʒ, *corsage*; dʒ, *savage*; ŋ, *orangutang*; j, *yak*; ʃ, *fish*; tʃ, *fetch*; 'l, *rabble*; 'n, *redden*. Complete pronunciation key appears inside front cover.

adjacent islands, now part of Papua New Guinea

Pap·u·an (pǽpjuːən) 1. *adj.* pertaining to the former territory of Papua or to its native peoples, or to a group of unclassified languages spoken in Papua and New Guinea, New Britain and the Solomon Is, not belonging to the Austronesian family 2. *n.* a member of any of the native races of Papua and New Guinea ‖ a language of the group spoken in Papua and New Guinea [fr. PAPUA fr. Malay *pepuah*, frizzled, from the hair of Papuans]

Papua New Guinea a country (total area 178,260 sq. miles, pop. 3,400,000) occupying the eastern half of New Guinea and outlying islands (Bismarck Archipelago, N. Solomon Is, Trobriand Is, D'Entrecasteaux Is, Louisiade Archipelago, Woodlark Is) and islets. Capital and chief port: Port Moresby. Official languages: English, Pidgin English, Motu. Livestock: cattle (in the north). Exports: copra and shell, rubber, coconut oil, coffee, cocoa, tropical hardwoods, small quantities of gold and other minerals. Imports: food, chemicals, manufactured goods. HISTORY. The territory of Papua was annexed (1883) by Queensland, became a British protectorate (1884), and has been ruled by Australia since 1905. The northeast of New Guinea was occupied (1914) by Australia, was mandated (1920) to Australia by the League of Nations, and was placed under Australian trusteeship (1946) by the United Nations. The two territories were given a common administration (1949). The country became self-governing in 1973 and gained full independence in 1975, as a member of the British Commonwealth. Michael Somare became prime minister (1972–80, 1982–)

pap·ule (pǽpjuːl) *n.* a pimple [fr. L. *papula*]

pap·y·ra·ceous (pæpiréiʃəs) *adj.* (*bot.*) of papery texture [fr. L. *papyrus*, paper fr. Gk.]

pa·py·rus (pəpáirəs) *pl.* **pa·py·ri** (pəpáirai), **pa·py·rus·es** *n.* *Cyperus papyrus*, fam. *Cyperaceae*, an aquatic plant indigenous to the Nile Valley. The pith, shredded and pressed into sheets, was used to write on, chiefly by the ancient Egyptians, Greeks and Romans ‖ this material ‖ a document written on papyrus [L. fr. Gk *papuros*]

par (par) 1. *n.* equality of value, status or condition, *on a par with* ‖ average or normal state, quality, physical condition etc., *to feel below par* ‖ (*commerce*) nominal value, *to sell at par* ‖ (*golf*) the ideal number of strokes in which a hole, or the course, should be played by a scratch golfer 2. *adj.* (*commerce*) at par ‖ average, normal [L.=equal, equality]

par *PARR

PAR or **par** (*mil. acronym*) perimeter acquisition radar, outermost radar antiballistic missile system *Cf* MSR

pa·ra (párə) *n.* a Turkish coin equal to about 1/40 of a piaster ‖ a Yugoslav unit of currency equal to 1/100 of a dinar ‖ a coin of this value [Turk. *pārah*, piece]

para- (pǽrə) *prefix* beside, beyond ‖ amiss, faulty, irregular ‖ somewhat resembling ‖ chemically related to or derived from [fr. Gk *para prep.*, beside]

par·a·bi·o·sis (pærəbaióusis) *n.* the anatomical and physiological conjunction of two organisms, e.g. in Siamese twins **par·a·bi·ot·ic** (pærəbaiótik) *adj.* [Mod. L. fr. *para-*, beside+*-biosis*, mode of life]

par·a·blast (pǽrəblæst) *n.* the yolk of a meroblastic ovum **par·a·blás·tic** *adj.* [PARA-+Gk *blastos*, sprout, germ]

par·a·ble (pǽrəb'l) *n.* a story designed to teach a moral or religious principle by suggesting a parallel [F. *parabole* fr. L. fr. Gk]

pa·rab·o·la (pərǽbələ) *n.* (*geom.*) a plane curve derived from the section of a cone by a plane parallel to its side, and obeying the law that any point on the curve is equidistant from a fixed point (the focus) and from a fixed straight line (the directrix) [Mod. L. fr. Gk *parabolē*, juxtaposition]

par·a·bol·ic (pærəbólik) *adj.* having the nature of a parabola ‖ (*geom.*) relating to or having the form of a parabola **par·a·ból·i·cal** *adj.* [fr. L.L. *parabolicus*]

par·ab·o·loid (pərǽbəlɔid) *n.* (*math.*) a quadric surface of which sections parallel to two coordinate planes are parabolas and sections parallel to the third plane are circles, ellipses or hyperbolas ‖ the equation of such a surface **pa·rab·o·lói·dal** *adj.* [PARABOLA]

par·a·ca·sein (pærəkéisiːn) *n.* casein (insoluble protein)

Par·a·cel·sus (pærəsélsəs), Philippus Aureolus (Theophrastus Bombastus von Hohenheim, 1493–1541), Swiss physician, alchemist and natural philosopher. Prominent in the Renaissance reaction against the medical doctrines of Galen and Avicenna, he combined the beginnings of a modern scientific spirit with a Neoplatonic pantheistic mysticism

par·a·chlor·o·phen·y·lal (pærəklɔrouféniləl) *n.* (*pharm.*) drug that reduces the brain's serotonin level, used experimentally in treating schizophrenia and tremors *abbr.* **PCPA**

pa·rach·ro·nism (pərǽkrənizəm) *n.* an error in dating, esp. the dating of an event later than is correct [fr. Gk *para*, beside+*chromos*, time]

par·a·chute (pǽrəʃuːt) 1. *n.* a collapsible umbrella-shaped contrivance of nylon or silk fabric used esp. in aeronautics. A person or thing suspended from it by cords can drop safely through the air because the fall is slowed by the resistance of the air gathered in the top ‖ (*zool.*) a patagium 2. *v. pres. part.* **par·a·chut·ing** *past and past part.* **par·a·chut·ed** *v.t.* to land (a person or thing) by parachute ‖ *v.i.* to descend by parachute [F.]

parachute spinnaker a very large spinnaker used by racing yachts

par·a·chut·ist (pǽrəʃuːtist) *n.* a person, esp. a soldier, who makes descents from aircraft by parachute

Par·a·clete (pǽrəkliːt) *n.* (*theol.*) the Holy Ghost as comforter or advocate [F. *paraclet* fr. L. fr. Gk fr. *para*, beside+*kalein*, to call]

pa·rade (pəréid) 1. *n.* an assembly of troops in strict order for inspection or drill ‖ a ceremonial procession, esp. of troops ‖ an area where troops assemble for inspection or drill ‖ a passing in review for appraisal, *a fashion parade* ‖ a pompous display, *to make a parade of one's learning* ‖ a place where people stroll for amusement, a promenade **on parade** exhibited for inspection 2. *v. pres. part.* **pa·rad·ing** *past and past part.* **pa·rad·ed** *v.t.* to make a display of, *to parade one's talents* ‖ to cause (soldiers) to be drawn up for inspection or drill ‖ *v.i.* to assemble for the purpose of, and take part in, a parade ‖ to stroll, promenade, in order to attract attention [F. fr. Ital. *parata*, Span. *parada*]

par·a·di·chlor·o·ben·zene (pærədaiklɔroubénziːn; pærədaiklɔuroubénziːn) *n.* a white crystalline compound, $C_6H_4Cl_2$, used mainly as a moth repellent [PARA-+DI-+*chloro*-, containing chlorine+BENZENE]

par·a·digm (pǽrədim, pǽrədaim) *n.* an example serving as a pattern, *a paradigm of virtue* ‖ (*gram.*) a conjugation or declension serving to demonstrate the inflections of a word **par·a·dig·mat·ic** (pærədigmǽtik) *adj.* **par·a·dig·mát·i·cal·ly** *adv.* [F. *paradigme* fr. L. fr. Gk fr. *paradeiknunai*, to show side by side]

paradigmatic *adj.* (*linguistics*) of one of the two relationships operating between an element at a given level between elements of a sentence; of a syntactically interchangeable element, *we* (or *they*) *are going Cf* SYNTAGMATIC

par·a·di·sa·ic (pærədiséiik) *adj.* paradisiacal **par·a·di·sá·i·cal** *adj.* [fr. PARADISE or fr. L. *paradisus*, paradise]

par·a·di·sal (pærədáis'l) *adj.* paradisiacal [fr. L. *paradisus*, paradise]

par·a·dise (pǽrədais) *n.* a place or state in which spiritual bliss is enjoyed after death, the Christian or Moslem heaven ‖ (*Bible*) an intermediate place or state in which, after death, the souls of the righteous await judgment ‖ any place of or offering perfect happiness, *a swimmer's paradise* **Par·a·dise** the garden of Eden [F. *paradise* fr. L. fr. Gk fr. O. Pers.]

par·a·dis·i·ac (pærədísiːæk) *adj.* paradisiacal **par·a·di·si·a·cal** (pærədisíak'l) *adj.* of, relating to or like paradise [fr. L. *paradisiacus* fr. Gk]

par·a·dos (pǽrədɒs) *pl.* **par·a·dos, par·a·dos·es** *n.* (*mil.*) an earthwork erected to protect a position from rear attack [F.]

par·a·dox (pǽrədɒks) *n.* a statement which, though true, seems false and selfcontradictory ‖ a statement which is selfcontradictory and false, though it may seem true or clever ‖ a person or thing displaying contradictory qualities **par·a·dóx·i·cal** *adj.* [fr. L. *paradoxum* fr. Gk *paradoxos* adj., contrary to accepted opinion]

paradoxical sleep (*physiol.*) period in sleep when dreams occur *also* rem sleep

par·a·drop (pǽrədrɒp) *n.* delivery by parachute of personnel or cargo from an aircraft in flight

par·af·fin (pǽrəfin) 1. *n.* an alkane ‖ a waxy, crystalline, white, odorless substance obtained by distilling wood, coal and esp. petroleum. It is a complex mixture of hydrocarbons, esp. alkanes, and is used as a stable and water-resistant coating or seal, and in candles etc. It is sometimes called paraffin wax ‖ kerosene (*Br.* paraffin oil) 2. *v.t.* to coat or saturate with paraffin [fr. L. *parum*, too little+*affinis*, skin (from the chemical saturation of these hydrocarbons)]

paraffin hydrocarbon an alkane

paraffin oil (*Br.*) kerosene

paraffin series the homologous series of alkanes

paraffin wax *PARAFFIN

par·a·foil (pǽrəfɔil) *n.* airfoil parachute capable of aiding a guided, gliding descent

par·a·glide (pǽrəglaid) *n.* kitelike device used for directing the landing of a reentering space vehicle. *also* parawing

par·a·go·ge (pærəgóudʒi) *n.* (*gram.*) the addition of a final letter or syllable to a word either so as to modify the meaning (e.g. 'ly' in 'worldly' fr. 'world'), or adventitiously (e.g. 'b' in 'limb' fr. O.E. 'lim') **par·a·gog·ic** (pærəgɒdʒik) *adj.* [L. fr. Gk *paragōgē*, a leading past]

par·a·gon (pǽrəgɒn, pǽrəgən) *n.* a model or pattern of something good, *a paragon of virtue* ‖ a perfect diamond of at least 100 carats ‖ (*printing, hist.*) a large size of type (about 20 point) [O.F. fr. Ital.]

par·a·gon·ite (pǽrəgənait) *n.* a form of mica with sodium replacing the potassium of the commoner type [fr. Gk *paragōn*, pres. part. of *paragein*, to mislead]

par·a·graph (pǽrəgræf, pǽrəgraf) 1. *n.* a distinct unit of writing (generally containing more than one sentence, but shorter than a chapter), usually a subsection dealing with a particular point. It is always begun on a new line and usually indented (symbol ¶) ‖ a brief article or item in a newspaper or magazine 2. *v.t.* to divide or arrange into paragraphs ‖ (*journalism*) to write a paragraph about ‖ *v.i.* to write paragraphs in a newspaper or magazine **pár·a·graph·er** *n.* a journalist who writes paragraphs **par·a·graph·ic** (pærəgrǽfik), **par·a·gráph·i·cal** *adjs* **par·a·graph·ist** (pǽrəgræfist, pǽrəgrafist) *n.* [F. *paragraphe* fr. L.L. fr. Gk]

paragraph loop (*figure skating*) a specified series of turns

Pa·ra·gua·ná (parəgwaná) a peninsula on the northwest coast of Venezuela, enclosing the Gulf of Venezuela on the east

Par·a·guay (pǽrəgwei, pǽrəgwai) the chief tributary (1,500 miles long) of the Paraná, flowing from the central Mato Grosso, Brazil, across Paraguay (forming the northeastern and southwestern borders) to the Paraná estuary. It is navigable by large vessels past Asunción and by small steamers in the rainy season into the Mato Grosso (900 miles)

Paraguay a republic (area 157,000 sq. miles, pop. 3,270,000) of central South America. Capital: Asunción. People: Spanish-Guaraní Indian mestizos (93%), with minorities of tribal Indians, Italians, Japanese and Germans. Religion: predominantly Roman Catholic. Languages: Spanish, Guaraní. The land is 54% forest, 4% arable, and 40% suitable for pasture. The River Paraguay divides the country. The west is flat and largely semidesert (the Gran Chaco), with some forest. The east (containing 95% of the population) is a rolling plain, cultivated in the south, with hills (rising to 2,800 ft) separating the Paraguay and Paraná basins, and great rain forests (the Selva) in the north. In the center, on both sides of the Paraguay, is the Campo: marshland and savanna (cattle raising). Average temperatures (F.): Asunción 62° (Jul.) and 80° (Jan.), the Chaco 70° (Jul.) and 100° (Jan.). Rainfall: 80 ins near Brazil, 50 ins east of Asunción, 44 ins in Asunción, 32 ins in the Chaco. Livestock: cattle, horses. Agricultural products (eastern region): manioc, corn, cotton, sugarcane, peanuts, sweet potatoes, beans, onions, yerba maté, rice, tobacco, coffee, fruit. Forest products: cedar, hardwoods, quebracho extract, petitgrain oil, tung oil. Mineral resources (largely unexploited): iron, manganese, copper, mica. Industries: rum, meat, textiles, lace, consumer goods. Exports: cotton, quebracho extract, lumber, hides, tobacco, meat, yerba maté, vegetable oils. Imports: food, textiles, vehicles, machinery, chemicals, fuels and oil, paper. Port: Asunción (on River Paraguay, over 900 miles from the sea). University:

CONCISE PRONUNCIATION KEY: **(a)** æ, cat; ɑ, car; ɔ fawn; ei, snake. **(e)** e, hen; iː, sheep; iə, deer; ɛə, bear. **(i)** i, fish; ai, tiger; əː, bird. **(o)** o, ox; au, cow; ou, goat; u, poor; ɔi, royal. **(u)** ʌ, duck; u, bull; uː, goose; ə, bacillus; juː, cube. x, loch; θ, think; ð, bother; z, Zen; ʒ, corsage; dʒ, savage; ŋ, orangutang; j, yak; ʃ, fish; tʃ, fetch; 'l, rabble; 'n, redden. Complete pronunciation key appears inside front cover.

Asunción (1889). Monetary unit: guaraní (100 centimos). HISTORY. Paraguay, inhabited by Guaraní Indians, was ruled by Spain (16th c.– 1811), which made it part of the viceroyalty of Río de la Plata (1776). It revolted, and declared its independence (May 14, 1811). Paraguay prospered under a series of dictatorships, but in the War of the Triple Alliance (1864–70) against Argentina, Brazil, and Uruguay it lost 305,000 out of a population of 525,000, and of the survivors only 28,000 were men. Its economy was shattered. Again in the Chaco War (1932–5) with Bolivia, it sustained 20,000 dead for the 20,000 sq. miles of borderland it gained in the wilderness of the Gran Chaco. The country remained neutral for most of the 2nd world war, and joined the U.N. (1945). Civil War (1947) and political instability were followed in 1954 by the election of Gen. Alfredo Stroessner. Ruling dictatorially, he introduced certain improvements, esp. in communications, and reforms, esp. women's suffrage (1963). He continued in power, being reelected to succeeding five-year terms

Paraguay tea maté

Pa·ra·i·ba (pərəí:bə) *JOÃO PESSOA

par·a·jour·nal·ism (pærədjó:rn'lizəm) *n.* tendentious reporting

parakeet *PARRAKEET

par·a·kite (pærəkait) *n.* (*sports*) a slitted parachute with a sportsman harnessed in, launched from the ground or water by a motor vehicle — **parakite** *v.* —**parakiting** *n.*

par·a·lan·guage (pærəlæŋgwidʒ) *n.* the inflections and other vocal and gestural nuances added to language to convey meaning, e.g., in sarcasm —**par·a·lin·guis·tic** *adj.* —**par·a·lin·guis·tics** *n.* the study

par·al·de·hyde (pærældəhaid) *n.* a polymer, (CH₃CHO)₃, of acetaldehyde, used in medicine as a hypnotic and sedative

par·a·le·gal (pæerəlí:g'l) *n.* a paraprofessional legal assistant; one trained to assist an attorney —**par·a·le·gal** *adj.*

par·a·lep·sis (pærəlépsis) *n.* paralipsis

par·a·lip·sis (pærəlípsis) *n.* a rhetorical device in which a speaker emphasizes something by professing not to speak of it (usually introduced by 'not to mention' or 'to say nothing of') [Gk *paraleipsis*]

par·al·lac·tic (pærəlæktik) *adj.* of, relating to or caused by parallax

par·al·lax (pærælæks) *n.* the apparent change of position or the difference in apparent direction of an object when viewed from two or more positions not on a line with the object. In astronomical calculations, parallax is expressed by the angle subtended at a celestial body by some suitably chosen standard base line (e.g. the equatorial radius of the earth, or the mean radius of the earth's orbit) [F. *parallaxe* fr. Gk *parallaxis*, alternation]

parallax-second *PARSEC

par·al·lel (pærəlel) **1.** *adj.* (of lines, curves or planes) equidistant from each other at all points and having the same direction or curvature ‖ (of a line, curved or plane) equidistant from another at all points, and having the same direction or curvature, *draw line AB parallel to CD* ‖ similar or analogous in tendency, purpose, time etc., *parallel situations* ‖ (*mus.*, of simultaneous melodic lines) maintaining a constant pitch difference ‖ (*mus.*, of intervals) moving consecutively, *parallel fifths* **2.** a line, curve or plane which is parallel to another ‖ a situation, event, narrative etc. which is similar to another ‖ similarity between situations etc., *strange parallels exist in their histories* ‖ a comparison, *to draw a parallel between two circumstances* ‖ the arrangement of electrical devices in a parallel circuit ‖ (*geog.*) a parallel of latitude ‖ (*printing*) a reference mark consisting of two vertical parallel lines (‖) ‖ (*mil.*) a long trench constructed parallel to a fortification etc. **3.** *v.t. pres. part.* **par·al·lel·ing**, *esp. Br.* **par·al·lel·ling** *past* and *past part.* **par·al·leled**, *esp. Br.* **par·al·lelled** to be parallel to ‖ to find or quote a fact, event, thing or circumstance that is similar to (another) [F. *parallèle* fr. L. fr. Gk *parallēlos*, beside one another]

parallel bars a gymnastic apparatus, consisting of two parallel horizontal bars of wood or tubular metal well above floor level, used for vaulting, balancing etc.

parallel circuit (*elec.*) a circuit arranged so that the positive poles or terminals are connected to one conductor and the negative poles or terminals to another

Parallel Development Doctrine British policy of racial separation urged for Rhodesia and South Africa prior to 1978

par·al·lel·e·pi·ped (pærələlepáipid) *n.* (*geom.*) a solid all of whose sides are parallelograms, opposite sides being parallel to one another [fr. Gk *parallēlepipedon* fr. *parellēlos*, parallel + *epipedon*, a plane surface]

par·al·lel·ism (pærəlelizəm) *n.* the quality or state or being parallel

parallel of latitude (*geog.*) any imaginary circle on the globe which forms the locus of points equidistant from the equator

par·al·lel·o·gram (pærəlélⱥgræm) *n.* (*geom.*) a four-sided plane figure, the opposite sides of which are equal and parallel to one another [F. *parallélogramme* fr. L. fr. Gk]

parallel processing, concurrent processing (*computer*) an operation simultaneously storing or executing more than one program *also* concurrent processing *Cf* MULTIPROCESSING, MULTIPROGRAMMING

parallel ruler an instrument for drawing parallel lines. It consists of two rulers hinged together in such a way that they always remain parallel

pa·ral·o·gism (pərælⱥdʒizəm) *n.* fallacious reasoning ‖ an instance of this **pa·ral·o·gis·tic** *adj.* [F. *paralogisme* fr. L.L. fr. Gk]

paralyse *PARALYZE

pa·ral·y·sis (pərælisiz) *pl.* **pa·ral·y·ses** (pæræli:si:z) *n.* inability to move a muscle or group of muscles, often coupled with lack of sensation in the affected area. It is usually caused by diseases of the nervous system, brain damage, apoplexy or poliomyelitis, but it may be caused by certain poisons or by hysteria ‖ inability to act or move [L. fr. Gk *paralusis*]

paralysis ag·i·tans (ædʒitænz) *n.* Parkinson's disease

par·a·lyt·ic (pærəlítik) **1.** *adj.* of, characterized by or affected with paralysis **2.** *n.* a person affected with paralysis **par·a·lyt·i·cal·ly** *adv.* [F. *paralytique*]

par·a·lyze, par·a·lyse (pærəlaiz) *pres. part.* **par·a·lyz·ing, par·a·lys·ing** *past* and *past. part.* **par·a·lyzed, par·a·lysed** *v.t.* to effect with paralysis [F. *paralyser*]

par·a·mag·net·ic (pærəmægnétik) *adj.* of or designating a substance that exhibits paramagnetism **par·a·mag·net·ism** (pærəmægnitizəm) *n.* the property (possessed by many substances having a magnetic permeability close to but greater than unity) of being weakly attracted by an external field. The degree of magnetization is proportional to the strength of the applied field

Par·a·mar·i·bo (pærəmæribou) *n.* the capital (pop. 67,718), chief port, and communications center of Suriname on the Suriname River estuary 15 miles from the coast, founded (1540) by the French

par·a·mat·ta (pærəmætə) *n.* a lightweight fabric of wool and cotton or silk [after *Paramatta*, town in New South Wales, Australia]

par·a·me·ci·um, par·a·moe·ci·um (pærəmí:siəm) *n.* (*zool.*) any of several ciliate protozoans of genus *Paramoecium*, fam. *Holotricha*, found freeswimming in stagnant pools [Mod. L. fr. Gk. *parammēkēs*, oval]

par·a·med·ic (pærəmédik) *n.* **1.** trained medical worker (usu. with 2 yrs of training) capable of performing basic emergency medical functions **2.** (*mil.*) parachuting member of the medical corps —**paramedical** *adj.*

par·a·men·stru·um (pærəménstruəm) *n.* (*med.*) period of four days before, and first four days during menstruation when women are most vulnerable to infection —**paramenstrual** *adj.*

pa·ram·e·ter (pəræmitər) *n.* (*math.*) a variable which is kept constant while others are being investigated ‖ (*math.*) a variable of which other variables are taken to be functions **par·a·met·ric** (pærəmétrik) *adj.* [Mod. L. fr. Gk *para*, beside + *metron*, measure]

par·a·met·ric (pærəmétrik) *adj.* (*math.*) of an equation in which there is a symbol representing an arbitrary constant—the symbol can be given any numerical value desired

par·am·ne·sia (pærəmní:ʒə) *n.* the illusion of remembering something which in fact one is experiencing for the first time [Mod. L.]

par·a·mo (pærəmou) *pl.* **par·a·mos** *n.* a high, treeless plateau, esp. in the northern Andes [Span.]

paramoecium *PARAMECIUM

par·a·morph (pærəmɔrf) *n.* (*mineral.*) a pseudomorph formed by physical but not chemical changes **par·a·mor·phic** *adj.* **par·a·mor·phism** *n.* [PARA- + Gk *morphē*, form]

par·a·mount (pærəmaunt) *adj.* supreme in rank, importance etc. [A.F. *paramont*, above fr. O.F.]

par·a·mour (pærəmuər) *n.* (*old-fash., rhet.*) a married man's mistress or married woman's lover [M.E. fr. O.F. *par amour*, by or because of love]

par·a·myx·o·vi·rus (pærəmiksouváirəs) *n.* (*med.*) a group of ribonucleic-acid-containing myxoviruses that cause mumps, measles, parainfluenza, etc.

Pa·ra·ná (pɑrɑná, pərɑná) a city (pop. 223,665) in E. Argentina, on the Paraná River 80 miles north of Rosario. It has a large river (oceangoing steamers) and railroad trade. Urquiza made it his capital, thus dividing Argentina between Buenos Aires and the rest

Pa·ra·ná (pɑrɑná) a river (2,040 miles long) flowing from S. central Brazil, around lower Paraguay (as the southeastern-southern border) and through N.W. Argentina to a delta on the Río de la Plata. It is navigable by river steamer to the Paraguay and by boat, between waterfalls, nearly to the Río Grande. With the Paraguay and the Pilcomayo it drains most of S. Brazil and N. Argentina, all of Paraguay and part of Bolivia. Headstreams: Paranaíba, Río Grande.

Pa·ra·na·í·ba (pærənɑí:bə) a headstream (530 miles long) of the Paraná, rising in the central highlands of S.E. Brazil

pa·rang (púrɑŋ) *n.* a short sword used in Malaysia and Indonesia as a weapon or tool [Malay]

par·a·noi·a (pærənɔiə) *n.* a mental disorder in which the sufferer believes that other people suspect, despise or persecute him or, less commonly, in which the sufferer has delusions of grandeur **par·a·noi·ac** (pærənɔiæk) *n.* and *adj.* **pár·a·noid** *n.* and *adj.* [Mod. L. fr. Gk fr. *paranoos*, distracted]

par·a·pet (pærəpit, pærəpet) *n.* a low wall at the edge of a bridge, flat roof, balcony etc. to prevent people from falling off ‖ (*mil.*) a defensive work of earth or stone in front of a trench or along the top of a rampart [F. or fr. Ital. *parapetto* fr. *parare*, to protect + *petto*, chest]

par·aph (pærəf) *n.* a flourish at the end of a signature, formerly used to make forgery more difficult [F. *paraphe*, *parafe*]

par·a·pha·sia (pærəféiʒə) *n.* (*med.*) a pathological condition in which the person affected uses words other than those intended [Mod. L. fr. *para*, beside + *-phasia*, speech]

par·a·pher·nal·ia (pærəfərnéiljə, pærəfənéiljə) *pl. n.* (sometimes construed as singular) miscellaneous personal belongings or equipment ‖ (*law*) a wife's personal possessions as distinct from her dowry [M.L. fr. *paraphernalia* (*bona*), wife's own (goods) fr. Gk]

par·a·phrase (pærəfreiz) *n.* a restatement in different words or free rendering of a text, passage etc. [F. fr. L. fr. Gk fr. *para-*, beside + *phrazein*, to tell]

paraphrase *pres. part.* **par·a·phras·ing** *past* and *past part.* **par·a·phrased** *v.t.* to make a paraphrase of ‖ *v.i.* to make a paraphrase [fr. F. *paraphraser*]

par·a·phras·tic (pærəfrǽstik) *adj.* having the nature of a paraphrase **par·a·phrás·ti·cal·ly** *adv.* [fr. M.L. *paraphrasticus* fr. Gk]

pa·raph·y·sis (pəræfisis) *pl.* **pa·raph·y·ses** (pəræfəsi:z) *n.* a sterile filament possessed by many cryptogamic plants [Mod. L. fr. *para*, beside + *phusis*, nature]

par·a·ple·gi·a (pærəplí:dʒiə) *n.* paralysis of both legs due to disease of or injury to the spinal cord **par·a·plé·gic** *adj.* and *n.* [Mod. L. fr. Gk *paraplēgia*, a stroke at the side]

par·a·po·di·um (pærəpóudiəm) *pl.* **par·a·po·di·a** (pærəpóudiːə) *n.* one of the unsegmented lateral locomotive processes on the body segments of certain annelid worms [PARA- + Gk *pous* (*podos*), foot]

par·a·po·lit·i·cal (pærəpolítik'l) *adj.* semipolitical

par·a·pro·fes·sion·al (pærəprəféʃən'l) *n.* one trained to assist a professional, esp. in teaching, nursing, etc; e.g., paramedical, paralegal — **par·a·pro·fes·sion·al** *adj.*

par·a·pro·tein (pærəpróuti:n) *n.* (*biochem.*) plasma protein with some qualities unlike normal protein, esp. some globulins —**par·a·pro·tein·e·mi·a** *n.* having abnormal amount of paraproteins

CONCISE PRONUNCIATION KEY: (a) æ, c*a*t; ɑ, c*a*r; ɔ f*aw*n; ei, sn*a*ke. (e) e, h*e*n; i:, sh*ee*p; iə, d*ee*r; ɛə, b*ea*r. (i) i, f*i*sh; ai, t*i*ger; ə:, b*i*rd. (o) o, *o*x; au, c*ow*; ou, g*oa*t; u, p*oo*r; ɔi, r*oy*al. (u) ʌ, d*u*ck; u, b*u*ll; u:, g*oo*se; ə, b*a*cill*u*s; ju:, c*u*be. x, lo*ch*; θ, *th*ink; ð, bo*th*er; z, *Z*en; ʒ, cor*s*age. dʒ, sava*g*e; ŋ, ora*ng*utan*g*; j, *y*ak; ʃ, fi*sh*; tʃ, fe*tch*; 'l, rabb*le*; 'n, redd*en*. Complete pronunciation key appears inside front cover.

par·a·psy·chol·o·gy (pærəsaikólədʒi:) *n.* the experimental study of psychic phenomena such as telepathy, clairvoyance etc.

par·a·quat [$C_{12}H_{14}N_2$] (pǽrəkwɒt) *n.* (*chem.*) herbicide used to spray marijuana fields; a weed killer

Pa·rá rubber (pɑrá) rubber obtained from South American trees, esp. from *Hevea braziliensis*, fam. *Euphorbiaceae* [after *Pará*, a state and city of Brazil]

par·a·sail (pǽrəseil) *n.* (*sports*) a maneuverable type of parachute

par·a·se·le·ne (pærəsilí:ni:) *pl.* **par·a·se·le·nae** (pærəsilí:ni:) *n.* a bright patch on a lunar halo [Mod. L. fr. Gk *para*, beside + *selēne*, moon]

par·a·sex·u·al·i·ty (pærəsekʃu:áeliti:) *n.* (*biol.*) capacity to reproduce with genes of different vegetative or somatic cells involving mitotic crossing over and loss of chromosomes, esp. among fungi —**par·a·sex·u·al** *adj.*

Para·shah (pɑ́rəʃɑ) *pl.* **Par·a·shoth** (pɑ́rəʃout) *n.* a reading from the Pentateuch in a synagogue, esp. on the sabbath and on feast days [Heb. = explanation]

par·a·site (pǽrəsait) *n.* an organism living in or on another living organism and deriving its nutriment partly or wholly from it, usually exhibiting some special adaptation, and often causing death or damage to its host (cf. SAPHROPHYTE, cf. SYMBIONT) ‖ someone who associates with a person or organization for the purpose of living at the expense of that person or group, without contributing anything to their or its well-being [fr. L. *parasitus* fr. Gk]

par·a·sit·ic (pærəsítik) *adj.* of, relating to, having the nature of or characteristic of a parasite **par·a·sit·i·cal** *adj.* [fr. L. *parasiticus*]

par·a·sit·i·side (pærəsítisaid) *n.* a substance that destroys parasites [fr. L. *parasitus*, parasite + *caedere*, to kill]

par·a·sit·ism (pǽrəsaitizəm) *n.* the association of parasite and host ‖ (*med.*) a diseased state caused by parasites

par·a·sol (pǽrəsɒl, pǽrəsɒl) *n.* an umbrella to give shade from the sun [F. fr. Ital.]

par·a·sta·tal (pærəstéit'l) *adj.* of one serving government in an auxiliary capacity, of an organization sponsored by the state, e.g., an authority

par·a·sym·pa·thet·ic (pærəsimpəθétik) *adj.* of or relating to the parasympathetic nervous system

parasympathetic nervous system (*physiol.*) the portion of the autonomic nervous system which has motor nerve fibers originating in the head and sacral regions of the spinal cord and generally maintains muscle tone, induces secretion and dilates blood vessels (cf. SYMPATHETIC NERVOUS SYSTEM)

par·a·syn·the·sis (pærəsínθisis) *n.* (*linguistics*) the formation of derivatives from compound words and their use to build up new words [Gk *parasunthesis* fr. *para*, beside + *sunthesis*, composition]

par·a·syn·thet·ic (pærəsinθétik) *adj.* (*linguistics*) relating to or formed by parasynthesis [fr. Gk *parasunthetos*]

par·a·tac·tic (pærətǽktik) *adj.* (*gram.*) of, relating to or characterized by parataxis **par·a·tac·ti·cal·ly** *adv.*

par·a·tax·is (pærətǽksis) *n.* (*gram.*) coordination of clauses etc. in succession without connectives, e.g. 'he went, she stayed' (cf. HYPOTAXIS) [Gk = a placing beside]

par·a·thy·roid (pærəθáirɔid) 1. *n.* one of (usually) four small endocrine glands, situated close to the thyroid gland or occasionally embedded in the gland, which produce a hormone regulating the metabolism of calcium and phosphorus 2. *adj.* concerning or produced by these glands

par·a·troop (pǽrətru:p) *adj.* of, relating to or involving paratroops [PARATROOPS]

par·a·troop·er (pǽrətru:pər) *n.* a member of a body of paratroops

par·a·troops (pǽrətru:ps) *pl. n.* troops transported by air and dropped, with their arms and equipment, by parachute [PARACHUTE TROOPS]

par·a·ty·phoid (pærətáifɔid) 1. *n.* an infectious enteric fever, resembling typhoid but milder 2. *adj.* of, involving or designating this fever

par·a·vane (pǽrəvein) *n.* a device with sharp teeth, fitted with vanes which control its depth, towed by warships to cut the moorings of floating mines

par·a·wing (pǽrəwiŋ) *n.* a sail shaped glider

parachute that unfurls during descent *Cf* PARA-FOIL

par·a·zo·an (pærəzóuən) 1. *n.* a member of the order *Parazoa*, the simplest animals of the sub-kingdom *Metazoa*. It denotes the grade of organization represented by sponges. Parazoans are a group of invertebrates of worldwide distribution, living and growing exclusively under water of any depth between several miles and a few inches and either salt or fresh 2. *adj.* pertaining to the order *Parazoa* or to a parazoan **par·a·zó·ic** *adj.* [Mod. L. fr. Gk fr. *para*, akin + *zoon*, animal]

par·boil (pɑ́rbɔil) *v.t.* to boil until partially cooked, usually as a preparation for roasting etc. [O.F. *parboillir*, *parbouillir*]

par·buck·le (pɑ́rbʌk'l) 1. *n.* a doubled rope, made fast above at its midpoint, each half forming a sling, used for lowering or hoisting a barrel, heavy gun etc. 2. *v.t. pres. part.* **par·buck·ling** *past and past part.* **par·buck·led** to hoist or lower with this device [older *parbunkle*, *parbuncle*, origin unknown]

Par·cae (pɑ́rsi:) (*mythol.*) the Roman name for the three Fates

par·cel (pɑ́rs'l) 1. *n.* one or more things secured by a string or wrapping to make a single object for handling and transport ‖ a number of things dealt with as a single unit, *a parcel of diamonds for sale* ‖ a portion, esp. of land forming part of a property 2. *v.t. pres. part.* **par·cel·ing**, esp. *Br.* **par·cel·ling** *past and past part.* **par·celed**, esp. *Br.* **par·celled** (with 'out') to distribute in portions ‖ (esp. with 'up') to make a parcel of ‖ (*naut.*) to wrap or cover with parceling **pár·cel·ing**, esp. *Br.* **pár·cel·ling** *n.* the act of making a parcel ‖ (*naut.*) a strip of canvas, usually covered with pitch, used to cover a caulked seam or to bind around a rope so as to keep moisture out [F. *parcelle*]

parcel post the branch of the postal system which deals with parcels as distinct from letters

par·ce·nar·y (pɑ́rsəneri:) *n.* (*law*) coparcenary [A.F. *parcenarie*, O.F. *parçonerie*]

par·ce·ner (pɑ́rsənər) *n.* (*law*) a coparcener [A.F. fr. O.F. *parçonier*]

parch (pɑrtʃ) *v.t.* to make dry by heating, esp. to excess ‖ to make very thirsty ‖ to dry (beans, grain etc.) by exposure to steady, intensive heat ‖ *v.i.* to become hot and dry [origin unknown]

parch·ment (pɑ́rtʃmənt) *n.* (esp. *hist.*) the skin of a calf, kid or sheep prepared for writing on ‖ a sheet of such prepared skin ‖ paper made to resemble this ‖ a document written or printed on this material [M.E. *perchemin* fr. F. *parchemin*]

par·don (pɑ́rd'n) *n.* a pardoning or being pardoned ‖ (*law*) an official release from a penalty, or the document granting this ‖ (*pl.*, *Roman Catholicism*) indulgences **to beg someone's pardon** to ask someone to excuse one, e.g. for some minor breach of manners [M.E. fr. O.F. *perdun*, *pardun* fr. *pardonner*, to pardon]

pardon *v.t.* to choose to let (a person) be unpunished or no longer punished for wrongful acts they have committed ‖ to require no punishment for (a fault) ‖ to excuse or forgive [O.F. *pardoner* and F. *pardonner* fr. L.L. *perdonare* fr. *per-*, through, fully + *donare*, to give]

par·don·a·ble (pɑ́rd'nəb'l) *adj.* (of a crime, fault etc.) capable of being pardoned [F. *pardonnable*]

par·don·er (pɑ́rd'nər) *n.* (*hist.*) a priest licenced to sell papal indulgences

pare (peər) *pres. part.* **par·ing** *past and past part.* **pared** *v.t.* to cut off the outer surface, skin or edge of, *to pare an apple* ‖ to cut off (the outer surface, skin or edge) from something ‖ to reduce the bulk of (something) by removing successive thicknesses or portions, *his profits were pared down by taxes* [F. *parer*, to prepare, trim]

par·e·gor·ic (pærəgórik, pærəgórik) *n.* camphorated tincture of opium, used to relieve pain, e.g. of diarrhea [fr. L.L. *paregoricus* adj., soothing pain]

pa·ren·chy·ma (pərénkəmə) *n.* (*bot.*) a simple plant tissue that consists typically of unspecialized thin-walled cells of simple form and structure (cf. PROSENCHYMA). It may serve for photosynthesis (*PALISADE PARENCHYMA), storage or conduction, and occurs throughout the plant body (e.g. fleshy parts of fruit, softer parts of leaves and other storage organs). Parenchyma cells with specialized secretory functions may occur in various tissues and parts of the plant (*COLLENCHYMA, *SCLERENCHYMA) ‖

the characteristic or distinctive tissue of an organ, or an abnormal growth as distinguished from its supporting portion **par·en·chym·a·tous** (pærenkímətəs) *adj.* [Gk *parenchuma* fr. *para*, beside + *enchuma*, infusion]

par·ent (péərənt, pǽrənt) *n.* someone who begets or gives birth to offspring ‖ an organism, thing or organization which is the source of a new one [O.F.]

par·ent·age (péərəntidʒ, pǽrəntidʒ) *n.* immediate or remoter ancestry [F.]

pa·ren·tal (pərént'l) *adj.* pertaining to, characteristic of, or like a parent [fr. L. *parentalis*]

parental generation (*biol.*) a generation of individuals who are crossbred to produce hybrids

pa·ren·the·sis (pərénθisis) *pl.* **pa·ren·the·ses** (pərénθisi:z) *n.* a word, phrase or sentence, usually having its own complete meaning, inserted into a sentence which is grammatically complete without this insertion, and marked off from it by punctuation, e.g. 'it was surprisingly effective', or 'it was, to our surprise, effective' ‖ either of the punctuation marks (or) used to contain such a word, phrase etc., or to mark off several qualities or elements in a formula, equation etc. as units to be treated as a whole **pa·rén·the·size** *pres. part.* **pa·ren·the·siz·ing** *past and past part.* **pa·rén·the·sized** *v.t.* to insert parentheses in (a speech etc.) ‖ to insert (a word etc.) in a sentence as a parenthesis ‖ to place parentheses around (a written word etc.) [M.L. fr. Gk fr. *para*, beside + *en*, in + *thesis*, a placing]

par·en·thet·ic (pærənθétik) *adj.* constituting a parenthesis ‖ containing a parenthesis **par·en·thét·i·cal** *adj.* [fr. M.L. *parentheticus* fr. Gk]

par·ent·hood (péərənthud, pǽrənthud) *n.* the state of being a parent

pa·rer·gon (pærɔ́:rgon) *pl.* **pa·rer·ga** (pærɔ́:rgə) *n.* a piece of work subsidiary to, or a by-product of, some main work [L. fr. Gk]

pa·re·sis (pərí:sis, pǽrisis) *n.* partial paralysis ‖ general paresis **pa·ret·ic** (pərétik) *n.* and *adj.* [Mod. L. fr. Gk = paralysis]

par ex·cel·lence (pæréksəlɑns) *adv.* preeminently [F. = by excellence]

par·fait (pɑrféi) *n.* a dessert of ice cream, fruits and fruit syrups arranged in layers in a tall glass and topped with whipped cream

par·get (pɑ́rdʒit) 1. *v.t. pres. part.* **par·get·ing**, **par·get·ting** *past and past part.* **par·get·ed**, **par·get·ted** to cover or coat with parget (plaster) 2. *n.* pargeting ‖ the plaster used in pargeting **pár·get·ing**, **pár·get·ting**, *n.* ornamentation of plaster on a wall, esp. with incised patterns [prob. fr. O.F. *pargeter*, *parjeter*, to throw or cast over a surface]

par·gy·line [$C_{11}H_{13}N$] (pɑ́rgili:n) *n.* (*pharm.*) drug for relief of high blood pressure; marketed as Eutonyl

par·he·li·a·cal (pɑrhiláiəkəl) *adj.* of or like a parhelion

par·he·lic (pɑrhí:lik, pɑrhélik) *adj.* parheliacal [PARHELION]

parhelic circle a luminous ring sometimes seen around the sun, caused by scattering of ice crystals in the earth's atmosphere

par·he·li·on (pɑrhí:li:ən) *pl.* **par·he·li·a** (pɑrhí:li:ə) *n.* a bright patch sometimes visible on a parhelic circle [fr. L. *parelion* fr. Gk fr. *para*, beside + *helios*, the sun]

Pa·ria, Gulf of (pɑ́rjə) an inlet (c. 100 miles long, 40 miles wide) between Trinidad and Venezuela, enclosed on the north by Paria peninsula, and connected with the Atlantic by two hazardous straits. Port of Spain. Trinidad, lies on this gulf

pa·ri·ah (pəráiə, pǽri:ə) *n.* a social outcast ‖ a member of a low caste in parts of S. India and Burma, usually employed as a servant or common laborer [fr. Tamil *paraiyar*, pl. of *paraiyan*]

pariah dog a mongrel dog of parts of N. Africa and Asia which lives by scavenging

Par·i·an (péəri:ən) 1. *adj.* of or pertaining to the island Paros, famous for fine white marble ‖ of or designating this marble 2. *n.* a native or inhabitant of Paros ‖ a white porcelain used for statuettes etc. [fr. L. *Parius*]

pa·ri·es (péəri:i:z) *pl.* **pa·ri·e·tes** (pəráiiti:z) *n.* (*biol.*, esp. *pl.*) a wall of a hollow organ, plant cell etc. [L. = wall]

pa·ri·e·tal (pəráiit'l) *adj.* of or relating to a wall of a body cavity etc. [F. *pariétal* fr. L.]

parietal bone either of two bones forming the upper part of the skull

pa·ri·e·tals (pəráiit'ls) *n.* rules regarding visitors of the opposite sex in a men's or women's dormitory

Pa·ri·ma, Serra (pərí:mɑ) a mountain range rising to 8,000 ft extending north and south along part of the Venezuela-Brazil boundary. It is the source of the Orinoco River

par·i·mu·tu·el (pæri:mjú:tʃu:əl) n. a betting system by which all bets are recorded, the sums wagered on each eventuality are totaled, and the total sum wagered (minus a percentage for running costs and tax) is divided, in proportion to the stake, among those who placed bets on the winner ‖ the machine that totalizes the bets [F.=mutual wager]

par·ing (péəriŋ) n. a strip of rind etc. that has been pared off something

Pa·ri·ni (parí:ni:), Giuseppe (1729–99), Italian lyric poet. His 'Odi' and 'Il Giorno' are among the classics of Italian poetry

Par·is (pǽris) the son of King Priam of Troy. His abduction of Helen led to the Trojan War

Paris, Matthew (c. 1200–59), English chronicler and monk of St Albans. His 'Chronica majora' is a continuation of Roger of Wendover's chronicle, and is a valuable source for the period 1235–59

Paris the capital (pop. 2,183,000, with agglom. 8,510,000), and economic and cultural center of France, on the Seine in the central Paris basin. It is the country's chief river port and communications center, and concentrates a quarter of France's industry: luxury goods (esp. fine furniture, leather goods, haute couture and readymade clothing, jewelry) in the city, heavy industry (mechanical, electrical and aeronautical engineering, motorcars, metallurgy, chemicals, food processing) in the suburbs. The city's geometric center and original site is the Île de la Cité in the Seine, containing the law courts, Sainte Chapelle (the Gothic chapel of St Louis, 1242–8) and Notre Dame. The left bank contains the university (or Latin) quarter, most of the remaining medieval buildings and, far west, the Eiffel Tower. The right bank, behind the Louvre and the Tuileries gardens, which stretch along the river, contains the financial and commercial section laced by the system of squares and boulevards laid out by Haussmann (19th c.): notably, the Place de l'Étoile (1836, surrounding the Arc de Triomphe) and the Place de la Concorde, with the Avenue des Champs-Élysées connecting them. Government buildings are spread throughout the center. Cultural institutions: university (1215), five national theaters, Louvre, Museum of Modern Art (1947), National Library, numerous other museums, academic and scientific institutes, and national schools. HISTORY. Paris developed as a Roman town (1st c. B.C.), and according to tradition, was saved from the Huns by St Geneviève (5th c.). It was temporarily the Merovingian capital under Clovis I and was besieged (885–7) by the Vikings. Its importance increased when Hugh Capet became king of France (987). The Sorbonne made it a center of theological learning (13th and 14th cc.). Louis XIV and Louis XV gave Paris some of its finest public buildings. Paris was the center of the French Revolution. It was besieged (1870–1) during the Franco-Prussian War, was shelled in the 1st world war, and was occupied by the Germans (1940–4) during the 2nd world war. It was the scene of the treaties (1947) between the Allies and Italy, Rumania, Bulgaria, Hungary and Finland after the 2nd world war. Massive urban renewal projects, such as the one at Beaubourg, have changed its face during the postwar period and plans are underway for major construction in Paris and the Paris Basin all the way to the mouth of the Seine River

Paris Commune *COMMUNE, THE

Pa·ris, é·cole de (eikɔldəpæri:) a name (invented c. 1925) for the painters and sculptors (e.g. Soutine, Chagall, Modigliani and Brancusi) who came to Paris from different countries and associated with the modern 20th-c. French school [F. = school of Paris]

Paris green a double salt of copper arsenite and copper acetate, used as a light green pigment and insecticide

par·ish (pǽriʃ) n. an administrative district of some churches, esp. a part of a diocese in the charge of a priest or minister ‖ (often construed as pl.) the residents of such a district ‖ the members of the congregation of a Protestant church ‖ a civil division in Louisiana, corresponding to a county [M.E. parissche, parosche fr. O.F. fr. L. fr. Gk paroikia, neighborhood, diocese]

parish clerk an official of a parish church appointed by the clergyman to perform certain duties

pa·rish·ion·er (pəríʃənər) n. someone who belongs to a parish [fr. M.E. parishion fr. O.F.+-ER]

parish register a record of baptisms, marriages, burials etc. kept at a parish church

Pa·ri·sian (pərí:ʒən, pəríʒən) 1. adj. of, pertaining to or characteristic of Paris, France 2. n. a native or resident of Paris [F. parisien]

Paris, Treaty of a treaty (1763) ending the Seven Years' War. Britain gained Canada and Cape Breton Is. and all French territory east of the Mississippi, and Florida from Spain. Control of India passed from France to Britain ‖ a treaty (1783) ending the Revolutionary War. The independence of the U.S.A. was recognized by Britain and the boundaries of the U.S.A. were fixed ‖ a treaty (1841) during the Napoleonic Wars after Napoleon's first abdication. It limited France to its boundaries of 1792 ‖ a treaty (1815) at the end of the Napoleonic Wars. It limited France to its boundaries of 1790 and imposed heavy reparations ‖ a treaty (1856) ending the Crimean War. The neutrality of the Black Sea was guaranteed ‖ a treaty (1898) ending the Spanish-American War. Spain 'relinquished' Cuba to the U.S.A. in trust for its inhabitants. Its provisions stressed the temporary character of U.S. occupation ‖ a treaty (1947) between the Allies and Italy, Finland, Rumania, Hungary and Bulgaria

par·i·ty (pǽriti:) n. equality in status, values etc. ‖ equality of purchasing power at a legally fixed ratio, between two convertible currencies at par ‖ equivalence (maintained by government price supports) between the current ratio of agricultural prices to the prevailing price structure and this ratio during a selected base period ‖ (computer) a redundant bit added to others to detect a bit inaccuracy ‖ (math.) odd or even function; oddness or evenness ‖ (nuclear phys.) the property that indicates whether an elementary particle has a mirror image in accordance with space reflection symmetry that holds that there is no fundamental difference between left and right ‖ (football) principle that all teams in a league exist in the same competitive class [fr. L. paritas fr. par. equal]

Park (pɑrk) Mungo (1771–1806), Scottish explorer. He made two expeditions to discover the course and mouth of the Niger (1795–7 and 1805–6). The first is described in his 'Travels in the Interior of Africa' (1799). In the second he died with all his party

Park, Robert Ezra (1864–1944), U.S. sociologist, secretary to Booker T. Washington. He studied the blacks and became an authority on race relations. His 'Introduction to the Science of Sociology' (1921, in collaboration with E. W. Burgess) promoted empirical research

park (pɑrk) 1. n. a very large area of land belonging to the government preserved in its natural state and accessible to the public ‖ (mil.) space allotted to artillery, stores etc. in an encampment, or the artillery, stores etc. themselves ‖ an enclosed area that is used for games or sports, a baseball park ‖ a tract of grassland, with widely spaced trees, paths, small lakes, beds of shrubs and flowers etc., adjoining or surrounding a mansion ‖ a similar tract laid out (e.g. in a city) for the general public ‖ an area set aside for oyster breeding, covered by the sea at high tide 2. v.t. to put or leave (a vehicle) temporarily by the roadside or in a space set aside for this purpose ‖ (pop.) to deposit for the time being in a certain place, park your baggage in the hall ‖ v.i. to put or leave a vehicle temporarily by the roadside or in a specially allotted space [O.F. parc fr. Gmc]

par·ka (pɑ́rkə) n. a long fur jacket with an attached hood, worn by Eskimos ‖ a similar garment of windproof fabric worn by campers, mountaineers etc. [Aleutian]

Par·ker (pɑ́rkər), Dorothy (1893–1967), U.S. writer and critic. Her often sardonic verse includes 'Enough Rope' (1926) and 'Not So Deep as a Well' (1936) and her short stories of social satire include 'Laments for the Living' (1930) and 'Here Lies' (1939)

Parker, Sir (Horatio) Gilbert (1860–1932), Canadian politician and writer, best known for his 'Pierre and His People' (1892) and other adventure stories of the Canadian northwest and of French Canada

Parker, Matthew (1504–75), English prelate,

the first archbishop of Canterbury (1559–75) under the Elizabethan settlement. He guided the Church of England on a moderate course between Catholicism and extreme Protestantism, defending episcopal organization, and checking the rise of Puritanism. He revised the Thirty-nine Articles (1562), supervised the preparation of the Bishops' Bible (1568) and wrote 'De antiquitate ecclesiae' (1572)

Parker, Theodore (1810–60), U.S. theologian. He set forth his liberal and transcendentalist views in his 'Discourse of Matters Pertaining to Religion' (1842). He was a leader of antislavery and other reform movements

parking lot (Am.=Br. car park) a space provided for the temporary parking of motor vehicles

parking orbit (aerospace) the orbit of a space vehicle while it is serving as a launching and/or recovery station for another space vehicle

Park·in·son's disease (pɑ́rkins'nz) paralysis agitans, a chronic nervous disease characterized by a progressive tremor and weakening of muscular tone [after James Parkinson (1755–1824), Eng. neurologist, who first diagnosed it]

Parkinson's Law in an organization, 'Work expands to fill the time available for completion,' and 'Staff increases at a fixed rate regardless of the amount of work produced'; by C. Northcote Parkinson, English historian and satirist

Park·man (pɑ́rkmən), Francis (1823–93), U.S. historian, best known for his multivolume series 'France and England in North America' (1865–92)

park·way (pɑ́rkwęi) n. a broad highway lined with trees and grass, sometimes landscaped in the middle and usually closed to heavy vehicles, usually having an imposed speed limit

par·lance (pɑ́rləns) n. way of speaking, esp. in regard to vocabulary and idiom [A.F. and O.F.]

par·lay (pɑ́rlei, pɑ́rli:) 1. n. a bet or series of bets made by parlaying 2. v.t. to lay (a former bet and its winnings) on a later race, contest etc. ‖ to make use of (some asset) to gain some greater advantage, to parlay a small income into a fortune [F. fr. Ital. paroli fr. paro, equal]

parle·ment (pǽrləmɑ̃) n. (F. hist.) any of the supreme judicial courts of the ancien régime, abolished in 1790 [F.]

par·ley (pɑ́rli:) 1. v.i. to confer, esp. to talk peace terms with an enemy 2. pl. par·leys n. an official conference, esp. for settling a dispute, e.g. one held under truce arrangements with an enemy [perh. fr. F. parler, to speak]

par·lia·ment (pɑ́rləmənt) n. the supreme legislative body of certain countries. The parliament of the United Kingdom comprises the sovereign, the lords spiritual and temporal assembled in the House of Lords, and the representatives of the counties, boroughs etc. meeting in the House of Commons [M.E. fr. O.F. parlement, a speaking]

—The English parliament developed out of the king's council of the 13th c., a feudal assembly of leading barons summoned at the king's will. Knights from each county were summoned to assemblies in 1213, 1227 and 1254, and Simon de Montfort's parliament (1265) also included representatives from the boroughs. Organization remained vague, however, even after Edward I's Model Parliament (1295). Parliament assumed the right to make laws (14th c.) and to control taxation (1340), and the division into Lords and Commons became permanent in the reign (1327–77) of Edward III. By 1377, parliament was claiming the right to examine public accounts and to impeach the king's officers, and by the end of the 15th c. its members claimed freedom of speech and freedom from arrest. The Commons increased their demands for privilege during the reign (1558–1603) of Elizabeth I, and serious constitutional conflicts marked the reigns of James I and Charles I. The Long Parliament (1640–53) opposed Charles in the Civil War (1642–52) and England was ruled (1653–60) under a written republican constitution. The Restoration (1660) renewed the problem of the relationship between king and parliament, and out of the opposition to the succession of James II arose the beginnings of the party division into Whigs and Tories. After the Glorious Revolution (1688), parliament was able to assert its supremacy in the Bill of Rights (1689) and the Act of Settlement (1701), though the administration and the executive remained in the hands of the sovereign. Parliament was enlarged by the Act of Union (1707) to represent Great Britain, and the 18th c. saw the development of political parties and of the cabinet. The office of prime minister also emerged at this time, though the prime minister was dependent on royal patronage to manage parliament. The Reform Act of 1832 slightly increased the electorate and began to redistribute seats, that of 1867 enfranchised urban workers, and that of 1884 virtually completed manhood suffrage. The ballot was introduced (1872) and the suffrage was extended (1918) to women of 30 and over, and (1928) to women of 21 and over. The Liberals (formerly the Whigs), the Conservatives (formerly the Tories) and, in the early 20th c., the Labour party developed nationwide organization. The Parliament Act (1911) limited the power of the House of Lords, giving legislative supremacy to the Commons and reduced the length of a parliament from seven years to five. The House of Lords admitted life peers and women (1958). Modern executive government is exercised, in the sovereign's name, by a cabinet and ministry represented in both Houses, and ultimately responsible to the Commons. The royal right to veto legislation has not been exercised since the 18th c.

par·lia·men·tar·i·an (pɑrləməntéəri:ən) *n.* a person well versed in parliamentary procedure ‖ (*hist.*) a supporter of parliament in the English Civil War, 1642–52 (cf. ROYALIST) **par·lia·men·tár·i·an·ism** *n.* the doctrine of government by a parliament

par·lia·men·ta·ry (pɑrləméntəri) *adj.* of or relating to parliament ‖ in accordance with the uses and practices of parliament ‖ (of language) permitted to be used in parliament ‖ (*Br. hist.*) of or belonging to or supporting parliament in the English Civil War (1642–52)

parliamentary privilege the rights and immunities enjoyed by a member of parliament, e.g. freedom from charges of libel and slander while in pursuit of his parliamentary duties

par·lor, *Br.* **par·lour** (pɑ́rlər) *n.* (*old-fash.*) the best reception room of a house, not usually used as a living room ‖ a shop or business establishment specially equipped to perform some specified service, *a funeral parlor* ‖ (*Br.*) a room in an inn with chairs and tables, where customers can talk in comfort over their drinks [M.E. fr. A.F. *parlur*, O.F. *parleor*]

parlor car a railroad passenger car fitted out like a living room

par·lor·maid, *Br.* **par·lour·maid** (pɑ́rlərmeid) *n.* (*old-fash.*) a woman employed in a home to wait on the table, answer the door, and do light housework

parlour *PARLOR

parlourmaid *PARLORMAID

par·lous (pɑ́rləs) *adj.* (*rhet.*) involving danger or risk [M.E. *perlous* fr. *perilous*]

Par·ma (pɑ́rmə) a market city (pop. 178,000) of Etruscan origin in Emilia-Romagna, Italy. Industries: food processing, mechanical engineering, textiles. Romanesque-Gothic cathedral (12th c.) and baptistry (1196–1260), palace (16th–17th cc.), theater, museums. University (1502). It was the capital of the duchy of Parma and Piacenza (1545–1860)

Par·men·i·des (pɑrménidi:z) (c. 504–450 B.C.), Greek Eleatic philosopher. He regarded movement and change as illusions, and the universe as single, continuous and motionless. He discovered the law of contradiction and the possibility of logical proof. His work has come down to us in some 25 fragments of a poem in hexameters

Par·me·san (pɑ́rmizæn, pɑ́rmizan) **1.** *adj.* of or relating to Parma **2.** *n.* a hard, dry, sharp Italian cheese often used grated over spaghetti etc. [F. *parmesan* and Ital. *parmigiano*]

Par·mi·gia·ni·no (pɑrmi:dʒɑní:nou) (Francesco Maria Mazzola, 1503–40), Italian mannerist painter. His frescos are chiefly in Rome and Parma. The long necks and long hands of his figures help to express spiritual intensity

Par·na·í·ba (pɑrnɑíːbə) a river (c. 900 miles long) in N.E. Brazil, flowing into the Atlantic

Par·nas·si·an (pɑrnǽsi:ən) **1.** *adj.* of, designating or characteristic of a 19th-c. school of French poets (incl. Leconte de Lisle, Gautier, Banville, Heredia, Sully Prudhomme and Coppée) who, in reaction against Romanticism, stressed perfection of poetic form and defended the notion of 'art for art's sake' (1866–76) ‖ of or relating to poetry as an art, esp. with regard to

form alone **2.** *n.* a poet of the Parnassian school [fr. L. *Parnassius, Parnasius,* of Mt Parnassus]

Par·nas·sus (pɑrnǽsəs) a mountain (summit 8,062 ft) between Phocis and Boeotia, Greece, overlooking the Gulf of Corinth. It was sacred in antiquity to Apollo and the Muses

Par·nell (pɑrnél), Charles Stewart (1846–91), Irish nationalist politician. He organized an agrarian boycott and obstructed business in the House of Commons until Gladstone passed the Irish Land Act (1881). His influence as leader of the Home Rule movement waned when he was unjustly accused of political murders (1887) and when he was named as correspondent in a divorce suit (1889)

pa·ro·chi·al (pəróuki:əl) *adj.* relating to a parish ‖ (of opinions, ideas) narrowly limited in scope, provincial **pa·ró·chi·al·ism** *n.* narrowness of opinions or ideas [O.F.]

parochial school a school supported by a Church, esp. by the Roman Catholic Church

par·o·dy (pǽrədi:) **1.** *pl.* **par·o·dies** *n.* an imitation of the characteristic style of a writer, composer etc. or of a literary, artistic or musical work, designed to ridicule ‖ a poor imitation, travesty **2.** *v.t. pres. part.* **par·o·dy·ing** *past* and *past part.* **par·o·died** to make (someone or something) the subject of parody [fr. Gk *parōdia,* a burlesque poem or song]

par of exchange the recognized value of one nation's money in terms of that of another, esp. when both use the same metal as a standard of value

pa·role (pəróul) **1.** *n.* a promise given by a prisoner of war that in return for liberty or a degree of liberty he will respect certain conditions ‖ the conditional release of a civil prisoner ‖ liberation gained by parole ‖ (*mil.*) a password used by officers only **2.** *v.t. pres. part.* **pa·rol·ing** *past* and *past part.* **pa·roled** to release on parole [F.=formal promise]

par·o·mo·my·cin (pærəmoumqisin) *n.* (*pharm.*) broad-spectrum antibiotic used in the treatment of amebiasis and bacillary dysenteries; marketed as Humatin

par·o·nym (pǽrənim) *n.* a paronymous word [fr. Gk *parónumon* neut. adj., paronymous]

pa·ron·y·mous (pəróniməs) *adj.* (of words) having the same root ‖ (of words) pronounced alike but having different meanings [fr. Gk *parónumos* fr. *para,* beside+*onoma,* name]

Par·os (péərɒs) an island (area 81 sq. miles, pop. 7,314) of the Cyclades, Greece, Famous for its white marble. Capital: Paros. Exports: wine, figs, wool

pa·ro·tic (pərótik) *adj.* (*anat.*) beside the ear [fr. Mod. L. *paroticus* fr. PARA-+Gk *ous* (*ōtos*), ear]

pa·rot·id (pərótid) **1.** *adj.* of or designating a salivary gland in front of and below each ear **2.** *n.* this gland [F. *parotide* or fr. L. *parotis* (*parotidis*) fr. Gk *para,* beside+Gk *ous* (*ōtos*), the ear]

par·o·ti·tis (pærətáitis) *n.* inflammation of the parotid glands, e.g. in mumps ‖ mumps [fr. L. *parotis* (*parotidis*), the parotid gland]

par·ox·ysm (pǽrəksizəm) *n.* a sudden and violent muscular contraction and relaxation ‖ periodic intensification of an illness ‖ a sudden explosive burst of laughter, rage etc. **pár·ox·ys·mal** *adj.* [F. *paroxysme* fr. M.L. fr. Gk]

par·pen (pɑ́rpən) *n.* a perpend [O.F. *parpain*]

par·quet (pɑrkéi, pɑrkét) **1.** *n.* flooring consisting of pieces of wood arranged in a pattern, e.g. of parquetry ‖ the lower floor of some theaters, or the front section of this, i.e. excluding the part beneath the balcony **2.** *v.t.* to provide (a room) with parquet flooring ‖ to make (a floor) of parquet [F.]

par·quet·ry (pɑ́rkitri:) *n.* woodwork of small, thin inlaid pieces arranged in esp. geometric patterns, used for flooring etc. [F. *parqueterie*]

Parr *CATHERINE PARR

parr, *Br.* also **par** (pɑr) *n.* a young salmon before it becomes a smolt ‖ a young individual of any of several other fishes [origin unknown]

par·ra·keet, par·a·keet (pǽrəki:t) *n.* any of various small, slender, long-tailed parrots [O.E. *paroquet,* Ital. *parrochetto*]

par·ri·cid·al (pærisáid'l) *adj.* of, relating to or guilty of parricide [fr. L. *parricidalis*]

par·ri·cide (pǽrisaid) *n.* someone who murders his father ‖ (*rhet.*) someone who murders his mother or another close relative ‖ any of these crimes [F. fr. L.]

par·rot (pǽrət) **1.** *n.* any of a great number of tropical birds of the order *Psittaciformes,* with a

strong, curved, hooked bill, and usually brilliant plumage. Many can be trained to imitate human speech and other sounds ‖ someone who repeats words or actions mechanically without using the intelligence **2.** *v.t.* to repeat mechanically, without using the intelligence [origin unknown]

parrot *n.* (*mil.*) transponder equipment used to identify friend or foe

parrot disease psittacosis

parrot fever psittacosis

parrot fish any of several brilliantly colored tropical marine fish, esp. of fam. *Scaridae,* having a beaklike projection of the jaw

Par·ry (pǽri:), Sir Charles Hubert Hastings (1848–1918), English composer. He is best known for his choral works, e.g. the cantata 'Blest Pair of Sirens'

par·ry (pǽri:) **1.** *v. pres. part.* **par·ry·ing** *past* and *past part.* **par·ried** *v.t.* to stop (a blow, weapon etc.) from striking by putting something in its path to change its direction ‖ to avert by interposing something, *to parry a question by asking another* ‖ *v.i.* to ward off a blow, weapon, unwelcome question etc. in that way **2.** *pl.* **par·ries** *n.* the act of parrying esp. in boxing, fencing etc. ‖ an instance of this [prob. fr. F. *parer,* to ward off]

parse (pɑrs, pɑrz) *pres. part.* **pars·ing** *past* and *past part.* **parsed** *v.t.* to define the grammatical function of (a word) by giving it the name of a part of speech ‖ to dissect (a sentence) according to the grammatical functions of its parts [fr. L. *pars* (*orationis*), part (of speech)]

par·sec (pɑ́rsek) *n.* (*astron.*) a unit of measurement equal to the distance giving rise to a heliocentric parallax of one second of arc (3.26 light-years) [PARALLAX+SECOND]

Par·see, Par·si (pɑ́rsi:) *n.* a member of a Zoroastrian sect descended from the Persians who fled to India (8th c.) to escape Moslem persecution. Today over 100,000 of them live in India, concentrated in Bombay, where the community has great influence in business. There are about 15,000 in Iran **Pár·see·ism, Pár·si·ism** *n.* [Pers. *Pársī,* Persian]

par·si·mo·ni·ous (pɑrsəmóuni:əs) *adj.* too careful and sparing with money or assets ‖ scanty, meager, *a parsimonious contribution* [fr. L. *parsimonia,* parsimony]

par·si·mo·ny (pɑ́rsəmouni:) *n.* the quality of being parsimonious [fr. L. *parsimonia*]

pars·ley (pɑ́rsli:) *n. Petroselinum crispum,* fam. *Umbelliferae,* a European aromatic herb with divided, curly or smooth leaves, native to the Mediterranean. It is widely cultivated for use as a garnish and for flavoring ‖ any of certain other plants of fam. *Umbelliferae* [O.E. *petersilie* fr. L. fr. Gk fr. *petros,* stone+*selinon,* parsley]

pars·nip (pɑ́rsnip) *n. Pastinaca sativa,* fam. *Umbelliferae,* a European biennial plant. Its long whitish taproot, consisting mainly of phloem cells filled with starch, in cultivated varieties develops a sweet flavor after exposure to cold, and is used as a vegetable ‖ the root itself ‖ any of several similar or related plants [M.E. *passenep, pasnepe* perh. fr. O.F]

par·son (pɑ́rs'n) *n.* a Protestant clergyman, esp. one holding a benefice [M.E. *persone* fr. O.F.]

par·son·age (pɑ́rs'nidʒ) *n.* the house of a parish parson ‖ the house of any minister of religion [M.E. *personnage* fr. O.F.]

Par·son·i·an Resembling Theories (pɑrsóuni:ən) (*social science*) theories hypothesizing (1) personalities and cultures can be analyzed as action systems; (2) each action system involves elements of maintenance of patterns, integration, goal attainment and adaptation; (3) societies evolve toward functional specialization; (4) social structures may be analyzed in terms of values, norms, collectivities and roles. These theories were developed by sociologist Talcott Parsons

par·son·ic (pɑrsónik) *adj.* of, like or characteristic of a parson **par·són·i·cal** *adj.*

Par·sons (pɑ́rs'nz), Sir Charles Algernon (1854–1931), British engineer. He invented the steam turbine (1884), which revolutionized marine engineering

Parsons, Per·sons (pɑ́rs'nz), Robert (1546–1610), English Jesuit. He worked with Campion for the reconversion of England to Catholicism (1580–1) and founded several seminaries abroad for training English priests

Parsons, Talcott (1902–79) U.S. sociologist. Considered the major theorist in American sociology through the 1950s and 1960s, he also

CONCISE PRONUNCIATION KEY: **(a)** æ, c*a*t; ɑ, c*a*r; ɔ f*aw*n; ei, sn*a*ke. **(e)** e, h*e*n; i:, sh*ee*p; iə, d*ee*r; ɛə, b*ea*r. **(i)** i, f*i*sh; ai, t*i*ger; ə:, b*i*rd. **(o)** o, *o*x; au, c*ow*; ou, g*oa*t; u, p*oo*r; ɔi, r*oy*al. **(u)** ʌ, d*u*ck; u, b*u*ll; u:, g*oo*se; ə, b*a*cillus; ju:, c*u*be. x, lo*ch*; θ, *th*ink; ð, bo*th*er; z, *Z*en; ʒ, corsa*g*e; dʒ, sava*g*e; ŋ, ora*ng*utang; j, *y*ak; ʃ, *fi*sh; tʃ, fe*tch*; 'l, rabb*le*; 'n, redd*en*. Complete pronunciation key appears inside front cover.

strongly influenced anthropology, psychology and, to a lesser degree, history. His functional approach to the study of society explained any society as a total system of inter-related institutions each fulfilling functions necessary for the continuing operation of the society. He founded (1946) and taught at Harvard University's department of social relations. His works include 'The Structure of Social Action' (1937) and 'The Social System' (1951)

part (part) **1.** *n.* that which is less than all, *to walk part of the way home* ‖ one of several equal amounts, numbers, quantities etc. which, when combined, constitute a whole, *fifteen minutes is a fourth part of an hour* ‖ one of several amounts, numbers, quantities etc. which are not necessarily equal, and which, when combined, constitute a whole ‖ any activity, function, duty etc. allotted to or performed by an individual and regarded as contributing to some enterprise, event etc., *he wants no part in this affair* ‖ the lines and actions assigned to a performer in a play, opera etc. ‖ the function or task of performing these lines and actions, *to audition for a part in a play* ‖ the printed or written lines of an actor ‖ one of the parties in a transaction, contest, dispute etc. ‖ an individual thing, organ, member etc. that constitutes an essential element in something, *the parts of a machine* ‖ one of the units of a serial publication ‖ (*mus.*) a series of notes, allotted to a particular type of voice or instrument in a composition, *sing the bass part* ‖ (*mus.*) an individual score on which this is written or printed ‖ (*Am.=Br.* parting) a dividing line formed where the hair is combed in opposite directions ‖ (*pl.*) regions, *foreign parts* ‖ (*pl., rhet.*) abilities, *a man of parts* **for my part** as far as I am concerned **in part** partly, *the house is furnished in part* **on my (his,** etc.**) part** for which I am (he is etc.) responsible, *it was a lapse on my part* **part and parcel** an essential element, *receptions are part and parcel of the mayor's job* **to play a part in** to contribute something towards the total effect or result or activity of, *saving plays a part in a sound economy* **to take in good part** to take no offense at, *he took the joke in good part* **to take part in** to participate in **to take someone's part** to side with (someone) in a dispute etc. **2.** *adv.* partly, *he is part Italian* [O.E. and F. fr. L. *pars* (*partis*)]

part *v.t.* to divide into parts, *the police parted the crowd* ‖ to separate, *he parted the fighting dogs* ‖ to comb (the hair) so as to make a part ‖ *v.i.* (with 'from', 'with') to go away, take one's leave, *he parted with her on bad terms* ‖ to leave one another, *we parted at midnight* ‖ (with 'with') to let go of the possession of something, *he hated parting with his piano* ‖ to draw apart, *the curtains parted* ‖ to separate into two or more pieces, *the rope parted in the middle* **to part company** to cease to associate [F. *partir*]

par·take (partéik) *pres. part.* **par·tak·ing** past **par·took** (partúk) *past part.* **par·tak·en** (partéik'n) *v.i.* (with 'in' or 'of') to take or receive a share in, to partake of someone's dinner ‖ (*rhet.*, with 'of') to eat (a meal), *he partook of his dinner alone* ‖ (with 'of') to have some of the qualities of something [fr. older *partaker*, participator, trans. of L. *particeps*]

part·ed (pártid) *adj.* (*bot.*, of a cleft leaf) having divisions extending almost to the base ‖ divided ‖ separated

par·terre (partéər) *n.* an ornamental part of a garden consisting of formal flower beds and walks ‖ the part of the ground floor of a theater which is behind the orchestra ‖ the rear part of this, beneath the balcony [F.]

par·the·no·gen·e·sis (pɔrθənoudʒénisis) *n.* reproduction from an egg unfertilized by a spermatozoon, esp. in some insects, worms, algae and fungi **par·the·no·ge·net·ic** (pɔrθinoudʒənétik) *adj.* [fr. Gk *parthenos*, virgin+*genesis*, origin]

Par·the·non (párθənɒn, párθənən) a Doric temple on the Acropolis in Athens, dedicated to Athena, erected (447–432 B.C.) under Pericles by Ictinus and Callicrates and decorated with sculptures by Phidias. It represents the culmination of Greek classical architecture

Par·thi·a (párθiːə) an ancient country of N.E. Iran. It was successively part of the empire of Assyria, Persia, Macedon and Syria before rebelling, under the Arsacid dynasty (c. 250 B.C.– c.226 A.D.), to form the Parthian Empire, which extended (1st c. B.C.) from Bactria and the Caspian Sea to the Euphrates and India. The empire (centered on Ctesiphon) and the dy-

nasty were overthrown (c. 226) by the Sassanids

Par·thi·an shot (párθiːən) a retort, hostile gesture etc., made in retreat [*Parthian*, of Parthia, whose cavalrymen turned to shoot their arrows while in real or feigned retreat]

par·tial (párʃəl) **1.** *adj.* of, affecting or involving only a part, *a partial explanation* ‖ having or showing a bias in favor of one of several disputants, contestants etc., *a partial judgment* ‖ (*pop.*, with 'to') fond of, *he is very partial to claret* **2.** *n.* (*mus.*) any note in the harmonic series [O.F. *parcial* fr. L.L.]

partial derivative (*math.*) the derivative of a function of more than one variable taken with respect to one variable while the others are considered as constants

partial fraction one of the fractions into which a given fraction may be separated, *1/6 and 3/12 are the partial fractions of 5/12*

par·ti·al·i·ty (parʃiːǽliti:, parʃǽliti:) *n.* bias, *his judgment showed partiality* ‖ (*pop.*) liking, fondness, *a partiality for sweets* [O.F. *parcialité, partialité*]

partial product (*math.*) the result of the multiplication of the unit figure of a multiplier by more than one digit

part·i·ble (pártəb'l) *adj.* (of property or an inheritance) able to be divided into parts [fr. L.L. *partibilis*]

par·tic·i·pant (partísəpənt) **1.** *n.* someone who participates **2.** *adj.* participating [fr. L. *participans* (*participantis*) fr. *participare*, to take part]

par·tic·i·pate (partísəpeit) *v.i. pres. part.* **par·tic·i·pat·ing** past and past part. **par·tic·i·pat·ed** (often with 'in') to be active or have a share in some activity, enterprise etc. [fr. L. *participare* (*participatus*)]

par·tic·i·pa·tion (partísəpéiʃən) *n.* the act of participating [F. fr. L.]

participatory theater theatrical presentations in which the audience takes part

par·ti·cip·i·al (partisípiːəl) *adj.* of or having the nature and function of a participle [fr. L. *participialis*]

par·ti·ci·ple (pártisip'l, pártisəpəl) *n.* (*gram.*) a derivative of a verb which shows tense and voice and which functions in various verb forms (e.g. to form the English present progressive 'I am writing') or as an adjective (e.g. 'a written text') or in absolute constructions (e.g. 'all things being equal'). A participle may take an object (e.g. 'they like singing songs'), and may be modified by an adverb (e.g. 'the loudly swearing boys'). The present participle may also function as an adverb (e.g. 'steaming hot') [O.F.]

par·ti·cle (pártik'l) *n.* a small portion, *particles of dust, not a particle of evidence* ‖ (*phys.*) an idealization in physics whereby a body is considered as having finite mass but infinitesimal size ‖ (*phys.*) a fundamental particle ‖ (*gram.*) a word used only in combination, or one that is not inflected ‖ (*eccles.*) one of the Hosts distributed to communicants [fr. L. *particula*]

particle accelerator any of several devices used to accelerate charged particles (e.g. electrons, protons, deuterons, or other light nuclei) to extremely high speeds and energies in order to study their interaction with matter or with other particles (*CYCLOTRON, *BETATRON, *SYN-CHROTRON, *VAN DE GRAAFF GENERATOR, *SYN-CHROCYCLOTRON, *LINEAR ACCELERATOR)

particle board board made of resin-bonded bits of material

particle physics the branch of physics that deals with breakdown of the atom *Cf* ATOMIC PHYSICS, NUCLEAR PHYSICS, QUANTUM CHEMISTRY

par·ti·col·ored, *Br.* **par·ti·col·oured** (párti:-kʌlərd) *adj.* partly of one color, partly of another [*parti* var. of PARTY *adj.*]

par·tic·u·lar (partíkjulər) **1.** *adj.* of, relating to or designating one thing singled out among many, *I wanted that particular book* ‖ unusual, special, *take particular care not to offend him* ‖ (*old-fash.*) concerned with details, minute, *a particular account of what occurred* ‖ fussy, fastidious, *she is very particular about what she eats* ‖ (*logic*, of a proposition) applicable to only some members of a class **2.** *n.* (*pl.*) details of information ‖ (*logic*) a particular proposition **in particular** specifically, specially, by contrast with others, *I remember one day in particular* [O.F. *particuler*]

particular average (*maritime insurance*) a partial loss which must be borne only by the

owner of the property in question, without the assistance of other interests (cf. GENERAL AVERAGE)

par·tic·u·lar·ism (partíkjulərizəm) *n.* (*theol.*) the doctrine that particular individuals are chosen by God for redemption ‖ narrow allegiance to a particular party, sect, interest etc. ‖ the political principle advocating individual rights and freedom for each state in a federation without regard to the interest of the whole

par·tic·u·lar·i·ty (partíkjulǽriti:) *pl.* **par·tic·u·lar·i·ties** *n.* the quality or state of being particular ‖ a particular feature or detail [F. *particularité*]

par·tic·u·lar·ize (partíkjuləraiz) *pres. part.* **par·tic·u·lar·iz·ing** *past* and *past part.* **par·tic·u·lar·ized** *v.t.* to state (details or items) separately ‖ *v.i.* to go into details [F. *particulariser*]

par·tic·u·lar·ly (partíkjulərli:) *adv.* in a particular manner ‖ in particular

Par·ti·do Re·vo·lu·cio·na·ri·o Feb·re·ris·ta (partí:ðɔrevɔlu:sjɔnári:ɔfebreri:sta) *FEBRERISTAS*

Par·ti·do Re·vo·lu·cio·na·rio In·sti·tu·cio·nal (partí:ðɔrevɔlu:sjɔnárjɔi:nsti:tu:sjɔnál) (Institutional Revolutionary Party), the governing party of Mexico since 1929 (then called the Partido Nacional Revolucionario). It is regularly returned with 90% of the popular vote. Though basically democratic, it regulates the opposition and permits presidents to pick their own successors ('el tapadismo') and, in effect, their legislators

part·ing (pártiŋ) *n.* separation or division ‖ a place where separation or division occurs ‖ (*Br.*) a part (line of division of the hair) [PART *v.*]

Par·ti Que·be·cois (partí: keibəkwá) *n.* in Quebec, Canada, the political party of French-speaking population desiring national independence for Quebec

par·ti·san, par·ti·zan (pártiz'n) **1.** *n.* someone who actively supports (a party, cause or principle) ‖ someone not in a regular army who engages in guerrilla warfare **2.** *adj.* of, relating to or characteristic of a partisan ‖ one-sided, biased **pár·ti·san·ship, pár·ti·zan·ship** *n.* [F. fr. Ital.]

par·tite (pártait) *adj.* (*bot.*, of a cleft leaf) divided nearly to the base ‖ (in compounds) divided into a specified number of parts, as in 'bipartite' [fr. L. *partitus*, divided]

par·ti·tion (partíʃən) **1.** *n.* a dividing into parts ‖ something that divides a room etc. into parts, esp. a thin wall ‖ one of the parts so separated ‖ (*law*) the sale of jointly owned property and distribution of the proceeds among the co-owners ‖ (*math.*) in set theory, the division of the members of the set into subsets such that each member belongs to one and only one of the subsets **2.** *v.t.* to divide into parts ‖ (esp. with 'off') to separate (one area from another) by erecting a partition [F.]

par·ti·tive (pártitiv) **1.** *adj.* serving or tending to divide into parts ‖ (*gram.*, of an adjective, article etc.) denoting only a part of a whole, e.g. 'some', 'any' **2.** *n.* a partitive word [fr. L. *partitivus*]

partizan *PARTISAN

part·ly (pártli:) *adv.* in part, not completely

part·ner (pártnər) **1.** *n.* someone associated with another in a common undertaking ‖ one of two or more persons who are associated in a business or other joint venture and share risks and profits ‖ (*naut., pl.*) a stout wooden frame surrounding a mast, pump etc., taking strain off the deck timbers **2.** *v.t.* to be the partner of [older *partener*, prob. var. of PARCENER]

part·ner·ship (pártnərʃip) *n.* the state of being a partner or partners ‖ the relationship between partners ‖ an association of persons who share risks and profits in a business or other joint venture ‖ the legal contract binding such persons

part of speech one of the traditional classes of the words of a language according to their function (adjective, adverb, conjunction etc.) ‖ a word regarded as belonging to one of these classes

par·ton (pártɒn) *n.* (*particle phys.*) hypothetical constituents of a proton and neutron that scatter high-energy electrons

partook *past* of PARTAKE

par·tridge (pártridʒ) *n.* any of certain plump gallinaceous game birds of *Perdix, Alectoris* and related genera, fam. *Phasianidae*, native to Europe, Asia and N. Africa, having short wings and tail, variegated grayish-brown plumage and unfeathered legs ‖ any of several somewhat similar gallinaceous game birds of North America, e.g. the bobwhite, the ruffed grouse ‖ the tinamou [M.F. *pertrich, partrich* fr. O.F. *perdriz* fr. L. fr. Gk]

part-song (pártsɒŋ, pártsɒŋ) n. (*mus.*) a usually homophonic choral composition for several different voice parts, esp. unaccompanied

part-time (párttaim) *adj.* entailing less than the full number of hours of work, attendance etc., *a part-time job* ‖ working, operating etc. for less than a full number of hours, *a part-time typist*

par·tu·ri·ent (pɑrtúəri:ənt, pɑrtjúəri:ənt) *adj.* giving birth or about to give birth ‖ of or relating to parturition [fr. L. *parturiens* (*parturientis*) fr. *parturire*, to be in labor]

par·tu·ri·tion (pɑrturíʃən, pɑrtjuríʃən, pɑrtʃuríʃən) n. the act of giving birth [fr. L. *parturitio* (*parturitionis*)]

part work one of a set of books published one part at a time

par·ty (párti:) *adj.* (*heraldry*, of a shield) divided into parts of different tinctures [F. *parti*, divided, separate]

party pl. **par·ties** n. a group of people united by some common interest or for some common purpose, *a party of tourists, a search party* ‖ a group of people united in support of a common cause, esp. a national political organization ‖ a gathering to which guests are invited in order to enjoy one another's company, *a cocktail party* ‖ one of the persons or groups of persons engaged in a dispute or legal action ‖ a person who knowingly assists, shares in or condones an action, *he refused to be a party to the deception* ‖ (*pop.*) a person [M.E. *partie, partye* fr. F. *partie*]

party line the official policy of a political party ‖ a single telephone line shared by two or more subscribers

party pooper one who fails to participate in an event designed for enjoyment

party wall a jointly owned wall dividing two properties

par·ve·nu (párvənu:, párvənju:) **1.** *n.* a person who has suddenly risen from comparative poverty or obscurity to wealth, power etc., esp. one who makes a vulgar, ostentatious display **2.** *adj.* like or characteristic of such a person [F. fr. past part. of *parvenir*, to arrive]

par·vis (párvis) *n.* an enclosed court in front of a building, esp. a church [F. *parvis*, O.F. *parecvis*]

par·y·lene (párəli:n) *n.* (*chem.*) plastic derived from paraxylene by polymerization; used as a thin, transparent insulator and protective covering

Pas·a·de·na (pæsədí:nə) a suburban residential city and winter resort (pop. 119,374) of S.W. California, 8 miles northeast of Los Angeles. California Institute of Technology (1891), Pasadena College (1902)

Pa·sar·ga·dae (pəsárgədi:) an ancient Persian city, founded (c. 550 B.C.) by Cyrus II. Ruins include his tomb

Pas·cal (pæskǽl), Blaise (1623–62), French scientist, mathematician, philosopher and writer. He wrote mathematical and scientific treatises of great importance making contributions to hydraulics, pure geometry etc., and laid the foundation of the theory of probability (upon which Leibniz was to build his theory of the calculus). But his chief work was in Christian apologetics. He came into contact with the Jansenists in 1646. On Nov. 23, 1654 he had a mystical experience: he withdrew to Port Royal, lived ascetically, and wrote the brilliant 'Provincial Letters' (1656–7) in defense of the Jansenists, with Jesuit casuistry as the special target for attack. His most famous work, the so-called 'Pensées' (1670), is a series of fragments of a work in which Pascal set himself to persuade free thinkers of the truth of Christianity, broadly by exploring the limits of reason and the function of the imagination and affirming that at a certain point a leap into faith has to be made (the 'wager', as he put it: if you win you win all, if you lose you lose all, but have nothing to lose). On the literary level the 'Pensées' are unsurpassed examples of French classical prose: lucid, subtle and powerful. They can be said to have contributed to that science of the human heart from which the greatest works of French classical literature sprang

pas·cal (pæskál) n. a SI unit of pressure equal to a force of 1 newton per sq m; for Blaise Pascal *also* **Pa**

PASCAL n. (*computer*) a high-level program language around which a microcomputer was developed, requiring an intermediate P-code, a structure similar to ALGOL

pas·chal (pǽskəl) *adj.* of or relating to the Jewish Passover or the Christian Easter [F. *pascal*]

Pas·chal II (pǽskəl) (d. 1118), pope (1099–1118). He was involved in the Investiture Controversy with Emperors Henry IV and Henry V. He was captured (1110) and forced to recognize lay investiture, but later renounced this

paschal lamb a lamb eaten at the Passover festival ‖ Christ

Pas·co·li (páskɔli:), Giovanni (1885–1912), Italian lyric poet, author of romantic verse expressing a mystical love of his native countryside. His works include 'Myricae' (1891), 'Primi Poemetti' (1903) and 'Poemi del Risorgimento' (1913)

Pas-de-Ca·lais (pædəkælei) a department (area 2,606 sq. miles, pop. 1,403,000) in N. France (*ARTOIS). Chief town: Arras

pa·se·o (paséiou) n. (*bullfighting*) procession preceding the fighting

pas·gang (pɑsgáŋ) n. (*skiing*) striding with a forward kick and pole push on the same side

pa·sha (páʃə, pəʃá, pæʃə) n. a former courtesy title denoting high rank or office, used after the holder's name, in some Near Eastern, Middle Eastern or N. African countries [Turk. *pāshā*]

pasque-flow·er (pæskflauər) n. *Anemone pulsatilla*, fam. *Ranunculaceae*, a low perennial European plant which puts out purple flowers at about Eastertime ‖ any of several other plants of genus *Anemone* [earlier *passe-flower* fr. F. *passefleur* fr. *passer*, to surpass+*fleur*, flower]

pass (pæs, pɑs) *v.i.* to move along, proceed ‖ to go by something in the course of moving, *keep to the left as you pass* ‖ to go from one place, quality, state etc. to another, *to pass into a liquid state* ‖ to cease, *wait till the danger passes* ‖ (*rhet.*) to occur ‖ (of time) to be spent, elapse, *days passed before news arrived* ‖ to circulate or be transferred among people or places, *the rumor passed through the crowd within minutes* ‖ to be interchanged, *angry letters passed between them* ‖ to be just barely acceptable, *his suit is shabby, but it will pass* ‖ to be judged satisfactory in an examination, inspection, course of study etc. ‖ (of a proposed bill etc.) to be approved by a legislative body ‖ (with 'for' or 'as') to be accepted (as something else), *a synthetic fiber that passes for wool, farthings no longer pass as legal tender in Britain* ‖ (*law*, of a jury, the court etc., with 'on', 'upon') to pronounce the verdict or judgment ‖ (*law*, of a judgment etc., with 'for' or 'against') to be pronounced, *judgment passed for the defendant* ‖ (*ball games*) to throw, kick etc. the ball to a teammate ‖ (*cards*) to decline one's turn to play, bid, take cards etc. ‖ *v.t.* to go by, beyond, over, through etc. and leave behind, *they passed my house on the way* ‖ to meet successfully the requirements of (an examination etc.) ‖ to judge as satisfactory (someone being examined, their performance etc.) ‖ to spend (time etc.), *we passed one night in Rome* ‖ (of a committee, legislative body etc.) to approve (a motion, bill etc.) ‖ to convey, esp. by handing, *please pass the butter* ‖ to cause to go or move in a particular way or direction, *pass the rope over the pulley* ‖ to cause to move past, *the general passed the troops in review* ‖ to pronounce (a sentence or judgment), *to pass the death sentence on a prisoner* ‖ to use (counterfeit money, invalid checks etc.) as if valid ‖ to expel (feces, urine etc.) from the body ‖ (*ball games*) to convey (the ball) to a teammate ‖ (*baseball*, of the pitcher) to walk (a batter) ‖ (*magic*) to transfer or manipulate (objects) by sleight of hand **to let** (or **allow to**) **pass** to permit (a statement, remark etc.) to be made without correcting or challenging it, in spite of one's reservations etc. **to pass away** to come to an end, cease ‖ to die **to pass off** to come to an end, disappear, *the headache soon passed off* ‖ to take place and be completed, *the demonstration passed off without violence* ‖ to palm off, induce a person to accept (something that is not what it is said to be), *he passed the story off as his own* ‖ to treat as unimportant, dismiss in an offhand way, *she passed off the accusation with a laugh* **to pass out** (*pop.*) to faint ‖ (*pop.*) to lose consciousness through drinking too much alcohol ‖ (*Br.*) to complete a course of instruction (esp. military) **to pass over** to consider and reject, *they passed him*

over for promotion **to pass through** to undergo, experience, *to pass through a crisis* **to pass up** (*pop.*) to decline (an offer) or decide not to take advantage of (an opportunity) [F. *passer*]

pass n. a mark sufficient for passing an examination or test ‖ a document which gives the holder permission to do what would otherwise be forbidden, or to enjoy a special privilege ‖ a free ticket ‖ (*ball games*) the passing of the ball to a teammate ‖ (*baseball*) a walk ‖ (*cards*) a declining of one's turn to play, bid etc. ‖ a quick movement of the hands, made by a conjurer to confuse or mystify his audience ‖ (*fencing*) a thrust with the weapon ‖ (*bullfighting*) the movement executed by a matador with his cape in order to cause the bull to charge **a pretty pass** a difficult or critical state of affairs **to make a pass at** to try to attract sexually ‖ to attempt to strike [F. *passe* and PASS v.]

pass n. a narrow way by which one can cross over or between mountains [M.E. *pas, paas,* pace fr. F. *pas*]

pass·a·ble (pæsəb'l, pásəb'l) *adj.* moderately good, adequate ‖ (of a river, stream etc.) capable of being crossed ‖ (of a road) capable of being traveled along **pass·a·bly** *adv.* [F.]

pas·sa·ca·glia (pæsəkáljə) n. (*mus.*) an instrumental composition, originally a dance tune, in which a theme is constantly repeated (usually as a ground bass) in slow and stately triple time ‖ (*hist.*) a Spanish or Italian dance which was the origin of this [Ital. fr. Span. *pasacalle*]

pas·sade (pəséid) n. (*manège*) a backward and forward movement of a horse over the same ground [F.]

pas·sage (pæsidʒ) n. a corridor in a building ‖ an alley, lane, channel, path or other way providing communication, *an underground passage* ‖ a passage from one place, state or thing to another ‖ a moving along, progressing, *the passage of time* ‖ the passing of a measure by a legislative body ‖ the right or opportunity to pass ‖ a journey by sea or air, *a smooth passage* ‖ a passenger's accommodation on board ship, *to book a passage* ‖ the charge made for this ‖ an esp. brief extract from a literary or musical work ‖ (*rhet.*) a conversation, dispute etc. between two persons ‖ a bowel movement ‖ (*manège*) a horse's controlled slow sideways walk or trot [F.]

passage pres. part. **pas·sag·ing** past and past part. **pas·saged** *v.i.* (*manège*, of a horse) to move sideways ‖ (*manège*, of a rider) to cause a horse to move sideways ‖ *v.t.* (*manège*) to cause (a horse) to move sideways [F. *passager* fr. Ital. *passegiare*, to walk]

pas·sage·way (pæsidʒwei) n. a way between two points, affording passage

pass·a·long (pæsalɒŋ) n. (*business*) price increase due to increase in costs

pas·sant (pæsənt) *adj.* (*heraldry*, of an animal) walking and looking towards the dexter side with the dexter forepaw upraised [F.]

Pas·sau, Treaty of (pæsau) a treaty (1552) between Maurice, elector of Saxony, and the future Emperor Ferdinand I. It granted full religious liberty to Lutherans and led on to the Peace of Augsburg (1555)

pass·book (pæsbuk, pásbuk) n. a small book supplied by a bank to the holder of an account, in which the bank enters his credits and debits ‖ a customer's book in which a storekeeper or merchant records the purchases not yet paid for

Pass·chen·dae·le, Battle of (pæʃəndeil, pásəndɑlə) *YPRES, BATTLE OF

pass degree (*Br.*) a university academic degree gained by passing an examination at a lower level than the honors degree

pas·sé (pæséi, pæsei) *adj.* no longer in style, out-of-date [F.=past]

passed ball (*baseball*) a pitch which the catcher fails to catch when he could be expected to do so, thus allowing a base runner to reach another base

passe·men·terie (pæsméntri:) n. decorative trimming or braid of gold thread, beads, silken cord, gimp etc. [F.]

pas·sen·ger (pæsindʒər) n. a person who travels in a vehicle, ship, boat, aircraft etc. but is not the driver, nor one of the crew [M.E. *passager* fr. F.]

passenger pigeon *Ectopistes migratorius*, an extinct North American pigeon, once abundant in the Mississippi Valley

passe-partout (pæspartú:) **1.** n. a type of picture frame in which the glass is attached to the backing by an edging of adhesive tape ‖ the tape used ‖ a mount surrounding a picture in a frame ‖ a master key 2. *v.t.* to frame with a passe-partout [F. fr. *passer*, to pass+*partout*, all around]

pass·er·by (pǽsərbái, pásərbái) *pl.* **pass·ers·by** *n.* someone who passes by, esp. by chance

pas·ser·ine (pǽsərain, pǽsərin) 1. *adj.* belonging to *Passeriformes*, an order of birds which perch, comprising more than half of all living birds 2. *n.* a passerine bird [fr. L. *passerinus* fr. *passer*, sparrow]

pass-fail (pǽsféil) *n.* (*education*) a system of grading with only the two grades, vs. letter or number grading, esp. for academic work — **pass-fail** *adj.*

Pass·field (pǽsfi:ld), 1st Baron *WEBB

pas·si·bil·i·ty (pǽsəbíliti:) *n.* the quality of being passible

pas·si·ble (pǽsəb'l) *adj.* capable of suffering or of feeling emotion [O.F.]

pas·sim (pásim, pǽsim) *adv.* (of references to a cited work) scattered throughout, *see chapter V passim* [L.]

pass·ing (pǽsiŋ, pásiŋ) l. *adj.* going past, *a passing taxi* ‖ transitory, *a passing whim* ‖ incidental, *a passing reference* ‖ (of a mark) indicating that one has passed an examination, course of study etc. 2. *n.* the act of someone who or something that passes ‖ (*rhet.*) death **in passing** by the way, incidentally [PASS v.]

passing bell a church bell tolled to mark a person's death

passing note (*mus.*) a note in a melody which forms a discord with the harmony but which serves as a transition between two others which are not discordant

passing tone (*mus.*) a passing note

pas·sion (pǽʃən) *n.* intense or violent emotion, esp. sexual desire or love, *intense anger* ‖ a great liking or enthusiasm, *a passion for swimming* ‖ a violent emotional outburst, *a passion of tears* ‖ the martyrdom of an early Christian **Pas·sion** the sufferings and death of Jesus Christ ‖ one of the Gospel accounts of this ‖ a musical work based on such an account

pas·sion·al (pǽʃən'l) *n.* a book containing accounts of the sufferings and martyrdom of Christian saints [fr. M.L. *passionale*, neut. of *passionalis* adj., relating to passion]

pas·sion·ate (pǽʃənit) *adj.* easily moved to strong emotion ‖ showing or inspired by strong emotion, *a passionate love letter* ‖ (of emotion) intense ‖ (*old-fash.*) easily angered [fr. M.L. *passionatus*]

pas·sion·flow·er (pǽʃənflauər) *n.* a member of *Passiflora*, fam. *Passifloraceae*, a genus of tropical American woody climbing plants. The parts of the flowers suggest the instruments of Christ's Passion (the stigmas suggesting the nails, the corona the crown of thorns, the anthers the five wounds). Some species produce edible fruit ‖ the flower of such a plant

passion fruit the edible fruit of a passion-flower

Pas·sion·ist (pǽʃənist) *n.* a member of an austere Roman Catholic order founded (1720) in Italy by St Paul of the Cross. The Passionists take a special vow to keep the memory of the Passion alive in the hearts of the faithful. There is an order of nuns, founded 1771

pas·sion·less (pǽʃənlis) *adj.* without passion, not moved by or showing emotion

Passion play a play based on Christ's Passion, e.g. a medieval mystery (*OBERAMMERGAU)

pas·sive (pǽsiv) 1. *adj.* acted upon by someone or something else ‖ not reacting to an external influence, inert ‖ offering no resistance ‖ (of a person) lacking initiative or drive ‖ (*gram.*) designating or expressed in a voice which denotes that the subject is also the object of the verb ‖ (*phys.*) of an instrument designed to reflect, but not record or amplify, energy impulses, e.g., transducer, filter 2. *n.* (*gram.*) the passive voice [fr. L. *passivus*]

passive homing (*mil.*) the capability of homing requiring only the natural emanations from the target, e.g., heat, light, sound, magnetism, exhaust

passive jamming (*mil.*) creating confusion in enemy signals or radar by use of reflectors

passive resistance resistance to civil law, military occupation etc. by nonviolent means

passive satellite a satellite that reflects only signals sent to it

pas·siv·i·ty (pǽsíviti:) *n.* the quality or state of being passive [fr. L. *passivus*]

pass·key (pǽski:, páski:) *pl.* **pass·keys** *n.* a master key ‖ any private key

Pass·o·ver (pǽsouvər, pásouvər) *n.* a Jewish feast commemorating the release of the Israelites from slavery in Egypt, celebrated on the 14th day of Nisan and continuing for seven or (in modern Israel) eight days (*JEWISH CALENDAR) [PASS v.+OVER prep., fr. the passing over of the Jews, i.e. their exemption from the curse bringing death on the firstborn in all Egyptian homes (Exodus xii)]

pass·port (pǽspɔrt, pǽspourt, páspɔrt, páspourt) *n.* a document certifying nationality, issued by the government of a country, to a citizen intending to travel abroad ‖ something that enables a person to achieve a desired end, *a passport to success* [F. *passeport*]

pass·word (pǽswərd, páswərd) *n.* a word or phrase used to show that one is authorized to enter, pass a barrier etc. ‖ a word used by members of a secret society etc. in recognition of one another

past (pǽst, pást) 1. *adj.* (of a period of time) just ended, *the past week has been very eventful* ‖ relating to an earlier time, *one's past life* ‖ (of a period of time, used post-positively) gone by, elapsed, *the time for talking is past* ‖ (of the holder of an office, position etc.) former, no longer in office, *a past president* ‖ (*gram.*) of or designating a tense that expresses an action or state in time that has gone by 2. *n.* time that has gone by ‖ the earlier part of a person's life or the earlier history of a community, country, institution etc. ‖ (*pop.*) a wild or discreditable earlier life, *a woman with a past* ‖ (*gram.*) the past tense 3. *prep.* beyond or further than (in time or place), *past his prime, just past the post office* ‖ (in time expressions) used to indicate the period after the hour, *10 past 8* ‖ going beyond or by, *he pushed past me, bullets whistled past our ears* ‖ beyond the scope, capacities or limit of, *those pants are past mending* 4. *adv.* in such a way as to pass by, *the car drove past* [alt. past part. of PASS]

pas·ta (pástə) *n.* an alimentary paste of wheat flour used in processed form (noodles, macaroni, spaghetti etc.) or as fresh dough (ravioli) [Ital.]

paste (peist) 1. *n.* a moist, fairly stiff mixture of liquid and a powdery substance ‖ a mixture of flour and butter, lard etc. used for pastry crust etc. ‖ a soft, creamy foodstuff made by pounding, grinding etc., *anchovy paste, almond paste* ‖ a hard, brilliant lead and glass substance used to make imitation jewels ‖ dampened clay used in making earthenware or porcelain ‖ an adhesive made typically from flour and water 2. *v.t. pres. part.* **past·ing** *past* and *past part.* **past·ed** to make (something) stick, using paste, *to paste a photograph onto a mount* ‖ to cover with paste ‖ (*pop.*) to deal a hard blow or blows to, *he pasted him in the eighth round* [O.F. *paste*]

paste·board (péistbɔrd, péistbourd) 1. *n.* a stiff material made by pasting together two or more sheets of paper 2. *adj.* made of pasteboard ‖ (*fig.*) unsubstantial, being merely a facade, *he can only create pasteboard characters*

paste job a literary work made up of patches of other works

pas·tel (pæstél, pǽstel) *n.* a powdered pigment mixed with gum, compressed into small, colored sticks for drawing ‖ a stick of this material ‖ the art of drawing with such sticks ‖ a drawing made with these ‖ (of color) light in tone **pas·tél·ist**, esp. *Br.* **pas·tél·list** *n.* [F. fr. Ital. *Pastello*, woad]

pas·tern (pǽstərn) *n.* the part of the foot of a horse or other equine animal between the fetlock and the hoof (corresponding to the human ankle) ‖ (*loosely*) a corresponding part in other animals [M.E. *pastron* fr. O.F. *pasturon*, a hobble]

Pas·ter·nak (pǽstərnæk), Boris Leonidovich (1890–1960), Russian writer. His poetry includes 'Above Barriers', (1917) and 'Second Birth' (1932). He is best known in the West for his novel about the Russian Revolution, 'Dr. Zhivago' (1958). He won the Nobel prize for literature (1958)

paste-up (péistʌp) *n.* a mock-up of printed matter, esp. of a magazine, made by pasting sample matter on sheets of paper or card, to show what the finished product is to look like

Pas·teur (pæstə:r), Louis (1822–95), French chemist and biologist. His researches showed that the fermentation of milk and wine was due to the multiplication of bacteria and other microorganisms led to the discovery of the role of microorganisms in human and animal disease.

From these findings, he developed immunization by inoculation of attenuated microbes, and the process of pasteurization. His work on asepsis greatly facilitated medical advances and he also established stereochemistry. The French government took up his work and created the Institut Pasteur (1888)

pas·teur·i·za·tion (pæstʃərizéiʃən, pæstərizéiʃən) *n.* a process which renders milk free of disease-producing bacteria and helps to prevent it from spoiling without destroying the vitamins or changing the taste. It involves heating the milk to 145°–150°F. for 30 minutes, or to 164°–168° for 15 seconds. It is also used in the production of other dairy products, wine and beer

pas·teur·ize (pǽstʃəraiz, pǽstəraiz) *pres. part.* **pas·teur·iz·ing** *past* and *past part.* **pasteur·ized** *v.t.* to sterilize by by pasteurization [after PASTEUR]

pas·tiche (pæstí:ʃ) *n.* a musical, literary or artistic work with elements borrowed from several sources ‖ a work which imitates or caricatures the work of someone else [F. fr. Ital. *pasticcio*]

past·ies (péisti:z) *n.* small adhesive covering for a woman's nipples, esp. to avoid laws against indecent exposure

pas·til (pǽstəl) *n.* a pastille

pas·tille (pǽstí:l) *n.* a flavored or medicated lozenge ‖ a small cone made of an aromatic paste, used to perfume or disinfect the air [F.]

pas·time (pǽstaim, pástaim) *n.* anything that serves as agreeable recreation [PASS+TIME]

pas·tis (pastí:) *n.* a licorice-flavored liqueur produced in France

past master someone who excels in an activity ‖ someone who has held the office of master in a guild, lodge etc.

Pas·to (pástɔ) a city (pop. 140,700) on a high plateau (8,400 ft) in S.W. Colombia: gold mines

pas·tor (pǽstər, pástər) *n.* a priest or minister in charge of a parish or congregation [M.E. and A.F. *pastour* fr. O.F. *pastor, pastur*, shepherd]

pas·to·ral (pǽstərəl, pástərəl) 1. *adj.* of, relating to or characterized by the care of grazing animals, esp. sheep and goats, *a pastoral economy* ‖ (of land) used for grazing ‖ dealing with idealized country life, *pastoral poetry* ‖ relating to the office and work of a minister of religion 2. *n.* a pastoral poem, play, opera etc. ‖ a circular letter sent by a bishop to his clergy, often to be read in all churches [fr. L. *pastoralis* fr. *pastor*, shepherd]

pas·to·rale (pæstərál, pæstəráel) *n.* a musical composition with themes suggestive of pastoral life [Ital.]

Pastoral Epistles *TIMOTHY AND TITUS

pas·tor·ate (pǽstərit, pástərit) *n.* the office or period of office of a pastor ‖ the clergy in general, or a particular body of ministers [fr. M.L. *pastoratus*]

pas·tor·ship (pǽstərʃip, pástərʃip) *n.* the office or period of office of a pastor

past participle (*gram.*) a participle which expresses an action that is completed, usually with the auxiliary verbs 'have' or 'be'

past perfect (*gram.*) the pluperfect tense

pa·stra·mi (pəstrámi:) *n.* highly spiced smoked shoulder of beef sliced thin and served hot in sandwiches or as a meat course [Yiddish fr. Rum. *pastramă* fr. *pastră*, to preserve]

pas·try (péistri:) *pl.* **pas·tries** *n.* dough consisting of flour, water or milk and a high proportion of butter etc., used baked as piecrust etc. ‖ baked goods consisting of this ‖ an individual tart, pie etc. made with this [prob. fr. PASTE]

pas·try·cook (péistri:kuk) *n.* a person hired by a restaurant etc. to make pastry ‖ a person who makes and sells pastries

pas·tur·a·ble (pǽstʃərəb'l, pástʃərəb'l) *adj.* (of land) suitable for pasture

pas·tur·age (pǽstʃəridʒ, pástʃəridʒ) *n.* grazing land, or grass for grazing ‖ the pasturing of cattle e.g. on common land [O.F. *pasturage*, Mod. F. *pâturage*]

pas·ture (pǽstʃər, pástʃər) *n.* grass or other vegetation that provides food for cattle, sheep, horses, goats etc. or for wild animals ‖ land which produces such vegetation ‖ a particular piece of such land [O.F. *pasture*, Mod. F. *pâture* fr. L.L. *pastura*, a grazing]

pasture *pres. part.* **pas·tur·ing** *past* and *past part.* **pas·tured** *v.t.* to cause (an animal) to feed on pasture ‖ *v.i.* (of an animal) to feed on pasture [O.F. *pasturer*, Mod. F. *pâturer*]

pas·ty (péisti:, pǽisti:) *pl.* **pas·ties** *n.* (esp. *Br.*) a

---

CONCISE PRONUNCIATION KEY: **(a)** æ, c*a*t; ɑ, c*a*r; ɔ f*aw*n; ei, sn*a*ke. **(e)** e, h*e*n; i:, sh*ee*p; iə, d*ee*r; ɛə, b*ear*. **(i)** i, f*i*sh; ai, t*i*ger; ə:, b*i*rd. **(o)** o, *o*x; au, c*ow*; ou, g*oa*t; u, p*oo*r; ɔi, r*oy*al. **(u)** ʌ, d*u*ck; u, b*u*ll; u:, g*oo*se; ə, b*a*cillus; ju:, c*u*be. x, lo*ch*; θ, *th*ink; ð, bo*th*er; z, *Z*en; ʒ, cor*s*age; dʒ, sava*g*e; ŋ, ora*ng*utang; j, *y*ak; ʃ, *f*ish; tʃ, fe*tch*; 'l, rabb*le*; 'n, redd*en*. Complete pronunciation key appears inside front cover.

small pie, consisting either of meat and vegetables or of fruit [M.E. *pastee* fr. O.F. *pastée*]

past·y (péisti:) *comp.* **past·i·er** *superl.* **past·i·est** *adj.* like paste in color or consistency ‖ pale, flabby, or unhealthy in appearance, *a pasty complexion* [PASTE]

pat (pæt) **1.** *n.* a gentle stroke or blow made with something flat (esp. with the hand) ‖ the sound of a gentle blow ‖ a small, neat piece of some soft substance, esp. butter **to give someone a pat on the back** to praise or congratulate someone **2.** *v.t. pres. part.* **pat·ting** *past* and *past part.* **pat·ted** to give a pat to, often as a sign of affection or sympathy, *to pat a dog* ‖ to shape with blows of the hands or of some flat implement, *pat the butter into half-pounds* **to pat on the back** to praise or congratulate [M.E. *pat, patte*, prob. imit.]

pat 1. *adv.* in exactly the right way or at exactly the right time, *his answer came pat* **2.** *adj.* glib, *a pat remark* **to stand pat** (*poker*) to play the hand as dealt without drawing further cards ‖ to stand firmly by what one has said, or the position one has taken [perh. fr. PAT v.]

pa·ta·gi·um (pətéidʒi:əm) *pl.* **pa·ta·gi·a** (pətéidʒi:ə) *n.* a membranous expansion between the fore and hind limbs of a bat, flying squirrel etc. ‖ the membranous skin in the angle of a bird's wing [M.L. fr. L. *patagium*, gold border on a tunic]

Pat·a·go·ni·a (pætəgóuni:ə) a region of S. Argentina, southernmost Chile and Tierra del Fuego, consisting of the E. Andes (ice-capped at this latitude and with several peaks over 10,000 ft) and arid tablelands stretching to the Atlantic. Temperatures and precipitation are low. Products: wool, petroleum. The native Indians are almost extinct

Pat·a·go·ni·an (pætəgóuni:ən) **1.** *adj.* of or relating to Patagonia or its inhabitants **2.** *n.* a native or inhabitant of Patagonia

Pa·tan (pútən) a Buddhist and Hindu pilgrimage place (pop. 135,000) and former capital (17th–18th cc.) of Nepal, near Katmandu: funeral mounds (3rd c. B.C.), temples

patch (pætʃ) **1.** *n.* a piece of material sewed on, let into, or otherwise attached to something in order to mend it ‖ any of the bits of cloth which, when sewn together, form patchwork ‖ a part of a surface, generally irregular in shape, which is in some way different from the rest, *the bald patch on his head* ‖ a small piece of adhesive tape used to cover a scratch, wound etc. ‖ (*computer*) insertion of an instruction in a program to correct, change, or add new material without destroying the routine, esp. an improvised patch ‖ a small piece of ground, esp. under a specified crop, *a potato patch* ‖ a passage in a literary or musical work ‖ (*mil.*) an emblem sewn on the sleeve of a soldier's uniform to indicate the unit to which he belongs ‖ (*Br.*) a period, stage, *going through a bad patch* ‖ a piece of cloth worn over an injured eye ‖ (*hist.*) a beauty spot worn on the face or neck **not a patch on** (esp. *Br.*) not nearly so good as **2.** *v.t.* to mend by putting a patch on or over, *to patch a hole* ‖ to make by sewing bits of cloth together, *to patch a quilt* **to patch up** to put together or mend in a makeshift way ‖ to put together out of odds and ends, *a book patched up out of old magazine articles* ‖ to become reconciled after (a quarrel etc.) [M.E. *pacche, patche*, origin unknown]

patch·board (pætʃbɔrd) *n.* (*electr.*) removable circuitry panel with multiple terminals adaptable to various electronic operations *also* patch panel

patch cord (*computer*) removable wire with connectors at both ends that can be inserted into proper sockets to create new circuits for input or output, esp. for punch-card operations —**patch plug** *n.* a cordless metal instrument capable of performing the function of a patch cord

Patch·en (pætʃən), Kenneth (1911–72), U.S. poet and novelist. His verse, concerned in the 1930s with social protest, includes 'Before the Brave' (1936) and 'First Will & Testament' (1939). His prose works include 'The Journal of Albion Moonlight' (1941) and the satirical 'Memoirs of a Shy Pornographer' (1945)

patch·i·ly (pætʃili:) *adv.* in a patchy way

patch·i·ness (pætʃi:nis) *n.* the quality or state of being patchy

patch·ou·li (pætʃuli:) *n. Pogostemon cablin,* fam. *Labiatae,* a heavy-scented plant cultivated in the Far East ‖ the essential oil distilled from

its leaves, used as a fixative for many heavy perfumes and as an insect repellent in the Far East [Tamil]

patch panel (*computer*) perforated panel, often portable, capable of receiving patch cords to create new circuit connections *also* patch board, plugboard

patch pocket a pocket made by sewing cloth to the outside of a garment

patch test a test for an allergy made by applying to the skin a small piece of cloth soaked in the substance believed to cause the allergy, and observing the skin for irritation

patch·work (pætʃwə:rk) *n.* needlework made of assorted small pieces of material sewn together at the edges to form regular or free patterns ‖ something made up of miscellaneous, jumbled elements

patch·y (pætʃi:) *comp.* **patch·i·er** *superl.* **patch·i·est** *adj.* consisting of or containing patches ‖ uneven in quality, *a patchy performance*

pate (peit) *n.* (*pop., old-fash.*) the head, *his bald pate was glinting in the sun* **pat·ed** *adj.* (*pop.,* in combinations) having a specified kind of head or mind, *bald-pated, addlepated* [origin unknown]

pâ·té (pɑtei) *n.* an edible paste of finely minced meat or fish ‖ a small meat pie or patty [F.]

pâ·té de foie gras (pɑteidəfwɑgrɑ) *n.* a rich paste of the fat livers of geese [F.]

paté *PATTÉE

pa·tel·la (pətélə) *pl.* **pa·tel·lae** (pətéli:), **pa·tel·las** *n.* (*anat.*) the kneecap ‖ (*anat., bot.*) any pan-shaped formation **pa·tél·lar, pa·tél·late** *adjs* [L.=little dish]

pat·en (pæt'n) *n.* (*eccles.*) a plate used to cover the chalice and receive the host in the Eucharist ‖ any thin, circular metal disk [O.F. *patène*]

pa·ten·cy (péit'nsi:) *n.* the quality or state of being evident ‖ (*med.*) the quality or state of being unobstructed [PATENT]

pat·ent 1. (pæt'nt, *Br.* also péit'nt) *n.* an official paper conferring a right, privilege etc., esp. one issued by a government, guaranteeing an inventor and his heirs exclusive rights over an invention, process etc. for a given length of time ‖ this invention or process ‖ a document issued by the government authorizing the sale or grant of public lands ‖ the land so sold or granted **2.** (pæt'nt, péit'nt) *adj.* (of an invention) protected by a patent, *a patent lock* ‖ made or sold under a registered trademark or trade name ‖ of or relating to the granting of patents, *patent attorney* ‖ original and individual as if protected by a patent, *a patent way of pickling onions* ‖ evident, obvious ‖ (*med.,* of a body passage) unobstructed ‖ (*hist.,* of a document) open to public view ‖ (*biol.*) patulous **3.** (pæt'nt, *Br.* also péit'nt) *v.t.* to obtain a patent for (an invention) **pat·ent·ée** *n.* the person to whom a patent has been granted [F. *patent* adj., open and fr. L. *patens (patentis)* adj., open]

patent leather leather sprayed with varnish to give a hard, very shiny surface. It is used for shoes, handbags etc.

pat·ent·ly (pæt'ntli:, péit'ntli:) *adv.* obviously, evidently

patent office the government office which examines inventors' claims and grants patents

patent rolls (*Br.*) the annual roll of patents issued. The rolls are preserved in the Public Record Office in London

Pa·ter (péitər), Walter Horatio (1839–94), English essayist and critic. His elegant prose heralds the aestheticism of the 1890s. He wrote 'Studies in the History of the Renaissance' (1873), 'Marius the Epicurean' (1885), and 'Imaginary Portraits' (1887)

pa·ter·fa·mil·i·as (péitərfəmíli:əs) *n.* the father of a family, regarded as head of the household [L.]

pa·ter·nal (pətə́:rn'l) *adj.* of or relating to a father ‖ having or showing fatherly qualities, e.g. benevolence, *to take a paternal interest in someone's welfare* ‖ related through the father, *one's paternal grandmother* **pa·tér·nal·ism** *n.* the principle or practice of governing a country or running an organization etc. in a way that suggests a father's authoritative deciding of what is in the best interest of his children **pa·ter·nal·ís·tic** *adj.* **pa·ter·nal·ís·ti·cal·ly** *adv.* [fr. L.L. *paternalis* fr. L. *paternus* fr. *pater*, father]

pa·ter·ni·ty (pətə́:rniti:) *n.* the state of being a father ‖ descent from a father, male parentage, *of unknown paternity* ‖ authorship or origin, *he*

didn't deny his paternity of the scheme [F. *paternité*]

pa·ter·nos·ter (péitərnóstər) *n.* the Lord's Prayer, esp. as recited in Latin ‖ one of the large beads of a rosary on which the Lord's Prayer is said [L.=our father]

Pat·er·son (pætərs'n) a manufacturing city (pop. 137,970) in N. New Jersey. It is famous for its silk industry ('Silk City'). Manufactures: cotton goods, revolvers, airplane motors, textile machinery, foundry products

path (pæθ, pɑθ) *pl.* **paths** (pæðz, pɑðz, pæθs, pɑθs) *n.* a narrow way or trail, esp. one formed by the frequent passage of people or animals ‖ (*computer*) the proper sequence for executing a routine ‖ a narrow way specially constructed, *garden paths* ‖ any way or space by which people may pass, *the police cleared a path through the crowd for him* ‖ the course of a moving person or thing, *the path of a planet* ‖ line of progress, *his path through life was hard* [O.E. *pæth*]

Pa·than (pətán) *n.* a member of the chief people inhabiting Afghanistan and N.W. Pakistan, famous as soldiers [Hind. *pathán*]

pa·thet·ic (pəθétik) *adj.* arousing pity or sympathetic sorrow ‖ arousing pitying contempt, *his incompetence is pathetic* **pa·thét·i·cal·ly** *adv.* [fr. L.L. *patheticus* fr. Gk fr. *paschein*, to suffer]

pathetic fallacy (in literature) the attribution of human emotions or characteristics to natural phenomena, e.g. 'the frowning cliffs'

Pa·thet Lao (pɑθet láou) North Vietnamese Communist-led forces in Laos

path·find·er (pæθfaindər, pɑθfaindər) *n.* someone who explores unknown regions ‖ someone who pioneers a new process or procedure etc. which has general applications ‖ (*mil.*) an aircraft sent ahead of a bombing force to find and mark the target by flares etc. ‖ the pilot of such an aircraft

path·less (pæθlis, pɑθlis) *adj.* having no paths ‖ unexplored

path·o·gen (pæθədʒen) *n.* an agent that produces disease, e.g. a bacterium or virus [fr. Gk *pathos*, suffering, disease+*genēs*, born of]

path·o·gene (pæθədʒi:n) *n.* a pathogen

path·o·gen·e·sis (pæθədʒénisis) *n.* the origin or development of a disease **path·o·ge·net·ic** (pæθədʒənétik), **path·o·gen·ic** (pæθədʒénik) *adjs* relating to pathogenesis ‖ causing or capable of causing a disease **pa·thog·e·ny** (pəθódʒəni:) *n.* pathogenesis [fr. Gk *pathos*, disease+*genesis*, origin]

pa·thog·no·mon·ic (pəθɒgnəmónik) *adj.* characteristic of or indicating with certainty the presence of a specific disease [fr. Gk *pathognōmonikos*, skilled in judging symptoms]

path·o·log·ic (pæθəlódʒik) *adj.* pertaining to pathology **path·o·lóg·i·cal** *adj.* pathologic ‖ involving or resulting from disease ‖ morbid, *his writings show a pathological vision of humanity* [fr. Gk *pathologikos* fr. *pathos*, disease+*logos*, word]

pa·thol·o·gist (pəθólədʒist) *n.* a specialist in pathology

pa·thol·o·gy (pəθólədʒi:) *n.* the study of disease and all its manifestations, esp. of the functional and structural changes caused by it ‖ all the manifestations of a disease, *the pathology of tuberculosis* [fr. Mod. L. or M.L. *pathologia* fr. Gk *pathos*, disease+*logos*, word]

pa·tho·mor·phol·o·gy (pæθəmɔrfólədʒi:) *n.* the science of abnormal diseases of the form and structure, e.g., histology, anatomy —**pa·tho·mor·phol·o·gic** *adj.* —**pa·tho·mor·pho·log·i·cal** *adj.*

pa·thos (péiθɒs) *n.* a quality in an experience, narrative, literary work etc. which arouses profound feelings of compassion or sorrow [Gk=suffering]

pa·tho·type (pæθətaip) *n.* an organism capable of causing disease

path·way (pæθwei, pɑθwei) *n.* a narrow way or footpath

Pa·ti·a·la (pʌti:álə) a former princely capital (pop. 125,000) now in the Punjab, India, producing cotton thread, textiles and metalwork

pa·tience (péiʃəns) *n.* the capacity to put up with pain, troubles, difficulties, hardship etc. without complaint or ill temper ‖ the ability to wait or persevere without losing heart or becoming bored ‖ (*Br.*) solitaire (card game) **out of patience with** unable to put up with any longer **to have no patience with** to feel nothing but irritation with or contempt for, be unable to

---

CONCISE PRONUNCIATION KEY: **(a)** æ, cat; ɑ, car; ɔ fawn; ei, snake. **(e)** e, hen; i:, sheep; iə, deer; εə, bear. **(i)** i, fish; ai, tiger; ə:, bird. **(o)** o, ox; au, cow; ou, goat; u, poor; ɔi, royal. **(u)** ʌ, duck; u, bull; u:, goose; ə, bacillus; ju:, cube. x, loch; θ, think; ð, bother; z, Zen; ʒ, corsage; dʒ, savage; ŋ, orangutang; j, yak; ʃ, fish; tʃ, fetch; 'l, rabble; 'n, redden. Complete pronunciation key appears inside front cover.

put up with [M.E. fr. O.F. *patience, pacience* fr. L.]

pa·tient (péiʃənt) **1.** *adj.* showing or having patience **2.** *n.* a person receiving medical attention ‖ a client of a doctor, dentist etc., whether sick or not [O.F. *pacient, passient* fr. L. *patiens* (*patientis*)]

pat·i·na (pǽt'nə) *n.* a surface formed on metal (esp. bronze) by long exposure to the air, or produced artificially by an acid ‖ a surface formed on wood by age or constant care and handling [L. *patina, patena,* a shallow bronze bowl]

Pa·ti·ño (patí:njɔ) Simón (1861–1947), Bolivian Indian who made himself a multi-millionaire from his tin-mining monopoly, although he was almost illiterate

pa·ti·o (pǽti:ou) *pl.* **pa·ti·os** *n.* an open courtyard enclosed by the walls of a house, characteristic of Spanish and Spanish-American houses ‖ an area, usually paved, adjoining a house, used esp. for outdoor cooking or dining [Span.]

Pat·more (pǽtmɔr, pǽtmọur), Coventry Kersey Dighton (1823–96), English mystical poet. His subject in 'The Angel in the House' (1858–62) and 'The Unknown Eros' (1877) is human love as an image of divine love

Pat·mos (pǽtmɒs) a Greek island (area 13 sq. miles, pop. 2,486) of the Dodecanese. There is a tradition that St John wrote Revelation here in exile. Monastery (1088)

Pat·na (pǽtnə) the capital (pop. 473,001) of Bihar, India, on the Ganges, center of a famous rice-growing district. Handicrafts: metalwork, glass, carpets, pottery, leatherwork. Mosques (15th, 16th and 17th cc.), Sikh temple. It was the capital of the Maurya Empire (325–184 B.C.)

pat·ois (pǽtwɑ) *n.* the speech or dialect peculiar to one part of a country, differing from the standard written or spoken language [F., origin unknown]

Paton (péit'n), Alan (1903–) South African writer and political figure. He gained international fame with his novels 'Cry, the Beloved Country' (1948) and 'Too Late the Phalarope' (1953), which explored racial conflict in South Africa long before it became an international issue. His later works include nonfiction ('The Land and the People of South Africa,' 1955), short-story collections ('Tales from a Troubled Land,' 1961; 'Knocking on the Door,' 1975), and the novel 'Ah, But Your Land Is Beautiful' (1982). He helped found the Liberal party of South Africa, an anti-apartheid political organization

Pa·tos, La·go·a dos (lɑgɔ́əðuʃpátus) a lake (150 miles long, 37 miles wide) in S. Brazil, separated from the Atlantic by a sandy peninsula

Pa·tras (pətrǽs) (*Gk* Patrai) a port (pop. 111,607) of the N.W. Peloponnesus, Greece

pa·tri·al (péitri:'l) *n.* a citizen by reason of birth or adoption — **pa·tri·al·i·ty** *n.* the condition

pa·tri·arch (péitri:ɑrk) *n.* the father or head of a family or tribe, esp. one of the founders of the Jewish people in the Old Testament (Abraham, Isaac, Jacob, ten of Jacob's sons and Joseph's two sons) ‖ (*rhet.*) any venerable head of a large family or tribe ‖ (*rhet.*) any very old and dignified man ‖ (*Roman Catholic and Uniate Churches*) a bishop who ranks in jurisdiction immediately below the pope ‖ a bishop of the Orthodox Eastern sees of Constantinople, Alexandria, Antioch and Jerusalem ‖ the spiritual head of any of certain Eastern Churches (e.g. the Syrian, Coptic or Russian Orthodox Churches) ‖ (*Mormon Church*) a high dignitary who has the power to invoke and pronounce blessings [O.F. *patriarche* fr. L. fr. Gk fr. *patria, clan*+*archēs,* ruler]

pa·tri·ar·chal (peitri:ɑ́rk'l) *adj.* relating to, like or ruled by a patriarch [fr. L.L. *patriarchalis*]

pa·tri·ar·chate (peitri:ɑrkit) *n.* the district ruled by an ecclesiastical patriarch or his residence, office or term of office ‖ a patriarchal system [fr. M.L. *patriarchatus*]

pa·tri·ar·chy (péitri:ɑrki:) *pl.* **pa·tri·ar·chies** *n.* a social system in which the chief authority is the father or eldest male member of the family or clan ‖ a community characterized by this system [fr. Gk *patriarchia,* office of a patriarch]

pa·tri·cian (pətríʃən) **1.** *n.* (*hist.*) a member of one of the privileged families of ancient Rome, who alone until the 4th c. B.C. had the right to hold office (cf. PLEBEIAN) ‖ a noble, esp. (*hist.*) in the Byzantine Empire and the medieval Italian city-states **2.** *adj.* noble, aristocratic ‖ having or exemplifying qualities and standards associ-

ated with the aristocracy, i.e. sense of style, refinement without weakness, noble sentiment etc. ‖ (*Rom. hist.*) of or relating to the patricians [fr. L. *patricius,* belonging to the rank of *patres,* senators of Rome]

pa·tri·ci·ate (pətríʃi:it, pətríʃi:eit) *n.* (*Rom. hist.*) the body or class of patricians ‖ the rank or dignity of a patrician [fr. M.L. *patriciatus*]

pat·ri·ci·dal (pǽtrisáid'l) *adj.* of, relating to or guilty of patricide

pat·ri·cide (pǽtrisaid) *n.* the murder of a father by his child ‖ someone who murders his father [fr. L. *pater,* father+*caedere,* to kill]

Pat·rick (pǽtrik), St (c. 385–461), the patron saint of Ireland. He brought Christianity to Ireland (432 onwards) and founded the see of Armagh (c. 444). He wrote 'The Letter to Coroticus' and 'Confessions', a moving account of his work. Feast: Mar. 17

pat·ri·lin·e·al (pætrilíni:əl) *adj.* tracing kinship through the father rather than the mother [fr. L. *pater,* father+LINEAL]

pat·ri·lo·cal (pætrilóuk'l) *adj.* at or taking place at the habitation of the husband's family or tribe [fr. L. *pater,* father+LOCAL]

pat·ri·mo·ni·al (pætrimóuni:əl) *adj.* pertaining to or constituting a patrimony

pat·ri·mo·ny (pǽtrimouni:) *pl.* **pat·ri·mo·nies** *n.* property, money etc. inherited from one's father or an ancestor ‖ anything valuable handed down by earlier generations and looked on as a trust, *our Roman patrimony* ‖ an endowment of an institution, e.g. a church or college [F. *patrimoine, patremoine* fr. L.]

pa·tri·ot (péitri:ət, péitri:ɒt, *Br.* also pǽtri:ət) *n.* a person who loves his native country and will do all he can for it [F. *patriote* fr. L.L. fr. Gk]

Patriot *n.* (*mil.*) U.S. air-defense, solid-fuel missile with command direction, under development

pa·tri·ot·ic (peitri:ɒ́tik, *Br.* also pætri:ɒ́tik) *adj.* inspired by, showing or aimed at arousing love of one's country, *a patriotic speech* — **pa·tri·ót·i·cal·ly** *adv.* [fr. L.L. *patrioticus* fr. Gk]

pa·tri·ot·ism (péitri:ətizəm, *Br.* also pǽtri:ətizəm) *n.* zealous love of one's country [PATRIOT]

pa·tris·tic (pətrístik) *adj.* of or relating to the Fathers of the Christian Church or to their writings — **pa·tris·tics** *n.* the study of these writings [fr. L. *patres* pl. of *pater,* father]

Pa·tro·clus (pətróukləs) Greek warrior and friend of Achilles at the siege of Troy. When Achilles, slighted by Agamemnon, refused to fight, Patroclus took his arms and, mistaken for Achilles, was killed by Hector. Achilles fought again to avenge his friend

pa·trol (pətróul) *pres. part.* **pa·trol·ling** *past and past part.* **pa·trolled** *v.t.* to go the rounds of (an army camp, town etc.) for the purpose of guarding, inspecting etc. ‖ *v.i.* to go the rounds of a place in order to guard it etc. [F. *patrouiller* fr. *patouiller,* to tramp in mud]

patrol *n.* a patrolling ‖ an instance of this, *his patrol lasted until dark* ‖ the men, aircraft, ships etc. engaged in patrolling, *the patrol captured two prisoners* ‖ a subdivision of a troop of boy scouts or girl scouts, usually having six to eight members [F. *patrouille*]

patrol car a squad car

pa·trol·man (pətróulmən) *pl.* **pa·trol·men** (pətróulmən) *n.* a policeman who patrols an assigned area

patrol wagon an enclosed motor vehicle used by the police to transport people under arrest

pa·tron (péitrən) *n.* a person or institution that gives practical (e.g. financial) support to a cause, individual or group regarded as deserving it ‖ a person who lends his name to a deserving institution or cause as an indication of his approval and support ‖ a patron saint of a specified person, place, group etc., *St Christopher is the patron of travelers* ‖ a customer, esp. a regular one, in a shop, restaurant etc. ‖ (*Church of England*) a person who has the right of presentation to a benefice [M.E. *patroun* fr. O.F. *patrun, patron* fr. L.]

pa·tron·age (péitrənidʒ, pǽtrənidʒ) *n.* the material help and encouragement given by a patron ‖ the special protection of a patron saint ‖ the power of putting people into advantageous positions, bestowing privileges etc., *he owed the job to political patronage* ‖ (*commerce*) the support or orders of a customer, *your patronage is solicited* ‖ the granting of favors in a condescending way ‖ (*Church of England*) the right of presentation to a benefice [F.]

pa·tron·al (péitrən'l) *adj.* of, relating to or characteristic of a patron or a patron saint

pa·tron·ess (péitrənis, pǽtrənis) *n.* a female patron [fr. M.L. *patronissa*]

pa·tron·ize (péitrənaiz, pǽtrənaiz) *pres. part.* **pa·tron·iz·ing** *past* and *past part.* **pa·tron·ized** *v.t.* (of a patron) to give material support or encouragement to ‖ to be a regular customer at (a shop etc.) ‖ to treat in an offensively superior, condescending manner — **pá·tron·iz·ing** *adj.* offensively condescending

patron saint a saint in the relationship of spiritual guardian to a person, group, place etc.

pat·ro·nym·ic (pætrənímik) **1.** *n.* a name derived from that of the father or paternal ancestor, esp. by the addition of a suffix or prefix ‖ a family name **2.** *adj.* of or relating to a patronymic [fr. L. *patronymicus* adj. fr. Gk fr. *patēr,* father+*onoma, onuma,* name]

pa·troon (pətrú:n) *n.* (*Am. hist.*) a landowner with manorial rights in New York or New Jersey dating from a Dutch grant of 1629 [Du.=patron]

pat·tée, pa·tée (pətéi) *adj.* (*heraldry*) of a cross whose four arms become much wider as they extend from the center [F. *patté, pattée,* pawed fr. *patte,* paw]

pat·ten (pǽt'n) *n.* (*hist.*) a clog or overshoe having a metal device under the sole to raise the wearer out of the mud [F. *patin*]

pat·ter (pǽtər) **1.** *n.* the quick talk or chatter of a comedian or entertainer, salesman etc. ‖ the slang or private language used by a particular group or class, *thieves' patter* ‖ mechanically repeated words, *his prayers were a meaningless patter* **2.** *v.t.* to repeat (words, prayers, a formula etc.) mechanically without considering the meaning ‖ *v.i.* to talk volubly but without much sense [fr. L. *paternoster,* our father, fr. the mechanical recitation of the Lord's Prayer in the rosary etc.]

patter 1. *v.t.* to make a series of short, light, rapid taps, *the rain was pattering on the roof* ‖ to run or move making a series of light tapping sounds, *she pattered up the aisle* **2.** *n.* the noise made by pattering [PAT v.]

pat·tern (pǽtərn) **1.** *n.* an orderly sequence consisting of a number of repeated or complementary elements, decorative motifs etc. ‖ a style of design or applied decoration, *these jugs come in several patterns* ‖ a model from which a copy can be made ‖ a sample of cloth, paper etc. showing the design or color, *take some from the seam as a pattern* ‖ a model to be followed as an example of excellence ‖ the model from which the mold is made for casting metal ‖ the way in which the shot or bullets are distributed on a target **2.** *v.t.* to make or form in imitation of another person or thing, *pattern yourself on him* ‖ to decorate with a pattern [M.E. *patron* fr. F.]

pat·tern·ing (pǽtərnin) *n.* **1.** (*med.*) technique of physical therapy utilizing biofeedback to control and modify nervous responses **2.** (*zool.*) behavior developed in imitation or response to education

Pat·ter·son (pǽtərsən), Joseph Medill (1879–1946), U.S. journalist. He became (1914) co-editor (with Robert McCormick) of the 'Chicago Tribune' and founded with McCormick (1919) the 'New York Daily News', the first successful tabloid newspaper in the U.S.A.

Pat·ton (pǽt'n), George Smith (1885–1945), American general. In the 2nd world war he was a commander in the Allied invasion of N. Africa (1942), led the U.S. invasion of Sicily (1943) and commanded the U.S. 3rd Army in the Normandy invasion (1944), advancing rapidly into Germany (1945)

pat·ty (pǽti:) *pl.* **pat·ties** *n.* a little pie, generally with a savory filling ‖ a small, flat, esp. fried cake of minced meat etc. [fr. F. *pâté,* O.F. *pasté,* a pasty]

pat·u·lous (pǽtʃuləs) *adj.* (*bot.,* e.g. of tree branches) spreading outward from a center ‖ distended [fr. L. *patulus* fr. *patere,* to be open]

pau·ci·ty (pɔ́siti:) *n.* smallness, esp. insufficiency, in number or amount, *a paucity of trained operators* [F. *paucité* or fr. L. *paucitas* fr. *paucus,* few, little]

Paul (pɔl), St (*d.* c. 64 or c. 67 A.D.), the first Christian missionary and apostle to the gentiles. Born a Jew of Tarsus in Cilicia, he inherited his father's Roman citizenship. He studied Mosaic law in Jerusalem, and was zealous in persecuting Christians, being present at the martyrdom of Stephen. He was converted to Christianity by a vision while on the road to Damascus (c. 35) and changed his name from

CONCISE PRONUNCIATION KEY: (**a**) æ, c*a*t; ɑ, c*a*r; ɔ f*aw*n; ei, sn*a*ke. (**e**) e, h*e*n; i:, sh*ee*p; iə, d*ee*r; ɛə, b*ea*r. (**i**) i, f*i*sh; ai, t*i*ger; ə:, b*ir*d. (**o**) o, *o*x; au, c*ow*; ou, g*oa*t; u, p*oo*r; ɔi, r*oy*al. (**u**) ʌ, d*u*ck; u, b*u*ll; u:, g*oo*se; ə, b*a*cillus; ju:, c*u*be. x, lo*ch*; θ, *th*ink; ð, bo*th*er; z, *Z*en; ʒ, corsa*g*e; dʒ, sava*g*e; ŋ, ora*ng*utang; j, *y*ak; ʃ, *fi*sh; tʃ, fe*tch*; 'l, rabb*le*; 'n, red*den*. Complete pronunciation key appears inside front cover.

Saul to Paul. His missionary journeys, recounted by Luke in the Acts of the Apostles, took him first to Cyprus and Asia Minor (c. 45–9). His preaching to the gentiles aroused controversy among Jewish Christians, and the first apostolic council took a compromise decision on the issue of gentile converts' submission to Jewish law (c. 50). His second journey (c. 50–3) was to Asia Minor, Macedonia, Athens and Corinth, and his third (c. 53–7) was to Ephesus, Macedonia and Corinth. Back in Jerusalem, he was arrested by the Roman authorities after a riot, was imprisoned for two years and was then sent to Rome, after appealing, as a Roman citizen, to Caesar. He was either martyred at this time (c. 64), or else was released, went to Spain, returned to Rome and was martyred c. 67. His letters to the early Churches include the Epistles to the Thessalonians, Corinthians, Galatians, Colossians, Philippians and Romans, and possibly the Epistle to the Ephesians. He did much to make Christianity a universal religion and was the first to enunciate the doctrine of justification by faith. Feast: June 29

Pau·li·cian (pɔlíʃən) *n.* a member of a dualistic heretical Christian sect (c. 7th c.–c. 11th c.) of Armenia

Pauli exclusion principle (*phys.*) a statement in quantum mechanics that since an electron is a fermion it cannot exist in a system containing other fermions that possess identical quantum numbers. The periodic system of the elements follows directly from this principle

Paul III (Alessandro Farnese, 1468–1549), pope (1543–49). Devoted to the cause of Catholic reform, he approved (1540) the founding of the Society of Jesus, and summoned (1545) the Council of Trent. He was a patron of the arts, and employed Michelangelo as architect, painter and sculptor at the Vatican. His pontificate marks the transition from the Renaissance to the Counter-Reformation

Paul·ine (pɔ́lain) *adj.* of St Paul, his writings or teaching [fr. L. *Paulinus*]

Paul·ist (pɔ́list) *n.* a member of an American community of Roman Catholic priests, founded (1858) for missionary work within the U.S.A.

Paul IV (Gian Pietro Carafa, 1476–1559), pope (1555–9). An extremist leader of the Counter-Reformation, he established (1559) the Index Librorum Prohibitorum and attempted to reform the clergy

Pau·low·ni·a (pɔlóuni:ə) *n.* a member of *Paulownia*, fam. *Scrophulariaceae*, a genus of ornamental trees with white or purple flowers, native to China and Japan, now widely cultivated in parks [after Anna *Paulovna*, daughter of Czar Paul I]

Paul V (Camillo Borghese, 1552–1621), pope (1605–21). He was a noted canon lawyer, and put Venice under interdict (1606) in an attempt to assert ecclesiastical supremacy over secular power

Paul VI (Giovanni Battista Montini, 1897–1978), pope (1963–78). He continued the 2nd Vatican Council convened by John XXIII. He made a pilgrimage to the Holy Land (1964), and he had discussions there with Patriarch Athenagoras I. He addressed the U.N. (1965) in New York and was the first pope to go to Latin America, when he visited (1968) a eucharistic congress at Bogotá. His encyclical 'Humanae Vitae' on married life (1968), reiterating the Roman Catholic Church's teaching against contraception, was called in question by many

Paul (1901–64), king of Greece (1947–64), brother of George II

Paul I (1754–1801), czar of Russia (1769–1801), son of Catherine II. He was mentally unstable. He reversed his mother's policy, revoking the privileges given to the nobility, improving the lot of the serfs and cutting off contacts with foreign countries. He took Russia into the French Revolutionary Wars against France (1798–9), but allied with France in 1801

Paul Bun·yan (bʌ́njən) (*Am. folklore*) a giant lumberjack, the hero of many tales in which he performs feats of strength and daring

Paul·ding (pɔ́ldiŋ), James Kirke (1778–1860), U.S. public official and writer who was one of the first to employ native American themes in literature. His 'The Lay of the Scottish Fiddle' (1813) satirized England's policy toward the U.S.A. during the War of 1812. In his play 'The Lion of the West' (1831) he introduced frontier humor to the stage, and the character of Davy Crockett

Pau·li (páuli:), Wolfgang (1901–58), Austrian physicist. He was awarded the Nobel prize (1945) for his work on atomic structure, esp. for his discovery of the exclusion principle. He also predicted (1931) the existence of the neutrino from his study of nuclear decay by beta-particle emission. This was confirmed in 1956

Pau·ling (pɔ́liŋ), Linus Carl (1901–), U.S. chemist and winner of the 1954 Nobel prize in chemistry for discovering the basic principles determining the structure of molecules, and their application to the explanation of the properties of matter. He was awarded the 1962 Nobel prize for peace

Pau·li·nus of No·la (pɔláinəsəvnóulə), St (353–431), bishop of Nola (409–31) and poet. His writings include poems to St Felix, metrical paraphrasings of the Psalms, and correspondence with Sts Augustine and Jerome. Feast: June 22

Paulinus of York, St (*d.* 644), 1st archbishop of York (632). He worked with St Augustine of Canterbury and temporarily converted Northumbria (625–32), but fled when Penda defeated King Edwin (632). Feast: Oct. 10

Paul of the Cross, St (Paolo Francesco Danei, 1694–1775), Italian priest, founder of the Passionists. Feast: Apr. 28

Paul the Deacon (c. 720–c. 799), Lombard historian. He wrote 'Historia Langobardorum', covering the history of the Lombards from the late 6th c. to the early 8th c.

paunch (pɔntʃ) *n.* a fat, protruding belly, esp. a man's || (*zool.*) the rumen [M.E. fr. O.N.F. *panche*]

pau·per (pɔ́pər) *n.* a completely destitute person, esp. one entirely dependent on public charity **pau·per·ism, pau·per·i·zá·tion** *ns* **páu·per·ize** *pres. part.* **pau·per·iz·ing** *past* and *past part.* **pau·per·i·zed** *v.t.* to reduce to the condition of a pauper [L. adj.=poor]

Pau·sa·ni·as (pɔséini:əs) (*d.* c. 470 B.C.), Spartan general. He commanded the Greek force which defeated the Persians at Plataea (479 B.C.)

Pausanias (2nd c. A.D.), Greek geographer. His 'Description of Greece' is an important source for the history and topography of ancient Greece

pause (pɔz) *n.* a short period of time when sound, motion or activity stops before starting again, *a pause in a conversation* || (*mus.*) the lengthening of a note, or the mark ⌒ or ⌒ indicating this **to give** (**someone**) **pause** to cause (someone) to hesitate or think again before taking action [F. fr. L. fr. Gk]

pause *pres. part.* **paus·ing** *past* and *past part.* **paused** *v.i.* to make a pause || to hesitate, stop to reflect [fr. PAUSE or fr. L. *pausare* or F. *pauser,* to cease]

pav·an (pǽvən) *n.* (*hist.*) a slow stately dance for couples, originating in Italy and popular in Tudor England || a musical composition in slow duple time, originally to accompany this dance [F. *pavane* fr. Span. or Ital.]

pa·vane (pəvǽn) *n.* a pavan

Pavarotti (pɑvɑroúti:), Luciano (1935–), Italian tenor, one of the principal singers with the Metropolitan Opera, La Scala and other leading companies. He made his debut (1961) as Rodolfo in Puccini's 'La Bohème' in Reggio Emilia and performed the same role in a film and in his Metropolitan Opera debut (1968). He has also achieved fame in such operas as 'Lucia di Lammermoor,' 'L'Elisir d'Amore,' and 'Rigoletto'

pave (peiv) *pres. part.* **pav·ing** *past* and *past part.* **paved** *v.t.* to cover (a road, path etc.) with a surface to walk or travel on **to pave the way for** (or **to**) to provide an easy road for (or to), *influential contacts paved the way to his success* [O.F. *paver*]

pa·vé (pɔvéi) *n.* a paved road or sidewalk || a setting of jewels close together so that the metal is completely covered [F. past part. of *paver,* to pave]

pave·ment (péivmənt) *n.* a paved street or road || any paved surface || the material used in paving || (esp. *Br.*) a sidewalk [O.F.]

pavement artist an artist who exhibits and sells his work on the pavement || (*Br.*) a sidewalk artist

pave·way (péivwei) *n.* (*mil.*) family of laser-guided bombs targeted by air or ground; produced by Rockwell International and developed in 1965

Pa·vi·a (pəví:ə) an agricultural center (pop. 84,000) of Lombardy, Italy, 20 miles south of Milan. Red brick Romanesque churches, town

hall (12th and 13th cc.), Gothic churches and castle (14th and 15th cc.). Cathedral (1488–1898). University (1361)

Pavia, Battle of a battle (1525) in which François I was defeated and captured by Emperor Charles V during the Italian Wars

pa·vil·ion (pəvíljən) *n.* a large tent, often open on one side || a light, elegant building or shelter in a garden, park etc. || one of several buildings into which a large institution, esp. a hospital is sometimes divided || (*Br.=Am.* field house) a building attached to a playing field, in which players change, equipment is stored, and where spectators may sometimes be accommodated || (*jewelry*) the lower part of a cut brilliant, below the girdle || (*anat.*) the auricle of the ear [M.E. fr. F. *pavillon,* tent]

pav·ing (péiviŋ) *n.* a sidewalk or other paved surface || material for a pavement [PAVE]

pav·ior, pav·iour (péivjər) *n.* a worker who lays paving || a ramming machine for setting paving stones || a specially hardened brick used for paving [older *pavier, pavyer* fr. PAVE]

Pav·lov (pǽvlɒv), Ivan Petrovitch (1849–1936), Russian physiologist. He worked on the simple reflex, showing by experiment with dogs how an original stimulus can be replaced by a secondary stimulus producing a 'conditioned reflex', and he showed the importance of such reflexes in the behavior patterns of animal and man. He also demonstrated the importance of the vagus nerve in controlling gastric and pancreatic secretion. Nobel prize (1904)

Pav·lo·va (pǽvlóuvə, pávlʌvɑ), Anna (1885–1931), Russian ballerina, the greatest solo dancer of her time

paw (pɔ) **1.** *n.* the foot of a four-footed animal having claws || (*pop.*) a hand, esp. a clumsy or dirty one || (of an animal) to strike, scrape or scratch with the hoof or paw || (of a person) to feel, touch or handle with the hands in a rude or clumsy way [M.E. fr. O.F. *powe, poue*]

pawl (pɔl) **1.** *n.* a hinged catch engaging with the teeth of a wheel to prevent reverse motion || a similar device on a capstan or windlass **2.** *v.t.* to hold firm with a pawl [etym. doubtful]

pawn (pɔn) **1.** *n.* the state of being pawned, *his suit is in pawn* || something pawned **2.** *v.t.* to hand over as a pledge or security for a loan of money [O.F. *pan, pant*]

pawn *n.* (*chess*) one of the men of least size and value, each player having eight. A pawn can move forward only one square at a time (two on the initial move if the player chooses), but captures only a piece that is one square diagonally in front of it || a person whom others use for their own ends [M.E. *poune* fr. A.F. and O.F.]

pawn·bro·ker (pɔ́nbroukər) *n.* a person licensed to lend money on articles pawned

Paw·nee (pɔní:) *pl.* **Paw·nee, Paw·nees** *n.* a member of a confederacy of North American Indians living in Nebraska, Oklahoma and Kansas || their language

pawn·shop (pɔ́nʃɒp) *n.* a shop or office at which articles may be pawned

pawn ticket a pawnbroker's receipt, held by the client until he redeems the goods pawned

pawpaw *PAPAW

pax (pǽks) *n.* (*eccles.*) a kiss given by the priest at High Mass to the deacon, and passed on to the subdeacon and others in the chancel and choir || (*hist.*) a tablet with a representation of Christ or the Virgin Mary, passed among the priests and to the congregation, being kissed by all in turn [L.=peace]

Pax·ton (pǽkstən), Sir Joseph (1801–65), English architect. His Crystal Palace was one of the sources of modern architecture based on rigid frames and glazing. He designed many private houses

pay (pei) **1.** *v. pres. part.* **pay·ing** *past* and *past part.* **paid** (peid) *v.t.* to give (someone) money in return for goods, work or services || to give (someone) money owed or due || to discharge (a debt), *to pay one's bills* || to give (a sum) in return for goods or services || to yield as a recompense, *the investment paid 5% last year* || to be rewarding to, *it will pay you to take that trip* || to make return for, repay, *she paid his sarcasm in kind* || to suffer (a penalty, consequences etc.) || to give or render (a service, visit, compliment etc.), *please pay attention* || *v.i.* to give money in return for goods, work or services || to be profitable, *it pays to buy good quality* **to pay for** to meet the cost of, *how can you pay for a new car?* || to suffer the consequences of, *make him pay for his rudeness* **to pay in** to deposit (money etc.) in an account **to pay off** to finish paying, *to pay off* *a mortgage* ‖ to give (someone) his wages and dismiss him ‖ (*naut.*) to cause or allow (a ship) to fall off to leeward ‖ to recompense for good or evil ‖ to turn out profitably, *it was a risk but it paid off* **to pay one's way** to pay one's share of costs or expenses ‖ to remain solvent **to pay out** to distribute (money etc.), *they paid out hundreds of dollars in prizes* ‖ (*past* and *past part.* **payed**) to pass along the slack of (a rope) **to pay up** to pay in full or on time **2.** *adj.* (of earth) yielding oil or valuable metals ‖ made available for use by the insertion of a coin or coins in a slot, *a pay toilet* [M.E. fr. F. *payer*]

pay *pres. part.* **pay·ing** *past* and *past part.* **payed, paid** *v.t.* (*naut.*) to coat with pitch etc. so as to make waterproof [O.N.F. *peier* fr. L. fr. *pix*, pitch]

pay *n.* money received as wages or salary for work or services (always used instead of 'wage' or 'salary' in the armed services) **in the pay of** receiving money from, in return for work or services (often with the suggestion of being bribed) [O.F. *paie*]

pay·a·ble (péiəb'l) *adj.* that must, can, should, or may be paid, *the rent is payable in advance* ‖ (of a mine etc.) profitable to work

pay-as-you-earn (péiəzju:ə́:rn) *n.* (*Br.*, *abbr.* P.A.Y.E.) the system of deducting income tax from wages before they are paid to the worker

pay·book (péibuk) *n.* (*Br.*) a serviceman's record of his pay and allowances

pay·ca·ble (péikéib'l) *n.* cable television programs for which a surcharge is made

pay·day (péidei) *n.* the day of the week or month on which wages or salary are regularly paid ‖ the day on which stock transfers are paid for in the London Stock Exchange

pay dirt earth containing enough ore to be profitably worked by a miner ‖ something that turns out to be a valuable source of information etc.

P.A.Y.E. *PAY-AS-YOU-EARN

pay·ee (peií:) *n.* a person to whom money is or should be paid, esp. a person to whom a check, money order etc. is made out

paying guest (*abbr.* P.G.) a boarder in a boardinghouse or in a private home

pay·load (péiloud) *n.* (*rocketry*) the warhead of a guided missile, or whatever is projected by it

pay·load (péiloud) *n.* the size and weight of cargo, instrumentation, and passenger capacity, but not including the fuel, of a plane or space vehicle

pay·mas·ter (péimæstər, péimɑstər) *n.* an official who pays troops, government employees etc.

paymaster general *pl.* **paymasters general, paymaster generals** (*Br.*) a government officer, nominally the head of the department responsible for arranging payments to most other government departments, but effectively free to assume any special responsibilities the prime minister may entrust to him

pay·ment (péimənt) *n.* a paying for work, services, goods bought, charges incurred, debts etc. ‖ the money etc. paid for work or services ‖ something given in return, or as a reward, punishment or revenge [F. *paiement*]

pay·off (péiɔf, péiɒf) *n.* a paying of wages, winnings etc. ‖ (*pop.*) a final reckoning, *the payoff came when Interpol closed in* ‖ (*pop.*) the climax of a dramatic situation or story

pay·o·la (peióulə) *n.* illegal or unethical payments for favors

pay·out ratio (péiautréiʃiːou) (*securities*) the ratio of corporate dividends to earnings

pay·roll (péiroul) *n.* a list of employees and their wages or salaries ‖ the whole body of people employed by a person or firm or institution ‖ the total amount regularly paid in wages and salaries

Pay·san·dú (paisandú:) an industrial city and port (pop. 61,000) of W. Uruguay, on the east bank of the Uruguay River: meat-packing and frozen meats

pay station a telephone booth

pay telephone a telephone operated by a coin-in-the-slot device

Paz (pɑs), Octavio (1914–), Mexican poet, writer and diplomat, author of 'Raíz del hombre', 'Libertad bajo palabra', and 'Luna silvestre'

PBB (*chem. acronym*) polybrominated biphenyl, a persistent toxic chemical used in a fire retardant

PCB (*chem. acronym*) polychlorinated biphenyls, a group of clear, slightly viscous nearly

indestructible and highly toxic industrial compounds used in transformers and capacitors

PCM (*computer*) **1.** (*acronym*) plug compatible manufacturer, equipment producers who manufacture equipment compatible with IBM software. **2.** (*abbr.*) punched card machine. **3.** (*abbr.*) pulse code modulation

PCP (*med. abbr.*) phencyclidine hydrochloride [C$_{17}$H$_{25}$N], a depressant

P-day (pí:dei) *n.* (*mil.*) the time when the rate of production of an item available for military consumption equals the rate at which the item is required by the armed forces

pea (pi:) *n. Pisum sativum*, fam. *Papilionaceae*, a climbing or bushy annual plant with large green pods whose fresh or dried seeds are valued as a vegetable. The pods and vines are used as green manure and forage ‖ one of the seeds of this plant ‖ any of several leguminous plants, e.g. the chick pea [older *pease* sing. and pl., taken as a pl., fr. O.E. *pise* fr. L. fr. Gk *pison*]

Pea·bod·y (pí:bɒdi:, pí:bədi:), George (1795–1869), U.S. merchant, financier and philanthropist. He established (1829) a banking and mercantile firm in London and amassed a fortune. He donated about $8.5 million to educational institutions and the poor

Peace (pi:s) a river (1,065 miles long) of British Columbia and Alberta, Canada rising in the Rocky Mtns, the main headstream of the Mackenzie

peace *n.* the condition that exists when nations or other groups are not fighting ‖ the ending of a state of war ‖ the treaty that marks the end of war ‖ friendly relations between individuals, untroubled by disputes ‖ freedom from noise, worries, troubles, fears etc., *peace of mind* **at peace** in a state of peace, friendliness or calm **the peace** or (*Br.*) **the king's** (or **queen's**) **peace** public order and security **to hold** (or **keep**) **one's peace** (*rhet.*) to be silent **to keep the peace** to prevent or avoid strife **to make** (**one's**) **peace** to put an end to a quarrel, become friendly again [M.E. *pais* fr. O.F. *pais*, Mod. F. *paix* fr. L. *pax* (*pacis*)]

peace·a·ble (pí:səb'l) *adj.* not given to fighting or quarreling ‖ in a state of peace, **péace·a·bly** *adv.* [M.E. *peisible* fr. O.F.]

Peace Corps a U.S. government agency established (1961) by President John Kennedy to 'help foreign countries meet their urgent needs for skilled manpower'. A volunteer, who must be a U.S. citizen and at least 18 years old, undergoes intensive training in the language, history, culture and customs of the country to which he is to be sent, normally for a two-year term. Once overseas, he works directly with the people of the host country, speaking their language and sharing their lives

peace·ful (pí:sfəl) *adj.* calm, quiet, untroubled, undisturbed by noise, worries, fears etc., *peaceful summer evenings* ‖ not warlike or violent, *to use peaceful means* ‖ not given to fighting or quarreling

peace-keep·ing force (pí:ski:pinfɔ́rs) *n.* a United Nations combat-ready force of member nations combined into military body to maintain peace in an area involved in dispute

peace·mak·er (pí:smeikər) *n.* a person who restores peace or friendly relations

peace·nik (pí:snik) *n.* antiwar activist

peace offering something given to show that one wishes to end a quarrel

Peace of God (*hist.*) a truce in feudal warfare enjoined by the Church periodically from the 9th c. until 1095, when, at the Synod of Clermont-Ferrand, it became an official institution of the Church

peace pipe the calumet as a symbol of peace

peace·time (pí:staim) *n.* the time when a country is not at war

peach (pi:tʃ) **1.** *n. Prunus persica*, fam. *Rosaceae*, a small tree of the temperate zone, native to China, having lanceolate leaves. The fruit is a sweet, juicy, yellow or white drupe occurring in clingstone and freestone varieties and having a thin, downy skin ‖ the fruit of this tree ‖ (*pop.*) any particularly excellent person or thing, *a peach of a house* ‖ a color resembling that of the fruit, a soft, pale, yellowish red **2.** *adj.* of the color peach [M.E. *peche* fr. F. *pêche*, O.F. *pesche*, *peche*]

peach *v.i.* (*pop.*) to turn informer [M.E. *apeche*, to impede, impeach]

Pea·cock (pí:kɒk), Thomas Love (1785–1866), English novelist and poet. 'Headlong Hall' (1816), 'Nightmare Abbey' (1818), and

'Crotchet Castle' (1831) are conversation pieces rather than novels. In a playful but effective way he wittily attacked both Romanticism and the myth of inevitable social progress. His 'Four Ages of Poetry' (1820) provoked Shelley into writing his 'Defense of Poetry'

pea·cock (pí:kɒk) *n.* a male member of *Pavo*, fam. *Phasianidae*, a genus of large gallinaceous birds, native to India and Asia but widely kept for their ornamental value. They occur in predominantly blue or white species. Their long, brilliantly colored tail coverts are marked with iridescent ocellate spots ('eyes'), and they display them in a vertical position fanned out magnificently ‖ (*loosely*) the male or female of any of these birds [M.E. fr. O.E. *pēa* fr. L.+COCK]

peacock blue a bright iridescent blue, as seen on the neck plumage of a peacock

peacock butterfly *Nymphalis io*, a European butterfly with markings on its wings like the eyes on the peacock's tail

pea·fowl (pí:faul) *pl.* **pea·fowls, pea·fowl** *n.* a peacock or peahen

pea green a light, yellowish-green color

pea·hen (pí:hen) *n.* the female of the peacock [M.E. *pehen, pehenne* fr. O.E. *pēa henne*]

pea jacket a short, double-breasted black or navy blue overcoat worn esp. by seamen [prob. fr. M.Du. *pīe*, coarse woolen coat+JACKET]

peak (pi:k) *n.* a pointed top or projection ‖ the pointed top of a mountain ‖ a high mountain, esp. one that stands alone ‖ the projecting brim at the front of a cap ‖ the highest point, maximum, *tourism is at its peak in August* ‖ (*elec.*) the maximum value of a varying quantity during a specified period ‖ (*naut.*) the forepeak or the afterpeak ‖ (*naut.*) the upper after corner of a fore-and-aft sail held by a gaff [var. of PIKE, sharp point]

peak *v.i.* (*old-fash.*) to be sickly and listless, become increasingly low in health and spirits [etym. doubtful]

peak *v.t.* (*naut.*) to raise (a yard, a gaff, oars) to or towards the vertical [fr. APEAK]

Peak District a plateau region of wild moors and crags in N. Derbyshire, England, a famous tourist area

peaked (pí:kt) *adj.* having a peak or point ‖ (pí:kid) looking sickly and thin

peak·y (pí:ki:) *comp.* **peak·i·er** *superl.* **peak·i·est** *adj.* peaked (sickly looking) [PEAK *n.*]

peal (pi:l) **1.** *n.* a loud ringing of a bell or bells ‖ a set of bells tuned to the notes of the major scale for ringing changes ‖ a complete set or part of a set of changes, rung on these ‖ a sudden burst of noise, *a peal of thunder* **2.** *v.i.* (of bells, thunder, laughter etc.) to ring out, burst into sudden noise ‖ *v.t.* (often with 'out') to sound vigorously in a peal, *the organ pealed out the wedding march* [M.E. *pele* fr. *apele*, appeal]

Peale (pi:l), Charles Willson (1741–1827), U.S. painter, best known for his portraits of leading figures of the Revolutionary period, incl. seven life portraits of George Washington. He founded (1784) Peale's Museum in Philadelphia, which held (1801) the first U.S. scientific exhibition, displaying the first complete skeleton of the American mastodon

Peale, Rembrandt (1778–1860), U.S. painter, who served (1808–10) as portrait painter at the court of Napoleon. He is best known for his portrait of Thomas Jefferson and his huge 'Court of Death' (1819)

pean *PAEAN

pea·nut (pí:nʌt) *n. Arachis hypogaea*, fam. *Papilionaceae*, a branched, trailing annual plant, probably indigenous to Brazil, but cultivated widely in warm regions for its oily, nutritious seeds ‖ its nutlike seed

peanut butter an edible paste made from ground roasted peanuts

peanut oil an oil expressed from peanuts and used as a salad oil, in soaps, and as a vehicle in medicines

pear (peər) *n. Pyrus communis*, fam. *Rosaceae*, a tree native to W. Asia and E. Europe. Many strains and hybrids are cultivated in all temperate regions ‖ its fruit, a fleshy, juicy, sweet pome, varying in color between yellow-green and russet, and usually tapering at the stem from a bulbous base [O.E. *pere* fr. L.]

Pearce (piərs), Charles Sprague (1851–1914), U.S. historical painter, best known for his 'The Beheading of John the Baptist' and 'The Arab

CONCISE PRONUNCIATION KEY: **(a)** æ, c*a*t; ɑ, c*a*r; ɔ f*aw*n; ei, sn*a*ke. **(e)** e, h*e*n; i:, sh*ee*p; iə, d*ee*r; ɛə, b*ear*. **(i)** i, f*i*sh; ai, t*i*ger; ə:, b*i*rd. **(o)** o, *o*x; au, c*ow*; ou, g*oa*t; u, p*oo*r; ɔi, r*oy*al. **(u)** ʌ, d*u*ck; u, b*u*ll; u:, g*oo*se; ə, bacill*u*s; ju:, c*u*be. x, lo*ch*; θ, *th*ink; ð, bo*th*er; z, *Z*en; ʒ, cor*s*age; dʒ, sa*v*age; ŋ, ora*n*gutang; j, *y*ak; ʃ, *f*ish; tʃ, *f*etch; 'l, ra*bble*; 'n, re*dden*. Complete pronunciation key appears inside front cover.

Jeweler', and for his mural decorations in the Library of Congress

pearl (pəːrl) **1.** *n.* a secretion, chiefly of calcium carbonate, produced by some mollusks ‖ a hard, lustrous, usually white, almost spherical deposit of this around a small solid irritant (e.g. a grain of sand) which finds its way into the mollusk's shell, or is put into it by man (*CULTURED PEARL), and is greatly prized for its luster, form and color ‖ something rare and precious, *his words are pearls of wisdom* ‖ (*printing*) a type roughly 5-point in size ‖ a very pale gray color with bluish overtones **to cast pearls before swine** to say wise or witty things to people unable to appreciate them **2.** *adj.* made of or resembling pearl [M.E. fr. F. *perle*]

pearl *v.t.* to ornament with pearls or with pearl-like drops ‖ to reduce (barley etc.) to hard, round grains by rubbing or grinding ‖ *v.i.* to seek for pearls by diving or fishing for pearl-bearing mollusks ‖ to form drops like pearls, *the perspiration pearled down his forehead* [F. *perler* or fr. PEARL n.]

pearl ash potassium carbonate, K_2CO_3, extracted from the ash of burned wood

pearl barley barley reduced to small, round grains by rubbing

pearl diver a person who dives for oysters or other mollusks in search of pearls

pearl fisher a pearl diver

Pearl Harbor a U.S. naval base in Hawaii. The Japanese attacked it treacherously and without warning (Dec. 7, 1941), destroying a large part of the U.S. Pacific fleet. As a result the U.S.A. entered the 2nd world war

pearl·ies (pə́ːrliːz) *pl. n.* (*Br.*) the traditional holiday dress of the London costermongers, decorated with hundreds of pearl buttons

pearl·ing *n.* (*surfing*) riding down a wave to a fall; from pearl diving

Pearl Islands a group of islands (area 450 sq. miles), belonging to Panama in the Gulf of Panama: pearl fisheries

pearl·ite (pə́ːrlait) *n.* a lamellar mixture of ferrite and cementite, a principal constituent of steel and cast iron ‖ perlite [PEARL]

pearl oyster any of several mollusks of genera *Aviculidae* and *Pinctada*, fam. *Pteriidae*, which often produce pearls. They are found chiefly in the Indian Ocean, the Persian Gulf, the S. Pacific, the Gulf of California and the Caribbean

pearl white bismuth oxychloride, used in cosmetics and as a white pigment ‖ any of several other white or pearly substances used in cosmetics etc.

pearl·y (pə́ːrliː) *comp.* **pearl·i·er** *superl.* **pearl·i·est** *adj.* of or like a pearl or mother-of-pearl ‖ decorated with mother-of-pearl or pearls ‖ abounding in pearls

pearly nautilus a nautilus of the genus *Nautilus*

Pear·son (píərs'n), Lester Bowles (1897–1972), Canadian statesman. He was secretary of state for external affairs (1948–57) and president of the U.N. General Assembly (1952–3). He was instrumental in settling the Suez Canal crisis (1956), and was awarded the Nobel peace prize (1957). He became leader of the Canadian Liberal party (1958) and was prime minister (1963–8)

Pea·ry (píəri:), Robert Edwin (1856–1920), American Arctic explorer. He made an expedition to Greenland (1886), crossed to the east coast of Greenland (1891–2), and was the first man to reach the North Pole (1909)

peas·ant (péz'nt) *n.* a hired farm laborer or the owner or tenant of a small farm or holding, in a country where the mass of farm workers and small farmers are very poor **péas·ant·ry** *n.* a body of peasants ‖ peasants collectively [A.F. *paisant*, O.F. *paisent, paisant*]

Peasants' Revolt a rebellion (1381) in East Anglia and S.E. England against the poll tax and the labor legislation following the Black Death. A mob led by Wat Tyler pillaged London and extracted promises of redress from Richard II, but the revolt was put down with great severity and Tyler was beheaded

Peasants' War a social, economic and religious revolt (1524–6) in Germany and Austria. The peasants demanded abolition of serfdom, freedom in selecting pastors, justice in the courts and restriction of labor dues. The revolt was brutally crushed with the approval of Luther, who had earlier been sympathetic toward the rebels

pea·shoot·er (pí:ʃu:tər) *n.* a toy blowpipe for shooting dried peas

pea soup thick soup made from dried peas ‖ (*Am. pop.=Br.* pea-souper) thick yellow fog or smog

pea-soup·er (pí:su:pər) *n.* (esp. *Br.*) pea soup (fog)

peat (pi:t) *n.* a dense accumulation of water-saturated, partially decayed vegetable tissue. The first stage in the formation of coal, it is itself, after drying, used as a fuel, esp. in Ireland and Russia. Peat is also dug into soil to increase its capacity to retain moisture and is a source of plant food [M.E. *pete*, origin unknown]

peat bog a marsh containing peat

peat moss sphagnum

peat·y (pí:ti:) *comp.* **peat·i·er** *superl.* **peat·i·est** *adj.* of, like, or consisting of peat

peau-de-soie (póudəswá) *n.* a smooth, satiny, silk or rayon fabric used esp. for dresses [F.=skin of silk]

pea·vey (pí:vi:) *n.* a stout pole with a sharp spike and a hinged metal hook, for handling logs [after Joseph *Peavey*, its inventor]

peb·ble (péb'l) **1.** *n.* a small stone, naturally rounded and worn smooth by the action of water ‖ transparent rock crystal, used instead of glass in spectacles ‖ a lens of this ‖ pebbled leather or its surface **2.** *v.t. pres. part.* **peb·bling** *past* and *past part.* **peb·bled** to pave or cover with pebbles set in cement, plaster etc. ‖ to give a roughly indented surface to (leather etc.) **péb·bly** *adj.* [O.E. *papolstān, popelstān*, pebble stone]

pe·can (pikǽn, pikán, pí:kæn) *n.* an edible, smooth-shelled, olive-shaped nut, the fruit of *Carya illinoensis*, a species of hickory often of great size, with rough bark and hard wood, found wild and cultivated in the southern U.S.A. and N. Mexico ‖ this tree ‖ the wood of this tree [older *paccan* fr. Algonquian]

pec·ca·dil·lo (pekədílou) *pl.* **pec·ca·dil·los, pec·ca·dil·loes** *n.* a trifling fault or transgression [Span.]

pec·cant (pékənt) *adj.* (*rhet.*) sinful ‖ (*rhet.*) offending against accepted rules or conventions ‖ (*med.*) diseased or causing disease [fr. L. *peccans* (*peccantis*) fr. *peccare*, to sin]

pec·ca·ry (pékəri:) *pl.* **pec·ca·ries** *n.* either of two members of *Tayassu*, fam. *Tayassuidae*, a genus of wild, gregarious, ungulate mammals of tropical America. They look like small, tusked pigs. Their tanned skins are used for gloves etc. [fr. Carib. *pakira, paquira*]

Pe·chen·ga (pətʃéŋgə) (*Finn.* Petsamo) an ice-free port (pop. 5,000) and naval base of the R.S.F.S.R., U.S.S.R. ‖ the territory (3,860 sq. miles) including it, ceded to the U.S.S.R. by Finland (1920)

Pe·cho·ra (pətʃórə) a river (1,125 miles long) of the northwest R.S.F.S.R., U.S.S.R., rising in the Urals and flowing through the Komi A.S.S.R. to the Barents Sea

peck (pek) *n.* a little-used dry measure, one quarter of a bushel, for measuring grain, equal to (*Am.*) 537.605 cu. ins or (*Br.*) 554.84 cu. ins ‖ a vessel holding this measure [M.E. *pek*, etym. doubtful]

peck 1. *v.t.* (of a bird) to strike or make holes in with the beak ‖ to make (a hole) by striking with a rapid movement ‖ to kiss perfunctorily ‖ *v.i.* (esp. with 'at') to make striking movements or holes in something with the beak or as if with the beak ‖ (with 'at') to nibble food without appetite **2.** *n.* an instance of pecking, *the bird gave him a nasty peck* ‖ a quick perfunctory kiss ‖ a little mark or hole made by or as if by pecking [prob. var. of PICK v.]

pecking order the natural hierarchy that exists in a flock of poultry, in which each bird is free to peck at another, less aggressive one without being pecked at by it, while having to submit to the pecking of another, more aggressive bird

peck·ish (pékiʃ) *adj.* irritable ‖ (esp. *Br.*, *pop.*) pleasantly hungry

Pe·cock (pí:kɒk), Reginald (c. 1395–c. 1460), English bishop. He is noted for his attempt to popularize theology and logic by writing in English. In his 'Repressor of Overmuch Blaming of the Clergy' (c. 1455) he tried to hold the Lollard movement in check by argument. He was himself accused of heresy (1457), for denying the doctrines of the Apostles' Creed. He recanted, and saw his books burned

Pe·cos (péikəs) a river (735 miles long) flowing through E. New Mexico across the Texas border and emptying into the Rio Grande River in S.W. Texas

Pécs (peitʃ) (G. Fünfkirchen) the center (pop. 173,396) of a coal-mining district in S.W. Hungary: metallurgy. Romanesque cathedral (11th c.). University (1367–1526, 1912)

pec·ten (péktən) *pl.* **pec·tens, pec·ti·nes** (péktəni:z) *n.* (*zool.*) any structure that suggests the teeth of a comb [L. *pecten* (*pectinis*), comb]

pec·tic (péktik) *adj.* relating to or derived from pectin [fr. Gk *pēktikos* fr. *pēktos*, congealed]

pec·tin (péktin) *n.* any of a group of polysaccharides occurring in plant tissues esp. in fruits, solutions of which readily form a gel. Added to jams or fruit juices, they induce setting into a jelly [PECTIC]

pec·ti·nate (péktineit) *adj.* divided into many lobes etc. like the teeth of a comb **péc·ti·nat·ed** *adj.* [fr. L. *pectinatus* fr. *pecten*, comb]

pec·to·ral (péktərəl) **1.** *adj.* of or relating to the chest or breast ‖ used in treating diseases of the chest or lungs ‖ worn on the chest or breast **2.** *n.* a pectoral muscle or fin ‖ a pectoral cross ‖ the decorated breastplate worn by the Jewish high priest ‖ a pectoral medicine [fr. L. *pectoralis* fr. *pectus* (*pectoris*), breast]

pectoral cross a cross worn on the chest by certain high Church dignitaries

pec·tose (péktous) *n.* any of several substances found with cellulose in plant tissue and converted into pectin by ripening [PECTIC]

pec·u·late (pékjuleit) *pres. part.* **pec·u·lat·ing** *past* and *past part.* **pec·u·lat·ed** *v.t.* to embezzle ‖ *v.i.* to embezzle money **pec·u·lá·tion, péc·u·la·tor** *ns* [fr. L. *peculari* (*peculatus*) fr. *peculium*, private property]

pe·cu·liar (pikjú:ljər) **1.** *adj.* odd, unusual, strange ‖ (often with 'to') belonging to or associated with a particular person, place, time, thing etc., *this word is peculiar to Scottish dialect* ‖ (*canon law*) independent of the authority of the bishop of the diocese, *a peculiar church* **2.** *n.* (*printing*) an unusual and little-used character, e.g. an unusual accent ‖ (*canon law*) a church or parish under peculiar jurisdiction **pe·cu·li·ar·i·ty** (pikju:li:ǽriti:) *pl.* **pe·cu·li·ar·i·ties** *n.* a distinctive characteristic, a feature peculiar to a particular person, place, thing etc. ‖ oddness, unusualness ‖ an odd, unusual characteristic [obs. F. *peculier* or fr. L. *peculiaris*, relating to private property fr. *peculium*, private property]

pe·cu·ni·ar·i·ly (pikjú:ni:ərili:) *adv.* as regards money

pe·cu·ni·ar·y (pikjú:ni:əri:) *adj.* consisting of money, *pecuniary reward* ‖ of or relating to money ‖ (of an offense) having a fine as penalty [fr. L. *pecuniarius* fr. *pecunia*, money]

pedagog *PEDAGOGUE

ped·a·gog·ic (pedəgɒdʒik, pedəgóudʒik) *adj.* of, characteristic of or like a pedagogue ‖ having to do with teaching **ped·a·góg·i·cal** *adj.* **ped·a·góg·ics** *n.* the science of teaching [fr. L. *paedagogicus* fr. Gk]

ped·a·gogue, ped·a·gog (pédəgɒg, pédəgɔg) *n.* a teacher, esp. a narrowminded pedant [O.F. *pedagoge, pedagogue* fr. L. fr. Gk fr. *pais* (*paidos*), child+*agein*, to lead]

ped·a·gog·y (pédəgoudʒi:, pédəgɔdʒi:) *n.* the science or profession of teaching [F. *pédagogie* fr. Gk]

ped·al (péd'l) **1.** *n.* a lever operated by the foot, e.g. to sound, sustain or dampen notes on a piano etc., work the brake etc. of a car, propel a bicycle etc. ‖ (*mus.*) a pedal point **2.** *v. pres. part.* **ped·al·ing**, esp. *Br.* **ped·al·ling** *past* and *past part.* **ped·aled**, esp. *Br.* **ped·alled** *v.t.* to operate by a pedal or pedals ‖ *v.i.* to operate a pedal or pedals [F. *pédale*]

ped·al (pí:d'l) *adj.* (*zool.*) of or relating to a foot, esp. of a mollusk ‖ (péd'l) of, relating to or involving the use of a pedal or pedals [fr. L. *pedalis* fr. *pes* (*pedis*), foot]

pe·dal·fer (pədǽlfər) *n.* soil lacking a layer of calcium and magnesium carbonates (cf. PEDOCAL) [fr. Gk *pedon*, ground+L. *alumen*, alum+L. *ferrum*, iron]

ped·al·o (pédəlou) *n.* raft with pedalmotivated paddle wheel

pedal point (*mus.*) a single note, esp. in the bass, sustained while harmonies change in the other voices

ped·ant (péd'nt) *n.* a person who makes a tedious show of dull learning ‖ an overprecise person who is unimaginative about using rules or knowledge **pe·dan·tic** (pədǽntik) *adj.* **pe·dán·ti·cal·ly** *adv.* [F. *pédant* or Ital. *pedante*, teacher]

ped·ant·ry (péd'ntri:) *pl.* **ped·ant·ries** *n.* the pedantic show or use of learning or knowledge ‖

an instance of this ‖ the quality or state of being pedantic [fr. Ital. *pedanteria*]

ped·ate (pédeit) *adj.* (*zool.*) having feet or foot-like extremities ‖ (*bot.*, of leaves) palmate, with divided lobes [fr. L. *pedatus* fr. *pes* (*pedis*), foot]

ped·dle (péd'l) *pres. part.* **ped·dling** *past* and *past part.* **ped·dled** *v.t.* to sell (goods) as one travels from place to place ‖ *v.i.* to travel around with goods to sell [perh. fr. PEDLAR]

ped·dler, Br. ped·lar (pédlər) *n.* someone who travels about peddling goods [possibly synonymous with earlier *pedder*, etym. doubtful]

ped·er·ast, paed·er·ast (pédəræst, pí:dəræst) *n.* a man who habitually practices pederasty

ped·er·as·ty, paed·er·as·ty (pédəræsti, pí:dəræsti:) *n.* sodomy [fr. Mod. L. *paederastia* fr. Gk fr. *pais* (*paidos*), boy+*erastes*, lover]

ped·es·tal (pédistəl) *n.* a separate base supporting a column, statue, large vase etc. **to place (someone) on a pedestal** to attribute ideal qualities to (someone) [F. *piédestal* fr. Ital.]

pe·des·tri·an (pidéstri:ən) **1.** *n.* a person going about on foot **2.** *adj.* of, for or relating to pedestrians ‖ dull, commonplace, lacking imagination, *a pedestrian performance* [fr. L. *pedester* (*pedestris*) adj., on foot]

pe·des·tri·an·i·za·tion (pidestri:ənizéifən) *n.* creating the condition of pedestrian dominance —**pe·des·tri·an·ize** *v.*

pe·di·at·ric, pae·di·at·ric (pi:diætrik) *adj.* of or relating to the medical care of children **pe·di·a·tri·cian, pae·di·a·tri·cian** (pi:diətrífən) *n.* a specialist in pediatrics **pe·di·at·rics, pae·di·at·rics** (pi:diætriks) *n.* the branch of medicine concerned with the health and illnesses of children [fr. Gk *pais* (*paidos*), child+*iatrikos* fr. *iatros*, physician]

ped·i·cel (pédisəl) *n.* (*bot.*) a short, slender stalk holding a flower or fruit ‖ (*zool.*) a stalk or stem-like structure [fr. Mod. L. *pedicellus*, dim. of *pediculus*, little foot]

ped·i·cel·lar·i·a (pedisəléəri:ə) *pl.* **ped·i·cel·lar·i·ae** (pedisəléəri:i:) *n.* (*zool.*) one of various minute pincerlike structures studding the surface of certain echinoderms. They keep the body free from debris and parasites [Mod. L. fr. *pedicellus*, pedicel]

ped·i·cel·late (pedisélit, pediséleit) *adj.* (*biol.*) having a pedicel or attached by a pedicel [fr. Mod. L. *pedicellus*, pedicel]

ped·i·cle (pédik'l) *n.* a pedicel [fr. L. *pediculus*, little foot]

pe·dic·u·lar (pədíkjulər) *adj.* of, pertaining to or infested with lice [fr. L. *pedicularis* fr. *pediculus*, louse]

pe·dic·u·late (pədíkjulit, pədíkjuleit) **1.** *adj.* belonging to *Pediculati*, an order of teleost fishes with elongated pectoral fins **2.** *n.* a pediculate fish [fr. L. *pediculus*, louse]

pe·dic·u·lo·sis (pədikjulóusis) *n.* infestation of the body with lice [fr. L. *pediculus*, louse]

pe·dic·u·lous (pədíkjuləs) *adj.* infested with lice [fr. L. *pediculosus*]

ped·i·cure (pédikjuər) *n.* chiropody ‖ a chiropodist ‖ (*loosely*) a cleaning, cutting and polishing of the toenails [F. *pédicure*]

ped·i·gree (pédigri:) *n.* a chart or table showing how and from whom a person or family is descended, a genealogical or family tree ‖ a table of descent of purebred animals ‖ ancestry **péd·i·greed** (of domestic animals) having a recorded pedigree [older *pedegru* fr. F. *pié de grue*, crane's foot, a three-lined symbol used in genealogical tables]

ped·i·ment (pédimənt) *n.* (*archit.*) the gable over the front of a building with a two-pitched roof, triangular in classical architecture, later (e.g. in baroque) arched or broken at the peak **ped·i·men·tal** (pədimént'l) *adj.* relating to, designating or like a pediment **péd·i·ment·ed** *adj.* having a pediment [older *peremint, periment*, perh. corrup. of PYRAMID]

pedlar *PEDDLER

ped·o·cal (pédəkæl) *n.* soil that has a hard layer of calcium and magnesium carbonates (cf. PEDALFER) [fr. Gk *pedon*, ground+L. *calx* (*calcis*), lime]

pedogenesis *PAEDOGENESIS

pe·dol·o·gy (pidólədʒi:) *n.* the scientific study of soils [fr. Russ. *pedologiya* fr. Gk *pedon*, ground+*logos*, word]

pe·dom·e·ter (pidómitər) *n.* an instrument which counts the number of steps taken by a person walking and measures the approximate distance covered [F. *pédomètre*]

Pe·dra·ri·as (peðrárjəs) (Pedro Arias Dávila, c. 1440–1531), Spanish conquistador. As gover-

nor of Darien (from 1514) he ordered (1517) the execution of Núñez de Balboa. He founded (1519) Panama City and directed important expeditions

Pe·dro I (péidrou) 'the Cruel' (1334–69), king of Castile and León (1350–69). His reign was a period of unbroken civil war, in which he was supported by the Black Prince

Pedro II (1174–1213), king of Aragon (1196–1213). He helped Alfonso VIII of Castile to defeat the Moors (1212) and was killed fighting in alliance with the Albigenses

Pedro III 'the Great' (c. 1236–85), king of Aragon (1276–85) and of Sicily (1282–5), son of James I. His seizure of Sicily after the Sicilian Vespers (1282) provoked a French invasion of Aragon

Pedro IV 'the Ceremonious' (1319–87), king of Aragon (1336–87). He supported Castile against the Moors, and regained Majorca (1343–4)

Pedro I (1320–67), king of Portugal (1357–67)

Pedro II (1648–1706), king of Portugal (1683–1706), son of John IV. He concluded the Methuen Treaty (1703) with England

Pedro III (1717–86), king of Portugal (1777–86), son of John V. He ruled jointly with his niece and wife, Maria I

Pedro IV king of Portugal *PEDRO I, emperor of Brazil

Pedro I (1798–1834), emperor of Brazil (1822–31) and, as Pedro IV, king of Portugal (1826), son of John VI of Portugal. He remained in Brazil after the Portuguese royal family's exile there, and became its first emperor. He abdicated the Portuguese throne in favor of his daughter, Maria II

Pedro II (1825–91), emperor of Brazil (1831–89), son of Pedro I. An enlightened liberal, he opened the Amazon to trade (1867) but his abolition of slavery (1888) was unpopular with landowners. He was deposed (1889) and a federal republic was established

pe·dun·cle (pidʌ́ŋk'l) *n.* (*biol.*) a pedicel ‖ (*anat.*) a stalklike band of white fibers joining different parts of the brain **pe·dun·cu·lar** (pidʌ́ŋkjulər) *adj.* [fr. Mod. L. *pedunculus*, footstalk, dim. of *pes* (*pedis*), a foot]

pe·dun·cu·late (pidʌ́ŋkjuleit, pidʌ́ŋkjulit) *adj.* having or growing on a peduncle **pe·dun·cu·lat·ed** (pidʌ́ŋkjələ̣eitid) *adj.* [fr. Mod. L. *pedunculatus*]

pee (pi:) **1.** *v.i.* (*pop.*) to urinate **2.** *n.* (*pop.*) the act of urinating ‖ (*pop.*) urine

Pee·bles (pí:b'lz) a former county in S.E. Scotland, site of Iron Age remains and Roman ruins

peek (pi:k) **1.** *v.i.* to peep, look, esp. in such a way as not to be seen **2.** *n.* a quick or furtive look [M.E. *pike, pyke*, origin unknown]

peek·a·boo (pí:kəbu:) *n.* a game played with in infant by someone who alternately hides and reveals himself or his face, crying 'peekaboo'

peek-a-boo *adj.* **1.** of a revealing woman's décolletage, esp. with eyelet holes. **2.** (*computer*) of a document retrieval system in which selection is made through cards with punched holes

Peel (pi:l), Sir Robert (1788–1850), British Tory statesman. He was secretary for Ireland (1812–18), and as home secretary (1822–7 and 1828–30) secured the passage of the Catholic Emancipation Act (1829). His legal reforms included the establishment (1829) of the London police. As prime minister (1834–5) he rallied the Tories in support of recent Whig reforms, and so laid the foundations of the Conservative party. In his second ministry (1841–6), he imposed an income tax (1842), lowered many tariffs and reorganized the banking system (1844). His repeal of the Corn Laws (1846) split the Conservative party into the Peelites, who supported the measure, and the followers of Disraeli, who opposed it

peel (pi:l) **1.** *v.t.* to remove the outer covering, skin, rind etc. from ‖ (with 'off') to remove (an outer covering, skin, rind etc.), *he peeled off his raincoat* ‖ *v.i.* (of an outer covering, skin etc.) to come off, flake off ‖ to shed an outer covering or skin **to peel off** (of aircraft flying in formation) to break away from the formation in orderly succession, turning sharply and losing height ‖ (of a warship or aircraft) to break away from a formation, e.g. to attack or investigate **to keep one's eyes peeled** to keep a sharp lookout, *keep your eyes peeled for a parking place* **2.** *n.* the rind or outer skin of a fruit or of some vegetables [older *pill*, prob. fr. O.E.]

peel *n.* a long-handled flat shovel for putting loaves into a bread oven and for taking them out [M.E. fr. O.F. *pele*]

peel *n.* (*hist.*) a 16th-c. fortified structure common on the Scottish border, housing the cattle on the ground floor and the family on the floor above [M.E. *pel, pele*, stake fr. A.F. and O.F.]

Peele (pi:l), George (c. 1558–c. 1596), English dramatist. 'The Old Wives' Tale' (1595) is his best-known work

peel·er (pí:lər) *n.* (*Br. hist.*) a policeman ‖ (*Br. hist.*) a member of the Irish constabulary [after Sir Robert *Peel* who founded the Irish constabulary (1818) and the London police (1829)]

peel·ings (pí:liŋz) *pl. n.* the peel of a fruit or vegetable when stripped off

Peel·ite (pí:lait) *n.* (*Br. hist.*) a member of a political group which supported Peel in repealing the Corn Laws (1846), thereby seceding from the Conservative party. Led by Gladstone, the Peelites allied themselves by 1868 with the Liberal party

peen (pi:n) **1.** *n.* the thin end of the head of a hammer **2.** *v.t.* to strike or work with a peen [older *pen*, etym. doubtful]

peep (pi:p) **1.** *v.i.* to take a look through a small hole, around a corner, over a wall etc., esp. in such a way as not to be seen ‖ to take a quick look ‖ (with 'out') to be visible briefly, incompletely or from a distance, *his toes peeped out through the holes in his socks* ‖ to come into view, as if from hiding, *the sun peeped through the clouds v.t.* (with 'out') to cause to protrude a bit, *to peep one's head out* **2.** *n.* the act of peeping ‖ a surreptitious, furtive glance ‖ (*rhet.*) the first sign, *at peep of dawn* [etym. doubtful]

peep **1.** *n.* the high, weak noise made by very young birds **2.** *v.i.* to utter a peep ‖ *v.t.* to utter in a high, weak voice [M.E. *pepe*, imit.]

peep·er (pí:pər) *n.* a person who looks furtively

peeper *n.* any of several frogs, esp. of fam. *Hylidae*, that make a peeping sound

peep·hole (pí:phoul) *n.* a small hole which one can look through without being seen

peeping Tom an erotic pervert who hides himself and watches loving couples or women undressing [after *Peeping Tom*, the legendary tailor of Coventry who peeped at Lady Godiva]

peep show a miniature exhibition inside a box, consisting of entertaining pictures or objects looked at through a small hole fitted with a lens

peep sight the aperture sight of a rifle

peepul *PIPAL

peer (piər) *v.i.* to look closely, attentively, or as if one had difficulty in seeing ‖ to come partly into view, peep out, *the moon peered out through the clouds* [etym. doubtful]

peer *n.* a member of one of the British degrees of nobility: a duke, marquis, earl, viscount, or baron ‖ a nobleman of any country ‖ someone having the same status in rank, age, ability etc. as another, *to be judged by one's peers* **péer·age** *n.* the peers of a country, esp. of Great Britain, as a body ‖ the rank of a peer ‖ a book containing the names of all the peers, with historical and genealogical details etc. **péer·ess** *n.* the wife or widow of a peer ‖ a woman who holds the rank of a peer in her own right **péer·less** *adj.* so excellent as to have no equal [M.E. *per, peere* fr. O.F.]

peer group a group who regard themselves of equal standing in the milieu in which they exist

peer of the realm a British peer, entitled to sit in the House of Lords after his majority

peer pressure influence of one's friends on morals

peet·weet (pí:twi:t) *n.* the spotted sandpiper [imit.]

peeve (pi:v) **1.** *v.t. pres. part.* **peev·ing** *past* and *past part.* **peeved** to make peevish **2.** *n.* (*pop.*) a peevish mood, *he got up in a peeve* **a pet peeve** some trivial, frequent source of annoyance [backformation fr. PEEVISH]

peev·ish (pí:vif) *adj.* irritable, apt to complain, grumble and be ill-tempered ‖ showing such crossness, *peevish gesture* [origin unknown]

pee·wee (pí:wi:) *n.* (*pop.*) an unusually small person, animal or thing ‖ *PEWEE [imit., after the bird's cry]

peewit *PEWIT

peg (peg) **1.** *n.* a small piece of wood, metal, plastic etc., generally cylindrical and slightly tapered, used to hold together two parts of a construction, to secure a joint, bung a hole,

CONCISE PRONUNCIATION KEY: **(a)** æ, c*a*t; ɑ, c*ar*; ɔ f*aw*n; ei, sn*a*ke. **(e)** e, h*e*n; i:, sh*ee*p; iə, d*eer*; εə, b*ear*. **(i)** i, f*i*sh; ai, t*i*ger; ə:, b*ir*d. **(o)** o, *o*x; au, c*ow*; ou, g*oa*t; u, p*oo*r; ɔi, r*oy*al. **(u)** ʌ, d*u*ck; u, b*u*ll; u:, g*oo*se; ə, b*a*cillus; ju:, c*u*be. x, lo*ch*; θ, *th*ink; ð, bo*th*er; z, *Z*en; ʒ, cor*s*age; dʒ, sava*ge*; ŋ, ora*n*gutang; j, *y*ak; ʃ, *f*ish; tʃ, fe*tch*; 'l, rabb*le*; 'n, redd*en*. Complete pronunciation key appears inside front cover.

hang things on, mark the score in cribbage or darts, fasten ropes to etc. ‖ a small screw for holding and adjusting the tension of the strings of a stringed instrument ‖ (*Br.*) a short drink of liquor ‖ a step or degree, *to move up a peg in an organization* ‖ something used as a pretext, *a peg to hang a claim on* ‖ (*Br.*) a clothes-peg ‖ one or the two end markers in croquet **a square peg in a round hole** (or **a round peg in a square hole**) a person who is out of place in the circumstances in which he finds himself **to take** (**someone**) **down a peg** to make (someone) less bumptious or self-satisfied **2.** *v. pres. part.* **peg·ging** *past* and *past part.* **pegged** *v.t.* to fasten, secure or attach with a peg or pegs ‖ to mark (a score) in cribbage etc. with pegs ‖ to mark (a distance) with pegs ‖ to fix or maintain (prices, wages etc.) at a certain level ‖ *v.i.* (with 'away', 'at' etc.) to work hard and steadily, *to peg away at one's thesis* ‖ (cribbage etc.) to keep score with pegs **to peg out** to mark out with pegs, *to peg out the site for a house* ‖ (croquet) to finish the game by hitting the peg with the ball [prob. fr. L.G.]

Peg·a·sus (pégəsəs) (*Gk mythol.*) a winged horse that sprang from the blood of Medusa. He caused the Hippocrene to spring forth on Mount Helicon ‖ a constellation of the northern hemisphere

peg·a·sus (pégəsəs) *n.* a member of *Pegasus* fam. *Pegasidae*, a genus of tropical marine fishes with a long snout, a small, toothless mouth and large, winglike fins

peg·board (pégbɔrd, pégbourd) *n.* a small board with holes in it into which pegs are stuck. It is used for scoring, esp. at cribbage

peg·leg (pégleg) *n.* an artificial leg, esp. a wooden one, fitted to the knee

peg·ma·tite (pégmətait) *n.* an exceptionally coarse-grained variety of granite **peg·ma·tit·ic** (pegmətítik) *adj.* [fr. Gk *pēgma* (*pēgmatos*), a thing joined together]

peg top a child's spinning top, wide at the top and narrowing to the point on which it spins

Pe·gu (pegú:) a river port and rail center (pop. 123,600) of S. Burma, a Buddhist pilgrimage place

Pé·guy (peigi:), Charles (1873–1914), French poet and essayist. He professed a mystical, patriotic socialism which opposed both anticlerical socialism and right-wing Catholicism. Most of his writings appeared in his 'Cahiers de la Quinzaine' from 1900. His poetry includes 'le Mystère de la charité de Jeanne d'Arc' (1910)

Pe·gu Yo·ma (pegú:jóumə) a mountain range in S. central Burma between the Irrawaddy and Sittang Rivers: Mt Popa, 4,981 ft

Pehlevi *PAHLAVI

Pei (pei), I(eoh) M(ina) (1917–), Chinese-American architect. Born in Canton, China, he came to the U.S.A. (1935) to study architecture and became a U.S. citizen in 1954. After practicing architecture in Boston, he founded his own firm in New York City (1955). One of the most prolific contemporary architects, he has designed such buildings as Denver's Mile High Center (1956), Washington, D.C.'s L'Enfant Plaza (1967), Boston's John Hancock Tower (1973), and the Fragrant Hill (Xiangshan) Hotel in Peking, China (1983)

peign·oir (penwár, pénwɑr) *n.* a negligee [F. fr. *peigner*, to comb]

Pei·ping (péipíŋ) *PEKING

Pei·pus (pí:pəs) (*Estonian* Peipsi, *Russ.* Chudskoe Ozero) a lake (area 1,356 sq. miles) of the U.S.S.R., on the boundary between Estonia and the R.S.F.S.R. It drains into the Gulf of Finland. In 1242 Alexander Nevski defeated the Teutonic Knights on the frozen lake

Peirce (piərs), Charles Sanders (1839–1914), U.S. philosopher, mathematician and physicist, best known as the founder of the pragmatic movement in American philosophy, in which he developed a criterion of meaning in terms of conceivable effects or consequences in experience and a view of beliefs as 'habits of action.' He also wrote in numerous other fields, as well as working as an astronomer at the Harvard Observatory and as a physicist for the U.S. Coast and Geodetic Survey

Peirce (piərs) *PRAGMATISM

Peisistratus *PISISTRATUS

Pei·xo·to (peiʃótu), Floriano (1842–95), Brazilian soldier and president (1891–4) after leading (with da Fonseca) the Revolution of 1889 which overthrew the Empire and established the Republic

pe·jo·ra·tive (pidʒɔ́rətiv, pidʒórətiv, pédʒərei-

tiv) **1.** *adj.* (of words or phrases) expressing disparagement **2.** *n.* a word or expression used in a pejorative sense [fr. L. *pejorare* (*pejoratus*), to make worse]

pek·an (pékən) *n.* the fisher (animal) [F., of Algonquian origin]

peke (pi:k) *n.* a pekingese

pe·kin (pi:kín) *n.* a usually striped, silk material, originally from China [after PEKING]

Pe·kin·ese (pi:kiní:z) *pl.* **Pe·kin·ese** *n.* a Pekingese

Pe·king (pi:kíŋ) (Beijing) the capital (pop. 9,230,687) of China, in N. Hopei (but administered directly by the government), 35 miles south of the Great Wall of China. It is an ancient communications center and traditionally China's center of learning. Industries: cotton milling, iron and steel, mechanical engineering, food processing, chemicals. It consists of the Inner, or Tatar, City (walls from 1437) and the Outer, or Chinese, City beside the south wall, enclosed in 1544. There are 16 gates. Within the Inner City, walls enclose the Imperial City, the former official district: Peking University, 1898, National Library, parks and monuments. Within this, purple walls enclose the Forbidden City, the former imperial precinct, a formal ensemble of palaces, temples, halls, gardens etc., now the seat of government. The Outer City, partly truck farms, contains the main commercial quarter and the old principal temples: the Altar of Heaven and the Temple of Agriculture (both 15th c.). Outside the Inner City are the Temples of the Earth (north), Moon (west) and Sun (east). A modern university (People's University, 1912) and residential quarter are outside the walls on the west, and the industrial district lies on the east. A city of great antiquity, Peking was destroyed (1215) by Genghis Khan and rebuilt, as a capital (1264), by Kublai Khan. It was the northern capital of China (1421–1928) and became the capital of the whole country in 1949 (*NANKING)

Pe·king·ese (pi:kiní:z, pi:kiŋí:s, pi:kiní:z, pi:kiní:s) **1.** *pl.* **Pe·king·ese** *n.* a native or inhabitant of Peking ‖ the Chinese dialect spoken in the Peking district ‖ a dog of an ancient, small breed, originally from China, popular as a pet. They have short legs, long silky hair, a flat nose, curled bushy tail, protruding eyes and a high-pitched yap **2.** *adj.* of or relating to Peking, its inhabitants, dialect etc.

Peking man an extinct man whose remains have been found near Peking, often regarded as a variety of pithecanthropus

Pe·kin·ol·o·gist or **Pe·king·ol·o·gist** (pi:kinóləd3i:st) *n.* expert in studies of the hierarchy of China —**Pe·kin·ol·o·gy** or **Pe·king·ol·o·gy** *n.*

pe·koe (pí:kou, *Br.* also pékou) *n.* a black tea of good quality made from selected young leaves picked with the down still upon them [Chinese *pek-ho* fr. *pek*, white + *ho*, down, hair]

pe·lage (pélid3) *n.* the fur or other coat of a mammal [F.]

Pe·la·gi·an (pəléidʒi:ən) **1.** *adj.* pertaining to Pelagius or Pelagianism **2.** *n.* a follower of Pelagius or upholder of Pelagianism [fr. L. *Pelagianus*]

Pe·la·gi·an·ism (pəléidʒi:ənizəm) *n.* the heresy originated by Pelagius. It denied original sin and the need for baptism, and held that grace was not necessary for salvation. It asserted that free will and the law are sufficient for man to live without sin. It arose is a reaction to gnosticism and Manichaeism, in the interests of a higher morality which Pelagius found lacking in Rome. Originally an attempt to heighten human responsibility, it fell into the extreme of diminishing divine grace. Opposed by St Augustine of Hippo, the heresy and Pelagius were condemned at several synods (411–18). A form of the heresy, with emphasis on free will, arose briefly (late 5th c.) in France but was condemned (528–9). Pelagianism long continued as a trend in Christian philosophy

pe·lag·ic (pəlǽd3ik) *adj.* of or occurring on the open sea. *pelagic navigation* ‖ (*zool.*) ocean-inhabiting (cf. DEMERSAL) [fr. L. *pelagicus* fr. Gk fr. *pelagos*, sea]

Pe·la·gi·us (pəléidʒi:əs) (c. 360–c. 422), English monk who settled in Rome (400). He was accused of heresy at several synods (411–18) and was banished from Rome (418) (*PELAGIANISM)

pel·ar·go·ni·um (pelɑrgóuni:əm) *n.* a member of *Pelargonium*, fam. *Geraniaceae*, a genus of

flowering plants native to S. Africa. Many varieties and hybrids are cultivated for their ornamental flowers and foliage (*GERANIUM) [Mod. L. fr. Gk *pelargos*, stork]

Pe·las·gi·an (pəlǽzdʒi:ən) **1.** *n.* one of the aboriginal non-Greek inhabitants of Greece, Asia Minor and the Aegean Islands before the Achaean invasion (c. 2000 B.C.) **2.** *adj.* of or characteristic of the Pelasgians or their language [fr. L. *Pelasgius* fr. Gk]

Pe·las·gic (pəlǽzdʒik) *adj.* Pelasgian [fr. L. *Pelasgicus*]

Pe·lé (pelé), Edson Arantes do Nascimento (1940–), Brazilian soccer star and national hero

pe·lec·y·pod (pəlésipɒd) *n.* (*zool.*) a lamellibranch [fr. Gk *pelekus*, hatchet + *pous* (*podos*), foot]

Pe·lée (pəléi) a volcanic mountain (4,428 ft) in N. Martinique. Its eruption (1902) destroyed St Pierre with the loss of 40,000 lives

Pel·e·liu Island (péləlju:, pəlálí:u:) one of the W. Caroline Is in the W. Pacific, site of a battle (1944) in the 2nd world war in which U.S. marines defeated Japanese forces and captured the island

pelf (pelf) *n.* (*rhet.*) money or riches referred to contemptuously, esp. to suggest they were dishonestly acquired

pel·i·can (pélikən) *n.* a member of *Pelecanus*, fam. *Pelecanidae*, a genus of large, web-footed, gregarious birds with a large wingspread. They are widely distributed in temperate and tropical zones. They are characterized by a very long bill, and a pouch in the upper throat in which they store the fish they catch before eating them [fr. L.L. *pelicanus, pecanus* fr. Gk]

Pe·li·on (pí:li:ən) a mountain of Thessaly, Greece. In Greek mythology, the giants in revolt against Zeus placed it on top of Mt Ossa in order to attack Mt Olympus

pe·lisse (pelí:s) *n.* (*hist.*) a man's or woman's long, fur-lined cloak ‖ (*hist.*) a woman's long, loose cloak or coat [F. fr. Ital. *pelliccia*, furred garment]

pe·lite (pí:lait) *n.* rock composed of minute bits of clay or mud [fr. Gk *pelos*, earth, clay]

pel·la·gra (pəléigrə, pelǽgrə) *n.* a disease, commonest in the Tropics, manifested by skin inflammation, diarrhea and nervous disorders. It is caused by a deficiency of niacin and protein [Ital. and Mod. L., perh. fr. Ital. *pelle*, skin + *agra*, tough]

pel·let (pélit) *n.* a little ball, e.g. of rolled-up paper ‖ a small piece of shot, fired singly from an air gun, or in groups packed into the cartridge of a shotgun [F. *pelote*]

Pell grants (pélgrænts) *n.* U.S. government student scholarships, varying in amount based on income, assets and expenses; named for Senator Claiborne Pell

pel·li·cle (pélik'l) *n.* (*biol.*) any thin skin or filmy protective covering ‖ the scum on a liquid ‖ any thin film or membrane **pel·líc·u·lar, pel·líc·u·late** *adjs* [fr. L. *pellicula*, dim. of *pellis*, skin]

pel·li·to·ry (pélitɔri:, pélitouri:) *pl.* **pel·li·to·ries** *n. Anacyclus pyrethrum*, a composite plant of S. Europe ‖ its roots, formerly used as an irritant, a salivant and a toothache remedy ‖ any of several plants resembling this plant, esp. feverfew and yarrow ‖ a member of *Parietaria*, fam. *Urticaceae*, a genus of plants allied to nettles [M.E. *peletre* fr. M.F. *piretre* fr. L. *pyrethrum*]

pell-mell (pélmel) **1.** *adv.* in great haste and confusion **2.** *adj.* confused, disorderly, *pell-mell haste* **3.** *n.* hurry and confusion, *the pell-mell of city life* [F. *pêle-mêle*]

pel·lu·cid (pelú:sid) *adj.* crystal clear, *pellucid waters* ‖ (of literary style, wording etc.) extremely clear **pel·lu·cíd·i·ty** *n.* [fr. L. *pellucidus*]

pel·met (pélmit) *n.* a valance or fitting at the top of a window to hide the curtain rod [origin unknown]

Pe·lop·i·das (pəlópidəs) (d. 364 B.C.), Greek general, friend of Epaminondas. He drove the Spartans out of Thebes (378 B.C.) but was killed at Cynoscephalae

Pel·o·pon·nese (peləpəní:s) the Peloponnesus

Pel·o·pon·ne·sian (pelopəní:ʒən, pelopəní:ʃən) **1.** *adj.* of or relating to the Peloponnesus, its people etc. **2.** *n.* a native or inhabitant of the Peloponnesus

Peloponnesian War a decisive war (431– 404 B.C.) between Sparta and Athens caused by Spartan fear of the growing power of Athens and her maritime empire. After an indecisive start, Athens wasted her financial and naval

---

CONCISE PRONUNCIATION KEY: **(a)** æ, c*a*t; ɑ, c*a*r; ɔ f*aw*n; ei, sn*a*ke. **(e)** e, h*e*n; i:, sh*ee*p; iə, d*ee*r; εə, b*ea*r. **(i)** i, f*i*sh; ai, t*i*ger; ə:, b*i*rd. **(o)** o, *o*x; au, c*ow*; ou, g*oa*t; u, p*oo*r; ɔi, r*oy*al. **(u)** ʌ, d*u*ck; u, b*u*ll; u:, g*oo*se; ə, b*a*cillus; ju:, c*u*be. x, lo*ch*; θ, *th*ink; ð, bo*th*er; z, *Z*en; ʒ, corsa*g*e; d3, sava*g*e; ŋ, ora*ng*utang; j, *y*ak; ʃ, *fi*sh; tʃ, fe*tch*; 'l, rabb*le*; 'n, redd*en*. Complete pronunciation key appears inside front cover.

superiority in a disastrous expedition to Sicily (415–413 B.C.). Sparta built a fleet with Persian aid, destroyed the remainder of the Athenian fleet at Aegospotami (405 B.C.) and Athens surrendered (404 B.C.). The war ruined Athens

Pel·o·pon·ne·sus (peləpɔní:səs) (*Gk* Morea) a mountainous peninsula forming S. Greece, connected to the continent by the isthmus of Corinth. The region comprises eight historical regions of Greece: Achaea, Arcadia, Argolis, Corinth, Elis, Laconia, Messenia and Sicyonia. It was the site of Sparta and Corinth

Pe·lops (pí:lops) (*Gk mythol.*) the son of Tantalus, who served Pelops's limbs to the gods as food. Pelops was revived by the gods and, grown to manhood, he murdered a friend, thus perpetuating the strain of evil which was to be more marked in his sons, Atreus and Thyestes

pe·lo·ta (pəlóutə) *n.* any of several similar Basque, Spanish or Latin American games, esp. jai alai ‖ the ball used in these games [Span.=ball]

pel·o·ton (péləton) *n.* ornamental glassware decorated with overlaid colored strands made in Italy. *also* Peloton glass

pelt (pelt) **1.** *v.t.* to strike by throwing things at continuously and in great quantity, *they pelted us with snowballs* ‖ to throw (objects) continuously, *to pelt snowballs at someone* ‖ *v.i.* (e.g. of rain) to pour or beat down continually with force ‖ (*pop.*) to run as fast as possible, *he came pelting around the corner* **2.** *n.* a hard blow ‖ a pelting **at full pelt** at full speed [origin unknown]

pelt *n.* the skin of an animal with the hair or wool on ‖ a raw hide after the hair or wool has been removed [perh. fr. PELTRY]

pel·tate (pélteit) *adj.* (*bot.*, of leaves) attached to the plant not at the edge or base but at the middle of the lower surface, e.g. in the nasturtium ‖ (*biol.*) shaped like a shield [fr. L. *peltatus* fr. *pelta*, shield]

Pel·tier effect (peltjéi) (*elec.*) the evolution or absorption of heat at a junction of two different metals in an electric circuit [after Jean *Peltier* (1785–1845), F. physicist]

pelt·ry (péltri) *n.* pelts (skins) collectively [A.F. *pelterie*, O.F. *peleterie*]

pel·vic (pélvik) *adj.* related to or situated at or near the pelvis [fr. L. *pelvis*, basin]

pelvic arch the pelvic girdle

pelvic fin one of the posterior pair of fins attached to the pelvic girdle of a fish

pelvic girdle an arch of bones or cartilage to which the hind limbs of vertebrates are attached, and which forms part of the pelvis

pel·vis (pélvis) *pl.* **pel·vis·es, pel·ves** (pélvi:z) *n.* (*anat., zool.*) a bony cavity in vertebrates, formed in man by the pelvic girdle together with the coccyx and sacrum ‖ the bones that form this cavity, collectively ‖ the expansion of the ureter at its junction with the kidney [L.=basin]

Pem·ba (pémbə) a coral island (area 380 sq. miles, pop. 164,300) in the Indian Ocean, 34 miles north of Zanzibar, forming part of Tanzania. Chief town: Chake Chake. Pemba produces five-sixths of the country's cloves

Pem·broke (pémbruk), Richard de Clare, 2nd earl of (c. 1130–76), also known as Richard Strongbow. He subdued (1170) and ruled much of Ireland in the name of Henry II of England

Pembroke, William Marshal, 1st earl of (c. 1146–1219), English nobleman. He was adviser to Henry II, regent (1190–4) for Richard I, adviser to King John, and regent (1216–19) for Henry III

Pembrokeshire *DYFED

pem·mi·can, pem·i·can (pémikən) *n.* dried meat, pounded and compressed with fat, as prepared by North American Indians ‖ a similar preparation of concentrated food, carried by explorers, mountaineers etc. [Cree *pimecan*, *pimekan* fr. *pime*, fat]

pem·o·line [$C_9H_8N_2O_2$] (pémoli:n) *n.* (*pharm.*) a central nervous system stimulant drug used for children; marketed as Cylert

pen (pen) *n.* a small enclosure, often outdoors, for farm animals ‖ the animals kept in this ‖ any small enclosure, e.g. a fortified dock for submarines [O.E. *penn*]

pen *n.* a female swan (cf. COB) [origin unknown]

pen 1. *n.* an instrument for writing in ink ‖ the nib of such a writing instrument ‖ a bird's feather, sharpened at the broad end and split to form a nib, formerly used for writing ‖ (*rhet.*) style or manner of writing, *he has a lively pen* ‖

professional writing, *a journalist lives by his pen* ‖ (*zool.*) the internal, feather-shaped shell of a squid **2.** *v.t. pres. part.* **pen·ning** *past and past part.* **penned** (*rhet.*) to write, *he penned a furious answer* [M.E. fr. O.F. *penne*, pen, feather]

pen *pres. part.* **pen·ning** *past and past part.* **penned** (with 'in', 'up') *v.t.* to shut up in a pen or other confined space [M.E. *pennen* fr. O.E.]

pe·nal (pí:n'l) *adj.* concerned with esp. legal punishment of crime, *penal code* ‖ constituting an esp. legal punishment for crime ‖ (of an offense) legally punishable **pé·nal·ize** *pres. part.* **pe·nal·iz·ing** *past and past part.* **pe·nal·ized** *v.t.* to inflict a penalty upon ‖ to subject to a disadvantage, *a tax on tobacco penalizes the smoker* **pe·nal·i·za·tion** *n.* a penalizing or being penalized [F. *pénal* fr. L. fr. Gk]

Penal Laws (*Eng. hist.*) the laws (1559–1829) banning Roman Catholics from civil office and imposing penalties on them for failing to conform with the Church of England. The discrimination ended (1829) with the passing of Catholic Emancipation

penal servitude a legal punishment consisting of imprisonment with hard labor

penal times (*Eng. hist.*) the period (1559–1829) during which the Penal Laws were in force

pen·al·ty (pén'lti) *pl.* **pen·al·ties** *n.* a punishment for breaking a law or otherwise committing an offense against established authority ‖ a disagreeable consequence suffered as a result of one's own folly or wrongdoing, *his hangover was a penalty for drinking too much* ‖ a fine, forfeit etc. incurred when some condition is not observed, some undertaking not fulfilled etc. ‖ (*games*) a disadvantage imposed as punishment for breaking the rules ‖ (*bridge*) the points added to the opponent's score when the declarer fails to make his contract **on** (or **upon** or **under**) **penalty of** with the certainty of incurring (some penalty) if a specified command or condition is not fulfilled, *no smoking under penalty of instant dismissal* [fr. M.L. *poenalitas* fr. *poenalis*, penal]

penalty area (*soccer and field hockey*) an area around the goal in which an offense by the defending side entitles the other side to a kick or hit at the goal defended only by the goalkeeper

pen·ance (pénəns) *n.* punishment or suffering undergone voluntarily to atone for sin or wrongdoing ‖ (*Roman Catholic and Orthodox Churches*) the sacrament by which the sins of those who sincerely repent, confess and perform the acts required by the priest are absolved ‖ the acts which a priest requires of a penitent **to do penance** (*Roman Catholic and Orthodox Churches*) to perform the acts required for absolution after confession ‖ to perform some act as atonement for sin or wrongdoing [O.F. *peneance, pennance* fr. L.]

Pe·nang (pi:næŋ, pi:náŋ) a state (pop. 706,000) of Malaysia in W. Malaya, consisting of Penang Is. (Prince of Wales Is., 108 sq. miles) and a strip of territory on the peninsula, Province Wellesley (area 280 sq. miles). Capital: Penang (pop. 250,578), Penang Is. The British settled (1786) on Penang Is. It was ceded (1791) to Britain by the Sultan of Kedah. Province Wellesley was ceded (1800). Penang formed (1826), together with Malacca and Singapore, the Straits Settlements. It joined (1946) the Union, later (1948) the Federation, of Malaya

Pe·ñas, Gulf of (pénjas) an inlet of the Pacific on the southwest coast of Chile south of the Taitao Peninsula

pe·nat·es (pənéiti:z) *pl. n.* (*Rom. mythol.*) the household gods revered as the guardians of the home, worshiped in conjunction with Vesta (*LARES*) [L.]

pence *PENNY

pen·chant (pént∫ənt, pã∫ã) *n.* an inclination towards, a liking for, *a penchant for ice cream* [F. fr. pres. part. of *pencher*, to slope]

pen·cil (pénsəl) **1.** *n.* an instrument for writing or drawing, consisting of a slim cylinder esp. of wood, with a core of graphite or black lead which can be sharpened to a point and which is sometimes mechanically retractable ‖ a drawing instrument with a colored core of chalk, wax etc. ‖ anything like such an instrument in shape or function, *a styptic pencil* ‖ a long, converging, narrow beam of light ‖ (*geom.*) a number of lines passing through the same point and lying on a plane **2.** *v.t. pres. part.* **pen·cil·ing**, esp. *Br.* **pen·cil·ling** *past and past part.* **pen·ciled**, esp. *Br.* **pen·cilled** to write, draw or mark in pencil [M.E. fr. O.F. *pincel*, brush]

pencil beam a searchlight beam reduced to, or set at its minimum width. *also* focused beam

Pen·da (péndə) (c. 577–655), king of Mercia (632–55). He extended his kingdom by conquest to include the whole of England's Midlands

pen·dant (péndənt) **1.** *n.* something suspended, *chandelier pendants* ‖ a piece of jewelry hanging from a brooch, necklace, chain etc. ‖ a hanging electric-light fitting ‖ a companion piece, e.g. a picture meant to be seen in conjunction with another ‖ (*naut.*) a short line hanging from a masthead, with an eye for attaching gear or tackle ‖ (*Br., naut.*, pénənt) a narrow tapering flag ‖ (*archit.*) a decorative finial or spiked ornament projecting downward from a ceiling or roof **2.** *adj.* pendent [F. fr. pres. part. of *pendre*, to hang]

pen·dent (péndənt) *adj.* (*rhet.*) hanging, *pendent branches* ‖ (*rhet.*) overhanging, *pendent cliffs* ‖ undetermined, pending [fr. L. *pendens* (*pendentis*) fr. *pendere*, to hang]

pen·den·tive (pendéntiv) *n.* (*archit.*) one of the spherical triangular pieces of vaulting forming the support for a dome resting on a square ‖ (*archit.*) that part of a groined vault rising from a pier or corbel [fr. F. *pendentif*, *pendentive* fr. L.]

pend·ing (péndiŋ) **1.** *adj.* in process of being decided, settled, arranged etc., *the court case is still pending* ‖ about to happen, *hold this over for the pending meeting* **2.** *prep.* during the wait for, until, *a temporary arrangement pending a final settlement* ‖ until the completion of, *pending the armistice discussions there are to be no troop movements* [formed after F. *pendant*, L. *pendens*, hanging]

Pendragon, Uther *UTHER PENDRAGON

pen·drag·on (pendrǽgən) *n.* an ancient title of a British or Welsh supreme leader or chief [Welsh *pen*, head+*dragon*, dragon, the standard of a band of warriors]

pen·du·lous (péndʒuləs, péndjuləs, péndʊləs) *adj.* hanging down, *a pendulous dewlap* ‖ (*bot.*, of ovules, branches, flowers etc.) bending down from the point of origin, overhanging ‖ swinging to and fro [fr. L. *pendulus*]

pen·du·lum (péndʒuləm, péndjuləm, péndʊləm) *n.* a body suspended from a pivot and able to swing to and fro as a result of gravitational force, when displaced from its position of rest. It is used to regulate clockwork movement etc. [Mod. L. fr. L. *pendulus*, hanging down]

Pe·nel·o·pe (pinéləpi:) the wife of Odysseus. She faithfully waited 20 years for his return from Troy. She put off her many suitors by saying she must first finish a certain piece of weaving, each night unraveling her day's work

pe·ne·plain, pe·ne·plane (pí:ni:plein) *n.* (*geol.*) an area of land worn almost flat by erosion [fr. L. *paene*, almost+PLAIN (PLANE)]

pen·e·tra·bil·i·ty (penitrəbíliti:) *n.* the quality or state of being penetrable

pen·e·tra·ble (pénitrəb'l) *adj.* capable of being penetrated **pén·e·tra·bly** *adv.* [fr. L. *penetrabilis*]

pen·e·tra·li·a (penitréili:ə) *pl. n.* (*rhet.*) the innermost or most sacred parts, esp. of a temple [L. pl. of *penetrale*]

penetralium *n.* the innermost part

pen·e·trance (pénitrəns) *n.* (*genetics*) frequency in which a dominant gene or a recessive gene in a homozygote appears in a phenotype

pen·e·trate (pénitreit) *pres. part.* **pen·e·trat·ing** *past and past part.* **pen·e·trat·ed** *v.t.* to go into by piercing, *a splinter penetrated his eye* ‖ to make or force a way through, *damp is penetrating the brickwork* ‖ to spread through, *the smell penetrated the whole house* ‖ to see through or into, *he tried to penetrate the darkness* ‖ to discern, *to penetrate the meaning of someone's words* ‖ *v.i.* to go into something by piercing it, *the nail penetrated all the way through the wood* ‖ to make or force a way, *the army penetrated into the interior* ‖ to have an effect on the mind or feelings, *nothing she says penetrates enough to make him ashamed* ‖ (with 'into', 'through' or 'to') to discern the truth or meaning of something obscure **pén·e·trat·ing** *adj.* [fr. L. *penetrare* (*penetratus*)]

pen·e·tra·tion (penitréi∫ən) *n.* the act of penetrating ‖ keenness of mind, insight ‖ (*mil.*) the depth to which a projectile penetrates into a target [fr. L.L. *penetratio* (*penetrationis*)]

pen·e·tra·tive (pénitreitiv) *adj.* penetrating [fr. M.L. *penetrativus*]

Peng·hu (pʌ́ŋgú:) *PESCADORES ISLANDS

Pengpu

Peng·pu (pángpú:) *FENGYANG

pen·guin (péngwin, péngwin) *n.* a member of *Spheniscidae,* order *Sphenisciformes,* a family of aquatic, flightless birds of Antarctic and subantarctic regions. They are characteristically whitebreasted with dark backs, scalelike fur and wings modified to flippers. They are gregarious and feed on fish and crustaceans [etym. doubtful]

pen·hold·er (pénhouldər) *n.* the part of a pen to which the nib is attached ‖ a device for holding a pen or pens

pen·i·cil·late (penisílit, penisíleit) *adj.* (*biol.*) of, designating or having a small tuft of hairs [fr. L. *penicillus,* painter's brush]

pen·i·cil·lin (penisílin) *n.* a mixture of antibiotic substances produced by molds of the genus *Penicillium,* preparations of which are widely used for their potent bacteriostatic action against a variety of pathogenic bacteria [fr. Mod. L. *Penicillium* fr. L. *penicillus,* painter's brush]

pen·i·cil·li·nase (penisílineis) *n.* (*biochem.*) an enzyme that opposes the action of penicillin on bacteria, found in penicillin resistant bacteria

pen·i·cil·li·um (penisíli:əm) *pl.* **pen·i·cil·li·a** (penisíli:ə) *n.* a member of *Penicillium,* fam. *Moniliaceae,* a genus of fungi comprising the familiar blue mold on cheese, jam etc. [Mod. L. fr. *penicillus,* painter's brush]

pen·in·su·la (pənínsulə, pənínsjulə) *n.* a piece of land that is almost an island, either connected to the mainland by a narrow neck or projecting into the sea, with the sea on three sides **pen·in·su·lar** *adj.* [L. *paeninsula* fr. *paene,* almost + *insula,* island]

Peninsular War a war (1808–14) fought in the Iberian peninsula by Britain, Portugal and Spain against France, forming part of the Napoleonic Wars. To encourage Portuguese and Spanish resistance to Napoleonic rule, Britain sent an army, which was evacuated (1809) from Corunna by Sir John Moore, but which returned to Lisbon under Wellington. After two years of defensive warfare based on the lines of Torres Vedras, Wellington led an offensive (1812–14) which drove the French from Iberia. The war was notable for the guerrilla tactics of the Portuguese and Spanish and, by keeping over 200,000 French troops occupied in Spain, it contributed to Napoleon's downfall

pe·nis (pí:nis) *pl.* **pe·nes** (pí:ni:z), **pe·nis·es** *n.* the male organ of copulation in mammals [L.]

pen·i·tence (pénitəns) *n.* the quality or state of being penitent [O.F. *pénitence*]

pen·i·tent (pénitənt) **1.** adj. feeling or showing sorrow for having sinned or done wrong **2.** *n.* a penitent person ‖ (*Roman Catholic and Orthodox Churches*) a person receiving the sacrament of penance [O.F. *pénitent* fr. L. fr. *paenitere,* to repent]

pen·i·ten·tial (peniténʃəl) *adj.* relating to, expressing or having the nature of penitence or penance [fr. M.L. *poenitentialis*]

penitential psalms Psalms vi, xxxii, xxxviii, li, cii, cxxx and cxliii, or vi, xxxi, xxxvii, l, ci, cxxix and cxlii in the Douai version

pen·i·ten·tia·ry (peniténʃari:) **1.** *pl.* **pen·i·ten·tia·ries** *n.* a prison for criminals ‖ such a prison, esp. a state or federal prison, in which the inmates are required to do labor ‖ (*Roman Catholicism*) a papal tribunal which deals with cases of conscience, dispensations, absolution of sins and indulgences **2.** adj. rendering liable to a prison sentence, *a penitentiary offense* ‖ relating to civil prisons ‖ of or relating to penance [fr. M.L. *poenitentiarius*]

Pen·ki (bántʃí:) a town (pop. 449,000) of S. Liaoning, China, on the S. Manchurian railroad: iron and steel, coal, machinery, building materials

pen·knife (pénnaif) *pl.* **pen·knives** (pénnaivz) *n.* a pocketknife, originally one used for making and repairing quill pens

pen·man (pénmən) *pl.* **pen·men** (pénmən) *n.* a professional copyist or scribe ‖ a person with regard to the quality of his penmanship ‖ someone who excels in penmanship

pen·man·ship (pénmənʃip) *n.* style, manner or skill in handwriting or calligraphy

Penn (pen), William (1644–1718), English Quaker and founder of Pennsylvania. His lifelong aim was to secure toleration for the Society of Friends. Receiving a gift of land from Charles II in payment of a debt, he established a colony at Philadelphia (1682). He formulated a progressive and idealistic constitution with legislation by an assembly elected by popular vote, and granted full religious toleration

pen name a writer's pseudonym

pen·nant (pénənt) *n.* a long, narrow, triangular or tapering flag used esp. on ships for signaling etc. ‖ a similar flag as a symbol of sports championship [fr. PENNON, influenced by PENDANT]

pen·nate (pénit) *adj.* (*bot.*) pinnate [fr. L. *pennatus,* winged fr. *penna,* feather]

pen·ni (péni:) *pl.* **pen·ni·a** (péni:ə), **pen·nis** *n.* one-hundredth of a markka ‖ a coin of this value [Fin.]

pen·ni·less (péni:lis) *adj.* having no money or virtually none

pen·nis (pénis) *n.* unit of currency in Finland, equal to 1/100th mark

pen·non (pénən) *n.* a long flag, usually triangular or swallow-tailed, esp. (*hist.*) one borne on the lance of a knight ‖ (*naut.*) a pennant ‖ a bird's pinion [M.E. fr. O.F. *penon, pennon*]

Penn., Penna. Pennsylvania

Pen·nine Alps (pénain) *ALPS

Pen·nines (pénainz) a range of hills in N. central England, extending south from the Cheviot Hills (Scottish border) to Derbyshire and N. Staffordshire (Cross Fell, 2,892 ft)

Penn·syl·va·ni·a (pensəlvéini:ə, pensəlvéinjə) (*abbr.* Pa., Penn., Penna.) a state (area 45,333 sq. miles, pop. 11,865,000) of the eastern U.S.A., just north of the Mason-Dixon line. Capital: Harrisburg. Chief cities: Philadelphia, Pittsburgh. Except for the southeastern plain it is in the Appalachians (Allegheny and smaller ranges). Agriculture: cereals (esp. buckwheat), dairy and beef cattle, poultry, cigar tobacco, mushrooms. Resources: anthracite coal (sole American producer), bituminous coal, oil, natural gas, building materials. Industries: iron and steel (leading American state producer), metal products, textiles, plastics, machinery, food processing. Chief universities: University of Pennsylvania (1791) at Philadelphia, Pennsylvania State (1855) at University Park, Carnegie Institute of Technology (1900) at Pittsburgh. Pennsylvania was founded (1682) as a Quaker colony by William Penn, was one of the Thirteen Colonies, and became (1787) the 2nd state of the U.S.A.

Pennsylvania Dutch (*pl.*) the descendants of Germans who migrated to E. Pennsylvania in the 18th c. ‖ a dialect of High German spoken by these people ‖ a style of decoration and architecture peculiar to them

Penn·syl·va·ni·an (pensəlvéini:ən, pensəlvéinjən) **1.** adj. relating to the state of Pennsylvania ‖ of the period or system corresponding to the later or upper Carboniferous (*GEOLOGICAL TIME) **the Pennsylvanian** the Pennsylvanian period or system of rocks **2.** *n.* an inhabitant of Pennsylvania

Pennsylvania, University of a U.S. private educational institution in Philadelphia, Pa. Originally planned (1740) as a charity school, it was transformed (1755), chiefly by Benjamin Franklin, into an academy (the College and Academy of Philadelphia), with Franklin as its first president. The present name dates from 1791. It established (1765) the first medical school in North America and (1881) the first business school and (1892) the first anatomical institute in all America

pen·ny (péni:) *pl.* **pen·nies,** *Br.* also **pence** (pens) (except when referring to a number of separate coins) *n.* (symbol [¢]) a U.S. or Canadian coin worth one cent ‖ (symbol d) a British bronze coin, 100 of which make up one pound **a penny for your thoughts** what are you thinking about so abstractedly? **a pretty penny** a large sum of money spent or gained, *advertising costs them a pretty penny* **to turn an honest penny** (*Br.*) to earn some money by real work [O.E. *penig*]

penny arcade (*Am.=Br.* amusement arcade) a covered passageway or hall with slot machines etc.

penny black one of the first British adhesive postage stamps (1840)

penny dreadful (esp. *Br.*) a cheap book with stories about crime, horror, ghosts etc.

pen·ny-far·thing (péni:fárðiŋ) *n.* (*Br.*) an ordinary (early type of bicycle) [from the proportions of the two wheels]

pen·ny-pinch·ing (péni:pintʃiŋ) *adj.* (*pop.*) stingy

pen·ny·roy·al (péni:rɔ́iəl) *n. Mentha pulegium,* fam. *Labiatae,* a plant native to Europe used in cooking ‖ *Hedeoma pulegioides,* fam. *Labiatae,* an American plant from which an insect repellent is extracted [prob. fr. older *pulyole, ryale* fr. A.F. *puliol,* thyme + *real,* royal]

pen·ny·weight (péni:weit) *n.* (*abbr.* dwt) a unit of troy weight equal to 24 grains or 1/20 of a troy ounce

pen·ny-wise (péni:waiz) *adj.* (usually in the phrase) **penny-wise and pound-foolish** sensible in dealing with small sums of money, but reckless or extravagant with larger ones

pen·ny·wort (péni:wə:rt) *n. Cotyledon umbilicus,* fam. *Crassulaceae,* a European plant with round, peltate leaves, often found growing in crevices of walls ‖ a member of either *Hydrocotyle* or *Centella,* fam. *Umbelliferae,* genera of round-leaved marsh plants

pen·ny·worth (péni:wə:rθ) *pl.* **pen·ny·worth, pen·ny·worths** *n.* (esp. *Br.*) the amount one can buy for a penny, *a pennyworth of chewing gum*

Pe·nob·scot (penóbskɔt) *n.* a member of a tribe of Algonquian Indians living around the Penobscot River and Bay in Maine

pe·nol·o·gist (pi:nólədʒist) *n.* a specialist in penology

pe·nol·o·gy (pi:nólədʒi:) *n.* the study of how to treat criminals and of how prisons or other establishments for their reform should be organized [fr. Gk *poinē,* punishment + *logos,* word]

pen·sile (pénsil) *adj.* (e.g. of nests) hanging ‖ (of birds) making a hanging nest [fr. L. *pensilis*]

pen·sion (pénʃən) **1.** *n.* a sum of money paid regularly to a person who no longer works because of age, disablement etc., or to his widow or dependent children, by the state, by his former employers, or from funds to which he and his employers have both contributed ‖ a similar sum paid, either by the state or by a firm or a private individual, to enable e.g. a research scientist or poet to live and carry on his work ‖ (pãsjõ) a boardinghouse or boarding school in European countries outside Great Britain ‖ (pãsjõ) the amount paid regularly for living in such an institution ‖ (pãsjõ) accommodation at such an institution, *full pension is 10 francs a day* **2.** *v.t.* to pay a pension to ‖ (with 'off') to dismiss and pay a pension to, *it's time the old man was pensioned off* **pén·sion·a·ble** adj. entitled to a pension ‖ entitling to a pension, *the job is not pensionable* [F.]

pen·sion·ar·y (pénʃənəri:) **1.** *pl.* **pen·sion·ar·ies** *n.* a person who receives a pension ‖ a hireling **2.** adj. of, consisting of, relating to or receiving a pension [fr. M.L. *pensionarius*]

pen·sion·er (pénʃənər) *n.* a person who receives a pension ‖ (*Cambridge Univ.*) a student who pays for his room, board etc. [A.F. *pensionner*]

pen·sive (pénsiv) *adj.* deep in serious thought ‖ showing this state, *a pensive look* [F. *pensif, pensive*]

pen·stock (pénstɔk) *n.* a sluice gate for controlling the flow of water ‖ a conduit or channel by which water is led to a mill wheel etc. to make it work

pent (pent) *adj.* (usually with 'up' or 'in') shut in, confined, *pent up in school* [past part. of *pend,* obs. var. of PEN, to shut up]

penta- (péntə) *prefix* five [fr. Gk *pente,* five]

pen·ta·cle (péntəkl) *n.* (*hist.*) an ancient, five-pointed, star-shaped magical symbol [M.L. *pentaculum*]

pen·tad (péntæd) *n.* a group of five ‖ a period of five days or years ‖ a pentavalent element, atom or radical [fr. Gk *pentas (pentados)* fr. *pente,* five]

pen·ta·dac·tyl (pentədǽktil) *adj.* having five digits on the hand or foot ‖ having five parts like fingers [fr. PENTA- + Gk *dactulos,* finger]

pen·ta·gas·trin (pentəgǽestrin) *n.* (*pharm.*) gastric-secretion stimulant often used to measure secretory capacity

pen·ta·gon (péntəgon) *n.* a plane figure with five angles and five sides **the Pentagon** a pentagonal building in Arlington, Virginia, headquarters of the U.S. Department of Defense **pen·tag·o·nal** (pentǽgən'l) *adj.* [fr. L. *pentagonum* fr. Gk]

Pentagon Papers the mainly top-secret findings of an official U.S. survey ordered by President Lyndon B. Johnson's secretary of defense, Robert McNamara. The survey covered the decision-making process in the Vietnam War up until 1968. Publication (1971) of a purloined copy by the 'New York Times' and the 'Washington Post' provoked the Richard Nixon administration to attempt to impose prior restraint

pen·ta·gram (péntəgræm) *n.* a pentacle [fr. Gk *pentagrammon, pentegrammon* fr. *pente,* five + *gramma,* letter]

pen·ta·he·dral (pentəhí:drəl) *adj.* (of a solid figure) having five plane surfaces **pen·ta·he·dron** *n.* such a solid figure [fr. PENTA-+Gk *hedra*, base, seat]

pen·tam·er·ous (pentǽmərəs) *adj.* (*biol.*) composed of five parts, esp. having whorls of five or a multiple of five parts [fr. PENTA-+Gk *meros*, part]

pen·tam·e·ter (pentǽmitər) *n.* a line of English verse, consisting of ten syllables forming five iambic feet ‖ a line of Latin or Greek verse, consisting of five feet [L. fr. Gk fr. *pente*, five+*metron*, measure]

pen·tane (péntein) *n.* one of three isomeric, low-boiling hydrocarbons, C₅H₁₂, found in petroleum. Two are liquid, one is a gas [fr. Gk *pente*, five]

pen·ta·pep·tide (pentəpéptaid) *n.* (*biochem.*) compound containing five amino acids linked by -CONH- (carbon, oxygen, nitrogen and hydrogen)

pen·ta·stich (péntəstik) *n.* a stanza or poem consisting of five lines [fr. Mod. L. *pentastichus* fr. Gk fr. *pente*, five+*stichos*, line of verse]

Pen·ta·teuch (péntətu:k, péntətju:k) *n.* the first five books of the Old Testament: Genesis, Exodus, Leviticus, Numbers and Deuteronomy. They are commonly attributed to Moses, but held by scholars to be a composite work of documents dating from the 9th c. B.C. to the 4th c. B.C. **Pén·ta·teuch·al** *adj.* [fr. L. *pentateuchus* fr. Gk fr. *pente*, five+*teuchos*, implement, book]

pen·tath·lon (pentǽθlon) *n.* an athletic competition in which each competitor has to take part in five events. In the present Olympic Games these are horseback riding, swimming, fencing, shooting and running [Gk fr. *pente*, five+*athlon*, competition]

pen·ta·va·lent (péntəveilənt, pentǽvələnt) *adj.* (*chem.*) having a valence of five (cf. QUINQUEVALENT) [fr. PENTA-+L. *valens* (*valentis*) fr. *valere*, to be strong]

pen·ta·zo·are [C₁₉H₂₇NO] (pentəzóuər) *n.* (*pharm.*) minimally addictive pain reliever used as a morphine substitute; marketed as Talwin

Pen·te·cost (péntikɔst, péntikɒst) *n.* the Jewish festival of Shabuoth ‖ the Christian festival celebrated on Whitsunday seven weeks after Easter in commemoration of the coming of the Holy Ghost (Acts ii) **Pen·te·cós·tal** *adj.* of Pentecost ‖ of or pertaining to the Holy Ghost [fr. L. *pentecoste* fr. Gk *pentēcostē (hēmera)*, the fiftieth (day)]

Pen·thes·i·le·a (penθesilí:ə) queen of the Amazons, killed by Achilles in the siege of Troy

pent·house (pénthaus) *pl.* **pent·hous·es** (pénthauziz) *n.* a shed or other structure built against a main building with its roof sloping away from the larger building's wall ‖ a sloping roof projecting from the wall of a building to form a shelter ‖ a rooftop apartment or other structure [fr. older *pentice* fr. M.E., prob. fr. O.F. *apentis*, small sacred building dependent on a larger church]

pen·tode (péntoud) *adj.* (*phys.*) of a thermionic valve which has five electrodes (anode, cathode, control grid, screen grid and suppressor grid) [fr. PENTA-+Gk *hodos*, way]

pen·to·mi·no (pentəmí:nou) *n.* a many-sided, shaped figure designed to cover five squares on a game board

pen·tose (péntous) *n.* any of a group of monosaccharides having five carbon atoms in the molecule

pe·nult (pí:nʌlt, pinʌ́lt) *n.* the last syllable but one of a word or verse [shortened fr. PENULTIMATE and fr. older *penultima*]

pe·nul·ti·mate (pinʌ́ltəmit) **1.** *adj.* last but one **2.** *n.* the last syllable but one [fr. L. *paene*, almost+ULTIMATE]

pe·num·bra (pinʌ́mbrə) *pl.* **pe·num·bras, pe·num·brae** (pinʌ́mbri:) *n.* the partial shadow cast by a body where light from a given source is not wholly excluded, e.g. in an eclipse ‖ the outer shaded part of a sunspot **pe·núm·bral** *adj.* [Mod. L. fr. L. *paene*, almost+*umbra*, shade]

pe·nu·ri·ous (pənúəri:əs, pənjúəri:əs) *adj.* poor or showing extreme poverty [fr. M.L. *penuriosus* fr. L. *penuria*, poverty]

pen·u·ry (pénjəri:) *n.* poverty ‖ lack, scarcity, *penury of ideas* [fr. L. *penuria, paenuria*]

Pe·nu·ti·an (pənú:ti:ən, pənú:ʃən) *n.* a North American Indian linguistic stock including several linguistic families and extending from British Columbia to Mexico. There are about 5,000 Penutian-speaking Indians

Pen·za (pénzə) a rail center and river port (pop. 500,000) of the central R.S.F.S.R., U.S.S.R., 350 miles southeast of Moscow: lumber, pulp and paper, food processing, textiles, mechanical engineering

pe·on (pí:ən, pí:ɒn) *n.* (in Latin America) a laborer, esp. formerly one compelled to work for a master in order to work off a debt ‖ (in India, pju:n) an Indian foot soldier, policeman or servant ‖ any laborer **pe·on·age** (pí:ənidʒ) *n.* the condition of a peon ‖ (*loosely*) servitude of any kind [Span. *peon* fr. Port. *peao*, pedestrian, F. *pion*, foot soldier fr. L. *pes*, foot]

pe·o·ny (pí:əni:) *pl.* **pe·o·nies** *n.* a member of *Paeonia*, fam. *Ranunculaceae*, a genus of usually herbaceous plants native to Europe and Asia, widely cultivated for their large, showy single or double red, pink, yellow or white flowers [O.E. *peonie* fr. L.L. fr. Gk]

peo·ple (pí:p'l) **1.** *pl. n.* human beings, *you can't treat people like cattle* ‖ other persons in general, *what will people say?* ‖ a collective group of persons, *village people* ‖ one's family or parents **a people** the members of a particular race or nation **the people** the working classes as contrasted with the privileged ‖ the electorate **2.** *v.t. pres. part.* **peo·pling** *past* and *past part.* **peo·pled** to populate ‖ to fill as if with people, *his memoirs are peopled with imaginary creatures* [A.F. *poeple*, people fr. L. *populus*, the populace]

people movers horizontal escalators; moving sidewalks

people sniffer chemical-electronic device for detecting persons

people's republic a Communist republic modeled on the U.S.S.R., such as was formed after the 2nd world war in many countries, e.g. in Albania, Bulgaria, Poland, China, North Korea

Pe·o·ri·a (pi:ɔ́ri:ə, pi:óuri:ə) an agricultural market city (pop. 124,160) of central Illinois: farm machinery, corn liquor

pep (pep) **1.** *n.* (*pop.*) energy, liveliness **2.** *v.t. pres. part.* **pep·ping** *past* and *past part.* **pepped** to put new life into, *to pep up a dull party* [shortened fr. PEPPER]

PEP (*acronym*) Positron Electron Project, 1½-mi. ring accelerator at Stanford University, established in 1980

Pé·pin I (pépin, peipḗ) 'the Elder' (c. 580–c. 639), mayor of the palace of Austrasia (c. 615–c. 639), and ancestor of the Carolingian dynasty

Pépin II 'of Héristal' (c. 640–c. 714), mayor of the palace of Austrasia (c. 680–c. 714), grandson of Pépin I. His victory (687) over Neustria gave him effective rule over all the Frankish kingdoms of the Merovingians

Pépin III 'the Short' (c. 714–68), first Carolingian king of the Franks (751–68), son of Charles Martel. In return for the pope's support in obtaining the throne, he conquered Rome (754) against the Lombards, and ceded to the pope the nucleus of the Papal States

pep·lum (pépləm) *n.* a short flounce joined to a waist or jacket and covering the hips [L. fr. Gk *peplos*, a large scarf worn around the body by women]

pe·po (pí:pou) *pl.* **pe·pos** *n.* the fleshy many-seeded fruit with firm rind of any plant of fam. *Cucurbitaceae*, order *Campanulales*, e.g. a pumpkin, melon or cucumber [L.=pumpkin]

pep·per (pépər) **1.** *n.* a product consisting of the dried, usually ground fruit of *Piper nigrum*, fam. *Piperaceae*, a plant native to the East Indies and cultivated in the Tropics. It is used universally as a culinary seasoning (*BLACK PEPPER, *WHITE PEPPER) ‖ this plant ‖ any of several similar condiments, e.g. cayenne pepper ‖ any of several plants of genus *Capsicum*, fam. *Solanaceae*, esp. *C. frutescens*, universally found in warm climates ‖ the fruit of any of these, e.g. the sweet pepper and the red pepper **2.** *v.t.* to season with the ground fruit of *Piper nigrum* ‖ to sprinkle or pelt as if with this [O.E. *pipor* fr. L. *piper* fr. Gk fr. an Oriental source]

pepper-and-salt *adj.* (of cloth or hair) having light and dark threads or hairs so closely mixed that they produce a speckled effect

pep·per·corn (pépərkɔrn) *n.* the dried berry of *Piper nigrum*, the pepper plant

peppercorn rent a purely nominal rent imposed to safeguard the rights of the owner

pepper gas riot-control gas that causes irritation of nose and throat. *also* pepper fog

pep·per·mint (pépərmint) *n. Mentha piperita*,

fam. *Labiatae*, a small, perennial, aromatic plant with toothed leaves and pale purple flowers, native to Europe, but now found wild and cultivated in most temperate zones ‖ an oil with an aromatic taste, distilled from its leaves, stems and flowers, used in confectionery etc. ‖ a candy flavored with this ‖ any of several related plants, e.g. *M. arvensis*

pepper pot a West Indian dish of stewed meat or fish and vegetables incl. red peppers ‖ a highly seasoned soup

pepper shaker a small container with holes in the top, for sprinkling pepper on food

pepper tree *Schinus molle*, fam. *Anacardiaceae*, a tropical American evergreen tree which bears pungent red berries

pep·per·y (pépəri:) *adj.* containing or tasting of pepper ‖ irascible ‖ (of language, words etc.) fiery, biting

pep·py (pépi:) *comp.* **pep·pi·er** *superl.* **pep·pi·est** *adj.* full of pep

pep·sin (pépsin) *n.* an enzyme secreted in the stomach of higher vertebrates which, together with diluted hydrochloric acid, aids digestion by converting proteins into peptones ‖ a preparation containing this enzyme extracted from the stomach of a hog, calf etc. and used as a digestive aid etc. [fr. Gk *pepsis*, digestion]

pep·tic (péptik) *adj.* helping digestion, esp. by the action of pepsin ‖ of, like or involving pepsin ‖ relating to digestion or to gastric juice [fr. Gk *peptikos*, able to digest]

peptic gland one of the glands secreting gastric juice

peptic ulcer an ulcer of the stomach or duodenum resulting from the abnormal action of pepsin and other gastric juices on the mucous membrane of these areas. The term includes gastric and duodenal ulcers

pep·tide (péptaid, péptid) *n.* an amide formed by the condensation of certain amino acids [PEPTONE]

pep·tone (péptoun) *n.* any of several substances, produced by the action of pepsin on proteins, which are soluble and can be absorbed by the bloodstream **pep·to·nize** *pres. part.* **pep·to·niz·ing** *past* and *past part.* **pep·to·nized** *v.t.* to convert into a peptone [fr. G. *pepton* fr. Gk neuter of *peptos* adj., cooked, digested]

Pepys (pi:ps), Samuel (1633–1703), English diarist and naval administrator. As secretary to the admiralty (1673–9 and 1684–9), he expanded and reformed the administration of the English navy, and played an important part in the political life of the Restoration. His 'Diary' provides a vivid account of events in the period 1660–9 and is an intimate record of the daily life of the time. He was president of the Royal Society (1684–6) and wrote 'Memoirs Relating to the Royal Navy' (1690)

Pe·quot War of 1637 (pí:kwɒt) a war between the settlers of the American colony of Connecticut and the Pequot Indians, precipitated by the murder of John Oldham (c. 1600–1636), an English trader, by the Pequots. The Indians where virtually exterminated, while those taken captive were enslaved

per- *prefix* through, throughout ‖ thoroughly, completely ‖ (*chem.*) containing a large or the largest possible proportion of a specified element or radical [L.]

per (pəːr, pər) *prep.* for each, *three dollars per person* ‖ by means of, *send it per diplomatic agent* [L.]

per·ad·ven·ture (pəːrədvéntʃər) *adv.* (*old-fash.*, *rhet.*) perhaps, possibly [M.E. *perauenture, parauenture* fr. O.F.]

Pe·rae·a (perí:ə) (*hist.*) the Roman name for Gilead

Pe·rak (péirʌk, pérə) a state (area 7,980 sq. miles, pop. 1,762,288) of Malaysia in N. Malaya, the chief tin-producing region. Capital: Ipoh. It became a British protectorate (1874) and joined the Federation of Malaya (1948)

per·am·bu·late (pərǽmbjuleit) *pres. part.* **per·am·bu·lat·ing** *past* and *past part.* **per·am·bu·lat·ed** *v.t.* (*rhet.*) to walk through, *to preambulate the countryside* ‖ *v.i.* (*rhet.*) to walk about, stroll [fr. L. *perambulare (perambulatus)*]

per·am·bu·la·tion (pərǽmbjuléiʃən) *n.* (*rhet.*) the act of perambulating ‖ (*rhet.*) a walk or stroll [A.F. and fr. M.L. *perambulatio (perambulationis)*]

per·am·bu·la·tor (pərǽmbjuleitər) *n.* (*Br.*) a baby carriage ‖ a wheeled odometer used by surveyors [fr. L. *perambulare (perambulatus)*, to walk about]

per·an·num (pərǽnəm) adv. (abbr. per an.) yearly, *he is paid $15,000 per annum* [L.]

per·brom·ic acid [HBrO₂₄] (pərbróumikǽsid) n. (chem.) bromine in its highest oxidation state; synthesized in 1968

per·cale (pərkéil) n. a smooth, closely woven cotton material [F. fr. Pers. *pargāl*]

per cap·i·ta (pərkǽpitə) adv. and adj. (abbr. per cap.) per head of population for each person [L.=by heads]

per·ceiv·a·ble (pərsí:vəb'l) adj. capable of being perceived or discerned **per·céiv·a·bly** adv.

per·ceive (pərsí:v) pres. part. **per·ceiv·ing** past and past part. **per·ceived** v.t. to become aware of through the senses, e.g. by hearing or seeing ‖ to become aware of by understanding, discern [fr. O.F. *perçoivre* fr. L.]

per·cent (pərsént) (abbr. p.c., pct, per ct. symbol %) **1.** adv. in a hundred, for each hundred, *prices have risen 6 percent in the past year* **2.** pl. **per·cent, per·cents** n. a hundredth part, *12 is 1 percent of 1,200* ‖ percentage, the amount or rate per hundred **per·cént·age** n. rate or proportion per hundred ‖ (loosely) a proportion, *a good percentage of the output goes to waste* **per·cen·tile** (pərséntail, pərséntil) n. (statistics) one of a hundred parts, each containing an equal number of members, into which a series of individual things, persons etc. has been divided **per·cents** pl. n. securities yielding a specified rate of interest, *to invest in 5 percents* [fr. L. per centum]

per cen·tum (pərséntəm) percent [L.]

per·cept (pá:rsept) n. (philos.) a product of perception, a recognizable mental impression of something perceived [fr. L. *perceptum*]

per·cep·ti·bil·i·ty (pərseptəbíliti:) n. the quality of being perceptible

per·cep·ti·ble (pərséptəb'l) adj. capable of being perceived **per·cép·ti·bly** adv. [fr. L.L. *perceptibilis* fr. *percipere* (*perceptus*), to perceive]

per·cep·tion (pərsépʃən) n. the act of perceiving, *visual perception* ‖ the ability to perceive, esp. to understand ‖ (philos.) the action of the mind in referring sensations to the object which caused them (cf. SENSATION) ‖ (psychol.) awareness through the senses of an external object ‖ (psychol.) a percept ‖ (law) the collection of rents etc. **per·cép·tion·al** adj. of or having the nature of perception [O.F. and perh. fr. L. *perceptio* (*perceptionis*)]

per·cep·tive (pərséptiv) adj. capable of perceiving ‖ having or showing keen understanding or insight **per·cep·tiv·i·ty** (pərseptíviti:) n. [fr. L. *percipere* (*perceptus*)]

per·cep·tu·al (pərséptʃuəl) adj. relating to or involving esp. sensory perception [fr. L. *percipere* (*perceptus*)]

Per·ce·val (pá:rsivəl), Spencer (1762–1812), British statesman, Tory prime minister of Britain (1809–12). He was assassinated

perch (pə:rtʃ) n. *Perca fluviatilis*, fam. *Percidae*, a small, edible European freshwater fish with a broad, laterally flattened body and spiny fins ‖ *Perca flavescens*, a related North American food fish ‖ any of several related freshwater and marine fishes [F. *perche* fr. L. fr. Gk]

perch n. anything on which a bird alights or rests, e.g. a horizontal bar in a cage ‖ any resting place, esp. an elevated or temporary one, *he had a good view from his perch on the rooftop* ‖ (esp. Br.) a rod (measure of length) ‖ (esp. Br.) a square rod (measure of area) ‖ any of several cubic measures for stone, used in building ‖ a central pole joining the front and rear axles of a carriage [F. *perche*]

perch v.i. (of a bird) to alight or sit ‖ to sit or settle on or as if on a perch, *the child perched on his knee* ‖ v.t. to place on or as if on a perch [F. *percher*]

perchance (pərtʃǽns, pərtʃáns) adv. (rhet.) perhaps, maybe [M.E. fr. A.F. *par chance*, by chance]

Perche (perʃ) an old French county west-southwest of Paris, finally united to the crown in 1525

perched water (envir.) ground water separated from underlying water table by a zone of impervious material. —**perched water table** n.

perch·er (pá:rtʃər) n. a passerine bird

Per·che·ron (pá:rtʃərɒn, pá:rʃərɒn) n. a strong, fast-trotting cart horse of a breed that originated in Perche, France [F.]

per·chlo·rate (pə:rklóreit, pə:rklóureit) n. a salt of perchloric acid

per·chlo·ric acid (pə:rklórik, pə:rklóurik) n. a strong, fuming, colorless acid, HClO₄, used in

chemical analysis, in electroplating and as a catalyst

per·chlo·ride (pə:rklóraid, pə:rklóuraid) n. a chloride having a relatively high proportion of chlorine

per·cip·i·ence (pərsípi:əns) n. power of perception **per·cíp·i·en·cy** n.

per·cip·i·ent (pərsípi:ənt) **1.** adj. readily capable of perceiving **2.** n. someone who perceives [fr. L. *percipiens* (*percipientis*) fr. *percipere*, to perceive]

per·co·late (pá:rkəleit) pres. part. **per·co·lat·ing** past and past part. **per·co·lat·ed** v.i. to seep through a porous substance ‖ to become diffused, *to allow a rumor to percolate* ‖ (of coffee) to be brewed in a percolator ‖ v.t. to cause to filter gradually through a porous substance ‖ (of a liquid) to permeate (a substance) in this way ‖ to prepare (coffee) in a percolator [fr. L. *percolare* (*percolatus*), to strain]

per·co·la·tion (pə:rkəléiʃən) n. a percolating or being percolated [fr. L. *percolatio* (*percolationis*)]

per·co·la·tor (pá:rkəleitər) n. a machine for percolating, esp. one for preparing coffee as a drink by passing boiling water repeatedly through the ground beans [fr. L. *percolare* (*percolatus*)]

per·cuss (pərkʌ́s) v.t. (med.) to tap (a part of the body) in order to make a diagnosis [fr. L. *percutere* (*percussus*), to strike]

per·cus·sion (pərkʌ́ʃən) n. the act of causing one body to make a sudden impact on another ‖ such an impact ‖ the sound produced by this ‖ (med.) the percussing of a body part ‖ (mus.) percussion instruments collectively, esp. as a section of an orchestra or band [fr. L. *percussio* (*percussionis*)]

percussion cap a small vessel containing a substance which initiates the explosion of the main body of explosive in the cartridge, shell, mine etc. to which it is fitted

percussion instrument a musical instrument in which the sound is produced by striking, e.g. a cymbal or drum

per·cus·sive (pərkʌ́siv) adj. of or characterized by percussion ‖ fr. L. *percutere* (*percussus*), to strike]

Per·cy (pá:rsi:), Sir Henry (1364–1403), called 'Harry Hotspur', English nobleman. He fought against the Scots, the French and the Welsh and was killed while leading a rebellion against Henry IV

Percy, Thomas (1729–1811), Bishop of Dromore and antiquarian. His 'Reliques of Ancient English Poetry' (1765) opened up the realm of ballads and folk literature to writers of the Romantic movement

Percy, Walker (1916–) U.S. novelist. He trained as a physician and practiced medicine for a year before contracting tuberculosis. During his convalescence he read existentialist philosophers, which influenced his writing in such novels as 'The Moviegoer' (1961; National Book Award, 1962), 'The Last Gentleman' (1966) and 'Love in the Ruins' (1971). Other novels include 'Lancelot' (1977), examining religious faith, and 'The Second Coming' (1980), dealing with mental breakdown

per di·em (pərdí:əm, pərdáiəm) **1.** adv. daily, by the day **2.** adj. daily, *a per diem allowance* **3.** n. the money allotted to someone, e.g. a salesman, for expenses incurred in connection with work [L.]

per·di·tion (pərdíʃən) n. damnation, eternal death [M.E. fr. O.F. *perdiciun*]

per·du·ra·bil·i·ty (pərduərəbíliti:, pərdjuərəbíliti:) n. the quality or state of being perdurable

per·du·ra·ble (pərduárəb'l, pərdjuárəb'l) adj. (theol.) eternal ‖ (rhet.) extremely durable **per·dúr·a·bly** adv. [O.F. *perdurable, pardurable* fr. L.L.]

per·e·gri·nate (périgrineit) pres. part. **per·e·gri·nat·ing** past and past part. **per·e·gri·nat·ed** v.i. (rhet.) to travel about on foot ‖ v.t. (rhet.) to travel through [fr. L. *peregrinari* (*peregrinatus*), to travel abroad]

per·e·gri·na·tion (perigrinéiʃən) n. (rhet.) a wandering about [F. *pérégrination* or fr. L. *peregrinatio* (*peregrinationis*)]

per·e·grine (périgrin, périgri:n) n. *Falco peregrinus*, fam. *Falconidae*, a bird of prey used in falconry. It is dark with a whitish breast, and has long pointed wings and tail. It is very swift in flight [fr. L. *peregrinus*, foreign (because peregrines were caught during migration)]

pe·rei·ra (pəréirə) n. *Geissospermum vellosii*, fam. *Apocynaceae*, a Brazilian tree yielding a

bark used as a tonic etc. ‖ the bark itself [after Jonathan *Pereira* (1804–53), Eng. professor]

Perelman (pá:rlmən), S(idney) J(oseph) (1904–79) U.S. humorist, playwright and screenwriter, who used parody, hyperbole, puns and an extensive vocabulary in his satirical works. He wrote regularly for 'The New Yorker' from 1931 and his books include 'The Road to Miltown; or, Under the Spreading Atrophy' (1957) and 'Eastwood Ha!' (1977). His most successful Broadway play was 'One Touch of Venus' (1943), written with Ogden Nash and Kurt Weill

per·emp·to·ri·ly (pərémptərili:) adv. in a peremptory manner

per·emp·to·ri·ness (pərémptəri:nis) n. the quality of being peremptory

per·emp·to·ry (pərémptəri:, pérəmptɔri:, pərəmptóuri:) adj. imperious, curtly authoritative ‖ that cannot be denied or refused, *a peremptory command* ‖ (law, pərəmptəri:) final, absolute [fr. L. *peremptorius*, destructive, decisive]

per·en·ni·al (pəréni:əl) **1.** adj. perpetual, longlasting, *a perennial source of amusement* ‖ (bot.) living more than two years ‖ (of a stream etc.) remaining active or lasting throughout the year **2.** n. perennial plant (cf. ANNUAL, cf. BIENNIAL) [fr. L. *perennis*, lasting through the year or years]

Peres (pérez), Shimon (1933–) Israeli political figure, a founder of the Labor party (1968) and prime minister (1984–). A protégé of David Ben-Gurion, he was elected to the Knesset (parliament) (1959) and held cabinet posts including that of defense minister (1974–7). He was leader of the opposition (1977–84)

Pé·rez Gal·dós (péreθguldós), Benito (1843–1920), Spanish novelist and dramatist. His 'Episodios Nacionales' (1873–1912) is a series of 46 novels based on Spanish history. His other works include the novels 'Doña Perfecta' (1876) and 'Fortunata y Jacinta' (1886–7). His objectivity and realism, together with his subtle observation and powers of characterization, make him a major figure in Spanish literature

Pé·rez Ji·mé·nez (péreshi:ménes), Marcos (1914–), Venezuelan soldier and dictator (1952–8) until his overthrow

per·fect (pá:rfikt) **1.** adj. complete or correct in every way, conforming to a standard or ideal with no omissions, errors, flaws or extraneous elements ‖ utter, absolute, *a perfect idiot* ‖ (gram., of a tense) expressing the completion of an action at the time of speaking or at the time indicated ‖ (bot., of a plant or its flowers) hermaphrodite ‖ (bot., of fungi) producing sexual spores ‖ (mus., of the intervals of fourth, fifth or octave) neither major nor minor in character, remaining unaltered in character when inverted **2.** n. (gram.) the perfect tense **3.** (pərfékt) v.t. to put the finishing touches to, make as good as possible, *to perfect one's piano technique* [M.E. *parfit* fr. O.F.]

per·fect·a (pərféktə) n. (horse racing) method of betting on horse racing, placing combined bet on both first and second places in a horse race. *Cf* EXACTA

perfect binding book-binding technique using glue to replace sewing. —**perfect bound** adj.

perfect cadence (mus.) a cadence consisting of a dominant chord leading to the tonic chord in root position

per·fect·i·bil·i·ty (pərfektəbíliti:) n. the quality of being perfectible

per·fect·i·ble (pərféktəb'l) adj. capable of being perfected

perfecting machine (Br.) a perfecting press

perfecting press (Am.=Br. perfecting machine) a printing machine that prints both sides of the paper before the paper leaves the machine

per·fec·tion (pərfékʃən) n. the quality or state of being perfect ‖ an instance of this, *she is tired of hearing about her mother-in-law's perfections* ‖ a perfecting or being perfected **to perfection** perfectly, *he mimics her to perfection* **per·féc·tion·ism** n. the theory of the moral perfectibility of man **per·féc·tion·ist** n. a person who is not content with anything less than the very best [O.F.]

per·fec·tive (pərféktiv) **1.** adj. (gram., e.g. in Russian) of a verbal aspect which expresses a completed action or state **2.** n. the perfective aspect ‖ a verb in this aspect

per·fec·to (pərféktou) pl. **per·fec·tos** n. a thick cigar that tapers at both ends [Span.=perfect]

per·fec·tor (pərféktər) n. a perfecting press [L.=someone who or something that perfects]

perfect participle (gram.) past participle

perfect pitch absolute pitch (ability to identify a note)

per·fer·vid (pərfə́:rvid) adj. (rhet.) very or excessively fervent [fr. Mod. L. perfervidus fr. L. per, very+fervidus, fervid]

per·fid·i·ous (pərfidi:əs) adj. characterized by, involving or guilty of perfidy [fr. L. perfidiosus]

per·fi·dy (pə́:rfidi) pl. **per·fi·dies** n. treachery, faithlessness ‖ an instance of this [F. perfidie]

per·fo·li·ate (pərfóuli:it, pərfóuli:eit) adj. (bot.) of a leaf) having the basal lobes united around the stem so that the stem appears to pierce through the leaf [PER-+L. folium, leaf]

per·fo·rate (pə́:rfəreit) pres. part. **per·fo·rat·ing** past and past part. **per·fo·rat·ed** v.t. to make a hole through, pierce, a perforated eardrum ‖ to make a row of holes through (paper etc.) so that it can easily be pulled into parts ‖ v.i. to make a perforation [fr. L. perforare (perforatus)]

per·fo·ra·tion (pə:rfəréiʃən) n. a perforating or being perforated ‖ a small hole cut or punched into something ‖ a series of holes made in paper etc. to facilitate division ‖ (philately) one of such a series of holes on a sheet of postage stamps ‖ (philately) one of the teeth left on a stamp after it has been torn off the sheet ‖ (philately) a classification according to the number of such teeth per 20 mm. [fr. L.L. perforatio (perforationis)]

per·fo·ra·tor (pə́:rfəreitər) n. a machine for making perforations [fr. L. perforare, to perforate]

per·force (pərfɔ́rs, pərfóurs) adv. (rhet.) through necessity [M.E. fr. O.F. parforce, by force]

per·form (pərfɔ́rm) v.t. to do, fulfill, carry out, accomplish (an action, obligation etc.) ‖ to render, execute (a stage role, play, piece of music, dance etc.), esp. before an audience ‖ v.i. to execute a stage role, play, piece of music etc., esp. in public, the soloist performed poorly ‖ to carry out, accomplish an action, function etc., the engine performs well in cold weather **per·fór·mance** n. the act of performing ‖ an instance of this, there will be no performance of the play tonight ‖ the quality or manner of performing, to judge a car's performance ‖ something performed, a deed, feat etc. [M.E. fr. O.F. parfourmer, perfourmer]

performance what is accomplished, contrasted with capability

per·form·a·tive (pərfɔ́rmətiv) adj. (linguistics) of a statement of performance; e.g., I go. Cf CONSTATIVE

per·fume (pə́:rfju:m, pərfjú:m) n. a sweet smell ‖ a sweet-smelling liquid for personal use prepared from essential oils from flowers or aromatic chemicals and fixed, e.g. with musk [F. parfum]

per·fume (pərfjú:m) pres. part. **per·fum·ing** past and past part. **perfumed** v.t. to give a sweet smell to ‖ to apply perfume to **per·fúm·er** n. a person who or firm that makes or sells perfumes **per·fúm·er·y** pl. **per·fum·er·ies** n. a place where perfumes are manufactured ‖ the technique or business of making perfume ‖ perfumes collectively [F. parfumer]

per·func·to·ri·ly (pərfʌ́ŋktərili) adj. in a perfunctory manner

per·func·to·ri·ness (pərfʌ́ŋktəri:nis) n. the quality of being perfunctory

per·func·to·ry (pərfʌ́ŋktəri) adj. behaving or performing in an offhand manner without any show of interest or concern ‖ done, given etc. in this way, a perfunctory kiss [fr. L.L. perfunctorius, done carelessly or superficially]

per·fuse (pərfjú:z) v.t. pres. part. **per·fus·ing** past and past part. **per·fused** v.t. to cover or suffuse with a liquid ‖ to cause (a liquid) to flow over or through something [fr. L. perfundere (perfusus)]

per·fu·sion (pərfjú:ʒən) n. the act or an instance of perfusing, esp. a pouring over of water in baptism [fr. L. perfundere (perfusus)]

Per·ga·mum (pə́:rgəməm) an ancient city of N.W. Asia Minor (modern Bergama, Turkey, pop. 20,000). It was a powerful Hellenistic city (3rd–2nd cc. B.C.), famous for its library. Remains include the acropolis, amphitheater and temples

per·go·la (pə́:rgələ) n. a bower or covered walk made by training climbing plants over a trellis or similar support [Ital.]

Per·go·le·si (pergɔlézi:), Giovanni Battista (1701–36), Italian composer. His known works

include the comic intermezzo 'La Serva Padrona' (1733), other operas, instrumental music and the 'Stabat Mater' (1736) for women's voices

per·haps (pərhǽps) adv. possibly, maybe [fr. PER+M.E. hap, chance, accident]

pe·ri (píəri) pl. **pe·ris** n. (Pers. mythol.) a good fairy (originally an evil one) descended from fallen angels and excluded from Paradise ‖ a fairylike creature [fr. Pers. pārī or pērī]

peri- (péri) prefix around, surrounding ‖ near [Gk prep. and adv.]

Per·i·an·der (péri:ændər) (d. 585 B.C.), Greek statesman, tyrant of Corinth (625–585 B.C.), one of the Seven Sages of Greece. Corinth reached a peak of prosperity and culture under his rule

per·i·anth (péri:ænθ) n. (bot.) the envelope of external floral whorls including calyx and corolla, esp. when these are not easily distinguished ‖ a cover or ring of cells surrounding the archegonium of certain bryophytes [fr. Mod. L. perianthum fr. Gk peri, around+anthos, flower]

per·i·ap·sis, pl -ses, -sides (periǽpsis) n. (astron.) point in a celestial orbit nearest the center of the attraction. Cf HIGHER APSIS, LOWER APSIS

per·i·apt (péri:æpt) n. something worn as a charm [F. périapte fr. Gk]

per·i·car·di·ac (perikárdi:æk) adj. pericardial

per·i·car·di·al (perikárdi:əl) adj. of or pertaining to the pericardium

per·i·car·di·um (perikárdi:əm) pl. **per·i·car·di·a** (perikárdi:ə) n. the conical membranous sac enveloping the heart in vertebrates ‖ the cavity surrounding the heart in invertebrates [fr. Gk perikardion fr. peri, around+kardia, the heart]

per·i·carp (périkarp) n. (bot.) the ripened walls of a plant ovary (*FRUIT) that may be more or less homogeneous or consist of up to three layers (*ENDOCARP, *MESOCARP, *EPICARP) [fr. Mod. L. pericarpium, fr. Gk perikarpion, pod, husk fr. peri, around+karpos, fruit]

per·i·chon·dri·um (perikɔ́ndri:əm) pl. **per·i·chon·dri·a** (perikɔ́ndri:ə) n. the layer of fibrous connective tissue covering the surface of cartilage except at joints [fr. PERI-+Gk chondros, cartilage]

per·i·clase (périkleis) n. oxide of magnesium, MgO, found commonly in metamorphosed magnesian limestones [fr. Mod. L. periclasia fr. Gk peri, very+klasis, breaking (from its perfect cleavage)]

Per·i·cle·an (perikliː́ən) adj. of or concerning Pericles or his time

Per·i·cles (périkli:z) (c. 495–429 B.C.), Athenian statesman, leader of the democratic party and ruler of Athens (c. 460–429 B.C.). He was noted for his oratory, his strong, reserved character and his successful policies. He strengthened the Athenian maritime empire, lavishly patronized the arts, notably music and the drama, adorned the Acropolis and democratized the regime. He foresaw and provoked the Peloponnesian War, having previously fortified Piraeus and reconstructed the navy. His name is given to the most brilliant age of Greek history, 'Periclean Athens' standing for one of the highest achievements of civilization

per·i·cra·ni·um (perikréini:əm) pl. **per·i·cra·ni·a** (perikréini:ə) n. the membrane externally surrounding the bony or cartilaginous cranium of a vertebrate [M.L. or Mod. L. fr. Gk fr. peri, around+kranion, cranium]

per·i·cy·cle (périsaik'l) n. (bot.) a thin layer of nonconducting parenchyma cells separating the endodermis from the stele in stems and roots of higher plants and associated with the development of cambium [fr. Gk perikuklos fr. peri, around+kuklos, circle]

per·i·cyn·thi·on (perisínθi:ən) n. point in a lunar orbit nearest the moon. also perilune. Cf APOCYNTHION, APOLUNE

per·i·derm (péridə:rm) n. (bot.) a protective layer developing in the epidermis of many roots, stems and other plant organs that in maturity consists of an initiating layer (phellogen), an inner parenchyma (phelloderm) and an external cork layer (phellem) ‖ (anat.) the outer layer of the epidermis, esp. of an embryo ‖ (zool.) the external cuticular layer of a hydroid [Mod. L. peridermis fr. Gk peri, around+derma, skin]

per·id·i·um (peridi:əm) pl. **pe·rid·i·a** (peridi:ə), **pe·rid·i·ums** n. the exterior wall which enve-

lopes the sporophore of many fungi [Gk. péridion, small wallet]

per·i·dot (péridot) n. olivine [F. péridot]

per·i·ge·al (peridʒí:əl) adj. perigean

per·i·ge·an (peridʒí:ən) adj. of or pertaining to the perigee

per·i·gee (péridʒi:) n. (astron.) the point in the orbit of the moon or another satellite of the earth when it is nearest to the earth (cf. APOGEE) [F. périgée fr. L.L. fr. Gk peri, around+gē, the earth]

per·ig·y·nous (perídʒinəs) adj. (bot., of flowers) having the sepals, petals and stamens on the rim of the receptacle containing the pistil ‖ (bot., of sepals, petals or stamens) borne on this rim [fr. Mod. L. perigynus fr. Gk. peri, around+gunē, woman (used for the pistil)]

per·i·he·li·on (perihí:li:ən, perihí:ljən) pl. **per·i·he·li·a** (perihí:li:ə, perihí:ljə) n. (astron.) the point of a comet's or planet's orbit when it is nearest to the sun (cf. APHELION) [fr. Mod. L. perihelium fr. Gk peri, around+hēlios, sun]

per·il (pérəl) n. risk of serious injury, destruction, disaster, etc. ‖ the state of being exposed to such risk **at** (or **to**) **one's peril** taking the risk and assuming the responsibility for the ill effects that are likely to result from it **in peril of** (rhet.) in danger of losing, in peril of one's life [F. péril]

per·il·ous (pérələs) adj. involving or exposing one to peril [A.E. perillous]

perilure *PERICYNTHION

Per·im (périm) an island (area 5 sq. miles, pop. 300) in the Strait of Bab El Mandeb. It is a dependency of the People's Democratic Republic of Yemen

pe·rim·e·ter (perímətər) n. the line bounding a closed plane figure or an area on the ground ‖ the length of this line ‖ an optical instrument for testing a person's field of vision **per·i·met·ric** (perimétrik) adj. [fr. L. perimetros fr. Gk fr. peri, around+metron, a measure]

per·i·ne·al (perini:əl) adj. pertaining to or situated in the perineum

per·i·ne·um (perini:əm) n. the region around the opening of the rectum and bladder [L.L. fr. Gk]

per·i·nu·clear (perinú:kli:ər) adj. (biol.) around a cell nucleus

pe·ri·od (píəri:əd) 1. n. a portion of time forming a division in a development, life, chronology, timetable, etc., the Elizabethan period of English history, Picasso's blue period, the school day is divided into 7 periods ‖ (phys.) the interval of time required for the completion of a single complete cycle of some periodic or cyclical phenomenon (e.g. the period of a planetary orbit or the period of a simple harmonic vibration), being equal to the reciprocal of the frequency (cf. WAVELENGTH, cf. WAVE NUMBER) ‖ (chem.) one of the divisions of the periodic table consisting of a sequence of elements of increasing atomic number beginning with an alkali metal and ending with an inert gas ‖ (gram.) a complete, esp. a complex, sentence ‖ a pause marking the completion of a sentence ‖ the symbol (.) denoting this pause, or following an abbreviation, or marking a decimal ‖ a single menstruation ‖ (mus.) a group of (usually) eight or 16 measures divided into two phrases and ending with a cadence, generally forming a statement within a larger composition ‖ (geol.) a division of geological time, part of an era ‖ (pl.) rhetorical language 2. adj. having the characteristics of a particular historical period, period furniture [F. période fr. L. fr. Gk fr. peri, around+hodos, way]

pe·ri·od·ic (pi:əri:ɔ́dik) adj. occurring again and again, at constant intervals ‖ recurring intermittently ‖ characterized by regularly recurring stages or processes, the periodic motion of the planets ‖ (gram., of a sentence) in which the grammatical form and the meaning are not complete until the end is reached **pe·ri·ód·i·cal** 1. adj. periodic ‖ (of a magazine etc.) published at regular intervals ‖ characteristic of or pertaining to such publications 2. n. a periodical publication [F. périodique fr. L. fr. Gk]

pe·ri·o·dic·i·ty (pi:əri:ədísiti) pl. **pe·ri·o·dic·i·ties** n. the quality or fact of recurring at constant intervals ‖ (elec.) frequency ‖ (chem.) the position of an element in the periodic table [F. périodicité]

periodic law a statement in chemistry: the chemical and physical properties of elements depend upon the structure of the atom and vary with the atomic number in a systematic and roughly periodic way (*PERIODIC TABLE)

periodic table (*chem.*) a tabular arrangement of the elements based upon atomic number and emphasizing the periodic recurrence of properties. The modern periodic table in long-period form contains horizontally a very short period of two elements, two short periods of eight elements each, two long periods of 18 elements each, a very long period of 32 elements, and an incomplete period. Vertically there are 16 columns (excluding the lanthanide series and incomplete actinide series) comprising eight groups divided into two subgroups each. Elements to the left and in the center are metals, those to the right nonmetals. Metallic properties are most pronounced for elements in the lower left-hand corner, and nonmetallic properties most pronounced for elements in the upper right-hand corner. Transition from metallic to nonmetallic properties is usually gradual and continuous from left to right. The structure of the periodic table and the periodic law follow directly from the quantized structure of the atom

per·i·os·te·al (peri:ósti:əl) *adj.* of the periosteum ‖ situated around a bone

per·i·os·te·um (peri:ósti:əm) *pl.* **per·i·os·te·a** (peri:ósti:ə) *n.* a fibrous membrane of connective tissue which closely surrounds all bones except at the joints [Mod. L. fr. Gk *peri*, around+*osteon*, bone]

per·i·ot·ic (peri:óutik) **1.** *adj.* of or designating the inner ear or the bony structure that surrounds it **2.** *n.* this bony structure [fr. PERI-+Gk *otikos* fr. *ous* (*ôtos*), ear]

per·i·pa·tet·ic (perəpətétik) *adj.* moving about from place to place **Per·i·pa·tet·ic 1.** *adj.* Aristotelian **2.** *n.* a follower of Aristotle, an Aristotelian (from Aristotle's habit of conversing with pupils while they walked in the Lyceum) **per·i·pa·tét·i·cal·ly** *adv.* [F. *péripatétique* fr. L. fr. Gk fr. *peri*, around+*patein*, to walk]

per·i·pe·tei·a, per·i·pe·ti·a (perəpitáiə) *n.* a sudden change or reversal of fortune in tragedy or real life [Gk *peripeteia* fr. *peri*, around+*piptein*, to fall]

pe·riph·er·al (pərífərəl) *adj.* of, concerning or constituting a periphery ‖ lying on a periphery ‖ (*computer*) of electronic or mechanical devices not part of the basic processor, e.g., card readers, printers, terminals, etc. ‖ (*anat.*) of those nerves which run outward from the brain and spinal cord to the tissues [fr. Gk *periphéres*, moving around]

pe·riph·er·y (pərífəri) *pl.* **pe·riph·er·ies** *n.* the line bounding a figure, esp. a rounded one ‖ the outermost part of something thought of as ringed or circled, *the periphery of consciousness* ‖ the boundary or outer surface of a space or body ‖ (*anat.*) the areas in which the nerves terminate [fr. L.L. *peripheria* fr. Gk fr. *peri*, around+*pherein*, to carry]

per·i·phor·ic (perifónik) *adj.* (*acoustics*) of a speaker system with several speakers placed facing various directions

pe·riph·ra·sis (pərífrəsis) *pl.* **pe·riph·ra·ses** (pərífrəsi:z) *n.* circumlocution or an instance of this [L. fr. Gk fr. *peri*, around+*phrazein*, to declare]

per·i·phras·tic (perifrǽstik) *adj.* expressed in a roundabout fashion ‖ (*gram.*) formed by the use of auxiliary verbs etc. instead of by inflection, e.g. 'it does do' for 'it does' **per·i·phrás·ti·cal·ly** *adv.* [fr. Gk *periphrastikos*]

per·i·scope (périskoup) *n.* a tubular optical device used in submarines etc. and in scientific observation, by which light received by an oblique mirror or prism at one end of the tube is reflected by another at the other end. An observer can thus see without being exposed, or see around an obstacle **per·i·scop·ic** (periskópik) *adj.* [fr. Gk *peri*, around+*skopos*, observer]

per·ish (périʃ) *v.i.* to suffer utter ruin or destruction, or die a violent death, *the whole family perished in the fire* ‖ to suffer spiritual death **perish the thought!** don't even consider the possibility of such a thing! **pér·ish·a·ble** *adj.* liable to decay or deterioration, *perishable foods* **pér·ish·a·bles** *pl. n.* perishable goods **pér·ish·ing** *adj.* (of cold, pain etc.) extreme ‖ (*pop.*) damned, blasted, *a perishing nuisance* [M.E. fr. O.F. *perir* (*periss*)]

pe·ris·so·dac·tyl (perisoudǽktəl) **1.** *adj.* having an odd number of toes, or toes placed evenly in relation to the axis of the foot ‖ of or belonging to *Perissodactyla*, an order of ungulate mammals having such toes, e.g. the horse, rhinoceros **2.** *n.* a mammal of this order [fr. Mod. L. *perissodactylus* fr. Gk *perissos*, uneven+*daktulos*, finger, digit]

per·i·stal·sis (peristólsis, peristǽlsis) *pl.* **per·i·stal·ses** (peristǽlsi:z) *n.* a series of muscular contractions of a hollow structure, esp. of the alimentary canal, which force the contents along ‖ one of these contractions [Mod. L. fr. Gk]

per·i·stal·tic (peristóltik, peristǽltik) *adj.* of, relating to or characterized by peristalsis [fr. Gk *peristaltikos* fr. *peristellein*, to send around]

per·i·stome (péristoum) *n.* (*bot.*) the fringe of teeth surrounding the opening of a moss capsule ‖ (*zool.*) the area around the mouth in certain invertebrates [fr. Mod. L. *peristomas* fr. Gk *peri*, around+*stoma*, mouth]

per·i·style (péristail) *n.* a row of columns enclosing a courtyard or building, esp. supporting the roof ‖ the space so surrounded [F. *péristyle* fr. L. fr. Gk fr. *peri*, around+*stulos*, pillar]

per·i·the·ci·um (periθí:si:əm) *pl.* **per·i·the·ci·a** (periθí:si:ə) *n.* (*bot.*) a flask-shaped case enclosing the fruiting body in certain fungi [Mod. L. fr. Gk *peri*, around+*thēkē*, box]

per·i·to·ne·al, per·i·to·nae·al (peritəní:əl) *adj.* of the peritoneum

per·i·to·ne·um, per·i·to·nae·um (peritəní:əm) *pl.* **per·i·to·ne·a, per·i·to·nae·a** (peritəní:ə) *n.* (*anat.*) the membrane lining the abdominal viscera and the interior of the abdominal wall [L. fr. Gk fr. *peri*, around+*teinein*, to stretch]

per·i·to·ni·tis (peritənáitis) *n.* inflammation of the peritoneum caused by the spreading of infection from a diseased or ruptured visceral body [Mod. L. fr. Gk fr. *peritonos*, stretched over]

pe·ri·tus, pl **-ti** (pérətas) *n.* **1.** Vatican Council adviser. **2.** a theological adviser

per·i·wig (périwig) *n.* (esp. *hist.*) a wig [earlier *perwyke* fr. F. *perruque*]

per·i·win·kle (périwiŋk'l) *n.* any member of *Littorina*, fam *Littorinidae*, a genus of edible sea snails found on shore or in shallow water [O.E. *pinewinclan* pl.]

periwinkle *n.* a member of *Vinca*, fam. *Apocynaceae*, a genus of European, North American and W. Asian often creeping, perennial, evergreen plants with glossy leaves and blue or white flowers, esp. *V. major* and *V. minor* [O.E. *peruince* fr. L.]

per·jure (pó:rdʒər) *pres. part.* **perjur·ing** *past and past part.* **per·jured** *v. refl.* to make (oneself) guilty of perjury [O.F. *parjurer*]

per·jur·er (pó:rdʒərər) *n.* a person guilty of perjury [A.F. *parjurour, perjurour*]

per·ju·ry (pó:rdʒəri) *pl.* **per·ju·ries** *n.* (*law*) the crime of swearing on oath that something is true which one knows is false, or of telling a lie when under oath to tell the truth ‖ failure to do what one has sworn on oath to do [A.F. *perjurie*]

perk (pə:rk) *v.t.* (with 'up') to restore good spirits or courage to, *a drink will perk him up* ‖ (with 'up') to make bright or gay in appearance, *to perk up a coat with a red scarf* ‖ *v.i.* (with 'up') to recover one's health, energy or good spirits after sickness, depression etc. [etym. doubtful]

perk *v.i.* (*pop.*), of coffee) to percolate

Perkins (pó:rkənz), Frances (1882–1965) U.S. secretary of labor, the first woman cabinet member. Serving (1933–45) in the administration of Franklin D. Roosevelt, she greatly strengthened the Labor Department, esp. in the bureaus of Labor Statistics, Women and Children as well as championing such reforms as social security, federal public works and relief and legislation for minimum wages and maximum hours and abolition of child labor

perk·man (pó:rkmæn) *n.* an official or businessman who receives substantial income in the form of perquisites of his job; coined by President Jimmy Carter in 1977

perk·y (pó:rki:) *comp.* **perk·i·er** *superl.* **perk·i·est** *adj.* lively and cheerful ‖ cocky [PERK]

perks (pə:rks) *pl. n* (*Br.*, *pop.*) perquisites

Perlis (pó:rlis) a state (area 316 sq. miles, pop. 147,726) of Malaysia in N.W. Malaya. Capital: Kangar. Part of Kedah until 1842, it was ruled by Siam (1842–1909), after which it was ceded to Britain. It joined the Federation of Malaya (1948)

per·lite (pó:rlait) *n.* an acid, glassy, volcanic rock marked with concentric cracks separating small globular portions formed by tension during cooling **per·lit·ic** (pərlítik) *adj.* [F. fr. *perle*, pearl]

Perm (pə:rm) (called Molotov 1940–57) a river port and industrial center (pop. 1,028,000) of the western R.S.F.S.R., U.S.S.R., on the Kama: metallurgy, mechanical engineering, oil refining. University (1916)

perm (pə:rm) *n.* (esp. *Br.*, *pop.*) a permanent wave

perm·al·loy (pə:rmǽləi, pó:rməlɔi) *n.* an iron-nickel alloy of high magnetic permeability, giving little loss of energy by hysteresis [trademark *Permalloy* fr. PERMEABLE+ALLOY]

per·ma·nence (pó:rmənəns) *n.* the quality or state of being permanent **pér·ma·nen·cy** *pl.* **per·ma·nen·cies** *n.* permanence ‖ someone or something that is permanent ‖ a permanent position [fr. M. L. *permanentia*]

per·ma·nent (pó:rmənənt) **1.** *adj.* continuing and enduring without change **2.** *n.* (*pop.*) a permanent wave [fr. L. *permanens* (*permanentis*) fr. *permanere*, to remain to the end]

permanent magnet a magnet, usually of cobalt steel or nickel steel, which retains its magnetism for a long time

permanent magnetism magnetism retained by a substance in the absence of any external magnetic field

permanent memory (*computer*) data that are retained when power is cut off

permanent press durable press chemical and steaming process for treating fabric to retain creases. *also* durable press

permanent wave a wave set in hair by chemicals and sometimes heat, and lasting a long time

permanent way (*Br.*) a railroad track designed to carry a train service for many years

per·man·ga·nate (pərmǽŋgəneit) *n.* a salt of permanganic acid, esp. potassium permanganate

per·man·gan·ic acid (pə:rmǽŋgænik) HMnO$_4$, a strong acid known only in solution and by its salts (permanganates)

per·me·a·bil·i·ty (pə:rmi:əbíliti:) *n.* the quality or state of being permeable (*MAGNETIC PERMEABILITY)

per·me·a·ble (pó:rmi:əb'l) *adj.* able to be permeated [fr. L. *permeabilis*]

per·me·ance (pó:rmi:əns) *n.* a permeating or being permeated ‖ the quality of being permeable

per·me·ase (pó:rmi:eis) *n.* (*biochem.*) **1.** bacterial system that facilitates transportation of soluble substances in the cell. **2.** an enzyme in a cell membrane that concentrates lactose

per·me·ate (pó:rmi:eit) *pres. part.* **per·me·at·ing** *past and past part.* **per·me·at·ed** *v.t.* to penetrate wholly, pervade, soak through, *a smell of baking permeated the house* ‖ *v.i.* to diffuse or spread through something **per·me·á·tion** *n.* [fr. L. *permeare* (*permeatus*), to pass through]

per men·sem (pə:rménsəm) *adv.* by the month [L.]

Per·mi·an (pó:rmi:ən) *adj.* of the latest period or system of the Paleozoic era, characterized by the decline of amphibians and development of reptiles, by extensive glaciation, and by red sandstone and shales (*GEOLOGICAL TIME) **the Permian** the Permian period or system or rocks [after *Perm*, former Russian province in the Urals]

per·mis·si·bil·i·ty (pərmisəbíliti:) *n.* the quality or state of being permissible

per·mis·si·ble (pərmísəb'l) *adj.* that may be permitted **per·mís·si·bly** *adv.* [O.F.]

per·mis·sion (pərmíʃən) *n.* freedom, power, privilege etc. which one person or authority grants to another, *he has her permission to park in the drive* ‖ a permitting, or being permitted [fr. L. *permissio* (*permissionis*)]

per·mis·sive (pərmísiv) *adj.* permitting, tolerating ‖ morally tolerant in a high degree [O.F. *permissif, permissive*]

per·mis·siv·ist or **per·mis·sion·ist** (pərmísivist) *n.* one who believes in policy of indulgence of behavior not generally acceptable

per·mit 1. (pərmít) *v. pres. part.* **per·mit·ting** *past and past part.* **per·mit·ted** *v.t.* to give voluntarily or officially to (someone or something) some right, opportunity, power etc., *he permitted them to stay away from school* ‖ to accept or agree to (something), *how can you permit such insolence?* ‖ to make possible, *the addition of a window permits better air circulation* ‖ *v.i.* to provide opportunity, *drop in when time permits* ‖ (with 'of') to admit of, *there were too many present to permit of any intimacy* **2.** (pó:rmit, pərmít) *n.* a written license issued by an authority [fr. L. *permittere*, to let go, surrender, permit]

per·mit·tiv·i·ty (pə;rmitíviti:) *n.* dielectric constant ‖ the ratio of the induced polarity in a dielectric substance to the electric force producing it

per·mu·ta·tion (pə;rmju:téiʃən) *n.* (*math.*) any of the different arrangements in linear order that can be made of a given set of objects (*COMBINATION) ‖ (*math.*) the act or process of making such variations ‖ a change or the process of changing [O.F. *permutacion*]

per·mute (pərmjú:t) *pres. part.* **per·mut·ing** *past* and *past part.* **per·mut·ed** *v.t.* to change the order of (esp. things in a series) [fr. L. *permutare*, to exchange, interchange]

pern (pə:rn) *n.* the honey buzzard [fr. Mod. L. *pernis* fr. Gk *pternis*, a kind of hawk]

Per·nam·bu·co (pə;rnəmbú:kou) *RECIFE

per·ni·cious (pərníʃəs) *adj.* destructive, extremely injurious, or deadly, *a pernicious pest* [fr. F. *pernicieux* fr. L.]

pernicious anemia, *Br.* **pernicious anaemia** a severe type of anemia characterized by the presence of large red blood cells. It is treated by the administration of vitamin B$_{12}$ and liver extract

per·nick·et·y (pərníkiti:) *adj.* (esp. *Br.*) persnickety [origin unknown]

Perón, Isabel (1931–) president of Argentina (1974–6). A dancer, she became the secretary, then the wife (1961) of the exiled Juan Perón. When Perón returned to Argentina and became president (1973) Isabel served as his vice-president and on his death she succeeded to the presidency. Unable to cope with severe economic problems and rising political violence, she was deposed in a military coup and placed under house arrest. Upon her release (1981) she went into exile in Spain

Pe·rón (perɔ́n, pəróun), Juan Domingo (1895–1974), Argentine general and statesman, nationalist dictator of Argentina (1946–55). With his wife Eva (1919–52), he did much to modernize Argentina and won the support of the trade unions, but instituted a police state. He was exiled by the army (1955) and settled in Spain, returning to Argentina (1973) for a short second tenure as president. He died after 9 months of a term marked by factionalism and violence and was succeeded by his third wife, Isabel, who was deposed by a military junta in 1976

per·o·ne·al (perəní:əl) *adj.* of or relating to the fibula [fr. Mod. L. *peronaeus* n., muscle connected with the fibula, fr. Gk *peronē*, fibula]

per·o·rate (pérəreit) *pres. part.* **per·o·rat·ing** *past* and *past part.* **per·o·rat·ed** *v.i.* to make or deliver a peroration [fr. L. *perorare* (*peroratus*)]

per·o·ra·tion (perəréiʃən) *n.* a protracted tedious speech, often pompously delivered ‖ the concluding portion of a speech, rhetorical composition etc. [fr. L. *peroratio* (*perorationis*), summing up]

per·ox·ide (pərɔ́ksaid) **1.** *n.* an oxide which yields hydrogen peroxide when combined with an acid ‖ an oxide containing a high proportion of oxygen ‖ hydrogen peroxide **2.** *v.t. pres. part.* **per·ox·id·ing** *past* and *past part.* **per·ox·id·ed** to bleach (the hair) with hydrogen peroxide

per·ox·y·a·cet·yl nitrate (perɔksiəsi:təl) (*envir.*) toxic element in smog, created by action of sunlight on hydrocarbon exhausts from automobiles

per·pend (pərpénd) *v.t. and i.* (*rhet.*) to ponder [fr. L. *perpendere*]

per·pend (pérpənd) *n.* a large stone extending through a wall from one side to another, to bind it

per·pen·dic·u·lar (pə;rpəndíkjulər) **1.** *adj.* (of a line, plane or surface) forming an angle of 90° with another line, plane or surface ‖ (of two lines, planes or surfaces) forming a 90° angle ‖ at right angles to the horizontal at any point on the earth's surface **Per·pen·dic·u·lar** (*archit.*) of an English Gothic style (14th–16th cc.) which succeeded the Decorated and is characterized by vertical lines, esp. in its window tracery **2.** *n.* a direction which is perpendicular, esp. as represented by a straight line, *draw a perpendicular to each side of the triangle* ‖ an instrument, e.g. a plumb line, for determining the perpendicular line from any point **per·pen·dic·u·lar·i·ty** (pə;rpəndikjulǽriti:) *n.* [O.F. *perpendiculer, perpendiculair* fr. L.]

per·pe·trate (pé:rpitreit) *pres. part.* **per·pe·trat·ing** *past* and *past part.* **per·pe·trat·ed** *v.t.* to commit, perform (something bad), *to perpe-* *trate a crime* **per·pe·tra·tion,** **pér·pe·tra·tor** *ns* [fr. L. *perpetrare* (*perpetratus*)]

per·pet·u·al (pərpétʃu:əl) **1.** *adj.* eternal, everlasting, *perpetual damnation* ‖ constant, continual, *he's in a perpetual bad temper* ‖ (*bot.*) flowering throughout the season **2.** *n.* a hybrid perpetual rose [F. *perpétuel*]

perpetual annuity an annuity under which payments cease only when the principal is repaid

perpetual calendar a table of calendar dates by which one can determine the day of the week of a given date within a wide range of years ‖ a mechanical calendar which can be set for any date within a period of several years

perpetual motion the motion of a hypothetical (but impossible) machine which would go on working forever without receiving energy from an outside source

per·pet·u·ate (pərpétʃu:eit) *pres. part.* **per·pet·u·at·ing** *past* and *past part.* **per·pet·u·at·ed** *v.t.* to make perpetual ‖ to cause to continue ‖ to save from oblivion, *a bronze plaque perpetuates his memory* **per·pet·u·a·tion, per·pét·u·a·tor** *ns* [fr. L. *perpetuare* (*perpetuatus*)]

per·pe·tu·i·ty (pə;rpitjú:iti:, pə;rpitú:iti:) *pl.* **per·pe·tu·i·ties** *n.* eternity ‖ the quality or state of being inalienable forever or for a period beyond certain limits ‖ (*law*) such an estate ‖ a perpetual annuity **in perpetuity** forever [M.E. *perpetuite* fr. F.]

per·phen·a·zine [C$_{21}$H$_{26}$ClN$_3$OS] (pə:rfénəzi:n) *n.* (*pharm.*) tranquilizer, antinauseant, and antiemetic; marketed as Trilafon

Per·pi·gnan (perpi:njã) the chief town (pop. 106,426) of Pyrénées-Orientales, France, and historic capital of Roussillon, 15 miles from Spain, an agricultural market. Cathedral (14th–15th cc.), fortress, and castle (14th–15th cc.)

per·plex (pərpléks) *v.t.* to make (someone) uncertain about the nature of, or the reason for or answer to, something difficult to understand ‖ to complicate (a situation etc.) [fr. obs. *perplex adj.* fr. L. *perplexus*, involved]

per·plex·i·ty (pərpléksiti:) *pl.* **per·plex·i·ties** *n.* the quality or state of being perplexed ‖ something which perplexes [fr. L.L. *perplexitas*]

per·qui·site (pé:rkwizit) *n.* an extra profit or item received over and above one's agreed wage ‖ a tip, gratuity [fr. L. *perquisitum* fr. *perquirere* (*perquisitus*), to seek carefully for]

Per·rault (perou), Charles (1628–1703), French author. His 'Contes de ma mère l'oye' (1697) included some of the most famous of all fairy tales (Tom Thumb, Cinderella, Little Red Ridinghood)

Per·ret (perei), Auguste (1874–1954), French architect born in Belgium. He innovated the architectural use of reinforced concrete (1902–3), and successfully coordinated its use in a neoclassical style

Per·ry (péri:), Matthew Calbraith (1794–1858), American naval officer. He led a naval expedition which forced the opening of Japan to Western trade (1854)

Perry, Oliver Hazard (1785–1819), U.S. naval officer. As commander of the flagship 'Niagara' during the War of 1812, he defeated the British at the Battle of Lake Erie

per·ry (péri:) *pl.* **per·ries** *n.* (esp. *Br.*) a drink made from fermented pear juice [M.E. *pereye* fr. O.F.]

Perse, Saint-John *SAINT-JOHN PERSE

per se (pərséi) *adv.* intrinsically, considered independently of other things [L.=by itself]

per·se·cute (pé:rsikju:t) *pres. part.* **per·se·cut·ing** *past* and *past part.* **per·se·cut·ed** *v.t.* to cause to suffer, esp. for religious or political reasons ‖ to vex, harass [F. *persécuter* fr. L. *persequi* (*persecutus*), to follow closely]

per·se·cu·tion (pə;rsikjú:ʃən) *n.* a persecuting or being persecuted [M.E. *persecucion* fr. O.F. fr. L.]

persecution complex persecution mania

persecution mania a delusion that one is being persecuted

per·se·cu·tor (pé:rsikju:tər) *n.* someone who persecutes [A.F. *persecutour* fr. L.]

Per·seph·o·ne (pərséfəni:) (*Gk mythol.*) the daughter of Zeus and Demeter. She was kidnapped by Pluto and made queen of the underworld, but was allowed to return to the earth every spring and summer

Per·sep·o·lis (pərsépəlis) the ancient residential capital (40 miles east of modern Shiraz) of the Achaemenid kings of Persia, sacked (331

B.C.) by Alexander III. Fine bas-reliefs cover the remaining palace walls

Per·se·us (pé:rsi:əs, pé:rsju:s) (*Gk mythol.*) son of Zeus and Danae. He cut off the head of Medusa, rescued and married Andromeda and founded Mycenae ‖ (*astron.*) a constellation of the northern hemisphere between Taurus and Cassiopeia

Perseus (c. 212–166 B.C.), last king of Macedon (179–168 B.C.), son of Philip V. He was attacked by the Romans (171 B.C.), overthrown (168 B.C.) and died a prisoner in Rome

per·se·ver·ance (pə;rsivíərəns) *n.* the quality of being persistent and persevering ‖ the act of persevering ‖ (*theol.*) a continuing in a state of grace leading to a state of glory [F.]

per·se·vere (pə;rsivíər) *pres. part.* **per·se·ver·ing** *past* and *past part.* **per·se·vered** *v.i.* to try hard and continuously in spite of obstacles and difficulties [F. *persévérer* fr. L.]

Per·shing (pé:rʃiŋ), John Joseph (1860–1948), American general. He was commander in chief (1917–18) of the U.S. forces in France in the 1st world war, and was U.S. chief of staff (1921–4)

Per·shing (pé:rʃiŋ) *n.* army surface-to-surface guided missile (XMGM-31A) utilizing a solid propellant, with a range of 400 nautical miles, and nuclear capability; developed in 1967 and manufactured by Martin Marietta

Per·sia (pé:rʒə, pé:rʃə) the ancient, and (since 1949) the official alternative name of Iran. For geography *IRAN. HISTORY. The Iranian plateau saw the growth of an early civilization at Elam (c. 4000 B.C.). The Persians, an Aryan people, settled in S. Persia (2nd millennium B.C.), while the Medes, also an Aryan people, settled N.W. Persia (1st millennium B.C.), coming into conflict with the Assyrians (9th c. B.C.). The Medes established a strong kingdom (7th c. B.C.) and conquered Assyria (c. 616–606 B.C.), but were themselves conquered by the Persians (mid- 6th c. B.C.) under Cyrus II. His successors, the Achaemenids, built up a vast empire extending from Egypt to the Punjab and from the Dardanelles to Samarkand. The empire, founded on Zoroastrianism, was remarkable for its efficient organization, based on that of the Assyrians, and for its art, influenced by Egypt and Babylonia. The empire was weakened by the dynastic disputes of Cambyses II and Darius I, and by the Greek victories over Darius I and Xerxes I during the Persian Wars (499–449 B.C.). It fell (331 B.C.) to Alexander the Great at Arbela, and power passed to the Seleucids. Parthia broke away (mid-3rd c. B.C.) and formed an empire which rivaled Rome and which in turn was replaced by the Sassanids (c. 226–c. 641 A.D.), under whom the arts again developed. The Arabs took Ctesiphon, the capital (c. 641), and brought Islam to the whole country. Persia prospered under the Umayyad and Abbasid caliphates. Under the latter, the Seljuk Turks gained control, and poetry, philosophy, mathematics and astronomy flourished (10th–13th cc.). Genghis Khan incorporated Persia in the Mongol domains (1220), and a period of anarchy and destruction ensued until the Safavids gained power (1502–1736). This dynasty was at its height under Abbas I, in whose reign (1587–1629) Persian territory was extended and the Portuguese driven from the bases they had established on the Persian Gulf. Ottoman, Russian and Afghan raids were put down (early 18th c.) by Nadir Shah, who ruled despotically (1736–47). A period of civil war was ended (1794) by the Kajar dynasty (1794–1925), under whom Persia was drawn into European power politics, forming treaties with France (1807) and Britain (1814), and ceding most of her territory in the Caucasus to Russia (1828). Britain and Russia guaranteed Persian independence (1834), but Britain forced Persia to withdraw from Afghanistan (1857). The discovery of oil (1901) increased Western financial interest in Persia. A liberal constitution was introduced (1905) and Russia and Britain agreed to divide Persia into two zones of influence (1907). An army officer, Reza Khan, staged a coup detat (1921), established a dictatorship, and assumed the title of Reza Shah Pahlavi (1925). Under his rule, Persia was rapidly modernized. The name of the country was changed (1935) to Iran

Per·sian (pé:rʒən, pé:rʃən) **1.** *adj.* of ancient Persia or modern Iran, its people, language etc. **2.** *n.* a native or inhabitant of Persia or Iran ‖

CONCISE PRONUNCIATION KEY: **(a)** æ, cat; ɑ, car; ɔ fawn; ei, snake. **(e)** e, hen; i:, sheep; iə, deer; ɛə, bear. **(i)** i, fish; ai, tiger; ə:, bird. **(o)** o, ox; au, cow; ou, goat; u, poor; ɔi, royal. **(u)** ʌ, duck; u, bull; u:, goose; ə, bacillus; ju:, cube. x, loch; θ, think; ð, bother; z, Zen; ʒ, corsage; dʒ, savage; ŋ, orangutang; j, yak; ʃ, fish; tʃ, fetch; 'l, rabble; 'n, redden. Complete pronunciation key appears inside front cover.

the Iranian language of Iran [M.E. *Persien* fr. F.]

Persian blinds persiennes

Persian cat a domestic cat of a breed having long, silky fur, stocky build and a round head

Persian Gulf an arm (area 77,000 sq. miles) of the Arabian Sea between Iran and Arabia: tideland oil wells, pearl fisheries

Persian lamb the skin of a Karakul lamb, with tight curly hair, used for coats etc. (cf. BROADTAIL, cf. ASTRAKHAN)

Persian Wars the struggle (499–449 B.C.) between the Greeks and the Persian Empire. Following the revolt of the Greeks of Ionia (499–494 B.C.), Darius I invaded Greece and was defeated at Marathon (490 B.C.). Xerxes I continued the campaigns, was victorious at Thermopylae (480 B.C.) and took Athens. But the Persian fleet was destroyed at Salamis (480 B.C.) and the army defeated at Plataea (479 B.C.), driving the Persians from the Aegean

per·si·ennes (pəːrziːénz) *pl. n.* outside window blinds with adjustable slats, similar to Venetian blinds [F. fr. *persien* adj., Persian]

per·si·flage (pə́ːrsiflaʒ) *n.* light-hearted and bantering speech, writing etc. [F.]

per·sim·mon (pərsímən) *n.* a member of *Diospyros*, fam. *Ebenaceae*, a genus of trees growing in hardwood forests and also cultivated, esp. *D. virginiana* of the southern and eastern U.S.A. and *D. kaki*, the Japanese persimmon. The ripe fruit, a large berry, is reddish orange and succulent ‖ the fruit of one of these trees [fr. Algonquian]

per·sist (pərsíst) *v.i.* to continue, esp. in spite of opposition or difficulties, *he persists in doing what he shouldn't* ‖ to continue to exist, *the tradition has persisted to this day* [fr. L. *persistere*, to remain]

per·sist·ence (pərsístəns) *n.* the quality or state of being persistent ‖ the act of persisting [F. *persistance*]

per·sist·en·cy (pərsístənsiː) *n.* persistence [fr. L. *persistens*]

per·sist·ent (pərsístənt) *adj.* continuing in spite of opposition ‖ enduring, lasting or recurrent, *a persistent cough* ‖ (*bot.*, of a leaf) not falling although withered ‖ (*zool.*, of horns, hair etc.) permanent, not disappearing or falling off ‖ (*chem.*, of toxic chemicals) nondegradable or slowly degradable ‖ (*med.*, of a disorder) not readily cured [fr. L. *persistens* (*persistentis*)]

per·sis·tron (pə́ːrsistrən) *n.* (*electr.*) display panel utilizing solid-state electroluminescent amplification

Per·si·us (pə́ːrsiːəs), Aulus Persius Flaccus (34–62), Roman poet and author of six satires extolling Stoic morality in private life

per·snick·et·y (pərsníkitiː) *adj.* fastidious, finicky, fussy ‖ complex, requiring careful, precise handling [alt. of PERNICKETY]

per·son (pə́ːrsn) *n.* a man, woman or child, regarded as having a distinct individuality or personality, or as distinguished from an animal or thing ‖ someone regarded patronizingly, *there's a strange person to see you* ‖ the body of a human being, *attacks on the person of the president* ‖ an individual's self or being ‖ (*gram.*) one of the three referents for pronouns and the corresponding verb forms in many languages (*FIRST PERSON, *SECOND PERSON, *THIRD PERSON) ‖ (*theol.*) one of the modes of being of the trinitarian Godhead ‖ (*law*) a human being or a collection of human beings considered as having rights and duties ‖ (*zool.*) a single zooid in a colony **in person** being physically present, *apply in person* [O.F. *persone*, Mod. F. *personne*, a part in a drama]

per·so·na (pərsóunə) *n.* (*in Jung's psychology*) the personality assumed by an individual in adaptation to the outside world [L.=actor's mask, character acted]

per·son·a·ble (pə́ːrsnəbˈl) *adj.* (*old-fash.*, of people) good-looking

per·son·age (pə́ːrsnidʒ) *n.* a person of eminence or importance ‖ a character in a play or novel [O.F.]

per·son·al (pə́ːrsnˈl) **1.** *adj.* belonging or particular to one person, private, *a personal opinion, personal belongings* ‖ done by oneself, in person, *a personal intervention* ‖ of or concerning the body, *personal cleanliness* ‖ referring to a person without proper respect for his privacy, *personal remarks* ‖ considered as a person with human faculties of reason etc., *a personal God* ‖ (*gram.*, of a verb ending or pronoun) denoting the first, second or third person **2.** *n.* (esp. *pl.*) newspaper paragraphs about individual per-

sons, or containing paid personal messages to individuals [O.F.]

personal distance the minimum distance from a person or animal subconsciously considered too close for comfort

personal equation the correction to be made in a reading, e.g. of a scientific instrument, in order to compensate for the tendency of an individual to err habitually in a particular direction

personal estate (*law*) personal property

per·son·al·ism (pə́ːrsn'lizəm) *n.* any philosophical system based on the assumption that the human person is the fundamental value

per·son·al·i·ty (pəːrsn'næliti) *pl.* **per·son·al·i·ties** *n.* the total of the psychological, intellectual, emotional and physical characteristics that make up the individual, esp. as others see him ‖ a person with regard to this total of characteristics, *he is a powerful personality* ‖ an eminent or famous person, *many personalities were at the banquet* ‖ the quality, state or fact of being a person ‖ pronounced individuality, *he lacks personality* ‖ (*pl.*) reference, esp. critical, to a person or people, *let us avoid personalities in this discussion* [O.F. *personalité*]

personality cult (in Marxist terminology) a deliberate, organized process of persuading a community that its leader has a supreme excellence in his personal qualities which entitles him to unquestioning loyalty

personality inventory (*psych.*) a psychological profile comparing certain personality traits and interests with the average. Cf MMPI

per·son·al·i·za·tion (pəːrsn'lizéiʃən) *n.* the quality or state of being personalized ‖ the act of personalizing or an instance of this

per·son·al·ize (pə́ːrsn'laiz) *pres. part.* **per·son·al·iz·ing** *past* and *past part.* **per·son·al·ized** *v.t.* to personify ‖ to make personal, e.g. by labeling with one's name, *personalized writing paper*

per·son·al·ly (pə́ːrsn'li) *adv.* in a personal way ‖ in person, not using an agent, *the manager personally conducted us* ‖ for one's part, so far as one is oneself concerned, *personally, I like him*

personal property (*law*) estate or property that consists of temporary or movable things, as opposed e.g. to land

personal tax a tax whose incidence falls directly on individuals, e.g., sales tax

per·son·al·ty (pə́ːrsn'lti) *n.* personal property [fr. A.F. *personaltie*]

persona non gra·ta (pərsóunənoungrátə) *pl.* **per·so·nae non gra·tae** (pərsóuniːnoungrátiː) a diplomat who is not acceptable to the government of the country he is accredited to ‖ any person who is not welcome in a particular group [L.]

per·son·ate (pə́ːrsnit, pə́ːrsneit) *adj.* (*bot.*, of a corolla) consisting of two lips with a projection of the lower lip closing the throat ‖ (*bot.*, of a flower, e.g. a snapdragon) having such a corolla [fr. L. *personatus*, masked]

personate (pə́ːrsneit) *pres. part.* **per·son·at·ing** *past* and *past part.* **per·son·at·ed** *v.t.* (*law*) to pretend to be (someone, or some kind of person, that one is not) for illegal purposes **per·son·a·tion, pér·son·a·tor** *ns* [fr. L. *personare* (*personatus*) fr. *persona*, mask]

per·son·day (pə́ːrsn'dei) *n.* unit of activity measurement of one person for one day

per·son·hood (pə́ːrsn'hud) *n.* the distinctive qualities that make up an individual

per·son·i·fi·ca·tion (pərsɒnifikéiʃən) *n.* the treating of an abstract quality or thing as if it had human qualities ‖ an instance of this ‖ a person regarded as the embodiment of a quality, *she is the personification of generosity*

per·son·i·fy (pərsónifai) *pres. part.* **per·son·i·fy·ing** *past* and *past part.* **per·son·i·fied** *v.t.* to treat (an abstraction, thing or inanimate object) as a person, *the Greeks personified the forces of nature as gods* ‖ to be the embodiment of, *he is urbanity personified* [F. *personnifier*]

per·son·nel (pəːrsnél) *n.* the body of employees in a service, business, factory etc., *military personnel* [F.]

Persons, Robert *PARSONS

per·spec·tive (pərspéktiv) *n.* the art of representing solid objects on a flat surface so that they seem to be in relation to one another in space just as the eye would see them ‖ a picture made using this technique ‖ the appearance of objects with reference to distance, relative position etc. ‖ relative importance, *to see problems in their true perspective* ‖ evaluation of events according to a particular way of looking at

them, *historical perspective* ‖ a view or prospect [fr. M.L. *perspectiva* (*ars*), (the science of) optics]

perspective *adj.* of, pertaining to or depicted according to perspective [fr. L.L. *perspectivus* fr. *perspicere*, to look through, view]

per·spex (pə́ːrspeks) *n.* a transparent acrylic resin, produced in England, essentially polymerized methyl methacrylate, used e.g. in aircraft (cf. LUCITE) [fr. *Perspex*, trademark]

per·spi·ca·cious (pəːrspikéiʃəs) *adj.* having clear insight, *a perspicacious judge of people* [fr. L. *perspicax* (*perspicacis*) fr. *perspicere*, to look through]

per·spi·cac·i·ty (pəːrspikǽsiti) *n.* the quality of being perspicacious [fr. L. *perspicacitas*]

per·spi·cu·i·ty (pəːrspikjúːiti) *n.* clearness of expression, lucidity [fr. L. *perspicuitas*]

per·spic·u·ous (pərspíkjuːəs) *adj.* clearly expressed so as to be easily understood, *a perspicuous explanation* ‖ (of a person) clearly intelligible in speech or writing [fr. L. *perspicuus*, clear, transparent]

per·spi·ra·tion (pəːrspəréiʃən) *n.* sweat ‖ the act of sweating [F.=a breathing out]

per·spi·ra·to·ry (pərspáirətəri, pərspáirətouri) *adj.* of, having the nature of or inducing perspiration [fr. L. *perspirare* (*perspiratus*), to perspire]

per·spire (pərspáiər) *pres. part.* **per·spir·ing** *past* and *past part.* **per·spired** *v.i.* and *t.* to sweat [fr. L. *perspirare*, to breathe through]

per·suad·a·ble (pərswéidəb'l) *adj.* able to be persuaded

per·suade (pərswéid) *pres. part.* **per·suad·ing** *past* and *past part.* **per·suad·ed** *v.t.* to cause (someone) to do something by reasoning, coaxing, urging etc., *to persuade a sick man to stay in bed* ‖ to cause (someone) to believe something by reasoning etc., *she persuaded him that she was telling the truth* [fr. L. *persuadere*]

per·sua·si·bil·i·ty (pərsweizəbíliti:) *n.* the quality of being open to persuasion

per·sua·si·ble (pərswéizəb'l) *adj.* persuadable [fr. L. *persuasibilis*]

per·sua·sion (pərswéiʒən) *n.* a persuading or being persuaded ‖ capacity or power to persuade, *he spoke with great persuasion* ‖ a strongly held conviction, esp. a sectarian belief ‖ a religious sect, *the Methodist persuasion* [fr. L. *persuasio* (*persuasionis*)]

per·sua·sive (pərswéisiv) *adj.* able or tending to persuade or convince [fr. M.L. *persuasivus*]

pert (pəːrt) *adj.* forward and self-confident, and not entirely respectful, *a pert answer* ‖ jaunty, *a pert little spring outfit* ‖ in good spirits, lively, *feeling quite pert again* [M.E. *apert*, open, fr. O.F.]

PERT (*management acronym*) program evaluation and review technique, a management and decision-making system defining objectives, steps for achieving them, and procedures for evaluating progress toward them

per·tain (pəːrtéin) *v.i.* (with 'to') to be a natural part, *the illnesses pertaining to childhood* ‖ (with 'to') to be suitable, *the politeness pertaining to a guest* ‖ (with 'to') to have reference, *criticisms pertaining to their smartness and discipline* [O.F. *partenir*, to belong]

Perth (pəːrθ) the capital and commercial center (pop. 89,700), with agglom., incl. the port of Fremantle, 558,000) of Western Australia. Industries: automobiles, food processing, building materials, light manufactures. University (1912)

Perth a county (area 2,493 sq. miles, pop. 128,600) of central Scotland ‖ its county town (pop. 44,100), an agricultural market on the Tay, formerly the capital of Scotland (9th–15th cc.)

per·ti·na·cious (pəːrtinéiʃəs) *adj.* persistent and determined, often to the point of stubbornness [fr. L. *pertinax* (*pertinacis*)]

per·ti·nac·i·ty (pəːrtinǽsiti) *n.* the quality or state of being pertinacious [F. *pertinacité*]

per·ti·nence (pə́ːrtinəns) *n.* the quality or state of being pertinent [PERTINENT]

per·ti·nen·cy (pə́ːrtinənsi:) *n.* pertinence [fr. L. *pertinens*]

per·ti·nent (pə́ːrtinənt) *adj.* (often with 'to') referring centrally to the matter being discussed or considered, *pertinent details, information pertinent to this problem* [fr. L. *pertinens* (*pertinentis*) fr. *pertinere*, to belong]

per·turb (pərtə́ːrb) *v.t.* to cause to be anxious [O.F. *perturber* fr. L. *perturbare*, to disturb physically]

per·tur·ba·tion (pəːrtərbéiʃən) *n.* a perturbing

CONCISE PRONUNCIATION KEY: **(a)** æ, cat; ɑ, car; ɔ fawn; ei, snake. **(e)** e, hen; iː, sheep; iə, deer; ɛə, bear. **(i)** i, fish; ai, tiger; əː, bird. **(o)** o, ox; au, cow; ou, goat; u, poor; ɔi, royal. **(u)** ʌ, duck; u, bull; uː, goose; ə, bacillus; juː, cube. x, loch; θ, think; ð, bother; z, Zen; ʒ, corsage; dʒ, savage; ŋ, orangutang; j, yak; ʃ, fish; tʃ, fetch; 'l, rabble; 'n, redden. Complete pronunciation key appears inside front cover.

or being perturbed ‖ an irregular variation or a deviation from the predicted or usual course, e.g. of a celestial body under the influence of a weak but significant force from a source that is unaccounted for [O.F.]

per·turb·a·tive (pəːrtə́rbətiv) *adj.* (*meteor.*) disturbances in the regular motions of celestial bodies

per·tus·sis (pərtʌ́sis) *n.* (*med.*) whooping cough [Mod. L. fr. L. *per*, thoroughly+*tussis*, cough]

Pe·ru (pərú:) a republic (area 496,093 sq. miles, pop. 17,031,200) of W. South America. Capital: Lima. People: 53% mestizo or white, 46% Indian (mainly Quechua and Aymará, with little-known smaller groups in the east), 1% Asian and African. Languages: Spanish (official), Indian languages. Religion: mainly Roman Catholic (75%), with Protestant (1%) and Animist minorities. The land is 55% forest, 1% cultivated (mainly irrigated). West of the Andes, which run the length of W. Peru, is a narrow coastal belt (the *costa*) rising to 5,000 ft, mainly desert (oil fields), but with irrigated valleys, containing 25% of the population. The eastern foothills and jungle-covered Ucayali (upper Amazon) basin comprise the *montaña* and contain 13% of the population. The *sierra* (the Andes) is highest (above 18,000 ft except in the north) along the western crest, with smaller ranges, high plateaus and steep valleys in the east, and contains 62% of the population and most of the mines. Highest peak: Huascarán (22,180 ft). The climate ranges from tropical to polar. Average temperatures (F.): Lima (costa) 65°, Iquitos (montaña) 76°, Cuzco (sierra) 53°. Rainfall: Lima 1.7 ins, montaña 20–130 ins, Cuzco 23 ins. Agriculture employs 62% of the people. Main crops: (costa) cotton, sugar, rice, fruit, market vegetables, olives, (montaña, largely undeveloped) coffee, rubber (gathered wild), cacao, lumber, other tropical products, (sierra) root vegetables, cereals, coca plants. Livestock (mainly *sierra*): sheep, cattle, goats, llamas, alpacas, horses, mules, hogs. Exports: fish (2nd world producer) and fishmeal, copper, iron ore, silver, lead, zinc, petroleum, hides and skins, wool, cotton, sugar, coffee, cocaine. Other products: textiles, building materials, consumer goods, chemicals, guano, vanadium, antimony, tungsten, bismuth, gypsum, coal, barite, gold. Imports: machinery, vehicles, metals, chemicals, food, fuels, textiles. Chief port: Callao. There are 8 universities, the oldest being Lima (1551) and Arequipa (1821). Monetary unit: sol (100 centavos). HISTORY. The center of the Inca Empire, Peru was invaded (1532) and conquered (1533) by a Spanish expedition under Pizarro. It was organized during the colonial period under a viceroy and comprised the Audiencias of Panama, Bogotá, Quito, Charcas, Chile, and Buenos Aires. Its importance declined in the 18th c. with the creation of Nueva Granada (1739) and the River Plate (1776). San Martín led a liberation movement and proclaimed the independence of Peru (July 28, 1821). Final Spanish resistance was defeated (1824) by Bolívar. Independence was followed by a succession of dictatorships and revolts, and by war (1863–71) with Spain. Peru was involved in war with Chile (1879–84) over the mining of nitrates in Bolivia, and lost much territory. Some economic progress was made (late 19th c.). A popular uprising which overthrew (1930) the dictatorship of Augusto B. Leguía y Salcedo introduced a radical reform party, the Alianza Popular Revolucionaria Americana (APRA), under the leadership of Víctor Raúl Haya de la Torre. Subsequently the Apristas were largely kept from power by the ruling conservative groups. Peru declared war (1945) on the Axis and joined (1945) the U.N. In 1948 a military junta installed Gen. Manuel A. Odría as president. The constitutional presidency of Manuel Prado y Ugarteche (1956–62) was followed (1962) by another military coup in order to prevent Haya de la Torre from assuming the presidency. After new elections in 1963 in which the Popular Action and Christian Democrat parties and the army's approval won the presidency for Fernando Belaúnde Terry, a new social reform program was introduced. This concentrated on building and communications, incl. a new highway cutting into the trans-Andean forests (it opened up 3,500 acres of land with each completed mile), on a vigorous (25% of the budget) attempt to reduce Peru's 45% illiteracy rate, and on an agrarian reform plan (1964) which drew about 2 million Peruvi-

ans, mostly Indians, into Cooperación Popular projects for village improvement. Such a program, beyond Peru's fiscal capacity, was further hurt by scandal and corruption. Belaúnde's failure to make good his promise to expropriate the U.S.-owned International Petroleum Co. (IPC, a subsidiary of Standard Oil Company, New Jersey), which had been drilling in Peru since 1924, and pressure from the rich landowners, brought about his overthrow (1968) by a junta headed by Gen. Juan Velasco Alvarado. Velasco introduced a vigorous agrarian reform program. His seizure of U.S. tuna clippers (1969) for violating Peru's territorial waters (extended unilaterally to 200 miles) angered the U.S.A. His confiscation, within six days of his inauguration, of most of IPC's property posed for the U.S. government the dilemma of having either to apply the Hickenlooper amendment or risk the alienation of all Latin America by waging 'economic aggression'. A compromise with the U.S.A. was worked out, and his reform program thus lost some of its impact. A violent earthquake ravaged (May 31, 1970) 300 miles of the Pacific coast region and killed 50,000 people. In 1975, with Peru facing spiraling inflation and massive foreign debt Velasco Alvarado's government was replaced by a military junta led by Gen. Francisco Morales Bermúdez. The constitution was suspended and the parliament dissolved. A new constitution was prepared by an assembly elected (1978) for the purpose and elections were held (1980) to return Peru to civilian government. Belaúnde Terry was returned to office, succeeded by Alan García Pérez (1985–), who moved to alleviate continuing economic problems and to fight cocaine trafficking

Peru–Bolivian Federation a federal state created (1836) by Gen. Santa Cruz, president of Bolivia, who declared himself its Protector (1836–9). The union was opposed by Chile, which defeated (1839) Santa Cruz in the Battle of Yungay, after which the federation was dissolved

Peru Current the Humboldt Current

Pe·ru·gia (pərú:dʒə) a city (pop. 143,089) of N. Umbria, Italy. Industries: textiles, mechanical engineering, pharmaceuticals, tourism. Etruscan and Roman city walls, palace and churches (12th and 13th cc.), Gothic cathedral (14th–15th cc.)

Pe·ru·gi·no (peru:dʒí:no) (Pietro di Vannucci, c. 1445–1523), Umbrian painter of religious subjects. His symmetrical compositions generally consist of well drawn, graceful figures contained in a landscape articulated with architectural elements. His work includes the Sistine Chapel fresco 'Christ Giving the Keys to St Peter' (1481) and the fresco 'Crucifixion with Saints' (1496, Sta Maria Maddalena de' Pazzi, Florence). He taught Raphael

pe·ruke (pərú:k) *n.* a wig, esp. one of those worn in the 17th to early 19th cc. [F. *perruque*]

pe·rus·al (pərú:z'l) *n.* the act or an instance of perusing

pe·ruse (pərú:z) *pres. part.* **pe·rus·ing** *past* and *past part.* **pe·rused** *v.t.* to read through carefully or critically [etym. doubtful]

Pe·ru·vi·an (pərú:vi:ən) **1.** *adj.* of Peru, its people, culture etc. **2.** *n.* a native or inhabitant of Peru [fr. Mod. L. *Peruvia*, Peru]

Peruvian bark cinchona

per·vade (pərvéid) *pres. part.* **per·vad·ing** *past* and *past part.* **per·vad·ed** *v.t.* to spread throughout and into every part of, *new ideas pervaded the nation* **per·va·sion** (pərvéiʒən) *n.*

per·va·sive (pərvéisiv) *adj.* pervading or tending to pervade [fr. L. *pervadere* (*pervasus*), to pass through]

per·verse (pərvə́:rs) *adj.* willfully doing what is wrong or unreasonable ‖ indicating such willfulness, *a perverse refusal* ‖ obstinate, intractable ‖ (*law*, of a verdict) contrary to the evidence or to judicial direction [F.]

per·ver·sion (pərvə́:rʒən) *n.* a perverting or being perverted ‖ a deviation from usual behavior, esp. from normal sexual behavior [fr. L. *perversio* (*perversionis*)]

per·ver·si·ty (pərvə́:rsiti:) *pl.* **per·ver·si·ties** *n.* the quality or state of being perverse ‖ an instance of this [F. *perversité* fr. L.]

per·ver·sive (pərvə́:rsiv) *adj.* perverting or tending to pervert [fr. L. *pervertere* (*perversus*), to pervert]

per·vert 1. (pərvə́:rt) *v.t.* to damage the mind or

will of (a person) so that he thinks or acts in an immoral way ‖ to cause to be misused, falsified, wrongly understood etc., *to pervert the course of justice* **2.** (pə́:rvərt) *n.* a person who is perverted, esp. someone given to homosexuality or other abnormal sexual practices [fr. F. *pervertir* fr. L. *pervertere*, to turn upside down]

per·vi·ous (pə́:rvi:əs) *adj.* capable of being permeated or passed through, e.g. by heat ‖ (with 'to') willing to be influenced (by something stipulated, e.g. reason) [fr. L. *pervius*, having a way through]

Pe·sach (péisax) *n.* the Passover [Heb.]

Pe·sa·ro (pézarɔ) an Adriatic port (pop. 84,373) in the Marches, Italy: celebrated ducal palace (15th–16th cc.)

pe·sa·wa (pəsáwə) *n.* one hundredth of a cedi ‖ a coin of this value [native word in Ghana]

Pes·ca·do·res Islands (peskədóriz, peskədóri:z) (or Penghu) a group of 64 islands (area 50 sq. miles, pop. 115,600) that are a dependency of Formosa and lie between Formosa and Fukien, China

pe·se·ta (pəséitə) *n.* the basic Spanish monetary unit ‖ a coin of this value [Span.]

Pe·sha·war (pəʃówər) a strategic communications center (pop. 268,366) of Pakistan in the valley leading to the Khyber Pass (11 miles west), a market for produce and handicrafts. Greek, Buddhist and Mogul remains

Pe·shi·to (pəʃí:tou) *n.* the Peshitta

Pe·shit·ta (pəʃí:tə) *n.* the principal Syriac version of the Bible [Syriac *p'shitâ p'shitô*, plain, simple]

pes·ky (péski:) *comp.* **pes·ki·er** *superl.* **pes·ki·est** *adj.* (*pop.*) annoyingly troublesome [perh. var. of *pesty* fr. PEST]

pe·so (péisou) *pl.* **pe·sos** *n.* the monetary unit of many South American republics and of the Philippines ‖ a coin of this value [Span.=a weight]

pes·sa·ry (pésəri:) *pl.* **pes·sa·ries** *n.* an instrument worn in the vagina to prevent displacement of the uterus or as a contraceptive ‖ a vaginal suppository [fr. M.L. *pessarium* fr. L. *pessum* fr. Gk *pessos*, an oval stone]

pes·si·mism (pésəmizəm) *n.* the tendency to expect the worst or to stress the worst aspect of things (opp. OPTIMISM) ‖ the belief that the world is fundamentally evil **pés·si·mist** *n.* someone who persistently takes the worst view of things ‖ someone who holds the metaphysical doctrine of pessimism **pes·si·mís·tic** *adj.* **pes·si·mís·ti·cal·ly** *adv.* [fr. L. *pessimus*, worst]

Pest (pest) *BUDAPEST

pest (pest) *n.* an animal (e.g. an insect or rodent) which is destructive to crops, stored food etc. ‖ a tiresome, annoying person ‖ (*hist.*) the plague [F. *peste*, plague fr. L.]

Pes·ta·loz·zi (pestalótsi:), Johann Heinrich (1746–1827), Swiss educational reformer, influential in the development of modern primary education

pes·ter (péstər) *v.t.* to annoy with persistent requests, questions etc. [perh. fr. O.F. *empestrer*, to shackle]

pest·house (pésthaus) *pl.* **pest·hous·es** (pésthauziz) *n.* (*hist.*) a hospital or other establishment for people with deadly epidemic diseases, e.g. plague

pes·ti·cide (péstisaid) *n.* a substance, e.g. an insecticide, used for destroying pests [fr. PEST+L. *caedere*, to kill]

pes·tif·er·ous (pestífərəs) *adj.* carrying infection ‖ socially or morally harmful [fr. L. *pestiferus*, pest-bearing]

pes·ti·lence (péstələns) *n.* a deadly epidemic disease, esp. (*hist.*) the bubonic plague ‖ something morally or socially pernicious [F. fr. L. *pestilentia*]

pes·ti·lent (péstələnt) *adj.* pestilential ‖ harmful to society, esp. in a moral sense ‖ tiresomely annoying [fr. L. *pestilens* (*pestilentis*) fr. *pestis*, plague]

pes·ti·len·tial (pestilénʃəl) *adj.* of, causing or having the nature of pestilence [fr. M.L. *pestilentialis*]

pes·tle (pés'l, péstəl) *n.* a blunt-ended implement for reducing hard substances to powder by pounding them in a mortar ‖ any of several instruments used for pounding or stamping [M.E. fr. O.F. *pestel, pesteil*]

pestle *pres. part.* **pes·tling** *past* and *past part.* **pes·tled** *v.t.* to pound or crush with a pestle ‖ *v.i.* to use a pestle [O.F. *pesteler*]

pes·tol·o·gy (pestóladʒi:) *n.* the scientific study of pests, esp. insect pests, and of their control [fr. PEST+Gk *logos*, word]

pet (pet) **1.** *n.* a tame animal kept as a companion or for fun, and affectionately cared for ‖ someone who is treated as a favorite **2.** *adj.* kept as a pet ‖ favorite, *he's off on his pet topic again* **3.** *v. pres. part.* **pet·ting** *past* and *past part.* **pet·ted** *v.t.* to pat or caress (e.g. a pet animal) ‖ to pamper ‖ *v.i.* (*pop.*) to caress someone of the opposite sex in sexual play [origin unknown]

pet *n.* a fit of resentful or peevish ill humor, *to be in a pet* [etym. doubtful]

peta- (petə) standard international combining prefix for 10¹⁵

Pé·tain (peitɛ̃), Henri Philippe (1856–1951), French soldier and statesman, marshal of France (1918–45). He defended Verdun (1916) and was the French commander in chief (1917–18). He became prime minister of France (1940), signed the armistice with Germany and was appointed head of state of the Vichy government (1940–4). He was tried for treason (1945) and condemned to death, but the sentence was commuted to life imprisonment

pet·al (pét'l) *n.* one of the colored, modified leaves forming part of the corolla of a flower **pét·aled, pét·alled** *adj.* [fr. Mod. L. *petalum* fr. Gk *petalon,* thin plate]

pet·al·oid (pét'lɔid) *adj.* (*bot.*) looking like or having the form of a petal ‖ (*biol.*) composed of petallike parts [fr. Mod. L. *petaloideus* fr. L. *petalum,* petal]

pe·tard (pitárd) *n.* (*hist.*) a kind of bomb once used to break down obstructions [F. *pétard*]

pet·cock (pétkɒk) *n.* a small cock or valve used to release air from a water pump or pipe, or to drain a steam cylinder, radiator etc.

Pe·tén, El (petén) a region of Central America, between N. Guatemala and S. Yucatán. It was one of the earliest centers of Mayan civilization and is known today for its archaeological ruins

Pe·ter (pí:tər), St (*d.* 64 or 67), chief of the 12 Apostles, brother of St Andrew. He was originally called Simon but Jesus gave him the Aramaic name 'Kepha', meaning rock, translated into Greek as 'Petros'. A fisherman on the Sea of Galilee, he was summoned by Jesus to be a disciple. Jesus's declarations to him recorded in Matthew xvi, 18–19 are the basis of the papal claim to supremacy in succession to Peter. Peter was present at Gethsemane, but afterwards he denied three times being a follower of Jesus. He was the first of the Apostles to whom Jesus appeared after the Resurrection, and became their acknowledged leader. He was imprisoned in Jerusalem and miraculously released. Peter preached in Asia Minor, and, according to tradition, went to Rome (c. 55) and was martyred under Nero. It is generally thought that he influenced the writing of the Gospel according to St Mark. Feast: June 29

pe·ter (pí:tər) *v.i.* (usually with 'out') to become gradually smaller in size or amount and finally cease to be, *her enthusiasm petered out* [origin unknown]

Peter I 'the Great' (1672–1725), czar of Russia (1682–1725). Assuming personal power (1689), he gave Russia an outlet to the Black Sea by capturing Azov from the Turks (1695–6). After extensive travels in Europe (1697–8), he began to Westernize Russian institutions. His victory over the Swedes (1709) in the Northern War gave Russia access to the Baltic. He moved the capital from Moscow to St Petersburg (1713). His other reforms included the reorganization of the army, the founding of a navy, the establishment of several hundred factories, the construction of canals and technical schools and the planning of the Russian Academy of Sciences. He established a new tax system and made the Church subject to the State. By often ruthless methods he made Russia an important European power

Peter III (1728–62), czar of Russia (1762). He was forced to abdicate in favor of his wife, Catherine II

Peter I (1844–1921), king of Serbia (1903–18) and of the country later called Yugoslavia (1918–21), grandson of Karageorge. On account of ill health, he made his son, Alexander I, regent (1914)

Peter II (1923–70), king of Yugoslavia (1934–45), son of Alexander I. After a regency under his cousin had formed an alliance with the Axis provoking a revolution, he seized personal power (1941) but went into exile when the Germans invaded (1941). The monarchy was abolished (1945)

Peter kings of Castile, León, Aragon and Portugal, and emperors of Brazil *PEDRO

Peter Ca·ni·sius (kənífəs), St (1521–97), Dutch Jesuit theologian who converted many Lutheran regions of W. and S. Germany to Catholicism. Feast: April 27

Peter Cla·ver (kléivər), St (Pedro Claver, c. 1581–1654), Spanish Jesuit missionary, known as the 'apostle of the blacks' for his ministering to W. African slaves in Colombia. Feast: Sept. 9

Peter Da·mi·an (déimiːən), St (Pietro Damiani, 1007–72), Italian monk and reformer. He was associated with Pope Gregory VII in promoting clerical reform, and scathingly attacked clerical abuses in his 'Liber Gomorrhianus' (c. 1050). Feast: Feb. 23

Peter, Epistles of the 21st and 22nd books of the New Testament, of uncertain authorship (late 1st and early 2nd cc.), the first of which deals with Christian duties and encourages the Christians of Asia Minor under persecution

Peter Lombard *LOMBARD

Pe·ter·loo (pí:tərlú:) (*Br. hist.*) the name derisively given to a public disturbance in Manchester (1819), in which the magistrates ordered the cavalry to charge a large crowd peaceably assembled to petition for the repeal of the Corn Laws. There were several hundred casualties. The government's action in congratulating the magistrates greatly increased the growth of radicalism and of the reform movement [after St *Peter's* Fields, where the meeting was held +WATERLOO]

Peter Principle tenet that employees advance to the level of their incompetence; satirically conceived by Lawrence Peter, Canadian educator

Pe·ters·burg (pí:tərzbə:rg) a city (pop. 41,055) and port of entry in S.E. Virginia. During the American Revolution it was captured (1781) by British troops. In the Civil War it was finally taken, after a long Union siege (1865), by a force under Gen. Ulysses S. Grant. The victory was followed within a week by Gen. Robert E. Lee's surrender at Appomattox

pe·ter·sham (pí:tərʃəm) *n.* corded ribbon for stiffening waistbands, hatbands etc. ‖ a rough woolen cloth used mainly for men's coats [after Viscount *Petersham,* 19th-c. English nobleman]

pe·ter·son·ics (pí:tərsóniks) *n.* (*acoustics*) the study of acoustic waves at microwave frequencies on solid substances (e.g., a railroad station, a house). *also* acoustoelectronics

Peter's pence a voluntary contribution paid annually by Roman Catholics for the expenses of papal administration ‖ (*hist.*) an annual tax of one penny formerly payable by every household in many European countries to the papal see

Peter the Hermit (c. 1050–1115), French preacher. After preaching the 1st Crusade (1096–9), he led a band of peasant followers through E. Europe, but had already left them before their defeat by the Turks. He reached the Holy Land in the company of other Crusaders

Peter Zeng·er Trial a landmark in British jurisprudence during the colonial period in America. Peter Zenger (1697–1746), a New York printer, was charged (1734) with seditious libel against the colonial government. His defense, Andrew Hamilton, denied that the alleged libels were false and set a precedent by upholding the right of publication of matters 'supported by truth.' Zenger was acquitted

pet·i·o·lar (péti:ələr) *adj.* (*biol.*) of, designating, like or attached to a petiole

pet·i·o·late (péti:əleit) *adj.* having a petiole **péti·o·lat·ed** *adj.*

pet·i·ole (péti:oul) *n.* (*bot.*) a stalk holding a leaf ‖ (*zool.*) something resembling this, esp. the slender stalk connecting thorax and abdomen in some insects, e.g. ants [fr. L. *petiolus,* little foot, stalk]

Pé·tion (peitjɔ̃) (Alexandre Sabès, 1770–1818), Haitian soldier and statesman. He founded (1807) a republic in S. Haiti, and served (1807–18) as its first president. He is known for his aid to Simón Bolívar's wars for independence

Pe·ti·pa (peti:pa), Marius (1822–1910), French dancer and choreographer. He was one of the chief creators of the Russian ballet and helped to make Diaghilev's achievements possible

pe·tite (pətíːt) *adj.* (of a person) small and neat in figure [F.]

pet·it·grain oil (péti:grein) a fragrant essential oil extracted from the leaves and branches of the Seville orange and other trees of genus *Citrus,* used in the production of soap and perfume [F. *petitgrain,* unripe bitter orange]

pe·ti·tion (pətíʃən) **1.** *n.* a formal request, esp. to a sovereign, a governing body etc., often a written one signed by a large number of people ‖ a solemn prayer to God, *the petitions of the litany* ‖ a formal written request to a court of law ‖ that which is requested, *your petition is granted* **2.** *v.t.* to make a petition to (someone) for something to be done ‖ to make a request for (something) ‖ *v.i.* to make a petition [F. *pétition* fr. L. fr. *petere,* to seek, request]

pe·ti·tion·a·ry (pətíʃəneri) *adj.* of, relating to or involving a petition [fr. M.L. *petitionarius*]

Petition of Rights (*Eng. hist.*) a declaration (1628) by parliament that unparliamentary taxation, arbitrary imprisonment, billeting of soldiers on citizens and declaration of martial law in peacetime were illegal practices. Charles I accepted the petition, but his subsequent violation of it led to the Civil War (1642–52)

pet·it ju·ry (péti:dʒúəri) a petty jury [F. *petit,* small]

pe·tit mal (pətí:mæl) *n.* mild epilepsy characterized by momentary loss of consciousness (cf. GRAND MAL) [F.=small evil or illness]

pet name a name other than a person's true name or nickname, used affectionately

pet·nap·ping (pétnæpiŋ) *n.* theft of pet animals for ransom or other reason. —**pet·nap·per** *n.*

Pe·tra (pí:trə) an ancient citadel and former center of the caravan trade, in the E. Great Rift Valley in S. Jordan. It was the capital of the Edomites and Nabataeans: Nabataean, Hellenistic and Roman tombs and temples carved in the cliffs, and Frankish fortifications

Pe·trarch (pí:trɑrk, pétrɑrk) (Francesco de Petrarca, 1304–74), Italian poet and scholar, famous for his sonnets, which quickly influenced poets writing in other European languages, and esp. for his 'Rime in Vita e Morte di Madonna Laura'. They were written in the main tradition of courtly love, but they embody a celebration of love freed from allegory and mysticism. He used the Tuscan dialect. He also wrote in Latin, esp. the epic poem 'Africa' (1341). In many ways he is one of the first men of the Renaissance: he translated and collected classical manuscripts, visited Rome for the ruins of antiquity rather than the splendors of the Church, and in his extensive letters and essays on religious, philosophical and political subjects frequently expressed a humanistic point of view

pet·rel (pétrəl) *n.* any of several rather small, web-footed sea birds of fam. *Procellariidae* and fam. *Hydrobatidae,* having mainly dark or dark and white plumage. They are nocturnal, feeding far out at sea on creatures swimming near the surface. They breed in crevices and holes in rocks, a single egg being laid [older *pitteral,* perh. fr. a L. dim. of *Petrus,* St Peter (because he walked on the waves)]

Pe·trie (pí:tri:), Sir William Matthew Flinders (1853–1942), British archaeologist. He carried out many excavations in Egypt (1881–1924), notably at Abydos (1899), and was a pioneer of modern archaeological method, esp. in the use of pottery for establishing dates and periods

pet·ri·fac·tion (pétrifækʃən) *n.* (of organic matter) a converting or being converted into stone ‖ a petrified mass [fr. PETRIFY]

pet·ri·fi·ca·tion (pétrifikéiʃən) *n.* petrifaction [F. *pétrification*]

pet·ri·fy (pétrifai) *pres. part.* **pet·ri·fy·ing** *past* and *past part.* **pet·ri·fied** *v.t.* to turn (an organic structure) into stone, or a substance hard as stone, through the replacement of organic tissues by deposited silica, agate or calcium carbonate in solution ‖ to render (a person) rigid or numb with fear or horror ‖ *v.i.* to be turned into stone or a stony substance [F. *pétrifier* fr. L. fr. *petra,* rock]

Pe·trine (pí:train, pí:trin) *adj.* of or like St Peter or the doctrines connected with him [fr. L. *Petrus,* Peter]

pet·ro·chem·i·cal (pétroukémik'l) *n.* a chemical derived from petroleum or natural gas or from one of their derivatives, e.g. ethyl alcohol [fr. Gk *petros,* stone and *petra,* rock+CHEMICAL]

pet·ro·dol·lars (pétroudɒlərz) *n.* oil earnings of petroleum-exporting countries in excess of their domestic needs, usu. deposited in dollars in Western European banks

pet·ro·glyph (pétrəglif) *n.* a rock carving esp. a prehistoric one **pet·ro·glyph·ic** *adj.* [fr. F.

CONCISE PRONUNCIATION KEY: **(a)** æ, c*a*t; ɑ, c*a*r; ɔ f*aw*n; ei, sn*a*ke. **(e)** e, h*e*n; i:, sh*ee*p; iə, d*ee*r; ɛə, b*ea*r. **(i)** i, f*i*sh; ai, t*i*ger; ə:, b*i*rd. **(o)** o, *o*x; au, c*ow*; ou, g*oa*t; u, p*oo*r; ɔi, r*o*yal. **(u)** ʌ, d*u*ck; u, b*u*ll; u:, g*oo*se; ə, b*a*cillus; ju:, c*u*be. x, lo*ch*; θ, *th*ink; ð, bo*th*er; z, *Z*en; ʒ, cor*s*age. dʒ, sava*g*e; ŋ, ora*ng*utang; j, *y*ak; ʃ, *fi*sh; tʃ, fe*tch*; 'l, rabb*le*; 'n, redd*en*. Complete pronunciation key appears inside front cover.

pétroglyphe fr. Gk *petra*, rock+*gluphē*, carving]

Pet·ro·grad (pétrəgræd) *LENINGRAD

pet·ro·graph·ic (petrəgræfik) *adj.* of or relating to petrography **pet·ro·gráph·i·cal** *adj.*

pe·trog·ra·phy (pətrógrəfi:) *n.* the scientific description and classification of rocks [fr. Gk *petra*, rock+*-graphos*, written]

pet·rol (pétrəl) *n.* (*Br.*) gasoline [F. *pétrole*]

pet·ro·la·tum (petrəléitəm) *n.* a yellowish and white gelatinous, tasteless hydrocarbon mixture derived from petroleum, used as a base for ointments, as a lubricant etc. [Mod. L. fr. M.L. *petroleum*, petroleum]

petrol bomb (*Br.*) Molotov cocktail

pe·tro·le·um (pətróuli:əm) *n.* an oily liquid mixture of complex hydrocarbons occurring naturally in the pores and fissures of sedimentary rock, usually in association with its gaseous form, natural gas [M.L. fr. L. *petra*, rock+*oleum*, oil]
—In the refining process, the crude oil is distilled, yielding fractions which constitute gasoline, kerosene, diesel fuel, fuel oil, lubricating oils and heavy fuel oils. The residue yields paraffin wax and asphalt. To increase the yield of motor fuel, the hydrocarbons in the heavier fractions are broken down by thermal or catalytic cracking. Petroleum is the source of petrochemicals used widely in manufacturing (plastics, synthetic fibers, drugs, detergents, fertilizers, insecticides and rust preventives). The chief petroleum producing areas of the world are the U.S.A., Venezuela, Russia and the areas bordering the Persian Gulf

petroleum jelly petrolatum

petroleum spirit (esp. *pl.*) white spirits

pet·ro·log·ic (petrəlódʒik) *adj.* of or pertaining to petrology **pet·ro·lóg·i·cal** *adj.*

pe·trol·o·gist (pətrólədʒist) *n.* a specialist in petrology

pe·trol·o·gy (pətrólədʒi:) *n.* the branch of geology dealing with the origin, occurrence, structure and composition of rocks, based on field and laboratory tests [fr. Gk *petra*, stone+*logos*, word]

Pe·tro·ni·us (pitróuni:əs) (d. 66), Roman satirist, author of the novel the 'Satyricon', and probably the same Petronius as the Arbiter Elegantiae (arbiter of taste) at Nero's court, who committed suicide for political reasons

Pe·tro·pav·lovsk (petroupávlɔfsk) an agricultural market and rail center (pop. 212,000) of N. Kazakhstan, U.S.S.R.: farm machinery, food processing, military equipment

Pe·tro·pav·lovsk-Kam·chat·ski (petrʌpávlʌfskkəmtʃátski) a port and naval base on the S.E. Kamchatka peninsula, U.S.S.R. Fish and shellfish canning factories

pet·ro·pol·i·tics (petroupólitiks) *n.* the backstage manipulations among oil-producing countries, companies and related political figures

pe·tro·sal (pətróus'l) **1.** *adj.* hard, rocklike ‖ belonging or near to the hard portion of the temporal bone or the capsule of the internal ear, e.g. of the otic bone of fish **2.** *n.* a petrosal bone [fr. L. *petrosus*, rocky]

pet·rous (pétrəs) *adj.* of or like rock ‖ of the pyramidal part of the temporal bone between the sphenoid and the occipital bones [fr. L. *petrosus*, rocky]

Pe·tro·za·vodsk (petrʌzavótsk) the capital (pop. 241,000) of the Karelian A.S.S.R., U.S.S.R., a port and rail center on Lake Onega: wood and machine industries

Pet·sa·mo (pétsamɔ) *PECHENGA

pet·ti·coat (péti:kout) *n.* an undergarment hanging from the waist, esp. one bedecked with lace, ruffles etc. to be worn under a skirt ‖ (*Br.*) a slip (dress-length undergarment) [earlier *petty coat*, little coat]

petticoat government domination by women in the home or in politics

petticoat insulator an insulator for high insulation, shaped like a number of superimposed inverted cups

pet·ti·fog·ger (péti:fɒgər) *n.* (old-fash.) a disreputable lawyer who handles petty cases ‖ someone given to pettifogging **pet·ti·fóg·ger·y** *n.* [fr. PETTY+(*obs.*) fogger, pettifogger, prob. fr. the FUGGER family]

pet·ti·fog·ging (péti:fɒgiŋ) **1.** *adj.* (of a person) quibbling over trivial details ‖ (of behavior) characteristic of such a person ‖ (of details) tiresomely trivial **2.** *n.* a quibbling over unimportant details [fr. PETTIFOGGER]

pet·ti·ly (péti:li:) *adv.* in a petty manner

pet·ti·ness (péti:nis) *n.* the quality of being petty ‖ an instance of this

pet·tish (pétiʃ) *adj.* sulking or apt to sulk and be peevish [PET, fit of bad humor]

pet·ti·toes (péti:touz) *pl. n.* pig's feet as food [etym. doubtful]

Pet·ty (péti:), Sir William (1623–87), English statistician and economist. He put forward the view that land and labor were the basis of value in his 'Treatise of Taxes and Contributions' (1662). He wrote many works on trade, industry and population from a statistical point of view

pet·ty (péti:) *comp.* **pet·ti·er** *superl.* **pet·ti·est** *adj.* minor, trivial, *petty grievances* ‖ (of a person) giving minor matters, esp. minor faults or grievances, unwarranted importance ‖ characteristic of such a person [M.E. *pety* fr. F. *petit*, small]

petty cash small amounts of money for incidental expenses ‖ a fund drawn on for these expenses

petty jury a jury of 12 people that hears evidence and gives a verdict in a criminal or civil case on trial (cf. GRAND JURY)

petty larceny theft of property valued at less than a stated sum (which varies between $10 and $200 according to jurisdiction) ‖ (*Br. hist.*) theft of property valued at less than 12d.

petty officer (*Am. navy*) a member of one of three classes of noncommissioned naval officer of lowest rating: petty officer first class, petty officer second class and petty officer third class ‖ (*Br. navy*) an officer of a rank corresponding to that of non-commissioned officer in the army

petty sessions the meeting of two or more justices of the peace or magistrates to try certain minor offenses summarily, without a jury

pet·u·lance (pétʃuləns) *n.* the quality or state of being petulant [F. *pétulance*]

pet·u·lant (pétʃulənt) *adj.* discontented and irritable over trifles [F. fr. L. *petulans* (*petulantis*), forward, insolent]

pe·tu·ni·a (pitú:njə, pitjú:njə) *n.* a member of *Petunia*, fam. *Solanaceae*, a genus of herbaceous plants native to South America and widely cultivated for their variously colored, funnel-shaped flowers [Mod. L. fr. obs. F. *petun*, tobacco fr. Guaraní]

pe·tun·tse (petúntsə) *n.* china stone [Mandarin *pai-tun-tze*, white stone]

Peul (pju:l) *n.* a member of the Fulani people ‖ the Fulani language

Pevs·ner (péfsnər), Antoine (1886–1962), French sculptor, born in Russia, an originator of constructivism

pew (pju:) *n.* a long bench with a back used as church furniture [M.E. *puwe*, *pywe*, *pewe* fr. O.F. *puye*, *poye*, balcony, parapet]

pe·wee, **pee·wee** (pí:wi:) *n.* any of several North American olive-green flycatchers, esp. *Contopus virens*, the wood pewee [imit.]

pe·wit, **pee·wit** (pí:wit) *n.* the pewee ‖ the lapwing [imit.]

pew·ter (pjú:tər) **1.** *n.* any of several gray alloys of tin, usually with lead in the proportion roughly 4 to 1, or sometimes with a small amount of antimony or copper to harden it, used (esp. formerly) for plates, mugs etc. Pewter is malleable and does not tarnish ‖ utensils made of this alloy **2.** *adj.* made of this alloy [M.E. fr. O.F. *peutre*, *peautre*, *peaultre*, origin unknown]

pe·yo·te (peióuti:) *n.* any of several cacti growing in the southwest U.S.A. and Mexico, esp. mescal ‖ a stimulant from mescal buttons used in some esp. Mexican Indian religious rituals [Span. fr. Nahuatl *peyotl*, caterpillar]

pfen·nig (fénig)*n.* one hundredth of a deutsche mark ‖ a coin of this value [G.]

PG 1. (*pharm. abbr.*) prostaglandin. **2.** a motion-picture rating indicating that parental guidance is suggested. *Cf* G, R, X

pH (*chem.*) a symbol signifying the negative logarithm (base 10) of the hydrogen ion concentration of a solution or pure liquid expressed in gram equivalents per liter. The range of values of pH extends from 0 to 14, 7 being the negative logarithm of the hydrogen-ion concentration in pure water at 25°C (1 x 10^{-7} gram liter) or neutrality. Smaller numbers signify increasing acidity, greater ones increasing basicity

Phae·dra (fí:drə, fédrə) (*Gk mythol.*) daughter of Minos, and wife of Theseus. She was seized by an unrequited passion for her stepson (*HIPPOLYTUS) and killed herself after causing his death

Phae·drus (fí:drəs) (c. 15 B.C.–c. 50 A.D.), Roman author of verse fables, largely based on Aesop, but told with originality and charm

Phaes·tus (féstəs) an ancient town of Crete with remains of a Minoan palace (c. 2200 B.C.)

Pha·ë·thon (féiəθən) (*Gk mythol.*) son of Helios. One day he drove the sun's chariot, and nearly set fire to the world when the horses bolted. Zeus struck him dead with a thunderbolt to save the world

pha·e·ton (féiitən) *n.* a light, fourwheeled, open carriage drawn by one horse or two [after PHAËTHON]

phag·o·cyte (fægəsait) *n.* any cell, esp. a leucocyte, able to ingest and destroy foreign particles harmful to the body **phag·o·cyt·ic** (fægəsítik) *adj.* **phag·o·cy·to·sis** (fægəsitóusis) *n.* the ingestion and destruction of harmful microorganisms, foreign matter and tissue debris, that in vertebrates is accomplished by leucocytes, and that serves as an important defense and waste-disposal mechanism [fr. Gk *phagein*, to eat+*kutos*, cell]

phag·o·some (fægəsoum) *n.* (*cytol.*) a vesicle in a cell holding material captured by ameboid cells

phal·ange (fæləndʒ, fəlændʒ) *pl.* **pha·lan·ges** (fəlǽndʒi:z) *n.* (*anat.*) a phalanx [F. *phalange* fr. L.]

pha·lan·ge·al (fəlǽndʒi:əl) *adj.* (*anat.*) of the bones of the fingers and toes [fr. Mod. L. *phalangeus* fr. L. *phalanx*, phalanx]

pha·lan·ger (fəlǽndʒər) *n.* a member of *Phalangeridae*, suborder *Diplotodontia*, a family of arboreal marsupials of Australia and New Guinea. They are mostly nocturnal, feeding on insects and fruit, and usually have a prehensile tail [Mod. L. fr. Gk *phalangion*, spider's web, from the structure of the hind feet]

phal·an·ster·y (fælənsteri:) *pl.* **phal·an·ster·ies** *n.* a community living together and sharing property after the plan of Charles Fourier [fr. F. *phalanstère* fr. *phalange*, phalanx]

pha·lanx (féilæŋks, fǽlæŋks) *pl.* **pha·lanx·es**, **pha·lan·ges** (fəlǽndʒi:z) *n.* (*Gk hist.*) a body of Greek infantry formed in close ranks with shields joined ‖ any body of people solidly grouped for defensive or offensive action ‖ (*anat.*) *pl.* **phalanges** each of the bones composing the segments of finger and toe ‖ a phalanstery [L. fr. Gk *phalanx* (*phalangos*)]

Phalanx *n.* (*mil.*) a close-in weapons system providing automatic, autonomous terminal defense against antiship cruise missiles, including self-contained search-and-track radars, weapons control and 20-mm M61 gun firing subcaliber penetrators

phal·a·rope (fæləroup) *n.* a member of *Phalaropodidae*, a family of small, lobate-toed wading birds of Europe and North America, breeding in the Arctic and wintering in warm climates. The female is more brightly colored than the male and conducts the courtship. The male incubates the egg [F. fr. Mod. L. *Phalaropus* fr. Gk *phalaris*, coot+*pous* (*podos*), foot]

phal·lic (fælik) *adj.* of or relating to a phallus or phallicism ‖ like a phallus **phal·li·cism** (fǽlisizəm) *n.* worship of the phallus as symbol of the generating force in nature [fr. Gk *phallikos* fr. *phallos*, phallus]

phal·lus (fæləs) *pl.* **phal·li** (fǽlai) *n.* a symbol of the penis, used in Dionysian cults and other religions to represent the generative force [L. fr. Gk *phallos*, penis]

phan·er·o·gam (fænərəgæm) *n.* a seed plant or flowering plant (cf. CRYPTOGAM) [F. *phanérogame* fr. Gk *phaneros*, visible+*gamos*, sexual union]

phan·er·o·gam·ic (fænərəgǽmik) *adj.* of or designating a phanerogam [fr. Mod. L. *phanerogamia*, former bot. division, fr. *phanerogamus*, phanerogamic]

phan·er·og·a·mous (fænərógəməs) *adj.* phanerogamic [PHANEROGAM]

phan·o·tron (fænətron) *n.* (*electr.*) a rectifier made of a hot cathode gas diode

phan·tasm (fæntæzəm) *n.* an illusion ‖ a ghostly apparition, esp. of a person, dead or alive ‖ (*philos.*) the mental image of a person or an object [F. *fantasme* fr. L. fr. Gk *phantasma*]

phan·tas·ma·go·ri·a (fæntæzməgóri:ə, fæntæzməóuri:ə) *n.* a constantly moving succession of real or imagined scenes, people or things, esp. characteristic of a dream or a fevered state

phan·tas·ma·gor·ic (fæntæzməgórik, fæntæzməóurik) *adj.* [fr. Gk *phantasma*, phantasm+(perh.) *agora*, assembly]

phan·tas·mal (fæntǽzməl) *adj.* of, involving or having the nature of a phantasm

phan·tas·mic (fæntǽzmik) *adj.* phantasmal

phantasy *FANTASY

phan·tom (fǽntəm) 1. *n.* something, esp. a ghost, that appears to be seen but that has no real physical existence ‖ someone who or something which is only apparently what they or it purports to be 2. *adj.* illusory [M.E. *fantosme, fantome* fr. O.F.]

phantom order a draft contract with an industrial establishment for wartime production of a specific product. It provides for necessary preplanning in peacetime and for immediate execution of the contract when proper authority is received

Phantom II (*mil.*) U.S. twin-engine, supersonic multipurpose jet fighter/bomber (F-4 and RF-4), operative from land and aircraft carriers and employing both air-to-air and air-to-surface weapons; made by McDonnell Douglas

phar·aoh (fέərou, fǽrou) *n.* the title of ancient Egyptian kings **phar·a·on·ic** (fεəreiónik) *adj.* [O.E. *pharaon* fr. L. fr. Gk fr. Heb. fr. Egypt.]

phar·i·sa·ic (færiséiik) *adj.* self-righteous and hypocritical **Phar·i·sa·ic** of, relating to or like the Pharisees **phar·i·sá·i·cal** *adj.* [fr. L. fr. Gk *pharisaïkos*]

phar·i·see (fǽrisi:) *n.* a hypocrite ‖ a self-righteous person **Phar·i·see** a member of a Jewish religious sect (2nd c. B.C.–2nd c. A.D.) which upheld strict obedience to the Torah, combined with traditional interpretations of it. The Pharisees were the opponents of the Sadducees [M.E. *pharise, farise* fr. O.F. fr. L. fr. Gk fr. Aram.]

phar·ma·ceu·tic (fɑːrməsúːtik) *adj.* of or relating to pharmacy **phar·ma·céu·ti·cal** *adj.* **phar·ma·céu·tics** *n.* the science of the preparation and use of medicines **phar·ma·céu·tist** *n.* a pharmacist [fr. L. fr. Gk *pharmakeutikos* fr. *pharmakon*, poison, medicine]

pharmaceutical chemist a chemist engaged in research in or the production of medical chemicals ‖ (*Br.*) a druggist

phar·ma·cist (fɑːrməsist) *n.* a person skilled or engaged in pharmacy

phar·ma·co·ge·net·ics (fɑːrməkoudʒənétiks) *n.* study of interaction of drugs and genetic reactions. —**phar·ma·co·ge·net·ic** *adj.* —**phar·ma·co·ge·net·i·cist** *n.*

phar·ma·co·log·i·cal (fɑːrməkəlódʒik'l) *adj.* of or relating to pharmacology

phar·ma·col·o·gist (fɑːrməkólədʒist) *n.* a person trained or engaged in pharmacology

phar·ma·col·o·gy (fɑːrməkólədʒi:) *n.* the study of the preparation, properties, use and effects of drugs [fr. Mod. L. *pharmacologia* fr. Gk *pharmakon*, poison, medicine+*logos*, word]

phar·ma·co·poe·ia (fɑːrməkəpíːə) *n.* a book, esp. an official reference book, listing the properties, effects, recommended dosages and ways of administration of chemicals, medicinal preparations and esp. drugs. It usually gives standards and tests for drugs ‖ a stock of drugs **pharma·co·póe·ial** *adj.* [fr. Gk *pharmakon*, poison, medicine+*poiein*, to make]

phar·ma·cy (fɑːrməsi:) *pl.* **phar·ma·cies** *n.* the art or profession of preparing and dispensing medicinal drugs ‖ a pharmacist's shop ‖ a drugstore [O.F. *farmacie, pharmacie* fr. L.L. fr. Gk fr. *pharmakon* poison, medicine]

Pha·ros, the (fέərɔs) a lighthouse on an island near Alexandria, completed (c. 280 B.C.) by Ptolemy II and destroyed by an earthquake (14th c.). It was one of the Seven Wonders of the World ‖ this island

Phar·sa·lus (fɑːrséiləs) an ancient city of Thessaly, near which Julius Caesar defeated Pompey (48 B.C.)

pha·ryn·gal (fəríŋg'l) *adj.* pharyngeal [fr. Mod. L. *pharynx*, pharynx]

pha·ryn·ge·al (fəríndʒi:əl, fəríndʒəl, færindʒíːəl) *adj.* of, pertaining to or near the pharynx [fr. Mod. L. *pharyngeus*]

pharynges alt. *pl.* of PHARYNX

phar·yn·gi·tis (færindʒáitis) *n.* inflammation of the pharynx [Mod. L. fr. Gk *pharunx* (*pharungos*), throat]

phar·ynx (fǽriŋks) *pl.* **phar·yn·ges** (fəríndʒi:z), **phar·ynx·es** *n.* in vertebrates, the cavity of the alimentary canal between the mouth and the esophagus, communicating with the nasal passages and ears ‖ the corresponding part in invertebrates [Mod. L. fr. Gk *pharunx* (*pharungos*), throat]

phase (feiz) 1. *n.* each of the successive aspects or stages in any course of change or development ‖ (*astron.*) an aspect in the cycle of chang-

ing form or quantity of illumination of the moon or of a planet ‖ (*chem., phys.*) a uniform, bounded portion of matter that is mechanically separable from a heterogeneous physico-chemical system (cf. STATE) ‖ (*phys.*) the progress of a cyclic harmonic motion in relation to some standard point of reference (in time or space), usually expressed in angular measure, 360 degrees representing a full period or cycle **in phase** in or of the same phase ‖ in a synchronized manner **out of phase** in or of different phases ‖ not in a synchronized manner 2. *v.t. pres. part.* **phas·ing** *past* and *past part.* **phased** to cause to be in phase **to phase in** to bring in in phases or as a phase **to phase out** to stop using or cause to cease by phases ‖ to cease by phases **phá·sic** *adj.* [fr. F. *phase* and fr. Mod. L. *phases* pl. of *phasis*, phase fr. Gk *phainein*, to show, appear]

phased array antenna antenna with dipoles with varied signals so arranged so that beams can be formed and scanned rapidly

phase·down (féizdɑun) *v.* to reduce in stages — **phase·down** *n.* —**phase out** *v.*

phase rule (*phys., chem.*) a law of heterogeneous systems in equilibrium: $P+F=C+2$, where P is the number of phases, C the number of components and F is the number of degrees of freedom

pheas·ant (féz'nt) *n.* a member of *Phasianus*, fam. *Phasianidae*, a genus of large, long-tailed gallinaceous game birds. The male has highly colored, varied plumage. They feed on insects, seeds and berries. They are native to Asia, but many species are now found in Europe and North America, esp. *P. colchicus* ‖ any of several related birds of fam. *Phasianidae*, e.g. the peacock, or any of several unrelated birds thought to resemble this, found in various parts of the world [M.E. fr. A.F. *fesant*, O.F. *fesan* fr. L. fr. Gk *phasianos* (*ornis*), Phasian bird, fr. R. *Phasis*]

phel·lem (féləm) *n.* (*bot.*) cork [fr. Gk *phellos*, cork]

phel·lo·derm (félədəːrm) *n.* (*bot.*) a secondary parenchymatous suberized cortex of trees, developed from the inner side of the phellogen (*PERIDERM) **phel·lo·dér·mal** *adj.* [fr. Gk *phellos*, cork+*derma*, skin]

phel·lo·gen (félədʒən) *n.* (*bot.*) a meristem (cork cambium) developing externally in dicotyledonous stems and giving rise to cork tissue and phelloderm **phel·lo·ge·nét·ic, phel·lo·gén·ic** *adjs* [fr. Gk *phellos*, cork+*genēs*, born of]

phen- (fi:n) *prefix* (*chem.*) relating to or derived from benzene [fr. Gk *phainein*, to show and *phainesthai*, to appear (from its originally denoting substances obtained in the manufacture of gas for lighting)]

phe·nac·e·tin, phe·nac·e·tine (finǽsitin) *n.* a white crystalline compound, $C_{10}H_{13}NO_2$, used medicinally to reduce pain or fever [PHEN-+*acetin*, acetic glycerin]

phen·cy·cli·dine [$C_{17}H_{25}N$] (fensáiklidi:n) *n.* (*pharm.*) a central-nervous-system depressant used by veterinarians

phe·net·ic (fenétik) *adj.* (*genetics*) of an organism classification method based on similarity of characteristics. —**phe·net·i·cist** *n.* —**phe·net·i·cal·ly** *adv.* —**phe·net·ics** *n.* Cf CLADISTIC

phen·for·min [$C_{10}H_{15}N_5$] (fenfɔ́rmin) *n.* (*pharm.*) an oral antidiabetic; marketed as DBI

Phenicia *PHOENICIA

Phenician *PHOENICIAN

phenix *PHOENIX

phe·no·bar·bi·tal (fiːnoubɑ́rbital, fiːnoubɑ́rbitɔl) *n.* a white crystalline powder, phenylethyl-barbituric acid, $C_{12}H_{12}N_2O_3$, used medicinally as a hypnotic and sedative

phe·nol (fíːnoul, fíːnɒl) *n.* a white crystalline solid, organic hydroxy acid, C_6H_5OH, with a characteristic smell, poisonous and corrosive, distilled from coal tar and used as a disinfectant and in the manufacture of dyes and plastics ‖ any of the hydroxy derivatives of benzene **phe·nó·lic** *adj.* [fr. Gk *phaino-*, shining fr. *phainein*, to show and *phainesthai*, to appear]

phe·nol·o·gy (finólədʒi:) *n.* (*biol.*) a study of periodic biotic events, e.g. flowering, breeding, migration, in relation to climatic and other factors [PHENOMENON+Gk *logos*, word]

phe·nol·phthal·e·in (fiːnoulθǽliːin) *n.* a white or yellowish compound, $C_{20}H_{14}O_4$, used as a laxative and as a chemical indicator. It turns red in basic solutions and loses its color in acid ones

phe·nom·e·nal (finómən'l) *adj.* (*philos.*) recognized by or experienced by the senses rather than through thought or intuition ‖ concerned with or constituting a phenomenon or phenomena ‖ extraordinary, unusual, *a phenomenal number of voters*

phe·nom·e·nal·ism (finómən'lizəm) *n.* (*philos.*) the theory that phenomena are the only things we can know and that everything else is either nonexistent or inaccessible to the human mind **phe·nóm·e·nal·ist** *n.* and *adj.* **phe·nom·e·nal·ís·tic** *adj.*

phe·nom·e·no·log·i·cal (finɒmən·lódʒik'l) *adj.* of, relating to or characterized by phenomenology ‖ (*philos.*) of, relating to or professing phenomenology

phe·nom·e·nol·o·gy (finɒmənɒlədʒi:) *n.* the observation and description of phenomena ‖ (*philos.*) a method of arriving at absolute essences through the analysis of living experience in disregard of scientific knowledge (*HUSSERL) [fr. PHENOMENON+Gk *logos*, word]

phe·nom·e·non (finómənɒn) *pl.* **phe·nom·e·na** (finómənə) *n.* (*philos.*) something known by sense perception rather than by thought or intuition ‖ any fact or event which can be described and explained in scientific terms ‖ an extraordinary or remarkable event, thing, person etc. [L.L. *phaenomenon* fr. Gk *phainomenon*, appearing, apparent fr. *phainesthai*, to appear]

phen·o·thi·a·zine [$C_{12}H_9NS$] (fenəθáiəzi:n) *n.* (*pharm.*) a deworming drug used by veterinarians

phe·no·type (fíːnətaip) *n.* the appearance of an organism due to the response of genotypic (inherited) characters to the environment ‖ all the individuals belonging to such a type (opp. GENOTYPE) **phe·no·týp·ic** (fiːnətípik), **phe·no·týp·i·cal** *adjs* [G. *phänotypus* fr. L. fr. Gk]

phen·tol·a·mine [$C_{17}H_{19}N_3O$] (fentóləmi:n) *n.* (*pharm.*) drug used to block action of the adrenal medulla used in diagnosis of tumors; marketed as Regitine

phen·yl (fén'l, fí:n'l) *n.* the monovalent radical, C_6H_5, of which benzene is the hydride. It is the basis of many aromatic derivatives [fr. Gk *phaino-*, shining fr. *phainein*, to show and *phainesthai*, to appear]

phen·yl·ke·to·nu·ri·a (fenilki:tounjú:ri:ə) *n.* (*med.*) genetic mental retardation due to inability of the body to metabolize the amino acid phenylalanine. *abbr.* PKU

pher·o·mone (fέərəmoun) *n.* (*biochem.*) chemical substance secreted to produce a response by others of the same species, particularly by insects, esp. in relation to sexual attraction. —**pher·o·mon·al** *adj.* Cf ECTOHORMONE

phi (fai) *n.* the twenty-first letter (Φ, ϕ = ph) of the Greek alphabet

phi·al (fáiəl) *n.* a small glass bottle, esp. for medicines [M.E. fr. O.F. *fiole, phiole* fr. L. fr. Gk *phialē*, a flat shallow bowl]

Phi Be·ta Kap·pa (fáibeitəkǽpə) *n.* a national academic honorary society of the U.S.A., founded in 1776. College and university students may be elected to membership, usually in their senior year [fr. initial letters of Gk *philosophia biou kubernētēs*, philosophy the guide of life, the society's motto]

Phid·i·as (fídi:əs) (c. 500–c. 431 B.C.), Greek sculptor who was appointed by Pericles to beautify Athens. His works include the sculptural decoration of the Parthenon and the monumental statue of Athene which it housed, as well as the statue of Zeus at Olympia which was one of the Seven Wonders of the World

Phil·a·del·phi·a (filədélfi:ə) the fourth largest city (pop. 1,688,210) of the U.S.A., an international port, commercial and industrial center on the Delaware River, E. Pennsylvania. Industries: food processing, mechanical engineering, chemicals, metallurgy, shipbuilding, publishing, textiles, petroleum. Colonial monuments include the courthouse (1732), State House, or Independence Hall (1732–53), numerous private houses. University of Pennsylvania (1791). The city was founded as a Quaker settlement (1682) by Penn, was the scene of the Continental Congresses (1774–83) and the signing of the Declaration of Independence (1776), and was the capital of the U.S.A. (1790–1800)

phi·lan·der (filǽndər) *v.i.* (of a man) to flirt ‖ (of a man) to have many but casual love affairs **phi·lan·der·er** *n.* [fr. Gk *philandros* *adj.*, (of a woman) loving men]

---

phil·an·throp·ic (filənθrópik) *adj.* doing good works, actively benevolent ‖ showing philanthropy **phil·an·thróp·i·cal** *adj.* [fr. F. *philanthropique* fr. Gk]

phi·lan·thro·pist (filǽnθrəpist) *n.* a humanitarian, esp. one who disinterestedly gives large gifts of money for particular causes

phi·lan·thro·py (filǽnθrəpi:) *pl.* **phi·lan·thro·pies** *n.* generous help or benevolence toward one's fellow men ‖ an instance of this [fr. L.L. *philanthropia* fr. Gk fr. *philos*, loving+*anthrōpos*, man]

phil·a·tel·ic (filətélik) *adj.* relating to philately **phi·lat·el·ist** (filǽt'list) *n.* an expert in philately ‖ a stamp collector

phi·lat·e·ly (filǽt'li:) *n.* the collection and study of postage stamps, envelopes bearing postmarks etc., usually as a hobby [fr. F. *philatélie* fr. Gk *philos*, loving+*ateleia*, tax exemption (taken as=postage stamp)]

Phi·le·mon and Bau·cis (filí:mən, failí:mən, bɔ́sis) (*Gk mythol.*) a peasant and his wife who gave hospitality to Zeus and Hermes traveling incognito on the earth. They became priest and priestess of Zeus and, when they had grown very old together, they were turned into intertwined trees. Their names are a symbol of conjugal love

Philemon, Epistle to (filí:mən) the 18th book of the New Testament. It is a personal letter written by St Paul to Philemon, a Colossian, asking him to forgive his runaway slave

phil·har·mon·ic (filharmónik, filərmónik) *adj.* loving music (only used in titles of orchestras, musical societies etc.) [F. *philharmonique* fr. Gk *philos*, loving+*harmonikos*, harmonic]

phil·hel·lene (filhéli:n) *n.* a person who admires Greece, its people, culture etc. ‖ (*hist.*) a supporter of the cause of Greek independence **phil·hel·len·ic** (filhəlénik) *adj.* **phil·hel·len·ism** (filhélinizəm) **phil·hél·len·ist** *ns* [fr. Gk *philellēn* adj. fr. *philos*, loving+*Hellēn*, Hellene]

Phil·ip (filip), St (*d.* c. 80), one of the 12 Apostles. Feast: May 1

Philip (Marcus Julius Philippus, 204–49), Roman emperor (244–9). The millennium of Rome's foundation was celebrated (248) during his reign

Philip II (382–336 B.C.), king of Macedon (359–336 B.C.). A great statesman and general, he unified his kingdom, favored Greek culture and created a highly skilled army. His defeat of Athens and Thebes (338) made Macedon the leading power in Greece. He was assassinated while preparing an expedition against the Persians, and was succeeded by his son Alexander the Great

Phi·lip·pic (filípik) *n.* any of a number of speeches in which Demosthenes warned his fellow-countrymen of the danger to which Greece was exposed by the expansion of Philip II of Macedon **phi·lip·pic** (*rhet.*) an angry tirade filled with invective

Phil·ip·pine (filipi:n) *adj.* of or relating to the Philippine Is or to the Republic of the Philippines

Philip V (238–179 B.C.), king of Macedon (221–179 B.C.), son of Demetrius II. He fought two wars against the Romans (215–205 B.C. and 200–197). He was defeated by Flamininus at Cynoscephalae (197)

Philip I (*Span.* Felipe) 'the Handsome' (1478–1506), king of Castile (1506), son of Emperor Maximilian I

Philip II (1527–98), king of Spain and the Two Sicilies (1556–98), of the Netherlands (1555–98) and, as Philip I, of Portugal (1580–98), son of Emperor Charles V. His reign was devoted to increasing the power of Spain and the Church. He married (1554) Mary I of England, but the English alliance ended with her death (1558). The Treaty of Cateau-Cambrésis (1559) left Spain as the dominant European colonial power, and Spain became still more powerful with the defeat of the Turks at Lepanto (1571). Philip governed repressively through the Inquisition. The northern provinces of the Netherlands rose (1567) against Alba, whom he had appointed governor, and were declared independent (1581). He unsuccessfully supported the Holy League against Henri IV, and failed in his attempt to invade England by the Armada (1588). He conquered Portugal (1580)

Philip III (1578–1621), king of Spain and the Two Sicilies (1598–1621) and, as Philip II, king of Portugal (1598–1621), son of Philip II of Spain. His reign marked the decline of the Spanish Empire, but was a golden age in

Spanish culture (Cervantes, Lope de Vega, El Greco)

Philip IV (1605–65), king of Spain and the Two Sicilies (1621–65) and, as Philip III, king of Portugal (1621–40), son of Philip III of Spain. He was forced to reaffirm the independence of the Netherlands in the Treaties of Westphalia (1648) and to cede Roussillon and Artois to France in the Treaty of the Pyrenees (1659)

Philip V (1683–1746), first Bourbon king of Spain (1700–46), grandson of Louis XIV. His designation by Charles II as successor to the Spanish throne precipitated the War of the Spanish Succession. The attempts of his minister, Alberoni, to regain the territory lost by the Treaty of Utrecht (1713) resulted in his defeat by the Quadruple Alliance (1720). He concluded the Family Compact with France (1733) and regained the Two Sicilies (1734)

Philip kings of France and dukes of Burgundy *PHILIPPE

Philip 'the Magnanimous' (1504–67), landgrave of Hesse (1509–67) and a leader of the Reformation in Germany. He was a prominent member of the Schmalkaldic League, established the first Protestant university (Marburg, 1527) and tried to reconcile Luther and Zwingli (1529)

Philip (*d.* 1676), American Indian leader in King Philip's War

Philip, Prince, duke of Edinburgh (1921–), consort of Elizabeth II

Philip Ne·ri (nέəri:), St (Filippo Romolo de' Neri, 1515–95), Italian priest. He founded the Congregation of the Oratory (1564). Feast: May 26

Phi·lippe I (filí:p) (1052–1108), king of France (1060–1108), son of Henri I. He enlarged his kingdom and supported Robert II of Normandy in his revolt against William I of England

Philippe III 'the Bold' (1245–85), king of France (1270–85), son of Louis IX. He gained possession of Toulouse, Auvergne and part of Poitou (1271), but died after an unsuccessful attempt to gain Aragon

Philippe IV 'the Fair' (1268–1314), king of France (1285–1314), son of Philippe III. He greatly increased royal authority, reduced feudal power and came into conflict with Pope Boniface VIII over clerical taxation. His stand against the papacy was approved by the States General, which he summoned for the first time (1302). He triumphed with the election to the papacy (1305) of the French Clement V, and the establishment (1309) of the papacy at Avignon. He acquired Navarre, Champagne, part of Flanders and Lyon for the French crown

Philippe V 'the Tall' (1294–1322), king of France (1316–22), son of Philippe IV. Appointed regent on the death (1316) of his brother Louis X, he proclaimed himself king on the death of Louis's posthumous son, Jean I, claiming that the succession was governed by Salic law. He frequently summoned the States General

Philippe VI (1293–1350), king of France (1328–50), the first of the Valois. His claim to the throne, based on Salic law, was disputed by Edward III of England, thus starting (1337) the Hundred Years' War. He was defeated at Crécy (1346) and lost Calais to the English. He acquired the Dauphiné (1343) and Montpellier (1349)

Philippe 'the Bold' (1342–1404), duke of Burgundy (1363–1404), son of Jean II. He distinguished himself in battle at Poitiers (1356). He was regent (1380–8) for Charles V, and was the effective ruler during much of Charles's reign

Philippe 'the Good' (1396–1467), duke of Burgundy (1419–67), son of Jean the Fearless. He supported the claims of Henry V of England to the French throne prior to making peace with Charles VII (1435). He extended his territories into the Netherlands, and founded (1429) the Order of the Golden Fleece

Philippe II Augustus (1165–1223), king of France (1180–1223), son of Louis VII. He allied himself (1189) with the future Richard I of England against Henry II, accompanied Richard on the 3rd Crusade (1190–1), and resumed the war against England. His victory over King John at Bouvines (1214) gained him Normandy, Anjou, Poitou, Maine and Touraine. His administrative reforms included the establishment of royal courts of justice. He fostered the growth of towns and trade, and was a founder of the University of Paris

Philippe E·ga·li·té (eigæli:tei) *ORLÉANS, Louis-Philippe Joseph, duc d'

Phi·lippe·ville (fi:li:pvi:l, fílipvil) *SKIKDA

Phi·lip·pi (filípai) an ancient town of Macedonia, near which Antony and the future Emperor Augustus decisively defeated Brutus and Cassius (42 B.C.)

Phi·lip·pi·ans, Epistle to the (filípi:ənz) the eleventh book of the New Testament, a letter of gratitude and advice written by St Paul during imprisonment either in Ephesus (c.53) or in Rome (c.60)

Philippine Islands the group of islands constituting the Republic of the Philippines

Philippine Sea, Battle of the a naval engagement (1944) during the 2nd world war in which a U.S. naval aviation force defeated the Japanese, paving the way for Gen. MacArthur's return to the islands

Phil·ip·pines, Republic of the (fílipi:nz) a republic (area 115,708 sq. miles, pop. 54,500,000) of S.E. Asia, comprising 7,107 islands, the northernmost part of the Malay Archipelago. Capital and chief town: Manila. Principal islands: Luzon, Mindanao, Mindoro, Palawan, and the Visayas. People: Filipino (Malay), 1% Chinese, small aborigine (pygmy) and Indonesian minorities. Language: Tagalog (official), 75 other Malayo-Polynesian languages. 35% also speak English, 2% Spanish. Religion: 75% Roman Catholic, with Protestant, Moslem, independent Catholic, Animist, Buddhist and other minorities. The islands are mountainous (few peaks over 5,000 ft) and largely volcanic, with fertile valleys. The land is 44% forest, 27% cultivated. Highest point: Mt Apo (9,540 ft), on Mindanao. Except for primitive tribes, the population is concentrated on the coasts. Average summer and winter temperatures (F.): coast 82° and 77°, interior mountains 70° and 60°. Rainfall: 40–120 ins. Rainy seasons: summer and autumn in W. Luzon and W. Visayas, winter in E. Luzon, E. Visayas, and N.E. Mindanao. Typhoons are frequent north of Samar. Livestock: water buffaloes (carabao), hogs, cattle, goats, poultry, horses. Crops: rice, abaca, copra, sugarcane, corn, coconuts, tobacco, coffee, sweet potatoes, fruit (esp. pineapples), vegetables. Forestry products: lumber, gums, resins, dyes, vegetable oils, rattan. Fisheries. Mineral resources: gold, copper, chromite, silver, lead, zinc, manganese, iron ore, mercury, coal, salt, nickel, uranium. Industries: textiles, tobacco, hydroelectricity, footwear, cement, wood products, plastics. coconut oil refining, rubber goods, embroidery, hats, mats, pottery. Exports: sugar, lumber, copra, minerals and metals, abaca, coconut oil. Imports: machinery, fuels and oil, textiles, cereals, vehicles, foodstuffs. Ports: Manila, Cebu, Iloilo, Davao, Zamboanga. There are 26 universities. Monetary unit: peso (100 centavos). HISTORY. Inhabited by Negritos, the islands were invaded by Indonesians (3rd millennium B.C.). They were visited by Japanese and Chinese traders (8th c. A.D.) and by Moslem Arab missionaries (14th–15th cc.). A Spanish expedition led by Magellan reached the Philippines (1521) and a Spanish settlement was founded (1565). Revolts against Spanish rule were unsuccessful until the Spanish-American War (1898), after which the Philippines were transferred to the U.S.A., which put down a Filipino rebellion (1899–1901). As trade with the U.S.A. developed, economic progress was made, and communications and education were improved. Quezon became (Sept. 1935) first president of the Philippines. The islands were occupied (1942–4) by the Japanese. The Philippines joined the U.N. (1945) and became a Republic (July 4, 1946), but continued to receive large amounts of U.S. aid to repair war damage and strengthen the economy. The Philippines joined the South East Asia Treaty Organization (1954). President Ramón Magsaysay (1953–7) ended the Communist-dominated Huk guerrilla movement. President Diosdado Macapagal (1961–5) tried unsuccessfully to confederate the Philippines with Malaya and Indonesia. President Ferdinand Marcos (1965–86) imposed martial law (1972–81) and changed the constitution (1981) to maintain his power after martial law was lifted. The assassination of the political opposition leader Benigno Aquino (1983) caused a political crisis. The opposition made substantial gains in the 1984 elections. After a court acquitted armed forces chief of staff Gen. Fabian Ver of complicity in the Aquino slaying,

CONCISE PRONUNCIATION KEY: **(a)** æ, c*a*t; ɑ, c*ar*; ɔ, f*aw*n; ei, sn*a*ke. **(e)** e, h*e*n; i:, sh*ee*p; iə, d*eer*; εə, b*ear*. **(i)** i, f*i*sh; ai, t*i*ger; ə:, b*i*rd. **(o)** o, *o*x; au, c*ow*; ou, g*oa*t; u, p*oo*r; ɔi, r*oy*al. **(u)** ʌ, d*u*ck; u, b*u*ll; u:, g*oo*se; ə, b*a*cillus; ju:, c*u*be. x, lo*ch*; θ, *th*ink; δ, bo*th*er; z, *Z*en; ʒ, corsa*g*e; dʒ, sava*g*e; ŋ, ora*ng*utan*g*; j, *y*ak; ʃ, fi*sh*; tʃ, fe*tch*; 'l, rabb*le*; 'n, redd*en*. Complete pronunciation key appears inside front cover.

criticism of Marcos and his government increased. A 1986 presidential election between Marcos and Aquino's widow, Corazon, led to widespread allegations of fraud and voter intimidation by the Marcos faction and ultimately led to Marcos's being deposed and forced to leave the country. Mrs. Aquino became president and attempted conciliation among all political groups in the country

Phil·ips (fílips), Ambrose (1674–1749), English poet, pioneer of sentimental landscape poetry in 'A Winter Piece' (1709) and 'Pastorals' (1710)

Phi·lis·ti·a (filísti:ə) the ancient region of Palestine inhabited by the Philistines

Phil·is·tine (fílisti:n, fílistain) n. a member of an ancient people who settled (c. 13th c. B.C.) in the coastal region of Palestine. They are thought to have spoken a Semitic language and to have originated in Crete. They were subdued by the Hebrews under Saul and David (10th c. B.C.) **phil·is·tine** 1. adj. lacking culture or having contempt for it 2. n. a person with uncultivated tastes **phíl·is·tin·ism** n.

Phil·lips (fíləps), Wendell (1811–84), leading U.S. abolitionist, orator and reformer. He advocated Union separation from the slave states, and, after emancipation, headed the American Antislavery Society until its dissolution. He also campaigned for temperance and women's rights

Phil·lips curve (fílips) (economics) a graphic presentation of correlation between inflation and unemployment, conceived by A. W. H. Phillips, British economist

phil·lu·men·ist (filú:menist) n. a collector of matchbooks and/or matchbox labels — **phil·lu·men·y** n. the hobby

Phi·lo (fáilou) Jewish-Hellenistic philosopher (c. 20 B.C.–c. 54 A.D.). He believed in the divinity of the Jewish law but elaborated an allegorical interpretation of the Bible, purporting to show that it embodies the ideas of Greek philosophy, esp. Plato. His main work is his massive exegesis of the Pentateuch

phil·o·den·dron (filədéndrən) pl. **phil·o·den·drons, phil·o·den·dra** (filədéndrə) n. any of various members of genus Philodendron, tropical American climbing plants. Many are cultivated as house plants [Mod. L. fr. Gk, neuter of philodendros adj., treeloving]

phil·o·log·ic (filələdʒik) adj. philological

phil·o·log·i·cal (filələdʒik'l) adj. of or relating to philology

phi·lol·o·gist (filóledʒist) n. a specialist in philology

phi·lol·o·gy (filóledʒi:) n. the study of language from the written texts by which it is known ‖ the study of texts and their transmission [fr. L. philologia, love of talk fr. Gk]

Phil·o·me·la (filəmí:lə) (Gk mythol.) daughter of the king of Athens. She was raped and had her tongue torn out by Tereus, king of Thrace, the husband of her sister Procne. The gods turned Philomela into a nightingale and her sister into a swallow

phil·o·pro·gen·i·tive (filouproudʒénitiv) adj. (rhet.) tending to produce many offspring (rhet.) loving one's offspring [fr. Gk philos, loving+L. progignere (progenitus), to beget]

phi·los·o·pher (filósəfər) n. a person who engages in the study of philosophy ‖ (pop.) a person who accepts misfortune with stoic calm [M.E. philosophre fr. O.E. fr. L. fr. Gk fr. philos, loving+sophos, wise]

philosopher's stone, philosophers' stone a mythical stone or substance much sought after by alchemists, who believed it had the power to change base metals into gold and to grant eternal youth

phil·o·soph·ic (filəsófik) adj. of or relating to philosophy ‖ (pop.) resigned in the face of troubles, wisely unemotional about what cannot be altered **phil·o·sóph·i·cal** adj. [fr. L.L. philosophicus]

phi·los·o·phize (filósəfaiz) pres. part. **phi·los·o·phiz·ing** past and past part. **phi·los·o·phized** v.i. to theorize ‖ (pop.) to moralize [fr. Gk philosophos, philosopher]

phi·los·o·phy (filósəfi:) pl. **phi·los·o·phies** n. the love or pursuit of wisdom, i.e. the search for basic principles. Traditionally, Western philosophy comprises five branches of study: metaphysics, ethics, aesthetics, epistemology and logic ‖ systematized principles of any subject or branch of knowledge, the philosophy of history ‖ an attitude towards life ‖ (pop.) calm resignation, he faced the situation with philosophy

[M.E. fr. O.F. philosophie fr. L. philosophia fr. Gk fr. philos, loving+sophos, wise, a wise man]

phil·ter, phil·tre (fíltər) n. a potion supposed to make a person fall in love ‖ any magic potion [F. philtre fr. L. philtrum fr. Gk fr. philein, to love]

phi me·son (faí mí:sʌn) n. (particle phys.) an unstable elementary meson particle with negative charge parity and a large mass (1019 MEV). also phi

Phips, Phipps (fips), Sir William (1651–95), the first royal governor (1692–5) of Massachusetts. He appointed a commission to try those accused of witchcraft

phle·bit·ic (fləbítik) adj. relating to or having phlebitis

phle·bi·tis (fləbáitis) n. inflammation of the veins, usually in the legs [Mod. L. fr. Gk phleps (phlebos)]

phle·bol·o·gy (flebólədʒi:) n. (med.) medical study of the veins

phle·bot·o·my (fləbótəmi:) pl. **phle·bot·o·mies** n. (hist.) the act or practice of opening a vein for the purpose of bloodletting as a cure for various ailments ‖ an instance of this [O.F. flebothomie fr. L. phlebotomia fr. Gk fr. phleps (phlebos), vein+tomos, a cutting]

phlegm (flem) n. mucus esp. when it occurs in excessive quantity in the respiratory passages ‖ (hist.) one of the four humors ‖ stoic self-possession, imperturbability **phleg·mat·ic** (flegmǽtik) adj. having or showing stoic self-possession, imperturbable **phleg·mát·i·cal** adj. [M.E. fleen, fleume, fleme fr. O.F. fr. L.L. fr. Gk phlegma, inflammation, phlegm]

phlo·em (flóuem) n. a complex tissue in the vascular system of higher plants, consisting of sieve tubes and companion cells and usually also parenchyma and sclerenchyma. It serves esp. in conduction. but also in support and storage [G. fr. Gk phloos, bark]

phlo·gis·tic (floudʒístik) adj. (med.) of or relating to inflammations ‖ (hist.) or relating to phlogiston [fr. Gk phlogistos, inflammable and fr. PHLOGISTON]

phlo·gis·ton (floudʒístɒn, floudʒístən) n. (hist.) a hypothetical substance formerly assumed to be present in all substances which burn, and to escape during combustion, leaving an ash (calx) behind [Mod. L. fr. Gk fr. phlogizein, to set on fire]

phlox (floks) n. a member of Phlox, fam. Polemoniaceae, a genus of herbaceous plants native to North America and widely cultivated, having clusters of white, pink or purple, salver-shaped flowers [L.=a kind of flower, flame, fr. Gk]

Phnom Penh (p'nóumpén) the capital (pop. 70,000) and chief river port of Cambodia, on the Mekong River, an agricultural market and communications (rail and air) center. Industries: food processing, brewing, distilling, textiles, wood manufactures. Handicrafts: jewelry, goldwork

pho·bia (fóubi:ə) n. morbid and often irrational dread of some specific thing [Mod. L. fr. Gk phobos, fear]

Pho·cis (óusis) a region of central Greece on the N.E. Gulf of Corinth. It formed a league of 20 city-states (7th c. B.C.) to guard the oracle at Delphi and was involved in a series of wars to defend it (c. 590 B.C., c. 448 B.C. and 355–346 B.C.), in the last of which Phocis was conquered by Macedon

Phoe·be (fí:bi:) (Gk mythol.) Artemis as goddess of the moon

phoe·be (fí:bi:) n. a member of Sayornis, a genus of North American flycatchers, esp. S. phoebe [imit.]

Phoe·bus (fí:bəs) (Gk mythol.) Apollo as god of the sun

Phoe·ni·cian, Phe·ni·cian (finíʃən, finí:ʃən) 1. adj. of Phoenicia, its colonies, people or language 2. n. a native of Phoenicia

—The Phoenicians, a Semitic people, settled in Phoenicia (c. 3000 B.C.). Centered on Byblos, Tyre and Sidon, they were at the height of their power c. 1200–c. 800 B.C., trading throughout the Mediterranean. They exported cedar wood, purple dye, textiles, glass, metalwork, spices and perfumes, and founded trading stations and colonies, notably at Carthage (c. 814 B.C.). Phoenician seamen sailed into the Atlantic, and are thought to have reached Britain and to have explored the west coast of Africa. The Phoenicians were the first to devise an alphabet. Phoenicia was conquered (6th c. B.C.) by

Persia, and Phoenicians made an important contribution to Persian sea power and craftsmanship

Phoe·ni·cia, Phe·ni·cia (finíʃə, finí:ʃə) an ancient country now forming the coastal region of Lebanon and part of Syria

Phoe·nix (fí:niks) the capital (pop. 764,911) and largest city of Arizona, center of an irrigated agricultural district: electrical and electronic engineering, farm machinery, aircraft, food processing, metallurgy, tourism

phoe·nix, phe·nix (fí:niks) n. (Egypt. mythol.) a bird of gorgeous plumage, sacred to the sun, reborn from the ashes of the funeral pyre which it made for itself when each life span of 500 or 600 years was over ‖ something or someone seen as resembling this bird, esp. with respect to its power of self-regeneration [O.E. and O.F. fenix fr. M.L. phenix, and L. phoenix fr. Gk phoinix]

Phoenix Islands eight coral islands (area 11 sq. miles, pop. 1,200), of which Canton and Enderbury have been jointly controlled by the U.S.A. and Great Britain since 1939, the rest being part of Kiribati

phon (fon) n. (phys.) a unit of loudness, equivalent to a sound intensity of 1 decibel [fr. Gk phōnē, sound, voice]

pho·nate (fóuneit) pres. part. **pho·nat·ing** past and past part. **pho·nat·ed** v.i. (physiol.) to produce a vocal sound **pho·na·tion** n. [fr. Gk phōnē, voice]

phone (foun) 1. n. a telephone 2. v.i. and t. pres. part. **phon·ing** past and past part. **phoned** to telephone [TELEPHONE]

phone n. (phon.) a simple speech sound [fr. Gk phōnē, voice]

phone-in (fóunin) n. a broadcast program inviting audience telephone participation with questions or comments

pho·neme (fóuni:m) n. a class of closely related speech sounds in a given language considered as forming a unit **pho·né·mic** adj. **pho·né·mi·cal·ly** adv. **pho·né·mics** n. the branch of linguistics dealing with the phonemes of a particular language [fr. F. phonème fr. Gk]

pho·net·ic (fənétik, founétik) adj. of or relating to vocal sounds and speech ‖ consistently representing sounds by the same symbols, phonetic spelling ‖ relating to phonetics **pho·nét·i·cal·ly** adv. **pho·ne·ti·cian** (founitíʃən) n. a specialist in phonetics **pho·nét·i·cist** n. a phonetist **pho·nét·ics** n. the branch of language study concerned with the production of speech sounds, alone or in combination, and their representation in writing ‖ the phonetic system of a given language [fr. Mod. L. phoneticus fr. Gk phōnētikos fr. phōnein, to utter sound]

pho·ne·tist (fóunitist) n. a phonetician ‖ someone who advocates phonetic spelling [fr. Gk phōnētos, to be spoken]

phoney *PHONY

phon·ic (fónik, fóunik) adj. of or relating to sound, esp. speech sounds [fr. Gk phōnē, voice]

phon·ics (fóniks) n. the use of sound-symbol (phoneme-grapheme) relationships in the teaching of reading

pho·no·an·gi·og·ra·phy (founouænʒi:ɒgrəfi:) n. (med.) analysis of blood flow by sound

pho·no·car·di·og·ra·phy (founoukɑrdi:ɒgrəfi:) n. (med.) the recording of heart sounds. —**pho·no·car·di·o·gram** n. the record —**pho·no·car·di·o·graph** n. the instrument used

pho·no·gram (fóunəgræm) n. a symbol representing a spoken word, sound or syllable, e.g. in shorthand [fr. Gk phōnē, sound, voice +gramma, letter, writing]

pho·no·graph (fóunəgræf, fóunəgraf) n. (Am.= Br. Gramophone) a machine for reproducing sounds recorded on a disk or cylinder **pho·no·graph·ic** (founəgrǽfik) adj. **pho·no·gráph·i·cal·ly** adv. [fr. Gk phōnē, sound+-graphos, written]

pho·nog·ra·phy (founógrəfi:) n. phonetic spelling or writing ‖ a phonetic shorthand system [fr. Gk phōnē, sound+graphia, writing]

pho·no·lite (fóun'lait) n. a gray or green volcanic rock giving a ringing sound when struck **pho·no·lit·ic** (founʼlítik) adj. [fr. Gk phōnē, sound+lithos, stone]

pho·no·log·ic (founʼlódʒik) adj. relating to or according to the principles of phonology **pho·no·lóg·i·cal** adj.

pho·nol·o·gist (founóledʒist, fənóledʒist) n. a specialist in phonology

pho·nol·o·gy (founóledʒi:, fənóledʒi:) n. the study of speech sounds, esp. of the theory and development of sound changes within a given language ‖ the system of phonetics of a language ‖ the study of phonetics or of phonemics [fr. Gk *phōnē*, voice, sound+*logos*, word]

pho·nons (fóunɒns) n. (*phys.*) a quantum of heat energy in the acoustic vibration of a crystal lattice

pho·no·pho·tog·ra·phy (fóunofətɒgrəfi:) n. photographic recording of vibrations created by speech. *Cf* VOICEPRINT

pho·nop·si·a (founɒpsi:ə) n. (*physiol.*) the visual perceptions of color resulting from sound

pho·no·tac·tics (fóunoutæktiks) n. (*linguistics*) analysis of sound structure and function in language. —**pho·no·tac·tice** adj.

pho·ny, pho·ney (fóuni:) comp. **pho·ni·er** superl. **pho·ni·est** 1. adj. (*pop.*) not genuine, counterfeit 2. pl. **pho·nies** n. (*pop.*) a person who is not what he pretends to be [origin unknown]

pho·ny mine (fóuni:) (*mil.*) an object of any available material, used to simulate a mine in a phony minefield (which see)

phony minefield (*mil.*) an area of ground used to simulate a minefield with the object of deceiving the enemy

pho·rate [C₇H₁₇O₂PS₃] (fóurait) n. (*chem.*) toxic biodegradable insecticide used esp. to protect seeds

phos·gene (fózdʒi:n) n. carbonyl chloride, COCl₂, a colorless, poisonous gas with a smell like musty hay, used in the dyestuff industry and in chemical warfare in the 1st world war **phos·ge·nite** (fózdʒinait) n. a mineral, Pb₂Cl₂CO₃, consisting of lead chloride and lead carbonate, occurring as tetragonal crystals [fr. Gk *phós*, light+*genēs*, born, produced]

phos·pham·i·don [C₁₀H₁₉ClNO₅P] (fosfǽmidɒn) n. (*chem.*) organophosophorus insecticide and miticide

phos·pha·tase (fósfəteis) n. any of many enzymes in body tissues, which break down compounds of carbohydrates and phosphates [PHOSPHATE+DIASTASE]

phos·phate (fósfeit) n. any salt or ester of phosphoric acid ‖ (pl.) any of several substances containing these (e.g. phosphate of calcium), used as fertilizer to supply phosphorus **phos·phat·ic** (fosfǽtik) adj. of or containing phosphates or phosphoric acid **phos·pha·tide** (fósfətaid) n. (*biochem.*) one of a class of complex esters of phosphoric acid and an alcohol containing more than one hydroxyl group (e.g. glycerol) and containing usually fatty acids and a nitrogen base. They are found in all living cells in association with fats **phós·pha·tize** pres. part. **phos·pha·tiz·ing** past and past part. **phos·pha·tized** v.t. to treat with a phosphate or phosphates ‖ to change into a phosphate [F.]

phos·phene (fósfi:n) n. the bright image formed as a result of mechanical stimulation of the retina in the absence (usually) of light, e.g. when pressure is put on the eyeball with the eyelid shut [fr. Gk *phós*, light+*phainein*, to show]

phos·phide (fósfaid, fósfid) n. (*chem.*) a binary compound consisting of phosphorus with another element or a radical [PHOSPHORUS]

phos·phine (fósfi:n, fósfin) n. a colorless, poisonous gas, PH₃, with a smell like garlic ‖ a basic orange dye [PHOSPHORUS]

phos·phite (fósfait) n. any salt or ester of phosphorous acid [F.]

phos·pho·e·nol·py·ru·vic acid (fosfoui:nɒlpairú:vik) (*biochem.*) high-energy phosphate that releases energy for muscular activity

phos·pho·fruc·to·ki·nase (fósfoufrʌktóukineis) n. (*biochem.*) an enzyme that catalyzes conversion of fructose in carbohydrate metabolism. — **phosphofructokinase disease** *med*

phos·pho·gly·cer·al·de·hyde [OHCCHOHCH₂-OPO₃H₂] (fósfouglisərǽldehaid) n. (*biochem.*) an intermediate product in the metabolism process of carbohydrates

phos·pho·lip·id (fósfoulípid, fósfouláipid) n. a phosphatide [PHOSPHORUS+LIPID]

phos·pho·lip·id (fósfoulípid) n. (*biochem.*) a lipid made up of an ester of phosphoric acid with an alcohol, a fatty acid and a nitrogen base, e.g., lecithin, sphingomyelin

phos·pho·pro·tein (fósfoupróuti:n, fósfoupróuti:in) n. a protein in which the protein molecule is combined with a phosphorus compound other than a nucleic acid or lecithin (e.g. caseinogen)

phos·phor (fósfər) n. any of a large number of naturally occurring or synthetic materials that are phosphorescent or fluorescent and that consist of sulfides, silicates, phosphates etc., often activated with a metallic impurity (e.g. copper, silver, lead). Phosphors are used for luminescent coatings in cathode-ray tubes, fluorescent lamps, luminous dials etc. [fr. L. *phosphorus*, phosphorus]

phosphor bronze a very hard, tough bronze containing a small amount of phosphorus. It is used in bearings, ships' propellers etc.

phos·pho·resce (fosfərés) pres. part. **phos·pho·resc·ing** past and past part. **phos·pho·resced** v.i. to exhibit phosphorescence [PHOSPHORUS]

phos·pho·res·cence (fosfərés'ns) n. a luminescence characterized by a temperature-dependent time rate of decay after the stimulation has been removed (cf. FLUORESCENCE), e.g. in many forms of bioluminescence [PHOSPHORESCENT]

phos·pho·res·cent (fosfərés'nt) adj. exhibiting phosphorescence [PHOSPHORUS]

phos·pho·ret·ed, phos·pho·ret·ted (fósfəretid) adj. combined with phosphorus

phos·phor·ic (fosfórik, fosfórik) adj. pertaining to phosphorus, esp. in compounds where this has a high valence [fr. F. *phosphorique*]

phosphoric acid a colorless, crystalline bitter acid, H₃PO₄, used in the manufacture of fertilizers, in sugar refining etc.

phos·pho·rism (fósfərizəm) n. phosphorus poisoning

phos·pho·rous (fósfərəs) adj. pertaining to phosphorus, esp. in compounds where this has a low valence [fr. F. *phosphoreux*]

phosphorous acid a crystalline acid, H₃PO₃, which absorbs oxygen easily, used as a reducing agent

phos·pho·rus (fósfərəs) pl. **phos·pho·ri** (fósfərai) n. a nonmetallic element (symbol P, at. no. 15, at. mass 30.9738) which can exist in several allotropic forms. White or yellow phosphorus is an unstable, poisonous, waxy substance which is highly inflammable, oxidizing with a faint glow in air at room temperature. Red phosphorus is a stable, less inflammable, nonpoisonous powder obtained by heating white phosphorus. Organic compounds of phosphorus are present in all living cells. Inorganic compounds are important constituents of minerals, soil, bones and teeth, and are used in the manufacture of matches [L. fr. Gk *phósphoros* adj. fr. *phós*, light+*phoros*, bringing]

phos·phu·ret·ed, phos·phu·ret·ted (fósferetid) adj. phosphoreted [fr. obs. *phosphuret*; phosphide fr. Mod. L. *phosphoretum*]

phot (fot, fout) n. a unit of illumination, being the illumination when 1 lumen is incident on 1 square centimeter of a surface [fr. Gk *phós* (*phótos*), light]

pho·tic zone (fóutik) (*envir.*) the region of aquatic environment in which the intensity of natural light is sufficient for photosynthesis

Pho·ti·us (fóuʃi:əs) (c. 820–c. 891), patriarch of Constantinople. A partisan of the Iconoclasts, he replaced St Ignatius as patriarch (858–67), but was not recognized by the papacy. He was again patriarch (877–86)

photo- (fóutou) prefix having to do with light ‖ having to do with photography or photographs [fr. Gk *phós* (*phótos*), light]

pho·to pl. **pho·tos** n. a photograph, esp. a snapshot

pho·to·au·to·troph (fóutoɔtoutrouf) n. (*biol.*) self-nourishing organism that utilizes light as an energy source, e.g., blue-green algae

pho·to·bi·ol·o·gy (fóutoubaiɒlədʒi:) n. study of effect of light on life. —**pho·to·bi·ot·ic** adj. — **pho·to·bi·ol·o·gist** n.

pho·to·bot·a·ny (fóutoubɒtəni:) n. branch of botany that deals with effect of light on plants

pho·to·cell (fóutousel) n. a photoelectric cell

pho·to·chem·i·cal (fóutoukémik'l) adj. of or relating to photochemistry ‖ of or relating to the action of light on chemical properties or reactions

pho·to·chem·is·try (fóutoukémistri:) n. the branch of chemistry dealing with the effects of electromagnetic radiation (esp. in the visible region of the spectrum) on chemical reactivity (e.g. in photography or photosynthesis)

pho·to·chro·mat·ic (fóutoukroumætik) adj. 1. of color photography. 2. of colored light.

pho·to·chrom·ism (fóutoukróumizəm) n. property of changing color under light or lack of light. —**pho·to·chrom·ic** adj.

pho·to·chron·o·graph (fóutəkrónəgræf, fóutəkrónəgruf) n. a camera taking exposures at timed intervals, used to record biological changes etc. ‖ a photograph taken by such a camera ‖ (*astron.*) a camera attached to a telescope and used to photograph a heavenly body at timed intervals ‖ (*phys.*) a device for recording small intervals of time

pho·to·co·ag·u·la·tion (fóutoucɒuægju:leiʃən) n. (*med.*) technique of causing tissue to coagulate under intense controlled light, e.g., in ophthalmological surgery. —**pho·to·co·ag·u·la·tive** adj. **pho·to·co·ag·u·la·tor** n. the instrument

pho·to·con·duc·tive (fóutoukəndʌktiv) adj. of, relating to or having the property of photoconductivity

pho·to·con·duc·tiv·i·ty (fóutoukɒndʌktíviti:) n. the property of certain substances (e.g. selenium) of having an electrical conductivity that depends upon the nature and intensity of the electromagnetic radiation impinging upon them (*PHOTOELECTRIC CELL)

photoconductivity cell a type of photoelectric cell

pho·to·cop·i·er (fóutoukɒpi:ər) n. a machine for making photocopies

pho·to·cop·y (fóutoukɒpi:) 1. pl. **pho·to·cop·ies** n. a photographic reproduction of a document, illustration, etc. 2. v.t. pres. part. **pho·to·cop·y·ing** past and past part. **pho·to·cop·ied** to make a photocopy of

pho·to·cube (fóutoukju:be) n. a plastic cube that holds a photograph to inside surface for display

pho·to·cur·rent (fóutoukə:rənt, fóutoukʌrənt) n. a photoelectric current, i.e. one produced by the action of electromagnetic radiation in a photoelectric effect

pho·to·de·tec·tor (fóutouditektər) n. (*electr.*) device sensitive to light, e.g., photodiodes, phototransistors, photoswitches. *also* photosensor

pho·to·do·sim·e·try (fóutoudousimetri:) n. the measurement of total radiation exposure through exposure of a photographic film

pho·to·dy·nam·ic (fóutoudainæmik) adj. of or relating to the toxic effect of light, esp. sunlight, on living organisms

pho·to·e·las·tic (fóutouilæstik) adj. relating to or having the property of photoelasticity

pho·to·e·las·tic·i·ty (fóutoui:læstísiti:) n. the property in certain transparent isotropic solids of becoming birefringent when submitted to stress

—Stresses in engineering components may be investigated by modeling them in glass or a transparent plastic and examining the stressed model by polarized light. The stressed regions in the model rotate the plane of polarization of the light and produce a visible pattern from which the direction and size of the stresses may be deduced

pho·to·e·lec·tric (fóutouiléktrik) adj. of any of the factors involved in the effect of electromagnetic radiation on the electrical behavior of matter

photoelectric cell one of three types of device utilizing a photoelectric effect: (a) a photoconductivity cell, consisting essentially of a photoconductive substance in a current-measuring circuit. It is used most often to measure the intensity or quantity of illumination falling on it. A change in conductivity caused by incident light results in a change in the current carried by the circuit, which is registered by an ammeter (*EXPOSURE METER) (b) a phototube, consisting of an evacuated glass bulb containing a photoemissive cathode and an anode held at a positive potential, which attracts the photoelectron produced in the cathode by incident light. The current so produced may be used to actuate other electrical devices (*ELECTRIC EYE, *PHOTOMULTIPLIER) (c) a photovoltaic cell, used to convert electromagnetic radiation to an electric current, e.g. in a solar battery

photoelectric effect any of several phenomena caused by the interaction of electromagnetic radiation with (usually metallic) substances (*PHOTOEMISSION, *PHOTOCONDUCTIVITY, *PHOTOVOLTAGE)

pho·to·e·lec·tric·i·ty (fóutouilektrísiti:, fóutoui:lektrísiti:) n. electricity produced by the action of electromagnetic radiation ‖ a branch of physics that deals with the physical effects of the interaction of light and matter

pho·to·e·lec·tron (fóutouiléktrɒn) n. an electron released by photoemission

pho·to·e·mis·sion (fóutouimíʃən) n. the process in which electromagnetic radiation incident upon a substance (usually a metal) causes the release of electrons. The process occurs only when the frequency of the radiation is greater than a threshold value characteristic of the substance. The kinetic energy of the photoelectrons is independent of the intensity of radiation, depending only on its frequency

pho·to·e·mis·sive (foutouimíssiv) *adj.* emitting electrons when exposed to radiation of certain wavelengths, or capable of doing so

pho·to·en·grave (foutouingréiv) *pres. part.* **pho·to·en·grav·ing** *past* and *past part.* **pho·to·en·graved** *v.t.* to make a photoengraving of **pho·to·en·gráv·er** *n.* [backformation fr. PHOTO-ENGRAVING]

pho·to·en·grav·ing (foutouingréiviŋ) *n.* (*printing*) a process by which a printing block is made from a photograph: the photograph is photographed onto metal and the parts not to be printed are then mechanically etched away (cf. PHOTOGRAVURE) ‖ a print taken from such a block

pho·to·es·say (foutouései) *n.* a study of a subject presented principally through photographs

pho·to·fab·ri·ca·tion (foutoufæbrikéifən) *n.* (*electr.*) 1. use of photographic process creating integrated circuits on silicon wafers. 2. (*computer*) manufacture of miniaturized semiconductor circuits by photographic reduction before chemical etching

photo finish the finish of a race so close that a photograph at the finish line is required to identify the winner ‖ the end of any very close contest

pho·to·fis·sion (foutoufíʃən) *n.* (*nuclear phys.*) photo-induced nuclear fission

pho·to·flash bomb (foutoufláʃ) (*mil.*) bomb designed to produce a brief and intense illumination for medium-altitude night photography

pho·to·flood (foutouflʌd) *n.* (*photog.*) an electric lamp to which excess voltage is supplied so that it emits especially bright light

pho·to·gen·ic (foutədʒénik) *adj.* photographing to advantage ‖ causing or producing light [fr. PHOTO-+Gk *genēs*, born, produced]

pho·to·gram·me·try (foutəgræmitri:) *n.* the art or process of making a survey or a map with the help of photographs taken esp. from the air [fr. *photogram*, var. of PHOTOGRAPH+Gk *metria*, a measuring]

pho·to·graph (foutəgræf, foutəgrʌf) 1. *n.* a reproduction, usually on photographic paper, made by photography 2. *v.t.* to take a picture of by photography ‖ *v.i.* to practice photography ‖ to appear (in a specified way) in a photograph, *she photographs badly* **pho·tog·ra·pher** (fətógrəfər) *n.* a person who practices photography, esp. as a profession [fr. PHOTO-+Gk *graphos*, written]

pho·to·graph·ic (foutəgræfik) *adj.* pertaining to photography ‖ resembling the process of photography, *a photographic memory* **pho·to·gráph·i·cal·ly** *adv.*

photographic paper a piece of paper that has been coated with an emulsion containing silver salts. When exposed to the light passed through a negative and developed (*PHOTOGRAPHY) it gives a (positive) photograph (cf. FILM)

pho·tog·ra·phy (fətógrəfi:) *n.* the art, process or occupation of producing photographs [fr. Gk *phōs* (*phōtos*), light+*graphia*, writing] —A photographic film is exposed to an image formed by the optical system of a camera, producing a latent image on the film. This image consists of regions exposed to variable quantities of light which render an amount of silver salts susceptible to reduction according to the degree to which they were exposed. Development of the film consists of chemical reduction of the exposed portions without affecting the unexposed ones. By means of the reduction, black, colloidal particles of metallic silver are deposited with a density corresponding to the amount of incident light. The film is then fixed, i.e. all unaffected silver salts are removed by chemical extraction. (To this point in the process all steps are carried out in the absence of light.) Fixing is accomplished by the action of hypo, which forms a water-soluble complex with silver salts, and the film is then washed with water. Finally the film is dried, giving a negative. A photograph may be produced at any time from the negative by allowing light that has passed through the negative to fall upon a piece of photographic paper which is then treated in the same way as the negative was, giving a photograph or print (*ENLARGER). Color photography depends upon a method of

confining the incident wavelengths to three ranges of the spectrum, usually by using filters. The reduction due to each range is specific to that range, subsequent transmission through the negative being therefore also specific and giving the corresponding color sensations

pho·to·gra·vure (foutəgrəvjúər) *n.* the process of printing from an etched copper plate (cf. PHOTOENGRAVING). A wiper removes all ink except that in the etched recesses, and these print in a tone related to their depth ‖ a print made by this process [F.]

pho·to·ki·ne·sis (foutoukiní:sis, foutoukainí:sis) *n.* movement in response to light **pho·to·ki·net·ic** (foutoukinétik, foutoukainétik) *adj.*

pho·to·lith·o (foutəlíθou) *pl.* **pho·to·lith·os** 1. *n.* a photolithograph 2. *v.t.* to photolithograph

pho·to·lith·o·graph (foutəlíθəgræf, foutəlíθəgrʌf) 1. *v.t.* to print by photolithography 2. *n.* a print made by protolithography [PHOTOLITHOGRAPHY]

pho·to·lith·o·graph·ic (foutəlíθəgræfik) *adj.* of or produced by photolithography [PHOTOLITHOGRAPHY]

pho·to·li·thog·ra·phy (foutouliθógrəfi:) *n.* a process of printing from a plate coated with a photographic film which has been exposed in a camera, developed, and made receptive to ink

pho·tol·y·sis (foutólisis) *n.* chemical decomposition effected by electromagnetic radiation [Mod. L. fr. Gk *phōs* (*phōtos*), light+*lusis*, a loosening]

pho·to·map (foutoumæp) *n.* mosaic of aerial photographs with identification markings

pho·to·me·chan·i·cal (foutoumək·kænik'l) *adj.* of any mechanical printing process using a plate prepared photographically **pho·to·me·chán·i·cal·ly** *adv.*

pho·tom·e·ter (foutómitər) *n.* (*phys.*) an instrument used to measure illuminating power by comparing two sources of light **pho·to·met·ric** (foutəmétrik) *adj.* **pho·tom·e·try** (foutómitri:) *n.* (*phys.*) the comparison of illuminating powers, esp. of one source of light with a standard source ‖ the science which deals with this [fr. Gk *phōs* (*phōtos*), light+METER]

pho·to·mi·cro·graph (foutoumáikrəgræf, foutoumáikrəgrʌf) *n.* a photograph made by photomicrography **pho·to·mi·crog·ra·phy** (foutoumaikrógrəfi:) *n.* the process of making photographs of the enlarged images, formed by a microscope, of very small objects [fr. PHOTO-+MICRO-+Gk *graphos*, written]

pho·to·mi·cros·co·py (foutoumaikróskəpi:) *n.* photomicrography

pho·to·mul·ti·pli·er (foutoumʌltiplaiər) *n.* an electron multiplier having a photoelectric emission as its first stage

pho·ton (fóutɒn) *n.* (*phys.*) a fundamental particle of rest mass 0 that is regarded as the quantum of radiant energy. The photon has spin quantum number 1 (*ELECTROMAGNETIC WAVE) [fr. Gk *phōs* (*phōtos*), light]

pho·to·off·set (foutouófset, foutouófset) *n.* (*printing*) a process whereby a photolithographic plate transmits an image to a roller which transfers the impression to paper

pho·to·pe·ri·od (foutəpíəri:əd) *n.* (*biol.*) the relative duration of periods of light and dark as these affect the growth or behavior of plants and animals (e.g. budding or bird migration) **pho·to·pe·ri·od·ic** (foutəpiəri:ódik) *adj.* **pho·to·pe·ri·ód·i·cal·ly** *adv.* **pho·to·pe·ri·o·dic·i·ty** (foutəpiəri:ədísiti:) **pho·to·pé·ri·od·ism** *n.* (*biol.*) the response of an organism to the photoperiod

pho·to·phile (fóutəfail) *adj.* photophilic **pho·to·phil·ic** (foutəfílik) *adj.* (*biol.*) flourishing in strong light **pho·toph·i·lous** (fətófələs) *adj.* photophilic **pho·tóph·i·ly** *n.* the quality or state of being photophilic [PHOTO-+Gk *philos*, loving]

pho·to·pho·bi·a (foutəfóubi:ə) *n.* (*med.*) abnormal dislike of or sensitivity to strong light [Mod. L. fr. Gk *phos* (*phōtos*), light+*phobia*, fear]

pho·to·pig·ment (foutoupígmənt) *n.* coloring material that changes under light

pho·to·po·la·rim·e·ter (foutoupoulærímitər) *n.* (*astron.*) device for examining features of planets utilizing telescopy, photography and polarized light

pho·to·pol·y·mer (foutoupólimər) *n.* (*chem.*) a photosensitive plastic

pho·to·print (fóutəprint) *n.* (*printing*) a reproduction made by any photomechanical process

pho·to·re·al·ism (foutouríːəlizəm) *n.* form of realistic painting life situations (esp. the worst) with photographic detail. —**pho·to·real·ist** *n.*

pho·to·re·sist (foutouri:zíst) *n.* plastic that softens under light, used as coating on integrated circuits

pho·to·scan (foutouskæn) *n.* a photographic record of radioactivity in various parts of a body. —**pho·to·scan** *v.* —**pho·to·scan·ner** *n.* the X-ray camera

pho·to·sen·si·tive (foutousénsitiv) *adj.* affected by the incidence of radiant energy, esp. light **pho·to·sen·si·tív·i·ty** *n.*

photosensor *PHOTODETECTOR

pho·to·sphere (fóutəsfiər) *n.* (*astron.*) the surface layer of the sun, consisting of a layer of gases of extremely low density at a very low pressure and high temperature (c. 6,000°C) in which heat-transfer processes produce many convective cells. They give this layer a granular appearance when photographed through a telescope (*CHROMOSPHERE, *CORONA) [fr. PHOTO-+Gk *sphaira*, sphere]

pho·to·stage (foutoustéidʒ) (*botany*) life stage of a seedling during which light is essential

pho·to·stat (fóutəstæt) 1. *n.* a machine used to make photographs of documents etc. to any desired scale ‖ a photograph thus made 2. *v.t. pres. part.* **pho·to·stat·ing**, esp. *Br.* **pho·to·stat·ting** *past* and *past part.* **pho·to·stat·ed**, esp. *Br.* **pho·to·stat·ted** to make a photostatic copy of **pho·to·stát·ic** *adj.* [fr. *Photostat*, a trademark]

pho·to·syn·the·sis (foutəsínθisis) *n.* the synthesis of chemical substances with the aid of light, esp. the formation of carbohydrates (e.g. in green plants) from carbon dioxide and water with the liberation of oxygen, in the presence of chlorophyll

pho·to·tax·is (foutətǽksis) *pl.* **pho·to·tax·es** (foutətǽksi:z) *n.* a taxis in response to light **pho·to·táx·y** *pl.* **pho·to·tax·ies** *n.* a phototaxis

pho·to·tel·e·graph (foutoutélægræf, foutoutélægrʌf) *n.* a picture or signal which has been transmitted by phototelegraphy **pho·to·tel·e·graph·ic** (foutoutelægræfik) *adj.*

pho·to·te·leg·ra·phy (foutoutælégrəfi:) *n.* the transmission of photographs by telegraphy ‖ transmission of signals by light, e.g. by a heliograph

pho·tot·o·nus (foutót'nəs) *n.* a tonic condition (e.g. in phototropic plants) induced by the proper light conditions [Mod. L. fr. Gk *phōs* (*phōtos*), light+*tonos*, tone, tension]

pho·to·tran·sis·tor (foutoutrænzístər) *n.* (*electr.*) semiconductor with three electrodes that induce and amplify a current induced by light

pho·to·troph (foutoutróuf) *n.* an organism that uses light to turn carbon dioxide into oxygen and carbon dioxide

pho·to·troph·ic (foutətrófik) *adj.* able to use carbon dioxide, in the presence of light, for metabolism (*PHOTOSYNTHESIS) [fr. PHOTO-+Gk *trophē*, food]

pho·to·trop·ic (foutətrópik) *adj.* of, by, or capable of undergoing phototropism [fr. PHOTO-+Gk *tropos*, turning]

pho·tot·ro·pism (fətótrəpizəm) *n.* a tropism in which light acts as a stimulus ‖ the reversible color change exhibited by certain substances when exposed to radiant energy

pho·to·tube (fóutətu:b, fóutətju:b) *n.* a type of photoelectric cell

pho·to·ty·po·graph·ic (foutoutaipəgræfik) *adj.* referring to or done by phototypography **pho·to·ty·po·gráph·i·cal** *adj.*

pho·to·ty·pog·ra·phy (foutoutaipógrəfi:) *n.* a printing process using photomechanical means at the composing stage as well as later

pho·to·volt·age (foutouvóultidʒ) *n.* the electromotive force developed in a conducting circuit when the boundary between certain dissimilar substances within the circuit is bathed in electromagnetic radiation ‖ any voltage generated in a photosensitive substance by electromagnetic radiation

pho·to·vol·ta·ic (foutouvɒltéiik) *adj.* photoelectric, *a photovoltaic cell*

phras·al (fréiz'l) *adj.* of or consisting of a phrase or phrases

phrase (freiz) 1. *n.* a sequence of words expressing a single idea, esp. (*gram.*) a group of words without a subject and predicate, functioning together within a sentence ‖ an expression that is pithy or idiomatic ‖ (*mus.*) a small group of notes forming a unit of melody, often forming half of a period ‖ (*dance*) a sequence of movements forming a choreographic pattern 2. *v.t. pres. part.* **phras·ing** *past* and *past part.* **phrased** to express in words, *this passage is badly phrased* ‖ (*mus.*) to divide or mark off into phrases, esp. in performance [fr. L.L. *phrasis*, diction fr. Gk fr. *phrazein*, to point out, tell]

phrase marker (freiz) (*linguistics*) a signal of the end of a phrase

phra·se·o·gram (fréizi:əgræm) *n.* a single written character representing a whole phrase, esp. in shorthand [fr. Gk *phrasis*, diction+*gramma*, letter, writing]

phra·se·o·graph (fréizi:əgræf, fréizi:əgraf) *n.* a phrase for which a phraseogram is used [fr. Gk *phrasis*, diction+*graphos*, written]

phra·se·o·log·i·cal (freizi:əlódʒik'l) *adj.* of, relating to or involving phraseology

phra·se·ol·o·gy (freizi:ólədʒi) *n.* manner of using and arranging words [fr. Mod. L. *phraseologia* fr. Gk fr. *phrasis*, diction+*logos*, word]

phras·ing (fréiziŋ) *n.* mode of expressing in words, *the phrasing of a request* ‖ (*mus.*) musical phrases with respect to composition or performance

phra·try (fréitri:) *pl.* **phra·tries** *n.* (*Gk hist.*) a subdivision of a phyle in the Athenian state ‖ a tribal or clan subdivision in primitive society [fr. Gk *phratria* fr. *phratēr*, member of the same clan]

phrenetic *FRENETIC

phren·ic (frénik) *adj.* (*anat.*) pertaining to the diaphragm [fr. Gk *phrēn* (*phrenos*), diaphragm]

phren·o·log·i·cal (frenˈlódʒik'l) *adj.* of or relating to phrenology

phre·nol·o·gist (frinólədʒist) *n.* a person who practices phrenology

phre·nol·o·gy (frinólədʒi:) *n.* a study based on the outdated theory that mental faculties and dispositions can be judged by observing the shape of the skull as a whole and the different parts of its surface [fr. Gk *phrēn* (*phrenos*), mind+*logos*, discourse]

Phryg·i·a (frídʒi:ə) an ancient country of central Asia Minor, peopled by Indo-Europeans (c. 12th c. B.C.). It fell to Lydia (c. 7th c. B.C.)

Phryg·i·an (frídʒi:ən. *n.* a native of Phrygia ‖ the Indo-European language of the ancient Phrygians **2.** *adj.* of or pertaining to Phrygia

Phrygian mode (*mus.*) a medieval authentic mode represented by the white piano keys ascending from E ‖ (*mus.*) an ancient Greek mode represented by the white piano keys descending from D

phthal·ein (θǽli:n, fθǽli:n) *n.* any of a group of organic dyes derived from a phenol and phthalic anhydride, e.g. phenolphthalein [PHTHALIC]

phthal·ic (θǽlik, fθǽlik) *adj.* of any of three isomeric acids, C₄H₄(COOH)₂, formed by oxidizing benzene derivatives ‖ of an anhydride, C₆H₄(CO)₂O, produced by oxidation of naphthalene, used in making certain resins, solvents, dyes etc. [NAPHTHALENE]

phthis·ic (tízik) *adj.* of, relating to, or affected by phthisis **phthis·i·cal** *adj.* [M.E. *tisik, tisike* n., a wasting lung disease, fr. O.F. fr. Gk]

phthi·sis (θáisis, fθáisis) *n.* tuberculosis of the lungs ‖ any wasting disease [L. fr. Gk fr. *phthinein*, to decay]

phut (fʌt) *adv.* (*Br.*, only in) **to go phut** to burst, collapse, cease suddenly to be in working order [fr. Hind. *phatna*, to burst]

phy·col·o·gy (faikólədʒi:) *n.* algology [fr. Gk *phukos*, seaweed+*logos*, discourse]

phy·co·my·cete (faikoumáisi:t) *n.* a member of *Phycomycetes*, a large class of fungi, both saprophytic and parasitic, whose thallus ranges from a simple protoplasmic mass to a complex mycelium usually consisting of tubular septae, and whose reproduction is frequently asexual (often by the formation of conidia or sporangia), but which may take a variety of sexual forms. Phycomycetes include a number of plant or animal parasites (e.g. the mildew responsible for the Irish potato famine, 1845-9) **phy·co·my·cé·tous** *adj.* [fr. Mod. L. *Phycomycetes* fr. Gk *phukos*, seaweed+*mukēs*, mushroom]

Phyfe (faif), Duncan (c. 1768–1854), American cabinetmaker and interpreter of fashionable European styles

phy·lac·ter·y (filǽktəri:) *pl.* **phy·lac·ter·ies** *n.* either of two small, square leather boxes containing slips of vellum, on which are written portions of the Mosaic Law, worn one on the head, another on the left arm, by orthodox and conservative Jewish men at prayer, in token of the duty to obey the Law ‖ an amulet [M.E. *phi-laterie* fr. L. fr. Gk *phulaktērion*, a fort]

phy·le (fáili:) *pl.* **phy·lae** (fáili:) *n.* (*Gk hist.*) an ancient Hellenic tribe ‖ a political subdivision

in the Athenian state ‖ (*Gk hist.*) a division in the Athenian army [Gk *phulē*]

phy·let·ic (failétik) *adj.* (*biol.*) of or relating to a phylum or to a line of descent [fr. Gk *phuletikos* fr. *phuletēs*, a tribesman]

phyl·lo·clad (fíləklæd) *n.* a phylloclade

phyl·lo·clade (fíləkleid) *n.* (*bot.*) a flattened or rounded stem which functions as a leaf, e.g. in cactus [fr. Mod. L. *phyllocladium* fr. Gk *phullon*, leaf+*klados*, branch]

phyl·lode (fíloud) *n.* (*bot.*) a flattened and expanded petiole functioning as a leaf, e.g. in the acacia [F. fr. Mod. L. fr. Gk *phullōdēs*, leaflike]

phyl·lo·tax·is (fílətæksis) *pl.* **phyl·lo·tax·es** (fílətæksi:z) *n.* (*bot.*) the arrangement of leaves on a stem ‖ the study of the principles governing this arrangement **phyl·lo·táx·y** *pl.* **phyl·lo·tax·ies** *n.* phyllotaxis [Mod. L. fr. Gk *phullon*, leaf+*taxis*, arrangement]

phyl·lox·e·ra (fílóksərə) *pl.* **phyl·lox·e·rae** (fílóksəri:), **phyl·lox·e·ras** *n.* a member of *Phylloxera*, fam. *Phylloxeridae*, a genus of plant lice very destructive esp. to grape vines, which spread from the U.S.A. to European countries [Mod. L. fr. Gk *phullon*, leaf+*xēros*, dry]

phy·lo·gen·e·sis (failədʒénisis) *n.* phylogeny [fr. Gk *phulon, phulē*, tribe+*genesis*, origin]

phy·log·e·ny (failódʒəni) *n.* the history of the development of a species or group of related organisms (cf. ONTOGENY) [G. *phylogenie* fr. Gk *phulon*, race+-*geneia*, birth, origin]

phy·lon (fáilon) *pl.* **phy·la** (fáilə) *n.* (*biol.*) a phylum [Mod. L. fr. Gk *phulon*, race]

phy·lum (fáiləm) *pl.* **phy·la** (fáilə) *n.* (*biol.*) the primary division of classification in the plant or animal kingdom, based on common characteristics and assumed common ancestry [Mod L. fr. Gk *phulon*, race]

phys·ic (fízik) **1.** *n.* a laxative **2.** *v.t. pres. part.* **phys·ick·ing** *past and past part.* **phys·icked** *v.t.* purge [M.E. *fisike* fr. O.F. *fisique* fr. L. *physica*]

phys·i·cal (fízik'l) *adj.* of or pertaining to matter or nature ‖ pertaining to the body (in contrast to the mind) ‖ of or pertaining to the science of physics [fr. M.L. *physicalis*]

physical anthropology the branch of anthropology concerned with the evolution and biological classification of human races, based on comparative anatomy and physiology (*SOCIAL ANTHROPOLOGY)

physical chemistry the branch of chemistry in which physical methods and theory are applied to chemical systems

physical culture exercises and treatment to develop and tone up the body

physical education education in the development and care of the body through sports and exercise

physical geography *GEOGRAPHY

physical optics the branch of optics that describes and explains optical phenomena by means of the wave theory or quantum mechanics (cf. GEOMETRICAL OPTICS)

physical science any of the sciences dealing with inanimate matter or energy, including physics, chemistry, geology, astronomy etc.

physical therapy physiotherapy

phy·si·cian (fizíʃən) *n.* a doctor of medicine, licensed to diagnose and treat diseases ‖ such a doctor as distinguished from a surgeon [M.E. *fisicien* fr. O.F. fr. L.]

physician's assistant one trained (2 yrs. of special study) to aid a physician under his direction. *acronym* PA

phys·i·cist (fízisist) *n.* a specialist in physics

phys·i·co·chem·i·cal (fizikoukémik'l) *adj.* physical and chemical ‖ relating to physical chemistry [fr. Gk *phusikos*, natural, physical+CHEMICAL]

phys·ics (fíziks) *n.* the science of matter and energy, and their interactions. It is essentially based on measurement and mathematical processes ‖ physical properties or processes, *the physics of gravitation* [fr. L. *physica*, neut. pl., trans. of Gk *ta phusika*, natural things]

phys·i·o·crat (fízi:əkræt) *n.* (*hist.*) an adherent of the economic theory put forward by the Frenchman François Quesnay (1694-1774) that land is the source of all wealth and that it alone should be taxed. The physiocrats held that economic law is immutable, and advocated total freedom of trade. Their views influenced Turgot and Adam Smith [F. *physiocrate* fr. Gk *phusis*, nature+*kratos*, rule]

phys·i·og·nom·ic (fizi:ɒgnómik, fizi:ənómik)

adj. of or relating to physiognomy or a physiognomy [fr. L.L. *physiognomicus* fr. Gk]

phys·i·og·no·my (fizi:ɒgnəmi, fizi:ónəmi:) *pl.* **phys·i·og·no·mies** *n.* the facial features as indicative of character ‖ the art of assessing character by studying the features of the face ‖ the general appearance of a landscape, situation etc. [M.E. *fisnomie* fr. O.F. fr. M.L. fr. Gk fr. *phusis*, nature+*gnōmōn*, judge]

phys·i·og·ra·pher (fizi:ógrəfər) *n.* a specialist in physiography

phys·i·o·graph·ic (fizi:əgræfik) *adj.* of, pertaining to or involving physiography **phys·i·o·gráph·i·cal** *adj.*

phys·i·og·ra·phy (fizi:ógrəfi) *n.* a scientific description of natural phenomena ‖ physical geography [fr. Gk *phusis*, nature+*graphia*, writing]

phys·i·o·log·ic (fizi:əlódʒik) *adj.* physiological **phys·i·o·lóg·i·cal** *adj.* of physiology ‖ characteristic of normal, healthy functioning (cf. PATHOLOGICAL) [PHYSIOLOGY]

phys·i·ol·o·gist (fizi:ólədʒist) *n.* a specialist in physiology

phys·i·ol·o·gy (fizi:ólədʒi:) *n.* the branch of biology concerned with the functions of living organisms ‖ the functions, collectively, of an organism or its parts, *the physiology of the starfish* [fr. L. *physiologia*, natural science fr. Gk fr. *phusis*, nature+*logos*, discourse]

phys·i·o·ther·a·pist (fizi:ouθérəpist) *n.* a specialist in physiotherapy

phys·i·o·ther·a·py (fizi:ouθérəpi:) *n.* treatment of bodily disease or injury by applying heat or massage, giving muscle training etc. [fr. Gk *phusis*, nature+THERAPY]

phy·sique (fizí:k) *n.* the form, structure, organization or constitution of a person's body, *a stocky physique* [F.]

phy·so·stig·mine (faisəstígmi:n) *n.* a poisonous alkaloid, C₁₅H₂₁N₃O₂, used medically for contracting the pupil of the eye. It is obtained from the calabar bean [fr. Mod. L. *Physostigma* fr. Gk *phusa*, bladder+*stigma*, mark]

phy·so·sto·mous (faisəstóuməs) *adj.* (of fish) having a swim bladder connected with the intestinal canal by a pneumatic duct [fr. Gk *phusa*, bladder+*stoma*, mouth]

phy·tane [C₂₀H₄₂] (fáitein) *n.* (*chem.*) hydrocarbon resulting from breakdown of chlorophyll, found as constituent of fossils 3 billion yrs. old

phy·to·gen·e·sis (faitədʒénisis) *n.* the origin, evolution or development of plants **phy·to·ge·net·ic** (faitədʒinétik) *adj.* [fr. Gk *phuton*, plant+GENESIS]

phy·to·gen·ic (faitədʒénik) *adj.* of or derived from plants [fr. Gk *phuton*, plant+*genēs*, born, produced]

phy·tog·e·ny (faitódʒini:) *n.* phytogenesis

phy·to·ge·og·ra·phy (faitoudʒi:ógrəfi:) *n.* the study of the geographical distribution of plants [fr. Gk *phuton*, plant+GEOGRAPHY]

phy·tog·ra·phy (faitógrəfi:) *n.* the description and (sometimes) systematic classification of plants [fr. Mod. L. *phytographia* fr. Gk *phuton*, plant+*graphia*, writing]

phy·to·pa·thol·o·gy (faitoupəθólədʒi:) *n.* the study of plant diseases, esp. parasitic diseases [fr. Gk *phuton*, plant+PATHOLOGY]

phy·toph·a·gous (faitófəgəs) *adj.* (esp. of insects) feeding on plants [fr. Gk *phuton*, plant+*phagos*, eating]

phy·tos·ter·ol (faitóstərəl) *n.* any of several sterols derived from plants, e.g. ergosterol [fr. Gk *phuton*, plant+STEROL]

phy·to·tron (fáitoutrɒn) *n.* (*botany*) an apparatus or laboratory for growing plants under controlled conditions

pi (pai) *n.* the sixteenth letter (Π, π=p) of the Greek alphabet ‖ the symbol (π) used to denote the ratio of the circumference of a circle to the diameter. π=3.14159 ‖ this ratio

pi, pie 1. *n.* (*printing*) type metal jumbled together instead of being sorted into the case **2.** *v. pres. part.* **pi·ing, pie·ing** *past and past part.* **pied** *v.t.* (*printing*) to jumble up (type) ‖ *v.i.* (*printing*, of type) to become jumbled [perh. fr. PIE, baked dish]

pi·ac·u·lar (paiǽkjulər) *adj.* (of a fault) requiring atonement ‖ expiatory [fr. L. *piacularis*, expiatory fr. *piaculum*, atonement]

piaffe (pjæf) **1.** *v.i. pres. part.* **piaff·ing** *past and past part.* **piaffed** (*manège*, of a horse) to perform a slow trot without advancing or retreating **2.** *n.* the movement so executed **píaff·er** *n.* [F. *piaffer*]

CONCISE PRONUNCIATION KEY: **(a)** æ, c*a*t; ɑ, c*a*r; ɔ f*aw*n; ei, sn*a*ke. **(e)** e, h*e*n; i:, sh*ee*p; iə, d*ee*r; εə, b*ea*r. **(i)** i, f*i*sh; ai, t*i*ger; ə:, b*i*rd. **(o)** o, *o*x; au, c*ow*; ou, g*oa*t; u, p*oo*r; ɔi, r*oy*al. **(u)** ʌ, d*u*ck; u, b*u*ll; u:, g*oo*se; ə, b*a*cillus; ju:, c*u*be. x, lo*ch*; θ, *th*ink; δ, *b*o*th*er; z, *Z*en; 3, corsa*g*e; dʒ, sava*g*e; ŋ, ora*n*gutang; j, *y*ak; ʃ, *f*ish; tʃ, fe*tch*; 'l, ra*bble*; 'n, re*dden*. Complete pronunciation key appears inside front cover.

Piaget (pjazei), Jean (1896–1980) Swiss psychologist, the most influential theorist in the history of developmental psychology and the study of human development. He wrote more than fifty books as well as articles and lectures on psychology, epistemology, philosophy, logic, biology, sociology and pedagogy

pi·a ma·ter (páiǝméitǝr) n. the highly vascular, delicate, innermost membrane of three which surround the brain and spinal cord (*MENINGES) [M.L.=tender mother]

pi·a·nis·si·mo (pi:ǝnísǝmou, pjɑní:ssi:mɔ) (mus., abbr. pp.) 1. adj. very soft 2. adv. very softly 3. pl. **pi·a·nis·si·mos** n. a pianissimo passage [Ital. superl. of piano, soft, softly]

pi·an·ist (pi:ǝnist, pjǽnist, pí:ǝnist) n. a person who plays the piano, esp. professionally **pi·a·nis·tic** (pi:ǝnístik) adj. relating to or suitable for performance on the piano **pi·a·nís·ti·cal·ly** adv. [fr. F. pianiste]

pi·a·no (pi:ɑnou) (abbr. p.) 1. adv. (mus.) softly 2. adj. (mus.) soft 3. pl. **pi·a·ni** (pi:áni:), **pi·a·nos** n. (mus.) a passage rendered softly [Ital.]

pi·an·o (pi:ǽnou, pjǽnou) pl. **pi·an·os** n. a musical stringed percussion instrument before which the player sits (as if at a table), playing on a horizontal keyboard. This usually has 88 keys, with corresponding wires (tuned by equal temperament) which are stretched over a sounding board inside the instrument. When a key is pressed down, its corresponding wires (usually 3 per key) are struck by a felt-covered wooden hammer to produce the note, which may be dampened or sustained by pedals. The keyboard consists of flat, white keys which correspond to the C major scale, with shorter, thinner, raised black ones which sound the other notes of the chromatic scale (*GRAND PIANO, *UPRIGHT PIANO) [Ital., shortened fr. pianoforte]

pi·an·o·for·te (pi:ǽnoufɔ́rti, pi:ǽnoufɔ́rtei) n. a piano [Ital. fr. piano, soft+forte, loud (from its capacity for producing wide variations in volume)]

pi·a·no·la (pi:ǝnóulǝ) n. a player piano ‖ a mechanical attachment operating this [fr. Pianola, a trademark]

pi·as·sa·ba, pi·a·sa·ba (pi:ǝsábǝ) n. piassava **pi·as·sa·va, pi·a·sa·va** (pi:ǝsávǝ) n. either of two South American palms, Attalea funefera and Leopoldinia piassaba, which yield a woody brown fiber ‖ the fiber of either of these, used in the manufacture of brooms, brushes etc. [Port. piassaba fr. Tupi]

pi·as·ter, pi·as·tre (pi:ǽstǝr) n. a monetary unit of varying value used in many countries, e.g. Turkey, Egypt, Lebanon, Libya, the Sudan ‖ a coin of the value of any of these [F. piastre fr. Ital.]

Pia·ve (pjáve) a river in N.E. Italy, flowing 137 miles from the E. Alps to the Adriatic above Venice

pi·az·za (pi:ǽzǝ, pi:ázǝ, pi:ǽtsǝ, pi:átsǝ) n. an open square in a town, closely surrounded by buildings, esp. in Italy ‖ (archit.) a portico or covered walk supported by arches ‖ a veranda [Ital.]

pi·broch (pí:brɒx) n. (mus.) a theme with a set of variations, usually martial but including dirges, played on the bagpipe [fr. Gael. piobaireachd, the art of playing the bagpipe]

pic (pik) pl. **pics, pix** (piks) n. a photograph ‖ (pop.) a movie [PICTURE]

pi·ca (páikǝ) n. (printing) a size of type equal to 12 point ‖ a typewriter face of 10 characters to the inch, 6 lines to the vertical inch [M.L.=directory]

pica n. (med.) a morbid craving to eat things not normally eaten, e.g. coal, chalk [Mod. L. or M.L.=magpie]

Pi·ca·bia (pi:kǽbjæ), Francis (1879–1953), French painter, an originator of dada and surrealism

pi·ca·dor (pí:kǝdɔr) (bullfighting) a horseman who prods the bull in the neck and shoulders with a lance to weaken it [Span. fr. picar, to prick]

Pi·card (pi:kær), Jean (1620–82), French astronomer. He was the first to measure precisely a degree of the earth's meridian, thus calculating the earth's radius. His values were used by Newton

Pic·ar·dy (píkǝrdi:) (F. Picardie) a former province of N. France on the English Channel, comprising Somme, most of Aisne, the coast of Pas-de-Calais and part of Oise. It is a fertile chalk plateau, cut by the Somme. Crops: wheat, sugar beets, market produce. Industries: textiles, fishing. Main towns: Amiens (the old capital), Boulogne, Abbeville. Feudal Picardy, composed of free cities and petty fiefs, included large parts of Flanders. Annexed by the Crown (12th–14th cc.), it was disputed with England (14th–15th cc.) and Spain (16th–17th cc.) before being secured (1659)

pic·a·resque (pikǝrésk) adj. of or written in a genre of episodic, usually satiric fiction originating in 16th-c. Spain, in which a rogue is the hero [fr. Span. picaresco fr. picaro, rogue]

pic·a·roon (pikǝrú:n) n. a rogue, esp. a pirate ‖ a pirate ship [Span. picarón fr. picaro, rogue]

Pi·cas·so (pikásou, pi:kɑssɔ) (Pablo Ruiz y Picasso, 1881–1973), Spanish painter, sculptor and ceramist. He migrated to Paris just at the time when the gains of the Postimpressionists in rendering space and solid form were being consolidated. His 'blue period' (1901–4) and 'rose period' (1905–7), in which these colors dominate his work, preceded the analytical and geometrical investigation (1908–14) with Braque leading to the development of cubism. 'Les demoiselles d'Avignon' (1907) is one of his first major works in this style (*CUBISM). To this period also belong experiments with collage, and pictures which show the influence of the 'simplifications' of Negro art. His period of 'classicism' (1920–6) was characterized by monumental human figures, and full-on or profile treatment of races and bodies. He then turned to surrealism and abstraction (1926–36). His 'Guernica' (1937) is a powerful symbolic illustration of the horrors of war. Throughout his career Picasso moved from style to style with ease, or from painting to etching, sculpture, pottery, theater décor for ballet or poster-design. From all this activity some themes stand out: the gypsies, acrobats and absinthe-drinkers of the melancholy blue period, the sober abstractions of the early cubist paintings (guitars, fruit, household objects, but also pierrots), the newspaper and wood-grain of the collages, and from the later periods the obsessive bulls, goats and shepherds of Mediterranean life, the minotaurs of Mediterranean mythology, the succession of women companions lovingly analyzed and re-created, the images of grief and violence from 1937–45, his children, the gay variations, in rather flat bright hard colors, of later years, and at all times a celebration of the natural creation

pic·a·yune (pikij:ú:n) 1. n. anything of little value 2. adj. of very small value ‖ picayunish **pic·a·yún·ish** adj. trivial ‖ too concerned with petty detail [F. picaillon, farthing fr. Prov. fr. picalho, money]

pic·ca·lil·li (píkǝlili:) pl. **pic·ca·lil·lis** n. a relish of chopped vegetables and pungent spices [origin unknown]

Pic·card (pi:kɑr), Auguste (1884–1962), Swiss physicist. He made balloon ascents into the stratosphere and underwater explorations to great depths in a bathyscaphe

pic·co·lo (píkǝlou) pl. **pic·co·los** n. a small flute pitched an octave higher than the standard flute [Ital.=small]

pice (pais) pl. **pice** n. a former monetary unit and coin in India and Pakistan, equal to ¼ anna ‖ a monetary unit and coin in Nepal equal to one hundredth of a rupee [fr. Hindi paisā]

pich·i·ci·a·go (pitʃisi:ágou) pl. **pich·i·ci·a·gos** n. Chlamydophorus truncatus, a small South American burrowing armadillo that lives entirely underground. It has protective plates attached only at the spine, and truncated hind parts [fr. Span. pichiciega, prob. fr. Guaraní pichey little armadillo+Span. ciego, blind]

Pi·chin·cha (pitʃí:ntʃa) a volcano (15,918 ft) in Ecuador, northwest of Quito. In a battle (1822) fought nearby, Sucre defeated the royalist Spanish troops. The victory of the patriots led to the immediate proclamation of independence of the Audiencia of Quito, which became part of the Republic of Gran Colombia

pick (pik) 1. v.t. to gather (a flower, fruit etc.) by severing it from the rest of the plant or tree ‖ to choose or select carefully ‖ to probe or scratch with an instrument or with one's fingers in order to remove extraneous matter from ‖ to steal from (the pockets of the clothes which someone is wearing) ‖ to pluck (a chicken etc.) ‖ to pierce or dig up (soil, rock etc.) by striking with a pick ‖ to pluck (the strings of a banjo, guitar etc.) ‖ to open (a lock) with a wire etc. instead of with a key, esp. for purposes of robbery ‖ to find an opportunity or pretext for, and begin (a quarrel, fight etc.) ‖ v.i. to work with a pick ‖ to eat sparingly or with small bites ‖ (of a bird, esp. a chicken) to tap at the ground or take bits of food up with the bill ‖ (of fruit etc.) to be or admit of being picked, these berries pick easily **to pick and choose** to be fastidious about making a choice, there's no time to pick and choose **to pick apart** to separate or rip into parts ‖ to find defects in (an argument etc.) **to pick at** to eat (one's food) in small bites and without appetite **to pick on** to choose, select ‖ to single out in order to attack, criticize or tease **to pick out** to select ‖ to distinguish from others, he hoped no one would pick him out in the crowd ‖ to cause to stand out, accentuate, important passages are picked out in red ‖ to play (a tune etc.) by searching hesitantly for the notes on a keyboard etc. **to pick up** to lift or take up ‖ to get or acquire, esp. by chance or casually, to pick up some useful information ‖ to meet casually and get to know (someone, esp. of the opposite sex) ‖ to increase (speed) ‖ to accelerate, the train picked up after the slope ‖ to improve in health, spirits or performance 2. n. the act of selecting ‖ the right or privilege of selecting, to have one's pick of the items ‖ the person or thing selected ‖ someone or something selected as the best, the pick of the lot ‖ the amount of a crop that is picked at one time [rel. to O.E. picung, a pricking]

pick n. a pickaxe ‖ any of several tools used for picking, e.g. an ice pick ‖ a plectrum [prob. var. of PIKE]

pick 1. v.t. (weaving) to throw (a shuttle) 2. n. (weaving) one of the weft threads ‖ (weaving) the blow that impels the shuttle [var. of PITCH v.]

pick·a·back (píkǝbæk) 1. adv. piggyback 2. n. a piggyback [origin unknown]

pick and roll (basketball) maneuver of defending a member of the team, then moving toward the goal to receive a pass

pick·ax, pick·axe (píkæks) pl. **pick·ax·es** n. a tool for breaking hard ground etc., consisting of a heavy iron or steel curved bar, having either two pointed ends or one end pointed and the other flattened to an edge, and having a long wooden handle that fits into its center [M.E. pikois, picois fr. O.F. picois]

pick·er (píkǝr) n. someone who picks, a fruit picker ‖ a tool or machine that picks, esp. a machine that separates and cleans fibers

picker n. (weaving) the instrument that impels the shuttle

pick·er·el (píkǝrǝl) pl. **pick·er·el, pick·er·els** n. any of several rather small fierce pikes of North America ‖ (Br.) a young pike, Esox lucius [dim. of PIKE]

Pick·er·ing (píkǝriŋ), Timothy (1745–1829), American Revolutionary general and statesman. As secretary of state (1795–1800), he was dismissed when President John Adams learned of his scheme with the Hamiltonian Federalists to steer the U.S.A. into war with France. He wrote 'Political Essays' (1812)

Pickering, William Henry (1858–1938), U.S. astronomer. He led (1878–1901) five solar eclipse expeditions and established several observatories and astronomical stations. He discovered (1899) the ninth satellite of Saturn, which he called Phoebe, and predicted (1919) the existence of a ninth planet, later named Pluto

pick·et (píkit) 1. n. a small group of soldiers posted against surprise attack or sent out to counter enemy reconnoitering parties ‖ a group of workers posted to dissuade other workers or clients from entering their place of work during a strike ‖ a member of such a group ‖ a group of demonstrators, or a member of such a group, carrying placards to advocate a cause or register a protest ‖ a pointed stake used e.g. as part of a fence or to mark positions in surveying 2. v.t. to protect by means of a picket fence ‖ to tether (an animal) to a stake driven into the ground ‖ to act as a picket at (a place of business etc.) ‖ to post (men) as a picket ‖ to guard (a military camp etc.) with a picket ‖ v.i. to act as a picket ‖ to set or place a picket [F. piquet, pointed stake]

picket fence (bowling) standing pins 1, 2, 4 and 7 or 1, 3, 6 and 10

picket ship (mil.) relay ship to extend range of radar signals in early-warning systems

Pick·ett (píkit), George Edward (1825–75), Confederate general, best known for 'Pickett's charge' in the Gettysburg Campaign, which resulted in the virtual annihilation of his division

pick·ings (píkiŋz) *pl. n.* scraps of good food left over, e.g. on a chicken after the meat has been carved ‖ (*fig.*) gleanings ‖ (*pop.*) goods or booty acquired dishonestly

pick·le (pík'l) 1. *n.* a liquid (brine, vinegar etc.) in which food is preserved ‖ food or a piece of food (e.g. a cucumber) so preserved ‖ an acid solution for cleaning metal articles ‖ (*pop.*) an awkward situation, sorry plight ‖ (*Br., pop.*) a mischievous child 2. *v.t. pres. part.* **pick·ling** *past* and *past part.* **pick·led** to preserve in, or treat with, a pickle, *to pickle walnuts* ‖ to give a bleached finish to (woodwork) [M.E. prob. fr. M. Du. *pekel, pekele*]

pick·lock (píklɒk) *n.* a device for picking locks ‖ a burglar

pick-me-up (píkmiˌʌp) *n.* (*pop.*) a drink, esp. an alcoholic one, taken to restore zest or energy

pick·pock·et (píkpɒkit) *n.* a person who picks people's pockets

pick·up (píkʌp) *n.* a picking up, e.g. of a ball from the ground, esp. just after its impact ‖ (*pop.*) recovery, *the stock market registered a good pickup* ‖ a device in a phonograph which converts the vibration of the needle into electrical impulses ‖ (*radio, television*) the reception of sound (or light) by the transmitter ‖ the apparatus used for this ‖ (*radio, television*) a place outside a studio where a broadcast originates ‖ the electrical system connecting the program from this place to the broadcasting station ‖ (*television*) the changing of light into electrical energy by the transmitter ‖ (*pop.*) a person whose acquaintance one makes casually, esp. for purposes of love-making ‖ acceleration, esp. of a car ‖ a light truck used esp. for deliveries

pick·y (píki:) *comp.* **pick·i·er** *superl.* **pick·i·est** *adj.* (*pop.*) choosy, finical, *a picky eater*

pi·clo·ram [C₆H₃Cl₃N₂O₂] (píklɔrɒm) *n.* (*chem.*) persistent defoliation herbicide used in Vietnam

pic·nic (píknik) 1. *n.* an outing in which the people involved eat a meal outdoors, brought along for the occasion ‖ the food prepared for this ‖ (*pop.*) something easy or pleasant to do or experience, *the climb was no picnic* 2. *v.i. pres. part.* **pic·nick·ing** *past* and *past part.* **pic·nicked** to have or participate in a picnic **pic·nick·er** *n.* [fr. F. *pique-nique*]

Pi·co Bo·lí·var (pí:kɒbɒlí:var) the highest point (16,000 ft) in Venezuela in the Cordillera Mérida, a spur of the Andes east of Lake Maracaibo

Pi·co del·la Mi·ran·do·la (pí:kɔdellɑmiːrándɔlɑ), Giovanni (1463–94), Italian philosopher and humanist. His encyclopedic learning, esp. in philosophy and languages, made him a typical man of the Renaissance. After meeting Ficino (1484) he joined the Neoplatonist school. His 'Conclusiones' (1486) are a compendium of contemporary philosophy and theology, and the first of these,'Oratio de hominis dignitate', is a manifesto of the Renaissance humanist spirit. He was condemned for heresy by the pope (1487), but was saved by Lorenzo de' Medici

pic·o·line (píkɔliːn) *n.* any of three isomeric bases, C₆H₇N, derived from pyridine and occurring in bones and coal tar. They are colorless liquids with a strong smell and are used as a sedative [fr. L. *pix* (*picis*), pitch+*oleum*, oil]

pic·o·line [C₅H₄N (CH₃)] (píkoliːn) *n.* (*chem.*) solvent for chemical synthesis, used to make nicotinic acid and for fabric waterproofing

pi·cor·na·vi·rus (píkɔrnæviⱳirəs) *n.* a group of small ether-resistant RNA viruses that include those causing poliomyelitis, Coxsackie foot-and-mouth disease and encephalomyocarditis

pi·cot (pí:kou) 1. *n.* a small loop of thread forming a part of an ornamental edging to ribbon, lace etc. 2. *v.t.* to give such edging to [F. dim. of *pic*, point]

pic·o·tee (pikətí:) *n.* a cultivated variety of carnation, sweet pea etc. with a dark-colored or spotted edge to the petals [F. *picoté, picotée*, spotted, pricked]

pic·rate (píkreit) *n.* a salt or ester of picric acid

pic·ric acid (píkrik) a bitter yellow crystalline acid, C₆H₂(NO₂)₃OH, used as a dye, in explosives etc. [fr. Gk *pikros*, bitter]

pic·rite (píkrait) *n.* a blackish-green igneous rock, largely composed of augite and olivine [fr. Gk *pikros*, bitter]

Pict (pikt) *n.* a member of a warlike people centered in N. and E. Scotland at the time of the

Roman occupation of Britain **Pict·ish** 1. *adj.* of, relating to or like the Picts 2. *n.* the language of the Picts [fr. L.L. *Picti*, perh. fr. L. *pictus*, painted]

pic·to·graph (píktəgræf, píktəgrɑf) *n.* a picture used to represent a thing, idea etc., e.g. in hieroglyphic writings ‖ a record consisting of such pictures **pic·to·graph·ic** (píktəgræfik) *adj.* **pic·tog·ra·phy** (piktɒgrəfi) *n.* [fr. L. *pictus*, painted+Gk *graphos*, written]

pic·to·ri·al (piktɔ́riːəl, piktóuriːəl) 1. *adj.* of, containing, expressing or illustrating by pictures ‖ suggesting a mental image, *a pictorial style of writing* 2. *n.* an illustrated periodical or newspaper [fr. L. L. *pictorius*]

pic·ture (píktʃər) 1. *n.* a representation or image on a surface, e.g. a painting, drawing, print or photograph, esp. as a work of art ‖ a perfect likeness, *he is the picture of his father* ‖ a type, symbol, *he is the picture of health* ‖ a mental image, idea, *his book gives an accurate picture of monastic life* ‖ a film, movie ‖ a situation as a combination of circumstances, *have you understood the picture?* ‖ a picturesque sight, *the roses were a picture this year* **in the picture** (of actions, events or persons) forming part of the circumstances under consideration, *his candidacy remains very much in the picture* ‖ (*Br.*) informed as to what is going on **the pictures** (*Br., pop.*) the movies **to take a picture** to record on film the image of an object by means of a camera 2. *v.t. pres. part.* **pic·tur·ing** *past* and *past part.* **pic·tured** to imagine, *picture yourself in his situation!* ‖ to depict, esp. in writing [M.E. fr. L. *pictura* fr. *pingere* (*pictus*), to paint]

picture hat a woman's large, wide-brimmed hat, worn esp. on dressy occasions

picture molding, *Br.* **picture moulding** a rod, wooden rail or molding running around the walls of a room, parallel to the ceiling and typically 2-3 feet below it, to take supports from which pictures hang

picturephone *VIDEOPHONE

picture postcard a postcard with a picture on one side of it

picture rail a picture molding

pic·tur·esque (piktʃərésk) *adj.* (of scenery, landscapes etc.) full of charm, esp. through having an irregular prettiness or quaintness or antique quality, rather than classical beauty, *a picturesque old village* ‖ (of language etc.) strikingly vivid **the picturesque** picturesqueness as an aesthetic concept [fr. F. *pittoresque* fr. Ital. *pittoresco*, in the style of a painter]

picture window a large window having a single pane of glass, which frames the scene outside

picture writing a form of record using pictorial symbols for things, ideas etc. ‖ pictures made in this kind of writing

pid·dle (píd'l) *pres. part.* **pid·dling** *past* and *past part.* **pid·dled** *v.i.* to trifle, waste time ‖ to urinate ‖ *v.t.* (with 'away') to pass (time etc.) wastefully **pid·dling** *adj.* trivial [etym. doubtful]

pid·dock (pídək) *n.* a member of *Pholas*, fam. *Pholadidae*, a genus of bivalve mollusks which characteristically bore holes in wood, clay, rocks etc. ‖ any mollusk of fam. *Pholadidae* [origin unknown]

pidg·in (pídʒin) *n.* any mixed language, spoken usually in trade, which uses the vocabulary of two or more languages and a simplified form of the grammar of one of them. Pidgin is used esp. in trading ports etc. ‖ pidgin English ‖ (*Br., pop.*, also **pigeon**) a strictly personal problem or concern, *that's his pidgin, not yours* [Chin. pronunciation of BUSINESS]

pidgin English a variety of pidgin used in the Far East between Chinese and English-speaking people ‖ a variety of pidgin used in Melanesia and N. Australia

pi-dog *PYE-DOG

pie (pai) *n.* a magpie [O.F.]

pie *PI

pie *n.* a dish of fruit, meat etc., baked with a pastry crust [etym. doubtful]

pie *n.* a former monetary unit and coin of India and Pakistan equal to 1/12 anna [Hindi *pāī*]

pie·bald (páibɔld) 1. *adj.* marked in patches of two different colors, esp. black and white 2. *n.* a piebald animal, esp. a horse [PIE, magpie+BALD]

piece (pi:s) 1. *n.* a distinct part, separated or broken off from a whole, *a piece of cake, a piece of broken china* ‖ a single example or unit of a

class of things, *a piece of furniture* ‖ a single unit belonging to a set, *a dinner service of 48 pieces* ‖ a coin of a specified kind, *a 50-cent piece* ‖ a musical or literary composition, esp. a short one, *play that piece again* ‖ a short recitation, esp. one rendered by a child ‖ (*checkers, chess* etc.) any of the men used in playing, esp. (*chess*) any man other than a pawn ‖ a cannon, field gun etc. ‖ a firearm ‖ a unit of manufactured goods, e.g. cloth or wallpaper, of a standard size **in one piece** integral, not being in nor consisting of separate pieces ‖ not broken **in pieces** broken in pieces or otherwise destroyed, *his plans are now in pieces* **of a piece** consistent, *his actions and principles are all of a piece* **to come to pieces** to be able to be disassembled into its component parts **to give (someone) a piece of one's mind** to rebuke (someone) severely and bluntly **to go to pieces** to lose control of oneself or suffer a nervous or emotional collapse **to take to pieces** to disassemble (something) into its component parts ‖ to come to pieces 2. *v.t. pres. part.* **piec·ing** *past* and *past part.* **pieced** to mend or patch by adding a piece ‖ (with 'together') to join (things) so that they make a whole ‖ (often with 'out' or 'together') to make by joining parts or pieces, *to piece a quilt, he pieced out the story from their statements* [M.E. fr. O.F.]

pièce de ré·sis·tance (pjɛsdəreizi:stɑs) *n.* the choice item in a collection or series, esp. the chief dish in a meal [F.]

piece goods textiles made and sold in standard lengths ‖ textiles sold by the retailer to the length a customer orders, cut from the bolt

piece·meal (pí:smiːl) 1. *adv.* by degrees, one part after another, *he conquered the territory piecemeal* 2. *adj.* done bit by bit, *the piecemeal conquest of the territory* [M.E. *pecemel* fr. *pece*, piece+*-mele*, by a (specified) measure]

piece of eight a former Spanish coin worth eight reals

piece of the action participation in a project, esp. the profits

piece·work (pí:swəːrk) *n.* work paid for by the amount done, not by the time taken (cf. TIME-WORK)

pie·crust (páikrʌst) *n.* the baked pastry of a pie

pied (paid) *adj.* parti-colored [PIE n., magpie]

Pied·mont (pí:dmɒnt) (*Ital.* Piemonte) a region (area 11,334 sq. miles, pop. 4,540,700) of N.W. Italy. Its center is the fertile basin (fodder crops, cereals, silk, wine) of the upper Po, open on the east toward the Lombardy plain, and surrounded north, west and south by the Graian, Cottian (forestry, cattle raising, hydroelectricity) and Ligurian Alps. Industry is centered in the chief city, Turin. By the 15th c. Piedmont was dominated by the dukes of Savoy, under whom it was joined (1748) to Sardinia. It was annexed (1798–1814) to France, was restored (1815) to Sardinia, and formed (1861) the nucleus of the new kingdom of Italy

Piedmont a plateau of the eastern U.S.A., extending from the coastal plain to the Appalachians and Blue Ridge Mtns, and from Alabama to New Jersey

Pien·chieng (bjéndʒiŋ) *KAIFENG

pie·pow·der, **pie·pou·dre**, **court of** (páipaudər) (*Eng. hist.*) a summary court held at medieval markets and fairs to enforce law merchant among intinerant traders [M. E.=M. L. *pede-pulverosus*, dusty-footed]

pier (piər) *n.* a breakwater of masonry ‖ a wooden-decked structure, supported on piles and built to extend for some distance into the sea or other body of water, used to give passengers access to vessels, now often containing places of entertainment, variety theaters etc. ‖ (*archit.*) a pillar or other structure supporting an arch or lintel or the span of ridge ‖ a buttress of masonry or brick ‖ a section of wall between two doors or other openings **pier·age** *n.* a toll paid for use of a pier or breakwater [M.E. *per* fr. M.L. *pera*, origin unknown]

Pierce (piərs), Franklin (1804–69), 14th president (1853–7) of the U.S.A., a Democrat. A dark-horse candidate for the presidency, he won the election by virtue of his moderate policies and his advocacy of the Compromise of 1850. His administration sponsored the Ostend Manifesto and ordered the bombardment of San Juan del Norte in Nicaragua. The West was further developed by the Gadsden Purchase. His efforts to reconcile the North and the South, notably the Kansas-Nebraska Bill (1854), were counter-productive

pierce (piərs) *pres. part.* **pierc·ing** *past* and *past part.* **pierced** *v.t.* to make a hole in or through (something) using a sharp implement || to affect (the senses, esp. the sense of hearing, or the emotions) intensely, *the whistle pierced his ears* || to make a way into or through, *the cold pierced his clothes* || to understand or see through, *to pierce a mystery* **pierc·ing** *adj.* penetrating sharply or deeply, *a piercing wind* [O.F. *percer*]

pier glass a large mirror, esp. one intended to go on the wall between two windows

Pi·e·ri·an (paiíəri:ən) *adj.* (*Gk mythol.*) of Pieria, a region of Thessaly where the Muses were worshiped || of the Muses

Pie·ro del·la Fran·ce·sca (pjérɔdéllafrantʃéska) (c. 1415–1492), Italian painter. His profound knowledge of perspective and use of its rules, his precise forms, grave faces and soft colors and his mastery of light and atmosphere combine spiritual majesty and a noble vision of Renaissance man. His most notable frescos include 'The Legend of the True Cross' (1452–9), 'The Resurrection' and 'The Flagellation'. Paintings include 'The Baptism', 'The Nativity', 'The Madonna della Misericordia' and 'The Brera Madonna' (c. 1472)

Pie·ro di Co·si·mo (pjérɔdikɔ́zi:mɔ) (1462–1521), Italian painter. His characteristic works have mythological or religious subjects with beautifully executed landscape backgrounds, esp. 'Death of Procris'

Pierre (piər) the capital (pop. 11,973) of South Dakota, on the Missouri

pi·er·rot (pi:əróu, pjérou) *n.* a comic character adopted from old French pantomime, with a floppy white costume and whitened face [F. dim. of *Pierre*, Peter (propername)]

pier table a low table placed between two windows

Pie·tà (pi:eitá, pjeitá) *n.* a painting or sculpture of the Virgin Mary mourning over the dead Christ. Very often Christ is lying across her knees [Ital.]

Pie·ter·ma·ritz·burg (pi:tərmǽritsbə:rg) the capital (pop. 178,972) of Natal, South Africa, an agricultural market 40 miles inland from Durban: metallurgy, rubber, leather, footwear. Natal University (1909)

pi·e·tism (páiitizəm) *n.* the stressing in religious devotion of personal feeling rather than dogma and intellectual truth, sometimes involving exaggerated or ostentatious piety **Pi·e·tism** the practice and principles of a Lutheran movement, originating in Germany and led by Philipp Jakob Spener, stressing the importance of personal experience of God and of Bible study rather than the forms and dogma of religion [fr. G. *pietismus* fr. *pietist*, pietist]

pi·e·tist (páiitist) *n.* a person whose religious observances are marked by pietism **Pi·e·tist** an adherent of Pietism **pi·e·tis·tic** *adj.* [G. fr. L. *pietas*, piety]

pi·e·ty (páiiti:) *pl.* **pi·e·ties** *n.* devotion and reverence for God || an act which shows this quality [O.F. *piete* fr. L.]

pi·e·zo·e·lec·tric (paiːzouiléktrik) *adj.* of, relating to, or characterized by piezoelectricity [fr. Gk *piezein*, to press+ELECTRIC]

pi·e·zo·e·lec·tric·i·ty (paiːzouiléktrísiti:) *n.* the property of some asymmetric crystals (e.g. quartz) of acquiring opposite electrical charges on opposing faces when they are subjected to pressure (conversely, an applied electric potential results in a change of volume). Thus quartz oscillators are used as frequency stabilizers and ultrasonic generators [fr. Gk *piezein*, to press+ELECTRICITY]

pi·e·zom·e·ter (paiizómitər) *n.* an instrument for measuring pressure by its effect in the volume of a liquid or solid **pi·e·zo·met·ric** (paiːzəmétrik) *adj.* **pi·e·zom·e·try** (paiizómitri:) *n.* the measurement of the effect of hydrostatic pressure on the behavior of ground water [fr. Gk *piezein*, to press+METER]

piff·le (pífəl) *n.* (*pop.*) twaddle, silly nonsense, *don't talk piffle!* **pif·fling** *adj.* (*pop.*) utterly trivial [perh. imit.]

pig (pig) **1.** *n.* a young hog less than 120 lbs in weight || (*Br.*) any domestic hog || a greedy, dirty or selfish person || an oblong mass of iron, lead etc. obtained when the molten metal from a furnace cools in a trough || a container for holding radioactive materials || one of the molds in which this metal is cast || pig iron **a pig in a poke** something which one buys or accepts without seeing it first, taking a chance on its being satisfactory **to make a pig of oneself** to

eat too much **2.** *v.i. pres. part.* **pig·ging** *past* and *past part.* **pigged** (of a sow) to bring forth young || (with "out") to gorge oneself [M.E. *pigge*, origin unknown]

pig bed a trough of sand into which molten metal from a furnace is run for cooling

pi·geon (pídʒən) *n.* a member of *Columbidae*, order *Columbiformes*, a large family of words of worldwide distribution having stout bodies, short legs, smooth plumage and small heads and beaks, esp. a member of a variety descended from *Columba livia*, the rock pigeon. Pigeons eat berries and seeds, and are often raised to eat. They utter a characteristic cooing sound. The fancy, specially bred varieties include carrier, fantail, tumbler and pouter pigeons || one of the larger, domesticated birds of fam. *Columbidae* as distinguished from smaller, wild doves || a clay pigeon [M.E. *pyjon, pejon* fr. O.F. *pijon, pyjoun*, young bird, young dove, and Mod. F. *pigeon*]

pigeon *PIDGIN (personal problem or concern)

pigeon breast a deformity consisting of a projecting sternum, often due to rickets **pi·geon-breast·ed** *adj.*

pigeon hawk *Falco columbarius*, an American falcon related to the merlin

pi·geon·hole (pídʒənhoul) **1.** *n.* a recess in a desk, cabinet etc. for keeping letters, papers etc. **2.** *v.t. pres. part.* **pi·geon·hol·ing** *past* and *past part.* **pi·geon·holed** to put away for future attention or indefinitely || to classify mentally || to put away (papers) in the pigeonholes of a desk

pi·geon-toed (pídʒəntoud) *adj.* having the toes turned inwards

pig·fish (pígfiʃ) *pl.* **pig·fish·es, pig·fish** *n.* any of several fish that make a grunting sound when taken out of the water [*GRUNT]

pig·ger·y (pígəri:) *pl.* **pig·ger·ies** *n.* (*Br.*) a pig farm || (*Br.*) a pigsty || (*Br.*) a filthy place || (*Br.*) filthiness

pig·gish (pígiʃ) *adj.* selfishly greedy

pig·gy (pígi:) *adj.* like a pig || piggish

pig·gy·back (pígi:bæk) **1.** *adj.* of a transport system by which road-haulage loads in their vehicles are carried by rail || of something carried along with another more important package **2.** *adv.* carried in this way || on the back and shoulders, *to carry a child piggyback* **3.** *n.* a ride made piggyback || a piggyback transport system

piggybacking funding of an organization already funded for a federal program, with an additional, related program

piggy bank a money box shaped like a pig, with a slot in the for the coins || any small money box

pig·head·ed (píghedid) *adj.* stupidly obstinate

pig iron the impure iron, with a large content of combined carbon, obtained directly from a blast furnace

pig Latin a jargon in which each word begins with its first vowel, any consonants at the beginning being placed at the end and followed by 'ay', e.g. 'igpay atinLay' for 'pig Latin'

pig·let (píglit) *n.* a young pig [dim. of PIG]

pig·ment (pígmənt) *n.* a coloring matter, esp. in dry powdered form, used in paints etc. || the coloring matter in the cells and tissues of an animal or plant [fr. L. *pigmentum* fr. *pingere*, to paint]

pig·men·tar·y (pígmənteri:) *adj.* of, relating to or containing pigment [fr. L. *pigmentarius*]

pig·men·ta·tion (pigməntéiʃən) *n.* (esp. *biol.*) coloring or discoloring, esp. in tissues, as a result of pigment [fr. L. *pigmentatus*, painted]

pigmy *PYGMY

pig·nut (pígnʌt) *n.* an earthnut, esp. tuber of *Conopodium denudatum*, fam. *Umbelliferae*, of S. Europe || any of several hickory nuts || a tree bearing such a nut, esp. *Carya glabra*

pig·pen (pígpen) *n.* a pigsty

pig·skin (pígskin) *n.* leather made from a hog's skin || (*pop.*) a football

pig·sty (pígstai) *pl.* **pig·sties** *n.* a partly covered enclosure in which pigs are kept || a filthy place

pig·tail (pígteil) *n.* a braid of hair

pi·ka (páikə) *n.* a member of *Ochotona*, fam. *Ochotonidae*, a genus of small, short-eared, tailless rodents of Asia and W. North America, closely related to the rabbit [Tungus *peeka*]

Pike (paik), Zebulon Montgomery (1779–1813), U.S. explorer and army officer. On an expedition (1806–7) in the Southwest he discovered the peak which now bears his name

pike (paik) *n.* (*hist.*) a pointed projection or

sharp tip, e.g. on the center of a shield or the head of an arrow [O.E. *piic, píc*, pickax]

pike *pl.* **pike, pikes** *n.* a member of *Esox*, fam. *Esocidae*, a genus of voracious freshwater fishes of the northern hemisphere, with narrow, elongated snout and sharp teeth, esp. *E. lucius*. They are prized as game fish and as food || any of several fishes resembling these, e.g. the barracuda and walleye pike [shortened fr. *pikefish* fr. PIKE, pointed projection (because of its pointed snout)]

pike *n.* (*hist.*) a weapon carried by a foot soldier, consisting of a long wooden shaft with a pointed metal head, superseded in the 18th c. by the bayonet [F. *pique*]

pike *n.* a gate or bar across a road where a toll is paid || a road, esp. one on which a toll is levied || a toll [short for TURNPIKE]

pike·let (páiklit) *n.* (*Br.*) a crumpet [shortened fr. older *barapicklet* fr. Welsh *bara pyglyd*]

pike·man (páikmən) *pl.* **pike·men** (páikmən) *n.* (*hist.*) a soldier armed with a pike

pike perch any of several fish of fam. *Percidae* resembling the pikes, e.g. the walleye pike and the sauger

pik·er (páikər) *n.* (*pop.*) someone who is mean with his money, and generally lacking in largeness of spirit [etym. doubtful]

Pikes Peak (paiks) a peak (14,110 ft) of the Rocky Mtns, in E. central Colorado, on the edge of the Great Plains

pike·staff (páikstæf, páikstɑf) *pl.* **pike·staffs, pike·staves** (páiksteivz) *n.* the wooden shaft of a pike || a staff with a sharp metal tip at the lower end, used as a walking stick

pi·laf, pi·laff, pi·lau (pí:lʌf, piláf) *n.* an Oriental dish of rice boiled with fish, meat or chicken and spices [Pers. *piláw*]

pi·las·ter (pilǽstər) *n.* (*archit.*) a rectangular column engaged in a wall and serving as a pier or as decoration [F. *pilastre* fr. Ital.]

Pi·late (páilət), Pontius, Roman procurator of Judea and Samaria (c. 26–c. 36 A.D.). He gave Christ up to the Jews to be crucified, in order to conciliate the Sanhedrin, though possibly against his own desire

pi·lau *PILAF

pil·chard (píltʃərd) *n. Sardinia pilchardus* (or *Sardinella pilchardus*), fam. *Clupeidae*, a small marine food fish like the related herring but smaller, found in great numbers along the coasts of Britain, and of Europe as far south as Portugal. The young are sardines [etym. doubtful]

Pil·co·ma·yo (pi:lkɔmájɔ) a river (1,000 miles long) flowing southeast from the Bolivian Andes above Potosí across the Gran Chaco (where it forms the Argentina-Paraguay border) to the River Paraguay just north of Asunción

pile (pail) **1.** *n.* a stout beam of wood or steel driven vertically into unfirm ground or the bed of a lake, river or sea, as a support for a superstructure, e.g. a house or causeway || (*heraldry*) a wedge-shaped charge issuing point downwards from the top of an escutcheon **2.** *v.t. pres. part.* **pil·ing** *past* and *past part.* **piled** to support with or furnish with piles || to drive piles into [O.E. *píl* fr. L. *pilum*, a heavy javelin, pestle]

pile 1. *n.* a number of things lying one upon another, or a quantity of material placed in or as if in layers forming an elevated mass, *a pile of books, a pile of gravel* || (*pop.*) a large amount of, *a pile of things to do* || a funeral pyre || (*elec.*) a battery of dry cells || a nuclear reactor || (*rhet.*) a large building or group of buildings **to make one's pile** to make a fortune **2.** *v. pres. part.* **pil·ing** *past* and *past part.* **piled** *v.t.* to place in a pile, *pile the books on top of each other* || (esp. with 'together' or 'up') to gather, accumulate || to cover with a pile or piles, *a table piled with books* || *v.i.* to crowd together, *they piled into his car* || (esp. with 'up') to come together in or as if in a pile, *his debts are piling up* **to pile arms** (*mil.*) to stand rifles together, with their butts on the ground, so that they support one another in a pyramid [F.]

pile *n.* a soft, furry or velvety raised surface consisting of threads standing out from the surface of a fabric or carpet, either singly or as loops || soft down, fur, hair or wool [fr. L. *pilus*, hair]

pile driver a machine used to drive piles into the ground with a drop hammer || a person who operates this machine

pile-driv·er (páildrɑivər) *n.* (*slang*) one who hits with great force

piles (pailz) *pl. n.* hemorrhoids [origin unknown]

pi·le·um (páili:əm) *pl.* **pi·le·a** (páili:ə) *n.* the top of a bird's head, from the nape to the bill [Mod. L. fr. L. *pileus*, felt cap]

pi·le·us (páiliːəs) *pl.* **pi·le·i** (páiliːai) *n.* (*biol.*) the umbrella-shaped structure in a mushroom or a jellyfish [L.=a felt hat]

pile·wort (páilwəːrt) *n.* the lesser celandine (*CELANDINE) [fr. its use in treating piles]

pil·fer (pílfər) *v.t.* to steal in small quantities ‖ *v.i.* to commit petty thefts [prob. fr. A.F. and O.F. *pelfrer*, to pillage]

pil·grim (pílgrim) *n.* a person who makes a journey to some sacred place as an act of religious devotion **Pil·grim** (*Am. hist.*) any of the Puritan refugees, mostly Brownists, who sailed from England in the 'Mayflower' (1620) and founded Plymouth Colony in New England [M.E. *pelegrim, pilegrim* fr. O.F.]

pil·grim·age (pílgrəmidʒ) *n.* a journey made by a pilgrim ‖ a journey made for sentimental reasons, e.g. to a poet's birthplace [M.E. *pelrimage* fr. O.F.]

Pilgrimage of Grace (*Eng. hist.*) a rising in Lincolnshire and Yorkshire (1536) against Henry VIII's religious innovations, notably the suppression of the monasteries, as implemented by Thomas Cromwell. The leaders were executed (1537)

Pilgrim Father (*Am. hist.*) one of the Pilgrims

pi·li (píːliː) *n. Canarium ovatum*, fam. *Burseraceae*, a Philippine tree bearing edible nuts ‖ the nut of this tree [Tagalog]

pi·lif·er·ous (pailífərəs) *adj.* (esp. *bot.*) having or producing hairs a covering of hair [fr. L. *pilus*, hair + -*fer*, bearing]

pil·ing (páiliŋ) *n.* the act of driving in piles ‖ (*collect.*) piles used in construction

Pi·li·pi·no (piləpíːnou) *n.* official language in the Republic of the Philippines, similar to Tagalog

pill (pil) 1. *n.* a small ball or pellet of medicine usually coated with sugar, which is swallowed whole ‖ (with 'the') an oral contraceptive ‖ something unpleasant that must be accepted ‖ (*pop., old-fash.*) a disagreeable person 2. *v.i.* (of a woolen sweater etc.) to form little balls of fiber on its surface [prob. fr. M. Du. and M.L.G. *pille* fr. L. *pilula*, little ball]

pill (preceded by 'the') an oral contraceptive pill

pil·lage (pílidʒ) 1. *n.* the act of taking goods by force, esp. by armed force in war 2. *v. pres. part.* **pil·lag·ing** past and past part. **pil·laged** *v.t.* to plunder (persons or places), esp. in wartime ‖ *v.i.* to make plundering raids [F. *pillage* n. fr. *piller* v.]

pil·lar (pílər) 1. *n.* (*archit.*) a vertical structure of masonry, metal etc., of much greater height than thickness, used as a support for a superstructure or as an ornament ‖ anything like this in shape or function, *a pillar of smoke, idealism is a pillar of his philosophy* ‖ a chief supporter of a cause or institution, *a pillar of the Church* **from pillar to post** from one place of refuge, resource etc. to another 2. *v.t.* to support or ornament with pillars [O.F. *piler*]

pillar box (*Br.*) a short, hollow metal pillar in a public place, for mailing letters etc.

Pillars of Hercules the two rocky promontories (Gibraltar in Europe and Gebel Musa in N. Africa) on either side of the Strait of Gibraltar. For the ancients they marked the finish of the civilized world at the western end of the Mediterranean. According to legend, they were parted by Hercules

pill·box (pílbɒks) *n.* a small round box used as a container for pills ‖ a small, round shallow hat, with no brim ‖ (*mil.*) a small gun shelter of reinforced concrete

pill·head (pílhed) *n.* one who is addicted to pills or hard drugs, esp. when not medically necessary

pil·lion (píljən) *n.* a saddle or spring seat for a second person at the back of a motorcycle or scooter ‖ a light saddle, esp. for a woman ‖ a pad placed behind a man's saddle for a woman to sit on **to ride pillion** (*Br.*) to ride on a pillion [prob. fr. Celt. fr. L. *pellis*, skin, pelt, felt]

Pill·nitz, Declaration of (pílnits) a statement issued (1791) by the Emperor Leopold II and Frederick William II of Prussia, calling on the European powers to restore Louis XVI's authority in France

pil·lo·ry (píləri) 1. *pl.* **pil·lo·ries** *n.* (*hist.*) a wooden framework with three holes into which the head and hands of an offender were locked, exposing him to public abuse and ridicule 2. *v.t. pres. part.* **pil·lo·ry·ing** past and past part. **pil-**

lo·ried (*hist.*) to set in a pillory ‖ to expose to public scorn [M.E. fr. O.F.]

pil·low (pílou) 1. *n.* a rest and support for the neck or head of a recumbent person (in Western countries a cushion stuffed with down, feathers or other soft material) ‖ (*engin.*) a block, e.g. of wood, used as a cushioning support ‖ a small cushion supporting the design in the making of pillow lace 2. *v.t.* to lay (the head etc.) on a pillow or on something serving as a pillow [O.E. *pylu, pyle*]

pil·low·case (píloukeis) *n.* a loose, removable cover of cotton or linen for a pillow

pillow lace handmade lace worked over bobbins on a pillow on which the pattern is marked out

pil·low·slip (pílouslip) *n.* pillowcase

pillow talk (*colloq.*) conversations about sex between partners, esp. in bed

pi·lo·car·pine (pailəkárpiːn, pailəkárpin) *n.* an alkaloid derived from jaborandi. It is used to contract the pupil of the eye, e.g. in counteracting effects of atropine [fr. Mod. L. *Pilocarpus* (genus) fr. Gk *pilos*, felt + *karpos*, fruit]

pi·lose (páilous) *adj.* covered with hair, esp. soft hair **pi·los·i·ty** (pailósiti) *n.* [fr. L. *pilosus* fr. *pilus.* hair]

pi·lot (páilət) 1. *n.* a person qualified to direct a vessel on its course into or out of a port, river mouth, canal etc., or along a coast, and taking over navigational control from the master of the vessel while so employed ‖ a person qualified to operate the flying controls of an aircraft ‖ someone who acts as a guide ‖ (*engin.*) a machine part which guides another part in its movement ‖ a pilot light 2. *adj.* serving as an experimental model for others to follow, *a pilot factory plant* ‖ (*engin.*) serving as a device to direct the operation of a larger device‖ serving as a guide, *a pilot dog* [older F. *pilotte, pilot* and Mod. F. *pilote* fr. Ital.]

pilot *v.t.* to act as the pilot of (a ship, aircraft etc.) ‖to guide (someone) [fr. PILOT n. or F. *piluter*]

pi·lot·age (páilətidʒ) *n.* the work of piloting ‖ the fee paid to a pilot [F.]

pilot balloon a small, unmanned balloon filled with hydrogen used to indicate the speed and direction of the wind

pilot boat a boat used to transport a pilot between a port and the vessel he is to pilot

pilot engine a locomotive sent ahead of a train to see if the track is clear

pilot fish either of two fishes of fam. *Carangidae, Seriola zonata* and *Naucrates ductor,* which follow sharks and ships for food, and were formerly thought to guide mariners. They are about 12 ins long and are found in warm waters

pi·lot·house (páiləthaus) *pl.* **pi·lot·hous·es** (páiləthauziz) *n.* the structure on a ship containing the wheel and navigating equipment

pilot lamp a small electric lamp in an electrical circuit, which shows by its light when the circuit is closed ‖ an electric lamp indicating the position of a switch or circuit breaker

pilot light a small burner kept alight to kindle a large burner when this is supplied with fuel, e.g. in a gas heater

pilot officer (*Br.*) an officer in the Royal Air Force ranking immediately below a flying officer

pi·lous (páiləs) *adj.* pilose [fr. L. *pilosus*, hairy]

Pil·sen (pílzen) (*Czech*. Plzeň) an industrial center (pop. 165,400) of Bohemia, Czechoslovakia: metallurgy, heavy machinery, armaments, automobiles, beer

Pił·sud·ski (pilsúːdskiː), Józef (1867–1935), Polish statesman and general. He commanded the Polish army in the service of Austria (1914–16). He declared Poland an independent republic (1918), with himself as head of state (1918–22). After a coup d'état, he ruled autocratically as premier (1926–8, 1930–5)

pil·u·lar (píljulər) *adj.* of or like a pill [fr. L. *pilula*, pill]

pil·ule (píljuːl) *n.* a small pill [F.]

Pi·ma (píːmə) *pl.* **Pi·ma, Pi·mas** *n.* a member of a people of S. Arizona and N. Mexico ‖ their Uto-Aztecan language

Pi·man (píːmən) *adj.* of, relating to or designating a family of Uto-Aztecan languages incl. Pima

pi·men·to (piméntou) *pl.* **pi·men·tos** *n.* allspice ‖ the pimiento [fr. Span. *pimienta*, Port. *pimenta*, pepper]

pi meson *PION

pi·mien·to (pimjéntou) *pl.* **pi·mien·tos** *n.* any of certain red sweet peppers used for stuffing olives, as a source of paprika etc. [Span. fr. *pimienta*, pepper]

pimp (pimp) 1. *n.* a male procurer of clients for a prostitute 2. *v.i.* to act as a pimp [etym. doubtful]

pim·per·nel (pímpərnel) *n.* a member of *Anagallis*, fam. *Primulaceae*, a genus of creeping plants with red, blue or white flowers, growing on cultivated land, by roadsides and on dunes. esp. *A. arvensis*, the scarlet pimpernel. The flowers close in bad weather [O.F. *pimprenele, pimpernelle* and F. *pimprenelle*]

pim·ple (pímp'l) *n.* a small, solid, rounded, raised area on the skin, caused by inflammation etc. **pim·pled, pim·ply** *adjs* [origin unknown]

pin (pin) 1. *n.* a short, very thin, sharp-pointed length of metal, with a small, flat or round head at one end, used to fasten textiles, paper etc., or one without a head, mounted on a badge or brooch to fasten it to clothing ‖ any of several other fastening devices, e.g. a hairpin or safety pin, or a wooden peg used in carpentry ‖ a peg for fastening things to, e.g. one that holds and maintains the tension of a string of a piano, harp etc. ‖ a brooch ‖ (*carpentry*) the tenon of a dovetail ‖ a bottle-shaped piece of wood bowled at in ninepins or tenpins ‖ a linchpin ‖ something of very small value, *not worth a pin* ‖ (golf) the flagpole marking a hole ‖ a small cask holding 1/2 firkin ‖ (*pl., pop.*) the legs, to *knock someone off his pins* 2. *v.t. pres. part.* **pin·ning** past and past part. **pinned** to fasten with or as if with a pin **to pin (someone) down** to hold (someone) down by force ‖ to cause (someone) to commit himself or to be specific, *you must pin him down to a particular day* **to pin (something) on someone** to put the blame for (something) on someone [O.E. *pinn*]

pi·ña co·la·da (píːnjəkouláːdə) *n.* drink with a pineapple juice base to which rum, coconut cream and ice are added

pin·a·fore (pínəfɔr, pínəfour) *n.* a sleeveless, apronlike garment fastened at the back and worn over good clothing, esp. by little girls

Pi·nar del Río (pinárðelríːɔ) the westernmost province (area 5,211 sq. miles, pop. 588,000) of Cuba. Capital: Pinar del Río (pop. 27,000). Chief occupations: agriculture (tobacco, coffee, sugarcane, pineapples), cattle raising, lumbering, mining. It includes Cuba's largest copper mine, and huge asphalt deposits

pin·ball (pínbɒl) *n.* a game played on a pinball machine

pinball machine (*Am.*=*Br.* pin table) a glass-covered slot machine used for amusement or gambling. Steel balls are projected up a slope, and when they roll back down they make electric contact with pins projecting in a pattern, causing bulbs to flash and a score to be indicated

pince-nez (pɛ̃snei, pɪ́nsnei) *pl.* **pince-nez** *n.* a pair of glasses, usually rimless, not hooked over the ears but simply held in place by a spring which grips the bridge of the nose [F.=pinch-nose]

pin·cer·like (pínsərlaik) *adj.* like pincers in function or action

pin·cers (pínsərz) *pl. n.* (sometimes construed as *sing.*) a tool consisting of two arms, hinged together not far from their curved gripping ends and serving as a pair of levers, used to crush, extract nails, grip etc. ‖ (*zool.*) an appendage for grasping, e.g. the chela of certain crustaceans [M.E. *pinsours* fr. A.F.]

pincers movement (*mil.*) a converging attack by two forces from opposed directions on a position

pinch (pintʃ) 1. *v.t.* to grip between the forefinger and thumb with a sudden, strong pressure, *to pinch someone's arm* ‖ to grip a portion of the flesh of (someone) in this way ‖ to squeeze, *he pinched his finger in the door* ‖ to cause pain to by pressing tightly, *do the new shoes pinch you?* ‖ to cause to become thin, worn, haggard etc., *pinched by poverty* ‖ (often passive and with 'for') to restrict to a narrow space or range of activity, spending etc., *pinched for cash* ‖ (*naut.*) to sail (a boat) with the sails close-hauled ‖ (*pop.*) to steal ‖ (*pop.*) to arrest ‖ *v.i.* to exert painful pressure by squeezing ‖ to overeconomize, be stingy, *the more he pinched, the hungrier we became* 2. *n.* the act or an instance of pinching between forefinger and thumb ‖ an amount which can be taken up between the forefinger

CONCISE PRONUNCIATION KEY: (**a**) æ, c*a*t; ɑ, c*a*r; ɔ f*aw*n; ei, sn*a*ke. (**e**) e, h*e*n; iː, sh*ee*p; iə, d*ee*r; ɛə, b*ea*r. (**i**) i, f*i*sh; ai, t*i*ger; əː, b*i*rd. (**o**) o, *o*x; au, c*ow*; ou, g*oa*t; u, p*oo*r; ɔi, r*oy*al. (**u**) ʌ, d*u*ck; u, b*u*ll; uː, g*oo*se; ə, b*a*cillus; juː, c*u*be. x, lo*ch*; θ, *th*ink; ð, bo*th*er; z, *Z*en; ʒ, corsa*g*e; dʒ, sava*g*e; ŋ, ora*ng*utan*g*; j, *y*ak; ʃ, *f*ish; tʃ, fe*tch*; 'l, rabb*le*; 'n, redd*en*. Complete pronunciation key appears inside front cover.

and thumb, *a pinch of salt* ‖ suffering caused by the pressure of poverty etc. **in a pinch** (*Am.=Br.* **at a pinch**) if absolutely necessary, *can you manage it in a pinch?* [O.N.F., origin unknown]

pinch·beck (píntʃbek) **1.** *n.* an alloy of copper and zinc used in cheap jewelry to imitate gold **2.** *adj.* made of pinchbeck ‖ false, sham [after Christopher *Pinchbeck*, Eng. jeweler who invented it]

pinch effect (*electr.*) the constricting effect that occurs in a fluid conductor, e.g., liquid metal, subject to a large electric current with magnetism tending to push electrons toward the axis of the current

pinch·ers (píntʃərz) *pl. n.* pincers

pinch·hit (píntʃhit) *pres. part.* **pinchhit·ting** *past* and *past part.* **pinch-hit** *v.i.* (*baseball*) to bat for the regular player ‖ (pop.) to act as substitute in an emergency [back-formation fr. PINCH HITTER]

pinch hitter (*baseball*) a player who pinch-hits for another ‖ (*pop.*) someone who acts as a substitute for another person

Pin·chot (píntʃou), Gifford (1865–1946), U.S. forester and public official. He headed (1898–1910) what became the federal forest service, and co-founded (1912) Theodore Roosevelt's Progressive party

Pinck·ney (píŋkni:), Charles (1757–1824), U.S. statesman and governor of South Carolina (1789–92, 1796–8, 1806–8). His outline for the federal constitution, submitted to the Constitutional Convention of 1787, strongly influenced the constitution's final form

Pinckney, Charles Cotesworth (1746–1825), U.S. minister to France during John Adams' administration, in the mission which led to the X-Y-Z Affair

Pinckney, Thomas (1750–1828), U.S. statesman. While minister to England (1792–6), he served (1794–5) as envoy extraordinary to Spain, where he negotiated the Pinckney Treaty

Pinckney Treaty a U.S.-Spanish treaty negotiated (1795) by Thomas Pinckney, in which Spain granted the U.S.A. the use of the Mississippi River and the right to deposit merchandise at New Orleans, and which defined the boundaries of E. and W. Florida and Louisiana

pin·cush·ion (píŋkuʃən) *n.* a small cushion in which pins and needles are stuck so as to be handy for use

Pin·dar (píndər) (c. 518–c. 438 B.C.), Greek lyric poet. He is best known for his choral odes celebrating the victors at the great Greek games and praising the gods

Pin·dar·ic (pindǽrik) **1.** *adj.* in the complex style of Pindar **2.** *n.* a Pindaric ode

Pin·dus (píndəs) a wooded mountain range (highest point 8,635 ft) running through N. Greece (between Epirus and Thessaly) and S.E. Albania

pine (pain) *n.* a member of *Pinus*, fam. *Pinaceae*, a genus of chiefly north temperate, coniferous, resinous trees with needlelike evergreen leaves, usually in clusters. There are over 90 species, widely cultivated for their easily worked lumber and for resinous products ‖ the wood of any of these trees [O.E. *pin* fr. L. *pinus*]

pine *pres. part.* **pin·ing** *past* and *past part.* **pined** *v.i.* (often with 'away') to lose vitality gradually through hunger, unhappiness etc. ‖ (with 'for') to long for, often so intensely as to suffer [O.E. *pinian*, to torment]

pin·e·al body (píni:əl) a small body lying behind the third ventricle of the brain in vertebrates. It is thought to be either a vestigial optical organ or an endocrine gland [F. *pinéal*, conical, shaped like a pinecone]

pineal eye an eyelike structure in some lizards, the tuatara etc., with a distinguishable retina and lens. It is an outgrowth of the roof of the forebrain

pineal gland the pineal body

pine·ap·ple (páinæp'l) *n. Ananas comosus*, fam. *Bromeliaceae*, a perennial tropical plant with spiny, recurved leaves and a short, thick stem, native to South America and widely cultivated for its fruit ‖ the edible fruit of this plant, which has juicy, yellowish flesh and a covering of floral bracts topped with short, stiff leaves ‖ (*archit.*) an ornament in the shape of this fruit

pine·cone (páinkoun) *n.* the cone of a pine tree

Pi·nel (pi:nel), Philippe (1745–1826), French physician. He pioneered in the humane treatment of the insane, esp. in his 'Traité médico-philosophique sur l'aliénation mentale' (1801)

pi·nene (páini:n) *n.* either of two oily unsaturated terpenes containing two rings, $C_{10}H_{16}$, obtained from oil of turpentine and occurring in many essential oils [PINE (tree)]

pine needle one of the aromatic, needlelike leaves of a pine

Pi·ne·ro (piníərou), Sir Arthur Wing (1855–1934), English playwright. His success between 1890 and 1900, notably in 'The Second Mrs Tanqueray' (1893), marked the break between the sentimentality and melodrama of the Victorian theater and the new realistic drama

Pi·ñe·ro (pi:njérɔ), Jesús Toribio (1897–1952), Puerto Rican farmer and public official, the first Puerto Rican to be appointed (1946) governor of Puerto Rico

pin·er·y (páinəri) *pl.* **pin·er·ies** *n.* a field or hothouse where pineapples are cultivated ‖ a pine grove or forest

Pines, Isle of (Painz) *CUBA

pine tar tar residue from the distillation of pine wood, used in roofing materials, paint etc., and in treating skin diseases

pine·tum (painí:təm) *pl.* **pi·ne·ta** (painí:tə) *n.* a plantation of pines of various species for scientific study or ornament [L.=pine grove]

pin·eyed (páinaid) *adj.* (*bot.*) having minute markings resembling eyes, esp. having concealed stamens, with the stigma visible within the corolla (cf. THRUM-EYED)

pin·feath·er (pínfeðər) *n.* a young feather, esp. one just emerging from the skin

pin-fire (pínfaiər) *v.* (*veterinary*) treatment of a horse for a leg ailment by use of electric needles applied to an anesthetized part affected

pin·fold (pínfould) **1.** *n.* a pound for confining stray animals **2.** *v.t.* to confine in a pinfold [O.E. *pundfald*]

ping (piŋ) **1.** *n.* a sharp ringing sound, e.g. of a pebble hitting a rock, a bullet flying through the air etc. **2.** *v.t.* to make this sound [imit.]

ping *v.i.* (*Am.=Br.* pink, of an internal combustion engine) to knock [imit.]

Ping-Pong (píŋpɒŋ) *n.* table tennis [Trademark]

Ping Pong 1. camera missile that takes pictures at predetermined heights and returns by parachute to the launching pad. **2.** requiring a patient, esp. insured or Medicaid-subsidized, to see various specialists or to bring in family members, ostensibly for diagnosis and treatment, but primarily for increasing the service charges

pin·guid (píŋgwid) *adj.* (*rhet.*) fatty or greasy ‖ (*rhet.*, of soil) rich, fertile [fr. L.]

pin·head (pínhed) *n.* the head of a pin ‖ a very small object ‖ (*pop.*) a person of very low intelligence

pin·hole (pínhoul) *n.* a hole in paper etc., made by or as if by a pin ‖ a hole into which a pin or peg fits

pin·ion (pínjən) *n.* the smallest and smallest-toothed of two or more gear wheels forming a train or set of gear wheels [fr. F. *pignon*]

pinion 1. *n.* a flight feather of a bird's wing ‖ the end joint of a bird's wing **2.** *v.t.* to cut off or bind the pinions or wings of (a bird) to prevent flight ‖ to bind (the arms) of a person so as to make him powerless ‖ to make (someone) powerless by binding his arms [O.F. *pignon*]

pi·nite (páinait) *n.* an amorphous mineral consisting of aluminum potassium silicate [fr. G. *pinit* after the *Pini* mine in Saxony]

pink (piŋk) *n.* (*hist.*) a sailing vessel with a particularly narrow stern [prob. fr. M. Du. *pincke*, *pinke*, small seagoing ship]

pink *n.* (*Br.*) a salmon or grayling at the parr stage

pink 1. *n.* a member of *Dianthus*, fam. *Caryophyllaceae*, a genus of plants native to E. Europe, widely cultivated in temperate zones for their fragrant, white, pale red or crimson flowers ‖ a pale, bluish-red color ‖ a pigment, fabric etc. of this color ‖ the scarlet coat of a fox hunter ‖ the scarlet color of this coat **in the pink of health** (or **condition**) in perfect health (or condition) **2.** *adj.* having the color pink, *pink cheeks* ‖ (*pop.*) tending towards communism [etym. doubtful]

pink *v.t.* to ornament (a fabric etc.) by making patterns of holes in it ‖ to make small scallops with indented edges or zigzags in the border of (cloth or paper) ‖ to thrust a sword lightly into, or wound superficially with a bullet, causing a

small amount of surface bleeding ‖ (often with 'out') to adorn, decorate gaily [etym. doubtful]

pink *v.i.* (*Br.*, of an internal combustion engine) to ping [imit.]

pink collar *adj.* **1.** of women workers in cosmetology. **2.** by extension, of jobs predominantly held by women

Pin·ker·ton (píŋkərtən), Allan (1819–84), U.S. detective and founder of the Pinkerton National Detective Agency. He headed (1861), under the name of E. J. Allen, an organization for obtaining military information on the southern states

Pinkerton National Detective Agency an organization founded (1850) in Chicago, Ill., by Allan Pinkerton, which specialized in railway theft cases. It thwarted (1861) an assassination plot against President-elect Lincoln in Baltimore, Md., and captured (1866) the ringleaders in a $700,000 Adams Express company theft. A Pinkerton man, James McParlan, broke up (1876) the Molly Maguires

pink·eye (píŋkai) *n.* a highly contagious form of conjunctivitis

Pin·kiang (biŋyán) *HARBIN

pink·ie, pink·y (píŋki) *n.* (*pop.*) the little finger [prob. fr. Du. *pinkje*, dim. of *pink*, the little finger]

pinking shears a dressmaker's toothed shears for pinking the edges of fabric

Pink·ney (píŋkni:), William (1764–1822), U.S. diplomat. As U.S. commissioner to England under the Jay Treaty, he secured (1796) a claim of $800,000 for Maryland against the Bank of New England for losses and damages to American merchants caused by the British government

pin·na (pínə) *pl.* **pin·nae** (píni:), **pin·nas** *n.* (*bot.*) a leaflet of a pinnate leaf ‖ (*zool.*) any of certain appendages, e.g. a wing, feather, fin or flipper ‖ (*anat.*) the broad upper part of the auricle of the ear or the whole auricle [Mod. L. fr. L.=feather, wing]

pin·nace (pínis) *n.* (*hist.*) a six-oared or eight-oared boat of a man-of-war ‖ a ship's boat for conveying the crew ashore etc. [F. *pinasse*, *pinace* prob. fr. L. *pinus*, pine tree]

pin·na·cle (pínæk'l) **1.** *n.* a slender, usually pointed, turret ornamenting a gable, tower etc. ‖ a slender peak of rock ‖ (*fig.*) the highest point, climax, *the pinnacle of fame* **2.** *v.t. pres. part.* **pin·na·cling** *past* and *past part.* **pin·na·cled** to ornament with a pinnacle or pinnacles ‖ to place on or as if on a pinnacle ‖ to be the pinnacle of [M.E. *pinacle* fr. O.F. and F.]

pin·nate (píneit, pínit) *adj.* (*bot.*, of a compound leaf) having leaflets on each side of the rachis ‖ (*zool.*) divided in a feathery manner with lateral processes [fr. L. *pinnatus* fr. *pinna*, feather, wing]

pin·nat·i·fid (pinǽtifid) *adj.* (*bot.*) having pinnately cleft leaves, the clefts reaching approximately halfway to the midrib [fr. L. *pinnatus*, pinnate]

pin·na·tion (pinéiʃən) *n.* the state or fact of being pinnate

pin·ni·ped (pínəped) **1.** *adj.* (*zool.*) of or belonging to *Pinnipedia*, a suborder of marine carnivores with flippers, including seals, sea lions and walruses **2.** *n.* an animal of this suborder [fr. Mod. L. *pinnipedia* fr. L. fr. *pinna*, fin+*pes* (*pedis*), foot]

pin·nu·late (pínjəleit) *adj.* having pinnules **pín·nu·lat·ed** *adj.*

pin·nule (pínju:l) *n.* (*bot.*) one of the secondary divisions of a bipinnate leaf ‖ (*zool.*) a winglike or finlike part or organ [fr. L. *pinnula*, little plume or wing]

Pinochet Ugarte (pi:nouʃ eiu:gártei), Augusto (1915–) Chilean general and president (1974–). He became commander of the army (1973) and led the right-wing military coup that deposed Salvador Allende that same year. His efforts to suppress dissent led to massive civil rights violations

pi·noch·le, pi·noc·le (pí:nʌk'l, pí:nɒk'l) *n.* a card game, similar to bezique, which uses 48 cards taken from two packs, all cards below the eight being discarded and aces being kept in ‖ the pairing and declaration of the queen of spades and the knave of diamonds in this game [origin unknown]

pi·no·cy·to·sis (pinəsaitóusis) *n.* a method by which some cells absorb outside material by forming a membrane around themselves retaining the material in a separate sac. —**pi·no·cy·tot·ic** *adj.* —**pi·no·cy·tot·i·cal·ly** *adv.*

pi·no·le (pinóuli:) *n.* flour made from ground

CONCISE PRONUNCIATION KEY: (**a**) æ, c*a*t; ɑ, c*a*r; ɔ f*aw*n; ei, sn*a*ke. (**e**) e, h*e*n; i:, sh*ee*p; iə, d*ee*r; ɛə, b*ea*r. (**i**) i, f*i*sh; ai, t*i*ger; ə:, b*i*rd. (**o**) o, *o*x; au, c*ow*; ou, g*oa*t; u, p*oo*r; ɔi, r*oy*al. (**u**) ʌ, d*u*ck; u, b*u*ll; u:, g*oo*se; ə, b*a*cillus; ju:, c*u*be. x, lo*ch*; θ, *th*ink; ð, bo*th*er; z, *Z*en; ʒ, cor*s*age; dʒ, sa*v*age; ŋ, ora*ng*utang; j, *y*ak; ʃ, *fi*sh; tʃ, fe*tch*; 'l, rabb*le*; 'n, red*den*. Complete pronunciation key appears inside front cover.

corn, mesquite beans etc. in the southwestern U.S.A. and Mexico [Span. fr. Nahuatl]

pi·ñon (pínjən, píːnjən) *n.* any of several low-growing pines of W. and S.W. North America, which bear edible nutlike seeds, e.g. *Pinus parryana, Pinus edulis* ‖ the seed of any of these trees [Span.]

Pi·no Suá·rez (píːnɔswáres), José María (1869–1913), Mexican lawyer, writer, politician, and vice-president under Francisco Madero. He was assassinated with Madero by agents of Victoriano Huerta

pin·point (pínpɔint) **1.** *n.* the pointed end of a pin **2.** *v.t.* to locate (e.g. a target) precisely ‖ to direct (an attack, bomb etc.) on a small objective with great accuracy **3.** *adj.* (of a bombing target) requiring extreme accuracy of aim ‖ extremely precise, *pinpoint accuracy*

pin·prick (pínprik) *n.* a very small puncture made by or as if by a pin ‖ a small vexation or irritation, esp. a malicious remark meant to hurt a person's self-esteem

pins and needles a pricking sensation in a limb caused by a partial stoppage of the circulation **on pins and needles** in a state of nervous anxiety

pint (paint) *n.* any of various liquid or dry units of capacity equal to 1/8 gallon, esp., *(Am.)* a unit equal to 28.875cu. ins, *(Br.)* a unit equal to 34.678 cu. ins ‖ a dry measure equal 33.600 cu. ins ‖ *(Br.)* a pint pot of beer, ale or cider [M.E. *pynte* fr. F. *pinte*]

pin·ta (píntə, píːntə) *n.* a contagious tropical American disease marked by blotches and loss of pigment in patches [Span.=spot]

pin table *(Br.)* a pinball machine

pin·tail (pínteil) *n. Anas acuta,* fam. *Anatidae,* a freshwater duck of North America, Europe and Asia. The male has long, pointed central tail feathers ‖ *Pedioecetes phasianellus,* fam. *Tetraonidae,* a large grouse of the western U.S.A. and Canada with long middle tail feathers ‖ *Pterocles alchata,* fam. *Pteroclididae,* a long-winged, long-tailed bird somewhat like a pigeon in build, native to Europe, Africa and Asia

pin·tle (pínt'l) *n.* a thick pin or bolt, esp. when used as a pivot, e.g. that on which a rudder turns [O.E. *pintel, penis*]

pin·to (píntou) *pl.* **pin·tos** *n.* a pony or horse that is mottled, esp. with blotches of two or more colors ‖ a pinto bean [Span. fr. *pinto adj.,* spotted, mottled]

pinto bean a variety of mottled kidney bean of the southwest U.S.A.

Pin·tu·ric·chi·o, Pin·to·ric·chi·o (piːntuːríːkkjɔ, piːntɔríːkkjɔ) (Bernardino di Betto, c. 1454–1513), Italian painter. His themes are religious, and their treatment notable for lively composition and brilliance of color. His chief works are fresco series, including 'The Dispute of St Catherine' (1492–5) in the Vatican, and 'Life of Pius II' (1503–8) in Siena

pin·up (pínʌp) *n. (pop.)* a picture of a pinup girl ‖ *(pop.)* a pinup girl

pinup girl *(pop.)* a sexually attractive young woman

pin·wheel (pínhwiːl, pínwiːl) *n.* (*Am.=Br.* whirligig) a child's toy consisting of a stick with miniature windmill sails which spin in the wind ‖ (*Am.=Br.* Catherine wheel) a rapidly rotating firework

pin·worm (pínwəːrm) *n.* any of several tiny, unsegmented worms of fam. *Oxyuridae* that infest the intestine and rectum, esp. of children

Pin·zón (piːnθón), Vicente Yáñez (d. 1523), Spanish explorer, captain of 'La Niña' during Columbus' voyage of discovery. With Juan Díaz de Solís he explored (1508–9) Yucatán and Venezuela and discovered (1500) the mouth of the Amazon River

pi·on (píːɒn) *n. (particle phys.)* the group of three mesons with charges of +1.0 and −1 times the proton charge, no spin, a mass of about 138 MEV, used to bombard cancer cells. *also* pi meson **—pi·on·ic** *adj.*

pi·o·neer (paiəníər) **1.** *n.* a person who experiments and originates, or plays a leading part in the early development of something, *a pioneer of flying* ‖ an early settler, *pioneers of the American West* ‖ a member of a military unit which clears the way in advance of the main body of troops, building bridges, roads, trenches etc. **2.** *v.t.* to prepare, initiate and champion, *to pioneer flew methods of engineering* ‖ to explore and be among the first to develop (a region etc.) ‖ *v.i.* to be a pioneer [F. *pionnier,* O.F. *paonier,* foot soldier, pioneer]

Pioneer Venus Orbiter NASA's spacecraft circling Venus beginning December 1978

pi·ous (páiəs) *adj.* devout or showing religious devotion ‖ designating or making a hypocritical show or pretense of virtue, propriety etc. [fr. L. *pius,* dutiful]

pip (pip) *n.* a disease of poultry and other birds consisting of the accumulation of thick mucus in the mouth and throat **the pip** *(Br., pop.)* a feeling of crossness or depression [prob. fr. M. Du. *pippe,* Du. *pip*]

pip *n.* one of the marks on dice or dominoes ‖ *(Br.)* a star on the shoulder of an army officer's uniform, rank being indicated by the number of stars present ‖ one of the segments on the rind of a pineapple ‖ the root or rootstock of certain plants, e.g. lily of the valley, peony etc. ‖ a single flower in a clustered inflorescence [older-peep, origin unknown]

pip *n.* the seed of an apple, orange, pear, grape etc. [prob. shortened fr. PIPPIN]

pip *pres. part.* **pip·ping** *past* and *past part.* **pipped** *v.t.* (of a bird) to break (the shell of its egg) when hatching ‖ *v.i.* (of a bird) to break through the eggshell when hatching ‖ (of a shell) to break as a bird hatches out [prob. var. of PEEP]

pip *pres. part.* **pip·ping** *past* and *past part.* **pipped** *v.t.* *(Br., pop.)* to defeat, e.g. in an athletic contest ‖ *(Br., pop.)* to spoil completely, ruin, *that's pipped it !* ‖ *(Br., pop.)* to hit (a target) with a shot ‖ *(Br., pop.)* to fail (someone) in an examination ‖ *(Br., pop.)* to fail (an examination) ‖ *(Br., pop.)* to blackball [etym. doubtful]

pip *n.* a short high-pitched sound, used, e.g. on the radio, as a signal [imit.]

pip·age (páipidʒ) *n.* transportation of oil, natural gas, water etc. by pipes ‖ the charge for such transportation ‖ the pipes used, collectively

pi·pal, pee·pul (píːpəl) *n.* the bo tree [Hindi *pīpal*]

pipe (paip) *pres. part.* **pip·ing** *past* and *past part.* **piped** *v.t.* to convey through pipes, *to pipe oil* ‖ to utter in a squeaky or shrill voice, *to pipe an answer* ‖ *(naut.)* to summon (a crew) by sounding a boatswain's whistle ‖ to play (a tune) on a pipe ‖ to furnish with pipes ‖ to ornament with piping ‖ *v.i.* to play a pipe, esp. the bagpipes ‖ to make squeaky or shrill sounds ‖ *(metall.,* e.g. of steel castings) to develop longitudinal cavities ‖ *(naut.)* to summon a ship's crew by sounding a boatswain's whistle **to pipe down** *(pop.)* to stop talking, or become quiet and subdued **to pipe up** to begin to sing or speak, *several children piped up with the answer* [O.E. *pīpian,* to blow a pipe, and M.E. *pipen,* to peep, chirp, fr. L.]

pipe *n.* a large cask, usually one containing 105 imperial gallons ‖ the amount held by this [O.F. and F.]

pipe *n.* a long hollow cylinder, used chiefly to convey fluids, gas etc. ‖ a musical wind instrument consisting of a hollow cylinder in which the air is made to vibrate, producing a note ‖ one of the hollow tubes in an organ, in which the note is produced in this way ‖ a tubular organ, vessel etc. in the body ‖ a device for smoking tobacco, opium etc. ‖ a quantity of tobacco etc. contained in the bowl of this device ‖ a session of smoking such a device ‖ *(naut.)* a boatswain's whistle or the sounding of it ‖ *(mining)* a cylindrical vein of ore ‖ the shrill sound of a bird ‖ *(pl.)* bagpipes [O.E. *pipe,* a musical tube fr. L.L.]

pipe bomb explosive device made of a pipe filled with explosives and a fuse

pipe clay fine, white plastic clay used to clean and whiten uniform belts etc., also to make clay tobacco pipes **pipe·clay** *v.t.* to clean and whiten with pipe clay

pipe dream a hope or fantastic plan far removed from reality

pipe·fish (páipfiʃ) *pl.* **pipe·fish, pipe·fishes** *n.* a member of *Syngnathus,* fam. *Syngnathidae,* and related genera of lophobranch fishes covered with bony plates, having long tapering bodies, and jaws united to form a tube

pipe·line (páiplain) *n.* a long line of pipes jointed together, with pumping stations at intervals, used to convey liquids or gases, esp. to convey the crude product from an oil field to a port or refinery ‖ a channel of communication or transport

pipe major the chief player in a band of bagpipes

pipe of peace the calumet as a symbol of peace

pipe organ an organ in which the sound is produced by air vibrating in pipes (*ORGAN, cf. REED ORGAN)

pip·er (páipər) *n.* someone who plays a pipe, esp. the bagpipes

pi·per·a·zine (pi:pérəzi:n, pi:pérəzin) *n.* a basic compound, $C_4H_{10}N_2$, which forms crystalline salts in the presence of organic and inorganic acids [PIPERINE+AZOTE]

pi·per·i·dine (pipéridi:n, pipéridin) *n.* a basic liquid, $C_5H_{11}N$, with the odor of pepper, derived from piperine [fr. L. *piper,* pepper]

pip·er·ine (pípəri:n, pípərin) *n.* a crystalline alkaloid, $C_{17}H_{19}NO_3$, obtained from black pepper, and the active constituent of it [fr. L. *piper,* pepper]

pipe roll *(Br. hist.)* any of the annual accounts of royal revenue and expenditure kept by the Exchequer

pi·per·o·nal (paipérənæl) *n.* a crystalline aldehyde, $(CH_2O_2)C_6H_3CHO$, with the odor of heliotrope, used in perfumery [G.]

pipe·stone (páipstoun) *n.* a pink, hard, clayey stone used by American Indians to make tobacco pipes

pi·pette, pi·pet (paipét, pipét) *n.* a slender glass tube, open at both ends or with a rubber bulb at one end, used esp. in laboratories to take up liquids by suction [F. dim. of *pipe,* pipe]

pip·ing (páipiŋ) **1.** *n.* the music of pipes ‖ a high-pitched, pipelike sound made by or as if by a bird ‖ a system of pipes ‖ material of which pipes can be made ‖ an ornamental fold of cloth sewn along an edge e.g. of a loose cover and often threaded with cord ‖ an ornamental ridge of icing on a cake **2.** *adj.* playing on a pipe ‖ high-pitched, shrill treble, *a child's piping voice* **3.** *adv.* (in the phrase) **piping hot** (of food or liquid) very hot

pip·it (pípit) *n.* a member of *Anthus,* fam. *Motacillidae,* a genus of small birds resembling the lark in coloring and behavior, esp. *A. pratensis,* the meadow pipit of Europe and Asia ‖ any bird of fam. *Motacillidae* [prob. imit.]

pip·kin (pípkin) *n.* a small earthenware pan or pot for cooking [etym. doubtful]

Pip·pin (pípin) Frankish rulers *PÉPIN

pip·pin (pípin) *n.* any of several varieties of dessert apple [M.E. fr. O.F. pepin, seed]

pip·sis·se·wa (pipsísəwə) *n. Chimaphila umbellata,* fam. *Pyrolaceae,* an evergreen plant with astringent leaves sometimes used medicinally as a tonic and diuretic [fr. Algonquian]

pip·squeak (pípskwi:k) *n. (pop.)* a person one regards as of no consequence [prob. imit., originally used of a small. high-speed German shell in the lst world war]

pi·quan·cy (pí:kənsi:) *n.* a piquant flavor or quality

pi·quant (pí:kənt) *adj.* sharply stimulating the sense of taste, *a piquant sauce* ‖ stimulating the curiosity or interest [F.]

pique (pi:k) *pres. part.* **piqu·ing** *past* and *past part.* **piqued** *v.t.* to cause resentment in, esp. by wounding the pride of, *he was piqued by her remark* ‖ to stimulate, arouse, *to pique someone's curiosity* [fr. F. *piquer,* to prick]

pique *n.* resentment caused by injured self-esteem [F.]

pique 1. *n.* a score of 30 in piquet made before one's opponent begins to count **2.** *v. pres. part.* **piqu·ing** *past* and *past part.* **piqued** *v.t.* to make this score against (one's opponent) ‖ *v.i.* to make this score [F. *pic*]

pi·qué (pikéi, pi:kéi) *n.* a rather stiff fabric of esp. cotton with a ribbed surface [F. fr. *piquer,* to prick]

pi·quet (pikét, pikéi) *n.* an elaborate l7th-c. card game for two players, using only the 32 cards above the six, incl. the aces [F.]

pi·ra·cy (páirəsi:) *pl.* **pi·ra·cies** *n.* robbery of ships at sea ‖ robbery on land by a descent from the sea by persons not acting under the authority of a state ‖ unauthorized use of a patented or copyrighted work ‖ an instance of any of these [fr. M.L *piratia* fr. Gk]

Pi·rae·us (pairí:əs, piréiəs) *(Gk* Peiraieus) the chief port and industrial center (pop. 500,000) of Greece, adjoining Athens; chemicals, shipbuilding, textiles, mechanical engineering, building materials, light manufacturing

pi·ra·gua (pirágwə, piːrǽgwə) *n.* a pirogue [Span. fr. Carib]

Pi·ran·del·lo (pirəndélou, piːrəndéllɔ), Luigi (1867–1936), Italian playwright, short-story writer and novelist. His novels include 'The Late Mattia Pascal' (1904). His short stories were collected as 'Novelle per un anno' (1922). His best plays are grotesque and scintillating tragedies, notably 'Six Characters in Search of an Author' (1921) and 'Henry IV' (1922), in which the leading ideas of multiple personality and the relativity of reality are convincingly exploited, and in which he consistently plays with the ambiguity of dramatic illusions

Pi·ra·ne·si (pi:ranézi:), Giambattista (1720–78), Italian architect and etcher. His etchings include the 'Vedute' (views of ancient Rome) and 'Carceri d'Invenzione' (imaginary prisons). The dramatic power of these, with their expressive use of light and shade, influenced neoclassical architecture

pi·ra·nha (piránjə) n. a member of *Serrasalmus*, fam. *Characidae*, a genus of small, voracious fishes found in lakes and rivers of South America. They attack men and animals in the water [Port. fr. Tupi]

pi·rate (páirət) 1. n. someone who commits piracy 2. v. *pres. part.* **pi·rat·ing** *past* and *past part.* **pi·rat·ed** v.t. to use (another's copyright material) for one's own profit without permission or without paying fees ‖ v.i. to practice piracy **pi·rat·ic** (pairǽtik), **pi·rát·i·cal** *adjs* [fr. L. *pirata* fr. Gk fr. *peiran*, to attack]

Pi·renne (pi:ren), Henri (1862–1935), Belgian historian. He wrote a 'History of Belgium' (1899–1932) and was a specialist in medieval economic history, esp. the growth of towns

pi·rogue (piróug) n. a dugout canoe [F. fr. Carib]

pir·ou·ette (piru:ét) 1. n. a rapid spin or whirl of the body on the point of the toe or ball of the foot, esp. in ballet 2. v.i. *pres. part.* **pir·ou·et·ting** *past* and *past part.* **pir·ou·et·ted** to execute a pirouette [F.=spinning top]

Pi·sa (pí:zə) a city (pop. 103,500) of Tuscany, Italy, on the Arno. Its chief monuments, in the Piazza del Duomo, are the cathedral (11th–13th cc.), baptistry (12th c.), 12th-c. campanile or 'leaning tower' (179 ft high, 14 ft off the perpendicular) and Campo Santo (1203). University (1338)

pis al·ler (pí:zælei) n. an expedient resorted to only because there is no better alternative [F.=to go worse]

Pi·sa·nel·lo (pi:zanéllo) (Antonio Pisano, c. 1395–c. 1450), Italian painter and medalist, influenced by Gentile da Fabriano and the international Gothic style. His extant works include 'The Annunciation' (c. 1424) and 'St George and the Princess' (c. 1437). Few of his frescos survive, but his portrait medals and his drawings, esp. his studies of animals, are masterly

Pi·sa·no (pi:záno), Andrea (c. 1270–1348), Italian sculptor. He carried on the work of Giotto on the campanile of Florence's cathedral, after working on the bronze doors of the baptistry (1330–6)

Pisano, Giovanni (c. 1245–after 1314), Italian sculptor and architect, son of Nicola Pisano. He worked toward a fusion of Gothic and classical elements, notably in his two pulpits, in St Andrea, Pistoia (c. 1297–1301) and in Pisa cathedral (1302–10)

Pisano, Nicola (c. 1220–c. 1287), Italian architect and sculptor. He initiated classical styles, making his influence felt throughout Italy. His best work includes pulpits in the baptistry at Pisa (1260) and in Siena cathedral (1265–8) and the fountains at Perugia (1278)

pis·ca·to·ri·al (piskətóri:əl, piskətóuri:əl) adj. piscatory

pis·ca·to·ry (pískətɔri:, pískətouri:) adj. of or relating to fishing or fishermen [fr. L. *piscatorius* fr. *piscator,* fisherman]

Pis·ces (páisi:z, písi:z) a southern constellation ‖ the twelfth sign of the zodiac, represented as a fish [L. pl. of *piscis,* fish]

pis·ci·cide (písisaid) n. 1. extermination of fish life. 2. the product used for the purpose —**pis·ci·cíd·al** adj.

pis·ci·cul·ture (písikʌltʃər) n. the breeding and rearing of fish [fr. L. *piscis,* fish+*cultura,* culture]

pis·ci·na (pisí:nə, pisáinə) pl. **pis·ci·nas, pis·ci·nae** (pisí:ni:, pisáini:) n. a stone basin with a drain, near the altar of a church, for carrying away water from liturgical ablutions [L.=tank, fishpond]

pis·cine (písain, písi:n) adj. of, relating to, like or characteristic of fish [fr. L. *piscis,* fish]

pis·civ·o·rous (pisívərəs) adj. (zool.) fish-eating [fr. L. *piscis,* fish+-*vorous,* devouring]

pi·si·form (páisifɔrm) adj. having the size and shape of a pea [fr. Mod. L. *pisiformis* fr. *pisum,* pea]

pisiform bone a small, rounded bone on the upper, outer side of the wrist

Pi·sis·tra·tus, Pei·sis·tra·tus (paisístrətəs) (c. 600–c. 527 B.C.), tyrant of Athens (c. 560–c. 527 B.C.). He gained power by a coup d'état and was twice exiled, but returned with increased power. He adorned Athens and encouraged art, commerce and farming

pis·mire (písmair) n. (rhet.) an ant [M.E. fr. PISS+*mire,* an ant (from the odor of anthills, caused by the formic acid discharged by ants)]

pi·so·lite (pízəlait, páisəlait) n. limestone formed of pea-shaped concretions **pis·o·lit·ic** (pizəlítik, paisəlítik) adj. [fr. Mod. L. *pisolithus* fr. Gk *pisos,* pea+*lithos,* stone]

piss (pis) 1. v.i. (pop.) to urinate 2. n. (pop.) urine [O.F. *pissier,* F. *pisser*]

Pis·sar·ro (pi:særou), Camille (1831–1903), French painter who specialized in landscapes in a wide range of media. One of the original Impressionists, he was represented in all eight Impressionist exhibitions

pis·ta·chi·o (pistǽʃi:ou, pistáʃi:ou) pl. **pis·ta·chi·os** n. *Pistacia vera,* fam. *Anacardiaceae,* a small dioecious tree native to W. Asia. Its fruit, a drupe, contains an edible seed, the pistachio nut, used as a flavoring in ice cream, confectionery etc. ‖ this nut ‖ the yellowish green color of the nut [fr. L. *pistacium* fr. Gk]

pis·til (pístil) n. (bot.) the female seedbearing organ of a flower, including the ovary, stigma and style **pis·til·late** (pístilit, pístileit) adj. having or bearing a pistil, esp. without a stamen [F. *pistil* and L. *pistillum*]

Pis·to·ia (pi:stɔ́jə) a city (pop. 84,700) in Tuscany, Italy: Romanesque cathedral (12th c.), baptistry (1337), medieval and Renaissance palaces and churches

pis·tol (pístəl) n. a small firearm held and fired with one hand [obs. F. *pistole*]

pis·tole (pistóul) n. any of several obsolete European gold coins, esp. a Spanish one [F.]

Pis·ton (pístən), Walter (1894–1976), American composer. His work includes symphonies, chamber music and a ballet, 'The Incredible Flutist' (1938)

pis·ton (pístən) n. a disk or short cylinder attached centrally to a rod and fitted closely inside a hollow cylinder, within which it can be driven up and down by fluid pressure (in engines) or create a partial vacuum on one side of it as the piston rod is moved up and down (in pumps or compressors) ‖ (mus.) a sliding valve in a brass wind instrument. When pressed, it causes an additional length of tubing to be opened, thus lowering the pitch [F. fr. Ital.]

piston ring an elastic, split metal ring surrounding a piston, giving a tighter fit inside the cylinder

piston rod a rod which moves or is moved by the piston to which it is attached

piston valve (mus.) a piston in a brass instrument

pit (pit) 1. n. a deep hole in the ground, either natural or made by digging for minerals ‖ a deep hole for refuse ‖ a covered hole in the ground used as a trap for animals ‖ a deep hole for carrying out some operation, e.g. a sawpit ‖ a coal mine, including the shaft and all the workings ‖ a small depression in a surface, e.g. one left in the skin by the pustules of smallpox ‖ a hole made in the floor of a garage or workshop enabling a car or machine to be examined or repaired from below ‖ an enclosed, often sunken area for fights between animals, esp. cocks ‖ (bot.) a specialized depressed region of the secondary wall of plant cells that plays a role in the intercellular transport of fluids ‖ (Am.=Br. orchestra pit) the space, often depressed, in front of the stage in a theater, where the orchestra sits ‖ (Br.) the ground floor of a theater auditorium, esp. the back part, under the gallery ‖ (Br.) the audience in this part of the theater ‖ (commerce) an area of an exchange devoted to a particular commodity, *wheat pit* 2. v. *pres. part.* **pit·ting** *past* and *past part.* **pit·ted** v.t. (with 'against') to match (one's strength, courage, willpower) against another's or against some natural force ‖ to make a pit in (the skin etc.), *a face pitted by smallpox* ‖ to set (one animal) to fight against another ‖ to put into a pit, usually for storage ‖ v.i. to become marked with pits [O.E. *pytt*]

pit 1. n. the stone of a peach, cherry, plum etc. 2.

v.t. *pres. part.* **pit·ting** *past* and *past part.* **pit·ted** to remove the pit from [Du.]

pi·ta (pí:tə) n. any of various plants yielding fiber, esp. the century plant ‖ the tough fiber obtained from such a plant, used for cordage ‖ flat, round bread used in the Middle East [Span.]

pit-a-pat (pítəpæt) 1. n. movement and sound suggested by the fast beating of the heart or by light, rapid footsteps 2. adv. in such a way as to make this sound, *her heart went pit-a-pat* 3. v.i. *pres. part.* **pit-a-pat·ting** *past* and *past part.* **pit-a-pat·ted** to move pit-a-pat ‖ (esp. of the heart) to go pit-a-pat [imit.]

Pit·cairn Islands Group (pítkɛərn), a British colony in the central S. Pacific, consisting of Pitcairn Is. (area 1.75 sq. miles, pop. 70) and three adjacent uninhabited islands. The inhabitants are descended from the 'Bounty' mutineers and Tahitians and speak their own idiom of English. Religion: Seventh-Day Adventist. Products: fruit, vegetables, curios. Pitcairn became a British colony (1838) and has been administered since 1970 from New Zealand

pitch (pitʃ) 1. n. a dark-colored, sticky, resinous substance, liquid when heated, hard when cold, which is a residue from distillation of tars, turpentine or fatty oils etc. and occurs naturally as asphalt. It is used for proofing wood or fabric, e.g. the hulls of boats or roofs, in the manufacture of soaps and plastics, and for road surfacing ‖ this substance as a criterion of blackness or obscurity ‖ a resin derived from certain conifers, sometimes considered to have medicinal properties 2. v.t. to coat or smear with pitch [O.E. *pic* fr. L.]

pitch 1. v.t. to fix and set up, *to pitch a tent* ‖ to set or place in a definite position ‖ to throw, toss, *to pitch hay* ‖ (baseball, cricket) to throw or deliver (the ball) to the batter or between ‖ (mus.) to set (a part, note etc.) in a scale or key or at a particular pitch ‖ to set in a particular style, manner, mood, feeling etc. ‖ v.i. to encamp ‖ (of a ship) to plunge or toss with bow and stern alternately rising and falling (cf. ROLL) ‖ to plunge headlong ‖ (cricket, of the ball) to fall in a specified way or place, *it pitched on the leg stump* ‖ to dip, slope, *the roof pitches steeply* ‖ (baseball) to throw the ball to the batter or be the player who throws the ball to the batter **to pitch in** to get down to work vigorously **to pitch into** (pop.) to attack violently **to pitch on** (or **upon**) (Br., pop.) to select arbitrarily, *when he needs a volunteer he always pitches on me* 2. n. the act of pitching or an instance of this ‖ a place claimed for doing business in an open market, for street performance or for camping, (Br.) playing a game etc. ‖ (baseball) the act of pitching or manner in which the ball is pitched ‖ (baseball) a turn at pitching, *it's your pitch now* ‖ (cricket) the part of the ground between and immediately around the two wickets (cf. INFIELD, cf. OUTFIELD) ‖ (cricket) the way a ball falls with respect to the batsman ‖ the quality of a sound with respect to the frequency of vibration of the sound waves ‖ degree of intensity, *feelings raised to a high pitch* ‖ the degree of slope something, e.g. of a roof ‖ (geol., mining) the dip of a vein or bed ‖ (mech.) the distance between a point on a gear tooth and the corresponding point on the next one, or between a point on a screw thread and the corresponding point on the adjacent thread in a line parallel with the axis ‖ the pitching motion of a ship ‖ the highest point of a falcon's soaring before diving on to its prey ‖ (pop.) a line of talk, e.g. of a salesman [etym. doubtful]

pitch and toss a game in which coins are thrown at a mark by various players. The one who throws nearest has the first turn at tossing all the coins and keeping all those that fall with the head uppermost, the other players following in turn

pitch-black (pítʃblǽk) adj. (esp. of darkness, night) as black as pitch

pitch·blende (pítʃblend) n. (mineral.) a massive form of uraninite from which uranium and radium are extracted [fr. G. *pechblende*]

pitch circle a hypothetical circle around teeth of a gear wheel at the place where they come in contact with the teeth of another gear wheel

pitch-dark (pítʃdárk) adj. pitch-black

pitched battle a battle in which the opposing troops have fixed, clearly defined positions, studied and arranged in advance

pitch·er (pítʃər) n. a jug for holding liquids, esp. one with a wide lip and a handle or ears ‖ the amount of liquid that this holds ‖ (*bot.*) a modified leaf of a pitcher plant, in which the petiole becomes tubular, with the blade forming a lid [M.E. *picher, pecher* fr. O.F.]

pitcher *n.* a person who pitches, esp. (*baseball*) the player who pitches the ball to the batter ‖ (*golf*) an iron with a blade lofted more than a mashie niblick but less than a niblick, used for short approach shots to the green ‖ (*Br.*) a brick-shaped granite paving stone

pitcher plant any of several insectivorous plants, e.g. a member of the American genus *Sarracenia*, fam. *Sarraceniaceae* or of the Malaysian genus *Nepenthes*, fam. *Nepenthaceae*, with leaves modified into tubular pitchers holding secretions for trapping and digesting their prey

pitch·fork (pítʃfɔrk) **1.** *n.* a longhandled fork with sharp, curved prongs for lifting and turning hay, straw etc. **2.** *v.t.* to shift with a pitchfork ‖ to thrust (someone) suddenly or forcibly or without preparation (into some job or position) [older *pickfork*, prob. fr. PICK (sharp tool)+FORK]

pitch·ing (pítʃiŋ) *n.* a stone paving or walled facing on a slope ‖ a foundation of coarse stone for a macadamized road

pitch pine any of several resinous pines which produce pitch, esp. *Pinus rigida* of E. North America ‖ the wood of such a pine

pitch pipe a small tuning pipe used for setting the pitch for unaccompanied singers or for tuning an instrument

pitch·y (pítʃi:) *comp.* **pitch·i·er** *superl.* **pitch·i·est** *adj.* of the quality or nature of pitch ‖ covered or smeared with pitch ‖ dark or black

pit·e·ous (píti:əs) *adj.* arousing pity, *piteous cries* [M.E. *pytos, pitous* fr. O.F. and A.F.]

pit·fall (pítfɔl) *n.* a hidden danger or difficulty

pith (piθ) **1.** *n.* the medulla or central region of parenchymatous cells in the stem of a vascular plant ‖ the soft white lining of e.g. orange peel ‖ any spongy tissue resembling the pith of a vascular plant, e.g. the spongy core of a feather ‖ the substance or gist of a matter ‖ forceful relevance, *comments full of pith* **2.** *v.t.* to kill (an animal) by piercing or severing the spinal cord ‖ to destroy the central nervous system by passing a wire up the vertebral canal of (e.g. a frog) ‖ to remove pith from (a plant) [O.E. *pitha*]

pith·e·can·thrope (pìθikǽnθroup) *n.* pithecanthropus

pith·e·can·thro·pus (pìθikǽnθrəpəs, pìθikǽn-θróupəs) *pl.* **pith·e·can·thro·pi** (pìθikǽnθrəpai, pìθikənθróupai) *n.* a member of the extinct genus *Pithecanthropus* of primitive men characterized by their small cranial capacity and apelike facial profile. Examples have been found in Java and, with slight variations, at Peking (*PEKING MAN*) [fr. Gk *pithēkos*, ape+*anthrōpos*, man]

pith·i·ly (píθili:) *adv.* in a pithy manner

pith·i·ness (píθi:nis) *n.* the quality of being pithy

pith·y (píθi:) *comp.* **pith·i·er** *superl.* **pith·i·est** *adj.* forcefully concise, tersely cogent ‖ of, like or containing pith

pit·i·a·ble (píti:əb'l) *adj.* arousing or deserving pity ‖ arousing or deserving pitying contempt **pit·i·a·bly** *adv.* [M.E. fr. O.F.]

pit·i·ful (pítifəl) *adj.* calling forth pity or compassion ‖ contemptible

pit·i·less (píti:lis, pítilis) *adj.* showing or feeling no pity

Pit·man (pítmən), Sir Isaac (1813–97), English inventer (1837) of a shorthand system based on phonetic principles rather than orthographic principles

pit·man (pítmən) *pl.* **pit·men** (pítmən) *n.* someone who works in a pit, esp. a coal miner ‖ (*mach.*, *pl.* **pit·mans**) a connecting rod

pi·ton (pí:tɒn) *n.* (*mountaineering*) an iron peg or spike driven into rock, used as a step or support, or as a belay for the rope [F.]

pi·tot tube (pí:tou, pi:tóu) a device to measure the pressure of a fluid flow, and so its velocity, that is essentially a tube (with an opening turned upstream) connected to a manometer [after H. *Pitot*, F. engineer]

pit·prop (pítprɒp) *n.* a piece of wood used as a temporary support for the roof of a mine

pit saw a long saw handled by two men, one above and one below the log being sawn into planks. The man below is usually in a pit (cf. TOP SAWYER)

Pitt (pit), William, 1st earl of Chatham (1708–78), known as the 'Elder Pitt' and as the 'Great Commoner', British statesman. He led the op-

position to Walpole and to George II's preoccupation with Hanover. As effective head of the administration (1756–61), he successfully directed British policy in the Seven Years' War (1756–63). He again formed an administration (1766–8) as lord privy seal, but suffered increasingly from mental and physical illness. His last years were devoted to urging the conciliation of the American colonies

Pitt, William (1759–1806), known as the 'Younger Pitt', British statesman, son of the Elder Pitt. He entered parliament (1781), was chancellor of the Exchequer (1782–3) and was appointed prime minister (1783–1801 and 1804–6) by George III. He refused to resign despite repeated Commons defeats during his first year in office, and gained a majority in the 1784 elections. A liberal Tory, he reduced the national debt and many tariffs, negotiated a commercial treaty with France (1786), placed India under government control (1784) and reorganized the government of Canada (1791). His free-trade policies were upset by the outbreak of the French Revolutionary Wars (1792–1802), in which he took the lead in organizing coalitions against the French (1793, 1798). He passed the Act of Union with Ireland (1800), but resigned when George III refused to approve Catholic Emancipation (1801). Recalled to office (1804), he organized another coalition against the French in the Napoleonic Wars, but died soon after the news of Napoleon's crushing victory at Austerlitz (1805)

pit·tance (pít'ns) *n.* a very small income wage or allowance [M.E. *pitance, pitaunce* fr. O.F. *pitance*, pity]

pit·ter-pat·ter (pítərpætər) **1.** *n.* a quick succession of light tapping sounds **2.** *adv.* with a quick succession of light taps **3.** *v.i.* to go pitter-patter [reduplication of PATTER]

Pitts·burgh (pítsbə:rg) a port (pop. 423,938, with agglom. 2,263,894) and industrial center in the coalfield of Pennsylvania, at the head of the Ohio River: iron and steel, chemical industries (esp. coal by-products), aluminum, glass, oil refining, food processing. Carnegie Institute of Technology (1900)

pi·tu·i·tar·y (pitú:iteri:, pitjú:ieri:) **1.** *adj.* of or relating to the pituitary gland **2.** *pl.* **pi·tu·i·tar·ies** *n.* the pituitary gland [fr. L. *pituitarius* fr. *pituita*, phlegm]

pituitary body the pituitary gland

pituitary gland a small vascular endocrine gland located at the base of the brain and found in most vertebrates. It consists of an anterior and posterior lobe. The posterior lobe secretes hormones affecting renal functions, contraction of smooth muscle and reproduction. The anterior lobe secretes hormones which control and regulate most of the other endocrine glands. Thus this gland directly or indirectly controls and regulates most basic body functions

pi·tu·i·trin (pitú:itrin, pitjú:itrin) *n.* an aqueous preparation of the pituitary glands of cattle, used as a source of pituitary hormones in the treatment of certain conditions in man [*Pituitrin*, a trademark]

pit viper any of several poisonous snakes esp. of the New World, belonging to fam. *Crotalidae*, incl. the rattlesnake, copperhead, water moccasin etc.

pit·y (píti:) **1.** *pl.* **pit·ies** *n.* a feeling of sympathy for the sufferings or privations of others ‖ a cause of sorrow or regret, *it's a pity that it's raining* **to have** (or **take**) **pity on** to act with compassion toward **2.** *v.t. pres. part.* **pit·y·ing** *past* and *past part.* **pit·ied** to feel pity for [M.E. *pite* fr. O.F. and Mod. F. fr. L.]

pit·y·ri·a·sis (pìtəráiəsis) *n.* any of several superficial skin diseases in man, characterized by the formation and shedding of thin scales ‖ a similar disease of domestic animals [Mod. L. fr. Gk fr. *pituron*, bran, dandruff]

Pi·us II (páiəs) (Enea Silvio de' Piccolomini, 1405–64), pope (1458–64). He was a distinguished humanist poet and author. He failed in his ambition to drive the Turks from Europe

Pius IV (Giovan Angelo de' Medici, 1499–1565), pope (1559–65). He convened the last part (1562–3) of the Council of Trent, and supported the Counter-Reformation

Pius V, St (Michele Ghislieri, 1504–72), pope (1566–72). He enforced the decisions of the Council of Trent and launched a ruthless attack on Protestantism, excommunicating Elizabeth I of England (1570). He helped to organize the

coalition which defeated the Turks at Lepanto (1571). Feast: May 5

Pius VI (Giovanni Angelo Braschi, 1717–99), pope (1775–99). He opposed the ecclesiastical measures of the French Revolution, but was forced to recognize the French republic and to cede territory after Napoleon invaded the Papal States (1796). He was deported to France (1798) and died in exile

Pius VII (Barnaba Chiaramonti, 1740–1823), pope (1800–23). He negotiated with Napoleon the Concordat of 1801, reestablishing Catholicism in France, and anointed Napoleon as emperor (1804). He was a prisoner of the French (1809–14). He restored the Society of Jesus (1814)

Pius IX (Giovanni Mastai-Ferretti, 1792–1878), pope (1846–78). His early liberal reforms were welcomed by Italian patriots, but were abandoned after revolution drove him to Gaeta (1848). He was restored to Rome (1850) and maintained there by a French armed force until 1870, when the French withdrew and Italy seized the remainder of the Papal States except Vatican City, to which the pope was thereafter confined. He promulgated the dogma of the Immaculate Conception (1854), and convened the 1st Vatican Council, which proclaimed papal infallibility (1870)

Pius X, St (Giuseppe Sarto, 1835–1914), pope (1903–14). He ordered the Church in France to surrender its property to the French government rather than submit to State control (1906). He condemned Modernism (1907). He encouraged frequent Communion (1905), reorganized the Curia (1908), revised the missal and breviary (1911), began a new codification of canon law, and encouraged the use of plainsong

Pius XI (Achille Ratti, 1857–1939), pope (1922–39). He established papal relations with Italy by the Lateran Treaty (1929). He condemned Fascism (1931), Nazism (1937) and Communism (1937). He was eloquent in his criticism of laissez-faire capitalism and urging of social reform, notably in the encyclical 'Quadragesimo Anno' (1931). He encouraged the laity to participate more in the work of the Church, and set up a radio station in the Vatican

Pius XII (Eugenio Pacelli, 1876–1958), pope (1939–58). He attempted to alleviate the suffering caused by the 2nd world war, and denounced Communist persecution of Christianity. He defined the dogma of the Assumption (1950)

piv·ot (pívət) *n.* a fixed shaft or pin having a pointed end which acts as the point of balance upon which a plate or bar can turn or oscillate ‖ the pointed end of such a shaft or pin ‖ the turning or oscillating movement of something mounted on such a shaft or pin ‖ a person, thing or fact on which a set of circumstances etc. depends, *this point is the pivot of the argument* [F.]

pivot *v.t.* to supply with or balance on a pivot ‖ *v.i.* to turn or oscillate on or as if on a pivot, *the whole movement pivots on him* [F. *pivoter*]

pivot *n.* (*sports*) the key participant in an action. —**pivotman** (*basketball*) the center

piv·ot·al (pívət'l) *adj.* of, relating to or having the nature of a pivot ‖ having vital importance for some activity or for what will develop from a set of circumstances etc.

pix *PIC

pix *PYX

pix·el (píksel) *n.* the picture element in a television image

pix·ie, pix·y (píksi:) *pl.* **pix·ies** *n.* a small, mischievous elf or fairy [etym. doubtful]

pix·i·lated, **pix·il·lat·ed** (píksəleitid) (*pop.*) slightly crazy ‖ (*pop.*) rather drunk [PIXIE]

pix·y *PIXIE

Pi·zar·ro (pizárou), Francisco (c. 1475–1541), Spanish conquistador. After two unsuccessful attempts to explore Peru (1524–5, 1526–8), he landed there (1532), captured Cuzco (1533) and executed Atahualpa, the Inca king. He faced rebellions both from the Incas and from his own followers, in the course of which he was murdered

pi·zazz (pizǽz) *n.* (*slang*) a provocative vitality

piz·za (pí:tsə) *n.* a large, round, flat, breadlike crust spread with tomatoes, cheese and sometimes other ingredients, e.g. shreds of meat, anchovies and herbs, and baked [Ital.]

piz·ze·ri·a (pì:tsərí:ə) *n.* a place where pizzas are made and sold [Ital.]

CONCISE PRONUNCIATION KEY: **(a)** æ, c*a*t; ɑ, c*a*r; ɔ f*aw*n; ei, sn*a*ke. **(e)** e, h*e*n; i:, sh*ee*p; iə, d*ee*r; ɛə, b*ea*r. **(i)** i, f*i*sh; ai, t*i*ger; ə:, b*i*rd. **(o)** o, *o*x; au, c*ow*; ou, g*oa*t; u, p*oo*r; ɔi, r*oy*al. **(u)** ʌ, d*u*ck; u, b*u*ll; u:, g*oo*se; ə, b*a*cillus; ju:, c*u*be. x, lo*ch*; θ, *th*ink; ð, bo*th*er; z, *Z*en; ʒ, corsa*g*e; dʒ, sava*g*e; ŋ, ora*n*gutang; j, *y*ak; ʃ, *fi*sh; tʃ, fe*tch*; 'l, rabb*le*; 'n, redd*en*. Complete pronunciation key appears inside front cover.

piz·zi·ca·to (pɪtsikátou) 1. *adj.* (*mus.*, of a note) played on a stringed instrument by plucking the strings with the finger instead of using the bow 2. *adv.* (*mus.*) in a pizzicato manner 3. *pl.* **piz·zi·ca·ti** (pɪtsikáti:), **piz·zi·ca·tos** *n.* (*mus.*) a note or passage played pizzicato [Ital.]

PKU (*med. abbr.*) phenylketonuria (which see)

plac·a·bil·i·ty (plækəbíliti:, pleikəbíliti:) *n.* the quality of being placable

plac·a·ble (plǽkəb'l, pléikəb'l) *adj.* capable of being placated, or easily placated ‖ showing tolerance or forgiveness, *in a placable mood* [M.E. fr. O.F. fr. L. *placabilis*]

plac·ard (plǽkɑrd, plǽkərd) 1. *n.* a notice for advertising or display purposes 2. *v.t.* to set up placards in or on ‖ to advertise by such means ‖ to display as a placard [O. F. *plackart, placard* and Mod. F. *placard* fr. O.F. *plaquier*, to lay flat, plaster]

pla·cate (pléikeit, plǽkeit) *pres. part.* **pla·cat·ing** *past* and *past part.* **pla·cat·ed** *v.t.* to pacify, esp. by making concessions **pla·ca·tion** (pleikéiʃən) *n.* **pla·ca·to·ry** (pléikətɔri:, plǽkətɔri:, pléikətɔuri:, plǽkətɔuri:) *adj.* [fr. L. *placare (placatus)*]

place (pleis) 1. *n.* a particular part of space, *this is the place where they first met* ‖ a particular spot or area on a surface, *a worn place on the carpet* ‖ a particular city, town, village, district etc., *it is one of the places he visited* ‖ position in space, or in some hierarchy, scale, orderly arrangement etc., *to lose one's place in a line* ‖ proper function that goes with status, *it's not your place to criticize* ‖ a building or area appointed for a specified purpose, *a place of worship* ‖ (in names) a square in a city ‖ (in street names) a short street ‖ (in names) a country mansion ‖ home, dwelling, *we ate supper at his place* ‖ a space, seat or other accommodation, in a theater, train etc. ‖ a particular passage in a book etc., *she always cries at the sad places* ‖ the point that one has reached in reading a book, etc. ‖ (*racing*) a position among the winners, esp. second or third ‖ an official position, *a place on the board* ‖ a stage or step in an argument or sequence, *in the first place we must define our terms* ‖ (*math.*) the position of a figure in relation to others in a series, esp. of decimals, *calculate to four decimal places* **in place** in the usual or correct place ‖ proper, appropriate **in place of** as a substitute for, rather than **out of place** inappropriate, unsuitable ‖ not in keeping with the surroundings etc., *he felt out of place in their company* **to give place to** to be succeeded by ‖ to yield one's position to **to go places** (*pop.*) to achieve worldly success or distinction **to know one's place** (*old-fash.*) to act humbly and respectfully in accordance with one's relatively low rank or standing **to take place** to occur, happen **to take the place of** to be a substitute for 2. *v. pres. part.* **plac·ing** *past* and *past part.* **placed** *v.t.* to put in a particular place, position, rank, office, condition etc. ‖ to identify by recalling the context or circumstances connected, *she knew his face but couldn't place him* ‖ to invest (money) ‖ to give (an order for goods etc.) ‖ (followed by 'in', 'on' or 'upon') to bestow (confidence, trust etc.) upon something or someone‖ to pitch (the voice) in singing or speech ‖ *v.i.* (*racing*) to be among the first three contestants to finish, esp. to finish second in a horse or dog race **to be placed** (*Br., racing*) to be among the first three to finish [M.E. fr. F. fr. L. fr. Gk *plateia* (*hodos*), broad (street)]

pla·ce·bo (pləsí:bou) *pl.* **pla·ce·bos, pla·ce·boes** *n.* an inactive but harmless preparation given to humor a patient ‖ (*Roman Catholicism*) the first antiphon of vespers for the dead [L.=I shall be pleasing (first word of Psalm cxiv, 9 in the Vulgate)]

place-kick (pléiskɪk) 1. *n.* (*football, rugby*) the act of kicking the ball after it has been placed on the ground for this purpose (in rugby, after a try has been scored or a free kick awarded) 2. *v.t.* to kick (the ball) in this way ‖ *v.i.* to perform such a kick

place·man (pléismən) *pl.* **place·men** (pléismən) *n.* (esp. *Br.*, used pejoratively) a person who holds or seeks some political office out of self-interest rather than to do public service

place mat a mat placed under the dishes and eating utensils of a person at a dining table on which no cloth is laid

place·ment (pléismənt) *n.* a placing or being placed ‖ the manner of placing or being placed ‖ the finding of employment for a worker ‖ (*foot-*

ball) the placing or position of the ball on the ground for a place-kick

pla·cen·ta (pləséntə) *pl.* **pla·cen·tas, pla·cen·tae** (pləsénti:) *n.* the vascular organ in most mammals which joins the fetus to the maternal uterus and acts as the site of metabolic exchange between them. The placenta arises from differentiated regions of the chorion and allantois brought into intimate relation with a specialized region of the uterine wall where fetal and maternal vascular systems are permitted to exchange nutriment and oxygen by diffusion without direct mixing of blood, the fetus being able to get rid of waste products ‖ any of various functionally similar organs in other animals ‖ (*bot.*) the part of the carpel bearing ovules [L.=cake fr. Gk]

pla·cen·tal (pləsént'l) *adj.* of, relating to or having a placenta [fr. Mod. L. *placentalis* fr. L. *placenta*]

plac·en·ta·tion (plæs'ntéiʃən) *n.* the development of the placenta ‖ the way the placenta is attached to the uterus ‖ (*bot.*) the way in which the placenta is attached to the pericarp [F.]

plac·er (pléisər) *n.* a deposit of sand or gravel e.g. in the bed of a stream, where gold or other valuable minerals can be obtained in particles [Span. *placer*, deposit]

placer mining the mining of placers by washing, dredging etc.

place value (*math*) the value of a digit due to its place as a numeral, e.g., units, tens, hundreds

plac·id (plǽsid) *adj.* (of temperament) not easily roused ‖ (of a person) having such a temperament **pla·cid·i·ty** (pləsíditi:) *n.* [fr. L. *placidus* fr. *placere*, to please]

plack·et (plǽkit) *n.* a slit or opening, e.g. one in the top of a skirt for convenience in putting on and fastening, or for getting at a pocket [perh. var. of PLACARD, (obs.) plate of armor]

plac·oid (plǽkɔid) 1. *adj.* (*zool.*, of the hard scales or dermal teeth of an elasmobranch fish) plate-shaped 2. *n.* (*zool.*) a fish having placoid scales [fr. *plax* (*plakos*), plate]

pla·gal (pléig'l) *adj.* (*mus.*, of certain medieval modes) having the fourth note of the range as keynote (cf. AUTHENTIC MODE) [fr. M. L. *plagalis* fr. *plaga*, plagal mode fr. Gk *plagios*, plagal, oblique]

plagal cadence (*mus.*) a cadence in which the subdominant chord resolves to the tonic chord

pla·gia·rism (pléidʒərizəm, pléidʒi:ərizəm) *n.* the act of plagiarizing or an instance of this ‖ a plagiarized idea etc. **pla·gia·rist** *n.* someone who plagiarizes [fr. L. *plagiarius*, a kidnapper]

pla·gia·rize (pléidʒəraiz, pléidʒi:əraiz) *pres. part.* **pla·gia·riz·ing** *past* and *past part.* **pla·gia·rized** *v.t.* to use and pass off (someone else's ideas, inventions, writings etc.) as one's own ‖ *v.i.* to take another's writings etc. and pass them off as one's own [PLAGIARY]

pla·gia·ry (pléidʒəri:, pléidʒi:əri:) *pl.* **pla·gia·ries** *n.* plagiarism ‖ a plagiarist [fr. L. *plagiarius*, a kidnapper]

pla·gi·o·clase (pléidʒi:əkleis) *n.* (*mineral.*) a triclinic feldspar with an oblique cleavage, esp. one containing sodium and calcium **pla·gi·o·clas·tic** (pleidʒi:əklǽstik) *adj.* [G. *plagioklas* fr. Gk *plagios*, oblique+*klasis*, cleavage]

pla·gi·o·tro·pic (pleidʒi:ətrɑpik) *adj.* (*bot.*, e.g. of most roots and lateral branches) having the longer axis inclined from the vertical **pla·gi·ot·ro·pism** (pleidʒi:ɑtrəpizəm) *n.* [fr. Gk *plagios*, oblique+*tropos*, a turning]

plague (pleig) 1. *n.* an epidemic, often fatal disease caused by the bacterium *Pasteurella pestis*, occurring in various forms, e.g. as bubonic plague. After the Black Death, the plague broke out sporadically in Europe (14th-18th cc.), notably decimating London in 1665. It remains endemic in parts of Asia ‖ a social scourge, *a plague of petty thieving* ‖ a nuisance, annoyance 2. *v.t. pres. part.* **pla·guing** *past* and *past part.* **plagued** to pester or harass, *plagued by insects* **plá·guey, plá·guy** 1. *adj.* (*pop.*) annoying, bothersome 2. *adv.* (*pop.*) plaguily **plá·gui·ly** *adv.* [M.E. *plage* fr. O.F.]

plaice (pleis) *pl.* **plaice** *n. Pleuronectes platessa*, fam. *Pleuronectidae*, a European edible marine flatfish, laterally compressed. Both eyes are on the upper side of the body. It lies on the sea bed, and swims on one side. It has no air bladder ‖ any of several American flatfishes [M.E. *plais, plaice* fr. O.F. fr. L. *plotessa*]

plaid (plæd) 1. *n.* a long piece of woolen cloth of tartan pattern worn esp. over the shoulder and breast by Scottish Highlanders ‖ cloth having a

tartan pattern 2. *adj.* made of cloth with a tartan pattern, *a plaid skirt* ‖ having a tartan pattern, *a plaid tablecloth* **pláid·ed** *adj.* wearing a plaid ‖ made of or wearing plaid [Gael. *plaide*]

plain (plein) 1. *adj.* easy to see or understand ‖ simple, not embellished or complicated ‖ absolute, complete, *plain madness* ‖ (of food) unelaborate, not having unusual or spicy ingredients ‖ bluntly frank ‖ unsophisticated ‖ lacking physical beauty, but not ugly 2. *n.* a large expanse of level, open country 3. *adv.* manifestly, *it's just plain wrong* ‖ clearly, candidly, *she told him plain* [O.F. fr. L.]

plain·chant (pléintʃænt, pléintʃɑnt) *n.* plain-song

plain·clothes·man (pléinklóuzmən, pléinklóuðzmən) *pl.* **plain·clothes·men** (pléinklóuzmən, pléinklóuðzmən) *n.* a police officer, esp. a detective who does not wear a uniform when on duty

plain dealing straightforwardness, honesty in business or social relations

plain-laid (pléinléid) *adj.* (of a rope) made by laying three strands together with a right-hand twist

plain sailing progress unimpeded by difficulties or obstacles, *once that is solved the rest will be plain sailing*

Plains Indian a member of any of the tribes of American Indians formerly inhabiting the prairies of the U.S.A., notably the Cheyennes, the Apaches, the Sioux, the Comanches, the Navahos, the Kiowas, the Arapahos and the Utes. As a result of the land grabs and the worst of the Indian Wars (1860-90), they lost the bison-hunting grounds on which they chiefly depended. Those who survived the conflict with the whites were concentrated on unfertile, game-poor reservations

plains·man (pléinzmən) *pl.* **plains·men** (pléinzmən) *n.* someone who lives in an area characterized by great plains

Plains of Abraham the Heights of Abraham

plain·song (pléinsɔŋ, pléinsɔŋ) *n.* an ancient nonmetrical modal type of chant without accompaniment for singing the Christian services, still used in the form of the Gregorian chant [trans. M.L. *cantus planus*]

plain-spo·ken (pléinspóukən) *adj.* frank and forceful in speech

plaint (pleint) *n.* (*law*, esp. *Br.*) a statement of grievance ‖ (*rhet.*) a complaint or lamentation [M.E. *plaint, plainte* fr. O.F.]

plain·tiff (pléintif) *n.* (*law*) a person who brings a lawsuit against another (cf. DEFENDANT) [O. F. *plaintif*]

plain·tive (pléintiv) *adj.* quietly mournful ‖ weakly complaining [M.E. fr. O.F. *plaintif, plaintive*]

plait (pleit, plæt) 1. *n.* a length of hair, straw, ribbon etc. consisting of at least three interlaced strands 2. *v.t.* to interlace at least three strands of (hair, ribbon etc.) to form a plait ‖ to make (a basket, mat etc.) by interlacing strands together [M.E. *pleyt, playt* fr. O.F. *pleit, ploit*, fold, crease]

plan (plæn) 1. *n.* a design for a construction, layout, system etc. ‖ a drawing representing a horizontal section of a solid object (cf. ELEVATION) ‖ a detailed diagram, *a plan of Paris* ‖ a formulated scheme setting out stages of procedure, *a plan for the production of a book* ‖ (often *pl.*) a proposed or intended course of action, *what are your plans for this weekend?* ‖ (*art*, in perspective) any of the imaginary perpendicular planes interposed between the represented object and the eye 2. *v. pres. part.* **plan·ning** *past* and *past part.* **planned** *v.t.* to make a design for (a building, garden, city etc.) ‖ to devise a program of action for, *a planned tour* ‖ to intend, *we plan to go there next summer* ‖ *v.i.* to make plans ‖ *PLANNED ECONOMY [F. fr. plan adj., flat fr. L.]

planch (plæntʃ) *n.* a flat slab, especially one of baked fireclay used in the kiln in enameling [F. *planche*, plank, slab]

planche (plæntʃ) *n.* (*gymnastics*) horizontal position supported on the hands

planch·et (plæntʃit) *n.* a plain disk of metal from which a coin is made [dim. of PLANCH]

plan·chette (plæntʃét) *n.* a small, usually heart-shaped board used in some spiritualistic seances. It is mounted on two castors and a pencil. It moves when lightly touched by a person's fingers, and is supposed to trace out significant words [F. dim. of *planche*, plank]

Planck (plaŋk), Max Karl Ernst Ludwig (1858–1947), German physicist. He propounded the quantum theory (1900). Nobel prize (1918)

Planck constant (*phys.*) the constant factor ($6.624 + 10^{-27}$ erg sec., symbol *h*) in the Planck radiation law and many other equations of quantum theory

Planck radiation law a law in physics relating the radiation associated with atomic processes to the energy changes involved (*SPECTROS-COPY). It may be expressed: Energy change=*h* (frequency of radiation) where *h* is the Planck constant ‖ a law in physics giving the distribution of energy over the range of wavelengths within a blackbody as a function of temperature (*QUANTUM THEORY)

plane (plein) *n.* a member of *Platanus*, fam. *Platanaceae*, a genus of tall, spreading trees of northern temperate regions, with large, simple, palmately lobed leaves and brittle bark which tends to flake away [F. fr. L. *platanus* fr. Gk]

plane 1. *n.* a carpenter's tool used for producing a smooth surface on wood by paring away irregularities. It consists of an adjustable blade fixed at an angle in a wooden or metal stock. Variations exist for cutting grooves, routing etc. **2.** *v. pres. part.* **plan·ing** *past* and *past part.* **planed** *v.t.* to work (wood) with this tool ‖ *v.i.* to work with this tool [F.]

plane 1. *adj.* flat, level ‖ (*math.*) lying on a surface which is a plane ‖ of such surfaces **2.** *n.* a level surface such that if any two points on it are joined by a straight line, every part of that line will lie in that surface ‖ an imaginary plane surface in which points or lines are regarded as lying, e.g., in perspective ‖ a level of development, existence, accomplishment, thought, value etc., *to consider a problem on the metaphysical plane* ‖ an aircraft ‖ one of the main supporting surfaces of an aircraft or hydroplane, for controlling balance and elevation in flight ‖ one of the natural faces of a crystal ‖ a main road in a mine [fr. L. *planus*]

plane *pres. part.* **plan·ing** *past* and *past part.* **planed** *v.t.* to glide ‖ to travel in an aircraft ‖ (of a boat or seaplane) to skim the surface of the water [F. *planer*]

plane chart a chart of a small area on which meridians and parallels of latitude are shown by equidistant straight lines on a flat surface

plane geometry that branch of geometry which deals with the properties and relations of plane figures

plane-po·lar·ized (pléinpóuləraizd) *adj.* (of a wave of light etc.) vibrating in a single plane (*POLARIZATION)

plane sailing a method of navigation which ignores the earth's curvature, treating its surface as a plane

plan·et (plǽnit) *n.* one of the bodies in space, other than a comet, meteor or satellite, which revolve around the sun of the earth's solar system, shining by reflected light from the sun ‖ any similar body revolving about a star (*ASTEROID, *MAJOR PLANET) [M.E. fr. O.F. *planete* fr. L. L. fr. Gk *planētēs*, wanderer]

plane table a drawing board with a ruler attached to its center, mounted on a tripod, used in making maps or surveys in the field by direct observation along the ruler

plan·e·tar·i·um (plǽnitéariəm) *pl.* **plan·e·tar·i·ums, plan·e·tar·i·a** (plǽnitéariə) *n.* a complex system of optical projectors by means of which the positions and relative motions of the planets and visible stars are displayed on the inner surface of a large dome within which observers are situated ‖ the building containing this ‖ an orrery [Mod. L. fr. L.L. *planetarius*, planetary]

plan·e·tar·y (plǽniteri:) *adj.* of or pertaining to a planet or the planets ‖ of or pertaining to the earth ‖ of or designating an epicyclic train of gear wheels, esp. the transmission gear of a car ‖ (*phys.*) moving like a planet, *planetary electrons* [fr. L.L. *planetarius*]

plan·e·tes·i·mal (plǽnitésəməl) **1.** *adj.* of or designating a small solid heavenly body thought to have existed in the early stages of the solar system's evolution **2.** *n.* such a body [PLANT+INFINITESIMAL]

planetesimal hypothesis the theory that the planets were formed by accretion of planetesimals

plan·et·oid (plǽnitɔid) *n.* an asteroid

Plan·et·o·khod (plǝnétoukɒd) *n.* (*aerospace*) U.S.S.R. vehicle for planetary exploration

plan·e·tol·o·gy (plǽnitólədʒi:) *n.* the study of

the natural solar sytem, its orbiting bodies, planets and meteorites. **—plan·e·to·log·i·cal** *adv.* **—plan·e·tol·o·gist** *n.*

planet wheel a gear wheel revolving around another with which it engages in an epicyclic train

plan·gen·cy (plǽndʒənsi:) *n.* the quality of being plangent

plan·gent (plǽndʒənt) *adj.* making a loud reverberating sound, or a loud plaintive, drawn-out sound [fr. L. *plangens* (*plangentis*) fr. *plangere*, to beat]

planigraphy *TOMOGRAPHY

pla·nim·e·ter (plǝnímitər) *n.* an instrument which measures the area of a plane figure when a tracer is moved along the perimeter **pla·nim·e·try** *n.* measurement of the area of a plane figure [fr. F. *planimétre*]

plan·ish (plǽniʃ) *v.t.* to flatten, smooth, polish or toughen (metal) by hammering or rolling [fr. obs. F. *planir* (*planiss-*), to make smooth]

plan·i·sphere (plǽnisfjər) *n.* (*geom.*) a projection of a sphere upon a plane surface, esp. one of a part of the heavens to show the relative positions and movements of the heavenly bodies [M.E. *planisperie* fr. M.L. *planisphaerium* fr. L. *planus*, plane + *sphaera* fr. Gk *sphaira*, sphere]

plank (plæŋk) **1.** *n.* a long, heavy board, usually at least 2 ins thick and at least 8 or 9 ins wide ‖ a main idea, principle etc. in an argument, political program etc. ‖ planking **to walk the plank** (*hist.*) to be made to walk blindfold along and off a plank projecting from a ship over the sea (a method of killing used by pirates) **2.** *v.t.* to cover or provide with planks ‖ to cook and serve on a wooden board, *a planked steak* ‖ (*pop.*, esp. with 'down') to put (something) on a counter, table etc. with force ‖ to put down (money) in payment on the spot **plank·ing** *n.* planks collectively [M.E. *planke* fr. O.N.F.]

plank·ton (plǽŋktən) *n.* minute plants (chiefly algae) and animals which float in great quantities near the surface of fresh or salt water. They provide the only source of food for many kinds of fish **plank·ton·ic** (plæŋktɒnik) *adj.* (*DIATOM, cf. NEKTON) [G. fr. Gk fr. *planktos* adj., drifting]

planned economy an economy in which government regulates labor, capital etc. in order to secure the success of an overall production plan, instead of leaving the forces of supply and demand to operate freely

planned obsolescence (*business*) quality in the design of a product that provides deterioration or outstyling before the end of the expected period of usefulness

planned parenthood * FAMILY PLANNING

planned shrinkage deliberate reduction in a population, esp. for the purpose of reducing necessary services

pla·no·con·cave (pléinoukɒnkéiv) *adj.* (esp. of a lens) flat on one side and concave on the other [fr. L. *planus*, flat+CONCAVE]

pla·no·con·vex (pléinoukɒnvéks) *adj.* (esp. of a lens) flat on one side and convex on the other [fr. L. *planus*, flat+CONVEX]

plant (plænt, plɑnt) *v.t.* to put the roots of (a plant) in the ground to enable it to grow, or to sow (seed) ‖ to stock with plants, *to plant a garden* ‖ to introduce (living things) in the hope that they will settle and multiply, *to plant settlers in a colony* ‖ to instill (ideas, principles etc.) in the mind ‖ to put firmly in position, *he planted himself in front of the door* ‖ (*pop.*) to place as a trap, *they planted marked bills to prove the man's guilt* ‖ (*pop.*) to deliver (a blow) ‖ (with 'out') to transplant (young plants) to the ground where they are to mature [O.E. *plantian* and O.F. *planter* fr. L.]

plant *n.* any organism belonging to the kingdom *Plantae* (cf. ANIMAL), characterized usually by lack of independent locomotion, absence of a central nervous system, cell walls composed of cellulose, and a nutritive system based on photosynthesis. Many plants exhibit a strong tendency to alternation of generations ‖ such an organism large enough to be handled, esp. one smaller than a shrub, bush or tree ‖ the assemblage of buildings, tools etc. used to manufacture some kind of goods or power ‖ mechanical equipment for a particular operation, *the power plant of a submarine* ‖ (*pop.*) a carefully planned swindle ‖ (*pop.*) a carefully planned trap laid to catch a wrongdoer [O.E. *plante* fr. L. *planta*]

Plan·tag·e·net (plæntǽdʒənit) an English royal dynasty founded by Geoffrey, count of Anjou (1113–51), father of Henry II. The Plantagenets ruled England (1154–1399, Henry II–

Richard II), and most of W. France (1154–1205). Their succession was disputed (1399–1485) by the claimants of York and Lancaster, the dispute culminating in the Wars of the Roses (1455–85)

plan·tain (plǽntin, plǽntein) *n.* a member of *Plantago*, fam. *Plantaginaceae*, genus of plants with a radical, ribbed rosette of leaves. They are cosmopolitan weeds. The inflorescence is a spike or head [M.E. fr. O.F.]

plantain *n. Musa paradisiaca*, fam. *Musaceae*, a species of banana plant native to India ‖ its fruit, starchy and green-skinned, a basic food in the Tropics, commonly baked, boiled or fried [older *platan*, *plantane* fr. Span. *plátano*, *plántano*]

plan·tar (plǽntər) *adj.* pertaining to the sole of the foot, *a plantar wart* [fr. L. *plantaris* fr. *planta*, sole]

plan·ta·tion (plæntéiʃən) *n.* a group of growing plants or trees, *a fir plantation* ‖ an estate, esp. in a tropical or warm region, on which a crop such as sugarcane, cotton, tea etc. is cultivated ‖ (*hist.*) the settling of a colony or new country ‖ (*hist.*) a colony or settlement [fr. L. *plantatio* (*plantationis*), a planting]

Plantation System a U.S. socioeconomic form of production unique to the South, esp. between c. 1800 and 1860 (though less than one–fifth of southern farms were plantations). It was characterized by huge farms which were worked by slave labor and which cultivated single crops for profit, notably cash crops, i.e. cotton, rice, sugar and tobacco. The plantations did much of their own manufuturing. The planter-aristocrat lived a life of ease, but he lived in isolation from urban life and even from his fellow planters

plant·er (plǽntər, plɑntər) *n.* a person who plants ‖ a machine used to plant ‖ a person who manages a plantation ‖ a container for potted or unpotted house plants ‖ (*hist.*) a colonist

plant·i·grade (plǽntigreid) **1.** *adj.* (*zool.*) walking on the soles of the feet, with the heel touching the ground (cf. DIGITIGRADE) **2.** *n.* (*zool.*) a plantigrade animal (e.g. man, bear etc.) [F. fr. L. *planta*, sole+-*gradus*, going, walking]

Plan·tin (plátɛ̃, *Eng.* plǽntin), Christophe (c. 1520–89), French printer. He established his printing press in Antwerp (1555). His masterpiece is the eight-volume 'Biblia Polyglotta' (c. 1568–c. 1572). Typefaces based on Plantin's are still very commonly used

plant louse an insect, esp. an aphid, which infests plants

plan·u·la (plǽnjulə) *pl.* **plan·u·lae** (plǽnjuli:) *n.* the usually flattened, ovoid, young free-swimming larva of a coelenterate [Mod. L., dim. of L. *planus*, flat]

plaque (plæk) *n.* a flat piece of metal, ivory etc. attached to a wall or inset in wood, either as an ornament or to record a fact of historical interest ‖ (*virology*) in a culture, an area destroyed by a virus ‖ (*med.*) an area of psoriasis ‖ a localized area of atherosclerosis ‖ any abnormal flat area in or on the body [F. fr. Du. *plakke*, a kind of coin]

plash (plæʃ) **1.** *v.t.* to agitate (water) so that it makes a gentle splashing sound ‖ to sprinkle or splash so as to speckle ‖ *v.i.* to make a gentle splashing noise **2.** *n.* the sound of water plashing ‖ a plashing movement [etym. doubtful]

plash *v.t.* (esp. *Br.*) to break partially, bend down and interweave (stems, branches and twigs) so as to form a hedge ‖ to make or mend (a hedge) in this way [O.F. *plaisser*, *plaissier*]

plash *n.* a muddy pond or pool ‖ a puddle **plash·y** *adj.* marshy, boggy [O.E. *plæsc*]

Plas·kett (plǽskit), John Stanley (1865–1941), Canadian astronomer, best known for his discovery (1922) of the dual star subsequently named 'Plaskett's twins'

plasm (plǽzəm) *n.* plasma

plas·ma (plǽzmə) *n.* (*biol.*) the viscous living matter of a cell surrounding the nucleus, the protoplasm ‖ the blood plasma ‖ (*mineral.*) a bright green variety of quartz allied to chalcedony, used as a semi-precious gem ‖ (*phys.*) an ionized gas produced at very high temperatures (e.g. in the stars) containing about equal numbers of positive and negative charges, which is a good conductor of electricity, and is affected by a magnetic field **plas·mat·ic** (plæzmǽtik), **plás·mic** *adjs* [L.L.=something shaped or molded, fr. Gk fr. *plassein*, to shape]

plasma engine a rocket engine utilizing thrust from magnetically accelerated ionized gases

CONCISE PRONUNCIATION KEY: **(a)** æ, c*a*t; ɑ, c*a*r; ɔ f*aw*n; ei, sn*a*ke. **(e)** e, h*e*n; i:, sh*ee*p; iə, d*ee*r; ɛə, b*ea*r. **(i)** i, f*i*sh; ai, t*i*ger; ə:, b*i*rd. **(o)** o, *o*x; au, c*ow*; ou, g*oa*t; u, p*oo*r; ɔi, r*o*yal. **(u)** ʌ, d*u*ck; u, b*u*ll; u:, g*oo*se; ə, b*a*cillus; ju:, c*u*be. x, lo*ch*; θ, *th*ink; ð, bo*th*er; z, *Z*en; ʒ, corsa*g*e; dʒ, sava*g*e; ŋ, ora*n*gutang; j, *y*ak; ʃ, *f*ish; tʃ, *f*etch; 'l, rabb*le*; 'n, redd*en*. Complete pronunciation key appears inside front cover.

plas·ma·gene (plǽzmədʒi:n) n. (genetics) one or a group of genes not in a chromosome. These can sometimes reproduce

plasma jet a stream of hot, ionized gas used in welding and satellite propulsion

plas·ma·pause (plǽzməpɔz) n. the upper parameter of the plasmasphere

plasma physics branch of physics dealing with the ionzied gas in thermonuclear activity and cosmic reactions —**plasma physicist** n.

plas·ma·sphere (plǽzməsfiər) n. (astron.) the layer of ionized gas surrounding a planet

plasma torch a device for producng ionized gas

plas·mid (plǽzmid) n. 1. (genetics) a self-reproducing particle of protoplasm, without a nucleus that determines hereditary characteristics. 2. (biol.) cell cytoplasm capable of self-reproduction. 3. (phys.) a section of plasma that has a distinct shape

plas·mo·di·um (plæzmóudi:əm) pl. **plas·mo·di·a** (plæzmóudi:ə) n. the vegetative stage in the life cycle of a slime mold, consisting of a motile mass of protoplasm containing several nuclei ǁ a member of Plasmodium, fam. Plasmodiidae, a genus of parasitic sporozoans including those causing malaria in man. [Mod. L. fr. PLASMA+Gk -ōdēs, like]

plas·mol·y·sis (plæzmólisis) n. (bot.) contraction of the plant cell wall and loss of protoplasm from the cell wall, caused by the withdrawal of water from plant cells by osmosis [fr. Gk plasma, form+lusis, loosing]

plas·mon (plǽzmʌn) n. (genetics) the hereditary factors in cytoplasm

Plas·sey, Battle of (plǽsi:, plúsi:) a battle (1757) in which Clive decisively defeated the nawab of Bengal and prepared the way for British rule in India

plas·ter (plǽstər, plústər) n. a mixture of slaked lime, sand and water, sometimes with hair or fibers added as binding material, applied wet to an interior wall or ceiling and hardening to a smooth surface when dry ǁ plaster of paris ǁ a medicinal preparation spread on a cloth and applied to the body, a mustard plaster [O.E. plaster and O.F. plastre fr. L. fr. Gk]

plaster v.t. to cover (a wall etc.) with wet plaster ǁ to put (something adhesive) on a surface, esp. in great quantity or with force ǁ to apply a medicinal plaster to ǁ to treat (wine) with plaster of paris to neutralize acidity ǁ to bomb or shell heavily [fr. PLASTER n. or older F. plaster]

plas·ter·board (plǽstərbɔrd, plǽstərbɔrd, plástərbourd, plástərbourd) n. a board made by compressing sheets of fiber separated by a layer of partly set plaster of paris and used esp. as a surface to be plastered

plaster cast a sculpture cast in plaster of paris ǁ a firm covering made of gauze and plaster of paris used e.g. for holding a fractured bone in place

plas·ter·er's putty (plǽstərərz, plástərərz) a white paste of slaked lime, used for finishing

plaster of paris a white or pinkish powder, essentially the hemihydrate of calcium sulfate, $2CaSO_4 \cdot H_2O$, obtained by calcining gypsum. With water it forms a quick-setting paste, drying to form a tough, hard solid. It is used for casts and molds and building materials

plas·tic (plǽstik) 1. adj. of material which changes shape when pressure is applied and retains its new shape when the pressure is removed (cf. ELASTIC) ǁ of the processes involved in using such materials to fashion things, the plastic arts ǁ of an object fashioned from such a material ǁ (art) of, relating to or characterized by three-dimensional movement, form and space ǁ pliable, easily influenced ǁ (biol.) capable of undergoing variation, growth, repair etc. ǁ (colloq.) unnatural, synthetic ǁ so changeable as to be phony 2. n. a plastic material **plás·ti·cal·ly** adv. [fr. L. plasticus, able to be molded, fr. Gk fr. plassein, to shape, form]

—A plastic material is a substance which, though stable in normal use, was plastic under pressure or heat (or both) at some stage during manufacture. Plastics are usually polymers. If they soften again when reheated, they are said to be thermoplastic. If, after fashioning, they resist further applications of heat, they are thermosetting. The raw materials of the plastics industry are by-products of oil refining, coal distillation etc. The plastics industry has great importance in industrialized countries (*BAKELITE, CELLULOID, *POLYSTYRENE, *POLYETYHLENE)

Plas·ti·cine (plǽstisi:n) n. a plastic substance used as a substitute for modeling clay, drying very slowly and not adhering to the fingers. It cannot be fired in a kiln [Trademark]

plas·tic·i·ty (plæstísiti:) n. the quality or state of being plastic ǁ (chem.) the quality of being displaced within a molecular sphere of action

plas·ti·cize (plǽstisaiz) pres. part. **plas·ti·ciz·ing** past and past part. **plas·ti·cized** v.t. to make plastic ǁ v.i. to become plastic **plás·ti·ciz·er** n. any of a number of substances added to a plastic to improve its physical properties, e.g. its flexibility

plastic memory tendency of some plastics to return to a former shape

plastic surgery the branch of surgery concerned with correcting disfigurements due to injury, age or congenital deformities, usually by transference of skin or bone

plastic zone *RUPTURE ZONE

plas·tid (plǽstid) n. a small body of specialized protoplasm within the cell of some organisms (e.g. a chloroplast) [G. fr. Gk fr. plassein, to form]

plas·tral (plǽstrəl) adj. (zool.) of or pertaining to a plastron

plas·tron (plǽstrɒn, plǽstrən) n. a padded breast shield worn by a fencer ǁ (hist.) a steel breastplate ǁ (zool.) the ventral part of the shell of a tortoise or turtle ǁ a similar part in other animals ǁ a dicky (for a shirt or blouse) [F. fr. Ital.]

plat (plǽt) 1. n. a small piece of land ǁ a detailed plan or map 2. v.t. pres. part. **plat·ting** past and past part. **plat·ted** to make a plan or map of [fr. PLOT]

Plata, Río de la *RÍO DE LA PLATA

Pla·tae·a, Battle of (plətí:ə) a battle fought (479 B.C.) during the Persian Wars. The Greeks, under Pausanias, destroyed a superior Persian army and forced the Persians to withdraw from Greece

plate (pleit) 1. n. a flat, shallow dish (usually circular, and typically of porcelain or earthenware) from which food is eaten ǁ the food served on such a dish ǁ the main course of a meal (meat, vegetables, salad etc.) all served on one plate ǁ a thin flat piece of metal for engraving on or bearing an inscription ǁ a full-page illustration (usually on coated paper or some paper other than what is used for the text) bound in a book ǁ (collect.) domestic utensils (esp. tableware) made of gold, silver etc., or plated ǁ a thin coating of precious metal put on base metal by electrolysis, the plate is wearing off these forks ǁ (photog.) a rectangular piece of metal or glass, coated with a sensitized emulsion, on which a photograph is taken ǁ a thin flat piece of metal etc. of uniform thickness, varying in size and serving various purposes, e.g. to join a fractured bone or forming part of a ship's armor ǁ (dentistry) that part of a denture which fits against the mouth and holds the artificial teeth in position ǁ (pop.) a set of false teeth ǁ a metal or wooden dish used for taking up the collection in church ǁ (printing) a sheet of metal, cast from type or engraved, from which impressions are taken ǁ a printed impression from this, e.g. of an engraving ǁ (archit.) a horizontal beam supporting or supported by vertical ones ǁ a horse race carrying a gold or silver cup etc. as prize for the winner, or the trophy awarded ǁ (hist.) sheets or one sheet of armor metal ǁ (baseball) home plate ǁ (baseball) a piece of rubber upon which the pitcher stands when delivering the ball to the batter ǁ a thin cut of beef from the forequarter, below the short ribs ǁ (anat., zool.) a thin layer or scale, e.g. of bone, horny tissue etc. ǁ (elec.) the anode or positive element of an electron tube toward which the stream of electrons flows 2. v.t. pres. part. **plat·ing** past and past part. **plat·ed** to cover with metal plates ǁ to cover with a thin layer (e.g. of metal) mechanically, chemically or electrically ǁ to make a solid plate of (type) for printing [M.E. fr. O.F. plate, a thin plate]

plate armor, Br. **plate armour** (hist.) armor consisting of steel plates riveted side by side with welded joints (cf. MAIL)

pla·teau (plætóu, Br. plǽtou) pl. **pla·teaus, pla·teaux** (plætóuz, Br. plǽtouz) n. a level, horizontal region at a considerable height above sea level or surrounding regions ǁ a roughly level section in a graph (e.g. of progress in production, showing little or no advance) [F.]

plate·ful (pléitful) pl. **plate·fuls** n. the amount of food etc. that fills a plate

plate glass thick polished glass made in large

sheets and used for shop windows, mirrors etc.

plate·lay·er (pléitleiər) n. (Br.) a tracklayer

plate·let (pléitlit) n. a microscopic, noncellular disk found in large numbers in vertebrate blood, that is involved in the activation of prothrombin. The rupture of blood vessels serves to initiate this process

plate mark a hallmark ǁ the rectangular depression surrounding an engraving where the metal plate has sunk into the paper

plat·en, Br. also **plat·ten** (plǽt'n) n. (printing) an iron plate in a hand press or platen press which presses the paper against the inked type ǁ the roller in a typewriter [M.E. plateyne, a flat plate of metal, fr. O.F. platine]

platen press a small printing press in which the type is secured in a vertical flat bed, and a platen brings the paper up into contact with it

plat·er (pléitər) n. someone who makes plates or applies them to ships etc. ǁ someone who plates with metals ǁ (racing) a horse only good enough to be entered for a selling race

plat·er·esque (plætərésk) adj. of a style of architecture of the early Spanish Renaissance characterized by rich ornamentation [fr. Span. plateresco fr. plata, silver]

Plate, River *RÍO DE LA PLATA

plate tracery (archit.) tracery consisting of flat surfaces of stone in which ornamental patterns have been traced, e.g. in early Gothic windows

plat·form (plǽtfɔrm) 1. n. a raised structure of planks on which a speaker or performer stands, acts etc. so that he can be seen by an audience ǁ a raised structure next to the track, by which passengers enter or leave a train in a station ǁ the open area at the end of a railroad passenger car, trolley car etc. ǁ a ledge, e.g. on a cliff face ǁ a flat structure on which a gun is mounted ǁ a flat, esp. raised, piece of ground ǁ a statement of aims and policies in the program of a person or party seeking electoral support 2. adj. of or designating a shoe sole from ½ in. to 3 ins. thick ǁ of or designating a shoe with such a sole [F. plateforme, flat form]

platform car (rail.) a flatcar

platform tennis paddleball game utilizing four walls of wire netting on an outdoor platform, similar to a small covered tennis court; usu. played in winter; developed in 1928 from paddle tennis

Plath (plæθ), Sylvia (1932–63) U.S. poet. Her first volume of verse 'Colossus,' was published in 1960. But it was only upon the posthumous publication of 'Ariel' (1965) that she became the most celebrated poet of her generation, based on her intense descriptions of extreme states of mind. Two other collections of verse were published following her suicide, 'Crossing the Water' (1971) and 'Winter Trees' (1971). She also wrote a semiautobiographical novel, 'The Bell Jar' (1963), an account of a young woman's struggle with mental breakdown

plat·ing (pléitiŋ) n. the process or result of covering with a plate or plates, esp. with a thin layer of metal ǁ the plates of a vessel, tank or other armored vehicle

pla·tin·ic (plətínik) adj. of or pertaining to platinum, esp. of compounds in which platinum is tetravalent (cf. PLATINOUS)

plat·i·nize (plǽt'naiz) pres. part. **plat·i·niz·ing** past and past part. **plat·i·nized** v.t. to coat with platinum black or combine or treat with platinum

plat·i·noid (plǽt'nɔid) 1. n. an alloy of copper (60%), zinc (24%), nickel (14%) and wolfram (2%), used as a substitute for platinum in resistances and thermocouples ǁ a metal related to platinum 2. adj. like platinum

pla·ti·no·tran (plǽt'noutræn) n. (electr.) device consisting of a microwave tube with a permanent magnet, used as a high-power saturated oscillator or amplifier in radar apparatus

plat·i·no·type (plǽt'noutaip) n. a photographic print of great lasting quality, in which platinum is used instead of silver ǁ the process of making such a print [PLATINUM+TYPE]

plat·i·nous (plǽt'nəs) adj. of or pertaining to platinum, esp. of compounds in which platinum is divalent (cf. PLATINIC)

plat·i·num (plǽt'nəm, plǽtnəm) n. a very heavy, ductile, malleable, silvery white metallic element (symbol Pt, at. no. 78, at. mass 195.09), very resistant to acids, heat and corrosion, and therefore used as a precious metal in jewelry and in some forms of chemical apparatus. An excellent conductor of electricity, the metal is used for electrical contacts etc. in the platinum resistance thermometer etc. The U.S.S.R. is the main producer [Mod. L. fr. Span. *platina*, platinum]

platinum black a black powder of finely divided platinum obtained by the reduction of platinum salts and used as a catalyst, esp. in hydrogenation or oxygenation

platinum blonde a woman with hair bleached silvery blond, or with hair naturally of this color

platinum metal any of six metallic elements including platinum and metals resembling or occurring with it: iridium, osmium, palladium, rhodium and ruthenium

plat·i·tude (plǽtitu:d, plǽtitju:d) *n.* a flat, stale or commonplace remark or statement uttered as if it were informative and important ‖ (in speech, writing, thinking) the quality of being dull or commonplace **plat·i·tú·di·nize** *pres. part.* **plat·i·tu·di·niz·ing** *past* and *past part.* **plat·i·tu·di·nized** *v.i.* to utter platitudes **plat·i·tú·di·nous** *adj.* [F. fr. *plat*, flat]

Pla·to (pléitou) (c. 428–c. 348 B.C.), Greek philosopher. At 20 he became a follower of Socrates. Their association continued until the death of Socrates, and thereafter Plato devoted his life to philosophy. In 388 he founded the Academy. Socrates was the crucial influence in his development as a philosopher, but Plato achieved a synthesis of all Greek thought that had preceded him. Plato's writings, mainly in dialogue form, deal with mathematics, politics, beauty, the laws of thought, education, love, friendship etc. But he never treated any specialized subject for its own sake: all are subordinated to his central interest, the Good, or virtue. Though he regarded mathematics as a valuable discipline to thought, he took little interest in science. His use of dialogue reflects his belief that man cannot find the truth alone, that he approaches it through discussion, through the clash of ideas and personalities. He often sets forth his ideas with the help of myths, some solemn, some playful, but always poetic. Socrates is the central character in all but the last dialogues. 'Apology' and 'Crito' deal with the trial and death of Socrates. Those that follow present the Socratic method of argument (*SOCRATIC IRONY). False ideas are exposed, but the main questions are left open. The personality of Socrates is most fully developed in 'Phaedo' and 'Symposium'. At the same time Plato begins to move away from the historical Socrates. His characteristic method of rising toward higher truth by a synthesis of antagonisms makes its appearance. He introduces his theory of ideas (*IDEA), and in the 'Republic' he formulates his conception of a perfect state. The late work ('Parmenides', 'Critias', 'Timaeus', 'Statesman', 'Laws') becomes increasingly expository, and the Socratic element disappears. The Platonic doctrine that has most influenced philosophy is the theory of ideas. But his enormous influence springs equally from his elaboration and clarification of the laws of reasoning, and perhaps most of all from his own person as an embodiment of the search for truth

Pla·ton·ic (plətónik) *adj.* of, pertaining to or characteristic of Plato or Platonism ‖ of or designating love as Plato described it, a desire for union with the beautiful, ascending in a scale of perfection from human passion to ecstasy in the contemplation of the ideal **pla·ton·ic** of or designating love for a person, usually of the opposite sex, that is free of carnal desire **Pla·tón·i·cal·ly, pla·tón·i·cal·ly** *adv.* [fr. L. *Platonicus* fr. Gk]

Pla·to·nism (pléit'nizəm) *n.* the Platonic philosophy in its philosophical developments and transformations since Plato. The earliest Platonism was that taught in the Academy. With Plotinus it underwent fundamental changes, and for the next thousand years Platonism was known as Neoplatonism. Through Augustine it became the dominant current in Christian philosophy and remained so until the 13th c., when it was superseded by Scholasticism, stressing Aristotle. In Renaissance Italy it regained its original character with the rediscovery of Plato by Ficino and Pico della Mirandola. It had another significant revival in 17th-c. England (*CAMBRIDGE PLATONISTS). It played an important part in the development of the German

idealist philosophers (Leibniz, Kant, Fichte and Hegel)

Pla·to·nist (pléit'nist) *n.* a follower of Plato or adherent of a Platonic philosophy [fr. M.L. *platonista*]

Pla·to·nize (pléit'naiz) *pres. part.* **Pla·to·niz·ing** *past* and *past part.* **Pla·to·nized** *v.t.* to interpret in a Platonic manner ‖ to make Platonic ‖ *v.i.* to philosophize in the manner of Plato, or be a Platonist [fr. Gk *platōnizein*]

pla·toon (plətú:n) *n.* (*mil.*) a tactical infantry unit, smaller than a company and under the command of a lieutenant [fr. F. *peloton*, little ball, platoon]

Platt (plæt), Orville Hitchcock (1827–1905), American legislator. He drew up the Platt Amendment (1905), which provided for U.S. intervention in Cuba

Platt Amendment a series of amendments to the Army Appropriations Bill of 1901, sponsored by U.S. Sen. Orville H. Platt, that defined U.S.-Cuba relations during the period 1901–34. The Platt Amendment essentially made Cuba a U.S. protectorate, limiting the island's treaty-making capacity, restricting its ability to contract public debt and giving the U.S.A. the right to maintain naval bases in Cuba and to intervene in Cuban affairs as necessary to preserve order or Cuba's independence. These provisions were appended to Cuba's constitution (1901), U.S. troops were withdrawn (1902) and the provisions were formalized by treaty (1903). Considered a symbol of 'Yankee imperialism,' the treaty was repealed by the U.S. (1934); however, the lease on the U.S. naval base at Guantánamo Bay was continued

Platt·deutsch (plátdɔitʃ) *n.* the vernacular Low German language spoken in N. Germany [G. *platt*, flat, low+*deutsch*, German]

Platte (plæt) a river (total length c. 930 miles) formed by the union of the North and South Platte Rivers in central Nebraska. The North Platte (618 miles long) rises in N. Colorado, flows across the Wyoming border into central Wyoming and turns east across the Nebraska border through central Nebraska, to unite with the South Platte River. The newly formed Platte (310 miles long) flows east and empties into the Missouri River

platten *PLATEN

plat·ter (plǽtər) *n.* a shallow, usually oval serving dish ‖ (*Br., old-fash.*) a plate or dish [M.E. *plater* fr. A.F. fr. *plat*, dish]

plat·y·hel·minth (plǽtihélminθ) *n.* a flatworm [fr. Mod. L. *Platyhelminthes*, name of the phylum fr. Gk *platus*, flat+*helmins* (*helminthos*), worm]

plat·y·pus (plǽtipəs) *n.* *Ornithorhynchus anatinus*, order *Monotremata*, a small, primitive aquatic Australian mammal, about 18 ins. long. It has thick blackish-brown fur, a flat, leathery bill like that of a duck, no lips, a long, flat tail and webbed feet. It lays eggs, but nurses its young [Mod. L. fr. Gk *platupous* fr. *platus*, flat+*pous*, foot]

plat·yr·rhine (plǽtirain) *adj.* having a broad, esp. flat-bridged nose ‖ of or belonging to *Platyrrhina*, a division of *Anthropoidea* including all the New World monkeys [fr. Mod. L. *platyrrhinus* fr. Gk *platus*, flat+*rhis* (*rhinos*), nose]

plau·dits (plɔ́dits) *pl. n.* (*rhet.*) praise or approval [fr. L. *plaudite* (said by a Roman cast at the end of a performance), 2nd person pl. imper. of *plaudere*, to applaud]

plau·si·bil·i·ty (plɔzəbíliti:) *n.* the quality of being plausible [fr. L. *plausibilis*, praiseworthy]

plau·si·ble (plɔ́zəb'l) *adj.* (of a statement, argument etc.) apparently true or reasonable, winning assent, *a plausible explanation* ‖ (of a person) genuine, trustworthy etc. in appearance, but probably not to be trusted **pláu·si·bly** *adv.* [fr. L. *plausibilis*, praiseworthy]

Plau·tus (plɔ́təs), Titus Maccius (or Maccus) (c. 254–184 B.C.), Roman playwright. He adapted Greek comedies for the Roman stage. His 21 extant plays, incl. 'Miles Gloriosus', 'Menaechmi', 'Amphitruo' etc., contain boisterous, low-comedy portrayals of middle-class and lower-class life

play (plei) *n.* movement or activity, esp. quick or unconstrained, *the play of light and shade on the water* ‖ activity or exercise performed for amusement (cf. WORK) ‖ freedom of movement, scope, *to give full play to one's imagination* ‖ (*games*) manner of playing, *defensive play* ‖ a maneuver in a game etc. ‖ a turn to play, in a game ‖ a dramatic stage performance ‖ the written or printed text for this ‖ gambling, *he lost a*

fortune in an hour's play **in play** as a joke, in fun, *he meant it in play* ‖ (*games*, of the ball) available for kicking etc. in accordance with the rules **out of play** (*games*, of the ball) not available for kicking etc. **to make a play for** to use various wiles in an effort to win the love, admiration, interest etc. of (someone) [O.E. *plega*]

play *v.t.* to take part in games or a game of, *to play tennis* ‖ to make music on (a musical instrument), *to play the piano* ‖ to perform (a piece of music) ‖ to perform the music of (a composer), *to play Beethoven* ‖ to act (a part) in a theatrical performance ‖ to perform the role of (a character) in such a performance ‖ to give a theatrical performance of, *they played 'Hamlet' to a full house* ‖ to perform in (a city etc.), *they played Brighton for a month* ‖ to accompany with music, *a band played the procession into the arena* ‖ to perform (a trick, joke etc.) ‖ (*ball games*) to strike or deliver, *he played the ball into the net* ‖ to direct (a jet of water, searchlight etc.), *the fireman played his hose into the flames* ‖ to take part in a game against, *England is playing Australia* ‖ to move, use, place etc. (a card, piece etc.) in a game, *he played his ace* ‖ to hazard, stake, *he played his last dollar* ‖ to place a bet on (something), *to play the horses* ‖ to include in a team, *England is playing three fast bowlers* ‖ to fill (a position) in a game, *he played center forward* ‖ to imitate or pretend to be, for fun, *to play pirates* ‖ to give (a fish) scope to exhaust itself by pulling against the line ‖ *v.i.* to engage in activity for amusement ‖ to trifle, toy, *stop playing with your food* ‖ to flutter, flit, in a light, erratic manner, *shadows played on the ceiling* ‖ to perform music on an instrument, *he played as only a virtuoso can* ‖ to give a (usually dramatic) performance, *they played to a full house* ‖ (of a fountain, jet of water etc.) to be in operation ‖ to take part in a game, *to play half-heartedly* ‖ (*games*, of ground) to be in a specified condition, *the court plays slowly after rain* ‖ to frolic, gambol ‖ to gamble ‖ to be serious in appearance but not in fact, *they're only playing* ‖ (of a play, film etc.) to be performed or be showing, *what's playing tonight?* ‖ (of a musical instrument) to respond to the performer, *the piano plays better now* ‖ (*mach.*) to show loose movement, *the steering plays badly* **to be played out** to be exhausted ‖ to be no longer effective ‖ to hold no more interest **to play around**, *Br.* also **to play about** to be active without doing anything useful ‖ (*pop.*) to engage in flirtation or illicit or promiscuous lovemaking **to play at** to take part in (some activity) in the spirit of make-believe or without being in earnest **to play back** to play and listen to (a recording which one has just made) **to play ball** to be cooperative **to play both ends against the middle** to set rivals or opposing interests against each other, to one's own advantage **to play by ear** to play a musical instrument without being able to read music or without reading the music ‖ to act in (a situation) as seems best while it is developing, rather than in accordance with some plan **to play down** to make (something) appear less important, worthy etc. than it really is **to play fair** to obey the rules ‖ to behave toward another person without cheating or deception **to play (someone) false** (*rhet.*) to deceive (someone) **to play for time** (*games*) to play out a game defensively, without risking real attack ‖ to seek to postpone an undesired event by dodges and delaying tactics **to play into someone's hands** to do something that gives one's opponent a sudden and overwhelming advantage **to play off** to play (one's allotted game or a particular stage) in a tournament etc. ‖ (*games*) to take part in a play-off to settle (a tie) **to play off one person against another** to set one person against another for one's own advantage **to play on** to take advantage of, exploit, *she won by playing on his weak points* ‖ (*cricket*) to put oneself 'out' by playing the ball on to the wicket **to play out** to play to its finish, *play out the game* ‖ to pay out, *to play out a line* **to play the field** to have dates or romantic involvements with many people, not confining one's interests to one person ‖ to operate over a broad area or range **to play the fool** to behave or act as if one were a fool **to play to the gallery** to seek to win admiration in a way that is beneath one, by appealing to those who will respond most easily **to play up** (*Br.*) to put all one's energy into a game ‖ to emphasize unduly, *the newspaper played up the issue* ‖ (*Br.pop.*) to be

CONCISE PRONUNCIATION KEY: **(a)** æ, c*a*t; ɑ, c*a*r; ɔ f*aw*n; ei, sn*a*ke. **(e)** e, h*e*n; i:, sh*ee*p; iə, d*ee*r; ɛə, b*ea*r. **(i)** i, f*i*sh; ai, t*i*ger; ə:, b*i*rd. **(o)** o, *o*x; au, c*ow*; ou, g*oa*t; u, p*oo*r; ɔi, r*oy*al. **(u)** ʌ, d*u*ck; u, b*u*ll; u:, g*oo*se; ə, b*a*cillus; ju:, c*u*be. x, lo*ch*; θ, *th*ink; ð, bo*th*er; z, *Z*en; ʒ, cor*s*age. dʒ, sava*g*e; ŋ, ora*n*guta*ng*; j, *y*ak; ʃ, *sh*; tʃ, fe*tch*; 'l, rabb*le*; 'n, redd*en*. Complete pronunciation key appears inside front cover.

nuisance to **to play up to** to insinuate oneself into the favor of by flattery [O.E. *plegan*]

play·a·ble (pléiəb'l) *adj.* able to be played or played on

play·act (pléiækt) *v.i.* to make a pretense, be false or insincere in conduct **pláy·act·ing** *n.*

play-ac·tion pass (pléiækʃən) *(football)* play involving a feinted hand-off by the quarterback before passing to someone else

play·back (pléibæk) *n.* a playing back of a recording || the part of a tape recorder etc. which serves to play back transcriptions

play·bill (pléibil) *n.* a poster or handbill advertising a theatrical performance || a theater program

play·book (pléibuk) *n. (football)* set of diagrams of team's plays

play·boy (pléibɔi) *n.* a rich young man who cares chiefly about having a good time

play-by-play (pléibaipléi) *adj.* describing each development of a game etc. as it occurs, *a play-by-play account*

play·er (pléiər) *n.* a person who plays in a game || a person who performs on a specified musical instrument || a device for operating a piano mechanically || *(old-fash.)* an actor

player piano a piano equipped with a mechanical attachment which depresses the keys by air pressure, reproducing notes that are represented by perforations on a paper roll

play·fel·low (pléifelou) *n. (old-fash.)* a playmate

play·ful (pléifəl) *adj.* tending or liking to play, *as playful as a kitten* || lighthearted and humorous, *a playful mood*

play·go·er (pléigouər) *n.* a person who often goes to the theater

play·ground (pléigraund) *n.* a piece of ground set apart for children to play on, often attached to a school || a favorite district for recreation, esp. as giving scope for some particular activity, *a climber's playground*

play·group (pléigru:p) *n.* an improvised neighborhood nursery school for child care

play·house (pléihaus) *pl.* **play·hous·es** (pléihauziz) *n.* (usually in titles) a theater || a little house for children to play in

playing card one of the cards in a pack of 52 used in playing games. They are small rectangular pieces of pasteboard, grouped into four suits (hearts, diamonds, clubs, spades), each having 13 cards which comprise the ace (marked A), cards numbered 2 to 10, and three cards bearing pictures of figures called king, queen and jack (or knave). Such cards are also used by fortune-tellers and conjurers

playing field a field (esp. one attached to a school) for games and recreation

play·list (pléilist) *n.* schedule of recordings to be played on a radio broadcast

play·mate (pléimeit) *n.* a child's friend with whom he plays

play-off (pléiɔf, pléiɒf) *n. (games)* a match played to decide a tie or where a previous game has given an inconclusive result

play on words a pun

play·pen (pléipen) *n.* a portable enclosure in which very young children can play safely. It usually consists of a small square base enclosed by a wooden or metal railing with vertical bars or netting

play·room (pléiru:m, pléirum) *n.* a room children use to play in, or a recreation room

play·thing (pléiθiŋ) *n.* something designed to be played with || *(rhet.)* a person treated as a toy by another or by fate etc.

play·time (pléitaim) *n.* a period set apart for play

play·wright (pléirait) *n.* a writer of theatrical plays

pla·za (plázə, plǽzə) *n.* a public square in a town or city [Span. fr. (assumed) pop. L. *plattia* fr. L. *platea*, courtyard]

plea (pli:) *n. (rhet.)* an appeal || *(rhet.)* a request || an argument used to excuse || *(law)* a statement made in court by either party in argument of his case [M.E. *plaid, plai* O.F.]

plea bargaining negotiation between defense attorney in a criminal action and the prosecutor for a reduced charge in exchange for a plea of guilty

pleach (pli:tʃ) *v.t.* to plash (interweave stems, branches etc.) [M.E. *pleche* fr. O.F.]

plead (pli:d) *pres. part.* **plead·ing** *past* and *past part.* **plead·ed, pled** *v.i.* to beg with emotion and at length, implore, *to plead for mercy* || *(law)* to state a plea || *(law)* to argue in court || *v.t. (law)* to cite (something) in legal defense, *he*

pleaded ignorance || *(law)* to argue (a case) in court **to plead (not) guilty** *(law)* to admit (deny) guilt, as a method of procedure [O. F. *plaidier*]

plead·ing (pli:diŋ) *n.* the act of making a plea || an instance of this || *(law)* the written statements setting forth the cause of the plaintiff and the response of the defendant

pleas·ant (pléz'nt) *adj.* agreeable, pleasing [O.F. *plaisant, pleisant*]

pleas·ant·ry (péz'ntri:) *pl.* **pleas·ant·ries** *n.* (in conversation) pleasant, goodhumored joking back and forth || an instance of this

please (pli:z) *pres. part.* **pleas·ing** *past* and *past part.* **pleased** *v.t.* to gratify, satisfy, give pleasure to || *v.i.* to desire and intend, *do as you please* || to make oneself pleasant, agreeable etc., *the desire to please* || to win favor, *dogs obey in order to please* || (in requests or commands) be good enough to, *please come along* **if you please** if you wish || expressing surprise (ironic), *then she turned on her heel, if you please* **please God** if it is God's wish || may it be God's wish **to please oneself** to do as one wishes **pleased, pleas·ing** *adjs* [M.E. *plaise, pleise, plese* fr. O.F.]

pleas·ur·a·ble (pléʒərəb'l) *adj.* giving or capable of giving pleasure **pleas·ur·a·bly** *adv.* [PLEASURE]

pleas·ure (pléʒər) *n.* a general feeling of satisfaction, enjoyment || something which causes this feeling, *your visit will be a pleasure* || self-gratification, *he lives for pleasure* [M.E. *plesir, plaisir* fr. O.F.]

pleat (pli:t) 1. *n.* a fold, esp. one made by doubling cloth etc. upon itself and pressing or stitching it in place or allowing it to hang free 2. *v.t.* to make a pleat or pleats in [var. of PLAIT]

ple·bei·an, ple·bi·an (pləbí:ən) 1. *n.* a member of the common people || *(Rom. hist.)* a member of the lowest class in ancient Rome, without privileges until the 4th c. B.C. (cf. PATRICIAN) 2. *adj.* of or characteristic of the common people, uncultured, vulgar [fr. L. *plebeius*, of the plebeians]

pleb·i·scite (plébisait, plébisit) *n.* a vote of the entire electorate on a national issue (e.g. constitutional change) || a vote of the people to decide whether a contested region should be attached to one country or another or, in some cases, become autonomous [F. *plébiscite*]

plec·tog·nath (pléktɒgnæθ) 1. *adj. (zool.)* of *Plectognathi*, an order of fishes covered with bony plates, spines etc. and having small mouths with powerful jaws 2. *n.* a member of this order, e.g. the globefish [fr. Gk *plektos*, plaited + *gnathos*, jaw]

plec·tron (pléktrɒn) *n.* a plectrum

plec·trum (pléktrəm) *pl.* **plec·tra** (pléktrə), **plec·trums** *n.* a small implement of ivory, wood, metal etc., used for plucking the strings of a mandolin, banjo etc. [L. fr. Gk *plēktron*, something to strike with]

pledge (pledʒ) 1. *n.* something of value left as security for a loan or as a guarantee that an obligation will be met || a solemn promise || the state of being pledged, *in pledge* || *(old-fash.)* a toast || a person who has agreed to become a member of a club, fraternity etc. but who has not yet been initiated **to take the pledge** to make a solemn promise to abstain from alcoholic drink 2. *v.t. pres. part.* **pledg·ing** *past* and *past part* **pledged** to hand over as security for a loan || to commit (oneself, one's reputation etc.) || to promise, to pledge allegiance to the flag || *(old-fash.)* to drink a toast to || to agree to become a member of (a club, fraternity etc.) || to cause to be a pledge in a club, fraternity etc. [O.F. *plege*, hostage, security]

Plé·iade (pláiəd, pléijæd) a group of French poets who under Henri II set out to freshen French poetry with new forms (esp. the sonnet), and to clear the language of useless rhetoric. They were: Ronsard, Du Bellay, Rémy Belleau (1528–77), Jodelle, Jean Dorat (1508–88), Baïf and Pontus de Tyard (1521–1605)

Ple·ia·des (pláiədi:z) the seven brightest stars in the constellation Taurus || *(Gk mythol.)* the seven daughters (Alcyone, Celaeno, Electra, Maia, Merope, Asterope, Taygete) of Atlas who were changed into stars by Zeus [L. fr. Gk *Pleias (Pleiados)*]

Pleiocene **PLIOCENE*

plei·ot·ro·py (plaiátrəpi:) *n. (genetics)* ability of a gene to produce various characteristics

Pleis·to·cene (pláistəsi:n) *adj.* of the earlier epoch or series of the Quaternary era, characterized by the formation of glaciers (**GEOLOGICAL*

TIME) **the Pleistocene** the Pleistocene epoch or series of rocks [fr. Gk *pleistos*, most + *kainos*, recent]

Plek·ha·nov (pljəkhánʌf), Georgi Valentinovich (1857–1918), Russian Marxist political philosopher. He was one of the founders of the Russian Social Democratic party (1898) and became the leader of the Mensheviks. He took refuge in Finland after the Bolshevik revolution (1917). His works include 'Anarchism and Socialism' (1896)

ple·na·ri·ly (plí:nərili:, plénərili:) *adv.* in a plenary manner

ple·na·ry (plí:nəri:, plénəri) *adj.* complete, absolute, *plenary powers* || (of a legislative body) attended by all members, *a plenary session* [fr. L.L. *plenarius*]

plenary indulgence *(Roman Catholicism)* an indulgence which remits in full the temporal punishment incurred by a sinner

plench (plentʃ) *n.* tool combining pliers and wrench operable from the handle; originally used on space vehicles

plen·i·po·ten·ti·ar·y (plenipəténʃi:eri:, plenipəténʃəri:) 1. *adj.* invested with unlimited power || of or relating to a plenipotentiary 2. *pl.* **plen·i·po·ten·ti·ar·ies** *n.* an ambassador or envoy with full powers of decision [fr. M.L. *plenipotentiarius* fr. *plenus*, full + *potens*, powerful]

plen·i·tude (plénitu:d, plénitju:d) *n.* completeness || *(rhet.)* abundance, *a plenitude of natural gifts* [O. F.]

plen·te·ous (plénti:əs) *adj. (rhet.)* plentiful [M.E. *plentifous, plentivous* fr. O.F.]

plen·ti·ful (pléntifəl) *adj.* abundant, *plentiful supplies* || producing or yielding abundantly, *a plentiful harvest*

plen·ty (plénti:) 1. *n.* prosperity, abundance, *years of plenty* || more than enough, *plenty of money* || a great quantity, *he lost plenty of money in the business* || (esp. with 'in') the quality or state of being plentiful, *compliments in plenty* 2. *adj.* abundant, *money was plenty but goods were scarce* 3. *adv. (pop.)* more than adequately, *it is plenty large enough* [M.E. *plente, plenteth* fr. O.F.]

ple·num (plí:nəm) *pl.* **ple·nums, ple·na** (plí:nə) *n.* the entirety of a space regarded as being filled with matter (opp. VACUUM) || (esp. of a legislative body) a full assembly [L. neuter of *plenus*, full]

ple·o·mor·phic (pli:oumórfik) *adj.*, characterized by pleomorphism

ple·o·mor·phism (pli:oumórfizem) *n. (biol.)* the occurrence of two or more distinct forms at different stages in one life cycle [fr. Gk *pleon*, more + *morphē*, form]

ple·o·nasm (plí:ənæzəm) *n.* the using of more words than necessary in expressing an idea, with redundancy || an instance of this or a redundant word or expression, e.g. 'falsely fraudulent' **ple·o·nas·tic** *adj.* **ple·o·nas·ti·cal·ly** *adv.* [fr. L. *pleonasmus* fr. Gk *pleon*, more]

ple·o·pod (plí:əpɒd) *n. (zool.)* one of the swimming appendages attached to the abdomen of a crustacean [fr. Gk *plein*, to swim + *pous (podos)*, foot]

ple·si·o·saur (plí:si:əsɔr) *n.* a Mesozoic marine reptile of the suborder *Plesiosauria*, order *Sauropterygia*, 40 ft or more in length, having four large paddlelike limbs [fr. Mod. L. *plesiosaurus* fr. *plesios*, near + *saurus*, lizard]

ples·sor (plésər) *n.* a plexor

Ples·sy v. Fer·gu·son (plési:, fə:rgəsən) a decision (1896) of the U.S. Supreme Court led by Melville W. Fuller, which enunciated the 'separate but equal' doctrine of racial segregation. It ruled that segregation was legal if equal facilities were offered for both races

pleth·o·ra (pléθərə) *n.* a great quantity, esp. more than desirable, *a plethora of examples* || an unhealthy physical condition caused by an excess of blood and characterized by a highly flushed complexion **pleth·or·ic** (pleθórik, pleθórik) *adj.* (esp. of speech, writing etc.) pretentious || having an excess of blood [M.L. fr. Gk *plēthōrē* fr. *plēthein*, to become full]

pleu·ra (plúərə) *pl.* **pleu·rae** (plúəri:), **pleu·ras** *n.* a thin serous membrane lining the chest cavity and surrounding each lung in most air-breathing mammals [M.L. fr. Gk *pleura*, rib, side]

pleu·ri·sy (plúərisi:) *n.* inflammation of the pleura, resulting in fever and sharp pain in the chest or side [O.F. *pleurisie*]

pleu·rit·ic (plurítik) *adj.* of or having pleurisy [fr. F. *pleurétique* or fr. L. *pleuriticus*]

CONCISE PRONUNCIATION KEY: (a) æ, c*a*t; ɑ, c*a*r; ɔ f*aw*n; ɔi, sn*a*ke. **(e)** e, h*e*n; i:, sh*ee*p; iə, d*ee*r; ɛə, b*ea*r. **(i)** i, f*i*sh; ai, t*i*ger; ə:, b*i*rd. **(o)** o, *o*x; au, c*ow*; ou, g*oa*t; u, p*oo*r; ɔi, r*oy*al. **(u)** ʌ, d*u*ck; u, b*u*ll; u:, g*oo*se; ə, b*a*cillus; ju:, c*u*be. x, lo*ch*; θ, *th*ink; ð, bo*th*er; z, *Z*en; ʒ, corsa*g*e; dʒ, sava*g*e; o, or*a*ngut*a*ng; j, *y*ak; ʃ, *fi*sh; tʃ, fe*tch*; 'l, rabb*le*; 'n, redd*en*. Complete pronunciation key appears inside front cover.

pleu·ro·dont (plúərədɒnt) 1. *adj.* (of some lizards) having the teeth consolidated with the inner edge of the jaw 2. *n.* a lizard having pleurodont teeth [fr. Gk *pleura*, rib, side+*odous* (*odontos*), tooth]

pleu·ro·pneu·mo·ni·a (plúərounu:móunjə, plúərounju:móunjə) *n.* a combination of pleurisy and pneumonia ‖ a severe, often fatal inflammation of the lungs of farm animals, esp. cattle [Mod. L. fr. Gk *pleura*, rib+PNEUMONIA]

Plev·en (plévən) an agricultural market (pop. 122,916) of N. central Bulgaria

Plex·i·glass, Plex·i·glas (pléksiglæs, pléksiglɑs) *n.* a clear transparent thermoplastic synthetic resin used for cast and molded transparent parts and for coatings [Trademark]

plex·im·e·ter (pleksímitər) *n.* a thin plate of ivory, hard rubber etc. which is placed on some part of the body to receive the blow of the plexor in medical percussion. Gk *plēxis*, stroke+*metron*, measure]

plex·or (pléksɔr) *n.* a small rubber-headed hammer used in medical percussion [fr. Gk *plēxis*, stroke]

plex·us (plékssəs) *n.* (*anat.*) a network of intertwining nerves or blood vessels, *the solar plexus* ‖ an exceedingly complex organization or network [L.=a twining, braid]

pli·a·bil·i·ty (plaiəbíliti:) *n.* the quality of being pliable

pli·a·ble (pláiəb'l) *adj.* readily bent, pliant ‖ readily influenced **pli·a·bly** *adv.* [F.]

pli·an·cy (pláiənsi:) *n.* the quality of being pliant

pli·ant (pláiənt) *adj.* (of materials) pliable ‖ (of people) readily yielding to influence [F.]

pli·ca (pláikə) *pl.* **pli·cae** (pláisi:) *n.* (*biol.*) a fold of skin, membrane etc. ‖ a crusty, matted condition of the hair caused by disease or vermin [M.L.=a fold]

pli·cate (pláikeit) *adj.* (*zool.*) folded ‖ (*bot.*) pleated, *a plicate leaf* **pli·cat·ed** *adj.* [fr. L. *plicare* (*plicatus*), to fold]

pli·ca·tion (plaikéiʃən) *n.* a folding or being folded ‖ a fold, esp. (*geol.*) a fold in a stratum [O.F.]

pli·ers (pláiərz) *pl. n.* small pincers with long jaws, used for handling small objects, for bending or cutting wire etc. [fr. older *ply* v., to fold]

plight (plait) *n.* a state of distress, predicament [M.E. *plit*, *plyt* fr. A. F.]

plight *v.t.* (*rhet.*) to pledge (esp. in) **to plight one's troth** to make a promise of marriage [O.E. *plihtan*, fr. *pliht*, danger]

Plim·soll line (plímsəl, plímsɒl, plímsɒl) (*naut.*) a diagram of lines on the hull of a cargo boat indicating the depth to which the vessel may be safely loaded (varying according to the season and the salinity of the water) in conformity with a British Merchant Shipping Act of 1876 [after Samuel *Plimsoll* (1824-98), Br. reformer who campaigned for this in the interest of crews]

Plimsoll mark a Plimsoll line

plim·solls (plímsəlz, plímsɔlz, plímsɒlz) *pl. n.* (*Br., old-fash.*) sneakers, tennis shoes [origin unknown]

plinth (plinθ) *n.* (*archit.*) the rectangular base of a column ‖ (*Br.*) the base of a wall which projects just above ground level ‖ a similar base on which a statue, vase etc. is placed [fr. L. *plinthus* fr. Gk]

Plin·y (plíni:) 'the Younger' (Gaius Plinius Caecilius Secundus, c. 62–c. 114), Roman author and administrator, nephew of Pliny the Elder. He served in several public offices and was consul (100). His one extant oration is a 'Panegyric on Trajan' (100). His 'Letters' (c. 97–c. 111) give a valuable account of contemporary upper-class life

Pliny 'the Elder' (Gaius Plinius Secundus, 23–79), Roman writer and administrator. Only his encyclopedic 37-volume 'Natural History' (77) survives. He died in the eruption of Vesuvius

Pli·o·cene (pláiəsi:n) *adj.* of the latest epoch or series of the Tertiary (*GEOLOGICAL TIME) **the Pliocene** the Pliocene epoch or series of rocks [fr. Gk *pleon*, more+*kainos*, new]

PLO (*acronym*) Palestine Liberation Organization (which see)

PL/I (*computer abbr.*) Programming Language One, used for simple general purposes

plod (plɒd) 1. *v.i. pres. part.* **plod·ding** *past and past part.* **plod·ded** to walk heavily and slowly ‖ to make slow, laborious progress when working, *to plod through a lesson* 2. *n.* a laborious tread or the sound of this **plód·der** *n.* someone

who works diligently and learns by hard work rather than by natural aptitude [prob. imit.]

Plo·es·ti (ploujéʃt) the chief petroleum-refining center (pop. 199,300) of Rumania, in Walachia, 34 miles north of Bucharest

Plom·bières Agreement (plɔbjɛər) a secret pact (1858) between Napoleon III and Cavour at Plombières in the Vosges, providing for French support for Piedmont in a war against Austria

plonk (plɒŋk) 1. *n.* a plunk 2. *v.t.* and *i.* to plunk

plop (plɒp) 1. *n.* the sound made when an object or body drops into a liquid 2. *v.i. pres. part.* **plop·ping** *past and past part.* **plopped** to make this sound ‖ to fall with a plop ‖ to let one's body fall wearily, *to plop into a chair* [imit.]

plot (plɒt) 1. *n.* a small piece of ground, esp. one used or to be used for a particular purpose, *a building plot* ‖ a ground plan ‖ a secret, usually evil, plan or conspiracy ‖ the plan of events in a novel, play etc. ‖ a chart showing the progress of a ship, submarine or aircraft, or any comparable chart, *a plot of the month's sales* ‖ a point of intersection marked on a chart 2. *v. pres. part.* **plotting** *past and past part.* **plot·ted** *v.t.* to plan secretly (esp. something evil) ‖ to make a plan or map of ‖ to mark (a position, course etc.) on a chart ‖ to construct the plan of (events in a novel, play etc.) ‖ to determine and mark (a point) e.g. on a graph, by working from coordinates ‖ to draw (a curve) by means of points so marked ‖ (*math.*) to represent (an equation) by means of such a curve ‖ *v.i.* to conspire [origin unknown]

Plo·ti·nus (ploutáinəs) (205-70), Roman philosopher of Egyptian birth. After studying in Alexandria, he established his Neoplatonic school in Rome (244). From 253 he wrote the 'Enneads' (published posthumously by his pupil Porphyry). He used the metaphysical myths of Plato (esp. the dialectic of love) to create a mystic religion of union with the One through contemplation and ecstatic vision. Through St Augustine his theory of the human spirit entered into the mainstream of Western philosophy

plot·ter (plɒtər) *n.* someone who makes a plot, conspirator ‖ someone who marks plots on a chart ‖ a device for marking plots ‖ (*computer*) a peripheral output device for data analysis

plough (plau) 1. *n.* *PLOW ‖ (*Br.*) land which has been plowed ‖ 2. *v.t.* *PLOW ‖ (*Br., old-fash.*) to fail (someone) in an examination ‖ (*Br., old-fash.*) to fail (an examination) ‖ *v.i.* (*Br., old-fash.*) to fail in an examination [O.E. *plōh*]

plough·boy *PLOWBOY

plough·man *PLOWMAN

plough·share *PLOWSHARE

Plov·div (plɔúdif) the second largest city (pop. 309,242) of Bulgaria, on the Maritsa, the market for a rich farm area: tobacco (national center), food processing, silk weaving. As Philippopolis, it prospered (4th c. B.C.) under Philip II of Macedon

plov·er (plávər, plóuvər) *n.* any of several small wading birds of fam. *Charadriidae*. They are cosmopolitan and gregarious and nest on the ground. Some species are edible and the eggs are considered a delicacy [O.F. *plovier*, plover, rain bird]

plow, esp. *Br.* **plough** (plau) 1. *n.* an agricultural implement drawn by a tractor, oxen, horses etc., used for cutting through and turning over soil, esp. in a field to be planted ‖ any implement or device resembling this ‖ (*bookbinding*) a device for cutting the edges of books ‖ (*carpentry*) a plane for making a groove etc. 2. *v.t.* to turn over, break up etc. (soil) with a plow ‖ to furrow as if with a plow, *to plow one's way through a crowd* ‖ (of ships) to cut through the surface of (water) ‖ (*carpentry*) to cut a groove etc. in with a plow ‖ (*bookbinding*) to cut the edges of (a book) with a plow ‖ *v.i.* to work with a plow ‖ (of a field etc.) to admit of plowing ‖ (with 'through', 'along' etc.) to cut a way as a plow does, *to plow through the snow* ‖ to proceed slowly and laboriously, *to plow through a dull book* ‖ to operate a bookbinder's or carpenter's plow **to plow back** to bury (a growing crop) by plowing through it so as to enrich the soil ‖ to use (profits) to develop the enterprise which yielded them **to plow into** to begin (work) with vigor and enthusiasm [O.E. *plōh*]

plow·boy, esp. *Br.* **plough·boy** (pláubɔi) *n.* a boy who leads the horse or horses of a horse-drawn plow

plow·man, esp. *Br.* **plough·man** (pláumən) *pl.* **plow·men**, esp. *Br.* **plough·men** (pláumən) *n.* someone who plows

plow·share, esp. *Br.* **plough·share** (pláuʃɛər) *n.* the cutting and turning blade of a plow [M.E.]

ploy (plɔi) *n.* a cunning tactic or gambit, e.g. in a game [origin unknown]

PLSS (*acronym*) portable life support system

pluck (plʌk) 1. *v.t.* to pull off or out with sudden sharp force, *to pluck feathers from a chicken* ‖ to pull the feathers from, *to pluck a chicken* ‖ to pull quickly at, *to pluck a harp string* ‖ to pick, *to pluck a flower* ‖ (*pop.*) to swindle ‖ *v.i.* (with 'at') to give a quick little pull, *to pluck at someone's sleeve* **to pluck up** to revive one's flagging spirits and courage **to pluck up one's courage** to overcome nervousness or timidity 2. *n.* an act of plucking ‖ the heart, lungs and liver of a slaughtered animal used for food ‖ courage **plúck·i·ly** *adv.* **plúck·y** *comp.* **pluck·i·er** *superl.* **pluck·i·est** *adj.* courageous [O.E. *pluccian*]

plug (plʌg) 1. *n* a piece of wood etc. used to fill a gap or hole ‖ (*Br.*) the release mechanism in the flushing system of a toilet ‖ smoking or chewing tobacco compressed into a solid cake ‖ a fireplug ‖ any electrical connection, esp. the male part ‖ a spark plug ‖ (*pop.*) the favorable mention of a product etc., esp. on a radio or television program ‖ the mass of igneous rock filling in the channel leading to a volcanic vent ‖ (*pop.*) an old, worn-out horse ‖ (*angling*) a lure that darts and dives, usu. used for catching pike 2. *v. pres. part.* **plug·ging** *past and past part.* **plugged** *v.t.* to insert a plug in ‖ (*pop.*) to publicize (something) frequently, esp. on a radio or television program ‖ *v.i.* (with 'up') to become obstructed, *drains that won't plug up* ‖ (*pop.*, with 'away') to persevere laboriously, *plugging away at geometry* **to plug in** to connect (an electrical device) to an outlet [M. Du. *plugge*, bung]

plug·o·la (plʌgóulə) *n.* special promotion for a product, e.g. a song, in exchange for a payment or favor

plug·ug·ly (plʌɡʌ́ɡli:) *pl.* **plug·ug·lies** *n.* (*old-fash.*) a tough guy, esp. a member of a gang using intimidation for political ends

plum (plʌm) *n.* *Prunus domestica*, fam. *Rosaceae*, a small tree widely cultivated in temperate regions ‖ the edible fleshy fruit of the tree, or of other trees of the same genus ‖ the bluish-red color of many varieties of this fruit ‖ (*pop.*) an opportunity, appointment etc. offering exceptional advantages [O.E. *plūme* fr. L. fr. Gk]

plum·age (plú:midʒ) *n.* the feathers of a bird [O.F.]

plu·mate (plú:meit, plú:mit) *adj.* (of bodily hairs, antennae etc.) having a main shaft that bears tiny hairs or threadlike parts [Mod. L. *plumatus*, covered with feathers fr. *pluma*, feather]

plumb (plʌm) 1. *n.* a small, heavy piece of metal, usually lead, attached to a line and used to indicate the vertical ‖ a similar contrivance for ascertaining the depth of water in a well etc. **out of plumb** not vertical 2. *adj.* vertical ‖ (*cricket*) (a wicket) perfectly level 3. *adv.* vertically 4. *v.t.* to ascertain the depth of (water etc.) by sounding ‖ to come to understand completely, *to plumb someone's mind* ‖ to test for verticality, *to plumb a wall* ‖ to do the work of a plumber on (something), *to plumb a joint* [fr. F. *plomb*, lead]

plum·ba·go (plʌmbéigou) *n.* graphite ‖ (*bot.*) a member of *Plumbago*, fam. *Plumbaginaceae*, a genus of perennial tropical woody plants, bearing spikes of blue and white flowers and having alternate leaves [L.]

plumb bob the metal weight on the end of a plumb line

plum·be·ous (plʌ́mbi:əs) *adj.* of or resembling lead ‖ lead-colored ‖ (*ceramics*) lead-glazed [fr. L. *plumbeus*]

plumb·er (plʌmər) *n.* a skilled worker who fits, repairs and maintains pipes, bathroom fixtures, cisterns, drains etc. [O.F. *plummier*, *plommier*]

plum·bic (plʌmbik) *adj.* containing or pertaining to lead ‖ (*chem.*) of compounds in which lead exerts a valence of 4 [fr. L. *plumbum*, lead]

plumb·ing (plʌ́miŋ) *n.* the craft of a plumber ‖ the entire water-supply and drainage system of a building ‖ the act of using a plumb [PLUMB]

plum·bism (plʌ́mbizəm) *n.* (*med.*) lead poisoning, esp. when chronic [fr. L. *plumbum*, lead]

plumb line a cord suspending a lead weight used in sounding || a similar device for determining verticality

plum·bous (plʌ́mbəs) adj. containing or pertaining to lead || (chem.) of compounds in which lead exerts a valence of 2 [fr. L. plumbosus, full of lead]

plumb rule a strip of wood fitted with a plumb line and bob, used esp. by carpenters

plum·bum (plʌ́mbəm) n. lead (the metal) [L.]

plum duff a flour pudding with raisins or currants, boiled or steamed

plume (plu:m) n. a feather, esp. a large feather || a cluster or tuft of feathers worn as an ornament or as a symbol of office, rank etc. || (envir.) visible emission from a chimney flue or volcano || (geol.) in plate tectonics, a hypothetical force of molten material from the earth's center that drives plates || anything having the lightness and form of a feather, a plume of smoke || (biol.) a featherlike appendage or part [O.F.]

plume pres. part. **plum·ing** past and past part. **plumed** v.t. to adorn with plumes || (of a bird) to dress the feathers of (itself) || (of a bird) to preen (its feathers) || (rhet., of a person) to feel pride in (oneself), he plumed himself on the way they had listened to him [O.F. plumer, to pluck (a bird)]

plum·met (plʌ́mit) 1. n. the weight attached to a plumb line, a sounding line or a fishing line || the line and bob together || a clock weight 2. v.i. to drop vertically downwards [O.F. plommet, plombet, plummet, a ball of lead]

plu·mose (plú:mous) adj. (zool.) having feathers || (biol.) plumate **plumos·i·ty** (plu:mósiti:) n. [fr. L. plumosus]

plump (plʌmp) 1. v.i. to fall heavily, to plump into a chair || (with 'for') to decide on (one of several courses of action, choices etc.) || to come or go suddenly with determination or in a huff, to plump out of a room || (Br.) to vote for one candidate only, even though entitled to vote for two or more || v.t. to drop, place, put down etc. heavily, she plumped the package on the table, or with abrupt unconcern, she plumped the baby in his cot 2. adv. suddenly and heavily downwards, it fell plump into the water 3. n. the act of falling heavily or the sound of this [M. Du. plompen]

plump 1. adj. (of people) pleasantly rounded, without being fat || (of animals) fleshy, a plump chicken 2. v.t. (with 'up') to knead (a pillow, cushion etc.) so as to shake up the feathers etc. in it || v.i. (with 'out', e.g. of sails) to become rounded or distended [M. Du. plomp, bulky]

plum pudding a rich suet pudding containing raisins, currants, candied citrus peel, eggs, nuts and spices, boiled or steamed, and eaten esp. at Christmas

plu·mule (plú:mju:l) n. (bot.) the primary bud of an embryo normally located on the apex of the hypocotyl (which develops into the primary shoot of a seedling) || a small or downy feather [fr. L. plumula, small feather]

plum·y (plú:mi:) comp. **plum·i·er** superl. **plum·i·est** adv. plumelike, feathery || covered with plumes

plun·der (plʌ́ndər) 1. v.t. to strip (a person or place) of goods by force, esp. in wartime || v.i. to commit robbery 2. n. the act of plundering || the goods obtained by plundering [G. plündern]

plun·der·age (plʌ́ndəridʒ) n. (maritime law) the embezzlement of goods on shipboard || the goods embezzled

plunge (plʌndʒ) 1. v. pres. part. **plung·ing** past and past part. **plunged** v.t. to thrust (something) forcefully into something else, to plunge a knife into someone's heart || to force (something or someone) into a new set of circumstances, attitudes liable to plunge us into war || v.i. to throw oneself into water, esp. headfirst || to go headlong, make one's way swiftly and resolutely, to plunge into a thicket || (esp. of a ship) to pitch 2. n. the act of plunging || a leap into or as if into water || (old-fash.) an act or instance of engaging in heavy gambling, reckless speculation etc. **to take the plunge** to decide to take a risk despite the possible consequences **plúng·er** n. (mech.) a moving machine part serving as a ram in a hydraulic press, a piston in a force pump etc. || a pistonlike part in a tire valve unit || a rubber suction cup attached to the end of a wooden rod and used to clear a blockage in a water pipe, drain etc. [O.F. plungier]

plunk (plʌŋk) 1. n. the dull, short sound made by the forceful impact of inelastic bodies || a twang || (pop.) a forceful blow 2. v.t. to put (something) down suddenly and heavily, he plunked his books on the table || to pluck the strings of

(e.g. a banjo) || v.i. to make a twanging sound || to fall or sink heavily 3. adv. with the sound of a plunk [imit.]

plu·per·fect (plu:pə́:rfikt) 1. adj. (gram.) expressing an action completed before a past time either spoken of or implied 2. n. (gram.) a pluperfect tense or form [shortened fr. L. plus quam perfectum, more than perfect]

plu·ral (plúərəl) 1. adj. of or including more than one || (gram.) of or designating more than one of the things referred to || (gram., in languages having dual number) involving more than two 2. n. (gram.) the plural number || the plural form of a word || a word in the plural form [O.F. plurel]

—The most common pattern for the formation of the written plural of English nouns is the addition of -s or -es. A final -es is added to words ending in -ss, -sh, -ch, -s, -x (e.g. masses, rashes, marches, gases, foxes), or to words ending in -y preceded by a consonant or by -qu, the -y being changed to -i- (e.g. navy- navies, soliloquy-soliloquies) or to some words ending in -o preceded by a consonant (e.g. tomato -tomatoes). -s alone is added to most words ending in -o preceded by a consonant, and to all words ending in -o preceded by a vowel (e.g. pianos, radios). The minor formations of plurals of English nouns include -s for many words ending in -f, the -f changing to -ve- (e.g. calf-calves). -en is added in some cases (e.g. ox-oxen), or -ren is added (e.g. child-children). Change of vowel is another formation (e.g. man-men, goose - geese). Sometimes the plural is the same as the singular (e.g. Chinese, sheep, moose). In some cases the plural may be different or may remain the same (e.g. fish-fishes or fish-fish). Some words have only one form, which may be singular or plural (e.g. scissors). Some Latin and Greek plurals are carried over into English (e.g. alumnus-alumni, analysis-analyses). Some other foreign plurals are also carried over (e.g. Hebrew seraph -seraphim). The plurals of letters, symbols etc. add -'s (e.g. two p's, a row of +'s)

plu·ral·ism (plúərəlizəm) n. the holding of more than one office, esp. of more than one ecclesiastical benefice, by the same person || (philos.) the doctrine that there is more than one universal principle (cf. MONISM, cf. DUALISM) **plú·ral·ist** n. **plu·ral·is·tic** adj.

plu·ral·i·ty (plurǽliti:) pl. **plu·ral·i·ties** n. the state of being plural || a great number || the holding of more than one office by one person || (eccles.) the holding of two or more benefices by one person || (in a political election involving three or more candidates) a number of votes obtained by one candidate exceeding that of any other candidate but not constituting an absolute majority [O.F. pluralité]

plural vote the casting of more than one vote or the right to cast more than one vote || the right to vote in more than one constituency

plus (plʌs) 1. prep. added to, 4 plus 2 is 6 || (pop.) in addition to, he arrived with a trunk plus a large suitcase 2. adj. indicating addition, the plus sign || positive, a plus quantity || (used postpositively) somewhat more than, a C plus mark || (pop., used predicately) having as an addition, he was plus $10 on the sale || (bookkeeping) credit, the plus side of an account || (elec.) positive 3. pl. **plus·es, plus·ses** n. a plus sign || a plus quantity || an additional quantity [L.=more]

plus fours men's loose, baggy trousers that overlap about 4 ins below the knees, worn esp. for golf

plush (plʌʃ) 1. n. a fabric resembling velvet, but having a longer, softer pile 2. adj. luxurious and expensive, a plush hotel [F. pluche]

plus sign (math.) the symbol (+) used to indicate addition

Plu·tarch (plú:tɑrk) (c. 46–c. 125), Greek essayist and biographer. He wrote 'Moralia', a group of dialogues and essays, but is most famous for his 'Parallel Lives of Illustrious Greeks and Romans', a book of great historical value. He portrayed character and its moral implications in a racy, anecdotal style

plu·tar·chy (plú:tɑrki:) pl. **plu·tar·chies** n. a plutocracy

Plu·to (plú:tou) (Gk mythol.) the god of departed spirits and of the underworld (*HADES) || the ninth planet of the solar system in order of distance from the sun. It is the second smallest planet of the system (diameter=3,600 miles, mass=1.76 x 10²⁰ tons). It has the greatest inclination and eccentricity in orbit of all the planets (sidereal period=248.430 earth years,

period of rotation=6.39 earth days, aphelion=4.6 x 10⁹ miles, perihelion=2.8 x 10⁹ miles). It has no known satellites

plu·toc·ra·cy (plu:tókrəsi:) pl. **plu·toc·ra·cies** n. rule by the rich || a ruling class of rich people **plu·to·crat** (plú:təkræt) n. a member of a plutocracy **plu·to·crát·ic** adj. [fr. Gk ploutokratia fr. ploutos, wealth+kratia, power]

plu·ton·ic (plu:tónik) adj. (geol.) of or relating to the theory that igneous rocks solidified from magmas far below the earth's crust || (of rock) solidified as accounted for by this theory [fr. Gk Plouton, Pluto]

plu·to·ni·um (plu:tóuni:əm) n. an artificial metallic element (symbol Pu), having up to 15 isotopes (mass of isotope of longest known half-life 242). The most important of these isotopes is Pu 239, which can be produced in large amounts in nuclear reactors. Pu 239 undergoes fission under slow nuclear bombardment and forms uranium 235 (*URANIUM. It is used as nuclear fuel and as a nuclear explosive [after PLUTO, the planet]

plu·vi·al (plú:vi:əl) adj. of, relating to or characterized by rain || (geol.) due to the action of rain, pluvial erosion [fr. L. pluvialis]

plu·vi·om·e·ter (plu:vi:ómitər) n. a rain gauge **plu·vi·o·met·ric** (plu:vi:əmétrik), **plu·vi·o·mét·ri·cal** adjs **plu·vi·om·e·try** (plu:vi:ómitri:) n. [fr. L. pluvia, rain+METER]

plu·vi·ous (plú:vi:əs) adj. of or pertaining to rain [fr. L. pluviosus]

ply (plai) pres. part. **ply·ing** past and past part. **plied** v.t. to use with vigor and diligence, to ply a needle || to work busily at, to ply a trade || to supply (someone) persistently, to ply someone with drink || to keep at (someone) constantly, to ply someone with questions || (of boats) to sail or row across (a river etc.) and back more or less regularly || v.i. to sail or go, usually regularly, between two places, the ship plies between London and Rotterdam || (e.g. of a taxi driver) to have a regular stand where one waits for customers, to ply for hire || (naut.) to make progress to windward by tacking [M.E. plye fr. aplie, aplye, to apply]

ply pl. **plies** n. one of the lengths of spun fiber which are twisted together to make rope, cord etc., two-ply wool || one of the thin wooden layers in plywood || one of several layers of fabric sewn or stuck together [F. pli, fold]

Plym·outh (plíməθ) a county borough and port (pop. 255,500) of S.W. Devonshire, England, with a fine harbor: naval base (at adjacent Stonehouse and Devonport), shipbuilding, fishing

Plymouth the town (pop. 35,913) in S.E. Massachusetts where the Pilgrims landed (1620) from the 'Mayflower'

Plymouth Brethren a Christian sect which originated (c. 1830) in Plymouth, England. Its members have no formal creed or regular ministry and regulate their lives solely by their literal interpretation of the Bible

Plymouth Colony a colony founded in 1620 on the coast of Massachusetts by the Pilgrims

Plymouth Rock the rock on which the Pilgrims are said to have landed in 1620

Plymouth Rock a hen of a U.S. breed characterized by its long yellow legs

ply·wood (pláiwud) n. a material used in light construction composed of thin layers of wood glued or cemented together, usually having the grain of one layer at right angles to that of the next

Plzen *PILSEN

p.m., P.M. *POST MERIDIEM

PNET (acronym) Peaceful Nuclear Explosions Treaty, negotiated between the U.S.A. and the U.S.S.R. regulating explosions carried out by both countries in locations other than nuclear-weapon test sites

pneu·mat·ic (numætik, njumætik) adj. of, pertaining to, or using air, wind or gas || operated by pressure of air, a pneumatic drill || filled with air, a pneumatic tire || (zool., of bones) characterized by air-filled cavities || (zool.) of the duct between the swim bladder and the alimentary tract in some fish **pneu·mát·i·cal·ly** adv.

pneu·mát·ics n. the branch of physics dealing with the mechanical properties of gases, esp. air, and certain elastic fluids [fr. L. pneumaticus fr. Gk]

pneu·ma·tol·o·gy (nu:mətólədʒi:, nju:mətóladʒi:) n. (theol.) the theory of the spirit or of the nature of the spirit || (theol.) the doctrine of the Holy Spirit [fr. Gk pneuma (pneumatos), air+logos, discourse]

pneu·ma·tol·y·sis (nu:mətólisis, nju:mətólisis) *n.* the formation of ores and rocks by steam or other vapors, or by superheated liquids under pressure [Mod. L. fr. Gk *pneuma (pneumatos)*, air+*lusis*, a loosening]

pneu·ma·to·lyt·ic (nu:mətoulítik, nju:mət'litik) *adj.* of ores or rocks formed by pneumatolysis [fr. Gk *pneuma (pneumatos)*, air+*lutikos*, able to loose]

pneu·ma·to·phore (nú:mətəfɔr, njú:mətəfɔr, nú:mətəfour, njú:mətəfour) *n.* (*zool.*) the air-filled sac serving as a float on a colony of siphonophores || (*bot.*) a root serving as a breathing organ for various swamp or marsh plants [fr. Gk *pneuma (pneumatos)*, air+*phoros*, bearing]

pneu·mo·coc·cal (nu:məkók'l, nju:məkók'l) *adj.* of or caused by pneumococci **pneu·mo·cóc·cic** *adj.*

pneu·mo·coc·cus (nu:məkókəs, nju:məkókəs) *pl.* **pneu·mo·coc·ci** (nu:məkóksai, nju:məkóksai) *n.* (*med.*) *Diplococcus pneumoniae*, a bacterium that causes one type of pneumonia [fr. Gk *pneumōn*, lung+*coccus*]

pneu·mo·co·ni·o·sis (nu:məkouni:óusis, nju:məkouni:ósis) *n.* a disease of the lungs caused by the inhalation of particles of dust, metals etc., common among miners [Mod. L. fr. Gk *pneumōn*, lung+*konia*, dust]

pneu·mo·cys·tic (nu:məsístik) *n.* an ice-free body of water formed amid vast ice fields off the coast off Antarctica during winter; believed to be warm-water ventilation from below the surface of the ocean

pneu·mo·gas·tric (nu:mougæstrik, nju:mougæstrik) **1.** *adj.* of or pertaining to the lungs and stomach || of or pertaining to the vagus nerve **2.** *n.* the vagus nerve [fr. Gk *pneumōn*, lung+GASTRIC]

pneu·mo·nec·to·my (nu:mənéktəmi:, nju:mənéktəmi:) *pl.* **pneu·mo·nec·to·mies** *n.* the surgical removal of a lung or part of a lung [fr. Gk *pneuma (pneumatos)*, air+Mod. L. *-ektomē*, a cutting out]

pneu·mo·nia (numóunjə, njumóunjə, numóuni:ə, njumóuni:ə) *n.* any of several diseases of the respiratory tract characterized by inflammation of the lungs and caused by bacteria, viruses or chemical irritants **pneu·mon·ic** (numónik, njumónik) *adj.* [Mod. L. fr. Gk *pneumōn*, lung]

pneu·mo·tho·rax (nu:mouθóræks, nju:mouθóræks, nu:mouθóuræks, nju:mouθóuræks) *n.* an accumulation of air or other gas in the pleural cavity, occurring naturally as a result of lung disease or induced artificially in order to collapse a lung in the treatment of pulmonary tuberculosis [fr. Gk *pneumōn*, lung+THORAX]

Po (pou) the longest river (418 miles, navigable for 337) of Italy, and chief river of the N. Italian plain, the country's main industrial and agricultural region. It flows from the Cottian Alps across Piedmont and Lombardy, and between Emilia Romagna and Veneto to the Adriatic. Transported sediment constantly raises its bed, causing disastrous floods

P.O. post office

poach (poutʃ) *v.t.* to cook (fish, chicken etc.) in a liquid that is never allowed to boil || to drop (an egg removed from its shell) into simmering water and let it cook until the white coagulates, or steam it in a special pan [O.F. *pochier*, to enclose in a bag]

poach *v.t.* to take (game or fish) illegally from another person's property || to soften or make holes in (ground) by trampling || *v.i.* (with 'on') to trespass (on another person's property) || to take game or fish illegally from another person's property || (*racket games*) to play a ball that should be played by one's partner || (of ground) to become soggy or full of holes when trampled **póach·er** *n.* someone who trespasses in order to steal or kill game || someone who takes or kills game illegally [F. *pocher* fr. Gmc]

Po·be·do·nos·tsev (pɔbjedʌnóstsjəf), Konstantin Petrovich (1827–1907), Russian statesman and jurist. As adviser to Alexander II and Nicholas II, he opposed liberal reforms and strengthened the autocracy

Po·ca·hon·tas (poukəhóntəs) (c. 1595–1617), a North American Indian princess reputed to have saved the colonist John Smith from being put to death

po·chard (póutʃərd) *pl.* **po·chards, po·chard** *n.* a member of *Aythya*, a genus of European

---

diving sea ducks, esp. *A. ferina*. The male has a dark chestnut head, black breast and pale gray body [etym. doubtful]

pock (pok) *n.* a pustule caused by smallpox and other diseases (*POX) [O.E. *pocc*]

pock·et (pókit) **1.** *n.* a small, baglike receptacle of fabric, leather etc., having the top or side open, inserted in or sewed on a garment, for carrying a handkerchief, small change etc. || a hollow place in which something has collected or could collect, *a pocket in a rock* || a deposit of material (e.g. gold, oil) found on or in the earth || (*football*) a wall of blockers surrounding a passer || *financial resources, living beyond one's pockets* || an air pocket || any of the pouches, usually of netting, at the sides or corners of a billiard table || (*mil.*) a body of soldiers almost completely hemmed in by the enemy, or the area they occupy || the external pouch of some animals **in one's pocket** under one's influence || virtually secured **out of pocket** (esp. *Br.*) in the condition of having lost money on a transaction etc., *he ended up $20 out of pocket on the day's races* **2.** *v.t.* to put into a pocket, *pocket the change* || to take (money etc.) dishonestly, *to pocket the deposits* || (*billiards*) to drive (a ball) into a pocket || to use the pocket veto on (a bill) || to suppress (pride, anger, scruples etc.) || to accept submissively, *to pocket an insult* **3.** *adj.* suitable for or adapted for carrying in a pocket, *a pocket notebook* || small, *a pocket revolution* [A.F. *pokete*]

pocket battleship (*hist.*) one of several fast German battleships of about 10,000 tons, built (1929) of weight-saving materials to come within Treaty of Versailles specifications

pocket billiards any of various games of billiards played usually with 15 object balls on a table having 6 pockets

pock·et·book (pókitbuk) *n.* a wallet for carrying paper money, papers etc. || a woman's purse or handbag

pocket book a paperback

pocket borough (*Br. hist.*) a parliamentary constituency of which the representation was controlled by a single person or family

pock·et·knife (pókitnaif) *pl.* **pock·et·knives** (pókitnaivz) *n.* a small knife having a blade or blades folding into the handle

pocket money money for small personal needs || (*Br.*) a regular allowance to children

pocket veto a method of indirect veto in which the president of the U.S.A. or the governor of a state leaves a bill presented to him within a few days of adjournment unsigned until Congress or the state legislature has adjourned

pock·mark (pókmɑrk) *n.* the pitlike scar left in the skin by the pustule of esp. smallpox **póck·-marked** *adj.* having or as if having pockmarks

po·co (póukou) *adv.* (*mus.*) somewhat, slightly [fr. L. *paucus*, little]

po·co a po·co (póukouɑpóukou) *adv.* (*mus.*) little by little

pod (pod) **1.** *n.* a dry dehiscent fruit that is either monocarpellary, e.g. legume, or consists of two or more carpels, e.g. the poppy || a protective envelope, e.g. a cocoon || a streamlined container attached to the wings or fuselage of an aircraft || (*aerospace*) a unit designed to detach from a space craft **2.** *v. pres. part.* **pod·ding** *past* and *past part.* **pod·ded** *v.i.* to swell into pods || to produce pods || *v.t.* to split and empty the pods of (peas etc.) [origin unknown]

pod 1. *n.* a school of seals, whales etc. **2.** *v.t. pres part.* **pod·ding** *past* and *past part.* **pod·ded** to drive (seals) into a pod [origin unknown]

pod *n.* the socket of a brace into which the bit is inserted || the channel or groove of an auger which holds the chips [origin unknown]

pod·a·gra (pódəgrə) *n.* (*med.*) gout, esp. in the foot **po·dag·ric** (pədægrik) *adj.* [fr. Gk *pous (podos)*, foot+*agra*, a seizure]

podg·i·ness (pódʒi:nis) *n.* the condition of being podgy [PODGY]

Pod·gor·ny (pódgʌrni:), Nikolai Viktorovitch (1903–83), Soviet statesman, head of state from 1965

podg·y (pódʒi:) *comp.* **podg·i·er** *superl.* **podg·i·est** *adj.* short and fat [var. of PUDGY]

po·di·a·trist (poudáiətrist) *n.* a chiropodist [fr. Gk *pous (podos)*, foot]

po·di·a·try (poudáiətri:) *n.* chiropody [fr. Gk *pous (podos)*, foot]

po·di·um (póudi:əm) *pl.* **po·di·a** (póudi:ə), **po·di·ums** *n.* (*archit.*) a low wall supporting a row

---

of columns or serving as a foundation for the wall of a building || (*hist.*) a low wall surrounding the arena of an ampitheater, serving as support for the seats || a dais, e.g. for an orchestra conductor || (*zool.*) the foot of an echinoderm [L. fr. Gk *podion*, dim. of *pous (podos)*, foot]

pod·o·phyl·lin (pɒdəfílin) *n.* a brown to greenish yellow resin extracted from the roots and rhizomes of *Podophyllum peltatum*, fam. *Berberidaceae*, the mayapple of North America, used esp. as a cathartic [fr. Mod. L. *Podophyllum* fr. Gk *pous (poudos)*, foot+*phullon*, leaf]

Poe (pou), Edgar Allan (1809–49), American short-story writer, poet and critic. He was the inventor of the ratio-cinative detective story, his most famous being 'The Murders in the Rue Morgue' (1841). Other stories, e.g. 'Tales of the Grotesque and Arabesque' (1840), are written around motifs that were for him an obsession: death, decay and madness. These motifs also thread through his poetry, which is mainly known for its musicality. The translation of some of his prose works by Baudelaire brought him wide acclaim in France. His critical studies had a powerful effect on Baudelaire's own writing, and served as inspiration for the Symbolists, esp. Mallarmé

po·em (póuəm) *n.* a piece of poetry [F. *poème* L. fr. Gk]

po·e·sy (póuisi:, póuizi:) *n.* (*rhet.*) the art of writing poetry || (*rhet.*) poetry in general [O.F. *poésie* fr. L. fr. Gk]

po·et (póuit) *n.* a person who writes poetry [O.F. *poète* fr. L. fr. Gk]

po·et·as·ter (póuitæstər) *n.* a writer of trivial or bad verse [Mod. L. fr. *poeta*, poet fr. Gk+L. *-aster*, inferior]

po·et·ess (póuitis) *n.* a female poet [POET]

po·et·ic (pouétik) *adj.* of, pertaining to or characteristic of poets or poetry || of the language or meaning of a poem or of poetry || composed in verse || having qualities associated with poetry, *poetic movements* [F. *poétique* fr. L. fr. Gk]

po·et·i·cal (pouétik'l) *adj.* poetic [fr. L. *poeticus*]

po·et·i·cize (pouétisaiz) *pres. part.* **po·et·i·ciz·ing** *past* and *past part.* **po·et·i·cized** *v.t.* to endow with poetic qualities

poetic justice justice which reveals itself in its mode of operation peculiarly appropriate, as though fate had shown itself

poetic license, poetic licence the right of a poet to deviate from the conventional rules of syntax, grammar etc.

po·et·ics (pouétiks) *n.* the theory of poetry || a treatise on poetry [POETIC]

po·et·ize (póuitaiz) *pres. part.* **po·et·iz·ing** *past* and *past part.* **po·et·ized** *v.t.* to treat poetically, *to poetize an experience* || *v.i.* to play the poet [fr. F. *poétiser*]

poet laureate *pl.* **poet laureates, poets laureate** the title given in Britain to a poet appointed to the Royal Household for life and having as his duty the celebrating of national or royal occasions in verse. The laureateship is now largely titular

po·et·ry (póuitri:) *n.* a type of discourse which achieves its effects by rhythm, sound patterns and imagery. Most characteristically, the poetic form evokes emotions or sensations, but it may also serve to convey loftiness of tone, or to lend force to ideas || poems || the quality of a poem || the quality of whatever arouses emotions comparable to those aroused by a poem [O.F. *poétrie*]

Pog·gio Brac·cio·li·ni (póddʒɔbrɑttʃolí:ni:), Gian Francesco (1380–1459), Italian author. He was lay secretary to the Curia (1404–50), during which time he discovered many valuable Latin manuscripts. He wrote moral essays, a 'History of Florence' and 'Liber Facetiarum', a collection of satiric stories

po·go (póugou) *n.* **1.** (*mil.*) in air intercept, a code meaning 'switch to communications channel number preceding "pogo" and if unable to establish communications, switch to channel number following "pogo" '. **2.** (*music*) a dance step consisting of jumping up and down, esp. by punk rock groups

Po·go·noph·o·ran (pougənófərən) *n.* (*zool.*) a marine worm of a phylum or class (*Pogonophora*) found at great ocean depths —**po·go·noph·o·ran** *adj.*

po·go stick (póugou) a toy consisting of a single stilt having two pedals and a spring, used to jump around on [origin unknown]

po·grom (pəgrám, pəgróm, póugrəm) *n.* an or

CONCISE PRONUNCIATION KEY: **(a)** æ, c*a*t; ɑ, c*a*r; ɔ f*aw*n; ei, sn*a*ke. **(e)** e, h*e*n; i:, sh*ee*p; iə, d*ee*r; ɛə, b*ea*r. **(i)** i, f*i*sh; ai, t*i*ger; ə:, b*i*rd. **(o)** o, *o*x; au, c*ow*; ou, g*oa*t; u, p*oo*r; ɔi, r*oy*al. **(u)** ʌ, d*u*ck; u, b*u*ll; u:, g*oo*se; ə, b*a*cillus; ju:, c*u*be. x, lo*ch*; θ, *th*ink; ð, bo*th*er; z, *Z*en; ʒ, cor*s*age; dʒ, sa*v*age; ŋ, ora*n*gutang; j, *y*ak; ʃ, *fi*sh; tʃ, fe*tch*; 'l, rabb*le*; 'n, redd*en*. Complete pronunciation key appears inside front cover.

ganized massacre, esp. of Jews in Russia (1881, 1903, 1905) [Russ.=devastation]

Po Hai (bóuhái) (formerly Gulf of Chihli) the northwest arm of the Yellow Sea, bordered by Liaoning, Hopei and Shantung, China

poign·an·cy (póinjənsi:) *n.* the quality or state of being poignant [POIGNANT]

poign·ant (póinjənt) *adj.* causing or marked by feelings of sadness || (of grief) deeply felt || stimulating, *of poignant interest* [O. F. *puignant, poignant*]

Poin·ca·ré (pwēkærei), Jules Henri (1854–1912), French mathematician, physicist and philosopher. He made important discoveries in the field of mathematical functions and wrote 'la Science et l'hypothèse' (1902), 'Science et Méthode' (1909)

Poincaré, Raymond (1860–1934), French statesman, president of France (1913–20). As prime minister (1912–13, 1922–4, 1926–9), he ordered the French occupation of the Ruhr (1923) in order to enforce German payment of reparations

poin·set·ti·a (pɔinséti:ə, pɔinsétə) *n.* any plant of the genus *Euphorbia*, fam. *Euphorbiaceae*, esp. *E. pulcherrima*, a Mexican and South American plant having feathery scarlet leaves surrounding small yellow flowers [Mod. L. after J. R. *Poinsett* (1779-1851), U.S. ambassador to Mexico]

point (pɔint) *n.* a specific place having a definite position in space but no definite size or shape, *a point of intersection* || a measurable position in a scale, *boiling point* || a definite, often decisive, moment in time, *turning point, at the point of death* || (of something spoken or written) the most prominent or important idea, *the point of a story* || the climax of a joke || a particular item in a speech, argument, exposition etc., *there were four main points in his proposal* || a distinguishing characteristic, *generosity is not one of her strong points* || purpose, *is there any point in going on?* || the sharp end of something, *a pencil point* || something having such a sharp end, e.g. a tool used in etching and engraving || a particular place, e.g. on a route, *points of interest* || a period (punctuation mark) || a decimal point || (*games*) a unit of counting in scoring || a unit of value used in quoting variations in cost of living, the prices of stocks etc. || a unit of academic credit || (*printing*) a unit for measuring size of type (1/72 in.) || a unit for assessing performance in boxing etc. || (in Semitic alphabets) a mark for indicating vowels || (*geog.*, esp. in place names) a piece of land projecting into the sea, *Start Point* || (*cricket*) a fielder's position on the off side of the batsman, fairly close to him and roughly in line with the popping crease || (*lacrosse*) the position to the right of the goal || (*securities*) the minimum price fluctuation, equal to 1/100 of one cent in most futures traded in decimal units, to ¼ of one cent in grains, $1 in stocks, $10 in $1,000 bonds || 1% of a sum, sometimes charged for a loan or other service || (*fencing*) a lunge || (*boxing*) the tip of the chin || (*ballet*) the tip of the toe || any of a number of types of lace worked with a needle, esp. needle-point lace || (of certain gundogs) the act of pointing || (*pl.*) the mane, tail and legs of a horse || a tine of an antler || a physical feature of an animal used esp. as a standard in judging its quality || (*pl.*) the characteristic facial markings of a Siamese cat || (*naut.*) any of the 32 marks around the circumference of a compass || (*naut.*) the difference of 11° 15′ between any such mark and the next to it || (*naut.*) that part of the horizon indicated by one of these marks || (*naut.*) any of the pieces of rope used in reefing a sail || (*hist.*) a cord for lacing parts of a garment together || (*pl.*) the two tapering, movable rails for turning a train from one track to another || (*mil.*) a small party leading an advance guard or following a rear guard || one of the raised dots used in printing for the blind || (*heraldry*) one of the nine divisions of a shield or escutcheon used for locating the position of a charge || (*Br.*) an outlet (of a wiring system) || (*elec.*) either of the two contacts serving to make or break the circuit in a distributor || (*hunting*) a straight run || (*hunting*) the spot to which the run is made || a useful suggestion **at all points** in every respect **beside the point** not relevant **in point of** in the matter of **in point of fact** in reality **to carry one's point** to establish an argument, proposition etc. by persuasion **to come to the point** to discard irrelevancies and get to the heart of the matter **to give points to** (*Br.*) to be better than **to make a point** to establish the

force of an idea, argument etc. **to make a point of** (with pres. infin.) to do with marked deliberateness, *to make a point of not answering rude letters* **on the point of** just about to **to stretch a point** to be indulgent in interpreting or applying a rule **to the point** relevant **to win on points** (*boxing*) to win by performance over the rounds fought, not by knockout [F. *point*, a dot and F. *pointe*, a sharp end]

point *v.t.* to give a point to, *to point a pencil* || (often with 'up') to give force or emphasis to, *to point a speech with jokes* || to cause (something) to be turned towards a particular person or object, or in a particular direction, *to point a gun at someone, he pointed the car south* || to fill the joints in (brickwork) with mortar etc. using a special trowel || to mark (Semitic vowels) with points || to mark (a printed text of the Psalms) with indications showing how to phrase when chanting || (of certain gundogs) to indicate the presence of (game) by staring fixedly towards it and assuming a rigid stance with one forepaw upraised and the tail extended || to reef (a sail) with points || *v.i.* (with 'at', 'to', 'towards' etc.) to indicate position or direction with or as if with a finger, *to point at a crack in the ceiling* || to be turned in a particular direction, *an arrow pointing to the south* || (*naut.*) to sail close to the wind || (of certain gundogs) to point game **to point out** to direct attention to || to explain, *he pointed out that it was not his fault* **to point to** (or *towards*) to be an indication of a specified probability, *everything points to his guilt* [O.F. *pointer*]

point balance a statement prepared by futures commodities commission merchants to show profit or loss on all open contracts by computing them to an official closing or settlement price, usu. at calendar month end

point-blank (póintblǽŋk) **1.** *adv.* with level aim || directly, *he accused her point-blank of lying* **2.** *adj.* (of a shot) fired at a very close target || (of a shooting range) so close that one takes level aim || direct, *a point-blank question* [POINT+BLANK fr. F. *blanc*, white point (center of a target)]

point d'Al·en·con (pwēdælɑ̃sɔ́) a needlepoint lace made in Alençon, France. Based on the lace of Venice, it was introduced in the mid 17th c.

point duty (*Br.*) the work of a police officer in directing traffic

Pointe-à-Pi·tre (pwētæpi:tr) the largest town (pop. 23,889) of Guadeloupe, a seaport on the southwest coast of Grande Terre Is.

point·ed (póintid) *adj.* having, or being given, a sharp point || (of a remark) sharply, though obliquely, critical || made deliberately obvious, *his rudeness was very pointed* || lively, piquant, *pointed wit* [POINT]

pointed arch (*archit.*) an arch the top of which forms a point, as in the Gothic style (esp. in contrast to the earlier rounded arch)

pointed fox the fur of the red fox dyed and treated to resemble that of the silver fox

Pointe Noire (pwētnwær) the chief port (pop. 141,700) of the Republic of the Congo, linked by rail to Brazzaville: shipyards

point·er (póintər) *n.* a person or thing that points, *the pointer on a dial* || a rod used for pointing, e.g. by a lecturer || a gundog of a breed having a smooth, usually white coat with brown or black spots, used for pointing game || a useful indication or suggestion [POINT]

Point Four Program a program proposed (1949) by U.S. President Harry Truman, which extended technical assistance and financial aid, previously channeled to rebuild war-torn Europe, to underdeveloped areas. It became a part of the Agency for International Development (AID)

poin·til·lism (pwǽnt'ljizəm, pwǽnti:lizəm) *n.* a method of painting developed by Seurat and used by certain other Postimpressionists, in which separated small dots of pure color applied to the picture surface become mixed by the viewer's eye, with an effect of increased luminosity **póin·til·list** *n.* a painter using this method [F. *pointillisme* fr. *pointiller*, to mark with dots]

point lace lace made entirely with a needle

point·less (póintlis) *adj.* having no point, esp. having no meaning or purpose

point of diminishing return the point after which an increased amount of land, labor or money devoted to a project does not give a proportionate increase in yield, or at which higher

prices or charges cease to produce proportionately higher revenue or profit

point of honor, *Br.* **point of honour** a matter to which one chooses to give the force of a principle involving one's honor

point of impact the point hit by a projectile

point of no return the point beyond which one's decisions or actions commit one irrevocably || the point on a cross-country flight after which one is nearer to the destination than to the starting point

point of order a question of debating procedure

point-of-sale (póintʌfséil) *n.* the place e.g., a retail store, where a product or service is offered to prospective customers. *abbr.* **POS**

point of view a mental position from which something is considered || an opinion

point-to-point (póinttəpóint) *n.* a cross-country steeplechase for amateur riders from a starting point to a distant but visible point

poise (pwaz) *n.* (*phys.*) the unit of absolute viscosity of a fluid [after Jean *Poiseuille* (1779-1869), French physicist]

poise (póiz) *n.* balance || carriage, bearing || emotional stability, self-possession [M.E. *poys* fr. O.F.]

poise *pres. part.* **pois·ing** *past* and *past part.* **poised** *v.t.* to balance, *to carry a jug poised on one's head* || to hold suspended for a moment, *to poise a javelin before hurling it* || to hold (the head) in a particular way || to put (esp. oneself) in a state of readiness, *to poise oneself for an ordeal* || *v.i.* to be balanced || to hang suspended or as if suspended, *a dancer poised in mid-air* [M.E. *poise* fr. O.F.]

Poi·seuille's law (pwæsə:jz) (*phys.*) the law stating that the rate of flow of a fluid through a tube varies directly with the pressure and the fourth power of the diameter of the tube, and inversely with the length of the tube and the coefficient of viscosity, for laminar (i.e. nonturbulent) flow [after Jean *Poiseuille* (1799-1869), F. physicist who formulated the law in 1844]

poi·son (póiz'n) **1.** *n.* a substance which, by its direct action on tissues, a mucous membrane etc., or after absorption into the circulatory system, can seriously injure an organism or destroy life completely || anything having a pernicious effect on the mind or character of an individual or individuals **2.** *adj.* poisonous [M.E. *poison, puison* fr. O.F.]

poison *v.t.* to injure or destroy by using a poison || to make poisonous, *to poison a well* || to exert a pernicious influence on (the mind or character of an individual or individuals) [M.E. *poisonen* fr. O.F.]

poison gas a poisonous gas used esp. in chemical warfare

poi·son·ing (póiz'niŋ) *n.* the condition produced by the application or absorption of a poison

poison ivy a member of *Rhus*, fam. *Anacardiaceae*, a genus of North American shrubs, esp. *R. toxicodendron*, common in the eastern and central U.S.A. These shrubs exude an irritating oil capable of causing a violently itchy skin rash

poison oak a shrubby variety of poison ivy || any of various poison sumacs

poi·son·ous (póiz'nəs) *adj.* having the properties or effects of a poison || impregnated with, or containing poison || as pernicious or deadly as a poison, *a poisonous influence* || (*pop.*) hateful, *a poisonous fellow*

poi·son-pen (póiz'npén) *adj.* written anonymously and with deliberate malice, *a poison-pen letter*

poison sumac, poison sumach *Rhus vernix,* fam. *Anacardiaceae*, a North American swamp sumac having pinnate leaves, greenish flowers and greenish-white berries. It produces an irritating oil like that of poison ivy

Pois·son (pwæsɔ́), Siméon Denis (1781–1840), French mathematician and physicist, noted for his contributions to electrostatics and mechanics

Poisson's ratio (*phys.*) the ratio between the lateral and longitudinal strains in a stretched wire or rod (symbol σ)

Poi·tiers (pwætjei) the chief town (pop. 81,313) of Vienne, France, and historical capital of Poitou. Gothic cathedral (12th–13th cc.), Romanesque and pre-Romanesque churches. University (1431)

Poitiers, Battle of a battle (732) in which Charles Martel repulsed the Moslem invasion of Europe || an English victory (1356) in the Hundred Years' War. The Black Prince fought

---

CONCISE PRONUNCIATION KEY: **(a)** æ, cat; ɑ, car; ɔ fawn; ei, snake. **(e)** e, hen; i:, sheep; iə, deer; ɛə, bear. **(i)** i, fish; ai, tiger; ə:, bird. **(o)** o, ox; au, cow; ou, goat; u, poor; ɔi, royal. **(u)** ʌ, duck; u, bull; u:, goose; ə, bacillus; ju:, cube. x, loch; θ, think; ð, bother; z, Zen; ʒ, corsage; dʒ, savage; ŋ, orangutang; j, yak; ʃ, fish; tʃ, fetch; 'l, rabble; 'n, redden. Complete pronunciation key appears inside front cover.

a brilliant defensive battle against the French, who greatly outnumbered his army

Poi·tou (pwætu:) a former province of W. France between the Paris and Garonne basins, comprising Vienne and Deux-Sèvres departments inland, and Vendée on the Atlantic, with parts of Charente (inland) and Charente-Maritime (coast). It consists largely of limestone plains, partly fertile, partly sandy. The coast is marshy. Agriculture: cereals, market produce, beef cattle, dairy farming. Historic capital: Poitiers. United with Aquitaine, it went to England through Henry II (1152), was taken back by the French, first in 1224, finally in 1369

poke (pouk) 1. *v. pres. part.* **pok·ing** past and past part. **poked** *v.t.* to thrust quickly the tip of some object, e.g. a finger, into (someone or something), *to poke someone in the ribs* ‖ to thrust (something) forward, or into or through an aperture, *to poke one's finger into a crack* ‖ to insert (an object) into something soft, *he poked his finger into the clay* ‖ to make (a hole) by doing this ‖ to stir up (a fire in a grate etc.) with a poker ‖ (*pop.*) to hit with a short, jabbing blow of the fist ‖ *v.i.* to make little digs or thrusts with a stick, finger etc. ‖ to be thrust forward through an aperture, *his head poked through the door* ‖ to go slowly, dawdle **to poke around** to examine things in a nosy or desultory way ‖ to busy oneself without any apparent purpose, *he is poking around in the garden* **to poke fun at** to make the object of ridicule 2. *n.* the act of poking ‖ (*old-fash.*) a poke bonnet ‖ (*pop.*) a short, jabbing blow with the fist ‖ a slow-moving person, slow coach [M.E. *poken*]

poke bonnet (*old-fash.*) a woman's bonnet having a projecting brim in the front

po·ker (póukər) *n.* a gambling game played with 52 cards (each player being dealt 5 or 7 cards), and based on the relative value of certain combinations of cards. To stay in the game a player must either equal or raise the bets made by other players. These bets, in the form of money or chips, constitute the pot, which is won by the possessor of the highest card combination shown. Bluffing plays an important part in the game

poker *n.* a heavy, usually iron, rod used to poke a fire [POKE v.]

poker face a face revealing no emotion whatsoever

poker work the art of making decorative designs on wood, leather, calabashes etc. by burning or scorching with a hot instrument ‖ this decoration, or articles so decorated

poke·sy (póukzi) *adj.* word combining 'pokey' and 'folksy'; meaning easygoing

poke·weed (póukwi:d) *n. Phytolacca americana,* fam. *Phytolaccaceae,* a North American perennial plant, having greenish-white flowers, poisonous purple berries and edible shoots

pok·y, pok·ey (póuki) *comp.* **pok·i·er** *superl.* **pok·i·est** *adj.* (of a small room, house etc.) inconveniently small ‖ (esp. of a town) small, drab and dull ‖ (of a person) slow, lazy

Po·land (póulənd) a republic (area 120,733 sq. miles, pop. 36,229,000) of central Europe on the Baltic. Capital: Warsaw. People: 98% Polish, with Ukrainian, Byelorussian and other minorities. Language: Polish. Religion: 95% Roman Catholic, 1.5% Orthodox, 5% Protestant, with smaller Old Catholic and Jewish minorities. The land is 54% arable, 13% pasture and 23% forest. It is largely a plain, rising to a slightly elevated (mainly 600–1,000 ft) plateau in the southwest quarter, the country's richest agricultural district, and to the wooded Sudeten and Carpathian Mtns (*BESKIDS, *TATRA MTNS) along the southern border. The north (with N. East Germany) forms part of the Baltic lake plateau (coastal lagoons, sandy soil, marshes, peat deposits, hundreds of lakes). Climate: continental. The Oder is frozen an average of 40 days a year, the Vistula 60. Average temperatures (F.): (Jan.) 26°, (July) 64°. Rainfall: Warsaw 18 ins, Carpathians 50 ins. Livestock: cattle, hogs, sheep, horses. Agricultural products: cereals, root vegetables, tobacco, hops, flax, silk, dairy goods. Main fisheries: cod, herring. Mineral resources: coal, lignite, iron ore, lead, zinc, petroleum, natural gas, salt, sulfur, potassium salts, silver, nickel, copper, arsenic. Manufactures and industries (rapidly developing): mining, iron and steel, motor vehicles, heavy machinery, rolling stock, electrical and optical equipment, precision instruments, tex-

tiles, lumber, chemicals, foodstuffs, leather, rubber goods, paper, cement, shipbuilding, glass, fertilizers, footwear, hydroelectricity. Exports: coal, rolling stock, coke, lignite, ships, chemicals, cement, machinery, iron and steel, sugar, wood and pulp, textiles, eggs. Imports: iron ore, oil and petroleum products, fertilizers, wheat, cotton, wool, zinc concentrates. Chief ports: Gdynia, Gdansk, Szczecin. There are 8 universities, including Krakow (1364) and Warsaw (1816). Monetary unit: zloty (100 groszy). HISTORY. The lower valleys of the Oder and the Vistula, inhabited by Slavs, were united in one duchy (10th c.) and the people became Christians. This territory was expanded to cover most of modern Poland until 1138, when it was split up into a number of duchies. The Teutonic Knights conquered East Prussia (13th c.), cutting off Poland's access to the Baltic. Poland was reunited (14th c.) under Casimir III, and became a refuge for the Jews expelled from W. Europe. Under Ladislaw II, the founder of the Jagiello dynasty, Lithuania was united to Poland (1386) and the Teutonic Knights were decisively defeated at Tannenberg (1410). The kingdom was enlarged to include parts of White Russia and the Ukraine, a constitutional monarchy was established, and a flourishing culture developed. The Reformation made some impact on the nobility, but Catholicism was reestablished by the end of the 16th c. After the death (1572) of the last Jagiello, an elective monarchy was instituted. This weakened the country by provoking civil wars, and involved Poland in wars with the Turks, Sweden and Russia. John III defeated the Turks at Vienna (1683), but by his death (1696) Poland had ceased to be a great power. It was further weakened by the War of the Polish Succession (1733–5) and was finally annihilated when Austria, Russia and Prussia agreed to partition Poland. In the 1st partition (1772) Prussia took northwestern Poland (except Gdansk), Austria took Galicia, and Russia took land east of the Dvina. In the 2nd partition (1793) Prussia and Russia took more than half of what remained. A revolt (1794) led by Kosciusko prompted the 3rd partition (1795), in which Austria, Prussia and Russia annexed all the remainder, and Poland completely disappeared. Napoleon formed the Grand Duchy of Warsaw (1807) but this was abolished (1815) by the Congress of Vienna and the land redistributed to Austria, Prussia and Russia. Polish revolts were harshly put down (1830, 1846, 1848 and 1863) but the independence movement remained strong. In the 1st world war, Pilsudski organized Polish legions to oppose Russia. Poland was reestablished as an independent state (1918) and given access to the Baltic through the Polish Corridor. Frontier disputes caused fighting with the Germans, the Czechs, the Russians and the Ukrainians until 1921. National minorities and the economic backwardness of the country were severe problems. Pilsudski established a dictatorship after a coup d'état (1926). Nazi Germany invaded Poland (Sept 1, 1939), provoking the 2nd world war, and the country was partitioned between Germany and the U.S.S.R. The population, esp. the Jews, were subject to mass deportation and extermination. A large underground resistance movement developed and a government in exile was formed in London. Many Polish exiles fought in the Allied forces. The German army was expelled by the Russians (1945) and the state of Poland was reestablished with the addition of former German territory east of the Oder-Neisse line and Russian territory west of the Curzon line. Communists immediately dominated the Polish government, and took it over completely (1947), establishing a people's republic. After mass riots (1956), Gomulka took power and the regime became more liberal. Poland's eastern frontiers were recognized (1970) 'de facto' by the West German government. A social and economic crisis (Dec. 1970) provoked riots. Gomulka was replaced by Gierek. An industrial boom in the early 1970's was followed by economic difficulties, which led to food-price riots (1976). Increases in food prices (1980) again led to unrest, culminating in a workers' takeover of the Gdańsk shipyards. Strikes spread to include 350,000 workers throughout Poland until the government granted pay increases and the right to form independent unions; the new unions subsequently became Solidarity, a single, nationwide organization.

Gierek was replaced by Stanislaw Kania, who announced economic reforms. Solidarity's call for a five-day work week (1981) was agreed to by the government, but following the settlement Premier Jozef Pinkowski (1980–1) was replaced by Defense Minister Gen. Wojciech Jaruzelski, who also replaced Kania as party leader later that year as strikes and protests about food shortages continued. Following a call by Solidarity for a referendum on the competence of the government, Jaruzelski imposed martial law and outlawed Solidarity. Martial law was not lifted until 1983, and the government still retained the power to restrict union activity. After a new parliament was elected (1985), Jaruzelski assumed the office of president, and handed the premiership over to Zbigniew Messner

po·lar (póulər) 1. *adj.* of or pertaining to the regions of the earth, or of the celestial sphere, located near the poles ‖ of or pertaining to the pole of a magnet, *polar force* ‖ of or pertaining to positive and negative electric charges ‖ (*chem.*) electrovalent ‖ (*chem., phys.*) having a dipole ‖ (*math.*) of a relationship to a fixed point (pole) ‖ opposite in nature, character etc., *polar views* ‖ (*rhet.*) guiding, *a polar principle* 2. *n.* (*math.*) a polar curve ‖ (*math.*) a line joining the intersections of tangents drawn from a pole to a conic section [fr. M.L. *polaris*]

polar bear *Thalarctos maritimus,* a powerful bear inhabiting the Arctic regions, having a long body (up to 9 ft), a narrow, pointed head, and shaggy yellowish-white fur. It feeds mainly on fish, seals and grasses

polar body a polocyte

polar cap the white region at each pole of the planet Mars

polar circle one of the circular zones parallel to the equator, and at a distance of 23° 27' from each pole (cf. ARCTIC CIRCLE, cf. ANTARCTIC CIRCLE)

polar climate a climatic regime of the Arctic, Antarctic and high mountain regions, characterized by continuous below-freezing temperatures, low precipitation and little seasonal variation

polar coordinates (*math.*) the distance *r* of a point from a pole (a fixed point of reference) and the angle θ made by the line joining the point and the pole with a fixed axis passing through the pole

polar curve a curve drawn in polar coordinates

polar distance the angular distance of a point on a sphere from the nearest pole

polar front the boundary between the cold climate of the polar regions and the warmer climate of the temperate latitudes

po·lar·im·e·ter (poulərímitər) *n.* an instrument used to measure optical rotation ‖ an instrument used to measure the degree of polarization of light in a partially polarized ray [fr. M.L. *polaris,* polar+METER]

Po·la·ris (pouléaris, pouláris) *n.* the polestar [Mod. L. short for *stella polaris,* polar star]

Polaris *n.* (*mil.*) an underwater/surface-launched, surface-to-surface solid-propellant, computer-guided ballistic missile (UGM-27), equipped with inertial guidance and nuclear warheads with ranges 1,200 to 2,500 nautical mi. It was replaced by Poseidon

po·lar·i·scope (pouláriskoup) *n.* a polarimeter used to measure optical rotation

po·lar·i·ty (pouláriti) *n.* the quality of having poles ‖ the state of having one or other of two opposite polar conditions, *positive or negative polarity* ‖ the tendency of bodies having magnetic poles to align them with the earth's poles [POLAR]

po·lar·i·za·tion (poulərizéiʃən, *Br.* pouləraizéiʃən) *n.* the act of polarizing ‖ the state of being polarized, used esp. of light and other transverse wave radiation to signify a special relation between the direction of propagation and the plane of vibration of the waves. In plane or linearly polarized radiation (e.g. light) the vibrations of the waves are confined to a single plane that includes the direction of propagation (as distinguished from nonpolarized light, where the planes of vibration of the waves may be any, including the direction of propagation). Light may be polarized by various means, e.g. by scattering, by its passage through a dichroic material, by its passage through birefringent materials or by reflection from nonmetallic surfaces ‖ the gradual decrease in the voltage of an electrolytic cell associated with the accumulation of gaseous materials on one or both electrodes (also called electrolytic polarization) ‖ the slight shifting of electrons with respect to nuclei in a dielectric or other substance when it is placed in an electric field (also called dielectric or induced polarization) ‖ magnetization

po·lar·ize (póuləraiz) *pres. part.* **po·lar·iz·ing** *past and past part.* **po·lar·ized** *v.t.* to produce polarization in or give polarity to ‖ to determine the relative importance of, or to fix the relative direction of, *to polarize the efforts of a team of researchers* ‖ *v.i.* to become concentrated around two opposites or extremes ‖ to serve as a point around which concentration takes place [F. *polariser*]

polarizing microscope a microscope employing polarized light, used to study crystal structure

po·lar·o·graph (poulǽrəgræf, poulǽrəgraf) *n.* an instrument to record the degree of electric polarization in an electrolyte, esp. in microanalysis [after *Polarograph*, a trademark fr. M.L. *polaris*, polar+Gk *graphos*, written]

po·lar·oid (póulərɔid) *n.* a film in which multitudes of polarizing minute crystals are orientated parallel to one another, so that the film polarizes the light it transmits. It is used in sunglasses to prevent glare and in a variety of optical instruments [after *Polaroid*, a trademark]

Polaroid *n.* trademark of Polaroid Corp., producer of Polaroid Land instant-picture cameras and of light-polarizing material, etc.

Po·la·vi·sion (póuləviʒən) *n.* trademark for instant motion picture-making device by Polaroid Corp.

pol·der (póuldər) *n.* an area of low lying land reclaimed from the sea or other large body of water and usually protected by dikes [Du.]

Pole (póul), Reginald (1500–58), English cardinal, archbishop of Canterbury (1556–8). He went into exile (1532) when he opposed Henry VIII's divorce, but returned (1553) as papal legate and attempted to restore Roman Catholicism in England during the reign of Mary I

Pole *n.* a native or inhabitant of Poland [G. fr. Pol. *poljane*, field-dwellers]

pole *n.* (*biol.*) either of two differentiated areas that lie at opposite ends of an axis, e.g. the ends of the spindle in mitosis or the animal and vegetal poles in an egg ‖ either of the terminals of a battery, cell or dynamo etc. between which a current will flow when connected by an external conductor (i.e. between which a potential difference exists) ‖ one of the two or more points in a magnet where most of the magnetic flux is concentrated ‖ one of two extremes, *the poles of an argument* ‖ a point of attraction **Pole** either end of the axis of a sphere, e.g. the North Pole or South Pole of the earth or the celestial sphere [fr. L. *polus* fr. Gk]

pole 1. *n.* a long, usually rounded piece of wood or other material, *tent pole, telegraph pole* ‖ the wooden shaft of a wagon or carriage attached to the front axle and extending between the wheelhorses ‖ a unit of length, esp. one measuring 16 ½ ft ‖ a unit of area measuring 30 ¼ square yards ‖ (*naut.*) a mast, esp. the upper end ‖ the tail of an otter 2. *v.t. pres. part.* **pol·ing** *past and past part.* **poled** to propel (a punt etc.) by using a pole ‖ to furnish with poles, *to pole beans* [O.E. *pāl* fr. L.]

pole·ax, pole·axe (póulæks) 1. *pl.* **pole·ax·es** *n.* (*hist.*) an ax set in a long handle used as a weapon ‖ (*hist.*) such an ax fitted with a hook, used for grappling an enemy vessel, cutting the ship's tackle etc. ‖ a long-handled, hammer-backed ax used for slaughtering cattle 2. *v.t. pres. part.* **pole·ax·ing** *past and past part.* **pole·axed** to kill or render unconscious by hitting with a poleax [M.E. *pollax* fr. *poll*, the head+*ax*, ax]

pole bean a climbing bean (cf. BUSH BEAN)

pole·cat (póulkæt) *n. Mustela putorius*, fam. *Mustelidae*, a European carnivorous mammal about 2 ft long, having brown and black fur and white head markings ‖ (*pop.*) a skunk [M.E. *polcat*, prob. fr. O.F. *pole*, a hen+CAT]

pole lamp lighting fixture with lamps on a pole, often from floor to ceiling

po·lem·ic (pəlémik, poulémik) 1. *adj.* of or pertaining to controversy 2. *n.* a disputation ‖ a person who takes part in a controversy, esp. a theological controversy **po·lem·i·cal** *adj.* **po·lem·i·cist** *n.* a person who engages in polemics **po·lem·ics** *n.* (construed as *sing.* or *pl.*) the art or practice of theological disputation [fr. Gk *polemikos* fr. *polemos*, war]

po·lem·ol·ogy (pouləmólədʒi:) *n.* study of wars

po·len·ta (pʊléntə) *n.* meal made of corn ‖ a form of mush made from this [Ital.]

pole position 1. (*sports*) in a race, the position closest to the infield, i.e., the one offering shortest circumference. 2. by extension, an outstandingly advantageous position

pole·star (póulstər) *n.* a bright star in the constellation Ursa Minor

pole strength a measure of the magnetic flux emanating from a given magnetic pole expressed in unit magnetic poles

pole vault a competitive athletic event in which a contestant vaults with the aid of a long pole of bamboo, aluminum etc. over a horizontal bar supported by two upright posts ‖ this vault

po·lice (pəlí:s) *pl.* **po·lice** *n.* a department of government responsible for the preservation of public order, detection of crime and enforcement of civil law ‖ the police force ‖ (*pl.*) members of the police force, *a squad of mounted police* ‖ any body of people whose job is to keep order and enforce regulations ‖ (*mil.*) the act or process of putting and keeping in order (e.g. the grounds of an army camp) ‖ (*mil.*) enlisted men assigned to perform a specific function (*KP) [F.]

police *pres. part.* **po·lic·ing** *past and past part.* **po·liced** *v.t.* to control, or maintain law and order in, by means of police ‖ to provide with police ‖ to exercise police control over (an area etc.) ‖ to control, regulate etc. as if by means of police ‖ (*mil.*, esp. with 'up') to clean and put in order (a camp, garrison etc.) [F. *policer* fr. L.L. fr. Gk and POLICE *n.*]

police constable (*Br.*) a rank-and-file member of the uniformed police force

police court a court of summary jurisdiction, presided over by a magistrate and dealing chiefly with minor offenses, but having the power to bind over for trial those guilty of more serious offenses

police dog a German shepherd (dog) ‖ a dog trained to help the police. e.g. as a tracker

police force the entire body of local or national police

po·lice·man (pəlí:smən) *pl.* **po·lice·men** (pəlí:smən) *n.* a male member of a police force

police state a country in which the government uses its power arbitrarily over citizens mainly through police, esp. secret police

police station the headquarters of a local section of the police force where arrested persons are taken and police reports written

po·lice·wom·an (pəlí:swumən) *pl.* **po·lice·wom·en** (pəlí:swimən) *n.* a female member of a police force

pol·i·cy (pólisi:) *pl.* **pol·i·cies** *n.* a selected, planned line of conduct in the light of which individual decisions are made and coordination achieved, *advertising policy* ‖ shrewdness in support of an aim, *would it be good policy to accept the invitation?* [O.F. *policie* fr. L. fr. Gk *politeia*, citizenship]

policy *pl.* **policies** *n.* a document containing the contract made between an individual and an insurance company ‖ the numbers (lottery, *NUMBER) [fr. F. *police*, bill of lading]

pol·i·cy·hold·er (pólisi:houldər) *n.* a person holding an insurance policy

policy matrix the side effects of a policy on other issues and areas, e.g. disarmament on employment, income tax receipts, etc.

Po·lig·nac (poli:njæk), Jules Armand, prince de (1780–1847), French statesman, prime minister of France (1829–30). His reactionary government precipitated the revolution of 1830

Polignac Memorandum an assurance given (1823) by the Prince de Polignac, then French ambassador to London, at the request of Prime Minister Canning, to the effect that France would not provide any assistance to Spain if Spain should attempt to recover any of her lost territories in America

pol·i·met·rics (pplimétriks) *n.* the study of statistics of political science. **—pol·i·me·tri·cian** *n.*

po·li·o·my·e·li·tis (póuli:oumaiəláitis) *n.* (*pop. abbr.* polio) a serious infectious virus disease, esp. of children, caused by inflammation of the gray matter of the spinal cord, and characterized by fever, motor paralysis and muscular atrophy, often resulting in permanent deformity [Mod. L. fr. Gk *polios*, gray+MYELITIS]

Polisario (*acronym*) Popular Front for the Liberation of Western Sahara, an Algerian- and Libyan-backed guerrilla group seeking the in-

dependence of territory in Western Sahara from Morocco

Po·lish (póuliʃ) 1. *adj.* of or pertaining to Poland, its inhabitants or their language 2. *n.* the Slavic language of Poland

pol·ish (póliʃ) 1. *v.t.* to make smooth and lustrous by rubbing, esp. by exerting a back-and-forth pressure on the waxed surface of ‖ to cause (a person, his speech, behavior etc.) to become more refined or cultivated ‖ to bring (a style, sentence etc.) nearer perfection ‖ *v.i.* to take a polish **to polish off** to consume quickly, *to polish off a meal* ‖ to dispose of completely, *to polish off an opponent* **to polish up** to make brighter by rubbing ‖ to revise and improve, *to polish up one's French* 2. *n.* a polishing or being polished ‖ the lustrous surface of something polished ‖ a preparation used in polishing ‖ personal refinement or cultivation [F. *polir* (*poliss*)]

Polish Corridor the strip of land which linked Poland to the Baltic Sea between the two world wars. Following the lower Vistula, it separated East Prussia from the rest of Germany, and was a cause of disputes between Germany and Poland on account of its German population and the status of Danzig as a free city

Polish Succession, War of the a war (1733–5) between France, supported by Spain and Sardinia, and Austria, supported by Russia, on behalf of rival candidates for the Polish throne. At the end of the war, France recognized the Austrian candidate, Augustus III, while Stanislaus Leszczynski received the Lorraine duchies until his death, when they were to be annexed to France. Spain regained the Two Sicilies

Po·lit·bu·ro (pəlítbjʊərou) *n.* (*hist.*) the former committee of the Russian Communist party for fixing policy between sessions of the Central Committee. It was replaced (1952) by a presidium **politburo** the policy-forming body and executive committee of a Communist party, e.g. of the Chinese [fr. Russ. *politicheskoe buro*, political bureau]

po·lite (pəláit, pouláit) *adj.* having good social manners ‖ characterized by refinement, *polite usage* [fr. L. *polire* (*politus*), to polish]

Po·li·tian (poulíʃən) (Angelo Poliziano or Angelus Politianus 1454–94), Florentine humanist and poet. He translated parts of the Iliad and wrote 'Orfeo' (1475), one of the earliest plays in the Italian language. His poems, written in the Tuscan dialect, are classical in tone

pol·i·tic (pólitik) *adj.* shrewdly judicious in support of an aim [F. *politique*]

po·lit·i·cal (pəlítik'l) *adj.* of or pertaining to politics ‖ engaged in politics, *a political figure* [fr. L. *politicus* fr. Gk]

political animal (*colloq.*) one who thinks and acts like a politician, esp. in relations with others

political economy economics (as an academic study)

political retrogression withdrawal from a political group or organization in protest against its activities

political science the study of the nature and functions of the state and of government

pol·i·ti·cian (pplitíʃən) *n.* a person engaged in politics and in the techniques of civil government ‖ (in a derogatory sense) a person engaged in politics merely for personal gain [POLITIC].

po·lit·i·ci·za·tion (pəlitəsəzéiʃən) *n.* the process of becoming responsive to political forces or issues **—po·lit·i·cize** *v.* **—po·lit·i·cized** *adj.*

pol·i·tics (pólitiks) *n.* the art and science of the government of a state ‖ public affairs or public life as they relate to this ‖ the opinions, principles or policies by which a person orders his participation in such affairs ‖ scheming and maneuvering within a group, *college politics* [POLITIC]

pol·i·ty (póliti:) *pl.* **pol·i·ties** *n.* organized government ‖ the form or constitution of a nation, state or community ‖ a politically organized nation, state or community [O.F. *politie* fr. L. fr. Gk]

Polk (pouk), James Knox (1795–1849), 11th president of the U.S.A. (1845–9), a Democrat. He reestablished the independent treasury system (1846) and a very low tariff. He accepted the 49th parallel as the Oregon frontier (1846). After the Mexican War (1846–8), he annexed Texas, California and most of Arizona, Colorado, Nevada, Utah, New Mexico and Wyoming

pol·ka (póulkə, póukə) 1. *n.* a lively dance in

CONCISE PRONUNCIATION KEY: (a) æ, *cat*; ɑ, *car*; ɔ *fawn*; ei, *snake*. **(e)** e, *hen*; i:, *sheep*; iə, *deer*; ɛə, *bear*. **(i)** i, *fish*; ai, *tiger*; ə:, *bird*. **(o)** o, *ox*; au, *cow*; ou, *goat*; u, *poor*; ɔi, *royal*. **(u)** ʌ, *duck*; u, *bull*; u:, *goose*; ə, *bacillus*; ju:, *cube*. x, *loch*; θ, *think*; ð, *bother*; z, Zen; ʒ, *corsage*; dʒ, *savage*; ŋ, orangutang; j, *yak*; ʃ, *fish*; tʃ, *fetch*; 'l, *rabble*; 'n, *redden*. Complete pronunciation key appears inside front cover.

duple time for couples, originating in Bohemia ‖ the music for this type of dance **2.** *v.i.* to dance the polka [F. and G. prob. fr. Czech *pulka,* half step]

polka dot one dot in a regular pattern of dots used as a design, esp. in textiles ‖ a material of this design

poll (poul) **1.** *n.* the number of votes cast in an election, *a heavy poll* ‖ the casting of votes ‖ (esp. *pl.*) the place where votes are cast and recorded ‖ the period of time during which votes may be cast ‖ a poll tax ‖ a canvassing of persons chosen at random or from a sample group in order to discover trends of public opinion ‖ the blunt end of a hammer, miner's pick etc. **2.** *v.t.* to receive (a number of votes) ‖ to record the votes of ‖ to canvass (people) in order to discover their opinions ‖ to cut off the horns of (cattle etc.) ‖ to pollard (a tree) ‖ *v.i.* to cast a vote [M.E. *pol, polle,* head fr. M. Du.]

pol·lack (pólǝk) *pl.* **pol·lack, pol·lacks** *n. Pollachius virens,* fam. *Gadidae,* a highly esteemed N. Atlantic food fish related to the cod, but having a longer lower jaw [etym. doubtful]

Pol·lai·uo·lo (pɔllaiwɔ́lo), Antonio (1429–98), Florentine painter, sculptor, goldsmith and engraver. He is famous for his muscular figures in action, and is said to have been the first painter to study anatomy by dissection. His brother Piero (1443–96) collaborated on many paintings

pol·lard (pólǝrd **1.** *n.* a tree cut back to the trunk so that a thick head of branches is formed by new growth ‖ a hornless variety of goat, ox, sheep etc. ‖ a feed for livestock consisting of a mixture of finely ground bran and coarse flour ‖ a coarse wheat bran **2.** *adj.* pollarded **3.** *v.t.* to cut back the branches of (a tree) so as to make a pollard [POLL]

pol·len (pólǝn) *n.* the male reproductive cells or microspores produced by and discharged from the anther of a seed plant [L.=fine flour]

pollen count the amount of pollen of a specific variety in a given volume of air at a specific time and place, useful in determining infective areas for sufferers from hay fever etc.

pol·lex (póleks) *pl.* **pol·li·ces** (pólisi:z) *n.* the thumb [L.]

pol·li·nate (pólineit) *pres. part.* **pol·li·nat·ing** *past* and *past part.* **pol·li·nat·ed** *v.t.* (of insects, wind etc.) to place pollen on the stigma of (a flower) **pol·li·na·tion** *n.* [fr. L. *poll (pollinis),* fine flour]

polling booth (*Br.*) a voting booth

pol·li·nif·er·ous (pɔllinífǝrǝs) *adj.* bearing or yielding pollen [fr. L. *pollen (pollinis),* fine flour +*-fer,* bearing]

pol·lin·i·um (pǝlíni:ǝm) *pl.* **pol·lin·i·a** (pǝlíni:ǝ) *n.* an agglutinated mass of pollen found esp. in the flowers of orchids [Mod. L. fr. *pollen (pollinis),* fine flour]

pol·li·wog (póli·wɔg) *n.* a tadpole [M.E. *polwygle* fr. *pol,* the head+WIGGLE]

Pol·lock (pólǝk), Sir Frederick (1845–1937), British jurist. His works include 'The History of English Law before the Time of Edward I' (with F. W. Maitland, 1895), 'The Principles of Contract' (1876) and 'The Law of Torts' (1887). His correspondence with Oliver Wendell Holmes was published as 'The Holmes-Pollock Letters' (1941)

Pollock, Jackson (1912–56), American painter, an originator of abstract expressionism. Using methods of automatism (e.g. dripping paint on canvas), he painted large, nonobjective compositions of rhythmic intensity

pol·lock (pólǝk) *pl.* **pol·lock, pol·locks** *n.* a pollack

poll tax a tax of a fixed amount per head levied on adults. In some states of the U.S.A. payment of a poll tax was formerly a prerequisite of voting but was declared unconstitutional by the U.S. Supreme Court (1966) in state elections, after the xxivth amendment (1964) to the U.S. constitution prohibited the requirement for federal elections

pol·lute (pǝlú:t) *pres. part.* **pol·lut·ing** *past* and *past part.* **pol·lut·ed** *v.t.* to make unhealthily impure, *factory waste may pollute rivers* ‖ to corrupt, *books which pollute the mind* ‖ to make ritually unclean [fr. L. *polluere (pollutus)*]

pol·lu·tion (pǝlú:ʃǝn) *n.* a polluting or being polluted [fr. L. *pollutio (pollutionis)*]

pol·lut·ive (pǝlú:tiv) *adj.* causing pollution

pollywog *POLLIWOG

Pol·lux (pólǝks) *DIOSCURI

Po·lo (póulou), Marco (1254–1324), Venetian traveler who went overland to China (1271–5)

across the Pamirs and the Gobi Desert. After 17 years of itinerant service for Kublai Khan he returned (1292–5) by sea via Sumatra to Persia and thence overland home. His 'Book of Marco Polo' is the earliest firsthand European account of Asia

po·lo (póulou) *n.* a game played on horseback by two teams of three or four players on a ground 300 yds by 160 or 200 yds. Mallets with long flexible handles are used to drive a ball of bamboo or willow root down the field, and through the goalposts ‖ water polo [prob. fr. Tibetan *pulu,* the ball]

po·lo·cyte (póulǝsait) *n.* one of the minute cells produced during the first and second meiotic division in maturation [fr. POLE (end of axis)+Gk *kutos,* hollow vessel]

pol·o·naise (pɔlǝnéiz, poulǝnéiz) *n.* a dignified dance in ¾ time, of Polish origin ‖ the music for this dance ‖ a woman's garment consisting of a bodice and a short skirt divided in front and looped back over a longer skirt [F. fem. of *polonais,* Polish]

po·lo·neck (póulouneķ) *n.* (*Br.*) a turtleneck or sweater with this type of neck

Po·lo·ni·a (pǝlóuni:ǝ) *n.* Poles in diaspora around the world

po·lo·ni·um (pǝlóuni:ǝm) *n.* (radium F) a radioactive element which emits alpha particles as it decays (symbol Po, at. no. 84, at. mass 210), appearing during the disintegration of radium [Mod. L. fr. *Polonia,* Poland (named by Marie Curie)]

po·lo·ny (pǝlóuni:) *pl.* **po·lo·nies** *n.* (*Br.*) a cooked, red-skinned sausage filled esp. with pork [corrup. of *Bologna* sausage]

polo shirt a man's knitted cotton sports shirt usually with a collar

Pol·ta·va (paltáva) an agricultural center (pop. 279,000) of the N. central Ukraine, U.S.S.R.: food processing, meat packing

pol·ter·geist (póultǝrgaist) *n.* a mischievous spirit which manifests its presence by throwing objects about noisily [G. fr. *polter,* uproar+*geist,* spirit]

pol·troon (pɔltrú:n) *n.* (*rhet.*) an abject coward

pol·troon·er·y *n.* (*rhet.*) cowardice [F. *poltron* fr. Ital.]

pol·y·a·cet·y·lene (pɔli:ǝsét'li:n) *n.* (*plastics*) a synthetic polymer capable of conducting electricity, used in making paper-thin batteries

pol·y·a·del·phous (pɔli:ǝdélfǝs) *adj.* (*bot.*) having stamens joined by the anthers into three or more bundles [fr. Gk *polu,* many+*adelphos,* brother]

pol·y·an·drous (pɔli:ǽndrǝs) *adj.* of or characterized by polyandry ‖ practicing polyandry ‖ (*bot.*) having many separate stamens [fr. Gk fr. *polu,* many+*anēr (andros),* man]

pol·y·an·dry (póli:ændri:, pɔli:ǽndri:) *n.* the state or practice of having more than one husband at the same time ‖ (*zool.*) the condition of having more than one male mate at a time ‖ (*bot.*) the presence of many separate stamens [fr. Gk *poluandria* fr. *polu,* many+*anēr (andros),* man]

pol·y·an·thus (pɔli:ǽnθǝs) *pl.* **pol·y·an·thus·es, pol·y·an·thi** (pɔli:ǽnθai) *n. Primula polyantha,* fam. *Primulaceae,* a hybrid supposedly derived from three primulas ‖ *Narcissus tazetta,* a narcissus having small umbellate yellow or white flowers [Mod. L. fr. Gk *polu,* many+*anthos,* flower]

pol·y·arch·y (póli:arki:) *n.* a free democratic, literate, decentralized, politically well-organized society with high economic and political mobility. Wealth and power rest with the rank and file

pol·y·ba·sic (pɔli:béisik) *adj.* (*chem.*. of acids) having more than one hydrogen atom replaceable by a basic atom or radical ‖ (of a salt) containing two or more atoms of a univalent metal [Gk *polu,* many+BASIC]

pol·y·ben·zim·id·a·zole (pɔli:benzimídǝzoul) a synthetic polymer that, as a fiber, creates a textile suitable for clothing, that does not melt, burn in air or become stiff when charred; developed by NASA. *abbr.* **PBI**

Po·lyb·i·us (pǝlíbi:ǝs) (c. 200–c. 125 B.C.), Greek historian. Sent as a hostage to Rome (168 B.C.), he gained the patronage of Scipio Aemilianus. He wrote a 'History' of the period 264–146 B.C. in 40 books, of which five survive complete and the rest in excerpts

pol·y·car·bon·ate (pɔli:kárbǝneit) *n.* (*chem.*) any of a group of hard thermoplastics with great resistance to impact and to softening

Pol·y·carp (póli:karp), St (c. 69–c. 155), bishop of Smyrna (c. 105–55) and martyr. A disciple of St John, he forms a link between the Apostolic period and the early Church Fathers. Feast: Jan. 26

pol·y·cen·trism (pɔli:séntrizǝm) *n.* the principle of having many political or management centers. —**pol·y·cen·tric** *adj.* —**pol·y·cen·trist** *n.*

pol·y·chaete, pol·y·chete (pɔlíki:t) **1.** *adj.* of or relating to *Polychaeta,* a large class of chiefly marine annelid worms, usually having well-developed parapodia and characterized by the numerous bristles on their appendages **2.** *n.* a member of this class [fr. Mod. L. *Polychaeta* fr. Gk *polu,* many+*chaitē,* bristle]

pol·y·cha·sium (pɔli:kéiʒǝm) *pl.* **pol·y·cha·sia** (pɔli:kéiʒǝ) *n.* (*bot.*) a cymose inflorescence in which each main axis produces three or more branches [Mod. L. fr. Gk *polu,* many+*chasis,* division]

polychete *POLYCHAETE

pol·y·chlo·rin·at·ed biphenyl (pɔli:klɔ́rineitid) (*chem.*) highly toxic, very persistent carcinogenic pollutant used in plastics and as an insulator in electrical devices. It has been banned since 1977. *abbr.* **PCB**

pol·y·chro·mat·ic (pɔli:kroumǽtik) *adj.* multicolored [fr. Gk *polu,* many+CHROMATIC]

polychromatic theory concept of seven types of vision color reception: crimson, orange, yellow, green, blue green, blue, and blue violet

pol·y·chrome (póli:kroum) **1.** *adj.* painted or printed in many colors **2.** *n.* a work of art, esp. a late 6th-B.C. Athenian vase, decorated in many colors **pol·y·chróm·ic** *adj.* **pól·y·chrom·y** *n.* [F. fr. Gk *polu,* many+*chrōma,* color]

pol·y·clin·ic (pɔli:klínik) *n.* a clinic or hospital where many sorts of disease are treated

Pol·y·cli·tus (pɔli:kláitǝs) Greek sculptor and architect (5th c. B.C.). A contemporary of Phidias, he excelled in bronze sculptures of the male nude. His theory of proportions as applied in the 'Doryphoros' (Spear Bearer) became a standard for other sculptors. No original works survive, but there are many Greek and Roman copies

pol·y·cot·y·le·don (pɔli:kɒtlí:d'n) *n.* (*bot.*) a plant, e.g. a conifer having more than two cotyledons **pol·y·cot·y·lé·don·ous** *adj.* [Mod. L. fr. Gk *polu,* many+COTYLEDON]

Po·lyc·ra·tes (pǝlíkrǝti:z) (d. c. 522 B.C.), tyrant of Samos (c. 540–c. 522 B.C.). After establishing himself as ruler, he built Samos into a major naval power. He gave Cambyses II strong support against the Egyptians in the Persian Wars

pol·y·crys·tal·line diamond (pɔli:krístǝlin) synthetic diamond substitutes bonded to tungsten carbide cutters, used as protective coatings for industrial cutting tools; developed by General Electric Co.

pol·y·dac·tyl (pɔli:dǽkt'l) **1.** *adj.* having more than the normal number of fingers and toes **2.** *n.* a polydactyl person or animal **pol·y·dác·tyl·ism, pol·y·dác·ty·ly** *ns* [fr. Gk *polu,* many+*daktulos,* finger]

pol·y·dae·mon·ism, pol·y·de·mon·ism (pɔli:dí:mǝnizǝm) *n.* the belief in or worship of many divinities, esp. those having evil powers [fr. Gk *polu,* many+*daimon,* divinity]

pol·y·e·lec·tro·lytes (pɔli:iléktrǝlaits) *n.* (*chem.*) synthetic chemicals that help solids to clump during sewage treatment

pol·y·em·bry·o·ny (pɔli:émbri:ɒni:) *n.* the condition of giving birth to genetically identical offspring (identical twins, triplets, etc.) —**pol·y·em·bry·on·ic** *adj.*

pol·y·es·tra·di·ol (pɔli:estréidi:ǝl) *n.* (*pharm.*) estrogen drug used in treatment of carcinoma of the prostate; marketed as Estradurin. *abbr.* **PEP**

pol·y·e·thers (pɔli:í:θǝrz) *n.* (*plastics*) a group of long-chain dihydric alcohols in a viscous liquid used in producing emulsifying agents, antistatic agents and polyurethane foam

pol·y·ethyl·ene (pɔli:éθǝli:n) *n.* one of a group of thermoplastics (-CH_2CH_2-)x, lightweight and varying in flexibility and having high resistance to chemicals, and good insulating properties, used in food packaging, insulation etc. [fr. Gk *polu,* many+ETHYLENE]

po·lyg·a·mist (pǝlígǝmist) *n.* a person who practices polygamy [POLYGAMY]

po·lyg·a·mous (pǝlígǝmǝs) *adj.* having more than one wife or husband ‖ (*zool.*) having more than one mate at the same time ‖ (*bot.*) bearing male, female or hermaphrodite flowers on the same plant [fr. Gk *polugamos*]

po·lyg·a·my (pəlígəmi:) n. the state or practice of being polygamous [F. *polygamie* fr. L. fr. Gk fr. *polu*, many + *gamos*, marriage]

pol·y·gen·e·sis (pɒli:dʒénisis) n. (biol.) the theory that the human races originate from a few primitive types taken as species

pol·y·ge·net·ic (pɒli:dʒənétik) adj. of or relating to polygenesis

pol·y·glass or polyglas (pɒli:glǽs) n. (plastics) a polyester fiber cord used in automobile tire belts in order to improve wear

pol·y·glot (pɒli:glɒt) 1. adj. speaking or writing several languages ‖ containing or made up of several languages, *a polyglot text* 2. n. a person who knows several languages ‖ a book, esp. the Bible, containing the same text in many languages [fr. Gk *poluglōttos* fr. *polu*, many + *glōtta*, tongue]

Polyglot Bible a Bible in which texts in several languages are printed in parallel columns. Such Bibles were produced by Origen (early 3rd c.), at Alcala (1502–17) by Cisneros, at Antwerp (1569–73), in Paris (1645) and in London (1654–7)

pol·y·gon (pɒli:gɒn) n. a plane figure enclosed by five or more straight lines **po·lyg·o·nal** (pəlígən'l) adj. [fr. L.L. *polygonum* fr. Gk fr. *polu*, many + *gōnia*, angle]

polygon law of vectors the statement that if any number of vectors are represented by straight lines, taken in order and having the same cyclic sense, they are equivalent to a single vector represented by the straight line, drawn in the opposite sense, needed to complete the polygon

polygraph *LIE DETECTOR

po·lyg·y·nous (pəlídʒinəs) adj. of, relating to, practicing or characterized by polygyny [fr. Mod. L. *polygynus*]

po·lyg·y·ny (pəlídʒini:) n. the state or practice of having several wives at the same time ‖ (zool.) the condition of having more than one female mate at a time ‖ (bot.) the condition of bearing male, female or hermaphrodite flowers on the same plant [fr. Gk *polu*, many + *gunē*, woman]

pol·y·he·dral (pɒli:hí:drəl) adj. of or relating to, or having the form of, a polyhedron [fr. Gk *poluedros* fr. *polu*, many + *hedra*, base]

pol·y·he·dron (pɒli:hí:drən) pl. **pol·y·he·dra** (pɒli:hí:drə), **pol·y·he·drons** n. (geom.) a figure or solid formed usually by seven or more plane faces [Gk *poluedron*]

Pol·y·hym·ni·a (pɒlihímni:ə) the Muse of sacred song [L. fr. Gk fr. *polu*, many + *humnia*, hymn]

poly I:C n. (physiol.) chemical resembling a two-stranded RNA that stimulates body production of interferon

pol·y·mer (pɒləmər) n. a natural or synthetic substance or mixture, usually of high molecular mass, whose molecules are formed repeated polymerization of identical sequence of identical chemical units (*HIGH POLYMER, *COPOLYMER). Cellulose, lignin, nucleic acids, hair and horn are among a vast number of naturally occurring polymers. Nylon, rayon and rubber are some important synthetic polymers **pol·y·mer·ic** (pɒləmérik) adj. **pol·y·mer·ism** (pɒlémərizəm) n. [fr. Gk *polu*, many + *meros*, part]

pol·ym·er·ase (páli:məreis) n. (physiol.) any of a group of enzymes that catalyze polymerization assisting in the formation of DNA or RNA

po·lym·er·i·za·tion (pəlìmərizéiʃən) n. a chemical reaction in which two or more small molecules react to form larger molecules, eventually resulting in long chains of identical repeating units (*COPOLYMER) ‖ the state of being combined in this way

po·lym·er·ize (pəlíməraiz) v.pres.part. **po·lym·er·iz·ing** past and past part. **po·lym·er·ized** v.t. to subject to polymerization ‖ v.i. to undergo polymerization

pol·y·mide resin (páli:maid) (chem.) a group of synthetic polymeric resins, strongly heat resistant, used in insulators, coatings, semiconductors and adhesives

pol·y·morph (páli:mɔrf) n. (biol.) a leucocyte having the nucleus complexly lobed ‖ (crystall.) a substance capable of being crystallized into various forms ‖ one of these forms **pol·y·mór·phic** adj. polymorphous **pol·y·mór·phism** n. (biol.) occurrence of different forms of individuals in the same species ‖ (biol.) occurrence of different forms, or different forms of organs, in the same individual at different periods of life (e.g. in some coelenterates) ‖ (crystall.) the quality of crystallizing into various forms [fr. Gk

polymorphos, multiform fr. *polu*, many + *morphē*, form]

pol·y·mor·phous (pɒli:mɔ́rfəs) adj. capable of assuming two or more forms [fr. Gk *polymorphos*, multiform]

Pol·y·ne·sia (pɒlini:ʒə, pɒlini:ʃə) the eastern division of Oceania, including French Polynesia, the Hawaiian Is, Samoa, Tonga, the Line, Cook, Phoenix and Ellice Is, and Easter Is.

Pol·y·ne·sian (pɒlini:ʒən, pɒlini:ʃən) 1. adj. of, relating to, or characteristic of Polynesia, its people or its languages 2. n. a native of the Polynesian islands ‖ the group of Austronesian languages spoken there

po·ly·ni·a (pəlíni:ə) n. a lakelike patch of clear water in floating ice, esp. if found in the same area every year [Russ. *poluinya*]

pol·y·no·mi·al (pɒlinóumi:əl) 1. adj. (math., of an algebraic expression) having two or more terms 2. n. an expression of this kind [fr. Gk. *polu*, many + NOMIAL]

pol·y·o·ma virus (pɒli:óumə) (med.) a DNA virus associated with cancer in mammals. also polyoma

pol·y·o·mi·no (pɒli:əmí:nou) n. a multisided shape capable of covering many squares on a game board Cf PENTOMINO

pol·yp (pɒlip) n. any of various coelenterates, such as those building coral reefs, having tubular, hollow bodies and an anterior mouth surrounded by tentacles ‖ a projecting growth of hypertrophied mucous membrane, e.g. in the nasal passages [F. *polype* fr. L. fr. Gk fr. *polu*, many + *pous (podos)*, foot]

pol·y·par·y (pɒlipəri:) pl. **pol·y·par·ies** n. the common base and connecting tissue of a colony of polyps [fr. Mod. L. *polyparium* fr. *polypus*, polyp]

pol·y·pep·tide (pɒli:péptaid) n. any combination of several amino-acid molecules [fr. Gk *polu*, many + PEPTIDE]

pol·y·pet·al·ous (pɒli:pét'ləs) adj. (bot.) having separate or distinct petals (opp. GAMOPETALOUS) [fr. Gk *polu*, many + PETA-LOUS]

pol·y·phase (pɒli:feiz) adj. (elec.) having or producing two or more phases [fr. Gk *polu*, many + PHASE]

Pol·y·phe·mus (pɒlifí:məs) a one-eyed giant or Cyclops in Homer's 'Odyssey', who kept Odysseus and his companions prisoners. He ate two of his prisoners each day, until Odysseus made him drunk and blinded him

pol·y·phon·ic (pɒli:fónik) adj. (mus.) comprising two or more melodies combined ‖ (of musical instruments, e.g. the piano) able to sound more than one note at a time ‖ consisting of many sounds ‖ (phon.) representing more than one vocal sound by the same symbol or group of symbols **po·lyph·o·nous** (pɒlífənəs) adj. [fr. Gk *poluphōnos* fr. *polu*, many + *phōnē*, sound]

po·lyph·o·ny (pɒlífəni:) n. (mus.) composition in two or more concurrent and harmonizing parts or voices (cf. HOMOPHONY) ‖ (phon.) the use of one written character to represent more than one sound [fr. Gk *poluphōnia*]

pol·y·phy·let·ic (pɒli:failétik) adj. (biol.) combining the characteristics of more than one ancestral line, e.g. by convergence [fr. Gk *polu*, many + *phuletēs*, of the same clan]

pol·y·pide (pɒli:paid) n. a single polyp, an individual of a zooid colony [POLYP]

pol·y·ploid (pɒli:plɔid) 1. adj. with a reduplication of the chromosome number, e.g. triploid, tetraploid etc., i.e. having three, four etc. times the normal haploid or gametic number 2. n. an organism with more than two sets of chromosomes **pol·y·plói·dic** (pɒli:plɔ́idik) adj. **pol·y·ploi·dy** n. a manifold arrangement of chromosomes, esp. when this is induced to enhance the size and vigor of plants [fr. Gk *polu*, many + *ploos*, fold]

pol·y·poid (pɒli:pɔid) adj. of or like a polyp [POLYP]

pol·y·pro·pyl·ene [C₃H₅] (pɒli:próupəli:n) n. a thermoplastic resin that is a moisture-resistant, hard, tough plastic used to make molded objects in plates, fibers, film, rope and toys; manufactured by Hercules, Inc.

pol·yp·ter·id (pɒlíptərid) n. a member of fam. *Polypteridae*, primitive, tropical African river fishes having long bodies, ganoid scales and one characteristic dorsal fin separated into a series of spines [fr. Mod. L. *Polypterus*, the type genus, fr. Gk *polu*, many + *pteron*, wing]

pol·y·pus (pɒləpəs) pl. **pol·y·pi** (pɒləpai), **pol·y·pus·es** n. a polyp (projecting growth) [L. fr. Gk *polu*, many + *pous (podos)*, foot]

pol·y·ri·bo·some (pɒli:ráibəsoum) n. a cluster of the cell particles held together by a single messenger RNA that synthesize proteins and enzymes. also polysome. —**pol·y·ri·bo·som·al** adj.

pol·y·sac·cha·ride (pɒli:sǽkəraid) n. one of a class of carbohydrates which are decomposable by hydrolysis into two or more molecules of monosaccharides and which include the oligosaccharides as well as high-molecular-weight polymeric substances of complex and often indeterminate structure (e.g. glycogen, starch, cellulose) [fr. Gk *polu*, many + SACCHARIDE]

pol·y·sor·bates (pɒli:sɔ́rbeits) n. (chem.) group of fatty-acid esters used as emulsifying, dispersing and solubilizing agents in production of certain foods and drugs

pol·y·sty·rene (pɒli:stáiri:n) n. a transparent rigid thermoplastic used in making containers and other molded products, e.g. refrigerators [fr. Gk *polu*, many + STYRENE]

pol·y·syl·lab·ic (pɒli:silǽbik) adj. having more than three syllables **pol·y·syl·láb·i·cal** adj. [fr. M.L. *polysyllabus* fr. Gk *polu*, many + *sullabē*, syllable]

pol·y·syl·la·ble (pɒlisíləb'l, pɒlisílɒb'l) n. a polysyllabic word [fr. M.L. *polysyllaba* fr. Gk fr. *polu*, many + *sullabē*, syllable]

polysystemicism (linguistics) *FIRTHIAN

pol·y·tech·nic (pɒli:téknik) 1. adj. of or pertaining to instruction in a number or technical subjects 2. n. a school giving instruction of this kind **pol·y·téch·ni·cal** adj. **pol·y·tech·ní·cian** n. [F. *polytechnique* fr. Gk fr. *polu*, many + an art]

pol·y·the·ism (pɒliθi:izəm, pɒliθí:izəm) n. belief in or worship of more than one god **pól·y·the·ist** n. **pol·y·the·ís·tic** adj. [F. *polythéisme* fr. Gk fr. *polu*, many + *theos*, god]

pol·y·thene (pɒliθi:n) n. polyethylene

pol·y·to·nal·i·ty (pɒli:tounǽliti:) n. (mus.) the simultaneous use of two or more keys, or the effect of this [fr. Gk *polu*, many + TONALITY]

pol·y·troph·ic (pɒli:trófik) adj. (bacteriol.) obtaining nourishment from more than one organic substance or organism [fr. Gk *polutrophos* fr. *polu*, many + *trophos*, feeder]

pol·y·un·sat·u·rate (pɒli:ʌnsǽtʃəreit) n. (chem.) an oil or fatty acid containing more than one double or triple bond and therefore cholesterol-defensive, e.g., certain fish and vegetable oils. —**pol·y·un·sat·u·rat·ed** adj.

pol·y·va·lence (pɒli:véiləns) n. the state of being polyvalent

pol·y·va·lent (pɒli:véilənt, pəlívələnt) adj. (bacteriol.) containing antibodies able to counteract more than one kind of microorganism ‖ (chem.) having a valence of more than 1 (cf. MULTIVALENT) [fr. Gk *polu*, many + VALENT]

polyversity *MULTIVERSITY

pol·y·vi·nyl (pɒli:váinil, pɒli:váin'l) adj. of a compound made by polymerizing a vinyl compound [fr. Gk *polu*, many + VINYL]

polyvinyl acetal any of several thermoplastic resins made by condensing polyvinyl alcohol with an aldehyde, and used chiefly in molded products and adhesives

polyvinyl acetate a polymer of vinyl acetate used esp. in adhesives, textile processes etc.

polyvinyl alcohol a polymer of vinyl alcohol, esp. a thermoplastic resin used in molded products, emulsifiers etc.

polyvinyl chloride a polymer of vinyl chloride, rigid unless plasticized, used for pipes, electrical insulation, films etc.

pol·y·zo·an (pɒli:zóuən) n. a bryozoan [fr. Gk *polu*, many + *zōon*, animal]

pol·y·zo·ar·i·um (pɒli:zouéari:əm) pl. **pol·y·zo·ar·i·a** (pɒli:zouéari:ə) n. (zool.) a bryozoan colony or its supporting skeleton [Mod. L. fr. *Polyzoa*, name of the class]

pol·y·zo·ic (pɒli:zóuik) adj. (zool.) comprising many zooids ‖ producing many sporozoites [fr. *Polyzoa*, name of the class of bryozoans]

pom·ace (pʌmis) n. a mass of apple pulp crushed for cider-making ‖ some other crushed or pulpy substance, e.g. seeds for oil [fr. L. *pomum*, apple]

po·ma·ceous (pouméiʃəs) adj. (bot.) of, relating to, or resembling a pome [fr. Mod. L. *pomaceus*]

po·made (pəméid, pəmáad) 1. n. a scented ointment for the hair 2. v.t. pres. part. **po·mad·ing** past and past part. **po·mad·ed** to apply pomade to [F. *pommade*]

po·man·der (poumǽndər, póumændər) n. (hist.) a ball of fragrant or aromatic substances carried as protection against infection ‖ (hist.) a metal ball containing this ‖ an orange pierced with cloves and dried, and hung in a wardrobe etc. for fragrance [earlier *pomamber* fr. O.F. *pomme d'embre*, apple of amber]

po·ma·to (pəméitou) *n.* (*agriculture*) hybrid potato and tomato

po·ma·tum (pəméitəm) *n.* a pomade [Mod. L. fr. L. *pomum*, apple, fruit]

Pom·bal (pɒmbál), Sebastião José de Carvalho e Mello, marquês de (1699–1782), Portuguese statesman. As foreign secretary (1750–77) to Joseph I, he was the effective ruler of Portugal. In an attempt to modernize the country, he limited the power of the Inquisition and the wealth of the Church, expelled the Jesuits (1759), encouraged trade and replanned Lisbon after the earthquake of 1755

pome (poum) *n.* (*bot.*) a fruit, e.g. an apple, having a seed-containing core enclosed within a cartilaginous capsule and surrounded by the fleshy, edible receptacle [O.F.=apple, fruit]

pome·gran·ate (pɒmgrænit, pɒmígrænit) *n. Punica granatum*, fam. *Punicaceae*, a small shrubby tree, native to Asia and Africa ‖ its edible, orange-sized fruit, consisting of a succulent crimson pulp containing many seeds and enclosed in a tough golden red rind [O.F. *pome grenade, grenate* fr. *pome*, apple, fruit+*grenade, grenate*, seeded, grained]

pom·e·lo (pɒ́məlou) *pl.* **pom·e·los** *n.* a shaddock ‖ a grapefruit [origin unknown]

Pom·er·a·ni·a (pɒməréini:ə) a region bordering the Baltic on both sides of the Oder in N.W. Poland and N.E. East Germany. It was inhabited by German tribes, and conquered by Slavs by the 10th c. The western part was colonized by Germans, became a duchy of the Holy Roman Empire (1181), passed to Sweden (1648) and was taken by Prussia (1720 and 1815). Most of this became the German state of Mecklenburg (1945). The eastern part passed to Prussia (1648) and was taken by Poland (1945)

Pom·er·a·ni·an (pɒməréini:ən) 1. *adj.* of or relating to Pomerania or its people 2. *n.* a native or inhabitant of Pomerania ‖ a small black, white or brown dog of a breed having a pointed muzzle, erect ears, upturned tail and long silky hair

pom·mel (pʌ́məl) 1. *n.* a knob on a sword hilt ‖ a knoblike projection on the front of a saddle 2. *v.t. pres. part.* **pom·mel·ing**, esp. *Br.* **pom·mel·ling** *past* and *past part.* **pom·meled**, esp. *Br.* **pom·melled** to pummel [O.F. *pomel*, dim. of *pome*, apple]

po·mo·log·i·cal (poumələ́dʒik'l) *adj.* of or relating to pomology

po·mol·o·gist (poumɒ́lədʒist) *n.* a person who cultivates fruit professionally [POMOLOGY]

po·mol·o·gy (poumɒ́lədʒi:) *n.* the science and practice of fruit cultivation [fr. Mod. L. *pomologia* fr. *pomum*, apple, fruit+Gk *logos*, word]

pomp (pɒmp) *n.* splendor in display, esp. ceremonial magnificence [F. *pompe* fr. L. fr. Gk *pompē*, procession]

Pom·pa·dour (pɔ̃pædu:r, pɒ́mpədɔr, pɒ́mpəduər), Jeanne Antoinette Poisson, marquise de (1721–64), mistress of Louis XV of France (from 1745), over whom and over whose government she wielded great influence. She is thought to have been instrumental in forming the Austrian alliance which involved France in the Seven Years' War. She spent prodigally, but patronized writers and artists, and founded the royal porcelain factory at Sèvres

pom·pa·dour (pɒ́mpədɔr, pɒ́mpədɔr, pɒ́mpəduər) *n.* a woman's hairstyle in which the hair is drawn in a high roll up over the forehead ‖ a man's hairstyle in which the hair is brushed straight up and back from the forehead [after the marquise de POMPADOUR]

pom·pa·no (pɒ́mpənou) *pl.* **pom·pa·no**, **pom·pa·nos** *n. Trachinotus carolinus.* fam. *Carangidae*, an edible fish of the S. Atlantic and Gulf coasts of North America [Span. *pámpano*]

Pom·peii (pɒmpéi, pɒmpéii:) an ancient Roman port and resort (now inland) in Campania, Italy, near Naples, buried by a sudden eruption of Vesuvius (79). Excavations have uncovered many buildings with their walls nearly intact, wall paintings, mosaics, furniture etc.

Pom·pei·us (pɒmpéiəs), Sextus (75–35 B.C.), Roman soldier, son of Pompey. He attempted to avenge his father's death, was defeated (36 B.C.) by the future Emperor Augustus, and killed

Pom·pey (pɒ́mpi:) (Gnaeus Pompeius Magnus, 106–48 B.C.), Roman soldier and statesman. He distinguished himself as a general and became consul (70 B.C.). He decisively defeated Mithridates VI (66 B.C.) and annexed Syria and Pales-

tine. He formed the 1st Triumvirate with Crassus and Caesar (60 B.C.) but broke with Caesar (54 B.C.), was defeated by him at Pharsalus (48 B.C.) and assassinated on arrival in Egypt. He had great military ability but was irresolute in politics

Pom·pi·dou (pɒmpi:du:), Georges (1911–74), French statesman. He was prime minister (1962–8) and president of the republic (1969–74). He died in office

pom·pom (pɒ́mpɒm) *n.* an automatic antiaircraft gun firing explosive shells, mounted on ships' decks in pairs, fours or eights

pom·pon (pɒ́mpɒn, pɔ̃pɔ̃) *n.* a small, brightly colored ball usually of yarn used for ornamenting women's and children's hats, sailors' caps etc. ‖ a dwarf cabbage rose ‖ any of several varieties of chrysanthemum or dahlia bearing small round flowers [F.=a tuft, topknot]

pom·pos·i·ty (pɒmpɒ́siti:) *pl.* **pom·pos·i·ties** *n.* the quality of being full of self-importance ‖ an instance of behavior revealing this [fr. M.L. *pompositas*]

pomp·ous (pɒ́mpəs) *adj.* (of people) full of ridiculous self-importance ‖ (of language) inflated, pretentious [O.F. *pompeux*]

Pon·ce (pɒ́nθe) the chief Caribbean port (pop. 188,219) of Puerto Rico. Industries: sugar, rum, textiles. Spanish fort, cathedral. University of Santa Maria (Roman Catholic, 1948)

ponce (pɒns) *n.* (*Br., pop.*) a pimp [origin unknown]

Pon·ce de Le·ón (pɒ́nθeðeleɔ́n, pɒ́nsdəlí:oun), Juan (c. 1460–1521), Spanish explorer. He was governor of Puerto Rico (1509–12) and explored the coast of Florida (1513), claiming it for Spain

pon·cho (pɒ́ntʃou) *pl.* **pon·chos** *n.* a Spanish-American cloak like a blanket with a central slit for the head ‖ a waterproof garment made like this [Span. fr. Araucan]

pond (pɒnd) *n.* a small area of still water, in a natural or contrived hollow‖ an area of water smaller than a lake [M.E. *ponde*, var. of POUND]

pon·der (pɒ́ndər) *v.i.* (often with 'on' or 'over') to meditate, be absorbed in thought ‖ *v.t.* to consider carefully, *to ponder a problem* [O. F. *ponderer*]

pon·der·a·bil·i·ty (pɒndərəbíliti:) *n.* the state or quality of being ponderable

pon·der·a·ble (pɒ́ndərəb'l) *adj.* able to be weighed ‖ able to be assessed, *a ponderable influence* [fr. L. L. *ponderabilis*]

pon·der·ous (pɒ́ndərəs) *adj.* (of style or manner) lacking ease and a light touch, *ponderous wit* ‖ (of movement) slow, lumbering ‖ (*rhet.*, of weights) very heavy [fr. F. *pondéreux*]

Pon·di·cher·ry (pɒndítʃéri:) (F. Pondichéry) a seaport (pop. 60,000) on the Coromandel coast of India comprising, with Karikal, Mahé and Yanaon, a Union Territory (total area 186 sq. miles, pop. 570,000) of India. Official language: French. Pondicherry was the chief settlement of French India (1674–1954), but was taken by the Dutch (1693–7) and by the British (1761–3, 1778–83, 1793–1802 and 1803–16)

Pon·do·land (pɒ́ndəlænd) *TRANSKEIAN TERRITORIES

pond scum any floating filamentous alga of fam. *Zygnemataceae*, esp. the genus *Spirogyra*

pond·weed (pɒ́ndwi:d) *n.* any of several species of *Potomogeton*, fam. *Potamogetonaceae*, a genus of aquatic plants

pone (poun) *n.* cornmeal bread shaped into ovals, then fried or baked [fr. Algonquian=bread]

pon·gee (pɒndʒí:, pʌndʒí:) *n.* a thin, soft, silk fabric of Chinese origin having its natural écru color [fr. N. Chin. *pun-chi*, domestic loom]

pons (pɒnz) *n.* the pons Varolii [L.=bridge]

pons as·i·no·rum (pɒnzæsinɔ́rəm, pɒnzæsinóurəm) *n.* the fifth proposition of the first book of Euclid ‖ anything that beginners find hard to understand

pons Va·ro·li·i (pɒnzvəróuli:ai) *n.* that part the brainstem (*BRAIN) at the anterior end of the medulla oblongata transmitting impulses between the cerebrum and cerebellum [Mod. L.=bridge of Varoli, after Costanzo *Varoli* (1542-75), Italian anatomist]

Pon·te·ve·dra (pɒntevédra) a province (area 1,695 sq. miles, pop. 859,897) of N.W. Spain (*GALICIA) ‖ its capital (pop. 47,000)

Pon·ti (pɒ́nti:), Gio (Giovanni Ponti, 1891–1979), Italian architect. He is best known for

the Pirelli skyscraper, Milan (1955–9), designed in collaboration with Nervi

Pon·ti·ac (pɒ́nti:æk) (c. 1720–69), Ottawa Indian chief who led (1763–5) Pontiac's Rebellion. This brought together the most powerful Indian coalition in Indian history to resist the white man. Pontiac signed (1766) a formal peace treaty with the British which permitted peaceful coexistence

Pon·ti·a·nak (pɒnti:ánɑk) the chief port and commercial center (pop. 217,555) of W. Kalimantan, Indonesia

pon·ti·fex (pɒ́nti:feks) *pl.* **pon·tif·i·ces** (pɒntífisi:z) *n.* (*Rom. hist.*) a priest of the principal college of priests (cf. FLAMEN) [L.]

pon·tiff (pɒntif) *n.* the pope ‖ a bishop ‖ a pontifex [F. *pontife*]

pon·tif·i·cal (pɒntífik'l) 1. *adj.* of or relating to a pontiff ‖ celebrated by a bishop, *pontifical mass* ‖ absurdly dogmatic or pretentious, *pontifical utterances* 2. *n.* a book setting out the forms for sacraments and rites performed by a bishop ‖ (*pl.*) vestments and insignia worn by a bishop when he celebrates a pontifical mass [fr. L. *pontificalis*]

pon·tif·i·cate 1. (pɒntífikeit) *v.i. pres. part.* **pon·tif·i·cat·ing** *past* and *past part.* **pon·tif·i·cat·ed** (of a pope or bishop) to officiate at a pontifical mass ‖ (of a person) to act in an absurdly solemn and dogmatic way 2. (pɒntífikit, pɒntífikeit) *n.* the office or term of office of a pope or bishop [fr. L. *pontificare* (*pontificatus*)]

pontifices *pl.* of PONTIFEX

pon·til (pɒ́ntil) *n.* a punty [F. fr. Ital. *pontello*, dim. of *punto*, point]

Pon·tine marshes (pɒ́ntain) (*Ital.* Agro pontino) a narrow plain near the coast of S. Latium, Italy, beginning 25 miles southeast of Rome. The Romans and various popes tried to drain its malarial marshes, but this was not achieved until 1926, under Mussolini

Pon·tius Pilate (pɒ́nʃəs) *PILATE, Pontius

pon·ton (pɒ́ntən) *n.* (*mil.*) a pontoon [F.]

pon·to·nier, pon·to·neer (pɒntəníər) *n.* (*mil.*) a military engineer who builds pontoon bridges [F. *pontonnier*]

pon·toon (pɒntú:n) *n.* a flat-bottomed boat or a metal cylinder used in quantity to support a temporary bridge ‖ in a low, flat boat carrying equipment for sinking shafts at sea, raising sunken ships etc. ‖ a float of an aircraft [F. *ponton*]

pontoon *n.* (*Br.*) blackjack (card game)

pontoon bridge (*mil.*) a temporary bridge supported by pontoons

Pon·tus (pɒ́ntəs) an ancient country of N.E. Asia Minor, occupying what is now the Turkish Black Sea coast east of the Kizil Irmak. It developed in the 4th c. B.C. and, under Mithridates VI (c. 115–63 B.C.), extended its power over all Asia Minor, but was crushed by the Romans (mid-1st c. B.C.)

po·ny (póuni:) *pl.* **po·nies** *n.* a small, sturdy horse of any of several breeds measuring up to 14 to 14 ½ hands in height, or (*Br.*) 13 hands or, in the case of polo ponies, 15 hands ‖ (*pop.*) a literal translation used by students, a crib ‖ (*pop.*) a small liqueur glass, or the amount it holds ‖ (*Br., pop.*) the sum of £25 [Scot. *powny*, prob. fr. F.]

pony car (*automobile*) a small, sporty, two-door hardtop named for an animal, e.g. Mustang, Pinto

pony express (*Am. hist.*) a system of mail transport and delivery by riders on fast ponies (esp. beween St Joseph, Mo. and Sacramento, Calif., 1860-1)

poo·dle (pú:d'l) *n.* a dog of a highly intelligent, playful breed, having tight-curling, solid-color hair. They make excellent gundogs, but are usually kept as pets. There are standard, miniature and toy varieties [G. *pudel* fr. L.G. *pudeln*, to splash in water]

pooh (pu:) *interj.* used to indicate contempt, impatience, disdain etc.

pooh-pooh (pu:pú:) *v.t.* to make light of, *he pooh-poohed her fears* ‖ to dismiss with contempt, *he pooh-poohed the suggestion* [pooh (an expression of contempt or impatience)]

pool (pu:l) *n.* a small body of fresh water ‖ a small body of standing water or other liquid, *a pool of blood* ‖ a deep, cool, quiet spot in a stream or river ‖ a swimming pool [O.E. *pōl*]

pool 1. *n.* (*gambling*) the total of sums staked and (sometimes) of fines paid in, all to be taken by the winner, or divided among several win-

CONCISE PRONUNCIATION KEY: **(a)** æ, c*at*; ɑ, c*ar*; ɔ f*aw*n; ei, sn*a*ke. **(e)** e, h*e*n; i:, sh*ee*p; iə, d*ee*r; ɛə, b*ea*r. **(i)** i, f*i*sh; ai, t*i*ger; ə:, b*i*rd. **(o)** o, *o*x; au, c*ow*; ou, g*oa*t; u, p*oo*r; ɔi, r*oy*al. **(u)** ʌ, d*u*ck; u, b*u*ll; u:, g*oo*se; ə, b*a*cillus; ju:, c*u*be. x, lo*ch*; θ, *th*ink; ð, bo*th*er; z, *Z*en; ʒ, cor*s*age; dʒ, sa*v*age; ŋ, ora*ng*utan*g*; j, *y*ak; ʃ, *f*ish; tʃ, fe*tch*; 'l, rabb*le*; 'n, redd*en*. Complete pronunciation key appears inside front cover.

ners ‖ **pocket billiards** ‖ (*Br.*) a game of billiards in which each player contributes to the stake, the winner gaining the whole ‖ (*commerce*) a combination of resources for some common enterprise or for removing competition, manipulating prices etc. ‖ (*commerce*) a fund common to various undertakings on a basis of shared profits and liabilities ‖ a source of supply to which members of a group or organization have access, *a transport pool, a typists' pool* ‖ (*fencing*) a competition in which each member of a team successively engages each member of another team **2.** *v.t.* to contribute (something) to a common fund, *pool resources, to pool ideas* [F. *poule*, stakes in a game]

Pool of London the Thames just below Tower Bridge, the furthest point up the river for oceangoing vessels. The Port of London begins here, with London Docks on the north side

pool·room (púːlruːm, púːlrum) *n.* a usually public room where pool and other games are played

pool table a billiard table equipped with pockets, on which various games of pool are played

Poo·na (púːnə) a commercial center (pop. 856,100) of W. Maharashtra, India, in the Deccan, 80 miles southeast of Bombay. Industries: textiles, paper, chemicals. Maratha palace, temples. University (1948)

poop (puːp) **1.** *n.* a raised, sometimes enclosed deck at the stern of a ship ‖ the stern of a ship **2.** *v.t.* (of a wave) to break over the stern of (a ship) ‖ to ship (a wave) over the stern [O.F. *pupe*, L.L. *puppa* for L. *puppis*, poop, stern]

poop·er-scoop·er (púːpərskúːpər) *n.* an instrument for manual removal of dog excrement from a sidewalk or street

Po·o·pó, Lake (pɔɔpɔ́) a lake (60 miles long) in W. central Bolivia, at 12,000 ft

poor (puər) **1.** *adj.* having little money, few possessions and no luxuries ‖ of, relating to, or characterized by poverty, *a poor place* ‖ meager, *poor attendance* ‖ showing small yield, *a poor harvest* ‖ (of soil) unproductive ‖ inferior, *a poor speaker, poor work* ‖ (of a person) failing to arouse respect ‖ to be pitied, *the poor child cried all night* ‖ in bad condition through underfeeding **2.** *n.* **the poor** poor people collectively [O.F. *povre, poure*]

poor boy a tightly fitting sweater with a ribbed weave

Poor Clares *CLARE, ST, *FRANCISCAN

poor·house (púərhaus) *pl.* **poor·hous·es** (púərhauziz) *n.* (*Am. hist.*) a public institution sheltering and caring for homeless and poor people

Poor Knights of Christ *KNIGHT TEMPLAR

poor·ly (púərliː) **1.** *adv.* inadequately, *poorly fed* **to think poorly of** to have a low opinion of **2.** *adj.* not in good health but not seriously ill

poor-mouth (púərmauθ) *v.* to portray oneself as a poor person

poor white a white person who lives in squalid poverty, esp. in the southern U.S.A.

pop (pɔp) **1.** *n.* a small, sharp, explosive sound, *the pop of a toy pistol* ‖ an effervescent nonalcoholic drink **in pop** (*Br., pop.*) in pawn **2.** *v. pres. part.* **pop·ping** *past* and *past part.* **popped** *v.t.* to cause to make a sharp explosive sound ‖ to cause to burst open with a sharp explosive sound, *to pop corn* ‖ to place quickly, *to pop a peanut into one's mouth* ‖ (*Br., pop.*) to pawn ‖ *v.i.* to move, come, enter etc., suddenly or unexpectedly or for a short time, *to pop in to see someone* ‖ (of the eyes) to protrude, or seem to protrude, from the sockets ‖ to explode with a sharp sound **to pop the question** (*pop.*) to propose marriage **3.** *adv.* with a pop ‖ like a pop [imit.]

pop *adj.* of or pertaining to popular music, *pop singer* or pop art [by shortening]

pop *adj.* (*pop.*) father [short for *poppa*, var. of PAPA]

pop art an art style derived from posters and comic strips and depicting objects of everyday life

pop·corn (pɔ́pkɔrn) *n. Zea mays everta*, a variety of corn, the kernels of which burst open with a pop when heated in butter or oil ‖ these popped kernels

Pope (poup), Alexander (1688–1744), English poet. The publication of 'An Essay on Criticism' (1711) established him as a master of didactic poetry and of the heroic couplet. 'The Rape of the Lock' (1712, 1714) is a mock-heroic epic ridiculing the society of his time. 'An Epistle to Dr Arbuthnot' (1735) is a bitter but scintillating

attack on Addison and 'The Dunciad' (1728, with an added book IV 1742) is a virulent satire on the literary critics of the day. Pope made the heroic couplet a supremely supple form. The repertory of diction provided e.g. by his translation of Homer (on which he worked 1715–26) was to be predominant up to the Romantic age. His poetry was essentially of the intellect, and in its conversational tone, moral concern and exuberant conceits of fancy it belongs in the tradition of Donne and Marvell. But another side of his work, seen e.g. in 'Windsor Forest' (1713) and 'Eloisa to Abelard', inspired sentiment of a kind which helped to bring in the Romantic movement

pope *n.* the head of the Roman Catholic Church ‖ (*Orthodox Eastern Church*) a parish priest [O.E. *pāpa* fr. L. fr. G k fr. *pappas*, father]

pop·er·y (póupəriː) *n.* a hostile term for the Roman Catholic religion and practices [POPE]

pop·eye (pɔ́pai) *n.* (*mil.*) in air intercept, a code meaning 'in clouds or area of reduced visibility'

pop·eyed (pɔ́paid) *adj.* having protruding eyes

pop·gun (pɔ́pgʌn) *n.* a toy gun which fires corks, pellets etc. by air compression

pop·in·jay (pɔ́pindʒei) *n.* (*rhet.*) a silly, mannered, conceited fop [M.E. *papegai, papejai* fr. O. F. *papegai*, parrot]

pop·ish (póupiʃ) *adj.* a hostile term for Roman Catholic [POPE]

Popish Plot *OATES, TITUS

pop·lar (pɔ́plər) *n.* a member of *Populus*, fam. *Salicaceae*, a genus of trees native to the northern hemisphere ‖ the wood of these trees, used for crates, paper pulp etc. [O.F. *poplier*]

pop·lin (pɔ́plin) *n.* a tightly woven fabric, frequently of mercerized cotton, used for shirts, pajamas etc. [F. *popeline* fr. Ital.]

pop·lit·e·al (pɔplítiːəl) *adj.* (*anat.*) of or relating to the hollow behind the knee joint [fr. L. *poples* (*poplitis*), the ham]

Po·po·ca·te·petl (poupoukátépet'l) a perpetually snowcapped volcano (17,887 ft) of central Mexico, visible from Mexico City 36 miles away

pop·out (pɔ́paut) *n.* book illustration that rises when the page is turned

Po·pov (pʌpɔ́f), Alexsandr Stepanovic (1859–1905), Russian physicist, a pioneer in radiotelegraphy. He invented a detector for wireless waves and was the first to use a suspended wire as an aerial

pop·o·ver (pɔ́pouvər) *n.* a puffy, light muffin having a hollow center caused by the intense heat of baking [it pops up over the rim of the baking tin]

pop·pet (pɔ́pit) *n.* (*Br.*) a term of endearment, esp. for a little child (*engin.*) a lathe head ‖ a valve that moves up out of and down into its port ‖ (*naut.*) any of several stout pieces of wood used for various purposes, e.g. to support the hull of a vessel before launching [M.E. *popet, popette* fr. Romanic *puppa* fr. L. *pupa*, a girl]

pop·ping crease (pɔ́piŋ) (*cricket*) a line 4 ft in front of the wicket and parallel to it, within which the batsman must stand to receive the ball

pop·ple (pɔ́p'l) **1.** *n.* a heaving or wild tumbling of water **2.** *v.i. pres. part.* **pop·pling** *past* and *past part.* **pop·pled** (of water) to toss or heave, e.g. in a choppy sea [prob. imit.]

pop·py (pɔ́piː) *pl.* **pop·pies** *n.* a member of *Papaver*, fam. *Papaveraceae*, a genus of annual, biennial and perennial plants usually containing white latex. They have showy white, yellow or red flowers, and many light seeds in a capsule ‖ the flower of any of these plants ‖ an extract made from poppy juice, used in pharmacy ‖ the color of a red poppy [O.E. *popæg* fr. L.]

pop·py·cock (pɔ́pikɔk) *n.* (*pop.*) nonsense, foolish talk [etym. doubtful]

pop·py·head (pɔ́pihed) *n.* (*archit.*) the raised ornament on the tops of ends of church seats in Gothic carving

poppy seed the seed of the poppy used esp. as a topping for rolls and other baked goods

POPS (*electr. acronym*) **p**antograph **o**ptical **p**rojection **s**ystem, a system for plotting radar data on a board by marking (with a grease pencil) the points of light in a projection of the target. *Cf* DOPS, TOPS

pop top *adj.* of a can with a self-contained ring that creates an opening when pulled. *also* ring top. *Cf* ZIP TOP

pop·u·lace (pɔ́pjuləs) *n.* (*rhet.*) the common people, the masses [F. fr. Ital.]

pop·u·lar (pɔ́pjulər) *adj.* liked or admired by people in general, *a popular actress*, or by a particular group or section, *a popular student* ‖ adapted to the tastes, understanding or needs of people in general, *popular science* ‖ (*commerce*) cheap, *popular prices* ‖ of, relating to or carried on by the people in general, *a popular election* ‖ commonly held, prevalent, *popular opinions* [fr. L. *popularis* fr. *populus*, people]

popular front a coalition of left-wing political parties usually against a common opponent

pop·u·lar·ist (pɔ́pjulərist) *adj.* of someone who appeals to a wide public

pop·u·lar·i·ty (pɔpjulæritiː) *n.* the state or quality of being popular [F. *popularité*]

pop·u·lar·i·za·tion (pɔpjulərizéiʃən) *n.* a popularizing or being popularized

pop·u·lar·ize (pɔ́pjuləraiz) *pres. part.* **pop·u·lar·iz·ing** *past* and *past part.* **pop·u·lar·ized** *v.t.* to cause (a commercial product) to become widely known and adopted ‖ to cause (a resort etc.) to become popular ‖ to present (e.g. a technical subject) in a form easily understood by people in general [POPULAR]

popular sovereignty the political concept that sovereign power is vested in the people ‖ (*Am. hist.*) the doctrine (introduced by Senator Lewis Cass of Michigan in opposition to the Wilmot Proviso as a means of settling the slavery question) stipulating that the citizens of each territory should decide for themselves whether or not slavery should be permitted in their territory. Its most famous champion was Stephen A. Douglas

pop·u·late (pɔ́pjuleit) *pres. part.* **pop·u·lat·ing** *past* and *past part.* **pop·u·lat·ed** *v.t.* to provide with inhabitants, *an effort to populate Siberia* ‖ to inhabit, *heavily populated bird sanctuaries* [fr. M.L. *populare* (*populatus*)]

pop·u·la·tion (pɔpjuléiʃən) *n.* the inhabitants of a country, town etc. ‖ the total number of these ‖ a specified group of people of a country or area, *the working-class population* ‖ the act or process of supplying with inhabitants ‖ (*statistics*) a group of individuals or items ‖ (*biol.*) all the organisms living in a particular area [fr. L.L. *populatio* (*populationis*)]

population explosion a rapid geometric increase in a population

population inversion (*phys.*) condition in which electrons of an atomic system are more numerous than electrons on an associated lower-energy state

Pop·u·list (pɔ́pjulist) *n.* (*Am. hist.*) a member of a political party (1891 - c. 1900) advocating the free coinage of silver, a graduated income tax and government control of railroads ‖ (*Russ. hist.*) a member of a political movement (c. 1870-81) which attempted to spread revolutionary socialist ideas among the peasantry

pop·u·lous (pɔ́pjuləs) *adj.* densely populated [fr. L. *populosus*]

pop wine sweet, fruit-flavored wine

por·bea·gle (pɔ́rbiːg'l) *n. Lamna nasus* or *L. cornubica*, fam. *Lamnidae*, a fierce, viviparous shark reaching 8 ft in length, found in northern seas, and distinguished by its crescent-shaped tail [Cornish, perh. fr. F.]

por·ce·lain (pɔ́rslin, póurslin) **1.** *n.* fine, translucent nonporous ceramic ware made of quartz, feldspar and kaolin, and used esp. for tableware ‖ (*pl.*) articles made of this **2.** *adj.* made of porcelain [F. fr. Ital.]

por·cel·la·ne·ous, **por·cel·la·ne·ous** (pɔrsəléiniːəs, poursəléiniːəs) *adj.* of, relating to, or resembling porcelain [fr. Ital. *porcellana*, porcelain]

por·cel·la·nous, **por·cel·la·nous** (pɔrsəléinəs, poursəléinəs) *adj.* porcelaneous

porch (pɔrtʃ) *n.* the covered entrance of a building jutting out from the main wall ‖ an open, roofed gallery extending along a side of a house, used for sitting out on, or giving access to rooms [O.F. *porche*]

por·cine (pɔ́rsain, pɔ́rsin) *adj.* of, relating to, or resembling a pig

por·cu·pine (pɔ́rkjupain) *n.* any of several vegetarian rodents constituting the Old World terrestrial fam. *Hystricidae* and the New World arboreal fam. *Erthizontidae*, measuring about 2 ft in length, and having the body covered with brown or black barbed spines intermixed with stiff hairs [M.E. *porkepyne, porke despyne* fr. O.F. *porc espin, porke despyne*]

pore (pɔr, pour) *pres. part.* **por·ing** *past* and *past part.* **pored** *v.i.* (only in) **to pore over** to study intently, *to pore over a manuscript* ‖ to think

CONCISE PRONUNCIATION KEY: **(a)** æ, c*a*t; ɑ, c*a*r; ɔ f*aw*n; ei, sn*a*ke. **(e)** e, h*e*n; iː, sh*ee*p; iə, d*ee*r; ɛə, b*ea*r. **(i)** i, f*i*sh; ai, t*i*ger; əː, b*i*rd. **(o)** o, *o*x; au, c*ow*; ou, g*oa*t; u, p*oo*r; ɔi, r*oy*al. **(u)** ʌ, d*u*ck; u, b*u*ll; uː, g*oo*se; ə, b*a*cillus; juː, c*u*be. x, lo*ch*; θ, *th*ink; ð, bo*th*er; z, *Z*en; ʒ, cor*s*age; dʒ, sava*g*e; ŋ, ora*n*gutan*g*; j, *y*ak; ʃ, *f*i*sh*; tʃ, fe*tch*; 'l, rabb*le*; 'n, redde*n*. Complete pronunciation key appears inside front cover.

deeply about, *to pore over a problem* [origin unknown]

pore *n.* a minute opening or interstice, esp. in mammalian skin, through which fluids, e.g. sweat, pass || a similar opening in plant tissue through which respiration etc. takes place [F. fr. L. fr. Gk]

por·gy (pórdʒi:) *pl.* **por·gies, por·gy** *n. Pagrus pagrus,* fam. *Sparidae,* a widely distributed edible fish, having a plump, oval body, crimson-colored and blue-spotted || any of various related marine fish [etym. doubtful]

po·rif·er·an (porífərən, pourífərən) 1. *n.* any of various members of the phylum *Porifera,* comprising the sponges 2. *adj.* of or belonging to this phylum [fr. L. *porus,* pore + -*fer,* bearing]

pork (pork, pourk) *n.* hog's flesh (fresh or cured) as food [O.F. *porc*]

pork barrel (*pop.*) funds appropriated from the federal treasury, e.g. for local improvements, primarily to ingratiate political representatives with their constituents

pork·er (pórkər, póurkər) *n.* a hog, esp. one bred and fattened for food

pork·pie (pórkpai, póurkpai) *n.* a hat with a round flat crown

porn (porn) *n.* (*slang*) short for pornography. — **porn, porno, porny** *adj.*

por·nog·ra·pher (pornágrəfər) *n.* a person who writes etc. pornography

por·no·graph·ic (pornəgræfik) *adj.* of, relating to, or characterized by pornography

por·nog·ra·phy (pornágrəfi) *n.* obscene literature, photographs, paintings etc., intended to cause sexual excitement || the treating of obscene subjects in art, literature etc. [fr. Gk *pornographos,* writing of harlots]

por·no·to·pia (pornətóupiːə) *n.* (*slang*) an idyllic place for sexual activities

po·ro·mer·ic (porəmérik) *adj.* (*chem.*) of a group of polyurethane-based, synthetic porous leathers used for upper parts of shoes, e.g., Corfam

Po·ron·gos Lakes (poróŋgos) a salt swamp area with no outlet, in N. central Argentina, north of Mar Chiquita

po·ros·i·ty (porósiti:, pourósiti:) *n.* the state or quality of being porous [fr. M.L. *porositas*]

po·rous (pórəs, póurəs) *adj.* full of pores, permeable [fr. L. *porus,* pore]

por·phy·rin (pórfərin) *n.* any of a group of naturally occurring complex heterocyclic compounds that play an important role in the respiratory processes of plants and animals. They are found (e.g. in chlorophyll or in the nonprotein portion of hemoglobin) usually in combination with metal ions (e.g. magnesium or iron) [fr. Gk *porphura,* purple]

por·phy·rit·ic (porfərítik) *adj.* of or relating to porphyry || (*geol.*) like porphyry [fr. M.L. *porphyriticus*]

Por·phy·ry (pórfəri:) (223–305), Greek philosopher. A pupil of Plotinus, he wrote a 15-volume treatise condemning Christianity. Only fragments of this survive

por·phy·ry (pórfəri:) *pl.* **por·phy·ries** *n.* (*hist.*) a hard rock once quarried in ancient Egypt, made up of white or red feldspar crystals embedded in a compact red or purple glassy base || (*geol.*) any igneous or unstratified rock made up of a homogeneous base in which mineral crystals are embedded [fr. Gk *porphuros,* purple]

por·poise (pórpəs) *n.* any of various members of *Phocaena,* fam. *Delphinidae,* a genus of toothed whales, 5-8 ft in length, having a blunt snout. *P. phocaena,* inhabiting the N. Atlantic and Pacific, is the most commonly known [M.E. *porpays, porpoys* fr. O.F.]

por·rect (pərékt) 1. *v.t.* (*eccles. law*) to submit, tender (a document) 2. *adj.* (*bot.*) extending forward [fr. L. *porrigere* (*porrectus*), to stretch forth]

por·ridge (póridʒ, pórridʒ) *n.* a soft food made by boiling oatmeal or other cereal substance in water or milk [fr. POTTAGE]

por·rin·ger (pórindʒər, pórrindʒər) *n.* an individual wide shallow bowl, usually having a handle, for porridge, soup etc. [alt. of older *potager*]

Porsena, Lars *LARS PORSENA

port (port, pourt) *n.* a harbor || a town or place with a harbor || a port of entry [O.E.]

port *n.* (*mil.*) the position taken up in porting arms [fr. the order 'port arms!']

port 1. *n.* the side of a ship or aircraft that is on the left of someone aboard facing the bow (opp. STARBOARD) 2. *v.t.* to turn (the helm) to the left [etym. doubtful]

port *n.* (*naut.*) a porthole || (*mech.*) an opening in

a cylinder through which the lubricating oil can pass || (*mech.*) a valve opening to allow the passage of steam, gases etc. [M.E. *porte, port,* gateway fr. F.]

port *n.* a fortified, sweet, rich red or white wine from Portugal || an imitation of this [fr. *Oporto,* a city in Portugal]

port *v.t.* (*mil.*) to carry (a rifle or other weapon) in an upward-sloping position close to and across the body from right to left, esp. for inspection [F. *porter,* to carry]

port·a·bil·i·ty (portəbíliti:, pourtəbíliti:) *n.* the condition or quality of being portable **port·a·ble** (pórtəb'l, póurtəb'l) 1. *adj.* easily carried or transported, *a portable radio* || that can be carried or transported 2. *n.* anything easily carried, esp. a portable typewriter [F.]

por·tage (pórtidʒ, póurtidʒ) 1. *n.* the carrying of boats or goods by land from one river etc. to another, around falls or rapids etc., or the place or route over which this is done 2. *v.t. pres. part.* **por·tag·ing** *past* and *past part.* **por·taged** to carry (boats or goods) [F.]

por·tal (pórt'l, póurt'l) *n.* a door, gateway or other entrance, esp. when large and imposing || a portal vein [obs. F. fr. M.L. *portale adj.* fr. L. *porta,* door]

portal *adj.* (*anat.*) of or relating to the transverse fissure of the liver, where most of the vessels enter || of, relating to, or being any large vein that collects and distributes blood from one part of the body to another [fr. M.L. *portolis,* of a door]

Por·ta·les (portáles), Diego (1793–1837), Chilean statesman and dictator (1830–7). He unleashed (1836) the war against the Bolivian-Peruvian Confederation

por·tal-to-por·tal (pórt'ltəpórt'l, póurt'ltəpóurt'l) *adj.* of or relating to the amount of time a workman spends in getting from the entrance of his place of employment, e.g. a mine, to his work site and, after work, from his work site to the entrance

portal vein a large vein conveying blood from the digestive organs and spleen to the liver

por·ta·men·to (portəméntou, pourtəméntou) *pl.* **por·ta·men·ti** (portəménti:, pourtaménti:) *n.* (*mus.*) a smooth gliding from one note to another in singing, or in playing esp. a trombone or a bowed stringed instrument [Ital.]

Port Arthur the chief port (pop. 38,000) for the Canadian prairies on Lake Superior in S.W. Ontario

Port Arthur *LUSHUN

por·ta·tive (pórtətiv, póurtətiv) *adj.* (*old-fash.*) portable [O.F. *portatif*]

Port-au-Prince (portouprés) the capital and chief port (pop. 862,900) of Haiti. Industries: sugar refining, rum. Cathedral (18th c.). University

port authority a governmental commission in charge of a port

port·cul·lis (portkʌ́lis, pourtkʌ́lis) *n.* (*hist.*) an iron grating suspended by chains and made to slide in grooves in the sides of a fortified gateway in order to block the cntrance [O.F. *porte coleïce,* sliding door]

Porte (port, pourt) *n.* the title of the government of the Ottoman Empire || the government of Turkey

Port Elizabeth a port (pop. 492,140) of S.E. Cape Province, South Africa: boots and shoes, automobile assembly, fishing, food processing, building materials

por·tend (porténd, pourténd) *v.t.* to give signs of (impending evil or catastrophe) || to indicate broadly (some coming change), *these events perhaps portend a closer link with Europe* [fr. L. *portendere,* to stretch forth]

por·te·ño (porténjo) *n.* a monied inhabitant of Buenos Aires, as opposed to a gaucho [Span.]

por·tent (pórtent, póurtent) *n.* an inexplicable event taken as an omen, esp. as an evil omen || a sign of some coming change for good or bad [fr. L. *portendere* (*portentus*), to stretch forth]

por·ten·tous (porténtəs, pourténtəs) *adj.* of the nature of a portent || (*rhet.*) highly significant, *portentous happenings* [fr. L. *portentosus*]

Por·ter (pórtər, póurtər), David (1780–1843), U.S. commodore. As captain of the 'Essex' during the War of 1812, he captured several British ships carrying troops to Halifax. He also attacked British whalers in the Pacific. He was defeated (1814) by British warships when a storm forced the 'Essex' into Valparaiso harbor

Porter, David Dixon (1813–91), U.S. admiral. During the Civil War he led (1862) the mortar

flotilla of David Farragut's fleet in the successful assault on New Orleans and aided (1863) Gen. U.S. Grant in the Vicksburg campaign

Porter, Katherine Anne (1890–1980), U.S. novelist and short story writer. Her first full-length novel, 'Ship of Fools' (1962), which is set aboard a German ship shortly before Hitler's rise to power, reflects the mood of impending disaster

Porter, William Sydney *HENRY, O.

por·ter (pórtər, póurtər) *n.* a dark brown beer brewed from browned or charred malt [short for porter's ale]

porter *n.* (esp. *Br.*) a gatekeeper || (esp. *Br.*) a doorkeeper, e.g. at a school, hotel, college etc. [A.F.]

porter *n.* a person employed in railroad stations, hotels, markets etc. to carry baggage or other loads || a man who cleans or does errands in a store etc. || an attendant in a parlor car or sleeping car [O.F. *porteour*]

por·ter·house steak (pórtərhaus, póurtərhaus) a choice steak cut from the thick end of the short loin of beef [fr. older *porterhouse,* where steaks and chops and porter were served]

port·fo·li·o (portfóuliːou, pourtfóuliːou) *pl.* **port·fo·li·os** *n.* a case for keeping loose papers, drawings, prints etc. || such a case for carrying state documents || the office and functions of a government minister || the securities etc. held by a bank, investment trust etc. [fr. Ital. *porta-fogli*]

Port Har·court (húrkərt) a port (pop. 242,000) and rail terminus of E. Nigeria, on the Niger delta. It is the capital of Rivers State

port·hole (pórthoul, póurthoul) *n.* an opening in a ship's side to admit light and air || an opening in a tank, fortification etc. to shoot through

por·ti·co (pórtikou, póurtikou) *pl.* **por·ti·coes, por·ti·cos** *n.* a colonnade or covered passageway in classical architecture [Ital.]

portiere, por·tière (portjéər, pourtjéər) *n.* a door curtain [F.]

Por·ti·na·ri (porti:nári:), Cândido (1903–62), Brazilian painter of murals. He decorated the entrance to the Hispanic Foundation in the Library of Congress in Washington, D.C.

por·tion (pórʃən, póurʃən) 1. *n.* a part of a whole, *a portion of the field was allotted to the sports club* || a helping of food || (*hist.*) a share of an estate received by inheritance or gift || (*old-fash.*) a dowry || (*rhet.*) one's lot in life [O.F. *portion*]

portion *v.t.* to divide into portions (with 'out') to share, *he portioned out the estate among his three sons* [O.F. *portionner*].

Port Jackson *SYDNEY

Port·land (pórtland, póurtland) the chief city (pop. 366,383) of Oregon, a seaport (on the Columbia 108 miles from the coast) and industrial center: food processing, textiles, sawmilling, pulp and paper, chemicals, aluminum

Portland the largest city (pop. 61,572) of Maine, a seaport

portland cement a cement made by grinding and mixing chalk and clay and burning it in a kiln [after the color of Portland stone, quarried at the Isle of *Portland,* Dorset, England]

port·li·ness (pórtli:nis, póurtli:nis) *n.* the state or quality of being portly [PORTLY]

Port Louis the capital, chief port and commercial center (pop. 146,844) of Mauritius: sugar refining, tobacco, rum

port·ly (pórtli:, póurtli:) *comp.* **port·li·er,** *superl.* **port·li·est** *adj.* (of adults) stout, corpulent [PORT n., (obs.) bearing]

port·man·teau (portmǽntou, pourtmǽntou) *pl.* **port·man·teaus, port·man·teaux** *n.* a traveling case for clothes, opening into two compartments [F. fr. *porter,* to carry + *manteau,* a cloak]

portmanteau word a word in which the sounds and meanings of two other words are combined, e.g. 'smog' (smoke and fog)

Port Mores·by (mórzbi:, móurzbi:) the capital and chief port (pop. 141,000) of Papua New Guinea, on the southeast coast

Pôr·to A·le·gre (pórtuolégrə) the chief port and industrial center (pop. 1,183,500) of S.E. Brazil, at the head of a great lagoon-estuary (Lagoa dos Patos). Industries: meat packing, tanning, wool textiles, food processing. Cathedral. Universities (1934, 1948)

port of call a place at which a ship makes regular stops for supplies, repairs etc.

port of entry a place, not necessarily a port, where foreign goods are cleared through customs offices

CONCISE PRONUNCIATION KEY: **(a)** æ, c*a*t; ɑ, c*a*r; ɔ f*a*wn; ei, sn*a*ke. **(e)** e, h*e*n; i:, sh*ee*p; iə, d*ee*r; ɛə, b*ea*r. **(i)** i, f*i*sh; ai, t*i*ger; əː, b*i*rd.
(o) o, *o*x; au, c*ow*; ou, g*oa*t; u, p*oo*r; ɔi, r*oy*al. **(u)** ʌ, d*u*ck; u, b*u*ll; u:, g*oo*se; ə, b*a*cillus; juː, c*u*be. x, lo*ch*; θ, *th*ink; ð, b*o*ther; z, *Z*en; ʒ, cor*s*age;
dʒ, sava*g*e; ŋ, ora*ng*utang; j, *y*ak; ʃ, *f*ish; tʃ, fe*tch*; 'l, rabb*le*; 'n, redd*en*. Complete pronunciation key appears inside front cover.

por·to·la·no (pɔrt'lɑ́nou, pourt'lɑ́nou) *pl.* **por·to·la·nos, por·to·la·ni** (pɔrt'lɑ́ni:, pourt'lɑ́ni:) *n.* a medieval sailing handbook and guide to harbors, illustrated with charts [Ital.]

Port-of-Spain (pɔ́rtəvspéin, póurtəvspéin) the capital (pop. 11,032) and commercial center of Trinidad and Tobago, a port on the gulf separating Trinidad from Venezuela: sugar refining

Por·to No·vo (pɔ́rtounóuvou, póurtounóuvou) the capital (pop. 104,000) of Benin, a seaport and rail terminus: palm oil refining

Por·to Ri·co (pɔ́rtourí:kou, póurtourí:kou) the former name for Puerto Rico

Por·to·vie·jo (pɔrtəvjého) a city (pop. 97,000) of W. Ecuador: Panama hats, baskets

por·trait (pɔ́rtrit, póurtrit) *n.* a painting, photograph, drawing etc. of a person, esp. of his face, usually made from life || a vivid verbal description of someone or something **pór·trait·ist** *n.* a person who makes portraits [F.]

por·trai·ture (pɔ́rtritʃər, póurtritʃər) *n.* the art, act or practice of making portraits || a portrait [O.F.]

por·tray (pɔrtréi, pourtréi) *v.t.* to paint etc. a portrait of || to describe vividly in words, so as to bring out the character of || to represent (a character) on the stage **por·tráy·al** *n.* [O.F. *portraire*]

Port Roy·al (pɔrtrɔ́iəl, pourtrɔ́iəl, pɔrrwǽjael) a convent of Cistercian nuns founded in 1204 near Chevreuse, France. It was reformed (1608) by Angélique Arnauld, and transferred (1625) to Paris. It came (1636) under the spiritual direction of Duvergier de Hauranne. It became, with an associated group of scholarly solitaries including Antoine Arnauld living at the Chevreuse convent, a center of Jansenism. A school, the Petites Écoles de Port Royal, was established (1638), and Racine was among the pupils. Some nuns returned to the old convent (1648) and the men took up residence on a nearby farm. It was here that Pascal retired (1654). As one of the measures to suppress Jansenism Louis XIV closed the old convent (1709), and it was razed (1712). The history of Port Royal is vital in the history of French religious thought in the 17th c. and the defense of orthodoxy

Port Sa·id (saɪ:d) a port and fueling station (pop. 262,760) of Egypt at the Mediterranean end of the Suez canal: fishing, salt works

Ports·mouth (pɔ́rtsməθ, póurtsməθ) a port and county borough (pop. 179,419) of Hampshire, England, on Spithead: naval base, cathedral (12th and 17th cc.)

Port Sudan the port of entry (pop. 132,631) of the Sudan, on the Red Sea, a rail terminus

Port Swet·ten·ham (swét'nəm) a port (pop. 11,000) of Malaysia in W. central Malaya, serving Kuala Lumpur

Por·tu·gal (pɔ́rtʃug'l, póurtʃug'l) a republic (area 34,831 sq. miles, pop. 10,056,000, incl. the Azores and Madeira) in S.W. Europe. Capital: Lisbon. Overseas territory: Macao. Language: Portuguese. Religion: mainly Roman Catholic. The land is 46% arable, 28% forest, 16% pasture. The coastal plain (fertile in delta regions), narrow in the north, widens gradually to cross the country in the far south. East of it is the Meseta, the central plateau (mainly 1,000–3,000 ft) of Iberia, cut by the Minho, Douro, Tagus and Guadiana Rivers. The Meseta is highest north of the Tagus, with mountain ranges (Serra da Estrella, 6,532 ft) running northwest southeast. Average temperatures (F.): (Jan.) 40° in the north, 50° in the south, (July) 70° in the north, 75° in the south. Rainfall: north of the Douro 40–60 ins, Serra da Estrella 110 ins, Lisbon 27 ins, south 20 ins. Principal occupation: agriculture (small holdings and mixed farming in the north, large cereal-growing estates in the center and south). Livestock: sheep, hogs, oxen, goats, donkeys, mules. Crops: cereals, root vegetables, olives, vines, fruit (esp. citrus), almonds. Minerals: coal, copper, kaolin, sulfur, wolfram, cassiterite. Exports: sardines, cork (1st world producer), wine (esp. port, sherry and madeira). olive oil, turpentine, resin, pyrites, wolfram, pulp, tires, embroidery. Other industries: food processing, hydroelectricity, iron and steel, cement, tourism. Imports: iron and steel, machinery, raw cotton, vehicles, wheat, sugar, fuels, oil seeds, coal, tobacco, coffee, chemicals. Chief ports: Lisbon, Oporto. Universities: Coimbra (1290), Lisbon (1911), Oporto (1911). Monetary unit: escudo (100 centavos). HISTORY. Originally inhabited by Iberians, Portugal was visited by Phoenician traders (9th c. B.C.). The Greeks founded colonies (6th–5th cc. B.C.), and the Romans made the area part of the province of Lusitania (2nd c. B.C.–5th c. A.D.). Together with the rest of the Iberian Peninsula, Portugal was overrun by the Visigoths (5th c.) and the Moors (8th c.). It was one of the first areas reconquered from the Moors (11th c.), was made a county (1095) by Alfonso VI, and became a kingdom (1143). By 1249 Portugal had expanded to approximately its modern extent. Under Ferdinand I and John I Portugal was at war with Castile and was supported by England. A permanent alliance was formed (1386) with England. The patronage of Henry the Navigator encouraged Portuguese geographers and navigators to explore the west coast of Africa and parts of South America. Prominent in this age of expansion were Dias, da Gama and Cabral. Portugal and Spain, as the leading colonial powers, divided the undiscovered world between themselves in the Treaty of Tordesillas (1494). By the mid-16th c., Portugal had acquired a vast empire which included Morocco, Brazil, and parts of East Africa and the East Indies. The climax of prosperity was reached under Manuel I and John III, but decline set in rapidly (mid-16th c.) as the economic effects of the expulsion of the Jews (1497) were felt and as Portugal's limited resources and tiny population were unable to compete with the rise of English and Dutch sea power. Philip II of Spain seized the throne (1580). Portugal suffered economically under Spanish rule and lost control of the East Indies to the Dutch. A revolt (1640) brought John IV to the throne. The Methuen Treaty (1703) helped to strengthen the economy, and the marquês de Pombal built up agriculture and trade with a strong mercantilist policy (mid-18th c.). When Portugal refused to obey Napoleon's embargo on trade with Britain, it was invaded by the French, the royal family fled to Brazil (1808) and the Peninsular War broke out. With the restoration of peace, the royal family returned but Brazil declared itself independent (1822). After political struggles between liberals and absolutists throughout the 19th c., Portugal became a republic (1910). The colonization of Mozambique and Angola (late 19th c.) caused ill feeling between Britain and Portugal, but Portugal joined the Allies in the 1st world war. Political and economic chaos worsened until Salazar was appointed finance minister (1928). Salazar became prime minister (1932), established a dictatorship, and kept Portugal neutral in the 2nd world war. Portugal joined NATO (1949), the U.N (1955) and the European Free Trade Association (1959). Attempts were made to modernize industry and agriculture (1950s). Salazar resigned (1968) on grounds of health. Portugal was widely criticized (1960s) for its dealings with Angola and Mozambique. Salazar's successor as premier, Marcello Caetano, was overthrown in a military coup (1974) led by Gen. António de Spínola, and democratic government was restored under a military junta. Portugal granted independence to its African colonies that same year. The constitution of 1976 committed the country to socialist goals and a minority socialist government under Mário Soares came to power (1976–8). After several short-lived successors, the right-centrist Democratic Alliance coalition, headed by Francisco Sá Carneiro, took over the government. After Sá Carneiro's death (1980) Francisco Pinto Balsemão became head of the Democratic Alliance and premier. He remained in office until 1982, and after a six-month political crisis, a new coalition headed by Soares was formed (1983)

Por·tu·guese (pɔrtʃugí:z, pourtʃugí:z, pɔrtʃugí:s, pourtʃugí:s) **1.** *adj.* of or relating to Portugal, its people, language, customs etc. **2.** *n.* a native or inhabitant of Portugal || the Romance languages spoken in Portugal, Madeira, the Azores and Brazil, and in the Portuguese territories, by a total of about 93 million people

Portuguese Guinea *GUINEA-BISSAU

Portuguese man-of-war any of several siphonophore coelenterates of the genus *Physalia*, fam. *Physalidae*, having a large air sac with a sail-like crest on the upper side, enabling them to float on the sea

Portuguese Timor formerly an overseas territory of Portugal, annexed by Indonesia (1976)

POS (*abbr.*) point-of-sale (which see)

pose (pouz) *n.* a way of standing or sitting, esp. the position held by a model etc. in posing || an attitude of mind, or manner of behavior assumed for its effect on others, *his brave words are merely a pose* [F.]

pose *pres. part.* **pos·ing** *past and past part.* **posed** *v.t.* to place (an artist's model, a person being photographed etc.) in a certain position for artistic effect || to state or present (a problem etc.) || *v.i.* to assume a certain position, e.g. in having one's portrait made || to represent oneself falsely, *he posed as a successful businessman* [F. *poser*, to place]

Po·sei·don (pəsáid'n) the Greek god of earthquakes, of the sea and of horses, the brother of Zeus and Pluto and identified with the Roman Neptune

Po·sei·don (pousáidən) *n.* (*mil.*) two-stage, solid propellant ICBM [UGM-73] capable of being launched from a specially configured submarine operating on the ocean surface or submerged, equipped with inertial guidance, nuclear warheads, and a maneuverable bus capable of carrying up to 14 reentry bodies that can be directed to many separate targets, with 290-mi range. It replaced Polaris. *Cf* POLARIS, TRIDENT

pos·er (póuzər) *n.* a difficult or baffling question or problem [POSE v.]

po·seur (pouzə́:r) *n.* a person who pretends to be what he is not, out of affectation, insincerity, guile or silliness [F.]

posh (pɒʃ) *adj.* (*pop.*) very smart, *posh clothes* || (*pop.*) high-class, *a posh hotel* [etym. doubtful]

Po·shan (pɔ́ʃan) *TZEPO

pos·i·grade (pózəgreid) *adj.* **1.** providing forward thrust. **2.** *n.* (*aerospace*) a supplementary rocket used to provide additional thrust. *Cf* RETROGRADE

pos·it (pózit) *v.t.* to postulate, assume || to set in context, *the problem posited in this way took on another aspect* [fr. L. *ponere* (*positus*), to place]

po·si·tion (pəzíʃən) **1.** *n.* the place occupied by a person or object in relation to another person or object || (*mil., chess*) strategical advantage, *to maneuver for position* || (*mil.*) a place held by troops, *to attack a position* || a way of looking at things, mental attitude, *to state one's position* || a person's relative rank or standing in the social or business world || exalted rank or standing, *a man of position* || financial circumstances, *in a position to marry* || office or employment, *a position as housemaid* || physical posture, *a comfortable position* || any of the formal postures of the feet and arms upon which all movements in ballet are based || any of the points on the fingerboard of a stringed instrument which when pressed by the fingers control the length of string free to vibrate and so allow various notes to be produced || (*sports*) a place in a team or on the playing field **in a (in no) position to** (not) enabled by circumstances to, *in no position to argue* || **in position** normally placed **out of position** abnormally placed **2.** *v.t.* to place in position, *to position troops* **po·sí·tion·al** *adj.* [F.]

position paper a statement of opinion on a particular question or issue

pos·i·tive (pózitiv) **1.** *adj.* leaving no doubt or question, *there is positive proof that he did it* || (of people) given to significant action || (of people) apt to be dogmatic || indicating affirmation, *a positive response* || (*philos.*) constructive as opposed to skeptical || (*photog.*) of a photographic print or transparency in which the distribution of light and dark areas corresponds to that of the original optical image || (*biol.*) moving toward a source of stimulation || (*bacteriol.*) showing the presence of a specific condition, disease etc. || explicit, *he had positive orders to do it* || downright, *he is a positive nuisance* || (*gram.*) designating an adjective or adverb in its simple uncompared degree, e.g. 'good' in contrast to 'better' or 'best' (cf. COMPARATIVE, cf. SUPERLATIVE) || of this degree || (*math.*, symbol+) greater than zero || (*phys.*) of an electric charge of the kind associated with the proton || (*elec.*) of an electrode (anode) of a cell or other electric device that is at the higher potential || of a magnetic pole attracted towards the magnetic north || of a counterclockwise moment or rotation || (*chem.*) of an ion formed by the loss of electrons || acting or moving in a direction conventionally or arbitrarily taken as that of increase, progress or superiority **2.** *n.* that which is positive || (*photog.*) a positive print or transparency || (*gram.*) the positive degree || (*elec.*) the plate of a cell at the higher potential (the anode) [F.]

---

positive discrimination (*Br.*) *AFFIRMATIVE ACTION

positive eugenics a policy of achieving race improvement by increasing genetic transmission of favorable traits

positive feedback *FEEDBACK

pos·i·tive·ly (pózitivli:) *adv.* in a positive way || (pɒzitívli) extremely, certainly

positive prescription (*law*) usage from time immemorial, or for a long period fixed by law, giving right or title || the right or title so acquired

positive ray a stream of positively charged ions traveling towards the cathode in a discharge tube

positive reinforcement (*psych.*) system of employee management technique based on positive rewards, e.g., praise, recognition; developed by Edward J. Feeney. *Cf* BEHAVIOR MODIFICATION, SKINNERISM

pos·i·tiv·ism (pózitivizəm) *n.* a philosophic system founded by August Comte, based on the assumption that truth is completely represented by observable phenomena and scientifically verified facts [fr. F. *positivisme*]

pos·i·tiv·ist (pózitivist) *n.* an adherent of positivism [fr. F. *positiviste*]

pos·i·tiv·i·ty (pɒzitíviti) *n.* the quality or state of being positive [POSITIVE]

pos·i·tron (pózitron) *n.* (*phys.*) the particle having the same mass and spin as the electron but opposite electric charge (i.e. +1) produced by the interaction of cosmic rays with matter [POSITIVE+ELECTRON]

pos·se (pósi) *n.* a force of men having legal authority, *a posse of police* [M.L.=power]

pos·sess (pəzés) *v.t.* to have as property, own, *to possess a car* || to have as a faculty, quality etc., *to possess endless patience* || to get control over, *what possessed him to act that way?* || to keep (oneself) in a condition of emotional or mental control, *to possess oneself in patience* || (of an evil spirit) to enter into in order to control, *to be possessed by a devil* || to command (a language other than one's own) **pos·séssed** *adj.* crazy || controlled by an evil spirit [O.F. *possessier*]

pos·ses·sion (pəzéʃən) *n.* a possessing or being possessed || that which is possessed || (*pl.*) property || a territory under the political and economic control of another country || (*law*) actual enjoyment of property not founded on any title of ownership **to take possession of** to begin to occupy as owner || to affect so as to dominate [O.F.]

pos·ses·sive (pəzésiv) 1. *adj.* (*gram.*, of a case, form, or construction) expressing possession or a comparable relationship, *possessive pronoun* (his, ours, yours etc.), *possessive adjective* (my, your, her etc.), *the possessive case of a noun* (expressed by 's, or ' after a plural ending in 's') || tending to want to concentrate all another's affections on oneself || jealously assertive of one's rights over something, *to be possessive about one's toys* 2. *n.* (*gram.*) a possessive case or form [fr. L. *possessivus*]

pos·ses·sor (pəzésər) *n.* a person who owns or controls || a person who holds property without title of ownership [late M.E. and A.F. *possessour*]

pos·ses·so·ry (pəzésəri:) *adj.* (esp. *law*) arising from, of the nature of, possession || of or being a possessor [fr. L.L. *possessorius*]

pos·set (pósit) *n.* (*hist.*) a drink made of sweetened hot milk curdled by wine, ale etc. and often spiced, taken as a remedy [M.E. *poshote*, origin unknown]

posset pot a vessel (esp. of the 17th and 18th cc.) with two handles, lid and spout, to make posset in

pos·si·bil·i·ty (pɒsəbíliti)*pl.* **pos·si·bil·i·ties** *n.* the fact or state of being possible || something that is possible [F. *possibilité*]

pos·si·ble (pósəb'l) 1. *adj.* that may exist, happen, be done etc. || potential, *a possible enemy* || reasonable, *the only possible explanation* || reasonably satisfactory, *he's quite possible as a bridge partner* 2. *n.* the highest attainable score, esp. in target shooting || a person whom it is reasonable to consider seriously for some position etc. **pós·si·bly** *adv.* by any possible means, *it can't possibly happen* || perhaps [F.]

pos·sum (pósəm) *n.* (*pop.*) an opossum **to play possum** (*pop.*) to pretend to be asleep or to be dead || to feign ignorance [after the habit of the opossum of feigning death when attacked]

post (poust) 1. *n.* a strong, usually square or cylindrical piece of wood, metal etc., fixed or meant to be fixed in an upright position, and serving as a support || something resembling this, e.g. one of the stakes in a fence || (*horse racing*) a pole marking the starting point or finishing point 2. *v.t.* to affix (a public notice, placard etc.) to a post, wall etc. || to put (a list of names etc.) on a bulletin board etc., *to post students' marks* || to warn trespassers to stay off (esp. private property) by placing notices around the boundaries, *to post some woods* || to publish (a name) in a public notice, *posted missing, a ship posted as missing* || to advertise (a show, speaker etc.) by poster [O.E. fr. L.]

post 1. *n.* (esp. *Br.*) the public organization dealing with the collection and delivery of correspondence and other postal matter || (esp *Br.*) the collection of letters etc. taken on one occasion from a collecting point || (esp. *Br.*) the letters etc. delivered on one occasion, *what's in the post?* (*hist.*) one of a series of stations furnishing horses for relays || (*hist.*) the distance between two successive stations in such a series || (*hist.*) one of a relay of men on horseback stationed along a road, each one carrying letters from his own station to the next || (*Br.*) a size of writing paper (16 x 20 ins) 2. *v.t.* (esp. *Br.*) to mail || (*bookkeeping*) to transfer (an item) from a record to a ledger || (bookkeeping, esp. with 'up') to complete (a ledger) by transferring and properly entering all items from preceding records || (*bookkeeping*, esp. with 'up') to transfer entries in (all books) || (often with 'up') to supply (a person) with the latest news, information etc., *to keep someone posted about a situation* || *v.i.* (*hist.*) to travel with relays of horses changed at successive stations [F. *poste* fr. Ital. *posta*, a station]

post 1. *n.* the position a soldier occupies, or the area he patrols when he is on duty || the place at which a soldier or body of troops is stationed || the body of troops occupying this place || a position being held by troops, *advance post*, or the troops themselves || a position to which a person is assigned || a position to which a person is appointed, *a post in the public service* || a trading post || a local branch of an army veterans' organization **first post, last post** (*Br.*, *mil.*) two bugle calls sounded at the hour of retiring to bed (the last post is also sounded at a soldier's grave after burial) 2. *v.t.* to station in a specific place, *to post men along the route* || (*mil.*) to assign (e.g. a sentry) to a specific station || (*Br.*, *mil.*) to appoint to a particular regiment etc. || (*Br.*, *naval*) to commission as captain [F. *poste* fr. Ital. *posto*, station, employment]

post-*prefix* after || behind [L.]

post·age (póustidʒ) *n.* the charge for conveying a letter or parcel by mail

postage meter (*Am.*=*Br.* franking machine) a machine which automatically stamps letters etc. and records the cost of postage

postage stamp a printed adhesive stamp, or a stamp imprinted on a letter etc., issued by postal authorities for use as evidence of payment of postage

post·al (póustəl) *adj.* of or relating to the post [F.]

postal order (*Br.*) a money order available in fixed denominations, payable at a post office

Postal Union, Universal *UNIVERSAL POSTAL UNION

post·bel·lum (poustbéləm) *adj.* occurring after a war, esp. (*Am. hist.*) after the Civil War [L. *post bellum*=after the war]

post·box (póustbɒks) *n.* a box into which letters etc. are put for collection

post·card (póustkɑrd) *n.* a card for correspondence

post chaise (póustʃeiz) *n.* (*hist.*) a hired covered carriage drawn by two or more horses, changed at successive posting stations

post·code (póustkoud) *n.* (*Br.*) ZIP code

post·com·mun·ion (poustkəmjú:njən) *n.* the prayer in the Mass said by the priest after communion [fr. M.L. *postcommunio* (*posicommunionis*)]

postconciliar (poustkənsíli:ər) *adj.* of the period after the 1962–65 Vatican ecumenical council. *Cf* PRECONCILIAR

post·date (poustdéit) *pres. part.* **post·dat·ing** *past and past part.* **post·dat·ed** *v.t.* to assign a later than actual date to (e.g. a check, event etc.) || to be later in time than (a certain date, event etc.)

post·de·ter·min·er (poustdité:rminər) the limiting modifier of a noun that appears after the noun

post·er (póustər) *n.* a placard displayed in public [POST, a piece of wood]

poste res·tante (póustrestánt) *n.* (esp. *Br.*) general delivery [F.=remaining post]

pos·te·ri·or (pɒstíəri:ər) 1. *adj.* located behind (cf. ANTERIOR) || (*anat.*) away from the head || (*human anat.*) dorsal || (*bot.*) facing or on the same side as the axis || (*bot.*) on the side next to the main stem || later in time 2. *n.* the buttocks [L. comp. of *posterus*, following]

pos·te·ri·or·i·ty (pɒstiəri:óriti, pɒstiəri:óriti) *n.* the quality or state of being later in time or sequence [fr. M.L. *posterioritas*]

pos·ter·i·ty (pɒstériti) *n.* the succssive descendants of a person || generations not yet born, *posterity will judge* [F. *postérité*]

pos·tern (póustə:rn) 1. *n.* (*hist.*, esp. of castles) a back or side door or gate || (*hist.*, fortification) an escape tunnel leading to the ditch and outworks 2. *adj.* (*hist.*, of a door or gate) at the back or side [O.F. *posterne*]

post·ex·il·i·an (poustegzíljən) *adj.* postexilic

post·ex·il·ic (poustegzílik) *adj.* relating to the period after the Babylonian Captivity of the Jews

post·fig·ur·a·tive (poustfígjurətiv) *adj.* of a society in which three generations live together, dominated by the ideas of the older members; defined by American anthropologist Margaret Mead. *Cf* CONFIGURATIVE, PREFIGURATIVE

post·fix 1. (póustfiks) *n.* (*gram.*) a suffix 2. (póustfíks) *v.t.* to attach as a suffix

post·free (póustfrí:) *adj.* (*Br.*) postpaid

post·gla·cial (poustgléiʃəl) *adj.* occurring after a glacial period, esp. the Pleistocene

post·grad·u·ate (poustgrǽdʒu:it) 1. *adj.* of or relating to studies that go beyond the first degree || of or relating to a student engaged in such studies 2. *n.* a student who continues his studies beyond a first degree

post·haste (póusthéist) *adj.* with the greatest possible speed

post·hu·mous (póstʃuməs) *adj.* published after the death of the author || (of a child) born after the death of the father || occurring after death, *a posthumous award* **póst·hu·mous·ly** *adv.* [fr. L. *postumus*, last]

pos·til (póstil) *n.* a marginal comment, esp. a marginal biblical comment [F. *postille*]

pos·til·ion, pos·til·lion (pəstíljən) *n.* a man who rides the near horse of the leading pair when two pairs or more are used to draw a carriage || a man who rides the near horse of a single pair when there is no driver on the box [F. *postillon*]

Post·im·pres·sion·ism (poustimpréʃənizəm) *n.* the various reactions in painting in the last decade of the 19th c. and the early 20th c. away from Impressionism. Cézanne, Gauguin, Van Gogh and Seurat were, each in his own way, Postimpressionists **Post·im·prés·sion·ist** *adj.* and *n.*

post·in·dus·tri·al society (poustindʌ́stri:əl) late 20th-century society in which theoretical knowledge as a source of innovation and policymaking is centralized in a professional and technical class, such knowledge serving to replace goods as major elements of production; defined by Daniel Bell

post·li·min·i·um (poustlimíni:əm) *n.* postliminy [L. fr. *post*, behind+*limen* (*liminis*), threshold]

post·lim·i·ny (poustlímini:) *n.* (*internat. law*) the law under which persons or property captured by an enemy revert to their original status and the rights relating to them are restored when they come under the jurisdiction of their own country again [fr. POSTLIMINIUM]

post·man (póustmən) *pl.* **post·men** (póustmən) *n.* someone employed to collect and deliver letters and other postal matter

post·mark (póustmɑrk) 1. *n.* an official post-office mark stamped on a piece of mail, recording the date, place and usually time of mailing, and serving to cancel the stamp 2. *v.i.* to stamp with a postmark

post·mas·ter (póustmæstər, póustmɑstər) *n.* a man in charge of a post office

postmaster general *pl.* **postmasters general**, **postmaster generals** the head of a national postal system

post·me·rid·i·an (poustmərídi:ən) *adj.* of or relating to the afternoon

post me·rid·i·em (poustmərídi:əm) *adv.* (*abbr.* p.m., P.M.) after noon and before midnight [L.]

post·mis·tress (póustmistris) *n.* a woman in charge of a post office

CONCISE PRONUNCIATION KEY: **(a)** æ, c*a*t; ɑ, c*ar*; ɔ f*aw*n; ei, sn*a*ke. **(e)** e, h*e*n; i:, sh*ee*p; iə, d*ee*r; ɛə, b*ear*. **(i)** i, f*i*sh; ai, t*i*ger; ə:, b*ir*d. **(o)** o, *o*x; au, c*ow*; ou, g*oa*t; u, p*oo*r; ɔi, r*oy*al. **(u)** ʌ, d*u*ck; u, b*u*ll; u:, g*oo*se; ə, bacill*u*s; ju:, c*u*be. x, lo*ch*; θ, *th*ink; ð, bo*th*er; z, *Z*en; ʒ, corsa*g*e; dʒ, sava*g*e; ŋ, ora*ng*utang; j, *y*ak; ʃ, *fi*sh; tʃ, fe*tch*; 'l, rabb*le*; 'n, redd*en*.   Complete pronunciation key appears inside front cover.

post·mor·tem (poustmórtəm) **1.** *adj.* of or relating to the period after death, *postmortem changes* ‖ after an event, a *postmortem analysis of a campaign* **2.** *n.* a postmortem examination ‖ an analysis after an event, esp. after a hand of bridge [L.]

postmortem examination an autopsy

post·na·tal (poustnéit'l) *adj.* after birth

post·ne·o·na·tal (poustni:ouneit'l) *adj.* of the first year after birth

post·nup·tial (poustnʌ́pʃəl) *adj.* after marriage

post·o·bit (poustóubit) **1.** *adj.* effective after death **2.** *n.* a bond payable after the death of a person from whom the borrower expects to inherit money [fr. L. *post obitum*, after death]

post office an office where the mail is received and sorted for distribution and other postal services are maintained **Post Office** the governmental department or ministry from which this service is administered

Pos·ton (póustən), Charles Debrill (1825–1902), U.S. explorer of the southwest U.S.A. Advocating territorial organization for Arizona, he served (1863–4) as superintendent of Indian affairs and (1864–5) as the first delegate to Congress from Arizona. His writings include 'Apache Land' (1878)

post·paid (póustpéid) *adj.* (Am.=Br. post-free) with the postage prepaid

post·paint·er·ly (poustpéintərli:) *adj.* of a painting style utilizing traditional techniques for nonobjective works with color that tends to blend with the environment. *also* color-field

post·pone (poustpóun, pouspóun) *pres. part.* **post·pon·ing** *past* and *past part.* **post·poned** *v.t.* to put off, defer, *to postpone a holiday* **post·pone·ment** *n.* [fr. L. *postponere* fr. *post*, after + *ponere*, to place]

post·po·si·tion (poustpəzíʃən) *n.* a particle or word placed after another word, esp. a particle or word having the function of a preposition, e.g. 'ward' in 'skyward' **post·pos·i·tive** (poustpózitiv) *adj.* after fr. L. *postponere* (*postpositus*), to place afterwards]

post·pran·di·al (poustprǽndi:əl) *adj.* of or relating to the period following a meal, esp. dinner [fr. POST- + L. *prandium*, meal]

post road (*hist.*) a road, used esp. by mounted mail carriers and mail coaches, having a series of inns that provided refreshment, fresh horses etc.

post·script (póustskript) *n.* (*abbr.* P.S.) a brief afterthought, or series of these, added to a letter below the signature ‖ a short section at the end of a book, often a commentary on what has gone before [fr. L. *postscriptum* fr. *post*, after + *scribere*, to write]

post-traumatic stress disorder psychological disorder following or resulting from trauma. It may develop after any traumatic experience, such as an accident, but it gained prominence in the U.S.A. in the 1970s as a result of the difficulties experienced by Vietnam War veterans in readjusting to civilian life. Symptoms begin with a feeling of numbness as the victim attempts to assimilate the traumatic experience. Other symptoms include irritability, depression, an unreasoned sense of guilt for having survived and emotional difficulties with relationships. Nightmares, flashbacks to the traumatic experience, overreaction to sudden noises and outbursts of violence can also occur. Treatment can include group or individual therapy as well as sedating drugs. *abbr.* PTSD

pos·tu·lant (póstʃulənt) *n.* a candidate for admission to a religious order who is not yet a novice ‖ (*Protestant Episcopal Church*) a candidate for ordination [F.]

pos·tu·late (póstʃulit) *n.* an assumption ‖ a hypothesis ‖ an essential condition for something ‖ (*geom.*) a statement that a construction etc. can be made [fr. L. *postulatum*, something demanded]

pos·tu·late (póstʃuleit) *pres. part.* **pos·tu·lat·ing** *past* and *past part.* **pos·tu·lat·ed** *v.t.* to demand, to require as an essential condition ‖ to assume without need to prove ‖ (*eccles. law*) to elect or nominate (a person) subject to acceptance by an ecclesiastical superior **pos·tu·la·tion** *n.* **pós·tu·la·tor** *n.* [fr. L. *postulare* (*postulatus*)]

pos·ture (póstʃər) **1.** *n.* the way a person holds himself ‖ the position held by a model in posing **2.** *v.i. pres. part.* **pos·tur·ing** *past* and *past part.* **pos·tured** to assume a physical posture, esp. for effect ‖ to behave in the studied one isn't, *posturing as an intellectual* [F.]

post·war (póustwɔ́r) *adj.* of or relating to the period after a war

po·sy (póuzi:) *pl.* **po·sies** *n.* (esp. *Br.*) a small bunch of flowers, esp. one arranged in a tight bunch so as to form a pattern ‖ a flower [shortened fr. POESY]

pot (pɒt) **1.** *n.* a container of earthenware, glass, metal etc. used for holding liquids or solids, for cooking, boiling etc. ‖ such a container with its contents ‖ a lobster pot ‖ a chamber pot ‖ (*card games*, pop. poker) the total of bets ‖ a large prize or sum to be won, e.g. in a contest ‖ (*pl.*, *pop.*) a lot of, *pots of money* ‖ (*Br.*, *pop.*) a silver cup awarded as a prize ‖ (esp. *Br.*) a chimney pot ‖ (*pop.*) marijuana **to go to pot** to go to ruin **2.** *v. pres. part.* **pot·ting** *past* and *past part.* **pot·ted** *v.t.* to set (e.g. a plant) in a flowerpot ‖ (*Br.*, *billiards*) to pocket (a ball) ‖ to preserve (meat, fish etc.) and pack it in pots ‖ to kill (an animal) by a potshot ‖ (*Br.*, *pop.*) to win, *he potted all the prizes* ‖ (of a potter) to make or shape (earthenware) ‖ *v.i.* to take potshots [O.E. *pott*]

po·ta·ble (póutəb'l) *adj.* suitable for drinking [F. fr. L.L. *potabilis*]

po·tash (pótæʃ) *n.* potassium carbonate, K_2CO_3, esp. in an impure form ‖ (*loosely*) a potassium salt or compound, *caustic potash* [fr. Du. *potasschen* fr. *pot*, pot + *asch*, ash]

po·tas·sic (pətǽsik) *adj.* of or relating to potassium ‖ containing potassium

po·tas·si·um (pətǽsi:əm) *n.* a silver-white univalent metallic element (symbol K, at. no. 19, at. mass 39.102) that oxidizes rapidly in the air. It occurs in plants and animals, and in combined form in minerals. In the compound potash it is one of the basic mineral fertilizers, and its salts are used extensively in chemical analysis, medicine etc. [Mod. L. fr. POTASH]

potassium alum *ALUM

potassium antimonyl tartrate tartar emetic

po·tas·si·um-ar·gon dating (pətǽsi:əmárgən) method of determining the age of geological or archeological specimens based on the measurement of radioactive decay from potassium to argon

potassium bitartrate cream of tartar

potassium carbonate the deliquescent crystalline salt K_2CO_3, used in glass and soap manufacturing ‖ the acid salt potassium bicarbonate. Both are potassium salts of carbonic acid

potassium chlorate $KClO_3$, a crystalline salt of potassium which readily yields oxygen on heating and is a basis of some explosive mixtures

potassium chloride KCl, a crystalline salt used chiefly as a fertilizer and in making other potassium compounds

potassium cyanide KCN, an intensely poisonous salt used chiefly in electroplating and as a weed killer

potassium dichromate $K_2Cr_2O_7$, a red, crystalline, poisonous salt used as an oxidizing agent, e.g. in safety matches, and in textile and leather finishing

potassium hydroxide KOH, a brittle white solid made usually by electrolysis of a solution of potassium chloride and used esp. in making soap and in bleaching

potassium nitrate KNO_3, a soluble crystalline salt used chiefly in curing meat and as a constituent of gunpowder

potassium permanganate $KMnO_4$, a deep purple, crystalline salt used as an oxidizing and bleaching agent, and in solution as a disinfectant

po·ta·to (pətéitou) *pl.* **po·ta·toes** *n. Solanum tuberosum*, fam. Solanaceae, a plant grown in most temperate regions for its edible tubers ‖ the starchy tuber eaten cooked as a vegetable, and used for stock feed and to produce alcohol ‖ (*loosely*) a sweet potato [Span. *patata*, var. of *batata*, sweet potato fr. Haitian]

potato beetle the Colorado beetle

potato chip (Am.=Br. crisp) a thin slice of potato fried until brown and brittle, often sold in quantity in packets ‖ *CHIP

potato ring an 18th-c. stand for a bowl, typically of silver or earthenware, of Irish provenance

Pot·a·wat·a·mi (pɒtəwótəmi:) *pl.* **Pot·a·wat·a·mi, Pot·a·wat·a·mis** *n.* a North American Indian people first encountered (early 17th c.) near Green Bay, Wis. They supported Pontiac's rebellion but sided with the British in the War of 1812. About 1,500 Potawatami live on reservations in Kansas, Michigan, Oklahoma and Wisconsin

pot·bel·lied (pótbeli:d) *adj.* having a potbelly

pot·bel·ly (pótbeli:) *pl.* **pot·bel·lies** *n.* a protuberant belly ‖ a person having a protuberant belly ‖ a heating stove having a rounded body

pot·boil·er (pótbɔilər) *n.* a work of art or literature, usually second-rate, produced merely to make money

pot culture life-style centered on use of marijuana

Po·tem·kin (poutémkin), Grigori Aleksandrovich (1739–91), Russian field marshal and statesman, favorite of Catherine II. He annexed the Crimea (1783), organized the colonization of S. Russia, reformed the army and navy, and wielded great influence in the Russian court

po·ten·cy (póut'nsi:) *pl.* **po·ten·cies** *n.* the state or quality of being potent ‖ degree of being potent ‖ capability [fr. L. *potentia*]

po·tent (póut'nt) *adj.* strong, powerful, *a potent drink* ‖ convincing, *potent arguments* ‖ (of a male) able to perform the act of sexual intercourse [fr. L. *potens* (*potentis*) fr. *posse*, to be able]

po·ten·tate (póut'nteit) *n.* a powerful monarch, ruler [fr. L.L. *potentatus*]

po·ten·tial (pəténʃəl) **1.** *adj.* existing but not fully developed, exploited etc., *a potential source of wealth* ‖ having the capacity to be, *a potential winner* ‖ (*gram.*) expressing possibility **2.** *n.* that which is potential ‖ potentiality ‖ (*gram.*) the mood of a verb which expresses possibility ‖ (*gram.*) a potential construction ‖ (*math.*) a potential function ‖ (*phys.*) electric potential **po·tén·tial·ize** *pres. part.* **po·ten·tial·iz·ing** *past* and *past part.* **po·ten·tial·ized** *v.t.* [fr. L.L. *potentialis*]

potential difference the difference in the electric potential function at two points in an electric field, esp. at two points in a circuit

potential energy (*phys.*) the energy of a body due to its position in a field

potential function (*math.*, *phys.*) a function the difference in whose values at two points in a force field measures the work done in moving a unit of mass, charge or magnetism from one position to the other, from which may be calculated the force at a point

po·ten·ti·al·i·ty (pətenʃi:ǽliti:) *pl.* **po·ten·ti·al·i·ties** *n.* the state or quality of being potential ‖ (*pl.*) possibilities of development [fr. M.L. *potentialitas*]

po·ten·tial·ly (pəténʃəli:) *adv.* with the possibility of becoming actual

po·ten·ti·om·e·ter (pətenʃi:ómitər) *n.* an instrument for precise measurement of electromotive force employing a voltage divider and a sensitive galvanometer to indicate equality between a standard emf and a known fraction of the unknown emf [fr. POTENTIAL + METER]

pot·head (póthed) *n.* (*colloq.*) a marijuana smoker

poth·er (póðər) *n.* (*old-fash.*) disturbance, commotion [etym. doubtful]

pot·herb (pótə:rb, póthə:rb) *n.* a herb, esp. a wild herb, boiled and eaten as a vegetable ‖ a cultivated herb, e.g. mint, used for seasoning

pot·hold·er (póthouldər) *n.* a square of heavy quilted cotton etc. used for picking up or holding the handles of hot pots, kettles etc.

pot·hole (póthoul) *n.* a roundish depression in a road surface, bed of a stream etc., caused by local erosion ‖ a deep cavity within a rock formation having its opening at the upper surface **pót·hol·ing** *n.* (*Br.*) spelunking

pot·hol·er (póthoulər) *n.* amateur cave explorer —**pothole** *v.*

pot·hook (póthuk) *n.* an S-shaped hook used for hanging pots over an open fire ‖ a stroke with a hook on it copied by children learning to write

po·tion (póuʃən) *n.* a dose of medicine or poison or drug in liquid form [O.F. *pocion*, potion]

pot lead (led) graphite used on the hull of a racing vessel to reduce friction **pot-lead** (pótled) *v.t.* to apply pot lead to

pot·luck (pótlʌk) *n.* what can be produced in the way of a meal for an unexpected guest or guests

Po·to·mac (pətóumək) a river (287 miles long) flowing from the Allegheny Mtns, West Virginia, to the Chesapeake Bay, forming the Maryland-Virginia border. Its estuary is navigable by large vessels to Washington, D.C.

Potomac, Army of the a huge Union army in the Civil War, organized (1861) by Gen. George McClellan. It served (1862) in the Peninsular

CONCISE PRONUNCIATION KEY: (**a**) æ, c*a*t; ɑ, c*a*r; ɔ f*aw*n; ei, sn*a*ke. (**e**) e, h*e*n; i:, sh*ee*p; i:, d*ee*r; iə, d*ee*r; ɛə, b*ea*r. (**i**) i, f*i*sh; ai, t*i*ger; ə:, b*i*rd. (**o**) o, *o*x; au, c*ow*; ou, g*oa*t; u, p*oo*r; ɔi, r*o*yal. (**u**) ʌ, d*u*ck; u, b*u*ll; u:, g*oo*se; ə, b*a*cillus; ju:, c*u*be. x, lo*ch*; θ, *th*ink; ð, bo*th*er; z, *Z*en; ʒ, cor*s*age; dʒ, sava*g*e; ŋ, ora*n*gutang; j, *y*ak; ʃ, *fi*sh; tʃ, fet*ch*; 'l, rabb*le*; 'n, redd*en*. Complete pronunciation key appears inside front cover.

Campaign and at Antietam. Although defeated (1862) at Fredericksburg and (1863) at Chancellorsville, it captured (1863) Gettysburg

Po·to·sí (pɔtɔsí:) a city (pop. 77,233) of Bolivia at 13,600 ft beside the Cerro (hill) de Potosí, famous for its now exhausted silver lode (worked 1545–19th c.). Tin is mined. Cathedral (16th c.). University

pot·pie (pótpái) n. a meat pie cooked in a deep dish

pot·pour·ri (poupurí:) n. dried flower petals and flavoring herbs stored in jars or displayed in bowls to scent a room ‖ a musical medley ‖ a literary anthology [F. pot-pourri, rotten pot, stew, trans. Span. olla podrida]

pot roast meat, usually beef, braised with vegetables **pót-roast** v.t. to cook (meat) in this way

Pots·dam (pótsdæm) a city (pop. 125,000) of East Germany 17 miles southwest of Berlin, the historical capital of Brandenburg and the Prussian royal and imperial residence. Industries: mechanical engineering, film making, precision instruments. Palaces and parks (mainly 18th c.) include Frederick II's Sans Souci (1745–7) ‖ the surrounding district (area 4,582 sq. miles, pop. 1,151,000)

Potsdam Conference a meeting (July 17–Aug. 2, 1945) of Truman, Stalin and Churchill (succeeded July 28 by Attlee) after Germany's collapse in the 2nd world war. The conference continued the work of the Yalta Conference in arranging zones of occupation in Germany, reparations and conditions to be imposed on Germany. An ultimatum was issued to Japan. It was agreed that Poland should occupy temporarily land to the east of the Oder-Neisse line

pot·sherd (pótʃə:rd) n. a piece of broken pottery [POT+SHARD]

pot·shot (pótʃɔt) n. an easy shot ‖ a shot at random

pott (pot) (Br.) adj. of a size of printing or writing paper, usually 15½×12½ ins [from the watermark of a pot]

pot·tage (pótidʒ) n. a thick soup made from vegetables or vegetables and meat [M.E. potage fr. F., lit.=something put in a pot]

Potter (pótər), Beatrix (1866–1943) English writer and illustrator of children's books. Best known for 'The Tale of Peter Rabbit' (1901), she wrote and illustrated about 28 children's stories, all involving animal characaters

Pot·ter (pótər), Paul or Paulus (1625–54), Dutch painter and etcher. He excelled in the painting of animals, e.g. 'The Bear Hunt' and the celebrated life-size 'Young Bull'

pot·ter (pótər) v.i. and t. (esp. Br.) to putter [O.E. potian, to push]

potter n. a person who makes pottery

Pot·ter·ies, the a district in N. Staffordshire, the center of the English china and earthenware industry, including the towns of Burslem, Hanley, Fenton, Tunstall, Stoke-on-Trent and Longton

potter's wheel a flat, revolving disk connected by a shaft to a flywheel, for the throwing of round forms in clay

pot·tery (pótəri:) pl. **pot·ter·ies** n. clay vessels, esp. earthenware ‖ the potter's craft ‖ the workshop of a potter [F. poterie]

Pott's disease tuberculosis of the spine [after Percivall Pott (1714–88), Eng. surgeon]

Pott's fracture a fracture of that part of the fibula nearest the ankle

pot·ty (póti) comp. **pot·ti·er** superl. **pot·ti·est** adj. (Br., pop.) trivial, pointless ‖ (Br., pop.) slightly crazy [origin unknown]

pouch (pautʃ) 1. n. a small bag, esp. for carrying tobacco or ammunition ‖ an abdominal receptacle for the young of a marsupial ‖ a baglike dilatation of the cheeks of some monkeys and rodents for storing food ‖ any baglike fold of skin, e.g. under the eyes ‖ a bag equipped with a lock for holding first-class mail or diplomatic papers ‖ a baglike plant part, e.g. the seed vessel of certain plants 2. v.t. to put into a pouch, esp. to put (first-class mail etc.) into a locked bag ‖ to store or carry in a cheek pouch ‖ to cause (skin) to form baglike folds, esp. under the eyes ‖ v.i. to form a pouch [O.N.F. pouche]

pouffe, pouf (pu:f) n. a large, tightly wadded cushion used as a seat [F.]

Pouil·let (pu:je), Claude Servais Mathias (1790–1868), French physicist. He invented the tangent galvanometer (1837) and the pyrheliometer (1837)

Pou·lenc (pu:lãk), Francis (1899–1963), French composer, member of 'Les Six'. He wrote many lyric piano pieces and songs, two operas ('les Mamelles de Tirésias', 1947 and 'Dialogue des Carmélites', 1957) and a ballet ('les Biches', 1924). His religious works include a Mass, many chorales, and the outstanding 'Stabat Mater' (1951)

poult (poult) n. a young turkey, pheasant, chicken or other fowl [F. poulet, pullet]

poul·ter·er (póultərər) n. a poultry dealer [fr. obs. poulter]

poul·tice (póultis) 1. n. a warm, soft, moistened mass, e.g. of bread, bran, linseed etc., spread on cloth and applied to a sore or inflamed part of the body to draw pus, act as a counterirritant etc. 2. v.t. pres. part. **poul·tic·ing** past and past part. **poul·ticed** to apply a poultice to [fr. L. puls (pultis), thick pap]

poul·try (póultri:) n. chickens, ducks, geese, turkeys and other domesticated birds raised for food

pounce (pauns) n. the talon of a bird of prey [etym. doubtful]

pounce n. (hist.) a fine powder, used to prevent ink from blotting on unsized paper, or to prepare a writing surface on parchment ‖ pulverized charcoal or chalk for transferring a stenciled pattern to a surface [F. ponce]

pounce 1. n. the act of pouncing ‖ the swooping, grabbing or springing motion made in pouncing 2. v.i. pres. part. **pounc·ing** past and past part. **pounced** (with 'at', 'on' or 'upon') to make a sudden swoop, spring or grasp, to pounce on the evening paper ‖ (with 'on' or 'upon') to seem to swoop, spring or grab, to pounce on an opponent [etym. doubtful]

pounce pres. part. **pounc·ing** past and past part. **pounced** v.t. to emboss (metal) by beating on the reverse side [M.E. pounsen, alt. of pounsonen fr. M.F. poinconer, to stamp]

pounce pres. part. **pounc·ing** past and past part. **pounced** v.t. to sprinkle, rub, or smooth over with pounce ‖ to transfer (a design) with pounce [F. poncer]

Pound (paund), Ezra (1885–1972), American poet. Pound began as an imagist, but his work soon transcended the limits of imagism. The most obvious feature is the delicate control of the rhythm, which conveys a tone of subtle witty comment. The element of elaborate artifice, even pedantry and sometime romantic archaism and mystification progressively took control in his work. His masterpiece, the still-unfinished 'Cantos' (begun 1919), is a brilliant though often obscure work woven of myth and legend in which he attempts to reconstruct the history of civilization. Other important works are 'Homage to Sextus Propertius' (1918) and 'Hugh Selwyn Mauberley' (1920)

pound n. an enclosure where stray or unlicensed animals are kept until they are claimed or disposed of ‖ an enclosure for trapping animals ‖ an enclosure for fish, esp. the inner compartment of a pound net ‖ a pound net ‖ a place where personal property is held until redeemed by the owner, a car pound [O.E. pundfald, pinfold]

pound 1. v.t. to thump with or as if with repeated blows, to pound a door with one's fists, to pound a typewriter ‖ to reduce to small particles by crushing, grinding etc., to pound cassava (with 'out') to produce with or as if with vigorous thumps, to pound out a tune on a piano, to pound out a letter on the typewriter ‖ (with 'in' or 'into') to cause someone to learn or remember (facts etc.) by constant repetition, to pound facts into someone's head ‖ v.i. to strike heavy, thumping blows, to pound on a door ‖ to make a thumping noise, the artillery pounded away for an hour ‖ (of a ship) to hit the water heavily and repeatedly ‖ (of the heart, an engine etc.) to throb violently ‖ to move quickly but heavily or with force or effort and a dull thudding sound **to pound away** to persevere in work calling for effort 2. n. a pounding ‖ a thud or blow or the sound of a thud or blow [O.E. pūnian]

pound pl. **pounds, pound** n. (abbr. lb.) the unit of mass equal to 16 oz. avoirdupois or to 12 oz. troy ‖ (symbol £) the pound sterling, the British monetary unit equal to 100 pence ‖ the monetary unit of various countries, e.g. Egypt, Ireland, Syria, Turkey [O.E. pund fr. L.]

pound·age (páundidʒ) n. charge of a percentage as a fee in pound sterling transactions ‖ payment regulated according to the weight of an object to be handled (e.g. of postal charges)

pound·al (páund'l) n. (phys.) a unit of force defined as that required to accelerate a mass of 1 lb by 1 ft per sec. per sec.

pound·er (páundər) n. (in compounds) something weighing a specific number of pounds, the fish was a good three-pounder ‖ a gun firing a shot weighing a specified number of pounds, a twenty-five pounder [POUND (unit of mass)]

pound-fool·ish (páundfú:liʃ) adj. *PENNY-WISE

pound-force (páundfɔrs, páundfóurs) n. (phys.) a unit of force in the foot-pound-second system, defined as the force required to accelerate a mass of 1 lb. at a rate equal to the acceleration of gravity

pound net a fish trap consisting of long net fences directing fish into an inner, completely meshed-in compartment from which they cannot escape

pound sterling the pound (British monetary unit)

pound-weight (páundwéit) n. the weight of a mass of 1 lb. at a place where the acceleration due to gravity is 32.19 ft per sec. per sec.

pour (pɔr, pour) 1. v.t. to send out in a stream, pour water over the flowers ‖ to discharge profusely, the river poured its waters through the breach ‖ (esp. with 'out') to send forth (words, music etc.) as if in a stream, to pour out one's feelings ‖ v.i. to flow in copious streams, blood poured out of the wound ‖ to flow out as if in a stream, the crowd poured out of the theater ‖ to rain heavily ‖ to preside at a tea table 2. n. the act of pouring ‖ a downpour ‖ (founding) a quantity of molten metal poured at one time [M.E. pouren, etym. doubtful]

Pous·sin (pu:sɛ̃), Nicolas (1594–1665), French painter who lived mainly in Rome. His early works, based on mythological and elegiac subjects, display dramatic and sensuous beauty, and show the influence of Titian and Veronese. The strict classicism which he went on to develop allowed no compromise with intellectual content: the moral statement of the picture must be fully served by color and composition. His themes are heroic, involving some dramatic moment of classical or biblical inspiration and a central psychological crisis. He sets down a vision of a world of dignity and nobility, with intense power. In landscape painting his ideal is in total contrast with that of Claude Lorrain

pout (paut) pl. **pout, pouts** n. Gadus luscus, fam. Gadidae, a small European cod having a biblike membrane on its head [O.E. pūta]

pout 1. v.i. to express displeasure, resentment, bad humor etc. by thrusting out the lower lip and looking sulky ‖ to sulk ‖ v.t. to thrust out (the lips) ‖ to utter with a pout 2. n. a sulky thrusting out of the lips ‖ (pl.) a fit of sulking [M.E. pouten, prob. fr. O.N.]

pout·er (páutər) n. a person who pouts ‖ a breed of domestic pigeon capable of inflating its crop to a great size [POUT]

po·ver·a (pəvérə) adj. of the art form that emphasizes the idea or process over the product, e.g., collage, fingerpainting

pov·er·ty (póvərti:) n. the condition or quality of being poor ‖ (of soil) unproductiveness ‖ deficiency in or inadequate supply of something, poverty of ideas ‖ monastic renunciation of the right to own, a vow of poverty [O.F. pouerte, poverté]

poverty line the marginal income level at which an adequate living standard is possible

pov·er·ty-strick·en (póverti:strikən) adj. poor ‖ exhibiting poverty, a poverty stricken town

pow·der (páudər) 1. n. a dry substance composed of fine particles ‖ a medicine in powdered form ‖ a scented cosmetic for the face or body ‖ gunpowder 2. v.t. to cover, sprinkle or dust with or as if with powder ‖ to convert to powder ‖ to apply cosmetic powder to (the face etc.) ‖ to decorate (a surface) with dots, small figures etc. ‖ v.i. to use cosmetic powder ‖ to become powder [F. poudre]

powder blue pale blue

powdered sugar confectioners' sugar

powder flask (Br., hist.) a case for carrying gunpowder

powder horn (hist.) a powder flask made of the horn of an ox or cow

Pow·der·ly (páudərli:), Terence Vincent (1849–1924), U.S. labor leader who headed (1879–93) the Knights of Labor

powder magazine (hist.) a place for storing gunpowder

powder metallurgy the process of reducing metals to powder and their use in molding small metal parts

powder monkey (hist.) a boy employed on a ship to carry gunpowder to the guns

---

powder puff a small, soft pad for applying cosmetic powder

powder room a rest room for women in a restaurant, night club etc.

pow·der·y (páudəri:) *adj.* resembling powder, *powdery snow* ‖ covered with powder ‖ apt to become powder

Pow·ell (páuəl), John Wesley (1834–1902), U.S. geologist and ethnologist. His 'Explorations of the Colorado River of the West' (1875) and his 'Canyons of the Colorado' (1895) describe his several expeditions to Arizona and Utah, especially his hazardous voyage through the Grand Canyon. He helped to establish (1879) the U.S. Geological Survey

Powell, Lewis F., Jr. (1907–　） U.S. Supreme Court justice. He practiced law in Richmond, Va., beginning in 1932 and was elected president of the American Bar Association (1964). He was appointed to the Supreme Court (1971) by Pres. Richard M. Nixon and usually voted as a moderate conservative. His opinion in 'University of California v. Bakke' (1978) was considered pivotal in the Court's decision on that case

pow·er (páuər) 1. *n.* an ability or faculty, *the power of motion, intellectual powers* ‖ physical strength ‖ control, *to be in someone's power* ‖ military strength ‖ controlling influence, *political power* ‖ authority, authorization, *the power to sign a document* ‖ a person of great influence or authority ‖ a country having international influence or authority ‖ mechanical or electrical energy ‖ (*phys.*) the rate at which work is done or energy transmitted ‖ (*math.*) the number of times a quantity is multiplied by itself, or the index denoting this, *10 to the power of 3 is 1,000* ‖ the magnifying capacity of a lens measured as the ratio between the dimensions of the image and the object (*MAGNIFICATION) ‖ the reciprocal of the focal length of a lens ‖ (*pl.*) an order of angels (*ANGEL) **in power** in authority or control 2. *v.t.* to supply with a source of power [M.E. *poer, poeir, pouer* fr. A.F.]

power base the center of support for a person or policy, esp. political support

pow·er·boat (páuərbɔut) *n.* a motor boat

power broker one who trades in influence, esp. political influence

power component the part of an alternating current which is in phase with the voltage

power dive (*aviation*) a descent with the thrust of the engines added to the pull of gravity

power down *v.* (*astronautics*) to lower the energy level of a spacecraft. *ant.* power up

power elite head of institutional hierarchies (business, military, political, religious) who make decisions of national consequence; originated by sociologist C. Wright Mills in 1956

pow·er·ful (páuərfəl) *adj.* having great power, *a powerful nation* ‖ physically strong ‖ (of drugs, medicine etc.) potent

power function (*math.*) an algebraic function of the form *f(x) = ax^n* where *a* and *n* are constants

pow·er·house (páuərhaus) *pl.* **pow·er·hous·es** (páuərhauziz) *n.* a building in which power is generated

pow·er·less (páuərlis) *adj.* without power ‖ (followed by an infinitive) unable, *powerless to intervene*

power of attorney a written authority, with an attested signature, authorizing a person to act as the attorney or agent of the person granting it

power point (*Br.*) an electrical outlet

power politics international political relations based on the achievement of aims through force or show of force rather than through peaceful negotiations

power station a powerhouse

power steering a steering system in which the engine power automatically amplifies the torque which the driver applies at the steering wheel

power structure where the group that makes basic political and economic decisions for an organization or community. *Cf* ESTABLISHMENT

power sweep (*football*) an end run supported by one or more linemen running interference for the player carrying the ball

POW, P.O.W. prisoner of war

Pow·ha·tan (pauhətǽn, pauhǽt'n) (c. 1550–1618), American Indian chief of the Powhatan tribe in Virginia, and father of Pocahontas

pow·wow (páuwau) 1. *n.* a North American Indian conjurer or medicine man ‖ a North American Indian ceremony marked by noise and feasting, performed to secure victory in war, the curing of a disease etc. ‖ a conference of or with North American Indians ‖ (*pop.*) any long talk or conference 2. *v.t.* to take part in a ceremonial powwow ‖ (*pop.*) to confer [fr. Algonquian]

pox (pɔks) *n.* any of various specified diseases characterized by pustules, e.g. chicken pox ‖ (*old-fash.*) syphilis [old pl. of POCK]

pox·vi·rus (pɔksvəirəs) *n.* (*med.*) a group of large, chemically complex DNA viruses covered with threads and tubules that cause smallpox, mousepox, and myxomatosis (mucous tumors in rabbits)

Po·yang Hu (póujáŋhú:) a lake (area 1,042 sq. miles) in N. Kiangsi, China, connected by a natural channel to the Yangtze-kiang

Poy·nings' Law (pɔ́iniŋz) (*Br. hist.*) an act of the Irish parliament (1495) extending English jurisdiction to Ireland and requiring English approval for the summoning of an Irish parliament. The law was repealed (1782) [after Sir Edward Poynings (1459–1521), English soldier and diplomat, lord deputy of Ireland (1494–6)]

Poyn·ting (pɔ́intiŋ), John Henry (1852–1914), English physicist. He carried out experiments to determine the gravitational constant and mean density of the earth by a balance method, and also did valuable research on electromagnetic energy

Poz·nan (pɔ́znaŋ) (*G. Posen*) a commercial and industrial center (pop. 527,000) of W. Poland on the Warta. Main industries: mechanical engineering, chemicals, textiles, food processing. Cathedral (15th–18th cc.), city hall (16th c.), university (1919)

poz·zo·la·na (pɔtsəlánə) *n.* a volcanic ash used in hydraulic cements [Ital. *pozzuolana* after *Pozzuoli*, a city in Italy near Naples]

poz·zuo·la·na (pɔtswəlánə) *n.* pozzolana

PPBS or **PPB** (*business acronym*) planning programming budgeting systems, a procedure for enlarging the information base in budgeting in which benefits are provided in proportion to costs, and alternatives evaluated based on costs

PPLO (*med. abbr.*) pleuropneumonia-like organism, any of a genus of nonmotile microorganisms without cell walls that are between viruses and bacteria, generally parasitic, found in body fluids (serums) of mammals, *also* mycoplasma

prac·ti·ca·bil·i·ty (præktikəbíliti:) *n.* the quality or condition of being practicable

prac·ti·ca·ble (præktikəb'l) *adj.* capable of being done, feasible, *a practicable experiment* ‖ capable of being used, *a practicable route* [F. *praticable*]

prac·ti·cal (præktik'l) *adj.* of, relating to, or obtained through practice or action, *practical experience* ‖ that can be put into practice, *a practical suggestion* ‖ able to apply theory, esp. in constructing, repairing etc., *a practical man* **prac·ti·cál·i·ty** *n.* [fr. older *practic* fr. F.]

practical joke a trick played upon a person, often at the expense of his dignity

prac·ti·cal·ly (præktik'li:) *adv.* in a practical way ‖ virtually, *she is practically deaf now*

practical nurse a nurse who is experienced but is without the training of a registered nurse

practical unit a unit of measurement which is a multiple or submultiple of an absolute unit, used for arithmetical convenience

prac·tice (præktis) 1. *v.* (*Am. also* **practise**, *Br.* only **practise**) *pres. part.* **prac·tic·ing** *past* and *past part.* **prac·ticed** *v.t.* to make a practice of, *to practice thrift* ‖ to follow or work at as a profession, *to practice medicine* ‖ to study, exercise one's skill in regularly or frequently so as to win greater command, *to practice a circus act, practice the violin* ‖ to practice a class in French pronunciation ‖ *v.i.* to perform an act or exercise a skill repeatedly in order to achieve greater command, *to practice on the flute* ‖ to be active in a profession, *does he still practice?* 2. *n.* (*Am. also* **practise**, *Br.* only **practice**) a customary action or customary code of behavior, *to make a practice of dining early* ‖ a way of behavior, *evil practices* ‖ repeated performance or systematic exercise for the purpose of learning or acquiring proficiency, *piano practice* ‖ the exercise of a profession, esp. law or medicine ‖ a professional business, *to sell one's practice* ‖ (*law*) the established method of conducting and carrying on suits and prosecutions **in practice** in a condition to be able to perform with skill as a result of exercise and repeated performance

out of practice not in this condition **to put into practice** to apply (theory etc.) in action **prác·ticed, prác·tised** *adj.* expert through long experience [O.F. *practiser*]

prac·ti·cian (præktíʃən) *n.* a person who practices a skill, art etc. ‖ a practitioner [F. *practicien*]

practise *PRACTICE

prac·ti·tion·er (præktíʃənər) *n.* a person who practices a profession, esp. a doctor [PRACTICIAN]

Pra·do (prádou) *MADRID

Pra·do y U·gar·te·che (práðɔi:ú:gartétʃe), Manuel (1889–1967), Peruvian engineer, statesman, and president (1939–45, 1956–62). He was overthrown by a military junta

prae·co·ces, pre·co·ces (prí:kəsi:z) *pl. n.* precocial birds [L., pl. of *praecox*, mature early]

praecocial * PRECOCIAL

prae·mu·ni·re (prí:mju:náiri:) *n.* (*Br. hist.*) a writ charging a sheriff to summon a person accused under the Statutes of Praemunire ‖ the offense of which the person is accused ‖ the penalty incurred by someone found guilty of such an offense [M.L.=to warn, used for L. *praemonire*, to forewarn]

Praemunire, Statute of (*Br. hist.*) any of several statutes enacted (1353, 1365, 1393) with the aim of preventing papal encroachments on royal rights. Charging with praemunire later became a political weapon, notably (1529) in Henry VIII's attack on Wolsey

prae·no·men, pre·no·men (prɪːnóumən) *pl.* **prae·no·mens, pre·no·mens, prae·nom·i·na, pre·nom·i·na** (prɪːnɔ́minə) *n.* the first of the three names making up an ancient Roman name, e.g. 'Gaius' in Gaius Julius Caesar (cf. AGNOMEN, cf. COGNOMEN, cf. NOMEN) [L.]

praesidium *PRESIDIUM

Praetorian Guard, Pretorian Guard (*Rom. hist.*) a member of the bodyguard of Roman emperors, disbanded (312 A.D.) after its influence had increased to the point where it could make and unmake emperors

praetor, pre·tor (prí:tər) *n.* (*Rom. hist.*) a magistrate, ranking below a consul **prae·to·ri·al, pre·to·ri·al** (prɪːtɔ́ri:əl, prɪːtɔ́uri:əl) *adj.* [L.]

prae·to·ri·an, pre·to·ri·an (prɪːtɔ́ri:ən, prɪːtɔ́uri:ən) 1. *adj.* of or relating to a praetor **Prae·to·ri·an** or relating to the Praetorian Guard 2. *n.* a man of praetorian status **Praetorian** a member of the Praetorian Guard [fr. L. *praetorianus*]

prae·tor·ship, pre·tor·ship (prí:tərʃip) *n.* the office of praetor or period of tenure of the office

prag·mat·ic (prægmætik) *adj.* of or relating to pragmatism ‖ dealing with events in the light of practical lessons or applications ‖ of or relating to state affairs **prag·mát·i·cal** *adj.* [fr. L. *pragmaticus* fr. Gk *pragmatikos*, active, businesslike]

prag·mat·ics (prægmætiks) *n.* (*semiotics*) the science of relationships between symbols, their interpretation and users

pragmatic sanction a royal decree having the force of fundamental law **Pragmatic Sanction** the Emperor Charles VI's settlement (1713) of the Austrian succession on his daughter Maria Theresa. It was guaranteed by most European sovereigns, but resulted in the War of the Austrian Succession

prag·ma·tism (prægmətizəm) *n.* a doctrine which tests truth by its practical consequences. Truth is therefore held to be relative and not attainable by metaphysical speculation. Pragmatism was first formulated by C. S. Peirce (1839–1914) and was developed by William James, John Dewey and others

Prague (*Czech.* Praha) the capital (pop. 1,176,000) and industrial, commercial and cultural center of Czechoslovakia, on the Moldau. Principal industries: metallurgy, heavy machinery, motor vehicles, chemicals, food processing, publishing. The old royal city (14th and 18th-cc. Hradčany castle, mainly 14th-c. Gothic cathedral, baroque palaces and churches) and medieval quarters are on the left bank, and the old town (14th-c. Gothic cathedral, ghetto, medieval monuments) is on the right bank. University (1348), national museums and theaters. The city was occupied (1968) by troops from the U.S.S.R. and other Warsaw Pact countries

Prague Spring (prag) political and economic liberalization movement in Czechoslovakia in 1968 under Communist Party Secretary Alexander Dubček. It was opposed by the Warsaw Pact nations by mid-July and crushed by a

CONCISE PRONUNCIATION KEY: (**a**) æ, c*a*t; ɑ, c*a*r; ɔ f*aw*n; ei, sn*a*ke. (**e**) e, h*e*n; i:, sh*ee*p; iə, d*ee*r; ɛə, b*ea*r. (**i**) i, f*i*sh; ai, t*i*ger; ə:, b*i*rd. (**o**) o, *o*x; au, c*ow*; ou, g*oa*t; u, p*oo*r; ɔi, r*oy*al. (**u**) ʌ, d*u*ck; u, b*u*ll; u:, g*oo*se; ə, b*a*cill*u*s; ju:, c*u*be. x, lo*ch*; θ, *th*ink; ð, bo*th*er; z, *Z*en; ʒ, corsa*g*e; dʒ, sava*g*e; ŋ, ora*ng*utang; j, *y*ak; ʃ, *fi*sh; tʃ, fe*tch*; 'l, rabb*le*; 'n, redd*en*. Complete pronunciation key appears inside front cover.

Soviet-led invasion in August of the same year

Prague, Treaty of a treaty (May 30, 1635) during the Thirty Years' War, between Emperor Ferdinand II and John George I, elector of Saxony ‖ a treaty (Aug. 23, 1866) between Prussia and Austria, ending the Seven Weeks' War. Italy gained Lombardy-Venetia. Austria was left intact, but had to withdraw from Germany. The North German Confederation was set up

pra·hu (préiu:) n. a prau

prai·rie (préəri:) n. a wide tract of treeless and gently undulating grassland in North America, esp. in the Mississippi valley [F. fr. L. *pratum*, meadow]

prairie chicken *Tympanuchus cupido pinnatus*, a North American grouse inhabiting the Mississippi valley from Manitoba to Texas, or a smaller grouse, *T. pallidicinctus*, of W. Texas ‖ *Pedioecetes phasianellus*, a grouse of the western U.S.A. and Canada

prairie dog a member of *Cynomys*, fam. *Sciuridae*, a plump North American rodent, esp. *C. ludovicianus*, having a doglike bark and measuring about 1 ft in length

prairie schooner (*Am. hist.*) a long covered wagon used by the pioneers in traveling westward

prairie wolf a coyote

praise (preiz) 1. *v.t. pres. part.* **prais·ing** *past* and *past part.* **praised** to speak of with approval or admiration ‖ to glorify (God or a deity) 2. *n.* a praising or being praised ‖ the act of glorifying God or a deity [O.E. *preisier*]

praise·wor·thi·ly (préizwə:rθili:) *adv.* in a praiseworthy manner

praise·wor·thi·ness (préizwə:rθi:nis) *n.* the quality of being praiseworthy

praise·wor·thy (préizwə:rθi:) *adj.* worthy of praise

Pra·krit (prάkrit) *n.* any of the popular ancient Indic languages, including Ardhamagadhi, Maharashtri, Sauraseni and Magadhi (cf. SANSKRIT) ‖ any of the modern Indic languages [fr. Skr. *prάkrta*, not refined]

pra·line (prάli:n, préili:n) *n.* a confection of almonds or other nuts browned in boiling sugar [F. after Comte du Plessis-*Praslin* (1598-1675), French marshal]

prall-trill·er (prάltrilər) *n.* (*mus.*) an ornament starting and stopping upon the main note with one sounding of the note above it heard in between, all three notes executed as swiftly as possible [G. fr. *prall*, elastic+*triller*, a trill]

pram (præm) *n.* (*Br., pop.*) a baby carriage [shortened fr. PERAMBULATOR]

prance (præns, prɑns) 1. *v. pres. part.* **prancing** *past* and *past part.* **pranced** *v.i.* (of a mettlesome horse) to leap up on the hind legs in a rearing motion, or to move forward by so doing ‖ to ride or drive a horse leaping in this way ‖ (of a person) to move in a gleeful or arrogant way ‖ *v.t.* to cause (a horse) to prance 2. *n.* a prancing movement [etym. doubtful]

prank (præŋk) *v.t.* (*rhet.*) to deck, adorn [etym. doubtful]

prank *n.* a piece of mischief **pránk·ish** *adj.* [perh. fr. PRANK v.]

Pra·sad (prəsάd), Rajendra (1884–1963), Indian statesman, first president of India (1950–62). He was president of the Indian National Congress (1934)

prase (preiz) *n.* a variety of leek-green, translucent quartz [F. fr. L. fr. Gk *prasios*, leek green]

pra·se·o·dym·i·um (preizi:oudími:əm, preisi:oudími:əm) *n.* a trivalent element (symbol Pr, at. no. 59, at. mass 140.907) of the rare-earth group [Mod. L. fr. Gk *prasios*, leek green+*didymium*, a mixture of rare-earth elements containing neodymium and formerly considered as an element]

Pras·lin (prɑlɛ̃) *SEYCHELLES

Prat Cha·cón (prάttʃakɔ́n), Arturo (1848–79), Chilean admiral and hero of the War of the Pacific

prate (preit) 1. *v.i. pres. part.* **prat·ing** *past* and *past part.* **prat·ed** (*rhet.*) to babble or chatter idly or nonsensically ‖ *v.t.* (*rhet.*) to utter (nonsensical chatter) 2. *n.* (*rhet.*) foolish talk [M.E. *praten* fr. M. Du.]

prat·in·cole (prætiŋkoul) *n.* any of several limicoline birds of genus *Glareola*, fam. *Glareolidae*, esp. *G. pratincola*, having a white abdomen, brown breast and brown upper parts, and measuring about 9 ins in length. It is found in parts of Europe, Asia and Africa [fr. Mod. L.

pratincola fr. *pratum*, meadow+*incola*, inhabitant]

pra·tique (prætí:k) *n.* permission granted to a ship that has complied with quarantine regulations etc. to carry on business with a port [F.]

Pra·to (prάtou) a town (pop. 154,400) of Tuscany, Italy, 10 miles northwest of Florence. Industry: wool textiles. Cathedral (12th c.) with works by Donatello, Lippi and Andrea Della Robbia, palace (13th–14th cc.)

Pratt (præt), Edwin John (1882–1964), the leading Canadian poet of his time. His works include 'The Cachalot' (1926), an imaginative and humorous account of a whale hunt, and 'Brébeuf and His Brethren' (1940), a chronicle of the martyrdom of Jesuit missionaries by the Iroquois. He turned during the 2nd world war to topical themes, esp. 'Dunkirk' (1941)

prat·tle (præt'l) 1. *v. pres. part.* **prat·tling** *past* and *past part.* **prat·tled** *v.i.* to talk incessantly, esp. to gossip ‖ to chatter *v.t.* to babble (gossip, nonsense etc.) 2. *n.* chatter, esp. childish chatter [PRATE]

prau (prau) *n.* a narrow Malayan boat up to 30 ft long, shaped like a canoe and usually equipped with oars, a large triangular sail, and an outrigger [fr. Malay *prau, prao*]

prawn (prɔn) *n.* any of several decapod crustaceans related to the shrimp and the lobster, having thin legs and long antennae. They are widely distributed in fresh and salt waters of warm and temperate regions and are highly esteemed as food [M.E. *prane*]

prax·is (præksis) *pl.* **prax·es** (præksi:z) *n.* a customary mode of behavior [Mod. L. fr. Gk *praxis*, doing]

Prax·it·e·les (præksít'li:z) (c. 370–c. 330 B.C.), Athenian sculptor famous for his statues of Aphrodite at Cos and Cnidus. His work survives mainly in Roman copies (*SATYR)

pray (prei) *v.i.* to enter into spiritual communion with God or an object of worship, *he prays constantly* ‖ to implore God or an object of worship, *to pray for their health* ‖ *v.t.* (*archaic*) to implore (God or an object of worship) ‖ (*rhet.*, contr. of 'I pray you') you must tell me, *what, pray, is the meaning of this behavior.?* [O.F. *preier*]

prayer (prɛər) *n.* a humble communication in thought or speech to God or to an object of worship expressing supplication, thanksgiving, praise, confession etc. ‖ that which is prayed for, *God granted him his prayer* ‖ the liturgical formulation of a communication to God or to an object of worship, *the Lord's Prayer* ‖ (esp. *pl.*) a public or private religious service consisting mainly of such formulations, *family prayers* ‖ the act or practice of praying ‖ (*rhet.*) an entreaty made to someone, *a prayer to the king for mercy* [O.F. *preiere*]

prayer book a book containing prayers and usually including set forms of worship

prayer·ful (prɛ́ərfəl) *adj.* given to frequent praying ‖ characterized by prayer ‖ expressive of prayer

prayer meeting a religious meeting for offering prayer

prayer rug a mat or small carpet used by Moslems to kneel on when praying

prayer shawl a tallith

prayer wheel a revolving cylinder inscribed with prayers used esp. by Tibetan Buddhists

pray-in (préiin) *n.* a protest gathering characterized by prayers and sermons, usu. held in a house of worship

praying mantis *Mantis religiosa*, the common mantis

pra·ze·pam [$C_{19}H_{17}CIN_2O$] (prázəpæm) *n.* (*pharm.*) benzodiazepine tranquilizer used as a muscle relaxant and antidepressant; marketed as Verstran

pra·zo·sin [$C_{19}H_{21}N_5O_4$] (prázousin) *n.* (*pharm.*) a drug used to reduce high blood pressure by relaxing muscles; marketed as Minipress

pre- (pri:) *prefix* earlier than, preceding ‖ beforehand ‖ preparatory to ‖ before, in front of (in location, order of importance or degree etc.) [L. *prae* adv. and *prep.*, before]

preach (pri:tʃ) *v.i.* to deliver a religious address publicly, esp. to expound the gospel ‖ to offer moral advice in a tiresome manner, *he does nothing but preach at his children* ‖ *v.t.* to advocate (*a course* or *principle*), *to preach moderation and prudence* **préach·er** *n.* someone who preaches, esp. a minister [O.F. *precher, préchier*]

preach·i·fy (prí:tʃifai) *pres. part.* **preach·i·fy·ing** *past* and *past part.* **preach·i·fied** *v.i.* to moralize endlessly [PREACH]

pre·ag·ri·cul·tur·al (pri:ægrikʌ́ltərəl) *adj.* of the period before human beings began to practice agriculture

pre·am·ble (prí:æmb'l) *n.* an introductory part of a speech or piece of writing, esp. the introductory part of a statute, ordinance etc. stating the reasons and purpose of the text that follows [F. *préambule*]

pre·ar·range (pri:ərĕindʒ) *pres. part.* **pre·ar·rang·ing** *past* and *past part.* **pre·ar·ranged** *v.t.* to arrange in advance

Pre·ax (prí:æks) *n.* trademark of synthetic heat-resistant fabric designed to replace asbestos; created by Gentex Corp. of Carbondale, Pa.

pre·ax·i·al (pri:ǽksi:əl) *adj.* (*anat.*) situated in front of the axis of the body

pre·bend (prébənd) *n.* a stipend paid out of cathedral revenue, e.g. to a member of the chapter ‖ the land or tithe which produces this revenue ‖ a prebendary **pre·ben·dal** (pribénd'l) *adj.* [O.F. *prebende*]

preb·en·dar·y (prébənderi:) *pl.* **preb·en·dar·ies** *n.* a cleric receiving a prebend ‖ (*Church of England*) an honorary canon (receiving no such stipend) [fr. M.L. *praebendarius*]

pre·bi·o·log·i·cal (pri:baiəlɔ́dʒik'l) *adj.* of the period before or precursors of the origin of life. **—pre·bi·o·log·ic** or **pre·bi·ot·ic** *adj.*

Pre·cam·bri·an (pri:kǽmbri:ən) *adj.* relating to the eras of geological history prior to the Cambrian (*PROTEROZOIC, *ARCHEOZOIC, *GEOLOGICAL TIME) the Precambrian these eras

pre·car·i·ous (prikέəri:əs) *adj.* uncertain, *to earn a precarious living* ‖ dangerous, *falling rocks made the ascent precarious* ‖ not firmly founded, *a precarious line of reasoning* [fr. L. *precarius*]

pre·cast (pri:kǽst, pri:kάst) *v.t.* (of concrete) to cast in blocks for subsequent construction

prec·a·tive (prékətiv) *adj.* precatory ‖ (*gram.*) of or relating to a verb form expressing a request [L.L. *precativus*]

prec·a·to·ry (prékətɔri:, prékətouri:) *adj.* of, relating to, or expressing request [fr. L.L. *precatorius*]

precatory trust a trust created by precatory words construed as having binding force

precatory words (*pl.*) words of request employed in a will, not always construed as binding

pre·cau·tion (prikɔ́ʃən) *n.* care with respect to the foreseeable future, *to invest with due precaution* ‖ a measure taken against some possible future evil or calamity or undesirable happening, *fire precautions* **pre·cáu·tion·ar·y, pre·cáu·tious** *adjs* [F. *précaution*]

pre·cede (prisí:d) *pres. part.* **pre·ced·ing** *past* and *past part.* **pre·ced·ed** *v.t.* to go before in rank, importance etc. ‖ to come before in time, *the stillness that precedes a storm* ‖ to go or come before or in front of, *twelve guards on motorcycles preceded the president's car* ‖ (with 'by' or 'with') to preface, *to precede a ceremony with a speech of welcome* ‖ *v.i.* to go or come before, *the days that preceded were filled with activity* [F. *précéder*]

prec·e·dence (présidəns, prisí:d'ns) *n.* the act, fact, right or privilege of preceding another or others, usually according to rank, esp. on ceremonial or highly formal social occasions [PRECEDENT]

prec·e·dent 1. (présidənt) *n.* a previous instance or case that may serve to justify a subsequent act, procedure etc. of a similar kind ‖ (*law*) a previous judicial decision, proceeding etc., taken as a rule in dealing with subsequent similar cases 2. (prisí:dənt) *adj.* (*rhet.*) coming before in order, time etc., *precedent judgments* **préc·e·dent·ed** *adj.* having an established precedent [F. *précédent*]

pre·cen·sor·ship (pri:sénsərʃip) *n.* censorship before publication or other public release, usu. of politically sensitive material. **—pre·cen·sor** *v.*

pre·cen·tor (priséntər) *n.* the leader of congregational singing in some churches ‖ a member of a cathedral staff responsible for all musical arrangements connected with cathedral worship [fr. L.L. *praecentor*]

pre·cept (prí:sept) *n.* a commandment or instruction intended as a rule of action or conduct ‖ a technical instruction [fr. L. *praecipere* (*praeceptus*), to teach]

pre·cep·tive (priséptiv) *adj.* of or relating to a precept ‖ mandatory [L.L. *praeceptivus*]

CONCISE PRONUNCIATION KEY: **(a)** æ, c*a*t; ɑ, c*a*r; ɔ f*aw*n; ei, sn*a*ke. **(e)** e, h*e*n; i:, sh*ee*p; iə, d*ee*r; ɛə, b*ea*r. **(i)** i, f*i*sh; ai, t*i*ger; ə:, b*i*rd. **(o)** o, *o*x; au, c*ow*; ou, g*oa*t; u, p*oo*r; ɔi, r*oy*al. **(u)** ʌ, d*u*ck; u, b*u*ll; u:, g*oo*se; ə, bacill*u*s; ju:, c*u*be. x, lo*ch*; θ, *th*ink; ð, bo*th*er; z, *Z*en; ʒ, corsa*g*e. **(o)** o, *o*x; ... dʒ, sava*g*e; ŋ, ora*n*guta*ng*; j, *y*ak; ʃ, *f*ish; tʃ, fe*tch*; 'l, rabb*le*; 'n, redd*en*. Complete pronunciation key appears inside front cover.

pre·cep·tor (priséptər) n. (archaic) a teacher ‖ (hist.) the head of a preceptory [L. praeceptor, teacher]

pre·cep·to·ry (priséptəri:) pl. **precep·to·ries** n. (hist.) a subordinate community of the Knights Templars ‖ the manor, estate etc. belonging to this [fr. M.L praeceptoria, estate of a preceptor]

pre·ces·sion (priséʃən) n. the motion of the axis of rotation of a spinning body (e.g. a gyroscope) about a line that makes an angle with it, so as to describe a cone. It is caused by a torque acting on the rotation axis to change its direction, and is a motion continuously at right angles to the plane of the torque causing it and the angular momentum vector of the spinning body **pre·ces·sion·al** adj. [fr. L.L. praecessio (praecessionis), a preceding]

precession of the equinoxes (astron.) the combined effect of lunisolar and planetary precessions on the movement of the equinoctial points, causing a slightly earlier occurrence of the equinoxes each year (a complete to-and-fro swing taking 25,800 terrestrial years)

pre·Chris·tian (pri:krístʃən) adj. of, relating to or being a time prior to the birth of Christ ‖ of, relating to or being a time before the introduction of Christianity

pre·cinct (prí:siŋkt) n. the space within the boundaries of a church, school or other building or place, the abbey precinct ‖ the boundary itself ‖ (pl.) the immediate surroundings of a place ‖ a subdivision of a county, city or city ward for police and election purposes [fr. M.L. praecinctum fr. praecingere (praecinctus), to surround]

pre·ci·os·i·ty (preʃi:ósiti:) n. excessive refinement, esp. the affected insistence on purity or nicety of language characteristic of a group of fashionable women of 17th-c. French society [O.F. preciosité]

pre·cious (préʃəs) 1. adj. of great material value, precious metals ‖ of great nonmaterial value, a precious friendship ‖ exhibiting preciosity ‖ (used as a term of endearment) beloved ‖ (pop.) complete, you have made a precious fool of yourself 2. adv. (pop.) extremely, I took precious good care not to let him know [O.F. precios]

precious metal a valuable metal, esp. gold, silver, platinum

precious stone a jewel, e.g. diamond, ruby etc., of great value

prec·i·pice (présəpis) n. the very steep or overhanging part of the face of a cliff, side of a mountain etc. [F. précipice]

pre·cip·i·tance (prisípitəns) n. precipitancy

pre·cip·i·tan·cy (prisípitənsi:) n. excessive, violent haste ‖ rashness, or an instance of this [PRECIPITANT]

pre·cip·i·tant (prisípitənt) 1. adj. precipitate 2. n. (chem.) that which causes precipitation to occur [fr. L. praecipitans (praecipitantis) fr. praecipitare, to precipitate]

pre·cip·i·tate 1. (prisípiteit) v. pres. part. **pre·cip·i·tat·ing** past and past part. **pre·cip·i·tat·ed** v.t. (rhet.) to hurl downward, throw violently, he precipitated himself into the melee ‖ to hasten, his illness precipitated the crisis ‖ (chem.) to cause (a soluble substance) to become insoluble and separate from a solution ‖ (meteorol.) to cause (vapor) to condense and fall as rain, snow etc. ‖ v.i. (chem.) to separate from a solution ‖ (meteorol.) to condense from a vapor and fall as rain, snow etc. 2. (prisípitit) adj. sudden, hasty, precipitate action ‖ rushing violently ‖ rash, headstrong 3. (prisípitit) n. (chem.) a solid substance separated from a solution as the result of a chemical reaction, esp. a crystalline solid that can be separated from the solution by filtration [fr. L. praecipitare (praecipitatus), to rush headlong]

pre·cip·i·ta·tion (prisipitéiʃən) n. a precipitating or being precipitated ‖ excessive or reckless haste ‖ (meteorol.) a deposit of water in either liquid or solid form, e.g. rain, snow, which reaches the earth from the atmosphere ‖ (meteorol.) the quantity deposited ‖ (chem.) a precipitate [F. précipitation]

pre·cip·i·ta·tor (prisípiteitər) n. (envir.) an air pollution control device that mechanically or electrically collects particles from an emission

pre·cip·i·tin (prisípitin) n. (med.) an antibody which forms a precipitate when reacting with its antigen [PRECIPITATE]

pre·cip·i·tous (prisípitəs) adj. resembling a precipice ‖ containing precipices ‖ hasty [fr. obs. F. precipiteux]

pré·cis (préisi:) pl. **pré·cis** (préisi:z) n. a brief summary of essential points etc. in a speech or writing [F.]

pre·cise (prisáis) adj. accurate in every detail, a precise account ‖ exact, precise measurement ‖ excessively attentive to detail, punctilious, precise manners ‖ very, at that precise moment he came in **pre·cise·ly** adv. [F. précis]

pre·ci·sian (prisíʒən) n. a person who adheres strictly to rules and forms, esp. in religious observances ‖ (hist.) an English Puritan [PRECISE]

pre·ci·sion (prisíʒən) n. the quality of being precise ‖ (computer) the exactness of a quantity, sometimes expressed in the number of significant digits in the solution [F.]

pre·clas·sic (pri:klǽsik) adj. preclassical

pre·clas·si·cal (pri:klǽsik'l) adj. of or relating to the period before the classical age, esp. in literature and art

pre·clin·i·cal (pri:klínik'l) adj. (med.) of or relating to the period before the appearance of symptoms

pre·clude (priklú:d) pres. part. **pre·clud·ing** past and past part. **pre·clud·ed** v.t. to prevent, illness precluded his visit ‖ to make practically impossible, esp. by anticipatory action, measures to preclude failure [fr. L. praecludere, to shut off]

pre·clu·sion (priklú:ʒən) n. a precluding or being precluded [fr. L. praeclusio (praeclusionis)]

preclusion order an order providing a choice of alternatives to punishment, e.g., public service

pre·clu·sive (priklú:siv) adj. tending to preclude [fr. L. praeclusus, shut off]

precoces *PRAECOCES

pre·co·cial, Br. **prae·co·cial** (prikóuʃəl) adj. designating birds whose young are able to look after themselves as soon as they are hatched [fr. L. praecox (praecocis), mature early]

pre·co·cious (prikóuʃəs) adj. displaying highly developed mental or physical characteristics at an early age, a precocious child ‖ done or made by someone having these characteristics, a precocious work ‖ (bot.) fruiting or flowering earlier than usual [fr. L. praecox (praecocis), mature early]

pre·coc·i·ty (prikósiti:) n. the condition or quality of being precocious [F. précocité]

pre·cog·ni·tion (pri:kɔgníʃən) n. foreknowledge [fr. L. praecognitio (praecognitionis)]

pre·Co·lum·bi·an (pri:kəlʌ́mbi:ən) adj. of or relating to the period before the discovery of America by Columbus

pre·con·ceive (pri:kənsí:v) pres. part. **pre·con·ceiv·ing** past and past part. **pre·con·ceived** v.t. to form (an idea or opinion) beforehand

pre·con·cep·tion (pri:kənsépʃən) n. the act of preconceiving or an instance of this ‖ a prejudice

pre·con·cert (pri:kənsə́:rt) v.t. to arrange beforehand by agreement, preconcerted plans

pre·con·cil·i·ar (pri:kənsíli:ər) adj. of the period before the second Vatican council, 1962–65. Cf POSTCONCILIAR

pre·co·nize (prí:kənaiz) pres. part. **pre·co·niz·ing** past and past part. **pre·co·nized** v.t. (Roman Catholicism) to confirm publicly the appointment of (a bishop etc.) by papal proclamation in consistory ‖ to proclaim, cite or summon publicly [fr. M. L. praeconizare]

pre·cur·sive (prikə́:rsiv) adj. precursory [fr. L. praecurrere (praecursus), to run before]

pre·cur·sor (prikə́:rsər) n. someone who prepares the way for another or who precedes him in office ‖ something which precedes something else, Sturm und Drang was a precursor of Romanticism [L. fr. praecurrere, to run before]

pre·cur·so·ry (prikə́:rsəri:) adj. preliminary ‖ indicating something to follow [fr. L. praecursorius]

pre·da·cious, **pre·da·ceous** (pridéiʃəs) adj. preying upon other animals **pre·dac·i·ty** (pridǽsiti:) n. the quality or condition of being predacious [fr. L. praedari, to prey upon]

pre·date (pri:déit) pres. part. **pre·dat·ing** past and past part. **pre·dat·ed** v.t. to happen before (a certain time or event or set of circumstances) ‖ to inscribe with a date earlier than the date on which the inscribing is done

pred·a·tor (prédətər) n. a predatory animal [L. praedator]

pred·a·to·ri·ly (prédətɔri:, prédətouri:) adv. in a predatory way

pred·a·to·ri·ness (prédətɔri:nis, prédətouri:nis) n. the quality or state of being predatory

pred·a·to·ry (prédətɔri:, prédətouri:) adj. (of persons) given to preying upon others ‖ predacious [fr. L. praedatorius fr. praedator fr. praedari, to prey upon]

pre·de·cease (pri:disí:s) pres. part. **pre·de·ceas·ing** past and past part. **pre·de·ceased** v.t. to die before (another person)

pred·e·ces·sor (prédisesər, predisésər, Br. esp. pri:disesər, pri:disésər) n. a person preceding another in an office, position etc. ‖ something which has been succeeded by something else [fr. F. prédécesseur]

pre·del·la (pridélə) pl. **pre·del·le** (pridéli:, prédélei) n. (eccles.) the step or platform on which an altar stands ‖ (eccles.) a painting or sculpture on the vertical face of this ‖ (eccles.) a secondary painting forming a border or pendant to the principal painting [etym. doubtful]

pre·des·ti·nar·i·an (pri:destinéəri:ən) 1. n. a person who accepts the doctrine of predestination 2. adj. pertaining to predestination [PREDESTINATE]

pre·des·ti·nate 1. (pri:déstineit) v.t. pres. part. **pre·des·ti·nat·ing** past and past part. **pre·des·ti·nat·ed** to predestine 2. (pri:déstinit) adj. determined beforehand [fr. L. praedestinare (praedestinatus)]

pre·des·ti·na·tion (pri:destinéiʃən) n. the act of predestinating ‖ (theol.) the doctrine that everything was determined by God from the beginning, esp. with reference to the play of divine omnipotence and human free will in determining the fate of the soul [fr. praedestinatio (praedestinationis) fr. praedestinare, to predestine]

pre·des·tine (pri:déstin) pres. part. **pre·des·tin·ing** past and past part. **pre·des·tined** v.t. to destine beforehand, esp. by divine decree [F. prédestiner]

pre·de·ter·mi·nate (pri:dité:rminit) adj. determined beforehand

pre·de·ter·mi·na·tion (pri:ditə:rminéiʃən) n. a predetermining or being predetermined

pre·de·ter·mine (pri:dité:rmin) pres. part. **pre·de·ter·min·ing** past and past part. **pre·de·ter·mined** v.t. to calculate or determine in advance ‖ to predestine ‖ to give a mental bias to, this predetermined me in his favor [fr. L. L. praedeterminare]

pre·de·ter·min·er (pri:dité:rminər) n. (grammar) a limiting noun modifier placed before a noun in a phrase. Cf POSTDETERMINER

pred·i·ca·bil·i·ty (predikəbíliti:) n. the state or quality of being predicable

pred·i·ca·ble (prédikəb'l) 1. adj. capable of being predicated 2. n. that which may be predicated ‖ (logic) any of Aristotle's five relationships (genus, species, difference, property, accident) used in predication [F. prédicable]

pre·dic·a·ment (pridíkəmənt) n. a situation involving a hard or unpleasant choice ‖ (Aristotelian logic) a category [fr. L. praedicamentum]

pred·i·cate 1. (prédikeit) v. pres. part. **pred·i·cat·ing** past and past part. **pred·i·cat·ed** v.t. to state as an assumed attribute, quality or property, to predicate the perfectibility of man ‖ to imply, connote, his attitude predicates self-interest ‖ (logic) to affirm or deny (something) about the subject of a proposition ‖ to base (a thesis, statement, attitude etc.) on, his conclusions are predicated on laboratory tests ‖ v.i. to make a statement 2. (prédikit) n. (logic) that which is affirmed or denied about the subject of a proposition ‖ (gram.) the words (verb with object or adverbial modifier, or copula with noun or adjective) which express what is stated of the subject of a clause or sentence [fr. M.L. praedicatum fr. praedicare, to proclaim]

pred·i·ca·tion (predikéiʃən) n. a predicating or being predicated [M.E. fr. O.F. predicaciun]

pred·i·ca·tive (prédikeitiv) adj. constituting a predicate or part of a predicate [fr. L. praedicativus]

pre·dict (pridíkt) v.t. to make known beforehand, foretell, to predict rain ‖ v.i. to foretell the future **pre·dict·a·ble** adj. [fr. L. praedicere (praedictus)]

pre·dic·tion (pridíkʃən) n. the action of predicting ‖ that which is predicted [fr. L. praedictio (praedictionis)]

pre·dic·tive (pridíktiv) adj. of or relating to prediction

pre·dic·tor (pridíktər) n. someone who or that which predicts ‖ an instrument used to control antiaircraft guns by allowing for the height and speed of the target

---

CONCISE PRONUNCIATION KEY: **(a)** æ, cat; ɑ, car; ɔ fawn; ei, snake. **(e)** e, hen; i:, sheep; iə, deer; ɛə, bear. **(i)** i, fish; ai, tiger; ə:, bird. **(o)** o, ox; au, cow; ou, goat; u, poor; ɔi, royal. **(u)** ʌ, duck; u, bull; u:, goose; ə, bacillus; ju:, cube. x, loch; θ, think; ð, bother; z, Zen; ʒ, corsage; dʒ, savage; ŋ, orangutang; j, yak; ʃ, fish; tʃ, fetch; 'l, rabble; 'n, redden. Complete pronunciation key appears inside front cover.

pre·di·gest (priːdidʒést, priːdaidʒést) v.t. to make (food) more digestible by artificial means **pre·di·gés·tion** n.

pre·di·lec·tion (priːdilékʃən, prɛdlékʃən) n. a special taste or liking, *a predilection for sparkling wines* [F. *prédilection*]

pre·dis·pose (priːdispóuz) pres. part. **pre·dis·pos·ing** past and past part. **pre·dis·posed** v.i. to make (someone) tend to act, feel, suffer etc. in a particular way or be prone, *his constitution predisposes him to colds*

pre·dis·po·si·tion (priːdispəzíʃən) n. the condition of being predisposed ‖ a tendency, susceptibility, *a predisposition to quarrelsomeness*

pre·dom·i·nance (pridóminəns) n. the quality or state of being predominant

pre·dom·i·nan·cy (pridóminənsiː) n. predominance

pre·dom·i·nant (pridóminənt) adj. most frequent, prevailing, *barley is the predominant crop here* [F. *prédominant*]

pre·dom·i·nate (pridómineit) pres. part. **pre·dom·i·nat·ing** past and past part. **pre·dom·i·nat·ed** v.i. to be most frequent, or lead in quality, status etc., *small farmers predominate in the region* [fr. M.L. *praedominari (praedominatus)*]

pre·e·mer·gent (priːimə́rdʒənt) adj. (botany) of seed below ground

pre·em·i·nence (priːéminəns) n. the quality or state of being preeminent [fr. L. L. *praeeminentia*]

pre·em·i·nent (priːéminənt) adj. superior to others, esp. in some specified quality or sphere, *he is preeminent in Shakespearean roles* [fr. L. *praeeminens (praeemiuentis)* fr. *praeeminere*, to excel]

pre·empt (priːémpt) v.t. to purchase before others have the opportunity to purchase ‖ (Am. hist.) to settle on (public land) in order to establish the right of preemption ‖ to acquire beforehand ‖ v.i. (bridge) to make a preemptive bid [PREEMPTION]

pre·emp·tion (priːémpʃən) n. the act or right of purchasing before others have a chance to purchase ‖ (Am. hist.) the preempting of public land ‖ a taking possession before others **pre·emp·tive** (priːémptiv) adj. (bridge) of, relating to, or constituting a bid that is higher than necessary, in order to discourage one's partner or opponents from bidding [etym. doubtful]

pre·emp·tive adj. occurring before, and in anticipation of, a situation developing, e.g., preemptive attack, preemptive seizure

preen (priːn) v.t. (of a bird) to trim (the feathers) with the beak ‖ (of a person) to make (oneself) trim in appearance ‖ to congratulate (oneself) mildly [var. of PRUNE v.]

pre·en·gi·neered (priːéndʒiniərd) adj. made of prefabricated units

pre·es·tab·lished harmony (priːistǽbliʃt) (philos.) a theory of Leibniz stating that a harmony between mind and matter was established eternally at the Creation

pre·ex·ist (priːigzíst) v.i. to exist previously (esp. of the soul before the birth of the body) ‖ v.t. to exist before (something) **pre·ex·ist·ence** n. previous existence, esp. the life of the soul before birth **pre·ex·ist·ent** adj.

pre·fab (priːfǽb) n. (pop.) a prefabricated building, esp. a house

pre·fab·ri·cate (priːfǽbrikeit) pres. part. **pre·fab·ri·cat·ing** past and past part. **pre·fab·ri·cat·ed** v.t. to construct sections of (e.g. a house) in a factory for assembly on a site elsewhere **pre·fab·ri·cá·tion** n.

pref·ace (préfis) 1. n. a written introduction to a book or the opening remarks of a speaker intended to elucidate the text or speech to follow ‖ a leading up to something ‖ (eccles.) the part of the Mass before the canon 2. v.t. pres. part. **pref·ac·ing** past and past part. **pref·aced** to introduce by or furnish with a preface ‖ to lead up to [F. *préface*]

pref·a·to·ri·al (prefətóriːəl, prefətóuriːəl) adj. prefatory

pref·a·to·ry (préfətɔːriː, préfətouriː) adj. of, relating to, or constituting a preface [fr. L. *praefari*, to say beforehand]

pre·fect (príːfekt) n. (Rom. hist.) a civil or military commander ‖ the civil governor of a department in France ‖ (in some schools) a senior pupil to whom some disciplinary authority is delegated **pre·fec·tó·ri·al** adj. [O.F.]

pre·fec·tur·al (priːféktʃərəl) adj. of or relating to a prefecture

pre·fec·ture (priːféktʃər) n. the office, official residence, jurisdiction or term of office of a prefect [fr. L. *praefectura*]

pre·fer (prifə́r) pres. part. **pre·fer·ring** past and past part. **pre·ferred** v.t. to like better, *I prefer this house to that one* ‖ to choose rather, *I prefer not to think about it* ‖ (law) to place (a charge, complaint etc.) against a person) before someone in authority ‖ (law) to give priority to (a creditor) **pref·er·a·ble** (préfərəbʼl) adj. **pref·er·a·bly** adv. [fr. L. *praeferre*, to place before]

pref·er·ence (préfərəns) n. a preferring or being preferred ‖ the person or thing preferred ‖ the right to choose, *to be allowed no preference* ‖ a system whereby lower import duties are levied on goods from certain countries ‖ (law) priority in the right to demand payment of a debt [F. *préférence*]

preference shares (Br.) preferred stock

pref·er·en·tial (prefərénʃəl) adj. relating to, or constituting preference [fr. M. L. *praeferentia*, preference]

preferential primary a presidential primary

preferential shop a firm which gives preference to union members, but is free to hire nonunion workers when the union is unable to supply its own workers

pre·fer·ment (prifə́rmənt) n. a preferring or being preferred ‖ promotion in office ‖ a position that confers advancement

preferred stock (Am.=Br. preference shares) a corporation's stock which has first claim on the distribution of assets and on the payment of a specified dividend

pre·fig·u·ra·tion (priːfigjəréiʃən) n. something that prefigures ‖ the act of prefiguring or the state of being prefigured [fr. L. *praefiguratio (praefigurationis)*]

pre·fig·u·ra·tive (priːfígjərətiv) adj. serving to prefigure ‖ of a society in which the parental role is nurturant until the child reaches the age when he or she can teach the society, and thereafter the child's values predominate; defined by American anthropologist Margaret Mead [fr. M.L. *praefigurativus*]

pre·fig·ure (priːfígjər) pres. part. **pre·fig·ur·ing** past and past part. **pre·fig·ured** v.t. to represent beforehand, serve as an image of, *Rome in the play prefigures the heavenly city* ‖ to picture to oneself beforehand [fr. L.L. *praefigurare*]

pre·fix 1. (priːfíks, príːfiks) v.t. (gram.) to place or put (a syllable, group of syllables or word) in front of a word to modify its meaning or form a new word 2. (príːfiks) n. (gram.) that which is placed in front in this way, e.g. 'un' in 'unable' [O.F. *prefixer*]

pre·form (priːfɔ́rm) v.t. to form beforehand **pre·for·má·tion** n. a forming beforehand ‖ (biol.) a formerly prevalent theory that the ovum of an animal contained a miniature individual and that only nourishment was needed for it to develop into a perfect adult [fr. L. *praeformare*]

Pregl (preig'l), Fritz (1869–1930), Austrian chemist. He developed microanalysis of organic compounds. Nobel prize (1923)

preg·na·ble (prégnəbʼl) adj. capable of being captured [M.E. *prenable* fr. F.]

preg·nan·cy (prégnənsiː) pl. **preg·nan·cies** n. the condition of being pregnant

preg·nant (prégnənt) adj. (of a female) carrying an unborn child or unborn young within the body ‖ deeply significant, *pregnant remarks*, or full of implication, *a pregnant silence* ‖ full of ideas, imaginative [fr. L. *praegnans (praegnantis)*]

pre·hen·sile (prihénsil, prihénsail) adj. (zool.) able to grasp and hold, *a prehensile tail* **pre·hen·sil·i·ty** (priːhensíliti:) n. [F. *préhensile*]

pre·hen·sion (prihénʃən) n. (zool.) the act of seizing or grasping ‖ mental apprehension [fr. L. *prehensio (prehensionis)* fr. *prehendere*, to grasp]

pre·his·tor·ic (priːhistórik, priːhistórik) adj. of or relating to the period before recorded history ‖ existing during this period, *prehistoric man* **pre·his·tór·i·cal·ly** adv.

pre·his·to·ry (priːhístəri:) n. the study of the period of history before there were written records, esp. the study of prehistoric man ‖ the period of history before there were written records

pre·ig·ni·tion (priːigníʃən) n. the premature explosion of the gas mixture in the cylinder of an internal-combustion engine

pre·in·i·ti·a·tion (priːiniʃi:éiʃən) n. (mil.) premature initiation of the fission chain reaction in the active material of a nuclear weapon

pre·judge (priːdʒʌ́dʒ) pres. part. **pre·judg·ing** past and past part. **pre·judged** v.t. to pass judgment on before all the evidence is known ‖ to form a premature opinion of **pre·júdg·ment**, **pre·júdge·ment** n. [fr. F. *prejuger*]

pre·ju·di·ca·tion (priːdʒuːdikéiʃən) n. the act of prejudging [fr. L. *praejudicare (praejudicatus)*, to judge beforehand]

prej·u·dice (prédʒudis) pres. part. **prej·u·dic·ing** past and past part. **prej·u·diced** v.t. to cause (someone) to have a prejudice, (of a thing) to prejudice a jury member ‖ to cause injury to ‖ (law) to impair the validity of (a right) [F. *préjuaicier*]

prejudice n. a preconceived opinion, usually unfavorable ‖ the holding of such an opinion ‖ an unjustified and unreasonable bias ‖ (law) injury due to some judgment or action of another, e.g. the disregard of a person's rights **without prejudice** (law) without detriment to a person's claims or rights [F. *préjudice*]

prej·u·di·cial (predʒudíʃəl) adj. injuring, or likely to injure, *his political views were prejudicial to his chances of success* [F. *préjudicial*]

prel·a·cy (prélɐsiː) pl. **prel·a·cies** n. (eccles.) the office, dignity or see of a prelate ‖ prelates collectively ‖ (used in a hostile sense) Church government by prelates [A.F. *prelacie*]

prel·ate (prélit) n. (eccles.) a high-ranking Church dignitary, e.g. an archbishop. bishop or patriarch **pre·lat·ic** (prilǽtik) adj. [M.E. *prelat* fr. O.F.]

prelate nullius n. pl. a Roman Catholic ecclesiastic in charge of an independent district not in any diocese

prel·a·ture (prélətʃər) n. the office, dignity or see of a prelate ‖ prelates collectively [F. *prélature*]

pre·lim·i·nar·i·ly (prilíminɛrili:) adv. in a preliminary way

pre·lim·i·nar·y (prilímineri:) 1. adj. introductory or preparatory, *a preliminary test* 2. pl. **pre·lim·i·nar·ies** n. a preliminary step, procedure etc. ‖ a preliminary examination ‖ (pl., abbr. prelims, Br.) front matter [fr. L. *prae*, before+*liminaris*, of a threshold]

prel·ude (prélju:d) 1. n. something serving to introduce, or set the mood for, some event, performance, action etc. to follow, *the discussions were a prelude to the treaty* ‖ a piece of music serving as an introduction to the theme of a fugue, an act of an opera etc. ‖ the title used by some composers for some self-contained pieces for piano and orchestra 2. v.t. pres. part. **prel·ud·ing** past and past part. **prel·ud·ed** to serve as a prelude to [F. *prélude*]

pre·ma·ture (priːmətúər, priːmətjúər, priːmətʃúər) adj. occurring, done, existing etc. before the proper time, *a premature crop* ‖ (of an infant) born before the 37th week of pregnancy or weighing less than 5½ lbs **pre·ma·túre·ly** adv. [fr. L. *praematurus*]

pre·ma·tu·ri·ty (priːmətúəriti:, priːmətjúəriti:, priːmətʃúəriti:) n. the state or quality of being premature [F. *prématurité*]

pre·max·il·la (priːmæksílə) pl. **pre·max·il·lae** (priːmæksíli:), **pre·max·il·las** n. (anat., zool.) one of a pair of bones in the upper jaw of vertebrates, between and in front of the maxillae **pre·max·il·lar·y** (priːmǽksələri:) adj.

pre·med·i·cal (priːmédik'l) adj. of or relating to the studies preceding the medical course proper

pre·med·i·tate (priːméditeit) v.t. pres. part. **pre·med·i·tat·ing** past and past part. **pre·med·i·tat·ed** to think about and plan beforehand

pre·med·i·ta·tion (priːmeditéiʃən) n. a premeditating, esp. (law) the degree of planning sufficient to show intent to commit an act [fr. L. *praemeditatio (praemeditationis)*]

pre·mier (primíər, primjíər, príːmjər) 1. adj. first in position, importance etc. ‖ bearing the oldest title within a degree of rank, *premier earl* 2. n. prime minister [F. =first]

pre·miere, pre·mière (primíər, primjíər, primjéər) n. the first public performance of a play or showing of a film ‖ the female star of a theatrical production [F.]

pre·mier·ship (primíərʃip, primjíərʃip, príːmjərʃip) n. the office of premier or tenure of office of a premier

prem·ise, prem·iss 1. (prémis) n. a fact, statement or assumption on which an argument is based or from which conclusions are drawn ‖ (esp. premiss, logic) one of the two propositions (major and minor) of a syllogism from which the conclusion is drawn ‖ (pl., law) the section of a deed stating the names of the parties involved and giving an explanation of the transaction ‖

(*pl.*) a piece of land and the house and buildings on it, *keep off the premises* 2. **prem·ise** (primáiz) *v.t. pres. part.* **prem·is·ing** *past* and *past part.* **prem·ised** to state or assume as a premise [F. *prémisse*]

pre·mi·um (prí:mi:əm) *n.* a prize or reward, esp. a sum paid addition to wages or salary ‖ a sum paid, either all at once or periodically, for an insurance contract ‖ the rate above nominal value at which something sells ‖ a fee paid for instruction or training in a trade etc. ‖ a sum given for a loan in addition to interest at a premium worth more than the nominal value ‖ very hard to get and therefore valuable **to put a premium on** to stress the importance of, put a high value on, *to put a premium on honesty* [L. *praemium*, profit, reward]

pre·mo·lar (prí:móulər) 1. *n.* a premolar tooth 2. *adj.* situated in front of the molar teeth

pre·mo·ni·tion (prj:mənífən, prɛmənífən) *n.* a forewarning ‖ a presentiment [fr. obs. F. *premonicion* fr. L.L. *praemonitio* fr. L. *praemonere*]

pre·mon·i·to·ry (primónitɔri:, primónitouri:) *adj.* giving warning beforehand, *premonitory signs of sickness* [fr. *premonitor*, something that forewarns fr. L.]

Pre·mon·stra·ten·sian (pri:mɒnstrəténfən) 1. *adj.* of a religious order of canons regular founded (1119) by St Norbert at Prémontré in N. France 2. *n.* a member of this order, or of its order of nuns, or of its third order [after *Prémontré*]

pre·morse (primɔ́rs) *adj.* (of a leaf or root) having the end truncated as if bitten off [fr. L. *praemordere* (*praemorsus*), to bite off in front]

Prem·y·slide (prémislid) *n.* a member of the Přemysl family who ruled Bohemia (9th–13th cc.)

pre·na·tal (pri:néit'l) *adj.* occurring or existing before birth

prenomen *PRAENOMEN

pren·tice (préntis) *adj.* of work showing incomplete command or skill ‖ of work done in order to learn, *prentice plays* [APPRENTICE]

pre·oc·cu·pa·tion (pri:ɒkjupéifən) *n.* a preoccupying or being preoccupied [fr. L. *praeoccupatio* (*praeoccupationis*)]

pre·oc·cu·pied (pri:ókjupaid) *adj.* completely engrossed, esp. in thought ‖ (*biol.*, of a generic or specific name) not available as a designation because already in use [PREOCCUPY]

pre·oc·cu·py (pri:ókjupai) *pres. part.* **pre·oc·cu·py·ing** *past* and *past part.* **pre·oc·cu·pied** *v.t.* to engage the attention or interest of (someone) almost completely

pre·or·dain (pri:ɔrdéin) *v.t.* to ordain beforehand

pre·or·gas·mic (pri:ɔrgæzmik) *adj.* 1. of one who has never had an orgasm. 2. of the arousal period preceding an orgasm

prep (prep) *n.* (*Br.*, *pop.*) homework (done by a schoolboy or schoolgirl)

prep·a·ra·tion (prepəréifən) *n.* a preparing or being prepared ‖ that which is prepared, esp. a chemical substance or medicine, for subsequent use ‖ (*pl.*) preparatory measures ‖ the work done in preparing school lessons ‖ (*mus.*) the leading up to a dissonance by sounding the dissonant note as a consonant note in the preceding chord ‖ (*mus.*) the note so sounded [F. *préparation*]

pre·par·a·tive (pripǽrətiv) 1. *adj.* preparatory 2. *n.* a preparation [F. *préparatif*]

pre·par·a·tor (pripǽrətər) *n.* someone who prepares specimens for scientific study or for display in a museum [L.L. *praeparator*]

pre·par·a·to·ry (pripǽrətɔri:, pripéərətɔri:, pripǽrətouri:, pripéərətouri:) *adj.* of that which prepares or introduces ‖ undergoing preliminary instruction, *a preparatory student* [fr. M. L. *praeparatorius*]

preparatory school (*abbr.* prep school) a private school for preparing students for college ‖ (*Br.*) a private school bringing children to public secondary school level at age 13½

pre·pare (pripéər) *v.t. pres. part.* **pre·par·ing** *past* and *past part.* **pre·pared** to make the necessary preparations for, *to prepare a meal* ‖ to get ready for by study, work, practice etc., *to prepare a speech, lesson etc.* ‖ to get (someone) ready ‖ to put (someone) in a receptive state of mind, *to prepare someone for a shock* ‖ to make (e.g. a chemical preparation), *to prepare a vaccine* ‖ (*mus.*) to lead up to (a dissonance) by sounding the dissonant note as a consonant note in the preceding chord ‖ (*mus.*) to lead up to (a note or ornament) by a preliminary note ‖ *v.i.* to take necessary previous measures, *to prepare for a journey* ‖ to make oneself ready in one's

mind, *to prepare for the worst* **to be prepared** to be willing to, *to be prepared to apologize* **pre·par·ed·ly** (pripéəridli:) *adv.* **pre·par·ed·ness** *n.* the state of being prepared, esp. of being prepared for war [F. *préparer*]

pre·pay (pri:péi) *pres. part.* **pre·pay·ing** *past* and *past part.* **pre·paid** *v.t.* to pay for in advance **pre·pay·ment** *n.*

pre·pense (pripéns) *adj.* (in the phrase) **malice prepense** (*law*) malice aforethought [alt. fr. *purpense* fr. O.F. *purpenser*]

pre·pon·der·ance (pripóndərəns) *n.* the condition of being preponderant

pre·pon·der·ant (pripóndərənt) *adj.* superior in weight, number, influence, power, importance etc. [fr. L. *praeponderans* (*praeponderantis*) fr. *praeponderare*, to outweigh]

pre·pon·der·ate (pripóndəreit) *pres. part.* **pre·pon·der·at·ing** *past* and *past part.* **pre·pon·der·at·ed** *v.i.* to be superior in weight, number, influence, power, importance etc. **pre·pón·der·at·ing·ly** *adv.* [fr. L. *praeponderare* (*praeponderatus*), to outweigh]

prep·o·si·tion (prepəzífən) *n.* (*gram.*) a word (in some languages) expressing the relationship between a noun, pronoun or noun phrase (which usually follows the preposition and is called the 'object' of the preposition) and another element of the sentence, e.g. a verb ('down' in 'he walked down the street'), a noun ('of' in 'the mother of twins') or an adjective ('for' in 'grateful for favors') ‖ a compound construction which functions as a preposition (e.g. 'on top of') **prep·o·si·tion·al** *adj.* [fr. L. *praepositio* (*praepositionis*)]

prepositional phrase a preposition and its object

pre·pos·i·tive (pri:pózitiv) *adj.* (*gram.*) prefixed or placed before a word [fr. L.L. *praepositivus*]

pre·pos·sess (pri:pəzés) *v.t.* to influence favorably in advance or at the outset

pre·pos·sess·ing (pri:pəzésiŋ) *adj.* making an immediate favorable impression, attractive

pre·pos·ter·ous (pripóstərəs) *adj.* grotesquely or comically ridiculous, *a preposterous hat* ‖ unreasonable, unlikely, *a preposterous proposal, a preposterous story* [fr. L. *praeposterus*, reversed]

pre·po·ten·cy (pri:póut'nsi:) *n.* the quality or condition of being prepotent ‖ (*biol.*) the capacity of one parent to transmit more characteristics to its offspring than the other parent ‖ fertilization of a flower by pollen from another flower in preference to pollen from its own stamens, when both are offered simultaneously [fr. L. *praepotentia*]

pre·po·tent (pri:póut'nt) *adj.* having superior power ‖ (*bot.*, of a flower) exhibiting a preference for cross-pollination ‖ (*biol.*) displaying prepotency [fr. L. *praepotens* (*praepotentis*) fr. *praeposse*, to be very powerful]

prep·pie (prépi:) *n.* one who attends or has attended a private secondary high school — **prep·pie** *adj.* of the typical appearance or characteristics of such a person

pre·peg (prí:peg) *n.* (*chem.*) a synthetic impregnated with resin before processing. **—pre·peg** *adj.*

pre·pref·er·ence (pri:préfərəns) *adj.* (*Br.*, of shares etc.) ranking before preference shares in a claim to dividend or repayment

pre·puce (prí:pju:s) *n.* the foreskin, or a similar fold of skin over the clitoris [F. *prépuce*]

Pre·Raph·a·el·ite (pri:ræfi:əlait) 1. *n.* a member or follower of the Pre-Raphaelite Brotherhood 2. *adj.* pertaining to such an artist or his work

Pre·Raphaelite Brotherhood a group of English painters, including William Holman Hunt, Millais and Dante Gabriel Rossetti, formed in London in 1848. In a broad sense they took their ideals from the painting of Italian masters prior to Raphael. They gave great importance to subject, and often took it from religion. Other characteristics include sensitive painting of elaborate detail, fondness for outdoor settings, and the use of bright color. Ruskin defended their ideas in 'Pre-Raphaelitism' (1851)

pre·req·ui·site (prirékwizit) 1. *adj.* requisite in an antecedent condition 2. *n.* that which is prerequisite

pre·rog·a·tive (prirógətiv) 1. *n.* an exclusive right or privilege possessed by a person or body of persons ‖ a right attached to an office or rank, *the royal prerogative* ‖ 2. *adj.* pertaining to a prerogative, arising from special privilege [F. *prérogative*]

pres·age 1. (présidʒ) *n.* that which foretells a future event ‖ a presentiment 2. (présidʒ, priséidʒ) *v.t. pres. part.* **pres·ag·ing** *past* and *past part.* **pres·aged** to foretell (a future event) [fr. L. *praesagium*, a foreboding]

pre·sanc·ti·fied (prj:sǽŋktifaid) *adj.* (*eccles.*, of the Host) consecrated at a previous celebration of the Mass

pres·by·o·pi·a (prezbi:óupi:ə, presbi:óupi:ə) *n.* (*med.*) a failure, due to age, of the muscles of the eye to adjust the focus of the crystalline lens for vision at different distances (*ACCOMMODATION), and to distinguish near objects sharply **pres·by·op·ic** (prezbi:ópik, presbi:ópik) *adj.* [Mod. L. fr. Gk *presbus*, old +*ops*, eye]

pres·by·ter (prézbitər, présbitər) *n.* (*eccles.*, *hist.*) an elder having lay authority in the early Christian Church ‖ a minister in certain Episcopal churches ‖ an elder in a Presbyterian Church, esp. a member of a presbytery [L.L. fr. Gk]

pres·by·ter·ate (prezbítərit, presbítərit) *n.* the office of a presbyter ‖ a body of presbyters [fr. M.L. *presbyteratus*]

pres·by·te·ri·al (prezbitíəri:əl, presbitíəri:əl) *adj.* of or relating to a presbyter, a body of presbyters, or a presbytery [fr. L.L. *presbyterialis*]

Pres·by·te·ri·an (prezbitíəri:ən, presbitíəri:ən) 1. *adj.* of or relating to a system of Church polity consisting of a series of four courts composed of ministers and elected elders 2. *n.* a member of a Church adhering to this form of government **Pres·by·té·ri·an·ism** *n.* [fr. L. *presbyterium*, presbytery] —Presbyterian polity was first established in Geneva by Calvin, who held that Church government by elders and ministers conformed with New Testament practice. This system was adopted by Knox (*CHURCH OF SCOTLAND) and the Huguenots, and is now found throughout the world. Most Presbyterian Churches also adhere to Calvinist doctrine

pres·by·ter·y (prézbitəri:, présbitəri:) *pl.* **pres·by·ter·ies** *n.* (*eccles.*) a district court of ministers and elders of a Presbyterian Church ‖ the district within which this court has jurisdiction ‖ (*archit.*) the eastern part of a church beyond the choir stalls ‖ (Roman Catholicism) the residence of a priest [O.F. *presbiterie*, a priest's house]

pre·school (pri:skú:l) *adj.* of or relating to the period of infancy prior to the age of compulsory school attendance

pre·science (prí:ʃi:əns, préʃi:əns, prí:ʃəns, préʃəns) *n.* foreknowledge ‖ an instance of foreknowledge [F.]

pre·scient (prí:ʃənt, préʃənt) *adj.* having foreknowledge [F.]

Pres·cott (préskɒt), William Hickling (1796–1858), American historian. He wrote a 'History of the Conquest of Mexico' (1842) and a 'History of the Conquest of Peru' (1847)

pre·scribe (priskráib) *pres. part.* **pre·scrib·ing** *past* and *past part.* **pre·scribed** *v.t.* to order with the force of authority ‖ to order the use of (a medicine or treatment) ‖ (*law*) to state (a prescriptive right or title) ‖ *v.i.* to lay down a rule ‖ to write a medical prescription ‖ (*law*) to claim a title etc. by a prescription [fr. L. *praescribere*, to write before]

pre·script (prí:skript) *n.* a command, rule [fr. L. *praescribere* (*praescriptus*), to write before]

pre·scrip·tion (priskrípʃən) *n.* the act of prescribing ‖ that which is prescribed, esp. (*med.*) a written statement, giving directions for making and using a medicine ‖ (*law*) negative prescription ‖ (*law*) positive prescription ‖ ancient custom, esp. when regarded as authoritative [F. or fr. L. *praescriptio* (*praescriptionis*), a prescribing]

pre·scrip·tive (priskríptiv) *adj.* that prescribes ‖ arising from, based on, or determined by prescription, *a prescriptive right* [fr. L.L. *praescriptivus*, pertaining to a legal exception]

pres·ence (préz'ns) *n.* the state or fact of being in a certain place, *his presence in the room was not noticed* ‖ the space immediately surrounding a person, *in the royal presence* ‖ distinction of bearing and demeanor ‖ the quality which marks a dominating personality, esp. the quality which enables a performer to dominate his audience, *to lack presence* ‖ an intangible spirit or mysterious influence felt to be present [O.F.]

presence of mind the ability to act quickly, intelligently and calmly in an emergency

pres·ent (préz'nt) *n.* a gift [O.F.]

present 1. *adj.* being in a specified place,

present in the room ‖ existing, being done, or occurring at this time, *the present moment, the present discussion* ‖ used as a form of reference to oneself, *the present writer* ‖ (*gram.*) of or designating a tense that expresses action now taking place, or state in time now existing **2.** *n.* this time ‖ (*gram.*) the present tense ‖ (*gram.*) a verb in the present tense ‖ (*pl., law*) present statements, *let it be known by these presents* **at present** at this time, *I cannot receive him at present* **for the present** at this time and for some little time to come, *that is enough for the present* [O. F.]

pre·sent (prizént) **1.** *v.t.* to bring (someone) to the notice of or into the presence of someone else, esp. a superior, *to present the candidates in Latin* ‖ to introduce (someone) formally at court ‖ (with 'with') to make a gift to ‖ (with 'with') to cause to face, *to present with a problem* ‖ to exhibit or offer to view or notice, *to present a fine appearance, to present a bold front* ‖ to offer as a public entertainment ‖ to submit for consideration or action, *to present an argument, to present a bill* ‖ (*law*) to bring a formal charge against ‖ (*law*) to lay (e. g. a charge) before a court etc. ‖ to aim or point (e.g. a gun) at someone or something ‖ to bring (a clergyman) to the notice of a bishop with a view toward his selection for a benefice ‖ to install (a clergyman) in a benefice ‖ *v.i.* (of a fetus) to be directed towards the opening of the womb ‖ (*med.*) to come forward as a patient **to present arms** (*mil.*) to display the rifle perpendicularly in front of the center of the body as a salute while in the position of attention **2.** *n.* the position of presenting arms **pre·sent·a·bil·i·ty** *n.* the condition or quality of being presentable **pre·sént·a·ble** *adj.* fit to be presented, shown, or offered, *a presentable appearance* **pre·sént·a·bly** *adv.* [O.F. *présenter*]

pres·en·ta·tion (prɛzentéiʃən, prɪ:zəntéiʃən) *n.* a presenting or being presented ‖ that which is presented, e.g. a theatrical performance ‖ a formal introduction, esp. an introduction at Court ‖ the act of presenting a benefice to a clergyman ‖ a formal presenting of a gift, usually before a gathering of people, *a presentation to the retiring chairman* ‖ (*med.*) the position of the fetus at birth ‖ (*philos.*) direct awareness (as distinct from association or reflection) as an element of cognition **pres·en·tá·tion·al** *adj.* **pres·en·tá·tion·ism** *n.* (*philos.*) the doctrine that the mind has immediate cognition of the objects of perception [O.F. *presentacion*]

pre·sent-day (préz'ntdéi) *adj.* belonging to the present time, *present-day standards*

pre·sen·tient (pri:sénʃənt) *adj.* (with 'of') feeling or perceiving beforehand [fr. L. *praesentiens* (*praesentientis*) fr. *praesentire*, to feel beforehand]

pre·sen·ti·ment (prizéntəmənt) *n.* a vague, usually uneasy sensing of an impending event [obs. F.]

pre·sen·tive (prizéntiv) *adj.* (of a word) presenting a thing directly to the mind (cf. SYMBOLIC)

pres·ent·ly (préz'ntli) *adv.* in a short time from now, *I'll write to him presently* ‖ in a short time from then, *presently the room began to fill*

pre·sent·ment (prizéntmənt) *n.* a theatrical presentation or artistic delineation ‖ the act of presenting to the mind, e.g. by statement or suggestion ‖ that which is presented ‖ (*law*) the statement made by members of a grand jury under oath of any offense based on their own knowledge or without any bill of indictment ‖ (*eccles.*) a complaint presented to a bishop by the parish authorities ‖ (*philos.*) presentation [O.F. *presentement*]

present participle (*gram.*) a participle which expresses an action that takes place in the present or at the same time as the finite verb in the sentence, formed in English by adding '-ing' to the verb stem

pres·er·va·tion (prɛzərvéiʃən) *n.* a preserving or being preserved [F. *préservation*]

pre·serv·a·tive (prizə́:rvətiv) **1.** *adj.* having the ability to preserve, *a preservative coat of lead paint* **2.** *n.* a substance added to preserve, esp. a chemical added to prevent food from decomposition [fr. M.L. *praeservativus*]

pre·serve (prizə́:rv) **1.** *v. pres. part.* **pre·serv·ing** *past* and *past part.* **pre·served** *v.t.* to prepare (fruit, vegetables, meat or fish) by boiling, salting, pickling etc. and packing into containers for future use ‖ to keep up, maintain, prevent from ruin or decay, *to preserve the coun-*

tryside ‖ to keep from decomposition by freezing, treating with chemicals etc. ‖ to retain (e.g. a quality), *to preserve one's dignity* ‖ to maintain and protect (fish or game) for private use ‖ *v.i.* to be suitable for preserving ‖ to make preserves **2.** *n.* a large area of land or body of water where game or fish is protected ‖ something, e.g. an occupation, place etc., regarded exclusively as one's own, *to trespass on someone's preserve* ‖ (esp. *pl.*) jam [F. *préserver*]

pre·set (pri:sét) *pres. part.* **pre·set·ting** *past* and *past part.* **pre·set** *v.t.* to set (e.g. a thermostat reading) in advance

pre·side (prizáid) *pres. part.* **pre·sid·ing** *past* and *past part.* **pre·sid·ed** *v.i.* to be in a position of control or authority, *to preside over a meeting* [F. *présider*]

pres·i·den·cy (prézidənsi:) *pl.* **pres·i·den·cies** *n.* the office or function of president ‖ the term of office of a president ‖ the region under the control of a president, esp. (*hist.*) one of the three regions of India administered by the East India Company (presidencies of Bengal, Bombay, Madras) [fr. M.L. *praesidentia*]

pres·i·dent (prézidənt) *n.* the elected head of government in the U.S.A. and many other republics ‖ a person elected to preside over an organization, *the president of the football club* ‖ the chief officer of a bank, company, corporation etc. ‖ the head of a college or university ‖ (*Br.*) the head of certain colleges within a university [F. *président*]

pres·i·den·tial (prɛzidénʃəl) *adj.* of or relating to a president or a presidency [M.L. *praesidentialis* fr. *praesidentia*, presidency]

presidential primary an election within a state political party in which the voters indicate choices for president of the U.S.A. either by vote or by the selection of delegates to the national nominating convention

Presidential Succession Act a U.S. Congressional act sponsored (1947) by President Harry Truman. It declared that, in the event of the death or incapacity of both the president and the vice president, succession would pass to the Speaker of the House, then to the President pro tempore of the Senate, and then in succession to the cabinet members in the order of the creation of their departments

pre·sid·i·um, prae·sid·i·um (prisídi:əm) *pl.* **pre·sid·i·a, prae·sid·i·a** (prisídi:ə), **pre·sid·i·ums, prae·sid·i·ums** *n.* an executive committee of the Supreme Soviet of the U.S.S.R. which exercises supreme authority between sessions of the latter ‖ a similar body in various administrative districts of the U.S.S.R., or within a Communist party [fr. L. *praesidium*]

Presley (prézli:), Elvis (1935–77) U.S. singer and film actor, credited with popularizing rock 'n' roll music during the 1950s. Known worldwide for his vocal style, sideburns and body gyrations, he was a phenomenal recording artist, receiving 28 gold-record awards, more than any other individual, by the time of his death. Some of his best-known recordings include 'Heartbreak Hotel' (1956), 'Hound Dog,' 'Don't Be Cruel' and 'Love Me Tender.' He also appeared in 33 films and in concerts and on television

pre·soak (pri:sóuk) *v.* to soak clothes prior to washing. **pre·soak** *n.* the solution in which the clothes are soaked, such a soaking

pre·sort (pri:sɔ́rt) *v.* to sort mail by ZIP code prior to posting, esp. in order to reduce postal costs

press (pres) *v.t.* to exert a steady force upon (something) by applying pressure ‖ to make flat by exerting such pressure, *to press flowers* ‖ to make smooth by applying pressure, *to press clothes* ‖ to try to persuade, *to press someone to stay* ‖ to put forward (a claim) with energy ‖ to squeeze (fruit etc.) in order to extract juice ‖ to make more forceful by insistence, *to press a point* ‖ to cause distress to (the mind or spirits), *pressed by poverty* ‖ to clasp or hold in an affectionate embrace, *to press someone's hand* ‖ to make (a phonograph record) ‖ *v.i.* to throng about someone or something, *the crowd pressed against the sentries* ‖ to force one's way ‖ to require immediate action, *the matter does not press* ‖ (of time) to suffice barely for what must be done ‖ (with 'for') to make an insistent demand or recommendation, *to press for higher wages* **pressed for** desperately short of (money, time, space etc.) **to press on** to advance with grim resolution [O.F. *presser*]

press *n.* a pressing or being pressed ‖ an instance of pressing ‖ an instrument or machine

by which a substance or material is shaped, smoothed, stamped, compressed etc. by the force of pressure, *a cheese press* ‖ a printing press ‖ an establishment for printing and publishing books etc. ‖ the personnel of such an establishment ‖ newspapers and periodicals collectively ‖ journalists collectively ‖ critical notice in newspapers etc., *the play received a good press* ‖ a cupboard in which linen, clothes etc. are kept ‖ a device for holding a tennis racket etc., in order to keep it from warping ‖ (old-fash.) a dense crowd, *the press at the gate* **in press, Br. in the press** in the process of being printed **off the press** just printed **to go to press** to print off the edition of a newspaper etc. [F. *presse*]

press 1. *v.t.* (*hist.*) to force into military or naval service **to press into service** to make use of (something) through urgent necessity, *a door was pressed into service as a stretcher* **2.** *n.* (*hist.*) forced enlistment ‖ (*hist.*) a commission to press men into the armed forces [fr. older *prest v.*, to hire, giving part payment in advance, fr. O.F. fr. *prester*, to make a loan]

press agent someone whose job is to see to the publicity for a film star, theater, company etc.

press availability in political public relations, an indication that a person will be available for questioning

press box a newspaper reporters' enclosure, esp. at sporting events

Press·burg (présburk) *BRATISLAVA

press-gang (présgæŋ) *n.* (*hist.*) a detachment of men used to compel men into military or naval service

press·ing (présiŋ) *adj.* requiring immediate attention, *a pressing need* ‖ (of a request, invitation etc.) very earnest ‖ very persistent, *pressing demands for payment*

press kit a package of releases, photographs and other material for distribution to the press

press·man (présmən) *pl.* **press·men** (présmən) *n.* a man who operates a printing press ‖ (esp. *Br.*) a journalist

press·mark (présmɑrk) *n.* (*Br.*) a call number

press money (*hist.*) a money reward paid to men enlisting for armed service

press of canvas press of sail

press of sail (*naut.*) as much sail as the wind permits

press·room (présru:m, présrum) *n.* that part of a printing plant which contains the printing presses

press-show (présʃóu) *v.* to display for the press before a public opening. **—press show** *n.*

press stud (*Br.*) a snap fastener

press-up (présʌp) *n.* (*Br.*) a push-up

pres·sure (préʃər) **1.** *n.* the action of pressing ‖ (*phys.*) the force acting per unit area ‖ (*elec.*) electromotive force ‖ atmospheric pressure ‖ interference, by an interested party, with someone's freedom in making a decision ‖ (*fig.*) a burden, *pressure of work* **2.** *pres. part.* **pres·sur·ing** *past* and *past part.* **pres·sured** to influence or force by using psychological pressure ‖ to pressurize [obs. F. fr. L. *pressura*]

pressure altitude (*meteor.*) an atmospheric pressure, expressed in terms of the altitude at which that pressure would be duplicated on the earth

pressure cabin a pressurized cabin in an aircraft

pressure cooker an airtight cooking pot for quick cooking by superheated steam under pressure

pressure gauge an instrument used to measure the pressure of a fluid ‖ an instrument used to measure the pressure of an explosive, e.g. in a gun barrel

pressure group a group of persons who cooperate in seeking to influence the policy of a legitive body etc.

pres·sur·ize (préʃəraiz) *pres. part.* **pres·sur·iz·ing** *past* and *past part.* **pres·sur·ized** *v.t.* to cause the air pressure within (an aircraft cabin etc.) to remain equal to atmospheric pressure at ground level whatever the external air pressure may actually be

press·work (préswə:rk) *n.* the work done by a printing press in making an ink impression ‖ the quality of the result of this work

Pres·ter John (préstər) a mythical Christian priest-king supposed by Europeans in the Middle Ages to rule some vast and rich Eastern country, but thought in the 14th c. to be the king of Abyssinia [M.E. *Prestre Johan* fr. O.F. *prestre*, priest + *Jehan*, John]

pres·ti·dig·i·ta·tion (prɛstidɪdʒitéifən) *n.* sleight of hand [PRESTIDIGITATOR]

pres·ti·dig·i·ta·tor (prɛstidídʒiteitər) *n.* someone skilled in sleight of hand [fr. F. *prestiaigitateur* fr. *preste*, nimble+L. *digitus*, finger]

pres·tige (prestíːʒ) *n.* widely acknowledged high reputation, as a source of power, credit or influence [F.]

prestige advertising (*Br.*) institutional advertising

pres·tig·ious (prestídʒəs, prestídʒi:əs, prestí:dʒəs, prestí:dʒi:əs) *adj.* held in high esteem [fr. L.L. *praestigiosus*, cheating, deceitful, illusory]

pres·tis·si·mo (prestísəmou) *adv.* and *adj.* (*mus.*) extremely fast [Ital. superl. of *presto*, presto]

prest money (prest) (*hist.*) press money [O.F. *prest*, a loan]

pres·to (préstou) *adv.* and *adj.* (*mus.*) fast [Ital.]

Pres·ton (préstən) a sea and river port and county borough (pop. 143,734) of W. central Lancashire, England: textiles, electrical appliances, aircraft

pre·stress (prí:strés) *v.* to process (e.g., steel, concrete) by placing under stress before completing manufacture —**pre·stress** *n.* —**prestressed** *adj.*

pre·stressed (prí:strest) *adj.* (of concrete) reinforced with wire strands to which stress has been applied

pre·sum·a·ble (prizú:məb'l) *adj.* that may be presumed **pre·súm·a·bly** *adv.*

pre·sume (prizú:m) *pres. part.* **pre·sum·ing** *past* and *past part.* **pre·sumed** *v.t.* to assume as true, take for granted ‖ (with *infin.*) to take upon oneself boldly or rashly, venture, *he presumed to criticize her performance* ‖ to imply, presuppose ‖ *v.i.* (with 'on', 'upon') to take advantage of or rely on something or someone more than is warranted [F. *présumer*, to usurp or fr. L. *praesumere*, to anticipate assume]

pre·sump·tion (prizámpfən) *n.* the act of presuming ‖ something presumed, a supposition ‖ unwarranted taking for granted of someone's approval, acquiescence etc. ‖ a too high opinion of oneself ‖ (*law*) a deduction made from known facts but lacking direct evidence [M.E. fr. O.F. *presumpcion, presompcion*]

pre·sump·tive (prizámptiv) *adj.* based on or justifying a presumption [F. *présomptif, présomptive*]

presumptive evidence circumstantial evidence

pre·sump·tu·ous (prizámptfu:əs) *adj.* displaying excessive self-confidence and taking liberties [O.F. *presuntuex, presumptuoux*]

pre·sup·pose (pri:səpóuz) *v.t. pres. part.* **pre·sup·pos·ing** *past* and *past part.* **pre·sup·posed** to assume beforehand, take for granted ‖ to imply the existence of, *the agreement presupposes certain conditions* [F. *présupposer*]

pre·sup·po·si·tion (pri:sʌpəzífən) *n.* the act of presupposing ‖ something presupposed [fr. M.L. *praesuppositio (praesuppositionis)*]

prêt à port·er (prétəpɔrtéi) *adj.* (Fr.) prepared-to-carry, ready-to-wear, e.g., clothing

pre·tax (prí:tǽks) *adj.* (*economics*) of a sum, esp. profit, before making provision for taxes

pre·teen (prí:tí:n) *n.* one who is under the age of 13 years, esp. between the ages of 9 and 12 — **preteen** *adj.*

pretence *PRETENSE

pre·tend (priténd) *v.t.* to allege falsely, make deliberately (a false impression), *to pretend ignorance* ‖ to claim, *he did not pretend to know much about it* ‖ to imagine in play or go through motions representing (an imaginary situation), *let's pretend that we're on an island* ‖ *v.i.* to make a pretense **to pretend to (something)** to lay claim to (some honor, quality etc.) [fr. L. *praetendere*, to stretch forth]

pre·tend·ed (priténdid) *adj.* put forward as being something it is not, *pretended kindness*

pre·tend·er (priténdər) *n.* a claimant to a throne without just title ‖ someone who pretends

Pretender, the Old *STUART, James Francis Edward

Pretender, the Young *STUART, Charles Edward

pre·tense, esp. *Br.* **pre·tence** (priténs, prí:tens) *n.* the deliberate creating of a false impression, *a pretense of friendship* ‖ something pretended, *his anger was all a pretense* ‖ pretentiousness ‖ claim, *no pretense to originality* [A. F. *pretensse*]

pre·ten·sion (priténfən) *n.* a claim, whether true or false ‖ the putting forth of a claim ‖ pretentiousness [prob. fr. M.L. *praetensio (praetensionis)*]

pre·ten·tious (priténfəs) *adj.* claiming to possess superior qualities or great importance, esp. without justification [fr. F. *prétentieux*]

pret·er·ite, pret·er·it (prétərit) **1.** *adj.* (*gram.*) of the form of a verb which denotes something done or existing in the past **2.** *n.* (*gram.*) the preterite tense of a verb, e.g. 'went' is the preterite of 'go' [fr. L. *praeterire (praeteritus)*, to pass by]

pret·er·i·tion (prɛterífən) *n.* a passing over or omitting ‖ the state of being so treated ‖ (*law*) the omission of the name of a possible heir by a testator ‖ (*theol.*) the Calvinist doctrine that God passes over all but the elect [fr. L.L. *praeteritio (praeteritionis)*]

pre·ter·mis·sion (pri:tərmífən) *n.* a pretermitting [fr. L. *praetermissio (praetermissionis)*]

pre·ter·mit (pri:tərmít) *pres. part.* **pre·ter·mit·ting** *past* and *past part.* **pre·ter·mit·ted** *v.t.* to pass over or omit ‖ to discontinue temporarily ‖ (*law*) to omit (a possible heir's name) in a will [fr. L. *praetermittere*, to let go by]

pre·ter·nat·u·ral (pri:tərnǽtfərəl) *adj.* beyond what is regarded as natural, *a preternatural gift for remembering faces* ‖ supernatural [fr. M.L. *praeternaturalis*]

pre·text 1. (prí:tekst) *n.* a false reason given to conceal the real reason for an action etc. **2.** (priték st) *v.t.* to advance (a pretext) for one's actions etc. [fr. L. *praetextus*, outward display]

pretor *PRAETOR

Pre·to·ri·a (pritóri:ə, pritóuri:ə) the capital (pop. 739,043) of South Africa and of the Transvaal, 30 miles northeast of Johannesburg: iron and steel, mechanical engineering, mining, chemicals, cement. Universities (1873, 1930)

pretorian *PRAETORIAN

Pretorian Guard *PRAETORIAN GUARD

Pre·to·ri·us (pritóri:əs, pritóuri:əs), Andries Wilhelmus Jacobus (1799–1853), Boer leader. He led the Great Trek (1835–6), defeated the Zulus in Natal (1838) and laid the foundations of the independent South African Republic, later the Transvaal

Pretorius, Martinus Wessel (c. 1818–1901), Boer statesman, son of Andries Pretorius. He was first president (1857–71) of the South African Republic, later the Transvaal, and president of the Orange Free State (1859–63)

pretorship *PRAETORSHIP

pret·ti·fy (prítifai) *pres. part.* **pret·ti·fy·ing** *past* and *past part.* **pret·ti·fied** *v.t.* to make pretty or depict prettily, esp. inappropriately or vapidly

pret·ti·ly (prítili:) *adv.* in a way that is charming to see or hear, *she curtsied prettily*

pret·ti·ness (príti:nis) *n.* the quality of being pretty

pret·ty (príti:) *comp.* **pret·ti·er** *superl.* **pret·ti·est 1.** *adj.* pleasing to see or hear, esp. on account of grace, delicacy or charm, but less than beautiful ‖ excellent, fine, good (used ironically), *a pretty mess* **2.** *adv.* (used as a mild intensive before another adv. or an adj.) rather, *pretty good, pretty awful* **sitting pretty** (*pop.*) well placed for taking advantage of a situation [O.E. *prættig*, crafty]

pret·ty-pret·ty (príti:príti:) *adj.* insipidly pretty

pret·zel (prétsəl) *n.* a cracker shaped like an open knot, glazed and salted [G. *brezel*]

pre·vail (privéil) *v.i.* (often with 'against', 'over') to be victorious ‖ to be the chief characteristic, predominate, *strong winds prevail in those regions* ‖ to be widespread or current, *strange customs prevail among the inhabitants* ‖ (with 'on', 'upon') to persuade **pre·vail·ing** *adj.* [M.E. *prevaylle, prevaile* fr. L. *praevalere*, to be very strong]

prev·a·lence (prévələns) *n.* the quality, state or fact of being prevalent [F. *prévalence*]

prev·a·lent (prévələnt) *adj.* widespread, generally used, followed, circulated etc., *the prevalent fashion* [fr. L. *praevalens (praevalentis)* fr. *praevalere*, to be very strong]

pre·var·i·cate (privǽrikéit) *pres. part.* **pre·var·i·cat·ing** *past* and *past part.* **pre·var·i·cat·ed** *v.i.* to speak or act evasively, hiding the truth [fr. L. *praevaricari (praevaricatus)*, to walk crookedly]

pre·var·i·ca·tion (privǽrikéifən) *n.* the act of prevaricating ‖ an instance of this [fr. L. *praevaricatio (praevaricationis)*]

pre·var·i·ca·tor (privǽrikeitər) *n.* someone who prevaricates [L. *praevaricator*]

pre·ven·ient (privíːnjənt) *adj.* preceding ‖ anticipating [fr. L. *praeveniens (praevenientis)* fr. *praevenire*, to come before]

prevenient grace (*theol.*) the grace which operates on a person's will and disposes him to repentance

pre·vent (privént) *v.t.* to cause not to do something, *illness prevented him from going* ‖ to cause not to happen, or not to be made or done, *the storm prevented an early departure* [fr. L. *praevenire (praeventus)*, to come before]

pre·vent·a·ble, pre·vent·i·ble (privéntəb'l) *adj.* capable of being prevented

pre·vent·a·tive (privéntətiv) **1.** *adj.* preventive **2.** *n.* a preventive

prevent defense (*football*) deep behind-the-line defense against a long forward pass

preventible *PREVENTABLE

pre·ven·tion (privénfən) *n.* the act of preventing ‖ something that serves as a preventive [fr. L.L. *praeventio (praeventionis)*]

pre·ven·tive (privéntiv) **1.** *adj.* preventing or intended to prevent something ‖ (*med.*) intended to prevent disease **2.** *n.* something that prevents or is intended to prevent something ‖ a medicament etc. used for preventing disease ‖ (*Br.*) of or pertaining to that department of Customs which is concerned with prevention of smuggling, *a preventive officer* [fr. L. *praevenire (praeventus)*, to come before]

preventive detention holding one suspected of a crime in order to prevent his or her commission of further crime (illegal in the U.S.A.)

pre·view (prí:vju:) **1.** *n.* a presentation of a film, book etc. to critics, press reporters etc. before it is presented to the general public ‖ a brief view or foretaste of something that is to come ‖ (also **prevue**) short extracts from a new film exhibited as advance publicity **2.** *v.t.* to see or show a preview of

pre·vi·ous (prí:vi:əs) **1.** *adj.* occurring or done earlier, *his previous attempts had been unsuccessful* ‖ (*pop.*) before the right time, *she was a little previous in announcing the engagement* **2.** *adv.* (with 'to') before, *did you test it previous to buying it?* [fr. L. *praevius*, going before]

previous question a motion in a legislative session to put some central matter under discussion to the vote immediately, without more debate or proposal of further amendments. In British usage, if the motion is not carried the matter is shelved, but in the U.S.A. the matter remains a live issue

pre·vi·sion (privíʒən) *n.* foresight **pre·vi·sion·al** *adj.* showing or characterized by prevision [fr. L. *praevidere (praevisus)*, to foresee]

pre·vo·ca·tion·al (pri:voukéifən'l) *adj.* of a course of study combining general education with preparation for vocational training

Pré·vost (preivou), l'Abbé (Antoine François Prévost d'Exiles, 1697–1763), French novelist. He is best known for his sentimental masterpiece of psychological analysis, 'Manon Lescaut' (1731)

prevue *PREVIEW

pre·war (prí:wɔr) *adj.* existing or occurring before a war recently over

prey (prei) (*sing.* and *collect.*) *n.* an animal or animals seized as food by another animal ‖ a victim or victims, *con men and their prey* [M.E. fr. O.F. *preie, booty*]

prey *v.i.* (of an animal, esp. with 'on', 'upon') to seek for or seize prey ‖ (with 'on', 'upon') to make raids in order to take booty ‖ (with 'on', 'upon') to have a destructively wearing effect, *his worries preyed on his mind* [M.E. fr. O.F. *preer, preier*]

Pri·am (práiəm) the last king of Troy, who reigned during its siege and was killed when the city was taken. He was the father of Hector, Paris, Cassandra etc.

pri·a·pism (práiəpizəm) *n.* persistent erection of the penis, caused esp. by disease [fr. L.L. *Priapismus* fr. Gk fr. *Priapizein*, to act the part of Priapus]

Pri·a·pus (praiéipəs) Greek god of fertility, son of Dionysus and Aphrodite, guardian deity of gardens, vineyards and herds. His cult spread to Greece during the time of Alexander. He personified male procreative power

Prib·i·lof (príbələf) (or Fur Seal Islands) a group of hilly islands in the southeast Bering Sea, Alaska, noted as fur-seal grounds

price (prais) *n.* that which is given or demanded in return for a thing, service etc. offered for sale or for barter ‖ (*rhet.*) that which must be done, sacrificed, suffered etc. in return for something,

CONCISE PRONUNCIATION KEY: (**a**) æ, c*a*t; ɑ, c*a*r; ɔ f*aw*n; ei, sn*a*ke. (**e**) e, h*e*n; i:, sh*ee*p; iə, d*ee*r; ɛə, b*ea*r. (**i**) i, f*i*sh; ai, t*i*ger; ə:, b*i*rd. (**o**) o, *o*x; au, c*ow*; ou, g*oa*t; u, p*oo*r; ɔi, r*o*yal. (**u**) ʌ, d*u*ck; u, b*u*ll; u:, g*oo*se; ə, b*a*cill*u*s; ju:, c*u*be. x, lo*ch*; θ, *th*ink; ð, bo*th*er; z, *Z*en; ʒ, cor*s*age. dʒ, sava*ge*; ŋ, ora*ng*utang; j, *y*ak; ʃ, *fi*sh; tʃ, fe*tch*; 'l, rabb*le*; 'n, redd*en*. Complete pronunciation key appears inside front cover.

his freedom was the price he paid for security **a price on someone's head** a reward offered for the capture or killing of someone **at a price** at an unusually high cost ‖ with great sacrifice **beyond** (or **without**) **price** of so great a value that no buyer could pay for it **to have one's price** to be willing to be bribed if the bribe is big enough **what price (something)?** what is the use or value of (something)?, *what price freedom now?* [M.E. fr. O.F. *pris*]

price *pres. part.* **pric·ing** *past* and *past part.* **priced** *v.t.* to state or ascertain the price or market value of ‖ to set the price of (something one is selling), *he prices his goods very high* [var. of older *prise* fr. O.F. *prisier*, F. *priser*]

price control governmental establishment of ceiling prices on basic commodities to combat inflation etc.

price-earn·ings ratio (práisó:rniŋz) (*securities*) the ratio of market price to earnings expressed as a simple number, e.g., 9 × *earnings*. *also* price-earnings multiple

price index (*Br.*) (*economics*) an economic measure based on annual Family Expenditure Surveys for the preceding three yrs. *Cf* CONSUMER PRICE INDEX

price·less (práislis) *adj.* too valuable to carry any price ‖ very valuable ‖ (*pop.*) very funny, ridiculous, *a priceless story*

prick (prik) *v.t.* to make a very small hole in with a sharp point ‖ to make (a hole) in something with a sharp point ‖ to deflate (a balloon etc.) by piercing its surface ‖ to wound by piercing with a sharp implement, *to prick one's finger* ‖ to pain mentally, esp. to goad as if with spurs, *his conscience pricked him* ‖ to mark (a surface) with little punctures or dots, esp. in tracing ‖ to form (a pattern etc.) on a surface with little punctures or dots ‖ to disable (a horse) by driving a nail into the quick in shoeing ‖ (with 'off') to mark (a name or item) on a list by putting a dot etc. next to it ‖ (with 'up') to cause (esp. the ears) to point upward or forward as a sign of sudden attention or interest ‖ (esp. with, 'out') to transplant (seedlings) ‖ *v.i.* (with 'up') to point upward or forward. *his ears pricked up* ‖ to have or cause a feeling of being pierced [O.E. *prician*]

prick *n.* the act or an instance of pricking ‖ a small puncture made by pricking ‖ the pain caused by pricking [O.E. *prica, pricca, price*]

prick-eared (príkiord) *adj.* (of a dog) having erect pointed ears

prick·er (príkor) *n.* a sharp instrument for pricking, e.g. an awl

prick·et (príkit) *n.* a sharp-pointed spike on which a candle is stuck ‖ a candlestick with such a sharp spike ‖ a buck in its second year when the horns are straight and unbranched [prob. fr. M.L. *prikettus*]

prick·le (prík'l) **1.** *n.* (*bot.*) a pointed process arising from epidermal tissue, e.g. of a bramble, rose etc., and which can be peeled off with the outer skin (cf. THORN) ‖ a tingling or prickling sensation **2.** *v. pres. part.* **prick·ling** *past* and *past part.* **prick·led** *v.i.* to feel a tingling or pricking sensation ‖ *v.t.* to pierce with or as if with a prickle ‖ to cause to feel a tingling or prickling sensation [O.E. *pricel*]

prick·li·ness (príkli:nis) *n.* the quality or state of being prickly

prick·ly (príkli:) *comp.* **prick·li·er** *superl.* **prick·li·est** *adj.* armed with prickles, *prickly leaves* ‖ feeling as if pricked by prickles ‖ causing such a feeling ‖ quick to take offense, very touchy

prickly ash *Zanthoxylum americanum*, fam. *Rutaceae*, a fragrant shrub or small tree with many prickles and yellowish flowers

prickly heat an inflammation of the sweat glands of the skin, accompanied by a rash and itching, common in hot and humid climates

prickly pear a member of *Opuntia*, fam. *Cactaceae*, a genus of jointed cactus with pear-shaped, edible fruit, native to America but widely distributed in warm regions ‖ the fruit of this cactus

prickly poppy a member of *Argemone*, fam. *Papaveraceae*, a genus of American plants with large flowers and prickles, esp. *A. mexicana*

pride (praid) **1.** *n.* excessive self-esteem ‖ behavior that shows this ‖ proper self-respect ‖ a source of great satisfaction for which one feels some responsibility, *he is his mother's pride* ‖ a sense of satisfaction with one's achievements etc. ‖ the best, *this one is the pride of his collection* ‖ (of a bird) the state of having the tail fully

displayed, *a peacock in his pride* ‖ (of lions) a group, often a family, in the wild state **to take pride in** to set oneself a high standard in (one's work etc.) ‖ for the satisfaction brings ‖ to be proud of (some achievement etc.) **2.** *v. refl. pres. part.* **prid·ing** *past* and *past part.* **prid·ed** to feel pride in some achievement or prowess [O.E. *prýtu, prýte*]

pride of place the first or most exalted position

Pride's Purge (*Eng. hist.*) the exclusion (Dec. 6, 1648) by a group of soldiers under Colonel Thomas Pride (*d.* 1658) of more than 100 members (mostly Presbyterians) from the Long Parliament. The remaining members formed the extremist Rump Parliament

prie-dieu (pri:djó:) *n.* a narrow desk or high-backed chair with a ledge on which one kneels to say prayers [F.]

priest (pri:st) *n.* (*Christian churches*) an ordained person trained and authorized by a bishop to be an intermediary between the people and God by conducting sacred rites. administering the sacraments, making intercession, pronouncing absolution and safeguarding sacred buildings and treasures ‖ any member of the clergy ‖ a minister of a non-Christian religion [O.E. *prēost* fr. L. *presbyter* fr. Gk]

priest·craft (prí:stkræft, prí:stkrɑft) *n.* worldly scheming by priests

priest·ess (prí:stis) *n.* a woman priest

priest·hood (prí:sthud) *n.* the office held by a priest ‖ the collective body of priests in a Church [O.E. *prēosthād*]

Priest·ley (prí:stli:), Joseph (1733–1804), British scientist and clergyman. He discovered oxygen (1774) independently of Scheele. He isolated and identified many new gases. He invented soda water (1772)

priest·ly (prí:stli:) *comp.* **priest·li·er** *superl.* **priest·li·est** *adj.* pertaining to a priest, his office or qualities ‖ like or characteristic of a priest

priest-rid·den (prí:strid'n) *adj.* (of a country or people) harmfully dominated by priests

priest's hole (*hist.*) a hidden room or other hiding place for Catholic priests during the times in which they were persecuted in England

Priests of the Mission, Congregation of the *LAZARIST

priest vicar (*Church of England*) a minor canon in some cathedrals

Prie·to (pri:éto), Guillermo (1818–97), Mexican politician, orator and romantic poet. His works include 'El romancero nacional', 'Musa callejera', and 'Memorias de mis tiempos'

prig (prig) *n.* a narrow-minded person who makes an annoying parade of being morally or culturally superior to others **prig·gish** *adj.* [origin unknown]

prim 1. *adj.* (prim) *comp.* **prim·mer** *superl.* **prim·mest** (of a person) stiff in manner, too clipped or precise in speech, too formal in dress, or narrow and intolerant in opinion ‖ (of manner or expression) stiff and formal **2.** *v.t. pres. part.* **prim·ming** *past* and *past part.* **primmed** to shape (the face or lips) into a prim expression [etym. doubtful]

pri·ma ballerina (prí:mə) the principal female dancer of a ballet company [Ital.]

pri·ma·cy (práiməsi:) *n.* the state or being first in rank, importance etc. ‖ (*eccles.*) the office or dignity of a primate [O.F. *primacie*]

pri·ma don·na (pri:mədònə, primədónə) *pl.* **pri·ma don·nas** *n.* the chief woman singer in an opera [Ital.]

primaeval *PRIMEVAL

pri·ma fa·cie (práiməféiʃi:) *adj.* (*law*, of evidence) having every appearance of proving a fact though it may not constitute certain proof [L.=at first appearance]

pri·mage (práimidʒ) *n.* a percentage of the freight charge, paid to the ship's owner in consideration of satisfactory loading or unloading [etym. doubtful]

pri·mal (práimal) *adj.* primitive or earliest in history, *primal customs* ‖ first in importance [fr. M.L. *primalis*]

pri·ma·ri·ly (praiméorili:, práimerili:. práimərili:) *adv.* principally ‖ originally

pri·ma·ry (práiməri:) **1.** *adj.* first in time of origin or order of development, *primary instincts* ‖ basic, fundamental ‖ first in a succession or series, *primary school* ‖ first in importance, *a primary consideration* ‖ not derived, *his diaries are a primary source for the history of the period* ‖ first in order of production, *gas, coke and tar*

are primary products of the coal-gas industry ‖ of or designating the large, stiff feathers on the end joint of a bird's wing ‖ (*elec.*) of or relating to or designating the inducing current, coil or circuit of a transformer or induction motor ‖ (*geol.*) relating to the Paleozoic or earlier eras ‖ (*chem.*) formed by the direct union of two atoms, or by the substitution of only one atom or group, *a primary compound* ‖ (of Latin, Greek or Sanskrit tenses) referring to present or future times **2.** *pl.* **pri·ma·ries** *n.* something which is primary ‖ a primary color ‖ (esp. *pl.*) a primary election ‖ a primary feather ‖ (*astron.*) a primary planet ‖ (*chem.*) a primary compound or product ‖ (*elec.*) a primary cell [fr. L. *primarius*, chief]

primary accent the first and main beat in a musical measure ‖ the strongest stress on a syllable in a polysyllabic word

primary cell (*elec.*) a device for producing by chemical changes an electromotive force which can be used to give an electric current (e.g. Leclanché or Daniell cell)

primary coil (*elec.*) the intake coil of an induction coil or transformer

primary color, Br. primary colour (*phys.*, of light) one of the three wave bands (red, green, bluish-violet) from which, by suitable combinations, all other colors can be obtained ‖ (of pigments) one of the three colored pigments (red, yellow, blue) which cannot be imitated by mixing other pigments

primary consumer the original primitive plant-eating organism in the food cycle

primary election a direct primary ‖ an election within a political party to choose delegates to a party's nominating convention or to select party officers

primary planet (*astron.*) any of the planets which move in orbit around the sun

primary sere (*botany*) the first plant in an area that has not produced vegetation in recent eras

primary service area (*broadcasting*) area capable of receiving consistently satisfactory broadcast transmission from a station

primary storage (*computer*) the storage unit in the main frame

primary structure (*aerospace*) **1.** the craft components that upon failing could destroy the aircraft, e.g., wings, tail, engine bearers. **2.** (*sculptural*) art reduced to simplest primary form with no embellishment. **—primary structurist** *n.* the artist

pri·mate (práimeit) *n.* (*eccles.*) an archbishop ‖ (*eccles.*) a bishop having authority over other bishops ‖ (*zool.*) a member of the order *Primates*, the highest order of mammals, including man, apes, monkeys, lemurs etc. [fr. L.L. *primas* (*primatis*) adj., first]

pri·ma·tial (praiméiʃəl) *adj.* characteristic of or having to do with a primate [F.]

prime (praim) **1.** *adj.* first in time, importance, quality or rank ‖ fundamental ‖ (*math.*, of a number) divisible only by itself and by 1, not by any other integer **2.** *n.* a minute of angle or the symbol (') for this ‖ (*math.*) a prime number ‖ a symbol (') used after a character to distinguish it from another, e.g. to distinguish A' from A ‖ (*fencing*) the first of eight parrying positions ‖ (*mus.*) the tonic ‖ (*mus.*) a unison ‖ (*mus.*) the fundamental note in a harmonic series [F. *prime* or fr. L. *primus*]

prime *n.* (*eccles.*) the first service of the day, held at sunrise or at 6 o'clock a.m. ‖ the time or hour of this service ‖ the best, most flourishing stage or state, *he has passed his prime* ‖ (*rhet.*) the earliest state, *the prime of the year* ‖ (*rhet.*) the best or chief part or member [O.E. *prím* fr.L. *prima* (*hora*), first (hour)]

prime *pres. part.* **prim·ing** *past* and *past part.* **primed** *v.t.* to fill (a pump) with water to initiate action ‖ to inject gasoline into the carburetor of (an engine) ‖ to fill pores of (wood etc.) with a first coat of paint etc. ‖ to provide (someone) with information etc. beforehand ‖ to ply (someone) with liquor ‖ (*hist.*) to put the charge in (a gun) ‖ *v.i.* (of a steam cylinder) to carry over water with the steam [etym. doubtful]

prime cost the cost of raw material and labor in producing an article (in contrast to the cost of advertising, distribution etc.)

prime meridian the meridian at 0° longitude, passing through Greenwich, England, from which longitude is measured

prime minister the leader of a government ‖ the leader of a cabinet or of an executive ‖ a chief minister

---

CONCISE PRONUNCIATION KEY: **(a)** æ, cat; ɑ, car; ɔ fawn; ei, snake. **(e)** e, hen; i:, sheep; iə, deer; ɛə, bear. **(i)** i, fish; ai, tiger; ə:, bird. **(o)** o, ox; au, cow; ou, goat; u, poor; ɔi, royal. **(u)** ʌ, duck; u, bull; u:, goose; ə, bacillus; ju:, cube. x, loch; θ, think; ð, bother; z, Zen; ʒ, corsage; dʒ, savage; ŋ, orangutang; j, yak; ʃ, fish; tʃ, fetch; 'l, rabble; 'n, redden. Complete pronunciation key appears inside front cover.

prime mover (*engin.*) a natural source of power (wind, water pressure etc.) a machine (a windmill, water wheel etc.) converting this power to useful purposes ‖ the first cause of all movement ‖ the person who originates a corporate action

prim·er (prímər, *Br.* esp. práimər) *n.* a simple book for children learning to read ‖ an elementary textbook, *Latin primer* [fr. M.L. *primarius*, a prayer book for the laity]

prim·er (práimər) *n.* something that primes ‖ a cap, cylinder etc. containing an explosive compound used to fire the charge of a gun

prime rate or **prime interest rate** (*banking*) the lowest rate of interest charged by a lending institution to its best-rated customers

prime time (*broadcasting*) the broadcast period during which the largest audiences are watching or listening, usu. from 6 PM to 10 PM or 11 PM

pri·me·val, pri·mae·val (praimí:vəl) *adj.* belonging to the earliest era of life on the earth, *primeval forest* [fr. L. *primaevus*]

prim·ing (práimiŋ) *n.* the act of someone who or something that primes ‖ something used for priming, e.g. a first coat of paint

priming of the tides an acceleration of the time of high and low tide occurring during the first and third quarters of the moon

pri·mip·a·ra (praimípərə) *pl.* **pri·mip·a·rae** (praimípəri:) *n.* a woman who or animal that has given birth once only ‖ an individual pregnant for the first time **pri·míp·a·rous** *adj.* [L. fr. *primus*, first + *parere*, to bring forth]

prim·i·tive (prímitiv) **1.** *adj.* of, pertaining to or characteristic of the earliest period or origin of something ‖ having the characteristics of the earliest stages of civilization, *they are a primitive tribe* ‖ roughly constructed, crude and simple ‖ without civilized accretions, *he lives a primitive life* ‖ (of a work of art or artist) of the period just before the Renaissance ‖ of modern (often deliberately) unsophisticated works of art, or artists painting in such a style ‖ (*math.*) of a figure, line etc. from which another is derived ‖ (*biol.*) of or pertaining to an early stage of development ‖ (*biol.*) showing little change from an early ancestral type ‖ (*geol.*) primary ‖ (*gram.*) of a root form in contrast to a derived word **2.** *n.* a primitive person ‖ a primitive work of art or artist ‖ (*math.*) a primitive line, figure etc. ‖ (*gram.*) a primitive form **prim·i·tiv·ism** *n.* primitivity ‖ primitive practices, customs etc. ‖ a belief in the superiority of a primitive way of life or of things primitive ‖ the style of a primitive (deliberately unsophisticated) artist **prim·i·tiv·i·ty** *n.* the quality or stage of being primitive [M.E. *primitif* fr. F. fr. L. *primitivus*, first of its kind]

Pri·mo de Ri·ve·ra (prí:mɔəri:vérɑ), Miguel, marqués de Estella (1870–1930), Spanish general and dictator (1923–30). His son, José Antonio (1903–36), founded Falangism (1933)

pri·mo·gen·i·tor (praimoudʒénitər) *n.* the earliest ancestor of whom anything is known ‖ (*loosely*) an ancestor [M.L. fr. L. *primo* adv., first + *genitor*, begetter]

pri·mo·gen·i·ture (praimoudʒénitʃər) *n.* the state or fact of being the firstborn of parents ‖ (*law*) this fact as conferring the right to inherit in the event of intestacy [fr. M.L. *primogenitura* fr. L. *primo* adv., first + *genitura*, birth]

pri·mor·di·al (praimɔ́rdiəl) *adj.* existing from the beginning, of that which was the first to be created, *primordial matter* ‖ fundamental, underived, *primordial rights* ‖ (*biol.*, of a species, organ, cell etc.) earliest developed [fr. L.L. *primordialis*, first of all]

primordial soup mixture of amino acids, purine, pyrimidine and phosphate, from which life first began. *also* prebiotic soup or protolicotic soup

primp (primp) *v.i.* to busy oneself fussily about one's dress or appearance, *she likes to primp before her mirror* ‖ *v.t.* to fuss over (one's hair, clothes etc.) so as to impress ‖ to put in order (a room etc.), esp. for visitors' eyes [perh. fr. PRIM]

prim·rose (prímrouz) *n. Primula vulgaris*, fam. *Primulaceae*, a plant having a rosette of leaves and a single flower ‖ the flower of this plant ‖ a light yellow color [M.E. *primerose*, rel. to O.F. *primerose* and to M.L. *prima rosa*, earliest rose]

primrose path a way of pleasure ‖ an easy way that leads to destruction etc.

prim·u·la (prímjulə) *n.* a member of *Primula*, fam. *Primulaceae*, a large genus of perennial

plants with white, yellow and pink flowers, found in temperate and mountainous parts of the northern hemisphere [M.L.]

pri·mum mo·bi·le (práimmmóubəli:) *n.* (*Ptolemaic astron.*) a sphere assumed to revolve from east west around the earth, carrying with it the heavenly bodies ‖ a prime mover [M.L. fr. L. *primus*, first + *mobilis* adj., movable]

Prince (prins), Morton (1854–1929), U.S. psychologist and physician who formulated such concepts as neurograms (the neurological record of psychological behavior) and the coconscious (a parallel, possibly rival, well-organized system of awareness comparable with ordinary consciousness). His 'The Dissociation of a Personality' (1906) is a study of a multiple personality

prince (prins) *n.* (*Br.*) a son or son's son of a ruling sovereign ‖ any male member in certain royal families ‖ the ruler of a principality ‖ a courtesy title in some countries, accorded to certain members of noble families ‖ a ruler ‖ a distinguished and powerful person in some walk of life, *a merchant prince* ‖ (*Roman Catholicism*) a cardinal [O.F.]

prince consort the husband of a reigning queen, who is himself a prince **the Prince Consort** *ALBERT

prince·dom (prínsdəm) *n.* a principality (state) ‖ the rank or dignity of a prince

Prince Edward Island an island (area 2, 184 sq. miles, pop. 124,600) in the Gulf of St Lawrence, forming a province of Canada. Capital: Charlottetown. It is a rolling, fertile lowland. Industries: farming (dairying, potatoes, hay, oats, fruit, furs), food processing, tourism. The island was settled by the French (17th c.) but captured by the English (1758). It became a separate colony (1769) and joined the Canadian Confederation (1873)

prince·ling (prínsliŋ) *n.* a minor prince

prince·ly (prínsli:) *comp.* **prince·li·er** *superl.* **prince·li·est** *adj.* worthy of a prince, splendid, *a princely reward* ‖ of or relating to a prince

prince of Wales a title conferred on the eldest son of a British sovereign

Prince of Wales, Cape the most westerly point of the North American mainland, on the Bering Strait at the west tip of the Seward Peninsula

prince regent *pl.* **prince regents** a title conferred on a royal prince appointed to act as regent **the Prince Regent** (*Br. hist.*) the title by which the future George IV was commonly styled while he was regent (1811-20) for George III

Prince Rupert a city (pop. 12,000) of W. British Columbia, Canada. It is the W. terminus of the Canadian National transcontinental railroad (completed 1914). Fisheries, sawmills, shipbuilding

prin·cess (prínsis, prínses, *Br.* also prinsés) *n.* a nonreigning female member of a royal family ‖ a daughter or granddaughter of a sovereign ‖ the wife of a prince [M.E. *princesse* fr. F.]

princess royal *pl.* **princesses royal** a title which may be conferred upon the eldest daughter of the British sovereign

Prince·ton University (prínstən) a private university at Princeton, New Jersey, chartered (1746) as the College of New Jersey. It consists of Princeton College, graduate schools and research centers. It shares facilities with the Institute for Advanced Study

prin·ci·pal (prínsəp'l) **1.** *adj.* first in importance **2.** *n.* a person having the chief authority or responsibility, *the principal of a school* ‖ a person employing another as his agent ‖ (*law*) a person actually committing or directly aiding in a crime ‖ the sum of money on which interest is earned ‖ a person playing a chief role in a play, film, ballet etc. ‖ the soloist in a concert ‖ (*mus.*) the chief metal stop of an organ, giving the octave above the open diapason ‖ (*mus.*) the subject of a fugue ‖ (*mus.*) the first player of any division of orchestral instruments except first violins (*LEADER) ‖ (*law*) someone who is primarily liable, as distinct from someone who stands surety or endorses ‖ (*building*) a roof truss ‖ one of the combatants in a duel [fr. L. *principalis*]

principal diagonal (*math.*) in a square matrix, the diagonal from lower right to upper left

principal focus the point at which a beam of rays parallel to the axis of a lens (*OPTICAL CENTER) is brought to a focus. Its distance from the optical center (i.e. the focal length of the lens) depends upon the algebraic sum of the recipro-

cals of the radii of curvature of the lens surface and the refractive index of the lens substance

prin·ci·pal·i·ty (prinsəpǽliti) *pl.* **prin·ci·pal·i·ties** *n.* any of certain small states whose ruler is called a prince, e.g. one which is or was within or subordinate to a kingdom or empire ‖ the rank, office or dignity of a prince ‖ (*pl.*) an order of angels (*ANGEL) [M.E. *principalite* fr. O.F *principalite, principaltee*]

principal parts (*gram.*) the inflected forms of a verb, including in English the infinitive, past tense and past participle, from which other inflected forms can be derived

prin·ci·pate (prínsəpit) *n.* (*Rom. hist.*) a form of government under the early emperors which retained some republican features ‖ the tenure of office of one of these emperors [fr. L. *principatus*, the first place]

Principe *SÃO TOMÉ AND PRINCIPE

prin·ci·ple (prínsəp'l) *n.* a law of nature as formulated and accepted by the mind, *Archimedes' principle* ‖ an essential truth upon which other truths are based ‖ the acceptance of moral law as a guide to behavior, *a man of principle* ‖ a rule by which a person chooses to govern his conduct, often forming part of a code, *a man of liberal principles* ‖ a fundamental implication, *he objects to the principle of the thing, not to the method* **in principle** as regards essentials, *we agree in principle but we dislike your procedure* **on principle** by virtue of the principles one accepts, *to agree on principle* [fr. F. *principe* or L. *principium*]

principle of inertia *LAW OF MOTION

principle of superposition a theorem in physics that permits the vectorial addition of effects if they are proportional to the causes and if the causes are also vectorially additive. Thus the resultant displacement produced by two or more waves intersecting at a point at a given time is equal to what the sum of the instantaneous displacement of each wave would be if each were acting alone at that point

prink (priŋk) *v.i.* and *t.* (often with 'up') to dress with elaborate care and finery [perh. related to PRANK v.]

print (print) **1.** *n.* a picture or design made by an inked impression of a block, engraved plate etc. ‖ a mark made on something by pressure ‖ a photograph made from a negative ‖ printed matter ‖ handwritten letters imitating typographical forms ‖ an object for making a mark by impression, a stamp, seal ‖ an object which has received such a mark, *a print of butter* ‖ a textile made with an applied colored or black and white pattern ‖ a dress made of this **in print** printed in a publication etc., *to see one's name in print* ‖ still available from the publisher **out of print** no longer available from the publisher [M.E. fr. O.F. *priente,preinte*, impression of a seal etc.]

print *v.t.* to make a mark on (a surface) by pressure or stamping ‖ to make (a mark) on a surface by pressing or stamping ‖ to make an impression on the surface of (paper, fabric etc.) by pressing inked blocks etc. on it ‖ to reproduce (a text, news etc.) by this process ‖ to write or draw (letters) in imitation of type forms ‖ to make (a photograph) from a negative ‖ to fix firmly (a memory, idea etc.) on the mind ‖ *v.i.* to practice the art of making inked impressions on paper etc. ‖ to write in characters resembling type forms **to print off** to go to press with (the edition) after proofing is finished **print·a·ble** *adj.* good enough or proper enough to be printed and published **print·er** *n.* someone who prints, esp. as a profession [M.E. *prenten, printen* fr. *prente,printe* n., a print]

printer's devil a person employed in a printing business as an apprentice or to do odd jobs

printer's imprint the name or identifying mark on printed matter of the printer, together with the place of printing, usually found on the back of the title page or on the last page of a book, or the foot of the last page of a newspaper

printer's ink a quick-drying ink used in printing newspapers, books etc.

printer's ream a ream of 516 sheets

print·ing (príntiŋ) *n.* the action of someone or something that prints ‖ the art or business of a printer ‖ the style or quality of that which is printed ‖ the total number of printed copies of a book etc. made at one time.

—The technique of printing was known to the Chinese as early as the 9th c. In the European Middle Ages pictures and playing cards were

CONCISE PRONUNCIATION KEY: (**a**) æ, c*a*t; ɑ, c*a*r; ɔ f*aw*n; ei, sn*a*ke. (**e**) e, h*e*n; i:, sh*ee*p; iə, d*ee*r; ɛə, b*ea*r. (**i**) i, f*i*sh; ai, t*i*ger; ə:, b*i*rd. (**o**) o, *o*x; au, c*ow*; ou, g*oa*t; u, p*oo*r; ɔi, r*oy*al. (**u**) ʌ, d*u*ck; u, b*u*ll; u:, g*oo*se; ə, b*a*cillus; ju:, c*u*be. x, lo*ch*; θ, *th*ink; δ, *b*o*th*er; z, *Z*en; ʒ, cor*s*age; dʒ, sava*g*e; ŋ, ora*ng*utang; j, *y*ak; ʃ, *fi*sh; tʃ, fe*tch*; 'l, rabb*le*; 'n, redd*en*. Complete pronunciation key appears inside front cover.

printed from wood blocks. It was not until c. 1436 that Gutenberg invented the technique of casting single metal letters (types) which could be assembled together to form a continuous text. The first book printed from movable types was probably the celebrated 42-line Bible produced (c. 1452-5) by Gutenberg in Mainz. The art quickly spread to Italy, Venice, Switzerland, France, the Low Countries, Spain and England. The Renaissance and Reformation almost coincided with the development of printing, and were greatly assisted by it. The spread of learning and the production of the works of the Reformers gave printers a crucial importance. At first books remained expensive, and were produced in small numbers, but editions of 1,500-3,000 became common in the 16th c. and prices fell.

Until the early 19th c. printing developed little. The old wooden printing press was improved but not substantially changed. Type was set, and paper made, by hand. In 1802 the first papermaking machine was invented. In 1811 the mechanical press, which could be driven by steam, was invented. In 1804 stereotyping was perfected, enabling casts to be taken of whole pages of type. The mechanization of printing coincided with the movement towards universal education. Vast audiences were thus created at the same time as the craft became one of mass production

printing press a machine used to print from type or metal plates etc.

print·out (príntɒut) n. (computer) the printed record of the solution to the program or of the contents of the computer memory —**print out** v.

Pri·or (práiər), Matthew (1664–1721), English poet and diplomat. His humorous poems and satires include 'Poems on Several Occasions' (1718)

pri·or (práiər) **1.** adj. earlier ‖ preceding in order or importance **2.** adv. (with 'to') earlier when we had not met prior to that occasion [L.=former, superior]

prior n. a superior of a religious order or house, esp. a priory ‖ the officer in a monastic order ranking next below an abbot [O.E. fr. L. prior adj., former, superior]

pri·or·ate (práiərit) n. the office, term of office or dignity of a prior [fr. L.L. prioratus]

pri·or·ess (práiəris) n. a nun whose rank in a woman's order or religious house corresponds to that of a prior [M. E. fr. O.F. prioresse, prieuresse]

pri·or·i·tize (praiɔ́ritaiz) v. to place in an order of priority

pri·or·i·ty (praiɔ́riti:, praiɔ́riti:) pl. **pri·or·i·ties** n. the quality or state of coming first in time, priority of claim ‖ something that comes first or among the first in importance ‖ the right or privilege of precedence over others, the job must be given top priority [M.E. fr. F. priorité]

prior restraint a court order against publishing, with a contempt citation as the penalty for violation

pri·o·ry (práiəri) pl. **pri·o·ries** n. a religious house governed by a prior or prioress, lower in status and smaller than an abbey [M.E. fr. A.F. priorie]

Pri·pet (prí:pet) (Russ. Pripyat) a river (500 miles long, navigable for 300) rising in the N.W. Ukraine. U.S.S.R., and curving east through Byelorussia to join the Dnieper north of Kiev ‖ a thickly wooded marshland (about 4,200 sq. miles) lying along its central course, largely impassable except when frozen

Pris·ci·an (prí∫i:ən) (Priscianus Caesariensis, 6th c.), Latin grammarian who taught in Constantinople. His 'Institutiones grammaticae' was the definitive Latin grammar of the Middle Ages

Pris·cil·lian (prisíljən) (d. 385), Spanish bishop. His teaching was suspected of containing Manichaean and Gnostic heresy. His execution, on the order of the Emperor Maximus, was the first instance of capital punishment for heresy by a Christian state

prise *PRIZE (leverage)

prism (prízəm) n. (geom.) a solid figure having two parallel polygonal faces, the other faces being parallelograms ‖ (crystall.) a crystal form having three or more faces parallel to one axis ‖ (optics) a device used to disperse light or change its direction, consisting of a transparent solid with two nonparallel plane faces ‖ an electric or magnetic field used to deviate or disperse a

beam of charged particles [fr. L.L. prisma fr. Gk]

pris·mat·ic (prizmǽtik) adj. of or resembling a prism ‖ formed, dispersed, refracted by, or using a prism ‖ orthorhombic [fr. Gk prisma (prismatos), something sawed]

prismatic compass a compass used in surveying: (a prism supplies an image of the reading in such a way that it can be read while the user sights through a telescope)

prismatic spectrum (phys.) a spectrum formed by dispersion by a prism

prism binoculars a pair of binoculars in which the path of the light entering the objective lenses is increased by the use of two totally reflecting prisms, allowing the use of an objective lens of longer focal length than the length of the tube itself would permit

prism spectrum a prismatic spectrum

pris·on (príz'n) n. a building used to confine offenders or suspects awaiting trial, or enemy captives ‖ imprisonment. prison is no cure for first offenders [M.E. fr. O.F. prisun, prison, the act of taking]

pris·on·er (príz'nər) n. a person who is confined in a prison ‖ a person who is in custody or under restraint ‖ a person who is captured or held captive [M.E. fr. F. prisonier]

prisoner of conscience one imprisoned for political reasons

prisoner of war a member of the armed forces captured by the enemy during a war

pris·sy (prísi) comp. **pris·si·er** superl. **pris·si·est** adj. (pop.) primly precise about little details of dress, behavior etc. ‖ prudish [PRECISE or PRIM+SISSY]

pris·tane [C₁₉H₄₀] (prístein) n. (chem.) hydrocarbon resulting from breakdown of chlorophyll in marine fossils; used as a lubricant and anticorrosion agent. also norphytane

pris·tine (prísti:n, prístain, pristí:n) adj. unspoiled, still in an uncorrupted state ‖ of or in ancient or original condition [fr. L. pristinus, former]

pris·tin·i·ty (pristí:niti:) n. the quality of being pristine

Pritchett (prít∫ət), V. S. (1900–) British author. Best known for his masterfully-crafted, comically ironic short stories, exemplified in 'Collected Stories' (1982) and 'More Collected Stories' (1983). He also wrote novels, literary essays, biographies of Turgenev and Balzac, travel books and several autobiographical works

pri·va·cy (práivəsi:, Br. prívəsi:) n. the quality or state of being hidden from, or undisturbed by, the observation or activities of other persons, there is no privacy in a barracks ‖ freedom from undesirable intrusions, to respect someone's privacy [PRIVATE]

pri·vate (práivit) **1.** adj. belonging to a particular person or group and not shared with others in any way, private property ‖ not holding public office, private citizen ‖ having nothing to do with one's official or public character, private life ‖ secret, hidden from others, private thoughts ‖ not available to or not supported by the general public, a private library **2.** n. a soldier in the U.S. army one grade above a new or recent recruit ‖ (Br.) a private soldier in private not openly, without witnesses [fr. L. privatus, not holding public office]

private bill a legislative bill conferring particular powers or benefits on an individual or body in excess of, and sometimes in conflict with, the general law (cf. PUBLIC BILL)

private detective a person who hires himself out to make confidential investigations into crime or into people's activities or who patrols a store on the lookout for shoplifters etc.

pri·va·teer (praivətíər) **1.** n. (hist.) an armed private vessel authorized by a government to engage in hostile acts against the enemy (*LETTERS OF MARQUE) ‖ the captain or a member of the crew of such a vessel **2.** v.i. to sail or act as a privateer

private first class a soldier in the U.S. army or Marine Corps ranking next above private

private hotel (Br.) a hotel catering esp. to resident guests and usually not having a liquor license

private income private means

private means income from investments etc., not from salary or fees

private member's bill (Br.) a parliamentary bill introduced by a member of parliament who does not hold office in the government

private practice practice of a profession (e.g. medicine, architecture) on one's own independent financial account ‖ the goodwill of the patients of a doctor having such a practice, to buy a private practice

private school a school owned and run by private individuals, not by the government, and usually charging fees for tuition etc.

private soldier (Br.) a soldier ranking below a noncommissioned officer

private view a showing of an exhibition to specially invited people, held before the general public is admitted

pri·va·tion (praivéi∫ən) n. complete or serious lack of the usual necessities of life (food, shelter, warmth etc.) ‖ an instance of this [fr. L. privatio (privationis) fr. privare, to deprive]

pri·vat·ism (práivətizəm) n. **1.** policy of not becoming involved in matters not personally essential. **2.** the desire for privacy —**pri·vat·is·tic** adj.

priv·a·tive (prívətiv) **1.** adj. causing privation ‖ of that which constitutes a lack ‖ (gram.) indicating negation or lack **2.** n. (gram.) a prefix or suffix denoting a negative meaning, e.g. 'un-' or '-less' [fr. L. privativus]

priv·et (prívit) n. Ligustrum vulgare, fam. Oleaceae, a quick-growing shrub, with small leaves, white flowers and black berries, native to S. Europe and N. Africa but widely grown as hedging ‖ any of several other plants of genus Ligustrum, grown as hedging [origin unknown]

priv·i·lege (prívəlidʒ) n. a benefit or advantage possessed by one person only or by a minority of the community, his seniority brings him many privileges ‖ any of the fundamental rights common to all persons under a modern constitutional government ‖ (law) a right or power conferred by a special law [fr. L. privilegium, a bill or law in favor of or against an individual]

priv·i·lege pres. part. **priv·i·leg·ing** past and past part. **priv·i·leged** v.t. to grant a privilege to [fr. F. privilégier fr. M. L. privilegiare]

priv·i·leged (prívəlidʒd) adj. enjoying a privilege [fr. PRIVILEGE n. or v.]

privileged communication (law) a defamatory communication made under circumstances such that it is not actionable as slander or libel ‖ (law) a communication made under circumstances such that a witness cannot be compelled to disclose it in court

priv·i·leg·es (prívəlidʒes) n. (securities) a contract whereby one party acquires the right, but not the obligation, to buy from or sell to another party a specified amount of a commodity or security at a predetermined price. also puts and calls

private automatic branch exchange a depot where telephone connections are made automatically or by remote control. abbr. **PABX**

priv·i·ly (prívəli:) adv. (rhet.) privately, esp. secretly [PRIVY]

priv·i·ty (príviti:) pl. **priv·i·ties** n. (law) a relationship between persons, esp. a mutual property interest, that is recognized in law, e.g. between lessor and lessee [M.E. privite, privete fr. O.F.]

priv·y (prívi:) **1.** adj. (in the phrase) **privy to** (rhet.) having private knowledge of, taken into the secret of ‖ (law) having a personal interest or part in **2.** pl. **priv·ies** n. (pop.) an outdoor toilet with no flushing mechanism ‖ (law) a party to a privity [M.E. prive, privy, intimate, familiar fr. F. privé]

privy council a British body which advises the Crown on matters of government, nominally comprising all ministers and ex-ministers and several people eminent in public life in the Commonwealth. It developed out of the king's council of the 13th c., and remained powerful until the 18th c., when most of its work was taken over by the cabinet. Its work is now restricted to formal matters, e.g. orders-in-council, royal proclamations etc., mostly carried out in a series of committees. It is presided over by the lord president of the council **privy councillor** a member of this body

privy purse money granted by the British parliament from public revenue for the personal use of the sovereign **Privy Purse** the officer in charge of this

privy seal (Br. hist.) the royal seal formerly affixed to documents to authorize the use of the great seal, or to documents not requiring the great seal. It was originally intended for the sovereign's private business (13th c.) but by the mid-14th c. had become a public department and had been replaced by the signet. It was abolished (1884), but the office of lord privy seal remains **Privy Seal** the lord privy seal ‖ his office

prize (praiz) **1.** *n.* something of value or satisfaction received in recognition of distinction ‖ such a thing offered to the winner of a competition, to the drawer of a lucky lottery ticket etc. ‖ something of value or satisfaction that is gained or worth gaining by an effort **2.** *adj.* awarded or worthy of receiving a prize, *a prize bull* ‖ awarded as a prize, *prize money* [M.E. *pris, prise,* price fr. O.F.]

prize *pres. part.* **priz·ing** *past* and *past part.* **prized** *v.t.* to value highly [M.E. fr. O.F. *prisier,* F. *priser,* to regard as worth (something))

prize 1. *n.* (also **prise**) leverage, *to get a prize on a weight to be lifted* ‖ a vessel or property captured at sea in wartime **2.** *v.t. pres. part.* **priz·ing** *past* and *past part.* **prized** to capture (a ship) as prize ‖ (also **prise** *pres. part.* **pris·ing** *past* and *past part.* **prised**) to leverage, to pry, force open or lift with or as if with a lever [M.E. *prise,* a taking hold fr. O.F.]

prize court (*law*) a court which assesses and distributes the value of a prize taken at sea during wartime

prize·fight (práizfait) *n.* a professional boxing match [back-formation fr. PRIZEFIGHTER]

prize·fight·er (práizfaitər) *n.* a professional boxer, esp. one taking part in a prizefight **prize·fight·ing** *n.* professional boxing

prize money money from the proceeds of a prize captured at sea, formerly distributed among the officers and crew of the vessel that had made the capture ‖ any money offered as a prize

prize ring the roped enclosure within which a boxing match takes place ‖ prizefighting

Pro (pro), Miguel Agustín (1891–1927), Mexican Jesuit priest. He was accused of an attempted assassination of President Álvaro Obregón, and was executed

pro (prou) *PRO AND CON [L.=for]

pro *n.* (*pop.*) a professional, esp. a professional athlete or coach

pro- *prefix* favoring or advocating ‖ taking the place of ‖ forward, to the front of ‖ before, in advance [L.]

P.R.O. (*abbr.*) public relations officer

pro·a (próuə) *n.* prau [fr. Malay *prau, prao*]

pro·ac·tive (prouǽktiv) *adj.* (*psych.*) of the dominance of material learned early in life, before the current process of change

pro·am (próuǽm) *adj.* (*sports*) of competition including both professionals and amateurs

pro and con *adv.* for and against **pros and cons** *pl. n.* the arguments for and against ‖ those persons who are, respectively, in favor of or opposed to a proposal or proposition ‖ their respective affirmative and negative votes [L. *pro,* for+*contra,* against]

prob·a·bi·lism (prɒbəb'lizəm) *n.* (*theol.*) the doctrine that where there is reasonable doubt in a matter of conscience, it is lawful to act as one thinks best, esp. when there seems to be some authority for acting thus ‖ (*philos.*) the doctrine that knowledge is uncertain and that probability is a sufficient basis for action [fr. L. *probabilis,* probable]

prob·a·bil·i·ty (prɒbəbíliti:) *pl.* **prob·a·bil·i·ties** *n.* the state or quality of being probable ‖ (*math.*) the likelihood of an event, based on the ratio between its occurrence and the average number of cases favorable to its occurrence, taken over an indefinitely extended series of such cases ‖ something regarded as probable, based on the experience that of two or more possible effects one tends to predominate **in all probability** quite probably [fr. F. *probabilité*]

probability distribution or **probability function** (*math.*) a frequency function, where the function values *f(x)* are interpreted as probabilities that a quantity will take the value *x*

prob·a·ble (prɒbəb'l) **1.** *adj.* likely though not certain to occur or to be true, *rain is probable today, it is probable that he was murdered* **2.** *n.* a person, horse etc. likely to participate in a race ‖ a person likely to be selected as a member of a team, or to participate in a competition, or to be a candidate in an election or examination [F. or fr. L. *probabilis*]

probable cause (*law*) reasonable grounds for supposing guilt in a person charged with a crime

prob·a·bly (prɒbəbli:) *adv.* very likely, with probability

pro·bate (próubeit) **1.** *n.* (*law*) the official establishing of the legal validity of a will ‖ (*law*) a copy of a will certified to be legally valid **2.** *v.t. pres. part.* **pro·bat·ing** *past* and *past part.* **pro·bat·ed** (*law*) to prove (a will) ‖ to put on probation [fr. L. *probatum,* something proved]

probate court a court for submitting wills to probate and administering estates

pro·ba·tion (proubéiʃən) *n.* a critical testing. esp. to discover a person's suitability for a job, membership of an organization or institution etc. ‖ a period of such testing ‖ the suspension of the sentence of a convicted offender, allowing him his freedom subject to regular supervision by a probation officer ‖ a period of such supervision **on probation** in the condition of being a probationer **pro·ba·tion·ar·y** *adj.* of or relating to probation ‖ undergoing probation **pro·ba·tion·er** *n.* a person undergoing probation [O. F. *probacion*]

probation officer an official who supervises a convicted offender on probation

pro·ba·tive (próubətiv, prɒbətiv) *adj.* proving, or tending to prove, *probative evidence* ‖ serving to test [fr. L. *probativus*]

probe (proub) **1.** *n.* a blunt surgical instrument used to explore and examine wounds or cavities in the body ‖ a device, e.g. a space satellite, used for scientific exploration and investigation ‖ an investigation **2.** *v. pres. part.* **prob·ing** *past* and *past part.* **probed** *v.t.* to investigate thoroughly ‖ to examine with a surgical probe ‖ *v.i.* to make a thorough investigation ‖ to make an examination with a surgical probe [fr. L.L. *proba,* proof]

Prob·eye (próubai) *n.* trademark of infrared viewer that creates pictures by sensing heat radiated by objects, e.g., used to locate energy losses

pro·bi·ty (próubiti:, prɒbiti:) *n.* scrupulous honesty [fr. L. *probitas*]

prob·lem (prɒbləm) **1.** *n.* a question whose answer is doubtful or difficult to find ‖ a question for discussion or consideration ‖ a matter that causes worry or perplexity ‖ (*math.*) a statement of what has to be done ‖ (*chess*) an arrangement of chessmen on a chessboard, in which a given result is to be achieved under given conditions, usually a certain number of moves **2.** *adj.* (of a play, novel etc.) presenting or dealing with a human or social problem ‖ that constitutes a problem or is difficult to deal with, *a problem child* [F. *problème*]

prob·lem·at·ic (prɒbləmǽtik) *adj.* constituting a problem ‖ open to question ‖ uncertain, *his success is very problematic* **prob·lem·at·i·cal** *adj.* [F. *problématique*]

pro·bos·cid·e·an, pro·bos·cid·i·an (proubasídi:ən, proubɒsidí:ən) **1.** *adj.* (*zool.*) pertaining to *Proboscidea,* an order of mammals having an elongated proboscis and some of the teeth adapted as tusks (e.g. the elephant, mammoth) **2.** *n.* a member of this order [fr. Mod. L. fr. Gk]

pro·bos·cis (proubɒsis) *pl.* **pro·bos·cis·es, pro·bos·ci·des** (proubɒsidi:z) *n.* a trunklike process of the head e.g. in many insects and annelids, and in elephants [L. fr. Gk fr. *pro,* in front+*boskein,* to feed]

proboscis monkey *Nasalis larvatus,* a monkey of Borneo with a long nose

pro·bu·col [$C_{31}H_{48}O_2S_3$] (próubu:kəl) *n.* (*pharm.*) a drug used to lower serum cholesterol; marketed as Lorelco

Pro·bus (próubəs), Marcus Aurelius (232–82), Roman emperor (276–82). He repelled barbarian invasions in many parts of the Roman Empire. He used soldiers on public works in peacetime, and was murdered by mutinous troops

pro·cain·a·mide or **procaine amide** [$C_{13}H_{21}N_3O$] (proukéinəmaid) *n.* (*pharm.*) a cardiac muscle depressant used to treat heart disease; marketed as Pronestyl

pro·cam·bi·al (proukǽmbi:əl) *adj.* of or derived from the procambium

pro·cam·bi·um (proukǽmbi:əm) *n.* (*bot.*) the tissue from which vascular bundles and cambium are developed [Mod. L. fr. Gk *pro,* before+ CAMBIUM]

procaryote *PROKARYOTE

pro·ca·the·dral (proukəθí:drəl) *n.* a church or other building used as a cathedral

pro·ce·dur·al (prəsí:dʒərəl) *adj.* of or relating to procedure

pro·ce·dure (prəsí:dʒər) *n.* an act or manner of proceeding, *he agreed with our purpose but crit-* icized *our procedure* ‖ a prescribed way of doing something, *legal procedure* ‖ rules of parliamentary practice ‖ a particular course of action [F. *procédure*]

pro·ceed (prəsí:d) *v.i.* to move forward, to go further, *to proceed on one's way* ‖ to continue, *proceed along these same lines* ‖ to begin some action and persist in it, *he proceeded to get angry* ‖ to come forth, arise, *the whole trouble proceeded from a misunderstanding* ‖ (*law,* with 'against') to begin action or take legal measures **pro·ceed·ing** *n.* the act of someone or something which proceeds ‖ a course of action, *an illegal proceeding* ‖ (*pl.*) transactions or negotiations ‖ (*pl.*) a record of the activities of a body or organization, *the proceedings of the last meeting* ‖ (*pl.*) a legal action ‖ (*pl.*) legal measures **proceeds** (próusi:dz) *pl. n.* the sum yielded by a sale or other money-raising transaction, *he is entitled to one half of the proceeds* [F. *procéder*]

proc·ess (próces, Br. esp. próuses) **1.** *n.* a series of acts or changes, proceeding from one to the next ‖ a method of manufacturing or conditioning something ‖ a moving forward, esp. as part of a progression or development, *the historical process* ‖ (*biol.*) an outgrowth or extension of an organ or an organism ‖ (*law*) legal proceedings, or the writ or summons beginning them **in process** in progress **in process of, in the process of** during the course of **2.** *v.t.* to submit (something) to a treatment, preparation or process, *to process milk* ‖ to submit (something) to a routine handling procedure, *his application was quickly processed* ‖ to submit (data etc.) to analysis ‖ (*printing*) to produce by a photomechanical process [F. *procès*]

process *v.t.* (*law*) to take legal action against by serving a writ [O.F. *processer,* to prosecute]

pro·cess (prəsés, prousés) *v.i.* (esp. *Br.*) to go in procession

process art art form involving ideas and effects, sometimes never executed and without completed objects. *also* conceptual art **—pro·cessor** *n.*

process engraving any method of engraving printing blocks other than by hand

pro·ces·sion (prəséʃən) *n.* an orderly line of persons, animals or things, singly or in rows, moving together in the same direction ‖ the act of moving thus, *the procession lasted five hours* ‖ (*theol.*) a divine issuing forth, *the procession of the Holy Ghost* [F.]

pro·ces·sion·al (prəséʃən'l) **1.** *adj.* of or pertaining to a procession, *a processional hymn* **2.** *n.* a musical composition, esp. a hymn, which accompanies a procession ‖ a service book containing hymns etc. to be sung in procession [fr. M. L. *processionale*]

processor (*computer*) *CENTRAL PROCESSING UNIT

process printing halftone printing in three or more superimposed colors, giving almost any desired color combination

process server (*law*) a person who serves legal documents, e.g. subpoenas

pro·claim (proukléim) *v.t.* to announce publicly or officially ‖ to declare (someone or something) officially to be, *the new state was proclaimed a republic* ‖ to declare (war, peace) ‖ to announce the accession to the throne of ‖ to reveal as, *his pretentious terminology proclaimed him a charlatan* [fr. L. *proclamare,* to cry out]

proc·la·ma·tion (prɒkləméiʃən) *n.* a proclaiming or being proclaimed ‖ an announcement, esp. an official one [F.]

pro·clam·a·to·ry (prəklǽmətɔri:, prəklǽmətouri:) *adj.* of or resembling a proclamation ‖ resembling the style of a person proclaiming

pro·clit·ic (prouklítik) **1.** *adj.* (*gram.*) of a monosyllabic word or particle with no accent of its own which is pronounced with the following word in ordinary speech (cf. ENCLITIC) **2.** *n.* a proclitic word or particle [fr. Mod. L. *procliticus* fr. Gk *proklinein,* to lean forward]

pro·cliv·i·ty (prouklíviti:) *pl.* **pro·cliv·i·ties** *n.* a tendency or inclination towards some habit, attitude of mind etc., esp. an undesirable one [F. *proclivité*]

Pro·clus (próukləs, prókləs) (c. 410–85), Greek philosopher. He combined metaphysics with Euclid's geometric method, to present Neoplatonism in its most complete and systematic form

Proc·ne (prókni:) *PHILOMELA

pro·con·sul (proukɒnsəl) *n.* (*Rom. hist.*) a governor of a province, with most of the powers of a

CONCISE PRONUNCIATION KEY: **(a)** æ, c**a**t; ɑ, c**a**r; ɔ f**aw**n; ei, sn**a**ke. **(e)** e, h**e**n; i:, sh**ee**p; iə, d**ee**r; ɛə, b**ea**r. **(i)** i, f**i**sh; ai, t**i**ger; ə:, b**i**rd. **(o)** o, **o**x; au, c**ow**; ou, g**oa**t; u, p**oo**r; ɔi, r**oy**al. **(u)** ʌ, d**u**ck; u, b**u**ll; u:, g**oo**se; ə, b**a**cillus; ju:, c**u**be. x, lo**ch**; θ, **th**ink; ð, **b**o**th**er; z, **Z**en; ʒ, corsa**g**e; dʒ, sava**g**e; ŋ, ora**ng**utang; j, **y**ak; ʃ, **fi**sh; tʃ, fe**tch**; 'l, rabb**le**; 'n, redd**en**. Complete pronunciation key appears inside front cover.

consul ‖ a deputy consul **pro·cón·su·lar** adj. [L.]

pro·con·su·late (proukónsəlit) n. the office or jurisdiction of a proconsul [fr. L. proconsulatus]

pro·con·sul·ship (proukónsəlʃip) n. the office or term of office of a proconsul

Pro·co·pi·us (proukóupi:əs) (c. 500–c. 562), Byzantine historian. His 'History of the Wars' (550–3) is a valuable account of the wars of Justinian I

Procopius 'the Great' (Andrew Prokop, c. 1380–1434), Czech Hussite leader. He succeeded Žižka as leader of the Hussites in Bohemia (1425), won several victories over Imperial forces, and ravaged Hungary, Silesia and Saxony

pro·cras·ti·nate (proukrǽstineit) pres. part. **pro·cras·ti·nat·ing** past and past part. **pro·cras·ti·nat·ed** v.i. to keep delaying and putting things off **pro·crás·ti·na·tor** n. [fr. L. procrastinare (procrastinatus)]

pro·cras·ti·na·tion (proukrǽstinéiʃən) n. the act or habit of procrastinating [fr. L. procrastinatio (procrastinationis)]

pro·cre·ant (próukri:ənt) adj. producing young ‖ of procreation [fr. L. procreans (procreantis) fr. procreare, to procreate]

pro·cre·ate (próukri:eit) pres. part. **pro·cre·at·ing** past and past part. **pro·cre·at·ed** v.t. to produce (offspring) ‖ v.i. to bear offspring **pró·cre·a·tive** adj. [fr. L. procreare (procreatus)]

pro·cre·a·tion (proukri:éiʃən) n. a procreating or being procreated [O.F. procreacion]

Pro·crus·te·an (proukrʌ́sti:ən) adj. of or relating to Procrustes ‖ fitting people, ideas or events forcibly into a rigid preconceived plan or pattern, Procrustean methods of reform [after PROCRUSTES]

Pro·crus·tes (proukrʌ́sti:z) (Gk mythol.) a brigand who tied his guests to an iron bed and then either stretched them or lopped off their legs to make them fit it

proc·tor (próktər) 1. n. (Am. = Br. invigilator) someone who supervises students at a written examination ‖ (Br.) a university official appointed from the academic staff to see that undergraduates observe the regulations ‖ a person who manages another's cause in a court of canon or civil law or admiralty law ‖ (Br.) a clergyman elected as a deputy to convocation of the Church of England 2. v.t. (Am.=Br. invigilate) to supervise students at (a written examination) **proc·tó·ri·al** adj. [alt. form of O.F. procuratour, procurator]

pro·cum·bent (proukʌ́mbənt) adj. (of plants) trailing along the ground [fr. L. procumbens (procumbentis) fr. procumbere, to fall forward]

pro·cur·a·ble (proukjúərəb'l) adj. able to be procured

pro·cur·ance (proukjúərəns) n. the act of procuring or bringing about

proc·u·ra·tion (prɔkjəréiʃən) n. procuring ‖ an instance of this ‖ the act of giving someone power of attorney ‖ a fee paid (to a broker) for the negotiation of a loan [F.]

proc·u·ra·tor (prókjəreitər) n. someone who manages another's legal affairs ‖ a proctor in a court of civil or canon law ‖ (hist.) a financial administrator in a province of the Roman Empire **proc·u·ra·tó·ri·al** adj. [O.F. procuratour or fr. L.]

proc·u·ra·to·ry (prókjərətɔːri:, prókjərətɔːuri:) n. legal authorization to act for another [fr. L.L. procuratorius, belonging to a procurator]

pro·cure (proukjúər) pres. part. **pro·cur·ing** past and past part. **pro·cured** v.t. to obtain, esp. as a result of some degree of effort ‖ to bring about, contrive, to procure someone's dismissal ‖ to obtain (women) for prostitution ‖ v.i. to obtain women for prostitution **pro·cúre·ment** n. [F. procurer]

pro·cur·er (proukjúərər) n. someone who procures (esp. women for prostitution) **pro·cúr·ess** n. a female procurer [A.F. procurour, procurator]

prod (prod) 1. v. pres. part. **prod·ding** past and past part. **prod·ded** v.t. to poke with a finger, stick or pointed instrument ‖ to goad, rouse, he occasionally needs prodding into activity ‖ v.i. (with 'at') to poke 2. n. a poke or sharp dig, she gave him a prod with her stick ‖ an urge to activity, a sharp reminder, her memory needs a prod ‖ a pointed instrument for prodding with [etym. doubtful]

prod·i·gal (pródig'l) 1. adj. given to reckless spending, wasteful ‖ (rhet.) lavishly generous 2. n. (rhet.) a spendthrift [obs. F.]

prod·i·gal·i·ty (prɔdigǽliti:) n. reckless spending, extravagance ‖ very great generosity ‖ abundance [F. prodigalité]

prodigal son a repentant waster [after the biblical parable (Luke xv, 11-32)]

pro·di·gious (prədídʒəs) adj. amazing, esp. marvelously great, a prodigious memory [fr. L. prodigiosus]

prod·i·gy (pródidʒi:) pl. **prod·i·gies** n. a person, esp. a child, with extraordinary talents ‖ an exceptional instance (of some quality), a prodigy of patience [fr. L. prodigium, portent]

prod·ro·mal (pródrəməl) adj. (med.) of or constituting a prodrome

pro·drome (próudroum, Br. pródrəm) n. (med.) a premonitory symptom of a disease [F. fr. Mod. L. fr. Gk prodromos, forerunner]

pro·duce 1. (prədú:s, prədjú:s) v. pres. part. **pro·duc·ing** past and past part. **pro·duced** v.t. to bring forward, present for inspection, to produce one's ticket ‖ to bring forth, cause to appear, he produced two apples from his pocket ‖ to create (a work of art), write (books etc.), this author has produced little in the last few years ‖ (of land, plants etc.) to bear, yield ‖ to give birth to ‖ to yield as an exportable product, Australia produces wool and meat ‖ to manufacture, the factory produces 1,000 cars a week ‖ to bring (a play) before the public, arranging financial backing etc. ‖ (Br.=Am. direct) to supervise the presentation of (a play), directing the actors etc. at rehearsals ‖ to assume overall responsibility for the making of (a film) ‖ (geom.) to extend (a line), produce the base BC of the triangle ABC ‖ to give rise to, cause, his arrival produced a sensation ‖ to cause to accrue, money invested produces interest ‖ v.i. to yield or manufacture economically valuable products 2. (pródu:s, pródju:s, próudu:s, próudju:s) n. agricultural or horticultural products, dairy produce ‖ a result (of efforts etc.) ‖ an amount produced **pro·dúc·er** n. a person who or a thing which produces ‖ a furnace for making producer gas [fr. L. producere, to lead forth]

producer gas a fuel gas which is a mixture of carbon monoxide, hydrogen and nitrogen, made by passing air over red-hot coke

producer goods goods, e.g. raw materials and tools, needed by a manufacturer to make other goods (cf. CONSUMER GOODS)

pro·duc·i·ble (prədú:səb'l, prədjú:'səb'l) adj. capable of being produced

prod·uct (pródəkt, pródʌkt) n. something produced, esp. something grown or manufactured ‖ an outcome, result, these evils were the product of laissez-faire ‖ (math.) the number obtained by multiplying numbers together ‖ (chem.) a new compound formed as a result of chemical change (cf. EDUCT) [fr. L. productum]

product differentiation (business) marketing strategy based upon the creation and promotion of product differences, which may be real or imagined, in the physical character of the product or in packaging, name or way it is being promoted

pro·duc·tion (prədʌ́kʃən) n. a producing or being produced ‖ something produced, esp. a literary, artistic or dramatic work [F.]

pro·duc·tive (prədʌ́ktiv) adj. able to produce or producing in abundance ‖ (with 'of') being the direct or indirect cause, these laws were productive of great hardship ‖ yielding results or profit, productive efforts ‖ (econ.) producing goods which have economic value, productive labor **pro·duc·tiv·i·ty** (proudʌktíviti:, prɔdəktíviti:) n. ability to produce ‖ productive yield, productivity and wage increases have not kept in step [fr. F. productif (productive)]

pro·em (próuem) n. a preface or introduction, e.g. to a book or speech **pro·e·mi·al** (prouí:mi:əl) adj. [O.F. proeme fr. L. fr. Gk]

prof·a·na·tion (prɔfənéiʃən) n. a profaning or being profaned [O.F. prophanation]

pro·fane (prəféin) adj. blasphemous, irreverent, profane language ‖ heathen, profane rites ‖ not connected with things sacred or biblical, sacred and profane literature ‖ (rhet.) not initiated into sacred mysteries, the profane multitude ‖ (rhet.) not possessing esoteric knowledge or tastes, his work is too subtle for the profane mass of readers [F.]

profane pres. part. **pro·fan·ing** past and past part. **pro·faned** v.t. to treat (something sacred) with irreverence, desecrate ‖ (rhet.) to treat disrespectfully, debase [fr. L. profanare]

pro·fan·i·ty (prəfǽniti:) pl. **pro·fan·i·ties** n. irreverence ‖ an irreverent act or utterance [fr. L. profanitas]

pro·fess (prəfés) v.t. to claim, he doesn't profess to be an expert ‖ to claim or declare falsely, he professed to be sorry but doesn't look it ‖ to declare one's faith in by observances and practices, to profess Christianity ‖ to follow as one's profession, to profess medicine ‖ to accept into a religious order ‖ v.i. to make a profession, esp. of religious vows **pro·féssed** adj. openly declared, self-acknowledged, a professed atheist ‖ pretended, claiming to be, professed friendship ‖ having taken religious vows, a professed nun **pro·fess·ed·ly** (prəfésidli:) adv. according to a person's own claims, he is professedly an authority on the subject [L. profiteri (professus), to profess]

pro·fes·sion (prəféʃən) n. one of a limited number of occupations or vocations involving special learning and carrying a certain social prestige, esp. the learned professions: law, medicine and the Church ‖ any vocation or occupation, a dancer by profession ‖ the people engaged in such an occupation, an insult to the profession ‖ open declaration, avowal, a profession of loyalty ‖ a declaration of religious belief ‖ a taking of religious vows **pro·fés·sion·al** 1. adj. of or relating to a profession ‖ showing a sound workman's command, a thoroughly professional novel ‖ engaging in some activity as a remunerated occupation, a professional football player (cf. AMATEUR) ‖ following some line of conduct as if it were one's profession, a professional agitator ‖ of or done by professionals, professional golf 2. n. someone who engages in an activity, esp. a sport, to earn money ‖ someone engaged in one of the learned or salaried professions **pro·fés·sion·al·ism** n. [F.]

pro·fes·sor (prəfésər) n. a university teacher of the highest rank in a faculty ‖ someone who declares or confesses views, a faith etc. **pro·fés·sor·ate** n. the office or term of office of a professor **pro·fes·so·ri·al** (proufəsɔːri:əl, prɔfəsɔːuri:əl) adj. **pro·fes·só·ri·ate** n. a body or professors **pro·fés·sor·ship** n. [fr. L. fr. profiteri, to profess]

prof·fer (prófər) n. an offer, a proffer of help [A.F. profre]

proffer v.t. to offer, tender, to proffer a bribe [O.F. proffrir]

pro·fi·cien·cy (prəfíʃənsi:) n. the state or quality of being proficient

pro·fi·cient (prəfíʃənt) adj. having or showing effective command in an art, skill, study etc. [fr. L. proficiens (proficientis) fr. proficere, to advance]

pro·file (próufail) 1. n. the shape of something, esp. the face, as seen from a side view ‖ a drawing of the side view of something, esp. the face ‖ a concise biographical description, a profile of the new prime minister ‖ any short historical, geographical or other descriptive sketch in writing, a profile of modern India ‖ a flat, cutout piece of stage scenery ‖ (archit., engin. etc.) a side elevation or a section 2. v.t. pres. part. **pro·fil·ing** past and past part. **pro·filed** to draw or write a profile of [fr. Ital. profilo]

prof·it (prófit) n. advantage, benefit, he gained a lot of profit from his visit ‖ financial gain, he says he writes for profit, not for pleasure ‖ (sing. or pl.) an excess of income over expenditure, esp. in a particular transaction or over a period of time ‖ the ratio of this annual excess to the amount of capital invested ‖ (econ.) net income [O.F.]

profit v.i. (with 'by' or 'from') to obtain financial gain or other benefit, to profit from an experience ‖ v.t. (old-fash.) to be of advantage to, it will not profit you to start an argument [F. profiter]

prof·it·a·ble (prófitəb'l) adj. yielding profit or a profit **prof·it·a·bly** adv. [F.]

profit and loss account (bookkeeping) an account in which receipts are credited and expenses debited so as to show the net profit or loss over any given period

profit center (business) division providing major source of profit for a company, such as a particular department or product line

prof·it·eer (prɔfitíər) 1. n. someone who makes extortionate profits, esp. in times of scarcity 2. v.i. to make such profits

prof·it·less (prófitlis) adj. yielding or offering no profit

profit sharing a system by which workers share in the profits of a business

prof·li·ga·cy (prófligəsi:) n. the state or quality of being profligate

prof·li·gate (prófligit) 1. adj. dissolute ‖ wildly

extravagant **2.** *n.* a profligate person [fr. L. *profligare* (*profligatus*), to ruin, destroy]

pro for·ma invoice (proufɔ́rmə) an invoice sent in advance of goods to show that they are being dispatched and what sum will figure on the invoice proper

pro·found (prəfáund) *adj.* searching into the deepest and most subtle problems or truths, *a profound thinker* ‖ possessing particular wisdom and shrewdness, *a profound statesman* ‖ requiring deep thought, *profound difficulties* ‖ very great, intense, *he made a profound impression* ‖ coming as if from a great depth, *a profound sigh of relief* [O.F. *profund, profond,* deep]

pro·fun·di·ty (prəfʌ́nditi:) *pl.* **pro·fun·di·ties** *n.* depth, intensity, *the profundity of his learning* ‖ something profound, *we could not follow him in these profundities* [O.F. *profundite*]

pro·fuse (prəfjú:s) *adj.* (of persons) lavish, very generous, *he was profuse in his thanks* ‖ (of things) very abundant, *profuse apologies* [fr. L. *profundere* (*profusus*), to pour forth]

pro·fu·sion (prəfjú:ʒən) *n.* the quality or state of being profuse ‖ great abundance, *flowers grew in profusion* [F.]

pro·gen·i·tive (proudʒénitiv) *adj.* able to produce offspring ‖ relating to the production of offspring [fr. L. *progignere* (*progenitus*), to beget]

pro·gen·i·tor (proudʒénitər) *n.* an ancestor of a person, animal or plant ‖ an originator of an idea, theory etc. [obs. F. *progeniteur*]

pro·gen·i·ture (proudʒénitʃər) *n.* offspring ‖ the begetting of offspring [fr. L. *progignere* (*progenitus*), to beget]

prog·e·ny (prɔ́dʒəni:) *pl.* **prog·e·nies** *n.* offspring, descendants [obs. F. *progenie*]

pro·ges·ter·one (proudʒéstəroun) *n.* a hormone produced by the ovaries, preparing the uterus for pregnancy [PROGESTIN+STEROL]

pro·ges·tin (proudʒéstin) *n.* progesterone [L. *pro,* for+GESTATION]

pro·glot·tis (prouglɔ́tis) *pl.* **pro·glot·ti·des** (prouglɔ́tidi:z) *n.* a reproductive body segment of a cestode formed by budding from the neck [Mod. L. fr. Gk *pro-,* forward+*glōssa, glōtta,* tongue]

prog·nath·ic (prognǽθik) *adj.* prognathous

prog·na·thism (prɔ́gnəθizəm, *Br.* also prognǽθizəm) *n.* the state of being prognathous

prog·na·thous (prɔ́gnəθəs) *adj.* having projecting jaws ‖ (of jaws) projecting [fr. Gk *pro-,* forward+*gnathos,* jaw]

prog·no·sis (prognóusis) *pl.* **prog·no·ses** (prognóusi:z) *n.* a doctor's assessment of the probable course of an illness and the prospects of recovery ‖ the act of making such an assessment ‖ a forecast [L.L. fr. Gk fr. *pro-,* before+*gnōsis,* knowledge]

prog·nos·tic (prognɔ́stik) *n.* an omen, sign ‖ a forecast [O.F. *pronostique* fr. L. fr. Gk]

prognostic *adj.* of or relating to prognosis or a prognostication [fr. M.L. *prognosticus*]

prog·nos·ti·cate (prognɔ́stikeit) *pres. part.* **prog·nos·ti·cat·ing** *past and past part.* **prog·nos·ti·cat·ed** *v.t.* to foretell, predict ‖ *v.i.* to make a prediction [fr. Mod. L. *prognosticare* (*prognosticatus*)]

prog·nos·ti·ca·tive (prognɔ́stikeitiv) *adj.* characterized by prognostication

prog·nos·ti·ca·tion (prognɔstikéiʃən) *n.* a prognosticating ‖ a forecast [O.F. *pronosticacion*]

prog·nos·ti·ca·tor (prognɔ́stikeitər) *n.* someone who prognosticates

pro·gram, esp. *Br.* **pro·gramme** (próugræm, próugrəm) **1.** *n.* a plan or sequence of things to be done, *a research program* ‖ a list of items planned to constitute a concert, dramatic performance, athletic meet etc., esp. a printed list giving the names of the participants etc. ‖ the performance itself, *last night's program was a great success* ‖ a complete item broadcast on radio or television ‖ a plan of the operations to be executed by a computer **2.** *v.t. pres. part.* **pro·gram·ing,** esp. *Br. and computer technol.* **pro·gram·ming** *past and past part.* **pro·gramed,** esp. *Br. and computer technol.* **pro·grammed** to work out a plan of the operations to be executed by (a computer) ‖ to plan the details of, esp. with respect to timing **pró·gram·mer** *n.* someone who programmes a computer [F. and fr. L. fr. Gk *programma,* a public notice]

programmable signal processor (*mil.*) digital computer device for U.S. fighter aircraft capable of performing 7.2 million operations per second, used in radar on F-18A Hornet, F-15 Eagle, and F-14 Tomcat. *abbr.* **PSP**

programmed instruction technique for arranging material to make learning of it easy, and for showing interconnection of the material, esp. with use of a computer. *Cf* TEACHING MACHINE

pro·gram·metry (prougrǽmitri:) *n.* (*computer*) the measurement of the performance of a program

programming language (*computer*) a series of codes to which a computer can respond

program music, esp. *Br.* **programme music** music whose primary intention is to evoke moods, suggest images or tell a story to the listener

prog·ress 1. (prɔ́gres, esp. *Br.* próugrəs) *n.* forward movement ‖ (*fig.*) movement nearer to some aim, *his research made slow progress* ‖ a forward course or development, *the progress of a disease* ‖ improvement, advancement, *he has made good progress in his job* ‖ a supposed gradual advancement or improvement in the condition of mankind, esp. seen from a scientific or material standpoint ‖ (esp. *hist.*) an official or ceremonial journey **in progress** going on now or at the time in question **2. pro·gress** (prəgrés, *Br.* esp. próugrés) *v.i.* to go forward or onward ‖ to go on, continue, *the demolition work progresses steadily* ‖ to develop, show improvement, *how is the boy progressing?* ‖ (*fig.*) to advance, move nearer to some aim, *space research has progressed greatly* [fr. L. *progredi* (*progressus*), to go forward]

pro·gres·sion (prəgréʃən) *n.* the act or process of going forward ‖ continuing development, *the narrative shows a sense of orderly progression* ‖ (*mus.*) a movement from one note or chord to another, or the series of notes or chords themselves ‖ (*astron.*) movement of the planets from west to east through the zodiac ‖ (*math.*) a series whose terms increase or decrease according to a rule (*ARITHMETIC PROGRESSION, *GEOMETRIC PROGRESSION, *HARMONIC PROGRESSION) ‖ a connected series, esp. showing continuity **pro·grés·sion·ist** *n.* someone who believes in human progress [F.]

pro·gres·sive (prəgrésiv) **1.** *adj.* moving forward or onward ‖ increasing in severity, intensity etc., *the progressive stages of an illness* ‖ increasing or advancing in stages or in series, *progressive taxation* ‖ having to do with, or favoring, political and social progress or reform ‖ of or favoring modern educational ideas which stress informal teaching methods and the encouragement of self-expression, *a progressive headmaster* ‖ (*gram.*) of or being a verbal form designating action going on (e.g. 'he is running') ‖ (*cards*) of a tournament in which there is a movement from table to table after each game so as to effect a change of partners ‖ (of a dance) in which there is a regular change of partners **Pro·gres·sive** (*Am. hist.*) of a Progressive party **2.** *n.* someone who is progressive (*printing, pol.*) progressive proofs **Progressive** (*Am. hist.*) a member of a Progressive party [F. *progressif* (*progressive*)]

Progressive party (*Am. hist.*) a Republican splinter group (1912–16) led by Theodore Roosevelt in opposition to Taft ‖ a Republican splinter group (1924–46) centered chiefly in Wisconsin ‖ a Democratic splinter group organized (1948) by H. A. Wallace

progressive proofs (*printing*) a set of individual color guides for inking and registration from which a color printer works in order to reproduce exactly the model proposed

pro·hib·it (prouhíbit) *v.t.* to forbid with authority, esp. by law ‖ to prevent or make impossible [fr. L. *prohibere* (*prohibitus*)]

pro·hi·bi·tion (prouəbíʃən) *n.* a prohibiting by authority ‖ a law that prohibits ‖ the forbidding by law of the manufacture or sale of liquor, or the law itself ‖ (*law*) a high-court writ prohibiting a lower court from proceeding in a case beyond its jurisdiction **Pro·hi·bi·tion** (*Am. hist.*) the forbidding, under the 18th amendment to the constitution, of the manufacture, sale, import or export of liquor throughout the U.S.A. The law was in force 1920-33. In spite of the Volstead Act (1919), the law proved impossible to enforce and was frequently evaded thanks to bootleggers and speakeasies **pro·hi·bi·tion·ist** *n.* an advocate of prohibition of the sale of liquor [F.]

Prohibition party the oldest of U.S. third political parties, founded (1869) in Chicago, Ill., to secure legislation to prohibit the manufacture, transportation and sale of intoxicating liquors. It strongly influenced the presidential election of 1892 and the passage (1919) of the Prohibition Amendment. After that its most effective work was in local and county elections

pro·hib·i·tive (prouhíbitiv) *adj.* serving to prohibit, *prohibitive laws* ‖ (of prices etc.) so high as to discourage purchase or use [F. *prohibitif, prohibitive*]

pro·hib·i·to·ry (prouhíbitɔri:, prouhíbitouri:) *adj.* prohibitive [fr. L. *prohibitorius*]

proj·ect (prɔ́dʒekt) *n.* a course of action intended or considered possible ‖ a systematic planned undertaking, *a research project* ‖ a set task for a class of schoolchildren in which, for a given period of time, subjects are taught with special reference to some chosen topic, and pupils are encouraged to make independent inquiries to supplement formal teaching

pro·ject (prədʒékt) *v.t.* to throw by mechanical means ‖ to cause (light, an image etc.) to fall on a certain surface, *the film was projected onto the screen* ‖ to have in mind as an intention or possibility, *to project a visit* ‖ to direct (the mind etc.), *to project one's thoughts into the future* ‖ to cause (oneself) to enter imaginatively, *to project oneself into the hero's situation* ‖ to externalize (one's own hopes, ideas, frustrations etc.) in something outside oneself or in some other person ‖ (*geom.*) to represent on a given plane or surface a point, line, surface or solid, as viewed from a particular direction or in accordance with a fixed correspondence ‖ to represent (e.g. a map of the earth or heavens) in this way ‖ *v.i.* to stick out, protrude ‖ (of an actor etc.) to establish effective sympathy with the audience [fr. L. *projicere* (*projectus*), to thrust forward]

project grant a contract with a government or private agency to perform certain tasks, esp. research

pro·jec·tile (prədʒéktil, prədʒéktail) **1.** *n.* a body projected, esp. a missile projected from a gun etc. **2.** *adj.* suddenly thrusting forward, *projectile force* ‖ capable of being projected with force [fr. Mod. L. *projectilis* fr. *projicere,* to thrust forward]

pro·jec·tion (prədʒékʃən) *n.* a projecting or being projected ‖ a system by which lines of longitude and latitude are translated onto a plane surface so as to represent the curved surface of the earth or the celestial sphere ‖ the result of projecting a geometrical figure ‖ (*psych.*) accusation of, or unconscious attribution to another of, one's own thoughts, feelings, or actions [fr. L. *projectio* (*projectionis*)]

projection booth (*Am.*=*Br.* projection room) a room at the rear of a movie house from which a movie is projected onto the screen

pro·jec·tion·ist (prədʒéktʃənist) *n.* the operator of a movie projector

projection room (*Br.*) a projection booth

pro·jec·tive (prədʒéktiv) *adj.* projecting ‖ of or relating to projection [fr. L. *projicere* (*projectus*), to thrust forward]

projective geometry the branch of geometry concerned with those properties of figures that are unaltered by projection

pro·jec·tor (prədʒéktər) *n.* an instrument for projecting a beam of light or for throwing an image or a series of images onto a screen

pro·jec·tu·al (prədʒéktʃu:əl) *adj.* of visual material suitable for projection on a screen, e.g., by an instructor. —**projector** *n.* the projectionist or the projecting machine

pro·kar·y·ote or **pro·car·y·ote** (proukǽri:out) *n.* (*biol.*) a primitive single-celled organism with no bound nucleus, e.g., blue-green alga, a bacterium. *Cf* EUCARYOTE

Pro·ko·fiev (prəkɔ́fi:ef), Sergei Sergeyevich (1891–1953), Russian composer and soloist. His work showed great rhythmic and percussive originality and humor. He wrote five piano and two violin concertos, ballet and film music, and seven symphonies, including the 'Classical Symphony' (1916–17). His 'Peter and the Wolf' (1936) is a popular descriptive guide to the orchestra

Pro·ko·pyevsk (prʌkɔ́pjəfsk) a coal-mining center (pop. 267,000) of the R.S.F.S.R., U.S.S.R., in the S. Kuznetsk Basin

pro·lapse (próulæps) **1.** *n.* (*med.*) a slipping down or out of place of some internal organ of the body, esp. the womb **2.** *v.i. pres. part.* **pro·laps·ing** *past and past part.* **pro·lapsed** (*med.*) to slip down (as in a prolapse) [fr. L. *prolabi* (*prolapsus*), to fall forward]

pro·lap·sus (proulǽpsəs) *n.* (*med.*) a prolapse [L.]

CONCISE PRONUNCIATION KEY: **(a)** æ, c*a*t; ɑ, c*a*r; ɔ f*aw*n; ei, sn*a*ke. **(e)** e, h*e*n; i:, sh*ee*p; iə, d*ee*r; ɛə, b*ea*r. **(i)** i, f*i*sh; ai, t*i*ger; ə:, b*i*rd. **(o)** o, *o*x; au, c*ow*; ou, g*oa*t; u, p*oo*r; ɔi, r*oy*al. **(u)** ʌ, d*u*ck; u, b*u*ll; u:, g*oo*se; ə, b*a*cillus; ju:, c*u*be. x, lo*ch*; θ, *th*ink; ð, bo*th*er; z, *Z*en; ʒ, cor*s*age; dʒ, sa*v*age; ŋ, ora*ng*uta*ng*; j, *y*ak; ʃ, *fi*sh; tʃ, fe*tch*; 'l, rabb*le*; 'n, redd*en.* Complete pronunciation key appears inside front cover.

pro·late (próuleit) *adj.* (*geom.*, of a spheroid) elongated in the direction of the longer axis (opp. OBLATE) [fr. L. *proferre* (*prolatus*), to extend]

pro·leg (próuleg) *n.* one of the fleshy legs found on the abdominal segments of the larvae of certain insects

pro·le·gom·e·non (prouləgómənən) *pl.* **pro·le·gom·e·na** (prouləgómənə) *n.* (esp. *pl.*) an introductory section, esp. to a learned work **pro·le·góm·e·nous** *adj.* [Gk=what is being said first, fr. *prolegein*, to say before]

pro·lep·sis (proulépsis) *pl.* **pro·lep·ses** (proulépsi:z) *n.* (in rhetoric) the anticipation of objections ‖ the figure of speech by which what is to follow is taken as already effective, e.g. the application for dramatic effect of an adjective to a noun to which it does not yet apply [Gk *prolēpsis* fr. *prolambanein*, to take before]

pro·le·tar·i·an (proulitéəriən) **1.** *n.* a member of the proletariat **2.** *adj.* of or relating to the proletariat [fr. L. *proletarius*, lowest-class citizen]

pro·le·tar·i·at (proulitéəriət) *n.* the lowest class in a modern society, esp. (in Marxist theory) industrial wage earners possessing neither property nor capital and living by the sale of their labor ‖ (*Rom. hist.*) the lowest class in ancient Rome [F. *prolétariat*]

pro-life movement (próuláif) antiabortion political pressure groups. *ant.* pro-choice movement

pro·lif·er·ate (proulífereit) *pres. part.* **pro·lif·er·at·ing** *past* and *past part.* **pro·lif·er·at·ed** *v.i.* (*biol.*) to grow or reproduce rapidly by cell division, budding etc. ‖ to multiply fast, grow by multiplying, *ideas proliferated in his mind* ‖ *v.t.* to cause to increase greatly in number [back-formation fr. PROLIFERATION]

pro·lif·er·a·tion (proulifəréiʃən) *n.* a proliferating or being proliferated [F. *prolifération*]

pro·lif·er·ous (proulífərəs) *adj.* (*bot.*) developing buds from a normally terminal organ (e.g. a leaf or flower) ‖ (*biol.*) reproducing by budding [fr. M.L. *prolifer*, bearing offspring]

pro·lif·ic (proulífik) *adj.* reproducing rapidly and in large numbers, *rabbits are very prolific* ‖ producing abundantly, *a prolific writer* ‖ abundant, *a prolific output* ‖ (*rhet.*, with 'in' or 'of') very productive **pro·lif·i·ca·cy** *n.* **pro·lif·i·cal·ly** *adv.* [fr. M. L. *prolificus*]

pro·lif·i·ca·tion (prouliftkéiʃən) *n.* (*biol.*) the quality or state of being proliferous ‖ (*bot.*) a proliferous growth [fr. M.L. *prolificatio* (*prolificationis*), production of offspring]

pro·lix (próuliks, proulíks) *adj.* tediously wordy, long-winded, verbose **pro·líx·i·ty** *n.* [F. *prolixe* or fr. L. *prolixus*, extended]

pro·loc·u·tor (proulókjutər) *n.* (*rhet.*) a spokesman ‖ a chairman, esp. (*Br.*) of the lower house of a convocation of the Church of England [L. fr. *proloqui* (*prolocutus*), to speak out]

prolog *PROLOGUE

pro·log·ize (proulɔgaiz, proulɔgaiz, prouləʤaiz) *pres. part.* **pro·log·iz·ing** *past* and *past part.* **pro·log·ized** *v.i.* to write or speak a prologue [fr. Gk *prologizein*]

pro·logue, pro·log (próulɔg, próulɒg) *n.* an introduction or preface, often in verse, to a literary work, esp. a play (cf. EPILOGUE) [O.F. fr. L. fr. Gk]

pro·logu·ize (próulɔgaiz, próulɒgaiz) *pres. part.* **pro·logu·iz·ing** *past* and *past part.* **pro·logu·ized** *v.i.* to prologize

pro·long (prəlɔ́ŋ, prəlɒ́ŋ) *v.t.* to make longer, extend, draw out (usually in time), *to prolong a visit* ‖ to lengthen the pronunciation of (a syllable etc.) [O.F. *prolonguer*]

pro·lon·ga·tion (proulɔŋgéiʃən, proulɒŋgéiʃən) *n.* a prolonging or being prolonged ‖ a linear extension [F.]

prom (prɒm) *n.* ‖ (*pop.*) a ball or dance given by a college or high school group or class ‖ (*Br.*, *pop.*) a promenade concert ‖ (*Br.*, *pop.*) a seafront promenade [shortened fr. PROMENADE]

prom·e·nade (prɒmənéid, prɒmənáːd) **1.** *n.* a slow walk or ride taken for pleasure, esp. for display or as a social custom ‖ a place suitable for this, esp. a paved walk along the seafront at a resort ‖ a series of walking steps in a square dance ‖ the opening of a formal ball in which all the guests participate in a stately march ‖ (*Am.*, *hist.*) a competitive walk or strut to music by couples **2.** *v. pres. part.* **prom·e·nad·ing** *past* and *past part.* **prom·e·nad·ed** *v.i.* to take a stroll ‖ to go on a promenade ‖ to perform a promenade in a dance ‖ *v.t.* to take a stroll through, *to promenade the streets* ‖ to take for a stroll or ride so as to display [F.]

---

promenade concert an orchestral concert where some members of the audience are not seated and may stroll around

promenade deck an upper deck of a liner, where passengers may stroll

Pro·me·the·an (prəmíːθiːən) *adj.* having to do with Prometheus, or like him in his skill or suffering

Pro·me·the·us (prəmíːθiːəs, prəmíːθjuːs) (*Gk mythol.*) son of the Titan Iapetus and brother of Atlas. He stole fire from the gods and gave it to man. In punishment, Zeus chained Prometheus to a rock and sent an eagle or vulture by day to eat out his liver, which was restored every night. He was eventually rescued by Heracles. In some myths, Prometheus appears as the giver of the arts and sciences to mankind

pro·me·thi·um (prəmíːθiːəm) *n.* a metallic element (symbol Pm, at. no. 61, weight of most important isotope 147) of the rare-earth series, produced during the fission of uranium [after PROMETHEUS]

prom·i·nence (prɒ́minəns) *n.* the state or quality of being prominent ‖ a hill, elevation etc. ‖ a solar prominence **próm·i·nen·cy** *n.* [F. *prominence*]

prom·i·nent (prɒ́minənt) *adj.* conspicuous, *a prominent landmark* ‖ jutting out, projecting, *a prominent nose* ‖ distinguished, eminent, *a prominent public figure* ‖ leading, *a prominent advocate of reform* [fr. L. *prominens* (*prominentis*) fr. *prominere*, to project, jut out]

prom·is·cu·i·ty (prɒmiskjúːiti:) *pl.* **prom·is·cu·i·ties** *n.* the fact or an instance of being promiscuous [fr. F. *promiscuité*]

pro·mis·cu·ous (prəmískjuːəs) *adj.* having sexual relations with many ‖ indiscriminate, *promiscuous borrowing from secondary sources* ‖ made up of various kinds indiscriminately mixed together, *a promiscuous gathering* [fr. L. *promiscuus*, mixed]

prom·ise (prɒ́mis) **1.** *n.* an assurance that one will do or refrain from doing a specified thing, *a promise to return soon* ‖ a firm prospect, *a promise of a good harvest* ‖ potential greatness or distinction, *a new writer of great promise* **2.** *v. pres. part.* **prom·is·ing** *past* and *past part.* **prom·ised** *v.t.* to make a promise (to do something, that something will be done etc.) ‖ to assure (someone) that he will receive, *to promise someone a warm welcome* ‖ to give cause for expectation of, *early mist promises a fine day* ‖ *v.i.* to make a promise ‖ (with 'well') to show potential good quality, *he promises well as a mathematician* [fr. L. *promittere* (*promissum*), to put forth, promise]

promised Land Canaan

prom·is·ee (prɒmisíː) *n.* (*law*) someone to whom a promise is made

prom·is·ing (prɒ́misiŋ) *adj.* giving hope of achievement or success in the future, likely to turn out well, *a promising pupil*

prom·i·sor (prɒ́misər) *n.* (*law*) someone who makes a promise

prom·is·so·ry (prɒ́misɔri:, prɒ́misɒuri:) *adj.* containing a promise [fr. M.L. *promissorius*]

promissory note a written and signed promise to pay unconditionally to a named person or body, or to bearer, a fixed sum of money either on demand or at some definite future time, e.g. a bank note

pro·mo (próumou) *n.* (*colloq.*) short for advertising promotion —**promo** *adj.*, *v.*

prom·on·to·ry (prɒ́məntɔri:, prɒ́məntɒuri:) *pl.* **prom·on·to·ries** *n.* a point of high land jutting out into an area of water ‖ (*anat.*) any one of certain protuberances [fr. M.L. *promontorium*]

pro·mote (prəmóut) *pres. part.* **pro·mot·ing** *past* and *past part.* **pro·mot·ed** *v.t.* to raise in rank or status ‖ to help forward, further, *to promote a scheme* ‖ to push the sales of by intensive advertising etc. ‖ to encourage, *to promote interest* ‖ to organize, present and secure financial backing for, *to promote a boxing match* ‖ to support actively, devote energy and influence to securing the passage of, *to promote a bill in Congress* ‖ (*chess*) to advance (a pawn) to the eighth rank and change it into a piece [fr. L. *promovere* (*promotus*), to move forward]

pro·mot·er (prəmóutər) *n.* a person who promotes the formation of a company etc. ‖ someone who organizes and secures financial backing (esp. for a sporting event) [A.F. *promotour*]

pro·mo·tion (prəmóuʃən) *n.* a promoting or being promoted ‖ advancement to higher rank or status, *to work for promotion* ‖ a striving to secure greater sales by intensive advertising

---

etc. ‖ the organization or setting up of an enterprise, *company promotion* **pro·mó·tion·al**, **pro·mó·tive** *adjs* [F.]

prompt 1. *adj.* quick to respond and act without delay, *prompt to obey* ‖ immediate, instant, *a prompt reply* **2.** *n.* (*commerce*) a time limit given for payment of the account for goods bought [F. or L. *promptus*, at hand]

prompt (prɒmpt) **1.** *v.t.* to move or rouse to action, *his anger prompted him to interrupt* ‖ to give rise to, inspire, *malice prompted that remark* ‖ to whisper to (an actor) words which he has forgotten ‖ to suggest words to (a hesitating speaker) **2.** *n.* the prompting of an actor or speaker ‖ the words said in prompting **prómpt·er** *n.* [fr. PROMPT *adj.* or fr. F. or L. *promere* (*promptus*), to make ready to do something]

promp·ti·tude (prɒ́mptituːd, prɒ́mptitjuːd) *n.* the quality of being prompt [F. or fr. L. *promptitudo*]

prompt side (*theater*) the side of the stage closest to the prompter, usually to the actor's right (in the U.S.A.) or left (in Britain) as he faces the audience

prom·ul·gate (prɒ́məlgeit, prouΛlgeit) *pres. part.* **prom·ul·gat·ing** *past* and *past part.* **prom·ul·gat·ed** *v.t.* to proclaim, make publicly known (a statute, decree, dogma etc.) **prom·ul·gá·tion**, **prom·ul·ga·tor** *ns* [fr. L. *promulgare* (*promulgatus*), to expose to public view]

pro·nate (próuneit) *pres. part.* **pro·nat·ing** *past* and *past part.* **pro·nat·ed** *v.t.* to turn (a hand) so that the palm is downward (cf. SUPINATE) [fr. L. *pronare* (*pronatus*), to bend forward]

pro·na·tion (prounéiʃən) *n.* a pronating or being pronated [fr. M.L. *pronatio* (*pronationis*), a bending forward]

pro·na·tor (prounéitər) *n.* a muscle in the forearm which performs pronation [M.L.]

prone (proun) *adj.* lying face down (opp. SUPINE) ‖ flat on the ground, prostrate, *the boxer lay prone for several seconds* ‖ (with 'to') inclined, liable, disposed, *prone to act rashly* [fr. L. *pronus*]

pro·neth·a·lol [$C_{15}H_{19}NO$] (prounéθaləl) *n.* (*pharm.*) drug that causes a blockage of the receptor of sympathomimetic agent. also *nethalide*

prong (prɔŋ, prɒŋ) **1.** *n.* a tine of a fork ‖ a fork for lifting hay etc. ‖ any thin pointed object, e.g. the point of an antler **2.** *v.t.* to pierce or lift (soil etc.) with a fork or prong [etym. doubtful]

prong·horn (prɔ́ŋhɔrn, prɒ́ŋhɒrn) *pl.* **prong·horn**, **prong·horns** *n. Antilocapra americana*, a North American ruminant mammal whose curved horns have an annually deciduous outer sheath and a short prong in front

pro·nom·i·nal (prounɒ́min'l) *adj.* (*gram.*) of, relating to or acting as a pronoun [fr. L.L. *pronominalis*]

pro·noun (próunaun) *n.* a word used to replace noun. It functions as a noun and represents a person or thing previously mentioned or known, or being asked about. Pronouns may be classified as demonstrative, distributive, indefinite, interrogative, personal, possessive, reflexive and relative

pro·nounce (prənáuns) *pres. part.* **pro·nounc·ing** *past* and *past part.* **pro·nounced** *v.t.* to make the sounds of, utter, articulate, *he pronounced every syllable with care* ‖ to utter or declare formally, *to pronounce sentence* ‖ to declare authoritatively, *the doctor pronounced him free from infection* ‖ *v.i.* to produce speech sounds, *she pronounces abominably* ‖ to give one's considered or authoritative opinion, *to pronounce on a matter* **pro·nóunced** *adj.* strongly marked, very noticeable, *a pronounced list to port* **pro·nóunce·ment** *n.* an official statement or announcement ‖ an opinion, decision etc. announced in a formal way [O.F. *pronuncier*]

pronouncing dictionary a dictionary which shows how words are pronounced

PRONTO (*computer acronym*) program for numerical tool operation, a computer program utilizing numerical machine tool language translated from drawings in order to position a cutting device; designed by General Electric

pro·nu·cle·us (prounúːkliːəs, prounjúːkliːəs) *pl.* **pro·nu·cle·i** (prounúːkliːai, prounjúːkliːai) *n.* (*biol.*) the haploid nucleus of a spermatozoon or egg (ovum) after maturation and fertilization

pro·nun·ci·a·men·to (prənΛnsiːəméntou, prə-nΛnʃiːəméntou) *pl.* **pro·nun·ci·a·men·tos** *n.* a proclamation or pronouncement, esp. one made by revolutionaries or by any self-appointed dictatorial body [fr. Span. *pronunciamiento*]

CONCISE PRONUNCIATION KEY: **(a)** æ, cat; ɑ, car; ɔ fawn; ei, snake. **(e)** e, hen; iː, sheep; iə, deer; εə, bear. **(i)** i, fish; ai, tiger; ɔː, bird. **(o)** o, ox; au, cow; ou, goat; u, poor; ɔi, royal. **(u)** Λ, duck; u, bull; uː, goose; ə, bacillus; juː, cube. x, loch; θ, think; ð, bother; z, Zen; ʒ, corsage; dʒ, savage; ŋ, orangutang; j, yak; ʃ, fish; tʃ, fetch; 'l, rabble; 'n, redden. Complete pronunciation key appears inside front cover.

pro·nun·ci·a·tion (prənʌnsi:éiʃən) n. the act of making the sounds of syllables, words etc. ‖ the way in which a word etc. is sounded ‖ the phonetic transcription of the way in which a word should be or is pronounced [fr. L. *pronuntiatio* (*pronuntiationis*)]

proof (pru:f) **1.** n. a proving or being proved ‖ convincing evidence, *his fingerprints were a proof of his guilt* ‖ (*law*) a document receivable as evidence ‖ (*law*) a written version of the evidence a witness is willing to give on oath in court ‖ the alcoholic content of a beverage compared with the standard for proof spirit ‖ (*printing*) an impression of composed type to verify correctness ‖ (*engraving*) an impression carefully taken, for approval before general printing proceeds ‖ (*photog.*) a test print ‖ (*geom.*) the operations which demonstrate and verify a proposition **2.** adj. (with 'against') able to resist, *proof against temptation* ‖ (in compounds) impenetrable by, *bulletproof* ‖ of proved strength, *proof armor* ‖ (of gold and silver) pure and serving as a standard for comparison (in a mint etc.). ‖ of a standard alcoholic strength, *duty charged on the proof gallon* **3.** v.t. to make (something) impervious (esp. to water), *to proof tent fabric* ‖ (*printing, engraving* etc.) to take a trial impression of ‖ to proofread [M.E. *preove, proeve, preve* fr. O. F.]

proof·ing (prú:fiŋ) n. the act of making proof ‖ a substance used for proofing (fabric) etc., esp. against water

proof·read (prú:fri:d) pres. part. **proof·read·ing** past and past part. **proof·read** (prú:fred) v.t. to read and correct (a printer's proof) ‖ v.i. to read and correct a printer's proof [back-formation fr. PROOFREADER]

proof·read·er (prú:fri:dər) n. a person employed to read and correct printers' proofs

proof spirit a mixture of alcohol and water, containing a standard amount of alcohol of (*Am.*) one half by volume, (*Br.*) 57.10% by volume. The alcoholic content of a drink is measured as a percentage of the standard proof spirit

prop (prɒp) n. (*theater*) a property

prop n. a propeller

prop 1. n. a support placed under or against something to hold it up ‖ any person or thing serving as a support **2.** v.t. pres. part. **prop·ping** past and past part. **propped** (often with 'up') to support with or as if with a prop, keep upright, *to prop up a drunken man* ‖ to make to stand or stay in a specified condition, *to prop a door open with a chair* [origin unknown]

pro·pae·deu·tic (proupi:dú:tik, proupi:djú:tikj **1.** adj. serving as introduction to higher study **2.** n. a preliminary study [fr. Gk *propaideuein*, to teach beforehand]

prop·a·gan·da (prɒpəgǽndə) n. information and opinions (esp. prejudiced ones) spread to influence people in favor of or against some doctrine or idea ‖ the spreading of such information and opinions **prop·a·gán·dist** n. someone who uses or spreads propaganda **prop·a·gán·dize** pres. part. **prop·a·gan·diz·ing** past and past part. **prop·a·gan·dized** v.t. to spread (ideas etc.) through propaganda ‖ to expose (a person or people) to propaganda ‖ v.i. to spread propaganda [Ital. fr. Mod. L. *Congregatio de propaganda fide*, Congregation for the propagation of the faith, the committee of cardinals formed (1622) by Gregory XV (1554-1623, pope 1621-3) to be in charge of foreign missions]

prop·a·gate (prɒpəgeit) pres. part. **prop·a·gat·ing** past and past part. **prop·a·gat·ed** v.t. to cause to multiply by natural reproduction, to reproduce, to propagate a species ‖ to transmit from one generation to another ‖ to spread, disseminate, make widely known, *to propagate the gospel of social service* ‖ to transmit (heat, light, sound etc.) ‖ v.i. to multiply by natural reproduction, *this plant propagates readily* [fr. L. *propagare* (*propagatus*), to multiply (plants) by means of layers]

prop·a·ga·tion (prɒpəgéiʃən) n. a propagating or being propagated [F. or fr. L. *propagatio*(*propagationis*)]

prop·a·ga·tor (prɒpəgeitər) n. someone who or something which propagates

pro·pane (próupein) n. a gaseous hydrocarbon, $CH_3CH_2CH_3$ [fr. PROPIONIC ACID+METHANE]

pro·par·il [$C_9H_9Cl_2NO$] (próupəril) n. (*chem.*) a weed killer, esp. used in rice cultivation

pro·pel (prəpel) pres. part **pro·pel·ling** past and past part. **pro·pelled** v.t. to push or drive forward or onward, *the earliest locomotives were propelled by steam* **pro·pél·lant, pro·pél·lent 1.**

adj. able or serving to propel **2.** n. a propelling agent, esp. a rocket fuel or an explosive which propels a bullet or shell from a gun **pro·pél·ler** n. something that propels, esp. a screw propeller [fr. L. *propellere*]

propeller shaft a shaft that transmits power from the engine to the driving device (e.g. wheels, propeller) of an automotive vehicle

pro·pene (próupi:n) n. propylene [fr. PROPIONIC ACID]

pro·pen·si·ty (prəpénsiti) pl. **pro·pen·si·ties** n. a natural disposition, tendency [fr. L. *propensio* (*propensionis*), inclination]

prop·er (prɒpər) **1.** adj. decent, seemly, *proper behavior* ‖ (*Br.*) real, genuine, *he wants a proper gun, not a toy one* ‖ (*Br., pop.*) utter, complete, thorough, *a proper fool* ‖ fitting, suitable, *the proper time to broach the matter* ‖ accurate, *in the proper sense of the word* ‖ (usually following the noun) strictly so-called, (excluding adjuncts etc., *Japan proper excludes the outlying islands* ‖ (with 'to') belonging particularly or exclusively, *the activities proper to a mayor* ‖ (*eccles.*) appointed for a certain day, *the proper Psalms* ‖ (*heraldry*) represented in its natural colors **2.** n. (*eccles.*) a special office, or part of one, appointed for a certain day [F. *propre*, own]

proper fraction (*math.*) a fraction less than unity in which the numerator is less than the denominator (cf. IMPROPER FRACTION)

prop·er·ly (prɒpərli:) adv. correctly, rightly, *she likes to do a thing properly* ‖ in a respectable way, with good manners, *you must learn to behave properly* ‖ (*Br., pop.*) thoroughly, completely, *you've properly messed it up*

proper motion (*astron.*) the motion through space of a star in relation to an imagined position of absolute rest (not to the earth) (cf. TANGENTIAL MOTION)

proper name a proper noun

proper noun a noun designating some single person, place etc. and usually spelled with a capital letter (cf. COMMON NOUN)

prop·er·tied (prɒpərti:d) adj. owning property, esp. land, *the propertied classes*

Pro·per·ti·us (proupə́:rʃi:əs), Sextus (c. 47–c. 15 B.C.), Roman lyric poet. He wrote four books of elegies mainly devoted to love, in the style of the Alexandrian poets

prop·er·ty (prɒpərti:) pl. **prop·er·ties** n. a thing or things owned ‖ real estate ‖ a piece of real estate ‖ abundant wealth, *a man of property* ‖ ownership, the exclusive right to possess and use something, *is private property in itself wrong?* ‖ an attribute, characteristic, *the properties of a magnet* ‖ virtue, quality, *the soothing property of an ointment* ‖ (*logic*) an attribute common to a whole class but not necessary to distinguish it from others ‖ (*theater, movie*) any piece of furniture or accessory used on the stage or set (excluding only fixed scenery and clothes actually worn by actors) [M.E. *proprete* fr. O.F.]

pro·phase (próufeiz) n. (*biol.*) the first events in mitosis and meiosis, consisting of the condensation of the dispersed chromosomes, the replication of these and the formation of the spindle. The prophase of the first meiotic division involves synapsis. That of the second meiotic division occurs without replication (*META-PHASE, *ANAPHASE, *TELOPHASE)

proph·e·cy (prɒ́fisi:) pl. **proph·e·cies** n. a prediction or foretelling of what is to come ‖ the power to speak as a prophet, *the gift of prophecy* ‖ something said by a prophet [O.F. *profecie* fr. L.L. fr. Gk]

proph·e·sy (prɒ́fisai) pres. part. **proph·e·sy·ing** past and past part. **proph·e·sied** v.t. to foretell by divine inspiration ‖ to predict ‖ v.i. to act as a prophet ‖ to make a prediction or predictions [O.F. *profecier*]

proph·et (prɒ́fit) n. a person who, by divine inspiration, declares to the world the divine will, judgments etc. ‖ a person who foretells the course or nature of future events ‖ a leader, founder or spokesman of a cause or party, *an early prophet of socialism* **Proph·et** one of the Old Testament writers of the prophetic books. The Major Prophets are Isaiah, Jeremiah, Ezekiel and (in Christian versions of the Old Testament) Daniel. The Minor Prophets are Hosea, Joel, Arnos, Obadiah, Jonah, Micah, Nahum, Habakkuk, Zephaniah, Haggai, Zechariah and Malachi **the Prophet** Mohammed **próph·et·ess** n. a woman prophet [F. *prophète* fr. L. fr. Gk]

pro·phet·ic (prəfétik) adj. foretelling, containing a prediction ‖ of or relating to a prophet or

prophecy **pro·phét·i·cal** adj. [F. *prophétique* or fr. L.L. *propheticus* fr. Gk]

pro·phy·lac·tic (proufəlǽktik, prɒfəlǽktik) **1.** adj. guarding against disease ‖ preventive, protective **2.** n. a prophylactic medicine ‖ anything which guards against disease [fr. Gk *prophulaktikos*]

pro·phy·lax·is (proufəlǽksis, prɒfəlǽksis) pl. **pro·phy·lax·es** (proufəlǽksi:z, prɒfəlǽksi:z) n. measures aiming to prevent disease ‖ the prevention of disease [Mod. L. fr. Gk *pro*, against+*phulaxis*, a guarding]

pro·pin·qui·ty (prəpíŋkwiti:) pl. **pro·pin·qui·ties** n. nearness in place or time ‖ nearness of kinship [O.F. *propinquite*]

pro·pi·on·ic acid (proupi:ɒ́nik) a pungent liquid acid, C_2H_5COOH, found in milk and its products. It is used in the form of its esters in the perfume industry and in the form of its salts (esp. of sodium and calcium) as a fungistatic agent [fr. F. *propionique* fr. Gk *pro-*, before+*pion*, fat]

pro·pi·ti·ate (prəpíʃi:eit) pres. part. **pro·pi·ti·at·ing** past and past part. **pro·pi·ti·at·ed** v.t. to gain the favor of by appeasement or conciliation [fr. L. *propitiare* (*propitiatus*)]

pro·pi·ti·a·tion (prəpiʃi:éiʃən) n. a propitiating or being propitiated ‖ an atoning sacrifice, esp. Christ as this [fr. L.L. *propitiatio* (*propitiationis*)]

pro·pi·ti·a·to·ry (prəpíʃi:ətɔ:ri:, prəpíʃi:ətouri:) adj. intended or serving to propitiate

pro·pi·tious (prəpíʃəs) adj. favorably disposed, *the fates were propitious* ‖ favorable, giving promise of success, *a propitious omen* ‖ advantageous, *a moment propitious for action* [O.F. *propicius*]

prop·o·lis (prɒ́pəlis) n. a sticky red resin which bees obtain from the buds of trees (e.g. the horse chestnut) and use to fix the combs to the hive and to stop up crevices [L. fr. Gk=suburb, bee glue]

pro·po·nent (prəpóunənt) n. a person who advocates or supports a proposal or idea ‖ (*law*) someone who propounds a will etc. [fr. L. *proponens* (*proponentis*) fr. *proponere*, to put forward]

Pro·pon·tis (prəpɒ́ntis) *MARMARA, SEA OF

pro·por·tion (prəpɔ́rʃən) n. a part, share (in relation to the whole), *a large proportion of the population is illiterate* ‖ relative size or number, ratio, comparative relation, *the proportion of deaths to births* ‖ satisfactory relation between things or parts as regards size, symmetry, balance, *the door is out of proportion with the windows* ‖ (*pl.*) dimensions, *a room of generous proportions* ‖ (*math.*) an equality of ratios between two pairs of numbers, as in the statement 2 is to 4 as 3 is to 6 [F. fr. L.]

proportion v.t. to adjust in proportion or suitable relation [O.F. *proporcioner*]

pro·por·tion·al (prəpɔ́rʃən'l, prəpóurʃən'l) **1.** adj. in proportion ‖ (*math.*) having the same or a constant ratio ‖ used in determining proportions, *proportional compasses* **2.** n. (*math.*) any number in a proportion **pro·por·tion·ál·i·ty** n. [fr. L. *proportionalis*]

proportional representation a system of election by which each party has a number of representatives in the governing body proportional to the number of votes cast for it

pro·por·tion·ate 1. (prəpɔ́rʃənit, prəpóurʃənit) adj. in proportion, proportionally adjusted **2.** (prəpɔ́rʃəneit, prəpóurʃəneit) v.t. pres. part. **pro·por·tion·at·ing** past and past part. **pro·por·tion·at·ed** to proportion [fr. L.L. *proportionatus*]

pro·po·sal (prəpóuz'l) n. a course of action put forward for consideration ‖ an offer of marriage ‖ the act of proposing

pro·pose (prəpóuz) pres. part. **pro·pos·ing** past and past part. **pro·posed** v.t. to offer for consideration, *to propose a plan* ‖ to intend, *she proposes to catch the early train* ‖ to put forward for approval (a person for office or as a new member of a society) ‖ to offer as a toast ‖ to expound the arguments in favor of, *to propose a motion in debate* ‖ v.i. to offer marriage [F. *proposer*]

prop·o·si·tion (prɒpəzíʃən) **1.** n. a proposal ‖ (*logic*) an expression or statement of which the subject can be affirmed or denied ‖ the point to be discussed in formal disputation, usually framed in a single sentence ‖ (*math.*) the statement of a theorem or problem to be demonstrated or solved ‖ a scheme, offer, usually commercial ‖ an invitation to sexual intercourse ‖ (*pop.*) any project, thing or person considered to be difficult to handle, *a tough proposition* **2.** *v.t.* to make a business proposal to ‖ to suggest sexual intercourse to **prop·o·si·tion·al** *adj.* [F.]

Proposition 13 1978 referendum passed in California that placed a ceiling on local taxes; promoted by Howard Jarvis

Proposition 2½ tax-cutting initiative defeated in Massachusetts in 1980; it limits property tax to 2½% of fair cash value and increases in government expenditures to 4% a year

pro·pound (prəpáund) *v.t.* to set forth (a problem, plan, interpretation etc.) for consideration ‖ (*law*) to produce (a will or other testamentary document) before the probate authority so as to establish its legality [fr. earlier *propone* fr. L. *proponere*, to set forward]

pro·prae·tor, pro·pre·tor (prouprí:tər) *n.* (*Rom. hist.*) a magistrate, having served as praetor in ancient Rome, sent out to govern a province [L.]

pro·pran·o·lol [$C_{16}H_{21}NO_2$] (prouprǽnəlɒl) *n.* (*pharm.*) a beta-adrenergic blocking drug that lowers the heart rate and increases end-diastolic pressure; marketed as Inderal

pro·pri·e·tar·y (prəpráiiteri) **1.** *adj.* relating to ownership, *he has a proprietary interest in the business* ‖ owning property, *the proprietary section of the community* ‖ legally made or distributed only by those holding patents or special rights, *proprietary medicines* **2.** *pl.* **pro·pri·e·tar·ies** *n.* a body of owners ‖ right of ownership, *a proprietary over the manufacture of a product* ‖ (*Am. hist.*) the owner of a proprietary colony [fr. L.L. *proprietarius*]

proprietary colony (*Am. hist.*) a colony in which extensive rights of government were granted to a person or persons

pro·pri·e·tor (prəpráiitər) *n.* a person who has legal rights of possession of land, an object, or a process of manufacture or distribution, an owner ‖ a person who has the temporary but not the absolute control and use of property ‖ (*Am. hist.*) a proprietary **pro·pri·e·tress** *n.* a woman proprietor [irregular fr. PROPRIETARY]

pro·pri·e·ty (prəpráiiti) *pl.* **pro·pri·e·ties** *n.* suitability, correctness, *the propriety of such a move is doubtful* ‖ accepted conventions of behavior or morals, *an offense against propriety* ‖ (*pl.*) details of correct conduct in polite society, *to observe the proprieties* [F. *propriété*, property]

pro·pri·o·cep·tive (pr[oup]ri:ouséptiv) *adj.* (*physiol.*) capable of receiving stimuli from within the organism, used in receiving these, or concerned with receiving these, e.g. through muscles, tendons and joints (cf. EXTEROCEPTIVE, cf. INTEROCEPTIVE) [fr. L. *proprius*, own+RECEPTIVE]

prop root a root growing outwards from the stem close to ground level and serving to support the plant (e.g. mangrove)

prop shaft a propeller shaft

prop·to·sis (prɒptóusis) *n.* (*med.*) protrusion, esp. of the eyeball [L.L. fr. Gk *proptōsis*, a fall forward]

pro·pul·sion (prəpʌ́lʃən) *n.* a propelling or being propelled ‖ a driving force [F.]

pro·pul·sive (prəpʌ́lsiv) *adj.* tending to propel, driving forward [fr. L. *propellere* (*propulsus*), to drive forward]

pro·pyl (próupil) *n.* the monovalent radical, C_3H_7, derived from propane [PROPIONIC ACID]

prop·y·lae·um (prɒpəlí:əm) *pl.* **prop·y·lae·a** (prɒpəlí:ə) *n.* (*archit.*) a porch or vestibule serving as entrance to a temple or public building **the Prop·y·lae·a** the entrance to the Acropolis in Athens [L. fr. Gk *propulaion*]

propyl alcohol a liquid alcohol, C_3H_7OH

pro·pyl·ene (próupəli:n) *n.* an inflammable gaseous hydrocarbon, $CH_3CH{=}CH_2$, obtained by breaking down petroleum hydrocarbons and used in the manufacture of detergents

prop·y·lite (próupəlait) *n.* a volcanic rock, an altered form of andesite, found in the vicinity of certain ore deposits, esp. silver [fr. Gk *propylon*, gateway (formerly considered to mark the opening of the Tertiary)]

pro ra·ta (prouréitə, prourátə) **1.** *adv.* at a proportionate rate, *costs are $100 per thousand and pro rata* **2.** *adj.* calculated at a proportionate rate [L.]

pro·rate (prouréit, prouṛeit) *pres. part.* **pro·rat·ing** *past and past part.* **pro·rat·ed** *v.t.* to assess pro rata ‖ to distribute proportionally ‖ *v.i.* to make a pro rata distribution

pro·ro·ga·tion (prouṛəgéiʃən) *n.* a proroguing or being prorogued

pro·rogue (prouróug) *pres. part.* **pro·rogu·ing** *past and past part.* **pro·rogued** *v.t.* to bring a session of (esp. a parliament) to a close by adjourning the next meeting to a particular day ‖ *v.i.* to be prorogued [F. *proroguer*]

pro·sa·ic (prouzéiik) *adj.* commonplace, without great imaginative gifts, *a prosaic young man* ‖ dull, ordinary, *a prosaic career* **pro·sá·i·cal·ly** *adv.* [L. *prosaicus*]

pro·sce·ni·um (prousí:ni:əm) *n.* (*theater*) that part of a stage between the curtain and the orchestra ‖ (*theater*) the proscenium arch and surrounding wall ‖ the stage in an ancient Greek or Roman theater [L. fr. Gk *proskēnion*]

proscenium arch (*theater*) the structure which frames the spectators' view of the stage

pro·scribe (prouskráib) *pres. part.* **pro·scrib·ing** *past and past part.* **pro·scribed** *v.t.* to outlaw (a person) ‖ to condemn or forbid (a practice) ‖ (*Rom. hist.*) to publish the name of (a person) as being condemned to death and to have his property confiscated [fr. L. *proscribere*, to write in front of]

pro·scrip·tion (prouskrípʃən) *n.* a proscribing or being proscribed ‖ a prohibition [fr. L. *proscriptio* (*proscriptionis*)]

pro·scrip·tive (prouskríptiv) *adj.* pertaining to proscription ‖ tending to proscribe [fr. L. *proscribere* (*proscriptus*), to write in front of]

prose (prouz) **1.** *n.* the language of ordinary speech ‖ this language artificially heightened for literary effect, in nonmetrical rhythms (cf. POETRY) ‖ dull, commonplace discourse or writing ‖ (*rhet.*) humdrum commonplace quality, *the prose of everyday life* ‖ (*eccles.*) a sequence **2.** *v.i. pres. part.* **pros·ing** *past and past part.* **prosed** to talk or write boringly and tediously [F.]

pros·e·cute (prósikju:t) *pres. part.* **pros·e·cut·ing** *past and past part.* **pros·e·cut·ed** *v.t.* to start legal proceedings against, *trespassers will be prosecuted* ‖ to start legal proceedings with reference to (a claim etc.) ‖ (*rhet.*) to carry on, *to prosecute a war* ‖ *v.i.* to start and continue legal proceedings ‖ to act as prosecutor [fr. L. *prosequi* (*prosecutus*), to follow, pursue]

prosecuting attorney the attorney who conducts proceedings in a court of law on behalf of the government against accused persons on criminal charges

pros·e·cu·tion (prɒsikjú:ʃən) *n.* a prosecuting or being prosecuted ‖ (*law*) the prosecuting party or his legal representatives ‖ (*law*) the bringing of formal criminal charges against an offender in court [O.F.]

pros·e·cu·tor (prósikjuːtər) *n.* a person who starts legal proceedings against another or others ‖ a prosecuting attorney ‖ (*Br.*) a public prosecutor [M.L.]

pros·e·lyte (prósəlait) **1.** *n.* an individual newly converted from one creed or belief to another, esp. a convert to Judaism **2.** *v.t. pres. part.* **pros·e·lyt·ing** *past and past part.* **pros·e·lyt·ed** to proselytize ‖ *v.i.* to proselytize ‖ to induce athletes to attend and play for a certain school **pros·e·lyt·ism** (prósəlitizəm) *n.* the practice of making converts ‖ the act, or fact, of becoming a convert **prós·e·lyt·ize** *pres. part.* **pros·e·lyt·iz·ing** *past and past part.* **pros·e·lyt·ized** *v.i.* to make or try to make converts ‖ *v.t.* to make a convert of [fr. L.L. *proselytus* fr. Gk]

pros·en·chy·ma (prɒsénkəmə) *n.* (*bot.*) any of several kinds of tissue, distinguishable in higher plants, consisting of elongated cells with pointed ends, containing little or no protoplasm and serving to support and to conduct (cf. PARENCHYMA) **pros·en·chym·a·tous** (prɒsənkímətəs) *adj.* [fr. Gk *pros*, toward+*enchuma*, infusion]

Pro·ser·pi·na (prousɜ́ːrpinə) Persephone
Pros·er·pine (prósərpain, prousɜ́ːrpini:) Persephone

pros·i·ly (próuzili:) *adv.* in a prosy way

pros·i·ness (próuzi:nis) *n.* the state or quality of being prosy

pro·sod·ic (prəsódik) *adj.* of or pertaining to prosody

pros·o·dist (prósədist) *n.* a person skilled in prosody

pros·o·dy (prósədi:) *pl.* **pros·o·dies** *n.* the rhythmic structure of sound in speech ‖ the study of versification ‖ a particular system of versification [fr. L. *prosodia* fr. Gk]

pro·so·ma (prousóumə) *n.* the anterior part of the body of some mollusks and some other vertebra [Mod. L.]

pros·o·pog·ra·phy (prɒsəpógrəfi:) *n.* biographical study of a group, esp. of an elite group—a method used in quantitative history

pro·so·po·poe·ia (prəsoupəpí:ə) *n.* (*rhet.*) introduction by an orator of an imaginary speaker, esp. the personification of an abstract concept, e.g. '… at this point Common Sense will retort…' [L. fr. Gk]

pros·pect 1. (próspekt) *n.* a wide or distant scenic view, *a splendid prospect over the bay* ‖ the scene itself, *admiring the prospect beneath them* ‖ the assumed course of the future, *their probable defeat is a grim prospect* ‖ a view of some specified eventuality, *the prospect for the harvest* ‖ reasonable expectation, *is there any prospect of a meeting?* ‖ a potential client or customer ‖ (*pl.*) social or financial expectations, *a job offering good prospects* ‖ (*mining*) property on which signs of mineral deposit are found ‖ (*mining*) a partly developed mine ‖ (*mining*) mineral extracted from a test sample **in prospect** likely to materialize, *he has a job in prospect* **2.** (próspekt, prəspékt) *v.i.* to explore a region in search of oil, gold, minerals etc. ‖ *v.t.* to explore (an area, mine) for minerals [fr. L. *prospectus*, view]

pro·spec·tive (prəspéktiv) *adj.* (of payments etc.) relating to the future (cf. RETROSPECTIVE) ‖ destined or expected to be, *her prospective father-in-law* [fr. F. *prospectif*]

pros·pec·tor (próspektər, prəspéktər) *n.* someone who prospects for oil, gold, minerals etc.

pro·spec·tus (prəspéktəs) *n.* a circular containing information or plans of enterprise, literary work, issue of securities etc., designed to win support [L.=lookout]

pros·per (próspər) *v.i.* to thrive ‖ to achieve financial success [F. *prospérer*]

pros·per·i·ty (prɒspériti) *n.* the condition of being prosperous, the condition of high economic activity [F. *prospérité*]

Pros·per of Aquitaine (próspər), St (c. 390–c. 460), Gallic theologian. He championed St Augustine of Hippo's doctrine of grace against Pelagian tendencies. Feast: July 7

pros·per·ous (próspərəs) *adj.* financially successful [obs. F. *prospereus*]

pros·ta·glan·din (prɒstəglǽndin) *n.* (*physiol.*) a potent compound that acts like a hormone, produced by enzyme action on fatty acids in mammals, highly concentrated in seminal fluid, important in metabolism reproduction, muscle contraction, transmission of nerve impulses and blood pressure control

pros·tate (prɒsteit) **1.** *adj.* of the partially muscular gland at the neck of the bladder surrounding the beginning of the urethra in male mammals **2.** *n.* this gland **pro·stat·ic** (proustǽtik) *adj.* [fr. M.L. *prostata* fr. Gk *prostatēs*, one who stands before]

pros·the·sis (prósθisis) *pl.* **pros·the·ses** (prósθisi:z) *n.* (*gram.*) the prefixing of a letter or syllable to a word, e.g. 'be' in 'bemoan' ‖ (*med.*) an artificial device to replace a missing part of the body (e.g. false teeth, an artificial limb) [L. fr. Gk *prosthesis*, addition]

pros·thet·ic (prɒsθétik) *adj.* of or relating to prosthesis or prosthetics ‖ (*biochem.*) relating to a group or radical of a different kind attached to or substituted in a compound, e.g. the nonprotein portion of a conjugated protein or the vitamin portion of certain enzymes **pros·thet·ics** *n.* the branch of surgery or dentistry which deals with artificial limbs, teeth etc. [fr. Gk *prosthetikos*]

pros·ti·tute (próstitu:t, próstitju:t) **1.** *n.* a woman who has promiscuous sexual intercourse for payment ‖ (*hist.*) a woman who has sexual intercourse as part of a religious cult ‖ a person who degrades his talents for money **2.** *v.t. pres. part.* **pros·ti·tut·ing** *past and past part.* **pros·ti·tut·ed** to degrade (a science, talents etc.), esp. for money [fr. L. *prostituere* (*prostitutus*), to offer for sale]

pros·ti·tu·tion (prɒstitú:ʃən, prɒstitjú:ʃən) *n.* the act, practice or profession of offering the body for sexual relations for money ‖ the degradation of some science, talent etc. for money [fr. L.L. *prostitutio* (*prostitutionis*)]

pros·trate 1. (próstreit) *v.t. pres. part.* **pros·trat·ing** *past and past part.* **pros·trat·ed** *v.t.* to cast to the ground face downwards ‖ to abase (oneself) in submission, worship etc. ‖ (*rhet.*) to reduce to utter submission, *to prostrate an enemy* ‖ to exhaust bodily, wear out ‖ to overcome with shock, grief etc. **2.** *adj.* lying full-length face downwards ‖ overcome with shock, grief etc. ‖ physically exhausted ‖ (*rhet.*) utterly defeated, *Carthage lay prostrate* ‖ (*bot.*) lying loosely along the surface of the ground [fr. L. *prosternere (prostratus)*, to lay flat]

pros·tra·tion (prɒstréiʃən) *n.* a prostrating or being prostrated [F.]

pro·style (próustail) **1.** *adj.* (*archit.*, of a classical temple) having a row of free columns in a portico across the whole front **2.** *n.* such a temple [L. *prostylos*, having pillars in front, fr. Gk]

pro·sum·er (prousú:mər) *n.* (*slang*) one who consumes what he or she produces

pros·y (próuzi) *comp.* **pros·i·er** *superl.* **pros·i·est** *adj.* dull, tedious, *a prosy speaker* [PROSE]

pro·tac·tin·i·um (proutæktíni:əm) *n.* a radioactive pentavalent element (symbol Pa, at. no. 91, mass of most important isotope 231) which is formed naturally by the radioactive decay of uranium 235, and which on disintegration yields actinium [Mod. fr. Gk *prōtos*, first+ACTINIUM]

pro·tag·o·nist (proutǽgənist) *n.* the principal character in a drama, story etc. ‖ someone who champions a cause [fr. Gk *prōtagōnistēs* fr. *prōtos*, first+*agōnistēs*, actor]

Pro·tag·o·ras (proutǽgoræs) (c. 485–c. 411 B.C.), Greek Sophist and philosopher, famous for his dictum 'Man is the measure of all things'. He was attacked by Plato in 'Protagoras' for his emphasis on rhetoric and his Sophist belief that there is no absolute good

pro·ta·mine (próutəmi:n) *n.* (*biochem.*) any of a class of basic proteins, occurring in the sperm of fish, soluble in ammonia, not coagulating in heat and yielding certain amino acids on hydrolysis [fr. Gk *prōtos*, first+AMINE]

pro·tan·drous (proutǽndrəs) *adj.* (*biol.*) having the male reproductive organs mature before the corresponding female organs are (cf. PROTOGYNOUS) [fr. PROTO- +Gk *anēr (andros)*, man]

prot·a·sis (prótəsis) *pl.* **prot·a·ses** (prótəsi:z) *n.* (*gram.*) a subordinate clause expressing condition in a conditional sentence (cf. APODOSIS) ‖ the introductory section of a play, preceding the epitasis [L.L. fr. Gk *protasis*, a stretching forward]

pro·te·an (próuti:ən, proutí:ən) *adj.* versatile ‖ extremely variable, often changing, *a protean policy* ‖ able to take on different shapes [after PROTEUS]

pro·te·ase (próuti:eis) *n.* (*biochem.*) any of a class of enzymes which hydrolyze proteins or peptides [PROTEIN]

pro·tect (prətékt) *v.t.* to shield or defend against danger, injury etc. ‖ (*econ.*) to guard (home producers) from foreign competition in the home market by imposing protective tariffs on imported goods ‖ (*commerce*) to guarantee the availability of funds to meet (a draft, note etc.) when it matures [fr. L. *protegere (protectus)*]

protected state a state under the protection of another, esp. one retaining its traditional form of government and control over domestic policy, which has signed a treaty with Britain whereby it receives British protection in return for placing its foreign affairs under British control

pro·tec·tion (prəték∫ən) *n.* a protecting or being protected ‖ a person who or a thing which protects ‖ (*econ.*) the theory, policy or system of helping home producers to face foreign competition by putting protective tariffs on imported goods ‖ money paid to gangsters under threat of damage to property etc. **pro·téc·tion·ism, pro·téc·tion·ist** *ns* [F.]

pro·tec·tive (prətéktiv) *adj.* giving or intended to give protection ‖ seeking to guard, *protective instincts*

protective coloring, *Br.* **protective colouring** coloring which enables animals to escape notice in their natural surroundings

protective custody detention of a person by the state in order to protect him, or on this pretext

protective tariff a tariff designed to secure protection for domestic producers from foreign competition (cf. REVENUE TARIFF)

pro·tec·tor (prətéktər) *n.* a person who or thing which protects ‖ (*Eng. hist.*) a regent ‖ (*Eng. hist.*) a lord protector **pro·téc·tor·al** *adj.* **pro·téc·tor·ate** *n.* government by a protector ‖ the office of protector ‖ authority assumed by a strong state over a weak or underdeveloped one, without direct annexation, for the defense of the latter from external enemies ‖ a state so

governed, esp. a territory ruled in foreign and domestic affairs by Britain, but not having the legal status of a colony ‖ the period of such government **the Protectorate** (*Eng. hist.*) the period of rule by the Cromwells (1653-9) [O.F. *protectour*]

pro·tec·tress (prətéktris) *n.* a woman protector

pro·té·gé (próutəʒei) *n.* someone who is under the patronage, care or guidance of another, esp. for help in his career **pro·té·gée** (próutəʒei) *n.* a female protégé [F.]

pro·tein (próuti:n) *n.* (*chem.*) any of a class of naturally occurring, usually colloidal, complex combinations of amino acids (containing carbon, hydrogen, oxygen, nitrogen, usually sulfur, occasionally phosphorus) which are essential constituents of all living cells, being responsible for growth and maintenance of all tissue, and the essential nitrogenous constituent of the food of animals. They can be synthesized from inorganic nitrogenous material by plants, but apparently not by animals **pro·tein·a·ceous, pro·téin·ic, pro·téin·ous** *adjs* [F. *protéine* and G. *protein* fr. Gk *prōteios*, primary]

pro·tein·oid (próutənɔid) *n.* (*biol.*) a compound of two or more amino acids united through the peptide linkage (CONH), hypothesized as an early stage in the evolution of life

pro tem·po·re (proutémpori:) *adv.* and *adj.* (*abbr.* pro tem.) for the time being [L.]

pro·te·ol·y·sis (prouti:ólisis) *n.* (*biochem.*) the hydrolysis of proteins to form simpler soluble products, e.g. in digestion **pro·te·o·lýt·ic** *adj.* [PROTEIN+Gk *lusis*, loosening]

pro·te·ose (próuti:ous) *n.* (*biochem.*) any of a class of substances, soluble in water, formed by the partial hydrolysis of proteins by digestive enzymes [PROTEIN]

Prot·er·o·zo·ic (prɒtərəzóuik) *adj.* of the era of geological history between the Archeozoic and the Paleozoic, and the rocks formed during this era, whose fossils indicate the contemporary existence of annelid worms and algae (*GEOLOGICAL TIME) **the Proterozoic** this era [fr. Gk *proteros*, former+*zōē*, life]

pro·test (próutest) *n.* a strong affirmation of, dissent from or disapproval of something done or some policy adopted ‖ a written declaration by a notary of an unpaid or unaccepted bill ‖ a written declaration by the master of a ship giving details of disaster, accident or injury at sea ‖ (in diplomacy) a solemn declaration of disapproval **to do (something) under protest** to do (something) having first stated one's disapproval [O.F.]

pro·test (prətést) *v.i.* to express strong dissent or objection ‖ *v.t.* to affirm emphatically, *to protest one's innocence* ‖ to write a declaration of nonpayment or nonacceptance of (a bill) ‖ to make a protest against, *to protest a witness* [F. *protester*]

Prot·es·tant (prótistənt) **1.** *n.* a member of any Christian body which separated from the Roman Catholic Church at the Reformation, or of any later offshoot of such a body, esp. the Anglican, Baptist, Congregationalist, Evangelical, Lutheran, Methodist, Reformed and Presbyterian Churches ‖ (*hist.*) one of the German princes who protested against an edict of the Diet of Speyer (1529) designed to crush the reform movement in the Church **2.** *adj.* relating to the doctrines or organizations of Protestants **prot·es·tant 1.** someone who protests **2.** *adj.* protesting [F.]

Protestant Episcopal Church the religious body which represents the Anglican Communion in the U.S.A. It adopted an organization separate from that of the Church of England in 1789, but is still linked with it through the Lambeth Conference.

Protestant ethic mores of early Americans, involving compliance with the law and placing importance on work, thrift, self-discipline, competition and making a profit

Prot·es·tant·ism (prótistəntizəm) *n.* the beliefs and practices of Protestants. These cover a very wide range, but have common roots in the refusal to accept any external, man-centered, ultimate authority in spiritual matters, and the rejection of any belief which implies the possibility of self-justification before God

Protestant Union an alliance of Protestant German states formed (1608) in opposition to the future Emperor Ferdinand II's attempt to revive and enforce the Peace of Augsburg. It collapsed (1621) early in the Thirty Years' War

prot·es·ta·tion (prɒtistéiʃən, proutestéiʃən) *n.* an emphatic affirmation, *protestations of friendship* ‖ a formal protest [F.]

Pro·te·us (próuti:əs, próutju:s) (*Gk mythol.*) a prophetic sea god who could assume different shapes so as to escape capture. He was shepherd of the flocks of seals for Poseidon

pro·te·us (próuti:əs, próutju:s) *n. Proteus anguinus,* fam. *Proteidae,* a blind, aquatic salamander with a long body and permanent gills, found in caves in S.E. Europe [after PROTEUS]

pro·tha·la·mi·um (prouθəléimi:əm) *n.* a marriage song sung to herald the wedding (cf. EPITHALAMIUM) [coined by Edmund SPENSER]

pro·thal·li·um (prouθǽli:əm) *pl.* **pro·thal·li·a** (prouθǽli:ə) *n.* the gametophyte of a fern, consisting usually of a small, flat, green thallus with rhizoid soil attachment that is differentiated into antheridia and archegonia ‖ any of various structures in seed plants that resemble or correspond to the prothallium of the pteridophytes [Mod. L. fr. Gk *pro,* before+*thallos,* young shoot]

pro·thal·lus (prouθǽləs) *pl.* **pro·thal·li** (prouθǽlai) *n.* a prothallium [L. fr. Gk]

proth·e·sis (próθisis) *n.* (*Orthodox Eastern Church*) preparation and offering of the Eucharistic bread and wine before the liturgy ‖ the table on which this is done ‖ (*gram.*) prosthesis in the part of the church where this stands ‖ (*gram.*) prosthesis **proth·et·ic** (prəθétik) *adj.* [L.L. fr. Gk *prothesis,* placing in public]

proth·et·e·ly (próθəteli:) *n.* (*zool.*) a condition in insects between nymph and adult resulting from dysfunction during metamorphosis — **proth·et·e·lic** *adj.*

pro·thon·o·tar·y (prouθónəteri:, prouθounóutəri:) *pl.* **pro·thon·o·tar·ies** *n.* a protonotary

pro·tho·rac·ic (prouθəræsik, prouθouræsik) *adj.* pertaining to the prothorax

prothoracic gland (*entomology*) one of a pair of glands that produce ecdysone to control molting in some insects

pro·tho·rax (prouθóræks, prouθóu·ræks) *pl.* **pro·tho·rax·es, pro·tho·ra·ces** (prouθórəsi:z, prouθóurəsi:z) *n.* the anterior segment of an insect's thorax

pro·throm·bin (prouθrómbin) *n.* (*biochem.*) a protein produced in the liver in the presence of vitamin K and present in blood plasma. Under the proper conditions (e.g. the presence of activators, *PLATELET) it is converted to thrombin, which initiates clot formation

pro·tist (próutist) *n.* (*biol.*) a member of *Protista,* a group of simple organisms, e.g. protozoans, not distinguished as animals or plants, though having some characters common to both [fr. Gk *prōtistos,* primary]

pro·ti·um (próuti:əm) *n.* (*nuclear physics*) a hydrogen isotope with a mass of 1, consisting of one proton and one electron. *Cf* DEUTERIUM, TRITIUM

proto- (próutou) *prefix* first in time, status or importance ‖ first in a series ‖ original, primitive [Gk fr. *prōtos,* first]

pro·to·ac·tin·i·um (proutouæktíni:əm) *n.* protactinium

pro·to·bi·ont (proutoubáiənt) *n.* an organism extant at the emergence of life on earth

pro·to·col (próutəkɔl) **1.** *n.* a code of precedence in rank and status and correct procedure in diplomatic exchange and state ceremonies ‖ a preliminary draft or memorandum of a diplomatic document, e.g. of resolutions arrived at in negotiation to be incorporated in a formal treaty, and signed by the negotiators ‖ official formulas at the beginning and end of a charter, papal bull etc. **2.** *v. pres. part.* **pro·to·col·ling, pro·to·col·ing** *past* and *past part.* **pro·to·colled, pro·to·cole** *v.t.* to record (something) in a protocol ‖ *v.i.* to draw up a protocol [O.F. *prothocole* fr. M.L. fr. Gk *prōtokollon,* flyleaf glued to a book]

pro·to·con·ti·nent (proutoukóntinənt) *n.* a hypothetical great landmass existing on the earth 60 million yrs ago, from which contemporary continents were created. *also* supercontinent

pro·to·gal·ax·y (proutougǽləksi:) *n.* (*ast·on.*) gas and dust in the process of hypothetical star formation

pro·tog·y·nous (proutódʒənəs) *adj.* (*biol.*) having the female reproductive organs mature before the corresponding male organs are (cf. PROTANDROUS) [PROTO-+Gk *gunē,* woman]

pro·to·his·to·ry (proutouhístəri:) *n.* period after prehistory, sometimes referred to, but not elucidated in, recorded history

---

CONCISE PRONUNCIATION KEY: **(a)** æ, c*a*t; ɑ, c*ar*; ɔ f*aw*n; ei, sn*a*ke. **(e)** e, h*e*n; i:, sh*ee*p; iə, d*ee*r; ɛə, b*ear*. **(i)** i, f*i*sh; ai, t*i*ger; ə:, b*i*rd. **(o)** o, *o*x; au, c*ow*; ou, g*oa*t; u, p*oo*r; ɔi, r*oy*al. **(u)** ʌ, d*u*ck; u, b*u*ll; u:, g*oo*se; ə, b*a*cillus; ju:, c*u*be. x, lo*ch*; θ, *th*ink; ð, bo*th*er; z, *Z*en; ʒ, cor*s*age; dʒ, sava*g*e; ŋ, ora*ng*utang; j, *y*ak; ʃ, *fi*sh; tʃ, fe*tch*; 'l, ra*bble*; 'n, re*dden*. Complete pronunciation key appears inside front cover.

pro·to·lith·ic (prəutəlíθik) *adj.* Eolithic [PROTO- +Gk *lithos*, stone]

pro·to·mar·tyr (prəutoumártər) *n.* the first martyr in any cause, esp. the first Christian martyr, St Stephen [M.E. *prothomartir* fr. O.F.]

pro·ton (próuton) *n.* (*phys.*) a baryon of mass 938.2+ 10^6 eV (1.672 x 10^{-24} gm) and net electric charge +1 that is a constituent of all atomic nuclei (the proton is the nucleus of the lightest hydrogen isotope). The proton is thought to be closely related to the neutron in structure, both having the same positive core of electrical charge, though the proton has a shell of positive charge thus rendering it positive ‖ a hydrogen ion of at. mass 1 [Gk, neuter of *prótos*, first]

proton decay (*nuclear phys.*) transmutation of one chemical into another by loss of a proton

pro·to·ne·ma (prəutəní:mə) *pl.* **pro·to·ne·ma·ta** (prəutəní:mətə) *n.* the early stage of the development of the gametophyte of a moss or liverwort. It often consists of a branching system of filaments arising directly from the asexual spore, and develops by budding into the moss plant proper or gives rise to the second stage of the gametophyte [PROTO-+Gk *nēma*, thread]

proton microscope (*nuclear phys.*) a microscope in which a beam of protons passing through a sample is absorbed in proportion to its density, providing an image by the emerging protons that is magnified and displayed on a fluorescent screen or photo film

pro·ton·o·tar·y (proutónətəri:, prəutounóutəri:) *pl.* **pro·ton·o·tar·ies** *n.* (*Br. hist.*) the chief clerk in the courts of Chancery, Common Pleas and King's Bench ‖ (*Roman Catholicism*) a protonotary apostolic ‖ (in some European courts) a chief secretary [fr. L.L. *protonotarius* fr. Gk]

protonotary apostolic (*Roman Catholicism*) one of the seven members of the highest college of prelates, authorized to sign papal bulls and keep papal records

pro·ton-syn·chro·tron (prəutonsínkrətron) *n.* a synchrotron that accelerates protons to extremely high energies by frequency modulation of the accelerating voltage

pro·to·phyte (próutəfait) *n.* a member of *Protophyta*, a division of the lower plants (esp. in former classifications) comprising unicellular plants incl. bacteria, yeasts, slime molds, blue-green algae and various simple green algae [fr. Mod. L. *Protophyta* fr. Gk *prótos*, first+*phuton*, a plant]

pro·to·plasm (próutəplæzəm) *n.* a viscous, translucent, colloidal substance constituting all living cells. It consists of compounds of oxygen, hydrogen, carbon and nitrogen and is usually differentiated into cytoplasm and nucleoplasm **pro·to·plás·mic** *adj.* [G. *protoplasma* fr. Gk *prótos*, first+*plasma*, form]

pro·to·plast (próutəplæst) *n.* the first formed example of any type, the original ‖ (*biol.*) a living unit of protoplasm **pro·to·plás·tic** *adj.* [F. *protoplaste* or fr. L.L. fr. Gk *prótos*, first+*plastos*, shaped]

protoplast *n.* (*cytol.*) the living part of a cell.

pro·to·ste·le (próutəsti:li:, próutəsti:l) *n.* (*bot.*) a solid stele, characteristic of most roots and some young stems (cf. SIPHONOSTELE) **pro·to·sté·lic** *adj.*

pro·to·tract (prəutətrǽkt) *v.* to move back and forth, e.g., the jaw

pro·to·troph·ic (prəutətrófik) *adj.* (of bacteria etc.) feeding on inorganic matter

pro·to·typ·al (próutətaip'l, prəutətáip'l) *adj.* of or relating to a prototype

pro·to·type (próutətaip) *n.* an original model or pattern from which subsequent copies are made, or improved specimens developed ‖ (*biol.*) an ancestral form or archetype **pro·to·typ·i·cal** (prəutətípik'l) *adj.* [F. fr. Mod. L. fr. Gk *prótos*, first+*tupos*, model, mold]

pro·to·vi·rus (próutəvairəs) *n.* a prototype of a virus that stimulates DNA production

pro·to·zo·an (prəutəzóuən) *n.* a member of *Protozoa*, a phylum of small (often microscopic) single-celled or colonial organisms. They are of worldwide distribution and are usually restricted to water. They include flagellates, sporozoans, ciliates and rhizopods **pro·to·zó·ic** *adj.* [PROTO-+Gk *zōē*, life]

pro·to·zo·ol·o·gy (prəutouzouólədʒi:) *n.* the study of protozoans

pro·to·zo·on (prəutəzóuən) *pl.* **pro·to·zo·a** (prəutəzóuə) *n.* a protozoan

pro·tract (proutrǽkt) *v.t.* to draw out in time,

prolong, *bad weather protracted the work* ‖ (*surveying*) to plot to scale **pro·trác·ted·ly** *adv.*

pro·trac·tile (proutrǽktil) *adj.* (*zool.*, of an organ etc.) capable of being pushed out, extended or lengthened [fr. L. *protrahere* (*protractus*), to prolong]

pro·trac·tion (proutrǽkʃən) *n.* a protracting or being protracted [F.]

pro·trac·tor (proutrǽktər) *n.* an instrument for measuring or drawing angles on a flat surface, often in the form of a semicircle graduated in 180 degrees ‖ (*zool.*) a muscle whose function extends a limb or part of the body [M.L. fr. *protrahere*, to prolong]

pro·trude (proutrú:d) *pres. part.* **pro·trud·ing** *past* and *past part.* **pro·trud·ed** *v.t.* to thrust forward or outward ‖ *v.i.* to stick out or project [fr. L. *protrudeve*, to thrust forward]

pro·tru·sile (proutrú:sil) *adj.* (of a limb or organ) so formed that it can be pushed outwards [fr. L. *protrudere* (*protrusus*), to thrust forward]

pro·tru·sion (proutrú:ʒən) *n.* a protruding or being protruded ‖ something which protrudes [F.]

pro·tru·sive (proutrú:siv) *adj.* protruding ‖ obtrusive [fr. L. *protrudere* (*protrusus*), to thrust forward]

pro·tu·ber·ance (proutú:bərəns, proutjú:bərəns) *n.* something that is protuberant ‖ the condition of being protuberant

pro·tu·ber·ant (proutú:bərənt, proutjú:bərənt) *adj.* bulging, swelling out [fr. L.L. *protuberans* (*protuberantis*) fr. *protuberare*, to bulge]

proud (praud) *adj.* manifesting inordinate self-esteem ‖ feeling proper satisfaction, *proud of his son's success* ‖ arousing or marked by feelings of great satisfaction, *a proud moment* ‖ having a proper sense of self-esteem, *too proud to give way to self-pity* ‖ (*rhet.*) splendid, glorious, *a proud heritage* ‖ (*rhet.*, of a horse) mettlesome **to do oneself proud** to indulge oneself lavishly **to do someone proud** to honor someone with lavish hospitality or attentions [O.E. *prút, prúd* fr. O.F.]

proud flesh (*med.*) excessive growth of granulation tissue around a wound or ulcer

Proud·hon (pru:dɔ̃), Pierre Joseph (1809–65), French anarchist philosopher. In his pamphlet 'Qu'est-ce que la propriété?' (1840) he declared that property was theft. He believed that the State should be replaced by a voluntary contract among individuals, and that labor should be the basis of value. He was strongly opposed to communism and socialism

Proust (pru:st), Joseph Louis (1754–1826), French chemist. He formulated the law of constant composition, stating that every compound always contains the same elements in the same proportion by mass

Proust, Marcel (1871–1922), French novelist. His 'A la recherche du temps perdu' (1913–27), in seven novels, recreates in fictional form Proust's own childhood in Paris and the Normandy countryside. In effect it re-creates the society, especially the upper-class society, of Paris at the turn of the century. Certain themes emerge: above all that of the transforming power of dominant love, and the effects it has on the lover's vision of the beloved and the world. But in a sense the whole work is about the transformation of the universe by the individual perceiving and suffering sensibility. The style reflects this characteristic of personal vision: it is highly poetic and complex, full of elaborate imagery. The work has had a profound influence on the art of the novel

Prout (praut), William (1785–1850), English chemist. He discovered that the stomach contains hydrochloric acid. He proposed (1815) on the basis of the effectively whole number values of the atomic masses of the elements that these were condensed forms of hydrogen

prove (pru:v) *pres. part.* **prov·ing** *past* and *past part.* **proved,** (*old-fash.* and *legal*) **prov·en** (prú:vən) *v.t.* to establish the truth of by evidence, *they proved his innocence* ‖ to show to be true by reasoning, *to prove a point in argument* ‖ (*math.*) to test (a calculation) ‖ to test for conformity to standard ‖ to test the alcoholic content of ‖ to establish the authenticity of (a legal document) ‖ to obtain probate of (a will) ‖ to test experimentally ‖ (*printing*) to proof, take proofs of (a block etc.) ‖ *v.i.* (sometimes with 'to be') to be shown by later knowledge to be, *the story proved quite false* [O.F. *prover*]

prov·e·nance (próvənəns) *n.* place of origin ‖ source of supply [F.]

Pro·ven·çal (prɔvãsæl) **1.** *adj.* of or pertaining to Provence or its inhabitants ‖ of or pertaining to Provençal **2.** *n.* the Romance language spoken in Provence proper, a form of langue d'oc ‖ a native or inhabitant of Provence [F.]

Pro·vence (prɔvãs) a former province of France in the S.E. Rhône valley and the southern slopes of the Maritime Alps. Provence proper comprises Bouches-du-Rhône (including the Camargue) in the fertile Rhône valley (fruit, market produce, cereals, livestock, wine), Var, largely in the mountains, and Alpes-de-Haute-Provence entirely so (olives, wine, lavender). Comtat-Venaissin (now Vaucluse department) was added in 1791 and the former countship of Nice (coastal Alpes-Maritimes) in 1860. The rich Mediterranean Riviera contrasts with the arid interior. The climate is Mediterranean. Main towns Marseille, Nice, Toulon, Aix-en-Provence (the old capital), Avignon, Arles. Provence was the first part of Gaul subdued by Rome (1st c. B.C.), and the last to surrender to the Germanic invasion (5th c.). It was overrun by the Arabs (8th c.), was reduced and annexed by the Carolingians, and was united with Burgundy. It passed to Aragon and Anjou before being attached to France (1486). Provençal is still spoken, though by few

prov·en·der (próvəndər) *n.* food for domestic animals [O.F. *provendre*]

pro·ve·ni·ence (prouví:ni:əns) *n.* (esp. *Am.*) provenance [fr. L. *proveniens* (*provenientis*) fr. *provenire*, to come forth]

pro·ven·tric·u·lus (prəuventríkjuləs) *pl.* **pro·ven·tric·u·li** (prəuventríkjulai) *n.* the glandular or true stomach of a bird ‖ (in many insects) a dilated part of the alimentary canal, in which food is ground up [Mod. L.]

pro·verb (próvə:rb) *n.* a brief familiar maxim of folk wisdom, usually compressed in form, often involving a bold image and frequently a jingle that catches the memory [F. *proverbe*]

pro·ver·bi·al (prəvé:rbi:əl) *adj.* characteristic of or expressed in proverbs or mentioned in a proverb, *proverbial wisdom* ‖ very well known, notorious, *his stinginess was proverbial* [fr. L.L. *proverbialis*]

Prov·erbs (próvə:rbz) a book of the Old Testament, containing a collection of didactic sayings

pro·vide (prəváid) *pres. part.* **prov·id·ing** *past* and *past part.* **pro·vid·ed** *v.t.* to supply, *the trees provide shade* ‖ to equip, *provided with helmets* ‖ (*law*) to stipulate, *the law provides that these buildings may not be demolished* ‖ *v.i.* to make advance preparations (for, against some eventuality), *I think we have provided for every possible hazard* ‖ to ensure a supply of the necessities of life, *to provide for one's family* **pro·vid·ed** *conj.* (sometimes with 'that') on condition that, on the understanding that, *they may swim provided an adult accompanies them* [fr. L. *providere*, to see before]

Prov·i·dence (próvidəns) the capital (pop. 156,840), chief port and commercial center of Rhode Island. Industries: textiles, jewelry, silverware. Colonial State House (1762). Brown University (1764)

prov·i·dence (próvidəns) *n.* prudent looking ahead, forethought ‖ thrift **Prov·i·dence** God as prescient guide and guardian of human beings ‖ divine care and guidance [F.]

prov·i·dent (próvidənt) *adj.* showing providence [fr. L. *providens* (*providentis*) fr. *providere*, to see before]

prov·i·den·tial (prɔvidénʃəl) *adj.* opportune, as if brought about by divine foresight ‖ of or determined by Providence [fr. L. *providentia*, providence]

Pro·vid·er (prəváidər) (*mil.*) an assault, twin-engine transport aircraft (C-123K or AC-123K) that can operate from short, unprepared landing strips

pro·vid·ing (prəváidiŋ) *conj.* (sometimes with 'that') provided

prov·ince (próvins) *n.* (*Rom. hist.*) a territory outside Italy ruled by a Roman governor ‖ an administrative division, sometimes overseas, of certain countries ‖ (*eccles.*) an area under the charge of an archbishop or metropolitan ‖ (*eccles.*) an administrative area of a religious order ‖ proper scope of professional or business action, *theater criticism is not my province* ‖ a particular sphere of learning ‖ (*pl.*, with 'the') the parts of a country beyond the capital [F.]

Province Wellesley *PENANG

pro·vin·cial (prəvínʃəl) **1.** *adj.* of or relating to a province ‖ characteristic of the provinces in manner, mode or speech ‖ taking or characterized by a limited view **2.** *n.* a native or inhabitant of a province or of the provinces ‖ (*eccles.*) a superintendent of the daughter houses of a religious order in a province, responsible to the general of the order **pro·vin·cial·ism** *n.* the narrow attitude of mind or the unpolished behavior held to be characteristic of the provinces ‖ a word, pronunciation, custom etc. peculiar to a province ‖ love of one's own region not enlarged into patriotism **pro·vin·ci·al·i·ty** (prəvinʃiːǽliti:) *n.* [F.]

proving ground a site for testing vehicles etc.

pro·vi·sion (prəvíʒən) **1.** *n.* a providing or being provided ‖ preparation, *make provision for six new arrivals* ‖ a clause in a legal document, esp. a proviso ‖ a supply or stock ‖ (*pl.*) food supplies **Pro·vi·sion** (*Eng. hist.*) a law issued (13th and 14th cc.) by the nobility or the king **2.** *v.t.* to supply with provisions **pro·vi·sion·al** *adj.* temporary, filling an interval until a definite decision is made, *a provisional government* ‖ requiring later confirmation, *provisional assent* [F.]

Provisions of Oxford *OXFORD, PROVISIONS OF

pro·vi·so (prəváizou) *pl.* **pro·vi·soes, pro·vi·sos** *n.* a condition, stipulation ‖ a clause containing this in a legal document [L.=it being provided]

pro·vi·so·ry (prəváizəri:) *adj.* conditional, containing a proviso ‖ provisional [fr. F. *provisoire*]

Pro·vo (próuvou) *n.* member of the Provisional Irish Republican Army

prov·o·ca·tion (prɒvəkéiʃən) *n.* a provoking or being provoked ‖ something which provokes [F.]

pro·voc·a·tive (prəvókətiv) *adj.* tending to provoke ‖ arousing annoyance deliberately ‖ involved in the planning stage of a crime; provocative of a crime [fr. L.L. *provocativus*]

pro·voke (prəvóuk) *pres. part.* **pro·vok·ing** *past* and *past part.* **pro·voked** *v.t.* to rouse to anger ‖ to incite, instigate, esp. deliberately, *their arrival provoked an international crisis* ‖ to excite, call forth, *to provoke an answer* [O.F. *provoker*]

prov·ost (próvəst, próuvoust) *n.* an administrative officer of high rank in some universities ‖ (*Br.*) the head of any of certain colleges ‖ (*eccles.*) the head of a chapter or religious community ‖ the mayor of a Scottish burgh ‖ (próuvou) a provost marshal ‖ (*Br.*, prəvóu) an officer in the military police [O E. *prafost, profost* fr. L.]

pro·vost marshal (próuvou) (*mil.*) the head of the military police in camp or in the field

prov·ost·ship (próvəstʃip, próuvoustʃip) *n.* the office or term of office of a provost ‖ the jurisdiction of a provost

prow (prau) *n.* the forepart of a boat or ship, the bow [F. *proue* fr. L. fr. Gk]

prow·ess (práuis) *n.* dexterity and daring ‖ great ability [O.F. *proece*]

prowl (praul) **1.** *v.i.* to roam stealthily in search of prey, or as if in search of prey ‖ *v.t.* to roam over (a place) in search of prey or as if searching for prey, *to prowl the streets* **2.** *n.* a prowling **on the prowl** prowling [M.E. *prollen*, origin unknown]

prowl car a squad car

prowl·er (práulər) *n.* someone who prowls, esp. a sneak thief

Prowler *n.* a twin-engine, quadruple-crew, all-weather turbojet aircraft (EA-6B), designed to operate from aircraft carriers

prox·em·ics (prɒksí:miks) *n.* study of the interaction of human beings with their environment

prox·i·mal (próksəməl) *adj.* (*anat.*, of a point on a limb or part of the body) situated at the end nearest the point of attachment (opp. DISTAL) [fr. L. *proximus*, nearest]

prox·i·mate (próksəmit) *adj.* (in space, time or kinship, or in a series of events) nearest, next ‖ approximate ‖ (of a cause) direct, immediate [fr. L.L. *proximare* (*proximiatus*), to approach]

prox·im·i·ty (prɒksímiti:) *n.* the state or quality of being near in space, time or kinship [F. *proximité*]

proximity fuze, esp. *Br.* **proximity fuse** an electronic device for detonating a projectile by means of radio waves reflected back off the target from a transmitter in the nose of the projectile, thus ensuring that detonation takes place only within effective range of the target

prox·i·mo (próksəmou) *adj.* (*commerce, abbr.* prox.) in or of the next month, *the meeting pro-*

posed *for the 18th prox.* [L. *proximo* (*mense*), in the next month]

prox·y (próksi:) **1.** *pl.* **prox·ies** *n.* authority given by one person to another to act for him, *to vote by proxy* ‖ the person thus authorized ‖ a document empowering a person to act for another **to stand proxy for** to act as proxy for **2.** *adj.* of an act done by a proxy, *a proxy vote* [contr. fr. obs. *procuracy* fr. M.L. *procuratia*, procuration]

PRS-7 (*mil.*) a U.S. Army land-mine detector

prude (pru:d) *n.* a person who affects an excessively rigid attitude in matters of personal modesty and proper conduct [F.]

pru·dence (prú:d'ns) *n.* foresight leading a person to avoid error or danger ‖ the virtue by which the practical reason distinguishes the things useful for salvation (*CARDINAL VIRTUES) ‖ practical discretion [F.]

pru·dent (prú:d'nt) *adj.* (of a person) exercising prudence ‖ (of behavior) guided by prudence [F.]

pru·den·tial (pru:dénʃəl) *adj.* of that which is characterized or actuated by prudence [fr. L. *prudentia*, prudence]

prudent investment 1. standard for investment, esp. for a fiduciary, involving a reasonable income and preservation of capital in a security. **2.** in some jurisdictions, a specified list of securities designated by the state. *Cf* BUSINESSMAN'S RISK

Pru·den·tius (pru:dénʃəs), Aurelius Clemens (348–c. 410), Latin poet born in Spain. He wrote Christian hymns and poems

prud·er·y (prú:dəri:) *n.* the quality or state of being prudish [fr. F. *pruderie*]

Pru·d'hon (prydɔ), Pierre-Paul (1758–1823), French painter, esp. of portraits, to which he gave a mysterious and poetic but rather vapid grace

prud·ish (prú:diʃ) *adj.* of or relating to a prude or the behavior of a prude

pru·i·nose (prú:inous) *adj.* (*bot.*) covered with a whitish powdery substance or bloom [fr. L. *pruinosus*, frosty]

prune (pru:n) *n.* a plum that has been dried without allowing fermentation to take place and that has a dark, wrinkled, pruinose skin [F.=plum, fr. L. fr. Gk]

prune *pres. part.* **prun·ing** *past* and *past part.* **pruned** *v.t.* to cut off from (a tree or bush) branches, twigs etc. which are diseased or not desired, so as to encourage fruiting or flowering, and to shape ‖ to reduce, cut down, *to prune expenses* ‖ *v.i.* to prune trees or bushes [O.F. *proignier*, to prune the vine]

pru·nus (prú:nəs) *n.* an ornamental shrub of the very large genus *Prunus*, fam. *Rosaceae* (which includes the sloe, plum, greengage, cherry, almond, apricot, peach etc.) [L.]

pru·ri·ence (prúəri:əns) *n.* the state or quality of being prurient **prú·ri·en·cy** *n.*

pru·ri·ent (prúəri:ənt) *adj.* (of people) excessively interested in or curious about sexuality ‖ (of ideas, books etc.) tending to excite such interest or curiosity [fr. L. *pruriens* (*prurientis*) fr. *prurire*, to itch]

pru·ri·go (pruráigou) *n.* (*med.*) a skin inflammation characterized by itching papules [L.=an itching]

pru·rit·ic (pruritik) *adj.* of or marked by pruritus

pru·ri·tus (pruráitəs) *n.* (*med.*) itching of the skin [fr. L. *prurire*, to itch]

Prus·sia (prʌ́ʃə) the former largest state of Germany (area in 1939 113,545 sq. miles, pop. 41,762,000). It extended from France and the Low Countries to the Baltic Sea and Poland, and included the provinces of East Prussia, Brandenburg, Berlin, Pomerania, Grenzmark, Silesia, Prussian Saxony, Schleswig-Holstein, Hanover, Westphalia, Hesse-Nassau, Rhine and the district of Hohenzollern. Historic capital: Berlin. HISTORY. The people known from the 10th c. onwards as Prussians were overrun and converted to Christianity (mid-13th c.) by the Teutonic Knights. Rebellion against the Knights (1454) brought Prussia under Polish suzerainty. The Knights' grand master, Albert of Ansbach and Bayreuth, a member of a branch of the Hohenzollern dynasty, became duke of Prussia (1525), which was converted to a secular duchy under the crown of Poland. The duchy passed (1618) to the house of Brandenburg and, under Frederick William, the Great Elector, gained full independence (1660) from Poland. The Reformation and the Treaties of Westphalia (1648) increased Prussian terri-

tory. Elector Frederick III of Brandenburg, duke of Prussia, was crowned (1701) King Frederick I of Prussia. Frederick William I (1713–40) built up a unified state founded on Junker power and developed a strong army. Under Frederick the Great (1740–86), Prussia started a policy of ruthless conquest, gaining Silesia from the War of the Austrian Succession (1740–8), and emerging from the Seven Years' War (1756–63) as the chief military power of the Continent. More territory was gained in the partitions of Poland (1772, 1793, 1795). Under Frederick William II (1786–97) Prussia entered the French Revolutionary War, but agreed by the Treaty of Basle (1795) to withdraw from the coalition. Frederick William III (1797–1840) reopened the struggle against France, but met with total defeat at Jena (1806) and humiliation in the Treaty of Tilsit (1807). Prussia was transformed by the social reforms of Stein and Hardenberg, the educational reforms of Humboldt and the army reforms of Scharnhorst and Gneisenau. Prussia again joined (1813) the coalition against France, participating in the defeat of Napoleon at the Battle of the Nations (1813) and Waterloo (1815). The Congress of Vienna increased Prussian territory considerably, notably along the Rhine, and incorporated Prussia in the German Confederation. Prussia's reactionary policy after entering the Holy Alliance was modified only by her organization (1834) of the Zollverein. Under Frederick William IV the 1848 revolution was put down, and the German Confederation revived, although Prussia was granted a constitution. Bismarck, appointed chancellor (1861) by Wilhelm I (1861–88), eliminated Austria from German affairs by fighting Denmark (1864) over Schleswig-Holstein, by the Seven Weeks War (1866), and by the Franco-Prussian War (1870–1). The king of Prussia was proclaimed emperor of the new German Empire (1871), which was dominated by Prussian control of foreign and military affairs. Prussia remained part of Germany until the collapse of the Third Reich (1945), when it was divided among the U.S.S.R., Poland, East Germany and West Germany

Prus·sian (prʌ́ʃən) **1.** *adj.* of or pertaining to Prussia **2.** *n.* (*hist.*) a native or inhabitant of Prussia

Prussian blue a dark blue crystalline salt, ferric ferrocyanide, $Fe_4[Fe(CN)_6]_3.xH_2O$, used as a pigment and a dye

prus·sic acid (prʌ́sik) hydrocyanic acid [fr. F. *prussique*, hydrocyanic]

Prut (pru:t) a river (500 miles long) flowing south from the E. Carpathians in the S.W. Ukraine, U.S.S.R., to form the border between Moldavia (Rumania) and Moldavia (U.S.S.R.)

pry (prai) *pres. part.* **pry·ing** *past* and *past part.* **pried** *v.i.* to look closely into something which is not one's own concern merely to satisfy one's curiosity, *to pry into someone's affairs* [M.E. *prien*, origin unknown]

pry 1. *v.t. pres. part.* **pry·ing** *past* and *past part.* **pried** to force open or lift with or as if with a lever ‖ (*fig.*) to extract with difficulty, *they pried his secret from him* **2.** *pl.* **pries** *n.* a lever used in prying [PRIZE]

P.S. postscript ‖ Public School

Psalm (sɑm) *n.* any of the sacred songs in the Book of Psalms (*PSALMS) ‖ a metrical version of any of these, for chanting **psalm** (*rhet.*) a song to God [O.E. *psealm, sealm* fr. L. fr. Gk *psalmos*, a song accompaniment]

psalm·ist (sɑ́mist) *n.* an author of sacred songs, esp. of one of the Psalms [fr. L. L. *psalmista*]

psal·mod·ic (sælmódik, sɑmódik) *adj.* of or relating to psalmody

psal·mo·dist (sǽlmədist, sɑ́mədist) *n.* a writer or singer of psalms

psal·mo·dy (sǽlmədi:, sɑ́mədi:) *pl.* **psal·mo·dies** *n.* the act or art of singing psalms, esp. in a religious service ‖ a collection of psalms in book form for liturgical use [fr. L.L. *psalmodia* fr. Gk]

Psalms (sɑmz) a book of the Old Testament containing 150 psalms attributed to King David. Most scholars detect a variety of authors, from widely differing periods. The final compilation was probably c. 150 B.C. The Psalms are widely used in both the Jewish and Christian liturgies

psal·ter (sɔ́ltər) *n.* a copy or version of the Psalms for liturgical use [O.E. *psaltere, saltere* fr. L. fr. Gk]

psal·te·ri·um (sɔltíəri:əm) *pl.* **psal·te·ri·a**

CONCISE PRONUNCIATION KEY: **(a)** æ, c*a*t; ɑ, c*a*r; ɔ f*aw*n; ei, sn*a*ke. **(e)** e, h*e*n; i:, sh*ee*p; iə, d*ee*r; ɛə, b*ea*r. **(i)** i, f*i*sh; ai, t*i*ger; ə:, b*i*rd. **(o)** o, *o*x; au, c*ow*; ou, g*oa*t; u, p*oo*r; ɔi, r*oy*al. **(u)** ʌ, d*u*ck; u, b*u*ll; u:, g*oo*se; ə, b*a*cillus; ju:, c*u*be. x, lo*ch*; θ, *th*ink; ð, bo*th*er; z, *Z*en; ʒ, cor*s*age; dʒ, sa*v*age; ŋ, ora*ng*utang; j, *y*ak; ʃ, *fi*sh; tʃ, fe*tch*; 'l, rabb*le*; 'n, redd*en*. Complete pronunciation key appears inside front cover.

(sɔltíəri:ə) n. an omasum [L.=psalter (fr. its resemblance to the leaves of a psalter)]

psal·ter·y (sɔ́ltəri) pl. **psal·ter·ies** n. an ancient and medieval stringed instrument resembling a dulcimer, played by plucking with the fingers or a plectrum [O.F. psalterie, sauterie fr. L. fr. Gk]

pse·phite (sí:fait) n. a coarse rock composed of pebbles [fr. Gk psēphos, pebble]

pse·phol·o·gist (si:fólədʒist) n. a specialist in psephology

pse·phol·o·gy (si:fólədʒi:) n. the study of elections and the scientific analysis of election results [fr. Gk psēphos, pebble+ logos, discourse (fr. the Greeks' use of pebbles for voting)]

pseud·ax·is (su:dǽksis) n. (bot.) a sympodium

pseud·e·pig·ra·pha (su:dipígrəfə) pl. n. writing falsely attributed to an author, esp. to a biblical author **pseud·e·píg·ra·phy** n. the ascription of false names of authors to writings [fr. Gk pseudepigrophos adj., with false title]

pseudo- (sú:dou) prefix sham || spurious || unreal || showing a superficial resemblance to || being an abnormal form of [Gk=false, falsely]

pseu·do·carp (sú:dəkɑrp) n. (bot.) a fruit including parts of the flower other than the ripened ovary (e.g. a pome) [fr. PSEUDO-+Gk karpos, fruit]

pseu·do·cho·lin·es·ter·ase (su:doukoulənéstər-eis) n. (physiol.) an enzyme that catalyzes the hydrolosis of choline esters and other esters, present in the human liver and in blood plasma. also cholinesterase

Pseu·do·Di·o·ny·si·us (sú:doudaiəníʃi:əs, sú:-doudaiənísi:əs) a pseudonym of Dionysius the Areopagite (c. 500)

pseu·do·morph (sú:dəmɔrf) n. a mineral resembling another in crystalline form **pseu·do·mór·phic** adj. **pseu·do·mór·phism** n. **pseu·do·mór·phous** adj. [fr. PSEUDO-+Gk morphē, form]

pseu·do·nym (sú:d'nim) n. a name other than one's own, assumed for some purpose **pseu·do·ným·i·ty** n. **pseu·don·y·mous** (su:dónəməs) adj. having or bearing a pseudonym [fr. Gk pseudōnumos, falsely named]

pseu·do·pod (sú:dəpɒd) n. a pseudopodium

pseu·do·po·di·um (su:dəpóudi:əm) pl. **pseu·do·po·di·a** (su:dəpóudi:ə) n. (biol.) a temporary, blunt protrusion of ectoplasm serving for locomotion and prehension in cain protozoans, e.g. in an amoeba [fr. PSEUDO-+Gk pōdion, dim. of pous (podos), foot]

pseu·do·ran·dom (su:dourǽndəm) adj. of numbers selected by a system that duplicates random selection

pshaw (ʃɔ) 1. interj. (old-fash.) used as a mild expression of irritation, disbelief etc. 2. n. (old-fash.) an exclamation of 'pshaw!'

psi (psai) n. the twenty-third letter (Ψ, ψ=psi) of the Greek alphabet

PSI (computer acronym) proto synthex indexing, a computer program for indexing each word in English based on semantic or morphological similarity; used in IBM 7090 and applied by System Development Corp.

psil·an·thro·pism (sailǽnθrəpizəm) n. (theol.) psilanthropy **psil·án·thro·pist** n. **psil·án·thro·py** n. (theol.) the doctrine that Christ was only human [fr. Gk psilos, bare, mere+anthrōpos, man]

psi·lo·cin [C₁₂H₁₆N₂O] (sáiləsin) n. (chem.) hallucinogenic compounds found in mushrooms

psi·lo·cy·bin [C₁₂H₁₇N₂O₂P] (sailəsáibin) n. (chem.) hallucinogenic compound found in mushrooms, Psilocybe mexicana

psi·lo·phyt·ic (sailəfítik) adj. (paleobiol.) of Psilophytales, an order of Paleozoic fossil plants

psi·lop·sid (sailópsid) n. a member of Psilopsida, a subphylum of mostly very old fossil plants but which includes two living genera of rootless, leafless plants having a branched, primitively vascular stem [fr. Mod. L. Psilopsida fr. Gk psilos, bare+Lycopsida (*LYCOPSID)]

psi particle *J PARTICLE

psit·ta·co·sis (sitəkóusis) n. (med.) a disease of birds, esp. parrots, communicable to man and causing high fever and pulmonary disorders [Mod. L. fr. Gk psittakos, parrot]

Pskov (pskɔf) a town (pop. 176,000) in the R.S.F.S.R., U.S.S.R., 160 miles southwest of Leningrad: textiles, rope. Kremlin (12th–16th cc.)

pso·as (sóuəs) pl. **pso·ai** (sóuai), **pso·ae** (soui:) n. (anat.) either of two muscles in the loin [fr. Gk psoa, loin muscle]

pso·ra·len [C₁₁H₆O₃] (sɔ́rələn) n. (chem.) a plant derivative, parts of which are used to darken human skin

pso·ri·a·sis (sɔráiəsis) n. (med.) a chronic skin disease, characterized by red patches covered with white scales **pso·ri·at·ic** (sɔri:ǽtik, souri:ǽtik) adj. [Mod. L. fr. Gk fr. psōra, an itch]

PSRO (acronym) Professional Standard Review Organization, created as part of Social Security Amendment in 1972 to oversee health services

P.S.T. Pacific standard time

psych or **psyche** (saik) v. to make one receptive for what is to come or not to come. —**psyched** adj. of one dominated by an idea

psy·chas·the·ni·a (saikəsθí:ni:ə) n. any of a variety of mental disorders involving irrational obsessions and fears

Psy·che (sáiki:) (Gk mythol.) a maiden, personifying the soul, loved by Eros

psy·che (sáiki:) n. the soul || (psychol.) the mind, both conscious and unconscious [Gk psuchē, soul]

psych·e·del·ic (saikidélik) adj. of a mental condition induced by certain drugs and characterized by an impression of greatly heightened sensory perception. It may be accompanied by feelings of elation or misery, by hallucinations, or by sharp perceptual distortion || of a drug inducing this state || of patterns, images etc. characteristic of this state [fr. PSYCHE+Gk dēlos, visible, evident]

psy·chi·at·ric (saiki:ǽtrik) adj. of psychiatry || using psychiatry

psychiatric nurse registered nurse trained to assist with mental health patients

psy·chi·a·trist (sikáiətrist, saikáiətrist) n. a doctor who specializes in psychiatry

psy·chi·a·try (sikáiətri:, saikáiətri:) n. the branch of medicine concerned with the treatment and study of mental and emotional disorders [fr. Gk psuchē, soul + iatreia, healing]

psy·chic (sáikik) 1. adj. nonphysical, psychic forces || of or pertaining to the mind or spirit || apparently able to respond to nonphysical influences, a psychic medium 2. n. a person seemingly sensitive to nonphysical influences || a person able to act as a medium **psy·chi·cal** (sáikik'l) adj. [fr. Gk psuchikos, of the soul]

psychic energizer (pharm.) a mental stimulant, e.g., amphetamine

psycho- (sáikou) prefix of or concerned with the mind or brain [fr. Gk fr. psuchē, soul]

psy·cho·ac·tive (saikouǽktiv) adj. (pharm.) of a drug or drugs that affect the mind or behavior. —**psy·cho·ac·tiv·i·ty** n. Cf PSYCHOCHEMICAL

psy·cho·a·nal·y·sis (saikouənǽlisis) n. a technique of psychotherapy which renders conscious the contents of the unconscious mind through a dialogue between analyst and analysand || the psychological system or doctrine elaborated from the results of this technique (both technique and doctrine owe much to Freud) **psy·cho·an·a·lyst** (saikouǽnəlist) n. a person who practices psychoanalysis **psy·cho·an·a·lýt·ic**, **psy·cho·an·a·lýt·i·cal** adjs **psy·cho·an·a·lýt·i·cal·ly** adv. **psy·cho·an·a·lyze**, **psy·cho·an·a·lyse** (saikouǽnəlaiz) pres. part. **psy·cho·an·a·lyz·ing**, **psy·cho·an·a·lys·ing** past and past part. **psy·cho·an·a·lyzed**, **psy·cho·an·a·lysed** v.t. to subject (someone) to psychoanalytic treatment

psy·cho·bi·og·ra·phy (saikoubaióɡrəfi:) n. a study of a person from a psychodynamic or psychoanalytical viewpoint. Cf PSYCHOHISTORY

psy·cho·chem·i·cal (saikoukémik'l) n. (pharm.) 1. a chemical that affects the nervous system, esp. to cause temporary ineffectuality, e.g., for chemical warfare. 2. a psychoactive chemical — **psychochemical** adj.

psy·cho·di·ag·nos·tics (saikoudaiəɡnóstiks) n. (psych.) analysis of personality based on mannerisms, gait, facial expressions, handwriting, or on response in inkblots

psy·cho·dra·ma (sáikoudrɑmə, sáikoudræmə) n. a form of psychiatric treatment in which the patient obtains emotional release by acting out his problem in an improvised dramatic play

psy·cho·gen·ic (saikoudʒénik) adj. belonging to or originating in the mind, mental, psychogenic disorder (cf. SOMATOGENIC) [PSYCHO-+Gk -genēs, born]

psy·cho·ger·i·at·ric (saikoudʒeri:ǽtrik) adj. (psych.) of mental illness in old age

psy·cho·his·to·ry (saikouhístəri) n. approach to history based in analysis of subconscious and private elements in the lives of participants: a psychodynamic view of the people involved in historic incidents. —**psy·cho·his·to·ri·an** n. — **psy·cho·his·to·ri·cal** adj. Cf PSYCHOBIOGRA-PHY

psy·cho·log·i·cal (saikəlódʒik'l) adj. of or pertaining to psychology || of or relating to the mind

psychological moment the moment when the individual or collective mind is most likely to respond positively to an action, statement, request etc.

psychological warfare actions designed to weaken the morale or loyalty of an enemy

psy·chol·o·gist (saikólədʒist) n. a specialist in psychology

psy·chol·o·gy (saikólədʒi:) n. the scientific study of human or animal behavior || the mental and behavioral characteristics of a person or group, mob psychology || the mental characteristics associated with a particular kind of behavior, the psychology of thieving [fr. Mod. L. psychologia fr. Gk psuchē, soul+logos, discourse]

psy·cho·met·ric (saikoumétrik) adj. of or relating to the measurement of mental data

psy·cho·met·rics (saikoumétriks) n. the science of applied psychometric techniques

psy·chom·e·trist (saikómitrist) n. a person who practices psychometrics

psy·chom·e·try (saikómitri:) n. divination, from personal, physical contact with an object, of the character etc. of the object or of people connected with it || psychometrics [fr. PSYCHO-+Gk -metria, measuring]

psy·cho·mi·met·ic (saikoumimétik) adj. (pharm.) of a drug that creates the symptoms of a hallucinogenic state. Cf PSYCHOTOMIMETIC

psy·cho·mo·tor (saikoumóutər) adj. (physiol.) of a muscular movement which results directly from a mental process

psy·cho·neu·ro·sis (saikounuróusis, saikounju-róusis) pl. **psy·cho·neu·ro·ses** (saikounuróu-si:z, saikounjuróusi:z) n. a nervous disorder of mainly psychic origin **psy·cho·neu·rot·ic** (sái-kounurótik, saikounjurótik) 1. adj. of, relating to, or afflicted by psychoneurosis 2. n. a person suffering from psychoneurosis

psy·cho·path (sáikəpæθ) n. a person suffering from a mental disorder (*CHARACTER DISORDER)

psy·cho·path·ic (saikəpǽθik) adj. of or characterized by mental disorder

psy·cho·path·o·let·ic (saikoupæθəlétik) adj. of a political system without roots or special values, unsure of its goals, usu. functioning at minimum effectiveness, and using force to ensure compliance with its rules

psy·cho·pa·thol·o·gy (saikoupəθólədʒi:) n. the scientific study of the psychological causes of mental illnesses

psy·chop·a·thy (saikópəθi:) n. character disorder

psy·cho·phar·ma·ceu·ti·cal (saikoufɑrməsú:ti-k'l) n. (pharm.) a drug that affects one's mental condition

psy·cho·pro·phy·lax·is (saikouproufəlǽksis) n. (med.) preparing women psychologically for childbirth, esp. natural childbirth. Cf LAMAZE

psy·cho·quack·er·y (saikoukwǽkəri:) n. the practice of psychology or psychiatry by an unqualified person —**psy·cho·quack** n.

psy·cho·sen·so·ry or **psy·cho·sen·so·ri·al** (saikousénsəri:) adj. (psych.) perceived either as something real or as a hallucination

psy·cho·sis (saikóusis) pl. **psy·cho·ses** (saikóu-si:z) n. serious mental derangement [fr. late Gk psuchōsis, animation]

psy·cho·so·mat·ic (saikousəmǽtik) adj. of, pertaining to or resulting from the interaction between mind and body

psy·cho·so·mat·o·graph (saikousoumǽtəɡræf) n. a device for measuring and recording muscular reactions to mental stimuli

psy·cho·sur·ger·y (saikousé:rdʒəri:) n. (med.) surgery performed on the brain for the purpose of changing the patient's personality, thought, emotions or behavior, rather than for the treatment of a physical disease

psy·cho·ther·a·pist (saikouθérəpist) n. a person who practices psychotherapy

psy·cho·ther·a·py (saikouθérəpi:) n. the treatment of mental illness by psychological methods, esp. psychoanalysis

psy·chot·ic (saikótik) 1. adj. of, relating to or

suffering from psychosis **2.** *n.* a psychotic person

psy·chot·o·gen (saikɒ́tədʒən) *n.* (*pharm.*) a drug affecting the mind psychotically. —**psy·chot·o·gen·ic**

psy·chot·o·mi·met·ic (saikɒtoumimétik) *adj.* (*psych.*) inducing or mimicking a psychosis. — **psy·chot·o·mi·met·ic** *n.* a psychotomimetic drug. *Cf* PSYCHOMIMETIC

psy·cho·tox·ic (saikoutóksik) *adj.* (*pharm.*) of a nonnarcotic drug with harmful effects, esp. on the mind

psy·cho·trop·ic drug (saikoutróupik) (*pharm.*) a drug affecting psychic function, behavior or experience

psy·chrom·e·ter (saikrómitər) *n.* (*phys.*) a hygrometer consisting of a wet-and-dry-bulb thermometer. The difference in the thermometer readings is a measure of the relative humidity of the atmosphere

psy-op (sáiɒp) *n.* (*mil.*) a psychological warfare operation

P-3 *ORION

ptar·mi·gan (tármigən) *pl.* **ptar·mi·gan, ptar·mi·gans,** *n.* any of several grouse of genus *Lagopus*, of the Arctic and northern temperate zones of Europe and America, characterized by completely feathered feet, and plumage that is brownish or blackish in summer and, in most species, largely white in winter [Gael. *tarmachan*, origin unknown]

PT boat a motor torpedo boat [fr. *patrol torpedo boat*]

pter·i·dol·o·gist (teridólədʒist) *n.* a specialist in pteridology

pter·i·dol·o·gy (teridólədʒi:) *n.* (*bot.*) the study of ferns [fr. Gk *pteris* (*pteridos*), fern+*logos*, discourse]

pte·rid·o·phyte (terídəfait) *n.* (in former classifications) a member of *Pteridophyta*, a subdivision of the plant kingdom coordinate with thallophytes, bryophytes and spermatophytes, including the ferns and fern allies (*PTEROPSID) [fr. Mod. L. *Pteridophyta* fr. Gk *pteris* (*pteridos*), fern+*phuton*, a plant]

pter·o·dac·tyl (terədǽktil) *n.* one of the pterosaurs. The flying mechanism was a large membrane between the body and a greatly developed fourth digit. Fossilized remains are found in strata from the Lower Jurassic to Late Mesozoic [fr. Mod. L. *Pterodactylus* fr. Gk *pteron*, wing+*daktulos*, finger]

pter·o·pod (térəpɒd) *n.* any of various mollusks of *Pteropoda*, a division of *Tectibranchia*, with the foot expanded into a wing-shaped paddle for swimming [fr. Gk *pteron*, wing+*pous* (*podos*), foot]

pte·rop·sid (terópsid) *n.* a member of *Pteropsida*, a large subphylum of green vascular land plants, comprising the ferns and flowering plants. The sporophytes possess roots, stems and often large leaves and are independent. In ferns the gametophyte generation is independent, but in the seed plants it is dependent upon the sporophyte for water and nutriment. The subphylum includes ferns, gymnosperms and angiosperms [fr. Gk *pteron*, wing+*opsio*, appearance]

pter·o·saur (térəsɔr) *n.* a member of *Pterosauria*, an extinct order of flying reptiles which included the pterodactyl

pter·y·goid (térigɔid) *adj.* of, pertaining to, or situated in the lower part of the sphenoid bone in the skull of man and other vertebrates [fr. Gk *pterugoeidēs*, like a wing]

Ptol·e·ma·ic (tɒləméiik) *adj.* of or pertaining to Ptolemy or to his theory of the universe ‖ of the Macedonian dynasty which ruled Egypt (304–30 B.C.)

Ptol·e·my (tóləmi:) (Claudius Ptolemaeus, 2nd c. A.D.), Greek astronomer and geographer of Alexandria, author of the famous 'Geography', which remained the standard geographic work throughout the Middle Ages, of the 'Optics', and of the 'Great Collection' or 'Almagest'. In this he gave a full account of Greek astronomy and propounded his own belief (unchallenged until Copernicus) that the earth is the center of the universe, and the sun, planets and stars revolve around it. Ptolemy divided the degree into minutes and seconds. He also determined the value of [π] (*PI)

Ptolemy I (*d.* 283 B.C.), king of Egypt (304.283 B.C.), founder of the Ptolemaic dynasty. He was a general of Alexander the Great, after whose death (323 B.C.) he seized power in Egypt

Ptolemy II (c. 308–c. 246 B.C.), king of Egypt (c.

285–c. 246 B.C.), son of Ptolemy I. He carried out economic reforms, completed the Pharos, was a patron of art and literature and, according to tradition, commissioned the Septuagint

Ptolemy III (*d.* c. 221 B.C.), king of Egypt (c. 246–c. 221 B.C.), son of Ptolemy II. He made war on Syria and extended his power to the coasts of Asia Minor and E. Greece

Ptolemy XI (*d.* 51 B.C.), king of Egypt (80–58 B.C. and 55–51 B.C.). He was overthrown (58 B.C.) by the Egyptians for misrule, but was restored (55 B.C.) with Roman support, giving Rome complete control of Egypt

pto·maine (tóumein, touméin) *n.* any of a number of alkaloids, some highly poisonous, formed by the action of bacteria on putrefying proteins [fr. Ital. *ptomaina* fr. Gk *ptōma*, corpse]

ptomaine poisoning poisoning by ptomaines ‖ (*pop.*) any food poisoning

pto·sis (tóusis) *n.* (*med.*) the drooping of an upper eyelid due to the paralysis of the muscle which lifts it [Gk *ptōsis*, a falling]

PTV (*acronym*) public television

pty·a·lin (táialin) *n.* (*biochem.*) an enzyme in human saliva which promotes the conversion of starch into sugar [fr. Gk *ptualon*, spittle]

pty·a·lism (táializəm) *n.* (*med.*) excessive flow of saliva [fr. Gk *ptualismos* fr. *ptualizein*, to expectorate]

p-type semiconductor (pí:taip) (*electr.*) a crystal material in a semiconductor that has been doped with an impurity that causes electronic holes that move from molecule to molecule, creating a condition as the major carrier of electric current

pub (pʌb) *n.* (*Br., pop.*) a public house

pu·ber·ty (pjú:bərti:) *n.* the period of life when the reproductive glands begin to function ‖ the condition of becoming able to reproduce [F. *puberté*]

pu·bes (pjú:bi:z) *n.* the hair that begins to grow on the lower hypogastric region at puberty ‖ the lower hypogastric region [L.]

pubes *pl.* of PUBIS

pu·bes·cence (pju:bésn's) *n.* the reaching of puberty ‖ (*biol.*, of some plants and certain insects) a downy or hairy covering **pu·bés·cent** *adj.* [F.]

pu·bic (pjú:bik) *adj.* of or pertaining to the pubis ‖ of or pertaining to the pubes

pu·bis (pjú:bis) *pl.* **pu·bes** (pjú:bi:z) *n.* the foremost of the three sections of the hipbone [L. (*os*) *pubis*, the groin (bone)]

pub·lic (pʌ́blik) **1.** *adj.* of or pertaining to the community as a whole, *the public good* ‖ for the use of the community at large and maintained at the community's expense, *public amenities* ‖ that is or can be known by all members of the community, *a public scandal* ‖ acting for the people, *public prosecutor* ‖ of or relating to the service of the community, *prominent in public life*, often receiving publicity, *a public figure* **2.** *n.* (usually with 'the') the members of a community in general ‖ a group or section of a community characterized by some common interest etc., *his television program reaches a wide public* **in public** in the state of being visible or accessible to the public [M.E. *publique* fr. F.]

public access 1. access to government-held information under the Freedom of Information Act. **2.** access to broadcast facilities, e.g., CATV, under licensing arrangements

public address system a microphone and amplifier system which enables a speaker etc. to be heard at a distance

pub·li·can (pʌ́blikən) *n.* (*Br.*) a person who manages a public house ‖ (*Rom. hist.*) a tax collector [F. *publicain*, a tax collector of ancient Rome]

pub·li·ca·tion (pʌblikéiʃən) *n.* a publishing or being published ‖ the issue of printed matter for public sale or free distribution ‖ a printed and published book, magazine, pamphlet etc. [M.E. *publicacion* fr. O.F.]

public bill a legislative bill affecting a whole country (cf. PRIVATE BILL)

public domain the realm of collective property (esp. property not protected by patent or copyright) to which any member of the public may lay claim, *Oscar Wilde's plays are in the public domain now* ‖ land belonging to, or controlled by, the government

public enemy a criminal at large whose liberty menaces the community, esp. one widely advertised as sought by the police

public house (*Br.*) an establishment licensed for the sale and consumption of alcoholic bever-

ages on the premises, sometimes also having a license permitting consumption off the premises. There is usually more than one bar, beer is the main drink, and food and lodging are sometimes provided. A public house is often the center of sociability in a community

pub·li·cist (pʌ́blisist) *n.* an expert in international law ‖ a person who writes on public affairs ‖ a person who publicizes ‖ a press agent [F. *publiciste*]

pub·lic·i·ty (pʌblísiti:) *n.* the whole of the methods and materials used in making an enterprise, product etc. known to the public with a view to increasing business ‖ the methods and materials used in making some noncommercial matter similarly known ‖ the disseminating of advertising or informative matter ‖ the condition of being exposed to the knowledge of the general public, esp. through newspaper reports, *the scandal was given full publicity* [fr. F. *publicité*]

pub·li·cize (pʌ́blisaiz) *pres. part.* **pub·li·ciz·ing** *past* and *past part* **pub·li·cized** *v.t.* to bring to public notice

public library a library usually run by a municipality from which books may be borrowed free

public opinion the consensus of people's views on a given issue, usually of a political, social or economic nature and on a national scale

public orator (*Br.*) the official spokesman of a university, who delivers addresses (usually in Latin) on official occasions (such as the conferring of honorary degrees)

public prosecutor an official who investigates and prosecutes a criminal act on behalf of the State ‖ (*Br.*) a legal officer who prosecutes on behalf of the State

public relations the promotion, by a firm, corporation, government department etc., of the goodwill of other organizations or the public by distributing information about policy etc. ‖ the degree of goodwill existing or created between organizations or between an organization and the public

public relations officer (*Br.*, *abbr.* P.R.O.) a person employed to promote good public relations

Public Safety, Committee of (*F. hist.*) the group of 12 men who ruled France Apr. 6, 1793–Oct. 27, 1795. Led (Sept. 1793–July 1794) by Carnot, Danton and Robespierre, the committee developed into a dictatorship under Robespierre, and was responsible for the Terror

public school an elementary or secondary school maintained by taxes, supervised by local authorities and offering education to the children of the district free of charge ‖ (*Br.*) a private secondary school whose headmaster is a member of the Headmasters' Conference, an independent professional body. Such schools are wholly or partly boarding, are administered by a governing body and meet some part of their upkeep from pupils' fees and income from endowments

public servant a person holding public office

public service service of the state ‖ that which serves a need of the public, e.g. a public transport system

pub·lic-spir·it·ed (pʌblikspíritid) *adj.* (of people) seeking the public good and acting accordingly ‖ (of actions) prompted by zeal for the public good

public television educational, cultural and informational television programs, without commercials, provided by nonprofit organizations

public trustee (*Br. law*) an official authorized and appointed by the State to act as trustee (e.g. in relation to the investment of charitable funds)

public utility *pl.* **public utilities** a business concern which provides and administers a public service, e.g. water, gas, electricity ‖ a stock or bond issued by such a concern

public works facilities such as roads, playgrounds etc. built with government funds for the use of the general public

pub·lish (pʌ́bliʃ) *v.t.* to arrange the printing and distribution of (books, newspapers etc.) for sale to the public ‖ (*loosely*) to be the author of (a work thus offered to the public), *he has just published his third novel* ‖ to make known to the public ‖ to announce publicly, *to publish banns of marriage* **pub·lish·er** *n.* someone who arranges for the multiplication of copies of a work (a book, record, sheet music etc.) and for

CONCISE PRONUNCIATION KEY: **(a)** æ, *cat*; ɑ, *car*; ɔ *fawn*; ei, *snake.* **(e)** e, *hen*; i:, *sheep*; iə, *deer*; ɛə, *bear.* **(i)** i, *fish*; ai, *tiger*; ə:, *bird.* **(o)** o, *ox*; au, *cow*; ou, *goat*; u, *poor*; ɔi, *royal.* **(u)** ʌ, *duck*; u, *bull*; u:, *goose*; ə, *bacillus*; ju:, *cube.* x, *loch*; θ, *think*; δ, *bother*; z, *Zen*; ʒ, *corsage*; dʒ, *savage*; ŋ, *orangutang*; j, *yak*; ʃ, *fish*; tʃ, *fetch*; 'l, *rabble*; 'n, *redden.* Complete pronunciation key appears inside front cover.

their handling by distributive agencies. He remunerates, or is remunerated by, the author (or performer etc.) according to the terms of the contract made between them [M.E. *publisen, publisshen* fr. O.F.]

publisher's imprint the name of the publisher, together with the place and date of publication, e.g. on the title page of a book

Puc·ci·ni (puːˈtʃiːni:), Giacomo (1858–1924), Italian operatic composer. His dramatic sense and his flow of sensuous melody made his operas popular. The best known are 'Manon Lescaut' (1893), 'la Bohème' (1896), 'la Tosca' (1900) and 'Madame Butterfly' (1904). 'Turandot', unfinished at his death, was first performed in 1926

puc·coon (pəkuːn) *n.* any of various North American plants (e.g. the bloodroot) which yield a red or yellow pigment [Algonquian]

puce (pjuːs) *n.* and *adj.* brownish purple [F.=flea]

Puck (pʌk) a mischievous goblin believed, esp. in the 16th and 17th cc., to roam the English countryside looking for pranks to play [O.E. *pūca*, a mischievous spirit]

puck *n.* a hard rubber disk used in ice hockey as the object to be shot into the goal [origin unknown]

puck·er (pʌkər) **1.** *v.t.* (often with 'up') to gather into narrow folds or wrinkles ‖ *v.i.* to become gathered into narrow folds or wrinkles **2.** *n.* a narrow fold or wrinkle, or a number of them together [prob. fr. POKE, (obs.) a bag]

puck·ish (pʌkiʃ) *adj.* mischievous, *puckish humor* [after PUCK]

pud·ding (pudiŋ) *n.* a sweet dessert, thick and soft, typically composed of flour and milk and eggs and sometimes fruit ‖ (*naut.*) a pad of rope etc. used as a fender [M.E. *poding, pudding*, origin unknown]

pudding stone conglomerate

pud·dle (pʌd'l) **1.** *n.* a small pool of liquid, esp. rainwater ‖ clay and sand kneaded together with water and used to construct a watertight lining for the bank of a canal, the bottom of a pond etc. **2.** *v. pres. part.* **pud·dling** *past* and *past part.* **pud·dled** *v.t.* to knead (clay, sand and water or concrete etc.) into an impervious mass‖ to stir (molten iron) in order to reduce its carbon content ‖ to make (water etc.) dirty ‖ *v.i.* to dabble in mud etc. ‖ to play about messily with paints, clay etc. **pud·dly** *adj.* having many puddles, *a puddly road* [M.E. *podel, puddel*, prob. dim. of O.E. *pudd*, ditch]

pu·den·da (pjuːˈdɛndə) *pl. n.* the external genital organs, esp. those of a woman [pl. of L. *pudendum*, that of which one ought to be ashamed]

pudge (pʌdʒ) *n.* (*pop.*) a short, fat person **púdg·i·ness** *n.* the quality of being pudgy **púdg·y** *comp.* **pudg·i·er** *superl.* **pudg·i·est** *adj.* short and fat [etym. doubtful]

Pue·bla (pweˈblə) a densely populated interior state (area 13,096 sq. miles, pop. 3,285,300) of Mexico, on the Anáhuac Plateau. Capital: Puebla. Main crops: coffee, sugarcane, fibers, corn, cereals. Its mountains yield onyx and gold and other metals. Rivers provide hydroelectric power. Puebla is an important corridor between Mexico City and Veracruz. There are many sites of archaeological interest

Puebla a city (pop. 710,833) of central Mexico, 130 miles southeast of Mexico City. Traditional crafts: pottery and tiles (it was the original center of Moorish style in Mexico), onyx carving. Industries: metallurgy, building materials, textiles. Cathedral (16th–17th cc.). University (1922)

pueb·lo (pweˈblou) **1.** *pl.* **pueb·los** *n.* a type of Indian village in the southwest U.S.A. and some parts of Latin America built as communal dwelling houses of adobe or stone **Pueb·lo** a member of certain Indian tribes of Arizona and New Mexico, e.g. the Zuñi and the Hopi, inhabiting such a village ‖ their languages **2. Pueb·lo** *adj.* of the Pueblo Indians or their culture [Span.=village, people]

'Pueblo', U.S.S. a U.S. vessel designed for espionage which became (1968) the center of an international crisis when North Korean vessels intercepted it in the Sea of Japan and escorted it to North Korea, where it was detained. The captain and crew were released (1969) when the U.S.A. agreed to admit what it officially denied: that at the time of capture the vessel was inside North Korean territorial waters

pu·er·ile (pjuːˈəril, pjuːˈərail) *adj.* (of an adult's ideas, behavior) not befitting an adult, childish

pu·er·il·i·ty (pjuːəˈriliti:) *n.* [fr. L. *puerilis*, pertaining to a child]

pu·er·per·al (pjuːˈɜrpərəl) *adj.* (*med.*) relating to the puerperium [fr. L. *puerperus*]

puerperal fever infection of the female reproductive organs following childbirth

pu·er·pe·ri·um (pjuːəˈrpiːriːəm) *n.* the period of confinement immediately after childbirth [L.=childbirth]

Puer·to Ca·bel·lo (pwertɔkɑbéjo) a seaport (pop. 90,000) in N. Venezuela, 70 miles west of Caracas

Puer·to Ri·can (pwertourí:kən, pórtourí:kən, póurtourí:kən) **1.** *adj.* of or pertaining to Puerto Rico or its inhabitants **2.** *n.* a native or inhabitant of Puerto Rico

Puer·to Ri·co (pwertourí:kou, pórtourí:kou, póurtourí:kou) the easternmost island (area 3,423 sq. miles, pop. 3,196,520) of the Greater Antilles, comprising, with Vieques, Culebra and Mona Is (total pop. 7,800), a territory of the U.S.A. Capital and chief port: San Juan. People: 80% European stock, with African and Mulatto minorities. Language: Spanish, 17% also speak English (both are official). Religion: mainly Roman Catholic, with Protestant and Spiritist minorities. The land is 38% arable, 37% pasture, and 12% forest (palms, tropical hardwoods). Reforestation is proceeding. The coast (sugar plantations) is flat, and the interior mountainous (highest point 4,398 ft). Mean annual temperature (F.) 76°. Rainfall: north 40–60 ins, south 20–40 ins. Exports: sugar, rum, tobacco, molasses, cotton textiles, pineapples, citrus fruit, light manufactures. The tourist industry is important. Territorial university (founded as a normal school, 1900) at Rio Piedras, near San Juan. Some land has been redistributed, but there is heavy emigration to the mainland, esp. New York City. HISTORY. Puerto Rico was inhabited by the Arawak and Carib Indians when Columbus landed there (1493) during his second voyage. The island was explored (1508) by Ponce de León, who founded the city of San Juan de Puerto Rico in the same year. During the colonial period it lay under the authority of the Audiencia de Santo Domingo and was subjected to numerous attacks by pirates, notably Drake, who set fire (1595) to San Juan. During the 18th c. Britain attempted on three occasions to take possession of the island and to annex it to Jamaica. Following several independence movements during the 19th c., the island was occupied by the U.S.A. in the Spanish-American War and was ceded to the U.S.A. (1898) in the Treaty of Paris. Government was at first in the hands of the military. In 1917 Puerto Ricans obtained U.S. citizenship. President Franklin Roosevelt initiated (mid-1930s) a New Deal measure, the Puerto Rico Reconstruction Administration (PRRA), which gave rise (1938) to the Popular Democratic party (PDP), led by Luis Muñoz Marín. It initiated reforms, notably land distribution, enforcement of minimum wage and hour laws and a progressive income tax law, and the establishment of an economic development program known as Operation Bootstrap, initiated in 1942. President Harry Truman named (1946) Jesús T. Piñero as the first Puerto Rican governor. The U.S. government permitted (in the Organic Act, 1947) the election of governors by popular vote, the first of whom (1948) was Muñoz Marín. Endorsing a proposal made by the U.S. government, he drafted a new constitution which went into effect in 1952 and which defined Puerto Rico as an internally self-governing commonwealth or associated free state. Muñoz Marín was reelected in 1956 and 1960 and was succeeded (1964–8) by his PDP lieutenant Roberto Sánchez Vilella. In 1968 the PDP lost to millionaire engineer and industrialist Luis Alberto Ferré, leader of the New Progressive party (NPP) which had been founded only one year earlier. Although Ferré had campaigned for statehood in a 1967 plebiscite which ratified (by about 60–40) the island's status as associated free state, he did not interpret his election as a mandate for statehood, but favored another plebiscite in 1971. By the early 1980s federal budget cuts, a worldwide recession, and an erosion of Puerto Rico's competitive advantages caused an economic slump that led to demands for greater autonomy, with or without change in commonwealth status. Debate continued among factions favoring commonwealth, statehood and independence

Puerto Rico Reconstruction Administration (PRRA), a New Deal agency established (mid-1930s) to readjust the distribution of economic power in Puerto Rico. It placed a restrictive quota on sugar production and enforced a law limiting corporation holdings to 500 acres. It established a cooperative sugar mill to compete with private mills, and catered to the long-neglected coffee and tobacco interests. The PRRA gave birth (1938) to the Popular Democratic party

puff (pʌf) **1.** *v.i.* to breathe quickly, esp. after exertion ‖ to emit steam, smoke etc. in a series of whiffs or puffs ‖ to blow in rapid gusts, whiffs or puffs ‖ (with 'up' or 'out') to swell, become inflated ‖ (with 'at' or 'on') to draw (on a pipe etc.) ‖ *v.t.* to blow or emit in whiffs or puffs ‖ to draw on (a pipe, cigar, or cigarette), emitting puffs of smoke ‖ (with 'out') to extinguish (a candle etc.) by blowing on it ‖ (with 'up' or 'out') to cause to swell, inflate ‖ (with 'out') to arrange (hair etc.) in a loose, fluffy mass ‖ (sometimes with 'up') to praise excessively ‖ (with 'up') to make conceited **2.** *n.* a short, light gust of air, steam, smoke etc. ‖ a small cloud, emission of smoke etc. ‖ a draw on a cigarette etc. ‖ a shell of soft light pastry etc. ‖ a fluffy mass ‖ a powder puff ‖ a quilt ‖ a laudatory critical notice written to publicize a work ‖ publisher's blurb ‖ (*genetics*) an intensely active portion of an enlarged chromosome [M.E. *puffen*]

puff adder a deadly poisonous S. African viper, *Bitis arietans*, which inflates the upper part of its body when excited

puff·ball (pʌfbɔl) *n.* any of several fungi of fam. *Lycoperdaceae* with a large round, white spore case which emits dustlike spores when stepped on or struck

puffed (pʌft) *adj.* swollen, puffy ‖ (*Br.*) out of breath

puf·fin (pʌfin) *n.* any of various marine birds of genera *Fratercula* or *Lunda*, fam. *Alcidae*, having a brightly colored, laterally flattened bill, which it partially sheds after the breeding season. It lives colonially in rabbit or shearwater burrows on cliffs or grassy islands on the N. Atlantic seaboard [origin unknown]

puff·i·ness (pʌfi:nis) *n.* the state or quality of being puffy

puff pastry light flaky pastry

puff·y (pʌfi:) *comp.* **puff·i·er** *superl.* **puff·i·est** *adj.* short of breath ‖ puffed out ‖ swollen, *puffy eyelids*

pug (pʌg) **1.** *n.* a large roll of clay prepared for working **2.** *v.t. pres. part.* **pug·ging** *past* and *past part.* **pugged** to mix (clay) into a working consistency ‖ to fill (a hollow floor or wall) with compacted material in order to absorb vibration and sound [etym. doubtful]

pug *n.* a dog of a small, short-haired breed having a broad, flat nose and short, tightly curled tail [origin unknown]

pug *n.* the footprint of a wild beast [Hindi *pag*, foot]

Pu·get (pyʒe), Pierre (1620–94), French sculptor. His classical subjects are treated with often violent realism and are full of power and movement

Pu·get Sound (pjú:dʒit) a branched inlet (80 miles long) of the Pacific in north and central Washington

pu·gil·ism (pjú:dʒəlizəm) *n.* boxing **pú·gil·ist** *n.* a boxer **pu·gil·is·tic** *adj.* [fr. L. *pugil*, boxer]

Pu·gin (pjú:dʒin), Augustus Welby Northmore (1812–52), English architect. He was one of the leaders of the Gothic Revival, esp. in its decorative detail, and was best known for his ecclesiastical architecture and his part in designing the Houses of Parliament in London

pug mark a pug (footprint)

pug mill a machine in which clay is pugged

pug·na·cious (pʌgnéiʃəs) *adj.* fond of fighting, aggressive [fr. L. *pugnax (pugnacis)*]

pug·nac·i·ty (pʌgnǽsiti:) *n.* the state or quality of being pugnacious [fr. L. *pugnacitus*]

pug nose a broad snub nose **pug·nosed** *adj.*

puis·ne (pjú:ni:) **1.** *adj.* (*law*) more recent, *a puisne mortgage* ‖ (*law*) of lower rank or importance **2.** *n.* (*law*) a puisne judge [O. F. fr. *puis*, after+*né*, born]

pu·is·sance (pjú:isəns, pju:ís'ns, pwís'ns) *n.* (*rhet.*) might, power [F. fr. *puissant*, puissant]

pu·is·sant (pjú:isənt, pju:ís'nt, pwís'nt) *adj.* (*rhet.*) mighty, powerful [F.]

puke (pju:k) **1.** *v. pres. part.* **puk·ing** *past* and

CONCISE PRONUNCIATION KEY: **(a)** æ, c*a*t; ɑ, c*a*r; ɔ, f*aw*n; ei, sn*a*ke. **(e)** e, h*e*n; i:, sh*ee*p; iə, d*ee*r; ɛə, b*ea*r. **(i)** i, f*i*sh; ai, t*i*ger; ə:, b*i*rd. **(o)** o, *o*x; au, c*ow*; ou, g*oa*t; u, p*oo*r; ɔi, r*oy*al. **(u)** ʌ, d*u*ck; u, b*u*ll; u:, g*oo*se; ə, b*a*cillus; ju:, c*u*be. x, lo*ch*; θ, *th*ink; δ, bo*th*er; z, *Z*en; ʒ, corsa*g*e; dʒ, sava*g*e; ŋ, ora*ng*utang; j, *y*ak; ʃ, *fi*sh; tʃ, fe*tch*; 'l, rabb*le*; 'n, redd*en*. Complete pronunciation key appears inside front cover.

past part. **puked** *v.i.* (*pop.*) to vomit ‖ *v.t.* (*pop.*) to vomit **2.** *n.* (*pop.*) vomit [origin unknown]

pul (pu:l) *pl.* **puls, pu·li** (pú:li:) *n.* a monetary unit of Afghani equal to one hundredth of an afghani ‖ a coin of the value of one pul [Pers. *pūl* fr. Turk.]

pu·la (púlə) *n.* unit of currency in Botswana

Pu·las·ki (pulǽski:), Kazimierz (Casimir) (1747–79), Polish patriot and U.S. general. He distinguished himself during the Polish anti-Russian insurrection of 1768 and in the American Revolution, when he led his Pulaski legion against the British

pul·chri·tude (pʎlkritu:d, pʎlkritju:d) *n.* (*rhet.*) physical beauty [fr. L. *pulchritudo*]

pule (pju:l) *pres. part.* **pul·ing** *past* and *past part.* **puled** *v.i.* (*rhet.*) to cry with weak, whimpering sounds [of imit. origin, perh. fr. F. *piauler*]

Pu·litz·er (pú:litsər, pjúltsər), Joseph (1847–1911), American newspaper publisher of Hungarian birth. He endowed a number of monetary prizes and scholarships which have been awarded annually in the U.S.A. since 1917 for distinction in journalism, letters and music

pull (pul) **1.** *v.t.* to apply a force to (something) in order to make it move towards the person or thing applying the force (opp. PUSH) ‖ to extract, *to pull a tooth* ‖ to strain (a muscle etc.) ‖ (sometimes with 'up') to uproot (vegetables etc.) ‖ to row (a boat) ‖ (*racing*) to check (a horse) by pulling the reins, and so prevent it from winning ‖ (*football*) to pull back from the scrimmage line and toward one side to protect the carrier ‖ (*golf, baseball, cricket* etc.) to hit (the ball) towards the side on which the player is standing ‖ (*printing,* often with 'up') to take (a proof) from the inked type, lithographic stone etc. ‖ to draw out (a knife, gun etc.) ready for use ‖ to draw off (beer) from a container ‖ (*pop.*) to accomplish with daring, *to pull a coup* ‖ (*pop.*) to assert (superiority) in order to obtain an advantage over someone ‖ (*pop.*) to attract (votes, support, an audience etc.) ‖ *v.i.* to apply a force to something in order to make it move towards the person or thing applying the force ‖ to be capable of being so moved, *the drawer won't pull* ‖ (often with 'away', 'ahead', 'into', 'out' etc.) to move by means of physical or mechanical energy ‖ (with 'at') to draw (on a pipe) ‖ (with 'at') to take a drink (from a bottle) ‖ (*golf, baseball, cricket* etc.) to pull the ball ‖ (of a horse) to strain against the bit ‖ to row a boat **to pull around** to handle (a person) roughly **to pull a fast one** to play an unfair trick **to pull apart, to pull to pieces** to tear apart ‖ to find great fault with (a piece of work etc.) **to pull down** to demolish (a building) ‖ to weaken in health **to pull for** (*pop.*) to encourage by shouting or cheering **to pull off** to be finally successful in (something difficult or chancy) **to pull oneself together** to regain control of one's emotions or behavior **to pull one's punches** (of a boxer) to abstain from hitting as hard as one can ‖ to criticize or accuse less forcibly than would be justifiable **to pull one's weight** to take one's full share of work or responsibility **to pull out** (of a vehicle) to move out from the side of the road or from the line of traffic ‖ (*pop.*) to leave, esp. to abandon some group effort **to pull over** (of a vehicle) to move suddenly across the road or move to the edge of the road **to pull through** to survive illness, danger etc. ‖ to enable (someone) to survive illness, danger etc. **to pull together** to cooperate in a task **to pull up** (of a moving vehicle, horse etc.) to come to a stop ‖ (*Br.*) to reprimand, *the manager pulled him up for his carelessness* ‖ to improve one's position relative to other competitors in a race **2.** *n.* the act of pulling ‖ an instance of this ‖ a force which pulls or attracts, *the pull of the tide* ‖ an effort necessary for forward or upward movement, *a hard pull up the hill* ‖ a draw on a cigarette, drink etc. ‖ (*golf, baseball, cricket* etc.) a stroke which pulls the ball ‖ the force needed to pull a bow or the trigger of a firearm ‖ an advantage due to influence, relationship etc. ‖ influence exerted to obtain a privilege or advantage ‖ a knob, handle etc. by which a drawer, bell etc. may be pulled ‖ (*printing*) a proof ‖ the checking of a horse by pulling on the bridle, esp. to prevent it from winning a race ‖ a row (in a boat etc.) ‖ a distance or period of time spent in rowing [O.E. *pullian,* origin unknown]

pull date a date recorded on a food product indicating the latest time at which it should be sold, e.g., on milk

pul·let (púlit) *n.* a hen before the first moult [F. *poulet,* chicken]

pul·ley (púli:) *pl.* **pul·leys** *n.* a wheel with a grooved rim, used to raise or lower a load attached to one end of a rope, chain etc. passing around the groove and pulled from the other end. The mechanical advantage of pulleys, mounted in the same block, enables a small effort exerted over a long distance to raise a heavy load through a short distance ‖ a wheel on a fixed shaft used to transmit power by means of a belt, chain etc. passing over its circumference [O.F. *polie* prob. fr. Gk]

Pullman (púlmən), George Mortimer (1831–97) U.S. industrialist, inventor of the railroad sleeping car. Working in Chicago from 1855, he first remodeled old railroad coaches and then built the first modern sleeping car (1863). Called the 'Pioneer,' it had a folding upper berth and seat cushions that could be extended to form a lower berth. He also developed other types of railroad cars, including the dining car (1868), and formed the Pullman Palace Car Company to manufacture his sleeping cars

Pull·man (púlmən) *n.* a railroad car with luxurious sleeping or dining accommodations [after George Mortimer *Pullman* (1831-97), American inventor who introduced such cars in the U.S.A.]

Pullman Strike a shutdown (1894) in the servicing of Pullman cars in Chicago, Ill., undertaken by the American Railway Union led by Eugene Debs. The strike was broken by the intervention of U.S. troops, and Debs and other leaders were arrested. Although defended at his trial by Clarence Darrow, Debs was convicted (1895) and imprisoned

pull·o·ver (púluvər) *n.* a sweater put on by being pulled over the head ‖ a shirt or blouse put on in this way

pull-through (púlθru:) *n.* a weighted cord with an oiled rag or a brush attached, used for cleaning the bore of a gun

pul·lu·late (pʎljuleit) *pres. part.* **pul·lu·lat·ing** *past* and *past part.* **pul·lu·lat·ed** *v.i.* (of a seed) to germinate ‖ to develop in great quantity, to swarm, **pul·lu·la·tion** *n.* [fr. L. *pullulare (pullulatus),* to sprout]

pul·mo·nar·y (púlməneri:) *adj.* of, like or affecting the lungs ‖ pulmonate ‖ of the artery conveying blood from the heart to the lungs ‖ of the vein conveying blood from the lungs to the heart [fr. L. *pulmonarius*]

pulmonary valve a valve in the heart of higher vertebrates between the right ventricle and the artery leading blood from the heart to the lungs

pul·mo·nate (púlməneit, púlmənit) **1.** *adj.* (*zool.*) having lungs or the equivalent of lungs ‖ belonging or relating to *Pulmonata,* an order of gastropod mollusks having a lung or respiratory sac **2.** *n.* a pulmonate gastropod [fr. Mod. L. *pulmonatus*]

pul·mon·ic (pulmónik) *adj.* pulmonary [F. *pulmonique*]

pulp (pʎlp) **1.** *n.* a soft, moist mass of animal or vegetable matter ‖ such a part of a fruit (e.g. of an orange) or of an animal body (e.g. of a tooth) ‖ soft pithy matter found in plant stems ‖ a mixture, made by mechanical or chemical treatment of wood, consisting of water and cellulose fibers, and used as the raw material in paper-making ‖ (*Am., pl.*) pulp magazines ‖ (*mining*) pulverized ore mixed with water ‖ (*mining*) dry crushed ore **2.** *v.t.* to make into a pulp ‖ *v.i.* to become a pulp **pulp·i·ness** *n.* the quality or state of being pulpy [F. *pulpe*]

pulp magazine a magazine, usually sensational, on cheap wood-pulp paper

pulp·wood (púlpwud) *n.* the wood of some trees, e.g. spruces, most suitable for converting into pulp for papermaking

pulp·y (púlpi:) *comp.* **pulp·i·er** *superl.* **pulp·i·est** *adj.* of, like or having the consistency of pulp

pul·que (pú:lke, púlki:) *n.* a Mexican fermented drink prepared from several species of agave, esp. *Agave atrovirens* [Span.]

pul·sar (púlsər) *n.* (*meteor.*) a source in space of strong, pulsating radio waves, believed to be the core of an exploded or rotating neutron star. *Cf* QUASAR

pul·sate (pʎlseit) *pres. part.* **pul·sat·ing** *past* and *past part.* **pul·sat·ed** *v.i.* to move rhythmi-cally to and fro, esp. to expand and contract in a regular way (e.g. of the heart) ‖ to be as if throbbing or vibrating, *the pulsating enthusiasm of the crowd* [fr. L. *pulsare (pulsatus),* to beat]

pul·sa·tile (pʎlsətil, pʎlsətail) *adj.* pulsating ‖ percussive [fr. M.L. *pulsatilis*]

pul·sa·tion (pʎlséiʃən) *n.* the action of pulsating ‖ a beat, throb [fr. L. *pulsatio (pulsationis)*]

pul·sa·tor (pʎlseitər, pʎlséitər) *n.* a device that works with a throbbing movement, e.g. a machine which agitates diamond-bearing earth and so separates out the diamonds, or an attachment on milking machinery [fr. L. *pulsare (pulsatus),* to beat]

pul·sa·to·ry (pʎlsətɔri:, pʎlsətɔuri:) *adj.* able to pulsate, throbbing

pulse (pʎls) **1.** *n.* the regular expansion and contraction of the arteries due to the rhythmical action of the heart in forcing blood through them ‖ the frequency with which the resultant throbs occur, *a rapid pulse* ‖ a single one of these throbs ‖ the magnitude of the arterial expansions and contractions, *a strong pulse* ‖ the beat in music or verse ‖ any rhythmical beat ‖ a disturbance of brief duration transmitted through a medium ‖ a transitory disturbance of voltage, current, pressure or some other normally constant quantity ‖ a generalized group sentiment divined rather than known by direct experience, *testing the political pulse of the South* **2.** *v. pres. part.* **puls·ing** *past* and *past part.* **pulsed** *v.i.* to pulsate ‖ *v.t.* to emit in a regular succession of pulses or waves [L. *pulsus* fr. *pellere (pulsum),* to beat]

pulse (pʎls) a leguminous plant (pea, bean etc.) ‖ the edible seeds of these plants [O.F. *pols, pouls*]

pulse-jet engine a jet engine to which the intake of air is intermittent (through valves), resulting in a pulsating thrust

pulse-jet or **pulse-jet engine** a jet-propulsion engine containing neither compressor nor turbine, equipped with valves in its front that open and shut and so create thrust intermittently, rather than continuously. *Cf* RAMJET

pul·sim·e·ter (pʎlsímitər) *n.* (*med.*) an instrument used to measure the rate and strength of the pulse

puls·ing (pʎlsiŋ) *n.* (*mil.*) in naval mine warfare, a method of operating magnetic and acoustic sweeps in which the sweep is energized by varying or intermittent current in accordance with predetermined schedule

pul·som·e·ter (pʎlsómitər) *n.* a vacuum pump operating by the intake and condensation of steam at regular intervals ‖ a pulsimeter

pul·ver·i·za·tion (pʎlvərizéiʃən) *n.* a pulverizing or being pulverized

pul·ver·ize (pʎlvəraiz) *pres. part.* **pul·ver·iz·ing** *past* and *past part.* **pul·ver·ized** *v.t.* to reduce to a fine powder ‖ to defeat with devastating effect, *to pulverize the opposition* ‖ *v.i.* to become powder **púl·ver·iz·er** *n.* someone or something which pulverizes ‖ a harrow for breaking soil into a fine tilth [fr. L.L. *pulverizare*]

pul·ver·u·lent (pʎlvérjulənt) *adj.* consisting of fine powder ‖ covered with fine powder ‖ (of a rock) disintegrating with ease into a fine powder [fr. L. *pulverulentus*]

pul·vil·lus (pʎlvíləs) *pl.* **pul·vil·li** (pʎlvílai) *n.* (*zool.*) a process or membrane on an insect's foot sometimes serving as an adhesive organ [L. fr. *pulvinulus,* dim. of *pulvinus,* pillow]

pul·vi·nus (pʎlváinəs) *pl.* **pul·vi·ni** (pʎlváinai) *n.* (*bot.*) a swelling at the base of a petiole [L.=pillow]

pu·ma (pjú:mə) *pl.* **pu·mas, pu·ma** *n.* a cougar ‖ the fur of the cougar [Span.]

pum·ice (pʎmis) **1.** *n.* a light, porous volcanic stone formed by the escape of steam or gas from cooling lava, used as an abrasive in cleaning, smoothing and polishing ‖ a piece of this **2.** *v.t. pres. part.* **pum·ic·ing** *past* and *past part.* **pum·iced** to clean, smooth or polish with pumice [O.F. *pomis, pumis*]

pum·mel (pʎməl) *pres. part.* **pum·mel·ing,** esp. *Br.* **pum·mel·ling** *past* and *past part.* **pum·meled,** esp. *Br.* **pum·melled** *v.t.* to strike or thump repeatedly, esp. with the fist or fists [var. of POMMEL]

pump (pʎmp) **1.** *n.* a device for raising or moving a liquid or gas by decreasing or increasing the pressure on it ‖ an act or the process of pumping **2.** *v.t.* to raise, move or eject by using a pump or as if with a pump ‖ (with 'out') to remove a liquid or gas from, *they pumped the well dry* ‖ to supply with air by means of a pump or bellows, *to pump an organ* ‖

CONCISE PRONUNCIATION KEY: **(a)** æ, c*a*t; ɑ, c*a*r; ɔ f*aw*n; ei, v*ei*n; i:, sh*ee*p; iə, d*ee*r; εə, b*ea*r. **(i)** i, f*i*sh; ai, t*i*ger; əː, b*i*rd. **(o)** o, *o*x; au, c*ow*; ou, g*oa*t; u, p*oo*r; ɔi, r*oy*al. **(u)** ʌ, d*u*ck; u, b*u*ll; u:, g*oo*se; ə, b*a*cillus; ju:, c*u*be. x, lo*ch*; θ, *th*ink; δ, *b*o*th*er; z, *Z*en; ʒ, cor*s*age; dʒ, sava*g*e; ŋ, ora*n*gutang; j, *y*ak; ʃ, *fi*sh; tʃ, fe*tch*; 'l, rabb*le*; 'n, red*den*. Complete pronunciation key appears inside front cover.

(usually with 'up') to inflate by means of a pump, *to pump up car tires* ‖ to inject (someone) with a stream of something, *he pumped him full of shots* ‖ to extract information from (a person) by subtle questions ‖ to move (something) energetically up and down as if working a pump handle, *to pump someone's hand* ‖ to invest (capital) heavily in a business, industry etc., *he pumped funds into the firm* ‖ *v.i.* to work a pump [M.E. *pumpe*]

pump *n.* (*old-fash.*) a man's light shoe fitting without laces or other fastening, esp. one of patent leather worn with evening dress ‖ (*Am.=Br.* court shoe) a lady's high-heeled shoe without fastenings [origin unknown]

pumped storage (*electr.*) system for storing energy by using surplus power to lift water into a reservoir so that it may be lowered to turn a generator to produce electricity when needed

pum·per·nick·el (pámpərniḵ'l) *n.* a very dark, close-textured German wholemeal rye bread [G.]

pump·kin (pámpkin) *n.* any of several members of *Cucurbita*, fam. *Cucurbitaceae*, a genus of vines bearing a large, edible, globular fruit with a firm yellowish-orange rind, esp. *C. pepo* ‖ the fruit of such a plant [fr. older *pumpion* fr. F. fr. L. fr. Gk]

pump room a large room in a spa where medicinal waters are supplied

pun (pʌn) 1. *n.* a witticism involving the playful use of a word in different senses or of words which differ in meaning but sound alike 2. *v.i. pres. part.* **pun·ning** *past* and *past part.* **punned** to make a pun [etym. doubtful]

pun *pres. part.* **pun·ning** *past* and *past part.* **punned** *v.t.* to pound (earth etc.) in order to form it into a hard, dense mass [var. of POUND]

Pu·na (pu:ná) an island (29 miles long) in the Gulf of Guayaquil, S.W. Ecuador

pu·na (pú:nə) *n.* a cold high plateau between two ranges of the Andes in Peru ‖ the cold prevalent wind of this region [Span. fr. Quechua]

Pu·na de A·ta·ca·ma (pú:naðeɑ:takáma) a highland region (mainly 7,000–13,500 ft) in N.W. Argentina, with border peaks above 21,000 ft

punch (pʌntʃ) 1. *v.t.* to indent or make a hole in (metal, paper etc.) using a punch ‖ to make (this indentation or hole) ‖ to strike with the closed fist ‖ to herd (cattle) 2. *n.* the action of punching ‖ a blow with the closed fist ‖ forcefulness, *the story lacks punch* [etym. doubtful]

punch *n.* a tool, usually cylindrical but tapered at one end, used to emboss or make holes in metal, paper etc. ‖ a tool for forcing a bolt from a hole ‖ a tool for driving the head of a nail beneath a surface ‖ a tool used to stamp a die or impress a design [etym. doubtful]

punch *n.* a drink composed of sugar, spice and fruit, usually mixed with wine or liquor, and drunk hot or cold [Hindi *panch*, five (from the original number of ingredients)]

Punch and Judy the hero and heroine of a farcical puppet show, which originated in Italian popular comedy, spread to France and England in the 17th c., gained widespread popularity in the 18th c., and spread to the U.S.A.

punch·ball (pántʃbɔl) *n.* (*Br.*) a punching bag ‖ a game resembling baseball in which the ball is struck with the fist

punch card a card having a pattern of perforations representing data for use in a computer

punch-drunk (pántʃdrʌŋk) *adj.* (of a boxer) dazed through brain injury after receiving many punches on the head

pun·cheon (pántʃən) *n.* a short vertical auxiliary strut used to hold up a roof, esp. in a mine ‖ a slab of wood or split log used in flooring etc. ‖ a patterned die used by goldsmiths, silversmiths etc. to punch an impression in metal [O.F. *poinçon, poinchon*]

puncheon *n.* a cask varying in capacity from 70 to 120 gallons ‖ the amount such a cask holds [O.F. *ponçon, poinchon*]

punching bag (*Am.=Br.* punchball) a large leather ball, suspended from or tethered to a flexible upright, used for exercising the muscles of the arm, shoulder and chest

punch press a machine used for working metal by cutting, shaping or various combination dies

punch-up (pántʃʌp) *n.* (*Br.*) a street fight

punc·tate (pánkteit) *adj.* (*biol.*) dotted or shallowly pitted ‖ covered with very small dots or holes (e.g. in some skin diseases) [fr. Mod. L. *punctatus* fr. *punctum*, a point]

punc·ta·tion (pʌnktéiʃən) *n.* the action of making or condition of being punctate ‖ a small dot or depression on a plant, animal etc.

punc·til·i·o (pʌnktíli:ou) *pl.* **punc·til·i·os** *n.* a point of detail in very correct behavior or in ceremony ‖ careful attention to such details [Span. *puntillo* and Ital. *puntiglio*, dim. *of punto*, point]

punc·til·i·ous (pʌnktíli:əs) *adj.* paying scrupulous attention to points of detail in behavior, ceremony or matters touching one's honor [fr. F. *pointilleux* fr. Ital.]

punc·tu·al (pánktʃu:əl) *adj.* occurring, arriving etc. at the agreed, right or stated time ‖ of or pertaining to a point ‖ having the nature of a point **punc·tu·al·i·ty** *n.* the quality of being punctual [fr. M.L. *punctualis*]

punc·tu·ate (pánktʃu:eit) *pres. part.* **punc·tu·at·ing** *past* and *past part.* **punc·tu·at·ed** *v.t.* to mark the divisions of (written matter) into sentences, clauses etc. or to indicate exclamation, interrogation, direct speech etc. by inserting punctuation marks ‖ to interrupt by, or intersperse with, sound or gesture, *his speech was punctuated by cheers* ‖ *v.i.* to use punctuation [fr. M.L. *punctuare (punctuatus)*, to prick, point]

punc·tu·a·tion (pʌnktʃu:éiʃən) *n.* a punctuating or being punctuated ‖ the act, practice or system of inserting the correct marks to punctuate written matter ‖ punctuation marks [fr. M.L. *punctuatio (punctuationis)*]

punctuation mark one of the marks used to punctuate written matter, esp. the period or full stop (.), comma (,), colon (:), semicolon (;), exclamation mark (!), question mark (?), hyphen (-), dash (—), brackets ([]), parentheses (()), inverted commas or quotation marks (" "), apostrophe (')

punc·ture (pánktʃər) 1. *n.* the act of making a hole in something by pricking ‖ a small hole made thus, esp. one made accidentally in a tire 2. *v. pres. part.* **punc·tur·ing** *past* and *past part.* **punc·tured** *v.t.* to make a small hole in by pricking ‖ to make (a hole, perforation etc.) by pricking ‖ to sustain a puncture in, *the cyclist punctured his front tire* ‖ to destroy as if by pricking and deflating, *to puncture someone's self-esteem* ‖ *v.i.* (of a tire etc.) to sustain a puncture [fr. L. *punctura*]

pun·dit (pándit) *n.* (*pop.*) an expert [fr. PANDIT]

pun·gen·cy (pándʒənsi:) *n.* the quality or condition of being pungent

pun·gent (pándʒənt) *adj.* pricking or stinging to the taste or smell ‖ (of speech or writing) sharply biting ‖ (of remarks, a speech etc.) forthright and very much to the point [fr. L. *pungens (pungentis)* fr. *pungere*, to prick]

Pu·nic (pjú:nik) 1. *adj.* (*hist.*) pertaining to the ancient city of Carthage or its inhabitants ‖ (of the Carthaginians as regarded by the Romans) treacherous 2. *n.* the language of ancient Carthage, related to Phoenician [fr. L. *Punicus*]

Punic Wars three wars between Rome and Carthage in which Rome became the leading power in the W. Mediterranean. Early relations had been friendly, but the Carthaginian occupation of Sicily, prompted by commercial interest, threatened the trade and security of Rome's allies, the Greek cities of S. Italy. Rome's intervention to help Messina led to the 1st Punic War (264–241 B.C.). The Romans built a fleet to challenge the naval strength of Carthage and reduced Sicily to a Roman province (241 B.C.). The Carthaginians under Hamilcar and Hannibal conquered Spain (237–219 B.C.). Hannibal's attack (219 B.C.) on Saguntum, a Roman ally in Spain, led to the 2nd Punic War (218–201 B.C.). Hannibal crossed the Rhône and the Alps into Italy and defeated the Romans at Trasimene (217 B.C.) and Cannae (216 B.C.). But worn down by the tactics of Fabius Cunctator, who avoided further pitched battles, and deprived of the help of Hasdrubal, who was defeated and killed on the Metaurus (207 B.C.), Hannibal was recalled (203 B.C.), Scipio Africanus had driven the Carthaginians from Spain (206 B.C.) and invaded Africa. After his defeat by Scipio Africanus at Zama (202 B.C.), Hannibal advised acceptance of the harsh Roman terms of peace. Carthage nevertheless made a quick economic recovery. On the pretext of a Carthaginian attack on one of Rome's allies, Rome opened the 3rd Punic War (149–146 B.C.) landed in Africa and, under Scipio Aemilianus, destroyed Carthage completely (146 B.C.), as Cato the Elder had long urged should be done

pu·ni·ness (pjú:ni:nis) *n.* the condition or quality of being puny

pun·ish (pániʃ) *v.t.* to cause to suffer for some offense committed ‖ to prescribe a form of suffering in penalty for (an offense), *the crime was punished by death* ‖ (*pop.*) to treat harshly, *to punish an engine* ‖ (*pop.*) to deal (someone) hard blows ‖ *v.i.* to inflict punishment **to take a punishing** to be subjected to rough treatment **pún·ish·a·ble** *adj.* deserving or capable of being, or liable to be, punished **pún·ish·ment** *n.* a punishing or being punished ‖ the suffering given or received, *the punishment was a fine* [F. *punir (puniss-)*]

pu·ni·tive (pjú:nitiv) *adj.* concerned with punishing, *a punitive expedition* ‖ harsh or severely discriminatory, *punitive taxation* [F. *punitif (punitive)*]

Pun·jab (pándʒɑb) (*hist.*) a region of N.W. British India bordering the Himalayas, and consisting mainly of the basin of the Sutlej, Beas, Ravi, Chenab and Jhelum Rivers. It was partitioned (1947) between India and Pakistan ‖ (formerly East Punjab) the state (area 47,205 sq. miles, pop. 47,000,000) of India comprised of the eastern part of the former Punjab with Patiala, crossed by the Beas and Sutlej. Capital: Chandigarh. Products: irrigated crops (cereals, sugarcane, cotton), lumber, resin. This was partitioned (1966) into a Punjabi-speaking state (Punjab) and a Hindi-speaking state (Haryana) ‖ (formerly West Punjab) a region and former province (area 62,245 sq. miles) of Pakistan comprised of the western part of the former Punjab, a rich agricultural area (cereals, sugarcane, cotton) crossed by the Sutlej, Ravi, Chenab and Jhelum. Chief towns: Lahore, Rawalpindi

Pun·ja·bi, Pan·ja·bi (pʌndʒáɑbi:) 1. *n.* a native of the Punjab, India ‖ the Indic language spoken in the Punjab 2. *adj.* of or relating to the Punjab or its inhabitants [Hind.]

pun·ji stick (pándʒi:) (*mil.*) a bamboo spike set in camouflaged trap to wound the enemy

punk (pʌŋk) 1. *n.* wood rotted by a fungus, sometimes used as tinder ‖ amadou [origin unknown]

punk 1. *n.* a person, esp. a young one, regarded as inferior 2. *adj.* (*pop.*) worthless, of poor quality [etym. doubtful]

punk rock hard rock music created by and for the working-class English, in the late 1970s and subsequently popular in the U.S.A. — **punk** *adj.* of punk rock music; of the style of dress associated with punk rock musicians and their admirers. *Cf* NEW WAVE

pun·ner (pánər) *n.* a heavy-headed tool used for punning earth etc.

pun·net (pánit) *n.* (*Br.*) a chip basket [origin unknown]

pun·ster (pánstər) *n.* a person who makes puns

punt (pʌnt) 1. *n.* a long, shallow, square-ended, flat-bottomed boat, usually propelled by thrusting a long pole with a two-pronged iron end on the riverbed 2. *v.t.* to propel (someone or something) in this way ‖ *v.i.* to go by punt [O.E. fr. L.]

punt 1. *v.t.* (*football, rugby*) to kick (the ball) as it drops from the hands and before it bounces on the ground ‖ *v.i.* to punt a football 2. *n.* a kick made in this way [etym. doubtful]

punt 1. *v.i.* (*gambling*) to bet against the bank ‖ (*Br.*) to gamble 2. *n.* (*gambling*) a bet made against the bank [fr. F. *ponter*]

Pun·ta A·re·nas (púntaɑrénɑs) a port (pop. 67,600) of Chile on the Strait of Magellan, the southernmost town in the world

Pun·ta del Es·te (pú:ntadeléste) a seaside resort in S. Uruguay, in the state of Maldonado. It served (1961) as site of the Inter-American Economic and Social Council Conference, which created the Alliance for Progress, and (1962) as site of the eighth foreign ministers conference which by a bare two-thirds majority suspended Cuba from membership in the Organization of American States

pun·ty (pánti:) *pl.* **pun·ties** *n.* an iron rod used in shaping hot glass [perh. fr. F. *pontil*]

pu·ny (pjú:ni:) *comp.* **pu·ni·er** *superl.* **pu·ni·est** *adj.* much below normal in development, size or strength [fr. PUISNE]

pup (pʌp) 1. *n.* a puppy ‖ a young seal 2. *v.i. pres. part.* **pup·ping** *past* and *past part.* **pupped** (of a bitch) to bring forth young **to sell someone a pup** to sell someone something which proves to be worthless

pu·pa (pjú:pə) *pl.* **pu·pae** (pjú:pi:), **pu·pas** *n.* the stage in the metamorphosis of an insect between the larva and the imago, in which the insect is enclosed in a hardened case ‖ an insect in this stage **pu·pal** (pjú:pəl) *adj.* **pu·pate** (pjú:peit) *pres. part.* **pu·pat·ing** *past* and *past part.* **pu·pat·ed** *v.i.* to pass into or through the pupal stage **pu·pá·tion** *n.* [Mod. L. fr. L. *pupa*, doll]

pu·pil (pjú:p'l) *n.* a person, esp. a child, receiving tuition ‖ (*Rom. and Scot. civil law*) a child under the age of puberty in the care of a guardian [F. *pupille*, an orphan who is a minor]

pupil *n.* the aperture in the iris of the eye, contracted or dilated by the muscles of the iris to control the amount of light entering the eye [F. *pupille*]

pu·pil·age, pu·pil·lage (pjú:p'lidʒ) *n.* the state or period of being a pupil

Pu·pin (pu:pí:n, pu:pí:n), Michael Idvorsky (1858–1935), U.S. physicist who invented devices to extend the range of long-distance telephony, and discovered (1896) secondary X-ray radiation

pu·pip·a·rous (pju:pípərəs) *adj.* (*zool.*, e.g. of certain parasitic insects) bringing forth young already developed to the pupal stage [fr. PUPA+L. *parere*, to bring forth]

pup·pet (pʌ́pit) *n.* a small model of a human being or an animal with mobile limbs controlled by strings or wires, or made in the form of a glove and operated by a hand inserted in it. Texts are written and miniature stages made for puppet shows ‖ a person whose actions are initiated and controlled by the will of another **pup·pet·eer** (pʌpitíər) *n.* a person who operates puppets **púp·pet·ry** *n.* the art of making or operating puppets [fr. POPPET]

puppet valve a valve operated by the vertical rise and fall of a disk, ball etc.

pup·py (pʌ́pi) *pl.* **pup·pies** *n.* a young dog ‖ (*old-fash.*) a bad-mannered, selfsatisfied young man as seen by an older person [perh. fr. F. *poupée*, doll]

puppy love calf love

pup tent a simple tent for shelter, without side walls, such as U.S. soldiers carry in their pack

Pu·ra·cé (pu:rasé) an active volcano (15,420 ft) in S.W. central Colombia

Pu·ra·nas (puránəz) a group of 18 sacred Sanskrit poems comprised chiefly of mythical and historical legends concerning the creation of the universe, the gods and the era of the lawgivers and patriarchs, in direct tradition with earlier Vedic literature and law books [Skr. =of former times]

Pur·beck marble (pə́:rbek) a fine-grained, metamorphosed limestone from Purbeck, Dorset, England, used for building

pur·blind (pə́:rblaind) *adj.* partially blind ‖ unable to understand or perceive the obvious truth [M.E. *pur blind*, quite blind]

Pur·cell (pə́:rs'l), Henry (1659–95), English composer. His many vocal and instrumental compositions include much important church music and music for state occasions. His works for the theater include 'King Arthur' (1691), 'The Fairy Queen' (1692) and the opera 'Dido and Aeneas' (c. 1689)

Pur·chas (pə́:rtʃəs), Samuel (c. 1575–1626), English author. His collections of travelers' tales 'Purchas his Pilgrimage' (1613) and 'Hakluytus Posthumus' (1625) are often inaccurate but contain valuable historical material

pur·chase (pə́:rtʃəs) 1. *v.t. pres. part.* **pur·chas·ing** *past* and *past part.* **purchased** to acquire by paying money ‖ to acquire at the cost of sacrifice, work, exposure to danger etc. ‖ (*law*) to become the owner of (real estate) otherwise than by inheritance ‖ to move or raise by means of a lever, pulley etc. 2. *n.* the act of purchasing ‖ a thing purchased ‖ (in assessing value) annual yield in rent, *worth 20 years' purchase* ‖ mechanical advantages gained by the use of a pulley, lever etc. ‖ a device, e.g. a lever or pulley, by which this may be gained ‖ a hold or position in which leverage may be applied [A.F. *porchacier*, to seek to obtain]

purchase tax (*Br.*) a tax levied at varying percentages on the sale of certain kinds of consumer goods

pur·dah (pə́:rdə) *n.* the practice of secluding women from the sight of all men except the head of the family, by screens and curtains in the home or by veils outside it, maintained esp. in India ‖ a curtain serving to secure this seclusion **in purdah** secluded in this way [Urdu and Pers. *pardah*, veil]

pure (pjuər) *comp.* **pur·er** *superl.* **pur·est** *adj.* (of a substance) free from the presence of any other substance, *pure gold* ‖ free from contamination or admixture, *pure drinking water* ‖ free from moral guilt, *pure intentions* ‖ (*fig.*) unalloyed, *pure stupidity, pure joy* ‖ chaste, *a pure girl* ‖ not lascivious, *pure thought* ‖ not turned or related to practical use, *pure mathematics* (cf. APPLIED) ‖ (*genetics*) homozygous ‖ (of an animal) with an unmixed ancestry ‖ (*phon.*, of a vowel) not diphthongized ‖ (of a language) free from foreign elements ‖ (*philos.*) a priori ‖ (*phys.*, of a note) due to one simple periodic vibration, unmixed with any overtones [O.F. *pur*]

pure·bred 1. (pjuərbréd) *adj.* of a recognized breed, unmixed by crossbreeding 2. (pjúərbred) *n.* an animal which is pure bred

pure culture (*bot.*) a culture containing one strain of e.g. algae or fungi

pu·rée (pjuréi, pjurí:) 1. *n.* a thick liquid prepared by forcing cooked fruit or vegetables through a sieve ‖ a thick soup prepared in this way 2. *v.t.* to make a purée of (fruits or vegetables) [F.]

pure·ly (pjúərli) *adv.* in a pure way ‖ only, merely, *purely by chance*

pur·ga·tion (pə:rgéiʃən) *n.* a purging or being purged ‖ the purging of sin, esp. the process of spiritual purification in purgatory [O.F. *purgacion*]

pur·ga·tive (pə́:rgətiv) 1. *adj.* having the quality of purging (esp. the bowels) 2. *n.* a medicine which has this quality [F. *purgatif* (*purgative*)]

pur·ga·to·ri·al (pə:rgətɔ́ri:əl) *adj.* serving to expiate sin ‖ of or like purgatory [fr. L.L. *purgatorius*]

pur·ga·to·ry (pə́:rgətəri:, pə́:rgətɔ:ri:) *pl.* **pur·ga·to·ries** *n.* a condition or place of purification, esp. (*Roman Catholicism*) the state or place where the souls of the departed, though in a condition of grace, are purified by suffering before they enter paradise ‖ a condition of suffering, *it was purgatory to have to listen* [M.L. *purgatorium*]

purge (pə:rdʒ) 1. *v. pres. part.* **purg·ing** *past* and *past part.* **purged** *v.t.* to cause (the bowels) to be evacuated by administering or taking a purgative ‖ to remove undesirable elements from, *to purge a political party* ‖ to make expiation for, *to purge a sin* ‖ to clear (oneself or another) of a charge or suspicion 2. *n.* a purging or being purged ‖ a purgative [O. F. *purgier*]

Pu·ri (púəri:) (formerly also Jagannath) a port (pop. 72,712) of Orissa, India, on the Bay of Bengal, among the most sacred of Hindu pilgrimage places. Temple (12th c.) to Krishna under the name of Jagannath (*JUGGERNAUT)

pu·ri·fi·ca·tion (pjuərifikéiʃən) *n.* a purifying or being purified **the Purification** the Church festival (Feb. 2 in the Western Church) commemorating the presentation of Christ in the Temple at the end of the ritual time of purification of the Virgin Mary [O.F.]

pu·ri·fi·ca·tor (pjúərifikeitər) *n.* someone who or that which cleanses, esp. (*eccles.*) a cloth used to wipe clean the chalice, the paten, and the fingers and lips of the celebrant of the Eucharist [fr. L. *purificare*, to purify]

pu·ri·fi·ca·to·ry (pjurífikətɔri:, pjurífikətɔ:ri:) *adj.* serving to purify [fr. L.L. *purificatorius*]

pu·ri·fy (pjúərifai) *pres. part.* **pu·ri·fy·ing** *past* and *past part.* **pu·ri·fied** *v.t.* to make pure by removing impurities ‖ to free from guilt or sin ‖ to free from corrupting elements [F. *purer*]

Pu·rim (púərim) *pl. n.* (construed as *sing.*) a Jewish festival commemorating the rescue of the Jews by Esther, celebrated on the 14th day of Adar (*JEWISH CALENDAR) [Heb. *pūrīm*, pl. of *pūr*, lot]

pu·rine (pjúəri:n) *n.* a crystalline heterocyclic nitrogen base ($C_5H_4N_4$) related to the pyrimidines and to uric acid ‖ any of a group of derivatives of purine, some of which (e.g. adenine and guanine) are hydrolysis products of nucleic acids [fr. G. *purin* fr. L.]

pu·rism (pjúərizəm) *n.* strict emphasis on purity, esp. in language ‖ an instance of this [fr. F. *purisme*]

pur·ist (pjúərist) *n.* a person who places great emphasis or overemphasis on linguistic purity (freedom from foreign words or bastard forms etc.) ‖ a person, who will admit no departures from some chosen method, technique or ideal of perfection [fr. F. *puriste*]

Pu·ri·tan (pjúəritən) *n.* (*hist.*) a member of a Protestant movement in England (16th and 17th cc.) which sought to purify worship in the Church of England by excluding everything for which authority could not be found in the Bible **pu·ri·tan** 1. *n.* a person who seeks to regulate his own way of life and that of the community by a narrow moral code, esp. someone who intolerantly denounces many usual pleasures as sinful or corrupting 2. *adj.* of or relating to the Puritans **pu·ri·tán·ic, pu·ri·tán·i·cal** *adjs* **Pú·ri·tan·ism, pú·ri·tan·ism** *ns* [L. *purus*, pure or *puritas*, purity]
—Puritanism arose (1560s) as a protest against the ecclesiastical settlement of Elizabeth I. Puritans objected to the liturgy, vestments and episcopal organization of the Church of England, as not being warranted by the Scriptures. Sharp divisions arose among those Puritans who would be content with moderate reform, the Presbyterians (who wanted to abolish episcopacy), and the Brownists (who favored Congregationalism). Puritanism grew more vociferous and took on political overtones at the end of Elizabeth's reign and under the early Stuarts, culminating in the English Civil War and triumphing under Cromwell. Episcopacy returned with the Restoration (1660) and the Puritans became known as dissenters. Meanwhile in New England the Pilgrims (1620) had founded the first of several successful Puritan settlements

Puritan Revolution (*Eng. hist.*) the constitutional conflicts of the reigns of James I (1603–25) and Charles I (1625–49) and the English Civil War

pu·ri·ty (pjúəriti:) *n.* the state or quality of being pure [O.F. *purte*]

Pur·kin·je (pə:rkíndʒi:), Johannes Evangelista (1787–1869), Czech physiologist and microscopist. He is particularly noted for his ophthalmological studies

purl (pə:rl) 1. *n.* a stitch in knitting in which the yarn is held in front of the work and the right needle is inserted into a stitch in front of the left needle to form a new stitch (cf. KNIT) ‖ (*Br.*) an edging of small loops on lace, ribbon etc. ‖ an edging of twisted gold or silver thread ‖ the gold or silver thread used in this 2. *v.t.* to invert (stitches) in knitting ‖ to make (a garment) in purl stitches ‖ to border or decorate with purl *v.i.* to do purl stitches [etym. doubtful]

purl 1. *v.i.* (of little streams) to flow in eddies, making pleasing soft sounds 2. *n.* the sound or movement of purling [akin to Norw. *purla*, to bubble up]

purl·er (pə́:rlər) *n.* (*Br.*, *pop.*) a heavy headlong fall

pur·lieu (pə́:rlu:, pə́:rlju:) *n.* (*Eng. hist.*) a tract of royal forest restored to private ownership but still subject to forest laws ‖ (*pl.*) the region immediately surrounding a town, city etc., the outskirts [A.F. *puralée*]

pur·lin, purline (pə́:rlin) *n.* a horizontal beam supported by the principals of a roof and itself supporting the common rafters [etym. doubtful]

pur·loin (pə:rlɔ́in, pə́:rlɔin) *v.t.* to steal [A. F. *purloigner*]

pur·ple (pə́:rp'l) 1. *n.* a composite deep color of red and blue ‖ a pigment, fabric etc. of this color ‖ Tyrian purple **the purple** royal or very noble rank 2. *adj.* of the color purple 3. *v. pres. part.* **pur·pling** *past* and *past part.* **pur·pled** *v.i.* to assume a purple color ‖ *v.t.* to make purple [O.E.]

Purple Heart a heart-shaped medal awarded to U.S. servicemen for wounds received in action

purple of Cassius a mixture of stannic oxide and colloidal gold, used as a purple pigment and in making ruby glass

purple passage (in a book, play etc.) a passage overcharged with emotive words and sentiments

purple patch a purple passage

pur·plish (pə́:rpliʃ) *adj.* having a purple tinge

pur·ply (pə́:rpli:) *adj.* purplish

pur·port 1. (pə:rpɔ́rt, pə:rpɔ́urt) *v.t.* (*rhet.*) to have as meaning or purpose, *what do his actions purport?* ‖ (with 'to be') to be meant to appear, *the letter purports to be in his writing* 2. (pə́:rpɔrt, pə́:rpɔurt) *n.* the meaning of a document, speech etc. [A.F. *purporter*]

pur·pose (pə́:rpəs) *pres. part.* **pur·pos·ing** *past* and *past part.* **pur·posed** *v.t.* (*old-fash.*) to have as intention (to do something) [O.F. *porposer*]

purpose *n.* a result which it is desired to obtain and which is kept in mind in performing an action ‖ (*old-fash.*) willpower, *weak of purpose* **on purpose** deliberately, intentionally ‖ with a specific intention, *he came on purpose to see them* **to no (little, good) purpose** with no (little, good) effect **to the purpose** relevant **púr·pose·ful** *adj.* serving or having a purpose **púr·pose·less** *adj.* **púr·pose·ly** *adv.* on purpose **púr·pos·ive** *adj.* purposeful [A.F.]

pur·po·siv·ism (pə́:rpəsivizəm) *n.* (*psych.*) approach to psychological analysis based on theory that behavior is purposeful and that a person is responsible for his or her condition and destiny

pur·pu·ra (pə́:rpjərə) *n.* the occurrence of multiple small purplish hemorrhages in the skin and mucous membranes, due to a variety of blood and blood vessel disorders **pur·pu·ric** (pə:rpjúərik) *adj.* [L.=purple]

pur·pure (pə́:rpjər) *n.* (*heraldry*) purple [O.E. fr. L.]

purr (pə:r) **1.** *n.* the soft, intermittent vibratory sound made by a contented cat ‖ a similar sound, *the purr of an engine* **2.** *v.i.* to make this sound [imit.]

purse (pə:rs) **1.** *n.* a small container for coins etc., carried in a pocket or handbag ‖ a handbag ‖ a sum of money collected for a charity, or offered as a gift or prize ‖ (*rhet.*) financial resources ‖ a baglike receptacle **to hold the purse strings** to control the money in a household etc. **2.** *v.t. pres. part.* **pursing** *past* and *past part.* **pursed** (sometimes with 'up') to pucker, *she pursed her lips in displeasure* [O.E. purs, prob. fr. L.L. *bursa*]

purs·er (pə́:rsər) *n.* a ship's officer responsible for accounts etc. and for the welfare of passengers on a passenger boat [PURSE n.]

purs·lane (pə́:rslin, pə́:rslein) *n. Portulaca oleracea,* fam. *Portulacaceae,* a garden annual, eaten raw in salads or boiled [O.F. *porcelaine*]

pur·su·ance (pərsú:əns) *n.* the act of pursuing an end, object etc. ‖ the carrying out of a plan etc.

pur·su·ant (pərsú:ənt) **1.** *adj.* (*rhet.*) pursuing **2.** *adv.* (with 'to') in accordance with, *pursuant to the act* [O.F. *porsuiant, poursuiant*]

pur·sue (pərsú:) *pres. part.* **pur·su·ing** *past* and *past part.* **pur·sued** *v.t.* to follow in order to capture, overtake etc., *to pursue a thief* ‖ to harass (someone) persistently, *bad luck pursued him* ‖ to inflict persistent attentions on (someone) ‖ to continue with, *to pursue one's studies* ‖ to engage in, *to pursue a hobby* ‖ to go on talking about, *we will not pursue the subject* ‖ *v.i.* to go in pursuit ‖ to resume an argument or narrative after interruption [O.F. *poursuir*]

pur·suit (pərsú:t) *n.* the act of pursuing‖ the act of proceeding with or towards an aim ‖ an occupation, *an aimless pursuit* [O.F. *poursuite*]

pur·sui·vant (pə́:rsivənt, pə́:rsiwvənt) *n.* (*heraldry*) an officer of arms of lower rank than a herald [O.F. *poursuivant,* following]

pur·sy (pə́:rsi:) *adj.* corpulent ‖ shortwinded [fr. PURSE]

pu·ru·lence (pjúəruləns, pjúərjuləns) *n.* the state of being purulent ‖ pus [fr. L.L. *purulentia*]

pu·ru·lent (pjúərulənt, pjúərjulənt) *adj.* consisting of, or exuding pus [fr. L. *purulentus*]

Pu·rús (pu:rú:s) a river (2,000 miles long) flowing from S.E. Peru into E. Brazil, joining the Amazon above Manaus. It is navigable for river steamers for 800 miles, and for small boats for most of its length

pur·vey (pə:rvéi) *v.t.* (*old-fash.*) to supply (groceries) as a commercial activity ‖ to provide (information) [A.F. *porveier, purveier*]

pur·vey·ance (pə:rvéiəns) *n.* the act of purveying ‖ that which is purveyed ‖ (*Eng. hist.*) the royal right to buy provisions, services and supplies at a price fixed by the purveyors [O.F. *porveaunce, purveaunce*]

pur·vey·or (pə:rvéiər) *n.* someone who deals in groceries, esp. on a large scale ‖ (*Eng. hist.*) a royal agent who bought supplies under the right of purveyance [A.F. *purveür, purveuor*]

pur·view (pə́:rvju:) *n.* the extent of the meaning of a document ‖ the extent of the knowledge, authority or responsibility etc. of a person, group etc., *the matter lies outside his purview* ‖ (*law*) that part of a statute which includes the enacting clauses [A.F.=provided]

pus (pʌs) *n.* yellowish-white fluid matter, produced by infected body tissue, and composed of bacteria and disintegrated tissue [L.]

Pu·san (pú:sán) (*Jap.* Fusan) the chief port (pop. 2,879,600) of South Korea, on the east coast, exporting rice, soybeans etc. Industries: shipbuilding, textiles, rubber, food processing. University

Pu·sey (pjú:zi:), Edward Bouverie (1800–82), British churchman. He became the leader of the Oxford movement after Newman had been received into the Roman Catholic Church

Pu·sey·ism (pjú:zi:izəm) *n.* the Oxford movement **Pú·sey·ite** *n.* an adherent of this [after E. B. *Pusey*]

push (puʃ) **1.** *v.t.* to apply a force to (something) in order to make it move away from the person or thing applying the force (opp. PULL) ‖ to move (something) away or forward by applying such a force, *to push a bicycle uphill* ‖ to make (a way) by forcing obstacles aside ‖ (with 'up', 'down', 'along' etc.) to cause to move by exerting pressure ‖ (with 'up') to cause (something) to increase as if under pressure, *the wage increase pushed up prices* ‖ to exert influence upon (someone) so that he acts in a desired way, *they pushed him into doing it* ‖ to force toward or beyond the limits of capacity or endurance, *they pushed the child too hard at school* ‖ to develop (an idea etc.), esp. to an extreme degree ‖ to urge the qualities of (a person or thing) in order to secure some advantage ‖ to stimulate (someone) in his will to succeed ‖ to make a steady effort to secure recognition for (a claim) ‖ *v.i.* to apply a force to something in order to make it move away from the person or thing applying the force ‖ to move by the application of such force ‖ to make a steady effort towards some end, *to push for more pay* ‖ to advance, esp. with persistence or energy **to be pushed for time** (or **money**) to be short of time (or money) **to push off** (*pop.*) to leave **to push on** to proceed, esp. with determination **to push one's luck** to act rashly, take a dangerous risk **2.** *n.* the act of pushing ‖ an instance of this ‖ a force which pushes ‖ (*mil.*) an offensive ‖ the ineluctable moment of decision, *when it came to the push* ‖ influence, *to use push* ‖ self-assertion, aggressive drive **at a push** (*Br.*) if absolutely necessary **to get the push** (*Br.*) to be dismissed **to give (someone) the push** (*Br.*) to dismiss (someone) [F. *pousser*]

push·ball (púʃbɔl) *n.* a game played by two teams of usually 11 each, in which a 50-lb ball, 6 ft in diameter, is pushed toward either of two opposite goals ‖ this ball

push button a device which, when pressed with the finger, makes or breaks an electrical circuit and so controls an electrical mechanism

push-button dialing making a telephone connection by pushing buttons, using Bell System Touch Tone or similar equipment

push·cart (púʃkɑrt) *n.* a hand-pushed cart used esp. by street vendors

push·chair (púʃtʃɛər) *n.* (*Br.*) a stroller (child's wheeled chair)

push·down, pushdown list, or **pushdown stack** (púʃdaun) *n.* (*computer*) a list on which the last item stored is the first item retrieved, and the first item is the second item, the second the third, etc.

push·er (púʃər) *n.* a person who is aggressive in furthering his own career ‖ (*colloq.*) one who sells drugs illegally

push·ing (púʃiŋ) *adj.* aggressively self-assertive, esp. for self-advancement

Push·kin (púʃkin), Alexander Sergeievich (1799–1837), Russian poet, novelist and short-story writer. Some of his most important poetical works are 'The Captive of the Caucasus' (1822), 'Boris Godunov' (1825) and 'Eugene Onegin' (1825–33). His best-known prose work is 'The Captain's Daughter' (1836)

push·o·ver (púʃouvər) *n.* (*pop.*) something very easy to accomplish, or very easily accomplished ‖ (*pop.*) a person easily persuaded, tricked etc.

push·pin (púʃpin) *n.* a short pin with a large, often colored, head, used to mark positions on a map etc.

push shot (*billiards*) a shot in which the cue stays in contact with the cue ball until it strikes the object ball or in which the cue strikes the cue ball twice

Push·tu, Pash·tu (pʌ́ʃtu:) *n.* the principal language of Afghanistan, an Iranian language spoken by about 4 millions [Pers. *Pashtō*]

push-up (púʃʌp) (*Am.=Br.* press-up) *n.* an exercise in which a person pushes himself up from a face-down prone position by placing his palms on the ground or floor at shoulder level and straightening his arms (while keeping the trunk and legs rigidly straight) and lets himself down by bending his arms

pu·sil·la·nim·i·ty (pju:sələnímiti:) *n.* the quality of being pusillanimous [F. *pusillanimité*]

pu·sil·lan·i·mous (pju:səlǽnəməs) *adj.* showing a lack of moral courage [fr. eccles. L. *pusillanimis* fr. *pusillus,* very small+*animus,* mind, spirit]

puss (pus) *n.* (pet name for) a cat [origin unknown]

puss·y (púsi:) *pl.* **puss·ies** *n.* (pet name for) a cat

puss·y·foot (púsi:fut) *v.i.* (*pop.*) to avoid committing oneself

pussy willow either of two species of willow bearing large silky catkins, *Salix capera* and *S. discolor*

pus·tu·lar (pʌ́stʃulər) *adj.* like pustules ‖ covered with pustules [fr. Mod. L. *pustularis*]

pus·tu·late 1. (pʌ́stʃulit) *adj.* covered with pustules **2.** (pʌ́stʃuleit) *v. pres. part.* **pus·tu·lat·ing** *past* and *past part.* **pus·tu·lat·ed** *v.t.* to cause to form into pustules ‖ *v.i.* to form into pustules [fr. L.L. *pustulare (pustulatus)*]

pus·tule (pʌ́stʃu:l) *n.* a tiny abscess on the skin surface ‖ (*zool.*) a warty excrescence on the skin, e.g. in toads ‖ (*bot.*) a small wart or swelling on a leaf, either natural or caused by parasitic influence [fr. L. *pustula*]

pus·tu·lous (pʌ́stʃuləs) *adj.* pustular [fr. L.L. *pustulosus*]

put (put) **1.** *v. pres. part.* **put·ting** *past* and *past part.* **put** *v.t.* to cause to be in a specified place, position etc., *put the books on the table* ‖ to cause to be in a specified condition, situation, relationship etc., *to put someone's mind at rest* ‖ to submit for attention or consideration, *to put a proposal before a committee* ‖ to cause to be voted on, *to put a motion* ‖ (followed by 'to') to subject, *to put someone to expense* ‖ (usually followed by 'in' or 'into') to formulate, *put it in writing* ‖ (followed by 'at') to cause (a horse) to attempt to clear an obstacle ‖ (followed by 'on', 'upon') to impose, *to put a tax on beer* ‖ (followed by 'to' or 'into') to apply, bring to bear, *to put one's mind to a problem* ‖ (followed by 'on') to lay (blame, responsibility etc.) ‖ (followed by 'to' and pres. part.) to set (someone) to work of a specified kind, *to put the troops to digging trenches* ‖ (followed by 'in' or 'into') to invest, *to put one's money in copper shares* ‖ (followed by 'on') to gamble (money), *he put his last penny on that horse* ‖ to estimate, *he put the price at five pounds* ‖ (followed by 'on' or 'upon') to attribute, ascribe, *to put a high value on someone's service* ‖ to fix (a limit etc.), *to put an end to something* ‖ to throw (the shot) with a thrust from the shoulder ‖ *v.i.* (of a ship) to take a specified course, *to put out to sea* **to put about** to change the course of (a boat) ‖ (of a boat) to go on the contrary tack **to put across** to convey effectively the meaning, dramatic effect etc. of **to put aside** to place to one side, esp. as of no immediate use or importance ‖ to save (money etc.) for later use **to put away** to place (something) where it should be when not in use ‖ to save (money etc.) for later use ‖ (*pop.*) to consume (food or drink) ‖ to have an animal killed painlessly **to put back** to restore (something) to its former place ‖ to move the hands of (a clock) backwards ‖ (of a boat) to return to harbor **to put by** to save (money etc.) for later use **to put down** to stop (a rebellion etc.) by force ‖ to commit to writing ‖ to pay as deposit ‖ to place (bottled wine) in a cellar for drinking later ‖ (*Br.*) to have (an animal) killed painlessly ‖ (*Br.*) to preserve (eggs) ‖ to attribute, *to put a remark down to bad humor* ‖ to enter (an item) on a bill, account etc. **to put forward** to submit (a proposal etc.) for attention or consideration ‖ to propose (someone or oneself) as a candidate **to put in** to present (a claim) ‖ to do (a specified amount of a specified activity), *to put in two hours' weeding* ‖ (of a boat) to enter a port **to put it across (someone)** (*Br., pop.*) to deceive (someone) **to put it on** to pretend **to put it over on (someone)** (*pop.*) to deceive (someone) **to put it past (someone) to do (something)** (*neg.* and *interrog.*) to consider (someone) morally incapable of doing (something) **to put off** to postpone (something planned) ‖ to postpone an engagement made with (someone) ‖ to cause (someone) to cease to like something ‖ to cause (someone) to be unable to concentrate on something ‖ to avoid giving a direct answer to (someone) ‖ undertaking (something) **to put on** to clothe oneself with ‖ to assume (an attitude, expression etc.) deceptively ‖ to apply (a brake etc.) ‖

cause (a light etc.) to work ‖ to increase (speed) ‖ to present (an entertainment) to the public ‖ to move the hands of (a clock) forwards ‖ to acquire extra (weight) **to put out** to extinguish (a flame, light or fire) ‖ to cause (someone) to feel affronted ‖ to inconvenience ‖ to produce industrially ‖ to gouge out (eyes) ‖ to publish ‖ (baseball) to retire (a batter or a runner) ‖ (cricket) to cause (a batsman) to be out ‖ to dislocate (a joint) ‖ to give (work) to be done off the premises **to put over** to convey effectively the meaning, dramatic effect etc. of ‖ to postpone ‖ to succeed in doing (something) by craft or against odds **to put through** to cause to undergo, *he put her through great suffering* ‖ to negotiate (a business deal) ‖ to make (a telephone call) ‖ to connect (a telephone caller) with the person he is calling **to put through it** (*Br.*) to cause (someone) to suffer or to make a great physical or mental effort **to put together** to assemble **to put up** to offer (resistance, a fight etc.) ‖ to increase (a price etc.) ‖ to offer (someone) as candidate ‖ to offer oneself as candidate ‖ to provide (someone) with lodging ‖ to be provided with lodging at a hotel etc. ‖ to provide (financial backing) ‖ to stake (money) ‖ to pack in containers ‖ to publish (banns) ‖ to cause (game) to leave cover ‖ to preserve (fruit, vegetables etc.) ‖ to construct ‖ to offer (for sale, auction etc.) ‖ (with 'to') to incite (a person) to some action, esp. to some mischief or crime **to put upon** to impose on **to put up with** to endure, esp. without resentment or complaint **2.** *n.* a throw of the weight or shot ‖ (*med.*) the outer, darker part of the lenticular nucleus of the brain **3.** *adj.* (in the phrase) **to stay put** to remain in the same position, condition, situation etc. [O.E. *putian*, to thrust]

pu·ta·men (pjuːtéimin) *pl.* **pu·tam·i·na** (pjuːtǽminə) *n.* (*bot.*) the hard stone of a drupe, e.g. of a plum [L.=that which falls off in pruning]

pu·ta·tive (pjúːtətiv) *adj.* commonly thought to be, reputed [F. *putatif* or fr. L.L. *putativus*]

put-down (pútdaun) *n.* an act or statement to embarrass or denigrate another —**put down** *v.*

put·log (pútlog, pútlɔg, pátlog, pútlog) *n.* a short horizontal beam supporting scaffolding planks, with one end resting on the scaffolding and the other in a hole left or made for it in a wall [etym. doubtful]

put-on (pútɔn) *n.* a tease or spoof —**put-on** *adj.* —**put on** *n.*

put on hold *v.* (*colloq.*) to delay momentarily, from the telephone operator's procedure

Pu·to Shan (púːtoufán) a Buddhist sacred island in the Chushan Archipelago China: temples, monasteries

put-out (pútaut) *n.* (*baseball*) the act of retiring a baserunner or batter

pu·tre·fac·tion (pjuːtrifǽkʃən) *n.* the chemical decomposition of animal or vegetable tissue, esp. proteins, caused by bacteria, fungi etc. [O. F. or fr. L. *putrefactio* [*putrefactionis*]]

pu·tre·fac·tive (pjuːtrifǽktiv) *adj.* of, relating to or causing putrefaction [F. *putréfactif*]

pu·tre·fy (pjúːtrifai) *v. pres. part.* **pu·tre·fy·ing** *past* and *past part.* **pu·tre·fied** *v.i.* to become putrid ‖ *v.t.* to cause to become putrid [F. *putréfier*]

pu·tres·cence (pjuːtrésns) *n.* the condition of being putrescent

pu·tres·cent (pjuːtrésnt) *adj.* becoming putrid ‖ of or relating to putrefaction [fr. L. *putrescens* (*putrescentis*)]

pu·tres·ci·ble (pjuːtrésəbl) *adj.* liable to be putrefied

pu·tres·cine (pjuːtrésiːn) *n.* a poisonous ptomaine, $NH_2(CH_2)_4NH_2$, formed by the decomposition of animal tissue

pu·trid (pjúːtrid) *adj.* rotten, decayed ‖ of, relating to or caused by decay **pu·trid·i·ty** *n.* [fr. L. *putridus*]

puts and calls *PRIVILEGES

putsch (putʃ) *n.* a coup d'etat [G.=push fr. Swiss dial.]

putt (pʌt) **1.** *v.t.* (*golf*) to strike (the ball) gently so that it rolls across the green towards the hole ‖ *v.i.* (*golf*) to play the ball in this way **2.** *n.* (*golf*) a stroke made in this way [akin to PUT *v.*]

put·tee (pʌti) *n.* a cloth strip wound firmly around the leg from the ankle to the knee ‖ a leather gaiter [Hind. *paṭṭi*, bandage]

putt·er (pʌtər) *n.* (*golf*) a short-shafted wood or iron with an almost vertical face, used for putting

put·ter (pʌtər) *v.i.* to busy oneself in an agreeable though somewhat aimless way ‖ to loiter, dawdle [alt. fr. POTTER]

put·ty (pʌti) **1.** *n.* powdered chalk mixed with linseed oil to form a highly malleable mass which hardens when the oil oxidizes, used e.g. to hold window glass in its frame ‖ any of several other malleable cements made with linseed oil ‖ impure tin oxide used for polishing by jewelers **2.** *v.t. pres. part.* **put·ty·ing** *past* and *past part.* **put·tied** to fix, fill or cover with putty [F. *potée*, a potful]

Pu·tu·ma·yo (puːtuːmájo) a tributary (980 miles long) of the Amazon. It flows from W. Colombia. forming most of the southern frontier, into N.E. Brazil (as the Ica)

put-up (pútʌp) *adj.* (*pop.*) prearranged with guile, esp. with the connivance of insiders

Pu·vis de Cha·vannes (pyviːdʃævæn), Pierre (1824–98), French painter, notably of large-scale murals and decorative panels including 'Life of St Geneviève' (1898)

Puy-de-Dôme (pwiːdədoum) a department (area 3,090 sq. miles, pop. 580,000) of France in the N. Massif Central (*AUVERGNE, *BOURBONNAIS). Chief town: Clermont-Ferrand ‖ the summit (4.806 ft) of les Puys, a chain of volcanic cones in the N. Massif Central

puz·zle (pʌzl) **1.** *v. pres. part.* **puz·zling** *past* and *past part.* **puz·zled** *v.t.* to perplex (someone) ‖ *v.i.* to make a great mental effort to find a solution or meaning, *to puzzle over a problem* **to puzzle out** to find (a solution or meaning) by means of great mental effort **2.** *n.* a question or device which sets a problem to be worked out by ingenuity ‖ something which puzzles ‖ the state of being puzzled [etym. doubtful]

pya (pjɑ, piːɑ́) *n.* a monetary unit of Burma equal to one hundredth of a kyat ‖ a coin of the value of one pya [Burmese]

pyaemia *PYEMIA

pyc·nid·i·o·spore (piknídiəspɔr, piknídiəspour) *n.* a spore formed in a pycnidium

pyc·nid·i·um (piknídiəm) *pl.* **pyc·nid·i·a** (piknídiə) *n.* (*bot.*) a small flasklike organ or spermagonium which forms pycnidiospores and conidiophores, e.g. in various fungi [Mod. L. fr. Gk *puknos*, thick+-*idion*, dim. suffix]

pyc·nom·e·ter, pyk·nom·e·ter (piknómitər) *n.* a graduated glass vessel used to determine the variation of density of a liquid with variation of temperature [fr. Gk *puknos*, thick+METER]

pye-dog, pi-dog (páidɔg, páidog) *n.* a mongrel dog which hangs around Indian and other Asian villages

py·e·li·tis (paiəláitis) *n.* (*med.*) inflammation of the pelvis of the kidney [Mod. L. fr. Gk *puelos*, trough]

py·e·mi·a, py·ae·mi·a (paiːmiːə) *n.* (*med.*) pus in the blood, a condition causing multiple abscesses throughout the body **py·é·mic, py·ǽ·mic** *adj.* [Mod. L. fr. Gk *puon*, pus+*haima*, blood]

py·gid·i·um (paidʒídiəm) *pl.* **py·gid·i·a** (paidʒídiə) *n.* a caudal shield covering the abdomen of certain arthropods ‖ the terminal abdominal segment in certain insects [Mod. L. fr. Gk *pugidion*, dim. of *pugē*, rump]

Pyg·ma·li·on (pigméiliən) (*Gk mythol.*) Cypriot king and sculptor who fell in love with the statue he had made of a girl. He successfully begged Aphrodite to bring the statue to life

Pygmalion legendary king of Tyre, brother of Dido

pyg·my, pig·my (pígmi) **1.** *pl.* **pyg·mies, pig·mies** *n.* a person of very small stature **Pyg·my, Pig·my** *pl.* **Pyg·mies, Pig·mies** a member of a Negrillo people of very small stature of equatorial Africa ‖ a member of a mythical race of dwarfs described by ancient Greek authors as inhabiting Ethiopia or India **2.** *adj.* of or relating to a person of very small stature **Pyg·my, Pig·my** of or relating to the Pygmies [fr. L. *pygmaeus* fr. Gk fr. *pugmē*, length from elbow to knuckles]

pyjamas *PAJAMAS

pyk·nic (píknik) *adj.* (*anthrop.*) having an endomorphic physique [fr. Gk *puknos*, compact]

pyknometer *PYCNOMETER

py·lon (páilɔn) *n.* a lofty structure, typically of open steelwork, used esp. to carry electric cables etc. over a long span ‖ (*archit.*) a large monumental gateway having two truncated pyramidal towers, esp. on an ancient Egyptian temple [Gk *pulōn*, gateway]

py·lor·ic (pailórik, pailórik) *adj.* of or relating to the pylorus

py·lo·rus (pailórəs, pailóurəs) *pl.* **py·lo·ri** (pailórai, pailóurai) *n.* (*anat.*) the opening from the stomach into the intestine of vertebrates, usually including a muscular valve ‖ (in some invertebrates) a posterior division of the stomach [L.L. fr. Gk *pulōros*, gatekeeper]

Py·los (páilɒs) an ancient port of Messenia, S.W. Greece

Pym (pim), John (c. 1583–1643), English parliamentarian, one of the leaders of the opposition to Charles I, notably in the Long Parliament

Pyong·yang (pjóŋján) the capital (pop. 1,700,000) and industrial center of North Korea, founded c. 1122 B.C. Industries: anthracite mining (nearby), iron and steel, mechanical engineering. textiles, sugar, cement, chemicals, railway stock, light manufacturing. Ruins: tombs (1st c. B.C.), gates and Buddhist temples. University (1946)

py·or·rhe·a, py·or·rhoe·a (paiəríːə) *n.* (*med.*) a discharge of pus, esp. from the gums [Mod. L. Gk *puon*, pus+*rhoia*, a flow]

pyr·a·mid (pírəmid) **1.** *n.* (*geom.*) a solid figure of which the base is a polygon and the other faces are triangles with a common vertex ‖ any of the very large square-based stone monuments of this form, constructed by the ancient Egyptians as royal burial places, esp. during the Old Kingdom (c. 2614-2181 B.C.), and by the Aztecs and Mayas as centers of ritual worship. The huge pyramid of Khufu at Giza was one of the Seven Wonders of the World ‖ anything shaped thus ‖ a group of things piled up or arranged in this form ‖ (*anat.*) any of various parts resembling this form ‖ the shape of a well-organized staffing structure in relation to levels of responsibility or to age distribution, or any comparable organizational structure ‖ (*crystall.*) any crystal form having inclined faces which intersect all three axes of symmetry ‖ the series of buying operations in which a speculator pyramids on an exchange **2.** *v.t.* to build up in the form of a pyramid ‖ *i.* to engage in a series of buying operations during a continued rise, buying out of the paper profits made on the transactions **py·ra·mi·dal** (pirǽmid'l) *adj.* [L. *pyramis* (*pyramidis*)]

Pyramids, Battle of the a victory (July 1798) in which Napoleon defeated the Mamelukes and gained control of Egypt

py·rar·gy·rite (pairárdʒərait) *n.* a naturally occurring silver antimony sulfide, Ag_3SbS_3, having a rhombohedral crystalline form [fr. Gk *pur*, fire+*arguros*, silver]

pyre (páiər) *n.* a heaped mass of material for the burning of a corpse [fr. L. *pyra* fr. Gk]

py·rene (páiriːn) *n.* a yellow, crystalline hydrocarbon, $C_{16}H_{10}$, derived by distillation from coal tar [fr. Gk *pur*, fire]

pyrene *n.* (*bot.*) the seed of a drupelet [fr. Mod. L. *pyrena* fr. Gk]

Pyr·e·nees (pírəniːz) (*F.* les Pyrénées) the mountain range (270 miles long, mainly 6,000–9,000 ft high in the center, lower toward the coasts) separating France from Spain. Two main roads and two railways cross them by passes over 5,000 ft, but other main routes follow the coasts. The higher peaks are rugged, with perpetual snowfields, but the lower slopes serve as cattle and sheep pasture. The Spanish side is drier and less populated than the French. Industries: hydroelectricity, tourism

Pyrénées, Basses- *PYRÉNÉES ATLANTIQUES

Pyrénées, Hautes- *HAUTES-PYRÉNÉES

Py·ré·nées-At·lant·iques (piːreineizatlɑntik) a department (area 2,977 sq. miles, pop. 534,700) of S.W. France (*BÉARN *NAVARE, *BASQUE COUNTRY). Chief town: Pau

Py·ré·nées-O·rien·tales (piːreineizɔrjɑ̃ntæl) a department (area 1,598 sq. miles, pop. 299,500) of S. France (*ROUSSILLON). Chief town: Perpignan

Pyrenees, Treaty of the a treaty (1659) between France and Spain, in which Spain ceded Roussillon and part of Flanders to France and the marriage of Louis XIV and the infanta of Spain was arranged

py·re·thrum (pairíːθrəm) *n.* *Chrysanthemum coccineum*, fam. *Compositae*, which yields insecticide, or any of several garden perennials derived from it ‖ an insecticide obtained from the dried powdered flowers of the pyrethrum [L. fr. Gk *purethron*, feverfew]

py·rex·i·a (pairéksiːə) *n.* (*med.*) fever **py·rex·i·al, py·rex·ic** *adjs* [Mod. L. fr. Gk *purexis*]

pyr·he·li·om·e·ter (paiərhiːliːómitər) *n.* an instrument used to determine the solar constant

CONCISE PRONUNCIATION KEY: (**a**) æ, c**a**t; ɑ, c**a**r; ɔ f**a**wn; ei, sn**a**ke. (**e**) e, h**e**n; iː, sh**ee**p; iə, d**ee**r; ɛə, b**ea**r. (**i**) i, f**i**sh; ai, t**i**ger; əː, b**i**rd. (**o**) o, **o**x; au, c**ow**; ou, g**oa**t; u, p**oo**r; ɔi, r**o**yal. (**u**) ʌ, d**u**ck; u, b**u**ll; uː, g**oo**se; ə, b**a**cillus; juː, c**u**be. x, lo**ch**; θ, **th**ink; ð, bo**th**er; z, **Z**en; ʒ, cor**s**age; dʒ, sava**g**e; ŋ, ora**ng**utang; j, **y**ak; ʃ, **sh**ip; tʃ, fe**tch**; 'l, rabb**le**; 'n, redd**en**. Complete pronunciation key appears inside front cover.

of radiation [fr. PYRO-+ Gk *hēlios*, sun+METER]

pyr·i·dine (píridi:n) *n.* a heterocyclic compound, C_5H_5N, with an unpleasant smell and taste, used to make methylated spirit unpalatable, and as the basis of compounds used in medicine [fr. Gk *pur*, fire]

pyr·i·form (pírifɔrm) *adj.* (esp. of the forward aperture of the nasal canal in the skull) pear-shaped [fr. Mod. L. *pyriformis* fr. *pirum*. pear]

py·ri·meth·a·mine [$C_{12}H_{13}C1N_4$] (pairəméθəmi:n) *n.* (*pharm.*) an antimalarial drug; marketed as Daraprim

py·rim·i·dine (pairímidi:n) *n.* a crystalline, weakly basic, heterocyclic compound ($C_4H_4N_2$) ‖ any of a group of derivatives of pyrimidine, some of which (e.g. thymine and cytosine) are hydrolysis products of nucleic acids [altered fr. PYRIDINE]

py·rite (páirait) *n.* iron disulfide, FeS_2 [fr. L. *pyrites*, firestone fr. Gk]

py·ri·tes (pairáiti:z, páiraits) *pl.* **py·ri·tes** *n.* (*mineral.*) one of several disulfides of metals, e.g. of iron or copper occurring as ores **py·rit·ic** *adj.* [L.=firestone fr. Gk]

pyro- (páirou) *prefix* fire ‖ heat ‖ producing or derived from fire or heat ‖ causing fever [fr. Gk fr. *pur*, fire]

py·ro·chem·i·cal (pairoukémik'l) *adj.* pertaining to chemical changes at high temperatures

py·ro·clas·tic (pairouklǽstik) *adj.* (*geol.*, of a rock) formed of igneous material subjected to fragmentation [fr. PYRO-+Gk *klastos*, broken]

py·ro·e·lec·tric (pairouiléktrik) *adj.* of, relating to or acquiring pyroelectricity

py·ro·e·lec·tric·i·ty (pairouilektrísiti) *n.* the electric charges produced in various crystals by heating

py·ro·gal·lol (pairougǽlɔl) *n.* a crystalline phenol, $C_6H_3(OH)_3$, used as a developer in photography [fr. Gk *pur*, fire+GALLIC ACID]

py·ro·gen·ic (pairoudʒénik) *adj.* producing or produced by heat ‖ igneous in origin ‖ producing or produced by fever [fr. PYRO-+-*genic*, produced]

py·ro·lig·ne·ous (pairoulígni:əs) *adj.* produced by the destructive distillation of wood [F. *pyroligneux* fr. Gk *pur*, fire+L. *lignium*, wood]

pyroligneous acid an acid liquid produced by the destructive distillation of wood, the chief source of commercial acetic acid

py·ro·lu·site (pairoulú:sait) *n.* naturally occurring manganese dioxide, MnO_2 [fr. PYRO-+Gk *lousis*, a washing]

py·rol·y·sis (pairɔ́lisis) *n.* chemical decomposition by heat [Mod. L. fr. PYRO-+Gk *lusis*, a loosing]

py·ro·lyt·ic incinerator (pairəlítik) an incinerator that requires little oxygen for burning, reducing pollution and producing gas suitable for burning

py·ro·ma·ni·a (pairouméini:ə) *n.* an irrational compulsion to destroy by fire **py·ro·ma·ni·ac** (pairouméini:æk) *n.* **py·ro·ma·ni·a·cal** (pairoumənáiak'l) *adj.*

py·rom·e·ter (pairómitər) *n.* an instrument used to measure temperatures too high for ordinary thermometers **py·ro·met·ric** (pairoumétrik), **py·ro·met·ri·cal** *adjs* **py·róm·e·try** *n.*

py·ro·mor·phite (pairoumɔ́rfait) *n.* a naturally occurring crystalline, usually colored, double chloride and phosphate of lead, $PbCl·Pb_4(PO_4)_3$ [G. *pyromorphit* fr. Gk *pur*, fire+*morphē*, shape]

py·rone (páiroun) *n.* an unsaturated heterocyclic ring compound, $C_5H_4O_2$, used as the basis of yellow dyes [fr. PYRO-+Gk -*ōnē*, patronymic suffix]

py·rope (páiroup) *n.* a dark red variety of garnet, used as a gem [fr. L. fr. Gk *purōpos*, fiery-eyed]

py·ro·phor·ic (pairəfɔ́rik, pairəfórik) *adj.* igniting spontaneously ‖ (of an alloy) emitting sparks when scraped or struck [fr. Gk *purophoros* fr. *pur*, fire+*pherein*, to bear]

py·ro·sis (pairóusis) *n.* (*med.*) heartburn [Mod. L. fr. Gk]

py·ro·some (páirəsoum) *n.* a member of *Pyrosoma*, fam. *Pyrosomaditae*, a genus of highly phosphorescent compound ascidians of tropical seas, which unite into a free-swimming colony in the form of a hollow cylinder closed at one end [fr. Mod. L. *Pyrosoma* fr. Gk *pur*-, fire+*sōma*, body] .

py·ro·stat (páirəstæt) *n.* any mechanical device which automatically warns of a fire, or which sets in operation an extinguisher [fr. PYRO-+Gk *statēs*, one that causes to stand]

py·ro·sul·fu·ric acid, py·ro·sul·phu·ric acid (pairousʌlfjúərik) a crystalline acid, $H_2S_2O_7$, formed by combining sulfur trioxide with sulfuric acid

py·ro·tech·nic (pairoutéknik) *adj.* of or relating to pyrotechnics **py·ro·tech·ni·cal** *adj.*

py·ro·tech·nics *n.* the art of making or displaying fireworks ‖ (*pl.*) a brilliant or witty display **py·ro·tech·nist**, **py·ro·tech·ny** *ns* [fr. PYRO-+Gk *technikos* fr. *technē*, art]

py·ro·tox·in (pairoutóksin) *n.* one of various toxins capable of causing fever

py·ro·tron (páirətrɔn) *n.* device using magnetic mirrors in a tube surrounded by electric coils used to reflect charged particles; prevents end leaks in fusion research

py·rox·ene (pairóksi:n) *n.* any of a class of double silicates (e.g. of calcium and magnesium) occurring widely in igneous rocks **py·rox·en·ic** (pairaksénik) *adj.* **py·rox·e·nite** (pairóksənait) *n.* an igneous rock composed chiefly of pyroxene, with no olivine [fr. Gk *pur*, fire+*xenos*, stranger]

py·rox·y·lin, py·rox·y·line (pairóksəlin) *n.* any of the lower nitrates of cellulose, dissolved in an organic solvent (usually alcohol and ether) and used in making lacquers, celluloid etc. [F. *pyroxyline* fr. Gk *pur*, fire+*xulon*, wood]

pyr·rhic (pírik) *n.* an ancient Greek war dance performed in armor [fr. L. *pyrrhica* or Gk *purrhichē*]

pyrrhic 1. *n.* a metrical foot of two short syllables **2.** *adj.* of or composed of pyrrhics [fr. L. *pyrrhichius* fr. Gk]

Pyrrhic victory a victory won with terrible loss of life or otherwise at too heavy a cost [after the victory of PYRRHUS at Asculum (279 B.C.)]

Pyr·rho (pírou) (c. 360–c. 270 B.C.), Greek philosopher, founder of skepticism. He thought it impossible to arrive at any certain knowledge

and held that the wise man should not judge but should aim at a balanced imperturbability

Pyr·rho·nism (pírənizəm) *n.* the skeptical philosophy taught by Pyrrho ‖ philosopical skepticism

pyr·rho·tite (pírətait) *n.* a bronze-colored sulfide of iron, often with some nickel, occurring naturally [fr. Gk *purrhotēs*, redness]

Pyr·rhus (pírəs) (c. 318–272 B.C.), king of Epirus (295–272 B.C.). He invaded Italy to assist Tarentum (modern Tarento) against Rome, and defeated the Romans at Heraclea (280 B.C.) and at Asculum (279 B.C.), although with very heavy loss to his own army. After being defeated by the Romans at Beneventum (275 B.C.) he withdrew to Greece, where he was killed besieging Argos

Pyrrhus a son of Achilles who killed Priam at the siege of Troy and carried off Andromache

pyr·role, pyr·rol (píroul) *n.* a liquid azole, C_4H_3N, that is both a weak acid and base, found naturally in coal tar [Gk *purros*, reddish]

Py·thag·o·ras (piθǽgərəs) (c. 580–c. 500 B.C.), Greek mathematician and philosopher. He founded the Pythagorean school which believed in metempsychosis, thought that the soul imprisoned in the body could be purified by study, and followed a strict discipline of purity and self-examination. Pythagoras discovered the numerical ratios of intervals in the musical scale, and believed that the elements of numbers were the elements of the world. The so-called Pythagorean theorem, that the square on the hypotenuse of a right-angled triangle is equal to the sum of the squares on the other two sides, is attributed to his school

Py·thag·o·re·an (piθægərí:ən) **1.** *adj.* pertaining to Pythagoras, his followers or his teachings **2.** *n.* a follower of Pythagoras

Pyth·i·an (píθi:ən) *adj.* (*Gk mythol.*) pertaining to the oracle at Delphi or to Apollo as its patron ‖ of the games held every four years near Delphi in honor of Apollo's slaying of the Python [fr. L. *Pythius* fr. Gk fr. *Puthō*, old name for Delphi]

py·thon (páiθon, páiθən) *n.* a member of *Python*, fam. *Boidae*, a genus of nonvenomous snakes up to 30 ft long, which kill their prey by constriction, native to the Old World tropics ‖ any of several large snakes which kill by constriction

Python (*Gk mythol.*) a monstrous serpent which lived in a cave near Delphi and was killed by Apollo [L. fr. Gk fr. *Puthō*, old name for Delphi]

py·tho·ness (páiθənis) *n.* (*Gk mythol.*) a priestess of Apollo at Delphi [O.F. *phitonise* fr. M.L.]

py·u·ri·a (paijúəri:ə) *n.* (*med.*) the presence of pus in the urine, causing pain and frequency of micturition [fr. Gk *puon*, pus+*ouron*, urine]

pyx (piks) *n.* (*eccles.*) a vessel in which the Host is reserved ‖ (also **pix**) a box at a mint in which sample coins are reserved for assay [fr. L. *pyxis*, box fr. Gk]

pyx·id·i·um (piksídi:əm) *pl.* **pyx·id·i·a** (piksídi:ə) *n.* (*bot.*) a fruit capsule (e.g. in plantain) whose upper portion is dehisced transversely [Mod. L. fr. Gk *puxidion*, dim. of *púxis*, a box]

CONCISE PRONUNCIATION KEY: (a) æ, c*a*t; ɑ, c*a*r; ɔ f*aw*n; ei, sn*a*ke. **(e)** e, h*e*n; i:, sh*ee*p; iə, d*ee*r; ɛə, b*ea*r. **(i)** i, f*i*sh; ai, t*i*ger; ə:, b*i*rd. **(o)** o, *o*x; au, c*ow*; ou, g*oa*t; u, p*oo*r; ɔi, r*oy*al. **(u)** ʌ, d*u*ck; u, b*u*ll; u:, g*oo*se; ə, b*a*cillus; ju:, c*u*be. x, lo*ch*; θ, *th*ink; ð, bo*th*er; z, *Z*en; ʒ, cor*s*age; dʒ, sa*v*age; ŋ, ora*n*gutang; j, *y*ak; ʃ, *fi*sh; tʃ, fe*tch*; 'l, rabb*le*; 'n, redde*n*. Complete pronunciation key appears inside front cover.

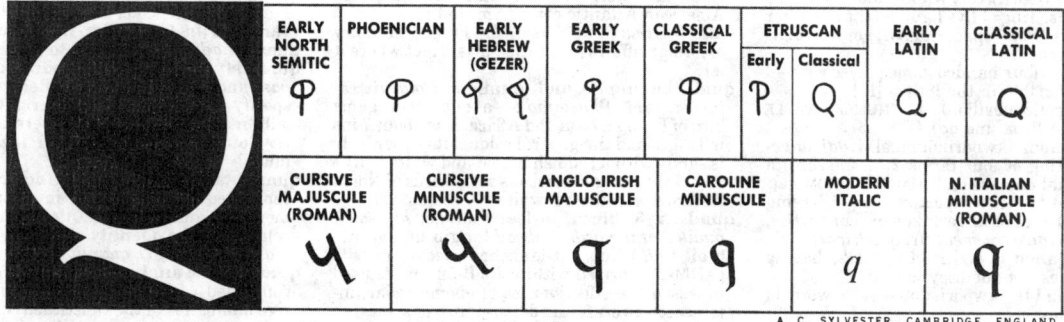

EARLY NORTH SEMITIC	PHOENICIAN	EARLY HEBREW (GEZER)	EARLY GREEK	CLASSICAL GREEK	ETRUSCAN		EARLY LATIN	CLASSICAL LATIN
					Early	Classical		

CURSIVE MAJUSCULE (ROMAN)	CURSIVE MINUSCULE (ROMAN)	ANGLO-IRISH MAJUSCULE	CAROLINE MINUSCULE	MODERN ITALIC	N. ITALIAN MINUSCULE (ROMAN)

A. C. SYLVESTER, CAMBRIDGE, ENGLAND

Development of the letter Q, beginning with the early North Semitic letter. Evolution of both the majuscule, or capital, letter Q and the minuscule, or lowercase, letter q are shown.

Q, q (kju:) the seventeenth letter of the English alphabet

Q *n.* **1.** symbol of one quadrillion [10^{18}] **2.** British terminal unit of heat equal to 1.055×10^{21} joules

Qaddafi, Muammar al- (muːɑmɑrɑlkɑdɑfiː) (1942–) Libyan head of state. An army colonel, he assumed power (1969) after leading a coup against King Idris I. He negotiated (1970) the removal of U.S. and British military bases. A Moslem fundamentalist, he instituted a cultural revolution (1973) that established the Koran as the basis of law. He took control of the Libyan oil industry (1973–4) and later abolished all private enterprise. A militant Arab nationalist, he has tried unsuccessfully to effect various mergers with Egypt, Syria, Tunisia, Chad and Morocco. Often accused by neighboring African countries of meddling in their internal political affairs, he also intervened militarily in a civil war in Chad. He has been accused of fostering international terrorism; various terrorist attacks around the world resulted in the U.S. bombing of Libya in 1986

Qajar *KAJAR

qat (kɒt) *n. Catha edulis,* fam. *Celastraceae,* a shrub cultivated in Arabia for the narcotic qualities of its leaves [Arab. *qāt*]

Qa·tar, Ka·tar (kútɑr) a sovereign independent state (area 4,000 sq. miles, pop. 250,000) occupying the Qatar peninsula on the west coast of the Persian Gulf. Capital: Doha (pop. 190,000). Port: Umm Said. Race and language: Arabic. Religion: Moslem. The land is a flat desert, with few oases. Traditional occupations: fishing, pearl diving. Industry: petroleum extraction (since 1949). Monetary unit: Saudi Arabian rial. Qatar was subject to Bahrain until 1868, and was under British protection (1916–71)

Qaz·vin, Kaz·vin (kɑzviːn) an agricultural market (pop. 138,527) of N.W. Iran at the foot of the Elburz Mtns. It was the capital of Persia (1514–90)

Q band (*electromag.*) band of radio frequency of 36–46 GHz

QC (*abbr.*) for **1.** quick-change convertible passenger-cargo jets **2.** quality control.

Q clearance the highest governmental security clearance, including availability to atomic secrets

Q fever (*med.*) an acute infectious disease caused by *Coxiella burnetii,* acquired by inhalation, ingestion, (milk) handling, and symptomized by fever, headache, malaise, and muscle pains

qi·vi·ut (kíːviːuːt) *n.* cashmerelike wool of the undercoat of the musk-ox

q-mes·sage (kjúmésidʒ) *n.* (*mil.*) a classified message relating to navigational dangers, navigational aids, mine areas, and searched or swept channels

Q point position and direction of a radar target, observed from two or more directions

Q rating system of measurement on tests of audience response to action

Q ratio ratio of the market value of a nonfinancial corporation to replacement cost of net assets

Q scale (*geol.*) unit of geological measurement of transverse waves of planetary tremors

QSO (*astron. acronym*) for quasi-stellar object

QSTOL (*acronym*) for quiet short takeoff and landing. *Cf* CTOL, STOL, VTOL

Q-switch (kjúswítʃ) *n.* a device that produces a powerful pulsed output from a laser after first creating a blockage. **—Q-switch** *v.* **—Q-switched** *adj.*

qua (kwei, kwɑ) *adv.* (*rhet.*) strictly in the capacity or character of, *the match qua match was a victory, but as sport it was lamentable* [L. abl. fem. sing. of *qui,* who]

Quaa·lude (kwáluːd) *n.* (*pharm.*) trade name and popular terms for methaqualone (which see). *also* lude

quack (kwæk) **1.** *n.* the call of a duck **2.** *v.i.* (of ducks) to utter this [imit.]

quack 1. *n.* a person who pretends to have medical knowledge ‖ a fraudulent person **2.** *adj.* fraudulent, bogus **quáck·er·y** *n.* [shortened fr. *quacksalver* fr. Du., perh. fr. *quacken.* to quack+*salf,* salve]

quad (kwɒd) *n.* (*printing*) a piece of type metal used for spacing etc., *an em quad* [abbr. of QUADRAT]

quad *n.* a quadrangle (courtyard or courtyard and its buildings) [abbr. of QUADRANGLE]

quad *adj.* of a size paper that is four times as large as the specified size, *quad demy* [abbr. or QUADRUPLE]

quad *n.* a quadruplet

quad·plex (kwɒ́dplɛks) *n.* a multiple dwelling consisting of four apartments. *also* fourplex

quad·ra·ge·nar·i·an (kwɒdrədʒənéəriːən) **1.** *n.* a person who is 40 years old or over but not yet 50 **2.** *adj.* having such an age [fr. L. *quadragenarius*]

Quad·ra·ges·i·ma (kwɒdrədʒésimə) *n.* the first Sunday in Lent [M.L. the forty days of Lent, fem. of *quadragesimus,* fortieth]

quad·ran·gle (kwɒ́dræŋgʼl) *n.* a plane figure with four sides, esp. a square or rectangle ‖ a courtyard surrounded by large buildings or the courtyard and its buildings **quad·rán·gu·lar** *adj.* [F.]

quad·rant (kwɒ́drənt) *n.* a quarter of a circle's circumference ‖ the area bounded by this and

the two radii drawn from its ends to the center of the circle ‖ a quarter of something, e.g. a sphere ‖ an instrument with a calibrated arc of 90°, used for measuring angles and formerly, before the sextant was developed, for measuring altitudes [fr. L. *quadrans (quadrantis),* fourth part]

Qua·dran·tids (kwɒdrǽntəds) *n.* (*astronomy*) a meteor shower with a small orbit; it occurs annually about January 31

quad·ra·phon·ic (kwɒdrəfónik) *adj.* of a sound system utilizing four channels to obtain high-fidelity sound reproduction. **—quadraphony** *n.*

quadraphonic recordings sound recordings made on four channels to provide high fidelity

quad·rat (kwɒ́drit) *n.* (*printing*) a quad [var. of older *quadraie* n., a square]

quad·rate (kwɒ́dreit) **1.** *v.i. pres. part.* **quad·rat·ing** *past* and *past part.* **quad·rat·ed** (with 'with') to conform, square, correspond **2.** *adj.* square or rectangular **3.** *n.* a quadrate bone [fr. L. *quadrare (quadraius),* to square]

quadrate bone a bone in birds and reptiles which articulates the lower jaw with the skull

quad·rat·ic (kwɒdrǽtik) **1.** *adj.* (*algebra*) of an expression which involves the square but no higher power of a term **2.** *n.* a quadratic expression or equation **quad·rát·ics** *n.* the branch of algebra dealing with quadratic equations [fr. L. *quadratus,* squared]

quad·ra·ture (kwɒ́drətʃər) *n.* (*math.*) the act of finding a square with an area exactly equal to that of a curvilinear figure ‖ (*astron.*) a position in which a celestial body is in a relation of 90° or 70° to another celestial body ‖ (*astron.*) one of two points on an orbit midway between the syzygies [fr. L. *quadratura,* a square]

quad·ren·ni·al (kwɒdréniːəl) *adj.* happening every four years ‖ lasting four years [fr. L. *quadriennium,* four-year period]

quad·ren·ni·um (kwɒdréniːəm) *pl.* **quad·ren·ni·ums, quad·ren·ni·a** (kwɒdréniːə) *n.* a four-year period [L. fr. *quadri-,* four+*annus,* year]

qua·dri- (kwɒ́driː) *prefix* four [=L. *quattuor,* four]

quad·ric (kwɒ́drik) **1.** *adj.* (*math.*) of the second degree **2.** *n.* (*math.*) a quantic of the second degree ‖ (*math.*) a surface whose equation is of the second degree [fr. L. *quadra,* square]

quad·ri·ceps (kwɒ́drisɛps) *n.* the large extension muscle of the thigh **quad·ri·cip·i·tal** (kwɒdrisípit'l) *adj.* [Mod. L. fr. QUADRI-+*caput (capitis),* head]

quad·ri·ga (kwədráigə) *pl.* **quad·ri·gae** (kwədráidʒiː) *n.* (*Rom. hist.*) a two-wheeled chariot drawn by four horses abreast [L.]

QRS

quad·ri·lat·er·al (kwɒdrilǽtərəl) **1.** *n.* a plane figure enclosed by four straight lines **2.** *adj.* having four straight sides [fr. L. *quadrilaterus*]

quad·ri·lin·gual (kwɒdrilíŋgwəl) *adj.* written in or involving four languages ‖ speaking or knowing four languages [fr. QUADRI- + L. *lingua*, tongue]

qua·drille (kwədríl) *n.* a square dance for four couples, consisting of five figures ‖ the music for such a dance [F. fr. Span. *cuadrilla* or Ital. *quadriglia*, a troop]

quadrille *n.* a four-handed game played with 40 cards, fashionable in the 18th c. [F.]

quad·ril·lion (kwɒdríljən) *n.* *NUMBER TABLE **quad·ril·lionth** *n.* and *adj.* [F.]

quad·ri·no·mi·al (kwɒdrinóumi:əl) **1.** *adj.* (*algebra*) consisting of four terms **2.** *n.* (*algebra*) a quadrinomial expression [QUADRI- + BINOMIAL]

quad·ri·par·tite (kwɒdripártait) *adj.* having four parts shared or undertaken by four parties, *a quadripartite agreement* [fr. *quadripartitus*]

quad·ri·syl·lab·ic (kwɒdrisilǽbik) *adj.* having four syllables ‖ of quadrisyllables

quad·ri·syl·la·ble (kwɒdrisíləb'l) *n.* a word of four syllables

quad·ri·va·lent (kwɒdrivéilənt) *adj.* (*chem.*) having four valencies (cf. TETRAVALENT) [fr. QUADRI- + L. *valens* (*valentis*) fr. *valere*, to be strong]

quad·riv·i·um (kwɒdrívi:əm) *pl.* **quad·riv·i·a** (kwɒdrívi:ə) *n.* (in medieval education) arithmetic, geometry, astronomy and music, the higher division of the seven liberal arts, studied for three years between the bachelor's and master's degree (cf. TRIVIUM) [L. = a place where four roads meet]

quad·ro (kwɒ́drɒu) *n.* in city planning, a section containing residential and commercial entities

quad·roon (kwɒdrú:n) *n.* a person of quarter Negro blood [fr. Span. *cuarteron* fr. *cuarto*, fourth]

qua·dru·ma·nous (kwɒdrú:mənəs) *adj.* (*zool.*, of primates except man) having hind feet as well as forefeet constructed like hands ‖ of or relating to such primates [fr. Mod. L. *quadrumana* fr. *quadrumanus*, four-handed]

quad·ru·ped (kwɒ́druped) **1.** *n.* a four-footed animal, esp. such a mammal **2.** *adj.* four-footed **quad·ru·pe·dal** (kwɒdrú:pid'l) *adj.* [fr. L. *quadrupes* (*quadrupedis*), four-footed]

quad·ru·ple (kwɒ́drup'l, kwɒdrú:p'l) **1.** *adj.* four times as much or as many ‖ having four parts or parties, *Quadruple Alliance* ‖ (*mus.*) having four beats to a measure **2.** *n.* a quantity or amount four times as large as another, *8 is the quadruple of 2* [F.]

quadruple *pres. part.* **quad·ru·pling** *past* and *past part.* **quad·ru·pled** *v.t.* to multiply by four ‖ *v.i.* to become four times as many or as much [fr. F. *quadrupler* or fr. L. *quadruplare*]

Quadruple Alliance the alliance (1718) of Britain, France, the Netherlands and Austria to oppose Spain's attempt to undo the Treaty of Utrecht (1713) ‖ the alliance (1815) of Britain, Austria, Russia and Prussia to maintain peace after the defeat of Napoleon ‖ the alliance (1834) of Britain, France, Spain and Portugal to support Isabella II against the Carlists

quad·ru·plet (kwɒ́druplit, kwɒdrú:plit) *n.* one of four offspring of a single birth [QUADRUPLE *adj.*]

quad·ru·pli·cate 1. (kwɒdrú:plikit) *adj.* repeated four times **2.** (kwɒdrú:plikit) *n.* one of four copies or specimens **in quadruplicate** in four copies **3.** (kwɒdrú:plikeit) *v.t. pres. part.* **quad·ru·pli·cat·ing** *past* and *past part.* **quad·ru·pli·cat·ed** to make four copies or specimens of ‖ to quadruple **quad·ru·pli·ca·tion** *n.* [fr. L. *quadruplicare* (*quadruplicatus*), to quadruple]

quaes·tor, ques·tor (kwéstər, kwí:stər) *n.* (*Rom. hist.*) a Roman official, originally a prosecutor, or judge in certain criminal cases, later a treasurer, paymaster etc. **quaes·to·ri·al, ques·to·ri·al** (kwestɔ́ri:əl, kwi:stɔ́ri:əl, kwi:stóuri:əl) *adj.* **quaes·tor·ship, quéstorship** *n.* [L. fr. *quaerere*, to seek]

quaff (kwɒf) **1.** *v.t.* (*rhet.*) to drink off or take long drinks at ‖ *v.i.* (*rhet.*) to take copious drinks **2.** *n.* (*rhet.*) a hearty drink [prob. imit.]

quag (kwæg) *n.* a quagmire (shaky, muddy ground) [perh. related to obs. *quag*, to shake]

quag·ga (kwǽgə) *pl.* **quag·gas, quag·ga** *n.* *Equus quagga*, fam. *Equidae*, an extinct ungulate mammal of southern Africa, related to the zebra. It had wide stripes on the head and foreparts [S. African]

quag·gy (kwǽgi:) *comp.* **quag·gi·er** *superl.* **quag·gi·est** *adj.* of or like a quagmire [QUAG]

quag·mire (kwǽgmaiər) *n.* shaky, muddy ground ‖ a piece of firm ground transformed by rain or flooding into a sea of mud ‖ a situation which threatens to become inextricable

qua·hog, qua·haug (kwóhɒg) *n. Mercenaria mercenaria,* fam. *Veneridae,* the common round clam, an edible mollusk found on the North American Atlantic coast [Am. Ind.]

Quai d'Or·say (keidɔrsei) the French ministry of foreign affairs [after the Paris street where it is]

quail (kweil) *pl.* **quail, quails** *n. Coturnix coturnix,* fam. *Phasianidae,* a migratory game bird of Europe, Asia and Africa. It is about 7 ins in length and the general color of its upper body is sandy with a reddish breast and white belly ‖ any of various gallinaceous game birds of North America, e.g. the bobwhite [O. F. *quaille*]

quail *v.i.* to flinch, to lose courage, *his spirit quailed at the ordeal ahead* [origin unknown]

Quail (*mil.*) an air-launched decoy missile [ADM-20] carried within the B-52 that is used to lessen the effectiveness of enemy radar, interceptor aircraft, air-defense missiles, etc.

quaint (kweint) *adj.* old and picturesque, *quaint thatched cottages* ‖ amusingly old-fashioned, *a quaint survival* ‖ odd in an interesting way, *a quaint sense of humor* [O.F. *queinte, cointe,* wise, crafty]

quake (kweik) **1.** *v.i. pres. part.* **quak·ing** *past* and *past part.* **quaked** to shake violently ‖ to shake inwardly **2.** *n.* a trembling or quaking ‖ an earthquake, e.g. the bobwhite [O. E. *cwacian*]

Quak·er (kwéikər) *n.* a member of the Society of Friends (*FRIENDS) **Quák·er·ism** *n.* [a nickname given by a judge to George Fox, who had told him to quake at the word of the Lord]

Quaker meeting a communal meeting of Friends for worship ‖ a congregation of Friends

quak·y (kwéiki:) *comp.* **quak·i·er** *superl.* **quak·i·est** *a* trembling, shaky ‖ having a tendency to quake [QUAKE V.]

qual·i·fi·ca·tion (kwɒlifikéiʃən) *n.* a limiting, narrowing down (e.g. of meaning, application etc.), reservation, *the statement needs some qualification,* or something that does this ‖ a skill, quality etc. fitting a person for particular work or a particular appointment ‖ a requirement which has to be met, *we can waive the qualifications in his case* ‖ a descriptive term, *opportunist is hardly the qualification applicable to their policy* **qual·i·fi·ca·to·ry** (kwɒlifikətɔːri:, kwɒlifikətouri:) *adj.* [fr. M. L. *qualificatio* (*qualificationis*)]

qual·i·fi·er (kwɒ́lifaiər) *n.* someone who or something that qualifies

qual·i·fy (kwɒ́lifai) *pres. part.* **qual·i·fy·ing** *past* and *past part.* **qual·i·fied** *v.t.* to render fit or competent, to entitle, *no experience doesn't qualify him to speak as an authority* ‖ to render legally capable or entitled, *residence qualifies you for membership* ‖ to describe by attributing a quality to, *could you qualify his behavior as offensive?* ‖ to modify, restrict, *to qualify a statement* ‖ to make less severe, mitigate, *to qualify a criticism* ‖ (*gram.*) to limit the meaning of, *adjectives qualify nouns* ‖ *v.i.* to be or become qualified ‖ (*sports*) to reach the required standard in preliminary contests [F. *qualifier*]

qual·i·ta·tive (kwɒ́liteitiv) *adj.* concerned with, relating to or involving quality (cf. QUANTITATIVE) [fr. L.L. *qualitativus*]

qualitative analysis the branch of chemistry concerned with the identifcation of the constituent elements in a compound mixture, e.g. by spectroscopic and spectrographic analysis (cf. QUANTITATIVE ANALYSIS)

qual·i·ty (kwɒ́liti:) *pl.* **qual·i·ties** *n.* grade, degree of excellence, *goods of the first quality* ‖ excellence, worth, *a tobacco of quality* ‖ trait, characteristic, attribute etc. ‖ (*hist.*) high social status, *a man of quality* ‖ (*logic,* of a proposition) the character of being affirmative or negative ‖ (*mus.*) timbre **the quality** (*hist.*) the nobility [M.E. *qualite* fr. F. *qualité*]

quality control (*business*) system for ensuring quality of output involving inspection, analysis, and action to make required changes

quality of life standard of living including health, entertainment, and subjective factors, e.g., social satisfaction

qualm (kwɑm, kwɔm) *n.* a twinge of guilt, a scruple, *qualms of conscience* ‖ a sudden feeling of anxiety or apprehension, *a qualm of fear* ‖ a

sudden sensation of nausea or faintness [etym. doubtful]

quan·da·ry (kwɒ́ndəri:) *pl.* **quan·da·ries** *n.* a dilemma, a state of perplexity [etym. doubtful]

quan·ta·some (kwɒ́ntəsɒum) *n.* (*botany*) the chlorophyll granule in chloroplast of plant cells, believed to be site of photosynthesis

quan·tic (kwɒ́ntik) *n.* (*math.*) a rational, integrally homogeneous function of two or more variables [fr. L. *quantus,* how much]

quantic *adj.* of or relating to a quantum

quan·ti·fy (kwɒ́ntifai) *pres. part.* **quan·ti·fy·ing** *past* and *past part.* **quanti·fied** (*logic*) to specify the application of (a term) by the use of 'all', 'many', 'some' etc. ‖ to determine the quantity of [M.L. *quantificare* fr. *quantus,* how much]

quan·ti·ta·tive (kwɒ́ntiteitiv) *adj.* relating to or concerned with quantity ‖ involving measurement or quantity (cf. QUALITATIVE) ‖ of or relating to the quantity of vowels, *quantitative scansion* [fr. M. L. *quantitativus*]

quantitative analysis the branch of chemistry concerned with the determination of the relative quantities of the constituent elements in a compound or mixture, e.g. by gravimetric and volumetric analysis (cf. QUALITATIVE ANALYSIS)

quan·ti·ty (kwɒ́ntiti:) *pl.* **quan·ti·ties** *n.* an amount, *a small quantity of cement* ‖ a great deal, *a quantity of jewelry was missing* ‖ the property of things that can be measured, *the science of pure quantity* ‖ the relative length or shortness of vowel sounds or syllables ‖ (*logic*) the extent of the application of a proposition ‖ (*math.*) anything which is measurable a figure or symbol used to represent this [O.F. *quantité*]

quantity surveyor someone who estimates the quantities that will be required for a building job, with their costs

quan·tize (kwɒ́ntaiz) *pres. part.* **quan·tiz·ing** *past* and *past part.* **quan·tized** *v.t.* to subdivide (energy) into quanta ‖ to impart a quantum to ‖ to express in multiples of an indivisible unit, e.g., age in whole years ‖ to treat or express in terms of quantum mechanics

Quan·trill (kwɒ́ntril), William C. (1837–65) American Confederate guerrilla leader during the Civil War. Known as Quantrill's Raiders, his guerrilla bands burned and looted Union strongholds in Kansas and Missouri, and on Aug. 21, 1863, they pillaged Lawrence, Kans., killing more than 150 civilians. Quantrill was mortally wounded by Union troops (May 1865) and died in prison in Louisville, Ky.

quan·tum (kwɒ́ntəm) *pl.* **quan·ta** (kwɒ́ntə) *n.* amount, quantity ‖ share ‖ one of the very small discrete packets into which many forms of energy are subdivided, and which are always associated with a frequency v such that the product of v and Planck's constant is equal to the quantum ‖ one of the small subdivisions of other quantized physical magnitudes (*QUANTUM NUMBER, *SHELL, *ORBITAL) [L. neut. of *quantus,* how much]

quantum chemistry the study of the mechanics of molecular physics applied to chemistry. — **quantum chemist** *n.*

quantum electronics the application of the mechanics of molecular physics to electronics, e.g., hydrogen maser, atomic beam resonator

quantum leap a sudden large advance or breakthrough

quantum mechanics the formal mathematical methods of wave mechanics and of matrix mechanics applied to physical problems

quantum number an integral or half integral number belonging to a set of four such numbers denoting the energy level, angular momentum, magnetic moment and spin of a particle, esp. an electron in an atom (*PAULI EXCLUSION PRINCIPLE). For such a particle, each of the above-mentioned quantities is quantized, the quantum numbers representing the discrete levels of each quantity in which the particle is to be found (*QUANTUM THEORY, *SHELL, *ORBITAL)

quantum physics an approach to physics based on the quantum theory

quantum theory a theory in physics and chemistry based on the assumption that the energy possessed by a physical system is quantized, i.e. it cannot take on a continuous range of values (permitted in classical physics) but is restricted to discrete ones that depend on its dimensions, masses and charges. This hypothesis, made first in the early 20th c. to explain certain per-

CONCISE PRONUNCIATION KEY: **(a)** æ, c*a*t; ɑ, c*a*r; ɔ f*aw*n; ei, sn*a*ke. **(e)** e, h*e*n; i:, sh*ee*p; iə, d*ee*r; ɛə, b*ea*r. **(i)** i, f*i*sh; ai, t*i*ger; ə:, b*i*rd. **(o)** o, *o*x; au, c*ow*; ou, g*oa*t; u, p*oo*r; ɔi, r*oy*al. **(u)** ʌ, d*u*ck; u, b*u*ll; u:, g*oo*se; ə, bac*i*llus; ju:, c*u*be. x, lo*ch*; θ, *th*ink; ð, *b*o*th*er; z, *Z*en; ʒ, corsa*g*e; dʒ, sava*g*e; ŋ, ora*ng*utang; j, *y*ak; ʃ, *f*ish; tʃ, *fe*tch; 'l, rabb*le*; 'n, redd*en*. Complete pronunciation key appears inside front cover.

plexing phenomena (*PLANCK RADIATION LAW, *PHOTOEMISSION*, *ATOMIC SPECTRUM), was incorporated in the 1920s into different but equivalent thematical formulations (*WAVE MECHANICS, *MATRIX MECHANICS) which are now regarded as providing a more general theoretical framework than that supporting classical mechanics. Indeed, the latter is considered a special case of quantum mechanics, applying to systems whose dimensions and energy are such as to allow them to exist in quantum states so close together that they may, for purpose of calculation, be regarded as continuous. The quantum theory has progressed to the point where it permeates the whole of physics and chemistry, permitting a unified and often quantitative treatment of a wide range of experimental facts. It has also revealed certain fundamental properties of nature (*UNCERTAINTY PRINCIPLE, *WAVE-PARTICLE DUALITY) that have profoundly affected current epistemology

quantum theory of fields a modern unified theory of force fields in which the field at some distance from its source is thought of as being carried to that point by a messenger or field quantum. For electrostatic fields this messenger is the photon, for gravitational fields it is the hypothetical graviton. Both these particles have 0 rest mass, travel with the speed of light, and therefore extend their effect to infinity. For the short-range forces observed in nuclei by means of scattering experiments, a type of meson with finite rest mass and therefore limited effective distance was postulated. Several such mesons have since been observed

quap (kwɒp) *n.* a hypothetical nuclear particle of a quark plus an antiproton

quar·an·tine (kwɔ́rənti:n, kwɒ́rənti:n) 1. *n.* a period of isolation imposed to lessen the risk of spreading an infectious or contagious disease ‖ a period of detention during which a ship suspected of carrying contagion is allowed no contact with the shore ‖ such a state of isolation imposed on an individual, ship etc. ‖ the place where the ship is detained ‖ a place, esp. a hospital, where people with contagious diseases are isolated. 2. *v.t. pres. part.* **quar·an·tin·ing** *past* and *past part.* **quar·an·tined** to put in quarantine, to isolate [fr. Ital. *quarantina* fr. *quaranta*, forty]

quark (kwɒrk) *n.* a hypothetical basic subatomic nuclear particle held to be the basic component of protons, neutrons, etc., or a mathematically convenient parameter of a model; coined by American physicist Murray Gell-Mann *Cf* ATOM SMASHER, BETATRON, PARTICLE ACCELERATOR, PEP, PETA

quar·rel (kwɔ́rəl, kwɒ́rəl) *n.* (*hist.*) a heavy square-headed arrow, esp. one used with a crossbow [O.F.]

quarrel *pres. part.* **quar·rel·ing**, esp. *Br.* **quar·rel·ling** *past* and *past part.* **quar·reled**, esp. *Br.* **quar·relled** *v.i.* to wrangle, to dispute angrily ‖ to find fault, to *quarrel with someone's suggestions* [O.F. *quereler*]

quarrel *n.* an angry dispute, altercation ‖ disagreement, *what is your quarrel with this definition?* ‖ a cause for complaint, *my real quarrel with him is the way he treats dogs* **quár·rel·some** *adj.* quick to quarrel [O.F. *querele, querelle*]

quar·ry (kwɔ́ri:, kwɒ́ri:) *pl.* **quar·ries** *n.* a diamond-shaped pane of glass ‖ a machine-made paving tile [var. of QUARREL (arrow)]

quarry *pl.* **quarries** *n.* the prey of an animal ‖ the victim of a hunt ‖ a person or thing pursued as though the victim of a hunt [fr. O.F. *cuirée, curée* fr. *cuir*, hide]

quarry 1. *pl.* **quar·ries** *n.* an open cavity where stone or slate is extracted 2. *v.t. pres. part.* **quar·ry·ing** *past* and *past part.* **quar·ried** to take from a quarry ‖ to make a quarry in ‖ to extract (information) from books, records etc. ‖ *v.i.* to search for information **quar·ry·man** (kwɔ́ri:mən, kwɒ́ri:mən) *pl.* **quar·ry·men** (kwɔ́ri:mən, kwɒ́ri:mən) *n.* a person who works in a quarry [fr. M.L. *quareia*]

quart (kwɔrt) *n.* any of various units of liquid or dry capacity esp. (*Am.*) one equal to ¼ liquid gallon or 57.75 cu. ins or (*Br.*) one equal to ¼ imperial gallon or 69.355 cu. ins ‖ a measure of dry capacity equal to 1/32 bushel or 67.200 cu. ins [F. *quart, quarte*]

quart *QUARTE

quar·tan (kwɔ́rt'n) 1. *n.* a type of fever characterized by a paroxysm reoccurring every 72 hours 2. *adj.* (of a fever) occurring every 72 hours [F. (*fièvre*) *quartaine*]

quarte (kart) *n.* (*fencing,* also **quart, carte**) the fourth parrying position ‖ a sequence of four cards in piquet [F.]

quar·ter (kwɔ́rtər) 1. *n.* one of four equal parts, a fourth part ‖ a fourth part of an hour ‖ the moment marking this ‖ a fourth part of a year ‖ a fourth of a lunar period ‖ the phase of the moon between the first and second quarter, or between the third and fourth quarter ‖ a period for instruction and study, usually equal to one fourth of an academic year ‖ (*sports*) one of the four periods of playing time into which certain games are divided ‖ a race over one fourth of a mile ‖ one of four parts, each including a limb, into which a carcass is divided by a butcher ‖ a district in a town, *the Chinese quarter* ‖ a region or direction corresponding to one of the cardinal points of the compass, *the wind is moving around to the opposite quarter* ‖ any point or direction of the compass, esp. a cardinal point or division ‖ a source of information, help etc.. *don't look for sympathy in that quarter* ‖ (*hist. or fig.*) mercy granted to an enemy or opponent in a contest‖ the fourth part of a hundredweight ‖ (*Br.*) a measure for grain etc. equal to about 8 bushels ‖ 25 cents, a fourth part of a dollar ‖ a coin of this value ‖ the lateral part of a horse's hoof between the heel and the toe ‖ (*naut.*) the fourth part of a fathom ‖ (*naut.*) the afterpart of a ship's side ‖ (*naut.*, esp. *pl.*) one of the stations where men are called for a specified activity, *battle quarters* ‖ (*shoemaking*) the side of a shoe from heel to vamp ‖ (*heraldry*) one of the four divisions of a quartered shield ‖ (*heraldry*) a charge occupying such a division placed in chief ‖ (*pl.*, esp. *mil.*) lodging‖ (of two machine parts) the condition of being at a 90° angle to one another **at close quarters** very near by **from all quarters, from every quarter** from all directions ‖ from everyone 2. *v.t.* to divide into four equal parts ‖ to lodge, assign accommodation to, *he quartered his troops in the school* ‖ to fix, adjust etc. (two parts of a machine) at right angles ‖ (*heraldry*) to bear or arrange (different coats of arms) quarterly on a shield ‖ (*heraldry*) to add (another's coat) to one's hereditary arms ‖ (*heraldry*, with 'with') to place in alternate quarters to ‖ (*heraldry*) to divide (a shield) into parts ‖ (of dogs) to search (the ground) thoroughly in all directions ‖ (*hist.*) to cut (a corpse) into four pieces 3. *adj.* consisting of or equal to a quarter ‖ (of a machine part) placed at a right angle to another part [O.F.]

quar·ter·back (kwɔ́rtərbæk) *n.* (*football*) the player whose position is behind the line of scrimmage with the fullback and the halfbacks, and who generally calls the signals for the plays

quarter binding a book binding in which the material covering the spine is different from that covering the sides. The material covering the spine extends over the boards up to a quarter of their width (cf. FULL BINDING, cf. HALF BINDING, cf. THREE-QUARTER BINDING)

quar·ter·bound (kwɔ́rtərbaund) *adj.* bound in quarter binding

quarter day a day on which a quarterly payment (of rent, interest etc.) is due and a quarterly tenancy begins or ends

quar·ter·deck (kwɔ́rtərdek) *n.* the after section of a ship's upper deck usually between stern and after mast

quar·ter·fi·nal (kwɔrtərfáin'l) *n.* the game or round before the semifinal of a tournament

quarter horse a horse of a U.S. breed developed for short-distance racing

quar·ter·ing (kwɔ́rtəriŋ) *n.* (*heraldry*) the arrangement of coats of arms on a shield to show family alliances [QUARTER *v.*]

Quartering Act of 1764 a British act of parliament during the ministry of George Grenville, which declared that the American colonists were required to pay for housing British troops in the colonies. It was re-enacted (1774) with the passage of the Intolerable Acts, which caused bitter colonial resentment

quar·ter·ly (kwɔ́rtərli:) 1. *adj.* occurring every quarter of a year 2. *adv.* once every quarter ‖ (heraldry) in quarters ‖ (*heraldry*) in diagonally opposite quarters 3. *pl.* **quar·ter·lies** a publication issued once every quarter

quar·ter·mas·ter (kwɔ́rtərmæstər, kwɔ́rtərmɑstər) *n.* (*naut.*) a petty officer in charge of steering, signals etc. ‖ (*mil.*, abbr. Q.M.) an officer who allots quarters to troops, deals with supplies etc.

quartermaster general (*mil.*, abbr. Q.M.G.) a staff officer in charge of the department dealing with quarters, supplies etc.

quarter note (*mus.*, *Am.*=*Br.* crotchet) a note (symbol ♩) equal to half a half note or two eighth notes

quarter plate (*Br.*) a photographic plate or film of the size 4½ x 3½ ins

quar·ter·saw (kwɔ́rtərsɔ) *pres. part.* **quar·ter·saw·ing** *past* **quar·ter·sawed** *past part.* **quar·ter·sawn** (kwɔ́rtərsɔn), **quar·ter·sawed** *v.t.* to saw (a log) into quarters and then each quarter into planks so that the grain shows to advantage i.e. with the growth rings at least 45° to the cut face) and warping is reduced

quarter section (*abbr.* q.s.) one fourth of a section of land

quarter session a local court in certain states, having limited criminal jurisdiction ‖ a British court of limited criminal and civil jurisdiction held quarterly and presided over by two justices of the peace or by a judge sitting with a jury in counties, and by recorders in boroughs

quarter tone (*mus.*) an interval equal to half a semitone

quar·tet, quar·tette (kwɔrtét) *n.* a musical composition for four voices or instruments ‖ a group of performers of such compositions [F. *quartette* fr. Ital.]

quar·tile (kwɔ́rtail, kwɔ́rt'l) *n.* (*statistics*) one of the three values in a frequency distribution which divides the items into four categories [fr. M.L. *quartilis* adj. fr. *quartus*, fourth]

quar·to (kwɔ́rtou) *n.* (*abbr.* 4to, 4°) the size of a sheet of paper folded into four ‖ a book of sheets so folded [L. (*in*) *quarto*, (*in*) *fourth*]

quartz (kwɔrts) *n.* a common and widely distributed form of silicon dioxide, SiO_2, occurring in hexagonal crystals and massive forms. Usually colorless and transparent (*ROCK CRYSTAL), it is also found in colored, translucent and opaque forms. It is more transparent than glass to ultraviolet waves, but polarizes the light it transmits. Having a very small coefficient of expansion, and high rigidity, it is used for making heat resistant apparatus. It exhibits piezoelectricity and so is used in radio transmitters and the mechanisms of astronomical clocks etc. [G. *quarz*]

quartz-i·o·dine lamp (kwɔ́rtsáiədain) (*electrical eng.*) a high-intensity incandescent lamp with a tungsten filament, and a quartz bulb containing an inert gas of iodine or bromine vapor. It is used in automobile lamps, movie projectors, etc.

quartz·ite (kwɔ́rtsait) *n.* a sandstone, often milky white in color, compacted into a solid rock by a deposit of crystalline quartz around its grains

quartz light (*med.*) a bactericidal cold-light lamp with a quartz lens, used for therapy

qua·sar (kwéizar) *n.* any of several very intense celestial radio sources, among the furthest known objects from the earth (10^9 light-years away). The size, optical and radio intensity, frequency of occurrence and distance of quasars are extremely unusual. Quasars are of primary importance in modern cosmological theories [*quasi-stellar* radio source]

quash (kwɒʃ) *v.t.* (*law*) to annul ‖ to dismiss summarily, *to quash an objection* ‖ to put down (a rebellion etc.) [fr. O.F. *quasser*]

qua·si- (kwázi:, kwéizai) 1. *adj.* seeming, *quasi humor* 2. *prefix* seeming, almost real, apparent, *the decision has an appearance of quasi-legality* ‖ semi-, more or less, *in a quasi-official capacity* [L.=if]

Qua·si·mo·do (kwɑzi:mɔ́dɔ), Salvatore (1901-68), Italian lyric poet. His works include 'La Vita non e sogno' (1949) and 'La Terra impareggiabile' (1958)

Qua·si·mo·do Sunday (kwɑzi:mɔ́dɔ) Low Sunday [fr. L. *quasi modo*, the opening words of the introit for this day]

qua·si-par·ti·cle (kwázi:pártik'l) *n.* (*phys.*) in solid-state physics, a unit of energy (sound, light, heat) with mass and momentum but that does not exist as a free particle, e.g., phonons

quasi-stellar object *QUASAR

quas·sia (kwɒ́ʃə) *n.* a drug obtained from the heartwood of several members of *Simaroubaceae*, a family of tropical trees. It is used as a tonic, a roundworm cure, and in insect control

quas·sin (kwɒ́s'n) *n.* the bitter essence of quassia [Mod. L. fr. Graman *Quassi*, a Surinam slave, who discovered. c. 1730) this drug]

CONCISE PRONUNCIATION KEY: **(a)** æ, c*a*t; ɑ, c*a*r; ɔ f*a*wn; ei, sn*a*ke. **(e)** e, h*e*n; i:, sh*ee*p; iə, d*ee*r; ɛə, b*ea*r. **(i)** i, f*i*sh; ai, t*i*ger; ə:, b*i*rd. **(o)** o, *o*x; au, c*ow*; ou, g*oa*t; u, p*oo*r; ɔi, r*oy*al. **(u)** ʌ, d*u*ck; u, b*u*ll; u:, g*oo*se; ə, b*a*cillus; ju:, c*u*be. x, lo*ch*; θ, *th*ink; ð, bo*th*er; z, *Z*en; ʒ, corsa*g*e; dʒ, sava*g*e; ŋ, ora*ng*utang; j, *y*ak; ʃ, *fish*; tʃ, fe*tch*; 'l, ra*bble*; 'n, re*dden*. Complete pronunciation key appears inside front cover.

qua·ter·cen·te·nar·y (kwɒtərséntənəri:) *pl.* **qua·ter·cen·te·nar·ies** *n.* a 400th anniversary [fr. L. *quater*, four times]

qua·ter·na·ry (kwɒtə́:rnəri:, kwátərneri:) **1.** *adj.* consisting of four ‖ arranged in groups of four **Qua·ter·na·ry** of the most recent period of geological time **2.** *n.* the number four ‖ a group of four **the Quaternary** the Quaternary period or system of rocks [fr. L. *quaternarius* fr. *quaterni*, by fours]

Quaternary *n.* (*geol.*) time period of the last 2 or 3 million yrs, i.e., the Pleistocene and Holocene eras. —**Quaternary** *adj.*

qua·ter·nate (kwətə́:rnit, kwútərneit) *adj.* being a set or sets of four ‖ having four parts [fr. L. *quaterni*, by fours]

qua·ter·ni·on (kwətə́:rni:ən) *n.* a set of four ‖ (*math.*) an operator, depending upon four irreducible elements, which changes one vector into another ‖ (*pl.*) the calculus of these [fr. L.L. *quaternio* (*quarternionis*) fr. *quaterni*, by fours]

quat·rain (kwótrein) *n.* a four-line stanza ‖ four lines of verse [F fr. *quatre*, four]

quat·rat (kwótrət) *n.* (*envir.*) area, usu. 1 sq m, used to sample vegetation. *Cf* QUADRAT

quat·re·foil (kǽtrəfɔil) *n.* a stylized ornament, used e.g. in tracery, representing a leaf or flower with four lobes [fr. O. F. fr. *quatre*, four+foil, leaf]

quat·tro·cen·to (kwɒtroutʃéntou) *n.* the 15th c. in Italy, esp. in relation to its art and literature [Ital.=four hundred, used for fourteen hundred]

quat·tu·or·de·cil·lion (kwɒtu:ɔ́rdisíljən) *n.* *NUMBER TABLE [fr. L. *quattuordim*, fourteen+MILLION]

Quauhtémoc *CUAUHTÉMOC

qua·ver (kwéivər) **1.** *v.i.* (*of* the voice) to shake, tremble ‖ to speak or sing tremulously ‖ *v.t.* to utter or sing with a tremulous voice **2.** *n.* a tremulous unsteadiness in speech ‖ (*mus.*) a trill in singing ‖ (*Br., mus.*) an eighth note **qua·ver·y** *adj.* shaky, tremulous [fr. older *quave* fr. M.E. *cwavier*, to shake]

quay (ki:) *n.* an artificially constructed wharf lying parallel to or projecting into the water, for loading and unloading ships **quay·age** (kí:idʒ) *n.* the charge for the use of a quay ‖ mooring space alongside a quay [alt. spelling of older *key*, a quay, after F. *quai*]

quea·si·ly (kwí:zili:) *adv.* uneasily [QUEASY]

quea·si·ness (kwí:zi:nis) *n.* the condition or quality of being queasy

quea·sy (kwi:zi:) *comp.* **quea·si·er** *superl.* **quea·si·est** *adj.* sick, qualmish, inclined to nausea ‖ nauseating, *the queasy rolling of the ship* ‖ fastidious, easily upset ‖ uneasy, uncomfortable in one's mind [perh. rel. to O.F. *coisier*, to hurt]

Que·bec (kwibék, F. keibek) the capital (pop. 166,474, with agglom. 576,075) of Quebec province, Canada, a port on the St Lawrence. Industries: textiles, leather, pulp and paper, mechanical engineering. Language: 90% French. Cathedrals (1647 and 1922), 17th-c. city walls. University (*LAVAL). The first French settlement in Canada, Quebec was founded (1608) by Champlain. The battle of the Heights of Abraham was fought here (1759). Quebec was the capital of Lower Canada (1791–1840)

Quebec a province (area 594,860 sq. miles, pop. 6,529,300, about 80% French-speaking of whom a quarter are bilingual) occupying most of E. Canada. Capital: Quebec. Largest city: Montreal. It lies almost wholly within the Canadian Shield, and settlement is concentrated in the fertile St Lawrence valley. Agriculture: beef and dairy cattle, hogs, poultry, fodder crops, fruit and vegetables, maple syrup. Resources: furs, fish, timber, asbestos, copper, iron ore, gold, building materials, hydroelectricity. Industries: pulp and paper, nonferrous-metal processing, wood industries, textiles and clothing, chemicals. food processing, aircraft, rolling stock. The city of Quebec was founded in 1608 and the area was part of New France until ceded to the English (1763). The province of Quebec was set up (1763–90), became Lower Canada (1791–1840) and joined the Canadian Confederation (1867). Its predominantly French culture fostered a separatist spirit which gave rise in the 1960s to both a moderate and a radical movement. The moderate Parti Québécois (founded 1968) demanded political separation from Canada. The radical Front de Libération du Québec (FLQ, founded 1962) sought the same end by terrorism. The Parti Québécois was elected in 1976 with René Lévesque as its leader, but a 1980 referendum defeated the proposal to negotiate the province's sovereignty with the federal government. In 1985, following Lévesque's resignation, Pierre Marc Johnson took office as premier and head of the Parti Québécois

Quebec Act a British act of parliament (1774) which guaranteed freedom of worship and maintenance of the French civil code to the former French colonies of Canada

Quebec Conference a meeting (Aug. 11–24, 1943) at Quebec between F. D. Roosevelt, Churchill, Mackenzie King and Tse-ven Soong. Lord Louis Mountbatten was made supreme Allied commander in S.E. Asia, and plans for the invasion of France were approved

que·bra·cho (keibrátʃou) *n.* any of various tropical American trees with very hard wood, esp. *Aspidosplierma quebracho*, fam. *Apocynaceae*, the white quebracho of Chile and Argentina, yielding a bark used medicinally and *Schinopsis* (*Lorentzii*, fam. *Anacardiaceae*, the red quebracho of Argentina, whose bark yields tannin used in dyeing the wood of a quebracho [Span. fr. *quebrar*, to break+*hacha*, axe]

Quech·ua (kétʃwə) *n.* a member of a group of Inca tribes ‖ the language of these tribes (still spoken among Indians of Peru and Ecuador)

Quech·uan **1.** *n.* Quechua **2.** *adj.* relating to the Quechuas, their language, culture etc.

queen (kwi:n) **1.** *n.* the wife of a king ‖ a female monarch ‖ (*rhet.*) a woman, creature or thing thought of as the foremost of its kind ‖ the fertile female of social insects, e.g. bees, wasps, ants and termites ‖ a playing card bearing a conventionalized picture of a queen ‖ (*chess*) the most mobile piece, able to move in a straight line in any direction for any number of squares **2.** *v.t.* (*chess*) to convert (a pawn) into a queen by advancing it to the opponent's end of the board ‖ *v.t.* (*chess, of* a pawn) to become a queen **to queen it** to be bossy, put on airs, and assume that other people are there to do one's bidding [O.E. *cwēn*, a woman, wife, queen]

Queen Anne (*archit.*) of an early 18th-c. English style of unpretentious elegance, usually employing red brick with restrained carved classical ornamentation, and used very successfully, esp. in domestic architecture ‖ (*furniture*) of an early 19th-c. English style showing Dutch influence, generally characterized by cabriole legs, generous but elegant comfort in the chairs, use of walnut, affection for marquetry, and use of upholstery

Queen Anne's lace *Dancus carota*, an umbelliferous widely distributed in North America. It has large, lacy umbels of white flowers, the central flower often being purple

Queen Anne's War the American aspect (1701–13) of the War of the Spanish Succession, fought by England and her American colonies against the French and the Indians, and settled by the Peace of Utrecht (1713)

Queen Charlotte Islands (ʃɑ́rlət) a wooded archipelago (land area 3,970 sq. miles, pop. 3,000) of British Columbia, Canada. The islands are mountainous, with the exception of Graham (the largest island). Minerals (largely unexploited): coal, copper, iron, gold. Occupations: fishing, farming, forestry

queen dowager the widow of a king

queen·li·ness (kwí:nli:nis) *n.* the quality of being queenly

queen·ly (kwí:nli:) *comp.* **queen·li·er** *superl.* **queen·li·est** *adj.* befitting a queen of or like a queen

Queen Maud Land (mɔd) a sector of Antarctica between 20° W and 45° E and south of 60° S., claimed by Norway

queen mother a queen dowager who is the mother of a reigning monarch

queen post one of two uprights on a tie beam, supporting the main rafters

Queens (kwi:nz) a residential and industrial borough (pop. 1,891,325) of New York City, on Long Island

Queen's Bench *KING'S BENCH

Queens·ber·ry rules (kwí:nzberi:) the code of rules governing modern boxing, introduced (1865) by John Sholto Douglas, 8th marquis of Queensberry (1844–1900), British sports enthusiast

Queen's Counsel *KING'S COUNSEL

Queen's county *LAOIGHIS

queen-size (kwí:nsaiz) *adj.* of a bed size, approximately 60 in by 80 in

Queens·land (kwí:nzlənd, kwí:nzlænd) the state (estimated area 667,000 sq. miles, pop. 2,275,700) comprising the northeastern part of Australia. Capital: Brisbane. The Great Dividing Range separates the wet coastal plain from the dry Great Artesian Basin in the south. The northern half is tropical. Agriculture: sugarcane, wheat, corn, sorghum, vegetables, fruits, dairy and meat cattle, sheep and pig farming. Resources: timber, coal, copper, uranium, gold, silver, lead, zinc, petroleum. Industries: agricultural processing, lumber, engineering, copper refining, rubber, clothing. University of Queensland (1909) at Brisbane

Queen's Proctor *KING'S PROCTOR

queen's shilling *KING'S SHILLING

queen substance (*zool.*) a pheromone secreted by queen bees, made up of 9-ketodecanoic acid, that is ingested by worker bees, suppressing their ovary development

Queen's War *DEVOLUTION, WAR OF

queer (kwiər) **1.** *adj.* strange, peculiar ‖ eccentric, odd ‖ arousing suspicion ‖ unwell, sick ‖ (*pop.*) homosexual **2.** *v.t.* to spoil, ruin **to queer someone's pitch** (esp. *Br.*) to spoil someone's plans, chances of success, schemings, etc. **3.** *n.* (*pop.*) a homosexual [origin unknown]

quell (kwel) *v.t.* to subdue, to overcome, *to quell someone's fears* ‖ to crush, to supress, *to quell an uprising* [O.E. *cwellan*, to kill]

Que·moy (kimɔ́i) an island (area 60 sq. miles, pop. 57,500) off the coast of Fukien, China, held by Formosa since 1949

quench (kwentʃ) *v.t.* (*rhet.*) to put out, extinguish, *to quench flames* ‖ to suppress, *to quench enthusiasm* ‖ to slake (thirst) ‖ to cool (heated steel etc.) by immersion in water or oil in order to harden it [M.E. *cwenken, quenchen*]

quench tank water tank used to cool hot materials in an industrial plant

Quen·tal (kentál), Antero de (1842–91), Portuguese poet, whose introspective works, usually in sonnet form, reflect his socialistic political philosophy

Quer·cia (kwértʃa), Jacopo della (c. 1367–1438), Italian sculptor. His tombs, fountains and religious works are characterized by vigorous rounded forms

quer·ci·tron (kwə́:rsịtrən) *n. Quercus velutina*, a black oak of N. America ‖ its bark, yielding a yellow dye ‖ this dye [fr. L. *quercus*, oak+CITRON]

Que·ré·ta·ro (keretɑrɔ) a central plateau state (area 4,544 sq. miles, pop. 355,000) of Mexico. Capital: Querétaro. The land is divided between mountainous areas (opals and mercury) and plains and fertile southern valleys (fruits, grain, medicinal plants, sweet potatoes). Fighting bulls are bred

Querétaro a town (pop. 680,700) in central Mexico, capital of Querétaro state. It was the site of the execution (1867) of Emperor Maximilian and his generals, and was the seat of the Constituent Congress of 1917

quern (kwə:rn) *n.* (*hist.*) a hand mill for grinding grain ‖a small hand mill for grinding spices [O.E. *cweorn*]

quer·u·lous (kwérulǝs, kwérjulǝs) *adj.* complaining, peevish, *querulous old age* [fr. L. L. *querulosus*]

que·ry (kwíəri:) **1.** *pl.* **que·ries** *n.* a question ‖ a doubt or objection, mental reservation ‖ a question mark, used to signalize a question about a text etc. **2.** *v.t. pres. part.* **que·ry·ing** *past* and *past part.* **que·ried** to question the truth or accuracy of ‖ to pose as a question ‖ to question (someone), *he queried several doctors on reactions to the drug* ‖ to mark as a query [Anglicized fr. L. *quaere*, imper. of *quaerere*, to ask a question]

Quesada *JIMÉNEZ DE QUESADA

Ques·nay (kenei), François *PHYSIOCRAT

quest (kwest) *n.* a pursuit, search, *a quest for riches* ‖ (in medieval romance) a search undertaken by a knight in selfless devotion, *the quest for the Holy Grail* **in quest of** (*rhet.*) in search of (adventure, treasure etc.) [O.F. *queste*]

quest *v.i.* (of gun dogs) to search for game ‖ (*rhet.*) to be on a quest ‖ *v.t.* (*rhet.*) to search for ‖ F. *quester*]

ques·tion (kwéstʃən) *n.* a word, phrase or sentence asking about a particular point, fact etc. ‖ a problem designed to test knowledge, *answer 7 out of 10 questions* ‖ doubt, *there's some question about his qualifications* ‖ a topic, esp. one involving a difficulty, *the question of capital* *punishment is sure to come up* ‖ a matter, *it's only a question of time* ‖ the subject for or under discussion ‖ a questioning, interrogation, *he broke down under question* **beyond question, beyond all question** without doubt, certainly **in question** in doubt ‖under consideration **out of the question** impossible, not to be thought of **to make no question** to have no doubts in one's mind **to put to the question** (*hist.*) to torture (in the exercise of justice) **without question** without doubt without challenge [A.F. *questium* fr. O.F. *question*]

question *v.t.* to ask (someone) a question or questions, to interrogate ‖ to dispute, to cast doubt upon, *we question the accuracy of the statistics v.i.* to ask a question or questions **question·a·ble** *adj.* open to doubt of a dubious, shady character **ques·tion·a·bly** *adv.* [O. F. *questionner*]

question mark a punctuation mark (?) after a question

ques·tion·naire (kwɛstʃənéər) *n.* a set of questions drawn up for answering by a number of people independently, usually to provide statistical information ‖ a paper containing such questions ‖ an inquiry using such questions [F.]

question time (*parliament*) a period in which ministers reply orally to written questions from members

questor **QUAESTER

Quet·ta (kwétə) a trade, road and rail center (pop. 156,000) of Baluchistan, Pakistan, near the passes leading to Iran and Afghanistan: wool textiles. It was largely rebuilt after the earthquake of 1935

quet·zal (ketsál) *n. Pharomachrus mocino*, fam. *Trogonidae*, a central American bird, with splendid metallic plumage, the male having long, streaming tail feathers. According to tradition, it is the bird of liberty and cannot live in captivity, though its plumage never fades in life or death. It has been taken as the emblem and monetary unit of Guatemala [Span. fr. Nahuatl]

Quet·zal·có·atl (ketsɑlkouátʼl) ('plumed serpent') a 9th-c. pre-Columbian deity of Mexico, king of the Toltecs, and poet-philosopher who discovered the supreme divine duality. He was deified as Ehecatl ('god of the winds', or 'god of air and water') and was reputed to have the power of giving life by his mere look. He taught men agriculture, metal work, the arts, and the calendar. Because he disapproved of the growing practice of offering human sacrifices he abandoned the Toltecs for the 'land of black and red' to the east (probably Yucatán), promising his faithful that he would return in another age and under a different guise. The Aztecs, who revered him as the animator of nature, regarded Hernán Cortés as the promised reincarnation

queue (kjú:) 1. *n.* (esp. *Br.*) a line of people etc. awaiting their turn ‖ (*computer*) the line-up of messages waiting to be processed, transmitted, or stored ‖ (*hist.*) a plait of hair hanging at the back of the head, esp. as formerly worn by Chinese men or found on men's wigs in Europe 2. *v.i. pres. part.* **queu·ing** *past* and *past part.* **queued** (esp. *Br.*, often with 'up') to form a queue (esp. *Br.*) ‖ to join a queue [F.]

queuing theory (*math.*) application of the probability theory relating to waiting time, order, and delays at a point where action is delayed in computers, esp. in handling information from diverse sources

Que·ve·do y Vi·lle·gas (keνéðoi:vi:ljégɑs), Francisco Gomez de (1580–1645), Spanish satirical writer, poet and author of political treatises. His picaresque novel 'Historia de la vida del Buscón llamado don Pablos' (1626) is one of the first to trace the psychological development of a hero from his youth

Que·zon (kéisɒn), Manuel Luis (1878–1944), Filipino statesman, first president of the Philippine Commonwealth (1935–44). He led his government-in-exile in the U.S.A. (1942–4) during the Japanese occupation of the Philippines

Quezon City former capital (pop. 1,165,865) of the Philippines, in central Luzon overlooking Manila, which it replaced as capital from 1948–76. University (1908)

quib·ble (kwíbʼl) 1. *n.* an evasion of the point at issue by petty argumentation, raising purely formal difficulties etc. ‖ a piddling piece of faultfinding 2. *v.i. pres. part.* **quib·bling** *past* and

past part. **quib·bled** to use a quibble or quibbles [perh. dim. of older *quib* fr. L. *quibus* ablative and dative pl. of *qui*, who, which]

Qui·be·ron Bay, Battle of (ki:brɔ̃) a sea battle (1759) of the Seven Years' War, in which the British under Hawke decisively defeated a French fleet preparing to invade Britain

Qui·che (ki:tʃei) *pl.* **Qui·che, Qui·ches** *n.* a member of an Indian people of S. central Guatemala ‖ their Mayan language [Span. *Quiché*]

quiche (ki:ʃ) *n.* a pastry shell filled with egg custard into which bits of ham and grated cheese have been added

quick (kwik) 1. *adj.* fast-moving, rapid hurried, *a quick look* ‖ lively, perceptive, alert, responsive, *a quick mind* ‖ prompt, *quick action* ‖ easily aroused, *a quick temper* ‖ hasty, impulsive, *a quick retort* ‖ (*Br.*) quickset 2. *n.* the sensitive living flesh, esp. the part under the nail **to hurt** (or **touch** or **wound**) **someone to the quick** to hurt someone's feelings very deeply **the quick and the dead** the living and dead 3. *adv.* quickly, *come as quick as you can* [O.E. *cwicu*, alive]

quick assets (*accounting*) ready cash and goods which can easily be marketed

quick bread a kind of bread, muffin etc. made with a leaven which allows it to be baked as soon as mixed

quick·en (kwíkən) *v.t.* to accelerate, *to quicken one's pace* ‖ (*rhet.*) to restore to life, *to quicken the dead* ‖ to stimulate, rouse, *to quicken someone's interest* ‖ *v.i.* to become faster ‖to reach the stage in pregnancy when the fetal movement is perceptible [QUICK *adj.*]

quick-fire (kwíkfɑiər) *adj.* firing or made for firing in quick succession **quickfir·ing** *adj.*

quick-freeze (kwíkfri:z) *pres. part.* **quick-freez·ing** *past* **quick-froze** (kwikfróuz) *past part.* **quick-fro·zen** (kwikfróuzʼn) *v.t.* to deep-freeze

quick grass couch grass

quick·ie (kwíki:) *n.* (*pop.*) anything made, produced or consumed quickly, esp. something not requiring much time or effort, e.g. a hastily made, cheap film

quick kick (*football*) a surprise punt made on the first, second, or third down

quick·lime (kwíklaim) *n.* lime (calcium oxide)

quick·sand (kwíksænd) *n.* a mass of unstable sand saturated with water, tending to suck down into it anyone or anything that comes on to it‖ such sand

quick·set (kwíksɛt) 1. *n.* live slips esp. of whitethorn or hawthorn, planted closely to make a hedge ‖ *Br.*) a quickset hedee 2. *adj.* (*Br.*, of a hedge etc.) made up of such slips planted in this way

quick·sil·ver (kwíksílvər) 1. *n.* mercury 2. *adj.* (of temperament) changing rapidly and without warning 3. *v.t.* to treat with quicksilver or a compound of this [O.E. *cwicseolfor* after L. *argentum vivum*]

quick·step (kwíkstɛp) *n.* (*mil.*) a step used in marching quick time ‖ music with this rhythm ‖ a quick dance step, esp. a fast fox-trot

quick-tem·pered (kwíktɛmpərd) *adj.* having a temper that flares up easily

quick time (*mil.*) a rate of marching reckoned as (*Am.*) 120 paces of 30 ins to the minute, (*Br.*) 128 paces of 33 ins to the minute

Quick-tran (kwíktræn) *n.* (*computer*) programming language for use on IBM 1050 terminal 7044 for time-sharing for concurrent access to up to 50 remote terminals

quick·trans (kwíktrænz) *n.* (*mil.*) long-term contract airlift service within continental U.S. for the movement of cargo in support of the logistic system for the military services. *Cf* LOGAIR

quick trick (*bridge*) a card or combination of cards that can be expected to win the first or second trick in a suit

quick-wit·ted (kwíkwítid) *adj.* having a ready wit ‖quick to understand

quid (kwid) *n.* a piece of chewing tobacco [var. of CUD]

quid *pl.* quid *n.* (*Br.*, *pop.*) a pound sterling **quids in** (*Br.*, *pop.*) full of winnings; a bet or a gamble [origin unknown]

quid·di·ty (kwíditi:) *pl.* **quid·di·ties** *n.* (*old-fash.*) the essence of a thing ‖ a quibble [fr. M.L. *quidditas* fr. *quid*, what]

quid pro quo (kwídproukwóu) *n.* something said or done in return for something else, esp. by way of retaliation [L.=something for something]

qui·es·cence (kwaiés'ns) *n.* the state or quality of being quiescent [fr. L.L. *quiescentia*]

qui·es·cent (kwaiés'nt) *adj.* at rest, dormant, inactive [fr. L. *quiescens* (*quiescentis*) fr. *quiescere*, to become quiescent]

qui·et (kwáiit) *n.* silence, stillness, the *quiet of the night* ‖ repose, *periods of quiet between bursts of activity* [fr. L. *quies* (*quietis*)]

quiet *adj.* peaceful, calm and undisturbed, *quiet waters* ‖ noiseless, the *machine room was quiet for once* ‖ not speaking at all, *to keep quiet* ‖ making little sound, *quiet footsteps* ‖ having little volume of sound, *a quiet voice* ‖ (of a person or the mind) free from anguish, worry etc. ‖ (of people) having a gentle, reserved manner ‖ (of colors) soft, unobtrusive ‖ (of feeling etc.) private, interior, *a mood of quiet happiness* ‖ tranquil, free from social pressures, *a quiet life* ‖ (of a social function) informal, attended by few people ‖ (*commerce*) characterized by relatively few sales or little business **on the quiet** (*pop.*) secretly ‖ stealthily [fr. L. *quietus* or O.F. *quiet*, *quiete*]

quiet *v.t.* to make quiet ‖ to soothe, *to quiet someone's fears* ‖ *v.i.* (usually with 'down') to become quiet [fr. M.L. *quietare*]

qui·et·en (kwáit'n) *v.t.* (*Br.*) to make quiet *v.i.* (*Br.*) to become quiet

qui·et·ism (kwáiitizəm) *n.* a Christian mystical doctrine of the 17th c., expounded chiefly by Molinos, Madame Guyon and Fénelon. It stressed the annihilation of the self in contemplation so as to allow free course to the divine will. It was ethically antinomian, and was condemned by Innocent XI (1687) and Innocent XII (1699) **qui·et·ist** *n.* **qui·et·is·tic** *adj.* [fr. Ital. *quietismo*]

qui·e·tude (kwáiitu:d, kwáiitju:d) *n.* (*rhet.*) stillness, calm [F. *quiétude*]

qui·e·tus (kwaii:təs) *n.* (*rhet.*) death, final dissolution [fr. M.L. *quietus est*, he is released (from a debt)]

quiff (kwif) *n.* (*Br.*) a flat curl on the forehead [origin unknown]

quill (kwil) 1. *n.* the hard, partly hollow stem of a bird's feather by which the feather is attached to the skin ‖ a long feather of a bird's wing or tail ‖ something, esp. a pen or a plectrum, made from the hard stem of a bird's feather ‖ the hollow spine of a porcupine ‖ (*weaving*) a spindle or bobbin ‖(*pharm.*) a roll of dried bark, e.g. of cinnamon or cinchona 2. *v.t.* (*weaving*) to wind (thread) onto a spindle or bobbin [etym. doubtful]

quil·lai (ki:jái) *n.* soapbark (tree or bark) [Span.]

Qui·lon (ki:lɔ̃) a port (pop. 100,000) of Kerala, India, on the Malabar coast. Industries: textiles, woodworking, chemicals, metallurgy

quilt (kwilt) 1. *n.* a bedcover made of feathers, flock or other padding between two pieces of fabric, held in place by lines of stitching ‖ an eiderdown ‖ (*esp. Br.*) a bedspread 2. *v.t.* to put padded material into ‖ to stitch or stitch together like a quilt ‖ to make (a quilt) ‖ *v.i.* to make a quilt **quilt·ing** *n.* the act of quilting ‖ padded material used esp. for making quilts and warm clothes [O.F. *cuilte*, *coilte*]

quin (kwin) *n.* (esp. *Br.*) a quintuplet [QUINTUPLET]

qui·nate (kwáinit) *adj.* (*bot.*, of a compound leaf) having five leaflets growing from one point [fr. L. *quini*, five each, like BINATE]

Qui·nault (ki:nou), Philippe (1635–88), French dramatist. He wrote libretti for Lully, e.g. 'Cadmus et Hermione' (1673), 'Armide' (1686) and 'Alceste' (1674)

quince (kwins) *n. Cydonia oblonga*, fam. *Rosaceae*, a small tree native to central and eastern Asia and cultivated in temperate climates. It bears solitary white flowers and pear-shaped, astringent yellow fruits, used cooked or preserved. The tree is also used as a dwarfing stock for grafting pears ‖ its fruit (orig. pl. of M.E. *qe*, a quince]

quin·cen·te·nar·y (kwinséntənɛri:) *pl.* **quin·cen·te·nar·ies** *n.* a 500th anniversary [fr. L. *quinque*, five+CENTENARY]

quin·cunx (kwíŋkʌŋks) *n.* an arrangement of five objects, e.g. the symbols on playing cards, with one at each corner and one in the center ‖ this as a planting unit, esp. for orchards [L. fr. *quinque*, five+*uncia*, a twelfth]

Quin·cy (kwínzi:, kwínsi:), Josiah (1772–1864), U.S. Federalist statesman and president (1829–45) of Harvard University. Appointed (1822) judge of the Boston Municipal Court, he was the first to rule that the publication of

CONCISE PRONUNCIATION KEY: **(a)** æ, c*a*t; ɑ, c*a*r; ɔ f*aw*n; ei, sn*a*ke. **(e)** e, h*e*n; i:, sh*ee*p; i:, sh*ee*p; iə, d*ee*r; ɛə, b*ea*r. **(i)** i, f*i*sh; ai, t*i*ger; əː, b*i*rd. **(o)** o, *o*x; au, c*ow*; ou, g*oa*t; u, p*oo*r; ɔi, r*oy*al. **(u)** ʌ, d*u*ck; u, b*u*ll; u:, g*oo*se; ə, b*a*cillus; ju:, c*u*be. x, lo*ch*; θ, *th*ink; ð, bo*th*er; z, *Z*en; ʒ, cor*s*age; dʒ, sava*g*e; ŋ, ora*ng*utan; j, *y*ak; ʃ, *fi*sh; tʃ, fet*ch*; 'l, rab*b*le; 'n, red*d*en. Complete pronunciation key appears inside front cover.

truth with good intent and for a justifiable end is not libel

quin·de·cil·lion (kwĭndĭsílʹjən) n. *NUMBER TABLE [fr. L. *quinque*, five+DECILLION]

Quine (kwaɪn), Willard Van Orman (1908–) U.S. philosopher and logician. Although influenced by such positivists as Rudolf Carnap, he deviated sharply from positivism with his denial of the distinction between analytic and synthetic statements and his view on the logical status of the problem of what exists. His belief that logic and language evolve as tools of inquiry reflect the pragmatism of Clarence Irving Lewis. His books include 'From a Logical Point of View' (1953), 'Word and Object' (1960), 'Philosophy of Logic' (1970) and 'Theories and Things' (1981)

quin·es·trol [$C_{25}H_{32}O_2$] (kwĭnástrol) n. (pharm.) estrogenic sex hormone; marketed as Estrovis

Qui·net (ki:neɪ), Edgar (1803–75), French republican writer. He wrote historical and philosophical works, including 'le Génie des religions' (1842), and imaginative works, including 'Ahasvérus' (1833), a prose poem

quin·i·dine [$C_{20}H_{24}N_2O_2$] (kwínədi:n) n. (pharm.) a cardiac depressant with actions similar to quinine in malaria; marketed as Cardioquin and Quinalglute

qui·nine (kwáinain, Br. esp. kwiní:n) n. an alkaloid $C_{20}H_{24}N_2O_2$, derived from the bark of the cinchona and used esp. as a febrifuge in antimalarial treatment ‖ a quinine salt [fr. Span. *quina* fr. Quechua *kina*, bark]

qui·no·a (ki:nóuə) n. *Chenopodium quinoa*, fam. Chenopodiaceae, a herbaceous plant native to the high Andes ‖ the seeds of this plant which, ground into meal, constitute a staple of the native diet [Span. fr. Quechua *kinua, kinoa*]

quin·o·line (kwínəli:n, kwínəlin) n. a colorless pungent, oily liquid, C_9H_7N, obtained from coal tar and bone oil, used in the manufacture of many dyes and medicines [fr. Span. *quina* fr. Quechua *kina*, bark]

qui·none (kwinóun) n. one of two compounds, $C_6H_4O_2$, derived from the benzene hydrocarbons, used in dyes [fr. Span. *quima* fr. Quechua *kina*, bark]

quin·qua·ge·nar·i·an (kwĭdkwədʒinéɑri:ən) 1. n. a person 50 years old or more but not yet 60 2. adj. having such an age [fr. L. *quinquagenarius* fr. *quinquaginta*, fifty]

Quin·qua·ges·i·ma (kwĭŋkwədʒe´simə) n. the Sunday before Lent [M.L. fr. *quinquagesimus*, fiftieth]

quin·que- (kwíŋkwei) prefix five [L. *quinque*, five]

quin·que·fo·li·o·late (kwĭŋkwifóuli:əleit) adj. (bot.) having five leaflets [QUINQUE-+L. *folium*, a leaf]

quin·quen·ni·al (kwĭŋkwéni:əl) 1. adj. taking place every five years ‖ of or lasting for a five-year period 2. n. a five-year period or term [fr. L. *quinquennis*]

quin·quen·ni·um (kwĭŋkwéni:əm) pl. **quin·quen·ni·ums, quin·quen·ni·a** (kwĭŋkwéni:ə) n. a five-year period [L. fr. *quinque*, five+*annus*, a year]

quin·que·va·lent, quin·qui·va·lent (kwĭŋkwivéilənt) adj. (chem.) exhibiting five different valencies (cf. PENTAVALENT) [fr. QUINQUE-+L. *valens* (*valentis*) fr. *valere*, to be strong]

quin·sy (kwínzi:) n. an abscess of the areas surrounding the tonsils, esp. when these are previously infected, giving rise to a very sore throat, difficulty in swallowing and fever [fr. M.L. *quinancia* fr. Gk *kunanchē* fr. *kun-*, dog+*anchein*, to throttle]

quint (kwint) n. a quintuplet [QUINTUPLET]

quint (kwint, kint) n. (piquet) a sequence of five cards [F. *quinte*]

quint (kwint, kint) n. a pipe-organ stop which causes a note to sound a fifth higher than the key depressed [F. *quint, quinte*]

quin·tain (kwíntin) n. (hist.) a device consisting of a vertical post surmounted by a pivoting horizontal bar with a board at one end and a bag of sand etc. at the other. It was used in a medieval sport in which a rider tilted at the board and tried to avoid being hit by the swinging bag [O.F. *quintaine*]

quin·tal (kwínt'l) n. a measure of weight which varies according to the country (in the U.S.A. 100 pounds, in England 112 pounds) ‖ a metric unit of weight equal to 100 kilograms [fr. O.F. fr. Arab. *quintar*]

Quin·ta·na Ro·o (ki:ntɑnɑrɔ´ɔ), Andrés (1787–1851), Mexican jurist, poet and patriot. He

served as president of the Congress of Chilpancingo (1813)

Quintana Roo a federal territory (area 19,630 sq. miles, pop. 209,858) of Mexico, on the eastern side of the Yucatán peninsula. Capital: Chetumal (pop. 8,000). Main products: chicle, copra. The hardwood forests are largely unexploited. The descendants of the Maya Indians, who form the bulk of the population, practice subsistence farming

quin·tar (kwíntar) n. one-hundredth of a lek [Albanian]

quin·tes·sence (kwintésʹns) n. the chief, purest or best part of anything, *the quintessence of the book is not in the film* ‖ someone or something perfectly exemplifying a quality ‖ (ancient and medieval philos.) the fifth and highest essence, present in all things, but distinct from the four elements of earth, water, air and fire **quin·tes·sen·tial** (kwĭntisénʹfəl) adj. [F. or fr. M.L. *quinta essentia*, fifth essence]

quin·tet, quin·tette (kwintét) n. (mus.) a composition for five performers ‖ a group of five instrumentalists or singers [F. *quintette*]

quin·tile (kwínt'l) n. (astron.) the aspect of two planets when distant 72° from one another (=360/5°) ‖ (statistics) one of the four values in a frequency distribution which divides the items into five categories [fr. L. *quintus*, fifth]

Quin·til·ian (kwintíljən) (Marcus Fabius Quintilianus, c. 35–95), Roman orator and teacher of rhetoric. His 'Institutio oratoria' (c. 95) describes the education of an orator and analyzes the composition, style and delivery of a classical speech

quin·til·lion (kwintíljən) n. *NUMBER TABLE **quin·til·lionth** n. and adj. [fr. L. *quintus*, fifth+MILLION]

quin·tu·ple (kwintjúː·p'l, kwintúː·p'l, kwintʌ´p'l) 1. adj. five times as much or as many ‖ having five parts (mus.) having five beats to a measure 2. n. a quantity or amount five times as large as another 3. v. pres. part. **quin·tu·pling** past and past part. **quin·tu·pled** v.t. to multiply by five ‖ v.i. to become five times as much or as many [F.]

quin·tu·plet (kwintʌ´plit, kwintú´plit, kwintjú´plit) n. one of five children born at a single birth [QUINTUPLE adj.]

quip (kwip) 1. n. a drily witty or sarcastic remark 2. v.t. pres. part. **quip·ping** past and past part. **quipped** to make (such a remark) ‖ v.i. to make such a remark or remarks [fr. older *quippy*, perh. fr. L. *quippe*, indeed]

qui·pu (kí:pu:) n. a device used by the ancient Peruvians for recording dates and events by knotting colored threads together [Quechua]

quire (kwáiər) n. a set of 24 or 25 matching sheets of paper ‖ four sheets of paper folded to form eight leaves ‖ a group of sheets folded one within the next in a book etc. **in quires** (of a book, manuscript etc.) in unbound folded sheets [O.F. *quaer, quaier*, a quire of six sheets]

Quir·i·nal (kwírin'l) one of the seven hills of Rome ‖ the former royal palace situated on it, now used by the president of Italy

Qui·ri·no (ki:rí:nɔ), Elpidio (1890–1956), second president (1948–53) of the Republic of the Philippines. His administration was marked by great progress in the post-war reconstruction

quirk (kwəːrk) n. a peculiar trait of character or kind of imagination ‖ a flourish with a pen in writing ‖ (archit.) a deep lengthwise groove in a molding [etym. doubtful]

Qui·ro·ga (ki:rɔ´ga), Horacio (1878– 1937), Uruguayan writer, best known for his short stories, notably 'Cuentos de la selva' (1918), 'Anaconda' (1921), 'El desierto' (1924), and 'Los desterrados' (1926)

Quiroga, Juan Facundo (1793–1835), Argentinian federalist. military adventurer, and virtual ruler (1820–30) of northeastern Argentina. His exploits earned him the nickname 'tiger of the llanos'. While governor of Buenos Aires (1834–5) he was assassinated

quirt (kwəːrt) 1. n. a short-handled riding whip, with a plaited leather lash 2. v.t. to lash with such a whip [Span. *cuarta*]

Quis·ling (kwízlɪŋ), Vidkun (1887–1945), Norwegian fascist politician. He led a puppet regime (1940–5) during the German occupation of Norway, and was executed for treason

quis·ling (kwízlɪŋ) n. person who collaborates with an enemy power occupying his country ‖ (loosely) a traitor [after V. QUISLING]

Quis·que·ya (kiskéijə) the original name of the island of Hispaniola

quit (kwit) adj. (usually followed by 'of') rid, free, *to be quit of an obligation* [M.E. *quite* fr. O.F.]

quit pres. part. **quit·ting** past and past part. **quit**, **quit·ted** v.t. to leave, go away from, *to quit the army* ‖ to resign (one's job) ‖ to discontinue (some activity), *to quit work* ‖ v.i. (Br., of a tenant) to leave a rented house, flat etc. ‖ to resign one's job ‖ to discontinue some activity [M.E. *quitten* fr. O.F.]

quitch (kwitf) n. couch grass [O.E. *cwice*, rh. related to *cwic*, quick]

quit·claim (kwítkleim) n. (law) a document by which the signatory renounces his rights to some title, claim or possession and gives this over to another person [M.E. *quitclaymie* fr. O.F.]

quitclaim v.t. to renounce one's rights to (a property, title etc.) by quitclaim [M.E. fr. A.F. and O.F. *quiteclamer, quiteclaimer*]

quite (kwait) adv. completely, entirely, *are you quite sure?, we are not quite there yet* ‖ very much, *he is quite an artist* rather, to an appreciable extent, *it's quite warm* ‖ (Br., as a response to a question or statement) true, yes **quite a few** a considerable number [M.E. fr. *quite, quit* adj.]

Qui·to (kí:tou) the capital (pop. 1,110,248) of Ecuador, in the N. Sierra at 9,300 ft, 170 miles from its port, Guayaquil. Earthquakes are frequent. Industries: textiles, food processing, light manufactures. Handicrafts: leatherwork, stone and wood carving, jewelry. It was a pre-Inca capital (10th–15th cc.). It was founded (1534) by Sebastián de Benalcázar with the name San Francisco de Quito. Cathedral (18th c.). University (1787)

quit·rent (kwítrɛnt) n. (hist.) a sum paid in commutation of feudal services

quits (kwits) adj. equal, on even terms as a result or repayment of a debt or injury, *to be quits (with someone)* **to call it quits** to agree to stop squabbling or competing without victory or defeat on either side, and with no ill feeling [QUIT adj.]

quit·tance (kwítʹns) n. acknowledgment of payment of a debt or the receipt for this [O.F. *quitance*]

quiv·er (kwívər) 1. v.i. to tremble, to shake with a slight, rapid movement, *leaves quivering in the breeze, to quiver with rage* ‖ v.t. to cause to tremble 2. n. a quivering ‖ a tremulous sound, *a quiver in his voice* [perh. imit.]

quiver n. a long case, suspended on a strap worn over one shoulder, to hold arrows ‖ the arrows themselves [A.F. *quiveir*, O.F. *quivre* fr. Gmc]

qui vive (ki:ví:v) n. (only in the phrase) **on the qui vive** on the alert, on guard or on the watch [F.=(long) live who?, originally a sentry's challenge]

quix·ot·ic (kwiksɔ́tik) adj. striving for or characterized by lofty ideals in a way that is ludicrous because totally unrealistic ‖ rashly altruistic **quix·ot·i·cal·ly** adv. [after Don Quixote, hero of a story by Cervantes]

quiz (kwiz) 1. pl. **quiz·zes** n. a short written or oral test of knowledge 2. v.t. pres. part. **quiz·zing** past and past part. **quizzed** to test (someone) by asking a series of questions [origin unknown]

quiz·zi·cal (kwízik'l) adj. interrogative, indicating a state of puzzlement, *a quizzical glance* ‖ teasing, gently mocking, *quizzical remarks* mildly eccentric or odd [QUIZ=(obs.) to make fun of]

Qum·ran (kumrán) a village of Jordan, northwest of the Dead Sea, the site of the ascetic community (2nd c. B.C.–1st c. A.D.) by whom the Dead Sea Scrolls were written

quo·drat (kwóudrət) n. (envir.) a sampling area, usu. 1 sq mi, used for analyzing vegetation. Cf QUATRAT

quoin (kɔin, kwɔin) 1. n. the external corner of a building, or one of the stones or bricks which form it (usually laid with their long axes in alternate directions) and which are distinguished from the material of the walls coming in to form the corner ‖ (printing) a wedge keeping type in its form ‖ a wedge used for various purposes, e.g. for raising a gun carriage 2. v.t. to secure or raise with a quoin [var. of COIN=(obs.) quoin, wedge] .

quoit (kɔit, kwɔit) n. a ring of rope, wood etc. used in a throwing game (pl.) a game in which such a ring is tossed towards a peg or small stake in an attempt to ring it [prob. fr. F.]

quon·dam (kwóndæm) *adj.* (*rhet.*) former, *a quondam colleague* [L.=formerly]

Quon·set hut (kwónsit) a prefabricated structure used for temporary army barracks etc. It has a cylindrical roof of corrugated iron curving down to form walls [Trademark]

quo·rum (kwórəm, kwóurəm) *n.* a number of people, fixed by rule, that must be present to make valid the proceedings of a committee, society, court etc. [L.=of whom]

quo·ta (kwóutə) *n.* an allotted share, to be either contributed or received, *each has his quota of work for the day* ‖ a numerical limit set on some class of things or persons, *a quota of immigrants* [M.L. *quota (pars)*, how great (a part)]

quo·ta·ble (kwóutəb'l) *adj.* which may be publicly repeated lending itself to quotation [QUOTE v.]

quota post an international post that a particular nation has accepted to fill indefinitely

quo·ta·tion (kwoutéiʃən) **1.** *n.* a passage or phrase quoted, esp. from printed literature ‖ the act of quoting ‖ the amount declared as the current price for a commodity etc. ‖ a contractor's estimate of the cost of a piece of work ‖ (*printing*) a large metal quad used for filling blanks [fr. M.L. *quotatio (quotationis)*, a reference to a passage in a manuscript etc.]

quotation marks single (") or double ("") punctuation marks signalizing direct speech, a quoted passage or phrase, book titles etc.

quote (kwout) **1.** *v. pres. part.* **quot·ing** *past* and *past part.* **quot·ed** *v.t.* to repeat in writing or speech (a passage or phrase previously said or written, esp. by someone else) ‖ to repeat in speech or writing a passage from, *to quote the Scriptures* ‖ to refer to (a person, work etc.) in support of a statement, *she quoted him as her authority* ‖ to enclose (a word or words) within quotation marks ‖ to state (the price) of a commodity etc. ‖ to state the price of (a commodity etc.) ‖ *v.i.* to make a quotation or quotations **2.** *n.*

a quotation ‖(*pl.*) quotation marks [fr. M.L. *quotare*, to mark the number of]

quo·tid·i·an (kwoutídiːən) **1.** *adj.* (*rhet.*) daily, occurring each day ‖ (of a fever) which occurs every day **2.** *n.* a quotidian fever [O.F. *cotidien, cotidian* or fr. L. *cotidianus, quotidianus*]

quo·tient (kwóuʃənt) *n.* the result obtained after dividing one number by another [fr. L. *quotiens*, how many times]

quo war·ran·to (kwọuwɔrǽntou) *n.* a writ issued by a court commanding a person to show by what warrant he holds an office, franchise etc. [Med. L.=by what warrant]

qu·rush (kʌrəʃ) *n.* a monetary unit of Saudi Arabia equal to one twentieth of a rial ‖ a coin of the value of one qurush

Q-val·ue (kjúvǽljuː) *n.* (*phys.*) quantity of energy released in a nuclear reaction, expressed in million electron volts, (MEV), or atomic mass units

	EARLY NORTH SEMITIC	PHOENICIAN	EARLY HEBREW (GEZER)	EARLY GREEK	CLASSICAL GREEK	ETRUSCAN Early	ETRUSCAN Classical	EARLY LATIN	CLASSICAL LATIN
R	٩	٩	٩٩	٩	P	٩	٩	R	R

CURSIVE MAJUSCULE (ROMAN)	CURSIVE MINUSCULE (ROMAN)	ANGLO-IRISH MAJUSCULE	CAROLINE MINUSCULE	VENETIAN MINUSCULE (ITALIC)	N. ITALIAN MINUSCULE (ROMAN)
٢	٧	℞	ɼ	ɼ	ɼ

A. C. SYLVESTER, CAMBRIDGE, ENGLAND

Development of the letter R, beginning with the early North Semitic letter. Evolution of both the majuscule, or capital, letter R and the minuscule, or lowercase, letter r are shown.

R, r (ɑr) the eighteenth letter of the English alphabet

R *adj.* motion picture rating of *restricted*, requiring that a person under the age of 18 (sometimes 17) be accompanied by an adult. *Cf* G, PG, X

Ra (rɑ) (*Egypt. mythol.*) the sun god and chief deity of ancient Egypt. He is usually represented as having the head of a hawk crowned with the solar disk

Raa·be (rúbə), Wilhelm (1831-1910), German novelist, best known for his 'Die Chronik aus der Sperlingsgasse' (1857) and 'Der Hungerpastor' (1864)

Rab (rɑb) a Yugoslav island (area 40 sq. miles, pop. 7,000), in the N. Adriatic: tourism

RABAL (*meteor. acronym*) for radiosonde balloon, a system of balloons at various altitudes that relay information about atmospheric conditions

Ra·ba·nus Mau·rus (rəbéinəsmɔ́rəs) (c. 780-856), German Benedictine theologian and scholar. As abbot of Fulda (822-42), he made the monastery a leading center of the Carolingian revival of learning

Ra·bat (rəbát) the capital (pop. 518,616) of Morocco, on the Atlantic: cotton spinning, weaving, leatherwork, carpets. Famous mosque (12th c.), palace, university

rab·bet (rǽbit) 1. *n.* a groove cut in a wooden board, panel etc. to fit the edge or a tongue on another piece of wood 2. *v.t.* to cut a rabbet in ∥ to join (two pieces of wood) with a rabbet [O.F. *rabat, rabbat* fr. *rabattre*, to beat down]

rab·bi (rǽbai) *n.* (*esp. hist.*) a teacher and scholar of Jewish civil and religious law ∥ an ordained leader of a Jewish congregation [Heb. *rabbî*, my master]

rab·bin (rǽbin) *n.* (*esp. hist.*) a rabbi (teacher) **rab·bin·ate** (rǽbinit, rǽbineit) *n.* the office or term of office of a rabbi ∥ (*collect.*) rabbis **rab·bín·ic** *adj.* of or pertaining to rabbis, their writings etc. ∥ of or pertaining to the rabbinate **Rab·bín·ic** 1. *adj.* of or pertaining to the rabbis of the period of the compilation and exegesis (c. 2nd c.–13th c.) of the Talmud 2. *n.* Rabbinic Hebrew [F. or fr. M.L. *rabbinus*]

rab·bin·i·cal (rəbínik'l) *adj.* **rabbinic Rab·bin·i·cal** *adj.* Rabbinic

Rabbinic Hebrew the Hebrew language as used by the rabbis in their writings, esp. during the Middle Ages

rab·bit (rǽbit) 1. *pl.* **rab·bits, rab·bit** *n. Oryctolagus cuniculus*, fam. *Leporidae*, a usually gray-brown, extremely prolific, herbivorous, burrowing lagomorph approximately 16 ins long. Native to W. Europe, it is now found in nearly all temperate regions. It has very long ears, a short round tail, and long hind limbs

and feet. It moves about by jumping. Rabbits yield meat good to eat and furs (*CONEY), poorer quality furs being made into felt ∥ the fur or pelt of a rabbit ∥ (*sports*) track-team member who sets a fast pace to induce competition to spend energy early in a long-distance race, to the advantage of a teammate ∥ (*Br., pop.*) someone who is very weak in games 2. *v.i.* to hunt rabbits [etym. doubtful]

rabbit ears *n. pl.* a V-shape indoor television antenna

rabbit punch (*boxing*) an illegal blow delivered with the outside edge of the hand to the base of the skull

rab·ble (rǽb'l) *n.* a large, disorderly mob of people **the rabble** (used contemptuously) the common people, lowest members of society [etym. doubtful]

rabble *n.* an iron rod bent at one end, used for stirring molten metal [F. *râble*]

Rab·e·lais (rǽblei), François (c. 1494–c. 1553), French writer and scholar. After a time in monasteries, he became a secular priest and a doctor. His great satirical work, usually known as 'Gargantua and Pantagruel', was published in parts (1532-64). 'Rabelaisian' has come to mean joyously coarse, for there is an enormous strain of hyperbolical bawdiness in Rabelais. It combines with his obvious love of life and its good things, and his extraordinary torrential style—punning, neologizing, alternately mockpedantic and earthy—to produce his special humor. He had a profound reverence and sympathy for the ideal of humanist learning. This is best expressed in the education devised for the philosophic monster Gargantua, and the description of the Abbey of Thelème. In contrast, monkish learning, the pedantries of medieval scholarship, and the bigotry which for Rabelais went with them, are derided. Yet the freedom and art of his grotesque humor places him firmly in the Middle Ages

Rab·e·lai·sian (rǽbəléizən) *adj.* (of humor) joyously coarse or gross ∥ of or pertaining to Rabelais [after RABELAIS]

Ra·bi (rúːbiː), Isidor Issac (1898-), U.S. physicist and winner of the 1944 Nobel prize in physics for discovering and measuring spectra in the radio-frequency range of atomic nuclei whose magnetic spin has been disturbed

rab·id (rǽbid) *adj.* affected with rabies ∥ pertaining to rabies ∥ violent, unreasoning, *a rabid reactionary* **ra·bid·i·ty** (rəbíditiː) *n.* [fr. L. *rabidus*, mad]

ra·bies (réibiːz) *n.* an acute virus disease of warm-blooded animals, esp. dogs. It is transmitted with infected saliva through the bite of a rabid animal (*HYDROPHOBIA)

Rabin (rabíːn), Yitzhak (1922-), Israeli statesman, prime minister (1974-7). He served as armed forces chief of staff (1964-8), during which time he directed the Six-Day War victory (1967), and as ambassador to the U.S.A. (1968-73) before being made prime minister. Pres. Shimon Peres named him defense minister in 1984

Ra·can (rækã), Honorat de Bueil, marquis de (1589-1670), French classical poet. 'Bergeries' (1625), a pastoral play, is his most important work

rac·coon, ra·coon (rækúːn) *pl.* **rac·coon, rac·coons, ra·coon, ra·coons** *n. Procyon lotor*, fam. *Procyonidae*, a North American carnivore about 32 ins in length, with grayish-brown fur and a bushy tail marked with black rings ∥ its fur [fr. Algonquian *ärähkun* fr. *ärähkunĕm*, he scratches with his hands]

race (reis) *n.* a distinct group of people, the members of which share certain inherited physical characteristics (skin color, form of the hair etc.) and transmit them ∥ all descendants of a person, family or a people, *the race of David* ∥ a group of people of the same profession or sharing some binding interest, *the race of actors* ∥ (*biol.*) a subdivision of a species ∥ (*biol.*) a permanent variety ∥ (*biol.*) a particular breed ∥ (*loosely*) a political, linguistic or nationalist group [F.]

race 1. *n.* a contest of speed in which runners, horses or yachts etc. try to reach a set goal first ∥ (*pl.*) a series of such contests for horses on a regular course ∥ (*astron.*) a set orbit ∥ a strong, swift current in water ∥ the channel of a stream, esp. one artificially constructed to create power for industrial use ∥ either of the rings of a ball bearing or a roller bearing between which the bearings rotate ∥ the groove along which a shuttle moves in a loom ∥ a slipstream 2. *v.i. pres. part.* **rac·ing** *past* and *past part.* **raced** to take part in a contest of speed ∥ to go swiftly ∥ (of an engine) to go very fast, either without the gears being engaged or because the load has been diminished *v.t.* to compete against in speed ∥ to cause (a horse etc.) to compete in a race ∥ to accelerate (an engine) very fast without engaging the gears ∥ to make (something or someone) move quickly [O.N. *rás*, a running]

racecourse (réiskɔrs, réiskɔurs) *n.* a racetrack **race·horse** (réishɔrs) *n.* a horse bred and trained for racing

ra·ceme (rəsíːm) *n.* an unbranched inflorescence having stalked flowers with the youngest growing at the tip (e.g. lupin, hyacinth) [fr. L. *racemus*, bunch of grapes]

race meeting (*Br.*) a number of horse races held at one place on one day or over several days

CONCISE PRONUNCIATION KEY: (**a**) æ, c*a*t; ɑ, c*a*r; ɔ f*aw*n; ei, sn*a*ke. (**e**) e, h*e*n; iː, sh*ee*p; iə, d*ee*r; ɛə, b*ea*r. (**i**) i, f*i*sh; ai, t*i*ger; əː, b*i*rd. (**o**) o, *o*x; au, c*ow*; ou, g*oa*t; u, p*oo*r; ɔi, r*oy*al. (**u**) ʌ, d*u*ck; u, b*u*ll; uː, g*oo*se; ə, b*a*cillus; juː, c*u*be. x, lo*ch*; θ, *th*ink; ð, bo*th*er; z, *Z*en; ʒ, corsa*g*e; dʒ, sava*g*e; ŋ, ora*ng*utan*g*; j, *y*ak; ʃ, *f*ish; tʃ, fe*tch*; 'l, rabb*le*; 'n, redd*en*. Complete pronunciation key appears inside front cover.

ra·ce·mic (rəsí:mik, rəsémik) *adj.* (*chem.*) of or pertaining to a compound or mixture having equal amounts of dextrorotatory and levorotatory forms of the same compound and which is therefore optically inactive to polarized light ‖ of or derived from racemic acid [F. *racémique*]

racemic acid racemic tartaric acid, obtained from grape juice

rac·e·mi·za·tion (ræsəmizéiʃən) *n.* the process of changing from an optically active substance to a racemic substance [RACEMIZE]

rac·e·mize (ræsəmaiz) *pres. part.* **rac·e·miz·ing** *past* and *past part.* **rac·e·mized** *v.t.* to cause to undergo racemization ‖ *v.i.* to undergo racemization [RACEMIC]

rac·e·mose (ræsəmous) *adj.* bearing a raceme or racemes ‖ of the nature of a raceme [fr. L. *racemosus*]

rac·er (réisər) *n.* a person or animal who races a car, bicycle etc. made and used for racing ‖ a circular rail on which a heavy coast artillery gun is traversed ‖ any of several snakes, esp. the black racer and the blue racer of North America [RACE]

race riot an outbreak of violence and fighting caused by racial hatred in a community

race suicide the gradual dying out of a race whose members deliberately fail to keep the birthrate as high as the death rate

race·track (réistræk) *n.* a course laid out, typically in an oval, for horse racing

Ra·chel (réitʃəl) (*Bible*) the wife of Jacob, and the mother of Joseph and Benjamin

ra·chis (réikis) *pl.* **ra·chis·es**, **ra·chi·des** (réikidi:z) *n.* the central stalk which bears the leaflets of a compound leaf ‖ (*bot.*) the axis of an inflorescence ‖ the shaft of a feather ‖ the spinal column [Mod. L. fr. Gk *rhachis*, spine]

ra·chit·ic (rəkítik) *adj.* suffering from or pertaining to rickets

ra·chi·tis (rəkáitis) *n.* rickets [Mod. L. fr. Gk *rhachitis*, inflammation of the spine]

Rach·ma·ni·noff (rækmáninɔf, ræxmáninɔf), Sergei Vassilievich (1873-1943), Russian composer, pianist and conductor who lived in the U.S.A. after 1918. The best-known of his highly romantic compositions are the piano preludes and the Second Piano Concerto (1901)

ra·cial (réiʃəl) *adj.* pertaining to or caused by the distinction between races **rá·cial·ism** *n.* race hatred or race discrimination

rac·i·ly (réisili:) *adv.* in a racy way

Ra·cine (ræsí:n), Jean (1639-99), French dramatist. He was as great a poet as he was a dramatist, developing the Alexandrine as an instrument for the direct expression of intense emotion, in language of great beauty. His plays are based on classical themes and they obey the classical unities and conventions. In the 24 hours of the action the fruit of years, or a lifetime, is reaped, so that the audience is filled with a profound sense of destiny. The motivating force is always love, which is presented as a destructive force dissolving the personality and bringing spiritual disaster. Racine's heroes and heroines analyze their failings with great lucidity, and this lucidity adds to the pathos and feeling of imminent disaster. Racine's greatest plays are: 'Andromaque' (1667), 'Britannicus' (1669), 'Bérénice' (1670) and 'Phèdre' (1677)

rac·i·ness (réisi:nis) *n.* the quality of being racy

racing form information printed in a newspaper or in a separate sheet, comprising data about horses, races, jockeys, odds etc.

rac·ism (réisizəm) *n.* the assumption that the characteristics and abilities of an individual are determined by race and that one race is biologically superior to another ‖ a political program or social system based on these assumptions **rác·ist** *n.* and *adj.*

rack (ræk) **1.** *n.* a mass of clouds driven by the wind **2.** *v.i.* (of scudding clouds) to fly before the wind [prob. fr. Scand.]

rack *n.* a framework of wooden or metal bars, pegs etc. for holding objects, often adapted to objects of a particular type, e.g. hats, plates ‖ a shelf of bars or cord mesh in a railroad car etc. to hold luggage ‖ a framework in a stable, paddock etc. holding hay or fodder ‖ a framework fitted on a wagon for carrying hay, straw etc. ‖ a bar or rail with teeth which gear into those of a cogwheel or worm ‖ (*printing*) a frame holding type cases ‖ a row or box of pigeonholes into which letters etc. are sorted ‖ (*pool games*) a triangular frame for setting up the balls at the beginning of a game [prob. M. Du. *rec* fr. *recken*, to stretch]

rack 1. *v.t.* (*hist.*) to torture by stretching on a rack ‖ to inflict extreme mental or physical pain upon ‖ to shake or strain severely, *a racking cough* ‖ (of a landlord) to exact an unjustly high rent from (a tenant) ‖ (of a landlord) to raise (rents) unjustly and exorbitantly **to rack one's brains** to think very hard ‖ to try very hard to remember **2.** *n.* (*hist.*) an instrument of torture consisting of a frame with rollers at each end, to which the victim's wrists and ankles were tied so that he was stretched as the rollers were turned **on the rack** in physical or mental anguish [prob. fr. M. Du. or Middle L.G. *recken*, to stretch]

rack *n.* (only in the phrase) **rack and ruin** utter destruction or decay [var. of WRACK]

rack 1. *n.* a fast gait in which a horse is supported on the right and left pairs of legs alternately **2.** *v.i.* (of a horse) to go at a rack [etym. doubtful]

rack *v.t.* to draw off (wine etc.) from the lees [fr. Prov. *arracar* fr. *raca*, stems and skins of grapes]

rack and pinion (*mechanics*) method of exchanging linear and rotary force by engagement between a straight-toothed rack and a small gear-wheel (pinion)

rack car a railroad freight car equipped with two or three levels for carrying automobiles

rack·et, **rac·quet** (rækit) *n.* (*games*) a bat formed by a long-handled oval wooden frame across which a mesh of catgut or nylon is stretched. Each game (tennis, squash etc.) played with a racket has its own special kind ‖ (*pl.*) a game not unlike squash played with rackets and a ball in a four-walled court by two or four players [F. *raquette*]

racket *n.* a considerable and usually continued clattering noise or similar disturbance ‖ (*pop.*) a fraudulent means of gaining money on a large or small scale ‖ (*pop.*) an easy way of making money which is lawful but not praiseworthy or respectable **to stand the racket** (*Br.*) to take the blame for an action [prob. imit.]

racket ball a small, hard, kid-covered ball used in rackets

rack·et·eer (rækitíər) *n.* a person who is engaged in fraudulent business or who extorts money by threats, blackmail etc.

rack·et·y (rækiti:) *adj.* noisy, causing a racket

rack railway a railway with an extra, cogged rail between the lines, which engages with a cogged wheel on the railway engine to prevent its sliding back on steep slopes

rack rent an unjustly large sum demanded as rent for property **rack-rent** *v.t.* to subject to such extortion

rac·on·teur (rækɒntə:r) *n.* a person who tells anecdotes well [F.]

ra·coon *RACCOON

racquet *RACKET

rac·y (réisi:) *comp.* **rac·i·er** *superl.* **rac·i·est** *adj.* spirited, lively, *written in a racy style* ‖ (of stories or conversation) wittily indecent

rad (ræd) *n.* (*phys.*) unit of absorbed radiation equal to 100 ergs per gram of irradiated material

RADAN (acronym) for radar doppler automatic navigation, an aircraft radar navigation system depending on Doppler effect, with no ground communication

ra·dar (réidɑr) *n.* a radio system which detects the presence, position and speed of such objects as ships, aircraft, vehicles etc. by emitting microwaves and measuring by electronic devices the speed with which they return after reflection from the object. It is also used e.g. for guiding ships and aircraft in fog etc. or by police for determining the speed of vehicles etc. [RAdio Detection And Ranging]

radar astronomy (*meteor.*) study of celestial bodies through use of radar signals sent from earth —**radar telescope** *n.* the instrument used

radar range distance at which a radar sighting may be made with 50% visibility

ra·dar·sonde (réidərsɒnd) *n.* **1.** (*meteor.*) a system for measuring atmospheric conditions automatically from high altitudes and transmitting data via a ground command signal **2.** a system to gauge the range, elevation, and azimuth of a radar target

Rad·cliffe (rædklif), Mrs Ann (1764-1823), British novelist. Her Gothic novels include 'The Mysteries of Udolpho' (1794)

rad·dled (ræd'ld) *adj.* (of aging women) grotesquely rouged, haggard under cosmetics [fr. older *raddle*, to ruddle]

Ra·detz·ky (rædétski:) Joseph, Graf Radetzky von Radetz (1766-1858), Austrian field marshal. He led the Austrian army against Sardinia (1848-9), winning brilliant victories at Custozza (1848) and Novara (1849)

Radhakrishnan (radəkríʃnən), Sir Sarvepalli (1888-1976), Indian statesman and educator, president (1962-7). He taught at Oxford (1936-9), Benares Hindu (1938-48) and Delhi (1953-62) universities; headed the Indian UNESCO delegation (1946-52); was ambassador to the U.S.S.R. (1949-52); and was vice-president (1952-62) before becoming president. His works include 'Indian Philosophy' (1923-7), 'An Idealist View of Life' (1932) and 'Indian Philosophy Religions and Western Thought' (1939)

ra·di·ac (réidiæk) *adj.* (*mil.* acronym) for radioactivity detection, indication, and computation of various types of radiological measuring instruments, or equipment. —**radiac dosimeter** *n.* an instrument used to measure the ionizing radiation absorbed by that instrument

ra·di·al (réidiəl) **1.** *adj.* pertaining to a radius ‖ arranged like or resembling radii ‖ having radiating lines, *radial engine* ‖ (*anat.*) pertaining to the radius ‖ moving along a radius **2.** *n.* a radial nerve or artery [fr. L.L. *radialis*]

radial, radial-ply tire, or **radial tire** *n.* a pneumatic tire made with ply casing cords parallel at right angles to the center line and rim

radial keratotomy (*med.*) surgical process involving a series of cuts into the transparent corneal tissue, causing a slight bulge, thus improving the focusing ability of nearsighted people; developed by U.S.S.R. scientist Svyatoslav Fydorov in 1980

radial symmetry the state of having an arrangement of similar parts around a median vertical axis, e.g. in jellyfish or starfish

ra·di·an (réidiən) *n.* a unit of angular measurement, the angle subtended at the center of a circle by an arc equal in length to the radius. Since the circumference of a circle equals 2π times its radius the total angle in a complete turn (360°) is 2π radians [RADIUS]

ra·di·ance (réidiəns) *n.* the state or quality of being radiant **rá·di·an·cy** *n.* [fr. L.L. or M.L. *radiantia*]

ra·di·ant (réidiənt) **1.** *adj.* emitting energy in the form of electromagnetic waves ‖ shining, bright ‖ bright with, or expressing, great joy, hope etc., *a radiant smile* **2.** *n.* (*astron.*) a point from which a meteor appears to proceed ‖ (*phys.*) a point which is a source of radiant energy [fr. L. *radians* (*radiantis*) fr. *radiare*, to emit rays]

ra·di·ate (réidi:eit) **1.** *v. pres. part.* **ra·di·at·ing** *past* and *past part.* **ra·di·at·ed** *v.t.* to emit (something) in all directions from a central point ‖ *v.i.* to lose energy by emission of waves or particles ‖ to proceed in all directions from a central point, *eight roads radiate from the marketplace* **2.** *adj.* radially symmetrical ‖ having ray flowers [fr. L. *radiare* (*radiatus*), to emit rays]

ra·di·a·tion (réidi:éiʃən) *n.* the act or process of radiating ‖ energy radiated in the form of waves or particles (e.g. the energy in the form of heat and light radiated from an incandescent source) [fr. L. *radiatio* (*radiationis*)]

radiation chemistry the study of the chemical effects of high-energy radiations on matter (cf. RADIOCHEMISTRY)

radiation genetics study of mutations produced by ionizing radiation. *also* radiogenetics

radiation sickness an illness caused by the action of high-energy radiation upon the body, resulting either from radiotherapy or from radioactive debris after an atomic-bomb explosion. Vomiting and fatigue are the first symptoms after exposure, and may be followed later by liability to infection, hemorrhage, prostration and death

ra·di·a·tor (réidi:eitər) *n.* any of various heating or cooling devices which work by radiating heat ‖ any object emitting radiant energy [RADIATE]

rad·i·cal (rædik'l) **1.** *adj.* relating to or affecting fundamentals, *a radical change* ‖ existing in the essential character of a person or thing, *radical differences* ‖ (*math.*) relating to the root of a number ‖ (*bot.*, e.g. of basal leaves or peduncles) arising from the rhizome, or rootlike stem ‖ (*gram.*) of or pertaining to a linguistic root ‖ (*esp. politics*) seeking to make drastic reforms in society as it is **2.** *n.* (*math.*) a number or quantity as the root of another number or quantity ‖

CONCISE PRONUNCIATION KEY: **(a)** æ, c*a*t; ɑ, c*a*r; ɔ f*aw*n; ei, sn*a*ke. **(e)** e, h*e*n; i:, sh*ee*p; iə, d*ee*r; εə, b*ea*r. **(i)** i, f*i*sh; ai, t*i*ger; ə:, b*i*rd. **(o)** o, *o*x; au, c*ow*; ou, g*oa*t; u, p*oo*r; ɔi, r*oy*al. **(u)** ʌ, d*u*ck; u, b*u*ll; u:, g*oo*se; ə, b*a*cillus; ju:, c*u*be. x, lo*ch*; θ, *th*ink; ð, bo*th*er; z, *Z*en; ʒ, cor*s*age; dʒ, sava*g*e; ŋ, ora*ng*utang; j, *y*ak; ʃ, *f*ish; tʃ, fe*tch*; 'l, rabb*le*; 'n, redd*en*. Complete pronunciation key appears inside front cover.

(*chem.*) an atom or group of atoms that retains its identity during chemical changes of the rest of the molecule ‖ (*chem.*) a free radical ‖ (*gram.*) the base or root of a word from which other words can be formed ‖ (*politics*) a person of radical views or sympathies [fr. L.L. *radicalis*]

rad·i·cal·ism (rǽdik'lizəm) *n.* the state or quality of being radical, esp. in politics ‖ the doctrines or practices of radicals, esp. political radicals

radical right (*U.S.*) extreme conservative movement in politics, e.g., fascism —**radical rightism** *n.* —**radical rightist** *n.*

radical sign the symbol √ or √‾, indicating that the square root is to be extracted from the quantity that follows the sign

radices alt. *pl.* of RADIX

rad·i·cle (rǽdik'l) *n.* the primary root developing in a seed ‖ a rootlet of a seedling ‖ (*chem.*) a radical ‖ (*anat.*) a small rootlike origin of a bodily part [fr. L. *radicula*, dim. of *radix*, root]

rad·i·es·the·sia (rædi:esθí:ʒə) *n.* 1. use of a divining rod, e.g., for water 2. the capability of using a divining rod 3. the study of the subject

Ra·di·guet (rædi:gei), Raymond (1903-23), French novelist, author of 'le Diable au corps' (1923) and 'le Bal du comte d'Orgel' (published 1924)

radii alt. *pl.* of RADIUS

ra·di·o (réidi:ou) 1. *n.* the transmission and reception of messages by electromagnetic waves ‖ broadcasting for public entertainment ‖ a radio receiving set ‖ a message sent by radio 2. *adj.* operated by radiant energy, esp. electromagnetic waves ‖ (of waves) having a frequency between about 10^4 and 3×10^{11} cycles ‖ of or relating to radio or a radio receiving set 3. *v.i.* to communicate by radio ‖ *v.t.* to send (a message) by radio [shortened from RADIOTELEGRAPHY] —Coded signals, speech, music etc. may be transmitted by superimposing the audible signals on an electromagnetic carrier wave of much higher frequency, so that they vary (modulate) the frequency of the amplitude of the carrier wave. In the receiver the superimposed signal is isolated and fed to a loudspeaker. The radio frequency band occupies a range of wavelengths from 10^5 to 10^{-3} meters

radio- *prefix* concerned with radiation ‖ radioactive ‖ radio [fr. L. *radius*, spoke, ray]

ra·di·o·ac·tin·i·um (rẹidi:ouæktíni:əm) *n.* (*phys.*) thorium isotope resulting from natural decay of actinium 227. *abbr.* RdAc

ra·di·o·ac·tive (rẹidi:ouǽktiv) *adj.* of, relating to or having radioactivity ‖ **ra·di·o·ac·tiv·i·ty** *n.* the property possessed by some natural elements (e.g. radium, uranium) and many synthetic elements (all those with atomic number greater than 92) of spontaneously undergoing nuclear decay, emitting either an alpha particle (reducing their atomic number by 2 and mass number by 4) or a beta particle (increasing their atomic number by 1, leaving their mass number unaltered). Emission of a beta particle is accompanied by the emission of a neutrino, the overall process obeying both energy and momentum conservation. Sometimes emission of either alpha or beta particles leaves the new nucleus in an excited state from which it falls with the emission of a gamma ray. The rates for such nuclear processes, usually indicated by the half-life, vary over a tremendous range (from a microsecond to a billion years or more). The half-life for a radioactive element is an important constant, characteristic of the element (*FISSION, *NUCLEAR ENERGY)

radioactive dating a technique for dating ancient objects by evaluating and comparing the ratio of radioisotopes contained in them —**radiocarbon age** *n.* Cf RADIOCARBON DATING

radioactive decay (*nuclear phys.*) the decrease in the radiation intensity of any radioactive material over time, generally accompanied by the emission of particles and/or gamma radiation

radioactive isotope or **radioisotope** (*nuclear chem.*) any of two or more natural or artificially produced chemical elements with the same atomic number but a different mass number, used for tracing in medicine and industry —**radioisotopic** *adj.* —**radioisotopically** *adv.*

radioactive tracer a preparation consisting of a radioisotope added to a nonradioactive material, to tag it in order that it can be followed in a living system or along an oil pipeline

radio astronomy a branch of astronomy dealing with electromagnetic radiation in the range of radio frequencies received (*RADIO TELESCOPE) from objects or regions outside the earth's atmosphere. Radio astronomy has been able, for example, to elucidate the structure of spiral galaxies, since these contain large quantities of hydrogen which emits a strong signal of wavelength 21 cm.

radio beacon a radio station which transmits a special identifying signal to enable esp. an aircraft to fix its position at night or in fog

radio beam a beam of radio-frequency electromagnetic radiation, emitted from a highly directional antenna, used in location and guidance systems

ra·di·o·car·bon (rẹidi:oukárbən) *n.* radioactive carbon, esp. carbon 14 (*CARBON)

radiocarbon dating a technique for determining the age of ancient material by measuring the proportion of 12C to residual 14C, a constant ratio formed by cosmic radiation in living organisms. 14C has a half-life of 5,740 yrs. *also* carbon dating, carbon 14 dating. Cf RADIOACTIVE DATING

ra·di·o·chem·is·try (rẹidi:oukémistri:) *n.* the chemistry of radioactive elements and compounds ‖ radiation chemistry

ra·di·o·chro·ma·tog·ra·phy (rẹidi:oukrọumətógrəfi:) *n.* measurement of isotope-labeled chemicals by their radioactivity —**radiochromatographic** *adj.*

ra·di·o·e·col·o·gy (rẹidi:ouikólədʒi:) *n.* the study of effects of radiation on plant and animal life —**radioecological** *adj.* —**radioecologically** *adv.* —**radioecologist** *n.*

radio frequency any of a range of electromagnetic wave frequencies used for carrier-wave radio and television transmission

radio galaxy (*astron.*) a group of celestial bodies from which radio energy emissions are detected

ra·di·o·gen·ic (rẹidi:oudʒénik) *adj.* (*nuclear phys.*) produced by radioactive transformation. Cf RADIATION GENETICS

ra·di·o·gram (réidi:ougræm) *n.* a radiograph ‖ a message sent by wireless telegraphy ‖ (*Br.*) a radiogramophone [fr. RADIO-+Gk *gramma*, letter]

ra·di·o·gram·o·phone (rẹidi:ougrǽməfoun) *n.* (*Br.*) a cabinet combining radio receiver and a record player

ra·di·o·graph (réidi:ougræf, réidi:ougrɑf) 1. *n.* an image produced on a fluorescent screen or photographic plate by rays other than those of light, esp. an X-ray photograph 2. *v.t.* to take an X-ray photograph of **ra·di·og·ra·pher** (rẹidi:ógrəfər) *n.* someone who takes X-ray photographs, esp. for medical purposes **ra·di·o·graph·ic** (rẹidi:ougrǽfik) *adj.* **ra·di·og·ra·phy** (rẹidi:ógrəfi:) *n.* the making of X-ray photographs [fr. RADIO-+Gk *-graphos*, written]

ra·di·o·im·mu·no·as·say (rẹidi:ouiṃmjunouǽsei) *n.* (*med.*) diagnostic technique utilizing radioisotopes to measure small quantities of hormones and enzymes present in blood and tissue —**radioimmunoassayable** *adj.* *abbr.* RIA. Cf IMMUNOASSAY

ra·di·o·i·so·tope (rẹidi:ouáisətoup) *n.* a radioactive isotope

ra·di·o·la·beled (rẹidi:ouléib'ld) *n.* a material into which a radioactive substance has been added for identification or tracing

ra·di·o·lar·i·an (rẹidi:ouléəri:ən) 1. *n.* a member of *Radiolaria*, an order of highly organized marine rhizopods, producers of almost indestructible siliceous skeletons. Their remains form an ooze on the Pacific and Indian Ocean bottoms 2. *adj.* of a radiolarian [fr. L.L. *radiolus*, dim. of *radius*, ray]

ra·di·o·lo·ca·tion (rẹidi:ouloukéiʃən) *n.* the science and practice of identifying distant objects, e.g. aircraft or ships, by radar

ra·di·ol·o·gist (rẹidi:ólədʒist) *n.* a specialist in radiology

ra·di·ol·o·gy (rẹidi:ólədʒi:) *n.* the study of radioactive substances and high-energy radiations (e.g. X rays, gamma rays), esp. their use in the diagnosis and treatment of disease [fr. RADIO-+Gk *logos*, word]

ra·di·om·e·ter (rẹidi:ómitər) *n.* a device to detect or measure electromagnetic radiation, commonly a pivoted set of vanes each with one black and one polished side [fr. L. *radius*, ray+METER]

ra·di·o·paque (rẹidi:oupéik) *adj.* opaque to radiation

ra·di·o·par·ent (rẹidi:oupǽrənt) *adj.* transparent to radiation

ra·di·o·phar·ma·ceu·ti·cal (rẹidi:oufɑrməsú:tik'l) *n.* a radioactive drug used in therapy, diagnosis, or research

radio pill (*med.*) capsuled radio transmitter used in medical diagnosis for monitoring physiological activity, e.g., pH values in animal digestion

ra·di·o·pro·tec·tive (rẹidi:ouprətéktiv) *adj.* of a shield that reflects or absorbs radiation to protect against exposure —**radioprotection** *n.* —**radioprotector** *n.*

ra·di·o·re·sis·tance (rẹidi:ourizístəns) *n.* capability of resisting the effects of radiation, e.g., certain cells. —**radioresistant,** *adj.*

ra·di·o·re·sis·tant (rẹidi:ourizístənt) *adj.* (esp. of cancer cells) not destroyed by radiation (cf. RADIOSENSITIVE)

ra·di·o·scop·ic (rẹidi:əskópik) *adj.* of or pertaining to radioscopy

ra·di·os·co·py (rẹidi:óskəpi:) *n.* the study of opaque material, esp. by X rays [fr. RADIO-+Gk *skopein*, to look at]

ra·di·o·sen·si·tive (rẹidi:ousénsitiv) *adj.* (esp. of cancer cells) able to be destroyed by radiation (cf. RADIORESISTANT)

ra·di·o·sonde (réidi:ousɒnd) *n.* a balloon equipped with a radio transmitter from which information is obtained about atmospheric conditions at high altitudes

radio spectrum the radio-frequency spectrum

radio stars (*astron.*) celestial bodies that are probably made up of turbulent gases and are identified by discrete radio emissions, e.g., a crab nebula, Cygnus A

ra·di·o·sterilization (rẹidi:ousterəlizéiʃən) *n.* process of sterilizing by use of radiation —**radiosterilize** *v.*

ra·di·o·tel·e·gram (rẹidi:outéligræm) *n.* a message sent by radiotelegraphy

ra·di·o·tel·e·graph (rẹidi:outéligræf, rẹidi:outéligrɑf) 1. *n.* radiotelegraphy 2. *v.t.* to transmit (a message) by means of radiotelegraphy

ra·di·o·te·leg·ra·phy (rẹidi:outəlégrəfi:) *n.* telegraphy by means of radio waves

ra·di·o·te·lem·e·try (rẹidi:outəlémitri:) *n.* measurement of distance by radio transmission. —**radiotelemetric** *adj.* Cf BIOTELEMETRY

ra·di·o·tel·e·phone (rẹidi:outélifoun) *n.* a transmitter for radiotelephony

ra·di·o·te·leph·o·ny (rẹidi:outəléfəni:) *n.* sound transmitted by radio waves. The sound is converted by a microphone into electrical impulses which are superimposed on a continuous carrier wave, esp. a microwave. The receiver, after amplification and rectification of the carrier wave, passes the resulting direct current through a telephone, which reconverts the impulses into sound

radio telescope an instrument for studying radio signals of cosmic origin (particularly the 21-cm. hydrogen radio line). It consists of an antenna (usually a large paraboloid, mounted on a heavy, vibration-free, mechanically steerable base) for capturing and focusing the cosmic signal, and a receiver for amplifying and rectifying it (*RADIO ASTRONOMY)

ra·di·o·tel·e·type (rẹidi:outélitaip) *n.* communication by radio-operated telegraphy connected to a typewriter *abbr.* RTTY

ra·di·o·ther·a·pist (rẹidi:ouθérəpist) *n.* a specialist in radiotherapy

ra·di·o·ther·a·py (rẹidi:ouθérəpi:) *n.* the treatment of malignant tumors and certain other diseases by means of X rays and radioactive substances

ra·di·o·thon (rẹidi:ouθón) *n.* a long-continuing radio program in support of a cause, usu. to raise funds

ra·di·o·tox·ic (rẹidi:outóksik) *adj.* of toxic effects of radiation —**radiotoxin** *n.* the poison in irradiated chemicals —**radiotoxologic** *adj.* of the study of radiotoxins

rad·ish (rǽdiʃ) *n. Raphanus sativus*, fam. *Cruciferae*, an annual plant with a basal rosette of leaves, and a tuberous taproot esteemed for its pungent, crisp flesh ‖ this root [O.E. *rædic, redic* fr. L.]

ra·di·um (réidi:əm) *n.* a shining white, divalent metallic element (symbol Ra, at. no. 88, mass of isotope of longest known half-life 226) which is strongly radioactive, disintegrating into radon. It was first isolated by Pierre and Marie Curie. It is used in radiography and radiotherapy and in the making of luminous paints etc. [Mod. L. fr. *radius*, ray]

ra·di·us (réidi:əs) pl. **ra·di·i** (réidi:ai), **ra·di·us·es** n. a straight line drawn from the center of a circle or sphere to any point on its periphery, or the length of this line ‖ a radiating part, e.g. a spoke of a wheel ‖ any of a number of lines diverging from a central point ‖ (pop.) an area measured or indicated by a radius, *he knows all the bars in a 15-mile radius* ‖ (anat.) the shorter of the two bones of the forearm in man, or the corresponding bone in an animal's forelimb or bird's wing. In some vertebrates it is fused with the ulna ‖ the ray or outer zone of petals of a composite flower, e.g. the daisy ‖ an insect-wing vein [L.=spoke, ray]

radius of gyration the square root of the mean squared distance of the particles of a pivoted body from the pivot point (*MOMENT OF INERTIA)

radius vector pl. **radii vec·to·res** (vektóri:z, vektóui:z) (math.) a line, or the length of a line, from a fixed point to a variable point ‖ (astron.) a straight line between a star or planet and a heavenly body describing an orbit around it

ra·dix (réidiks) pl. **rad·i·ces** (rædisi:z, réidisi:z), **ra·dix·es** n. a number or value used as the basis for a scale of numeration, measurement etc., *10 is the radix of the decimal system* ‖ (bot.) the root of a plant ‖ (anat.) a radicle [L.=root]

RADNO (acronym) (transposed) for *No Radio*, fadeout of reception in arctic areas believed to be the result of solar explosions

Rad·nor·shire (rædnərʃiər) (abbr. Radnor.) a county (area 471 sq. miles, pop. 18,000) in N. Wales. County town: Presteigne (pop. 1,000). Administrative center: Llandrindod Wells (pop. 3,000)

Ra·dom (rúdɔm) a town (pop. 183,600) in Poland, 60 miles south of Warsaw: metallurgy, chemicals, tanning, mechanical engineering

ra·dome (acronym) for radar dome, a radar antenna housing made of insulation material that permits passage of radio frequency radiation

ra·don (réidɒn) n. a radioactive gaseous element (symbol Rn, at. no. 86, mass of isotope of longest known half-life 222) formed by the disintegration of radium ‖ a radioactive gas released from the earth, esp. before an earthquake [RADIUM]

rad·u·la (rædʒulə) pl. **rad·u·lae** (rædʒuli:) n. a short broad strip of membrane bearing rows of chitinous teeth, found in the mouths of most gastropod mollusks [L.=scraper]

Rae·burn (réibərn), Sir Henry (1756-1823), Scottish portrait painter who made many paintings of contemporary leading Scottish figures, esp. in Edinburgh

Raetia *RHAETIA

raf·fi·a (ræfi:ə) n. the fiber obtained from the leaves of *Raphia ruffia*, the low-growing raffia palm of Madagascar. It is used for matting, tying up plants etc. [Malagasy]

raf·fi·né (ræfi:néi) adj. (Fr.) highbrow, ultra-refined

raf·fish (ræfiʃ) adj. (of appearance) flashily attractive without breeding or style ‖ (esp. of men) somewhat disreputable, in a flashy way [fr. older *raff*, a low fellow]

raf·fle (ræfəl) 1. n. a lottery in which numbered tickets are sold to a large number of people, the holder of a ticket selected at random qualifying for a prize 2. v. pres. part. **raf·fling** past and past part. **raf·fled** v.t. (usually with 'off') to sell by raffle ‖ v.i. to take part in or conduct a raffle [F. *rafle*, a dice game]

raffle n. (naut.) a jumble of ropes, canvas etc. [perh. fr. O.F. *rafle* used in phrase *rifle ou rafle*, anything at all]

Raf·fles (ræfəlz), Sir Thomas Stamford Bigley (1781-1826), British colonial administrator. He was lieutenant governor of Java (1811-16). He acquired Singapore for Britain (1819)

raft (ræft, raft) 1. n. a floating platform used for transportation over water or moored as a diving platform or landing stage ‖ a number of casks, logs etc. lashed together for floating down a river ‖ a mass of floating driftwood, ice etc. 2. v.t. to transport on a raft ‖ to make into a raft ‖ to cross (a river) on a raft ‖ v.i. to work a raft ‖ to go by raft [O.N. *raptr*, rafter]

raft n. (pop.) a lot, large number [fr. older *raff*, a jumble]

raf·ter (ræftər, ráftər) n. one of the sloping beams forming the framework of a roof [O.E. *ræfter*]

raft·er n. a man who forms rafts out of logs

rafts·man (ræftsmən, ráftsmən) pl. **rafts·men** (ræftsmən, ráftsmən) n. someone who works a raft or works on a raft

rag (ræg) n. a torn, tattered or worn scrap, piece of cloth, article of clothing etc. ‖ (pl.) shabby, tattered clothing ‖ a small piece of used cloth for cleaning or polishing ‖ (pop., pejorative) a newspaper [M.E. *ragge*]

rag 1. v. pres. part. **rag·ging** past and past part. **ragged** v.t. to tease ‖ to scold ‖ (Br., pop.) to play practical, esp. rough, jokes upon ‖ v.i. (Br., pop.) to engage in horseplay 2. n. (Br., pop.) a show of horseplay by students, with dressing up and fooling around to get money for some charity [origin unknown]

rag n. a large roofing slate with one rough surface ‖ any of various kinds of hard, coarse stone which split into thick, flat slabs [perh. RAG (scrap)]

rag·a·muf·fin (rægəmʌfin) n. a ragged, disreputable person, esp. a street urchin [prob. fr. RAG (scrap)]

rag-and-bone man (Br.) a man who with a cart or car goes through the streets collecting old clothes or junk

rag·a·rock (rægərɒk) n. a mixture of rock 'n roll and Indian musical forms, often played with a sitar

rag bolt a bolt having barbs on its shaft which prevent its easy withdrawal

rage (reidʒ) n. violent and uncontrolled anger, or a fit of this ‖ (rhet.) the violence of a natural element ‖ (rhet.) passionate desire for something, *the rage for conquest* ‖ intense emotion, passion, *a rage of grief* ‖ an object of modish enthusiasm, *big hats were the rage* [F. *raige, rage*]

rage v.i. pres. part. **rag·ing** past and past part. **raged** (often with 'at', 'over' or 'against') to utter with violent and uncontrolled anger ‖ (of a storm, sea, battle, disease, passion etc.) to be unchecked in its violence [fr. F. *rager*]

rag·ged (rægid) adj. (of fabric, clothes etc.) torn or frayed ‖ (of hair, fur etc.) rough, hanging in tufts ‖ having a broken, jagged outline or surface ‖ written or performed in an uneven way ‖ (of people) dressed in torn or frayed clothes

ragged robin *Lychnis floscuculi*, fam. *Caryophyllaceae*, a perennial plant with small pink flowers with five narrow-lobed and ragged-looking petals

rag·gee, rag·i (rægi:) n. *Eleusine coracana*, fam. *Graminaceae*, a cereal cultivated in India and Africa for flour [Hindi *rägi*]

Rag·lan (ræglən), Fitzroy James Henry Somerset, 1st Baron (1788-1855), British field marshal. He commanded (1854-5) the British troops in the Crimean War

rag·lan (ræglən) adj. (of sleeves) made with the seams running from the underarm to the neck so that there are no shoulder seams ‖ (of coats etc.) having such sleeves [after Lord *Raglan*]

rag·man (rægmæn, rægmən) pl. **rag·men** (rægmen, rægmən) n. a man who collects or deals in rags, old newspapers etc.

ra·gout (rægú:) n. a highly seasoned dish of stewed meat and vegetables [F.]

rag paper high-quality paper made from rags

rag·pick·er (rægpikər) n. a person who picks up rags and other refuse for a living

rag·tag (rægtæg) n. (pop.) a crowd of poor, dirty people **ragtag and bobtail** the rabble, the riff-raff

rag·time (rægtaim) n. a type of early jazz popular in the two decades before the 1st world war. It derived from black folk music and is marked by persistent syncopation [=ragged time]

Ra·gu·sa (rɑgú:zɑ) *DUBROVNIK

rag·weed (rægwi:d) n. ragwort ‖ a member of *Ambrosia*, fam. *Compositae*, a genus of plants whose pollen may cause hay fever and asthma

rag·wort (rægwə:rt) n. a member of *Senecio*, fam. *Compositae*, a genus of plants growing in fields and hedgerows, with lyrate leaves and clusters of bright yellow flowers, esp. *S. jacobaea*

Rahman, Tunku Abdul *ABDUL RAHMAN

raid (reid) 1. n. a swift, sudden military attack with a limited objective, esp. by a detachment ‖ air raid ‖ a swift, sudden robbery of money, goods, cattle etc., esp. in broad daylight ‖ a sudden swoop on suspected premises by law-enforcement officers to arrest criminals, seize contraband etc. ‖ (stock exchange) an attempt by dealers to force prices down 2. v.t. to make a raid upon ‖ v.i. to make a raid [orig. Scot. fr. O.E. *rād*, road]

rail (reil) 1. n. a horizontal bar of wood or metal etc. used e.g. to hang things on or from, for a support in climbing stairs etc. or for a guard or

barrier ‖ a horizontal piece in a fence or in paneling ‖ the fence on either side of a racetrack ‖ a line of a track on which, or suspended from which, a vehicle moves ‖ (naut.) the wide wooden bar along the top of the bulwarks **by rail** by railroad train **on the rails** progressing satisfactorily, going along well **over the rail** over a ship's side **to go off the rails** (Br.) to stop behaving with propriety 2. v.t. (with 'in', 'off') to separate from an adjoining or surrounding space by a rail [O.F. *reille*]

rail v.i. (rhet.) (with 'against' or 'at') to utter curses and lamentations, *to rail against fate* (with 'at') to shout abuse [F. *railler*, to banter]

rail n. any of various wading birds of temperate regions, with thin bodies, strong legs and short wings, constituting a subfamily of fam. *Rallidae*. They have a raucous cry [F. *râle*]

rail chair one of the iron clamps fastened to the sleepers which hold the tracks of a railroad

rail·gun (réilgʌn) n. device under development for projecting a plastic missile (bullet, rocket) utilizing a magnetic flux generator with a direct current linear motor fired by a pulse of high-voltage electrical energy with 10 times the power of a rifle

rail·head (réilhed) n. the furthest point reached by a railroad under construction ‖ (mil.) the point on a railroad at which supplies are unloaded and sent up to front-line troops by other means

rail·ing (réiliŋ) n. a fence, barrier, or support consisting of rails or a rail ‖ material for rails

rail·ler·y (réiləri) n. good-humored teasing [F. *raillerie*]

rail·road (réilroud) 1. n. (Am.=Br. railway) a road or system of roads of easy gradient on which parallel rails are laid, and held in position by being bolted to ties, for trains to run on 2. v.t. to transport by railroad train ‖ (pop.) to rush (something) through quickly so that it cannot receive careful consideration ‖ (pop.) to cause (someone) to be sent to prison on a false charge
—The first surface railroad designed for passenger transport was constructed between Stockton and Darlington, in England, in 1825 (*STEPHENSON). U.S. railroads began effectively with the Baltimore and Ohio Railroad (1830)

rail·way (réilwei) n. (Br.) the organization concerned with running a regional system of railroads ‖ the tracks of such a regional system ‖ a rail line which carries equipment over a relatively small area

rai·ment (réimənt) n. (rhet.) clothing, esp. of fine quality [fr. older *arrayment* fr. ARRAY]

rain (rein) n. a multitude of falling drops of water formed by the coalescing of droplets in a cloud ‖ the fall of such drops ‖ a fall of other liquid drops, dust particles, bullets etc. ‖ (pl.) the season of heavy rain, esp. in countries with a monsoon climate [O.E. *regn, rēn*]

rain v.i. (usually impersonal) to fall as rain, *it is raining* ‖ to fall like pouring rain ‖ v.t. to cause to fall like pouring rain **to rain cats and dogs** to rain very hard [O.E. *regnian*]

rain·bow (réinbou) 1. n. a circle (usually observed as an arc) of concentric bands in the atmosphere in the colors of the spectrum, due to the reflection and refraction of sunlight in drops of water 2. adj. colored like a rainbow ‖ many-colored [O.E. *regnboga*]

rainbow pill (med.) a capsule containing drugs of several colors, each of which usually becomes effective at various times

rainbow trout *Salmo gairdnerii*, fam. *Salmonidae*, a brightly colored trout, native to the mountain streams and the rivers of the Pacific coast of North America

rain check a ticket which a spectator can use for readmission to a game, e.g. baseball, which has been called off or stopped because of rain ‖ an agreement that a person can exercise an unfulfilled privilege, favor etc. sometime in the future

rain·coat (réinkout) n. a rainproof coat

rain·drop (réindrɒp) n. a drop of rain

rain·fall (réinfɔl) n. a fall of rain ‖ the precipitation of a given period on a region as measured by the depth (in inches or centimeters) of water in a rain gauge which collects the rain, snow or hail

rain forest a hot, wet, equatorial forest characterized by high, broadleaved, evergreen trees and absence of undergrowth

rain gauge, rain gage an instrument for measuring the amount of rainfall at a given time and place

---

CONCISE PRONUNCIATION KEY: **(a)** æ, c*a*t; ɑ, c*a*r; ɔ f*aw*n; ei, sn*a*ke. **(e)** e, h*e*n; i:, sh*ee*p; iə, d*ee*r; ɛə, b*ea*r. **(i)** i, f*i*sh; ai, t*i*ger; ə:, b*i*rd. **(o)** o, *o*x; au, c*ow*; ou, g*oa*t; u, p*oo*r; ɔi, r*oy*al. **(u)** ʌ, d*u*ck; u, b*u*ll; u:, g*oo*se; ə, b*a*cillus; ju:, c*u*be. x, lo*ch*; θ, *th*ink; δ, *b*other; z, *Z*en; ʒ, corsa*g*e; dʒ, sava*g*e; ŋ, ora*ng*utang; j, *y*ak; ʃ, *f*ish; tʃ, fe*tch*; 'l, rabb*le*; 'n, redd*en*. Complete pronunciation key appears inside front cover.

Rai·nier III (reiniər, *F.* renjei) (1923-), prince of Monaco since 1950

Rai·nier (rəniər, réiniər) the highest peak (14,410 ft) of the Cascade Range, in W. central Washington

rain·out (réinaut) *n.* radioactive material in the atmosphere brought to earth by precipitation

rain·proof (réinpruːf) 1. *adj.* (of materials) not letting the rain come through 2. *v.t.* to make rainproof

rain shadow the area to the leeward of mountains where little rain falls

rain·storm (réinstɔrm) *n.* a heavy fall of rain

rain·wa·ter (rainwɔtər, réinwɔtər) *n.* water recently fallen as rain and free of the dissolved salts often present in water which has percolated through chalk, soil, rocks etc.

rain·y (réini) *comp.* **rain·i·er** *superl.* **rain·i·est** *adj.* during or in which much rain falls, *the rainy season* ‖ (of clouds, wind etc.) bringing rain ‖ wet with rain

rainy day a future time or period when one will experience some want or urgent need, *put money away for a rainy day*

Rai·pur (ráipur) a rail center (pop. 140,000) of E. Madhya Pradesh, India: food processing, sawmills, mechanical engineering

raise (reiz) 1. *v.t. pres. part.* **rais·ing** *past* and *past part.* **raised** to cause to rise or come to a vertical or standing position ‖ to rouse, enliven, *to raise one's spirits* ‖ to incite, *to raise a revolt* ‖ to stir up (a person or persons) to some action ‖ to call up, evoke (the spirit of a deceased person) ‖ to bring back to life ‖ to build up or construct (a building etc.) ‖ to give rise to, *to raise a smile* ‖ to give vent to (a loud cry, shout etc.) ‖ to institute, initiate (a claim, complaint etc.) ‖ to bring up (a question, objection etc.) for consideration ‖ to elevate, cause to be on or at a higher level ‖ to exalt in rank, position etc. ‖ to make rise according to some accepted scale, *to raise the temperature* ‖ to cause (the voice) to rise in pitch or strength ‖ to cause to rise in amount, size, value, price etc., *to raise the cost of living* ‖ to cause (dough) to rise or lighten ‖ (*dyeing*) to make (a color) brighter ‖ to give (cloth) a nap ‖ to collect together, *to raise an army, to raise money* ‖ to abandon, give up (a blockade, siege etc.) ‖ to end (a blockade, siege etc.) by forcing the besieging troops to retire ‖ to remove (an embargo, injunction etc.) ‖ to increase (a bid or wager) ‖ (*cards*) to go one better than (a previous player) ‖ (*naut.*) to come in sight of (land, another ship etc.) ‖ (*naut.*) to make (land, another ship etc.) seem higher by approaching it ‖ to bring up (children) ‖ to breed (animals) ‖ to cause to grow, *to raise corn* ‖ to flush (game) ‖ (*math.*) to multiply (a quantity) by itself a given number of times ‖ to increase fraudulently the face value of (a money order, check etc.) by altering the figures **to raise hell** (or **the devil**) to make a great disturbance ‖ to make a furious protest **to raise one's voice** to give expression to one's disapproval or disagreement 2. *n.* an act of raising ‖ an increase of stakes or the amount increased ‖ (*Am.=Br.* rise) an increase in salary [O.N. *reisa*]

rai·sin (réiz'n) *n.* any of various kinds of grape dried either in the sun or artificially [O.F. *razin, raizin,* grape]

rai·son d'ê·tre (réizɔndétrə, *F.* rezɔ̃detr) *n.* the justifying reason for the existence of something [F.]

rai·son·neur (reizɔné:r) *n.* (*Fr.*) one who comments on the actions of others, esp. a character in a literary work

raj (radʒ) *n.* (in India) rule, reign [Hindi *rāj*]

ra·ja, ra·jah (rádʒə) *n.* an Indian prince ‖ someone who holds a Hindu title of nobility ‖ the title of an Indian noble or dignitary or of a Malay or Javanese prince [Hindi *rājā*]

Ra·ja·mun·dry (radʒəmúndri:) a city (pop. 130,000) of N.W. Andhra Pradesh, India, on the Godavari River: aluminum, metallurgy, lumber, food processing

Ra·ja·sthan (rádʒəstən) a state (area 132,152 sq. miles, pop. 28,401,000) of N.W. India, in the Thar and the central plateau. Capital: Jaipur. Resources: mica, gypsum, salt. Agriculture: livestock, wheat, sugar, cotton, pulses. Industries: sugar refining, cotton textiles. State university (1947) at Jaipur

Raj·kot (rádʒkout) a former princely capital (pop. 300,612) in the Kathiawar Peninsula, Gujarat, India, a rail center: food processing, tanning

Raj·put (rádʒput) *n.* a member of a landowning and military caste of the former Rajputana

states of N. India, now part of Rajasthan. The Rajputs ruled much of central India (7th–18th cc.) [Hindi *rājpūt*]

rake (reik) *n.* a hand tool consisting of a pole ending in a short crossbar set with prongs, for smoothing out loose soil or gravel, collecting fallen leaves etc. ‖ a farm machine for collecting hay into lanes ‖ any of a variety of tools similar to a garden rake, used e.g. by a croupier or a bookbinder [O.E. *raca*]

rake *n.* a thoroughly dissolute man, esp. one in fashionable society [shortened fr. older *rakehell*]

rake *pres. part.* **rak·ing** *past* and *past part.* **raked** *v.t.* to collect with a rake, *to rake leaves* ‖ (often with 'up') to gather (e.g. facts) by hard work ‖ to make clean, smooth, loosen etc. with a rake ‖ (with 'up') to search out and expose, *to rake up a scandal* ‖ to bank up (a fire) for slow burning ‖ to search minutely ‖ (*pop.*, usually with 'in') to take in a great deal of (money) ‖ to sweep the length of (a ship, column of troops etc.) with shots ‖ (of a hawk) to attack while flying ‖ *v.i.* to use a rake ‖ to search with a rake or as if with a rake [O.N. *raka,* to scrape]

rake 1. *v. pres. part.* **rak·ing** *past* and *past part.* **raked** *v.t.* to cause to be set off at an angle from the perpendicular ‖ *v.i.* to be at such an angle ‖ (*naut.*) to project at the bow or stern beyond the keel 2. *n.* a slant from the perpendicular ‖ (*naut.*) the projection of a ship's bow or stern over the keel ‖ an upward slope of the stage or auditorium of a theater from the horizontal ‖ the angle given to the face of a cutting tool [etym. doubtful]

rake-off (réikɔf, réikɔf) *n.* a percentage of profits or winnings kept, often illegally or covertly, by a party to a transaction [RAKE (garden tool)+OFF]

rak·ish (réikiʃ) *adj.* (esp. of ships) looking as though built for speed ‖ jaunty [etym. doubtful]

rakish *adj.* of or like a rake (dissolute man)

rale, *Br.* **râle** (ræl, rɑːl) *n.* any abnormal breathing sound heard through a stethoscope, indicating lung disorder [F.]

Ra·leigh, Ra·legh (rɔ́li:), Sir Walter (c. 1552-1618), English courtier, explorer and author. The favorite of Elizabeth I, he sent expeditions (1584-9) to colonize the coast of North America, founding an unsuccessful settlement in Virginia. He led (1595) an expedition to the Orinoco in search of gold. He fell from favor on the accession of James I and was imprisoned (1603-16) in the Tower of London, where he began his 'History of the World'. After the failure of a second expedition to the Orinoco (1617), he was executed

Raleigh the capital (pop. 150,255) of North Carolina: tobacco, cotton, textiles

ral·len·tan·do (rɑlentɑndou) *n.* (*mus.*) a direction to play or sing more slowly ‖ (*mus.*) a passage becoming gradually slower in tempo [Ital.]

ral·ly (ræli:) 1. *v. pres. part.* **ral·ly·ing** *past* and *past part.* **ral·lied** *v.t.* to gather together (what was disunited or disordered, e.g. troops) ‖ to cause to regain vigor, *to rally one's spirits* ‖ to summon together for a common purpose ‖ *v.i.* to come back to a state of order ‖ to come together for a common purpose, *to rally to a cause* ‖ to regain strength of body or mind ‖ (*tennis*) to take part in a rally ‖ (of stocks etc.) to rise again in price after a fall 2. *pl.* **ral·lies** *n.* the act of rallying a gathering of persons with a common purpose, *a political rally* ‖ (*tennis*) a sustained to-and-fro succession of strokes by opposing players [F. *rallier*]

ral·ly *pres. part.* **ral·ly·ing** *past* and *past part.* **ral·lied** *v.t.* (*old-fash.*) to tease or chaff [F. *railler*]

ram (ræm) *n.* a male sheep ‖ the dropweight of a pile driver or steam hammer ‖ the compressing piston of a hydrostatic press or force pump ‖ a battering ram ‖ a device for raising water from a running stream ‖ (*hist.*) a steel beak jutting from the prow of a ship for piercing the side of an enemy ship, or a ship thus equipped [O.E. *ram, ramm*]

ram *pres. part.* **ram·ming** *past* and *past part.* **rammed** *v.t.* to pound (earth) so as to make it firm ‖ to crash head-on into ‖ to drive or force down or into by heavy blows, pressure etc. ‖ to fill or stuff with tightly pressed material ‖ to force (a charge) into a gun ‖ to force acceptance of (e.g. an idea), *to ram facts into someone's head* ‖ (*hist.*, of a ship) to attack (another ship) with a ram ‖ *v.i.* (of something in movement) to crash

violently into an obstacle ‖ to pound earth in order to make it firm **to ram something down someone's throat** to force someone to accept an unwelcome fact [M.E. *rammen*]

RAM 1. (*computer acronym*) for random-access memory 2. (*mil. acronym*) for reentry antimissile

Ra·ma (rámə) (*Hindu mythol.*) the sixth, seventh or eighth avatar of Vishnu, esp. Ramachandra

RAMAC (*acronym*) for random-access method of accounting and control, a computerized accounting system designed by IBM

Ra·ma·chan·dra (rəmətʃándrə) the seventh, most famous avatar of Vishnu [Skr. *Rāmacandra*]

Ram·a·dan (ræmədán) *n.* the ninth month of the Moslem year, during which strict fasting is observed from dawn until sunset ‖ this fast [Arab. *ramadān*]

Ra·ma·krish·na (rəməkríʃnə) (1836-86), Hindu reformer and founder of the Ramakrishna Mission. Having practiced Hindu, Moslem and Christian rites, he taught that all religions are one, but suit man's needs differently. His disciples were taught to see God in all men, and to serve mankind accordingly

Ramakrishna Mission an order of monks dedicated to chastity, poverty and charity, founded by Ramakrishna

Ra·man (rámən), Sir Chandrasekhara Venkata (1888-1970), Indian physicist, who discovered the Raman effect. Nobel prize (1930)

Raman effect (*phys.*) a change in frequency experienced by radiation scattered while traversing a transparent substance. The amount of the change is determined by the substance. The Raman effect is the principle underlying a spectroscopic technique (*SPECTROSCOPY) that employs a monochromatic beam in the infrared, which upon scattering produces new frequencies characteristic of the material [after Sir Chandrasekhara RAMAN]

Ra·ma·nu·ja (rámánujə) Brahmin commentator on the Upanishads, writing c. 1017. He taught, in contrast with the more usual monistic teaching of Hinduism, that individual selves are dependent on the Highest Self for their existence, yet are distinct from him, and can enter into a relationship of love with him

RAMARK (*acronym*) for radar marker, a beacon that emits continuous radar waves as a navigation guide

Ra·ma·ya·na (rəmájənə) one of the two great Sanskrit poems of Hinduism (*MAHABHARATA), written c. 5th c. B.C. Its 24,000 couplets in seven books record the deeds of Rama

ram·ble (ræmb'l) 1. *v.i. pres. part.* **ram·bling** *past* and *past part.* **ram·bled** to go for a long, unplanned walk purely for enjoyment ‖ to talk or write without any clear thread 2. *n.* the act of rambling **rám·bler** *n.* someone who rambles ‖ any of several climbing roses having large clusters of small flowers **rám·bling** *adj.* seeming to be constructed on no clear plan, *a rambling house* ‖ wandering, disconnected, *rambling thoughts* [origin unknown]

Ram·bouil·let (rūbu:jei), Catherine de Vivonne, marquise de (1588-1665), French noblewoman. Her salon, which included Mme de Sévigné, Descartes, La Rochefoucauld and Bossuet, was the first of its kind and influenced the development of the French language and French literature

ram·bunc·tious (ræmbʌ́nkʃəs) *adj.* boisterous, noisy, difficult to control [prob. altered fr. RUMBUSTIOUS]

ram·bu·tan (ræmbúːt'n) *n. Nephelium lappaceum,* fam. *Sapindaceae,* a Malaysian and Indonesian tree cultivated for its fruit ‖ this fruit, covered with soft, red hair [Malay]

Ra·meau (ræmou), Jean-Philippe (1683-1764), French classical composer. His 'Traité de l'harmonie' (1722) helped to establish the theories of modern harmony. His operas include 'les Indes galantes' (1735) and 'Castor et Pollux' (1737). He also wrote church music, chamber music, cantatas and works for the harpsichord

ram·e·kin, ra·me·quin (ræməkin) *n.* cheese, with bread crumbs, eggs etc. baked in an individual dish ‖ a dish for baking and serving this [F. *ramequin*]

Ram·e·ses (ræmsi:z) Ramses

ram·ie (ræmi:) *n.* a strong, absorbent, lustrous fiber obtained from *Boehmeria nivea,* fam. *Urticaceae,* a bushy plant of E. Asia, now cultivated in the southeastern U.S.A. ‖ this plant [Malay *rāmī*]

ram·i·fi·ca·tion (ræmifikéiʃən) *n.* the process of branching ‖ the way in which branches are arranged ‖ a branch or offshoot ‖ (*biol.*) a branched structure ‖ a development or outgrowth of something which has expanded as though by branching, *the ramifications of the plot are hard to follow* [fr. M.L. *ramificare* (*ramificatus*), to ramify]

ram·i·fy (ræmifai) *pres. part.* **ram·i·fy·ing** *past* and *past part.* **ram·i·fied** *v.t.* to cause to form or produce branches or subdivisions ‖ *v.i.* to spread out by branching [F. *ramifier*]

Ram·il·lies, Battle of (ræmili:z, ræmiˌji:) a victory (1706) of Marlborough, commanding allied British, Dutch and Danish armies, during the War of the Spanish Succession

Ra·mí·rez (ɾɑmí:res), Ignacio (1818-97), Mexican politician, writer and poet, of pure Indian stock, who styled himself 'El nigromante' (the necromancer). When not inflamed by politics he wrote classical love sonnets, notably 'Al amor', 'A sol', and 'A mi musa'

ram·jet (ræmdʒet) *n.* a jet engine in which the stream of air used for fuel combustion is compressed by the forward motion of the engine ‖ (*mil.*) U.S. missile containing no oxidizer, reaching speeds up to 3,000 mph, with a range of 300–400 mi

Ra·món y Ca·jal (ramón:i:kɑhál), Santiago (1852-1934), Spanish physician and biologist, and winner (1906) of the Nobel prize for medicine

ra·mose (ræmóus, rəmóus) *adj.* composed of or having branches [fr. L. *ramosus*]

ramp (ræmp) *n.* a sloping path or way joining different levels of a building, road etc. ‖ (*archit.*) a difference in level in the opposite abutments of a rampant arch ‖ an upward bend in a stair rail etc. ‖ a passenger stairway for boarding or leaving an aircraft [F. *rampe*]

ramp *n.* (*Br., pop.*) a racket, swindle [etym. doubtful]

ramp *v.i.* to slope up or down to a different level ‖ (*heraldry*, of a lion) to stand rampant ‖ *v.t.* to provide with a ramp [O.F. *ramper*, to creep]

ram·page 1. (ræmpéidʒ) *v.i. pres. part.* **ram·pag·ing** *past* and *past part.* **ram·paged** to behave violently, be in a storm of anger 2. (ræmpeidʒ) *n.* violent or uncontrolled behavior, esp. in the phrase **on the rampage** furiously active, esp. punitively or destructively **ram·pá·geous** *adj.* [Scot., etym. doubtful]

ram·pan·cy (ræmpənsi) *n.* the state or quality of being rampant

ramp·ant (ræmpənt) *adj.* (*heraldry*, of a lion) on the hind legs with forepaws menacingly or aggressively outstretched and the head in profile ‖ holding extremist views and proclaiming them aggressively, *a rampant militarist* ‖ (of crime, disease etc.) rife ‖ (of roses, weeds etc.) growing unchecked ‖ (*archit.*, of an arch) with one abutment higher than the other [F., *pres. part.* of *ramper*, to ramp]

ram·part (ræmpɑrt) 1. *n.* (*hist.*) a broad-topped embankment, usually with a stone parapet, constructed for defense ‖ something compared to this 2. *v.t.* to protect with a rampart or as though with a rampart [fr. F. *rempart*, *rampart*]

Ram·pur (rámpur) a town (pop. 135,000) of N. Uttar Pradesh, India: damask, chemicals, electrical goods, jewelry

ram·rod (ræmrɒd) *n.* (*hist.*) a long, straight rod of iron used to force the gunpowder and bullets down the barrel of a muzzle-loading gun ‖ a rod for cleaning the bore of a rifle or gun ‖ a keen disciplinarian

Ram·say (ræmzi:), Sir William (1852-1916), Scottish chemist. He discovered the line spectrum of helium in uranium and thorium ores. With Lord Rayleigh he discovered argon (1894) and was also one of the discoverers of neon, krypton and xenon. Nobel prize (1904)

Rams·den (ræmzdən), Jesse (1735-1800), British optician and instrument maker. He devised the equatorial mounting for telescopes and invented a machine for graduating instruments

Ram·ses II (ræmsi:z) (*d. c.* 1223 B.C.), king of Egypt (c. 1290–c. 1223 B.C.), of the 19th dynasty. He extended Egyptian rule over Ethiopia and part of Arabia, and was at war with the Hittites for 15 years. He had many monuments built, esp. at Thebes

Ramses III (*d. c.* 1158 B.C.), king of Egypt (c. 1190–c. 1158 B.C.) of the 20th dynasty. He won military successes in Nubia and Syria

ram·shack·le (ræmʃæk'l) *adj.* (of a structure, machine etc.) so old or badly made or in such disrepair that it is in danger of falling to pieces [fr. older *ramshackled*]

ram·son (ræms'n, ræmz'n) *n. Allium ursinum*, fam. Liliaceae, a species of garlic with broad leaves ‖ (*pl.*) the root of this plant, used esp. in salads [O.E. *hramsan*, pl. of *hramsa*, wild garlic]

ram·til (ræmtil) *n. Guizotia abyssinica*, fam. Compositae, a plant cultivated in India for its seeds, from which an oil is expressed [Hindi *rāmtil*]

ram·u·lose (ræmjulous) *adj.* having numerous small branches [fr. L. *ramulosus*]

Ra·mus (réiməs), Petrus (Pierre de la Ramée, 1515-72), French philosopher. He opposed Aristotelian scholasticism and encouraged skeptical thought. He was converted to Calvinism and was killed in the Massacre of St Bartholomew

ra·mus (réiməs) *pl.* **ra·mi** (réimai) *n.* (*biol.*) a branchlike structure, e.g. the barb of a feather, the mandible or its proximal part of a vertebrate, or a branch of a nerve [L.=branch]

ran *past* of RUN

Ran·cé (rɑ̃séi), Armand Jean le Bouthillier de (1626-1700), French religious reformer. His reform of the Cistercian order (c. 1662) gave rise to the Trappists

ranch (ræntʃ) 1. *n.* a farm, esp in the southwest and western U.S.A. and S.W. central Canada, for breeding and raising cattle, horses or sheep ‖ the people living and working on a ranch 2. *v.i.* to manage a ranch ‖ *v.t.* to raise (an animal) on a ranch ‖ to use (land) as a ranch **ranch·er** *n.* a person who owns or manages a ranch, or a ranch hand [fr. Span. *rancho*, a mess (group dining together)]

ran·che·ro (ræntʃérou) *n.* (esp. in the southwest U.S.A. and Mexico) a rancher [Span.]

ranch·ette (ræntʃét) *n.* 1. a small ranch 2. small ranch-type house

ranch house a house built on one level, sometimes with adjoining half levels. *Cf* BILEVEL

Ran·chi (rántʃi:) a town (pop. 122,000) in Bihar, India, in Chota Nagpur: silk weaving, lacquer

ranch·man (ræntʃmən) *pl.* **ranch·men** (ræntʃmən) *n.* a rancher

ran·cid (rænsid) *adj.* (esp. of food) smelling or tasting foul because of chemical change, esp. due to age **ran·cid·i·ty** *n.* [fr. L. *rancidus*]

ran·cor, *Br.* **ran·cour** (ræŋkər) *n.* bitter, lasting hatred or malignant spite **rán·cor·ous** *adj.* [O.F. *rancour*]

Rand (rænd), Ayn (1905-82), U.S. writer, originator of objectivism, born in Russia. Her philosophy encompassed self-interest as a reason for action, self-fulfillment as a responsibility and productivity as the ultimate. She wrote 'The Fountainhead' (1943) and 'Atlas Shrugged' (1957) and edited her own newsletter (1962-82)

rand (rænd) *n.* the strip of leather or similar material between the heel and sole of a shoe or boot [O.E. *rand, rond*, a border, margin]

rand *n.* (*abbr.*) the basic monetary unit of the republic of South Africa, divided into 100 cents ‖ a coin of the value of one rand

R & B *RHYTHM AND BLUES

R & D (*acronym*) for research and development

rand·i·ness (rændi:nis) *n.* the quality or state of being randy

ran·dom (rændəm) 1. *n.* (only in the phrase) **at random** in an unplanned way, without any predetermined direction, purpose or method 2. *adj.* haphazard, *random bombing* ‖ made or chosen at random, *a random guess* ‖ (*math.*, of numbers) as likely to come up as any others in a set [O.F. *randon* fr. *randir*, to run fast, gallop]

random access (*computer*) capability of obtaining stored information in any order — **random-access** *adj.* —**random-access memory (RAM)** *n.*

R and R (*acronym*) 1. rest and recreation; 2. rest and recuperation

Rand, the (rænd) *WITWATERSRAND

Randolph (rændolf, rændəlf), Asa Philip (1889-1979), U.S. labor leader, organizer of the Brotherhood of Sleeping Car Porters (1925), vice-president of the AFL-CIO from 1955. He was a major influence in the organization of the federal Fair Employment Practices Committee and worked for civil rights in industry and government, directing the March on Washington for Jobs and Freedom (1963)

Randolph, Edmund (1753-1813), U.S. statesman. A delegate to the Constitutional Convention of 1787, he presented his Virginia Plan. He served (1789-94) as the first attorney general of the U.S.A.

Randolph, John (1773-1833), U.S. orator and Congressman from Virginia who vigorously supported the cause of states' rights

rand·y (rændi:) *comp.* **rand·i·er** *superl.* **rand·i·est** *adj.* lecherous [prob. fr. obs. *rand*, var. of RANT]

ranee *RANI

rang *past* of RING

range (reindʒ) *n.* a row, file or rank of things ‖ a group of mountains considered as forming a connected system ‖ a cooking stove, esp. one fired by solid fuel ‖ grazing land for cattle, sheep etc., usually not fenced in ‖ freedom to roam at will, *to give free range to one's imagination* ‖ a maximum attainable distance, *the missile has a range of 2,000 miles* ‖ field, scope, *within one's range of vision* ‖ the distance of a target from a gun etc. or this as a setting on a sight ‖ the maximum distance which an aircraft etc. can travel without refueling ‖ a place for practicing shooting ‖ (*statistics*) the area of magnitude within which a variable lies ‖ an order or class, *the upper ranges of society* ‖ extent between limits, area of activity, experience or knowledge, *within the income range of $4–5,000, temperature range, a wide range of interests* ‖ the scope of the voice or an instrument ‖ the region over which a plant or animal is distributed ‖ one of the north-south rows of a township numbered east-west from the principal meridian of a public-land survey [O.F.]

range *pres. part.* **rang·ing** *past* and *past part.* **ranged** *v.t.* to place in a line or orderly pattern, *trees were ranged along the roadside* ‖ to wander through, *to range the countryside* ‖ to sail along or through ‖ to pasture (cattle etc.) on a range ‖ (*Br., printing*) to set (type) so that the start or end of the line or word falls directly under some other part of the matter being set, *range the author's name under the last word of the title* ‖ (*Br., printing*) to make (lines of type, margins etc.) straight ‖ to put in a class etc., *he ranged himself with the opposition* ‖ to fire and observe single rounds from (a gun or guns) in an attempt to bracket a target ‖ (*naut.*) to arrange (an anchor cable) so that the anchor can descend without difficulty ‖ *v.i.* to stretch in a line, *the peaks ranged as far as he could see* ‖ to go about, move freely, *they range through the desert, his speech ranged over a number of topics* ‖ (*biol.*) to be found over a specific region ‖ to vary within limits, *the temperature ranges between 0° C and 30° C* ‖ (*Br., printing*) to line up, lie in the same line ‖ (of artillery) to fire and observe single rounds in an attempt to bracket a target ‖ to use a range finder [fr. F. *ranger*]

range finder an instrument for establishing the distance between an observer and a point (e.g. a target) ‖ (*photog.*) a camera attachment for measuring the distance between a camera and what is to be photographed

rang·er (reindʒər) *n.* an officer who patrols a public forest ‖ a soldier trained for close-range fighting ‖ (*Br.*) an official who supervises a royal forest or park ‖ (*Br.*) a senior girl scout

Ran·goon (ræŋgú:n) the capital (pop. 3,662,300) and chief port of Burma, on River Rangoon. Industries: food processing (esp. rice), wood working, oil refining. It is dominated by the gilded pagoda of Shwe Dagon (18th c.). University (1920)

rang·y (reindʒi:) *comp.* **rang·i·er** *superl.* **rang·i·est** *adj.* tall, slim and loose-limbed [RANGE *n.* or *v.*]

ra·ni, ra·nee (ráni:) *n.* an Indian princess ‖ the wife of a raja [Hind. *rānī*]

Ran·jit Singh (rándʒitsíŋ) (1780-1839), Sikh ruler. He conquered Kashmir and the Punjab, allied himself with the British and united the Punjab into the most powerful state in India

rank (ræŋk) 1. *n.* a homogeneous line or row of persons or things ‖ a level of relative excellence, *writing of the very first rank* ‖ position in a hierarchy ‖ high social position, *a man of rank* ‖ a row of soldiers standing or marching abreast ‖ (*pl.*) the body of private soldiers, *to rise from the ranks* ‖ (*chess*) one of the horizontal lines extending across a chessboard 2. *v.t.* to arrange in a rank or ranks ‖ to ascribe a level or position in a hierarchy to, *to rank something very highly* ‖ to hold a higher rank than, *a major ranks a lieutenant* ‖ *v.i.* to form a rank or ranks ‖ to belong to a category in a hierarchy, *he ranks with our finest poets* ‖ to be in the top rank,

CONCISE PRONUNCIATION KEY: **(a)** æ, c*a*t; ɑ, c*a*r; ɔ f*aw*n; ei, sn*a*ke. **(e)** e, h*e*n; i:, sh*ee*p; iə, d*ee*r; ɛə, b*ea*r. **(i)** i, f*i*sh; ai, t*i*ger; ə:, b*i*rd. **(o)** o, *o*x; au, c*ow*; ou, g*oa*t; u, p*oo*r; ɔi, r*oy*al. **(u)** ʌ, d*u*ck; u, b*u*ll; u:, g*oo*se; ə, b*a*cillus; ju:, c*u*be. x, lo*ch*; θ, *th*ink; ð, bo*th*er; z, *Z*en; ʒ, corsa*g*e; dʒ, sava*g*e; ŋ, ora*ng*utang; j, *y*ak; ʃ, *f*ish; tʃ, fe*tch*; 'l, rabb*le*; 'n, redd*en*. Complete pronunciation key appears inside front cover.

ranking officers of the corporation [obs. O.F. *ranc*, perh. fr. Gmc]

rank *adj.* excessively luxuriant in growth, *rank weeds* ‖ coarse in growth, *rank grass* ‖ gross, crude, *rank behavior* ‖ smelling like damp, partly rotted vegetation ‖ complete, utter, *a rank outsider* [O.E. *ranc*, strong proud]

rank and file private soldiers, as distinguished from their officers ‖ ordinary people, as distinguished from their leaders

Ran·ke (rúŋkə), Leopold von (1795-1886), German historian. His works include 'German History in the Time of the Reformation' (1839-47), 'The Roman Popes in the Last Four Centuries' (1834-7) and a 'History of the World' (1880-8). He was a pioneer of objective method in historical research

ran·kle (ræŋk'l) *pres. part.* **ran·kling** *past* and *past part.* **ran·kled** *v.i.* to be a source of prolonged emotional pain or distress, *his unkind remark rankled in her mind* ‖ *v.t.* to cause bitter feelings in, *it rankled him to think of her ingratitude* [O. F. *rancler*, *raoncler*]

Rann of Kutch (ræn) a salt marsh (about 9,000 sq. miles) along the frontier between Pakistan and Gujarat, India. It is dry Oct.-Feb. By arbitration c. 300 square miles formerly administered by India passed (Feb. 1968) to Pakistan

ran·sack (rænsæk) *v.t.* to search thoroughly, *he ransacked his pockets for the ticket* ‖ to steal everything valuable from [O.N. *rannsake* fr. *rann*, house+*skæja*, to search]

ran·som (rænsəm) *v.t.* to secure the release of by paying a ransom ‖ to demand a ransom for ‖ to release on payment of a ransom [O. F. *ransonner*, *rançonner*]

ransom *n.* money paid or demanded for the release of a person held captive ‖ a release by payment of this **to hold (someone) in** (*Br.* **to**) **ransom** to keep (someone) captive until a ransom is paid [O.F. *rançon*, *raençon*]

rant (rænt) **1.** *v.i.* to use bombastic language, esp. in public speaking ‖ (of an actor) to be declamatory in a ludicrously exaggerated way ‖ to be noisily angry ‖ *v.t.* to utter with exaggerated emphasis **2.** *n.* a piece of ranting [obs. Du. *randten*, to rave]

ra·nun·cu·lus (rənΛŋkjuləs) *pl.* **ra·nun·cu·lus·es, ra·nun·cu·li** (rənΛŋkjulai) *n.* a member of *Ranunculus*, fam. *Ranunculaceae*, a genus of plants including about 200 species, e.g. the buttercup, found chiefly in northern temperate latitudes [L. dim. of *rana*, frog]

Ra·oult (ræu:), François Marie (1830-1901), French chemist. He demonstrated for dilute solutions that the depression of the freezing point and the elevation of the boiling point were related to the molecular mass and the concentration of the solute

rap (ræp) **1.** *n.* a sharp, quick blow ‖ the sound of such an impact **to take the rap** to take blame or punishment, esp. unjustly, or agree to be held responsible **2.** *v. pres. part.* **rap·ping** *past* and *past part.* **rapped** *v.t.* to strike with a quick sharp blow ‖ (with 'out') to express (something) quickly and forcefully, *to rap out a command* ‖ *v.i.* (usually with 'at' or 'on') to knock sharply [imit.]

rap *n.* (only in the phrase) **not to care** (or **give**) **a rap** not to care the least bit [fr. its 18th-c. meaning: a counterfeit halfpenny. Origin unknown]

rap *n.* (*colloq.*) **1.** a free, open, and unorganized conversation **2.** a conversation that stimulates spontaneity —**rap** *v.* —**rap group** *n.* —**rap·per** *n.* —**rap session** *v.*

ra·pa·cious (rəpéiʃəs) *adj.* grasping, avid for wealth or gain ‖ living by preying ‖ ravenous, *a rapacious appetite* [fr. L. *rapax (rapacis)*, grasping]

ra·pac·i·ty (rəpæsiti:) *n.* the quality of being rapacious [fr. L. *rapacitas, rapacitatis*]

Ra·pal·lo, Treaty of (rəpǽlou) a treaty (1920) between Italy and Yugoslavia, agreeing to establish a free state of Fiume ‖ a treaty (1922) between Germany and the U.S.S.R. canceling pre-war debts and war claims and providing for trade agreements

rape (reip) *n.* (*law*) illicit sexual intercourse with a woman without her consent (by force, deception, while she is asleep etc.) ‖ (*rhet.*) the doing of violence, e.g. to a city or country, esp. in war [A.F. *rap, rape*]

rape *pres. part.* **rap·ing** *past* and *past part.* **raped** *v.t.* to commit rape on [prob. fr. L. *rapere*, to seize]

rape *n. Brica napus*, fam. *Cruciferae*, an annual plant cultivated in Europe and America as forage for sheep and hogs and for the oil expressed from rapeseeds [fr. L. *rapa, rapum*, turnip]

rape *n.* (often *pl.*) the substance which remains after the juice has been pressed out of grapes, used as a filter in making vinegar [F. *rape*, grape stalk]

rape cake cattle food made of the compressed residue when the oil from rapeseed has been extracted

rape oil an oil obtained from rapeseed and turnip seed, used e.g. as a lubricant and food

rape·seed (réipsi:d) *n.* the seed of rape

Raph·a·el (ræfi:əl, réifi:əl) (Raffaello Sanzio, 1483-1520), Italian Renaissance painter and architect. He was a pupil of Perugino. His greatest paintings were done in Florence and Rome. By 1511 he had finished the frescos for the Stanza della Segnatura of the Vatican, and at the age of 28 he ranked with the greatest painters of the time. In 1514 he was appointed chief architect of St Peter's. He also worked on paintings for the Sistine Chapel. His finely drawn compositions, though sometimes elaborate, are subtly unified and the poses of his figures are profoundly expressive. His colors are of extreme delicacy. His portraits are perhaps the first in European art in which the spirituality of the sitter is expressed as well as his likeness. Raphael expresses, in both his religious and classical subjects, a vision of idealized beauty in a harmoniously ordered universe

ra·phe (réifi:) *n.* (*anat.*) a line of union like a seam, e.g. in the perineum, scrotum, tongue, medulla oblongata etc. ‖ (*bot.*) a line of junction, suture ‖ (*biol.*) the slitlike median line in a diatom valve [Mod. L. fr. Gk *raphē*, seam]

ra·phide (réifid) *n.* (*bot.*) a needleshaped crystal, usually of calcium oxalate, developed as a metabolic by-product in plant cells [F. fr. Gk *rhaphis (rhaphidos)*, a needle]

rap·id (ræpid) **1.** *adj.* occurring, done or acting with speed ‖ characterized by speed **2.** *n.* (esp. *pl.*) that part of a river where the water flows swiftly and turbulently over a shallow, usually rocky, bed **rap·id·i·ty** (rəpíditi:) *n.* the state or quality of being rapid [fr. L. *rapidus*]

ra·pi·er (réipi:ər) *n.* a light, straight, thin, two-edged sword [F. *rapière*, origin unknown]

ra·pine (ræpin) *n.* (*rhet.*) plundering, despoiling others of their property [F.]

rap·ist (réipist) *n.* a person who has committed rape

rap music (*music*) personal lyrics sung with no melody in a syncopated beat —**rapper** *n.*

RAPCON (acronym) for radar approach control, a system of radar control of aircraft in their approach to the airport

rapid eye movement *n.* a rapid movement of the eyes during sleep when dreams occur and special forms of relaxation occur. *acronym* REM. *Cf* REM SLEEP

rap·pen (ræpin) *pl.* **rap·pen** *n.* a Swiss centime [G. fr. *rappe*, raven]

rap·port (ræpór, ræpóur) *n.* sympathetic connection, harmony, *to be in rapport with one's surroundings* [F.]

rap·proche·ment (ræprɔʃmá) *n.* a renewal of friendly relations, esp. between states or parties [F.]

rap·scal·lion (ræpskǽljən) *n.* (*old-fash.*) a rascal, good-for-nothing [earlier *rascallion* fr. RASCAL]

rapt (ræpt) *adj.* carried away in imagination from the reality of one's environment ‖ of the mental or emotional state or activity accompanying this condition, *rapt attention* [fr. L. *rapere (raptus)*, to seize]

rap·to·ri·al (ræptóri:əl, ræptóuri:əl) *adj.* (of claws) adapted for seizing prey ‖ of or relating to birds of prey [fr. L. *raptor*, one that seizes]

rap·ture (ræptʃər) *n.* an emotional state in which intense joy, love etc. possesses the mind to the exclusion of every other emotion or consideration ‖ a fulsome expression of approval or satisfaction **ráp·tur·ous** *adj.* characterized by rapture [fr. past part. of obs. *rapt*, to carry away]

rare (rɛər) *adj.* infrequently found, seen or experienced, *a rare event, a rare species* ‖ (of a gas, air etc.) not dense, not having the components massed closely together ‖ unusually good, appealing etc. ‖ (*pop.*) intense, extreme, *a rare fright* [fr. L. *rarus* or F. *rare*]

rare *adj.* (of meat) cooked very lightly [fr. older *rear* fr. O.E. *hrēr*, lightly boiled]

rare·bit (rɛ́ərbit) *n.* Welsh rabbit

rare earth any of a group of oxides of the lanthanide elements that usually occur together naturally and have very similar properties (*PERIODIC TABLE)

rare-earth element one of the lanthanide series (*PERIODIC TABLE)

rare-earth metal a rare-earth element

rar·e·fac·tion (rɛərəfǽkʃən) *n.* a rarefying or being rarefied [fr. L. *rarefacere (rarefactus)*, to rarefy]

rar·e·fac·tive (rɛərəfǽktiv) *adj.* causing rarefaction ‖ characterized by rarefaction [fr. L. *rarefacere (rarefactus)*, to rarefy]

rar·e·fy, rar·i·fy (rɛ́ərəfai) *pres. part.* **rar·e·fy·ing, rar·i·fy·ing** *past* and *past part.* **rar·e·fied, rar·i·fied** *v.t.* to make (a gas etc.) rare ‖ to refine, make more subtle, *rarefied notions* ‖ *v.i.* (of gases etc.) to become rare [F. *raréfier*]

rare gas an inert gas belonging to group 0 of the periodic table

rare·ly (rɛ́ərli:) *adv.* very infrequently

rarity *RAREFY

rar·ing (rɛ́əriŋ) *adj.* (*pop.*, used with an infinitive) full of eagerness, *raring to go*

rar·i·ty (rɛ́əriti:) *pl.* **rar·i·ties** *n.* something which is rare ‖ something highly valued because it is rare ‖ the quality or fact of being rare [fr. L. *raritas*]

ras·cal (ræskəl) **1.** *n.* a rogue, trickster ‖ an endearingly mischievous person, esp. a child **ras·cal·i·ty** (ræskælíti:) **2.** *n.* the quality of being a rascal or behaving like a rascal [O.F. *rascaille*, rabble]

ra·schel knit (ræʃəl) fabric made on latch needles, with 1 to 32 warp or thread systems, with warps mounted in a stationary position

rase *RAZE

rash (ræʃ) *adj.* made or done hastily without considering the possible consequences or attendant risks ‖ acting in a hasty inconsidered manner, or given to acting in this way [M.E. *rasch*, active, vigorous]

rash *n.* an eruption or collection of spots or small red patches on the skin [perh. fr. O.F. *rache, rasque*]

rash·er (rǽʃər) *n.* a thin slice of bacon or ham, usually for frying [etym. doubtful]

rasp (ræsp, rɑsp) *v.t.* to remove unevennesses etc. from by rubbing with a rasp ‖ to grate harshly upon (the nerves) ‖ *v.i.* to make a rough scraping sound ‖ to grate [prob. O.F. *rasper*]

rasp *n.* a type of coarse file with individual, hard, raised teeth set very close together ‖ a machine used for rasping ‖ a noise made by rasping or as if by rasping ‖ a machine that grinds waste into a manageable material and helps prevent odor [O.F. *raspe* fr. *rasper*, to rasp]

ras·pa·to·ry (ræspətɔri:, ræspətɔuri:) *pl.* **ras·pa·to·ries** *n.* a surgical rasp [fr. M.L. *raspatorium* fr. *raspare*, to rasp]

rasp·ber·ry (ræzbɛri:, rázbɛri:) *pl.* **rasp·ber·ries** *n.* any of several members of *Rubus*, fam. *Rosaceae*, a genus of tall-growing shrubs having annually renewed canes usually covered with fine, prickly hairs, and bearing succulent red or black aggregate fruits, each composed of many small drupes and set on a conical receptacle ‖ the fruit of this shrub ‖ the color or flavor of the fruit of the red raspberry ‖ (*pop.*) a rude sound made by vibrating the tongue between the lips, to show contempt or derision [fr. older *rasp*, raspberry+BERRY]

raspberry sawfly *Blennocampa rubi*, fam. *Tenthredinidae*, a small, black sawfly with a reddish abdomen. Its pale green larvae feed on the leaves of raspberries and blackberries

Ras·pu·tin (ræspjú:tin), Grigori Yefimovich (1871-1916), Russian monk and adventurer. He exercised a hypnotic fascination on the czarina and influenced the policies of Nicholas II. Hated by the nobility for his debauchery and abuse of power, he was assassinated

Ras-Sham·ra (rús̆æmrə) *UGARIT

Ras Ta·fa·ri (ræstəfúri:) a black, back-to-Africa movement in Jamaica organized by Marcus Garvey. It makes Ethiopia's Emperor Haile Selassie (Ras Tafari is the original name of Haile Selassie) the object of a cult, and compares the 'heaven' of Ethiopia with the 'hell' of Jamaica

Ras Ta·fa·ri·an (ræstəféəri:ən) *n.* an adherent of the Ras Tafari movement

Rastafarian *n.* Jamaica-based sect devoted to Haile Selassie (former Emperor of Ethiopia) espousing love, peace, ganja (marijuana); noted for reggae music and for members' hair worn in dread locks, ropelike boyo strands

Ras·tatt, Treaty of (ráʃtat) a treaty (1714) between Austria and France at the end of the War of the Spanish Succession, complementing the Peace of Utrecht (1713)

rast·er (ræstər) *n.* the part in the cathode-ray tube of a television set on which the image is reproduced [G.=screen]

raster display (*computer*) a graphic presentation of data created on a screen in fixed sequence, usu. from left to right

rat (ræt) 1. *n.* any of various omnivorous rodents of *Rattus* and related genera of fam. *Muridae.* They are approximately 8 ins long with a scaly tail 8–9 ins in length. Rats live in drains, sewers and rubbish piles and have spread throughout the world on ships. They are highly destructive and are the carriers of many diseases, esp. bubonic plague ‖ (*pop.*) a contemptible person, esp. one who betrays or deserts associates ‖ a tapered coil, esp. of hair, over which a woman's hair may be arranged ‖ **to smell a rat** to suspect some trap, piece of trickery, treachery etc. 2. *v. pres. part.* **rat·ting** *past* and *past part.* **rat·ted** *v.i.* to hunt rats ‖ (often with 'on') to desert or betray one's associates [O.E. ræt]

ra·ta (rúta) *n.* either of two New Zealand trees, *Metrosideros robusta* and *M. lucida,* fam. *Myrtaceae,* yielding a hard, red wood ‖ this wood [Maori]

rat·a·ble, rate·a·ble (réitəb'l) *adj.* liable to be rated ‖ able to be rated in accordance with some scale **rát·a·bly, ráte·a·bly** *adv.*

rat·a·fi·a (rætafí:ə) *n.* a liqueur flavored with almonds or with peach, apricot or cherry kernels [F., origin unknown]

rat·al (réit'l) *n.* (*Br.*) the amount on which local property taxes are assessed

ratan *RATTAN

rat-bite fever a febrile disease caused by the bacterium *Spirillum minus* and transmitted by the bite of a rat. An ulcer forms at the site of the wound, the lymph glands swell, and there is usually a bluish-red rash

ratch (rætʃ) *n.* a ratchet ‖ a toothed bar with which a pawl engages to prevent reverse motion

ratch·et (rætʃit) *n.* a detent, catch or pawl for retaining or activating a ratchet wheel ‖ a ratchet wheel and pawl working together ‖ (*Br.*) the notched, tapering teeth set on certain wheels and bars which may engage with a pawl to prevent reverse motion [F. *rochet,* lance head, bobbin]

ratchet wheel a wheel having teeth with which a detent, catch or pawl engages to prevent reverse motion or to activate forward motion

rate (reit) 1. *n.* the amount of something in relation to some other thing, *absentee rate of 2 men and 5 women per 1,000 employees* ‖ a fixed ratio between two things, quantities etc., *rate of exchange* ‖ speed of motion or change, *drive at a moderate rate* ‖ (*pl., Br.*) a local property tax levied on buildings etc. in proportion to an estimated annual rental value ‖ a fixed charge per unit of a commodity, service etc. ‖ (*insurance*) a premium charge per unit ‖ a charge asked or paid for a service etc. ‖ (*naut.*) a class of vessel, esp. of warships **at any rate** at least, in any case, *at any rate he didn't forget* **at this** (or **that**) **rate** given the present (or those) conditions 2. *v. pres. part.* **rat·ing** *past* and *past part.* **rat·ed** *v.t.* to assess the quality or worth of ‖ (*Br.*) to assess (property) for local tax purposes ‖ to consider (someone or something) as something, *they rate him as a public menace* ‖ to deserve, merit, *this essay rates a low grade* ‖ (*naut.*) to determine the relative rank or class of ‖ *v.i.* to be considered, *he rates as a fine workman* [O.F.]

rate (reit) *pres. part.* **rat·ing** *past* and *past part.* **rat·ed** *v.t.* to scold severely ‖ *v.i.* (usually with 'at') to deliver a scolding [etym. doubtful]

rateable *RATABLE

ra·tel (réit'l) *n.* a member of *Mellivora,* fam. *Mustelidae,* a genus of burrowing carnivores, esp. *M. capensis* of S. Africa and *M. indica* of India. Ratels are about 3 ft long, including an 8–9-in. tail, and have thick coarse fur, gray on top and black underneath. They destroy wild bees' nests for their honey [Afrik.]

rate·me·ter (réitmi:tər) *n.* an instrument that indicates the rate at which radiation is being absorbed by a human

rat·er (réitər) *n.* (only in compounds) a person of a certain class or rating, *a second-rater*

rath·er (ræðər, ráðər) *adv.* more willingly, preferably, *we would rather go for a walk than stay indoors* ‖ more truthfully, more exactly, *it was a*

foolish rather than a malicious remark ‖ on the contrary, *it wasn't damp, rather it was too dry* ‖ in some measure, *he is rather tiresome* ‖ (ræðə:r, raðə:r) (*Br., pop.,* in answering a question) yes, most certainly [comp. of older *rathe,* quickly]

rat·i·cide (rætisaid) *n.* a chemical or other preparation for exterminating rats [fr. RAT+L. *caedere,* to kill]

rat·i·fi·ca·tion (rætifikéiʃən) *n.* a ratifying or being ratified

rat·i·fy (rætifai) *pres. part.* **rat·i·fy·ing** *past* and *past part.* **rat·i·fied** *v.t.* to confirm (something done or promised), esp. formally, *to ratify a treaty* [F. *ratifier*]

ra·tine (rætí:n) *n.* ratiné

rat·i·né (ræt'néi) *n.* a coarse woolen, cotton or rayon cloth, woven so as to have a rough, knotted surface [F.=tufted]

rat·ing (réitin) *n.* a man's class in a warship's crew, or in the army ‖ (*Br.*) a sailor below commissioned rank classification, e.g. of engines by horsepower, yachts by tonnage etc. ‖ (*commerce*) the estimated credit and reliability of a business concern ‖ an estimate of achievement, status etc. ‖ (*Br.*) the amount fixed as a rate to be paid on property

ra·ti·o (réiʃiou, réiʃou) *n.* the relation between two quantities which is expressed by dividing the magnitude of one by that of the other, *the ratio between selling price and cost price is 3 to 1* [L.=reason]

ra·ti·oc·i·nate (ræʃi:ósineit) *pres. part.* **ra·ti·oc·i·nat·ing** *past* and *past part.* **ra·ti·oc·i·nat·ed** *v.i.* (*rhet.*) to reason, argue logically [fr. L. *ratiocinari* (*ratiocinatus*)]

ra·ti·oc·i·na·tion (ræʃi:psinéiʃən) *n.* (*rhet.*) the reasoning process [fr. L. *ratiocinatio* (*ratiocinationis*)]

ra·ti·oc·i·na·tive (ræʃi:ósineitiv) *adj.* (*rhet.*) of or marked by ratiocination [fr. L. *ratiocinativus*]

ra·tion (ræʃən, réiʃən) 1. *n.* an amount (of food, time etc.) which one permits oneself or which one is permitted ‖ (*pl.*) provisions (esp. of food or drink) allotted 2. *v.t.* to fix the amount of (something) which each individual is permitted to consume ‖ to allow to consume only a certain amount of something ‖ (with 'out') to give out as a ration [F. or fr. L. *ratio* (*rationis*), ratio]

ra·tion·al (ræʃən'l) *adj.* of or relating to reason ‖ based on and in accordance with reason or reasoning ‖ well suited to its purpose, *rational dress* ‖ endowed with reason, *man is a rational animal* ‖ (*pop.*) sensible, sound-minded ‖ (*math.*) not requiring a radical for its expression [fr. L. *rationalis*]

ra·tion·ale (ræʃənæl) *n.* the logical justifying grounds for something ‖ a statement or exposition of principles or reasons [L. neut. of *rationalis,* rational]

ra·tion·al·ism (ræʃən'lizəm) *n.* the belief that all knowledge and truth consist in what is ascertainable by rational processes of thought and that there is no supernatural revelation ‖ (*philos.*) the doctrine that true and absolute knowledge is found only in reason **ra·tion·al·ist** *adj.* and *n.* **ra·tion·al·ís·tic** *adj.*

ra·tion·al·i·ty (ræʃənæliti:) *n.* the quality or state of being rational [fr. L.L. *rationalitas*]

ra·tion·al·i·za·tion (ræʃən'lizéiʃən) *n.* a rationalizing or the result of this ‖ (*business*) reducing costs of industrial production to meet competition, esp. in world markets

ra·tion·al·ize (ræʃən'laiz) *pres. part.* **ra·tion·al·iz·ing** *past* and *past part.* **ra·tion·al·ized** *v.t.* to discover and express the reason for (conduct etc.), esp. in order to justify ‖ to put a natural explanation in place of a supernatural one for (something) ‖ to make (a production or an industry) more efficient and less costly ‖ (*math.*) to reduce (an expression) to finite terms

Ra·tis·bon (rætizbɔn) *REGENSBURG

rat·ite (rætait) 1. *adj.* of a member of *Ratitae,* a group of flightless, running birds with a flat sternum and rudimentary wings (e.g. emu, ostrich) 2. *n.* a member of *Ratitae* [fr. L. *ratis,* raft]

rat·line (rætlin) *n.* (*naut.,* esp. *pl.*) one of the small lines rope across the shrouds of a ship, forming a ladder ‖ the thin rope so used ‖ (*mil.*) an organized effort for clandestine movement of personnel and/or material across a denied area or border [etym. doubtful]

rat·o·mor·phic (rætəmɔ́rfik) *adj.* research conclusions based on the reactions of rats

ra·toon, rat·toon (rætú:n) 1. *n.* a new shoot growing from the root or crown of a perennial, e.g. sugarcane, after the old growth has been

cut down 2. *v.i.* to send up new shoots in this way ‖ *v.t.* to cut back (a plant) to encourage ratoons to sprout [fr. Span. *retoño,* a sprout]

rat race (*pop.*) a hectic rush, frantic scramble (used esp. of the struggle to earn a living in an industrial economy under conditions which tend to dehumanize)

rat racer *n.* (*colloq.*) participant in competitive society

rat·tan, ra·tan (rætǽn) *n.* any of various climbing palms, esp. of genera *Calamus* and *Daemonothops,* growing in India and S.E. Asia ‖ a part of the long stem of this plant used for wickerwork, chair seats, rope etc. ‖ a walking stick fashioned from such a stem [Malay *rōtan* fr. *rāut,* to pare]

rat·ter (rætər) *n.* a dog good at catching rats

rat·tle (ræt'l) 1. *v. pres. part.* **rat·tling** *past* and *past part.* **rat·tled** *v.i.* to emit a rapid succession of short, sharp sounds, *the shutter rattled in the wind* ‖ to move emitting such sounds, *the old car rattled down the road* ‖ to move rapidly, *the car rattled along at great speed* ‖ (often with 'on') to talk rapidly, incessantly and often rather foolishly ‖ *v.t.* to cause (something) to make a rattling sound ‖ (often with 'off') to express in rapid, usually emotionless, speech, *he rattled off the poem* ‖ to cause to become confused and lacking in confidence, *the questions rattled the witness* 2. *n.* the sound made by something which rattles ‖ such a sound made in a mucus-clogged throat ‖ a contrivance or baby's toy designed to make this sound ‖ the horny rings on a rattlesnake's tail [M.E. *ratelen,* prob. imit.]

rat·tle·brain (ræt'brein) *n.* an emptyheaded person **rát·tle·brained** *adj.*

rat·tler (rætlər) *n.* a rattlesnake

rat·tle·snake (ræt'lsneik) *n.* a member of *Sistrurus* or *Crotalus,* fam. *Crotalidae,* genera of North American poisonous snakes having horny sheaths towards the end of the tail which make a rattling sound

rat·tle·trap (ræt'ltræp) 1. *n.* something old and dilapidated, esp. a noisy, rattling automobile, wagon etc. ‖ (*Br., old-fash.*) someone who chatters incessantly 2. *adj.* old and dilapidated

rat·tling (rætlin) *adj.* (*pop.*) decidedly good, *a rattling success* ‖ (*pop.*) lively, brisk, *a rattling pace*

rat·tly (rætli:) *adj.* tending to rattle ‖ having a noisy sound like a rattle

rattoon *RATOON

rat·trap, rat-trap (rǽttræp) *n.* a trap for catching rats

rau·cous (rɔ́kəs) *adj.* hoarse, grating, roughsounding, *raucous laughter* [fr. L. *raucus*]

raun·chy (rɔ́ntʃi:) *adj.* bawdy —**raunchiness** *n.*

Rau·schen·berg (ráuʃənbə:rg), Robert (1925-), U.S. painter, known esp. for his 'combine-drawings' depicting themes drawn from American folklore and using a juxtaposition of collage, ink, pencil and photography

rav·age (rævidʒ) *n.* devastation ‖ (*pl.*) ill effects, *the ravages of time* [F.]

rav·age *pres. part.* **rav·ag·ing** *past* and *past part.* **rav·aged** *v.t.* to lay waste to ‖ *v.i.* to do ruinous damage [F. *ravager*]

rave (reiv) 1. *v.i. pres. part.* **rav·ing** *past* and *past part.* **raved** to talk or act wildly or incoherently, *he raved in his delirium* ‖ (with 'about' or 'over') to express or feel exaggerated admiration, *she raves about that singer* ‖ *v.t.* to express wildly or incoherently, *to rave obscenities* 2. *n.* the act of raving or an instance of this ‖ (*pop.*) an excessively enthusiastic criticism, esp. of a play [perh. O.F. *raver*]

Ra·vel (rævel), Maurice (1875-1937), French composer. He explored a highly chromatic and sensuous harmony. His art is rigorously precise, but also full of tenderness and fantasy, e.g. 'Ma mère l'Oye' (1908) and the operas 'l'Heure espagnole' (1907) and 'l'Enfant et les sortilèges' (completed in 1925). His mastery of orchestration, e.g. the suites from the ballet 'Daphnis and Chloe' (1908), is famous. Other works include the piano suite 'Gaspard de la nuit' (1908), two piano concertos, chamber music and songs

rav·el (rævəl) 1. *v. pres. part.* **rav·el·ing,** esp. *Br.* **rav·el·ling** *past.* and *past part.* **rav·elled,** esp. *Br.* **rav·elled** *v.t.* to separate the threads of ‖ to cause (the edge of a fabric) to fray ‖ *v.i.* to become tangled or confused ‖ to become untwisted ‖ to fray 2. *n.* a frayed end or loose thread ‖ something tangled, esp. a tangled situation [prob. fr. Du. *ravelen, rafelen,* to make tangled]

rave·lin (rǽvlin) *n.* (*hist.*) a detached part of a system of fortifications (15th–16th cc.) outside the curtain, its two embankments forming a salient [F. fr. Ital.]

rav·el·ing, esp. *Br.* **rav·el·ling,** (rǽvəliŋ) *n.* a thread that has come loose from a fabric and hangs from the surface

ra·ven (réivən) **1.** *n. Corvus corax,* fam. *Corvidae,* a large, black, omnivorous and occasionally predatory bird about 2 ft long with a wingspread of 3 to 4 ft. It has a black bill, a wedge-shaped tail and a deep, harsh croak. It nests on cliffs or in very tall trees **2.** *adj.* glossy black [O.E. *hræfn*]

rav·en·ing (rǽvəniŋ) *adj.* (*rhet.*) hungrily searching for prey [pres. part. of *raven,* to search for prey, fr. O.F. *raviner*]

Ra·ven·na (rəvénə) a town (pop. 137,093) of Emilia Romagna, Italy, an ancient port, now 6 miles from the Adriatic. Industries: sugar refining, textiles, oil refining. Cathedral (18th c.). Romano-Byzantine and Byzantine mausoleums, baptistry and churches (5th-11th cc.), some containing celebrated mosaics (esp. those of San Vitale and Sant' Apollinare Nuovo, both 6th c.). Ravenna was the capital of the Western Roman Empire (402-76), of the Ostrogoths (493-526), and of an exarchate (584-751). It was given to the papacy (754) by Pépin III

rav·en·ous (rǽvinəs) *adj.* fiercely hungry ‖ consuming or devouring greedily [O.F. *ravineux,* addicted to plundering]

Ra·vens·brück (réivənzbruk, rɑvənsbryk) the site in S. Mecklenburg, East Germany, of a Nazi concentration camp for women (1934-45)

Ra·vi (rɑ́viː) a tributary (400 miles long) of the Chenab, rising in S. Kashmir and forming part of the border between the Indian Punjab and the Pakistani Punjab. It joins the Chenab above Multan

ra·vine (rəvíːn) *n.* a long, deep, narrow hollow, usually made by a torrent deepening its bed [F.=flood, torrent]

rav·ing (réiviŋ) **1.** *adj.* talking wildly or incoherently, *a raving lunatic* ‖ worthy of being raved about, *a raving beauty* **2.** *adv.* to the extent of raving, *raving mad* **3.** *n.* (esp. *pl.*) incoherent talk or an item of such talk, *lucid moments in her ravings* [RAVE]

ra·vi·o·li (rævi:óuli:, rɒvi:óuli:) *pl. n.* small cases of pasta filled with meat, spinach etc. cooked and served with a sauce [Ital.]

rav·ish (rǽviʃ) *v.t.* (*rhet.*) to rape **ráv·ish·ing** *adj.* so beautiful as to cause rapture [F. *ravir (raviss-)*]

raw (rɔ) **1.** *adj.* (of foodstuffs) uncooked ‖ (of other material) unprocessed, unrefined, or unfinished, *raw silk, raw spirit* ‖ untrained, inexperienced, *raw recruits* ‖ (of a wound or part of the body) having the skin partly or wholly removed ‖ (of weather) cold and damp ‖ (*pop.*) indecent, *a raw joke* ‖ (*photog.*) unexposed **2.** *n.* (in the phrases) **to touch on the raw** (*Br.*) to cause painful emotions to **in the raw** in the original state, *nature in the raw* ‖ (*pop.*) naked [O.E. *hrēaw* fr. Gk]

Ra·wal·pin·di (rɔlpíndi:) a city (pop. 928,000) of Pakistan in the N. Punjab, a commercial center and military base, temporary headquarters of the national government (1959-60): oil refining, chemicals, rail yards

raw·boned (rɔ́bound) *adj.* having little flesh covering the bones

raw deal an instance of unfair or unjust treatment

raw·hide (rɔ́haid) *n.* untanned cattle hide ‖ a whip made of this

ra·win (réiwən) *n.* (*meteor. acronym*) for radar wind sounding, **1.** a radar system for determining wind direction and velocity above a station utilizing a balloon-borne radiosonde and radio; or **2.** the information so collected

ra·win·sonde (réiwənsɒnd) *n.* (*meteor.*) a method of determining and evaluating wind speed, direction, air pressure and humidity

Rawlings (rɔ́liŋz), Jerry (1947-   ), leader of Ghana (1981-95). An armed forces officer, he overthrew Lt.-Gen. Frederick W. K. Akuffo (1979), briefly led the country before installing a civilian government and then staged another coup in 1981

Raw·lin·son (rɔ́linsən), Sir Henry Creswicke (1810-95), British administrator and Orientalist. He deciphered (1835-46) the Assyrian cuneiform inscription of Darius I at Behistun and was a founder of Assyriology

raw material the basic matter from which processed or manufactured goods are made

RAWOL (*mil. acronym*) for radar without line of sight, a system of radar detection of targets obscured by intervening hills.

raw sienna sienna that has not been calcined ‖ the brownish-orange color of this

Raws·thorne (rɔ́sθɔrn), Alan (1905-71), English composer. His works include three symphonies, piano and violin concertos, chamber music etc.

raw umber umber that has not been calcined ‖ the dark yellowish-brown color of this (cf. BURNT UMBER)

Ray (rei), John (1627-1705), English naturalist. He and Willughby planned a complete classification of animal and vegetable life. His 'Catalogus plantarum Angliae' (1670) was the first systematic account of English flora

Ray, Man (1890-1976), U.S. painter of the Dada movement, and photographer. He invented the 'rayograph', a photograph obtained by the direct application of objects of varying opacity to a light-sensitive plate

ray (rei) **1.** *n.* a line constructed perpendicular to a wave front in which light is propagated, representing the path of light in geometrical optics. It is considered a beam of infinitesimally small cross section ‖ a line of light that appears to radiate from some light-producing or light-reflecting objects ‖ a stream of particles travelling along the same path ‖ any of several lines radiating from a center (e.g. the radii of a circle) ‖ a portion or organ of a plant or animal having a number of like parts diverging from a common center, e.g. a vascular ray, the arm of a starfish or any of the supporting bones of the fins of some fishes ‖ a slight manifestation, e.g. *of hope or intelligence* ‖ (*bot.*) the outer whorl of florets of a composite flower **2.** *v.i.* to issue in rays [O.F. *rai*]

ray *n.* a member of *Hypotremata,* an order of flattened, cartilaginous fish similar to the skate (*STING RAY, ELECTRIC RAY)

ray (*mus.*) *RE

Rayburn (réibərn), Samuel Taliaferro (1882-1961), U.S. politician, Speaker of the House of Representatives (1940-7; 1949-53; 1955-61). A Democrat from Texas, he served in the House (1913-61) and was elected majority leader in 1937. He was instrumental in the drafting of New Deal legislation

ray·dist (réidist) *n.* a navigation system involving a continuous signal to several ground stations, which compare, compute, and report position

ray floret one of the marginal flowers going around the head of disk florets in e.g. the daisy, or making up the head in composites having no disk florets

ray flower a ray floret

Ray·leigh (réili:), John William Strutt, 3rd Baron (1842-1919), English physicist. He contributed largely to the study of vibratory motion. With Ramsay he discovered argon, and he worked on the standardizing of electrical units. Nobel prize (1904)

Ray·leigh wave or **R wave** (réili:) **1.** (*seismology*) surface vibrations with retrograde, elliptical ground motion. **2.** (*mechanics*) parallel waves in the surface of a solid

Ray·naud's phenomenon (reinóuz) (*med.*) obstruction in bloodstream resulting in discoloration (white or blue) of hands

ray·on (réiɒn) *n.* a textile fiber made by forcing various solutions of naturally occurring cellulose through fine holes and solidifying in a chemical bath or warm air ‖ any of various textiles made of such fibers [coined fr. RAY]

raze, rase (reiz) *pres. part.* **raz·ing, ras·ing** *past and past part.* **razed, rased** *v.t.* to destroy completely, *to raze a city* [F. *raser,* to shave]

ra·zor (réizər) *n.* an instrument with a very sharp rigid cutting edge, or fitted with a blade having this, used esp. to shave hair from the skin (*STRAIGHT RAZOR) [O.F. *rasor, rasour*]

ra·zor·back (réizərbæk) *n.* a rorqual whale ‖ a thin, long-legged, semiwild hog of the southern U.S.A.

ra·zor·bill (réizərbil) *n. Alca torda,* fam. *Alcidae,* a black and white auk of the N. Atlantic, approx. 16 ins long with a very sharp bill

razor clam a member of *Solenidae,* a family of bivalve mollusks having a very long, narrow, curved shell

razor cut a haircut given with a razor

razor fish a razor clam

razor shell a razor clam ‖ the shell of a razor clam

razz (ræz) *v.t.* (*pop.*) to tease

RBE (*abbr.*) for relative biological effectiveness, a factor for comparison of radiation effects on organisms

R.C. Roman Catholic

RC-135 *n.* (*mil.*) U.S. strategic reconnaissance plane with altitude capability of 40,000 ft, replacing the U-2

Rd. Road

R.D. rural free delivery

RDX *CYCLONITE

Re (rei) Ra

re (ri:) *prep.* (*law, commerce,* etc.) in the matter of, as regards [L. ablative of *res,* thing]

re, *Br.* also **ray** (rei) *n.* (*mus.*) the note D in the fixed-do system of solmization ‖ the second note of any diatonic scale in movable-do solmization [Ital.]

re- (ri:) *prefix* again, another time. Re-compounds are hyphenated when confusion might occur between identical forms, e.g. re-ally and really. The hyphen is also employed when the second part of the word begins with a capital letter, e.g. re-Christianize ‖ back, to a former state or condition [L.]

reach (ri:tʃ) **1.** *v.t.* to arrive at, *to reach the end of a journey, to reach the age of 30* ‖ to extend so as to touch (a particular point or place), *the rubber plant reaches the ceiling* ‖ to extend, *to reach out one's hand* ‖ to succeed in touching or grasping with an outstretched limb ‖ to pass with the hand, *just reach me that book* ‖ to get in touch with, *we tried to reach them by cable* ‖ to touch the mind or feelings of, *her words failed to reach him* ‖ *v.i.* to extend in dimension, scope etc., *the woods reach as far as the river* ‖ (of the voice, eye etc.) to carry, penetrate, *as far as the eye can reach* ‖ to put or stretch out a hand or foot, *reach for the bell* ‖ (*naut.*) to sail on a reach **2.** *n.* the act of stretching out or reaching, or an instance of this ‖ the extent of such a reach ‖ intellectual or imaginative range, *an idea not within his reach* ‖ an uninterrupted expanse, e.g. a straight part of a river or a length of canal between locks ‖ (*naut.*) a tack sailed with the wind abeam ‖ the pole coupling the rear axle of a wagon to the transverse bar over the front axle [O.E. *rǣcan*]

re·act (ri:ǽkt) *v.t.* to act again

re·act (ri:ǽkt) *v.i.* to act in response to a stimulus etc., *he did not react to the treatment* ‖ to act contrary to a stimulus etc., *he reacted against my suggestion* ‖ to undergo chemical change

re·ac·tance (ri:ǽktəns) *n.* (*elec.*) the portion of impedance in an alternating current circuit that results from capacitance or inductance or both. It is expressed in ohms [REACT]

re·ac·tion (ri:ǽkʃən) *n.* a response to a stimulus ‖ opposition caused by an act, proposal etc., *the workers' reaction against automation* ‖ the tendency to favor extremely conservative social or political policies ‖ (*phys.*) the equal and opposing force which is always called into play by a force ‖ a chemical change involving two or more substances **re·ác·tion·ar·y 1.** *adj.* characterized by reaction, esp. in politics **2.** *n. pl.* **re·ác·tion·ar·ies** a reactionary person **re·ác·tion·ist** *n.* a reactionary

reaction time (*psychol.*) the time which elapses between the start of the application of a stimulus and the start of the response it evokes

re·ac·ti·vate (ri:ǽktəveit) *pres. part.* **re·ac·ti·vat·ing** *past* and *past part.* **re·ac·ti·vat·ed** *v.t.* to cause to be active again ‖ *v.i.* to be active again

re·ac·tive (ri:ǽktiv) *adj.* of or characterized by reaction or reactance ‖ tending to react

re·ac·tor (ri:ǽktər) *n.* a person or thing that reacts (e.g. a chemical reagent or a subject of a physiological test reacting to a stimulus) ‖ a low-resistance coil of high inductance used to suppress alternating current or change its phase ‖ a vessel or other piece of equipment in which a chemical reaction is carried out, esp. on a large scale ‖ a device in which a fission chain reaction is initiated and controlled. In general it includes a fuel (a source of neutrons) such as uranium or plutonium, a moderator such as graphite or heavy water (which slows the neutrons to a speed permitting the maximization of capture by other nuclei) and a set of control rods (usually made of cadmium or boron) which absorb neutrons readily and which are brought into play to arrest the reaction if and when there is a danger of its going out of control. The energy produced (*NUCLEAR ENERGY) in a reactor may be converted to electricity (via steam turbines) or to mechanical energy (e.g. in nuclear ships). The nuclear reaction can be used as a source of neutrons producing further radioactive material (*BREEDER REACTOR) [REACT]

read (ri:d) 1. *v. pres. part.* **read·ing** *past and past-part.* **read** (red) *v.t.* to understand the meaning of (symbols, signs, gestures etc.) by looking at them and assimilating them mentally, *to read a book, to read music, to read French* || to learn in this way, *he read that sterling had been protected* || to say aloud (written or printed material that one sees and understands in this way), *read this story to us* || (*Br.*) to study (a subject) at a university || to touch (Braille symbols) and understand them || to observe a measurement shown by (an instrument), *to read a pressure gauge* || (of an instrument) to show (a measurement), *the thermometer reads 30 degrees* || to consider (something) to have a certain meaning, *she read his letter to mean that he didn't intend to come* || to give (a word, phrase etc.) as a reading in a particular passage, *for 'marry' this copy reads 'merry'* || to cause (a word, phrase etc.) to be substituted in a particular passage, *read 'marry' for 'merry'* || to discover the meaning of (someone's thoughts, expressions etc.) by observation || to predict (the future, someone's fortune etc.) || to explain or interpret (riddles, magic symbols, palms etc.) || to go over (printer's proofs), marking corrections on them || *v.i.* to be engaged in reading something || to be able to read books etc. || to say audibly what one is reading, *he is reading to the children* || to make a specified impression on a reader, *his letter reads well* || to contain certain words, *the constitution reads as follows . . .* || to suggest a meaning, *his letter reads as if he doesn't intend to come* || to learn or study by reading, *he likes reading about ancient peoples* || to have a specified stylistic quality, *it reads jerkily* **to read out** to read (something) aloud || to expel (someone) from an organization by publicly reading the notice of dismissal **to read (someone) like a book** to understand perfectly the intentions, motives etc. of (someone) without his explaining them or even if he tries to hide them **to read into** to attach to (something) a meaning which is neither stated nor intended **to read oneself in** (Church of England) to assume the office of incumbent by reading aloud publicly the Thirty-nine Articles || (*Br.*) to familiarize oneself with the files etc. before attempting to make decisions, initiate work etc. 2. *n.* (*Br.*) a period of reading, *to enjoy a read after dinner* **read** (red) *adj.* (often in compounds) learned or informed through reading, *a well-read critic* **to take as read** to accept as accurate without having read aloud, *to take the minutes as read* || to assume to be true **réad·a·ble** *adj.* easy or pleasant to read || legible [O.F. *rēdan*]

re·ad·dress (ri:ədrés) *v.t.* to alter the address on (e.g. a letter)

Reade (ri:d). Charles (1814-84), British novelist. His works include the historical novel 'The Cloister and the Hearth' (1861)

read·er (ri:dər) *n.* a person able to read || a book for children learning to read || a book containing selections for reading for a beginner, esp. in another language || a person who reads, esp. one who reads a particular book or periodical, *this newspaper has over a million readers* || a person very fond of reading || someone who reads and criticizes manuscripts for a publisher, literary agent etc. || a proofreader || someone, esp. a graduate student, who marks examination papers || a person selected to read aloud, e.g. in a religious service || (*Br.*) a member of a university staff ranking between a senior lecturer and a professor **réad·er·ship** *n.* the office of a university reader || the collective body of readers of a newspaper or periodical

read·i·ly (rédili:) *adv.* easily, *one can readily imagine this* || willingly, *to admit a mistake readily* [READY]

read·i·ness (rédi:nis) *n.* the state of being ready || willingness, lack of hesitation, *readiness to offer help*

Read·ing (rédiŋ) the county town (pop. 132,037) of Berkshire, England. Industries: biscuit-making, brewing, mechanical engineering, seed nurseries. University (1926)

read·ing (ri:diŋ) 1. *n.* the act of one who reads || the ability to read, *reading comes slowly* || the material a person is reading, *means to read or has read* || the extent to which a person has read, *a man of wide reading* || a public entertainment

at which passages from a book, stories, poems etc. are read aloud || a textual version, *the manuscripts offer four variant readings of the passage* || a measurement shown by an instrument, *the reading is 30°C* || understanding, *my reading of the situation differs somewhat* || (*parliament*) the presentation of a bill for debate. The first reading serves as a general and formal introduction. The second reading provides an opportunity for debate on the purpose of the measure and the means proposed to put it into effect. The third reading is a review of the final form of the bill 2. *adj.* of or for reading or readers

reading desk a raised stand on which a book etc. being read is placed

read·just (ri:ədʒʌ́st) *v.t.* to adjust or arrange again || to change or rearrange (the terms of a company's debts, stocks etc.) through the voluntary action of shareholders, esp. so as to take advantage of new business opportunities **re·ad·júst·ment** *n.* a readjusting or being readjusted

read-on·ly (ri:dóunli:) *n.* (*computer*) device that stores basic operational data that cannot be altered by programmed instructions

read·out (ri:dqut) *n.* (*computer*) 1. information taken from storage for transcription and recording 2. the processor output. —**readout** *v.* to produce a readout. —**read-out device** *n.* the device

read·y (rédi:) 1. *adj. comp.* **read·i·er** *superl.* **read·i·est** in a state fit for immediate action, use etc. || immediately available whenever needed, *a ready source of supplies* || in an emotional state adapted to a possible set of circumstances, willing, *she is ready to suffer in order to stay slim* || quick and easy, *a ready wit* || forward, prompt, *he is very ready with his criticism* || reduced to the point of being likely (to do something indicated), *she looked ready to drop* 2. *n.* (*mil.*, esp. of firearms) the state of being fit or poised for immediate action or use, *rifles at the ready* 3. *v.t. pres. part.* **read·y·ing** *past and past part.* **read·ied** (esp. *reflex.*) to prepare, *he readied himself for the blow* [M.E. *rædi, readi, redi,* prob. fr. O.E. *rǣde*]

ready cap (*mil.*) fighter aircraft in condition of 'standby.'

read·y-made (rédi:méid) *adj.* (of clothes) made to a stock size, not to individual requirements || lacking freshness and originality, *ready-made excuses*

ready reckoner a book of mathematical tables

read·y-to-wear (rédi:təwéər) *adj.* (of clothes) ready-made

re·af·firm (ri:əfə́:rm) *v.t.* to affirm again

re·af·for·est (ri:æfórist, ri:æfórist) *v.t.* (*Br.*) to reforest **re·af·for·est·á·tion** *n.*

Reagan (réigən), Ronald Wilson (1911-), U.S. statesman and actor, 40th president (1981-). Born in Tampico, Ill., he went to Eureka College and then to Hollywood (1937) where he appeared in 53 films and also served as president of the Screen Actors' Guild (1952, 1959-60). He also hosted the TV series 'Death Valley Days' (1961-2). Finding that his views had become more conservative, he ran for governor of California on the Republican ticket in 1966 and, defeating incumbent Democrat Pat Brown, served in that post for eight years (1967-75). He opposed tax increases and government spending and left office with a considerable budget surplus. The Republican nominee in the 1980 presidential election, he chose George Bush as his running mate, won by a near-landslide victory and was decisively reelected in 1984. As president he worked to revamp the U.S. economy, stem inflation, produce tax cuts and increase the country's defenses, and he took a firm stand against the Soviet Union and terrorist tactics. An assassination attempt (1981) by John W. Hinckley, Jr., hospitalized him briefly, as did the early discovery of intestinal cancer in 1985. He was married to actress Jane Wyman (1940-9) and Nancy Davis (1952-)

re·a·gent (ri:éidʒənt) *n.* a substance used to bring about a chemical reaction in another substance

re·al (ri:əl, ríəl) 1. *adj.* existing in fact, not merely seeming, *his pain is real, not imaginary* || natural, not artificial, *a real pearl* || proper, *this is real summer weather* || (used merely for emphasis) great, *a real surprise* || (*philos.*) relating to objective things in the physical world || (*law*) of or relating to real estate || (*math.*, of

numbers) not imaginary || (of wages) measured by their purchasing power (cf. NOMINAL) 2. *adv.* (*pop.*) really, *a real good time* 3. *n.* **the real** that which exists objectively in the physical world [O.F. *real, réel* or L.L. *realis*]

re·al (reiál) *pl.* **re·als, re·a·les** (reiáleis) *n.* a former Spanish silver coin and money of account [Span.=royal]

real estate (*law*) immovable property, e.g. land or houses, as opposed to temporary, movable personal property

real estate investment trusts mutual funds holding real property or mortgages on real property as principal assets. *acronym* REIT

re·al·gar (ri:ǽlgər) *n.* a naturally occurring mineral, As_4S_4 or AsS, arsenic sulfide, used in fireworks [M.L. fr. Arab. *rehj al-ghār*, powder of the cave]

real image an optical image formed of the points of convergence of light coming from an object

realise *REALIZE

re·al·ism (ri:əlizəm) *n.* an attitude based on facts and reality as opposed to emotions, imaginings etc. || (*philos.*) the doctrine that ideas, or universals, have an absolute existence outside the mind || (*philos.*) the belief that the objects of sense perception have real existence || (in art, literature etc.) fidelity to life as perceived and experienced (cf. NATURALISM)

re·al·ist (ri:əlist) *n.* an exponent of realism in art, philosophy etc. || a practical person who concerns himself with facts as they are known to him rather than with things as they might be **re·al·ís·tic** *adj.* of, characterized by, or relating to, realism **re·al·ís·ti·cal·ly** *adv.*

re·al·i·ty (ri:ǽliti:) *pl.* **re·al·i·ties** *n.* the state or quality of being real or of existing in fact || someone or something that is real or exists in fact || (*collect.*) the real world, e.g. considered as a force or pressure || the true or actual nature of something **in reality** actually, in fact, really [fr. M.L. *realitas* or F. *réalité*]

re·al·iz·a·ble (ri:əlaizəb'l) *adj.* able to be realized

re·al·i·za·tion (ri:əlaizéiʃən) *n.* a realizing or being realized || that which is realized

re·al·ize (ri:əlaiz) *pres. part.* **re·al·iz·ing** *past and past part.* **re·al·ized** *v.t.* to be aware of the truth of, recognize as real, *he realized that she was in danger* || to make real or actual (something imagined, hoped for etc.), *her wish was realized at last* || to convert (other forms of property) into money, *to realize investments* || to acquire, gain, *to realize profits* || (of property) to bring as proceeds, *the sale of the house realized a large profit* [fr. REAL after F. *réaliser*]

re·al·ly (ri:əli:, ri:li:) *adv.* in reality || (emphatic) truly, *a really steep hill*

realm (relm) *n.* (*hist., law* or *rhet.*) kingdom, *the laws of the realm* || province, domain, *the realm of fancy* [O.F. *realme, reaume*]

re·al·po·li·tik (reiálpoulití:k) *n.* politics which deal solely in terms of national interests and the realities of the situation, being neither doctrinaire nor idealistic and not concerned with ethics [G.=real politics]

real property real estate

real tennis (*Br.*) court tennis

real time *n.* (*computer*) 1. (*mil.*) the absence of delay, except for the time required for transmission by electromagnetic energy, between the occurrence of an event or the transmission of data, and the knowledge of the event, or reception of the data at some other location 2. (*computer*) the actual time for a physical operation or process to take place 3. the adequate performance of a computation in the actual time to solve a problem. —**real-time** *adj.* 1. of the time necessary to perform a computation 2. of a data-processing system that produces data not later than is required, e.g., a reservations system

re·al·tor (ri:əltər) *n.* (*Am.=Br.* estate agent) someone who sells or lets land or houses on behalf of the owner, manages estates, collects rents, draws up leases etc. and often surveys and values properties, esp. someone who is a member of the National Association of Real Estate Boards [REALTY]

re·al·ty (ri:əlti:) *n.* real estate

real wage insurance President Carter's proposed anti-inflation program (October 1978) providing bonus of up to 3% of annual wage, to be paid by the government to offset the difference between the percentage increase in the consumer price index over 7% and any proposed wage settlement

CONCISE PRONUNCIATION KEY: **(a)** æ, c*a*t; ɑ, c*a*r; ɔ f*aw*n; ei, sn*a*ke. **(e)** e, h*e*n; i:, sh*ee*p; iə, d*ee*r; ɛə, b*ea*r. **(i)** i, f*i*sh; ai, t*i*ger; ə:, b*i*rd. **(o)** o, *o*x; au, c*ow*; ou, g*oa*t; u, p*oo*r; ɔi, r*oy*al. **(u)** ʌ, d*u*ck; u, b*u*ll; u:, g*oo*se; ə, b*a*cillus; ju:, c*u*be. x, lo*ch*; θ, *th*ink; δ, *b*o*th*er; z, *Z*en; ʒ, corsa*g*e. dʒ, sava*g*e; ŋ, orangutan*g*; ʒ, ya*l*:; ʃ, *fi*sh; tʃ, fe*tch*; 'l, rabb*le*; 'n, red*den*. Complete pronunciation key appears inside front cover.

re·an·i·mate (ri:ǽnəmeit) *pres. part.* **re·an·i·mat·ing** *past* and *past part.* **re·an·i·mat·ed** *v.t.* to cause to be animate again || to cause to be animated again, put fresh spirit into

ream (ri:m) *n.* a unit of measure for paper usually equal to 20 quires or 480 sheets || a unit of measure for paper for printing, being 211 quires or 516 sheets || (usually *pl.*) a huge amount (esp. of written matter), *to write reams* [M.E. *rem, rim* fr. Arab. *rizmah,* bundle]

ream *v.t.* to widen or shape (an opening of a hole in metal) with a reamer || to widen the bore of (a gun) with a reamer || (*naut.*) to open (a seam) for caulking || to extract (fruit juice) with a reamer || to extract the juice (of fruit) with a reamer || (*Br.*) to turn over the edge of (a metal cap)

réam·er *n.* a rotating tool with cutting edges for reaming a gun's bore or a hole || a lemon squeezer || (*Br.*) a tool used to turn over the edge of a metal cap [etym. doubtful]

reap (ri:p) *v.t.* to cut (ripe grain etc.) || to gather (a crop) || to cut the crop of (a field) || to receive as the result of one's own acts **réap·er** *n.* someone who reaps || a machine for reaping grain without binding into sheaves [O.E. *rīpan, reopan*]

rear (riər) 1. *n.* the back of something || the position or space behind something || the part of a procession, army, fleet, military column etc. furthest from the front || (*pop.*) the buttocks || (*Br., pop.*) a latrine **to bring up the rear** to be the last person in a line etc. 2. *adj.* located at or toward the rear [fr. older *arrear,* that which is behind]

rear (riər) *v.t.* to erect, *to rear a monument* || to raise, esp. to great or unusual height, *to rear one's head* || to bring up, *to rear a family* || to cultivate, *to rear a crop* || to breed, *to rear dogs* || *v.i.* (of a horse) to rise up on its hind legs || (*rhet.*) to rise high up, *the mountain reared above the village* [O.E. *rǣran*]

rear admiral a naval officer ranking below a vice admiral and above a commodore

rear guard a body of troops protecting the rear of a military force, esp. in a withdrawal

re·arm (ri:ɑ́rm) *v.t.* (*mil.*) to arm again, esp. with new or better arms || *v.i.* to become so equipped **re·ár·ma·ment** *n.*

rear·most (ríərmoust) *adj.* farthest behind

re·ar·range (rí:əréindʒ) *v.t. pres. part.* **re·ar·rang·ing** *past* and *past part.* **re·ar·ranged** to arrange again, esp. in a different way **re·ar·ránge·ment** *n.*

rear·ward (ríərwərd) 1. *adj.* being at or towards the rear 2. *adv.* towards the rear **réar·wards** *adv.*

rea·son (rí:z'n) *n.* the ability to think logically, to understand, and to draw inferences, *his reason has shown him the right course* || the cause that makes a phenomenon intelligible, *she understands the reason for his behavior* || sound thinking, *it is contrary to reason* || (Kantian *philos.*) the faculty which provides a priori principles (as opposed to the understanding, which is the mere ability to think logically) **in reason** reasonably || within reasonable limits **to have (good) reason to** to have sufficient (strong) cause for **to listen to reason** to be persuaded out of one's obstinacy **to stand to reason** to be obviously true **within reason** within reasonable limits [O.F. *resun, reisun, reson, reison*]

reason *v.i.* to think or talk logically || to argue persuasively with someone || *v.t.* to analyze by reasoning (usually with 'out') || to think out (something) by reasoning || to persuade (someone) by reasoning [fr. O.F. *raisonner*]

rea·son·a·ble (rí:z'nəb'l) *adj.* ready to listen to reason or act according to reason, *a reasonable person* || in accord with reason, *a reasonable excuse* || not expensive, *a reasonable rent* || neither more nor less than normal or expected, *the book had a reasonable success* **réa·son·a·bly** *adv.* [O.F. *raisonable, raisonnable*]

rea·son·ing (rí:z'niŋ) *n.* the act of someone who reasons or an instance of this

re·as·sem·ble (rí:əsémb'l) *pres. part.* **re·as·sem·bling** *past* and *past part.* **re·as·sem·bled** *v.t.* to put together again || *v.i.* to come together again

re·as·sur·ance (rí:əʃúərəns) *n.* a reassuring or being reassured || something which reassures

re·as·sure (rí:əʃúər) *pres. part.* **re·as·sur·ing** *past* and *past part.* **re·as·sured** *v.t.* to restore confidence to (someone), esp. in a matter of judgment || to reinsure

Ré·au·mur scale (réiəmjuər) (*abbr.* R) a temperature scale on which the freezing point of water at 1 atmosphere is 0° and its boiling point 80° at the same pressure, i.e. 1°C=0.8°R [after

René Antoine Ferchault de *Réaumur* (1683–1757), French physicist]

re·bate (rí:beit, ribéit) *n.* a deduction from an amount to be paid, usually as a courtesy discount [fr. F. *rabat* fr. *rebattre,* to rebate]

rebate *pres. part.* **re·bat·ing** *past* and *past part.* **re·bat·ed** *v.t.* to make a rebate of (a sum) || to give a rebate to (a person) || (*heraldry*) to remove a portion of (a charge) [O.F. *rabattre*]

rebate (rí:beit, rǽbit) 1. *n.* a rabbet 2. *v.t. pres. part.* **re·bat·ing** *past* and *past part.* **re·bat·ed** to rabbet

Re·bec·ca-Eu·re·ka system (ri:békə ju:rí:kə) a preset homing aircraft system utilizing a ground beacon (Eureka) and an airborne interrogator (Rebecca)

reb·el (réb'l) 1. *n.* a person who resists authority || a person who opposes the lawful government by force of arms 2. *adj.* rebellious of or pertaining to rebels [F. *rebelle*]

re·bel (ribél) *pres. part.* **re·bel·ling** *past* and *past part.* **re·belled** *v.i.* to disobey or oppose someone in authority || to resist the lawful government by force of arms || to feel or show aversion [fr. F. *rebeller*]

re·bel·lion (ribéljən) *n.* an organized attempt to overthrow a lawful government by force of arms || open opposition to any authority [F. *rébellion*]

re·bel·lious (ribéljəs) *adj.* defying authority or control || engaged in rebellion || stubbornly defying control or treatment, *rebellious curly hair* [fr. L. *rebellis*]

re·birth (ri:bə́rθ) *n.* a second birth || a renewal, e.g. of energy or strength || a renaissance

re·bound (ribáund) 1. *v.i.* to reverse direction after an impact || to bounce back as if on impact 2. (ríbaund) *n.* a rebounding || a rebounding ball **on the rebound** in a state of hasty emotional reaction to some setback or blow to one's pride etc. [fr. O.F. *rebondir*]

re·buff (ribʌ́f) *v.t.* to give a rebuff to (someone or someone's suggestion, idea etc.) [fr. obs. F. *rebuffer* fr. Ital.]

re·buff (ribʌ́f, rí:bʌf) *n.* a curt rejection (esp. of an expressed desire) causing injury to a person's self-esteem, *his suggestion met with a rebuff* [obs. F. *rebuffe* fr. Ital.]

re·buke (ribjú:k) 1. *v.t. pres. part.* **re·buk·ing** *past* and *past part.* **re·buked** to tell (someone) severely that his conduct or action is wrong or unsatisfactory 2. *n.* a rebuking or being rebuked, or the words uttered or written [A.F. *rebuker*]

re·bus (rí:bəs) *n.* a word or series of words represented by pictures of objects, symbols etc. || a puzzle or riddle made up of such pictures, symbols etc. [ablative pl. of L. *res,* thing]

re·but (ribʌ́t) *pres. part.* **re·but·ting** *past* and *past part.* **re·but·ted** *v.t.* to refute, esp. in formal or legal argument **re·bút·tal** *n.* a rebutting **re·bút·ter** *n.* (*law*) a defendant's answer in matters of fact to a plaintiff's surrejoinder [A.F. *reboter*]

re·cal·ci·trance (rikǽlsitrəns) *n.* the quality or state of being recalcitrant || recalcitrant behavior

re·cal·ci·trant (rikǽlsitrənt) 1. *adj.* refusing to submit to authority, rules etc. || (of a substance or a machine) resisting efforts at control || (*med.*) unresponsive to treatment 2. *n.* a recalcitrant person [F. fr. L. *recalcitrans* (*recalcitrantis*) fr. *recalcitrare,* to kick back]

re·ca·les·cence (rikəlés'ns) *n.* the process of becoming hot again, esp. in iron and steel which, when allowed to cool from white heat, suddenly glow more brightly for a short time at their critical temperature [fr. L. *recalescere.* to grow hot again]

re·call 1. (rikɔ́l) *v.t.* to order to return, *to recall an ambassador* || to cause to return, *the edition was recalled from the booksellers* || to recollect, remember, *she recalls meeting him last year* || to revive the memory or thought of, *the scene recalled her childhood* 2. (rikɔ́l, rí:kɔl) *n.* the act of recalling or an instance of this || the process or right of removal of a public official from office before the end of his term by a vote of the people || (*business*) offer by a manufacturer to repair or replace a defective part of a product || (*mil.*) a signal to call troops back to ranks or camp || (*naut.*) a flag used to signal a ship to return to a squadron **beyond recall** impossible to undo, revoke, rescind etc.

recall ratio (*computer*) ratio of data retrieved to the total

re·cant (rikǽnt) *v.t.* to retract or renounce (an opinion, belief, statement etc.) || *v.i.* to declare

publicly that one has been wrong, or held a mistaken belief, esp. religious or political **re·can·ta·tion** (ri:kæntéiʃən) *n.* [fr. L. *recantare*]

re·cap (rí:kæp, ri:kǽp) *pres. part.* **re·cap·ping** *past* and *past part.* **re·capped** *v.t.* (*pop.*) to recapitulate [by shortening]

re·cap (rí:kæp) *n.* a recapitulation [by shortening]

re·cap 1. (ri:kǽp) *v.t.* to put a strip of prepared rubber on the worn tread of (a tire) and vulcanize it 2. (rí:kæp) *n.* a tire refurbished in this way (cf. RETREAD)

re·ca·pit·u·late (ri:kəpítʃuleit) *v.t. pres. part.* **re·ca·pit·u·lat·ing** *past* and *past part.* **re·ca·pit·u·lat·ed** to repeat or go over again briefly, summarize [RE-+CAPITULATE, (obs.) to draw up under headings]

re·ca·pit·u·la·tion (ri:kəpitʃuléiʃən) *n.* a recapitulating or an instance of this || (*biol.*) the repetition of phylogenetic development in an individual || (*mus.,* esp. of sonata form) a repetition of themes introduced earlier but which in the interval have undergone development [O.F. *recapitulacion* or fr. L. *recapitulatio* (*recapitulationis*)]

re·cap·ture (ri:kǽptʃər) 1. *v.t. pres. part.* **re·cap·tur·ing** *past* and *past part.* **re·cap·tured** to capture again || to get or give the illusion of by remembering or imitating, *to recapture the atmosphere of the past* 2. *n.* a recapturing or being recaptured || the taking by a government of a certain portion of earnings or profits over a fixed amount

re·cast 1. (ri:kǽst, ri:kɑ́st) *v.t.* to cast (metal) again || to get a new cast for (a play etc.) || to put into a new form, to remodel, *to recast the plot of a novel* || to add up again 2. (rí:kæst, rí:kɑst) *n.* a recasting || that which is obtained by recasting

re·cede (ri:sí:d) *pres. part.* **re·ced·ing** *past* and *past part.* **re·ced·ed** *v.i.* to draw back, *the floods slowly receded from the fields* || to become more distant, *the shore gradually receded* || to slope backwards, *a receding chin* || to become less, *the volume of trade has receded* || (usually with 'from') to withdraw from a position, promise etc. [fr. L. *recedere*]

re·ceipt (ri:sí:t) 1. *n.* the act of receiving || a formal written acknowledgment that something has been received, *a receipt for payment* || (*oldfash.*) a recipe || (esp. *pl.*) something received, e.g. goods, money 2. *v.t.* to sign a receipt for || to sign (a bill) as a receipt || *v.i.* (with 'for') to give a signed receipt [M.E. *receit, receite*]

re·ceiv·a·ble (ri:sí:vəb'l) *adj.* that can be accepted or received, esp. as legal, *receivable bonds* || (of bills etc.) on which money is due or callable, *accounts receivable* **re·céiv·a·bles** *pl. n.* accounts, bills or business notes becoming due on a fixed date, or due from others

re·ceive (ri:sí:v) *pres. part.* **re·ceiv·ing** *past* and *past part.* **re·ceived** *v.t.* to be given, awarded or sent, *to receive a good education, to receive a letter through the mail* || to take into one's hands or one's mind || to accept (something offered) || to be subjected to, *to receive bad advice,* or have inflicted on one, *to receive a wound* || to experience, undergo, *to receive a shock to the nerves* || to be accorded, *to receive acceptance* || to welcome (someone as a visitor or guest) into one's presence, one's home etc. || to admit into membership, *to be received into a club* || to give a reception of a specified kind to, *they received him with cheers* || to act as a receptacle for, *this pit receives the juice from the grapes* || to accept and pay for (stolen goods), esp. in order to resell them || to take the force of, *the buttresses receive the weight of the stone roof* || (esp. *past part.*) to accept as authoritatively sound and valid || to take (Communion) from the priest || *v.i.* to be a recipient or receiver || to take Communion || to act as host or hostess, *to receive on Thursday* || (*radio, television*) to transform incoming electromagnetic waves into sound or light [O.N.F. *receivre*]

re·ceiv·er (ri:sí:vər) *n.* a person who receives, e.g. a fence || something that receives, e.g. a receptacle for collecting and containing a chemical distillate || (*law*) a person appointed by a court to administer a bankrupt's property or property under litigation || the earpiece of a telephone || a television or radio receiving set [M.E. fr. A.F. *receivour*]

re·ceiv·er·ship (ri:sí:vərʃip) *n.* (*law*) the condition of being in the receiver's hands || (*law*) the position of being a receiver

re·cen·cy (ri:s'nsi:) *n.* the state or quality of being recent

re·cen·sion (riséncʃən) n. a revising of a text ‖ a version thus produced [fr. L. recensio (recensionis), a review]

re·cent (ríːsnt) adj. of or pertaining to a time not long before the present, in recent months, footprints of recent origin ‖ done or made during such a time, a recent housing development **Recent** (geol.) Holocene [fr. L. recens (recentis) or F. récente]

re·cep·ta·cle (riséptək'l) n. a container, have a receptacle ready before you open the vent ‖ (bot.) the part of a plant stem containing germinal buds, sporangia etc. [fr. L. receptaculum]

re·cep·tion (risépʃən) n. a receiving or being received ‖ the admission of a person into a religious organization, hospital, club etc. ‖ a formal social gathering during which guests are received ‖ a welcoming or greeting in a specified manner ‖ the receiving of radio or television signals or the quality of these **re·cép·tion·ist** n. a person, usually a woman, whose job is to fix appointments for, and receive, the patients or clients of her employer [F.]

reception room a room used for receiving the patients of a doctor, dentist etc. ‖ a room for receiving guests, e.g. in a hotel, institution etc. ‖ (Br.) realtor's term) a living room as distinct from a bedroom

re·cep·tive (riséptiv) adj. markedly able and willing to receive and retain impressions, ideas etc. ‖ (of a sensory end organ) able to receive and send stimuli ‖ of or relating to sense organs **re·cep·tiv·i·ty** (rìːseptíviti) n. [fr. M.L. receptivus]

re·cep·tor (riséptər) n. (physiol.) a specialized cell or tissue sensitive to a specific stimulus, e.g. a sense organ or sensory nerve ending [M.E. receptour]

receptor n. (cytol.) a specialized structure portion of a cell that is capable of combining with molecules (hormones, toxins, etc.) in a physiological process, e.g., in a nerve terminal

re·cess (risés, ríːses) 1. n. an alcove, window recess, or a natural feature suggesting this ‖ (esp. fig.) an obscure or secret place, the recesses of the mind ‖ an interval of time during which an activity ceases, e.g. in business or parliament ‖ a period between school classes, usually devoted to play ‖ (anat.) a fossa, sinus, cleft or hollow space 2. v.t. to construct a recess in (a wall) ‖ to put into a recess, set back ‖ v.i. to go into recess [fr. L. recedere (recessus), to recede]

re·ces·sion (riséʃən) n. a receding or withdrawing ‖ a receding part ‖ a return procession, esp. of clergy and choir after a service ‖ (econ.) a temporary falling off of business activity, less serious than a depression **re·cés·sion·al** 1. adj. of or relating to the recession of the clergy and choir from the chancel after a service ‖ (Br.) of or relating to a parliamentary recess 2. n. a hymn sung during the recession of the clergy and choir [fr. L. recessio (recessionis)]

re·ces·sive (risésiv) 1. adj. receding or tending to recede ‖ (of stress or accent) tending to move from the last toward the first syllable of a word ‖ (biol.) of a character possessed by one parent which in a hybrid is masked by the corresponding alternative or dominant character derived from the other parent (opp. DOMINANT) 2. n. (biol.) a recessive character ‖ (biol.) an organism having such characters [fr. L. recedere (recessus), to recede]

re·cher·ché, re·cher·che (rəʃéərʃei) adj. uncommon, out of the ordinary ‖ affected, precious, recherché language [F.]

re·cid·i·vism (risídiviʒəm) n. constant falling back or the tendency to fall back into criminal, delinquent or antisocial habits in spite of punishment or treatment [RECIDIVIST]

re·cid·i·vist (risídivist) n. a person marked by recidivism [fr. F. récidiviste]

Re·ci·fe (rəsíːfə) (formerly Pernambuco) a port (pop. 1,249,800) in Brazil, the commercial center of the northeast, founded in 1548. Food industry, university (1946)

rec·i·pe (résəpi) n. a list of ingredients and set of cooking directions for a dish ‖ a course of action recommended for producing some result, a recipe for fitness [L. imper. of recipere, to receive, take]

re·cip·i·ence (risípiːəns) n. the quality of being recipient

re·cip·i·en·cy (risípiːənsi) n. recipience

re·cip·i·ent (risípiːənt) 1. n. someone who or something which receives 2. adj. receiving or able to receive [fr. L. recipiens (recipientis) fr. recipere, to receive]

re·cip·ro·cal (risíprək'l) 1. adj. mutual, reciprocal feelings of affection ‖ of something in an inverse relationship to something else ‖ (of two things) corresponding, complementary ‖ (gram.) expressing mutual relation, one another is a reciprocal pronoun ‖ (math.) of a quantity which is reciprocal 2. n. a thing that has a reciprocal relation to something else ‖ (math.) a quantity which when multiplied by a given quantity produces unity, 1/6 is the reciprocal of 6 [fr. L. reciprocus]

reciprocal ohm the mho

re·cip·ro·cate (risíprəkeit) pres. part. **re·cip·ro·cat·ing** past and past part. **re·cip·ro·cat·ed** v.t. to give in return (affection, good wishes etc.) ‖ (mech.) to cause to move backwards and forwards alternately ‖ to give and receive mutually, the negotiators reciprocated formal expressions of goodwill ‖ v.i. to return in kind something done, given etc. ‖ to be correspondent ‖ (mech.) to move backwards and forwards [fr. L. reciprocare (reciprocatus)]

reciprocating engine an engine in which a piston or pistons move to and fro (*ROTARY ENGINE)

re·cip·ro·ca·tion (risìprəkéiʃən) n. a reciprocating or an instance of this [fr. L. reciprocatio (reciprocationis)]

rec·i·proc·i·ty (resəprósiti) n. the state of being reciprocal ‖ an exchange of trade between nations etc., based upon privileges granted to both [fr. F. réciprocité]

re·cit·al (risáit'l) n. an enumerating or relating of facts, events etc. ‖ something which is so enumerated or related ‖ a reciting of poetry before an audience ‖ (mus., dancing) a performance given by one person or a small group ‖ (law) the reciting of facts in a document [RECITE]

rec·i·ta·tion (resitéiʃən) n. an enumerating of facts, events etc. ‖ a reciting, esp. before an audience, or an instance of this ‖ (old-fash.) the reciting of a lesson to satisfy the teacher or the answering of the teacher's questions on a prepared lesson [fr. L. recitatio (recitationis)]

rec·i·ta·tive (resitətíːv) 1. n. musical declamation of the narrative parts of opera and oratorio 2. adj. of or in this style [fr. Ital. recitativo]

re·cite (risáit) pres. part. **re·cit·ing** past and past part. **re·cit·ed** v.t. to repeat aloud (something memorized), esp. before an audience ‖ (old-fash.) to repeat aloud or answer the teacher's questions about (a lesson) ‖ to enumerate ‖ (law) to set out (facts) in a document ‖ v.i. to repeat aloud something memorized, esp. before an audience ‖ (old-fash.) to repeat aloud or answer the teacher's questions about a lesson [F. réciter or fr. L. recitare]

reck (rek) v.t. (archaic, neg. or quasi-neg. and interrog. only) to take heed of (danger, expense etc.), or to care about, he little recks what the outcome may be [O.E. reccan]

reck·less (réklis) adj. wildly careless, reckless driving ‖ indifferent to danger, reckless courage [O.E. recceléas, rēceléas]

Reck·ling·hau·sen (réklinghauz'n) a town (pop. 119,600) of North-Rhine-Westphalia, West Germany, in the Ruhr: coal mining, mechanical engineering, textiles, chemicals

reck·on (rékən) v.t. (often with 'up') to work out, calculate, reckon how much you have spent ‖ to arrive at (a number, answer etc.) by calculating, he reckoned 400 persons attended ‖ to include as one of a number, she reckons him among her best friends ‖ (pop.) to think, suppose ‖ to estimate, they reckon him to be the best worker ‖ v.i. (with 'with') to make a reckoning, he'll reckon with you later ‖ to count, calculate, she reckoned on her fingers ‖ (with 'on' or 'upon') to count on having something or on some event, we are reckoning on a devaluation of the franc **to reckon with** (without) to take into (leave out of) account [O.E. gerecenian, recenian]

reck·on·er (rékənər) n. someone who reckons ‖ a ready reckoner

reck·on·ing (rékəniŋ) n. the act of counting or calculating, or an instance of this ‖ the manner of doing this ‖ the process of doing this or the result arrived at ‖ (naut.) a calculation of a ship's position by astronomical observations and reference to logged information ‖ (naut.) a position so determined ‖ a settling of accounts, differences etc., or an instance of this

re·claim (riléim) 1. v.t. to reform, salvage from a life of vice, crime etc. ‖ to bring back (land suitable for human use) into service, e.g. by draining or irrigation ‖ to obtain (something useful) from a waste product 2. n. a reclaiming or being reclaimed [fr. O.F. reclamer]

re·claim (riːkléim) v.t. to claim back, to recover possession of

re·clam·a (rikléemə) n. (mil.) a request to authority to reconsider a decision or proposed action

rec·la·ma·tion (rekləméiʃən) n. a reclaiming or being reclaimed [F.]

rec·li·nate (réklineit) adj. (bot.) curving downward, a reclinate leaf [fr. L. reclinare (reclinatus), to recline]

re·cline (rikláin) pres. part. **re·clin·ing** past and past part. **re·clined** v.i. (usually with 'on' or 'upon') to lie at ease ‖ to lean back comfortably ‖ v.t. to lay (one's head etc.) back [fr. L. reclinare]

re·cluse (riklúːs, réklus) n. someone who lives alone and avoids the company of others ‖ such a person acting out of self-discipline on religious grounds [fr. F. reclus, recluse fr. reclure, to shut up]

rec·og·ni·tion (rekəgníʃən) n. a recognizing or being recognized ‖ acknowledgment, in recognition of his services ‖ (internat. law) acknowledgment of the status of an independent state [fr. L. recognitio (recognitionis)]

rec·og·niz·a·ble (rékəgnaizəb'l) adj. able to be recognized **rec·og·níz·a·bly** adv.

re·cog·ni·zance (rikógnizəns) n. (law) a bond entered into before a court or magistrate by which one undertakes to do something ‖ the sum pledged as a surety for the performance of such an obligation [O.F. reconissance, reconuissance, recognussance]

rec·og·nize (rékəgnaiz) pres. part. **rec·og·niz·ing** past and past part. **rec·og·nized** v.t. to identify (something known or perceived before), to recognize a handwriting ‖ to acknowledge, to recognize a debt ‖ to admit acquaintance with (someone) by a sign etc., he recognized us with a wave ‖ (law) to acknowledge the status of (e.g. a newly independent state or a new government) ‖ to give (someone) the opportunity to speak in a legislature, public meeting etc. ‖ (law) to obligate (someone) by a recognizance ‖ v.i. (law) to enter into a recognizance [O.F. reconoistre (reconuiss-, recognoiss-)]

re·coil (rikóil) v.i. to start back in repugnance ‖ to shrink away ‖ (of a piece of artillery) to slide back when the charge explodes ‖ (of a rifle or shotgun) to kick ‖ (of a spring) to spring back when released ‖ to retreat, to fall back before the enemy 2. (rikóil, ríːkoil) n. the sliding back or kick of a gun when the charge explodes ‖ the distance of such a backward movement ‖ a physical or mental shrinking away [fr. O.F. reculer]

rec·ol·lect (rekəlékt) v.t. to call to mind, remember [fr. L. recolligere (recollectus), to gather again]

re·col·lect (rìːkəlékt) v.t. to gather together again ‖ to regain control of, collect (oneself, one's thoughts etc.) [fr. L. recolligere (recollectus), to gather again]

rec·ol·lec·tion (rekəlékʃən) n. the act of remembering ‖ a memory ‖ the span or power of a person's memory, within my recollection ‖ a spiritual gathering of oneself together **rec·ol·léc·tive** adj. [F. récollection]

re·com·bi·nant DNA (riːkómbənənt) (genetics) a technique for splicing strands of genetic material (DNA) from different organisms and inserting the resultant combination into a host virus or bacterium. Cf GENE SPLICING

re·com·mence (rìːkəméns) pres. part. **re·com·menc·ing** past and past part. **re·com·menced** v.i. to begin again ‖ v.t. to cause to begin **re·com·ménce·ment** n. [fr. F. recommencer]

re·com·mend (rekəménd) v.t. to write or speak in favor of (someone, something) to another person, as deserving employment, patronage etc. ‖ to advise, he recommended a long holiday ‖ to render pleasing, the property has little to recommend it ‖ (rhet.) to commend, he recommended his soul to God [M.L. recommendare]

rec·om·men·da·tion (rekəmendéiʃən) n. the act of recommending a person or thing ‖ a letter which recommends a person to a prospective employer ‖ advice ‖ a quality which predisposes in favor of someone or something, ease of access is a strong recommendation for the site [O.F. or fr. M.L. recommendatio (recommendationis)]

rec·om·pense (rékəmpens) n. a gift or remuneration in recognition of a service rendered ‖ a payment or compensation for an injury done or received [O.F.]

recompense pres. part. **rec·om·pens·ing** past and past part. **rec·om·pensed** v.t. to give a recompense to [fr. O.F. recompenser]

rec·on·cil·a·ble (rekənsáiləb'l) *adj.* able to be reconciled **rec·on·cíl·a·bly** *adv.*

reconcilable neglect governmental and political practices based on disregard of new conditions and ideas, and the belief that inadequacies will somehow be self-correcting; suggested by American journalist Walter J. Raymond

rec·on·cile (rékənsail) *pres. part.* **rec·on·cil·ing** *past and past part.* **rec·on·ciled** *v.t.* to bring together again in love or friendship || to induce (someone) to accept something disagreeable || to make or show to be consistent || to reach a compromise agreement about (differences) **réc·on·cile·ment** *n.* [fr. F. *réconcilier* or L. *reconciliare*]

rec·on·cil·i·a·tion (rekənsili:éiʃən) *n.* a reconciling or being reconciled [F. or fr. L. *reconciliatio* (*reconciliationis*)]

rec·on·dite (rékəndait, rikóndait) *adj.* obscure, little known || concerned with something obscure and little known || difficult to understand [fr. L. *recondere* (*reconditus*), to put away]

rec·on·di·tion (ri:kəndíʃən) *v.t.* to restore (something) to sound condition by cleaning, repairing etc.

re·con·fig·ure (ri:kənfigjər) *v.* to rearrange

rec·on·nais·sance (rikónisəns) *n.* a survey of an enemy-held area to obtain military information concerning the enemy's position, strength, intentions etc. || any preliminary survey || (*engin.*) a general survey of a territory before proceeding with a more specialized one || (*geol.*) a preliminary examination of a particular region [F.]

rec·on·noi·ter, esp. *Br.* **rec·on·noi·tre** (ri:kə-nóitər) 1. *v. pres. part.* **rec·on·noi·ter·ing,** esp. *Br.*, **rec·on·noi·tring** *past and past part.* **re·con·noi·tered,** esp. *Br.* **rec·on·noi·tred** *v.t.* to make a reconnaissance of || *v.i.* to make a reconnaissance 2. *n.* a reconnaissance [obs. F. *reconnoitre*, to recognize]

rec·on·sid·er (ri:kənsídər) *v.t.* to consider again, esp. with a view to changing one's opinion, *to reconsider a decision* || *v.i.* to consider a matter again **re·con·sid·er·á·tion** *n.*

rec·on·sti·tute (ri:kónstitu:t, ri:kónstitju:t) *pres. part.* **rec·on·sti·tut·ing** *past and past part.* **rec·on·sti·tut·ed** *v.t.* to reconstruct, *to reconstitute an antique poem from fragments* || to reorganize in a changed form, *to reconstitute the cabinet* || to restore the composition of (dried or concentrated foods or juices) by adding water **re·con·sti·tú·tion** *n.*

rec·on·struct (ri:kənstrʌ́kt) *v.t.* to rebuild || to re-create mentally or in fact the known conditions, actions etc. surrounding (a crime, battle etc.) in the hope that this will lead to better understanding

rec·on·struc·tion (ri:kənstrʌ́kʃən) *n.* a reconstructing || something reconstructed **Re·con·struc·tion** (*Am. hist.*) the period in the Southern states between the end of the Civil War (1865) and the withdrawal of federal troops (1877)

Reconstruction Finance Corporation (RFC), a U.S. government agency created (1932) by President Herbert Hoover to revive economic activity in the Depression by granting loans totaling $50 billion. It was abolished (1953) by act of Congress, on the grounds that it had been used for political favoritism

re·con·ver·sion (ri:kənvə́:rʒən) *n.* a reconverting or being reconverted, esp. a going back from a wartime to a peacetime basis || a period of reconverting

re·con·vert (ri:kənvə́:rt) *v.t.* to convert back to a former state || *v.i.* to go back, esp. from a wartime to a peacetime basis

rec·ord (rékərd) 1. *n.* a recording or being recorded || a document or other piece of historical evidence || an account made in permanent form, *he will not keep records of his telephone conversations* || a minute or official text, *he keeps the records of the society's proceedings, he asked for it to go on record that he took no part in the discussion* || (*law*) an official copy of the proceedings of a case which will be accepted as authentic evidence subsequently || a public register, monument etc. where historical or legal evidence is recorded || the facts concerning the past performance etc. of a person or thing, *he has an excellent war record* || a memento, *he gave it to her as a record of her visit* || the best performance so far recorded || a circular plate to which sound has been transferred, esp. electronically. When the record is played through a phonograph, the sound is reproduced **off the record** private and not to be repeated or made

publicly known **on record** recorded or publicly declared **to go on record** to keep a written statement of a decision, opinion etc. 2. *adj.* of that which is the best so far officially recorded, *a record jump* [O.F.]

re·cord (rikɔ́rd) *v.t.* to set down in some permanent form, esp. in writing || (*law*) to commit to writing as authentic evidence of || to transcribe (sound) in some permanent form, e.g. on tape || (esp. of an instrument) to make a graph or chart of || to serve as evidence of, *this gift will serve to record our appreciation* || to register, *to record a vote* || *v.i.* to make a record, esp. a phonograph record || to be able to be recorded [fr. O.F. *recorder*]

re·cord·er (rikɔ́rdər) *n.* someone who or something which records || an official appointed or elected to keep records of deeds etc. || (*Br.*) a magistrate of a city or borough who presides over the court of quarter sessions and has a limited criminal and civil jurisdiction || (*mus.*) a simple woodwind instrument somewhat similar to a flute and popular, esp. in the 16th–18th cc. It is blown from an end mouthpiece and held downwards not transversely || the recording device in certain machines, e.g. in a cash register

re·cord·er·ship (rikɔ́rdərʃip) *n.* the office or duration of office of a recorder

re·cord·ing (rikɔ́rdiŋ) *n.* the act of making a record || the process of preserving sound on a record, cylinder, tape etc. || a phonograph record or a tape etc. on which something is recorded || that which is recorded

Record Office (*Br.*) a state department responsible for the safe custody of public documents || (*Br.*) the place housing these documents

record player an instrument for playing phonograph records by means of a pickup and one or more amplifiers

re·count (rikáunt) *v.t.* to relate, narrate in detail [A.F. *reconter*]

re·count 1. (ri:káunt) *v.t.* to count again 2. (rí:kaunt, ri:káunt) *n.* a second or additional counting, esp. of votes

re·coup (rikú:p) *v.t.* to make good, get back the equivalent of (a loss) || to compensate (oneself) for losses, expenses etc. || to get back, *to recoup one's fortune* || (*law*) to deduct or withhold (part of a sum due) **re·cóup·ment** *n.* [fr. F. *recouper*, to cut back]

re·course (ri:kórs, ri:kóurs, rí:kɔrs, rí:kours) *n.* someone or something to which one turns for help, *the only recourse was prayer* || a turning to someone or something for help **to have recourse to** to turn to when in need of help **without recourse** the words added to a bill by the endorser to show that he does not take responsibility for nonpayment [F. *recours*]

re·cov·er (rikʌ́vər) 1. *v.t.* to get back possession of, *to recover a stolen car, to recover consciousness* || to regain the composure, control, balance etc. of (oneself) || to make good (a loss) || (*law*) to obtain by a court decision etc. || to reclaim (e.g. land from the sea) || to obtain (a useful substance) from a waste product || *v.i.* to return to normal health after illness || to return to a normal condition of prosperity etc., *to recover from civil war* || to regain one's composure, balance etc. || (*law*) to obtain a favorable judgment in a suit || (*fencing*) to return to the normal posture of defense || (*rowing*) to return to a position of readiness for the succeeding stroke 2. *n.* (*fencing, rowing*) a recovery [A.F. *recouvrer*]

re·cov·er (ri:kʌ́vər) *v.t.* to provide with a new cover

re·cov·er·y (rikʌ́vri) *pl.* **re·cov·er·ies** *n.* the act or an instance of recovering || a returning to normal health or prosperity || the regaining of one's balance or control after e.g. a stumble or mistake || a return to financial well-being after a depression || (*fencing*) the return to a position of guard after a thrust || (*rowing*) the return to a position of readiness in preparation for the next stroke || (*law*) the obtaining of a right to something by verdict or judgment || the salvaging of useful material from waste products [A.F. *recoverie*]

rec·re·an·cy (rékri:ənsi:) *pl.* **rec·re·an·cies** *n.* (*rhet.*) the quality of being recreant or an instance of this

rec·re·ant (rékri:ənt) 1. *adj.* (*rhet.*) cowardly || (*rhet.*) apostate, unfaithful 2. *n.* (*rhet.*) a coward || (*rhet.*) a deserter || (*rhet.*) a betrayer [O.F.=one who gives up his cause]

rec·re·ate (rékri:eit) *pres. part.* **rec·re·at·ing** *past and past part.* **rec·re·at·ed** *v.t.* (*rhet.*) to put fresh life into, esp. by some kind of amusement

or relaxation after work [fr. L. *recreare* (*recreatus*), to refresh]

re·cre·ate (ri:kri:éit) *pres. part.* **re·cre·at·ing** *past and past part.* **re·cre·at·ed** *v.t.* to create again

rec·re·a·tion (rekri:éiʃən) *n.* a leisure-time activity engaged in for the sake of refreshment or entertainment || (*loosely*) a pastime, *her favorite recreation is spying on her neighbors* [fr. L. *recreatio* (*recreationis*)]

re·cre·a·tion (ri:kri:éiʃən) *n.* a re-creating or being re-created || that which is re-created

re·crim·i·nate (rikrímineit) *pres. part.* **re·crim·i·nat·ing** *past and past part.* **re·crim·i·nat·ed** *v.i.* to make counter accusations [fr. L. *recriminari* (*recriminatus*)]

re·crim·i·na·tion (rikriminéiʃən) *n.* a recriminating || a counter accusation [F. *récrimination*]

re·crim·i·na·tive (rikrímineitiv) *adj.* recriminating **re·crim·i·na·to·ry** (rikríminətɔri, rikríminatɔuri:) *adj.*

re·cru·desce (ri:kru:dés) *pres. part.* **re·cru·desc·ing** *past and past part.* **re·cru·desced** *v.i.* (of an illness, sore etc.) to break out afresh **re·cru·dés·cence** *n.* **re·cru·dés·cent** *adj.* [fr. L. *recrudescere*]

re·cruit (rikrú:t) *v.t.* to enlist (recruits) || to enlist men for (an army) || to recover (strength, health etc.) || to recover the strength, health etc. of (oneself) || *v.i.* to enlist recruits || to recuperate, recover strength, health **re·crúit·ment** *n.* [fr. F. *recruter*]

recruit *n.* a newly enlisted member of the armed forces, esp. of the army || a new member or supporter of a society, cause etc. [fr. obs. F. *recrute*]

rec·tal (réktəl) *adj.* of, relating to, or near the rectum

rec·tan·gle (réktæŋg'l) *n.* a plane quadrilateral figure with four right angles **rec·tan·gu·lar** (rektǽŋgjulər) *adj.* shaped like a rectangle || right-angled || at right angles **rec·tan·gu·lar·i·ty** (rəktæŋgjulǽriti:) *n.* [fr. L.L. *rectangulum*, a right-angled triangle]

rec·ten·na (rekténə) *n.* an antenna used to convert microwave power to DC power, including rectifying elements

rec·ti·fi·a·ble (réktifáiəb'l) *adj.* able to be rectified

rec·ti·fi·ca·tion (rektifikéiʃən) *n.* a rectifying or being rectified [F. or fr. L.L. *rectificatio* (*rectificationis*)]

rec·ti·fi·er (réktifaiər) *n.* someone who or something that rectifies || (*elec.*) a device for converting an alternating current into a direct current

rec·ti·fy (réktifai) *pres. part.* **rec·ti·fy·ing** *past and past part.* **rec·ti·fied** *v.t.* to put right, *to rectify an error* || to set (a trajectory, orbit etc.) right by computation and mechanical adjustment || to replace by something more right or just, *he rectified the earlier judgment* || (*chem.*) to purify by repeated distillation || (*elec.*) to convert (an alternating current) to a direct current || (*math.*) to measure (the length of a curve) [fr. F. *rectifier*]

rec·ti·lin·e·al (rektilíni:əl) *adj.* rectilinear [fr. L.L. *rectilineus*]

rec·ti·lin·e·ar (rektilíni:ər) *adj.* in a straight line || bounded by straight lines || characterized by straight lines [fr. L.L. *rectilineus*]

rec·ti·tude (réktitu:d, réktitju:d) *n.* moral uprightness, integrity [F.]

rec·to (réktou) *n.* (*printing*) the righthand page of an open book || (*printing*) the front of a leaf (opp. VERSO) [fr. L. *recto* (*folio*), on the right (leaf)]

rec·tor (réktər) *n.* (*Church of England*) a clergyman to whom the parish tithes were formerly payable (cf. VICAR) || (*Protestant Episcopal Church* and *Episcopal Church of Scotland*) a minister in charge of a parish || (*Roman Catholicism*) the head priest of a parish || the head of some universities, colleges, schools or religious institutions **réc·tor·ate** *n.* **rec·tor·i·al** (rektóri:əl, rektóuri:əl) *adj.* **rec·tor·ship** (réktərʃip) *n.* [L.=one who rules]

rec·to·ry (réktəri:) *pl.* **rec·to·ries** *n.* a rector's house || the benefice of a rector [fr. M.L. *rectoria*]

rec·trix (réktriks) *pl.* **rec·tri·ces** (rektrisi:z) *n.* (usually *pl.*) one of a bird's long stiff tail feathers used in steering [L. fem. of *rector*=one who rules]

rec·tum (réktəm) *pl.* **rec·tums, rec·ta** (réktə) *n.* (*anat.*) the portion of the large intestine nearest to the anus [L. neut. of *rectus*, straight]

CONCISE PRONUNCIATION KEY: **(a)** æ, cat; ɑ, car; ɔ fawn; ei, snake. **(e)** e, hen; i:, sheep; iə, deer; ɛə, bear. **(i)** i, fish; ai, tiger; ə:, bird. **(o)** o, ox; au, cow; ou, goat; u, poor; ɔi, royal. **(u)** ʌ, duck; u, bull; u:, goose; ə, bacillus; ju:, cube. x, loch; θ, think; ð, bother; z, Zen; ʒ, corsage; dʒ, savage; ŋ, orangutang; j, yak; ʃ, fish; tʃ, fetch; 'l, rabble; 'n, redden. Complete pronunciation key appears inside front cover.

re·cum·ben·cy (rikʌ́mbənsi:) n. the state or position of being recumbent

re·cum·bent (rikʌ́mbənt) adj. lying down, reclining ‖ (biol.) of or relating to a part which leans on the part from which it grows [fr. L. recumbens (recumbentis) fr. recumbere, to lie down]

re·cu·per·ate (rikú:pəreit, rikjú:pəreit) pres. part. **re·cu·per·at·ing** past and past part. **re·cu·per·at·ed** v.t. to regain (esp. one's health, one's losses) ‖ v.i. to make such a recovery [fr. L. recuperare (recuperatus)]

re·cu·per·a·tion (riku:pəréiʃən, rikju:pəréiʃən) n. the restoration of health ‖ the recovery of losses [fr. L. recuperatio (recuperationis)]

re·cu·per·a·tive (rikú:pərətiv, rikjú:pərətiv) adj. of or promoting recuperation [fr. L.L. recuperativus]

re·cur (rikə́:r) pres. part. **re·cur·ring** past and past part. **re·curred** v.i. to return, come back, the idea recurred to my mind ‖ to occur again, esp. after some lapse of time ‖ (of a problem etc.) to present itself repeatedly for consideration [fr. L. recurrere]

re·cur·rence (rikə́:rəns, rikʌ́rəns) n. the act or fact of recurring [RECURRENT]

re·cur·rent (rikə́:rənt, rikʌ́rənt) adj. recurring from time to time, a recurrent fever ‖ (anat., of a vein, nerve etc.) running back in the opposite direction [fr. L. recurrens (recurrentis) fr. recurrere, to run back]

recurring clause (insurance) a provision in a health insurance policy that specifies a period of time during which the recurrence of a condition is considered a continuation of a former disability or hospital confinement rather than a separate illness

recurring decimal a decimal fraction with the same figure or figures repeated indefinitely in the same order, e.g. 1.6666 (also written 1.6)

re·cur·sion formula or **recursion relation** (rikə́:rʒən) (math.) an algorithm that allows a series of quantities to be computed —**recur·sive** adj.

re·cur·sive (rikə́:rsiv) adj. 1. capable of being used again, or of being returned to after an interruption 2. (computer) of a method of calculation in steps, each of which establishes more elementary values, used in ALGOL and LISP, but otherwise not acceptable as a procedure

re·cur·vate (rikə́:rveit) adj. recurved [fr. L. recurvatus]

re·curved (rikə́:rvd) adj. curved backward

rec·u·san·cy (rékjuzənsi:) n. the state or condition of being a recusant

rec·u·sant (rékjuzənt) 1. n. someone who refuses to conform ‖ (Eng. hist.) a person, esp. a Roman Catholic, who refused to attend Church of England services when attendance was compulsory 2. adj. refusing to conform or submit to authority ‖ (Eng. hist.) refusing to attend the services of the Church of England [fr. L. recusans (recusantis) fr. recusare, to refuse]

re·cy·cle (ri:sáik'l) v. 1. to process so that basic raw material may be used again, e.g., to recycle aluminum cans to obtain the metal for reuse 2. to repeat a series of operations —**recyclable** n. —**recyling** n.

red (red) 1. comp. **red·der** superl. **red·dest** adj. of the color sensation stimulated by the wavelengths of light in that portion of the spectrum, ranging from orange to infrared, being the color e.g. of blood flowing from a vein ‖ flushed with blood, red cheeks ‖ (of the eyes) bloodshot or with sore or swollen lids ‖ of the tawny or chestnut color of the coat of some animals or the hair of some persons **Red** of or pertaining to a Red or to a country, group etc. of communist political persuasion 2. n. a red color, pigment, fabric etc. ‖ a red object, e.g. the red ball in billiards **Red** a communist **in** (**out of**) **the red** (pop.) in (not in) debt **to see red** to be made suddenly very angry [O.E. rēad]

re·dact (ridǽkt) v.t. to edit, to prepare for publication ‖ to draw up (a document etc.) [fr. L. redigere (redactus), to bring back]

re·dac·tion (ridǽkʃən) n. the preparing of written material for publication, or an instance of this ‖ the work so prepared [F. rédaction]

re·dac·tor (ridǽktər) n. an editor [F. rédacteur]

red admiral Vanessa atlanta, fam. Nymphalidae, a purplish-black butterfly, with white spots on the front wings, and orange bands across the front wings and bordering the hind wings

red alert 1. signal of imminent danger 2. the period of such danger

re·dan (ridǽn) n. a fortification with two parapets forming a salient angle [F.]

Red Army faction guerrilla group responsible for terrorism in West Germany, 1976–1980. Cf BAADER-MEINHOF GANG

Red Basin of Szechwan *SZECHWAN

red·bird (rédbə:rd) n. Richmondena cardinala, the cardinal

red blood cell an erythrocyte

red·blood·ed (rédblʌ́did) adj. (of writing) full of strong action ‖ (of people) vigorous, lusty

red·breast (rédbrest) n. a European or American robin ‖ an American knot (sandpiper)

Red Brigade Italian left-wing terrorist organization

red·cap (rédkæp) n. a porter in a railroad station etc. ‖ (Br., pop.) a military policeman

Red Cat theory hypothesis of Chinese political economy that the source of technical know-how is unimportant, from It is irrelevant if the cat is red or not, as long as it catches the mouse; expressed by Deng Xiaoping, Chinese leader

red cent (pop.) a trifling sum of money, it isn't worth a red cent

Red Cloud (red klaud) (1822–1909), U.S. Indian chief of the Sioux Oglala Lakota tribe, born as Makhpiya Luta. He fought the white settlers of the West, esp. around Ft. Laramie, Wy., and along the Bozeman Trail so that by 1868 the trail was no longer used by the whites. He signed a peace treaty (1868), settled on a reservation and, after accusations that he had 'sold out' to the whites, stepped down as head chief

red·coat (rédkout) n. (hist.) a British soldier, esp. during the Revolutionary War

red cross St George's cross, the national emblem of England **Red Cross** a red Greek cross on a white ground, adapted from the Swiss flag, used to mark hospitals, ambulances etc. as a symbol of neutrality in time of war ‖ the International Red Cross

red currant a shrub of genus Ribes, bearing red, edible berries ‖ its fruit

red deer Cervus elaphus, the common European and Asian deer related to the wapiti, measuring about 4 ft from shoulders to ground and weighing about 300 lbs. ‖ the Virginia deer in its summer markings

red·den (réd'n) v.i. to become red ‖ to become flushed ‖ v.t. to make red

red·dish (rédiʃ) adj. somewhat red, tinged with red

red·dle (réd'l) 1. n. ruddle 2. v.t. pres. part. **red·dling** past and past part. **red·dled** to ruddle

red dye #2 a former food and cosmetic coloring agent made from coal, found to be carcinogenic and now banned for any use

re·deem (ridí:m) v.t. to get back full possession of, esp. by repaying the sum of money secured by the thing being recovered, to redeem a pawned ring ‖ to change or convert (bonds etc.) into cash ‖ to fulfill (a promise) ‖ to recover from captivity, by ransom ‖ (theol.) to free from the bondage of sin ‖ to save from being a total failure, this quality redeemed him of her opinion **re·deem·a·ble** adj. **the Re·deem·er** Jesus Christ [fr. F. rédimer or L. redimere]

re·demp·tion (ridémpʃən) n. a redeeming or being redeemed ‖ something which redeems ‖ (theol.) salvation from sin and its consequences

re·demp·tive (ridémptiv) adj. [F. or fr. L. redemptio (redemptionis)]

Re·demp·tor·ist (ridémptərist) n. a member of the Congregation of the Most Holy Redeemer, a Roman Catholic order founded (1732) by St Alphonsus Liguori for missionary work among the poor [F. Rédemptoriste]

red ensign a red flag with the Union Jack in one corner, flown by British merchant ships

Red·eye [M4 1E2] (rédai) n. (mil.) a lightweight, portable, shoulder-fired air defense artillery weapon with infrared guidance for low altitude air defense, widely used in NATO

red·fish (rédfiʃ) pl. **red·fish**, **red·fish·es** n. any of various reddish fishes, esp. the sockeye ‖ (Br.) a male salmon in spawning condition, when it assumes a red color

red fox a fox, esp. Vulpes vulpes, having reddish-brown fur, with considerable variation in color (*SILVER FOX)

red giant (astron.) a large star, hundreds of times the size of the sun, with a cool, low density (less than the air on earth), that is nearing the end of its life, e.g., Betelgeuse in the constellation Orion

red grouse Lagopus scoticus, fam. Tetraonidae, a ptarmigan of the British Isles which does not turn white in winter

Red Guard 1. the masses of young Chinese who actively promoted the Great Proletarian Cultural Revolution, Mao Zedong's movement during 1965–1968 to reestablish the egalitarian values of the Chinese revolution 2. a member of the group —**Red Guardism** adj. Cf CULTURAL REVOLUTION

red-hand·ed (rédhǽndid) adj. actually engaged in a crime or bearing clear signs of having just committed a crime

red·head (rédhed) n. a person with red hair **réd·head·ed** adj.

redheaded woodpecker Melanerpes erythrocephalus, fam. Picidae, a North American woodpecker with chiefly black and white plumage and a red head and neck

red herring a dried, salted smoked herring ‖ a subject introduced into talk to divert attention from the truth or from the matter at issue

red-hot (rédhót) adj. (of a metal) so hot as to emit red light ‖ (of news etc.) the very latest ‖ (of a story) sensational ‖ (pop.) full of pep, a red-hot band

re·di·a (rí:di:ə) pl. **re·di·ae** (rí:di:i:) n. a larva of some trematodes growing inside the sporocyst [Mod. L. after Francesco Redi (1626–98), Italian naturalist]

Red Indian a North American Indian

red·in·gote (rédiŋgout) n. (hist.) a long double-breasted overcoat formerly worn by men ‖ a woman's lightweight coat which is cut away below the waist or worn open [F. fr. Eng. riding coat]

re·di·rect examination (ri:dirékt) the further questioning of one's own witness after his cross-examination by the opposing lawyer

re·dis·trict (ri:dístrikt) v.t. to divide into new districts, esp. into new political divisions

red lead the tetroxide Pb_3O_4 (*LEAD OXIDE)

red-letter day a very fortunate day [from the marking of festivals and holy days in red letters on Christian calendars]

red-light district a district where brothels are situated in a town

red·lin·ing (rédlainiŋ) n. a policy of many financial institutions of refusing to lend money on properties in certain areas, esp. those with a predominantly black and/or Hispanic population

red man (rhet.) a North American Indian

red mullet any of several small fish of fam. Mullidae, usually red or gold in color, with two long barbels on the chin. They are highly valued as food

red ocher, red ochre a red form of hematite, used as a pigment ‖ the color of this

red·o·lence (réd'ləns) n. the quality or state of being redolent [O.F.]

red·o·lent (réd'lənt) adj. (of an odor) sweet or aromatic ‖ (with 'of' or 'with') smelling, having a strong fragrance ‖ (rhet., with 'of' or 'with') suggestive, evocative, the place was redolent of vanished glories [O.F.]

Re·don (rədɔ́n), Odilon (1840–1916), French symbolist painter and illustrator

Re·don·da (rədóndə) an island (area 1 sq. mile) of the Leeward Is, a dependency of Antigua

re·dou·ble (ri:dʌ́b'l) 1. v. pres. part. **re·dou·bling** past and past part. **re·dou·bled** v.t. (bridge) to double (one's opponent's double) ‖ v.i. (bridge) to double a bid which one's opponent has already doubled 2. n. (bridge) an instance of redoubling

re·dou·ble (ri:dʌ́b'l) pres. part. **re·dou·bling** past and past part. **re·dou·bled** v.t. to intensify, to redouble one's efforts ‖ v.i. to become more intense, more frequent etc. [F. redoubler]

re·doubt (ridáut) n. a temporary isolated fortification without flanking defenses [F. redoute, ridotte]

re·doubt·a·ble (ridáutəb'l) adj. formidably hard to resist or conquer, a redoubtable adversary [F. redoutable]

re·dound (ridáund) v.i. (with 'to') to contribute (to someone's credit or discredit) ‖ (with 'on' or 'upon', of honor, disgrace etc.) to recoil [fr. F. rédonder, to overflow]

re·dox (rí:dɒks) n. (chem.) oxidation reduction [REDUCTION+OXIDATION]

red pepper cayenne pepper ‖ any pepper which is red when ripe

red·poll (rédpoul) n. any of several small finches of genus Carduelis of N. Europe, Asia and America. They are streaked gray-brown on the back and sides and the males have a red crown and sometimes a reddish breast [RED+M.E. pol, polle, head]

Red Power American Indian slogan urging political unity, comparable to Black Power. *Cf* BROWN POWER

re·draft 1. (ri:dræft, ri:dráft) *v.t.* to make another draft of **2.** (rí:dræft, rí:draft) *n.* a second or later draft ‖ a draft on the endorser of a protested bill of exchange for the amount of the bill plus charges

re·dress (ridrés) *v.t.* to put right (e.g. a fault) ‖ to make amends for, *to redress wrongs* ‖ to readjust, *to redress the balance* [fr. F. *redresser*]

re·dress (rí:dres, ridrés) *n.* the reparation of a wrong ‖ a redressing [A.F. *redresse*]

Red River (*Vietnamese* Songkoi) a river (500 miles long) flowing from Yunnan, China, across northern Vietnam to the Gulf of Tonkin, navigable to the Chinese border. Chief port: Hanoi

Red River a river (1,020 miles long) flowing from N.W. Texas (forming the Texas borders with Oklahoma and Arkansas) through S.W. Arkansas and across Louisiana to the Mississippi. It is navigable to Shreveport

Red River of the North a river (about 310 miles long) flowing north from W. Minnesota to form the Minnesota-North Dakota boundary, crossing the Canadian border and continuing north to Lake Winnipeg, Canada

Red Sea a long arm (area 178,000 sq. miles) of the Arabian Sea between Arabia and Africa, joined to the Mediterranean by the Suez Canal

red·shank (rédʃæŋk) *n. Tringa totanus*, fam. *Scolopacidae*, a European shore bird about 11 ins long, with pale red legs and feet

red shift (*astron.*) the shift of light of receding galaxies toward the red end of the spectrum. This is interpreted as a Doppler effect or shift, lending confirmation to the theory of an expanding universe

red·shirt (rédʃəːrt) *n.* (*sports*) a college athlete whose eligibility to play is extended by exclusion for varsity competition for a year — **redshirt** *v.* —**redshirting** *n.*

red·skin (rédskin) *n.* a North American Indian

red snow arctic or alpine snow reddened by the presence of various algae, esp. *Chlamydomonas nivalis*

red·start (rédstart) *n. Setophaga ruticilla*, a N. American warbler. The male has black plumage with white belly and bright orange on the sides, wings and tail ‖ *Phoenicurus phoenicurus*, fam. *Sylviidae*, a small European singing bird about 5 ½ ins long. It has a black face with white forehead and a chestnut breast and tail [fr. RED + O.E. *steort*, tail]

red tape the rigid application or observance of rules and regulations in all their minute detail without regard for the end they were designed to achieve ‖ such rules and regulations [fr. the tape tied around legal documents]

red tide (*zool.*) seawater discolored by a proliferation of plankton, usu. red in color, that kills large numbers of fish and other marine life. The proliferation is sometimes stimulated by the addition of nutrients

re·duce (ridú:s, ridjú:s) *pres. part.* **re·duc·ing** *past* and *past part.* **re·duced** *v.t.* to make smaller or less in size, weight, condition etc., *to reduce prices* ‖ to change to a different form, *to reduce a stone to powder, to reduce one's ideas to writing* ‖ to separate into its elements ‖ to bring to a certain state, *to reduce to silence* ‖ to lower in rank ‖ to conquer by assault, or bring under control ‖ to compel by force of circumstances, *reduced to begging* ‖ to make physically weak ‖ to thin (paint etc.) ‖ to reduce the volume of (a sauce etc.) by boiling ‖ (*chem.*) to combine with or subject to the action of hydrogen ‖ to add one or more electrons to (a compound, radical or ion) and thus change the oxidation state to a lower positive or higher negative number ‖ (*math.*) to express in another form without changing the value of, *to reduce acres to square yards* ‖ (*surg.*) to restore (a broken or dislocated bone or organ) to its original position ‖ (*biol.*) to cause (a cell) to undergo meiosis ‖ (*photog.*) to make (a negative) less dense ‖ *v.i.* to become reduced ‖ to lose weight by dieting ‖ to limit the air intake into a kiln so that fuel gases are not completely burned ‖ to undergo meiosis **re·dúced** *adj.* decreased in size, cost etc. ‖ (*phys.*, *chem.*) of a variable (e.g. temperature, pressure, volume) of the state of a system or substance divided by the critical value of that variable [fr. L. *reducere*, to lead back]

reduced circumstances comparative poverty experienced by someone used to having plenty of money

re·duc·er (ridú:sər, ridjú:sər) *n.* (*chem.*) a substance that acts as a reducing agent ‖ (*mech.*) a pipe fitting for connecting two different sizes of pipe ‖ (*photog.*) a developing agent ‖ (*photog.*) an agent that reduces the density of negatives ‖ a paint thinner

re·duc·i·bil·i·ty (ridu:səbíliti:, ridju:səbíliti:) *n.* the quality of being reducible

re·duc·i·ble (ridú:səb'l, ridjú:səb'l) *adj.* able to be reduced

re·duc·tion (ridʌkʃən) *n.* a reducing or being reduced ‖ the result of reducing, e.g. a lower price ‖ the amount by which something is reduced ‖ limitation of the air intake into a kiln so that there is incomplete combustion of fuel gases ‖ (*chem.*) the process by which electrons are added to a substance to reduce it, e.g. the conversion of a metallic oxide or sulfide to the free metal (cf. OXIDATION, *OXIDATION-REDUCTION) ‖ (*math.*) an expression in simpler form or in another denomination ‖ (*photog.*) the lessening of the opacity of a negative ‖ (*biol.*) meiosis [F. *réduction* or fr. L. *reductio* (*reductionis*)]

reduction division the first of two meiotic divisions in maturation

re·duc·tion·ism (ridʌkʃənizəm) *n.* (*biol.*) theory that all biological processes follow the same laws as do chemistry and physics

reductivism *MINIMAL ART

re·dun·dance (ridʌndəns) *n.* redundancy [fr. L. *redundantia*]

re·dun·dan·cy (ridʌndənsi:) *pl.* **re·dun·dan·cies** *n.* the state or quality of being redundant ‖ something or (*Br.*, *administration*) someone redundant [fr. L. *redundantia*]

re·dun·dant (ridʌndənt) *adj.* unnecessarily repetitive or superfluous, *redundant phrases* ‖ of a back-up system duplicating the function of a device, e.g., in a space vehicle ‖ (*Br.*, *administration*), of a workman or his work) surplus to requirements [fr. L. *redundans* (*redundantis*) fr. *redundare*, to redound]

re·du·pli·cate (ridú:plikeit, ridjú:plikeit) *pres. part.* **re·du·pli·cat·ing** *past* and *past part.* **re·du·pli·cat·ed** *v.t.* to repeat, esp. unnecessarily ‖ (*gram.*) to repeat (a letter or syllable) so as to form an inflected or derived form, sometimes with change of vowel etc., e.g. 'dilly-dally' ‖ (*gram.*) to form (words) in this way [fr. M.L. *reduplicare* (*reduplicatus*)]

re·du·pli·cate (ridú:plikit, ridjú:plikit) *adj.* reduplicated ‖ (*bot.*, of petals) having the edges curving outward [fr. L.L. *reduplicatus*]

re·du·pli·ca·tion (ridu:plikéiʃən, ridju:plikéiʃən) *n.* a reduplicating or being reduplicated ‖ a word produced by reduplicating ‖ the part of the word added in reduplicating [fr. L.L. *reduplicatio* (*reduplicationis*)]

re·du·pli·ca·tive (ridú:plikeitiv, ridjú:plikeitiv) *adj.* of, relating to, formed or characterized by reduplication [fr. L. *reduplicare* (*reduplicatus*), to double]

red warbler *Acrocephalus scirpaceus*, a small brown and white European warbler frequenting the reeds of a river's edge or marsh

red·wing (rédwiŋ) *n. Turdus musicus* (or *T. iliacus*) the smallest common European thrush, having chestnut-red feathers on the underpart of its wings and tail ‖ the redwing blackbird

redwing blackbird *Agelaius phoeniceus*, fam. *Icteridae*, a North American bird about 9 ins in length. The male is jet black, with a bright red patch on the upper part of each wing

red·wood (rédwud) *n. Sequoia sempervirens*, fam. *Taxodiaceae*, a giant Californian conifer often reaching a height of 300 ft and having a diameter of up to 28 ft ‖ the hard reddish wood of this tree ‖ any of various trees with reddish wood, or their wood

Reed (ri:d), Thomas Brackett (1839-1902), U.S. legislator. As Speaker of the House (1889-91, 1895-9), he introduced the 'Reed Rules' (1890). One of these determined the House quorum by the count of members present rather than by the count of those voting. His use of the Speaker's power of recognition to thwart obstructive tactics by the minority earned him the nickname 'Tsar Reed'

Reed, Walter (1851-1902), U.S. army surgeon. He proved that yellow fever was caused by a virus transmitted by a mosquito. His findings enabled W. C. Gorgas to eradicate the disease in Cuba and in the Canal Zone. His name is given to the army medical center in Washington, D.C.

reed (ri:d) **1.** *n.* any of several varieties of tall-growing, erect grasses, found in water or swamps ‖ (*collect.*) a quantity of these growing or cut and dried ‖ material of cut reeds used as a thatch etc. ‖ a musical pipe made of one or more hollow reed stems ‖ a thin strip of cane or metal which vibrates when agitated by air pressure and thus emits sound, e.g. in a harmonium, or when attached to a pipe, e.g. in a clarinet ‖ a musical instrument fitted with a reed or reeds ‖ (*archit.*) a semicircular molding, usually one of a number set parallel in a line ‖ (*weaving*) a device for separating the threads of the warp and beating up the weft **2.** *v.t.* to thatch with reed ‖ to furnish with reed or reeds ‖ (*weaving*) to draw (yarn) through a reed **reed·ing** *n.* (*archit.*) a reed ‖ (*collect.*) decoration made with a series of these ‖ the grooves around the edge of a coin [O.E. *hrēod*]

reed mace the cattail

reed organ a keyboard wind instrument in which the sound is produced by the action of wind on free metal reeds

reed pipe the pipe of a pipe organ in which the tone is produced by an air current striking a vibrating reed (cf. FLUE PIPE)

reed stop a set of reed pipes (usually imitating some instrument of the orchestra) controlled by a single stop of a reed organ

re·ed·u·cate (ri:édʒukeit, ri:édjukeit) *pres. part.* **re·ed·u·cat·ing** *past* and *past part.* **re·ed·u·cat·ed** *v.t.* to educate again, esp. to rehabilitate by special training

reeducation camps a euphemism for detention camps in which some nations 'reorient' certain members of their population to the government's political and social philosophy, e.g., Cambodia, China

reed·y (ríːdiː) *comp.* **reed·i·er** *superl.* **reed·i·est** *adj.* abounding in reeds ‖ thin, reedlike in form ‖ like a reed instrument in quality

reef (ri:f) *n.* a line of rocks, sand, small stones etc., just above or near the surface of the water ‖ (*mining*) a vein of ore [akin to O.N. *rif*, reef of a sail]

reef 1. *n.* a part of a sail which can be rolled up to expose less surface to the wind **2.** *v.t.* to take in or roll up a reef in (a sail) ‖ to shorten (a topmast) by taking part of it down or (a bowsprit) by taking part of it in ‖ to fold up or roll, as though folding a sail [O.N. *rif*]

reef·er (ríːfər) *n.* **1.** a refrigerator **2.** a railroad freight car, ship, aircraft, or other conveyance, so constructed and insulated as to protect commodities from either heat or cold **3.** a thick, close-fitting, double-breasted jacket **4.** (*pop.*) a cigarette containing marijuana

reef knot (*naut.*) a square knot used in reefing a sail

reek (ri:k) *n.* a very strong, unpleasant smell ‖ mist, vapor [O.E. *rēc*]

reek *v.i.* to give off thick smoke ‖ to give off an unpleasant smell ‖ to have an undesirable quality in abundance, *it reeks of hypocrisy* [O.E. *rēocan, rēcan*]

reel (ri:l) **1.** *n.* a revolving, often cylindrical device for winding up or letting out yarn, cord, wire etc. ‖ the quantity of material contained on such a device ‖ a small revolving device attached to a fishing rod for winding in and letting out the line ‖ the quantity of line contained on it ‖ (*Br.*) a spool or bobbin for sewing thread ‖ a spool onto which photographic film is wound for use in a camera ‖ a strip of film or given length so wound or able to be so wound **off the reel** straight off, without interruption, *he recited their names and dates off the reel* **2.** *v.t.* to wind on a reel ‖ (with 'in') to bring in by reeling **to reel off** to recite easily without pause or interruption, *he reeled off the verses* [O.E. *hrēol*]

reel 1. *v.i.* to sway unsteadily (from a blow, drunkenness etc.) ‖ to be attacked by vertigo ‖ to be shaken physically or mentally by the shock of grief or astonishment ‖ to whirl around or to seem to whirl around **2.** *n.* a reeling movement [perh. fr. REEL, to wind]

reel 1. *n.* a lively Scottish dance, performed by facing couples who move around one another in a series of figures of eight ‖ the Virginia reel ‖ the music for these dances **2.** *v.i.* to dance a reel [perh. fr. REEL, to wind]

re·e·lect (ri:ilékt) *v.t.* to elect for another term **re·e·lec·tion** *n.*

re·en·force (ri:enfórs, ri:enfóurs) *pres. part.* **re·en·forc·ing** *past* and *past part.* **re·en·forced** *v.t.* to reinforce

re·en·ter (ri:éntər) *v.t.* to enter again

---

re·en·trant (ri:éntrənt) 1. *adj*. pointing inward, *a reentrant angle* 2. *n*. something reentrant, esp. (*mil.*) *a* part of a defense line which projects away from the enemy ‖ an angle at the side of a valley where a secondary valley joins the main one

re·en·try (ri:éntri) *pl.* **re·en·tries** *n*. the act of entering again ‖ (*law*) the act of taking possession again, esp. of leased property ‖ (*bridge*) a card with which a player is assured of recapturing the lead ‖ (of a rocket, spaceship etc.) the act of returning from space to the earth's atmosphere

reeve (ri:v) *n*. (*Eng. hist.*) a royal agent in Anglo-Saxon times ‖ (*Eng. hist.*) the chief magistrate of a town or district ‖ (*Eng. hist.*) an officer of a medieval manor ranking below a bailiff ‖ (*Canada*) the president of a local council ‖ [O.E. *geréfa*]

reeve *n*. the female of the ruff (sandpiper) [etym. doubtful]

reeve *pres. part.* **reev·ing** *past* and *past part.* **rove** (rouv), **reeved** *v.t.* (*naut.*) to pass (the end of a rope) through a hole in a block, cleat etc. ‖ to thread (a block, cleat etc.) with a rope ‖ to attach a rope, block etc. to by reeving [etym. doubtful]

re·ex·am·i·na·tion (rị:igzæminéiʃən) *n*. a reexamining or being reexamined

re·ex·am·ine (rị:igzǽmin) *pres. part.* **re·ex·am·in·ing** *past* and *past part.* **re·ex·am·ined** *v.t.* to examine again ‖ (*law*) to examine a witness after cross-examination

re·ex·port (rị:ikspɔ́rt, rị:ikspóurt, ri:éksport, rị:ékspourt) 1. *v.t.* to export (something previously imported) 2. *n*. something reexported ‖ a reexporting

re·face (ri:féis) *pres. part.* **re·fac·ing** *past* and *past part.* **re·faced** *v.t.* to renew the front surface of (e.g. a building)

re·fec·tion (rifékʃən) *n*. (*rhet.*) a light meal [F. *réfection*]

re·fec·to·ry (riféktəri) *pl.* **re·fec·to·ries** *n*. a room used for meals by a religious community [fr. M.L. *refectorium*]

refectory table a long, narrow dining table, massively built

re·fer (rifə́:r) *pres. part.* **re·fer·ring** *past* and *past part.* **re·ferred** *v.i.* to speak or write of something in the course of dealing with some other or larger topic ‖ to relate, *this statement refers to remarks by his opponent* ‖ to turn for information etc., *to refer to the dictionary* ‖ *v.t.* to transfer (something) for the attention or action of someone else ‖ to direct (someone) to a source of information etc. ‖ to assign to a specific place, period etc., *historians refer the fall of Rome to 410 A.D.* ‖ to regard as caused by, *he referred his depressions to his childhood illness* **ref·er·ee** (rèfəri:) 1. *n*. a person to whom something in dispute is referred for his opinion or decision ‖ (*law*) a person appointed to examine, take testimony and give judgment on a matter ‖ (*Br.*) someone who furnishes a character reference etc. for another ‖ (*in many sports*) a person appointed to make sure that a game is played or match fought according to the rules 2. *v.i. pres. part.* **ref·er·ee·ing** *past* and *past part.* **ref·er·eed** to act as a referee ‖ *v.t.* to be the referee of **ref·er·ence** (rèfrəns, rèfərəns) 1. *n*. a referring or being referred or an instance of this ‖ the state of being related, *all the parts have reference to one another* ‖ an indication in a work of some other work to be consulted ‖ the work cited ‖ a mark directing the reader to a footnote etc. ‖ a person who, on request, will testify to the ability, qualities, character etc. of an applicant e.g. for employment ‖ a written testimony as to the character, ability etc. of another person ‖ a source of information taken as authoritative **in** (or **with**) **reference** to concerning 2. *v.t. pres. part.* **ref·er·enc·ing** *past* and *past part.* **ref·er·enced** to furnish (a book etc.) with references [fr. O.F. *referer* or L. *referre*, to carry back]

reference beam (*holography*) guiding laser beam aimed at the film

reference book a book consulted for information, e.g. a dictionary ‖ a book in a library to be used only on the premises

reference library a library in which books may be consulted on the premises but not taken away

ref·er·en·dum (rèfəréndəm) *pl.* **ref·er·en·da** (rèfəréndə), **ref·er·en·dums** *n*. the submission of a particular measure or question of national importance to the whole electorate (rather than just to their representatives) as a single issue on which to vote ‖ such a vote ‖ a similar proce-

dure in an organized group for discovering its general will ‖ a note sent by a diplomat to his government asking for instructions [L.=a carrying back]

re·fill 1. (rí:fil) *n*. a replacement for the expendable contents of a container intended for reuse 2. (ri:fíl) *v.t.* to fill again

re·fine (rifáin) *pres. part.* **re·fin·ing** *past* and *past part.* **re·fined** *v.t.* to remove impurities or coarse elements from ‖ to make (manners, language, taste, expression etc.) more delicate or polished ‖ to make more subtle and efficient, *refined methods of cataloging* ‖ *v.i.* (with 'on' or 'upon') to achieve greater subtlety or purity in meaning or effect, *to refine on a definition* **re·fined** *adj.* **re·fine·ment** *n*.

re·fin·er·y (rifáinəri:) *pl.* **re·fin·er·ies** *n*. a place or apparatus for refining or for purifying e.g. sugar, petroleum or pig iron

re·fit 1. (ri:fít) *v. pres. part.* **re·fit·ting** *past* and *past part.* **re·fit·ted** *v.t.* to supply (a ship) with new equipment, appointments etc. ‖ *v.i.* (of a ship) to be reequipped and made fit for service again 2. (rí:fit) *n*. a refitting or being refitted

re·flect (riflékt) *v.t.* to cause or permit the collision of (a beam of particles or a wave) with a surface, resulting in its partial or complete return into the medium originally traversed (*LAW OF REFLECTION) ‖ to show as an image, *they gazed at the stars reflected in the lake* ‖ (with 'on', 'upon') to cause (contributory credit or discredit) to be ascribed to, *his success reflects credit on his trainer* ‖ to be in accordance with and give an insight into, *his behavior reflects his upbringing* ‖ (*biol.*) to bend back, *reflected petals* ‖ *v.i.* (of a beam of particles or wave) to become reflected ‖ to act as a reflector ‖ (with 'on' or 'upon') to think back, *to reflect on one's past* ‖ to ponder, meditate, *give them time to reflect* ‖ (with 'on' or 'upon') to bring discredit, *such an act reflects upon him* [O.F. *reflecter* or L. *reflectere*]

re·flec·tance (rifléktəns) *n*. (*phys.*) a measure of a surface's ability to reflect radiant energy, equal to the ratio of the intensity of the reflected radiation to that of the incident radiation

reflecting telescope a telescope whose objective is a mirror (*NEWTONIAN TELESCOPE, *CASSEGRAINIAN TELESCOPE). Since there is no refractive medium through which the light from the object must pass, chromatic aberrations are eliminated. By utilizing a paraboloidal mirror rather than a spherical one, the spherical aberrations are eliminated as well. Reflecting telescopes are used mainly as astronomical telescopes (cf. REFRACTING TELESCOPE)

re·flec·tion, re·flex·ion (riflékʃən) *n*. a reflecting or being reflected ‖ something (e.g. light, heat or an image) reflected ‖ an organ or tissue bent or folded back ‖ an opinion arrived at after consideration, *we are waiting to hear his reflections on the book's merits* ‖ (often *pl.*) adverse criticism, *to cast reflections on someone* **on reflection** after consideration [F. *réflexion*]

reflection coefficient reflectance

reflection factor reflectance

re·flec·tive (rifléktiv) *adj.* inclined to be thoughtful, meditative ‖ concerning thinking habits or faculties ‖ causing, relating to, or caused by reflection, *reflective surfaces*

re·flec·tor (rifléktər) *n*. any surface which reflects, esp. a highly polished curved surface which reflects light or heat as a coherent beam ‖ a reflecting telescope

re·flex (rí:fleks) 1. *n*. (*physiol.*) an automatic or involuntary response to a stimulus (*REFLEX ARC) ‖ (*pl.*) the ability to respond in this way, *his reflexes are failing* ‖ an automatic mental reaction, *it had become a reflex to say 'no'* 2. *adj.* reflected, bent back ‖ (*math.*) of an angle greater than 180° but less than 360° ‖ (*physiol.*) of an automatic or involuntary response to a stimulus, *a reflex action* [fr. L. *reflectere* (*reflexus*), to bend back]

reflex arc the complete nerve path of a reflex action. The simplest is a sensory impulse conducted by an afferent neuron to a nerve center and a motor impulse conducted by an efferent neuron to an effector, e.g. a muscle, e.g. in the case of a hand touching a hot iron

reflex camera a camera equipped with two objective lenses (or with one objective lens and a movable mirror), one of which forms an image on the film and the other forms an image on a ground-glass plate. The latter is identical with the former and is used to focus and compose the image

reflex force (*mil.*) the part of the Air Force alert forces maintained overseas or domestic forward bases by scheduled rotations

reflexion *REFLECTION

re·flex·ive (rifléksiv) 1. *adj.* (*gram.*) denoting an action by the subject upon itself, e.g. of a verb whose subject and direct object are the same ('dressed' in 'he dressed himself'), or of a pronoun which is the object of such a verb ('himself' in 'he dressed himself') ‖ of or relating to or consisting of a reflex or reflexes ‖ able to bend back 2. *n*. a reflexive verb or pronoun [M.L. *reflexivus*, reflected fr. L. *reflectere* (*reflexus*), to bend back, reflect]

reflexology *FOOT REFLEXOLOGY

ref·lu·ence (réflu:əns) *n*. reflux [fr. L. *refluere*, to flow back]

ref·lu·ent (réflu:ənt) *adj.* flowing back ‖ ebbing [fr. L. *refluens* (*refluentis*) fr. *refluere*, to flow back]

re·flux (rí:flʌks) *n*. a flowing back, *the flux and reflux of the tide*

re·for·est (ri:fɔ́rist, rị:fóurist) *v.t.* (*Am.*=*Br.* reafforest) to plant (denuded land) with trees again **re·for·est·a·tion** *n*.

re·form (rifɔ́rm) *v.t.* to improve by removing faults and weaknesses or by strengthening good qualities ‖ to put an end to (an evil, abuse etc.) ‖ to correct, *Pope Gregory reformed the calendar* ‖ to persuade (a person) to change his ways for the better ‖ *v.i.* to become reformed [fr. O.F. *reformer* or L. *reformare*]

reform 1. *n*. a reforming ‖ a measure intended to reform something 2. *adj.* of, pertaining to or advocating reform [REFORM v. or fr. F. *réforme*]

re-form (rị:fɔ́rm) *v.t.* to form again ‖ *v.i.* to take form again ‖ to form up or gather together again

Re·for·ma, Guer·ra de la (gérəðelarefɔ́rma) the internal struggle (1858-61) in Mexico between the conservatives and the liberals under Benito Juárez, victory going to the latter. The 'Leyes de Reforma' refer to the laws establishing the separation of Church and State

ref·or·ma·tion (rèfərméiʃən) *n*. a reforming or being reformed **the Reformation** a 16th-c. religious movement against abuses in the Roman Catholic Church, ending in the formation of the Protestant Churches [fr. L. *reformatio* (*reformationis*)]

—Although the Reformation was a religious movement in origin, its course was much influenced by political and economic factors. Wyclif and Hus had prepared the way for it, and by the end of the Middle Ages many were convinced that the Church needed reforming. Circumstances favorable to the Reformation included: humanism and the Renaissance (which encouraged a new critical spirit), the invention of printing (which aided the spread of ideas), the reaction of princes and jurists against the temporal encroachments of the papacy, the growing wealth of the clergy (esp. in Germany) and the religious and moral shortcomings of certain sections of the clergy. The leaders of the Reformation sought to restore Christianity to its early purity by submitting ecclesiastical tradition to the test of Scriptural authority.

The Reformation was begun in Germany (1517) by Luther, who at first thought reform possible without schism. His attack on the papacy and his refusal to recant led to his excommunication (1521). The Augsburg Confession (1530) defined Lutheran doctrine, of which the main points were justification by faith and the sovereign authority of the Scriptures in matters of faith. The German nobles adopted the new ideas, enabling themselves to appropriate Church property and to challenge the authority of the Emperor as members of the Schmalkaldic League. On Luther's death (1546), his followers were condemned by the Council of Trent and defeated in the Schmalkaldic War. The Peace of Augsburg (1555) recognized the legal existence of Lutheranism in Germany. The conflict later became merged in the Thirty Years' War.

From Saxony, Lutheranism spread into Prussia and the Slav provinces of the Baltic, and was adopted by Denmark, Sweden, Norway and Iceland. The Reformation was preached in Switzerland by Zwingli and in France by Calvin, who added to it the doctrine of predestination. Protestants did not win religious freedom in France until the end of the Wars of Religion. Calvinism was victorious in the Protestant cantons of Switzerland, in Scotland under Knox, and in Flanders and the Netherlands despite the persecutions of Philip II. England rejected papal control (1534) under Henry VIII, veered towards Calvinism under Edward VI, and, after the Catholic reaction under Mary I, adopted the compromise of the Elizabethan Church settlement (*CHURCH OF ENGLAND).

The Reformation tended to increase the growth of nationalism and to strengthen the economic position of the mercantile class. Within the Roman Catholic Church it led to the Counter-Reformation

re·form·a·tive (rifórmətiv) adj. producing or likely to produce reform [fr. L. reformare (reformatus), to reform]

re·form·a·to·ry (rifórmətəri:, rifórmətouri:) **1.** n. pl. **re·form·a·to·ries** an institution to which young offenders may be sent for rehabilitation **2.** adj. reformative [fr. L. reformare (reformatus), to reform]

Re·formed (rifórm'd) adj. of or relating to Protestant theology ‖ of or relating to a Reformed Church

Reformed Church any of the group of Protestant Churches which follow the doctrines of Zwingli and Calvin rather than those of Luther, and which are Presbyterian in Church government. The first Reformed Church was set up by Zwingli in Zurich (1519) under the influence of Erasmus. Zurich broke with Roman Catholicism in 1523, followed by Geneva (site of Calvin's theocracy) in 1541. The movement spread to Strasbourg (1521) and thence to Germany, the Netherlands (1522), France and England. Its doctrine and orders were defined by the Heidelberg Catechism (1563). The French Huguenots were the first to apply Presbyterian Church polity on a national scale, closely followed by Scotland (1561-7 under Knox), Hungary (1567) and the Netherlands (1584). The movement reached the U.S.A. in the 1640s. Politically the movement lost ground in England (from 1660) and was crushed by the Counter-Reformation in Bohemia (1620). Hungary (mid-17th c.) and France (1685). Its religious influence dwindled under the incursions of rationalism in the successive forms of Socinianism, Arminianism and Unitarianism, but in the 20th c. its orthodoxy was redefined by Karl Barth. There are about 50 million adherents of the Reformed or Presbyterian Churches. They are strong in North America (16 million), Scotland (1 million), the Netherlands (4 million), Switzerland (3 million), and South Africa (1½ million). They form important minorities in Hungary (2 million), Rumania (800,000), Czechoslovakia (530,000), France (750,000), Indonesia (2 million), Korea (500,000), Australasia (1½ million), Brazil (500,000), Lesotho (200,000), Cameroun (300,000), Central Africa (500,000), and Ghana (200,000), and smaller ones in Italy (Waldensians), Poland, the Malagasy Republic and Togo. In Germany they are united with the Lutherans

Reformed Episcopal Church a U.S. Protestant community formed (1873) as a result of a division in the Protestant Episcopal Church. It was established by George David Cummings, a leader of the evangelical episcopalians, who stressed the difference in points of faith between Anglicanism and Roman Catholicism

re·form·er (rifórmər) n. someone who reforms or favors reform **Re·form·er** a leader of the 16th-c. Protestant Reformation

reform school a reformatory

re·fract (rifrǽkt) v.t. to subject (waves of light, sound etc.) to refraction ‖ to measure the refraction of (an eye or a lens) [fr. L. refringere (refractus)]

refracting telescope a telescope whose objective is a lens or lens system (*GALILEAN TELESCOPE). Modern refractors are equipped with compound achromatic objective lenses and are used for astronomical and terrestrial observations (cf. REFLECTING TELESCOPE)

re·frac·tion (rifrǽkʃən) n. a refracting or being refracted ‖ the ability of the eye to refract light ‖ the technique of determining the refractive condition of the eye ‖ the change in direction of the path followed by electromagnetic waves (e.g. a ray of light) or other energy-bearing waves in passing obliquely from one medium to another in which its velocity is different (*SNELL'S LAW OF REFRACTION) ‖ the change in the apparent position of a celestial body caused by the passage of light from it through the earth's atmosphere ‖ the determination of the refractive index of the eye or a lens [fr. L.L. refractio (refractionis)]

re·frac·tive (rifrǽktiv) adj. of or pertaining to refraction ‖ caused by refraction ‖ able to refract [fr. L.L. refractiuus or REFRACT]

refractive index (phys.) the ratio of the velocity of light, or other radiation, in one medium (usually taken to be a vacuum) to its velocity in a second medium (*SNELL'S LAW)

re·frac·tom·e·ter (ri:fræktómitər) n. (phys.) an instrument for measuring refractive indices

re·frac·tor (ri:frǽktər) n. a device (e.g. a refracting telescope) that causes refraction, i.e. one utilizing a lens as the focusing device

re·frac·to·ry (rifrǽktəri) **1.** adj. resisting discipline, a refractory child ‖ (of injuries, diseases etc.) not benefiting from treatment ‖ (of substances) resisting high temperature **2.** pl. **re·frac·to·ries** n. any of various nonmetallic ceramic substances that resist great heat, e.g. oxides of silicon, aluminum or magnesium and certain plastics [older refractary fr. L. refractarius]

re·frain (rifréin) n. a phrase or line in poetry or song repeated at regular intervals ‖ the music for such a phrase or line [O.F. refrein, refrain]

refrain v.i. to abstain from doing something, he refrained from making any criticism [O.F. refrener, to hold back]

re·fran·gi·bil·i·ty (rifrændʒəbíliti:) n. the quality of being refrangible

re·fran·gi·ble (rifrǽndʒəb'l) adj. able to be refracted [altered fr. L. refringere, to bend]

re·fresh (rifréʃ) v.t. to make (someone) feel restored and freshened, e.g. by rest or food ‖ to recall to (the mind) **re·fresh·er** n. something that refreshes, e.g. a cool drink ‖ (Br.) an extra fee paid to counsel in a prolonged law case ‖ a refresher course [O.F. refrescher]

refresher course a course of study to bring one's knowledge of something up to date

re·fresh·ment (rifréʃmənt) n. a refreshing or being refreshed ‖ something that refreshes ‖ (pl.) light food and drink, refreshments will be served after the meeting [O.F. refreschement]

re·frig·er·ant (rifrídʒərənt) **1.** adj. cooling ‖ alleviating fever or bodily heat **2.** n. a substance used in a refrigerating cycle or directly (e.g. ice) for cooling ‖ a medicine, ointment etc. used in reducing fever [F. réfrigérant or fr. L. refrigerans (refrigerantis) fr. refrigerare, to cool]

re·frig·er·ate (rifrídʒəreit) pres. part. **re·frig·er·at·ing** past and past part. **re·frig·er·at·ed** v.t. to cool, make or keep cold ‖ to keep (food) at a low temperature in order to preserve it [fr. L. refrigerare (refrigeratus)]

re·frig·er·a·tion (rifrídʒəréiʃən) n. a refrigerating or being refrigerated [fr. L. refrigeratio (refrigerationis)]

refrigeration cycle a sequence of compression and expansion stages of a working substance (e.g. freon, ammonia) induced by mechanical means that permits the continuous transfer of heat from one region (the source) to another region (the sink), where it is either dissipated (e.g. in a refrigerator) or is utilized for heating (e.g. in a heat pump)

refrigeration machine a refrigerator utilizing a refrigeration cycle

re·frig·er·a·tive (rifrídʒəreitiv, rifrídʒərətiv) adj. refrigerating, used to refrigerate

re·frig·er·a·tor (rifrídʒəreitər) n. any of several devices used to maintain a low temperature in a container or a room, for preserving food or other articles

re·frig·er·a·to·ry (rifrídʒərətəri:, rifrídʒərətouri:) adj. refrigerative [fr. L. refrigeratorius]

re·frin·gent (rifríndʒənt) adj. refractive [fr. L. refringens (refringentis) fr. refringere, to refract]

ref·uge (réfju:dʒ) n. shelter or protection from danger, distress or difficulty ‖ a place offering this ‖ a person, thing, or course of action offering protection, tears were her usual refuge **to take refuge** to put oneself in a place or state that affords protection [F.]

ref·u·gee (refju:dʒí:, réfju:dʒi:) n. a person who flees, esp. to a foreign country, to escape e.g. an oppressive government, religious persecution or an invading army [fr. F. réfugié]

re·ful·gence (rifʌ́ldʒəns) n. the state or quality of being refulgent [fr. L. refulgentia]

re·ful·gent (rifʌ́ldʒənt) adj. shining brightly [fr. L. refulgens (refulgentis) fr. refulgere, to shine]

re·fund 1. (rifʌ́nd) v.t. to pay back (money spent) ‖ to reimburse (someone) ‖ v.i. to make repayment **2.** (rí:fʌnd) n. a repayment [fr. O.F. refunder or L. refundere, to pour back]

re·fur·bish (ri:fʌ́rbiʃ) v.t. to make bright or fresh again, renovate

re·fus·al (rifjú:z'l) n. the act of refusing ‖ the right or opportunity to have the offer of something before it is offered to another, he has the refusal of the property

re·fuse (rifjú:z) pres. part. **re·fus·ing** past and past part. **re·fused** v.t. to decline to accept, he refused my offer, or to submit to, he refused the lie-detector test ‖ to decline to grant or give (something) to someone, to refuse readmittance to former members ‖ to decline (to do something), he refused to shake hands ‖ (of a fabric) to fail to be affected by (a dye) ‖ (of a horse) to decline to jump (a fence etc.) ‖ (cards) to be unable to play a card of (the suit led) ‖ v.i. to make a refusal ‖ (cards) to fail to play a card of the suit led [fr. F. refuser]

re·fuse (réfju:s) **1.** n. remains having no value or use **2.** adj. rejected as of no value or use [fr. O.F., past part. of refuser, to refuse]

ref·u·ta·ble (réfjutəb'l, rifjú:təb'l) adj. able to be refuted **réf·u·ta·bly** adv. [fr. L.L. refutabilis]

ref·u·tal (rifjú:t'l) n. a refutation [REFUTE]

ref·u·ta·tion (refjutéiʃən) n. a refuting ‖ something which refutes [fr. L. refutatio (refutationis)]

re·fute (rifjú:t) pres. part. **re·fut·ing** past and past part. **re·fut·ed** v.t. to prove (an assertion or argument) to be untrue or incorrect ‖ to prove (a person) wrong [fr. L. refutare]

re·gain (rigéin, ri:géin) v.t. to get back (something lost), to regain one's composure ‖ to get back to (a place) [fr. F. regagner]

re·gal (rí:g'l) adj. befitting a king ‖ of or pertaining to a king [O.F. or L. regalis]

re·gale (rigéil) pres. part. **re·gal·ing** past and past part. **re·galed** v.t. to entertain (someone) richly ‖ to amuse and entertain, he regaled her with the latest gossip ‖ to feast (oneself) ‖ v.i. to feast [fr. F. régaler, Ital. regalare]

re·ga·lia (rigéiljə) pl. n. objects symbolizing kingship ‖ emblems of office

re·gal·i·ty (rigǽliti:) n. royal jurisdiction [O.F. regalité]

re·gard (rigárd) n. esteem, he stands high in their regard ‖ consideration, sympathetic concern, he shows little regard for others ‖ (old-fash.) a long, steady look ‖ attention, heed, without regard for danger ‖ (pl.) a conventional expression of kindly feeling, esteem etc., give him my best regards **in** (or **with**) **regard to** concerning [F.]

regard v.t. (usually with 'as') to consider (someone or something) as being a specified thing, possessing specified qualities etc. ‖ to concern, insofar as it regards them . . . ‖ to look closely at [F. regarder]

re·gard·ant (rigárd'nt) adj. (heraldry) looking backward [F.]

re·gard·ful (rigárdfəl) adj. (old-fash.) heedful, mindful ‖ (old-fash.) respectful

re·gard·ing (rigárdiŋ) prep. in or with regard to, concerning

re·gard·less (rigárdlis) **1.** adj. (usually with 'of') paying no heed or attention, he went regardless of the risk **2.** adv. (pop.) without consideration of the situation, consequences etc., we'll go regardless

re·gat·ta (rigǽtə, rigátə) n. a series of rowing or sailing races, organized as a sporting and social event [Ital.=gondola race]

re·ge·late (rí:dʒileit) pres. part. **re·ge·lat·ing** past and past part. **re·ge·lat·ed** v.i. (of water or ice) to freeze again when the pressure is released after partial, local melting due to pressure **re·ge·la·tion** n. [fr. RE-+L. gelare (gelatus), to freeze]

re·gen·cy (rí:dʒənsi:) **1.** pl. **re·gen·cies** n. the office of a regent ‖ the authority of a regent ‖ the period of power of a regent ‖ a commission exercising such power ‖ the region controlled by a regent or body of regents **Re·gen·cy** (Br. hist.) the period (1811–20) during which the future George IV was regent for George III ‖ (F. hist.) the period (1715–23) during which Philippe, duc d'Orléans was regent for Louis XV **2.** **Re·gen·cy** adj. of a transitional style of French furniture developed c. 1715–23 and characterized by scrollwork, curves and graceful decorative motifs ‖ of a style of English furniture, architecture etc. prevalent c. 1811–30, characterized by fine proportions, classical elements, the use of stucco in buildings and often decorative use of iron [fr. M.L. regentia]

re·gen·er·a·cy (ridʒénərəsi:) n. the state or quality of being regenerate

re·gen·er·ate 1. (ridʒénəreit) *v. pres. part.* **re·gen·er·at·ing** *past* and *past part.* **re·gen·er·at·ed** *v.t.* to give new life or vigor to ‖ to restore to moral or spiritual health ‖ (*biol.*) to grow (a new part) to replace a lost or injured one ‖ *v.i.* to become regenerate **2.** (ridʒénərit) *adj.* having new life or vigor ‖ spiritually or morally revived or restored ‖ (*biol.*) reformed or grown again [fr. L. *regenerare* (*regeneratus*), to be reborn]

re·gen·er·a·tion (ridʒənəréiʃən) *n.* a regenerating or being regenerated ‖ a spiritual rebirth ‖ (*biol.*) the regrowth or renewal of an organ, tissue or substance that has been lost or damaged [fr. F. *régénération* or L. *regeneratio* (*regenerationis*)]

re·gen·er·a·tive (ridʒénərətiv, ridʒénəreitiv) *adj.* of regeneration ‖ regenerating [fr. F. *régénératif* or M.L. *regenerativus*]

re·gen·er·a·tor (ridʒénəreitər) *n.* a device which uses the heat of combustion in a furnace to raise the temperature of the inflowing air or combustible gas

Re·gens·burg (réigənsbuːrx) (*Eng.* formerly Ratisbon) a communications center (pop. 131,800) of E. Bavaria, West Germany, on the Danube. Industries: mechanical engineering, light manufactures. Gothic cathedral (13th-16th c.), town hall (14th c.). University

re·gent (ríːdʒənt) **1.** *adj.* (placed after the noun) acting as regent, *a prince regent* **2.** *n.* a person appointed to rule during the minority, absence or physical or mental disability of a monarch ‖ one of a governing board, esp. of a university [F. *régent* or fr. L. *regens* (*regentis*) fr. *regere*, to rule]

Re·ger (réigər), Max (1873-1916), German composer, esp. for the organ. He also wrote chamber and orchestral music. He adapted classical forms to the Romantic idiom

reg·gae (régei) *n.* Jamaican rock music with pulsating blues style, often with a political or religious message derived from Rastafarian beliefs. *Cf* RASTAFARIAN

Reg·gio di Ca·la·bria (réddʒɔdi:kɑlábrjɑ) a port (pop. 150,000) of Calabria, Italy, on the Straits of Messina, rebuilt after an earthquake (1908). Manufactures: perfumes, silk goods

Reg·gio nell' E·mi·lia (réddʒɔnelemɪ́ːlja) an agricultural market (pop. 130,159) of Emilia-Romagna, Italy, in the Po Valley: food processing, mechanical engineering, clothing

reg·i·cid·al (redʒisáid'l) *adj.* pertaining to regicide or a regicide

reg·i·cide (rédʒisaid) *n.* a person who kills a monarch, esp. the monarch to whom he is subject ‖ the crime of killing a monarch **Reg·i·cide** (*Eng. hist.*) any of the judges who condemned Charles I to death (1649) ‖ (*F. hist.*) any of the members of the National Convention who voted (1792) for the execution of Louis XVI [fr. L. *rex* (*regis*), king + *caedere*, to kill]

re·gime, ré·gime (reiʒíːm, rəʒíːm) *n.* a system of rule or government, *a republican regime* ‖ any systematic organizational control ‖ the length of time during which such a system or organization is in force ‖ a recurring pattern of prevailing conditions, activity etc., *climatic regime* ‖ the character of a river with respect to its rate of flow ‖ a regimen [F.]

reg·i·men (rédʒəmen, rédʒəmən) *n.* (*med.*) a regulated course of diet, exercise etc. for restoring strength and health or for keeping the body fit [L.=rule]

reg·i·ment 1. (rédʒəmənt) *n.* (*mil.*) an army unit, commanded by a colonel, and containing subunits: troops, batteries, battalions etc. ‖ a large number, *a regiment of ants* **2.** (rédʒiment) *v.t.* (*mil.*) to form into a regiment ‖ to assign to a regiment ‖ to subject to stultifying organization, *children should not be regimented* [fr. L. L. *regimentum*, rule, government]

reg·i·men·tal 1. *adj.* of a military regiment **2.** *n.* (*pl.*) the uniform worn by a regiment [REGIMENT *n.*]

reg·i·men·ta·tion (redʒəməntéiʃən) *n.* the act of regimenting, esp. so as to produce a dull uniformity and stifle individual initiative ‖ a being so regimented

Re·gi·na (ridʒáinə) the capital (pop. 162,613) of Saskatchewan, Canada, an agricultural market: farm machinery, oil refining

Re·gi·o·mon·ta·nus (riːdʒiːoumɒntéinəs) (Johann Müller, 1436-76), German astronomer. He advanced the study of algebra and trigonometry and introduced the use of tangents. He published his astronomical observations and calculations in his 'Ephemerides' for the years 1474-1506

re·gion (ríːdʒən) *n.* a large part of space, land, sea or air which has certain distinctive characteristics (e.g. of boundary, temperature, fauna or flora, configuration), *the solar regions, the arctic region* ‖ the space or area surrounding a specified place, *the London region* ‖ an area which is a unit of administration ‖ an area surrounding an organ of the body, *the lumbar region* **ré·gion·al** *adj.* **ré·gion·al·ism** *n.* [A.F. *regiun*]

regional planning coordination of more than one governmental agency in an area to meet common problems

reg·is·ter (rédʒistər) *n.* an official or formal list, *Lloyd's Register of Ships* ‖ an official record of births, marriages and deaths ‖ a book in which a record is kept, *a hotel register* ‖ an official document issued to the owner of a ship as evidence of her nationality etc. ‖ an automatic cash till, recording sums as they are paid in ‖ (*mus.*) the range of a voice or an instrument, or a part of this, *the chest register* ‖ (*mus.*) a set of pipes in an organ controlled by one stop ‖ a movable plate for regulating the draft into a furnace, fire grate etc. ‖ registration, registry, *port of register* ‖ an instrument recording speed, force etc. ‖ (*computer*) a short-term storage of limited capacity used to facilitate operations ‖ (*printing*) the correctness of fall in relation to one another of successive printings on a single sheet, or of the recto and verso of a leaf in relation to each other ‖ (*photog.*) correspondence in position between the focusing screen and the surface of the sensitive film or plate ‖ (*art, archit.*) a strip or layer e.g. of sculptural relief [F. *registre* or M.L. *registrum, registrum*]

register *v.t.* to place on formal or official record ‖ to express or show (a feeling or emotion) ‖ to send (a letter etc.) through the mail under a system whereby for a fee the postal authority gives the sender a certificate of receipt and demands a certificate of receipt on delivery ‖ (of gauges, meters etc.) to record ‖ (*printing, photog.*) to make correspond exactly ‖ *v.i.* to enter one's name on a formal or official record ‖ to have one's name entered on a voters' list by following the procedure prescribed ‖ (*mus.*) to select pipe organ stops suitable for the piece to be played ‖ (*pop.*) to penetrate the mind, *he heard, but did it register?* ‖ (*printing, photog.*) to be in register, correspond exactly [fr. F. *registrer* or M.L. *registrare*]

registered nurse (*abbr.* R.N.) a fully qualified nurse who has passed a state examination ‖ (*Br.*) a state-registered nurse

register office a place where registration is made

register ton a unit of internal capacity for ships equal to 100 cu. ft

reg·is·tra·ble (rédʒistrəb'l) *adj.* able to be registered

reg·is·trar (rédʒistrɑr, redʒistrár) *n.* an official in charge of a register, e.g. in a university, or one responsible for recording births, marriages, deaths **reg·is·trar·ship** *n.*

reg·is·trate (rédʒistreit) *pres. part.* **reg·is·trat·ing** *past* and *past part.* **reg·is·trat·ed** *v.i.* to register pipe organ stops [fr. M.L. *registrare* (*registratus*)]

reg·is·tra·tion (redʒistréiʃən) *n.* a registering or being registered ‖ an entry in an official register ‖ a number of persons registered ‖ the selecting and adjusting of organ stops for a piece of music to be performed, or the selection made [fr. M.L. *registratio* (*registrationis*)]

reg·is·try (rédʒistri) *pl.* **reg·is·tries** *n.* registration ‖ a register office ‖ (*Br.*) a registry office

registry office (*Br.*) a place where registration is made and where civil marriages take place

re·gius (ríːdʒəs) *adj.* (of a professorship at Oxford or Cambridge or certain Scottish universities) founded by the monarch, or requiring royal consent for an appointment to it to be made ‖ designating a professor holding such a chair [L.=royal]

reg·let (réglit) *n.* (*archit.*) a flat, thin molding [F. *réglet*]

reg·nal (régnəl) *adj.* of or pertaining to a reign or a monarch [fr. M.L. *regnalis*]

regnal day the anniversary of a monarch's accession to the throne

regnal year (used in dating State documents) the year dating from a monarch's accession

reg·nant (régnənt) *adj.* (of a queen, always following the noun) reigning as sovereign in her own right, not as consort [fr. L. *regnans* (*regnantis*) fr. *regnare*, to rule]

Re·gnard (renjær), Jean-François (1655-1709), French dramatist. His lively comedies include 'le Joueur' (1696)

Re·gnault (renjou), Victor (1810-78), French physicist and chemist. He made extremely precise measurements for his study of the physical, esp. thermal, properties of fluids. He also worked in the field of organic chemistry

Ré·gnier (reinjei), Henri de (1864-1936), French writer. His volumes of poetry include 'Sites' (1887) and 'les Médailles d'argile' (1900). His best known novel is 'la Double Maîtresse' (1900)

Ré·gnier, Mathurin (1573-1613), French poet. His satires imitated the Latin poets, esp. Horace and Juvenal

reg·o·lith (régəliθ) *n.* mantlerock [fr. Gk *rhēgos*, blanket + *lithos*, stone]

re·gress 1. (ríːgres) *n.* a going back or returning ‖ a tendency to decline **2.** (rigrés) *v.i.* to move backwards ‖ to retrogress [fr. L. *regredi* (*regressus*), to go back]

re·gres·sion (rigréʃən) *n.* a regressing ‖ a reversion to earlier stages of personality development or to objects of infantile attachment ‖ (*biol.*) the return to an earlier or less complex form ‖ (*astron.*) movement of a heavenly body in a direction contrary to normal, esp. movement of a planet from east to west in the solar system [fr. L. *regressio* (*regressionis*)]

re·gres·sive (rigrésiv) *adj.* regressing or tending to regress ‖ (*biol.*) of, marked by, or caused by regression

re·gret (rigrét) *n.* the emotion arising from a wish that some matter or situation could be different from what it is. The emotion may be accompanied by sadness, remorse, disappointment, dissatisfaction etc., and may arise from something done or said or from some failure to do or say something, or be a response to a general situation, or be felt on behalf of someone else ‖ an expression of this emotion ‖ (*pl.*) a conventional expression of disappointment, esp. at refusing an invitation [F.]

regret *pres. part.* **re·gret·ting** *past* and *past part.* **re·gret·ted** *v.t.* to feel or express regret for **re·gret·ful, re·gret·ta·ble** *adjs.* [fr. F. *regretter*, origin unknown]

reg·u·lar (régjulər) **1.** *adj.* conforming to a rule of equal disposition in space or time, *houses built at regular distances from one another, occurring at regular times of the day* ‖ conforming to some standard pattern of proportion or symmetry *the crystal has a regular form* ‖ conforming to rules of procedure etc. ‖ customary, *this is not his regular job* ‖ disciplined, *regular habits* ‖ (*pop.*) real, complete, *a regular nuisance* ‖ (*eccles.*) subject to monastic vows or discipline, *the regular clergy* ‖ (*gram.*) having the normal type of inflection, formation etc., *a regular verb* ‖ (*math.*) obeying the same law throughout ‖ (*math.*) having equal sides and angles ‖ (of a customer, visitor etc.) frequently received over a long period ‖ (*bot.*) radially symmetrical, actinomorphic ‖ not varying, *keep up a regular stroke* ‖ (*internat. law*, of soldiers) recognized as legitimate combatants in warfare ‖ (*mil.*) of the standing army of a country **2.** *n.* one of the regular clergy ‖ a regular soldier **reg·u·lar·i·ty** (reġjuláriti) *n.* [O.F. *reguler* fr. L. *regularis* fr. *regula*, rule]

reg·u·lar·i·za·tion (reġjulərizéiʃən) *n.* a regularizing or being regularized ‖ an instance of regularizing

reg·u·lar·ize (régjuləraiz) *pres. part.* **reg·u·lar·iz·ing** *past* and *past part.* **reg·u·lar·ized** *v.t.* to make regular, cause to conform to a rule, principle etc.

reg·u·late (régjuleit) *pres. part.* **reg·u·lat·ing** *past* and *past part.* **reg·u·lat·ed** *v.t.* to control by rule, system etc. ‖ to adjust so as to make accurate, *to regulate a watch* ‖ to adjust as regards amount, rate etc., *they regulate the flow of water by the sluice gate* ‖ to arrange so as to adapt, *she regulates her hours to fit in with his* **reg·u·la·tion 1.** *n.* a regulating or being regulated ‖ a rule **2.** *adj.* correct, prescribed, *regulation dress* **rég·u·la·tive** *adj.* **rég·u·la·tor** *n.* something which regulates ‖ a device in a timepiece for making it run faster or slower ‖ a mechanical device controlling temperature, pressure, the admission of steam or water etc. **rég·u·la·to·ry** *adj.* [fr. L.L. *regulare* (*regulatus*)]

regulatory gene (*genetics*) class of genes that specify whether a structural gene will function. *Cf* OPERATOR

Reg·u·lus (régjuləs), Marcus Atilius (*d. c.* 250 B.C.), Roman general, consul (267 B.C. and 256

CONCISE PRONUNCIATION KEY: **(a)** æ, c*a*t; ɑ, c*a*r; ɑ: f*aw*n; ei, sn*a*ke. **(e)** e, h*e*n; iː, sh*ee*p; iə, d*ee*r; ɛə, b*ea*r. **(i)** i, f*i*sh; ai, t*i*ger; əː, b*i*rd. **(o)** o, *o*x; au, c*ow*; ou, g*oa*t; u, p*oo*r; ɔi, r*oy*al. **(u)** ʌ, d*u*ck; u, b*u*ll; uː, g*oo*se; ə, b*a*cillus; juː, c*u*be. x, lo*ch*; θ, *th*ink; ð, bo*th*er; z, *Z*en; ʒ, corsa*g*e; dʒ, sava*g*e; ŋ, orangutan*g*; j, *y*ak; ʃ, fi*sh*; tʃ, fe*tch*; 'l, rabb*le*; 'n, red*den*. Complete pronunciation key appears inside front cover.

B.C.). Captured (255 B.C.) by the Carthaginians in the 1st Punic War, he is said to have been sent on parole to Rome to negotiate peace but to have advised the senate against accepting the Carthaginian terms. On his return to Carthage he was tortured to death

reg·u·lus (régjuləs) *pl.* **reg·u·lus·es, reg·u·li** (régjulai) *n.* the impure metallic mass formed under the slag when ores are smelted ‖ the substance of such a mass [L. dim. of *rex* (*regis*), king]

re·gur·gi·tate (rigś:rdʒiteit) *pres. part.* **re·gur·gi·tat·ing** *past* and *past part.* **re·gur·gi·tat·ed** *v.t.* to bring up (what has been swallowed) ‖ *v.i.* (*rhet.*) to gush or surge back

re·gur·gi·ta·tion (rigə:rdʒitéiʃən) *n.* a regurgitating or being regurgitated [fr. M.L. *regurgitatio* (*regurgitationis*)]

re·hab (rí:hæb) *v.* to rehabilitate a real property as a business or for one's own use. —**rehab·bing** *n.*

re·ha·bil·i·tate (ri:həbíliteit, ri:əbíliteit) *pres. part.* **re·ha·bil·i·tat·ing** *past* and *past part.* **re·ha·bil·i·tat·ed** *v.t.* to restore to rank, privileges, rights etc. lost or forfeited ‖ to vindicate, restore the reputation of ‖ to restore (e.g. something damaged, decayed or not functioning) to its previous good condition ‖ to restore (e.g. a disabled person or a criminal) to physical or mental health through training **re·ha·bil·i·ta·tion** *n.* [fr. M.L. *rehabilitare* (*rehabilitatus*)]

re·hash 1. (ri:hǽʃ) *v.t.* to serve up the same (food, arguments, ideas etc.) in a new guise **2.** (rí:hæʃ) *n.* the act or process of rehashing ‖ something which is the result of rehashing

re·hears·al (rihə́:rs'l) *n.* a rehearsing ‖ a trial performance

re·hearse (rihə́:rs) *pres. part.* **re·hears·ing** *past* and *past part.* **re·hearsed** *v.t.* to practice (a play etc.) before performing it for an audience ‖ to enumerate, *to rehearse a list of complaints* ‖ *v.i.* to practice a play etc. [O.F. *rehercer*, to harrow again]

Rehnquist (rénkwist), William Hubbs (1924-), U.S. Supreme Court associate justice (1971-86) and chief (1986-) justice. He graduated from Stanford Law School (1952) and practiced law privately in Phoenix, Ariz. from 1953. An assistant U.S. attorney general (1969-71), he was nominated to the Supreme Court by Pres. Richard M. Nixon in 1971. A conservative, Pres. Ronald Reagan nominated him to be chief justice in 1986, upon the retirement of Chief Justice Warren Burger. As an associate justice he wrote the majority opinions in 'Edelman v. Jordan' (1974) and 'Fitzpatrick v. Bitzer' (1976), both of which denied retroactive benefits for welfare recipients, and in 'Rostker v. Goldberg' (1981), which dealt with excluding women from the draft. In 'New York v. Quarles' (1984) and 'Hunter v. Underwood' (1985) he wrote for the Court regarding civil rights

Re·ho·bo·am (ri:əbóuəm) (*d.* c. 914 B.C.), king of the Hebrews (c. 932–c. 914 B.C.), son of Solomon. During his reign, the northern tribes seceded under Jeroboam I to form the kingdom of Israel

Reich (raik), Wilhelm (1897-1957), Austrian psychoanalyst known for his controversial theory of orgastic potency—that emotions of love and the pleasurable sensations form the basis of mental health. He taught in Vienna and Berlin (1927-33). During the 1940s and 1950s, in the U.S.A., he maintained that orgone energy was the basis of life energy and invented the orgone energy accumulator, a device that was banned. When he defied the ban he was arrested, convicted and imprisoned. He wrote 'Character Analysis' (1933) and 'The Mass Psychology of Fascism' (1933)

Reich *THIRD REICH

Reichs·rat (ráixsrɑt) the lower chamber of the German parliament (1871-1934)

Reich·stadt (ráixʃtɑt), duke of *NAPOLEON II

Reichs·tag (ráixstɑx) the diet of the Holy Roman Empire ‖ the lower chamber of the parliament of the North German Confederation ‖ the lower chamber of the German parliament (1871-1945). The deliberate destruction by fire (1933) of the building in which this met was used by Hitler as a pretext for measures against the Communist party

Reid (ri:d), Thomas (1710-96), British philosopher. His teaching opposed both the idealism of Berkeley and the skepticism of Hume. His main work is 'Inquiry into the Human Mind on the Principles of Common Sense' (1764)

re·i·fy (rí:ifai) *pres. part.* **re·i·fy·ing** *past* and *past part.* **re·i·fied** *v.t.* to treat (an abstraction) as a real thing [fr. L. *res*, thing]

reign (rein) *n.* the power of a monarch ‖ some other power compared with this, *the reign of law* ‖ the period during which a monarch reigns [O.F. *regne, reigne*]

reign *v.i.* to hold royal office, to be monarch ‖ to be predominant, prevail, *confusion reigned* [O.F. *regner*]

re·ig·ni·tion (ri:igníʃən) *n.* (*electr.*) **1.** a process by which several counts are generated within a radiation-counter tube by a single ionization **2.** renewal of ionization after cessation of conduction

Reign of Terror *TERROR, the

re·im·burse (ri:imbə́rs) *pres. part.* **re·im·burs·ing** *past* and *past part.* **re·im·bursed** *v.t.* to compensate (a person) for money expended ‖ to repay (expenses) **re·im·búrse·ment** *n.* [fr. RE- + L. *inbursare*, to put into a purse]

re·im·port (ri:impɔ́rt, ri:impóurt) **1.** *v.t.* to import again (something previously exported in a raw state) **2.** *n.* a reimporting ‖ something reimported **re·im·por·tá·tion** *n.*

re·im·pres·sion (ri:impréʃən) *n.* a reprint from the original plates or type without correction

Reims (ri:s) (*Eng.* Rheims, ri:mz) the chief town (pop. 177,369) of Marne department, France. Industries: champagne, wool textiles, mechanical engineering. Gothic cathedral (12th–late 13th cc.), Romanesque and Gothic abbey (11th-12th cc.), both damaged during the 1st world war. University (1547-1793, refounded 1961)

rein (rein) **1.** *n.* one of the two leather straps or ropes fastened to the sides of a horse's bit as a means of control ‖ a similar device used to control other animals ‖ (*Br., pl.*) a harness used to keep a small child close to its mother etc. when walking ‖ (*pl.*) a means of control or restraint, *the reins of government*, or power to control, *to hold the reins* **to draw rein** to halt one's horse **to give rein to** to allow (a horse, a person, one's imagination or desire etc.) to proceed without restraint **to keep a tight rein on** to keep under one's strict control **2.** *v.t.* (usually with 'in', 'up') to bring (a horse) to a halt or to a slower gait [O.F. *rene*]

re·in·car·nate 1. (ri:inkɑ́rneit) *pres. part.* **re·in·car·nat·ing** *past* and *past part.* **re·in·car·nat·ed** *v.t.* to cause to be reborn in a new body or a new form **2.** (ri:inkɑ́rnit) *adj.* born again in a new form **re·in·car·ná·tion** *n.* a reincarnating or being reincarnated

rein·deer (réindiər) *pl.* **rein·deer, rein·deers** *n.* any of several large subarctic deer of the genus *Rangifer*, inhabiting Northern Europe, Asia and America. They are domesticated, esp. in Lapland, and are used to draw sleighs and to provide meat and leather. Both the male and female have antlers, those of the male being broader and more sweeping [O.N. *hreindȳri*]

Reindeer Lake (réindiər) a lake (area 2,436 sq. miles) on the northern section of the Saskatchewan-Manitoba boundary in central Canada

reindeer moss *Cladonia rangiferina*, fam. Cladoniaceae, a gray, tufted lichen that is the main food of reindeer and caribou in winter and is sometimes eaten by man

re·in·dus·tri·al·i·za·tion (ri:indʌstriəlizéiʃən) *n.* 1980 government policy designed to make American industry competitively more efficient

re·in·force (ri:infɔ́rs, ri:infóurs) *pres. part.* **re·in·forc·ing** *past* and *past part.* **re·in·forced** *v.t.* to strengthen by the addition of something ‖ to support (an argument, suggestion) with facts, evidence etc. ‖ (*behavioral psych.*) to strengthen a tendency to act in a desired manner, esp. by a system of rewards

reinforced concrete concrete strengthened by having wire mesh, metal bars etc. embedded in it

re·in·force·ment (ri:infɔ́rsmənt, ri:infóursmənt) *n.* a reinforcing or being reinforced ‖ something that reinforces ‖ (*pl.*) extra men or material to strengthen a military force

Rein·hardt (ráinhɑrt), Max (1873-1943), Austrian theatrical producer, naturalized American (1943). He led (c. 1903-32) the German romantic school of producers and directed works by Shakespeare, Molière, Goethe, Strindberg, Ibsen and Shaw. His spectacular production of 'The Miracle', first presented in 1911, was one of his greatest successes

Reinsch (rainʃ), Paul Samuel (1869-1923), U.S. educator and diplomat. As U.S. minister to China (1913-9), he was highly respected by the

new republican regime, which appointed him (1919) legal adviser

re·in·state (ri:instéit) *pres. part.* **re·in·stat·ing** *past* and *past part.* **re·in·stat·ed** *v.t.* to restore to a former position, state etc. **re·in·státe·ment** *n.*

re·in·sur·ance (ri:inʃúərəns) *n.* a reinsuring ‖ insurance taken out by an insuring company against loss ‖ the amount of this

re·in·sure (ri:inʃúər) *pres. part.* **re·in·sur·ing** *past* and *past part.* **re·in·sured** *v.t.* to insure again by transferring (a risk) to another company in whole or in part ‖ to insure again by accepting (such a transferred risk)

REIT (*acronym*) for real estate investment trusts (which see)

re·it·er·ate (ri:ítəreit) *pres. part.* **re·it·er·at·ing** *past* and *past part.* **re·it·er·at·ed** *v.t.* to repeat several times [fr. L. *reiterare* (*reiteratus*)]

re·it·er·a·tion (ri:itəréiʃən) *n.* a reiterating or being reiterated [fr. L. *reiteratio* (*reiterationis*)]

re·it·er·a·tive (ri:ítərətiv, ri:ítəreitiv) *adj.* repetitious [REITERATE]

re·ject 1. (ridʒékt) *v.t.* to refuse to accept, *to reject an offer* ‖ to cast or set aside as being unacceptable, faulty or useless, *the machine rejects badly worn coins* ‖ to eject from the stomach **2.** (rí:dʒekt) *n.* someone or something rejected [fr. L. *reicere, rejicere* (*rejectus*), to throw back]

re·ject·ant (ridʒéktənt) *n.* a natural insect-repellent substance in plants

re·jec·tion (ridʒékʃən) *n.* a rejecting or being rejected ‖ something rejected ‖ the action of the body to destroy foreign matter, e.g., transplanted tissue [F. *réjection* or fr. L. *rejectio* (*rejectionis*)]

rejectivism *MINIMALISM —**rejectivist** *n.*

re·joice (ridʒ́ɔis) *pres. part.* **re·joic·ing** *past* and *past part.* **re·joiced** *v.i.* to feel joy ‖ *v.t.* to cause to feel joy **re·jóic·ing** *n.* joyfulness, esp. shared with others ‖ the action of someone who rejoices ‖ (esp. *pl.*) an instance or expression of joyfulness [O.F. *rejoir* (*rejoiss-*)]

re·join (ridʒɔ́in) *v.t.* to join again [fr. F. *rejoindre* (*rejoign-*) or fr. RE-+JOIN]

re·join (ridʒɔin) *v.t.* to reply, to retort ‖ *v.i.* (*law*) to reply to a charge, esp. to the plaintiff's replication [fr. F. *rejoindre* (*rejoign-*)]

re·join·der (ridʒɔ́indər) *n.* a reply, retort ‖ (*law*) the defendant's answer to the replication of the plaintiff [F. *rejoindre*, to join again]

re·jus·ti·fy (ri:dʒʌ́stifai) *n.* (*computer*) a command to justify the margins of the input after additions and deletions have been made

re·ju·ve·nate (ridʒú:vineit) *pres. part.* **re·ju·ve·nat·ing** *past* and *past part.* **re·ju·ve·nat·ed** *v.t.* to make as though young again ‖ (*geol.*) to restore (a stream), e.g. by uplift of the surrounding land, to a state of active erosion ‖ *v.i.* to become as though young again **re·ju·ve·ná·tion** *n.*

re·ju·ve·nes·cence (ridʒu:vinés'ns) *n.* a reviving, renewing of youthful characteristics **re·ju·ve·nés·cent** *adj.* [fr. older *rejuvenesce*, to become young again]

re·lapse 1. (rilǽps) *v.i. pres. part.* **re·laps·ing** *past* and *past part.* **re·lapsed** to fall back into ill health, crime or heresy **2.** (rilǽps, rí:læps) *n.* a relapsing or an instance of this [fr. L. *relabi* (*relapsus*), to slip back]

relapsing fever any of several related acute infectious diseases characterized by recurring fever and muscular pains. The fever occurs esp. in the tropics and is caused by a spirochete transmitted by lice and tick bites

re·late (riléit) *pres. part.* **re·lat·ing** *past* and *past part.* **re·lat·ed** *v.t.* to tell the story of, recount, narrate ‖ to show or establish a relation between ‖ *v.i.* to have or be in relation, *anything relating to his welfare concerns you* **re·lát·ed** *adj.* (of two or more things) having or bearing a relationship, *related subjects* ‖ in the same family through birth or by marriage, *distantly related* ‖ (*mus.*, of one key, chord etc. and another) in harmonic relation [fr. L. *referre* (*relatus*), to carry back, refer]

re·la·tion (riléiʃən) *n.* a recounting or narrating ‖ that which is recounted or narrated ‖ a relative by birth or marriage ‖ relationship by blood or marriage ‖ the way in which one thing is associated with another, *the two are in a simple relation numerically* ‖ the fact of being so associated, *he sees no relation between the two events* ‖ (*Br. law*) the laying of information before the attorney general by a plaintiff ‖ (*pl.*) the terms on which one person (state etc.) has dealings

CONCISE PRONUNCIATION KEY: (**a**) æ, c*a*t; ɑ, c*a*r; ɔ f*aw*n; ei, sn*a*ke. (**e**) e, h*e*n; i:, sh*ee*p; iə, d*ee*r; ɛə, b*ea*r. (**i**) i, f*i*sh; ai, t*i*ger; ə:, b*i*rd. (**o**) o, *o*x; au, c*ow*; ou, g*oa*t; u, p*oor*; ɔi, r*oy*al. (**u**) ʌ, d*u*ck; u, b*u*ll; u:, g*oo*se; ə, b*a*cillus; ju:, c*u*be. x, lo*ch*; θ, *th*ink; ð, bo*th*er; z, *Z*en; ʒ, cor*s*age; dʒ, sava*g*e; ŋ, orangutan*g*; j, *y*ak; ʃ, fi*sh*; tʃ, fe*tch*; 'l, rabb*le*; 'n, red*den*. Complete pronunciation key appears inside front cover.

with another person (state etc.) **in** (or **with**) **relation to** concerning, so far as concerns **re-la·tion·al** adj. (gram., of conjunctions, prepositions etc.) showing syntactic relation [F.]

re·la·tion·ship (riléiʃənʃip) n. the state of being related ‖ the mutual exchange between two people or groups who have dealings with one another ‖ kinship

rel·a·tive (rélətiv) **1.** adj. of something (a quantity, quality, truth, idea etc.) considered in reference to something else, *the mass of the earth, relative to that of the sun, is very small* ‖ comparative, not absolute ‖ pertinent ‖ (gram.) of a word that introduces a subordinate clause and refers to an antecedent, e.g. ‘whom’ is a relative pronoun in the phrase ‘the man whom she saw’ ‖ (gram.) of a clause introduced by such a word ‖ (mus., of a minor key or scale) having the same key signature as a specified major key or scale ‖ (mus., of a major key or scale) having the same key signature as a specified minor key or scale **2.** n. a person connected by birth or marriage with another person ‖ something that is relative ‖ (gram.) a relative pronoun [fr. F. *relatif* or L. *relativus*]

relative aperture the effective diameter of a camera lens expressed as a fraction of its focal length (*f-NUMBER) or as the ratio of the aperture to the focal length. Thus a lens with an aperture that is one eleventh of its focal length has a relative aperture of f/11 or 1:11

relative humidity the ratio between the actual amount of moisture in the air and that which would be needed to saturate the air at the same temperature, expressed as a percentage

rel·a·tive·ly (rélətivli) adv. in a relative way, to a qualified degree or extent

rel·a·tiv·ism (rélətivizəm) n. (philos.) the doctrine that all we can know about things is the relations between them, i.e. that all knowledge is relative

rel·a·tiv·i·ty (relətíviti:) n. the state or quality of being relative ‖ a theory first formulated by Einstein (1905), and usually called the special theory of relativity (special relativity), which deals with the question of what may properly be understood by space and time, restricting the analysis to systems at rest or those moving with uniform motion (nonaccelerated) in a region free from gravitation. Its fundamental assumptions are (a) that the laws of physics are the same in any system regardless of its velocity and (b) that the velocity of light is a constant, independent of its source and of the system in which it is measured. By defining two systems, one at rest and one in motion, in terms of their space coordinates and their time coordinates, Einstein was able to show the relation between the usual physical quantities in the two systems, i.e. the effect of relative motion on observations of time, length etc. He found that; (1) the mass of a body depends upon its velocity (2) mass and energy are interconvertible (*MASS-ENERGY EQUATION) (3) a body moving with a given velocity appears to an observer at rest to be shortened in the direction of motion (*FITZGERALD CONTRACTION). The condition of nonaccelerated and hence gravitation-free systems in the special theory is too restrictive. When applied to gravitational systems it is found that no set of coordinates exists in which special relativity holds throughout a finite region. Einstein therefore sought to present the theory in a form that would include gravitation and be independent of the choice of coordinates. The result, the general theory of relativity (general relativity), presents a set of equations which meet these requirements and which show that the space described by them is curved in a way which depends upon the distribution of mass and energy in it, so that space and time near concentrations of mass differ from space and time great distances away. The general theory has been confirmed in a number of its predictions, esp. in astrophysics and astronomy

re·lax (riléks) v.t. to loosen, *to relax a hold* ‖ to make less strict, *to relax discipline* ‖ to lower nervous tension in, *to relax the upper torso* ‖ to diminish, *to relax one's efforts* ‖ v.i. to become less tense, esp. in nerves and muscles ‖ to become less strict, esp. in matters of discipline ‖ (of a person) to become less restrained, esp. in social relationships ‖ to cease to work, take relaxation [fr. L. *relaxare*]

re·lax·a·tion (ri:lækséiʃən) n. a relaxing or being relaxed ‖ a partial remission of a duty, punishment etc. ‖ a recreation, *driving fast cars*

was his main relaxation [fr. L. *relaxatio* (*relaxationis*)]

re·lax·er (riléksər) n. a curly-hair straightener

re·lay (rí:lei) n. a fresh supply of people, animals or materials used to take the place of others when these are exhausted or have completed their assigned tasks ‖ (elec.) a device which enables a current in one circuit to open or close another circuit to the flow of a current ‖ a local battery used to enable telegraphic or telephonic signals to be transmitted over long distances ‖ a relaying, passing on ‖ a relay race or one of its divisions [fr. O.F. *relais*, a fresh supply of hunting hounds or horses]

re·lay (rí:lei, riléi) v.t. to pass on, *relay the news* ‖ (radio) to transmit (a program received from another transmitting station) ‖ (elec.) to control by using a relay ‖ to arrange in or supply with relays [fr. F. *relayer*]

re·lay (rj:léi) pres. part. **re·lay·ing** past and past part. **re·laid** v.t. to lay again

relay race a race between teams in which each team member, after covering a certain distance, is relieved by another team member

re·lease (rilí:s) n. a setting free or being set free from e.g. pain, duty or imprisonment ‖ a document stating that one is free, e.g. from prison ‖ a putting of information or a new film before the public ‖ something (e.g. information or a new film) put before the public ‖ (law) the surrender of a claim, right etc. to someone else ‖ (law) the document containing this surrender ‖ something which releases, e.g. a mechanical contrivance, *the release in an alarm clock* [O.F. *reles, relais*]

release pres. part **re·leas·ing** past and past part. **re·leased** v.t. to free (someone or something) from whatever had limited his or her freedom to act, move etc., *to release a prisoner* ‖ to free from care, pain, anxiety etc. ‖ (law) to surrender (property, a right etc.) to another ‖ to put (information, a new film etc.) before the public [fr. O.F. *relesser, relaissier*]

releasing factor (physiol.) a hormone that triggers the secretion of other hormones

rel·e·gate (réligeit) pres. part. **rel·e·gat·ing** past and past part. **rel·e·gat·ed** v.t. to demote to some inferior or obscure place, *the officer was relegated to the ranks* ‖ to pass (a matter requiring a decision) to someone else ‖ to assign or refer to a particular class or kind [fr. L. *relegare (relegatus)* fr. re-, again + *legare*, to send with a commission]

rel·e·ga·tion (religéiʃən) n. a relegating or being relegated ‖ an instance of relegating [fr. L. *relegatio (relegationis)* fr. re-, again + *legare*, to send with a commission]

re·lent (rilént) v.i. to become less severe in one's attitude, intention, judgment etc., esp. under the influence of love or pity **re·lént·less** adj. unmoved by love or pity ‖ unceasing, as if without mercy, *relentless pressure of work* [fr. L. re-, again + *lentus*, pliable]

rel·e·vance (rélivəns) n. the state or quality of being relevant **rél·e·van·cy** n.

relevance or **relevance ratio** (computer) the ratio of the number of items retrieved by an instruction to the number retrieved by a standard query. Cf RECALL RATIO

rel·e·vant (rélivənt) adj. closely related to a matter under consideration [fr. M.L. *relevans (relevantis)* fr. *relevare*, to raise again]

re·li·a·bil·i·ty (rilaiəbíliti:) n. the state or quality of being reliable

re·li·a·ble (rilái·ə·b'l) adj. able to be relied on **re·li·a·bly** adv.

re·li·ance (rilái·əns) n. a relying ‖ readiness to believe in and depend on the good qualities of someone or something, *do not put too much reliance on his honesty*

re·li·ant (rilái·ənt) adj. having reliance ‖ trusting [RELY]

rel·ic (rélik) n. the material evidence of something which has ceased to exist ‖ a trace of something no longer in existence, practiced, believed etc. ‖ the body or a part of the body of a saint or martyr or something associated with him, set apart after his death for veneration ‖ (pl., rhet.) the remains of a dead person [F. *relique*]

rel·ict (rélikt) n. (rhet.) a widow ‖ (ecology) a species which has the characteristics of an earlier stage of evolution and has survived unchanged [fr. L. *relinquere (relictus)*, to relinquish]

re·lief (rilí:f) n. a freeing from military siege ‖ a freeing from or alleviating of oppression, danger, distress, pain etc. ‖ the sensation of being

set free from emotional tension, anxiety, fear etc., *a sigh of relief* ‖ something which breaks or relieves monotony, emotional tension etc. ‖ a release from work or duty ‖ someone to whom a person's work is handed over, esp. to insure continuity ‖ something, esp. money, food or clothing, given by state agencies or private persons to alleviate privation, *famine relief* [O.F.]

relief n. the extent to which, in a three-dimensional carving, sculpture, map etc., features are represented as raised above the general plane, *low relief* ‖ the quality of being or appearing to be raised thus, *lettering in relief* ‖ a carving etc. having this quality ‖ the appearance of solidity and spatial dimension in a painting ‖ (geog.) the parts of a land surface raised above the surrounding lowlands ‖ the difference of level between the top of the works and the bottom of the ditch in a fortification [fr. Ital. *rilievo* and F. *relief*]

relief map a map which indicates altitude, either by actual three-dimensional representation or by using colors, shading etc.

re·lieve (rilí:v) pres. part. **re·liev·ing** past and past part. **re·lieved** v.t. to alleviate (pain, distress, anxiety etc.) ‖ to free (someone) from pain, distress, anxiety etc. ‖ to rescue (a besieged city) ‖ (pop., with 'of') to rob, *to relieve someone of his wallet* ‖ to provide a contrast, make less monotonous ‖ to replace (someone on duty), *to relieve a sentry* ‖ to give relief to (oneself) by passing water or emptying the bowels [fr. O.F. *relever*]

re·li·gion (rilídʒən) n. man's expression of his acknowledgment of the divine ‖ a system of beliefs and practices relating to the sacred and uniting its adherents in a community, e.g. Judaism, Christianity ‖ adherence to such a system, *a man without religion* ‖ something which has a powerful hold on a person's way of thinking, interests etc., *football is his religion* ‖ monastic life, *his name in religion was Damian* [A.F. *religiun* and O.F. *religion* or fr. L. *religio (religionis)*]

—The major extant religions emerged in the following order: Hinduism (in India) and Shintoism (in Japan) 3rd millennium B.C., Judaism (in Palestine) 13th c. B.C., Zoroastrianism (in Persia) 7th c. B.C., Taoism and Confucianism (in China) and Jainism and Buddhism (in India, with roots in Hinduism) 6th c. B.C., Christianity (in Palestine with roots in Judaism) 1st c. A.D., Islam (in Arabia, with roots in Judaism) 7th c., Sikhism (in India, with roots in Hinduism) 16th c., Bahaism (in Persia, with roots in Islam) 19th c.

Religion, Wars of a series of civil wars (1562-3, 1567-8, 1568-70, 1572-3, 1574-6, 1576-7, 1580, 1585-98) in France. Basically a Huguenot struggle for freedom of worship, they developed into political wars between the monarchy and the houses of Guise and Bourbon. The main Huguenot leaders were Condé, Coligny and Henri de Navarre (later Henri IV). The Catholics were led by Henri, duc de Guise, who formed (1576) the Holy League. Catherine de' Medici and her sons, François II, Charles IX and Henri III, intrigued mainly on behalf of the Catholics. Many Huguenots were killed in the Massacre of St Bartholomew (1572), but the Huguenot cause triumphed after Henri IV succeeded to the throne (1589). Freedom of worship was granted in the Edict of Nantes (1598)

re·li·gi·os·i·ty (rilidʒi:ɒsiti:) n. morbid or excessive concern with religion in its formal expressions, or the practice of a merely superficial religion [fr. L.L. *religiositas*]

re·li·gious (rilídʒəs) **1.** adj. of, pertaining to, or concerned with religion ‖ faithful in religion ‖ associated with the practice of religion, *a religious rite* ‖ (of behavior) governed by principles adhered to as strictly as if they were those of a religion, *a religious regard for accuracy* ‖ of or pertaining to a monastic order **2.** pl. **re·li·gious** n. someone who has made monastic vows [A.F. *religius*, O.F. *religiosus* or fr. L. *religiosus*]

re·lin·quish (rilíŋkwiʃ) v.t. to give up, renounce, *to relinquish a right* ‖ to let go of, cease to hold in the hand **re·lín·quish·ment** n. [fr. O.F. *relinquir (relinquiss-)*]

rel·i·quar·y (rélikwɛri) pl. **rel·i·quar·ies** n. a receptacle in which a sacred relic or relics are kept [F. *reliquaire*]

rel·ish (réliʃ) **1.** v.t. to take pleasure in (food or drink) ‖ to enjoy heartily, *to relish a good joke* **2.** n. keen enjoyment, *to do something with relish* ‖ a savory embellishment (e.g. chutney, pickles) to a dish [O.F. *reles, relais*, something remaining]

re·luc·tance (rilʌ́ktəns) *n.* an emotional or mental opposition to a course of action, *he did it with reluctance* ‖ the property of a magnetic circuit expressed by the ratio of the magnetic potential difference to the magnetic flux. It is analogous to the resistance of an electric circuit

re·luc·tant (rilʌ́ktənt) *adj.* marked by or showing reluctance [fr. L. *reluctans (reluctantis)* fr. *reluctari*, to resist]

re·ly (rilái) *pres. part.* **re·ly·ing** *past* and *past part.* **re·lied** *v.i.* (with 'on' or 'upon') to depend absolutely, *they relied on the weekly boat for their supplies* ‖ to place one's complete confidence in and make no alternative provision, *he relied on his subordinate to prepare the report* [fr. O.F. *relier*, to bind together]

rem (*acronym*) for roentgen equivalent man, a unit of measurement of ionizing radiation that, when absorbed by a human being or other mammal, produces a physiological effect equivalent to that produced by the absorption of one roentgen of X-ray or gamma radiation

REM (*acronym*) for rapid eye movement (which see)

re·main (riméin) *v.i.* to stay behind ‖ to stay in the same place ‖ to be left, *nothing remains to be done* ‖ to continue in a certain state, *to remain calm in a crisis* [A.F. *remeyn-, remayn-*, stem of O.F. *remanoir*]

re·main·der (riméindər) 1. *n.* the portion which remains when part has been taken away ‖ (*math.*) the number remaining after subtraction or division ‖ (*law*) the right to inherit a title, rank etc. upon the death of the holder ‖ (*law*) an interest in property which comes to someone upon the termination of a previous estate and that was devised at the same time as the estate ‖ a copy of a book withdrawn from normal sale and offered for sale at a reduced price 2. *v.t.* to withdraw (books) from normal sale and offer them for sale at a reduced price [A.F.]

re·mains (riméinz) *pl. n.* the part which is left after the ravages of e.g. time, weather or destruction, *the remains of an ancient fort* ‖ the part which is left over, *the remains of a meal* ‖ (in funeral contexts) a dead human body ‖ the writings left unpublished at the time of an author's death, *literary remains* [O.F. *remain*]

re·make 1. (ri:méik) *v.t. pres. part.* **re·mak·ing** *past* and *past part.* **re·made** (ri:méid) to make again, esp. in a new form or to a new plan ‖ (*movies*) to make (a film) using the same story as that of an old film 2. (rí:meik) *n.* (*movies*) a remade film

re·man (ri:mǽn) *pres. part.* **re·man·ning** *past* and *past part.* **re·manned** *v.t.* to furnish (e.g. a ship) with a new complement of men

re·mand (ri:mǽnd, ri:mánd) 1. *v.t.* to order back into custody until brought before a court of law for trial ‖ to release on bail pending trial ‖ (*law*) to order back for further action, *the appellate court remanded the case to the trial court* 2. *n.* a remanding or being remanded ‖ an order to remand a person [fr. F. *remander*]

re·ma·nence (rémənəns) *n.* (*phys.*) the residual magnetism of a ferromagnetic substance when the magnetizing field is reduced to zero (cf. COERCIVE FORCE) [fr. L. *remanens (remanentis)* fr. *remanere*, to remain]

re·mark (rimárk) *n.* a brief spoken or written statement expressing an opinion on something noticed or observed **to escape remark** to pass unnoticed [fr. F. *remarque*]

remark *v.t.* to make as a remark [fr. F.] ‖ *v.i.* (with 'on' or 'upon') to make a remark [fr. F. *remarquer*]

re·mark·a·ble (rimárkəb'l) *adj.* exceptional, unusual enough to arouse notice, *remarkable linguistic ability, remarkable obstinacy* **re·mark·a·bly** *adv.* [fr. F. *remarquable*]

Remarque (rəmárk), Erich Maria (1898-1970), German writer whose well known work 'All Quiet on the Western Front' (1929) dealt with the 1st world war. The Nazis banned his books in 1933, and when they revoked his citizenship in 1938, he emigrated to the U.S.A. His other works include 'The Road Back' (1931), 'Three Comrades' (1938), 'Arc de Triomphe' (1946), 'Spark of Life' (1952) and 'The Night in Lisbon' (1963)

re·marque (rimárk) *n.* a mark, usually a marginal sketch, indicating the stage reached in engraving a plate ‖ an impression taken from a plate bearing such a mark [F.]

Rem·brandt (rémbrænt, rémbrɑnt) (Rembrandt Harmenszoon van Rijn, 1609-69),

Dutch baroque painter and etcher, one of the greatest masters of European art. He became famous and successful esp. as a portrait painter in the rich bourgeois society of 17th-c. Holland. But as his art matured the portraits became less flattering, less obviously brilliant, and patronage declined. The most obvious characteristic of Rembrandt's art is the use of a single, hidden source of light falling like a shaft into spacious shadows, creating a single focus, or reflected from a few highlights. The tones are somber but more jewellike because of the contrast of light and shade. The subject is often motionless, but again made more dramatic by this contrast. There is a love of exotic costume (turban, golden helmet, plume, rich robe) and of striking architecture (vault or pillar lost in shadow at the top of the picture and dramatically defining the human groups below), but these are used as settings for human experience. No artist saw more clearly or realized more deftly the poignant human meaning of a biblical scene. The drama is never merely theatrical. It is felt as truth and marvelously captured, especially in the easy, amazingly fast line of the drawing, or the etchings. The bodily pose and facial expression belie in their homeliness and truth the grandeur of the trappings. Especially in portraits of the aging, and in his many self-portraits, he saw the battered vessel of a hard-won spirituality, beyond pity

re·me·di·a·ble (rimí:di:əb'l) *adj.* able to be remedied [fr. F. *remédiable* or fr. L. *remediabilis*]

re·me·di·al (rimí:di:əl) *adj.* of that which serves to remedy, *remedial treatment*

rem·e·dy (rémidi) *pl.* **rem·e·dies** *n.* something which corrects a fault, error or evil ‖ a medicine or application which relieves or cures a disease or other physical affliction ‖ (*coinage*) the margin of tolerance permitted as to weight or purity ‖ (*law*) legal redress, restitution [A.F. *remedie*]

rem·e·dy (rémidi) *pres. part.* **rem·e·dy·ing** *past* and *past part.* **rem·e·died** *v.t.* to correct by removing a fault, error or evil ‖ to heal or cure [O.F. *remedier*]

re·mem·ber (rimémbər) *v.t.* to bring back to mind by an effort of will, *he could not remember your name* ‖ to have (something) come into one's memory again by chance, *she suddenly remembered that the kettle was on* ‖ to retain in the conscious mind, *remember to keep your shoulders back* ‖ to bear (a person) in mind as deserving a gift, attention etc., *to remember a friend on his birthday* ‖ to leave (a person) a legacy, *he remembered her in his will* ‖ to mention (a person) to another as sending greetings, *please remember me to him* ‖ to give a gratuity to [fr. O.F. *remembrer*]

re·mem·brance (rimémbrəns) *n.* a remembering ‖ the condition of retaining in the conscious mind, *to have something in remembrance* ‖ memory, the ability to recall the past ‖ the period over which the memory extends ‖ something which recalls a person, event etc. to the memory, *please accept this as a remembrance of me* ‖ (*pl.*) greeting conveyed on one's behalf [F.]

Re·mem·branc·er (rimémbrənsər) *n.* (*Br.*) an officer of the Supreme Court of Judicature whose duty is to collect debts owed to the sovereign

Rem·en·dur (rémendər) *n.* a cobalt-iron-vanadium alloy with high magnetic retention (remanence) that is malleable and ductible, developed by Bell Laboratories

re·mex (rí:meks) *pl.* **rem·i·ges** (rémidʒi:z) *n.* one of the primary or secondary quill feathers of a bird's wing [L.= a rower]

Re·mi (reimi), St (c. 437-c. 533), bishop of Reims (c. 458-c. 533), apostle of the Franks. He baptized Clovis (c. 496). Feast: Oct. 1

re·mind (rimáind) *v.t.* to cause (a person) to remember **re·mind·er** *n.*

Rem·ing·ton (rémiŋtən), Eliphalet (1793-1861), U.S. inventor, gunsmith, and arms manufacturer. He supplied the U.S. army with rifles in the Mexican War and his firm held many government contracts during the Civil War. The firm began (1870) to manufacture sewing machines and (1873) typewriters

Remington, Frederic Sackrider (1861-1909), U.S. artist whose works depicted the Wild West. After traveling through the West as a young man, he settled (1891) in New Rochelle, N.Y., and painted and sculpted in clay for bronze casting, taking time out to serve as an illustrator and correspondent in Cuba for a

magazine during the Spanish-American War (1898). His works include numerous book illustrations and the sculptures 'Trooper of the Plains' (1868), 'Bronco Buster' (1895) and 'Comin' through the Rye' (1902)

rem·i·nisce (reminís) *pres. part.* **rem·i·nisc·ing** *past* and *past part.* **rem·i·nisced** *v.i.* to recall memories of past events, esp. in relating them to others [REMINISCENCE]

rem·i·nis·cence (reminís'ns) *n.* something which is remembered ‖ (*pl.*) personal memories of past events ‖ reminiscing, *evenings given up to reminiscence* ‖ something which reminds one of someone or something else [F. *réminiscence* or fr. L.L. *reminiscentia*]

rem·i·nis·cent (reminís'nt) *adj.* indulging in memories ‖ (with 'of') apt to call up memories, *it is reminiscent of his earlier book* [fr. L. *reminiscens (reminiscentis)* fr. *reminisci*, to remember]

re·mise (rimí:z) 1. *n.* (*fencing*) the second of two thrusts made on one lunge 2. *v. pres. part.* **re·mis·ing** *past* and *past part.* **re·mised** *v.i.* (*fencing*) to make a remise ‖ (rimáiz) *v.t.* (*law*) to give or release (property) to another person [F.=restoration]

re·miss (rimís) *adj.* neglectful of doing one's duty or work efficiently ‖ marked by such negligence [fr. L. *remittere (remissus)*, to send back]

re·mis·si·ble (rimísəb'l) *adj.* able to be remitted [F. *rémissible* or fr. L. *remissibilis*]

re·mis·sion (rimíʃən) *n.* forgiveness, *the remission of sins* ‖ a decrease in the magnitude of a force etc. ‖ a remitting of a debt, fine etc. [O.F.]

re·mis·sive (rimísiv) *adj.* characterized by remission [fr. M.L. *remissivus*]

re·mit (rimít) *pres. part.* **re·mit·ting** *past* and *past part.* **re·mit·ted** *v.t.* to send (e.g. a decision or a report) to an authority for further consideration ‖ to return (a case) to a lower court ‖ to postpone ‖ to forgive (a sin) ‖ to waive (a debt, fine, penalty etc.) ‖ to send (money) by mail or other means ‖ *v.i.* to become less in force, intensity etc. [fr. L. *remittere*, to send back]

re·mit·tal (rimít'l) *n.* a remission [REMIT]

re·mit·tance (rimít'ns) *n.* the sending of money ‖ the money sent [REMIT]

remittance man (esp. *Br.*) a man living abroad on money sent to him from home

re·mit·tent (rimít'nt) *adj.* abating at intervals; *a remittent fever* [fr. L. *remittens (remittentis)* fr. *remittere*, to send back]

re·mit·ter (rimítər) *n.* (*law*) the substitution of a more valid claim to property than the claim under which a person is holding it ‖ (*law*) the remitting of a case to another court [fr. REMIT, (obs.) to surrender (a claim or property)]

rem·nant (rémnənt) *n.* a small remaining part, number, amount etc., *the last remnants of his self-control* ‖ a piece, esp. the end piece, of a roll of fabric remaining unused or unsold [fr. older *remenant* fr. O.F. *remenoir*, to remain]

re·mod·el (ri:mɔ́d'l) *v.t. pres. part.* **re·mod·el·ing**, esp. *Br.* **re·mod·el·ling** *past* and *past part.* **re·mod·eled**, esp. *Br.*, **re·mod·elled** to give new shape or form to

Re·món Can·te·ra (remɔ́nkɑntéra), José Antonio (1908-55), Panamanian soldier and president of the Republic (1952-5). He was assassinated

re·mon·e·ti·za·tion (ri:mʌnitizéiʃən, ri:mɔniti-zéiʃən) *n.* a remonetizing or being remonetized

re·mon·e·tize (ri:mʌ́nitaiz, ri:mɔ́nitaiz) *pres. part.* **re·mon·e·tiz·ing** *past* and *past part.* **re·mon·e·tized** *v.t.* to make (a metal) legal again as the basis of coinage

re·mon·strance (rimɔ́nstrəns) *n.* a remonstrating or an instance of this ‖ (*Br. hist.*) a formal public statement of protest against wrongs (*GRAND REMONSTRANCE) **Re·mon·strance** (*hist.*) the document in which 46 Dutch Arminians set out their differences from the Reformed Church, addressing it to the States General of the Netherlands (1610) [O.F.]

Re·mon·strant (rimɔ́nstrənt) 1. *n.* an Arminian of the Dutch Reformed Church deriving from those who presented the Remonstrance of 1610. The Remonstrants were banned in the Netherlands (1619-25) and were recognized as an independent Church (1795) 2. *adj.* of or pertaining to these Arminians [fr. M.L. *remonstrans (remonstrantis)* fr. *remonstrare*, to remonstrate]

re·mon·strate (rimɔ́nstreit) *pres. part.* **re·mon·strat·ing** *past* and *past part.* **re·mon·strat·ed**

v.i. to express opposition or disapproval ‖ *v.t.* to say or urge in protest **re·mon·stra·tion** (rɪ:mɒnstréiʃən) *n.* **re·mon·stra·tive** (rimɒnstrə-tiv) *adj.* [fr. M.L. *remonstrare* (*remonstratus*), to remonstrate]

re·mon·tant (rimɒ́ntənt) 1. *adj.* (of a rose bush) blooming more than once in a year 2. *n.* a remontant rose bush [F. fr. *remonter*, to climb back up]

rem·o·ra (rémərə) *n.* any of several carnivorous fishes of *Echeneis* and related genera which attach themselves by a sucking disk to sharks and other large fishes and to ships. They inhabit warm seas [L. fr. *re*, back+ *mora*, delay]

re·morse (rimɔ́rs) *n.* the emotion associated with painful recollection of something one would prefer not to have done or said, usually because it hurt others **re·mórse·ful** *adj.* **re·mórse·less** *adj.* without remorse, without mercy ‖ not ceasing to cause pain or discomfort, a *remorseless wind* [O.F. *remors*]

re·mote (rimóut) *adj.* at a great distance in space or time ‖ far removed from a place, person etc. ‖ out-of-the-way, rarely frequented ‖ exhibiting great differences, *remote theories* ‖ (of an idea, intention, possibility etc.) very slight ‖ not closely related, *a remote cousin* [fr. L. *removere* (*remotus*), to move back]

remote bath (*computer*) data stored in peripheral units

remote control control exercised from some distance, usually by using an electrical circuit or radio waves ‖ a device by which this is effected

remote sensing data gathering from a great distance by infrared photography, radar, and other techniques

re·mount 1. (ri:máunt) *v.t.* to mount again 2. (rí:maunt, ri:máunt) *n.* a fresh horse

re·mov·a·bil·i·ty (rimu:vəbíliti:) *n.* the state or quality of being removable

re·mov·a·ble (rimú:vəb'l) *adj.* able to be removed from a place or office

re·mov·al (rimú:vəl) *n.* a removing or being removed ‖ a discharge from office ‖ (*Br.*) the moving of furniture and possessions out of one's old home to a new one ‖ a change of residence

re·move (rimú:v) 1. *pres. part.* **re·mov·ing** *past* and *past part.* **re·moved** *v.t.* to move from a place ‖ to eliminate, *he removed all traces of having been there* ‖ to take off, *remove your hat* ‖ to dismiss from office or to transfer to another post ‖ (*Br.*) to transfer (one's personal effects) from one dwelling to another ‖ *v.i.* (*Br.*) to change one's place of residence 2. *n.* (fig.) a degree of difference, *it is many removes from what he would like* ‖ a specified distance in relationship, *a cousin at first remove* **re·móved** *adj.* distant by a specified number of degrees of relationship, *a second cousin once removed* ‖ remote, distant **re·móv·er** *n.* [O.F. *remeuvoir*, *remouvoir*]

Rem·scheid (rémʃait) a town (pop. 129,300) of North Rhine-Westphalia, West Germany, in the Ruhr: tool and dye making, cutlery, metallurgy, chemicals

Rem·sen (rémsən), Ira (1846-1927), U.S. chemist, best known for his research in organic chemistry, esp. on saccharin. He founded the department of chemistry at Johns Hopkins and served (1901-13) as the university's second president

REM sleep (*physiol.*) deep sleep pattern in which rapid eye movement takes place, characterized by sudden electroencephalograph arousal, slowing of heart rate, and dreams. *also* paradoxical sleep

re·mu·ner·ate (rimjú:nəreit) *pres. part.* **re·mu·ner·at·ing** *past* and *past part.* **re·mu·ner·at·ed** *v.t.* to pay money, or make a gift, to (someone) in return for his services ‖ to compensate for (an expenditure of time, trouble or money) **re·mu·ner·á·tion** *n.* a remunerating ‖ the money or gift received by the person remunerated **re·mú·ner·a·tive** *adj.* paying, producing a good profit or carrying a good salary [fr. L. *remunerari* (*remuneratus*), to reward]

Remus *ROMULUS AND REMUS

ren·ais·sance (rénisans, rɛnisáns, rənesás) *n.* a revival or rebirth **Ren·ais·sance** 1. *n.* the artistic, literary and scientific revival which originated in Italy in the 14th c. and which influenced the rest of Europe in a great variety of ways in the next two centuries. Broadly, it was typified by the spread of humanism, a return to classical values and the beginning of

objective scientific inquiry ‖ this period of history, considered as intermediate between the Middle Ages and modern times 2. *adj.* of or relating to the Renaissance or its style in art, architecture, music etc. [F.]
—The term 'Renaissance' was given currency in the 19th c. by Burckhardt, who emphasized the contrast between the Church-centered culture of the Middle Ages and the new sense of the primacy of personality of 14th-c. Italy. More recent research sees the Italian Renaissance as the result of gradual change rather than as a break with the past, and emphasizes earlier cultural revivals in the Middle Ages. The political and economic situation of Italy in the 14th c. was peculiarly favorable to the development of the Renaissance. The presence of a wealthy leisured class of merchants and bankers made secular patronage of men of genius possible. The city-states were ruled by families (e.g. Medici, Sforza, Este) for whom lavish patronage of the arts was often a means of justifying their otherwise weak title to political power. In Florence in the 14th c., Petrarch and Boccaccio revived interest in humanist and classical learning, while Giotto brought a new realism to art. In the 15th c. the invention of printing, and the founding of libraries and academies by princes and popes, helped to spread the new ideas. Uccello, Fra Angelico, Botticelli and Pollaiuolo excelled in painting, Donatello and Ghiberti in sculpture and Brunelleschi in architecture. The Renaissance reached its height in the 16th c., esp. under the patronage of Julius II and Leo X, with Michelangelo, Leonardo da Vinci and Raphael in Rome and Giovanni Bellini and Titian in Venice. Ariosto and Tasso used Italian for epic poetry, and Machiavelli brought a new approach to political thought. Palestrina was the glory of Renaissance music. The Italian Wars (1494–1559) ended political stability, but were effective in spreading the Renaissance to other parts of Europe. In France the Renaissance gave rise, under the patronage of François I, to the chateaus of the Loire valley and to the writings of Ronsard and Rabelais, and, later, to those of Montaigne. In Germany and the Netherlands, the dominant literary figure was Erasmus, while the critical spirit of the Renaissance may be said to have contributed to the development of the Reformation. Dürer, Holbein and the Bruegel family dominated in the arts. In Spain the leading figures were El Greco, Cervantes and Lope de Vega. In England the influence of the Renaissance is seen in Colet and More as well as in Shakespeare and Marlowe. The new scientific spirit of inquiry was fruitful esp. in astronomy with the work of Copernicus and Galileo, and in the new studies of psychology, ethics, anatomy and philology. The Renaissance created a culture which, though based in large part on the imitation of the ancients, freed men to prove and enjoy the world in a way not possible under the medieval Church's dispensation. In this release lay the way of development of the modern world

Renaissance man a man of wide knowledge in many fields

Renaissance woman a woman of wide knowledge in many fields

re·nal (rí:n'l) *adj.* pertaining to or near the kidneys [F. *rénal* or fr. L.L. *renalis*]

Re·nan (rənã), Joseph Ernest (1823-92), French historian and critic. He studied for the priesthood but lost his faith and instead devoted himself to the history of languages and religions, and to scientific studies. His exegetical work strengthened him in his rationalism and his faith in science ('l'Avenir de la science', 1890, 'Histoire des origines du Christianisme', 1863-81). In his 'Vie de Jésus' (1863) he describes Christ as an 'incomparable man', but man only, not divine. He had great influence on students and young writers in the 1880s. He also wrote the autobiographical 'Souvenirs d'enfance et de jeunesse' (1883)

Re·nard (rənær), Jules (1864-1910), French writer. His bitter attacks on middle-class society are relieved by passages of poignant tenderness. His best-known novel is 'Poil de carotte' (1894)

re·nas·cence (rinǽs'ns) *n.* a renaissance, revival **Re·nas·cence** the Renaissance **re·nás·cent** *adj.* coming into existence again, *renascent militarism* [fr. L. *renascens* (*renascentis*) fr. *renasci*, to be born again]

rend (rend) *pres. part.* **rend·ing** *past* and *past part.* **rent** (rent) *v.t.* to split or tear violently ‖ to

pull away, wrench out with great force ‖ to cause emotional pain to ‖ to divide into bitter factions ‖ *v.i.* to become torn or split **to rend the air** (of screams, bullets etc.) to pierce or shatter the silence [O.E. *rendan*]

rend·er (réndər) 1. *v.t.* to give (what is due), *to render thanks to God* ‖ to submit (a bill) for payment ‖ to do (a service) ‖ to cause to become, *the blow rendered him unconscious* ‖ to melt (fat) ‖ to clarify (a fat) by melting ‖ to extract the fat from by melting ‖ (*building*) to cover with a render ‖ to translate ‖ to interpret, express artistically 2. *n.* (*building*) a first thin coat of plaster or cement applied to a wall ‖ (*hist.*) a return in money, kind or service made by a tenant to his lord **rénd·er·ing** *n.* the process of melting or extracting fat ‖ (*building*) the application of a render ‖ an artistic version or interpretation ‖ a translation ‖ an architect's perspective drawing for a building [A.F.=to give back]

ren·dez·vous (rándivu:, róndivu:) 1. *pl.* **rendez·vous** (rándivu:z, róndeivu:z) *n.* an agreement to meet ‖ a place agreed upon for a meeting ‖ a meeting at an agreed time and place ‖ a place where people habitually gather, *a gourmets' rendezvous* 2. *v.i.* to meet at an agreed time and place ‖ *v.t.* (esp. *mil.*) to assemble (e.g. troops, ships) at an agreed time and place [F. *rendez vous*, present or take yourselves]

ren·di·tion (rendíʃən) *n.* a translation ‖ an artist's interpretation of a dramatic part or piece of music [obs. F. fr. *rendre*, to render]

ren·e·gade (rénigeid) *n.* (used esp. in apposition) someone who throws over authority or allegiance and gives himself to another, usually opposed, allegiance, *a renegade priest*, *a renegade socialist* [fr. Span. *renegado*, an apostate]

re·nege (riníg, riní:g, rinég) 1. *v.i. pres. part.* **re·neg·ing** *past* and *past part.* **re·neged** to go back on a promise ‖ to go back on an agreement, position etc. ‖ (*cards*) to revoke 2. *n.* (*cards*) a revoke [fr. M.L. *renegare*, to deny]

re·new (rinú:, rinjú:) *v.t.* to make new again or as if new ‖ to begin again after an interval of time, *to renew one's efforts* ‖ to revive, reawaken, *to renew one's interest* ‖ to make (a contract) valid for a further period, *to renew a lease* ‖ to replace, replenish, *to renew stock* ‖ *v.i.* to become new or as if new again **re·néw·al** *n.* a renewing or being renewed

re·new·a·ble (rinú:əb'l) *adj.* replaceable naturally or by human activity, e.g., of forests

Ren·frew (rénfru:) a county (area 239 sq. miles, pop. 339,000) of S.W. Scotland. County town: Renfrew (pop. 18,000). Administrative center: Paisley

Reni *GUIDO RENI

re·ni·form (rí:nifɔrm, réniform) *adj.* (*bot.*) kidney-shaped [fr. Mod. L. *reniformis* fr. L. *ren* (*renis*), kidney + *forma*, form]

re·nin (rí:nin) *n.* a protein occurring in the kidney thought to increase blood pressure [fr. L. *ren* (*renis*), kidney]

Rennes (ren) the chief town (pop. 234,000) in Ille-et-Vilaine, France, the old capital in Brittany. Industries: mechanical engineering, textiles, food processing. Courthouse (17th c.), the former parliament of Brittany. University (1735)

ren·net (rénit) *n.* curdled milk from the stomach of an unweaned calf, used to curdle milk by coagulating the protein ‖ the membrane lining the stomach, esp. the abomasum of some young animals, esp. the calf, or a prepared extract of such a membrane. They are both used for curdling milk ‖ any natural or artificial product used for this purpose ‖ rennin [fr. obs. *renne* fr. RUN]

rennet casein casein (insoluble protein)

Ren·nie (réni:), John (1761-1821), Scottish civil engineer. He designed and built several bridges and docks in London

ren·nin (rénin) *n.* an enzyme of the gastric juice of young animals which coagulates the protein in milk [RENNET]

Re·no (rí:nou) a city (pop. 100,756) in Nevada on the Truckee River. Industries: mining, gambling, tourism (largely owing to the relative liberality of the state divorce laws). University of Nevada (1886)

re·no·gram (rí:nəgræm) *n.* a photographic record of the movement of a tagged radioactive renal excretion. *also* nephrogram —**renogra·phy** *n.* the process

Re·noir (rənwær), Jean (1894-1979), French film director. Among his films are: 'la Grande

Illusion' (1937), 'la Bête humaine' (1939), 'la Règle du jeu' (1941), 'The River' (1952)

Renoir, Pierre Auguste (1841-1919), French Impressionist painter. Working with Monet in the late 1860s, he painted from nature and also developed the broken-color technique (*MONET). His early paintings include many kinds of subject: portraits, flowers, nudes, modern life, landscapes. After 1882, when he first went to Italy, he supplemented the techniques of Impressionism with much careful working out of the elements of the picture, exploitation of limited (pink and red) color ranges etc. His later subjects are mostly female nudes. These differ from other Impressionist nudes in that there is a fine fleshiness in them, a solidity, and indeed sensuality

re·nounce (rináuns) 1. *v. pres. part.* **re·nounc·ing** *past and past part.* **re·nounced** *v.t.* to refuse to have anything to do with, repudiate || to give up, *to renounce a claim* || to decline or abandon (a legal right) || *v.i.* (*cards*) to fail to follow suit through inability to do so || (*cards*) to revoke 2. *n.* (*cards*) an instance of renouncing || (*cards*) a revoking [fr. F. *renoncer*]

ren·o·vate (rénəveit) *pres. part.* **ren·o·vat·ing** *past and past part.* **ren·o·vat·ed** *v.t.* to make as good as new, *to renovate a house* [fr. L. *renovare* (*renovatus*)]

ren·o·va·tion (renəvéiʃən) *n.* a renovating or being renovated [F. *rénovation* or fr. L. *renovatio* (*renovationis*)]

ren·o·va·tor (rénəveitər) *n.* someone who renovates or restores (e.g. paintings or furniture)

re·nown (rináun) *n.* public recognition, fame [A.F. *renoun, renun*]

re·nowned (rináund) *adj.* famous || widely known, *renowned for his generosity* [fr. O. F. *renoumer*, to make famous]

rent (rent) *n.* a payment made usually at fixed intervals to an owner of land or property in return for the right to occupy or use it [O.F. *rente*]

rent *v.t.* to occupy or use (land or property owned by another), paying rent for doing so || to allow another to occupy or use (one's land or property) in return for payment || *v.i.* to command rent, *the house rents at a high sum* [fr. O.F. *renter*]

rent *past and past part.* of REND

rent *n.* the result of rending, e.g. a tear, hole or gap || a schism [fr. obs. *rent* v., *var.* of REND]

rent·al (rént'l) 1. *n.* a sum paid as rent || income from rents || a house etc. offered for rent || a renting 2. *adj.* pertaining to rent [A.F.]

rental library a library lending books for a fee

rent·er (réntər) *n.* someone who pays rent || someone who permits occupation or use of his land or property in return for rent || (*Br.*) a distributor in the movie business

rent-free (réntfri:) 1. *adv.* without payment of rent 2. *adj.* occupied or used without payment of rent

ren·tier (rätjei) *n.* someone whose income is drawn from his investments or from rents on property [F.]

rent-roll (réntroul) *n.* a list of properties which bring in an income from rent || the total of this income, esp. as an indication of market value

Rentsch·ler (réntʃlər), Harvey Clayton (1881-1949), U.S. physicist. He pioneered (1922) in refining pure uranium from uranium salts. During the 2nd world war, while employed at Westinghouse Electric Corporation, he was the only man who could provide the three tons of pure uranium needed for the atomic bomb project

rent strike a protest action (as against lack of services) by tenants by withholding rents or placing the rents into a special fund, such rents to be paid upon the landlord's compliance with tenants' demands

re·nun·ci·a·tion (rinʌnsi:éiʃən) *n.* a renouncing, esp. the giving up of a pleasure or of a claim, right etc. || very strict self-denial || (*Br.*) a written statement embodying the giving up of a claim or right **re·nun·ci·a·to·ry** (rinʌnsi:ətɔri:, rinʌnsi:ətɔuri:) *adj.* [fr. L. *renunciatio* (*renunciationis*)]

Ren·wick (rénwik), James (1792-1863), U.S. educator and engineer who became (1853) the first professor emeritus of Columbia University. He constructed the Morris Canal, connecting the Hudson and Delaware Rivers, and surveyed (1840) the disputed boundary between the U.S.A. and New Brunswick, Canada, which led to the Webster-Ashburton Treaty

re·o·pen (ri:óupən) *v.t.* to open again || to make a fresh start on

re·or·der (ri:ɔ́rdər) 1. *v.t.* to give as a reorder || to reorganize || *v.i.* to give a reorder 2. *n.* a repeat order for goods previously supplied

re·or·gan·i·za·tion (ri:ɔrgənizéiʃən) *n.* a reorganizing or being reorganized

re·or·gan·ize (ri:ɔ́rgənaiz) *pres. part.* **re·or·gan·iz·ing** *past and past part.* **re·or·gan·ized** *v.t.* to organize again, usually by rearranging

re·o·vi·rus (rí:ouvairəs) (*med. acronym*) for respiratory enteric orphan virus, any of a group of relatively large (72 millimicrons) RNA viruses, that are parasitic for humans and most animals, and believed to cause intestinal ailments and tumors

rep, repp (rep) *n.* a strong fabric with a finely corded surface, used chiefly in upholstery [fr. F. *reps*, origin unknown]

re·paint 1. (ri:péint) *v.t.* to paint again 2. (rí:peint) *n.* a repainting || something repainted || a repainted golf ball

re·pair (ripéər) *v.i.* (*rhet.*) to go to a specified place, esp. often as a party [O. F. *repeirer, repairer*]

repair 1. *v.t.* to make (something) good, strong, whole etc. after damage, injury etc. || to right (a wrong) or make good (a loss) 2. *n.* a repairing or being repaired || (often *pl.*) an instance of repairing or the result of this || a state of good condition, *to keep in repair* **in good (bad)** **repair** in good (bad) condition [O.F. *reparer*]

re·pand (ripænd) *adj.* (of a leaf) having a wavy margin [fr. L. *repandus*, bent back]

rep·a·ra·ble (répərəb'l) *adj.* able to be repaired or remedied

rep·a·ra·tion (repəréiʃən) *n.* a putting into good condition again or being so repaired || a righting of a wrong || something done or paid as compensation for a wrong || (*pl.*) the money or services paid by a defeated nation as compensation for the destruction and loss it has inflicted [O.F. *reparacion*]

rep·ar·tee (repartí:, repartéi) *n.* quick, witty exchange between two speakers, in which each speaker makes a reply which neatly destroys the force of what the other has just said || the practice or art of making such replies [fr. F. *repartie* fr. *repartir*, to set out again]

re·par·ti·mien·to (reparti:mjénto) *n.* an official act of distribution of Indian workers to Spanish colonists in Latin America, after the decline of the encomienda [Span.]

re·par·ti·tion (ri:partíʃən) *n.* distribution || a fresh distribution

re·pass (ri:pǽs, ri:pás) *v.t.* to pass again || to cause to pass again || *v.i.* to pass again, esp. in the opposite direction **re·pas·sage** (ri:pǽsidʒ) *n.* a repassing || the right to repass [F. *repasser*]

re·past (ri:pǽst, ri:pást) *n.* (*rhet.*) a meal || (*rhet.*) the food eaten at a meal [O.F.]

re·pa·tri·ate 1. (ri:péitri:eit, ri:pǽtri:eit) *v. pres. part.* **re·pa·tri·at·ing** *past and past part.* **re·pa·tri·at·ed** *v.t.* to send back to the country of origin || *v.i.* to go back to the country of origin 2. (ri:péitri:it, ri:pǽtri:it) *n.* a repatriated person **re·pa·tri·a·tion** *n.* [fr. L.L. *repatriare* (*repatriatus*)]

re·pay (ri:péi) *pres. part.* **re·pay·ing** *past and past part.* **re·paid** (ri:péid) *v.t.* to pay back (money) || to pay (someone) back || to return (e.g. a service), *to repay someone's kindness* || to recompense, *to be repaid for one's trouble* || to requite, *he repaid the trick by setting his dog on them* || *v.i.* to make repayment **re·pay·a·ble** *adj.* able or due to be repaid **re·pay·ment** *n.* a paying back or an instance of this || the sum repaid [fr. O.F. *repaier, rapaier*]

re·peal (ripí:l) *n.* a repealing or an instance of this [A.F. *repel*]

repeal *v.t.* to cancel, revoke (a decision or enactment previously made) [fr. A.F. *repeller, repeler*]

re·peat (ripí:t) 1. *v.t.* to say again, *to repeat a statement* || to do or make again, *to repeat a visit* || to say from memory or after someone else || to say to another (what one has oneself been told), *to repeat gossip* || to undergo again, *to repeat an experience* || to cause or allow to recur, *the second room repeats the decorative motif* || (of a student) to take (a course or term) again because of previous failure || *v.i.* to say or do something again || to occur again || to vote more than once in an election **not to bear repeating** to be unworthy of being repeated **to repeat oneself** to say, write or do again what one has already said etc., or something very like it 2. *n.*

a repeating || something repeated || (*mus.*) a passage to be played twice || (*mus.*) the symbol for this (:||) **re·peat·ed·ly** *adv.* over and over again, *she told him repeatedly* **re·peat·er** *n.* someone or something that repeats || a repeating watch or clock which strikes the last hour, quarter hour and the subsequent number of minutes when a spring is released || a rifle, shotgun or pistol which can fire a number of times without reloading || a person who repeats in an election || a student who has to repeat a class or term || (*telegraphy*) an automatic relay for switching a message from a weak circuit to a strong one [fr. F. *répéter*]

repeating decimal a recurring decimal

re·pel (ripél) *pres. part.* **re·pel·ling** *past and past part.* **re·pelled** *v.t.* to exert a force tending to move (a body) further away, *like magnetic poles repel one another* || to drive back, *to repel an attack* || to repress, *to repel a desire to turn and run* || to discourage, *to repel an offer of friendship* || to cause not to adhere, penetrate etc., *to repel moisture* || to cause to feel aversion, to repulse, *the sight of such luxury repelled him* [fr. L. *repellere*]

re·pel·lent (ripélənt) 1. *adj.* repelling, driving back || causing aversion 2. *n.* a preparation for repelling insects or pests || a solution which makes a fabric resist moisture, liquids, etc. [fr. L. *repellens* (*repellentis*) fr. *repellere*, to drive back]

re·pent (rí:pənt) *adj.* (*bot.*) creeping || (*zool.*) crawling [fr. L. *repens* (*repentis*) fr. *repere*, to crawl]

re·pent (ripént) *v.i.* to grieve for sins committed or for things sinfully left undone || (often with 'of') to feel extreme regret for what one has done or forgotten or omitted to do, *he repented of his decision to lend the boy his car* || to change one's mind and regret the original decision, *he thinks he has been clever but he will live to repent* || *v.t.* to think with contrition of or do penance for, *to repent one's sins* [fr. F. *repentir*]

re·pent·ance (ripéntəns) *n.* the act of repenting || a feeling of contrition or act of penance for sins committed [F.]

re·pent·ant (ripéntənt) *adj.* feeling repentance || indicating repentance [F.]

re·peo·ple (ri:pí:p'l) *pres. part.* **re·peo·pling** *past and past part.* **re·peo·pled** *v.t.* to furnish (a region) again with people

re·per·cus·sion (ri:pərkʌ́ʃən) *n.* a recoil, e.g. of a gun || a reverberation, echo || a usually unanticipated and indirect reaction to some event, *nonratification of the treaty would have grave repercussions* || (*mus.*, in a fugue) the reappearance of the subject and answer after an episode [F. *répercussion* or fr. L. *repercussio* (*repercussionis*)]

rep·er·toire (répərtwar, répərtwɔr) *n.* a collection of anecdotes, songs, plays, pieces of music etc. which a person or group of persons is able to present or perform || an inventory of capabilities || (*computer*) the operations that can be contained in a specific code [F. *répertoire*]

rep·er·to·ry (répərtɔri, répərtouri:, *Br.* répətri) *pl.* **rep·er·to·ries** *n.* a repertoire || any store or stock (e.g. of information) that can be drawn on [fr. L. *repertorium*, catalog, storehouse]

repertory theater, *Br.* **repertory theatre** a theater where a permanent acting company presents its repertoire of plays

rep·e·ti·tion (repitíʃən) *n.* a repeating or being repeated || something done or said again || the ability of a keyboard instrument to respond to the striking of the same note in rapid succession [O.F. *repeticion* or fr. L. *repetitio* (*repetitionis*)]

rep·e·ti·tious (repitíʃəs) *adj.* full of repetition, esp. boringly so [fr. L. *repetere* (*repetitus*), to repeat]

re·pet·i·tive (ripétitiv) *adj.* repeating or tending to repeat || repetitious [fr. L. *repetere* (*repetitus*), to repeat]

re·phrase (ri:fréiz) *pres. part.* **re·phras·ing** *past and past part.* **re·phrased** *v.t.* to express again in a different way

re·pine (ripáin) *pres. part.* **re·pin·ing** *past and past part.* **re·pined** *v.i.* (*rhet.*, often with 'at') to feel or express discontent

re·pique (ri:pí:k) 1. *n.* (*piquet*) the scoring of 30 points from the cards held before play begins 2. *v. pres. part.* **re·piqu·ing** *past and past part.* **re·piqued** *v.t.* to make this score against || *v.i.* (*piquet*) to make this score [fr. F. *repic*]

re·place (ripléis) *pres. part.* **re·plac·ing** *past and past part.* **re·placed** *v.t.* to put back (something) in its original place ‖ to take the place of (someone or something), *Smith replaced Brown* ‖ to fill the place of (someone or something) with another, *he replaced Brown by Smith* **re·pláce·ment** *n.* a replacing or being replaced ‖ someone or something that replaces ‖ a person immediately available for assignment to a military or naval unit

re·plead·er (ri:plí:dər) *n.* (*law*) a second pleading ‖ (*law*) the right to a second pleading

re·plen·ish (riplénif) *v.t.* to fill again, *to replenish a glass* ‖ to get a new supply of, *to replenish one's stores* **re·plén·ish·ment** *n.* [fr. O.F. *repliner (repleniss-)*]

re·plete (riplí:t) *adj.* gorged, *replete with food* ‖ richly supplied or imbued, *replete with humor* ‖ completely filled **re·plé·tion** *n.* [F. *replet* or fr. L. *replere (repletus)*, to fill again]

re·plev·in (riplévin) 1. *n.* (*law*) a replevying ‖ (*law*) an action for replevying ‖ (*law*) the writ by which goods or property are replevied 2. *v.t.* (*law*) to replevy [A.F.]

re·plev·y (riplévi:) 1. *v. pres. part.* **re·plev·y·ing** *past* and *past part.* **re·plev·ied** *v.t.* (*law*) to take possession of (disputed goods or property) subject to an undertaking to submit the dispute to a court and surrender the property if the court so decrees ‖ *v.i.* (*law*) to take possession of goods, or property by replevin 2. *n.* (*law*) a replevin

rep·li·ca (réplikə) *n.* an accurate copy of a painting, statue etc., esp. one made by the artist who made the original ‖ someone or something very closely resembling someone or something else [Ital.]

rep·li·case (réplikeis) *n.* an enzyme that synthesizes RNA from DNA. **also** RNA polymerase — **replicate** *v.* —**replicative** *adj.* Cf DNA POLYMERASE, RIBONUCLEASE

rep·li·cate 1. (réplikit) *adj.* folded back on itself 2. (réplikit) *n.* (*mus.*) a tone which is one or more octaves above or below another 3. (réplikeit) *v.t. pres. part.* **rep·li·cat·ing** *past* and *past part.* **rep·li·cat·ed** (*biol.*) to repeat or duplicate (e.g. a procedure or experiment) **rép·li·cat·ed** *adj.* replicate [fr. L. *replicare (replicatus)*, to fold back]

rep·li·ca·tion (réplikéifən) *n.* (*law*) the plaintiff's reply to the defense ‖ (*biol.*) a replicating or being replicated ‖ repetition of an experiment under the same conditions, e.g., to verify the results ‖ (*biol.*) reproduction of bacteriophage in order to enlarge itself ‖ (*biol.*) division of cells for reproduction [O.F.]

rep·li·somes (réplisoumz) *n.* (*genetics*) fixed points in chromosomes at which genetic factors are transferred

re·ply (riplái) 1. *v. pres. part.* **re·ply·ing** *past* and *past part.* **re·plied** *v.t.* to say or write (something) in return, after a question, letter etc. ‖ *v.i.* to say or write something in return ‖ to act by way of a return, *he replied with a round of shots* ‖ (*law*) to plead so as to deal with the case put forward by a defendant 2. *pl.* **re·plies** *n.* a replying ‖ something said, written or done in replying to a question, letter, action etc. ‖ (*law*) the plaintiff's reply to the defense [fr. O.F. *replier*]

re·ply-paid (ripláipéid) *adj.* (of a telegram) having a reply by telegram paid for in advance by the sender ‖ (of a letter or postcard, used esp. in publicity drives) for which the person to whom it is addressed bears the postage

re·port (ripórt, ripóurt) *n.* something reported, esp. a formal account of what has been said, seen or done ‖ an unsubstantiated item of information or news ‖ (*rhet.*) repute, *of good report* ‖ a loud explosive noise, *the report of a firearm* ‖ a periodic statement of a student's academic rating and sometimes his school conduct, sent to his parents [O.F. *report, raport*]

report 1. *v.t.* to give information about or relate (e.g. what one has seen or heard) ‖ to repeat (a message) ‖ to register a complaint about to someone in authority, *he reported the driver to the foreman* ‖ to make known to the correct authority, *to report a theft to an insurance company* ‖ to write an account of (some event etc.), esp. for publication ‖ to tell about following inquiry, investigation etc., *to report the results of research* ‖ to give a formal statement of ‖ *v.i.* to make a report ‖ to work as a reporter ‖ to make one's arrival or presence known by presenting oneself, *he reported to the office at noon* [O.F. *reporter*]

report card a periodic report on a student's academic achievement etc. sent to his parents

re·port·ed·ly (ripórtidli) *adv.* on the authority of what people are saying

re·port·er (ripórtər, ripóurtər) *n.* a person who reports, esp. one who writes an account of formal proceedings for the record ‖ a person who writes accounts of events for publication, esp. in a newspaper

report stage the stage reached in parliamentary practice when a committee has considered a bill and reports its findings to the full assembly, between the second and third readings

re·pose (ripóuz) *n.* a state or condition of rest, esp. after work, activity or excitement ‖ sleep ‖ a state of tranquillity ‖ a restful attitude ‖ a restful effect, e.g. in painting [F. *repos*]

repose *pres. part.* **re·pos·ing** *past* and *past part.* **re·posed** *v.i.* to rest ‖ to lie in a restful position ‖ (*rhet.*) to lie in death, *to repose in state* ‖ (with 'on' or 'upon') to have as a support or basis [fr. F. *reposer*]

repose *pres. part.* **re·pos·ing** *past* and *past part.* **re·posed** *v.t.* (usually with 'in') to place (trust, confidence etc.) in someone or something [fr. L. *reponere (repositus)*, to replace]

re·pos·i·to·ry (ripózitəri:, ripózituri:) *pl.* **re·pos·i·to·ries** *n.* a place where things are put for safekeeping ‖ (*rhet.*) a burial vault ‖ anything thought of as a place of storage [fr. obs. F. *repositoire* or L. *repositorium*]

re·pos·sess (ri:pəzés) *v.t.* to possess again ‖ to put in possession again **re·pos·ses·sion** (ri:pəzéfən) *n.*

re·pous·sé (rəpu:séi) 1. *adj.* (of sheet metal) having a pattern in relief made by hammering the reverse face ‖ of a pattern or design formed in this way 2. *n.* metalwork so ornamented ‖ the art of ornamenting metal in this way [F.]

repp *REP

rep·re·hend (reprihénd) *v.t.* to reprimand ‖ to blame, be critical of [fr. L. *reprehendere*]

rep·re·hen·si·ble (reprihénsib'l) *adj.* (of an act or of conduct) that ought to be blamed or punished [fr. L.L. *reprehensibilis*]

rep·re·hen·sion (reprihénfən) *n.* a reprehending [fr. L. *reprehensio (reprehensionis)*]

rep·re·sent (reprizént) *v.t.* to present an image of, *this drawing represents a rocking horse* ‖ to describe as being of a certain kind, *he represented the hovel as 'a desirable residence'* ‖ (*rhet.*) to point out, *he represented to them the folly of such a move* ‖ to act on behalf of, *a lawyer represents his client* ‖ to be the delegate of, esp. to a legislative assembly ‖ to be a fair sample of, *his opinion represents that of the majority* ‖ to be a symbol for, *∞ represents infinity* ‖ to correspond to, *these notes represent eight hours' work* [fr. O.F. *representer* or L. *repraesentare*]

re·pre·sent (ri:prizént) *v.t.* to present again

rep·re·sen·ta·tion (reprizentéifən) *n.* a representing or being represented ‖ something which represents ‖ (*law*) a statement accepted as true and as a reason for entering into a contract **rep·re·sen·tá·tion·al** *adj.* [F. or fr. L. *repraesentatio (repraesentationis)*]

rep·re·sen·ta·tive (reprizéntətiv) 1. *adj.* serving to represent, esp. as being an example of or having the general character of some whole, *this painting is representative of his work* ‖ of, marked by or based on a system of representation by elected delegates, *representative government* 2. *n.* someone or something regarded as characteristic or serving to exemplify ‖ a person who is appointed to act and speak for another person or for a country, company, group etc. ‖ a traveling salesman ‖ in the U.S.A., a member of the elected lower house of Congress (House of Representatives) or of a state legislature (capitalized when used with the representative's name) [fr. F. *représentatif* or M.L. *repraesentativus*]

re·press (riprés) *v.t.* to put down, *to repress an uprising* ‖ to keep back, *to repress tears* ‖ to hinder the natural expression or development of, *to repress a child* ‖ (*psychol.*) to prevent (an idea, desire, memory etc.) from reaching the consciousness [fr. L. *reprimere (repressus)*]

re·pres·sion (ripréfən) *n.* a repressing or being repressed ‖ an instance of repressing ‖ (*psychol.*) a process by which unattainable or unacceptable desires, impulses etc. are repressed ‖ (*psychol.*) a desire, impulse etc. so repressed [fr. L. *repressio (repressionis)*]

re·pres·sive (riprésiv) *adj.* repressing or tending to repress

re·pres·sor (riprésər) *n.* (*genetics*) the product of a metabolic process between a regulator gene

and a genetic operator that tends to halt synthesis of enzymes —**repress** *v.* —**repressible** *adj.* —**repressibility** *n.* Cf ENDUCER

re·prieve (riprí:v) 1. *v. pres. part.* **re·priev·ing** *past* and *past part.* **re·prieved** *v.t.* to suspend the punishment of (a person), esp. by death ‖ to give temporary relief or respite to, e.g. from pain 2. *n.* a reprieving or being reprieved ‖ a revoking or commuting of a punishment, esp. of a death sentence ‖ a document authorizing such a revocation or commutation ‖ a temporary relief from pain or other ill [fr. older *repry*, prob. fr. F. *repris*, past part. of *reprendre*, to take back]

rep·ri·mand (réprimænd, réprimɑnd) *n.* a severe rebuke, esp. by someone in authority [fr. F. *réprimande*]

reprimand *v.t.* to rebuke severely, esp. using authority [fr. F. *réprimander*]

re·print 1. (ri:prínt) *v.t.* to print again 2. (rí:print) *n.* a new copy of an article, book etc. made by printing it again without altering the type ‖ an impression in quantity of a work made in this way ‖ an edition of a work printed by a publisher other than the original one and made without alteration of the text ‖ an offprint

re·pris·al (ripráiz'l) *n.* an injury inflicted in return for one suffered, or as vengeance ‖ the act or practice of using some means of coercion other than war against another nation in order to secure redress against real or imagined injustices an instance of this [O.F. *reprisaille*]

re·prise (ripráiz, riprí:z) *n.* (*law*) an annual payment made as rent or other charge on an estate ‖ (*mus.*) a repeated phrase, after an intervening section has been played [F.]

re·proach (ripróutf) *v.t.* to tell (someone) that he has acted wrongly, esp. when one would not have expected him to do so or because one feels hurt [F. *reprocher*]

reproach *n.* a reproaching ‖ an expression of such reproaching ‖ something which merits reproaching **to bring reproach on** to cause to feel disgraced **the Reproaches** part of the Good Friday ceremonies in Roman Catholic and some Anglican churches, consisting of antiphons and responses which recall what Christ did for man **re·próach·ful** *adj.* [F. *reproche*]

rep·ro·bate (réprəbeit) 1. *adj.* of someone who pursues evil in preference to good ‖ (*theol.*) condemned by God to eternal damnation 2. *n.* a reprobate person 3. *v.t. pres. part.* **rep·ro·bat·ing** *past* and *past part.* **rep·ro·bat·ed** to condemn severely, esp. as being evil ‖ (*theol.*, of God) to condemn to eternal damnation **rep·ro·bá·tion** *n.* [fr. L. *reprobare (reprobatus)*, to reprove]

re·pro·duce (ri:prədú:s, ri:prədjú:s) *pres. part.* **re·pro·duc·ing** *past* and *past part.* **re·pro·duced** *v.t.* to repeat exactly or very closely, *to reproduce Georgian furniture* ‖ to produce (a new individual or new individuals of the same species) by sexual or asexual methods ‖ to cause (a lost part or organ) to be replaced by the growth of a new one ‖ to re-create (e.g. a memory) mentally ‖ to quote the exact text of in writing or printing, *he reproduces extracts from her letters in his autobiography* ‖ to make a copy of, esp. by mechanical means, and use the copy e.g. to illustrate a text ‖ *v.i.* to produce a new individual or new individuals of the same species ‖ (of music, paintings etc.) to be susceptible of recording, printing etc. by mechanical means, *the second movement reproduces very well*

re·pro·duc·i·ble (ri:prədú:sib'l, ri:prədjú:sib'l) *adj.* able to be reproduced

re·pro·duc·tion (ri:prədʌkfən) *n.* a reproducing or being reproduced ‖ a painting, piece of furniture etc. which is a replica of an original ‖ the sexual or asexual process by which animals or plants produce new individuals

reproduction factor the ratio in a nuclear reactor between the number of neutrons produced and the number which vanish. If the factor exceeds unity, the chain reaction builds up until it is maintained at a constant level by reducing the factor to unity again

re·pro·duc·tive (ri:prədʌktiv) *adj.* of or concerned with reproducing or reproduction [REPRODUCE]

reproductive system the system in man and other vertebrates, plants and some invertebrates relating to and effecting reproduction. In the human male it comprises the following organs: the testicles, the two epididymides and vasa deferentia and the penis. In the human female it comprises the two ovaries, the Fallopian tubes, the uterus and the vagina

re·pro·graph·ics (riːprəgrǽfiks) *n.* the field of reproduction of documents, including input, editing, photocomposing, and reproduction; esp. for official use

re·prog·ra·phy (riprógrəfiː) *n.* document reproduction by electronic techniques, e.g., by photocopying —**reprographic** *adj.*

re·proof (riprúːf) *n.* a reproving or an instance of this [O.F. *reprove, reprouve*]

re·prove (riprúːv) *pres. part.* **re·prov·ing** *past and past part.* **re·proved** *v.t.* to rebuke (someone) [fr. O.F. *reprover*]

rep·tant (réptant) *adj.* (*biol.*) creeping or crawling [fr. L. *reptans (reptantis)*]

rep·tile (réptail, réptil) **1.** *n.* a member of *Reptilia*, a class of cold-blooded vertebrates incl. snakes, lizards, crocodiles and turtles etc. They have lungs, a heart with three chambers, and a skin covered with tough scales or plates. Some creep on their bellies, others crawl on very short legs **2.** *adj.* of, like or having the characteristics of a reptile **rep·til·i·an** (reptíljən, reptíliə:n) *adj. and n.* [fr. L.L. *reptilis*, creeping]

re·pub·lic (ripʌ́blik) *n.* a form of government in which the head of state is an elected president rather than a monarch ‖ a form of government in which the sovereign power is widely vested in the people either directly or through elected representatives ‖ a state with either of these forms of government ‖ a society whose members are equally engaged in the same activity, *the republic of letters* [fr. F. *république* or L. *respublica* fr. *res*, affair +*publicus*, public]

re·pub·li·can (ripʌ́blikən) **1.** *adj.* pertaining to, characteristic of or having the nature of, a republic ‖ favoring a republic **Re·pub·li·can** of or belonging to the Republican party **2.** *n.* a person who supports the form of government of a republic **Re·pub·li·can** a member of the Republican party

Republican party one of the two main political parties of the U.S.A. (cf. DEMOCRATIC PARTY). It was formed (1854) by antislavery groups to oppose the Kansas-Nebraska Act, and attracted many Whigs, Free-Soilers and those Know-Nothings who opposed slavery. It rapidly gained power in the North and held its first national convention in 1856. Lincoln became the first Republican president (1861). The Republicans held the presidency from then until 1913, with the exception of the administrations (1885-9 and 1893-7) of Cleveland. They were weakened by the secession of the Liberal Republicans (1872) and the Mugwumps (1884). In the late 19th c. the Republican party favored protective tariffs and the gold standard. After the administrations of Theodore Roosevelt and Taft, the secession of the Progressive party split the Republicans (1912). They returned to power (1921-33) under Harding, Coolidge and Hoover, but were blamed for the economic crisis of 1929 and were out of office until the administration (1953-61) of Eisenhower. They lost (1961-9) the presidency, regaining it with the administration (1969-74) of Richard Nixon. Vice President Gerald Ford assumed the presidency following Nixon's resignation but lost the 1976 election to Democrat Jimmy Carter. The Republicans regained the presidency with Ronald Reagan's landslide victory in 1980, and they controlled the Senate for the first time since 1955. Democrats held control of the House through the 1984 elections, when Reagan was reelected

Republic of Ireland *IRISH REPUBLIC

re·pu·di·ate (ripjúːdiːeit) *pres. part.* **re·pu·di·at·ing** *past and past part.* **re·pu·di·at·ed** *v.t.* to refuse to be concerned with or responsible for (someone) ‖ to refuse to accept (something) as valid or true ‖ to refuse to pay (e.g. a debt or claim) [fr. L. *repudiare (repudiatus)*, to divorce]

re·pu·di·a·tion (ripjuːdiːéiʃən) *n.* a repudiating or being repudiated [fr. L. *repudiatio (repudiationis)*]

re·pug·nance (ripʌ́gnens) *n.* extreme dislike, aversion [F. *répugnance* or fr. L. *repugnantia*]

re·pug·nant (ripʌ́gnənt) *adj.* producing the feeling of repugnance [F. or fr. L. *repugnans (repugnantis)*]

re·pulse (ripʌ́ls) *n.* a repulsing or being repulsed [fr. L. *repulsa* or *repulsus* fr. *repellere (repulsus)*, to drive back]

repulse *pres. part.* **re·puls·ing** *past and past part.* **re·pulsed** *v.t.* to drive back by force ‖ to refuse or reject, *to repulse an offer of help* ‖ to fill

with repulsion [fr. L. *repellere (repulsus)*, to drive back]

re·pul·sion (ripʌ́lʃən) *n.* a repulse ‖ a feeling of repugnance ‖ (*phys.*) the force tending to drive two bodies further apart [fr. L. L. *repulsio (repulsionis)*] ·

re·pul·sive (ripʌ́lsiv) *adj.* causing feelings of repulsion ‖ (*phys.*) tending to repel [REPULSE v.]

re·pu·nit (répjuːnit) *n.* (*math.*) a number consisting entirely of integers, 11, 111, etc., or 99, 999, etc.

re·pur·chase (riːpə́ːrtʃəs) *pres. part.* **re·pur·chas·ing** *past and past part.* **re·pur·chased** **1.** *v.t.* to buy back **2.** *n.* a repurchasing

rep·u·ta·bil·i·ty (repjuːtəbíliti:) *n.* the state or quality of being reputable

rep·u·ta·ble (répjutəb'l) *adj.* having a good reputation ‖ reliable, *a reputable source* **rép·u·ta·bly** *adv.* [fr. older *repute*, to consider fr. F. *réputer* or L. *reputare*]

rep·u·ta·tion (repjutéiʃən) *n.* the general opinion held by people about the merits or demerits of a person or thing ‖ the state or fact of being highly thought of or esteemed ‖ the good name of a person or thing earned through merit and distinction ‖ (usually with 'of') a specified manner, quality etc. generally ascribed to someone or something, *he has the reputation of being an excellent horseman* [fr. L. *reputatio (reputationis)*, consideration]

re·pute (ripjúːt) **1.** *n.* reputation, esp. good reputation, *a writer of repute* **2.** *v.t. pres. part.* **re·put·ing** *past and past part.* **re·put·ed** (esp. used passively) to consider, accord a certain character etc. to, *he is reputed to be rich* **re·pút·ed** *adj.* held in high esteem ‖ generally supposed, *its reputed origin goes back to Roman times* **re·pút·ed·ly** *adv.* by or according to reputation [fr. older *repute*, to consider fr. F. *réputer* or L. *reputare*]

re·quest (rikwést) *n.* an act of requesting something or an instance of this ‖ something requested ‖ the fact or state of being requested, *available on request* **by request** because of or following a request or requests **in request** asked for by many persons, popular [O.F. *requeste*]

request *v.t.* attempt to obtain (something) by making one's wants or desires known in speech or writing ‖ to attempt to get (someone) to do or give something that one wants by making this known in speech or writing ‖ to attempt in speech or writing to obtain permission (to do something) [fr. O.F. *requester*]

req·ui·em (rékwiːəm, ríːkwiːəm) *n.* a Mass for the repose of a deceased person ‖ the musical setting of such a Mass [L., accusative of *requies*, rest (the first word of the introit of the Roman Catholic requiem)]

re·quire (rikwáiər) *pres. part.* **re·quir·ing** *past and past part.* **re·quired** *v.t.* to stipulate, *the law requires that the report must be made annually* ‖ to place an obligation on (someone), *the law requires you to report annually* ‖ to need, *this requires careful consideration* **re·quíre·ment** *n.* something stipulated or demanded ‖ something needed [O. F. *requerre (requer-, requier-)*]

req·ui·site (rékwizit) **1.** *adj.* required **2.** *n.* something required or necessary [fr. L. *requirere (requisitus)*]

req·ui·si·tion (rekwizíʃən) **1.** *n.* a formal taking of control over goods or services under authority, esp. by an army in the field or by the State in a war or other catastrophe ‖ the condition of being taken over for use in this way, *to be on requisition* ‖ a written request or formal demand for goods or supplies under a centralized system of supply **2.** *v.t.* to take control of under authority, *to requisition a house* ‖ to require (someone or something) to provide, *householders were requisitioned to provide shelter for the victims* ‖ to request (goods, supplies etc.) under a centralized system of supply [F. *réquisition* or L. *requisitio (requisitionis)*]

re·quit·al (rikwáit'l) *n.* a requiting or being requited ‖ something given in return for services or retaliation

re·quite (rikwáit) *pres. part* **re·quit·ing** *past and past part.* **re·quit·ed** *v.t.* to repay (someone) for a benefit, injury etc. ‖ to give (something) in return for a benefit, injury etc., *to requite good for evil* [fr. RE- + *quite*, var. of QUIT]

re·ra·di·a·tion (riːreidiːéiʃən) *n.* (*communications*) unwanted radio signals in a receiving instrument

re·ra·di·a·tive (riːréidiːətiv) *adj.* having the ability to reflect radiation

rere·dos (ríərdos) *n.* an ornamental screen behind an altar [A.F. fr. *rere*, back + *dos*, back]

re·run 1. (riːrʌ́n) *v. pres part.* **re·run·ning** *past* **re·ran** (riːrǽn) *past part.* **re·run** *v.t.* to run (esp. a race, movie or television show) again **2.** (riːrʌn) *n.* a replayed T.V. show ‖ the public showing of a movie after withdrawing it from circulation for a time, or the movie itself

Re·sa·ca de la Pal·ma (resákəðelapálma), a valley of the Rio Grande in Texas, site of the second battle (1846) of the Mexican War. Mexican troops under Gen. Mariano Arista, retreating south after the battle of Palo Alto, were defeated by U.S. forces under Gen. Zachary Taylor

re·sale (ríːseil, riːséil) *n.* a selling again or an instance of this

re·scind (risínd) *v.t.* to cancel (a previous decision, regulation etc.) **re·scínd·a·ble** *adj.* [fr. L. *rescindere*]

re·scis·sion (risíʒən) *n.* the act of rescinding [fr. L. *rescissio (rescissionis)*]

re·scis·so·ry (risísəri:, risíʒəri:) *adj.* rescinding [fr. L.L. *rescissorius*]

re·script (ríːskript) *n.* (*hist.*) a written reply by a Roman emperor or a pope to a question of jurisprudence ‖ any official order or announcement by a ruler or government ‖ a rewriting ‖ something rewritten [fr. L. *rescribere (rescriptus)*, to rewrite, to write back]

res·cue (réskjuː) **1.** *pres. part.* **res·cu·ing** *past and past part.* **res·cued** *v.t.* to deliver from danger, harm, evil, violence, imprisonment etc. or the threat of any of these ‖ (*law*) to free from legal custody by force **2.** *n.* the act of rescuing ‖ (*law*) release by force from legal custody [O.F. *rescourre*]

re·search (risə́ːrtʃ) *v.i.* to engage in research [fr. obs. F. *recercher*]

research (risə́ːrtʃ, ríːsəːrtʃ) *n.* a systematic search for facts ‖ scientific investigation [fr. obs. F. *recerche*]

re·seat (riːsíːt) *v.t.* to seat (oneself, a person) again ‖ (*mech.*) to refit in its setting, *to reseat a valve* ‖ to provide (a chair) with a new seat

re·sect (risékt) *v.t.* (*surg.*) to remove a portion of (an organ etc.) [fr. L. *resecare (resectus)*, to cut off]

re·se·da (risíːdə) *n.* a member of *Reseda*, fam. *Resedaceae*, a genus of plants including mignonette, chiefly native to the Mediterranean region, having cleft petals and numerous stamens in their racemose flowers ‖ (also *rézidə*) the greenish-yellow color of some mignonette flowers [fr. L. *resedare*, to assuage (fr. the use of the plants as a charm for curing tumors)]

re·seg·re·ga·tion (riːsegrigéiʃən) *n.* to segregate after having desegregated

re·sem·blance (rizémbləns) *n.* the state, fact or quality of resembling, similarity

re·sem·ble (rizémb'l) *pres. part.* **re·sem·bling** *past and past part.* **re·sem·bled** *v.t.* to be similar to, have the same appearance or nature as [fr. O.F. *resembler*]

re·sent (rizént) *v.t.* to take strong exception to (what is thought to be unjust, interfering, insulting, critical etc.) **re·sént·ful** *adj.* **re·sént·ment** *n.* [fr. F. *ressentir*, to feel the result of]

res·er·va·tion (rezərvéiʃən) *n.* a reserving ‖ something that is reserved ‖ a limitation or qualification, *mental reservation* ‖ (*eccles.*) the practice of keeping in the sanctuary a portion of the consecrated Host ‖ (*eccles.*) the keeping back of the right of granting absolution in certain cases ‖ the engaging in advance of a hotel room, theater seat etc. ‖ a record of such an engaging ‖ a tract of land set aside for some special use [O.F.]

re·serve (rizə́ːrv) *n.* something set aside for future use ‖ limitation, reservation or qualification, *to accept a statement with reserve* ‖ an instance of this ‖ avoidance of familiarity in social relationships ‖ self-restraint in action or speech ‖ (in religious instruction and casuistry) suppression of a part of the truth ‖ (*mil.*, usually *pl.*) troops temporarily withheld from action so that they may be available for special use ‖ (*mil.*) the trained men of a country not in active service, but subject to call in case of war or emergency ‖ one of these men ‖ (*finance*) profit added to capital rather than being paid out to shareholders ‖ (*banking*) assets kept available as cash ‖ (*central banks*) assets held as gold or foreign exchange ‖ a reservation (tract of land) **in reserve** put aside for future use **without**

CONCISE PRONUNCIATION KEY: **(a)** æ, *cat*; ɑ, *car*; ɔ *fawn*; ei, *snake*. **(e)** e, *hen*; iː, *sheep*; iə, *deer*; ɛə, *bear*. **(i)** i, *fish*; ai, *tiger*; əː, *bird*. **(o)** o, *ox*; au, *cow*; ou, *goat*; u, *poor*; ɔi, *royal*. **(u)** ʌ, *duck*; u, *bull*; uː, *goose*; ə, *bacillus*; juː, *cube*. x, *loch*; θ, *think*; ð, *bother*; z, *Zen*; ʒ, *corsage*; dʒ, *savage*; ŋ, *orangutang*; j, *yak*; ʃ, *fish*; tʃ, *fetch*; 'l, *rabble*; 'n, *redden*. Complete pronunciation key appears inside front cover.

reserve (of something sold by auction) not subject to a fixed minimum price [F. *réserve*]

reserve *pres. part.* **re·serv·ing** *past* and *past part.* **re·served** *v.t.* to keep back for future use, *to reserve part of profit for reinvestment* ‖ (esp. with 'for') to set aside or apart for *a* specific use, *this room is reserved for chess players* ‖ to retain legal control of, *author's rights reserved* ‖ to book in advance, *to reserve train seats* ‖ (*eccles.*) to set apart (a portion of the consecrated Host), e.g. for communion of the sick ‖ to retain control of (some power, e.g. to pronounce absolution) [O.F. *reserver*]

reserve bank one of the 12 principal banks of the Federal Reserve System in the U.S.A.

reserve clause (*sports*) provision in a professional athlete's contract that gives a renewal option to the club for the athlete's effective playing life until he or she is traded, sold, etc.

re·served (rizá:rvd) *adj.* disciplined not to exhibit emotion or express opinions or to welcome intimate contact with others ‖ set apart or retained for future use ‖ booked in advance

Reserve Officers Training Corps (ROTC), an organization of the U.S. Department of Defense, established (1916) by the National Defense Act to develop a reserve of trained officers available for service in national emergencies

re·serv·ist (rizá:rvist) *n.* a member of a military reserve force

res·er·voir (rézərvwɑr, rézərvwɔr) *n.* a place, esp. an artificial lake, where a large quantity of water is collected and stored to be piped to a city or used for irrigation, hydroelectric power etc. ‖ any container for a store of liquid or gas, *the ink reservoir of a fountain pen* ‖ a sac or cavity in a plant or animal in which fluid collects or is secreted [F. *réservoir*]

re·set 1. (ri:sét) *pres. part.* **re·set·ting** *past* and *past part.* **re·set** *v.t.* to set anew (a diamond, broken arm, hair etc.) ‖ (*printing*) to compose (a book, type) afresh 2. (rí:set) *n.* a resetting ‖ something that is reset

re·ship (ri:ʃíp) *pres. part.* **re·ship·ping** *past* and *past part.* **re·shipped** *v.t.* to put on board again (goods which had been unloaded from the same or another ship) *v.i.* to go on board again, after disembarking from the same or another ship ‖ to sign up again as a member of a ship's crew

re·sid or **residual oil** (rizíd) *n.* the elements of petroleum remaining after its valuable portions are removed

re·side (rizáid) *pres. part.* **re·sid·ing** *past* and *past part.* **re·sid·ed** *v.i.* to have one's home in a particular place for a considerable length of time ‖ (of qualities) to lie, be present, *its virtue resides in its clarity and brevity* ‖ (of rights etc.) to be vested [fr. F. *résider* or L. *residere*]

res·i·dence (rézidəns) *n.* the act or fact of living in a particular place for a considerable length of time ‖ the period during which one lives at a place ‖ the act or fact of residing ‖ the place where one lives, esp. the official house of a dignitary, or a dwelling house of some size or pretension **in residence** living in a place where one fulfills certain duties, e.g. at a hospital inhabiting an official residence, *the palace flag flies when the queen is in residence* ‖ (*chem.*) the persistence of an undesired element in a solution [F. *résidence*]

res·i·den·cy (rézidənsi:) *pl.* **res·i·den·cies** *n.* (*hist.*) a territory in a protected state where a resident agent of the protecting power has authority ‖ (*hist.*) the official residence of such an agent ‖ (*med.*) the position of a resident in a hospital, or the period during which he holds the position [fr. L. *residentia*]

res·i·dent (rézidənt) 1. *adj.* residing ‖ involving residence, *a resident year in college* ‖ living in residence, *a resident teacher* ‖ (of birds etc.) non-migratory 2. *n.* a person who resides for a considerable length of time in a certain place, *the local residents* ‖ (*hist.*) the governor of a residency ‖ a qualified physician in residence at a hospital, usually as the final part of his medical training [fr. L. *residens* (*residentis*) fr. *residere*, to reside]

res·i·den·tial (rézidénʃəl) *adj.* occupied mainly by private houses, esp. of some standing ‖ (esp. *Br.*) requiring the holder of a post to reside at his place of work, *a residential post* ‖ of or relating to residence, *residential qualifications* [RESIDENCE]

res·i·den·tiary (rezidénʃəri:, rezidénʃi:eri:) 1. *adj.* (esp. *eccles.*, usually following the noun) obliged to be in residence for a stipulated pe-

riod, *a canon residentiary* 2. *pl.* **res·i·den·tiar·ies** *n.* an ecclesiastic bound to live in residence for a certain period [fr. M.L. *residentiarius*]

re·sid·u·al (rizídʒu:əl) 1. *adj.* remaining, left over ‖ of or relating to something which so remains ‖ remaining in a body cavity after maximum elimination ‖ (*math.*) remaining after subtraction 2. *n.* (*phys.*) the difference between a theoretical and an experimental value, an *error in the residual* ‖ a substance or product left over after a chemical process, distillation etc. ‖ fee for each repetition (after its first showing) of a performance paid to a participant, esp. in television commercials [fr. L. *residuum*, residue]

re·sid·u·ar·y (rizídʒu:eri:) *adj.* of, relating to, or consisting of a residuum [RESIDUUM]

residuary legatee (*law*) someone who inherits what remains of an estate after specific bequests and charges on the estate have been met

res·i·due (rézidu:, rézidju:) *n.* that which remains after something has been taken away, separated out etc., *evaporation left a white residue in the dish* ‖ (*law*) that part of an estate remaining after the paying of all debts, bequests etc. [fr. F. *résidu*]

re·sid·u·um (rizídʒu:əm) *pl.* **re·sid·u·a** (rizídʒu:ə), **re·sid·u·ums** *n.* that which remains, esp. (*chem.*) that which remains after other substances have been removed by evaporation, filtration etc. ‖ (*law*) the residue of an estate [L. neuter of *residuus*, remaining]

re·sign (rizáin) *v.t.* to leave (an occupation, office, post) of one's own volition, *he resigned his post last week* ‖ to relinquish, *he resigned his rights under the patent* ‖ *v.i.* (esp. with 'as' or 'from') to leave an office, post etc. of one's own volition, *to resign as chairman* **to resign oneself to** to accept as unavoidable, *he resigned himself to a long wait* [fr. O.F. *resigner*]

re·sign (ri:sáin) *v.t.* to sign again

res·ig·na·tion (rezignéiʃən) *n.* the act of resigning ‖ a formal letter, notice etc. affirming that one has resigned or wishes to resign a position, office etc. ‖ the state of being mentally resigned, *to accept a situation with resignation* [F. *résignation*]

re·signed (rizáind) *adj.* accepting what cannot be avoided [RESIGN]

re·sil·ience (rizíljəns) *n.* the quality of being resilient

re·sil·ien·cy (rizíljənsi:) *n.* resilience

re·sil·ient (rizíljənt) *adj.* (of a body or material) capable of resuming its shape, position etc. after being subjected to stress, elastic ‖ (of human temperament) capable of recovering rapidly, esp. from an emotional shock [fr. L. *resiliens* (*resilientis*) fr. *resilire*, to spring back]

res·in (rézin) 1. *n.* any of various amorphous plant secretions (e.g. from pine, fir and tropical trees) used chiefly in varnishes, printing ink, plastics etc. as a binder ‖ any of a large class of synthetic products usually with some physical properties similar to the natural resins but which are different chemically. The synthetic resins are prepared by polymerization and are used as plastics, varnishes, in adhesives and in ion exchange 2. *v.t.* to treat with resin **res·in·ate** *pres. part.* **res·in·at·ing** *past* and *past part.* **res·in·at·ed** *v.t.* to impregnate with resin ‖ to flavor with pine resin **res·in·if·er·ous** (rezinífərəs) *adj.* of a tree or plant which secretes resin **rés·in·oid** 1. *adj.* somewhat resinous 2. *n.* a gum resin **rés·in·ous** *adj.* of, pertaining to or obtained from resin [fr. F. *résine*]

re·sist (rizíst) 1. *v.t.* to oppose (a physical force, chemical change, mental influence etc.) ‖ *v.i.* to oppose a physical force etc. 2. *n.* a substance used to protect a surface from change, e.g. wax to protect parts of a piece of pottery not to be affected by a glaze or slip [fr. F. *résister* or L. *resistere*]

re·sist·ance (rizístəns) *n.* a resisting ‖ the opposing force used in resisting, *the resistance of the air to a body moving through it* ‖ (*elec.*) opposition offered by a substance (e.g. a conductor) to the flow of an electric current (*OHM'S LAW) or that which offers such resistance (e.g. a coil of wire) **Re·sist·ance** (often with 'the') an organized, usually underground, movement of fighters engaged in acts of sabotage etc. against occupying forces [F. *résistance*]

resistance, resistance level, or **resistance area** (*securities*) trading price range at which notable amounts of buying or selling appear

resistance thermometer a temperature-measuring device that depends upon the known variation of the electrical resistance of a substance (usually a platinum wire) with temperature, to give temperature readings by measurements of electrical resistance

re·sist·ant, re·sist·ent (rizístənt) 1. *adj.* resisting 2. *n.* someone who resists

re·sist·i·bil·i·ty (rizistəbíliti:) *n.* the quality or state of being resistible

re·sist·i·ble (rizístəb'l) *adj.* capable of being resisted

re·sis·tive (rizístiv) *adj.* resistant ‖ of, relating to, or having electrical resistance

re·sis·tiv·i·ty (ri:zistíviti:) *n.* (*elec.*) the property of a substance that determines the electrical resistance of a body made of that substance ‖ the electrical resistance per unit length of a uniform bar of unit cross-sectional area ‖ the ability to resist

re·sist·less (rizístlis) *adj.* of that which cannot be resisted, *the resistless onset of age* ‖ unable to resist

re·sis·to·jet (rizístədʒet) *n.* (*aerospace*) engine fueled by electrically heated hydrogen or ammonia, used to change a spacecraft's direction

re·sis·tor (rizístər) *n.* (*elec.*) an electrical resistance used in a circuit to control the current

re·sol·u·ble (ri:sólju'l) *adj.* able to be dissolved again (e.g. silver oxide when excess of ammonium hydroxide is added)

re·sol·u·ble (rizólju'l) able to be resolved [fr. L.L. *resolubilis*]

res·o·lute (rézəlu:t) *adj.* not turned from a purpose by difficulties or opposition or risk etc. [fr. L. *resolvere* (*resolutus*), to resolve]

res·o·lu·tion (rezəlú:ʃən) *n.* a resolving or being resolved ‖ something resolved ‖ the quality of not allowing difficulties or opposition to affect one's purpose ‖ the degree to which an analysis (e.g. in chemical, spectral, optical or statistical analysis) is capable of distinguishing between similar substances, properties, events, adjacent parts etc. (*RESOLVING POWER) ‖ a formal statement of opinion or decision, agreed to after the consideration of a motion ‖ (*med.*) dissipation, e.g. of an inflammation ‖ (*mus.*) the consonance in which a dissonance is resolved [O.F.]

Resolution 242 a resolution of the United Nations Security Council adopted November 22, 1967, advocating Israeli withdrawal from occupied territories, acknowledgment of the sovereignty of each state in the area, an end to belligerency, and settlement of the Palestinian refugee problem

re·solve (rizólv) 1. *v. pres. part.* **re·solv·ing** *past* and *past part.* **re·solved** *v.t.* to separate (something) into component parts, *to resolve a compound or mixture into its constituents* ‖ to render (adjacent parts, e.g. lines of a spectrum, or objects or light sources imaged by a microscope or telescope) distinguishable ‖ to decompose (a vector) into two or more components along specific (usually orthogonal) directions ‖ (*med.*) to cause (e.g. an inflammation) to dissipate ‖ to find a solution to (a question or problem) ‖ to convert by resolution, *the assembly resolved itself into a committee* ‖ (*mus.*) to convert (a discord) into a concord ‖ to decide, determine, to *resolve not to go* ‖ (of a committee) to agree to (a course of action or expression of opinion) by formal resolution ‖ *v.i.* (with 'on' or 'upon') to determine, *to resolve on a less violent course of action* ‖ to become separated into constituent parts ‖ (*mus.*) to pass from discord to concord 2. *n.* something resolved ‖ firmness of purpose ‖ a formal resolution [fr. L. *resolvere*]

resolving power the ability of an optical system or instrument (e.g. a microscope, telescope, or the lenses of a camera) to form distinct magnified images of adjacent features on the object being observed ‖ the degree to which photographic film is able to reproduce the fine features of an optical image

res·o·nance (rézənəns) *n.* the prolongation, amplification or modification of a sound by vibration ‖ (*phys.*) the increase in amplitude of an oscillation in a mechanical or electrical system, under the influence of an external periodic impulse of similar frequency to the original vibration ‖ this modified oscillation ‖ the state of adjustment of a system that results in this ‖ (*med.*) the sound produced by the chest on percussion ‖ (*chem.*) the phenomenon in certain molecules, ions or radicals to which two or more structures that differ in their electron distribution can be assigned, that results in greater stability and different bond lengths than in the

---

CONCISE PRONUNCIATION KEY: **(a)** æ, c*a*t; ɑ, c*a*r; ɔ f*aw*n; ei, sn*a*ke. **(e)** e, h*e*n; i:, sh*ee*p; iə, d*ee*r; ɛə, b*ea*r. **(i)** i, f*i*sh; ai, t*i*ger; ə:, b*i*rd. **(o)** o, *o*x; au, c*ow*; ou, g*oa*t; u, p*oo*r; ɔi, r*oy*al. **(u)** ʌ, d*u*ck; u, b*u*ll; u:, g*oo*se; ə, b*a*cillus; ju:, c*u*be. x, lo*ch*; θ, *th*ink; ð, b*o*ther; z, *Z*en; ʒ, cor*s*age; dʒ, sava*g*e; ŋ, ora*ng*utang; j, *y*ak; ʃ, *f*ish; tʃ, fe*tch*; 'l, rabb*le*; 'n, redd*en*. Complete pronunciation key appears inside front cover.

hypothetical structures, and that is attributed to the fact that the electrons in the system are no longer localized ‖ (*particle phys.*) a short-lived elementary particle or group of particles, e.g., rho mesons; undetectable temporary state of mesons or hyperons during a nuclear reaction; the particles themselves [O.F.]

res·o·nance particle any of a group of extremely short-lived fundamental particles of high mass and variable charge and angular momentum that are as yet incompletely understood, but which appear to play the role of field quanta (*QUANTUM THEORY OF FIELDS)

res·o·nant (rézənənt) *adj.* resounding ‖ causing sound to be reinforced or prolonged ‖ (of a sound) loud and rich in overtones ‖ (*phys.*) of or exhibiting resonance [fr. L. *resonans* (*resonantis*) fr. *resonare*, to resound]

res·o·nate (rézəneit) *pres. part.* **res·o·nat·ing** *past* and *past part.* **res·o·nat·ed** *v.i.* to exhibit resonance ‖ to react as if by resonance ‖ *v.t.* to make resonant **rés·o·na·tor** *n.* a device used to give resonance to sounds ‖ (*radio*) the system of antennae, or other high-frequency circuit, of a receiver [fr. L. *resonare*, to resound]

re·sorb (risórb, rizórb) *v.t.* to absorb again **re·sórb·ent** *adj.* [fr. L. *resorbere*]

res·or·cin·ol (rezórsinol, rezórsinoul) *n.* a crystalline phenol, $C_6H_4(OH)_2$, obtained in its natural state from various resins and tannins, and also prepared synthetically. It is used in the manufacture of dyes and in lotions for some skin diseases [RESIN + ORCIN]

re·sorp·tion (risórpʃən, rizórpʃən) *n.* a resorbing or being resorbed [fr. L. *resorbere* (*resorptus*), to resorb]

re·sort (rizórt) *v.i.* (often with 'to') to have recourse, *to resort to violence* ‖ (often with 'to') to go, esp. to go often and in great numbers [fr. O.F. *resortir*, to rebound]

resort *n.* a place to which people go frequently or habitually for rest, pleasure etc., *a seaside resort* ‖ a habitual or general going to a place, *a place of public resort* ‖ a person to whom or a thing to which one applies for aid ‖ the action of applying for aid [O.F.]

re·sound (rizáund) *v.i.* to sound loudly and with rich quality ‖ to re-echo ‖ to be filled with sound, *the hall resounded with applause* ‖ *v.t.* to utter with enthusiasm (someone's praises etc.) [fr. L. *resonare*]

re·source (risórs, risóurs, rí:sɔrs, rí:sours) *n.* a source of supply or support ‖ quick-wittedness in mastering a difficult situation ‖ something to which one resorts for comfort or help or to gain an end, *tears are her main resource when she is thwarted* ‖ (*pl.*) means of diversion, *he soon exhausted the resources of the place* ‖ (*pl.*) natural assets (of a country) ‖ (*pl.*) assets, wealth **without resource** having nothing to fall back on **re·sóurce·ful** *adj.* [fr. F. *ressource*]

re·spect (rispékt) 1. *n.* the special esteem or consideration in which one holds another person or thing ‖ the state or quality of being esteemed etc., *to be held in respect* ‖ aspect, detail, *the plan is faulty in every respect* ‖ (*pl.*) conventional expressions of esteem, sympathy etc. **in respect of, with respect to** as regards, concerning, *he wants to talk to you with respect to your journey* 2. *v.t.* to feel or show respect or consideration for [fr. L. *respicere* (*respectus*), to look (back) at]

re·spect·a·bil·i·ty (rispèktəbíliti:) *n.* the state or quality of being respectable

re·spect·a·ble (rispéktəb'l) *adj.* conforming to the standards of what one considers proper, socially acceptable etc. ‖ fairly large in amount, size, quantity etc., *a respectable sum of money* ‖ tolerably good, *a respectable performance* ‖ of good standing or acceptable appearance etc., *a respectable hotel* **re·spéct·a·bly** *adv.*

re·spect·ful (rispéktfəl) *adj.* showing respect, *a respectful silence*

re·spect·ing (rispéktiŋ) *prep.* considering ‖ regarding

re·spec·tive (rispéktiv) *adj.* concerning each of two or more persons or things taken in relationship to the other or others, *check the respective parts of the ignition according to the procedure laid down* ‖ proper to each individual of two or more persons or things of a group under consideration, *they all went off to their respective jobs* **re·spéc·tive·ly** *adv.* each considered in the order indicated, *Dick, John and Bill made the journey by car, train and on foot respectively* ‖ in a way which regards each of two or more persons or things in relation to the other or others,

consider respectively their prices and the uses they can be put to [fr. L.L. *respectivus*]

re·spell (ri:spél) *pres. part.* **re·spell·ing** *past* and *past part.* **re·spelled**, (esp. *Br.*) **re·spelt** (ri:spélt) *v.t.* to spell again, e.g. in a phonetic system so as to indicate pronunciation

Re·spi·ghi (respí:gi:), Ottorino (1879-1936), Italian composer. He is mainly known for his orchestral suites, esp. 'Fontane di Roma' (1917) and for his ballet music for 'la Boutique fantasque' (1917-18) arranged from airs by Rossini

re·spir·a·ble (réspərəb'l, rispáiərəb'l) *adj.* capable of, or suited for, being respired

res·pi·ra·tion (respəréiʃən) *n.* any of various processes by which an organism takes in air or dissolved gases, uses one or more of them in energy-producing chemical changes, and expels both the gaseous by-products of the changes and the unused part of the air or gas. Animals and plants use oxygen, expelling carbon dioxide formed by the oxidation of carbon compounds in the system. Green plants in daylight can use the carbon dioxide of the air to form starch, expelling oxygen as a by-product [fr. L. *respiratio* (*respirationis*)]

res·pi·ra·tor (réspəreitər) *n.* a device worn over the mouth and nose to filter poisonous substances from the air breathed in ‖ (*Br.*) a gas mask ‖ a device for inducing artificial respiration [fr. L. *respirare*, to breathe]

res·pi·ra·to·ry (réspərətəri:, réspərətouri:, rispáiərətɔri:, rispáiərətouri:) *adj.* of or relating to respiration ‖ serving for respiration [fr. Mod L. *respiratorius*]

re·spire (rispáiər) *pres. part.* **re·spir·ing** *past* and *past part.* **re·spired** *v.i.* to breathe ‖ *v.t.* to breathe (air etc.) in and out [L. *respirare*, to breathe]

res·pite (réspit) *n.* an interval of relief during a period of work, suffering etc. ‖ the postponement of the fulfilling of some obligation ‖ the postponement of the carrying out of a death sentence [O.F. *respit*]

respite *pres. part.* **res·pit·ing** *past* and *past part.* **res·pit·ed** *v.t.* to grant a respite to (someone) ‖ to delay the execution of (a sentence or punishment etc.) [O.F. *respiter*]

re·splend·ence (rispléndəns) *n.* the state or quality of being resplendent

re·splend·en·cy (rispléndənsi:) *n.* resplendence

re·splend·ent (rispléndənt) *adj.* brightly glowing with light or color [fr. L. *resplendens* (*resplendentis*)]

re·spond (rispónd) *n.* (*archit.*) a half-column or half-pier in a wall, used to support an arch ‖ (*eccles.*) a response (words said or sung by the congregation in answer) [O.F.]

respond *v.i.* to reply ‖ to show an effect due to a force, influence or stimulus, *the illness responded to treatment* ‖ (*eccles.*) to make a response in a liturgy [fr. L. *respondere*]

re·spond·ent (rispóndənt) 1. *adj.* (*law*) in the position of a defendant 2. *n.* (*law*) a defendant, esp. in a divorce case [fr. L. *respondens* (*respondentis*) fr. *respondere*, to answer]

re·sponse (rispóns) *n.* a reply, *he failed to make any response, a good response to the appeal* ‖ something answered, esp. (*eccles.*) words said or sung by the congregation or choir in answer to the priest ‖ (*eccles.*) a responsory ‖ (*mus.*) an answer ‖ the reaction to a stimulus **in response to** in answer to [O.F. *respons, response* and L. *responsum*]

re·spon·si·bil·i·ty (rispònsəbíliti:) *pl.* **re·spon·si·bil·i·ties** *n.* the state or quality of being responsible ‖ a person for whom or a thing for which one is responsible **to take responsibility for** to consider oneself answerable for

re·spon·si·ble (rispónsəb'l) *adj.* (of a person or persons) placed in control and having to give satisfaction, *he is responsible for the success or failure of the experiment* ‖ (of a position) held by such a person or persons ‖ fit to be placed in control, *a responsible man* ‖ capable of acting rationally, *he is not responsible* ‖ causing a particular result, *the rain was responsible for the poor attendance* **re·spón·si·bly** *adv.* [obs. F. fr. L. *responsus*, to pledge in return]

Re·spon·sions (rispónʃənz) *pl. n.* the first examination for a B.A. degree at Oxford University in certain faculties [F. or Fr. L.L. *responsio* (*responsionis*), answer]

re·spon·sive (rispónsiv) *adj.* giving a response, e.g. to a stimulus ‖ (of persons and things) quick to respond ‖ (*eccles.*) involving or consisting of responses [F. *responsif*]

re·spon·so·ry (rispónsəri:) *pl.* **re·spon·so·ries** *n.* (*eccles.*) an anthem said or sung by soloist and choir alternately after a reading from the Bible [fr. L.L. *responsoria*]

rest (rest) *n.* the state of being motionless ‖ the state of being inactive, esp. after physical exertion ‖ a period of being inactive, during which one gets back one's energy ‖ a period of sleep, *a good night's rest* ‖ (*mus.*) a short period of silence of an indicated time value ‖ (*mus.*) any of various symbols indicating this period and the length of the period ‖ something serving as a support for something else, *the fork of a tree made a rest for his back* ‖ a caesura ‖ (*billiards*) a bridge ‖ (*rhet.*) mental tranquillity **at rest** having no motion ‖ free from worries etc. ‖ in a state of repose **to come to rest** to cease moving, *the ball came to rest at the edge of the hole* **to lay to rest** to bury (a dead person) **to set (someone's) mind at rest** to cause (someone) to be free of worries etc. [O.E. *ræste, reste*]

rest *v.i.* to be motionless, *the ball rested at the edge of the hole* ‖ to refrain from activity, esp. in order to recover energy ‖ (of the mind etc.) to be or become tranquil ‖ to be fixed or supported, *the vase rests on a pedestal* ‖ (with 'on' or 'upon') to be founded, *the charge rests on the evidence of one witness* ‖ to remain in abeyance, *to let a matter rest* ‖ (with 'on' or 'upon') to be steadily directed, *his eyes rested on the ceiling* ‖ *v.t.* to place on or against a support, *to rest a ladder against a wall* ‖ to direct (e.g. the eyes), *to rest one's gaze on the ceiling* ‖ to give a period of rest to, *to rest one's feet after a march* ‖ to give tranquillity to, *to rest one's mind* ‖ to base (e.g. a case), *to rest one's defense on a plea of insanity* ‖ (*law*) to cease voluntarily the introduction of evidence in (a case) [O.E. *ræstan, restan*]

rest *n.* the portion which remains after part has been taken away ‖ (constr. as *pl.*) the others, the remaining group, *some of the guests went to church, the rest stayed at home* [F. *reste*]

rest *n.* (*hist.*, of armor) an attachment projecting from the right side of the cuirass for supporting the butt end of the lance [older *arest, arrest n.*]

re·state (ri:stéit) *pres. part.* **re·stat·ing** *past* and *past part.* **re·stat·ed** *v.t.* to state again or in other words **re·státe·ment** *n.*

res·tau·rant (réstərənt, réstərant) *n.* a place where meals are served, for payment, to members of the public [F.]

res·tau·ra·teur (rèstərətá:r) *n.* a person who owns or manages a restaurant [F.]

rest·ful (réstfəl) *adj.* enabling a person to rest his body or mind, *a restful holiday* ‖ having a calming effect, esp. on the senses, *restful colors*

Res·tif (or **Re·tif**) **de la Bre·tonne** (reiti:fdələbretɔn), Nicolas Edmé (1734-1806), French writer. He wrote some 250 volumes, many of which he illustrated and most of which were pornographic. They provide insight into the life of the poor in 18th-c. France

res·ti·form body (réstifɔrm) (*anat.*) one of the two cordlike bundles of fibers which connect the medulla oblongata with the cerebellum [Mod. L. *restiformis* fr. *restis*, cord + -*forma*, form]

rest·ing (réstiŋ) *adj.* (*biol.*) dormant ‖ (of actors) temporarily without an engagement

res·ti·tu·tion (restitú:ʃən, restitjú:ʃən) *n.* the act of giving back to a rightful owner ‖ a giving of something as an equivalent for what has been lost, damaged etc. ‖ a returning of something to its original state or condition ‖ (*phys.*, of an elastic body) a going back to its original form after deformation [O.F.]

res·tive (réstiv) *adj.* (of a person) having too much energy to be willing to remain at rest or to submit to control ‖ (of a horse) resisting control ‖ (of a crowd, audience etc.) uneasy or beginning to show displeasure [O.F. *restif*]

rest·less (réstlis) *adj.* agitatedly moving about, not composed ‖ not accompanied by unbroken sleep, *a restless night* ‖ in continual motion, *the restless sea* ‖ (of a person) constantly seeking change

rest mass the mass of a body which has no relative motion in regard to the observer ‖ (*nuclear phys.*) the mass of a particle (exclusive of mass acquired in movement) while moving at less than the speed of light

res·to·ra·tion (restəréiʃən) 1. *n.* a restoring or being restored ‖ a representation of what the original form of a building etc. may be supposed to have been **the Restoration** (*Eng. hist.*) the reestablishment of the monarchy on the accession (1660) of Charles II ‖ the period immediately following this ‖ (*F. hist.*) the reestablishment of the monarchy on the accession (1814) of Louis XVIII ‖ (*F. hist.*) the period 1814–30, interrupted by the Hundred Days (Mar. 20–June 18, 1815) **2.** *adj.* **Res·to·ra·tion** of or belonging to the Restoration

re·stor·a·tive (ristórətiv, ristóurətiv) **1.** *adj.* capable of restoring one's health or strength **2.** *n.* something which restores someone to consciousness, health etc. [O.F. *restoratif*]

re·store (ristór, ristóur) *pres. part.* **re·stor·ing** *past* and *past part.* **re·stored** *v.t.* to give back, *to restore stolen jewels to the owner* ‖ to make (something) look as it looked originally by repairing, retouching etc., *to restore a painting* ‖ to re-create the original form of (something no longer existing, or existing as a ruin), *to restore an amphora* ‖ to put back (a deposed monarch) on the throne or bring back (the monarchy) ‖ to bring back to a previous rank, dignity etc. ‖ to bring back to a healthy state ‖ to bring into use or being again, *the old custom has been restored, to restore order* ‖ (*rhet.*) to put back into place ‖ to add or correct (missing or illegible words or letters) to or in a text **re·stór·er** *n.* someone who restores ‖ an agent said to promote growth or activity, *a hair restorer* [O.F. *restorer*]

re·strain (ristréin) *v.t.* to prevent from doing something, *the dog was restrained from attacking the man* ‖ to set limits to (expansion, ambition etc.) ‖ to repress (emotions, a sigh etc.) ‖ to deprive of physical liberty, *restrained by a straitjacket* [O.F. *restraindre* (*restraign, restrain*)]

re·straint (ristréint) *n.* a restraining or being restrained ‖ something which restrains, *the natural restraints on conduct imposed by small communities* ‖ confinement, esp. because of madness, *to be placed under restraint* ‖ avoidance of exaggeration, shocking effects etc. in any form of expression **without restraint** freely, with no holding back [O.F. *restrainte*]

Res·tre·po (restrépɔ), Carlos E. (1868-1937), Colombian politician and president of the Republic (1910-14). He reformed (1910) the constitution and briefly restored constitutional government

re·strict (ristríkt) *v.t.* to keep within certain limits, *to restrict someone's movements, to restrict someone's freedom of choice* **re·strict·ed** *adj.* limited, *restricted supply* ‖ limited to a certain group or groups, esp. (used as a racist euphemism) limited e.g. to white non-Jews ‖ (of documents) not for general circulation, for reasons of security, although not classified as secret ‖ (*mil.*) of or relating to an area from which military personnel are excluded for reasons of security [fr. L. *restringere* (*restrictus*)]

re·stric·tion (ristríkʃən) *n.* a restricting or being restricted ‖ something which restricts [F.]

re·stric·tive (ristríktiv) *adj.* restricting or tending to restrict [F. *restrictif*]

restrictive clause (*gram.*) a relative clause, usually not set off by commas in English, which identifies the antecedent

rest room a room equipped with toilets, washbasins etc. for the use of employees, clients etc. in a department store or other building

result (rizʌ́lt) **1.** *v.i.* (with 'from') to be the effect of something, *his death resulted from injuries* ‖ (with 'in') to have a specified effect, *his injuries resulted in his death* **2.** *n.* an effect arising from something ‖ a solution arrived at by calculation or reasoning ‖ the success or benefit obtained from a course of action, *his efforts had some result* ‖ the outcome of an examination, election or similar contest ‖ (*pl.*, of sports) published or announced scores and winners etc. [fr. L. *resultare*, to spring back]

re·sult·ant (rizʌ́ltənt) **1.** *adj.* resulting, being a result **2.** *n.* that which is a result ‖ (*phys.*) a vector which is equivalent to or the sum of two or more other vectors taken together [fr. L. *resultans* (*resultantis*) fr. *resultare*, to spring back]

re·sume (rizúːm) *pres. part.* **re·sum·ing** *past* and *past part.* **re·sumed** *v.t.* to take back, or again, to resume possession of property ‖ to begin again, *to resume occupation of a house* ‖ to go back to using, *to resume a maiden name* ‖ to sum up, *to resume the main points of an argument* [fr. O.F. *resumer* or L. *resumere*, to take back]

ré·su·mé (rézumei, ręzuméi) *n.* a summary ‖ a curriculum vitae [F.]

re·sump·tion (rizʌ́mpʃən) *n.* the act or fact of beginning again, *a resumption of work* [F. *résumption*]

re·su·pi·nate (risúːpineit) *adj.* (*bot.*) so arranged that parts appear upside down, e.g. the flower of an orchid [fr. L. *resupinare* (*resupinatus*), to bend back]

re·sur·face (riːsə́ːrfis) *pres. part.* **re·sur·fac·ing** *past* and *past part.* **re·sur·faced** *v.t.* to give a new surface to

re·sur·gence (risə́ːrdʒəns) *n.* a rising again, *a resurgence of anger in the crowd*

re·sur·gent (risə́ːrdʒənt) *adj.* rising or seeming to rise again [fr. L. *resurgens* (*resurgentis*) fr. *resurgere*, to rise again]

res·ur·rect (rezərékt) *v.t.* to bring back to life ‖ to bring back to memory or into use, *don't resurrect that old tale* ‖ to resurrect an old custom ‖ to bring back to the surface by erosion ‖ (*hist.*) to steal (a body) from the grave ‖ *v.i.* to rise from the dead [RESURRECTION]

res·ur·rec·tion (rezərékʃən) *n.* the act of rising again after death ‖ a bringing back into use, memory etc. **the Resurrec·tion** (*theol.*) the rising of Christ from the dead ‖ (*theol.*) the rising of all the dead at the Last Judgment **res·ur·réc·tion·ist** *n.* (*hist.*) a body snatcher [O.F.]

re·sur·vey (riːsəːrvéi) **1.** *v.t.* to survey again **2.** (also riːsə́ːrvei) *n.* a fresh survey

re·sus·ci·ta·tion (risʌsitéiʃən) *n.* a resuscitating or being resuscitated [fr. L.L. *resuscitatio* (*resuscitationis*)]

re·sus·ci·tate (risʌ́siteit) *pres. part.* **re·sus·ci·tat·ing** *past* and *past part.* **re·sus·ci·tat·ed** *v.t.* to bring (someone unconscious or seemingly dead) to life or consciousness again ‖ (*fig.*) to revive (what had been discarded or forgotten), *to resuscitate old rumors* ‖ *v.i.* (esp. *fig., rhet.*) to come to life again, revive **re·sús·ci·ta·tor** *n.* someone or something that resuscitates ‖ an apparatus which, by forcing oxygen (or oxygen and carbon dioxide) into the lungs of an asphyxiated person induces respiration

ret (ret) *pres. part.* **ret·ting** *past* and *past part.* **ret·ted** *v.t.* to soak (flax etc.) in water in order to loosen the fibers from the woody stem by the action of bacteria ‖ *v.i.* (of flax) to undergo this soaking [etym. doubtful]

re·ta·ble (ríːteibl) *n.* (*eccles.*) a ledge or shelf above the back of an altar, used for supporting the ornaments ‖ (*eccles.*) a framework behind the altar enclosing a decorated panel [F. *rétable, retable*]

re·tail (ríːteil) **1.** *n.* the sale of goods in small quantities directly to consumers (opp. WHOLESALE) **2.** *adj.* of, relating to, or engaged in the sale of goods in this way, *retail price* **3.** *adv.* by retail sale **4.** (riːtéil) *v.t.* to sell in small quantities ‖ to repeat (a story) in detail to others ‖ *v.i.* to be sold in small quantities directly to consumers, *these goods retail at 20 francs a dozen* [O.F.]

re·tain (ritéin) *v.t.* to keep in one's possession or control, *he retained his vitality to the end* ‖ (*law*) to keep available the services of (an attorney or barrister) in case of need by paying a preliminary fee ‖ to keep securely in place ‖ to keep in one's memory, *to have difficulty in retaining names* **re·táin·er** *n.* something which retains, e.g. a device for keeping the balls or rollers of a bearing spaced correctly ‖ (*hist.*) a person serving someone of high rank ‖ (used to connote long and faithful service) a servant ‖ (*law*) the engaging by a client of the services of an attorney ‖ (*law*) a fee paid to an attorney or barrister to retain his services in case of need ‖ a similar fee or salary paid to any professional adviser [fr. O.F. *retenir*]

retaining fee a retainer (fee paid)

retaining wall a wall built to hold back water or the earth of an embankment

re·take 1. (riːtéik) *v.t. pres. part.* **re·tak·ing** *past* **re·took** (riːtúk) *past part.* **re·tak·en** (riːtéikən) to take back ‖ to recapture, *the fugitive was retaken* ‖ (*movies*) to rephotograph (a scene) **2.** (ríːteik) *n.* (*movies*) a refilming of a scene or the scene refilmed

re·tal·i·ate (ritǽliːeit) *pres. part.* **re·tal·i·at·ing** *past* and *past part.* **re·tal·i·at·ed** *v.i.* to return blow for blow, insult for insult, harm for harm ‖ *v.t.* to return (a blow, insult etc.) **re·tal·i·a·tion** *n.* **re·tal·i·a·tive, re·tal·i·a·to·ry** (ritǽliːətɔri:, ritǽliːətɔuri:) *adjs.* [fr. L. *retaliare* (*retaliatus*)]

re·tard (ritárd) *v.t.* to slow down the advance of, delay, *the storm retarded his arrival by an hour, solitude retarded her mental development* ‖ (*mech.*) to adjust the timing of (ignition) so that the spark ignites the fuel later in the stroke with respect to top dead center ‖ *v.i.* (of tides, or the movement of heavenly bodies) to occur later

than the normal or calculated time [fr. F. *retarder*]

re·tard·ate (ritárdeit) *n.* someone who is mentally retarded [fr. L. *retardare* (*retardatus*), to retard, delay]

re·tar·da·tion (riːtɑːrdéiʃən) *n.* a retarding or being retarded ‖ the amount by which something is retarded ‖ the state of being backward in mental development ‖ (*mus.*) a suspension ‖ (*mus.*) a slowing down of the tempo [F.]

re·tard·a·tive (ritárdətiv) *adj.* relating to or causing retardation

re·tard·a·to·ry (ritárdətɔri:, ritárdətɔuri:) *adj.* tending to retard

re·tard·ed (ritárdid) *adj.* (esp. of children) physically or mentally backward

re·tard·er (ritárdər) *n.* (*photog.*) a chemical which retards the action of a developer ‖ a substance which delays the setting of cement etc.

retch (retʃ) **1.** *v.i.* to try to vomit but fail to do so **2.** *n.* the act of retching [var. of *reach* fr. O.E. *hrēcan*]

re·ten·tion (riténʃən) *n.* a retaining or being retained ‖ the capacity of retaining ‖ (*med.*) the retaining in a bodily sac, canal etc. of some fluid meant to be eliminated ‖ a remembering or a keeping in the memory [O.F. *retencion*]

re·ten·tive (riténtiv) *adj.* tending or serving to retain or having the power or capacity of retaining ‖ having the ability to remember **re·ten·tiv·i·ty** (riːtentíviti:) *n.* [O.F. *retentif, retentive*]

re·think (riːθíŋk) *v.* to reconsider in depth

ret·i·cence (rétisəns) *n.* an inclination to be reserved in speech or behavior ‖ an instance of this [F.]

ret·i·cent (rétisənt) *adj.* characterized by reticence [fr. L. *reticens* (*reticentis*) fr. *reticere*, to be silent]

ret·i·cle (rétikl) *n.* a system of fine lines, cross hairs etc. in the focus of the lens of an optical instrument to assist observation [fr. L. *reticulum*, a little net]

re·tic·u·lar (ritíkjulər) *adj.* netlike ‖ (*rhet.*) intricate [fr. Mod. L. *reticularis*]

re·tic·u·late (ritíkjuleit) **1.** *v. pres. part.* **re·tic·u·lat·ing** *past* and *past part.* **re·tic·u·lat·ed** *v.t.* to divide so as to look like or form a mesh or network ‖ to construct with a reticle ‖ *v.i.* to be divided into a mesh or network or so divided as to resemble a mesh or network **2.** *adj.* (*biol.*) possessing crossing veins or fibers resembling a network **re·tic·u·lat·ed** *adj.* **re·tic·u·la·tion** (ritikjuléiʃən) *n.* [fr. L. *reticulatus* fr. *reticulum*, a little net]

ret·i·cule (rétikjuːl) *n.* a reticle ‖ (*old-fash.*) a lady's small handbag [F. *réticule*]

re·tic·u·lum (ritíkjuləm) *pl.* **re·tic·u·la** (ritíkjulə) *n.* the second stomach of a ruminant mammal ‖ a network structure, esp. in the dense protoplasm of cells [L.=a little net]

re·ti·form (ríːtifɔrm, rétifɔrm) *adj.* having the form of a net [fr. Mod. L. *retiformis*]

ret·i·na (rétnə) *pl.* **ret·i·nas, ret·i·nae** (rétniː) *n.* the membrane which forms the inner lining of the back wall of the vertebrate eye, constituted of two kinds of cell which respond to the stimulus of light and send nervous impulses to the brain through the optic nerve **rét·i·nal** *adj.* **ret·i·ni·tis** (retꞌnáitis) *n.* (*med.*) inflammation of the retina [M.L.]

ret·i·nal [$C_{20}H_{28}O$] (rétꞌnl) *n.* the visual pigment (derived from retinol, or vitamin A) in the disk of the retina essential to color perception

retinol *RETINAL

ret·i·nue (rétꞌnjuː, rétꞌnuː) *n.* the persons following someone as attendants [O.F. *retenue*]

re·tire (ritáiər) *pres. part.* **re·tir·ing** *past* and *past part.* **re·tired** *v.i.* to give up active participation in a business or other occupation, esp. because of advanced age ‖ to draw back or seem to do so ‖ to draw back from an area of combat, danger etc. ‖ (*cricket*) to cease batting although not out, e.g. because of being hurt ‖ to seek privacy ‖ to go to bed ‖ *v.t.* to withdraw (money) from circulation or (bonds, stocks) from the market ‖ to cause (troops) to fall back ‖ (*baseball*) to put out (a batter, side etc.) ‖ to cause to go into retirement **re·tired** *adj.* no longer taking an active part in a profession or other occupation, *a retired actress* ‖ of or relating to a person or persons no longer active in a profession etc., *the retired list, retired pay* ‖ (*old-fash.*) secluded, *a retired corner of the garden* **re·tíre·ment** *n.* a retiring or being retired **re·tír·ing** *adj.* (of persons) reserved, preferring seclusion [fr. F. *retirer*, to draw back]

retook *past* of RETAKE

CONCISE PRONUNCIATION KEY: (**a**) æ, c*a*t; ɑ, c*a*r; ɔ f*aw*n; ei, sn*a*ke. (**e**) e, h*e*n; iː, sh*ee*p; iə, d*ee*r; ɛə, b*ea*r. (**i**) i, f*i*sh; ai, t*i*ger; əː, b*i*rd. (**o**) o, *o*x; au, c*ow*; ou, g*oa*t; u, p*oo*r; ɔi, r*oy*al. (**u**) ʌ, d*u*ck; u, b*u*ll; uː, g*oo*se; ə, b*a*cillus; juː, c*u*be. x, lo*ch*; θ, *th*ink; ð, bo*th*er; z, *Z*en; ʒ, corsa*g*e; dʒ, sava*g*e; ŋ, ora*ng*utang; j, *y*ak; ʃ, *fi*sh; tʃ, fe*tch*; 'l, rabb*le*; 'n, redd*en*. Complete pronunciation key appears inside front cover.

re·tool (ri:tú:l) *v.t.* to reequip (a factory) with tools and machine || *v.i.* to reequip a factory with tools and machines

re·tort (ritórt) *n.* a vessel of metal etc. used for distilling metals, e.g. for extracting zinc from zinc ore || a refractory chamber in which coal is carbonized by heating the outside of the chamber || a vessel usually of glass with a long slanting tube, used in distillation [F. *retorte*]

retort 1. *v.i.* to make a retort || to retaliate || *v.t.* to turn (an argument, insult etc.) against the user **2.** *n.* a quick witty or sarcastic reply countering a remark by a previous speaker [fr. L. *retorquere* (*retortus*), to bend back]

re·tor·tion (ritórʃən) *n.* the act of retorting || a bending back || (*internat. law*) retaliation in kind by a country against the citizens of the state which has provoked it [fr. M.L. *retortio* (*retortionis*), a bending back]

re·touch 1. (ri:tʌ́tʃ) *v.t.* to improve by making small alterations in || to change the details on (a photographic print or negative or an engraved plate), esp. so as to hide blemishes or allow for process effects **2.** (ri:tʌtʃ, rit:ʌ́tʃ) *n.* a retouching || a detail which has been changed in retouching || a photograph etc. which has been retouched [F. *retoucher*]

re·trace (ritréis) *pres. part.* **re·trac·ing** *past* and *past part.* **re·traced** *v.t.* to go over again, *to retrace one's path* || to discover by going back in time step by step, *to retrace a genealogy* || to review step by step in memory, *to retrace one's childhood* [F. *retracer*]

re·tract (ritrǽkt) *v.t.* to take back, withdraw (a criticism, accusation etc.) || *v.i.* to draw back, shrink back || to recant [fr. L. *retractare*, to draw back]

retract *v.t.* (*zool.*) to draw (the head, body or limbs) back into the shell || (*zool.*) to draw (the claws) back into their sheaths || (*mach.*) to draw (e.g. wheels) up into the body || *v.i.* (*zool.*, of a head, body or limb) to able to be drawn back into the shell || (*zool.*, of claws) to be able to be drawn back into their sheaths || (*mach.*, of a wheel) to go up into the body [fr. L. *retrahere* (*retractus*), to draw back]

re·trac·tile (ritrǽktil) *adj.* (of claws etc.) that can be retracted [F. *rétractile*]

re·trac·tion (ritrǽkʃən) *n.* a retracting or being retracted || the act of withdrawing something said or promised etc. || the statement made in doing this [fr. L. *retractio* (*retractionis*)]

re·trac·tor (ritrǽktər) *n.* a muscle which causes an organ or part to retract || a surgical instrument for holding back the tissues around an incision during an operation

re·tral (rí:trəl) *adj.* at the back, posterior [fr. L. *retro*, backward]

re·tread 1. (ri:tréd) *v.t.* to supply a (tire) with a new tread after removing the old **2.** (rí:tred) *n.* a tire thus renewed (cf. RECAP)

re·treat (ritrí:t) *n.* (*mil.*) the withdrawal of troops from enemy territory or before invading forces after a defeat or when defeat appears imminent || (*hist.*) the signal for this || the act of absenting oneself temporarily from the dangers or difficulties of life || something which allows one to do this, *the world of books was his retreat* || a place to which one withdraws for peace, safety etc., *a country retreat* || (*mil.*) a signal given by a bugle (sometimes accompanied by drums) at sunset, announcing the ceremony of flag lowering || (*mil.*) this ceremony || (*eccles.*) a period during which a person or group of persons withdraws from worldly activities to e.g. a monastery for spiritual recollection under instruction and discipline [O. F. *retret, retrete*]

retreat *v.i.* to make a retreat || (esp. of the wing tip of an airplane) to slope backward || *v.t.* (*chess*) to move (a piece) back [fr. O.F. *retraiter*]

re·trench (ritréntʃ) *v.i.* to cut down expenses, live more cheaply || *v.t.* to reduce amount of, curtail, esp. in order to economize, *the government retrenched its expenditure on education* || (*mil.*) to furnish with a retrenchment **re·trénch·ment** *n.* a retrenching || (*mil.*) an inner line of defense (e.g. a ditch and parapet) to which troops can retreat if the outer line is breached [fr. F. *retrencher*]

ret·ri·bu·tion (retrəbjú:ʃən) *n.* merited punishment || the meting out of reward or punishment according to one's deserts, esp. (*theol.*) in the hereafter || something given in recompense [O.F.]

re·trib·u·tive (ritríbjutiv) *adj.* of, relating to or involving retribution, *retributive justice* [fr. L. *retribuere* (*retributus*), to give, assign]

re·triev·al (ritrí:vəl) *n.* a retrieving **beyond** (or **past**) **retrieval** lost without chance of recovery

re·trieve (ritrí:v) **1.** *pres. part.* **re·triev·ing** *past* and *past part.* **re·trieved** *v.t.* (of dogs) to find and bring back (fallen game) || to get back possession of || to win back (something almost lost), *to retrieve a reputation* || to save, *to retrieve a situation* || to put right, *to retrieve a mistake* || (*games*) to return (a difficult ball) || *v.i.* (of dogs) to bring back fallen game **2.** *n.* (*games*) the return of a difficult ball **beyond** (or **past**) **retrieve** beyond (or past) retrieval **re·triev·er** *n.* a dog of any of various breeds trained to recover fallen game [fr. O.F. *retrover, retrouver*]

ret·ro·act (retrouǽkt) *v.i.* to have effect as from a stipulated date in the past || to act in a way which affects the past **ret·ro·ác·tion** *n.* **ret·ro·ác·tive** *adj.* [fr. L. *retroagere* (*retroactus*)]

ret·ro·cede (retrousí:d) *pres. part.* **ret·ro·ced·ing** *past* and *past part.* **ret·ro·ced·ed** *v.t.* to cede (territory) back to a country [fr. F. *rétrocéder*]

retrocede *pres. part.* **ret·ro·ced·ing** *past* and *past part.* **ret·ro·ced·ed** *v.i.* to recede, move back [fr. L. *retrocedere*]

ret·ro·ces·sa·tion (retrouseséiʃən) *n.* a ceding back [fr. F. *rétrocession*]

ret·ro·ces·sion (retrouséʃən) *n.* a moving backward [fr. L.L. *retrocessio* (*retrocessionis*)]

ret·ro·choir (rétrəkwaiər) *n.* the area behind the high altar in a large church or cathedral [fr. M.L. *retrochorus*]

ret·ro·en·gine (retrouéndʒin) *n.* (*aerospace*) a reverse thrust engine

ret·ro·fit (retroufít) *v.* **1.** to modify equipment to include improvements in design and use **2.** to install new equipment in an old structure

ret·ro·flex (rétrəfleks) *adj.* (*biol.*) bent sharply backwards || (*phon.*, of the tip of the tongue) raised and bent back || (*phon.*, of a vowel) articulated in this manner **rét·ro·flexed** *adj.* [fr. M.L. *retroflectere* (*retroflexus*), to bend back]

ret·ro·flex·ion (retrəflékʃən) *n.* the act of bending back || the state of being bent backwards, esp. (*med.*) of the uterus upon the cervix || (*phon.*) retroflex articulation [fr. Mod. L. *retroflexio* (*retroflexionis*)]

ret·ro·gra·da·tion (retrougreidéiʃən) *n.* retrogression || (*astron.*) regression [fr. L. *retrogradatio* (*retrogradationis*)]

ret·ro·grade (rétrəgreid) **1.** *v.i. pres. part.* **ret·ro·grad·ing** *past* and *past part.* **ret·ro·grad·ed** to go from a better to a worse condition || (*astron.*) to move in a direction contrary to normal, esp. (of a planet) to appear to move from east to west in the solar system **2.** *adj.* moving or directed backwards || involving something worse or less desirable, *a retrograde step* || inverse, esp. of an alphabet that is written from right to left || (*astron.*) showing regression || (*aerospace*) of rotation of more than 90 degrees in the opposite direction to that of the launching point [fr. L. *retrogradi* or *retrogradare*, to go backward]

ret·ro·gress (retrəgrés) *v.i.* to revert to an inferior state [fr. L. *retrogradi* (*retrogressus*), to go backwards]

ret·ro·gres·sion (retrəgréʃən) *n.* (*astron.*) regression || a reversion to an inferior state, esp. (*biol.*) a reverting to a lower state in the evolutionary process of the individual or race || the subsiding of symptoms of a disease [fr. L. *retrogradi* (*retrogressus*), to retrograde]

ret·ro·gres·sive (retrəgrésiv) *adj.* retrograde

ret·ro·pack (rétroupæk) *n.* (*aerospace*) a group of retroengines on a spacecraft

ret·ro·re·flec·tive (retrourifléktiv) *adj.* of reflection of light to its source **—retroreflect** *v.* **—retroflection** *n.* **—retroflector** *n.* the device

ret·ro·rock·et (rétrourɒkit) *n.* a spacecraft's auxiliary rocket engine with a thrust opposing the vehicle's motion, so as to bring about deceleration, or for separating rocket stages, etc.

retro-rocket *n.* (*aerospace*) a rocket on an aircraft that provides reverse thrust for deceleration **—retrofire** *v.*

re·trorse (ritrórs) *aaj.* (*biol.*) turned or directed backwards or downwards [fr. L. *retrorsus*]

ret·ro·spect (rétrəspekt) *n.* an instance of looking back on past activities or events (cf. PROSPECT) **in retrospect** the past being looked at afresh, *in retrospect, the meeting was more successful than we had imagined* **ret·ro·spéc·tion** *n.* the act or process of reviewing the past || an instance of this **ret·ro·spéc·tive** *adj.* of, relating to or indulging in retrospection, *a retrospective exhibition* || (of payments etc.) retroactive,

applying to past enactments (cf. PROSPECTIVE) [fr. L. *retrospicere* (*retrospectus*), to look back upon]

retrospective *n.* a comprehensive presentation of accomplishments over a period of years, esp. of an artist **—retrospective** *adj.*

ret·rous·sé (rətrú:sei, rətru:séi) *adj.* (of a nose) turned up at the tip [F.]

ret·ro·ver·sion (rətrové:rʒən, rətrəvé:rʃən) *n.* the act or process of turning back || (*med.*) a retroflexion of the uterus || a retrogression in development or condition [fr. L. *retrovertere* (*retroversus*), to turn backward]

re·turn (ritá:rn) **1.** *n.* the act of returning to or from another place or condition || the act of returning something to a former place or condition || something returned, e.g. (*pl.*) unsold newspapers sent back to the publisher for refund || profit from business etc., esp. this in relation to its source || (*pl.*) an official report, announced or printed, of the results of balloting || a report of statistics, *tax returns* || (*Br.*) election, *the return of the same members is likely* || (*pl.*) the mail received in answer to an advertising campaign || (*archit.*) a wall etc. made to run in a different direction from the facade or from the direct line of building, esp. one turned back through 90° || (*card games*) a card played in answer to a partner's lead || (*fencing*) a riposte || (*tennis, handball* etc.) the act of returning a ball || (*baseball* and *cricket*) the sending back of a fielded ball || a pipe, channel etc. for conveying liquid etc. back to its starting point || (*Br.*) a return ticket **in return** by way of reward or retaliation **many happy returns (of the day)** a birthday greeting wishing the person greeted a long, happy life **2.** *adj.* of or pertaining to a return or a returning, *a return trip* || given or done in return, *a return blow* || used for returning, *a return pipe* [A.F. *retorn, retourn*]

return *v.i.* to go or come back to the same place, condition, person etc. || to go back mentally, *thoughts constantly returning to childhood* || to revert, *to return to my original theme* || to occur again, *the fits return at intervals* || *v.t.* to bring, give, put etc. (someone or something) back to a former place, condition or person, *return the book to the library, his departure returned us to normalcy, return the pipe to its owner* || to give back by way of thanks or retaliation, *to return a call* || to express as an answer or retort, *to return an oath* || to repay (a loan) || to pronounce (a verdict) || (*Br.*) to elect by voting || to yield (e.g. a profit) || to cast back (e.g. sound) || to submit (a set of statistics) required by authority || to render (thanks) in prayer || to cause (a wall etc.) to change in direction, esp. back through 90° || (*card games*) to respond to (a partner's lead) by the expected lead || (esp. *tennis*) to play back (the ball) || (esp. *baseball* and *cricket*) to send back (a fielded ball) || (*mil.*) to put (e.g. a weapon) back in its proper place [fr. O.F. *retorner, retourner*]

re·turn·a·ble (ritá:rnəb'l) *adj.* that may be returned || (*law*) required to be returned [A.F. *retournable*, O.F. *retournable*]

re·turn·ee (ritə:rní:, ritá:rni:) *n.* a soldier returning to the U.S.A. after service overseas

return game a return match

return match a second game played between the same opposing teams or players so that the loser of the first game may have a chance to recoup the loss

return ticket (*Br.*) a round-trip ticket, i.e. for a journey to a destination and back over the same route || the part of such a ticket valid for the trip back to the point of departure

re·tuse (ritú:s, ritjú:s) *adj.* (*biol.*) obtuse, with a broad shallow notch in the middle [fr. L. *retundere* (*retusus*), to beat]

re·type (ri:táip) *pres. part.* **re·typ·ing** *past* and *past part.* **re·typed** *v.t.* to type again

Retz (rets), Jean-François Paul de Gondi, cardinal de (1613-79), French politician and prelate. An enemy of Mazarin, he was a leader of the Fronde. He was nominally archbishop of Paris (1654-62) but was in exile until the death of Mazarin (1661), after which he was reconciled with Louis XIV. His 'Mémoires' vividly touch off men and situations

Reu·ben (rú:bən) Hebrew patriarch, the eldest son of Jacob || the Israelite tribe of which he was the ancestor

Reu·ben sandwich (rú:bən) three-deck sandwich with corned beef, turkey, and Swiss cheese

Reuch·lin (róixlən), Johann (1455-1522), German humanist. His 'De rudimentis Hebraicis'

CONCISE PRONUNCIATION KEY: **(a)** æ, cat; ɑ, car; ɔ fawn; ei, snake. **(e)** e, hen; i:, sheep; iə, deer; εə, bear. **(i)** i, fish; ai, tiger; ə:, bird. **(o)** o, ox; au, cow; ou, goat; u, poor; ɔi, royal. **(u)** ʌ, duck; u, bull; u:, goose; ə, bacillus; ju:, cube. x, loch; θ, think; ð, bother; z, Zen; ʒ, corsage; dʒ, savage; ŋ, orangutang; j, yak; ʃ, fish; tʃ, fetch; 'l, rabble; 'n, redden. Complete pronunciation key appears inside front cover.

(1506), a grammar and dictionary, was a major contribution to Hebrew scholarship. His defense of Hebrew literature caused a bitter feud between reformers and conservatives in the Church

re·u·ni·fi·ca·tion (ri:ju:nifikéiʃən) *n.* the restoration of a divided country to unity

re·u·ni·fy (ri:jú:nifai) *pres. part.* **re·u·ni·fy·ing** *past* and *past part.* **re·u·ni·fied** *v.t.* to restore (e.g. a divided country) to unity

Ré·u·nion (reiynjɔ̃) *a* mountainous, volcanic island (area 970 sq. miles, pop. 515,814) in the Indian Ocean between Mauritius and Madagascar, forming an overseas department of France. Chief town: Saint-Denis. People: Creole, with mulatto, Indian and African minorities. Highest point: Piton des Neiges (10,069 ft). Mean annual temperature: 69°. Rainfall: windward side over 100 ins, leeward side 30 ins. Exports: sugar (80% of exports, grown on coastal plantations), rum, tobacco, essential oils, fruit. Subsistence crops: corn, vegetables, vines. The island was discovered by the Portuguese (1513) and occupied by the French (17th c.). It became an overseas department in 1946

re·un·ion (ri:jú:njən) *n.* a reuniting or being reunited ‖ a meeting of former associates or of members of a family separated for a long time ‖ any social gathering held more or less regularly

re·u·nite (ri:ju:náit) *pres. part.* **re·u·nit·ing** *past* and *past part.* **re·u·nit·ed** *v.t.* to unite again after a period of separation ‖ *v.i.* to be united again [fr. M.L. *reunire* (*reunitus*)]

Reu·ters (rɔ́itərz) an independent international news agency founded (1851) in London by Baron Paul Julius von Reuter

Reuther (rú:θər), Walter Philip (1907-70), U.S. labor leader, president of the United Auto Workers (UAW) (1946-70). As a factory worker he became involved in the unions and quickly rose in the ranks. He also served as president of the Congress of Industrial Organizations (CIO) (1952-5) and, after its merger with the American Federation of Labor (AFL), as vice-president of the AFL-CIO (1955-68)

rev (rev) 1. *n.* (*pop.*) a revolution of an engine 2. *v. pres. part.* **rev·ving** *past* and *past part.* **rev·ved** *v.t.* (*pop.*, usually with 'up') to increase the number of revolutions per minute of (an engine) ‖ *v.i.* (*pop.*, of an engine, usually with 'up') to turn over faster [REVOLUTION]

Re·val (réival) *TALLINN

re·val·or·i·za·tion (ri:vælərizéiʃən) *n.* a revalorizing or being revalorized **re·val·or·ize** *pres. part.* **re·val·or·iz·ing** *past* and *past part.* **re·val·or·ized** *v.t.* to alter the value of (a currency or assets)

re·val·ue (ri:vælju:) *pres. part.* **re·val·u·ing** *past* and *past part.* **re·val·ued** *v.t.* to give a new value to (e.g. currency) ‖ to set a new estimate of worth on

re·vamp (ri:væmp) *v.t.* to put a new vamp on (an old shoe) ‖ to refurbish, revise and improve, *to revamp a play*

re·vas·cu·lar·ize (ri:væskjuləri:z) *v.* (*med.*) 1. to substitute arteries from other parts of the body for clogged or diseased arteries 2. to reestablish of blood supply, esp. after destruction of arteries —**revascularization** *n. Cf* CORONARY BYPASS

re·veal (ri:ví:l) *n.* (*archit.*) the thickness of a wall as shown by a doorway, aperture or window [fr. M.E. *revale*, to bring down]

reveal *v.t.* to make known, manifest, *to reveal one's real intention*, *God revealed his will to the Israelites* ‖ to expose to view (something that was hidden) ‖ to divulge (a secret) [fr. O.F. *reveler* or L. *revelare*]

revealed religion a religion based upon divine revelation (cf. NATURAL RELIGION)

re·veil·le (réveli:) *n.* (*mil.*) as signal sounded esp. by a bugle, to wake members of the forces in the morning ‖ (*mil.*) the first assembly of the day [fr. F. *réveillez* (-*vous*), wake up]

Re·vel (réival) *TALLINN

rev·el (réval) *n.* (*hist., pl.*) the games and dances etc. of a festive occasion [O.F.]

revel *pres. part.* **rev·el·ing**, esp. *Br.* **rev·el·ling** *past* and *past part.* **rev·eled**, esp. *Br.* **rev·elled** *v.i.* (with 'in') to take intense pleasure, *she revels in ballet* ‖ to be festive, *to revel all night long* [O.F. *reveler*]

Rev·e·la·tion (revəléiʃən) the 27th and last book (late 1st or early 2nd c.) of the New Testament, of uncertain authorship. It contains apocalyptic visions of the victory of God over Satan and was apparently written to strengthen persecuted Christians

rev·e·la·tion (revəléiʃən) *n.* a revealing ‖ something revealed ‖ (*theol.*) God's manifestation of himself to man ‖ something revealed to man by God ‖ something which brings a shock of surprise, *the revelation of hearing one's recorded voice* [O.F.]

rev·el·ry (révəlri:) *pl.* **rev·el·ries** *n.* the act of reveling

re·ven·di·ca·tion (rivendikéiʃən) *n.* (*law*) a formal claim for the recovery of property ‖ (*law*) the recovery of property by formal claim [F.]

re·venge (rivéndʒ) 1. *v.t. pres. part.* **re·veng·ing** *past* and *past part.* **re·venged** to inflict injury etc. in return for (injury etc.) ‖ to avenge (oneself or another person) 2. *n.* a revenging ‖ something done in revenging, *his revenge was to set the papers on fire* ‖ a desire to inflict injury etc. in return for an injury etc. suffered, *to be full of revenge* ‖ (*games*) a chance to win after a previous defeat, e.g. in a return match [obs. F. *revenger*]

rev·e·nue (révanu:, révanju:) *n.* return from investments, property etc. ‖ (*pl.*) items of income collectively ‖ the annual or periodic income, from taxes, customs and excise etc., collected by a government, state etc. for public use ‖ a government department in charge of collecting such income [O.F.]

revenue sharing policy of subsidizing taxes received by the federal government with states and/or municipalities

revenue stamp a stamp used on documents etc. as evidence that a tax has been paid

revenue tariff a tariff designed primarily to secure public revenue (cf. PROTECTIVE TARIFF)

re·verb (ri:vé:rb) *n.* an echo effect in a musical recording —**reverb** *n.* device for creating an echo effect

re·ver·ber·ate (rivé:rbəreit) *pres. part.* **re·ver·ber·at·ing** *past* and *past part.* **re·ver·ber·at·ed** *v.t.* to reflect (light etc.) ‖ to throw back (sound) ‖ to deflect (e.g. heat in a furnace) ‖ to subject to the heat of a reverberatory furnace ‖ *v.i.* to reecho ‖ to be reflected ‖ (*metall.*, of flame or heat, with 'upon' or 'over') to be forced to strike [fr. L. *reverberare* (*reverberatus*)]

re·ver·ber·a·tion (rivə:rbəréiʃən) *n.* a reechoing of sound ‖ a reflecting of light etc. ‖ a deflection of heat etc. ‖ subjection to the action of a reverberatory furnace ‖ something reverberated [O.F.]

re·ver·ber·a·tive (rivé:rbərətiv, rivé:rbəreitiv) *adj.* reverberating or tending to reverberate ‖ of the nature of reverberation

re·ver·ber·a·tor (rivé:rbəreitər) *n.* something that produces reverberation, e.g. a reflector

re·ver·ber·a·to·ry (rivé:rbərətɔ:ri:, rivé:rbərətɔuri) 1. *adj.* acting by reverberation 2. *pl.* **re·ver·ber·a·to·ries** *n.* a reverberatory furnace

reverberatory furnace a furnace or kiln in which the ore, metal etc. is melted not by direct contact with flame, but by the heat of flames radiated from the roof

Re·vere (riviər), Paul (1735-1818), American patriot. By a famous night ride (Apr. 18, 1775) he warned the Massachusetts colonists of the arrival of British troops at the start of the Revolutionary War

re·vere (riviər) *pres. part.* **re·ver·ing** *past* and *past part.* **re·vered** *v.t.* to regard with affectionate awe or veneration [fr. F. *révérer* or L. *revereri*]

rev·er·ence (révərəns, révrəns) 1. *n.* a revering, *teach them reverence for truth* ‖ the condition or state of being revered, *to be held in reverence* ‖ (*old-fash.*) a bow or curtsy 2. *v.t. pres. part.* **rev·er·enc·ing** *past* and *past part.* **rev·er·enced** to revere [O. F.]

Rev·er·end (révərənd, révrənd) *adj.* (*abbr.* Rev., preceded by 'the') used as a title for a clergyman (his surname being preceded by Mr. or Dr. or by his Christian name) [O.F.]

rev·er·ent (révərənt, révrənt) *adj.* feeling or showing due reverence [fr. L. *reverens* (*reverentis*) fr. *revereri*, to revere]

rev·er·en·tial (revərénʃəl) *adj.* showing reverence [fr. L. *reverentia*, reverence]

rev·er·ie (révəri:) *n.* the state of being absorbed in dreamlike contemplation ‖ an idea, theory etc. characteristic of such contemplation [F.]

re·vers (riviər) *pl.* **re·vers** (riviərz) *n.* a fold in a piece of tailoring work showing the inside lining of a facing ‖ a lapel on women's jackets, coats etc. [F.]

re·ver·sal (rivé:rsəl) *n.* a reversing or being reversed ‖ (*law*) a revoking or overthrowing of a legal proceeding

re·verse (rivé:rs) *pres. part.* **re·vers·ing** *past* and *past part.* **re·versed** *v.t.* to change the direction, arrangement, nature etc. of (something) to its opposite ‖ to turn (a reversible garment) inside out ‖ to turn upside down, *to reverse an hourglass* ‖ to change (a trend, opinion etc.) to the opposite ‖ to cause to go or move backwards, *to reverse a car* ‖ (*law*) to annul, make void (a decision etc.) ‖ *v.i.* to move, turn or go backwards ‖ (*dancing*) to go in the opposite direction ‖ to put an engine etc. in reverse [F. *reverser*]

reverse 1. *adj.* opposite, *the reverse side of the cloth* ‖ backward, *reverse motion* ‖ causing backward movement, *reverse gear* 2. *n.* the opposite of something, *what you say is the reverse of what I believed* ‖ the back side of a coin, medal etc. (opp. OBVERSE) ‖ a change from good fortune to bad, *a financial reverse* ‖ (*mil.*) a defeat ‖ a mechanism, e.g. a gear, for causing a motor etc. to run backwards **in reverse** in reverse gear ‖ (of a vehicle) moving backwards ‖ in the reverse order [O.F. *revers*, reverse]

reverse discrimination discrimination against one group (e.g., white people) alleged to result from affirmative action for another group (e.g., black people)

reverse mortgage mortgage funds withdrawn in installments from a lender, e.g., as a source of living expenses

reverse osmosis the pumping of a solvent through a semipermeable membrane to counter osmosis

re·vers·i·bil·i·ty (rivə:rsəbíliti:) *n.* the state or quality of being reversible

re·vers·i·ble (rivə:rsəb'l) *adj.* able to be reversed ‖ (of a fabric) having the full pattern on both sides ‖ (of a garment) made so that either the inside or outside can be worn outermost ‖ (*chem.*) of a reaction in which a change from one state to another can occur in either direction **re·vers·i·bly** *adv.*

re·ver·sion (rivé:rʒən, rivé:rʃən) *n.* return to a former condition, belief etc. or an instance of this ‖ (*biol.*) atavism ‖ (*biol.*) an atavistic organism or individual ‖ (*law*) the right to own something when it is relinquished by the present owner ‖ (*law*) the returning of property to its previous owner at the end of a period during which it was the temporary possession of someone else ‖ a reversionary annuity **re·ver·sion·al** *adj.* **re·ver·sion·ar·y** (rivé:rʒəneri:, rivé:rʃəneri) *adj.* **re·ver·sion·er** (rivé:rʃənər) *n.* (*law*) someone who has a reversion [O.F.]

re·vert (rivé:rt) *v.i.* to return to a former belief, opinion, condition etc., *the tribe reverted to paganism* ‖ to return to a topic, *to revert to your earlier remark...* ‖ (*law*) to return to a former owner by reversion ‖ (*biol.*) to undergo reversion **re·vert·i·ble** *adj.* subject to reversion [O.F. *revertir*]

re·ver·tant (rivé:rtənt) *n.* (*genetics*) a mutated organism that returns to a previous condition, e.g., a hybrid returning to a wild form — **revertant** *adj.*

re·vet (rivét) *pres. part.* **re·vet·ting** *past* and *past part.* **re·vet·ted** *v.t.* to face (an embankment, trench etc.) with supporting material **re·vét·ment** *n.* a retaining wall or other support for a trench or embankment [fr. F. *revêtir*]

re·view (rivjú:) 1. *n.* a looking over, considering, studying etc. again ‖ a general consideration of past events or situations, *a review of one's life* ‖ a ceremonial inspection of troops etc. ‖ (*law*) a reexamination of a decision etc. ‖ a critical evaluation of a book, concert, theatrical performance etc. in mass media ‖ a periodical containing critical evaluations and articles on specific subjects, *a science review* ‖ a brushing up (on work learned earlier) **re·view·al** *n.* **re·view·er** *n.* a person who writes reviews of books, plays etc. for publication 2. *v.t.* to consider again, *to review a manuscript in the light of criticism* ‖ to inspect ceremonially, *to review troops* ‖ to pass over (past events etc.) in one's mind ‖ to write a critical evaluation of (a book, theatrical performance etc.) ‖ (*law*) to reexamine judicially ‖ to brush up (something learned earlier) ‖ *v.i.* to write reviews of books, plays etc.

re·vile (riváil) *pres. part.* **re·vil·ing** *past* and *past part.* **re·viled** *v.t.* to use abusive language to or about ‖ *v.i.* to speak abusively [O.F. *reviler*]

re·vis·al (riváiz'l) *n.* a revising or being revised

re·vise (riváiz) 1. *v.t. pres. part.* **re·vis·ing** *past* and *past part.* **re·vised** to reexamine, esp. in

---

CONCISE PRONUNCIATION KEY: **(a)** æ, cat; ɑ, car; ɔ fawn; ei, snake. **(e)** e, hen; i:, sheep; iə, deer; εə, bear. **(i)** i, fish; ai, tiger; ə:, bird. **(o)** o, ox; au, cow; ou, goat; u, poor; ɔi, royal. **(u)** ʌ, duck; u, bull; u:, goose; ə, bacillus; ju:, cube. x, loch; θ, think; ð, bother; z, Zen; ʒ, corsage; dʒ, savage; ŋ, orangutang; j, yak; ʃ, fish; tʃ, fetch; 'l, rabble; 'n, redden. Complete pronunciation key appears inside front cover.

order to discover and amend errors in (a text etc.) ‖ to brush up (something learned earlier) so as to refresh the memory **2.** *n.* (*printing*) a proof of corrected type [F. *reviser*]

Revised Standard Version a revision (1946-57) by a committee of American biblical scholars of the American Standard edition (1901) of the Revised Version of the Bible. Designed for use in public worship, it succeeded largely in preserving the beauty of the Authorized (King James) Version

Revised Version (*abbr.* R.V., Rev. Ver.) a revision of the Authorized (King James) Version (1611) of the Bible, made by a committee of English and American scholars. The New Testament was published in 1881 and the Old Testament in 1885

re·vi·sion (riví$\mathfrak{z}$ən) *n.* a revising or being revised ‖ the result of revising, e.g. a revised text **re·ví·sion·al** *adj.* [fr. L.L. *revisio* (*revisionis*)]

re·vi·sion·ism (riví$\mathfrak{z}$ənizəm) *n.* a movement among socialists to modify Marxian revolutionary doctrine **re·vi·sion·ist** *n.*

re·vi·so·ry (riváizəri:) *adj.* of or relating to revision ‖ having the power to revise, *a revisory body*

re·viv·al (riváivəl) *n.* a reviving or being revived ‖ (of the mind or body) a coming back to health or consciousness ‖ an awakening of religious fervor, esp. by evangelism ‖ an evangelistic meeting or series of meetings ‖ the reappearance of a past mode, esp. the reappearance of Gothic architecture in the 19th c. ‖ a restaging of a play, esp. of one long neglected **re·vív·al·ism, re·vív·al·ist** *ns.*

Revival of Learning the literary aspect of the Renaissance

re·vive (riváiv) *pres. part.* **re·viv·ing** *past and past part.* **re·vived** *v.i.* to come back to consciousness ‖ to recover strength, vigor, spirits etc., *he revived after a rest and some food* ‖ (*chem.*, of a metal) to recover the metallic state ‖ *v.t.* to restore to consciousness, strength, vigor, spirits etc. ‖ to produce (an old play) again ‖ to make valid again, *why revive harsh laws?* ‖ to bring (old memories) to mind again ‖ to bring back into fashion ‖ (*chem.*) to restore (a metal) to the metallic state [fr. F. *revivre*]

re·viv·i·fi·ca·tion (rivivifikéi$\mathfrak{s}$ən) *n.* a revivifying or being revivified

re·viv·i·fy (rivívifai) *pres. part.* **re·viv·i·fy·ing** *past and past part.* **re·viv·i·fied** *v.t.* to restore to strength or vigor [fr. F. *revivifier*]

re·vi·vor (riváivər) *n.* (*Br.*, *law*) proceedings to revive a lawsuit after its lapsing (due to a death etc.)

rev·o·ca·bil·i·ty (rẹvəkəbíliti:) *n.* the state or quality of being revocable

rev·o·ca·ble, rev·o·ka·ble (révəkəb'l, rivóukəb'l) *adj.* that can be revoked [O.F. or fr. L. *revocabilis*]

rev·o·ca·tion (rẹvəkéi$\mathfrak{s}$ən) *n.* a revoking or being revoked ‖ a repealing or annulling [O.F.]

rev·o·ca·to·ry (révəkətɔ̣ri:, révəkətouri:) *adj.* revoking, tending to revoke [fr. L. L. *revocatorius*]

revokable *REVOCABLE

re·voke (rivóuk) **1.** *v. pres. part.* **re·vok·ing** *past and past part.* **re·voked** *v.t.* to cancel, withdraw, *to revoke permission* ‖ *v.i.* (*cards*) to fail to follow suit when one can and should do so **2.** *n.* (*cards*) a failure to follow suit when one could have done so [O.F. *revoquer*]

re·volt (rivóult) *n.* an opposing of authority, esp. by armed rebellion ‖ such rebellion ‖ the mental state of a person or group of persons likely to express itself by rebellion **in revolt** (of a person or group) in a state of rebellion [F. *révolte*]

revolt *v.i.* to turn actively against the government, esp. in armed rebellion ‖ to rebel against other authority ‖ (with 'at' or 'against') to feel disgust, *the mind revolts at such an idea* ‖ *v.t.* to disgust, *the scene revolted him* **re·vólt·ing** *adj.* disgusting ‖ rebelling [fr. F. *révolter*]

rev·o·lute (révəlu:t) *adj.* (*bot.*, esp. of leaves) having the margins or tips rolled backward or downward [fr. L. *revolutus*, rolled back]

rev·o·lu·tion (rẹvəlú:$\mathfrak{s}$ən) *n.* the act of revolving ‖ one complete turn in the action of revolving, *45 revolutions a minute* ‖ an unconstitutional overthrow of an established government ‖ a fundamental social change, *the Industrial Revolution* ‖ any fundamental complete change ‖ (of heavenly bodies) the action of going around in an orbit ‖ (of heavenly bodies) the time taken to complete this action **rev·o·lú·tion·ar·y 1.** *adj.* of or relating to a revolution, esp. a political or social revolution ‖ tending toward, or seeming

to tend toward, a revolution, *a revolutionary speech* **2.** *pl.* **rev·o·lu·tion·ar·ies** *n.* a revolutionist [O.F.]

Revolutionary War (*Am.*=*Br.* War of American Independence) the struggle (1775-83) of the Thirteen Colonies of America for independence from British rule. The war was caused by British attempts to tax the colonies for revenue without representation in Parliament and to make them pay for a standing army. The colonies' dependence on Britain was lessened when the Treaty of Paris (1763) removed the French and Indian threat. The colonies revolted (1775) under Washington and declared their independence (1776). Burgoyne's surrender at Saratoga (1777) encouraged France to declare war on Britain (1778), followed by Spain (1779) and the Netherlands (1780). Britain lost command of the sea, and her army was finally defeated at Yorktown (1781). Britain regained naval supremacy (1781-2) and the war ended with the Treaty of Paris (1783), in which the independence of the U.S.A. was recognized. The war discredited George III's government, weakened France financially, and served as an inspiration for the French Revolution and for revolutions in Spanish colonies in America

rev·o·lu·tion·ist (rẹvəlú:$\mathfrak{s}$ənist) *n.* a person who takes part in a revolution or who advocates revolution

rev·o·lu·tion·ize (rẹvəlú:$\mathfrak{s}$ənaiz) *pres. part.* **rev·o·lu·tion·iz·ing** *past and past part.* **rev·o·lu·tion·ized** *v.t.* to change completely as if by a revolution, *the invention of the reaper revolutionized harvesting*

Revolution of 1789 *FRENCH REVOLUTION
Revolution of 1830 *FRANCE
Revolution of 1848 *FRANCE, *GERMANY, *HUNGARY, *ITALY
Revolution of 1905 *RUSSIA
Revolution of 1917 *RUSSIA

re·volve (rivólv) *pres. part.* **re·vol·ving** *past and past part.* **re·volved** *v.t.* to cause to turn around an axis or center, *to revolve a prayer wheel* ‖ (*rhet.*) to ponder, *to revolve a problem* ‖ *v.i.* to move around or as if around an axis or center ‖ to recur, *the revolving seasons* ‖ (*rhet.*, of a problem etc.) to present itself for consideration under various aspects, *the subject was revolving in his mind* [fr. L. *revolvere*]

re·volv·er (rivólvər) *n.* a pistol with a revolving feeding mechanism enabling several cartridges to be discharged without reloading

revolving door a door, e.g. of a public building, consisting of two or more panels, normally of glass, attached to a central axis to allow free rotation usually in one direction

re·vue (rivjú:) *n.* a stage spectacle consisting of sketches, songs etc. in which parody and satire predominate [F.]

re·vul·sion (rivÁl$\mathfrak{s}$ən) *n.* a sudden, violent antipathy, *a revulsion against a person* ‖ disgust, *he shrank away in revulsion* [F.]

rev up or **rev** *v.* to get started by turning an airplane propeller

re·ward (riwɔ́rd) *n.* something given or promised in recognition of service rendered or in requital for ill-doing ‖ money offered for information leading to the capture of a criminal, the recovery of lost property etc. [O.N.F.]

reward *v.t.* to give a reward to (a person) ‖ to give a reward for (a service, merit etc.) **re·wárd·ing** *adj.* giving personal satisfaction, *a rewarding occupation* [O.N.F. *rewarder*]

re·wire (ri:wáiər) *pres. part.* **re·wir·ing** *past and past part.* **re·wired** *v.t.* to furnish (an electric circuit) with new wires ‖ to furnish (a house etc.) with a rewired electric circuit

re·word (ri:wɔ́rd) *v.t.* to express in other words

re·write 1. (ri:ráit) *v.t. pres. part.* **re·writ·ing** *past* **re·wrote** (ri:róut) *past part.* **re·writ·ten** (ri:rít'n) to alter or improve the style or wording of, *rewrite the section on accountancy*, esp. (*journalism*) to make (material turned in by a reporter) suitable for publication **2.** (rí:rait) *n.* a piece of writing treated in this way

Re·yes (réjes), Alfonso (1889-1959), Mexican humanist writer and diplomat. He exerted a major influence on the intellectual life of Latin America. His prose works, inspired by Greek and Roman civilization and by national themes, include 'Cuestiones estéticas', 'Homero en Cuernavaca', and 'Visión de Anáhuac'

Reyes, Neftalí *NERUDA

Reyes syndrome (raiz), a children's disease, first described (1963) by Australian pathologist R.D.K. Reye, that occurs most often as a result

of influenza or chicken pox. Symptoms include high fever, headache, vomiting and central nervous system disorders. It is thought that aspirin, often prescribed for the initial sickness, can trigger Reyes syndrome

Rey·kja·vik (réikjəvi:k) the capital and chief port (pop. 87,309) of Iceland, on the southwest coast. Industries: fishing, fish processing, codliver oil refining, shipbuilding. University (1911), national museums. It was settled by Vikings (late 9th c.) and became the capital of Iceland in 1918

Rey·les (réiles), Carlos (1868-1938), Uruguayan novelist, the author of 'Beba', 'La Raza de Caín', 'El embrujo de Sevilla', 'El gaucho Florido', and 'El terruño'

Rey·naud (reinou), Paul (1878-1966), French statesman. Appointed prime minister (Mar. 1940), he resigned (June 1940) when the Germans invaded France. He was a prisoner in Germany (1943-5)

Reyn·olds (rénəldz), Sir Joshua (1723-92), English portrait painter. He was a founding member and first president (1769) of the Royal Academy of Arts, London. His annual addresses to the Academy, published as his 'Discourses', have become classics in the field of art criticism. His portraits and historical paintings are notable for their richness of color. Reynolds was a member of the famous dining club which included Johnson, Gibbon, Burke, Garrick, Sheridan, Goldsmith and others

Reynolds, Osborne (1842-1912), British engineer. He developed the theory of the radiometer, and invented a high-lift centrifugal pump

Re·zai·yeh (rezajá) (formerly Urmia) a salt lake (area 1,500-2,300 sq. miles, depending on season) in N.W. Iran, near Tabriz

Reza Shah Pahlavi *PAHLAVI, REZA SHAH

R factor unit of measurement of **1.** a material's resistance to heat loss, used in stating the effectiveness of insulation, e.g., 6 in of fiberglass equals R-19 **2.** bacterial resistance to antibiotics in cells

R.F.D. rural free delivery

RF energy the energy of alternating current in the frequency range to 10 kHz and 300 GHz

RF-4 *PHANTOM II

RGM-84 *HARPOON

RGM-66D *STANDARD SSM (ARM)

rhab·do·vi·rus (rᴂbdouváirəs) *n.* (*med.*) any of a group of viruses associated with animal-bite diseases, e.g., rabies

rhachis *RACHIS

Rhad·a·man·thine (rᴂdəmᴂnθain, rᴂdəmᴂnθin) *adj.* (*rhet.*) sternly just [after *Rhadamanthus*, (Gk mythol.) son of Zeus and Europa and a judge in the lower world]

Rhae·ti·a, Rae·ti·a (rí:fi:ə) (*hist.*) a region of what is now E. Switzerland and W. Austria, annexed (c. 15 B.C.) as a province by the Romans

Rhae·tic (rí:tik) *n.* (*geol.*) the uppermost division of the European Triassic, disclosed in the Rhaetian Alps [fr. L. *Rhaeticus*, Rhaetian]

Rhae·to·Ro·man·ic (ri:touroumᴂnik) *n.* a Romance language of the Tyrol and the cantons of S.E. Switzerland and N. Italy

rhap·sod·ic (rᴂpsódik) *adj.* of, resembling or having the form of rhapsody ‖ extravagantly enthusiastic **rhap·sód·i·cal** *adj.* [fr. Gk *rhapsōdikos*]

rhap·so·dist (rᴂpsədist) *n.* a professional reciter of epic poetry in ancient Greece [fr. Gk *rhapsōdos* fr. *rhaptein*, to put together and *ōdē*, an ode]

rhap·so·dize (rᴂpsədaiz) *pres. part.* **rhap·so·diz·ing** *past and past part.* **rhap·so·dized** *v.i.* to speak or write in an extravagantly enthusiastic manner

rhap·so·dy (rᴂpsədi:) *pl.* **rhap·so·dies** *n.* an epic poem of ancient Greece, or a portion of one, suitable for recitation ‖ extravagant enthusiasm in speaking or writing ‖ (*mus.*) a title given to some usually single-movement compositions having no fixed form and often based on existing themes [fr. L. *rhapsodia* fr. Gk]

rhat·a·ny (rᴂt'ni:) *pl.* **rhat·a·nies** *n.* the dried root of *Krameria triandra* or *K. argentea*, fam. *Papilionaceae*, two South American shrubs, used in medicine as an astringent ‖ either of these shrubs [fr. Mod. L. *rhatania*]

Rhe·a (rí:ə) (Gk mythol.) one of the Titans, wife of Cronus, mother of Zeus, Poseidon etc. She was identified with Cybele

rhe·a (rí:ə) *n.* a member of *Rhea*, order *Rheiformes*, a genus of ostrichlike, flightless South

American birds, esp. *R. americana* [L. after RHEA]

Rhee (ri:), Syngman (1875-1965), South Korean leader. He campaigned for self-rule (1910-19) and was president of the exiled provisional government. He was president of the Republic of South Korea (1948-60). He opposed the truce of 1953 which partitioned Korea. In Apr. 1960 riots and the resignation of his cabinet forced him to resign

Rheims (ri:mz) *REIMS

Rhen·ish (réniʃ) *adj.* of or pertaining to the Rhine or the Rhine valley [fr. L. *Rhenus*, Rhine]

rhe·ni·um (rí:ni:əm) *n.* a rare, heavy polyvalent metallic element (symbol Re, at. no. 75, at. mass 186.2) having a high melting point (3,167°C.), used esp. in thermocouples [Mod. L. fr. *Rhenus*, Rhine]

rhe·ol·o·gy (ri:ólədʒi:) *n.* the study of the deformation and flow of matter [fr. Gk *rheos*, stream + *logos*, word]

rhe·o·stat (rí:əstæt) *n.* a variable resistance for the strength of an electric current **rhe·o·stat·ic** *adj.* [fr. Gk *rheos*, stream + *statos*, standing still]

rhe·o·tax·is (ri:ətǽksis) *pl.* **rhe·o·tax·es** (ri:ətǽksi:z) *n.* (*biol.*) a locomotor response to the stimulus of a current, usually of water [Mod. L. fr. Gk *rheos*, stream + *taxis*, arrangement]

rhe·o·trope (rí:ətroup) *n.* an instrument for changing the direction of an electric current [fr. Gk *rheos*, stream + *tropos*, a turning]

rhe·ot·ro·pism (ri:ɒ́trəpizəm) *n.* (*biol.*) curvature or growth response to the influence of a water current [fr. Gk *rheos*, stream + TROPISM]

rhe·sus (rí:səs) *n. Macaca mulata*, a small light brown Indian monkey [Mod. L. fr. a proper name]

rhesus factor (*abbr.* Rh factor) an inherited sex-linked agglutinating factor sometimes present in human red blood cells, which is capable of causing an intense antigenic reaction in certain circumstances (a Rh negative mother carrying a Rh positive fetus). Those having this factor are Rh positive. Those not having it are Rh negative

rhe·tor (rí:tər) *n.* a teacher of rhetoric, esp. in ancient Greece and Rome [L. fr. Gk *rhḗtōr*]

rhet·o·ric (rétərik) *n.* the art or science of communication in words ‖ this art or science practiced or taught as a formal discipline, esp. the doctrine formulated by Aristotle and taught throughout the Middle Ages ‖ overornate or ostentatious language ‖ language held by many to be proper to elevated written style but not normally used in everyday speech (indicated by *rhet.* in this book) **rhe·tor·i·cal** (ritórik'l, ritórik'l) *adj.* [O.F. *rethorique* fr. L. fr. Gk]

rhetorical question a question posed for rhetorical effect, emphasis etc. and not meant to be answered. Its context supplies its own answer by suggestion and admits of no others

rhet·o·ri·cian (retəríʃən) *n.* a teacher of or expert in the art of rhetoric ‖ a rhetorical speaker or writer [O.F. *rethoricien*]

rheum (ru:m) *n.* a discharge from the mucous membranes of the eyes or nose [O.F. *reume* fr. L. fr. Gk]

rheu·mat·ic (rumǽtik) **1.** *adj.* relating to rheumatism ‖ affected by or suffering from rheumatism **2.** *n.* someone afflicted with rheumatism [O.F. *reumatique* fr. L. fr. Gk]

rheumatic fever a disease, often recurrent, which sometimes follows an infected throat, occurring mainly in children or young adults. It is characterized by fever, pains and swelling in and around the joints and inflammation of the pericardium and valves of the heart

rheu·ma·tism (rú:mətizəm) *n.* any of various conditions characterized by pain and swelling in and around the muscles and joints [fr. L.L. *rheumatismus*]

rheu·ma·toid (rú:mətɔid) *adj.* of or resembling rheumatoid arthritis ‖ affected with rheumatoid arthritis [fr. Gk *rheuma* (*rheumatos*), catarrh]

rheumatoid arthritis a chronic relapsing disease of unknown cause, characterized by pain and stiffness of the joints, esp. those of the limbs. It tends to be a progressive disease and may cause permanent deformity

rheumatoid factor (*med.*) an antiglobulin (gamma globulin) often found in the blood serum of rheumatoid arthritics

RH-53 *SEA STALLION

rheum·y (rú:mi:) *comp.* **rheum·i·er** *superl.* **rheum·i·est** *adj.* exuding rheum ‖ (of weather) damp and tending to cause rheumatic troubles, catarrh etc.

Rheydt (rait) a textile manufacturing town (pop. 101,500) in North Rhine-Westphalia, West Germany, adjoining München-Gladbach

Rh factor *RHESUS FACTOR

rhi·nal (ráin'l) *adj.* of or relating to the nose [fr. Gk *rhis* (*rhinos*), nose]

Rhin (Bas-) *BAS-RHIN

rhi·nen·ceph·a·lon (rainenséfələn) *pl.* **rhi·nen·ceph·a·la** (rainenséfələ) *n.* (*anat.*) the part of the forebrain forming most of the cerebral hemispheres in fishes, amphibia and reptiles, and comprising chiefly the olfactory lobes in man [fr. Gk *rhis* (*rhinos*), nose + ENCEPHALON]

rhine·stone (ráinstoun) *n.* a colorless artificial gem usually cut to resemble a diamond [trans. F. *caillou du Rhin*]

Rhine wine any of the light, dry, white wines produced in the valley of the Rhine

Rhin (Haut-) *HAUT-RHIN

Rhine (rain) (G. Rhein, Du. Rijn) the chief river (824 miles long) of W. Europe, flowing from the Swiss Alps south of Lake Constance, through W. West Germany and the Netherlands to a delta on the North Sea, forming the frontiers of Switzerland with Liechtenstein, Austria and West Germany, and of West Germany with E. France. It is navigable to Basle. Chief ports: Strasbourg, Mannheim, Cologne, Duisburg, Rotterdam. Principal tributaries: the Aar, Main, Moselle, Ruhr and Meuse. Canals link it to the Danube, Rhône, Marne, Ems, Weser and Elbe. It flows through mountains between Bonn and Mainz, in a gorge of great scenic splendor, lined with vineyards and topped with castles

Rhine, Confederation of the a military and political confederation (1806-13) created by Napoleon, including Bavaria, Württemberg, Baden, Hesse-Darmstadt and other German states, as a bastion against Prussia and Austria

Rhine·land (ráinlænd, ráinlənd) the region of West Germany along both banks of the middle Rhine

Rhine·land-Pa·lat·i·nate (ráinlænd-pəlǽt'nit) (G. Rheinland-Pfalz) a state (area 7,654 sq. miles, pop. 3,638,700) of West Germany between the middle Rhine and the western frontier, partly wooded and largely mountainous. Agricultural products: wine (Moselle valley), cereals, root vegetables, fruit, tobacco (Rhine plain). Main industries: hydroelectricity, mining, chemicals. Chief towns: Mainz (the capital), Ludwigshafen, Koblenz. The state was formed (1945) out of the S. Prussian Rhine province (*NORTH RHINE-WESTPHALIA), the Rhine Palatinate and W. Hesse-Nassau

Rhine Palatinate *PALATINATE

rhi·ni·tis (raináitis) *n.* inflammation of the mucous membrane of the nose [fr. Gk *rhis* (*rhinos*), nose]

rhi·no (ráinou) *n.* (*pop.*) a rhinoceros

rhi·noc·er·os (rainɒ́sərəs) *pl.* **rhi·noc·er·os·es**, **rhi·noc·er·os** *n.* any of various herbivorous mammals of fam. *Rhinocerotidae*, native to Africa and S.E. Asia, weighing from 2 to 3½ tons and having a very thick gray or blackish gray knobby hide and either one or two horns curving up from the snout [Mod. L. fr. Gk fr. *rhis* (*rhinos*), nose + *keras*, horn]

rhi·nol·o·gist (rainɒ́lədʒist) *n.* a physician specializing in rhinology

rhi·nol·o·gy (rainɒ́lədʒi:) *n.* the study of the nose and its diseases [fr. Gk *rhis* (*rhinos*), nose + *logos*, word]

rhi·no·plas·tic (rainouplǽstik) *adj.* of or relating to rhinoplasty

rhi·no·plas·ty (ráinouplæsti:) *n.* plastic surgery of the nose [fr. Gk *rhis* (*rhinos*), nose +*-plastia*, formation]

rhi·no·scope (ráinəskoup) *n.* an instrument for examining the interior of the nose **rhi·nos·co·py** (rainɒ́skəpi:) *n.* examination of the nasal cavity and passages [fr. Gk *rhis* (*rhinos*), nose + *skopein*, to observe]

rhi·no·vi·rus (rainouváirəs) *n.* (*med.*) one of the small viruses in the picornavirus group, associated with the common cold. Cf PICORNOVIRUS

rhi·zo·bi·um (rizóubi:əm) *pl.* **rhi·zo·bi·a** (rizóubi:ə) *n.* a rod-shaped nitrogen-fixing bacterium living in the nodules of certain leguminous plants, e.g. the bean [Mod. L. fr. Gk *rhiza*, root + *bios*, life]

rhi·zo·car·pous (raizoukárpəs) *adj.* having a perennial root or rootlike process but annual stems and foliage [fr. Gk *rhiza*, root + *karpos*, fruit]

rhi·zo·ceph·a·lous (raizouséfələs) *adj.* of or relating to a parasitic crustacean of the order *Rhizocephala*, allied to the cirripeds [fr. Gk *rhiza*, root + *kephalē*, head]

rhi·zo·gen·ic (raizoudʒénik) *adj.* (*bot.*) producing roots indigenously (from the pericycle of seed plants) [fr. Gk *rhiza*, root + *genes*, born of]

rhi·zog·e·nous (raizɒ́dʒənəs) *adj.* rhizogenic

rhi·zoid (ráizoid) **1.** *n.* a rootlike filamentous outgrowth of the thallus of the gametophyte generation of many pteridophytes that serves to anchor the organism to the soil and function as an absorptive organ ‖ a similar organ in some thallophytes **2.** *adj.* rootlike [fr. Gk *rhiza*, root]

rhi·zom·a·tous (raizɒ́mətəs, raizóumətəs) *n.* of or having rhizomes

rhi·zome (ráizoum) *n.* a thickened, usually horizontal underground stem or branch of a plant that stores food, producing roots below and leafy shoots above, and that differs from a root in having buds and scaly leaves [fr. Mod. L. *rhizoma* fr. Gk]

rhi·zo·morph (ráizəmɔrf) *n.* a twisted strand of fungal hyphae that in many basidiomycetes serves for the transport of liquids and as a means by which the fungus spreads **rhi·zo·mór·phous** *adj.* formed like a root, rootlike [fr. Gk *rhiza*, root + *morphē*, shape, form]

rhi·zo·pod (ráizəpɒd) *n.* a member of *Rhizopoda*, a subclass of protozoans characterized by pseudopodia. Some form external shells or internal stiffening skeletons. Most are free-living, some parasitic. The subclass includes foraminifers, radiolarians, amoebas etc. **rhi·zop·o·dan** (raizɒ́pədən) *n.* and *adj.* **rhi·zóp·o·dous** *adj.* [fr. Gk *rhiza*, root + *pous* (*podos*), foot]

rho (rou) *n.* the seventeenth letter (P, ρ = r) of the Greek alphabet

Rhode Island (roud) (*abbr.* R.I.) the smallest state (area 1,214 sq. miles, pop. 958,000) of the U.S.A., on the northeast coast. Capital: Providence. The indented coastline is backed by a wooded coastal plain and hilly upland in the northwest. It is primarily industrial (textiles, machinery and metalwork, electronics, jewelry). Agriculture: dairy farming, poultry, nurseries. Resources: building materials. Chief universities: Brown (1764) at Providence, University of Rhode Island (1892) at Kingston. Rhode Island was settled by the English (17th c.), was one of the Thirteen Colonies, and became (1790) the 13th state of the U.S.A.

Rhodes (roudz) (Gk Rhodos) a mountainous Greek island (area 538 sq. miles, pop. 66,606), southernmost and largest of the Dodecanese. Products: barley, oranges, olives, wine ‖ its chief town and port (pop. 27,000): medieval city walls, palaces of the Knights Hospitalers. The island was settled (c. 1000 B.C.) by Dorian Greeks and reached the height of its prosperity in the 3rd c. B.C. Rhodes was ruled by Rome (1st c. B.C.-395 A.D.), the Byzantine Empire (395-1204), local lords (1204-48), Genoa (1248-50), Nicaea (1256-82), the Seljuk Turks (1282-1309), the Knights Hospitalers (1309-1522), the Ottoman Empire (1522-1912) and Italy (1912-47), after which it was ceded to Greece (*COLOSSUS OF RHODES)

Rhodes, Cecil John (1853-1902), British statesman and financier. After emigrating to South Africa (1870), he amassed a fortune from the Kimberley diamond mines and the Transvaal gold mines. He became a leading advocate of British imperialist expansion in Africa, entered the Cape Colony parliament (1881), obtained the British annexation of Bechuanaland (1884), and gained a monopoly of mineral rights (1888) in the Matabele lands later known as Southern Rhodesia. He was prime minister of Cape Colony (1890-6), resigning after popular criticism of the Jameson Raid. His connection with the raid was censured by the British House of Commons and he retired to Southern Rhodesia

Rhodes, James Ford (1848-1927), U.S. historian, author of 'History of the United States from the Compromise of 1850' (7 vols, 1893-1906)

Rho·de·sia former colony of Britain, then an independent country *ZIMBABWE

Rhodesia and Nyasaland, Federation of the Central African Federation

rho·di·um (róudi:əm) *n.* a metallic element (symbol Rh, at. no. 45, at. mass 102.905) resembling platinum, used in very hard alloys, as a catalyst, and in thermocouples [Mod. L. fr. Gk *rhodon*, a rose (from the reddish color of some of its compounds)]

rho·do·den·dron (roudədéndrən) *n.* a member of *Rhododendron*, fam. *Ericaceae*, a genus of evergreen shrubs bearing large pink, red, purplish or white flowers, native to the cool areas of the northern hemisphere [L. fr. Gk fr. *rhodon*, rose + *dendron*, tree]

rho·do·nite (róud'nait) *n.* a rose-red silicate of manganese (MnSiO₃), used as an ornamental stone [G. *rhodonit* fr. Gk *rhodon*, rose]

Rhod·o·pe Mountains (ródəpi:) a wooded mountain range running along the Bulgarian-Greek frontier. Occupations: livestock, mining (iron, lead, zinc). Highest peak: Musala (9,595 ft), in S.W. Bulgaria

rho·dop·sin (roudópsin) *n.* (*physiol.*) a red or purple photosensitive pigment occurring in the rods of the retina of marine fishes and most higher vertebrates, facilitating vision in dim light. Absence of it causes night blindness (*NYCTALOPIA). Vitamin A favors its formation [fr. Gk *rhodon*, rose + *opsis*, appearance]

rhomb (rɒm, rɒmb) *n.* a rhombus ‖ a rhombohedron [fr. L. *rhombus* fr. Gk]

rhom·ben·ceph·a·lon (rɒmbenséfələn) *pl.* **rhom·ben·ceph·a·la** (rɒmbenséfələ) *n.* the developed hindbrain

rhom·bic (rɒmbik) *adj.* having the shape of a rhombus ‖ orthorhombic

rhom·bo·he·dral (rɒmbəhí:drəl) *adj.* of or having the form of a rhombohedron

rhom·bo·he·dron (rɒmbəhí:drən) *pl.* **rhom·bo·he·drons, rhom·bo·he·dra** (rɒmbəhí:drə) *n.* a six-sided figure whose faces are equal rhombuses ‖ a crystal having this form [fr. Gk *rhombos*, rhomb + *hedra*, seat, base]

rhom·boid (rɒmbɔid) 1. *n.* a parallelogram having unequal adjacent sides and oblique angles 2. *adj.* shaped like a rhombus ‖ rhomboidal [fr. F. *rhomboide* fr. L. fr. Gk]

rhom·boi·dal (rɒmbɔid'l) *adj.* shaped like a rhomboid [fr. Mod. L. *rhomboidolis*]

rhom·bus (rɒmbəs) *pl.* **rhom·bus·es, rhom·bi** (rɒmbai) *n.* an equilateral parallelogram other than a square [L.]

rho meson (*particle phys.*) a short-lived vector meson with isospin of 1, hypercharge 0, negative charge, mass of 750 MEV, detected in high-energy colliscope, reclassified principally as mu meson as a result of additional research. *Cf* MU MESON

rho·met·al (róumetəl) *n.* an alloy of iron and nickel highly resistant to magnetism and used in high-frequency electrical circuits

rhon·chal (rɒŋk'l) *adj.* of or relating to a rhonchus ‖ caused by a rhonchus or by rhonchi

rhon·chi·al (rɒŋki:əl) *adj.* rhonchal

rhon·chus (rɒŋkəs) *pl.* **rhon·chi** (rɒŋkai) *n.* a whistling or wheezing sound heard on auscultation of the chest, due to partial blockage of the bronchi [L.=a snoring, fr. Gk]

Rhon·dda (rónðə, hrónðæ) the chief town (pop. 100,000) of a coal-mining valley (the Rhondda Valley) of Glamorganshire, Wales

Rhône (roun) a department (area 1,104 sq. miles, pop. 1,429,600) in E. central France (*LYONNAIS, *BEAUJOLAIS). Chief town: Lyon

Rhône a river (505 miles long) flowing from a glacier on the St Gotthard massif, Switzerland, through the Lake of Geneva and the S. Jura into France, where it flows south between the Massif Central and the Alps to a delta on the Mediterranean. It receives the Saône at Lyon. Rapidity and shifting sandbanks make navigation difficult, but it is a great source of hydroelectric power

rhu·barb (rú:barb) *n.* a member of *Rheum*, fam. *Polygonaceae*, a genus of perennial, large-leaved plants. The cultivated garden varieties, esp. *R. rhaponticum*, have large, fleshy, reddish stems which are peeled and cooked and used in making pies, preserves etc. [O.F. *reubarbe, rubarbe*]

rhu·barb·ing (rú:barbiŋ) *n.* (*Br.*) the mutterings of actors to simulate background talk

rhumb (rʌm) *n.* a rhumb line ‖ the angular distance (11° 15') between two successive compass points [fr. F. *rumb* or Span. *rumbo*, Port. *rumbo, rumo*]

rhumba *RUMBA

rhumb line the curve followed by a ship keeping to one course, cutting all meridians at the

same angle ‖ a line of the surface of the earth cutting all meridians at the same angle

rhyme (raim) *n.* identity or similarity in the sounds of word endings, employed usually at the ends of lines in order to please the ear and to assist in the construction of a poem ‖ verse in which this occurs ‖ a word presenting such identity with or similarity to another, *cat is a rhyme for rat* **without rhyme or reason** having no system or sense [O.F. *rime* fr. L. fr. Gk]

rhyme *pres. part.* **rhym·ing** *past* and *past part.* **rhymed** *v.i.* to form a rhyme, *'stoat' rhymes with 'moat'* ‖ to use or embody a technique or pattern of rhymes, *how do Milton's sonnets rhyme?* ‖ (*old-fash.*) to write verse ‖ *v.t.* to use as a rhyme ‖ (*old-fash.*) to put into verse [fr. O.F. *rimer*]

rhyme royal a stanza of 7 decasyllabic lines rhyming a b a b b c c

rhyming dictionary a dictionary which groups words by the rhymes which their last syllables provide

rhyming slang a kind of slang spoken by cockneys in which monosyllabic words are replaced by pairs of words (totally unrelated in meaning), the second of which rhymes with the original word, e.g. 'trouble and strife'= wife, 'butcher's hook'=look. In practice when rhyming slang is spoken the first, non-rhyming word is usually the only one pronounced

rhyn·cho·ce·pha·lian (rɪŋkousiféiljən) 1. *adj.* of or relating to *Rhynchocephalia*, an order of lizardlike reptiles now extinct except for the tuatara 2. *n.* a reptile of this order [fr. M.L. fr. Gk *rhunchos*, snout + *kephalē*, head]

rhy·o·lite (ráiəlait) *n.* an acid volcanic rock showing the effect of lava flow and containing quartz, orthoclase etc. [fr. G. *ryholit* fr. Gk *rhuax*, stream + *lithos*, rock]

rhythm (ríðəm) *n.* (in language) the irregular alternation of stress, duration or pitch, tending with heightened emotion towards meter ‖ a particular instance of such a pattern, *Skeltonic rhythm* ‖ (in music) the pattern produced by the relative duration and stress of notes ‖ (in art) the pattern of movement produced by the relationships between the parts of a work ‖ such a pattern in the movements of nature, the course of events etc., *the rhythm of the seasons* [fr. L. *rhythmus*]

rhythm and blues a mixture of rock 'n' roll and blues music. *abbr.* **R & B**

rhyth·mic (ríðmik) *adj.* having or using rhythm [fr. F. *rhythmique*]

rhyth·mi·cal (ríðmik'l) *adj.* of or relating to rhythm ‖ rhythmic

rhyth·mics (ríðmiks) *n.* the science or theory of rhythm

rhythm method a method of birth control in which continence is practiced during the period when fertilization is most likely to occur

rhythm section the instruments of a dance or jazz band which beat out the rhythm, e.g. drums, piano, double bass, guitar

R.I. Rhode Island

ri·al (ri:ál, ri:ɔ́l) *n.* the basic monetary unit of Iran and Saudi Arabia ‖ a coin or note representing one rial [Pers. fr. Arab.]

Ri·al·to (ri:æltou) an island in Venice, Italy where the exchange was located ‖ the bridge (1590) spanning the middle of the Grand Canal in Venice

Riau *RIOUW ARCHIPELAGO

rib (rib) 1. *n.* one of the paired, curved bones that form the bony cage which encloses and protects the thoracic cavity of most vertebrates. The ribs are articulated with the spine at the dorsal end, and are either joined to the sternum at the ventral end or free to move with the expansion and contraction of the lungs. In man there are normally 12 pairs ‖ (*archit.*) a raised molding on a ceiling, esp. of an arched roof ‖ (Gothic and Romanesque *archit.*) any of the intersecting arches of a vault ‖ (*bot.*) the principal vein of a leaf ‖ (*zool.*) a vein in an insect's wing ‖ (*zool.*) the quill of a feather ‖ a hinged, usually metal, rod supporting and shaping the fabric of an umbrella ‖ a vertical ridge in a woven or knitted fabric ‖ a curved timber supporting the frame of a ship ‖ any of the light, transverse pieces placed along the length of an airplane wing ‖ a pillar of ore or coal serving to support the roof of a mine ‖ a vein of ore ‖ (bookbinding) one of the raised bands where stitching goes across the spine of a book or such a band used ornamentally ‖ a cut of meat including a rib or ribs 2. *v.t. pres. part.* **rib·bing** *past* and *past part.* **ribbed** to furnish or strengthen with a rib

or ribs ‖ to make (a rib) in knitting ‖ (*pop.*) to tease (someone) [O.E. *rib, ribb*]

rib·ald (ríbəld) *adj.* (of wit or language) broad, indecent ‖ (of a person) wittily indecent or coarse **rib·ald·ry** (ríbəldri) *n.* ribald wit or language [fr. O.F. *ribaud, ribault*, a menial]

Ri·baut, Ri·bault (ri:bou), Jean (c. 1520-65), French colonist. On the orders of Coligny, he established a Huguenot colony in South Carolina (1562)

rib·band (ríbənd, ríbbænd) *n.* a narrow flexible slat of wood or metal fastened to a ship's frame while it is being built, to hold the ribs in position

Rib·ben·trop (ríbəntrɒp), Joachim von (1893-1946), German foreign minister (1938-45). He helped to form the Rome-Berlin Axis and to plan Nazi aggression, and negotiated the RussoGerman nonaggression pact of 1939. He was convicted as a war criminal and hanged

rib·bing (ríbiŋ) *n.* ribs collectively, esp. ribbed fabric ‖ (*pop.*) a teasing

rib·bon (ríbən) *n.* a narrow strip of satin, silk, velvet etc. used e.g. for tying the hair, or for trimming or decoration, or as a bookmark, or made up into a badge etc. as a symbol of achievement in a competition ‖ material sold in such strips ‖ anything resembling such a strip, *ribbons of light* ‖ (*pl.*) torn or ragged strips of anything, *the flag was in ribbons* ‖ a narrow strip used as a badge of a knightly order or to indicate membership in an athletic team etc. ‖ (*mil.*) a colored strip of material indicating that the wearer has received a particular medal or decoration ‖ a roll of narrow inked fabric used in a typewriter ‖ a radula [O.F. *riban, ruban*, perh. fr. Gmc]

ribbon development urban expansion along a highway

rib·bon·fish (ríbənfiʃ) *pl.* **rib·bon·fish, rib·bon·fish·es** *n.* any of various members of *Equetus*, fam. *Sciaenidae*, a genus of fishes having gray and black ribbonlike markings ‖ any of various fishes of fam. *Cepolidae*, having narrow elongated bodies

ribbon foil a cheaper substitute for gold leaf etc. applied in decorative work, e.g. in bookbinding

Ri·be·ra (ri:béra), José (called Spagnoletto, 1588-1652), Spanish painter. After 1616 he lived mainly in Naples. His early work depends much on chiaroscuro for its effects, and its subjects are often brutal. Later his style softened and his subjects are devotional with the fervor typical of the Counter-Reformation

ri·bo·fla·vin (raiboufléivən) *n.* vitamin B₂ (*DIET)

ri·bo·nu·cle·ase (raibounú:kli:eis) *n.* (*physiol.*) enzyme, present in body tissue, that polymerizes ribonucleic acid. *abbr.* RNase or RNAse

ri·bo·nu·cle·ic acid (raibounu:klí:ik, raibounju:klí:ik) (*abbr.* RNA) a nucleic acid similar to deoxyribonucleic acid but having a sugar residue, ribose (containing an additional oxygen atom) instead of deoxyribose. It serves as an intermediary in protein synthesis

ri·bose (ráibous, ráibouz) *n.* a pentose sugar, C₅H₁₀O₅, obtained by hydrolysis from certain nucleic acids (*RIBONUCLEIC ACID, *DEOXYRIBONUCLEIC ACID) [fr. *ribonic* fr. G.]

ri·bo·som·al RNA (raibəsóum'l) the part of RNA that combines with proteins to form cell ribosomes linked to messenger RNA to help synthesize proteins and enzymes —**ribosomal** *adj. Cf* MESSENGER RNA, RIBONUCLEIC ACID, TRANSFER RNA

Ri·car·di·an (rikárdi:ən) 1. *adj.* of or concerned with the political economist Ricardo 2. *n.* a supporter of Ricardo's economic theories

Ri·car·do (rikárdou), David (1772-1823), British economist. He applied the deductive logic of his mentor, James Mill, to the analysis of monetary principles and in 'Principles of Political Economy and Taxation' (1817) elaborated the labor theory of value, the division of incomes, and the function of wages, rent and trade. He was the founder of the classical school of economics, and his philosophy influenced Marx, Malthus, J. S. Mill, Henry George, Alfred Marshall and many others

Rice (rais), Elmer (1892-1967), American dramatist whose plays include 'The Adding Machine' (1923) and 'Street Scene' (1929)

rice (rais) 1. *n. Oryza sativa*, fam. *Gramineae*, an annual cereal grass widely cultivated for its seed, used for human food. It is one of the world's most important food crops. Rice is grown in Asian countries, esp. China and India, in parts of the Middle East (e.g. Egypt), in Russia, South America, Canada and the U.S.A. It is produced mainly in the deltas of rivers, on irrigated or flooded coastal plains, or on terraced hillsides. In Asia, dried rice stalks are used to make paper, sandals, hats etc., and to thatch roofs. Fermented rice kernels are sometimes used in making spirits, wine and beer, and in some countries rice hulls are fed to livestock ‖ the seeds or grains of this grass **2.** *v.t. pres. part.* **ric·ing** *past* and *past part.* **riced** to pass through a ricer [M.E. *ris, rys* fr. O.F. fr. Ital. fr. L. fr. Gk fr. an Oriental source]

rice paddy *pl.* **rice paddies** a field in which rice is grown

rice paper paper made from the pith of the shrub *Tetrapanax papyriferum,* fam. *Araliaceae.* It is widely used in China, Japan etc.

ric·er (ráisər) *n.* a utensil with a sievelike container through which boiled potatoes etc. are pressed so that they emerge in small strings about the thickness of a rice grain

Rich (ritʃ), Edmund *EDMUND RICH

rich 1. *adj.* possessing great wealth, *a rich man* ‖ having many natural resources, *a rich country* ‖ abundant, *a rich harvest* ‖ costly, precious, *rich jewels* ‖ (with 'in') abounding, *rivers rich in fish* ‖ fertile, *rich soil* ‖ (of food) containing a high proportion of fat, esp. butter, *a rich cake* ‖ (of voices) deep and mellow ‖ (of colors) vivid, deep and intense ‖ (of odors) strongly redolent ‖ producing abundantly, *a rich mine* ‖ (of materials or workmanship) elaborate, *rich brocade, rich carving* ‖ (*pop.*) humorous ‖ (*pop.*) absurd **2.** *n.* **the rich** rich people in general [O.E. *rīce*]

Rich·ard I (rítʃərd) 'Cœur de Lion' (1157-99), king of England (1189-99), son of Henry II, with whom he was at war (1173 and 1189). He spent almost his entire reign outside England. Returning from the 3rd Crusade (1190-2), he was imprisoned (1192-4) by the emperor of Austria, and ransomed (1194). He prevented his brother John from usurping his throne (1194), and was at war (1194-9) with Philippe II of France. His continual wars and huge ransom necessitated heavy taxation in England. Many acts of cruelty marred his reputation for chivalry

Richard II (1367-1400), king of England (1377-99), son of Edward the Black Prince. During his minority (1377-83), the government was in the hands of his uncle, John of Gaunt, but the young king showed great courage in dealing with the Peasants' Revolt (1381). He was forced to submit to a baronial faction known as the lords appellant (1387-8), whom he eliminated (1397). His subsequent tyrannical rule alienated his supporters, who deserted him when his cousin Henry of Lancaster forced him to abdicate (1399) and succeeded him as Henry IV. Richard died or was murdered shortly afterwards in prison

Richard III (1452-85), king of England (1483-5), younger brother of Edward IV, on whose death (1483) he was appointed protector of his nephews Edward V and his brother Richard. He usurped the throne (1483) and the young princes were murdered shortly afterwards in the Tower of London, almost certainly at his instigation. A rebellion under Stafford was put down (1483), but Henry Tudor, the Lancastrian claimant to the throne, invaded (1485), defeating and killing Richard at Bosworth Field. Henry assumed the crown as Henry VII

Richard, earl of Cornwall (1209-72), titular king of the Romans (1257-72), son of King John of England

Rich·ards (rítʃərdz), Dickinson Woodruff (1895-1973), U.S. physician, co-winner (with Werner Forssman and André Cournand) of the 1965 Nobel prize in medicine and physiology

Richards, Theodore William (1868-1928), U.S. chemist. He received the 1914 Nobel prize in chemistry for his research on atomic weights

Rich·ard·son (rítʃərdsən), Henry Hobson (1838-86), U.S. architect, known both as an initiator of the Romanesque revival, epitomized in his Trinity Church, Boston (1872-7), and as a pioneer of an indigenous, modern American style, exemplified by parts of the capitol at Albany, N.Y.

Richardson, Sir Owen Willans (1879-1959), English physicist, noted for his researches on the emission of charged particles by hot bodies. Nobel prize (1928)

Richardson, Samuel (1689-1761), English novelist. He wrote 'Pamela' (1740-1), the enormously popular 'Clarissa' (1747-8) and 'The History of Sir Charles Grandison' (1753-4). Unlike his contemporaries, who were principally

interested in simple narrative, social criticism and the humorous aspects of character, Richardson used the novel as a way of exploring psychological subtleties and moral issues

Rich·e·lieu (ri:ʃˈljə:), Armand-Jean du Plessis de (1585-1642), French cardinal and statesman. Through the influence of Marie de' Medici, he was appointed secretary of state (1616), cardinal (1622) and chief minister (1624) to Louis XIII. His domestic policy aimed at destroying the political power of the Huguenots, whom he successfully besieged (1628) in their stronghold of La Rochelle. Feudal nobles were suppressed, and their fortresses demolished. He obtained (1630) Marie de' Medici's banishment from court. Richelieu's foreign policy aimed at humbling the Hapsburgs in the Thirty Years' War. He made alliances with the Netherlands, the German states and Sweden, and took France into the war (1635), which caused financial crises but gained Catalonia and Roussillon from Spain. One of France's greatest statesmen, Richelieu carried out financial, military and legal reforms, encouraged manufactures, colonial trade and commerce, patronized the arts and founded the French Academy (1635)

rich·es (rítʃiz) *pl. n.* wealth, abundance ‖ precious possessions [orig. sing. fr. O.F. *richesse*]

Richler, (rítʃlər) Mordecai (1931-), Canadian writer whose novels concentrate on being Jewish in Montreal. His works include 'The Acrobats' (1954), 'The Apprenticeship of Duddy Kravitz' (1959), 'Saint Urbain's Horseman' (1971), 'Joshua Then and Now' (1980) and 'Home Sweet Home' (1984)

rich·ly (rítʃli) *adv.* in a rich way ‖ thoroughly, *he richly deserved the punishment*

Rich·mond (rítʃmənd) an industrial and residential borough (pop. 219,214) of New York City, consisting of Staten Island and adjacent islets

Richmond the capital (pop. 220,000) of Virginia, a river port and industrial center (tobacco, paper, printing, textiles, chemicals). It figured prominently during the Revolution, and was the Confederate capital during the Civil War

Rich·ter (ríxtər) *JEAN-PAUL

Rich·ter scale (ríktər) (*seismology*) a logarithmic scale for measuring the magnitude of a seismic disturbance in which the smallest detectable movement is 1.5 and 8.5 is the most devastating; after American seismologist Charles R. Richter

rick (rik) **1.** *n.* an outdoor stack of hay or straw etc., usually thatched **2.** *v.t.* to stack into a rick [O.E. *hrēac*]

rick 1. *v.t.* (*Br.*) to sprain or twist (an ankle, knee etc.) **2.** *n.* (*Br.*) a sprain or twist [M.E. *wrikken,* to move jerkily]

Rick·en·back·er (ríkənbækər), Edward Vernon (1890-1973), U.S. adventurer and airline executive. As a racing driver he set (1917) a world speed record of 134 m.p.h. at Daytona Beach, Fla. During the 1st world war he became America's 'ace' fighter pilot. He developed (from 1935) Eastern Air Lines into a major international air-transport system

rick·ets (ríkits) *pl. n.* (*sing.* in construction) a disease characterized by a softening and sometimes bending of bone structure in the pelvis and leg bones of infants and children. It is caused by a deficiency of vitamin D or lack of sunlight [etym. doubtful]

rick·ett·si·a (rikétsi:ə) *pl.* **rick·ett·si·ae** (rikétsi.i:) *n.* a member of *Rickettsia,* fam. *Rickettsiaceae,* a genus of microorganisms inhabiting the cells of certain biting arthropods. When transmitted to man by the bite of the host they can cause typhus and other serious diseases **rick·ett·si·al** *adj.* [after H.T. *Ricketts* (1871-1910), U.S. pathologist]

rick·et·y (ríkiti:) *adj.* suffering from rickets ‖ weak in the joints, *a rickety old man* ‖ shaky, insecure, *a rickety chair*

rick·rack (ríkræk) *n.* a zigzag braid trimming

rick·shaw, rick·sha (ríkʃɔ) *n.* a jinricksha

rick·yard (ríkjɑrd) *n.* a stackyard

rick·y-tick (ríki:tík) *n.* a jazz music style of the 1920s —**ricky-ticky** *adj.*

ric·o·chet (ríkəʃei, rìkəʃéi) **1.** *n.* the skipping or glancing off at a tangent of a bullet or other missile after hitting a flat surface which it does not penetrate **2.** *v.i. pres. part.* **ric·o·chet·ing,** esp. *Br.* **ric·o·chet·ting** (ríkəʃeiiŋ, rìkəʃéiiŋ) *past* and *past part.* **ric·o·cheted,** esp. *Br.* **ric·o·chetted** (ríkəʃeid, rìkəʃéid) (of a missile) to glance off, to rebound [F.]

ric·tus (ríktəs) *pl.* **ric·tus, ric·tus·es** *n.* the gape of a mouth, beak etc. [L.=open mouth]

rid (rid) *v.t. pres. part.* **rid·ding** *past* and *past part.* **rid, rid·ded** to free of a nuisance or something unwelcome, *to rid a house of rats* **to be rid of** to be freed from **to get rid of** to get free from ‖ to do away with ‖ (*pop.*) to cause (someone) to go away **rid·dance** (ríd'ns) *n.* a ridding or being rid **good riddance!** an expression of satisfaction or relief at getting rid of someone or something [O.N. *rythja*]

rid·a·ble, ride·a·ble (ráidəb'l) *adj.* capable of being ridden ‖ able to be ridden over, *a ridable track*

rid·del (ríd'l) *n.* one of the side curtains of an altar [M.E. *ridel, riddel,* perh. fr. *riddil, a riddle* (sieve)]

ridden *past part.* of RIDE

rid·dle (ríd'l) **1.** *n.* a question or problem phrased obscurely but correctly and posed to test the ingenuity of the person trying to find the answer ‖ a puzzling person or thing **2.** *v. pres. part.* **rid·dling** *past* and *past part.* **rid·dled** *v.i.* to speak in riddles ‖ *v.t.* to solve, explain (a riddle) [O.E. *rǣdels, rǣdelse*]

riddle 1. *n.* a coarse sieve for gravel, cinders etc. **2.** *v.t. pres. part.* **rid·dling** *past* and *past part.* **rid·dled** to sieve through a riddle ‖ to fill with holes, esp. by shooting ‖ to find flaws in (an argument etc.) [O.E. *hriddel*]

Ride, (raid) Sally Kirsten (1951-), U.S. astronaut, the first American woman in space. She graduated from Stanford University (1977) and became an astronaut in 1978. Her first space flight (June 18-24, 1983) was followed by the 13th shuttle mission (Oct. 5-13, 1984)

ride (raid) **1.** *v. pres. part.* **rid·ing** *past* **rode** (roud) *past part.* **rid·den** (ríd'n) *v.i.* to sit in a car, train etc. and be carried along ‖ to sit on and be carried along by a horse or other animal while controlling its movements ‖ to be carried as if on a horse, *to ride on someone's back* ‖ to turn or move on or in something, *the stud rides in the groove* ‖ (of a ship) to lie at anchor ‖ (of a ship) to move over or float on water ‖ (of the moon, sun etc.) to seem to float through the sky ‖ to be in a specified condition for riding or being ridden, *the ground rides hard* ‖ (of clothing, with 'up') to work upward out of place, *trousers that tend to ride up* ‖ (*pop.*) to continue without change, solution, interference etc., *to let a problem ride* ‖ (of a male animal) to mount in copulation ‖ *v.t.* to sit on (an animal) or on or in (a vehicle) and be carried along while controlling its movements ‖ to move along on and be supported by, *to ride the waves* ‖ to give a ride to, *to ride a baby on one's back* ‖ to engage in or do by riding, *to ride a race* ‖ (*horse racing*) to urge (a horse) to the point of exhaustion ‖ to keep (a ship) at anchor ‖ to rest on (something), e.g. by overlapping ‖ (esp. *past part.* in combination) to dominate completely, *fear-ridden* ‖ (*pop.*) to tease ‖ (of a male animal) to mount (the female) in copulation ‖ (*lacrosse*) to charge (an opponent in possession of the ball) **legally to ride down** (*horse racing*) to exhaust (a horse) by riding it too hard ‖ to overtake by riding ‖ to allow one's mount or vehicle to hit and knock down (a person or thing) **to ride for a fall** to court disaster **to ride out** to come through safely, *to ride out a storm, to ride out a crisis* **to ride (someone) on a rail** to cause (someone) to leave town **2.** *n.* a riding, esp. a journey made by riding ‖ a road for horseback riding, esp. one cut through a forest ‖ a machine to ride on for fun in an amusement park etc., e.g. a Ferris wheel **to take (someone) for a ride** (*pop.*) to deceive or trick (someone) by fooling or cheating him [O.E. *rīdan*]

rideable *RIDABLE

rid·er (ráidər) *n.* someone who rides, esp. someone who rides a horse ‖ an additional clause or amendment added to a legislative bill, document etc. ‖ (*Br., law*) an opinion, recommendation etc. added to a verdict ‖ (*math.*) a problem which is subsidiary to a theorem ‖ a piece of machinery, apparatus etc. that rests on or surmounts another, e.g. the movable weight on a balance beam ‖ (*naut., pl.*) an extra set of timbers or plates used to strengthen a ship's frame [O.E. *rīdere*]

rid·er·ship (ráidərʃip) *n.* those who ride in a particular vehicle or system

ride shotgun *v.* to protect or ensure, e.g., the successful completion of a project, from the stage-coach riders in the Old West

ridge (ridʒ) **1.** *n.* the horizontal angle at the junction of two slopes ‖ the top edge of a roof

CONCISE PRONUNCIATION KEY: **(a)** æ, c*a*t; ɑ, c*a*r; ɔ f*aw*n; ei, sn*a*ke. **(e)** e, h*e*n; i:, sh*ee*p; iə, d*ee*r; ɛə, b*ea*r. **(i)** i, f*i*sh; ai, t*i*ger; ə:, b*i*rd. **(o)** o, *o*x; au, c*ow*; ou, g*oa*t; u, p*oo*r; ɔi, r*oy*al. **(u)** ʌ, d*u*ck; u, b*u*ll; u:, g*oo*se; ə, b*a*cillus; ju:, c*u*be. x, lo*ch*; θ, *th*ink; ð, bo*th*er; z, *Z*en; ʒ, corsa*g*e. dʒ, sava*g*e; ŋ, ora*n*gutang; j, *y*ak; ʃ, fi*sh*; tʃ, fe*tch*; 'l, rabb*le*; 'n, redd*en*. Complete pronunciation key appears inside front cover.

where two sloping sides meet ‖ a long, narrow elevation of land, *a ridge of hills* ‖ a narrow, raised line on the surface of cloth etc. ‖ the raised earth thrown up between furrows ‖ (*Br.*) a raised hotbed for the cultivation of cucumbers, melons etc. ‖ (*meteorol.*) a wedge-shaped area of high atmospheric pressure (cf. TROUGH) 2. *v. pres. part.* **ridg·ing** *past* and *past part.* **ridged** *v.t.* to form into a ridge or ridges ‖ to mark with ridges ‖ (*Br.*) to plant (cucumbers etc.) in ridges ‖ *v.i.* to form into ridges [O.E. *hrycg*]

ridge-piece (rídʒpiːs) *n.* (*Br.*) a ridgepole (beam in a roof)

ridge·pole (rídʒpoul) *n.* the horizontal beam in a roof supporting the upper ends of the rafters ‖ the pole supporting the roof of a tent

ridge tile a curved tile used in quantity to form the ridge covering of a roof

Ridg·way (rídʒwei), Matthew Bunker (1895-), American general. He commanded the U.N. forces in Korea (1951-2)

rid·i·cule (rídikjuːl) 1. *n.* contemptuous laughter, *his suggestion met with ridicule by the others* 2. *v.t. pres. part.* **rid·i·cul·ing** *past* and *past part.* **rid·i·culed** to treat with ridicule, cause (someone, something) to be an object of ridicule [F.]

ri·dic·u·lous (ridíkjuləs) *adj.* provoking derisive laughter, *a ridiculous fellow* ‖ unworthy of consideration, unreasonable, *a ridiculous excuse, a ridiculous charge* [fr. L. *ridiculus*]

rid·ing (ráidiŋ) *n.* one of the three administrative divisions (East, West, North) of Yorkshire, England [fr. O.N. *thrithjungr*, third part]

riding 1. *n.* the act of a person who rides ‖ (*Br.*) a track for riders, esp. a grassy one through or along woods 2. *adj.* used in or for riding, *riding horses, a riding habit*

riding master a man who teaches horsemanship

Rid·ley (rídli:), Nicholas (c. 1500-55), English bishop. A Protestant, he helped to revise the liturgy under Edward VI and, refusing to recant after the accession of Mary I, was burned at the stake as a heretic

Rie·go y Nún·ez (rjégɔi·núːnjeθ), Rafael del (1785-1823), Spanish general. He and his force of 22,000, about to sail for America, mutinied (1820) at Cabezas de San Juan near Seville, forcing Ferdinand VII to capitulate. Following the French intervention (1823) he was hanged and quartered. The 'Hymn of Riego' became the national anthem of the Second Spanish Republic

Rieka *RIJEKA*

Riel (rjel), Louis (1844-85), French-Canadian political leader. He led (1869) a rebellion composed of Franco-Scottish métis of the Hudson Bay Company's territories, who opposed attempts (1868-9) by the Canadian government to transfer the area to Canada. He presided over a provisional government which established (1870), by an act of Parliament, the province of Manitoba. He led (1884) the Second Riel Rebellion of métis of the Saskatchewan Valley but was defeated (1885) by Canadian government forces, convicted of treason, and executed. His death increased racial and religious tensions in Canada, severely damaged the Conservative party in Quebec, and gave rise to a French-Canadian nationalist movement

ri·el (ríːəl) *n.* the basic monetary unit of Cambodia, divided into 100 sen [origin unknown]

Rie·mann (ríːman), Georg Friedrich Bernhard (1826-66), German mathematician. He is best known for his discussion of the foundations of geometry and his development of forms of geometry which do not assume Euclid's axiom about parallel lines

Rie·men·schnei·der (ríːmənʃnaidər), Tilmann (c. 1460-1531), German sculptor in stone and wood. His work can be seen in tombs and altars at Würzburg, Bamberg and other cathedrals and churches

rif·am·pi·cin or **rif·am·pin** (rifémpisin) *n.* (*pharm.*) any of a group of semisynthetic antibiotic and antiviral drugs that inhibit enzyme action; used in the treatment of pulmonary tuberculosis; marketed as Rifadin, Rimactane; and others

rif·a·my·cin (rifəmáisin) *n.* any of a group of substances resulting from fungal fermentation, some of which have antibiotic and antiviral capacity

rife (raif) *adj.* (*rhet.*, used only predicatively) widespread, prevalent [O.E. *rȳfe*]

Riff, Rif (rif) *n.* a Berber inhabitant of the Rif

riffed (rift) *adj.* dismissed from a job on the basis of reduction in force. —**riff** *v.*

riffle zone (*envir.*) shallow rapids in an open stream caused by submerged obstructions

riff·raff (rífræf) *n.* people regarded as worthless or disreputable [fr. M.E. *riff and raff* fr. O.F. *rif et raf*, one and all]

rif·fle (rífəl) 1. *n.* any of various devices, e.g. slats or blocks of wood, stones etc. which, when laid across the bottom of a mining sluice, form a series of grooves or ridges serving to catch and hold gold particles as the ore is washed ‖ one of these grooves or ridges ‖ a shallow in the bed of a stream across which the water flows rapidly, producing small choppy waves ‖ one of these waves ‖ the act or practice of riffling cards ‖ the sound of cards being riffled 2. *v. pres. part.* **rif·fling** *past* and *past part.* **rif·fled** *v.t.* to put (e.g. ore) through a riffle ‖ to form a riffle or riffles in (water) ‖ to leaf through (e.g. the pages of a book) rapidly, causing a slight rustling sound ‖ to shuffle (cards) by holding part of the pack in each hand and letting some cards slip between others as the two sets are quickly flicked together [fr. F. *riffler*]

ri·fle (ráifəl) 1. *v.t. pres. part.* **ri·fling** *past* and *past part.* **ri·fled** to steal everything of value from (a safe, a pocket etc.) ‖ to carry off as booty ‖ to cut spiral grooves in (the bore of a gun) so as to make the bullet spin in flight 2. *n.* a gun (usually fired from the shoulder) having spiral grooves cut in the bore ‖ (*pl.*, in regimental names) troops armed with rifles [O.F. *rifler, riffler*, to scratch]

ri·fle·man (ráifəlmən) *pl.* **ri·fle·men** (ráifəlmən) *n.* a soldier armed with a rifle ‖ a person with respect to his skill in using a rifle

rifle range a place for rifle practice

ri·fling (ráifliŋ) *n.* the act or process of cutting spiral grooves into a gun bore ‖ the spiral grooving itself

Rif, Riff (rif) the coastal strip of N. Morocco

rift (rift) *n.* a crack, fissure, e.g. in the earth ‖ a clearing or opening, e.g. in clouds or mist ‖ (*geol.*) a fault ‖ a break in friendship [of Scand. origin]

rift saw a saw for cutting lumber into planks

rift valley a valley which has been formed by the sinking of land between two roughly parallel faults. The best known example is the Great Rift Valley

Rift Valley fever (*med.*) livestock disease carried by mosquitoes that can cause blindness in humans; discovered in Africa in 1978

rift zone (*geol.*) a zone where plates of earth's crust tend to separate

rig (rig) 1. *v.t. pres. part.* **rig·ging** *past* and *past part.* **rigged** to fit (a ship) with ropes, spars and all necessary tackle ‖ to fit (shrouds, stays etc.) to a mast or yard ‖ to assemble and align the wings, fuselage etc. of (an airplane) ‖ (esp. with 'out') to provide with clothes, esp. outlandish clothes, *to rig someone out like a gypsy* ‖ (esp. with 'up') to put (something) together quickly as a temporary arrangement, *to rig up a hut in the garden* ‖ to provide with proper equipment, tools etc., *a boat rigged for trawling* 2. *n.* the manner in which a ship's sails, masts etc. are arranged, *schooner rig* ‖ (*pop.*) distinctive dress, esp. when designed for a special purpose, *a beefeater's rig* ‖ any specific tackle or machinery, esp. the equipment used in drilling an oil well [origin unknown]

rig *pres. part.* **rig·ging** *past* and *past part.* **rigged** *v.t.* to prearrange fraudulently, *the fire was rigged to make suspicion fall on the caretaker* ‖ to manipulate dishonestly, *to rig an election* [origin unknown]

Ri·ga (ríːgə) the capital, chief port and industrial center (pop. 835,000) of Latvia, U.S.S.R., on the Western Dvina near the head of the Gulf of Riga, an inlet (approx. 100 miles long, 60 miles wide) of the Baltic. Industries: mechanical engineering, metallurgy, textiles, oil refining, wood, fishing, fish packing. University (1919)

rig·a·doon (rigədúːn) *n.* a spirited dance popular in the 17th and 18th cc. ‖ the music for this dance [etym. doubtful]

rig·a·ma·role (rígəməroul) *n.* rigmarole

Ri·gaud (ríːgou), Hyacinthe (1659-1743), French painter. He specialized in portraits and in historical paintings. He is best known for his portraits of Bossuet and Louis XIV

rig·ger (rígər) *n.* someone who rigs, esp. someone who rigs ships or aircraft ‖ (in combination)

a ship rigged in a specified way, *a square-rigger*

rig·ging (rígiŋ) *n.* all the ropes, chains etc. used for supporting a ship's masts and spars and for hoisting and lowering the sails

right (rait) 1. *adj.* obeying the moral law, *in the circumstances his conduct was right* ‖ correct, *the right answer* ‖ true, logically sound, *the right conclusion* ‖ appropriate, opportune, *the right time to act* ‖ suitable, *the right man for the position* ‖ of or on the side of the body away from the location of the heart, on this side of a person's vertical axis of symmetry ‖ on or to this side as perceived by an observer ‖ (of a river bank) on this side of an observer facing downstream ‖ (of solid figures) involving a right angle ‖ of or pertaining to the finished side or surface of something, *the right side of the chintz* ‖ mentally sound ‖ physically healthy **Right** belonging to or associated with the Right **in one's right mind** in full possession of one's mental faculties 2. *n.* that which is morally right, *to fight for the right* ‖ that to which one is morally or legally entitled ‖ that which one judges to be the most suitable, correct etc. ‖ the right side or direction ‖ (*boxing*) the right hand or a blow with this hand ‖ (*marching, dancing* etc.) the right foot **the Right** that section of a political party, system of political parties, organization, group etc. which associates itself with traditional authority or opinion and which in legislative bodies is seated traditionally to the right of the presiding officer **in one's own right** through one's own authority, title etc. **in the right** having justice, legality or the facts on one's side **to put** (or **set**) **to rights** to make orderly or correct [O.E. *riht*]

right *adv.* in conformity with the moral law ‖ correctly, accurately, *to add a column of figures right* ‖ in a right-hand direction, *turn right* ‖ completely, *right on to the end* ‖ immediately (in time), *right after breakfast* ‖ immediately (in position), *right by the church* ‖ in a suitable way, *to turn out right* ‖ directly, *go right home* **right away** immediately **right off** right away [O.E. *rehte, rihte*]

right *v.t.* to restore to, or set in, the proper position, *to right a boat* ‖ to put (oneself) back into balance, *to right oneself after stumbling* ‖ to redress (a wrong) ‖ to put to rights ‖ *v.i.* to return to a correct or upright position, *the boat righted on the next wave* [O.E. *rihtan*]

right about, right-a·bout (ráitəbaut) 1. *n.* the position reached by turning to the right so as to face in the opposite direction ‖ a right-about-face 2. *adj.* pertaining to this movement 3. *adv.* in a right-about way, *to turn right about*

right-a·bout-face (ráitəbautféis) 1. *n.* (*mil.*) a turning to the opposite direction ‖ a reversal of opinion, attitude etc. 2. *interj.* turn right about! 3. *v.i.* to execute a right-about-face

right angle the angle (90°) between two radii which bound one quarter of a circle ‖ the angle between two lines perpendicular to one another **at right angles** perpendicularly **right-án·gled** *adj.*

right ascension (*astron.*) the angular distance eastwards along the celestial equator (or equinoctial) between the first point of Aries and the point where the circle of declination of a heavenly body cuts the equinoctial. It is one of the two data which determine position in the celestial sphere, corresponding with terrestrial longitude (*DECLINATION)

right·eous (ráitʃəs) *adj.* conforming to or in conformity with the moral law, *a righteous ruler, a righteous cause* ‖ caused by outrage against injustice, *righteous anger* [O.E. *rihtwīs*]

right field (*baseball*) the right-hand part of the outfield (as seen from home plate) ‖ the position of the player defending this

right·ful (ráitfəl) *adj.* having a just claim, *the rightful heir* ‖ owned by just claim, *rightful inheritance* ‖ proper, as befits a person's rank, merit etc., *to take one's rightful place in society* [late O.E. *rihtful* fr. *riht*, right]

right-hand (ráithænd) *adj.* on or to the right side ‖ (of a screw or thing to be used by a right-handed person) right-handed

right-hand·ed (ráithændid) 1. *adj.* using the right hand more efficiently than the left hand ‖ of or for someone who does this ‖ (of a screw) having a clockwise thread ‖ (of a rope) right-laid 2. *adv.* with the right hand

right-hand man someone's most relied-on assistant

Right Honourable (*Br.*) a title used in referring to a peer holding a rank lower than marquis, or to a privy councillor etc.

Right·ist (ráitist) 1. *n.* someone who belongs to the Right or tends to hold the views of the Right 2. *adj.* of, associated with or belonging to the Right

right-laid (ráitléid) *adj.* (of a rope) having strands twisted counterclockwise

right·ly (ráitli:) *adv.* correctly ‖ in the right way ‖ justly, fairly [O.E. *rihtlíce*]

right-mind·ed (ráitmáindid) *adj.* thinking and judging according to correct principles

right of search (*maritime law*) the right of a nation at war to stop any neutral vessel at sea to search her for contraband etc.

right-of-way, *Br.* also **right of way** (ráitəvwéi) *n.* the right of one vehicle to take precedence over another as laid down by traffic regulations ‖ the right of using a path or thoroughfare over another person's property ‖ the path or thoroughfare used ‖ the land over which an electric power line or natural-gas pipeline etc. passes

right-on (ráitɔn) *adj.* (*slang*) correct; honest; real —**right on** interjection indicating approval or encouragement

Right Reverend a title used in referring to a bishop

Rights, Bill of *BILL OF RIGHTS

Rights of Man, Declaration of the (*F. hist.*) a statement of the basic principles of civil society, drawn up (Aug. 17-26, 1789) by the Constituent Assembly

right-to-die (ráittədái) *n.* concept of patient's right to refuse life-prolonging measures if he or she is terminally ill

right-to-know law *FREEDOM OF INFORMATION ACT

right-to-life (ráittəláif) *n.* slogan of antiabortion proponents indicating a supposed right of the unborn from the moment of conception

right-to-work law (ráittəwə:rk) law forbidding the refusing of employment to one who does not belong to a union

right whale *Balaena mysticetus,* fam. *Balaenidae,* a genus of whalebone whales having no dorsal fin and no furrows on the throat

right wing the section of a political party, government, group etc. holding the views of the Right **right-wing** *adj.* **right-wing·er** *n.*

rig·id (rídʒid) *adj.* (*phys.*) strongly resisting deformation ‖ stiffly set, *a rigid stare* ‖ rigorous, *rigid discipline* ‖ inflexible, *too rigid a regard for the rules* ‖ (of an airship) having the gas chambers enclosed within a fixed framework **ri·gíd·i·ty** *n.* the state or quality of being rigid (*MODULUS OF RIGIDITY) [L. *rigidus*]

rig·ma·role (rígməroul) *n.* a long, disconnected narration, with no clear meaning ‖ a protracted, tiresome procedure or ceremonial, *I'm not going through all that rigmarole again just to get a visa* [etym. doubtful]

rig·or (rígər) *n.* (*med.*) a shivering fit often preceding an onset of fever ‖ (*physiol.*) a state of rigidity affecting living organs or tissues, due e.g. to shock or an accumulation of toxic substances [L. =stiffness]

rig·or, *Br.* **rig·our** (rígər) *n.* uncompromising firmness ‖ an instance of this ‖ extreme precision in the application of a rule, principle etc., *the rigor of the law* ‖ (of climate and season) extreme harshness ‖ (*pl.*) hardships ‖ (*math., logic*) severe precision of method [O.F. *rigor, rigour*]

rig·or mor·tis (rígərmɔ́rtis, ráigɔrmɔ́rtis) *n.* the stiffening of the muscles after death [L.]

rig·or·ous (rígərəs) *adj.* characterized by rigor ‖ (of climate or season) inclement ‖ precise, accurate [O.F.]

rigour *RIGOR

Rig-Ve·da (rigvéidə) the oldest and most important of the sacred Vedas

Ri·je·ka, Ri·e·ka (ri:jékə) (*Ital.* Fiume) the chief port (pop., with adjacent Sušak, 132,600) of Yugoslavia, in N.W. Croatia. Industries: shipbuilding, paper, oil refining, electrical engineering, food processing. Roman arch (1st c.), 18th-c. churches and palace. It was Austro-Hungarian before the 1st world war, but in 1919 was seized by d'Annunzio for Italy, whose possession was confirmed only in 1924. It passed to Yugoslavia in 1947

Rijswijk, Treaty of *RYSWICK, TREATY OF

rile (rail) *pres. part.* **ril·ing** *past* and *past part.* **riled** *v.t.* to arouse anger or resentfulness in ‖ to roil (a liquid) [var. of ROIL]

Ri·ley (ráili:), James Whitcomb (1849-1916), U.S. poet who wrote in the dialect of his native Indiana

Ril·ke (rílkə), Rainer Maria (1875-1926), German lyric poet born in Czechoslovakia of German parents. One of his great preoccupations was the quality of European life, which he saw as menaced by an encroaching mechanistic utilitarianism symbolized by the U.S.A. The two greatest of his works were the 'Sonnets to Orpheus' (1923) and the 'Duino Elegies' (1923), which are both a sustained meditation and a series of variations on certain themes, or indeed on the whole of life: a life without the Christian god, in which a religious attitude has to be re-created. Meaning and value are restored through the contemplation in particular of what artists, lovers and the great dead have made of life and of death, by the contemplation at the humbler level of the accumulated treasure of significance with which all the past has loaded every object in an old continent, and by the acceptance of death as the other side of life. But the themes are not to be divorced from the verse, which is richly metaphorical, the originality of the language springing directly from the forms and natural workings of German. He surrendered himself, he thought, to visitations in his verse, and he was perhaps the last and one of the greatest exponents of the romantic theory of inspiration

rill (ril) *n.* a small brook or stream [of Gmc origin]

rille, rill (ril) *n.* (*astron.*) a long narrow valley on the moon's surface [G. *rille,* groove]

rill·et (rílet) *n.* a little rill

rim (rim) 1. *n.* the outer edge of a circular, oval or otherwise curved object, often beveled, thickened etc. ‖ a curved frame, e.g. of a wheel or surrounding a lens in a pair of glasses etc. 2. *v.t. pres. part.* **rim·ming** *past* and *past part.* **rimmed** to furnish with a rim ‖ (of a ball) to roll around the rim of (esp. a golf hole) [O.E. *rima*]

RIM-8 *TALOS
RIM-7 *SPARROW
RIM-67 *STANDARD MISSILE
RIM-66 *STANDARD MISSILE
RIM-24 *TARTAR
RIM-2 *TERRIER

Rim·baud (rēbou), Arthur (1854-91), French poet. His literary works, including 'le Bateau ivre' (1871), 'les Illuminations' (published in 1886) and 'Une saison en enfer' (1873), were all written before he was 20. The last 16 years of his life were spent mainly in Ethiopia, where he became a trader. His influence has been profound: as a type of the world-forsaking visionary artist, of the inspired youthful genius, of the 'outcast' or scandalous bohemian, and of the poet as oracle. His poetry sprang from, as he said, a systematic transformation of the function of the senses, and a naturally oblique and figurative habit of expression

rime (raim) 1. *n.* white hoarfrost 2. *v.t. pres. part.* **rim·ing** *past* and *past part.* **rimed** to cover with or as if with rime [O.E. *hrīm*]

Rim·i·ni (rí:mini:) a resort and fishing port (pop. 125,800) of Emilia-Romagna, Italy, on the Adriatic: Roman bridge and arch (1st c.), 15th-c. cathedral (the Malatesta temple)

ri·mose (ráimous) *adj.* (*bot.,* esp. of bark) having many intersecting clefts or fissures **ri·mous** (ráiməs) *adj.* rimose [fr. L. *rimosus*]

Rim·sky-Kor·sa·kov (rímski:kɔ́rsəkɔf), Nikolay Andreyevich (1844-1908), Russian composer. One of his best-known works is the orchestral suite 'Schéhérazade' (1888). His operas on Russian themes, e.g. 'le Coq d'or' (performed 1910), brought him great acclaim in Russia

rim·y (ráimi:) *comp.* **rim·i·er** *superl.* **rim·i·est** *adj.* covered with rime

rind (raind) *n.* peel ‖ the outer layer of tree bark ‖ a hard skin or outer covering, e.g. of bacon or cheese [O.E.]

rin·der·pest (ríndərpest) *n.* a virulent infectious disease, affecting ruminant mammals, esp. cattle. It is characterized by fever, dysentery and inflammation of the mucous membranes [G. fr. *rinder* pl. of *rind,* ox]

ring (riŋ) 1. *v. pres. part.* **ring·ing** *past* **rang** (ræŋ) *past part.* **rung** (rʌŋ) *v.i.* to cause a bell to ring ‖ to give a sound suggestive of a bell ‖ to sound a bell as a summons, *to ring for a servant* ‖ to resound, *the room rang with laughter,* or seem to resound, *the country rang with his praise* ‖ (of the ears or head) to have or seem to

have a buzzing sensation ‖ *v.t.* to cause (a bell) to sound ‖ (esp. *Br.,* often with 'up') to telephone ‖ (with 'in' or 'out') to usher by the sound of bells, *to ring in the New Year* ‖ to test the purity of (a coin etc.) by striking it against a hard object **to ring a bell** to evoke a vague memory, sound remotely familiar **to ring down the curtain** to lower the curtain or give a signal for lowering the curtain in a theater etc. **to ring false** (**true**) to sound false (true) **to ring off** (esp. *Br.*) to end a telephone call **to ring the bell** to be successful **to ring up** to record (a sale etc.) on a cash register **to ring up the curtain** to raise the curtain or give a signal for raising the curtain in a theater etc. 2. *n.* the sound of a bell ‖ a sound resembling this, *the ring of laughter* ‖ a sound or tone suggesting a specified quality, *a ring of pride* ‖ a telephone call, *to give someone a ring* ‖ a set of church bells ‖ the act of ringing a bell [O.E. *hringan*]

ring 1. *n.* a circular band, usually of precious metal and often set with precious or semiprecious stones, worn on a finger as an ornament or symbol, *wedding ring* ‖ a circular band worn as an ornament elsewhere on the body, *nose ring* ‖ a circular band of metal, wood, plastic etc. used for holding, attaching etc., *key ring* ‖ anything having a more or less circular form, *smoke ring* ‖ the rim of a circular object ‖ the circular arena in which the acts of a circus are performed ‖ the square enclosure in which boxing and wrestling matches are held ‖ a bullring ‖ a piston ring ‖ an annual ring ‖ a cut around the trunk or limb of a tree ‖ (*horse racing*) an enclosure in which betting takes place ‖ a group of persons or things arranged in a circle ‖ a circular course ‖ a group of persons working together, often illicitly, e.g. in order to gain control of a market, political party etc. ‖ (*chem.*) a number of atoms united in such a way that they can be represented graphically in cyclic form **to make** (or **run**) **rings around** to surpass with ease **to throw one's hat in the ring** to announce that one is a candidate in a political contest 2. *v.t.* to encircle, *a lake ringed by trees* ‖ to fit with a ring, *to ring a bull* ‖ to prevent (cattle, game etc.) from straying or escaping by riding around them in a circle ‖ to cut a ring in the bark of (a tree) ‖ (in some games, e.g. quoits) to encircle (a peg etc.) with a ring ‖ *v.i.* to form into a ring or rings ‖ to move in a ring ‖ (esp. of a bird) to rise in a spiral [O.E. *hring*]

ring·bolt (ríŋboult) *n.* (*naut.*) an iron bolt having a ring through an eye at one end, through which a rope can be passed and tied

ring·bone (ríŋboun) *n.* (*vet.*) a deposit of bony matter on the pastern bones of a horse, usually causing lameness

ring compound (*chem.*) a compound in which some or all of the atoms of the molecule are linked to form a closed ring, e.g. benzene

ring·dove (ríŋdʌv) *n. Columba palumbus,* a European pigeon having a patch of white on each side of its neck ‖ *Streptopelia risoria,* a turtledove native to Asia and S.E. Europe having a ring of black around its neck

ringed (riŋd) *adj.* encircled by or as if by a ring or rings ‖ shaped like a ring or rings ‖ wearing a ring or rings ‖ decorated with a ring or rings

Ring·el·mann chart (ríŋgəlmɒn) (*envir.*) a series of shaded illustrations used to measure the opacity of air-pollution emissions, ranging from light gray (number 1) through black (number 5), used to set and enforce emission standards

ring·er (ríŋər) *n.* a person who, or thing which, rings a bell ‖ (*pop.,* often with 'dead') a person who strongly resembles another, *he is a dead ringer for his brother* ‖ a person or horse etc. entered in a competition under false identity or false representation

ringer *n.* a quoit that lodges correctly around a pin or peg

ring fence a fence completely enclosing a large piece of land, esp. grazing land

ring·lead·er (ríŋli:dər) *n.* a leader of a group of people engaged in unlawful or objectionable acts

ring·let (ríŋlit) *n.* a long lock of curly hair

ring·mas·ter (ríŋmæstər, ríŋmɑstər) *n.* an official in charge of the various acts in a circus

ring ou·zel (ú:z'l) *Turdus torquatus,* fam. *Turdidae,* a thrushlike bird allied to the European blackbird and American robin, having a white band on the breast. It breeds in the mountainous areas of N. Europe

ring-pull (ríŋpul) *n.* a metal ring on the top of a can that creates an opening when pulled off — **ring-pull** *adj.* Cf POP-TOP, ZIP-TOP

CONCISE PRONUNCIATION KEY: **(a)** æ, c*a*t; ɑ, c*a*r; ɔ f*aw*n; ei, sn*a*ke. **(e)** e, h*e*n; i:, sh*ee*p; iə, d*ee*r; ɛə, b*ea*r. **(i)** i, f*i*sh; ai, t*i*ger; ə:, b*i*rd. **(o)** o, *o*x; au, c*ow*; ou, g*oa*t; u, p*oo*r; ɔi, r*oy*al. **(u)** ʌ, d*u*ck; u, b*u*ll; u:, g*oo*se; ə, b*a*cillus; ju:, c*u*be. x, lo*ch*; θ, *th*ink; ð, bo*th*er; z, *Z*en; ʒ, corsa*g*e; dʒ, sava*g*e; ŋ, ora*ng*utang; j, *y*ak; ʃ, *f*ish; tʃ, fe*tch*; 'l, rabb*le*; 'n, redd*en.* Complete pronunciation key appears inside front cover.

ring road (*Br.*) a belt highway

ring·side (ríŋsaid) *n.* the area immediately outside a boxing or circus ring where a good view is afforded

ring vaccination (*med.*) universal inoculation of those who have been in the close vicinity of a sick person

ring·way (ríŋwẹi) *n.* (*Br.*) beltway; a road around a community, avoiding the city center

ring·worm (ríŋwərm) *n.* any of various contagious diseases of hair, skin and nails caused in man and domestic animals by fungi, esp. genera *Trichophyton* and *Microsporum*, marked by ring-shaped patches of discoloration in the skin

rink (riŋk) *n.* an area of natural or artificial ice used for ice-skating ‖ a wooden or asphalt floor used for roller-skating ‖ a building or enclosure containing an area for ice-skating or roller-skating ‖ a stretch of ice used for the game of curling or hockey ‖ a section of a bowling green wide enough for a match ‖ (*curling* and *bowling*) a team of four players [prob. O.F. *renc*, row, rank]

rink·y-dink or **rinky-tinky** (ríŋki:díŋk) *adj.* (*slang*) old-fashioned and dilapidated —**rinky dink, rinky tink** *n.*

rinse (rins) 1. *v.t. pres. part.* **rins·ing** *past* and *past part.* **rinsed** to remove the soap, dirt etc. from (clothes etc.) with clear water ‖ to remove (soap etc.) in this way ‖ to wash superficially in clear water 2. *n.* a rinsing or being rinsed ‖ a solution that tints the hair temporarily [F. *rincer*, origin unknown]

Ri·o·bam·ba (ri:ɔbámbɔ) a city (pop. 61,000) in central Ecuador. The first constitution of the Republic of Ecuador was proclaimed (1830) here

Río Bravo *RIO GRANDE

Rí·o de Ja·nei·ro (rí:oudɔdʒɔnéɔrou) the chief port of entry (pop. 4,857,700) of Brazil, on the southeast coast. Manufactures and industries: chemicals, pharmaceuticals, food processing, consumer goods. Built on the coastal plain and hills rising from Guanabara Bay, and flanked by crescent beaches, it is backed by a row of steep granite peaks, notably Pão de Açúcar (Sugarloaf, 1,296 ft) jutting into the bay, and Corcovado (Hunchback, 2,310 ft). Its modern architecture is often spectacular. Its colonial monuments include the 18th-c. cathedral and churches, botanical gardens (1808), National University (1920), library, museums and academies. The site was explored (1502) by the Portuguese, and settlement was begun by French Huguenots (1555). Rio de Janeiro was the capital of Brazil (1763-1960)

Rí·o de la Pla·ta (rí:ɔðelɑplátɔ) (*Eng.* River Plate) an estuary (170 miles long, 20-120 miles wide) between Uruguay and Argentina, formed by the Paraná and Uruguay Rivers. Chief ports: Montevideo, Buenos Aires. Its basin is one of the most fertile regions of South America

Rí·o de Oro (rí:ɔðeɔrɔ) *SPANISH SAHARA

Rí·o Gran·de (rí:ugrándɔ) a headstream (680 miles long) of the Paraná, rising in the coastal highlands of S.E. Brazil

Rí·o Gran·de (rí:ougrǽndi:, ri:ougrǽnd) (*Span.* Río Bravo or Río Grande del Norte) a river (1,800 miles long) flowing south from the Rocky Mtns in S. Colorado, through New Mexico to El Paso, Texas, then southeast, forming the Texas-Mexico border, to the Gulf of Mexico

Rio Grande de Santiago *SANTIAGO

ri·om·e·ter (ri:ɔ́mitər) (*acronym*) for relative ionospheric opacity meter, a device that records cosmic radio noise through changes in absorption rate of electromagnetic waves in the ionosphere

Rí·o Mu·ni (rí:oumú:ni:), or Mbini, the mainland (area incl. offshore islands 10,047 sq. miles, pop. 183,000) part of Guinea-Bissau. Capital: Bata. People: Fang (Bantu-speaking), 2% European. It is mountainous except for a narrow coastal strip. Highest point: 4,920 ft. Exports: cocoa, palm oil, coffee, hardwoods, fruit. Río Muni was occupied by Spain (1844) and became part of Equatorial Guinea (now Guinea-Bissau) (1959)

Rí·o Ne·gro (rí:onégrɔ) a river (1,400 miles long) rising (as the Guainía) in E. Colombia, flowing southwest along the Venezuelan border, then west through Brazil to the Amazon at Manaus

Rí·o Pie·dras (rí:ɔpjeðrɔs) a town (pop. 132,000) in N. Puerto Rico, main seat of the University of Puerto Rico

Rí·os Mo·ra·les (rí:ɔsmɔráles), Juan Antonio (1888-1946), Chilean statesman, president (1942-6). He followed a policy of neutrality in the 2nd world war

ri·ot (ráiɔt) *n.* a public tumult, often in defiance of authority and the law and sometimes destructive of life or property ‖ a profuse display or growth, *a riot of color, a riot of tropical vegetation* ‖ a hound's following of a scent other than that of the animal being hunted ‖ (*pop.*) a very funny person or entertainment **to read the riot act** to order someone to desist peremptorily on pain of punishment **to run riot** to act without control or restraint ‖ (of plants) to grow in wild profusion [O.F. *riote, riot*]

riot *v.i.* to take part in a riot ‖ to grow in undisciplined profusion, *roses rioted everywhere in the garden* ‖ (of a hound) to follow the scent of an animal other than the one it is supposed to be hunting ‖ *v.i.* (with 'away') to spend (time, money etc.) wantonly [O.F. *rioter*]

Riot Act an act of the British parliament, passed (1715) as a result of the rioting which followed the accession of George I. The act made it a felony if an unlawful assembly of 12 or more people fails to disperse within an hour of the reading of a prescribed proclamation by a magistrate or other law officer

Rí·o Tin·to (rí:ɔtí:ntɔ) a town (pop. 7,000) in Huelva, Spain, the site of copper mines (Minas de Río Tinto) exploited by the Phoenicians and Romans and, in modern times, since the 18th c., but now nearly exhausted

ri·ot·ous (ráiətɔs) *adj.* marked by rioting ‖ noisy and disorderly ‖ profligate, *riotous living* ‖ profuse, *riotous color* [O.F.]

Rio Treaty *INTERAMERICAN TREATY OF RECIPROCAL ASSISTANCE

Ri·ouw Archipelago (rí:ou) (*Indonesian* Riau) a group of islands (land area 2,279 sq. miles, pop. 77,000) in Indonesia, in S.E. Malaya. Main islands: Bintan, Bantam, Rempang. Chief town: Pakan Baru. Products: copra, bauxite

rip (rip) 1. *v. pres. part.* **rip·ping** *past* and *past part.* **ripped** *v.t.* to break the fibers of (e.g. cloth) by a sudden pull, tear, cut etc. ‖ (with 'off', 'out', 'away') to remove by pulling suddenly, *they ripped off his medals* ‖ to give a sudden pull or pulls to so as to bring into a specified condition, *to rip open a parcel* ‖ to split or saw (wood) in the direction of the grain ‖ *v.i.* to be suddenly torn, cut, split etc. ‖ (*pop.*) to move at a great speed **to rip into** (*pop.*) to attack suddenly with angry words **to rip out** to utter (an oath, threat etc.) violently 2. *n.* the act of ripping ‖ a tear or rent made by ripping [etym. doubtful]

rip *n.* a tide rip ‖ a tidal or river current caused by water moving over an irregular bottom [perh. fr. RIP v.]

rip *n.* (*pop.*) a dissolute person [perh. var. of REP]

ri·par·i·an (raipéəri:ən, ripéəri:ən) *adj.* of or relating to a riverbank, *riparian rights* ‖ located on a riverbank, *riparian land* [L. *riparius*]

rip cord a cord for opening a parachute ‖ a cord for opening the gasbag of a balloon for a rapid descent

ripe (raip) *adj.* ready to be harvested, *the corn is ripe* or to be eaten, *a ripe plum* ‖ having reached full flavor, e.g. by aging, *a ripe cheese* ‖ (of a plan etc.) ready to be put into action, execution etc. ‖ (of time) at a propitious juncture ‖ mature, *ripe judgment* ‖ far on in years, *the ripe age of 82* ‖ (of a boil etc.) ready to open **ri·pen** *v.i.* to become ripe ‖ *v.t.* to cause to become ripe [O.E. *ripe*]

rip-off (rípɔf) *n.* (*slang* or *colloq.*) an unethical, cheating practice —**rip off** *v.* —**rip-off** *adj.*

Rip·on Falls (rípən) a low waterfall marking the exit of the Nile from its source in Lake Victoria, Uganda. It has become virtually submerged by the nearby hydroelectric scheme at Owens Falls

Ripon Society an organization of liberal Republicans founded (1960s) to research for liberal Republican candidates. It is privately financed

ri·poste, ri·post (ripóust) *n.* a quick return thrust in fencing ‖ a quick, sharp retort [F. *riposte* fr. Ital. *risposta*, reply]

riposte, ripost *pres. part.* **ri·post·ing** *past* and *past part.* **ri·post·ed** *v.i.* to make a riposte [fr. F. *riposter*]

rip·per (rípɔr) *n.* a device for ripping, e.g. a ripsaw ‖ the operator of a ripsaw

rip·ple (ríp'l) 1. *v. pres. part.* **rip·pling** *past* and *past part.* **rip·pled** *v.i.* (of water) to have the surface disturbed by ripples ‖ to make the sound

of ripples ‖ to cause ripples, *the rippling movement of the boat* ‖ (of fabric etc.) to fall in ripplelike folds ‖ *v.t.* to cause ripples in, give a wavy appearance to 2. *n.* a small wave spreading outwards from a point where the surface of water etc. is disturbed ‖ a small wave made by the action of wind on water ‖ anything resembling this in appearance, *ripples in the grass* ‖ the sound made by small waves or the action of the wind on waves ‖ a sound compared with this, *a ripple of laughter* ‖ a ripple mark [etym. doubtful]

ripple 1. *v.t. pres. part.* **rip·pling** *past* and *past part.* **rip·pled** to draw (flax etc.) through a ripple in order to separate out the seeds 2. *n.* a comb used for separating the seeds from flax [M.E. *ripelen*]

ripple mark a wavy line or ridge produced by the action of wind or waves or both on the surface of sand etc.

rip·plet (ríplit) *n.* a little ripple

rip·ply (rípli:) *comp.* **rip·pli·er** *superl.* **rip·pli·est** *adj.* having ripples ‖ rippling

rip·rap (rípræp) 1. *n.* a foundation or wall of stones thrown together loosely and irregularly, used e.g. on slopes to prevent erosion ‖ stones used for this purpose 2. *v.t. pres. part.* **rip·rap·ping** *past* and *past part.* **rip·rapped** to strengthen with a riprap ‖ to build a riprap in or upon

rip-roar·ing (rípròriŋ, rípròuriŋ) *adj.* (*pop.*) (used as an intensive) very great, *a rip-roaring success, a rip-roaring time*

rip·saw (rípsɔ) *n.* a coarse-toothed saw for cutting wood along the grain

rip·snort·er (rípsnɔrtər) *n.* something very powerful, impressive or remarkable **ríp·snórt·ing** *adj.*

rip·tide (ríptaid) *n.* a powerful surface current flowing away from shore

Rip·u·ar·i·an (ripju:éəri:ən) 1. *adj.* of or relating to the southern division of the Franks, united (late 5th c.) with the Salian Franks under Clovis 2. *n.* a Ripuarian Frank [M.L. *Ripuarius*]

rise (raiz) 1. *v. pres. part.* **ris·ing** *past* **rose** (rouz) *past part.* **ris·en** (ríz'n) *v.i.* to come to a vertical position after sitting, kneeling, lying etc. ‖ to get up after sleeping, *to rise early* ‖ to extend upwards, *the mountain rises abruptly* ‖ to move upwards, *the balloon rose in the air* ‖ to be restored to life, *to rise from the dead* ‖ (of birds) to soar up from the ground in alarm ‖ (of a heavenly body) to appear above the horizon, *the moon rose* ‖ to increase in degree, quantity, volume, price etc., ‖ to become louder, *her voice rose in indignation* ‖ (of emotions) to become intensified, *indignation rose in him* ‖ to swell, puff up, *a blister rose on his thumb, the bread is rising* ‖ to advance in rank, acquire a higher social status etc., *to rise in a profession* ‖ to become elated, stirred, animated etc., *his spirits rose when he heard the news* ‖ to begin, *the river rises in the mountains* ‖ to revolt, *to rise against a king* ‖ to come into being, *the idea rose from my knowledge of him* ‖ (of the wind) to begin to blow ‖ (of the wind) to blow with greater force ‖ (of fish) to come towards the surface of the water to take food or bait ‖ to end a meeting, *the committee rose at 7* ‖ to be in the process of being erected, *a skyscraper is rising in the river area* ‖ to become, or seem to become, erect, *fear caused his hair to rise* ‖ *v.t.* to cause (birds) to soar up from the ground ‖ to cause (fish) to come towards the surface of the water **to rise above** to dominate by moral effort, *to rise above one's misfortunes* **to rise to** to show oneself capable of meeting (challenging circumstances, occasions etc.) 2. *n.* an upward-sloping piece of ground ‖ advancement in rank, social status etc. ‖ the original source of something, e.g. a river ‖ the emergence and early growth of something, e.g. a civilization or industry, *the rise of the Roman Empire* ‖ an increase in price, rate, value, volume etc. ‖ (of a body of water) a coming to a higher level or the amount of this ‖ (*Br.*) a raise (increase in salary or wages) ‖ the appearance of fish near the surface of water **to get a rise out of (someone)** to get a hoped-for reaction from (someone) by teasing or otherwise provoking **rís·er** *n.* the vertical piece connecting two stair treads **an early (late) riser**, a person who gets up early (late) in the morning [O.E. *rīsan*]

rise time (*telecommunications*) the time required for a pulse signal to go from 10% to 90% of maximum amplitude. *also* build-up time

ris·i·bil·i·ty (rizəbíliti:) *pl.* **ris·i·bil·i·ties** *n.* (*rhet.*) laughter, *to excise risibility* ‖ (*pl., rhet.*) responsiveness to what excites laughter

ris·i·ble (rízəb'l) *adj.* (*rhet.*) exciting laughter ‖ (*rhet.*) of or relating to laughter ‖ (*rhet.*) used in laughing, *risible muscles* ‖ (*rhet.*) easily disposed to laugh [fr. L.L. *risibilis*]

ris·ing (ráiziŋ) **1.** *adj.* of or relating to someone who, or something which, rises, *the rising sun, a rising man in his profession, the rising generation* ‖ (*Br.*) nearing a stated age, *he must be rising 12 by now* **2.** *n.* the act or process of someone who, or something which, rises ‖ a rebellion ‖ (*naut.*) one of the narrow strakes of wood on which the thwarts rest

risk (risk) **1.** *n.* the possibility of danger, injury, loss etc. ‖ (*insurance*) the possibility of loss in the case of goods covered by an insurance policy ‖ (*insurance*) the probability of such loss ‖ (*insurance*) a person or thing with reference to the hazard involved in insuring him or it, *a good risk* **at owner's risk** (*commerce*) on condition that the owner bears the risk in case of loss etc. **to run** (or **take**) **a risk** to expose oneself or be exposed to danger, injury, loss etc. **2.** *v.t.* to expose to danger, injury, loss etc., *to risk one's neck* ‖ to run or take the risk of, *to risk a battle* [F. *risque* fr. Ital.]

risk·i·ly (rískili:) *adv.* in a risky way

risk·i·ness (ríski:nis) *n.* the state or quality of being risky

risk retention self insurance, esp. by a cooperating group in a common situation

risk·y (ríski:) *comp.* **risk·i·er** *superl.* **risk·i·est** *adj.* involving risk

Ri·sor·gi·men·to (ri:sɔrdʒi:méntɔ) the rising (1815-70) of the people of Italy against Austrian domination. Among its leaders were Mazzini, who founded (1831) the 'Young Italy' movement, Garibaldi and Cavour

ri·sot·to (risótou, risótou) *n.* rice cooked in meat stock, with onions, bits of cooked meat etc. [Ital.]

ris·qué (riskéi) *adj.* close to being indecent, *a risqué story* [F.]

ris·sole (rísoul, risóul) *n.* a small ball of minced meat or fish coated with bread crumbs etc. and fried [O.F.]

ri·tar·dan·do (ri:tardándou) *n.* (*mus.*, *abbr.* rit., ritard.) a direction to go gradually slower [Ital.]

rite (rait) *n.* a religious ceremony or formal act of worship ‖ any ceremonial observance or procedure ‖ (often **Rite**) the liturgical form adopted by a church, *the Roman Rite* ‖ (often **Rite**) a division of a Church using such liturgical form [fr. L. *ritus*, ceremony]

ri·tor·nel·lo (ri:tornélou) *pl.* **ri·tor·nel·li** (ri:tornéli:) *n.* (*mus.*) a purely orchestral passage, esp. a refrain, in a vocal composition [Ital.]

rit·u·al (rítʃu:əl) **1.** *adj.* of or relating to or practiced as a rite or rites **2.** *n.* a strictly ordered traditional method of conducting and performing an act of worship or other solemn ceremony ‖ a book setting out this method ‖ (*loosely*) any method of doing something in which the details are always faithfully repeated, *to make a ritual of welcoming one's guests* **rit·u·al·ism** *n.* excessive observance of religious ritual ‖ the study of religious ritual **rit·u·al·ist** *n.* a person who practices or advocates ritualism **rit·u·al·is·tic**, *adj.* **rit·u·al·is·ti·cal·ly** *adv.* [fr. L. *ritualis*]

ritz wrap (rítzræp) (*cosmetology*) hair-styling device made with fabric-covered wire, to put up long hair into an elevated style

Ri·va·da·via (ri:vadávja), Bernardino (1780-1845), Argentinian politician and first president of the Republic (1826-7). He was forced to resign, and lived the remainder of his life in exile

ri·val (ráivəl) **1.** *n.* a person in competition with another or others, e.g. in love or business ‖ someone or something which equals or nearly equals another in some desirable quality, *he has no rival in Shakespearean roles* **2.** *adj.* competitive, *rival firms* **3.** *v.t.* *pres. part.* **ri·val·ing**, esp. *Br.* **ri·val·ling** *past* and *past part.* **ri·valed**, esp. *Br.* **ri·valled** to be in competition with ‖ to equal or approach equality with, *to rival someone in intelligence* **ri·val·ry** *pl.* **ri·val·ries** *n.* competition ‖ an instance of this [fr. L. *rivalis*, orig. a person living on the opposite riverbank from another person]

Ri·va Pa·la·cio (ri:vapalásjo), Vicente (1832-96), Mexican historical novelist and patriot. His 'Calvario y tabor' depicts the French intervention, against which he fought. His 'Mexico a través de los siglos' is an epic history of Mexico from its origins

rive (raiv) *pres. part.* **riv·ing** *past* **rived** *past part.* **rived**, **riv·en** (rívən) *v.t.* (rare except in

past part.) to split apart, a *riven oak* [O.N. *rífa*]

riv·er (rívər) *n.* a usually voluminous stream of fresh water flowing either permanently or seasonally in a natural channel into another body of water, e.g. a sea or a lake ‖ a voluminous flow of something, *a river of mud* **to sell** (**someone**) **down the river** to cause (someone) to come to ruin or near ruin by some kind of betrayal [O.F. *rivere, riviere*]

Ri·ve·ra (ri:véra), Diego (1886-1957), Mexican painter, esp. of murals depicting past and present social injustices and the reform achievements of the Mexican Revolution (1910-19)

Rivera, José Eustasio (1889-1928), Colombian writer, author of a collection of sonnets, 'Tierra de promisión' (1921), and of the novel 'La vorágine' (1924). The latter depicts Amazon jungle life, centered around the rubber industry, as one which debases all who come into contact with it, but which presents a challenge to the hero

Rivera, José Fructuoso (1788-1854), Uruguayan general, independence leader, and first president (1830-4, 1839-43)

Rivera, Primo de *PRIMO DE RIVERA

Rivera a town (pop. 40,000) in N. Uruguay on the Brazilian border

riv·er·bank (rívərbæŋk) *n.* the bank of a river

riv·er·bed (rívərbed) *n.* the channel in which a river flows or formerly flowed

Riv·er·i·na (rívərí:na) an extensively irrigated district in New South Wales, Australia, watered by the Lachlan, Murrumbidgee and Murray Rivers: wheat, wool, fruit, vegetables, cattle

riv·er·ine (rívərain, rívərin) *adj.* situated on or living on the banks of a river ‖ of or relating to a river, *riverine traffic*

riv·er·side (rívərsaid) *n.* the ground beside a river

riv·et (rívit) **1.** *n.* a metal pin or bolt, with a large head at one end, inserted into two or more metal plates etc., the headless end then being hammered out flat (often while hot) to hold the plates etc. firmly together **2.** *v.t.* *pres. part.* **riv·et·ing, riv·et·ting** *past* and *past part.* **riv·et·ed, riv·et·ted** to join with rivets ‖ (with 'on') to fix (the attention eyes, gaze etc.) [O.F. fr. *river*, to clinch]

Riv·i·e·ra (ri:vi:éəra) the Mediterranean coast between Toulon, France and La Spezia, Italy, a famous resort area

ri·vière (rivjéər, rivi:éər) *n.* a necklace of precious stones, esp. a necklace of diamonds [F. = a river]

riv·u·let (rívjulit) *n.* a small stream [perh. fr. Ital. *rivoletto*]

Ri·yadh (ri:jád) the chief city (pop. 667,000) of Nejd and capital of Saudi Arabia, and principal commercial center or the interior, in a cultivated oasis on the pilgrimage road from Iran to Mecca: Great Mosque (center for the Wahhabi sect), royal palace. University

ri·yal (ri:ál, ri:ɔ́l) *pl.* **ri·yal, ri·yals** *n.* the basic monetary unit of the Yemen ‖ a coin of the value of one riyal

Riz·zio (rítsi:ou), David (c. 1533-66), Italian musician and favorite of Mary Queen of Scots. He was murdered by Darnley, Mary's husband

RM-47 *U-2

RNA *RIBONUCLEIC ACID

RNA polymerase *REPLICASE

RNAse or **RNAase** (*physiol. abbr.*) for ribonuclease (which see)

RO *adj.* (*computer abbr.*) for receive only, used in reference to a printer that only receives data

roach (routʃ) *n.* a cockroach

roach *pl.* **roach, roach·es** *n. Rutilus rutilus*, fam. *Cyprinidae*, a European freshwater fish about 10-12 ins long and weighing up to 1 lb ‖ any of various American sunfishes of fam. *Centrarchidae* [O.F. *roche*]

roach *n.* (*naut.*) a curving edge at the foot of a square sail [origin unknown]

road (roud) *n.* a strip of smoothed, cleared land, usually provided with a hard surface, for the passage from place to place of vehicles, riders, pedestrians etc. ‖ a roadstead ‖ the way to get somewhere, *the road to Rome, the road to success* ‖ (*pop.*) a railroad **on the road** (of a salesman) traveling from place to place selling goods ‖ (esp. of a theatrical company) touring [O.E. *rād*]

road agent (*Am. hist.*) a highwayman on the stagecoach routes

road·bed (róudbed) *n.* the foundation of a road ‖ that part of a road surface upon which vehicles travel ‖ the bed of a railroad on which rails and sleepers are laid

road·block (róudblɒk) *n.* (*mil.*) a barricade constructed to impede the advance of an enemy ‖ a barrier set up by police to halt traffic

road·craft (róudkræft) *n.* (*Br.*) autodriving skill

road hog a driver of a vehicle who stays in or near the middle of the road and so prevents others from passing him

road·house (róudhaus) *pl.* **road·hous·es** (róudhauziz) *n.* a country inn ‖ a nightclub located outside the limits of a city

road·ie (róudi:) *n.* a road-show manager

road·man (róudmən) *pl.* **road·men** (róudmən) *n.* a worker employed in building and maintaining roads

road metal the broken stone etc. used in constructing a road

road racing (*sports*) motorcycle or auto racing on public roads or on simulations of public roads

road·run·ner (róudrʌnər) *n.* the chaparral cock

road·side (róudsaid) **1.** *n.* the side of a road **2.** *adj.* located along a roadside, *a roadside inn*

road·stead (róudsted) *n.* a sheltered water where ships may ride at anchor

road·ster (róudstər) *n.* an open car, with a front seat only, and room for luggage in the back or a rumble seat

road·way (róudwei) *n.* a road, esp. its central area ‖ the part of a bridge used by vehicular traffic

road·wor·thy (róudwə:rθi:) *adj.* fit for being driven on the road

roam (roum) **1.** *v.i.* to walk or travel with no particular goal ‖ *v.t.* to wander through, *to roam the streets* **2.** *n.* a roaming, ramble [etym. doubtful]

roan (roun) **1.** *adj.* (of an animal's coat, esp. a horse's coat) having the prevailing color, esp. when this is reddish-brown, deeply flecked with white or gray hairs **2.** *n.* a roan horse or other animal ‖ a reddish-brown color [O.F. *roan, rouen*, origin unknown]

roan *n.* a sheepskin treated to resemble morocco, used esp. for bookbinding [perh. F. *Roan*, old form of ROUEN]

roar (rɔr, rour) **1.** *v.i.* to emit the loud, deep sound characteristic of some savage or enraged beasts, e.g. a lion or bull ‖ to talk, sing or laugh loudly and boisterously ‖ (e.g. of flood water or the sea) to emit a loud, deep, confused, sometimes rumbling, noise ‖ (of a tunnel or other confined place) to resound noisily ‖ to go with a roaring noise, *cars roar past their houses* ‖ (of a horse afflicted with roaring) to breathe raspingly ‖ *v.t.* to utter or express with a roar ‖ (with 'down') to silence by roaring **2.** *n.* a roaring noise **róar·ing 1.** *n.* the sound made by someone who or something which roars ‖ (*vet.*) a disease of horses causing them to emit rasping breathing sounds during exercise **2.** *adj.* that roars ‖ (*pop.*) extremely successful, *a roaring trade* [O.E. *rārian*]

roaring forties either of two ocean areas between latitudes 40° and 50° N. and S., where very strong westerly winds prevail

roast (roust) **1.** *v.t.* to cook (meat etc.) by exposing it to the radiant heat from a fire, or the dry heat of an oven ‖ to cook (e.g. potatoes) in hot ashes etc. ‖ to dry and partly scorch (esp. coffee beans) ‖ to heat excessively, *the sun was roasting us* ‖ (*metall.*) to heat without melting, in order to burn away impurities ‖ (*pop.*) to criticize mercilessly, *to roast a performance* ‖ *v.i.* to be roasted ‖ to feel extremely hot **2.** *n.* a cut of meat roasted or ready for roasting ‖ a roasting or being roasted ‖ an outdoor social gathering in which the principal item of food is roasted, usually over an open fire, *a wiener roast* **róast·er** *n.* a chicken, pig, rabbit etc. suitable for roasting ‖ an oven for roasting ‖ a furnace used for roasting coffee etc. [fr. O.F. *rostir*]

rob (rɒb) *pres. part.* **rob·bing** *past* and *past part.* **robbed** *v.t.* to take property from (a person) illegally ‖ (*law*) to do this to (someone) with force or threat of force ‖ to take money, valuables etc. from (a place) illegally, *to rob a bank* ‖ to deprive (a person) of something desired or due, *fear robbed him of speech* ‖ to engage in robbery [fr. O.F. *robber, rober* fr. Gmc]

rob·a·lo (roubálou, róubəlou) *pl.* **rob·a·los, rob·a·lo** *n.* the snook (*Centropomus undecimalis*) [Span. *róbalo*]

rob·ber (róbər) *n.* a person who robs

robber baron (*hist.*) a feudal noble who lived by robbing people passing through his territory or holding them for ransom ‖ (*Am. hist.*) any late 19th-c. capitalist who grew rich by exploitation

rob·ber·y (róbəri:) *pl.* **rob·ber·ies** *n.* the act or practice of robbing [O.F. *roberie*]

Rob·bia (róbbja), Luca della (c. 1400-82), Florentine sculptor, one of a large and distinguished family. His most famous work was a series of singing angels and dancing boys, called the 'Cantoria' ('The Singing Gallery') made for the cathedral in Florence, Italy. He perfected a technique of applying colored lead glazes to terra cotta: typically, white figures on a clear blue ground. His work was continued by other members of the family, notably by his nephew, Andrea della Robbia (1435-1528)

Rob·bins (róbinz), Frederick Chapman (1916-   ), U.S. pediatrician and co-winner (with J. F. Enders and T. H. Weller) of the 1954 Nobel prize in medicine and physiology for cultivation of the poliomyelitis viruses in tissue culture

robe (roub) **1.** *n.* a long, loose outer garment worn as a symbol of profession or position, *academic robes, judge's robe* ‖ a skin or rug tucked around the legs while riding in a car etc. ‖ a dressing gown **2.** *v. pres. part.* **rob·ing** *past* and *past part.* **robed** *v.t.* to put a robe or robes on ‖ *v.i.* to put on robes or a robe [O.F.]

Rob·ert I (róbərt) (c. 865-923), French king (922-3)

Robert II (c. 970-1031), king of France (996-1031), son of Hugh Capet. He ruled jointly with his father after 987

Robert I (*d.* 1035), duke of Normandy (1027-35). He was the father of William the Conqueror

Robert II 'Curthose' (c. 1054-1134), duke of Normandy (1087-1106), son of William I of England. He rebelled against his father, was at war (1091-6) with his brother William II, and was defeated and captured by Henry I at Tinchebrai (1106)

Robert I 'the Bruce' (1274-1329), king of Scotland (1306-29). He was crowned in defiance of Edward I, and consolidated his hold on Scotland during the weak reign of Edward II, whom he heavily defeated at Bannockburn (1314). His title to the throne and the independence of Scotland were officially recognized (1328)

Robert II (1316-90), king of Scotland (1371-90), founder of the Stuart dynasty, grandson of Robert I. He was regent (1334-41 and 1346-57) for David II. His reign was spent in war with England

Ro·bert (róber), Hubert (1733-1808), French painter. His landscapes usually incorporated architectural features, often ruins, in the standard romantic vein

Ro·bert Guis·card (róbergi:skær) (c. 1015-85), Norman conqueror of Naples and Sicily. Between attempts (1081-2 and 1085) to conquer the Byzantine Empire, he defended (1084) Pope Gregory VII from a siege by Henry IV of Germany

Rob·erts (róbərts), Sir Charles George Douglas (1860-1943), Canadian writer. His prose works include 'History of Canada' (1897) and animal stories, notably 'The Kindred of the Wild' (1902) and 'Neighbours Unknown' (1911). His verse includes 'In Divers Tones' (1887) and 'The Vagrant of Time' (1927)

Roberts, Frederick Sleigh, 1st Earl Roberts of Kandahar, Pretoria and Waterford (1832-1914), British field marshal. He relieved Kandahar (1880) during the war between Britain and the Afghans (1878-80), was commander in chief in India (1885-93) and commanded (1899-1900) the British forces in the Boer War

Roberts, Owen Josephus (1875-1955), U.S. associate justice of the Supreme Court (1930-45). He was a special U.S. attorney (1924-30) during which time he was involved in the investigation of the Teapot Dome scandal before being appointed to the Court by Pres. Herbert Hoover. He was known as a conservative, generally opposed to Pres. Roosevelt's New Deal programs. He wrote the majority opinions in 'Nebbia v. New York' (1934), 'Railroad Retirement Board v. Alton Railroad Co.' (1935), 'Grovey v. Townsend' (1935) and 'United States v. Butler' (1936). After his resignation from the Court in 1945 he served as president of the University of Pennsylvania Law School (1948-51)

Robert (the) Bruce *ROBERT I

Robe·son (róubsən), Paul (1898-1976) U.S. black singer and actor. His rich bass voice is esp. associated with his repertory of spirituals. He was the star of New York productions 'Emperor Jones' (1924) and (1943) 'Othello', which established the longest Shakespearean run in the U.S.A.

Robes·pierre (rɔbzpjɛər), Maximilien François Marie-Isidore de (1758-94), French revolutionist. A provincial lawyer, he became the leader of the Jacobins during the French Revolution, and led the Mountain in overthrowing the Girondists (1793). As a member of the Committee of Public Safety (July 1793-July 1794) he was the virtual dictator of France, establishing the Terror, and eliminating his rivals Hébert and Danton. His measures, based on the doctrines of Rousseau, became increasingly extremist. He instituted the Cult of the Supreme Being (a mixture of deism and nationalism). He was overthrown and executed in the coup d'état of Thermidor (1794)

rob·in (róbin) *n. Erithacus rubecola,* fam. *Turdidae,* a small, plump European thrush having a dark olive-colored back and a yellowish-red throat and breast ‖ *Turdus migratorius,* fam. *Turoidae,* a large (9-10 ins in length) North American thrush having an olive-gray back, a black throat streaked with gray, and a dull-red breast [O.F. familiar form of ROBERT]

Rob·in Good·fel·low (róbingúdfelou) Puck

Robin Hood (róbinhụd) a medieval English outlaw of Sherwood Forest, the subject of many legends. His exploits are sometimes associated with the reign of Richard I

Rob·in·son (róbinsən), Edward (1794-1863), U.S. biblical scholar. His 'Biblical Researches in Palestine, Mount Sinai, and Arabia Petraea' (1841) and 'Later Biblical Researches in Palestine and the Adjacent Regions' (1856) were pioneer efforts in biblical geography

Robinson, Edwin Arlington (1869-1935), U.S. narrative poet. His best known works are 'The Man Against The Sky' (1916), 'Tristram' (1927) and 'Cavender's House' (1929). The residents of his 'Tilbury Town' were modeled after his boyhood hometown in Maine

Robinson, Henry Crabb (1775-1867), English diarist. He was a friend of Wordsworth, Southey, Coleridge, Lamb etc. and his vivid recollections make his 'Diary, Reminiscences and Correspondence' (1869) a valuable source book

Robinson, Jackie (Jack Roosevelt Robinson, 1919-72), U.S. baseball player, the first black to play (1947) in the major leagues. He became (1962) the first black to gain admission to the National Baseball Hall of Fame

ro·bot (róubɒt róubət) *n.* a mechanical device designed to do the work or part of the work of one or more human beings, esp. such a device activated by radiant energy, sound waves etc. ‖ an efficient but unfeeling person [fr. Czech *robota,* compulsory service, used in Karel Capek's play 'R.U.R.']

ro·bot·ics (roubótiks) *n.* the science of automated devices (robots) used to replace live workers, esp. in factories

ro·bot·o·mor·phic (roubɒtəmórfik) *adj.* of robotlike behavior

Rob Roy (róbrói) (Robert MacGregor, 1671-1734), Scottish outlaw. He ran an extortion racket, demanding money from his neighbors for the return of stolen cattle

Rob·son, Mt (róbsən) the highest point (12,972 ft) of the Canadian Rocky Mtns, in E. British Columbia

ro·bust (roubʌst, róubʌst) *adj.* strong, esp. in resisting fatigue, illness etc. ‖ requiring muscular strength, *a robust game* ‖ coarse, *robust humor* ‖ (esp. of a plant) hardy [fr. L. *robustus*]

roc (rɒk) *n.* an enormous legendary bird thought to inhabit the region around the Indian Ocean [fr. Arab. *rokh, rukhkh*]

Ro·ca (róka), Julio Argentino (1843-1914), Argentinian general, leader in the Paraguay Campaign, conqueror (1879) of Patagonia, and president (1880-6, 1898-1904)

roc·am·bole (rókemboul) *n. Allium scorodoprasum,* fam. *Liliaceae,* a European leek, used as a seasoning [etym. doubtful]

Ro·cham·beau (rɔʃābou), Jean-Baptiste Donatien de Vimeur, Comte de (1725-1807), French marshal. As commander of the French troops sent to aid the American patriots during the Revolutionary War, he contributed to the victory at Yorktown (1781)

Ro·chelle salt (rɔʃél) $KNaC_4H_4O_6·4H_2O$, a crystalline salt used as a mild laxative and in the silvering of mirrors [after *La Rochelle,* France, where it was discovered]

roches mou·ton·nées (rɔʃmu:tonéi) *pl. n.* knobs or hillocks of rock commonly occurring in upland regions, which have been formed and smoothed by glacial action [F. = sheeplike rocks]

Roch·es·ter (rótʃistər) a port (pop. 241,741) in N.W. New York State, on Lake Ontario. Industries: optical and other precision instruments, electrical equipment. University (1848)

Rochester, John Wilmot, 2nd earl of (1647-80), English poet and satirist. His best-known work is 'A Satire Against Mankind' (1675)

roch·et (rótʃit) *n.* (*eccles.*) a white linen vestment resembling a surplice. It is worn chiefly by bishops [O.F.]

rock (rɒk) *n.* (*geol.*) an aggregate of particles composed of one or more minerals, forming the major part of the earth's crust (*IGNEOUS ROCK, *METAMORPHIC ROCK, *SEDIMENTARY ROCK) ‖ a large, usually jagged, mass of this material protruding from the surface of the land or from a body of water ‖ a piece broken off from such a mass ‖ (*fig.*) a firm foundation or support ‖ (*Br.*) a stick of candied sugar flavored with peppermint etc. **on the rocks** in desperate financial straits ‖ (of drinks, esp. whiskey) served neat over ice cubes ‖ in or into a condition of disruption or ruin, *a marriage going on the rocks* ‖ short for rock 'n roll [O.F. *roke*]

rock 1. *v.t.* to cause to move to and fro, *to rock a baby's cradle* ‖ to bring into a specified condition by doing this, *to rock a baby to sleep* ‖ to cause to shake, vibrate, sway etc. violently ‖ to disturb emotionally ‖ (*mining*) to wash (sand or gravel) in a rocker ‖ (in mezzotint engraving) to prepare the surface of (a plate) by scraping it with a cradle ‖ *v.i.* to move to and fro ‖ to sway violently **2.** *n.* the act of rocking ‖ the movement involved in this act [O.E. *roccian*]

rock·a·bil·ly (rókəbɪli:) *n.* a combination of pop, rock, and country and western music styles

rock and roll, rock-'n-roll (rókənroụl) a style of popular music of Afro-American origin, characterized by an insistent, heavily accented syncopated rhythm and the obsessive repetition of short musical phrases, tending to build up tension in an audience and induce a state of group frenzy when played very loud

rock bass *Ambloplites rupestris,* fam. *Centrarchidae,* a North American sunfish found esp. in the Great Lakes region and the upper Mississippi valley ‖ the striped bass ‖ any of several sea basses of genus *Paralabrax* widely distributed in the coastal waters of California and Mexico

rock bottom the lowest point or level, *sales have reached rock bottom* **at rock bottom** fundamentally **róck-bót·tom** *adj.*

rock candy sugar in large, hard, clear crystals

rock crystal the purest and most transparent form of quartz

rock dove the rock pigeon

Rock·e·fel·ler (rókifelər), John Davison (1839-1937), American industrialist and philanthropist. He acquired a near-monopoly of oil refining in the U.S.A. He endowed an institute for medical research with 500 million dollars (1901), and also gave generously to educational, scientific and religious funds

Rockefeller, Nelson Aldrich (1908-79), U.S. statesman, vice-president (1974-7), governor of New York (1959-73), grandson of John D. Rockefeller. He served as coordinator of inter-American affairs (1940-4), assistant secretary of state (1944-5), head of the International Development Advisory Board (1953-4) and special assistant to Pres. Dwight D. Eisenhower (1954-5). As New York's governor he expanded social welfare and education programs. He was appointed vice-president when Gerald Ford succeeded Richard Nixon as president

Rockefeller Foundation a philanthropic organization chartered (1913) by John D. Rockefeller, Sr. Its objectives are the conquest of hunger, the solution to the problems of population, university development, equality of opportunity, and cultural development

rock·er (rókər) *n.* either of the curved pieces on which a rocking chair or cradle rocks ‖ a rocking chair ‖ a cradle for washing sand or gravel ‖ a cradle used by a mezzotint engraver ‖ a skate with a curved blade

rocker *n.* a rock musician

rocker arm a lever, usually pivoted near its midpoint, used to transmit motion to a valve stem from a cam

rock·er·y (rókəri:) *pl.* **rock·er·ies** *n.* a rock garden

rock·et (rókit) **1.** *n.* a projectile driven by the reaction to the rearward expulsion of gases which are produced by burning a fuel inside it. It is the only known form of propulsion which can operate in a vacuum, and is therefore used in space vehicles. Rockets range in size from toy fireworks up to the very large ones used to launch earth satellites etc. Rockets are also used to throw the line in marine lifesaving appliances and to propel military warheads **2.** *v.i.* to rise very rapidly, *prices rocketed when the news was heard* || (of game birds) to fly straight when flushed [F. *roquet* or fr. Ital. *rocchetta*]

rocket *n.* a member of *Hesperis*, fam. *Cruciferae*, a genus of plants having spikes of white or purple flowers which are fragrant at night, esp. *H. matronalis* || *Eruca sativa*, fam. *Cruciferae*, a European annual grown mainly for salad [F. *roquette* fr. Ital.]

rocket astronomy the science involving analysis of high-altitude data accumulated by rocket instruments

rock·et·drome (rókitdrɒum) *n.* a rocket airport

rock·et·ry (rókitri:) *n.* the study of or use of rockets

rock·fish (rókfiʃ) *pl.* **rock·fish, rock·fish·es** *n.* any of several food fishes living among rocks in deep or shallow water, e.g. the striped bass and various groupers

rock garden an arrangement of large stones set in soil, in which various alpine plants, dwarf shrubs etc. are grown

Rock·ies (róki:z) the Rocky Mtns

rock·i·ness (rókinis) *n.* the state or quality of being rocky

rocking chair a chair mounted on rockers

Rock·ing·ham (rókiŋəm), Charles Watson-Wentworth, 2nd marquis of (1730-82), English statesman who led Whig ministries (1765-6 and 1782)

rocking horse a wooden horse mounted on rockers, for children to ride on

rock·oon (rɒkkú:n) *n.* (*aerospace*) a system for high-altitude exploration utilizing a balloon from which a small, solidpropellant research rocket is launched near maximum altitude

rock pigeon *Columba livia*, fam. *Columbidae*, a bluish-gray European and Asian wild pigeon living along rocky coasts

rock rabbit the hyrax

rock·rose (rókrɒuz) *n.* any of various low-growing plants of fam. *Cistaceae*, esp. of genera *Cistus, Helianthemum* and *Crocanthemum*, growing mainly on rocky slopes and bearing roselike single flowers || the flower of any of these plants

rock salmon any of various tropical fishes, esp. *Lutjanus argentimaculatus*, fam. *Lutjanidae*, a variety of red or pink snapper of the Pacific || (*Br.*) the dogfish as sold by fish dealers

rock salt common salt occurring in stratified layers

rock·shaft (rókʃæft, rókʃɑft) *n.* a shaft that rocks back and forth on its journals (rather than revolving)

Rockwell (rókwel), Norman (1894–1978), U.S. illustrator, known for his 'Saturday Evening Post' covers (1916–63) depicting whimsical, humorous views of Middle America as well as events of the day. His best-known work is the 'Four Freedoms' mural, which was used on posters during the 2nd world war

rock wool a fibrous material formed by passing a jet of steam through limestone, siliceous rock etc. It is used for heat and sound insulation

rock·y (róki:) *comp.* **rock·i·er** *superl.* **rock·i·est** *adj.* full of rocks || made of rock || hard as rock

rocky *comp.* **rock·i·er** *superl.* **rock·i·est** *adj.* (of something which ought to be firm) shaky or weak, *a rocky table* || (*pop.*) feeling unwell

Rocky Mountain goat the mountain goat

Rocky Mountains a mountain system of W. North America, running from British Columbia and Alberta, Canada, through Montana, Idaho, Wyoming, Utah and Colorado to Arizona and New Mexico. The peaks are characteristically massive and barren, only lower slopes being forested. The system is rich in minerals. Highest point: Mt Elbert (14,431 ft) in Colorado || the entire axial mountain system of North America, running from the Bering Strait to the Andes, including, with the Rocky Mtns proper,

the Alaska, Cascade, Sierra Nevada, Sierra Madre, Central American and lesser ranges

Rocky Mountain spotted fever a serious febrile disease characterized by chills, fever, pains in the muscles and joints, and a dark reddish-purple rash. It is caused by rickettsia transmitted by the bite of the Rocky Mountain wood tick

ro·co·co (rəkóukou, roukóukou) **1.** *n.* a highly ornamental style in architecture, interior decoration etc., characterized by asymmetrical arrangements of curved lines and elaborate scrollwork, developed in France from the baroque, and prevalent in Europe in the 18th c. **2.** *adj.* of or relating to painting, music, literature etc. of this same period having similar ornately decorative characteristics [F.]

Roc·roi, Battle of (rɔkrwæ) a battle (1643), during the Thirty Years' War. The French army under Louis II de Condé decimated the Spanish infantry

rod (rɒd) *n.* a slender, sometimes extensible bar, shaft, pole, staff etc. in wood, cane, metal, glass etc., *a curtain rod, a fishing rod* || a connecting rod || a staff or wand carried as a symbol of office, authority etc. || a stick used to measure with || a measure of length equal to 5 ½ yds or 16 ½ ft || a square rod || one of the rod-shaped cells in the retina of the eye sensitive to dim light || a rod-shaped bacterium **the rod** corporal punishment [O. E. *rodd*]

rode past of RIDE

ro·dent (róud'nt) **1.** *n.* a small gnawing mammal of the order *Rodentia* including rats, mice, squirrels, marmots etc. All rodents have a single pair of large chisellike incisors in the upper jaw. These keep growing from the roots as they wear away at the tips **2.** *adj.* of or relating to a rodent [fr. L. *rodens* (*rodentis*) fr. *rodere*, to gnaw]

ro·de·o (róudi:ou, roudéiou) *n.* a roundup (of cattle) || an area where cattle are enclosed || a public exhibition of skill by cowboys, e.g. in riding, lassoing etc., often in competition [Span.=a going around]

Rod·er·ick (ródərik) (*d.* c. 711), last king of the Visigoths in Spain (c. 710–c. 711). He was killed fighting the Moors

Ro·dil (rɔdí:l), José Ramón (1789-1853), Spanish general. In spite of the definitive defeat of Spanish forces at Ayacucho, he held the port of El Callao until the following year (1825)

Ro·din (rodɛ̃), Auguste (1840-1917), French sculptor. The sensitive, almost flickering surfaces of his bronzes render both the internal life and energy of the subject and the modeler's own creative energy. The subjects start from the human form, but tend toward a more abstract 'thought'. They thus form a bridge between the 'literary' symbolism of Rodin's own time and the more abstract formal art of the 20th c. His most frequent themes are human aspiration and creativity ('The Thinker', 'Balzac'), the anguish of humanity which knows its own mortality ('The Burghers of Calais'), and the related theme of erotic love ('The Kiss' etc.)

Rod·ney (ródni:), George Brydges, 1st Baron Rodney (1718-92), British admiral. He won victories over the Spanish and French fleets in the Revolutionary War

Ro·dó (rodóu), José Enrique (1872-1917), Uruguayan essayist and moralist. His most important works are his essay on Rubén Darío (1899), 'Ariel' (1900) and 'Motivos de Proteo' (1909)

rod·o·mon·tade (rɒdəmɒntéid, rɒdəmɒntɑ́d, rɒudəmɒntéid, rɒudəmɒntɑ́d) **1.** *n.* bluster, boasting **2.** *adj.* boastful **3.** *v.i.* **pres. part. rod·o·mon·tad·ing** *past* and *past part.* **rod·o·mon·tad·ed** to boast [F. fr. Ital. after the character *Rodomonte* in Ariosto's 'Orlando Furioso']

Rod·rí·guez (rɔdri:ges), José Gaspar *FRANCIA

rod storage (*computer*) cylindrical rods or wires, 1/10th-in long, utilized as a static magnetic storage unit in some computers in place of ring-shape cores

roe (rou) *n.* a mass of fish eggs, esp. when enclosed in the ovarian membrane || the eggs or ovaries of certain crustaceans, e.g. the coral of a lobster [prob. fr. O.N. *hrogn*]

roe *pl.* **roe, roes** *n.* a roe deer [O.E. *rāha, ræge*]

Roeb·ling (róubliŋ), John Augustus (1806-69), U.S. civil engineer and designer of suspension bridges, notably the Brooklyn Bridge in New York

roe·buck (róubʌk) *n.* the male roe deer

roe deer *Capreolus capreolus*, a species of small, graceful, European and Asian deer, having forked antlers. They are reddish-brown in summer, grayish in winter

roent·gen, rönt·gen (réntgən, réntʃən) *n.* (*phys.*) a unit of X-ray or gamma radiation, defined as the amount which will produce ions in 1 cc. of dry air at standard temperature and pressure that carry 1 electrostatic unit of charge [after Wilhelm Konrad *Roentgen* (1845-1923), G. discoverer of X rays]

roent·gen·o·gram (réntgənəgræm, réntʃənəgræm) *n.* an X-ray picture, radiograph

Roentgen ray an X-ray

ro·ga·tion (rougéiʃən) *n.* (*eccles., pl.*) the litanies sung on Rogation Days || (*Rom. hist.*) a law proposed by consuls or tribunes for ratification by the people [fr. L. *rogatio* (*rogationis*), supplication]

Rogation Days the three days preceding Ascension Day

rog·a·to·ry (rógətɔ:ri:, rógətɔuri:) *adj.* (*law*) demanding information, esp. authorized to question witnesses [fr. F. *rogatoire*]

rog·er (ródʒər) *interj.* (in radio communication) your message has been received and understood || your instruction will be complied with

Rog·er I (ródʒər) (c. 1031-1101), Norman count of Sicily (1072-1101), brother of Robert Guiscard. He conquered Sicily from the Arabs and made it a strong feudal state

Roger II (c. 1095-1154), count (1101-30) and king (1130-54) of Sicily, son of Roger I. He defeated (1139) the forces of Innocent II and extended his conquests to N. Africa

Rog·ers (ródʒərz), Robert (1731-95), American frontiersman. A popular hero during the French and Indian Wars, he led daring expeditions in the British cause. He directed (1760s) a secret expedition to discover the Northwest Passage, was arrested on a charge of conspiring with foreign governments to establish an independent state, but was acquitted

Rogers, Will (William Penn Adair Rogers, 1879-1935), U.S. humorist, known as the 'cowboy philosopher' for his freewheeling comments on the political and social scene through the media of radio, movies, books, and a syndicated newspaper column

rogue (roug) **1.** *n.* a man who gets along in life by cheating, deceiving, and taking advantage of others || a mischievous child or person || (*hort.*) an abnormal or inferior plant displaying a variation from the standard || a rogue elephant || any enraged, large animal which has left the herd **2.** *adj.* resembling a rogue elephant [16th-c. thieves' slang]

rogue elephant an enraged elephant which leaves the herd to live alone

ro·guer·y (róugəri:) *pl.* **ro·guer·ies** *n.* roguish behavior || a roguish act

rogues' gallery a collection of photographs of criminals, used by police for purposes of identification

ro·guish (róugiʃ) *adj.* of, relating to or acting like a rogue || mischievous, *a roguish look*

roil (rɔil) *v.t.* to stir up sediment in (a liquid) and make it turbid || to vex, irritate **róil·y** *comp.* **roil·i·er** *superl.* **roil·i·est** *adj.* turbid [etym. doubtful]

roist·er (rɔ́istər) *v.i.* (*rhet.*) to engage in noisy, carefree, drunken revelry [fr. F. *rustre*]

Ro·kos·sov·sky (rɒkɔssɔ́fski:), Konstantin Konstantinovitch (1896-1968), Russian army officer. He commanded the defense of Moscow (1941-2) and Stalingrad (1943). He was minister of defense in Poland (1949-56)

ro·la·mite (róuləmait) *n.* a device for minimizing sliding friction on rollers by use of a flexible loop over the rollers, used in miniaturized nuclear weapons, developed by American physicist Donald F. Wilkes

Ro·land (róulənd) *n.* (*mil.*) U.S. air-launched cruise missile made by Boeing

Ro·land, Chanson de (rɔlɑ̃) a *Chanson* (*CHANSON DE GESTE), written two or three hundred years after the event, describing the death of Roland (who was a historical character, one of Charlemagne's knights) at Roncesvalles. Charlemagne had invaded Spain in 778 and, after capturing Pamplona, had been recalled home by news of a Saxon revolt on the Rhine. Roland was in charge of the rear, which was ambushed by the Saracens in a pass in the Pyrenees and destroyed. He blew his magic horn, which Charlemagne duly heard, but by the time he had returned Roland was dead. The *Chanson* is one of the finest examples of the heroic French epic

Ro·land de la Pla·tière (rɔlɑ̃dəlæplætjɛər), Manon (Manon Phlipon, 1754-93), French revolutionist. She influenced Girondist policy through her salon, a brilliant intellectual center

role, rôle (roul) *n.* the part in which an actor or singer is cast in a play, opera etc. ‖ the part a person or thing plays in a specific situation, operation etc., *the role of cement in modern building* [F. *rôle*, a roll, the scroll on which an actor's part was written]

Rolfe (rolf), John (1585–1622), English settler in America. He settled in Jamestown, Va., married Pocahontas, an Indian princess, in 1614 and worked at farming tobacco, which became the main crop of Virginia. He died fighting the Powhatan Indians

roll (roul) *n.* a quantity of cloth, wrapping paper, wallpaper etc., rolled up in the form of a cylinder ‖ a rounded mass of something, *rolls of fat, a roll of hair* ‖ any of variously shaped pieces of baked dough ‖ a scroll (of parchment or paper) ‖ an official list of names or catalog of items ‖ a muster roll ‖ (*Br.,* esp. *pl.*) a list of solicitors qualified to practice ‖ (*bookbinding*) a wheel-like tool for making decorative lines on book covers ‖ (*bookbinding*) the decoration produced ‖ a tobacco twist done up in cylindrical form ‖ (*archit.*) a curved molding ‖ (*pop.*) a wad of paper money **to strike off the rolls** (*Br.*) to disqualify (a solicitor) from practicing ‖ to disqualify (someone) from membership [O.F. *role, rolle*]

roll 1. *v.i.* to move along a surface by turning over and over, *the marble rolled across the floor* ‖ (of a wheeled vehicle) to move, *the car rolled down the slope* ‖ to flow forward in undulations, streams, etc., *the smoke rolled across the sky* ‖ (esp. of land) to have an undulating surface ‖ to make a long, deep sound varying in loudness, *the thunder rolled* ‖ (of a bird) to trill ‖ (of a ship) to move with a heavy side-to-side motion ‖ (of a person) to walk in this manner ‖ to acquire a spherical or cylindrical shape by curling over and over on itself or on something else ‖ (of the eyes) to turn from side to side and seem to rotate in their sockets ‖ to move or proceed smoothly, *the work keeps rolling along* ‖ *v.t.* to make (something) move along a surface by causing it to turn over and over, *to roll a marble* ‖ to cause to move on wheels, rollers etc., *to roll a wheelbarrow down a road* ‖ to shape by movements inducing roundness, *to roll a cigarette* ‖ to move (the eyes) from side to side, causing them to seem to rotate ‖ to level, smooth, flatten etc. with a roller or something resembling a roller ‖ to beat a roll upon (a drum) ‖ to throw (dice) ‖ to envelop (someone or something) in a covering, *to roll a baby in a blanket* ‖ (*printing*) to ink (a form etc.) with a roller ‖ to utter (the letter 'r') with a trill-like sound ‖ to drive forward with a sweeping motion, *the waves rolled the bathers toward the shore* ‖ (*pop.*) to rob (someone) while he is asleep, unconscious etc. **to roll around** (of a cyclical event) to recur, *spring rolled around again* **to roll back** to reduce (a price or prices) by government control ‖ to cause (a crowd etc.) to retreat **to roll in** to arrive in large numbers ‖ (*pop.*) to have a great deal of (money) **to roll out** to make flat or thin by using a roller, *to roll out pastry* ‖ to unroll 2. *n.* a rolling movement, e.g. of a ship in heavy seas ‖ (of a person) a rolling walk ‖ a long, deep sound varying in loudness, *the roll of thunder* ‖ a succession of rapid beats on a drum ‖ (*aeron.*) a complete revolution of an aircraft around its longitudinal axis with little or no change in the horizontal direction of flight ‖ the trill of some birds ‖ one of a set of grooved cylinders in a steel mill used for shaping white-hot ingots [fr. O.F. *roler*]

Rol·land (rɔlɑ̃), Romain Edmé Paul Emile (1866-1944), French author. In his works he exalts an ideal of energy without violence. His best-known work is 'Jean Christophe' (10 vols, 1904-12), the fictitious biography of a German-born musician

roll·a·thon (róuləθɔn) *n.* (*sports*) marathon race in which participants roller skate

roll·a·way bed (róuləwei) a bed that folds up and can be rolled out of sight when not in use

roll·back (róulbæk) *n.* a reduction in prices by government control

roll bar a heavy steel bar on top of a motor vehicle, esp. a convertible, to protect riders from being crushed should the vehicle overturn — **roll cage** *n.* a roll bar for a racing car

roll call the act of calling out names from a list in order to ascertain those present ‖ the fixed time at which this is done ‖ (*mil.*) the signal for a roll call

Rolle (roul), Richard, of Hampole (c. 1300–c. 1349), English hermit and mystic. He was one of the first religious authors to write in the vernacular as well as in Latin. He is the author of 'Meditation of the Passion'

roll·er (róulər) *n.* a revolving cylinder over or on which something is rolled, e.g. the cylinder on which a roller towel is placed ‖ a revolving cylinder used for pressing, crushing or smoothing a road surface, soil etc. ‖ a cylinder on which heavy objects are moved ‖ a revolving cylinder for applying paint to a flat surface or (*printing*) for spreading ink on a form ‖ either of the revolving cylinders in a mangle or wringer between which linen is pressed flat or wrung out ‖ someone who operates rolling machinery ‖ a large, long wave that rolls over as it breaks ‖ a roll for flattening metal etc. ‖ a tumbler pigeon [ROLL V.]

roller *n.* any of various nonpasserine Old World birds of fam. *Coraciidae,* esp. *Coracius garrulus,* a European species having blue or green plumage and a reddish-brown back [G. fr. *rollen,* to roll]

roller bearing a bearing consisting of hardened steel cylinders revolving in a cylindrical housing

roller coaster (*Am.=Br.* switchback) a usually circular railway high up in an amusement park, consisting of very steep alternate ascents and descents, along which small, open cars hurtle

roller hockey (*sports*) hockey played on roller skates

roller skate a skate mounted on small wheels **ról·er-skate** *pres. part.* **roll·er-skat·ing** *past and past part.* **roll·er-skat·ed** *v.i.* to skate on a pair of these

roller towel an endless towel suspended from a rotating roller

rol·lick (rólik) 1. *v.i.* to move or act with exuberant gaiety 2. *n.* a burst of exuberant gaiety **ról·lick·ing** *adj.* [origin unknown]

rolling mill a plant where metal etc. is rolled into sheets, bars etc. ‖ the machine used for this purpose

rolling pin a usually wooden cylinder used for rolling out pastry, dough etc.

rolling stock the wheeled vehicles of a railroad, collectively ‖ a road carrier's fleet of vehicles

Rol·lo (rólou) (or Hrolf, c. 860–c. 931), first duke of Normandy (911-27). A Viking leader, he was granted (911) the fief of Normandy by Charles III of France

roll-on (róulɔn) *adj.* of a movable ball-shaped applicator in the top of a container that dispenses a substance, e.g., deodorant

roll·out (rouláut) *v.* (*football*) to carry the ball behind the scrimmage line to one flank separating from blockers in order to throw a pass or feint for a pass —**rollout** *n.*

roll-top desk (róultɔp) a writing desk having a slatted cover which slides open and shut

roll·way (róulwei) *n.* a road or path used esp. for rolling logs down to a stream ‖ a pile of logs by a stream awaiting transport

ro·ly-po·ly (róuli:póuli:) 1. *adj.* (of a person or an animal) round and plump 2. *pl.* **ro·ly-po·lys, ro·ly-po·lies** *n.* a roly-poly person or animal ‖ a dough spread with jam etc., rolled up and steamed or baked ‖ a weighted toy which, when pushed down, returns to an erect position [etym. doubtful]

ROM (*computer abbr.*) for read-only memory

Ro·ma·gna (roumánjə) (*hist.*) a region on the Adriatic coast of Emilia-Romagna, Italy, under the rule of the Papal States (early 13th c.–1860)

Ro·ma·ic (rouméiik) 1. *adj.* of or pertaining to modern Greece ‖ of or pertaining to the language of modern Greece 2. *n.* modern Greek [fr. Gk *Rhōmaïkos,* Roman]

ro·maine (rouméin) *n.* (*Am. = Br.* cos) a variety of crisp lettuce with long leaves [F.]

Ro·mains (rɔmɛ̃), Jules (Louis Farigoule, 1885–1972), French poet, novelist and playwright. His works include the farce 'Knock' (1923) and the cycle of novels 'les Hommes de bonne volonté' (1932-47)

Ro·man (róumən) 1. *adj.* of or pertaining to the city of Rome, its history, its people, its language etc. ‖ of or pertaining to the Roman Catholic Church or the Latin rite ‖ of or pertaining to the type normally used for printed narrative and

based on the forms used in Roman inscriptions (cf. ITALIC, cf. BOLDFACE) ‖ (of a nose) having a highly arched bridge 2. *n.* a resident or native of Rome ‖ (used disparagingly) a member of the Roman Catholic Church ‖ (*printing*) Roman type ‖ the dialect spoken in Rome [O.E. fr. L.]

Roman alphabet an alphabet of the classical Latin period consisting of 23 letters (J, U and W were added later) from which most modern European alphabets are derived

Roman arch a semicircular arch

Roman candle a candle-shaped firework emitting sparks and globes of fire

Roman Catholic 1. *adj.* of or pertaining to the Roman Catholic Church 2. *n.* a member of this Church

Roman Catholic Church that part of the Christian Church which accepts the authority of the pope, in distinction to the Orthodox Eastern Church, which separated from it in 1054, and to the Protestant Churches, which broke away in the 16th c. (For the early history of the Church *CHRISTIANITY.) The Roman Catholic Church rose to be a great political force in the Roman Empire (4th c.) and dominated Western Europe throughout the Middle Ages. Attacks on the Church culminated in the Reformation. The Counter-Reformation produced administrative and educational reforms within the Church, and missionary activities were extended under the Jesuits in the Far East and America. From the Council of Trent (1545-63) to the Vatican Council (1869-70) the Church was on the defensive against the incursions of rationalism, enlightenment, liberalism and revolution. In the 20th c. it has begun to reconsider its ideological traditions and to participate in the ecumenical movement. The excommunication of the Orthodox Eastern Church was annulled (1965). Distinctive tenets of Roman Catholicism are the authority of ecclesiastical tradition, transubstantiation, the seven sacraments, papal infallibility, purgatory, the Immaculate Conception (1854) and the Assumption (1950) of the Virgin Mary. Theology is based on natural and divine law as established by Thomas Aquinas. The clergy are celibate, though in E. Europe and the Middle East there are Roman Catholic Churches with Uniate rites and noncelibate clergy. Many religious orders exist. There are several hundred million Roman Catholics in the world. They preponderate (over 85%) in Spain, Ireland, Luxembourg, Belgium, Portugal, Italy, Latin America, Austria, Poland and France. They form large minorities (over 30%) in the Netherlands, Czechoslovakia, Hungary, Switzerland, West Germany, Lebanon, Yugoslavia, the Philippines, Canada and the U.S.A. Smaller minorities exist in Australia, New Zealand, East Germany, Rumania, Great Britain and the U.S.S.R.

Roman Catholicism the doctrine and organization of the Roman Catholic Church

ro·mance (roumǽns, róumæns) 1. *n.* a medieval literary form, initially old French or Provençal, dealing with deeds of chivalry or with historical or mythological events seen in the perspective of a medieval court ‖ an example of this ‖ an imaginative story of idealized love ‖ the type of literature comprising such stories ‖ a love affair ‖ the quality of being romantic ‖ a pure exaggeration, falsehood ‖ (*mus.*) a term loosely used for various sorts of composition predominantly tender or intimate in mood 2. *v. pres. part.* **ro·manc·ing** *past* and *past part.* **ro·manced** *v.i.* to indulge in highly exaggerated stories ‖ *v.t.* to give a made-up version of, *romanced biography*

Ro·mance *adj.* of or relating to the Romance languages [O.F. *romans, romanz*]

Romance languages a group of languages developed from Latin, incl. French, Italian, Provençal, Portuguese, Rumanian, Spanish, Catalan, Rhaeto-Romanic, Sardinian and the now-extinct Dalmatian

ro·man cour·tois (rɔmɑ̃ku:rtwæ) *pl.* **ro·mans cour·tois** (rɔmɑ̃ku:rtwæ) a medieval romance, based on classical or legendary themes. They were usually in verse and were intended to be read aloud, whereas the Chansons de Geste were written to be sung [F.]

Roman de la Rose *LORRIS, GUILLAUME DE, *JEAN DE MEUNG

Ro·man de Re·nart (rɔmɑ̃dərənær) a collection of verse stories by unknown authors, in which animals—and their 'wives'—have experiences which satirize or parallel human behavior. The stories, of which the best date from the 13th c., seem to have originated near the borders of modern France, but there are Flemish, Dutch and German versions

Roman Empire *ROME

Ro·man·esque (roumənésk) **1.** *n.* (*archit.*) a style developed between the Roman and Gothic periods in former Roman European territories. It is characterized by round arches, decorative arcades, and elaborately carved ornament, esp. on capitals and moldings **2.** *adj.* of, relating to, or constructed in the Romanesque style [F.]

Romania *RUMANIA

Ro·man·ic (roumǽnik) **1.** *adj.* of or relating to the Romance languages **2.** *n.* the Romance languages [fr. L. *Romanicus*]

Ro·man·ism (róumənizəm) *n.* (used disparagingly) the doctrine and usages of the Roman Catholic faith **Ró·man·ist** *n.* and *adj.*

Roman law the system of jurisdiction of ancient Rome and of the Roman and Byzantine Empires, esp. to the death (565) of Justinian I

Roman numerals letters of the Roman alphabet used as symbols for numbers until the 10th c. A.D. Those still used, e.g. on clock faces or in classifications, are I = 1, V = 5, X = 10, L = 50, C = 100, D = 500, M = 1,000. A letter placed in front of one of greater value is subtracted from it, a letter placed after it is added, e.g. XCIV = 94

Ro·ma·nov (róumənɔf) the Russian ruling dynasty from the accession (1613) of Michael until the enforced abdication (1917) of Nicholas II

Romans, Epistle to the the sixth book of the New Testament, written (c. 58) by St Paul to the Church at Rome. It proclaims the possibility of salvation for all men through Christ

Ro·mansh, Ro·mansch (roumǽnʃ, roumánʃ) *n.* Rhaeto-Romanic as spoken esp. in Graubünden, Switzerland [native name]

ro·man·tic (roumǽntik) **1.** *adj.* of or pertaining to romance, *a romantic novel, a romantic situation* ‖ susceptible to romance, *a romantic person* ‖ not based on fact, fanciful or exaggerated, *a romantic rendering of the facts* ‖ (*loosely*) farfetched, not very practical, *a romantic scheme* **Ro·man·tic** of, relating to or having the characteristics of Romanticism **2.** *n.* a romantic person **Ro·man·tic** an exponent of Romanticism **ro·mán·ti·cal·ly** *adv.* **ro·mán·ti·cism** *n.* the quality or state of being romantic **Ro·man·ti·cism** a movement in literature, philosophy and art which developed in Europe in the late 18th and early 19th cc. Starting from the ideas and attitudes of Rousseau in France and from the Sturm und Drang movement in Germany, it held that classicism, dominant since the 16th c., denied expression to man's emotional nature and overlooked his profound inner forces. Romanticism is above all an exaltation of individual values and aspirations above those of society. The movement looked to the Middle Ages and to direct contact with nature for inspiration, and it was responsible for the national liberation movement of 19th-c. Europe. The leading Romantic poets were Byron, Keats, Shelley, Wordsworth, Hugo, Musset, Heine and Novalis. In painting its chief exponent was Delacroix. Beethoven, Schubert, Berlioz and Bizet were great Romantic composers. Through its concern with the hidden forces in man, Romanticism exerted a profound influence on modern thought, and opened the way e.g. to psychoanalysis. In art, the same current led to expressionism and surrealism **ro·mán·ti·cist** *n.* **Ro·man·ti·cist** a Romantic **ro·mán·ti·cize** *pres. part.* **ro·man·ti·ciz·ing** *past and past part.* **ro·man·ti·cized** *v.t.* to treat or interpret romantically, esp. to falsify so as to make more pleasing [fr. obs. *romant*, romance fr. O.F.]

Ro·ma·nus II (rouméinəs) (939-63), Byzantine emperor (959-63), son of Constantine VII. His reign was notable for the military successes of Nicephorus II Phocas

Rom·a·ny (róməni:, róuməni:) *pl.* **Rom·a·nies 1.** *n.* a gypsy ‖ the Indic language of the gypsies **2.** *adj.* of or relating to gypsies, or to their language

Rome (roum) (*Ital.* Roma) the capital (pop. 2,897,800) of Italy and ancient capital of the Roman Empire, in Latium, 16 miles up the Tiber. Industries: light manufacturing, esp. luxury goods (haute couture, leatherwork etc.), chemicals, food processing, printing and publishing, film making, tourism. The left bank (with Trastevere, a section of the right bank included by the Aurelian wall, 2nd c.), now a region of narrow streets opening on to squares cut by occasional wide avenues, is still the center of the city. The Vatican City is on the upper right bank. Surviving ancient structures include the Forum (remains of temples, 5th c. B.C.–3rd c. A.D., triumphal arches and columns of the emperors), the Pantheon, and the Colosseum or amphitheater (1st c.). Each age has employed, in its buildings, elements left by past ones. Monuments of the Romano-Byzantine period (4th-9th cc.) include numerous churches and basilicas, many partially restored, e.g. St John Lateran (4th c.), and Santa Maria Maggiore (4th-5th cc., with 5th-c. mosaics). Renaissance Rome survives in churches, palaces and piazza architecture, e.g. the Vatican, the Farnese Palace (1514–mid-16th c.), St Peter's and the Square of the Capitol (designed by Michelangelo). The baroque period (16th-late 18th c.) is rich in churches, squares, fountains and facades, e.g. the church of Il Gesù (1568-84, the first of the Jesuit style), the portico (1667) of St Peter's, the Trevi fountain (1632-62), the Spanish Steps (completed in 1725), the facades of St Peter's, St John Lateran etc. Principal cultural institutions: the Vatican Museum, Gallery and Library, the National Library, galleries, and museums of antiquities (the Terme and Villa Giulia), the university (1303), and numerous academies. HISTORY. Traditionally founded by Romulus in 753 B.C., Rome grew as a group of villages on seven hills on the east bank of the Tiber, and was ruled until 510 B.C. by seven kings, of whom the last three are thought to have been Etruscan. After the last of these, Tarquinius Superbus, had been expelled, a republic was set up (510 B.C.), ruled by a senate and two consuls. The dominant power of the patricians was increasingly challenged by the plebeians, until by 300 B.C. the latter had obtained the right to hold any office. The political organization was expanded to include tribunes, quaestors, aediles, censors and praetors. A code of law was drawn up (451 B.C.) by the decemvirs. Rome extended its power to neighboring peoples in Italy (5th-3rd c. B.C.), defeated Carthage in the Punic Wars (264-241 B.C., 218-201 B.C. and 149-146 B.C.) and gained territory in Spain, Sicily, Sardinia, Corsica and N. Africa. Macedon was made a Roman province (146 B.C.) and the whole of Greece was subdued by 27 B.C. The task of governing the Mediterranean world resulted in class dissension in Rome, notably when the brothers Gracchus attempted to reform the agrarian laws (2nd c. B.C.). Civil war broke out, and the republic was further weakened by the rivalry between Marius and Sulla and by that between Pompey and Caesar. After the collapse of the 1st Triumvirate, Caesar established a dictatorship (48-44 B.C.). On his assassination, civil war was resumed and the 2nd Triumvirate was formed. This dissolved in war between Antony and Octavian, and the republic collapsed when the latter took absolute power as emperor with the title of Augustus (27 B.C.). In the two centuries after the reign of Augustus the Roman Empire reached its greatest extent, encircling the Mediterranean, reaching north to the Rhine, the Danube and central Scotland and spreading into Armenia and Mesopotamia. The empire was united by a well-developed system of communications, the use of Latin as a universal language, and the growth of trade and industry. Augustus' successors, Tiberius, Caligula, Claudius and Nero, continued to develop the civil service and provincial administration (14-68). In the civil war of 68-9, provincial armies successively made Galba, Otho and Vitellius emperors. Stability was restored by Vespasian and his sons Titus and Domitian. Rome reached the height of its prosperity under Trajan, Hadrian, Antoninus Pius and Marcus Aurelius, but decline set in during the reign (180-92) of Commodus. Civil war followed his murder and the Praetorians began to exercise the dominating influence in the choice of emperors. Septimius Severus established a new dynasty (193) supported by the army, and under Caracalla, his son, Roman citizenship was extended to free men throughout the empire. Military anarchy followed the murder (235) of Alexander Severus and provincial armies made emperors in rapid succession. The frontiers came under increasing pressure from the Sassanids in Persia, and from the Alemanni, the Franks and the Goths in the north. These incursions were halted by the capable emperors Claudius II, Aurelian and Probus. During the reign (284-305) of Diocletian, the empire was divided into four administrative units. It was temporarily reunited by Constantine I, who moved its capital to Constantinople (330). Christianity, which had spread throughout the empire, won toleration (313) and became official (380) under Theodosius I. On Constantine's death (337) the division between east and west reappeared. It became final on the death (395) of Theodosius I, Arcadius inheriting the east (*BYZANTINE EMPIRE) and Honorius the west. To deal with increasing barbarian attacks, the capital of the Western Roman Empire was moved to Ravenna (402). Rome was sacked by the Visigoths under Alaric I (410) and by the Vandals under Genseric (455). Attila was prevented from sacking it by Pope Leo I, and papal influence over the city began to increase. The last Roman emperor, Romulus Augustulus was deposed (476) by Odoacer. The Roman Empire had brought urban civilization and a high degree of material prosperity as well as Roman law, the Latin language and the Christian religion to a large part of Europe. Rome now came to be disputed between the Byzantine Empire and the barbarians, and later between the papacy and the Holy Roman Empire. As capital of the Papal States (after 756), it became the spiritual center of W. Europe during the Middle Ages. It was several times devastated by invading armies but began to recover in the second half of the 15th c. and became a center of the Renaissance. It became the capital of Italy (1871)

Ro·me·ro (romérɔ), Francisco (1891-1962), Argentinian philosopher, author of 'Filosofía de la persona' (1944), 'El hombre y la cultura' (1950), and 'Teoría del hombre' (1952)

Rom·il·ly (rómili:, rámili:), Sir Samuel (1757-1818), British lawyer and social reformer. He worked all his life for the reform of the criminal code. Many of his proposals were put into effect later in the 19th c.

Rom·mel (rómel), Erwin (1891-1944), German field marshal. He led the German army in N. Africa (1941) and drove the British army back to Alamein (1942), but was then forced to retreat to Tunisia. He was briefly commander in chief of the German armies in N. Europe (1944). His sympathy with the July 1944 plot against Hitler led to his enforced suicide

Rom·ney (rómni:, rámni:), George (1734-1802), English portrait painter. He was esp. famous for his paintings of Lady Hamilton

romp (romp) **1.** *v.i.* to be in high spirits and play boisterously **to romp home** (or in) (esp. of a racehorse) to win easily **2.** *n.* the act of romping **rómp·ers** *pl. n.* a child's one-piece garment combining top and bloomers [perh. var. of RAMP]

Rom·u·lus and Re·mus (rómjuləs, rí:məs) (*Rom. mythol.*) twin sons of Mars. They were exposed in infancy, but were suckled by a she-wolf and then brought up by a shepherd. According to tradition, Romulus was the founder of Rome (753 B.C.)

Romulus Au·gus·tu·lus (ɔgástjuləs) (*d.* after 476), last Roman emperor (475-6). He was deposed by Odoacer and spent the rest of his life in retirement

Ron·ces·valles (rɔnθesváljes, *Eng.* rónsəvælz) a pass in the Pyrenees, where, according to the Chanson de Roland, the rear of Charlemagne's army was attacked and Roland was killed (778)

ron·deau (róndou, rɔndóu) *pl.* **ron·deaux** (róndouz, rɔndóuz) *n.* a form of verse consisting of 15 usually octosyllabic lines arranged in three stanzas. It uses the opening words twice as a refrain and permits only two rhymes: aabba, aab refrain, aabba refrain ‖ a poem in this form [F.]

ron·del (róndl) *n.* a form of verse having two rhymes only, consisting of usually 14 lines arranged in three stanzas. The first two lines of the first stanza serve as a refrain for the second and third stanzas ‖ a poem in this form [F.]

ron·do (róndou, rɔndóu) *pl.* **ron·dos** *n.* a musical composition in which the principal theme is repeated three or more times. It often forms the last movement of a sonata [Ital.]

Ron·dón (rɔndón), Cándido (1865-1957), Brazilian general who opened up vast regions of the Brazilian interior. An Indian himself, he founded the Service for the Protection of the Indians, which forbade its personnel to carry arms into the interior

Ron·sard (rɔ̃sær), Pierre de (1524-85), French poet, leader of the Pléiade. Ronsard and his fol-

CONCISE PRONUNCIATION KEY: **(a)** æ, c*a*t; ɑ, c*a*r; ɔ f*aw*n; ei, sn*a*ke. **(e)** e, h*e*n; i:, sh*ee*p; iə, d*ee*r; ɛə, b*ea*r. **(i)** i, f*i*sh; ai, t*i*ger; ə:, b*i*rd. **(o)** o, *o*x; au, c*ow*; ou, g*oa*t; u, p*oo*r; ɔi, r*oy*al. **(u)** ʌ, d*u*ck; u, b*u*ll; u:, g*oo*se; ə, bacill*u*s; ju:, c*u*be. x, lo*ch*; θ, *th*ink; ð, bo*th*er; z, *Z*en; ʒ, corsa*g*e; dʒ, sava*g*e; ŋ, ora*n*gutan*g*; j, *y*ak; ʃ, *f*ish; tʃ, fe*tch*; 'l, rabb*le*; 'n, redd*en*. Complete pronunciation key appears inside front cover.

lowers wished to make French—as Petrarch had made Italian—a literary language, rich, supple and elegant, capable of a poetry which would rival that of Greece and Rome. Though Ronsard's verse is characterized by a Renaissance courtliness and elegance, it also retains some of the directness and naïve freshness of the Middle Ages

röntgen *ROENTGEN

rood (ru:d) n. a crucifix, esp. one mounted on a rood screen ‖ (in England and Scotland) a quarter of an acre [O.E. *rōd*]

rood loft a gallery above the rood screen

rood screen a carved wooden or stone screen separating the nave from the choir in a church and usually having a crucifix raised up on it

roof (ru:f, ruf) 1. *pl.* **roofs** n. the structure which covers the top of a building, typically of shingles, slates, tiles, concrete etc., together with the load-carrying elements above the walls ‖ something compared to this, *the roof of a cave, the roof of the mouth* ‖ the hard or canvas top of an automobile etc. ‖ (*rhet.*) a home or house as affording shelter and hospitality ‖ (*mining*) the overhanging part of an excavation or tunnel ‖ (*mining*) the rock above a bed of coal etc. **to raise the roof** (*pop.*) to create a noisy disturbance due to anger, discontent, enthusiasm etc. 2. *v.t.* to furnish with a roof **roof·age** (rú:fidʒ) n. roofing [O.E. *hróf*]

roof garden a restaurant on the roof of a building ‖ a flat roof of a building used as a terrace

roof·ing (rú:fiŋ, rúfiŋ) n. the material used to surface a roof

roof·less (rú:flis, rúflis) adj. having no roof ‖ without a home or any shelter

roof·tree (rú:ftri:, rúftri:) n. the ridgepole of a roof

rook (ruk) 1. n. *Corvus frugilegus*, fam. *Corvidae*, an Old World bird (about 18 ins in length), resembling a crow in color, form and habits. With age, the skin around the base of its bill becomes gray and scabby ‖ (*pop.*) a cheat, esp. in gambling 2. *v.t.* (*pop.*) to cheat, esp. in gambling ‖ (*Br.*) to overcharge [O.E. *hróc*]

rook n. (*chess*) a castle-shaped piece having the power to move over any number of unoccupied, consecutive squares either horizontally or vertically [O.F. *roc* fr. Pers.]

rook·er·y (rúkəri:) *pl.* **rook·er·ies** n. a colony of rooks or the group of trees containing their nests ‖ a breeding place or colony of seals, penguins and other gregarious birds or beasts

rook·ie (rúki:) n. (*pop.*) a raw army recruit ‖ a raw recruit of any sort ‖ (*baseball*) a player in his first season with a major league team

room (ru:m, rum) 1. n. a space within a building enclosed by walls, ceiling and floor, *hotel room, assembly room* ‖ space regarded as available to contain something, or something more, *make some room on the shelf,* or as affording the opportunity to act, move etc., *scarcely room to breathe* ‖ opportunity or scope, *room for improvement, room to expand* ‖ (*pl.*) a suite in a private house, boarding house etc., rented for a period ‖ a roomful of people, *the room was hushed* ‖ one of the chambers where coal is mined **to make room for** to move so as to leave space for 2. *v.i.* to lodge in someone's house, or with someone else, sharing accommodation [O.E. *rúm*]

room·er (rú:mər, rúmər) n. someone who rents a room in someone else's house

room·ful (rú:mful, rúmful) n. as much as a room will contain ‖ the people, objects etc. in a room

room·i·ness (rú:mi:nis, rúmi:nis) n. the quality or state of being roomy

rooming house a lodging house

room·mate (rú:mmeit, rúmmeit) n. someone with respect to a person with whom he shares a room

room·y (rú:mi:, rúmi:) *comp.* **room·i·er** *superl.* **room·i·est** adj. having plenty of room, *a roomy trunk*

Roon (ru:n), Albrecht Theodor Emil, Graf von (1803–79), Prussian general and minister of war (1839–73). His army reforms provoked parliamentary hostility, but were largely responsible for the victories of Prussia over Austria (1866) and France (1870–1)

Roosevelt (róuzəvelt, rú:zəvelt), Anna Eleanor (1884–1962), U.S. First Lady (1933–45) and social activist. She married her cousin, Franklin D. Roosevelt, and when he became crippled (1921) by polio she represented him on the campaign trail. As First Lady she undertook her special causes, esp. youth employment and civil

rights for minorities, and continued working for these causes after her husband's death. She was a U.S. delegate to the U.N. (1945–52, 1961–2) and was instrumental in drafting the U.N. Declaration of Human Rights. She wrote 'This I Remember' (1949) and 'The Autobiography of Eleanor Roosevelt' (1961)

Roo·se·velt, Franklin Delano (1882-1945), 32nd president (1933-45) of the U.S.A., a Democrat. Beginning with a general 'bank holiday', he initiated the New Deal in order to restore the economy after the great depression of 1929. His 'fireside chats', broadcast by radio to the nation, helped him to maintain the support and confidence of the American people. He led the U.S.A. away from isolationism with his goodneighbor policy toward Latin America, his recognition (1933) of the U.S.S.R., and his lend-lease support (1941) for Britain. He became (1940) the first U.S. president to run for a third term in office. With Churchill he drafted (1941) the Atlantic Charter and, as the power of the Axis increased, he augmented U.S. military strength and preparedness, issuing the first peacetime selective service act in U.S. history. With the Japanese attack (1941) on Pearl Harbor, he brought the U.S.A. into the 2nd world war. He attended conferences with Allied leaders at Casablanca (1943), Quebec (1943 and 1944), Cairo (1943), Tehran (1943) and Yalta (1945). He has been criticized for making too many territorial concessions to the U.S.S.R. at Yalta. He died a month before Germany's surrender. His wife Eleanor (1884-1962) continued his humanitarian policies as a delegate to the U.N.

Roosevelt, Theodore (1858-1919), 26th president (1901-9) of the U.S.A., following the assassination of President McKinley. He was a Republican. During the Spanish-American War he organized the regiment of volunteers known as the Rough Riders, and gained wide fame as a cavalry colonel in Cuba (1898). As president he launched an extensive 'trust-busting' campaign, promoted the conservation of natural resources, and through his Roosevelt Corollary to the Monroe Doctrine he maintained the right of the U.S.A. to intervene in the internal affairs of Latin American countries for the maintenance of law and order. He also pursued a policy of 'dollar diplomacy', notably in the Caribbean. He used the U.S. Navy (1903) to ensure that Panama gained independence from Colombia, and secured the right to construct the Panama Canal. He received the Nobel peace prize (1906) for his mediation in the Russo-Japanese War (1904-5). At his initiative the Algeciras Conference (1906) was called. Opposed to the reelection of conservative Republican President Taft, he organized (1912) the Progressive or 'Bull Moose' party, running as its candidate in the 1912 presidential elections and thus splitting Republican ranks, which allowed a Democratic victory. During the 1st world war he vigorously attacked President Wilson's initial policy of neutrality

Roosevelt Corollary an extension of the Monroe Doctrine issued (1904) by President Theodore Roosevelt and Elihu Root. It asserted U.S. right to intervene in the internal affairs of Latin America to maintain peace and order. It is the most imperialistic interpretation of the Monroe Doctrine

roost (ru:st) 1. n. the perch of a bird or fowl ‖ the part of a hen house or other building where fowls roost **to rule the roost** to be the dominating person (esp. in a household) 2. *v.i.* to be perched for the night ‖ to settle down as if on a perch, *to roost on a park bench* **róost·er** n. a male domestic fowl [O.E. *hróst*]

Root (ru:t), Elihu (1845-1937), U.S. lawyer, political leader and diplomat. As secretary of war (1899-1903) under Presidents McKinley and T. Roosevelt he strongly influenced the Foraker Act of 1900 and the Organic Act of 1902. His military reforms included the transformation of the state National Guard into the organized militia of the U.S.A. and the creation of the Army War College. As secretary of state (1905-9) under President Theodore Roosevelt, he negotiated the Root-Takahira agreement and settled the dispute with the British over the North Atlantic coast fisheries. He received the 1912 Nobel prize for peace

root (ru:t, rut) 1. n. that part of a plant which in most species penetrates the earth. It absorbs moisture, stores food, and also serves as an

anchor and support ‖ a plant, e.g. a carrot, in which this part is fleshy and edible ‖ (*Br.*) a young, esp. herbaceous, plant suitable for transplanting ‖ (*physiol.*) the part of an organ etc. by which it is attached to the body, *the root of a tooth* ‖ a fundamental or essential part, *the root of a problem* ‖ the original cause of something, *his selfishness was the root of the trouble* ‖ (*math.*) a quantity which, when multiplied by itself a certain number of times, produces a given quantity, *2 is the square root of 4 or the cube root of 8* ‖ (*math.*) a value of an unknown which satisfies an equation ‖ (*linguistics*) that part of a word remaining after removal of prefixes, suffixes, inflectional endings etc. ‖ (*mus.*) the lowest note of a chord when the chord is in its normal position **to take root** to grow roots ‖ to become firmly fixed by or as if by roots, *the idea gradually began to take root* 2. *v.i.* to grow roots ‖ to become firmly fixed by or as if by roots ‖ *v.t.* to cause to root ‖ (*fig.*) to fix firmly, *rooted in one's memory* ‖ to attach by or as if by roots **to root out** (or **up**) to remove (a plant) completely by pulling it, with its roots, out of the ground ‖ to remove (a habit, idea etc.) completely [O.E. *rōt* fr. O.N.]

root *v.i.* (esp. of swine) to turn up the earth with the snout looking for food ‖ to search around (among papers, in closets etc.) for something ‖ *v.t.* (with 'up') to turn up with the snout [O.E. *wrōtan*]

root *v.i.* (*pop.*) to give encouragement by shouting or cheering, *to root for one's team* or simply give moral support [perh. fr. *rout*, to shout]

root beer a carbonated soft drink made of various roots and herbs and flavored with cloves, anise etc.

root cap the protective cap of tissue at the apex of a root

root hair (*bot.*) one of many epidermal outgrowths behind the root cap, having absorptive functions

roo·tle (rú:t'l, rút'l) *pres. part.* **roo·tling** *past* and *past part.* **roo·tled** *v.i.* (*pop.*, esp. of swine) to root

root·let (rú:tlət, rútlət) n. a small root

root nodule a small swelling on the root of a leguminous plant, containing nitrogen-fixing bacteria

root pressure the force by which water is made to rise from the roots to the stem of a plant

root·stalk (rú:tstɔk, rútstɔk) n. a rhizome

root·stock (rú:tstɔk, rútstɔk) n. the rhizomatous underground part of a stem

Root-Takahira Agreement (1908), a U.S.-Japanese agreement, under which the U.S.A. acknowledged Japan's right to annex Korea and its special position in Manchuria in return for Japan's promise not to grant exit visas to laborers

rope (roup) 1. n. a thick cord made of twisted strands of hemp, flax, wire etc. ‖ (*pl.*) the ropes enclosing a boxing ring ‖ a row of things strung together, *a rope of pearls, a rope of onions* ‖ a viscous stringy formation in wine, beer etc. caused by contamination by bacteria ‖ a lasso **at the end of one's rope** at the limit of what one can bear **to know the ropes** to know how an organization works, what procedures to follow etc., in circumstances which would be strange to the uninitiated **to give someone plenty of rope, to give someone enough rope to hang himself** to allow someone to continue unchecked until he brings about his own downfall 2. *v. pres. part.* **rop·ing** *past* and *past part.* **roped** *v.t.* to fasten or secure with a rope ‖ (with 'off') to mark off or enclose with ropes ‖ to lasso ‖ (of climbers) to link together by attachment to a common rope ‖ *v.i.* to become viscous **to rope somebody in** to secure somebody's help or support (usually in spite of his reluctance) [O.E. *ráp*]

rope·danc·er (róupdænsər, róupdɑnsər) n. a dancer who performs on a tightrope

rope ladder a ladder having rope sides and rope, wood or metal rungs

rope walk a long covered walk where ropes are twisted ‖ a building containing a rope walk

rope·walk·er (róupwɔkər) n. an acrobat who walks on a tightrope

rop·y (róupi:) *comp.* **rop·i·er** *superl.* **rop·i·est** adj. viscous like rope, stringy

Roque·fort (róukfərt) n. a cheese made from ewes' milk, impregnated with a special mold, and ripened in caves [after *Roquefort*, French town in the Aveyron]

ro·quet (roukéi) 1. *v.t. pres. part.* **ro·quet·ing** (roukéiiŋ) *past* and *past part.* **ro·queted**

CONCISE PRONUNCIATION KEY: (**a**) æ, c*a*t; ɑ, c*a*r; ɔ f*aw*n; ei, sn*a*ke. (**e**) e, h*e*n; i:, sh*ee*p; iə, d*ee*r; ɛə, b*ea*r. (**i**) i, f*i*sh; ai, t*i*ger; ə:, b*i*rd. (**o**) o, *o*x; au, c*ow*; ou, g*oa*t; u, p*oo*r; ɔi, r*o*yal. (**u**) ʌ, d*u*ck; u, b*u*ll; u:, g*oo*se; ə, b*a*cillus; ju:, c*u*be. x, lo*ch*; θ, *th*ink; δ, *b*other; z, *Z*en; ʒ, cor*s*age; dʒ, sava*g*e; ŋ, ora*n*gutang; j, *y*ak; ʃ, *f*ish; tʃ, fe*tch*; 'l, rabb*le*; 'n, redd*en*. Complete pronunciation key appears inside front cover.

(roukéid) (*croquet*) to make one's ball hit (another ball) ‖ (*croquet*) (of a ball) to hit (another ball) **2.** *n.* (*croquet*) the act of roqueting [formed fr. CROQUET]

Ro·rai·ma, Mt (ruráimə) *PACARAIMA

ro·ro ship (róuróu) a freighter that carries loaded trucks and trailers

ror·qual (rórkwəl) *n.* a member of *Balaenoptera*, fam. *Ballaenopteridae*, a genus of whalebone whales having a dorsal fin and many furrows on the throat [F. fr. Norw. *røyrkval*]

Ror·schach test (rórʃæk, róurʃæk) a psychological test in which the subject is presented with a series of blots of ink of standard designs. The responses of the subject yield useful, if not always specific, information about his intelligence and emotional state [after Hermann *Rorschach* (1884–1922), Swiss psychiatrist]

Ro·sa (róza), Salvator (1615-73), Italian painter, etcher and poet. He is best known for his large battle scenes and romantic landscapes

Rosa a massif in the Pennine Alps on the Swiss-Italian border. Summit: Dufourspitze (15,217 ft), the highest point in Switzerland

Ro·sa·rio (rɔsárjɔ) a port and commercial center (pop. 750,455) in N. Argentina on the Paraná. Industries: meat packing, flour milling, sugar refining, tanning. University (1920)

ro·sa·ry (róuzəri) *pl.* **ro·sa·ries** *n.* a rose garden ‖ a string of beads for keeping count of the prayers of the Rosary ‖ **the Rosary** a Roman Catholic devotion to the Virgin Mary consisting of 5 or 15 decades of Aves, each preceded by a paternoster and ended by a gloria (Gloria Patri) [fr. L. *rosarium*]

Ro·sas (rósɑs), Juan Manuel de (1793-1877), Argentinian general and dictator, leader (after 1828) of the Federal Party. With the aid of a force of vaqueros, which he made the most efficient fighting force in Argentina after independence, he served as governor and dictator (1829-32 and 1835-52) of the province of Buenos Aires. Despite hostilities with Paraguay, Chile, Peru, Brazil, Uruguay, France, and England, from which he had scarcely a moment's freedom, he waged a war of extermination against the leaders of the interior provinces who sought to combine against him or to set themselves up as independent rulers. A coalition of his disaffected generals and Brazil brought about his defeat (1852) at Monte Caseros. He fled to exile in England (*SARMIENTO). He was dictatorial, but greatly contributed to the unification of Argentina

Ros·ce·lin (rɔslē) (*Lat.* Roscellinus, c. 1050–c. 1120), French scholastic philosopher, the founder of nominalism

Ros·com·mon (rɔskɔ́mən) an island county (area 951 sq. miles, pop. 53,519) in Connacht, Irish Republic ‖ its county seat (pop. 2,000)

rose (rouz) **1.** *n.* a member of *Rosa*, fam. *Rosaceae*, a genus of erect, climbing or creeping shrubs, usually with prickles, native to the northern hemisphere, but grown throughout the temperate regions in hundreds of varieties. They have compound leaves and usually fragrant red, rose, pink, yellow or white flowers ‖ the flower of any of these shrubs ‖ the dark pinkish color characteristic of some of these flowers ‖ a representation of the flower, e.g. in heraldry or (*Eng. hist.*) as an emblem of the houses of York and Lancaster (*ROSES, WARS OF THE) ‖ a form in which many gems are cut, consisting of a double tier of triangular facets rising to a point from a round, flat base ‖ a gem, esp. a diamond, cut in this way ‖ the perforated nozzle of a hose, watering can etc. ‖ (*naut.*) the card of the mariner's compass ‖ a rose window ‖ a rosette (ornamental fixture or other decoration) ‖ (*pl.*) a healthy glow, esp. in the cheeks **2.** *adj.* of or relating to a rose ‖ scented or flavored with roses ‖ having a rose color [O.E. fr. L. fr. Gk]

rose *past of* RISE

ro·se·ate (róuzi:it, róuzi:eit) *adj.* (*rhet.*) flushed pink, *the roseate hue of dawn* ‖ (*rhet.*), of a viewpoint etc.) optimistic [fr. L. *roseus*]

Rose·ber·y (róuzbəri), Archibald Philip Primrose, 5th earl of (1847-1929), British Liberal statesman. As foreign secretary (1886 and 1892-4) and prime minister (1894-5) he advocated imperial federation

Rose Bowl (*football*) postseason college game played in Pasadena, CA

rose·bud (róuzbʌd) *n.* the bud of a rose

rose·bush (róuzbuʃ) *n.* a shrub bearing roses

rose-col·ored,　rose-col·oured (róuzkʌlərd) *adj.* of a warm pink color ‖ (of opinions etc.) optimistic, hopeful **to see life through rose-colored glasses** (or **spectacles**) to view things optimistically

Rose·crans (róuzkræns), William Starke (1819-98), U.S. Union general during the Civil War. His excessive cautiousness earned him official displeasure. Pressured to assume the offensive, he was saved from complete disaster at Chickamauga and Chattanooga only by the stand of Gen. George Thomas

rose geranium any of several S. African plants of the genus *Pelargonium*, fam. *Geraniaceae*, esp. *P. graveolens*, having fragrant leaves and small pink flowers

rose mallow the hibiscus ‖ the hollyhock

rose·mar·y (róuzmɛəri:) **rose·mar·ies** *n.* *Rosmarinus officinalis*, fam. *Labiatae*, an evergreen shrub grown esp. in the Mediterranean area. The pungent leaves are used as a culinary herb and in making perfume, soap etc.

Ro·sen·bach (róuz'nbæk), Abraham Simon Wolf (1876-1952), U.S. book and manuscript collector and dealer. He founded (1902) the Rosenbach Company which became probably the largest book dealer in the world. He willed his estate to the Rosenbach Foundation, established (1950) to foster interest in books, paintings, and objets d'art

Ro·sen·berg Trial (róuz'nbə:rg) a U.S. federal espionage trial, in which Julius and Ethel Rosenberg and their associates were convicted (1951) of revealing to the Soviet Union secret information concerning the construction of the atomic bomb. The Rosenbergs were executed (1953). They were the first U.S. civilians to receive the death penalty for treason

Ro·sen·wald (róuz'nwɔld), Julius (1862-1932), U.S. merchant and philanthropist. As president (1910-25) of Sears Roebuck & Company, he created a fund (1917) for the education of blacks which helped to construct more than 5,000 schools in 15 Southern states. His donations exceeded $22 million

rose of Jericho *Anastatica hierochuntica*, fam. *Cruciferae*, an Asiatic plant which curls up in a dry wickerlike ball when dry and opens out when moistened

rose oil an essential oil distilled from roses, esp. attar of roses

ro·se·o·la (rouzí:ələ) *n.* (*med.*) a mild disease affecting babies and very young children, characterized by a three-day fever followed by a rose-colored rash [Mod. L. fr. *roseus*, rosy]

Roses, Wars of the (*Eng. hist.*) an intermittent civil war (1455-85) between the houses of York and Lancaster for possession of the throne, so called because of the white rose emblem of York and the red rose of Lancaster. Prompted by the incapacity and French failures of the Lancastrian Henry VI, the Yorkists took up arms (1455), deposed Henry (1461) and replaced him by the Yorkist Edward IV. Henry was briefly restored (1470-1) by Warwick 'the Kingmaker', but Edward regained the throne (1471). His son Edward V was overthrown (1483) by Richard III, who was defeated and killed (1485) at Bosworth Field by the Lancastrian claimant Henry Tudor. The latter, as Henry VII, married (1486) the daughter of Edward IV, thus uniting the rival houses. The wars demonstrated the danger of allowing too powerful nobles to build up private armies

Ro·set·ta stone (rouzétə) a large piece of black basalt bearing an inscription in Egyptian hieroglyphics, in demotic script and in Greek. Jean-François Champollion and Thomas Young, working independently, found the key to the deciphering of ancient Egyptian hieroglyphics from it. The stone was found by some of Napoleon's soldiers in 1799 near Rosetta, on the western mouth of the Nile. It is in the British Museum

ro·sette (rouzét) *n.* a knot of ribbon or other small decoration in the shape of a rose ‖ (*archit.*) a formal representation of the wild rose used as an ornament ‖ (*Br.*) a rose window ‖ (*bot.*) a cluster of leaves arising in close circles from a central axis ‖ (*bot.*) any of several plant diseases affecting the leaves and due to an attack of fungi, nutritional deficiencies etc. ‖ any of various ornamental fixtures resembling a rose, e.g. the head of a screw for fastening mirrors [F.]

rose water a solution distilled from rose petals and used as a perfume

rose window (*archit.*) a circular window with radiating tracery

rose·wood (róuzwud) *n.* a dark red cabinet wood obtained from various tropical trees ‖ a tree producing such wood, esp. *Dalbergia nigra*, fam. *Papilionaceae*

Rosh Ha·sha·nah (rouʃəʃánə, rouʃəʃɔnə) the Jewish New Year celebrated on the first two days of Tishri (cf. JEWISH CALENDAR) [Mishnaic Heb. *rosh hashānāh*, beginning of the year]

Ro·si·cru·cian (rouzikrú:ʃən, rɔzikrú:ʃən) **1.** *n.* a member of a secret society which flourished in the 17th and early 18th cc. and was concerned with occult symbols and other secret lore, the transmutation of metals etc. It is said to have been founded in the late 15th c. by a man named Christian Rosenkreuz ‖ a member of any of several groups descended from this society **2.** *adj.* of or pertaining to Rosicrucians or Rosicrucianism **Ro·si·cru·cian·ism** *n.* [fr. L. *rosa*, rose and *crucis*, of the cross (to give a Latinized form of *Rosenkreuz*)]

ros·i·ly (róuzili:) *adv.* with a rosy color ‖ brightly, cheerfully

ros·in (rózin) **1.** *n.* the resin obtained from the oleoresin of pine by the removal of the volatile turpentine or as a by-product in the production of chemical pulp **2.** *v.t.* to rub (esp. a violin bow) with rosin ‖ to add rosin to [O.F. *rosine, resine*, resin]

ros·i·ness (róuzi:nis) *n.* the state or quality of being rosy

Ross (rɔs, rɒs), Betsy (Elizabeth Griscom Ross, 1752-1836), American flagmaker at the time of the American Revolution. She was for long credited with designing and creating the first U.S. national flag, but this is now generally refuted

Ross, Edward Alsworth (1866-1951), U.S. pioneer sociologist, best known for his 'Social Control' (1901) and 'Social Psychology' (1908)

Ross, Harold Wallace (1892-1951), U.S. journalist, founding-editor (from 1925) of 'The New Yorker'

Ross, Sir James Clark (1800-62), British explorer. He located the North magnetic pole (1831). He led an expedition to Antarctica (1839-43), during which he discovered Ross Sea and explored the Ross Ice Shelf

Ross, Sir Ronald (1857-1932), British physician. He established (1897) the presence of the malarial parasite in the stomach of the anopheles mosquito. Nobel prize (1902)

Ross and Crom·ar·ty (krómərti:) a former county (area 3,089 sq. miles, pop. 57,000) in N. Scotland. County town: Dingwall (pop. 4,000)

Ross Barrier *ROSS SEA

Ross·by (rósbi:), Carl-Gustaf Arvid (1898-1957), Swedish-U.S. meteorologist, best known for his research in atmospheric circulation, for his discovery of the 'Rossby Waves' (the long waves in the upper westerlies) and of the jet stream, and as a leader of international research teams in atmospheric chemistry and radioactivity

Ross Dependency a sector of Antarctica between 160° E. and 150° W. south of 60° S., claimed by Britain under New Zealand jurisdiction

Ros·sel·li·no (rɔsəlí:nou), Antonio (c. 1427–c. 1478), Italian sculptor. His greatest work (1459-61) is the tomb of the cardinal prince of Portugal in the church of San Miniato, Florence, Italy

Rossellino, Bernardo (1409-64), Italian sculptor, eldest brother of Antonio. His principal work (c. 1444) is the tomb of Leonardo Bruni in Santa Croce, Florence, Italy

Ros·set·ti (rouséti:), Christina Georgina (1830-94), English Pre-Raphaelite poet. Her work, mainly lyrical, is combined with a strong element of mystical or religious feeling. She shared her sense of color and atmosphere with her brother Dante Gabriel and other Pre-Raphaelites. 'Goblin Market and other Poems' was published in 1862

Rossetti, Dante Gabriel (Gabriel Charles Dante, 1828-82), English poet and painter, son of an Italian exile, brother of Christina. With Millais and Holman Hunt he formed the Pre-Raphaelite Brotherhood. In its passionate feeling, its sense of color and its preoccupation with medieval themes and atmosphere, his poetry creates the haunted, autumnal dream world of a group of artists who had turned away from society. Among his best poems are 'The Blessed Damozel' (1847), 'Sister Helen' (1870) and the sonnet sequence 'The House of Life', included in his collection 'Ballads and Sonnets' (1881). His best-known paintings are 'Ecce Ancilla Domini'

CONCISE PRONUNCIATION KEY: **(a)** æ, c*a*t; ɑ, c*a*r; ɔ f*aw*n; ei, sn*a*ke. **(e)** e, h*e*n; i:, sh*ee*p; iə, d*ee*r; ɛə, b*ea*r. **(i)** i, f*i*sh; ai, t*i*ger; ə:, b*i*rd. **(o)** o, *o*x; au, c*ow*; ou, g*oa*t; u, p*oo*r; ɔi, r*oy*al. **(u)** ʌ, d*u*ck; u, b*u*ll; u:, g*oo*se; ə, b*a*cillus; ju:, c*u*be. x, lo*ch*; θ, *th*ink; ð, bo*th*er; z, *Z*en; ʒ, cor*s*age; dʒ, sava*g*e; ŋ, ora*n*gutang; j, *y*ak; ʃ, *f*ish; tʃ, *f*etch; 'l, rabb*le*; 'n, redd*en*. Complete pronunciation key appears inside front cover.

(1849), 'Beata Beatrix' (1863), 'Dante's Dream' (1871)

Ross Ice Shelf *ROSS SEA

Ros·si·ni (rɒsíːniː, rɒssíːniː), Gioacchino Antonio (1792-1868), Italian composer. He began to compose when he was 18 and it is said that he wrote 40 operas in as many years. Some of the best known of these are 'The Barber of Seville' (1816), 'La Cenerentola' (1817), 'Semiramis' (1823) and 'William Tell' (1829). After 1829 he wrote no more operas, and few works of any kind apart from the 'Stabat Mater' oratorio (1842). Rossini's greatest gifts were his feeling for the theater and his brilliant bravura pieces

Ross Sea an arm of the S. Pacific in Ross Dependency, Antarctica, ending at about 78° S. in the Ross Ice Shelf or Ross Barrier, a permanent layer of ice (50-200 ft high) ending in mountains at about 85° S.

Ros·tand (rɒstɑ̃), Edmond (1868-1918), French playwright. 'Cyrano de Bergerac' (1897) and 'l'Aiglon' (1900), his best-known works, are distinguished by their wit and brilliance

ros·tel·late (rɒsteleit, rɒstəlit) adj. (biol.) having a rostellum

ros·tel·lum (rɒsteləm) pl. **ros·tel·la** (rɒstélə) n. (biol.) a small rostrum || a beaklike structure developed from the stigmatic surface of an orchid || a round prominence on the scolex of the tapeworm || the sucking mouthpart of a louse [L. dim. of rostrum, beak]

ros·ter (rɒstər) n. a list, esp. of officers or men, setting out the duties of groups or individuals, together with the times or dates for performing these || any itemized list or roll [fr. Du. rooster, a list]

Ros·tock (rɒstɒk) the chief port (pop. incl. Warnemünde, its outport, 220,900) of East Germany, in former Mecklenburg. Industries: shipbuilding, fishing, mechanical engineering, chemicals. University (1419) || the surrounding district (area 2,730 sq. miles, pop. 849,000)

Ros·tov-on-Don (rɒstɒ́fɒndɒn, rɒstɒ́fəndɒn) (Russ. Rostov-na-Donu) a seaport and communications center (pop. 934,000) in the R.S.F.S.R., U.S.S.R., on the Don 25 miles above the Sea of Azov. Industries: textiles, shipbuilding, heavy engineering, metallurgy, chemicals, food processing. University

ros·tral (rɒstrəl) adj. (zool.) of, relating to, resembling or being a rostrum || (Rom. hist., of historical monuments) adorned with rostrums [fr. L.L. rostralis]

ros·trate (rɒstreit, rɒstrit) adj. (zool.) having a rostrum || (Rom. hist., of historical monuments) rostral **ros·trat·ed** (rɒstreitid) adj. (zool.) rostrate [fr. L. rostratus fr. rostrum, beak]

Rostropovich (rɒstrəpóuvitʃ), Mstislav (1927–), Russian-American cellist and conductor. After establishing his career as a cellist in the U.S.S.R., he was forced to flee to the U.S.A. because his association with dissidents and his outspokenness had put him in disfavor with the Soviet government. He directed (1974–) the National Symphony Orchestra in Washington, D.C.

ros·trum (rɒstrəm) pl. **ros·trums**, **ros·tra** (rɒstrə) n. a platform from which a speaker addresses his audience || (Rom. hist.) the beaked prow of an ancient war galley || (biol.) a beak or a beaklike process, esp. of many insects and arachnids [L. = beak]

ros·y (róuziː) comp. **ros·i·er** superl. **ros·i·est** adj. like a rose || having a healthy, rose-colored complexion || hopeful, promising, a rosy future || optimistic, to take a rosy view

rot (rɒt) pres. part. **rot·ting** past and past part. **rot·ted** v.i. to decay || (with 'away', 'off' etc.) to become impaired or detached by decay || to degenerate morally || (esp. of plants) to suffer from rot || v.t. to cause to decay || to affect (sheep) with rot || to ret (flax etc.) [O.E. rotian]

rot 1. n. a rotting or being rotten || something rotting or rotten || a parasitic liver disease in sheep caused by the liver fluke || (pop.) rubbish, nonsense || a process of decline 2. interj. rubbish [prob. Scand.]

ro·ta (róutə) n. (Br.) a roster **Ro·ta** the supreme court of the Curia [L. = wheel]

Ro·tar·i·an (routéəriən) n. a member of the Rotary movement of international clubs (*ROTARY INTERNATIONAL)

ro·ta·ry (róutəriː) 1. adj. rotating, turning on an axis || working by rotation 2. pl. **ro·ta·ries** n. a rotary machine, e.g. a rotary press || a traffic circle [fr. L.L. rotarius]

Rotary Club a local branch of the Rotary International

rotary engine an engine, e.g. a turbine, in which the turning movement results from the direct application of a force to vanes etc. (cf. RECIPROCATING ENGINE)

Rotary International an international organization of clubs for business and professional men. It was founded in Chicago, Illinois (1905). Local club members each represent a different business or profession. It aims at serving the community and promoting international friendship

rotary press a printing press on which the type, in the form of a curved plate, is mounted on a cylinder rotating at high speed against a continuously moving reel of paper

ro·tate (róuteit) adj. having flat, radiating, spokelike parts [fr. L. rota, wheel]

rotate pres. part. **ro·tat·ing** past and past part. **ro·tat·ed** v.i. to turn around an axis || to turn on a pivot with a circular movement || to happen in regular cyclical succession, the rotating seasons || v.t. to cause to revolve || to cause to move on a pivot in a circular movement || to cause to recur in a cycle, to rotate crops [fr. L. rotare (rotatus)]

ro·ta·tion (routéiʃən) n. a rotating or being rotated || a repetitive arrangement or occurrence, each becomes chairman in rotation **ro·ta·tion·al** adj. [fr. L. rotatio (rotationem)]

rotation of crops the order in which different crops are grown so that each contributes to the soil constituents or conditions needed by its successors

ro·ta·tive (róuteitiv) adj. causing rotation || characterized by rotation || occurring in regular succession

ro·ta·tor (routéitər, róuteiter) n. anything that rotates || (anat., pl. **ro·ta·tors**, **ro·ta·to·res** (routətɔ́ːz, routətóuriːz) a muscle that rotates a limb etc. [L.]

ro·ta·to·ry (róutətɔriː, róutətɔuriː) adj. of, relating to or causing rotation

rote (rout) n. (only in) by rote (of the process of learning) by memory only, without intelligent understanding and assimilation [etym. doubtful]

Roth (rɒθ), Philip Milton (1933–), U.S. writer, known for his stories of American Jewish life. His novels include 'Letting Go' (1962), 'When She Was Good' (1967), 'Portnoy's Complaint' (1969), 'The Great American Novel' (1973), 'The Professor of Desire' (1977), 'The Ghost Writer' (1979), 'Zuckerman Unbound' (1981) and 'The Anatomy Lesson' (1983). His short stories are collected in 'Goodbye, Columbus' (1959)

Roth·er·mere (róðərmiər) * NORTHCLIFFE

Roth·ko (róθkou), Mark (1903-70), American painter born in Russia, an originator of abstract expressionism. His vast compositions, usually employing two or three colors, achieve intensity by their strong tones and extreme simplicity of form

Roth·schild (rɒθfaild, rɔ́θstfaild, róɔθfaild, róɔθstfaild), Meyer Anselm (1743-1812), German Jewish banker. He founded a family of international bankers who dominated European finance in the 19th c.

ro·ti·fer (róutifər) n. a member of Rotifera, a class of usually microscopic, many-celled aquatic animals of phylum Aschelminthes. The anterior end bears one or two rings of cilia, used esp. for swimming, which seem to rotate like spinning wheels [Mod. L. fr. rota, wheel+ -fer, bearing]

ro·tis·ser·ie (routísəriː) n. an electric cooking appliance fitted with a rotating spit for broiling fowl etc. [F.]

ro·to·flec·tor (róutəflɛktər) n. a radar reflector shaped elliptically so that it reflects radar beams at a right angle

ro·to·gra·vure (routəgrəvjúər) n. a process of photogravure using etched cylinders fixed to the rollers of a rotary press || a print reproduced by this method || the section of a newspaper containing these reproductions [fr. L. rota, wheel+ GRAVURE]

ro·tor (róutər) n. the rotary part of an electrical machine || (aeron.) a system of rotating airfoils producing lift

ro·to·va·tor (róutəveitər) n. (Br.) a power-driven soil tiller —**rotovate** v.

Ro·trou (rɒtru:), Jean de (1609-50), French poetic dramatist. A contemporary of Corneille, he contributed to the founding of French classical drama. His best-known works are 'Saint Genest' (1646) and 'Venceslas' (1647)

rot·ten (rɒt'n) adj. decayed, decomposed || having a bad smell because of decay || (of rocks) friable || morally corrupt || (of a sheep) affected with rot || (pop.) completely unsatisfactory, a rotten idea! || (pop.) very unpleasant, rotten weather [O.N. rotinn]

rotten borough (Br. hist.) a parliamentary constituency which possessed the right to elect members of parliament even though its population had dwindled or was nonexistent. The rotten boroughs were abolished in 1832

rot·ten·stone (rɒt'nstoun) n. a friable siliceous limestone, used for polishing metals

rot·ter (rɒtər) n. a person having no moral integrity whatsoever

Rot·ter·dam (rɒtərdæm, rɔtərdæm) the second largest city (pop. 568,167) and chief port of the Netherlands, serving much of W. Europe, on the Rhine delta in South Holland. Industries: oil refining, mechanical engineering, distilling, shipbuilding, chemicals, food processing. The city has been rebuilt in modern style after being almost totally destroyed (May 14, 1940) in a German bombing attack

ro·tund (routʌnd) adj. round, plump || (of speech) florid, rhetorical [fr. L. rotundus, round]

ro·tun·da (routʌndə) n. a circular building, esp. one with a dome or cupola || a large circular room [fr. earlier rotonda fr. Ital. rotonda fem. adj., round]

ro·tun·di·ty (routʌ́nditiː) pl. **ro·tun·di·ties** n. the state or quality of being rotund || a rotund phrase [fr. L. rotunditas]

Rou·ault (ru:ou), Georges (1871-1958), French expressionist painter, etcher and lithographer, briefly associated with Fauvism. His works, ranging in subject from Christ's Passion and biblical themes to grotesque judges, clowns and prostitutes, reveal his love of Christ and his compassion for his fellow men in the face of social injustice and human suffering. He knew the technique of making stained glass, and his style was greatly influenced by this. He designed (1945) windows for the church at Assy, Haute-Savoie, France. His 'Miserere' etchings (1917-27) were published in 1948

Rou·baix (ru:bei) a textile manufacturing center (pop. 109,797) of Nord department, France

Rou·bi·liac (ru:bi:ljæk) (Louis François Roubillac, c. 1695-1762), French sculptor. He lived in England from about 1720. His works include many fine tombs in Westminster Abbey, and busts in Trinity College Library, Cambridge

rouble *RUBLE

rou·é (rú:ei, ru:éi) n. a sexually debauched man, esp. one who is no longer young [F. past part. of rouer, to break on the wheel]

Rou·en (rwã) the chief town (pop. 114,925) of Seine-Maritime, France, and historic capital of Normandy, a sea and river port on the Lower Seine. Main industries: metallurgy, shipbuilding, mechanical engineering. Half the town was destroyed (1944) in the 2nd world war, but the cathedral (12th-16th cc.), churches (14th and 15th cc.) and other monuments remain, partly restored

rouge (ru:ʒ) 1. n. a cosmetic for heightening the color of the cheeks || jewelers' rouge 2. v. pres. part. **roug·ing** past and past part. **rouged** v.t. to color with rouge || v.i. to use rouge [F.=rouge, red]

rouge et noir (rú:ʒeinwær) (gambling) a card game in which two rows of cards are dealt, one row designated as red, the other as black. The players bet on which row will come closer to the count of 31 [F.=red and black]

Rou·get de Lisle (ru:ʒeidəli:l), Claude Joseph (1760-1836), French army officer. He wrote both words and music of the 'Marseillaise' (1792)

rough (rʌf) 1. adj. having a surface which is uneven or marked by protuberances or other irregularities || difficult to make one's way over or through, rough country || (of cloth) having a coarse texture || (of an animal's coat) coarse and shaggy || turbulent, a rough sea, a rough crossing || (of sound) harsh and rasping || (of wine, cider etc.) harsh and acid to the taste || approximate, a rough guess || hasty and not worked up, rough notes || unrefined, a rough manner || full of oaths, rough language || boisterous, rough play || requiring strength rather than intelligence, rough work || (of behavior) characterized by violence || crudely executed, rough garden furniture || (pop.) severely trying, a rough time || (esp.

of gems) unpolished || lacking luxuries, comfort etc., *a rough camping holiday* || (*phon.*) aspirate **to be rough on** to be harsh with || (*impers.*) to involve hardship for, *it was rough on her having to work on Saturdays* **2.** *adv.* (esp. with *past part.*) roughly, *rough shaped* **3.** *n.* uneven, stony ground || (*golf*) the ground bordering the fairway || anything in a rough, unfinished state, esp. an uncut gem || a tough || a spike in a horseshoe to prevent the horse from slipping **in the rough** in a crude, unfinished state **to take the rough with the smooth** to accept life as it comes, good or bad **4.** *v.t.* to make rough || (esp. with 'up') to put a spike or spikes into (a horseshoe) **to rough in** to add (provisional detail) to a sketch, plan etc. **to rough it** to live without the comforts and amenities of civilized life **to rough out** to make (a diagram, plan etc.) in broad outline, without detail **róugh·age** *n.* the rough or refuse part of grain etc. used as food for domestic animals || (*dietetics*) the bran of cereals or vegetable fibers, which stimulates the action of the alimentary canal [O.E. *rūh*]

rough-read·y (rʌ́fənrédi:) *adj.* (of a thing) good enough for its purpose, though not well designed or finished || (of a person) crude, vigorous and outspoken || (of method) crude but adequate

rough-and-tum·ble (rʌ́fəntʌ́mb'l) *n.* an unorganized fight, brawl or scuffle in which anyone joins who wants to

rough breathing *BREATHING

rough·cast (rʌ́fkæst, rʌ́fkɑst) **1.** *n.* a coarse plaster usually of mortar and small stones used on outside walls || a rough, preliminary model **2.** *v.t.* to coat (a wall) with roughcast || to construct in a rough preliminary form

rough diamond an uncut diamond || (*Br.*) a diamond in the rough

rough·dry (rʌ́fdrái) **1.** *v.t.* pres. part. **rough·dry·ing** past and past part. **rough·dried** to dry (laundry) without ironing it **2.** *adj.* (of laundry) dried but not ironed

rough·en (rʌ́fən) *v.t.* to make rough || *v.i.* to become rough

rough·hew (rʌ́fhjú:) *pres. part.* **rough·hew·ing** *past* **rough·hewed** *past part.* **rough·hewn** (rʌ́fhjú:n), **rough·hewed** *v.t.* to cut into shape without smoothing or polishing || to make a preliminary shape or rough model of **róugh·héwn** *adj.* left as it was hewn, not smoothed or polished || (of a person) uncultivated

rough·house (rʌ́fhaus) **1.** *n.* play that has gotten out of hand and turned into brawling **2.** *v. pres. part.* **rough·hous·ing** (rʌ́fhausin, rʌ́fhauz-ing) *past* and *past part.* **rough·housed** (rʌ́fhaust, rʌ́fhauzd) *v.i.* to create or take part in a roughhouse || *v.t.* to give (someone) a rough handling (sometimes in fun, sometimes in earnest)

rough·ly (rʌ́fli:) *adv.* in a rough way || approximately, *the price is roughly 600 francs*

rough·neck (rʌ́fnek) *n.* (*pop.*) a tough, rowdy man or boy || the lowest member of an oil-rig crew, doing manual work only

rough·rid·er (rʌ́fraidər) *n.* a person who rides untrained horses, or breaks them to the saddle **Rough·rid·er** (*Am. hist.*) a member of the 1st U.S. Volunteer Cavalry regiment in the Spanish-American War (1898), commanded by Theodore Roosevelt

rough·shod (rʌ́fʃɒd) *adj.* (of a horse) having shoes with spikes in them to prevent slipping **to ride roughshod over** to show no regard for

rough-spo·ken (rʌ́fspoukən) *adj.* using blunt or coarse language

rou·lade (ru:lɑ́d) *n.* (*mus.*) an ornamental passage of running notes usually sung to one syllable [F.]

rou·leau (ru:lou) *pl.* **rou·leaus, rou·leaux** (ru:lóuz) *n.* a roll of coins packeted in paper [F.]

rou·lette (ru:lét) **1.** *n.* a gambling game played with a ball on a revolving disk which brings a ball to rest against a numbered red or black compartment || a toothed wheel for making dots or incisions, e.g. in engraving || a series of small slits separating rows of postage stamps **2.** *v.t.* pres. part. **rou·let·ting** past and past part. **rou·let·ted** to make incisions in or on with a roulette [F.]

Roumania *RUMANIA
Roumanian *RUMANIAN

round (raund) **1.** *adj.* having a circular or roughly circular shape || having a spherical or roughly spherical shape || having a circular cross section, cylindrical || involving a circular

movement || plump, *round cheeks* || pronounced with the lips rounded || brisk, *a round pace* || (of the voice, a sound etc.) full-toned and even || (of handwriting) curved rather than angular || expressed in tens, hundreds, thousands etc. || expressed as a whole number, not fractional || full, complete, *a round dozen* || approximate, *a round estimate* || loud and clear, *a round oath* || (of a blow) delivered with a swinging motion of the arm **2.** *n.* the rung of a ladder || (esp. *pl.*) a route or course habitually taken. e.g. by a milkman, watchman, a doctor visiting patients in a hospital etc. || (*mil.*) a patrol whose main function is to keep the sentinels alert, esp. at night || (*mil.*) the route taken by this patrol || (*mil.*) a single shot fired from a weapon or from each gun of a troop, battery etc. || a single outburst of applause, cheers etc. || a circular movement || a succession of events, actions etc., *a round of parties* || the rounded part of the thigh of beef, or a slice cut from this || a round slice of bread, sausage etc. || (*archery*) a given number of arrows shot from a given distance at the target || (*boxing*) one of the periods into which a match is divided || (*golf*) the playing of all the holes of the course || (*mus.*) a usually short vocal canon in which the voices enter in turn and sing the melody at the same pitch or at the octave || (*card games*) a unit of play in which each player has a turn || a drink of liquor served at the same time to each member of a group of people || (*archit.*) a rounded molding **in the round** in which sculptured figures are three-dimensional and not attached to a background || (*theater*) with a central stage, surrounded by seats **out of round** distorted from true roundness **to go the round of** to go, ask etc. all through (a group of people), *he went the round of the class asking the same question* **to go the round** (or **rounds**) (of gossip, rumor etc.) to be circulated about and widely repeated **3.** *v.t.* to make round || to pronounce with rounded lips || to pass esp. by making a circuit of, *to round the Cape, to round a corner* || to make full or plump || to polish (phrases or style) || *v.i.* to become round || to make a circular course || to become full or plump || (with 'into') to develop fully, *the plan rounded into shape* || to reverse direction by turning around, *he rounded on his heel* **to round off** to complete, put the finishing touches to **to round on** to betray, inform against || to make an unexpected verbal attack on **to round out** to make full or round || to furnish with detail **to round to** (*naut.*) to come about in order to heave to **to round up** to drive (cattle) together || (*pop.*) to collect (people) together || to bring in (e.g. criminals or suspects) for questioning **4.** *adv.* in a circle or in a circular course, *to run round* || on every side, *gather round* || from beginning to end, *all year round* || in various places, *scattered round* || with a revolving movement, *the wheel whirled round* || in circumference, *the tower is 60 ft round* || on a circuit, *the milkman comes round at 10* || so as to face, go etc. in the opposite direction, *turn round*, or so as to hold an opposite or different view, *to talk someone round* || to everyone present, *pass the muffins round* || to someone or some place understood, *send round for more beer* || in the area, *search round* || so as to encircle, *wrap round* || so as to see the sights, inspect a property etc., *to show someone round* || back to consciousness, *to bring someone round* **5.** *prep.* on every side of, *the wind blew round the house* || so as to encircle, *put it round your wrist* || so as to revolve about, *the earth turns round its axis* || near, *he lives round here somewhere* || on a circuit of, *he went round his diocese* || throughout, *it works all round the clock* || here and there in, *he looked round the room* || on the border, edge or outer part of, *a pattern of roses round the saucers* || so as to go in a curved or circular path about, *ski round the trees* || located beyond the circuit of, *the house round the corner* || (of a specified time, date or season) at about, *round 1830* || in different parts of, *public telephones were put all round the town* **round the clock** for 24 hours nonstop [O.F. *rund-, rond-, round-*]

round·a·bout (ráundəbaut) **1.** *adj.* circuitous, indirect, *a roundabout way of getting somewhere* || circumlocutory, *a roundabout way of saying something* **2.** *n.* (*Br.*) a merry-go-round || (*Br.*) a traffic circle

roun·del, roun·dle (ráundl) *n.* a small, round disk, form or figure || (*poetry*) an English version of the French rondeau || a circular medallion, panel or window [O.F. *rondel*]

roun·de·lay (ráundəlei) *n.* a short song, part of which is repeated as a refrain [fr. F. *rondelet*]

round·ers (ráundərz) *n.* (*Br.*) a game resembling baseball played esp. by children [ROUND n. and v.]

Round·head (ráundhed) *n.* (*Br. hist.*) a Puritan or parliamentarian in the English Civil War, 1642-52 (cf. CAVALIER)

round·house (ráundhaus) *pl.* **round·hous·es** (ráundhauziz) *n.* (*hist.*) a cabin on the afterpart of the quarterdeck of a ship || (*hist.*) a building where prisoners were kept temporarily || a circular building where railroad engines are stored or repaired

roundle *ROUNDEL

round·ly (ráundli:) *adv.* violently, *to abuse someone roundly* || openly, without circumlocution, *he roundly declared himself satisfied* || thoroughly, completely, *roundly condemned*

round robin a letter, petition or protest bearing a number of signatures in a circle so that none heads the list || a letter addressed to a group. When the first person to receive it has read it he sends it on to the next, perhaps adding information or comment, and so on until all have seen it

round-shoul·dered (ráundʃouldərd) *adj.* having the shoulders slouched forward and the upper part of the back rounded

rounds·man (ráundzmən) *pl.* **rounds·men** (ráundzmən) *n.* (*Br.*) a man employed to deliver milk, bread etc. to customers

Round Table King Arthur's assembly of knights, in the Arthurian legend

round table conference a conference so arranged that none of the participants takes precedence

round trip a journey to and from a place over the same route || (*Br.*) a circular journey, not covering the same ground twice

round turn (*naut.*) a single turn of a rope around a post or bollard made in order to check the motion of a ship abruptly

round·up (ráundʌp) *n.* the collecting of scattered cattle || men and horses who collect such cattle || a collecting of scattered people, esp. of criminals by police

round·worm (ráundwəːrm) *n.* a nematode worm, as distinguished from a flatworm or tapeworm

roup (ru:p) *n.* one of various poultry diseases, esp. fowl pox [etym. doubtful]

rouse (rauz) *pres. part.* **rous·ing** past and past part. **roused** *v.t.* to awaken from sleep || to cause to become active || to provoke, *the sight roused him to anger* || (*naut.*, with 'in', 'out' or 'up') to pull with great force

rouse·a·bout (ráuzəbaut) *n.* (*Austral.*) a handyman on a sheep farm

rous·ing (ráuzin) *adj.* exciting, *a rousing speech* || very enthusiastic, *a rousing welcome*

Rous·seau (ru:sou), Henri 'le Douanier' (1844-1910), French painter. Much of his work re-creates a childish vision of a luxuriant, strangely ordered jungle, through which elegant beasts menacingly approach the spectator. His view of contemporary France and his portraits have the same direct, naïve character

Rousseau, Jean-Jacques (1712-78), French writer born in Geneva. A man of volatile emotions but keen mind, he rebelled against many dominant values of his time and quarreled with a striking number of contemporaries, e.g. Voltaire, Grimm, Diderot and Hume. He rejected absolutism, rationalism, the moderation as well as the rigidity of waning classicism, coercive education and formal gardens. Prefiguring the main trends which were to converge in Romanticism, he glorified nature, including human nature (the greater part of his work stems from his belief in the natural goodness of men), favored feeling and emotion as against reason, and advocated a method of education in which the pupil would be helped to develop freely in accordance with his own inborn nature. In 'le Contrat social' (1762), he developed a theory of the State based on a contract by which free individuals freely entrust a part of their freedom to the body politic. His political ideas played an important part in the development of modern democracy. Other important works are: 'Discours sur l'origine de l'inégalité' (1755), 'Julie ou la Nouvelle Héloïse' (1761), 'Emile ou Traité de l'Education' (1762) and 'Confessions' (published posthumously)

Rousseau, Théodore (1812-67), French landscape painter, one of the leaders of the Barbizon school

Rous·sel (ru:sel). Albert (1869-1937), French composer. He wrote four symphonies (of which the second is the best known). Of his four ballets, the most famous is 'le Festin de l'araignée'(1912). Other works include the symphonic poem 'Evocations' (1910-11), chamber music, songs etc.

Rous·sil·lon (ru:si:jɔ̃) a former province of France in the Pyrenees, bordering Spain and the Mediterranean, forming the modern Pyrénées-Orientales. Historic capital: Perpignan. Industries: agriculture (early vegetables, fruit, wine), fishing, tourism. It was disputed by French and Spanish powers from the 8th c., when the Franks took it from the Arabs, until 1659, when France definitively annexed it. Catalan is widely spoken

roust·a·bout (ráustəbaut) n. a dock laborer ‖ a deckhand ‖ an unskilled laborer ‖ a laborer in a circus ‖ (*Austral.*) a rouseabout [ROUSE+ ABOUT]

rout (raut) 1. *n.* a disorderly flight, e.g. of defeated troops **to put to rout** to defeat utterly 2. *v.t.* to rout (an army) to rout. [obs. F. *route*]

rout *v.i.* (of swine) to root ‖ to rummage, *to rout about in a drawer* ‖ *v.t.* (with 'out') to make (someone) come out or get up ‖ (with 'out') to search for and discover ‖ to dig out (metal or wood) with a router

route (ru:t, raut) 1. *n.* a course of travel, esp. between two distant points ‖ a way of progress, *to reconnoiter a route through a minefield* ‖ a regularly followed course, *a map of the main shipping routes to Africa* ‖ a specific area covered regularly by a specific person, *postal route* 2. *v.t. pres. part.* **rout·ing** *past* and *past part.* **rout·ed** to send (goods, troops etc.) by a certain route, or to plan such a route for (someone or something) [F.]

rout·er (ráutər) n. a carpenter's plane used to cut grooves, moldings etc. ‖ a machine for routing out wooden or metal surfaces

rou·tine (ru:tí:n) 1. *n.* a regularly repeated course of action or standard practice, *a hospital routine* ‖ (*dancing*) a set series of steps ‖ an act (feature in a show), *a comedy routine* 2. *adj.* in accordance with a routine, *routine duties* [F.]

roux (ru:) *pl.* **roux** a mixture of fat and flour browned together and used to thicken sauces [F. = red, browned]

rove (rouv) *pres. part.* **rov·ing** *past* and *past part.* **roved** *v.i.* and *t.* to roam [etym. doubtful]

rove n. a small metal plate or ring, through which a screw or nail is passed and held fast, used in boat building ‖ a burr (small washer) [O.N. *rõ*]

rove 1. *v.t.pres. part.* **rov·ing** *past* and *past part.* **roved** to form into roves 2. *n.* a thin strand of cotton, wool or silk drawn out and slightly twisted [etym. doubtful]

rove *past* and *past part.* of REEVE

rove beetle a member of *Staphylinidae*, a large family of swift-running, long-bodied beetles having very short wing cases. They are found in decaying animal and vegetable matter

rov·er (róuvər) n. a person who shuns a settled life ‖ (*Br.*) a senior boy scout ‖ (*archery*) a fixed mark for long-distance shooting, also one chosen at random ‖ (*croquet*) a ball that has passed through all its wickets, but is continued in play rather than being allowed to peg out ‖ (*croquet*) the person playing this ball

ro·ver·back (róuvərbæk) n. (*football*) linesman who plays linebacker and cornerback

rov·ing (róuviŋ) n. a rove (thin strand of cotton etc.)

row (rou) 1. *v.t.* to propel (a boat) by using oars ‖ to participate in (a race) by doing this ‖ to compete against in a race ‖ to employ (a specified number of oars) ‖ to take (passengers) in an oar-propelled boat, *to row someone across a river* ‖ *v.i.* to use oars ‖ to be an oarsman ‖ to be propelled by or as if by oars 2. *n.* a journey in a rowboat [O.E. *rõwan*]

row (rou) n. an orderly line of persons or things near, or touching, one another, *a row of houses* ‖ a line of seats in a theater etc. ‖ (esp. *Br.*, used chiefly in street names) a small street each side of which is lined with houses **a hard** (or **long**) **row to hoe** a wearisome, difficult task to perform [perh. O.E. *rãw*]

row (rau) n. (esp. *Br.*) a loud, harsh noise ‖ a quarrel or disturbance, esp. a noisy one **to**

make (or **kick up**) **a row** to make a lot of noise ‖ to protest strongly [origin unknown]

row·an (róuən, ráuən) n. *Sorbus aucuparia*, a tree of Europe and Asia bearing corymbs of small white flowers. The fruits are red, berry-like pomes [of Scand. origin]

row·boat (roubout) n. (*Am.= Br.* rowing boat) a small, shallow boat propelled by oars

row·di·ness (ráudi:nis) n. the state or quality of being rowdy

row·dy (ráudi:) 1. *comp.* **row·di·er** *superl.* **row·di·est** *adj.* disorderly and noisy 2. *pl.* **row·dies** n. a disorderly, noisy person **rów·dy·ism** n. [etym. doubtful]

row·el (ráuəl) n. the spiked wheel on a spur [fr. O.F. *roel, rouel*]

row·ing boat (róuiŋ) n. (*Br.*) a rowboat

Row·land (róulənd), Henry Augustus (1848-1901), American physicist. He made valuable experiments in electricity and invented a dividing apparatus for ruling diffraction gratings

Row·land·son (róuləndsən), Thomas (1756-1827), English painter and caricaturist. Though his drawings reveal a brutal and gross world, the seamy side of 18th-c. civilization, they display a sublime sense of the ridiculous coupled with delicate tone and brilliant line

row·lock (rólək, róulɒk) n. an oarlock

Ro·xas y A·cu·ña (rójasi:akú:nja), Manuel (1892-1948), first president (1946-8) of the Republic of the Philippines

Rox·burgh (róksbrə) a former county (area 670 sq. miles.) of S. Scotland. County town: Jedburgh. Administrative center: Newtown St Boswells

roy·al (rɔ́iəl) 1. *adj.* of or relating to a king or queen ‖ of or belonging to the family of a king or queen, *the royal governess* ‖ having the rank of a king or queen ‖ fit for a king or queen, *a royal welcome* ‖ very imposing, splendid, majestic etc. ‖ (of a mast, sail or yard) next above the topgallant ‖ (*printing*) folded from royal paper, *royal octavo* **Roy·al** (*Br.*) the descriptive title of a place or institution under the patronage of a king or queen or given a charter under the monarch's hand etc., *the Royal Borough of Tunbridge Wells, the Royal College of Physicians* 2. *n.* a stag at least 8 years old having 12 or more points on its antlers ‖ a sail set on the royal mast ‖ (*pl.*) a size of paper measuring 24 ins x 19 ins (for writing) or 25 ins × 20 ins (for printing) [O.F. *roial*]

Royal n. U.S. government secrecy classification more restrictive than 'top secret,' established September 1980

royal assent the British sovereign's formal ratification of an act of parliament

royal blue a deep, vivid blue

Royal Canadian Mounted Police (RCMP) the federal police force of Canada, originally instituted (1873) to establish law and order between the Manitoba border and the Rocky Mtns. In the 1900s it tracked down murderers, horse thieves, and desperadoes, contained the Sioux Indians, and assisted thousands of new settlers unfamiliar with the wilderness. It is the only police force in the Yukon and Northwest Territories. In the 1930s the marine and air divisions and the first crime detection laboratories were added. Its many duties include ceremonial parades and national security

roy·al·ism (rɔ́iəlizəm) n. monarchism

roy·al·ist (rɔ́iəlist) 1. *n.* a person who supports the institution of monarchy ‖ (*Br. hist.*) a Cavalier, or supporter of the king in the English Civil War, 1642-52 (cf. PARLIAMENTARIAN) ‖ (*hist.*) a supporter of George III's government at the time of the Revolutionary War ‖ (in France) a supporter of the Bourbons at any time during and since the French Revolution 2. *adj.* of royalism or pertaining to a royalist

royal jelly a jellylike substance secreted from the pharyngeal glands of the honey bee and fed to very young larvae and to all queen larvae

royal palm a member of *Roystonea*, fam. *Palmaceae*, a genus of tall, ornamental palms, esp. *R. regia*, a native to Florida and Cuba, grown in many tropical regions

royal purple a rich reddish-purple color

Royal Society British scientific society. It is an independent, private body of scientific scholars, founded in 1660. There are more than 900 fellows and foreign members; elections of new members are made each year. The Royal Society promotes scientific research, advises the government, and represents Britain internationally in scientific matters. It publishes its learned 'Proceedings' and 'Philosophical

Transactions'. It receives an annual government subsidy

royal standard a square banner bearing the royal arms, flown to indicate the presence of the sovereign in a castle or on a ship and as a naval flag of command

roy·al·ty (rɔ́iəlti:) *pl.* **roy·al·ties** n. the office or dignity of a sovereign ‖ a person having royal rank ‖ royal persons collectively ‖ the sum, e.g. a percentage of the sales figure, paid to the owner of a literary etc. property by the person who exploits it commercially, or the sum paid to the owner of a patent for the use of his patent ‖ (*pl., hist.*) a right or prerogative granted by a sovereign [O.F. *roialté*]

Royce (rɔis), Josiah (1855-1916), U.S. philosopher. Espousing a monistic idealism, he held that moral order in the world takes the form of man's loyalty to the great community, or to collective individuals

RPG (*computer abbr.*) for report program generator, a computer language used to display data or prepare a desired business report

rpm, r.p.m revolutions per minute

R.R. railroad

R.S.F.S.R. *RUSSIAN SOVIET FEDERAL SOCIALIST REPUBLIC*

R.S.V.P. (used in formal invitations) please reply [F. *répondez s'il vous plait*]

Ru·an·da-U·run·di (ru:ándəu:rú:ndi:) a former territory of central Africa. It was incorporated in German East Africa (1890) and was administered by Belgium as a mandate (1919-46) and as a trustee territory (1946-62). It divided (July 1, 1962) into the separate independent states of Rwanda and Burundi

rub (rʌb) 1. *v. pres. part.* **rub·bing** *past* and *past part.* **rubbed** *v.t.* to move (something), using pressure, over a surface, *to rub ointment on one's leg* ‖ to apply such moving pressure to, *to rub one's leg with ointment* ‖ to clean or polish with a pressing motion ‖ to chafe, *to rub one's shin on a rail* ‖ to take a rubbing of (an incised design) ‖ to move in contact causing friction, *to rub one's hands together* ‖ *v.i.* to be subjected to friction ‖ to chafe, *shoes that rub* ‖ (*lawn bowling*) to be deflected or slowed down by an uneven piece of ground **to rub along** to make a barely adequate living ‖ to manage to avoid undue friction in social relationships **to rub down** to dry the sweat off (a horse) after exercise or a race **to rub in** to cause to penetrate by rubbing **to rub it in** to emphasize, and continue to emphasize, a person's shortcomings, failures, mistakes etc. **to rub off** to remove (something) by rubbing ‖ to be removable by rubbing **to rub out** to erase ‖ to become erased **to rub shoulders** (**elbows**) (esp. with 'with') to associate with someone whom one would not normally expect to associate with, *to rub shoulders with the gentry* **to rub (someone) the wrong way,** *Br.* to **rub (someone) up the wrong way,** to offend the susceptibilities of (someone) and so irritate him **to rub up** (*Br.*) to refresh one's memory of, *to rub up one's French* 2. *n.* a rubbing, *give the silver a rub* ‖ (*lawn bowling*) unevenness or inequality in the surface of the ground affecting the course of a bowl ‖ a hindrance or obstacle, esp. one having metaphysical overtones [origin unknown]

Rub al Kha·li (rʌbælxáli:) *GREAT SANDY DESERT*

ru·ba·to (ru:bátou) 1. *adj.* (*mus.*) played with some freedom as regards tempo 2. *pl.* **ru·ba·ti** (ru:báti:), **ru·ba·tos** n. (*mus.*) a tempo varied at discretion to express changes of mood [Ital.]

rub·ber (rʌ́bər) n. an elastic substance obtained from the latex of many tropical plants, esp. *Hevea brasiliensis*, fam. *Euphorbiaceae*, and *Ficus elastica*, fam. *Moraceae* ‖ a substance for this made synthetically ‖ (*Am.=Br.* galosh) a low rubber overshoe worn in wet weather ‖ someone who or something which rubs ‖ (*Br.*) an eraser ‖ an overshoe [RUB v.]

rubber n. three successive games of bridge or of certain other games, or the first two only if the same side wins both

rubber band an endless band of rubber used to hold bundles, papers etc. together

rub·ber·ize (rʌ́bəraiz) *v.t. pres. part.* **rub·ber·iz·ing** *past* and *past part.* **rub·ber·ized** to coat with rubber, impregnate with rubber solution

rub·ber·neck (rʌ́bərnek) 1. *n.* (*pop.*) a very inquisitive person ‖ an indefatigable sightseer 2. *v.i.* (*pop.*) to stare out of curiosity

rubber plant any of several plants which yield rubber, esp. *Ficus elastica*, fam. *Moraceae*, an Asian tree which grows to 100 ft or more and is the source of Assam rubber. A dwarfed variety is popular as an indoor plant

rubber ring (*Br.*) a rubber band ‖ (*Br.*) a rubber washer for a jar ‖ (*Br.*) an inflatable device worn around the waist by someone learning to swim

rubber stamp a rubber device which is inked and used on documents etc. for dating, endorsing, signing etc. **rúb·ber stámp** *v.t.* to stamp with this ‖ (*pop.*) to approve as a matter of routine, without real consideration

rub·ber·y (rʌ́bəri:) *adj.* like rubber in consistency, appearance etc.

rub·bish (rʌ́biʃ) *n.* waste material, refuse ‖ worthless or inferior ideas, goods etc. ‖ (*pop.*) nonsense **rúb·bish·y** *adj.* [etym. doubtful]

rub·ble (rʌ́b'l) *n.* pieces of broken brick, stone etc., usually from demolition and used for foundations etc. ‖ (*masonry*) rough stones for filling in ‖ rubblework‖ (*geol.*) loose fragments of stone or rock lying beneath alluvium [M.E., etym. doubtful]

rub·ble·work (rʌ́b'lwəːrk) *n.* coarse masonry of roughly dressed stones

Rub·bra (rʌ́brə), Edmund (1901-), English composer and pianist. His works include seven symphonies, two masses, much chamber music, songs and choral works

rub·down (rʌ́bdaun) *n.* the act of rubbing down the body, e.g. a brisk toweling after swimming or bathing ‖ a massage given to athletes to improve circulation

rube (ru:b) *n.* (*pop.*) a bumpkin [shortened fr. *Reuben*, a man's name]

ru·be·fa·cient (ru:biféiʃənt) 1. *adj.* causing redness 2. *n.* (*med.*) a salve etc. which causes the skin to redden **ru·be·fac·tion** (ru:bifǽkʃən) *n.* [fr. L. *rubefaciens* (*rubefacientis*) fr. *rubefacere*, to redden]

ru·bel·la (ru:bélə) *n.* German measles [Mod. L.]

ru·bel·lite (rú:belait, ru:bélait) *n.* a variety of tourmaline in various shades of red [fr. L. *rubellus*, reddish]

Ru·bens (rú:binz), Sir Peter Paul (1577-1640), Flemish painter. His patrons included the Gonzaga family, Marie de' Medici, Philip IV of Spain, and Charles I of England. After work and study in Italy (1600-3, 1604-8), where he steeped himself in the classic style of the high Renaissance and the naturalism of Caravaggio, he returned to Antwerp and established himself as a portrait painter and master of allegorical and mythological subjects. His large compositions reduce an enormous number of component parts to a unified composition, and yet remain full of light and air and above all of life and energy. His swift brushwork was extraordinarily fluent in rendering surface textures, above all that of flesh. The breadth of his drawings, the freedom of his technique and the warmth of his color make him one of the greatest of decorative painters. Among his masterpieces are 'The Raising of the Cross' (1610) and 'The Descent from the Cross' (1612) both in Antwerp Cathedral

ru·be·o·la (ru:bí:ələ, ru:bi:óulə) *n.* measles [Mod. L., neut. pl. of *rubeolus*, reddish]

ru·bes·cent (ru:bésənt) *adj.* growing or becoming red [fr. L. *rubescens* (*rubescentis*) fr. *rubescere*, to redden]

ru·bi·celle (rú:bisel) *n.* a yellow or reddishorange ruby spinel [F.]

Ru·bi·con (rú:bikɒn) a small river which marked the boundary between Italy and Cisalpine Gaul. Caesar's crossing of the Rubicon in Italy against the orders of the senate (49 B.C.) marked the opening of the civil war with Pompey

ru·bi·cund (rú:bikənd) *adj.* (of complexions) ruddy [F. *rubicond* or fr. L. *rubicundus*]

ru·bid·i·um (ru:bídi:əm) *n.* a soft silvery metallic element (symbol Rb, at. no. 37, at. mass 85.47) resembling sodium both physically and chemically [Mod. L. fr. L. *rubidus*, red]

ru·big·i·nous (ru:bíd3inəs) *adj.* rust-colored [fr. L. L. *rubiginosus*]

Rubinstein (rú:bənstain) Arthur (1887-1982), U.S. pianist, born in Poland. He debuted in Berlin (1899) and gave concerts in Europe and Russia, debuting in the U.S.A. in 1906. He was esp. known for his interpretation of such composers as Chopin, Brahms, Mozart and Grieg. A world concert tourer, he became a U.S. citizen in 1946

ru·ble, rou·ble (rú:b'l) *n.* the Russian monetary unit ‖ a coin representing a ruble [F. fr. Russ. *rubli*]

ru·bric (rú:brik) *n.* the heading of a chapter or section printed or written in special lettering (originally red), or a section so indicated ‖ a liturgical direction in a prayer book **rú·bri·cal** *adj.* [fr. F. *rubrique* or L. *rubrica*]

ru·bri·cate (rú:brikeit) *pres. part.* **ru·bri·cating** *past* and *past part.* **ru·bri·cat·ed** *v.t.* to mark with red ‖ to print or write in red ‖ to provide with rubrics **ru·bri·ca·tion, rú·bri·ca·tor** *ns* [fr. L. *rubricare* (*rubricatus*)]

ru·bri·cian (ru:bríʃən) *n.* an expert in liturgical rubrics

ru·by (rú:bi:) 1. *pl.* **ru·bies** *n.* a precious stone of red corundum ‖ something shaped like this, e.g. the jewel of a watch ‖ the red wine cr of ruby ‖ (*Br., printing*) agate 2. *adj.* of the color of ruby [O.F. *rubi, rubis*]

ruby laser a laser based on a rod-shape ruby crystal to which optical pumping is applied, producing a narrow beam of red light

ruby maser a maser utilizing a ruby crystal

ruby spinel a spinel used as a gem

ruche (ru:ʃ) 1. *n.* a frill, pleat or ruffle of lace, net etc. 2. *v.t. pres. part.* **ruch·ing** *past* and *past part.* **ruched** to trim with ruching [F.]

ruch·ing (rú:ʃiŋ) *n.* material used in making a ruche or ruches

ruck (rʌk) *n.* the ordinary run of persons or things [prob. of Scand. origin]

ruck 1. *n.* a crease, wrinkle 2. *v.i.* (esp. with 'up') to become wrinkled ‖ *v.t.* (esp. with 'up') to wrinkle [O.N. *hrukka*]

ruck *v.* (*Br.*) to seek the ball aggressively in rugby

Rück·ert (rýkərt), Friedrich (1788-1866), German poet and Orientalist. He wrote many imitations of Oriental poetry, as well as 'Kindertotenlieder' (1834) set to music by Mahler

ruck·sack (rʌ́ksæk, rúksæk) *n.* a knapsack [G.]

ruck·us (rʌ́kəs) *n.* a noisy disturbance, argument etc. [prob. fr. RUCTION + RUMPUS]

ruc·tion (rʌ́kʃən) *n.* (*pop.*, often *pl.*) a row, noisy disturbance [origin unknown]

rud·beck·i·a (rʌdbéki:ə) *n.* a member of *Rudbeckia*, fam. *Compositae*, a genus of North American perennial plants cultivated for their showy, usually yellow, flowers ‖ one of these flowers [after Olof *Rudbeck* (1630–1702), Swedish botanist]

rudd (rʌd) *n. Scardinius erythrophthalmus*, fam. *Cyprinidae*, a small common European freshwater fish having red irises and red fins [perh. O.E. *rudu*, red]

rud·der (rʌ́dər) *n.* a flat piece of wood or metal hinged vertically to a vessel's sternpost, used for steering ‖ a similar device for controlling the direction of an aircraft's flight [O.E. *rôther*]

rud·di·ly (rʌ́dili:) *adv.* with a ruddy color

rud·di·ness (rʌ́di:nis) *n.* the quality or state of being ruddy

rud·dle (rʌ́d'l) 1. *n.* red ocher, esp. that used for marking sheep 2. *v.t. pres. part.* **rud·dling** *past* and *past part.* **rud·dled** to mark or color with ruddle [fr. older *rud*, red color, redness]

rud·dy (rʌ́di:) *comp.* **rud·di·er** *superl.* **rud·di·est** *adj.* red-tinted ‖ glowing healthily, *ruddy cheeks* [O.E. *rudig*]

ruddy duck *Oxyura jamaicensis rubida*, an American broad-billed duck having a wedge-shaped tail and, in the drake, reddish upper parts

rude (ru:d) *comp.* **rud·er** *superl.* **rud·est** *adj.* very impolite, *rude behavior* ‖ vulgar, *a rude story* ‖ roughly put together, *rude carpentry* ‖ crude, *a rude plow* ‖ unexpectedly unpleasant, *a rude awakening, a rude shock* ‖ (*rhet.*) uneducated, uncivilized ‖ (*rhet.*, esp. of the wind or the sea) violent ‖ (of health) vigorous [O.F. *ruide, rude*]

ru·di·ment (rú:dəmənt) *n.* (esp. *pl.*) a basic principle of a subject, *the rudiments of orchestration* ‖ (esp. *pl.*) the merest beginning of something capable of being developed, *the rudiments of a plot* ‖ (*biol.*) a part or organ beginning to develop ‖ (*biol.*) a part or organ whose development has been arrested ‖ (*biol.*) a vestigial part or organ **ru·di·men·ta·ri·ly** (ru:dəméntərili:) *adv.* **rud·i·men·ta·ri·ness** (ru:dəméntəri:nis) *n.* **ru·di·men·ta·ry** (ru:dəméntəri:, ru:dəméntri:) *adj.* very elementary ‖ (*biol.*) in an early or arrested stage of development ‖ (*biol.*) vestigial [L. *rudimentum*, beginning]

Ru·dolf (rú:dɒlf) a lake (area 3,500 sq. miles) extending from the southwest corner of Ethiopia through N.W. Kenya. It has no outlet and is surrounded by desert

Rudolf I (1218-91), king of Germany (1273-91), founder of the Hapsburg dynasty. He enlarged his kingdom at the expense of Ottocar II of Bohemia, whom he defeated (1278)

Rudolf II (1552-1612), Holy Roman Emperor (1576-1612), king of Hungary (1572-1608) and of Bohemia (1575-1611), son of Maximilian II. Unable to deal with attacks from Turkey and revolts in Hungary and Bohemia, he ceded his kingdoms to his brother Matthias

rue (ru:) *n. Ruta graveolens*, fam. *Rutaceae*, a perennial evergreen European shrub bearing yellow flowers. Its strongly scented, bitter leaves were formerly used as a narcotic and stimulant [F. fr. L. fr. Gk]

rue *pres. part.* **ru·ing** *past* and *past part.* **rued** *v.t.* (*old-fash.*) to regret, to repent of **to rue the day** to regret bitterly a particular moment, *you'll live to rue the day you left him* **rué·ful** *adj.* regretful, sorrowful ‖ arousing sorrow or regret [O.E. *hrēowan*, to grieve]

ru·fes·cence (ru:fés'ns) *n.* the state or quality of being rufescent

ru·fes·cent (ru:fés'nt) *adj.* red-tinged [fr. L. *rufescens* (*rufescentis*) fr. *rufescere*, to become red]

ruff (rʌf) *n.* a natural growth of hair or feathers around the neck of a bird or beast ‖ (*hist.*) a broad starched collar of fluted linen or muslin worn by both men and women, esp. in the 16th c. [perh. fr. ROUGH *adj.*]

ruff *n. Acerina cernua*, fam. *Percidae*, a small, freshwater European fish [perh. fr. ROUGH because of its prickly scales]

ruff *n. Philomachus pugnax*, fam. *Scolopacidae*, a sandpiper of Europe and Asia. The male is about 11 ins long, the female (reeve) is smaller. In the breeding season, the male develops an enormous ruff of erectile feathers [perh. rel. to RUFF (growth of hair or feathers)]

ruff 1. *n.* (card games) the act of trumping 2. *v.i.* to play a trump card ‖ *v.t.* to trump [fr. O.F. *roffle, rouffle*, a card game]

ruffed grouse (rʌft) *Bonasa umbellus*, fam. *Tetraonidae*, a North American reddish-black and gray game bird. The male (about 17 ins in length) has tufts of long black feathers on each side of its neck, and drums loudly with its wings during the mating season

ruf·fi·an (rʌ́fjən, rʌ́fi:ən) *n.* a man who is coarse, tough, brutal, and prepared to break the law ‖ a boisterous, rascally boy **rúf·fi·an·ism** *n.* **rúf·fi·an·ly** *adj.* [O.F. *rufien, ruffian*]

ruf·fle (rʌ́fəl) 1. *v. pres. part.* **ruf·fling** *past* and *past part.* **ruf·fled** *v.t.* to destroy the smoothness or regularity of, *the breeze ruffled her hair* ‖ to disturb the self-possession of ‖ (of a bird) to stiffen and to raise (the feathers) e.g. in fright or astonishment ‖ to pucker up, gather (cloth, ribbon etc.) into a ruffle ‖ *v.i.* to become disordered, broken up into little waves etc. ‖ to become disturbed or confused 2. *n.* an ornamental frill attached to a garment, esp. at the neckline or wrists ‖ something resembling this, e.g. the ruff of a bird ‖ a ripple on the surface of water [etym. doubtful]

ruffle 1. *n.* (*mil.*) a low throbbing drumbeat 2. *v.i. pres. part.* **ruf·fling** *past* and *past part.* **ruf·fled** (of a drum) to beat a ruffle [prob. imit.]

ru·fous (rú:fəs) *adj.* reddish-brown (used esp. of the color of animals) [fr. L. *rufus*]

rug (rʌg) *n.* a mat usually of thick wool used esp. to cover part of a floor ‖ a mat made of an animal pelt placed directly on the floor over a carpet ‖ a thick blanket used as a bed covering or for wrapping around the knees when traveling etc. [perh. of Scand. origin]

rug·by (rʌ́gbi:) *n.* rugby football

rugby football a game which originated (1823) at Rugby School, England. It is played by two teams of 15 men (in Rugby Union) or 13 men (in Rugby League), with an elliptical football, on a rectangular field (110 yds by 75 yds) having an H-shaped goal at either end. Players may kick the ball or run with it in their hands, but may not pass, throw or knock it forwards. Tackling is allowed, and scrums are a feature of the game. Scoring is by points: in Rugby Union, 3 for a try, 5 for a try converted into a goal (the 3 for the try being discounted) and 3 for any other goals; in Rugby League, 3 for a try and 2 for any goal

Rü·gen (rýgən) an island (area 358 sq. miles, pop. 86,216) of Rostock district, East Germany. Industries: agriculture (livestock, cereals, sugar beets), fishing, tourism

rug·ged (rʌ́gid) *adj.* (of country) wild and broken ‖ (of ground) very rough-surfaced ‖ (of men's faces) having well-marked, usually irregular features suggesting a strong, generous character || (of style) lacking polish || (of a way of life) hard and austere || hardy and vigorous, *rugged pioneers* [prob. of Scand. origin]

rug·ger (rʌ́gər) *n.* (*Br.*) rugby football

ru·gose (rú:gous) *adj.* (*bot.*, of leaves) wrinkled-looking because of having sunken veins and the spaces between them elevated **ru·gos·i·ty** (ru:gɔ́siti:) *n.* [fr. L. *rugosus*]

Ruhr (rúər, ru:r) a tributary (144 miles long) of the lower Rhine || the district of North Rhine-Westphalia, West Germany, through which it flows, containing the largest concentration of industry on the mainland of Europe, based on vast local hard-coal deposits and iron ore from Sweden, Spain and France (Lorraine). Centers: Essen, Düsseldorf, Dortmund, Duisburg, Wuppertal, Gelsenkirchen, Bochum, Oberhausen, Cologne. The Ruhr was occupied (1923-5) by the French as a result of the Franco-German dispute over reparations

ru·in (rú:in) *n.* a state of advanced destruction or decay (physical or moral), *the house fell into ruin, drink led to his ruin* || something or someone in this state, *the mansion is now a ruin* || something which causes such a state, *this flood will be the ruin of the harvest* || (*pl.*) the remains of something which has been destroyed or fallen into decay, *they wandered among the ruins of the old city* || financial disaster [O.F *ruine*]

ruin *v.t.* to cause to become a ruin, *an earthquake ruined the city* || to destroy, *it ruined his chances of success* || (*loosely*) to spoil, *the rain ruined her hair* || to wreck financially, *the inflation ruined him* [fr. F. *ruiner*]

ru·in·a·tion (ru:inéiʃən) *n.* a ruining or being ruined || a cause of ruin

ru·in·ous (rú:inəs) *adj.* causing or likely to cause ruin, *ruinous expense* || ruined, dilapidated, *a ruinous estate* [F. *ruineux*]

Ruis·dael, Ruys·dael (ráizdɑl, ráisdɑl), Jacob van (c. 1628-82), Dutch landscape painter. He excelled in the painting of trees and woodlands beneath skies in which dark clouds are a foil to bright light. Little appreciated in his lifetime, his work was deeply influential on later Romantic landscape painting

Ru·iz (ru:í:θ), José Martínez *AZORIN

Ru·iz de A·lar·cón y Men·do·za (ru:í:sðeɑlɑrkɔ́ni:mendɔ́sɑ), Juan (c. 1581-1639), Mexican dramatist. His works include 'comedias de caracteres' (notably 'La verdad sospechosa', which was the inspiration of Corneille's 'le Menteur', and 'Las paredes oyen'), plays depicting social vices, and plays portraying the national hero-figure

rule (ru:l) *n.* control by authority || the reign of a monarch || an accepted method of behavior or procedure, *rules of conduct, the rules of arithmetic* || something which prevails generally or occurs normally, *after a victory, free drinks are the rule* || a code of regulations setting forth the discipline under which members of a religious order live, *the Benedictine rule* || (*pl.*) the body of official regulations setting forth the method of play in a sport, or the method of procedure in some other group activity || (*law*) a regulation governing court procedure || a ruler (strip of wood etc.) || (*printing*) a thin metal strip used for making ornamental borders, separating headings etc. **as a rule** usually **to work to rule** (*Br.*, of organized labor) to obey in detail all the rules laid down, e.g. on safety, as a method of slowing production and so bringing force to bear on an employer [O.F. *riule, rule*]

rule *pres. part.* **rul·ing** *past* and *past part.* **ruled** *v.t.* to exercise authority or dominion over, *to rule a country* || to exercise power over, esp. in enforcing obedience to one's own ideas of what is desirable, *to rule a household, to rule one's life with austerity* || to decide or decree with authority || to mark with straight lines, *ruled paper* || to draw (a line) with a ruler || *v.i.* to exercise authority or power || to be the governing condition, *silence ruled in the assembly* || (of prices) to be prevalent || to decide a point of law or lay down a formal ruling **to rule (something) out** to exclude (something) from further consideration [O.F. *riuler, ruler*]

rule·mon·ger (rú:lmʌ̀ŋgər) *n.* a strict constructionist and strong enforcer of written rules, esp. in an authoritarian regime

rule-of-rum·mage (rú:ləvrʌ́midʒ) *n.* Supreme Court decision permitting police with warrants to search newspaper offices, etc., for informa-

rule of the road the rules governing vehicles or ships in their movements

rule of three a rule for finding the fourth term of a proportion where only three are given. The rule states that the product of the means equals the product of the extremes

rule of thumb a rough guide or principle, adequate working method

ru·ler (rú:lər) *n.* a sovereign || someone who commands or dominates || a strip of wood, metal etc., marked off in inches or centimeters, used in drawing straight lines, measuring etc.

ru·ling (rú:liŋ) **1.** *adj.* exercising sovereignty || predominant, controlling, *a ruling passion* **2.** *n.* the act of someone who rules || the drawing of a line or lines || the line or lines drawn || an authoritative decision, esp. (*law*) a decision of a judge or court

ru·ly English (rú:li:) English language adapted so that each word has a single meaning and each meaning a single word, utilized with a set of ambiguity-avoiding rules, esp. for patents, computer commands

rum (rʌm) *n.* an alcoholic liquor prepared by fermenting molasses, sugarcane etc. and distilling it. It is produced mainly in the West Indies [etym. doubtful]

rum *comp.* **rum·mer** *superl.* **rum·mest** *adj.* (*Br.*, *pop.*) odd, queer [etym. doubtful]

Ru·ma·nian, Rou·ma·nian (ru:méinjən, ru:méini:ən) **1.** *n.* the Romance language of Rumania || a native or inhabitant of Rumania **2.** *adj.* of or pertaining to Rumania, Rumanians or the Rumanian language

Ru·ma·ni·a, Rou·ma·nia (ru:méinjə, ru:méini:ə) a republic (area 91,671 sq. miles, pop. 22,510,000) in S.E. Europe. Capital: Bucharest. People and languages: 86% Rumanian, 9% Magyar, 2% German, Ukrainian, Gypsy, Yugoslav, Russian and other minorities. Religion: 80% Orthodox, 6% Roman Catholic, 5% Calvinist, 2% Lutheran, small Jewish, Moslem and Protestant minorities. The land is 44% arable, 17% pasture and 27% forest (mainly evergreen). The E. Carpathians (Pietros, 7,568 ft) and the Transylvanian Alps (Negoi, 8,346 ft) cross the country diagonally from north and south meeting in the east center. With the Bihor massif (6,000 ft) in the west they enclose the cultivated Transylvanian plateau (1,000-1,600 ft). The mountains are surrounded northwest, west, south, and east, by the Hungarian, Banat, Walachian and Moldavian plains. The Black Sea coast (Dobruja) is flat. The Danube, cutting through the Transylvanian Alps at the Iron Gate, forms most of the southern border. Average temperatures (F.): Bucharest 9° (Jan.) and 72° (July). Rainfall: 10-20 ins in Dobruja, Moldavia and Walachia, 20-30 ins in the west and the central basin, 30-60 ins in the mountains. Livestock: cattle, sheep, hogs, poultry, horses. Agricultural products: cereals, potatoes, root vegetables, tobacco, grapes, plums and other fruit. Fishing is important in the Danube delta and the Black Sea. Mineral resources: oil (esp. Ploesti), coal, natural gas, salt, iron ore, lignite, copper, bauxite, chromium, other metals. Other resources: timber, hydroelectricity. Manufactures and industries: iron and steel, mining, machinery, oil refining, shipbuilding, chemicals, paper, cement, sugar, edible oils, textiles, light manufactures, electrical equipment, vehicles. Exports: oil, cement, lumber, tractors, machinery, ships, oilfield and factory equipment, corn, foodstuffs. Imports: iron ore, metals, industrial plant, coke, electric cables, diesel engines. Chief ports: Constanta, Galati. Universities: Iasi (1860), Bucharest (1864), Cluj (1872), Timisoara (1945). Monetary unit: leu (100 bani). HISTORY. The region formed the Roman province of Dacia (2nd-3rd cc.), was invaded by Visigoths, Huns, Lombards and Avars (4th-5th cc.) and was settled by Slavs (6th c.) and Bulgarians (7th c.). It became divided (late 13th c.) into the principalities of Moldavia and Walachia, which became vassals of the Ottoman Empire (15th and 16th cc.), were briefly united (early 17th c.) and were involved in the Russo-Turkish Wars. Revolutions were put down (1821) by the Turks and the principalities were occupied (1829-34) by the Russians after the Treaty of Adrianople. More revolutions failed (1848) and the principalities were jointly occupied by the Turks and the Russians. Conflicts over navigation rights on the Danube were a cause of the Crimean War. Moldavia and Walachia formed a personal union (1859) and were officially united as Rumania (1861). Un-

der Carol I constitutional and economic progress was made and, after the Congress of Berlin (1878), the country became an independent kingdom (1881). Rumania gained S. Dobruja after the 2nd Balkan War (1913) and joined the Allies (1916) in the 1st world war, after which it received Transylvania, Bukovina, Banat and Bessarabia. Agrarian reforms broke up most of the large estates, but political chaos weakened the country. Carol II established (1930) a fascist dictatorship, but was deposed (1940) and Antonescu became dictator, supporting the Axis in the 2nd world war. King Michael overthrew Antonescu (1944) and formed an alliance with the Allies. Communists gained a majority (1946), Michael abdicated (1947) and Rumania became a people's republic. It joined the U.N. and the Warsaw Pact (1955); it is also a member of COMECON. It became a socialist republic (1965) but maintains a foreign policy independent of the Soviet Union

rum·ba, rhum·ba (rʌ́mbə, rúmbə) *n.* an Afro-Cuban dance || a ballroom version of this || the music for this dance [Span.]

rum·ble (rʌ́mb'l) **1.** *v. pres. part.* **rum·bling** *past* and *past part.* **rum·bled** *v.i.* to make a dull, rolling sound, *the thunder rumbled in the distance* || to move with such a sound, *the cart rumbled slowly down the street* || *v.t.* to utter in a deep, gruff voice, *to rumble a reply* || to polish (small metal parts) in a tumbling box **2.** *n.* a rumbling sound || a tumbling box [imit.]

rumble seat (*Am.=Br.* dickey) an open-air seat at the back of some automobiles

rum·bus·tious (rʌmbʌ́stʃəs) *adj.* (*pop.*) rambunctious [fr. earlier *robustious*, robust]

Ru·me·lia (ru:mí:ljə, ru:mí:li:ə) a former region of the Ottoman Empire, comprising the provinces of Thrace and Macedonia. Eastern Rumelia was made an autonomous province (1878) and was annexed (1885) by Bulgaria

ru·men (rú:min) *pl.* **ru·mi·na** (rú:minə), **ru·mens** *n.* the first chamber of a ruminant's stomach [L.=throat]

Rum·ford (rʌ́mfərd), Benjamin Thompson, Count (1753-1814), American scientist who spent the major part of his life in England. He is known chiefly for his measurements on the production of heat by mechanical work

Ru·mi·ña·hui (ru:minjáwi:) (d. 1534), Inca cacique, adviser and general of Atahualpa, upon whose death he proclaimed himself sovereign. His stubborn resistance to the conquistadores ended in his execution

ru·mi·nant (rú:minənt) **1.** *n.* any member of the order *Artiodactyla*, suborder *Ruminantia*, e.g. the sheep, cow, camel, llama, goat, giraffe, deer. These animals are all even-toed and hoofed, and all chew the cud and have a stomach consisting of four chambers **2.** *adj.* of or relating to one of these animals || meditative [fr. L. *ruminans (ruminantis)* fr. *ruminare*, to ruminate]

ru·mi·nate (rú:mineit) *pres. part.* **ru·mi·nat·ing** *past* and *past part.* **ru·mi·nat·ed** *v.i.* to chew the cud || to reflect at length || *v.t.* to ponder over [fr. L. *ruminari (ruminatus)*]

ru·mi·na·tion (ru:minéiʃən) *n.* the act or process of ruminating [fr. L. *ruminatio (ruminationis)*]

ru·mi·na·tive (rú:mineitiv) *adj.* ruminating or apt to ruminate

rum·mage (rʌ́midʒ) **1.** *v. pres. part.* **rum·mag·ing** *past* and *past part.* **rum·maged** *v.i.* to make a search, esp. by turning things over or otherwise creating disorder, *to rummage in a drawer* || *v.t.* to search through (a place etc.) thoroughly, ransack **2.** *n.* things found or turned up by rummaging, odds and ends || a search made by rummaging [origin unknown]

rummage sale a sale of odds and ends, usually to raise money for charity

rum·mer (rʌ́mər) *n.* a large upright drinking vessel, esp. for wine [Du. *romer, roemer*]

rum·my (rʌ́mi:) *n.* a simple card game won by the first player to match all his cards into sets, sequences of three etc. by drawing cards from the stock and discarding others and declaring the sets he has made

ru·mor, *Br.* **ru·mour** (rú:mər) **1.** *n.* an unauthenticated story or report put into circulation, *an idle rumor* **2.** *v.t.* to spread or report by rumor [O.F.]

rump (rʌmp) *n.* the upper hindquarters of an animal || the posterior of a bird || a cut of beef between the loin and the round || the buttocks || a remnant, esp. of a parliament or other body [prob. of Scand. orig.]

rum·ple (rʌ́mp'l) 1. *v. pres. part.* **rum·pling** *past and past part.* **rum·pled** *v.t.* to make (hair, clothes etc.) disorderly, wrinkled etc. || *v.i.* to become wrinkled 2. *n.* a wrinkle in clothes etc. [fr. M. Du. *rompelen*]

Rump Parliament (*Eng. hist.*) the name given to the Long Parliament after Pride's Purge (1648) had reduced it to about 50 antiroyalists who ordered the execution (1649) of Charles I

rum·pus (rʌ́mpəs) *n.* (*pop.*) an uproar, disturbance, row [origin unknown]

run (rʌn) 1. *v. pres. part.* **run·ning** *past* **ran** (ræn) *past part.* **run** *v.i.* (of persons and animals) to move rapidly over the ground with long, usually even, strides in such a way that for a moment the feet are off the ground || to escape by moving in this way, *he grabbed the gun and ran* || to go rapidly, *run for the doctor* || to move about without restraint, *the lions ran loose in the streets* || to compete in a race || to finish a race in a specified place, *who ran third?* || to be a candidate in an election || (with 'up', 'down' etc.) to make a quick, casual trip, *to run up to London for a day* || to move on or as if on wheels || to move with a smooth, gliding motion, *the rope runs in the pulley* || to go regularly between two places, *the ferry runs every three hours* || to circulate, *rumors ran through the crowd* || to flow rapidly, *water ran down the pipe* || to melt and flow, *the ice cream is starting to run* || to be covered with a flow, *her eyes were running with tears, the gutters are running with water* || (of a sore etc.) to discharge pus etc. || (of the nose) to exude mucus || (esp. with 'through' or 'in') to force itself again and again into the conscious mind, *the song kept running through his head* || (of a theatrical production) to be presented, *the play ran for six months* || (of fish) to swim in migration || to be in operation, *the motor is still running* || (with 'by' or 'into') to elapse, *the years ran by, the weeks ran into months* || to be impelled, *the ship ran on a rock* || to continue in effect, *the contract has two more years to run* || to average a specified size, *trout are running large this year* || to be at a specified level or average, *casualties are running high, sales are running just above last year's figures* || (with 'in') to be a hereditary feature, *insanity runs in the family* || (of liquids, e.g. ink) to spread on being applied to a surface || (of colors in a fabric) to spread or become mixed together when washed or moistened || to extend in time, *the holiday ran into a third week* || to proceed, *the poem runs like this* || to merge, *the two towns run into one another* || to extend in a certain direction or course, *bookshelves run across the left side of the room, the road runs through mountains* || to proliferate unchecked, *dry rot ran all through the roof* || (of vines) to creep and climb || to pass lightly and rapidly, *fire ran through the stubble* || (with 'into') to pass into a specified situation, condition etc., *to run into trouble, to run into debt* || (of a stocking etc.) to develop a vertical flaw because of the breaking of a longitudinal thread || *v.t.* to cause to move, operate etc., *to run a tractor* || to cause (e.g. a vehicle) to go in a specified direction, *to run a car into a ditch* || to enter (a horse) in a race || to enter (someone) as a candidate in an election || to do by or as if by running, *to run a race, to run an errand* || to traverse by or as if by running, *he ran the full length of the room, let the situation run its course* || to roam about in, *to run the streets* || to hunt, *to run a fox to earth* || to smuggle || (with 'into' or 'through') to cause to pierce, *to run a needle into one's finger* || (with 'into' or 'against') to cause to be thrust, *to run one's head into a wall* || to force or contrive one's way through, or attempt to get through (a blockade etc.) || (of a newspaper) to publish (e.g. a story) || to cause (a liquid) to flow, *run the water into that ditch* || to manage or control, *to run a factory* || to cause to extend in a particular direction or manner, *run the rope between those two trees* || to cause to pass quickly over, along etc., *to run one's fingers over a shelf* || to cast (e.g. bullets) in a mold || to convey in a ship or vehicle || to bring to a specific state by or as if by running, *to run oneself to death, to run someone into debt* || to sew with rapid stitches, *run a hem around the cuff* || to have (an account) which is allowed to accumulate for a certain length of time **to run across** to meet by chance **to run after** to chase, *to run after a thief* || (*pop.*) to pursue amorously, *to run after girls* **to run around** to go out a great deal, esp. in pursuit of pleasures, esp. through casual sexual adventures **to run a temperature** to have a fever **to run away** to

flee || to elope || (esp. of children) to leave home without parental consent || (esp. of a horse being driven or ridden) to get completely out of control **to run away with** to take over emotional control of, *his temper ran away with him* **to run down** (of a clock) to become in need of winding || to run against and knock down || (*pop.*) to disparage or abuse || (*baseball*) to tag out (a base runner) between bases **to run dry** to become empty of water or other liquid || to cease to have ideas, inspiration etc. **to run foul of** to come into conflict with, *to run foul of the law* **to run free** (*naut.*) to sail with the wind coming from behind the beam **to run in** (*pop.*) to arrest || to operate (new machinery, e.g. an automobile engine) over a specified period at restricted speed so as to adjust bearing surfaces to one another || (*printing*) to run on || to pay a quick, usually casual, visit **to run into** to collide with || to meet by accident, *to run into an old classmate* || to amount to, *it ran into hundreds of dollars* **to run low** to become depleted or scarce, *money was running low* **to run off** to print (an edition or specified number of copies) || to cause (a race) to be run || to flee, *he snatched the package and ran off* **to run on** to continue || to talk continuously || (*printing*) to set (typeset matter) on the same line as what precedes **to run out** to come to an end, *his patience has run out* || to cause to leave by force || (*cricket*) to put (a batsman) out while he is running between the wickets || (*cricket, of a batsman*) to leave the crease and go up the pitch to hit a ball being bowled **to run out of** to come to the end of, esp. prematurely **to run out on** (*pop.*) to desert, leave, forsake, *to run out on one's wife* **to run over** to drive or ride over, *to run over a dog* || to flow over the edge of || to make a rapid review of, *to run over some notes* || to flow over the edge of a container **to run short** to begin to cease to be plentiful || to be left with less than enough **to run short of** to come to have less than enough of **to run (some-one) ragged** to exhaust (someone) physically **to run through** to transpierce || to spend quickly and completely, *to run through a fortune* || to examine rapidly, *to run through the accounts* || to rehearse (e.g. a play) without pausing **to run to** (*Br.*) to be sufficient for, *his income won't run to two holidays a year* || (*Br.*) to be able to afford, *we can't run to a new car this year* **to run up** to make rapidly (by sewing), *to run up a skirt in an afternoon* || to add (figures) rapidly || to construct hastily, *to run up a shed in the garden* || to accumulate, *his debts ran up over the years* **to run wild** to run riot || to grow in disorderly confusion, *roses running wild* 2. *n.* an act or period of running || the distance covered in running || the time spent in running || (of a theatrical production) a continuous succession of performances || a prolonged period of being in a specified condition, *a run of good luck* || a continuous series or sequence of similar or identical things, *a run of misprints* || a mass withdrawal of funds by depositors, usually provoked by panic, *a run on a bank* || an abnormally high demand from buyers for some article or class of articles, *a run on sugar* || a kind or class, e.g. of goods, *the ordinary run of ski boots* || the average or usual level of people or things, *he is above the run of politicians* || (with 'the') unrestricted access to a place, *he gave them the run of the library* || a track used habitually by animals, *a rat run* || an enclosure for livestock large enough for them to exercise in || a number of fish migrating together || a vertical flaw in a stocking caused by the breaking of a longitudinal thread || a short, usually quick, journey || the regularly traveled route or course covered by a train, ship etc. || the distance covered in a period of sailing etc. || general tendency, *the run of the market* || general direction, *the run of the streets is away from the river* || a rush of tidal water || a small stream || the period in which a machine is in operation || an amount of work turned out in one operation || (*printing*) an edition size, *a run of 20,000 copies* || (*baseball*) the point scored by a player in completing a circuit of the bases || (*cricket*) the point scored by a batsman in moving without penalty from one popping crease to the other || (*mil.*) the part of a bombing sortie during which the bomber approaches the target and releases its bombs || (*naut.*) the bottom of a ship where it rises from the keel and bilge, narrowing in to the stern || (*mining*) a sudden fall of a mass of earth || (*mining*) an inclined passage between levels || a downward course, e.g. for skiing || a track, course, channel etc. on or along which something moves || the bower of a bower-

bird **in the long run** measured over a prolonged period of time **on the run** retreating in disorderly haste || trying to escape capture, e.g. by police [partly fr. O.E. *rinnan*, partly fr. O.N. *rinna, renna*]

run·a·bout (rʌ́nəbaut) *n.* a small, easily parked, economical automobile used for short journeys, shopping expeditions etc. || a small motorboat used for pleasure trips || a person who goes out a great deal in pursuit of pleasure, esp. through casual sexual adventures

run·a·way (rʌ́nəwei) 1. *n.* a fugitive || a horse running out of control || a runaway race, victory etc. 2. *adj.* escaping || (of a marriage) achieved by eloping || (of a race, victory etc.) easily won || (of prices etc.) rising very rapidly

runaway shop business that relocates in a distant area to avoid labor difficulties, esp. with unions

run·ci·nate (rʌ́nsinit, rʌ́nsineit) *adj.* (of leaves) pinnate with their other divisions pointing towards the base (e.g. in the dandelion) [fr. L. *runcina*, a plane]

run-down (rʌ́ndaun) *adj.* in poor health || exhausted || dilapidated || (of clocks) stopped because not wound **run-down** (rʌ́ndaun) *n.* a summary || (*baseball*) the act of running down a base runner

Rund·stedt (rúntʃtet), Karl Rudolf Gerd von (1875-1953), German field marshal. He commanded a group of armies in Poland, France and Russia (1939-41). In command of the German western front (1942-4), he was the effective military ruler of France. His Ardennes counteroffensive (Dec. 1944) failed

rune (ruːn) one of the characters of an ancient alphabet used for making inscriptions and magic signs by the Germanic peoples, esp. the Scandinavians and Anglo-Saxons. The characters were supposedly formed by adapting Greek or Roman letters for carving on wood || a Finnish poem or a division of one || an ancient Norse poem [O.N. *rún*]

rung (rʌŋ) *n.* a crosspiece in a ladder || a bar joining the legs of a chair || a spoke in a wheel [O.E. *hrung*]

rung *past part.* of RING

ru·nic (rúːnik) *adj.* of or relating to a rune or runes || consisting of runes, *runic poetry* [fr. Mod. L. *runicus* fr. O.N. *rún*, a rune]

run-in (rʌ́nin) *n.* (*pop.*) a minor altercation, *a run-in with the milkman* || (*printing*) an additional insertion in copy or typeset material

run·let (rʌ́nlit) *n.* a small stream

run·nel (rʌ́n'l) *n.* a small channel || a small stream [O.E. *rynel*]

run·ner (rʌ́nər) *n.* a person who or animal which runs, esp. in a race || a person who runs errands, esp. for a brokerage house || a smuggler || a ship carrying smuggled goods || (*bot.*) a stolon || (*bot.*) a plant that creeps by means of these || (loosely) any of various twining plants || the blade of an ice skate || a decorative strip of cloth, lace etc. to be laid on a table, dresser etc. || a long strip or carpet for a corridor, staircase etc. || either of the pieces on which a sled or sledge slides || (*naut.*) a rope with a hook at one end rove through a single block and run around a tackle block || a groove along which something (e.g. a drawer) slides || a roller for moving a heavy object || (*metall.*) the trough through which molten metal flows on its way to the mold || a run in a stocking || the water rail || the revolving stone of a pair of millstones [M.E. *rennere* fr. *rennen*, to run]

runner bean (*Br.*) a string bean

run·ner-up (rʌ́nərʌp) *pl.* **run·ners-up** *n.* a competitor or team coming second in a contest etc.

run·ning (rʌ́niŋ) 1. *n.* the act of a person or thing that runs **in (out of) the running** having a good chance (no chance) of winning a competition 2. *adj.* moving at a run || done while running, *a running fight* || performed with a run, *a running play* || uninterrupted, *running fire* || flowing, *running water* || sliding, able to slip, *a running knot* || (of machines) operating || discharging pus, *a running sore* || measured in a straight line, *per running foot* 3. *adv.* successively, *three months running*

running board a footboard on either side of a vehicle

running commentary a verbal (esp. broadcast) description of the events of a game etc. as they occur

running dog lackey; collaborator

---

running fix (*mil.*) the intersection of two or more position lines, not obtained simultaneously, adjusted to a common time

running head a running title

running mate a horse entered in a race to set the pace for another expected to win || a candidate competing for a subordinate place, esp. the office of vice-president

running title a short heading or title printed at the top of each text page or at the top of each left-hand text page

Run·ny·mede (rʌ́nimiːd) a meadow on the south bank of the Thames, three miles downstream from Windsor, where Magna Carta was signed (1215)

run·off (rʌ́nɔf, rʌ́nɒf) *n*. a final contest, made necessary because a previous contest was drawn or without a result || water drained from surface soil

run-of-the-mill (rʌ́nəvðəmíl) *adj*. not outstanding in quality, ordinary, *a run-of-the-mill group of students*

run·on (rʌ́nɔn, rʌ́nɒn) *adj*. (*printing*) immediately appended without any break || (*poetry*) continuing without pause from one line into the next

runt (rʌnt) (*Br.*) an ox or cow of a small breed || any small animal, esp. the smallest in a litter of pigs || (*pop.*, used disparagingly) an undersized person [etym. doubtful]

run·up (rʌ́nʌp) *n*. (*Br.*) prelude

run-up area (*mil.*) a zone within the maneuvering area reserved for testing aircraft engines prior to take-off

run·way (rʌ́nwei) *n*. a strip on an airfield for taking off or landing || a gangway || a slope down which logs are slid || the trail made by animals in going to and from their regular feeding places ||an enclosed area in which chickens etc. are kept

Run·yon (rʌ́njən), (Alfred) Damon (1884-1946), U.S. writer of humorous short stories, notably 'Guys and Dolls' (1931), 'Blue Plate Special' (1934), and 'Money from Home' (1935), which portray underworld characters in New York City

ru·pee (ruːpíː, rúːpiː) *n*. the monetary unit of India, Pakistan, Ceylon and Nepal || the monetary unit of Mauritius, Seychelles and some areas of the Arabian peninsula || a coin worth one rupee [fr. Urdu *rūpiyah*]

Ru·pert (rúːpərt), Prince (1619-82), count palatine of the Rhine, duke of Bavaria, nephew of Charles I of England. He distinguished himself as a royalist cavalry leader in the English Civil War and, later, as an admiral in the Dutch Wars

ru·pi·ah (ruːpíːə) *pl.* **ru·pi·ah, ru·pi·ahs** *n*. the basic monetary unit of Indonesia || a note worth one rupiah [Hindi *rūpaiyā*, rupee]

rup·ture (rʌ́ptʃər) 1. *n*. a drastic break in harmonious relations between individuals or nations || a hernia || the tearing apart of a muscle or other bodily part || a breaking apart || the state of being broken apart 2. *v. pres. part.* **rup·tur·ing** *past and past part.* **rup·tured** *v.t.* to cause a break in || to cause a hernia in || *v.i.* to suffer a rupture [F.]

rupture zone (*mil.*) the region immediately adjacent to the crater boundary after an explosion characterized by the appearance of numerous radial cracks of various sizes. *Cf* PLASTIC ZONE

RUR-5A *ANTISUBMARINE ROCKET

ru·ral (rúərəl) *adj*. of, relating to, or characteristic of the country or of people living in the country (opp. URBAN) [F. or fr. L. *ruralis*]

rural dean a clergyman ranking below an archdeacon and responsible for a district containing a number of rural parishes

rural free delivery (*abbr*. R.F.D., R.D.) the free delivery, by postal employees, of mail in rural areas

ru·ri·de·ca·nal (ruəridikéin'l, ruəridékan'l) *adj*. of or relating to a rural dean or rural deanery [fr. L. *rus* (*ruris*), country+DECANAL]

Ru·rik (rúərik) (*d.* 879), Varangian chief. He established control over Novgorod (*c.* 862). His descendants ruled Russia until 1598

Ru·ri·ta·nian (ruəritéinjən, ruəritéiniːən) *adj*. of or like the imaginary European kingdom of Ruritania, where all is romantic gaiety and adventure, court intrigue and royal splendor [after the setting of two novels by Anthony Hope (Sir Anthony Hope Hawkins, 1863-1933), Eng. novelist]

rurp (*acronym*) for released ultimate reality piton, a sharp, pointed tool, used in mountaineering

Ru·se (rúːsei) (formerly Ruschuk) the chief inland port (pop. 170,594) of Bulgaria, on the Danube

ruse (ruːz) *n*. a piece of cunning, *a ruse to escape taxation* || cunning, *ruse and influence got him the appointment* [F.]

Rush (rʌʃ), Benjamin (1745-1813), U.S. physician. He became (1769) the first professor of chemistry in the U.S.A., at what became the University of Pennsylvania, where he introduced clinical instruction. He pioneered in the treatment and care of mental patients, and his 'Medical Inquiries and Observations Upon the Diseases of the Mind' (1812) was the first systematic U.S. work on the subject

Rush, Richard (1780-1859), U.S. statesman and diplomat, son of Benjamin Rush. Attorney general (1814-17) under President James Madison, and temporary secretary of state (1817), he negotiated with Charles Bagot the Rush-Bagot Treaty providing for the demilitarization of the Great Lakes. As minister to Great Britain (1817-25), he negotiated the Convention of 1818. He helped to found (1836) the Smithsonian Institution

rush (rʌʃ) 1. *v.i.* to move with speed and violence, *the boys rushed down the corridor* || to hasten, *he rushed to help her* || to appear or seem to appear swiftly, *tears rushed to her eyes, the idea rushed into his mind* || to act swiftly with too little reflection, *don't rush into divorce* || *v.t.* to cause to move or be moved with great speed, *they rushed the child to the doctor* || to cause to decide or act hastily, *to rush someone into marriage* || to get past or over with violent movement, *they rushed the barrier* || to take by sudden attack, *to rush an enemy position* || (*football*) to carry (the ball) forward in a running play || (*football*) to move in on (a player) in order to block a kick or pass || (*pop.*) to court (a girl) assiduously || to entertain (a prospective member of a sorority or fraternity) as a means of persuasion into membership **to rush at** to charge **to rush into print** to publish after too little work or experience **to rush someone off his feet** to make a person do too much in too short a time || to upset or try to upset a person's judgment by harrying him 2. *n*. a violent forward movement or the sound of it, *the rush of water* || a movement of many people to a place or region to be occupied or exploited, *a rush for the corner seats* || feverish movement, *the rush of city life* || a sudden burst of activity, *a rush of work* || the state of being busy and pressed for time, *she was always in a rush* || violent inflow, *a rush of blood to the head* || (of an emotion) a sudden access, *a rush of tenderness* || the first surge of pleasures produced by a drug || (with 'on') a great demand for a commodity || (*soccer*) a sudden attack by several players || (*football*) the act of carrying the ball during a game || (*movies*, esp. *pl.*) the first print of a sequence of filming, for inspection by the director etc. 3. *adj*. needing to be dealt with or done very quickly, *a rush order* || characterized by enormous bustle and activity, *the rush hour* [A.F. *russher*]

rush *n*. any of various members of *Juncus,* fam. *Juncaceae,* or *Scirpus,* fam. *Cyperaceae,* plants having cylindrical and often hollow stems which are used for making chair seats, mats, baskets etc. [O. E. *risc, risce*]

rush·light (rʌ́ʃlait) *n*. a rude candle made by dipping the peeled pith of various rushes in grease

Rush·more, Mount (rʌ́ʃmɔr, rʌ́ʃmʊər) a peak in the Black Hills of South Dakota which has 60-ft busts of Washington, Jefferson, Lincoln and Theodore Roosevelt carved in it by John Gutzon Borglum (1867-1941)

Rusk (rʌsk), (David) Dean (1909–), U.S. secretary of state (1961-8) under Presidents John Kennedy and Lyndon Johnson. He advocated negotiation with Communist powers from a position of national strength and more extensive aid to underdeveloped countries

rusk (rʌsk) *n*. a slice of crisp, twice-baked bread often sweetened [Span. *rosca,* a twisted roll of bread]

Rus·kin (rʌ́skin), John (1819-1900), English critic and essayist. He made his name as an art critic with the first part of 'Modern Painters' (1843), begun as a defense of Turner. Visits to Switzerland and Italy—esp. to Venice—led to 'The Seven Lamps of Architecture' (1849) and 'The Stones of Venice' (1851-3). 'Modern Painters' continued to appear until 1860. In 1853 Ruskin began his career as a lecturer, mainly on art but later also on economic, social and general cultural subjects. 'Sesame and Lilies' (1865) was the most popular collection. Later works include 'Fors Clavigera' (1871-84), a series of letters to the working men of England, and 'Praeterita' (1885-9), his autobiography. He was a profound critic of art, and his range was wide, though he had little sympathy for 'advanced' contemporary work. He was also a profound social critic, emphasizing the distinction between mere wealth and true social welfare, and between mechanical labor and craftsmanship. Like Dickens and Morris, he laid his finger on the defects of the new industrial society

Rus·sell (rʌ́s'l), Bertrand, 3rd Earl Russell (1872-1970), British philosopher. His 'Principles of Mathematics' (1903) led to 'Principia Mathematica' (1910-13, in collaboration with Whitehead), a research into symbolic logic. Other writings include 'An Outline of Philosophy' (1927) and 'Philosophy and Politics' (1947)

Russell, Henry Norris (1877-1957), U.S. astronomer. He invented (1913, with Ejnar Hertzsprung of Denmark) the Russell diagram, which determined the distances from the solar system of double stars which are telescopically observed to be in revolution about their common center of gravity

Russell, Lord John, 1st Earl Russell (1792-1878), British Whig statesman. A liberal reformer, he supported the Catholic Emancipation Act (1829) and was largely responsible for the Reform Act of 1832. He brought in other reforms as home secretary (1835-9) and was prime minister (1846-52 and 1865-6)

Russell, Lord William (1639-83), English statesman. One of the leaders of the Whig campaign to exclude the future James II from the succession, he was unjustly executed for alleged complicity in the Rye House Plot

rus·set (rʌ́sit) 1. *n*. a color between red and brown || a variety of rough-skinned russet-colored eating apple || (*hist.*) coarse homespun cloth worn by peasants 2. *adj*. reddish-brown [O.F. *rousset*]

Rus·sia (rʌ́ʃə) a former country of E. Europe and Asia which developed out of the grand duchy of Moscow, and which became (1917) the Union of Soviet Socialist Republics. The name is loosely used for the U.S.S.R., but is properly applied only to the R.S.F.S.R., esp. the European part. HISTORY. The Scythians, inhabiting the steppes from before the 7th c. B.C., were displaced (3rd c. B.C.) by the Sarmatians. The steppes were successively invaded by the Goths (3rd c. A.D.), the Huns (4th c.) and the Avars (6th c.). The Khazars established an empire in the southeast (7th–early 11th cc.) and the Bulgars founded a state (8th-13th cc.) in the region of the Volga. The Eastern Slavs settled in the Ukraine (c. 9th c.). A Russian state originated in the conquests (9th c.) of the Varangians, Viking warriors who established their capital at Kiev. Greek Orthodox Christianity became the official religion (c. 988). Trade with Scandinavia, Byzantium and the Middle East prospered but, after the attacks of the Cumans (11th c.), Kiev declined (12th c.). Russia was overrun (1237-40) by the Golden Horde and under the rule of the Tatars Moscow emerged as the dominant principality (14th c.). During the reign (1462-1505) of Ivan III, Novgorod and much of N. Russia were conquered, and Moscow asserted its independence against the Tatars (1480). Ivan IV's reign (1533-84) brought conquests in the lower Volga, extending Muscovite territory south to the Caspian. Ivan took the title of czar, established an autocracy, and did much to reduce the power of the boyars. Boris Godunov seized power on the death (1598) of Ivan's weak-minded son, and faced the opposition of the boyars and the Cossacks, and the threat of pretenders to the throne. Disorder followed Godunov's death (1605) and Sigismund III of Poland, in alliance with the boyars and the Cossacks, occupied Moscow (1610-12). After a national uprising (1612), Michael Romanov was elected czar (1613). Order was restored but, despite the growth of trade with the West, Moscow remained largely isolated from Europe. Colonization began to spread toward the Pacific. The nobles' rights over the serfs were increased, until serfdom was little better than slavery (17th c.). Rule of the czars became even more absolute. Peter I, who had traveled widely in Europe, began to westernize and modernize the country during his reign (1689-

1725). The army was reorganized and a navy founded. The Church was made subject to the State, and the capital was moved from Moscow to St Petersburg (1713). The upper classes were forced to adopt Western clothes, and educational institutions were founded on Western lines. The Northern War (1700-21) resulted in the acquisition of Livonia and other Baltic territories. The Russo-Turkish Wars enabled Russia to expand toward the Balkans. After Peter's death (1725), Russian participation in European affairs continued to increase. Russia supported Austria in the War of the Polish Succession (1733-5) and, under Elizabeth, fought Prussia in the Seven Years' War (1756-63). During the reign (1762-96) of Catherine II, Russia became a leading European power, gaining vast territories in the partitions of Poland (1772, 1793, 1795), by the Treaty of Kuchuk Kainarji (1774), and by the annexation of the Crimea (1783). After a rising of Cossacks and serfs (1773), the central autocracy was strengthened. Under the influence of the French Enlightenment, literature and the arts flourished. Catherine's son and successor, the mentally unstable Paul I, was assassinated (1801), and succeeded by Alexander I. Russia opposed France in the Napoleonic Wars, but was forced to make peace at Tilsit (1807). Russian territory expanded with the acquisition of Finland (1809), Bessarabia (1812) and Caucasia (1813). Russian reluctance to adhere to the Continental System led to an unsuccessful Napoleonic invasion (1812). Russia took a leading part in the Congress of Vienna (1814-15) and in the establishment of the reactionary Holy Alliance (1815). On Alexander's death (1825), the liberal Decembrist movement failed in its attempt to prevent his brother Nicholas I from succeeding to the throne, and a period of repression began. Russian troops put down risings in Poland (1830-1) and revolution in Hungary (1848-9), but Russia's attempt to extend its influence toward Constantinople met with a severe defeat in the Crimean War (1853-6). This was followed by a period of liberal reform during the reign (1855-81) of Alexander II. The serfs were emancipated (1861), but agrarian conditions failed to improve. The courts were reformed, and a limited form of self-government was provided by the introduction of zemstvos (1864). Under Gorchakov, Russia's foreign policy concentrated on expansion into Caucasia and central Asia, but renewed attempts to expand at the expense of Turkey were crushed at the Congress of Berlin (1878). The late 19th c. saw rapid industrial progress as the construction of railroads enabled Russia's vast resources to be brought into use. Siberia was opened up by the Trans-Siberian Railroad, begun in 1891. A Populist conspiracy resulted in the assassination (1881) of Alexander II, but his successor, Alexander III, proved more reactionary. Increasing rivalry led to the Russo-Japanese War (1904-5). Marxist doctrines spread among the small but rapidly growing urban proletariat, and a revolution broke out (1905) in St Petersburg, spreading to the Black Sea fleet. It was followed by a series of strikes and peasant riots, and by the formation of soviets. Police repression included pogroms of the Jews. The czar granted a measure of parliamentary government by creating a duma, but its meetings were dissolved when it opposed the regime. Stolypin brought in belated agrarian reforms to distribute land to the peasants. Russia allied with France and Britain in the Triple Entente. Russian support of Pan-Slavism contributed to the outbreak of the 1st world war, which Russia entered very ill-prepared. Its first offensive against the Germans was halted at Tannenberg (Aug. 1914) and a series of reverses followed, with heavy casualties. Popular feeling turned against Nicholas II and his court. A revolution took place in Petrograd and spread throughout the country (Feb. 1917), the duma assumed real power, and the czar was forced to abdicate (Mar. 15, 1917). A provisional government was organized under the leadership (July-Nov. 1917) of Kerenski. This was overthrown (Nov. 7, 1917) by the Bolsheviks, led by Lenin, who had been allowed to return to Russia by the German government. The dictatorship of the proletariat was announced, and Russia went out of the 1st world war under the humiliating terms of the Treaty of Brest-Litovsk (1918). (For subsequent history *UNION OF SOVIET SOCIALIST REPUBLICS)

Russia leather a hard-wearing leather used esp. for bookbinding and made by tanning skins of various kinds with the barks of birch, willow or oak and then soaking them in birch-tar oil to protect them against insects

Rus·sian (rʌʃən) 1. *adj.* of or relating to Russia, its inhabitants, language, customs etc. 2. *n.* a native or inhabitant of Russia || a member of the Slavic-speaking Great Russian ethnic group || the official language of the U.S.S.R.

Russian Orthodox Church the largest of the Orthodox Eastern Churches. It dates officially from the baptism in 988 of Vladimir, grand duke of Kiev. Its life from 1051-1240 was centered in the monastic stronghold of Kiev. After the fall of Constantinople (1453), the patriarchate of Moscow assumed the leadership of Orthodoxy. Peter I abolished the patriarchate (1721) and put the Church under State control. It thus became associated with czarism, to its cost in the Communist revolution. But thanks to its patriotic action during the 2nd world war the patriarchate was restored (1943)

Russian Soviet Federal Socialist Republic (*abbr.* R.S.F.S.R.) the chief constituent republic (area 6,500,000 sq. miles, pop. 137,552,000) of the U.S.S.R. Capital: Moscow. The Urals divide the European R.S.F.S.R., or European Russia (pop. 100,000,000), from Siberia, the Asian section (area approx. 4,887,000 sq. miles), whose native Finnic, Turkic and Mongol tribal peoples are outnumbered by Russian and Ukrainian settlers. The western half of the republic, comprising the rolling plain of the European R.S.F.S.R. (drained by the Volga and Pechora systems) and the flat plain of W. Siberia (drained by the Ob), rises above 1,000 ft only in the Kola Peninsula, the Caucasus and the Urals. The north is tundra and forest (mixed evergreen and deciduous), the center (the 'Black Earth' region) and south are steppe, largely cultivated. Central (or Eastern) Siberia, between the Yenisei and the lower Lena and Amur, is a plateau (1,000–3,000 ft), largely evergreen forest, with tundra in the north and scattered steppe lands in the south. The Pacific coast region (or Far East) is mountainous (few peaks over 7,000 ft), with tundra covering half the country in the east. The center and south are heavily forested. Climate: *U.S.S.R. Crops: (European R.S.F.S.R. and W. Siberia) cereals, flax, root vegetables, hemp, sunflower seed, (central Siberia) cereals, (Pacific region, south of the Amur) cereals, incl. rice, soybeans, kaoliang. Livestock: dairy and beef cattle (mainly European R.S.F.S.R.), sheep, reindeer. Resources (fully exploited only in European R.S.F.S.R. and W. Siberia): coal (esp. Kuznetsk Basin), iron (esp. E. Volga basin and Urals), oil (esp. E. Volga basin and Urals, N. Caucasia, E. Siberia), lead, zinc, tin, tungsten, salt, gold and most other known minerals, fish, furs. timber, hydroelectricity. The R.S.F.S.R. contains two thirds of Soviet industry (expanding in Siberia as hydroelectricity is developed). Main industries: chemicals, building materials, iron and steel, oil refining, mechanical and aeronautical engineering. Industrial centers: Moscow, Leningrad, Volga basin, Urals, Novosibirsk, Omsk, Novokuznetsk, Krasnoyarsk, Irkutsk, Khabarovsk, Vladivostok. Ports: Leningrad, Vladivostok

Russian wolfhound a dog of a tall (28 to 31 ins), long-haired, long-legged breed of Russian origin, originally bred for coursing wolves

Rus·si·fi·ca·tion (rʌsəfikéiʃən) *n.* practice of requiring study of Russian language and culture by all ethnic groups in the U.S.S.R.

Rus·so-Jap·an·ese War (rʌsoudʒæpəni:z, rʌsoudʒæpəni:s) a war fought (1904-5) between Russia and Japan over a conflict of interests in Manchuria and Korea. Rapid Japanese victories gave Japan control of Manchuria and Korea, and established her as a world power. Russia's loss of prestige was a chief cause of the Russian revolution of 1905

Rus·so·phil (rʌ́səfil) *n.* a Russophile

Rus·so·phile (rʌ́səfail) *n.* a person who admires Russia or Russian civilization

Rus·so·phobe (rʌ́səfoub) *n.* a person who dislikes Russia or Russian civilization

Rus·so-Tur·kish Wars (rʌ́soutə́:rkiʃ) a series of wars (17th-19th cc.) between Russia and Turkey, caused by Russia's desire to take advantage of Turkey's weakness and to expand toward the Black Sea and the Balkans. The main wars were those of 1677-81, 1686-1700, 1736-9, 1768-74 (settled by the Treaty of Ku-

chuk Kainarji), 1787-92, 1806-12, 1828-9 (settled by the Treaty of Adrianople), 1853-6 (the Crimean War) and 1877-8 (settled by the Treaty of San Stefano and the Congress of Berlin) (*EASTERN QUESTION)

rust (rʌst) 1. *n.* a hydrated oxide of iron, $Fe_2O_3 \cdot H_2O$, formed when iron is exposed to air and moisture || the reddish-brown color of this substance || a stain that looks like iron rust || any of several diseases of grasses and other plants caused by phycomycetes || the parasitic fungus producing rust 2. *v.i.* to become coated with, or converted into, rust || to deteriorate through lack of use || *v.t.* to cause to be coated with or converted into rust [O.E. *rūst*]

rus·tic (rʌ́stik) 1. *adj.* of, relating to, or characteristic of the country or countryside, *a rustic scene* || characteristic of the qualities ascribed to country life, country people etc., *rustic simplicity, rustic speech* || robust and simple in workmanship || made of untrimmed wood, *a rustic seat* || (*archit.*) with roughened surface or chamfered joints || (*rhet.*) rural 2. *n.* (*rhet.*) a person born and bred in the country and quite unsophisticated **rús·ti·cal·ly** *adv.* [fr. L. *rusticus*]

rus·ti·cate (rʌ́stikeit) *pres. part.* **rus·ti·cat·ing** *past* and *past part.* **rus·ti·cat·ed** *v.i.* (*rhet.*) to retire to live in the country || *v.t.* (*Br.*) to suspend for a time from a university or college as punishment || (*archit.*) to produce a rustic effect by roughening the surface or sinking the joints of (stone) **rus·ti·ca·tion** *n.* [fr. L. *rusticari* (*rusticatus*), to live in the country]

rus·tic·i·ty (rʌstísiti:) *n.* the state or quality of being rustic [fr. F. *rusticité* or L. *rusticitas*]

rus·tle (rʌ́s'l) 1. *v. pres. part.* **rus·tling** *past* and *past part.* **rus·tled** *v.i.* to make light sounds like those of stirring leaves etc., *her dress rustled as she moved* || (*pop.*) to move busily and energetically || to steal cattle || *v.t.* to cause to make light sounds like those of stirring leaves, *he rustled his newspaper* || to get by making energetic efforts || to steal (cattle) **to rustle up** (*pop.*) to get together by or as if by foraging, *to rustle up a meal* 2. *n.* the sound made by something that rustles **rús·tler** *n.* a cattle thief [imit.]

rus·ty (rʌ́sti:) *comp.* **rus·ti·er** *superl.* **rus·ti·est** *adj.* coated with rust, *a rusty knife* || having the color of rust || deteriorated by disuse, *his French has grown rusty* || (of a voice) hoarse, esp. from old age || stiff from age or neglect || (of black clothes) discolored by age || out-of-date, behind the times

rut (rʌt) 1. *n.* a groove made by wheels in soft ground || a way of life so fixed in routine as to be dreary, *to get into a rut* 2. *v.t. pres. part.* **rut·ting** *past* and *past part.* **rut·ted** to make a rut or ruts in [etym. doubtful]

rut 1. *n.* the periodic sexual excitement of male deer and some other animals || (often with 'the') the period during which this occurs 2. *v.i. pres. part.* **rut·ting** *past* and *past part.* **rut·ted** to be affected with this [O.F.]

ru·ta·ba·ga (ru:təbéigə) *n.* (*Am.=Br.* swede) *Brassica napobrassica*, fam. *Cruciferae*, a turnip having a large yellowish root used as food by humans and livestock [Swed. dial. *rotabagge*]

Ru·te·beuf (rytəbə:f) 13th-c. French trouvère. He wrote fabliaux and satires, mainly in vigorous rhyming octosyllabics, and some plays

Rut·gers University (rʌ́tgərz) the State University of New Jersey, the eighth colonial college in British America, at New Brunswick, N. J. It was chartered (1776) by George III in response to a petition of the Dutch Reformed Church. It became a university in 1924

Ruth (ru:θ) a book of the Old Testament which tells the story of Ruth, a Moabite widow who accompanied her mother-in-law, Naomi, to Bethlehem and married Boaz, a Hebrew

Ruth (ru:θ), 'Babe' (George Herman Ruth, 1895-1948), the most popular baseball player in U.S. history and holder (1927) of the home-run record of 60 in a 154-game season

Ru·the·ni·a (ru:θí:ni:ə) a former region of E. Europe. It became a province of Czechoslovakia (1919) and part of the Ukraine (1945)

Ru·the·ni·an (ru:θí:ni:ən) *n.* a member of a people living in the former region of Ruthenia, now part of the Ukraine || the Ukrainian language, esp. as spoken in the former region of Ruthenia

ru·then·ic (ru:θí:nik, ru:θénik) *adj.* of or relating to ruthenium || derived from ruthenium

ru·the·ni·um (ru:θí:ni:əm) *n.* a rare metallic element of the platinum group (symbol Ru, at. no.

44, at. mass 101.07) [Mod. L. fr. *Ruthenia*, Russia]

Ruth·er·ford (rʌðərfərd), Ernest, Baron (1871-1937), British physicist, born in New Zealand. His major achievements included the identification of the alpha and beta particles and gamma rays formed in radioactive decay, the discovery of the atomic nucleus (1919) and the artificial transmutation of one element into another. Nobel prize in chemistry (1908)

ruth·er·ford·i·um (rʌðərfərdi:əm) *n.* element 104 as proposed to honor English physicist Lord Ernest Rutherford. *Cf* KURCHOTOVIUM

ruth·less (rú:θlis) *adj.* merciless, *a ruthless tyrant* [fr. older *ruth*, compassion]

ru·tile (rú:ti:l, rú:tail) a crystalline mineral, titanium dioxide, that is usually reddish-brown with a brilliant metallic luster ‖ a synthetic gem of the same composition as the mineral [F. or G. *rutil* fr. L.]

ru·tin (rú:t'n) *n.* a glycoside ($C_{27}H_{30}O_{16}$), found in buckwheat, tobacco leaves and other plants, used mainly for treating hypertension and radiation injuries [G. fr. L.]

Rut·land (rʌtlənd) a county (area 152 sq. miles, pop. 24,000) of England, in the E. Midlands. County town: Oakham

Rut·ledge (rʌtlidʒ), Ann (c. 1813-35), daughter of an innkeeper of New Salem, Illinois. Evidence for the story of Abraham Lincoln's romance with her is generally thought too slight to be taken seriously

Rutledge, John (1739-1800), U.S. political leader and jurist. He served (1776-8) as president and (1779-82) as the first governor of South Carolina. At the Constitutional Convention he championed slavery, the division of society into classes as a basis for representation, and the restriction of office-holders to those owning large property. Nominated (1795) chief justice of the Supreme Court, he failed to win confirmation by the Senate

rut·ty (rʌti:) *comp.* **rut·ti·er** *superl.* **rut·ti·est** *adj.* full of ruts

Ru·vu·ma (ru:vú:mə) a river (400 miles long) rising in S.W. Tanganyika, Tanzania, and flowing east, forming the border with Mozambique, to the Indian Ocean

Ru·wen·zo·ri (ru:wənzɔ́ri:, ru:wənzóuri:) a snow-capped massif on the border between Uganda and Zaïre. Highest peak: Mt Stanley, with two summits (16,750 ft and 16,791 ft)

Ruys·broeck (róisbryk), Jan Van (1293-1381), Flemish mystic. Among his best-known writings are 'The Seven Steps of the Ladder of Spiritual Love', 'The Adornment of the Spiritual Marriage', 'The Book of the Highest Truth', 'The Mirror of Blessedness'

Ruysdael *RUISDAEL

Ruy·ter (róitər), Michiel Adriaanszoon de (1607-76), Dutch admiral. He distinguished himself in the Dutch Wars, notably by leading a fleet up the Thames (1667)

RV (*abbr.*) **1.** reentry vehicle, i.e., from space **2.** recreational vehicle, e.g. a trailer

R-val·ue (ɔ́rvælju:) **1.** (*phys.*) unit of measure of resistance to heat flow **2.** (*nuclear phys.*) decrease in the density of reactor fuel for 1% burn-up. *Cf* S-VALUE

Rwan·da (ruɑ́ndə) (formerly Ruanda) a republic (area 10,169 sq. miles, pop. 5,111,000) in central Africa. Capital: Kigali. People: mainly Bahutu, with Watutsi and Batwa (pygmy) minorities. Languages: Kinyarawanda (Bantu) and French (both official), Swahili for trading. Religion: mainly local African and Roman Catholic, with a Moslem minority. The Nile-Congo dividing range (rising to 9,000 ft) and a volcanic chain (Karisimbi, 14,825 ft) rise sharply from the Great Rift Valley (Lake Kivu) in the west. The east (5,000–7,000 ft) is part of the E. African plateau. Little woodland remains. Average temperature (F.): 63°-80°. Rainfall: northeastern plateau 40 ins, Lake Kivu 70 ins. Main industries: subsistence agriculture (beans, palm products, peanuts, cassava, cereals), coffee growing, cattle raising, mining (cassiterite, tin, gold), hydroelectricity, brewing. Exports: coffee, cassiterite. University college at Butare (1963). Monetary unit: Rwanda-Burundi franc. Formerly part of Ruanda-Urundi, Rwanda became independent July 1, 1962. The Bahutu had risen against Watutsi domination (1959). They massacred several thousand (1964) and caused thousands of others to emigrate to neighboring countries. Habyarimana led a coup that put him in power July 5, 1973 and he has since been reelected to successive 5-year terms

ry·a (ráiə) *n.* **1.** a colorful, handwoven, flat pile Scandinavian rug with characteristic patterns **2.** a similarly made bed cover —**rya** *adj.* of the weave typical of the rug

Ry·a·zan (ri:əzǽn) a city (pop. 453,000) of the central European R.S.F.S.R., U.S.S.R.: mechanical engineering, food processing, shoes

Ry·binsk (ríbinsk) (called Shcherbakov 1946-57) an inland port (pop. 243,000) of the N. European R.S.F.S.R., U.S.S.R., on the Rybinsk Reservoir (formed by damming the upper Volga). Industries: engineering, shipbuilding, food processing, sawmilling

Ry·der (ráidər), Albert Pinkham (1847-1917), U.S. painter, best known for his moonlit landscapes, seascapes and allegorical scenes, notably 'Siegfried', 'The Race Track' and 'Toilers of the Sea'

rye (rai) *n. Secale cereale*, fam. *Gramineae*, a tall-growing cereal with dark-colored grain. It is cultivated mainly in N. Europe and North America ‖ its grain, used in making bread and for the distilling of rye whiskey, and fed to poultry and farm animals ‖ rye whiskey [O.E. *ryge*]

rye·grass (ráigræs, ráigrɒs) *n.* a member of *Lolium*, fam. *Gramineae*, a genus of European perennial grasses used for lawn grass, hay and pasture

Rye House Plot (*Eng. hist.*) an unsuccessful conspiracy (1683) to assassinate Charles II and his brother, the future James II. The Whig leaders Russell and Sidney were unjustly held responsible for the plot, and executed

ry·o·kan (ri:óukɑn) *n.* (*slang*) a traditional Japanese inn

Rys·brack (ráisbræk), John Michael (1693-1770), sculptor. He was Dutch by parentage but worked in England from 1720. His works include tombs in Westminster Abbey and of the Marlboroughs at Blenheim

Rys·wick, Treaty of (ráizwik) the treaty (1697) which ended the War of the Grand Alliance. Louis XIV lost most of his conquests and William III was recognized king of England. Spain acknowledged the French invasion of Hispaniola and ceded the western part of the island (Haiti) to France. England's promise to refrain from sacking Spanish towns put an end to buccaneering in the West Indies

Ry·u·kyu Islands (ri:ú:kju:) a volcanic archipelago (land area excluding islands included in Japan 848 sq. miles, pop. 1,118,000) in the N.W. Pacific, stretching 600 miles between Kyushu, Japan and Formosa. Chief town: Naha, on Okinawa. Language: Ryukyu (akin to Japanese). The larger of the several dozen islands are mountainous, the smaller are coral atolls. Climate: tropical, with typhoons. Products: fish, sugarcane, sweet potatoes, rice, pineapples, market produce. University at Shuri, Okinawa (1949). The islands were invaded (7th c.) by the Chinese. They were tributary to China (14th-17th cc.). Japan and China have disputed them since the 17th c. They were formally incorporated (1879) with Japan. They were placed (1945) under a U.S. military governor. The Japanese were given sovereignty (1951) over the islands, but the U.S.A. retained actual control. The islands were returned (by 1968) to Japan, with the exception of Okinawa, which the U.S.A. handed back in 1972, maintaining bases

---

	EARLY NORTH SEMITIC	PHOENICIAN	EARLY HEBREW (GEZER)	EARLY GREEK	CLASSICAL GREEK	ETRUSCAN Early / Classical	EARLY LATIN	CLASSICAL LATIN
S	≢ (s) / 〜(sh–s)	≢ (s) / W (sh–s)	≢ (s) / W W (sh — s)	∫	Σ	∫ / ∫	∫	S

CURSIVE MAJUSCULE (ROMAN)	CURSIVE MINUSCULE (ROMAN)	ANGLO-IRISH MAJUSCULE	CAROLINE MINUSCULE	VENETIAN MINUSCULE (ITALIC)	N. ITALIAN MINUSCULE (ROMAN)
∫	∨	S	S	δ	S

A. C. SYLVESTER, CAMBRIDGE, ENGLAND

Development of the letter S, beginning with the early North Semitic letter. Evolution of both the majuscule, or capital, letter S and the minuscule, or lowercase, letter s are shown.

S, s (es) the 19th letter of the English alphabet ‖ an object shaped like this letter

S, S. South, Southern

's (es *after a vowel and after most voiced consonant sounds,* z *after most unvoiced consonant sounds,* iz *after* s, ∫, t∫, z, ʒ, dʒ) possessive ending for singular nouns, *Brown's dog,* some pronouns, *anyone's,* noun word groups, *the man in the corner's hat,* and of plural nouns not ending in s, *the children's toys* [older *-es,* genitive sing. suffix of many masculine and feminine nouns and adjectives]

S (*abbr.*) for siemens, a unit of electrical conductance

Saa·le (zálə) a tributary (226 miles long, navigable for 100 miles) of the Elbe, flowing from the Thüringer Wald through Thuringia and Saxony-Anhalt, East Germany

Saar, the (zɑr, sɑr) the industrial region of Saarland

Saar·brück·en (zɑrbrýkən) the capital (pop. 198,900) of Saarland, West Germany, center of its coal basin: iron and steel

Saa·ri·nen (sárinən), Eero (1910-61), naturalized American architect, born in Finland. He experimented with modern materials and techniques, attempting to reconcile external forms of maximum simplicity and originality with complex functional requirements. Among his best-known works are General Motors Technical Center, Warren, Michigan (1951-5), Kresge Auditorium, Massachusetts Institute of Technology, Cambridge, Massachusetts (1955), and Trans World Airlines Terminal Building, Kennedy International Airport, New York City (1962)

Saar·land (zárlɑnt) a state (area 991 sq. miles, pop. 1,081,000) of West Germany in the southwestern hills bordering France (Lorraine), a great industrial region based on coal reserves. Industries: coal mining, iron and steel (using iron ore from Lorraine), engineering. Capital: Saarbrücken. It was formed (1919) from Bavarian and Prussian territories and put under League of Nations control, but reverted to Germany after a plebiscite (1935). Part of the French zone from 1945, it was attached economically to France (1948) but returned under Franco-German agreement to West Germany (1957)

Sa·a·ve·dra (sɑɑvéðrɑ), Cornelio de (1761–1829), Argentinian soldier. Following the declaration (1810) in Buenos Aires by a cabildo abierto that the viceroyalty was now vacant, he served as president of a junta acting in the name of the king

Saavedra La·mas (lámɑs), Carlos (1880-1959), Argentine lawyer, professor, diplomat, who received the 1936 Nobel peace prize. He is best known for his 'Por la Paz de las Américas' (1937)

Sa·ba (séibə) (*Bible* Sheba) an ancient country of S. Arabia, including modern Yemen and Hadhramaut (*SABAEAN)

Sa·ba (séibə, sɑ́bɑ) an island (area 5 sq. miles, pop. 1100) in the N.W. Leeward Is, part of the Netherlands Antilles. It is the cone (2,851 ft) of an extinct volcano

Sa·ba·dell (sɑbɑdél) a textile-manufacturing center (pop. 159,408) in Barcelona Province, Spain

Sa·bae·an, Sa·be·an (səbí:ən) 1. *adj.* of or relating to Saba, its people or its language 2. *n.* an inhabitant of Saba. The Sabaeans developed a flourishing kingdom (c. 930–c. 115 B.C.) and acquired great wealth from a monopoly of the spice trade through S. Arabia. Many inscriptions from the 7th c. B.C. in an alphabet resembling the Phoenician have been found ‖ the language of the Sabaeans

Sa·bah (sɑ́bɑ) (formerly North Borneo) a state (area 29,545 sq. miles, pop. 967,000, incl. adjacent islands) of Malaysia, occupying the northeast corner of Borneo. Capital: Kota Kinabalu. The population includes a large Chinese minority (23%). Languages: Malay, Chinese, English, Dusun. Religions: Animist, Moslem, with a 17% Christian minority. Highest point: Mt Kinabulu (13,455 ft). Exports: hardwoods, rubber, cutch, hemp, tobacco, fish. Other products: building materials. Imports: foodstuffs (incl. rice), machinery, textiles. Chief ports: Victoria (on Labuan Is.), Kota Kinabalu. HISTORY. Britain established trading links with the area (19th c.) and proclaimed it a protectorate as North Borneo (1888). Rubber cultivation was introduced (late 19th c.). North Borneo was occupied by the Japanese (1942-5), and became a British colony (1946). It became independent and, as Sabah, joined Malaysia (1963)

Sa·ba·tier (sæbætjei), Paul (1854-1941), French chemist known for his method of hydrogenating organic compounds. Nobel prize (1912)

sab·ba·tar·i·an (sæbətéəri:ən) 1. *adj.* of the sabbath or its observance ‖ of the doctrines of the sabbatarians 2. *n.* a Jew who observes Saturday as holy ‖ a Christian who keeps strict observance of Sunday as the holy day of the week **sab·ba·tár·i·an·ism** *n.* [L. *sabbatarius*]

sab·bath (sǽbəθ) *n.* the seventh day of the Jewish week (from sundown on Friday until sundown on Saturday), set apart by Moses (Exodus xx, 8–9) as a holy day of rest and worship commemorating the completion of the Creation (Genesis ii, 1–3) ‖ Sunday, the first day of the Christian week, set apart for worship in memory of Christ's resurrection ‖ a day of the week set apart regularly for worship in any of certain other religions, e.g. Friday in the Moslem week [fr. L. *sabbatum* fr. Gk fr. Heb.]

sab·bat·i·cal (səbǽtik'l) 1. *adj.* of, relating to or characteristic of the sabbath ‖ of an extended period of free time, esp. one available for special study given to teachers by some schools etc. 2. *n.* such an extended period

Sabean *SABAEAN

sa·ber, *Br.* **sa·bre** (séibər) 1. *n.* a heavy cavalry sword with a curved blade ‖ (*fencing*) a light weapon heavier than a foil 2. *v.t. pres. part.* **sa·ber·ing,** *Br.* **sa·bring** *past* and *past. part.* **sa·bered,** *Br.* **sa·bred** to wound or kill with a saber [F. fr. older G. *sabel*]

sa·ber-toothed tiger, *Br.* **sa·bre-toothed tiger** (séibərtu:θt) one of several large, extinct felines with long, swordlike, curved upper canine teeth

sa·bil·iz·ing (séibəlaiziŋ) *n.* (*cosmetology*) hair coloring technique that darkens the ends of light-colored hair

Sa·bin (séibin), Albert Bruce (1906-), U.S. physician who developed (c. 1959) a live-virus vaccine against poliomyelitis. It protects not only against paralyzation (as with the Salk vaccine) but also infection, and provides longer immunity

Sa·bine (séibain), Sir Edward (1788-1883), British physicist and astronomer. The discovery of the effect of sunspots on the earth's magnetic field arose from his work

Sabine 1. *n.* (*hist.*) a member of an ancient people of the Apennines northwest of Rome. It was said that during a festival the Sabine women were seized by the men of Romulus, and that when the Sabines attacked Rome the women placed themselves between the armies to stop the battle. By the 3rd c. B.C. the Sabines had become fully Romanized ‖ their Italic language 2. *adj.* of the Sabines or their language [fr. L. *Sabinus*]

sa·ble (séib'l) *n. Martes zibellina,* fam. *Mustelidae,* a small carnivorous mammal related to the weasel, native to arctic and subarctic Europe and Asia, highly valued for its lustrous dark brown fur ‖ the fur or pelt of this animal ‖ any of several related animals ‖ a garment of sable fur [O.F. prob. fr. Slavonic]

sable 1. *n.* (*heraldry*) black ‖ (*rhet.*) black clothing, esp. as a sign of mourning 2. *adj.* (*heraldry*) of the color sable [F.]

sable antelope *Hippotragus niger,* a large antelope of E. and S. Africa having long curved horns and a little mane. The male is shiny black

Sa·ble, Cape (séib'l) a swampy, mangrove-covered peninsula (c. 20 miles long, 5-10 miles wide) in S.W. Florida, the southernmost point of the U.S. mainland

CONCISE PRONUNCIATION KEY: **(a)** æ, c*a*t; ɑ, c*a*r; ɔ f*aw*n; ei, sn*a*ke. **(e)** e, h*e*n; i:, sh*ee*p; iə, d*ee*r; ɛə, b*ea*r. **(i)** i, f*i*sh; ai, t*i*ger; ə:, b*i*rd. **(o)** o, *o*x; au, c*ow*; ou, g*oa*t; u, p*oo*r; ɔi, r*oy*al. **(u)** ʌ, d*u*ck; u, b*u*ll; u:, g*oo*se; ə, b*a*cillus; ju:, c*u*be. x, lo*ch*; θ, *th*ink; ð, bo*th*er; z, *Z*en; ʒ, cor*s*age; dʒ, *s*avage; ŋ, ora*n*gutang; j, *y*ak; ∫, fi*sh*; t∫, fe*tch*; 'l, rabb*le*; 'n, redd*en*. Complete pronunciation key appears inside front cover.

sa·bot (sǽbou) *n.* a clog made from a single piece of wood, worn esp. in rural France, Belgium, the Netherlands and Germany ‖ a leather work shoe with a wooden sole ‖ (*mil.*) a disk of wood or metal attached to a spherical projectile to make it fit the bore [F.]

Sabot *n.* (*mil.*) lightweight carrier in which a subcaliber projectile is centered to permit firing the projectile in a larger caliber weapon, the carrier filling the bore of the weapon from which the projectile is fired

sab·o·tage (sǽbətɑʒ, sæbətɑ́ʒ) **1.** *n.* deliberate damage done to property, installations etc., e.g. by enemy agents or by hostile employees, or (*fig.*) to plans, enterprises etc. **2.** *v.t. pres. part.* **sab·o·tag·ing** *past* and *past part.* **sab·o·taged** to commit sabotage upon [F.]

sab·o·teur (sæbətɔ́:r) *n.* a person who commits sabotage [F]

sabre *SABER

SABRE *n.* an electronic seat-reservation system created for American Airlines by IBM

sa·bre·tache (séibɑrtæʃ, sǽbɑrtæʃ) *n.* a leather case hung on the left side from a cavalry officer's sword belt [F. fr. G. *säbeltasche* fr. *säbel*, saber + *tasche*, pocket]

sabre-toothed tiger *SABER-TOOTHED TIGER

Sac (sæk, sɔk) *n.* a Sauk Indian

sac (sæk) *n.* (*biol.*) a part shaped like a pouch in an animal or plant, often filled with a fluid [F. or fr. L. *saccus*, sack]

SAC *n.* (*mil. acronym*) for Strategic Air Command, U.S. Air Force agency charged with air-defense strategy and maintenance of long-range aircraft and missiles

Sacagawea (sǽkədʒəwí:ə) (c. 1788–1884), American Shoshoni Indian woman, interpreter and guide for the Lewis and Clark expedition (1804–5). A captive of the Hidatsa tribe of North Dakota, she and her baby accompanied the expedition party in the Pacific Northwest and, on the return journey, remained with Shoshoni in Wyoming

sac·cade (sækád) *n.* a jerky eye movement

sac·cate (sǽkit, sǽkeit) *adj.* (*biol.*) shaped like a sac ‖ encysted [fr. M.L. *saccatus*]

sac·cha·rate (sǽkəreit) *n.* (*chem.*) a salt of saccharic acid

sac·char·ic (səkǽrik) *adj.* of or obtained from saccharine compounds [fr. M.L. *saccharum*, sugar]

saccharic acid a solid diacid, HOOC(CHOH)₄COOH, obtained from glucose and its derivatives

sac·cha·ride (sǽkəraid, sǽkərid) *n.* a sugar, polymerized sugar or combination of sugars [fr. M.L. *saccharum*, sugar]

sac·cha·rim·e·ter (sækərímitər) *n.* an instrument used to find the concentration of sugar in a solution by measuring the angle through which the plane of vibration of polarized light is turned by the solution [F. *saccharimètre* fr. Gk *sakchari*, *sakcharon*, sugar + *metron*, measure]

sac·cha·rin (sǽkərin) *n.* a white crystalline extremely sweet substance, C₆H₄ (SO₂)(CO)NH, prepared from toluene, and used as a sugar substitute, e.g. by diabetics. It has no food value

sac·cha·rine (sǽkərin, sǽkərain) *adj.* very sweet, esp. (*fig.*) sickeningly cloying, *saccharine sentiment* **sac·cha·rin·i·ty** (sækəríniti) *n.* [fr. M.L. *saccharum* or Gk *sakcharon*, sugar]

sac·cha·roid (sǽkərɔid) *adj.* (*geol.*, of rocks) granular in structure, like sugar [fr. Gk *sakcharon*, sugar]

sac·cha·rom·e·ter (sækərómitər) *n.* a hydrometer calibrated to show the concentration of sugar in a solution as it affects the density [fr. Gk *sakcharon*, sugar + *metron*, measure]

sac·cha·rose (sǽkərous) *n.* sucrose [fr. Gk *sakcharon*, sugar]

Sac·co-Van·zet·ti Case (sǽkouvænzéti:) a U.S. murder trial held (1920-7) in Massachusetts. The defendants, Nicola Sacco and Bartolomeo Vanzetti, two Italian immigrants, were accused of murdering F. A. Parmenter, paymaster of a shoe factory, and Alessandro Berardelli, the accompanying guard, to secure the payroll they were carrying. After their conviction and execution, worldwide demonstrations protested that they were convicted for their radical, anarchist beliefs, and not because there was clear evidence of guilt on the murder charge. Subsequent investigations suggested that others might have committed the crime, but their convictions were never overturned

sac·cu·late (sǽkjuleit) *adj.* formed of or divided into saccules **sác·cu·lat·ed** *adj.* [SACCULUS]

sac·cule (sǽkju:l) *n.* a small sac, esp. the smaller division in the membranous labyrinth of the ear [SACCULUS]

sac·cu·lus (sǽkjuləs) *pl.* **sac·cu·li** (sǽkjulai) *n.* a saccule [L. dim. of *saccus*, sack]

sac·er·do·tal (sæsərdóut'l) *adj.* pertaining to priests or the priesthood ‖ of doctrines asserting great or excessive spiritual authority in priests **sac·er·dó·tal·ism** *n.* the assuming of spiritual powers by priests as intermediaries between man and God, or the ascribing of excessive authority to priests [F.]

sa·chem (séitʃəm) *n.* (among certain peoples) a North American Indian chief ‖ an officer of the Tammany Society [Algonquian]

sa·chet (sæféi, sǽfei) *n.* a small bag, esp. one containing perfumed powder or dried herbs, placed among clothes and linen [F., dim. of *sac*, bag]

Sachs (zɑks), Hans (1494-1576), German meistersinger and playwright. Wagner made him the central figure of 'Die Meistersinger von Nürnberg'

Sachs (sæks), (Leonie) Nelly (1891–1970), German poet whose poetry spoke out against Nazism and the Holocaust, co-winner of the Nobel Prize for literature (1966). She fled from Germany to Sweden in 1940. Her poems are collected in 'O the Chimneys' (1967)

sack (sæk) **1.** *n.* a large receptacle, typically oblong and made of a coarse fabric, for storing or conveying goods ‖ such a receptacle with its contents ‖ the amount it holds, sometimes used as a unit of measurement ‖ a woman's loose-fitting straight dress ‖ (*hist.*, also **sacque**) a woman's loose gown, or a train hanging from its shoulders ‖ (*pop.*) summary dismissal, esp. from employment, *to get the sack* **2.** *v.t.* to put into a sack or sacks ‖ (*pop.*) to dismiss, esp. from employment [O.E. *sacc* fr. L. *saccus* fr. Gk fr. Heb.]

sack *n.* (*hist.*) any of various kinds of dry white wine imported into England from Spain and the Canary Islands in the 16th and 17th cc. [earlier (*wyne*) *seck* fr. F. (*vin*) *sec*, dry (wine)]

sack 1. *n.* the violent plundering by soldiers of a captured town, city etc. **2.** *v.t.* to plunder and lay waste (a captured town, city etc.) [F. *sac* fr. Ital.]

sack·but (sǽkbʌt) *n.* a medieval wind instrument, ancestor of the trombone ‖ (*Bible*) a trigon (harp) [F. *saquebute*, prob. fr. O.N.F. *saqueboute*, a hooked lance]

sack·cloth (sǽkklɔθ, sǽkklɒθ) *n.* sacking ‖ penitential or mourning clothing of coarse cloth

sack·ful (sǽkful) *pl.* **sack·fuls** *n.* the amount a sack will hold

sack·ing (sǽkiŋ) *n.* coarse cloth, e.g. of hemp or jute, for making sacks

sack race a race in which each contestant has his legs or the lower half of his body in a sack

sacque *SACK (loose gown)

sa·cral (séikrəl) *adj.* (*anat.*) of or near the sacrum [fr. Mod. L. *sacralis*]

sacral *adj.* of or for sacred ceremonies [fr. L. *sacrum*, sacred thing]

sac·ra·ment (sǽkrəmənt) *n.* any of certain Christian rites held to have been instituted by Christ and to convey God's grace to man. In the Roman Catholic and Orthodox Eastern Churches these are: baptism, penance, the Eucharist, confirmation, ordination, matrimony and Extreme Unction. In most Protestant Churches, baptism and the Eucharist are the only sacraments **the Sacrament** the Eucharist ‖ any ceremony or act symbolizing a deep spiritual reality ‖ a solemn oath or pledge ‖ (*Roman Catholicism*) the Host [F. *sacrement* fr. L. *sacramentum* fr. *sacrare*, to consecrate]

sac·ra·men·tal (sækrəmént'l) **1.** *adj.* of, relating to or having the nature of a sacrament ‖ (of religious doctrine) affirming the validity and indispensability of the sacraments **2.** *n.* a religious rite resembling a sacrament but not regarded as having been instituted by Christ **sac·ra·mén·tal·ism, sac·ra·mén·tal·ist** *ns.* [obs. F. or fr. L.L. *sacramentalis*]

sac·ra·men·tar·i·an (sækrəmentéəri:ən) **1.** *adj.* pertaining to the sacraments or a sacrament ‖ pertaining to the sacramentarians **2.** *n.* (*hist.*) Luther's name for Zwingli and other Protestant theologians who claimed that God was present in the bread and wine of the Eucharist only in a symbolic sense ‖ someone who asserts the inherent efficacy of the sacraments in conveying grace to the soul of a recipient [fr. eccles. L. *sacramentarius*]

Sac·ra·men·to (sækrəméntou) the capital (pop. 275,741) of California, in the central valley, a distributing center of a rich agricultural region. The discovery of gold nearby (1848) started the California gold rush

Sacramento the largest river (382 miles long) in California, rising in N. California and flowing into the east arm of San Francisco Bay. It is navigable for 180 miles. Its valley was the site of the Gold Rush of 1848

sa·cred (séikrid) *adj.* consecrated, holy ‖ set apart, esp. for the service or worship of God or a deity ‖ hallowed by religious association ‖ having a religious, not a profane character, *a sacred picture* ‖ to be held in reverence ‖ (of a person or his office) inviolate [past part. of obs. *sacre*, to consecrate fr. F. *sacrer*]

Sacred College the College of Cardinals

sacred mushroom any hallucinogenic mushroom used in ceremonies by some American Indians

sac·ri·fice (sǽkrəfais) **1.** *n.* an offering, e.g. of animal life, food or incense, made to a deity etc. as propitiation, thanksgiving etc. ‖ the act or practice of making such an offering ‖ (*theol.*) Christ's offering of himself in the Crucifixion ‖ the act of depriving oneself of something for the sake of attaining some goal or for the sake of someone else, *he made many sacrifices for his son's education* ‖ the thing given up in this way ‖ (*baseball*) a sacrifice bunt or fly which does not count as an official time at bat **2.** *v. pres. part.* **sac·ri·fic·ing** *past* and *past part.* **sac·ri·ficed** *v.t.* to offer as a sacrifice ‖ to deprive oneself of (something valued) for the sake of another person, purpose or ideal ‖ *v.i.* to make a sacrifice [F.]

sacrifice bunt (*baseball*) a bunt which enables a base runner to advance although the batter is put out

sacrifice fly (*baseball*) a fly ball to the outfield which enables a base runner to advance although the batter is put out

sac·ri·fi·cial (sækrifíʃəl) *adj.* of or pertaining to sacrifice [fr. *sacrificium* + Eng. -*al* fr. L. -*alis*, of the kind of]

sac·ri·lege (sǽkrəlidʒ) *n.* the violation of a sacred building, or stealing, misuse, destruction etc. of a sacred object [O.F.]

sac·ri·le·gious (sækrəlídʒəs, sækrəli:dʒəs) *adj.* guilty of sacrilege ‖ having the nature of sacrilege [fr. L. *sacrilegium*]

sa·cring bell (séikriŋ) a small bell rung at the Elevation during the Mass ‖ the tolling of the church bell at the moment of the Elevation [fr. obs. *sacre*, to consecrate fr. F. *sacrer*]

sac·rist (sǽkrist, séikrist) *n.* a sacristan [O.F. *sacriste*]

sac·ris·tan (sǽkristən) *n.* the official who looks after the sacristy of a church [fr. M. L. *sacristanus*]

sac·ris·ty (sǽkristi:) *pl.* **sac·ris·ties** *n.* a room in or attached to a church, in which the sacred vessels, vestments etc. are kept [F. *sacristie*]

sac·ro·il·i·ac (sækrouíli:æk, seikrouíli:æk) **1.** *n.* the region of juncture of the sacrum and the ilium of the spinal column **2.** *adj.* of or pertaining to the sacroiliac

sac·ro·sanct (sǽkrousæŋkt) *adj.* (of a person, place, oath, right etc.) most holy, inviolable **sac·ro·sánc·ti·ty** *n.* [fr. L. *sacrosanctus*]

sac·rum (sǽkrəm, séikrəm) *pl.* **sac·ra** (sǽkrə, séikrə), **sac·rums** *n.* a triangular bone composed of fused vertebrae that is part of the spinal column and forms the back of the pelvis [fr. L. (*os*) *sacrum*, sacred (bone), because it was used in religious rites]

Sac·sa·hua·mán (saksawɑmán) an Inca fortress and arsenal on a hill north of Cuzco, Peru

sad (sæd) *comp.* **sad·der** *superl.* **sad·dest** *adj.* grieving ‖ depressed in spirits ‖ causing sorrow or depression ‖ showing sorrow, *a sad expression* ‖ deplorable, *a sad example to set* ‖ (of color) dark, drab **sad·den** (sǽd'n) *v.t.* to make sad ‖ *v.i.* to become sad [O.E. *sæd*, sated, weary]

Sadarm System (sǽdɑrm) *n.* U.S. sense and destroy missile guidance system, in development as of 1981

Sa·dat (sɑdát), Anwar (1918-81), Egyptian statesman. He succeeded (1970) Nasser as president of the United Arab Republic. He expelled about 20,000 Soviet advisers and military personnel from the country (1972) and launched a war against Israel (1973). In 1977 he flew to Israel to initiate peace negotiations, which culminated (1979) in an historic Egypt-Israel peace treaty, for which he shared the Nobel peace prize (1978) with Manachem Begin, but

CONCISE PRONUNCIATION KEY: **(a)** æ, c*a*t; ɑ, c*a*r; ɔ f*aw*n; ei, sn*a*ke. **(e)** e, h*e*n; i:, sh*ee*p; iə, d*ee*r; ɛə, b*ea*r. **(i)** i, f*i*sh; ai, t*i*ger; ə:, b*i*rd. **(o)** o, *o*x; au, c*ow*; ou, g*oa*t; u, p*oo*r; ɔi, r*oy*al. **(u)** ʌ, d*u*ck; u, b*u*ll; u:, g*oo*se; ə, b*a*cillus; ju:, c*u*be. x, lo*ch*; θ, *th*ink; ð, bo*th*er; z, *Z*en; ʒ, corsa*g*e; dʒ, sava*g*e; ŋ, ora*ng*utang; j, *y*ak; ʃ, *fi*sh; tʃ, *fe*tch; 'l, rabb*le*; 'n, redd*en*. Complete pronunciation key appears inside front cover.

which made Egypt unpopular with the Arab world. Sadat was assassinated (1981) by members of a militant Moslem fundamentalist group

sad·dle (sǽd'l) *n.* a seat, generally of padded leather, for the rider of a horse, camel etc. ‖ the seat on a bicycle, tractor etc. ‖ the part of a draft horse's harness to which the shafts are attached ‖ an object resembling a riding saddle, esp. a ridge between two mountain peaks ‖ a marking resembling a horse's saddle, on the back of an animal ‖ a cut of mutton or venison including both loins and part of the back ‖ the movable tool carriage of a lathe [O.E. *sadol, sadul*] **saddle** *pres. part.* **sad·dling** *past* and *past part.* **sad·dled** *v.t.* to put a saddle on ‖ to place a burdensome duty, responsibility etc. on [O.E. *sadolian*]

sad·dle·back (sǽd'lbæk) *n.* (*archit.*) a roof with a gable at each end or one sloping upwards at each end ‖ a saddlebacked hill ‖ an animal with markings which suggest a saddle, e.g. a black hog of either of two British breeds with a white saddle across the shoulders **sád·dlebacked** *adj.* (*archit.*) having a saddleback ‖ (of a horse) having a hollow in the back behind the withers ‖ having a concave upper outline

sad·dle·bag (sǽd'lbæg) *n.* a large bag or one of a pair, hanging from a saddle ‖ a small bag or one of a pair, hung at the rear wheel of a bicycle or motorcycle

sad·dle·bow (sǽd'lbou) *n.* the arched front of a saddle

sad·dle·cloth (sǽd'lklɔθ, sǽd'lklɒθ) *pl.* **sad·dle·cloths** (sǽd'lklɔðz, sǽd'lklɒðz, sǽd'lklɔðs, sǽd'lklɒðs) *n.* a cloth placed underneath a saddle

saddled prominent a moth (*Heterocampo guttivitta*) that in the larval state, defoliates hardwood trees in the eastern and midwestern U.S.

saddle horse a horse used for riding

sad·dler (sǽdlər) *n.* someone who makes, repairs or sells saddles, harness etc. **sád·dler·y** *pl.* **sád·dler·ies** *n.* the saddles, harness etc. sold by a saddler ‖ a saddler's trade or shop

saddle roof a saddleback roof

saddle shoe an oxford, usually white, having a band of contrasting leather (usually brown or black) across the instep

saddle soap a mild soap for cleaning and treating leather

sad·dle·tree (sǽd'ltri:) *n.* the framework of a saddle ‖ *Liriodendron tulipifera*, the tulip tree

Sad·du·ce·an (sædʒusí:ən, sædjusí:ən) *adj.* of or characteristic of the Sadducees [fr. L. L. *Sadducaeus,* Sadducee]

Sad·du·cee (sǽdʒusi:, sǽdjusi:) *n.* a member of a Jewish religious sect (2nd c. B.C.–1st c. A.D.) believing in free will and denying belief in the resurrection of the dead or the existence of spirits. The Sadducees were the opponents of the Pharisees [fr. L.L. *Saddacaeus* fr. Gk fr. Heb. *Çaddūqī*]

Sade (sæd), Donatien Alphonse François, comte de (known as the marquis de Sade, 1740-1814), French writer after whom sadism was named. His works contain descriptions of sexual perversions

sad·hu (sádu:) *n.* a Hindu ascetic holy man [Skr.=holy man]

Sa'di (sɑdí:) (c. 1184-1291), one of the most popular Persian poets, author of the long didactic works 'Būstān' (Fruit Garden, 1257) and 'Gulistān' (Rose Garden, 1258), partly in verse and partly in prose, containing stories, lyrics, aphorisms etc.

sad·i·ron (sǽdaiərn) *n.* a solid flatiron pointed at each end [SAD, (obs.) heavy]

sad·ism (sǽdizəm, séidizəm) *n.* the deriving of pleasure from inflicting pain on another, esp. as a form of sexual perversion (cf. MASOCHISM) **sád·ist** *n.* **sa·dis·tic** (sədístik, sædístik, seidistík) *adj.* **sa·dís·ti·cal·ly** *adv.* [fr. F. *sadisme* after the marquis de SADE]

Sa·do (sádou) an island (area 331 sq. miles, pop. 126,000) of Japan off W. Honshu: gold and silver mines

Sa·do·wa, Battle of (sádɔvɑ) a decisive Prussian victory over Austria (July 3, 1866), also known as the Battle of Königgrätz, fought near Hradec Králové on the upper Elbe, Czechoslovakia

Sá·enz (sáens), Manuela ('La Sáenz', 1793-1859), a patriot of Quito and mistress of Simón Bolívar. In 1828 she saved Bolívar from conspirators in Bogotá. On his death she remained in Bogotá and protected his papers

sa·fa·ri (səfári:) *pl.* **sa·fa·ris** *n.* a hunting expedition, esp. in E. Africa [Swahili fr. Arab. *safara,* to travel]

Sa·fa·vid (safáwi:d) a member of a Moslem dynasty which ruled Persia (1502-1736)

safe (seif) *comp.* **saf·er** *superl.* **saf·est** *adj.* out of danger ‖ not presenting or involving any danger or risk, *a safe policy* ‖ uninjured, *the car crashed but they were safe* ‖ (*baseball*) of a batter or base runner who reaches a base without being put out **on the safe side** covered so as to reduce or avoid risk ‖ (of an estimate etc.) conservative, *with a margin in hand* [M.E. *sauf* fr. F.]

safe *n.* a fireproof and burglarproof container for valuables ‖ a ventilated cupboard or chest in which foods are stored [older *save* fr. SAVE v.]

safe·break·er (séifbreikər) *n.* (*Br.*) a safecracker

safe·con·duct (seifkóndʌkt) *n.* the privilege granted by an authority to an otherwise unauthorized person of traveling through a zone or territory without being arrested or molested ‖ the document conveying this authorization

safe·crack·er (séifkrækər) *n.* a person who breaks open and robs safes

safe·crack·ing (séifkrækiŋ) *n.* the breaking open and robbing of safes

safe deposit (*Br.*) a place, e.g. the vault of a bank, where individual safes can be hired for the deposit of valuables

safe-deposit box a metal container for the safe storage of valuables, e.g. one kept in a bank

safe·guard (séifgɑrd) 1. *n.* someone who or something that serves as protection 2. *v.t.* to provide with something intended as a protection against a possible risk or danger [M.E. *savegarde* fr. F. *sauvegarde*]

safe haven (*mil.*) 1. designated area to which noncombatants, commercial vehicles, and matériel can be evacuated during an emergency 2. temporary storage provided the Department of Energy for classified shipments of nuclear material, including parking for commercial vehicles containing Class A or Class B explosives

safe·keep·ing (séifki:piŋ) *n.* the act of keeping safe or secure ‖ the state of being kept safe or secure ‖ custody, *the money is in his safekeeping*

safe·ty (séifti:) *pl.* **safe·ties** *n.* the condition of being safe from risk or danger ‖ the quality or state of not presenting or involving risk or danger ‖ the condition of a weapon when the safety catch is on, *at safety* ‖ (*baseball*) a base hit ‖ (*football*) a play in which the player grounds the ball behind his goal line (cf. TOUCHDOWN) [M.E. *sauvete* fr. F. *sauveté*]

safety belt a belt or strap fastening an occupant to the seat of an aircraft or vehicle, to prevent or minimize injury if there is an accident ‖ a strong belt securing a man working high above ground, fastened to a rigid support

safety catch a device fitted to a firearm, which, when engaged, prevents the trigger from releasing the firing pin ‖ any of various safety devices on machinery

safety curtain a fireproof curtain which can cut off the stage of a theater from the auditorium in case of fire

safety fuse a fuse made of a slow-burning material, for exploding detonators from a safe distance ‖ (*elec.*) a fuse (short length of wire in an electric circuit)

safety glass strong, tempered glass, treated in such a way that, if broken, it will not shatter or produce jagged fragments

safety lamp a lamp, esp. a Davy lamp, constructed so as not to ignite gas in the surrounding atmosphere

safety man or **safety** (*football*) a defense back whose function is to prevent a long gain by the opposing team

safety match a match which lights only when rubbed on a specially prepared surface

safety net U.S. federal assistance programs designed to assure minimum subsistence for the very poor even under the budget cutbacks proposal by Pres. Ronald Reagan

safety pin a pin for fastening clothing, doubled back on itself so as to form a spring, and having its point secured and covered by a guard

safety razor a razor fitted with a guard so that the blade cannot cut deeply

safety valve a valve automatically opening to release steam or gas from a boiler etc. when the pressure reaches a certain point ‖ something

which serves to release excess emotion, energy etc. in a harmless way

safety zone an island in the middle of a busy street where pedestrians can stand until it is safe to cross

saf·flow·er (sǽflauər) *n. Carthamus tinctorius,* fam. *Compositae,* a thistlelike plant cultivated esp. in Asia, bearing large orange or red flowers which yield a light red dye ‖ this dye [Du. *saffloer* fr. O.F. *saffleur* fr. Ital.]

saf·fron (sǽfrən) *n. Crocus sativus,* a crocus cultivated for its flowers, whose stigmas yield an orange substance used for coloring and flavoring food ‖ this substance ‖ the color of this substance [O.F. *safran* fr. Arab.]

saf·ing (séifiŋ) *v. pres. part* (*mil.*) as applied to weapons and ammunition, the changing from a state of readiness to fire to a safe condition

saf·ra·nin (sǽfrənin) *n.* safranine

saf·ra·nine (sǽfrəni:n, sǽfrənin) *n.* any of several aniline dyes [fr. F. *safran,* saffron]

saf·role (sǽfroul) *n.* a poisonous oil, $C_{10}H_{10}O_2$, obtained from oil of sassafras, and used for perfuming and flavoring [fr. F. *safron,* saffron]

sag (sæg) 1. *v.i. pres. part.* **sag·ging** *past* and *past part.* **sagged** to bend, hang or sink in the center as a result of weight or pressure, *the plank sagged under his weight* ‖ to bend, hang or sink as if giving way to pressure, *his shoulders sagged from weariness* ‖ (of sales or market prices) to fall ‖ (*naut.*) to drift, *to sag to leeward* ‖ to cease to hold interest 2. *n.* a sagging ‖ a depression, *a sag in the road* ‖ the amount by which a thing sags from normal position ‖ (*naut.*) a drift to leeward [perh. related to M. Du. *zakken,* Norw. *sakka,* to subside]

sa·ga (ságə) *n.* a prose epic narrating the history of the early heroes or families of Iceland or Norway ‖ any long narrative story tracing the fortunes of a family through several generations [O.N.=narrative]

—The Icelandic sagas were passed on orally for generations by the descendants of the 9th-c. exiles from Norway, before they began to be written down in the 12th c. By this time their character had become established: the terse simplicity of the language, free from the influence of Latin literature, and the anonymity of the narration, free from subjective commentary, lent great power to the violent, often tragic events related. By the late 13th c. the saga began to decline, depending increasingly upon foreign influences and fictional subjects. The great sagas include the 'Egilssaga' (c. 1200), the 'Laxdaelasaga' (mid-13th c.), the 'Njálssaga' (late 13th c.) and the 'Völsungasaga' (late 13th c.). The 'Heimskringla' was probably by Snorri Sturluson (1179–1241)

sa·ga·cious (səgéiʃəs) *adj.* keen and perceptive, having or showing discernment in judgment [fr. L. *sagax (sagacis)*]

sa·gac·i·ty (səgǽsiti:) *n.* the quality of being sagacious [fr. F. *sagacité*]

sag·a·more (sǽgəmɔr, sǽgəmour) *n.* a secondary chief of certain North American Indian tribes [fr. Penobscot *sagamo*]

Sa·gan (séigən) Carl Edward (1934-), U.S. scientist, known for popularizing science and for his research on the possibility of extraterrestrial life. He was a professor of astronomy and director of the Laboratory for Planetary Studies at Cornell University (1968-). He wrote 'Life in the Universe' (1966), with Josif Shlovsky, 'The Cosmic Connection' (1973), 'The Dragons of Eden' (1977, Pulitzer Prize), 'Broca's Brain' (1979), 'Cosmos' (1980) and 'Contact' (1985)

Sage (seidʒ), Russell (1816-1906), U.S. financier. In association with Jay Gould, he amassed a fortune by his control of railroad systems in New York City and the western U.S.A., and of the Western Union Telegraph Company. His wife Margaret Olivia Slocum Sage (1828-1918), to whom he left his fortune, established (1907) the Russell Sage Foundation in New York City, for 'the improvement of social and living conditions' in the U.S.A.

sage (seidʒ) *n. Salvia officinalis,* fam. *Labiatae,* an aromatic herb native to Europe and North America, whose leaves are used to flavor food [M.E. *sauge* fr. F.]

sage 1. *comp.* **sag·er** *superl.* **sag·est** *adj.* having or showing great wisdom and sound judgment 2. *n.* a very wise man, e.g. a philosopher of ancient times [F.]

SAGE *n.* (*mil. acronym*) for semiautomatic ground environment, a system that correlates surveillance data for air defense and guides interceptor aircraft

sage·brush (séidʒbrʌʃ) n. a member of *Artemisia*, fam. *Compositiae*, a genus of bushy, aromatic plants growing wild on the western plains of North America, esp. *A. tridentata*

sagebrush rebellion campaign by Western states in 1970s and 1980s to force federal relinquishment of public lands to states —**sagebrush rebel** n.

Sagger AT-3 n. U.S.S.R. anti-tank missile with 2 clusters of 3 missiles

sag·ger, sag·gar (sǽgər) n. a fireclay container in which porcelain or stoneware is enclosed during firing ‖ the clay of which this container is made [prob. contr. of SAFEGUARD]

Sag·i·naw Bay (sǽginɔ) an inlet (60 miles long, 15-25 miles wide) of Lake Huron on the coast of E. central Michigan

sa·git·ta (sədʒítə) n. (math.) the distance from the midpoint of an arc to that of its chord [Mod. L. fr. L. =arrow]

sag·it·tal (sǽdʒit'l) adj. of, pertaining to or lying in the median plane dividing any animal body into right and left halves, or any plane parallel to this ‖ of or relating to the median suture between the parietal bones of the skull ‖ of or resembling an arrow or arrowhead [fr. Mod. L. *sagittalis* fr. L. *sagitta*, arrow]

Sag·it·ta·ri·us (sædʒitéəriəs) a southern constellation ‖ the ninth sign of the zodiac, represented as an archer

sag·it·tate (sǽdʒiteit) adj. (bot., of a leaf) shaped like an arrowhead [fr. Mod. L. *sagittatus* fr. L. *sagitta*, arrow]

sa·go (séigou) n. a starch extracted from the pith of certain tropical palms, esp. of genus *Metroxylon*, used as a food and for textile finishing ‖ a plant yielding this starch [Malay *sāgū*]

sa·gua·ro (sɑgwárou, səwárou) pl. **sa·gua·ros** n. *Carnegiea gigantea*, a large cactus of Mexico and the southwestern U.S.A., growing to a height of 60 ft. It has white flowers and an edible fruit [Span. fr. native name]

sag wagon (cycling) vehicle which follows a race and picks up those who fall behind

Sa·ha·gún (saɑgúːn), Fray Bernardino de (c. 1499-1590), a Spanish Franciscan missionary and historian in Mexico. His chief work is 'A History of Ancient Mexico' (published 1829, Eng. trans. Vol. I, 1932)

Sa·har·a (səhǽrə, səhárə) the largest desert (area about 3,500,000 sq. miles) in the world, covering most of N. Africa (the bulk of Mauritania, Morocco, Western Sahara, Tunisia, Algeria, Libya and Egypt, with the north of Mali, Niger, Chad and the Sudan). It includes the Libyan, Arabian and Nubian deserts. Average elevation: 1,000 ft. A mountain system, running from the Ahaggar Mtns, S.E. Algeria, to the W. Sudan, rises over 11,000 ft (*TIBESTI MTNS). Surface types: erg (sandy desert), reg (gravel plains), hammada (rocky plateaus). Highest recorded temperature: 133° F. Rainfall: mainly under 5 ins. Large oases are mainly in the north, but there are skeletal river systems. Principal resources: natural gas, oil, salt (all mainly in the south). Population is estimated at 2,000,000 incl. nomads and oasis farmers

Sa·ha·ran·pur (səhárənpur) a town (pop. 185,000) in N. Uttar Pradesh, India: railroad shops, paper, wood carving

sa·hel (sáhel) n. a climatic transition zone of tropical Africa south of the Sahara, between the desert and the savanna. It is characterized by low, scattered vegetation (tamarisk, gum acacia etc.) and supports a limited agriculture (millet, peanuts) [F. fr. Arab. *sahil*]

sa·hib (sáib, sáːib) n. (hist.) a title of address used by Indians to European men

said past and past part. of SAY

Sa·i·da (sáːidɑ) *SIDON

Sai·gon (*HO CHI MINH CITY (saigón, sǽiːgɔ̃) a city (pop. with its mainly Chinese suburb of Cholon 1,825,297) of Vietnam, a seaport (Saigon River) 60 miles from the sea, European in aspect. Industries (largely concentrated in Cholon): shipbuilding, food (esp. rice, sugar) and rubber processing, textiles. University

sail (seil) n. a piece of canvas or other cloth suspended from the spars of a boat or ship to catch or deflect the wind and drive the vessel along ‖ such sails collectively ‖ a ship, esp. a sailing ship, *not a sail in sight* ‖ a voyage by ship, *a five-day sail from the nearest port* ‖ something like a ship's sail in form or purpose, *the sails of a windmill* ‖ (zool.) a fin, tentacle or wing ‖ a windsail **in full sail** with all sails spread **to set**

sail to hoist a boat's sails ‖ to begin a sea voyage **to take in sail** to reduce the amount of sail spread ‖ to curb one's ambitions **under sail** with sails spread [O.E. segl, segel]

sail v.i. to travel in a boat or ship with sails ‖ to make or start a sea voyage, *the liner sails tomorrow* ‖ to move or glide effortlessly in the air ‖ to walk in a stately manner, *the duchess sailed into the room* ‖ v.t. to travel over (a body of water) in a ship ‖ to manage (a boat or ship with sails) ‖ to cause to move or glide through the air **to sail against the wind** to sail in a direction other than or contrary to that of the wind ‖ to act or work under difficulties or opposition **to sail in** to sail into a task etc. **to sail into** to begin (a task etc.) with energy and enthusiasm ‖ to attack with words or blows **to sail near (or close to) the wind** to sail against the wind ‖ (Br.) to come close to breaking a law or rule, e.g. in a business deal [O.E. *siglan, seglian*]

sail arm an arm of a windmill

sail·board (séilbɔrd) n. (sports) an unsinkable flat boat with a single mast, usu. with no cockpit, for one or two passengers

sail·boat (séilbout) n. (Am.=Br. sailing boat) a boat normally propelled by sail, though often having an auxiliary engine

sail·cloth (séilklɔθ, séilklɒθ) n. canvas cloth used for sails, tents, casual clothes etc.

sail·er (séilər) n. a ship considered with reference to the way it sails, *a fast sailer*

sail·fish (séilfiʃ) pl. **sail·fish, sail·fish·es** n. any of various large fishes of genus *Istiophorus*, fam. *Istiophoridae*, related to the swordfish, and having a large dorsal fin ‖ the basking shark

sail·ing (séiliŋ) n. the act or skill of navigating a boat under sail ‖ the sport of navigating a boat under sail ‖ a ship's scheduled departure on a voyage

sailing boat (Br.) a sailboat

sailing orders instructions about a voyage given to the ship's captain

sailing ship a ship with sails

sail·or (séilər) n. a man professionally trained in the operating of a ship, or a member of a ship's crew below the rank of officer **a good (bad) sailor** a person who is rarely (often) seasick [alt. of older *sailer*]

sailor hat a round, flat-topped straw hat with a narrow brim

sail·plane (séilplein) **1.** n. a light glider **2.** v.i. pres. part. **sail·plan·ing** past and past part. **sail·planed** to glide in a sailplane

sain·foin (séinfɔin) n. *Onobrychis viciaefolia*, fam. *Papilionaceae*, a pink-flowered perennial Eurasian plant grown for fodder [F. fr. *sain*, wholesome+*foin*, hay]

saint (seint, Br., when used in combination, s'nt) **1.** n. a soul gone to heaven, esp. (Roman Catholic and Orthodox Churches) a person whose holiness has been attested by miracles after his death and who has been officially recognized (canonized) by the Church as worthy of veneration and to receive intercession ‖ (abbr. S. or St, pl. SS. or Sts) the title of a canonized person or of one receiving the same veneration ‖ (pop.) a person of great charity, patience, purity and meekness **2.** v.t. to canonize [O.F.]

SAINT n. (mil.) U.S. satellite inspector system. U.S.S.R. equivalent is ASAT

St Agnes's Eve the night of Jan. 20, when a young girl, upon performing certain ceremonies, expected to have a vision of her future husband

St Al·bans (ɔ́lbənz) a city (pop. 125,600) in Hertfordshire, S.E. England: Roman mosaics and theater. Norman abbey (793, largely rebuilt late 11th c.)

St An·drews (ǽndruːz) a town (pop. 13,100) on the northeast coast of Fife, Scotland. It contains Scotland's oldest university (1411). Famous golf courses

St Andrew's cross a cross in the shape of an X ‖ (heraldry) an ordinary consisting of such a cross, usually white on a blue ground. It is the cross of Scotland

St Anthony's cross a cross in the shape of a T

St Anthony's fire any of certain diseased conditions of the skin, esp. erysipelas or ergotism

St Au·gus·tine (ɔ́gəstiːn) a city (pop. 11,985) in N.E. Florida, the oldest in the U.S.A. It was founded in 1565 by the Spanish

St Bartholomew a mountainous island (area

9.5 sq. miles, pop. 2,200) in the Antilles, a dependency of Guadeloupe

St Bartholomew, Massacre of *BARTHOLOMEW, MASSACRE OF ST

St Ber·nard (bəːrnárd, Br. esp. bə́ːnəd) n. a dog of a large, powerful breed, famous for its use esp. at the hospice of Great St Bernard in the Swiss Alps for rescuing lost travelers

St Bernard, Great and Little two passes over the Alps. The Great St Bernard (8,111 ft), in the Pennine Alps 15 miles east of Mont Blanc, links the Rhône valley and Valais, Switzerland, with Valle d'Aosta, Italy. The Little St Bernard (7,178 ft), in the Graian Alps 10 miles south of Mont Blanc, links the Isère valley, Savoie, France, with Valle d'Aosta. Each shows traces of a Roman road and has a hospice and monastery founded by St Bernard de Menthon (11th c.)

St Christopher and Nevis *ST KITTS—NEVIS

Saint Clair, Lake (klɛər) a lake (area 460 sq. miles) between S.E. Michigan and S. Ontario, Canada. The U.S.A.-Canadian boundary passes through it. Rivers join it to Lake Huron and Lake Erie

St Croix (krɔi) (or Santa Cruz) the largest island (area 82 sq. miles, pop. 49,013) of the Virgin Is of the U.S.A., south of St. Thomas Is. West Indies. It was purchased (1917) from Denmark by the U.S.A.

Saint-Cy·ran (sɛ̃siːrã), l'abbé de *DUVERGIER DE HAURANNE

St-De·nis (sɛ̃dəniː) a northern industrial suburb (pop. 90,000) of Paris, with a Gothic abbey church (12th-13th cc.), the burial place of the majority of French sovereigns

Sainte-Beuve (sɛ̃bəːv), Charles-Augustin (1804-69), French critic. He is best known for his articles on French literature collected in 'Causeries du Lundi' (1851-62) and 'Nouveaux Lundis' (1863-70). His 'Port Royal' (1840-59) is a classic study in depth of the relation, in Jansenism, of literature, society and religion

St E·li·as, Mt (iláiəs) a peak (18,008 ft) in the St Elias Range on the boundary between S.E. Alaska and the S.W. Yukon Territory, Canada

St Elias Range a mountain range (c. 250 miles long) in E. Alaska and the S.W. Yukon Territory, Canada, containing great glaciers on its Alaskan slopes. Highest peak: Mt Logan (19,850 ft)

St El·mo's fire (élmouz) a flamelike discharge sometimes seen on ships' masts etc. during storms, similar in cause to brush discharge

St-É·tienne (sɛ̃teitjen) the chief town (pop. 218,289) of Loire department, France: coal mining, iron and steel, mechanical engineering, metalwork, textiles

St Eu·sta·tius (juːstéiʃəs) an island (area 11.8 sq. miles, pop. 1020) in the Leeward Is, part of the Netherlands Antilles

Saint-Ev·re·mond (sɛ̃tevrəmɔ̃), Charles de Marguetel de Saint-Denis de (c. 1614-1703), French satirical writer and essayist. His writings include literary and dramatic criticism and a voluminous correspondence

Saint-Ex·u·pé·ry (sɛ̃tegzypeiri:), Antoine de (1900-44), French writer and pilot, author of 'Vol de nuit' (1931), 'Terre des hommes' (1939), 'Pilote de guerre' (1942), 'le Petit Prince' (1943) and 'Citadelle' (1948)

St Gal·len (gǽlən) (G. Sankt Gallen, F. St Gall) a German-speaking canton (area 777 sq. miles, pop. 391,995) of N.E. Switzerland ‖ its capital (pop. 75,847): cathedral (14th c., restored in the 18th c.), formerly part of the Benedictine abbey of St Gall, famous (9th-11th cc.) as a leading center of art and literature

Saint-Gau·dens (seintgɔ́d'nz) Augustus (1848-1907), U.S. sculptor, born in Ireland, known for his monuments of heroic figures. He came to the U.S.A. at a young age and learned the art of cameo cutting to support his art lessons. After studying with François Jouffroy in Paris (1867) he began sculpting; by 1881 his bronze sculpture 'Admiral David Farragut' stood in Madison Square Park in New York City. Other works include 'Abraham Lincoln' (1887, Lincoln Park, Chicago), a shrouded seated woman in Rock Creek cemetery, Washington, D.C., (1886-91) and 'General William Tecumseh Sherman' (1897-1903, Central Park, New York City)

St George's cross a Greek cross, red on a white ground, the cross of England

St-Ger·main, Treaty of (sɛ̃ʒermɛ̃) a treaty (1919) between the Allies and Austria, dissolving the dual monarchy of Austria-Hungary. It recognized the independence of Hungary, Czechoslovakia, Poland and the country that was later called Yugoslavia, and made Austria a republic

St Got·thard (gótərd) a massif (highest peak 10,490 ft) in the Lepontine Alps, where the Rhône, Rhine and Ticino rise. The St Gotthard pass (6,808 ft) links Lake Lucerne (Switzerland) with Lake Maggiore (Italy), and the St Gotthard tunnel (completed 1882) links the Swiss and Italian railroads

St He·le·na (həlí:nə) a mountainous volcanic island (area 47 sq. miles, pop. 5,584) in the S. Atlantic 1,200 miles west of Angola, forming, with Ascension I. and Tristan da Cunha, a British Crown Colony. Capital: Jamestown. It was discovered by the Portuguese (1502), then from 1659 held by the East India Company under charter until 1834, when it came directly under the Crown. Napoleon was imprisoned here from 1815 until his death

St Hel·ens (hélinz) a town (pop. 98,769) and county borough in S.W. Lancashire, England: glass, metallurgy, chemicals

saint·hood (séinthud) *n.* the state or quality of being a saint ‖ saints collectively

St James's Palace the London residence of British sovereigns from 1697 to 1837. The British court, to which ambassadors are accredited, is still officially called the Court of St James's

St John (síndʒən), Henry, 1st Viscount Bolingbroke *BOLINGBROKE

St John (seintdʒón, *Br.* s'ntdʒón) the chief town (pop. 80,521) of New Brunswick, one of Canada's chief winter ports

St John (seintdʒón) a river (450 miles long) rising in N.W. Maine and flowing northeast to form a section of the Maine-New Brunswick boundary, then bending southeasterly to the Bay of Fundy. It was named by Champlain on the day of St John the Baptist (1604)

St John of Jerusalem, Order of the Hospital of *KNIGHT HOSPITALER

Saint-John Perse (síndʒənpɛ́:rs, sɛ́dʒɔnpɛərs) (Alexis Saint-Léger Leger, 1887-1975), French lyric poet. His works included 'Eloges' (1911), 'Anabase' (1924), 'Exil' (1942), 'Vents' (1946), 'Amers' (1957) and 'Oiseaux' (1962). His work is extremely difficult for the reader, full of obscurities, but the nobility and musicality of the language and the force of imagination in the poetry have irresistible power. He wrote a cadenced prose, using forms peculiar to himself. 'Anabase' is generally considered his masterpiece. He received the Nobel prize for literature (1960)

St John's (seintdʒónz, *Br.* s'ntdʒónz) the capital (pop. 80,000) of Newfoundland, Canada, a fishing port

St-John's-wort (seintdʒónzwə:rt) *n.* a member of *Hypericum*, fam. *Gutiferae*, a genus of wild and garden plants with bright yellow flowers

Saint-Just (sɛ́ʒyst), Louis de (1767-94), French revolutionist. A fervent believer in the teachings of Rousseau, he collaborated with Robespierre in the Committee of Public Safety (1793-4), and shared Robespierre's fall

St Kitts-Ne·vis (kits-ní:vis), officially Saint Christopher and Nevis, independent state (area 103 sq. miles, pop. 44,000) in the Leeward Islands, West Indies. Capital: Basseterre (pop. 14,725). Language: English. People: African descent. Mountainous islands with volcanic peaks (Mount Misery, St Kitts, 3,793 ft. and Nevis Peak, Nevis, 3,232 ft.), the country has dense vegetation surrounded by beaches. Products: sugar processing, cotton, salt, copra. Exports: sugar, molasses, cotton. HISTORY. First settled by English colonists in the 1620s, it became, with Anguilla, a state in association with Britain (Feb. 27, 1967). Anguilla subsequently declared its independence and St Kitts-Nevis became an independent state within the Commonwealth in 1983

Saint-Lau·rent (sɛ́lərã), Louis Stephen (1882-1973), Canadian statesman, Liberal prime minister of Canada (1948-57)

St Law·rence the river system joining the Great Lakes (U.S.A. and Canada) and linking them with the Atlantic, to form in all a waterway 2,100 miles long from the source of its headstream in N. Minnesota. Chicago, Detroit and Montreal are the chief ports. The St Lawrence was opened to oceangoing traffic (1959) by the St Lawrence Seaway (114 miles long), a canal system bypassing shoals and rapids be-

tween Lake Ontario and Montreal. The St Lawrence River proper (760 miles long) flows from Lake Ontario, forming the Ontario-New York state border, to the Gulf of St Lawrence. It was discovered by Cartier (1534)

St Lawrence, Gulf of a gulf of the Atlantic Ocean off the east coast of Canada, bounded by Cape Breton Is. and Newfoundland. It receives the St Lawrence

St Lawrence Seaway *ST LAWRENCE

St Leg·er (lédʒər) an annual English horse race run at Doncaster, Yorkshire, in September

saint·li·ness (séintli:nis) *n.* the quality or state of being saintly

St Lou·is (lú:is, lú:i:) the largest city (pop. 453,085, with agglom. 2,355,276) in Missouri, on the Mississippi, 16 miles below its confluence with the Missouri. It is a river port, rail center and market (furs, hides, wheat). Industries: mechanical engineering, automobiles, shoes, chemicals, food processing. Washington University (1857)

St Louis (sɛ́lwi) a port (pop. 81,204) of Senegal, on St Louis I., at the mouth of the Senegal River

St Lu·cia (lú:ʃə, lu:sí:ə) a mountainous, largely jungle-covered island republic (area 238 sq. miles, pop. 120,000) of the Windward group, West Indies. Capital: Castries (pop. 45,000). Highest point: 3,145 ft. People: mainly of African origin. Exports: bananas, copra, cocoa, coconut oil. The island was visited by the English (1605), claimed by the French (1642) and ceded to Britain (1814). It became a state in association with Britain (Mar. 3, 1967) and gained its independence in 1979

saint·ly (séintli:) *comp.* **saint·li·er** *superl.* **saint·li·est** *adj.* holy, like a saint ‖ of or pertaining to a saint

St Ma·lo (sɛ́mælou) a walled fishing port (pop. 46,270) on an island joined to the coast of Ille-et-Vilaine, France: tourism

St Mar·tin (sɛ́mɑrtɛ̃) (*Du.* Sint Maarten) an island (area 37 sq. miles, pop. 10,300) of the Leeward group, West Indies. Two thirds belong to the French department of Guadeloupe, the remainder to the Netherlands Antilles. Chief port: Marigot (French), a free port

Saint-Mi·hiel (sɛ́mi:jel) a town (pop. 5,000) in the Meuse department of France, site of a 1st world war battle in which U.S. forces under Gen. Pershing defeated (1918) the Germans, capturing the vital Verdun-Toul-Nancy rail link. It was the first victory in the 1st world war of the U.S. army fighting as an independent unit

St Mo·ritz (mɔríts) a health and winter sports resort (elevation approx. 6,000 ft, pop. 7,400) in the upper Engadine, S.E. Graubünden, Switzerland

St Na·zaire (sɛ́næzɛər) a port (pop. 69,251) of Loire-Atlantique, France, at the mouth of the Loire, the outport for Nantes

Sain·tonge (sɛ́tɔ̃ʒ) a former province of France in the N. Aquitaine basin, largely forming Charente-Maritime. It is mainly pasture (dairy cattle, sheep), with salt marshes and oyster beds along the Atlantic. Crops: cereals, vines (for cognac). Old capital: Saintes. Included in Aquitaine, it was recovered from England in 1371 and annexed by the Crown (1375)

St Paul the capital (pop. 270,230) of Minnesota, on the Mississippi opposite Minneapolis, a rail center and livestock market. Industries: meat packing, automobiles, mechanical engineering

saint·pau·lia (seintpɔ́li:ə) *n.* a member of *Saintpaulia*, fam. *Gesneriaceae*, a genus of E. African plants, esp. *S. ionantha*, which is much cultivated as a house plant [Mod. L. fr. Baron Walter von *Saint Paul* (*d.* 1910), G. colonial administrator]

St Peter's the basilica (1450-1626) of Vatican City, Rome: floor plan by Bramante and Raphael, dome by Michelangelo, portico by Bernini

St Pe·ters·burg (pí:tərzbə:rg) *LENINGRAD

St Petersburg a winter resort city (pop. 236,893) in W. central Florida: fruit, vegetables, fish

Saint-Pierre (sɛ́pjer) a town (pop. 6,000, formerly 26,000) in Martinique, destroyed (1902) by the eruption of Mt Pelée

St Pierre and Mi·que·lon (pjɛər, mĭkələn, *F.* sɛ̃pjɛr, mi:klɔ̃) an overseas territory of France off S. Newfoundland, consisting of 2 main islands and 6 islets (total area 93 sq. miles, pop. 6,272), mainly bare rock. Industries: cod fish-

ing, fur farming. The islands were claimed for France (1536) by Cartier

Saint-Saëns (sɛ̃sãs), Camille (1835-1921), French composer. His works include five symphonies, five piano concertos, three violin concertos, the opera 'Samson and Delilah' (1877), 'Carnival of Animals' (1886) for two pianos and orchestra, 'Dance Macabre' (1874) for orchestra, symphonic poems, chamber and church music, songs etc.

Saints, Battle of the a battle fought (1782) off Antigua, in which Admiral Rodney defeated the French admiral, François de Grasse (1722-88)

saint's day a day of commemoration in honor of a saint

Saint-Si·mon (sɛ̃si:mɔ̃), Claude-Henri, comte de (1760-1825), French philosopher and political economist. He was opposed to political authority and believed that society should be organized along the principles of a workshop, individual reward being strictly in proportion to productive merit. One of his principal works is 'le Système industriel' (1823-4)

Saint-Simon, Louis de Rouvroy, duc de (1675-1755), French courtier and writer. His 'Mémoires' provide a penetrating description of the French court (1691-1723)

Saint-Si·mo·ni·an (sɛ̃tsimóuni:ən) **1.** *adj.* of or advocating the ideas of Claude-Henri Saint-Simon **2.** *n.* an advocate of these ideas **Saint-Si·mó·ni·an·ism** *n.*

St So·phi·a (sɔfáiə) *ISTANBUL

St Thomas *VIRGIN ISLANDS OF THE UNITED STATES

St Tro·pez (sɛ́trɔpei) a popular resort (pop. 6,000) in Var, France, on the Riviera

St Vin·cent and the Gren·a·dines (seint vínsənt; grénədi:nz) independent state (area 153 sq. miles, pop. 138,000) consisting of St Vincent Island and the northern Grenadine Islands in the Caribbean Sea. Capital: Kingstown (pop. 23,959). Language: English. People: African descent. Wooded, mountainous islands, originally volcanic, the highest point is 4,048 ft. Products: arrowroot, bananas, coconuts. Exports: processed food. HISTORY. The island of St Vincent, whose inhabitants were Carib Indians, was disputed between the French and British (18th c.), ceded to Britain (1783), made a Crown Colony (1877) and part of the Windward Is colony (1885). It became a separate colony (1960), then a state in association with Britain (1960) and gained independence in 1979. A volcanic eruption in 1979 destroyed most of the banana crop and much of the agricultural land

St Vitus's dance chorea

Sai·pan (saipǽn) *U.S. TRUST TERRITORY OF THE PACIFIC

Saipan Island, Battle of a 2nd world war engagement in the W. Pacific, in which U.S. forces defeated (1944) the Japanese. Afterwards the island was used as a base for air attacks on the Japanese mainland

Sa·is (séiis) an ancient city of Egypt on the Nile delta. Princes of Saïs governed Egypt under the 24th, 26th and 28th-30th dynasties. It was the center of a brilliant civilization

Sa·ite (séiait) *adj.* of or pertaining to Saïs ‖ of or pertaining to the 26th dynasty of Egypt, founded by a native of Saïs

saith (seθ) *archaic 3rd pers. sing. pres.* of SAY

Sa·it·ic (seií:tik) *adj.* Saïte

Sa·kai (sakai) a town (pop. 810,000) in S. Honshu, Japan, on Osaka Bay: engineering, chemicals, textiles

sa·ke, sa·ké, sa·ki (sáki:) *n.* a Japanese liquor made from fermented rice [Jap.]

sake (seik) *n.* (in phrases) **for the sake of** (**someone** or **something's**) and **for** (**someone's** or **something's**) **sake** for the benefit of (someone or something), *she did it for the sake of her health* ‖ for the purpose of attaining, achieving etc. (something), *he said it just for argument's sake* [O.E. *sacu*, cause lawsuit]

sa·ker (séikər) *n. Falco cherrug* (or *F. sacer*), a large falcon used in hawking, esp. the female [F. *sacre* fr. Span. and Port. *sacro* fr. Arab.]

sa·ker·et (séikərit) *n.* the male saker, smaller than the female [F. *sacret*, dim. of *sacre*, saker]

Sa·kha·lin (sǽkəli:n, sʌxalí:n) a wooded mountainous island (area 24,560 sq. miles, pop. 655,000) off S.W. Siberia, U.S.S.R., 25 miles north of Hokkaido, Japan, part of the R.S.F.S.R. Products: coal, oil, gold, fish. The southern half

---

CONCISE PRONUNCIATION KEY: (a) æ, c*a*t; ɑ, c*a*r; ɔ f*aw*n; ei, sn*a*ke. (e) e, h*e*n; i:, sh*ee*p; iə, d*ee*r; ɛə, b*ea*r. (i) i, f*i*sh; ai, t*i*ger; ə:, b*i*rd. (o) o, *o*x; au, c*ow*; ou, g*oa*t; u, p*oo*r; ɔi, r*oy*al. (u) ʌ, d*u*ck; u, b*u*ll; u:, g*oo*se; ə, b*a*cillus; ju:, c*u*be. x, lo*ch*; θ, *th*ink; ð, *b*o*th*er; z, *Z*en; ʒ, cor*s*age; dʒ, sava*g*e; ŋ, ora*n*gutang; j, *y*ak; ʃ, *f*ish; tʃ, fe*tch*; 'l, rabb*le*; 'n, redd*en*. Complete pronunciation key appears inside front cover.

of the island was administered (1905-45) by Japan, but was ceded to the U.S.S.R. in 1945

Sa·kha·rov (səkórəf) Andrei Dimitriyevich (1921-), Soviet scientist, whose advocacy of nuclear disarmament and democracy brought internal exile to Gorky, winner of the Nobel peace prize (1975). A physicist, he helped to develop the Soviet H-bomb but was ostracized when he criticized the Soviets' violation of the Nuclear Test Ban Treaty in 1961. In following years he criticized the Soviet government's treatment of political prisoners and dissidents and called for nuclear arms reduction. He and his wife Dr. Yelena G. Bonner were sent into exile in Gorky in 1980 but his criticisms continued. They were released in Dec. 1986.

Sa·ki (sáki:) (Hector Hugh Munro, 1870-1916), British writer, best known for his witty, ironic short stories. Collections of these include 'Reginald' (1904), 'Reginald in Russia' (1910), 'Beasts and Superbeasts' (1914) etc.

sa·ki (sǽki:, sáki:) n. any of certain South American monkeys of fam. *Cebidae*, with long, non-prehensile tails, well-developed thumbs and neck ruffs. They are gregarious and nocturnal [F. fr. Tupi]

saki *SAKE

sal (sal) n. *Shorea robusta*, fam. *Dipterocarpaceae*, a tree of E. India, whose resin is used in varnishes ‖ its valuable hardwood [Hindi *sāl*]

sa·laam (səlám) 1. n. an Oriental greeting, in India usually accompanied by a low bow and the placing of the right palm on the forehead ‖ this bow 2. v.i. to make a salaam ‖ v.t. to greet with a salaam [Arab. *salām* fr. Heb. *shalom*, peace]

sal·a·bil·i·ty, sale·a·bil·i·ty (seiləbíliti) n. the quality or state of being salable

sal·a·ble, sale·a·ble (séiləb'l) adj. capable of being sold or fit to be sold

sa·la·cious (səléiʃəs) adj. arousing lewd thoughts ‖ lewd in character [fr. L. *salax* (*salacis*), fond of leaping, lustful]

sa·lac·i·ty (səlǽsiti) n. the quality or state of being salacious [fr. L. *salacitas*]

sal·ad (sǽləd) n. a cold dish of (esp. raw, green) vegetables etc., usually with a salad dressing ‖ a cold dish of which this forms a substantial part, *lobster salad* ‖ vegetables grown for salad, esp. lettuce [O.F. *salade* fr. Prov.]

salad days days of raw, inexperienced youth [after Shakespeare's 'Antony and Cleopatra' I, v]

salad dressing a sauce of oil, vinegar, mustard etc. for salad

Sal·a·din (sǽlədin) (Salāh-al-Dīn, 1138-93), sultan of Egypt and Syria, founder of the Ayyubid dynasty. His capture (1187) of Jerusalem led to the 3rd Crusade, in which he distinguished himself as the adversary of Richard I of England

Sa·la·do del Nor·te (saláðɔ͝ɔðelnórte) (or Salado) a river (1,120 miles long) of N. Argentina, flowing from the Andes across the eastern plain to the Paraná at Santa Fé

Sa·la·do del Sud (saláðɔ͝ɔðelsú:d) (or Salado) a river (850 miles long) of central Argentina, rising (as the Desaguadero) in the Andes and flowing the length of the Pampas. It joins the smaller Colorado before reaching the Atlantic

Sal·a·man·ca (sæləmǽŋkə, salamáŋka) a province (area 4,829 sq. miles, pop. 368,055) of W. Spain (*LEÓN) ‖ its capital (pop. 167,131): Roman bridge, two cathedrals (12th-13th and 16th-18th cc.), medieval and Renaissance monasteries, churches etc., central square (18th c.). University (early 13th c.)

sal·a·man·der (sǽləmændər) n. a mythical creature believed to live in fire and delight in it ‖ a member of *Caudata*, an order of amphibians superficially like lizards but with a soft, moist, brightly colored skin and no scales. The order includes newts and hellbenders. The adults are terrestrial and many are viviparous ‖ a hot iron plate for browning the tops of puddings, pastries etc. **sal·a·mán·dri·an** adj. [F. *salamandre* fr. L. fr. Gk]

sal·a·man·drine (sæləmǽndrin) adj. of or like a salamander [fr. L. *salamandra*, salamander]

sal·a·mi (səlámi:) n. a highly seasoned sausage of pork and beef [Ital.]

Sal·a·mis (sǽləmis, sɑlamí:s) an island (area 36 sq. miles, pop. 18,317) just off the coast of Attica, Greece, west of Piraeus

Salamis, Battle of the decisive victory (480 B.C.) of the Greek fleet over the Persians, fought off Salamis during the Persian Wars

sal ammoniac (sæl) n. ammonium chloride [L. *sal*, salt+AMMONIAC]

sal·an·gane (sǽləngæn) n. any of several swifts of Asia and Oceania, which make edible nests (*BIRD'S NEST SOUP) [F. or fr. Mod. L. *salangana* fr. *salamga*, the birds' name in Luzon]

sa·lar·i·at (səlǽri:æt) n. salary earners as a class

sal·a·ried (sǽləri:d) adj. receiving a salary

sal·a·ry (sǽləri) pl. **sal·a·ries** n. a fixed regular payment made esp. to nonmanual workers (cf. WAGE, cf. FEE) [A.F. *salarie*]

Sa·la·zar (sɑlazár), Antonio de Oliveira (1889-1970), Portuguese statesman. As finance minister (1928-32), he restored economic order. As prime minister (1932-68), he established a dictatorship on fascist lines (1933)

Sa·la·zar y Es·pi·no·za (sɑlaθári:espi:nóθa), Juan de (b. 1508), Spanish conquistador. With Gonzalo de Mendoza he founded (1537) Asunción, Paraguay

sale (seil) n. a selling or being sold, *to arrange for the sale of one's books* ‖ the amount of goods sold, *sales of wine have gone up* ‖ a public selling by auction ‖ a selling of surplus or out-of-date stock at reduced prices **for sale** offered for purchase **on sale** displayed for purchase [O.E. *sala* prob. fr. O.N.]

saleability *SALABILITY

saleable *SALABLE

Sa·lem (séiləm) a town (pop. 308,716) in N. central Madras, India: textiles, paper, mining (iron ore, manganese)

Salem a seaport and seaside resort (pop. 38,220) in the northeast corner of Massachusetts. Witchcraft trials (1692) led to the execution of 19 'witches'

Salem the capital (pop. 89,233) of Oregon. It is a processing center for the area's livestock, fruit, nut and vegetable farms. Paper and textiles are also produced. Site of Willamette University (1842)

sa·lep (sǽlep) n. a starchy food prepared from the dried tubers of certain orchids, esp. *Orchis mascula* [F. fr. Turk. fr. Arab. fr. *khus.a ath·tha'lab*, the fox's testicles]

sal·e·ra·tus (sæləréitəs) n. sodium bicarbonate, NaHCO3, or potassium bicarbonate, KHCO3, used for leavening [Mod. L. *sal*, salt+*aeratus*, aerated]

Sa·ler·no (sɑlérnə, *Eng.* səlé:rnou) a port and agricultural market (pop. 161,997) of Campania, Italy, 32 miles south of Naples on the Gulf of Salerno, a wide inlet of the Tyrrhenian Sea. Cathedral (11th c.). It had a famous school of medicine (flourished 9th-13th cc.). During the 2nd world war it was the site (1943) of a flanking maneuver by Allied landing forces that was bitterly resisted by German forces

sale·room (séilru:m, séilrum) n. (*Br.*) a room where goods are displayed and sold esp. by auction

sales clerk a man or woman who sells goods in a store

sales·girl (séilzgə:rl) n. a saleswoman

Sa·le·sian (səli:ʒən, səli:ʃən) 1. n. a member of the Society of St Francis of Sales, founded (c. 1851) by St John Bosco to educate poor children 2. adj. of or pertaining to this order

sales·la·dy (séilzleidi:) pl. **sales·la·dies** n. a saleswoman

sales·man (séilzmən) pl. **sales·men** (séilzmən) n. someone whose job is to sell goods, whether in a store or by traveling to visit potential buyers

sales·man·ship (séilzmənʃip) n. skill in the technique of selling goods

sales resistance resistance by a potential customer to the persuasive influence of a salesman or of advertisements etc.

sales·room (séilzru:m, séilzrum) n. any room where goods are displayed and sold ‖ (*Br.*) a saleroom

Sales, St Francis of *FRANCIS OF SALES, ST

sales tax a tax levied on retail sales and collected by the retailer

sales·wom·an (séilzwumən) pl. **sales·wom·en** (séilzwimən) n. a girl or woman employee who sells goods, esp. in a store

Sal·ford (sǽlfərd, sɔ́lford) a port and county borough (pop. 98,024) in S.E. Lancashire, England, adjoining Manchester, on the Manchester Ship Canal: textiles, engineering, dyeing, rubber goods, paper

Sa·li·an (séili:ən, séiljən) 1. adj. of or relating to the northern division of the Franks, united (late 5th c.) with the Ripuarian Franks under

Clovis 2. n. a Salian Frank [fr. L.L. *Salii*, a division of Franks, fr. R. Sala (now the IJssel)]

Sal·ic (sǽlik, séilik) adj. Salian [fr. F. *salique* or Med. L. *Salicus*]

sal·i·cet (sǽliset) n. an organ stop of soft tone, resembling the salicional but of 4-ft or 2-ft pitch [G. fr. L. *salix* (*salicis*), willow, with reference to the tone of a willow pipe]

sal·i·cin (sǽlisin) n. a bitter white crystalline substance, C13H18O7, obtained from the bark of the willow and poplar and used in the treatment of rheumatism and neuralgia [fr. F. *salicine*]

sa·li·cion·al (səlíʃən'l) n. a soft-toned organ stop, sounding somewhat like the strings of the orchestra and usually of 8-ft pitch [G. fr. L. *salix* (*salicis*), willow, with reference to the tone of a willow pipe]

Salic law a law excluding succession by or through females, adopted in the Middle Ages by several European royal and noble houses and mistakenly thought to have been part of the laws of the Salian Franks. It was invoked (14th c.) in France and contributed to the outbreak of the Hundred Years' War. It was also responsible for the separation of Hanover and Britain on the accession (1837) of Queen Victoria

sa·lic·y·late (səlísəleit, sælisíleit) n. a salt or ester of salicylic acid [SALICYLIC ACID]

sal·i·cyl·ic acid (sælisílik) a colorless crystalline acid, HOC6H4COOH, formerly obtained from willow bark but now manufactured from phenol. It is used in the preparation of dyestuffs, and as a strong antiseptic, and in medicine as an analgesic and antirheumatic, usually in the form of its acetyl ester, aspirin [fr. F. *salicyle* fr. L. *salix* (*salicis*), willow]

sa·li·ence (séili:əns, séiljəns) n. the quality or state of being salient ‖ a striking feature, detail etc. **sá·li·en·cy** pl. **sa·li·en·cies** n.

sa·li·ent (séili:ənt, séiljənt) 1. adj. being most prominent or of the most importance, *the salient points in a speech* ‖ pointing outwards, *a salient angle* ‖ (*heraldry*) shown in a leaping posture 2. n. that which is salient, esp. (*mil.*) a part of a defense line which projects into enemy territory [fr. L. *saliens* (*salientis*) fr. *sal*, to leap]

sa·li·en·ti·an (seili:éntʃi:ən) 1. n. a member of *Salientia*, an order of amphibians which are tailless in the adult stage, with powerful long hind limbs for swimming and leaping. The order includes frogs, toads and tree toads 2. adj. pertaining to salientians [fr. Mod. L. fr. L. *saliens* (*salientis*) fr. *salire*, to leap]

sa·lif·er·ous (səlífərəs) adj. (*e.g.* of geological strata) impregnated with salt [fr. L. *sal*, salt+*ferre*, to bear]

sal·i·fy (sǽlifai) pres. part. **sal·i·fy·ing** past and past part. **sal·i·fied** v.t. to cause to become a salt ‖ to combine or impregnate with salt ‖ v.i. to become a salt [fr. F. *salifier*]

sa·li·na (səláinə, səli:nə) n. a salt lake or marsh (e.g. in the Argentine plains) [Span.]

sa·line (séilain, séili:n) 1. adj. of or containing salt, *a saline solution* ‖ salty in taste ‖ relating to or having the nature of chemical salts ‖ (*med.*) containing salts of alkaline metals or magnesium 2. n. a salina ‖ a salt spring ‖ a natural deposit of salt ‖ a saline solution ‖ a saline cathartic or other metallic salt **sa·lin·i·ty** (səlíniti:) n. [fr. L. *sal*, salt]

Sal·in·ger (sǽlindʒər), J(erome) D(avid) (1919-), U.S. novelist. He is best known for his 'The Catcher in the Rye' (1951). Other works include 'Franny and Zooey' (1961) and 'Raise High the Roof Beam, Carpenters' and 'Seymour: An Introduction' (1963, published in one volume)

sal·i·nom·e·ter (sælinómitər) n. an instrument for determining salinity, e.g. the salinity of the seawater in marine boilers, by measuring the density

Salis·bur·y (sɔ́lzbəri:, sɔ́lzbəri:), Robert Arthur Talbot Gascoyne-Cecil, 3rd marquis of (1830-1903), British Conservative statesman. As foreign secretary (1878-80), he attended the Congress of Berlin (1878). He was prime minister (1885-6, 1886-92, 1895-1902) and was also foreign secretary during most of the period. At home, he led the opposition to Irish Home Rule, and abroad was primarily concerned with African affairs, notably the Fashoda crisis (1898-9) and the Boer War (1899-1902). His avoidance of major foreign alliances has been described as 'splendid isolation'

Salisbury *HARARE

Salisbury a city (pop. 100,929) in Wiltshire, England, at the southern end of Salisbury Plain. Early Gothic cathedral (1220-58)

CONCISE PRONUNCIATION KEY: **(a)** æ, c*a*t; ɑ, c*a*r; ɔ f*aw*n; ei, sn*a*ke. **(e)** e, h*e*n; i:, sh*ee*p; iə, d*ee*r; ɛə, b*ea*r. **(i)** i, f*i*sh; ai, t*i*ger; ə:, b*i*rd. **(o)** o, *o*x; au, c*ow*; ou, g*oa*t; u, p*oo*r; ɔi, r*oy*al. **(u)** ʌ, d*u*ck; u, b*u*ll; u:, g*oo*se; ə, bacill*u*s; ju:, c*u*be. x, lo*ch*; θ, *th*ink; ð, bo*th*er; z, *Z*en; ʒ, corsa*g*e. dʒ, sava*g*e; ŋ, ora*ng*utang; j, *y*ak; ʃ, *fish*; tʃ, fe*tch*; 'l, rabb*l*e; 'n, redd*en*. Complete pronunciation key appears inside front cover.

Salisbury Plain a treeless chalk plateau (area 300 sq. miles) in Wiltshire, England, the site of Stonehenge and other ancient monuments

sa·li·va (səláivə) *n.* a colorless viscous fluid secreted into the mouth from special glands, helping by its chemical composition to predigest food and, by keeping the mouth and throat moist, to facilitate swallowing **sal·i·vant** (sǽlivənt) **1.** *adj.* promoting the secretion of saliva **2.** *n.* an agent that promotes secretion of saliva [L.]

sal·i·var·y (sǽliveri:) *adj.* pertaining to or secreting saliva [fr. L. *salivarius*]

sal·i·vate (sǽliveit) *pres. part.* **sal·i·vat·ing** *past* and *past part.* **sal·i·vat·ed** *v.i.* to secrete saliva (esp. in excess) ‖ *v.t.* to cause an excessive flow of saliva in, e.g. by the use of mercury **sal·i·va·tion** *n.* [fr. L. *salivare* (*salivatus*)]

Salk (sɔːlk, sɔk), Jonas Edward (1914-), U.S. authority on virus diseases. He developed (1947) a dead-virus vaccine which protects against paralyzation in poliomyelitis. His research was further developed by Albert Sabin (1906-), whose live-virus oral vaccine largely replaced Salk's

sal·let (sǽlit) *n.* a light helmet of the 15th c. [F. *salade* fr. Span. or Ital. perh. fr. L. (*galea*) *caelata,* an engraved (helmet)]

sal·low (sǽlou) **1.** *adj.* (esp. of complexion) dull yellow or pale brown **2.** *v.t.* to make sallow [O.E. *salo*]

sallow *n.* any of several low, shrubby Old World varieties of willow, esp. *Salix caprea* ‖ a willow shoot [O.E. *sealh*]

Sal·lust (sǽləst) (Gaius Sallustius Crispus, 86–c. 34 B.C.), Roman historian. His 'Bellum Catilinarium' (43 B.C.) and his 'Bellum Jugurthinum' (c. 41 B.C.) are important for the character sketches they contain, rather than as accurate history

sal·ly (sǽli:) **1.** *pl.* **sal·lies** *n.* a brief and clever or fanciful witticism ‖ a burst of activity or outburst expressing emotion ‖ (*mil.*) a sudden attack made from a fortified position ‖ a little trip, *a sally into the hills* **2.** *v.i. pres. part.* **sally·ing** *past* and *past part.* **sal·lied** (with 'forth' or 'out') to leave home, or a temporary stopping place, for a short journey ‖ (*mil.*) make a sally [F. *saillie* fr. *saillir,* to rush forth]

Sal·ly Lunn (sǽli:lʌn) a sweet tea cake, eaten hot and buttered [perh. after *Sally Lunn,* a street hawker in Bath, c. 1800]

sal·ma·gun·di (sælməgʌ́ndi:) *n.* a mixed dish of chopped meat, anchovies, eggs, oil, vinegar etc. [F. *salmigondis,* origin unknown]

sal·mi, sal·mis (sǽlmi:) *n.* a seasoned stew of game birds in wine or rich brown sauce [F. *salmis* perh. fr. *salmigondis, salmagundi*]

salm·on (sǽmən) *pl.* **salm·on, salm·ons** *n. Salmo salar,* fam. *Salmonidae,* a large N. Atlantic game fish prized for its flesh as food ‖ the orange-pink color of its flesh ‖ any fish of fam. *Salmonidae,* esp. of genus *Oncorhynchus,* living and breeding in N. Pacific waters ‖ any of certain fishes of families other than *Salmonidae,* having the reddish flesh of a true salmon [A.F. *salmoun, saumoun*]
—The silvery salmon adults feed in the sea, but ascend rivers in winter to spawn in shallow, gravel-based streams. In 120–140 days the newly hatched salmon escape. In the second or third spring after hatching, when uniformly bluish-silver and about 7 ins long, they descend to the sea and feed voraciously. They may return to spawn 18 months after descent (*GRILSE, * PARR, *SMOLT)

salmon ladder a fish ladder

salmon leap a fish ladder

salmon stair a fish ladder

salmon trout *Salmo trutta,* a European sea trout ‖ any of certain other trout or salmon

Sa·lo·me (səlóumi:) (c. 14–c. 62), daughter of Herodias. Herodias prompted her to ask Herod Antipas to consent, in reward for her dancing, to the death of John the Baptist (Matthew xiv. 8)

sa·lon (səlɔ́n, sæló) *n.* a living room or drawing room in a French home ‖ an assembly of wits, artists, writers or other men and women of society, meeting in the house of a society lady, esp. (*hist.*) in 17th-c. and 18th-c. France ‖ a room in which hairdressers, dressmakers etc. receive their clients ‖ an exhibition of paintings etc., esp. in Paris [F.]

Sa·lon·i·ca (səlónikə) (*Gk* Thessaloniki) a port (pop. 406,413) of central Macedonia, Greece, at the head of the Gulf of Salonica, a narrow inlet of the Aegean. Industries: textiles, tobacco. Greek and Roman ruins, Byzantine churches and fortifications. University

sa·lon·ist (sɔ́lənist) *n.* one who frequents social gatherings of interesting people *syn.* sallonard

sa·loon (səlúːn) *n.* a room, usually public, for some special purpose, *a billiards saloon* ‖ a lounge or other public room on a passenger ship ‖ (*Br.*) a large cabin for a first-class passenger ‖ a public room or establishment where alcoholic drinks are served ‖ (*Br.*) a saloon bar ‖ (*Br.*) a luxurious railroad car without compartments, often having a specified function, *dining saloon* ‖ (*Br.*) a sedan (automobile) [F. *salon* fr. Ital.]

saloon bar (*Br.*) a well-appointed bar in a public house, where prices are higher than in the public bar

saloon deck a ship's deck reserved for first-class passengers occupying saloon cabins, or the deck on which a saloon is located

sa·loon·keep·er (səlúːnkiːpər) *n.* the owner or manager of a public bar

Sal·op (sǽləp) Shropshire [fr. A.F. *Sloppesberie* fr. O.E. *Scrobbesbyrig* Shrewsbury (the county town)]

sal·pi·glos·sis (sælpiglɔ́sis, sælpiglósis) *n.* a member of *Salpiglossis,* fam. *Solanaceae,* a genus of Chilean plants bearing handsome variegated flowers superficially resembling petunias [Mod. L. fr. Gk *salpinx,* trumpet+*glōssa,* tongue]

sal·pinx (sǽlpiŋks) *pl.* **sal·pin·ges** (sælpíndʒi:z) *n.* a Eustachian tube ‖ either of the Fallopian tubes [Gk=trumpet]

sal·si·fy (sǽlsəfi:) *pl.* **sal·si·fies** *n. Tragopogon porrifolius,* a European biennial composite plant, whose tubular white roots are eaten as a vegetable [F. *salsifis* prob. fr. Ital.]

sal soda (sæl) crystallized sodium carbonate, $Na_2CO_3 \cdot 10H_2O$, used in washing and bleaching fabrics

salt (sɔlt) **1.** *n.* a white crystalline compound, NaCl, which occurs widely in nature both as a solid and in seawater (2.6%). It is used as a food seasoning, as a preservative for meat and fish, as a raw material for the manufacture of many chemicals and in the manufacture of glass and soap. Salt is found in all animal fluids and plays an important role in maintaining the health of the animal and plant body. It is obtained commercially by the evaporation of brine or from solid deposits ‖ (esp. *pl.*) any of various naturally occurring substances, either mineral or saline mixtures, used as aperients or cathartics ‖ (*chem.*) one of a class of compounds derived from acids by the replacement of one or more acid hydrogens by a metal or by a radical acting like a metal. It may be produced by the reaction of an acid with a base or with a metal or metal oxide, or by the direct combination of its elements. Salts are usually crystalline solids that melt at high temperatures and that in the fused state or in solution conduct electricity ‖ a saltcellar ‖ (*pop.*) an experienced sailor ‖ something that adds piquancy, interest etc. **the salt of the earth** people or a person of simple goodness whom one regards as eminently worthy of respect **to take with a grain (or pinch) of salt** to have doubts about, regard as exaggerated **2.** *adj.* impregnated with or preserved in salt ‖ tasting of salt ‖ of or relating to salt water [O.E. *sealt*]

salt *v.t.* to flavor, treat or preserve with salt ‖ to enliven, *to salt a speech with racy anecdotes* ‖ to make (a mine) seem richer than it is by scattering valuable bits of ore in it **to salt down** (or **away**) to preserve in salt ‖ to store away (money etc.) [O.E. *sealtan*]

SALT *n.* (acronym) for strategic arms limitation talks, extensive negotiating sessions between the U.S. and the U.S.S.R. on the limitations on strategic nuclear weapons. SALT I opened in Helsinki in November 1969 and expired in 1970 without violation. SALT II, begun in Geneva in November 1972, attempted to achieve a comprehensive agreement on limiting strategic weapons, but it was not approved by the U.S. SALT III is the name for the prospective negotiations for qualitative and quantitative reduction in offensive nuclear arms

sal·ta·rel·lo (sæltərélou, sɔltərélou) *pl.* **sal·ta·rel·los** *n.* an Italian dance characterized by a skip at the beginning of each measure ‖ the music for this dance [Ital.]

sal·ta·tion (sæltéifən) *n.* (*rhet.*) a leaping ‖ a sudden change in the course of evolution [fr. L. *saltatio* (*saltationis*)]

sal·ta·to·ri·al (sæltətɔ́ri:əl, sæltətóuri:əl) *adj.* saltatory ‖ (*zool.*) adapted for leaping [fr. L. *saltatorius*]

sal·ta·to·ry (sǽltətɔri:, sæltətóuri) *adj.* (*rhet.*) of or relating to dancing ‖ proceeding by or characterized by sudden changes [fr. L. *saltatorius*]

salt·box (sɔ́ltbɒks) *n.* a New England frame house, esp. in colonial times, usually having two stories in front but only one at the back, the back slope of the gable roof continuing down over this lower part

salt cake sodium sulfate, Na_2SO_4, used in processing wood pulp and in making glass and chemicals

salt·cel·lar (sɔ́ltselər) *n.* a vessel for containing salt, used at table

salted weapon (*mil.*) a nuclear weapon that has certain elements or isotopes capturing neutrons at the time of explosion and producing radioactive products in excess of the usual debris *Cf* MINIMUM RESIDUAL RADIOACTIVITY WEAPON, NEUTRON BOMB

salt·er (sɔ́ltər) *n.* a person who handles, sells or makes salt ‖ a person who salts meat, fish etc.

salt·ern (sɔ́ltərn) *n.* a place where salt is obtained by evaporation or by boiling salt water [O.E. *sealtærn*]

salt glaze a stoneware glaze formed by the reaction of sodium chloride and silica when common salt is burned in the kiln towards the end of the firing

sal·ti·grade (sǽltəgreid) **1.** *adj.* having legs adapted for leaping **2.** *n.* a member of *Salticidae,* a family of saltigrade spiders [fr. L. *saltus,* a leap+*gradi,* to walk]

Sal·ti·llo (sɑltíːjɔ) the capital (pop. 245,738) of the Mexican state of Coahuila, 430 miles north of Mexico City, a commercial and communications center. Manufactures: woolen fabrics, knitted goods. Gold, silver, lead, zinc, copper, iron and coal are mined

sal·tine (sɔltíːn) *n.* a thin cracker baked with a salt topping [fr. SALT+-INE]

salt·i·ness (sɔ́lti:nis) *n.* the quality or state of being salty

sal·tire (sǽltaiər, sæltaiər, sɔ́ltiər, sɔ́ltaiər) *n.* (*heraldry*) an ordinary having the form X [O.F. *sautoir, salteur*]

Salt Lake, Great *GREAT SALT LAKE

Salt Lake City the capital (pop. 163,033) of Utah, in the W. Rocky Mtns near Great Salt Lake, a communications center and market for the Great Basin. Industries: metallurgy (esp. copper), meat packing, food processing. Mormon Tabernacle (1863-7). University of Utah (1850)

salt lick a place where salt occurs naturally or is placed, and which is visited by animals when they crave salt

salt marsh a marsh impregnated with salt water and partly covered by it at high tide

salt mine a mine where rock salt is hewn from a natural deposit

Sal·to (sǽltɔ) a commercial and shipping center (pop. 80,000) in N.W. Uruguay, at the head of the Uruguay River: meat salting and canning

salt pan a natural depression near the sea, or a shallow vessel, in which salt water gathers and from which salt is obtained by evaporation

salt·pe·ter, salt·pe·tre (sɔltpíːtər) *n.* potassium nitrate ‖ chile saltpeter [older *salpetre* fr. O.F.]

salt pit a pit into which seawater comes and from which salt is obtained by evaporation

Salt Range a mountain range (average elevation 3,500 ft) in Pakistan between the Jhelum and the Indus

salt·shak·er (sɔ́ltfeikər) *n.* a container having a perforated top for sprinkling salt on food

salt spoon a tiny spoon used for helping oneself to salt at the table

salt water water containing salt, esp. seawater

salt·water (sɔ́ltwɔtər, sɔ́ltwɔːtər) *adj.* of or pertaining to or living in salt water

salt·wort (sɔ́ltwəːrt) *n.* a member of *Salsola,* fam. *Chenopodiaceae,* a genus of plants with sessile succulent leaves, growing in saline habitats, and used for making soda ash ‖ any of several other plants growing in saline soil

salt·y (sɔ́lti:) *comp.* **salt·i·er** *superl.* **salt·i·est** *adj.* containing or tasting of salt ‖ smelling like the sea ‖ (*fig.*) pungent, piquant

sa·lu·bri·ous (səlúːbri:əs) *adj.* good for the health, *a salubrious climate* ‖ morally wholesome [fr. L. *salubris*]

CONCISE PRONUNCIATION KEY: **(a)** æ, c*a*t; ɑ, c*a*r; ɔ f*aw*n; ei, sn*a*ke. **(e)** e, h*e*n; iː, sh*ee*p; iə, d*ee*r; ɛə, b*ea*r. **(i)** i, f*i*sh; ai, t*i*ger; əː, b*i*rd. **(o)** o, *o*x; au, c*ow*; ou, g*oa*t; u, p*oo*r; ɔi, r*oy*al. **(u)** ʌ, d*u*ck; u, b*u*ll; uː, g*oo*se; ə, b*a*cillus; juː, c*u*be. x, lo*ch*; θ, *th*ink; ð, bo*th*er; z, *Z*en; ʒ, cor*s*age; dʒ, sa*v*age; ŋ, ora*ng*utang; j, *y*ak; ʃ, *f*ish; tʃ, fet*ch*; 'l, rabb*le*; 'n, redd*en*.   Complete pronunciation key appears inside front cover.

sa·lu·bri·ty (səlú:briti:) *n.* the quality of being salubrious [fr. L. *salubritas*]

Sa·lu·ki (səlú:ki:) *n.* a dog of a swift, tall, slender Middle Eastern breed, used for hunting gazelles [Arab.]

sal·u·re·sis (sæljurí:sis) *n.* (*med.*) excretion of salt in urine —**saluretic** *n.* the drug which facilitates —**saluretic** *adj.* —**saluretically** *adv.*

sal·u·tar·i·ly (sæljutərəli:, sæljutéərili:) *adv.* in a salutary way

sal·u·tar·i·ness (sæljutəri:nis) *n.* the quality of being salutary

sal·u·tar·y (sæljutəri:) *adj.* producing a good result, beneficial, esp. to the health ‖ designed to effect improvement, *salutary punishment* [fr. F. *salutaire* or L. *salutaris*, good for the health]

sal·u·ta·tion (sæljutéiʃən) *n.* the act of saluting, or of giving greeting ‖ something done or said in greeting ‖ the conventional opening of a letter or speech, e.g. 'Dear Sir', 'Ladies and Gentlemen' [O.F. *salutacion*]

sa·lu·ta·to·ri·an (səlu:tətóri:ən, səlu:tətóuri:ən) *n.* a student, usually the one with the second highest marks, who delivers an oration opening the graduating exercises in high school or college (cf. VALEDICTORIAN)

sa·lu·ta·to·ry (səlú:tətɔri:, səlú:tətóuri:) 1. *adj.* having the nature of a salutation ‖ relating to or designating the oration of a salutatorian 2. *pl.* **sa·lu·ta·to·ries** *n.* the oration of a salutatorian [fr. L. *salutatorius* fr. *salutare*, to salute]

sa·lute (səlú:t) *pres. part.* **sa·lut·ing** *past* and *past part.* **sa·lut·ed** *v.t.* to address with some sign of respect or spoken formula of greeting ‖ to make a prescribed gesture of respect to (a military superior), esp. by raising the right hand to the cap ‖ *v.i.* to make a salute [fr. L. *salutare* fr. *salus* (*salutis*), health]

salute *n.* the gesture, position, act or form of words used in saluting ‖ (*fencing*) a set of movements made before engaging [F. *salut*]

Sal·va·dor (sælvədɔr) (or Bahía) a port (pop. 1,027,100) of Brazil, 750 miles northeast of Rio de Janeiro, the country's oldest city and first capital (1549-1763). Industries: tanning, tobacco and food processing. Cathedral (16th c.), colonial churches and houses. University (1946)

Salvador, El *EL SALVADOR

sal·vage (sælvidʒ) 1. *v.t. pres. part.* **sal·vag·ing** *past* and *past part.* **sal·vaged** to rescue from ruin, fire, shipwreck etc. 2. *n.* things salvaged ‖ the act of salvaging ‖ the value of insured goods saved from a catastrophe etc. ‖ the money paid for saving a ship or cargo from loss at sea [F.]

sal·va·tion (sælvéiʃən) *n.* the act of saving from destruction or catastrophe, esp. the saving of the soul from sin or its consequences ‖ the condition of being saved ‖ something that saves, *the hut was his salvation in the storm* [O.F. *salvatiun*]

Salvation Army a worldwide Christian organization, founded by William Booth in 1865, devoted to evangelism and social work among the poorest and most wretched. It has a quasi-military form of organization

Salvation Islands three islands off the coast of French Guiana. With the mainland prison of St Laurent, they served (up to 1946) as an escape-proof exile center. About 75,000 of France's worst criminals are sent there. The islands include Devil's Is (used for political prisoners, of whom Alfred Dreyfus was the most famous), Ile Royale (for dangerous prisoners), and Ile St Joseph (for incorrigibles who, if they continued to make trouble, were guillotined and tossed to the sharks)

Sal·va·tion·ist (sælvéiʃənist) *n.* a member of the Salvation Army

salve (sæv, sav, *Br.* esp. sælv) *n.* a healing ointment ‖ something that soothes hurt feelings or a guilty conscience [O.E. *sealf*]

salve *pres. part.* **salv·ing** *past* and *past part.* **salved** *v.t.* to soothe or set at ease (feelings or the conscience) [O.E. *sealfian*, to apply a salve to (a wound etc.)]

sal·ver (sælvər) *n.* a tray, esp. an ornamental one of silver etc., used for presenting letters, drinks etc. [fr. F. *salve* fr. Span. *salva*, the tasting of food before serving]

Sal·ve Re·gi·na (sálveirìdʒí:nə) *n.* (Roman Catholicism) an antiphon to the Virgin Mary, recited after Divine Office from Trinity Sunday to Advent ‖ the music for this [L.=hail, queen (the opening words)]

sal·vi·a (sælvi:ə) *n.* a member of *Salvia*, fam.

Labiatae, a large genus of widely distributed annual or perennial plants of warm and temperate climates. They have lipped flowers, and are protandrous. Many varieties are cultivated, e.g. sage [L.=sage]

sal·vo (sælvou) *pl.* **sal·vos, sal·voes** *n.* a simultaneous discharge of guns, explosion of bombs, or burst of cheers [earlier *salva* fr. Ital.]

sal vo·la·ti·le (sælvoulæt'li:) *n.* ammonium carbonate ‖ an aromatic solution of this used as smelling salts [Mod. L.=volatile salt]

sal·vor (sælvər) *n.* a person or ship effecting a salvage [SALVAGE]

Sal·ween (sælwi:n) a river (1,750 miles long) rising in E. Tibet and flowing through Yunnan, China, and E. Burma to the Indian Ocean

Salz·burg (zál/tsburg, sɔ́lzbə:rg) a city (pop. 138,213) of N. central Austria in the lower Alps. Industries: chemicals, metallurgy, tourism. It was Mozart's birthplace, and is esp. famous for its annual music festival. Castle (11th-17th cc.), baroque cathedral (17th c.), medieval, Renaissance and baroque churches etc. University (1928) ‖ the province (area 2,762 sq. miles, pop. 347,000) of which it is the capital

SAM *n.* (*mil.*) U.S.S.R. surface-to-air missile. SAM-3, named Sandal by NATO, with a range of 1,500 miles; involved in the 1958 Cuban missile crisis. SAM-6, battlefield missile with a range of 20 miles. SAM-9, mobile-mounted, heat-seeking missile with a range of 5 miles

Sa·main (sæmɛ̃), Albert Victor (1858-1900), French poet. His verse (e.g. 'Au jardin de l'infante,' 1893) showed symbolist influence

Sa·mar (sámər) an island (area 5,050 sq. miles, pop. 1,019,358) of the central Philippines (Visayas)

Sa·ma·ra (səmárə) * KUIBYSHEV

sam·a·ra (sæmərə, səmǽrə) *n.* (*bot.*) a dry, winged, indehiscent fruit, usually having one seed, e.g. the fruit of the ash or elm [Mod. L. fr. L.=elm seed]

Sa·mar·i·a (səmɛ́əri:ə) the ancient capital (c. 932–c. 722 B.C.) of Israel. It is modern Sebastyeh (pop. 800) in Jordan, near Nablus, with Israelite, Assyrian and Roman ruins ‖ the region of W. Jordan containing this

Sa·mar·i·tan (səmǽrit'n) 1. *adj.* pertaining to Samaria 2. *n.* a native of Samaria, esp. a member of a Hebrew sect differing from the Jews in accepting only the Pentateuch. A dwindling number survive in Nablus, Jordan ‖ a Good Samaritan [O.E. fr. L.L. fr. Gk]

sa·mar·i·um (səmɛ́əri:əm) *n.* a metallic element in the rare-earth group (symbol Sm, at. no. 62, at. mass 150.35), discovered spectroscopically in 1879 [Mod. L. fr. SAMARSKITE]

Sam·ar·kand (sæmərkǽnd, səmɑrkánt) (ancient Marcanda) a city (pop. 476,000) of W. Uzbekistan, U.S.S.R., the commercial center of an oasis region. Industries: food processing, cotton and silk spinning. Medieval city walls, Moslem colleges, tombs and mosques of Timur and his successors. From ancient times, Samarkand dominated the trade route between the Near East and China. It was taken (1220) by Genghis Khan, and became the capital of the empire of Timur (14th c.), who made the city splendid with gardens, palaces and mosques

sa·mar·skite (səmárskait) *n.* a velvet-black orthorhombic mineral with a vitreous luster [after Col. *Samarski*, 19th-c. Russ. mining official]

sam·ba (sæmbə, sámbə) *n.* a lively Brazilian dance of African origin ‖ a ballroom dance derived from it [Port.]

sam·bar, sam·bur (sæmbər, sámbər) *n.* any of certain large Asiatic deer with strong antlers, esp. *Cervus unicolor unicolor* of India [Hindi *sābar, sāmbar*]

sam·bo (sæmbou) *n.* (*sports*) wrestling judo style

Sam Browne belt (sæmbráun) an army officer's light leather belt with an attached shoulder strap [after Gen. Sir *Samuel J. Browne* (1834–1901), Br. army officer]

sambur *SAMBAR

Sam D *n.* (*mil.*) an army air-defense artillery surface-to-air missile system under development to replace Nike Hercules and the improved Hawk systems

same (seim) 1. *adj.* (with 'the' or a demonstrative adjective having one individuality or self, *she wore the same dress all week, the cooking and the eating took place in that same small room* ‖ (with 'the') being of one kind, having one nature or set of characteristics, *several women had on the same dress at the party, the two*

houses look very much the same ‖ (with 'the') corresponding, *it was hotter at the same time last year* ‖ (with 'the') not changing or showing change, *the same old routine* ‖ (with 'the' or a demonstrative adj.) being the one already mentioned, *that same boy was to become prime minister* 2. *adv.* (with 'the') in the same way, *they both feel the same about it* **all the same** nevertheless, *all the same you should apologize* ‖ a matter of indifference, *if it's all the same to you, let's go tomorrow* **just the same** nevertheless ‖ exactly alike ‖ in the same way 3. *pron.* (with 'the') the same person or thing, *the same applies to the rest of you, I'll have some more of the same, please* [M.E. fr. O.N.]

sam·el (sæməl) *adj.* (of bricks, tiles etc.) soft, from being fired in the outer part of the kiln and hence insufficiently fired [etym. doubtful]

sameness (séimnis) *n.* the state or quality of being the same ‖ monotonous lack of variety

Sa·mi·an (séimi:ən) 1. *adj.* of Samos or its people 2. *n.* a native or inhabitant of Samos [fr. L. *Samius*]

sam·iel (səmjél) *n.* the simoom [Turk. *samyel* fr. Arab.]

sam·i·sen (sæmisen) *n.* a Japanese three-stringed musical instrument played by plucking [Jap. fr. Chin. *san hsien*, three strings]

sam·ite (sæmait, séimait) *n.* (*hist.*) a medieval heavy silk fabric, sometimes interwoven with gold or silver thread [O.F. *samit* fr. Gk]

sa·miz·dat (sæmi:zdæt) *n.* (Russian, *self-publication*) unauthorized, typewritten works, clandestinely circulated to avoid legal censorship, e.g., *The First Circle*, by Alexander Solzhenitsyn —**samizdat** *n.* the system for publishing and circulating

sam·let (sæmlit) *n.* a young salmon [contr. and dim. of SALMON]

Sam·nite (sæmnait) 1. *n.* an inhabitant of ancient Samnium, subjugated (4th–3rd cc. B.C.) by the Romans 2. *adj.* pertaining to the Samnites [fr. L. *Samnites*]

Sam·ni·um (sæmni:əm) an ancient country of central and S. Italy inhabited by the Samnites

Sa·mo·a (səmóuə) a mountainous archipelago (14 inhabited islands, with offshore islets) of volcanic origin in the central Pacific (Polynesia), divided into Western Samoa and American Samoa. The larger islands are circled by coral reefs and largely covered by rain forest. Average temperature (F): 70°-90°. Rainfall: 193 ins (esp. Dec.-Mar.). Main occupations: agriculture (yams, taro, breadfruit, pineapples, oranges, bananas), fishing. Livestock: hogs, cattle, poultry. The islands, inhabited by Polynesians, were discovered (1722) by the Dutch. Possession was disputed (19th c.) by the U.S.A., Britain and Germany until 1899

Samoa, American an overseas territory (land area 76 sq. miles, pop. 32,395) of the U.S.A., comprising E. Samoa. Chief port and capital: Pago Pago (pop. 1,500), on the largest island, Tutuila. Highest point: 2,141 ft. Exports: canned tuna, copra, handicraft products (*SAMOA). The islands came under U.S. control in 1899. A local legislature was established (1960). In 1977, American Samoa voters elected their own governor

Sa·mo·an (səmóuən) 1. *n.* a native of Samoa ‖ the Polynesian language of Samoa 2. *adj.* pertaining to Samoa, its language, people etc.

Samoa, Western an independent state (land area 1,097 sq. miles, pop. 159,000) comprising the westernmost and largest islands (Savai'i and Upolu) of Samoa, with offshore islets. Chief port and capital: Apia. People: Polynesian, with 7% of mixed race, and small European and Chinese minorities. Official languages: Samoan, English. Religion: about 80% Protestant, 20% Roman Catholic. Highest point: 6,094 ft, on Savai'i. Main exports: copra, bananas, cocoa. Main imports: meat, sugar, cotton textiles. Monetary unit: Samoan pound (*SAMOA). The islands were under German control (1899-1914) and then under New Zealand trusteeship (1920-61). They gained independence Jan. 1, 1962, but maintain special treaty relations with New Zealand. Western Samoa became (1970) a member of the Commonwealth

Sa·mos (séimɒs, sǽmous, sámɔs) a mountainous Greek island (area 180 sq. miles, pop. 41,709) in the Aegean, 1 mile off W. Turkey. Products: wine, tobacco, olives, fruit. Remains of the temple of Hera (16th c. B.C.). It was at the height of its prosperity in the 6th c. B.C.

Sam·o·thrace (sæməθreis) (Gk *Samothraki*) a

CONCISE PRONUNCIATION KEY: (**a**) æ, c*a*t; ɑ, c*a*r; ɔ f*aw*n; ei, sn*a*ke. (**e**) e, h*e*n; i:, sh*ee*p; iə, d*ee*r; ɛə, b*ea*r. (**i**) i, f*i*sh; ai, t*i*ger; ə:, b*i*rd. (**o**) o, *o*x; au, c*ow*; ou, g*oa*t; u, p*oo*r; ɔi, r*oy*al. (**u**) ʌ, d*u*ck; u, b*u*ll; u:, g*oo*se; ə, b*a*cillus; ju:, c*u*be. x, lo*ch*; θ, *th*ink; ð, bo*th*er; z, *Z*en; ʒ, corsa*g*e; dʒ, sava*g*e; ŋ, ora*ng*utang; j, *y*ak; ʃ, *fi*sh; tʃ, fe*tch*; 'l, rabb*le*; 'n, redd*en*. Complete pronunciation key appears inside front cover.

mountainous Greek island (area 70 sq. miles, pop. 3,012) in the N.E. Aegean. The famous marble Winged Victory of Samothrace (now in the Louvre) was erected here c. 305 B.C. to mark a naval victory by Demetrius I Poliorcetes

sam·o·var (sǽmǝvar, sæmǝvár) n. a Russian tea urn in which the water is heated by charcoal burning slowly in an inner container [Russ.=self-boiler]

Sam·o·yed (sæmǝjéd) n. a member of a Mongolian people of the northern U.S.S.R. ‖ a group of Uralic languages spoken by these people ‖ any of these languages ‖ (sǝmɔ́ied) a dog of a medium-sized, white, Siberian breed used for pulling sleds **Sam·o·yéd·ic** adj. of or relating to the Samoyed people or languages [Russ.=self-eater]

samp (sæmp) n. coarsely ground corn ‖ porridge made of this [Algonquian nasaump, softened by water]

sam·pan (sǽmpæn) n. a flat-bottomed boat used on rivers and in harbors in China, Japan, Vietnam etc., usually propelled by oars [Chin. san-pun, boat]

sam·phire (sǽmfaiǝr) n. Crithmum maritimum, fam. Umbelliferae, a plant which grows in crevices in sea cliffs and has aromatic fleshy leaves which can be pickled for use as a condiment [earlier sampere, sampire fr. F. (herbe de) St. Pierre, St Peter's (herb)]

sam·ple (sǽmp'l, sámp'l) 1. n. an individual portion by which the quality of more of the same sort is to be deduced or judged, to examine a sample of dress material 2. v.t. pres. part. **sampling** past and past part. **sam·pled** to judge the quality etc. of (the whole) by examining a part [earlier essample, example]

sampler (sǽmplǝr, sámplǝr) n. a decorative piece of embroidery showing samples of different kinds of stitches and exhibited as evidence of the embroiderer's skill ‖ someone who tests quality by inspecting samples [fr. O.F. essamplaire, model]

sam·pling (sǽmpliŋ, sámpliŋ) n. the act or process of selecting a sample ‖ the sample selected ‖ a system of statistical analysis in which samples are assumed to give a reasonably accurate picture of the whole

Samp·son (sǽmpsǝn), William Thomas (1840-1902), U.S. admiral who commanded the U.S. North Atlantic squadron during the Spanish-American War. He conducted the blockade of Cuba and ordered the destruction of Spanish vessels at Santiago

Sam·son (sǽmsǝn) an Israelite Judge, of the tribe of Dan. A man of phenomenal physical strength, he was betrayed to the Philistines by Delilah, his mistress (Judges xiii-xvi)

Sam·u·el (sǽmju:ǝl) a Hebrew Judge and prophet (11th c. B.C.) who chose Saul as first king of the Hebrews and David as his successor ‖ either of two books of the Old Testament which relate the history of the Hebrews from the birth of Samuel to the death of David

Sam·u·el·son (sǽmju:ǝlsǝn), Paul Anthony (1915-), U.S. economist. He was awarded the 1970 Nobel prize for economics for his 'outstanding efforts to raise the level of scientific analysis in economic theory'

sam·u·rai (sǽmurai) pl. **sam·u·rai** n. (hist.) a member of a class of knights of feudal Japan who served their clan chiefs according to the bushido code of loyalty, honor and self-sacrifice. They were prominent in the overthrow of the Tokugawa shogunate (1867) and in the creation of modern Japan [Jap.]

Sa·n'a (saná) the capital (pop. 277,817) of Yemen, an ancient, walled trading center on the central plateau at 7,260 ft, 90 miles northeast of its port, Hodeida. Crafts: weaving, metalwork

San An·to·ni·o (sænæntóuni:ou) the commercial and communications center (pop. 785,410) of S. Texas, in a rich agricultural region and oilfield. Industries: oil refining, meat packing, chemicals, metallurgy, cotton textiles, tobacco. Spanish mission churches, palace (18th c.), the Alamo

san·a·tar·i·um (sænǝtéǝri:ǝm) pl. **san·a·tar·i·ums, san·a·tar·i·a** (sænǝtéǝri:ǝ) n. a sanatorium (residential building for patients)

san·a·tive (sǽnǝtiv) adj. (rhet.) healing [O.F. sanatif or M.L. sanativus]

san·a·to·ri·um (sænǝtɔ́ri:ǝm, sænǝtóuri:ǝm) pl. **san·a·to·ri·ums, san·a·to·ri·a** (sænǝtɔ́ri:ǝ, sænǝtóuri:ǝ) n. a residential establishment for patients undergoing treatment (e.g. for alcoholism or tuberculosis), or one for convalescents ‖

(Br.) an infirmary in a school etc. [Mod. L. fr. L. sanare, to heal]

san·a·to·ry (sǽnǝtɔri:, sænǝtóuri:) adj. (rhet.) sanative [fr. L.L. sanatorius]

san·be·ni·to (sænbenítou) pl. **san·be·ni·tos** n. (hist., Spanish Inquisition) either of two robes: one marked with a red St Andrew's cross, worn by heretics who renounced their heresy and were reconciled to the Church, or a black one bearing a design of devils and flames, worn by an impenitent heretic at the auto-da-fé [Span. fr. San Benito, St Benedict]

Sán·chez (sántʃes), Francisco del Rosario (1817-61), Dominican general, patriot, and (with Juan Pablo Duarte and Ramón Matías Mella) a hero of Dominican independence. He rebelled against Santana and was executed

Sán·chez Car·ro (sántʃeskárrɔ), Luis Miguel (1894-1933), Peruvian general and president (1930-3). He was assassinated by shock troops (búfalos) of the APRA movement, which he had persecuted

San·chi (sæntʃi:) a village near Bhopal, Madhya Pradesh, India, celebrated for several Buddhist stupas, with elaborate carving, built about 250 B.C.

San Cris·tó·bal (sɑnkristóbal) a city (pop. 241,000) in W. Venezuela, 100 miles south of Lake Maracaibo near the Colombian border. It is a commercial center

sanc·ti·fi·ca·tion (sæŋktifikéiʃǝn) n. a sanctifying or being sanctified [fr. eccles. L. sanctificatio (sanctificationis)]

sanc·ti·fy (sæŋktifai) pres. part. **sanc·ti·fy·ing** past and past part. **sanc·ti·fied** v.t. to make holy ‖ to reverence as holy ‖ to give authority to, sanctified by long custom [M.E. seintefie fr. O.F. saintifier fr. eccles. L. sanctificare fr. L. sanctus, holy]

sanc·ti·mo·ni·ous (sæŋktǝmóuni:ǝs) adj. making a pretense of holiness [fr. L. sanctimonia, sanctimony]

sanc·ti·mo·ny (sæŋktǝmouni:) n. the quality of being sanctimonious [O.F. sanctimonie]

sanc·tion (sæŋkʃǝn) 1. n. explicit permission given by someone in authority ‖ a measure taken by a state or states with a view to coercing another state which has failed to comply with internationally agreed forms ‖ a factor, e.g. a penalty for violation, tending to secure obedience to a rule of conduct or law ‖ ratification of a law by a supreme authority ‖ (hist.) a law or ecclesiastical decree 2. v.t. to permit ‖ to approve of, give encouragement to ‖ to ratify ‖ to attach a penalty to the violating of (a law) [F. or fr. L. sanctio (sanctionis), law or decree]

sanc·ti·ty (sæŋktiti) pl. **sanc·ti·ties** n. holiness ‖ the quality of being sacred, the sanctity of an oath ‖ (pl.) things held sacred, rights and obligations or feelings [O.F. sainteté fr. L. sanctitas]

sanc·tu·ar·y (sæŋktʃu:ɛri:) pl. **sanc·tu·ar·ies** n. a sacred place ‖ (eccles.) that part of a church which contains the altar ‖ a place set apart as a refuge, a bird sanctuary ‖ (hist.) a church or other building where, in the Middle Ages, certain categories of lawbreaker could take refuge from pursuers and be inviolate ‖ the immunity thus taken or given [O.F. sainctuarie]

sanc·tum (sæŋktǝm) pl. **sanc·tums, sanc·ta** (sæŋktǝ) n. a sacred place ‖ a private room where someone can be undisturbed [L. neut. of sanctus, holy]

sanc·tum sanc·to·rum (sæŋktǝmsæŋktɔ́rǝm, sæŋktǝmsæŋktóurǝm) n. the holy of holies in the temple in Jerusalem ‖ a sanctum (private room) [L.=holy of holies, trans. of Heb.]

Sanc·tus (sæŋktǝs) n. the last phase of the preface of the Mass or Eucharist, beginning with the words 'sanctus, sanctus, sanctus' or 'holy, holy, holy' ‖ the music for this [L.=holy]

Sanctus bell a bell rung at the Sanctus

Sand (sænd, F. sã), George (Aurore Dupin, baronne Dudevant, 1804-76), French writer. Her best-known novels are the 'rustic' or pastoral ones, e.g. 'la Mare au diable' (1846) and 'François le Champi' (1847-8), and those reflecting her mystical humanitarianism, e.g. 'Consuelo' (1842-5)

sand (sænd) 1. n. small grains of quartz resulting from the breaking down of siliceous rocks, the grains being often rounded by the action of water or wind. It is used as an abrasive, is mixed with lime or cement in making mortar or concrete, and is a constituent of glass ‖ (often pl.) a stretch of this, e.g. on the seashore ‖ (pl.) a sandbank 2. v.t. to abrade with sand or sandpaper ‖ to sprinkle with sand, e.g. (hist.) as a way

of drying the ink on a document ‖ to cover, fill or treat with sand ‖ to add sand to for purposes of fraud, to sand sugar [O.E. sand, sond]

san·dal (sænd'l) n. sandalwood [M.L. sandalum fr. Skr. candana]

sandal n. a sole attached to the foot by straps ‖ an openwork slipper **sán·daled**, esp. Br. **sán·dalled** adj. wearing sandals [fr. L. sandalium fr. Gk]

san·dal·wood (sænd'lwud) n. the fragrant, close-grained wood of Santalum album, fam. Santalaceae, an Indian parasitic tree, used in cabinetmaking ‖ the fragrant wood of various other trees resembling this ‖ one of these trees

sandalwood oil a fragrant oil extracted from sandalwood and used in perfumery

san·da·rach, san·da·rac (sændǝræk) n. Callitris articulata, fam. Pinaceae, a large Moroccan evergreen tree whose wood is used in building and is the source of a resin used in making varnishes ‖ this resin [fr. L. sandaraca fr. Gk prob. fr. Assyrian]

sand·bag (sændbæg) 1. n. a bag filled with sand or soil. Such bags are used in quantity to give protection from bullets, flood water or drafts, or for ballast etc. ‖ a bag filled with sand used to stun a person 2. v.t. pres. part. **sand·bag·ging** past and past part. **sand·bagged** to stun with a sandbag ‖ to put sandbags against, bank up with sandbags ‖ (pop.) to coerce, to sandbag someone into doing something

sand·bank (sændbæŋk) n. a bank or raised portion of the bed of a sea or river, made of sand accumulated by waves or currents

sand·bar (sændbɑr) n. a bank of sand built up at the mouth of a river or along a shore

sand bath a shallow vessel containing heated sand, used for heating glass vessels evenly, and in the tempering of steel

sand·blast (sændblæst, sændblɑst) 1. n. a high-speed jet of sand used to engrave or cut glass, polish a metal surface or strip a surface of paint, rust etc. ‖ the machine used for this 2. v.t. to clean, polish, cut or engrave with a sandblast

sand·box (sændbɒks) n. a box containing sand, e.g. one carried in a locomotive for sprinkling sand on slippery rails ‖ (Am.=Br. sandpit) a large container of sand in which little children can play

Sand·burg (sændbǝ:rg), Carl (1878-1967), American poet and biographer. His poetry catches the primitive quality of a rapidly expanding America. His biography of Abraham Lincoln (6 vols, 1926-39) won wide acclaim

sand·cast (sændkæst, sændkɑst) pres. part. **sand·cast·ing** past and past part. **sand·cast** v.t. to make (a casting) by pouring molten metal into a sand mold

Sand Creek the site in Colorado of an atrocity committed (1864) by U.S. troops. Cheyenne and Arapaho women and children were bayoneted, although they were friendly toward the U.S.A.

sand dollar any of several varieties of flat, round sea urchins, esp. Echinarachnius parma, which lives on the sandy bed of the sea on the east coast of the U.S.A.

sand dune a dune

San·deau (sãdou), Jules (1811-83), French novelist, author of 'Mademoiselle de la Seiglière' (1848)

sand eel a member of Ammodytes, fam. Ammodytidae, a genus of small, narrow marine fishes that bury themselves in the sand when the tide goes out

sand·er (sændǝr) n. a machine that sprinkles sand or abrades with sand ‖ a person who operates such a machine or who cleans, polishes etc. by hand with sand or sandpaper

sand·er·ling (sændǝrliŋ) n. Crocethia alba, a small sandpiper with chiefly gray and white plumage. It breeds in the Arctic but migrates south and is common on most shores [etym. doubtful]

sand flea a flea found on beaches ‖ Tungo penetrans, the chigoe

sand fly any of several biting flies, esp. a member of genus Phlebotomus, fam. Psychodidae

sand·fly fever a disease of short duration caused by a virus introduced by the bite of Phlebotomus papatasii, a sand fly

sand·glass (sændglæs, sændglɑs) n. a device similar to an hourglass, designed to measure a specific amount of time

san·dhi (sǽndi:, sándi:) pl. **san·dhis** n. (linguistics) modification of the sound of a word or affix because of phonetic context (e.g. 'the' in 'the girl' and 'the only girl for me') [Skr. sandhī, a placing together]

Sand·hoff's disease (sǽndhɒfs) a form of lipidosis affecting the nervous system, similar to Tay-Sachs disease, characterized by paralysis, dementia, occasionally blindness

sand·hog (sǽndhɒg, sǽndhɔg) n. a workman employed in underground or underwater construction projects which use pneumatic caissons

sand hopper any of several small crustaceans of fam. Orchestiidae, commonly found leaping in great numbers on the sand of a seashore after the tide has gone out

Sand·hurst (sǽndhə:rst) the popular name for the Royal Military Academy (1802) of Great Britain, formerly at Sandhurst, Berkshire, now (since 1947) at Camberley, Surrey

San Di·e·go (sændi:éigou) a port and naval base (pop. 875,504) in S. California, on a protected bay: aeronautical engineering, tuna fishing and packing. Spanish mission church (1769)

San·di·nis·ta (sɑndi:ní:stɑ) n. revolutionary group, Sandinista National Liberation Front [FSLN], that replaced the government of Anastasio Debayl Samoza in Nicaragua in 1979; named for General Augusto Cesar Sandino

San·di·no (sɑndí:nɔ), Augusto César (1895-1934), Nicaraguan farmer, mining engineer, and caudillo who led (1927-33) Nicaraguan resistance to the U.S. occupation. He was murdered by agents of Gen. Anastasio Somoza

sand launce, sand lance a sand eel

sand·lot (sǽndlɒt) n. a vacant lot, sometimes sand-covered, where city children often play

S and M (abbr.) for sadomasochism

sand·man (sǽndmæn) pl. **sand·men** (sǽndmɛn) n. an imaginary man of folklore, who puts children to sleep at night by sprinkling sand in their eyes

sand martin (Br.) the bank swallow

sand mold, esp. Br. sand mould a mold for casting, made of sand

sand painting a ceremonial design made of colored sands and finely powdered minerals, used by some Navaho and Pueblo Indian tribes in healing rites and other ceremonies

sand·pa·per (sǽndpeipər) 1. n. stiff paper covered with sharp grains of sand which are bound to it by an adhesive, used as an abrasive 2. v.t. to scour with sandpaper

sand·pi·per (sǽndpaipər) n. a small shore bird resembling the plover but having a longer bill, esp. the European Actitis hypoleucos and A. macularia, the spotted sandpiper of North America

sand·pit (sǽndpit) n. (Br.) a sandbox

sand·shoe (sǽndʃu:) n. (Br.) a light canvas shoe with a sole usually of rubber

sand sink n. technique for removing oil spills at sea by adding chemically treated sand that adheres to oil, causing it to sink

sand·stone (sǽndstoun) n. a porous rock consisting of grains of sand cemented together by substances such as clay or silica which give it characteristic colors. Some sandstones containing considerable quartz are used as grindstones, building stones and furnace linings. If soft they are crushed to sand for commercial purposes

sand·storm (sǽndstɔrm) n. a storm of sand-laden wind

sand table a table with raised edges, having a layer of sand which can be manipulated to create landscapes, used to study military tactics etc.

sand·wich (sǽndwitʃ, sǽnwitʃ) 1. n. two slices of buttered bread put face together with meat, fish, salad or vegetables etc. between them 2. v.t. insert between two other things, places, persons etc., he sandwiched a visit to them in between two jobs [after John Montagu, 4th earl of Sandwich (1718-92), who was said to have eaten these to avoid leaving the gaming table]

sandwich bar restaurant counter specializing in sandwiches

sandwich board the two boards worn by a sandwich man

sandwich course (education) technical college courses programmed to alternate with a period of practical work experience

Sandwich Islands the former name of Hawaii

sandwich man a man hired to walk through the streets wearing advertising boards slung one in front of him and one behind him

sandwich shop small restaurant serving a limited menu of light meals

sand·y (sǽndi:) comp. **sand·i·er** superl. **sand·i·est** adj. full of or covered with sand ‖ like sand ‖ (esp. of hair) of the color of sand

sand yacht a beach vehicle with sails, usu. with three wheels also land yacht —**sand yachting** n.

sane (sein) comp. **san·er** superl. **san·est** adj. (of a person) in full possession of the mental faculties, not insane ‖ (of the mind) sound ‖ (of opinions, plans etc.) sensible [fr. L. sanus, healthy]

SA-N-4 U.S.S.R. ship-to-air missile. SA-N-6, named Gainful by NATO

San Fran·cis·co (sænfrænsískou) the chief port and financial and commercial center (pop. 678,974, with agglom. 3,252,721) of the western U.S.A. in N. California, on the southernmost of two hilly peninsulas protecting San Francisco Bay, which ranks among the world's largest natural harbors (area 456 sq. miles). Industries: food processing, chemicals, mechanical engineering, printing and publishing, metal goods. White-collar industries very much predominate, however, and the city's skyline has many high-rise office buildings, notably the Transamerica Building and the Bank of America tower. The city is also a major cultural and educational center, with three universities and three museums. Spanish mission church (1782). San Francisco was founded by the Spanish (1776) and grew rapidly at the time of the California gold rush (1849). It was the scene of the conference which established the U.N. and the International Court of Justice (1945) and of the treaty of peace between the Allies and Japan (1951) after the 2nd world war. Its Haight-Ashbury district was the home of the 'flower children' of the 1960s

San Francisco Bay a large landlocked bay (40 miles long, 3-12 miles wide) on the west central coast of California, connecting with the Pacific through the Golden Gate. San Francisco is situated at its entrance and Oakland on its northeast shore

San Francisco Conference the conference held (1945) in San Francisco, Calif., which promulgated the charter of the United Nations

sang past of SING

San·gal·lo (sɑngállɔ), Antonio 'the Younger' (1483-1546), Italian architect, nephew of Giuliano. He built the Farnese palace in Rome

Sangallo, Giuliano da (1445-1516), Italian architect. He worked with Raphael on the building of St Peter's in Rome

san·ga·ree (sæŋgərí:) n. a sweetened, spiced, usually iced drink of wine and water [fr. Span. sangria]

Sang·er (sǽŋər), Margaret (1883-1966), U.S. social activist, founder of the National Birth Control League (1914). A nurse in the slums of New York City, she saw the consequences of self-induced abortions and pioneered the birth-control movement in the U.S.A., eventually winning the right for doctors to inform their patients of birth-control methods. She was the first president of the International Planned Parenthood Federation (1953)

sang·froid (sâfrwǽ) n. calm self-possession at a time of danger or stress [F. fr. sang, blood+froid, cold]

San·grail (sæŋgréil) n. the Holy Grail (*GRAIL) [O.F. Saint Graal]

san·gri·a (sæŋgrí:ə) n. a wine punch with fruit juices

Sang·ster (sǽŋstər), Sir Donald B. (1911-67), Jamaican statesman, leader of the Jamaican Labor party, minister of finance (1963), acting prime minister (1965-7) and prime minister (Feb.-Mar. 1967)

san·gui·nar·i·ly (sæŋgwinérili:) adv. in a sanguinary way

san·gui·nar·i·ness (sæŋgwənéri:nis) n. the quality or state of being sanguinary

san·gui·nar·y (sǽŋgwəneri:) adj. accompanied by much bloodshed ‖ wanting to shed blood, murderous, a sanguinary nature ‖ (of laws) exaggerating the use of the death penalty [fr. L. sanguinarius fr. sanguis, blood]

san·guine (sǽŋgwin) 1. adj. (esp. of complexion) ruddy ‖ cheerfully optimistic 2. n. a reddish drawing crayon, esp. of red hematite ‖ a drawing made with red crayon or chalk [F. sanguin]

san·guin·e·ous (sæŋgwíni:əs) adj. pertaining to blood ‖ blood-red ‖ bloodthirsty [fr. L. sanguineus]

San·he·drim (sǽnhidrim, sǽnidrim) the Sanhedrin

San·he·drin (sænhédrin, sǽnhí:drin, sǽnhidrin, sǽnidrin) (hist.) the Jewish supreme council and court of justice in New Testament times, consisting of 71 priests, scribes and elders

san·i·cle (sǽnik'l) n. a member of Sanicula, fam. Umbelliferae, a genus of perennial plants found in woods. Its roots were formerly used medicinally ‖ any of several other plants supposed to have healing powers [O.F.]

sa·ni·es (séini:i:z) n. a watery discharge of blood and pus from ulcers or infected wounds **sá·ni·ous** adj. [L.]

San Il·de·fon·so, Treaty of (sæniɪldifónsou, sɑniːldéfɔnsɔ) a Franco-Spanish treaty (1800) dictated by Napoleon Bonaparte in Segovia, Spain. France regained Louisiana from Spain in exchange for a promise that Napoleon would give an Italian kingdom to a member of the Spanish royal family. Napoleon planned to use the Louisiana territory as a supply base in his drive to reconquer the French West Indies and revive the French New World empire. Disregarding the treaty's provision never to cede Louisiana, he abandoned his designs with the Louisiana Purchase (1803)

san·i·tar·i·um (sænitéəri:əm) pl. **san·i·tar·i·ums, san·i·tar·i·a** (sænitéəri:ə) n. a sanatorium (residential establishment for patients) [fr. L. sanitas, health]

san·i·tar·y (sǽniteri:) adj. concerned with, promoting or conducive to the preservation of health [fr. F. sanitaire]

sanitary napkin (Am.=Br. sanitary towel) a pad of absorbent cotton worn by women during menstruation to absorb the menstrual flow

sanitary towel (Br.) a sanitary napkin

san·i·ta·tion (sænitéiʃən) n. the provision of means whereby health is protected, esp. the arrangements for the disposal of sewage

san·i·tize (sǽnitaiz) v. to revise a report or document in order to prevent identification of information sources, of the actual persons and places with which it is concerned, or of the means by which it was acquired

san·i·ty (sǽniti:) n. the quality or state of being sane [F. sanité]

San Ja·cin·to, Battle of (sændʒəsíntou) an engagement (1836) in S. Texas, in which Gen. Sam Houston's Texan troops defeated the Mexicans under Gen. Santa Anna, and so won independence for Texas

San Jor·ge, Gulf of (sɑnhɔ́rhe) an inlet (145 miles long, 100 miles wide) of the Atlantic on the east coast of S. Argentina

San Jo·se (sænhouzéi) a computer center and agricultural market (pop. 636,550) in N. central California: fruit canning and packing, wine making, and the U.S.A.'s largest computer and electronics industry, which has led to the San Jose area's being nicknamed 'Silicon Valley'

San Jo·sé (sɑnhɔsé) the capital (pop. 250,079) of Costa Rica, in the central plateau, commercial center of an agricultural region. Spanish cathedral, palace (18th c.). University (1843), national theater

San José Declaration a declaration issued at a meeting of consultation of foreign ministers of the American Republics under the Rio Treaty, held (1960) at San José, Costa Rica. It condemned 'the intervention, or the threat of intervention, even when conditional, by an extra-continental power in the affairs of the American Republics'. It was aimed at the Sino-Soviet powers

San Jose scale Aspidiotus perniciosus, a scale insect of warm and temperate climates which destroys fruit trees [after SAN JOSE, California, the first place of entry into the country]

San Juan (sɑnhwún, sænwún) a commercial center (pop. 112,582) of N.W. Argentina at the foot of the Andes in a rich farming and mining region, founded in 1562 but rebuilt after an earthquake in 1944

San Juan the capital and chief port (pop. 424,600) of Puerto Rico, on two islets joined to the northeast coast, founded (1521) by the Spanish. Industries: sugar refining, tobacco, plastics, light manufacturing. Spanish cathedral (16th-19th cc.), castle (17th c.)

San Juan del Nor·te (sɑnhwúndelnɔ́rte) the settlement in Nicaragua, at the mouth of the San Juan River, where a British force laid claim (1740) to sovereignty over Nicaragua

San Juan Hill, Battle of an engagement (1898) in E. Cuba during the Spanish-American War, in which Spanish troops were routed by Theodore Roosevelt and his Rough Riders

sank *past* of SINK

San·ka·ra (sáŋkərə) a commentator on the Upanishads and the Bhagavadgita, writing c. 800 A.D. An upholder of traditional monistic Hinduism, he developed the doctrine of illusion (maya): not only the variety of sense apprehensions is illusory, but sense apprehension itself, and all human 'knowing' is mere hallucination

San·khya (sǽŋkjə) *n.* a dualistic system of Hindu philosophy [Skr. *sāmkhya*]

San Lo·ren·zo, Cape (sɑnlɔrénsɔ) a cape on the west central coast of Ecuador

San Lu·is Po·to·sí (sɑnluːíspɔtɔsíː) a leading mining state (area 24,266 sq. miles, pop. 1,670,637) in Mexico, in the central high plateau region. Capital: San Luis Potosí. Agriculture: wheat, corn, beans, cotton, sugar, coffee, tobacco and fruit. Mining: primarily silver (also gold, copper, zinc and bismuth). Stock raising

San Luis Potosí the capital (pop. 327,333) of the state of San Luis Potosí, Mexico, 215 miles northwest of Mexico City. It is the hub of a rich silver-mining and agricultural region and a leading manufacturing center: rope, brushes, shoes, cotton, woolen textiles, clothing

San Mar·cos, University of *UNIVERSIDAD DE SAN MARCOS

San Ma·ri·no (sænməríːnou) a republic (area 23 sq. miles, pop. 21,622) in the E. Apennines, forming an enclave in Italy between Emilia-Romagna and the Marches. Language: Italian. Industries: agriculture, tourism. Exports: wine, postage stamps. The republic dates probably from the mid-4th c. It entered into a customs union and treaty of friendship with Italy (1862) ‖ its walled capital (pop. 1,500): 14th-c. church

San Mar·tín (sɑnmartíːn), José de (1778-1850), Argentinian general and politician. He fought as general in the struggles for independence of Argentina (1814-6) and led across the Andes the army which liberated Chile (1817) and Peru (1821) from Spanish rule. As Protector of Peru (1821-2), he abolished slavery. He retired in favor of Bolívar

San Ma·tí·as, Gulf of (sɑnmatíːɑs) an inlet (115 miles long, 60-100 miles wide) of the Atlantic in S. central Argentina

San·ni *GOA

San Pe·dro Su·la (sɑnpéɔrɔsúːlɑ) a town (pop. 342,900) in N. Honduras, the economic center of Honduras

San Re·mo (sænríːmou, sænréimou, sɑnrémɔ) a resort (pop. 53,200) of Liguria, Italy, on the Riviera near the French frontier: Romanesque cathedral (13th c.)

San Sal·va·dor (sænsǽlvədɔr, sɑnsɑlvɑðór) the capital (pop. 500,000) of El Salvador, at the foot of a volcano in the central highlands. Industries: textiles, food processing, tobacco. University. Founded in 1525, the city has been destroyed several times by earthquakes and floods

San Sal·va·dor (sænsǽlvədɔr) (or Watling Is.) an island (area 60 sq. miles, pop. 776) of the Bahamas, southeast of Cat Is. Columbus first made landfall (1492) in the New World here

sans-cu·lotte (sǽkylɔt) *n.* (*F. hist.*) a working-class republican in Paris during the French Revolution [F.=without breeches. (Breeches were discarded in favor of long pants by this class)]

San Se·bas·tián (sænsibǽstʃən, sɑnsebɑstján) the capital (pop. 175,576) of Guipúzcoa, Spain, and summer capital of the country, a port and resort on the Bay of Biscay. Industries: chemicals, metallurgy, glass

san·sei (sánséi) *pl.* **san·sei, san·seis** *n.* an American citizen whose grandparents were Japanese immigrants to the U.S.A. and who is educated mostly in the U.S.A. (cf. NISEI, cf. KIBEI, cf. ISSEI) [Jap. = third generation]

sanserif *SANS SERIF

San·skrit (sǽnskrit) *n.* the ancient language of India, belonging to the Indo-European family. The oldest literary period of Sanskrit is the Vedic (c. 1500–c. 200 B.C.). The classic period was c. 200 B.C.–c. 1100 A.D. Some of the oldest Indo-European texts are in Sanskrit. The comparison of Sanskrit with European languages at the end of the 18th c. was the starting point of scientific language study

sans ser·if, san·ser·if (sǽnsérif) *n.* a printing

---

type with no serifs [fr. F. *sans*, without+SERIF]

San Ste·fa·no, Treaty of (sɑnstéfɑnɔ) a treaty (1878) ending the Russo-Turkish War (1877-8). It created a large independent state of Bulgaria, and confirmed the independence of Serbia, Montenegro and Rumania. Russia gained land in the Caucasus and a large war indemnity. The treaty roused British and Austrian opposition, and was rapidly quashed by the Congress of Berlin (1878)

San·ta An·a (sántɑɑnɑ) a commercial center (pop. 109,300) of N. central El Salvador: textiles, tobacco

Santa Ana the highest volcanic peak (8,300 ft) in El Salvador

San·ta An·na (sántɑɑnɑ, sǽntɑǽnɑ), Antonio Lopez de (c. 1794-1876), Mexican general and politician. By political opportunism he became president of Mexico (1833-6, 1841-4, 1846-7 and 1853-5)

San·ta Bar·ba·ra Islands (sǽntəbárbərə, sǽntəbárbrə) a chain of islands and islets extending about 160 miles along the S. California coast, divided into a northern and a southern group. They are separated from the mainland by channels and are sometimes called the Channel Islands

San·ta Cla·ra (sántəklárɑ, sǽntəklérə) a city (pop. 525,402) of W. central Cuba. It is the capital of its province and an important railroad, sugar, and tobacco center. Port: Cienfuegos

San·ta Claus (sǽntəklɔz) the legendary friend of children, identified with St Nicholas, now usually depicted as a fat, jolly old man with a white beard wearing red, who brings children presents on Christmas Eve (or on St Nicholas' Day in some European countries) [fr. Du. dial. *Sante Klaas* fr. *Sant Nikolaas*, St Nicholas]

San·ta Cruz (sántɑkrúːs), Andrés de (c. 1792-1865), Bolivian marshal and president of the Republic (1829-36). He created (1836) the Peru-Bolivian Federation and served (1836-9) as its Protector. He was defeated (1839) at Yungay by Chilean forces

Santa Cruz an agricultural market (pop. 255,568) of central Bolivia on the plain and the terminus of a railroad to São Paulo, Brazil

San·ta Cruz de Te·ne·ri·fe (sántɑkrúːsðeteneríːfe) a province (area 1,528 sq. miles, pop. 653,833) of Spain comprising the W. Canary Is ‖ its capital (pop. 179,600), the chief port of Tenerife: oil refining

Santa Cruz Is. *ST CROIX

San·ta Cruz y Es·pe·jo (sántɑkrúːsiespéhɔ), Francisco Javier Eugenio de (1740-95), Ecuadorian encyclopedist, physician and patriot, the author of 'El nuevo Luciano o Despertador de los ingenios'

San·ta E·le·na (sántɑeléna) a peninsula in W. Ecuador, on the north side of the Gulf of Guayaquil. Its tip is La Puntilla

Santa Elena Bay a bay in W. Ecuador on the north side of the Santa Elena peninsula: the site of most of Ecuador's oil fields

San·ta Fé (sántɑfé) a river port (pop. 244,655) in Argentina on the eastern edge of the Pampa at the confluence of the Paraná and the Salado del Norte, founded in 1573. University (1920)

San·ta Fe (sǽntəféi) the capital (pop. 48,899) of New Mexico, in the upper Rio Grande valley, founded by the Spanish c. 1610. Spanish churches (17th and 18th cc.). Indian pueblos. It is a health resort and tourist center

Santa Fe Trail an overland trade route from W. Missouri to Santa Fe, New Mexico, which flourished from 1822 until the coming of the railroad in the 1880s

San·ta I·sa·bel (sántɑisɑbél) the capital (pop. 37,237) of Equatorial Guinea, a port on Fernando Poo exporting cacao and coffee

Santa María la Antigua del Darién *DARIÉN

San·ta Mar·ta (sántɑmárta) the oldest city (pop. 128,577) in Colombia, on the Caribbean, founded by the Spanish in 1525, now among the world's largest banana ports. Simón Bolívar died here

San·ta·na (santána), Pedro (1801-64), Dominican general who led the liberation (1844) from Haiti and served (1844-8, 1853-6, 1858-61) as president of the Republic. In 1861 he decreed the reannexation of his country to Spain as a province. This lasted until 1865

San·tan·der (sɑntandér), Francisco de Paula (1792-1840), Colombian general and politician. He joined Bolívar's army and won victories at Paya, Pantano de Vargas, and Boyacá. As vice-

---

president of Cundinamarca (1819-26), he participated in a rebellion against Bolívar for which he was condemned to death, but the sentence was commuted to exile. As president of Nueva Granada (1832-7) he initiated advances in education and civics

Santander a province (area 2,108 sq. miles, pop. 432,000) of N. Spain (*OLD CASTILE) ‖ its capital (pop. 170,700) a port and resort on the Bay of Biscay. Industries: fishing, metallurgy, dairy processing. Gothic cathedral (14th-15th cc.)

San·ta·ya·na (sɑnti:ǽnə, sɑntɑjúnə), George (1863-1952), American philosopher and poet. In 'The Life of Reason' (1905), 'Scepticism and Animal Faith' (1923) and 'The Realm of Essence' (1928) he restated Aristotelian principles in mechanistic materialist terms. He wrote one novel, 'The Last Puritan' (1935)

San·tia·go (santjágo, sɑnti:ágou) the capital and economic center (pop. 3,448,700, with agglom. 4,111,800) of Chile, in the center, at the foot of the W. Andes. It was founded (1541) by the Spanish. Industries (over 50% of national production): textiles, food processing, light manufacturing. Cathedral (1748). National university (1747), museum and library. One quarter of the population of Chile lives here

Santiago (Río Grande de Santiago) a river rising 18 miles west of Mexico City and flowing through Lake Chapala into the Pacific (340 miles long below Lake Chapala). It is called the Lerma River above Lake Chapala

Santiago a port (pop. 276,000) of S.E. Cuba, the capital of Oriente province: metallurgy, tobacco, sugar refining. Spanish cathedral (16th c.)

Santiago, Declaration of a declaration (1959) drafted by the Fifth Meeting of Consultation of Foreign Ministers, in Santiago, Chile. It proclaimed that the existence of anti-democratic regimes violated the principles on which the Organization of American States was founded and represented a threat to the peace of the hemisphere. It resulted in the creation of the Inter-American Commission on Human Rights

San·tia·go de Com·po·ste·la (santjágoðekɔmpostéla) a town (pop. 65,000) in La Coruna, Spain. Its cathedral (mainly 1078-1188, now with a baroque facade), built over the supposed grave of St James the Greater, was one of the chief pilgrimage places of medieval Christianity

Santiago de Cuba, Battle of a naval engagement (1898) outside Santiago, Cuba, during the Spanish-American War, in which a U.S. squadron destroyed a Spanish fleet

San·tia·go de los Ca·ba·lle·ros (santjágoðelɔskɑbɑjérɔs) a commercial center (pop. 242,000) of the N. central Dominican Republic, founded in 1524 but often destroyed by earthquakes: tobacco industries

San·ti·lla·na (santi:ljána), Iñigo López de Mendoza, marqués de (1398-1458), Spanish soldier, scholar, statesman and writer. He introduced the Italian sonnet into Spain

Santo Do·min·go (sántɔdɔmíːŋgɔ) (1930-61 Ciudad Trujillo) the capital, chief port and economic center (pop. 1,103,425) of the Dominican Republic, on the southeast coast, the oldest European town of the Americas, founded in 1496 by Bartolomé Colón. It was made (1511) the seat of an audiencia embracing the Caribbean and Venezuela. Industries: sugar refining, brewing, distilling. Spanish cathedral and churches (16th c.). University (1538)

san·ton·i·ca (sæntɔ́nikə) *n. Artemisia pauciflora*, fam. *Compositae*, a European wormwood ‖ its dried unopened flower buds used as a drug to destroy intestinal worms [L. fr. (*herba*) *Santonica*, (herb) of the Santones, a people of Aquitania]

san·to·nin (sǽntənin) *n.* a poisonous crystalline compound, $C_{15}H_{18}O_3$, derived from santonica and related plants and used to destroy intestinal worms [fr. L. (*herba*) *Sontonica*, santonica]

san·to·rin (sæntərí:n) (*Gk* Thera) the southernmost inhabited island (area 27 sq. miles, pop. 20,000) of the Cyclades, Greece, consisting largely of a volcanic cone (last active 1866): Mycenaean remains

San·tos (sǽntɔs, sántus) the chief export port (pop. 395,700) of Brazil, 45 miles southeast of São Paulo: iron and steel. It is the world's leading port for the exportation of coffee

---

CONCISE PRONUNCIATION KEY: (a) æ, c*a*t; ɑ, c*a*r; ɔ f*aw*n; ei, sn*a*ke. **(e)** e, h*e*n; i:, sh*ee*p; iə, d*ee*r; ɛə, b*ea*r. **(i)** i, f*i*sh; ai, t*i*ger; ə:, b*i*rd. **(o)** o, *o*x; au, c*ow*; ou, g*oa*t; u, p*oo*r; ɔi, r*oy*al. **(u)** ʌ, d*u*ck; u, b*u*ll; u:, g*oo*se; ə, b*a*cillus; ju:, c*u*be. x, lo*ch*; θ, *th*ink; ð, bo*th*er; z, *Z*en; ʒ, corsa*g*e; dʒ, sava*g*e; ŋ, ora*ng*utang; j, *y*ak; ʃ, *f*ish; tʃ, fe*tch*; 'l, rabb*le*; 'n, redd*en*. Complete pronunciation key appears inside front cover.

San·tos-Du·mont (sátusdymɔ̃), Alberto (1873-1932), Brazilian aviation pioneer. He made (1901) the first roundtrip flight from Saint-Cloud to the Eiffel Tower, erected (1903) at Neuilly the first airship station, and designed (1909) his 'demoiselle' or 'grasshopper' monoplane, the forerunner of the modern light plane

SA-N2 *GUIDELINE

Sa·nu·si, Se·nus·si (sənú:si:) *pl.* **Sa·nu·si, Sa·nu·sis, Se·nus·si, Se·nus·sis** *n.* a member of a militant Moslem sect founded in 1837 in N. Africa by Mohammed Ibn Ali as-Sanusi (*d.* 1859), Algerian religious leader

São Fran·cis·co (sáufrʌnsí:sku) a river (1,600 miles long) flowing north and east from the highlands of E. central Brazil to the Atlantic 300 miles below Recife, navigable, between rapids, for most of its length

São Francisco an island (20 miles long) off the southeast coast of Brazil

São Luís (sáulwí:s) a port (pop. 330,311) of N. Brazil: textiles, food processing. Portuguese cathedral (17th c.)

Saône (soun) the chief tributary (280 miles long, navigable for 190) of the Rhône, flowing from the Vosges to Lyon, E. France

SA-1 *GUILD

Saône, Haute- *HAUTE-SAÔNE

Saône-et-Loire (souneilwar) a department (area 3,330 sq. miles, pop. 569,800) of E. central France (*BURGUNDY). Chief town: Mâcon

São Pau·lo (sáupáulu) the chief industrial center (pop. 7,033,529, increasing rapidly) of Brazil, on a hilly plateau (2,500 ft) 200 miles south of Rio de Janeiro, and the market for a great agricultural region (coffee). Main industries: textiles, machinery, automobiles, chemicals, food processing. Port: Santos. University (1934). São Paulo was founded (c. 1552) by Jesuits

São Ro·que, Cape (sáurɔ́kə) a cape in N.E. Brazil, north of Natal

São To·mé and Prin·ci·pe (sáutɔmé, pri:nsi:pə) an African country consisting of two mountainous, fertile volcanic islands in the E. Gulf of Guinea with offshore islets (area 372 sq. miles, pop. 89,000). Capital: São Tomé. People: mulatto (native inhabitants), African (contract laborers), small European minority. Products: cocoa, copra, coconuts, coffee, palm oil, bananas, fish. Exports: cocoa, copra, coffee, palm oil. HISTORY. The islands were discovered by the Portuguese in 1471. São Tomé became a Portuguese colony in 1522 and Principe in 1573. The islands were a Portuguese overseas territory from 1951 until they achieved their independence in 1975

São Vi·cen·te (sauvi:sénte) the first Portuguese colony in America, established (1532) on the coast near Santos, in the state of São Paulo, Brazil

sap (sæp) **1.** *n.* the solution of raw materials and organic products of metabolism which circulates in a plant or tree ‖ (*pop.*) a stupid person easily fooled **2.** *v.t. pres. part.* **sap·ping** *past* and *past part.* **sapped** to drain (a tree) of its sap [O.E. *sæp*]

sap *n.* a deep trench or tunnel dug in order to undermine [older *zappe, sappe* fr. Ital. *zappa* and F. *sappe*, sap, spade]

sap *pres. part.* **sap·ping** *past* and *past part.* **sapped** *v.t.* to dig beneath, e.g. in order to lay an explosive beneath (an enemy fortification) ‖ to undermine (strength, energy etc.) [F. *saper*]

sap·a·jou (sæpədʒu:) *n.* a capuchin monkey ‖ a spider monkey [F. fr. Tupi]

sapanwood *SAPPANWOOD

sap·head (sæphɛd) *n.* (*pop.*) a sap (stupid person)

sap·id (sæpid) *adj.* (*rhet.*) having a strong, agreeable taste [fr. L. *sapidus* fr. *sapere*, to taste]

sa·pi·ence (séipi:əns) *n.* (*rhet.*) wisdom [O.F.]

sa·pi·ent (séipi:ənt) *adj.* (*rhet.*) wise, knowledgeable [O.F. or fr. L. *sapiens* (*sapientis*) fr. *sapere*, to be wise]

sapient *n.* any early ancestor of man

sa·pi·en·tial (seipi:énʃəl) *adj.* characterized by knowledge or wisdom [F.]

sapiential books the biblical books Proverbs, Ecclesiastes, Ecclesiasticus, Wisdom, Song of Solomon

Sa·pir (səpíər), Edward (1884-1939), U.S. linguist, anthropologist, and specialist in American Indian languages, best known for his 'Language: an Introduction to the Study of Speech' (1921)

sap·ling (sæpliŋ) *n.* a young tree ‖ a greyhound less than 12 months old

sap·o·dil·ia (sæpədílə) *n. Achras zapota*, fam. *Sapotaceae*, a tropical American evergreen tree, yielding chicle ‖ its durable reddish wood ‖ its edible, sweet-fleshed fruit [Span. *zapotilla* fr. Nahuatl]

sap·o·na·ceous (sæpənéiʃəs) *adj.* of, pertaining to, consisting of or resembling soap [fr. Mod. L. *saponaceus* fr. *sapo* (*saponis*), soap]

sa·pon·i·fi·ca·tion (səppnnifikéiʃən) *n.* the chemical process of converting fats into soap, involving the hydrolysis of a fat, usually accomplished by the action of alkali with the formation of glycerol and fatty acid salts ‖ the hydrolysis by alkali of any ester with an alcohol and an acid or its salt [F.]

sa·pon·i·fy (səpónifai) *pres. part.* **sa·pon·i·fy·ing** *past* and *past part.* **sa·pon·i·fied** *v.t.* to convert into soap by saponification ‖ *v.i.* to undergo the process of saponification [fr. F. *saponifier*]

sap·o·nin (sæpənin) *n.* any of several naturally occurring water-soluble glucosides, able to form a lather. A mixture of saponins is used as a foam producer in fire extinguishers, as a detergent, in beverages etc. [F. *saponine*]

sap·o·nite (sæpənait) *n.* hydrated aluminum magnesium silicate, occurring in soft, soapy masses in the veins of serpentine etc. [fr. L. *sapo* (*saponis*), soap]

sa·por, *Br.* also **sa·pour** (séipər, séipɔr) *n.* (in scientific contexts) a distinctive flavor ‖ a quality which affects the sense of taste, e.g. sweetness **sap·o·rous** (sæpərəs) *adj.* [L. fr. *sapere*, to have a taste]

sap·pan·wood, sap·an·wood (səppænwʊd) *n. Caesalpinia sappan*, fam. *Papilionaceae*, an East Indian tree ‖ its red dyewood [fr. Malay *sapang*+ WOOD]

sap·per (sæpər) *n.* (*mil.*) any member of a corps of engineers, trained in sapping and in other forms of military engineering ‖ (*Br.*) a private in a corps of engineers

Sap·phic (sæfik) **1.** *adj.* pertaining to Sappho ‖ of the poetic meter used by Sappho (esp. three pentameters followed by a verse in two feet) **2.** *n.* this meter ‖ (*pl.*) verse in Sapphic meter [F. *saphique* fr. L. *Sapphicus* fr. Gk]

sap·phire (sæfaiər) **1.** *n.* a precious stone of transparent blue corundum, whose color is due to traces of cobalt ‖ any of certain other varieties of corundum of various colors, some of which are used commercially to tip the needles of record players ‖ the deep blue color of the true sapphire **2.** *adj.* of this blue color **sap·phir·ine** (sæfirain) **1.** *adj.* resembling the sapphire in color **2.** *n.* a pale blue or green magnesium aluminum iron silicate [M.E. *saphyr, safir* fr. O.F. *safir*]

Sap·pho (sæfou), Greek lyric poetess of Lesbos (late 7th–early 6th c. B.C.). Only very little of her work survives, written in a variety of meters, using vivid language, and showing great love of nature. It includes love poems of passionate intensity, some of which are addressed to women, and a hymn to Aphrodite

Sap·po·ro (sapɔro) the chief town (pop. 1,307,600) of Hokkaido, Japan, near the east coast. Industries: food processing, flax, hemp, rubber manufactures. University (1918)

sap·py (sæpi:) *comp.* **sap·pi·er** *superl.* **sap·pi·est** *adj.* (of a plant) full of sap ‖ (*pop.*) foolish or foolishly sentimental

sap·ro·gen·ic (sæproudʒénik) *adj.* of, pertaining to, or producing putrefaction [fr. Gk *sapros*, putrid+*genēs* fr. *gignesthai*, to become]

sap·ro·phyte (sæprofait) *n.* a plant living on nonliving organic matter (opp. AUTOPHYTE, cf. HETEROPHYTE, cf. HETEROTROPH, cf. PARASITE) **sap·ro·phyt·ic** (sæprofítik) *adj.* pertaining to an organism, usually a plant, that obtains its food by absorbing nonliving organic matter [fr. Gk *sapros*, rotten+*phuton*, plant]

sap·suck·er (sæpsʌkər) *n.* any of several small American woodpeckers, esp. of genus *Sphyrapicus*, which feed partly on the sap of trees

sap·wood (sæpwʊd) *n.* the outer living portion of the xylem of vascular plants. It consists of radial vascular rays and longitudinal systems of tracheid fibers and vessels and associated parenchyma (cf. HEARTWOOD)

sar·a·band, sar·a·bande (sérəbænd) *n.* a slow, stately court dance of the 17th and 18th cc., originating from a lively Spanish dance ‖ the music for this, in triple time with a stress on the second beat, esp. as a movement in the classical suite [fr. F. *sarabande* fr. Span.]

Sar·a·cen (sérəs'n) *n.* (*ancient hist.*) one of the nomads of the Syro-Arabian desert ‖ (*hist.*) a Moslem, esp. an Arab. The Saracens invaded France (8th c.) and Sicily (9th c.), and fought against the Crusaders to retain Jerusalem [O.F. *Sarazin* fr. L.L. fr. Gk]

Sar·a·gos·sa (særəgósə) (*Span.* Zaragoza) a province (area 6,726 sq. miles, pop. 760,000) of E. central Spain (*ARAGON) ‖ its capital (pop. 547,300), the ancient capital of Aragon, on the Ebro. Industries: mechanical and electrical engineering, textiles, food processing. Medieval city walls, bridges. Romanesque-Gothic and baroque cathedrals. University (1474)

Sar·ah (séərə) (*Bible*) the wife of Abraham and mother of Isaac

Sarah Lawrence College a U.S. educational institution chartered (1926) at Bronxville, N.Y., originally for women only, now coeducational. It is known for its creative arts program

Sa·ra·je·vo (særəjéivou, sárajəvɔ) the capital (pop. 244,000) of Bosnia-Herzegovina, Yugoslavia. Industries: food processing, building materials. Crafts: carpetmaking, metalwork. Mosques (16th c.), old Moslem quarters. The assassination here (June 28, 1914) of Archduke Franz Ferdinand precipitated the 1st world war

Sar·a·kolle (særəkɒl, særəkɔ́l) *n.* a light-skinned people of W. Africa, speaking a Mandingo dialect ‖ a member of this people

Sa·ra·mac·ca (sɑrəmákə) a river (c. 250 miles long) in central and north central Suriname, flowing into the Atlantic

sarangi (səréndʒi:) *n.* Indian stringed instrument played with a bow, controlled with fingernails

Sar·a·to·ga, Battle of (særətóugə) the first major American victory (1777) of the Revolutionary War. Burgoyne's surrender with 5,000 British troops heartened the American patriots and encouraged France to enter the war

Saratoga Springs a health resort (pop. 23,906) and sporting center (horse racing) in E. New York state: over 150 mineral springs and wells. Skidmore College (1911)

Sa·ra·tov (sɑrátəf) a city (pop. 864,000) of the W. central R.S.F.S.R., U.S.S.R., on the Volga: shipbuilding, engineering, oil, printing. Baroque cathedral (1697). University

Sa·ra·wak (səráwɑk, səráwə) a state (area 48,342 sq. miles, pop. 1,294,753) of Malaysia in N. central Borneo. Capital: Kuching. People: 33% Chinese, 29% Sea Dyaks (Iban), 18% Malays, 8% Land Dyaks, with minorities of other indigenous tribes, Asians and Europeans. Languages: Iban, Chinese, Malay, English. Religion: Moslem, Buddhist, Christian, Animist. Rivers are the chief thoroughfares. Highest peak: 7,950 ft. Industries: oil refining, rubber and food processing. Exports: oil, rubber, sago, pepper, cutch, lumber. Other products: fish, rice, gold, bauxite, coal. Imports: crude oil (from Brunei), foodstuffs, machinery. Ports: Miri, Kuching. HISTORY. Sarawak formed part of the sultanate of Brunei until ceded (1841) by the sultan to James Brooke. He and his descendants administered it as an independent state until 1888, and then as a British protectorate until the Japanese occupation (1942-5). It became a British colony (1946) and joined Malaysia (1963)

sar·casm (sárkæzəm) *n.* a cruelly humorous statement or remark made with the intention of injuring the self-respect of the person to whom it is addressed, usually by drawing attention to one of his weaknesses and often associated with irony ‖ the making of such remarks ‖ the character of such remarks [fr. L.L. *sarcasmus* fr. Gk fr. *sarkazein*, to tear flesh, speak bitterly]

sar·cas·tic (sɑrkæstik) *adj.* having the nature of or involving sarcasm ‖ using or given to using sarcasm **sar·cás·ti·cal·ly** *adv.* [fr. Gk fr. *sarkazein*, to tear flesh, speak bitterly]

sarce·net, sarse·net (sársnit) *n.* a fine fabric of soft silk, used esp. for ribbons and linings [A.F. *sarzinet*, prob. dim. of *sarzin*, Saracen]

sar·co·carp (sárkoukɑrp) *n.* (*bot.*) the fleshy part of a fruit ‖ a fleshy fruit [fr. Gk *sarx* (*sarkos*), flesh+*karpos*, fruit]

Sar·co·di·na (sɑrkoudí:nə) *pl. n.* a class of protozoans characterized by pseudopodia [Mod. L. fr. Gk *sarkōdēs*, fleshy part]

sar·co·ma (sɑrkóumə) *pl.* **sar·co·mas, sar·co·ma·ta** (sɑrkóumətə) *n.* a malignant growth or tumor developing in bony or fibrous tissues

CONCISE PRONUNCIATION KEY: **(a)** æ, c*a*t; ɑ, c*ar*; ɔ f*aw*n; ei, sn*a*ke. **(e)** e, h*e*n; i:, sh*ee*p; iə, d*ee*r; ɛə, b*ea*r. **(i)** i, f*i*sh; ai, t*i*ger; ə:, b*i*rd. **(o)** o, *o*x; au, c*ow*; ou, g*oa*t; u, p*oo*r; ɔi, r*oy*al. **(u)** ʌ, d*u*ck; u, b*u*ll; u:, g*oo*se; ə, b*a*cillus; ju:, c*u*be. x, lo*ch*; θ, *th*ink; ð, bo*th*er; z, *Z*en; ʒ, cor*s*age; dʒ, sava*g*e; ŋ, ora*ng*utang; j, *y*ak; ʃ, *fi*sh; tʃ, fe*tch*; 'l, rabb*le*; 'n, redd*en*. Complete pronunciation key appears inside front cover.

sar·co·ma·tous (sɑrkóumətəs, sɑrkómətəs) *adj.* [Mod. L. fr. Gk *sarkōma* fr. *sarkoun*, to become fleshy]

sar·coph·a·gus (sɑrkófəgəs) *pl.* **sar·coph·a·gi** (sɑrkofədʒai), **sar·coph·a·gus·es** *n.* a stone coffin usually ornamented [L. fr. Gk *sarkophagos*, flesh-eating (fr. the idea that the limestone of which it was made decomposed the corpse)]

sar·co·plasm (sárkəplæzəm) *n.* the cytoplasmic mass in which fibrils of striated muscle are embedded [Mod. L. fr. Gk *sarx* (*sarkos*), flesh+*plasma*, form]

sar·cous (sárkəs) *adj.* (*anat.*) pertaining to flesh or muscle [fr. Gk *sarx* (*sarkos*), flesh]

sard (sɑrd) *n.* a yellow or orange-red variety of chalcedony used as a gem [prob. F. *sarde* fr. L. *sarda, sardius*]

sar·dine (sɑrdíːn) *pl.* **sar·dines, sar·dine** *n. Sardinia pilchardus*, a young pilchard cured and preserved in oil ‖ any of several related small or immature fishes treated in the same way [F. fr. Ital.]

Sar·din·i·a (sɑrdíniːə, sɑrdínjə) (*Ital.* Sardegna) a mountainous deforested island (area 9,302 sq. miles, pop. 1,568,000) in the Mediterranean, just south of Corsica, forming an autonomous region of Italy. Capital: Cagliari. Language: Sardinian and Italian. Highest peak: 4,468 ft. Except for fertile plains in the southwest and along the coasts it is largely scrub-covered. Industries: mining (a quarter of Italian production, esp. lead, zinc, antimony, copper, manganese, coal), fishing, agriculture (cork, beans, cereals, fruit, olives, vines). Livestock: sheep. Universities: Cagliari (1626), Sassari (1677). HISTORY. Sardinia was conquered by Rome (238 B.C.), by Vandals (5th c.) and Saracens (8th c.), by Genoa and Pisa (1022), and by Aragon (1323). It passed (1720) to the dukes of Savoy, who took the title of king of Sardinia. After the Napoleonic Wars the kingdom was reconstituted (1815) to include Sardinia, Piedmont, Savoy, Nice and Liguria. The reign (1831-49) of Charles Albert saw the granting of a liberal constitution (1848) and an unsuccessful attempt (1848-9) to free northern Italy from the Austrians. Victor Emmanuel II and Cavour obtained French help in defeating (1859) the Austrians. Other Italian states then allied with Sardinia to form (1861) the kingdom of Italy

Sar·din·i·an (sɑrdíniːən, sɑrdínjən) 1. *n.* a native or inhabitant of Sardinia ‖ the Romance language of Sardinia 2. *adj.* of Sardinia, its inhabitants, culture etc.

Sar·dis (sárdis) the ancient capital of Lydia. It flourished (7th c. B.C. to mid-6th c. B.C.) and was taken by the Persians (546 B.C.)

sar·di·us (sárdiːəs) *n.* (*hist.*) one of the gems worn by the Jewish high priest, possibly a sard or sardonyx ‖ a sard [L. fr. Gk *sardios* fr. *Sardeis*, Sardis]

sar·don·ic (sɑrdónik) *adj.* expressing bitterness or ironic mockery under laughter **sar·dón·i·cal·ly** *adv.* [F. *sardonique* fr. L. fr. Gk]

sar·don·yx (sárdóniks, sárd'niks) *n.* a variety of onyx in which there are layers of orange-red sard and of a white chalcedony, used as a gem [L. fr. Gk]

Sar·dou (særduː), Victorien (1831-1908), French dramatist. His successes included the popular historical dramas 'Fedora' (1887) and 'Robespierre' (1902)

sar·gas·so (sɑrgǽsou) *pl.* **sar·gas·sos** *n.* gulfweed ‖ a floating mass of this [Port. *sargaço*]

Sargasso Sea a part (area 2,000,000 sq. miles) of the Atlantic Ocean between the West Indies and the Azores, a calm center in the midst of the Gulf Stream. Its name derives from the sargasso floating on it, in which many varieties of marine life thrive

sar·gas·sum (sɑrgǽsəm) *n.* gulfweed [Mod. L. fr. Port.]

Sar·gent (sárdʒənt), John Singer (1856-1925), American painter who lived in England from 1885. He is best known for his many society portraits

Sar·gon I (sárgɒn) (c. 2600 B.C.), founder of the Semitic kingdom of Akkad in Babylonia

Sargon II (d. 705 B.C.), king of Assyria (721-705 B.C.), founder of the last Assyrian dynasty. He destroyed the kingdom of Israel (c. 722 B.C.), captured Samaria (721-717 B.C.), deported its inhabitants and devastated Armenia (714 B.C.)

sa·ri (sáːri) *pl.* **sa·ris** *n.* the robe of a Hindu woman, consisting of a long piece of cotton or silk fabric wrapped around the body and draped over the head or shoulder [Hindi *sārhī, sārī*]

Sark (sɑrk) the smallest island (area 2 sq. miles, pop. 600) of Great Britain's Channel Islands, comprising Great and Little Sark, connected by an isthmus. It is an autonomous dependency of Guernsey under a hereditary seigneur

Sar·ma·ti·an (sɑrméiʃiːən, sɑrméiʃən) 1. *n.* a member of the nomadic Indo-European people who displaced the Scythians (3rd c. B.C.) on the lower Don. First the enemies and then the allies of Rome, they were displaced by the Goths (3rd c. A.D.) 2. *adj.* of the Sarmatians or the area they inhabited

sar·men·tose (sɑrméntous) *adj.* (*bot.*) having or producing prostrate shoots which root at their nodes [fr. L. *sarmentum*, pruned twig]

Sar·mien·to (sɑrmjéntɔ), Domingo Faustino (1811-88), Argentinian writer, politician, and president of the Republic (1868-74). During the dictatorship of Rosas, which he depicts in his masterpiece 'Facundo o Civilización i barbarie' (1845), he lived in Chile. He returned to join the ranks of Urquiza, but again went into exile (1852-5). Succeeding Mitre as president, he brought the war with Paraguay to an end. He founded the Astronomical Observatory of Córdoba and the military and naval academies

sa·rong (sərɔ́ŋ, sərɒ́ŋ) *n.* an ankle-length garment worn by men and women in the Malay Archipelago, consisting of one long strip of cotton or silk wrapped around the body and tucked in at the waist [Malay *sārung*]

Sa·roy·an (sərɔ́iən), William (1908-81), U.S. writer. His works include the plays 'My Heart's in the Highlands' (1939) and 'The Time of Your Life' (1939); a novel, 'The Human Comedy' (1943); short stories collected in 'The Daring Young Man on the Flying Trapeze' (1934); and his autobiographical works 'My Name is Aram' (1940), 'Places Where I've Done Time' (1972), 'Chance Meeting' (1978) and 'Obituaries' (1979)

sar·ra·ce·ni·a (særəsíːniːə) *n.* a member of *Sarracenia*, fam. *Sarraceniaceae*, a genus of pitcher plants [Mod. L. after D. *Sarrazin* (17th c.), Canadian physician]

sar·sa·pa·ril·la (sɑrsəparílə, sɑrspərílə, sæspərílə) *n.* any of several members of *Smilax*, fam. *Liliaceae*, a genus of American vines ‖ an extract from the dried roots of these, used as a tonic and as a flavoring in beverages ‖ a carbonated beverage flavored with this [Span. *zarzaparrilla*]

sarsenet *SARCENET

Sarthe (sært) a department (area 2,410 sq. miles, pop. 490,400) of N.W. France (*MAINE). Chief town: Le Mans

Sar·to (sártɔ), Andrea del (1486-1531), Florentine painter. Both in his splendid color and in his composition he was exceptional in the Florence of his period. His frescos include the 'Birth of the Virgin' in the cloister of SS. Annunziata, Florence. His paintings include the 'Holy Family' in the Louvre, 'Madonna of the Harpies' in the Uffizi, and the 'Holy Family' in the Metropolitan Museum, New York

sar·to·ri·al (sortóriːəl, sɑrtóuriːəl) *adj.* of or pertaining to men's clothes ‖ of tailors or their trade [fr. L. *sartorius* fr. *sartor*, tailor]

sar·to·ri·us (sɑrtóriːəs, sɑrtóuriːəs) *pl.* **sar·to·ri·i** (sɑrtóriːai, sɑrtóuriːəs) *n.* the long thigh muscle, the longest in man, which enables the knee to be flexed and adducted [Mod. L. fr. L. *sartor*, tailor (fr. the tailor's traditional cross-legged posture when stitching)]

Sar·tre (særtr), Jean-Paul (1905-80), French philosopher, novelist and playwright. Sartre was the leading French exponent of existentialism (strictly speaking, the proposition that existence, i.e. the concrete historical situation, precedes essence. Among his philosophical works are 'l'Etre et le Néant' (1943), and 'Critique de la raison dialectique' (1960). His novels include 'la Nausée' (1938), 'les Chemins de la liberté' (1945). His plays include 'Huis clos' (1944), 'les Mouches' (1943), 'les Mains sales' (1948) and 'Nekrassov' (1955). His works explore the situation of 'anguish' which precedes 'commitment' to a course of action. He won but declined to accept the Nobel prize for literature (1964)

Sar·um use (séərəm) *n.* (*eccles.*) the order of divine service used before the Reformation in the diocese of Salisbury, England, and currently followed in some Anglican churches [M.L. *Sarum*, Salisbury]

SAS (*abbr.*) for British Special Air Service, an antiterrorist commando unit

SASE (*abbr.*) for self-addressed stamped envelope

Sa·se·bo (sásəbɔ) a port (pop. 254,313) and naval base of N.W. Kyushu, Japan

sash (sæʃ) *n.* a framework holding glass, in a window or greenhouse etc. ‖ a movable frame of a sash window [fr. F. *châssis*, frame]

sash *n.* a broad ribbon, often of silk, worn as a sign of office or honor ‖ a broad ribbon worn as an adornment around the waist [older *shash* fr. Arab. *shāsh*, turban, muslin]

sa·shay (sæʃéi) *v.i.* (*pop.*) to walk nonchalantly ‖ (*pop.*) to swagger about in an attention-catching way ‖ (*pop.*) to move sideways or in a zigzag course [fr. *chassé*, a gliding sideways dance step, fr. F.]

sash cord a strong cord attached to the sash of a sash window, passing over a pulley and carrying a counterweight, by means of which the sash is held in equilibrium in any position

sash window a window having glazed frames that slide up and down

sa·sin (séisin) *n.* the black buck [Nepalese]

Sask. Saskatchewan

Sas·katch·e·wan (sæskǽtʃəwɒn) a province (area 251,700 sq. miles, pop. 1,000,000) of central Canada. Capital: Regina. The north is part of the Canadian Shield and has important mineral resources. The south consists of fertile prairies. Agriculture: wheat (leading producer) and other cereals, beef and dairy cattle. Resources: copper, uranium, cadmium, zinc, gold, oil, coal, sodium sulfate, salt, potash. Industries: food processing, oil refining. University: Saskatoon. The Hudson's Bay Company promoted trade in furs with the Indians of the area (17th c.) and established permanent settlements (1774). The area was included in the Northwest Territories (1870) and became a province of Canada (1905)

Saskatchewan a navigable river (340 miles long) flowing from E. Saskatchewan, Canada, into Lake Winnipeg. It is formed by the confluence of the North Saskatchewan (760 miles long) and the South Saskatchewan (865 miles long), both rising in the Rocky Mtns in Alberta

Sas·ka·toon (sæskətúːn) a communications center and market (pop. 154,210) of central Saskatchewan, Canada, on the South Saskatchewan River: agricultural machinery, flour milling, meat packing. University (1907)

sas·ka·toon (sæskətúːn) *n.* a Juneberry, esp. *Amelanchier alnifolia* of Canada and the northern and western U.S.A.

Sas·quatch (sáskwatʃ) *n.* hypothetical humanlike animal said to inhabit the Pacific Northwest

sass (sæs) 1. *n.* (*pop.*) impudent talk 2. *v.t.* (*pop.*) to speak impudently to [SASSY]

sas·sa·by (sǽsəbi:) *pl.* **sas·sa·bies** *n. Damaliscus lunatus*, a large S. African antelope [Bantu]

sas·sa·fras (sǽsəfræs) *n.* a member of *Sassafras*, fam. *Lauraceae*, a genus of North American and Asian trees, esp. *S. albidum* of E. North America ‖ the dried bark of the roots of *S. albidum*, used as an aromatic stimulant and yielding a volatile oil used in perfumes [Span. *sasafras*]

Sas·sa·ni·an (səséiniːən) 1. *n.* a member of the Sassanid dynasty 2. *adj.* of or relating to the Sassanids

Sas·sa·nid (səsánid, səsǽnid) *pl.* **Sas·sa·nids, Sas·sa·ni·dae** (səsánidi:, səsǽnidi:) *n.* a member of a Persian dynasty of kings (c. 226–c. 641) who overthrew (c. 226) the kingdom of Parthia, and who were conquered (c. 641) by the Arabs. The dynasty's capital was Ctesiphon

Sas·sa·ri (sássari:) a commercial center (pop. 117,300) in N.W. Sardinia, Italy. Romanesque church (13th c.). University (1677)

Sas·se·nach (sǽsənəx, sǽsənæk) *n.* (the Gaelic or Erse term for) an Englishman, Saxon or Lowlander [fr. Gael. *Sasunnach*]

Sas·set·ta (sassétta), Stefano di Giovanni (c. 1392-1450), Italian painter. He worked in Siena and continued the mystical tradition of 14th-c. Sienese painting, but was influenced by the new Renaissance modes. His main work, now scattered, is the St Francis altarpiece painted for S. Francesco, Sansepolcro (1437-44)

sas·sy (sǽsi:) *comp.* **sas·si·er** *superl.* **sas·si·est** *adj.* (*pop.*) impudent, sometimes with coyness, *a sassy answer* [var. of SAUCY]

sat *past* and *past part.* of SIT

Sat. Saturday

Sa·tan (séit'n) *n.* the chief of the rebel angels (*LUCIFER) and the anthropomorphic personification of evil, the Devil

sa·tang (sətǽn) *n.* a monetary unit of Thailand, one hundredth of a baht ‖ a coin of the value of one satang [Thai *satān*]

sa·tan·ic (seitǽnik, sətǽnik) *adj.* of, pertaining to or characteristic of Satan [fr. SATAN fr. Heb. *sātān*, enemy]

Sa·tan·ism (séit'nizəm) *n.* worship of Satan, using rites which travesty Christian rites

satch·el (sǽtʃəl) *n.* a bag of leather or stout canvas, usually fastened by a strap and buckle, carried by hand or slung over the shoulder by strap [O.F. *sachel*]

Sat·com *n.* (*acronym*) for satellite communications center *Cf* EARTH STATION

sate (seit) *pres. part.* **sat·ing** *past* and *past part.* **sat·ed** *v.t.* to satisfy totally (the appetite or a desire) ‖ to satisfy so fully as to induce a revulsion of feeling [prob. fr. *sade*, to become or make weary fr. O.E.]

sa·teen, sa·tine (sætí:n) *n.* a cotton fabric given a glossy surface in imitation of satin [fr. SATIN]

sat·el·lite (sǽt'lait) *n.* a natural or man-made body moving in orbit around the moon or one of the planets etc. ‖ a state economically and politically dependent on another, although apparently independent ‖ a person in constant servile attendance upon another [F.]

satellite city an urban area outside a larger urban area, usu. created by municipal plan

satellite town separated residential (sometimes industrial) center associated with an urban center that provides jobs, services, entertainment *Cf* SATELLITE CITY

sa·ti·ate (séiʃi:eit) *pres. part.* **sa·ti·at·ing** *past* and *past part.* **sa·ti·at·ed** *v.t.* to satisfy (a desire or someone), esp. so fully that desire gives place to a revulsion of feeling **sa·ti·a·tion** *n.* [L. *satiore* (*satiatus*), to satisfy]

Sa·tie (sæti:), Erik Alfred Leslie (1886-1925), French composer. He was an experimentalist, analyzing the elements of music and reassembling them in a way which naturally associated him with cubism in art. His work includes piano solos and duets, the symphonic drama 'Socrates', ballets and a Mass

sa·ti·e·ty (sətáiiti:) *n.* the state of being sated [fr. F. *saiteté*]

sat·in (sǽt'n) **1.** *n.* a fabric of silk with a glossy surface on one side ‖ a fabric of nylon, rayon etc. resembling this **2.** *adj.* made of satin ‖ smooth and glossy, like satin [F. perh. fr. Ital. fr. L. *seta*, silk]

SATIN sage air traffic integration, air traffic control system that coordinates with SAGE; designed by Mitre Corporation

sat·i·net, sat·i·nette (sæt'nét) *n.* a glossy fabric of cotton with silk or wool, or of synthetic fiber, made to imitate satin [F. *satinet*]

satin stitch a long embroidery stitch worked in close, parallel bands to give a smooth, satiny appearance

sat·in·wood (sǽt'nwud) *n. Cloroxylon Swietenia*, fam. *Meliaceae*, an East Indian tree, the lustrous, light-colored wood of which is used in cabinetmaking ‖ this wood ‖ any of several trees whose wood resembles this ‖ the wood of these trees

sat·in·y (sǽt'ni:) *adj.* like satin in glossy smoothness or softness

sat·ire (sǽtaier) *n.* a literary genre in which ridicule is thrown upon something by stressing its worst features, often by the use of irony, thus assuming or affirming a norm by which aberrations are judged ‖ a literary work in this genre [F. or fr. L. *satira*]

sa·tir·ic (sətírik) *adj.* of, containing or characterized by satire ‖ writing satire, *a satiric poet* [fr. F. *satirique*]

sa·tir·i·cal (sətírik'l) *adj.* of, containing or characterized by satire ‖ given to the use of irony, ridicule or sarcasm [fr. L.L. *satiricus*]

sat·i·rist (sǽtərist) *n.* a writer of satires

sat·i·rize (sǽtəraiz) *pres. part.* **sat·i·riz·ing** *past* and *past part.* **sat·i·rized** *v.t.* to treat in a satirical way [fr. F. *satiriser*]

sat·is·fac·tion (sætisfǽkʃən) *n.* a satisfying or being satisfied ‖ a source or cause of pleasure, fulfilment or gratification ‖ a payment or other compensation for damage, injury etc. ‖ an opportunity to vindicate one's honor by fighting a duel, *he demanded satisfaction for the insult* ‖

(*theol.*) performance of the penance imposed by the priest on a penitent [F.]

sat·is·fac·to·ri·ly (sætisfǽktərili:) *adv.* in a satisfactory manner

sat·is·fac·to·ri·ness (sætisfǽktəri:nis) *n.* the quality or state of being satisfactory

sat·is·fac·to·ry (sætisfǽktəri:) *adj.* adequate ‖ giving satisfaction [fr. F. *satisfactoire*]

sat·is·fy (sǽtisfai) *pres. part.* **sat·is·fy·ing** *past* and *past part.* **sat·is·fied** *v.t.* to cause (someone) to be happy or free from some desire or need by supplying what he desires, needs or demands ‖ to provide what is required by (a need, obligation, standard etc.), *to satisfy the requirements for graduation* ‖ to provide all that is needed by (appetite, thirst etc.), *the meal did not satisfy his hunger* ‖ to pay (a creditor) ‖ to counter (misgiving, arguments etc.) convincingly ‖ to convince or persuade of some specified fact, *he satisfied the police that he was innocent* ‖ (*math.*) to be, or provide, the solution for (an equation) ‖ *v.i.* to give satisfaction [O.F. *satisfier* fr. L. *satisfacere* fr. *satis*, enough+*facere*, to do]

Sa·to (sou), Eisaku (1901-75), Japanese statesman, prime minister of Japan (1964-75)

Sat·pu·ra Range (sátpurə) a range of hills (average height 3,000 ft) in Madhya Pradesh, India, between the Narbada and Tapti Rivers

sa·trap (séitræp, sǽtræp) *n.* (*hist.*) a provincial ruler in ancient Persia ‖ (*rhet.*) a subordinate ruler or petty official, esp. one who is tyrannical [fr. L. *satrapes* fr. Gk fr. O. Pers.]

sa·trap·y (séitrəpi:, sǽtrəpi:) *pl.* **sa·trap·ies** *n.* the dignity, office or jurisdiction of a satrap [F. *satrapie*]

Sa·tsu·ma (sátsumə) *n.* a cream-colored variety of Japanese pottery [after *Satsuma*, former province of Kyushu]

sat·u·rate (sǽtʃəreit) *pres. part.* **sat·u·rat·ing** *past* and *past part.* **sat·u·rat·ed** *v.t.* to fill completely, *to saturate a market with orders* ‖ to transform some or all of the multiple bonds in (an unsaturated substance) by chemical addition ‖ to cause (a substance) to become impregnated to the point where it can absorb no more ‖ to steep or soak, esp. by immersion ‖ to destroy (an area) with a very high concentration of bombs or projectiles ‖ to magnetize (a substance) till further increase in magnetizing force produces no further increase in magnetization ‖ to increase the voltage to (an electron tube) to the point where further increase of voltage produces no change of current ‖ to dissolve in (a solvent) as much of a solute as can be held in solution at a given temperature and pressure **sat·u·rat·ed** *adj.* (*chem.*, of a solution) having the highest concentration of a solute possible at a given temperature and pressure ‖ (*chem.*, of a compound) having only single bonds between adjacent atoms (used esp. of carbon compounds) and hence not tending to form additional compounds ‖ (of a rock) having the greatest possible amount of combined silica [fr. L. *saturare* (*saturatus*)]

saturated vapor, esp. *Br.* **saturated vapour** (*phys.*) a vapor which is in equilibrium with its own liquid form

sat·u·ra·tion (sætʃəréiʃən) *n.* a saturating or being saturated ‖ the quality of a color that depends on the amount of achromatic color mixed with it (*COLOR)

saturation diving or **saturated diving** remaining underwater for a maximum period, thus requiring maximum decompression at the time of return to the surface —**saturation dive** *v.* —**saturated diver** *n.*

Sat·ur·day (sǽtərdi:, sǽtərdei) *n.* the seventh and last day of the week [O.E. *Sæterndæg*, Saturday, the day of Saturn]

Saturday night special *n.* (*slang*) an inexpensive, easily obtained handgun

Sat·urn (sǽtərn) (*Rom. mythol.*) the god of agriculture, father of Jupiter ‖ the sixth planet from the sun (mean orbital diameter=8.87 X 10^8 miles) and the second largest in the solar system (mass = 5.58 X 10^{23} tons, diameter=approx. 74,500 miles), 95 times more massive than the earth. It revolves about the sun with a sidereal period of 29.6 years and rotates on its axis with a period that depends on latitude (between 10 hrs 14 mins and 10 hrs 38 mins). In the telescope it appears as a yellowish disk, with belts similar to those of Jupiter but less well defined and yellow to green in color. Its atmosphere consists mostly of hydrogen and helium, with traces of methane, ammonia, ethine, phosphine and acetylene. The gas density gradually decreases downward and the gas

becomes a liquid and then metallic. A small core of silicate material probably is at the center. Saturn has a system of seven thin, concentric rings lying in the plane of its equator and varying in width (between 10,000 and 16,000 miles). The rings are composed of dust, of a density varying with the ring, orbiting about the planet. The dust is thought to be the remains of satellites or comets, which, when in the molten state, were disintegrated by tidal motions on approaching the planet. Saturn has at least 22 satellites

sat·ur·na·li·a (sætərnéili:ə, sætərnéiljə) *pl.* **sat·ur·na·li·a, sat·ur·na·li·as** *n.* a period of orgiastic revelry **Sat·ur·na·li·a** (*hist.*) the festival of Saturn, held in December in ancient Rome and characterized by unrestrained revelry **sat·ur·ná·li·an** *adj.* orgiastic **Sat·ur·na·li·an** of or characteristic of the Saturnalia (L., neut. pl. of *Saturnalis*, pertaining to Saturn)

Sa·tur·ni·an (sətó:rni:ən) *adj.* pertaining to Saturn, esp. to his supposed former reign, thought by ancient Romans to have been marked by peace and prosperity [fr. L. *Saturnius*]

sat·ur·nine (sǽtərnain) *adj.* gloomy, surly [fr. M.L. fr. *Saturnus*, Saturn. People born under the planet's influence were thought to be cold and gloomy in temperament]

sa·tyr (séitər, sǽtər) *n.* (*Gk* and *Rom. mythol.*) a god of the woods given to Bacchic revelry and lechery, often depicted with a horse's or goat's tail and a goat's legs and ears ‖ (*rhet.*) a lecher ‖ any of several butterflies of fam. *Satyridæ*, usually brown and gray and often having ocelli on the wings [fr. L. *satyrus* fr. Gk]

sa·tyr·ic (sətírik) *adj.* of or like a satyr **sa·týr·i·cal** *adj.* [fr. L. *satyricus* and Gk *satirikos*]

sauce (sɔs) **1.** *n.* a preparation, usually liquid or soft, added to food e.g. to make it more piquant ‖ (*fig.*) something which lends piquancy ‖ (*pop.*) impertinence, impudence **2.** *v.t. pres. part.* **sauc·ing** *past* and *past part.* **sauced** to add sauce to ‖ (*pop.*) to be impertinent to [F.]

sauce·boat (sɔ́sbout) *n.* a vessel in which sauce is served

sauce·pan (sɔ́spæn) *n.* a metal pot with a long handle, used to boil or stew food

sau·cer (sɔ́sər) *n.* a small, shallow dish, used as a stand in which to place a cup and to receive any overspill ‖ anything of this shape [O.F. *saussier*, dish for serving sauces]

sau·ci·ly (sɔ́sili:) *adv.* in a saucy manner

sau·ci·ness (sɔ́si:nis) *n.* the quality of being saucy

sau·cy (sɔ́si:) *comp.* **sau·ci·er** *superl.* **sau·ci·est** *adj.* impudent, sometimes with coyness, *a saucy answer* ‖ smart, gaily stylish

Sa·u·di Arabia (saú:di:, sáudi:, sɔ́di:) a kingdom (area approx. 600,000 sq. miles, pop. approx. 9,795,000, 50% Beduins) occupying most of Arabia and comprising the former kingdom of Hejaz (capital: Mecca) and former sultanate of Nejd (capital: Riyadh), with their dependencies. It has joint control with Iraq over 7,000 sq. miles and with Kuwait over 5,770 sq. miles of neutral territory. Language: Arabic. Religion: Islam (official), mainly Sunnites (Wahhabi sect in Nejd), with a Shi'ite minority in al-Hasa. It is largely an arid plateau (1,500–6,000 ft), with a lowland strip along the Red Sea coast and a wider plain along the Persian Gulf and in the southeast. Mountains between the western coastal strip and the interior rise to 5,000 ft north of Jedda and to 9,000 ft south of Mecca (highest in Asir). The Nafud and Great Sandy deserts occupy the northern center and the southeast. The rest of the country has seasonal vegetation. Average temperatures Jan. and July (F.): Jedda 70° and 90°, Riyadh 60° and 80°. Rainfall: 10 ins in oases, 4 ins and under elsewhere. Exports: crude and refined petroleum (the country contains 10% of known world deposits). Other industries: oasis farming (dates and other fruits, cereals), livestock raising (camels, horses, donkeys, sheep), the Mecca pilgrimage trade, building materials, food processing. Imports: piece goods, cereals, foodstuffs, vehicles, building materials, machinery, chemicals. Communications: chiefly by air services or by camel caravan. Ports: Dammam and Ras Tanura on the Persian Gulf, Jedda on the Red Sea. The trans-Arabian pipeline connects the oil fields with the Mediterranean. Universities: Riyadh, Mecca and Medina. Monetary unit: rial (20 qurush). HISTORY. (For early history *ARABIA) Hejaz and Nejd were united (1925) as a result of the Wahhabi conquest under ibn Saud, and adopted the name of Saudi

---

CONCISE PRONUNCIATION KEY: **(a)** æ, c**a**t; ɑ, c**a**r; ɔ f**aw**n; ei, sn**a**ke. **(e)** e, h**e**n; i:, sh**ee**p; iə, d**ee**r; ɛə, b**ea**r. **(i)** i, f**i**sh; ai, t**i**ger; əː, b**i**rd. **(o)** o, **o**x; au, c**ow**; ou, g**oa**t; u, p**oo**r; ɔi, r**oy**al. **(u)** ʌ, d**u**ck; u, b**u**ll; uː, g**oo**se; ə, b**a**cillus; juː, c**u**be. x, lo**ch**; θ, **th**ink; δ, **b**o**th**er; z, **Z**en; ʒ, cor**s**age; dʒ, **s**avage; ŋ, ora**n**gutang; j, **y**ak; ʃ, **f**ish; tʃ, fe**tch**; 'l, rabb**le**; 'n, redd**en**. Complete pronunciation key appears inside front cover.

Arabia (1932). Vast oil reserves were discovered (1930s) and were developed by an American firm. Saudi Arabia joined the U.N. and the Arab League (1945) and formed a military, economic and political alliance with Jordan (1962). Saud, son of ibn Saud, ruled the country (1953-64), and was succeeded by Faisal. Profits from the oil industry made possible improvements in irrigation, education and communications. Faisal was assassinated (1975) and was succeeded by Khalid, who ruled until his death (1982) and was succeeded by Crown Prince Fahd. Saudi Arabia acts as a 'conservative' force in the Middle East and is a leader of OPEC

Sa·ud ibn Ab·dul A·ziz (saú:di:b'nabdúlazí:z) (1902-69), king of Saudi Arabia (1953-64), son of ibn Saud. He was deposed in favor of Faisal

sau·er·kraut (sáuərkraut) *n.* shredded cabbage fermented under pressure in its own juices, with added salt, in large stone jars [G. fr. *sauer, sour+kraut,* cabbage]

sau·ger (sógər) *n. Stizostedion canadense,* a small North American pike perch, valued as a food fish

Sauk (sɔk) *pl.* **Sauk, Sauks** *n.* a North American Indian people from the Fox River valley and Green Bay area in Wisconsin ‖ a member of this people ‖ the dialect

Saul (sɔl) (*d.* c. 1012 B.C.), first king of the Hebrews (c. 1040-c. 1012 B.C.). A Benjamite, he was anointed king by Samuel, and successfully united the Hebrews against the Philistines. He committed suicide after a military defeat, and was succeeded by his son-in-law David (I Samuel x-xxxi)

Saul of Tarsus *PAUL, ST

Sault Sainte Ma·rie (sú:seintmərí:) an industrial city (iron and steel, shipbuilding, pulp and paper mills), port of entry and resort (pop. 14,448) in S. Ontario, Canada

Sau·mur (soumyr) a town (pop. 34,191) in Maine-et-Loire, France, on the lower Loire: castle (15th c.), cavalry school

sau·na (sóna, sáuna, sáuna) *n.* a Finnish steam bath ‖ the building in which such baths are taken [Finn.]

saun·ter (sóntər, sántər) **1.** *v.i.* to walk in a leisurely manner, with no particular aim in view **2.** *n.* a leisurely walk ‖ the leisurely gait at which one saunters [etym. doubtful]

Sau·ra·se·ni (saurəséini:) *n.* one of the Prakrit languages of India

sau·ri·an (sóri:ən) **1.** *adj.* pertaining to lizards **2.** *n.* a lizard ‖ a reptile resembling a lizard [fr. Mod. L. *Sauria,* former name of a division of reptiles, fr. Gk *saura,* lizard]

sau·ro·pod (sórəpɔd) *n.* a member of *Sauropoda,* order *Saurischia,* a suborder of gigantic herbivorous dinosaurs of the Jurassic and Cretaceous [fr. Mod. L. *Sauropoda* fr. Gk *sauru,* lizard+*pous (podos),* foot]

sau·ry (sóri:) *pl.* **sau·ries** *n. Scombresox saurus,* fam. *Scombresocidae,* a marine fish with a long body and long beak, found in temperate parts of the Atlantic, off S. Africa, and elsewhere [prob. fr. Mod. L. *saurus,* lizard]

sau·sage (sósidʒ) *n.* a quantity of finely minced meat, salted and spiced and forced into a thin-walled tube (usually a prepared intestine) which is hermetically sealed by tying its ends and may be divided into short lengths by twisting ‖ one such short length [M.E. *sausige* fr. O.N.F. *saussiche*]

sausage meat the mixture used to make sausages

sausage roll (*Br.*) a small quantity of sausage meat enclosed in flaky pastry and baked

Saus·sure (sousyr), Ferdinand de (1857-1913), Swiss Indo-European scholar and teacher, founder of modern linguistics

Saussure, Horace Bénédict de (1740-99), Swiss physicist and alpine traveler. He did important research in alpine metereology and geology

sau·té (soutéi, sóti) **1.** *adj.* fried quickly in a pan with a little hot butter or other fat **2.** *v. t. pres. part.* **sau·tée·ing** (soutéiɪŋ, sóteiɪŋ) *past and past part.* **sau·téed** (soutéid, sóteid) to fry in this way **3.** *n.* a dish prepared in this way [F. past part. of *sauter,* to leap]

Sau·terne, Sau·ternes (soutə́:rn, sótə:rn, *F.* soutern) *n.* a white wine, usually semi-sweet, from Sauternes, a region north of Bordeaux, France

Sau·veur (souvé:r), Albert (1863-1939), U.S. metallurgist whose research into the crystal structure of metals produced methods of improving the quality of steel. He devised (late 1800s) the technique of making photomicrographs

Sa·va (sáva) the chief river (450 miles long, navigable for 360) of Yugoslavia, flowing from the Julian Alps (Italian border) across Slovenia and Croatia (forming the border with Bosnia-Herzegovina) to the Danube at Belgrade

Sava, St (c. 1175-1235), Serbian monk, patron saint of Serbia, son of Stevan Nemanja. Feast: Jan. 14

sav·age (sǽvidʒ) **1.** *adj.* primitive, uncivilized, *a savage tribe* ‖ characteristic of a primitive, uncivilized people, *savage customs* ‖ uncultivated, *savage country* ‖ wild and ferocious, *a savage beast* ‖ extremely cruel, *savage criticism* ‖ (*pop.*) violently angry **2.** *n.* an uncivilized human being, esp. one who has not learned the art of cultivating the soil ‖ a person who behaves in a violent, cruel or uncultivated way **3.** *v.t. pres. part.* **sav·ag·ing** *past and past part.* **sav·aged** to attack and bite, claw, rend etc. [F. *sauvage*]

sav·age·ry (sǽvidʒri:) *pl.* **sav·age·ries** *n.* a savage act ‖ savage behavior ‖ the quality or state of being savage

Sa·van·nah (səvǽnə) the oldest and second largest city (pop. 141,390) in Georgia, in the southeast part of the state. It is an important shipping point for cotton, naval stores, and tobacco. Georgia State College (1890)

Savannah a navigable river (314 miles long) rising in N.W. South Carolina and flowing into the Atlantic at Savannah, forming the Georgia-South Carolina boundary: hydroelectric power

sa·van·na, sa·van·nah (səvǽnə) *n.* tropical or subtropical grassland containing scattered trees or bushes characteristic of tropical America and much of tropical Africa ‖ a treeless plain, esp. in the southeastern U.S.A. [older *zavanna* fr. Span. perh. fr. Carib]

sa·vant (sævánt, sǽvənt, sævǽ) *n.* (*rhet.*) a man of great erudition [F.]

save (seiv) **1.** *v. pres. part.* **sav·ing** *past and past part.* **saved** *v.t.* to keep alive, free, safe or in good condition, esp. when this state is in danger of being changed, *the gifts saved many from starvation* ‖ to make unnecessary or avoidable, *it will save trouble if we start early* ‖ to economize, *he saves his bus fares and walks* ‖ to work the spiritual salvation of ‖ (sometimes with 'up') to reserve for future use, enjoyment etc., *I'm saving that last chapter for tomorrow* ‖ to prevent (a game) from being lost ‖ *v.i.* to put aside for future use money that one would otherwise spend **to save face** to avoid injury to one's pride or public disgrace in some difficult situation **to save the situation** to act in a way which averts disaster or embarrassment **2.** *n.* (*games*) an action which directly prevents the opposing side from scoring [M.E. *salve, sauve* fr. O.F. *salver, sauver*]

save 1. *prep.* except, *they were all unhurt save the pilot* **2.** *conj.* (with 'that') except [fr. SAFE *adj.* and F. *sauf*]

Sav·ile (sǽvil), George, 1st marquis of Halifax *HALIFAX

sav·in, sav·ine (sǽvin) *n. Juniperus sabina,* a small, bushy juniper native to Europe and W. Asia, bearing bluish-green berries. The bitter tops yield an oil, used medicinally [O.F. *savine*]

sav·ing (séiviŋ) **1.** *adj.* making an exception, *a saving clause* ‖ outweighing faults, *a saving grace* ‖ securing salvation for the soul **2.** *n.* the act of someone or something that saves ‖ a desirable economy in time, money etc. ‖ (*pl.*) money saved ‖ (*law*) a reservation **3.** *prep.* excepting **4.** *conj.* (esp. with 'that') except

savings account (*Am.*=*Br.* deposit account) a bank account on which checks are not drawn and which earns some interest (cf. CHECKING ACCOUNT)

savings and loan association a financial organization under federal or state law for the promotion of thrift and private home ownership, first organized in 1831 after the pattern of the British building societies

savings bank a public or private bank which accepts small savings on deposit and pays interest on them

savings bond a nontransferable U.S. government bond in denominations of $25 to $1,000

sav·ior, esp. *Br.* **sav·iour** (séivjər) *n.* someone who saves a person or thing from destruction or injury **the Sav·ior,** esp. *Br.* **the Sav·iour** Christ [M.E. fr. O.F. *sauveour*]

Sa·voie (sævwa) a department (area 2,388 sq. miles, pop. 305,100) of E. France (*SAVOY). Chief town: Chambéry

Savoie, Haute- *HAUTE-SAVOIE

sa·voir faire (sǽvwarféər) *n.* tact and easy assurance in social relationships [F.]

Sav·o·na·ro·la (sævənəróulə), Girolamo (1452-98), Italian religious reformer. Prior of the Dominican monastery of St Mark in Florence (1491-8), he preached with great ardor against the moral corruption in Church and State that was an aspect of the Renaissance. When the Medici were exiled from the town (1494), he instituted a republic of terrifying severity until he was excommunicated by Alexander VI (1497) and lost the confidence of the citizens. He was hanged and burned for heresy

sa·vor, esp. *Br.* **sa·vour** (séivər) *n.* tastiness ‖ a smell of cooking which promises well ‖ the taste of something ‖ the characteristic quality of something [O.F. *savur, savour*]

savor, esp. *Br.* **savour** *v.t.* to give a distinctive taste to ‖ to have the distinctive taste of ‖ to have the characteristic quality of ‖ to have experience of ‖ to take pleasure in the taste, smell or characteristic quality of ‖ *v.i.* to have a distinctive taste or smell ‖ (with 'of') to have a quality suggestive of something specified, *his criticisms savor of jealousy* [O.F. *savourer*]

sa·vor·y, esp. *Br.* **sa·vour·y** (séivəri:) **1.** *adj.* having a pleasant and piquant taste and smell, *a savory dish* ‖ (esp. in negative constructions) morally edifying, *it is not a very savory affair* **2.** *n. pl.* **sa·vou·ries** (*Br.*) a small portion of savory food taken esp. as the last course of a dinner [M.E. *savure* prob. fr. O.F. *savouré*]

savory *n.* any of several members of *Satureia,* fam. *Labiatae,* a genus of aromatic mints native to S. Europe, esp. *S. hortensis* (summer savory) and *S. montana* (winter savory), the leaves of which are used in cooking [fr. L. *satureia*]

savour *SAVOR

savoury *SAVORY

Sa·voy (səvɔ́i) (*F.* Savoie) an alpine region forming the French departments of Savoie and Haute-Savoie, on the Italian and Swiss borders. It includes Mont Blanc. Occupations: cattle breeding, farming (cereals, vines), forestry, varied industry (based on abundant hydroelectricity), tourism. Historic capital: Chambéry. Principal resorts: Megève, Saint-Gervais, Chamonix, Annecy. Savoy was an independent county (11th c.) then a duchy (1416), including large regions of modern France and Switzerland which were lost in the 15th and 16th cc. Attached to Sardinia (1720), it was annexed by France (1792-1815) and finally ceded in 1860. The house of Savoy ruled Italy 1861-1946

sa·voy (səvɔi) *n.* a hardy cabbage with rough, wrinkled leaves and a compact head [F. (*chou de*) *Savoie,* (cabbage of) Savoy]

Sa·voy·ard (səvɔ́iərd, sǽvɔiárd) *n.* a native of Savoy [F.]

Savoyard *n.* an actor in or producer of the Gilbert and Sullivan operas ‖ a devotee of these operas [after the *Savoy,* London theater where most of the operas were first produced]

saw (sɔ:) **1.** *n.* a steel cutting tool with a toothed edge ‖ (*zool.*) a part of an animal which consists of a series of teeth like this tool, e.g. the snout of a sawfish or the ovipositor of a sawfly **2.** *v. pres. part.* **saw·ing** *past* **sawed** *past part.* **sawed, sawn** (sɔn) *v.t.* to cut with a saw ‖ to make by using a saw, *to saw a keyhole* ‖ to make movements as if using a saw, *to saw the air* ‖ (*pop.*) to play (a tune) on a bowed stringed instrument ‖ (*bookbinding*) to make cuts in (the leaves) to receive the threads with which they are sewn together ‖ *v.i.* to use a saw ‖ (of a saw) to cut ‖ to be able to be cut with a saw, *this wood saws easily* ‖ (*pop.*) to play with a bow on a stringed instrument [O.E. *sage*]

saw *n.* a maxim [O.E. *sagu*]

saw *past* of SEE

saw·bill (sóbil) *n.* any of several birds with a serrated bill, esp. the merganser

saw·buck (sóbʌk) *n.* a sawhorse [Du. *zaagbok*]

saw·dust (sódʌst) *n.* the small particles of wood torn off by the teeth of a saw as it cuts through wood, used esp. as packing material

saw·fish (sófiʃ) *pl.* **saw·fish, saw·fish·es** *n.* any of several viviparous fishes of fam. *Pristidae,* having an elongated snout with teeth on both edges. They are found in shallow seas of tropical Africa and America

saw·fly (sóflai) *pl.* **saw·flies** *n.* any of several members of *Tenthredinoidea,* a superfamily of hymenopterous insects. The female has an ovi-

CONCISE PRONUNCIATION KEY: **(a)** æ, c*a*t; ɑ, c*ar*; ɔ f*aw*n; ei, sn*a*ke. **(e)** e, h*e*n; i:, sh*ee*p; iə, d*eer*; ɛə, b*ear*. **(i)** i, f*i*sh; ai, t*i*ger; ə:, b*ir*d. **(o)** o, *o*x; au, c*ow*; ou, g*oa*t; u, p*oor*; ɔi, r*oy*al. **(u)** ʌ, d*u*ck; u, b*u*ll; u:, g*oo*se; ə, b*a*cillus; ju:, c*u*be. x, lo*ch*; θ, *th*ink; ð, bo*th*er; z, *Z*en; ʒ, cor*s*age; dʒ, sava*g*e; ŋ, ora*ng*utang; j, *y*ak; ʃ, *f*ish; tʃ, fe*tch*; 'l, rabb*le*; 'n, redd*en*. Complete pronunciation key appears inside front cover.

positor with sawlike teeth for cutting slits in leaves, within which the eggs are laid

saw·horse (sóhɔrs) *n.* a wooden rack resting on splayed end supports, on which lumber is laid for sawing

saw·mill (sómil) *n.* a factory furnished with power-driven machines which saw and plane lumber

sawn *alt. past part.* of SAW

saw·pit (sópit) *n.* a pit across which a log is laid to be sawed by a two-man saw, one man standing in the pit and the other raised above the log

saw set a tool used to slant a saw's teeth at desired angles

saw·tooth (sótu:θ) *pl.* **saw·teeth** (sóti:θ) 1. *n.* a tooth of a saw or of a sawlike formation 2. *adj.* saw-toothed **sáw-toothed** *adj.*

saw·yer (sójər) *n.* a man whose craft is sawing logs into planks or sawing up lumber in other ways ‖ (*zool.*) any woodboring insect larva, esp. any of several large beetles [altered fr. *sawer*, someone who saws]

sax (sæks) *n.* a tool for trimming slates, with a pointed end for making nail holes in them [O.E. *seax*, knife]

sax *n.* (*pop.*) a saxophone

sax·a·tile (sæksɔtil) *adj.* (*biol.*) saxicolous [F. or fr. L. *saxitilis* fr. *saxum*, rock]

Saxe (sæks), Hermann Maurice, comte de (1696-1750), marshal of France. He distinguished himself in the War of the Austrian Succession, notably at Fontenoy (1745)

Saxe blue a light, slightly greenish-blue color [F. *Saxe*, Saxony]

Saxe-Co·burg-Go·tha (sækskóubər:ggóuθə) the name (1901-17) of the British royal house, after the German duchy from which Albert, Victoria's consort, took his title. The name was changed (1917) to Windsor by George V

sax·horn (sækshɔrn) *n.* one of a family of brass wind instruments ranging from soprano to bass, having a long winding tube and valves. They are used in bands [after Antoine Joseph Sax (1814–94), Belgian inventor of the instrument]

sax·ic·o·lous (sæksíkələs) *adj.* (*biol.*) living among or growing on rocks [fr. Mod. L. *saxicola* fr. L. *saxum*, rock]

sax·i·frage (sæksifridʒ) *n.* a member of *Saxifraga*, fam. *Saxifragaceae*, a large genus of usually perennial plants native to northern temperate and arctic regions, and widely cultivated in rock gardens [O.F. fr. L. *saxifraga* (*herba*), rockbreaking (plant)]

sax·i·tox·in [$C_{10}H_{17}N_7O_4$2HCl] (sæksətáksən) *n.* (*chem.*) nonprotein poison found in red tide algae and mollusks

Sax·on (sæksən) 1. *n.* a member of a north-central German race living near the mouth of the Elbe early in the Christian era. They spread over N.W. Germany (6th–9th cc.) ‖ a member of that part of the race which settled in England in the 5th and 6th cc. A.D., an Anglo-Saxon ‖ a native of Saxony ‖ Old Saxon ‖ the German dialect of modern Saxony 2. *adj.* pertaining to the ancient Saxons ‖ English or Anglo-Saxon ‖ of modern Saxony [F.]

Sax·o·ny (sæksəni) (G. Sachsen) a former state of East Germany on the central plateau, bordering Czechoslovakia on the south (Erzgebirge Mtns), now included in Leipzig, Dresden and Karl-Marx-Stadt districts. The north is a loess-covered agricultural region (cereals, root vegetables). Minerals: lignite, hard coal, uranium, salt. It is the most densely populated part of the republic, highly industrialized (chiefly textiles, chemicals, metallurgy) since the 19th c. The old duchy of Saxony (9th-12th cc.) included most of the land between the Rhine and the Elbe (largely modern Lower Saxony). It was broken (1180) into smaller fiefs. One of these, Saxe-Wittenberg (on the middle Elbe), became an electorate (1356). With the land south of it it became the basis of the later duchy, which became a kingdom (1806-1918) but lost large territories to Prussia (1815). It joined the German Empire in 1871. Historic capital: Dresden

sax·o·ny (sæksəni:) *n.* a fine knitting yarn ‖ a fine woolen cloth woven from this, originally made in Saxony

Sax·o·ny-An·halt (sæksəni:ánhalt) (G. Sachsen-Anhalt) a former state of East Germany in the northern plain around the middle Elbe, now included in the districts of Halle, Magdeburg and Erfurt. Crops: root vegetables, hops. Minerals: potash (world's biggest known deposits, in

the Harz Mtns), salt, lignite (around Halle), supporting large chemical industries. The state was formed (1945) from the Prussian province of Saxony (the region gained from Saxony in 1815) and the small state (former duchy) of Anhalt, around Dessau

Saxony, Lower (G. Niedersachsen) a state (area 18,290 sq. miles, pop. 6,732,000) of West Germany, extending from the North Sea and lower Elbe to the central highland (Harz Mtns in the southeast). The partly reafforested plain, crossed by the Ems and Weser, produces cereals, potatoes and sugar beets. Industry (mechanical and electrical engineering, textiles) is now more important than agriculture. Main towns: Hanover (the capital), Brunswick. It was formed (1945) from the states of Hanover, Oldenburg, Brunswick and Schaumburg-Lippe

sax·o·phone (sæksəfoun) *n.* (*abbr.* sax) any of a family of instruments classified as woodwinds because they have a reed like a clarinet's, but having a long, usually curved metal body. They have finger keys, range from soprano to bass, and are used mainly in military, jazz and dance bands **sáx·o·phon·ist** *n.* [after Antoine Joseph Sax (1814–94), Belgian inventor of the instrument+Gk *phonos*, voiced]

Say (sei), Thomas (1787-1834), U.S. Quaker naturalist. His books include 'American Entomology' (1824-8) and 'American Conchology' (1830-4)

say (sei) 1. *v. pres. part.* **say·ing** *past* and *past part.* **said** (sed) *v.t.* to utter (specified words), '*it's time to go home*', *he said* ‖ to express (an idea, meaning or statement) vocally, in writing etc., *the papers say exports are down, the clock says 11:10* ‖ to promise, *he said he would come today* ‖ to allege, *don't believe everything people say* ‖ (*imperative*) to assume, suppose, *say x equals the unknown quantity* ‖ to declare, assert, *she says it is true* ‖ to order (something), *do as he says you are to do* ‖ to recite in words, *to say one's prayers* ‖ *v.i.* to make a statement, *you don't say so* ‖ (*imperative*) used parenthetically to indicate that what has just been said is a supposition or estimate, *a third of the population, say, is illiterate* **to go without saying** to be assumed because self-evident, *it goes without saying that they will both come* **to say nothing of** without mentioning or considering (something even more important), *the place is full of insects, to say nothing of the snakes* 2. *n.* what one wants to say, *let him say his say now* ‖ the opportunity to express one's ideas etc., *it is time I had my say* ‖ a role in the making of a decision, *he had no say in the matter* ‖ (with 'the') the power to decide, *he's the one with the say* **sáy·ing** *n.* a maxim [O.E. *secgan*]

say-so (séisou) *pl.* **say-sos** *n.* (*pop.*) the right to decide or the exercise of this right ‖ (*pop.*) an unsupported assertion

SBA (*abbr.*) for Small Business Administration

S-band *n.* ultrahigh radio frequencies (1,550 to 5,200 MHz) *Cf* L-BAND

SBIC (*abbr.*) for Small Business Investment Corporation

SBN (*abbr.*) for Standard Book Number

scab (skæb) 1. *n.* a tough crust of dried serum and blood formed over a sore or wound ‖ a form of scabies affecting some animals, esp. sheep ‖ any of certain fungoid or bacterial diseases of plants in which rough spots are formed ‖ one of these spots ‖ a worker who refuses to join the union or who works for less than union pay or conditions ‖ a person who works when his fellow workers are on strike or who works in the place of a striking worker 2. *v.i. pres. part.* **scab·bing** *past* and *past part.* **scabbed** to become covered with a scab ‖ to work or act as a scab [M.E. fr. O.N.]

scab·bard (skæbərd) *n.* the sheath of a sword, dagger or similar weapon [A.F. *escauberge* prob. fr. Gmc]

scab·ble (skæb'l) *pres. part.* **scab·bling** *past* and *past part.* **scab·bled** *v.t.* to work, shape or dress (stone) roughly [older *scapple* fr. O.F. *escapeler*]

scab·by (skæbi:) *comp.* **scab·bi·er** *superl.* **scab·bi·est** *adj.* encrusted with or consisting of scabs ‖ (of an animal) having scab

sca·bies (skéibi:z) *n.* a contagious skin disease caused by a mite [L. fr. *scabere*, to scratch]

sca·bi·ous (skéibi:əs) *n.* a member of *Scabiosa*, fam. *Dipsacaceae*, a genus of Old World plants bearing showy flowers at the end of tall stalks [fr. M.L. *scabiosa*, fem. of *scabiosus*, mangy

(from its being thought effective as a remedy for scabies)]

scab·rous (skæbrəs, esp. *Br.* skéi:brəs) *adj.* salacious, indecent ‖ (*biol.*) having a rough surface with raised points, scales etc. [fr. L. *scaber*, rough]

scads (skædz) *pl. n.* (*pop.*) a great number or amount, *scads of money* [prob. altered fr. dial. *scald*]

scaf·fold (skæfəld, skæfould) 1. *n.* a platform put on a temporary structure of poles or suspended by ropes, used by men building, repairing etc. at a height ‖ a raised platform constructed for the execution of criminals 2. *v.t.* to provide with a scaffold or scaffolding **scáf·fold·ing** *n.* a scaffold or number of connected scaffolds ‖ the poles, planks and ties used in constructing a scaffold [Northern F. related to O.F. *shaffaut, eschafaut*]

scagl·io·la (skæljóulə) *n.* an imitation of marble, made of gypsum and glue with marble or granite dust etc. set in it and polished [Ital. *scagliuola*]

scal·a·ble (skéiləb'l) *adj.* able to be scaled

scal·age (skéilidʒ) *n.* the margin allowed for loss by shrinkage ‖ the act of scaling in dimensions, quantity etc. ‖ the estimated yield in board feet of logs or timber [SCALE (arrangement of marks in measuring)]

sca·lar (skéilər) 1. *adj.* (*math.*, *phys.*) of a quantity which is fully described by a number 2. *n.* a quantity that has magnitude but is undirected, e.g. mass, temperature etc. (cf. VECTOR) [fr. L. *scalaris*, of a ladder]

sca·lar·i·form (skəlǽrifɔrm) *adj.* (*biol.*, e.g. of some structures of cells, veins, etc.) having the appearance of a ladder or markings like a ladder's rungs ‖ (*biol.*) of or designating conjugation between parallel filaments in an alga [fr. Mod. L. *scalariformis* fr. L. *scalaris*, of a ladder]

scal·a·wag (skæləwæg) *n.* a scallywag

scald (skɔld) 1. *v.t.* (of a very hot liquid or vapor) to burn, *the escaping steam scalded his hand* ‖ to heat (liquid) almost to boiling ‖ to cook (food) lightly in steam or hot water ‖ to clean (a vessel) by using boiling water ‖ *v.i.* to be heated almost to boiling, *heat the milk till it scalds* 2. *n.* the injury to the skin caused by scalding [O.N.F. *escalder, escauder*]

scale (skeil) 1. *n.* an arrangement of accurately spaced marks representing a series of numerical values, used in measuring lengths, angles, temperature etc. ‖ a measuring instrument having such marks ‖ an ordered series of graduated quantities, values, degrees etc., *scale of salaries, decimal scale* ‖ the proportion of a representation to the object it represents, *a map to the scale of one inch to the mile* ‖ a line on a map etc. with marks dividing it to show this proportion ‖ relative magnitude, *business on a large scale* ‖ (*mus.*) a series of notes in ascending or descending order of pitch in accordance with a system of successive intervals, *minor scale* ‖ the notes of such a series covering the range of an octave, *the scale of F sharp* 2. *v. pres. part.* **scal·ing** *past* and *past part.* **scaled** *v.t.* to apply a scale to ‖ (with 'down' or 'up') to reduce or increase in magnitude according to a fixed scale ‖ to ascend by or as if by a ladder, *to scale a cliff* ‖ to measure or estimate the yield in board feet of (logs or standing timber) ‖ *v.i.* (of two or more things) to have the same scale [fr. Ital. *scala* or L. *scala*, ladder]

scale 1. *n.* the suspended dish or pan of a simple beam balance ‖ a balance (instrument for measuring weight) ‖ (*pl.*) a pair of scales **to turn the scales** to decide an issue previously in doubt, *his past record turned the scales in his favor* 2. *v.t. pres. part.* **scal·ing** *past* and *past part.* **scaled** to amount to (a certain weight) ‖ to weigh on scales [O.N. *skál*, bowl, weighing pan]

scale 1. *n.* one of the thin, horny, bony or chitinous plates serving to protect the skin of fishes or reptiles or the legs of birds etc. ‖ a modified part of a leaf, bract etc. resembling this ‖ a small, loosely adhering, hardened flake or flat piece, e.g. of skin ‖ a scale insect ‖ a flaky deposit, e.g. of tartar on the teeth, of oxide formed on the surface of metal, or of lime deposited on the inner surface of a boiler 2. *v. pres. part.* **scal·ing** *past* and *past part.* **scaled** *v.t.* to remove scale or the scales from ‖ to throw (a flat stone) at a body of water in such a way that it skips on the water's surface ‖ *v.i.* to form scales ‖ to come off in scales ‖ to shed scales [O.F. *escale*]

CONCISE PRONUNCIATION KEY: **(a)** æ, c*a*t; ɑ, c*a*r; ɔ f*aw*n; ei, sn*a*ke. **(e)** e, h*e*n; i:, sh*ee*p; iə, d*ee*r; ɛə, b*ea*r. **(i)** i, f*i*sh; ai, t*i*ger; ə:, b*i*rd. **(o)** o, *o*x; au, c*ow*; ou, g*oa*t; u, p*oo*r; ɔi, r*oy*al. **(u)** ʌ, d*u*ck; u, b*u*ll; u:, g*oo*se; ə, b*a*cillus; ju:, c*u*be. x, lo*ch*; θ, *th*ink; ð, bo*th*er; z, *Z*en; ʒ, cor*s*age; dʒ, sava*ge*; ŋ, ora*ng*utang; j, *y*ak; ʃ, *fish*; tʃ, fe*tch*; 'l, rabb*le*; 'n, redd*en*. Complete pronunciation key appears inside front cover.

scale·board (skéilbɔrd, skéilbourd, skǽlbɔrd) *n.* thin board used for veneers ‖ the thin wooden sheet protecting the back of a picture in its frame

scale insect any of several homopterous insects which suck the sap of plants and have the appearance of small scales on the plant's surface

scale leaf (*bot.*) a leaf resembling a scale, e.g. a bud scale

sca·lene (skéili:n) *adj.* (of a triangle) having unequal sides ‖ of or relating to the scaleni [fr. L.L. *scalenus*, scalenus]

sca·le·nus (skeilí:nəs) *pl.* **sca·le·ni** (skeilí:nai) *n.* (*anat.*) any of a set of triangular muscles on either side of the neck, extending from the cervical vertebrae to the first or second rib [Mod. L. fr. Gk *skalēnos*]

scal·er (skéilər) *n.* an electronic instrument used for recording high-speed impulses ‖ someone who scales logs or timber ‖ (*computer*) a circuit that requires a directed number of inputs for each output

scal·er-ten·sor theory (skéilərténsər) (*phys.*) hypothesis that electromagnetic waves passing through a gravitational field should slow and curve less than indicated by Einstein's general theory

Scal·i·ger (skǽlidʒər) (Giulio Cesare Scaligero, 1484-1558), Italian Renaissance scholar, philologist and doctor. His son Joseph Justus (1540-1609) was also a great scholar and established a scientific basis for ancient chronology in his 'De emendatione temporum' (1583)

scal·i·ness (skéili:nis) *n.* the quality or state of being scaly

scaling ladder a ladder used in climbing walls, e.g. by firemen

scal·la·wag (skǽləwæg) *n.* a scallywag

scal·lion (skǽljən) *n.* the shallot ‖ the leek ‖ a green onion, pulled for eating before the bulb has swollen [A.F. *scalun*, *scaloun* fr. O.F. *eschaloigne*]

scal·lop (skóləp, skǽləp) 1. *n.* any of several marine bivalve mollusks of fam. *Pectinidae* having a fan-shaped fluted shell with an undulating margin ‖ the edible adductor muscle of such a mollusk ‖ a single shell of one of these mollusks, used for serving certain fish dishes ‖ (*hist.*) this shell worn as a badge by pilgrims returning from the Holy Land ‖ a thin, boneless slice of white meat, e.g. veal, turkey ‖ one of the rounded projections forming an undulating edging of cloth, metal etc. 2. *v.t.* to ornament with an edging of scallops ‖ to cook in a casserole etc. with sauce and a topping of bread crumbs **scal·lop·ing** *n.* a scalloped edging [O.F. *escalope* Gmc]

scal·ly·wag (skǽli:wæg) *n.* a scamp, rogue ‖ (*Am. hist.*) a Southerner willing to fraternize with the victorious enemy after the Civil War [etym. doubtful]

scalp (skælp) 1. *n.* the skin on the top and back of the head ‖ (*hist.*) this skin, with the hair attached, torn from an enemy by a North American Indian as a trophy ‖ a small profit made by scalping 2. *v.t.* to tear off the scalp from ‖ to buy and sell (securities and commodities) in order to make small profits on quick returns ‖ (*pop.*) to sell (theater tickets etc.) as a scalper ‖ *v.i.* to buy and sell stocks (or theater tickets etc.) in order to make quick returns [M.E. prob. of Scand. origin]

scal·pel (skǽlpəl) *n.* a small very sharp precision knife used in surgery [fr. L. *scalpellum*]

scalp·er (skǽlpər) *n.* a person who buys and sells for quick profit, esp. one who buys up theater tickets and sells them for more than the established price

scalp lock a tuft of hair left on the shaved crown by certain North American Indian warriors

scal·y (skéili:) *comp.* **scal·i·er** *superl.* **scal·i·est** *adj.* having, covered with or consisting of scales or a scale ‖ shedding scales or flakes ‖ resembling scales or a scale ‖ infested with scale insects

scaly anteater a pangolin

scam (skæm) *n.* (*slang*) an illegal operation, usu. a confidence racket, involving a sum of money

scam·mo·ny (skǽməni:) *pl.* **scam·mo·nies** *n.* *Convolvulus scammonia*, fam. *Convolvulaceae*, an Asiatic twining plant ‖ the dried root of this plant ‖ gum resin obtained from this root, used as a purgative [fr. L. *scammonia*, *scammonium* fr. Gk]

scamp (skæmp) *n.* a mischievous rogue [prob. fr. older *scamp* v., to rob on the highway, prob. related to SCAMPER]

scamp *v.t.* to perform (work etc.) carelessly [etym. doubtful]

scamp·er (skǽmpər) 1. *v.i.* to dart about with nimble, precipitate movements, esp. playfully ‖ to make a dash, *they scampered for shelter* 2. *n.* a scampering [perh. fr. Ital. *scampare*, to decamp]

scam·pi (skǽmpi:) *n., s. & pl.* Italian shrimp dish

scan (skæn) *pres. part.* **scan·ning** *past and past part.* **scanned** *v.t.* to examine closely or carefully, *to scan the horizon* ‖ to determine the meter (of verse) by analyzing it ‖ the path periodically followed by a radiation beam ‖ (*med.*) to examine a body by X-ray or other radioactive material ‖ (*computer*) to examine stored material for a purpose ‖ (*computer*) to examine channels for input-output activity ‖ to glance at hastily, *scan the headlines* ‖ *v.i.* to have the correct meter, *these lines do not scan* ‖ to examine verse in order to determine the meter ‖ (*television*) to pass a beam of light or electrons over a surface in order to transmit and reproduce the picture [fr. L. *scandere*, to climb]

scan·dal (skǽnd'l) *n.* a serious breach of the moral or social code which becomes widely known ‖ someone who or something that causes general indignation ‖ the indignation so caused ‖ malicious gossip [M.E. *scandle* fr. O.N.F. *escandle* fr. L. fr. Gk]

scan·dal·ize (skǽnd'laiz) *pres. part.* **scan·dal·iz·ing** *past and past part.* **scan·dal·ized** *v.t.* to give offense to (others) by acting contrary to their ideas of what is morally or socially right [F. *scandaliser*]

scan·dal·mon·ger (skǽnd'lmʌŋgər, skǽnd'lmɒŋgər) *n.* a person who makes up scandal or who passes it on [fr. SCANDAL + *monger*, a dealer]

scan·dal·ous (skǽnd'ləs) *adj.* of the nature of scandal, offensive and shocking [F. *scandaleux*]

Scan·der·beg (skǽndərbeg) (George Castriota, c. 1404-68), Albanian national hero who led his country's resistance (1443-68) against the threat of Turkish domination

Scan·di·na·vi·a (skændinéivi:ə) the region of N.W. Europe embracing Sweden, Norway and Denmark. Iceland is often included, on ethnic grounds, and Finland sometimes, on geographical and historical grounds ‖ the peninsula formed by Norway and Sweden

Scan·di·na·vi·an (skændinéivi:ən) 1. *adj.* pertaining to Scandinavia, its inhabitants, languages etc. 2. *n.* a native of Scandinavia ‖ the North Germanic group of languages spoken in Scandinavia (*SWEDISH, *NORWEGIAN, *DANISH, *ICELANDIC)

scan·di·um (skǽndi:əm) *n.* a metallic element (symbol Sc, at. no. 21, at. mass 44.956) occurring in some Scandinavian minerals [fr. L. *Scandia*, Scandinavia]

scan·ner (skǽnər) *n.* someone who or something that scans ‖ (*television*) a device used for scanning ‖ (*radar*) an electronic apparatus for traversing a region with a beam

scanning electron microscope *n.* a device for providing a three-dimensional image on a screen of an irregular surface, used for examining and photographing tissue

scan·sion (skǽnʃən) *n.* the scanning of verse [fr. L. *scansio* (*scansionis*) fr. *scandere*, to climb]

scan·so·ri·al (skænsóri:əl, skænsóuri:əl) *adj.* (*zool.*, esp. of the feet of certain birds) adapted for climbing ‖ (*zool.*) having such feet [fr. L. *scansorius*, used for climbing]

scant (skænt) 1. *adj.* meager ‖ less than enough ‖ barely enough ‖ just short of a specific measure, quantity etc., *a scant cup of sugar* 2. *v.t.* to provide (someone or something) with too small a supply or quantity ‖ to be stinting in the supply of (something) ‖ to treat inadequately [O.N. *skamt*, short]

scant·i·ly (skǽntili:) *adv.* in a scanty way

scant·i·ness (skǽnti:nis) *n.* the quality or state of being scanty

scant·ling (skǽntliŋ) *n.* a beam or timber of small cross section, esp. one less than 2–4 ins. wide and 2–4½ ins. thick ‖ small beams or timbers collectively ‖ (*shipbuilding*) a set of fixed dimensions [fr. older *scantillon*, a measuring rod fr. O. F. *escantillon*]

scant·y (skǽnti:) *comp.* **scant·i·er** *superl.*

scant·i·est *adj.* barely enough ‖ meager ‖ not quite enough

Sca·pa Flow (skápə, skǽpə) a protected harbor (15 miles long, 8 miles wide) formed by Great Britain's S. Orkney Is. It was the main British naval base during the 1st world war, and the scene of the scuttling of the German fleet in 1919

scape (skeip) *n.* (*archit.*) the shaft of a column, or a hollow curve in the shaft at the top or base, where it expands to meet the fillet ‖ (*biol.*) the basal joint of the antenna of an insect ‖ (*bot.*) a leafless peduncle arising at the surface of the ground or underground ‖ (*zool.*) the shaft of a feather [fr. L. *scapus*, stem, column shaft]

scape·goat (skéipgout) *n.* a person made to bear the blame which should fall on others ‖ (in ancient Jewish ritual) a goat on whose head the high priest symbolically laid the sins of the people on Yom Kippur, and which was then allowed to escape into the wilderness [fr. obs. *scape*, contr. of ESCAPE + GOAT]

Scapegoat *n.* (*mil.*) U.S.S.R. two-stage strategic, solid-fuel 32-ft-long nuclear missile (SS-14) with a 2,500-mi range

scape·grace (skéipgreis) *n.* a person who is always getting into trouble [fr. *scape*, obs. contr. of ESCAPE + GRACE]

scape wheel an escape wheel [fr *scape*, obs. contr. of ESCAPE]

scaph·oid (skǽfɔid) 1. *adj.* (*anat.*) navicular 2. *n.* a navicular bone [fr. Mod. L. *scaphoides* fr. Gk *skaphoeidēs* fr. *skaphē*, a boat + *eidos*, shape]

sca·pose (skéipous) *adj.* of, relating to or resembling a scape

scap·u·la (skǽpjulə) *pl.* **scap·u·lae** (skǽpjuli:), **scap·u·las** *n.* (*anat.*) either shoulder blade ‖ (*zool.*) any of several structures in insects suggestive of a shoulder blade [L. = shoulder, shoulder blade]

scap·u·lar (skǽpjulər) *n.* (*zool.*) any of a bird's feathers lying over the base of the wing ‖ (*zool.*) a scapula ‖ a sleeveless coat worn by certain monks, falling from the shoulders (usually almost to the feet) at the front and back ‖ a badge of membership of some religious orders, consisting of two pieces of cloth worn on the chest and back and joined by strips over the shoulders [fr. L. *scapulare* fr. *scapula*, shoulder]

scapular *adj.* of or relating to a scapula ‖ designating the scapulars of a bird [fr. Mod. L. *scapularis* fr. *scapula*, scapula]

scap·u·lar·y (skǽpjuleri:) *pl.* **scap·u·lar·ies** *n.* (*eccles.*) a scapular ‖ a scapular feather [fr. M.L. *scapularium* var. of *scapulare*, a scapular]

scar (skɑr) 1. *n.* a permanent mark on the skin or other tissue, consisting of fibrous tissue formed where a wound, ulcer etc. heals ‖ a permanent effect left by an emotional wound ‖ (*bot.*) a mark left on a stem etc. by the fall of a leaf or on a seed by the separation of the funicle 2. *v. pres. part.* **scar·ring** *past and past part.* **scarred** *v.t.* to mark with a scar ‖ *v.i.* to form a scar [fr. O.F. *escare* fr. L.L. fr. Gk]

scar *n.* a bare rocky side of a mountain [prob. fr. O.N. *sker*, a rock in the sea]

scar·ab (skǽrəb) *n.* any of several stout-bodied, lamellicorn beetles of fam. *Scarabaeidae*, esp. *Scarabaeus sacer*, a dung beetle of Mediterranean regions ‖ a conventionalized carving of *S. sacer*, common in ancient Egypt as a symbol of resurrection and worn as a charm or for ornament, or buried with the dead [fr. F. *scarabée*]

scar·a·bae·id (skærəbí:id) *n.* a scarab or related beetle [fr. Mod. L. *scarabaeidae* fr. L. *scarabaeus*, scarab]

scarce (skeərs) *comp.* **scarc·er** *superl.* **scarc·est** *adj.* present or available in very limited or insufficient amount, *food was scarce in the region* to **make oneself scarce** (*pop.*) to keep away from others or go away **scarce·ly** *adv.* barely, only just, *he is scarcely 21* ‖ not at all, *I scarcely think he could have done it* ‖ most improbably, *he will scarcely come at this hour* [M.E. *scarce* fr. O.N.F.]

scarce·ment (skéərsmənt) *n.* a setback in the thickness of a wall or bank of earth [prob. fr. obs. *scarce*, to become or make less]

scar·ci·ty (skéərsiti:) *pl.* **scar·ci·ties** *n.* the quality or state of being scarce ‖ a limited or insufficient supply [O.N.F. *escarceté*, frugality]

scare (skeər) 1. *v. pres. part.* **scar·ing** *past and past part.* **scared** *v.t.* to arouse fear in, *the idea scares her* ‖ (with 'away', 'off') to cause to flee in fear, *the noises scared them off* ‖ *v.i.* to become afraid, *he doesn't scare easily* **to scare up** (*pop.*)

CONCISE PRONUNCIATION KEY: **(a)** æ, cat; ɑ, car; ɔ *faw*n; ei, sn*a*ke. **(e)** e, h*e*n; i:, sh*ee*p; iə, d*ee*r; ɛə, b*ea*r. **(i)** i, f*i*sh; ai, t*i*ger; əː, b*i*rd. **(o)** o, *o*x; au, c*ow*; ou, g*oa*t; u, p*oo*r; ɔi, r*oy*al. **(u)** ʌ, d*u*ck; u, b*u*ll; u:, g*oo*se; ə, b*a*cillus; ju:, c*u*be. x, lo*ch*; θ, *th*ink; ð, bo*th*er; z, *Z*en; ʒ, cor*s*age; dʒ, sava*ge*; ŋ, ora*ng*utan*g*; j, *y*ak; ʃ, fi*sh*; tʃ, fe*tch*; 'l, rabb*le*; 'n, redd*en*. Complete pronunciation key appears inside front cover.

to manage to find or get quickly, *see if you can scare up some matches* **2.** *n.* an instance of being scared, *to give someone a scare* ‖ a widespread alarm, panic [M.E. *skerre* fr. O.N. *skirra*]

scare·crow (skéərkrou) *n.* a figure stuffed with straw and dressed in ragged old clothes, set up on a pole in a field to scare birds away from the crops ‖ a shabbily and untidily dressed person, esp. a very thin one

scared straight program for exposing experimental students to life in prison, as a crime deterrent

scare·head (skéərhed) *n.* (*pop.*) an extravagant, sensational newspaper headline in very large print, esp. one meant to cause alarm

scare·mon·ger (skéərmʌŋgər, skéərmɒŋgər) *n.* a person who spreads alarming false or exaggerated reports [fr. SCARE+*monger*, a dealer]

scarf (skɑrf) *pl.* scarfs, esp. *Br.* **scarves** (skɑrvz) *n.* a piece of material wrapped around the neck, head or shoulders for warmth or decoration ‖ a strip of cloth placed on a dresser or table ‖ (*mil.*) a sash [prob. fr. O.N.F. *escarpe*]

scarf 1. *pl.* **scarves** (skɑrvz), **scarfs** *n.* a joint made by scarfing lumber, metal or leather ‖ a groove cut along a whale's body **2.** *v.t.* to join (two pieces of lumber, metal or leather) by beveling or chamfering each so that they overlap, and then securing them, e.g. by bolting, gluing, brazing or sewing them together ‖ to cut scarfs in and remove the skin and blubber of (a whale) [perh. fr. Swed. *skarf* and Norw. *skarv*, piece added to lengthen a board or garment]

scar·i·fi·ca·tion (skærifikéiʃən) *n.* a scarifying or being scarified ‖ a mark or marks made by scarifying [fr. L.L. *scarificatio* (*scarificationis*) fr. *scarificare*, to scarify]

scar·i·fi·ca·tor (skǽrifikeitər) *n.* a surgical instrument for making superficial cuts in the skin [Mod. L. fr. L.L. *scarificare*, to scarify]

scar·i·fi·er (skǽrifaiər) *n.* a machine for loosening soil ‖ a machine for breaking up a road surface before resurfacing ‖ a scarificator

scar·i·fy (skǽrifai) *pres. part.* **scar·i·fy·ing** *past* and *past part.* **scar·i·fied** *v.t.* (*surgery*) to make superficial cuts in (the skin) ‖ to loosen (topsoil) with a scarifier ‖ to make incisions in the coat of (a seed) to bring on germination faster [F. *scarifier* fr. L.L. *scarificare*]

scar·i·ous (skéəriəs) *adj.* (*bot.*, of some bracts) thin, dry and membranous in texture [fr. F. *scarieux*]

scar·la·ti·na (skɑrlətí:nə) *n.* scarlet fever ‖ (*pop.*) a mild form of this [Mod. L. fr. Ital. *scarlattina* fr. *scarlatto*, scarlet]

Scar·lat·ti (skɑrlátti:), Alessandro (1660-1725), Italian composer, one of the founders of 18th-c. Italian opera. He wrote over 100 operas, 600 cantatas for solo voice and continuo, oratorios, Masses etc.

Scarlatti, Domenico (1685-1757), Italian composer, son of Alessandro. He wrote over 550 harpsichord 'sonatas', single-movement works in binary form, often characterized by harmonic and rhythmic variety and by brilliance

scar·let (skɑrlit) **1.** *n.* a brilliant red color ‖ red cloth or clothes, e.g. the red coat traditionally worn at a hunt **2.** *adj.* of the color scarlet ‖ (*rhet.*, of a sin or crime) flagrantly wicked [fr. O.F. *escarlate*, perh. fr. Pers. *saqalāt*, a kind of rich cloth]

scarlet fever an acute contagious disease caused by a streptococcus and characterized by fever, inflammation of the nose and throat and a reddish skin rash

scarlet pimpernel *PIMPERNEL

scarlet runner *Phaseolus coccineus*, fam. *Papilionaceae*, a climbing bean of tropical American origin, having large red flowers and red and black edible seeds in edible pods, cultivated esp. in Great Britain

scarlet tanager *Piranga olivacea*, a common tanager of the U.S.A., the male of which has a scarlet body and black wings and tail, the female and young being mainly olive in color

scarp (skɑrp) **1.** *n.* a steep slope ‖ the inner wall of a fortified ditch (cf. COUNTERSCARP) **2.** *v.t.* to cut so as to form a scarp [fr. Ital. *scarpa*]

Scar·ron (skær5), Paul (1610-60), French novelist, best known for his 'le Roman comique' (1651). His wife later became Mme de Maintenon

scarves alt. *pl.* of SCARF (piece of material)

scar·y (skéəri:) *comp.* **scar·i·er** *superl.* **scar·i·est** *adj.* (*pop.*) alarming, causing fright ‖ (*pop.*) easily frightened, timid

scat (skæt) *pres. part.* **scat·ting** *past* and *past part.* **scat·ted** *v.i.* (used esp. in *imperative*) to go away quickly [origin unknown]

scat *n.* (*zool.*) fecal droppings of animals

scathe (skeið) *pres. part.* **scath·ing** *past* and *past part.* **scathed** *v.t.* to attack with bitterly severe criticism, invective or denunciation **scáth·ing** *adj.* [O.N. *skatha*, it hurts]

scat·o·log·i·cal (skæt'lódʒik'l) *adj.* of, pertaining to or characterized by scatology

sca·tol·o·gy (skətólədʒi:) *n.* preoccupation with or treatment of excrement, defecation etc., esp. in literature ‖ literature characterized by this ‖ the scientific study of animal droppings or coprolites [fr. Gk *skōr* (*skatos*), dung+*logos*, discourse]

scat·ter (skǽtər) **1.** *v.t.* to cause to break up and go in different directions or be widely separated or distributed, esp. at random, *mud was scattered all over their clothes, his dog scattered the flock* ‖ to sow or distribute by handfuls, *to scatter fertilizer* ‖ to distribute or sprinkle something in or over (something), *she scatters her novels with French words* ‖ (*phys.*) to reflect diffusely ‖ (*phys.*) to diffuse (a radiation beam) in a random fashion as a result of collision ‖ (of a gun or cartridge) to cause (shot) to spread ‖ *v.i.* to separate widely in different directions, esp. at random, *the crowd scattered when the police charged* **2.** *n.* something scattered, *a scatter of foam on the sand* ‖ the extent of scattering, e.g. of shot [etym. doubtful]

scat·ter·brain (skǽtərbrein) *n.* a flighty person whose ideas are not properly organized and who forgets or confuses detail **scát·ter·brained** *adj.*

scat·tered (skǽtərd) *adj.* of objects placed at some distance from one another and at random, *a few scattered villages survived*

scat·ter·ing (skǽtəriŋ) **1.** *adj.* dispersed and in no order ‖ going in different directions, widely separated **2.** *n.* a small number of scattered individuals ‖ (*phys.*) the process of being scattered

scat·ter·om·e·ter (skǽtərómitər) *n.* radar equipment with many aerials to receive from a wide area

scatter rug one of a number of small rugs placed here and there in a room

scat·ter·site housing (skǽtərsait) low-income public housing dispersed to avoid concentration in one area

scaup (skɔp) *pl.* **scaups** *n.* a scaup duck [perh. var. of SCALP]

scaup duck a duck of genus *Aythya*, esp. *A. marila nearctica*, the greater scaup, and *A. affinis*, the lesser scaup, both native to North America

scav·enge (skǽvindʒ) *pres. part.* **scav·eng·ing** *past* and *past part.* **scav·enged** *v.t.* to gather up and remove (refuse) ‖ (of animals) to seek out and devour (refuse or dead organic matter) ‖ to remove refuse or impurities from ‖ to search for usable refuse in (a place) ‖ to remove the burned gases from (an internal-combustion machine) ‖ *v.i.* to seek among refuse for objects of some use ‖ to remove refuse, waste, impurities etc. from a place or thing [back-formation fr. SCAVENGER]

scav·en·ger (skǽvindʒər) *n.* an animal which feeds on dead organic matter ‖ (esp. *Br.*) a person employed to remove refuse [older *scavager* fr. *scavage*, toll levied on nonresident merchants, fr. A.F. *scawage, schawage*, inspection]

sca·zon (skéiz'n) *n.* a limping satiric meter in classical verse, esp. an iambic trimeter ending with a spondee or trochee [L. fr. Gk fr. *skazein*, to limp]

sce·na (ʃéinə, ʃéinɑ) *n.* a scene from an opera ‖ a composition for solo voice with accompaniment, usually a dramatic recitative. It may be either part of an opera or an independent entity [Ital.]

sce·nar·i·o (sinéəriou, sinɑ́riou) *n.* a brief summary of the scenes and story of a play, opera etc. ‖ a synopsis of a plan of action in specified situation ‖ a detailed outline of a movie, giving directions for actors etc. **sce·nár·ist** *n.* a writer of movie scenarios [Ital. fr. *scena*, scene]

scene (si:n) *n.* the place where some event occurs ‖ the place where the action of a play, novel etc. is supposed to take place ‖ a division of an act in a play ‖ theater scenery ‖ a display of strong emotion, e.g. of anger, *don't make a scene* ‖ (*colloq.*) the situation ‖ the world of activity ‖ a view, episode etc. seen by an observer as though in a theater **behind the scenes** where the public cannot see or know what goes on ‖ in the

discreet absence of all publicity [F. *scène* fr. L. *scena* fr. Gk *skēnē*, tent, stage]

scen·er·y (sí:nəri:) *pl.* **scen·er·ies** *n.* the painted flats etc. used in a theater to represent the place of action ‖ natural geographical features with regard to their beauty or picturesqueness [fr. obs. *scenary*, scenario fr. Ital. *scenario*]

scene-shift·er (sí:nʃiftər) *n.* someone who changes scenes during a theatrical production

sce·nic (sí:nik, sénik) *adj.* of or connected with stage scenery or effects ‖ (of natural scenery) (of a landscape etc.) beautiful or picturesque **scé·ni·cal·ly** *adv.* [F. *scénique* fr. L. *scenicus*]

scenic easement (*envir.*) right to use, or control use of, an area in order to preserve its natural characteristics

scenic railway a short railway of small gauge constructed to pass between artificial scenic views as an amusement at fairs, amusement parks etc.

scent (sent) **1.** *v.t.* to perceive by the sense of smell, *the buffalo scented our approach* ‖ to begin to have an awareness or suspicion of, *to scent a mystery* ‖ to give an odor to, *scented soap* **2.** *n.* a smell, usually pleasing ‖ (esp. *Br.*) perfume ‖ the smell remaining after an animal has passed ‖ a trace followed in hunting ‖ the way leading to detection of a crime ‖ the power of smelling or of detecting or discovering, *a keen scent* ‖ the paper trail laid in hare and hounds [M.E. *sent*, to scent game fr. F. *sentir*, to feel, smell]

scent·om·e·ter (sentómitər) *n.* breath-analyzing instrument for measuring pollutants in the breath

scepsis *SKEPSIS

scep·ter, esp. *Br.* **scep·tre** (séptər) *n.* a staff carried by a sovereign as symbol of authority **scép·tered,** esp. *Br.* **scép·tred** *adj.* [M.E. *ceptre, septre, sceptre* fr. O.F. fr. L. *sceptrum* fr. Gk]

sceptic *SKEPTIC

scepticism *SKEPTICISM

sceptre *SCEPTER

schad·en·freud·e (ʃádnfrɔidə) *n.* delight at the misfortune of another person [G. fr. *schaden*, damage+*freude*, joy]

Schaff (ʃæf, ʃɑf), Philip (1819-93), U.S. theologian and advocate of church unity. He believed that Roman Catholicism and Protestantism would blend eventually into an evangelical Catholicism. His works include 'History of the Christian Church' (7 vols, 1858-92)

Schaff·hau·sen (ʃɑfháuz'n) the northernmost canton (area 115 sq. miles, pop. 148,000) of Switzerland, German-speaking and mainly Protestant, and heavily industrialized ‖ its capital (pop. 69,413), near celebrated Rhine waterfalls (hydroelectric). Industries: mechanical and precision engineering, watchmaking, metallurgy, textiles. Romanesque abbev (11th c.)

Scharn·horst (ʃárnhɔrst), Gerhard Johann David von (1755-1813), Prussian general. He reformed the Prussian army after the Treaty of Tilsit, basing it on universal conscription and a national reserve

Schech·ter (ʃéktər), Solomon (1847-1915), U.S. Jewish theologian and talmudist. He discovered (1896) in Cairo over 90,000 manuscripts of great significance to biblical and rabbinical research. He served (1902-15) as president of the Jewish Theological Seminary of America in New York City, which he made a center of Jewish research, and founded (1913) the United Synagogue of America

Schechter Poultry Corp. v. United States a unanimous decision (1935) of the U.S. Supreme Court led by Charles Evan Hughes. It ruled that the codes concerning wages and hours outlined in the National Industrial Recovery Act of President Franklin Roosevelt exceeded the powers of Congress under the interstate commerce clause, and that the National Recovery Administration was thus illegal

sched·ule (skédʒu:l, skédʒul, skédʒuːəl, *Br.* ʃédju:l) **1.** *n.* a written or printed list, often appended to a document such as a will ‖ a timed program of procedure ‖ a timetable for trains etc. ‖ the list of occupations the Department of Labor considers to be in short supply throughout the U.S., and for which it grants certification for immigration **2.** *v.t. pres. part.* **sched·uling** *past* and *past part.* **sched·uled** to make a list of ‖ to work out a program or timetable for ‖ to assign in advance a time or date for (an event), *their departure was scheduled for 5:00 p.m.* [O. F. *cedule, sedule*, written slip fr. L.L.]

Schee·le (ʃéilə), Karl Wilhelm (1742-86), Swedish chemist who discovered oxygen (1773) independently of Priestley. He produced phosphorus from bone ash, studied the reduction of silver salts by light, and studied photosynthesis

Scheele's green a yellowish-green compound of copper and arsenic used as an insecticide and as a pigment

scheel·ite (ʃéilait), ʃí:lait) *n.* native calcium tungstate, CaWO4, one of the sources of tungsten [after K. W. SCHEELE]

Scheldt (skelt, ʃelt) (*Flem.* Schelde, *F.* Escaut) a river (270 miles long, navigable for 200) rising in Aisne, N.E. France, and flowing across W. Belgium through a double estuary into the S.W. Netherlands to the North Sea. By the Treaties of Westphalia (1648) the Dutch obtained the right to close the mouth of the Scheldt, with disastrous effects on Antwerp. Navigation was made free in 1863

Sche·ler (ʃéilər), Max (1874-1928), German phenomenologist philosopher. His main works include 'Der Formalismus in der Ethik und die materiale Wertethik' (1913-16), 'Wesen und Formen der Sympathie' (1923) and 'Die Stellung des Menschen im Kosmos' (1927, 1928)

Schel·ling (ʃélin), Friedrich Wilhelm Joseph von (1775-1854), German idealist philosopher. He was profoundly influential in German thought. In 'Vom Ich als Prinzip der Philosophie' (1795) he follows Fichte, acknowledging only one reality, the infinite and absolute Ego, of which the universe is the expression. In the 'natural philosophy' that marks his middle period he makes nature an absolute being, working unconsciously though purposively toward self-consciousness, man alone being in full possession of this faculty. His later writings were marked by Neoplatonist and theosophist speculations

sche·ma (skí:mə) *pl.* **sche·ma·ta** (skí:mətə) *n.* a plan, outline ‖ a diagram ‖ (*logic*) a syllogistic abstract figure ‖ (*Kantian philos.*) the imaginative form through which a particular perception is taken up into a category [Gk *schēma*, form, figure]

sche·mat·ic (ski:mǽtik) *adj.* of, like or having the nature of a schema **sche·mát·i·cal·ly** *adv.* [fr. Mod. L. *schematicus*]

sche·ma·ti·za·tion (skị:mətizéiʃən) *n.* a schematizing or being schematized ‖ an instance of this

sche·ma·tize (skí:mətaiz) *pres. part.* **sche·ma·tiz·ing** *past* and *past part.* **sche·ma·tized** *v.t.* to arrange in a scheme ‖ to conventionalize, stylize [fr. Gk *schēmatizein*]

scheme (ski:m) 1. *n.* a detailed plan or system, *a scheme for lodging the extra guests* ‖ a carefully constructed arrangement, *a color scheme* ‖ a secret, dishonest or malicious plot or plan (esp. *Br.*) an official project or plan, *a governmental hydroelectric scheme* 2. *v.i. pres. part.* **scheming** *past* and *past part.* **schemed** to form plans or schemes **schém·er** *n.* someone who devises secret, dishonest or malicious plans **schém·ing** *adj.* intriguing, full of guile [M.L. *schema* fr. Gk]

Scher·ba·kov *RYBINSK

scher·zan·do (skertsándou) 1. *adv.* (*mus.*) in a lively, playful manner 2. *adj.* (*mus.*) lively, playful 3. *n.* (*mus.*) a scherzando movement or passage [Ital.]

scher·zo (skértsou) *pl.* **scher·zos, scher·zi** (skértsi:) *n.* (*mus.*) a lively composition, esp. one in ternary form and in triple time, often constituting a movement following a slow movement in a classical sonata or symphony etc. [Ital.= a jest, scherzo]

Schia·pa·rel·li (skjɑpərélli:), Giovanni Virginio (1835-1910), Italian astronomer who discovered the canals on Mars, the asteroid Hesperia and the connection between comets and meteorites

Schick Gu·tié·rrez (ʃígku:tjérres), René (1910-66), Nicaraguan lawyer, politician, and president of the Republic (1963-6). He died in office

Schick test (ʃik) a test for diphtheria immunity, in which diphtheria toxin is injected into the skin. If the skin reacts by reddening etc., then the subject is susceptible to the disease [after Béla *Schick* (1877–1967), U.S. pediatrician]

Schie·dam (sxi:dám) a town (pop. 74,223) of South Holland, Netherlands, near Rotterdam

Schil·ler (ʃílər), Johann Christoph Friedrich von (1759-1805), German poet, playwright, his-

torian and critic. He achieved instant fame with his Romantic drama 'Die Räuber' (1781). His historical works include 'The History of the Thirty Years' War' (1791-3). The later historical dramas, e.g. 'Wallenstein' (1799), 'Maria Stuart' (1800) and 'Wilhelm Tell' (1804), showed a mature treatment of the themes of freedom, idealism and heroic achievement, and the same idealism is found in the poems (e.g. the 'Hymn to Joy', which Beethoven set to music in the last movement of the 9th Symphony). Collaboration with Goethe at Weimar produced important work in the editing of literary journals and in aesthetic philosophy

schil·ler (ʃílər) *n.* the sheen or iridescence of some minerals [G.=color play]

schil·ling (ʃílin) *n.* the basic monetary unit of Austria, subdivided into 100 groschen [G.]

schip·per·ke (skípərki:, skípərkə) *n.* a small, black dog of a Belgian breed, with a pointed head, prick ears and a piercing bark [Du. dial.=little boatman (fr. its use as a barge watchdog)]

schism (sízəm) *n.* a destruction of the unity of a Church through disagreement on doctrine or practice, resulting in the Church's regrouping into separate parts ‖ one of the sects so formed ‖ the offense of causing this to occur ‖ a division of any party etc. into differing factions [M.E. *scisme* fr. O.F. fr. eccles. L. *schisma* fr. Gk]

schis·mat·ic (sizmǽtik) 1. *adj.* of the nature of schism ‖ causing schism 2. *n.* a person who causes or fosters schism **schis·mát·i·cal** *adj.* [M.E. *cysmatyke, scismatik* fr. O.F. fr. eccles. L. *schismaticus* fr. Gk]

schist (ʃist) *n.* a metamorphic crystalline rock, much coarser than gneiss. It contains minerals such as mica and talc but no essential feldspar, and is easily split into thin flakes **schis·tose** (ʃístous) *adj.* of, relating to or having the characteristics of schist [F. *schiste* fr. L. *schistos*, easily split fr. Gk]

Schis·to·so·ma ja·pon·i·cum (skitəsóuməjæpónikəm) (*med.*) species of flukes that are found in the veins of the intestines, esp. in China and Japan

schis·to·some (ʃístəsoum) *n.* a fluke of fam. *Schistosomatidae*, esp. of genus *Schistosoma*, living as a parasite in mammals, snails and mollusks **schis·to·so·mi·a·sis** (ʃistəsoumáiəsis) *n.* bilharzia [fr. Mod. L. *Schistosoma* fr. Gk *schistos*, cleft+*sōma*, body]

schiz·an·thus (skizǽnθəs) *n.* a member of *Schizanthus*, fam. *Solanaceae*, a genus of plants native to Chile, with divided leaves and white, red or violet showy flowers [Mod. L. fr. Gk *schizein*, to split+*anthos*, flower]

schiz·o·carp (skízəkɑrp) *n.* (*bot.*) a compound fruit which splits when ripe into several indehiscent portions, each having one seed **schiz·o·cár·pous** *adj.* [fr. Gk *schizein*, to split+*karpos*, fruit]

schiz·o·gen·e·sis (skizədʒénisis) *n.* (*biol.*) reproduction by fission [Mod. L. fr. Gk *schizein*, to split+*genesis*, origin]

schiz·oid (skítsoid, skízoid) 1. *adj.* characteristic of schizophrenia or of split personality ‖ having personality traits associated with schizophrenia, e.g. reserve, emotional inhibition, introversion etc. 2. *n.* a schizoid person [fr. Gk *schizein*, to split]

schiz·o·my·cete (skizoumaisí:t) *n.* (in some classifications) a member of *Schizomycetes*, a class of unicellular or noncellular organisms comprising the bacteria grouped usually with the fungi [fr. Mod. L. *Schizomycetes* fr. Gk *schizein*, to split+*mukēs* (*pl. mukētes*), fungus]

schiz·o·my·co·phyte (skizəmáikəfait) *n.* a thallophyte of the phylum *Schizomycophyta* comprising the bacteria and sometimes the blue-green algae [fr. Mod. L. *Schizomycophyta* fr. Gk *schizein*, to split+*mukēs*, fungus+*phuton*, plant]

schiz·o·phrene (skítsəfri:n) *n.* a person who has schizophrenia

schiz·o·phre·ni·a (skitsəfrí:ni:ə, skizəfrí:ni:ə) *n.* a common mental disease whose characteristics may include separation of the intellect from the emotions, inappropriate emotional reactions, distortions in normal logical thought processes, withdrawal from social relationships, delusions and hallucinations [*CATATONIA, *HEBEPHRENIA, *PARANOIA] **schiz·o·phren·ic** (skitsəfrénik, skizəfrénik) *adj.* and *n.* [Mod. L. fr. Gk *schizein*, to split+*phrēn*, mind]

schiz·o·phyte (skízəfait) *n.* a schizomycophyte [fr. Mod. L. *Schizophyta* fr. Gk *schizein*, to split+*phuton*, plant]

schiz·zy or **schiz·y** (skítsi:) *adj.* (*slang*) schizophrenic

Schle·gel (ʃléig'l), August Wilhelm von (1767-1845), German translator and critic, one of the earliest of the Romantics. He translated Shakespeare, Calderón, Tasso, Petrarch, Ariosto and others

Schlegel, Friedrich von (1772-1829), younger brother of August, poet and scholar and one of the founders of German Romanticism

Schlei·er·mach·er (ʃláiərmɑxər), Friedrich Daniel Ernst (1768-1834), German mystical theologian who strongly influenced Protestant thought. Under the impetus of the Romantic movement he defined religion in terms of feeling and intuition and rejected dogma ('Discourse on Religion', 1799)

schlepp (ʃlep) (*slang*) (from the Yiddish) *v.* to move with difficulty or reluctance —**schlepper** *n.*

Schles·in·ger (slésinɡər), Frank (1871-1943), U.S. astronomer. His use of long-focus telescopes for photographic measurements of the distances of stars was a major contribution to knowledge of the scale of the universe beyond the solar system

Schles·wig-Hol·stein (ʃléisvixhólʃtain) the northernmost state (area 6,057 sq. miles, pop. 2,276,000) of West Germany: Main towns: Kiel (the capital), Lübeck. It is a largely marshy and sandy lowland, forming the neck of the Jutland peninsula (between the Elbe and Denmark), and includes the North Frisian Is. It is heavily industrialized (shipbuilding, mechanical engineering, textiles, fishing). Crops: cereals, root vegetables. HISTORY. The duchies of Schleswig and Holstein became the personal possessions of the king of Denmark in 1460, though the population was largely German. Holstein was included in the German Confederation (1815). Prussia intervened (1848) to stop a Danish attempt to annex the duchies and, with Austria, forced Denmark to give them up (1864), Austria taking Holstein and Prussia Schleswig. A dispute in Holstein was used by Bismarck as a pretext for the Seven Weeks' War against Austria (1866), after which Prussia took both Schleswig and Holstein. N. Schleswig was returned to Denmark (1920)

Schlief·fen (ʃlí:fən), Alfred, graf von (1833-1913), German field marshal. As chief of the German general staff (1891-1906), he devised (1905) a plan for defeating France by a massive flanking movement through the Low Countries. This was put into effect in a modified form in 1914, and was also followed in 1940

Schlie·mann (ʃlí:man), Heinrich (1822-90), German archaeologist. On a private expedition (1870-2) he first excavated Troy. He also excavated Mycenae (1876-8)

schlie·ren (ʃlí:rən) *pl. n.* streaks of different composition within an igneous rock ‖ (*phys.*) layers of differing refractive index, due to differences of pressure within a medium, esp. within the air, which enable sound waves and the air disturbances due to a fast-moving body to be photographed [G.]

schlieren photography technique for photographing changes in gas density occurring in wind tunnels as a result of shock or sound

schlock (ʃlok) (from the Yiddish) *n.* (*slang*) something of poor quality —**schlock** *adj.*

Schmal·kal·dic League (ʃmɑlkáldik) a league of Protestant German princes formed (1531) at Schmalkalden, Thuringia, for the defense of the Reformation after the Augsburg Confession. It was crushed during the Schmalkaldic War (1546-7) by Emperor Charles V

schmaltz (ʃmalts, ʃmɔlts) *n.* (*pop.*) extremely sentimental music ‖ (*pop.*) anything extremely sentimental **schmáltz·y** *comp.* **schmáltz·i·er** *superl.* **schmáltz·i·est** [Yiddish *shmalts*, rendered fat]

schmeer or **schmear** (from the Yiddish) (ʃmiər) *n.* (*slang*) the package, e.g., 'the whole schmeer'

Schmidt (ʃmit), Helmut (1918-), West German statesman, chancellor (1974-82). He joined the Social Democrat party in 1946, was elected to the lower house of parliament (Bundestag) in 1953 and was his party leader in the Bundestag (1967-9). He served as defense minister (1969-72) and finance minister (1972-4). He worked for better relations between the U.S.S.R. and the West and to strengthen West Germany's economy

Schmitt (ʃmit), Florent (1870-1958), French composer. His works, dense in texture, include

CONCISE PRONUNCIATION KEY: **(a)** æ, c*a*t; ɑ, c*a*r; ɔ f*aw*n; ei, sn*a*ke. **(e)** e, h*e*n; i:, sh*ee*p; iə, d*ee*r; ɛə, b*ea*r. **(i)** i, f*i*sh; ai, t*i*ger; əː, b*i*rd. **(o)** o, *o*x; au, c*ow*; ou, g*oa*t; u, p*oo*r; ɔi, r*oy*al. **(u)** ʌ, d*u*ck; u, b*u*ll; u:, g*oo*se; ə, b*a*cillus; ju:, c*u*be. x, lo*ch*; θ, *th*ink; ð, bo*th*er; z, *Z*en; ʒ, corsa*g*e; dʒ, sava*g*e; ŋ, ora*n*gutang; j, *y*ak; ʃ, *f*ish; tʃ, fe*tch*; 'l, rabb*le*; 'n, redd*en*. Complete pronunciation key appears inside front cover.

a choral setting of Psalm XLVI, a piano quintet, and much other symphonic, vocal and chamber music

schmuck (ʃmʌk) *n.* (*slang*) usu. considered vulgar (from the Yiddish) a stupid, or ignorant person

Schmuck·er (ʃmʌ́kər), Samuel Simon (1799-1873), U.S. liberal Lutheran theologian. He established (1820) the General Synod, a first united Lutheran Church of district synods in America, and published (1834) 'Elements of Popular Theology', a first systematic treatment in English of American Lutheran theology. He and his liberal movement were undermined (mid-19th c.) by pressure groups of conservative Lutheran immigrants

schnapps (ʃnɑps, ʃnæps) *n.* any of several distilled liquors of high alcoholic content, e.g. hollands [G.]

schnau·zer (ʃnáuzər) *n.* a short-haired terrier of a German breed, with a heavy head, heavy eyebrows and beard, and small ears [G.]

Schnitz·ler (ʃnítslər), Arthur (1862-1931), Austrian writer, author of novels, short stories, and of 'Anatol' (1893), a series of short dramatic sketches

schnook (ʃnuk) *n.* (*slang*) an easy mark

schnor·kel (ʃnɔ́rk'l) *n.* a snorkel

Schoel·cher (ʃelʃer), Victor (1804-93), French statesman. As Deputy from Martinique and Guadeloupe, he drafted (1848) the decree abolishing slavery in all French territories

Schoenberg, Arnold *SCHÖNBERG

schol·ar (skɒ́lər) *n.* a learned person ‖ a person who has made a thorough study and acquired a wealth of knowledge of a subject ‖ (*esp. Br.*) a student at a school, college or university who is supported financially, usually as the result of distinction in examination ‖ a school pupil **schol·ar·ly** *adj.* of or like a scholar ‖ having the quality characteristic of the work of a scholar, *a scholarly essay* **schol·ar·ship** *n.* the command of learning displayed by a scholar ‖ the methods by which scholars work ‖ the body of learning with which a subject is invested, *historical scholarship* ‖ a financial award to someone seeking to pursue his studies, usually on the result of a competitive examination [O.E. *scolere, scoliere* fr. L.L. *scholaris adj.*, of a school]

scho·las·tic (skəlǽstik) *adj.* pertaining to school education **Scho·las·tic** 1. *adj.* pertaining to the Schoolmen and to their methods of discussion 2. *n.* a Schoolman **Scho·lás·ti·cism** *n.* the synthesis of Aristotelian philosophy and Christian revelation in medieval European thought. It sought to resolve the conflicts of faith and reason and of nominalism and realism, and to establish proof of the existence of God. St Augustine of Hippo, in seeking to reconcile Platonic thought and Christian dogma, had stressed the illumination of faith by reason. The philosophical implications of Christianity were actively explored in Europe from the 11th c. onwards, notably by Anselm and Abelard. The debate was increased by the arrival (12th c.) in the universities of the work of Aristotle through the Arabian commentators Avicenna and Averroes. The Averroist doctrine that faith and reason might not be complementary brought Aristotelianism into disrepute until St Thomas Aquinas powerfully vindicated it in his 'Summa theologica', separating philosophy and theology and exploring the relationship between them. Other defenders of Aristotle were St Albertus Magnus and St Bonaventura. Thomism was opposed notably by Duns Scotus and William of Occam. By the time of the Renaissance, philosophy and theology had become separate studies. A Thomist revival took place in the late 19th and 20th cc. (*NEOTHOMISM)

scho·li·ast (skóuliæst) *n.* a commentator, esp. one of ancient times who annotated the classics [fr. L.L. *scholiasta* fr. Gk]

scho·li·um (skóuliəm) *pl.* **scho·li·a** (skóuliə) *n.* an explanatory note, esp. one made to a classic by a scholiast [M.L. fr. Gk]

Schön·berg, Schoen·berg (ʃɔ́ːnbəːrg), Arnold (1874-1951), Austrian composer, who lived in the U.S.A. after 1933 and became a U.S. citizen (1940). After a period as a romantic, showing the influence of Wagner, Brahms and Mahler (e.g. in 'Verklärte Nacht', 1899, a tone poem for string sextet), he began to explore the possibilities of atonal music, e.g. in the song cycle with instruments 'Pierrot Lunaire' (1912). By the early 1920s he had developed the theory and practice of twelve-tone music, which was to have a profound influence. Those he influenced

include Berg and Webern. His works comprise lieder, four string quartets, a piano concerto, a violin concerto, operas and many other chamber and orchestral works

Schon·gau·er (ʃóungauər), Martin (c. 1450-92), German engraver and painter. His work showed the influence of the Flemish painters, esp. of Van der Weyden. His 115 engravings on religious subjects had a great influence on the development of the art of engraving and of German art. His only certain extant painting is the 'Madonna of the Rosehedge' (1473, St Martin's Church, Colmar)

school (skuːl) 1. *n.* a community of those who teach and those who are taught, esp. one for the education of children, usually housed in a building designed and equipped for this purpose ‖ the building itself ‖ the pupils as distinct from the teachers, *the school will assemble in the hall* ‖ the period or session during which classes occur, *school is over at 4:30* ‖ a teaching community devoted to particular studies, often part of a university, *medical school* ‖ formal education, *he only had three years of school* ‖ the conditions of gaining skill or knowledge, *brought up in a hard school* ‖ a group sharing methods, opinions, teachings etc., *painters of the Impressionist school, a gentleman of the old school* ‖ (*pl.*) the medieval universities ‖ (*Br., pl.*) the honors courses of study at Oxford University or the examinations taken at the end of them **to teach school** to be a professional schoolteacher 2. *v.t.* to train or discipline, *he schooled himself to keep silent* [O.E. *scōl* fr. L. *schola* fr. Gk *scholē*, school, leisure]

school *n.* a number of fish or aquatic mammals keeping together while feeding or migrating [Du.]

school·book (skúːlbuk) *n.* a book written for and used by those attending school

school·boy (skúːlbɔi) *n.* a boy attending school

school·child (skúːltʃaild) *pl.* **school·children** (skúːltʃildrən) *n.* a boy or girl attending school

School·craft (skúːlkræft, skúːlkrɑft), Henry Rowe (1793-1864), U.S. ethnologist, explorer, and early specialist of the American Indian. He discovered (1832) Lake Itasca, then thought to be the source of the Mississippi

school·girl (skúːlgəːrl) *n.* a girl attending school

school·house (skúːlhaus) *pl.* **school·hous·es** (skúːlhauziz) *n.* the building in which a school is conducted, esp. a school for children ‖ (*Br.*) the house in which the schoolmaster or schoolmistress of a small school lives

school·ing (skúːliŋ) *n.* the act of someone who schools ‖ school education, *he had little schooling* ‖ disciplined training acquired elsewhere than in a school

School·man (skúːlmən) *pl.* **School·men** (skúːlmən) *n.* (*hist.*) an exponent of Scholasticism in a medieval university

school·mas·ter (skúːlmæstər, skúːlmɑstər) *n.* a man who teaches in a school

school·mate (skúːlmeit) *n.* a person who is educated at the same school as another

school·mis·tress (skúːlmistris) *n.* a woman who teaches in a school

school of thought an opinion or point of view on a subject, held by some but not constituting the only reasonable opinion or point of view, *there are several schools of thought on how to make coffee* ‖ the group holding such an opinion or point of view

school·room (skúːlruːm, skúːlrum) *n.* a room in which pupils are taught, in school or in a private house

school·teach·er (skúːltʃiːtʃər) *n.* a person who teaches in a school

school·work (skúːlwəːrk) *n.* work done to a schoolteacher's requirements, either at home or at school

school year the academic period making up one year of a school's administration

schoon·er (skúːnər) *n.* (*naut.*) a fore-and-aft vessel with two or more masts [etym. doubtful]

schooner *n.* a tall beer glass [origin unknown]

Scho·pen·hau·er (ʃóupənhauər), Arthur (1788-1860), German philosopher. In 'The World as Will and Idea' (1818), he stated that the will is the key to reason. His statement that without the will 'before us there is nothing' is regarded as a classic expression of pessimism. He

counted Buddhism and a world-denying mysticism as superior to current Christian theology

schorl (ʃɔrl) *n.* tourmaline, esp. of a black variety [G. *schörl*]

schot·tische (ʃótiʃ) *n.* a round dance in duple time resembling a slow polka ‖ the music for this dance [G. *schottische* (*tanz*), Scottish (*dance*)]

Schrö·ding·er (ʃrǿːdiŋər), Erwin (1887-1961), Austrian physicist who developed the theory of wave mechanics. Nobel prize (shared with Dirac, 1933)

Schrödinger equation the wave equation

schtick or **shtick** (ʃtik) *n.* (*slang*) (from the Yiddish) 1. a piece, esp. a theatrical piece 2. a hobby or characteristic

Schu·bert (ʃúːbəːrt), Franz Peter (1797-1828), Austrian composer. His early work shows a debt to Beethoven but he soon acquired his own style, marked everywhere by abundant lyrical invention and a great gift for sustained melody, with a characteristically subtle use of harmony and modulation. He wrote over 600 incomparable songs (*LIED), 9 symphonies, 15 complete string quartets, a quintet with viola, the 'Trout' piano quintet, piano sonatas and much other chamber and piano music as well as orchestral, choral and operatic works

Schu·man (ʃumɑ́), Robert (1886-1963), French statesman. French prime minister (1947-8) and foreign minister (1948-53), he proposed (1950) the establishment of a coal and steel pool in W. Europe, and is regarded as a founder of the European Economic Community

Schu·mann (ʃúːman), Robert Alexander (1810-56), German composer. His most characteristic music is for the piano. It is spontaneous, lyrical and in the main exquisitely brief: most often melancholy, nostalgic and tender. In addition to his many piano works he wrote many deeply expressive songs (*LIED) incl. the cycle 'Dichterliebe' (1840), 4 symphonies, 3 string quartets, a piano concerto, other chamber works etc.

Schurz (ʃuərts), Carl (1829-1906), U.S. political leader and reformer. He led (1884) the Mugwumps, who opposed the Republican party's nomination of James G. Blaine as presidential candidate

schuss (ʃus) 1. *n.* a straight run in skiing 2. *v.i.* to ski at high speed on a straight course [G.]

Schütz (ʃyts), Heinrich (1585-1672), German composer, one of the great masters of the German school. His work shows the influence of Gabrieli and Monteverdi. It includes the first German opera, 'Daphne' (1627, no longer extant), and noble and moving church music, notably four 'Passions' (1665-88)

Schutz·pan·zer Marder (ʃútzpɑnzər) *n.* (*mil.*) armored personnel carrier of the German Federal Republic

schwa (ʃwɑ) *n.* (*phon.*) an unstressed mid-central vowel, e.g. the 'o' in 'atom' ‖ the symbol ə used to represent this quality [G. fr. Heb.]

Schwann (ʃvɑn), Theodor (1810-82), German physiologist. He founded the cell theory of living organisms and recognized that the ovum is a cell

Schwarz·en·berg (ʃvá:rtsənberk), Felix, Fürst zu (1800-52), Austrian statesman. With the aid of Windischgrätz he put down revolutions in Austria and Bohemia (1848) and restored the authority of the Hapsburgs. As prime minister (1848-52) he humiliated Prussia in the Treaty of Olmütz (1850)

Schwarz·schild radius (ʃvártsʃild) (*astron.*) twice the minimum black hole mass times a gravitational force, divided by the speed of light. It is hypothesized in a solution to theory of general relativity concept of a nonrotating black hole *Cf* BLACK HOLE

Schweit·zer (ʃwáitsər, ʃváitsər), Albert (1875-1965), French physician, theologian and musician. He devoted his life after 1913 to a medical mission at Lambaréné, Gabon, originally financing it largely by organ recitals of Bach's music. His theological writings gave a new emphasis to the study of eschatology in New Testament interpretation. Nobel peace prize (1952)

Schweitzer's reagent cuprammonium solution [after Matthias *Schweitzer* (19th c.), G. chemist]

Schwe·rin (ʃveirí:n) the former capital (pop. 113,000) of Mecklenburg, East Germany. Gothic cathedral (15th c.), palace (19th c.) ‖ the surrounding district (area 3,343 sq. miles, pop. 623,000)

Schwit·ters (ʃvítərs), Kurt (1887-1948), German painter and poet, active in dada. He produced collages of considerable beauty out of scraps of wastepaper and rubbish

Schwyz (ʃviːts) a German-speaking, mainly Catholic canton (area 350 sq. miles, pop. 97,354) of Switzerland on the Lake of Lucerne ‖ its capital (pop. 11,000)

sci·at·ic (saiǽtik) adj. pertaining to the hip, esp. to the great nerve at the back of the thigh [F. sciatique fr. M.L. sciaticus]

sci·at·i·ca (saiǽtikə) n. pain due to irritation of the sciatic nerve [M.L. fr. sciaticus, sciatic]

sci·ence (sáiəns) n. knowledge acquired by careful observation, by deduction of the laws which govern changes and conditions, and by testing these deductions by experiment ‖ a branch of study, esp. one concerned with facts, principles and methods, the science of language ‖ a technique based on training, the science of fencing ‖ natural science or a branch of this [F. fr. L. scientia, knowledge]

science fiction fiction in which scientific fancy provides plots for adventure stories concerning esp. the future condition of man and society

sci·en·tial (saiénʃəl) adj. of or relating to knowledge or science [fr. M.L. scientialis]

sci·en·tif·ic (saiəntífik) adj. pertaining to science, esp. to natural science ‖ of or using methods based upon well-established facts and obeying well-established laws, scientific management ‖ using the knowledge made available by scientists, scientific farming ‖ (loosely) thorough and accurate **sci·en·tif·i·cal·ly** adv. [fr. L.L. scientificus fr. L. sciens (scientis), knowing + facere, to make]

sci·en·tist (sáiəntist) n. a specialist in science, esp. in a natural science

Sci·en·tol·o·gy (saiəntóləʤiː) n. founded 1952 by L. Ron Hubbard, a religious movement that teaches immortality and reincarnation and claims a psychotherapeutic method for freeing the individual from personal problems

sci-fi (sáifái) adj. of science fiction

scil·i·cet (síliset) adv. (abbr. sc., scil.) namely [L. fr. scire licet, it is permitted to know]

scil·la (sílə) n. a member of Scilla, fam. Liliaceae, a genus of wild and cultivated bulbous plants native to N. Europe and Asia, having esp. blue flowers [L.]

Scil·ly Isles (síli) a group of 140 islets (total area 10 sq. miles, pop. 2,428), five of them inhabited, off S.W. England. Capital: Hugh Town. Products: early fruit, vegetables, flowers

scim·i·tar (símitər) n. a short, curved, Oriental sword, with a sharp edge on the convex side only [F. cimeterre and Ital. scimitarra, origin unknown]

scin·til·ia (sintílə) n. (fig.) a light trace ‖ a spark [L. = spark]

scin·til·lant (síntˈlənt) adj. scintillating [fr. L. scintillans (scintillantis)]

scin·til·late (síntˈleit) pres. part. **scin·til·lat·ing** past and past part. **scin·til·lat·ed** v.i. to sparkle or twinkle like a star ‖ to be brilliant in conversation ‖ to emit sparks ‖ v.t. to give off in the form of sparks, twinkles etc. **scin·til·la·tion** n. a sparkling, esp. (astron.) the sparkling of a celestial body as the result of turbulence in the earth's atmosphere ‖ (phys.) a quantum of electromagnetic radiation as emitted e.g. by radioactive material [fr. L. scintillare (scintillatus)]

scintillation camera device for detecting and recording discrete emissions of radioactive substances, esp. in following isotopes in body scanning

scintillation counter a device for detecting and recording the presence of ionizing radiation, e.g. radioactive material (*GEIGER COUNTER)

sci·o·lism (sáiəlizəm) n. pretension to scholarship supported only by superficial knowledge [SCIOLIST]

sci·o·list (sáiəlist) n. someone who has only superficial knowledge but who pretends to have more **sci·o·lis·tic** adj. [fr. L. L. sciolus]

sci·on (sáiən) n. a shoot or branch used for grafting ‖ a young member or a descendant of a family, esp. of a noble family [O.F. cion, sion, etym. doubtful]

Scip·i·o Ae·mil·i·a·nus (sípi:oui:mili:éinəs), Publius Cornelius (185-129 B.C.), Roman soldier and statesman, adopted by the eldest son of Scipio Africanus. Commander in the 3rd Punic War, he destroyed Carthage (146 B.C.), making Africa a province. He subsequently destroyed Numantia (133 B.C.). At Rome he opposed the agrarian reforms of his brother-in-law Tiberius Gracchus

Scip·i·o Af·ri·ca·nus (sípi:ouæfrikéinəs), Publius Cornelius (c. 235-183 B.C.), Roman statesman and soldier. He defeated the Carthaginians in Spain during the 2nd Punic War, invaded Africa, and finally defeated Hannibal at Zama (202 B.C.). He trained the Roman army in new tactics and made it more professional

scir·rhoid (skírɔid, sírɔid) adj. like a scirrhus

scir·rhous (skírəs, sírəs) adj. of or having the nature of a scirrhus [fr. F. scirreux, scirrheux]

scir·rhus (skírəs, sírəs) pl. **scir·rhi** (skírai, sírai), **scir·rhus·es** n. a hard, cancerous tumor, esp. characterized by much fibrous tissue [Mod. L. fr. Gk skiros, skirros, hard covering, hard tumor]

scis·sile (sísil) adj. able to be cut or split with ease [L. scissilis fr. scindere, to split]

scis·sion (síʒən, síʃən) n. a cutting or splitting ‖ a division or split [F.]

scis·sor (sízər) v.t. to cut with scissors

scis·sors (sízərz) pl. n. a cutting tool consisting of two sharp-edged beveled blades which are pivoted near two handles through which finger and thumb are passed ‖ gymnastic movement of the legs like those of scissors in use ‖ (wrestling) a hold, by the legs, of the opponent's head or body [M.E. sisours, cysowres fr. O.F. cisoires]

scissors kick (swimming) a kick used in the sidestroke and trudgen. The upper leg is swung forward from the hip and the lower leg bent back from the knee, both legs then being sharply brought together

SCLC (abbr.) for Southern Christian Leadership Conference

scle·ra (sklíərə) n. the outer fibrous capsule of the eye, forming the white (*EYE) [Mod L. fr. Gk sklēros, hard]

scle·re·id (sklíəri:id) n. (bot.) a cell, composing one kind of sclerenchyma, that is roughly spherical. Sclereids occur throughout the plant body but esp. in the cortex, phloem, and in both hard and fleshy fruits (*FIBER) [fr. Gk sklēros, hard]

scle·ren·chy·ma (sklirénkəmə) pl. **scle·ren·chy·mas**, **scle·ren·chy·ma·ta** (sklirénkímətə) n. (bot.) a simple plant tissue (*PARENCHYMA, *COLLENCHYMA) that consists of thick-walled cells serving in support and protection. There are two principal types: fibers and sclereids ‖ the calcareous walls of certain coral cells [Mod. L. fr. Gk sklēros, hard + enchuma, infusion]

scle·rite (sklíərait, sklírait) n. (zool.) a chitinous plate ‖ (zool.) a calcareous plate or spicule [fr. Gk sklēros, hard]

scle·ro·der·ma·tous (sklíərədɛ:rmətəs, sklírədɔ:rmətəs) adj. (zool.) covered with hard outer scales or plates [fr. Gk sklēros, hard + derma (dermatos), skin]

scle·roid (sklíərɔid, sklírɔid) adj. (biol.) hard in texture [fr. Gk sklēros, hard]

scle·rom·e·ter (sklirómətər) n. a device used to determine the hardness of a material [fr. Gk sklēros, hard + metron, measure]

scle·ro·pro·tein (sklíəroupróuti:n, sklíroupróuti:in) n. one of a class of fibrous proteins which constitute many animal tissues, e.g. hair, horn, nail (*KERATIN, *COLLAGEN) [fr. Gk sklēros, hard + PROTEIN]

scle·rosed (sklíroust, sklíərouzd, sklírouzd) adj. suffering from sclerosis [SCLEROSIS]

scle·ro·sis (sklíróusis) pl. **scle·ro·ses** (sklíróusi:z) n. (med.) the pathological hardening of tissue produced by the overgrowth of connective tissue (*ARTERIOSCLEROSIS, *MULTIPLE SCLEROSIS) [Mod. L. fr. Gk sklēros, hard]

scle·ro·tes·ta (skliroutéstə) n. (botany) the middle layer of the outer covering (the pit in a fruit) of a seed

scle·rot·ic (sklirótik) 1. n. (anat.) the sclera (*EYE) 2. adj. of, relating to or having sclerosis ‖ of the sclera [fr. Mod. L. and M.L. scleroticus fr. Gk]

sclerotic coat the sclera

scle·rous (sklíərəs, sklírəs) adj. hardened, sclerous tissue [fr. Gk sklēros, hard]

scoff (skɔf, skaf) 1. v.i. to adopt a disbelieving or contemptuously mocking attitude towards something, to scoff at old wives' tales 2. n. an expression of such mockery [M.E. scof, skof n., etym. doubtful]

scold (skould) 1. v.t. to rebuke angrily and often noisily, to scold a child ‖ v.i. (often with 'at') to utter angry, noisy language or expressions 2. n. (old-fash.) a person, esp. a woman, who habitually scolds [prob. fr. O.N. skāld n., poet]

sco·lex (skóuleks) pl. **sco·le·ces** (skouli:si:z), **scol·i·ces** (skólisi:z, skóulisi:z) n. the head of a

larval or adult tapeworm [Mod. L. fr. Gk skōlex, worm]

sco·li·o·sis (skouli:óusis, skɔli:óusis) n. lateral curvature of the spine (*KYPHOSIS, *LORDOSIS)

sco·li·ot·ic (skouli:ótik) adj. [Mod. L. fr. Gk fr. skolios, bent]

scol·lop (skóləp) 1. n. a scallop 2. v.t. to scallop

sconce (skɒns) 1. a holder attached to a wall, for a candle or candles ‖ a flat candlestick with a handle [fr. O.F. esconse, lantern]

sconce 1. n. (Br., at Oxford University) a fine, to be paid in beer or ale, for an offense against good form when dining in hall, imposed by fellow students 2. v.t. pres. part. **sconc·ing** past and past part. **sconced** to impose this fine upon [origin unknown]

scone (skoun, skɒn) n. a small, soft cake of wheat or barley flour (baked originally on a griddle) [perh. fr. M.Du. schoonbrot and M.L.G. schonbrot, fine bread]

scoop (sku:p) 1. n. any implement for holding or removing liquids or loose solids, e.g. the bucket of an earth-moving machine or dredge or a little shovel for flour etc. ‖ a small concave holder with a handle for serving ice cream etc. ‖ a cutting or gouging instrument with a spoon-shaped blade ‖ (geog.) a basin-shaped depression ‖ a surgical implement used to gather and remove matter from the body ‖ a quantity gathered by using a scoop, a large scoop of ice cream ‖ (surfing) the upturned nose of the surfboard ‖ the act of scooping ‖ (pop.) a large profit made by a single transaction ‖ a piece of news obtained and published by a journalist or newspaper exclusively or before it has been published by a rival 2. v.t. to dip into, gather and transfer, by using a scoop ‖ to make (a hole etc.) by scooping ‖ to hollow out ‖ to empty out (water) by bailing ‖ (pop.) to get and publish a piece of news before (one's rivals) [M.E. scope fr. M.Du. schôpe, schoepe, vessel for bailing out water, and M.Du. schoppe, shovel]

scoot (sku:t) v.i. (pop.) to go quickly or go away quickly **scoot·er** n. a child's vehicle consisting of a low board fitted with a wheel at each end and a steering handle attached to the axle of the front wheel. The child stands with one foot on the board, thrusting against the ground with his other foot ‖ a low-powered, small-wheeled motorcycle, the driver of which sits as if on a chair, not astraddle [etym. doubtful]

sco·pa (skóupə) pl. **sco·pae** (skóupi:), **sco·pas** n. (zool.) a bunch of small hairs, e.g. the hairs which gather pollen on a bee's legs [L. scopae pl., twigs, broom]

Sco·pas (skóupəs) (4th c. B.C.), Greek sculptor who rebuilt the temple of Athena at Tegea and made the sculptures for it

sco·pate (skóupeit) adj. (zool.) brushlike [fr. L. scopae pl., twigs, broom]

scope (skoup) n. the area covered by an activity, plan, study etc., such subjects are not within the scope of this book ‖ room or opportunity for free activity, thought etc., he needs more scope for displaying his gifts ‖ (fig.) limit of capacity, beyond the scope of his imagination [fr. Ital. scopo, aim, fr. Gk skopos, mark for shooting at]

Scopes Trial (skoups) a U.S. civil liberty trial in which John Scopes, a Tennessee schoolteacher of biology, was indicted (1925) for teaching the doctrine of evolution. The trial attracted the participation of fundamentalist William Jennings Bryan for the prosecution and of Clarence Darrow for the defense. Scopes was convicted. In an appeal to the state supreme court Scopes was cleared, although the 1925 law was held constitutional

sco·pol·a·mine (skəpóləmi:n, skəpóləmin, skoupəlæmin) n. an alkaloid, $C_{17}H_{21}NO_4$, extracted from certain plants of fam. Solanaceae, esp. of genus Scopolia, and used as a sedative in surgery and obstetrics in conjunction with morphine and in the prevention of airsickness, seasickness etc. [fr. Mod. L. Scopolia, plant genus]

scop·u·la (skópjulə) pl. **scop·u·las**, **scop·u·lae** (skópjuli:) n. (zool.) the tuft of hairs on the feet and chelicerae of spiders used in making the web ‖ (zool.) a scopa **scop·u·late** (skópjuleit, skópjulit) adj. [L.L. dim. of scopa, broom]

scor·bu·tic (skɔrbjú:tik) adj. of, pertaining to or affected by scurvy [fr. Mod. L. scorbuticus fr. scorbutus, scurvy]

scorch (skɔrtʃ) 1. v.t. to apply such intense heat to (something) as to dry it up, fields scorched by *the summer sun* ‖ to burn (something) just enough to affect its color or taste, *the iron scorched the sheet* ‖ to criticize very harshly ‖ *v.i.* to become slightly discolored by being partially burned ‖ to become dried up by intense heat ‖ (*pop.*) to drive a vehicle very fast **2.** *n.* a discoloration caused by scorching [etym. doubtful]

scorched-earth policy the policy of destroying everything (buildings, bridges, crops etc.) that could help an enemy force to advance

scorch·er (skórtʃər) *n.* (*pop.*) a very hot day ‖ (*pop.*) a biting criticism ‖ (*pop.*) a very fast driver

score (skɔr, skour) *n.* a notch or line cut or scratched in the surface of something, *the scores of tribal markings* ‖ the number of points gained by a player or team in a game, or by the respective teams, *the score is 20 to 5 in our favor* ‖ a record of this ‖ the making of a point in a game or competition ‖ the point so made ‖ an act or remark which puts an opponent at a disadvantage ‖ a reason, motive, *he stayed away on the score of ill health* ‖ (*pl.* **scores, score**) a set of twenty (things, people etc.) ‖ (*pl.*) a great number, *scores of people had to be shut out* ‖ (*mus.*) a copy of a piece of music showing all the parts ‖ a number symbolizing the degree of success in a test ‖ (*pop.*) the facts and prospects of a situation, *to know the score* **to pay off** (or **settle**) **a score** to avenge a wrong [O.E. *scoru* fr. O.N. *skor*, notch, tally, four hundred, Icel. twenty]

score *pres. part.* **scoring** *past* and *past part.* **scored** *v.t.* to mark with cuts, lines, scratches etc. ‖ to make (a point) or win (a goal etc.) in a game ‖ to keep a record or account of by or as if by making notches or marks in a tally ‖ to count as, *an ace scores 10* ‖ (*mus.*) to arrange (a composition) for performance by certain instruments etc., *the piece is scored for two flutes and viola* ‖ to grade (an examination or a candidate) ‖ to criticize harshly ‖ *v.i.* to keep a score ‖ to win a point or points in a game ‖ to gain an advantage, *to score over a rival* ‖ (*pop.*) to make a success, be a hit, *an actor who scores every time* [O.N. *skora*, to make an incision, count by tallies]

score·board (skórbɔrd, skóurbourd) *n.* a large board visible to the spectators at a match, setting out the state of play

score·card (skórkɑrd, skóurkɑrd) *n.* a card identifying players and giving relevant information about a match and which can be used to record the score

score·keep·er (skórki:pər, skóurki:pər) *n.* an official who records the score throughout the progress of a sports contest

sco·ri·a (skóri:ə, skóuri:ə) *pl.* **sco·ri·ae** (skóri:i:, skóuri:i:) *n.* lava with a cellular structure ‖ a piece of such lava ‖ the residue from molten metals ‖ clinker **sco·ri·a·ceous** (skɔri:éiʃəs, skouri:éiʃəs) *adj.* [L. fr. Gk *skória*, refuse]

sco·ri·fi·ca·tion (skɔrifikéiʃən, skourifikéiʃən) *n.* a scorifying or being scorified ‖ something scorified

sco·ri·fy (skórifai, skóurifai) *pres. part.* **sco·ri·fy·ing** *past* and *past part.* **sco·ri·fied** *v.t.* to convert into [SCORIA]

scorn (skɔrn) *n.* a feeling of extreme contempt, often accompanied by anger or irritation ‖ a manifesting of this feeling, *her scorn wounded him deeply* **to laugh** (**someone** or **something**) **to scorn** to ridicule (someone or something) [M.E. *skarn, scharne* fr. O.F. *escarn, escharn* fr. Gmc]

scorn *v.t.* to reject with scorn, *to scorn an offer* ‖ to feel scorn for ‖ (with *infin.*) to refuse, out of a feeling of scorn or self-respect, *he scorned to answer their insults* [M.E. *scarne, schorne* fr. O.F. *escarnir, escharnir* fr. Gmc]

scorn·ful (skórnfəl) *adj.* feeling or showing scorn

Scor·pi·o (skórpi:ou) a southern constellation ‖ the eighth sign of the zodiac, represented as a scorpion [L.= scorpion]

scor·pi·oid (skórpi:ɔid) *adj.* (*bot.*, of an inflorescence) circinate ‖ like a scorpion [fr. Gk *skorpioeidēs*, like a scorpion]

scor·pi·on (skórpi:ən) *n.* a member of *Scorpionida*, an order of viviparous, carnivorous nocturnal arachnids of warm and tropical regions. They have an elongated abdomen forming a tail with a terminal poisonous sting which is rarely fatal to man. They may be as long as 6 or 8 ins [O.F. fr. L. fr. Gk]

scor·zo·ne·ra (skɔrzənérə) *n.* a member of *Scorzonera*, fam. *Compositae*, a genus of European plants with solitary heads of yellow flow-

---

ers on long peduncles. The roots of some species are edible, esp. those of black salsify [Ital.]

Scot (skɒt) *n.* a native of Scotland ‖ (*pl.*) the Gaelic-speaking tribe which emigrated from N. Ireland to Scotland (early 6th c. A.D.) [O.E. *Scottas* pl., fr. L.L. *Scottus*]

scot (skɒt) *n.* (*hist.*) a sum of money levied as a tax or imposed as an assessment ‖ one's share in the entertainment expenses of a group, *to pay one's scot* [a form of O.E. *sceot, gesceot, shot*]

Scotch (skɒtʃ) **1.** *adj.* (used esp. outside Scotland) Scottish **2.** *n.* (usually **scotch**) whiskey distilled in Scotland or a drink of this ‖ (non-Scottish term for) the Scottish variety of English **the Scotch** (non-Scottish term for) the Scots [contr. of SCOTTISH]

scotch *v.t.* to put down, crush, *to scotch a conspiracy* ‖ to wound without killing, disable [etym. doubtful]

scotch 1. a block or wedge used to prevent a wheel, barrel etc. from rolling **2.** *v.t.* to prevent from rolling by inserting a scotch [etym. doubtful]

Scotch-I·rish (skótʃáiriʃ) *adj.* of mixed Scotch and Irish descent ‖ of a group of people of Scottish descent living in N. Ireland ‖ of a group of people of Scottish descent who emigrated from N. Ireland to the U.S.A. prior to 1846, or of their descendants

Scotch·man (skótʃmən) *pl.* **Scotch·men** (skótʃmən) *n.* (non-Scottish term for) a Scot

Scotch terrier a Scottish terrier

Scotch whisky *SCOTCH

Scotch·wom·an (skótʃwʊmən) *pl.* **Scotch·wom·en** (skótʃwɪmin) *n.* (non-Scottish term for) a Scotswoman

sco·ter (skóutər) *pl.* **sco·ters, sco·ter** *n.* any of several large sea ducks of genera *Melanitta* and *Oidemia*, native to the northern coasts of Europe and North America [etym. doubtful]

scot-free (skótfri:) *adj.* not sentenced to any punishment ‖ quite unhurt [SCOT (sum of money)+FREE]

sco·tia (skóuʃə) *n.* a hollow molding near or at the base of a column [L. fr. Gk *skotia* fr. *skotos*, darkness (fr. the shadow in the molding)]

Sco·tism (skóutizəm) *n.* the philosophy of Duns Scotus [SCOTIST]

Sco·tist (skóutist) **1.** *n.* a follower of the philosophy of Duns Scotus **2.** *adj.* of or pertaining to this philosophy or its followers [fr. M.L. *Scotista*]

Scot·land (skótlənd) a country (area 30,405 sq. miles, pop. 5,130,735) occupying the north of Great Britain. It is a division of the United Kingdom. Capital: Edinburgh. Largest town: Glasgow. Language: English, with 1.5% also speaking Gaelic. Church membership: 25% Church of Scotland (Presbyterian), 15% Roman Catholic, with Nonconformist and Church of England minorities. The educational, judicial and financial systems retain many distinctive features. The land is 17% arable, 8% pasture, 16% forest, and much of the rest is rough grazing land. It is divisible into three natural zones: the Highlands, the Lowlands and the southern uplands. The Highlands in the north (1,000–over 4,000 ft, highest point: Ben Nevis, 4,406 ft) are a rocky, sparsely inhabited mountainous plateau (*CAIRNGORM MTNS, *GRAMPIANS), largely moorland, with a coastline deeply indented, esp. in the west, by firths. The Lowlands in the center are comprised mostly of the Forth and Clyde valleys (coal and iron fields, dairy pasture) and contain most of the industry and population. The southern uplands, a rolling moorland (mainly 800–2,000 ft), are cut by small fertile river valleys. Scotland has about 800 islands, including the Orkneys, Shetlands and Hebrides, and hundreds of lakes. Average temperatures (F.): (Jan.) 40°, (Jul.) 56°. Rainfall: under 30 ins along the east coast, over 80 ins along the west coast. Chief ports: Glasgow, Greenock, Leith, Aberdeen. Universities: St Andrews (1411), Glasgow (1451), Aberdeen (1494), Edinburgh (1582), Strathclyde (1964). HISTORY. The earliest inhabitants of Scotland are thought to have been of Iberian stock, and to have mingled with invading Celts (7th c. B.C.). The Romans, who named the northern part Caledonia and its inhabitants Picts, conquered the south (c. 80 A.D.) under Agricola, but were forced to withdraw behind Hadrian's Wall (early 2nd c.). The Scots, a Celtic tribe from Ireland, settled in the west (early 6th c.) and conquered the southern Picts (9th c.). The east coast was raided by Germanic tribes (4th and 5th cc.) and formed part of Northumbria. After

---

the Roman evacuation of Britain, a Romanized British kingdom was left in Strathclyde on the west coast. St Columba brought Christianity to the Picts (6th c.). The Scots, under Kenneth I, defeated the Picts (c. 841) and established a kingdom covering most of Scotland. He and his successors were involved in warfare with raiding Vikings, with Northumbria and with Strathclyde until the 10th c. Norse kingdoms were established in the Hebrides until 1266 and in Orkney and Shetland until 1472. During the reign (1057-93) of Malcolm III and his wife, St Margaret, the Scottish Church was reorganized. Feudalism was introduced in the Lowlands, while the Highlands maintained the clan system (11th c.). Scotland remained united despite sporadic wars with England caused by Norman claims to sovereignty over Scotland and by the intervention of David I in the war between Matilda and Stephen. Scotland became the feudal vassal of England (1174-89). A disputed succession to the throne (1290) enabled Edward I of England to intervene on behalf of John de Baliol, but when Baliol formed an alliance with France (1295) Edward deposed him (1296) and proclaimed himself king. The Scots revolted under Wallace and under Robert the Bruce, who claimed the throne (1306), defeated Edward II at Bannockburn (1314), and gained recognition of Scottish independence (1328). On the death (1371) of David II, Robert II became king, founding the Stuart dynasty. During the Hundred Years' War the Scots supported the French against the English. Scotland was weakened by baronial feuds and was heavily defeated at Flodden Field (1513), when James IV attempted to invade England. During the regency (1554-60) of Mary of Guise, many of the nobility became converted to Protestantism as a result of the work of Knox, and political and religious issues forced Mary Queen of Scots to abdicate (1567) in favor of her Protestant son, James VI. The latter inherited the throne of England (1603) as James I, by virtue of his descent from Margaret Tudor. The union of the two thrones remained a personal one, Scotland maintaining its own institutions and its Presbyterian religious tradition. Charles I's attempt to force the English liturgy on the Presbyterian Scots provoked the formation (1638) of the National Covenant and the outbreak of the Bishops' Wars (1639 and 1640). The Covenanters supported Cromwell in the English Civil War, but Cromwell's forced union of England and Scotland (1654) caused much resentment among the Scots, and a personal union was resumed at the Restoration. The religious policy of Charles II and James II was unpopular in Scotland. To guarantee the Hanoverian succession, Scotland and England were united by the Act of Union (1707), under which Scottish representatives would sit in the British parliament, but Scotland would keep its own laws and the Presbyterian Church. Scotland remained a center of the Jacobite cause until the mid-18th c. (For subsequent history *GREAT BRITAIN)

Scotland Yard the familiar name for the British Criminal Investigation Department of the Metropolitan Police

sco·to·ma (skoutóumə) *pl.* **sco·to·mas, sco·to·ma·ta** (skoutóumətə) *n.* a dark or blind spot in the field of vision [L.L. fr. Gk fr. *skotos*, darkness]

sco·to·pho·bin (skoutoufóubin) *n.* (*biochem.*) substance believed to encode fear-of-the-dark in the brain

sco·to·phor (skóutoufɔr) *n.* (*chem.*) a material that darkens or bleaches when exposed to X-rays, cathode rays, heat, or photons

Scots (skɒts) **1.** *adj.* Scottish **2.** *n.* the English spoken in Scotland [older *Scottis*, var. of Scottish]

Scots·man (skótsmən) *pl.* **Scots·men** (skótsmən) *n.* a Scot

Scots·wom·an (skótswʊmən) *pl.* **Scots·wom·en** (skótswɪmən) *n.* a Scottish woman

Scott (skɒt), Dred (c. 1795-1858), American Negro slave whose suit for freedom, based on his having spent a period in a non-slave state, led the U.S. Supreme Court to declare the Missouri Compromise unconstitutional (*DRED SCOTT DECISION). Scott himself was set free (1857) although technically he had lost his suit

Scott, Sir George Gilbert (1811-78), English architect. His work includes the Martyrs' Memorial at Oxford (1841), and the Albert Memorial

CONCISE PRONUNCIATION KEY: **(a)** æ, c**a**t; ɑ, c**a**r; ɔ f**aw**n; ei, sn**a**ke. **(e)** e, h**e**n; i:, sh**ee**p; iə, d**ee**r; ɛə, b**ea**r; **(i)** i, f**i**sh; ai, t**i**ger; əː, b**i**rd; **(o)** o, **o**x; au, c**ow**; ou, g**oa**t; u, p**oo**r; ɔi, r**oy**al. **(u)** ʌ, d**u**ck; u, b**u**ll; u:, g**oo**se; ə, b**a**cillus; ju:, c**u**be. x, lo**ch**; θ, **th**ink; δ, bo**th**er; z, **Z**en; ʒ, cor**s**age. dʒ, sava**ge**; ŋ, ora**ng**utang; j, **y**ak; ʃ, **fi**sh; tʃ, **fe**tch; 'l, rabb**le**; 'n, redd**en**. Complete pronunciation key appears inside front cover.

(1863-72) and St Pancras station (1865) in London. He is known chiefly for his restoration work in cathedrals and churches. He was foremost in the Victorian neo-Gothic revival

Scott, Sir Giles Gilbert (1880-1960), English architect, grandson of Sir George. His most striking work is the neo-Gothic Anglican cathedral at Liverpool, England

Scott, James Brown (1866-1943), U.S. jurist, publicist, and educator, and an influential leader in the international peace movement of the 20th c. He became (1906) founding editor of the first English-language international law periodical, and helped to establish (1914) the Academy of International Law at The Hague and (1921) the Permanent Court of International Justice

Scott, Robert Falcon (1868-1912), British naval officer and Antarctic explorer. He led two expeditions to Antarctica (1901-4 and 1909-12). On the first he carried out surveys of the Ross Sea and on the second he led a sledge journey from the Ross Sea to the South Pole, which he reached Jan. 18, 1912, shortly after Amundsen. He and his four companions died on the return journey

Scott, Sir Walter (1771-1832), Scottish poet and novelist. His work displayed his passion for the history of his country. His narrative poems, e.g. 'The Lay of the Last Minstrel' (1805), 'Marmion' (1808) and 'The Lady of the Lake' (1810), were immensely popular. The novel 'Waverley' (1814) was the first of a long series, published anonymously, including 'The Heart of Midlothian' (1818), 'Ivanhoe' (1820) and 'The Talisman' (1825). His influence can be traced in all romantic art of the early 19th c. which took balladry and folklore as its theme

Scott, Winfield (1786-1866), U.S. general, and Whig candidate for the presidency in 1852. As general officer commanding (1841-61) the U.S. Army, he won several victories during the Mexican War, notably at Veracruz, Cerro Gordo, and Chapultepec, by which he forced (1858) Mexico's surrender

Scot·ti·cism (skótisizəm) *n.* a turn of phrase, use of a word etc. characteristically Scottish [fr. L.L. *Scoticus*]

Scot·tish (skótiʃ) 1. *adj.* of or pertaining to Scotland, its people or customs, the variety of English spoken there etc. 2. *n.* the English language as spoken in Scotland [O.E. *Scottisc*]

Scottish Gaelic *GAELIC

Scottish terrier a terrier of a breed having a strong stocky build, with a large head, prick ears, short legs and thick, rough coat

Scotus, Duns *DUNS SCOTUS

scoun·drel (skáundrəl) *n.* a man who acts with shameful lack of principle **scóun·drel·ly** *adj.* [origin unknown]

scour (skáuər) 1. *v.t.* to clean by rubbing hard, esp. with an abrasive, or by flushing with a rapid flow of water ‖ to remove (dirt etc.) in this way ‖ to free from impurities, *to scour raw wool* ‖ to purge ‖ to wear away by erosion etc., *the torrent scoured a channel in the hillside* ‖ *v.i.* to perform a cleaning, removing or eroding action 2. *n.* a scouring ‖ a place eroded by scouring, *a scour in the hillside* ‖ (*pl.*) diarrhea, esp. in cattle [prob. M. Du. or M.L.G. *schuren*]

scour *v.t.* to move rapidly through or over, esp. in search of something, *she scoured the whole town for it* ‖ *v.i.* to move in this way, *scouring over the hills for bluebells* [etym. doubtful]

scourge (skə:rdʒ) *n.* (*rhet.*) a whip used to punish people ‖ someone or something causing misery, esp. on a large scale ‖ any cause of distress thought of as divine punishment [A.F. *escorge, escurge*]

scourge *pres. part.* **scourg·ing** *past* and *past part.* **scourged** *v.t.* (*rhet.*) to whip ‖ (*rhet.*) to cause extreme misery to [O.F. *escorgier*]

scout (skaut) 1. *n.* a soldier sent ahead to reconnoiter or gain information ‖ anyone whose job is to search, *a talent scout* ‖ a boy scout ‖ a girl scout ‖ a person who observes and reports on the abilities of players of rival professional or university teams ‖ the act of scouting, lookout, *on the scout for good young players* ‖ (*Br.*) a man employed by a motorists' association to assist motorists on the road ‖ (*pop.*) a fellow, *be a good scout* 2. *v.i.* to make a reconnaissance ‖ to make a search ‖ *v.t.* to observe as a scout ‖ to reconnoiter (a territory etc.) [F. *escoute,* the action of listening]

scout *n.* (*Br., hist.*) a college student's manservant at Oxford University [origin unknown]

scout *v.t.* to reject (a suggestion, statement etc.)

as being absurd or clearly untrue [of Scand. origin]

scout·ing (skáutiŋ) *n.* scouts' activities

scout·mas·ter (skáutmæstər, skáutmɑstər) *n.* a man responsible for training a troop of boy scouts

scow (skau) *n.* a large flat-bottomed boat with square ends, used esp. to transport gravel, sand etc. in bulk [Du. *schouw*]

scowl (skaul) 1. *v.i.* to frown angrily or sullenly ‖ *v.t.* to express by frowning, *he scowled his dissatisfaction* 2. *n.* an angry or sullen frown [prob. of Scand. origin]

SCP (*biol. abbr.*) for single-celled protein

scrab·ble (skræb'l) *pres. part.* **scrab·bling** *past* and *past part.* **scrab·bled** *v.i.* to make scratching movements with the fingers, hands or feet ‖ to make random, scrawling marks ‖ to climb with hasty struggling movements [Du. *schrabbelen*]

Scrabble *n.* word game played with evaluated lettered disks on a board with the object of forming words adjoining those already melded, utilizing maximum evaluations

scrag (skræg) 1. *n.* a scrawny person or animal ‖ the lean end of a neck of mutton or veal 2. *v.t. pres. part.* **scrag·ging** *past* and *past part.* **scragged** (*pop.*) to kill by hanging or by wringing or breaking the neck ‖ (*pop.*) to tackle by the neck or handle (someone) roughly [prob. altered fr. older *crag,* the neck]

scrag·gi·ly (skrǽgili:) *adv.* in a scraggy manner

scrag·gi·ness (skrǽgi:nis) *n.* the quality of being scraggy

scrag·gly (skrǽgli:) *comp.* **scrag·gli·er** *superl.* **scrag·gli·est** *adj.* sparse and unkempt, *a scraggly beard* ‖ rough and uneven, *a scraggly path* [SCRAG]

scrag·gy (skrǽgi:) *comp.* **scrag·gi·er** *superl.* **scrag·gi·est** *adj.* scrawny ‖ rough and rugged, *scraggy rocks* [SCRAG]

scram (skræm) *pres. part.* **scram·ming** *past* and *past part.* **scrammed** *v.i.* (*pop.*) to go away quickly [perh. shortened fr. SCRAMBLE]

scram·ble (skræmb'l) 1. *v. pres. part.* **scram·bling** *past* and *past part.* **scram·bled** *v.i.* to climb or move about with hasty or struggling movements, esp. on all fours, *he scrambled up the steep bank* ‖ to engage in a hasty struggle in order to obtain something desired also by others, *they scrambled for the best seats* ‖ (*football*) to carry the ball without blocker protection ‖ *v.t.* to jumble ‖ to mix thoroughly together, *scramble the cards* ‖ to superimpose other frequencies (a radio signal etc.) so that the message cannot be understood by an enemy etc. ‖ to cook (eggs) by beating them and then stirring them in a pan while they cook 2. *n.* the act or an instance of scrambling, *the way down is quite a scramble, a scramble for coins* **scrám·bler** *n.* someone who or something that scrambles, esp. a device which scrambles radio signals [etym. doubtful]

scram·jet (skrǽmjet) *n.* jet engine that depends on air pressure created by its high speed to mix with fuel to produce thrust

Scran·ton (skrǽntən) a commercial and industrial city (pop. 88,117) in N.E. Pennsylvania: textiles (esp. silk), laces, shoes, mattresses, furniture, mining machinery. It is an anthracite coal-mining center

scrap (skræp) 1. *n.* a small bit or piece torn out or broken off something, *a scrap of paper* ‖ (*pl.*) paragraphs, pictures etc. cut out of a newspaper etc. as worth keeping or suitable for pasting into an album ‖ a written or printed excerpt ‖ pieces, chips etc. of material left over or discarded, *the floor was littered with scrap* ‖ metal or other raw material recovered from old ships, cars etc. ‖ a least bit, *not a scrap of truth in it* ‖ (*pl.*) leavings, esp. leftovers of food ‖ (*pl.*) residue from fats after the oil has been pressed out 2. *v.t. pres. part.* **scrap·ping** *past* and *past part.* **scrapped** to discard as useless ‖ to break up into scrap [O.N. *skrap,* scraps, trifles]

scrap 1. *n.* (*pop.*) a fight, struggle or quarrel of short duration 2. *v.i. pres. part.* **scrap·ping** *past* and *past part.* **scrapped** (*pop.*) to engage in a scrap [origin unknown]

scrap·book (skrǽpbuk) *n.* a book with blank pages, usually with a hard cover, in which one pastes photos, clippings etc.

scrape (skreip) 1. *v. pres. part.* **scrap·ing** *past* and *past part.* **scraped** *v.t.* to remove by rubbing with a rough or sharp-edged object, *scrape the paint off the door* ‖ to bring into contact with something hard or rough in such a way as to

injure or graze, *he scraped his knee* ‖ to rub the surface of with a rough or sharp object ‖ to make smooth or clean by rubbing with an abrasive or sharp tool, *scrape the floor before applying the varnish* ‖ to cause (something) to make a harsh sound while pulling or rubbing it along a surface, *to scrape furniture across the floor* ‖ (esp. with 'out') to play (music, a tune) on a bowed stringed instrument, producing harsh, grating sounds ‖ to dig (e.g. a hole) with great difficulty, esp. with the nails ‖ (esp. with 'up' or 'together') to gather in small amounts or with difficulty, *to scrape up a team* ‖ *v.i.* to move against something roughly or graze it ‖ to clean or smooth something with an abrasive or sharp tool ‖ to make a harsh grating noise, *his chalk scraped on the blackboard* ‖ to draw back the foot in making a bow ‖ to make or save money in small amounts, with a struggle ‖ (with 'along', 'by' or 'through') to succeed barely or proceed with difficulty, *he scraped through his examination* **to bow and scrape** to make a display of deference, be obsequious 2. *n.* the act or noise of scraping ‖ an awkward or unpleasant situation, *he's always in scrapes at school* ‖ a scraped place, spot, hole etc., *a scrape on the elbow* **scráp·er** *n.* a tool used to scrape ‖ a device for scraping mud off one's shoes before going indoors ‖ (*archaeol.*) a flint implement used by prehistoric man for scraping the flesh and hair from skins [M.E. perh. fr. O.E. *scrapian*]

scrap·ple (skræp'l) *n.* a dish made by boiling together meat scraps, chopped vegetables and corn meal. They are then cooled in a mold, and fried before serving [SCRAP (small bit or piece)]

scrap·py (skrǽpi:) *comp.* **scrap·pi·er** *superl.* **scrap·pi·est** *adj.* assembled from bits and pieces, disconnected and insubstantial, *a scrappy speech* [SCRAP (small bit or piece)]

scrap·py *adj.* fond of a scrap (fight or quarrel) [SCRAP *n.*, fight, struggle]

scratch (skrætʃ) 1. *v.t.* to cut into (a surface) by forcing something hard and sharp along it ‖ to mark (something) on a surface by doing this, *he scratched his name on the post* ‖ to draw claws or nails over (the skin etc.) lightly, *to scratch one's head* ‖ to scrape with a grating noise ‖ to remove (writing etc.) by crossing out etc., *scratch his name from the list* ‖ to cancel (a match, race etc.) or to withdraw (a horse or competitor) from a race or competition ‖ (with 'together' or 'up') to gather with difficulty ‖ to divide (one's vote) or mark (a ballot) so as to divide one's vote between parties ‖ to reject (a candidate) by crossing out his name on a ballot ‖ *v.i.* to dig with the nails or claws ‖ to draw the nails etc. lightly over the skin, e.g. to relieve itching ‖ to give out a scraping noise ‖ to withdraw from a race or contest ‖ (*billiards*) to make a scratch ‖ (with 'along', 'by' or 'through') to manage with difficulty to get along or succeed 2. *n.* a mark or long, irregular, shallow cut made by scratching ‖ the noise made when a surface is scratched ‖ a slight wound, *it is only a scratch* ‖ the act of scratching, *dogs enjoy a good scratch* ‖ a line from which non-handicapped competitors start in a race etc. ‖ (*pl.*) a disease of horses resulting in scabs between the heel and pastern joint ‖ (*billiards*) a shot resulting in a penalty ‖ a meaningless mark made by a pen, pencil etc. **to start from scratch** to begin from nothing with no advantage, *he started his business from scratch* **up to scratch** reaching the required standard, *her performance was not up to scratch* 3. *adj.* assembled in a haphazard way, *a scratch team* ‖ of a competitor who has no handicap, allowance etc. [prob. fr. obs. *scrat,* to scratch+obs. *cratch,* to scratch]

scratch paper rough paper on which one jots messages, notes etc.

scratch test a test for allergy made by applying the suspected substance to a scratch in the skin

scratch·y (skrǽtʃi:) *comp.* **scratch·i·er** *superl.* **scratch·i·est** *adj.* covered with scratches ‖ causing surface irritation or itching, *scratchy wool* ‖ making a harsh, grating noise

scrawl (skrɔːl) 1. *v.* to write (something) with badly formed letters, esp. hurriedly ‖ (esp. with 'over') to cover with irregular marks or badly shaped writing 2. *n.* a piece of scrawled writing, *his signature is just a scrawl* ‖ scrawled writing **scrawl·y** *comp.* **scrawl·i·er** *superl.* **scrawl·i·est** *adj.* [perh. fr. obs. *scrawl,* to spread the limbs in a sprawling manner]

scrawn·y (skrɔ́ːni:) *comp.* **scrawn·i·er** *superl.* **scrawn·i·est** *adj.* thin and rawboned or under-nourished-looking [var. of dial. *scranny,* rel. to Norw. *skran,* lean]

scream (skri:m) 1. *v.i.* to utter a sudden high-pitched, loud cry because of fear, pain or shock ‖ to make a similar sound in laughter etc. ‖ to speak in a shrill, loud manner, esp. in anger or hysteria ‖ to produce a strident effect, *posters screamed outside the theater* ‖ *v.i.* to utter in a loud, high-pitched tone, esp. in anger or hysteria, *to scream insults* ‖ (often *refl.*) to bring to a specified state by uttering loud, high-pitched cries, *the baby screamed itself to sleep* 2. *n.* the sound made in screaming ‖ (*pop.*) someone who or something which is very funny **scréam·ing** *adj.* uttering screams ‖ strident or sensational in effect ‖ extremely funny, *a screaming farce* [M.E. *scrœmen, screamen* perh. fr. O.E.]

scree (skri:) *n.* loose fallen fragments of rock piled up against a hillside ‖ a pile of this [O.N. *skritha,* landslide]

screech (skri:tʃ) 1. *v.i.* to give a short, shrill scream ‖ to make a noise like a scream, *the brakes screeched* ‖ *v.t.* to utter with such a scream 2. *n.* the act or sound of screeching ‖ an instance of this [var. of older *scritch,* of imit. origin]

screech owl the barn owl ‖ any of several owls which screech and do not hoot

screed (skri:d) *n.* a tiresomely long discourse ‖ a long, chatty letter or other informal piece of writing ‖ a long list ‖ a strip of plaster put on a surface as a guide to the thickness of the whole plaster layer to be applied ‖ an implement of wood or metal used as a guide in surfacing a concrete pavement [var. of SHRED]

screen (skri:n) 1. *n.* a movable partition, often folding, made of wood, metal, cloth on a frame etc., used to shut off drafts etc. or to subdivide an area ‖ a fixed structure of wood, metal etc. partly separating one room or section of a building from another, e.g. a rood screen ‖ a window screen ‖ anything giving protection, esp. from observation, *a smoke screen* ‖ (*mil.*) a body of men covering the movement of troops etc. ‖ (*navy*) a formation of smaller vessels serving as a protection to a formation of larger vessels ‖ (*phys.*) a device for shielding from electric, magnetic or other interference ‖ a mesh for separating coarse and fine parts ‖ a transparency with very fine ruled lines used in halftone printing ‖ (*Br.*) a bulletin board ‖ a white surface on which filmstrips, movies etc. are projected ‖ the movie industry, *stars of stage and screen* ‖ the surface on which a television image or radar pattern is produced in a television or radar receiver ‖ (*cricket*) a large, white movable structure placed on or behind the boundary to enable the batsman to get a clear view of the ball as it leaves the bowler's hand 2. *v.t.* to shelter or conceal with or as if with a screen ‖ (*mil. and navy*) to protect with a screen ‖ to sift with a coarse mesh ‖ to make (a story etc.) into a movie ‖ to project (a movie) ‖ to subject (candidates) to exhaustive tests in order to be satisfied as to reliability, capability etc. ‖ (esp. with 'out') to separate (candidates) in this way ‖ to subject (letters, books etc.) to a similar test, e.g. for censorship purposes ‖ *v.i.* to be capable of being made into a film, *this book will screen well* **scréen·ings** *pl. n.* material separated during screening of coal, coke etc. [M.E. *skrene, skreene* perh. fr. F. *écran* and O.F. *escran*]

screen·play (skrí:nplei) the script for a movie, including stage directions, dialogue etc.

screen·wash·er (skrí:nwɒʃər) *n.* (*Br.*) a windshield wiper

screw (skru:) 1. *n.* a device for fastening things, consisting of a cylindrical or conical pin, with its surface cut in a spiral groove, which fits into a nut or bites securely into wood etc. by being turned ‖ one turn of this device ‖ a female screw ‖ a screw propeller ‖ (*games*) a turn or swerve of a ball struck so that it rotates in addition to its forward motion ‖ (*Br., pop.*) a miser ‖ (*Br., pop.*) salary, wages ‖ (*pop.*) an old broken-down horse **to have a screw loose** to be a little crazy **to put the screws** (*Br.* **screw**) **on** to increase coercive pressure on (someone) 2. *v.t.* to fasten, compress or tighten, using a screw or screws ‖ to twist ‖ (often with 'up') to contort, *to screw up one's face* ‖ (*pop.*) to extract forcefully or with difficulty, *to screw a dollar out of someone* ‖ *v.i.* to be put together or taken apart with a screw or screws, *the rack screws on to the wall* ‖ to be joined to or separated from something in the manner of a screw, *the top screws on to the jar* ‖ to rotate like a screw **to screw up one's courage** to brace oneself in order to face an ordeal,

danger etc. [prob. O.F. *escroue,* female screw, nut]

screw·ball (skrú:bɔl) 1. *n.* (*baseball*) a pitched ball which breaks in the opposite way to a curve ‖ (*pop.*) a person who is a little crazy in his behavior 2. *adj.* (*pop.*) somewhat crazy

screw coupling a collar with a female screw used to join pipes furnished with male screws (right-handed and left-handed) at their ends

screw·driv·er (skrú:draivər) *n.* a tool for tightening or loosening screws, having a thin, wedge-shaped end which fits into the groove in a screw's head

screw pine a member of *Pandanus,* fam. *Pandanaceae,* a widespread genus of trees native to tropical Asia. They have prominent prop roots, stems like those of palms, and branches with a terminal crown of long leaves

screw propeller the propeller of a ship, aircraft etc., consisting of a number of blades, each forming part of a helical surface, mounted symmetrically on a central hub at the end of a rotating shaft, so that their pressure on the water or air has a driving reaction on the vessel

screw thread the spiral ridge between the grooves of a screw ‖ the length of one turn of this ridge

screw·y (skrú:i) *comp.* **screw·i·er** *superl.* **screw·i·est** *adj.* (*pop.*) crazy ‖ (*pop.*) fantastically absurd

Scria·bin (skri:ábin, skrjábin), Alexander Nicholaevich (1872-1915), Russian composer. His work is emotionally highly charged, and he developed advanced theories of harmony to express his theosophical beliefs. His piano music includes 10 sonatas and many other works. His orchestral work includes 'Prometheus, the Poem of Fire' (1909-10)

scrib·ble (skríb'l) 1. *v.t.* and *i. pres. part.* **scrib·bling** *past* and *past part.* **scrib·bled** to write hastily and carelessly or in a hurried, badly constructed style 2. *n.* a piece of hasty writing ‖ bad handwriting or literary composition [prob. fr. M.L. *scribillare*]

scribble *pres. part.* **scrib·bling** *past* and *past part.* **scrib·bled** *v.t.* to card (wool) coarsely [prob. fr. L.G.]

scrib·bler (skríblər) *n.* a person who writes rapidly and in great quantities ‖ (*old-fash.*) a worthless writer

scribbler *n.* a machine that scribbles wool

Scribe (skri:b), Augustin Eugène (1791-1861), French playwright, master of light drama. He wrote 350 plays, as well as opera librettos for Auber, Meyerbeer etc.

scribe (skraib) 1. *n.* a person skilled in handwriting, esp. one who copied out manuscripts before the invention of printing ‖ a professional copyist or clerk ‖ an ancient Jewish interpreter of the Law ‖ a scriber 2. *v.t. pres. part.* **scrib·ing** *past* and *past part.* **scribed** to mark with a scriber ‖ to make (a line) with a scriber ‖ *v.i.* to act as a scribe **scrib·er** *n.* a pointed tool for marking wood, metal etc. with lines showing where it is to be cut [fr. L. *scriba* fr. *scribere,* to write]

scrim (skrim) *n.* a loosely woven, thin cotton fabric used in upholstering, clothing, curtains etc. ‖ (*theater*) a transparent drop curtain [etym. doubtful]

scrim·mage (skrímidʒ) 1. *n.* a confused struggle ‖ (*football*) the struggle for possession of the ball after it has been put into play by the center ‖ (*football*) practice between teams 2. *v.i. pres. part.* **scrim·mag·ing** *past* and *past part.* **scrim·maged** to engage in a scrimmage [altered fr. SKIRMISH]

scrimp (skrimp) *v.t.* to make too small, short etc. ‖ to treat stingily ‖ *v.i.* to be frugal **scrimp·y** *comp.* **scrimp·i·er** *superl.* **scrimp·i·est** *adj.* excessively meager [etym. doubtful]

scrim·shaw (skrímʃɔ) 1. *v.t.* to carve (whalebone, ivory, shells etc.) or decorate (these) with carved designs ‖ *v.i.* to engage in this work 2. *n.* a piece of such work ‖ the art or practice of scrimshawing [etym. doubtful]

scrip (skrip) *n.* (*hist.*) a small bag or satchel carried by a pilgrim or traveler [prob. O.F. *escrepe*]

scrip *n.* a provisional certificate of ownership of stock, property etc. ‖ such certificates collectively [SUBSCRIPTION]

scrip *n.* (*hist.*) paper money having a face value of less than a dollar, formerly in circulation [prob. alt. of SCRAP (small bit or piece)]

scrip dividend a dividend paid in the form of scrip (provisional certificates), not money

scrip·oph·i·ly (skripáfɪli:) *n.* (*securities*) the collection and care of bonds and stock certificates

Scripps (skrips), Edward Wyllis (1854-1926), U.S. newspaper publisher whose Cleveland Penny Press introduced (1878) into the U.S.A. the low-priced 'chain' newspaper. With his partners George Scripps and Milton McRae, he organized (1897) what eventually became the United Press. He established the Newspaper Enterprise Association, the first newspaper syndicate to serve a chain of newspapers

script (skript) *n.* handwriting as distinguished from print ‖ printer's type which imitates handwriting ‖ a style of handwriting, *Carolingian script* ‖ the printed or written text of a play, broadcast etc. ‖ (*Br.*) the written work of an examination candidate [fr. L. *scriptun,* something written]

scrip·to·ri·um (skriptóri:əm, skriptóuri:əm) *pl.* **scrip·to·ri·ums,** **scrip·to·ri·a** (skriptóri:ə, skriptóuri:ə) *n.* a room set apart for the scribes in a monastery [M.L.]

scrip·tur·al (skríptʃərəl) *adj.* pertaining to or contained in the Bible, *scriptural authority* [fr. Mod. L. *scripturalis*]

Scrip·ture (skríptʃər) *n.* (often in *pl.*) the Bible (usually omitting the Apocrypha) ‖ a passage in the Bible ‖ the study of the Bible ‖ the sacred writing or books of any religion [fr. L. *scriptura,* a writing]

script·writ·er (skríptraitər) *n.* a writer of radio or television programs or of dialogue for films

scriv·en·er (skrívnər) *n.* (*hist.*) a notary ‖ (*hist.*) a professional scribe [fr. obs. *scrivein,* professional scribe fr. O.F. *escrivein*]

scro·bic·u·late (skroubíkjulit, skroubíkjuleit) *adj.* (*biol.*) having many small furrows or depressions [fr. Mod. L. *scrobicula* or L.L. *scrobiculus,* small pit or depression]

scrod (skrɒd) *n.* a young cod. esp. one cut into strips for cooking [perh. fr. obs. Du. *schrood* and M. Du. *schrode,* a piece cut off]

scrof·u·la (skrɒfjulə) *n.* (*hist.*) tuberculosis of the lymph glands, esp. of the neck **scróf·u·lous** *adj.* afflicted with scrofula ‖ morally corrupt [after L.L. *scrofulae,* swelling of the glands, and after M. L. *scrofula*]

Scroggs (skrɒgz, skrogz) Sir William (c. 1623-83), English jurist. As lord chief justice (1678-81), he was notorious for his brutal judgments on the victims of the Popish Plot

scroll (skroul) 1. *n.* a length of parchment or paper rolled into a cylinder, esp. an ancient manuscript preserved in this form ‖ anything, esp. an ornament, having the form of a partly opened scroll of paper, e.g. the head of a violin, the legend of a decorative map etc. ‖ the volute of an Ionic or Corinthian capital 2. *v.t.* to form into a scroll ‖ to decorate with scrolls ‖ *v.i.* to roll up like scroll [earlier *scrowle, scrow* fr. O.F. *escrowe*]

scroll saw a saw consisting of a taut ribbon of steel with a toothed edge, used for sawing curves

scroll·work (skróulwə:rk) *n.* ornamental work having scrolls as its chief feature ‖ thin wood cut into designs with a scroll saw

Scrooge (skru:dʒ) *n.* (*mil.*) U.S.S.R. strategic solid-fuel nuclear missile (SS-15) with a 3,700-mi range

scro·tal (skróut'l) *adj.* of the scrotum [fr. Mod. L. *scrotalis*]

scro·tum (skróutəm) *pl.* **scro·ta** (skróutə), **scro·tums** *n.* the muscular sac containing the testicles [L.]

scrounge (skraundʒ) *pres. part.* **scroung·ing** *past* and *past part.* **scrounged** *v.t.* (*pop.*) to get by cadging ‖ (*pop.*) to get by hunting around for ‖ (*pop.*) to pilfer ‖ *v.i.* (*pop.,* esp. with 'around') to search around [etym. doubtful]

scrub (skrʌb) *n.* thick undergrowth and stunted trees etc. growing together, generally in poor soil or sand ‖ land covered with such growth ‖ a tract of such land ‖ a stunted tree or shrub ‖ (*sports*) a player not one regular team, or a team made up of such players ‖ an undersized, insignificant person or animal [var. of SHRUB]

scrub 1. *v. pres. part.* **scrub·bing** *past* and *past part.* **scrubbed** *v.t.* to clean by rubbing hard, esp. with a brush, soap and water ‖ to cleanse (a gas) so as to remove impurities ‖ *v.i.* to engage in scrubbing 2. *n.* an act or instance of scrubbing **scrub·ber** *n.* a person or thing that scrubs, esp. a device for cleansing gases, e.g. by passing them through a liquid [etym. doubtful]

scrub·ber (skrʌbər) *n.* an air-pollution-control

CONCISE PRONUNCIATION KEY: **(a)** æ, c*a*t; ɑ, c*a*r; ɔ f*aw*n; ei, sn*a*ke. **(e)** e, h*e*n; i:, sh*ee*p; iə, d*ee*r; ɛə, b*ea*r. **(i)** i, f*i*sh; ai, t*i*ger; əː, b*i*rd. **(o)** o, *o*x; au, c*ow*; ou, g*oa*t; u, p*oo*r; ɔi, r*oy*al. **(u)** ʌ, d*u*ck; u, b*u*ll; u:, g*oo*se; ə, b*a*cillus; ju:, c*u*be. x, lo*ch*; θ, *th*ink; ð, bo*th*er; z, *Z*en; ʒ, cor*s*age; dʒ, sava*ge*; ŋ, ora*ng*utang; j, *y*ak; ʃ, *fi*sh; tʃ, fe*tch*; 'l, rabb*le*; 'n, redd*en.* Complete pronunciation key appears inside front cover.

device that uses a spray of water to trap pollutants and to cool emissions

scrub oak any of several North American oaks of shrubby habit that grow on dry, rocky soil

scrub·by (skrʌ́bi:) *comp.* **scrub·bi·er** *superl.* **scrub·bi·est** *adj.* stunted ‖ covered with scrub ‖ inferior, shabby

scruff (skrʌf) *n.* the nape of the neck [corrup. of older *scuff* etym. doubtful]

scruff·y (skrʌ́fi:) *comp.* **scruff·i·er** *superl.* **scruff·i·est** *adj.* unkempt, grubby and neglected-looking ‖ (of terrain) dry, with a loose, flaky, dusty topsoil and without vegetation [var. of SCURF]

scrum (skrʌm) *n.* (*rugby*) a formation of the forwards of each team, crouching so that the two front rows meet shoulder to shoulder, and pushing in order to gain possession of the ball [abbr. of SCRUMMAGE]

scrum half (*rugby*) the halfback who puts the ball into the scrum ‖

scrum·mage (skrʌ́midʒ) 1. *n.* (*rugby*) a scrum 2. *v.i. pres. part.* **scrum·mag·ing** *past and past part.* **scrum·maged** (often with 'down') to form a scrum [var. of SCRIMMAGE]

scrump·tious (skrʌ́mpʃəs) *adj.* (*pop.*) delicious ‖ (*pop.*) delightful [etym. doubtful]

scrunch (skrʌntʃ, skrʌntʃ) 1. *v.t.* to crunch ‖ *v.i.* to make a crunching sound ‖ to crouch, esp. in a confined space 2. *n.* the sound of scrunching, *the scrunch of footsteps on gravel* [var. of CRUNCH]

scru·ple (skrú:p'l) 1. *n.* a feeling of uneasiness, doubt, objection or reluctance based on principle or propriety 2. *v.i. pres. part.* **scru·pling** *past and past part.* **scru·pled** (usually with *infin.*) to hesitate because of scruples, *he would not scruple to lie* [fr. F. *scrupule* fr. L. *scrupulus*]

scruple *n.* a unit of apothecaries' weight (=20 grains or one-third dram) [fr. L. *scrupulus*]

scru·pu·los·i·ty (skru:pjulósiti:) *pl.* **scru·pu·los·i·ties** *n.* the quality of being scrupulous, esp. to excess ‖ an instance of this [F. *scrupulosité* or fr. L. *scrupulositas*]

scru·pu·lous (skrú:pjuləs) *adj.* strictly honest and adhering to moral principles ‖ painstakingly thorough [fr. F. *scrupuleux* or L. *scrupulosus*]

scru·ti·neer (skru:t'níər) (*Br.*) a canvasser (person who checks the validity of ballot papers)

scru·ti·nize (skrú:t'naiz) *pres. part.* **scru·ti·niz·ing** *past and past part.* **scru·ti·nized** *v.t.* to examine with care and in detail [SCRUTINY]

scru·ti·ny (skrú:t'ni:) *pl.* **scru·ti·nies** *n.* close, searching examination ‖ an instance of this ‖ a steady, penetrating gaze ‖ (*Br.*) a fresh count and examination of ballot papers in an election [fr. L.L. *scrutinium* fr. L. *scrutari*, to search carefully, examine]

scu·ba (skú:bə) *n.* a breathing apparatus for free-swimming divers, consisting of a tank of compressed air strapped to the back and connected by a hose to the diver's mouth [SELF-CONTAINED UNDERWATER BREATHING APPARATUS]

scud (skʌd) 1. *v.i. pres. part.* **scud·ding** *past and past part.* **scud·ded** (esp. of a ship running before a gale) to go swiftly 2. *n.* a scudding ‖ thin clouds driven by a strong wind ‖ a gust of wind ‖ a brief shower of rain ‖ ocean spray etc. driven by the wind [etym. doubtful]

Scud (skʌd) *n.* (*mil.*) NATO name for SS-1, a U.S.S.R. mobile land missile with nuclear capability

Scu·dé·ry (skydeiri:), Madeleine de (1607–1701), French novelist. She collaborated with her brother Georges (1601–68) in sentimental novels with historical backgrounds, e.g. 'Clélie' (1654–61). The characters give an insight into 17th-c. society

scuff (skʌf) 1. *v.i.* to walk by scraping or dragging the feet along the ground instead of lifting them ‖ to become worn, chipped etc. ‖ repeated friction, *this surface scuffs easily* ‖ *v.t.* to scrape or drag (the feet) in walking ‖ to cause wear to by repeated friction, *to scuff one's shoes* 2. *n.* a scuffling or a scuffling sound ‖ a worn spot ‖ a soft, flat house slipper without a heel [perh. imit. or rel. to SCUFF]

scuf·fle (skʌ́f'l) 1. *v.i. pres. part.* **scuf·fling** *past and past part.* **scuf·fled** to struggle or scrap in a confused way at close quarters ‖ to move about hurriedly with confused sounds 2. *n.* a confused struggle or scrap at close quarters ‖ the act or sound of scuffling [perh. fr. Scand.]

scuffle hoe a hoe sharpened on both front and

rear edge for cutting by pushing or pulling under the surface of soil

scull (skʌl) 1. *n.* one of a pair of short oars used by one person in rowing a boat ‖ a single oar used at the stern in propelling a boat ‖ a sculler (boat) 2. *v.t.* to propel (a boat) using sculls or a scull ‖ to convey (a person etc.) in a boat which one sculls, *he sculled them back to shore* ‖ *v.i.* to use sculls or a scull in propelling a boat ‖ (of a boat) to be able to be propelled with a scull or sculls **scúll·er** *n.* a person who sculls ‖ a boat designed for sculling [etym. doubtful]

scul·ler·y (skʌ́ləri:) *pl.* **scul·ler·ies** *n.* a room adjacent to a kitchen, equipped and used for washing and cleaning cooking utensils, cleaning and preparing vegetables etc. [O.F. *escuelerie*]

scul·lion (skʌ́ljən) *n.* (*hist.*) a servant of low status who did the work in a scullery [perh. alt. of F. *souillon*, dirty person]

scul·pin (skʌ́lpin) *pl.* **scul·pin, scul·pins** *n.* any of several Atlantic sea fishes of fam. *Cottidae*, order *Scleroparei*, having large, spiny heads [etym. doubtful]

sculpt (skʌlpt) *v.i.* to make a sculpture or practice sculpture ‖ *v.t.* to sculpture (a figure etc.) [fr. F. *sculpter*]

sculp·tor (skʌ́lptər) *n.* a person who makes sculptures **scúlp·tress** *n.* a female sculptor [L.]

sculp·tur·al (skʌ́lptʃərəl) *adj.* of or pertaining to sculpture ‖ having the qualities of sculpture

sculp·ture (skʌ́lptʃər) 1. *n.* the making of three-dimensional works of art in stone, clay, metal, wood etc. ‖ one of these works ‖ such works collectively ‖ (*biol.*) markings in relief 2. *v.t. pres. part.* **sculp·tur·ing** *past and past part.* **sculp·tured** to represent by, or ornament with, sculpture ‖ to make sculpture out of (stone, clay, metal etc.) ‖ to carve [fr. L. *sculptura* fr. *sculpere*, to carve]

scum (skʌm) 1. *n.* impurities which rise to the surface of a liquid and collect on it, esp. during fermentation or boiling ‖ the light, floating skinlike mass so formed ‖ the residue of oxides etc. which floats on a molten metal ‖ people of a class that one regards with profound contempt 2. *v. pres. part.* **scum·ming** *past and past part.* **scummed** *v.i.* to become covered with scum ‖ *v.t.* to cover with scum [M.L.G. *schûm* and M. Du. *schume*]

scum·ble (skʌmb'l) 1. *v.t. pres. part.* **scum·bling** *past and past part.* **scum·bled** to lay a thin coat of opaque or nearly opaque color on (color or a painting) in order to break up the surface and render it less brilliant ‖ to apply (color) for this purpose ‖ to soften the lines or colors of (a drawing) by lightly rubbing them 2. *n.* the effect produced by scumbling ‖ the material used for scumbling [perh. fr. SCUM]

scum·my (skʌ́mi:) *comp.* **scum·mi·er** *superl.* **scum·mi·est** *adj.* of, like or covered with scum

scun·cheon (skʌ́ntʃən) *n.* (*archit.*) an arch etc. put across the corners of a square tower to give the additional supports for an octagonal spire ‖ (*archit.*) a splay etc. in an embrasure [O.F. *escoinson*]

scup (skʌp) *n.* either of two edible sea fish, *Stenotomus chrysops* and *S. aculeatus*, fam. *Sparidae*, found on the Atlantic coast of the U.S.A. [fr. Narragansett *mishcup*]

scup·per (skʌ́pər) 1. *n.* an aperture which enables water to escape overboard from the deck of a ship 2. *v.t.* (*Br.*, *pop.*) to sink (a ship) ‖ (*Br.*, *pop.*) to wreck or spoil (a plan etc.) [etym. doubtful]

scup·per·nong (skʌ́pərnɔŋ, skʌ́pərnɒŋ) *n.* any of several large, yellowish-green muscadine grapes of the southeastern U.S.A., esp. the fruit of *Vitis rotundifolia* ‖ a wine made from these grapes [after the *Scuppernong* River, North Carolina]

scurf (skə:rf) *n.* small flakes of dry skin, easily becoming detached, esp. on the scalp ‖ any scaly surface matter **scúrf·y** *comp.* **scurf·i·er** *superl.* **scurf·i·est** *adj.* like scurf ‖ covered with scurf [O.E.]

scur·ril·i·ty (skəríliti:) *pl.* **scur·ril·i·ties** *n.* the quality of being scurrilous ‖ scurrilous language or a scurrilous remark [F. *scurrilité* or fr. L. *scurrilitas*]

scur·ril·ous (skə́riləs) *adj.* expressed in or using language which is offensively or indecently abusive [fr. obs. *scurrile* fr. F. or fr. L. *scurrilis*, like a buffoon]

scur·ry (ská:ri:, skʌ́ri:) 1. *v.i. pres. part.* **scur·**

ry·ing *past and past part.* **scur·ried** to move along quickly, esp. with hurried little steps 2. *pl.* **scur·ries** *n.* a hurried moving along, or an instance of this ‖ gust, a *scurry of rain* [perh. fr. HURRY-SCURRY]

scur·vi·ly (ská:rvili:) *adv.* in a scurvy manner

scur·vi·ness (ská:rvi:nis) *n.* the quality of being scurvy

scur·vy (ská:rvi:) 1. *comp.* **scur·vi·er** *superl.* **scur·vi·est** *adj.* (*rhet.*) meriting contempt, vile, *a scurvy trick* 2. *n.* a disease characterized by skin spots, swollen gums, bleeding in the mucous membranes and general debility, caused by a deficiency of vitamin C in the diet for a long period of time [SCURF]

scurvy grass *Cochlearia officinalis*, an Arctic cress with pleasantly sharp-tasting leaves, said to prevent scurvy

scut (skʌt) *n.* the short tail of a rabbit, hare, deer etc. [etym. doubtful]

scu·tage (skjú:tidʒ) *n.* (*hist.*) a feudal tax paid by the tenant of a knight's fee in lieu of military service [fr. M.L. *scutagium*]

scu·tal (skjú:t'l) *adj.* of or having the nature of a scute or scutum [fr. Mod. L. *scutalis* fr. L. *scutum*, shield]

Scu·ta·ri (skú:tari:) (*Turk.* Uskudar) *ISTANBUL

Scutari *SHKODËR

Scutari, Lake *SHKODËR

scu·tate (skjú:teit) *adj.* (*zool.*) protected by large scales or horny plates ‖ (*bot.*) shaped like a shield [fr. L. *scutatus* fr. *scutum*, shield]

scutch (skʌtʃ) *v.t.* to remove the woody fibers from (flax, hemp etc.) by beating [O.F. *escousser*, to shake]

scutch *n.* a scutcher ‖ a tool used by bricklayers in cutting and shaping [O.F. *escouche*]

scutch·eon (skʌ́tʃən) *n.* an escutcheon ‖ a scute ‖ the frame or cover of a keyhole [ESCUTCHEON]

scutch·er (skʌ́tʃər) *n.* a tool or machine for scutching [SCUTCH v.]

scute (skju:t) *n.* (*zool.*) an external hard scale, esp. of a reptile, fish or scaly insect (cf. SCUTUM) [fr. L. *scutum*, shield]

scu·tel·late (skju:télit, skju:téleit, skjú:t'leit) *adj.* (*biol.*) flat, with a round or oval shape like a shield ‖ (*zool.*) having small plates or scales

scu·tel·lat·ed (skjú:t'leitid) *adj.* (*zool.*) scutellate **scu·tel·la·tion** (skju:t'léiʃən) *n.* (*zool.*) the manner in which scales or plates are arranged [fr. Mod. L. *scutellatus* fr. L. *scutella*, platter]

scu·tel·lum (skju:téləm) *pl.* **scu·tel·la** (skju:télə) *n.* (*zool.*) a small scale or plate, e.g. one of the tarsal scales of a bird ‖ (*bot.*) the shield-shaped cotyledon which separates the embryo from the endosperm in the seeds of grasses [Mod. L. fr. L. *scutella*, platter]

scu·ti·form (skjú:tiform) *adj.* (*biol.*) shaped like a shield [fr. Mod. L. *scutiformis* fr. L. *scutum*, shield]

scut·ter (skʌ́tər) 1. *v.i.* (*Br.*) to scurry 2. *n.* (*Br.*) a scurrying [perh. fr. SCUTTLE]

scut·tle (skʌ́t'l) 1. *v.i. pres. part.* **scut·tling** *past and past part.* **scut·tled** to scurry 2. *n.* a scuttling pace [etym. doubtful]

scuttle *n.* a small container holding coal, coke etc. for replenishing a fire [O.E. *scutel*, a dish, fr. M.L. *scutila* and L. *scutella*]

scuttle 1. *n.* (*naut.*) a hole in the side or deck of a ship, furnished with a movable cover ‖ the cover itself ‖ a similar opening in the roof or floor of a building, or the cover for this 2. *v.t. pres. part.* **scut·tling** *past and past part.* **scut·tled** to make or open holes in (a ship) below water level in order to sink it [etym. doubtful]

scu·tum (skjú:təm) *pl.* **scu·ta** (skjú:tə) *n.* (*zool.*) a horny, bony or chitinous plate, esp. the second of four parts which make up the upper surface of a thoracic segment in an insect (cf. SCUTE) [L.=shield]

scut work (skʌt) (*slang*) hospital staff term for unpleasant work, esp. trivial chores, paperwork, or work that could be done by someone else

Scyl·la and Charybdis (sílə) (*Gk mythol.*) the personification of a rock (Scylla) and a whirlpool (Charybdis), navigation hazards flanking Italy's narrow straits of Messina **between Scylla and Charybdis** in great difficulties no matter which of two alternative courses of action is chosen

scy·pho·zo·an (saifəzóuən) 1. *n.* a member of *Scyphozoa*, a class of coelenterates including many jellyfish of large size 2. *adj.* of or relating to this class [fr. Mod. L. *Scyphozoa* fr. Gk *skuphos*, cup + *zōon*, animal]

scy·phus (sáifəs) *pl.* **scy·phi** (sáifai) *n.* an an-

CONCISE PRONUNCIATION KEY: **(a)** æ, c*a*t; ɑ, c*a*r; ɔ f*aw*n; ei, sn*a*ke. **(e)** e, h*e*n; i:, sh*ee*p; iə, d*ee*r; ɛə, b*ea*r. **(i)** i, f*i*sh; ai, t*i*ger; ə:, b*i*rd. **(o)** o, *o*x; au, c*ow*; ou, g*oa*t; u, p*oo*r; ɔi, r*oy*al. **(u)** ʌ, d*u*ck; u, b*u*ll; u:, g*oo*se; ə, b*a*cillus; ju:, c*u*be. x, lo*ch*; θ, *th*ink; ð, *b*other; z, *Z*en; ʒ, cor*s*age; dʒ, sa*v*age; ŋ, ora*n*gutang; j, *y*ak; ʃ, *f*ish; tʃ, *f*etch; 'l, rabb*le*; 'n, redd*en*. Complete pronunciation key appears inside front cover.

cient Greek drinking cup with two handles || (*bot.*) a cup-shaped part, e.g. the corona of certain flowers [L. fr. Gk *skuphos*]

scythe (saið) 1. *n.* a long, curved blade with a sharp edge on the inner side of the curve, fitted to a long wooden handle, used by a person standing up to cut long grass etc. with steady, sweeping pulls 2. *v.t. pres. part.* **scyth·ing** *past and past part.* **scythed** to cut with a scythe [O.E. *sīthe*]

Scyth·i·a (síθi:ə) an ancient region of S.E. Europe and Asia, inhabited by the Scythians, centered north of the Black Sea on the lower Don and Dnieper

Scyth·i·an (síθi:ən) 1. *n.* a member of a nomadic Indo-European people who settled in Scythia before the 7th c. B.C. and were displaced (3rd c. B.C.) by the Sarmatians. They were specially noted in warfare for their mounted archers and in art for their rich gold ornaments || their Iranian language 2. *adj.* of Scythia, its people or its language

S. D. South Dakota

S. Dak. South Dakota

SDI (*computer abbr.*) for selective dissemination of information, program to distribute material based on recipient's declaration of interests

SDR (*economics abbr.*) of special drawing rights by nations from the International Monetary Fund *Cf* PAPER GOLD

SDS (*abbr.*) for Students for a Democratic Society, a radical organization originally formed in 1962 at the University of Michigan and later on college campuses throughout the U.S.; active during the late 1960s and early 1970s *Cf* NEW LEFT, WEATHERMAN

SE, S.E. Southeast, Southeastern

sea (si:) *n.* the continuous body of salt water covering most of the earth's surface || a named portion of this body of water, smaller than an ocean, sometimes partly or wholly enclosed by land || (only in names) a vast inland lake of salt or fresh water, e.g. the Sea of Galilee || the surface condition of the ocean with respect to the degree or type of movement of the waves, *a rough sea* || movement of the ocean's surface, *there is a strong sea running between the islands* || a heavy swell or wave || a vast expanse, quantity or mass, *a sea of memoranda* **at sea** on the sea || not knowing how to act or proceed, bewildered **to go to sea** to become a sailor [O. E. *sǣ*]

sea anchor a drag anchor

sea anemone a member of *Actiniaria*, an order of polyps of varied, often brilliant colors, living fixed to shore rocks. They have tentacles around the mouth which are armed with stinging cells for preying on small animals

sea bass any of many sea fishes of fam. *Serranidae*, esp. *Centropristes striatus*, of the Atlantic coast of the U.S.A., which is valued as a food fish

Sea·bee (síːbiː) *n.* a member of any of the construction battalions of the Civil Engineer Corps of the U.S. Navy, responsible for building bases, harbors etc. [fr. the pronunciation of the initials of 'construction battalion']

sea·bird (síːbərd) *n.* any of various birds, e.g. gulls and petrels, that fly over the open sea and frequent the seashore

sea·board (síːbɔrd, síːbourd) 1. *n.* the strip of land nearest to a seacoast 2. *adj.* bordering on the sea

Sea·borg (síːbɔrg), Glenn Theodore (1912-), U.S. physical chemist and cowinner (with Edwin M. McMillan) of the 1951 Nobel prize in chemistry for the discovery of eight new elements with atomic numbers 94-101, notably plutonium (94)

sea·borne (síːbɔrn, síːbourn) *adj.* carried on or conveyed by the sea

sea bream any of several edible seafishes of the suborder *Percoidea*, order *Percomorphi*

sea breeze a cool breeze from over the sea, replacing hotter air rising over the land

sea calf *Phoca vitulina*, a common seal of the N. Atlantic coasts, about 4 ft long

sea coal (*hist.*) (so called because it was transported by sea, esp. to London, from the mines of N.E. England)

sea·coast (síːkoust) *n.* the edge or strip of land adjacent to the sea

Sea Cobra (*mil.*) a single-rotor light attack helicopter (AH-1) armed with a variety of machine guns, rockets, grenade launchers, and antitank missiles

sea cow any large herbivorous aquatic mam-

mal of the order *Sirenia*, e.g. the manatee and the dugong || a walrus || a hippopotamus

sea cucumber a holothurian

sea dog an old, experienced sailor || (*hist.*) a pirate || a dogfish || the sea calf

Sea Dyak *DYAK

sea eagle any of several eagles which feed on fish, e.g. *Haliaëtus albicilla* || the osprey

sea-ear (síːjər) *n.* a haliotis

sea elephant an elephant seal

sea fan a member of *Gorgonia*, fam. *Gorgoniidoe*, a genus of corals with fanlike branches

sea·far·er (síːfɛərər) *n.* a mariner, or anyone traveling by sea

sea·far·ing (síːfɛəriŋ) 1. *n.* the occupation of a sailor || travel by sea 2. *adj.* working as a sailor || traveling on the sea || relating to seafaring

sea farming *v. pres. part.* cultivation of plants and animals in the ocean *also* mariculture

sea·flow·er (síːflauər) *n.* a sea anemone

sea-foam (síːfoum) *n.* the foam formed by turbulent seawater || meerschaum

sea·food (síːfuːd) *n.* food extracted from the sea, esp. shellfish

sea·front (síːfrʌnt) *n.* that part of a town etc. directly facing the sea

Se·aga (si:úgə), Edward Phillip George (1930-), Jamaican politician, prime minister (1980-). As a member of the House of Representatives he was minister of development and welfare (1962-7) and of finance and planning (1967-72). He worked to stabilize the economy and fostered ties with the U.S.A.

sea·girt (síːgəːrt) *adj.* (esp. *rhet.*) surrounded by sea

sea·go·ing (síːgouiŋ) *adj.* (of a vessel) designed for sailing on the sea, not built only for river or harbor use

sea grass any of certain plants growing by or in the sea, esp. eelgrass

sea green a bluish-green or yellow-green color **séa-green** *adj.* having such a color

sea gull a gull

sea hare a number of *Tethys*, fam. *Tethyidae*, a genus of large gastropod mollusks of sluglike appearance, with a prominent front pair of tentacles

sea holly *Eryngium maritimum*, fam. *Umbelliferae*, a prickly evergreen plant common among sand dunes

sea horse a member of *Hippocampus*, fam. *Syngnathidae*, a genus of small tropical or subtropical bony, lophobranch fishes having a body shaped like the head and arched neck of a horse, ending with a prehensile tail || a walrus || (*mythol.*) a creature half horse and half fish

Sea Island cotton a long-fibered cotton originally grown in the Sea Islands of the Atlantic, off the southern U.S.A., now also grown in the West Indies and on the southern U.S. coast

sea kale *Crambe maritima*, a European cruciferous perennial plant, native to northern temperate coasts. It is cultivated for its large leaves which are eaten as a vegetable

sea king a Norse pirate chief in the Middle Ages

Sea-King *n.* (*mil.*) a single-rotor medium-lift helicopter (SH-3) utilized for air/sea rescue and personnel/cargo transport

seal (siːl) 1. *pl.* **seals, seal** *n.* any of several fish-eating mammals of fam. *Phocidae* (lacking external ears) and fam. *Otariidae* (having external ears), suborder *Pinnipedia*. They have a thick, smooth coat and limbs like flippers adapted for swimming. They are hunted for their hide, for their pelt, and for their oil-yielding blubber || the valuable pelt of one of these animals, used for coats etc. || leather made from their hide 2. *v.i.* to hunt seals [O. E. *seolh*]

seal *n.* a device, e.g. a metal die or semiprecious stone, having a design which can be impressed into a plastic material (wax, lead etc.) || the design on this device used as a personal or official emblem || the piece of plastic material thus impressed, attached to a document as a sign of its authenticity, or covering a join in an envelope or wrapping so that it cannot be opened without the seal being broken || anything which serves to keep something secured or closed, e.g. a water seal in a pipe || an absolute obligation, *to put someone under the seal of secrecy* || a decorative adhesive stamp other than a postage stamp, put on an envelope etc. || a sign or guarantee of authority, approval etc., *he gave it the seal of his consent* [O.F. *seel*]

seal *v.t.* to attach or mark with a seal, *to sign and seal a document* || to close up thoroughly, *to seal a crack with putty* || to confirm the validity,

authenticity etc. of, *they sealed the bargain with a handshake* || (*fig.*) to make certain, irrevocable etc., *that fact sealed his doom* || to stamp (e.g. merchandise) as official evidence of standard quality, weight, capacity etc. [O.F. *seeler, seieler*]

Sealab *n.* underwater habitat for U.S. navy researchers

seal·ant (síːlənt) *n.* (*dentistry*) liquid plastic filler

sea lavender a member of *Limonium*, fam. *Plumbaginaceae*, a genus of maritime plants having spikes or panicles of white, pink or yellow flowers

sea lawyer (*pop.*) someone subject to discipline, esp. a sailor, who is given to quoting glibly from the regulations to avoid work or protect his own rights or privileges

sealed orders orders, e.g. to a ship's captain, which must not be opened or read until a fixed place or time has been reached

sea legs the ability to maintain balance and feel well on board ship at sea

seal·er (síːlər) *n.* a person or vessel engaged in seal hunting

sealer *n.* someone who or something which seals || an official who sets a seal on an article he has judged acceptable as to quality, weight etc. || a coat of material applied to a surface to prevent the top layer of paint or varnish from sinking in

sea level the horizontal line midway between high and low water, used as a line of reference from which to measure the altitude of positions on land

sea lily any crinoid, esp. one having a stalk

sealing wax a mixture of shellac, turpentine and pigment which is hard and brittle at room temperature but softens and becomes plastic when heated. It is used to seal documents, letters etc.

sea lion any of several large seals of the Pacific Ocean, having ears

seal point a Siamese cat of a strain having a fawn or creamy body and brown points (cf. BLUE POINT)

seal ring a signet ring

seal·skin (síːlskin) *n.* the skin of a seal, esp. with the soft fur || a coat or jacket made from this

Seal·y·ham (síːliːhæm, síːliːəm) *n.* a terrier of a Welsh breed with short legs, long head and long body, noted for its high spirits [after *Sealyham, Wales*]

seam (siːm) 1. *n.* a line of stitches where two pieces of cloth have been sewn together || any visible line, fold or ridge showing where two parts of a surface are joined || such a line etc. showing where two surfaces have been divided, e.g. a thin layer of coal etc. between two strata of rock || a scar or wrinkle of the skin || (*knitting*) a line of purled stitches making or resembling a seam 2. *v.t.* to join by a seam || to make an ornamental seam in, e.g. with purl stitch in knitting || to mark with a scar or wrinkle, *a face seamed with care* [O. E. *sēam*]

sea·man (síːmən) *pl.* **sea·men** (síːmən) *n.* a sailor below the rank of officer **séa·man·like** *adj.* characteristic of or like a good seaman **séa·man·ship** *n.* the art and skill of handling a vessel, esp. of navigating

sea·mark (síːmɑrk) *n.* an object on land, visible from the sea, serving to guide navigators of vessels || a line on the shore marking the upper limit of the tide

sea mew a gull, esp. *Larus canus*, a common gull of Europe

sea mile a nautical mile

sea mouse a member of *Aphrodite*, fam. *Aphroditidae*, a genus of marine polychaete worms, inhabiting deep water. They have iridescent setae fringing the sides of their bodies

seam·stress (síːmstris, *Br.* esp. sémstris) *n.* a woman who makes her living by sewing [O.E. *sēamestre*]

seam·y (síːmiː) *comp.* **seam·i·er** *superl.* **seam·i·est** *adj.* having seams **the seamy side** the sordid aspect of something

Sean·ad Éir·eann (sænədɛərən) the Senate of the Irish Republic, the upper house of the legislature

sé·ance (séiɑns) *n.* a meeting of persons for some purpose, esp. a spiritualist meeting [F. = a sitting]

sea onion a squill

sea otter *Enhydra lutris*, fam. *Mustelidae*, a rare marine mammal, sometimes reaching 6 ft in length, living on some coasts of the N.

CONCISE PRONUNCIATION KEY: **(a)** æ, c*a*t; ɑ, c*ar*; ɔ f*aw*n; ei, sn*a*ke. **(e)** e, h*e*n; iː, sh*ee*p; iə, d*ee*r; ɛə, b*ear*. **(i)** i, f*i*sh; ai, t*i*ger; əː, b*ir*d. **(o)** o, *o*x; au, c*ow*; ou, g*oa*t; u, p*oo*r; ɔi, r*oy*al. **(u)** ʌ, d*u*ck; u, b*u*ll; uː, g*oo*se; ə, b*a*cillus; juː, c*u*be. x, lo*ch*; θ, *th*ink; ð, bo*th*er; z, *Z*en; ʒ, corsa*g*e. dʒ, sava*g*e; ŋ, ora*ng*utang; j, *y*ak; ʃ, *fi*sh; tʃ, fe*tch*; 'l, rabb*le*; 'n, redd*en*. Complete pronunciation key appears inside front cover.

Pacific. It has short legs, webbed hind feet and feeds on shellfish ‖ its extremely valuable dark brown fur

sea pen a member of *Pennatula*, fam. *Pennatulidae*, or related genera of alcyonarians, the colonies of which have a feathery form

sea·plane (síːplein) *n.* an airplane having floats which enable it to rest on, take off from, and come down on water

sea·port (síːpɔrt, síːpourt) *n.* a town on a seacoast, or connected by river with the coast, having a harbor, docks etc., used by seagoing vessels

sea power naval strength ‖ a nation which has great naval strength

sea purse the horny egg case of certain rays, sharks or skates. It has filaments by which it becomes attached, e.g. to seaweed

sear (siər) *v.t.* to wither by applying heat and thus drying ‖ to burn or scorch ‖ to brown quickly the outside of (a piece of meat) so as to seal in the juices ‖ to cauterize [O.E. *sēarian*]

sear *n.* the catch which holds the hammer of a firearm at half cock or full cock [etym. doubtful]

sear *adj.* *SERE

search (səːrtʃ) *n.* an investigation or scrutiny, in order to find something, gain information etc. ‖ (*maritime law*) the exercise of the right of search **in search of** looking for, searching for [A.F. *serche* and O.F. *cerche*]

search *v.t.* to go or look into, over or through in order to find something, gain information etc., *he searched the records for their address* ‖ to examine the clothing and body of (a person) to see if he is concealing something ‖ *v.i.* to make a search **search·ing** *adj.* thorough, *a searching examination* ‖ (*fig.*) penetrating, *searching glances* [O.F. *cerchier*]

search-and-de·stroy (səːrtʃænddistrói) *adj.* of the antiguerrilla warfare tactic of clearing an area of the enemy forces

search·light (səːrtʃlait) *n.* a device whereby light from a source of great illuminating power is reflected from a paraboloidal mirror as an almost parallel beam, losing little intensity by spreading and thus brightly illuminating an object in the area which it sweeps. It is used to discover hostile aircraft, ships etc. at night

search warrant a written authorization, given to the police by a court, to enter specified private premises in order to make a search for stolen goods, fugitives from justice etc.

Seasat *n.* 5,000-lb research satellite devoted to ocean observation, with 14 daily orbits of earth

sea·scape (síːskeip) *n.* a painting or drawing in which the sea is a prominent feature

sea scout (*Br.*) a boy scout in a unit which gives training in seamanship

sea serpent a sea snake ‖ a mythological sea monster

sea·shell (síːʃel) *n.* the shell of any marine animal

sea·shore (síːʃɔr, síːʃour) *n.* the land immediately adjacent to the sea ‖ (*law*) the ground between low-water and high-water marks

sea·sick (síːsik) *adj.* suffering from seasickness **séa·sick·ness** *n.* nausea and vomiting caused by reaction to the motion of a vessel at sea

sea·side (síːsaid) 1. *n.* the seacoast, esp. as a place for holidays 2. *adj.* at or pertaining to the seaside

sea skimmer *n.* (*mil.*) a missile designed to transit at less than 50 ft above the surface of the sea

sea slug a holothurian ‖ a nudibranch

sea snail any marine gastropod mollusk with a spiral shell, e.g. a whelk ‖ any of several small slimy fishes of fam. *Liparididae* having a sucker

sea snake any of several poisonous aquatic fish-eating snakes of fam. *Hydrophidae*, inhabiting esp. tropical seas

sea·son (síːzn) *n.* a period in the year regarded as having its own characteristic weather, length of days etc., esp. any of the four divisions of the year (spring, summer, autumn and winter) running from equinox to solstice and from solstice to equinox ‖ a period during which something flourishes, or the period most favorable or suitable for something, *the strawberry season, this is not the season for harvesting* ‖ the period during which a specified activity is or may be engaged in, in which a specified event, festival etc. takes place, or during which something is active, *hunting season, Christmas season, the orchestra's season lasts 40 weeks* ‖ a period of great activity of a specified nature, *the*

social season ‖ the period of greatest social activity in a specified place, *the London season* ‖ (*Br.*) a season ticket **in good season** early enough **in season** (of fruit, vegetables, shellfish etc.) being harvested after growing under natural climatic conditions and hence available fresh at relatively cheap prices ‖ (of game) legally open to hunting ‖ (of a bitch etc.) in heat ‖ at the proper time **out of season** not in season [M.E. *seson* fr. O.F. *seson, seison*]

season *v.t.* to dry out and harden (lumber) for use, by exposure or heat ‖ to make more suitable for efficient use or bring into good condition by long, slow usage, *a seasoned pipe* ‖ to give long experience to, *a seasoned veteran* ‖ to add condiments or spices to (food) in order to enhance the flavor ‖ to make more tolerable or pleasant, *to season adverse comments with compliments* ‖ *v.i.* to go through the process of being seasoned by exposure, heat etc. [O.F. *saisonner*]

sea·son·a·ble (síːzənəb'l) *adj.* suitable to the season, *seasonable weather* ‖ opportune, *seasonable advice* **séa·son·a·bly** *adv.*

sea·son·al (síːzən'l) *adj.* characteristic of a season or the seasons, *seasonal storms* ‖ occurring at, determined by or active during a certain season or seasons, *seasonal work*

sea·son·ing (síːzəniŋ) *n.* something (e.g. salt, spices etc.) added to food to enhance the flavor ‖ something which seasons

season ticket a ticket entitling one to admission, service etc., for use over an extended specified period

Sea Sparrow *n.* (*mil.*) Navy solid-fuel, radar-directed 500-lb missile, with a 25-mi range *Cf* SPARROW

Sea Sprite *n.* (*mil.*) a single-rotor light-lift helicopter (SH-2), utilized for air/sea rescue, personnel/cargo transport and antisubmarine operations from ships

sea squirt a simple ascidian (so called because it contracts and squirts water when touched)

Sea Stallion *n.* (*mil.*) a single-rotor heavy-lift helicopter (CH-53 and RH-53) utilized for personnel/cargo transport

seat (siːt) 1. *n.* anything on which one sits or may sit ‖ that part of a chair etc. which supports the weight of the person sitting ‖ the place where one habitually sits, *that is the old man's seat* ‖ that part of a structure which acts as a support ‖ the buttocks ‖ the part of a pair of pants or skirt which covers the buttocks ‖ posture on horseback, *he has a good seat* ‖ a country mansion ‖ a center of some activity etc., *a seat of learning* ‖ the place at which some condition originates, *the seat of the trouble* ‖ the right of membership in an administrative or legislative body, *a seat on the board* **to take a seat** to sit down **to take one's seat** to sit down in the seat allotted to one (at table, in a theater etc.) ‖ to assume membership formally in Parliament 2. *v.t.* to cause to sit down ‖ to provide seats for, *the theater seats 1,000 people* ‖ to allot a seat or seats to in a certain place, *they had been seated behind a pillar* ‖ to furnish (a chair etc.) with a seat, or a new seat ‖ (*mech.*) to give a seating to, *to seat an axle* **to be seated** to sit down ‖ to be sitting **séat·ed** *adj.* sitting ‖ situated or established in a specified way or place **séat·er** *n.* (in compounds) something having a specified number of seats, *his new car is a two-seater* **séat·ing** *n.* the provision made for people to sit ‖ material for covering chair seats etc. ‖ the arrangement of seats ‖ (*mech.*) a surface on which something is supported [O.N. *sæti*]

seat belt a strap by which a passenger in a vehicle can secure himself to his seat as a safety precaution

SEATO (síːtou) *SOUTH EAST ASIA TREATY ORGANIZATION

sea trout any of several trouts that live in the sea as adults but ascend rivers to spawn

Se·at·tle (siːǽt'l) the chief city and port (pop. 490,077) of the northwestern U.S.A., on Puget Sound in W. central Washington, dominated by Mt Rainier. Industries: aeronautical and mechanical engineering, shipbuilding, food processing, brewing, fishing, lumber, pulp and paper. University of Washington (1861)

sea urchin an echinoderm of the class *Echinoidea*, possessing a calcareous boxlike exoskeleton with movable spines used for walking. The edible sea urchin is *Echinus esculenta*

sea·van (síːvæn) *n.* commercial or government-owned (or -leased) shipping con-

tainers without bogey wheels attached, i.e., lifted on and off the ship

sea·wall (síːwɔl) *n.* a wall built to prevent encroachment by the sea

sea walnut a ctenophore, e.g. of genus *Mnemiopsis*, shaped like a walnut

sea·ward (síːwərd) 1. *n.* the direction from a coast towards the open sea 2. *adj.* directed or situated toward the sea 3. *adv.* in the direction of the sea **séa·wards** *adv.*

sea·wa·ter (síːwɔtər, síːwɔtər) *n.* the water of the sea, containing in solution, on the average, 2.8% sodium chloride and other salts

sea·way (síːwei) *n.* a route over the sea ‖ a deep inland river up which an oceangoing vessel can sail ‖ (*naut.*) a vessel's progress ‖ a rough sea

sea·weed (síːwiːd) *n.* any marine plant, esp. a marine alga. Seaweeds are widely distributed in the oceans and are found floating or attached at considerable depth by specialized anchoring attachments. They are an important source of food, fertilizer and minerals (esp. iodine) ‖ seaweeds collectively

sea·wor·thi·ness (síːwəːrθiːnis) *n.* the quality or state of being seaworthy

sea·wor·thy (síːwəːrθiː) *adj.* (of a vessel) in a fit condition to go to sea and to survive storms

sea wrack a mass of coarse seaweed ‖ a plant tending to form such a mass ‖ eelgrass

se·ba·ceous (sibéiʃəs) *adj.* (of glands, ducts etc.) containing or secreting fatty oily matter ‖ consisting of such matter, *sebaceous secretions* [fr. L. *sebaceus* fr. *sebum*, tallow]

Se·bas·tian (sibǽstʃən), St (*d.* c. 288), Christian martyr in Rome, usually depicted as a nude youth pierced by arrows. Feast: Jan. 20

Sebastian (*Port.* Sebastião, 1554-78), king of Portugal (1557-78), grandson of John III. He was killed, and his army massacred, in a disastrous battle against the Moors in N. Africa

Se·bas·tia·no del Piom·bo (sɛbastjánɔdelpjómbɔ) (1485-1547), Italian painter. He was a Venetian, but worked in Rome after 1511, much influenced by Michelangelo

Se·bas·to·pol (sibǽstəpoul) Sevastopol

se·bum (síːbəm) *n.* the fatty matter secreted by the sebaceous glands to keep the skin and hair supple [L.=tallow, grease]

SECAM *n.* a color television system developed in France and used in U.S.S.R., East Germany, Czechoslovakia, and Lebanon in which each color is broadcast separately on 650 sequential lines

se·cant (síːkænt, síːkənt) 1. *adj.* (*math.*) intersecting 2. *n.* a straight line which intercepts a curve ‖ (*math.*, *abbr.* sec) the reciprocal of the cosine [fr. L. *secans* (*secantis*) fr. *secare*, to cut]

sec·a·teurs (sékətəːrz) *pl.* *n.* (*Br.*) steel shears used for pruning, cutting roses and grapes etc. [F. *sécateur*]

Sec·chi Disk (séki) device to determine clarity of seawater, usu. on underwater sites

se·cede (sisíːd) *pres. part.* **se·ced·ing** *past* and *past part.* **se·ced·ed** *v.i.* to withdraw formally from membership of some body, esp. from a state, federation etc. [fr. L. *secedere*, to go away]

se·ces·sion (siséʃən) *n.* the act of seceding **se·cés·sion·ism** *n.* the doctrines of those who favor secession from some body **se·cés·sion·ist** *n.* [fr. L. *secessio* (*secessionis*)]

se·clude (siklúːd) *pres. part.* **se·clud·ing** *past* and *past part.* **se·clud·ed** *v.t.* to keep (someone) apart from others, isolate **se·clúd·ed** *adj.* shut off, isolated, *a secluded garden, she lives a secluded life* [fr. L. *secludere*, to shut up apart]

se·clu·sion (siklúːʒən) *n.* a secluding or being secluded [fr. M.L. *seclusio* (*seclusionis*)]

se·clu·sive (siklúːsiv) *adj.* tending to seclude ‖ seeking seclusion [fr. L. *secludere* (*seclusus*), to seclude]

SECO *n.* (*computer acronym*) for sequential control, a system for controlling the sequence of teletype message transmissions of stored data

sec·ond (sékənd) *n.* a unit of time equal to 1/60 of a minute or 1/86,400 of a mean solar day ‖ a unit of angular measure (symbol ″) equal to 1/60 of a minute or 1/3,600 of a degree ‖ an undefined very short time, *it will just take me a second* [F. *seconde* fr. M.L. *secunda* (*minuta*), second (minute), denoting the second operation of sexagesimal division]

second 1. *adj.* being number two in a series (*NUMBER TABLE) ‖ next after the first in importance, quality, rank etc. ‖ being another of the same kind as the first, *a second Shakespeare* ‖ (*mus.*, of an instrument or voice) having a part generally lower in pitch than that of the first instrument or voice of the same kind, *second violin* ‖ of the gear immediately above first in a vehicle **2.** *n.* the person or thing next after the first ‖ someone who attends a principal in a boxing match, duel etc. ‖ (*Br.*) a grading in the second class of an examination ‖ a second prize in a race or other contest ‖ the gear immediately above first in a vehicle ‖ the second day of a month ‖ (*mus.*) the interval between two successive diatonic notes ‖ (*mus.*) one of these notes in relation to the other ‖ (*mus.*) a combination of these notes ‖ (*pl.*) substandard or inferior goods ‖ (*pl., pop.*) a second helping of food **3.** *v.t.* to give formal support to (a motion) before it is open to general discussion ‖ to express one's agreement with (a remark) ‖ to aid or encourage (someone's efforts) ‖ (sikónd, *Br., mil.*) to transfer (an officer) temporarily to another post, unit or rank **4.** *adv.* in the second place ‖ (followed by a superlative) except one, *the second biggest* [F. fr. L. *secundus*, following, next, second]

Second Advent the return of Christ to the world as judge on the last day **Sécond Advent-ist** a member of a Protestant sect which stresses this day of judgment

Second Amendment (1791) amendment to the U.S. Constitution, part of the Bill of Rights, that protects the right of citizens to maintain a state militia and to 'keep and bear arms.' State militias are represented by National Guard units, regulated by the state governments. The right to keep and bear arms does not necessarily apply to individuals for individual purposes and does not preclude state regulation of arms

sec·ond·ar·y (sékəndęri:) **1.** *adj.* being second in succession, rank importance etc. ‖ immediately derived from what is primary, *secondary colors* ‖ (*gram.*, of a tense in Greek etc.) referring to time in the past ‖ (*chem.*) formed by replacing two atoms or radicals, *a secondary compound* ‖ (*geol.*) Mesozoic ‖ (*bot.*) originating from elsewhere than the chief growing point ‖ (*zool.*) of or designating a quill on the second section of a bird's wing, or this section itself **2.** *pl.* **sec·ond·ar·ies** *n.* a secondary process in a (*zool.*) a secondary quill of a bird ‖ (*zool.*) an insect's hind wing [fr. L. *secundarius*, of the second class]

secondary accent a stress (shown in this book under the line) weaker than the primary stress

secondary cell (*elec.*) a storage cell

secondary color, *Br.* **secondary colour** a color made by a mixture of two primary colors

secondary education formal education below university level, following elementary education

secondary emission (*phys.*) the emission of electrons by a metal surface (e.g. the anode of a thermionic valve) when it is bombarded by rapidly moving electrons

secondary planet a celestial satellite that revolves around a planet

secondary school a school offering secondary education

second base (*baseball*) the base that must be touched second by the runner ‖ the player stationed at this base

second best something next below the best in quality, desirability etc. ‖ something inferior accepted or offered as a substitute for what is preferred **to come off second best** to be the loser in a dispute **sécond-bést** *adj.*

second chamber the upper house in a two-chamber parliament

second childhood dotage

sec·ond-class (sékəndklǽs, sékəndklás) **1.** *adj.* of or in a class next below the first ‖ of mediocre quality **2.** *adv.* by second-class accommodation etc., *to travel second-class*

Second Coming the Second Advent

second cousin the grandchild of a brother or sister of one of one's grandparents

second cousin once removed the child of one's second cousin

sec·ond-de·gree burn (sékənddigrí:) a burn involving blistering and superficial destruction of the dermis

se·conde (sikónd, səgɔ́d) *n.* (*fencing*) the second of eight parrying positions [F.]

Second Empire (of style in furniture, dress etc.) characteristic of the style of Napoleon III's

French empire of 1852–71, or imitating that ornate style

second fiddle (in phrase) **to be** (or **play**) **second fiddle** to have a secondary position or role

second hand (in the phrase) **at second hand** (of getting information) through an intermediary, *to hear an account at second hand* **sécond-hánd 1.** *adj.* used by a previous owner or owners, *secondhand clothes* ‖ not original, derivative, *secondhand ideas* **2.** *adv.* after use by someone else, *we bought it secondhand* ‖ (*pop.*) indirectly, *he acquired his education secondhand*

second hand the hand marking the seconds on a clock or watch

second intention (*med.*) the healing of a wound slowly and with much scar formation

second lieutenant an officer of the U.S. army, air force or marine corps ranking below a first lieutenant ‖ (*Br.*) an army officer ranking below a lieutenant

sec·ond·ly (sékəndlí:) *adv.* (used in enumeration) in the second place

second mortgage a mortgage secured on what will remain of the property when the first mortgage is redeemed

second nature acquired habits or characteristics that have become automatic

second papers an alien's final application papers for U.S. citizenship

second person (*gram.*) the person spoken to as shown in the form of a verb or pronoun

sec·ond-rate (sékəndréit) *adj.* inferior, of poor quality

second sight ability to look into the future

sec·ond-strike (sękəndstráik) *adj.* (*mil.*) of a capacity to withstand an initial nuclear attack and retaliate

sec·ond-string (sékəndstrín) **1.** *adj.* serving as a replacement, e.g. for another player in a game ‖ inferior or minor **2.** *n.* (*Br.*) an alternative recourse, esp. one kept in reserve

second thought (*pl.*) a change of mind as a result of thinking again about a matter, *to have second thoughts on* (or *upon*) **second thought** on reconsideration, *on second thought, he decided to wait*

second wind the recovery of breath after initial exhaustion during exercise ‖ (*fig.*) the strength for a renewed effort

SECOR *n.* (*acronym*) for sequential collation of range, navigation and surveying system for locating points on earth, utilizing an orbiting satellite and four ground stations

se·cre·cy (sí:krisi:) *pl.* **se·cre·cies** *n.* the state of being secret, *done in secrecy* ‖ the ability to keep a secret, *you can rely on his secrecy* ‖ the habit of being secretive [alt. of obs. *secretee*, *secretie* prob. fr. obs. *secre*, secret or SECRET *adj.*]

se·cret (sí:krit) **1.** *adj.* kept from the knowledge of others, *a secret agreement* ‖ hidden, *a secret drawer* ‖ known only to the initiated, *secret signs* **2.** *n.* something kept from the knowledge of others, *the process is a secret* ‖ something which has not been explained ‖ a hidden or not obvious explanation, *what is the secret of his success?* ‖ (*eccles.*) a prayer said very quietly by the celebrant just before the preface at Mass **in secret** secretly **to keep a secret** to refrain from communicating a secret to others [F.]

secret agent a person engaged in espionage or similar undercover work, esp. for a government

se·cre·taire (sękritéər) *n.* a secretary (desk) [F.]

sec·re·tar·i·al (sękritéəri:əl) *adj.* of or relating to a secretary ‖ characteristic of a secretary's work [fr. M.L. *secretarius*]

sec·re·tar·i·at, **sec·re·tar·i·ate** (sękritéəri:ət) *n.* that department of a large concern, administrative body etc. which handles the paper work ‖ the persons, collectively, who work in this department ‖ the position of secretary [F. *secrétariat*]

sec·re·tar·y (sékritęri:, *Br.* sékrətri) *pl.* **sec·re·tar·ies** *n.* a person responsible for dealing with the correspondence and records of an organization or individual employer ‖ (in titles) a minister in charge of a government department, *secretary of state* ‖ a desk fitted with drawers, having a shelf which hinges forward to work on [fr. M.L. *secretarius*, confidant, secretary]

secretary bird *Sagittarius serpentarius*, fam. *Sagittariidae*, a long-legged S. African bird which eats reptiles. It has a strong beak and long tail, and has a crest of long feathers which look like pens stuck in behind the ears

secretary-general *pl.* **secretaries-general** *n.* the principal administrative officer of a secretariat

Secretary of State, U.S. the chief adviser to the president on foreign affairs, in charge of the State Department, and responsible for the execution of foreign policy

se·crete (sikrí:t) *pres. part.* **se·cret·ing** *past and past part.* **se·cret·ed** *v.t.* (*physiol.*) to produce and emit (a secretion) ‖ *v.i.* (*physiol.*) to produce and emit a secretion [fr. L. *secernere* (*secretus*), to separate]

secrete *pres. part.* **se·cret·ing** *past and past part.* **se·cret·ed** *v.t.* to conceal [alteration of obs. *secret* v.]

se·cre·tin (sikrí:tin) *n.* a hormone secreted in the intestine, which stimulates the pancreas and the liver [prob. fr. SECRETION]

se·cre·tion (sikrí:ʃən) *n.* a substance (e.g. saliva) elaborated by a gland or other organ or by a plant, for use by the organism or for excretion ‖ the act of elaborating such a substance [F. *sécrétion*]

secretion *n.* a hiding or concealing

se·cre·tive (sí:kritiv, sikrí:tiv) *adj.* fond of or given to having secrets ‖ unduly reticent [back-formation fr. *secretiveness*, the quality of being secretive, after F. *secrétivité*]

se·cre·tor (sikrí:tər) *n.* a gland etc. which secretes

se·cre·to·ry (sikrí:təri:) *adj.* producing or having to do with a secretion or secretions ‖ produced by secretion [fr. L. *secernere* (*secretus*), to separate]

secret service government investigation or espionage

Secret Service, U.S. a bureau of the treasury department created in 1865. Its duties include the protection of the U.S. president and his family, the president-elect, and the vice-president, as well as the solution of crimes relating to coins, paper money, checks and securities of U.S. or foreign governments, and of violations of laws relating to the Federal Deposit Insurance Corporation, federal land banks, joint-stock land banks and national farm loan associations

secret society a group of people associated together for some common interest (e.g. religious, magical, social or political) under conditions of secrecy

sect (sekt) *n.* a body of people, sharing religious, philosophic or political opinions, who have broken away from a larger body (often used as a term of disapproval) ‖ a particular school of thought in politics etc. [F. *secte* or fr. L. *secta*]

sec·tar·i·an (sektéəri:ən) **1.** *adj.* of or relating to a sect or sects ‖ narrow-minded and ready to quarrel over petty differences of opinion **2.** *n.* a member of a sect ‖ a narrow-minded or bigoted adherent of a sect **sec·tár·i·an·ism** *n.* adherence to the interests of a sect rather than to those requiring wider sympathies [SECTARY]

sec·ta·ry (séktəri:) *pl.* **sec·ta·ries** *n.* a sectarian **Sec·ta·ry** (*Eng. hist.*) a Nonconformist of the 17th and 18th cc. [fr. F. *sectaire* or M.L. *sectarius*]

sec·tion (sékʃən) **1.** *n.* a part cut off or separated by cutting, splitting etc., *a section of an orange* ‖ a division or part, *the woodwind section of an orchestra* ‖ (esp. *med.*) separation by cutting ‖ a division of written or printed matter, *a section of an act* ‖ the symbol (§) denoting this division ‖ a part joined or designed to be joined to others to make a complete structure, *the hut consists of five sections to be bolted together* ‖ a distinct part of a community, country etc., *the industrial section of the nation* ‖ a thin slice prepared for study through a microscope ‖ (*mil.*) a subdivision of a platoon etc. ‖ (*geom.*) the plane figure produced by the cutting of a solid by a plane ‖ a drawing or description of any object as it would look if cut through by a plane ‖ one square mile of land forming 1/36 of a township ‖ (*rail.*) a division of a sleeping car, consisting of an upper and a lower berth ‖ (*bookbinding*) a signature (sheet of pages) **2.** *v.t.* to cut into or arrange in sections [F. or fr. L. *sectio* (*sectionis*), a cutting]

sec·tion·al (sékʃən'l) *adj.* relating to or characteristic of a particular section of something ‖ divided into sections **séc·tion·al·ism** *n.* exaggerated loyalty to a particular section of a country, inordinate local fervor

sec·tor (séktər) **1.** *n.* the plane figure bounded by two radii of a circle and the intercepted arc ‖ a mathematical instrument consisting of two rulers marked off in several scales and hinged

CONCISE PRONUNCIATION KEY: **(a)** æ, c*a*t; ɑ, c*a*r; ɔ f*aw*n; ei, sn*a*ke. **(e)** e, h*e*n; i:, sh*ee*p; iə, d*ee*r; ɛə, b*ear*. **(i)** i, f*i*sh; ai, t*i*ger; ə:, b*ir*d. **(o)** o, *o*x; au, c*ow*; ou, g*oa*t; u, p*oo*r; ɔi, r*oy*al. **(u)** ʌ, d*u*ck; u, b*u*ll; u:, g*oo*se; ə, b*a*cillus; ju:, c*u*be. x, lo*ch*; θ, *th*ink; ð, bo*th*er; z, *Z*en; ʒ, cor*s*age; dʒ, sava*g*e; ŋ, ora*ng*utang; j, *y*ak; ʃ, *f*ish; tʃ, fe*tch*; 'l, rabb*le*; 'n, redd*en*. Complete pronunciation key appears inside front cover.

together ‖ a division or section, e.g. a subdivision of a military zone, or a distinct part of an economy ‖ an astronomical instrument for measuring angles, consisting of a graduated arc with a telescope at its center **2.** *v.t.* to divide into sectors ‖ *v.i.* (of bacteria and fungi) to form colonies of different sectors [L.L.]

sec·to·ri·al (sektóríːəl, sektóríːəl) **1.** *adj.* (esp. of one of the premolar teeth) designed for cutting **2.** *n.* a sectorial tooth [fr. Mod. L. *sectorius*]

sectorial *adj.* of, relating to or consisting of a sector ‖ (*biol.*, of a chimera) made up of different tissues, a section of one kind of tissue being inserted in the main body [SECTOR]

sec·u·lar (sékjulər) **1.** *adj.* of or concerned with temporal, worldly matters rather than with religion ‖ profane (as distinct from sacred), *secular music* ‖ (*eccles.*) not belonging to a religious order (cf. REGULAR) ‖ not under the control of a religious body, *secular schools* ‖ of a change or event which occurs once during a century or other long period of time ‖ lasting or continuing over such a long period **2.** *n.* (*eccles.*) a member of the secular clergy **séc·u·lar·ism** *n.* the belief that religious influence should be restricted, and in particular that education, morality, the state etc. should be independent of religion **séc·u·lar·ist** *n.* **sec·u·lar·is·tic** *adj.* [O.F. *seculer* and fr. L. *saecularis*]

secular humanism belief in rational man as a source of his own salvation and a rejection of the supernatural; used esp. by the so-called New Right during the early 1980s

sec·u·lar·i·ty (sekjulǽriːí) *pl.* **sec·u·lar·i·ties** *n.* the quality or state of being secular ‖ a matter or affair that is secular [F. *sécularité* or fr. M.L. *saecularitas*]

sec·u·lar·i·za·tion (sekjulərizéiʃən) *n.* a secularizing or being secularized [fr. F. *sécularisation*]

sec·u·lar·ize (sékjuləraiz) *pres. part.* **sec·u·lar·iz·ing** *past* and *past part.* **sec·u·lar·ized** *v.t.* to make secular, to transfer from the control or use of the Church to that of the State [A.F. *séculariser*]

se·cund (síːkʌnd, sékʌnd) *adj.* (*biol.*, e.g. of a plant's flowers) arranged on one side only ‖ (*biol.*) having some part (e.g. the flowers) on one side only [fr. L. *secundus*, following]

se·cure (sikjúər) **1.** *adj.* completely safe ‖ sure, certain ‖ fixed firmly **2.** *v. pres. part.* **se·cur·ing** *past* and *past part.* **se·cured** *v.t.* to make secure against injury, loss etc., *he secured the prisoner with ropes* ‖ to make firm, *to secure a fastening* ‖ to guarantee, *to secure a loan* ‖ to get possession of, *to secure a good seat* ‖ *v.i.* (of a ship) to tie up, berth [fr. L. *securus*]

Securities and Exchange Commission (*abbr.* SEC) (1934) U.S. federal agency that oversees the securities and financial markets. Mandated by the Securities Act of 1933, the SEC requires registration statements with 'full and fair disclosure' for all offerings. It regulates securities exchanges and sets the rules for activities such as selling short, stock options, floor trading and specialists' and odd-lot dealers' transactions. The SEC was empowered to regulate electric and gas utility holding companies by the Public Utility Holding Company Act (1935), mutual funds by the Investment Company Act (1940) and investment counselors' practices by the Investment Advisers Act (1940). It is governed by five commissioners (one of whom is appointed chairman), appointed by the President with Senate approval

se·cu·ri·ty (sikjúəriːí) *pl.* **se·cu·ri·ties** *n.* freedom from danger or anxiety ‖ something given or pledged as a guarantee, for the payment of a debt ‖ a person who stands as guarantor ‖ something which guarantees or safeguards ‖ protective measures against espionage ‖ (esp. *pl.*) a bond, stock certificate etc. given as evidence of a debt or of property [fr. L. *securitas*]

Security Council the executive organ of the U.N., with primary responsibility for international peace and security. It has 11 members, of which China, France, Britain, the U.S.A. and the U.S.S.R. are permanent and the other six are elected for terms of two years. On all matters other than procedural ones, its decisions must not have a negative vote of any of the five permanent members

Se·daine (sədɛn), Michel-Jean (1719-97), French dramatist. His best-known play is 'le Philosophe sans le savoir' (1765)

Se·dan (sədã) a town (pop. 22,000) of N.E. France, in Ardennes department. It was the

scene of the surrender (1870) of the French army to the Prussians in the Franco-Prussian War. The German army broke through here (1940), turning the Maginot line

se·dan (sidǽn) *n.* (*Am.=Br.* saloon) an automobile with a large closed body, a hard roof, and no internal partitions ‖ (*hist.*) a sedan chair [etym. doubtful]

sedan chair (*hist.*) a canopied chair for one person, carried on poles by two bearers, one before the passenger and one behind, in use in the 17th and 18th cc.

se·date (sidéit) *adj.* characterized by or showing calm dignity, without any appearance of haste, excitement or confusion [fr. L. *sedare* (*sedatus*), to settle]

se·da·tion (sidéiʃən) *n.* (*med.*) a calming or being calmed, esp. by the use of a sedative [F. *sédation* or fr. L. *sedatio* (*sedationis*)]

sed·a·tive (sédətiv) **1.** *adj.* soothing, reducing excitement or nervousness **2.** *n.* something that soothes in this way, esp. a drug [F. *sédatif* or fr. M.L. *sedativus*]

sed·en·tar·i·ly (sed'ntéərilíː, séd'nterili) *adv.* in a sedentary way

sed·en·tar·i·ness (séd'nteríːnis) *n.* the quality or state of being sedentary

sed·en·tar·y (séd'nterí) *adj.* involving a great deal of sitting, *a sedentary occupation* ‖ accustomed, or compelled to sit for much or all of the time, *the accident made him sedentary* ‖ (*zool.*, e.g. of a mollusk) remaining attached by a base to a solid surface ‖ (*zool.*) remaining in the same region, not migratory [fr. F. *sédentaire*]

Se·der (séidər) *n.* a Jewish ceremonial dinner held esp. at home, on the first night of Passover, to commemorate the Exodus. It is repeated on the second night by most Orthodox Jews [Heb. *sēdher*, order, division]

sedge (sedʒ) *n.* any of several members of *Cyperaceae*, a family of coarse, solid-stemmed grasses growing in swampy places, esp. a member of genus *Carex* ‖ these plants collectively [O.E. *secg*]

Sedge·moor, Battle of (sédʒmuər) a battle (1685) in which James II of England defeated a rebellion led by the duke of Monmouth

sedge warbler *Acrocephalus schoenobaenus*, a small, brown and white warbler of Europe and Asia, nesting in dense, swampy thickets. Its song is loud and sweet

se·dil·i·a (sedíliːə) *sing.* **se·di·le** (sedəíli) *pl. n.* a set of (usually three) seats on the south side of the chancel of a church, for the use of officiating clergy during intervals of the service [L. fr. *sedere*, to sit]

sed·i·ment (sédəmənt) *n.* matter that, because of its greater density, sinks to the bottom of an undisturbed liquid with which it was previously mixed ‖ (*geol.*) matter or a mass of matter deposited by wind, glaciers etc. **sed·i·men·ta·ry** (sedəméntərí) *adj.* of matter thus deposited [F. *sédiment*]

sedimentary rock rock formed from fragments of other rocks, by precipitation from solutions, or by organic secretion (cf. IGNEOUS ROCK, cf. METAMORPHIC ROCK)

sed·i·men·ta·tion (sedəməntéiʃən) *n.* the act or process of settling as a sediment ‖ the movement of finely divided solid particles through a fluid, under the influence of a gravitational or other force (*CENTRIFUGE)

se·di·tion (sidíʃən) *n.* the inciting of hostility against the government, likely to cause rebellion or insurrection, but not amounting to treason [O.F. fr. L. *seditio* (*seditionis*)]

se·di·tious (sidíʃəs) *adj.* of, tending toward or guilty of sedition [fr. O.F. *séditieux*]

se·duce (sidúːs, sidjúːs) *pres. part.* **se·duc·ing** *past* and *past part.* **se·duced** *v.t.* to cause by persuasion or enticement (someone, esp. a girl who is a virgin) to have sexual intercourse with one ‖ to persuade (someone) to act contrary to the principles by which he normally abides [fr. L. *seducere*, to lead aside or away]

se·duc·tion (sidʌkʃən) *n.* a seducing or being seduced ‖ something seductive, *the seductions of wealth* [F. *séduction* or fr. L. *seductio* (*seductionis*)]

se·duc·tive (sidʌktiv) *adj.* tempting [fr. L. *seducere* (*seductus*), to lead aside or away]

se·du·li·ty (sidúːliti, sidjúːliti) *n.* the quality of being sedulous ‖ sedulous behavior [fr. L. *sedulitas*]

sed·u·lous (sédʒuləs) *adj.* diligent, painstaking, assiduous [fr. L. *sedulus*]

se·dum (síːdəm) *n.* a member of *Sedum*, fam. *Crassulaceae*, a genus of fleshy-leaved plants,

cultivated for their foliage and their yellow, pink or white flowers [L. = houseleek]

see (siː) *n.* a bishop's diocese, or his office [O.F. *sé, sed*]

see *pres. part.* **see·ing** *past* saw (sɔ) *past part.* **seen** (siːn) *v.t.* to perceive with the eye ‖ to form a mental picture of ‖ to understand, *I see your point* ‖ to imagine as having the character or capacities necessary for some specified activity, position etc., *I can't see her as an actress* ‖ to find out, *go and see what he wants* ‖ to attend as a spectator, *to see a baseball game* ‖ to watch on television, *did you see the fight last night?* ‖ to examine, *let me see your papers* ‖ to receive (a person), *the doctor will see you now* ‖ to call on, arrange to be received by (a person), *you must see your dentist* ‖ to meet, *I'll see you at the races* ‖ (with 'that') to make sure by taking care, *see that you pay attention* ‖ to escort, *to see someone home* ‖ to have or obtain knowledge or experience of, *she has seen a lot of life* ‖ (*cards*) to accept (a bet) by betting an equal sum ‖ (*cards*) to meet the bet of (another player) in this way ‖ *v.i.* to have the power of perceiving things with the eye ‖ to perceive objects, colors etc., e.g. at a given distance ‖ to understand, *now do you see?* ‖ to try to find out something to reflect about something, *let me see* **to see about** to attend to ‖ to make inquiries about **to see after** to attend to, *see after the dinner* **to see into** to investigate ‖ to perceive true nature of **to see (someone) off** to escort (someone) to the point of departure **to see out** to wait till the end of ‖ to finish, complete **to see through** to be undeceived and understand the true meaning or nature of (something) without being misled, *to see through someone's fine phrases* ‖ to help (someone) to overcome a difficulty, *he promised to see his client through the lawsuit* ‖ to finish, *you must see the task through, once you start* [O.E. *sēon*]

See·beck effect (síːbek, zéibek) (*phys.*) the generation of an electric current in a circuit consisting of two different metals in successive contact when the junctions are at different temperatures. It is the principle of the thermoelectric thermometer, thermopile etc. [after Thomas Johann *Seebeck*, G. physicist and inventor of the thermocouple]

seed (siːd) **1.** *pl.* **seed, seeds** *n.* the fertilized ovule of a plant and its covering. The seed contains a miniature plant capable of independent development into a plant similar to the one which produced it ‖ a spore or dry seedlike fruit ‖ seeds collectively ‖ (*rhet.*) semen ‖ a beginning or source, *seeds of discontent* ‖ (*Bible*) descendants, *the seed of David* ‖ seed oysters ‖ (*chem.*) a small crystal added to a solution to induce crystallization **to go** (or **run**) **to seed** (of a plant) to develop seeds at the expense of foliage or further flowers ‖ (of a person) to become lazy, feckless, slovenly etc. by gradual loss of self-respect **2.** *v.t.* to take the seeds out of (fruit) ‖ to sow with seed ‖ to sprinkle with seed ‖ to sprinkle chemicals in (clouds) in order to induce rain to fall ‖ (*sports*, esp. *tennis*) to select (players) so that those likely to be matched in the later stages do not play against one another in the early stages of a tournament ‖ *v.i.* (of a plant) to arrive at the stage when seed matures ‖ to shed seed **3.** *adj.* (of a crop) grown for production of seed or set aside for use as seed [O.E. *sǣd*]

seed·bed (síːdbed) *n.* a bed of soil in which seedlings are raised

seed·cake (síːdkeik) *n.* cake flavored with caraway or other seeds

seed·case (síːdkeis) *n.* a pod

seed coat the covering of a seed

seed drill a drill (agricultural machine)

seed·er (síːdər) *n.* a device that sows seed ‖ a device used to remove seed from fruit

seed·i·ly (síːdiliː) *adv.* in a seedy manner

seed·i·ness (síːdíːnis) *n.* the quality or state of being seedy

seed leaf a cotyledon

seed·ling (síːdliŋ) *n.* a young plant grown from seed (rather than from a cutting etc.) ‖ a young tree under 3 ft in height

seed·man (síːdmən) *pl.* **seed·men** (síːdmən) *n.* a seedsman

seed money funds to initiate a business or non-profit undertaking under the assumption that major financing will be forthcoming later

seed oyster a young oyster ready for transplanting

seed pearl a pearl weighing less than ¼ grain

seed plant a spermatophyte
seeds·man (sí:dzmən) *pl.* **seeds·men** (sí:dzmən) *n.* a dealer in seeds and other horticultural supplies
seed vessel a pericarp
seed·y (sí:dí:) *comp.* **seed·i·er** *superl.* **seed·i·est** *adj.* having abundant seeds ‖ having run to seed ‖ shabby and in an uncared-for state ‖ in rather poor health
see·ing (sí:iŋ) 1. *n.* the power or faculty of vision ‖ the act of someone who sees 2. *adj.* able to see 3. *conj.* (usually with 'that') since, considering, *seeing that it is so late you had better go*
seek (si:k) *pres. part.* **seek·ing** *past and past part.* **sought** (sɔt) *v.t.* to try to find, *to seek shelter* ‖ to ask for, *to seek advice* ‖ to try to obtain, *he seeks recognition of his work* ‖ (with *infin.*) to try, *to seek to establish a fact* ‖ *v.i.* (with 'for') to try to find, *I am seeking for information* [O.E. *sēcan*]
Seek Bus (*mil.*) a coordinated communications system for all U.S. armed forces linking intelligence and weapons systems for tactical purposes
seeker *n.* (*mil.*) a homing device that locates its target by heat or other radiation
seem (si:m) *v.i.* to give the impression of being something of a specified kind or of having a specified attribute, *she seems a complete fool, he seems happy* ‖ (with *infin.*) to give an impression of something specified, *he seems to have a cold* ‖ (with *infin.*) to have an impression that one is doing or being something specified, *I seem to smell something burning, I seem to be tired today* ‖ to have the appearance of being true, *it seems he died rich* ‖ (in constructions beginning with 'there') to have the appearance of existing, *there seems no reason for believing him* **seem·ing** 1. *adj.* having the false appearance of being, *a seeming friend though a secret enemy* 2. *n.* appearance, esp. false appearance **seem·ing·ly** *adv.* as far as can be judged [M.E. *seme* fr. O.N. *sǣma*]
seem·li·ness (sí:mlí:nis) *n.* the quality or state of being seemly
seem·ly (sí:mlí:) *comp.* **seem·li·er** *superl.* **seem·li·est** *adj.* conforming to accepted standards of behavior or appearance [M.E. fr. O.N. *sǣmiligr*]
seen *past part.* of SEE
seep (si:p) 1. *v.i.* (of a fluid) to pass slowly through a porous body 2. *n.* a place where water or petroleum seeps up out of the ground to form a pool **seep·age** *n.* the act or an instance of seeping ‖ fluid that has seeped through something [perh. fr. O.E. *sipian*, to soak]
se·er (sí:ər, sír) *n.* (*rhet.*) a wise man gifted with powers of divination [SEE v.]
seer·suck·er (síərsʌkər) *n.* a thin linen, cotton or rayon fabric with a crinkly surface, often having thin stripes with a flat surface [E. Indian corrup. of Pers. *shīr o shakkar*, milk and sugar, a striped linen garment]
see·saw (sí:sɔ) 1. *n.* a plank balanced in the center with its ends free to rise and fall alternately so that a person sitting at one end rises up in the air as one sitting at the other end sinks towards the ground ‖ this alternate rising and falling as a children's amusement ‖ a back-and-forth or up-and-down movement ‖ any situation in which two factors alternately rise and fall or take leading and inferior positions, *the seesaw of supply and demand* 2. *v.i.* to rise and fall alternately on or as if on a seesaw ‖ *v.t.* to cause to do this 3. *adj.* moving up and down as if on a seesaw [reduplication of SAW v.]
see-saw principle (*mil.*) tendency of defensive weapons development to overtake offensive weapons development, and vice versa
seethe (sí:ð) *pres. part.* **seeth·ing** *past and past part.* **seethed** *v.i.* to bubble violently as if boiling, *seething waters* ‖ to be in a state of rage or turmoil ‖ to be in restless commotion, *seething crowds* [O.E. *sēothan*]
seg academies (seg) *n.* private secular schools established to evade desegregation laws affecting public schools
Se·gal (sí:gəl), George (1924-), U.S. sculptor known for his life-size, lifelike, white plaster figures of people, usually set in everyday situations. Part of the 'New Realist' school of artists of the 1960s, he exhibited in significant shows of that time. His works include 'Cinema' (1963), a man changing a movie marquee, and 'The Diner' (1964-6), figures on stools at a counter
seg·gar (ségər) *n.* (*Br.*) a saggar
seg·ment (ségmənt) 1. *n.* a part, esp. a part separable at a natural junction (e.g. at a joint) ‖

(*geom.*) the part of a circle cut off by a chord, or of a sphere cut off by a plane ‖ (*geom.*) the finite part of a line between two points in the line 2. *v.t.* to separate (something) into segments ‖ *v.i.* to separate into segments ‖ (*biol.*) to undergo cleavage **seg·men·tal** (segmént'l), **seg·men·tar·y** (ségmənteri:) *adjs* **seg·men·ta·tion** (segməntéiʃən) *n.* separation into segments, e.g. in the cleavage of a cell or ovum [fr. L. *segmentum*]
Se·go·vi·a (segóvjə) a province (area 2,635 sq. miles, pop. 149,286) of N. Central Spain (*OLD CASTILE) ‖ its capital (pop. 41,880): Roman aqueduct. Romanesque churches, 16th-c. cathedral
Se·grè (segrèi), Emilio Gino (1905-), U.S. physicist and co-winner (with Owen Chamberlain) of the 1959 Nobel prize in physics for his discovery of the antiproton
seg·re·gate (ségrəgeit) *pres. part.* **seg·re·gat·ing** *past and past part.* **seg·re·gat·ed** *v.t.* to separate from others of a group, esp. to oblige (racial groups) to carry on their activities, schooling etc. separately ‖ *v.i.* to be or become segregated ‖ (*biol.,* of chromosome genes) to separate in meiosis **ség·re·gat·ed** *adj.* conforming to a policy of racial segregation [fr. L. *segregare* (*segregatus*), to set apart from the flock]
seg·re·ga·tion (segrigéiʃən) *n.* a segregating or being segregated ‖ a segregated part, group etc. ‖ (*biol.*) the separation of genes of chromosomes at meiosis **seg·re·ga·tion·ist** *n.* a person who believes in racial segregation [fr. L.L. *segregatio* (*segregationis*), a setting apart]
seg·re·ga·tive (ségrigeitiv) *adj.* relating to, causing or characterized by segregation [fr. M.L. *segregativus*]
se·gui·dil·la (seigidí:ljə, seigədí:jə) *n.* a Spanish poem of a form employing four to seven short lines ‖ a Spanish dance accompanied by castanets ‖ the music for it, in triple time [Span. fr. *seguida,* sequence]
sei·cen·to (seitʃéntou, setʃéntɔ) *n.* the 17th century in Italian art or literary history [Ital.=six hundred, used for sixteen hundred]
seiche (seiʃ) *n.* an oscillation of the surface in a lake, caused by barometric pressure changes [F. perh. fr. G.]
Seid·litz powder (sédlits) a preparation consisting of two powders, one of tartaric acid, the other of a mixture of sodium bicarbonate and Rochelle salt, which effervesce when mixed together in water, the effervescing liquid being drunk as a mild aperient **Seid·litz powders** Seidlitz powder [after *Seidlitz,* town in Czechoslovakia]
sei·gneur (senjə:r, senjə:r) *n.* (*hist.*) a feudal lord in France or Canada ‖ a lord of the manor in the Channel Is **sei·gneur·i·al** (seinjə:rí:əl) *adj.* [F.]
sei·gneur·y (séinjəri:) *pl.* **sei·gneur·ies** *n.* (*hist.*) the territory or estate of a feudal lord, esp. an estate held in Canada by feudal tenure (up to 1854), or the manor house itself ‖ the domain of a seigneur in the Channel Is [fr. F. *seigneurie*]
sei·gnior (séinjor) *n.* (*hist.*) the feudal lord of a manor [A.F. *segnour,* O.F. *seignor*]
sei·gnior·age, **sei·gnor·age** (séinjəridʒ) *n.* (*hist.*) seigniorial prerogative, e.g. the royal right to a percentage levy on bullion used for coinage ‖ the profit made in coining, resulting from the difference between a coin's intrinsic and its face value, as a source of revenue to a government [O.F. *seignorage*]
sei·gnio·ri·al, **sei·gno·ri·al** (seinjórí:əl, seinjóurí:əl) *adj.* of or pertaining to a seignior or sovereign
sei·gnior·y, **sei·gnor·y** (séinjəri:) *pl.* **sei·gnior·ies**, **sei·gnor·ies** *n.* (*hist.*) the dominion or rights of a seignior [O.F. *seignorie*]
seignorage *SEIGNIORAGE
seignorial *SEIGNIORIAL
Seine (sen, *Eng.* sein) a river (485 miles long) rising near Dijon, E. France, and flowing northwest to the English Channel. Canals link it with the Scheldt, Meuse, Rhine, Saône, Rhône and Loire. Ports: Le Havre, Rouen, Paris
seine (sein) 1. *n.* a large fishing net, with floats on one edge and weights on the other to make it hang upright in the water. The fish are enclosed in the net when the ends are brought together 2. *v.t.* and *i. pres. part.* **sein·ing** *past and past part.* **seined** to fish with a seine [O.E. *segne*]
Seine-et-Marne (seineimærn) a department (area 2,275 sq. miles, pop. 755,800) in N. France (*ILE-DE-FRANCE). Chief town: Melun
Seine-Ma·ri·time (senmari:ti:m) a department

(area 2,448 sq. miles, pop. 1,082,300) in N. France (*NORMANDY). Chief town: Rouen
seise (*law*) *SEIZE
seisin *SEIZIN
seis·mal (sáizməl, sáisməl) *adj.* seismic
seis·mic (sáizmik, sáismik) *adj.* relating to, characteristic of or produced by an earthquake or earthquakes **séis·mi·cal** *adj.* **seis·mism** *n.* phenomena characteristic of earthquakes [fr. Gk *seismos,* earthquake]
seis·mo·gram (sáizməgræm, sáisməgræm) *n.* a record made by a seismograph [fr. Gk *seismos,* earthquake +*gramma,* a letter]
seis·mo·graph (sáizməgræf, sáisməgrɑf, sáisməgræf, sáisməgrɑf) *n.* an instrument for recording the period, magnitude and direction of earth tremors **seis·mo·graph·ic** (saizmogræfik, saismogræfik) *adj.* **seis·mog·ra·phy** (saizmógrəfi, saismógrəfi:) *n.* [fr. Gk *seismos,* earthquake + *graphos,* written]
seis·mo·log·ic (saizməlódʒik, saisməlódʒik) *adj.* of or relating to seismology **seis·mo·lóg·i·cal** *adj.*
seis·mol·o·gy (saizmólədʒi:, saismólədʒi:) *n.* the scientific study of earthquakes or of artificially induced earth tremors [fr. Gk *seismos,* earthquake+*logos,* discourse]
seis·mom·e·ter (saizmómitər, saismómitər) *n.* an instrument, usually part of a seismograph, which supplies data for measurement of actual ground movements of an earthquake [fr. Gk *seismos,* earthquake + *metron,* measure]
seiz·a·ble (sí:zəb'l) *adj.* able to be seized (used esp. of goods that may lawfully be seized)
seize (si:z) *pres. part.* **seiz·ing** *past and past part.* **seized** *v.t.* to take suddenly and hold firmly ‖ to take by force, *he seized his sister's toy* ‖ (*law*) to take legal possession of, *to seize contraband* ‖ (*law*) to put in possession of ‖ to overwhelm mentally, take sudden mental possession of, *panic seized him* ‖ (often with 'on' or 'upon') to make instant use to one's advantage of (some chance, occasion, opportunity etc.), *to seize upon an excuse* ‖ to arrive at an immediate or sudden understanding of (a meaning etc.), *to seize a point* ‖ (*naut.*) to fasten with ropes **to seize up** (of moving mechanical parts) to become locked together because of undue heat, pressure or friction [O.F. *saisir, seisir*]
sei·zin, sei·sin (sí:zin) *n.* (*law*) possession or taking possession of land by freehold ‖ (*law*) the land so possessed [F. *saisine*]
seiz·ing (sí:ziŋ) *n.* (*naut.*) a fastening together with cords ‖ (*naut.*) cords used for this
sei·zor (sí:zər, sí:zɔr) *n.* (*law*) a person who takes possession of a freehold estate
sei·zure (sí:ʒər) *n.* a seizing or being seized ‖ a sudden attack of an illness, e.g. of epilepsy
se·jant (sí:dʒənt) *adj.* (*heraldry,* of an animal) sitting with the forelegs upright [older *seiant* fr. O.F.]
Sek·on·di-Ta·ko·ra·di (sekəndí:tɑkərádi:) a seaport and commercial center (pop. 160,900) of W. Ghana with an artificial deep-water harbor
se·lah (sí:lə, séfə) *n.* (*Bible*) a word, possibly denoting a musical rest, found at the end of a stanza in Psalms and in Habakkuk [Heb.]
Se·lan·gor (səlángor, səlóngour) a state (area 3,167 sq. miles, pop. 1,467,441) of Malaysia in W. Malaya. Capital: Kuala Lumpur. Selangor came under British protection (1874) and joined the Federation of Malaya (1948)
sel·dom (séldəm) *adv.* not often, rarely, *seldom at a loss* [O.E. *seldan*]
se·lect (silékt) 1. *v.t.* to take (something or someone preferred, most suitable etc.) from among a number, *to select a book from the shelf* 2. *adj.* having been selected as the most preferred ‖ socially exclusive, *a select resort* ‖ selecting carefully, discriminating, *select in his choice of books* [fr. L. *seligere* (*selectus*), to collect]
select committee a group of members of a legislative body chosen to study and report on a particular matter
Selected Reserve (*mil.*) the portion of the Ready Reserve consisting of units and individual Reservists required to participate in paid inactive-duty training periods and annual training
se·lec·tion (silékʃən) *n.* a selecting or being selected ‖ something selected ‖ (*biol.*) the natural or artificial process by which some members of a species reproduce while others do not, the result being a perpetuation of the characteristics of those who do reproduce (*NATURAL SELECTION) [fr. L. *selectio* (*selectionis*)]
selection fee a finder's fee

CONCISE PRONUNCIATION KEY: **(a)** æ, c*a*t; ɑ, c*ar*; ɔ f*aw*n; ei, sn*a*ke. **(e)** e, h*e*n; i:, sh*ee*p; iə, h*ere*; ɛə, b*ear*. **(i)** i, f*i*sh; ai, t*i*ger; ə:, b*ir*d. **(o)** o, *o*x; au, c*ow*; ou, g*oa*t; u, p*oor*; ɔi, r*oy*al. **(u)** ʌ, d*u*ck; u, b*u*ll; u:, g*oo*se; ə, b*a*cillus; ju:, c*u*be. x, lo*ch*; θ, *th*ink; ð, b*o*ther; z, *Z*en; ʒ, corsa*ge*; dʒ, sava*ge*; ŋ, ora*ng*utang; j, *y*ak; ʃ, *fi*sh; tʃ, fe*tch*; 'l, rabb*le*; 'n, redd*en*. Complete pronunciation key appears inside front cover.

selection pressure the magnitude of evolutionary pressure, separately measured as the rate at which one allele replaces another; coined by J. B. S. Haldane and R. A. Fisher

se·lec·tive (siléktiv) *adj.* discriminating, tending to select, *he is selective in the towns he visits* || (*radio*) of or designating the ability of a circuit to eliminate all unwanted frequencies

selective service compulsory military service according to age, physical fitness, occupation etc.

Selective Training and Service Act (1940), a U.S. Congressional act which adopted peacetime conscription for the first time in the U.S.A.

se·lec·tiv·i·ty (silektíviti:) *n.* the quality of being select || the extent to which a radio is selective

se·lect·man (siléktmən) *pl.* **se·lect·men** (siléktmən) *n.* an elected member of an administration board in towns of New England

Se·le·ne (silí:ni:) (*Gk mythol.*) the goddess of the moon, identified with the Roman Luna, and later with Artemis

se·le·nic (silí:nik, silénik) *adj.* of or containing selenium, esp. of compounds where this has a higher valence than in selenious compounds

selenic acid an acid, H_2SeO_4, resembling concentrated sulfuric acid in appearance, but so powerful an oxidizer when concentrated that it attacks gold and platinum

se·le·ni·ous (silí:ni:əs) *adj.* of or containing selenium, esp. of compounds where this has a valence lower than in selenic compounds

selenious acid a colorless crystalline acid, H_2SeO_3, an oxidizing agent yielding selenium

sel·e·nite (sélənait, silí:nait) *n.* a transparent crystalline variety of gypsum [fr. L. *selenites* fr. Gk *sēlēnitēs* (*lithos*), moon (stone)]

selenite *n.* a salt or ester of selenious acid [SELENIUM]

se·le·ni·um (silí:ni:əm) *n.* a nonmetallic element (symbol Se, at. no. 34, at. mass 78.96) obtained as a by-product of the refining of copper by electrolysis, and used in its crystalline form in the photoelectric cell, since its electrical resistance varies with the intensity of its illumination [Mod. L. fr. Gk *selēnē*, moon]

sel·en·o·de·sy (selənódəsi:) *n.* (*math.*) the branch of applied mathematics that determines, by observation and measurement, the positions of points and areas of portions of the moon's surface and the shape and size of the moon —**selenodetic** *adj.* —**solenodesist** *n.*

sel·e·nog·ra·pher (selənógrəfər) *n.* a specialist in selenography

se·le·no·graph·ic (silì:nəgræfik) *adj.* relating to selenography

se·le·nog·ra·phy (selənógrəfi:) *n.* the scientific study of the moon's physical features [fr. Mod. L. *selenographia* fr. Gk *selēnē*, moon + *-graphos*, written]

sel·e·nol·o·gy (selənólədʒi:) *n.* the branch of astronomy dealing with the moon [fr. Gk *selēnē*, moon + *logos*, discourse]

Se·leu·cia (silú:ʃə) the ancient capital of the Seleucids, and then of the Parthians, near Baghdad. It was founded (c. 312 B.C.) by Seleucus I

Se·leu·cid (silú:sid) a member of a Macedonian dynasty (312–65 B.C.) in Syria and western Asia, founded by Seleucus I. Under the Seleucids, Greek language and culture were introduced into Syria. Their rule ended when Antiochus XIII was defeated by Pompey (65 B.C.) and Syria became a Roman province

Se·leu·cus I (silú:kəs) (*d.* 280 B.C.), king of Syria (312–280 B.C.). One of Alexander the Great's generals, he received Babylonia when the Macedonian Empire broke up (312 B.C.), extended his power over much of Asia Minor and Syria, and founded the Seleucid dynasty

self- (self) *prefix* of, by, to, with or for oneself or itself || automatic || independent [O.E. *self-*, *sylf-*]

self 1. *adj.* (*bot.*) being of the same color throughout || of the same kind, material, color etc. as the rest **2.** *n. pl.* **selves** (selvz) the individuality or nature of a person or thing || a person's nature or an aspect of it, as revealed by his behavior etc., *he showed his true self* || a person with respect to his full mental or physical health, *he is his old self again* || personal advantage, *to put oneself to others before self* || (*biol.*) an individual resulting from self-fertilization || (*biol.*) a self-colored individual **3.** *pron.* myself, himself or herself, *a struggle to keep self and family going* [O.E. *self*, *selfa*]

self-a·ban·don·ment (sélfəbændənmənt) *n.* the act or state of forgetting selfish desires || an emotional state in which the self is heedless of its proper good

self-a·base·ment (sélfəbéismənt) *n.* a humbling of oneself

self-ab·ne·ga·tion (sélfæbnəgéiʃən) *n.* the quality of acting counter to one's desires for oneself in order to serve someone else, others, a cause etc.

self-a·buse (sélfəbjú:s) *n.* masturbation

self-act·ing (sélfæktiŋ) *adj.* automatic, acting by itself

self-ac·tu·al·i·za·tion (selfæktʃu:əlizéiʃən) *n.* (*psych.*) the process of understanding oneself and developing one's capacities and talents; coined by Abraham Maslow

self-ad·dressed (sélfədrést) *adj.* (of an envelope) addressed by the sender to himself, and enclosed with a letter so as to facilitate or solicit a reply

self-ad·he·sive (sélfədhí:siv) *adj.* (of an envelope) able to be sealed without any moistening of the surfaces treated with an adhesive

self-ap·point·ed (sélfəpóintid) *adj.* acting without outside authority, usually for the pleasure of bestowing blame or criticism

self-as·ser·tion (sélfəsə́:rʃən) *n.* behavior asserting one's claims or rights, expressing confidence in one's proper merit or aggressively asserting the superior quality of one's own mind or body **self-as·sér·tive** *adj.*

self-as·sur·ance (sélfəʃúərəns) *n.* self-confidence **self-as·súred** *adj.*

self-cen·tered *Br.* **self-cen·tred** (sélfséntərd) *adj.* thinking primarily or solely of what concerns oneself, seeing oneself as at the center of a situation

self-col·ored *Br.* **self-col·oured** (sélfkʌlərd) *adj.* (of animals, flowers, fabrics etc.) of one color throughout

self-com·mand (sélfkəmænd, sélfkəmúnd) *n.* self-control

self-com·pla·cen·cy (sélfkəmpléis'nsi:) *n.* self-satisfaction **self-com·plá·cent** *adj.*

self-com·posed (sélfkəmpóuzd) *adj.* having one's emotions under control

self-con·ceit (sélfkənsí:t) *n.* the quality of having too high an opinion of oneself

self-con·fi·dence (sélfkónfidəns) *n.* reliance on one's capacities **self-cón·fi·dent** *adj.*

self-con·scious (sélfkónʃəs) *adj.* thinking of one's own appearance or behavior as these may be assessed by others || embarrassed in the thought that one is making a poor impression in one's social relations || (of artistic style) knowingly artificial

self-con·tained (sélfkəntéind) *adj.* complete in itself || (*Br.*, of an apartment etc.) having its own entrance and all necessary living facilities || (of a person) not offering or dependent on contact with others

self-con·tra·dic·tion (sélfkɒntrədíkʃən) *n.* a proposition which contains within itself two statements which contradict one another || contradiction of oneself **self-con·tra·díc·to·ry** *adj.*

self-con·trol (sélfkəntróul) *n.* the ability to exercise the will so as to prevent oneself from expressing strong emotion or acting impulsively

self-de·ceit (sélfdisí:t) *n.* self-deception

self-de·cep·tion (sélfdisépʃən) *n.* the act or state of deceiving oneself

self-de·feat·ing (sélfdiffí:tiŋ) *adj.* initiated by oneself but having the effect of making one's purposes hard or impossible to attain

self-de·fense, *Br.* **self-de·fence** (sélf-diféns) *n.* a defending of one's life, property or reputation || (*law*) the right to defend oneself with the necessary force against violence or a threat of violence **self-defén·sive** *adj.*

self-de·lu·sion (sélfdilú:ʒən) *n.* self-deception

self-de·ni·al (sélfdináiəl) *n.* the deliberate refusal to satisfy one's desires, as a method of disciplining oneself or making it possible to help others, e.g. financially

self-de·ny·ing (sélfdináiiŋ) *adj.* showing self-denial

self-de·struct *v.* to destroy itself —**self-de·struct** *adj.*

self-de·struc·tion (sélfdistrʌ́kʃən) *n.* destruction of oneself, esp. suicide

self-de·ter·mi·na·tion (sélfditə:rminéiʃən) *n.* (*internat. law*) the right of a people to decide its own form of government or political status || the free determining of one's own actions **self-de·tér·min·ing** *adj.*

self-de·vo·tion (sélfdivóuʃən) *n.* devotion of oneself to some cause or to the needs, comfort etc. of some other person, usually involving personal sacrifice

self-dis·ci·pline (sélfdísəplin) *n.* the process of training one's emotions and impulses so that they conform to a certain standard of behavior in all circumstances

self-dis·trust (sélfdistrʌ́st) *n.* lack of confidence in one's own abilities, judgment etc.

self-driv·en (sélfdrívən) *adj.* driven by its own motive power

self-ed·u·cat·ed (sélfédʒukeitid) *adj.* having been educated by one's own efforts, without formal teaching

self-ef·face·ment (sélfiféismənt) *n.* the quality or practice of keeping modestly or discreetly in the background

self-em·ployed (sélfemplóid) *adj.* earning a living by working directly for oneself, without being tied to a regular employer by wage or salary

self-es·teem (sélfistí:m) *n.* one's good opinion of one's dignity or worth

self-ev·i·dent (sélfévidənt) *adj.* needing no proof of its truth

self-ex·am·i·na·tion (sélfigzæminéiʃən) *n.* thinking about one's own behavior and motives, esp. to judge them according to an ideal standard

self-ex·e·cut·ing (sélféksikju:tiŋ) *adj.* (of laws) coming into operation independently of any other legislation

self-ex·ist·ence (sélfigzístəns) *n.* the quality of being self-existent

self-ex·ist·ent (sélfigzístənt) *adj.* (of God) existing independently of any other cause or circumstance

self-ex·plain·ing (sélfiksptéiniŋ) *adj.* self-explanatory

self-ex·pla·na·to·ry (sélfiksplǽnətɔ:ri:, sélfiks-plǽnətɔuri:) *adj.* (of a statement) containing within itself all that is necessary for the understanding of it

self-ex·pres·sion (sélfiksspréʃən) *n.* expression of one's personality, e.g. in artistic form or through educational technique etc., esp. as a way of realizing one's individuality more fully

self-fer·ti·li·za·tion (sélffə:rt'lizéiʃən) *n.* fertilization of a hermaphrodite plant or animal by its own male elements

self-for·get·ful (sélffərgétfəl) *adj.* unselfish || characterized by self-abandonment

self-ful·fill·ment, *Br.* **self-ful·fil·ment** (sélfful-fílmənt) *n.* the complete realization of the potentialities of one's personality || (*loosely*) the satisfaction of one's creative impulses

self-gov·ern·ing (sélfgʌ́vərniŋ) *adj.* (of a state) administering its own government without interference from any other state **sélf-góv·ern·ment** *n.*

self-grat·i·fi·ca·tion (sélfgrætifikéiʃən) *n.* the act of satisfying one's desires

self-hard·en·ing (sélfhárd'niŋ) *adj.* (*metall.*, of steel) that hardens when raised to a high temperature and then cooled in air

self-help (sélfhélp) *n.* the practice of satisfying one's needs by one's own efforts, without drawing from the resources of the community or state

self-hood (sélfhud) *n.* unique identity, individuality

self-im·por·tance (sélfimpórt'ns) *n.* an exaggerated estimate of one's worth || behavior manifesting this **self-im·pór·tant** *adj.*

self-im·prove·ment (sélfimprú:vmənt) *n.* cultivation of the mind by steady application

self-in·duced (sélfindú:st, sélfindjú:st) *adj.* resulting from one's own or its own activity || (*elec.*) produced by self-induction

self-in·duc·tion (sélfindʌ́kʃən) *n.* (*elec.*) the production of an induced electromotive force in a circuit by changes in the magnetic field resulting from changes in the current flowing in the circuit. The induced electromotive force is proportional to the rate of change of the current

self-in·dul·gence (sélfindʌ́ldʒəns) *n.* a weakening of one's moral strength by satisfying one's desires and appetites too readily **sélf-in·dúl·gent** *adj.*

self-in·ter·est (sélfíntərist, sélfíntrist) *n.* primary concern for what is to one's own advantage, as a motive of behavior **self-in·ter·est·ed** *adj.*

self·ish (sélfiʃ) *adj.* concerned only to satisfy one's own desires and prepared to sacrifice the feelings, needs etc. of others in order to do so || caused by such concern

self-knowl·edge (sélfnólidʒ) *n.* knowledge of one's own nature, abilities, weaknesses etc.

CONCISE PRONUNCIATION KEY: **(a)** æ, c*a*t; ɑ, c*a*r; ɔ f*aw*n; ei, sn*a*ke. **(e)** e, h*e*n; i:, sh*ee*p; iə, d*ee*r; ɛə, b*ea*r. **(i)** i, f*i*sh; ai, t*i*ger; ə:, b*i*rd. **(o)** o, *o*x; au, c*ow*; ou, g*oa*t; u, p*oo*r; ɔi, r*oy*al. **(u)** ʌ, d*u*ck; u, b*u*ll; u:, g*oo*se; ə, b*a*cillus; ju:, c*u*be. x, lo*ch*; θ, *th*ink; ð, bo*th*er; z, *Z*en; ʒ, corsa*g*e; dʒ, sava*g*e; ŋ, ora*n*gutang; j, *y*ak; ʃ, *fi*sh; tʃ, fe*tch*; 'l, rabb*le*; 'n, redd*en*. Complete pronunciation key appears inside front cover.

self·less (sélflis) *adj.* concerned for others and not for one's own advantage, pleasure, comfort etc.

self·liq·ui·dat·ing (sélflíkwideitiŋ) *adj.* of a business transaction in which stock is swiftly turned into money or in which the original investment is quickly paid off

self·load·ing (sélflóudiŋ) *adj.* (of firearms) semiautomatic

self·love (sélflÁv) *n.* love of oneself || (*philos.*) proper concern for one's own well-being

self·made man (sélfmeid) a man who has materially succeeded in life by his own efforts and capacity without advantages of influential connections etc.

self·mas·ter·y (sélfmǽstəri:, sélfmÁstəri:) *n.* self-control

self·mov·ing (sélfmú:viŋ) *adj.* able to move under its own power

self·o·pin·ion·at·ed (sélfəpínjəneitid) *adj.* maintaining one's opinions in conceited obstinacy

self·or·dained (sélfɔrdéind) *adj.* designated by oneself, not by anyone else

self·pit·y (sélfpíti:) *n.* pity for oneself, esp. the belief that one is suffering as the innocent victim of circumstances

self·pol·li·nat·ed (sélfpólineitid) *adj.* pollinated by the transfer of pollen from anther to stigma of the same flower

self·pos·sessed (sélfpəzést) *adj.* having or showing self-possession

self·pos·ses·sion (sélfpəzéʃən) *n.* serene self-control || presence of mind

self·pres·er·va·tion (sélfprezərvéiʃən) *n.* the instinct to avoid being injured or killed

self·pro·nounc·ing (sélfprənáunsiŋ) *adj.* having diacritical marks of pronunciation applied to the original spelling instead of being rewritten in a phonetic transcription

self·pro·pelled (sélfprəpéld) *adj.* (of a gun) mounted on a tank or other armored vehicle and fired from it || (of a missile) propelled by its own fuel || (of a vehicle) driven by its own motor

self·pro·tec·tion (sélfprətékʃən) *n.* protection of oneself or one's interests

self·rais·ing (sélfréiziŋ) *adj.* (*Br.*) self-rising

self·re·al·i·za·tion (sélfri:əlizéiʃən) *n.* self-fulfillment

self·re·cord·ing (sélfrikɔ́rdiŋ) *adj.* (of an instrument) making an automatic record of its own operations

self·re·gard (sélfrigárd) *n.* concern for oneself

self·re·li·ance (sélfrilÁiəns) *n.* confidence in one's own abilities, power of judgment etc. **self·re·li·ant** *adj.*

self·re·nun·ci·a·tion (sélfrinÁnsiéiʃən) *n.* a sacrificing of one's own wishes or interests

self·re·proach (sélfripróutʃ) *n.* a reproaching or blaming of oneself, or an expression of this

self·re·spect (sélfrispékt) *n.* the proper esteem in which one holds oneself **self·re·spéct·ing** *adj.*

self·re·straint (sélfristréint) *n.* the ability to keep one's temper or desires in check

self·right·eous (sélfráitʃəs) *adj.* regarding oneself as more virtuous than others, or revealing this attitude

self·ris·ing (sélfráiziŋ) *adj.* (*Am.*=*Br.* self-raising, of flour) needing no further addition of baking powder etc.

self·sac·ri·fice (sélfsǽkrəfais) *n.* action intended to benefit others or to further an ideal, done in the knowledge that it is to one's own disadvantage **self·sác·ri·fic·ing** *adj.*

self·same (sélfseim) exactly the same, *both accidents happened at the selfsame spot*

self·sat·is·fac·tion (sélfsætisfǽkʃən) *n.* the belief that one's own actions, achievements or qualities are excellent

self·sat·is·fied (sélfsǽtisfaid) *adj.* having or showing self-satisfaction

self·seal·ing (sélfsí:liŋ) *adj.* made of a substance that automatically seals itself if holed, punctured etc. || (of envelopes etc.) having two treated surfaces which adhere on contact

self·seek·er (sélfsí:kər) *n.* a person who puts his own advantage above other considerations

self·seek·ing (sélfsí:kiŋ) 1. *adj.* characteristic of a self-seeker 2. *n.* the behavior of a self-seeker

self·serv·ice (sélfsə́:rvis) 1. *adj.* of a restaurant or shop where the customer selects and himself takes what he wants from the counter or shelf, paying when he leaves the counter or at the exit || of this method of supplying goods to customers 2. *n.* such a restaurant or shop

self·sown (sélfsóun) *adj.* sown by some natural process of dispersal, not by man

self·start·er (sélfstártər) *n.* a device for starting an engine without having to crank it || (*pop.*) someone who can be relied on to act on his own initiative

self·styled (sélfstáild) *adj.* (of a title etc.) assumed by oneself without authorization

self·suf·fi·cien·cy (sélfsəfíʃənsi:) *n.* the quality of being self-sufficient

self·suf·fi·cient (sélfsəfíʃənt) *adj.* accepting or needing no outside help

self·suf·fic·ing (sélfsəfáisiŋ) *adj.* self-sufficient

self·sup·port (sélfsəpɔ́rt, sélfsəpóurt) *n.* financial support of oneself without outside help **sélf·sup·pórt·ing** *adj.* earning one's own living || (of an enterprise) economically viable

self·sur·ren·der (sélfsəréndər) *n.* spiritual or passionate abandonment of oneself

self·sus·tain·ing (sélfsəstéiniŋ) *adj.* maintaining life or livelihood by oneself or itself

self·taught (sélftɔ́t) *adj.* taught by oneself with no formal instruction

self·will (sélfwíl) *n.* determination to follow one's own wishes, esp. when opposed to those of others **sélf·willed** *adj.*

self·wind·ing (sélfwáindiŋ) *adj.* (of a watch) winding itself automatically as the result of the kinetic energy imparted to it by moving it

Se·lim I (sí:lim, selí:m) (1467-1520), Ottoman sultan (1512-20). He massacred 40,000 of his own Shi'ite subjects for political reasons and conquered Persia (1514), Syria and Egypt (1516-17). He assumed the caliphate, was an able ruler, and was a patron of writers

Sel·juk (seldʒú:k, séldʒu:k) a member of any of several Turkish dynasties who ruled in Persia (11th-12th cc.), Syria (11th-12th cc.) and Asia Minor (11th-13th cc.)

Sel·kirk (sélkə:rk) a former county (area 267 sq. miles) of S.E. Scotland. Major towns: Selkirk, Galashiels

sell (sel) 1. *v. pres. part.* **sell·ing** *past* and *past part.* **sold** (sould) *v.t.* to dispose of the ownership of (goods, property or rights) to another or others in exchange for money, *he sold his house to them* || to effect such a transfer as an agent, *he sold their house for them* || to offer for sale, *he sells antiques* || to lead to the sale of, *advertising sold a million copies* || to betray for a reward, *he sold them to the police* || (*pop.*) to persuade others to accept, *to sell an idea* || (*pop.*) to cheat, deceive, *he was sold over the deal* || *v.i.* to offer something for sale, *is he thinking of selling?* || to find a buyer, *these goods sell quickly* **to sell off** to sell (what remains) at a reduced price **to sell out** to sell all the goods one has || to be completely sold, *the edition sold out overnight* || to sell one's stocks or shares, *to sell out before the market falls* || (*pop.*) to betray (a cause, partners in crime etc.) **to sell up** (*Br.*) to sell one's property, esp. in order to pay off debts 2. *n.* (*Br.*, *pop.*) a deception or disappointment, *the scheme proved a sell* || (*pop.*) salesmanship or sales appeal **séll·er** *n.* a person who sells || a product with respect to its rate of sale, *a poor seller* [O.E. *sellan*]

sellers' market a market in which, because of the scarcity of goods and intense demand, prices are generally high

selling plate a selling race

selling race a horse race in which the winning horse is sold by auction

sell·out (sélaut) *n.* (*pop.*) a betrayal || (*pop.*) a show etc. for which all the tickets are sold || (*pop.*) the sale of the entire stock of something as a result of popular demand

sel·vage, sel·vedge (sélvidʒ) *n.* the edge of cloth so woven as to prevent unraveling || the edge plate of a lock which permits the bolt to obtrude and engage [SELF+EDGE]

selves *pl.* of SELF

se·man·tic (simǽntik) *adj.* of meaning in language || of or in accordance with the science of semantics **se·man·tics** *n.* the branch of linguistic science which deals with the meanings of words and esp. with development and change in these meanings [fr. Gk *sēmantikos*, significant]

sem·a·phore (séməfɔr, séməfour) 1. *n.* a signaling device using movable arms || a system of signaling by flags or lights 2. *v. pres. part.* **sem·a·phor·ing** *past* and *past part.* **sem·a·phored** *v.t.* to send (a message) by semaphore || *v.i.* to signal using semaphore **sem·a·phor·ic** (seməfórik, seməfórik) *adj.* [fr. Gk *sēma*, sign +*pherein*, to bear]

Se·ma·rang (səmáraŋ) the chief port and commercial center (pop. 646,590) of central Java, Indonesia, on the Java Sea: shipbuilding, textiles, mechanical and electrical engineering. University

se·ma·si·o·log·i·cal (simeisi:əlódʒikəl, simeizi:əlódʒikəl) *adj.* semantic

se·ma·si·ol·o·gy (simeisi:ólədʒi:, simeizi:ólədʒi:) *n.* (*linguistics*) semantics [fr. Gk *sēmasia*, meaning of a word + *logos*, discourse]

se·mat·ic (simǽtik) *adj.* (*biol.*) of color, marking, odor etc. serving as a signal to attract or warn off [fr. Gk *sēma* (*sēmatos*), a sign]

sem·blance (sémbləns) *n.* just enough outward show to be plausible, *a semblance of gratitude* || a wilfully deceptive appearance, *under a semblance of friendship* [F.]

se·mé (səméi) *adj.* (*heraldry*) covered or sprinkled with many small bearings, e.g. flowers or stars [F.]

se·mei·ol·o·gy (sɪ:maiólədʒi:) *n.* (*philos.*) the science of signs or sign language || (*med.*) symptomatology [fr. Gk *sēmeion*, sign + *logos*, discourse]

se·mei·et·ic (sɪ:maiótik, sɪ:mi:ótik, semaiótik, semi:ótik) *adj.* (*med.*) of or relating to symptoms [fr. Gk *sēmeiōtikos* fr. *sēmeion*, a sign]

se·men (sí:men) *n.* the fluid secreted by the male's testes and accessory glands, containing spermatozoa [L.=a seed]

se·mes·ter (siméstər) *n.* one of the two divisions of the academic year in some universities, esp. in Germany and the U.S.A. [G. fr. L. (*cursus*) *semestris*, (period) of six months]

semi- (sémi:, sémai) *prefix* half || in part, to some extent || partial, not complete, full or perfect || partially, not completely, fully or perfectly || occurring twice within a specified period [L.]

sem·i·an·nu·al (semi:ǽnju:əl) *adj.* occurring every half year

sem·i·ar·id (semi:ǽrid) *adj.* receiving little annual rainfall, usually 10 to 20 ins

sem·i·au·to·mat·ic (semi:ɔtəmǽtik) *adj.* partly automatic || (of a firearm) that ejects spent cartridges and reloads automatically but that requires the trigger to be released and pressed for each shot

sem·i·breve (sémi:bri:v) *n.* (*Br.*, *mus.*) a whole note

sem·i·cir·cle (sémi:sə:rk'l) *n.* half a circle as divided by a diameter, or half a circle's circumference || an arrangement of objects roughly in this way, *a semicircle of chairs* [fr. L. *semicirculus*]

sem·i·cir·cu·lar (semi:sə́:rkjulər) *adj.* having the shape of a semicircle [fr. M.L. *semicircularis*]

semicircular canal any of the curved tubes of the inner ear that serve to maintain bodily equilibrium

sem·i·co·lon (sémi:koulən) *n.* a punctuation mark (;) separating two related sentences, esp. of some length or complexity, without suggesting the nature of the relationship

sem·i·con·duc·tor (semi:kəndÁktər) *n.* any of a group of materials (e.g. germanium, selenium, copper oxide, cadmium sulfide) having an electrical conductivity between that of metals and insulators. They are used in transistors, rectifiers, photoelectric cells and as thermometers

sem·i·con·scious (semi:kónʃəs) *adj.* not fully conscious

sem·i·con·serv·a·tive (semi:kənsé·rvətiv) *adj.* (*genetics*) of replication in which some molecular strands separate and combine with other molecules

sem·i·de·tached (semi:ditǽtʃt) *adj.* (of a house) having a common dividing wall with one other house

sem·i·di·ur·nal (semi:daié·rn'l) *adj.* occurring twice a day || lasting half a day

sem·i·farm·ing (semi:fɑrmiŋ) *n.* part-time farming activity

sem·i·fi·nal (semi:fáin'l) 1. *adj.* of a game or match played immediately before the final one of an eliminating series 2. *n.* such a game or match **se·mi·fí·na·list** *n.* a contestant in a semifinal

sem·i·flu·id (semi:flú:id) 1. *adj.* viscous 2. *n.* a viscous fluid

sem·i·lu·nar (semi:lú:nər) *adj.* crescent-shaped

sem·i·month·ly (semi:mÁnθli:) 1. *adj.* occurring, appearing, etc. twice a month 2. *pl.* **sem·i·month·lies** *n.* a paper, magazine etc. issued twice a month 3. *adv.* twice a month

sem·i·nal (sémin'l) *adj.* of seed or semen || constituting a source of later developments, *Coleridge was one of the seminal minds of the 19th century* [F. *séminal*]

seminal fluid semen excepting the spermatozoa ‖ semen

sem·i·nar (séminɑr) n. a group of advanced students working in association under the guidance of a teacher ‖ a course for or meeting of such a group [G. fr. L. *seminarium*, seedbed]

sem·i·nar·i·an (seminéəriən) n. a seminarist

sem·i·nar·ist (séminerist) n. a student at a seminary

sem·i·nar·y (sémineri:) pl. **sem·i·nar·ies** n. a place where intending priests, ministers or rabbis are trained ‖ (old-fash.) an educational institution [fr. L. *seminarium*, seedbed]

sem·i·nif·er·ous (seminífərəs) adj. bearing seed ‖ producing or carrying semen [fr. L. *semen* (*seminis*), seed +-*fer*, bearing]

Sem·i·nole (séminoul) pl. **Sem·i·nole, Sem·i·noles** n. a member of a Muskogean tribe of American Indians, which separated (18th c.) from the Creeks and settled in Florida. They were at war with the U.S.A. (1817–18 and 1835–42)

sem·i·of·fi·cial (semi:əfíʃəl) adj. derived from official sources but not having official authority

se·mi·ol·o·gy (si:mi:ólədʒi:, si:maiólədʒi:, semi:-ólədʒi:, semaiólədʒi:) n. semeiology

se·mi·ot·ic (si:mi:ótik, si:maiótik, semi:ótik, semaiótik) 1. adj. (mathematical logic) relating to the theory of symbols ‖ semeiotic 2. n. the theory of symbols **se·mi·ót·ics** n. semiotic

semiotics study of patterned human communication behavior, including auditory/vocal and facial expression, body talk (kinestics), touch (proxemics), signs, symbols (semiology) Cf ZOO-SEMIOTICS

sem·i·o·vip·a·rous (semi:ouvípərəs) adj. bearing young which are incompletely developed when born

sem·i·pal·mate (semi:pǽlmeit, semi:pǽlmit) adj. (zool., of some shore birds) having the anterior toes only partly webbed

sem·i·per·me·a·ble (semi:pə́:rmi:əb'l) adj. (phys.) of a membrane through which some substances (e.g. solvents) can pass, but not others (e.g. solutes) (*OSMOSIS)

sem·i·po·lar bond (semi:póulər) a coordinate bond

sem·i·por·ce·lain (semi:pɔ́rsəlin, semi:póursə-lin) n. a coarse type of porcelain

sem·i·pre·cious (semi:préʃəs) adj. (of a gem) valued for use in ornaments, but not having the commercial value of precious stones

sem·i·qua·ver (sémi:kwęivər) n. (Br., mus.) a sixteenth note

Se·mir·a·mis (simírəmis) legendary Assyrian queen, traditionally the founder of Babylon and Nineveh, worshiped as a dove and later identified with Ishtar

sem·i·sol·id (semi:sólid) 1. adj. having a thick viscous consistency 2. n. such a substance

Sem·ite (sémait, esp. Br. sí:mait) n. a member of any of the peoples speaking Semitic languages [fr. Mod. L. *semita* fr. L.L. fr. Gk *Sēm*, Shem (Noah's eldest son, eponymous ancestor of the Semites)]

Se·mit·ic (səmítik) adj. of, like, or concerning the Semites ‖ belonging to or concerned with the group of languages including E. Semitic (Akkadian), N.W. Semitic (Phoenician, Punic, Aramaic, Hebrew, Modern Hebrew etc.) and S.W. Semitic (Arabic, Amharic) **Se·mít·ics** n. the study of the Semitic languages, cultures etc.

Sem·i·tism (sémitizəm) n. a Semitic characteristic ‖ a Semitic expression or idiom ‖ ideas, cultural ideals etc., thought of as essentially Jewish [fr. Mod. L. *semiticus*]

sem·i·tone (sémi:toun) n. (mus.) the smallest interval in a diatonic scale, represented on a keyboard instrument by the interval between any two adjacent keys, e.g. between C and D♭

sem·i·trop·i·cal (semi:trópik'l) adj. subtropical

sem·i·vow·el (sémi:vǫuəl) n. a vowel sound which functions as a consonant, e.g. w and y in English

sem·i·week·ly (semi:wí:kli:) 1. adj. occurring twice a week 2. pl. **sem·i·week·lies** n. a paper, magazine etc. issued twice a week 3. adv. twice a week

sem·o·li·na (seməlí:nə) n. the small hard grains of *Triticum durum* or other hard wheat left after sieving and used to make macaroni, puddings etc. [fr. Ital. *semolino*]

sem·pi·ter·nal (sempitə́:rn'l) adj. (rhet.) eternal [F. *sempiternel*]

semp·stress (sémpstris, sémstris) n. a seamstress

sen (sen) pl. **sen** n. one hundredth of a yen, or a coin representing this [Jap. fr. Chin.]

sen pl. **sen** n. one hundredth of a riel [native Cambodian name]

sen pl. **sen** n. one hundredth of a rupiah, or a coin representing this [native name in Indonesia]

Se·nan·cour (sənɑ̃ku:r), Etienne Pivert de (1770-1846), French writer. His introspective epistolary novel 'Obermann' influenced other Romantic writers

sen·ate (sénit) n. (hist.) the governing body in ancient Athens, ancient Rome, and of certain medieval free cities etc. ‖ the upper legislative assembly in France, the U.S.A. etc. ‖ the governing body of certain U.S. universities and of the Universities of Cambridge (England) and London [O.F. *senat. senaz*]

sen·a·tor (sénətər) n. a member of a senate [O.F. *senateur*]

sen·a·to·ri·al (senətóri:əl, senətóuri:əl) adj. of, relating to, or befitting a senate or senator [fr. L. *senatorius*]

sen·a·tor·ship (sénətərʃip) n. the office or dignity of a senator

send (send) v. pres. part. **send·ing** past and past part. **sent** (sent) v.t. to cause (a person) to go to a specified place, in a specified direction or for a specified purpose, *she sent him to the store for some milk* ‖ to cause (a thing) to go or to be taken to another place, *to send a letter* ‖ (of God, fate etc.) to cause to happen, *trials sent from above* ‖ to cause to be on a divine mission, *a prophet sent to lead his people* ‖ to cause to behave or move in a specified way, *the blow sent him spinning* ‖ (Br.) to drive, cause to be in a specified state, *the noise sent him crazy* ‖ (radio) to transmit, *send it in code* ‖ v.i. (often with 'away', 'off') to send a letter asking for something ‖ (often with 'out') to send someone to fetch something, *he sent out for some beer* ‖ to send someone as a messenger, *she sent to inquire after you* ‖ (radio) to transmit a message **to send down** (Br.) to suspend or expel from a university **to send for** to ask for (someone or something) to come or be brought **to send in** to cause (a letter, bill etc.) to be delivered esp. to some large or central organization etc. **to send off** to dispatch ‖ to cause to go away ‖ to give a send-off to **to send on** to cause to be forwarded to someone after his departure to another place **to send out** to emit ‖ to put forth ‖ to distribute, dispatch **to send packing** to dismiss without ceremony [O.E. *sendan*]

Sen·dai (séndái) a city (pop. 618,700) of N. Honshu, Japan, a handicraft center (silk, pottery, lacquerware, woodwork). Castle (17th c.). University (1907)

sen·dal (sénd'l) n. (hist.) a fine silk fabric of medieval times [O. F. *cendal*]

send·er (séndər) n. a person who sends something ‖ (radio) a transmitter

send-off (séndɔf, séndɒf) n. a friendly demonstration of good wishes to a person or people going away

Sen·e·ca (sénikə), Lucius Annaeus 'the Elder' (c. 55 B.C.–c. 39 A.D.), Roman writer on rhetoric

Seneca, Lucius Annaeus (c. 4 B.C.–65 A.D.), Roman orator, statesman and philosopher, son of Seneca the Elder. He was tutor to Nero from 49 and an influential adviser during the early part of Nero's reign. Implicated in a conspiracy against Nero, he was forced to commit suicide. He wrote works on Stoic philosophy, the 'Apocolocyntosis' (a satire on the deification of Claudius) and nine tragedies on classical subjects

Sen·e·ca (sénəkə) n. a member of a tribe of Iroquois Indians who lived in W. New York State

Sen·e·gal (senigɔ́l) a republic (area 76,124 sq. miles, pop. 6,541,000) and member of the French Community, in W. Africa. Capital: Dakar. People: Wolof (24%), Fulani (10%), Serer, Toucouleur, Mandingo, Sarakolle and other African groups, 2% European. Languages: French, tribal languages (mainly Sudanic). Religion: 80% Moslem, 15% local African, 5% Christian. Coastal dunes give way to a rolling plain (rising above 700 ft only in the southeast near the Fouta Djallon of Guinea), semi-desert in the north, savanna and desert in the center and rain forest south of the Gambia. Average temperature (F.): 84° (higher in the northeast). Rainfall: under 20 ins in the north, over 20 ins in the center, tropical in the south. Livestock: cattle, sheep, goats, donkeys, horses, hogs, camels. Agricultural products: peanuts, millet, corn, rice, gum, palm nuts, manioc, beans. Mineral resources: phosphates, titanium, bauxite,

iron ore. Industries: fishing (esp. tuna), peanut oil refining, chemicals, textiles building materials, engineering. Exports: peanuts (85% of exports), peanut oil, oil cake, phosphates, hides and skins. Imports: wheat, rice, sugar, petroleum products, cement, textiles, machinery, chemicals. University: Dakar (1957). Monetary unit: CFA franc. HISTORY. A native kingdom developed (c. 9th c.) and was converted to Islam (11th c.). The area formed part of the empire of Mali (13th-15th cc.). The coast was explored by the Portuguese (late 15th c.) and the French established trading posts (17th c.). French control was strengthened (19th c.) and Senegal became part of French West Africa (1895). It became an autonomous republic within the French Community (1958) and was briefly part of the Mali Federation (1959-60). It became fully independent (Aug. 20, 1960) and joined the U.N. (1960). Senegal and Gambia formed the federation of Senegambia (1981) to coordinate their defense and economic and foreign policies

Senegal a river (1,000 miles long, navigable for 600 miles in the rainy season) flowing from S.W. Mali to the Atlantic at St Louis, Senegal, forming the Senegal-Mauritania frontier. Railroads link it to the Niger system

Sen·e·ga·lese (senigalí:z, senigɔlí:s, senəgalí:z, senəgalí:s) 1. adj. of or pertaining to Senegal or its people 2. pl. **Sen·e·ga·lese** n. a native or inhabitant of Senegal

se·nes·cence (sənésəns) n. the process or state of growing old [SENESCENT]

se·nes·cent (sənésənt) adj. growing old [fr. L. *senescens* (*senescentis*) fr. *senescere*, to grow old]

sen·e·schal (sénəʃəl) n. (hist.) the majordomo of a great medieval household or steward of an estate [O.F. fr. Gmc]

Sen·ghor (sǣgɔr), Léopold Sédar (1906-), Senegalese statesman, poet and essayist. He was president of Senegal (1960-80). In 1984 the Académie Français admitted him as the first black

se·nile (sí:nail, sénail) adj. of old age ‖ arising from old age, *senile decay* ‖ having the infirmities of old age ‖ (geog.) (of a river valley etc.) nearing the end of an erosion cycle **se·nil·i·ty** (sinílíti:) n. [fr. L. *senilis*]

sen·ior (sí:njər) 1. adj. indicating the older of two, *John Brown senior* (as distinguished from a younger John Brown, esp. a son) ‖ of higher rank, longer service etc., *the senior staff of a school* ‖ of or relating to a student in the graduating class of a school 2. n. someone who is senior by age, rank, length of service etc. ‖ a student in the graduating class of a school [L. comp. of *senex*, old]

senior citizen 1. a retired person 2. one over age 65, in some situations over age 55

senior high school a high school comprising the 10th, 11th and 12th grades, which follows junior high school

sen·ior·i·ty (si:njóriti:, si:njóriti:) n. the quality or state of being senior

senior wrangler (Br., Cambridge University) the person winning the highest first-class honors in the mathematical tripos

sen·na (sénə) n. a member of *Cassia*, fam. *Papilionaceae*, a genus of tropical shrubs and trees, whose leaves are dried for use as a laxative ‖ the dried leaves of these plants [Mod. L. fr. Arab.]

Sen·nach·er·ib (senǽkərib) king of Assyria (705-681 B.C.), son of Sargon II. He ravaged Judah (701 B.C.), destroyed Babylon (689 B.C.) and rebuilt Nineveh

se·ñor (seinjór, Span. senjór) pl. **se·ñors,** Span. **se·ñor·es** (senjóres) n. a courtesy title for a Spanish man (the equivalent of 'Mr') and (without the surname) a term of address [Span.]

se·ñor·a (seinjórə, Span. senjórɑ) pl. **se·ñor·as** (seinjóraz, Span. senjórɑs) n. a courtesy title for a married Spanish woman (the equivalent of 'Mrs') and (without the surname) a term of address [Span.]

se·ñor·i·ta (seinjəri:tə, Span. senɔrí:tɑ) pl. **se·ñor·i·tas** (seinjəri:təz, Span. senjorí:tus) n. a courtesy title for an unmarried Spanish girl or woman (the equivalent of 'Miss') and (without the surname) a term of address [Span.]

sen·sa·tion (senséiʃən) n. the activity of the senses ‖ (philos.) the immediate result of this activity before the combination with other data (cf. PERCEPTION) ‖ a state of emotional excitement, *the news caused a sensation* ‖ the cause of such a state of emotional excitement, *she was a sensation as Cleopatra* **sen·sá·tion·al** adj. sen–

sá·tion·al·ism *n.* the use of methods, e.g. in journalism, by which inordinate, foolish or harmful emotional responses are produced ‖ (*philos.*) the doctrine that all knowledge is acquired through the senses **sen·sá·tion·al·ist** *n.* [fr. M.L. *sensatio* (*sensationis*)]

sense (sens) **1.** *n.* any of the bodily faculties (hearing, sight, smell, taste or touch) by which an organism becomes aware of certain elements in its surroundings, when impulses are conveyed through the nervous system to the brain ‖ a conscious perception or sensation derived through these senses or through the intellect, *a sense of danger* ‖ the ability to judge external conditions, *a sense of direction* ‖ an ability to appreciate some quality, *a sense of honor* ‖ the meaning, nature or significance of a thing or idea, *the sense of someone's remarks* ‖ practical wisdom, the ability to perceive and act or judge soundly ‖ an apparent majority opinion, *the sense of the meeting* ‖ a meaning of a word, expression etc., as distinguished from its other meanings, *he was using the word in a different sense* ‖ (*pl.*) normal control of mental processes, *to bring someone to his senses* **in a sense** from one point of view **to make sense** to have a clear meaning or be rational **to make sense of** to understand the meaning of **2.** *v.t. pres. part.* **sens·ing** *past* and *past part.* **sensed** to perceive, esp. by intuition, *she sensed that he was hiding something* ‖ to read (computer data etc.) mechanically, electrically etc. **sénse·less** *adj.* unconscious, *he knocked her senseless* ‖ foolish, irrational, *a senseless thing to do* [F. *sens*]

sen·sei (sensei) *n.* a teacher of judo and karate

sense organ an organ, e.g. the eye, ear etc., adapted to receive stimuli

sense perception perception resulting from a stimulus received by a sense organ

sen·si·bil·i·ty (sensəbíliti:) *pl.* **sen·si·bil·i·ties** *n.* the ability to respond to a sense stimulus ‖ emotional responsiveness, esp. to the pathetic ‖ extreme refinement of taste ‖ (*pl.*) feelings easily hurt [fr. L. *sensibilitas*]

sen·si·ble (sénsəb'l) *adj.* showing good sense, being reasonable, practical, *a sensible precaution* ‖ appreciable, large enough to be perceived, *a sensible improvement*, ‖ capable of being perceived, *sensible phenomena* ‖ (*old-fash.*) sensitively aware, *he was sensible of the honor being done to him* [F.]

sen·si·bly (sénsəbli:) *adv.* in a sensible way

sen·si·tive (sénsitiv) *adj.* able to respond to a stimulus, *sensitive to light* ‖ able to respond to a very slight stimulus, *a sensitive instrument* ‖ keenly aware of the moods and feelings of others ‖ easily hurt emotionally, too readily affected by the feelings or imagined feelings of others with regard to oneself, *sensitive to criticism* ‖ (of a part of the body) liable to be painful ‖ quick to react to external influences, *a sensitive market* [F. *sensitif* (*sensitive*)]

sensitive plant *Minos pudica*, a common tropical American weed whose leaves droop and leaflets temporarily close when they are touched, due to changes in the pulvinus

sen·si·tiv·i·ty (sensitíviti:) *pl.* **sen·si·tiv·i·ties** *n.* the state or quality of being sensitive

sensitivity group (*psych.*) participants in a therapeutic group designed to promote understanding of personal emotions

sensitivity training (*psych.*) program designed to sharpen individual self-awareness

sen·si·ti·za·tion (sensitizéiʃən) *n.* a sensitizing or being sensitized

sen·si·tize (sénsitaiz) *pres. part.* **sen·si·tiz·ing** *past* and *past part.* **sen·si·tized** *v.t.* (*photog.*) to render (film, paper etc.) sensitive to light ‖ (*med.*) to render sensitive to a serum by using a series of injections

sen·si·tom·e·ter (sensitómitər) *n.* an instrument for measuring sensitivity, e.g. of the eye, of a film etc.

sen·so·ri·um (sensóriəm) *n.* (*biol.*) the sensory system

sen·so·ry (sénsəri) *adj.* of or relating to sensation ‖ (*physiol.*) carrying nerve impulses from the sense organs to the central nervous system

sen·su·al (sénʃuəl) *adj.* pertaining to the body and the senses as distinct from the intellect ‖ pertaining to the satisfaction of bodily desires, *sensual pleasures* ‖ (of people) having great liking for bodily pleasure, esp. sexual pleasure ‖ showing sensuality, *a sensual mouth* ‖ (*philos.*) relating to the doctrine of sensationalism **sén·su·al·ism** *n.* sensuality ‖ (*philos.*) sensationalism ‖ (*aesthetics*) the view that the beauty of an

object depends mainly on its sensuous qualities ‖ (*ethics*) the belief that the gratification of the senses is the highest good **sén·su·al·ist** *n.* **sen·su·al·is·tic** *adj.* [fr. L.L. *sensualis*]

sen·su·al·i·ty (senʃuːǽliti:) *n.* great liking for sensual pleasures [F. *sensualité*]

sen·su·ous (sénʃu·əs) *adj.* relating to, derived from, or affected by, the senses [fr. L. *sensus, sense*]

sent *past* and *past part.* of SEND

sen·tence (séntəns) **1.** *n.* (*gram.*) a word or group of words which states, asks, commands or exclaims something. It usually includes a subject and a predicate, is conventionally written with a capital letter at the beginning, and ends with a punctuation mark (period, question mark etc.) ‖ (*law*) the statement of a judicial decision to punish, *to pronounce sentence* ‖ the penalty which forms a part of such a statement, *he has served half his sentence* ‖ (*mus.*) a period [F.]

sentence *pres. part.* **sen·tenc·ing** *past* and *past part.* **sen·tenced** *v.t.* to state the penalty to be paid by (a person) [fr. F. *sentencier*]

sentence bargaining arrangement to have a defendant plead guilty in return for a lighter sentence

sentence stress the vocal stress put upon words in a sentence in order to make the meaning more clear. In English it is usually placed on the noun elements of the subject and on the object or complement

sen·ten·tious (senténʃəs) *adj.* making excessive or pompous use of statements of moral principles or of high-sounding phrases ‖ terse, pithy [fr. L. *sententiosus*]

sen·ti (sénti:) *n.* unit of currency in Tonga, equal to 1/100th pa'anga

sen·tience (sénʃəns) *n.* the state or quality of being sentient

sen·tien·cy (sénʃənsi:) *n.* sentience

sen·tient (sénʃənt) *adj.* capable of feeling, having the power of sense perception [fr. L. *sentiens* (*sentientis*) fr. *sentire*, to feel]

sen·ti·ment (séntəmənt) *n.* a group of emotions and opinions associated with and aroused by an idea ‖ susceptibility to emotional appeal ‖ expression of emotional ideas in art, music or literature ‖ (*loosely*) sentimentality ‖ a short, usually banal, expression of feeling, e.g. on a greeting card **sen·ti·men·tal** (sentəmént'l) *adj.* characterized by excessive emotional show ‖ influenced by feeling rather than reason ‖ feeling, or characterized by, tenderness **sen·ti·mén·tal·ism**, **sen·ti·mén·tal·ist**, **sen·ti·men·tal·i·ty** (sentəmentǽliti:) *n.* **sen·ti·mén·tal·ize** *pres. part.* **sen·ti·men·tal·iz·ing** *past* and *past part.* **sen·ti·men·tal·ized** *v.i.* and *t.* [O.F. *sentement*]

sen·ti·nel (séntin'l) *n.* a soldier posted on guard ‖ someone who keeps watch **to stand sentinel** to guard [F. *sentinelle* fr. Ital.]

Sentinel *n.* (*mil.*) proposed system for defense of 50 states against ICBMs utilizing radar-directed antiballistic missiles for interception

sen·try (séntri:) *pl.* **sen·tries** *n.* a soldier on guard duty [perh. fr. *centrinel*, older var. of SENTINEL]

sentry box a tall wooden box to shelter a sentry

sentry go duty as a sentry

Se·nu·fo (sinú:fou) *pl.* **Se·nu·fo, Se·nu·fos** *n.* a member of a W. African people of Mali and the Ivory Coast

Se·nus·si (senú:si:) *pl.* **Se·nus·sis** *SANUSI

sen·za·la (sénzələ) *n.* a set of slave quarters near the master's house in N.E. Brazil [Port.]

Seoul (soul, saú:l) the capital (pop. 9,454,825) and commercial and industrial center of South Korea, near the northwest coast. Industries: mechanical and railroad engineering, automobiles, textiles, tobacco, food processing, brewing. Port: Inchon. Palaces (14th c.). University

se·pal (sí:p'l) *n.* (*bot.*) a protective leaflike division of the calyx of a flower [fr. F. *sépale*]

sep·a·ra·bil·i·ty (sepərəbíliti:) *n.* the state or quality of being separable

sep·a·ra·ble (sépərəb'l) *adj.* capable of being separated [F. *séparable*]

sep·a·rate 1. (sépəreit) *v. pres. part.* **sep·a·rat·ing** *past* and *past part.* **sep·a·rat·ed** *v.t.* to cause (things or people which were joined together or mixed) to be no longer joined or mixed, *to separate wheat from chaff* ‖ to form a boundary between, *the fence separates the two gardens* ‖ to distinguish between, *you can't separate the rights and wrongs of the case* ‖ to cause (man and wife) to cease to live together ‖ *v.i.* to cease

to be connected or associated, go in different directions, *they separated when they reached the crossroads* ‖ (of man and wife) to cease to live together ‖ (with 'from') to withdraw ‖ to become disconnected ‖ to become separate **2.** (sépərit) *adj.* not joined to or mixed with something else ‖ existing independently of other things ‖ regarded as being individual ‖ isolated ‖ not shared **3.** (sépərit) *n.* an offprint ‖ (*pl.*) women's clothes (blouses, skirts etc.) meant for wearing either in combination with one another or with other alternatives [fr. L. *separare* (*separatus*)]

sep·a·ra·tion (sepəréiʃən) *n.* a separating or being separated ‖ a place where a division occurs ‖ something that separates ‖ a legal agreement by which man and wife do not live together [O.F.]

separation of powers the division of constitutional government in a democracy between three separate, independent branches: legislative, executive and judicial

sep·a·ra·tist (sépərətist, sépəreitist) *n.* someone in favor of separation (e.g. of a minority group from a large body) ‖ a member of a political or religious minority favoring secession **Sep·a·ra·tist** (*hist.*) a Brownist

sep·a·ra·tive (sépəreitiv, sépərətiv) *adj.* tending to separate or to cause separation [F. *séparatif* (*séparative*)]

sep·a·ra·tor (sépəreitər) *n.* a device which separates a mixture into constituent parts, e.g. a machine which separates cream from milk centrifugally [L.L.]

Se·phar·dic (səfárdik) *adj.* of or relating to the Sephardim

Se·phar·dim (səfárdim, səfardí:m) *pl. n.* (*hist.*) the Jews who settled in Spain and Portugal before the Inquisition and who spread to England, Greece, the Americas etc. (cf. ASHKENAZIM) ‖ their descendants [Heb.]

se·pi·a (sí:piːə) *n.* the black inky secretion of cuttlefish ‖ a dark brown pigment prepared from this and used in inks and watercolors ‖ a rich dark brown color ‖ a photograph reproduced in this color ‖ or drawing made in sepia ink [L. fr. Gk]

se·poy (sí:pɔi) *n.* (*hist.*) an Indian soldier in the British-Indian army [fr. Urdu]

Sepoy Rebellion the Indian Mutiny

sep·pu·ku (sepú:ku:) *n.* hara-kiri [Jap. fr. Chin.]

sep·sis (sépsis) *n.* pus formation in an infected part of the body resulting in blood poisoning [Mod. L. fr. Gk *sepsis*, putrefaction]

sept (sept) *n.* a clan, esp. one of ancient Ireland [prob. var. of SECT]

Sept. September

septa *pl.* of SEPTUM

sep·tal (séptəl) *adj.* of a septum or septa

sep·tar·i·um (septéariːəm) *pl.* **sep·tar·i·a** (septéariːə) *n.* (*geol.*) a nodule, esp. of limestone, crisscrossed by cracks which are filled with other deposits [Mod. L. fr. *septum*, partition]

sep·tate (sépteit) *adj.* (*biol.*) partitioned by or provided with a septum or septa [fr. Mod. L. *septatus*]

sep·ta·va·lent (septəvéilənt) *adj.* having seven valences [fr. *septa-* fr. L. *septem*, seven + *valens* (*valentis*) fr. *valere*, to be strong]

Sep·tem·ber (septémbər) *n.* (*abbr.* Sept., Sep.) the ninth month of the year, having 30 days [L. fr. *septem*, seven (being the seventh month in the Roman year)]

September massacres (*F. hist.*) the slaughter of political prisoners in French prisons Sept. 2-6, 1792, provoked partly by the news of the Prussian invasion

Sep·tem·brist (septémbrist) *n.* (*F. hist.*) a person who took part in the September massacres

sep·te·nar·y (séptənəri:) **1.** *adj.* of or relating to seven ‖ numbered in sevens **2.** *pl.* **sep·te·nar·ies** *n.* a seven-foot verse [fr. L. *septenarius*]

sep·ten·de·cil·lion (septendisíljən) *n.* *NUMBER TABLE [fr. L. *septendecim*, seventeen + MILLION]

sep·ten·ni·al (septéniːəl) *adj.* lasting seven years ‖ occurring once every seven years [fr. L. *septennium*, period of seven years]

sep·tet, sep·tette (septét) *n.* a set of seven objects or people, esp. musicians ‖ a musical composition for seven instruments or voices [Gk fr. L. *septem*, seven]

sep·tic (séptik) *adj.* causing to putrefy, *septic activity of bacteria* ‖ due to putrefaction, *septic poisoning* [fr. L.L. *septicus* fr. Gk]

sep·ti·ce·mi·a, sep·ti·cae·mi·a (septisí:miːə) *n.* blood poisoning **sep·ti·cémic, sep·ti·cæmic**

adj. [Mod. L. fr. Gk *sēptikos*, putrefactive+*haima*, blood]

septic tank a tank in which sewage is broken down by anaerobic bacterial activity

sep·til·lion (septíljən) *n.* *NUMBER TABLE [fr. F. fr. L. *septem*, seven+MILLION]

sep·time (sépti:m) *n.* (*fencing*) the seventh of eight parrying positions [fr. L. *septimus*]

Septimius Severus *SEVERUS

sep·tu·a·ge·nar·i·an (septʃu:ədʒənɛ́əri:ən) **1.** *adj.* between 70 and 80 years of age **2.** *n.* someone of this age [L. *septuagenarius*]

Sep·tu·a·ges·i·ma (septʃu:ədʒésəmə) *n.* the third Sunday before Lent [L. (fem.)=seventieth (this Sunday is about 70 days before Easter)]

Sep·tu·a·gint (séptʃu:ədʒint) *n.* (symbol LXX) the Greek version of the Old Testament, including the Apocrypha, traditionally said to have been made by about 70 translators. Produced for the library of Alexandria in the 3rd and 2nd cc. B.C., this translation was popular with the Jews of the Diaspora, whose language was Greek, and it was often preferred to the Hebrew version by the early Fathers of the Christian Church. It was the first vernacular version of the Bible and is still used in the Orthodox Eastern Church [fr. L. *septuaginta*, seventy]

sep·tum (séptəm) *pl.* **sep·ta** (séptə), **sep·tums** *n.* (*biol.*) a partition separating two cavities (e.g. the nostrils) or masses of tissue (e.g. in fruits) [L.=a partition]

sep·tu·ple (séptup'l, séptjup'l, septú:p'l, septjú:p'l, septʌ́p'l) **1.** *adj.* sevenfold **2.** *v. pres. part.* **sep·tu·pling** *past* and *past part.* **sep·tu·pled** *v.t.* to make seven times as great ‖ *v.i.* to become seven times as great [fr. L. L. *septuplus*]

sep·ul·cher, esp. Br. **sep·ul·chre** (sépəlkər) *n.* a tomb, esp. one cut in rock, a burial vault [O.F. *sepulcre*]

se·pul·chral (sipʌ́lkrəl) *adj.* relating to the burial of the dead, *sepulchral rites* ‖ suggestive of the tomb, *a sepulchral voice* [fr. L. *sepulcralis*]

sepulchre *SEPULCHER

sep·ul·ture (sépəltʃər) *n.* (*rhet.*) burial, entombment [O.F.]

se·quel (sí:kwəl) *n.* something which follows a continuation (esp. of a story) ‖ a result or aftereffect [O.F. *sequelle*]

se·que·la (sikwí:lə) *pl.* **se·que·lae** (sikwí:li:) *n.* that which follows as a consequence, esp. (*med.*) the aftermath of a disease [L.]

se·quence (sí:kwəns) *n.* a succession of things which are connected in some way, *the sequence of events which led to his downfall* ‖ a series of poems connected by form and theme, *a sonnet sequence* ‖ (*cards*) three or more consecutive cards in a suit ‖ (*movies*) one complete scene in a film ‖ (*eccles.*) a hymnlike non-biblical text preceding the reading of the Gospel at High Mass or a Requiem Mass ‖ (*mus.*) a succession of phrases repeated at different pitches [fr. L.L. *sequentia*]

se·quent (sí:kwənt) **1.** *adj.* succeeding, following in time or order ‖ following as a natural result **2.** *n.* a result, consequence [O.F. fr. L. *sequens* (*sequentis*) fr. *sequi*, to follow]

se·quen·tial (sikwénʃəl) *adj.* characterized by or constituting a sequence ‖ occurring as a result [fr. L.L. *sequentia*, sequence]

sequential marketing (*business*) marketing strategy involving introduction of a product or service in one market segment at a time

sequentials *n.* (*pharm.*) estrogen-based pills prescribed in series to minimize side effects *also* sequential contraceptive pills

se·ques·ter (sikwéstər) *v.t.* (*law*) to seize (property etc.) until the owner pays a debt or satisfies some other demand ‖ to seize, confiscate by public authority ‖ (*rhet.*) to place apart from society **se·qués·tered** *adj.* withdrawn from social intercourse, *a sequestered life* ‖ in rural isolation, *a sequestered cottage* [fr. L.L. *sequestrare*, to commit for safekeeping]

se·ques·trate (sikwéstreit) *pres. part.* **se·ques·trat·ing** *past* and *past part.* **se·ques·trat·ed** *v.t.* to sequester ‖ (*Br.*, *law*) to divert income from (property) from the owner or owners to another or others for a period of time [fr. L.L. *sequestrare* (*sequestratus*), to commit for safekeeping]

se·ques·tra·tion (si:kwestréiʃən, sikwestréiʃən) *n.* a sequestering or being sequestered [fr. L.L. *sequestratio* (*sequestrationis*)]

se·ques·tra·tor (sí:kwestreitər, sikwéstreitər) *n.* someone who sequestrates ‖ (*law*) a person appointed to administer sequestrated property [L.L.]

se·ques·trum (sikwéstrəm) *pl.* **se·ques·tra** (sikwéstrə), **se·ques·trums** *n.* (*med.*) a piece of dead tissue, esp. bone, which remains in its place although separated from the living tissue [Mod. L. = something separated, neut. of *sequester*, standing apart]

se·quin (sí:kwin) *n.* a small circular piece of glittering metal etc. sewn on to cloth for ornamentation ‖ (*hist.*) a Venetian gold coin [F. fr. Ital. fr. Arab.]

se·quoi·a (sikwóiə) *n.* a member of *Sequoia*, fam. *Taxodiaceae*, a genus of very large North American coniferous trees including the redwood. The tallest reach more than 300 ft and the thickest have a trunk diameter of up to 35 ft [Mod. L. after *Sequoya*, Cherokee Indian leader who reduced the Cherokee language to writing]

Sequoia National Park a reservation (386,863 acres) in the Sierra Nevada Mtns of California, established (1890) by a U.S. Congressional act to protect giant sequoia groves

Se·quoya (sikwóiə), (c. 1760-1843), American Cherokee Indian warrior credited with inventing the Cherokee written language (talking leaves), born George Guess. Having learned Spanish, French and English, and resenting the takeover of tribal lands by the whites, he developed a Cherokee alphabet to record and preserve the Cherokee culture. By 1821 he had developed 86 symbols for sounds. The syllabary was used in the newspaper 'Cherokee Phoenix' from 1828

se·rac (sirǽk) *n.* (*geol.*) a pinnacle of ice formed by the crossing of crevasses where a glacier breaks at a fall [Swiss F. *sérac*, orig. the name of a cheese]

se·ragl·io (sirǽljou, sirá:ljou) *pl.* **se·ragl·ios** *n.* a harem ‖ a Turkish palace enclosed by walls [Ital. *serroglio*, enclosure]

se·rа·i (sərái:, serái) *pl.* **se·ra·is** *n.* a caravanserai [Turk.]

Se·ram·pur (serəmpúr) (or Serampore) a resort (pop. 75,000) in West Bengal, India, on the Hooghly River near Calcutta. It was a Danish settlement (Frederiksnagar), 1755-1845

se·ra·pe (sərápi:) *n.* a woolen blanket, often brightly colored, worn as a cloak by Spanish-Americans [Span.]

ser·aph (sérəf) *pl.* **ser·aphs**, **ser·a·phim** (sérəfim) *n.* a member of the highest order of angels (*ANGEL) [M.L. fr. Heb.]

se·raph·ic (sirǽfik) *adj.* of or like a seraph ‖ angelic, *a seraphic smile* **se·ráph·i·cal** *adj.* [fr. eccles. L. *seracus*]

Se·ra·pis (siréipis) Egyptian deity whose cult flourished in the Ptolemaic and Roman periods. He was a god of healing, frequently identified with Osiris, Asclepius, Zeus and Dionysus

ser·a·ton·in [$C_{10}H_{12}ON_2$] (serətóunin) *n.* (*biochem.*) sleep-related hormone, derived from L-tryptophan, present in blood and nerve tissue, used to stimulate smooth muscles and nerves. Seratonin is believed to affect neurotransmission

Serb (sə:rb) **1.** *adj.* Serbian **2.** *n.* a member of a Slavic people of Serbia and adjacent regions ‖ their language

Ser·bi·a (sə́:rbi:ə), the largest and most populous constituent republic (area including Vojvodina and Kosovo-Metohija 36,937 sq. miles, pop. 8,860,000) of Yugoslavia. Capital: Belgrade. Serbia proper (pop. 4,900,000) is mainly mountainous, broken up by the broad valleys of the Morava and its tributaries. Crops: corn, cereals. Livestock: cattle. Mineral resources: lignite, copper, antimony. Hydroelectricity. HISTORY. Serbia emerged as a principality in the 9th c., but remained subject to the Byzantine Empire until consolidated (12th c.) by Stevan Nemanja. His son was crowned the first king of Serbia (1217). During the reign (1331-55) of Stevan Dušan, Serbia became the dominant power in the Balkans, but it was overthrown (1389) by the Turks at Kosovo Polje, and made a vassal state. It was fully incorporated in the Ottoman Empire (1459). Serbia revolted (1804) under Karageorge and was recognized by Turkey as independent (1828). Its independence was fully guaranteed by the Congress of Berlin (1878). Serbia acquired much of Macedonia after the Balkan Wars (1912-13), and became (1918) part of the kingdom later called Yugoslavia

Ser·bi·an (sə́:rbi:ən) **1.** *adj.* of or relating to Serbia, the Serbs, or their language **2.** *n.* Serbo-Croatian as spoken in Serbia

Ser·bo-Cro·a·tian (sə:rboukrouéiʃən) **1.** *n.* a S. Slavic language spoken by about 8,500,000 people in Yugoslavia and by minorities in Italy, Rumania and Hungary. Serbo-Croatian is divided into three main dialects. The literary language shows a strong Italian influence. The Croats use the Latin alphabet and the Serbs use the Cyrillic **2.** *adj.* of this language ‖ of the people who speak it

sere, sear (siər) *adj.* (*rhet.*) withered, dried up [O.E. sēar]

ser·e·nade (serənéid) **1.** *n.* a piece of music played or sung at night (cf. AUBADE) in the open air, esp. by a lover beneath his mistress' window ‖ a musical composition for several instruments in a number of movements **2.** *v. pres. part.* **ser·e·nad·ing** *past* and *past part.* **ser·e·nad·ed** *v.t.* to entertain with a serenade ‖ *v.i.* to perform a serenade [F. fr. Ital.]

se·re·na·ta (serənátə) *pl.* **ser·e·na·tas, ser·e·na·te** (serənátei) *n.* (*hist.*) a semioperatic cantata ‖ an orchestral serenade [Ital.]

ser·en·dip·i·ty (serəndípiti:) *n.* the gift of being able to make delightful discoveries by pure accident [coined by Horace Walpole after 'The Three Princes of Serendip', a fairy tale]

se·rene (sərí:n) *adj.* (of the weather) fine, clear and calm ‖ (of a person) tranquil, at peace with himself ‖ (of facial expression) expressing tranquility, inner calm ‖ used in the titles of certain members of some royal families, *His Serene Highness* [fr. L. *serenus*]

se·ren·i·ty (səréniti:) *n.* the state or quality of being serene ‖ calmness ‖ clearness **Se·ren·i·ty** *pl.* **Se·ren·i·ties** a title of respect used for certain members of some royal families [F. *sérénité*]

serf (sə:rf) *n.* (*hist.*) a feudal laborer bound to an estate **sérf·age, sérf·dom, sérf·hood** *ns.* [O.F.]

serge (sə:rdʒ) *n.* a hard-wearing twilled worsted fabric used for clothing [O.F. *serge, sarge*, a silk stuff]

ser·geant (sárdʒənt) *n.* (*mil.*) a noncommissioned officer ranking immediately above a corporal ‖ a police officer ranking immediately below (*Am.*) captain or lieutenant or (*Br.*) inspector ‖ a sergeant-at-arms [O.F. *sergent, serjant*, a servant]

Sergeant *n.* (*mil.*) a mobile, inertially guided, solid-propellant, surface-to-surface missile (MGM-29A), with nuclear warhead capability and a range of 75 nautical miles

ser·geant-at-arms, Br. **ser·jeant-at-arms** (sárdʒəntətármz) *n.* an officer in a legislature whose main responsibility is the preservation of order

sergeant first class a noncommissioned army officer ranking below a master sergeant and above a staff sergeant

sergeant major the highest-ranking noncommissioned army or Marine Corps officer

se·ri·al (síəri:əl) **1.** *adj.* being, being arranged as, or forming a series ‖ (of a story, radio or television program etc.) appearing regularly in a series of parts ‖ of a serial or serials, *serial rights* ‖ (*mus.*) pertaining to twelve-tone composition **2.** *n.* a serial story, radio or television program etc. **sé·ri·al·ize** *v.t. pres. part.* **se·ri·al·iz·ing** *past* and *past part.* **se·ri·al·ized** [fr. Mod. L. *serialis* fr. *series*, a row, order]

serial access *n.* (*computer*) method of access to information based on physical location of the data

serial number the separate item number given to a unit of a series for identification

serial printer *n.* (*computer*) an output printer in which each character is printed in sequence by type bars, type balls, daisy wheel, etc. *also* character printer *Cf* LASER PRINTER, LINE PRINTER

se·ri·ate (síəri:it, síəri:eit) *adj.* arranged in a series [fr. Mod. L. *seriatus* fr. *series*, row, order]

se·ri·a·tim (siəri:éitim, seri:éitim) *adv.* point by point, one after another in order [M.L.]

se·ri·a·tion (siəri:éiʃən) *n.* arrangement in an order

se·ri·ceous (sirí:ʃəs) *adj.* (*biol.*) covered with fine silky hairs [fr. L. *sericus*]

ser·i·cin (sérisin) *n.* a gelatinous protein that cements together the fibroin filaments in silk [L. *sericum*, silk]

ser·i·cul·ture (sérikʌltʃər) *n.* the breeding of silkworms for the production of raw silk [shortened fr. F. *sériciculture*]

se·ri·e·ma (seri:í:mə, seri:éimə) *n.* *Cariama cristata*, fam. *Cariamidae*, a long-legged, crested S. Brazilian bird feeding on snakes, lizards etc. ‖

Chunga burmeisteri, a related bird of Argentina [Mod. L. fr. Tupi]

se·ries (síəri:z) *pl.* **se·ries** *n.* a number of similar things occurring one after another, in space or time, in an orderly way, esp. in such a way that each has a similar relation to the one preceding it, *a pagoda with a series of six progressively narrower roofs* ‖ a number of successive events of the same kind, *a series of accidents* ‖ (*bibliography*) a number of volumes, articles etc. published successively and falling under one general title ‖ (of stamps and coins) a complete set ‖ (*chem.*) a group of substances (usually compounds) related by structure and properties, *a homologous series* ‖ (*geol.*) a division of rocks, formed during an epoch ‖ (*math.*) the sum obtained by adding the terms of a mathematical sequence ‖ (*chem.*) a period or a portion of a period of the periodic table, e.g. the lanthanide series **in series** (*elec.*) of cells or circuits so arranged that the current flows through each in succession (cf. PARALLEL) [L.=row, order]

ser·if (sérif) *n.* a small terminal line across the top or bottom of a main stroke of a printed or written letter [etym. doubtful]

ser·in (sérin) *n. Serinus canarius,* fam. *Fringillidae,* a small finch of central Europe related to the canary [F.]

se·rin·ga (səríŋgə) *n.* a member of *Hevea,* fam. *Euphorbiaceae,* a genus of Brazilian rubber trees ‖ syringa [F.]

se·ri·o·com·ic (siəri:oukómik) *adj.* neither wholly serious nor wholly comic but partly both **se·ri·o·cóm·i·cal** *adj.*

se·ri·ous (síəri:əs) *adj.* of great importance, *a serious decision* ‖ (of people) grave and thoughtful in manner ‖ scholarly and thought-provoking, *a serious book* ‖ in earnest ‖ firmly devoted, *a serious bridge player* ‖ alarming, critical, *a serious situation* [fr. F. *sérieux*]

ser·jeant (sárdʒənt) *n.* a sergeant-at-arms ‖ a serjeant at law [O.F. *sergent, serjant,* a servant]

serjeant-at-arms *SERGEANT-AT-ARMS

serjeant at law (*hist.*) a member of the highest rank of barristers, prior to 1880, from which Common Law judges were appointed

ser·mon (sármən) *n.* an address delivered by a priest or minister to instruct or exhort a congregation ‖ (*pop.*) a serious reproof or exhortation expressed at tedious length **sér·mon·ize** *pres. part.* **sér·mon·iz·ing** *past* and *past part.* **sér·mon·ized** *v.t.* and *i.* [A.F. *sermun*]

Sermon on the Mount Christ's discourse on the Mosaic Law. It includes the Beatitudes and the Lord's Prayer (Matthew v, vi, vii)

se·rol·o·gy (sirólədʒi:) *n.* the scientific study of serums and their reactions, esp. the behavior of antibodies and antigens [fr. SERUM + Gk *logos,* word]

se·ros·i·ty (sirósiti:) *n.* the quality or state of being serous

se·rot·i·nous (sirót'nəs) *adj.* (*biol.*) appearing or blooming late in the season [fr. L. *serotinus* fr. *sero,* late]

se·ro·type (síərətaip) *v.* to classify microorganisms according to their antigens

se·rous (síərəs) *adj.* of or like serum ‖ thin, watery [fr. F. *séreux*]

serous membrane a thin tissue that lines or encloses some organs and that produces serum, e.g. the pericardium

Se·row·e (seiróuei) a trade center (pop. 30,000) of E. Botswana

ser·pent (sárpənt) *n.* a snake ‖ (*Bible*) the devil, Satan ‖ (*mus., hist.*) an early bass wind instrument with a long, coiled tube [O.F.]

ser·pen·tine (sárpənti:n, sárpəntain) **1.** *adj.* of or like a serpent ‖ twisting, winding **2.** *n.* a hydrated magnesium silicate, usually dark green, with mottled coloring, used for ornaments [O.F. *serpentin* fr. L. *serpentinus*]

Ser·ra (sérra), Miguel José (in religion, Junípero, 1713-84) Spanish Franciscan priest, apostle to California

Ser·ra A·ca·ra·hy (sérrɑɑkɑɾɑí:) (Serra Acaraí) a mountain range rising to 2,500 ft and forming the boundary between Guyana and Brazil

Ser·ra da Es·trel·la (sérrədəistrélɑ) a mountain range in N. central Portugal: highest point 6,532 ft

ser·rate (sérit, séreit) *adj.* (of the edge of a leaf or other structure) having notches or teeth like the cutting edge of a saw **ser·rat·ed** (seréitid) *adj.* **ser·rá·tion** *n.* [fr. L. *serratus* fr. *serra,* a saw]

ser·ried (séri:d) *adj.* close set, arranged closely side by side, *serried ranks of spectators* ‖ ridged [*past part.* of older *serry* v. fr. F. *serrer,* to close]

ser·ro·dyn·ing (sɛərədáiniŋ) *n.* (*mil.*) technique to prevent enemy radar from discerning the velocity of approaching craft, achieved by varying the voltage of communications in a sawtooth pattern and varying frequency, so that counter equipment loses contact

ser·ru·late (sérjulit, sérjuleit, séralit, séraleit) *adj.* finely notched, finely serrate **sér·ru·lat·ed** *adj.* **ser·ru·lá·tion** *n.* [fr. Mod. L. *serrulatus* fr. *serrula,* a little saw]

ser·tão (sertáu) *n.* the semi-arid, thinly populated interior of N.E. Brazil [Port.]

Ser·to·ri·us (sərtóri:əs, sərtóuri:əs), Quintus (c. 123-72 B.C.), Roman general, a supporter of Marius in the civil war against Sulla. He gained control of most of Spain (83-76 B.C.), and organized a senate and a school for the sons of native chiefs. Checked by Pompey, he was murdered at Huesca

Ser·tür·ner (zertýrnər), Friedrich Wilhelm (1783-1841), German chemist. He discovered morphine (1805), isolating it from opium

se·rum (síərəm) *pl.* **se·rums, se·ra** (síərə) *n.* the colorless liquid remaining after blood has clotted ‖ the watery part of any animal fluid after coagulation (cf. PLASMA) ‖ blood serum. In serum therapy an animal serum with specific antibodies is injected into the bloodstream of a human being to immunize him against a particular disease [L.=watery fluid]

ser·val (sárvəl) *n. Felis capensis* or *F. serval,* fam. *Felidae,* a long-legged, blackspotted African wildcat [Mod. L. fr. Port. *lobo cerval,* lynx]

serv·ant (sárvənt) *n.* a person paid to wait on another or others, esp. to do work in or around a house ‖ an official, *a public servant* ‖ someone devoted to a cause etc., *a faithful servant of the Church* [F.]

serve (sárv) **1.** *v. pres. part.* **serv·ing** *past* and *past part.* **served** *v.t.* to be a servant to ‖ to satisfy the needs or requirements of (a person, organization etc.), *his old car has served him well* ‖ to render service to (one's country) under arms ‖ (of store employees) to supply (customers) with goods ‖ (of store employees) to supply (goods) to customers ‖ (*law*) to deliver (a writ, summons etc.) ‖ (*law*) to present (someone) with a writ, summons etc. ‖ to bring (food etc.) to the table for distribution, *lunch is served* ‖ to distribute (food etc.) at a meal, *to serve the vegetables* ‖ to distribute food etc. to, *to serve one's guests* ‖ to undergo (a term of imprisonment) ‖ to work through (a term of apprenticeship, training etc.) ‖ to act as server at (Mass) ‖ to assist (a priest) as server ‖ to fulfill (a requirement), *any heavy object will serve the purpose* ‖ to supply a service to, *two libraries serve the town* ‖ to treat, *fate served her badly* ‖ (*animal husbandry*) to mate with (a female animal) ‖ to keep in operation (a large gun) ‖ (*naut.*) to protect (a rope) with a binding ‖ (*tennis etc.*) to hit (the ball) to an opponent to start play ‖ *v.i.* to be a servant ‖ to do military service ‖ to carry out orders or duties, *to serve is to learn how to command* ‖ to act as server at the Eucharist ‖ to function, *this box can serve as a table* ‖ to be sufficient for a particular need, *this cushion will serve* ‖ to distribute food etc. at the table ‖ to wait on the table ‖ (of store employees) to supply goods to customers ‖ (*tennis etc.*) to start play by hitting the ball to an opponent **to serve someone right** to be the punishment someone deserves **2.** *n.* (*tennis etc.*) a service **sérv·er** *n.* someone who serves. esp. an assistant to the celebrant at the Eucharist ‖ (*tennis etc.*) the player whose turn it is to serve ‖ a salver, spoon etc. used in serving [O.F. *servir*]

Ser·ve·tus (sərví:təs), Michael (Miguel Serveto, 1511-53), Spanish doctor and theologian, burned alive on the orders of Calvin at Geneva for denying Christ's divinity and the Christian doctrine of the Trinity

Ser·vice (sárvis), Robert William (1874-1958), Canadian writer, born in England. Known for his ballads, he wrote 'The Spell of the Yukon' (1907) in which were the ballads 'The Shooting of Dan McGrew' and 'The Cremation of Sam McGee'; 'Ballad of a Cheechako' (1909); 'Rhymes of Rolling Stone' (1912) and 'Rhymes of a Red Cross Man' (1916). His autobiography is a two-volume work, 'Ploughman of the Moon' (1945) and 'Harper of Heaven' (1948)

serv·ice (sárvis) **1.** *n.* the occupation of being a servant ‖ government employment ‖ a branch of government employment, *the diplomatic service* ‖ a branch (army, navy etc.) of the armed forces, or the armed forces as a career or occupation ‖ the performance of military duties, esp. in war, *he saw service on several fronts* ‖ (*pl.*) the products of an employee's or professional man's paid activities, *to dispense with someone's services* ‖ assistance or advantage given to another ‖ the benefit derived from this ‖ use, *still in service* ‖ a set form of public worship or the music written for this ‖ (*law*) notification of legal action by delivery of a summons, writ etc. ‖ (*tennis etc.*) the act or manner of serving the ball ‖ (*tennis etc.*) a turn to serve ‖ (*tennis etc.*) a ball served ‖ (*Br., pl.*) utilities, e.g. gas, water and electricity, as supplied to a building ‖ the act or manner of serving food, esp. in a restaurant ‖ maintenance, repairs etc. provided by a dealer for items bought from him ‖ the cups, plates, dishes etc. used in serving a particular meal, drink etc., *a tea service* ‖ (*econ., esp. pl.*) a product of human activity (e.g. transport, research) meant to satisfy a human need but not constituting an item of goods ‖ scheduled public transportation, *an hourly bus service* ‖ the time and route of a bus, airplane etc. operating to a public transportation schedule, *summer services resume next week* ‖ attendance on a client, esp. with respect to quality ‖ (*animal husbandry*) the serving of a female animal by a male **2.** *adj.* of or for servants or service, *service entrance* ‖ of or for the armed forces ‖ (*mil., of a uniform*) for use in ordinary service ‖ providing services **3.** *v.t. pres. part.* **serv·ic·ing** *past* and *past part.* **serv·iced** to provide maintenance facilities for (cars, machinery etc.) ‖ to provide a service for [O.F. *servise, service*]

service *n.* the service tree ‖ its fruit [O.E. *syrfe* fr. L. *sorbus*]

serv·ice·a·bil·i·ty (sə:rvisəbíliti:) *n.* the quality of being serviceable

serv·ice·a·ble (sá:rvisəb'l) *adj.* able to be of use though old, damaged etc. ‖ durable, suited for hard use [O.F. *serviçable, servisable*]

serv·ice·ber·ry (sá:rvisbɛri:) *pl.* **serv·ice·ber·ries** *n.* a Juneberry plant ‖ its fruit

serv·ice·man (sá:rvismæn, sá:rvismən) *pl.* **serv·ice·men** (sá:rvismen, sá:rvismən) *n.* a member of the military forces ‖ a man who services machinery, equipment etc.

service medal a medal awarded for long military service or service in a particular war or campaign

service module in a spacecraft, the area containing propulsion, fuel, and other consumables *abbr.* **SM** *Cf* COMMAND MODULE, LUNAR MODULE

service pipe a pipe which links a main pipe, e.g. a gas or water main, to a building

service road a road branching off a main road and usually running parallel to it, providing access to stores, houses etc. and used exclusively by such local traffic

service station a filling station with a staff for servicing, but without garage or workshop facilities

service stripe (*mil.*) a stripe worn on the sleeve to indicate length of service

service tree *Sorbus domestica,* fam. *Rosaceae,* a European tree bearing small, edible, pear-shaped fruit ‖ *S. torminalis,* fam. *Rosaceae,* a similar tree bearing bitter fruit

ser·vi·ette (sə:rvi:ét) *n.* (esp. *Br.*) a table napkin [F.]

ser·vile (sá:rvil, sá:rvail) *adj.* like a slave or like the state of slavery ‖ showing oneself to be in complete submission to another ‖ having or showing no originality whatever, *servile imitation* **ser·vil·i·ty** (sə:rvíliti:) *n.* [fr. L. *servilis*]

serv·ing (sá:rviŋ) **1.** *n.* the act of one who or that which serves ‖ a portion of food or drink **2.** *adj.* used in holding or passing out food or drink, *a serving table*

Ser·vite (sá:rvait) *n.* a member of a mendicant order of friars founded (1233) in Florence and devoted to the service of the Virgin Mary

ser·vi·tor (sá:rvitər) *n.* (*hist.*) a male attendant or servant [O.F.]

ser·vi·tude (sá:rvitu:d, sá:rvitju:d) *n.* slavery, bondage ‖ (*law*) a right in respect of land or other property in virtue of which the property is subject to use or enjoyment in a specified way by another person [F.]

ser·vo con·trol (sá:rvou) an automatic device which aids a pilot's effort in controlling the airfoils of an aircraft

---

CONCISE PRONUNCIATION KEY: **(a)** æ, c*a*t; ɑ, c*a*r; ɔ f*aw*n; ei, sn*a*ke. **(e)** e, h*e*n; i:, sh*ee*p; iə, d*ee*r; ɛə, b*ea*r. **(i)** i, f*i*sh; ai, t*i*ger; ə:, b*i*rd. **(o)** o, *o*x; au, c*ow*; ou, g*oa*t; u, p*oo*r; ɔi, r*oy*al. **(u)** ʌ, d*u*ck; u, b*u*ll; u:, g*oo*se; ə, b*a*cillus; ju:, c*u*be. x, lo*ch*; θ, *th*ink; ð, bo*th*er; z, *Z*en; ʒ, cor*s*age; dʒ, sava*ge*; ŋ, ora*n*gutang; j, *y*ak; ʃ, *fi*sh; tʃ, fe*tch*; 'l, rabb*le*; 'n, redd*en*. Complete pronunciation key appears inside front cover.

ser·vo·mech·an·ism (séːrvoumękənɪzəm, səːrvoumékənɪzəm) *n.* a device by which one mechanism controls the movement of another, independently powered one. Its operation depends on feedback: a signal proportional to the difference in action between master and slave mechanisms is amplified and applied as a correction to reduce the difference ‖ (*eng.*) a control device that operates automatically to adjust to the desired end when input varies, e.g., a thermostat ‖ (*eng.*) a double-sided vacuum-based device to provide pressure in hydrostatic brakes ‖ (*computer*) the mechanical motion device in a computer system used to control the position of the output

ses·a·me (sésəmiː) *n. Sesamum indicum,* fam. Pedaliaceae, a herbaceous tropical and subtropical plant with small flat seeds, used as food and yielding a bland, pale yellow oil used in salads, margarine and soap and as a laxative [fr. L. *sesamum*]

ses·a·moid (sésəmɔɪd) **1.** *adj.* (of a bone or cartilage) of or being a nodular mass in a tendon passing over a joint (e.g. the patella) or bony structure **2.** *n.* such a bone or cartilage [fr. L. *sesamoides,* shaped like a sesame seed, fr. Gk]

ses·qui·cen·ten·ni·al (seskwisenténiəl) **1.** *adj.* of or relating to a century and a half **2.** *n.* a 150th anniversary [fr. L. *sesqui-,* a half in addition+ CENTENNIAL]

ses·qui·ox·ide (seskwiːɔ́ksaid, seskwiːɔ́ksaid) *n.* an oxide containing three atoms of oxygen in combination with two of the other atoms constituting the molecule

ses·sile (sésɪl, sésaɪl) *adj.* (*bot.,* of leaves etc.) attached directly at the base, with no intervening support such as a pedicel, peduncle or stalk ‖ (*anat., zool.*) stationary, permanently fixed ‖ (*anat., zool.*) attached directly by its base [L. *sessilis,* sitting down]

ses·sion (séʃən) *n.* the sitting of a court, parliament or other assembly for official business ‖ a single meeting of such a body ‖ the period between the opening and prorogation of parliament ‖ an academic year or term ‖ a period of time spent in some activity ‖ (in Presbyterian churches) the governing body of an individual congregation composed of elders and the minister **sés·sion·al** *adj.* [F.]

Ses·sions (séfənz), Roger (1896-1985), American composer. He wrote three symphonies, chamber music, songs, the opera 'The Trial of Lucullus' and the cantata 'Turn O Libertad'

ses·terce (séstərs) *n.* an ancient Roman coin worth a quarter of a denarius [L.]

ses·ter·ti·um (sestɔ́ːrʃiəm, sestɔ́ːrʃəm) *pl.* **sester·ti·a** (sestɔ́ːrʃiə, sestɔ́ːrʃə) *n.* an ancient Roman monetary unit equal to 1,000 sesterces [L.]

ses·tet (sestét, séstet) *n.* the last six lines of a sonnet [fr. Ital. *sestetto*]

ses·ti·na (sestíːnə) *pl.* **ses·ti·nas, ses·ti·ne** (sestíːnei) *n.* a poem with six six-line stanzas, each having the same six line-end words though not in the same order, and a three-line envoy containing these six words [Ital.]

Set (set) (*Egypt. mythol.*) the god of evil, represented with an animal's head and long snout

set 1. *v. pres. part.* **set·ting** *past* and *past part.* **set** *v.t.* to cause to occupy a certain position, *set the bowl in the center* ‖ to put (a hen etc.) on eggs to hatch them ‖ to put (eggs) to hatch ‖ (often with 'out') to plant (seedlings, bulbs etc.) ‖ to put (one's jaw or shoulders) into a position showing determination, *he set his shoulders squarely* ‖ to decorate, encrust e.g. with gems ‖ to bring (a lighted match) into contact with something else, *set a match to the leaves* ‖ to cause to be in a specified condition or state, *to set leaves on fire, to set someone thinking* ‖ to cause to be arranged in readiness or in working order, *to set a trap* ‖ to adjust, regulate, *to set a clock* ‖ to fix in a desired position, *set the pointer at 20* ‖ to bring together the parts of (a broken bone) in a position for healing, mending etc. ‖ to curl or wave (hair) by arranging it damp with hairpins or curlers and letting it dry ‖ to put (a seal) on paper ‖ to put (words) to music ‖ (*printing,* often with 'up') to compose (type) ‖ (*printing,* often with 'up') to put (manuscript) into type ‖ to lay (a table) ‖ to fix (a sail) so as to catch the wind ‖ to cause (a blade) to have a sharp edge ‖ to adjust the teeth of (a saw) ‖ to fix (e.g. one's mind, purpose or heart) firmly on something ‖ to cause (e.g. a jelly) to become firm in consistency ‖ to make (a color) fast ‖ to cause to go in a specified direction, *they set their horses towards home* ‖ to fix (a time, date etc.) for an event,

they set midnight for the escape ‖ to fix (limits etc.), *to set a term for a project* ‖ to establish (a standard in performance or a record in competition) ‖ to furnish (a precedent or an example) ‖ to station (someone) for a specific duty, *to set sentries at the gate* ‖ to put (someone) to work on a specified task ‖ to assign or allot (a lesson, task etc.) ‖ (*Br.*) to stipulate the written or practical work for (an examination, homework etc.) ‖ to fix (an amount of work etc.) ‖ to begin to apply (oneself) to a task etc., *he set himself to his chores* ‖ to fix (an amount, price etc.), *the club set $100 as the membership fee* ‖ to fix at an amount, price etc., *they set the goal at $1,000* ‖ to place (value) on something or someone, *she sets great store by him* ‖ to value (someone or something) in a certain way, *to set honor before glory* ‖ to place (a scene of a play, novel etc.) in some locality ‖ to arrange (scenery) in a certain way on the stage ‖ to arrange scenery on (the stage) ‖ (*baking*) to put aside (dough) to rise ‖ *v.i.* to become firm in consistency ‖ (of colors) to become fast ‖ (of a hen) to sit on eggs ‖ (of the sun etc.) to appear to descend below the horizon ‖ to go in a specified direction, *the current sets to the north* ‖ (of a broken bone) to become whole again, mend ‖ (of clothes) to fit in a specified way ‖ (of a flower, seed or fruit) to develop while still attached to the parent plant ‖ (of a gundog) to indicate the presence of game by assuming a rigid attitude ‖ (*square dancing*) to dance facing one's partner **to set about** to begin to cope with **to set against** to make unsympathetic or hostile toward ‖ to place (something) in juxtaposition to something else for contrast or balance **to set apart** to put to one side, reserve ‖ to cause to be seen to be different, outstanding etc. **to set aside** to put aside, esp. temporarily ‖ to reject, dismiss, esp. from the mind ‖ to annul **to set back** to check the progress of ‖ to put (a timepiece) to an earlier time **to set down** to put in writing or in print ‖ (with 'as') to record one's opinion of (someone or something), *they set him down as unfit* **to set forth** to give an account of ‖ to begin a journey **to set in** to insert ‖ (*naut.*) to sail (a boat) toward land ‖ (of weather or a natural catastrophe) to begin to be prevalent ‖ (*naut.*) to go toward land **to set off** to start (on a journey) ‖ to bring into prominence by contrast, *the red scarf set off the dark tweed* ‖ to cause to explode ‖ to cause (someone) to begin an activity (e.g. laughing or talking) **to set on** to attack ‖ to cause to attack, pursue etc. **to set out** to begin a journey ‖ to have a specified intention in beginning some undertaking, *he sets out to prove that Shakespeare was a woman* ‖ to arrange as a display, *to set out merchandise on a counter* **to set to** to begin a fight ‖ to begin a piece of work with determination **to set up** to start in business etc., *to set up as a grocer* ‖ to institute, establish (e.g. an organization) ‖ to put (a drink) in front of a customer ‖ to treat (somebody) to something, *he set them all up with ice cream* ‖ to place in an upright position ‖ to arrange (a machine etc.) in a state in which it can be used, *to set up a sewing machine* ‖ to elate, make happy, *the compliment set her up for the day* **to set upon** to attack with murderous violence **2.** *adj.* located, *a house set in a hollow* ‖ fixed, *a set date* ‖ determined, *a set purpose, set on becoming an actress* ‖ routine, invariable, *a set practice* ‖ rigid, immovable ‖ (of opinions) tenaciously held ‖ firm in consistency ‖ (of a book) prescribed for examination ‖ (of a topic) specified ‖ (of someone's ways) inflexible, unchanging ‖ (of a speech, answer etc.) prepared beforehand ‖ stereotyped, *a set formula* ‖ ready, *set for trouble* ‖ ready and keen, *all set to go* ‖ (of a fight or battle) pitched **3.** *n.* a number of things related to one another by similarity (e.g. of nature, appearance or use), considered as a whole and without regard to the order in which they are arranged in space or time, *a set of carpenter's tools, a tea set, a set of teeth* ‖ a number of people having similar interests, occupations etc. or the same friends ‖ a television or radio receiver ‖ (*tennis*) a group of games counting as a unit toward a match. It is constituted by the winning of six games before the opponent has won more than four. If the opponent wins more than four, play continues until one side is two games up ‖ the direction of motion e.g. of a current or wind ‖ the way clothing fits or hangs ‖ the posture or position of the body or a part of the body, *the set of his jaw* ‖ a deflection from a straight line or usual form because of some sort of strain or pressure ‖ the deflection in alternate directions of the teeth of a saw, or the amount of this ‖ the setting of hair

by arranging it damp with hairpins or curlers and letting it dry ‖ a young plant or rooted cutting ready for transplanting ‖ a little bulb, corm or tuber for planting out ‖ (*printing*) the spacing between words with regard to closeness ‖ (*printing*) the width of the shank of a piece of type ‖ a badger's burrow ‖ a clutch of eggs ‖ the act of a gundog that sets ‖ the flats, drops, furniture, props etc. used in the theater or in film making to set a scene ‖ (*square dancing*) the number of persons required to execute the figures in a dance ‖ (*square dancing*) the figure formed at the start of a dance [O.E. *settan*]

se·ta (síːtə) *pl.* **se·tae** (síːtiː) *n.* (*biol.*) any of various bristlelike structures ‖ (*bot.*) the stalk of the sporogonium of mosses and liverworts ‖ (*zool.*) a bristle or stiff hair, e.g. in earthworms [L. = bristle]

se·ta·ceous (sitéiʃəs) *adj.* (*biol.*) having or resembling bristles [fr. Mod. L. *setaceus*]

set-a·sides (sétəsaids) *n.* minimum quotas for special groups, esp. black, small business, in affirmative action programs

set·back (sétbæk) *n.* an unwelcome reversal of fortune ‖ an impeding of progress ‖ (*archit.*) a setting back of a building or part of a building behind the building line to give adequate daylight to adjacent buildings or streets

Se·ti I (síːtai, séiti) (*d. c.* 1290 B.C.), king of Egypt (*c.* 1303–*c.* 1290 B.C.), of the 19th dynasty. He conquered Palestine and Libya, and built a temple to Osiris at Abydos

Se·tif (seitíːf) a commercial center (pop. 94,000) in Algeria in the northeastern plateau at 3,600 ft

set·line (sétlain) *n.* a strong fishline having hooks on short lines attached to it at frequent intervals. It is put out at low tide, or strung out in a river

set·off (sétɔf, sétɒf) *n.* something counterbalancing something else ‖ (*law*) the balancing of a debt by money owed by the creditor to the debtor ‖ (*archit.*) an offset ‖ (*printing*) an image smudged on the back of a printed sheet from the freshly printed sheet beneath it, through failure of the ink to dry

Se·ton (síːt'n), Elizabeth Ann (née Bayley, 1774-1821), U.S. founder (1812) of the American Sisters of Charity, an organization of Catholic nuns, who laid the foundations of the parochial school system in the U.S.A. She was canonized (1975), becoming the first native-born American to be named a saint

se·ton (síːt'n) *n.* (*vet.*) threads or horsehairs passed beneath a section of skin and left with the ends protruding to form an issue from, or to promote drainage of, a wound [fr. M.L. *seto* (*setonis*), silk]

Se·to Nai·kai (sétounáikái) *INLAND SEA

set·screw (sétskruː) *n.* a screw passed through one part of a machine into another part, or tightly against it, to prevent relative motion

set square a flat, triangular piece of wood, metal etc. with angles of 90°, 60° and 30° or 90°, 45° and 45°, for drawing lines at angles

set·tee (setíː) *n.* a long, usually padded seat or couch with a back and often with arms, for two people or for three

set·ter (sétər) *n.* a large long-haired gundog of any of various breeds trained to stand rigid on scenting game

set theory the division of mathematics or symbolic logic that treats the nature and relationships of groups

set·ting (sétɪŋ) *n.* the act of someone who, or something which, sets ‖ the frame in which a gem is set ‖ the background against which a person or thing is seen, *she looks at home in that setting* ‖ the local or historical background of a story ‖ the music to which words are to be sung ‖ the contrived or natural background against which actors play ‖ the position at which the indicator is set on a scale ‖ a clutch of eggs

set·tle (sét'l) *pres. part.* **set·tling** *past* and *past part.* **set·tled** *v.i.* to cease to move around and come quietly or gently to rest, *a bird settled on the bough* ‖ take up permanent residence, *on retiring he settled in a village* ‖ (often with 'out') to sink slowly and come to rest, *a sediment settled at the bottom of the bottle* ‖ (of a turbid liquid) to become clear when the suspension sinks to the bottom ‖ (of a building etc.) to sink very slowly ‖ to come to a decision after hesitation between alternatives ‖ to end a dispute or difference by dealing with one's opponents, *to settle out of court* ‖ to adjust accounts, *we will settle with you later* ‖ (of a fog etc.) to descend on the landscape ‖ (of silence etc.) to descend on a group or person ‖ (of a disease etc.) to become localized ‖ to pay what is owing or agree on a sum of money to be paid out ‖ (of the ground) to become firm, esp. after severe rain or frost ‖ *v.t.* to cause to cease to move around ‖ to cause to take up permanent residence ‖ to provide (a region) with settlers ‖ to take up residence in as settlers ‖ to clarify (a liquid) by causing suspended matter to sink to the bottom ‖ to pay (a debt) ‖ to end (an argument, conflict, doubt etc.) by reaching a decision ‖ to fix definitely (a price, hour etc.) by mutual agreement ‖ to put in order, arrange ‖ to make stable ‖ (*old-fash.*) to establish in marriage, business etc. ‖ to make (the nerves, stomach, mind etc.) calm ‖ to decide (a legal dispute) out of court **to settle down** to adopt a quiet, regular way of life ‖ to become quiet and peaceful ‖ to apply oneself **to settle up** to arrange differences ‖ to adjust accounts **to settle (something) upon** (or **on**) **someone** to make over (property etc.) to someone by legal means [O.E. *setlan*]

settle *n.* a long wooden seat with arms and a high, straight back [O.E. *setl*, a seat]

set·tle·ment (sét'lmənt) *n.* a settling or being settled ‖ a choice or decision made to end a controversy ‖ a region in which settlers live, esp. that small part of it in which they have their homes ‖ a small, isolated hamlet or village ‖ the conveyance of property etc. settled on a person, e.g. at marriage ‖ the property etc. so conveyed ‖ an institution established and maintained esp. in the poorer sections of a large city to provide e.g. educational and recreational facilities for those in the area

Settlement, Act of (*Eng. hist.*) a law passed (1701) by parliament, fixing the succession to the throne on the house of Hanover should William III and Anne die without heirs. George I owed his succession (1714) to this law

set·tler (sétlər) *n.* a colonist, esp. an early colonist in any area

settling day the fortnightly payday on the London Stock Exchange

set-to (séttu:) *pl.* **set-tos** *n.* (*pop.*) a verbal quarrel ‖ a scuffle, a fight

Se·tú·bal (situ:bɑl) a fishing port and agricultural market (pop. 64,531) in Portugal, 20 miles southeast of Lisbon. Gothic church, castle (16th c.)

set-up (sétʌp) *n.* (*pop.*) all the arrangements, installations etc. that enable some activity to be carried on ‖ (*pop.*) the way in which the component parts make it possible for a mechanical etc. system to work

Seu·rat (sə:ræ), Georges (1859-91), French Post-impressionist painter. His consuming interest in theories of color was based on analysis of the mechanism of the eye's perception of the effects of light and led to his use of pointillism. He also developed equally brilliant methods of composition, based on the golden section ('le Chenal de Gravelines un soir'). His 'Baignade' (1884) and 'Un dimanche d'été à la Grande-Jatte' (1886) are generally considered his greatest works

Se·vas·to·pol (səvǽstəpoul, sevʌstɔ́pʌlj) a port, resort and naval base (pop. 328,000) in the Crimea, S. Ukraine, U.S.S.R., on the Black Sea. It withstood an Allied siege for 11 months (1854-5) during the Crimean War, and a German siege for eight months (1941-2) during the 2nd world war

se·ven (sévən) **1.** *adj.* being one more than six (*NUMBER TABLE) **2.** *n.* six plus one ‖ the cardinal number representing this (7, VII) ‖ seven o'clock ‖ a playing card marked with seven spots [O.E. *seofon*]

Seven Days Battles a Confederate counteroffensive (1862) during the Civil War, led by General Robert E. Lee. For two years it saved Richmond, Va., from Union attack

seven deadly sins pride, covetousness, lust, gluttony, anger, envy, sloth

Sev·en·er (sévənər) *n.* an Isma'ili

Seven Sages, the seven political philosophers and politicians of ancient Greece, usually taken as Bias, Chilon, Cleobulus, Periander, Pittaeus, Solon and Thales

seven seas, the (*rhet.*) the navigable waters of every part of the globe

Seven Sisters a group of long-established, distinguished colleges of the eastern U.S.A., comprising Vassar, Radcliffe, Sarah Lawrence, Wellesley, Mt Holyoke, Barnard, and Smith, all formerly exclusively for women ‖ (*colloq.*) a nickname for the major oil producers Exxon, Royal Dutch-Shell, Texaco, Standard Oil Co. of

California (Socol, marketed as Chevron), Mobil, Gulf, British Petroleum

sev·en·teen (sév'ntí:n) **1.** *adj.* being one more than 16 (*NUMBER TABLE) **2.** *n.* ten plus seven ‖ the cardinal number representing this (17, XVII) [O.E. *seofontíene, seofontēne, seofontȳne*]

sev·en·teenth (sév'nti:nθ) **1.** *adj.* being number 17 in a series (*NUMBER TABLE) ‖ being one of the 17 equal parts of anything **2.** *n.* the person or thing next after the 16th ‖ one of 17 equal parts of anything (1/17) ‖ the 17th day of a month [O. E. *seofontēotha*]

Seventeenth Amendment (1913) an amendment to the U.S. Constitution that provides for the election of senators by popular vote. Vacancies can be filled by appointment, but only temporarily, until an election can take place

sev·enth (sév'nθ) **1.** *adj.* being number seven in a series (*NUMBER TABLE) ‖ being one of the seven equal parts of anything ‖ **2.** *n.* the person or thing next after the sixth ‖ one of seven equal parts of anything (1/7) ‖ the seventh day of a month ‖ (*mus.*) the note seven steps above or below a given note in a diatonic scale, inclusive of both notes ‖ (*mus.*) the interval between these notes ‖ (*mus.*) a combination of these notes **3.** *adv.* in the seventh place ‖ (followed by a superlative) except six, *the seventh biggest* [O.E. *seofunda, siofunda*]

Seventh Amendment (1791) an amendment to the U.S. Constitution that guarantees the right to trial by jury, part of the Bill of Rights. It has been defined by the Supreme Court as requiring twelve members of the jury (later (1973) six-member juries were made possible) before a judge. The verdict must be unanimous for acquittal or conviction

Seventh-Day Adventist a member of an Adventist sect, founded (1844) in the U.S.A., which keeps Saturday as the sabbath

seventh heaven a state of supreme bliss

sev·en·ti·eth (sévanti:iθ) **1.** *adj.* being number 70 in a series (*NUMBER TABLE) ‖ being one of the 70 equal parts of anything **2.** *n.* the person or thing next after the 69th ‖ one of 70 equal parts of anything (1/70) [SEVENTY]

sev·en·ty (sévanti:) **1.** *adj.* being ten more than 60 (*NUMBER TABLE) **2.** *pl.* **sev·en·ties** *n.* seven times ten ‖ the cardinal number representing this (70, LXX) **the seventies** (of temperature, a person's age, a century etc.) the span 70-9 [O.E. *seofontig, hundseofontig*]

sev·en·ty-five (sévanti:fáiv) *n.* (*mil.*) a 75-mm. gun, esp. the famous French field gun of this caliber used in the 1st world war

Seven Weeks' War the Austro-Prussian war of 1866, provoked by Bismarck over the Schleswig-Holstein controversy. Prussia was supported by Italy, while Austria was allied with Saxony, Hanover and several S. German states. The Prussian army under von Moltke won rapid victories, ending with the decisive Battle of Sadowa (July 3, 1866) and the Treaty of Prague (Aug. 23, 1866)

Seven Wonders of the World seven monuments considered by the ancient world as remarkable for their size and splendor. They were usually listed as: the hanging gardens of Babylon, the pyramid of Khufu at Giza, the temple of Artemis at Ephesus, Phidias's statue of Zeus at Olympia, the Colossus of Rhodes, the tomb of Mausolus at Halicarnassus and the Pharos at Alexandria

Seven Years' War a war (1756-63) fought in Europe, North America and India between Prussia, with British financial support, and a coalition of Austria, Russia and France. It was provoked by Austrian attempts to regain Silesia after the War of the Austrian Succession (1740-8), and by colonial rivalry between France and Britain. The war was settled by the Treaty of Hubertusburg. In North America (*FRENCH AND INDIAN WAR), Britain gained Canada and other territories from France, and Florida from Spain (*PARIS, TREATY OF, 1763). French power in India was destroyed and Britain became the world's chief colonial power

sev·er (sévər) *v.t.* to cut completely through ‖ to divide from the main part ‖ to cut (esp. a part of the body) into two pieces, *to sever a nerve* ‖ to break off, bring to an end, *to sever a friendship* ‖ *v.i.* to become divided or ended in this way **sév·er·a·ble** *adj.* capable of being severed ‖ (of a contract etc.) capable of being divided into distinct rights or obligations [A.F. *severer*, O.F. *sevrer*, to wean]

sev·er·al (sévərəl, sévrəl) **1.** *adj.* being more than two but not many, *we met several times* ‖ separate, individual, *they went their several ways* **2.** *n.* (followed by 'of') a small number of persons or things, *several of the children were in the garden* **3.** *pron.* a small number of persons or things, *several were in the garden* **sév·er·al·ly** *adv.* each by itself, apart from others, separately [A.F.]

sev·er·al·ty (sévərəlti:, sévrəlti:) *pl.* **sev·er·al·ties** *n.* (*law*, usually with 'in') possession by a single individual only, *an estate held in severalty* ‖ (*law*) land or property so possessed [A.F. *severalte, severaute*]

sev·er·ance (sévərəns, sévrəns) *n.* a severing or being severed [A.F.]

se·vere (siví:ər) *adj.* having no sympathy for, and making no concessions to, what are regarded as human weaknesses, *a severe critic* ‖ harsh, *severe punishment* ‖ austere, *severe architecture* ‖ difficult to endure, *a severe pain* ‖ difficult and trying, *a severe test* [F. *sévère* or fr. L. *severus*]

se·ver·i·ty (sivériti:) *pl.* **se·ver·i·ties** *n.* the state or quality of being severe ‖ an instance of being severe [F. *sévérité*]

Sev·ern (sévərn) a river (210 miles long, navigable for 178 miles) rising in central Wales and following in a semicircle through W. central England to a wide estuary forming the head of the Bristol Channel

Se·ver·na·ya   Zem·lya (sjévərnɑjəzjəmljá) (North Land) an uninhabited archipelago (area 14,300 sq. miles) consisting of three large islands off the Taimyr Peninsula, U.S.S.R., discovered in 1913

Severus, Alexander *ALEXANDER SEVERUS

Se·ve·rus (sivíərəs), Lucius Septimius (146-211), Roman emperor (193-211). He was proclaimed emperor by his troops, and defeated two other usurpers (193 and 194). He took Byzantium (196), defeated another rival (197) and drove the Parthians from Mesopotamia (198)

Se·vier (siví:ər), John (1745-1815), American frontiersman, Revolutionary War soldier, and first governor (1796-1801, 1803-9) of the state of Tennessee

Sé·vi·gné (seivi:njei), Marie de Rabutin-Chantal, marquise de (1626-96), French letter writer. Her letters to her daughter Madame de Grignan and to her friends were the literary work of an intelligent, devoted and witty woman, very human and generous. They tell of events and manners of the day, of court, city and country life and of the things of the heart

Se·ville (savíl, sévil) (*Span.* Sevilla) a province (area 5,428 sq. miles, pop. 1,477,428) of S.W. Spain (*ANDALUSIA) ‖ its capital (pop. 616,900), historic capital of Andalusia, a sea and river port on the Guadalquivir 50 miles from its mouth. Industries: textiles, chemicals, earthenware. Alcazar (Almohad palace, begun 1181), Gothic cathedral (15th c.), other Moorish, Renaissance and baroque monuments. University (1502). It has a famous Holy Week festival. Iberian in origin, Seville was a Roman city, and was a center of Arab culture before the Castilian reconquest in 1248. From 1503 to 1717 it had the monopoly of trade with Spanish America

Seville orange (sévil) a bitter orange, used for making marmalade ‖ *Citrus aurantium,* the tree bearing this orange [after SEVILLE Spain]

Sè·vres (sevr) *n.* porcelain made at Sèvres, France, on the outskirts of Paris. The classic type of tableware is ornamented with painted designs and gilding (*POMPADOUR, MARQUISE DE)

Sèvres, Deux- *DEUX-SÈVRES

sew (sou) *pres. part.* **sew·ing** *past* **sewed** *past part.* **sewn** (soun), **sewed** *v.t.* to join or fasten by stitches made with a needle and thread ‖ to make or repair (garments etc.) in this way ‖ to bind (the sheets of a book) in this way (cf. STITCH) ‖ *v.i.* to use a needle and thread ‖ to earn one's living as a seamstress or tailor **to sew up** to close a gap in (a fabric) by sewing the edges together ‖ to enclose by sewing ‖ (*pop.*) to attend to all the detail of (something, e.g. a contract) and finish it [O.E. *siwan, siowan*]

sew·age (sú:idʒ) *n.* the waste matter that is carried away through sewers

sewage farm a farm where sewage is treated and used to fertilize and irrigate

Sew·all (sú:əl), Samuel (1652-1730), American colonial judge and diarist. He was one of the special commissioners presiding (1692) over the Salem witchcraft trials, which sentenced 19

persons to death. He later (1697) acknowledged his mistake. His diary illustrates the mind and way of life of the American Puritan

Sew·ard (súːwərd), William Henry (1801-72), U.S. secretary of state (1860-9) under Presidents Abraham Lincoln and Andrew Johnson. His purchase (1867) of Alaska from Russia for $7.2 million was dubbed at the time 'Seward's Folly'

Seward Peninsula a peninsula (c. 180 miles long, 130 miles wide) in W. Alaska, with Cape Prince of Wales, the most westerly point of the North American mainland, at its west tip. It contains rich gold deposits

sew·er (súːər) **1.** *n.* an underground tunnel that carries off the drainage and waste matter from a house or town **2.** *v.t.* to provide with sewers **séw·er·age** *n.* the system of sewers or drainage of a town ‖ sewage [A.F. fr. O.F. *seuwiere*, a canal for draining off excess water in a fish-pond]

sew·ing (sóuiŋ) *n.* the act or method of someone who sews ‖ something sewn, being sewn, or waiting to be sewn

sew·ing machine (sóuiŋ) a machine for seaming and for making a variety of stitches. Its needle may be worked by an electric motor or be operated by hand or by treadle

sewing press an appliance used by bookbinders for stretching the cords of a book being sewn by hand

sewn alt. *past part.* of SEW

sex (seks) **1.** *n.* the sum of characteristic structures and functions by which an animal or plant is classed as male or female ‖ male or female as a classification, *which sex is the chicken?* ‖ the area of human behavior concerning sexual activity ‖ sexual desires and instincts and their expression **2.** *v.t.* to identify the sex of (e.g. day-old chicks) [fr. L. *sexus*]

sex·a·ge·nar·i·an (seksədʒənέəriːən) **1.** *adj.* in the age span 60-9 **2.** *n.* a sexagenarian person [fr. L. *sexagenarius*, of sixty]

sex·ag·e·nar·y (seksǽdʒəneri) *adj.* of or relating to the number 60 ‖ advancing by units of 60 [fr. L. *sexagenarius*]

Sex·a·ges·i·ma (seksədʒésəmə, seksədʒéizəmə) *n.* the second Sunday before Lent [eccles. L.. fem. of *sexagesimus*, sixtieth]

sex·a·ges·i·mal (seksədʒésəməl) *adj.* of or relating to the number 60 ‖ calculating or proceeding in units of 60, e.g. in spherical and time calculations ‖ (*math..* of a fraction) having a denominator of 60 or a multiple of 60 [fr. M.L. *sexagesimalis*]

sex appeal physical attractiveness to the opposite sex

sex·cen·te·nar·y (seksséntənəri:, sekssenténəri:) **1.** *adj.* related to 600, or 600 years **2.** *pl.* **sex·cen·te·nar·ies** *n.* a celebration of 600 years of existence or a 600th anniversary [fr. L. *sex*, six +CENTENARY]

sex chromosome a chromosome whose presence, absence or particular form may determine the sex of an organism. A fertilized egg containing two X chromosomes (one from each parent) develops into a female. One containing an X and a Y chromosome (male germ cells carry either one or the other) develops into a male

sex·de·cil·lion (seksdisíljən) *n.* *NUMBER TABLE [fr. L. *sesdecim*, *sexdecim*, sixteen + MILLION]

sexed (sekst) *adj.* having sexuality in a specified degree, *highly sexed*

sex·en·ni·al (sekséniːəl) *adj.* enduring for six years ‖ happening every six years [fr. L. *sexennis* or *sexennium*]

sex·i·ly (séksili) *adv.* in a sexy manner

sex·i·ness (séksi:nis) *n.* the state or quality of being sexy

sex·ism (séksizəm) *n.* **1.** attitudes and institutions, often unconscious, that judge human worth on the grounds of gender or sex roles **2.** prejudice or discrimination, usu. against women, based on their gender —**sexist** *n.* Cf MALE CHAUVINISM

sex·i·va·lent (seksəvéilənt) *adj.* (*chem.*) having six valences (cf. HEXAVALENT) [fr. L. *sex*, six + *valens* (*valentis*) fr. *valere*, to be strong]

sex·less (sékslis) *adj.* without sex ‖ (*pop.*) lacking normal sexual desire or attractiveness

sex linkage a genetic determinant, esp. X chromosome, that is carried by members of only one sex, e.g., hemophilia through females

sex·linked (séksliŋkt) *adj.* (of those factors which are due to the sex chromosomes

sex·ol·o·gy (seksólədʒi:) *n.* the study of sexual behavior in humans [fr. SEX+Gk *logos*, discourse]

sex·ones (séksounz) *n.* sex odors believed to affect human sexuality

sex·ploi·ta·tion (seksploitéiʃən) *n.* (*slang*) promotion based on eroticism —**sexploiter** *n.*

sext (sekst) *n.* the fourth of the seven canonical hours, falling at noon or just before noon ‖ the service held at this time each day [fr. L. *sexta* (*hora*), sixth hour]

sex·tant (sékstənt) *n.* an instrument with a graduated arc of 60 degrees, used for measuring the angle subtended by two distant objects. It is used in navigation to measure the altitude of the sun, moon or a star above the horizon, so that, in conjunction with a chronometer and the nautical almanac, latitude and longitude can be determined [fr. L. *sestans* (*sextantis*), a sixth part]

sex·tet, **sex·tette** (sekstét) *n.* a musical composition for six instruments or voices ‖ a group of six players or singers performing together [altered fr. SESTET after L. *sex*, six]

sex therapy treatment of sexual dysfunction by psychological therapy and other means

sex·til·lion (sekstíljən) *n.* *NUMBER TABLE [fr. F. fr. L. *sex*, six + MILLION]

sex·to·dec·i·mo (sekstoudésəmou) *n.* (*abbr.* 16 mo) a book made of sheets each folded into 16 leaves ‖ this method of folding ‖ a sheet folded thus [L., abl. of *sextus decimus*, sixteenth]

sex·ton (sékstən) *n.* a person who acts as a caretaker of a church and its contents and often also acts as bell ringer, gravedigger etc. [A.F. *segerstaine*]

sex·tu·ple (sekstúːpʹl, sekstjúːpʹl, sékstupʹl, sékstjupʹl, sekstΛpʹl) **1.** *adj.* six times as much or as many ‖ (*mus.*) having six beats in a bar **2.** *n.* the product of a number multiplied by six **3.** *v. pres. part.* **sex·tu·pling** *past* and *past part.* **sex·tu·pled** *v.t.* to multiply by six ‖ *v.i.* to increase by six times as much or as many [prob. fr. L.L. *sextuplus* fr. L. *sex*, six]

Sex·tus Em·pir·i·cus (sékstəsempírikəs) (2nd c. A.D.) Greek physician and philosopher. His works are valued chiefly because they contain the only full account of skeptical philosophy in antiquity

sex·u·al (sékʃuːəl) *adj.* pertaining to sex, to difference of sex or to the satisfaction of the sex instinct ‖ (*biol.*) having sex ‖ (*biol.*) of reproduction by the union of male and female germ cells

sex·u·al·i·ty (sekʃuːǽliti:) *n.* the quality of being sexual ‖ (*biol.*) the state of being either male or female ‖ sexual desires and their gratification [fr. L.L. *sexualis*]

sexual revolution loosening of social mores regarding sexual behavior

sex·y (séksiː) *comp.* **sex·i·er** *superl.* **sex·i·est** *adj.* exciting sexual desire

Sey·chelles (seiʃél, seiʃélz) republic consisting of an archipelago, comprising 85 islands and islets, in the W. Indian Ocean (area 87 sq. miles, pop. 64,000). Chief islands: Mahé, Praslin. Capital and chief port: Victoria (pop. 23,334), on Mahé. People: mulatto, with Chinese, Indian and European minorities. Languages: Creole (official). Highest point: 2,970 ft, on Mahé. Exports: copra, cinnamon and cinnamon oil, vanilla, salted fish. Monetary unit: rupee (100 cents). HISTORY. The islands were occupied by the French (mid-18th c.), were contested by the British during the Napoleonic Wars, and were ceded to Britain (1814). They were administered jointly with Mauritius until 1903, when the Seychelles became a separate Crown Colony. Certain atolls became (1965) part of the British Indian Ocean Territory. Seychelles became an independent republic (1976), but the government was overthrown and a one-party state was declared (1979)

Sey·fert (síːfəːrt) *n.* (*astron.*) a group of galaxies of small stars with compact nuclei and high energy emissions discovered in 1940s; named for Carl K. Seyfert *Cf* N GALAXY

Seymour, Jane *JANE SEYMOUR

Sfax (sfaks) the chief export port (pop. 171,297) of Tunisia, on the east coast

Sfor·za (sfórtsa) an Italian family which ruled Milan (15th and 16th cc.). Lodovico Sforza (1451-1508), duke of Milan (1494-9), was a patron of Leonardo da Vinci and Bramante

sfor·zan·do (sfortsándou) **1.** *adv.* (*mus.*, *abbr.* sf., sfz., *symbol* >, Λ) with sudden energy or emphasis **2.** *adj.* to be played in this way [Ital.]

sfor·za·to (sfortsátou) *adj.* and *adv.* sforzando [Ital.]

's Gra·ven·ha·ge (sxrɑvənháːxə) *HAGUE, THE

Sha·ba (ʃáːbə) *KATANGA

shab·bi·ly (ʃǽbili:) *adv.* in a shabby manner

shab·bi·ness (ʃǽbi:nis) *n.* the state or quality of being shabby

shab·by (ʃǽbi:) *comp.* **shab·bi·er** *superl.* **shab·bi·est** (of clothing) looking badly worn ‖ wearing badly worn clothing ‖ shameful or mean in a petty way, *a shabby trick* ‖ poor in quality, *a shabby lot of recruits* [fr. older *shab*, a scab]

Sha·bu·oth (ʃɑbuːóːt, ʃəvúːəs) *n.* the Jewish harvest festival, celebrated on the 50th day after the second day of Passover [Heb. *shābhŭ'ŏth* pl. of *shābhūa'*, week]

shack (ʃæk) *n.* a crudely made hut, esp. one to live in [etym. doubtful]

shack·le (ʃǽkʹl) **1.** *n.* a chain or ring used to prevent the free movement of arms or legs ‖ any of certain fastening devices, e.g. the link that couples with the staple of a padlock or a U-shaped metal piece closed by a heavy pin ‖ (*pl.*) something considered to impede or prevent free movement, *matrimonial shackles* **2.** *v.t. pres. part.* **shack·ling** *past* and *past part.* **shack·led** to fasten with a shackle or shackles ‖ to impede the freedom of action or expression of [O.E. *sceacul*]

Shack·le·ton (ʃǽkʹltən), Sir Ernest Henry (1874-1922), British explorer in Antarctica. He was a member of Scott's expedition of 1901-4 and commanded his own expeditions (1907-9, 1914-17 and 1921-2). He located the south magnetic pole (1909)

shad (ʃæd)pl. **shad**, **shads** *n.* a member of *Alosa*, fam. *Clupeidae*, a genus of widely distributed marine food fishes that are closely related to herring and spawn in rivers, esp. *A. sapidissima*, the North American species [O.E. *sceadd*]

shad·ber·ry (ʃǽdberi:) *pl.* **shad·ber·ries** *n.* the fruit of the shadbush ‖ the shadbush [after SHAD, because the bush flowers when the shad appear in U.S. rivers]

shad·bush (ʃǽdbuʃ) *n.* the Juneberry (plant)

shad·dock (ʃǽdək) *n.* a large pear-shaped citrus fruit, resembling coarse or spongy grapefruit, found in the East Indies and introduced to the West Indies ‖ *Citrus grandis*, fam. *Rutaceae*, the tree which bears this fruit [after Captain *Shaddock*, English naval officer who introduced it into Barbados (1696)]

shade (ʃeid) **1.** *n.* a color containing some black (*COLOR, cf. TINT) ‖ a place partly sheltered from the full light or heat of the sun ‖ this quality of sheltering, *the place lacks shade* ‖ an eyeshade ‖ a lampshade ‖ a window blind ‖ comparative darkness, *the light and shade of a picture* ‖ a variation of individual depth or brightness of a color, *a shade of pink* ‖ a slight variation, *a shade of meaning* ‖ a slight degree, *a shade to the left* ‖ (*rhet.*) a disembodied spirit ‖ (*pl.*, *rhet.*) the dimming darkness of twilight, *shades of evening* ‖ (*pl.*, *rhet.*) the place where the spirits of the dead are **to put someone** (or something) **in the shade** to be so much better than someone (or something) that attention is withdrawn from him (or it) **2.** *v. pres. part.* **shad·ing** *past* and *past part.* **shad·ed** *v.t.* to shelter from the full light or heat of the sun ‖ to darken (parts of a drawing etc.) in order to suggest relief or differences of brightness etc. ‖ *v.i.* to change gradually, esp. in color [O.E. *sceadu*, *scead*]

shad·i·ly (ʃéidili:) *adv.* in a shady manner

shad·i·ness (ʃéidi:nis) *n.* the state or quality of being shady

shad·ing (ʃéidiŋ) *n.* a provision of shade ‖ the representation of degrees of light or dark in a drawing or painting or the strokes etc. used ‖ (*mus.*) a subtle dynamic modification for interpretive effect

sha·doof, **sha·duf** (ʃadúːf) *n.* a device consisting of a bucket and a pivoted pole with a balancing weight, used to raise water, esp. in Egypt [Arab. *shādūf*]

sha·dow (ʃǽdou) *n.* a region of relative darkness caused by the interception of the light of the sun etc. by an opaque or semiopaque body ‖ the image of an opaque body projected on a surface elsewhere illuminated ‖ a mere semblance, *a shadow of his former self* ‖ something insubstantial, *worn to a shadow* ‖ trace, hint, *not a shadow of doubt* ‖ an inseparable companion ‖ (*rhet.*) a foreshadowing, *shadows of events to come* ‖ (*rhet.*) protection, *under the shadow of his wings* ‖ the relatively dark or shaded portion of a painting etc. [O.E. *sceaduwe*, *sceadwe*, oblique case of *sceadu*, shade]

shadow *v.t.* to throw into shadow, darken, *the*

CONCISE PRONUNCIATION KEY: **(a)** æ, c*a*t; α, c*a*r; ɔ f*aw*n; ei, sn*a*ke. **(e)** e, h*e*n; iː, sh*ee*p; iə, d*ee*r; εə, b*ea*r. **(i)** i, f*i*sh; ai, t*i*ger; əː, b*i*rd. **(o)** o, *o*x; au, c*ow*; ou, g*oa*t; u, p*oo*r; ɔi, r*oy*al. **(u)** Λ, d*u*ck; u, b*u*ll; uː, g*oo*se; ə, bacill*u*s; juː, c*u*be. x, lo*ch*; θ, *th*ink; ð, bo*th*er; z, *Z*en; ʒ, cor*s*age; dʒ, sava*g*e; ŋ, ora*ng*utang; j, *y*ak; ʃ, *fi*sh; tʃ, fe*tch*; 'l, rabb*le*; 'n, redd*en*. Complete pronunciation key appears inside front cover.

canyon was shadowed by steep cliffs ‖ to follow and watch in secret ‖ (often with 'forth' and 'out') to suggest obscurely (what is to follow) [O.E. *sceadwian* fr. *sceadu*, shade]

sha·dow·box (ʃǽdoubɒks) *v.i.* to go through the movements of sparring with an imaginary boxing opponent as a method of training ‖ to deal warily with a person so as to cover up ignorance, avoid a decision, play for an advantage in argument etc.

shadow cabinet (esp. *Br.*) a group of parliamentary opposition leaders who constitute a prospective cabinet against the time when their party may be returned to power

shad·ow·graph (ʃǽdougræf, ʃǽdougrɑf) *n.* an image or a picture formed by shadows, e.g. as thrown on a wall by a hand lit from behind

shad·ow·i·ness (ʃǽdoui:nis) *n.* the state or quality of being shadowy

shadow play a play presented in images or pictures formed by shadows on a screen, e.g. of puppets lit from behind

shadow prices (*economics*) the maximum price level attainable if an extra unit of a resource were made available

shad·ow·y (ʃǽdoui:) *adj.* full of shadows ‖ like a shadow, indistinct or fleeting ‖ shaded

shaduf *SHADOOF

shad·y (ʃéidi:) *comp.* **shad·i·er** *superl.* **shad·i·est** *adj.* offering shade ‖ in shade ‖ (*pop.*) very probably dishonest, *a shady deal*

shaft (ʃæft, ʃɑft) *n.* a long, smooth-surfaced piece of wood or metal of roughly the same thickness throughout its length and usually of roughly circular cross section, e.g. the handle of an axe or golf club or the body of an arrow ‖ a long rod supporting a part of a machine or transmitting motion to a part of a machine ‖ (*archit.*) the part of a column separating the capital and the base ‖ a long, more or less vertical, hollow space, e.g. a mine shaft or ventilation shaft ‖ (*rhet.*) an arrow ‖ (*biol.*) the straight, cylindrical part of a long bone ‖ the distal part of a feather's stem ‖ a beam of light ‖ a bolt (of lightning) ‖ a remark or piece of verbal wit that scores off the person or thing to which it refers ‖ (*pl.* **shaves** ʃeivz) one of the bars between which a horse is harnessed when drawing a vehicle, a rotating axle etc. [O.E. *sceaft*, spear shaft]

Shaf·ter (ʃǽftər, ʃɑftər), William Rufus (1835-1906), U.S. general during the Spanish-American War. After the destruction of the Spanish fleet, he captured (1898) Santiago de Cuba

Shaftes·bur·y (ʃǽftsbəri:, ʃɑftsbəri:), Anthony Ashley Cooper, 3rd earl of (1671-1713), English philosopher. In his 'Characteristics of Men, Manners, Opinions and Times' (1711), he developed his view of moral sense as a harmony between the desires of society and those of the individual

Shaftesbury, Anthony Ashley Cooper, 7th earl of (1801-85), British Tory philanthropist and social reformer. He was responsible for much reforming legislation, including the prohibiting of the employment of women and children in mines (1842) and the limitation of the working day in factories to 10 hours (1847)

shag (ʃæg) *n.* coarse, rough-cut, shredded pipe tobacco ‖ thick, matted hair or wool ‖ the long nap on certain types of cloth or wool [O.E. *sceacga*]

shag *n. Phalacrocorax aristotelis*, a long-billed, shaggy-crested British cormorant (about 30 ins). Flocks fly in V formation like geese [perh. fr. *shag*, (*obs.*) mat of hair]

shag·bark (ʃǽgbɑrk) *n. Carya ovata*, fam. *Juglandaceae*, a white hickory tree found in the eastern and central U.S.A., yielding a sweet edible nut. Its light gray bark often peels back in rough strips ‖ the wood of this tree, used esp. for tool handles

shag·gi·ly (ʃǽgili:) *adv.* in a shaggy manner

shag·gi·ness (ʃǽgi:nis) *n.* the state or quality of being shaggy

shag·gy (ʃǽgi:) *comp.* **shag·gi·er** *superl.* **shag·gi·est** *adj.* rough-haired ‖ (of hair) thick, dense and (often) unkempt ‖ having a rough surface ‖ (of countryside) covered with a rough growth of shrubs and trees

shaggy-dog story a funny story with a calculatedly feeble ending. It is told at length with exasperating detail

sha·green (ʃəgrí:n) *n.* a type of leather prepared from the untanned hide of a horse, camel or ass, grained with rough raised spots and usually dyed green ‖ leather prepared from the rough skin of sharks and dogfish etc. and usually dyed green [var. of older *chagrin* fr. F.]

shah (ʃɑ) *n.* formerly the sovereign of Iran (Persia) or his title [Pers. *shāh*, king]

Sha·hap·ti·an (ʃɑhǽpti:ən) *n.* a member of an Indian people of the northwestern U.S.A. and British Columbia

Shah Ja·han, Shah Je·han (ʃɑdʒəhán) (c. 1592-1666), Mogul emperor (1627-58), son of Jahangir. His reign was especially noted for its magnificent architecture, incl. the Taj Mahal and Agra and Delhi mosques

shake (ʃeik) **1.** *v. pres. part.* **shak·ing** *past* **shook** (ʃuk) *past part.* **shak·en** (ʃéik'n) *v.t.* to cause to move rapidly up and down or from side to side of the normal position of rest ‖ to cause to vibrate or quiver ‖ to weaken (belief or confidence), *his lying shook my faith in him* ‖ to shock or jar the equilibrium of, *the fall shook me* ‖ to brandish (a weapon) etc., *to shake one's fist at someone* ‖ (*mus.*) to trill (a phrase) ‖ to agitate (dice) before casting them ‖ (*pop.*) to get rid of (someone or something), *to shake bad habits* ‖ *v.i.* to move rapidly to and fro about a normal position of rest ‖ to vibrate or quiver ‖ (*mus.*) to make a trill **to shake down** to cause to fall or descend by shaking ‖ (*pop.*) to extract money from ‖ to cause to settle by shaking ‖ to improvise a temporary bed or lodging ‖ to adjust to new conditions **to shake hands** to give someone a handshake ‖ to clasp hands in greeting, farewell etc. **to shake off** to get rid of (someone or something unwelcome) **to shake out** to shake in order to clean, open, restore to its proper shape or position etc. ‖ to cause to come out by shaking **to shake up** to mix by shaking ‖ to shock, agitate ‖ to destroy the complacency of **2.** *n.* a shaking or being shaken ‖ a tremble or quiver ‖ a crack in a tree parallel to the growth rings ‖ a shingle split by hand from a log ‖ (*pop.*) a milkshake ‖ (*mus.*) a trill **no great shakes** not of great quality or significance [O.E. *scacan*]

shake·down (ʃéikdaun) *n.* an improvised bed ‖ (*pop.*) an extorting of money ‖ a period of adjustment

shaken *past part.* of SHAKE

shak·er (ʃéikər) *n.* someone or something that shakes ‖ a container in which something is shaken, e.g. a cocktail shaker **Shak·er** a member of a sect (1747) the English founders of which emigrated to America after secession from the Quakers. They received their name because of their trembling when filled with religious ecstasy. The sect lives in celibate communities and by mid-20th c. had a few dozen remaining adherents

Shake·speare (ʃéikspiər), William (1564-1616), the greatest English poet and playwright. He was born and died at Stratford-upon-Avon. He was in London as actor, poet and playwright (with occasional visits to his home town) from about 1592 to about 1616, but there is a gap of 8 to 10 years before 1592 concerning which scarcely anything is known.

His greatest period was between 1600 and 1607, during which he produced the comedies 'As you Like It' and 'Twelfth Night' (1600-1), the tragedies 'Hamlet' (1602-3), 'Othello' (1604), 'King Lear' (1605-6), and 'Macbeth' (1606) as well as 'Antony and Cleopatra' (1607-8) and at least four other plays. The 'Sonnets' date from 1609.

Various ages have found various things in Shakespeare. The 18th c. saw in him 'just observation of general nature' (Johnson) or truth-to-life. The Romantics admired his freedom from literary convention, the sweep and grandeur of historical conflict, his parabolic insight into the extremes of the human predicament. The later 19th c. (e.g. Bradley) admired the delicate and complicated psychological insight of his characterization. All ages have admired his command of language, and our own age has presented a picture of Shakespeare as a conscious symphonic artist, producing in his greatest plays an elaborate structure in which theme answers theme and in which the whole, like music, is its own meaning, which any paraphrase denatures. He is presented by modern critics as deeply concerned with the moral basis of life. 'Nature', 'right', 'order', 'truth', the key concepts, are as it were both created and tested in the conflicts which form the plays

Shake·spear·e·an, Shake·spear·i·an (ʃeikspíəri:ən) **1.** *adj.* of or concerning Shakespeare **2.** *n.* a specialist in the works of Shakespeare

shake-up (ʃéikʌp) *n.* a shaking up, esp. a jolting of someone's complacency or an administrative reorganization for greater efficiency

Shakh·ty (ʃáxti:) a city (pop. 214,000) of the R.S.F.S.R., U.S.S.R., in the Donets Basin: anthracite mining, pig iron

shak·i·ly (ʃéikili:) *adv.* in a shaky manner

shak·i·ness (ʃéiki:nis) *n.* the state or quality of being shaky

shaking table a machine with a wide vibrating rubber belt used for dressing ores

shak·o (ʃǽkou, ʃéikou) *pl.* **shak·os, shak·oes** *n.* a stiff, high, cylindrical, peaked military headgear, with a plume [Hung. *csakó*]

sha·ku·ha·chi (ʃɑkuːhɑtʃiː) *n.* (*music*) Japanese bamboo recorder

shak·y (ʃéiki:) *comp.* **shak·i·er** *superl.* **shak·i·est** *adj.* unsteady, apt to shake, *a shaky old table* ‖ trembling, infirm, *a shaky old man* ‖ shaking, not even or smooth, *a shaky voice* ‖ wavering, *shaky faith* ‖ weak, not firmly based, *a shaky argument* ‖ (of a tree) marked by shakes

shale (ʃeil) *n.* a fine-grained sedimentary rock readily splitting into thin plates or layers [perh. a use of older *shale*, a shell, fr. O. E. *scealu*]

shale oil an oil distilled from bituminous shale

shall (ʃæl) *past* **should** (ʃud) *auxiliary v.* used to express futurity, *we shall see*, or promise, intention or command, *you shall go to the theater tomorrow, I shall see to it, you shall do what I say* (cf. WILL, cf. SHOULD, cf. WOULD) [O.E. *sceal, sculon*]

shal·lop (ʃǽləp) *n.* a small open boat using oars or sail, for shallow waters [F. *chaloupe* prob. fr. Du.]

shal·lot (ʃəlót) *n. Allium ascalonicum*, fam. *Liliaceae*, a perennial producing clusters of small bulbs, resembling the common onion, used in cooking [fr. older *eschalot* fr. F.]

shal·low (ʃǽlou) **1.** *adj.* having relatively little distance between the top and bottom or front and back surfaces, *shallow streams, a shallow colonnade* ‖ superficial, *a shallow mind* **2.** *n.* (*pl.*) a shallow part of a body of water **3.** *v.t.* to make shallow ‖ *v.i.* to become shallow or shallower [M.E. *schalowe* prob. rel. to O. E. *sceald*]

Shal·ma·ne·ser III (ʃælməní:zər) (*d.* c. 824 B.C.), king of Assyria (858–c. 824 B.C.). He made war on neighboring peoples, and fought an indecisive battle (c. 853 B.C.) against Ahab of Israel

Sha·lom A·lei·chem (ʃɑlóuməléixəm) (Salomon Rabinowitz, 1859-1916), Ukrainian author of short stories, plays and novels written in Yiddish

shal·y (ʃéili:) *comp.* **shal·i·er** *superl.* **shal·i·est** *adj.* pertaining to or like shale

sham (ʃæm) **1.** *v. pres. part.* **sham·ming** *past* and *past part.* **shammed** *v.i.* to make pretense ‖ *v.t.* to simulate, *to sham death* **2.** *n.* someone who pretends to be what he is not ‖ something pretended to be other than it is ‖ a shamming **3.** *adj.* having the appearance of being what it is not, *a sham fight* [etym. doubtful]

sha·man (ʃámən, ʃéimən, ʃæmən) *n.* a priest or witch doctor among some Ural-Altaic peoples. He uses magic to propitiate gods and spirits, foretell the future, heal etc. **Shá·man·ism** *n.* the religion practiced by a shaman ‖ a similar religion, e.g. among North American Indians [G. *schamane*, Russ. *shaman* fr. Tungus]

sham·ble (ʃǽmb'l) **1.** *v.i. pres. part.* **sham·bling** *past* and *past part.* **sham·bled** to walk awkwardly, with unorganized movements of the limbs and dragging the feet **2.** *n.* a shambling walk [etym. doubtful]

sham·bles (ʃǽmb'lz) *pl. n.* (*hist.*) a slaughterhouse ‖ a scene of great destruction ‖ (*pop.*) extreme disorder or a scene of this [O.E. *scamul. sceamul*, a bench]

shame (ʃeim) *n.* a painful emotion aroused by the recognition that one has failed to act, behave or think in accordance with the standards which one accepts as good ‖ the same feeling aroused by similar failure in others with whom one identifies oneself ‖ utter disgrace, *a life of shame* ‖ someone or something that causes disgrace ‖ (*pop.*) something unfair, *it's a shame that he got off scot-free* ‖ (*pop.*) something regrettable, *it was a shame that the rain spoiled your holiday* **for shame!** you ought to be ashamed! **to put (someone) to shame** to cause (someone) to feel shame by exposing his failures or misdeeds ‖ to cause (someone) to feel inadequate by surpassing him [O.E. *sceamu, scamu*]

shame *v.t. pres. part.* **sham·ing** *past* and *past part.* **shamed** to cause (someone) to feel shame ‖ to bring shame or disgrace on ‖ to impel (someone) to do something by making him feel shame, *to shame someone into doing something* ‖ to put (someone) to shame by displaying superior ability, behavior etc. [O.E. *sceamian, scamian*]

shame·faced (ʃéimfeist) adj. exhibiting shame ‖ painfully abashed **shame·fac·ed·ly** (ʃéimféisidli:, ʃéimféistli:) adv. **shame·fac·ed·ness** n.

shame·ful (ʃéimfəl) adj. causing shame ‖ offending one's sense of what is right or just

shame·less (ʃéimlis) adj. lacking modesty ‖ showing lack of modesty ‖ imprudent

Sha·mir (ʃəmíər), Yitzhak (c. 1915-), Israeli statesman, prime minister (1983-4), born in Poland. He emigrated (1935) to Palestine and led a guerrilla group against the British. He was foreign minister (1980-3) before leading his Likud coalition into power in the elections of 1984. Under a power-sharing arrangement with the rival Labor party, it was agreed that he would resume the prime ministership in late 1986

sham·mash (ʃáməs, *Heb.* ʃamáʃ) pl. **sham·ma·shim** (ʃamʃsim, *Heb.* ʃamaʃí:m) n. the candle used for lighting the other candles of the menorah ‖ the sexton of a synagogue [Yiddish *Shames* and *Heb. shámmāsh* fr. Aram. *shěmmāsh*, to serve]

sham·my (ʃámi:) pl. **sham·mies** n. (pop.) chamois (leather) [altered fr. CHAMOIS]

sham·poo (ʃæmpú:) 1. v.t. pres. part. **sham·poo·ing** past and past part. **sham·pooed** to wash (the hair) 2. n. a washing of the hair or an instance of this ‖ a usually liquid or powder preparation for washing the hair [prob. Hind. *haček* imper. of *čampnā*, to press]

sham·rock (ʃámrɒk) n. any of several clovers commonly regarded as the national emblem of Ireland, esp. *Trifolium dubium*, which has small yellow flowers

Shamrock n. code name of one of two operations that permitted screening of overseas telegrams by the National Security Agency, a practice later discontinued

Shan (ʃɑn, ʃæn) a state (area 57,816 sq. miles, pop. 1,950,000) of E. Burma on a mountainous plateau, comprised of former Shan principalities and Wa states. Capital: Taunggyi. The Shans, a Thai people, ruled most of Burma (1287-1531), retained the best land in the east, and economically are advanced over other minorities

shan·dy (ʃándi:) n. beer mixed with lemonade or ginger beer [short for SHANDYGAFF]

shan·dy·gaff (ʃándi:gæf) n. shandy [origin unknown]

Shang·hai (ʃæŋhái, ʃáŋhái) the largest city (pop. 11,859,748) and chief industrial and commercial center of China, a port in the Yangtze-kiang delta, Kiangsu. Industries: textiles, metallurgy, mechanical and electrical engineering, rolling stock, chemicals, rubber processing. Shanghai was the center of European trade in China (1842-1949). It consists of an old walled city with the former French concession and international settlement, surrounded by modern quarters. University (1905)

shanghai v.t. (hist.) to drug or otherwise stupefy and take aboard a ship to serve as a sailor ‖ (pop.) to force (someone) by guile to do something [after SHANGHAI]

shank (ʃæŋk) 1. n. the part of the leg in man between knee and ankle ‖ the corresponding part in various animals ‖ the leg in man ‖ the straight connection between the handle and working part of a tool etc. ‖ the long, roughly straight, portion of an object (e.g. a pin, nail, anchor) between its extremities ‖ the back loop on a button ‖ the narrow part of a shoe sole under the instep ‖ (printing) the body of a type ‖ the later part of the afternoon or evening) 2. v.i. (of a flower) to drop by reason of decay in the stalk ‖ v.t. (golf) to strike with the heel of the club [O.E. *scanca, sceanca*]

Shan·non (ʃánən) the chief river (240 miles long) of Ireland, flowing from the central Irish Republic to a long estuary below Limerick, linked by canal to Dublin: hydroelectricity

shan·ny (ʃáni:) pl. **shan·nies** n. *Blennius pholis*, fam. *Blennidae*, a smooth, spineless, olive-green European blenny [etym. doubtful]

Shan·si (ʃánsí:) a province (area 60,300 sq. miles, pop. 28,904,423) of E. Central China, with vast coal deposits. Capital: Taiyuan

shan't (ʃænt, ʃɑnt) contr. of SHALL NOT

Shan·tung (ʃæntʌ́ŋ, ʃándún) a province (area 56,944 sq. miles, pop. 74,419,054) of E. China,

partly formed by a large peninsula of the same name. Capital: Tsinan

shan·tung (ʃæntʌ́ŋ) n. a silk woven from coarse silk yarn and having a somewhat rough surface [after SHANTUNG]

shan·ty (ʃánti:) pl. **shan·ties** n. a chantey [perh. F. *chantez* imper. of *chanter*, to sing]

shanty pl. **shan·ties** n. a small shack of crude construction [Canad. F. *chantier*, workshop]

shan·ty·town (ʃánti:taun) n. a town, or part of a town, consisting of shanties

shape (ʃeip) n. the way in which an object is seen or felt to be extended as to its length, breadth and depth ‖ this as conforming to an ideal or pattern or original, *it has lost its shape* ‖ the outward appearance of a person's body as distinct from his facial appearance ‖ a dimly perceived form, *weird shapes in the fog* ‖ satisfactory arrangement, *to put a speech into shape* ‖ state, condition, *his business was in bad shape* ‖ a mold, e.g. for headcheese or jellies ‖ a jelly, headcheese etc. made in such a mold ‖ form, embodiment, *reward in the shape of an extra holiday* ‖ false appearance, semblance, *a troublemaker in the shape of a friend* ‖ nature, *the shape of things to come* **to take shape** to develop, esp. in an orderly or regular way [O.E. *gesceap*, creation, creature]

shape pres. part. **shap·ing** past and past part. **shaped** v.t. to cause to take on a certain shape, *to shape dough into loaves* ‖ to produce by manipulating, *to shape figures out of clay* ‖ to order, *to shape one's future* ‖ to make suitable or fit, *to shape a boy for his career* ‖ to cut (a garment) so as to fit the figure closely ‖ v.i. to acquire a particular shape ‖ to develop, *clouds shaping on the horizon* [O.E. *scieppan*]

shaped charge (mil.) a charge shaped so as to concentrate its explosive force in a particular direction

shape·less (ʃéiplis) adj. having no regular shape

shape·li·ness (ʃéipli:nis) n. the state or quality of being shapely

shape·ly (ʃéipli:) comp. **shape·li·er** superl. **shape·li·est** adj. well proportioned

shap·er (ʃéipər) n. someone or something that shapes, esp. a machine for producing a particular shape

shape up v. to get into proper condition; by extension, to conform

Sha·pi·ro (ʃəpíərou), Karl (1913-), U.S. poet and critic. His works, which present the poet as cultural spokesman, include 'Poems of a Jew' (1958) and 'In Defense of Ignorance' (1960)

Shap·ley (ʃápli:), Harlow (1885-1972), U.S. astronomer. As director (1921-52) of the Harvard College Observatory, he led pioneer research into the structure of the Milky Way and the universe beyond

shard (ʃɑrd) n. a broken piece of brittle material, esp. a potsherd ‖ (zool.) the wing case of a beetle [O.E. *sceard*, a gap]

share (ʃɛər) 1. n. a part shared, *he kept a share for the dog* ‖ the part to which one is entitled, *he gave you your share, you which is required of one, he did her share of the work* ‖ the part one receives or contributes ‖ (commerce) one of the equal parts into which the capital of a corporation is divided **to go shares** to share equally **to have a share in** to be partly responsible for 2. v. pres. part. **shar·ing** past and past part. **shared** v.t. (often with 'out') to distribute parts of (something) among others ‖ (often with 'with') to retain one part of (something) and give the rest or part of the rest to another or others, *he will share the winnings with you* ‖ to take or use a part of (something) with someone or something, *may she share your umbrella?* ‖ to do or experience (something) with others ‖ v.i. to join with others in doing or experiencing something, *he shared in the planning of it* [O.E. *scearu*, cutting, division]

share n. a plowshare [O.E. *scear, scær*]

share·crop (ʃéɑrkrɒp) pres. part. **share·crop·ping** past and past part. **share·cropped** v.t. to work (land) as a sharecropper ‖ v.i. to work as a sharecropper

share·crop·per (ʃéɑrkrɒpər) n. a tenant farmer, esp. in the southern U.S.A., given certain credits and a share in crops and charged for certain incidentals of upkeep

shared appreciation mortgage (banking) loan secured by property made at a reduced interest rate with provision that lender share in price appreciation of property, usu. when sold

share·hold·er (ʃéɑrhouldər) n. someone who

owns shares in a company or other shared property or business

Sha·ri (ʃári:) (F. Chari) a river (length excluding headstreams: 700 miles) flowing north from the S. Central African Republic through S.W. Chad to Lake Chad

sha·rif, she·rif (ʃərí:f) n. a descendant of Fatima and Ali ‖ a title used by certain princes of Islam ‖ the chief magistrate in Mecca [Arab *sharif*, noble]

shark (ʃɑrk) n. any of several large, voracious, elasmobranch fishes, armed with several rows of serrated teeth and having tough, scaly skins. They are particularly abundant in the warmer oceans ‖ a man who makes his living by swindles and trickery or by overcharging or otherwise exploiting in an antisocial way [etym. doubtful]

shark·skin (ʃárkskin) n. shagreen leather made from a shark's skin ‖ smooth worsted material in twill or basket weave, with two-color or two-tone designs woven in ‖ a rayon or cotton fabric with a smooth, sleek look, used esp. for sportswear

Sha·ron (ʃárən) the biblical name for the coastal plain of Israel from Jaffa to south of Haifa

Sharp (ʃɑrp), Granville (1735-1813), British philanthropist and pioneer in the struggle for the abolition of slavery. In 1772 he obtained the famous judgment making slavery illegal in Britain

sharp (ʃɑrp) 1. comp. **sharp·er** superl. **sharp·est** adj. well adapted to cut or pierce ‖ having a thin edge, *a sharp ridge*, or a pointed shape, *a sharp peak* ‖ making an acute or sudden angle, *a sharp bend in the road* ‖ as if cut with a knife, *a sharp outline, sharp features* ‖ piercing suddenly, *a sharp pain* ‖ (of a taste) acid ‖ (of air) cold ‖ (of a sound or voice) strong and shrill ‖ alert, attentive, *a sharp lookout* ‖ swiftly rebuking, *a sharp retort* ‖ (Br.) quick, *we must be sharp if we are to catch the train* ‖ brisk, energetic, *a sharp run* ‖ hotly contested, *a sharp fight* ‖ (of the senses, intelligence etc.) acute, keen, *sharp vision* ‖ quick-witted ‖ (pop.) clever, expert, *a sharp engineer* ‖ quick to look after one's own interests, *a sharp man of business* ‖ dishonest, *sharp practices* ‖ (mus., of a note or tone) raised a semitone in pitch ‖ (mus.) above true pitch ‖ (mus., of a key) having a sharp or sharps in the signature 2. adv. to a sharp point or edge ‖ punctually, *at 3 o'clock sharp* ‖ at a sudden angle, *turn sharp left* ‖ (mus.) above true pitch 3. n. (mus.) a note that is a semitone above a specified note ‖ the sign for this (#) ‖ a sharp piece of diamond used for cutting or for engraving gems 4. v.t. (mus., Am. = Br. sharpen) to raise a semitone ‖ v.i. (mus., Am.= Br. sharpen) to sing or play above true pitch **sharp·en** v.t. (Br., mus.) to sharp ‖ to make sharp or sharper ‖ v.i. (Br., mus.) to sharp ‖ to become sharp or sharper **sharp·er** n. (pop.) a swindler, esp. at cards [O.E. *scearp*]

sharp-eyed (ʃárpaid) adj. having acute sight ‖ quick to notice little details

sharp·ie (ʃárpi:) n. (hist.) a long, pointed, flat-bottomed boat with one or two masts each having a triangular sail ‖ a sharper

sharp sand sand with angular, not rounded grains

Sharps·burg (ʃárpsbə:rg) *ANTIETAM

sharp-set (ʃárpset) adj. placed at a sharp angle ‖ presenting sharp edges, *a sharp-set saw*

sharp·shoot·er (ʃárpʃu:tər) n. (U.S. army) a proficiency rating of marksmanship, above a marksman and below an expert ‖ a soldier with this rating ‖ a person who is a good shot

sharp-sight·ed (ʃárpsáitid) adj. sharp-eyed

sharp-wit·ted (ʃárpwítid) adj. having a quick, intelligent mind

Shas·tri (ʃástri:), Lal Bahadur (1904-66), Indian statesman, prime minister of India (1964-6)

Shatt-al-A·rab (ʃætælárab) a river (120 miles long) formed by the confluence of the Tigris and Euphrates in S.E. Iraq, flowing into the Persian Gulf

shat·ter (ʃátər) v.t. to cause to break suddenly into fragments ‖ to destroy suddenly and totally, *to shatter one's hopes* ‖ v.i. to break into fragments ‖ to become suddenly and totally destroyed [etym. doubtful, rel. to SCATTER]

shatter cones (geol.) distinctive striated rock fragments shaped like cones believed produced by an intense force

shave (ʃeiv) 1. v. pres. part. **shav·ing** past **shaved** past. part. **shaved, shav·en** (ʃéiv'n) v.t.

to remove using a sharp cutting edge, *to shave the bristles from a pig's back* ‖ to remove hair from (the skin) with a razor ‖ to remove thin slices from (leather, wood etc.) with a sharp tool ‖ to pass very closely without touching ‖ to graze, rub against lightly ‖ *v.i.* to remove hair with a razor 2. *n.* a shaving or being shaved ‖ a thin slice ‖ a tool used for shaving leather, wood etc. **sháv·er** *n.* an electric device for shaving ‖ someone who shaves ‖ (*pop.*) a young or small boy **sháv·ing** the act of one who shaves ‖ a thin slice shaved off wood, metal etc. [O.E. *sceafan*]

Sha·vi·an (ʃéiviːən) 1. *adj.* characteristic or imitative of the works of George Bernard Shaw 2. *n.* a devotee of Shaw, his writings and opinions [fr. *Shavius*, Latinized form of SHAW]

Shaw, George Bernard (1856-1950), Irish playwright and critic. His plays cover a wide range of modes: history ('Caesar and Cleopatra', 1901, 'Saint Joan', 1924), philosophy ('Man and Superman', 1903, 'Back to Methuselah', 1921), political fantasy ('The Apple Cart', 1929) etc. All his plays are linked by a uniform style of paradoxical volubility. They are entertaining and often acute. What Shaw stood for is hard to define, though he was a progressive in his own anarchic way (*FABIAN SOCIETY). Within his own style of verbal exchange he was a great theatrical craftsman. His best-made comedies include 'Arms and the Man' (1898), 'Major Barbara' (1905) and 'Pygmalion' (1913)

Shaw, Henry Wheeler *BILLINGS, JOSH

Shaw, Lemuel (1781-1861), chief justice (1830-60) of the supreme judicial court of Massachusetts. His decisions include 'Farwell v. Railroad' (in which he made the fellow-servant rule, that an employer is not liable for injuries caused by the negligence of a fellow servant, a principle of American law), 'Commonwealth v. Hunt' (in which he freed unions from the abusive application of the law of conspiracy), and 'Roberts v. Boston' (in which he ruled that racial segregation in public schools did not create unconstitutional inequalities)

shawl (ʃɔl) *n.* a square, oblong or triangular covering for the shoulders or head worn by women and girls ‖ a woolen wrap for babies [Pers. *shāl*]

shawm (ʃɔm) *n.* an obsolete musical instrument akin to the oboe [M.E. *shallemelle* fr. O.F.]

Shaw·nee (ʃɔní:) *pl.* **Shaw·nee, Shaw·nees** *n.* a member of a North American Algonquian Indian tribe originally of the eastern U.S.A. and now living in Oklahoma

Shays (ʃaiz), Daniel (c. 1747-1825), American soldier. He led an unsuccessful rebellion (1786-7) against high land taxes, legal costs and officials' salaries

Shcher·ba·kov (ʃtʃerbakɔ́f) *RYBINSK

she (ʃi:) 1. *pron., 3rd person sing., nominative case* a female person, animal or personified thing already mentioned 2. *adj.* (*prefixed*) female, *a she-devil* 3. *n.* a female, *is it a she or a he?* [prob. altered fr. O.E. *sío*, *sēo*, *sīe*]

shea (ʃi:) *n. Butyrospermum parkii*, fam. *Sapotaceae*, a tropical African tree, whose large nuts yield shea butter [Mandingo *si, se, sye*]

shea butter the vegetable fat yielded by the crushed nuts of the shea tree

shead·ing (ʃí:diŋ) *n.* any of the six administrative units of the Isle of Man [var. of *shedding*, pres. part. of SHED, (obs.) to divide]

sheaf (ʃi:f) 1. *pl.* **sheaves** (ʃi:vz) *n.* cut stalks of grain bundled together in an orderly way ‖ a quiverful of arrows, usually 24 ‖ a collection of things put together, *a sheaf of papers* 2. *v.t.* to make into a sheaf or sheaves [O.E. *scéaf*]

shear (ʃíər) 1. *v. pres. part.* **shear·ing** past **sheared** past part. **sheared, shorn** (ʃɔrn) *v.t.* to cut or clip with shears, esp. to clip the wool from (a sheep) ‖ (esp. *past part.*, with 'of') to deprive of, *shorn of his power* ‖ (*mech.*) to deform by causing to undergo a shear ‖ *v.i.* to use shears ‖ (*mech.*) to suffer deformation through a shear 2. *n.* a shearing or being sheared ‖ (esp. *Br.*) this used in designating the age of a sheep, *a sheep of four shears* ‖ something shorn off, esp. the wool cut off in one shearing ‖ (*mech.*) a deformation within a body in which two adjacent planes tend to move in a parallel direction relative to one another while remaining parallel ‖ (esp. *pl.*) a hoist of two or more poles joined at the top and steadied by guys, used e.g. for placing a ship's masts or engines in position ‖ (*geol.*) a change in direction of a stratum due to lateral pressure [O.E. *sceran*]

shear legs a shear (hoist)

shear·ling (ʃíərliŋ) *n.* (esp. *Br.*) a sheep shorn once only

shears (ʃíərz) *pl. n.* a pair of sharp cutting blades, larger than, but similar to, those of scissors, and often joined by a spring [O.E. *scérero* and O.E. *scéar*]

shear·wa·ter (ʃíərwɒtər, ʃíərwɔtər) *n.* any of several species of oceanic birds, esp. of genus *Puffinus*, fam. *Procellariidae*, that visit land only when breeding. They are blackish, with slender bills. They bank and glide and skim over the waves on long, narrow, stiff wings

sheat·fish (ʃí:tfiʃ) *pl.* **sheat·fish·es, sheat·fish** *n. Silurus glanis* fam. *Siluridae*, a large catfish (up to 10 ft) common in the Danube and some other European rivers [etym. doubtful]

sheath (ʃi:θ) *pl.* **sheaths** (ʃi:ðz) *n.* a cover fitting closely over the blade of a weapon or tool ‖ (*biol.*) a protective membrane covering ‖ (*bot.*) a leaf base surrounding the stem ‖ a close-fitting straight dress [O.E. *scǣth, scéath*]

sheath·bill (ʃí:θbil) *n.* a member of *Chionididae*, a family of sea birds found in the southern hemisphere. They have a horny sheath over the base of the upper mandible

sheathe (ʃi:ð) *pres. part.* **sheath·ing** past and past part. **sheathed** *v.t.* to put into a sheath, scabbard etc. ‖ to protect in a case ‖ to retract (claws) ‖ to provide (e.g. a roof, a ship's bottom) with sheathing **shéath·ing** *n.* a placing in a sheath ‖ a protective covering, e.g. on the hull of a wooden ship or the waterproof layer on a wooden roof [SHEATH]

sheave (ʃi:v) *pres. part.* **sheav·ing** past and past part. **sheaved** *v.t.* to gather into sheaves

sheave (ʃiv, ʃi:v) *n.* a grooved wheel or pulley, or one of several, for running a rope through a pulley block or set of pulley blocks [M.E. *sheve, shive*, a sheave, slice]

sheaves *pl.* of SHEAF *n.*

She·ba (ʃí:bə) *SABA

she·bang (ʃəbǽŋ) *n.* (*pop.*, esp. with 'the whole') a thing, matter, affair, place etc., *he wrecked the whole shebang* [origin unknown]

She·chem (ʃí:kem, ʃékem) *NABLUS

Shechinah *SHEKINAH

shed (ʃed) 1. *v. pres. part.* **shed·ding** past and past part. **shed** *v.t.* to throw off, *to shed one's wet clothes* ‖ to throw off by repelling, *this cloth sheds water* ‖ to become separated from, *some trees shed their leaves* ‖ to pour forth, *to shed tears* ‖ to cause (blood) to flow by injury ‖ to cause (blood) to flow by violence ‖ to spread around (e.g. favors, misery) [O.E. *scádan, scéadan*]

shed *n.* a small hut, lean-to or light shelter for boats, bicycles etc. ‖ a large storage warehouse, e.g. in docks [var. of SHADE n.]

she'd (ʃi:d) *contr.* of SHE HAD, SHE WOULD

sheen (ʃi:n) *n.* brightness, shininess **shéen·y** *comp.* **sheen·i·er** *superl.* **sheen·i·est** *adj.* [O. E. *scíene*, beautiful]

sheep (ʃi:p) *pl.* **sheep** *n.* a member of *Ovis*, fam. *Bovidae*, a genus of gregarious, ruminant animals, many breeds of which have been domesticated for the sake of their wool, flesh (*LAMB, *MUTTON) and skin (*SHEEPSKIN) ‖ a timid, easily led person **a wolf in sheep's clothing** someone who disguises his evil nature by appearing to be harmless and virtuous **to make sheep's eyes at** to keep making shy, amorous glances at [O.E. *scéap, scép*]

—The three main classes of wool-bearing sheep are fine, coarse and medium. The very fine-wooled merino flourish in dry, warm climates (e.g. Australia, S. Africa and parts of South America). Very coarse-wooled sheep are found mainly in Asia and in mountainous regions, parts of the fleece being used for carpets. Medium-wooled breeds are subdivided into long wools and short wools, and their fleeces are used for cloth. Medium-wooled breeds also form the chief supply of mutton and lamb, either pure or crossed with other types. Mutton rams are mated with ewes of breeds kept on richer grassland, where the cost of production of fat lamb is cheaper. In the Mediterranean area, where grazing for cattle is in short supply, milking sheep are kept, mostly for making cheese

sheep·cot (ʃí:pkɒt) *n.* (esp. *Br.*) a sheepfold

sheep·cote (ʃí:pkout) *n.* (esp. *Br.*) a sheepfold

sheep·dip (ʃí:pdip) *n.* a liquid containing disinfectants, into a solution of which sheep are immersed for a few moments in order to cleanse

and disinfect their wool and skin ‖ the enclosure where sheep are dipped in this solution

sheep dog a dog, esp. a collie, trained to herd sheep and to guard them from other animals

sheep·fold (ʃí:pfould) *n.* an enclosure, bounded by hurdles or rough stone walls, for the protection of sheep in severe weather, in the lambing season etc.

sheep·herd·er (ʃí:phɜːrdər) *n.* a shepherd

sheep·ish (ʃí:piʃ) *adj.* shy and embarrassed, esp. through consciousness of being in the wrong and feeling a little foolish about it

sheep ked *Melophagus ovinus*, fam. *Hippoboscidae*, a wingless, dipteran fly that feeds on sheep and carries sheep trypanosomiasis

sheep·man (ʃí:pmən) *pl.* **sheep·men** (ʃí:pmən) *n.* a person whose business is raising sheep on a large scale

sheep·shank (ʃí:pʃæŋk) *n.* a knot or hitch tied to shorten a rope

sheep·shear·er (ʃí:pʃiərər) *n.* a person who shears sheep ‖ a tool or machine used in shearing sheep

sheep·shear·ing (ʃí:pʃiəriŋ) *n.* the act of shearing sheep ‖ the time for shearing sheep ‖ a festival at this time

sheep·skin (ʃí:pskin) *n.* the skin of a sheep, esp. used, with the wool attached, as a rug or in a coat, slippers, gloves etc. ‖ leather prepared from the skin itself, used for bookbinding etc. ‖ parchment made from the skin of a sheep ‖ (*pop.*) a diploma written on such parchment

sheep·walk (ʃí:pwɒk) *n.* (esp. *Br.*) a pasture for sheep

sheer (ʃíər) 1. *adj.* complete, utter, *sheer nonsense* ‖ perpendicular, without intervening ledges or slopes, *a sheer drop* ‖ almost transparent, *sheer stockings* 2. *adv.* perpendicularly, *it rises sheer out of the sea* [M.E. *schere*]

sheer *v.i.* to deviate from a course ‖ *v.t.* to cause to turn aside from a course **to sheer off** (*Br.*) to go away abruptly so as to avoid work or avoid a person [perh. var. of SHEAR V.]

sheer *n.* (*naut.*) the fore-and-aft line of a ship curving upward to bow and stern [perh. var. of SHEAR N.]

sheer *n.* (*naut.*) a deviation from course ‖ (*naut.*) the oblique position of a ship riding at a single anchor [SHEER V.]

sheer *n.* a shears (a hoist, *SHEAR)

sheer·legs (ʃíərlegz) *pl. n.* shears (a hoist, *SHEAR)

sheet (ʃi:t) 1. *n.* a large rectangle of woven cotton, linen or silk etc. used esp. in pairs as bed linen between the mattress and the blankets ‖ a rectangular or square piece of paper ‖ a large, thin, flat piece of metal, glass etc. ‖ a wide expanse of water, ice etc. ‖ (*philately*) a complete page of stamps from one printing **in sheets** (of printed matter) not folded or bound **three sheets in the wind** drunk 2. *v.t.* to cover with, or form into, a sheet ‖ *v.i.* (*pop.*) to flow as if in a sheet, *the rain sheeted down* [O.E. *scíete, scéte*]

sheet 1. *n.* (*naut.*) a rope fastened to the lower corner of a sail and used to control the sail ‖ (*naut., pl.*) the spaces in an open boat fore or aft of the thwarts 2. *v.t.* **to sheet home** (*naut.*) to haul upon (the topsail) so that it is fully extended against the wind [O.E. *scéata*]

sheet anchor a large anchor slung amidships and used in an emergency ‖ something that in time of danger is a sure resource when other things have failed

sheet bend (*naut.*) a knot or hitch fastening one rope to the loop of another

sheet flow (*envir.*) water flowing in a thin layer over a land surface, usu. a storm runoff

sheet·ing (ʃí:tiŋ) *n.* the fabric in bulk from which sheets are made ‖ a material, e.g. a plastic or metal, formed in sheets and used e.g. as a protective covering or lining

sheet lightning lightning which is a discharge from cloud to cloud, giving wide flashes of reflected light

sheet metal metal in the form of a thin sheet

sheet music music printed on unbound sheets of paper

Shef·field (ʃéfi:ld) a town and county borough (pop. 547,400) in the West Riding of Yorkshire, England: cast iron, high-grade steel and steel manufactures, esp. cutlery, celebrated silver plate. University (1905)

sheikh, sheik (ʃi:k, ʃeik) *n.* a title of respect used by Arabs ‖ an Arab chief, head of a family, or headman of a village **shéikh·dom, shéik·dom** *n.* [Arab. *shaikh*, old man]

shek·el (ʃékʹl) *n.* any of several weight units used by the ancient Hebrews, Babylonians and Phoenicians ‖ an ancient coin of such a weight, esp. one used by the Hebrews ‖ (*pl.*, *pop.*) money as riches ‖ unit of currency in Israel, equal to 10 pounds [Heb. *sheqel*]

She·ki·nah, She·chi·nah (ʃikíːnə, ʃíkáinə) *n.* (*Heb. theol.*) the immanence of Jehovah as seen or felt or manifested [Heb.]

Shel·burne (ʃélbərn), William Petty Fitzmaurice, 2nd earl of (1737-1805), British statesman. He led a progressive but unpopular ministry (1782-3)

shel·drake (ʃéldreik) *pl.* **shel·drakes shel·drake** *n.* a member of *Tadorna*, fam. *Anatidae*, a genus of large wild duck found on coasts of Europe, Asia and N. Africa, esp. *T. tadorna*, the European species. It is about 24 ins long and is mainly black and white, with a green head and neck and a red bill having a prominent knob on it [prob. fr. older *sheld* adj., variegated+DRAKE]

shel·duck (ʃéldʌk) *pl.* **shel·ducks, shel·duck** *n.* the female sheldrake [prob. fr. older *sheld* adj., variegated+DUCK]

shelf (ʃelf) *pl.* **shelves** (ʃelvz) *n.* a horizontal board, stone slab etc. mounted against a perpendicular surface, to put things on ‖ such a support in a cabinet, bookcase etc. ‖ a projecting, roughly horizontal, layer of rock ‖ a roughly horizontal, narrow part of an otherwise steep cliff ‖ a ridge of rock or sand near the surface of a sea or other expanse of water [perh. fr. L.G. *schelf*, shelf or set of shelves]

shelf ice an extensive sheet of ice forming part of a land glacier or a frozen bay, stretching out to sea where it floats

shell (ʃel) **1.** *n.* the hard outer covering of an animal or fruit, or the calcareous, siliceous, bony, horny or chitinous covering of an organism, esp. the outer covering of a bird's egg ‖ a gutted building or one of which only the walls have been built ‖ (*mil.*) a cylindrical projectile containing an explosive within a metal container and exploded by impact or by a time fuse, or the container itself ‖ a cartridge or a cartridge case ‖ (*phys.* and *chem.*) a quantized energy level in an atom (*QUANTUM THEORY). In atoms the shells are denoted by the letters K, L, M,..., K representing the innermost and lowest energy level with quantum number (called the principal quantum number) 1, L with principal quantum number 2, M with 3 etc. In each shell except the K shell there are further subdivisions (orbitals). Each shell is associated with a region centered on the nucleus within which an electron of that shell spends most of its time, the effective diameter of the region getting larger with increasing principal quantum number. The number of atomic electrons that may exist in a given shell is equal to $2n^2$, where n is the principal quantum number ‖ (*rowing*) a light racing boat ‖ a baked unfilled pastry case, esp. the bottom crust of a pie **2.** *v.t.* to take out of the shell, *to shell peas* ‖ to separate the kernels of (wheat, corn etc.) from the ear ‖ (*mil.*) to fire shells at ‖ *v.i.* to become detached in scales ‖ to become free of the containing shell [O.E. *sciell*, *scill*]

she'll (ʃiːl) *contr.* of SHE SHALL, SHE WILL

shel·lac, shel·lack (ʃəlǽk) **1.** *n.* purified lac resin used in varnishes, stiffening agents, phonograph records, insulators etc. **2.** *v.* *pres. part.* **shel·lack·ing** past and past part. **shel·lacked** *v.t.* to coat with shellac ‖ (*pop.*) to defeat by a very large margin [trans. of F. *laque en écailles*, lac in fine plates]

Shel·ley (ʃéliː), Percy Bysshe (1792-1822), English poet. He was the most idealistic and uncompromising of Romantics. His works include longer poems, e.g. 'Queen Mab' (1813), 'The Revolt of Islam' (1818) and 'Prometheus Unbound' (1820), lyrics ('The Skylark', 'Ode to the West Wind', 'Ozymandias') and 'Adonais' (1821), a lament for Keats

shell·fire (ʃélfaiər) *n.* the firing of shells, e.g. at enemy positions, or the exploding shells

shell·fish (ʃélfiʃ) *pl.* **shell·fish, shell·fish·es** *n.* an aquatic invertebrate with a shell, e.g. a crab, lobster or oyster [O.E. *scilfisc*]

shell game a version of thimblerig, using walnut shells etc.

shell gland an organ from whose walls material for forming a shell is secreted

Shell Oil Company a U.S. petroleum industry company, one of the largest U.S. companies. It is connected with the Royal Dutch-Shell international group

shell·proof (ʃélpruːf) *adj.* not penetrable by shellfire or bombs

shell shock combat fatigue **shéll-shocked** *adj.*

shell·y (ʃéliː) *comp.* **shell·i·er** *superl.* **shell·i·est** *adj.* covered with shells ‖ like or consisting of a shell or shells

shel·ter (ʃéltər) **1.** *n.* something providing protection from danger or injury, esp. from rain and wind ‖ protection, *to afford shelter* **to take shelter** to go to a place affording protection ‖ to go under cover so as not to be rained on **2.** *v.t.* to protect from danger, injury, rain or wind ‖ to protect as if by shelter, shield, *he sheltered her from gossip* ‖ *v.i.* to take refuge, esp. from bad weather [etym. doubtful]

sheltered workshop a place of work for persons not fully adjusted to private life, e.g., retarded, recently released mental patients *Cf* HALFWAY HOUSE

shelve (ʃelv) *pres. part.* **shelv·ing** past and past part. **shelved** *v.t.* to put on a shelf ‖ to supply or fit with shelves ‖ to defer for the moment, *to shelve a decision* ‖ to relegate as if to a shelf [fr. SHELVES (pl. of SHELF)]

shelve *pres. part.* **shelv·ing** past and past part. **shelved** *v.i.* (of a road surface etc.) to slope gradually [etym. doubtful]

shelves *pl.* of SHELF

shelv·ing (ʃélviŋ) *n.* shelves

Shen·an·do·ah (ʃenəndóuə) a river (170 miles long) rising in N. Virginia, flowing across the tip of West Virginia into the Potomac River. It was an important avenue for several Civil War campaigns

Shenandoah National Park a U.S. reservation (193,646 acres) in the Blue Ridge Mtns of Virginia. It was established in 1935

Shenandoah Valley Campaigns military operations in the Shenandoah Valley of Virginia during the Civil War. The valley served as the avenue for Confederate attempts to invade the North and as a chief supply source for General Robert E. Lee's army. The maneuvers included Stonewall Jackson's campaign (1862), the Gettysburg campaign (1863), and Jubal A. Early's raid (1864). Laying the region waste, General Philip Sheridan's troops drove out (1865) the Confederates

she·nan·i·gans (ʃənǽnigənz) *pl. n.* trickery ‖ spirited carryings-on, high jinks [origin unknown]

Shen·si (ʃénsiː) a province (area 75,580 sq. miles, pop. 26,000,000) of N. central China. Capital: Sian

Shen·yang (ʃʌ́njáŋ) (Mukden 17th c. -1911) the capital (pop. 4,400,000) of Liaoning, S. Manchuria, China, a communications and industrial center (mechanical engineering, textiles, paper, chemicals). Manchu palaces (17th c.). It was the Manchu capital (1625-44)

She·ol (ʃíːoul) *n.* (*Jewish theol.*) the subterranean place of the dead [Heb.]

Shep·ard (ʃépərd), Sam (1943-   ), U.S. playwright and actor whose plays fused the past with the future and myth with reality. His plays include 'Operation Sidewinder' (1970), 'The Tooth of Crime' (1972), 'Buried Child' (1978, Pulitzer Prize), and 'A Lie of the Mind' (1985). He appeared in several movies

shep·herd (ʃépərd) **1.** *n.* a man whose occupation is tending sheep and watching over their safety **2.** *v.t.* to act as shepherd to ‖ to conduct, guide (a group of people) and prevent them from lagging or straying [O. E. *scēaphirde*, *scēaphyrde*]

shepherd's pie a pie of already cooked chopped meat, covered with mashed potatoes and baked in an oven

shepherd's purse *Capsella bursapastoris*, fam. *Cruciferae*, an annual cosmopolitan weed. It has a basal rosette of leaves, a raceme of small white flowers and a quantity of seed in its purse-shaped seedpods

Sher·a·ton (ʃérətən), Thomas (c. 1751-1806), English furniture designer. He is esp. famous for his slender, graceful shapes and use of inlay, and for his ingenious construction of combination pieces. He wrote 'The Cabinet Maker's and Upholsterer's Drawing Book' (1791-4)

sher·bet (ʃə́ːrbit) *n.* a cooling Oriental fruit drink ‖ a frozen dessert made of sugar, water, milk, egg white and fruit flavoring ‖ an effervescent drink made from a powder of sodium bicarbonate, tartaric acid, sugar and flavoring, or this powder [Turk., Pers. *sherbet* fr. Arab. *sharbah*]

Sher·brooke (ʃə́ːrbruk) a town (pop. 74,075) in S.E. Quebec, Canada, market for a mining and logging region. University (1954)

sherd (ʃəːrd) *n.* a shard

Sher·i·dan (ʃéridən), Philip Henry (1831-88), Union cavalry general during the Civil War. He drove out (1865) the Confederate forces from the Shenandoah Valley and destroyed supply and communication sources, rendering the valley useless to the South

Sheridan, Richard Bridsley Butler (1751-1816), Irish dramatist and politician. He had written his best work for the stage, 'The Rivals' (1775) and 'The School for Scandal' (1777), by the age of 26. Thereafter he concerned himself mainly with the management of his Drury Lane Theater and with parliament, where he shone as an orator. His plays have both wit and humor and are among the few late-18th-c. plays to become classics

sherif *SHARIF

sher·iff (ʃérif) *n.* a usually elected officer responsible for law and order in his county ‖ (*Br.*) the chief administrative officer in charge of courts, elections etc. in a county [O.E. *scīrgerēfa*, shire reeve]

Sher·man (ʃə́ːrmən), John (1823-1900), U.S. Senator (1861-77, 1881-97) from Ohio, secretary of the treasury (1877-81) under President Hayes, and secretary of state (1897-8) under President McKinley. Although both the Anti-Trust Act of 1890 and Silver Purchase Act (1890) bear his name, he gave them only qualified approval

Sherman, William Tecumseh (1820-91), Union general in the American Civil War. During his famous 'march to the sea' through Georgia (Nov.-Dec. 1864), he encouraged his troops to pillage and devastate

Sherman Anti-Trust Act a U.S. Congressional act (1890), named after Senator John Sherman. It declared illegal every contract, combination, or conspiracy in restraint of interstate and foreign trade. It was supplemented (1914) by the Clayton Anti-Trust Act

Sherman Silver Purchase Act a U.S. Congressional act (1890), named after Senator John Sherman, which required the U.S. government almost to double the amount of its silver purchases. When it threatened to undermine the U.S. treasury's gold reserves, it was repealed (1893) by the Grover Cleveland administration

Sher·pa (ʃérpə, ʃə́ːrpə) *pl.* **Sher·pa, Sher·pas** *n.* a member of a Buddhist people of Mongolian origin living in N.E. Nepal, in the foothills of the Himalayas. They are noted as guides and porters on mountaineering expeditions (*TENZING NORKAY)

Sher·ring·ton (ʃériŋt'n), Sir Charles Scott (1861-1952), British physiologist whose work on reflexes, 'Integrative Action of the Nervous System' (1906), paved the way for modern understanding of the activity of the central nervous system. Nobel prize (1932)

sher·ry (ʃériː) *pl.* **sher·ries** *n.* a fortified Spanish wine varying in color from light yellow to dark brown ‖ a wine of this type produced elsewhere [older *sherris* fr. *Xeres* (now *Jerez*), Spain]

Sher·wood (ʃə́ːrwud), Robert Emmet (1896-1955), U.S. playwright. His plays include 'The Road to Rome' (1927), 'Abe Lincoln in Illinois' (1939) and 'There Shall Be No Night' (1941)

Sherwood Forest a former royal forest, of which little remains, in W. Nottinghamshire, England. It covered 150 sq. miles. It was the home of Robin Hood

she's (ʃiːz) *contr.* of SHE IS, SHE HAS

Shet·land Islands (ʃétlənd) an archipelago (some 100 islands and islets, 21 inhabited) 50 miles northeast of the Orkney Is, forming a Scottish county, Zetland (land area 550 sq. miles, pop. 20,400). Main islands: Mainland, Yell, Unst. County town: Lerwick, on Mainland. Industries: knitting, weaving, fishing, farming (oats, barley, root vegetables). Livestock: cattle, sheep, Shetland ponies

Shetland pony a member of a breed of small (32–46 ins), stocky ponies originating in the Shetland Is

shew·bread, show·bread (ʃóubred) *n.* twelve loaves of consecrated unleavened bread formerly displayed in the Jewish temple (one for each tribe) and renewed each sabbath. It symbolized gratitude to Yahweh as the giver of all things [after G. *schaubrot*]

CONCISE PRONUNCIATION KEY: (a) æ, cat; ɑ, car; ɔ fawn; ei, snake. (e) e, hen; iː, sheep; iə, deer; ɛə, bear. (i) i, fish; ai, tiger; əː, bird. (o) o, ox; au, cow; ou, goat; u, poor; ɔi, royal. (u) ʌ, duck; u, bull; uː, goose; ə, bacillus; juː, cube. x, loch; θ, think; ð, bother; z, Zen; ʒ, corsage; dʒ, savage; ŋ, orangutang; j, yak; ʃ, fish; tʃ, fetch; 'l, rabble; 'n, redden. Complete pronunciation key appears inside front cover.

Shi·a (ʃíːə) *n.* a member of the Shi‘ite Moslem sect ‖ this sect [Arab.= sect]

Shi·at·su (ʃiːátsu:) *n.* Japanese massage technique using finger pressure at critical acupuncture points

shib·bo·leth (ʃíbəliθ, ʃíbələθ) *n.* (*Bible*) a test word which betrayed the members of the tribe of Ephraim because it was hard for them to pronounce [Judges xii.] ‖ any such test word ‖ any word, formula etc. used by adherents to a cause and considered by them a distinguishing mark [Heb. = flood]

Shi·de·ha·ra (ʃiːdehara), Kijūrō (1872-1951), Japanese statesman, prime minister (1945-6)

shied *past and past part.* of SHY

shield (ʃiːld) **1.** *n.* (*hist.*) a broad piece of leather and metal, or metal only, gripped with the hand by a thong or handle at its back and held to protect the body from arrows, spear thrusts, blows etc. ‖ a plate, screen etc. which serves to protect, e.g. a gunner from blast or a worker from the moving parts of a machine ‖ (*zool.*) a protective body covering, e.g. one of the plates forming the shell of a turtle ‖ (*heraldry*) a flat, three-sided area or surface, most commonly horizontal at the top with curved sides tapering to a point, on which a coat of arms is displayed ‖ someone or something thought of as serving to defend **2.** *v.t.* to protect with or as if with a shield [O.E. *sceld*]

shield law 1. legislation or rules designed to protect a domestic market from imports, e.g., quality controls on imports, antidumping laws **2.** legislation protecting a journalist from disclosing information sources

shier *alt. comp.* of SHY

shiest *alt. superl.* of SHY

shift (ʃift) *n.* a change of position, place, direction or condition ‖ a substituting of one thing for another, *a shift of scenery* ‖ an ingenious expedient adopted in a time of need or emergency ‖ a tricky ruse, artifice or maneuver ‖ a group of workers who work in turn with another group or other groups ‖ the period during which such a group works, *the night shift* ‖ a woman's straight dress ‖ (*mining*) a fault, e.g. in a vein ‖ (*mus.*, esp. of a violin) a change in the position of the hand not holding the bow ‖ (*linguistics*) a phonetic change or system of changes **to make shift with** to do the best one can with (what is available) [M.E. *schift*]

shift *v.t.* to exchange for or replace by another similar thing or things, *to shift scenery* ‖ to alter the position, place, direction or condition of ‖ to alter (a place, position etc.), *to shift the location of a factory* ‖ to accomplish, get through (a job or task) ‖ to change (gears) from one speed to another ‖ (*linguistics*) to change phonetically ‖ *v.i.* to move from one position, place, direction or condition to another ‖ to change gears ‖ (*linguistics*) to undergo phonetic change **to shift for oneself** to get along as well as one can unaided [O.E. *sciftan*]

shift·i·ly (ʃíftili:) *adv.* in a shifty manner

shift·i·ness (ʃífti:nis) *n.* the state or quality of being shifty

shift·less (ʃíftlis) *adj.* lazy and inefficient ‖ incapable of using determination and ingenuity in order to surmount some difficulty or achieve some purpose ‖ showing such lack of determination and ingenuity [fr. SHIFT *n.*, (*obs.*) resourcefulness]

shift register (*computer*) a peripheral device for storing data in a form in which it may be manipulated

shift·y (ʃífti:) *comp.* **shift·i·er** *superl.* **shift·i·est** *adj.* mean and untrustworthy, deceitful [fr. SHIFT *n.*, (*obs.*) resourcefulness]

shift·y-eyed (ʃífti:aid) *adj.* having an air of dishonesty and low cunning

Shi·ga·tse (ʃíːgatse) a trade center (pop. 15,000) in S. central Tibet, China, on the Tsangpo (Brahmaputra), at 11,000 ft. Lamasery (1446)

Shih·kia·chwang (ʃə́ːrdʒjúdʒwán) a textile industry center (pop. 598,000) of S.W. Hopei, China

Shi·‘ism (ʃíːizəm) *n.* the doctrine and beliefs of the Shi‘a sect

Shi·‘ite (ʃíːait) *n.* a member of a branch of Islam which separated from the orthodox Sunnites in 679. Shi‘ites hold that the historical succession of the caliphate passes through Ali, Mohammed's son-in-law, and Ali's sons, Hasan and Husein, whom they revere as martyrs and imams. They differ from the Sunna. Splinter groups of Shi‘ites later founded the Isma‘ili, Twelvers, Fatimite and Assassin sects. The Shi‘ites played a large part in the development

of Sufism. They constitute about 15% of Moslems. They are found mainly in Iran, where Shi‘ism is the state religion, and in Iraq, where half the Moslems are Shi‘ites. Minorities exist in India, Syria, Lebanon, Egypt, Yemen and Oman [Arab. fr. *Shi‘a*, a sect]

Shi·ko·ku (ʃiːkoku:) the smallest island (area 7,246 sq. miles, pop. 4,097,000) of Japan's four main islands. Chief town: Matsuyama. Main industries: agriculture (rice, wheat, sugarcane, tea, mulberry trees), mining (*JAPAN)

Shillelagh (ʃiléili:) *n.* (*mil.*) a missile system (MBM-51) with infrared target guidance, mounted on the main battle tank and assault reconnaissance vehicle

shil·le·lagh, shil·la·lah (ʃəléili:) *n.* a cudgel of oak or blackthorn, cut from a sapling and left rough [after *Shillelagh*, a town in Wicklow, Ireland]

shil·ling (ʃíliŋ) *n.* a British nickel alloy coin worth £ .05 ‖ the basic monetary unit of Tanzania, Kenya and Uganda, divided into 100 cents [O.E. *scilling*]

Shil·long (ʃílɔ̃ŋ) the capital (pop. 87,659) of Assam, India, an agricultural market and health resort at 4,980 ft

Shil·luk (ʃílʌk) *pl.* **Shil·luk, Shil·luks** *n.* a Nilotic people of Sudan living primarily on the west bank of the White Nile ‖ a member of this people ‖ their Nilotic language

shil·ly-shal·ly (ʃíli:ʃæli:) **1.** *v.i. pres. part* **shil·ly-shal·ly·ing** *past and past part.* **shil·ly-shal·lied** to waver continually between two opinions **2.** *pl.* **shil·ly-shal·lies** *n.* indecision, or an instance of it [originally *shill I, shall I*, alteration of 'shall I, shall I']

Shi·loh, Battle of (ʃáilou) a victory (Apr. 6-7, 1862) of the Union army under Grant, during the American Civil War

shim (ʃim) **1.** *n.* a sliver of wood, metal etc., often tapered, used in adjusting levels or to take up wear in machinery **2.** *v.t. pres. part.* **shim·ming** *past and past part.* **shimmed** to fit or pack with this [origin unknown]

shim·mer (ʃímər) **1.** *v.i.* to shine with glistening, tremulous light **2.** *n.* such a light **shim·mer·y** *adj.* [O.E. *scymrian*]

shim·my (ʃími:) **1.** *pl.* **shim·mies** *n.* a dance of the 1920s accompanied by a shaking of the body ‖ a wobble, e.g. in the front wheel of a car **2.** *v.i. pres. part.* **shim·my·ing** *past and past part.* **shim·mied** to dance a shimmy ‖ to oscillate abnormally [perh. fr. older *shimmy*, woman's

Shi·mo·no·se·ki (ʃimənəséiki:) a port (pop. 269,000) at the southwest tip of Honshu, Japan: shipbuilding, building materials, fishing

Shin (ʃin, ʃiːn) a Japanese Buddhist sect, numbering about 13,000,000 adherents

shin (ʃin) **1.** *n.* the lower part of the front of the leg, above the ankle (in beef cattle) the lower part of the foreleg **2.** *v.i. pres. part.* **shin·ning** *past and past part.* **shinned** to climb by using the hands and legs [O.E. *scinu*]

Shi·na·no (ʃiːnɑnɔ) the longest river (230 miles) of Japan, flowing from central Honshu to the Sea of Japan at Niigata

shin·bone (ʃínboun) *n.* the tibia [O.E. *scinbān*]

shin·dig (ʃíndig) *n.* (*pop.*) a social gathering, esp. a very large one, on which no expense is spared [prob. alt. of SHINDY]

shin·dy (ʃíndi:) *pl.* **shin·dies** *n.* (*pop.*) an uproar, commotion (*pop.*) a doctor or lawyer ‖ *shinty*, an obsolete game like hockey

shine (ʃain) **1.** *v. pres. part.* **shin·ing** *past and past part.* **shone** (ʃoun), **shined** *v.i.* to emit or reflect light ‖ to glow (e.g. with pleasure, happiness or rapture) ‖ to show great aptitude, *he doesn't shine in mathematics* ‖ *v.t.* to cause to shine, esp. by cleaning and polishing **to shine up to** (*pop.*) to lavish attentions on **2.** *n.* the quality of shining ‖ a finish given by polishing ‖ (*pop.*) a shoeshine **to take a shine to** (*pop.*) to take a liking to **shin·er** *n.* (*pop.*) a black eye ‖ any of various small, silvery, North American, freshwater fish ‖ something that shines or some one who shines [O.E. *scīnan*]

shin·gle (ʃíŋg'l) **1.** *n.* a wedge-shaped tile, esp. of wood, used esp. in roofing ‖ (*pop.*) a small signboard bearing the name esp. of a doctor or lawyer and hung outside his door ‖ a mannish style of women's hairdo, cut short esp. at the nape of the neck and tapering **to hang out one's shingle** (*pop.*, esp. of a doctor or lawyer) to start a professional practice **2.** *v.t. pres. part.* **shin·gling** *past and past part.* **shin·gled** to cover (e.g. a roof) with shingles ‖ to cut (a

woman's hair) in a shingle [M.E. *scincle, shyn-gle*]

shingle *n.* an accumulation of rounded pebbles found on some seashores [etym. doubtful]

shin·gles (ʃíŋg'lz) *n. Herpes zoster*, a painful but transient virus infection of a nerve, resulting in blisters over a restricted part of the body [alt. fr. M.L. *cingulus*, var. of *cingulum*, a girdle]

shin·gly (ʃíŋgli:) *adj.* consisting of shingles (rounded pebbles)

Shin·gon (ʃíŋgɑn) a Japanese Buddhist sect, numbering about 8,000,000 adherents

shin·i·ly (ʃáinili:) *adv.* in a shiny manner

shin·i·ness (ʃáini:nis) *n.* the state or quality of being shiny

shin·ing (ʃáiniŋ) *adj.* gleaming, *shining silver* ‖ splendid, *a shining example*

shin·ny (ʃíni:) *pres. part.* **shin·ny·ing** *past and past part.* **shin·nied** to shin

Shin·to (ʃíntou) *n.* an ancient religion of Japan, without a historical founder or organized body of teachings. Its chief features are the worship of national heroes and family ancestors and belief in the divinity of the Emperor. Mingled with and superseded by Buddhism (6th c.), it was revived in the 17th c. and was the state religion (1867–1945) **Shin·to·ism, Shin·to·ist** *ns* [Jap. fr. Chin. *shin*, god + *tao*, way or law]

shin·y (ʃáini:) *comp.* **shin·i·er** *superl.* **shin·i·est** *adj.* emitting or reflecting light ‖ polished, *shiny shoes* ‖ so worn as to be smooth and glossy, *shiny trousers* [SHINE]

ship (ʃip) **1.** *n.* (*hist.*) a large seagoing sailing vessel with a bowsprit and three square-rigged masts, divided each into lower mast, topmast and topgallant mast, sometimes with higher masts ‖ any large seagoing vessel ‖ the crew of such a vessel ‖ (*pop.*) an aircraft **when one's ship comes home** (or **in**) when one comes to have plenty of money **2.** *v. pres. part.* **ship·ping** *past and past part.* **shipped** *v.t.* to put in a ship ‖ (*naut.*) to put in place ready to use ‖ to take on (crew) ‖ to send (goods) by sea or (*pop.*) by any means of transport ‖ to lift (oars) out of the water and lay them in the boat or let them rest in the oarlocks with the blades in the boat ‖ to have (water) enter over the side of the vessel ‖ *v.i.* to go by ship ‖ to join a ship's crew [O.E. *scip*]

-ship *suffix* indicating state or quality, as in 'friendship' ‖ indicating office, as in 'chancellorship' ‖ indicating ability, as in 'horsemanship' [O.E. *-sciepe, -scipe, -scype*]

ship biscuit hardtack

ship·board (ʃípbɔrd, ʃípbourd) *n.* (in the phrase) **on shipboard** on or in a ship

ship·break·er (ʃípbreikər) *n.* a person who breaks up obsolete ships to sell the scrap metal, fittings etc.

ship broker an agent who transacts a ship's business when the ship is in port ‖ someone who buys, sells, charters or insures ships

ship·build·er (ʃípbildər) *n.* someone whose business is to construct ships

ship·build·ing (ʃípbildiŋ) *n.* the construction of ships

ship canal a canal deep and broad enough for seagoing vessels

ship chandler a dealer in ships' canvas, cordage and other small equipment

ship·load (ʃíploud) *n.* the total quantity of goods, passengers etc. loaded or able to be loaded into a ship

ship·mas·ter (ʃípmæstər, ʃípmɑstər) *n.* the captain of a merchant ship

ship·mate (ʃípmeit) *n.* someone in relation to oneself or to a third person serving or traveling in the same ship

ship·ment (ʃípmənt) *n.* the loading of goods, esp. on a ship ‖ the goods so shipped

ship money (*Eng. hist.*) an ancient tax levied in coastal areas to provide ships, revived and extended by Charles I, and abolished in 1640

ship of the line (esp. *hist.*) a warship carrying heavy guns and forming part of the line of battle at sea

ship·own·er (ʃípounər) *n.* an owner or part owner of a ship or ships

ship·per (ʃípər) *n.* someone who ships goods, esp. as a profession

ship·ping (ʃípiŋ) *n.* the act of putting on board ship, going on board ship, or sending by ship or other means of transport ‖ (*collect.*) all the ships of a country or port ‖ ships in general

shipping articles the terms of contract signed by sailors on joining a ship's crew

---

CONCISE PRONUNCIATION KEY: **(a)** æ, c*a*t; ɑ, c*a*r; ɔ f*a*wn; ei, sn*a*ke. **(e)** e, h*e*n; i:, sh*ee*p; iə, d*ee*r; ɛə, b*ea*r. **(i)** i, f*i*sh; ai, t*i*ger; ə:, b*i*rd. **(o)** o, *o*x; au, c*ow*; ou, g*oa*t; u, p*oo*r; ɔi, r*oy*al. **(u)** ʌ, d*u*ck; u, b*u*ll; u:, g*oo*se; ə, b*a*cillus; ju:, c*u*be. x, lo*ch*; θ, *th*ink; ð, bo*th*er; z, *Z*en; ʒ, cor*s*age; dʒ, sava*g*e; ŋ, ora*ng*utang; j, *y*ak; ʃ, *fi*sh; tʃ, fe*tch*; 'l, rabb*le*; 'n, redd*en*. Complete pronunciation key appears inside front cover.

shipping clerk (*Br.*) a clerk employed by a shipping line ‖ a person employed in packing and sending goods

shipping commissioner (*Am.*=*Br.* shipping master) an official responsible for signing on and paying off a crew

shipping master (*Br.*) a shipping commissioner

shipping room a room, e.g. in a factory, from which goods are dispatched

ship's articles *SHIPPING ARTICLES

ship's biscuit hardtack

ship's chandler a ship chandler

ship's company the crew of a ship exclusive of the officers

ship·shape (ʃípʃeip) *adj.* tidy, orderly

ship's papers the documents relating to the nationality, ownership and cargo of a ship

ship·way (ʃípwei) *n.* a timber-built slope used for building and launching ships etc. ‖ a ship canal

ship·worm (ʃípwəːrm) *n.* any of various long, thin marine clams, esp. of fam. *Teredinidae*, which bore into submerged wood and do heavy damage to piles, harbor installations, wooden ships etc.

ship·wreck (ʃíprek) 1. *n.* destruction of a ship at sea by being sunk in stormy seas or being stranded, esp. by being driven on rocks ‖ destruction as though by foundering at sea 2. *v.t.* to cause to undergo shipwreck

ship·wright (ʃíprait) *n.* a carpenter who specializes in building and repairing ships ‖ (*hist.*) a naval architect

ship·yard (ʃípjɑrd) *n.* the premises where ships are built and repaired

Shi·raz (ʃiːráz) a communications center and agricultural market in S.W. Iran in the Zagros Mtns, producing wines, carpets, silks and mosaics. Mosques (notably 9th and 18th cc.), mausoleums (15th-16th cc.)

Shi·re (ʃíːrei) a river flowing 370 miles from Lake Malawi through Malawi and Mozambique to the Zambezi, navigable except at Murchison Falls

shire (ʃáiər) *n.* (*Eng. hist.*) an Anglo-Saxon administrative district coinciding with the modern county ‖ (*Br.*) any of the British counties whose name ends in 'shire' **the Shires** Leicestershire, Northamptonshire and Rutland, noted for foxhunting [O.E. *scīr*, office, charge]

Shire Highlands an area of high ground in the south of Malawi, east of the Shire River, containing the capital, Zomba

shire horse a member of a breed of powerful draft horses, originally raised in the Midland counties of England

shirk (ʃəːrk) *v.t.* to avoid (e.g. work, responsibility or obligation), esp. out of indolence or selfishness ‖ *v.i.* to avoid work, responsibility etc., esp. out of indolence or selfishness [perh. fr. G. *schurke*, rascal]

Shir·ley (ʃə́ːrliː), William (1694-1771), colonial governor (1741-60) of Massachusetts. During King George's War he led the capture (1745) of Louisburg, but, as commander (1755-60) of the British forces in America, he failed in an expedition against Fort Niagara

shirr (ʃəːr) 1. *n.* a gathering in a piece of cloth to create fullness and elasticity 2. *v.t.* to make shirrs in ‖ to bake (eggs) in a dish with cream **shirr·ing** (ʃə́ːriŋ) *n.* [origin unknown]

shirt (ʃəːrt) *n.* a man's loose-fitting cloth garment covering the torso and usually having a collar and either long or short sleeves. It is often worn with a tie under a jacket ‖ a woman's tailored blouse **to lose one's shirt** to lose virtually all one's money [O.E. *scyrte*]

shirt·front (ʃə́ːrtfrʌnt) *n.* the starched part of a dress shirt covering the chest

shirt·ing (ʃə́ːrtiŋ) *n.* fabric used for making shirts

shirt·sleeve (ʃə́ːrtsliːv) *adj.* of down-to-earth (white-collar) work or worker

shirt·waist (ʃə́ːrtweist) *n.* a woman's tailored blouse ‖ a dress with this kind of top attached

Shiva *SIVA

shiv·er (ʃívər) 1. *v.i.* to shake esp. with cold or fear 2. *n.* the act or sensation of shivering [M.E. *chivere*, etym. doubtful]

shiver 1. *n.* a small fragment resulting from the breakage of a brittle substance 2. *v.t.* to break (something) into shivers ‖ *v.i.* to be smashed into shivers [M.E. *scifre*]

shiv·er·y (ʃívəriː) *adj.* feeling shivers ‖ causing shivers

Shi·zu·o·ka (ʃiːzuóka) a city (pop. 329,000) and tea market of central E. Honshu, Japan: alumi-

num, textiles, food processing, handicrafts (lacquerware, bamboo)

Shko·dër (ʃkódər) (*Ital.* Scutari) a city (pop. 65,000) of Albania on Lake Shkodër. Manufactures: textiles, cement, cigarettes. Venetian citadel (15th c.) ‖ (*Yugoslav Skadarsko, Ital.* Scutari) a lake (area varying between 150 and 200 sq. miles) in N.W. Albania and W. central Montenegro, Yugoslavia: fisheries

shoal (ʃoul) 1. *n.* a part of a river, sea, lake etc. where the water is very shallow ‖ a sandbank etc. causing such shallow water 2. *adj.* (of water) shallow 3. *v.i.* (of water) to become shallow ‖ *v.t.* (of a ship etc.) to move into a shallower depth of (water) [earlier *shoal* adj., shallow fr. O.E. *sceald*]

shoal 1. *n.* a school of fish ‖ (*pop.*) a large number or group, *a shoal of tourists* 2. *v.i.* to gather together to form a shoal [perh. fr. M.Du. *schole*]

shoal·y (ʃóuliː) *comp.* **shoal·i·er** *superl.* **shoal·i·est** *adj.* full of shoals (shallow areas of water)

shoat *n.* (*zool.*) hybrid sheep and goat *syn.* geep

shoat, shote (ʃout) *n.* a young pig, esp. one which has been weaned [M.E.]

shock (ʃɔk) *n.* a force of great magnitude applied suddenly, *the shock of a collision* ‖ a sudden conduction of electric current through a person's body ‖ a temporary but dangerous condition caused by pain, strong emotion or loss of blood and manifested by pallor, cold sweats and drowsiness which may pass into coma ‖ a sudden arousing of emotion or disturbance of mental stability by something unexpected, offensive or unwelcome ‖ something which causes this [F. *choc*]

shock *v.t.* to cause an emotional or mental shock to ‖ to give painful offense to ‖ to cause an electrical shock to ‖ to affect with physical shock [F. *choquer*]

shock *n.* a thick, untidy mass of hair [etym. doubtful]

shock 1. *n.* a number of sheaves stood leaning against one another to dry 2. *v.t.* to pile together in this way [M.E.]

shock absorber a device for protecting from shock by interposing something which converts the energy of the applied force into stresses within itself, e.g. into the stresses of a compressed spring or those of air or water compressed in a tube

shock·er (ʃókər) *n.* (*pop.*) a sensational novel or story, esp. one badly written ‖ (*pop.*) someone or something that shocks

shock front (*mil.*) the boundary between the pressure disturbance created by an explosion (in air, water, or earth) and the ambient atmosphere, water, or earth

shock·head (ʃókhed) *n.* a head of thick untidy hair **shóck·head·ed** *adj.*

shock·ing (ʃókiŋ) *adj.* causing shock, esp. to the emotions associated with what is thought to be morally right, *shocking behavior* ‖ (*pop.*) very bad, *a shocking mistake*

Shock·ley (ʃókliː), William Bradford (1910-   ), U.S. physicist and co-winner (with John Bardeen and Walter H. Brattain) of the 1956 Nobel prize in physics for the invention and development of the junction transistor. From the late 1960s, Shockley became a controversial figure by supporting the view of Arthur Jensen and others that intelligence capacity is a genetic trait of races

shock rock rock'n'roll music accompanied by outrageous lyrics, costumes, lights, or other effects

shock therapy the treatment of mental disorder, esp. schizophrenia, by administering a shock (e.g. electrical shock or heavy insulin dosage)

shock treatment shock therapy

shock troops highly trained and disciplined troops used for offensive combat operations, esp. for leading attacks

shock wave a narrow region of high density, temperature, pressure and velocity formed in a medium around the leading surface of an object traveling through it at a speed greater than that of sound in that medium. The very high temperatures generated by shock waves have been used to study chemical reaction at extreme conditions of temperature and pressure

shod *past* and *past part.* of SHOE

shod·dy (ʃódiː) 1. *comp.* **shod·di·er** *superl.* **shod·di·est** *adj.* made of poor material ‖ mean, shabby, *a shoddy trick* 2. *pl.* **shod·dies** *n.* fabric woven of yarn from the shredded fiber of other

fabric which has already been worn or used ‖ this yarn [origin unknown]

Shodop (*mil. acronym*) for short range doppler, system for measuring the trajectory of short-range missiles utilizing Doppler frequency shift as computed by ground stations

shoe (ʃuː) *n.* a foot covering of leather or other material which does not extend as far as the ankle, with a base or sole strong enough to be durable when worn out of doors, and giving some protection to the instep ‖ a horseshoe ‖ a wooden block placed under a wheel to prevent or retard its motion ‖ something fitted to and placed at the bottom, foot or end of another object, or under it, e.g. a metal tip on the end of a cane, staff etc. or a metal band fastened to the bottom of the runner of a sled ‖ the part of a bridge on which the superstructure rests ‖ the part of a brake which presses on an upper part of a wheel to slow it down ‖ the sliding contact which picks up current from a live rail ‖ a metal plate between a moving and a stationary part of a machine ‖ the outer cover of an automobile tire **if the shoe fits** (*Am.* =*Br.* if the cap fits) an expression used to indicate that a general remark is true for some particular person ('wear it' being understood) **in someone else's shoes** in the position or circumstances, or with the imaginative outlook, of someone else **where the shoe pinches** the cause of the trouble [O.E. *scōh*]

shoe *pres. part.* **shoe·ing** *past* and *past part.* **shod** (ʃɔd), **shoed** (ʃuːd) *v.t.* to supply or fit with shoes ‖ to attach a protective cover to the bottom or end [O.E. *scōgan*]

shoe·black (ʃúːblæk) *n.* a bootblack

shoe·horn (ʃúːhɔrn) *n.* a narrow, curved instrument of e.g. horn or polished metal, inserted at the back of the shoe, to enable the foot to slide in easily

shoe·lace (ʃúːleis) *n.* a lace or cord used to fasten the uppers of a shoe together over the instep

shoe·mak·er (ʃúːmeikər) *n.* someone whose business is to make or repair shoes **shóe·mak·ing** *n.* the trade of a shoemaker

shoe·shine (ʃúːʃain) *n.* a shine or polish applied to the shoes

shoe·string (ʃúːstriŋ) *n.* a shoelace **on a shoestring** on a very small budget, *living on a shoestring, making films on a shoestring*

shoe tree a metal or wooden device placed inside a shoe to help to keep it supple and preserve its shape

sho·far, sho·phar (ʃóufɑr, ʃoufɑ́r) *pl.* **sho·fars, sho·phars, sho·froth, sho·phroth** (ʃoufrɔ́t) *n.* a ram's horn formerly used by the ancient Hebrews as a battle signal and now blown in synagogues before and during Rosh Hashanah and at the end of Yom Kippur

sho·gun (ʃóugʌn, ʃóuguːn) *n.* (*hist.*) any of the hereditary military commanders who ruled Japan (1192–1867) **sho·gun·ate** (ʃóugʌnit, ʃóuguːnit) *n.* the rank or position of a shogun ‖ government by a shogun or shoguns [Jap. fr. Chin. *chiang chün*, to lead an army]

Sho·la·pur (ʃóuləpur) a commercial center (pop. 398,361) of S.E. Maharashtra, India: silk and cotton textiles

shone *past* and alt. *past part.* of SHINE

shoo (ʃuː) 1. *interj.* a cry meaning 'move along!', used in driving an animal away 2. *v. pres. part.* **shoo·ing** *past* and *past part.* **shooed** *v.t.* to drive (an animal, child etc.) away, esp. by crying 'shoo!' ‖ *v.i.* to make this cry in order to drive away animals etc.

shook (ʃuk) *n.* a set of staves and headings arranged ready for a cask to be built ‖ a set of pieces of wood prepared for making into a box ‖ a shock of sheaves [prob. var. of SHOCK]

shook *past* of SHAKE

shoot (ʃuːt) 1. *v. pres. part.* **shoot·ing** *past* and *past part.* **shot** (ʃɔt) *v.t.* (of a person) to cause (a projectile) to be projected, *to shoot an arrow* ‖ (of a gun etc.) to cause (a projectile) to be projected ‖ to fire (a gun etc.) ‖ to kill by doing this, *to shoot a rabbit* ‖ to wound by doing this, *he shot him in the leg* ‖ to put to death with a bullet as a punishment, *he was shot at dawn* ‖ to hunt (game etc.) ‖ to hunt the game on (land) ‖ (usually with 'away', 'down', 'out' or 'off') to destroy or remove with a projectile from a gun etc., *to shoot down an airplane* ‖ to go quickly through, under, over etc., *to shoot rapids* ‖ to project (someone or something) forward, out, towards etc., *he shot them onto the back seat and drove off* ‖ to direct (e.g. a reply question, glance etc.) with the rapidity of a moving bullet ‖ (with 'through' or

CONCISE PRONUNCIATION KEY: **(a)** æ, c*a*t; ɑ, c*a*r; ɔ f*aw*n; ei, sn*a*ke. **(e)** e, h*e*n; iː, sh*ee*p; iə, d*ee*r; ɛə, b*ea*r. **(i)** i, f*i*sh; ai, t*i*ger; əː, b*i*rd. **(o)** o, *o*x; au, c*ow*; ou, g*oa*t; u, p*oo*r; ɔi, r*oy*al. **(u)** ʌ, d*u*ck; u, b*u*ll; uː, g*oo*se; ə, b*a*cillus; juː, c*u*be. x, lo*ch*; θ, *th*ink; ð, bo*th*er; z, *Z*en; ʒ, corsa*g*e; dʒ, sava*g*e; ŋ, oranguta*ng*; j, *y*ak; ʃ, *f*ish; tʃ, fet*ch*; 'l, rabb*le*; 'n, redd*en*. Complete pronunciation key appears inside front cover.

'with') to streak with another color or colors ‖ to send (a letter, refuse etc.) down a chute or something resembling a chute ‖ (*games*) to drive (a ball etc.) in the direction of a goal ‖ (*basketball*) to score (a goal) ‖ to put (a marble) into action by a flick of the thumb ‖ to detonate (a blast) ‖ (esp. *movies*) to photograph ‖ (*naut.*) to take the altitude of (the sun etc.) ‖ to play (dice) ‖ *v.i.* to go, arrive or move with great speed like a moving projectile, *he shot past me on his bicycle* ‖ (with 'up') to grow quickly, *the boy has shot up during the last year* ‖ (of a plant) to begin to grow or put out young sprouts ‖ to hunt with a gun ‖ (of a person) to send forth a projectile, esp. from a gun or bow ‖ (of a gun etc.) to send forth a projectile ‖ to hunt with a gun ‖ (esp. *movies*) to photograph ‖ to jut out ‖ (*games*) to propel a ball, marble etc. toward the objective ‖ (*cricket*, of a ball) to increase in speed after hitting the ground ‖ (of a star, meteor etc.) to flash across the sky ‖ to dart painfully in or through a part or parts of the body ‖ 2. *n.* a slope down which something can glide quickly, a chute ‖ a young outgrowth of a tree etc. ‖ land used for shooting over ‖ a number of persons engaged in shooting game ‖ the game shot ‖ the right to shoot ‖ a place where rubbish is thrown [O.E. *scēotan*]

shooting box (*Br.*) a shooting lodge

shooting brake (*Br.*) a station wagon

shooting gallery a place for target practice with firearms ‖ a booth at a fairground where persons pay to shoot at targets for prizes

shooting lodge a country lodge or cabin used as quarters by hunters during the shooting season

shooting star a meteor

shop (ʃɒp) **1.** *n.* (esp. *Br.*) a store (building where retail trade is carried on) ‖ a workshop or establishment where machines or goods are made or repaired **to set up shop** to open a shop, business etc., esp. for the first time in a particular place **to shut up shop** to cease to be in business ‖ **to talk shop** to discuss the techniques etc. of one's profession or trade **2.** *v.i. pres. part.* **shop·ping** *past* and *past part.* **shopped** to go to a shop or shops in order to buy goods [O.E. *sceoppa*, a place where goods are made and sold]

shop assistant (*Br.*) someone who serves in a retail store

Shope virus or **Shope papilloma** (*med.*) a virus causing warts (*papillomatosis*); named for Dr. R. E. Shope

shophar *SHOFAR

shop·keep·er (ʃɒpkiːpər) *n.* a person who owns and manages a store

shop·lift·er (ʃɒplɪftər) *n.* someone who, pretending to be a customer, steals goods displayed for sale in a store **shop·lift·ing** *n.*

shop·per (ʃɒpər) *n.* a person who buys in a store ‖ a person hired by a store to do this for others ‖ a person hired by a store to check prices, quality of goods etc. in a rival store or stores

shop·ping (ʃɒpɪŋ) *n.* the action of someone who shops ‖ the goods bought

shopping center a complex consisting of food markets, stores of various kinds, parking facilities etc., designed to serve the needs of a local community

shop·soiled (ʃɒpsɔild) *adj.* (*Br.*) shopworn

shop steward a person chosen by his fellow trade unionists in an industrial establishment to speak for them to the management and to watch over their interests

shop·talk (ʃɒptɔːk) *n.* chat or conversation narrowly limited to one's trade or profession

shop·walk·er (ʃɒpwɔːkər) (*Br.*) a floorwalker

shop·worn (ʃɒpwɔːrn) *adj.* (of goods) slightly damaged or dirty from long exposure for sale ‖ too familiar or overused to be stimulating or interesting, *shopworn ideas*

shor·an (ʃɔːræn) *n.* (*mil.* acronym) for short-range electronic navigation system used in precision bombing

shore (ʃɔːr, ʃour) *n.* the land forming the edge of a large expanse of water ‖ (*law*) the land between high and low water marks ‖ land as opposed to water [M.E. *schore* prob. fr. M.L.G. or M. Du.]

shore **1.** *n.* a length of lumber or metal, resting firmly on the ground or other unyielding surface and adjusted usually at an angle with the vertical so as to support a structure above it **2.** *v.t. pres. part.* **shor·ing** *past* and *past part.* **shored** (with 'up') to support by using a shore [M.E. *schore* fr. M. Du. or M.L.G.]

shore·bird (ʃɔːrbəːrd, ʃourbəːrd) *n.* a member of *Charadrii*, a suborder of birds that live along

the seashore, e.g. the plover, snipe and sandpiper

shore leave leave granted to members of a ship's crew for going ashore

shore·line (ʃɔːrlain, ʃourlain) *n.* where the shore ends and the water begins

shore patrol the U.S. Navy or Coast Guard military police on shore

shorn alt. *past part.* of SHEAR

short (ʃɔːrt) **1.** *adj.* having a relatively smaller length, range, scope etc. than others of its kind, type etc. or of being the shorter or shortest in dimension, *the short side of the room* ‖ not lasting a long time ‖ not tall ‖ (of a mode of address, manner or treatment) less friendly or generous than true courtesy would require ‖ easily aroused, *a short temper* ‖ (of pastry) crumbly due to the high proportion of shortening used ‖ (*phon.*, of syllables, vowels etc.) comparatively brief in duration ‖ (*prosody*, of a syllable) not stressed ‖ (esp. *classical prosody*, of a syllable) of relatively little duration ‖ (*finance*) not in possession of the securities or commodities at the time of sale ‖ (*finance*) being or pertaining to a sale of securities or commodities not in possession of the seller ‖ (of memory) not retentive ‖ less than a correct or sufficient degree or amount, *short weight* ‖ (usually with 'of' or 'in') lacking the correct or sufficient amount of what is required, *short of funds* ‖ not extending to or reaching a particular point or objective ‖ (of an alcoholic beverage) served in a small glass ‖ (*pop.* with 'on') equipped with an inadequate amount of, *short on acceleration* **short for** being an abbreviation or contraction of **to make short work of** to dispose of very quickly **2.** *adv.* unexpectedly and suddenly, *to stop short* ‖ in a brusque, discourteous manner ‖ on the near side of a given point or objective ‖ without actually owning the securities etc. sold, *to sell short* **3.** *n.* (*movies*) a movie of one reel ‖ (*elec.*) a short circuit ‖ (*finance*) someone who sells short ‖ (*pl.*) short pants covering the body from the waist to above the knees ‖ (*pl.*) underpants ‖ (*pl.*) a byproduct of wheat milling consisting of wheat germ, bran and flour ‖ (*pl.*) the waste materials of various manufacturing processes ‖ (*prosody*) a short syllable ‖ (*baseball*) shortstop or a shortstop **for short** by way of abbreviation or contraction **in short** by way of summary **4.** *v.t.* and *i.* to short-circuit [O.E. *scort, sceort*]

short account the account of a person who sells short ‖ the total, at any time, of such accounts in a commodity or in the market

short·age (ʃɔːrtidʒ) *n.* the fact that there is less of something than is required, or the amount by which what is available falls short

short·bread (ʃɔːrtbred) *n.* a crisp, short, sweet cooky made with butter, flour, sugar etc.

short·cake (ʃɔːrtkeik) *n.* a dessert consisting of a crisp, short biscuit which is split, filled with fresh fruit and topped with more fruit and often cream ‖ this biscuit ‖ (*Br.*) shortbread

short·change (ʃɔːrttʃeindʒ) *pres. part.* **short·chang·ing** *past* and *past part.* **short·changed** *v.t.* (*pop.*) to give (a customer) less than the correct change

short circuit a connection, usually accidental, between two points at different potentials in an electric circuit of relatively low resistance **short·cir·cuit** *v.t.* to make a short circuit in ‖ *v.i.* to make a short circuit

short·com·ing (ʃɔːrtkʌmiŋ) *n.* a failure to reach an expected or desired standard of conduct

short·cut (ʃɔːrtkʌt) *n.* a shorter, quicker way to a place or objective than the customary road or course of action

short·en (ʃɔːrtn) *v.t.* to make shorter ‖ (*naut.*) to reduce the spread of (sail) by reefing or furling ‖ *v.i.* to become shorter ‖ (of odds) to decrease **short·en·ing** *n.* the act of making or becoming shorter ‖ butter, fat etc. used to make pastry or cake crisper or flakier

short·hand (ʃɔːrthænd) **1.** *n.* a rapid way of writing by using symbols to represent syllables or complete words or phrases **2.** *adj.* of, relating to or consisting of shorthand

short·hand·ed (ʃɔːrthændid) *adj.* having fewer persons available for work than is necessary or desirable

short head (*Br.*, racing) a distance less than the length of a horse's head, separating two horses in a race

short·head (ʃɔːrthed) *n.* a brachycephalic person **short·head·ed** *adj.*

Short·horn (ʃɔːrthɔːrn) *n.* one of a breed of beef or dairy cattle with short curving horns that

originated in N. England and that are red, white or roan

short hundredweight the U.S. hundredweight of 100 lbs

short leg (*cricket*) a fielder occupying a position near to the batsman on the leg side ‖ this position

short list (*Br.*) the remaining list of candidates after a preliminary weeding out **short-list** *v.t.* (*Br.*) to place on a short list

short-lived (ʃɔːrtlaivd, ʃɔːrtlivd) *adj.* not living or continuing long

short·ly (ʃɔːrtli) *adv.* in a few words ‖ soon ‖ discourteously, brusquely

short of *prep.* not quite up to, *short of the goal* ‖ without going as far as, *he would do anything short of murder that you asked*

short order an order for food that is quickly prepared after it has been ordered in a restaurant **in short order** with no delay **short-order** *adj.* preparing food in this way, *a short-order restaurant*

short-range (ʃɔːrtreindʒ) *adj.* limited in range ‖ concerned only with the near future, not the long term

short ribs a cut of beef taken from the ends of the ribs

short shrift summary treatment through lack of sympathy etc., *to make short shrift of something, to give someone short shrift*

short-sight·ed (ʃɔːrtsaitid) *adj.* myopic ‖ not taking into account the probable future results of one's behavior or actions

short slip (*cricket*) a position, or the fielder occupying it, in the slips but close to the batsman

short-spo·ken (ʃɔːrtspoukən) *adj.* curt

short·stop (ʃɔːrtstɒp) *n.* (*baseball*) the infielder between second and third base ‖ his position

short story a story in prose varying widely in length, but shorter than either a novel or a novelette, and concentrating on a single effect which the writer wants to achieve

short-tem·pered (ʃɔːrttémpərd) *adj.* quick-tempered

short-term (ʃɔːrttəːrm) *adj.* happening over or entailing only a brief period ‖ (*finance*) of or relating to a gain, loss, transaction etc. based on a relatively short period of time (usually less than a year)

short ton (*U.S.A., Canada* and *South Africa*) a unit of weight equal to 2,000 lbs, used for coal

short-wave (ʃɔːrtweiv) **1.** *n.* an electromagnetic wave having a 60-meter wavelength or less **2.** *adj.* of, pertaining to, or using shortwaves **3.** *v.t. pres. part.* **short-wav·ing** *past* and *past part.* **short-waved** to transmit by shortwaves

short-wind·ed (ʃɔːrtwindid) *adj.* out of breath or easily out of breath

Sho·sho·ne·an (ʃouʃóuniːən, ʃouʃəníːən) *pl.* **Sho·sho·ne·an, Sho·sho·ne·ans** *n.* a linguistic family of the Uto-Aztecan group ‖ a member of an Indian people speaking a Shoshonean language ‖ any such people

Sho·sho·ni, Sho·sho·ne (ʃouʃóuni) *pl.* **Sho·sho·ni, Sho·sho·nis, Sho·sho·ne, Sho·sho·nes** *n.* a group of Shoshonean peoples of the western U.S.A. ‖ their language ‖ a member of this group

Sho·sta·ko·vich (ʃɒstəkóuvitʃ), Dmitri (1906-75), Russian composer. His style is eclectic and he has incurred the disapproval of Soviet critics at various times. His work includes symphonies, operas, ballets, songs, chamber music and music for the movies. The authenticity of his autobiography, 'Testimony: The Memoirs of Dmitri Shostakovich' (1979) was disputed by family members

shot (ʃɒt) **1.** *n.* an act of shooting ‖ a discharge of a firearm, cannon or gun ‖ the range or distance able to be passed over by a discharged missile, *within shot* ‖ (*collect.*) small spherical pieces of hardened lead packed into a cartridge ‖ a single piece of this ‖ (*hist.*) a solid, nonexplosive ball designed to be shot from a cannon ‖ an attempt to hit by shooting ‖ an attempt, *to have a shot at something* ‖ a guess ‖ an opportunity or chance to achieve or get something ‖ an obliquely critical remark, *that was a shot at you* ‖ a marksman ‖ (*movies*) a scene or portion of a scene photographed by one camera without stopping or cutting ‖ (*games*) a stroke, throw, drive etc., *a shot at a goal* ‖ a photograph ‖ an injection of a drug ‖ (*pop.*) a small quantity of whiskey or other liquor ‖ (*athletics*) a heavy metal ball, weighing up to 16 lbs, thrown by contestants in the shot put field event **like a shot** with great alacrity ‖ very willingly **to pay one's shot** (*Br.*) to pay one's share of the cost **2.** *v.t. pres. part.* **shot·ting** *past* and *past part.* **shot·ted** to load or weight with shot [O.E. *sceot, scot, gesceot, gescot*]

shot *past* and *past part.* of SHOOT *adj.* (of silk or other fabric) closely woven with a warp of one color and weft of another color so that it exhibits its different colors and shades when viewed at different angles ‖ (*pop.*) worn out, broken, *this saucepan is shot* ‖ (*pop.*) ruined, in a useless state, *his nerves are shot*

shote *SHOAT

shot·gun (*ʃótgʌn*) *n.* a short-range, smooth-bore firearm, often with two barrels, from which shot is projected by the explosion of a cartridge, the shot spreading in a cone shape as it travels from the muzzle

shot put an athletic contest in which competitors put the shot ‖ a put of the shot in this contest

should (*ʃud*) *past* of SHALL *auxiliary v.* used to express moral obligation, necessity etc., *you should work harder*, or probability, *it should rain tonight if the wind drops*, futurity in indirect quotations to replace 'will' and 'shall' in direct quotations, *we said we should be happy to come*, futurity in polite requests or statements with implications of doubt, *I should think she will come*, or future condition, *if that should happen would you be able to go?* or past condition, *I should have been late if I hadn't taken a taxi* (cf. SHALL, cf. WOULD) [O.E. *sceolde, scolde*]

shoul·der (*ʃóuldər*) **1.** *n.* the joint connecting the arm or forelimb with the upper part of the body ‖ that part of the body to which is connected the arm of a person, the foreleg of a quadruped, or the wing of a bird ‖ (*pl.*) the upper part of a person's back and the two shoulders ‖ a cut of meat including the upper part of the foreleg and the part to which it is attached ‖ the part of a garment which covers the shoulder ‖ the part of a hide corresponding to an animal's shoulders ‖ a part of something thought of as like a shoulder, esp. in the way it projects, *the shoulder of a mountain* ‖ (*printing*) the flat top of the body of a type on which the bevel rises to the face ‖ either side of a road, off the roadway **shoulder to shoulder** standing side by side, close together ‖ acting closely together, helping one another to the utmost **straight from the shoulder** direct and frank, without qualification or reserve, esp. in expressing criticism **to put one's shoulder to the wheel** to make a great effort to further a project or piece of work **2.** *v.t.* to push with the shoulder ‖ to take or carry on the shoulder ‖ to accept (a burden of responsibility), *to shoulder the blame* ‖ *v.i.* to push with the shoulder **to shoulder arms** (*mil.*) to hold (a rifle) so that the barrel rests on the shoulder and the butt is supported in the palm of the hand [O.E. *sculdor*]

shoulder belt or **shoulder harness** across-the-chest restraint used in motor vehicles to hold back passengers in case of accidental impact

shoulder blade one of the two large flat bones of the upper back

shoulder loop a strap of cloth running from a button at the collar to the shoulder seam on Army, Air Force and Marine Corps uniforms. Commissioned and warrant officers' insignia of rank are attached to it

shoulder strap a band of ribbon etc. supporting a woman's dress or slip etc. across the shoulders ‖ a strap of cloth running from a button at the collar to the shoulder seam on a uniform

should·n't (*ʃúd'nt*) *contr.* of SHOULD NOT

shout (*ʃaut*) **1.** *n.* a loud, often wordless cry uttered in order to attract attention or to express some very strong emotion **2.** *v.i.* to utter this cry, *the shout to warn me* ‖ to speak very loudly, *she had to shout because he was deaf* ‖ *v.t.* to express by a shout, *he shouted a warning* **to shout (someone) down** to silence (a speaker) by shouting [M.E. *shouten*, etym. doubtful]

shove (*ʃʌv*) **1.** *v. pres. part.* **shov·ing** *past* and *past part.* **shoved** *v.t.* to push (someone or something) hard ‖ *v.i.* to push **to shove off** to push (a boat) away from shore ‖ (*pop.*) to leave **2.** *n.* a hard push [O.E. *scúfan*]

shove-half·pen·ny (*ʃʌvhéipəni, ʃʌvhéipini:*) *n.* a game in which coins (halfpennies etc.) are made to slide across scoring lines on a marked board by resting them at the edge and striking with the ball of the thumb ‖ (*Br.*) shuffleboard (disk and cue game)

shov·el (*ʃʌv'l*) **1.** *n.* a tool consisting of a large shallow concave head attached to the end of a long handle, used for lifting loose material and moving it elsewhere ‖ the quantity it holds **2.** *v.t. pres. part.* **shov·el·ing**, esp. *Br.* **shov·el·ling** *past* and *past part.* **shov·eled**, esp. *Br.* **shov·elled** to lift and move with a shovel ‖ to dig out or clear (e.g. a path) with a shovel [O.E. *scofl*]

shov·el·board (*ʃʌv'lbɔrd, ʃʌv'lbourd*) *n.* shuffleboard (disk and cue game) ‖ (*Br.*) shovehalfpenny (coin game)

shov·el·er, esp. *Br.* **shov·el·ler** (*ʃʌvələr, ʃʌvlər*) *n. Anas clypeata*, fam. *Anatidae*, a freshwater duck with a huge spatulate beak

shovel hat a shallow black hat with a broad brim turned up at the sides, formerly worn by pastors and clergymen

shov·el·head (*ʃʌvlhɛd*) *n. Sphyrna tiburo*, fam. *Sphyrnidae*, a shark related to the hammerhead shark, but smaller

shoveller *SHOVELER

show (*ʃou*) **1.** *v. pres. part.* **show·ing** *past* **showed** *past part.* **shown** (*ʃoun*), **showed** *v.t.* to cause to be seen, *he showed his books to me* ‖ to guide, conduct, *she showed me to my seat* ‖ to offer for public view, *the firm showed its new designs* ‖ to put on view for entertainment, *they are showing a new movie* ‖ to indicate, give to understand, *his letter shows why he did not come* ‖ to point out, *he showed her why she ought to do it* ‖ to establish, prove, *the evidence showed that he was sane at the time, it showed him that he was right* ‖ (*law*) to plead, present in a court, *to show just cause* ‖ to give evidence of (feelings, character, disposition), *he showed no pity* ‖ to bestow (favor etc.) ‖ to register, *the farm showed a profit* ‖ to present (a message) to the eye or mind, *the signal showed all clear* ‖ to depict, *the account shows him as a scoundrel* ‖ *v.i.* to be visible ‖ to be seen, *to show to advantage* ‖ to have a specified appearance ‖ (*pop.*) to prove a point, *it just goes to show* ‖ (of a movie) to be on view ‖ (*pop.*) to finish third, esp. in a horse race **to show off** to make a show of one's virtues or skills ‖ to demonstrate so as to reveal the qualities of **to show up** to reveal the true character (usually unworthy) of ‖ to put in an appearance ‖ to appear in a specified way ‖ to be conspicuous **2.** *n.* a display, *a show of grief* ‖ a demonstration, *a show of strength* ‖ a public exhibition, *a flower show*, esp. one of paintings or sculpture, a *one-man show* ‖ a public presentation of entertainment, e.g. a play, a radio program ‖ a visible trace, *no show of fatigue* ‖ pretense, *he made a show of not hearing me* ‖ a chance to reveal quality, *it got no sort of show* ‖ performance, *to put up a good show* ‖ (*pop.*) an undertaking, business etc., *he wrecked the whole show* ‖ (*pop.*) third place, esp. in a horse race ‖ **for show** in order merely to attract attention [O.E. *scéawian*, to look at]

show bill an advertising poster

show·boat (*ʃóubout*) *n.* a river steamer with actors or entertainers on board giving a show ‖ (*colloq.*) a show-off

showbread *SHEWBREAD

show·case (*ʃóukeis*) *n.* a glass-fronted cupboard, fitted with shelves, in which goods are set out on view for sale or objects for exhibition

show·down (*ʃóudaun*) *n.* the last stage in a dispute immediately preceding a settlement ‖ (*poker*) a laying down of the cards face up

show·er (*ʃáuər*) **1.** *n.* a brief fall of rain, hail or sleet ‖ a thick but brief fall of objects, *a shower of confetti* ‖ a shower bath ‖ a festive gathering at which presents are given to a prospective bride or mother **showers of** a great many, *showers of compliments* **2.** *v.t.* to cover as if in a shower ‖ *v.i.* to fall in or as if in a shower ‖ to take a shower bath [O.E. *scúr*]

shower bath a bath taken standing up under a spray of water from an overhead nozzle ‖ the apparatus installed for such baths ‖ the room etc. where such baths are taken

show·er·y (*ʃáuəri:*) *adj.* with rain falling briefly and frequently ‖ like a shower, *showery pink blossoms*

show·i·ly (*ʃóuəli:*) *adv.* in a showy manner

show·i·ness (*ʃóui:nis*) *n.* the state or quality of being showy

show·ing (*ʃóuiŋ*) *n.* the act of offering for public view ‖ an exhibition for display, *a private showing of a film* ‖ performance in a competition, *to make a good showing* ‖ evidence, *on present showing we should finish next year*

show·man (*ʃóumən*) *pl.* **show·men** (*ʃóumən*) *n.* the owner or manager of a circus, menagerie or

other lesser form of public entertainment ‖ someone who has a flair for putting something before the public effectively, esp. by using theatrical techniques, *the parson is something of a showman* **shów·man·ship** *n.*

shown *past* and *alt. past part.* of show

show-off (*ʃóuɔf, ʃóuɒf*) *n.* the act of showing off ‖ (*pop.*) a person who shows off for admiration

show of hands a raising of one hand by each member of a group as a method of voting, showing approval etc.

show·piece (*ʃóupi:s*) *n.* something being exhibited or that would exhibit well

show·room (*ʃóuru:m, ʃóurum*) *n.* a room set apart for showing samples of goods for sale

show window a store display window

show·y (*ʃóui:*) *comp.* **show·i·er** *superl.* **show·i·est** *adj.* ostentatious ‖ making attractive display, *showy blooms*

shrank *past* of SHRINK

shrap·nel (*ʃrǽpn'l*) *n.* bullets and jagged pieces of metal sprayed by a bursting shell ‖ a projectile fired for this effect [after Henry *Shrapnel* (1761-1842), British general]

shred (*ʃred*) *n.* a small piece torn or cut from something, usually in the form of a thin strip ‖ a small amount, *shreds of evidence* [O.E. *scréade*]

shred *pres. part.* **shred·ding** *past* and *past part.* **shred·ded, shred** *v.t.* to tear or cut into shreds [O.E. *scréadian*]

Shreve·port (*ʃri:vpɔrt, ʃri:vpourt*) a port and industrial town (pop. 205,815) of N.W. Louisiana: oil refining, chemicals, sawmilling

shrew (*ʃru:*) *n.* a member of *Soricidae*, a family of small, mouse-like, insectivorous, nocturnal animals with a long tail and a soft hairy coat ‖ a bad-tempered woman [O.E. *scréawa, scréwa*]

shrewd (*ʃru:d*) *adj.* intelligent and worldly-wise, *a shrewd businessman* ‖ clever and true or very near the truth, *a shrewd guess* [M.E. *shre-wede* fr. SHREW, (obs.) an evil person]

shrew·ish (*ʃrú:iʃ*) *adj.* (of a woman) bad-tempered, bullying

shriek (*ʃri:k*) **1.** *v.i.* to utter a shrill, sharp cry, esp. from pain, fear etc. ‖ to laugh in a shrill, high-pitched way ‖ *v.t.* to utter in a sharp, shrill way **2.** *n.* such a cry or laugh [etym. doubtful]

shriev·al·ty (*ʃri:vəlti*) *pl.* **shriev·al·ties** *n.* (*Br.*) the office, tenure of office or jurisdiction of a sheriff

shrift (*ʃrift*) *n.* (*archaic*) confession to a priest in the sacrament of penance ‖ (*archaic*) the remission of sins pronounced by a priest to a penitent ‖ *SHORT SHRIFT [O.E. *scrift*]

shrike (*ʃraik*) *n.* any of various hook-billed songbirds of fam. *Lanidae*, esp. of genus *Lanius*, that feed mainly on insects which they impale on thorny bushes [O.E. *scríc, scréc*, a bird with a shrill cry]

Shrike *n.* (*mil.*) an air-launched antiradiation missile (AGM-45) designed to home on and destroy radar emitters

shrill (*ʃril*) **1.** *adj.* (of a voice or sound) high-pitched and piercing ‖ made in or accompanied by such sounds, *shrill demands* **2.** *v.t.* to utter in a shrill voice ‖ *v.i.* to make shrill cries [M.E. *shrille*]

shrimp (*ʃrimp*) **1.** *pl.* **shrimps, shrimp** *n.* any of various members of *Natantia*, a suborder of small, edible, chiefly marine crustaceans having 10 legs and a long slender body ‖ (*pop.*) a tiny or undersized person, esp. one who is unimposing **2.** *v.i.* to fish for shrimps [M.E. *schrimpe*]

shrimp boat a plastic chip placed on radarscope in air traffic control to track aircraft

shrine (*ʃrain*) *n.* a box of stone, metal or wood used to hold sacred relics ‖ a tomb, chapel or other place held sacred because of the presence of such relics ‖ a place which is hallowed because it has special associations [O.E. *scrin* fr. L.]

shrink (*ʃriŋk*) **1.** *pres. part.* **shrink·ing** *past* **shrank** (*ʃræŋk*), **shrunk** (*ʃrʌŋk*) *past part.* **shrunk**, (only in *adj.* uses) **shrunk·en** (*ʃrʌŋk'n*) *v.i.* to become smaller, e.g. from heat, cold etc. ‖ (of cloth or clothing) to become smaller after being washed or thoroughly drenched ‖ to draw back in fear or unwillingness, *she shrank from the idea of meeting him* ‖ (e.g. of value) to lessen ‖ *v.t.* to cause to shrink **2.** *n.* the act of shrinking **shrink·age** *n.* the act, process or extent of shrinking [O.E. *scrincan*]

shrink-wrap (*ʃríŋkræp*) *n.* plastic film packaging that shrinks under heat to conform to shape of contents, e.g., a book —**shrink wrap** *v.*

---

shrive (ʃraiv) *pres. part.* **shriv·ing** *past* **shrove** (ʃrouv), **shrived** *past part.* **shriv·en** (ʃrív'n), **shrived** *v.i.* (*archaic*) to confess to a priest and receive absolution || *v.t.* (*archaic*) to hear the confession of and absolve [O.E. *scrifan*]

shriv·el (ʃrív'l) *pres. part.* **shriv·el·ing**, esp. *Br.* **shriv·el·ling** *past and past part.* **shriv·eled**, esp. *Br.* **shrivelled** *v.i.* (often with 'up') to become smaller, with the surface becoming wrinkled || *v.t.* to cause to become smaller and wrinkled [origin unknown]

shriven *alt. past part.* of SHRIVE

Shrop·shire (ʃrópʃiər, ʃrópʃər) (*abbr.* Salop) a county (area 1,347 sq. miles, pop. 380,400) of England on the Welsh border. County town: Shrewsbury (pop. 58,826)

shroud (ʃraud) **1.** *n.* a long sheet wound around a corpse || something which conceals or clouds, *a shroud of mist* || (*naut.*) one of the ropes attached to the sides of a ship and the lower mastheads, to keep the mast in position **2.** *v.t.* to wind in a shroud || to conceal or cloud, *her background was shrouded in mystery* [O.E. *scrūd*, garment]

shroud-laid (ʃráudleid) *adj.* (of a rope) having four strands and a core

shrove *alt. past* of SHRIVE

Shrove·tide (ʃróuvtaid) *n.* the three days before Ash Wednesday (Quinquagesima and the following Monday and Tuesday), when pre-Lent confessions are made and pre-Lent festivities are held [rel. to SHRIVE, origin unknown]

shrub (ʃrʌb) *n.* a plant with several branching woody stems and no main trunk, smaller than most trees **shrúb·ber·y** *pl.* **shrub·ber·ies** a number of shrubs growing close together || (*collect.*) shrubs **shrúb·by** *comp.* **shrub·bi·er** *superl.* **shrub·bi·est** *adj.* composed of shrubs || like a shrub [O.E. *scrybb*, shrubbery]

shrug (ʃrʌg) **1.** *v. pres. part.* **shrug·ging** *past and past part.* **shrugged** *v.t.* to lift (the shoulders) as a gesture expressing doubt, rejection of an idea, ignorance of the answer to a question etc. || *v.i.* to lift the shoulders in this way **2.** *n.* this gesture [origin unknown]

shrunk *alt. past and past part.* of SHRINK

shrunken *alt. past part.* of SHRINK

shtetl or **shte·tel** (ʃtet'l) *n.* (*Yiddish*) small Jewish town or village in Eastern Europe during the 19th and 20th century until World War II

SH-3 *SEA KING

SH-2 *SEA SPRITE

shuck (ʃʌk) **1.** *n.* a shell or husk **2.** *v.t.* to extract (e.g. peas, fruit, nuts) from pods or shells || to remove (oysters) from their shells **shucks** *interj.* an expression of disappointment, annoyance etc. [origin unknown]

shuck (*slang*) **1.** *n.* a sham **2.** *v.* to con or deceive verbally

shud·der (ʃʌdər) **1.** *v.i.* to experience a sudden and forceful muscular contraction throughout the body, arising from horror or disgust **2.** *n.* one of these muscular contractions || the act of shuddering [M.E. *shodre, shoddre*]

shuf·fle (ʃʌf'l) **1.** *v. pres. part.* **shuf·fling** *past and past part.* **shuf·fled** *v.t.* to move (things) about, changing their positions relative to one another, *to shuffle cards* || to slide (the feet) around continually on the ground || to jumble together into a disordered state || to change, shift, push, esp. in a clumsy way || *v.i.* to move while dragging or sliding the feet instead of lifting them || to dance in this way || (with 'in', 'into' or 'out of') to get into or out of a position, state etc. by shifty or evasive means, *to shuffle out of a situation* || to shift around from one position to another || to shuffle cards **2.** *n.* the act of shuffling || a shuffling of the feet || a shuffling gait || the rearranging of a pack of cards || one's turn to do this [prob. L.G. *schüffeln*, to walk clumsily]

shuf·fle·board (ʃʌf'lbɔrd,ʃʌf'lbourd) *n.* a game in which players use a cue to push large disks into sections marked out on a flat, smooth surface || (*Br.*) shove-halfpenny (coin game)

shuf·fler (ʃʌflər) *n.* (esp. in *cards*) a person who shuffles || a scaup duck

Shu·fu (ʃúːfúː) *KASHGAR

shun (ʃʌn) *pres. part.* **shun·ning** *past and past part.* **shunned** *v.t.* to keep clear of, avoid, *to shun publicity* [O.E. *scunian*]

shun·pike (ʃʌnpaik) *v.* to travel on secondary roads avoiding expressways —**shunpiker** *n.*

shunt (ʃʌnt) **1.** *v.t.* to move (a train etc.) to a different track || (*elec.*) to divert (a current) to a different direction || (*elec.*) to provide with a shunt || to cause (someone) to divert his thoughts, interests, attention etc. in another direction || *v.i.* (of trains) to move to a different track || (*elec.*, of a current) to be diverted by a shunt **2.** *n.* a shunting || (*elec.*) a conductor attached to a circuit at two points, reducing the amount of current flowing through the circuit || (*rail.*) a switch || (*auto racing*) an accident, esp. involving two or more cars [M.E. *shunten*]

shunt-wound (ʃʌntwáund) *adj.* (*elec.*) designating a coil of an armature wound so that some of the current travels around the field magnet

shush (ʃʌʃ) **1.** *interj.* hush! be silent! **2.** *v.t.* to cause (someone) to be silent

shut (ʃʌt) *pres. part.* **shut·ting** *past and past part.* **shut** *v.t.* (sometimes with 'up' or 'down') to cause (something) to come together with another surface so that there is no space between them, *to shut a door* || to fasten (a door etc.) with a catch, bolt etc. || to prevent passage through by imposing a barrier, *to shut a road to all traffic* || (sometimes with 'up') to bring together the parts of (the eye, mouth etc.) so that there is no space between them || (often with 'up') to prevent exit from or entrance to *to shut a house for the winter* || (sometimes with 'up') to confine, *shut the dog in the kitchen* || (often with 'up') to stop or stop temporarily the business or operation of *he will have to shut the shop* || (with 'up') to put away in a container, esp. in a safe place || (with 'up') to cause (someone) to stop talking || *v.i.* to be or become shut || (often with 'up') to stop or stop temporarily the business or operation of a store, factory etc. || (with 'up') to stop talking **to shut down** to cause (a factory etc.) to cease to work **to shut in** to prevent from coming out || to surround, *the house is shut in by trees* **to shut off** to prevent (water, gas, steam etc.) from flowing || to stop (machinery) from working by shutting off the power || to keep from human contact, *he is shutting himself off from society* || (of machinery) to stop working because the power has been cut off **to shut out** to prevent from entering || to prevent the possibility of, *this shuts out any danger of fire* || (*sports*) to keep (an opponent or opposing team) from scoring [O.E. *scyttan*]

shut-in (ʃʌtin) *n.* an invalid unable to leave his bed, room or house

shut-out (ʃʌtaut) *n.* a lockout || (*sports*) prevention from scoring in a game || (*sports*) a game with no score on one side

shut·ter (ʃʌtər) **1.** *n.* a cover, often consisting of wooden boards or slats, used to secure a window against unlawful entry or to allow air but not sunlight to enter || a mechanical device that acts to admit light into a camera or other optical instrument during a specified time interval. In cameras the shutter may be built into the lens system or may act in the focal plane. In motion-picture cameras it usually consists of a rotating device synchronized with the rate of passage of the film before the lenses || a device for opening and closing the swell box of an organ **2.** *v.t.* to provide with a shutter or shutters || to close the shutter or shutters of [SHUT]

shuttered fuse a fuse in which inadvertent initiation of the detonator will not initiate either the booster or the burst charge

shut·tle (ʃʌt'l) **1.** *n.* a device enclosing the bobbin which a weaver passes between the threads of the warp in order to make the weft || the holder of the lower thread of a sewing machine || a small device for holding the thread in tatting etc. || a passenger train, plane or bus which travels back and forth over a short route between two places at scheduled intervals || such a traveling back and forth **2.** *v. pres. part.* **shut·tling** *past and past part.* **shut·tled** *v.t.* to cause to move back and forth || *v.i.* to move back and forth [O.E. *scytel*, a dart]

shuttle bombing (*mil.*) bombing of targets located between two friendly bases

shut·tle·cock (ʃʌt'lkɒk) *n.* a cork, winged with feathers, struck with a battledore in the game of battledore and shuttlecock, or with a racket in badminton || the game of battledore and shuttlecock

shuttle diplomacy continuous travel between two disputing countries for the purpose of mediation

shuttle service a transport service consisting of vehicles which move back and forth between two places, esp. in short, scheduled trips || regular air transport service, usu. hourly, between two centers, with guaranteed seating for all comers

shy (ʃai) **1.** *comp.* **shy·er, shi·er** *superl.* **shy·est, shi·est** *adj.* (of persons) finding it hard to overcome selfconsciousness and establish personal relations with others, and therefore seeking to avoid notice || (of animals) easily frightened || showing timidity or reserve, *a shy smile* || (with 'about') wary of or reserved about doing something || (*poker*) not having paid one's ante || (with 'of') || short, not having a sufficiency, *shy of money* || short of money **to fight shy of** to try to avoid **2.** *v.i. pres. part.* **shy·ing** *past and past part.* **shied** (of a horse etc.) to move suddenly to one side when startled **3.** *pl.* **shies** *n.* an act of shying [O.E. *scēoh*]

shy (ʃai) **1.** *v.t. pres. part.* **shy·ing** *past and past part.* **shied** to throw (a stone, ball etc.) **2.** *pl.* **shies** *n.* a throw (*pop.*) a try, attempt [etym. doubtful]

shy·ster (ʃáistər) *n.* (*pop.*) a person, esp. a lawyer, who is unscrupulous in the practice of his profession [etym. doubtful]

si (siː) *n.* (*mus.*) the note B in the fixed-do system of solmization || ti, the seventh note of the scale in movable-do solmization [*SOLMIZATION]

SI *SI UNITS

si·al·a·gog·ic (saiələgódʒik) **1.** *adj.* (*med.*) stimulating the flow of saliva **2.** *n.* (*med.*) a sialagogic agent [SIALAGOGUE]

si·al·a·gogue (saiæləgɒg, saiǽləgɒg) *n.* (*med.*) an agent promoting the flow of saliva [F. fr. Gk *sialon*, saliva+*agōgos*, leading]

Si·al·kot (siːálkout) a commercial center (pop. 185,000) in Pakistan in the N. Punjab. Manufactures: sporting goods, musical and surgical instruments. Ancient fortress, mausoleum of Nanak

Si·am (saiæm, sáiæm) *THAILAND

si·a·mang (síːəmæŋ) *n. Symphalangus syndactylus*, a large black gibbon of Sumatra [Malay *siāmang, siyāmang*]

Si·a·mese (saiəmíːz, saiəmíːs) **1.** *adj.* of or relating to Thailand, its people or language **2.** *pl.* **Si·a·mese** *n.* a native of Thailand || the Sino-Tibetan language of Thailand

Siamese cat a cat of a short-haired, blue-eyed breed (*BLUE POINT, *SEAL POINT) noted for its sinewy delicacy

Siamese twins twins born joined together at some point [from the twins In and Jun (1811–74), born in Siam, who were the first widely publicized instance of this condition]

Si·an (síːán, ʃíːán) (medieval Changan or Singan and called Siking 1936-49) the capital (pop. 2,500,000) of Shensi, N. China. Industries: textiles, chemicals. Nestorian monument (c. 780), Ming dynasty walls. University

Siang·tan (sjáŋtán, ʃjáŋtán) an industrial center and river port (pop. 184,000) in E. Hunan, China: metallurgy, mechanical engineering, textiles

sib (sib) *n.* a blood relative, esp. a sibling || kindred, relatives || (*anthrop.*) a unilateral, usually exogamous kin group based on common descent whether matrilineal or patrilineal (cf. CLAN, cf. SEPT) [O.E. *sib, sibb*, kinship]

Si·be·li·us (sibéiliːəs, sibéiljəs), Jean (1865-1957), Finnish composer. His work is fundamentally nationalistic. His symphonies seem to spring from a consciousness of the sternness of man's relation with nature in the far north. They have a considerable formal interest and a characteristic melodic style

Si·be·ri·a (saibíəriːə) the Asiatic part (area c. 4,887,000 sq. miles) of the R.S.F.S.R., U.S.S.R. extending from the Urals to the Pacific. Geography: *R.S.F.S.R., *U.S.S.R. HISTORY. Siberia was the starting point for the Hun and Mongol invasions. It was annexed by Russia under Ivan IV in the 16th c. and became a place of political exile (17th c.). The building (1892-1905) of the Trans-Siberian Railroad led to colonization on a large scale, and the region is being industrialized rapidly

Si·be·ri·an (saibíəriːən) **1.** *adj.* of or relating to Siberia **2.** *n.* a native or inhabitant of Siberia

sib·i·lance (síbələns) *n.* a sibilant quality || a sibilant sound

sib·i·lan·cy (síbələnsi) *n.* sibilance

sib·i·lant (síbələnt) **1.** *adj.* having or making a hissing sound || uttered with a hissing sound **2.** *n.* a sibilant speech sound or the symbol for it (e.g. s, z, ʃ, ʒ) [fr. L. *sibilans* (*sibilantis*) fr. *sibilare*, to hiss]

sib·i·late (síbəleit) *pres. part.* **sib·i·lat·ing** *past and past part.* **sib·i·lat·ed** *v.t.* to pronounce with a hissing sound || *v.i.* to make an initial hissing sound when pronouncing **sib·i·lá·tion** *n.* [fr. L. *sibilare* (*sibilatus*), to hiss]

Si·biu (siːbjúː) (*G.* Hermannstadt) a commercial center (pop. 156,854) of central Transylvania, Rumania

---

CONCISE PRONUNCIATION KEY: (a) æ, c*a*t; ɑ, c*a*r; ɔ f*aw*n; ei, sn*a*ke. **(e)** e, h*e*n; iː, sh*ee*p; iə, d*ee*r; ɛə, b*ea*r. **(i)** i, f*i*sh; ai, t*i*ger; ə:, b*i*rd. **(o)** o, *o*x; au, c*ow*; ou, g*oa*t; u, p*oo*r; ɔi, r*oy*al. **(u)** ʌ, d*u*ck; u, b*u*ll; uː, g*oo*se; ə, b*a*cillus; juː, c*u*be. x, lo*ch*; θ, *th*ink; ð, bo*th*er; z, *Z*en; ʒ, corsa*g*e; dʒ, sava*g*e; ŋ, orangutan*g*; j, *y*ak; ʃ, *fi*sh; tʃ, fe*tch*; 'l, rabb*le*; 'n, redd*en*. Complete pronunciation key appears inside front cover.

sib·ling (síblıŋ) n. a person in relation to someone having the same parents or having one parent in common

Sib·yl (síb'l) n. one of various women in antiquity (e.g. in Greece, Rome and Egypt) believed to possess prophetic powers through divine inspiration **sib·yl** a prophetess [O.F. Sibile or fr. M.L Sibilla fr. L. fr. Gk]

Sib·yl·line (síbəli:n, síbəlain, síbəlin) adj. of, relating to or uttered by a Sibyl **sib·yl·line** oracular, obscurely prophetic, a sibylline utterance [fr. L. Sibyllinus]

Sibylline books a collection of oracles bearing on the worship of the gods and the policy of Rome, fabled to have been bought from a Sibyl by Tarquinius Superbus, and used in ancient Rome for guidance in matters of law

sic (sik) adv. thus (added in brackets after a word or expression in a quotation which looks wrong or absurd, to show that it has been quoted correctly) [L.]

sic, sick (sik) pres. part. **sick·ing** past and past part. **sicked** v.t. (esp. of a dog, used esp. in imper.) to set upon, chase to incite (a dog) to attack [var. of SEEK]

sic·ca·tive (síkativ) 1. adj. promoting drying 2. n. a substance promoting drying, esp. one mixed with oil paint, printing ink etc. [fr. L.L. siccativus]

Si·cil·ian (sisíljən) 1. adj. relating to Sicily or its inhabitants ‖ relating to the Italian dialect of Sicily 2. n. a native or inhabitant of Sicily ‖ the Italian dialect spoken in Sicily

Sicilian Vespers (hist.) a revolt (1282) against French rule in Sicily. It broke out at Palermo. The ringing of the vesper bell on Easter Monday was the signal for the people to kill or drive out the French. Sicily was joined to Aragon

Sic·i·lies, Kingdom of the Two (sísəli:z) (Ital. hist.) a former state consisting of Sicily and the southern portion of Italy. After the fall of Rome (476) this area was occupied by the Ostrogoths, and then by the Byzantines (535). The Saracens took Sicily (827-78), and Germans, Greeks and Arabs fought for the region until it was conquered (mid-11th c.) by Robert Guiscard and the Normans. The throne passed (1266) to the house of Anjou until the Sicilian Vespers (1282), when the house of Aragon took Sicily. The kingdom was reunited (1504) under the Spanish crown. After war with Austria, the Spanish Bourbons captured the kingdom (1734), and were restored (1815) after the Napoleonic Wars. Their despotic rule ended (1860) when Garibaldi invaded and joined (1861) the Two Sicilies to the kingdom of Italy

Sic·i·ly (sísəli:) (Ital. Sicilia) a mountainous, deforested island (area 9,815 sq. miles, pop. 4,884,000) off S.W. Italy, forming, with Pantelleria, the Lipari Is and other nearby islets, an autonomous region (area 9,928 sq. miles, pop. 4,936,200) of Italy. Capital: Palermo. Highest peak: 10,850 ft (*ETNA). The coasts are fertile, esp. in the north, and populous, the interior largely barren and sparsely inhabited. Main industries: agriculture (citrus fruit, bananas, olives, almonds, vines, cork, cotton), fishing, mining (sulfur), petroleum extraction (90% of Italian production) and refining, tourism. Universities: Catania (1434), Messina (1549), Palermo (1805). Part of the Mycenaean civilization of Crete, Sicily became a prosperous Greek colony (9th-5th cc. B.C.), was invaded by the Carthaginians, and fell (241 B.C.) to the Romans. After the fall of Rome (476) it became part of the Kingdom of the Two Sicilies

sick (sik) 1. adj. not physically healthy ‖ not healthy mentally, morally or spiritually ‖ so consumed with passion as to have a feeling of illness, sick with envy ‖ likely to vomit, to feel sick ‖ suffering an attack of vomiting, sick three times ‖ betraying that a person is not in good health, a sick look ‖ of or for people not in good health, sick leave, ‖ (pop.) feeling disgusted, his manners make me sick ‖ feeling weak and depressed, sick at heart ‖ (with 'of') disgusted by having or being subjected to too much of something, sick and tired of complaints ‖ (pop.) weak, of relatively poor quality, his painting looks pretty sick by comparison with yours ‖ (of humor, jokes) sadistic or suggesting heartlessness ‖ (rhet., with 'for') longing, sick for home ‖ forced, sickly, a sick smile **to go sick** (mil.) to report oneself as being ill 2. n. **the sick** people not in good health [O.E. sēoc]

sick v.t. *SIC

sick bay quarters in a naval vessel, military establishment, or some institutions, where the sick are treated

sick·bed (síkbed) n. (rhet.) the bed where someone lies ill

sick·en (síkən) v.i. to become ill ‖ v.t. to cause to feel sick **sick·en·ing** adj. nauseating, revolting ‖ distressing

Sick·ert (síkərt), Walter Richard (1860-1942), English painter. He was greatly influenced by Degas in composition and subject matter, esp. theater interiors

sick headache a migraine ‖ a condition of headache accompanied by intermittent feelings of nausea

Sick·ing·en (zíkiŋən), Franz von (1481-1523), German knight and Protestant military leader

sick·le (sík'l) n. a tool with a curved blade and a short handle, used for cutting long grass or trimming rough hedges etc. **the Sickle** a sickle-shaped group of six stars in the constellation Leo [O.E. sicol perh. fr. L.]

sick leave leave of absence from duty granted because of illness

sick·li·ness (síkli:nis) n. the state or quality of being sickly

sick·ly (síkli:) comp. **sick·li·er** superl. **sick·liest** adj. prone to illness, weak in health, a sickly child ‖ caused by, or suggestive of illness, a sickly complexion ‖ weak because forced, a sickly smile ‖ causing sickness, mildly nauseating, the sickly smell of ether

sick·ness (síknis) n. illness, being sick ‖ a disease ‖ (esp. Br.) vomiting or the desire to vomit

sick-out (síkaut) n. job action in which employees call in sick, esp. where a strike is not feasible

sick·room (síkru:m, síkrum) n. the room in which someone who is sick is being looked after

sid·dur (si:dú:r, sídər) pl. **sid·du·rim** (si:duri:m), **sid·durs** n. the Jewish daily prayer book, containing both Hebrew and Aramaic prayers [Heb. siddūr, order, arrangement]

side (said) 1. n. any one of the flat or relatively flat surfaces of an object, a cube has six sides ‖ one of the vertical or relatively vertical surfaces of an object as distinguished from the top or bottom, the side of a hill, the side of a box ‖ such a surface, but also excluding front and back, the side of a house ‖ one of the two surfaces of something flat and thin, write on both sides of the paper ‖ (math.) one of the lines bounding a figure ‖ the right or left part of a person's body, esp. between armpit and hip ‖ the right or left part of an animal's body, esp. between foreleg and hindleg as cut for meat, a side of bacon ‖ one of the two halves of an object, place or space or one of the two directions to the right and left of a real line or a line in the mind of the observer, the right side of the road, the debit side of an account book ‖ a part of an object, place or space away from the central part, the sides of the room ‖ a space or direction in a certain relation to a person or thing, arrows came at him from all sides ‖ an aspect or view that is not complete, or that differs from other aspects, he has many sides to his character ‖ one of the contrasting aspects of something as it affects a person, keep your side of the bargain ‖ one of two teams or sets of opponents in sport, war politics etc. ‖ a position nearer than, or beyond, some dividing line, stay on this side of the hedge ‖ a line of descent traced through one parent, a cousin on his father's side ‖ (billiards) the spin imparted to a ball by striking it on the side ‖ (Br., pop.) conceit or snobbishness **on the side** as a secondary occupation ‖ in addition to the main course of a meal **side by side** close together, esp. for mutual support **to take sides** to support one of the sides in a dispute 2. adj. of, on, by, from or towards a side, side wind ‖ subordinate, side road, side issue ‖ indirect, oblique, a side glance 3. v. pres. part. **sid·ing** past and past part. **sid·ed** v.t. to furnish with sides v.i. (with 'with' or 'against') to give sympathy to or support one party in a dispute [O.E. sīde, the long part or view of something]

side arm a weapon (e.g. sword, pistol or bayonet) worn at the side

side·board (sáidbɔrd, sáidbourd) n. a piece of furniture, with cupboards and drawers, placed against the wall of a dining room or living room, and used to store dishes etc. or to put them on when meals are being served

side·burns (sáidbə:rnz) pl. n. the short hair growing on a man's face in front of the ears when the beard is shaved off [after Gen. A. E. Burnside (d. 1881), U.S. general]

side·car (sáidkɑr) n. a small one-wheeled car for a passenger, attached to the side of a motorcycle ‖ an iced cocktail consisting of a mixture of orange-flavored liqueur, brandy and lemon juice

side dish an extra dish at a meal, subsidiary to the main dish

side-dress (sáiddres) v.i. to apply fertilizer to plants by working it into the soil along one side of each row ‖ v.t. to apply fertilizer (to plants etc.) in this way (cf. TOP-DRESS) **side-dress·ing** n. the fertilizer so used

side drum a snare drum

side·head (sáidhed) n. a subheading placed to the side of the text, usually to the left of the first line of a paragraph

side·kick (sáidkik) n. (pop.) someone who associates with another as a partner, assistant or companion, esp. as a subordinate

side·light (sáidlait) n. a small lamp on the side of a ship or vehicle ‖ an anecdote or piece of information which indirectly reveals the nature of someone or something ‖ light from a side ‖ a window or opening at the side of a wall, door etc.

side·line (sáidlain) n. a kind of goods sold in addition to one's regular and more important stock ‖ a job done in addition to one's regular occupation ‖ (sports) a line marking the boundary at the side of a football field, tennis court etc. ‖ (pl., sports) the space along the outside of the lines at the side of an athletic field ‖ (pl.) the point of view of those not actually participating, from the sidelines it looked like a complete accident

side·long (sáidlɔŋ, sáidlɒŋ) 1. adv. obliquely, to glance sidelong 2. adj. oblique, directed sideways, a sidelong glance

side-look·ing airborne radar (sáidlukiŋ) (mil.) airborne radar with reception from right and left, used to map a territory from its perimeter at altitudes up to 70,000 ft. (acronym SLAR)

side·piece (sáidpi:s) n. a piece forming the side of something

si·de·re·al (saidíəri:əl) adj. of or relating to the fixed stars or constellations, esp. as they are used in measures of time [fr. L. sidereus]

sidereal day the interval between successive transits of the March equinox over the upper meridian of a place: it is equal to 23 hours 56 minutes 4.09 seconds of mean solar time

sidereal time time based on the sidereal day consisting of 24 sidereal hours

sidereal year the period during which the earth makes a complete revolution in its orbit around the sun, with respect to the fixed stars: it is equal to 365 days 6 hours 9 minutes 9.54 seconds of mean solar time

sid·er·ite (sídərait) n. native ferrous carbonate, $FeCO_3$, a valuable ore of iron ‖ a meteorite largely consisting of iron **sid·er·it·ic** (sidərítik) adj. [F. sidérite or fr. siderites fr. Gk]

sid·er·o·lite (sídərəlait) n. a meteorite containing large proportions of metal and stone [fr. Gk sídēros, iron +lithos, stone]

sid·er·o·sis (sidəróusis) pl. **sid·er·o·ses** (sidəróusi:z) n. pneumoconiosis peculiar to iron workers resulting from the breathing in of iron particles ‖ iron pigment deposits in a tissue [Gk sídēros, iron]

side·sad·dle (sáidsæd'l) 1. n. a saddle for a woman on which she sits with both legs on one side of the horse 2. adv. mounted thus, to ride sidesaddle

side·show (sáidʃou) n. a small show or entertainment as part of a larger one ‖ an event or activity of less importance than the principal one

side·slip (sáidslip) 1. n. a slip sideways, e.g. in a car or on skis ‖ (aeron.) a slip sideways, and broadside on, in a downward direction, usually caused by low air speed in a turn 2. v.i. pres. part. **side·slip·ping** past and past part. **side·slipped** to make a sideslip

sides·man (sáidzmən) pl. **sides·men** (sáidzmən) n. an Anglican Church officer who shows members of the congregation to their seats, takes up the collection etc.

side·split·ting (sáidsplitiŋ) adj. hilariously funny

side·step (sáidstep) pres. part. **side·step·ping** past and past part. **side·stepped** v.t. to avoid by stepping sideways ‖ to be evasive about (an issue)

side·stroke (sáidstrouk) n. a stroke made when swimming on one's side, both arms moving in alternate forward and backward strokes and the legs moving in a scissors kick. The sidestroke is esp. useful for long distances

side·swipe (sáidswaip) **1.** v.t. pres. part. **side·swip·ing** past and past part. **side·swiped** to strike with a glancing blow along the side **2.** n. a sideswiping or an instance of this ‖ (pop.) an oblique scathing remark

side·track (sáidtræk) **1.** n. a siding **2.** v.t. to shunt into siding ‖ to lead (someone) away from the proper subject ‖ to prevent action on (a matter) by diversionary tactics

side·walk (sáidwɔk) n. a hard-surfaced pedestrian way along the side of a street

sidewalk artist (Am.= Br. pavement artist) a person who chalks pictures on the sidewalk in the hope that passers-by will give him money

side·ward (sáidwərd) adv. and adj. toward one side **side·wards** adv. sideward

side·way (sáidwei) **1.** adv. and adj. sideways **2.** n. a byway

side·ways (sáidweiz) **1.** adv. to the side, look sideways ‖ from the side, viewed sideways ‖ on the side, with the side first, carry it in sideways **2.** adj. to one side, a sideways look

side·whisk·ers (sáidhwiskərs, sáidwiskərs) pl. n. long whiskers on the side of the face

Side·wind·er (sáidwáindər) n. (mil.) solid-propellant, air-to-air missile (AIM-9) with nonnuclear warhead, and infrared, heat-seeking homing with speed of Mach 2

side·wise (sáidwaiz) adv. and adj. sideways

Si·di-bel-Ab·bès (sí:di:beləbés) an agricultural market (pop. 151,148) of N.W. Algeria: cereals, vines, fruit, vegetables

sid·ing (sáidiŋ) n. a short railroad track beside and connected with the main line, used for shunting, loading and unloading goods, laying up rolling stock etc. ‖ (collect.) boards forming the exposed surface of the outside walls of a frame building

si·dle (sáid'l) **1.** v.i. pres. part. **si·dling** past and past part. **si·dled** to go forward with a sideways motion, the fox sidled over the field ‖ (with 'up to', 'over to' etc.) to make a rather furtive approach **2.** n. the act or movement of sidling [back-formation fr. obs. sideling adv., sidelong]

Sid·mouth (sídməθ), Henry Addington, 1st Viscount (1757-1844), British Tory statesman, prime minister (1801-4). As home secretary (1812-21), he was responsible for much repressive legislation (1817-19)

Sid·ney (sídni:), Sir Philip (1554-86), English poet, critic, courtier and soldier. His works, published posthumously, include the pastoral prose romance 'Arcadia' (1590 and 1593), the sonnet sequence 'Astrophel and Stella' (1591) and a defense of poetry against utilitarian philistinism, 'The Defence of Poesie' (1595). He is often considered as the ideal Renaissance man

Sid·ney, Syd·ney, Algernon (1622-83), English statesman. A republican, he was one of the leaders of the Whig opposition, and was executed for alleged complicity in the Rye House Plot

Si·don (sáid'n) an ancient seaport (modern Saida, Lebanon, pop. 50,000) in Phoenicia, which flourished in the 2nd millennium B.C. as a center for Phoenician trade and colonization

SIDS n. (med. abbr.) for sudden infant death syndrome (which see)

siege (si:dʒ) n. the isolating of a fortified place by an attacking force in order to make it surrender ‖ a long, persistent attempt to force or persuade someone to do something ‖ a long, exhausting experience or period, esp. of ill health **to lay siege to** to begin the siege of **to raise a siege** to abandon a siege [O.F.]

Sieg·fried (sí:gfri:d, zí:kfri:t) a hero of Germanic legend, esp. of the 'Nibelungenlied'

sie·mens (sí:mənz) n. unit of conductance equal to 1 ampere per volt; named for Ernst Werner von Siemens, German electrical engineer

Sie·mens (sí:mənz, zí:mɑns), Ernst Werner von (1816-92), German electrical engineer and inventor. He invented an electroplating process (c. 1841) and the self-excited electric dynamo. With his brother, Sir William Siemens (1823-83), he was responsible for a process of steelmaking (1866), which, with some adaptation, became the open-hearth process

Si·e·na (si:énə, sjénɑ) a walled city (pop. 61,888) of central Tuscany, Italy. Its shell-shaped piazza is dominated by the tower of the Gothic town hall (1297-1310). Romanesque-Gothic marble cathedral (mainly 12th-14th cc.), art museums. University (1300). Siena was a rich independent republic from the 12th c. until it was captured (1555) by Emperor Charles V

Si·en·ese (sí:əni:z, sí:əni:s) **1.** adj. of or pertaining to Siena or the people who live there **2.** pl. **Si·en·ese** n. an inhabitant of Siena

si·en·na (si:énə) n. earth, consisting of clay colored by iron and manganese, used as pigment (*BURNT SIENNA, *RAW SIENNA) [Ital. (terra di) Siena, (earth of) Siena]

si·er·ra (si:érə) n. a mountain chain with sharp peaks, esp. in Spain and the Americas [Span.]

Si·er·ra de Gua·dar·ra·ma (sjérrɑðegwaðarráma) a mountain range in central Spain between Old and New Castile. Summit: Peñalara (7,900 ft)

Si·er·ra Le·o·ne (si:éroli:óuni:, si:érəli:óun) a republic (area 27,925 sq. miles, pop. 3,474,000), and member of the British Commonwealth, in W. Africa. Capital: Freetown. People: 26% Mende, 22% Temne, with Creole (descended from freed slaves) and Syrian-Lebanese minorities. Language: English (official), Krio, Mandingo, Mende, other local African languages. Religion: mainly local African, 20% Moslem, 4% Christian. The coastal plain is mainly deforested and cultivated, with mangrove swamps along the coast. The Sierra Leone peninsula, on the northern coast, rises to 2,912 ft and the northeastern plateau (mainly 1,000–3,000 ft) to 6,390 ft (Loma Mtns). Several navigable rivers flow southwest from the plateau to deep estuaries on the Gulf of Guinea. Average temperatures (F.): 75°-85° on the coast, 69°-95° inland. Rainfall: Freetown 150 ins, northeast 80 ins. Livestock: cattle, goats, sheep, poultry. Agricultural products: palm kernels and oil, piassava, rice and other cereals, cocoa, coffee, peanuts, ginger, kola nuts, cassava, coconuts, manioc, sweet potatoes. Mineral resources: diamonds, iron ore, bauxite, rutile. Manufactures and industries: fishing (esp. tuna), palm oil, rice milling, lumber, furniture, weaving. Exports: diamonds, iron ore, palm kernels, coffee, cocoa, piassava. Imports: cotton fabrics, oil, clothing and footwear, foodstuffs, vehicles, machinery, synthetic fibers, chemicals. University: University Colleges of Sierra Leone (1959) and of Njala (1964). Monetary unit: leone (100 cents). HISTORY. The area was inhabited by the Temne and other African peoples when the Portuguese explored the coast (c. 1462). The English raided it for slaves (16th c.), but a British abolitionist society founded Freetown (1787) as a settlement for freed American slaves. This became a British colony (1808) and the surrounding region became a British protectorate (1896). It gained independence within the Commonwealth (Apr. 27, 1961) and joined the U.N. (1961). Successful army coups d'état were mounted (1967 and 1968); the country's prime minister Siaka Stevens, although named premier in 1967, did not assume office until after the coups. Stevens became the country's first president (1971-85)

Sier·ra Ma·dre (sjérrɑmáðre) the principal mountain system of Mexico, running the length of the country. It comprises the Eastern Range (Orizaba, 18,700 ft) and the Western Range (over 10,000 ft in the south) enclosing the central plateau, and the Southern Range running along the southwestern coast (*ROCKY MTNS)

Sier·ra Ma·es·tra (sjérrɑmaéstrɑ) a mountain range in E. Cuba, containing the highest point in Cuba: Pico Turquino (6,500 ft)

Sier·ra Mén·dez (sjérrɑméndes), Justo (1848-1912), Mexican romantic poet, author of 'Playeras', 'A Dios', and 'El funeral bucólico'. He is also known for his work in education

Sier·ra Mo·re·na (sjérrɑmorénɑ) a mountain range (summit 4,305 ft) in S.W. Spain between the Guadalquivir and Guadiana Rivers, separating Andalusia from central Spain. Chief pass: Despeñaperros

Sier·ra Ne·va·da (sjérrɑnevɑ́ðɑ) a snow-capped massif (60 miles long) of S.E. Andalusia, Spain, near Granada (Mulhacén, 11,420 ft)

Sier·ra Ne·vad·a (si:éronevǽdɑ, si:érənevɑ́dɑ) a mountain range of E. California. Summit: Mt Whitney (14,495 ft). Chief pass: Donner (7,017 ft), linking San Francisco with Reno, Nevada

Sier·ra Ne·va·da de San·ta Mar·ta (sjérrɑnevɑ́ðɑðesɑ́ntamɑ́rta) a mountain range rising to 19,030 ft on the Caribbean coast in N. Colombia

si·es·ta (si:éstə) n. a short rest taken in the hottest part of the day, esp. by Latin peoples [Span.]

sieve (siv) **1.** n. a utensil with a fine wire-mesh bottom used for straining substances, for reducing substances to a finer consistency or for separating finer from coarser particles **2.** v.t. pres. part. **siev·ing** past and past part. **sieved** to put through a sieve ‖ to screen (candidates) [O.E. sife]

sieve cell (bot.) an elongate, tapering, thinwalled cell with a protoplast but without a nucleus when mature, and with areas of its walls closely perforated with minute openings. It is characteristic of the phloem and is variously modified to serve in sieve tubes and for storage and support

sieve tube a phloem vessel consisting of sugarconducting sieve cells in vascular plants, sometimes associated with companion cells achieving protoplasmic continuity by sievelike perforated end walls

Sie·yès (sjejes), Emmanuel Joseph (1748-1836), French statesman. He emerged as a leader of the third estate with his pamphlet 'Qu'est-ce que le tiers état?' (1789). He was a member of the Directory and of the Consulate

sift (sift) v.t. (often with 'out') to separate or strain the finer from the coarser particles of (a material) by passing through a sieve, sifter or riddle ‖ to sprinkle through a sifter or other perforated utensil, to sift sugar onto a cake ‖ to examine and evaluate, to sift evidence ‖ v.i. to fall, or pass, as if through a sieve, the sunlight sifted through the curtains ‖ to use a sieve, sifter etc. **sift·er** n. a small cylindrical container with a fine wire mesh bottom through which flour, sugar etc. is passed to separate the finer particles from the coarser or to reduce the substance to a finer texture [O.E. siftan, syftan]

sig·a·to·ka (sigətóukə) n. a disease of bananas, caused by Cercospora musae, a sooty mold

Si·ge·bert I (sígəbərt) (c. 535-75), king of Austrasia (561-75), son of Clotaire I. He overran Neustria, but was murdered by Fredegund

sigh (sai) **1.** v.i. to expel a deep audible breath, expressing relief, contentment, or sadness, weariness, resignation etc. (rhet., with 'for') to think with regret of the loss or passing of something, to sigh for the days of one's youth ‖ to make a sound like sighing, the wind sighed in the trees ‖ v.t. to utter with a sigh or sighs **2.** n. a sighing ‖ the sound made in sighing [M.E. sihen, sighen]

sight (sait) **1.** n. the power of seeing ‖ the act of seeing ‖ a way of considering something in one's mind, he can do no wrong in her sight ‖ range of vision, within sight ‖ something seen or visible, a beautiful sight ‖ (pl.) something worth seeing, e.g. famous buildings, monuments etc., the sights of London ‖ a display, poppies make a fine sight ‖ something odd, absurd or ugly to look at, what a sight you look in those slacks! ‖ (pop.) a great deal, you're a sight better off as you are ‖ a device for guiding the eye when aiming a gun or directing a quadrant etc. ‖ aim, take careful sight ‖ observation with an instrument, to take a sight **at first sight** when first seen, before being examined closely **at (or on) sight** as soon as seen, to shoot on sight **at (or from) sight** (mus.) without previous study of the music **to catch sight of** to get (someone or something) suddenly within one's vision **to get sight of** to manage to see **to know by sight** to know (someone) by appearance only, not to talk to **to lose sight of** to cease to see **2.** v.t. to see, get a sight of, esp. by approaching, to sight land ‖ to observe with the aid of sights, to sight a star ‖ to provide with sights ‖ to adjust the sights of ‖ to aim by means of sights ‖ v.i. to take aim or an observation through a sight [O.E. sihth fr. sih-, stem of séon, to see]

sight draft a draft ordering payment on presentation

sight·less (sáitlis) adj. not having vision

sight·li·ness (sáitli:nis) n. the state or condition of being sightly

sight·ly (sáitli:) comp. **sight·li·er** superl. **sight·li·est** adj. of pleasing appearance

sight·read·ing (sáitri:d) pres. part. **sight-read·ing** past and past part **sight-read** (sáitred) v.t. to read (music, a passage for translation, etc.) without preparation ‖ v.i. to read music etc. in this way

sight·see·ing (sáitsi:iŋ) *n.* the act of going around looking at places of interest, famous buildings etc. **sight·se·er** (sáitsi:ər) *n.*

sight translation (*Am.=Br.* unseen) a passage, not previously seen, set for translation

sight unseen without previous inspection, *to buy something sight unseen*

sig·il·late (sídʒəleit, sídʒəlit) *adj.* (of pottery) with impressed patterns ‖ (*bot.*, of certain rhizomes and roots) having marks like those made with a seal or signet [fr. L.L. *sigillatus* fr. *sigillum*, seal, signet]

Sig·is·mund (sígismund) (1368-1437), Holy Roman Emperor and German king (1411-37), king of Hungary (1387-1437) and of Bohemia (1420-37), son of Charles IV. Having summoned the Council of Constance in an effort to end the Great Schism, he was responsible for the burning (1415) of Hus

Sigismund I (1467-1548), king of Poland (1506-48). His reign saw the development of the Renaissance in Poland

Sigismund II (1520-72), king of Poland (1548-72), son of Sigismund I. He transformed (1569) the personal union of Poland and Lithuania into a political union and was the last of the Jagiello dynasty to rule in Poland. His reign saw the spread of the Reformation in Poland

Sigismund III (1566-1632), king of Poland (1587-1632) and of Sweden (1592-9). Deposed from his Swedish throne on account of his refusal to tolerate Protestantism, he began a series of wars between Poland and Sweden (1621-9). He took advantage of Russia's weakness after the death of Boris Godunov, and invaded Moscow (1610-12)

sig·ma (sígmə) *n.* the eighteenth letter (Σ, σ, s = s) of the Greek alphabet **sig·mate** (sígmit, sígmeit) *adj.* curved like an S [L., Gk]

sigma factor (*genetics*) regulator of RNA polymerase *also* sigma protein *Cf* REPLICASE

sigma particle (*nuclear phys.*) a short-lived (10⁻¹⁰ sec) hyperon triplet with a rest mass of 1,189.5 MEV, an isotopic spin of 1, and a lifetime of 8.1 × 10⁻¹¹ sec —**sigmic** *adj.*

sig·ma·tron (sígmətron) *n.* (*phys.*) a cyclotron and a betatron operating in tandem, producing billion-volt rays

sig·moid (sígmɔid) *adj.* curved like a C ‖ **sigmate** ‖ of or relating to the sigmoid flexure of the large intestine [fr. Gk *sigmoeidēs*]

sigmoid flexure the part of the large intestine between the colon and the rectum ‖ (*zool.*) an S-shaped double curve such as characterizes e.g. the neck of some birds

sign (sain) *v.t.* to mark with a sign, esp. with one's name ‖ to accept as legally binding by doing this, *to sign an agreement* ‖ to write (one's name) ‖ to mark with the sign of the cross, e.g. in blessing or consecrating ‖ (often with 'up' or 'on') to engage (esp. an athlete) by written agreement ‖ to intimate (something) by gestures ‖ *v.i.* to write one's name **to sign away** (or **over**) to sign a written agreement to convey ownership (of something) to another **to sign off** (of a radio or television station) to stop broadcasting after making station identification **to sign on** to accept employment, esp. as a regular soldier ‖ to engage as an employee **to sign up** to enlist in some organization, esp. in military service ‖ to agree to some obligation by signing, e.g. a contract ‖ to cause (someone) to accept a commitment by getting his signature, e.g. to a contract [fr. F. *signer* or L. *signare*]

sign 1. *n.* a mark or gesture which conveys an idea or meaning, *plus and minus signs, deaf-mutes converse by signs, he nodded as a sign of agreement* ‖ something having symbolic character, *an outward and visible sign of an inward and spiritual grace* ‖ a mark or gesture adopted as a method of recognition ‖ (*med.*) an indication of a disease that is noted and interpreted by a doctor (cf. SYMPTOM) ‖ indication or evidence, *she saw no sign that he would change his mind* ‖ trace, vestige, *no sign of life anywhere* ‖ (*rhet.*) portent, *signs from heaven* ‖ a notice or device advertising, admonishing, identifying etc. ‖ a board, placard etc. bearing such a notice or device ‖ one of the divisions of the zodiac ‖ (*pl.* **sign**) the tracks of a wild animal or animals, *deer sign* [F. *signe*]

sig·nal (sígnəl) **1.** *n.* a usually prearranged or generally recognizable sign giving information, *distress signal*, or an order, *the signal to attack*

2. *v. pres. part.* **sig·nal·ing**, esp. *Br.* **sig·nal·ling** *past* and *past part.* **sig·naled**, esp. *Br.* **sig·nalled** *v.t.* to order by signal, *he signaled the advance* ‖ to order (someone) by signal to do something, *he signaled them to advance* ‖ to give information of by using a sign, *to signal the surrender* ‖ *v.i.* to make a signal or signals ‖ (esp. *mil.*) to send a signal [F.]

signal *adj.* remarkable, noteworthy [fr. L. *signum*, sign, after F. *signalé*]

signal box (*Br.*) a signal tower

sig·nal·er, esp. *Br.* **sig·nal·ler** (sígnələr) *n.* someone who signals ‖ (*mil.*) someone responsible for communications in the field

sig·nal·ize (sígnəlaiz) *pres. part.* **sig·nal·iz·ing** *past* and *past part.* **sig·nal·ized** *v.t.* to treat as noteworthy or memorable, mark specially ‖ to point out

sig·nal·ler *SIGNALER

sig·nal·ly (sígnəli:) *adv.* notably, to a remarkable degree or in a remarkable way

sig·nal·man (sígnəlmən) *pl.* **sig·nal·men** (sígnəlmən) *n.* a man who operates railroad signals ‖ a military signaler

signal tower (*Am.=Br.* signal box) a building for men operating railroad signals

sig·na·to·ry (sígnətɔri, sígnətɔuri:) **1.** *adj.* signing or having signed a document, *the signatory powers* **2.** *pl.* **sig·na·to·ries** *n.* a party signing a document, esp. a state which has signed a treaty [fr. L. *signatorius*, to do with sealing]

sig·na·ture (sígnətʃər) *n.* a person's name written by himself in signing a letter or document ‖ the act of signing one's name ‖ (*mus.*) the sign used to denote key or rhythm, placed to the right of the clef ‖ (*bookbinding*) a letter or number at the foot of the first page on an unfolded sheet of printed pages, used as a guide in folding, assembling and binding such a sheet ‖ the portion of a medical prescription instructing the patient how to take the prescribed medicine ‖ a signature tune [F. or fr. M.L. *signatura*]

signature tune a special, easily recognizable tune used by a performer or group of performers, or to identify a radio program etc.

sign·board (sáinbɔrd, sáinbɔurd) *n.* a board on which is printed an advertisement, directions, the name of an inn, an announcement etc.

sig·net (sígnit) *n.* a personal seal used to show the authenticity of documents, often in addition to the signature ‖ (*Br.*) a royal seal formerly used to authenticate letters patent, grants etc. ‖ the mark or impression made by a signet [O.F. or fr. M.L. *signetum*]

signet ring a finger ring set or engraved with the monogram, sign or initials of the owner, formerly used as a seal

sig·nif·i·cance (signífikəns) *n.* real or inner meaning, *the significance of your remark escaped me for the moment* ‖ importance, *a matter of no significance* [O.F. or fr. L. *significantia*]

sig·nif·i·cant (signífikənt) *adj.* having or conveying a meaning, *a word is a significant grouping of sounds* ‖ important and influential, *a significant contribution to knowledge* ‖ marked, *he placed significant emphasis on the word* ‖ expressive, heavy with implication, *a significant look* ‖ suggesting some specific cause, not due merely to chance, *a significant increase in population* [fr. L. *significans* (*significantis*) fr. *significare*, to signify]

significant figures the figures of a number, which are considered to give correct or sufficient information on its accuracy, that are read from the first non-zero digit on the left to the last non-zero digit on the right, unless a final zero expresses greater known accuracy

sig·ni·fi·ca·tion (signifikéiʃən) *n.* meaning or sense ‖ the act of signifying [O. F. or fr. L. *significatio* (*significationis*)]

sig·nif·i·ca·tive (signífikeitiv) *adj.* offering evidence, indicative, *significative of approval* having sense or meaning [O.F. fr. L.L. *significativus*]

sig·ni·fy (sígnifai) *pres. part.* **sig·ni·fy·ing** *past* and *past part.* **sig·ni·fied** *v.t.* to make known, communicate by some sign, *to signify assent* ‖ to be a sign of, indicate, *a nod signifies agreement* ‖ *v.i.* to be significant, have meaning [fr. F. *signifier*]

sign language a system of communication by gestures, e.g. that used by deaf and dumb people

sign manual *pl.* **signs manual** a personal signature, esp. the royal signature on grants, letters patent etc.

sign of the cross a sacramental movement of the hand outlining a cross to recall that of Christ, used in blessing, prayer or worship

sign on *v.* (*broadcasting*) to announce the beginning of the day's programming —**sign-on** *n.* the announcement

si·gnor (sí:njɔr, *Ital.* si:njɔ́r) *pl.* **signors**, *Ital.* **si·gno·ri** (si:njɔ́ri:) *n.* a courtesy title for an Italian man (the equivalent of 'Mr') and term of address (without the surname) [Ital., reduced form of *signore*, sir]

si·gno·ra (si:njɔ́rə, *Ital.* si:njɔ́rɑ) *pl.* **si·gno·ras**, *Ital.* **si·gno·re** (si:njɔ́re) *n.* a courtesy title for an Italian married woman (the equivalent of 'Mrs') and term of address (without the surname) [*Ital.*, fem. of *signore*, sir]

Si·gno·rel·li (si:njɔrélli:), Luca (c. 1450-1523), early Italian Renaissance painter, esp. noted for his fresco painting on a vast scale (Orvieto cathedral)

si·gno·ri·na (si:njɔrí:nə, *Ital.* si:njɔrí:nɑ) *pl.* **si·gno·ri·nas**, *Ital.* **si·gno·ri·ne** (si:njɔrí:ne) *n.* a courtesy title for an unmarried Italian girl or woman (the equivalent of 'Miss') and term of address (without the surname) [*Ital.*, dim. of *signora*]

sign·post (sáinpoust) *n.* a post at a crossroad or junction, with arms showing directions and sometimes distances to places

sign·writ·er (sáinraitər) *n.* a person who letters display signs for storekeepers, advertisers etc.

Sigs·bee (sígzbi:), Charles Dwight (1845-1923), U.S. admiral who commanded (1897-8) the 'Maine' at the time of her destruction in Havana harbor prior to the Spanish-American War

Si·ha·nouk (sí:ənuk), Prince Norodom (1922-), Cambodian statesman. He was king (1941-55), then prime minister (1955-60), and became (1960) chief of state. He was overthrown (Mar. 1970) by a right-wing coup d'état and set up, in Peking, a Government of National Union. He served again as nominal head of state (1975-6) then resigned and disappeared from public view until 1978, where he reappeared in China. He supported the Pol Pot regime against the Vietnamese invasion of Cambodia (1978) and appealed unsuccessfully to the U.N. Security Council for a halt to the invasion (1979)

Si·ha·nouk·ville (sí:ənukvil) *KOMPONG SOM

Si·kang (ʃí:kɑ́ŋ) a former province (1914-55) of S.W. China, partitioned (1955) between Szechwan and Tibet

Sikh (si:k) **1.** *n.* a member of the religion founded in the 16th c. by Nanak, a Punjabi Hindu strongly influenced by Islam. There are about eight million Sikhs in India and Pakistan. In the 17th c. the Sikhs were persecuted, and from this time springs the martial discipline which is still characteristic of them. Their sacred book, the Granth Sāhib, was compiled by Gobind Singh (1675–1708). Sikhs owe their monotheism to Islam, but hold such basic Hindu doctrines as karma and reincarnation **2.** *adj.* relating to the Sikhs or their religion **Sikh·ism** *n.*

Sikh War either of two wars in India between the Sikhs and the British. After the first (1845-6) the Sikhs were forced to cede Kashmir and pay an indemnity. After the second (1848-9), Britain annexed the Punjab

Si·kiang (ʃí:kjɑ́ŋ) (or Si) the longest river (1,200 miles) and major waterway of S. China. It rises in Yunnan as two streams which join in Kwansi-chuang, and flows across Kwangtung to the Yellow Sea. Its delta, around Kwangchow, is formed by three rivers (the Si, the Pei and the Tung) and is one of China's most densely populated regions

Sik·kim (sikim) a former principality and Indian protectorate, now a state of India (area 2,818 sq. miles, pop. 314,999) in the Himalayas. Capital: Gangtok (pop. 36,768). People: Nepalese (75%), Bhutia, Lepcha. Languages: Nepali, Lepcha. Religion: 30% Lamaist, 60% Hindu, small Jain, Sikh and Christian minorities. Elevation: 700 ft (southern border) to 28,146 ft (Kanchenjunga). The northern mountains are cut by deep river valleys. Intense cultivation up to 6,500 ft gives way to forest (9,000–12,000 ft) and permanent snow (15,000 ft). Strategic trade routes to Tibet cross at 13,000–15,000 ft. Rainfall: Gangtok 137 ins. Livestock: cattle, yak, sheep, goats. Agricultural products: rice and other cereals, cardamom, oranges, apples, lumber, pineapples, vegetables. Minerals: copper, graphite, gypsum, iron ore, gold, silver. Industries: foodstuffs, weaving, copper ware,

---

CONCISE PRONUNCIATION KEY: **(a)** æ, c*a*t; ɑ, c*a*r; ɔ f*aw*n; ei, sn*a*ke. **(e)** e, h*e*n; i:, sh*ee*p; iə, d*ee*r; εə, b*ea*r. **(i)** i, f*i*sh; ai, t*i*ger; ə:, b*i*rd. **(o)** o, *o*x; au, c*ow*; ou, g*oa*t; u, p*oo*r; ɔi, r*oy*al. **(u)** ʌ, d*u*ck; u, b*u*ll; u:, g*oo*se; ə, b*a*cill*u*s; ju:, c*u*be. x, lo*ch*; θ, *th*ink; ð, bo*th*er; z, *Z*en; ʒ, cor*s*age; dʒ, sava*g*e; ŋ, oranguta*ng*; j, *y*ak; ʃ, *f*ish; tʃ, fe*tch*; 'l, rabb*le*; 'n, redd*en*. Complete pronunciation key appears inside front cover.

wooden goods. Exports: cardamom, oranges, apples, potatoes. Imports (from India): cotton goods, foodstuffs. Monetary unit: Indian rupee. HISTORY. Sikkim was established (1641) as a principality by a Tibetan family. British interest in the area dates from the early 19th c. A British protectorate over it was recognized (1890) by China and lasted until 1947, when Sikkim became independent. It signed a treaty (1950) giving India control of the country's defense, foreign relations and communications; India's role was extended after India's border war with China (1962) and strengthened (1974) after elections in Sikkim diminished the power of the Chogyal (ruler). Sikkim merged with India (1975) and became a state

Si·king (ʃiːdʒín) *SIAN

Si·kor·ski (sikórski:), Wladyslaw (1881-1943), Polish general and statesman. He was prime minister (1922-3) and war minister (1924-5), and was head of the exiled Polish government (1939-43) organizing Polish forces in the 2nd world war

si·lage (sáilidʒ) *n.* green fodder packed in a silo without drying and fermented by anaerobic lactic-acid bacteria often assisted by the addition of molasses, to preserve it for winter use [ENSILAGE]

si·lence (sáiləns) **1.** *n.* a not speaking or making any noise ‖ an abstaining from replying to a speech or letter, *his silence indicates disapproval* ‖ taciturnity ‖ a not betraying of some confidence, *can I rely on your silence?* ‖ deliberate or accidental failure to mention something ‖ stillness, quiet, *he can't work unless he has silence* ‖ (*rhet.*) oblivion **2.** *v.t. pres. part.* **si·lenc·ing** *past* and *past part.* **si·lenced** to cause to be quiet ‖ to quiet (fears, doubts, anxieties etc.) ‖ to compel to stop expressing an opinion ‖ to knock out (enemy guns) **si·lenc·er** *n.* (*Br.*) a muffler in the exhaust pipe of an engine ‖ a device for muffling the noise of a gun [O.F.]

si·lent (sáilənt) *adv.* making no sound, *a silent spectator* ‖ free from sound, *a silent house* ‖ not accompanied by audible speech or sound, *a silent prayer* ‖ taciturn, speaking little ‖ so smooth in action as to make scarcely any sound, *a silent car* ‖ (of a letter or group of letters) written but not pronounced, e.g. 'b' in doubt ‖ uninformative, *history is silent about what followed* ‖ witholding information, *he was silent about what he had seen* ‖ (of a motion picture) without any sound track ‖ (of a volcano) inactive but not extinct [fr. L. *silens* (*silentis*) fr. *silere*, to be silent]

silent butler a small metal receptacle, with a handle and hinged lid, for clearing away crumbs from the table and the contents of ash trays

silent majority the portion of the public not strongly committed to either side of a (right-left) controversy; citizens whose political opinions are seldom heard

silent partner a financial partner with no voice in the management of a business

silent spring hypothetical time when plant, bird, and insect life are destroyed by industrial pollutants; from *The Silent Spring*, by Rachel Carson, 1962

Si·le·nus (sailíːnəs) (*Gk mythol.*) an old, bearded, woodland satyr attendant upon Dionysus

Si·le·sia (silíːʒə, silíːʃə, sailíːʒə, sailíːʃə) a region around the upper and middle Oder in S.W. Poland. Colonized by Germans in the Middle Ages, it came under the Bohemian crown in the 14th c. and under the Hapsburgs in 1526. In 1742, Frederick the Great of Prussia took the whole of it except for a small part which in 1918 became Czech (*MORAVIA-SILESIA). In 1921, after a plebiscite, a large part of the economically important coal-mining and industrial area of Upper Silesia in the southeast was ceded to Poland. The latter annexed the whole of German Silesia after the 2nd world war

sil·hou·ette (siluːét) **1.** *n.* a portrait in profile, showing the outline only, and filled in with black, or cut out of black paper ‖ a similar representation of the outlines of any object ‖ a person or object seen against the light, with this effect **2.** *v.t. pres. part.* **sil·hou·et·ting** *past* and *past part.* **sil·hou·et·ted** to represent in silhouette ‖ to cause to show up thus against a background, *the cathedral was silhouetted against the sunset* [after Etienne de Silhouette (1709–67), French finance minister (1759) under Louis XV (in whose reign the silhouette

became popular as a cheap kind of portrait), in satirical allusion to his extreme economy]

sil·i·ca (silikə) *n.* silicon dioxide, SiO₂, one of the commonest minerals, occurring as quartz, agate, jasper, flint etc., and abundant in sandstone and other rocks. In the form of quartz sand, it is a main constituent of glass **sil·i·cate** (silikit, silikeit) *n.* a metal salt of a very large class, usually insoluble, containing silicon and oxygen in the anion. They constitute with silica the largest portion of the earth's crust, and are the principal constituent of cement, glass, bricks and other building materials ‖ a salt or ester of a silicic acid [Mod. L. fr. *silex* (*silicis*), flint]

silica gel (*chem.*) highly absorbent silica dehumidifier and dehydrating agent, used as a powder insecticide

si·li·ceous (silíʃəs) *adj.* of, pertaining to, like or containing silica growing in or needing soil containing silica [fr. L. *siliceus*]

si·lic·ic acid (silísik) any of several weak acids formed as solution or as gel-like masses by dissolving alkaline silicates in acids or obtained as salts or esters

si·lic·i·fy (silísifai) *pres. part.* **si·lic·i·fy·ing** *past* and *past part.* **si·lic·i·fied** *v.t.* to impregnate with silica ‖ to turn into silica ‖ *v.i.* to become impregnated with or turned into silica

sil·i·cle (silik'l) *n.* (*bot.*) a short, flat silique [fr. F. *silicule* or L. *silicula*]

sil·i·con (silikan, silikən) *n.* a gray, brittle, tetravalent, nonmetallic element (symbol Si, at. no. 14, at. mass 28.086) occurring abundantly in nature, always in compounds. Next to oxygen it is the chief elementary constituent of the earth's crust. Silicon compounds are much used in industry (e.g. sand and glass making) and the element itself is used in the production of very hard alloys

silicon dioxide silica

sil·i·cone (silikoun) *n.* any of a large class of polymers of R₂SiO where R is a hydrocarbon. Silicones are used as lubricants, as heatresisting resins and varnishes, as waterresisting films etc.

sil·i·co·sis (silikóusis) *n.* a disease of the lungs caused by inhaling silica dust over a long period of time [SILICA]

si·lic·u·la (silíkjulə) *n.* (*bot.*) a silicle [L., dim. of *siliqua*, pod]

si·lic·u·lose (silíkjulous) *adj.* (*bot.*) having silicles ‖ resembling a silicle [fr. Mod L. *siliculosus*]

si·lique (silíːk, sílik) *n.* a long cylindrical dry, dehiscent fruit (two carpels) divided into two by a false septum, and containing the seeds. It is characteristic of the fam. *Cruciferae*, e.g. mustard [F.]

silk (silk) **1.** *n.* a very fine, soft, lustrous fiber spun by the silkworm (*Bombyx mori*) as its cocoon ‖ a thread or fabric made of this fiber ‖ a garment made of this fiber ‖ a fiber spun by some arachnids ‖ (*Br., pop.*) a silk barrister's gown worn by a King's (or Queen's) Counsel ‖ corn silk ‖ (*pl., horse racing*) the distinctively colored cap and jacket worn by a jockey **to take silk** (*Br.*) to become a King's or Queen's Counsel **2.** *adj.* of, made of, or like silk **3.** *v.i.* (of corn) to blossom or be on the verge of blossoming [O.E. *sioloc*]

silk cotton a silky fiber, esp. kapok, obtained from the seeds of a silk-cotton tree

silk-cotton tree a member of *Bombaceae*, a family of tropical trees which produce silk cotton. They have palmate leaves and large fruit containing seeds which yield oil when crushed

silk·en (silkən) *adj.* soft and lustrous, *silken skin* ‖ soft and delicate, *a silken touch* ‖ smooth, suave, *a silken voice* ‖ (*rhet.*) made of silk, *silken fabrics*

silk·i·ness (silki:nis) *n.* the state or quality of being silky

silk·ing (sílkiŋ) *n.* (*cosmetology*) technique of temporary hair straightening using pressing combs

silk-screen (sílkskriːn) **1.** *adj.* of or relating to the silk-screen process **2.** *v.t.* to reproduce or print by the silk-screen process **silk screen** the screen, esp. of silk or organdy, used in the silkscreen process

silk-screen process a stencil process in which coloring matter is forced through the meshes of a silk screen on which all the areas not to be printed have been blocked out by an impermeable substance

silk·worm (sílkwəːrm) *n.* the larva of any of various moths that spin cocoons of silk, esp. the larva of *Bombyx mori*, fam. *Bombycidae*. The female lays 300–500 eggs on the leaves of a mulberry, esp. *Morus alba*. The caterpillar feeds voraciously, molting several times. Then it spins its pupa case of silk thread, from which after three weeks it emerges as an adult moth. Silk thread from one cocoon may be from 400 to over 3,000 yards long

silk·y (sílki) *comp.* **silk·i·er** *superl.* **silk·i·est** *adj.* soft and glossy like silk

silky terrier a toy terrier with blue and tan silky coat, a cross bred from Yorkshire terrier and an Australian terrier

sill (sil) *n.* a ledge at the bottom of a window, outside or inside ‖ a stone or wooden threshold of a door ‖ (*geol.*) a layer of intrusive igneous rock [O.E. *syll*, *sylle*]

sillabub *SYLLABUB

sil·li·man·ite (síləmənait) *n.* an aluminum silicate, Al₂SiO₅, in orthorhombicrystals [after Benjamin *Silliman* (1779–1864), U.S. chemist]

sil·li·ness (sííːnis) *n.* the state or quality of being silly ‖ a silly act or series of such acts

Sil·li·toe (sílitou), Alan (1928-), British writer, one of the 'Angry Young Men' of the 1950s. His works, which exemplify the working class and show contempt for the middle class, include 'Saturday Night and Sunday Morning' (1958), 'The Loneliness of the Long-Distance Runner' (1959), 'This Foreign Field' (1970), 'The Widower's Son' (1977) and 'Her Victory' (1982)

Sills (silz), Beverly (1929-), U.S. soprano, born Belle Silverman. She made her opera debut in 1948 at the Philadelphia Civic Opera and joined the New York City Opera (1953), where she was made director upon her retirement from the stage (1980). She sang the heroine role in over 50 operas; one of her first and most well-known was Cleopatra in 'Julius Caesar'

sil·ly (síli:) *comp.* **sil·li·er** *superl.* **sil·li·est** **1.** *adj.* lacking or seeming to lack common sense (*pop.*, used post-positively) stunned, *to be knocked silly* **2.** *pl.* **sil·lies** *n.* (*pop.*) a foolish person [fr. older *seely*, lucky, happy, blessed]

silly point (*cricket*) a fielding position close to the batsman on the off side

si·lo (sáilou) **1.** *pl.* **si·los** *n.* a pit or tall cylindrical structure that can be made air-tight, used for making silage ‖ a tall cylindrical structure used for storing grain ‖ a subterranean shelter for guided missiles **2.** *v.t. pres. part.* **si·lo·ing** *past* and *past part.* **si·loed** to put or store in a silo [Span.]

Si·lo·ne (silóuni:, si:lóne), Ignazio (1900-78), Italian Socialist writer. He had a great influence on the realist writers of the 1930s. His best-known novels are 'Fontamara' (1933), 'Bread and Wine' (1936) and 'The Story of a Humble Christian' (1968)

silt (silt) **1.** *n.* mud, soil etc. deposited esp. by a river ‖ particles of minerals, soil etc. suspended in water, esp. in a river **2.** *v.t.* (with 'up') to block or choke with silt ‖ *v.i.* (with 'up') to become blocked or choked with silt [perh. of Scand. origin]

Sil·u·res (síljuri:z) *pl. n.* the ancient inhabitants of S.E. Wales conquered by the Romans, c. 80 A.D. **Si·lu·ri·an** (silúəri:ən, sailúəri:ən) *adj.* of the Silures or their territory ‖ (*geol.*) of the period or system of the Paleozoic era characterized by abundant marine invertebrates and coral reefs (*GEOLOGICAL TIME) **the Silurian** the Silurian period or system of rocks [L.]

Sil·va (síːlva), José Asunción (1865-96), Colombian poet and precursor of modernism and symbolism, known esp. for his 'Nocturnos'. He influenced Rubén Darío and others

silvan *SYLVAN

Silva Xavier, Joaquim José de *TIRADENTES

sil·ver (sílvər) **1.** *n.* a white, stable, malleable, ductile, usually monovalent (rarely bivalent) metallic element (symbol Ag, at. no. 47, at. mass 107.870) that occurs naturally in an uncombined or combined state. It is the best-known conductor of heat and electricity and is resistant to oxidation. It is used for electrical contacts, for lining certain chemical equipment and for backing mirrors, in electroplating, coinage, photography and in jewelry and silverware ‖ coins minted from this metal or from an alloy resembling this ‖ silverware ‖ a somewhat shiny whitish-gray color **2.** *adj.* made of silver ‖ like silver, esp. in color ‖ of soft, clear tones ‖ (of a jubilee, wedding or other anniversary) twenty-fifth **3.** *v.t.* to coat with silver, usually by electrolysis ‖ to give (a surface) the appearance of silver, e.g. by using an amalgam of tinfoil and mercury ‖ *v.i.* to take on the color of silver [O.E. *seolfor*]

silver age a period, esp. of literary history, thought of as inferior only to a preceding golden age

silver anniversary a 25th anniversary

silver birch *Betula alba*, a birch of cold and temperate Old World regions, with silvery or parchment-colored bark

sil·ver·fish (sílvərfiʃ) *pl.* **sil·ver·fish, sil·ver·fish·es** *n.* any of several members of *Thysanura*, an order of insects, esp. the small, silvery, primitive, wingless *Lepisma saccharina*, fam. *Lepismatidae*. They are omnivorous feeders and domestic pests ‖ any of various silver fish, e.g. the tarpon

silver fox a fox valued for its black white-tipped fur. It is the American red fox in one color phase, but it can be bred stable

silver gilt silver covered with a thin coating of gold ‖ a yellow-lacquered imitation of this

silver glance argentite

silver gray, silver grey *n.* a light, lustrous gray color **sil·ver-gráy, sil·ver-gréy** *adj.*

silver iodide a naturally occurring compound, AgI, which can also be synthetically produced, used in photography and medicine etc.

silver lining the ultimately hopeful aspect of a situation that causes gloom

silver maple *Acer saccharinum*, a maple of North America. Its leaves are light green above, silvery below ‖ the hard wood of this tree

silver nitrate a colorless, crystalline salt, AgNO₃, obtained by dissolving silver in nitric acid and evaporating. It is used in photography as a chemical reagent, in medicine as an antiseptic, and in marking inks

silver paper tinfoil ‖ a fine white tissue paper for wrapping silver

silver plate a thin coating of silver (*collect.*) articles having such a coating **sil·ver-pláte** *pres. part.* **sil·ver-plát·ing** *past and past part.* **sil·ver-plát·ed** *v.t.* to apply a thin coating of silver to, usually by electrolysis **sil·ver-plát·ed** *adj.*

sil·ver·point (sílvərpɔint) *n.* a process of drawing on prepared paper with a silver-tipped pencil ‖ a drawing made by this process

silver side (*Br.*) the upper and best part of a round of beef

sil·ver·smith (sílvərsmiθ) *n.* a craftsman who works silver

silver-tongued (sílvərtʌŋd) *adj.* (*rhet.*, of an orator) wonderfully eloquent

sil·ver·ware (sílvərwçər) *n.* tableware, esp. knives, forks and spoons, made of silver or silver plate

silver wedding the 25th anniversary of a wedding

sil·ver·y (sílvəri) *adj.* of or like silver ‖ soft and clear in tone ‖ coated with or containing silver

Silvester *SYLVESTER I

sil·vex [C₆H₇O₃Cl₃] (sílveks) *n.* (*chem.*) herbicide used esp. against weeds in turf, aquatic plantings, and food crops

sil·vi·chem·i·cal (sílvəkéməkəl) *n.* chemical derived from trees

sil·vi·cul·ture, syl·vi·cul·ture (sílvikʌltʃər) *n.* a branch of the science of forestry dealing with the development, cultivation and reproduction of forest trees [fr. L. *silva, sylva*, a wood + F. *culture*, cultivation]

si·ma·zine [C₇H₁₂N₅Cl] (sáiməziːn) *n.* (*chem.*) moderately toxic herbicide used esp. to control weeds in farming, esp. for corn, alfalfa, and fruit

Sim·birsk (sjimbjírsk) *ULYANOVSK

Sim·e·on (símiːən) Hebrew patriarch, son of Jacob ‖ the Israelite tribe of which he was the ancestor

Sim·fe·ro·pol (simfjirópəl) a city (pop. 314,000) of the Ukraine, U.S.S.R., in the Crimea. Industries: food processing, mechanical engineering. Tatar mosque (16th c.)

sim·i·an (símiːən) **1.** *adj.* like, or having the characteristics of, an ape or monkey **2.** *n.* an ape or monkey, esp. an anthropoid ape [fr. L. *simia*, ape]

sim·i·lar (símələr) *adj.* like, much the same, *the two rooms are of similar size* ‖ (*geom.*, of figures) having the same shape **sim·i·lar·i·ty** (síməlǽriːti) *pl.* **sim·i·lar·i·ties** *n.* the state of

being similar ‖ a point of resemblance [fr. F. *similaire* or M.L. *similaris*]

sim·i·le (síməli) *n.* a figure of speech in which one thing is likened to another in one respect by the use of 'like', 'as' etc., e.g. 'his explanation was as clear as crystal' (cf. METAPHOR) [L., neut. of *similis*, like]

si·mil·i·tude (similítuːd, similítjuːd) *n.* resemblance, *similitude of character* ‖ semblance, *in the similitude of an angel* [O.F.]

Sim·la (símlə) the capital (pop. 55,326) of Himachal Pradesh, India, a health resort in the Himalayas at 7,000 ft

sim·mer (símər) **1.** *v.i.* to be just below boiling point ‖ (of liquids) to make a steady, low, bubbling sound while heated just to or just below boiling point ‖ to be near an emotional explosion, *to simmer with rage* ‖ *v.t.* to bring to, and cause to remain, just below boiling point **to simmer down** to become calm, esp. after anger **2.** *n.* a state of simmering [fr. earlier *simper*, prob. imit.]

Sim·nel (símn'l), Lambert (c. 1472-c. 1534), English pretender. Claiming to be Edward, earl of Warwick, the Yorkist heir, he led an unsuccessful rebellion (1687) against Henry VII. He was pardoned and given employment in the royal household

sim·nel cake (símn'l) (*Br.*) a rich fruit cake, associated with Easter and mid-Lent [O.F. *simenel, seminel*]

Si·mon (sáimən), St (1st c.), one of the 12 Apostles. Feast: Oct. 28

Si·mon (siːmɔ̃) Claude (1913-), French writer, winner of the Nobel prize for literature (1985). A proponent of the 'new novel', he usually disregarded chronology. His works include 'The Taut Rope' (1947), 'The Flanders Road' (1960) and 'The World About Us' (1975)

si·mo·ni·ac (simóuniːæk) *n.* someone who practices simony **si·mo·ni·a·cal** (sáimənáiək'l), simənáiək'l) *adj.* of or relating to simony [fr. M.L. *simoniacus*]

Si·mon·i·des (saimónidiːz) (c. 556-468 B.C.), Greek lyric poet, celebrated for his epigrams, elegies and scholia

Si·mon Ma·gus (sáimənméigəs) a magician prominent in early Christian history and legend. The Apostle Philip (Acts viii, 9-24) converted him, but when Peter and John came to Samaria he offered them money (*SIMONY) in return for being taught what he believed was the magic of the gift of the Spirit through the laying on of hands. Rebuked by Peter, he begged him to intercede with God on his behalf, and appears no more in Acts. Later literature shows him reappearing in Rome in the time of Claudius in a new movement of his own, curiously combining Christian and pagan elements, and in which he figures as a god

Simon Peter *PETER, ST

Si·mons·town (sáimənztaun) a port and naval base (pop. 8,000) in Cape Province, South Africa, on the Cape of Good Hope

si·mo·ny (sáimoni:, símoni:) *n.* the offense of buying or selling positions in the Church (*SIMON MAGUS) [O.F. *simonie*]

si·moom (simúːm) *n.* a hot, dry, dust-laden wind, esp. in the Arabian desert [Arab. *semūm*]

si·moon (simúːn) *n.* a simoom

sim·per (símpər) **1.** *v.i.* to smile foolishly and self-consciously ‖ *v.t.* to express with a simper **2.** *n.* an affected smile [origin unknown]

sim·ple (símp'l) **1.** *comp.* **sim·pler** *superl.* **sim·plest** *adj.* consisting of only one kind, part etc. ‖ consisting of few parts, *a simple device* ‖ easy to deal with, understand etc., *a simple problem* ‖ (*chem.*) elementary ‖ (*chem.*) composed of basically similar components ‖ (*law*) unconditional ‖ without any or much ornamentation, sophistication or complexity ‖ bare, mere, *the simple truth* ‖ of low rank or position, *a simple workman* ‖ unpretentious, *he is a simple man and a great scholar* ‖ possessed of little understanding, *he is simple about money matters* ‖ guileless ‖ half-witted **2.** *n.* (*archaic*) a medicine derived from only one plant ‖ (*archaic*) a plant gathered for this [O.F.]

simple eye (*zool.*) an eye having only one lens

simple fraction a fraction containing an integer in the numerator and the denominator (cf. COMPLEX FRACTION)

simple harmonic motion a vibratory motion in which the acceleration of the object is proportional to and in a direction opposite to the displacement from a point of equilibrium, and that is characterized by a single frequency and

amplitude. Thus, the projection of a point moving in uniform circular motion on the diameter of its trajectory moves with simple harmonic motion

sim·ple-heart·ed (símp'lhártid) *adj.* gladly accepting persons and things at their face value with sincerity, free of sophistication

simple interest (*finance*) interest calculated on principal only

simple leaf a lobed or unlobed leaf whose blade is not divided at the midrib

simple machine one of the elementary mechanisms, e.g. lever, pulley, wheel, inclined plane, screw, wedge, axle

sim·ple-mind·ed (símp'lmáindid) *adj.* simple-hearted ‖ of subnormal intelligence

simple sentence a sentence having only one main clause and no subordinate clauses

sim·ple·ton (símp'ltən) *n.* a person who lacks common sense or is easily deceived

sim·plic·i·ty (simplísiti:) *pl.* **sim·plic·i·ties** *n.* the quality or state of being simple ‖ a simple idea or fact [O.F. *simplicité* or fr. L. *simplicitas*]

sim·pli·fi·ca·tion (simplifikéiʃən) *n.* a simplifying or being simplified ‖ a result of this [F.]

sim·pli·fy (símplifai) *pres. part.* **sim·pli·fy·ing** *past and past part.* **sim·pli·fied** *v.t.* to make less complex, *to simplify a structure* ‖ to make easier to do or solve, *to simplify a problem* ‖ to make easier to understand, *to simplify an explanation* [fr. F. *simplifier*]

Sim·plon (sɛ̃plɔ̃) a pass (summit 6,578 ft) in the Lepontine Alps connecting the upper Rhône valley, Switzerland, with Lake Maggiore, Italy. Its railroad tunnel (12.5 miles long) was opened in 1906

sim·ply (símpli:) *adv.* in a simple way ‖ merely ‖ (*pop.*) completely, utterly, *the play was simply awful* ‖ (*pop.*) in point of fact, *there simply isn't anyone she can spare*

Simp·son (símps'n), Sir James Young (1811-70), Scottish physician. He was the first to use chloroform as an anesthetic

Sims (simz), William Sowden (1858-1936), U.S. admiral whose improvements in ship design, fleet tactics, and naval gunnery were a major contribution to modernizing the U.S. Navy

sim·u·la·crum (simjuléikrəm) *pl.* **sim·u·la·cra** (simjuléikrə), **sim·u·la·crums** *n.* something made to resemble some other thing ‖ an inferior or deceptive likeness [L.]

Sim·u·la-In (símjulaín) *n.* (*computer*) process-oriented, discrete simulation language based on Algol

sim·u·late (símjuleit) *pres. part.* **sim·u·lat·ing** *past and past part.* **sim·u·lat·ed** *v.t.* to assume the appearance of falsely, *to simulate death* (cf. DISSIMULATE) ‖ to pretend to have, *to simulate a headache* ‖ (*computer*) to reproduce a social or physical activity in computer terms to arrive at a solution [fr. L. *simulare* (*simulatus*)]

sim·u·la·tion (simjuléiʃən) *n.* a simulating ‖ a superficial resemblance ‖ a representation of a product, condition, or process in a different medium, e.g., computer, statistical chart, mock-up, esp. for the purpose of analysis [O.F.]

si·mul·cast (sáiməlkæst, sáiməlkɑst, síməlkæst, síməlkɑst) **1.** *v.t. pres. part.* **si·mul·cast·ing** *past and past part.* **si·mul·cast** to broadcast by radio and television at the same time **2.** *n.* a simultaneous broadcast by radio and television [SIMULTANEOUS+BROADCAST]

si·mul·ta·ne·i·ty (saiməltəní:iti:, siməltəni:iti:) *n.* the state or quality of being simultaneous

si·mul·ta·ne·ous (saiməltéini:əs, siməltéini:əs) *adj.* being or occurring at the same time [fr. L. *simul*, at the same time]

simultaneous equations (*math.*) a set of equations satisfied by the same values of the variables

sin (sin) *n.* an action contrary to the law of God ‖ a state to be condemned in the light of God's law, *a life of sin* ‖ (*loosely*) an offense against any widely accepted standard, *sins against propriety* ‖ (*pop.*) an offense against good sense, *it's a sin to have a garden and then neglect it* [O. E. *syn*, *synn*]

sin *pres. part.* **sin·ning** *past and past part.* **sinned** *v.i.* to offend against a law of God ‖ (*loosely*) to offend against any law, convention, standard of taste or reason [O.E. *syngian*]

Si·nai (sáinai, sáini:ai) a peninsula (area 11,055 sq. miles) at the head of the Red Sea between the gulfs of Suez and 'Aqaba, forming part of Egypt. It is mainly desert, with mountains in the south, incl. Mt Sinai (modern Gebel Musa, 7,363 ft), where God gave Moses the Ten Commandments (Exodus xix-xxxiv), and Gebel Katherina (*KATHERINA GEBEL). It is sparsely inhabited by nomadic Arab tribes

Si·na·lo·a (sɪːnɑlóə) a coastal state (area 22,582 sq. miles, pop. 1,882,200) of Mexico, on the Gulf of California and Pacific Ocean, with 400 miles of western coastline, and mountains on its eastern border. Capital and commercial center: Culiacán (pop. 302,229). Wheat, chickpeas, cotton, tobacco, sugarcane and fruits and vegetables are grown in the isolated valleys, mainly under irrigation. Industries: fishing (chiefly sharks), mining (salt, graphite, gold, silver), tourism

since (sins) **1.** *adv.* at some time between a point in the past and now, *he moved away three years ago but she has seen him since* ‖ (often preceded by 'ever') throughout the time between a point in the past and now, *he came in 1950 and has stayed ever since* ‖ ago, *he has married long since* **2.** *prep.* during the time between a point in the past and a more recent point or now, *they had not met since childhood* ‖ during the time between a point in the past and now, *they have been working since 10 o'clock* **3.** *conj.* during a period following a time when, *much has happened since they last met* ‖ continuously from some time in the past when, *he has not seen her since she was a child* ‖ because, *since you are so sure of it he will believe you* [fr. older *sithence* fr. *sithen* fr. O.E. *siththan,* subsequently to that, or fr. older *sith* adv., since]

sin·cere (sinsíər) *comp.* **sin·cer·er** *superl.* **sin·cer·est** *adj.* utterly honest and genuine, *a sincere friend* [fr. L. *sincerus,* clean, pure]

sin·cer·i·ty (sinséritі:) *pl.* **sin·cer·i·ties** *n.* the quality or state of being sincere [fr. L. *sinceritas*]

Sin·clair (sinkléər), Upton (1878-1968), U.S. social novelist. His 'The Jungle' (1906) fictionalizes his personal investigation into the Chicago stockyards. Later works include 'Dragon's Teeth' (1942)

Sind (sind) a region and former state of Pakistan, a flat, mainly arid region around the lower Indus Valley. Chief town: Hyderabad. Irrigated crops: cereals, hemp, cotton, indigo

Sin·dhi, Sin·di (síndi:) *pl.* **Sin·dhi, Sin·dhis, Sin·di, Sin·dis** *n.* a chiefly Islamic people inhabiting Sind ‖ a member of this people ‖ their Indic language

sine (sain) *n.* (*math., abbr.* sin) a measure of the magnitude of an angle expressed as the constant ratio of the side opposite the angle in a right-angled triangle to the hypotenuse [fr. L. *sinus,* curve, trans. Arab. *jaib*]

si·ne·cure (sáinəkjuər, sínəkjuər) *n.* a position offering profit or honor but carrying few or no duties ‖ (*hist.*) a benefice without cure of souls [fr. L. *sine cura,* without cure, care]

sin·ew (sínju:) *n.* a ligament ‖ (*rhet.*) physical strength ‖ (*pl., rhet.*) sources of strength, *sinews of war* **sin·ew·y** *adj.* of or like sinew ‖ having many or large sinews, muscular ‖ (of prose style) spare, strong and vigorous [O.E. *sinu, sionu*]

sin·fo·ni·a (sinfouní:ə) *pl.* **sin·fo·ni·e** (sinfouní:ei) *n.* a symphony [Ital.]

sin·ful (sínfəl) *adj.* marked by or full of sin ‖ (*pop.*) reprehensible, *a sinful waste*

sing (sіŋ) **1.** *v. pres. part.* **sing·ing** *past* **sang** (sæŋ) *past part.* **sung** (sʌŋ) *v.i.* to utter musical sounds with the voice ‖ to utter words in a musical succession usually set to music ‖ to make a small shrill sound, *bullets sang past our ears* ‖ (*rhet.*) to celebrate something in verse ‖ (of birds, insects, brooks etc.) to produce sounds thought of as tuneful ‖ (of the ears) to be full of a whining noise ‖ *v.t.* to utter (a song, musical note etc.) ‖ (*rhet.*) to celebrate in verse, *poets sang her beauty* **to sing out** to answer, call out **to sing to sleep** to lull to sleep by singing **2.** *n.* (*pop.*) a singing in company ‖ a small shrill sound, esp. of a bullet in flight [O.E. *singan*]

Si·ngan (sí:ŋán) *SIAN

Sin·ga·pore (síŋgəpɔr, síŋgəpour) a republic (area 225 sq. miles, pop. 2,503,000), and member of the British Commonwealth, off the southern tip of the Malay peninsula, consisting of Singapore Is. (224 sq. miles) and nearby islets (15 sq. miles). People: 76% Chinese, 15% Malay and Indonesian, 8% Indian and Pakistani, small European and Eurasian minorities. Main languages: English, Chinese, Malay, Tamil. Religions: Buddhist, Taoist, Confucianist, Moslem, Christian, Hindu, Sikh. Average temperature (F.): 75°-87°. Rainfall: 95 ins. Crops: vegetables, fruit, rubber, toba--o. Tin, rubber,

fruit, petroleum, tobacco, soybeans and palm oil are imported, processed and reexported. Other industries: fishing, engineering, textiles, building materials, light manufacturing. The island is a major air and naval base ‖ its capital (pop. 1,327,500), a great port, entrepôt and commercial center. University: National University of Singapore (1980). Monetary unit: Singapore dollar. HISTORY. Singapore was a prosperous commercial center (13th-14th cc.), and was destroyed (1377) by the Javanese. The British established a trading station (1819). Singapore was ceded (1824) to the British East India Company, and was administered (1826-1946) as part of Straits Settlements. After Japanese occupation (1942-5), it became a separate British colony (1946) and gained internal self-government (1959). It was part of Malaysia (1963-5) and became fully independent (Aug. 9, 1965). It became a republic within the Commonwealth (Dec. 22, 1965). Since independence Singapore has become an industrial and financial power with one of the highest standards of living in Asia

singe (sindʒ) **1.** *v.t. pres. part.* **singe·ing** *past* and *past part.* **singed** to burn slightly on the surface ‖ to burn off bristles or small feathers from (an animal carcass) ‖ to burn the ends of (hair) ‖ to burn off the excess fibers from (cloth) **2.** *n.* a slight burn ‖ the act of singeing [O.E. *sengan*]

Sing·er (síŋər), Isaac Bashevis (1904-), U.S.-Yiddish writer, born in Poland, winner of the Nobel prize for literature (1978). His stories concern the Jewish communities in eastern Europe before the 2nd world war. Novels include the trilogy 'The Family Moskat' (1950), 'The Manor' (1967) and 'The Estate' (1970). He is best known for his short stories, among them 'Gimpel the Fool' (1957) and 'The Spinoza of Market Street' (1961); they are collected in 'Passions and Other Stories' (1975), 'Collected Stories of Isaac Bashevis Singer' (1982) and 'The Image and Other Stories' (1985), among others. Autobiographical works are 'In My Father's Court' (1966) and 'Love and Exile' (1984)

Singer, Isaac Merrit (1811-75), U.S. inventor (1851) of the first practical domestic sewing machine. The Singer sewing machine company became (1860) the largest in the world

sing·er (síŋər) *n.* someone who sings, esp. as a professional ‖ a bird that sings

Sin·gha·lese (siŋgəlí:z, siŋgəlí:s) *SINHALESE

sing-in (síŋin) *n.* audience participation in a musical event

sin·gle (síŋg'l) **1.** *adj.* one and one only, *a single spectator remained* ‖ sole, only, *the single letter was found in the mailbox* ‖ individual, taken in isolation, *every single person present, the most important single influence* ‖ being or behaving as though one only, *we are single in our aim* ‖ (of a bed or room) for one person of the unmarried state ‖ unmarried ‖ being a complete whole, *three small towns became a single city* ‖ not double or compound, *a single plow* ‖ (*bot.,* of a flower) having only one row or set of floral leaves (cf. DOUBLE) ‖ (*bot.,* of a plant) bearing such flowers (cf. DOUBLE) ‖ (*Br.,* of a ticket) valid for a journey in one direction only **not a single** (**person or thing**) not even one (person or thing), *not a single mistake* **2.** *n.* one individual person or thing ‖ (*cricket*) one run scored ‖ (*baseball*) a hit by which the batter gets no farther than first base ‖ (*Br.*) a one-way ticket ‖ (*pl., golf*) a match between two players ‖ (*pl., tennis*) a game with only one player on each side ‖ (*slang*) an unmarried person **3.** *v. pres. part.* **sin·gling** *past* and *past part.* **sin·gled** *v.t.* (sometimes with 'out') to thin out (seedlings) ‖ (with 'out') to choose (one) from many, esp. for special treatment or as having special quality ‖ *v.i.* (baseball) to make a hit by which the batter gets no farther than first base [O.F.]

sin·gle-act·ing (síŋg'lǽktiŋ) *adj.* acting in one direction only, not reciprocating

sin·gle-ac·tion (síŋg'lǽkʃən) *adj.* of a firearm whose hammer must be cocked by hand before the weapon can be fired ‖ single-acting

sin·gle-bar·reled, esp. *Br.* **sin·gle-bar·relled** (síŋg'lbǽrəld) *adj.* (of a gun) having one barrel

single blind in an experimental situation, the condition in which only the one conducting the experiment understands the objectives **—sin·gle-blind** *adj.* Cf DOUBLE BLIND

sin·gle-breast·ed (síŋg'lbréstid) *adj.* (of a coat, waistcoat etc.) buttoned down the middle with a single row of buttons

single combat combat between two persons

single entry a method of bookkeeping by which debts owed to and by a firm are recorded once only in the ledger

single file a line of persons or animals arranged or moving one behind the other

sin·gle-foot (síŋg'lfut) **1.** *n.* the rack (horse's gait) **2.** *v.i.* (of a horse) to go at a rack

sin·gle-hand·ed (síŋg'lhǽndid) *adj.* done without assistance ‖ used with one hand only, *a single-handed sword* ‖ having only one hand

sin·gle-heart·ed (síŋg'lhártid) *adj.* devoted without reservation to one person, cause etc. ‖ marked by or resulting from such devotion

sin·gle-mind·ed (síŋg'lmáindid) *adj.* giving undivided effort to a single purpose ‖ without guile, utterly honest

single parents unmarried, divorced, or widowed mothers or fathers of nonadult children

sin·gle-phase (síŋg'lfeiz) *adj.* (*elec.*) of a circuit having an alternating current in which the two conductors differ in phase by 180°

singles bar (*colloq.*) a dating bar

sin·gle-screw (síŋg'lskru:) *adj.* (of a ship) having one screw propeller (cf. TWIN-SCREW)

sin·gle·stick (síŋg'lstik) *n.* a stick of sword length used in a form of fencing ‖ the sport of fencing with singlesticks

sin·glet (síŋglit) *n.* (*Br.*) a man's sleeveless vest ‖ (*Br.*) an athletic jersey

sin·gle·ton (síŋg'ltən) *n.* (*cards*) the only card of its suit held in a hand [SINGLE]

sin·gle·tree (síŋg'ltri:) *n.* a whiffletree

sin·gly (síŋgli:) *adv.* separately, one at a time, *singly or in pairs*

sing·song (síŋsɔŋ, síŋsɒŋ) **1.** *n.* a monotonous chanting tone of voice ‖ (*Br.*) a sing (in company) **2.** *adj.* in or marked by a monotonous rising and falling tone **3.** *v.i.* to speak or sing in a singsong way ‖ *v.t.* to utter in a singsong

sin·gu·lar (síŋgjulər) **1.** *adj.* (*gram.*) of or denoting one person or thing (cf. PLURAL, cf. DUAL NUMBER) ‖ very remarkable, *singular beauty* ‖ eccentric, *singular behavior* ‖ extraordinary, *a singular experience* **2.** (*gram.*) the form of a word expressing one only ‖ (*gram.*) the singular number [O.F. *singuler* and *singulaire* or fr. L. *singularis*]

sin·gu·lar·i·ty (siŋgjulǽriti:) *pl.* **sin·gu·lar·i·ties** *n.* the state or quality of being very distinctive or unusual ‖ a peculiar characteristic [fr. F. *singularité* or L.L. *singularitas*]

Sin·hai (jínhái) *SINHAILIEN

Sin·hai·lien (jínhái·ljén) or Sinhai, formerly Tunghai) a city (pop. 208,000) in N.W. Kiangsu, China, near the Yellow Sea: salt works

Sin·ha·lese, Sing·ha·lese (sinhəlí:z, sinhəlí:s) **1.** *n.* a member of the principal race of Ceylon ‖ its Indic language **2.** *adj.* of or belonging to this race, its language, culture etc.

sin·is·ter (sínistər) *adj.* evil or suggestive of evil, *a sinister face* ‖ (*rhet.*) disastrous or suggestive of misfortune, *sinister events* (heraldry) on the left of a shield (the viewer's right) [O.F. *sinistre* or L. *sinister,* left-hand]

sin·is·tral (sínistrəl) *adj.* (of spiral shells) having the whorls going from right to left ‖ (of flatfish) left side uppermost [O.F. or fr. M.L. *sinistralis*]

sin·is·tror·sal (sinistrórsəl) *adj.* sinistrorse

sin·is·trorse (sínistrɔrs, sínistrɔrs, sinistrórs) *adj.* (*bot.*) twining spirally upward from right to left ‖ (of spiral shells) sinistral [fr. L. *sinistrorsus*]

sink (siŋk) **1.** *v. pres. part.* **sink·ing** *past* **sank** (sæŋk) *past part.* **sunk** (sʌŋk), (only in adj. uses) **sunk·en** (sʌ́ŋkən) *v.i.* to move or settle slowly down, *to sink into a chair* ‖ (of a heavenly body) to disappear below the horizon ‖ to slope gradually downwards, *the hills sank to the sea's edge* ‖ to move down through or under water, snow etc. ‖ (of a ship etc.) to go to the bottom of the sea, a river etc. ‖ to become lower in level, *the city is steadily sinking* ‖ (usually with 'in' or 'into') to penetrate, esp. gradually, *the knife sank into his flesh, the facts don't seem to sink into his head* ‖ (with 'into') to drift into a specified condition, e.g. sleep, silence or despair ‖ to become lower according to some scale, *her opinion of him sank* ‖ (of the wind) to die down ‖ (of sound) to drop to a lower tone or pitch ‖ to lose courage or hope, *his heart sank* ‖ (with 'in' and 'into') to go down in social position, condition etc. ‖ to go down in value, amount etc. ‖ (of a sick person) to approach death ‖ (of the cheeks or eye sockets)

CONCISE PRONUNCIATION KEY: (**a**) æ, c*a*t; ɑ, c*a*r; ɔ f*aw*n; ei, sn*a*ke. (**e**) e, h*e*n; i:, sh*ee*p; iə, d*ee*r; ɛə, b*ea*r. (**i**) i, f*i*sh; ai, t*i*ger; ə:, b*i*rd. (**o**) o, *o*x; au, c*ow*; ou, g*oa*t; u, p*oo*r; ɔi, r*oy*al. (**u**) ʌ, d*u*ck; u, b*u*ll; u:, g*oo*se; ə, b*a*cillus; ju:, c*u*be. x, lo*ch*; θ, *th*ink; ð, bo*th*er; z, *Z*en; ʒ, corsa*g*e. dʒ, sava*g*e; ŋ, orangutan*g*; j, *y*ak; ʃ, *fi*sh; tʃ, fe*tch*; 'l, rabb*le*; 'n, redd*en.* Complete pronunciation key appears inside front cover.

to become as if shrunken or hollow ‖ *v.t.* to cause (e.g. a ship) to go to the bottom ‖ to cause to go down to a lower level ‖ to countersink (a screw) ‖ to wreck, ruin (someone or a plan etc.) ‖ to fix in below ground level, *to sink a gatepost* ‖ to make (a well, mineshaft etc.) by digging, drilling etc. ‖ to reduce the intensity, volume etc. of, *she sank her voice to a whisper* ‖ to invest (capital) ‖ to pay off (a debt) ‖ (*billiards*) to pocket ‖ (*golf*) to putt (the ball) into the hole **2.** *n.* a fixed basin of stone, stoneware or metal with a water supply and a drainpipe, esp. one in a kitchen in which tableware is washed ‖ a place of vice or corruption ‖ a preliminary excavation for a shaft, pit etc. ‖ (*geog.*) an area of depressed land, esp. where water has collected to form a saline lake without an outlet ‖ a body or substance by which heat or liquid is dissipated in a thermodynamic or hydrodynamic process **sink·er** *n.* someone or something that causes a sinking ‖ a weight used to sink a fishing line or net etc. [O. E. *sincan*]

sink·hole (síŋkhoul) *n.* a place where drainage collects, esp. with an opening to an underground channel ‖ a place of filth, misery, vice etc.

Sin·kiang-Ui·ghur (ʃínkjáŋwí·gúr) an autonomous region (area 705,950 sq. miles, pop. 13,081,681) of China in central Asia, consisting mainly of the Dzungaria and Tarim basins, separated by the Tien Shan. Capital: Urumchi. People: mainly Turkic (Uighur, Kazak, Kirghiz), with Mongol, Tibetan and other minorities. Religion: mainly Sunni Moslem, with Shi'ite and Buddhist minorities. It is largely desert (*TURFAN, *TAKLA MAKAN), with large oases around Urumchi, Kashgar, Khotan and Yarkand. The inhabitants are nomadic herdsmen and oasis farmers. Livestock: camels, horses, sheep, goats. Crops: cereals, cotton, fruit. Formerly part of Turkestan, it became (1881) a Chinese province

Sin·king (ʃíndʒíŋ) *CHANGCHUN

sinking fund a sum of money formed by periodically setting aside revenue to accumulate at interest, used to reduce a debt

sin·ner (sínər) *n.* someone who sins

Sinn Fein (ʃínféin) an Irish nationalist movement organized (1905) as a political party by Arthur Griffith. It triumphed (1921) when the Irish Free State was set up [Ir. Gael. =we ourselves]

Si·no-Jap·a·nese (sáinoudʒæpəníːz, sínoudʒæpəníːz, sáinoudʒæpəníːs, sínoudʒæpəníːs) *adj.* relating to both China and Japan

Sino-Japanese War either of two wars between China and Japan. The first (1894-5) was fought for control of Korea, spread into Manchuria and resulted in the defeat of China (1895), which recognized the independence of Korea, paid an indemnity, and ceded Formosa, the Pescadores Is and the Liaotung peninsula to Japan. In the second (1931-45), Japan occupied Manchuria (1931), Peking and Tientsin (1937), and captured the eastern coastal region of China (1940). The Japanese bombing of Pearl Harbor (1941) merged the conflict in the 2nd world war

si·no·log·i·cal (sainəlódʒik'l, sinəlódʒik'l) *adj.* of sinology [SINOLOGUE]

si·nol·o·gist (sainólədʒist, sinólədʒist) *n.* a sinologue [prob. fr. F. *sinologie*, sinology]

si·no·logue (sáinəlɔg, sáinəlɔg, sínəlɔg, sínəlɔg) *n.* a specialist in sinology [F. fr. Gk *Sinai*, the Chinese+*logos*, discourse]

si·nol·o·gy (sainólədʒiː, sinólədʒiː) *n.* the study of the language, history and culture of China [prob. fr. F. *sinologie* fr. Gk *Sinai*, the Chinese+*logos*, discourse]

Si·no-Ti·bet·an (sáinoutibét'n, sinoutibét'n) *n.* a group of languages including Chinese, Tibetan and usually Thai

SINS *n.* (*acronym*) for ships inertial navigation system, sonar and guidance system for a submarine to determine a ship's position and speed in relation to the ocean bottom

sin·ta·ki (sintáki) *n.* circular Greek folk dance with variations by individuals

sin·ter (síntər) **1.** *n.* (*geol.*) a deposit of calcareous or siliceous material precipitated from the water of a lake etc., which was previously held in solution ‖ the product of sintering **2.** *v.t.* to cause to form a fused mass by heating ‖ *v.i.* to become a fused mass from heating [G.]

sintering *n.* (*metallurgy*) process by which fine particles are held together when heated —**sin·ter** *v.* —**sintered conductor** *n.*

sin·u·ate (sínjuːit, sínjuːeit) *adj.* (esp. *bot.*, e.g. of the edges of some leaves) bending or winding in and out [fr. L. *sinuare* (*sinuatus*) to bend]

sin·u·a·tion (sinjuːéiʃən) *n.* (esp. *bot.*) a bending or winding in and out [fr. L.L. *sinuatio* (*sinuationis*) fr. *sinuare*, to bend]

sin·u·os·i·ty (sinjuːósitiː) *pl.* **sin·u·os·i·ties** *n.* the quality of winding or curving ‖ a curve, bend [F. *sinuosité*]

sin·u·ous (sínjuːəs) *adj.* winding, *a sinuous road* ‖ having many curves ‖ (*bot.*) sinuate [fr. L. *sinuosus*]

si·nus (sáinəs) *pl.* **si·nus·es** *n.* one of the airfilled cavities within the bones of the face and skull, in communication with the nose and mouth ‖ (*med.*) a channel for drainage from a pus-filled cavity ‖ (*bot.*) an indentation between the lobes of a leaf [L.=fold, curve]

si·nus·i·tis (sainəsáitis) *n.* (*med.*) inflammation of a sinus, esp. of the skull

si·nus·oi·dal projection (sainəsóidʼl) an equal-area representation of the surface of the earth having a straight equator and a straight central meridian that is one half the equator's length. The other lines of longitude are curved. The lines of latitude are straight, and parallel to the equator [F. *sinusoïde*]

sinus ve·no·sus (vənóusəs) *n.* the main cavity of each auricle in the heart ‖ the posterior chamber of the tubular heart of an embryo ‖ (in lower vertebrates, e.g. the frog) a corresponding structure receiving venous blood and opening into the auricle

Siou·an (súːən) *n.* a group of North American Indian languages formerly spoken in West central U.S.A., central Canada and parts of Virginia and the Carolinas ‖ the Sioux ‖ a member of the Sioux

Sioux (suː) *pl.* **Sioux** (suː, suːz) *n.* the North American Indian peoples speaking Siouan, esp. the Dakotas ‖ a member of these peoples [F. contr. of *Nadowessioux* fr. Am. Ind. *Nadowessi*, little snake]

Sioux Falls a city (pop. 81,343) in southeastern S. Dakota, a commercial and industrial center and port. Livestock market, meat processing

sip (sip) **1.** *v. pres. part.* **sip·ping** *past* and *past part.* **sipped** *v.t.* to drink by taking in a very slight quantity with the lips, esp. repeatedly ‖ *v.i.* to drink in this way **2.** *n.* a small amount of liquid taken in by the lips ‖ the act of sipping [perh. alteration of SUP (to drink)]

si·phon, sy·phon (sáifən) **1.** *n.* a tube bent so that it has two roughly vertical and parallel legs of unequal length, used to transfer a liquid from a vessel placed at a higher level to a vessel at a lower level. The tube is filled with the liquid (e.g. by suction) and the shorter leg immersed in the liquid to be transferred. The longer leg is placed in or just above the lower vessel. The difference of the pressure in the shorter leg and at the lower end of the longer leg results in a continuous flow ‖ *SYPHON (bottle) ‖ (*zool.*) a tubular part in certain animals, e.g. clams, for drawing in or ejecting liquids **2.** *v.t.* to cause to flow out through a siphon ‖ *v.i.* to flow through a siphon **si·phon·age** *n.* [fr. L. *sipho* (*siphonis*), tube, pipe fr. Gk]

siphon bottle a syphon

si·pho·net (saifənét) *n.* (*zool.*) one of the abdominal tubes used by an aphid to exude honeydew [SIPHON]

si·pho·no·phore (sáifənəfɔr, sáifənəfour, saifónəfɔr, saifónəfour) *n.* a member of *Siphonophora*, an order of usually transparent, brightcolored, colonial, marine hydrozoans that float or swim [fr. Mod. L. *Siphonophora* fr. Gk *siphōn*, pipe, tube+*-phoros*, bearer]

si·pho·no·stele (saifənəstiːl, sáifənousti·l) *n.* (*bot.*) a hollow stele, e.g. in the stem of a fern (cf. PROTOSTELE)

si·phun·cle (sáifʌŋk'l) *n.* (*zool.*) a tube of skin, partly calcareous, connecting the compartments of a cephalopod shell [fr. L. *siphunculus* dim. of *sipho*, siphon]

sip·pet (sípit) *n.* a small piece of fried bread or toast for soaking in soup etc., or used for garnishing ‖ a morsel, *sippets of information* [prob. fr. SOP (piece of bread)]

SIPROS *n.* (*computer acronym*) for simultaneous processing operating system, used in management of computer equipment and programs selection; designed by Control Data Corp.

Si·quei·ros (siːkéirɔs), David Alfaro (1898-1974), Mexican painter. His striking murals and frescoes are violent social protests

sir (səːr) **1.** *n.* a form of polite address to men ‖ a form of address used in writing to strangers or in business letters ‖ a title preceding the first name of a knight or baronet **2.** *v.t. pres. part.* **sir·ring** *past* and *part part.* **sirred** to address (someone) as sir [shortened from SIRE]

sire (saiər) **1.** *n.* the male parent of a quadruped, esp. a stallion ‖ (*archaic*) a form of address to a king **2.** *v.t. pres. part.* **sir·ing** *past* and *past part.* **sired** (esp. of quadrupeds) to beget [O.F.]

si·ren (sáirən) **1.** *n.* an instrument for producing a loud, penetrating sound as a warning, e.g. a signal for opening and closing a day's work at a factory etc., operated by revolving a perforated disk over a jet of compressed air or steam ‖ (*Gk* and *Roman mythol.*) a woman, or part-woman part-bird, who lured ships onto rocks by enchanting the sailors with her singing ‖ (*pop.*) an extremely seductive woman ‖ a member of *Sirenidae*, a family of eel-shaped amphibians with small forelimbs but without hind limbs or pelvis, having a compressed tail, and gills as well as lungs **2.** *adj.* of or relating to a siren [L.L. fr. L. fr. Gk *Seirēn*]

si·re·ni·an (sairíːniːən) **1.** *n.* a sea cow of order *Sirenia* **2.** *adj.* of or relating to such a sea cow [fr. Mod. L. *Sirenia* fr. L. *siren*, a siren]

Si·ri·o·no (síəriːonou) *pl.* **Si·ri·o·no, Si·ri·o·nos** *n.* a Bolivian people inhabiting the tropical forests of E. Bolivia ‖ a member of this people ‖ their language

Sir·i·us (síriːəs) the brightest star in the sky. It is in *Canis Major*, a southern constellation

sir·loin (səːrlɔin) *n.* the upper part of a loin of beef including the meat above and under the bone [fr. O.F. fr. *sur*, over+*longe*, loin]

si·roc·co (siróu) *pl.* **si·roc·cos** *n.* a hot, dustladen wind from N. African deserts reaching S. Europe, esp. Italy, Malta and Sicily [Ital. *sirocco, scirocco* fr. Arab. *sharq*, east]

sirup *SYRUP

si·sal (sáisəl, sísəl) *n.* a strong fiber used for making twine, cordage etc., obtained from the leaves of *Agave sisalana*, fam. *Amaryllidaceae* ‖ this plant, widely cultivated e.g. in Java, E. Africa and Mexico ‖ a similar fiber obtained from various agaves, e.g. henequen

sis·kin (sískin) *n. Spinus spinus*, a small yellowish-green finch of temperate Europe and Asia related to the goldfinch. The male has a black crown and chin [fr. G. dial. *sisschen*]

Sis·ley (siːslei), Alfred (1839-99), French impressionist landscape painter, esp. of river scenes

sis·sy, *Br.* also **cis·sie, cis·sy** (sísiː) *pl.* **sis·sies**, *Br.* also **cis·sies** *n.* (*pop.*) an effeminate boy or man, esp. one who shows fear [shortened fr. SISTER]

sissy bar a support bar behind the rider or passenger of a two-wheeled vehicle

sis·ter (sístər) *n.* a daughter in her relationship to another child of the same parents ‖ (*Br.*) a senior hospital nurse, usually one in charge of a ward ‖ a member of a religious community of women [O.E. *sweoster, swuster*]

sis·ter-ger·man (sístərdʒɔ́·rmən) *pl.* **sisters-german** *n.* one's sister born of the same two parents [SISTER+*german*, akin fr. O.F. *germain*]

sis·ter·hood (sístərhud) *n.* the state of being a sister ‖ the relationship between sisters ‖ a religious community of women

sis·ter-in-law (sístərinlɔ) *pl.* **sis·ters-in-law** *n.* the sister of one's husband or wife, or the wife of one's brother

sis·ter·ly (sístərliː) *adj.* of or like a sister

sister ship one of two or more ships having the same constructional characteristics and usually belonging to the same steamship line

Sis·tine Chapel (sístiːn, sístin, sístain) the pope's private chapel in the Vatican, Rome, built by Sixtus IV and famous for Michelangelo's frescoes

sis·trum (sístrəm) *pl.* **sis·trums, sis·tra** (sístrə) *n.* an ancient Egyptian percussion instrument of metal rings which rattled against a metal frame when jangled [L. fr. Gk *seistron*]

Sis·y·phus (sísəfəs) (*mythol.*) king of Corinth, feared for his cruelty and acts of brigandage. He was condemned in Hades eternally to push a rock to the top of a hill. It always rolled down again short of the top

sit (sit) **1.** *v. pres. part.* **sit·ting** *past* and *past part.* **sat** (sæt) *v.i.* to rest the body on the buttocks ‖ (of birds and many other animals) to rest with the legs huddled up to the body ‖ (of birds) to stay covering eggs so as to hatch them ‖ to be situated, *the cottage sits in a hollow* ‖ to take up,

CONCISE PRONUNCIATION KEY: **(a)** æ, *cat*; ɑ, *car*; ɔ *fawn*; ei, *snake.* **(e)** e, *hen*; iː, *sheep*; iə, *deer*; ɛə, *bear.* **(i)** i, *fish*; ai, *tiger*; əː, *bird.* **(o)** o, *ox*; au, *cow*; ou, *goat*; u, *poor*; ɔi, *royal.* **(u)** ʌ, *duck*; u, *bull*; uː, *goose*; ə, *bacillus*; juː, *cube.* x, *loch*; θ, *think*; ð, *bother*; z, *Zen*; ʒ, *corsage*; dʒ, *savage*; ŋ, *orangutang*; j, *yak*; ʃ, *fish*; tʃ, *fetch*; 'l, *rabble*; 'n, *redden.* Complete pronunciation key appears inside front cover.

or be in, a position to be painted, *to sit for a portrait* ‖ (of clothes) to fit (well or badly), esp. across the shoulders ‖ (*fig.*) to rest in a specified way, *his new authority sits heavily on him* ‖ (of courts, parliament, committees etc.) to be in session or to hold sessions ‖ to have a position as a member, *he sits on the board* ‖ (esp. *Br.*) to undergo an examination as candidate, *to sit for one's finals* ‖ to remain in the same condition, esp. idle or unused, *the scooter is sitting by the roadside* ‖ to look after a child, invalid etc. on behalf of a parent etc. ‖ (of the wind) to blow from a specified quarter ‖ *v.t.* to cause (someone) to take a seat, esp. to position (someone) at table, *sit him on her left* ‖ to place (oneself) in a sitting posture ‖ to ride (a horse), esp. with respect to carriage or capacity to stay in the saddle ‖ (*Br.*) to undergo (a written examination) ‖ to accommodate on chairs, *the table sits eight* ‖ **to sit down** to take a seat **to sit down under** (*Br.*) to accept without protest **to sit on** to consider (a case) with a view to deciding it ‖ (*pop.*) to cause to be less bumptious **to sit out** to choose not to dance (a dance) ‖ to stay until the end of ‖ to refrain from dancing **to sit up** to move from a lying to a sitting position ‖ to sit with one's back straight and shoulders held back ‖ to stay up late and not go to bed ‖ (of some animals, esp. a dog) to rest on its haunches with the body upright and front paws raised, esp. in order to beg for food [O.E. *sittan*]

si·tar (sitár) *n.* a lute-like instrument of India with a long fretted neck, two resonating gourds, and a set of sympathetic strings below the playing strings [Hindi *sitār*]

sit·com (sítkɔm) *n.* (*acronym*) for situation comedy, a television or radio series of usu. unconnected episodes with a continuing background and the same characters *Cf* SOAP OPERA

sit-down strike (sítdaun) a strike in which workers refuse to go away from their place of work

site (sait) 1. *n.* the geographical situation in the past, present, or future of a town or building, *the site of ancient Carthage, a site for the new factory* ‖ the scene of a specified event, *the exact site of the battle* 2. *v.t. pres. part.* **sit·ing** past and past part. **sit·ed** to fix in a location [A.F. or fr. L. *situs*]

sit-in (sítin) *n.* a group protest in which participants sit down in a public place, e.g. a racially segregated restaurant and stay there until their demands are considered or until they are removed by force

Sit·ka (sítkə) a town (pop. 7,803) on an island in the Alexander Archipelago off S.E. Alaska. In the 19th c. it was the headquarters of Russian America and the chief commercial center on the Pacific coast of North America. It was the capital of Alaska (1867-1900) after the U.S.A. purchased it

sit·ter (sítər) *n.* someone who poses for a portrait ‖ a baby-sitter ‖ a broody hen ‖ (esp. *Br., pop.*) an easy target

sit·ting (sítiŋ) 1. *n.* the act of someone who sits ‖ a continuous period of time during which one sits over some occupation, *she read the novel at one sitting* ‖ the act of posing for a portrait, *the portrait required three sittings* ‖ a meeting, esp. of parliament or a court of law ‖ any of two or more consecutive eating sessions served in a canteen, dining room etc. too small to seat all the diners at one time ‖ a brooding of a hen on eggs ‖ the clutch of eggs on which a broody hen is sitting 2. *adj.* being in office ‖ (of a target) very easy to hit ‖ (of a hen) on a clutch of eggs to hatch them ‖ (*Br.*, of a tenant) in occupancy

Sitting Bull (c. 1831-90), North American Indian warrior and principal chief of the Sioux nation. His refusal to be confined to a reservation led to many battles with the U.S. Army, notably Little Bighorn (1876). Starved into submission, he agreed to live (from 1883) on a reservation in S. Dakota. He was killed while being arrested for inciting the Sioux against the white man, in protest against expropriation of tribal lands

sitting room a living room in a house, furnished for sitting at leisure or sharing informal family activities

sit·u·ate (sítʃu:eit) *pres. part.* **sit·u·at·ing** past and *past part.* **sit·u·at·ed** *v.t.* to locate or site ‖ to fix in a particular set of circumstances or category, *she situates her characters in upper middle-class society* **sit·u·at·ed** *adj.* located or sited, *a house situated on a hill* ‖ placed in particular circumstances, *how are they situated*

financially? [fr. M.L. *situare* (*situatus*), to place]

sit·u·a·tion (sitʃu:éiʃən) *n.* the manner in which something is situated, esp. with regard to aspect, view, accessibility etc., *the house has a fine situation* ‖ the circumstances in which someone is placed ‖ state of affairs, *the political situation*, esp. a crucial state of affairs, *what a situation to be in !* ‖ a paid occupation, esp. one in a household as maid, governess etc. (wider usage being restricted to journal advertisements) [F. or fr. M.L. *situatio* (*situationis*)]

situation ethics thesis that what is right in a moral problem is more dependent on the immediate situation than on a general code

situation room (*mil.*) a center where reports are received on a current operation

sit-up (sítup) *n.* an exercise in which a person lying on his back raises his torso until he is in a sitting position, without bending his knees

sitz bath (sits, zits) a bath tub in which one sits up and cannot recline, used esp. in medical therapy ‖ a bath so taken [part trans. fr. G. *Sitzbad* fr. *sitzen*, to sit]

sitz·fleisch (sítsflaiʃ) *n.* (*German; usu. italics*) ability to sit and wait

SI units (*phys. abbr.*) for Système International d' Unités, i.e., International System of Units, for length, time, mass, electric current, temperature, luminous intensity, and molecular weight; recommended by General Conference on Weights and Measures

Si·va, Shi·va (ʃíːvə) the Hindu god of destruction and rebirth, the third god of the Hindu trinity (*VISHNU, *BRAHMA) [Skr.=the auspicious one]

Si·va·ji (sivádʒiː) (1627-80), Maratha leader. He established (1674) the Maratha empire

Si·vas (si:vás) a city (pop. 172,864) in N. central Turkey on the Kizil Irmak: textiles, copper mining. Mosque (12th c.)

Si·wa·lik Hills (si:wálik) a range (averaging 3,000 ft) of foothills of the Himalayas, running through N.W. India and S.W. Nepal, remarkable for their fossil beds

six (siks) 1. *adj.* being one more than five (*NUMBER TABLE) 2. *n.* twice three ‖ the cardinal number representing this (6, VI) ‖ six o'clock ‖ a playing card (domino etc.) marked with six symbols ‖ (*cricket*) a hit from which six runs are scored or made ‖ a team of six members, esp. in rowing or ice hockey **at sixes and sevens** in a state of confusion [O.E. *sex, six*]

Six-Day War (síksdei) the 1967 war between Egypt, Syria, Jordan and Israel

Six, les (leis:s) a group of young musicians including Darius Milhaud, Arthur Honegger, Francis Poulenc, Georges Auric, Louis Durey and Germaine Tailleferre, who in 1918 in France banded together in reaction against the influence of Debussy and sought greater simplicity in music. They were influenced by Erik Satie

six·pence (síkspəns) *n.* (*Br.*) the sum represented by six pennies ‖ (*Br.*) a coin worth 2½ new pence

six-shoot·er (síksʃú:tər) *n.* a revolver that can be fired six times without reloading

sixte (sikst) *n.* (*fencing*) the sixth of eight parrying positions [F.]

six·teen (sikstí:n) 1. *adj.* being one more than 15 (*NUMBER TABLE) 2. *n.* ten plus six ‖ the cardinal number representing this (16, XVI) [O.E. *syxtine, sixtyne, sextyne*]

six·teen·mo (sikstí:nmou) *pl.* **six·teen·mos** *n.* a sextodecimo (*abbr.* 16mo)

six·teenth (sikstí:nθ) 1. *adj.* being number 16 in a series (*NUMBER TABLE) ‖ being one of the 16 equal parts of anything 2. *n.* the person or thing next after the 15th ‖ one of 16 equal parts of anything (1/16) ‖ the 16th day of a month

Sixteenth Amendment (1913) an amendment to the U.S. Constitution that established the federal income tax. The levying of taxes as provided in the Constitution (Article 1, Sections 2 and 9) was controversial and caused many disputes between the federal government and the states. The 16th Amendment accorded Congress the right to tax incomes without regard to state apportionment or census

sixteenth note (*mus., Am.=Br.* semiquaver) a note (symbol ♪) equal in duration to half an eighth note

sixth (siksθ) 1. *adj.* being number six in a series (*NUMBER TABLE) ‖ being one of the six equal parts of anything 2. *n.* the person or thing next after the fifth ‖ one of six equal parts of anything (1/6) ‖ the sixth day of a month ‖ (*mus.*)

the note six steps above or below a given note in a diatonic scale, inclusive of both notes ‖ (*mus.*) the interval between these notes ‖ (*mus.*) a combination of these notes 3. *adv.* in the sixth place ‖ (followed by a superlative) except five, *the sixth biggest* [O.E. *sixta*]

Sixth Amendment (1791) an amendment to the U.S. Constitution, part of the Bill of Rights, that guarantees a speedy trial, an impartial jury and other rights to those accused in a criminal proceeding

six·ti·eth (síksti:θ) 1. *adj.* being number 60 in a series (*NUMBER TABLE) ‖ being one of the 60 equal parts of anything 2. *n.* the person or thing next after the 59th ‖ one of 60 equal parts of anything (1/60) [O.E. *sixteogotha*]

Six·tus IV (síkstəs) (Francesco della Rovere, 1414-84), pope (1471-84). A patron of letters and the arts, he sponsored the building of the Sistine Chapel. He consented to the establishment of the Inquisition in Spain

Sixtus V (Felice Peretti, 1521-90), pope (1585-90). He repressed civil disorder in the Papal States and was responsible for much new building in Rome

six·ty (síksti:) 1. *adj.* being ten more than 50 (*NUMBER TABLE) 2. *pl.* **six·ties** *n.* six times ten ‖ the cardinal number representing this (60, LX) **the sixties** (of temperature, a person's age, a century etc.) the span 60-9 [O.E. *siextig, syxtig, sextig*]

six·ty-fourth note (síksti:fɔ́rθ, síksti:fóurθ) (*mus., Am.=Br.* hemidemisemiquaver) a note equal in duration to half a thirty-second note

siz·a·ble, size·a·ble (sáizəb'l) *adj.* rather large, *a sizable majority*

siz·ar (sáizər) *n.* (*Br.*) the title of certain scholars in certain colleges at Cambridge University (England) and Trinity College (Dublin) [fr. SIZE *n.* (*obs.*) a portion of bread or ale]

size (saiz) 1. *n.* the length, area, volume or dimensions of something or someone as compared with a specific or arbitrary standard, *this book is twice the size of that, a crowd of considerable size* ‖ one of a number of standards used for such comparison, *size 9 shoes* ‖ the total quantity, *the size of an order* ‖ magnitude, *bears of some size* ‖ (of things) scope, *defense projects of astounding size* ‖ intellectual capacity and force of character, *it is not a job for a man of his size* ‖ (*pop.*) true account, *that's about the size of it* **of a size** of equal size 2. *v.t. pres. part.* **siz·ing** past and *past part.* **sized** to sort or arrange according to size, *to size potatoes* ‖ to make in a certain size or in a series of certain sizes **to size up** to estimate the size of ‖ to estimate the character or qualities of (someone) ‖ to estimate the importance or nature of (something) ‖ to compare in respect to size [O.F. *sise, cise* fr. *assise, assize*]

size 1. *n.* a thin gelatinous liquid used in glazing or for stiffening paper, textiles etc. 2. *v.t. pres. part.* **siz·ing** past and *past part.* **sized** to apply this liquid to **siz·ing** *n.* liquid size ‖ the process of applying it [perh. fr. SIZE *n.*]

sizeable *SIZABLE

siz·zle (síz'l) 1. *v.i. pres. part.* **siz·zling** past and *past part.* **siz·zled** to make a hissing sound, esp. in being fried 2. *n.* a noise so made **siz·zling** *adj.* very hot [imit.]

Sjael·land (ʃéllan) *ZEALAND

Ska·dar·sko (skádarskɔ) *SHKODËR

Skag·er·rak (skǽgəræk, skágərak) an arm (150 miles long, 80 miles wide) of the North Sea between Denmark, Norway and W. Sweden

skald, scald (skɔld, skald) *n.* a composer of elaborate courtly poetry in Old Norse, late 8th c. The poetry, notable for its metrical virtuosity, reached its highest point in Iceland (11th-11th cc.) **skáld·ic, scáld·ic** *adj.* [O.N., Icel. *skáld*, origin unknown]

skat (skat, skæt) *n.* a card game played by three people using 32 cards, bearing some resemblance to piquet [G.]

skate (skeit) *pl.* **skates, skate** *n.* a member of *Rajidae*, a family of cartilaginous fish related to rays, esp. genus *Raja*. Skates are peculiarly flattened, and rather rhomboidal in outline, having the mouth at one corner of a long snout and the anus at the opposite corner of the body [O.N. *skáta*]

skate 1. *n.* an ice skate ‖ a roller skate 2. *v. pres. part.* **skat·ing** past and *past part.* **skat·ed** *v.i.* to move or glide along on skates ‖ *v.t.* to go (one's way or a distance) on skates [fr. Du. *schaats* fr. O.N.F. *escache*, stilt]

skate·board (skéitbɔrd, skéitbourd) *n.* a piece of wood mounted on skate wheels and used by children for riding on

skating rink an area of ice artificially produced and preserved for ice skating ‖ an area of other hard, smooth surface used for roller skating

ske·dad·dle (skidǽd'l) 1. *v.i. pres. part.* **ske·dad·dling** *past* and *past part.* **ske·dad·dled** (*pop.*) to go away very quickly, run off 2. *n.* (*pop.*) a hurried flight [etym. doubtful]

skeet (ski:t) *n.* trapshooting at targets which simulate the speed and angle of flight of birds

skein (skein) *n.* a length of yarn, thread, wool or silk, looped many times and then twisted ‖ a flock of wild geese in flight ‖ something thought of as full of coils and windings, *the skein of events* [fr. O.F. *escaigne*, origin unknown]

skel·e·tal (skélit'l) *adj.* of, relating to or being part of a skeleton ‖ like a skeleton

skeletal muscle a muscle attached to the skeleton (cf. SMOOTH MUSCLE, cf. CARDIAC MUSCLE, cf. STRIATED MUSCLE)

skel·e·ton (skélitən) *n.* a hard framework, internal or external, supporting or protecting the soft tissues and organs of a man, animal or plant. Vertebrates have an endoskeleton consisting mainly of cartilage at first, replaced by bone during growth. Invertebrates have an exoskeleton which is often calcareous or chitinous ‖ the dried bones of a dead man or animal, esp. assembled as in life ‖ a framework, e.g. of a building ‖ the essential nucleus of an organization, esp. what remains after the period of full activity is over ‖ an outline, *the skeleton of a novel* ‖ a very thin person or animal **a skeleton in the closet** (*Br.* **cupboard**) a secret of which a family is ashamed [Mod. L. *sceleton, skeleton* fr. Gk *skeleton* (*sōma*), dried up (body)]

skeleton key a key made so as to fit many locks

skeleton shrimp a member of *Caprella* or a related genus of amphipod crustaceans. They have a cylindrical body and swim by wriggling movements

Skel·ton (skéltən), John (c. 1460-1529), English poet and satirist, esp. of the clergy. He used an alliterative, shortlined, much-rhyming, tumbling verse (Skeltonics)

skep (skep) *n.* any of various kinds of farm basket ‖ any of these as a measure of quantity ‖ a straw or wicker beehive [O.N. *skeppa*]

skep·sis, esp. *Br.* **scep·sis** (sképsis) *n.* philosophical skepticism [Gk *skepsis*, inquiry, doubt]

skep·tic, esp. *Br.* **scep·tic** (sképtik) *n.* a person who doubts the truth of anything, esp. of that which others accept as true **Skeptic**, esp. *Br.* **Sceptic** (*hist.*) a member of the Greek philosophical school founded by Pyrrho **skép·ti·cal**, esp. *Br.* **scép·ti·cal** *adj.* [fr. F. *sceptique* or L.L. *scepticus* fr. Gk]

skep·ti·cism, esp. *Br.* **scep·ti·cism** (sképti·sizəm) *n.* an attitude of doubt ‖ the philosophical view that nothing can be known with certainty [fr. Mod. L. *scepticismus* fr. L.L. *scepticus*, skeptic]

sketch (sketʃ) 1. *n.* a quickly made drawing ‖ a drawing preliminary to more careful work ‖ a brief, slight story, account or description ‖ a preliminary outline of a literary work ‖ a slight, short (usually one-scene) comedy, often musical ‖ a descriptive musical composition of one movement ‖ (*pop., old-fash.*) someone who looks ridiculous or one whose jokes and antics cause general hilarity 2. *v.t.* to make a sketch of ‖ *v.i.* to make a sketch or sketches (fr. Du. *schets* or G. *skizze* fr. Ital. fr. L. prob. fr. Gk]

sketch·book (skétʃbuk) *n.* leaves of drawing paper arranged in a book so as to be detachable ‖ a notebook of finished sketches ‖ a collection of short literary sketches

sketch·i·ly (skétʃili:) *adv.* in a sketchy manner **sketch·i·ness** (skétʃi:nis) *n.* the state or quality of being sketchy

sketch·y (skétʃi:) *comp.* **sketch·i·er** *superl.* **sketch·i·est** *adj.* lacking detail, slight, *a sketchy account*

skeu·o·mor·phic (skju:oumɔ́rfik) *adj.* of an object copied in a form materially different from its original, e.g., a candy ax, a hammer reproduced in clay **skeumorph** *n.* the object — **skeumorphism** *n.* the copying

skew (skju:) 1. *v.t.* to cut or set slantingly ‖ to give a bias to, *the account was skewed in favor of the police* ‖ (*statistics*) to cause (a frequency distribution or its curve) to lack symmetry ‖ (*pop.*) to twist, *to skew one's head around* ‖ *v.i.* to twist around 2. *adj.* running at an angle, oblique ‖

(*statistics*, of a frequency distribution or its curve) lacking symmetry 3. *n.* a slant, oblique direction ‖ (in cloth) a deviation from the proper straight line of a weave [fr. O.N.F. *eskiuwer, eskiuer, escuer*]

skew·back (skjú:bæk) *n.* a sloping face of masonry taking the thrust of an arch

skew·bald (skjú:bɔld) 1. *adj.* (of horses) having patches of white and another color, esp. other than black 2. *n.* a skewbald horse (cf. PIEBALD)

skew·er (skjú:ər) 1. *n.* a metal or wooden pin for holding meat together while cooking 2. *v.t.* to pierce with, or as if with, a skewer [var. of SKIVER]

skew·eyed (skjú:aid) *adj.* (*Br.*) squinting

ski (ski:) 1. *pl.* **skis, ski** *n.* one of a pair of long, narrow, wooden, metal or plastic strips which curve up and taper to a point at the front end. They are used for gliding downhill over snow at speeds up to 50 m.p.h. or more ‖ a similar device used in water-skiing 2. *v.i. pres. part.* **ski·ing** *past* and *past part.* **skied** to move on skis [Norw.]

ski·bob (skí:bɔb) *n.* (*sports*) a bicyclelike sled mounted on two short skis, one behind the other, the forward ski maneuvered by handbars, an upholstered seat over the rear ski, with rider balanced by miniature skis —**skibob** *v.* —**skibobber** *n.*

skid (skid) 1. *n.* a sideways slip or slide of a wheel through failure to grip the ground ‖ a block of wood or metal to prevent a wheel from turning, esp. on a slope ‖ one of a pair or set of bars etc. down which things can be slid or rolled ‖ (*aeron.*) a runner used as part of an airplane's landing gear ‖ (*naut.*, esp. *pl.*) a wooden bar hung over a ship's side to protect her when cargo is loaded or unloaded ‖ one of a number of timbers etc. used to shore up a boat, construction etc. 2. *v. pres. part.* **skid·ding** *past* and *past part.* **skid·ded** *v.i.* (of a wheel) to slide without gripping, e.g. on slippery ground ‖ to slide sideways ‖ *v.t.* to use skids for protecting, moving or checking movement ‖ to cause to slip sideways [etym. doubtful]

skid·board·ing (skídbɔrdiŋ) *n.* surfing on a coated plywood disk, introduced in England in 1960

ski-doo (skidú:) *n.* (*Br.*) ski-scooter, motorized snow-ice vehicle with endless tracks in rear and movable skis in front

skid pad a slick area of oiled asphalt used to test motor vehicles for skidding potential

ski·er (skí:ər) *n.* someone who skis

skiff (skif) *n.* a small rowing boat [fr. F. *esquif*, Span. or Port. *esquife* or Ital. *schifo*]

skif·fle (skíf'l) *n.* (*Br.*) mixture of rock 'n' roll and country music, with a blues rhythm, played on nonstandard, usu. homemade, instruments, e.g., washboards, combs, furniture; popular in English coffee shops during late 1950s

ski·jor·ing (skí:jɔriŋ) *n.* competitive skiing in which competitors are pulled by horses or motor vehicles

ski jump a jump made on skis ‖ a course prepared for jumping on skis and furnished with an elevated take-off platform or mound

skilful *SKILLFUL

ski lift a device consisting of a motordriven, overhead, endless cable with suspended seats for carrying skiers or sightseers up a mountain slope (cf. SKI TOW)

skill (skil) *n.* ability to do something well, esp. as the result of long practical experience ‖ a particular technique, *the work calls for various skills* ‖ tact, *to manage a person with skill* ‖ **skilled** *adj.* having skill ‖ requiring skilled workmen, *skilled trades* [O.N. *skil*, discernment]

skil·let (skílit) *n.* a frying pan ‖ (*Br.*) a small long-handled saucepan usually with short legs [origin unknown]

skill·ful, esp. *Br.* **skil·ful** (skílfəl) *adj.* having, showing or done with skill

skim (skim) 1. *v. pres. part.* **skim·ming** *past* and *past part.* **skimmed** *v.t.* to remove floating matter from the surface of (a liquid) ‖ to throw (a stone) so that it skips across a surface of water ‖ to pass lightly over, *to skim the ground* ‖ to read superficially or hastily, *to skim the headlines* ‖ to form a thin covering over ‖ *v.i.* to go fast and smoothly on or just above some surface, *skimming along at treetop height* ‖ to make a hasty superficial reading, *to skim through an index* ‖ to become coated with a thin covering 2. *n.* the act of skimming ‖ **skim milk** ‖ a thin covering ‖ the practice in health programs paid on a pre-

payment or capitation basis of seeking to enroll only the healthiest people as a way of controlling costs ‖ the practice in such of denying or delaying the provision of services to enrolled members as a way of controlling costs ‖ the practice of removing a portion of cash receipts from an accounting for tax evasion or cheating ‖ the use of a machine to remove oil or scum from the surface of bodies of water [fr. O.F. *escumer*]

skim·board (skímbɔrd) *n.* (*surfing*) a board, usu. circular, for skimming over shallow water

skim·mer (skímər) *n.* an implement, esp. a perforated, flat ladle, used for skimming liquids ‖ a member of *Rhynchops*, a genus of North American birds that skim over the water and scoop up small fish

skim milk milk from which the cream has been removed

skimp (skimp) 1. *v.t.* to allow an inadequate or hardly adequate quantity of (something), *she skimped the material for the curtains* ‖ to keep (someone) in short supply, *they are skimped for pocket money* ‖ to do (a piece of work) without proper care and effort ‖ *v.i.* to economize, esp. by making do on short supplies **skimp·i·ly** *adv.* **skimp·i·ness** *n.* **skimp·y** *comp.* **skimp·i·er** *superl.* **skimp·i·est** *adj.* unsatisfactory because of insufficiency in some respect, e.g. short on material, *skimpy curtains* [origin unknown]

skim sweeping (*mil.*) in naval mine warfare, the technique of wire sweeping to a fixed depth above deep-laid mines to cut any mines shallow enough to endanger shipping

skin (skin) 1. *n.* the membrane, of complex structure, which forms the outer covering of a human or animal body, or one of the layers of which it is composed (*EPIDERMIS, *DERMIS) ‖ such a membrane of an animal, esp. a small animal (cf. HIDE), when removed from the body, with or without the hair ‖ a container made of animal skin, e.g. a wine skin ‖ the outer covering of something, e.g. of a fruit, ship etc. ‖ an elastic film resembling skin, e.g. that forming on the surface of boiled milk **by the skin of one's teeth** with no margin to spare, *he escaped by the skin of his teeth* **to get under (someone's) skin** (*pop.*) to have an irritating effect on someone **to save one's skin** to avoid capture, death, punishment or injury 2. *v. pres. part.* **skin·ning** *past* and *past part.* **skinned** *v.t.* to provide with a covering of skin ‖ to remove the skin from, *to skin a rabbit* ‖ (with 'off') to strip off (close-fitting clothes) ‖ (*pop.*) to take all the money or other property from ‖ *v.i.* (e.g. of a wound when healing, or milk when boiled) to acquire a skin [O.N. *skinn*]
—The human skin is self-repairing, heat-resistant and water-resistant, and elastic. It serves as a protection for the flesh and bones. It has pores used for breathing and others used for perspiring, thus stabilizing bodily temperature. The inner skin, fed from small blood vessels, is the seat of nerve ends, through which the sense of touch operates. The hairs on the skin increase its heat-insulating and touch-sensitive properties

skin-deep (skíndí:p) *adj.* (of wounds) slight, affecting the skin only ‖ (of experiences, emotions etc.) not affecting a person at all deeply

skin diver someone who engages in skin diving

skin diving the sport of underwater swimming with a light, self-contained oxygen unit, goggles and rubber flippers

skin effect (*elec.*) the tendency of high-frequency alternating current to have greater density at the outer surface of a conductor than in the center, resulting in increased resistance

skin flick (*slang*) a motion picture containing much nudity; pornographic movie

skin·flint (skínflint) *n.* a mean, miserly person

skin game (*pop.*) a fraudulent trick or game of chance

skin·head (skínhed) *n.* (*Br.*) a young working-class street tough with cropped hair —**skinheadism** *n. also* agro-boy

skink (skiŋk) *n.* a member of *Scincidae*, a family of short-limbed lizards that creep or burrow. They are found in sandy desert areas [obs. F. *scinc* or fr. L. *scincus* fr. Gk]

Skin·ner (skínər), B(urrhus) F(rederick) (1904-), U.S. psychologist, developer of the Skinner Box for his use in the study of behaviorism. He developed the theory of conditioning of behavior by reinforcement with associative rewards.

His works include 'Science and Human Behavior' (1953), 'Verbal Behavior' (1957), 'Technology of Teaching' (1968) and 'Beyond Freedom and Dignity' (1971)

skinner *n.* someone who strips skins or prepares them for market ‖ (*pop.*) a swindler

Skinner box (*psych.*) a device used in training animals to press levers in order to gain a reward or avoid a punishment, developed by B. F. Skinner *Cf* SKINNERIAN

Skin·ner·i·an (skinéri:ən) *adj.* (*psych.*) of the behavior-modification theories (effected by means of rewards and reinforcements) developed by American psychologist B. F. Skinner *Cf* BEHAVIOR MODIFICATION, MOTIVATION HYGIENE, MOTIVATION RESEARCH, SKINNER BOX

skin·ni·ness (skíni:nis) *n.* the state or quality of being skinny

skin·ny (skíni:) *comp.* **skin·ni·er** *superl.* **skin·ni·est** *adj.* thin, with no superfluous fat

skin·ny-dip (skíni:dip) *v.* to swim in the nude — **skinny-dipping** *n.*

skin paint (*mil.*) a radar indication caused by the radar signal reflected by an object

skin-pop·ping or **skin-pop** (skínppɒpiŋ) *v.* (*slang*) a subcutaneous injection of a drug — **skin-pop** *v.* —**skin-popper** *n. Cf* MAINLINING

skin·tight (skintáit) *adj.* (of clothes) fitting closely to the body

skin tracking (*mil.*) the tracking of an object by means of a skin paint

skip (skip) 1. *v. pres. part.* **skip·ping** *past* and *past part.* **skipped** *v.i.* (of a person) to move along with a series of short, quick hops, first on one foot then on the other ‖ (of a lamb) to cavort with tense, springy movements ‖ (*Br.*) to jump rope ‖ to go over the top with a single hop, *to skip over a fence* ‖ to turn one's attention quickly, *to skip to another question* ‖ to read through a text hastily, omitting whole sections ‖ to omit whole sections, *the story skips to 20 years later* ‖ (of a missile) to skim along, grazing and jumping off a surface ‖ (*pop.*) to disappear quickly and secretly, *the bookie had skipped* ‖ *v.t.* to go up faster than is normal in a ladder of promotion by jumping (the grade next above one's own) and going straight to the one above that, *to skip a class in school* ‖ to omit deliberately to do (something normally done regularly), *they skipped the weekly visit this Sunday* ‖ to omit to attend, *to skip a lecture* ‖ to omit to read, notice or mention (something) ‖ to cause (a stone) to bounce on the surface of water by skimming it ‖ (*pop.*) to leave (town) quickly and secretly, esp. when wanted by the police or a creditor 2. *n.* the act of skipping ‖ an omission (esp. in reading) [M.E. *skippen* prob. of Scand. origin]

skip *n.* the captain of a side in some games, e.g. lawn bowling or curling [shortened fr. SKIPPER]

skip *n.* a cage in which men or materials are raised or lowered in mines [VAR. of SKEP, (obs.) a skip]

skip bombing (*mil.*) a method of aerial bombing in which a bomb is released from such a low altitude that it slides or glances along the surface of the water or ground and strikes the target —**skip bomb** *v.*

skip distance (*radio*) the minimum distance at which waves from a transmitter, reflected from the Kennelly-Heaviside layer, can be received

skip·jack (skípdʒæk) *pl.* **skip·jacks, skip·jack** *n.* any of several kinds of tropical or subtropical fish which play near the surface of the water and often leap out of it ‖ an elater (beetle)

skip·per (skípər) *n.* the captain or master of any small vessel ‖ the chief pilot of an aircraft ‖ (*pop.*) someone who leads or directs, esp. in games 2. *v.t.* to act as skipper of [fr. M.Du. or M.L.G. *schipper*]

skipping rope (*Br.*) a jump rope

skip rope a jump rope

skirl (skə:rl) 1. *n.* the shrill, musical sound characteristic of bagpipes 2. *v.i.* to make this sound [prob. of Scand. origin]

skir·mish (ská:rmiʃ) *n.* a brief fight between small forces of soldiers ‖ a slight quarrel or argument [fr. O.F. *escaramuche*]

skirmish *v.i.* to take part in a skirmish [fr. O.F. *escaramucher* fr. Ital. and O. F. *eskirmir* (*eskirmiss*) fr. O.H.G.]

skirr (skə:r) 1. *v.i.* to move, esp. to fly hastily, with a rushing sound 2. *n.* the sound so made [etym. doubtful]

skir·ret (skírit) *n. Sium sisarum*, fam. *Umbelliferae*, an Asiatic plant, a perennial species of which is grown in Europe as an annual produc-

ing bunched, grayish, edible tuberous roots [M.E. *skirwhit* alt. of O.F. *eschervis*]

skirt (skə:rt) 1. *n.* a woman's outer garment hanging from the waist ‖ the part of a coat, petticoat or dress that hangs from the waist ‖ anything hanging like a skirt, e.g. one of the flaps at the side of a saddle 2. *v.i.* to be on or move around the edge, *the road skirts around the park* ‖ *v.t.* to surround or be situated along, *woods skirt the town on all sides* ‖ to move around or at a distance from, esp. to avoid danger or detection, *the soldiers skirted the town* [O.N. *skyrta*, shirt]

skirting board (*Br.*) a baseboard

skish (skiʃ) *n.* (*angling*) competition using a standard plug cast twice at each of 10 targets

skit (skit) *n.* a short burlesque or satirical story or theatrical sketch [fr. older *skit*, to taunt, prob. fr. O.N.]

ski touring *n.* cross-country touring on skis

ski tow a power-driven endless cable which skiers grasp to be hauled up a short mountain slope (cf. SKI LIFT)

skit·ter (skítər) *v.i.* (of small animals or children) to scurry ‖ (e.g. of ducks landing in water) to skim along the surface ‖ to draw bait along the surface of the water with twitches of the line [fr. older *skit*, to jump or dart around, of Scand. origin]

skit·tish (skítiʃ) *adj.* (of a person) playful, esp. in a coy way ‖ (of a horse) nervous, restive and easily frightened

skit·tle (skít'l) 1. *n.* a bottle-shaped piece of wood bowled at in English ninepins or tenpins ‖ (*pl.*, construed as sing.) English ninepins 2. *v.t. pres. part.* **skit·tling** *past* and *past part.* **skit·tled** to knock down (a skittle) ‖ (*cricket*, with 'out') to dismiss (batsmen) in quick succession [origin unknown]

skive (skaiv) *pres. part.* **skiv·ing** *past* and *past part.* **skived** *v.t.* to cut off (leather, rubber etc.) in thin layers **skiv·er** *n.* a knife or machine for skiving ‖ thin, soft, dressed leather from the grain side of a sheepskin, tanned in sumac and dyed [O.N. *skífa*]

ski·wear (skí:wɛər) *n.* clothing designed to be worn while skiing

Skop·je (skópje) (or Skoplje, Turk. Üsküb) the capital (pop. 312,092) of Macedonia, Yugoslavia, a communications and commercial center. The old (medieval and Turkish) city was destroyed by earthquake (1963). University

sku·a (skjú:ə) *n.* a member of *Stercorariidae*, a family of large (18-24 ins), dark, hawklike seabirds of northern climates, with a white streak on the wing and central elongated tail feathers. They steal the prey of other birds [fr. Faroese *skúgvur*]

skul·dug·ger·y (skʌldʌ́gəri:) *n.* trickery, dishonest dealings [Scot. *sculdudrie*]

skulk (skʌlk) *v.i.* to hang around, under cover of doorways etc., in a sinister way or to avoid detection [M.E. *skulken* prob. of Scand. origin]

skull (skʌl) *n.* the bony covering of the head of a vertebrate that encloses the brain and the principal sense organs and consists of the cranium, jaws, and sockets for eyes, ears and nose ‖ (*pop.*) the mind of someone regarded as very obtuse [etym. doubtful]

skull and crossbones an emblem of death, having a skull surmounting crossed thighbones, formerly associated with pirate flags and now used in danger signs

skull·cap (skʌ́lkæp) *n.* a small, brimless, close-fitting cap

skunk (skʌŋk) 1. *pl.* **skunks, skunk** *n.* any of various North American omnivorous mammals constituting a subfamily of *Mustelidae*. They are bushy-tailed, are striped black and white, and are about the size of a cat. They spray a stink from a secretion of the anal glands when they are attacked or fear attack. They are hunted for their fur ‖ the fur of any of these animals ‖ (*pop.*) a contemptible person 2. *v.t.* (*pop.*) to defeat utterly (esp. an opponent at cards, so that he makes no score) [fr. Am. Indian *segankw* or *segongw*]

skunk cabbage *Symplocarpus foetidus*, fam. *Araceae*, a perennial plant growing in eastern North America and parts of Asia. Its early-flowering, purplish spathe emits a foul smell

skurfing *SKATEBOARDING

sky (skai) 1. *pl.* **skies** *n.* (often *pl.*) the atmosphere above the earth, with or without clouds ‖ the apparent enclosing dome which this atmosphere forms ‖ (*rhet.*) heaven **to praise to the skies** to praise very highly 2. *v.t. pres. part.* **sky·ing** *past* and *past part.* **skied, skyed** (*pop.*)

to hit (a ball) up high ‖ to hang (a picture) high on the wall, esp. in an exhibition [O.N. *ský*, cloud]

sky blue the light to medium blue of the sky on a clear day **sky-blúe** *adj.*

sky·div·ing (skáidaiviŋ) *n.* (*sports*) jumping from a plane at a moderate altitude and delaying the opening of the parachute, while the jumper performs acrobatics —**sky diver** *n.* — **sky-dive** *v.*

Skye (skai) the largest island (area 670 sq. miles, pop. 7,372) of the Inner Hebrides, Scotland. Chief town: Portree

Skye terrier a terrier of a Scottish breed having a long body, short legs and a long, hard gray or fawn coat and bred originally for digging out foxes and badgers

Skyhawk *n.* (*mil.*) single-engine, turbojet reconnaissance/attack aircraft (A-4) designed to operate from aircraft carriers or short, unprepared fields, capable of being air refueled and of delivering nuclear and/or nonnuclear weapons; manufactured by McDonnell Douglas

sky-high (skáihái) 1. *adv.* very, very high ‖ (*pop.*) to bits, *to blow someone's arguments sky-high* ‖ enthusiastically, *to praise someone sky-high* 2. *adj.* very high or excessive, *sky-high prices*

sky·jack (skáijæk) *v.* to assume control of an aircraft by force or threat of force, usu. in order to divert it from its original destination —**sky·jacker** *n.* —**skyjacking** *n. Cf* HIJACK

Sky·lab (skáilæb) *n.* U.S. unmanned research space station orbiting earth, launched in 1973, lost falling to earth, July 12, 1979

sky·lark (skáilɑrk) 1. *n. Alauda arvensis*, a European lark having brown, beige and white plumage and characterized by its high-pitched song uttered while soaring 2. *v.i.* to be full of mischief and have fun

sky·light (skáilait) *n.* a window in a roof and level with it or one set into a flat roof as a dome etc.

sky·line (skáilain) *n.* the visible horizon ‖ objects seen against it, *a skyline of mountains*

Sky·loft (skáiloft) *n.* a textured yarn created by passing the yarn through an air jet, causing its filaments to become wavy and intertwined; trade-name product of Arkzona Corporation

sky·lounge (skáilaunʒ) *n.* a vehicle that collects airline passengers and is then carried by helicopter to the airport

sky marshal an armed federal plainclothes security guard assigned to prevent skyjackings

sky·rock·et (skáirɒkit) 1. *n.* a fire work that consists of a rocket which explodes high in the air in a dazzling cascade of colored sparks 2. *v.i.* to rise very rapidly, rocket

Sky·ros (skáirɒs, skáirous, skí:rɒs) the largest island (area 81 sq. miles, pop. 2,352) of the N. Sporades, Greece: marble

sky·sail (skáiseil, skáis'l) *n.* (*naut.*) the sail above the royal of a square-rigged ship

sky·scrap·er (skáiskreipər) *n.* a very tall, narrow building with many stories

sky·ward (skáiwərd) 1. *adv.* towards the sky 2. *adj.* directed towards the sky **skȳ·wards** *adv.*

sky wave a radio wave transmitted by means of the ionosphere (cf. GROUND WAVE)

sky·writ·ing (skáiraitiŋ) *n.* the forming of words etc. in the air by smoke from an aircraft

SLA (*abbr.*) for Symbionese Liberation Army (which see)

slab (slæb) 1. *n.* a thick, flat, oblong piece of something, *a slab of pie* ‖ the outside piece cut away when a log is squared 2. *v.t. pres. part.* **slab·bing** *past* and *past part.* **slabbed** to put on thickly, *to slab paint on canvas* ‖ to remove a slab from (a log) [origin unknown]

slab·ber (slæbər) 1. *n.* slobber ‖ a machine for removing the outside slabs from lumber 2. *v.t.* and *i.* to slobber [prob. fr. Du. or L.G. origin]

slack (slæk) *n.* minute particles of coal, coal dust [origin unknown]

slack 1. *adj.* not under any tension, *a slack rope* ‖ lacking in diligence, *a slack official* ‖ involving little work, *a slack job* ‖ inactive, *slack trade* ‖ (of tides, winds) slow-moving 2. *v.i.* to be or become lazy ‖ to slacken ‖ *v.t.* to slacken ‖ to slake (lime) **to slack off** to slacken **to slack up** to become less diligent 3. *n.* the loose part of a rope, *haul in the slack* ‖ (*commerce*) a period of little trade ‖ any interval of inactivity ‖ (*pl.*) men's or women's long pants for casual wear ‖ a period of slow movement in the tide when it is turning **slack·en** *v.t.* to make slower, *to slacken speed* ‖ to make looser, *to slacken a rope* ‖ to slake (lime) ‖ *v.i.* to become less energetic or less diligent **slack·er** *n.* (pop.) someone who is lazy, or shirks a duty [O.E. *sleac, slæc*]

slag (slæg) 1. *n.* nonmetallic waste matter obtained when ore is smelted ‖ scoriaceous lava from a volcano 2. *v.i. pres. part.* **slag·ging** *past* and *past part.* **slagged** to form as slag **slag·gy** *adj.* [M. L.G. *slagge*]

slain *past part.* of SLAY

slake (sleik) *pres. part.* **slak·ing** *past* and *past part.* **slaked** *v.t.* to quench (a thirst, fire) ‖ to satisfy (a passion) ‖ (*chem.*) to hydrate (lime) [O.E. *slacian*]

slaked lime calcium hydroxide, Ca(OH)$_2$

sla·lom (slálɘm, slálɘum) 1. *n.* in skiing, a downhill race in which skiers zigzag between spaced markers 2. *v.i.* to ski in such a race [Norw.]

slalom canoe (*sports*) canoe, usu. with a deck, designed for slalom racing

slam (slæm) 1. *v. pres. part.* **slam·ming** *past* and *past part.* **slammed** *v.t.* to shut noisily and violently, *to slam a door* ‖ to cause (something) to strike against something violently and often frequently, *the wind slammed the shutters* ‖ to hit very hard, *to slam a ball* ‖ to bring into action violently, *to slam the brakes* ‖ (pop.) to condemn in criticism ‖ *v.i.* to shut with a loud noise, *the door slammed* ‖ to move in a violent fashion, *he slammed down the hall* **to slam the door on** to dismiss (a proposal) outright **to slam through** to promote vigorously and secure agreement for (a proposal), *the committee slammed the new legislation through* 2. *n.* a loud bang, esp. of something being shut, *the slam of a door* ‖ (pop.) a harshly critical notice ‖ (*cards*) the bidding and winning of all tricks in a hand of bridge (grand slam) or all but one (little slam) [etym. doubtful]

slam-bang (slæmbæŋ) 1. *adv.* with noise and commotion 2. *adj.* (pop.) done really well, giving carefree pleasure

slam dunk *DUNK SHOT

slam·mer (slæmɘr) *n.* (slang) a jail, prison, or penitentiary

slan·der (slændɘr) *n.* (pop.) any false and insulting statement ‖ (*law*) an oral statement which without due cause has the result, or is intended to have the result, of bringing its subject into disrepute (cf. LIBEL) [fr. A.F. *esclaundre*, O.F. *esclandre*]

slander *v.t.* to write or say a slander against [fr. O.F. *esclondrer*]

slan·der·ous (slændɘrɘs) *adj.* having the quality of slander ‖ given to speaking slander [late M.E.]

slang (slæŋ) 1. *n.* currently widely used and understood language, consisting of new meanings attributed to existing words or of wholly new words, generally accepted as lying outside standard polite usage. Originating from the attempt to introduce fresh expression into a language, slang will either usually pass out of usage in time or be accepted into standard usage ‖ a conventional language that is peculiar to a group, profession or social class, *thieves' slang, schoolboy slang* 2. *adj.* having the character of slang 3. *v.t.* (esp. *Br., pop.*) to assail with coarse, slangy language ‖ *v.i.* to use slang or coarse language [origin unknown]

slang·i·ly (slæŋili:) *adv.* in a slangy manner

slang·i·ness (slæŋi:nis) *n.* the state or quality of being slangy

slang·y (slæŋi:) *comp.* **slang·i·er** *superl.* **slang·i·est** *adj.* relating to, or being, slang ‖ fond of using slang

slant (slænt, slant) 1. *v.t.* to be at an angle with a given line or surface, esp. horizontal or vertical, *the floor slants* ‖ *v.t.* to cause to slant 2. *n.* the angle made with the given line ‖ the act or state of making such an angle, *the table is on a slant* ‖ an aspect, *the affair took on a new slant* 3. *adj.* slanting, *slant eyes* **slant-ways, slant-wise** *advs* [fr. older *slent* v., to slope]

slant range (*mil.*) the line of sight distance between two points on different elevations

slap (slæp) 1. *v. pres. part.* **slap·ping** *past* and *past part.* **slapped** *v.t.* to strike with the open hand, *she slapped his face* ‖ to put, place etc. with energetic force, *he slapped his hand on his thigh* ‖ *v.i.* to sound with the noise of such a striking, *the waves slapped against the boat* 2. *n.* a blow thus given ‖ the sound of such a blow ‖ an insult, affront ‖ a piece of sharp criticism **a slap in the face** a remark or action that comes as a shock and that hurts one's pride **a slap on the back** congratulations, *the critics gave the author a slap on the back* **to have a slap at** (pop.)

to make an attempt at (something one believes difficult) ‖ (pop.) to attack (someone or something) in criticism 3. *adv.* suddenly and violently, like such a blow, *she ran slap into him* [L.G. *slapp*, imit.]

slap-bang (slæpbæŋ) 1. *adv.* with great force and suddenness, *to run slap-bang into someone* 2. *adj.* characterized by rough, good-natured, blustering force in style, manner or method, *a slap-bang salesman*

slap-dash (slæpdæʃ) 1. *adj.* carelessly hasty, *slapdash work* 2. *adv.* carelessly 3. *n.* slapdash carelessness

slap·jack (slæpdʒæk) *n.* a cake cooked on a griddle, a flapjack ‖ a card game

slap shot (ice hockey) a swinging shot at a puck that usually causes it to fly over the ice

slap·stick (slæpstik) 1. *n.* fast, farcical comedy dominated by physical boisterousness 2. *adj.* of or relating to slapstick, *slapstick humor* [fr. Harlequin's cudgel in the commedia dell' arte, a slatted stick that made a loud noise when banged against someone's bottom]

SLAR *n.* (*mil.* acronym) for side-looking airborne radar

slash (slæʃ) 1. *v.t.* to make a long cut in, esp. by striking violently and with wide sweeps ‖ to strike with a whip, or with the edge of a sword etc. ‖ to cut a slit in (a garment) so that the garment or lining beneath is partly revealed ‖ to criticize severely ‖ to reduce (prices etc.) greatly ‖ *v.i.* to use a whip, sword, scissors etc. in order to slash something 2. *n.* the act of slashing ‖ a long cut made by slashing ‖ a slit in an article of clothing to show what lies beneath ‖ a great reduction in costs, prices, numbers etc. ‖ a clearing made in a forest by felling trees, before the branches etc. are removed from the site ‖ such debris [M.E. *slaschen* prob. fr. O.F.]

slash *n.* an area of soggy, esp. brush-covered swampland [origin unknown]

slat (slæt) *pres. part.* **slat·ting** *past* and *past part.* **slat·ted** *v.t.* (of sails etc.) to flap noisily against ‖ *v.i.* to move noisily with a flapping sound [M.E., origin unknown]

slat 1. *n.* a thin, narrow piece of wood, a lath 2. *v.t. pres. part.* **slat·ting** *past* and *past part.* **slat·ted** to furnish with slats ‖ to construct with slats [fr. O.F. *esclat*, splinter]

slate (sleit) 1. *n.* a laminated rock which is readily split along parallel planes of cleavage into large, thin, impervious pieces which, after trimming, are used to cover a timbered roof. Thicker masses, having a smooth, easily cleaned surface, are used as windowsills, doorsteps etc. ‖ a piece of split slate, used as a roofing tile or as a writing surface ‖ the blueblack or blue-gray color of slate ‖ a list of candidates drawn up by a political party 2. *v.t. pres. part.* **slat·ing** *past* and *past part.* **slat·ed** to cover (a roof) with slates ‖ to list or designate for an appointment, appearance, activity etc., *the next man slated to appear* [fr. O.F. *esclate*, splinter]

slate *pres. part.* **slat·ing** *past* and *past part.* **slat·ed** *v.t.* (esp. *Br.*) to criticize severely [origin unknown]

slat·ing (sléitiŋ) *n.* (*Br.*) a severe reprimand ‖ (*Br.*) a harshly critical notice [fr. SLATE v., to criticize]

slating *n.* the work of a man who lays slates ‖ slates collectively or material for slates [fr. SLATE v., to cover with slates]

slat·tern (slætɘrn) *n.* a woman of unkempt appearance and sluttish habits [prob. fr. dial. *slatter*, to be wasteful]

slat·tern·li·ness (slætɘrnli:nis) *n.* the state or quality of being slatternly

slat·tern·ly (slætɘrnli:) 1. *adj.* like a slattern, dirty, untidy 2. *adv.* in a slatternly way

slat·y (sléiti:) *comp.* **slat·i·er** *superl.* **slat·i·est** *adj.* having the quality of slate ‖ slate-colored

slaugh·ter (slɔtɘr) 1. *n.* the killing of animals for food ‖ a massacre 2. *v.t.* to kill mercilessly ‖ to kill in large numbers ‖ to kill (animals) for food [M.E. *slahter* fr. O.N.]

slaugh·ter·house (slɔtɘrhaus) *pl.* **slaugh·ter·hous·es** (slɔtɘrhauziz) *n.* a place where animals are killed for market

slaugh·ter·ous (slɔtɘrɘs) *adj.* of or characterized by slaughter

Slav (slav, slæv) 1. *n.* a member of a group of Eastern European peoples, usually subdivided into Eastern Slavs (Great Russians, Ukrainians and Byelorussians), Western Slavs (e.g. Poles, Moravians, Czechs, Slovaks) and Southern Slavs (e.g. Serbs, Croats, Slovenes, Bul-

gars) 2. *adj.* Slavic [older *sclave* fr. M. L. *sclavus*]

slave (sleiv) 1. *n.* a person who is the property of, and completely subject to, another ‖ a person victimized by another ‖ a person dominated by some habit etc., *a slave to alcohol* 2. *v.i. pres. part.* **slav·ing** *past* and *past part.* **slaved** to work like a slave [fr. O.F. *esclave*]

slave driver a hard taskmaster ‖ a person who directs the work of slaves

slave flash a photographic flash triggered by light from a master flash

slave·hold·er (sléivhouldɘr) *n.* a person who owns slaves

slave·hold·ing (sléivhouldiŋ) 1. *n.* possession of slaves 2. *adj.* having or owning slaves

slav·er (sléivɘr) *n.* a person trading in slaves ‖ a slave ship

slav·er (slævɘr, sléivɘr, slávɘr) 1. *v.i.* to let spittle drip from the mouth ‖ *v.t.* to cover with spittle 2. *n.* spittle dripping from the mouth ‖ senseless talk, drivel [M.E. *slaveren* prob. of Scand. origin]

Slave River (sleiv) *MACKENZIE RIVER

slav·er·y (sléivɘri:) *n.* the condition of a slave ‖ total subjection to a master ‖ slaveholding ‖ hard, grinding work ‖ addiction

slave ship (*hist.*) a ship engaged in the slave trade

slave state a totalitarian state ‖ (*hist.*) any of the 15 U.S. states south of the Mason-Dixon line, in which slavery was legal before the Civil War: Alabama, Arkansas, Delaware, Florida, Georgia, Kentucky, Louisiana, Maryland, Mississippi, Missouri, North Carolina, South Carolina, Tennessee, Texas, Virginia

slave trade the buying and selling of slaves, esp. the former transportation of Africans for sale in America

Slav·ic (slávik, slævik) 1. *adj.* of the Slavs, their languages etc. 2. *n.* a major branch of the Indo-European family of languages. It includes East Slavic (Great Russian, Ukrainian, Byelorussian), West Slavic (Polish, Serbian, Czech, Slovak), and South Slavic (Old Church Slavonic, Bulgarian, Serbo-Croatian, Slovene)

slav·ish (sléiviʃ) *adj.* of, like or befitting a slave ‖ showing no independence or originality, *slavish imitation* ‖ grindingly meticulous, *slavish attention to detail*

Slav·ism (slávizɘm, slævizɘm) *n.* Slavic character, culture etc. ‖ a word characteristically Slavic occurring in some other language

Sla·vo·ni·a (slɘvóuni:ɘ) a northeastern region of the Yugoslavian republic of Croatia, between the Drava and Sava valleys, largely forest and mountains: wine, lumber, cereals, cattle

Sla·vo·ni·an (slɘvóuni:ɘn) 1. *n.* an inhabitant of Slavonia ‖ the group of Slavic languages 2. *adj.* belonging to Slavonia ‖ Slav

Sla·von·ic (slɘvónik) 1. *adj.* of the Slavs or their languages 2. *n.* the group of Slavic languages [fr. M.L. *sclavonicus, slavonicus* fr. *Sclavonia, Slavonia*, land of the Slavs]

slaw (slɔ) *n.* coleslaw [fr. Du. *sla*, shortened form of *salade*, salad]

slay (slei) *pres. part.* **slay·ing** *past* **slew** (slu:) *past part.* **slain** (slein) *v.t.* (*rhet.*) to kill violently ‖ (pop.) to cause (someone) to be overcome by laughter, admiration etc. [O.E. *slēan*]

SLBM (*mil. abbr.*) for submarine-launched ballistic missile

SLCM (*mil. abbr.*) for sea-launched cruise missile

slea·zi·ly (slí:zili:, sléizili:) *adv.* in a sleazy way

slea·zi·ness (slí:zi:nis, sléizi:nis) *n.* the state or quality of being sleazy

slea·zy (slí:zi:, sléizi:) *comp.* **slea·zi·er** *superl.* **slea·zi·est** *adj.* (of materials) lacking substance, of poor texture ‖ tawdry, vulgar, of poor quality ‖ squalid, shabby [origin unknown]

sled (sled) 1. *n.* a vehicle mounted on runners for use on snow or ice, esp. a small, light one used by children to slide down hills 2. *v.i. pres. part.* **sled·ding** *past* and *past part.* **sled·ded** to ride on a sled [M. Flem. or M.L.G. *sledde*]

sledge (sledʒ) 1. *n.* a low sled used to transport usually heavy loads ‖ (esp. *Br.*) a child's sled 2. *v. pres. part.* **sledg·ing** *past* and *past part.* **sledged** *v.i.* to ride on a sledge ‖ *v.t.* to make (one's way) or convey by sledge [M. Du *sleedse*]

sledge 1. *n.* a sledgehammer 2. *v.i. pres. part.* **sledg·ing** *past* and *past part.* **sledged** to use a sledgehammer [O.E. *slecg*]

sledge·ham·mer (slédʒhæmɘr) 1. *n.* a large, heavy hammer usually swung with both hands

2. *v.t.* to strike with or as if with a sledgehammer ‖ *v.i.* to wield a sledgehammer **3.** *adj.* very powerful, *a sledgehammer blow*

sleek (sliːk) **1.** *adj.* smooth, soft and shiny, *sleek hair*, esp. this as evidence of good condition in animals ‖ very neat and polished, *a sleek appearance* ‖ stylish, elegant, *a sleek car* ‖ (*pop.*, of a person or his manners) smoothly polite in a way that displeases **2.** *v.t.* to groom (hair) so that it is sleek [altered fr. M.E. *slike*, slick]

sleep (sliːp) *pres. part.* **sleep·ing** *past* and *past part.* **slept** (slept) *v.i.* to be in the natural and regular state of inactivity in which (in man and most other animals) consciousness ceases and the bodily functions slow down or cease, or (in plants) the normal processes of development cease or almost cease ‖ to be in a state resembling sleep (e.g. torpor, unconsciousness) ‖ *v.t.* to slumber in (a specified kind of sleep), *to sleep a deep sleep* ‖ to spend (time) sleeping, *she slept the night in the attic* ‖ to provide sleeping accommodation for, *this hotel sleeps 50 guests* **to sleep away** to get rid of by sleeping, *to sleep away one's cares* **to sleep in** (of a domestic servant) to sleep at the place of work **to sleep off** to recover from by resting in sleep, *to sleep off one's fatigue* [O.E. *slēpan, slǣpan*]

sleep *n.* the state of sleeping ‖ a period of sleeping ‖ (*bot.*) nyctitropism [O.E. *slēp, slǣp*]

sleep around *v.* (*colloq.*) to be sexually promiscuous

sleep·er (slíːpər) *n.* someone who sleeps ‖ a large horizontal beam used as a support, esp. (*Br.*) a railroad tie ‖ a railroad sleeping car ‖ a child's sleeping garment ‖ a book, racehorse etc. which achieves unexpected success ‖ an intelligence agent who remains inactive and undercover for many years before becoming involved in any activity or risk ‖ (*bowling*) a pin left hidden behind another

sleep·i·ly (slíːpili:) *adv.* in a sleepy manner

sleep-in (slíːpin) *n.* overnight occupation of a public place, esp. as a protest

sleep·i·ness (slíːpi:nis) *n.* the state or quality of being sleepy

sleeping bag a sack-shaped, padded bag, used for sleeping outdoors or where there is no bed available

sleeping car a railway coach with berths for sleeping

sleeping partner (*Br.*) a silent partner

sleeping pill a pill, esp. a barbiturate, for inducing sleep

sleeping sickness a chronic disease occurring in tropical Africa, caused by the parasites *Trypanosoma gambiense* and *T. rhodesiense* and carried by the tsetse fly. It causes fever, bodily and mental lethargy and, very often, death. It also occurs in Central America ‖ (*Am.=Br.* sleepy sickness) encephalitis lethargica (**ENCEPHALITIS*)

sleep-learning (slíːplɜːrniŋ) *n.* process of receiving instruction through recordings while asleep *also* hypnopedia *Cf* SLEEP-TEACHING

sleep·less (slíːplis) *adj.* without sleep, *a sleepless night* ‖ without cessation, *sleepless activity*

sleep-teaching (slíːptiːtʃiŋ) *n.* technique for instruction through recordings while learner is asleep *Cf* SLEEP-LEARNING

sleep·walk·er (slíːpwɔːkər) *n.* someone who walks while asleep

sleep·walk·ing (slíːpwɔːkiŋ) *n.* walking while asleep

sleep·y (slíːpi:) *comp.* **sleep·i·er** *superl.* **sleep·i·est** *adj.* feeling ready to go to sleep ‖ without much activity, *a sleepy countryside* ‖ lethargic, lacking alertness ‖ tending to cause sleep ‖ (of fruit, esp. a pear) overripe and beginning to rot

sleep·y·head (slíːpi:hed) *n.* a term of endearment for someone very sleepy, esp. a very sleepy child

sleepy sickness (*Br.*) sleeping sickness (encephalitis lethargica)

sleet (sliːt) **1.** *n.* frozen or partly frozen rain ‖ hail or snow mixed with rain (*Am.=Br.* glaze) ice formed by rain falling on objects below freezing temperature **2.** *v.i.* to shower in the form of sleet **sleet·y** *adj.* *slete* prob. fr. O.E.]

sleeve (sliːv) **1.** *n.* the part of a garment covering the arm ‖ a slipcase for a phonograph record ‖ a tube or part that fits over another part to **have something up one's sleeve** to keep something (e.g. an argument) secretly in reserve to be used to advantage at the right moment **2.** *v.t.* *pres. part.* **sleev·ing** *past* and *past part.* **sleeved** to furnish or cover with a

sleeve **sléeved** *adj.* (esp. in compounds) provided with sleeves, *short-sleeved* **sléeve·less** *adj.* [O.E. *slīefe, slyf*]

sleeve nut a long nut used for drawing together pipes or shafts, having screw threads in opposite directions at its ends

sleeve valve a valve in the form of a sleeve or sleeves fitting inside the cylinder and controlling the opening of the inlet and exhaust ports as it slides with the piston

sleigh (slei) **1.** *n.* a sled, esp. a large one drawn by a horse or horses and carrying passengers **2.** *v.i.* to ride on or in a sleigh [fr. Du. *slee*]

sleight of hand (slait) deft manual skill, esp. in performing conjuring tricks [fr. O. N. *sloegth*, dexterity]

slen·der (sléndər) *adj.* small in cross section as compared with length, *a slender stalk* ‖ gracefully slim, *a slender waist* ‖ slight, small, *a slender income* **slén·der·ize** *pres. part.* **slen·der·iz·ing** *past* and *past part.* **slen·der·ized** *v.t.* to make slender ‖ to cause to seem more slender [M.E. *slendre* prob. fr. A.F.]

slept *past* and *past part.* of SLEEP

Sles·vig (slésvix) *SCHLESWIG-HOLSTEIN

sleuth (sluːθ) **1.** *n.* a detective **2.** *v.i.* to act as a sleuth ‖ *v.t.* to investigate the doings of or track (someone) [O.N. *slōth*, track]

sleuth·hound (slúːθhaund) *n.* a bloodhound ‖ (*old-fash.*) a detective

slew (sluː) *n.* a slough (swamp) [variant spelling]

slew, slue *n.* (*pop.*) a large number or amount [Ir. Gael. *sluagh*, a host]

slew *past* of SLAY

slew *SLUE

slice (slais) *pres. part.* **slic·ing** *past* and *past part.* **sliced** *v.t.* to cut into slices, *to slice a loaf* ‖ to cut with a slicing movement, *to slice the air* ‖ (*golf*) to strike (the ball) across its center line so that it goes off to the right of a righthanded player or to the left of a lefthanded player (cf. HOOK) ‖ *v.i.* to make cutting movements as though cutting slices [fr. O.F. *esclier*, to splinter]

slice *n.* a thin, flat piece, e.g. of bread or meat, cut from a larger piece ‖ a share of land, money etc. ‖ an instrument for lifting fish etc. from a frying pan ‖ (*golf*) a sliced stroke [fr. O.F. *esclice*, splinter]

slice of life (*advertising*) copy based on incidents from a life-style **—slice-of-life** *adj.*

slick (slik) **1.** *adj.* admirably deft, *slick fielding* ‖ clever and suave, *a slick young lawyer* ‖ slippery, *a slick surface* **2.** *adv.* smoothly ‖ smartly **3.** *v.t.* (*pop.*) to sleek, *to slick one's hair* ‖ to smarten (oneself, one's appearance) ‖ to make smooth **4.** *n.* a smooth or slippery surface ‖ an oil slick ‖ a tool for smoothing **slick·er** *n.* (*pop.*) a swindler ‖ an oilskin or raincoat ‖ a device for smoothing esp. leather ‖ (*pop.*) a natty city dweller [etym. doubtful]

slide (slaid) *pres. part.* **slid·ing** *past* and *past part.* **slid** (slid) *v.i.* to move with continuous contact and little friction over a smooth surface ‖ to slip so as to fall or nearly fall ‖ to move quietly and with great ease, *she slid across the stage* ‖ to move without attracting attention, *he slid into the room* ‖ to run up to a smooth flat surface and then let one's momentum carry one over it, keeping upright, or to slither down an inclined smooth surface on one's bottom ‖ to change slowly for the worse, *sliding into bad habits* ‖ *v.t.* to cause to slide, *he slid the book across the table* ‖ to add (a remark, clause, condition etc.) in a manner designed not to attract attention, *he slid a saving clause into the contract* **to let things slide** to make no effort to dominate a situation or keep up standards **to slide over** to gloss over, hardly mention (a topic) **2.** *n.* the act of sliding ‖ a smooth surface, esp. ice, on which to slide ‖ a smooth slope down which things can be slid, or down which children can slide on their bottoms ‖ (*mus.*) a portamento ‖ (*photog.*) a transparency ‖ a glass plate, on which the specimen is mounted, to be slid onto a platform in front of the objective of a microscope ‖ the fall of a mass (e.g. of rock, snow) down a mountainside ‖ such a mass ‖ (*Br.*) a decorative clip for the hair ‖ (of instruments, esp. the trombone) that section of the tube which, when pushed in or out, alters the pitch of the notes [O.E. *slīdan*]

slide fastener a zipper

Slide Mountain (slaid) the highest peak (4,204 ft) in the Catskill Mountains, S.E. New York State

slide rule an instrument used in mathematical calculation comprising a ruler with a sliding bar along the middle, both graduated with similar logarithmic scales labeled with corresponding antilogarithms. Multiplication and division thus become addition and subtraction and can be performed rapidly by reading the scales

slide valve a machine part which slides to and fro, opening and closing apertures in a steam cylinder etc.

sliding scale a scale varying in accordance with variation in a scale or scales to which it is geared, *the tuition fees are on a sliding scale according to income*

sliding scale deductible an insurance policy deductible amount that varies according to income, e.g., 25% of income deductible before medical insurance takes effect

slight (slait) **1.** *adj.* very little (in amount or importance), *a slight difference, a slight indisposition* ‖ (of a person) lightly built and not very tall **2.** *v.t.* to treat as of very little importance, *he slighted my efforts* ‖ to treat with indifference or calculated rudeness ‖ to do in a careless or negligent way, *to slight one's work* **3.** *n.* an instance of slighting something or someone **slight·ly** *adv.* [M.E. *slight, sleght* fr. O. Scand.]

Sli·go (sláigou) a county (area 693 sq. miles, pop. 55,474) of the N.W. Irish Republic (**CONNACHT*) ‖ its county seat (pop. 17,232)

slily *SLYLY

Slim (slim), William Joseph, 1st Viscount Slim (1891-1970), British field marshal and statesman. He commanded British operations in Burma (1943-5), and was governor general of Australia (1953-60)

slim (slim) **1.** *comp.* **slim·mer** *superl.* **slim·mest** *adj.* not thick, *a slim rod* ‖ not fat, *a slim figure* ‖ meager, *a slim chance* **2.** *v.* *pres. part.* **slim·ming** *past* and *past part.* **slimmed** *v.i.* to make oneself thinner, by dieting, exercises, drugs etc. ‖ *v.t.* to make slim or to give an appearance of slimness, *lines that slim the waist* [Du. or L.G. *slim, bad*]

slime (slaim) **1.** *n.* fine, moist mud or similar substance ‖ mucus exuded by slugs, snails etc. **2.** *v.* *pres. part.* **slim·ing** *past* and *past part.* **slimed** *v.t.* to cover with slime ‖ *v.i.* to become slimy [O.E. *slīm*]

slime mold, *Br.* **slime mould** a saprophytic plant of the phylum *Myxomycophyta* having a complex variable life cycle, the vegetative phase of which is a motile plasmodium. After a period of feeding this produces characteristic fruiting bodies, which give rise to spores. Upon germination these produce one or two small cells that swim by means of flagella. Fusion of these cells results in the plasmodium, completing the cycle

slim·i·ly (sláimili:) *adv.* in a slimy manner

slim·i·ness (sláimi:nis) *n.* the state or quality of being slimy

slim·nas·tics (slimnǽstiks) *n.* a weight-reducing exercise regimen

slim·y (sláimi:) *comp.* **slim·i·er** *superl.* **slim·i·est** *adj.* of or like slime ‖ covered with slime ‖ (*Br.*) marked by despicable lack of candor, *a slimy trick* ‖ (*Br.*) of a person who seeks to insinuate himself into one's favor by obsequiousness and flattery ‖ filthy, disgusting

sling (sliŋ) *n.* a drink made of liquor, water, sugar, and sometimes lemon, served hot or iced [etym. doubtful]

sling 1. *v.t.* *pres. part.* **sling·ing** *past* and *past part.* **slung** (slʌŋ) to suspend by, or transport in, a sling ‖ to throw from, or as if from, a sling, *he slung a stone at it* **2.** *n.* a loop of leather, rope, chain etc., used to suspend an object, *a rifle sling* ‖ (*naut.*, *pl.*) the rope or chain supporting the middle part of a yard ‖ an instrument for casting missiles, consisting of a loop of leather with strings attached to each end, which when swung rapidly projects the missile by centrifugal force ‖ a large, triangular bandage hung around the neck to support an injured arm or hand [etym. doubtful]

sling·shot (slíŋʃot) *n.* (*Am.=Br.* catapult) a forked stick with elastics and a leather sling attached, used with small stones as ammunition

slingshot *n.* (*auto racing*) **1.** a drag car in which its driver sits behind the rear wheels **2.** a maneuver by a trailing car to take the lead by use of its reserve power

slink (sliŋk) *pres. part.* **slink·ing** *past* and *past part.* **slunk** (slʌŋk) *v.i.* to move stealthily in fear or shame **slink·y** *comp.* **slink·i·er** *superl.*

slink·i·est adj. stealthy, *slinky as a fox* ‖ (of women's clothes) fitting the figure closely and attractively ‖ (of a woman's figure) slim and sinuous [O.E. *slincan*, to creep]

slip (slip) *pres. part.* **slip·ping** *past* and *past part.* **slipped** *v.i.* to move in a sliding motion, *his hand slipped over the windowsill* ‖ to lose one's balance by sliding on a slippery surface ‖ to slide from its or one's support or from one's grasp and fall, *the jug slipped to the floor* ‖ to move easily and rapidly, esp. without attracting attention, *he slipped from the room, the time slipped by* ‖ to sink a little from a previous standard of ability, health etc., *he used to be efficient but has been slipping lately* ‖ (often with 'up') to make a mistake, *he slipped up when he made that decision* ‖ to put a garment on quickly, *to slip into a jacket* ‖ to escape from one's consciousness or memory, *his name slipped from my mind* ‖ *v.t.* to cause (something) to slip or move quickly or easily, *she slipped a ring on her finger* ‖ to give in a manner which does not draw attention, *he slipped me a note* ‖ to escape from, *she slipped her pursuers, it had slipped his mind* ‖ to let loose, *to slip a hound* ‖ to release, *to slip a catch* ‖ to change (a stitch) from one needle to another without knitting it ‖ (of an animal) to give birth prematurely to ‖ to allow (the anchor) to run out too fast and so lose it ‖ to get rid of (an anchor) instead of hauling it in ‖ to dislocate, *to slip a disk* ‖ to molt, *the snake slipped its skin* **to slip it** (or **one**) **over on somebody** to cheat or deceive someone by catching him off his guard 2. *n.* a slipping ‖ a small unintentional mistake ‖ a covering which is easily slipped on and off, *a pillow slip* ‖ a dress-length undergarment, usually having adjustable shoulder straps ‖ a galley proof ‖ a sloping surface down which a vessel is slipped into the water, or on which it is built, repaired or laid up ‖ (*cricket*) a fielder on the offside of and close behind the batsman ‖ (*pl., cricket*) the part of the field in which these fielders stand ‖ a dog's leash that can be inserted for protection with **give someone the slip** to get away from someone without his noticing at the moment [perh. fr. M. L.G. *slippen*]

slip 1. *n.* (*hort.*) a plant cutting ‖ a long, narrow piece of wood, paper etc. ‖ a small person, esp. when not quite grown up, *a slip of a girl* 2. *v.t. pres. part.* **slip·ping** *past* and *past part.* **slipped** to take cuttings from (a plant) [perh. M. Du. or M. L.G. *slippe*, cut, strip]

slip *n.* liquid clay used for coating partly dried ceramic ware in order to have more than one color, or for joining leather-hard clay components together, or for casting ‖ (*envir.*) downhill movement of a soil mass [O.E. *slipa, slype*]

slip·case (slípkeis) *n.* a stiff container into which a book can be inserted for protection with only its spine visible ‖ a record jacket

slip·cov·er (slípkʌvər) *n.* (*Am.=Br.* loose cover) a removable, usually fitted, decorative cover for an upholstered chair etc. ‖ a book slipcase

Sli·pher (sláifər), Vesto Melvin (1875–1969), U.S. astronomer whose research culminated in the first observational evidence for the expanding universe theory. He determined by spectroscopic methods the rotation periods of the planets, discovered molecular bands in the planetary spectrum and the existence in space of interstellar sodium and calcium, and demonstrated that many diffuse nebulae shine by the reflected light of adjacent stars

slip·knot (slípnɒt) *n.* a knot that can move along the string or rope around which it was made

slip law in Congress, the final version of an act and its first official publication, usu. with the legislative history of the act

slip·per (slípər) *n.* a light, comfortable item of indoor footwear ‖ a drag for a vehicle to break its speed

slip·per·i·ness (slípərinis) *n.* the state or quality of being slippery

slip·per·y (slípəri:, slípri:) *comp.* **slip·per·i·er** *superl.* **slip·per·i·est** *adj.* of a surface offering so little friction that slipping easily occurs on it ‖ difficult to hold in one's grasp, *a slippery eel* ‖ difficult to hold to an agreement or to a point in discussion, *a slippery customer* ‖ requiring very tactful and attentive handling, *a slippery problem* ‖ untrustworthy, deceitful [O.E. *slipor*]

slippery elm *Ulmus rubra*, fam. *Ulmaceae*, a species of North American elm ‖ the wood of this tree ‖ its fragrant, sticky bark, used medicinally

slip·py (slípi:) *adj.* (*Br., pop.*) quick, alert, *look slippy about it* ‖ (*pop.*) slippery

slip ring a conducting ring in a generator or motor used by the brushes to take or deliver electric current

slip·shod (slípʃɒd) *adj.* negligent, careless, *slipshod work* ‖ wearing heels trodden down on one side

slip·stream (slípstri:m) 1. *n.* air or water recovering its normal volume after being compressed and displaced by some solid body (aircraft, ship, projectile etc.) which has passed through it ‖ (*auto racing*) the low-pressure area behind a speeding car 2. *v.* to drive in another's slipstream

slip·up (slípʌp) *n.* (*pop.*) a slip, mistake

slip·ware (slípwɛər) *n.* earthenware using colored slips and usually lead glazes

slip·way (slípwei) *n.* a launching slope on which a ship is built or repaired

slit (slit) 1. *v.t. pres. part.* **slit·ting** *past* and *past part.* **slit** to cut or tear lengthwise ‖ to cut or tear into slips ‖ to make a long, thin opening in 2. *n.* a long cut or tear ‖ a long, thin opening [rel. to O.E. *slītan*]

slith·er (slíðər) 1. *v.i.* to slide, esp. with imperfect control of balance ‖ to move with a smooth and slightly sinuous motion ‖ *v.t.* to cause to slide or move in such a way 2. *n.* a smooth, slightly sinuous motion ‖ the sound of something moving on a slippery surface **slith·er·y** *adj.* slippery [var. of older *slidder* fr. O.E. *sliderian*]

slit skirt woman's midlength skirt with side slit

slit trench a narrow trench, often quite shallow, which a soldier digs for protection from flying fragments

sliv·er (slívər) 1. *n.* a splinter of wood ‖ a very thin piece cut or torn off something, *a sliver of bacon* ‖ a piece sliced off a fish for use as bait ‖ a strand of cotton fiber from a carding or combing machine ready for twisting ‖ wool from a carding machine 2. *v.t.* to cut or tear into very thin pieces ‖ *v.i.* to slice or shred [fr. older *slive* v. fr. O.E. *slifan*, to split]

sliv·o·vitz (slívəvits) *n.* a colorless plum brandy made in the Balkan countries [Serbo-Croation *sljivovica* fr. *sljva, sliva*, plum]

slob (slɒb) *n.* (*pop.*) a boorish, vulgar or slovenly person [Irish *slab*, mud]

slob·ber (slɒbər) 1. *v.i.* to let saliva run from the mouth ‖ to gush sentimentally ‖ *v.t.* to wet or smear with dribbling saliva 2. *n.* dribbling saliva ‖ feebly sentimental talk, writing or emotion **slób·ber·y** *adj.* [prob. fr. Du. *slobberen*]

sloe (slou) *n. Prunus spinosa*, fam. *Rosaceae*, a widely distributed, spiny shrub bearing white flowers and small dark blue, very astringent plums ‖ this fruit, used for making sloe gin

sloe-eyed (slóuaid) *adj.* having dark blue or purplish-black, eyes ‖ having slant eyes

sloe gin liqueur made of gin flavored with sloes in place of juniper berries, and sweetened

slog (slɒg) 1. *v. pres. part.* **slog·ging** *past* and *past part.* **slogged** *v.t.* to hit hard, slug, esp. (*Br.*) in boxing or cricket without care for style ‖ to make (one's way) through difficult country or a long, difficult or tedious job, by sheer determination ‖ *v.i.* to push one's way forward persistently, esp. on foot, through hard country ‖ to grind away at a long, hard or tedious job 2. *n.* a hard blow lacking style, esp. in boxing, baseball or cricket ‖ something involving long hard effort, esp. at what is tedious [origin unknown]

slo·gan (slóugən) *n.* a catchword used by an advertiser in sales promotion ‖ a pithy phrase used by a political party or by any other group to indicate a party line on a topic [fr. Gael. *sluaghghairm* fr. *sluagh*, host + *gairm*, cry]

sloop (slu:p) *n.* a small fore-and-aft-rigged vessel with one mast ‖ a small armed vessel [fr. Du. *sloep* perh. fr. F.]

sloop of war a war vessel armed with guns only on the upper deck and larger than a gunboat

slop (slɒp) 1. *n.* (*pl.*) dirty water, esp. that a person has washed in or that dishes have been washed in ‖ (*pl., Br.*) dregs of tea left in a cup ‖ (*esp. pl.*) liquid food as taken by invalids ‖ (*esp. pl.*) swill fed to hogs 2. *v. pres. part.* **slop·ping** *past* and *past part.* **slopped** *v.i.* (of a liquid) to flow over the edge of a vessel ‖ to plod through mud, flood water etc. ‖ (of water) to make a slapping sound ‖ *v.t.* to pour or splash (liquid), *slop some paint on a canvas* ‖ to splash (someone) with liquid ‖ to serve or take (food or drink) clumsily [O. E. *sloppe*]

slop basin (*Br.*) the little bowl in a tea service into which dregs are emptied before a cup is refilled

slope (sloup) 1. *n.* a natural or artificial incline ‖ the degree or nature of such an incline, *a slope of 30°, a gentle slope* ‖ (*mil.*) the position of a rifle carried on the shoulder, *at the slope* 2. *v. pres. part.* **slop·ing** *past* and *past part.* **sloped** *v.i.* to be inclined at an angle with the horizontal, *the roof slopes steeply* ‖ (*pop.*) to walk, esp. in a casual manner ‖ *v.t.* to cause to make an angle with the horizontal **to slope arms** (*formerly*) to bring the rifle as a drill movement so that it is held in the left hand with the barrel on one's left shoulder and the muzzle sloping to the back of the shoulder **to slope off** (*pop.*) to go away so as to avoid having to work, pay etc., or just without announcing one's departure [fr. *aslope* fr. O.E. *aslopen* past part. of *aslupan*, to slip away]

slop·pi·ly (slópili:) *adv.* in a sloppy way

slop·pi·ness (slópi:nis) *n.* the state or quality of being sloppy

slop·py (slópi:) *comp.* **slop·pi·er** *superl.* **slop·pi·est** *adj.* wet with slopped-over liquid ‖ excessively liquid, *sloppy porridge* ‖ weakly sentimental, *sloppy talk* ‖ slovenly, *a sloppy soldier* ‖ careless, *sloppy work*

sloppy joe a hot, open sandwich, usu. on a whole bread or bun, with seasoned chopped or smoked meat in a spicy sauce

slops (slóps) *pl. n.* clothes etc. supplied to sailors from ship's stores [etym. doubtful]

slosh (slɒʃ) 1. *v.i.* to move through water, mud etc. with splashing, sucking and gurgling noises ‖ to flow with splashing noises and movement ‖ *v.t.* to apply (paint) thickly and without care ‖ to splash (something) around energetically ‖ to splash (liquid) freely ‖ (*Br., pop.*) to strike (someone, a ball etc.) hard [imit.]

slot (slɒt) 1. *n.* a groove or channel into which something fits or slides ‖ a narrow opening ‖ a slit in a machine for the insertion of a coin ‖ allocation in a program or budget, e.g., for a salaried position ‖ (*football*) a gap in the defense line, usu. between end and tackle 2. *v.t. pres. part.* **slot·ting** *past* and *past part.* **slot·ted** to provide with openings ‖ to cut a groove in [fr. O.F. *esclot*, hollow of the breast]

slot *n.* the track of an animal [fr. O.F. *esclot*, hoofprint, prob. fr. O.N.]

slot·back (slótbæk) *n.* (*football*) the offensive halfback placed between end and tackle, but behind the line of scrimmage

slot car (*games*) a remote-controlled electric toy racing car operating on metal strips —**slot racer** *n.* —**slot racing** *n.*

sloth (slɒθ, *Br.* esp. slouθ) *n.* laziness, esp. habitual laziness ‖ spiritual apathy, failure to pursue virtue ‖ any of several tropical South and Central American edentate mammals, slowmoving and exclusively arboreal, which have gray or brown hairy bodies, long forelimbs with either two toes (in *Choloepus*) or three (in *Bradypus*), and only a rudimentary tail. They like hanging (face upwards) from branches [M.E. *slāwthe, slowthe* fr. *slāw, slōw*, slow]

sloth bear *Melursus labiatus*, fam. *Ursidae*, a black, shaggy bear of India and Ceylon, feeding on fruit, honey and insects

sloth·ful (slɒθfəl, slóuθfəl) *adj.* lazy ‖ spiritually apathetic

slot machine (*Am.= Br.* fruit machine) a coin-operated gambling machine ‖ (*Br.*) a machine (esp. one selling candy, cigarettes etc., or one used for playing a mechanical game) set in operation by the insertion of a coin in a slot

slouch (slautʃ) 1. *n.* a bad posture or manner of walking, with drooping back and shoulders and loose, lax muscles and limbs ‖ a lazy or incompetent person ‖ the downward bend of the brim of a hat 2. *v.i.* to hold oneself or move with a drooping posture ‖ (of a hat brim) to droop downward ‖ *v.t.* to cause (one's shoulders) to droop ‖ to pull down (one's hat) so that it partly hides one's face [origin unknown]

slouch hat a soft felt hat with a wide drooping brim

slouch·i·ly (sláutʃili:) *adv.* in a slouchy manner

slouch·i·ness (sláutʃi:nis) *n.* the state or quality of being slouchy

slouch·y (sláutʃi:) *comp.* **slouch·i·er** *superl.* **slouch·i·est** *adj.* slouching, esp. in posture

slough (slʌf) 1. *n.* any part that an animal casts or molts, esp. a snake's cast-off skin ‖ dead outer skin that comes away when a wound heals 2.

CONCISE PRONUNCIATION KEY: **(a)** æ, c*a*t; ɑ, c*a*r; ɔ f*aw*n; ei, sn*a*ke. **(e)** e, h*e*n; i:, sh*ee*p; iə, d*ee*r; ɛə, b*ea*r. **(i)** i, f*i*sh; ai, t*i*ger; ə:, b*i*rd. **(o)** o, *o*x; au, c*ow*; ou, g*oa*t; u, p*oo*r; ɔi, r*oy*al. **(u)** ʌ, d*u*ck; u, b*u*ll; u:, g*oo*se; ə, b*a*cillus; ju:, c*u*be. x, lo*ch*; θ, *th*ink; δ, bo*th*er; z, *Z*en; ʒ, cor*s*age; dʒ, sava*g*e; ŋ, ora*ng*uta*ng*; j, *y*ak; ʃ, *fish*; tʃ, fe*tch*; 'l, rabb*le*; 'n, redd*en*. Complete pronunciation key appears inside front cover.

v.t. to throw off, shed ‖ *v.i.* to shed a skin etc. ‖ to be shed [M.E. *slouh*]

slough (slau, slu:) *n.* a marshy, muddy place or swamp ‖ a state of hopeless dejection [O.E. *slōh*]

Slo·vak (slóuvæk, slóuvak) 1. *n.* a member of a Slavic people of Slovakia ‖ their W. Slavic language, related to Czech 2. *adj.* of Slovakia, the Slovaks or their language

Slo·va·ki·a (slouváki:ə, slouvǽkiə) the eastern region of Czechoslovakia, containing the western Carpathians (Gerlachovka, 8,737 ft). Chief town: Bratislava. Slovakia is chiefly agricultural (wheat, corn, wine and cattle raising in the mountains), but industry is being developed (textiles, lumber products, paper, hydroelectricity, metal working). Slovakia was settled (c. 6th c.) by Slavs and conquered by the Magyars (10th c.). It remained part of Hungary until 1918, when it became part of Czechoslovakia. It became a Nazi puppet state (1939), and was returned to Czechoslovakia (1945)

Slo·va·ki·an (slouváki:ən, slouvǽki:ən) *n.* and *adj.* Slovak

slov·en (slʌ́vən) *n.* a person who is habitually untidy in appearance, slipshod or lazy in his work and mental outlook, and dirty in his habits [etym. doubtful]

Slo·vene (slóuvi:n, slouví:n) 1. *n.* a member of a Slavic people in Slovenia ‖ their Slavic language 2. *adj.* of Slovenia, the Slovenes, their language etc. [G.]

Slo·ve·ni·a (slouví:ni:ə) the northernmost constituent republic (area 7,837 sq. miles, pop. 1,792,000) of Yugoslavia. Capital: Ljubljana. It is largely mountainous, rising to 9,393 ft in the northwest (Julian Alps). Crops: cereals, potatoes, wine, fruit, hops and flax. Livestock: cattle. Minerals: coal, mercury, petroleum. Industries: iron and steel, textiles, wood industries, tourism. Slovenia was under Hapsburg domination from the 13th c. until the collapse of Austria-Hungary (1918), when it became part of the kingdom later called Yugoslavia

Slo·ve·ni·an (slouví:ni:ən) *n.* and *adj.* Slovene

slov·en·li·ness (slʌ́vənli:nis) *n.* the state or quality of being slovenly

slov·en·ly (slʌ́vənli:) comp. **slov·en·li·er** superl. **slov·en·li·est** *adj.* of or like a sloven ‖ loose, undisciplined, *slovenly thinking*

slow (slou) 1. *adj.* taking more time than is regarded as normal, *a slow response to a stimulus, slow combustion* ‖ acting, changing, moving etc. in such a way that more time is occupied than is usual, *a slow train, a slow worker* ‖ long drawn out, *a slow recovery* ‖ not easily roused, *a slow audience* ‖ not hasty, *slow to take offense* ‖ dilatory, in a way that shows lack of prudence, *slow to grasp an opportunity* ‖ (of business) not active, slack ‖ (of a timepiece) indicating a time behind the actual time ‖ needing more time than is usual to grasp, memorize or deal with ideas, *a rather slow boy* ‖ failing to amuse, interest or stimulate, *the party was a slow affair* ‖ (of a fire or oven) burning or heating very moderately ‖ (of a pitch, wicket, court, track etc.) soft and causing a slowing down 2. *v.t.* (with 'down' or 'up') to reduce the speed or rate of production of, *to slow up a machine* ‖ *v.i.* (with 'down' or 'up') to move or act at a reduced speed, *he slowed down at the crossroads* 3. *adv.* slowly **to go slow** (*Br.*) to work at less than full production as a way of enforcing a demand [O.E. *slāw*]

slow coach a person who thinks or acts slowly

slow·down (slóudaun) *n.* (*Am.=Br.* go-slow) a deliberate slowing down in production by workers, to put pressure on management

slow·ly (slóuli:) *adv.* in a slow way

slow match a match or fuse used for firing blasting charges, made to burn slowly and evenly at a given rate

slow-mo·tion (slóumóuʃən) 1. *adj.* of a film taken at an accelerated rate of exposures per second, which produces very slow action when projected at normal speed ‖ of a film projected at a greatly reduced speed 2. *n.* this action or speed

slow-mov·ing (slóumú:viŋ) *adj.* moving slowly ‖ (*commerce*, of stock) slow in selling

slow·ness (slóunis) *n.* the state or quality of being slow

slow·poke (slóupouk) *n.* (*pop.*) a person who thinks or acts with irritating slowness

slow virus (*med.*) a virus that remains latent for many years, believed to be causative agent in rheumatoid arthritis and in multiple sclerosis, kuru, and other nervous disorders

slow-worm (slóuwə:rm) *n.* a blindworm [O.E. *slāwyrm*]

slub (slʌb) 1. *n.* a lump in yarn, either accidental or contrived ‖ (*slang*) a badly developed suburban area comprising cheap housing and commercial or industrial properties 2. *v.t. pres. part.* **slub·bing** past and past part. **slubbed** to draw out (wool) and twist it slightly, in preparation for spinning [origin unknown]

sludge (slʌdʒ) *n.* a thick suspension of solid matter in a liquid, e.g. the mud on a riverbed, or carbonaceous mixture with oil as the waste product of an internal-combustion engine ‖ the treated solid matter of sewage after drying, used as a fertilizer ‖ floating (partly melted) ice or snow **slúdg·y** *adj.* [origin unknown]

slue *n.* *SLEW

slue (slu:) *n.* a slough, swamp

slue, slew 1. *v.i. pres. part.* **slu·ing, slew·ing** past and past part. **slued, slewed** to swing or turn in an arc, esp. about a point or axis ‖ *v.t.* to cause to swing around 2. *n.* a movement of this kind [origin unknown]

slug (slʌg) *n.* any roughly shaped piece of metal, esp. the head of a bullet ‖ (*printing*) a line of linotype type ‖ (*printing*) a strip of metal for spacing between lines ‖ (*printing*) a short title of one line used by compositors, editors etc. to identify a piece in process of going to press ‖ a token for an automatic machine ‖ a piece of metal put fraudulently into an automatic machine instead of the proper coin [etym. doubtful]

slug *n.* a usually terrestrial gastropod mollusk, having a much reduced shell or the shell represented by calcareous granules only. The lower surface is a creeping organ. Slugs are herbivorous and are often destructive to cultivated plants. They are widely distributed in tropical and temperate regions [etym. doubtful]

slug 1. *v.t. pres. part.* **slug·ging** past and past part. **slugged** (*pop.*) to hit hard, esp. with the fist 2. *n.* a heavy blow [etym. doubtful]

slug·gard (slʌ́gərd) *n.* a lazy, slow, inactive person

slug·ger (slʌ́gər) *n.* a hard-hitting boxer or baseball batter

slug·gish (slʌ́giʃ) *adj.* slow to act or move, *a sluggish engine, sluggish liver* ‖ (*commerce*) with few transactions taking place, *a sluggish market*

sluice (slu:s) 1. *n.* an artificial waterway with a gate or other device to control the flow and level of the water ‖ the device itself ‖ the stream on either side of the device ‖ any channel which drains off surplus water ‖ an inclined trough for floating down logs or washing ores, esp. such a trough with a grooved bottom to hold quicksilver for catching gold 2. *v. pres. part.* **sluic·ing** past and past part. **sluiced** *v.t.* to flood or cleanse with water from a sluice ‖ to wash thoroughly ‖ to transport (logs etc.) by the stream of a sluice ‖ to wash (ores) in a sluice ‖ *v.i.* to pour through, or as if through, a sluice [fr. O.F. *escluse*]

sluice·way (slú:swei) *n.* an artificial channel controlled by a sluice gate, a sluice

Sluis, Battle of (slɔis) a naval battle (1340) off the coast of the Low Countries, in which the fleet of Edward III of England defeated that of Philippe VI of France. It was the first important battle of the Hundred Years' War

slum (slʌm) 1. *n.* a heavily populated urban area of dilapidated buildings characterized by poverty and filth 2. *v.i. pres. part.* **slum·ming** past and past part. **slummed** to visit a poor neighborhood in search of amusement [cant origin]

slum·ber (slʌ́mbər) 1. *n.* (*rhet.*) sleep ‖ a light sleep 2. *v.i.* (*rhet.*) to sleep ‖ to sleep lightly ‖ *v.t.* (with 'away') to spend or waste (time) in sleep or as if in sleep **slum·ber·ous** (slʌ́mbərəs), **slum·brous** (slʌ́mbrəs) *adjs* [M.E. *slumeren*]

slum·lord (slʌ́mlɔrd) *n.* (pejorative) a landlord who neglects or abandons urban properties

slump (slʌmp) 1. *v.i.* to fall suddenly, e.g. into a bog or water or through ice ‖ to fall bodily, *he slumped to the floor* ‖ (*commerce*) to fall suddenly in value or activity 2. *n.* a sudden or continued drop in prices or stagnation in economic activity (cf. RECESSION) **in a slump** in a period of low spirits or flagging inspiration [prob. imit.]

slump-in·fla·tion (slʌ́mpinfléiʃən) *n.* (*economics*) a period of combined recession and inflation *Cf* STAGFLATION

slung past and past part. of SLING

slunk past and past part. of SLINK

slur (slə:r) 1. *v. pres. part.* **slur·ring** past and past part. **slurred** *v.i.* to speak indistinctly by running sounds together ‖ (with 'over') to make deliberately unemphatic reference, *he slurred over the facts and figures in his argument* ‖ *v.t.* to utter (speech sounds) indistinctly by running them together ‖ to speak of someone in such a way as to throw doubt on (his reputation) ‖ (*mus.*) to sing or play legato, or mark (notes) for performance in this way 2. *n.* the act of slurring ‖ a remark which throws doubt on a reputation ‖ (*mus.*) a sign showing that the notes should be sung or played legato ‖ (*printing*) an indistinct, blurred impression [fr. dial. *slur*, thin watery mud]

slurb (slə:rb) *n.* (*slang*) a poorly designed, constructed, and/or maintained suburb *Cf* SLUB

slur·ry (slə́:ri:) *pl.* **slur·ries** *n.* a thin mixture of water and insoluble matter, e.g. clay, lime or cement [M.E. *slory*]

slur·vi·ar (slə́:rvi:ər) *n.* slurred speech

slush (slʌʃ) *n.* watery mud ‖ melting snow ‖ a greasy mixture used to prevent rust or to lubricate machinery ‖ (*pop.*) sickly sentiment, gush [origin unknown]

slush fund a fund for use in bribery or other corrupt practices in favor of a private interest

slush·y (slʌ́ʃi:) comp. **slush·i·er** superl. **slush·i·est** *adj.* of or having the character of slush ‖ covered with or full of slush

slut (slʌt) *n.* a dirty, slovenly woman ‖ a loose woman, esp. a prostitute [origin unknown]

Slu·ter (slú:tər) Claus (c. 1350-1406), sculptor of the Burgundian school. He brought the Renaissance ideal of lifelikeness and natural expressiveness in pose into the sculpture of Gothic Europe. The 'Well of Moses' (Dijon) is his masterpiece

slut·tish (slʌ́tiʃ) *adj.* characteristic of a slut ‖ (of a woman) very dirtily and untidily dressed

sly (slai) comp. **sly·er, sli·er** superl. **sly·est, sli·est** *adj.* clever at concealing one's intention, artful, *a sly rogue* ‖ showing clever underhandedness, *a sly trick* ‖ crafty, mischievous, *sly wit* **on the sly** slyly, *he did it on the sly* **sly·ly, sli·ly** *adv.* [fr. O.N. *slœgr*]

slype (slaip) *n.* a covered passage between a transept in an English cathedral and the chapter house or deanery [perh. fr. W. Flem. *slipe, slijpe*, secret path]

smack (smæk) 1. *n.* a slight characteristic taste or flavor, *a smack of cinnamon in the sauce* ‖ a very small quantity, *give each of them just a smack out of your glass* 2. *v.i.* (with 'of') to have a taste or flavor, *this vegetable smacks of aniseed* ‖ to have a hint or suggestion, *his stories smacked of the sea* [O.E. *smæc*]

smack 1. *n.* a slap, a quick blow with the open hand or other flat surface ‖ the sound of such a blow ‖ the sharp noise made by compressing and suddenly opening the lips, expressing enjoyment or anticipation, esp. of food or drink ‖ a loud kiss 2. *v.t.* to slap loudly ‖ to part (the lips) with a sharp sound, in anticipation or enjoyment, esp. of food or drink ‖ to put, throw or bring into contact with a smack, *he smacked his hand against the pillar* ‖ *v.i.* to strike against something with the noise of a smack 3. *adv.* with sudden direct violence, *he drove smack into a tree* ‖ completely, directly, *each shot was smack on the bull's-eye* [prob. imit.]

smack *n.* a fishing boat rigged fore and aft and having a well for keeping the catch alive [prob. fr. Du. *smak*]

smack·er (smǽkər) *n.* (*pop.*) a loud kiss ‖ a heavy blow

small (smɔl) 1. *adj.* restricted in size by comparison with most others of the same kind or class etc., *a small garden* ‖ more restricted in quality, amount, value, duration etc. than some standard of comparision, *a small spoonful* ‖ of little importance, *a small matter* ‖ of inferior rank or influence ‖ not prominent, modest, *in a small way* ‖ acting or doing business on a limited scale, *a small investor* ‖ small-minded, petty, (of sound or the voice) weak **to feel small** to feel humiliated 2. *adv.* in small pieces 3. *n.* the small, narrow part of something, *the small of the back* ‖ (*Br., pl.*) small articles of clothing or laundry, esp. underclothes [O.E. *smæl*]

small arms firearms which can be carried on one's person

small beer a beer weak or poor in quality ‖ someone or something of little importance

small bond a baby bond

CONCISE PRONUNCIATION KEY: **(a)** æ, c*a*t; ɑ, c*a*r; ɔ f*aw*n; ei, sn*a*ke. **(e)** e, h*e*n; i:, sh*ee*p; iə, d*ee*r; ɛə, b*ea*r. **(i)** i, f*i*sh; ai, t*i*ger; ə:, b*i*rd. **(o)** o, *o*x; au, c*ow*; ou, g*oa*t; u, p*oo*r; ɔi, r*oy*al. **(u)** ʌ, d*u*ck; u, b*u*ll; u:, g*oo*se; ə, b*a*cillus; ju:, c*u*be. x, lo*ch*; θ, *th*ink; ð, bo*th*er; z, *Z*en; ʒ, cor*s*age; dʒ, sava*g*e; ŋ, orangutan*g*; j, *y*ak; ʃ, *fish*; tʃ, fe*tch*; 'l, rabb*le*; 'n, redd*en*. Complete pronunciation key appears inside front cover.

small-bore (smólbɔr, smólbour) *adj.* of or involving firearms having a relatively small bore, esp. a caliber of .22 in.

small bower **BOWER (either of two anchors)

small business an enterprise eligible for special consideration in dealing with government agencies because of limitation in volume of business and number of employees, such limitation varying by industry

small change coins, esp. of low denomination

small fruit (*Am.=Br.* soft fruit) strawberries, raspberries and red, black or white currants, or similar fruit for the table growing on plants or low bushes

small fry children ‖ people of minor importance

small·hold·er (smólhoulder) *n.* (*Br.*) a person who works a small holding

small holding (*Br.*) a piece of land small enough to be farmed by one man and usually rented

small hours (with 'the') the hours from midnight to approximately 4 a.m.

small intestine the narrow upper part of the intestines lined with a glandular mucous membrane which secretes enzymes responsible for the digestion of food and through which digested nutrients pass into the blood and lymph. It is divided into three parts, the duodenum, jejunum and ileum

small·mind·ed (smólmáindid) *adj.* narrow in outlook and sympathies ‖ petty

small nettle *Urtica urens,* an annual stinging weed found in Europe and North America

small of the back the hollow part of the back just above the hips

small pica an old size of type (approx. 11 point)

small potatoes (*pop.*) a person or thing of trivial importance

small·pox (smólppks) *n.* a severe and contagious virus disease causing fever, prostration, skin pustules and in many cases death

small stuff (*naut.*) small rope, usually designated by the number of threads it contains

small·sword (smólsɔrd, smólsourd) *n.* a light tapering sword for thrusting only and used, esp. in the 18th c., for duels and fencing

small talk light conversation about insignificant matters

small·time (smóltáim) *adj.* (*pop.*) insignificant, petty ‖ (*pop.*) of amateur standing

small·town (smóltáun) *adj.* of or characteristic of a small town

smalt (smɔlt) *n.* blue glass made by the fusion of potash, cobalt oxide and silica ‖ the deep-blue pigment ground from this [F. fr. Ital.]

sma·rag·dite (smærægdait) *n.* a green variety of hornblende [F. fr. Gk]

smarm·y (smármi:) *adj.* fulsomely flattering [etym. doubtful]

Smart (smɑrt), Christopher (1722-71), English poet. He is best known for his 'A Song to David' (1763)

smart (smɑrt) 1. *adj.* sharp, severe, *a smart rebuke* ‖ brisk, lively, *a smart pace* ‖ clever in an impudent way, *don't get smart with me* ‖ intelligent, *a smart student* ‖ showing lively intelligence, *a smart piece of investigation* ‖ shrewd in a selfish or dishonest way, *a smart politician* ‖ well styled, *a smart car* ‖ fashionable, *a smart nightclub* ‖ well cut, *a smart suit* ‖ well groomed and carefully dressed 2. *adv.* (*pop.*) smartly [O.E. *smeart*]

smart 1. *v.i.* to cause a sharp, stinging pain ‖ to feel such a pain ‖ (with 'under') to suffer mental pain, *smarting under a sense of injustice* 2. *n.* a sharp, stinging pain ‖ mental pain, esp. because of hurt pride [O.E. *smeortan*]

smart al·eck, smart-al·ec (smártælik) *n.* someone who shows off in an obnoxiously conceited way

smart bomb (*mil.*) an airborne missile capable of being directed to its target by laser beams, television, or other homing device

smart·en (smárt'n) *v.t.* to make smart ‖ *v.i.* (with 'up') to become smart, esp. in appearance

smart instrument (*mil.*) device equipped with infrared, radar, or similar guidance that makes possible automatic selection of objectives

smart·ly (smártli) *adv.* in a smart way

smart·ness (smártnis) *n.* the quality of being smart

smash (smæʃ) 1. *v.t.* to break violently to pieces, to shatter ‖ to hurt or damage very badly, *he smashed his hand in the door* ‖ to destroy or wreck ‖ to defeat, *to smash an attack* ‖ to ruin, esp. to cause to become bankrupt ‖ to hit or throw violently, *I smashed it on the head with a hammer, he smashed a brick through the window* ‖ (*tennis*) to hit (the ball) sharply downwards with a hard overhand stroke ‖ *v.i.* to come into violent collision, *my car smashed into the bridge* ‖ to break into many pieces ‖ to progress with violent effort so as to overcome obstacles, *they smashed through the jungle* ‖ to be ruined or go bankrupt 2. *n.* the act or noise of breaking into pieces ‖ a heavy blow with the fist ‖ (*tennis*) a hard overhand hit ‖ (*Br.*) a collision with another car etc. ‖ ruin, complete financial failure 3. *adv.* (*pop.*) smack, *we went smash into a tree* **smash·ing** *adj.* crushing, *a smashing blow on the chin* ‖ (*esp. Br.*) very impressive, *a smashing victory* [imit.]

smash hit a play or film which has an enormous success

smash·up (smǽʃʌp) *n.* a violent collision between motor vehicles ‖ a sudden, disastrous collapse in health, business, national economy, human relationships etc.

smat·ter·ing (smǽtəriŋ) *n.* (with 'of') a slight, superficial knowledge, *a smattering of French* [origin unknown]

smear (smiər) *v.t.* to spread, daub (a greasy, oily or sticky substance) over an area, *to smear butter on bread* ‖ to spread (something) with a greasy, oily or sticky substance, *to smear bread with butter* ‖ to spread (e.g. wet ink or paint) beyond its proper outline by rubbing, *he smeared the paint with his hand* ‖ to soil or stain (something) in this manner ‖ to spoil the good reputation of (someone), esp. falsely ‖ to prepare as a smear for microscopic examination ‖ (*pop.*) to defeat overwhelmingly [O.E. *smerian*]

smear *n.* a mark on a surface made by smearing ‖ a preparation of a substance for microscopic examination ‖ something which casts a slur on someone's good reputation, esp. falsely [O.E. *smeoru, smeru*]

smell (smel) 1. *v. pres. part.* **smel·ling** *past and past part.* **smelled, smelt** (smelt) *v.t.* to perceive or recognize by means of the nose and olfactory nerves ‖ to sniff the odor of (something) either to enjoy it or to identify it ‖ to detect or discover as if by smell ‖ *v.i.* to emit a smell, *the pastry smells good* ‖ (with 'of') to emit a characteristic smell, *the old man smelled of whiskey* ‖ to have a sense of smell **to smell out** to look for or discover as if by smell **to smell up** to fill up with a (usually bad) odor 2. *n.* the sensation which results when the olfactory organs respond to the stimulation of some gases, vapors or very fine solid suspensions in the air ‖ the sense by which odor is perceived ‖ the act of smelling ‖ the characteristic odor of a substance ‖ an air or hint of something bad, *a smell of corruption lingers about the name* [M.E. *smellen* prob. fr. O.E.]

smelling salts ammonium carbonate mixed with ammonia water and various aromatic substances, whose fumes can be inhaled as a stimulant or restorative

smell·y (sméli) *comp.* **smell·i·er** *superl.* **smell·i·est** *adj.* having an unpleasant smell

smelt (smelt) *pl.* **smelts, smelt** *n.* a member of *Osmerus,* fam. *Osmeridae,* a genus of small food fishes that resemble the salmon in structure. They are found in the northern hemisphere. They are a translucent greenish color above, are silvery on the sides, and average 8 to 10 ins in length [O.E.]

smelt *alt. past and past part.* of SMELL

smelt *v.t.* (*metall.*) to fuse (an ore), usually with chemical reducing agents (e.g. coke), in order to separate out the metal in a molten form **smelt·er** *n.* someone who smelts ‖ the owner or operator of a smelting works ‖ the works itself **smelt·er·y** *pl.* **smelt·er·ies** *n.* a smelting works [prob. fr. M.Du. or M.L.G. *smelten*]

Sme·ta·na (smét'nə, smétanə), Bedřich (1824-84), Czech composer. His best-known work is 'Ma Vlast' ('My Fatherland'), a set of six orchestral tone poems (1874-9). His successful operas include 'The Bartered Bride' (1866)

sme·tan·e sauce (smétanə) sauce with sour cream, white wine, and onions, and seasoned with salt and pepper, that is served with chicken, veal, or game

smew (smju:) *n. Mergus albellus,* fam. *Anatidae,* a N. European and Asian duck which is the smallest of the merganser group. The male is black and white with a white crest. The female is smaller and grayer. They frequent lakes, reservoirs, rivers and sometimes sea estuaries and are very expert at diving [etym. doubtful]

smid·gen (smídʒən) *n.* (*pop.*) a very small amount [origin unknown]

smi·lax (smáilæks) *n.* a member of *Smilax,* fam. *Liliaceae,* a genus of widely distributed climbing plants with tough, tuberous roots and evergreen leaves. Many species yield sarsaparilla and are cultivated in Mexico, Honduras, Costa Rica, Ecuador, Peru and Jamaica ‖ *Asparagus asparagoides,* fam. *Liliaceae,* a climbing South African plant, with ovate, bright green cladophylls, much cultivated in greenhouses and used by florists for bouquets [L. fr. Gk=bindweed]

smile (smail) 1. *v. pres. part.* **smil·ing** *past and past part.* **smiled** *v.i.* to make a facial expression which may show amusement, satisfaction, affection, irony or derision etc. and which is characterized by a lateral and upward movement of the lips and cheeks and a bright sparkle in the eyes ‖ (with 'at', 'on' or 'upon') to look with this expression ‖ (*rhet.*) to look with favor, *fortune smiled on them* ‖ (*rhet.*) to look welcoming and delightful, *a smiling landscape* ‖ *v.t.* to express with a smile, *to smile a welcome* ‖ to affect or change by smiling, *to smile someone back into good spirits* 2. *n.* the act of smiling ‖ the facial expression made in smiling ‖ (*rhet.*) favorable aspect, *smiles of fortune* [M.E. *smilen* perh. fr. M.L.G.]

smirch (sməːrtʃ) 1. *v.t.* to smear (esp. a reputation) 2. *n.* something which smears, esp. a reputation [prob. fr. O.F. *esmorcher,* to torment]

smirk (sməːrk) 1. *v.i.* to smile in a conceited or affected way 2. *n.* such a smile [O.E. *smearcian, smercian*]

smite (smait) 1. *v.t. pres. part.* **smit·ing** *past* **smote** *past part.* **smit·ten** (smít'n) (*rhet.*) to deliver a powerful, sudden blow to ‖ (*rhet.*) to inflict a crushing defeat on ‖ (esp. *past part.*) to arouse an intense emotion in, *smitten with remorse* ‖ (esp. *past part.*) to afflict with, *smitten with arthritis* 2. *n.* (*rhet.*) a tremendous blow [O.E. *smitan*]

Smith (smiθ), Adam (1723-90), Scottish economist. His 'Wealth of Nations' (1776), surveying the new world of industry and commerce, founded modern classical economics, substituting economic liberalism for mercantilist protection. He condemned unwarranted state control and monopoly and upheld private enterprise, competition, free trade and the laissez-faire state as the right and efficient way of producing maximum wealth and happiness. His ideas dominated the whole of industrial Europe and America until the revival of the opposing theories of state control and protection

Smith, Alfred Emanuel (1873-1944), U.S. politician and governor (1918-20, 1922-8) of New York. He was the first Roman Catholic to run (1928) for the U.S. presidency. He lost to Herbert Hoover, but polled the largest (c. 15 million) popular vote given to a Democrat up to that time

Smith, David (1906-65), U.S. painter and sculptor. He changed (c. 1933) from painting to sculpture, and was a pioneer in working with metal

Smith, Sir Francis Pettit (1808-74), English inventor. He devised and patented the screw-propelled boat (1836) adopted by the British Navy in 1844

Smith, Ian Douglas (1919-), Rhodesian politician, leader of a white supremacist party, prime minister of Southern Rhodesia (1964-5) and Rhodesia (1965-79). After leading his country in a unilateral declaration of independence from the United Kingdom (1965), he was forced to accept the formation of a multiracial coalition government (1978). Black majority rule was established (1980), and Rhodesia became Zimbabwe

Smith, John (1580-1631), English colonist. He was one of the original settlers of Jamestown (1607), and was the colony's leader (1608-9). He mapped the New England coast (1614)

Smith, Joseph (1805-44), American religious leader, founder (1830) of the Church of Jesus Christ of Latter-Day Saints (*MORMON)

Smith, Walter Bedell (1895-1961), U.S. general and diplomat. As chief of staff (1942-5) to Gen. Dwight D. Eisenhower, he negotiated for the Allies the surrender (1943) of Italy and (1945) that of Germany

smith (smiθ) *n.* someone, e.g. a blacksmith or silversmith, who works metal [O.E.]

Smith Act a U.S. Congressional act (1940) passed during the 2nd world war. It made it a crime to advocate, or belong to a group that

---

advocated, the violent overthrow of the U.S. government

Smith College the private women's college founded (1871) in Northampton, Mass., under the will of Sophia Smith (1796-1870) of Hatfield

smith·er·eens (smɪðərí:nz) *pl. n.* (*pop.*) small fragments [SMITHERS+Ir. dim. ending]

smith·ers (smíθərz) *pl. n.* (*pop.*) smithereens [origin unknown]

smith·er·y (smíθəri) *pl.* **smith·er·ies** *n.* the work of a smith ‖ a smithy

Smith·so·ni·an Institution (smiθsóuni:ən) an educational institution in Washington, D.C., founded (1846) by an act of Congress which accepted a trust bequeathed by James Smithson (1765-1829), a British scientist, providing for its establishment. Its governing board of regents includes the U.S. vice-president. The institution conducts activities in all branches of science

smith·son·ite (smíθsənait) *n.* natural zinc carbonate, ZnCO₃ ‖ (*Br.*) a former name for hemimorphite [after James *Smithson* (1765–1829), British chemist and mineralogist]

smith·y (smíθi:, smíði:) *pl.* **smith·ies** *n.* a blacksmith's workshop, forge [fr. O.N. *smithja*]

smitten *past part.* OF SMITE

smock (smɒk) **1.** *n.* a loose outer garment, resembling a long shirt, worn esp. by children and artists to protect their clothes **2.** *v.t.* to ornament with smocking **smóck·ing** *n.* decorative needlework used to gather cloth and make it hang in folds [O.E. *smoc*]

smock·mill (smɒ́kmil) *n.* a windmill with revolving cap and stationary body

smog (smɒg, smɔg) *n.* heavy fog injurious to health because it contains smoke and gases produced by the partial combustion of fuels [SMOKE+FOG]

smog·out (smɒ́gaut) *n.* (*meteor*) a condition of nonvisibility because of smog

smoke (smouk) *n.* fine solid particles, usually carbon, resulting from incomplete combustion suspended in the air and carried by air currents ‖ (*phys. chem.*) a suspension of solid particles in a gas ‖ any vapor resembling smoke ‖ the act of smoking tobacco ‖ something to smoke, esp. a cigarette **to go up in smoke** to be pure waste ‖ to have no useful outcome [O.E. *smoca*]

smoke *pres. part.* **smók·ing** *past* and *past part.* **smoked** *v.i.* to draw smoke into the mouth or lungs and exhale it ‖ to emit smoke by virtue of being in action ‖ to emit smoke by reason of faulty burning or improper draft, *the fire is smoking badly* ‖ to emit any vapor resembling smoke ‖ *v.t.* to cover with carbon particles by exposing to smoke, *to smoke glass* ‖ to cure (meat etc.) by exposure to smoke ‖ to draw smoke from (tobacco, a pipe etc.) into the mouth or lungs and then exhale it ‖ to bring to a given condition by smoking, *to smoke oneself to death* ‖ to fumigate **to smoke out** to expose to smoke so as to be rid of (a nuisance), *to smoke out a wasps' nest* ‖ to force (someone) from concealment with, or as if with, smoke, *to smoke out the enemy* [O.E. *smocian*]

smoke bomb a missile which, when it explodes, frees canisters of chemical smoke to act as a screen or marker

smoke·house (smóukhaus) *pl.* **smoke·hous·es** (smóukhauziz) *n.* a room or building where meat or fish is cured by means of smoke ‖ a room in a tannery used for softening hides by smoke from spent tanbark

smoke·in *n.* a gathering in which participants publicly smoke marijuana to protest the drug's legal status

smoke·less (smóuklis) *adj.* making little or no smoke, *smokeless fuel* ‖ free from smoke

smok·er (smóukər) *n.* someone or something which smokes ‖ a person who smokes tobacco habitually ‖ a railroad car in which passengers are permitted to smoke ‖ a social gathering for men only

smoke screen a dense cloud of smoke produced by chemicals, used to hide military or naval movements or positions from the enemy

smoke·shade *n.* **1.** standard for measuring air pollution **2.** air pollutants *Cf* COEFFICIENT OF HAZE, SOILING INDEX

smoke·stack (smóukstæk) *n.* a chimney or funnel which conveys the smoke from a fire to a high level before it escapes into the air

smok·i·ly (smóukili:) *adv.* in a smoky manner

smok·i·ness (smóuki:nis) *n.* the state or quality of being smoky

smok·y (smóuki:) *comp.* **smok·i·er** *superl.*

smok·i·est *adj.* of or like smoke ‖ giving off smoke, esp. more than is desired or expected ‖ filled with smoke ‖ soiled by smoke ‖ of the color or smell of smoke

Smoky Mountains *GREAT SMOKY MOUNTAINS

smoky quartz cairngorm

smol·der, smoul·der (smóuldər) **1.** *v.i.* to burn slowly at a low heat without flames ‖ to betray feelings one is trying hard to suppress, *his eyes smoldered with indignation* ‖ to exist in a suppressed state, *smoldering resentment* **2.** *n.* the state of smoldering [origin unknown]

Smo·lensk (smoulénsk, smʌljénsk) a communications and industrial center (pop. 305,800) in the R.S.F.S.R., U.S.S.R., on the upper Dnieper. Industries: textiles, engineering, woodworking, food processing. Its famous kremlin (16th c.) and cathedral (17th c.) were largely destroyed in the 2nd world war

Smol·lett (smɒ́lət), Tobias George (1721-71), Scottish novelist. His racy, picaresque novels include 'Roderick Random' (1748), 'Peregrine Pickle' (1751) and 'Humphry Clinker' (1771)

smolt (smoult) *n.* a two-year-old salmon, about 7 ins long, with newly acquired silvery scales, heading seaward from the river for the first time (cf. PARR, cf. GRILSE) [origin unknown]

SM-1 (*mil.*) U.S. surface-to-air solid-fuel missile

smooth (smu:ð) **1.** *adj.* having an even surface which is free from bumps, projections etc., not rough, *a smooth tabletop* ‖ having a surface which offers little frictional resistance when a body slides or rolls over it ‖ homogeneous, not granular, in structure, *a smooth paste* ‖ even in flow ‖ free from obstacles or difficulties ‖ free from hair, beard etc. ‖ suave, ingratiating, *smooth talk* ‖ marked by calm even progress ‖ not jolting, *a smooth crossing* ‖ having a surface leveled down by wear, *a smooth tire* ‖ (of sound) not grating, rasping or loud ‖ (*phon.*) not aspirated **2.** *v.t.* to make smooth ‖ to free from difficulty, *he smoothed the way for us* **to smooth over** to handle (e.g. a situation) in such a way as to reduce or avoid anger, ill will etc. **3.** *n.* an act of smoothing ‖ *ROUGH [O.E. *smóth*]

Smoot-Haw·ley Tariff Act (smú:thɔ́li:) a U.S. Congressional act (1930) of President Hoover's administration. Initiated by U.S. Senator Reed Smoot (1862-1941) from Utah, it provided for a U.S. tariff at the highest protective level in the nation's history. It provoked retaliatory tariff acts from foreign countries, causing a sharp decline in U.S. foreign trade

smooth·bore (smú:ðbɔr, smú:ðbour) **1.** *n.* a gun whose barrel is not rifled **2.** *adj.* (of a gun) having no rifling

smooth breathing *BREATHING

smooth·en (smú:ðən) *v.t.* to make smooth ‖ *v.i.* to become smooth

smooth-faced (smú:ðféist) *adj.* cleanshaven ‖ (*Br.*) smooth but insincere in manner ‖ having a smooth surface

smoothing plane a small, finely set carpenter's plane used in finishing

smooth muscle contractile tissue, lacking cross striations, associated with the walls of hollow viscera, e.g. the stomach and bladder, in the vertebrate body (cf. STRIATED MUSCLE, cf. CARDIAC MUSCLE, cf. SKELETAL MUSCLE)

smooth-spo·ken (smú:ðspóukən) *adj.* speaking in a pleasing, polished manner, sometimes with a hint of deception

smooth-tongued (smú:ðtʌ́ŋd) *adj.* smooth-spoken, esp. saying only what is accepted with pleasure and without question

smor·gas·bord (smɔ́rgəsbɔrd, smɔ́rgəsbourd) *n.* a buffet meal at which a great variety of dishes is offered [Swed. *smörgåsbord*]

smote *past* of SMITE

smoth·er (smʌ́ðər) **1.** *v.t.* to cover so completely, esp. with a mass of little density, that air or light is excluded, *to smother a fire with ash* ‖ to kill by depriving of air ‖ to suppress and hide (e.g. laughter, oaths, a yawn, rage etc.) by an effort of the will, *to smother a yawn* ‖ to give to in profusion, *to smother with kisses* ‖ to cover thickly, *to smother a steak in mushrooms* ‖ (*pop.*) to overcome (opponents) or win (a game) overwhelmingly ‖ *v.i.* to die for lack of air ‖ to be unable to breathe freely **2.** *n.* something which smothers, esp. a thick cloud of dust, gas, vapor etc. [M.E. *smorther* fr. O.E.]

smoul·der *SMOLDER

smudge (smʌdʒ) **1.** *v. pres. part.* **smudg·ing** *past* and *past part.* **smudged** *v.t.* to blur (ink,

paint, a piece of writing or painting) ‖ to soil by touching with something dirty ‖ to smoke (an orchard) against frost or insects ‖ *v.i.* to become smudged ‖ to be susceptible to becoming smudged, *pastel smudges easily* **2.** *n.* a mark made by smudging ‖ heavy smoke used to protect an orchard against frost or repel insects etc.

smudg·i·ly *adv.* **smúdg·i·ness** *n.* **smúdg·y** *comp.* **smudg·i·er** *superl.* **smudg·i·est** *adj.* [origin unknown]

smudge pot a burner put in an orchard, for producing smudge

smug (smʌg) *comp.* **smug·ger** *superl.* **smug·gest** *adj.* very self-satisfied and showing this by manner or appearance [origin unknown]

smug·gle (smʌ́gl) *pres. part.* **smug·gling** *past* and *past part.* **smug·gled** *v.t.* to import or export (goods liable to customs duty) without paying duty ‖ to convey secretly in defiance of the law or of prohibitions, *he smuggled the letter out of the country* ‖ *v.i.* to engage in smuggling **smúg·gler** *n.* someone who smuggles, esp. for gain [prob. of L.G. or Du. origin]

smut (smʌt) **1.** *n.* a small piece of solid, usually unburned carbon, carried off from burning fuel by the uprush of hot air and gases ‖ the black mark made by a smut ‖ a disease of cereal or other plants, affecting the seed-bearing stem and the seed itself and turning them black, caused by basidiomycete fungi ‖ such a fungus ‖ indecent talk, pictures etc. **2.** *v. pres. part.* **smut·ting** *past* and *past part.* **smut·ted** *v.t.* to mark with smuts ‖ to infect with smut ‖ to blacken ‖ *v.i.* to become infected by smut [akin to M.H.G. *smutzen*]

Smuts (smʌts), Jan Christiaan (1870-1950), South African statesman and field marshal. A Boer guerrilla leader in the Boer War (1899-1902), he supported Botha's postwar policy of Anglo-Boer cooperation and played a leading part in the establishment of the Union of South Africa (1910). He served as a general in the 1st world war and as a member of the British war cabinet (1917-18). He helped to found the League of Nations. He was prime minister of South Africa (1919-24 and 1939-48). Smuts commanded the South African army in the 2nd world war and became a British field marshal (1941). He drafted the preamble to the U.N. charter and had much influence on the development of the British Commonwealth. He is the author of 'Holism and Evolution' (1926), a philosophical study of evolution

smut·ti·ly (smʌ́tili:) *adv.* in a smutty way

smut·ti·ness (smʌ́ti:nis) *n.* the state or quality of being smutty

smut·ty (smʌ́ti:) *comp.* **smut·ti·er** *superl.* **smut·ti·est** *adj.* soiled with smut ‖ (of plants) affected with smut ‖ indecent

Smyr·na (smɔ́:rnə) *IZMIR

snack (snæk) *n.* a very slight, hurried meal, esp. between regular meals [prob. fr. M.Du.]

snaf·fle (snǽfəl) **1.** *n.* a bridle bit jointed in the middle and having no curb **2.** *v.t. pres. part.* **snaf·fling** *past* and *past part.* **snaf·fled** to fit with or control with a snaffle ‖ (*Br., pop.*) to filch [perh. akin to Du. or L.G. *snavel*, horse's muzzle]

snag (snæg) **1.** *n.* the roughly pointed piece left when a tree trunk, branch, tooth etc. is unevenly broken off ‖ a submerged tree or branch in a river etc. which may impede navigation or damage the hull of a boat ‖ a difficulty which at first is not seen to exist but which emerges ‖ any sharp projection ‖ a small tear, broken thread etc. made by such a projection **2.** *v.t. pres. part.* **snag·ging** *past* and *past part.* **snagged** to catch (a boat etc.) on a snag [prob. of Scand. origin]

snag·gle·tooth (snǽg'ltu:θ) *pl.* **snag·gle·teeth** (snǽg'lti:θ) *n.* the sharp, broken stump of a tooth ‖ a tooth that sticks out past the others

snag·gle·toothed (snǽg'ltu:θt, snǽg'ltu:ðd) *adj.* [fr. dial. *snaggle*, irregularly shaped tooth +TOOTH]

snail (sneil) *n.* one of many species of gastropod mollusks with a spiral protective shell into which it can withdraw its body. The lower surface of the body is a creeping organ. Snails have a mantle cavity that acts as a type of lung. There are marine, freshwater and terrestrial forms. Some species are edible ‖ an irritatingly slow person [O.E. *snægel*]

snail darter (*biol.*) endangered species of small fish native to, and believed unique to, the Little Tennessee River

Snake (sneik) a river (1,038 miles long, navigable for 180 miles) rising in N.W. Wyoming, crossing Idaho, and flowing through Hell's Can-

---

CONCISE PRONUNCIATION KEY: (**a**) æ, c*a*t; ɑ, c*a*r; ɔ f*aw*n; ei, sn*a*ke. (**e**) e, h*e*n; i:, sh*ee*p; iə, d*ee*r; ɛə, b*ea*r. (**i**) i, f*i*sh; ai, t*i*ger; ə:, b*i*rd. (**o**) o, *o*x; au, c*ow*; ou, g*oa*t; u, p*oo*r; ɔi, r*oy*al. (**u**) ʌ, d*u*ck; u, b*u*ll; u:, g*oo*se; ə, b*a*cillus; ju:, c*u*be. x, lo*ch*; θ, *th*ink; ð, bo*th*er; z, *Z*en; ʒ, corsa*g*e; dʒ, sava*g*e; ŋ, orangutа*ng*; j, *y*ak; ʃ, *fi*sh; tʃ, fe*tch*; 'l, rabb*le*; 'n, redd*en*. Complete pronunciation key appears inside front cover.

yon (40 miles long, greatest depth 7,000 ft) in Oregon and Washington before entering the Columbia

snake (sneik) **1.** *n.* any member of the suborder *Ophidia* (or *Serpentes*), order *Squamata*, limbless reptiles with epidermal scales which move by alternately contracting and stretching the body segments ‖ a treacherous, malevolent person **2.** *v.i. pres. part.* **snak·ing** *past* and *past part.* **snaked** to move or twist and turn like a snake ‖ *v.t.* to haul (a log) by a chain or rope ‖ to skid (logs) [O.E. *snaca*]

—More than 2,000 varieties of snake are known. They abound esp. in tropical and subtropical regions. A few, e.g. the poisonous adder and the harmless grass snake, are common in temperate regions. The snake's eyelids are fused near the eye, forming a transparent membrane. Its wide jaws enable it to swallow prey much larger than its own diameter, its body being very extensible and the skin elastic. Some varieties have poisonous fangs, others kill their prey by constriction. Most snakes are oviparous and most are terrestrial, but there are aquatic and arboreal varieties. Snakes slough their skin whole. They are useful to man as destroyers of vermin

snake·bird (snéikbə:rd) *n.* a member of *Anhinga*, a genus of several fish-eating birds with small heads and sharp bills. They are esp. characterized by long slender necks, and are allied to the cormorant

snake·bite (snéikbait) *n.* the bite of a snake ‖ the poisoned condition resulting from the injection of venom by a snake

snake charmer a person who can control (usually poisonous) snakes chiefly by rhythmic movements while playing quiet music on a wind instrument

snake in the grass a secret, treacherous enemy, esp. a secretly faithless friend

snake mode (*mil.*) a control mode in which the pursuing aircraft flies a programmed weaving flight path to allow time to accomplish identification functions

snake muishond *Poecilogale albinucha*, a small, burrowing African muishond

snak·y (snéiki:) *comp.* **snak·i·er** *superl.* **snak·i·est** *adj.* resembling a snake ‖ infested with snakes, *snaky undergrowth* ‖ having the qualities of a snake in the grass

snap (snæp) **1.** *v. pres. part.* **snap·ping** *past* and *past part.* **snapped** *v.t.* to close or open with a sudden rapid movement or action, *to snap a lid on* ‖ to seize with the jaws or as if with the jaws ‖ to cause to make a snapping sound, *to snap one's fingers* ‖ to break with a sharp sound, *to snap a twig in two* ‖ (with 'out', 'back') to utter very fast, esp. in anger, *she snapped back a retort* ‖ to take a snapshot of ‖ (*football*) to put (the ball) in play by sending it back with a quick movement ‖ *v.i.* to break suddenly ‖ to speak sharply, *don't snap at the boy* ‖ to take sharp quick bites, *the fish snapped at the bait* ‖ (with 'at') to snatch eagerly, *he snapped at the chance to go* ‖ to make a sudden sharp sound ‖ to close sharply with such a sound ‖ to move suddenly and fast, *he snapped into action* **to snap one's fingers at** to take no heed of, defy (authority etc.) **to snap out of it** to make an effort of the will and dominate one's lethargy, self-pity etc. **to snap someone's head off** to speak crossly and impatiently to someone **to snap up** to seize (e.g. seats in a theater, bargains, offers etc.) by quick, decisive action **2.** *n.* the act or sound of snapping ‖ the act, or sound, of breaking suddenly ‖ a snap fastener ‖ a snapshot ‖ a short period of unpleasant weather, *a cold snap* ‖ a children's card game in which players simultaneously turn up cards in succession and when two alike are exposed the first to shout 'snap' takes all the exposed cards ‖ (*pop.*) vigor, *put plenty of snap into it* ‖ a kind of crisp, hard cooky, *a ginger snap* (*Am.=Br.* snip) ‖ an easy task giving sure promise of success **3.** *adj.* done quickly without deliberation, *a snap decision* ‖ done quickly, without preparation or warning, *a snap vote* ‖ of something which closes with a snap, *a snap fastener* ‖ (*pop.*) simple, easy **4.** *adv.* with a snap [prob. fr. M.Du. or M.L.G. *snappen*]

snap bean any bean of genus *Phaseolus* of which the entire young green pod is eaten

snap·drag·on (snǽpdrægən) *n.* a member of *Antirrhinum*, fam. *Scrophulariaceae*, a genus of flowering garden plants of Mediterranean origin. The lipped petals meet, and only bees are strong enough to force an entrance

snap fastener (*Am.=Br.* press stud) a fastening device for openings in garments etc. It is in two pieces, the one being a small knob and the other a socket into which this fits when the opening is to be closed

snap·per (snǽpər) *pl.* **snap·per, snap·pers** *n.* any of various carnivorous food or game fishes of fam. *Lutjanidae*, growing up to 2 or 3 ft in length and living in warm seas ‖ a snapping turtle ‖ a click beetle ‖ a snappish irritable person

snap·pi·ly (snǽpili:) *adv.* in a snappy manner

snap·pi·ness (snǽpi:nis) *n.* the state or quality of being snappy

snapping turtle any of several large, ferocious turtles, fam. *Chelydridae*, which inhabit freshwater streams of North America. They seize their prey with a snap of their powerful jaws. They are considered a food delicacy

snap·pish (snǽpiʃ) *adj.* frequently cross, testy ‖ (of dogs) liable to bite

snap·py (snǽpi:) *comp.* **snap·pi·er** *superl.* **snap·pi·est** *adj.* short-tempered ‖ lively, snappy conversation ‖ (*pop.*) fast and stylish, *a snappy sports car*

snap·shot (snǽpʃɒt) *n.* a photograph taken with a very short exposure, usually of unposed subjects

snap shot a quick shot with a rifle or other firearm without sighting

snare (snɛər) **1.** *n.* a device, usually a slip noose, used for catching birds and animals ‖ an artifice for deceiving somebody ‖ (*pl.*) twisted strings of gut, leather or wire, stretched inside a drumhead in order to make a rattling sound ‖ one of these ‖ a wire loop or noose used to remove tonsils, small tumors etc. **2.** *v.t. pres. part.* **snar·ing** *past* and *past part.* **snared** to catch in a snare ‖ to deceive (a person) into acting to his own disadvantage [O.N. *snara*]

snare drum a small drum hung with its head horizontal at the drummer's side in a military band, or used in an orchestra for martial music

snarl (snɑrl) **1.** *v.i.* (of a dog or some other animals) to growl fiercely, usually with bared teeth ‖ to show anger or resentment in a growling manner **2.** *n.* the act or sound of snarling [fr. older *snar*, prob. imit.]

snarl **1.** *n.* a tangle of threads, hair etc. ‖ an entanglement **2.** *v.t.* to entangle ‖ to emboss the upper surface of (metal) by hammering with a snarling iron ‖ *v.i.* to become entangled (prob. fr. SNARE)

snarling iron a long-beaked tool used in embossing metal. Vibrations caused by hammering on it are transmitted to the working end of the tool, which is in contact with the inner surface of the ware being shaped

snarl-up (snɑ́rlʌp) *n.* delay caused by confusion —**snarl up** *v.i.*

snatch (snætʃ) **1.** *v.t.* to seize suddenly, esp. without permission ‖ to use an opportunity suddenly offered in order to enjoy, *to snatch an hour's sleep* ‖ to remove suddenly from or out of something, *they snatched the drowning man from the river* ‖ to put (a rope) in a snatch block **to snatch at** to try to grab ‖ to take quick advantage of **2.** *n.* a snatching, sudden grab ‖ a portion of talk, song etc. of short duration, *snatches of conversation* **in snatches** in short, sharp bursts, *to work in snatches* [origin unknown]

snatch block (*naut.*) a block of which one side can be opened to receive, and closed to grip, the bight of a rope

snatch squad (*Br.*) military unit assigned to defuse a disturbance by arresting its leaders

snatch·y (snætʃi:) *adj.* done in snatches

SNCC (*abbr.*) for Student Nonviolent Coordinating Committee, a predominantly black splinter group from Students for a Democratic Society (SDS) in the 1960s *Cf* NEW LEFT

sneak (sni:k) **1.** *v.i.* to move stealthily or furtively ‖ *v.t.* to transfer, carry, do etc. in a stealthy manner, *he sneaked the papers into his desk, to sneak a look* ‖ (*pop.*) to steal **2.** *n.* someone who sneaks ‖ an act of sneaking **3.** *adj.* happening without warning, *a sneak attack* [origin unknown]

sneak·ers (sní:kərz) *pl. n.* light, rubber-soled, canvas shoes worn for sports, esp. tennis

sneak·ing (sní:kiŋ) *adj.* of, or characteristic of a sneak ‖ obstinately lurking in the mind, *a sneaking suspicion* ‖ sometimes entertained in thought but never openly declared, *a sneaking desire*

sneak path *PATH

sneak preview an unannounced film shown to the public before general release in order to get the reaction of the audience

sneak thief someone who steals what they can get without using violence or breaking into a place

sneak·y (sní:ki:) *comp.* **sneak·i·er** *superl.* **sneak·i·est** *adj.* of or like a sneak

sneer (sniər) **1.** *v.i.* to make a scornful or contemptuous grimace ‖ to express contempt or derision in writing etc. ‖ *v.t.* to utter in a scornfully derisive way **2.** *n.* the act of sneering ‖ an expression of scornful derision [prob. imit.]

sneeze (sni:z) **1.** *v.i. pres. part.* **sneez·ing** *past* and *past part.* **sneezed** to expel air from the nose and mouth suddenly (often with a loud noise) as a result of irritation of the inner nasal membrane **not to be sneezed at** worthy of serious consideration **2.** *n.* the act or sound of sneezing [prob. alteration of older *fnese* v.]

sneeze·wort (sní:zwə:rt) *n. Achillea ptarmica*, fam. *Compositae*, a perennial plant with creeping woody stock, white ray florets and greenish-white disk florets. Its leaves are used in snuff

snell (snel) *n.* a short line of gut, horsehair etc. used to attach hooks to a fishline [origin unknown]

Snell's law (snelz) (*phys.*) a law of refraction, which states that the ratio of the sines of the angles of incidence and of refraction is equal to the ratio of the velocities of the disturbance (at constant frequency) in the first and second media. It follows that the refractive index may be measured by a simple measurement of these angles [after Willebrord *Snell* (1591–1626), Du. mathematician]

SNG (*abbr.*) for **1.** synthetic natural gas; **2.** substitute natural gas

snick (snik) **1.** *v.t.* to make a small cut in ‖ (*cricket*) to strike (a ball) with a light, glancing blow **2.** *n.* a snicking ‖ a small cut made by snicking ‖ (*cricket*) a snicked ball [etym. doubtful]

snick·er (sníkər) **1.** *v.i.* to laugh in a sly, half-suppressed manner, esp. at an indecent joke **2.** *n.* this kind of laugh [imit.]

snide (snaid) *adj.* mean, cheap ‖ obliquely malicious, *snide remarks* [formerly=counterfeit, fr. thieves' cant]

sniff (snif) **1.** *v.i.* to inhale suddenly and so forcefully through the nose that the action is audible ‖ *v.t.* to draw forcibly into the nostrils ‖ to test the smell of by sniffing ‖ to become aware of (as if by sniffing), *to sniff danger in the air* **not to be sniffed at** not to be treated with contempt **2.** *n.* the sound or act of sniffing ‖ something sniffed, *a sniff of new-mown hay* [imit.]

snif·fle (snifəl) **1.** *v.i. pres. part.* **snif·fling** *past* and *past part.* **snif·fled** to sniff repeatedly because one's nose is blocked with catarrh or as a result of weeping **2.** *n.* the act or sound of sniffling **the sniffles** a slight head cold [imit.]

snif·fy (snifi:) *comp.* **snif·fi·er** *superl.* **snif·fi·est** *adj.* (*pop.*) disdainful

snif·ter (sníftər) *n.* a wide brandy glass on a short stem, tapered at the opening to facilitate inhaling the bouquet ‖ (*pop.*) a small drink of liquor [imit.]

snift·ing valve (sníftiŋ) a valve in the cylinder of a steam engine, permitting air and condensed moisture to escape

snig·ger (snígər) **1.** *v.i.* to snicker **2.** *n.* a snicker [imit.]

snip (snip) **1.** *v. pres. part.* **snip·ping** *past* and *past part.* **snipped** *v.t.* to cut with scissors or shears using quick short strokes in a snappy action **2.** *n.* one cut made with scissors or shears ‖ the act or sound of snipping ‖ a piece snipped off ‖ (*pop.*) an impertinent person ‖ (*Br., pop.*) a steal (real bargain) ‖ (*Br., pop.*) a snap (easy task) [prob. of Du. or L.G. origin]

snipe (snaip) **1.** *pl.* **snipe, snipes** *n.* a member of *Capella*, a genus of long-billed brown marsh birds, related to the woodcock. They have a characteristic swift zigzag flight and a hoarse rasping cry **2.** *v. pres. part.* **snip·ing** *past* and *past part.* **sniped** *v.i.* to shoot snipe ‖ to fire single shots from cover at an enemy ‖ *v.t.* to shoot at (the enemy) in this way **snip·er** *n.* [akin to O.N. *snipa*]

snip·er·scope (snáipə:rskoup) *n.* snooperscope attached to a rifle *Cf* SNOOPERSCOPE

snip·pet (snípit) *n.* a fragment cut off ‖ (*pl.*) scraps, fragments (of knowledge, news etc.)

snip·pet·y *adj.* made esp. of snippets ‖ snobbishly curt [dim. of SNIP]

snip·py (snípi:) *comp.* **snip·pi·er** *superl.* **snip·pi·est** *adj.* snappish ‖ sniffy, supercilious

snitch (snitʃ) 1. *v.t.* (*pop.*) to steal (something of small value) ‖ *v.i.* (*pop.*, esp. with 'on') to give evidence against someone, inform 2. *n.* (*pop.*) an informer [origin unknown]

sniv·el (snívəl) *pres. part.* **sniv·el·ing**, esp. *Br.* **sniv·el·ling** *past* and *past part.* **sniv·eled**, esp. *Br.* **sniv·elled** 1. *v.i.* to have mucus running from the nose ‖ to breathe audibly through nostrils made wet with mucus or with tears ‖ to whine and make a pretense of weeping, esp. as a sign of contrition 2. *n.* the act of sniveling [fr. O.E. *snofl*, mucus]

snob (snɒb) *n.* a socially exclusive person ‖ someone deriving simple pleasure from being in the company of his social betters or who likes to think of himself as belonging to the social class next above his own ‖ a knowing person, e.g. about art or a branch of scholarship, who despises those less well informed, *an intellectual snob* **snób·ber·y** *n.* **snób·bish** *adj.* [origin unknown]

SNOBOL (*computer acronym*) for string oriented symbolic language, a programming language adapted for processing strings of symbols

snoek (snu:k) *n.* a member of *Thyrsites* (*BARRACOUTA) and other genera of large, edible S. African fish [Du.=pike]

sno·far·i (snoufári:) *n.* a hunting or other expedition into a snow-covered area

snood (snu:d) *n.* a ribbon or net bag worn to keep the hair at the back of a woman's head in place ‖ a part of a hat resembling this ‖ a snell [O.E. *snōd*]

snook (snuk, snu:k) *n.* (in the phrase **to cock a snook at** (*Br.*) to thumb one's nose in derision at [origin unknown]

snook (snu:k, snuk) *pl.* **snook, snooks** *n.* *Centropomus undecimalis*, fam. *Centropomidae*, a large game and food fish, resembling the pike and inhabiting warm seas ‖ any of various other fishes of this family [fr. Du. *snoek*, pike]

snook·er (snúkər) 1. *n.* a form of pool played with a number of colored billiard balls, of differing score value 2. *v.t.* to leave (an opponent) with a ball between the cue ball and ball he is to aim at **snóok·ered** *adj.* unable to play a direct shot because of an intervening ball ‖ (*pop.*) in a difficult situation where one is thwarted [origin unknown]

snoop (snu:p) 1. *v.i.* to pry in a sneaking or interfering way 2. *n.* someone who snoops **snóop·er** *n.* a snoop [fr. Du. *snoepen*]

snoop·er·scope (snú·pərskoup) *n.* an infrared image converter that permits viewing in the dark *Cf* ELECTRON TELESCOPE, SNIPERSCOPE

snoot (snu:t) *n.* (*pop.*) the nose ‖ (*pop.*) a snob [var. of SNOUT]

snoot·i·ly (snú·tili:) *adv.* (*pop.*) in a snooty manner

snoot·i·ness (snú·ti:nis) *n.* (*pop.*) the state or quality of being snooty

snoot·y (snú·ti:) *comp.* **snoot·i·er** *superl.* **snoot·i·est** *adj.* (*pop.*) snobbish ‖ (*pop.*) supercilious

snooze (snu:z) 1. *v.i. pres. part.* **snooz·ing** *past* and *past part.* **snoozed** to sleep lightly for a short time, esp. in the daytime 2. *n.* a short, light sleep, esp. in the daytime [cant word]

snopes (snoups) *n.* unscrupulous politicians or businessmen in the southern U.S.; from characters created by American novelist William Faulkner

snore (snɔr, snour) 1. *v.i. pres. part.* **snor·ing** *past* and *past part.* **snored** to breathe through the open mouth and the nose when asleep, producing a harsh noise by the vibration of the soft palate ‖ *v.t.* (esp. with 'away') to pass or waste (time) in this manner, *he snored away the afternoon* 2. *n.* the sound made by snoring [prob. imit.]

snor·kel (snɔ́rk'l) *n.* a pair of intake and outlet tubes pushed above water level by a submerged submarine in order to obtain fresh air and discharge exhaust fumes etc. ‖ an air tube enabling a swimmer to breathe under the surface of the water [G. *schnörkel*, spiral]

Snor·ri Stur·lu·son (snɔ́ri:stá·rləsən) (1179–1241), Icelandic poet and historian. His 'History of the Norwegian Kings' and his 'Prose Edda' are valuable sources for Norse mythology and history

snort (snɔrt) 1. *v.i.* to expel air suddenly and loudly through the nostrils, expressing (in people) anger or contempt, (in a horse etc.) fear or excitement ‖ to make a similar noise (e.g. of a steam engine) ‖ to express by or with a snort ‖ (*slang*) to inhale drugs, esp. cocaine 2. *n.* the

sound or act of snorting ‖ (*Br.*) a submarine's snorkel ‖ (*Am.*, *pop.*) a small drink of liquor, esp. swallowed in one gulp **snórt·er** *n.* a violent gale ‖ (*pop.*) something very powerful, impressive or remarkable [prob. imit.]

snot (snɒt) *n.* mucus in the nose [M.E. *snotte*, *snot*]

snot·ty (snɒ́ti:) 1. *adj. comp.* **snot·ti·er** *superl.* **snot·ti·est** dirty with snot ‖ (*pop.*) contemptible ‖ (*pop.*) snooty 2. *pl.* **snot·ties** *n.* (*Br.*, *pop.*) a midshipman

snout (snaut) *n.* the nose of a hog or of various other animals ‖ (*pop.*) the human nose, esp. when large and ugly ‖ a projection resembling the snout of an animal [M.E. *snūt, snūte*]

snow (snou) 1. *n.* frozen water vapor which falls to the earth in soft, white crystalline flakes ‖ a fall of snow ‖ a deposit of fallen snow, *tracks in the snow* ‖ (*slang*) cocaine ‖ (*slang*) heroine 2. *v.i.* (*impers.*) to be forming a fall of snow, *it is snowing* ‖ *v.t.* (*impers.*) to be forming a mass of (something compared with snow), *to be snowing invitations* **snowed in** or **up** prevented from going outdoors or traveling etc. because of snow **snowed under** overwhelmed (by correspondence, things to do etc.) [O.E. *snāw*] —A sufficiently large and sudden cooling of the air at some height above the ground can cause the water vapor to pass directly into the solid state in the form of small hexagonal ice crystals, without first liquefying. Since the vapor pressure of ice is low, these suspended crystals grow by accretion, in aggregates of small crystals which have regular geometrical patterns of structure (snowflakes), until their mass causes them to fall through the air and they are deposited on the ground. The air trapped between the small crystals of these aggregates causes internal reflection of light at the crystal surfaces, giving snow a sparkle and a pure white color. The air trapped in this way, and between the flakes themselves as they settle, makes the deposit of snow a very bad conductor of heat. The ground, and its animal and plant life, are thus protected from further loss of heat by radiation. The conversion of vapor into solid also releases latent heat, causing an appreciable rise of air temperature

snow·ball (snóubɔl) 1. *n.* a handful of snow, pressed or rolled and shaped into a ball ‖ the guelder rose 2. *v.i.* to grow rapidly larger, at an ever increasing rate, *the rumors snowballed into a major scandal* ‖ to throw snowballs ‖ *v.t.* to throw snowballs at

snow·bank (snóubæŋk) *n.* a great heap of snow

snow·ber·ry (snóuberi:, snóubəri:) *pl.* **snow·ber·ries** *n.* a member of *Symphoricarpos*, fam. *Caprifoliaceae*, a species of cultivated ornamental shrub, esp. the North American species, *S. albas*, bearing pink flowers in terminal racemes. The fruits are globose white berries

snow·bird (snóubə:rd) *n.* any of various North American finches of genus *Junco*

snowbirds 1. Northern residents who vacation in southern regions, esp. Florida 2. (*slang*) cocaine users 3. (*slang*) heroin users *Cf* SNOW-FLAKES

snow-blind (snóublaind) *adj.* afflicted with snow blindness **snow blindness** temporary blindness caused by overstimulation of the retina through prolonged exposure to the white light reflected from expanses of snow or ice

snow·blink (snóubliŋk) *n.* glaring reflection from fields of ice in polar regions (*ICEBLINK)

snow·bound (snóubaund) *adj.* forced to stay where one is because of snow

snow bunting *Plectrophenax nivalis*, a small finch which breeds in the Arctic and migrates farther south in winter. It is largely of white plumage and common in Europe and North America

snow-capped (snóukæpt) *adj.* (of a mountain) having snow on its summit

Snow·don (snóud'n) a mountain in N. Wales with five peaks, rising to 3,560 ft

Snow·do·ni·a (snoudóuni:ə) the massif in Caernarvonshire and Merioneth, N. Wales, of which Snowdon is the highest mountain

snow·drift (snóudrift) *n.* a heaped mass of snow, driven by the wind from more exposed places

snow·drop (snóudrɒp) *n.* *Galanthus nivalis*, fam. *Amaryllidaceae*, a small, early blossoming, bulbous plant which bears one white, nodding flower early in the year

snow·fall (snóufɔl) *n.* a fall of snow ‖ the amount of snow falling during a stated period of time

snow·field (snóufi:ld) *n.* a smooth and fairly level expanse of snow, esp. such a mass at the head of a glacier

snow·flake (snóufleik) *n.* a single crystal of snow ‖ a member of *Leucojum*, fam. *Amaryllidaceae*, a genus of cultivated plants of Mediterranean origin growing from a large bulb and having one or several nodding flowers ‖ the snow bunting

snowflakes Northerners who commute to southern regions on weekends, esp. to Florida

snow goose *pl.* **snow geese** a small white goose of genus *Chen* with black-tipped wings, indigenous to the Arctic and migrating south

snow leopard the ounce

snow line the altitude on a mountain slope above which the snow never completely melts during the year

snow·mak·er (snóumeikə:r) *n.* device for making artificial snow

snow·man (snóumæn) *pl.* **snow·men** (snóumen) *n.* a rough likeness of a man made by rolling and heaping snow

snow·mo·bile (snóumoubi:l) *n.* motor vehicle for travel on snow —**snowmobile** *v.* —**snow·mobiler** *n.* —**snowmobilist** *n.*

snow·plow, *Br.* **snow·plough** (snóuplau) *n.* any plowlike device used for cleaning snow from a road or railroad ‖ (*skiing*) a maneuver in which the tips of the skis are pointed inward, causing one to brake

snow·shoe (snóuʃu:) *n.* a light lattice, in a frame, worn under the shoes or boots, enabling a person to walk on soft snow without sinking

snow·slide (snóuslaid) *n.* an avalanche of snow

snow·storm (snóustɔrm) *n.* a heavy fall of snow, esp. when accompanied by a strong wind ‖ something resembling this, e.g. an electrical disturbance of a television screen image

snow-white (snóuhwáit, snóuwáit) *adj.* as white as snow, pure white

snow·y (snóui:) *comp.* **snow·i·er** *superl.* **snow·i·est** *adj.* covered by, or abounding in, snow, *a snowy landscape* ‖ as white as snow, *snowy hair*

Snowy Mountains the highest part of the Australian Alps, in New South Wales and Victoria: Mt Kosciusko (7,316 ft)

snub (snʌb) 1. *v.t. pres. part.* **snub·bing** *past* and *past part.* **snubbed** to refuse to notice the presence of (someone) ‖ to stave (someone) off deliberately by refusing to respond to a friendly approach ‖ to check the movement of (e.g. a horse or boat) by a rope attached to a stationary object ‖ (*naut.*) to check suddenly (e.g. a rope or chain) that is running out 2. *n.* the act or an instance of snubbing [O.N. *snubba*, to rebuke]

snub nose a short, slightly turned-up nose

snuff (snʌf) 1. *v.t.* to inhale through the nose usually in order to smell, to sniff ‖ *v.i.* to inhale through the nostrils in a noisy fashion 2. *n.* the act of snuffing ‖ powdered tobacco inhaled into the nose [prob. fr. M.Du. *snoffen, snuffen*, to snuffle]

snuff 1. *v.t.* to cut off the snuff of (a candle) ‖ (with 'out') to put out (a candle) ‖ (with 'out') to put an end to (a conspiracy etc.) 2. *n.* the charred end of a candle wick [origin unknown]

snuff-box (snʌ́fbɒks) *n.* a small, usually ornamented box for holding snuff

snuf·fer (snʌ́fər) *n.* a device used for snuffing out candles, consisting of a hollow cone attached to a handle ‖ (*pl.*) a pair of scissors used for clipping the snuff off a candle

snuff film violent, illegal sex film in which the female participant is actually murdered

snuf·fle (snʌ́fəl) 1. *v. pres. part.* **snuf·fling** *past* and *past part.* **snuf·fled** *v.i.* to breathe noisily through the nose when this is partly obstructed by mucus or moisture ‖ *v.t.* to say with such snuffling 2. *n.* the sound or act of snuffling **the snuffles** a congestion of mucus in the nose causing difficulty in breathing or talking ‖ a respiratory disease in rats, pigs etc. [prob. fr. Du. and Flem. *snuffelen*]

snug (snʌg) 1. *comp.* **snug·ger** *superl.* **snug·gest** *adj.* safe and comfortable (esp. warm) ‖ small but comfortably arranged ‖ close-fitting, *a snug jacket* ‖ (*naut.*) trim and seaworthy ‖ (of income) certain and sufficient to ensure comfort 2. *v.t. pres. part.* **snug·ging** *past* and *past part.* **snugged** (*naut.*, with 'down') to prepare (a ship) for a storm by reducing sail, fastening down movables etc. **snúg·ger·y** *pl.* **snug·ger·ies** *n.* (*Br.*) a place where one can be undisturbed and at ease, esp. a small, warm room of one's own [origin unknown]

snug·gle (snʌg'l) *pres. part.* **snug·gling** *past* and *past part.* **snug·gled** *v.i.* to lie closely for warmth, protection, affection etc. ‖ *v.t.* to move (oneself, one's head etc.) close to someone or something for warmth, protection etc. [fr. SNUG V., (obs.) to nestle closely]

so (sou) **1.** *adv.* in a certain way, *it must be done so* ‖ to a certain degree, *you may only go so far* ‖ to a large degree, *he was so angry* ‖ as a result, *she wrapped up well and so so warm* ‖ also, *she wants to leave and so do I* ‖ then, *so that's what you think* ‖ in a manner previously mentioned, *the wall is painted green and has been so for some time* ‖ (in comparative constructions) as, *it won't be so bad as you think* **and so on** et cetera ‖ and continuing in the same way **so as** in order to, *he left early so as not to be tired* **so . . . as** so great in quantity or number that a specified result follows, *cars so numerous as to block traffic for hours* **2.** *conj.* in order that, *I'll show you so you can see how it's done* ‖ (pop.) with the result that, *I covered him so he kept warm* ‖ therefore, *you aren't listening so I'll shut up* **3.** *pron.* approximately that much, *can you lend me a dollar or so?* ‖ as has been described or as will be understood, *he was ill but did not seem so* **4.** *adj.* true, *is that so?* **5.** *interj.* used to express surprise, understanding or indifference [O.E. *swa, swā*]

soak (souk) *v.i.* to be or become thoroughly wet by lying immersed in fluid ‖ (pop.) to penetrate the mind, *the idea hasn't soaked into his head* ‖ (of a liquid) to enter through pores or interstices ‖ *v.t.* to make very wet, *the rain soaked my clothes* ‖ (esp. with 'up') to take in (liquid) by absorbing ‖ to place (something) in a liquid in order to saturate it ‖ (with 'out') to cleanse or drain (something) by soaking, *to soak out stains* ‖ (pop.) to absorb mentally **sóak·age** *n.* the process of soaking ‖ the liquid soaked up by a porous body or lost by leaking **sóak·ers** *pl. n.* a pair of light woolen pants put on over a baby's diaper [O.E. *socian*]

so-and-so (sóuənsou) *pl.* **so-and-sos** *n.* an unnamed or undetermined person or thing ‖ (a euphemism for) a bastard (harsh or unjust person)

Soane (soun), Sir John (1753-1837), English architect. He was a leader of the classical revival with a highly imaginative personal style. His most important building is the Bank of England. The Soane Museum in London houses some of his designs as well as his collection of pictures, furniture and sculpture

soap (soup) **1.** *n.* a cleaning or emulsifying agent usually made from fats by saponification. It consists of a mixture of alkali metal salts of fatty acids, soluble in water, and various additions such as perfume or coloring agents, disinfectants etc. ‖ a metallic salt of a fatty acid **2.** *v.t.* to treat with soap [O.E. *sāpe*]

soap·bark (sóupbɑrk) *n. Quillaja saponaria,* fam. *Rosaceae,* a Chilean tree whose bark contains saponin and gives a soapy lather when rubbed in water. It is used in cleaning and emulsifying fluids ‖ any of several tropical shrubs of the genus *Pithecolobium,* fam. *Leguminosae,* which have saponaceous bark

soap·ber·ry (sóupbɛri:, sóupbəri:) *pl.* **soap·ber·ries** *n.* a tree of genus *Sapindus,* fam. *Sapindaceae,* whose fruit is used as a cleansing agent, and which yields gum as well as saponin ‖ the fruit of this tree

soap·box (sóupbɒks) **1.** *n.* an improvised platform used by a free-lance open-air orator with a pet subject to expound to anyone he can persuade to listen **2.** *adj.* of or relating to such oratory or orators

soap bubble an iridescent bubble of soapy water

soap opera radio or television serial drama or dramas of ongoing romantic and domestic crises; from its original sponsorship by soap manufacturers *Cf* SITCOM

soap plant *Chlorogalum pomeridianum,* fam. *Liliaceae,* a California plant yielding saponin

soap·root (sóupru:t, sóuprut) *n.* any of various S. European plants of genus *Gypsophilia,* fam. *Caryophyllaceae,* whose roots are used as soap

soap·stone (sóupstoun) *n.* steatite

soap·suds (sóupsʌdz) *pl. n.* the mass of soap bubbles in a solution of soap and water

soap·wort (sóupwə:rt) *n. Saponaria officinalis,* fam. *Carophyllaceae,* a plant whose leaves lather when rubbed with water

soap·y (sóupi:) *comp.* **soap·i·er** *superl.* **soap·i·est** *adj.* resembling, mixed or covered with soap ‖ (of a person) ingratiating, smooth

soar (sɔr, sour) **1.** *v.i.* to rise high into the air ‖ (of birds) to float high in the air while moving forward ‖ *(aeron.,* of a glider) to fly gaining height using rising air currents ‖ (of prices, profits etc.) to rise to a very high level ‖ (of hopes, thoughts etc.) to become more spiritual **2.** *n.* the act of soaring ‖ the height or distance attained in soaring [fr. F. *essorer*]

Soa·ve (swávei) *n.* a dry, white wine from the Soave area in Italy

sob (sɒb) **1.** *v. pres. part.* **sob·bing** *past* and *past part.* **sobbed** *v.i.* to weep violently with convulsive catches of the breath ‖ to make a sound like sobbing ‖ *v.t.* to utter thus ‖ to bring (oneself) thus to a certain condition, *she sobbed herself to sleep* **2.** *n.* the sound of sobbing ‖ the convulsive catch of the breath in sobbing [prob. imit.]

so·ber (sóubər) **1.** *adj.* not drunk ‖ not given to drinking alcohol excessively ‖ temperate in the use of all sources of pleasure ‖ staid, sedate, *sober habits* ‖ thought out with proper care, *a sober judgment* ‖ showing discretion and moderation ‖ serious, grave, *sober aldermen* ‖ giving cause for gravity, *a sober thought* ‖ not ornamented, not fanciful, *a sober style* ‖ subdued, *sober colors* **2.** *v.t.* to make sober ‖ *v.i.* to become sober [O.F. *sobre*]

so·ber·sides (sóubərsaidz) *n.* (pop.) a too earnest, serious-minded person

So·bies·ki (soubjéski:), John *JOHN III SOBIESKI

so·bri·e·ty (səbráiiti:, soubráiiti:) *n.* the quality or state of being sober [fr. F. *sobriété* or L. *sobrietas*]

so·bri·quet (sóubrəkei, sóubrəket, soubrəkéi, soubrəkét) *n.* an epithet ‖ a nickname [F.]

sob sister (pop.) a journalist who writes sentimental human-interest stories

sob story (pop.) a sentimental story intended to arouse sympathy

soc·age, soc·cage (sókidʒ) *n. (hist.)* the holding and use of land under the feudal system in return for payment of rent or some service other than military service [A.F.]

so-called (sóukɔ́ld) *adj.* popularly named, esp. improperly or undeservedly so, *a so-called liberal*

soccage *SOCAGE

soc·cer (sókər) *n.* a game developed in Britain since 1863. It is played by two teams each of 11 men, with a round football, on a rectangular field (120 yds x 80 yds) having a goal 8 yds wide and 8 ft high at either end. Players kick, dribble and pass the ball with their feet, though the head and trunk may be brought into play as well. Only the goalkeeper may handle the ball. A goal is scored when the ball is sent between the opponent's goalposts

So·che (sótʃʌ) *YARKAND

so·cia·bil·i·ty (souʃəbíliti:) *pl.* **so·cia·bil·i·ties** *n.* the quality or state of being sociable ‖ an instance of being sociable

so·cia·ble (sóuʃəb'l) *adj.* fond of the company of others and apt to seek or welcome it ‖ friendly, *a sociable gathering* [F. or fr. L. *sociabilis*]

so·cial (sóuʃəl) **1.** *adj.* relating to human society, *social legislation* ‖ living in communities, *social insects* ‖ enjoyed or taken in company ‖ sociable ‖ relating to or designed for social activities, *a social club* ‖ relating to rank in the community, *social equals* ‖ (bot.) growing in clumps **2.** *n.* an informal community gathering [F. or fr. L. *socialis*]

social anthropology the science which studies the culture and social structure of primitive peoples through their language, law, technical ability, religion etc. (*PHYSICAL ANTHROPOLOGY, *ANTHROPOLOGY)

social climber a person who tries to be accepted into a higher social milieu than the one to which he belongs

social compact a proposal by 1974 British Labour Government to trade unions, promising price subsidies, and price and dividend controls in exchange for restrained wage demands

Social Credit the theory that the profits of industry should be distributed to all consumers by a system of dividends so as to ensure a high level of consumption and allay the possibilities of economic depression. The theory was originated by C. H. Douglas

social democracy the political principles of those who hold that socialism should be achieved as an economic and political form of human society in place of capitalism, and that it should be done through the normal workings of democracy

social democrat an advocate of social democracy **Social Democrat** a member of a Social Democratic party

Social Democratic party any of several European political parties advocating gradual transition to a socialist society through the normal workings of democratic government ‖ *(Am. hist.)* a U.S. political party (founded c. 1897) which merged with dissident members of the Socialist Labor party to become (1901) the Socialist party

Social Democratic Party British political party that splintered from the Labor Party in 1980; generally regarded as expounding middle-of-the-road policies

social disease venereal disease ‖ a disease, e.g. tuberculosis, whose incidence is related directly to social conditions

so·cial·ism (sóuʃəlizəm) *n.* a political and economic theory advocating collective ownership of the means of production and control of distribution. It is based on the belief that all, while contributing to the good of the community, are equally entitled to the care and protection which the community can provide. The theory assumes different forms according to the relative stress laid on its social, economic and political corollaries. Thus Marxian socialism is concerned very largely with the economic issues, and postulates the communal ownership and control of the means of production, distribution and exchange. Christian socialism stresses the social aspect, making of the theory a way of life. Democratic socialism stresses the political aspect, accepting a compromise in the economic field between state and private enterprise. All forms of the theory agree in being opposed to uncontrolled capitalism and in seeking equality of opportunity for all members of the community [F. *socialisme* or fr. SOCIAL]

so·cial·ist (sóuʃəlist) **1.** *n.* a person who advocates socialism **So·cial·ist** a member of a socialist party **2.** *adj.* of, relating to, based on or favoring socialism **so·cial·ist·ic** *adj.*

socialist pluralism political socialism in its various manifestations, e.g., as practiced in the U.S.S.R., China, Yugoslavia

socialist realism 1. didactic use of the arts for the development of social consciousness and the enhancement of the socialist state **2.** official art of the Communist Party, esp. in U.S.S.R. *Cf* SOCIAL REALISM

socialist republic a title adopted by certain people's republics (e.g. Czechoslovakia, Yugoslavia, Rumania) denoting a more advanced stage in the transition from capitalism to communism

so·cial·ite (sóuʃəlait) *n.* (pop.) someone prominent in fashionable, affluent society

so·cial·i·za·tion (souʃəlaizéiʃən) *n.* a socializing or being socialized

so·cial·ize (sóuʃəlaiz) *pres. part.* **so·cial·iz·ing** *past* and *past part.* **so·cial·ized** *v.t.* to bring under public ownership and control, *to socialize an industry* ‖ *v.i. (Am., pop.)* to be active in social affairs

socialized medicine medical and hospital care made available for all members of a community, district or nation through funds obtained by taxation, philanthropy assessments or other means

social learning *(psych.)* concept that cognitive, vicarious, and self-regulatory factors in human behavior can best be learned from observation of others, as contrasted with expected rewards and punishments; coined by A. Bandura *Cf* SKINNERIAN

so·cial·ly (sóuʃəli:) *adv.* in a social way ‖ with respect to society

social mobility *(sociology)* movement of individuals from one social group to another social group, e.g., from the working class to the middle class, or vice versa

social promotion *(education)* automatic advancement in school without regard to grades or ability

social psychology that part of psychology which studies the relationships and reciprocal influences between individuals and between the individual and society

social realism realistic art works that depict contemporary social problems *Cf* SOCIALIST REALISM

social register a list of persons considered as belonging to the top ranks of society

social science the study of human society, esp. of its organization and of the relationship of individual members to it ‖ any of several studies, e.g. history, political science, economics, which treat an aspect of human society

social security a system, or the theory and legislation behind it, whereby individual members of the community can count on some degree of care and protection provided by the community as a whole (e.g. health insurance or unemployment and retirement benefits)

social service welfare work

Social War a war fought (90-88 B.C.) between Rome and its allies of S. and central Italy. The war was caused by the allies' demands for the privileges of Roman citizenship and was ended by the promise that the privileges would be granted to all who had not borne arms against Rome

social work any of various professional services, kinds of material assistance and organized activities etc. concerned with the treatment of social problems, esp. in the underprivileged classes

social worker a person who does social work

so·ci·e·ty (səsáiiti:) *pl.* **so·ci·e·ties** *n.* the state of living in organized groups ‖ any number of people associated together geographically, racially or otherwise with collective interests ‖ any stage in the development of a community, *a primitive society, feudal society* ‖ an association of people with some interest in common and some central discipline, *a debating society* ‖ a civil or business association organized under law and endowed by it with a moral personality ‖ that part of a community considered to be the élite by birth, wealth or culture etc. ‖ personal association, companionship, *he enjoys the society of younger people* ‖ (*biol.*) a group of organisms forming a community ‖ (*bot.*) a community of plants other than dominants within an association [fr. O.F. *societe*]

Society Islands (*F.* Îles de la Société) the principal archipelago (land area 650 sq. miles, pop. 75,000) of French Polynesia, comprising the Windward Is (*F.* Îles du Vent), including Tahiti, Moorea and islets, and the Leeward Is (*F.* Îles Sousle-Vent), made up of Huahine, Raiatea, Bora Bora and islets. They are mountainous (of volcanic origin), wooded, and circled by reefs. Chief town and port: Papeete. People: Polynesian, French, Chinese. Religion: Protestant, Roman Catholic. Exports: copra, vanilla (*TAHITI). Tahiti was discovered (1767) by the British, and the group was named after the Royal Society. The French established a protectorate over Tahiti (1843) and annexed it (1880). The other islands were annexed in 1887

Society of Friends *FRIENDS, THE SOCIETY OF

Society of Jesus *JESUS, SOCIETY OF

So·cin·i·an (sousíni:ən) 1. *n.* an adherent of Socinianism 2. *adj.* of or to do with the doctrine of Socinus **So·cin·i·an·ism** *n.* the doctrine of Laelius and Faustus Socinus

So·ci·nus (sousáinəs), Laelius (Lelio Sozzini, 1525-62), Italian theologian. His anti-Trinitarian rationalistic teachings resemble those of modern Unitarians, and were spread into Poland, Hungary and the Netherlands by his nephew, Faustus Socinus (Fausto Sozzini, 1539-1604)

so·ci·o·bi·ol·o·gy (sousi:oubaióləd͡ʒi:) *n.* 1. study of social behavior in nonhuman animal life 2. study of behavioral traits supposedly affected by hereditary factors

so·ci·o·ec·o·nom·ic (sousi:ouɛkənómik, souʃi:ouɛkənómik) *adj.* of or relating to combined social and economic conditions

so·ci·o·lin·guis·tics (sousi:oulɪŋgwístiks) *n.* study of language as determined or affected by sociocultural factors, e.g., education —**sociolinguist** *n.* —**sociolinguistic** *adj.*

so·ci·o·log·i·cal (sousi:əlód͡ʒik'l, souʃi:əlód͡ʒik'l) *adj.* of sociology ‖ of human society and its development and organization [fr. F. *sociologique*]

sociological jurisprudence theory that laws alone cannot regulate the conflict between social interests and values, but that the courts must decide some issues

so·ci·ol·o·gist (sousi:óləd͡ʒist:, souʃi:óləd͡ʒist:) *n.* a specialist in sociology

so·ci·ol·o·gy (sousi:óləd͡ʒi:, souʃi:óləd͡ʒi:) *n.* the study of the origin, the history and the structure of human society and its institutions [fr. F. *sociologie*]

so·ci·o·re·li·gious (sousi:ouri:líd͡ʒəs) *adj.* involving both religious and social influences

sock (sɒk) *n.* a wool, cotton or nylon etc. covering for the foot, ankle and lower part of the leg ‖ a light, removable inner sole worn in a shoe ‖ a

wind sock ‖ (*Gk* and *Rom. hist.*) a shoe worn by comic actors **to pull up one's socks** (*Br.*) to try harder [O.E. *socc*]

sock 1. *v.t.* (*pop.*) to hit hard with the fist or a heavy object 2. *n.* (*pop.*) such a blow [origin unknown]

sock·et (sɒkit) *n.* a hollow part or piece adapted or contrived to receive and hold something, *a bone socket, an electrical socket* ‖ *BALL AND SOCKET JOINT [A.F. *soket* dim. of *soc*, plowshare]

socket wrench (*Am.*=*Br.* box spanner) a hollow tubular wrench designed to fit over a nut and be turned by a tommy bar set into it at right angles (for getting at nuts inaccessible to an ordinary wrench)

sock·eye (sɒkai) *n.* Oncorhynchus nerka, fam. Salmonidae, a small N. Pacific salmon of economic importance. It reaches a weight of about 5 lbs

so·cle (sɒk'l, sóuk'l) *n.* (*archit.*) a simple, low, rectangular block of stone serving as a support for a pedestal, statue, wall etc. (*PLINTH) [F. fr. Ital. *zoccolo*]

So·co·tra, So·ko·tra (sóukóutrə, sókətrə) (*Arab.* Suqutra) a mountainous island (area 1,400 sq. miles, pop. 15,000) in the Indian Ocean near the entrance to the Gulf of Aden. It is a dependency of the People's Democratic Republic of Yemen. Highest point: 4,686 ft. Chief town (residence of the sultan): Tamridah. Exports: dates, gum, incense, ghee

Soc·ra·tes (sɒkrəti:z) (c. 470-399 B.C.), Greek philosopher of Athens. Most of his mature life was devoted to philosophy, although he developed no formal doctrine, founded no school and wrote nothing. His life, thought and method are known to us chiefly through Plato and Xenophon. He was familiar with the natural philosophers but they dissatisfied him by their lack of interest in human conduct. He studied the methods of the Sophists but attacked them for their indifference to virtue. He himself held that virtue is understanding and that no man knowingly does wrong. A strong patriot, he believed that a citizen is bound by conscience to obey the laws of the state. Thus, when (at the age of 70) he was imprisoned and condemned to death for irreligion and for corrupting the young men of Athens, he made no attempt to escape, despite the entreaties of his friends. More than any other philosopher, Socrates lived his philosophy. Several divergent schools of thought looked to him as their founder, and he has been widely regarded as the type and embodiment of the philosopher

So·crat·ic (səkrǽtik, soukrǽtik) 1. *adj.* pertaining to Socrates or his philosophy 2. *n.* a follower of Socrates **So·crat·i·cal·ly** *adv.*

Socratic irony the simulating of ignorance in argument in order to lead an opponent on to affirm something that reveals the absurdity of his position. This method was employed by Socrates in his teaching and plays an important part in Plato's earlier dialogues

sod (sɒd) 1. *n.* surface soil with grass growing on it ‖ a piece of this, dug out or otherwise removed 2. *v.t. pres. part.* **sod·ding** *past* and *past part.* **sod·ded** to lay sods on (an area) in order to make it a lawn [prob. fr. M.Du. *sode*]

sod *n.* (*pop.* used esp. as a general term of abuse or with a qualifying adjective) someone one considers peculiarly harsh, mean, silly etc. [abbr. of SODOMITE]

so·da (sóudə) *n.* crystalline sodium carbonate ‖ sodium bicarbonate ‖ sodium hydroxide ‖ soda water ‖ an ice-cream soda [M.L., origin unknown]

soda ash anhydrous sodium carbonate, Na_2CO_3, a product of the alkali industry

soda biscuit a biscuit made by baking a mixture of flour and buttermilk or sour milk, leavened with baking soda ‖ a soda cracker

soda cracker a crisp wafer leavened with bicarbonate of soda and cream of tartar

soda fountain a counter where sundaes, sodas, sandwiches, soft drinks etc. are served ‖ a device for delivering soda water into a drinking vessel

soda jerk (*pop.*) someone who serves at a soda fountain

soda lime a granular mixture prepared by slaking calcium oxide with sodium hydroxide and/or potassium hydroxide. It is used as an absorbent of moisture and acid gases

so·da·lite (sóud'lait) *n.* a compound of aluminum silicate, sodium silicate and sodium chlo-

ride, occurring in some igneous rocks as a transparent or translucent mineral

so·dal·i·ty (soudǽliti:, sədǽliti:) *pl.* **so·dal·i·ties** *n.* a fellowship, community or organized society ‖ (*Roman Catholicism*) a lay society formed for devotional or mutual aid purposes [F. *sodalité* or fr. L. *sodalitas*]

soda niter, *Br.* **soda nitre** sodium nitrate

soda water water charged under pressure with carbonic acid gas. It is used as a beverage, release of the excess pressure causing bubbles of gas to form, rise and burst ‖ a similar beverage consisting of sodium bicarbonate in a weak solution to which a little acid has been added to cause effervescence

sod·den (sɒd'n) *adj.* saturated with moisture ‖ (of bread etc.) too moist and doughy because not baked enough ‖ dulled and stupid from frequent drunkenness [old irregular past part. of SEETHE]

Sod·dy (sɒdi:), Sir Frederick (1877-1956), English scientist who predicted (1902) the formation of helium as the end product of atomic degradation, verified this in 1904, and discovered the isotopes of lead (1913). He was awarded a Nobel prize (1921) for his discovery of the laws of radioactivity

so·di·um (sóudi:əm) *n.* a metallic element (symbol Na, at. no. 11, at. mass 22.9898), of small density (0.971), oxidizing rapidly when exposed to the air and reacting violently with water to liberate hydrogen and give a solution of sodium hydroxide. It is widely distributed in compounds, esp. common salt. It is essential to bodily health, the body needing a balance between potassium and sodium. Its salts are of great industrial importance [fr. SODA+Mod. L. -*ium*]

sodium bicarbonate a weakly basic salt, $NaHCO_3$, which liberates carbon dioxide on heating and when combined with acids. It is used in baking powder, effervescent salts, as an antacid and in fire extinguishers

sodium carbonate a white crystalline salt, $Na_2CO_3 \cdot 10H_2O$, used to give an alkaline solution with water, to soften water (by precipitating calcium carbonate) and in soapmaking etc. ‖ soda ash

sodium chloride salt (NaCl)

sodium fluoride the poisonous crystalline salt NaF produced by the reaction of hydrofluoric acid with soda ash and used in the fluoridation of water and in rat and insect poisons etc.

sodium hydroxide a brittle, white deliquescent solid, NaOH, with a soapy feel. It dissolves in water to form a strongly alkaline solution. It is widely used in the manufacture of soap, detergents, rayon and cellulose etc.

sodium lamp an electric discharge tube filled with sodium vapor under low pressure, emitting a powerful yellowish light and often used for street lighting

sodium nitrate the deliquescent salt, $NaNO_3$, occurring naturally as caliche, or made by the reaction of nitric acid and soda ash. It is used as a fertilizer, in explosives etc.

sodium palmitate [$NaC_{16}H_{31}O_2$] *SODIUM STEARATE

sodium potassium tartrate Rochelle salt

sodium pump or **sodium potassium pump** (*biochem.*) an intramembranous transport system that expels selected sodium through a membrane while concentrating potassium inside a cell, utilizing energy from hydrolysis of adenosine triphosphate

sodium silicate any of various water-soluble substances obtained esp. by melting silica with a sodium compound. They are used e.g. in detergents

sodium stearate [$C_{17}H_{35}COONa$] (*chem.*) with sodium palmitate the basis of soap and detergent used for laundry, cosmetics, and toothpaste

sodium thiosulfate a salt, usually in the form of the hydrate $Na_2S_2 \cdot 5H_2O$, used in photography as a fixing agent

sodium-vapor lamp a sodium lamp

Sod·om (sɒdəm) a city of ancient Palestine in the lower Jordan valley, destroyed by God, with Gomorrah, because of the vices of its inhabitants (Genesis xviii-xix)

So·do·ma, Il (i:lsódəmə) (Giovanni Antonio Bazzi, 1477-1549), Sienese painter. His work includes a series of frescoes at Monte Oliveto near Siena, and frescoes for the Villa Farnesina, Rome

sod·om·ite (sódəmait) *n.* a person who practices sodomy [O.F.]

CONCISE PRONUNCIATION KEY: (a) æ, c*a*t; ɑ, c*ar*; ɔ f*aw*n; ei, sn*a*ke. (e) e, h*e*n; i:, sh*ee*p; iə, d*eer*; ɛə, b*ear*. (i) i, f*i*sh; ai, t*i*ger; əː, b*ir*d. (o) o, *o*x; au, c*ow*; ou, g*oa*t; u, p*oo*r; ɔi, r*oy*al. (u) ʌ, d*u*ck; u, b*u*ll; uː, g*oo*se; ə, b*a*cillus; juː, c*u*be. x, lo*ch*; θ, *th*ink; ð, bo*th*er; z, *Z*en; ʒ, corsa*g*e; d͡ʒ, sava*g*e; ŋ, oranguta*ng*; j, *y*ak; ʃ, *fish*; t͡ʃ, fe*tch*; 'l, rabb*le*; 'n, red*den*. Complete pronunciation key appears inside front cover.

sod·om·y (sódəmi:) *n.* sexual intercourse between males or (*law*) between members of the same sex or with animals, or unnatural sexual intercourse between a man and a woman [O.F. *sodomie* after SODOM]

Soerabaya *SURABAYA

Soerakarta *SURAKARTA

so·fa (sóufə) *n.* a long, upholstered seat, often with a raised back and raised arms or a raised end [F. fr. Arab.]

sofa bed a sofa that can be opened into a bed, e.g. by folding the back down

Sofala (soufála) (formerly Beira) a chief town (pop. 113,770) of Mozambique. A seaport on the Pungwe River estuary, it is connected by rail with Malawi, Zambia and Zimbabwe, for which it is the nearest port

so·far (sóufər) *n.* (*acronym*) for sound fixing and ranging, a system of determining a subsurface explosion at sea by triangulation

sof·fit (sófit) *n.* (*archit.*) the under surface of an arch, balcony, cornice etc. [F. *soffite* fr. Ital.]

So·fi·a (sóufi:ə, soufí:ə) the capital (pop. 1,047,920) and industrial center of Bulgaria, in the W. Balkan Mtns. Industries: mechanical and electrical engineering, automobile assembly, rolling stock, textiles, food processing. Roman baths (now a chapel), medieval churches, mosques, synagogue. Cathedral (late 19th c.). University (1880). Sofia was founded by the Romans (2nd c.) and was taken by the Bulgars (9th c.). It was under Turkish rule 1382-1878, and became the capital in 1879.

soft (soft, soft) *adj.* offering little resistance to pressure, *a soft bed* (opp. HARD) ‖ not hard of its kind, *soft butter* ‖ mild, *a soft climate* ‖ (*pop.*, of jobs) not requiring much effort ‖ not providing a strong sense stimulus, *a soft light, soft colors* ‖ not loud ‖ not sharp in outline, *soft contours* ‖ (*pop.*) of weak intellect, feeble-minded, *soft in the head* ‖ (*pop.*) foolishly sentimental ‖ (*pop.*) easily put upon ‖ (of words) smooth, insinuating ‖ weak ‖ (*phon.*) sibilant, *c is soft in 'cement', g is soft in 'gelatin'* ‖ (*phon.*) lenis or lenis and voiced ‖ (of certain Slavic consonants) palatalized ‖ (of drinks) nonalcoholic ‖ (of diet) bland ‖ (of metal) malleable ‖ (*phys.*) of electromagnetic waves which have little penetrating power ‖ (of water) containing no dissolved bicarbonates or sulfates of calcium, magnesium or iron and therefore giving an immediate lather with soap without the formation of an insoluble curd ‖ (of securities etc.) weakening in price because of selling activity ‖ (of currency) that cannot be converted into gold and is not backed by gold reserves ‖ (of currency) freely available for borrowing at a low rate of interest ‖ (of currency) not easily convertible into foreign currency ‖ (*bookbinding*) using paper, not board ‖ (*photog.*) having very subtle tone gradations (cf. CONTRASTY) [O.E. *sófte*]

soft answer an answer designed not to arouse anger

soft art 1. art form considered psychologically or technically unfinished **2.** tentative art using pliable material *Cf* SOFT SCULPTURE

soft·ball (sóftbol, sóftbɔl) *n.* a variety of baseball, played with a softer, larger ball and on a smaller diamond ‖ the ball used in this game

soft·boiled (sóftbóild, sóftbóild) *adj.* (of an egg) boiled in its shell for not more than 3 minutes so that the yolk does not set

soft·bound (sóftbaund) *adj.* bound in paper, e.g., a paperback book *also* soft-cover *Cf* HARDBOUND

soft coal bituminous coal

soft copy (*computer*) output that leaves no permanent record, e.g., the display in a cathode-ray tube

soft-core (sóftcor) *adj.* of pornography, not as explicit or prurient as hard-core *Cf* HARDCORE, R-RATED, X-RATED

soft dollars the portion of an investment that can be taken as a income-tax deduction *Cf* TAX SHELTER

soft drink a nonalcoholic drink, esp. a carbonated one

soft drug a nonaddictive drug, e.g., marijuana *Cf* HARD DRUG

sof·ten (sófən, sófən) *v.t.* to make soft or softer, *to soften a blow* ‖ (with 'up') to wear down the opposition or resistance of (esp. an opponent) ‖ *v.i.* to become soft or softer

soft fruit (*Br.*) *SMALL FRUIT

soft furnishings (*Br., commerce*) materials for curtains, chair covers etc.

soft goods (*commerce*) textiles

soft-heart·ed (sófthɑrtid, sófthɑrtid) *adj.* very ready to sympathize with others and act accordingly

soft ice cream ice cream that has been aerated while in a semiviscous state, to approximately double its original volume, then refrigerated

soft iron iron almost free from carbon, unable to retain magnetism in the absence of a magnetizing agent and therefore used as the core of an electromagnet

soft landing the landing of a space vehicle on a celestial body without damage to the vehicle

soft lens porous-plastic contact lens said to be less irritating than a glass lens

soft line a flexible domestic or international political policy —**soft-line** *adj.* —**soft-line** *v.* — **soft-liner** *n. Cf* HARD LINE

soft loan a no-interest loan granted to a developing country, esp. by the International Development Association

soft news news without immediacy, e.g., feature stories *Cf* HARD NEWS

soft palate the soft, fleshy part of the palate located behind the hard palate

soft-paste porcelain a porcelain made of glass or grit and china clay, and used for making esp. household china. It is fired at a lower temperature than true porcelain

soft pedal a pedal on a piano, operated by the right foot, which lessens the volume by causing fewer strings to be hit (per note) or by bringing the hammers nearer the strings so they cannot hit so forcefully **soft-ped·al** *pres. part.* **soft-ped·al·ing**, esp. *Br.* **soft-ped·al·ling** *past and past part.* **soft-ped·aled**, esp. *Br.* **soft-ped·alled** *v.t.* to reduce emphasis on ‖ to soften the tone of by using a soft pedal

soft rock sophisticated, low-keyed rock 'n' roll with a less defined rhythm than hard rock *Cf* HARD ROCK

soft roe milt

soft science a science dealing with human behavior, e.g., psychology, economics, sociology *Cf* HARD SCIENCE, NATURAL SCIENCE

soft sculpture sculpture utilizing pliable materials, e.g., plastic, foam rubber, cloth, or papier-mâché *Cf* SOFT ART

soft sell a sales technique using persuasion and suggestion (cf. HARD SELL)

soft soap a soap in semiliquid form made by the action of potassium hydroxide on fats ‖ (*pop.*) flattery **sóft-sóap** *v.t.* (*pop.*) to flatter

soft solder an alloy of lead and tin, melting at a low temperature

soft-spo·ken (sóftspóukən, sóftspóukən) *adj.* suave in speech

soft spot (*pop.*) a sentimentally affectionate feeling towards another person

soft state an inefficient sovereign government unresponsive to its people's needs *Cf* HARD STATE

soft·ware (sóftwçər, sóftwçər) *n.* (*electronics*) the system of general programs which simplifies and links the work of computer and user ‖ (*computer*) nonhardware properties, e.g., programs, languages, routines, instructions etc., utilized in operations ‖ in other technologies, nondurable supplies and equipment, e.g., fuel, plans, housekeeping materials (cf. HARDWARE)

soft·wood (sóftwụd, sóftwụd) *n.* any soft, light-textured wood, esp. the wood of a coniferous tree (cf. HARDWOOD)

soft·y (sófti:, sófti:) *pl.* **soft·ies** *n.* (*pop.*) a sentimental, unintelligent or weak person

sog·gy (sógi:) *comp.* **sog·gi·er** *superl.* **sog·gi·est** *adj.* soft and heavy because impregnated with water, *soggy ground* [fr. dial. *sog*, a swamp]

Sog·ne (sóŋnə) the longest fiord (115 miles) of Norway, on the west coast, north of Bergen

soh (sou) *n.* (*Br., mus.*) sol

So·ho (sóuhou, souhóu) a cosmopolitan quarter of London, noted for its restaurants and bohemian life

So·ho (sóuhou) *n.* area in Manhattan between Houston and Canal Streets, where many factory buildings have been converted to artists' residences and studios, galleries, restaurants, and boutiques

soi·gné (swɑnjéi) *adj.* (of a woman) elegantly and carefully dressed ‖ showing evidence of great care and attention to detail [F.]

soil (soil) *n.* the uppermost stratum of the earth's crust, esp. the top few inches from which plants and ultimately man derive food ‖ (*rhet.*) land, country, *on native soil* [A.F.]
—Soils vary enormously in composition. Basically they consist of an inorganic portion, the silicates of aluminum, iron, calcium, magnesium, silica etc., derived from the original rock by weathering and producing characteristic soil types (sands, silts, clays, loam), together with an organic portion produced by decomposed plants and animals as a result of the activity of innumerable microorganisms, particularly bacteria. Air and water are additional elements, the whole forming a biological entity whose proper balance is dependent on external environmental factors. Most soils belong to one of two great groups: the lime-rich pedocals or lime-poor pedalfers. Soils may also be classified as zonal, where climate and vegetation are the dominant influence on development, or azonal, where the influence of climate and vegetation is not dominant, or intrazonal, where the influence of local factors (relief, parent material, age) is more determinant than climate and vegetation

soil 1. *v.t.* to make dirty, to stain ‖ to tarnish or harm (a reputation etc.) ‖ *v.i.* to become stained or dirty **2.** *n.* a dirty mark ‖ refuse, esp. excrement [fr. O.F. *soillier*]

soil *v.t.* to feed (cattle etc.) on freshly cut green fodder in order to fatten them [perh. fr. SOIL (dirty mark), (obs.) pool used by wild boar]

soil bank U.S. Government-sponsored program providing compensation to farmers for leaving portions of land fallow, designed to control overproduction and conserve soil fertility *also* land retirement

soil·borne (sóilborn) *adj.* carried in or through soil, e.g., diseases, fungi

soiling index (*envir.*) measure of soiling properties of particles suspended in air, measured through a Whatman number 4 filter for a specified period, expressed as coefficient of haze [CoH] ÷ 1,000 linear ft *Cf* COEFFICIENT OF HAZE, SMOKE SHADE

soil pipe the pipe connecting a house etc. with a main sewer

soi·ree, soi·rée (swɑréi) *n.* a formal evening party or gathering [F.]

so·ja bean (sóiə) a soybean

so·journ 1. (sóudʒə:rn, soudʒə́:rn) *v.i.* (*rhet.*) to stay or dwell for a time in a place or among certain people **2.** (sóudʒə:rn) *n.* (*rhet.*) a temporary stay [O.F. *sojorner*]

soke (souk) *n.* (*Br. hist.*) the right to hold a local court of justice and receive certain fees and fines ‖ the district over which this right extended [fr. M.L. *soca* fr. O.E. *sōcn*]

So·ko·to (sóukoutou, soukoutóu, sokɑtú:) the capital (pop. 108,565) of North Western State, Nigeria, a trading center ‖ an ancient kingdom of W. central Africa, esp. powerful 16th-19th cc.

Sokota *SOCOTRA

Sol (sɒl) the Roman Sun god, or (in rhetorical use) the Sun

sol (sɒl, soul) *n.* a fluid colloidal system (cf. GEL)

sol (soul, sɒl) *n.* (*mus.*) the note G in the fixed-do system of solmization ‖ the fifth note of any diatonic scale in movable-do solmization

sol (soul, sɒl, *Span.* sɔl) *pl.* **sols**, *Span.* **so·les** (sóles) *n.* the basic monetary unit of Peru, divided into 100 centavos ‖ a coin or note worth one sol

sol·ace (sólis) **1.** *n.* that which lessens disappointment or grief or loneliness **2.** *v.t. pres. part.* **sol·ac·ing** *past* and *past part.* **sol·aced** to lessen the disappointment, grief or loneliness of [O.F. *solas*]

so·lan goose (sóulən) *n. Sula bassana* or *Moris bassana*, a large white gannet with black-tipped wings [older *soland* fr. O.N. *sūla*, gannet + -*and*, -*and*, duck]

so·la·num (souléinəm) *n.* a member of *Solanum*, fam. *Solanaceae*, a large genus of plants, trees and shrubs. They include the eggplant and the potato [L.=nightshade]

so·lar (sóulər) *adj.* of or relating to the sun, *a solar eclipse* [fr. L. *solaris*]

solar battery a thermopile or photovoltaic pile that uses radiation from the sun or its heating effect to produce an electrical current

solar cell (*electr.*) a photoelectric cell capable of converting photons from the sun's energy into electrical energy; used as a power or heat source *Cf* SOLAR PANEL

solar coalition a group of members of U.S. Congress advocating development of solar energy, esp. as an inexpensive alternative energy source

solar flare a transient explosive brightening originating from special bright areas in the solar chromosphere. Solar flares often occur in

CONCISE PRONUNCIATION KEY: (a) æ, c*a*t; ɑ, c*ar*; ɔ f*aw*n; ei, sn*a*ke. **(e)** e, h*e*n; i:, sh*ee*p; iə, d*ee*r; ɛə, b*ear*. **(i)** i, f*i*sh; ai, t*i*ger; ə:, b*ir*d. **(o)** o, *o*x; au, c*ow*; ou, g*oa*t; u, p*oo*r; ɔi, r*oy*al. **(u)** ʌ, d*u*ck; u, b*u*ll; u:, g*oo*se; ə, b*a*cill*u*s; ju:, c*u*be. x, lo*ch*; θ, *th*ink; ð, bo*th*er; z, *Z*en; ʒ, cor*s*age; dʒ, sava*ge*; ŋ, orangutan*g*; j, *y*ak; ʃ, *f*ish; tʃ, fe*tch*; 'l, rabb*le*; 'n, red*den*. Complete pronunciation key appears inside front cover.

association with explosive activity of solar prominences and sunspots

so·lar·i·um (souléari:əm, səléari:əm) *pl.* **so·lar·i·ums, so·lar·i·a** (souléari:ə, səléari:ə) *n.* a room or building so constructed as to be exposed to the radiant energy of the sun and to trap much of this energy, esp. one used for therapeutic purposes [L.]

solar month one twelfth of a solar year

solar panel a group of solar cells used as a power source, e.g., in a spacecraft *Cf* SOLAR SAIL

solar plexus a group of ganglia situated behind the stomach || (*pop.*) the upper front part of the abdomen just below the rib cage

solar pond body of water with a salted lower layer producing energy through tendency of denser bottom water to retain heat without rising to top. The water's heat is funneled into coiled tubes of a heat exchanger

solar prominence any of several types of incandescent gaseous mass containing hydrogen and metallic ions that circulate between the sun's chromosphere and corona along gently curved trajectories. Prominences occasionally erupt violently outward and are found esp. in regions containing sunspots

solar sail a flat sheet capable of receiving thrust from solar radiation, used as a power source e.g., in a spacecraft *Cf* SOLAR PANEL

solar system the sun, its nine planets (Mercury, Venus, Earth, Mars, Jupiter, Saturn, Uranus, Neptune, Pluto, in order of distance from the sun) and other celestial bodies (e.g. asteroids, comets and meteors) held to orbits around it by gravitation

solar wind (*meteor.*) a continuous stream of charged plasma protons emitted from the sun at 250 to 800 kms, causing distortion of earth's magnetic field and acceleration in comets *Cf* STELLAR WIND

solar year the average time taken by the earth to complete one orbit around the sun (=approx. 365¼ days)

sold *past* and *past part.* of SELL **to be sold on** to be thoroughly convinced about the excellence of (something)

sol·der (sódər, *Br.* esp. sóldə) **1.** *n.* a metallic alloy which, melted between clean metal surfaces, itself alloys with these and so bonds them together **2.** *v.t.* to join (metal surfaces) thus [M.E. *soudour* fr. O.F.]

soldering iron an iron tool, heated and used to melt solder

sol·dier (sóuldʒər) **1.** *n.* a man serving in an army || such a man who is not an officer || *ANT* **2.** *v.i.* to serve as a soldier **sól·dier·ly** *adj.* of or befitting a good soldier, *a soldierly bearing* [M.E. *soldiour, soudiour* fr. O.F.]

soldier of fortune an adventurous person prepared to earn his livelihood as a soldier wherever he will be well paid || a person who seeks an adventurous life in whatever circumstances chance offers

sol·dier·y (sóuldʒəri:) *n.* a specified body of soldiers || (*collect.*) soldiers || soldiering as a technique, *the art of soldiery*

sole (soul) *adj.* only, *the sole survivor* || unshared, exclusive, *sole right* [O.F. *sol*]

sole *n.* any of several varieties of edible flatfish, fam. *Soleidae*, esp. the European *Solea solea* [O.F.]

sole **1.** *n.* the undersurface of the foot || the part of a shoe etc. which meets the ground, esp. forward from the heel || the lower part or surface of something, e.g. of a golf club, plowshare etc. **2.** *v.t. pres. part.* **sol·ing** *past* and *past part.* **soled** to provide (a shoe, sock etc.) with a sole || (*golf*) to place (the club) on its sole in preparation for a stroke [O.F.]

sol·e·cism (sólisizəm) *n.* a grammatical or syntactical deviation from what is conventionally regarded as correct speech || a deviation from what are regarded as good social manners [fr. L. *solœcismus* fr. Gk]

sole·ly (sóulli:) *adv.* only, exclusively

sol·emn (sóləm) *adj.* arousing or expressing serious or profound thoughts and feelings of reverence, *solemn music* || accompanied by or performed according to religious rites, *a solemn ceremony* || (of an oath) made in a form and under circumstances such as to render it legally binding || (*eccles.*) celebrated with full liturgy, *a solemn high mass* || of grave significance, *solemn pronouncements* || earnest and gloomy, *don't look so solemn!* || pompous, *he's a solemn ass* [M.E. *solempne* fr. O.F.]

sol·em·ni·ty (səlémniti:) *pl.* **so·lem·ni·ties** *n.* solemn expression, behavior or character || a solemn rite || (*law*) a formality required to validate an act [M.E. *solempnite* fr. O.F.]

sol·em·ni·za·tion (sóləmnizéiʃən) *n.* a solemnizing or being solemnized

sol·em·nize (sóləmnaiz) *pres. part.* **sol·em·niz·ing** *past* and *past part.* **sol·em·nized** *v.t.* to perform (a religious marriage ceremony) || to perform, invest or honor with ceremony [fr. O.F. *solempniser*]

so·le·noid (sóulənɔid) *n.* a cylindrical coil of wire which creates a magnetic field within itself when an electric current is passed through it and so can draw a core of iron or steel into itself **so·le·nói·dal** *adj.* [F. *solénoïde* fr. Gk]

solenoid sweep (*mil.*) a magnetic mine sweep consisting of a horizontal axis coil wound on a floating iron tube

So·lent (sóulənt) the channel (15 miles long, ¾ mile–4 miles wide) between Hampshire and the Isle of Wight, England: yacht racing

sol-fa *TONIC SOL-FA, *SOLMIZATION

sol·fa·ta·ra (sɔulfətára, sɔlfatára) *n.* a vent from which issue volcanic gases rich in sulfur dioxide, indicating that the volcano is nearly extinct [name of a volcano near Naples fr. *solfo, sulfur*]

sol·fège (sɔlfɛʒ) *n.* solfeggio [F.]

sol·feg·gio (sɔlfédʒou, sɔlfédʒi:ou) *pl.* **sol·feg·gi** (sɔlfédʒi:), **sol·feg·gios** *n.* a vocal exercise in sol-fa syllables || application of sol-fa syllables to notes [Ital.]

Sol·fe·ri·no, Battle of (sɔlfərí:nɔ) a French and Sardinian victory (1859) over Austrian forces in northern Italy, after which Lombardy joined Sardinia

so·lic·it (səlísit) *v.t.* to beg for, canvass, appeal for (favor, help, a vote etc.) || to importune, approach with appeals || (of a prostitute) to propose sexual intercourse to in return for money || *v.i.* (of a prostitute) to propose sexual intercourse to someone in return for money [fr. O.F. *soliciter, solliciter*]

so·lic·i·ta·tion (səlisitéiʃən) *n.* the practice, or an act, of soliciting [O.F. or fr. L. *sollicitatio* (*sollicitationis*)]

so·lic·i·tor (səlísitər) *n.* a lawyer who acts as official law officer for a city, department etc. || (*Br.*, *law*) a lawyer qualified to advise clients in all legal matters, to prepare wills and deeds etc., to instruct counsel in cases for the higher courts and to appear on behalf of clients in some lower courts || a professional canvasser for money for a fund, trade, support etc. [fr. O.F. *solliciteur, soliciteur*]

solicitor general *pl.* **solicitors general** the federally appointed assistant to the attorney general or the chief law officer in certain states || a chief legal adviser to any of certain governments

so·lic·i·tous (səlísitəs) *adj.* attentive, full of anxious concern || (with *infin.*) eager [fr. L. *sollicitus, solicitus*]

so·lic·i·tude (səlísitu:d, səlísitju:d) *n.* anxious concern [O.F. or fr. L. *sollicitudo, solicitudo*]

sol·id (sólid) **1.** *adj.* having the properties of a solid, nonfluid || having three dimensions || unyielding, *solid conviction* || continuous, *a solid line of houses* || without openings, *solid jungle* || (of time) unbroken, *he waited two solid hours* || real, sound, *solid grounds for belief* || homogeneous, *a solid mass of red* || (of gold etc.) containing no more alloy than is specified by law to ensure hardness || dense, thick, *a solid cloud of smoke* || not hollow, not loosely packed, filled with matter, *a solid foot of snow* || firm and compact, *solid ground* || cubic, *a solid foot* || (of structures, furniture etc.) firmly built, stout and strong || (of compound words) written or printed without a hyphen || sound, serious, but not inspired, *solid work* || full, complete, *a solid day's work* || unanimous, *a solid vote of approval* || staunch, dependable, *a solid friend* || (*printing*) having no leads separating the lines of type **2.** *n.* a substance which when acted upon by moderate forces tends to retain its shape and volume, i.e. a substance that has little or no tendency to flow (cf. FLUID) || a figure having three spatial dimensions || (*pl.*) food which is not liquid [O.F. *solide*]

solid angle the angular spread of the vertex of a cone, expressed as the area of its intercept on the surface of the sphere of unit radius described about the vertex, the total solid angle subtended by such a sphere being 4π. Unit solid angle subtends an area of r^2 on a sphere of radius r

sol·i·dar·i·ty (sɔlidǽriti:) *pl.* **sol·i·dar·i·ties** *n.* common interest and active loyalty within a group [fr. F. *solidarité*]

Solidarity *n.* a worker-run trade union, established in Poland in 1980

solid geometry the branch of geometry dealing with three-dimensional figures

so·lid·i·fi·ca·tion (səlidifikéiʃən) *n.* a solidifying or being solidified

so·lid·i·fy (səlídifai) *pres. part.* **so·lid·i·fy·ing** *past* and *past part.* **so·lid·i·fied** *v.t.* to make hard and nonfluid || (*fig.*) to make clear and compact, *to solidify conclusions* || *v.i.* to become solid [fr. F. *solidifier*]

so·lid·i·ty (səlíditi) *n.* the quality or state of being solid || moral or financial soundness [fr. F. *solidité*]

solid laser a laser in which a solid (ruby, neodymium-doped yttrium-aluminum garnet) is excited by optical pumping to provide an intense, narrow beam

sol·id-state (sólidstéit) *adj.* (*electr.*) of semiconducting material connected to electrodes used to control flow of electricity, e.g., transistor, thrysistor *Cf* SEMICONDUCTOR, SOLID-STATE PHYSICS

solid-state memory (*computer*) a memory utilizing a metal-oxide semiconductor for storage

solid-state physics branch of physics dealing with the properties of crystal lattice in arrangement of atoms, dislocations and defects in this arrangement, esp. in connection with the conductance of heat and electricity, semiconductors, and the energy bands that insulate and conduct electricity —**solid-state** *adj.*

sol·i·dus (sólidəs) *pl.* **sol·i·di** (sólidai) *n.* a gold coin introduced by the Roman Emperor Constantine. The *s.* used to denote a shilling or shillings is an abbreviation of this word || the diagonal stroke used sometimes to divide pounds, shillings and pence, as in £1/7/6, or the stroke e.g. in and/or || a solidus curve [L.]

solidus curve a curve, usually expressing the temperature-composition relationship of a mixture, that corresponds with the liquidus, and which indicates the temperatures below which only the solid phase exists

so·lil·o·quist (səlíləkwist) *n.* a person who soliloquizes

so·lil·o·quize (səlíləkwaiz) *pres. part.* **so·lil·o·quiz·ing** *past* and *past part.* **so·lil·o·quized** *v.i.* to deliver a soliloquy || *v.t.* to address in a soliloquy

so·lil·o·quy (səlíləkwi:) *pl.* **so·lil·o·quies** *n.* the act of speaking one's thoughts aloud in solitude || a speech in a play through which a character reveals his thoughts to the audience, but not to any of the other characters, by voicing them aloud, usually in solitude [fr. L. *soliloquium*]

So·li·mões (sɔlimwɛ́s) *AMAZON

So·ling·en (zóuliŋən) a town (pop. 169,600) of North Rhine-Westphalia, West Germany, celebrated for its cutlery, metalwork and surgical instruments

sol·ip·sism (sóləpsizəm) *n.* (*philos.*) the view that only the self can be known to exist **sól·ip·sist** *n.* [fr. L. *solus*, alone+*ipse*, self]

So·lís (sɔlí:s), Juan Díaz de (*d.* 1516), Spanish explorer. With Vicente Yáñez Pinzón he explored (1508) the Yucatán and the Amazon and discovered (1516) the Rio de la Plata

sol·i·taire (sólitɛər) *n.* a single gem, usually a diamond, set alone, e.g. in a ring || a game played on a board by one person with marbles or pegs, which are moved by jumping. The object is to clear the board of all but one of the pieces (*Am.=Br.* patience) any of certain card games, generally for a single player, in which the cards are taken as they happen to fall and are arranged into set patterns for as long as this proves possible [F.]

sol·i·tar·i·ly (sólitərili:) *adv.* in a solitary way

sol·i·tar·i·ness (sólitəri:nis) *n.* the state or quality of being solitary

sol·i·tar·y (sólitəri:) **1.** *adj.* one alone, without others, *a solitary straggler* || preferring seclusion, not gregarious || lonely, without company, *a solitary life* || unfrequented, characterized by lack of human life || (of insects) not social **2.** *pl.* **sol·i·tar·ies** *n.* a recluse, someone who prefers to live remote from human contacts || (*pop.*) solitary confinement [fr. L. *solitarius*]

solitary confinement the confinement of a prisoner in a place where he is kept from contact with other prisoners

---

CONCISE PRONUNCIATION KEY: **(a)** æ, c*a*t; ɑ, c*ar*; ɔ f*aw*n; ei, sn*a*ke. **(e)** e, h*e*n; i:, sh*ee*p; iə, d*eer*; ɛə, b*ear*. **(i)** i, f*i*sh; ai, t*i*ger; ə:, b*ir*d. **(o)** o, *o*x; au, c*ow*; ou, g*oa*t; u, p*oor*; ɔi, r*oy*al. **(u)** ʌ, d*u*ck; u, b*u*ll; u:, g*oo*se; ə, b*a*cillus; ju:, c*u*be. x, lo*ch*; θ, *th*ink; ð, bo*th*er; z, *Z*en; ʒ, cor*s*age; dʒ, sava*g*e; ŋ, ora*ng*uta*ng*; j, *y*ak; ʃ, fi*sh*; tʃ, fe*tch*; 'l, rabb*le*; 'n, red*den*. Complete pronunciation key appears inside front cover.

sol·i·tude (sɔ́litju:d, sólitju:d) *n.* the state of being solitary ‖ loneliness ‖ isolation ‖ a lonely place, *Arctic solitudes* [O.F.]

sol·ler·et (sɔ́leret, sɔlərét) *n.* (*hist.*) a pliable steel shoe forming part of a 14th-c. or 15th-c. suit of armor [O.F.]

sol·mi·za·tion (sɔlmizéiʃən) *n.* (*mus.*) the application of syllabic names (*do, re, mi, fa, sol, la, si* or *ti*) to the notes of the C-major scale, to facilitate sight-singing (fixed-do system), developed from Guido d'Arezzo's 11th-c. system ‖ the application of these syllables to the tones of any scale, *do* always representing the tonic, *re* the second note etc. (movable-do system) (*TONIC SOL-FA) [fr. F.]

so·lo (sóulou) **1.** *n. pl.* **so·los, so·li** (sóuli:) a passage of music to be performed by one instrument or voice, with or without subordinate accompaniment ‖ any performance by one person ‖ a game of cards for four persons in which one player attempts to score a declared point on which he has wagered over the other three ‖ an airplane flight alone without passengers or instructor **2.** *adj.* alone, without accompaniment ‖ performed, made or done alone **3.** *v.i.* to fly an airplane alone, esp. for the first time without an instructor [Ital.]

So·logne (sɔlɔnj) a wooded, sandy region south of the Loire comprising parts of Loiret, Cher and Loir-et-Cher: hunting, forestry

so·lo·ist (sóulouist) *n.* a person who performs a solo

Sol·o·mon (sɔ́ləmən) (c. 986–c. 932 B.C.), king of the Hebrews (c. 972–c. 932 B.C.), son of David and Bathsheba. Famous for his wisdom and his wealth, he established foreign alliances and made trading agreements, and built the first Temple in Jerusalem. The Books of Proverbs and Ecclesiastes, and the Song of Solomon, are attributed to him, though modern scholarship disputes this attribution

Solomon Islands an archipelago (land area 16,120 sq. miles, pop. 273,000) in the W. Pacific, comprising eight mountainous, volcanic, forested islands, with 40-odd islets and atolls. People: Melanesian, with Polynesian and Micronesian minorities. The westernmost islands (Bougainville, Buka and islets) belong to Papua New Guinea. The remainder (main islands: Guadalcanal, Malaita) form an independent state within the British Commonwealth (area 11,500 sq. miles, capital Honiara, on Guadalcanal). People: predominantly Melanesians. Religions: Anglican, Roman Catholic, Protestant. University of the Pacific (1977). Crops: cocoa, coconuts, yams, bananas, pineapples. Main exports: fish, lumber, copra, pine, shell. The archipelago was visited by a Spanish expedition (1568). The various islands were formed into a British protectorate (1893-1900). Self-government was achieved (1976) and full independence was granted (1978)

Solomon's seal *Polygonatum multiflorum,* fam. *Liliaceae,* a genus of perennial plants with terminal inflorescences of white, tubular, pendulous flowers. There are seal-like scars on the rhizome ‖ a magic figure composed of two triangles interlaced to form a star [trans. M.L. *sigillum Salomonis*]

So·lon (sóulən) (c. 640–c. 558 B.C.), Athenian statesman and lawgiver, one of the Seven Sages of Greece. As archon (594-3 B.C.) he issued a new humane code of laws and reformed the constitution, defining the rights of the people's assembly, and establishing a senate and popular courts

so long (*pop.*) goodbye

So·lo·thurn (zóuloturn) a German-speaking, mainly Catholic canton (area 305 sq. miles, pop. 218,102) of N.W. Switzerland, in the Jura ‖ its capital (pop. 17,708)

sol·stice (sɔ́lstis, sóulstis) *n.* either of the two points in the sun's apparent annual orbit in relation to the fixed stars (the ecliptic) at which it is furthest from the equator (i.e. June 21–2, the summer solstice, Dec. 21–2, the winter solstice, which are correspondingly the longest and shortest days in the year, for the northern hemisphere) [O.F.]

sol·sti·tial point (sɔlstíʃəl, soulstíʃəl) the point in its ecliptic reached by the sun at the time of solstice

sol·u·bil·i·ty (sɔljubíliti) *n.* the quality of being soluble ‖ the amount of a substance (the solute) that will dissolve in a given amount of another substance (the solvent) to give a saturated solution, usually expressed as the mass of solute per 100 parts by mass or volume of the solvent, at specified temperature and pressure

solubility product (*abbr.* S.P.) the product of the concentrations of the ions of a dissolved electrolyte when the latter is in physical equilibrium with its solid state

sol·u·ble (sɔ́ljub'l) *adj.* capable of being dissolved ‖ capable of being solved or explained [O.F.]

sol·ute (sɔ́lju:t, sóulu:t) *n.* a substance which is dissolved, esp. the component in the lower concentration in a solution (cf. SOLVENT) [fr. L. *solvere* (*solutus*), to loosen]

so·lu·tion (səlú:ʃən) *n.* a homogeneous mixture of two (or more) substances in which a solid, liquid or gas forms a single phase with another liquid (or sometimes a gas or solid), and which has the same physical and chemical properties throughout at any given concentration up to its saturation point ‖ the act by which a substance is put into solution ‖ the state of being thus put into solution ‖ the answer to a problem ‖ the act, method or process by which such an answer is obtained [O.F. or fr. L. *solutio* (*solutionis*)]

solv·a·bil·i·ty (sɔlvəbíliti) *n.* capability of being solved

solv·a·ble (sɔ́lvəb'l) *adj.* capable of being solved

Sol·vay process (sɔ́lvei) the manufacturing process by which carbon dioxide (from heated limestone) and ammonia precipitate sodium bicarbonate from a solution of common salt (sodium chloride), the bicarbonate is converted into carbonate (washing soda) by heat and the ammonia is recovered by the action of quicklime on the residual solution. The process is the basis of the alkali industry [after Ernest *Solvay* (1838–1922), Belgian chemist]

solve (sɔlv) *pres. part.* **solv·ing** *past* and *past part.* **solved** *v.t.* to find the answer to, work out (e.g. a problem) [fr. L. *solvere,* to loosen]

sol·ven·cy (sɔ́lvənsi:) *n.* the state or quality of being solvent (having enough money)

sol·vent (sɔ́lvənt) **1.** *adj.* having enough money to pay all debts ‖ able to dissolve **2.** *n.* a substance, usually a liquid, capable of dissolving other substances, esp. the component in the higher concentration in a solution (cf. SOLUTE) ‖ something that solves, *no solvent has been found for the problem of unemployment* [fr. L. *solvens* (*solventis*) fr. *solvere,* to loosen]

Sol·zhe·ni·tsyn (sʌlʒəní:tsin), Aleksandr (1918–), Soviet writer. In his novels, including 'One Day in the Life of Ivan Deniscovich' (1962), 'Cancer Ward' (1968) and 'The First Circle' (1968) he describes the injustice and degradation suffered by millions of Russians in the Stalinist concentration camps. He won the Nobel Prize (1970). Publication of the first volume of 'August 1914' (1971) and the first volume of 'The Gulag Archipelago' (1973) as well as his outspoken criticism of the Soviet treatment of writers, led to his exile to the West (1974), first to Switzerland and later to the U.S.A., where he completed 'The Gulag Archipalego' (1974-8) and wrote 'The Oak and the Calf' (1975) and other works

so·ma (sóumə) *pl.* **so·ma·ta** (sóumətə), **so·mas** *n.* an animal or plant body as a whole, with the exception of the germ cells [Gk *sōma,* body]

So·ma·li (soumáli:, səmáli:) *pl.* **So·ma·lis, So·ma·li** *n.* a member of the principal people of Somaliland ‖ the Cushitic language spoken by this race

So·ma·li·a (soumáli:ə, soumáljə) (or Somali Republic) a republic (area 246,135 sq. miles, pop. 3,640,000) in N.E. Africa. Capital: Mogadiscio. People: Somali (6 tribal confederacies), with minorities of related groups, small Bantu and other Negroid peoples, Arabs, Indians and Europeans. The population is 80% nomadic. Languages: Somali, Arabic (both official), minority languages. Religion: Sunni Moslem. The land is 28% potentially arable (with irrigation), 31% pasture and grazing and 17% desert. The north (except for a narrow coastal plain) and west belong to the central African plateau, with mountains in the north rising to 7,900 ft. The low-lying semidesert of the east and south includes the flood plains of the Webbe Shibeli and Juba Rivers. Average temperatures (F.): 70°-100° along the coast. Rainfall: Mogadiscio 15 ins, highlands 20 ins, elsewhere 0-15 ins. Livestock: cattle, sheep, goats, camels. Agricultural products: sugarcane, bananas, durra, corn, sorghum, sesame, oil seeds, cotton, tobacco, beans, fruit, gum arabic, myrrh. Minerals: salt, iron ore, gypsum, beryl, columbite. Industries: fishing, meat and fish canning, tanning, footwear, weaving, woodwork, textiles, sugar. Exports: fresh fruit and vegetables, livestock, hides and skins, wood and charcoal. Imports: manufactures, machinery, foodstuffs, vehicles, oil, chemicals. Ports: Berbera, Mogadiscio. University institute: Mogadiscio. Monetary unit: Somali shilling or Somalo (100 cents). HISTORY. The area was settled (13th and 14th cc.) by Somali tribes. A Moslem kingdom waged war on Ethiopia (15th and 16th cc.). Egypt occupied several places on the coast (1874-84). Britain established (1884) the protectorate of British Somaliland in the north. Italy established (1889) the protectorate of Italian Somaliland along the east coast, to which was added (1924) a region west of the Juba, ceded by Kenya. Italian Somaliland was incorporated (1936) in Italian East Africa. Italy invaded British Somaliland (1940), but the British conquered both protectorates (1941). Italian Somaliland was restored to Italian control (1950-60). British Somaliland became independent (June 26, 1960) and united with Italian Somaliland to form the independent republic of Somalia (July 1, 1960). By 1978, Somalia had regained most of the Ogaden region from Ethiopia, which had been given it by Britain although most of its inhabitants are Somalis; however Ethiopia retook it in 1978. Conflict continued, and famine and a serious refugee problem ensued

So·ma·li·land (soumáli:læand, səmáli:læand) a region of East Africa incl. Somalia, the Djibouti coast, E. Ethiopia and N.E. Kenya (to the Tana)

So·man (sóumən) *n.* (*mil.*) U.S.S.R. nerve gas that causes nausea, shortness of breath, blindness, paralysis, and death depending on the amount inhaled

so·mat·ic (soumætik, səmætik) *adj.* of or relating to the body and body cells as contrasted with the reproductive or germ cells ‖ relating to the body as distinguished from the soul or mind [fr. Gk *sōmatikos*]

somatic cell one of the cells composing the tissues, organs etc. of a body (*GAMETE)

so·ma·to·gen·ic (soumətədʒénik, səmætədʒénik) *adj.* developing from, affecting, or acting through the somatic cells (cf. PSYCHOGENIC) [fr. Gk *sōma* (*sōmatos*), body+*gen,* born]

so·ma·to·log·ic (soumət'lɔ́dʒik, səmæt'lɔ́dʒik) *adj.* of somatology **so·ma·to·lóg·i·cal** *adj.*

so·ma·tol·o·gy (soumətɔ́lədʒi:) *n.* physical anthropology [fr. Gk *sōma* (*sōmatos*), body+*logos,* word]

so·ma·tome (sóumətoum) *n.* a somite

so·ma·to·sen·so·ry (soumətousénsəri:) *adj.* of sensations received by the body proper, excluding the eyes, ears, tongue, and nose

so·ma·to·stat·in (soumətoustæt'n) *n.* (*med.*) a brain hormone made synthetically by gene splicing that is used for the treatment of diabetes, gastric bleeding, and other body ailments

so·ma·to·ther·a·py (soumətouθéərəpi:) *n.* treatment of mental and/or emotional disorders by physical means —**somatotherapist** *n.*

so·ma·to·tro·phic hormone (soumətoutróufik) pituitary hormone that regulates growth and influences metabolism, esp. of carbohydrates, fats, proteins (*abbr.* STH) *also* growth hormone

som·ber, esp. *Br.* **som·bre** (sɔ́mbər) *adj.* depressingly dark and shadowy ‖ conveying or giving rise to feelings of gloom or melancholy, or experiencing such feelings [F.]

som·bre·ro (sɔmbréərou) *pl.* **som·bre·ros** *n.* a large felt or straw hat with a wide and often upturned brim originally worn in Mexico, Spain and South America [Span.]

some (sʌm) **1.** *adj.* of a person or persons not known or specified, *some people can't make up their minds* ‖ being an unspecified amount or proportion of a whole or quantity, *leave us some oranges* ‖ of a person or persons only vaguely or implicitly determined, *some fool left the light on* ‖ (with 'other') one or several of a number of unspecified alternatives, *they must have found some other way* ‖ a considerable amount, *they had been waiting some time* ‖ (with 'only') a relatively small number or amount, *they finished only some of the food* ‖ (*pop.*) remarkable, notable, striking, *that was some game!* **2.** *pron.* an indefinite quantity or indefinite number of people or things, *the flowers are out, but some have died already* **3.** *adv.* (with a number) approximately, *some six months ago* [O.E. *sum*]

-some *suffix* used added to numbers to indicate a group, as in 'foursome'

CONCISE PRONUNCIATION KEY: **(a)** æ, c*a*t; ɑ, c*a*r; ɔ f*aw*n; ei, sn*a*ke. **(e)** e, h*e*n; i:, sh*ee*p; iə, d*ee*r; ɛə, b*ea*r. **(i)** i, f*i*sh; ai, t*i*ger; ə:, b*i*rd. **(o)** o, *o*x; au, c*ow*; ou, g*oa*t; u, p*oo*r; ɔi, r*oy*al. **(u)** ʌ, d*u*ck; u, b*u*ll; u:, g*oo*se; ə, b*a*cillus; ju:, c*u*be. x, lo*ch*; θ, *th*ink; ð, bo*th*er; z, *Z*en; ʒ, cor*s*age; dʒ, sava*g*e; ŋ, orangutan*g*; j, *y*ak; ʃ, *f*ish; tʃ, fe*tch*; 'l, rabb*le*; 'n, redd*en*. Complete pronunciation key appears inside front cover.

-some *suffix* being or tending to be, as in 'loathsome'

some·bod·y (sámbɒdi, sámbʌdi, sámbədi:) 1. *pron.* an unspecified or unknown person, *will somebody please light the lamp?* 2. *pl.* **some·bod·ies** *n.* a person of importance, *he must be somebody to receive a welcome like that*

some·day (sámdei) *adv.* at some indefinite, usually distant, future time

some·how (sámhau) *adv.* (often with 'or other') by some means unknown or undefined, *we shall manage somehow* ‖ for some unknown cause or reason, *somehow it seems strange*

some·one (sámwʌn, sámwən) *pron.* somebody

some·place (sámpleis) *adv.* (pop.) somewhere

som·er·sault, sum·mer·sault (sámərsɒlt) 1. *n.* a forward roll executed by putting the head on the ground in a tucked-in position and rolling forward so that the back of the neck, shoulders and back all touch the ground successively and the feet pass above them ‖ a leap in which this forward roll is performed in the air 2. *v.i.* to perform a somersault [fr. O.F. *sombresaut*]

Som·er·set (sámərset, sámərsit), Edward Seymour, duke of (c. 1506-52), protector of England (1547-51) during the minority of Edward VI. The virtual ruler of England, he successfully invaded Scotland (1547), but was overthrown (1551) and executed (1552) by John Dudley, earl of Warwick

Somerset, Fitzroy James Henry *RAGLAN

Somerset a county (area 1,620 sq. miles, pop. 424,988) of S.W. England. County town: Taunton

some·thing (sámθiŋ) 1. *pron.* (often with 'or other') a thing, act or quality undefined or unspecified, *there must be something we can do* ‖ (with 'like' and a number) some number near to the one stated, *something like six weeks* ‖ (often with 'quite' or 'really') a thing which can be regarded as a minor achievement, *it is quite something to have persuaded him to speak* ‖ somewhat 2. *adv.* in a limited degree, *something more than pretense* **something like** something which nearly approximates an understood or specified ideal

some·time (sámtaim) 1. *adv.* at some indefinite time in the future or past 2. *adj.* former, *the sometime mayor*

some·times (sámtaimz) *adv.* occasionally, now and then

some·way (sámwei) *adv.* somehow, in some way

some·ways (sámweiz) *adv.* someway

some·what (sámhwɒt, sámhwʌt, sámwɒt, sámwʌt) 1. *adv.* to a certain degree, rather, *the speech was somewhat pompous* 2. *pron.* some previously mentioned person or thing having to some degree the nature of something specified, *it was somewhat of an ordeal*

some·where (sámhwɛər, sámwɛər) 1. *adv.* in or to some place unknown or unspecified, *you will find her somewhere around* ‖ (with 'between' and numbers) approximately, *somewhere between two and three months*

so·mi·tal (sóumit'l) *adj.* of or having a somite or somites

so·mite (sóumait) *n.* a longitudinal segment of an animal body, esp. a primitive segment in the early developmental stage of higher segmented animals **so·mit·ic** (soumítik) *adj.* [fr. Gk *soma*, body]

Somme (sɔm) a river (147 miles long) of N. France, navigable past Amiens. It was the scene of heavy fighting in both world wars, esp. in July-Oct. 1916, when a French and British offensive pushed back the German lines at very heavy cost to both sides, but relieved the Verdun front. In June 1940 an attempt was made to halt the German drive south

Somme a department (area 2,443 sq. miles, pop. 538,500) of N. France (*PICARDY). Chief town: Amiens (pop. 110,000), the only town with a population over 30,000

som·nam·bu·late (sɒmnǽmbjuleit) *pres. part.* **som·nam·bu·lat·ing** *past* and *past part.* **som·nam·bu·lat·ed** *v.i.* to walk when asleep **som·nám·bu·lism, som·nám·bu·list** *ns* [fr. L. *somnus,* sleep+*ambulare* (*ambulatus*), to walk]

som·no·lence (sómnələns) *n.* the inclination or longing for sleep **sóm·no·len·cy** *n.* [O.F. *somnolence* or fr. L. *somnolentia*]

som·no·lent (sómnələnt) *adj.* inclined to sleep, drowsy ‖ inducing sleep [O.F. *sompnolent* or fr. L. *somnolentus*]

So·mo·za (sɒmósa), Anastasio (1896-1956), Nicaraguan general and president (1937-47, 1950-6). After his assassination the presidency passed to his sons Anastasio Somoza Debayle and Luis Somoza Debayle or to a candidate approved by the Somoza family until 1979

So·mo·za De·bay·le (sɒmósaðebáile), Anastasio (1925-80), Nicaraguan soldier and politician, son of Anastasio Somoza, and president (1967-74) and again from 1979 until his overthrow by the left-wing Sandinistas (1979)

Somoza Debayle, Luis Anastasio (1922-67), Nicaraguan politician, son of Anastasio Somoza, and president (1956-63) after the assassination of his father

son (sʌn) *n.* a male human being in relation to his parents ‖ (*pl., rhet.*) male descendants ‖ a form of address from an older man or woman to a young man or boy ‖ (*rhet.*) a male person considered as the product of his native land, his school etc. **the Son** (*theol.*) the second person of the Trinity ‖ Jesus Christ [O.E. *sunu*]

so·nance (sóunəns) *n.* the state or quality of being sonant [fr. L. *sonare,* to sound]

so·nant (sóunənt) 1. *adj.* having sound ‖ (*phon.,* of speech sounds) voiced 2. *n.* (*phon.*) a voiced speech sound (opp. SURD) ‖ a speech sound used as a syllabic ‖ (in Indo-European) a voiced syllabic consonant [fr. L. *sonans* (*sonantis*) fr. *sonare,* to sound]

so·nar (sóunɑr) *n.* an apparatus which locates a submerged object by emitting high-frequency sound waves and registering the vibrations reflected back from the object. It is used for detecting submarines, shoals of fish etc., and for finding ocean depths [fr. initial letters of *sound navigation ranging*]

so·na·ta (sɒnáta) *n.* a musical composition for piano, or solo instrument usually accompanied by piano, consisting of three or four movements of varying mood and speed but related in key. Pre-18th-c. sonatas were sometimes in one movement only. A double sonata is one written for two solo instruments [Ital.]

sonata form a pattern of musical composition derived from that of the first movement of a sonata. A work in sonata form opens with an exposition (a statement of the first and second subjects or themes) followed by a development (of the subjects) and ends with a recapitulation (of the subjects) and coda. Sonatas, quartets, concertos, symphonies etc. may all use sonata form

son·a·ti·na (sɒnətí:na) *pl.* **son·a·ti·nas, son·a·ti·ne** (sɒnətí:nei) *n.* a shorter form of sonata, sometimes simpler to play [Ital.]

sonde (sɒnd) *n.* a device for testing atmospheric conditions at high altitudes [F.]

Son·der·bund (zóndərbunt) a league (1845-7) of seven Catholic cantons of Switzerland. It was formed to protect the interests of the cantons against the growing strength of the radicals. After the Sonderbund had been defeated in a short civil war (1847), Switzerland adopted a federal constitution

son et lu·mi·ère (sɔ̃n ei lu:myéər) *n.* (*Fr.,* often italics) sound-and-light spectacle including music and narration presented at some historic sites

song (sɒŋ, sɔŋ) *n.* the act or art of singing, *to burst into song* ‖ a short composition in which words and music together form a unity ‖ the utterance of some birds and certain other creatures ‖ (*rhet.*) a pleasing characteristic sound, *the song of the waves* ‖ (*rhet.*) poetry, verse **a song and dance** (*pop.*) an involved explanation, not necessarily true, designed to confuse or put someone off, *he gave me a song and dance about his absences* **for a song** (*pop.*) for a disproportionately small amount of money, *she sold the necklace for a song* **to make a song and dance** (*Br.*) to make a fuss [O.E. *sang, song*]

song·bird (sóŋbəːrd, sɔ́ŋbəːrd) *n.* a singing bird

song cycle a group or sequence of songs generally unified by theme or subject

Song·hai (sɒŋhái) *n.* a people of the W. African middle Niger region ‖ a member of this people ‖ their language
—The kingdom of Songhai was a W. African state based on the middle Niger, founded c. 700. Islam became its official religion (c. 1000). It reached its greatest territorial extent in the late 15th and early 16th cc., but was destroyed (1591) by the Almohades

Song·koi (sɒŋkɔ́i) *RED RIVER

Song of Solomon a Hebrew love poem (probably 5th-4th cc. B.C.) included among the sacred books of the Old Testament. Its imagery has been interpreted as an allegory of God's love for Israel or of Christ's love for his Church. It is also known as the Song of Songs and as Canticles

song-sce·na (sóŋʃeina, sɔ́ŋʃeina) *n.* (*mus.*) a scena (composition for solo voice)

song sparrow *Melospiza melodia,* a common brown and white North American sparrow

song·ster (sóŋstər, sɔ́ŋstər) *n.* a songbird **song·stress** (sóŋstris, sɔ́ŋstris) *n.* a woman singer of light popular music [O.E. *sangestre*]

song thrush *Turdus ericetorum,* a brown and white Old World thrush

song·writ·er (sóŋraitər, sɔ́ŋraitər) *n.* someone who composes either the words or the music of a song, or both

son·ic (sónik) *adj.* of sound waves which can be heard by the human ear ‖ of or relating to the speed of sound in air (about 1,087 feet per second, or about 738 m.p.h. at sea level) [fr. L. *sonus,* sound]

sonic alarm device that responds to disturbances of sonic field by emitting a loud noise or making an electrical contact with other devices used for security

son·i·ca·tion (sɒnikéiʃən) *n.* use of high-frequency sound waves for physical therapy, cleaning, separating solid materials, etc. — **sonicate** *v.* —**sonicator** *n.*

sonic bang (*Br.*) a sonic boom

sonic barrier the sound barrier

sonic boom a loud booming sound produced when the shock wave formed at the nose of a supersonic aircraft reaches the ground

so·nif·er·ous (sɒnífərəs, sounífərəs) *adj.* making or carrying sound [fr. L. *sonus,* sound+*ferre,* to carry]

son-in-law (sáninlɔ) *pl.* **sons-in-law** *n.* a daughter's husband

son·net (sónit) *n.* a poem of 14 lines (the number varied in its early development) written to a regular rhyme scheme, of which there are many patterns. It was invented in Italy in the early 13th c. Dante was the first great poet to use it, Petrarch the first to write a great sonnet cycle. The form lends itself to the concise expression of contemplative thought and emotion. The Petrarchan (or Italian) sonnet, used also by Milton, has an octave rhyming *abba abba* and a sestet freely using 3 rhymes. The Shakespearean (or English or Elizabethan) sonnet consists of three quatrains, *abab cdcd efef* or *abba cddc effe,* and a couplet *gg.* English sonnets are normally in 10-syllable lines, Italian in 11 and French in 12 [F. or fr. Ital. *sonetto*]

son·net·eer (sɒnitíər) *n.* (*old-fash.*) someone who writes sonnets ‖ (*old-fash.*) someone dismissed contemptuously as a mere versifier, not a poet of quality [fr. Ital. *Sonettiere* or fr. SONNET+-*eer,* suffix denoting someone concerned with]

son·ny (sáni:) *n.* a friendly or patronizing form of address by an older person to a boy

son·o·chem·is·try (sɒnoukémǝstri:) *n.* the study of the effects of ultrasonic waves on chemicals —**sonochemical** *adj.*

So·no·ra (sɒnóra) a northwest state (area 70,484 sq. miles, pop. 1,614,000) of Mexico, bounded on the north by the U.S.A. and on the west by Lower California and the Gulf of California. Capital: Hermosillo (pop. 264,073), situated within a flourishing cotton district. Winter vegetables, cereals, cotton, tobacco and corn are grown under irrigation. It was a famous colonial mining center, and still yields quantities of copper, gold, and silver. The Seri Indians live primitively on the offshore island of Tiburón

so·nor·i·ty (sɒnóriti:, sǝnóriti:) *pl.* **so·nor·i·ties** *n.* the state or quality of being sonorous [F. *sonorité* or fr. L. *sonoritas*]

so·no·rous (sɒnórǝs, sǝnóurǝs, sónǝrǝs) *adj.* giving out sound, esp. ringing or resonant and full sound ‖ impressive, lofty (or intended to be so), *sonorous rhetoric* [fr. L. *sonorus*]

Sons of Liberty a secret organization formed (1765) in the American colonies to protest the Stamp Act. The organization evoked a colonial spirit of liberty, supported the nonimportation agreement, and helped to convoke the Continental Congress of 1774

Soo·chow (sú:tʃáu, sú:dʒóu) *WUHSIEN

soon (su:n) *adv.* in a short time from now, *it will soon begin* ‖ close after a stated time or event, *soon after 12, soon after the accident* ‖ quickly, *he will soon set things straight* ‖ willingly, *I would as soon do it by myself* ‖ early, *you needn't leave so soon* **as soon as** at the moment when, *as soon as she saw him she remembered him* ‖ as quickly or early as, *come as soon as you*

---

can **no sooner . . . than** as soon as, *no sooner had he arrived than he began to complain* **no sooner said than done** it was put into effect as soon as it was decided or suggested **sooner or later** inevitably but with no certainty when, *sooner or later you will be glad of it* [O.E. *sōna*]

Soong (suŋ), Tse-ven (1894-1971), Chinese statesman. He was foreign minister of China (1941-5) and prime minister (1945-9)

soot (sut, su:t) 1. *n.* black particles of carbon formed by the incomplete combustion of carbonaceous fuel (coal, oil etc.) which contains enough hydrocarbon gases to carry these particles upward by convection. Soot contains an admixture of other volatile elements, some of which are valuable trace elements in soil 2. *v.t.* to cover or treat with soot [O.E. *sōt*]

soothe (su:ð) *pres. part.* **sooth·ing** *past and past part.* **soothed** *v.t.* to calm, reassure, *to soothe an anxious child* ‖ to smooth, *to soothe ruffled feelings* ‖ to alleviate (e.g. pain) **sóoth·ing** *adj.* [O.E. *sōthian*, to confirm]

sooth·say·er (sú:θseiər) *n.* (*hist.*) a person whose profession was telling the future [M.E. *sothseyer*, one who speaks the truth]

soot·y (súti:, sú:ti:) *comp.* **soot·i·er** *superl.* **soot·i·est** *adj.* having the color of soot ‖ covered with, or full of soot ‖ of or like soot

sop (sɒp) *n.* a piece of bread, cake etc. soaked in liquid before it is eaten ‖ something given to soothe or propitiate or as a concession, *a sop to one's pride* [O.E. *sopp*]

sop *pres. part.* **sop·ping** *past and past part.* **sopped** *v.t.* to soak (in soup, milk etc.) ‖ (with 'up') to absorb [O.E. *soppian*]

soph·ism (sɒfizəm) *n.* a piece of plausible but false reasoning intended either to deceive or to display intellectual virtuosity [O.F. *sophisme* fr. L. fr. Gk]

Soph·ist (sɒfist) *n.* a paid itinerant professional teacher of logic, philosophy and rhetoric in ancient Greece. The most famous were Gorgias and Protagoras. The Sophists were the first to systematize the laws of thought, and were forerunners of the Socratic dialectic and of Aristotelian logic. Later Sophists emphasized material success and the ability to argue any case irrespective of its truth **soph·ist** someone who uses sophistry, e.g. to make the worse cause appear the better [fr. L. *sophista, sophistes* fr. Gk]

so·phis·tic (səfístik) *adj.* of or characteristic of sophists using sophistry **so·phís·ti·cal** *adj.* **so·phís·ti·cal·ly** *adv.* [fr. L. *sophisticus* fr. Gk]

so·phis·ti·cate (səfístikeit) *pres. part.* **so·phís·ti·cat·ing** *past and past part.* **so·phís·ti·cat·ed** *v.t.* to deprive of simplicity or sincerity by making artificial or affected ‖ to make complex ‖ to alter (a text) without authority **so·phís·ti·cat·ed** *adj.* having the worldly wisdom characteristic of fashionable life ‖ adapted to this way of life, *a sophisticated style* ‖ elaborated, made complex ‖ too affected or artificial, lacking in naiveté or naturalness ‖ (of peoples, societies) no longer primitive **so·phis·ti·cá·tion** *n.* [fr. M.L. *sophisticare* (*sophisticatus*) fr. *sophisticus*, sophistic]

soph·ist·ry (sɒfistri:) *pl.* **soph·ist·ries** *n.* a piece of plausible but false reasoning, sophism ‖ the use of sophisms **Soph·ist·ry** the methods of the ancient Greek Sophists

Soph·o·cles (sɒfəkli:z) (c. 496-406 B.C.) Greek poetic dramatist, author of about 123 plays of which seven complete tragedies survive: 'Antigone', 'Electra', 'Trachiniae', 'Oedipus Rex', 'Ajax', 'Philoctetes' and 'Oedipus at Colonus'. Sophocles modified contemporary dramatic form and extended the range of emotion that could be portrayed in plays, by introducing a part for a third actor and by cutting down the commenting role of the chorus, though he increased the size of the chorus. He made the destinies of his characters dependent on their faults rather than on the actions of the gods

soph·o·more (sɒfəmɔr, sɒfəmour, sɒfmɔr, sɒfmour) *n.* a second-year student at a college or secondary school **soph·o·mor·ic** (sɒfəmɔrik, sɒfəmórik) *adj.* of or relating to a sophomore ‖ immature, brash [prob. fr. Gk *sophom*, sophism]

sop·o·rif·ic (sɒpərifik, soupərifik) 1. *adj.* inducing sleep ‖ showing or characterized by sleepiness 2. *n.* something which induces sleep, esp. a drug [fr. L. *sopor*, sleep]

sop·ping (sɒpiŋ) *adj.* soaked through, thoroughly wet

sop·py (sɒpi:) *comp.* **sop·pi·er** *superl.* **sop·pi·est** *adj.* soaked ‖ (*Br., pop.*) foolishly sentimental, *a soppy smile*

so·pran·o (səprǽnou, səprǽnou) 1. *n.* the highest singing voice in women, boys or castrati, ranging approx. from middle C to two octaves above it ‖ a singer with such a voice ‖ the musical part written for such a voice 2. *adj.* of or relating to a soprano ‖ (of an instrument in a family of instruments) having roughly the range of the soprano voice, *a soprano saxophone* [Ital.]

So·pron (ʃóprɔn) (G. *Ödenburg*) a town (pop. 43,000) in W. Hungary: Gothic churches

so·ra (sɔ́rə, sóurə) *n. Porzana carolina*, a small edible North American marsh bird of the rail family [perh. fr. Am. Ind.]

sora rail a sora

Sorb (sɔrb) *n.* a Wend ‖ Wendish [fr. G. *Sorbe*]

sorb (sɔrb) *n.* the service tree ‖ the rowan ‖ the fruit of either [F. *sorbe*]

sorb apple the fruit of the service tree or the rowan ‖ either of these trees

sor·bet (sɔ́rbət) *n.* a sherbet [F. fr. Ital. fr. Turk.]

Sor·bi·an (sɔ́rbi:ən) 1. *adj.* of or relating to the Sorbs or their language 2. *n.* a Sorb ‖ the language of the Sorbs ‖ Wendish

Sor·bonne (sɔrbón, sɔrbɑ́n, F. sɔrbɔn) the part of the University of Paris housing the faculties of science and letters. It was founded (1257) by Robert de Sorbon (1201-74), the chaplain and confessor of Louis IX, as a theological college, and became in effect the theological faculty of the university. In the 16th c. it was hostile to the Jesuits, in the 17th c. it condemned the Jansenists, in 1792 it was suppressed, and in 1808 given formally to the university. The present buildings (17th c.) were restored in the late 19th c.

sor·cer·er (sɔ́rsərər) *n.* a person who practices sorcery [earlier *sorcer* fr. O.F. *sorcier*]

sor·cer·ess (sɔ́rsəris) *n.* a female sorcerer [A.F. *sorceresse*]

sor·cer·y (sɔ́rsəri:) *pl.* **sor·cer·ies** *n.* the use of magic powers derived from evil spirits ‖ an instance of this [O.F. *sorcerie*]

sor·did (sɔ́rdid) *adj.* dirty, squalid, *sordid dwellings* ‖ dealing with squalor or moral degradation, *a sordid story* ‖ mean, contemptible, *sordid squabbles* [F. *sordide*]

sor·di·no (sɔrdí:nou) *pl.* **sor·di·ni** (sɔrdí:ni:) *n.* (*mus., abbr.* sord.) a mute [Ital.]

sore (sɔr, sour) 1. *comp.* **sor·er** *superl.* **sor·est** *adj.* painful, *a sore finger* ‖ causing painful emotions, *a sore memory* ‖ (*pop.*) feeling wounded in one's pride, *he is sore about not being promoted* ‖ hard to bear, *a sore disappointment* ‖ (*rhet.*) grievous, *in sore need* 2. *n.* a sore place on the body, esp. one where the skin has been broken 3. *adv.* (*archaic*) sorely, *sore afraid* [O.E. *sār*]

sore·head (sɔ́rhed, sóurhed) *n.* (*pop.*) someone who is aggrieved or disgruntled, angry etc., or easily made so

So·rel (sɔrel), Georges (1847-1922), French syndicalist philosopher, author of 'Réflections sur la violence' (1908)

sore·ly (sɔ́rli:, sóurli:) *adv.* painfully ‖ in a great degree, *sorely wanted* [O.E. *sārlīce*]

sore·ness (sɔ́rnis, sóurnis) *n.* the quality or state of being sore ‖ something painful

Sör·en·sen (sə́rənsən), Sören Peter Lauritz (1868-1939), Danish biochemist. He devised the pH scale of hydrogen ion concentration (1909)

sor·ghum (sɔ́rgəm) *n.* a member of *Sorghum*, fam. *Gramineae*, a genus of tropical grasses including several types used as cash crops, e.g. durra. Other species yield fiber, and some yield sugar ‖ the syrup obtained from a sorghum grown for sugar. Sorghum is most widely grown in Africa, but is also cultivated in India, China and the U.S.A. [Mod. L. fr. Ital. *sorgo*]

So·ria (sɔ́rja) a province (area 3,983 sq. miles, pop. 98,803) in N. central Spain (*OLD CASTILE*) ‖ its capital (pop. 19,000)

sor·ites (sɔráiti:z, souráiti:z) *pl.* **sor·ites** *n.* (*logic*) a series of syllogistical propositions in which the predicate of the first becomes the subject of the next, and so on, until it is concluded that the predicate of the last proposition can also be the predicate of the first [L. fr. Gk *sōreitēs* fr. *sōros*, heap]

so·ror·i·cide (sərɔ́risaid, sərɔ́risaid) *n.* the killing of one's sister ‖ someone who kills his sister [fr. L. *soror*, sister + *caedere*, to kill]

so·ror·i·ty (sərɔ́riti:, sərɔ́riti:) *pl.* **so·ror·i·ties** *n.* (esp. in U.S. colleges) a private, often residen-

tial social club of female students [fr. M.L. *sororitas* fr. *soror*, sister]

so·ro·sis (səróusis) *pl.* **so·ro·ses** (səróusi:z) *n.* (*bot.*) a compound fruit formed by the fusion of fleshy axis and flowers, e.g. the mulberry, pineapple [Mod. L. fr. Gk *sōros*, heap]

sorp·tion (sɔ́rpʃən) *n.* the process of taking up and holding a substance by absorption or adsorption

sor·rel (sɔ́rəl, sɔ́rəl) 1. *adj.* of a reddish brown or chestnut color 2. *n.* a reddish brown or chestnut color ‖ a sorrel-colored horse [O.F. *sorel*]

sorrel *n.* a member of *Rumex*, fam. *Polygonaceae*, a genus of plants with sour juice, of which 150 species are known in temperate regions. Some have rhizomes. They have whorled inflorescences with small inconspicuous flowers [O.F. *surele, sorele*]

sor·ri·ly (sɔ́rili:, sɔ́rili:) *adv.* in a sorry manner

sor·ri·ness (sɔ́ri:nis, sɔ́ri:nis) *n.* the state or quality of being sorry

sor·row (sɒrou, sɔ́rou) *v.i.* to grieve, to feel sorrow ‖ (*rhet.*) to express grief [O.E. *sorgian*]

sorrow *n.* grief, sadness ‖ a cause of grief, *he is a sorrow to his parents* **sór·row·ful** *adj.* [O.E. *sorh, sorg*]

sor·ry (sɒri:, sɔ́ri:) *comp.* **sor·ri·er** *superl.* **sor·ri·est** *adj.* feeling pity, *he was sorry for the poor man* ‖ feeling sympathy, *I am sorry that it hurts you* ‖ feeling regret, *I am sorry that I troubled you* ‖ (*rhet.*) arousing pity or contempt, *a sorry sight* [O.E. *sārig*, in pain fr. *sār*, sore]

sort (sɔrt) 1. *n.* a group having its own special qualities, *different sorts of flowers* someone having the qualities characteristic of a group, *he is not the sort to complain* ‖ (*printing*) a letter, figure etc. of a particular font **of a sort, of sorts** of a not very good kind, *it unfolds into a bed of sorts* **out of sorts** a little unwell ‖ cross, in a bad humor 2. *v.t.* to separate into groups having special qualities, *to sort apples according to size* ‖ (with 'out') to select (one, or some) of a particular kind ‖ to arrange (postal matter) in a suitable order for delivery ‖ (*computer*) to segregate into groups according to an instructed pattern [O.F. *sorte*]

sor·tie (sɔ́rti:) *n.* a sally of troops from a besieged position ‖ a mission or raiding flight by a single plane or ship [F.]

sor·ti·lege (sɔ́rt'lidʒ) *n.* divination by casting lots ‖ sorcery [O.F. or fr. M.L. *sortilegium*]

so·rus (sɔ́rəs, sóurəs) *pl.* **so·ri** (sɔ́rai, sóurai) *n.* a cluster of stalked sporangia on the undersurface of a fern frond ‖ a cluster of spores on lower plants [fr. Mod. L. fr. Gk *sōros*, heap]

SOS (ésoués) *n.* an internationally recognized signal (three dots, three dashes, three dots in Morse code) used in radiotelegraphy to call for help in distress ‖ (*pop.*) any call for help in need

so-so (sóusou) 1. *adj.* neither good nor bad, middling, *his health is only so-so* 2. *adv.* passably ‖ not very well

sos·te·nu·to (sɒstənú:tou, soustənú:tou) *adv.* (*mus.*) in a sustained, smooth manner [Ital.]

SOSUS (*mil. acronym*) for sound surveillance system, in which sonar devices are mounted on the ocean floor to sound an alert of submarine approach

sot (sɒt) *n.* a habitual drunkard [O.E. = fool]

so·te·ri·o·log·i·cal (sətiəri:ələdʒik'l) *adj.* of or relating to soteriology

so·te·ri·ol·o·gy (sətiəri:ólədʒi:) *n.* the branch of theology concerned with the doctrine of salvation through Christ [fr. Gk *sōtēria*, salvation]

So·thic (sóuθik, sóθik) *adj.* (ancient Egypt) of a year of 365 ¼ days as compared with the ordinary Egyptian year of 365 days ‖ of a period of 1,460 Sothic years (=1,461 solar years) [fr. Gk *sōthis*, an Egyptian name for the dog star]

sot·tish (sɒtiʃ) *adj.* of or like a sot

sot·to vo·ce (sɒtouvóutʃi:) 1. *adv.* in a low or soft voice ‖ (*mus.*, of the voice or an instrument) very softly indeed, just audibly 2. *adj.* very quietly spoken [Ital.]

sou (su:) *n.* a former French coin worth 5 centimes ‖ a former French coin worth 10 centimes ‖ (*pop.*) the least little bit of money, *they haven't a sou* [F.]

sou·a·ri (su:úri:) *n.* a member of *Caryocar*, fam. *Caryocaraceae*, a genus of South American tropical trees, producing large, rich, thick-shelled nuts, resembling large Brazil nuts, and durable lumber. The woody capsule may weigh 25 lbs. The nuts yield an oil used in cooking [F. *saouari* fr. native name in Guiana]

sou·brette (su:brét) *n.* a maid or servant girl, usually frivolous or intriguing, in a play or

CONCISE PRONUNCIATION KEY: **(a)** æ, c*a*t; ɑ, c*a*r; ɔ f*aw*n; **(e)** e, h*e*n; i:, sh*ee*p; iə, d*ee*r; ɛə, b*ea*r. **(i)** i, f*i*sh; ai, t*i*ger; ə:, b*i*rd. **(o)** o, *o*x; au, c*ow*; ou, g*oa*t; u, p*oo*r; ɔi, r*oy*al. **(u)** ʌ, d*u*ck; u, b*u*ll; u:, g*oo*se; ə, bacill*u*s; ju:, c*u*be. x, lo*ch*; θ, *th*ink; ð, bo*th*er; z, *Z*en; ʒ, corsa*g*e; dʒ, sava*g*e; ŋ, orangutan*g*; j, *y*ak; ʃ, *f*ish; tʃ, fet*ch*; 'l, rabb*le*; 'n, red*den*. Complete pronunciation key appears inside front cover.

opera ‖ an actress or singer taking such a part [F.]

sou·bri·quet (sú:brikei, sú:briket) n. a sobriquet

Sou·dan (su:dǽn, F. su:dã) *MALI

souf·flé (su:fléi, sú:flei) 1. n. a light, baked dish made by adding whipped egg whites to a sweet or savory mixture 2. adj. (cooking) of a dish, or of pastry, in which beaten egg whites are incorporated ‖ (of pottery) decorated with small spots of color that have been blown on [F.]

sough (sau, sʌf) 1. n. a murmuring sighing sound, as of wind through trees 2. v.i. to make such a sound [O.E. swōgan, to sound]

sought past and past part. of SEEK

sought·af·ter (sɔ́tæftər, sɔ́tɑftər) adj. much in demand or desired

souk, suq (su:k) n. (in Arab countries) a market [Arab. sūq]

soul (soul) 1. n. the immortal part of man, as distinguished from his body ‖ the moral and emotional nature of man, as distinguished from his mind ‖ the vital principle which moves and animates all life ‖ a human being, not a soul in sight ‖ personification or embodiment, he was the soul of honor ‖ (pop.) emotional expressiveness that appeals for emotional response in others, his performance lacks soul like a lost soul utterly forlorn to be the life and soul of (Br.) to make (a party) gay by one's own animation 2. adj. (pop.) characteristic of or associated with blacks, soul music **soul·ful** adj. expressing or appealing to the emotions, often with sentimentality **soul·less** adj. having no soul ‖ lacking nobility of mind ‖ deadening, rousing no enthusiasm, a soulless job [O.E. sāwol, sāwl]

soul brother a fellow black person (male) Cf SOUL SISTER

soul food traditional food of American blacks in the South (now nationwide), e.g., chitterlings, ham hocks, pigs feet, collard greens

soul music traditional rhythm and blues-related music of American blacks based on gospel songs that is direct, immediate, and of immense vitality

Sou·louque (su:lu:k), Faustin (1782-1867), Haitian black, emperor of Haiti (1849-59) under the name of Faustin I. His despotism led to his being overthrown

soul sister a fellow black person (female) Cf SOUL BROTHER

Soult (su:lt), Nicolas Jean de Dieu (1769-1851), French marshal. He distinguished himself in the Napoleonic Wars, notably at Austerlitz (1805). He was minister of war (1830-4) and nominal head (1840-4) of the conservative government effectively led by Guizot

sound (saund) v.t. to cause to emit sound, to sound a trumpet ‖ to signal or indicate with usually drum, trumpet, horn or bugle, to sound the retreat ‖ to pronounce, give sound to, articulate, sound your consonants clearly ‖ to test (something, e.g. the ground) by causing it to emit sounds ‖ to test (e.g. the heart) by auscultation ‖ v.i. to emit sound ‖ to convey a specified impression, it sounds silly **to sound off** (pop.) to speak out openly in a somewhat pugnacious manner ‖ (mil.) to count cadence while marching [fr. O.F. suner, soner]

sound n. the sensation experienced when the brain interprets vibrations within the structure of the ear caused by rapid variations of air pressure ‖ such a sensation understood as due to a particular source, the sound of wheels ‖ the distance over which something can be heard, within sound of the sea ‖ mere noise, or noise as distinguished from sense ‖ an impression gained from what one is told or learns about something, I don't like the sound of it [A.F. soun]

sound n. a narrow channel of water connecting two seas or a sea and a lake etc. ‖ a long, rather broad ocean inlet ‖ the air bladder of a fish ‖ (med.) a probe for investigating esp. cavities in the body [O.E. or O.N. sund]

sound 1. adj. not diseased or injured ‖ firm and solid ‖ wise, reliable, sound advice, a sound character ‖ financially satisfactory, a sound investment ‖ thorough, a sound thrashing ‖ deep, a sound sleep ‖ valid, convincing, a sound argument ‖ legally valid ‖ (of religious or political tenets etc.) orthodox 2. adv. (with 'sleep' or 'asleep' and used in combination) soundly [O.E. sund]

sound v.t. to measure the depth of (usually water) by using a rod or weighted line ‖ to examine (the ocean floor etc.) with a lead that brings up samples ‖ (sometimes with 'out') to ask (a per-

son) discreet questions in order to discover how he feels or thinks ‖ to investigate (feelings or ideas) in this way ‖ (med.) to examine (a person's body) with a sound ‖ v.i. to use a line etc. for measuring the depth of water ‖ to examine the ocean floor etc. with a lead that brings up samples ‖ (of a whale) to dive deeply and suddenly [fr. O.F. sonder]

sound and light *SON ET LUMIÈRE

sound barrier a sudden large increase in aerodynamic resistance to objects moving at speeds approaching that of sound

sound·board (sáundbɔrd, sáundbourd) n. the sounding board of a musical instrument

sound bow (bou) the thick part of a bell that the clapper strikes

sound box a mechanism in a nonelectric phonograph which converts into sounds the vibrating movements of the needle or stylus in the record grooves ‖ the hollow boxlike part in a musical instrument (e.g. a violin) which augments its resonance

sound·ing (sáundiŋ) adj. resonant ‖ making a sound ‖ (rhet.) high-sounding

sounding n. the act of someone who sounds ‖ a measurement or investigation made by sounding ‖ a part of the bottom of the sea or of a river etc. which can be reached by sounding ‖ (pl.) the depth of water in the sea or a river measured by sounding ‖ (pl.) entries of these depths in a logbook

sounding balloon a balloon used in recording the temperature, pressure etc. of the atmosphere

sounding board a thin board or plate in a musical instrument which resonates to amplify the notes ‖ a board placed above a pulpit etc. to reflect a speaker's voice to his audience ‖ an agency which gives greater force, scope etc. to various opinions, the government used the press as its sounding board

sounding line (naut.) a rope, wire etc., with a lead sinker, used for sounding depths

sound·ly (sáundli:) adv. wisely, prudently, she advised them soundly ‖ thoroughly, he thrashed them soundly ‖ deeply, she slept soundly all through the journey

sound·ness (sáundnis) n. the state or quality of being sound

sound pollution *NOISE POLLUTION

sound post a small wooden peg in a violin etc. supporting the belly and transmitting vibrations to the back of the instrument

sound·proof (sáundpru:f) 1. adj. impenetrable to sound waves 2. v.t. to make soundproof **sóund·proof·ing** n. the material used in making something soundproof ‖ the act or process of making something soundproof

sound ranging (mil.) the location of an enemy gun by taking bearings on a detonation and measuring how long it takes the sound to reach surveyed positions

sound·scape (sáundskeip) n. the overall feeling in music; a sound panorama

sound track the side strip of a motion-picture film on which sound is electrically recorded by tracks of variable density or variable width

sound wave (phys.) a periodic progression of alternations between high and low pressure through an elastic medium

soup (su:p) 1. n. a liquid food, usually savory, made by stewing ingredients such as meat, vegetables, fish or game, often in a stock and with seasoning **from soup to nuts** (pop.) from beginning to end, everything included **in the soup** (pop.) in a difficult position ‖ a chemical mixture, often a residual or waste product ‖ the white water remaining after a wave 2. v.t. **to soup up** (pop.) to increase the horsepower of (a car) [fr. F. soupe]

soup·çon (su:psɔ̃, sú:psɔ̃) n. a trace, suspicion, suggestion ‖ a very small quantity of something [F.=suspicion]

soup kitchen a place where food (not only soup) is provided without charge to people in need through poverty, a natural disaster etc.

sour (sáuər) 1. adj. tasting or smelling acid, sharp or biting, sour fruit ‖ changed, e.g. by fermentation, to an acid, esp. spoiled in this way, sour milk ‖ morosely angry or embittered, or expressing such a condition, a sour look ‖ (of soil) acid in reaction 2. v.t. to make sour ‖ v.i. to become sour 3. n. a cocktail of a specified liquor made acid with lemon or lime juice and a slice of orange, a whiskey sour [O.E. sūr]

source (sɔrs) n. the spring, or starting point, of a stream or river ‖ the place or thing from which, or person because of whom, something

begins or arises, the source of the trouble ‖ a person, book, document etc. consulted for information or providing initial inspiration [O.F. sors, source]

source language (computer) the language in which a program is written before translation into a language that the processor can utilize Cf TARGET LANGUAGE

sour cream cream soured by lactic acid bacteria

sour·dine (suərdí:n) n. (mus.) a mute, sordino [F.]

sour·dough (sáuərdou) n. an old inhabitant of Alaska or N.W. Canada ‖ fermented dough from one baking set aside to start the next [from the prospectors' practice of carrying fermented dough for breadmaking]

sour grapes the disparagement of something out of chagrin at not being able to get it [from a fable by Aesop]

sour·sop (sáuərsɔp) n. Annona muricata, fam. Annonaceae, a tree native to the West Indies which bears large, ovoid, pulpy, edible fruit, resembling the sweetsop but more acid in taste ‖ the fruit of the soursop tree

Sou·sa (sú:zə), John Philip (1854-1932), American composer. Besides his famous marches, e.g. 'Stars and Stripes Forever', 'Washington Post', he composed comic operas, songs and suites

Sou·sa (sóuzə), Martim Affonso de (c. 1500-1564), Portuguese explorer. He led (1530) the first expedition to Brazil, organized (1531) the Portuguese settlement against the incursions of Spaniards, French and Dutch, and founded (1532) São Vicente

sou·sa·phone (sú:zəfoun, sú:səfoun) n. a large tubalike instrument used in American brass bands [after J. P. Sousa, the originator]

souse (saus) 1. n. pickled food ‖ a preparation used for pickling ‖ a soaking ‖ a drunkard 2. v.t. pres. part. **sous·ing** past and past part. **soused** to pickle ‖ to soak or drench **soused** adj. pickled ‖ (pop.) very drunk [O.F. sous, souce, pickle fr. O.H.G.]

Sousse (su:s) (Arab. Susa) a walled port (pop. 255,000) in N.E. Tunisia: fortified Moslem convent (9th c.), Christian catacombs (2nd-3rd cc.). It was a Phoenician city, was destroyed by the Vandals (434) and rebuilt by Justinian

sou·tache (su:tǽʃ) n. a narrow braid used for trimming or ornamenting fabric [F. fr. Hung. szuszak, a curl of hair]

sou·tane (sú:tán) n. a Roman Catholic priest's cassock [F. fr. Ital.]

south (sauθ) 1. adv. toward the south 2. n. (usually with 'the') one of the four cardinal points of the compass (abbr. S., *COMPASS POINT) ‖ the direction to the right of a person facing east **the South** the southern part of a country, esp. the states of the U.S.A. south of the Mason-Dixon line which fought against the Union in the Civil War (*CONFEDERATE STATES OF AMERICA) 3. adj. of, belonging to or situated toward the south ‖ facing south, a south window ‖ (of winds) blowing from the south [O.E. sūth]

South Africa a republic (area 471,445 sq. miles, pop. 32,465,000) occupying the southern tip of Africa. Administrative capital: Pretoria. Seat of legislature: Cape Town. Largest city: Johannesburg. People: 68% African, 19% European, 9% Coloured, 3% Asian (mainly Indian). Racial segregation (*APARTHEID) is enforced. Native reservations occupy 12% of the land. Language: Bantu languages (mainly Xhosa, Zulu, Sotho, Tswana, Ciskei), Afrikaans (spoken by 57% of Europeans and most Coloured), English (39% of Europeans and most Asians), Indian languages. Religion: 50% local African religions, 42% Protestant (incl. Dutch Reformed, Methodist, Anglican and Native Separatist Churches), with Roman Catholic, Hindu, Moslem and Jewish minorities. The land is 8% cultivated and 1% forest. Broad, flat plateaus, broken by kopjes (dry ridges and gulleys), cover most of the country, sloping from the High Veld (mainly 5,000-7,000 ft) in the S. Transvaal, E. Orange Free State and N.E. Cape Province, to under 2,000 ft in the west. Mountains in the east (*DRAKENSBERG) and south (with the Great and Little Karoos) separate the plateaus from the Indian Ocean coastal plain. The plateaus are savanna (veld) in the east, semidesert in the west and north (*KALAHARI). The coastal plain is desert in the west, Mediterranean in the south and tropical in the east. Average temperatures (F.) in Jan. and July: Durban 75° and 65°, Mozambique border 92° and 79°, Johannesburg 80° and 38°, Kimberley 91° and 66°, Cape

Town 70° and 55°. Rainfall: N. Natal 45-50 ins, Drakensberg 68 ins, High Veld 20-30 ins, Johannesburg and Port Elizabeth 33 ins, Kimberley 16 ins, Cape Town 25 ins, northwest coast 2 ins. Livestock: cattle, sheep, goats, hogs, poultry, horses, mules, donkeys. Agricultural products: corn, Kaffir corn, wheat, other cereals, sugarcane, peanuts, sunflower seed, fruit (esp. oranges, apples, grapes and pears), dairy products, tobacco, potatoes, cotton, wool. Fisheries: esp. pilchards, lobsters, whales. Mineral resources: gold, uranium, coal, diamonds, asbestos, copper, manganese ore, iron ore. Industries: mining, ranching, subsistence farming (native reserves), iron and steel, foodstuffs, metals, machinery, chemicals, clothing and footwear, textiles, wines and spirits, furniture, vehicles, transport equipment, bark extract, soap, cement, bricks, tires, tourism. Exports: minerals, wool, cereals, hides and skins, machinery, oils and paints, citrus fruits, textiles, sugar, wines and spirits, bark extract. Imports: vehicles, drugs and fertilizers, cotton goods, rough diamonds, wood products, fuels and oil, jewelry and fancy goods, tea, rubber. Ports: Durban, Cape Town, Port Elizabeth, East London. There are nine universities for Europeans, and five university colleges for non-Europeans. Monetary unit: rand (100 cents). HISTORY. South Africa was inhabited by Bushmen and Hottentots when Dias discovered the Cape of Good Hope (1487). After Vasco da Gama rounded the Cape (1497), South Africa became important as a supply station on the route to the East Indies. The Dutch East India Company established a settlement at Cape Town (1652). Settlement extended inland to form Cape Colony (18th c.), giving rise to many wars with Bantu tribes (18th-19th cc.). The colony prospered with slave labor, largely imported from the Dutch East Indies. Britain annexed the colony (1806) to protect its route to India, an act officially recognized by the Netherlands in 1814. Increasing numbers of British settlers arrived (1820s), and to escape British domination the Boers moved northward in the Great Trek (1835-6) to Natal, the Transvaal and the Orange Free State, defeating the Zulus (1838). Britain annexed Natal (1843) but recognized the independence of the Transvaal (1852) and the Orange Free State (1854). Relations between the British colony and the Boer republics deteriorated, esp. when Britain annexed (1871) Griqualand, an area of the Orange Free State where diamonds had been discovered (1867). An attempt to annex the Transvaal (1877) resulted in war between Britain and the Boers (1880-1) in which Britain was defeated, and the Transvaal's independence was recognized. But the discovery (1886) of gold at Witwatersrand brought many new immigrants, known as Uitlanders, to the Transvaal. Kruger's refusal to give them the franchise and the Jameson Raid (1895) provoked the Boer War (1899-1902). After the British victory, the Transvaal and the Orange Free State became British colonies (1902) and were united with Cape Province and Natal to form the Union of South Africa (1910). Led by Botha and Smuts, South Africa fought Germany in the lst world war and received German South West Africa as a mandate (1920). In opposition to Smuts's policy of promoting cooperation between the British and Boer elements, the Nationalist party was formed, advocating Boer supremacy and secession from the Commonwealth. Despite Nationalist opposition, South Africa took an active part in the 2nd world war. The Nationalists came to power (1948) under Malan, put apartheid into practice, and virtually annexed South West Africa (1949). European supremacy was enforced by government control of electoral districts and the judicature and by strict segregation of residential areas and educational establishments. Amid mounting pressure from other African states, the U.N. and the Commonwealth to abandon apartheid, South Africa withdrew from the Commonwealth, as a republic (May 31, 1961). The U.N. terminated (1966) the mandate over South West Africa (Namibia), but South Africa described this as illegal and continued its administration. Between 1964 and 1985 some 3.5 million blacks were resettled into ten African 'homelands,' four of which, Transkei (1976), Bophuthatswana (1977), Venda (1979) and Ciskei (1981), were granted independence by South Africa, although no other country recognized them as nations. Op-

position to apartheid in South Africa grew, intensifying in 1976 when rioting broke out in several cities, including Soweto, a black township of Johannesburg. The death while in police custody of Stephen Biko, a young black detained in a government crackdown following the riots, caused international protests. Under pressure the government began to amend some apartheid laws from 1978, and in 1984 Coloureds and Asians were offered a limited role in the central government, although blacks were still excluded. Bishop Desmond Tutu, head of the South African Council of Churches, received the Nobel peace prize (1984) for his efforts to gain a nonviolent end to apartheid. Violence continued, however, leading the government to declare a state of emergency (1985-6) and to grant blacks a few concessions. Some of South Africa's trading partners imposed limited sanctions on South Africa to increase pressure on the government. South Africa continued to exert control over Namibia, despite continuous international pressure

South African 1. adj. of or relating to South Africa **2.** n. a native or inhabitant of South Africa esp. one of European origin

South African Dutch *AFRIKAANS

South African Republic the name (1856-81) of the Transvaal

South African War *BOER WAR

South America the fourth largest continent (area 7,035,340 sq. miles) comprising Argentina, Bolivia, Brazil, Chile, Colombia, Ecuador, French Guiana, Guyana, Paraguay, Peru, Suriname, Uruguay and Venezuela and including Curaçao, the Falkland and Galapagos Is, Trinidad and Tobago, and adjacent smaller islands (*AMERICA). (For history see articles on separate countries)

South American Indians *LATIN AMERICAN INDIANS

South·amp·ton (sauθǽmptən, sauθhǽmptən) a passenger port and county borough (pop. 207,500) in Hampshire, England. Industries: shipbuilding, oil refining, chemicals, engineering. University (1952)

South Arabia, Federation of *YEMEN, PEOPLES DEMOCRATIC REPUBLIC OF

South Australia a state (area 380,070 sq. miles, pop. 1,302,400) in S. central Australia. Capital: Adelaide. It is low-lying and arid except in the south. Agriculture: wheat, barley, fruit (mainly in irrigated areas along the Murray), sheep, some cattle. Resources: iron ore, pyrites, gypsum, salt, coral. Industries: metallurgy, textiles, chemicals, food processing, engineering. University (1874), at Adelaide

south by east S. 11° 15′E., one point east of due south (abbr. S. b. E., Br. esp. S by E., *COMPASS POINT)

south by west S. 11° 15′W., one point west of due south (abbr. S. b. W., Br. esp. S. by W., *COMPASS POINT)

South Canadian River *CANADIAN RIVER

South Car·o·li·na (kærəláinə) (abbr. S.C.) a state (area 31,055 sq. miles, pop. 3,203,000) on the S.E. Atlantic coast of the U.S.A. Capital: Columbia. It lies largely in the coastal plain and Appalachian piedmont plateau, rising to 3,548 ft in the northwest (Blue Ridge Mtns). It is primarily industrial. Agriculture: tobacco, cotton, soybeans, peaches, corn, hogs, cattle. Resources: building materials, timber. Industries: textiles, chemicals, forest products. State university (1801) at Columbia. South Carolina was colonized by the Spanish (16th c.) and the English (late 17th c.), was one of the Thirteen Colonies, and became (1788) the 8th state of the U.S.A.

South China Sea *CHINA SEA

South Dakota (abbr. S.D.) a state (area 77,047 sq. miles, pop. 691,000) of the N. central U.S.A. in the Great Plains, with the rugged Black Hills (summit 7,242 ft) and badlands in the southwest. Capital: Pierre. Agriculture: beef cattle, hogs, corn, fodder crops. Resources: gold (leading state producer), beryl, silver, sand, gravel. Industries: meat packing, butter making. State university (1882) at Vermillion. South Dakota was settled in the 19th c. and became (1889) the 40th state of the U.S.A.

South·down (sáuθdaun) n. a sheep of a hornless breed, with fine soft wool, valued chiefly for its meat [after the South Downs of Sussex and Hampshire, England, where the breed originated]

South Downs *DOWNS

south·east (sauθí:st) **1.** adv. toward the southeast **2.** n. (usually with 'the') the compass point or direction midway between south and east (abbr. S.E., *COMPASS POINT) **the Southeast** the southeastern part of a country **3.** adj. of, belonging to or situated toward the southeast ‖ (of winds) blowing from the southeast [O.E. súthēast]

South East Asia Treaty Organization (abbr. SEATO) an organization set up (1954) by the U.S.A., Great Britain, Australia, France, New Zealand, Pakistan, the Philippines and Thailand, as a bulwark against Chinese Communism after the Korean War. It was dissolved in 1977

southeast by east S. 56° 15′E., one point east of due southeast (abbr. S.E. b. E., Br. esp. S.E. by E., *COMPASS POINT)

southeast by south S. 33° 45′ E., one point south of due southeast (abbr. S.E. b. S., Br. esp. S.E. by S., *COMPASS POINT)

south·east·er (sauθí:stər) n. a strong wind or storm from the southeast

south·east·er·ly (sauθí:stərli:) **1.** adj. and adv. in or toward the southeast ‖ (of winds) from that direction **2.** pl. **south·east·er·lies** n. a wind blowing from the southeast

south·east·ern (sauθí:stə:rn) adj. situated, facing or moving toward the southeast ‖ of or relating to the southeast or the Southeast

south·east·ward (sauθí:stwərd) adv. and adj. toward the southeast **south·east·wards** adv.

South·end (sáuθend) (or Southend-on-Sea) a resort and county borough (pop. 156,683) in Essex, England, on the Thames estuary, providing the nearest beach to London (43 miles away). Industries: electrical equipment, chemicals

south·er·ly (sʌðərli:) **1.** adj. and adv. in or toward the south ‖ (of winds) from that direction **2.** pl. **south·er·lies** n. a wind blowing from the south

south·ern (sʌðərn) adj. situated, facing, or moving toward the south **South·ern** of or relating to the South [O.E. sútherne]

Southern Alps a mountain range along the west central coast of South Island, New Zealand (Mt Cook, 12,350 ft), with gorges and glaciers

Southern Bug (bu:g, Russ. bu:k) a river (520 miles long, mostly unnavigable) of the U.S.S.R., which flows through the S.W. Ukraine to the Black Sea (Dnieper estuary)

Southern Cross a cross-shaped constellation in the southern hemisphere with a bright star at each extremity

South·ern·er (sʌðərnər) n. a native or inhabitant of the South, esp. of the Southern part of the U.S.A.

southern hemisphere the half of the earth south of the equator

south·ern·most (sʌðərnmoust) adj. farthest south

southern pea black-eyed pea

Sou·they (sáuði:, sʌði:), Robert (1774-1843), English poet and man of letters. From 1803 he lived in the Lake District, met Wordsworth, and himself became one of the Lake poets. He was poet laureate from 1813. With Coleridge he attempted to found a utopian community, but the idea failed for lack of funds. Of his poems, only the shorter ones are now read, though his early works are long narrative poems. Of his many prose works, his 'Life of Nelson' (1813) is the best known

South Georgia an island (area 1,600 sq. miles, pop. 400 in the whaling season) in the S.W. Atlantic, part of the Falkland Islands Dependencies. Highest point: 9,200 ft. Capt. Cook took possession of it in 1775

South Holland *HOLLAND

south·ing (sáuθiŋ) n. (naut.) a sailing towards the south ‖ (naut.) the distance thus sailed since the last point of reckoning ‖ (astron.) the distance, in degrees, of any heavenly body south of the celestial equator

South Island *NEW ZEALAND

South Korea *KOREA, REPUBLIC OF

South Orkney Islands an uninhabited archipelago (land area 240 sq. miles) in the S.W. Atlantic and Antarctic Oceans, part of the Falkland Islands Dependencies. They were claimed by the British in 1821

south·paw (sáuθpɔ) **1.** adj. (pop.) left-handed **2.** n. (pop.) a left-handed person, esp. a pitcher in baseball or a boxer

South Platte a river (424 miles long) rising in central Colorado, flowing across the Nebraska boundary to join the North Platte River in central Nebraska and form the Platte River

South Pole the southern end of the earth's axis, in Antarctica. The first man to reach this point was Amundsen (1911) **south pole** the zenith of the heavens as viewed from the south terrestrial pole ‖ the pole of a magnet that points to the south when the magnet is allowed to rotate freely in the earth's magnetic field (cf. NORTH POLE)

South·port (sáuθpɔrt, sáuθpɔurt) a town (pop. 89,745) and resort in Lancashire, England, on the Irish sea

South Sandwich Islands an uninhabited volcanic archipelago (land area 130 sq. miles) in the S. Atlantic, part of the Falkland Islands Dependencies

South Sea Islands Oceania

South Seas a name given to the oceans of the southern hemisphere (excluding the Antarctic Ocean), esp. the S. Pacific

South Shetland Islands a group of uninhabited islands (land area 1,800 sq. miles) off the Antarctic Peninsula, part of the Falkland Islands Dependencies. They were discovered (1819) by William Smith, an English mariner

South Shields a county borough and resort (pop. 87,203) in Durham, England, at the mouth of the Tyne: glass and chemical industries

south-south-east (sáuθsauθíːst) 1. *adv.* toward south-southeast 2. *n.* S. 22° 30′ E., a compass point midway between south and southeast (*abbr.* S.S.E., *COMPASS POINT) 3. *adj.* of or situated toward south-southeast ‖ (of winds) blowing from south-southeast

south-south-west (sáuθsauθwést) 1. *adv.* toward south-southwest 2. *n.* S. 22° 30′ W., a compass point midway between south and southwest (*abbr.* S.S.W., *COMPASS POINT) 3. *adj.* of or situated toward south-southwest ‖ (of winds) blowing from south-southwest

South Tirol *TRENTINO-ALTO ADIGE

south·ward (sáuθwərd, sáðərd) 1. *adv. and adj.* toward the south 2. *n.* the southward direction or part **sóuth·wards** *adv.*

South·well (sáuθwəl), Robert (c. 1561-95), English Jesuit, religious tract writer and poet. He was imprisoned, tortured, tried and hanged for his faith. In 1929 he was beatified. His best-known poem is 'The Burning Babe'

south·west (sauθwést) 1. *adv.* toward the southwest 2. *n.* (usually with 'the') the compass point or direction midway between south and west (*abbr.* S.W., *COMPASS POINT) **the Southwest** the southwestern part of a country 3. *adj.* of, belonging to or situated toward the southwest ‖ (of winds) blowing from the southwest [O.E. *súthwest*]

South West Africa *NAMIBIA

southwest by south S. 33° 45′ W., one point south of due southwest (*abbr.* S.W. b. S., *Br.* esp. S.W. by S., *COMPASS POINT)

southwest by west S. 56° 15′ W., one point west of due southwest (*abbr.* S.W. b. W., *Br.* esp. S.W. by W., *COMPASS POINT)

south·west·er (sauθwéstər) *n.* a strong wind or storm from the southwest ‖ a sou'wester

south·west·er·ly (sauθwéstərli:) 1. *adj. and adv.* in or toward the southwest ‖ (of winds) from that direction 2. *n. pl.* **south·west·er·lies** a wind blowing from the southwest

south·west·ern (sauθwéstərn) *adj.* situated, facing or moving toward the southwest ‖ of or relating to the southwest or the Southwest

southwestern corn borer (*entomology*) a moth (*Diatraea grandiosella*) whose larva bore into corn stalks, thereby causing crop damage

south·west·ward (sauθwéstwərd) *adv. and adj.* toward the southwest **south·wést·wards** *adv.*

South Yemen, People's Republic of *YEMEN, PEOPLE'S DEMOCRATIC REPUBLIC OF

Sou·tine (suːtíːn), Chaïm (1894-1943), French painter born in Lithuania. His violently expressionist works include turbulent landscapes, studies of carcasses, and moody portraits charged with emotion

sou·ve·nir (suːvəníər, súːvəniər) *n.* something that serves to recall the past [F.]

sou'west·er (sauwéstər) *n.* a waterproof hat with a broad flap at the back to protect the neck, worn esp. by sailors, fishermen etc. [SOUTHWESTER]

Sou·za (suːsa), Tomé de (16th c.), Portuguese politician, first governor (1549-53) of Brazil. He founded Salvador, Bahia

sov·er·eign (sóvrin, sóvərin, sávrin, sávərin) 1. *adj.* of or relating to a sovereign ‖ having undisputed right to make decisions and act accordingly, *a sovereign state* ‖ unlimited, absolute, *sovereign power* ‖ (of a remedy) very effective 2. *n.* a person or body of persons supreme in a state ‖ a British gold coin worth 20 shillings, first struck in 1489 and last issued in 1931 ‖ a coin of Saudi Arabia worth 40 rials [O.F. *soverain, souverein*]

sov·er·eign·ty (sóvrinti:, sávrinti:) *pl.* **sov·er·eign·ties** *n.* undisputed political power ‖ the state or quality of being sovereign ‖ the status or authority of a sovereign ‖ a sovereign state [A.F. *sovereyneté*]

So·vetsk, So·vietsk (sʌvjétsk) (formerly Tilsit) a port (pop. 38,000) of the R.S.F.S.R. (Kaliningrad enclave), U.S.S.R., on the lower Niemen, on the Lithuanian border

so·vi·et (sóuvi:et, sóuvi:it, souvi:ét) *n.* an elected governing council in the U.S.S.R. ‖ any of the associated republics of the U.S.S.R. **So·vi·et** *adj.* of or relating to the U.S.S.R. **só·vi·et·ism** *n.* the soviet system of government **so·vi·et·i·zá·tion** *n.* **só·vi·et·ize** *pres. part.* **so·vi·et·iz·ing** *past and past part.* **so·vi·et·ized** *v.t.* to bring under the soviet system [Russ.=council]

—Soviets were originally revolutionary committees elected by factory workers after the revolution of 1905. At the time of the revolution of 1917, soviets were elected throughout Russia by workers, peasants and soldiers. The term was then applied to the primary units of government in the U.S.S.R., at local, provincial and national levels. The national soviet is called the Supreme Soviet, comprising delegates from all the Soviet Republics

So·vi·et·ol·o·gy (souvi:ətóləʒi:) *n.* the study of mores and politics of leadership in the U.S.S.R.
—**Sovietologist** *n. also* Kremlinology

Soviet Russia the Union of Soviet Socialist Republics

Sovietsk *SOVETSK

Soviet Union the Union of Soviet Socialist Republics

sow (sau) *n.* an adult female hog ‖ the female of certain other animals, e.g. the badger ‖ a main trough into which molten iron is poured and from which it flows into subsidiary molds to form pigs ‖ the large block of iron that hardens in this main trough [O.E. *sugu*]

sow (sou) *pres. part.* **sow·ing** *past* **sowed** *past part.* **sown** (soun), **sowed** *v.t.* to scatter or bury (seed) on or in the soil, so that it may germinate and grow ‖ to scatter seed in (land), *to sow a field with barley* ‖ to implant or spread (unrest, discontent etc.) ‖ to introduce (anchovies, oysters etc.) into an environment for cultivation ‖ (*mil.*) to lay (mines) in a stretch of water or land ‖ *v.i.* to scatter seed [O.E. *sáwan*]

sow bug (sau) a wood louse

sown *alt. past part.* of sow

sow thistle (sau) a member of *Sonchus,* fam. *Compositae,* a genus of tall grasses with copious latex. They are like thistles but have no prickles

sox (spks) *pl. n.* socks (articles of clothing)

soy (sɔi) *n.* an Oriental piquant sauce made from soybeans fermented and then treated in brine ‖ the soybean [Jap. fr. *shōyu* fr. Chin.]

soy·a bean (sɔiə) *SOYBEAN

soy·bean (sɔibi:n) *n.* (*Am.=Br.* soya bean) *Glycine max,* fam. *Papilionaceae,* a plant native to Asia, now cultivated in many parts of the world. The edible, highly nourishing seeds are used as a source of oil, flour and meal. The plant is used for fodder and for soil improvement

soybean cyst nematode (*entomology*) a long, thin worm (*Heterodera glycines*) that stunts and yellows soybeans

Soyinka (sɔiíŋkə), Wole (1934-), Nigerian playwright and poet, whose works, written in English, combine Western culture with African traditions. Plays include 'The Swamp Dwellers' (1958), 'Death and the King's Horseman' (1975), 'Opera Wonyosi' (1979) and 'A Play of Giants' (1984). 'A Shuttle in the Crypt' (1972) is a collection of poems written during a prison term (1967-9) for opposition to the war in Biafra. His autobiography 'Aké: The Years of Childhood' was published in 1982

soy·milk (sɔimilk) *n.* milklike substance derived from soybeans

soy sauce *SOY

So·yuz (soujúːs) *n.* (*aerospace*) U.S.S.R. spacecraft with 2–3 man crew for earth orbit, first launched in 1967 and modified in 1979

Soz·zi·ni (sɔttsíːni:) *SOCINUS

spa (spa) *n.* a resort where there is a spring of mineral water ‖ a spring of mineral water ‖ a hotel that features weight-reducing diets, exercise, massage, and water therapy [after *Spa,* in Belgium]

Spaak (spak), Paul Henri (1899-1972), Belgian socialist statesman. He was Belgian foreign minister (1936-8, 1939-45, 1946-50, 1954-7 and 1961-6) and prime minister (1938-9, 1946 and 1947-50). He was the first president of the U.N. General Assembly (1946) and secretary-general of NATO (1957-61), and helped to plan the European Economic Community

space (speis) 1. *n.* (without the article) that which contains and surrounds all material bodies ‖ the distance between two points, objects etc. ‖ a time interval, *within the space of half an hour* ‖ (without the article) the region outside the earth's atmosphere ‖ a limited extent or area for a specific purpose, *write your name in the blank space* ‖ (*printing*) a piece of metal used to separate words or letters, or lines of type ‖ (*mus.*) one of the degrees on the staff between lines *to gaze into space* to stare, normally for a long time and with the eyes unfocused on anything, as though into the infinite distance 2. *v.t.* *pres. part.* **spac·ing** *past and past part.* **spaced** to arrange at regular or suitable distances or time intervals ‖ (*printing, typing* etc.) to separate (words, lines etc.) by spaces [fr. O.F. *espace*]

—Space is the idea which each person forms and develops, as the result of his sense perceptions, that there exist 'things' other than himself, and that his own body consists of 'parts', and that these bear an orderly relationship to one another which he describes in terms of position in space and distance from one another. Experience associates with this idea the quality of being the same always, and thus the idea of time is also involved. The interrelationship of space and time as a condition of being is treated mathematically in the study of the space-time continuum. The idea 'space', like the idea 'time', is a relative concept, since it is based solely upon sensory experience

space·borne (spéisbɔrn) *adj.* carried beyond the earth's atmosphere

space charge (*phys.*) the negative charge created by the stream of electrons from the filament of a thermionic valve, opposing the motion of the electrons

space·craft (spéiskræft, spéiskrɑft) *pl.* **space·craft** *n.* a vehicle designed to travel beyond the earth's atmosphere

spaced-out (speisdáut) *adj.* (*slang*) under the influence of a narcotic or nonnarcotic drug, as shown, e.g., in disorientation, inappropriate affect

space exploration the exploration of space by instrumented and manned spacecraft from 1957. When the Soviet Union's 'Sputnik I' with cosmonaut Yuri Gagarin aboard was successfully launched and orbited the earth (1957), the Space Age had begun and the U.S.A. formed the National Aeronautics and Space Administration (NASA) (1958). The Mercury program saw John Glenn rocket into space (1962) in 'Friendship 7'; the Gemini program produced the first walk in space (1965) by Edward H. White; and the Apollo program sent Neil Armstrong, Edwin Aldrin and Michael Collins to the Moon (1969). As a cooperative venture a Soviet Soyuz spacecraft and an American Apollo spacecraft docked in space in 1975. By 1981 the space shuttle was in operation, but flights were suspended temporarily when 'Challenger' exploded (1986) (*SPACE SHUTTLE). Unmanned space exploration saw Earth satellites, lunar probes and interplanetary probes studying the Earth's radiation belts, atmosphere and ionosphere, as well as other planets (1962-) including Mercury, Venus, Mars, Jupiter, Saturn and Uranus

spacelab laboratory and workshop built by 10 European countries, all but one members of the European Space Agency, for the U.S. space shuttle. Begun in 1973, it consists of two adaptable modules—one a laboratory, the other a flat platform on which equipment can be exposed directly to space. Spacelab is carried in the cargo bay of the shuttle and is used to conduct various experiments. Its first flight aboard a space shuttle was in 1983

space lattice the geometrical arrangement of atoms in a crystal, esp. as revealed by X-ray spectroscopy

space·man (spéismæn, spéismən) *pl.* **space·men** (spéismɛn, spéismən) *n.* (esp. *science fic-*

CONCISE PRONUNCIATION KEY: **(a)** æ, c*a*t; ɑ, c*a*r; ɔ f*aw*n; ei, sn*a*ke. **(e)** e, h*e*n; iː, sh*ee*p; iə, d*ee*r; ɛə, b*ea*r. **(i)** i, f*i*sh; ai, t*i*ger; əː, b*i*rd. **(o)** o, *o*x; au, c*ow*; ou, g*oa*t; u, p*oo*r; ɔi, r*oy*al. **(u)** ʌ, d*u*ck; u, b*u*ll; uː, g*oo*se; ə, b*a*cill*u*s; juː, c*u*be. x, lo*ch*; θ, *th*ink; ð, bo*th*er; z, *Z*en; ʒ, corsa*g*e; dʒ, sava*g*e; ŋ, oranguta*n*g; j, *y*ak; ʃ, *fi*sh; tʃ, fe*tch*; 'l, rabb*le*; 'n, redd*en*. Complete pronunciation key appears inside front cover.

tion) a man who travels in space ‖ a visitor from outer space ‖ an astronaut

space plane prototype plane designed to serve as shuttle between space satellites and earth *Cf* SPACE SHUTTLE

space-ship (spéiʃip) *n.* a spacecraft

space shuttle reusable space launcher and carrier vehicle, consisting of the orbiter, external tank and solid rocket launch, that lands on a runway. U.S. astronauts John Young and Robert Crippen made the first orbit (1981) in 'Columbia.' 'Challenger' made 9 flights (1983-5) before exploding within 2 minutes of takeoff on its 10th mission (Jan. 28, 1986). All shuttle flights were cancelled pending investigation and reorganization of safety procedures. Four operational shuttles—'Challenger,' 'Columbia,' 'Discovery' and 'Atlantis'—made 24 flights before the 'Challenger' accident

space sickness physical maladjustment during space flight

space station a long-term earth-orbiting satellite, manned or unmanned, for observation or communication *also* **space platform**

space suit a pressurized suit worn by astronauts to protect them in outer space

Space Telescope U.S. satellite with optical instruments

space-time continuum (*phys.*) the concept of a space of four dimensions, arising from the theory of relativity. The presence of a body in space not being independent of time, a time axis must be added to the three axes of space dimensions in order to locate it

Spacetrack *n.* (*mil.*) a global system of radar, optical, and radiometric sensors linked to a computation and analysis center in the North American Air Defense Command complex *Cf* SPADATS

space walk *v.* to move beyond a craft in space as from one spaceship to another—**spacewalk** *n.* —**spacewalker** *n.* —**spacewalking** *n.*

spacial *SPATIAL

spac-ing (spéisiŋ) *n.* the arrangement of spaces ‖ the space between printed words in a line of type ‖ the act of someone who spaces

spa-cious (spéiʃəs) *adj.* roomy, giving or having ample space ‖ marked by ease, comfort, leisure, opportunity etc. [fr. L. *spatiosus*]

spa-cis-tor (speisístər) *n.* (*electr.*) a solid-state transistorlike device with several terminals, designed to generate an electron flow through layers in a germanium wafer

Spadats (*acronym*) a space detection and tracking system, for detecting and tracking space vehicles and reporting their orbital characteristics to a central control facility, designed as an early warning system of enemy ICBMs *Cf* SPACETRACK

spade (speid) **1.** *n.* a long-handled tool with a broad, flat blade, used for digging ‖ a tool of similar shape with a sharp edge to the blade, used for cutting turf, whale blubber etc. ‖ a spadelike part on the trail of a gun carriage. It is planted in the ground to check the recoil of the carriage **to call a spade a spade** to name bluntly what one might choose to refer to by a euphemism **2.** *v.t. pres. part.* **spad-ing** past and *past part.* **spad-ed** to dig or cut with a spade [O.E. *spadu*]

spade *n.* the mark of one of the four suits of playing cards (♠) ‖ (*pl.*) the suit of cards so marked ‖ a card of this suit [fr. Ital. *spade* pl. of *spada*, a sword]

spade-work (spéidwəːrk) *n.* laborious preparatory work

spa-di-ceous (speidíʃəs) *adj.* having a spadix ‖ being a spadix ‖ bright clear brown in color [fr. Mod. L. *spadiceus*]

spa-dix (spéidiks) *pl.* **spa-di-ces** (speidáisiːz) *n.* (*bot.*) a racemose inflorescence with sessile flowers, elongated axis and enveloping spathe, e.g. the arum lily [Mod. L. fr. L.=a leaf torn off a palm tree, fr. Gk]

spa-ghet-ti (spəgéti:) *n.* pasta in the form of very thin, long, solid rods, a little thicker than vermicelli, which are boiled and normally served with a sauce [Ital.]

spaghetti Western motion picture about the American West made in Italy

spa-hi (spáːhi:) *pl.* **spa-his** *n.* (*hist.*) a member of a largely irregular Turkish cavalry corps, organized on a more or less feudal basis and disbanded after 1826 ‖ (*hist.*) a member of an Algerian native cavalry corps serving under the French Government. The corps was disbanded after 1962 [fr. Turk. *sipāhi*]

Spain (spein) a state (area incl. the Balearic and Canary Is 194,945 sq. miles, pop. 37,746,260) of S.W. Europe, occupying most of the Iberian Peninsula. Capital: Madrid. Overseas possessions: Ceuta, Melilla and small offshore islands. Language: Spanish, with Catalan, Basque and Galician minorities. Religion: Roman Catholic, with 26,000 Protestants, 1,000 Jews. The land is 32% arable, 50% pasture and grazing, and 8% forest. The core of Spain is the dry, deforested central Iberian plateau, or Meseta (mainly 1,500-3,000 ft), divided into north (Old Castile and León) and south (New Castile and Estremadura) by the Sierra de Gredos (to 8,504 ft) and Sierra de Guadarrama, west and north of Madrid. The Meseta is bordered on the north, northeast and south by the Cantabrian Mtns, Iberian Mtns and Sierra Morena. Outside the Meseta lie the wooded hills of Galicia, the Pyrenees and Catalonian Mtns (separated from the Iberian Mtns by the Ebro basin) and the Andalusian ranges (Mulhacén, 11,420 ft), separated from the Sierra Morena by the Guadalquivir. Intensive agriculture is largely confined to the well-watered coastal strips (where industry is also concentrated) and the valleys of the Ebro, Douro, Tagus, Guadiana and Guadalquivir. The center (where large estates predominate) is mainly devoted to stock raising and cereals. Irrigation projects are under construction. Average temperatures (F.): (Jan.) south coast and Andalusia over 50°, other coasts 42°-50°, central Spain 36°-42°, mountains under 36°, (July) Alicante and Andalusia over 80°, S. Spain and Ebro basin 72°-80°, N. Spain and southern mountains 64°-72°, northern mountains, incl. Galicia, under 64°. Rainfall: N. Meseta, Ebro basin and Mureia under 16 ins, Galicia, Asturias and Basque coast over 30 ins. Livestock: sheep, goats, cattle, hogs, mules, donkeys, horses. Agricultural products: cereals, olives, oranges, potatoes, rice, vines, onions, lemons, almonds and raisins, esparto, flax, hemp, pulses, silk, tobacco, sugarcane, sugar beets, cotton. Forest products: cork, pine lumber, resin, eucalyptus. Mineral resources: coal, iron ore, iron pyrites, copper, lead, mercury, manganese, potash, salt, tin, zinc, wolfram, ilmenite, silver, gold, quartz, sulfur, titanium, cobalt, nickel, bismuth, antimony. Industries: mining, iron and steel, textiles, fishing, machinery and chemicals, fertilizers, explosives, paper, aluminum, shipbuilding, foodstuffs, wine, sugar, cork, oil refining, cement, vehicles, hydroelectricity, tobacco, footwear, pottery, glass, leather, tourism. Exports: vegetable products, foodstuffs, wine, tobacco, minerals, fats and oils, metals, textiles. Imports: minerals and metals, machinery, vehicles, cotton, foodstuffs, chemicals. Ports: Cádiz, Barcelona, Bilbao. There are 13 universities, the oldest being Salamanca (c. 1230). Monetary unit: peseta (100 céntimos). HISTORY. There is much evidence, notably the cave paintings at Altamira, of Stone Age habitation in Spain. Celts invaded (1st millennium B.C.) and mingled with the native Iberians. Colonies were established in Andalusia by the Phoenicians (11th c. B.C.) and on the east coast by the Greeks (6th c. B.C.). The Carthaginians under Hamilcar Barca conquered Spain (3rd c. B.C.) but were expelled by the Romans after the 2nd Punic War (218-201 B.C.). Roman control was established over the whole peninsula by the 1st c. A.D., the economy prospered, and Christianity was introduced. Spain was a center of Roman culture, and produced Seneca, Lucian, Trajan, Hadrian, Martial and Quintilian. It was overrun (5th c.) by the Vandals and the Visigoths, under whom a legal code was evolved and ecclesiastical learning flourished, notably with Orosius and Isidore of Seville. The Moors overran most of the peninsula (711) and Cordova became a splendid center of the Umayyad caliphate (756-1031). Irrigation works were constructed, new crops were introduced and crafts and trade flourished. Portugal became an independent kingdom (1143). Spain was gradually reconquered by the Christians, working first from Asturias, and then from the new kingdoms of León, Navarre, Castile and Aragon. These kingdoms merged by conquest and marriage, culminating in the union (1479) of Castile and Aragon. Ferdinand V and Isabella I completed the reconquest of Spain by driving the Moors from Granada, their last stronghold (1492). In the same year, Columbus claimed America for Spain, and Spaniards explored much of Mexico, Central America, the West Indies and South America (16th c.), building up a vast empire which yielded great quantities of gold. The Inquisition was introduced (1478), the Jews were expelled (1492), with severe consequences for Spanish commerce, and the Moors were forcibly converted to Christianity (16th c.) and expelled (1609). Spain was victorious in the Italian Wars (1494-1559) and reached the height of its power under its first Hapsburg ruler, Emperor Charles V. His son, Philip II, inherited the Kingdom of the Two Sicilies, the Netherlands, Sardinia, Milan and Franche-Comté as well as Spain and its colonies. Portugal was under Spanish rule (1580-1640). The northern provinces of the Netherlands rebelled successfully (1581), and Spain was involved in protracted warfare in the southern provinces until 1648 (*THIRTY YEARS' WAR). Spain defeated the Turkish fleet at Lepanto (1571) but failed in its attempt to invade England with the Armada (1588). The Treaties of Westphalia (1648) and the Pyrenees (1659) were unfavorable to Spain, and the Spanish decline was hastened by the War of Devolution and the War of the Grand Alliance. The death (1700) of Charles II without direct heir, and the rivalry of Austria and France, provoked the War of the Spanish Succession. The resultant Peace of Utrecht (1713) deprived Spain of its European possessions and transferred Gibraltar to British rule. The attempts of Philip V and Alberoni to regain these losses were defeated by the Quadruple Alliance (1720). Under Bourbon rule (1700-1931), Spain entered the Family Compacts with France and regained (1734) the Two Sicilies in the War of the Polish Succession. By the Treaty of Paris (1763), Spain gained Louisiana and lost Florida. It regained the latter by the Treaty of Paris (1783), and sold it to the U.S.A. (1819). During the reign (1759-88) of Charles III, Floridablanca carried out much-needed economic reforms, but the expulsion (1767) of the Jesuits had an adverse effect on education. Spain was involved in the French Revolutionary Wars and the Napoleonic Wars, was forced to accept Joseph Bonaparte as king (1808), and was devastated during the Peninsular War. Ferdinand VII was restored (1814) under a constitutional regime, but his reactionary rule led to the loss of the Latin American colonies and an unsuccessful revolution (1820). His daughter, Isabella II, was deposed after a reactionary reign (1833-68), and disorder broke out, with fighting between Carlists and republicans. Under Alfonso XIII (1886-1931), the Spanish-American War resulted in the loss of Cuba, Puerto Rico and the Philippines (1898). Primo de Rivera brought off a coup d'état (1923) and established a military dictatorship (1923-30). The growth of republicanism resulted in the overthrow of the monarchy (1931). The ensuing republic was strongly anticlerical and hostile to the landowners, and was overthrown by the Falangists under Franco in the Spanish Civil War (1936-9). Franco established a Fascist dictatorship (1939) and kept Spain neutral in the 2nd world war though friendly to the Axis powers. The Falange was declared the only legal party, Church property and privileges were restored, and Spain was declared a monarchy (1947) with Franco as regent for life. The U.S.A. supplied much economic and technical aid (1950s). Spain joined the U.N. (1955) and the Organization for European Economic Cooperation (1959). The Spanish government renewed its claim to Gibraltar (1964) by imposing frontier restrictions. The Cortes approved (1969) General Franco's proposal that on his death or retirement Prince Juan Carlos of Bourbon should become king of Spain, which he did (1975). Under a 1978 constitution Spain became a hereditary, constitutional monarchy. An attempted military coup (1981) was suppressed. Although the election of regional parliaments gave the regions more autonomy, Basque separatist groups demanded greater self-rule

spake *archaic past* of SPEAK

Spa-la-to (spalátou) *SPLIT

spall (spɔl) **1.** *n.* a fragment split off stone, concrete etc. or one separated from a rock by weathering **2.** *v.t.* to chip or break up (ore) for sorting or crushing ‖ *v.i.* to split off in particles or chips [etym. doubtful]

Spal-lan-za-ni (spɑllantsáni:), Abbé Lazzaro (1729-99), Italian biologist who first advocated artificial insemination

---

CONCISE PRONUNCIATION KEY: **(a)** æ, c*a*t; ɑ, c*a*r; ɔ f*aw*n; ei, sn*a*ke. **(e)** e, h*e*n; i:, sh*ee*p; iə, d*ee*r; ɛə, b*ea*r. **(i)** i, f*i*sh; ai, t*i*ger; əː, b*i*rd.
(o) o, *o*x; au, c*ow*; ou, g*oa*t; u, p*oo*r; ɔi, r*oy*al. **(u)** ʌ, d*u*ck; u, b*u*ll; u:, g*oo*se; ə, b*a*cillus; ju:, c*u*be. x, lo*ch*; θ, *th*ink; δ, bo*th*er; z, *Z*en; ʒ, corsa*g*e;
dʒ, sava*g*e; ŋ, ora*ng*utang; j, *y*ak; ʃ, *fi*sh; tʃ, fe*tch*; 'l, rabb*le*; 'n, redd*en*. Complete pronunciation key appears inside front cover.

span (spæn) **1.** *n.* (*naut.*) a rope with both ends fastened forming a loop ‖ a pair of animals used together, esp. a matched pair of horses **2.** *v.t. pres. part.* **span·ning** *past* and *past part.* **spanned** (*naut.*, sometimes with 'in') to make fast with ropes [Du. and L.G.]

span 1. *v. pres. part.* **span·ning** *past* and *past part.* **spanned** *v.t.* to extend from side to side of (a wide object) or over (a distance or period of time), esp. so as to be a link, *his life spanned three reigns* ‖ to form an arch across, *to span a river with a bridge* ‖ to measure, using the extended hand as a unit ‖ to encircle with the hand or hands in, or as if in, measuring ‖ *v.i.* to move by making successive stretching movements like a caterpillar ‖ (of whales) to swim under water, rising for breath at regular intervals **2.** *n.* the distance between two extremities, e.g. the piers of an arch, the ends of a bridge, the tips of wings etc. ‖ the interval between two points in time, *the normal span of human life* ‖ the distance between tips of the little finger and thumb (=approx. 9 ins) when the hand is extended [O.E. *spann*]

span dogs a pair of clawed iron bars for hoisting logs in lumbering

span·drel (spændrəl) *n.* (*archit.*) the space between the outer curve of an arch and the rectangular molding that frames it ‖ the space between the exterior curves of adjoining arches and the horizontal molding etc. above [prob. rel. to A.F. *spaundre*, to expand]

span·gle (spæng'l) **1.** *n.* a tiny disk of glittering material, esp. one sewn onto a garment **2.** *v. pres. part.* **span·gling** *past* and *past part.* **spangled** *v.t.* to adorn with spangles ‖ *v.i.* to glitter with or as if with spangles [M.E. *spangel* dim. of O.E. *spang*, buckle]

Span·glish (spænglish) *n.* mixture of Spanish and English, common in Latin America and Southwest U.S. *Cf* FRINGLISH, HINGLISH, JAPLISH

Span·iard (spænjərd) *n.* a native or inhabitant of Spain

span·iel (spænjəl) *n.* a dog of any of several breeds with large drooping ears and a silky coat, used as sporting dogs for flushing or retrieving game, or kept as pets [fr. O.F. *espaigneul*, Spanish dog]

Span·ish (spænish) **1.** *adj.* of or relating to Spain, its people or language **2.** *n.* the Romance language of Spain and Spanish America, including Aragonese, Asturian, Andalusian and Castilian dialects. In all, Spanish is spoken by over 100,000,000 people **the Spanish** the people of Spain

Spanish America the countries in Central and South America and the Caribbean islands where Spanish is the chief language

Spanish-American *adj.* of Spain and America ‖ of Spanish America or its people **Spanish American** *n.* a native or inhabitant of Spanish America

Spanish-American War a war fought (1898) in Cuba, the Philippines and Puerto Rico by the U.S.A. and Cuban revolutionaries against Spain to free Cuba from Spanish control. Spanish fleets were rapidly defeated, and by the Treaty of Paris (1898), the Philippines, Guam and Puerto Rico were ceded by Spain to the U.S.A. Cuba was placed provisionally under U.S. military occupation

Spanish Armada *ARMADA

Spanish bayonet a yucca with spiky swordlike leaves, found in the southern U.S.A. and tropical America

Spanish Civil War *CIVIL WAR, SPANISH

Spanish fly *Lytta vesicatoria*, fam. *Meloidae*, a bright golden-green blister beetle ‖ cantharides

Spanish Guinea *EQUATORIAL GUINEA

Spanish Inquisition *INQUISITION

Spanish Main the name given in the 16th and 17th cc. to the Spanish possessions along the coast of South America from the Isthmus of Panama to the Orinoco. The name was also applied to the Caribbean Sea

Spanish moss *Tillandsia usneoides*, fam. *Usneaceae*, a mossy plant which grows in long green-gray festoons on many trees in the southern U.S.A. and West Indies ‖ *Ramalina reticulata*, fam. *Usneaceae*, a lichen that grows in large laced nets on various trees in coastal areas of the western U.S.A.

Spanish onion a large, juicy, mild-flavored onion of any of a great many varieties

Spanish Sahara *WESTERN SAHARA

Spanish Succession, War of the the war

(1701-14) fought between England, the Netherlands and most of the German states against France, Spain, Bavaria, Portugal and Savoy. It was precipitated by Louis XIV's proclamation (1700) of his grandson as Philip V of Spain, and by his invasion (1701) of the Spanish Netherlands. The victories of Marlborough and Eugene at Blenheim (1704), Ramillies, Turin (1706), Oudenarde, Lille (1708) and Malplaquet (1709) crushed French military supremacy. The war was ended by the Peace of Utrecht (1713) and subsidiary settlements at Rastatt and Baden (1714)

Spanish West Africa a former overseas territory of Spain divided (1958) into the overseas provinces of Ifni and Spanish Sahara (now Western Sahara)

spank (spæŋk) *v.i.* to move briskly when riding or driving [prob. back-formation fr. SPANKING]

spank 1. *v.t.* to smack or slap (someone) on the bottom **2.** *n.* a smack or slap on someone's bottom [imit.]

spank·er (spæŋkər) *n.* a fast horse, esp. one that trots briskly and stylishly ‖ (*naut.*) a fore-and-aft sail set on the after side of the mizzenmast

spank·ing (spæŋkiŋ) *adj.* of unusually fine quality or impressive for its size, freshness or vigor ‖ (of a breeze) strong ‖ (of pace) quick, brisk, lively [origin unknown]

spanking *n.* a series of slaps on the bottom with the open hand, to punish a child etc.

span·ner (spænər) *n.* (*Br.*) a wrench for tightening or loosening nuts etc. **to throw a spanner in the works** (*Br.*, *pop.*) to spoil or thwart esp. the plans of others deliberately [G. fr. *spannen*, to fix, fasten, draw tight]

span roof a common form of roof, with two sides sloping downward from a central ridge

spansule (*pharm.*) *TIMED CAPSULE

span·worm (spænwə:rm) *n.* a looper

spar (spɑr) **1.** *n.* a pole used e.g. as a mast, yard or boom of a ship ‖ one of the longitudinal members of an aircraft wing into which the struts are set **2.** *v.t. pres. part.* **spar·ring** *past* and *past part.* **sparred** to supply with spars [M.E. *sperre*, *sparre*]

spar *n.* any of various lustrous, crystalline minerals, cleaving easily into flakes or chips [rel. to O.E. *spæran*, gypsum]

spar 1. *v.i. pres. part.* **spar·ring** *past* and *past part.* **sparred** (*boxing*) to make the motions of attack and defense without landing a blow, so as to draw the opponent or to seek protection or time ‖ (*boxing*) to fight practice rounds ‖ (of fighting cocks) to strike with the feet or spurs ‖ to try to score verbally in argument **2.** *n.* the act or a session of sparring [origin obscure]

spar·a·ble (spærəb'l) *n.* a small headless nail used in shoemaking [altered fr. *sparrow bill*, with reference to its shape]

spar deck the upper deck above the main deck of a ship

spare (speər) **1.** *v.t. pres. part.* **spar·ing** *past* and *past part.* **spared** to conserve (one's strength or energy) ‖ to leave unhurt or undamaged, let go free, let live, *the prisoner was spared* ‖ to refrain from injuring or distressing or punishing, *she spared his feelings* ‖ to omit, exclude, *spare the details, nothing was spared for his comfort* ‖ to part temporarily with, or give away, without inconvenience, *can you spare 5 dollars?* ‖ to relieve (a person) of the necessity of doing something, *he was spared answering* ‖ to make available, *can you spare the time to help me?* ‖ to refrain from making use of, to use frugally or economically, *don't spare the wine* ‖ to show consideration for by relieving of work, *he spares neither himself nor his employees* ‖ to have left over as a margin or surplus, *it fitted tightly with no room to spare, we arrived with no time to spare* **2.** *adj.* held in reserve for future use, *spare cash* ‖ left over, more than needed, *some of the food was spare* ‖ thin, esp. without excess flesh, *of spare build* ‖ meager, frugal, thin, *spare diet* **3.** *n.* a surplus, superfluous object ‖ a duplicate kept in reserve ‖ (*bowling*) the act of knocking down all the pins with two consecutive rolls of the ball ‖ the score so made ‖ a spare part, esp. of a machine [O.E. *sparian*]

spare part a duplicate part of a machine for use as a replacement

spare-part surgery (*med.*) popular term for the branch of surgery dealing with transplants of organs or with prosthetic devices

spare·ribs (speərribz) *pl. n.* a cut of pork consisting of the ribs with little meat left on them because the fleshy part has been cut off for bacon

sparge (spɑrdʒ) *pres. part.* **sparg·ing** *past* and *past part.* **sparged** *v.t.* (*brewing*) to sprinkle (the mash) with water heated to about 180° F. after the sweetwort has been drained off ‖ to plaster, roughcast ‖ to sprinkle, splash (water etc.) ‖ *v.i.* to sprinkle water [prob. fr. O.F. *espargier*]

spar·ing (speəriŋ) *adj.* using or taking little, because of shortage, for economy, out of abstemiousness or out of meanness

Spark (spɑrk), **Muriel** (1918-), British writer. She wrote 'The Prime of Miss Jean Brodie' (1961), also a play (1964) and movie (1969). Other novels include 'Memento Mori' (1959), 'The Mandelbaum Gate' (1965), 'The Public Image' (1968), 'The Driver's Seat' (1970), 'The Takeover' (1976) and 'Territorial Rights' (1979). Her short stories are collected in 'The Stories of Muriel Spark' (1985)

spark (spɑrk) **1.** *n.* a particle e.g. thrown off from a burning log, which is so hot that it emits light as well as heat, or such a particle produced by the striking of flint or steel etc. on another hard substance ‖ (*elec.*) a discharge of static electricity which raises the air, gas or vapor to incandescence ‖ (*elec.*) the light produced by this discharge ‖ (*elec.*) such a discharge in the spark plug of an internal-combustion engine ‖ a small or momentary indication of something thought of as like this, esp. with respect to its latent possibilities, *a spark of humor* ‖ (*old-fash.*, usually with 'bright' or 'bright young') a quick-witted young fellow **2.** *v.i.* to emit sparks ‖ (of an internal-combustion engine) to produce sparks correctly ‖ *v.t.* (with 'off') to initiate (a process) as if by using a spark, *the trouble was sparked off by an apparently harmless phrase* [O.E. *spœrca*, *spearca*]

spark arrester a safety device to prevent sparks from escaping from a smokestack (e.g. of a steam locomotive) ‖ a device to prevent sparking where the continuity of a circuit is broken

spark chamber an instrument for defining the tracks of high-energy particles. It contains a gas and a series of metal plates that can be electrically charged to such a potential that a spark is almost caused to pass from one plate to an adjacent one. If a track of ions is formed by an ionizing particle the spark follows the track and can be photographed

spark coil (*elec.*) an induction coil used to induce an electromotive force large enough to spark across a gap between conductors

spark gap (*elec.*) the gap between the electrodes (e.g. of an induction coil) across which a spark passes

sparking plug (*Br.*) a spark plug

spar·kle (spɑrk'l) **1.** *v.i. pres. part.* **spar·kling** *past* and *past part.* **spar·kled** to give off flashes of reflected light ‖ to give off flashes of wit or gaiety ‖ (of eyes) to show animation, intelligence, wit, pleasure, mischief etc. by their brightness ‖ (of wine) to effervesce with bubbles of carbon dioxide ‖ (of a performer or a performance) to be brilliant **2.** *n.* a flash of reflected light ‖ brilliance of performance, conversation etc. ‖ animation **spár·kler** *n.* an indoor firework, consisting of a piece of wire (which can be held in the hand) having part of its length coated with a substance which produces a shower of tiny sparks when lit **spár·kling** *adj.* glittering ‖ lively, vivacious ‖ (of wine) effervescent

sparkling water soda water

spark plug (*Am.*=*Br.* sparking plug) a device fitted into the cylinder of an internalcombustion engine, consisting of two electrodes between which the battery passes a spark which ignites the mixture of gasoline vapor and air

sparring partner someone employed to fight with a boxer during training ‖ a partner with whom one can argue amicably to sharpen one's wits

spar·row (spærou) *n.* a member of *Passer*, fam. *Fringillidae* (*FINCH), esp. the house sparrow [O.E. *spearwa*]

Sparrow *n.* (*mil.*) an air-to-air, solid-propellant missile (AIM-7) with nonnuclear warhead, electronic-controlled homing, and a range of 25 km *Cf* SEA SPARROW

sparrow hawk *Accipiter nisus*, fam. *Accipitri-*

CONCISE PRONUNCIATION KEY: **(a)** æ, c*a*t; ɑ, c*a*r; ɔ f*aw*n; ei, sn*a*ke. **(e)** e, h*e*n; i:, sh*ee*p; iə, d*ee*r; ɛə, b*ea*r. **(i)** i, f*i*sh; ai, t*ig*er; ə:, b*i*rd. **(o)** o, *o*x; au, c*ow*; ou, g*oa*t; u, p*oo*r; ɔi, r*oy*al. **(u)** ʌ, d*u*ck; u, b*u*ll; u:, g*oo*se; ə, b*a*cillus; ju:, c*u*be. x, lo*ch*; θ, *th*ink; ð, bo*th*er; z, *Z*en; ʒ, cor*s*age; dʒ, sava*ge*; ŋ, ora*ng*utang; j, *y*ak; ʃ, *fi*sh; tʃ, fe*tch*; 'l, rabb*le*; 'n, red*den*. Complete pronunciation key appears inside front cover.

dae, a bird (11–15 ins) of N. Europe and Asia related to the buzzard, but with short rounded wings and long tail. It preys on small birds. In flight it alternates several rapid wingbeats with short glides ‖ *Falco sparverius*, fam. *Falconidae*, a small North American falcon closely related to the kestrel. It feeds on insects, small birds and game

sparse (spars) *adj.* occurring at widely separated places or times, without any regularity, *sparse vegetation* ‖ not thickly grown, *a sparse beard* **spar·si·ty** (spársiti:) *n.* [fr. L. *spargere* (*sparsus*), to scatter]

Spar·ta (spártə) (Lacedaemon) ancient city of the S. central Peloponnesus, Greece, adjacent to the modern town (pop. 8,000) of the same name (*Gk* Sparti): remains of temples (9th, 6th and 2nd cc. B.C.). After 600 B.C. Sparta was governed by a stern military constitution attributed to Lycurgus, and it became the predominant power in the Peloponnesus. Sparta played a leading part (480-479 B.C.) in repulsing the Persian invasions during the Persian Wars, and defeated the growing empire of Athens in the Peloponnesian War (431-404 B.C.). Sparta was defeated by Thebes (4th c. B.C.) and its power declined

Spar·ta·cus (spártəkəs) (d. 71 B.C.), Roman gladiator. He led an unsuccessful revolt of slaves against Rome (73-71 B.C.)

Spar·tan (spárt'n) 1. *adj.* of or relating to Sparta ‖ hardy, austere, *a Spartan character* ‖ rigorous, offering no comfort, *Spartan living conditions* 2. *n.* a native of Sparta ‖ someone of Spartan endurance **Spár·tan·ism** *n.* [fr. L. *Spartanus*]

Spartan *n.* (*mil.*) a nuclear surface-to-air guided missile formerly deployed as part of the Safeguard ballistic missile defense weapon system, designed to intercept strategic ballistic reentry vehicles in the exoatmosphere

spasm (spǽzəm) *n.* a sudden, strong, involuntary muscular contraction, esp. one that is painful or convulsive ‖ a short, violent effort, *he works in spasms* [O.F. *spasme* or fr. L. *spasmus* fr. Gk]

spas·mod·ic (spæzmódik) *adj.* of, affected or marked by, or relating to, spasms ‖ intermittent, not sustained, *he takes a spasmodic interest in the child* **spas·mód·i·cal·ly** *adv.* [fr. M.L. or Mod. L. *spasmodicus* fr. Gk]

spas·tic (spǽstik) 1. *adj.* of, relating to or characterized by a spasm or spasms tightly contracted as though by a prolonged spasm ‖ of a long-standing paralysis of some or many muscles, esp. caused by injury at birth ‖ suffering from such paralysis 2. *n.* someone who suffers from such paralysis **spás·ti·cal·ly** *adv.* [fr. L. *spasticus* fr. Gk]

spat (spæt) *n.* a short gaiter covering the upper part of the foot and the ankle, and fastened under the shoe [short for SPATTERDASH]

spat *alt. past and past part.* of SPIT

spat 1. *pl.* spat, spats *n.* the spawn or young of bivalve mollusks, esp. of oysters 2. *v.i. pres. part.* **spat·ting** *past and past part.* **spat·ted** to spawn [perh. rel. to SPIT]

spat 1. *n.* (*pop.*) a brief, trifling quarrel ‖ a little splash, *a spat of rain* 2. *v. pres. part.* **spat·ting** *past and past part.* **spat·ted** *v.t.* to strike with a sound like that made by a splash of rain ‖ *v.i.* (*pop.*) to engage in a trifling quarrel [prob. imit.]

spatch·cock (spǽtʃkɒk) 1. *n.* a fowl killed and dressed hastily and cooked at once split open on a grill 2. *v.t.* to cook (a fowl) in this way ‖ to fit (extra matter) into a text, esp. too hurriedly or inappropriately [etym. doubtful]

spate (speit) *n.* a river flood ‖ a rapid flow, a gush, *a spate of words* ‖ a large amount or number, *a spate of articles* **in spate** in flood [etym. doubtful]

spa·tha·ceous (spəθéiʃəs) *adj.* having a spathe ‖ like a spathe [Mod. L. *spathaceus*]

spathe (speið, speiθ) *n.* (*bot.*) a large enveloping leaf, green or petaloid, enveloping a spadix [fr. L. *spatha* or Gk *spathē*, broad blade]

spath·ic (spǽθik) *adj.* of or like spar (mineral) [G. *spath*, *spat*, spar]

spath·ose (spǽθous) *adj.* spathic

spa·tial, spa·cial (spéiʃəl) *adj.* of or relating to space **spá·tial·ly, spá·cial·ly** *adv.* [fr. L. *spatium*, space]

spatial summation the total effect of stimuli from different sources converging simultaneously at a sensory receptor

spat·ter (spǽtər) 1. *v.t.* to project (a fluid, e.g. water, mud etc.) in drops, *the wheels spattered*

the mud on all sides ‖ to project drops of a fluid onto, *the car spattered him with mud as it passed* ‖ *v.i.* to fall in drops, *the rain spattered down* 2. *n.* a short fall of rain etc. ‖ the act or sound of spattering ‖ a spot caused by this [prob. fr. Du. or L.G. *spatten*, to burst]

spat·ter·dash (spǽtərdæʃ) *n.* (*hist.*) a long legging or gaiter worn as a protection from mud ‖ roughcast

spatter glass a glass of mixed colors resembling an amalgam of the day's scraps in a factory, used decoratively *also* end-of-day glass

spat·u·la (spǽtʃulə) *n.* an instrument with a broad, flexible, usually dull-edged blade, used for mixing, scooping or spreading soft substances such as paint etc. ‖ (*med.*) an instrument used in the examination of certain parts of the body [L. dim. of *spatha*, broad blade fr. Gk]

spat·u·late (spǽtʃulit) *adj.* with a broad rounded end, *a spatulate table leg* ‖ markedly broad at the tip, *spatulate fingers* ‖ (*biol.*) spoonshaped [fr. Mod. L. *spatulatus*]

spav·in (spǽvin) *n.* a disease of the hock in horses, marked by a bony enlargement caused by strain ‖ this enlargement **spáv·ined** *adj.* [fr. O.F. *espavain*]

spawn (spɔn) 1. *n.* the mass of eggs deposited by fish, bivalve mollusks, batrachians and some other aquatic animals ‖ the mycelium of some fungi, esp. of cultivated mushrooms 2. *v.t.* to produce (spawn) ‖ (*pop.*) to produce (something, e.g. books) in great numbers ‖ *v.i.* to deposit spawn ‖ (*pop.*) to produce young in great numbers [fr. A.F. *espaundre*]

spay (spei) *v.t.* to remove the ovaries of (an animal) [fr. A.F. *espeier*]

speak (spi:k) *pres. part.* **speak·ing** *past* **spoke** (spouk), *archaic* **spake** (speik) *past part.* **spo·ken** (spóukən), *archaic* **spoke** *v.i.* to utter words with the ordinary voice, *he speaks clearly* ‖ to talk, *she was too upset to speak* ‖ to make a speech, *I am going to speak at the meeting* ‖ (with 'about') to speak, *we spoke about the need for economy* ‖ (with 'about') to rebuke or reprimand, *will you speak to her about her laziness?* ‖ (*rhet.*) to sound, *the organ spoke* ‖ (*rhet.*) to be expressive of opinions, ideas, emotions etc., *his face spoke of suffering* ‖ *v.t.* to express (an idea) by speaking, *she spoke the truth* ‖ to use (a language) in speaking, *he can speak German* ‖ to utter orally ‖ to express (opinions, ideas, emotions etc.) without using words, *her eyes and smile spoke a warm welcome* ‖ (*naut.*) to communicate with (a ship), *he spoke to S.S. Orontes* **so to speak** if the expression is admissible **to speak for** to recommend, *I hope you will speak for him* ‖ to reserve, *this table is spoken for* **to speak of** to mention, *he was speaking of you yesterday* ‖ (usually in negative constructions) of any significance, *he has no problems to speak of* **to speak one's mind** to be completely frank **to speak out** (or up) to speak openly and with conviction, *she always speaks out against injustice* **to speak up** to speak rather loudly, to raise the voice, *you must speak up if you are to be heard* **to speak well of** (or for) to be favorable evidence of, *it speaks well of his good nature that he took no offense* [O.E. *sprecan*, later *specan*]

speak·eas·y (spí:kʌzi:) *pl.* **speak·eas·ies** *n.* (*pop. hist.*) a place where alcoholic drink was sold illegally (esp. associated with Prohibition)

speak·er (spí:kər) *n.* someone who speaks ‖ someone who makes a speech, gives a talk etc. ‖ a loudspeaker **Speak·er** the presiding officer of the U.S. House of Representatives, the British House of Commons, and of certain other legislative bodies

speak·er·phone (spí:kərfoun) *n.* device containing microphone and speaker often attached to a telephone, permitting all within range to listen and speak over the system to which it is attached

speak·ing (spí:kiŋ) 1. *adj.* (of a likeness) close, immediately perceptible ‖ seeming to speak, eloquent, vivid, *a speaking glance* ‖ involving speaking or talking, esp. as opposed to singing, *his speaking voice is low-pitched, she took the only speaking part in the opera* 2. *n.* the act of one who speaks **generally speaking** usually, in most cases **on speaking terms** on terms friendly enough to permit the exchange of conversation **strictly speaking** in the strict sense of the words

spear (spiər) 1. *n.* a thrusting, hurling or stabbing weapon consisting of a long shaft with a

pointed blade ‖ a similar weapon for stabbing fish 2. *v.t.* to pierce with a spear, or as if with one [O.E. *spere*]

spear *n.* a thin pointed shoot of grass or wheat etc. ‖ a sapling [var. of SPIRE]

spear·head (spíərhed) 1. *n.* the pointed head or blade of a spear ‖ the foremost person, or body of troops, in an attack ‖ the most forceful element, *the spearhead of the opposition* 2. *v.t.* to be the vital thrusting force of, *he spearheaded the opposition* ‖ (*mil.*) to precede in (an attack or advance)

spear·ing (spíəriŋ) *n.* (*hockey*) an illegal jab

spear·man (spíərmən) *pl.* **spear·men** (spíərmən) *n.* a warrior armed with a spear

spear·mint (spíərmint) *n.* *Mentha spicata*, fam. *Labiatae*, common garden mint. It yields the essential oil, carvone

spec (spek) *n.* (*Br., pop.*) a commercial speculation **on spec** (*Br., pop.*) in the hope that things will turn out as one wishes but without certainty that they will [short for SPECULATION]

spe·cial (spéʃəl) 1. *adj.* particular in kind, *each spice imparts a special flavor* ‖ superior, *a special brand* ‖ serving a particular purpose, *a special tool* ‖ specialized, *it requires special knowledge* ‖ (of friends) intimate, close 2. *n.* a train run in addition to the scheduled trains, for a special occasion ‖ a special edition of a newspaper ‖ a special offer for some regularly stocked item, e.g. of food ‖ (*television*) a featured program that is not part of a series ‖ something specially singled out and featured [fr. O.F. *especial*]

special constable (*Br.*) a man employed as a policeman on special occasions

special court-martial a military court for offenses less serious than those warranting a general court-martial. It is composed of three or more officers, the judge advocate and defense counsel, and can impose only certain limited fines or punishment

special delivery (*Am.*=*Br.* express post) the system of delivering mail for a special fee without waiting for the next regular delivery ‖ (*Am.*=*Br.* express letter) a letter sent by this system

Special Drawing Rights international reserve units created by the International Monetary Fund in 1969 to supplement the limited supplies of gold and dollars, which had been the prime stable international monetary assets *abbr.* **SDRs** *also* paper gold

spe·cial·ism (spéʃəlizəm) *n.* a specializing in a particular branch of study or in a particular field of a profession ‖ such a branch or field

spe·cial·ist (spéʃəlist) *n.* someone who devotes himself to a particular branch of study, or (esp. a doctor) to a particular branch of his profession

spe·ci·al·i·ty (speʃi:ǽliti:) *pl.* **spe·ci·al·i·ties** *n.* (*Br.*) a specialty ‖ some particular distinguishing feature [fr. O.F. *specialite*]

spe·cial·i·za·tion (speʃəlizéiʃən) *n.* a specializing or being specialized

spe·cial·ize (spéʃəlaiz) *pres. part.* **spe·cial·iz·ing** *past and past part.* **spe·cial·ized** *v.i.* to become a specialist, to restrict one's studies, interests, activities etc. to a particular branch or field, *he specializes in modern languages* ‖ to become specialized ‖ (*biol.*) to adapt an organ for a particular purpose ‖ *v.t.* to restrict, to limit, to specialize one's interests [fr. F. *spécialiser*]

special licence (*Br.*) a license giving permission to marry without the usual preliminaries of public notice and residence, and in a place or at a time other than those legally appointed

spe·cial·ly (spéʃəli:) *adv.* in a special manner for a special purpose, with a special intention

Special Mission Fleet U.S. Air Force unit assigned to transport government officials and visiting dignitaries

special pleading (*law*) the introduction of fresh matter into a plea, as opposed to the denial of allegations made by the other side, esp. to avoid damaging admissions ‖ an argument used for persuasion rather than for truth's sake, one supporting an arguable point of view

special relativity *RELATIVITY

special revenue sharing *REVENUE SHARING

spe·cial·ty (spéʃəlti:) *pl.* **spe·cial·ties** *n.* something in which one has special skill or special interest ‖ something for which a district, restaurant, store etc. is particularly well known ‖ (*law*) a contract under seal

special verdict (*law*) a verdict which sets out the facts on the material issues of a case as found by the jury, but which leaves the court to reach the legal conclusions from the facts so found

spe·cie (spíːʃiː) n. money in coin **in specie** in coin ‖ in kind [L. abl. of *species*, shape, kind]

spe·cies (spíːʃiːz) pl. **spe·cies** n. (biol.) a group of individuals closely related in structure, capable of breeding within the group but not normally outside it ‖ (biol.) a systematic unit including geographical races and varieties and included within a structure of more comprehensive classification (e.g. a genus) ‖ (logic) a group having certain attributes in common and given a common name ‖ (Roman Catholicism) the outward form of the consecrated bread and wine ‖ (pop.) a sort, kind [L.=appearance, form, kind]

spe·ci·fi·a·ble (spésifaiəbˈl) adj. that can be specified

spe·cif·ic (spisífik) 1. adj. clearly distinguished, stated or understood, *he had no specific reason for coming* ‖ of a species, *specific name* ‖ characteristic of something, *specific properties* ‖ (phys.) being an arbitrary constant ‖ (of a disease) caused by a particular infection ‖ (of a remedy) having particular influence on a particular disease or particular part of the body 2. n. (med.) a remedy for a particular ailment **spe·cif·i·cal·ly** adv. [fr. M.L. *specificus*]

specific address (computer) permanent location of data in a computer storage *also* absolute address

spec·i·fi·ca·tion (spesifikéiʃən) n. the act of specifying ‖ a detailed item, something specified ‖ (often pl.) a list of materials supplied and work done by a builder, engineer etc. or required for a project to be carried out ‖ a detailed description of a person's invention submitted by an inventor when applying for a patent [fr. M.L. *specificatio* (*specificationis*)]

specific gravity (phys.) the numerical ratio between the weight, at any chosen place, of a given volume of a substance and the weight, at the same place, of an equal volume of water at 4°C., i.e. the ratio of the density of a substance to the density of water at 4°C. (or other standard)

specific heat (phys.) the amount of heat required to raise the temperature of 1 gram of a substance through 1°C.

specific inductive capacity (abbr. s.i.c.) *DIELECTRIC CONSTANT

spec·i·fic·i·ty (spesifísiti) n. the quality or state of being specific

spec·i·fy (spésifai) pres. part. **spec·i·fy·ing** past and past part. **spec·i·fied** v.t. to name or mention explicitly ‖ to include in a specification [O.F. *specifier*]

spec·i·men (spésəmən) n. a part or individual taken to typify the whole or the class, esp. for the purpose of scientific investigation, a sample ‖ (pop., used pejoratively) an individual of a specified sort, *he's a nasty specimen* [L. fr. *specere*, to look, look at]

specimen page a sample of a manuscript or other copy set up in type to establish the format, typeface, conventions etc. to be used when the complete work is printed

spec·i·os·i·ty (spiːʃiːósiti) n. the state or quality of being specious [fr. L.L. *speciositas*]

spe·cious (spíːʃəs) adj. apparently sound and reasonable, but fallacious [fr. L. *speciosus*, beautiful]

Speck (spek), Frank Gouldsmith (1881-1950), U.S. anthropologist and authority on Indian tribes of eastern North America, especially the Algonquian and Iroquois. His works include 'Ethnology of the Yuchi Indians' (1909) and 'Penobscot Man: the Life History of a Forest Tribe in Maine' (1940)

speck (spek) 1. n. a small bit, a particle, *a speck of dust* ‖ a small spot or stain ‖ a spot indicating decay, e.g. in blemished fruit ‖ something made to appear very small by distance, *he was a speck on the horizon* 2. v.t. to mark with specks [O.E. *specca*]

speck·le (spékˈl) 1. n. a small spot or mark, esp. a natural one on skin etc. 2. v.t. pres. part. **speck·ling** past and past part. **speck·led** to mark with speckles

specs (speks) pl. n. (pop.) a pair of spectacles

spec·ta·cle (spéktəkˈl) n. a display, usually on a large scale, which attracts attention ‖ someone who, by his appearance or behavior, is seen to be ludicrous ‖ (pl.) a pair of lenses, mounted in a light frame which rests on the bridge of the nose and hooks or rests behind the ears, designed to correct certain defects of vision or to protect the eyes **spéc·ta·cled** adj. wearing spec-

tacles ‖ (of animals) having a marking suggesting spectacles [O.F.]

spec·tac·u·lar (spektǽkjulər) 1. adj. impressive to see, *a spectacular dive* ‖ of a kind to attract attention or relating to a spectacle 2. n. a long, lavish television show or movie [fr. L. *spectaculum*, a spectacle]

spec·ta·tor (spékteitər, spektéitər) n. an onlooker, someone who watches (a show, display etc.) [L.]

spec·ter, esp. Br. **spec·tre** (spéktər) n. the spirit of someone dead made visible, esp. with a terrifying appearance ‖ a threatening vision of something to come, *the specter of famine* [F. or fr. L. *spectrum*]

spectinomycin *ACTINOSPECTOCIN

spec·to·graph (spéktəgræf) n. a device for recording voiceprints *Cf* VOICEPRINT

spec·tral (spéktrəl) adj. of or resembling a specter ‖ of or relating to a spectrum or spectra

spectral type (astron.) the classification to which a star belongs on the basis of its spectrum. This system of classification comprises 10 categories which depend on the color, the observed relative prominence of spectral lines and bands, and the inferences obtained from these concerning surface temperature

spectre *SPECTER

spec·tro·graph (spéktrəgræf, spéktrəgrɑf) n. a spectroscope equipped with a device for photographing or otherwise recording the spectrum produced (*SPECTROMETER) [SPECTRUM+GRAPH]

spec·trom·e·ter (spektrómitər) n. a spectroscope equipped with some form of detector that measures the intensity of light falling on it and that is used to produce a record of the emission or absorption of radiation as a function of wavelength (cf. MASS SPECTROMETER) ‖ an instrument used to measure refractive indices [SPECTRUM+METER]

spec·tro·pho·tom·e·ter (spektroufoutómitər) n. a spectroscope equipped with a photometer for measuring the intensities of radiation in different parts of the spectrum, usually compared with a standard beam of the same frequency [SPECTRUM+PHOTOMETER]

spec·tro·scope (spéktrəskoup) n. any of various instruments used to disperse a beam of electromagnetic radiation into narrow wave bands (*RESOLVING POWER). A spectroscope consists of a source of radiation (in emission spectroscopy it is the material being studied), a collimator, a prism or diffraction grating for separating the narrow wave bands, and an optical system for bringing these to a focus. The optics and mechanics of spectroscopes vary widely, depending upon the kind of radiation employed (*SPECTROMETER, *SPECTROGRAPH, *SPECTROPHOTOMETER) **spec·tro·scop·ic** (spektrəskópik), **spec·tro·scop·i·cal** adjs **spec·tro·scóp·i·cal·ly** adv. **spec·tros·co·pist** (spektróskəpist) n. **spec·tros·co·py** n. (phys., chem.) the study of the interaction of electromagnetic radiation with matter by means of the production and analysis of spectra. Modern models of matter picture the particles of which it is composed as being in a state of continuous vibrational, rotational and translational motion. Underlying most spectroscopic techniques is the fact that these atomic and subatomic particles are capable (since they bear charges) of absorbing and emitting energy in the form of electromagnetic radiation. Furthermore, depending upon the energy (and hence the frequency, *PLANCK RADIATION LAW) of this radiation, different portions of the atomic or molecular structure are involved (*INFRARED SPECTRUM, *ULTRAVIOLET SPECTRUM, *VISIBLE SPECTRUM, *MICROWAVE SPECTRUM). Quantum theory requires that e.g. a spinning molecule or circulating electron can possess energy only in certain definite, permitted amounts: it follows that in absorbing or emitting energy only those transitions that bring the system from one allowed state to another can occur, and therefore only certain wavelengths of electromagnetic radiation will be emitted or absorbed.

Generally there are two methods of studying these interactions: the production of emission spectra and of absorption spectra. Emission and absorption spectra are further subdivided according to the character of the radiation employed, different optical and mechanical systems being required for handling each band.

Spectroscopy finds increasingly wide use as an analytic tool in theoretical studies and is a potent means of identifying the components of

complex mixtures and of unknown substances. Thus the infrared absorption spectrum of a pure substance is accepted as a proof that the substance is present, and it provides an extremely useful clue to the structure of the substance (cf. NUCLEAR MAGNETIC RESONANCE, *MASS SPECTROSCOPY) [G. *spektroskop*]

spec·trum (spéktrəm) pl. **spec·tra** (spéktrə), **spec·trums** n. an arrangement of the components of a beam, wave band or sound separated and displayed in order according to some varying factor, e.g. energy, charge-to-mass ratio, wavelength ‖ the band of colors (red, orange, yellow, green, blue, indigo, violet) into which a beam of light is decomposed by a prism ‖ the image retained on the retina when the eyes are turned away after staring at a bright colored object (*MASS SPECTRUM, *MOLECULAR SPECTRUM, *SPECTROSCOPY) [F. or fr. L. *spectrum* fr. *specere*, to look]

spectrum of war (mil.) 1. the full range of a conflict 2. cold, limited, and general war

spec·u·lar (spékjulər) adj. of, pertaining to or having the qualities of a mirror ‖ (of a surface) producing an image, i.e. reflecting coherently [fr. L. *specularis*]

spec·u·late (spékjuleit) pres. part. **spec·u·lat·ing** past and past part. **spec·u·lat·ed** v.i. to consider possibilities and probabilities, *it is idle to speculate about what might have happened* ‖ to undertake commercial transactions involving serious risk for the sake of possible large winnings, esp. to buy and sell in the hope of profiting from fluctuating prices, sometimes in an antisocial way [fr. L. *speculari* (*speculatus*), to watch]

spec·u·la·tion (spekjuléiʃən) n. theorizing, conjecture, *her departure gave rise to speculation* ‖ commercial activity involving serious risk in the hope of large profits ‖ an enterprise involving such activity [fr. L.L. *speculatio* (*speculationis*)]

spec·u·la·tive (spékjuleitiv, spékjulətiv) adj. of or concerning speculation ‖ given to speculating [O.F. *speculatif*]

spec·u·la·tor (spékjuleitər) n. someone who speculates [L. fr. *speculari*, to watch]

spec·u·lum (spékjuləm) pl. **spec·u·la** (spékjulə) **spec·u·lums** n. an instrument for examining body cavities ‖ a mirror of polished metal, used in telescopes etc. ‖ a colored patch on the wing of some birds [L. =mirror]

speculum metal an alloy, principally of copper and tin, which takes a very high polish and is used for making reflecting surfaces

sped alt. past and past part. of SPEED

speech (spiːtʃ) n. the ability to speak, *he lost his speech* ‖ the act of speaking, *she broke into speech* ‖ that which is spoken, esp. an address to an audience ‖ a group of lines given to a character in a play ‖ manner of speaking, *country speech* ‖ the theory of oral communication, e.g. as studied in some colleges ‖ (mus.) the sounding of an instrument, esp. of an organ pipe [O.E. *sprǣc*, later *spǣc*]

speech community all the people who speak a mutually intelligible language or dialect

speech day (Br.) the day when parents attend a school to witness the presentation of prizes to the pupils, and to hear speeches

speech·i·fy (spíːtʃifai) pres. part. **speech·i·fy·ing** past and past part. **speech·i·fied** v.i. to make unnecessary speeches, holding forth in a tedious or pompous manner

speech·less (spíːtʃlis) adj. without the ability to speak ‖ temporarily unable to speak because of some emotional shock or injury ‖ silent

speech pathology *SPEECH THERAPY

speech processing technique for changing characteristics of voice to improve intelligibility for transmission

speech synthesis artificial simulation of speech, e.g., electronically, by computer — **speech synthesizer** n.

speech therapy the study, examination, and treatment of defects and diseases of the voice, and of spoken and written language *also* speech pathology —**speech pathologist** n. —**speech therapist** n.

Speed (spiːd), John (c. 1552-1629), English antiquarian and cartographer. His 'Theatre of the Empire of Great Britaine' (1611) is a valuable collection of detailed maps of the English counties

speed (spiːd) n. rate of motion ‖ (phys.) the magnitude of a velocity vector irrespective of its direction ‖ a transmission gear ‖ the rate at which something proceeds or is done ‖ (*photog.*) the rapidity with which a sensitized surface is acted on by light, usually expressed by a number ‖ (*photog.*) the time during which the shutter of a camera is open [O.E. *sped*]

speed *pres. part.* **speed·ing** *past and past part.* **sped** (sped), **speed·ed** *v.i.* to move, act, change, pass etc. at a high speed ‖ to drive a vehicle more rapidly than is safe or legal ‖ *v.t.* to cause to move at a high speed ‖ to set (an engine) to run at a certain speed **to speed up** to increase the speed of ‖ to go faster [O.E. *spēdan*]

speed (*slang*) a stimulant drug, esp. methamphetamine

speed·ball (spíːdbɔl) *n.* (*sports*) a field ballgame of 11 players on each team, combining elements of basketball and football, invented in 1921 by Elmer D. Mitchell

speed·boat (spíːdbout) *n.* a motorboat capable of traveling at high speed

speed freak (*slang*) a habitual speed user

speed·i·ly (spíːdili) *adv.* with speed, quickly

speed·i·ness (spíːdinis) *n.* the state or quality of being speedy

speed·om·e·ter (spidómitər) *n.* a device that shows the speed at which a vehicle is traveling

speed·read·ing (spiːdríːdiŋ) *n.* technique and practice of rapid reading accomplished by extending sight and comprehension span to include several words or passages at one glance —**speed-read** *v.* —**speed-reader** *n.*

speed shop (*automobile*) a hot-rodders' supply store

speed·up (spíːdʌp) *n.* the act of speeding up ‖ (esp. in factories) an increase in speed and output not accompanied by an increase in salary

speed·way (spíːdwei) *n.* a racetrack, esp. for motorcycles ‖ a road on which fast driving is permitted

speed·well (spíːdwel) *n.* a member of *Veronica*, fam. *Scrophulariaceae*, a genus of plants native to the temperate regions of both hemispheres, many species of which are cultivated as garden flowers

speed·y (spíːdi) *comp.* **speed·i·er** *superl.* **speed·i·est** *adj.* swift, having a good capacity for speed ‖ prompt, *it gives speedy relief*

speiss (spais) *n.* a compound of arsenic, nickel, copper etc. produced in smelting certain lead ores [fr. G. *speise*, amalgam]

Speke (spiːk), John Hanning (1827-64), British explorer. He accompanied Sir Richard Burton to Somaliland (1854) and to E. Africa (1857-9). After they had discovered Lake Tanganyika (1858), Speke went on to discover Lake Victoria (1858), claiming it as the source of the Nile. In 1860-3 he traced the White Nile from its source, through the Sudan, to its mouth

spe·le·ol·o·gist (spiːliːó/lədʒist) *n.* someone who specializes in speleology

spe·le·ol·o·gy, *Br.* also **spe·lae·ol·o·gy** (spiːliː-ólədʒi:) *n.* the scientific study of caves ‖ spelunking [fr. L. *spelaeum*, cave+Gk *logos*, discourse]

spell (spel) **1.** *v.t.* (*pop.*) to relieve (a person) by taking a turn at work ‖ *v.i.* to rest from work for a period **2.** *n.* a turn at work, a shift ‖ a short period, *a spell in the country* ‖ (*Austral.*) a period of relaxation, rest from work ‖ a bout or period (of illness, depression etc.), *he's going through a bad spell* [etym. doubtful]

spell *pres. part.* **spell·ing** *past and past part.* **spelled,** esp. *Br.* **spelt** (spelt) *v.t.* to name or write the letters of (a word) in order ‖ (of specified letters) to make up (a word), *c-a-t spells cat* ‖ to signify, *the drought spells disaster for thousands* ‖ *v.i.* to form words by letters, *her typing is good, but she spells badly* **to spell out** to make out the meaning of (words, a written passage etc.) with difficulty ‖ to read out letter by letter ‖ to explain in full detail [fr. O.F. *espeller, espeler*]

spell *n.* an incantation, words which properly chanted or uttered are supposed to have magical effect ‖ the power to charm or fascinate, *the spell of Ireland* ‖ a state of enchantment, *putting on the light broke the spell* [O.E. *spel, spell,* a story]

spell·bind (spélbaind) *pres. part.* **spell·bind·ing** *past and past part.* **spell·bound** (spélbaund) *v.t.* to put a spell upon ‖ to enchant, fascinate **spéll-bind·er** *n.* a speaker or entertainer who has strong power over an audience **spell·bound** *adj.* entranced ‖ bound as if by a spell, esp. rendered motionless or speechless

spell·ing (spéliŋ) *n.* the act of one who spells ‖ orthography

spelling bee a spelling competition

spelt (spelt) *n. Triticum spelta,* German wheat, a variety of wheat grown in Germany and Switzerland [O.E. fr. L.L. *spelta*]

spelt alt. *past* and *past part.* of SPELL

spel·ter (spéltər) *n.* commercial zinc, about 97% pure, lead being the main impurity [rel. to pewter]

spe·lunk·er (spilʌ́ŋkər) *n.* (*pop.*) a spelunking enthusiast

spe·lunk·ing (spilʌ́ŋkiŋ) *n.* (*Am.=Br.* potholing) the sport of exploring underground caves [fr. L. *spelunca*, cave]

Spen·cer (spénsər), Herbert (1820-1903), English philosopher. His chief work was 'Synthetic Philosophy' (1860-1900) in several volumes, each treating a different branch of knowledge. He was the founder of an evolutionist philosophy, and an exponent of laissez-faire social philosophy

Spencer, Sir Stanley (1891-1961), English painter. His works include landscapes, portraits and nudes, but he is best known for his paintings on religious themes, which are often on a very large scale and show much distortion and some private symbolism. His pictures often show Christ in a 20th-c. English setting

spen·cer (spénsər) *n.* a fore-and-aft sail that serves as a trysail [etym. doubtful]

spencer *n.* a woman's close-fitting jacket (waist-length) or bodice ‖ (*hist.*) a man's double-breasted tailless coat or jacket of the late 18th c. and early 19th c. [after the 2nd Earl *Spencer* (1758–1834)]

spend (spend) *pres. part.* **spend·ing** *past and past part.* **spent** (spent) *v.t.* to pay out (money) for purchases ‖ to exhaust, wear out (oneself or itself) ‖ to pass (time) ‖ *v.i.* to pay out money [O.E. *spendan* fr. L. *expendere*]

spend·thrift (spéndθrift) **1.** *n.* someone who spends too much and spends wastefully **2.** *adj.* spending too much, wasteful

Speng·ler (ʃpéŋlər), Oswald (1880-1936), German philosopher. In his chief work, 'The Decline of the West' (2 vols, 1918, 1922), he predicts the end of Western civilization by examining aspects of it (politics, mathematics, art etc.) and finding analogies with declining civilizations of the past

Spen·ser (spénsər), Edmund (c. 1552-99), English poet. His most celebrated poem is 'The Faerie Queene' (1589, 1596), an allegorical, chivalric, epic romance originally conceived in 12 books, of which only the first six and fragments of a seventh were written. Spenser's other works include 'The Shepheardes Calender' (1579), 'Epithalamion' (1595) and 'Prothalamion' (1596) and many sonnets. He enriched poetic diction by introducing into his own poetry foreign loanwords, archaisms, pseudo-archaisms and dialect words. He adapted contemporary sonnet form, writing three linked quatrains and a couplet, and in 'The Faerie Queene' perfected a new stanza form which became known as the Spenserian stanza. Many of his poems contain thinly disguised references to contemporary political figures: thus the faerie queene served by the knights in the poem is, at one level of the allegory, Queen Elizabeth. Spenser's poetry influenced Milton, Wordsworth and Keats, and cast a spell on those for whom poetry was the creation of another world, a dream world of romance and enchantment, largely insulated from the realities of human life

Spen·se·ri·an (spensíəriən) *adj.* of or characteristic of Edmund Spenser or his poetry

Spenserian stanza a nine-lined stanza perfected by Edmund Spenser, who used it in 'The Faerie Queene'. It was later employed by Byron, Shelley and Keats. It is suitable only for long narrative poems. Eight iambic pentameters are followed by an alexandrine and are rhymed a b a b b c b c c

spent *past part.* of SPEND ‖ *adj.* exhausted ‖ devoid of further energy ‖ (of shells, cartridges etc.) exploded ‖ having lost its elasticity, plasticity or other active principle

sperm (spɜrm) *n.* semen ‖ a spermatozoon [fr. O.F. *esperme* or L. *sperma* fr. Gk]

sper·ma·ce·ti (spɜːrməséti:) *n.* a glistening white fatty, waxy substance, chiefly cetyl palmitate, $C_{15}H_{31}COOC_{16}H_{33}$, found in sperm oil and used in the preparation of textile finishes, cosmetics, candles etc. [M.L. fr. L.L. *sperma*, sperm (for which it was mistaken)+*ceti*, gen. of *cetus*, whale]

sper·mar·y (spɜ́ːrməri) *pl.* **sper·mar·ies** *n.* an organ in which spermatozoa are produced, e.g. a testis ‖ an antheridium

sper·mat·ic (spəːrmǽtik) *adj.* (*zool.*) relating to spermatozoa ‖ relating to a testis [fr. M.L. *spermaticus*]

spermatic cord a cord on which a testis hangs and which contains vessels and nerves

spermatic fluid semen

sper·ma·tid (spɜ́ːrmətid) *n.* a nonmotile and otherwise immature male germ cell produced by the second meiotic division and leading to the mature spermatozoon by cytoplasmic differentiation (*SPERMATOGENESIS) [fr. Gk *sperma* (*spermatos*), seed]

sper·ma·ti·um (spəːrméiʃiːəm) *pl.* **sper·ma·ti·a** (spəːrméiʃiːə) *n.* a nonmotile male gamete in red algae ‖ a cell functioning as a male gamete in various lichens and fungi [Mod. L. fr. Gk *spermation* dim. of *sperma*, seed]

sper·mat·o·cyte (spəːrmǽtəsait) *n.* an immature male germ cell (the primary spermatocyte) just prior to the first maturation division, or each cell (secondary spermatocyte) formed during that process and transformed into a spermatid by the second maturation division (*MEIOSIS, *SPERMATOGENESIS) [fr. Gk *sperma* (*spermatos*), seed+*kutos*, receptacle]

sper·ma·to·gen·e·sis (spəːrmətədʒénisis) *n.* the entire process of formation and maturation of the male gamete from spermatogonium through primary and secondary spermatocytes and spermatid to spermatozoon **sper·ma·to·ge·nét·ic** *adj.* [Mod. L. fr. Gk *sperma* (*spermatos*), seed+*genesis*, origin]

sper·ma·to·go·ni·um (spəːrmətəgóuniːəm) *pl.* **sper·ma·to·go·ni·a** (spəːrmətəgóuniːə) *n.* a primordial male germ cell (*SPERMATOGENESIS) [Mod. L. fr. Gk *sperma* (*spermatos*), seed+*gonē*, offspring]

sperm·a·toph·o·ral (spəːrmətófərəl) *adj.* of or having to do with a spermatophore

sper·mat·o·phore (spəːrmǽtəfɔːr, spəːrmǽtə-fouːr) *n.* a capsule or mass containing spermatozoa ejaculated by male mollusks, annelids and other animals [fr. Gk *sperma* (*spermatos*), seed+*-phoros*, bearing]

sper·mat·o·phyte (spəːrmǽtəfait) *n.* a member of *Spermatophyta*, plants producing seeds **sper·ma·to·phyt·ic** (spəːrmətəfítik) *adj.* [fr. Gk *sperma* (*spermatos*), seed+*phuton*, plant]

spermatozoa *pl.* of SPERMATOZOON

sper·ma·to·zo·al (spəːrmətəzóuəl) *adj.* of or having to do with spermatozoa

sper·ma·to·zo·an (spəːrmətəzóuən) *adj.* spermatozoal

sper·ma·to·zo·ic (spəːrmətəzóuik) *adj.* spermatozoal

sper·ma·to·zo·id (spəːrmətəzóuid) *n.* the motile male gamete or sexual cell of a plant freed in the water from the antheridium in which it has developed

sper·ma·to·zo·on (spəːrmətəzóuɒn) *pl.* **sper·ma·to·zo·a** (spəːrmətəzóuə) *n.* a motile male reproductive haploid cell (*SPERMATOGENESIS, *FERTILIZATION) [Mod. L. fr. Gk *sperma* (*spermatos*), seed+*zōon*, animal]

sper·mo·go·ni·um (spəːrməgóuniːəm) *pl.* **sper·mo·go·ni·a** (spəːrməgóuniːə) *n.* the receptacle or capsule of spermatia in certain lichens and fungi [Mod. L. fr. Gk *sperma*, seed+*gonē*, offspring]

sperm oil a liquid wax, not a true oil, light yellow in color and contained in the large head cavities of the sperm whale. When the spermaceti in it has been extracted, sperm oil is used as a lubricant and, in conjunction with other marine oils, as a leather dressing (cf. WHALE OIL)

sperm whale *Physeter catodon* or *P. macrocephalus,* fam. *Physeteridae,* a genus of toothed whales, measuring up to 60 ft in length, having a closed head cavity containing spermaceti and oil. A large sperm whale may yield up to 100 barrels of sperm oil and 24 barrels of spermaceti [short for *spermaceti whale*]

Sper·ry (spéri:), Elmer Ambrose (1860-1930), American inventor of the gyroscopic compass

sper·ry·lite (spérəlait) *n.* platinum arsenide, $PtAs_2$, the only natural compound of platinum. It occurs in white crystals and granular form [after Francis L. *Sperry*, 19th-c. Canadian chemist, its discoverer]

spew (spjuː) **1.** *v.t.* (*rhet.*) to vomit ‖ (*rhet.*, usually with 'out') to pour out (curses etc.) with abhorrence or disgust ‖ *v.i.* to vomit **2.** *n.* vomit [O.E. *spīwan, spēowan*]

Spey (spei) a river of N.E. Scotland, flowing northeast 110 miles from Loch Spey, in the

CONCISE PRONUNCIATION KEY: **(a)** æ, c*a*t; ɑ, c*a*r; ɔ f*aw*n; ei, sn*a*ke. **(e)** e, h*e*n; iː, sh*ee*p; iə, d*ee*r; ɛə, b*ea*r. **(i)** i, f*i*sh; ai, t*i*ger; əː, b*i*rd. **(o)** o, *o*x; au, c*ow*; ou, g*oa*t; u, p*oo*r; ɔi, r*oy*al. **(u)** ʌ, d*u*ck; u, b*u*ll; uː, g*oo*se; ə, b*a*cillus; juː, c*u*be. x, lo*ch*; θ, *th*ink; ð, bo*th*er; z, *Z*en; ʒ, cor*s*age; dʒ, sa*v*age; ŋ, ora*ng*utan*g*; j, *y*ak; ʃ, *f*ish; tʃ, fe*tch*; 'l, rabb*le*; 'n, redd*en*. Complete pronunciation key appears inside front cover.

Inverness highlands, to the North Sea: salmon fishing

Spey·er, Diet of (ʃpáiər) the Imperial Diet (1529) at which toleration was refused to Lutherans in Catholic states and to Zwinglians and Anabaptists

sphag·num (sfǽgnəm) pl. **sphag·na** (sfǽgnə), **sphag·nums** n. a member of Sphagnum, a genus of soft mosses, the only representative of the order Sphagnaceae. The plants are colored by chlorophyll and brown, yellow or red pigments, but are pale on account of air-containing tissues. Their remains, with other plant debris, form peat [Mod. L. fr. Gk sphagnos, a kind of moss]

sphal·er·ite (sfǽlərait) n. zinc blende [fr. Gk sphaleros, deceptive]

sphene (sfi:n) n. titanite [F. sphène fr. Gk]

sphe·no·don (sfí:nədon) n. the tuatara [fr. Gk sphēn, a wedge+odous (odontos), tooth]

sphe·noid (sfí:nɔid) 1. adj. (anat.) of the compound bone at the base of the cranium ‖ sphenoidal 2. n. a wedge-shaped crystal with four equal isosceles triangles as faces ‖ the sphenoid bone **sphe·nói·dal** adj. wedge-shaped [fr. Mod. L. sphenoides fr. Gk fr. sphēn, a wedge+eidēs, form]

sphe·nop·sid (sfi:nópsid) n. a member of Sphenopsida, a subphylum of chlorophyll-bearing, vascular plants (the horsetails) and many much larger fossil forms that flourished in the Carboniferous [fr. Mod. L. Sphenopsida fr. Gk sphēn, a wedge+opsis, vision, appearance]

sphere (sfiər) n. (geom.) the solid figure generated when a circle rotates about a diameter, every point on its surface being thus equidistant from the center of this circle (called the center of the sphere). The surface area of a sphere = 4π (radius)$_2$, the volume of a sphere = $4/3\pi$ (radius)$_3$ ‖ (loosely) anything of approximately this shape ‖ a limited domain within which something is effective, sphere of influence ‖ a range of knowledge, it lies outside my sphere ‖ a group of people in the social hierarchy (with respect to belonging or not belonging to it), he moves in more exalted spheres than they do ‖ (hist.) any of the hollow concentric transparent globes once conceived as moving around the earth and carrying in them the sun, planets and fixed stars and producing music by their vibrations ‖ (hist.) the path, within one of these concentric globes, followed by the sun, planets or fixed stars [O.F. espere fr. L.L. fr. Gk]

spher·ic (sférik) adj. spherical **sphér·i·cal** adj. shaped like a sphere ‖ relating to a sphere [fr. L.L. sphericus, sphaericus fr. Gk]

spherical aberration the distortion of an image produced by a spherical lens or mirror because of the different focal points for rays incident upon the central region and those incident upon the outer margins

spherical angle (math.) the angle between two intersecting arcs of great circles on a sphere measured between the tangents at the point of intersection

spherical polygon a figure formed by arcs of great circles on a sphere

spherical triangle the three-sided enclosed figure formed on the surface of a sphere which is bounded by the arcs of three great circles

sphe·ric·i·ty (sfirísiti:) n. the quality or state of being spherical [fr. Mod. L.]

spher·ics (sfériks) n. spherical geometry and spherical trigonometry

sphe·roid (sfíərɔid) n. a figure resembling a sphere, esp. an ellipsoid **sphe·roi·dal** (sfiərɔíd'l) adj. **sphe·roi·dic·i·ty** (sfiərɔidísiti:) n. [fr. L. sphaeroides fr. Gk]

sphe·rom·e·ter (sfirómitər) n. an instrument used to measure the curvature of a spherical or cylindrical surface [fr. F. sphéromètre]

spher·o·plasts (sfíərəplæst) n. (cytol.) mitochondria or other cytoplasmic bodies, threadlike bodies in the protoplasm of cells, involved in the enzyme processes also chondriosomes

spher·u·lar (sférjulər) adj. having the form of a spherule

spher·ule (sférju:l) n. a small sphere [fr. L. sphœrula]

spher·u·lite (sférjulait) n. a spherical crystalline concretion, esp. of quartz and feldspar, found in some rocks **spher·u·lit·ic** (sférjulítik) adj. [L.]

sphinc·ter (sfíŋktər) n. (anat.) a ring-shaped muscle which, by its contraction, is able to close or narrow an orifice **sphínc·ter·al** adj. [L. fr. Gk sphinktēr, band]

sphing·o·lip·i·do·sis (sfiŋoulipədóusis) n. (med.)

a metabolic disorder in which certain glycolipids and phospholipids accumulate in tissue, e.g, Tay-Sachs disease, Gaucher's disease, Nieman-Pick disease

sphinx (sfíŋks) pl. **sphinx·es, sphin·ges** (sfíndʒi:z) n. a compound creature having (in its most common form) a lion's body and a human head, either male or female. It originated in Egypt and the concept of the sphinx spread throughout the ancient world. Representations of the sphinx are found in Egyptian, Assyrian, Greek, Mayan and Roman art and sculpture. They are usually recumbent, may or may not be winged, and sometimes have a ram's or hawk's head. The heads of Egyptian sphinxes are usually royal portraits, and the lion bodies represent the pharaoh's strength. In Greek mythology, the Sphinx of Thebes had the head of a woman, the feet and tail of a lion and the wings of a bird. It devoured everyone who could not answer the riddle it asked, but when this was finally solved by Oedipus, the Sphinx killed itself ‖ an inscrutable person ‖ a member of Sphinx, a genus of hawkmoths **the Sphinx** the great sphinx of Giza, 187 ft long, the head and body of which are carved of living rock [L. fr. Gk prob. fr. sphingein, to bind together]

sphra·gis·tic (sfrədʒístik) adj. of or relating to engraved seals **sphra·gis·tics** n. the study of engraved seals or signet rings [fr. Gk sphragistikos]

sphyg·mo·graph (sfígməgræf, sfígməgrɑf) n. an instrument for recording the arterial pulse rate on a graph [fr. Gk sphugmos, the pulse+GRAPH]

sphyg·mo·ma·nom·e·ter (sfigmoumənómitər) n. an instrument for measuring blood pressure, esp. of the arteries [fr. Gk sphugmos, the pulse+MANOMETER]

sphyg·mom·e·ter (sfigmómitər) n. an instrument for measuring the strength of the pulse [fr. Gk sphugmos, the pulse+METER]

spi·cate (spáikeit) adj. (bot.) having spikes ‖ (biol., e.g. of an inflorescence) arranged in the form of a spike or spikes [fr. L. spicatus, furnished with spikes]

spic·ca·to (spikátou) adj. (mus.) with springy bowing (the bow rebounding off the strings in the achieving of a series of rapid detached notes) [Ital.]

spice (spais) 1. n. any of many vegetable substances, mostly plant parts from which the essential oils have not been extracted, used to impart their strong and aromatic flavors to food, and formerly to preserve foodstuffs from decay (e.g. cinnamon, cloves, nutmeg etc.) ‖ these substances collectively ‖ something which stimulates agreeably, variety is the spice of life 2. v.t. pres. part. **spic·ing** past and past part. **spiced** to flavor by adding spice ‖ to make more interesting, a description spiced with humor [fr. O.F. espicer]

spice·bush (spáisbuʃ) n. Lindera bezoin, fam. Lauraceae, an aromatic shrub having yellow flowers and scarlet or yellow berries

Spice Islands *MOLUCCAS

spic·i·ly (spáisili:) adv. in a spicy manner

spic·i·ness (spáisi:nis) n. the quality of being spicy

spick-and-span (spíkənspæn) adj. cleaned up or turned out to look extremely smart ‖ all fresh and new [fr. older spick and span new extension of spannew fr. O.N. spănn, chip+n̄yr, new]

spic·u·late (spíkjulit) adj. (biol.) covered with, having or consisting of spicules ‖ needlelike [fr. L. spiculatus]

spic·ule (spíkju:l) n. (zool.) a minute needlelike body, siliceous or calcareous, found in some invertebrates, e.g. in sponges and radiolarians ‖ (bot.) a small spike ‖ any small needlelike formation, esp. of a hard material, e.g. ice [F.]

spic·y (spáisi:) comp. **spic·i·er** superl. **spic·i·est** adj. having the flavor of spices ‖ stimulating the imagination, spicy adventures ‖ stimulating erotically, spicy stories

spi·der (spáidər) n. an animal of the order Araneida, subclass Arachnida, having eight legs, a large unsegmented abdomen, jaws often equipped with poison glands for paralyzing insect prey, usually four pairs of compound eyes, and spinnerets from which a very fine thread is drawn and woven into a web. The web is used as a nest or, rendered sticky by a secretion, as a trap for flying insects, though some species catch their prey by running and capturing. There are at least 20,000 species ‖ any of several contrivances with long, thin structural parts ‖ a frying pan, originally one supported on

three legs ‖ a light phaeton with big, thin wheels [O.E. spīthra]

spider hole (mil.) a disguised foxhole, esp. one used by a sniper

spider monkey one of many South American monkeys, esp. of genus Ateles, with long, slender, flexible limbs, prehensile tail and slender bodies (*MONKEY)

spider web a web made by a spider

spi·der·wort (spáidərwə.rt, spáidərwɔrt) n. a member of Tradescantia, fam. Commelinaceae, cultivated plants with usually blue or violet flowers. The six slender stamens are covered with hairs

spi·der·y (spáidəri:) adj. resembling or suggesting the appearance of a spider, esp. its long thin legs, spidery handwriting ‖ like a cobweb in formation, spidery lace ‖ infested with spiders

spie·gel·ei·sen (ʃpí:gəlaizən) n. pig iron containing manganese used in making steel by the Bessemer process [G. fr. spiegel, mirror+eisen, iron]

spiel (spi:l) 1. n. (pop.) a speech or story, usually delivered volubly and with intent to persuade 2. v.t. (pop., with 'off') to recite or utter volubly, usually with intent to persuade ‖ (pop., with 'off') to recite at length (something memorized) ‖ v.i. to talk volubly and often extravagantly [G. spielen, to play]

Spiel·berg (spí:lbə:rg), Steven (1947-   ), U.S. film director, known for his adventure and fantasy films. He directed 'Jaws' (1975), 'Close Encounters of the Third Kind' (1977), 'Raiders of the Lost Ark' (1981), 'E.T.: The Extraterrestrial' (1982), 'Indiana Jones and the Temple of Doom' (1984) and 'The Color Purple' (1985)

spig·ot (spígət) n. a device which controls the flow of a fluid from or through a pipe or from a container ‖ a peg or plug for the vent of a barrel or cask ‖ the end of one pipe fitting into the socket of another [prob. fr. Prov. espigot]

spike (spaik) 1. n. a thin, sharp-pointed piece of metal, rock or other hard material ‖ a sharply pointed rod or shaft set with the point upward, e.g. on a wall, as an obstacle ‖ a pointed nail set (in small quantity) into the soles of climbing boots or running shoes to prevent slipping ‖ a large nail used to fasten a rail to a railroad tie ‖ a single antler of a young deer ‖ an ear of grain, e.g. wheat ‖ (Br.) a spindle (filing device) ‖ (bot.) an inflorescence with sessile flowers along the stem, the youngest towards the tip 2. v. pres. part. **spik·ing** past and past part. **spiked** v.t. to furnish, fasten or pierce with a spike or with spikes ‖ to render (a gun) useless to an enemy who captures it ‖ to thwart, to spike someone's plans ‖ to put an end to (e.g. a rumor) ‖ (baseball etc.) to injure (a player) with the spikes of one's shoes ‖ (pop.) to add liquor to (a nonalcoholic drink) ‖ v.i. to form a spike, or project like one [fr. L. spica, ear of grain]

spike·let (spáiklit) n. (bot.) a small spike, bearing few flowers, esp. in certain sedges and grasses

spike·nard (spáiknɑrd) n. Nardostachys jatamansi, fam. Valerianaceae, an East Indian plant with fragrant rhizomes ‖ (hist.) a costly ointment prepared from these rhizomes ‖ Aralia racemosa, an American plant like sarsaparilla [fr. M.L. or L.L. spica, ear of grain+nardi, gen. of nardus, aromatic root]

spik·y (spáiki:) comp. **spik·i·er** superl. **spik·i·est** adj. having a spike or spikes ‖ having the shape of a spike ‖ (Br.) being touchy and aggressive

spile (spail) 1. n. a small peg or plug to stop the vent in a barrel or cask ‖ a timber pile driven into the earth as a support ‖ a spout inserted in a sugar maple tree to drain off sap 2. v.t. pres. part. **spil·ing** past and past part. **spiled** to make a vent in (a cask) ‖ to empty through a spile ‖ to furnish (a barrel etc.) with a spile or spiles ‖ to plug (a hole) with a spile [M.Du.=a splinter]

spill (spil) n. a thin wooden strip, or folded strip of paper, for lighting a pipe etc. ‖ a small peg or plug for stopping up holes, a spile ‖ a splinter [var. of SPILE]

spill 1. v. pres. part. **spill·ing** past and past part. **spilled, spilt** (spilt) v.t. to lose or waste (a fluid etc.) by causing or permitting it to fall out of or escape from its container ‖ (naut.) to empty (a sail) of wind ‖ (rhet.) to shed (blood) in violence ‖ (pop.) to divulge (information), he spilled the whole story ‖ (pop.) to cause (someone) to fall from a horse, vehicle etc. ‖ v.i. (of a liquid etc.) to fall out of or escape from a container and so be lost or wasted ‖ (of waves, with 'onto') to break gently ‖ to descend as though overflowing ‖ (with 'out') to overflow **to spill the beans** (*pop.*) to divulge information **2.** *n.* a fall from a saddle, vehicle, wall etc. [O.E. *spillan*, to destroy]

spill·back (spílbæk) *n.* traffic condition in which motorists become trapped in an intersection when the light turns red, preventing drivers on cross streets from passing through

spill·li·kin (spílikin) *n.* a jackstraw **spil·li·kins** *n.* the game of jackstraws [dim. of SPILL *n.*, a splinter]

spill·way (spílwei) *n.* a passage for the overflow of water from a reservoir etc. ‖ the part of a dam over which water flows

spi·lo·site (spáiləsait) *n.* greenish, schistose rock spotted with chlorite [G. *spilosit* fr. Gk *spilos*, spot]

spilt alt. *past* and *past part.* of SPILL

spin (spin) **1.** *v. pres. part.* **spin·ning** *past* and *past part.* **spun** (spʌn) *v.i.* to turn rapidly about an internal axis ‖ (*aeron.*) to dive in a spiral ‖ to engage in the process of drawing out and twisting cotton, silk etc. into a long, continuous thread ‖ (of spiders and silkworms) to secrete a thread or threads ‖ to move very fast ‖ (of ideas, thoughts etc.) to become wildly confused ‖ (*fishing*) to fish using a spinner ‖ *v.t.* to cause to spin, *to spin a top* ‖ to draw out and twist (cotton, silk etc.) into a long, continuous thread ‖ to secrete threads to make (a cocoon, web etc.) ‖ to give a round shape to, by using a lathe etc. ‖ to tell (a story) at great length ‖ (*fishing*) to fish for, using a spinner **to spin a yarn** to tell a rather long involved story, esp. in order to deceive **to spin out** to cause to last or seem to last for a long time, *to spin out a vacation* **2.** *n.* the act of spinning ‖ a rapid rotating movement, *to put spin on a ball*, or such a motion downwards, *the aircraft went into a spin* ‖ (*old-fash.*) a short, rapid journey for pleasure, *to go for a spin on a motorcycle* ‖ a state of wild mental confusion ‖ (*phys.*) the rotation of an electron or other fundamental particle about its own axis, producing a magnetic moment and associated with an angular momentum. Electron spin is mainly responsible for the magnetic properties of matter. In quantum theory an electron has an angular momentum whose space orientation is quantized taking on two values, designated by the spin quantum number (*abbr.* s, where s=½±, the sign indicating the sense of the motion) (*BOHR MAGNETON) [O.E. *spinnan*]

spi·na bi·fi·da (spáinə báifədə) *n.* (*med.*) an inherited defect in the closure of the vertebral canal allowing the meninges to protrude

spin·ach (spínitʃ) *n. Spinacia oleracea*, fam. Chenopodiaceae, a herbaceous annual native to S.W. Asia, introduced to Europe after Roman times. Its dark green, crisp leaves are cooked as a vegetable [fr. O.F. *espinage, espinache, spinache*]

spinach beet *Beta vulgaris cicla*, a variety of beet, the leaves of which are eaten as a substitute for spinach

spi·nal (spáin'l) *adj.* in the region of, pertaining to, or like the spinal column, spinal cord or spinal canal [fr. L.L. *spinalis*]

spinal canal the canal, formed by the neural arches of the vertebrae, which encloses and protects the spinal cord

spinal column the series of vertebrae extending from the base of the skull through the median dorsal part of the body to the tail. It serves to protect the spinal cord and acts as a principal supporting structure in virtually all vertebrates. Flexible cartilaginous intervertebral disks allow the vertebrae to move with some degree of freedom with respect to one another. The vertebrae are joined by ligaments allowing for considerable flexibility (*NOTOCHORD)

spinal cord the dorsal cord of neural tissue continuous with the medulla oblongata that lies within the spinal canal in vertebrates. In man there are 31 pairs of nerves along the spinal cord, which acts as a pathway for sensory and motor impulses to and from the brain and as a system of reflex centers often independent of the brain

spin·ar (spínɑr) *n.* (*astron.*) a heavenly body spinning very rapidly

spin·dle (spínd'l) **1.** *n.* a thin cylindrical rod which serves as an axis of rotation or itself rotates ‖ the thin rod in a spinning wheel serving to twist and wind the thread ‖ the rod bearing a bobbin in a spinning machine ‖ a measure of length for yarn (15,120 yds of cot-

ton, 14,400 yds of linen) ‖ (*naut.*) a long vertical iron rod set up on a rock as a navigational aid ‖ (*biol.*) the thin rod-shaped portion of the nucleus formed during the prophase of meiosis and mitosis along which the chromosomes are distributed to daughter nuclei ‖ a shaft in a lathe, capstan etc. ‖ the fixed spike on a phonograph turntable over which the record fits ‖ (*Am.*=*Br.* spike) a filing device consisting of a mounted nail or hook on which receipts, bills etc. are impaled **2.** *v.i. pres. part.* **spin·dling** *past* and *past part.* **spin·dled** (esp. of a plant which develops a stem rather than a flower or fruit) to grow long and thin ‖ *v.t.* to impale on a spindle ‖ to give the form of a spindle to [O.E. *spinel*]

spin·dle-leg·ged (spínd'llegid, spínd'llegd) *adj.* having thin or scrawny legs

spin·dle-legs (spínd'llegz) *n.* someone who has long scrawny legs ‖ (*pl.*) long thin legs

spin·dle-shanks (spínd'lʃæŋks) *n.* (of a person or his legs) spindlelegs

spindle tree *Euonymus europaeus*, fam. Celastraceae, a small tree or shrub whose hard wood is used for skewers etc. The inconspicuous green flowers produce red four-valved capsules, enclosing seeds with orange arils

spin·dling (spíndliŋ) *adj.* spindly

spin·dly (spíndli:) *comp.* **spin·dli·er** *superl.* **spin·dli·est** *adj.* very long and thin, esp. (in a person) suggesting weakness or scrawniness from overgrowth

spin·drift (spíndrift) *n.* fine spray blown from the surface of water [alt. fr. *spoondrift*, etym. doubtful]

spine (spain) *n.* the spinal column ‖ (*bot.*) a sharp-pointed outgrowth, e.g. from the stem or leaf of a thistle ‖ (*zool.*) a similar protective outgrowth, e.g. one of the quills of a porcupine ‖ (*anat.*) any of the thin, pointed processes of various bones ‖ a ridge of land, rock etc. resembling a backbone ‖ (*printing*) the back of a bound book, on which title and author are usually given **spined** *adj.* having a spine or spines [fr. O.F. *espine* or L. *spina*, thorn]

spi·nel (spinél) *n.* any one of a group of minerals of composition $MO·M^1_2O_3$ where M is a divalent metal, M^1 a trivalent metal [F. *spinelle*]

spine·less (spáinlis) *adj.* invertebrate ‖ having no spines or thorns ‖ without determination and strength of character

spi·nes·cent (spainésənt) *adj.* (*bot.*) tending to be spinous [fr. L. *spinescens (spinescentis)* fr. *spinescere*, to grow thorny]

spin·et (spínit) *n.* a small stringed musical instrument resembling a harpsichord ‖ a small electronic organ ‖ an upright piano of reduced dimensions, esp. for use in limited space [Ital. *spinetta* prob. after Giovanni *Spinetti*, the 16th-c. inventor]

spin·na·ker (spínəkər) *n.* (*naut.*) a large triangular sail, carried by a yacht on a long, light pole, on the side opposite the mainsail. It is used when running before the wind [etym. doubtful]

spin·ner (spínər) *n.* a person or machine which spins ‖ a manufacturer engaged in spinning ‖ (*fishing*) a bright metal vane which spins as the line is drawn through the water, used as a lure ‖ (*fishing*) a kind of fly used in trout fishing ‖ (*games*) a ball made to spin so that it rebounds obliquely when it hits the ground ‖ (*football*) a feint, in which the ball carrier spins around when about to play the ball ‖ a nightjar ‖ (*surfing*) a stunt of making a complete turn while the board continues its forward movement

spin·ner·et (spinərét) *n.* a process or organ found on the abdomen of the larvae of certain silk-producing insects and on the abdomen of a spider. From this organ are exuded the secretions of the silk glands, which usually fuse to form a single thread used e.g. for making a web or cocoon [dim. of SPINNER]

spin·ney (spíni:) *n.* (*Br.*) a small group of trees with undergrowth [fr. O.F. *espinei*, a place full of thorns]

spin·ning (spíniŋ) *n.* the process of making thread or yarn from natural or man-made fibers ‖ (in spiders and certain silk-producing insect larvae) the process of exuding a secretion through the spinnerets which hardens into a thread

spinning jenny a power-driven machine, fitted with many spindles, invented (1764) by James Hargreaves

spinning wheel a machine for domestic spin-

ning fitted with a single spindle driven by a wheel worked by the hand or foot

spin-off (spínɔf, spínɒf) *n.* things derived as useful by-products from some larger and more or less unrelated whole, activity etc., *spin-off from space research includes many medical inventions* ‖ an example of such derivations ‖ divestment of a subsidiary company by a parent corporation

Spi·no·la (spi:nɔ́lɑ), Ambrosio, marquis of (1569-1630), Italian general. He distinguished himself in the service of Spain in capturing Ostend (1604) and in the Thirty Years' War

spi·nose (spáinous) *adj.* spinous (covered with spines)

spi·nous (spáinəs) *adj.* covered with or full of spines or thorns ‖ having the form of a spine or thorn [fr. L. *spinosus*]

spin-out (spínaut) *n.* **1.** uncontrolled movement of an automobile, esp. at a turn, causing it to run off the highway **2.** a spin in a complete circle

Spi·no·za (spinóuzə), Baruch (1632-77), Dutch philosopher. In his 'Tractatus theologico-politicus' (1670) he develops a religious rationalism. In his 'Ethics' (1677), written in a strictly mathematical form, he expounds a theory of human salvation as knowledge of God, and also analyzes the human soul. His system is a pantheistic doctrine, according to which God is a substance constituted by an infinity of attributes, of which we know only two: thought and extension. The world is the sum of modes of these two attributes. Man is a collection of modes of thought and extension. The distinction between God and the created world can be reduced to a point of view ('Deus sive Natura'). He was a firm believer in political democracy as a reflection of reason

spin resonance *MAGNETIC RESONANCE

spin-scan (spínskæn) *n.* an infrared radiometer that provides a picture of cloud cover, day or night

spin·ster (spínstər) *n.* an unmarried woman ‖ an old maid **spin·ster·hood** *n.* (fr. SPIN V.]

spin·to (spí:ntou) *n.* (usu. ital.) the capacity to both sing and act—said of an opera singer — **spinto** *adj.*

spi·nule (spáinju:l) *n.* a very small spine [fr. L. *spinula*]

spi·nu·lose (spáinjulous) *adj.* having or covered with spinules ‖ shaped like a spinule [fr. Mod. L. *spinulosus*]

spin wave (*nuclear phys.*) a wave caused by change in direction of the spin of electrons *Cf* MAGNON

spin·y (spáini:) *comp.* **spin·i·er** *superl.* **spin·i·est** *adj.* covered with spines ‖ shaped like a spine or thorn ‖ difficult to overcome, troublesome, perplexing, *a spiny problem*

spiny anteater the echidna

spi·ra·cle (spáirak'l) *n.* (*zool.*) a breathing orifice, e.g. the lateral branchial opening in tadpoles or blowhole in cetaceans ‖ a vent for lava etc. **spi·rac·u·lar** (spairǽkjulər) *adj.* having one or more spiracles [fr. L. *spiraculum*, breath]

spiraea *SPIREA

spi·ral (spáirəl) **1.** *adj.* of a curve which continuously changes its plane, and sometimes its curvature, in relation to a fixed axis ‖ curving in this way, *a spiral staircase* ‖ of a curve in a fixed plane which changes its curvature as it steadily increases or diminishes its distance from a fixed central point **2.** *n.* a curve of either of these forms ‖ something having either of these forms ‖ a tendency to decrease or esp. increase steadily, *the wage spiral* ‖ a single coil or turn in something spiral ‖ a descent or an ascent in a spiral path ‖ (*football*) a kick or pass which makes the ball rotate on its long axis **3.** *v. pres. part.* **spi·ral·ing**, esp. *Br.* **spi·ral·ling** *past* and *past part.* **spi·raled**, esp. *Br.*, **spi·ralled** *v.i.* to move, esp. to ascend or descend, in a spiral ‖ *v.i.* to cause to move or evolve in a spiral, *inflation spiraled prices* [fr. M.L. *spiralis*]

spiral galaxy a galaxy that can be seen, when viewed through a telescope, to possess a central nucleus with curved, radiating arms. The nucleus sometimes possesses a barred structure from which the arms extend

spiral nebula a spiral galaxy

spi·rant (spáirənt) *n.* (*phon.*) a consonantal sound which is articulated with the oral cavity partly closed and is not a stop, i.e. it can be prolonged (e.g. f, v, s, z) [L. *spirans (spirantis)* fr. *spirare*, to breathe]

spire (spáiər) *n.* (*archit.*) a tall thin structure

CONCISE PRONUNCIATION KEY: **(a)** æ, c*a*t; ɑ, c*a*r; ɔ f*aw*n; ei, sn*a*ke. **(e)** e, h*e*n; i:, sh*ee*p; iə, d*ee*r; ɛə, b*ea*r. **(i)** i, f*i*sh; ai, t*i*ger; ə:, b*i*rd. **(o)** o, *o*x; au, c*ow*; ou, g*oa*t; u, p*oo*r; ɔi, r*oy*al. **(u)** ʌ, d*u*ck; u, b*u*ll; u:, g*oo*se; ə, b*a*cillus; ju:, c*u*be. x, lo*ch*; θ, *th*ink; ð, bo*th*er; z, *Z*en; ʒ, corsa*g*e; dʒ, sava*g*e; ŋ, ora*ng*utang; j, *y*ak; ʃ, *f*ish; tʃ, fe*tch*; 'l, rabb*le*; 'n, redd*en*. Complete pronunciation key appears inside front cover.

surmounting a tower, esp. of a church, and being of conical or pyramidal form and of very small diameter in relation to its length ‖ anything compared with this, esp. with regard to its tip only, *spires of young wheat* [O.E. *spīr*]

spire *n.* a spiral ‖ a single turn in a coil ‖ (*zool.*) the upper part of a spiral shell [F. fr. L. fr. Gk]

spi·re·a, spi·rae·a (spairí:ə) *n.* a member of *Spiraea*, fam. *Rosaceae*, a genus of shrubs found in temperate regions bearing small pink or white flowers, e.g. the meadowsweet [L. fr. Gk *speiraia*, meadowsweet]

spi·ril·lum (spairíləm) *pl.* **spi·ril·la** (spairílə) *n.* a member of *Spirillum*, a genus of bacteria having the form of a spiral thread, sometimes with flagella ‖ any of various other microorganisms with a similar form [Mod. L. dim. of *spira*, a coil]

spir·it (spírit) *n.* the intelligent or immaterial part of man as distinguished from the body ‖ the animating or vital principle in living things ‖ the moral nature of a man ‖ a disembodied soul ‖ a supernatural being, usually regarded as invisible but as having the power to become visible at will ‖ a specified mental or emotional attitude characterizing words, actions, opinions etc., *she said it in a forgiving spirit* ‖ a person animated by a specified quality, *he was one of the braver spirits* ‖ the emotional attitude or frame of mind characteristic of a group of people, *team spirit*, or of people at a particular time, *the spirit of the age* ‖ the essential character of something, *he considered the spirit of the law as more important than the letter of the law* ‖ cheerful or assertive liveliness, *full of spirit* ‖ (often *pl.*) mood or temperamental state, *in high spirits, in poor spirits* ‖ (esp. *pl.*) liquor of high alcoholic content ‖ (esp. *pl.*) a volatile distillate ‖ (*pharm.*) the alcoholic solution of a volatile ingredient **the Spirit,** the Holy Ghost **2.** *adj.* of spirits or spiritualism, *the spirit world* ‖ (of lamps, engines etc.) using alcohol as a fuel **3.** *v.t.* (with 'off', 'away') to cause (something) to be removed unseen, with mysterious rapidity **spir·it·ed** *adj.* lively, *a spirited argument* ‖ showing creative energy, *spirited brushwork* ‖ (of a horse) keen, eager, full of energy and courage ‖ having a strong, assertive personality ‖ (in hyphenated compounds) having a specified character, quality etc., *public-spirited* [A.F. or fr. L. *spiritus*, breath]

spir·it·ism (spíritizəm) *n.* spiritualism ‖ the belief that natural objects have indwelling spirits **spír·it·ist** *n.*

spir·it·less (spíritlis) *adj.* having little or no animation ‖ lacking boldness and resolution

spirit level a short glass tube of alcohol containing a bubble, usually enclosed in a wooden or metal casing, used in testing whether a surface is horizontal. The bubble rests midway in the tube if the surface is accurately horizontal (cf. PLUMB LINE)

spi·ri·to·so (spiritóusou) *adj.* (*mus.*) played, sung etc. with animation [Ital.]

spirit rapping alleged communication with spirits of the dead by the interpretation of rapping noises allegedly made by them in answer to questions

spirits of salt (commercial name of) hydrochloric acid

spirits of wine alcohol obtained by distilling wine

spir·it·u·al (spíritʃu:əl) **1.** *adj.* of, relating to or concerned with the soul or spirit (opp. TEMPORAL) ‖ relating to religious or sacred matters, *spiritual counsel* ‖ full of spirituality ‖ having a relationship based on sympathy of thought or feeling, *she considered him as her spiritual father* ‖ (*Br.*) of the archbishops and bishops with seats in the House of Lords, *the Lords spiritual* **2.** *n.* a religious song, asserting a strong simple faith, sung originally by blacks of the Southern U.S.A. Spirituals are characterized by strong rhythm and vivid narrative [O.F. *spirituel* or fr. L. *spiritualis*]

spiritual home the place where a person feels the fullest sympathy with his surroundings

spir·it·u·al·ism (spíritʃu:əlizəm) *n.* the doctrine that the spirit, surviving after the death of the body, can communicate with persons still living, esp. through the agency of a medium ‖ spiritualistic practices ‖ (*philos.*) the doctrine that spirit exists independently of matter (opp. MATERIALISM) ‖ spiritual quality **spir·it·u·al·ist** *n.* a person who believes in or practices spiritualism ‖ a person who believes in philosophical spiritualism

spir·it·u·al·i·ty (spiritʃu:æliti:) *pl.* **spir·it·u·al·i·ties** *n.* attachment to all that concerns the life of the soul ‖ the quality of being spiritual ‖ (*eccles. law*) something which belongs to the Church or to a priest of the Church [O.F. *spiritualite*]

spir·it·u·al·i·za·tion (spiritʃu:əlizéiʃən) *n.* a spiritualizing or being spiritualized

spir·it·u·al·ize (spíritʃu:əlaiz) *pres. part.* **spir·it·u·al·iz·ing** *past* and *past part.* **spir·it·u·al·ized** *v.t.* to make spiritual ‖ to give a spiritual meaning to

spir·it·u·ous (spíritʃu:əs) *adj.* containing alcohol derived from distillation [fr. L. *spiritus*, spirit]

spir·i·tus as·per (spíritəsæspər) (*Gk gram.*) rough breathing [L.]

spir·i·tus le·nis (spíritəslí:nəs, spírítəsléinəs) (*Gk gram.*) smooth breathing

spi·ro·chete, spi·ro·chaete (spairəkí:t) *n.* a bacterium of the order *Spirochaetales*. Many are important pathogenic species (causing e.g. syphilis and relapsing fever). Spirochetes are slender spiral organisms, many of which are normally aquatic [fr. L. *spira*, coil+Gk *chaitē*, long, flowing hair]

spi·ro·gy·ra (spairədʒáirə) *n.* any plant of *Spirogyra*, fam. *Zygnemataceae*, a genus of filamentous green freshwater algae, with spiral chloroplasts containing large starch-storage bodies [Mod. L. fr. Gk *speira*, coil+*guros*, ring]

spi·ro·no·lac·tone [$C_{21}H_{32}O_4S$] (spairounouláektoun) *n.* (*pharm.*) steroid diuretic drug that counteracts sodium, retaining action of aldosterone; marketed as Aldactazide and Aldactone

spirt *SPURT

spit (spit) **1.** *v. pres. part.* **spit·ting** *past* and *past part.* **spit, spat** (spæt) *v.t.* to get rid of (saliva etc.) from the mouth by a forceful muscular action of the tongue and lips ‖ to emit or eject as though spitting, *the guns spat fire* ‖ to express anger, scorn, hatred or malice by uttering (words) vehemently and explosively and sometimes with a sound imitative of the action of spitting ‖ *v.i* to eject saliva from the mouth ‖ to do this as a means of expressing anger, scorn, hatred or malice ‖ to make sounds imitative of this or to imitate this action, *the fire was spitting* ‖ (of angry or threatened cats etc.) to make a hissing sound ‖ (esp. *Br.*) to rain in scattered, infrequent drops ‖ (of a pen point) to catch in the paper and throw off spatters of ink **to spit it out** to divulge some piece of information that one has been slow to give **2.** *n.* saliva ‖ the act or an instance of spitting ‖ the frothy secretion of some insects ‖ (*pop.*, esp. in **spit and image**) exact physical resemblance of somebody else, *he's the spit and image of his grandfather at that age* [O.E. *spittan*]

spit 1. *n.* a metal skewer on which meat to be roasted is impaled and slowly turned over an open fire, or an electric device based on this principle ‖ a thin projection of land into the sea, lake or river ‖ a shoal or reef extending from the shore **2.** *v.t. pres. part.* **spit·ting** *past* and *past part.* **spit·ted** to fix (meat) on a spit [O.E. *spitu*]

spit *n.* (*Br.*) the depth of the blade of a spade ‖ (*Br.*) the quantity of earth lifted by a spade [M.Du., M.L.G.]

spit and polish extreme cleanliness and order ‖ (*mil.*) irksome preparation for ceremonial parades

spit·ball (spítbɔl) *n.* a missile consisting of a piece of moist paper crushed into a ball ‖ (*baseball, hist.*) a pitch in which the ball is made to curve after being moistened on one side

spitch·cock (spítʃkɒk) **1.** *v.t.* to split and broil, fry or grill (an eel) **2.** *n.* an eel split and cooked in one of these ways [etym. doubtful]

spite (spait) **1.** *n.* animosity towards a person which results in a desire to do him petty injury ‖ a specific feeling of resentment, a grudge, *a spite against intellectuals* **in spite of,** regardless of, notwithstanding, *he did it in spite of our efforts to stop him* **2.** *v.t. pres. part.* **spit·ing** *past* and *past part.* **spit·ed** to injure out of spite, *he did it to spite me* **to cut off one's nose to spite one's face** to injure one's own interests knowingly in seeking to injure another's **spite·ful** *adj.* [fr. DESPITE]

spit·fire (spítfaiər) *n.* someone, esp. a woman or girl, very quick to become angry

Spit·head (spíthéd) the eastern entrance (4-5 miles wide) of the Solent, England, an anchorage used for naval displays

spit·ting (spítiŋ) *n.* (*mil.*) in air intercept, a code meaning *I am about to lay, or am laying, sonobuoys. I may be out of radio contact for a few minutes.* If transmitted from a submarine, it indicates that the submarine has launched a sonobuoy

spitting image someone who exactly resembles someone else addressed or referred to (*SPIT *n.*)

spit·tle (spít'l) *n.* saliva, esp. when spit out ‖ the frothy secretion of some insects [O.E. *spittan*]

spit·toon (spitú:n) *n.* a round, flat vessel of earthenware, brass etc. on the floor to receive spit

spitz (spits) *n.* a dog of a medium-sized breed with a pointed muzzle and pointed ears and very thick double coat, usually white, and having the tail curved back over the body ‖ a pomeranian ‖ a chow chow ‖ a samoyed [G. *spitz*, pointed]

spitz dog a spitz

spiv (spiv) *n.* (*Br.*) a man who lives by trading in ways of doubtful honesty, does no hard work, and dresses flashily [etym. doubtful]

splash (splæʃ) **1.** *v.t.* to cause to receive the impact of drops of liquid and so be made wet or stained, *a car splashed her with mud as it passed* ‖ to cause (liquid) to move through the air in separate drops, *the car splashed mud on his clothes* ‖ to cause (something) to agitate and scatter a liquid, *to splash one's toes in the water* ‖ to make (one's way) by splashing thus ‖ to apply (paint etc.) in a careless or lavish way ‖ to decorate (e.g. a canvas) thus ‖ to drive (logs) by releasing water from a dam ‖ to make a display of (money, news) ‖ *v.i.* to agitate a liquid and scatter it or cause it to fly around in drops ‖ (of a liquid) to be suddenly and violently thrown up or off in drops ‖ to move through or into a liquid so that it is thrown around in this way, *we splashed through the waves* **2.** *n.* the act or sound of splashing ‖ the liquid which is splashed ‖ a spot made by splashing ‖ a bright patch of color ‖ (*Br.*) a small quantity of soda water squirted from a siphon ‖ the act of driving logs by releasing water from a dam **to make a splash** to make an ostentatious display [etym. doubtful]

splash·board (splǽʃbɔrd, splǽʃbourd) *n.* a fender ‖ a board or panel behind a sink to receive the splashes made in the sink ‖ a device for closing a dam

splash·down (splǽʃdaun) *n.* the landing of a spacecraft or missile on a body of water ‖ the moment of this landing

splashed *n.* (*mil.*) in air intercept, a code meaning *Enemy aircraft shot down* (followed by number and type)

splash·y (splǽʃi:) *comp.* **splash·i·er** *superl.* **splash·i·est** *adj.* causing splashes ‖ very showy, *a splashy front page* ‖ marked by splashes of color

splat (splæt) *n.* a single, broad, flat piece of wood forming the central upright of a chair back, e.g. in a Queen Anne dining chair ‖ a piece of wood performing the same function placed horizontally [etym. doubtful]

splat·ter (splǽtər) **1.** *v.t.* to spatter ‖ *v.i.* to become spattered **2.** *n.* a spatter [perh. fr. SPLASH+SPATTER]

splay (splei) **1.** *n.* (*archit.*) a sloping surface or bevel, e.g. at the side of a lancet window ‖ a spreading **2.** *adj.* turned outwards, broad and flat, *splay feet* **3.** *v.t.* to spread, *to splay one's elbows* ‖ to bevel, to set oblique ‖ *v.i.* to be or become splayed [fr. DISPLAY]

splay·foot (spléifut) *pl.* **splay·feet** (spléifi:t) *n.* a flattened foot turned outwards **splay·foot·ed** *adj.*

spleen (spli:n) *n.* a soft fleshy organ in the upper left abdomen, chiefly concerned with the formation and purification of blood. It becomes enlarged and hard in certain blood diseases such as malaria, kala-azar and leukemia ‖ (*old-fash.*) ill temper, *a fit of spleen* **spleen·ful** *adj.* [fr. O.F. *esplen* or L. *splen* fr. Gk]

spleen·wort (splí:nwət, splí:nwɔrt) *n.* a fern of the genus *Asplenium* ‖ a fern of the genus *Athyrium*

splen·dent (spléndənt) *adj.* (*mineral.*) having a bright metallic luster [fr. L. *splendens* (*splendentis*) fr. *splendere*, to shine]

splen·did (spléndid) *adj.* magnificent, gorgeous, sumptuous, *splendid palaces* ‖ exciting admiration by its fine or noble quality, *a splendid performance* [fr. L. *splendidus* fr. *splendere*, to be bright]

CONCISE PRONUNCIATION KEY: **(a)** æ, c*a*t; ɑ, c*a*r; ɔ f*aw*n; ei, sn*a*ke. **(e)** e, h*e*n; i:, sh*ee*p; iə, d*ee*r; ɛə, b*ea*r. **(i)** i, f*i*sh; ai, t*i*ger; ə:, b*i*rd. **(o)** o, *o*x; au, c*ow*; ou, g*oa*t; u, p*oo*r; ɔi, r*oy*al. **(u)** ʌ, d*u*ck; u, b*u*ll; u:, g*oo*se; ə, b*a*cillus; ju:, c*u*be. x, lo*ch*; θ, *th*ink; ð, *th*is; z, *Z*en; ʒ, cor*s*age; dʒ, *sa*vage; ŋ, ora*ng*utang; j, *y*ak; ʃ, *fi*sh; tʃ, fe*tch*; 'l, rabb*le*; 'n, redd*en*. Complete pronunciation key appears inside front cover.

splen·dor, *Br.* **splen·dour** (spléndər) *n.* the quality of being splendid ‖ great brilliance ‖ display of wealth or magnificence **the sun in splendor** (*heraldry*) a sun represented as having a human face and emitting golden rays [fr. A.F. *esplendour, splendor* or fr. L. *splendor*]

sple·net·ic (splinétik) **1.** *adj.* (*med.*) of or relating to the spleen ‖ apt to be peevishly or morosely ill-tempered **2.** *n.* a person apt to be peevishly or morosely ill-tempered **sple·nét·i·cal·ly** *adv.* [fr. L.L. *spleneticus*]

splen·ic (splénik, splí:nik) *adj.* (*med.*) splenetic [fr. L. *splenicus* fr. Gk]

splice (splais) **1.** *v.t. pres. part.* **splic·ing** *past* and *past part.* **spliced** to join together (two rope ends) by first unraveling both a little way and then twisting the strands of each around those of the other to form one continuous length ‖ to unite two parts of the same rope (forming a loop) by interweaving the partially unraveled strands of one end into those of another part ‖ to join together the ends of (two pieces of wood) by thinning them, making them overlap and fastening the overlaps together ‖ to join (film, tape etc.) at the ends ‖ to make (the handle of a tennis racket etc.) a better shock absorber by laminating it with layers treated in this way **to get spliced** (*pop.*) to get married **to splice the main brace** (*naut.*) to serve out an extra ration of rum **2.** *n.* a join made by splicing ‖ the part of a cricket-bat handle which fits into the blade [fr. M.Du. *splissen*]

spline (splain) **1.** *n.* a thin, narrow strip of wood, plastic or metal ‖ a flexible lath, or strip of rubber, used by draftsmen to trace arcs of large radius ‖ (*mech.*) a rectangular key fitting permanently into slots in two parts of a mechanism, e.g. a shaft and wheel, ensuring that these revolve together and giving maximum strength ‖ either of these slots **2.** *v.t. pres. part.* **splin·ing** *past* and *past part.* **splined** to fit with a spline ‖ to provide with a groove for a spline [perh. rel. to SPLINTER]

splint (splint) **1.** *n.* a strip of wood etc. which, bound to a limb, keeps broken bones from moving apart ‖ a strip of wood used in the same way in grafting fruit trees etc. ‖ a thin flexible strip of wood or cane woven with others to make a chair seat, basket etc. ‖ (*esp.* of a horse) a morbid bony growth on the splint bone ‖ (*armor*) one of the flexibly overlapping metallic plates for protecting esp. the elbows **2.** *v.t.* to secure with a splint [M.Du. *splinte*]

splint bone one of two small metacarpal bones in the foreleg of a horse (and related animals), lying behind and in close contact with the cannon bone or shank

splin·ter (splíntər) **1.** *n.* a thin, sharp piece of wood etc. broken or split off, esp. as the result of violent impact **2.** *v.i.* to break off in thin, sharp pieces, esp. as the result of violent impact ‖ *v.t.* to break or split into thin, sharp pieces, esp. by violent impact **3.** *adj.* (of a political or religious group) broken off from and independent of a larger or primary organization, esp. because of violent disagreement [M.Du.]

splin·ter·y (splíntəri) *adj.* of or like a splinter

Split (spli:t) a port (pop. 193,600) on the Dalmatian coast, Croatia, Yugoslavia. It dates from the 7th c. and is built within the ruined 4th-c. palace of Diocletian, incorporating its walls, gates, mausoleum and temples. Industries: shipbuilding, plastics, building materials, tourism, fishing

split (split) **1.** *v. pres. part.* **split·ting** *past* and *past part.* **split** *v.t.* to divide, separate, cleave, burst or force apart the layers of (a solid), esp. along its grain or length and esp. with force or violence, *the lightning split the tree* ‖ to divide into parts, *they split the profit between them* ‖ to cause division in (a group of people) so that those holding one view are opposed to those holding another, *the abdication split the country* ‖ (*gram.*) to separate the two parts of (an infinitive) by an adverb, as in 'to carelessly write' ‖ (*chem.*) to decompose (a compound) ‖ (*phys.*) to break (a molecule) into atoms ‖ (*phys.*) to produce nuclear fission in (an atom) **to split one's vote** (or **ticket**) to vote for candidates of more than one party at the same election ‖ *v.i.* to become divided, separated, cleft or forced apart, esp. along a grain or seam, or lengthwise ‖ to separate into groups holding opposing views ‖ to part, break asunder ‖ (*Br., pop.*) to divulge information (sometimes unintentionally) **2.** *n.* the act or result of splitting ‖ a separation into groups holding different views ‖ something that has been split, e.g. a split osier used in basket-

making or a single thickness of split leather ‖ (*Br.*) a bun opened up to be filled with jam and cream ‖ a dessert made of sliced fruit, ice cream and syrup with nuts added, *a banana split* ‖ (also *pl.*) the acrobatic feat of sitting down with the legs straight and in the same line either right and left of the body or in front and behind ‖ (*bowling*) an arrangement of the pins after the first bowl, esp. one that makes a spare almost impossible ‖ a small bottle of some drink, usually about half the normal size for such a drink **3.** *adj.* that has undergone the process of splitting ‖ divided into layers ‖ separated ‖ torn by bursting ‖ (of a stock exchange quotation) given in sixteenths, not in eighths [M.Du. *splitten*]

split-brain (splítbréin) *n.* (*neuropsychology*) concept of separation of right and left hemispheres of the brain, each functioning independently, in which the left is dominant in language and verbal recognition, the right in spatial recognition and motor activity

split end (*football*) an end position at some distance from an interior linesman *also* spread end

split-lev·el (splítlévəl) **1.** *adj.* of a building so constructed that the floor level of one part is roughly midway between those of adjoining parts **2.** *n.* a house constructed in this way

split personality a schizophrenic condition in which a person appears to be inhabited by two internally consistent but irreconcilable characters

split pin a securing pin split at one end for some distance along its length so that it may be spread open to keep it in position after insertion

split ring a metal ring consisting of two complete turns of a spiral pressed flat together. A metal loop (esp. of a key) can be forced between them and worked around till the ring and loop are freely but securely linked

split screen (*cinematography*) the presentation of two scenes on the screen at the same time, each having a different portion of the screen

split second an almost imperceptible moment of time

split·ting (splítiŋ) *adj.* that splits ‖ (of pain) very severe, causing one to feel as though being split, *a splitting headache* ‖ very funny, producing violent laughter

split vertical photography the process of taking photographs simultaneously by two cameras mounted at an angle from the vertical, one tilted to the left and one to the right, to obtain a small side overlap —**split cameras** *n. pl.* an assembly of two cameras disposed at a fixed overlapping angle relative to each other *Cf* FAN CAMERA

splodge (splɒdʒ) (*Br.*) **1.** *n.* a splotch of some thick heavy material, e.g. mud, which is not usually absorbed **2.** *v.t. pres. part.* **splodg·ing** *past* and *past part.* **splodged** to mark with a splodge or splodges **splódg·y** *comp.* **splodg·i·er** *superl.* **splodg·i·est** *adj.* [imit.]

splotch (splɒtʃ) **1.** *n.* an irregular, usually unintentional, displeasing patch of paint, stain etc. **2.** *v.t.* to mark with a splotch or splotches **splótch·y** *comp.* **splotch·i·er** *superl.* **splotch·i·est** *adj.* marked with such patches [imit.]

splurge (splə:rdʒ) **1.** *n.* (*pop.*) a showy effect, esp. as the result of lavish spending **2.** *v.i. pres. part.* **splurg·ing** *past* and *past part.* **splurged** to make a splurge [imit.]

splut·ter (splʌtər) **1.** *v.i.* to speak rapidly with bad articulation, sometimes spitting particles of saliva while doing so ‖ (e.g. of a car engine) to make a sound resembling this manner of speaking ‖ to splash, spatter, *the rain spluttered against the window* ‖ *v.t.* to express in this way, *he spluttered a hasty apology* ‖ to cause to spatter **2.** *n.* the sound of spluttering [imit.]

Spock (spɒk), Benjamin (1903-   ), U.S. pediatrician and leader of the anti-war movement during the Vietnam War

Spode (spoud), Josiah (1754-1827), English potter. In 1799 he first produced the fine bone china which bears his name

spod·u·mene (spɒ́djumi:n, spɒ́dʒumi:n) *n.* (*mineral.*) LiAlSi$_2$O$_6$, a monoclinic aluminum and lithium silicate occurring in various colors, often in very large crystals, e.g. kunzite [F. ult. fr. Gk *spodousthai*, to be burned to ashes]

spoil (spɔil) *pres. part.* **spoil·ing** *past* and *past part.* **spoiled, spoilt** (spɔilt) *v.t.* to take away the pleasure from, *quarreling spoiled the picnic* ‖ to fail to make as good as possible, *she spoiled the curtains by skimping the material* ‖ to damage or ruin, *spilled ink spoiled the cloth* ‖ to

impair, detract from, *her ridiculous gestures spoiled her singing* ‖ to injure (esp. a child or domestic animal) with respect to character during the formative period by overindulgence or too much leniency ‖ to pamper and make much of ‖ *v.i.* to become less good, valuable, enjoyable or useful ‖ to become unfit for use ‖ (*pop.*) to be eager for aggressive action, *spoiling for a fight* [fr. O.F. *espoillier*]

spoil *n.* (esp. *pl.*) goods taken from a defeated enemy, *spoils of war* ‖ goods acquired by theft ‖ (*pl.*) special privileges and rewards resulting from success in winning political office ‖ waste material resulting from mining etc. [fr. O.F. *espoille*]

spoil·age (spɔ́ilidʒ) *n.* unavoidable waste, e.g. of raw material in the initial stage of using a machine ‖ waste through decay, e.g. of fruit and vegetables ‖ goods spoiled ‖ the process of decay in foods through bacteria or fungi

spoil·er (spɔ́ilər) *n.* **1.** (*politics*) a candidate who enters a race principally for the purpose of splitting the votes of the opposition **2.** (*automobile*) a device on a motor vehicle to deflect air upward in order to provide additional stability at high speeds

spoils·man (spɔ́ilzmən) *pl.* **spoils·men** (spɔ́ilzmən) *n.* a politician actuated by desire to share in the spoils

spoil·sport (spɔ́ilspɔrt spɔ́ilspɔurt) *n.* someone who willfully prevents others from having fun

spoils system the system whereby offices, incomes and privileges once belonging to a defeated party are considered to be rightly distributed among members of the political party come to power

spoilt *alt. past* and *past part.* of SPOIL

Spo·kane (spoukǽn) an agricultural market town (pop. 171,300) in E. Washington: wood industries, flour mills, metallurgy, meat packing

spoke (spouk) **1.** *n.* a radial rod transmitting stress from the rim to the hub of a wheel ‖ something resembling this ‖ a rung of a ladder ‖ (*naut.*) a radial handle of a steering wheel **2.** *v.t. pres. part.* **spok·ing** *past* and *past part.* **spoked** to furnish with spokes **to put a spoke in someone's wheel** to prevent the success of his plan [O.E. *spāca*]

spoke *past* of SPEAK

spo·ken (spóukən) *past part.* of SPEAK ‖ *adj.* oral as opposed to written ‖ (in compounds) having a specified kind of voice or manner of speaking, *softspoken, plainspoken*

spoke·shave (spóukʃeiv) *n.* a plane with a handle on each side of a small blade, drawn or pushed along wood to give a curved surface

spokes·per·son (spóukspə:rsən) *n.* one who speaks for another person, a group, or a cause, esp. for public consumption

spokes·wom·an (spóukswumən) *pl.* **spokes·wom·en** (spóukswimən) *n.* a female spokesman

spok·ing (spóukiŋ) *n.* (*radar*) periodic flashes on a radial display for abnormal periods due to radar malfunction, sometimes caused by mutual interference

Spo·le·to (spolétɔ) a walled town (pop. 37,396) in Umbria, Italy: Roman basilica, arch, theaters, Romanesque cathedral (12th c., restored 15th and 17th cc.)

spo·li·a·tion (spouliéiʃən) *n.* the seizing of goods belonging to others, esp. the goods of neutrals in wartime ‖ (*law*) the alteration or mutilation of a document to prevent its use in evidence ‖ (*eccles.*) the taking of the emoluments of a benefice without legal entitlement to do so [fr. L. *spoliatio* (*spoliationis*)]

spon·da·ic (spɒndéiik) *adj.* of or characterized by a spondee ‖ constituting a spondee [fr. F. *spondaïque* or L. *spondaicus*]

spon·dee (spɒ́ndi:) *n.* a metrical foot consisting of two long or stressed syllables [F. *spondée* or fr. L. *spondeus* fr. Gk]

spon·dy·li·tis (spɒnd'láitis) *n.* inflammation of a vertebra or vertebrae [fr. Gk *spondulos*, a vertebra]

sponge (spʌndʒ) **1.** *n.* a parazoan and member of the phylum *Porifera*. Sponges vary greatly in shape, size and color and live permanently attached (e.g. to a rock) either alone or in colonies. They consist of two layers of cells surrounding a central cavity and have skeletons of a calcareous or siliceous substance or of spongin. These skeletons are traversed by a system of canals through which food-bearing water is circulated by flagellated cells lining the canal walls. Sponges reproduce either sexually or asexually ‖ the macerated, highly porous, elastic, spongin skeleton of a sponge of genera *Spongia* or *Hippospongia*, used commercially, esp. for its ability to absorb fluids and yield them again on pressure ‖ (without article) the material of which this is composed ‖ a synthetic substitute for this material ‖ (*Br.*) a sponge cake or sponge pudding ‖ a sterile cotton gauze used for sponging and wiping in surgical operations ‖ raised bread dough ‖ (*pop.*) a heavy drinker ‖ someone who tries to live parasitically ‖ a wash or rubdown with a sponge **to throw up** (or **in**) **the sponge** to admit defeat or failure 2. *v. pres. part.* **spong·ing** past and past part. **sponged** *v.t.* to moisten, clean or wipe with a wet sponge ‖ (with 'out') to efface with, or as if with, a sponge ‖ (with 'up') to absorb with, or as if with, a sponge ‖ (*pop.*) to get without cost by imposing oneself on someone, *to sponge a meal* ‖ *v.i.* (with 'on') to prey on other people's good nature parasitically, *he is always sponging on her for meals* ‖ to harvest sponges [O.E. *sponge, spunge* fr. L. fr. G]

sponge bag (*Br.*) a waterproof bag used to carry toilet accessories, esp. when one is traveling

sponge cake a light, sweet cake, made without fat, and spongy in texture, in which eggs are the leavening agent

sponge iron (*metallurgy*) high-grade ore, usu. from scrap. necessary for use with electric arc furnace

sponge pudding a pudding made of spongecake mixture

spong·er (spʌndʒər) *n.* a person who harvests sponges or a boat used for this ‖ someone who lives or tries to live parasitically

sponge rubber rubber given a very porous structure and used as a soft but elastic cushioning material

sponges *n.* temporary employees of a nuclear energy plant hired especially to perform a small task where exposure to radiation is involved *also* steam generator jumpers, jumpers

sponge·ware (spʌndʒweər) *n.* ceramics produced by applying glaze with a sponge to create a mottled surface, common in early American ware

spon·gin (spʌndʒin) *n.* the scleroprotein which chiefly forms the skeleton of commercial sponges

spong·i·ness (spʌndʒinis) *n.* the state or quality of being spongy

spong·gy (spʌndʒi:) *comp.* **spong·i·er** *superl.* **spong·i·est** *adj.* having the porous, absorbent, elastic properties of a sponge ‖ (of a metal) in a finely porous, absorbent condition, *spongy lead* (in a storage battery), *spongy platinum* (used as an adsorber of gases)

spongy parenchyma a tissue of the mesophyll, usually on the lower side of the leaf blade. It consists of a meshwork of cellular strands with large intercellular spaces. The spongy parenchyma also contains very many chloroplasts (*PALISADE PARENCHYMA)

spon·sion (spʌnʃən) *n.* the act of going surety ‖ (*internat. law*) an undertaking given on behalf of a state by an agent who is not directly authorized to do so [fr. L. *sponsio* (*sponsionis*) fr. *spondere*, to promise solemnly]

spon·son (spʌnsən) *n.* a projection of the side of a warship or tank to give a gun a greater arc of fire ‖ (*aeron.*) a projection from the wing of a hydroplane enabling it to rest steadily on water ‖ an air chamber along the gunwale of a canoe giving it greater stability [etym. doubtful]

spon·sor (spʌnsər) 1. *n.* someone who accepts personal responsibility for another ‖ a godparent ‖ (*radio, television*) a person or firm paying for a broadcast during which time will be allowed to advertise his or its wares 2. *vt.* to act as sponsor for **spon·so·ri·al** (sponsɔ́ːriəl, sponsóuriəl) *adj.* **spón·sor·ship** *n.* [L.=surety]

spon·ta·ne·i·ty (spontəníːiti, sponteneíiti:) *n.* the state or quality of being spontaneous [fr. L. *spontaneus* adj.]

spon·ta·ne·ous (spontéiniːəs) *adj.* arising from impulse, not suggested by another and not premeditated, *a spontaneous offer to help* ‖ happening without external cause or control, *the movements of the heart are spontaneous* ‖ growing without human intervention, in the wild state [fr. L. *spontaneus*]

spontaneous combustion combustion arising with no direct application of spark or flame. It is due to an internal rise of temperature to the

ignition point, usually caused by a slow oxidation process

spontaneous generation abiogenesis

spoof (spuːf) 1. *v.i.* (*old-fash., pop.*) to fool, pretend ‖ *v.t.* (*old-fash., pop.*) to deceive (someone) 2. *n.* (*old-fash., pop.*) a hoax ‖ a humorous, light, but telling parody [name of a game, invented (c. 1889) by Arthur Roberts, Eng. comedian]

spoof·er (spúːfəːr) *n.* (*mil.*) in air intercept, a contact employing electronic or tactical deception measures

spook (spuːk) *n.* (a seriocomic word, meeting the supernatural with joking awe) a specter ‖ (*slang*) an intelligence agent **spóok·y** *comp.* **spook·i·er** *superl.* **spook·i·est** *adj.* [Du.]

spool (spuːl) 1. *n.* a short cylinder, with a rim or head at each end and usually a hole up the middle for a spindle, on which thread or yarn is wound ‖ a reel on which e.g. a photographic film or an angler's line is wound 2. *v.t.* to wind on a spool [fr. M. Du. *spoele*]

spoon (spuːn) 1. *n.* a domestic utensil consisting of a shallow, oval or round bowl at the end of a handle, used for eating liquid or semiliquid food, and for mixing, stirring etc. ‖ something shaped like this utensil, esp. a spinner (fishing lure) ‖ (*golf*) a wood with a lofted face, used for long, high shots 2. *v.t.* to gather up with a spoon (domestic utensil) ‖ (*cricket, golf* etc.) to loft (a ball) with the bat, club etc. ‖ *v.i.* to fish with a spinner ‖ (*old-fash., pop.*) (of lovers) to hug and kiss [O.E. *spōn*]

spoon·bill (spúːnbil) *n. Platalea leucorodia*, fam. *Plataleidae*, a wading bird of S. Europe, N. Africa and Asia, resembling a small stork or heron. It is crested, has snow-white plumage and a long spatulate bill, and breeds colonially in reed beds

spoo·ner·ism (spúːnərizəm) *n.* the transposition with bizarre effect of (usually) the initial sounds of words adjacent in a phrase, esp. 'a half-warmed fish' for 'a half-formed wish' [after the Rev. W.A. *Spooner* (1844–1930), Warden of New College, Oxford]

spoon·fed (spúːnfed) *adj.* indulged by being given all that is needed without having to make any effort to get it ‖ fed with a spoon

spoon·ful (spúːnful) *pl.* **spoon·fuls** *n.* the amount a spoon will hold

spoor (spuər) 1. *n.* the footprints and other signs of the passage of an animal, esp. a game animal 2. *v.i.* to follow a spoor ‖ *v.t.* to track (an animal) by its spoor [Du.]

Spor·a·des (spóːrədiːz, spɒ́rədiːz) two groups of Greek islands in the Aegean: the N. Sporades, off Thessaly, and the S. Sporades (consisting largely of the Dodecanese), off S.W. Asia Minor

spo·rad·ic (spərǽdik) *adj.* occurring at infrequent and irregular intervals in time or space, *sporadic outbursts of plague* ‖ occurring in isolated or single instances **spo·rád·i·cal·ly** *adv.* [fr. M.L. *sporadicus* fr. Gk]

sporan *SPORRAN

spo·ran·gi·al (spɒrǽndʒiəl, spourǽndʒiəl) *adj.* of or like a sporangium ‖ characterized by sporangia

spo·ran·gi·um (spɒrǽndʒiəm, spourǽndʒiəm) *pl.* **spo·ran·gi·a** (spɒrǽndʒiə, spourǽndʒiə) *n.* a capsule in which spores are produced or carried in algae, fungi, bacteria, ferns and mosses [Mod. L. fr. Gk *spora*, seed+*angeion*, vessel]

spore (spɔr, spour) 1. *n.* a minute one-celled reproductive or resistant resting body produced usually by lower forms of plant and animal life and often adapted to withstand unfavorable environmental conditions. When these conditions improve the spore can produce a new vegetative individual 2. *v.i. pres. part.* **spor·ing** past and past part. **spored** to bear or develop spores [fr. Mod. L. *spora* fr. Gk]

spore case a sporangium

spo·ro·carp (spóːrəkɑrp, spóurəkɑrp) *n.* a structure in which or on which spores are reproduced [fr. Gk *spora*, seed+*karpos*, fruit]

spo·ro·cyst (spóːrəsist, spóurəsist) *n.* a stage in spore formation prior to sporogony ‖ the encysted sporozoan [fr. Gk *spora*, seed+*kustis*, sac]

spo·ro·gen·e·sis (spɒrədʒénisis, spourədʒénisis) *n.* reproduction by spores ‖ spore formation [Mod. L. fr. Gk *spora*, seed+L. *genesis*, origin]

spo·rog·e·nous (spɒród͡ʒənəs, spouród͡ʒənəs) *adj.* producing or able to produce spores ‖ reproducing by spores [fr. SPORE+Gk -*genes*, born of]

spo·rog·e·ny (spɒród͡ʒəni:, spouród͡ʒəni:) *n.* sporogenesis

spo·ro·go·ni·um (spɒrəgóuniːəm, spourəgóuni-əm) *pl.* **spo·ro·go·ni·a** (spɒrəgóuniːə, spourə-góuni:ə) *n.* the sporophyte of a moss or liverwort consisting typically of a stalk bearing a sporangium [Mod. L. fr. Gk *spora*, seed+*gonos*, offspring]

spo·rog·o·ny (spɒród͡ʒəni:, spouród͡ʒəni:) *n.* sporogenesis ‖ spore formation in a sporozoan by encystment and subsequent division of a zygote [fr. Gk *spora*, seed+-*gonia*, product]

spo·ro·phore (spóːrəfɔr, spóurəfour) *n.* a sporebearing structure, esp. in fungi [fr. Gk *spora*, seed+-*phoros*, bearing]

spo·ro·phyll, spo·ro·phyl (spóːrəfil, spóurəfil) *n.* a sporangium-bearing leaf [fr. Gk *spora*, seed+*phullos*, leaf]

spo·ro·phyte (spóːrəfait, spóurəfait) *n.* (in plants which exhibit alternation of generations) the individual or generation that bears asexual spores [fr. Gk *spora*, seed+*phuton*, plant]

spo·ro·pol·len·in (spɒrəpɒlenin) *n.* the outer covering of pollen or spores

spo·ro·zo·an (spɒrəzóuən, spourəzóuən) 1. *n.* a parasitic protozoan, of the class *Sporozoa*. They are usually without locomotory structures, and pass through a complicated life cycle often (as with the malaria parasites) involving two dissimilar hosts 2. *adj.* of or belonging to this class [fr. Mod. L. fr. Gk *spora*, seed+*zōon*, animal]

spo·ro·zo·ite (spɒrəzóuait, spourəzóuait) *n.* a small, elongate, usually motile, infective stage of some sporozoans

spor·ran, spor·an (spɒ́rən) *n.* a large pouch made of skin, usually with the hair left on, used as a purse and worn by Scottish Highlanders with the kilt. It is slung around the waist to hang down in front [Scot. Gael. *sporan*, Ir. Gael. *sparan*, purse]

sport (spɔrt, spourt) 1. *n.* the playing of games or participation in competitive pastimes involving physical exertion and skill, esp. those played outdoors ‖ any such game or pastime ‖ (*esp. Br.*) such games collectively ‖ the pleasure and satisfaction derived from such games or pastimes or from hunting etc., *it was good sport* ‖ an activity pursued for pleasure involving the hunting, taking or killing of wild animals, game or fish, *blood sports* ‖ (*pl.*) athletics (track events, jumping etc.) ‖ (*Br., pl.*) an organized meeting for these ‖ a person who has the qualities of sportsmanship ‖ (*biol.*) an animal or plant differing greatly from the normal ‖ (*bot.*) a bud variation **in sport** as a joke or for fun, not in earnest **to make sport of** to cause to look silly 2. *v.i.* (*rhet.*) to play ‖ (*rhet.*) to joke ‖ (*rhet.*) to gambol, frolic ‖ (*biol.*) to differ greatly from the normal ‖ (*bot.*) to show bud variation ‖ *v.t.* to wear esp. in order to show off, *to sport a new tie* ‖ (*biol.*) to produce as a sport **to sport one's oak** (*Oxford* and *Cambridge Universities*) to shut one's door as an indication that one is out or does not wish to be disturbed 3. *adj.* sports [shortened fr. M.E. *desport, disport*]

sport·ing (spɔ́rtiŋ, spóurtiŋ) *adj.* pertaining to sport ‖ involving risk but offering some possibility of success, *a sporting chance* ‖ sportsmanlike in conduct

spor·tive (spɔ́rtiv, spóurtiv) *adj.* (*old-fash.*) playful

sports (spɔrts, spourts) *adj.* concerned with, suitable for or devoted to sports, *sports page, sports instructor* ‖ (of clothes) comfortable and casual, for informal wear

sports car an automobile for traveling fast on public roads. Sports cars are usually open or convertible and seat two

sports·man (spɔ́rtsmən, spóurtsmən) *pl.* **sports·men** (spɔ́rtsmən, spóurtsmən) *n.* a person who practices a sport ‖ a person who behaves generously in defeat or victory **spórts·man·ly** *adj.*

sports·man·like (spɔ́rtsmənlaik, spóurtsmən-laik) *adj.* showing the moral qualities of a good sportsman

sports·man·ship (spɔ́rtsmənʃip, spóurtsmən-ʃip) *n.* generous behavior befitting a good sportsman

sports·wear (spɔ́rtsweər, spóurtsweər) *n.* (*commerce*) clothes for outdoor sports ‖ (*commerce*) casual, comfortable clothes for informal wear

sports·wom·an (spɔ́rtswumən, spóurtswumən) *pl.* **sports·wom·en** (spɔ́rtswimin, spóurtswimin) *n.* a woman who takes part in sports

sports·writ·er (spɔ́rtsraitər, spóurtsraitər) *n.* a journalist who writes about sports

sport·y (spɔ́rti, spóurti:) *comp.* **sport·i·er** *superl.* **sport·i·est** *adj.* (*old-fash.*) sportsmanlike

CONCISE PRONUNCIATION KEY: **(a)** æ, *cat*; ɑ, *car*; ɔ *fawn*; ei, *snake*. **(e)** e, *hen*; iː, *sheep*; iə, *deer*; ɛə, *bear*. **(i)** i, *fish*; ai, *tiger*; əː, *bird*. **(o)** o, *ox*; au, *cow*; ou, *goat*; u, *poor*; ɔi, *royal*. **(u)** ʌ, *duck*; u, *bull*; uː, *goose*; ə, *bacillus*; juː, *cube*. x, *loch*; θ, *think*; δ, *bother*; z, *Zen*; ʒ, *corsage*. dʒ, *savage*; ŋ, *orangutang*; j, *yak*; ʃ, *fish*; tʃ, *fetch*; 'l, *rabble*; 'n, *redden*. Complete pronunciation key appears inside front cover.

suitable for, or affording good sport, *a sporty little model* || (of a girl or woman) too fond of sports to be very feminine, but with strong sportsmanlike qualities

spor·u·late (spɔ́rjuleit, spóurjuleit) *pres. part.* **spor·u·lat·ing** *past* and *past part.* **spor·u·lat·ed** *v.i.* to undergo sporulation

spor·u·la·tion (spɔrjuléiʃən, spourjuléiʃən) *n.* (*biol.*) the formation of spores

spor·ule (spɔ́rjuːl, spóurjuːl) *n.* a very small or secondary spore [Mod. L. *sporula*, dim. of *spora*, seed]

spot (spɒt) **1.** *n.* a small disfiguring mark of dirt etc. || a small, usually round, decorative mark of different color or texture from its background, *the leopard's spots* || (on human skin) a pimple || a dark area on the face of the sun, moon or a planet || (*rhet.*) a blemish on a good reputation, character, name etc. || a place, *the spot where the crash occurred, good in spots* || (*esp Br.*) a drop of a liquid, esp. water, *spots of rain* || (*Br., pop.*) a small amount, *a spot of supper* || (*billiards*) the mark on the upper end of the table where the red ball is placed or one of two other marked places on the table || *Leiostomus xanthurus*, a fish found off the northeast coast of the U.S.A., with a black spot behind the shoulders || (*bot.*) a mark on a leaf etc. produced by a fungus || a small, usually round mark used as a distinguishing device || (*pop.*) a spotlight || (*radio, television*) a short interval set aside in a broadcast for announcements or advertisements, or the announcement or advertisement itself || a situation **in a spot** in a difficult situation **on the spot** at once || on the site where something happened, is happening or is expected to happen || alert, quick to grasp a situation **to put on the spot** (*pop.*, esp. of gangsters) to threaten with real intent to murder (a person or persons) || to force to justify oneself, give information or an answer etc. **2.** *v. pres. part.* **spot·ting** *past* and *past part.* **spot·ted** *v.t.* to look out for with the purpose of recording information, *the boys were spotting trains* || to mark or discolor with spots || to blemish || to pick out beforehand, *spot the winner* || to catch sight of, *she spotted him across the room* || to notice, *did you spot the errors?* || (*mil.*) to discover the exact position of || to place (things or people) in scattered strategic positions || (*pop.*) to allow as a handicap, *I'll spot you three points* || *v.i.* to become stained or soiled || to cause a spot or spots **3.** *adj.* involving immediate payment, *spot cash* || made at random, *a spot check* || (of a broadcast or broadcasting) done from a local station || (*radio*) of an announcement made between programs || (*commerce*) ready for delivery, *spot wheat* [prob. M.Du. *spotte*]

spot ball (*billiards*) the cue ball, having a black spot on it

spot·less (spɒ́tlis) *adj.* (*rhet.*, of character) irreproachable || (of a thing) perfectly clean

spot·light (spɒ́tlait) *n.* a bright, narrow beam of light used e.g. to illuminate a small part of a theater stage || a lamp used to project such a beam || public attention **2.** *v.t.* to throw the beam of a spotlight upon || to draw attention to, *to spotlight a social problem*

Spots·wood (spɒ́tswud), Alexander (1676–1740), American colonial governor (1710–22) of Virginia. He established and promoted the state's iron industry at Germanna, a German settlement in Spotsylvania County, which is named after him

spot·ted (spɒ́tid) *adj.* marked with spots

spotted alfalfa aphid a destructive aphid (*Therioaphis maculata*), established in southern and southwestern U.S., that stunts and yellows plants, esp. alfalfa

spotted fever any of various febrile diseases, resulting in spots on the skin, esp. Rocky Mountain spotted fever or typhus

spotted sandpiper *Actitis macularia*, a common North American sandpiper whose underparts, in the adult, have black spots in the summer

spot·ter (spɒ́tər) *n.* someone who watches out for esp. airplanes or trains, in order to record information about their identification and movements etc. || a pilot, or the airplane he uses, sent up to locate enemy positions || (*mil.*) someone who finds the position of a military objective || a device attached to a train to enable defects in the track to be discovered

spot·ti·ness (spɒ́tinis) *n.* the state or quality of being spotty

spot·ty (spɒ́ti) *comp.* **spot·ti·er** *superl.* **spot·ti·est** *adj.* marked with spots || occurring in spots ||

---

irregular, uneven in quality, *a spotty performance*

spouse (spaus) *n.* (*old-fash. except in legal contexts*) a husband or wife [O.F. *spous*]

spout (spaut) **1.** *v.t.* to force (a fluid) out of an aperture under pressure, *the volcano spouted lava* || (*pop.*) to utter (esp. something declamatory) volubly and at some length and esp. without subtleties of expression || *v.i.* to gush (as if under pressure) || to talk or recite, esp. at length in a voluble and declamatory manner **2.** *n.* a tubular projection for conducting e.g. rain off a roof, or pouring e.g. tea from a teapot || a column of fluid ejected by pressure || a column of water raised by a whirlwind || the spiracle of a whale || that which the whale ejects from its spiracle || a trough for carrying and discharging grain, flour etc. **up the spout** (*pop.*) in an irremediable situation, beyond help [etym. doubtful]

sprag (spræg) **1.** *n.* a length of wood or metal used to support the roof of a mine gallery, or to lock the wheel of a vehicle || a projection that prevents the movement of platforms or pallets in the side guidance rails in an aircraft cabin **2.** *v.t. pres. part.* **sprag·ging** *past* and *past part.* **spragged** to support with sprags || to check the motion of with a sprag [etym. doubtful]

sprain (sprein) **1.** *v.t.* to injure (a muscle or joint) by a sudden violent twist **2.** *n.* the injury thus caused [etym. doubtful]

sprang alt. *past* of SPRING

sprat (spræt) *n. Clupea sprattus*, fam. *Clupeidae*, a small sea fish allied to the herring but much smaller, found in the Atlantic and the Mediterranean || a young herring [O.E. *sprot*]

sprawl (sprɔl) **1.** *v.i.* to slump with the limbs stretched out in an ungainly way || to spread out in a disorderly way, *London sprawls over miles of suburbs* || *v.t.* to stretch out (the limbs) in an ungainly and relaxed way || to cause to spread out in an irregular straggling way **2.** *n.* the posture of sprawling || unplanned development of open land, e.g., urban sprawl [O.E. *spreawlian*]

spray (sprei) **1.** *n.* liquid moving in the air in the form of fine drops that have been thrown, blown or projected under pressure || the stream of fine drops ejected by an atomizer || a device for ejecting such a stream || the liquid used in this device **2.** *v.t.* to shoot out or apply in the form of spray, *to spray lacquer on hair* || to treat or cover with a spray, *to spray hair with lacquer* || *v.i.* to shoot out a spray || to shoot out in a spray [M. Du. *sprayen* prob. fr. L.G.]

spray *n.* a small branch with attached leaves, flowers etc., used as a decoration || a bouquet in a linear, trailing arrangement || an ornament resembling either of these, *a spray of diamonds* [etym. doubtful]

spray dome the mount of water spray thrown into the air when the shock wave from an underwater nuclear detonation reaches the surface

sprayed printed circuit an electrical circuit applied by spraying metal particles on a base

spray gun a device using air pressure for spraying paint, insecticides etc.

spray steel steel treated with oxygen sprays to remove impurities, while the molten metal is being poured

spread (spred) **1.** *v. pres. part.* **spread·ing** *past* and *past part.* **spread** *v.t.* to open out more or less fully, *she spread the clothes to dry* || to display for sale, *the potter spread his wares* || (esp. with 'out') to cause to occupy more space by unfurling or smoothing out, *he spread out the newspaper* || to distribute in a layer, *he spread varnish on the wood* || to overlay (something) esp. extensively, *she spread the floor with rugs* || to distribute so as to cover, *to spread papers on a desk* || to prepare (a table) for a meal || to put (food) on a table, stretch (esp. limbs), *the eagle spread its wings* || to allow (e.g. energies, interests etc.) to range widely || to disseminate or cause to extend, esp. over a wide area or among many people, *to spread happiness* || to make known (news etc.) to many people || to cause or allow (e.g. work) to occupy longer time than normal || to share (something burdensome) || to push apart, esp. by bearing down with weight or force, to distend || (*printing*) to display (matter) widely across two columns or two pages || to fan out a hand (of cards) || to display (cards) face upwards || to expand, unfurl or set (sails) || *v.i.* to become widely distributed or scattered, *the dust spread over the books* || (esp. with 'out') to extend in length and breadth,

---

the woods spread out as far as the eye could see || (with a preposition) to flow outwards and cover, swamp, saturate etc., *the syrup spread over the table, the damp spread into the next room* || (of news, disease, emotion etc.) to become widely or more widely shared, known, suffered etc. || to increase esp. in growth or numbers, *weeds spread all over the garden* || to admit of being distributed in a layer, *it will spread better if it is warmed* || to move apart under the effect of force, *the chair legs spread under his weight* || (*pop.*) to grow stout **to spread oneself** to make a great display || to busy oneself with a variety of activities **2.** *n.* the act of spreading or being spread, *the spread of disease* || the quality of being spread out, *the spread of the city* || the distance, area or time over which something is spread || a soft food for spreading on bread etc. || a bedspread || (*pop.*) increase in girth, *middle-age spread* || (*pop.*) a lavish, sumptuous meal or feast || (*aeron.*) wingspan || (*printing*) two facing pages used for display || printed matter running across more than one column or across two pages || (*stock exchange*) an option in which put and call price differ || the difference between these prices [O.E. *sprǣdan*]

spread city a large urban-suburban area with uncontrolled, random zoning

spread eagle the representation of an eagle with legs and wings outspread, e.g. the emblem of the U.S.A.

spread-ea·gle (sprédíːgˈl) **1.** *adj.* like a spread eagle || of exaggerated, aggressive patriotic sentiment for the U.S.A. **2.** *v.t. pres. part.* **spread-ea·gling** *past* and *past part.* **spread-ea·gled** to straddle or extend over or across (something) so as to have the arms and legs stretched out or sprawling

spread end (*football*) *SPLIT END

Sprech·stim·me (ʃpréxstimə) *n.* (*German*) the portion of a musical presentation that is recited instead of sung

spree (spriː) *n.* an outing in pursuit of pleasure or fun and usually involving lavish spending or drinking, *a shopping spree* [etym. doubtful]

sprig (sprig) **1.** *n.* a short or pretty little spray from a shrub or tree, *a sprig of rosemary* || an ornament resembling this || a small headless nail **2.** *v.t. pres. part.* **sprig·ging** *past* and *past part.* **sprigged** to adorn with sprigs || to drive brads into [etym. doubtful]

spright·li·ness (spráitliːnis) *n.* the state or quality of being sprightly

spright·ly (spráitliː) *comp.* **spright·li·er** *superl.* **spright·li·est** *adj.* brisk and lively in movement or manner, often unexpectedly so [var. of SPRITE]

spring (spriŋ) **1.** *n.* the action of springing || the ability to spring || an instance of springing || in latitudes where the climate is seasonal, the season of the year following winter and preceding summer || a place where water or natural oil is forced out of the ground by its own pressure || resilience || a device of bent or coiled metal etc. e.g. in watches, cars or mattresses, which, because of its elasticity, can store and release energy when bent or twisted || an origin or cause of action || (*rhet.*) a beginning period characterized by growth and abundant life, *the spring of life* || a crack, split, warp etc., e.g. in a ship's mast or spar || (*archit.*) the point at which an arch or vault rises from its support **2.** *adj.* of, appearing in or planted in the spring of the year || supported on springs || coming from a spring [O.E.]

spring *pres. part.* **spring·ing** *past* **sprang** (spræŋ), **sprung** (sprʌŋ) *past part.* **sprung** *v.i.* to make a bound upwards or in a curve || to rise suddenly and rapidly from a sitting or lying position || to come, appear or arise suddenly and quickly || to move as a result of elasticity, to *spring back into position* || (*rhet.*) to be descended, *his family sprang from northern stock* || to originate, *the quarrel sprang from a casual remark* || to begin to grow or put out leaves etc., *the winter wheat is springing* || (of winds, storms etc., with 'up') to begin to blow, be felt or have effect || (of wood) to warp or split || (of a mine) to explode || to appear to have a strong upward movement, *the arch springs from that slender pillar* || *v.t.* to jump over or across, *the dog sprang the gate* || to release the spring of, *to spring a trap* || to produce unexpectedly, *to spring a surprise* || to cause (a mine) to explode || to develop (a leak) suddenly || to cause (wood) to warp or split || to cause (game) to leave cover [O.E. *springan*]

spring balance an instrument for measuring

CONCISE PRONUNCIATION KEY: **(a)** æ, c*a*t; ɑ, c*a*r; ɔ f*aw*n; ei, sn*a*ke. **(e)** e, h*e*n; iː, sh*ee*p; iə, d*ee*r; ɛə, b*ea*r. **(i)** i, f*i*sh; ai, t*i*ger; əː, b*i*rd. **(o)** o, *o*x; au, c*ow*; ou, g*oa*t; u, p*oo*r; ɔi, r*oy*al. **(u)** ʌ, d*u*ck; u, b*u*ll; uː, g*oo*se; ə, b*a*cillus; juː, c*u*be. x, lo*ch*; θ, *th*ink; ð, *b*o*th*er; z, *Z*en; ʒ, corsa*g*e; dʒ, sava*g*e; ŋ, ora*n*gutang; j, *y*ak; ʃ, *fi*sh; tʃ, fe*tch*; 'l, rabb*l*e; 'n, redd*en*. Complete pronunciation key appears inside front cover.

weight in terms of the compression or extension of a coiled spring

spring·board (spríŋbord, spríŋbourd) *n.* a resilient board which, by releasing the energy which has bent it, assists a jumper, diver etc. to gain height. The board is fixed at one end and acts about a fulcrum ‖ something used as a starting point for further progress, *the job was a springboard to one with more scope*

spring·bok (spríŋbok) *n. Antidorcas euchore,* fam. *Boridae,* a S. African antelope closely allied to the gazelle, noted for its high perpendicular leaps in play or when alarmed. The horns are lyre-shaped [Af. fr. *springen,* to spring + *bok,* antelope]

spring bolt a bolt released by pressure and closed by a spring when the pressure is removed

spring-clean (spríŋklí:n) 1. *n.* (*Br.*) a spring-cleaning 2. *v.t.* to do a spring-cleaning of ‖ *v.i.* to do a spring-cleaning

spring-clean·ing (spríŋklí:niŋ) *n.* a particularly thorough cleaning given to a house or room to remove the accumulation of winter dirt

springe (sprindʒ) 1. *n.* a noose or other snare used to catch small animals 2. *v. pres. part.* **spring·ing** (spríndʒiŋ) *past* and *past part.* **springed** *v.t.* to catch in this way ‖ *v.i.* to set springes [M.E., etym. doubtful]

spring·er (spríŋər) *n.* a springer spaniel ‖ (*archit.*) the first stone (voussoir) of an arch at the point where it springs

springer spaniel a medium-sized gundog of a breed used for flushing game. They are usually black and white

Spring·field (spríŋfí:ld) the capital (pop. 99,637) of Illinois. An important agricultural, wholesale and industrial center. Home and burial place of Abraham Lincoln

Springfield a city (pop. 152,319) in S.W. Massachusetts: electric equipment, arms, tools, gasoline pumps, pack machinery, magnetos, plastics. Springfield College (1885), American International College (1855)

spring·head (spríŋhed) *n.* a source, fountain

spring·i·ly (spríŋili:) *adv.* in a springy manner

spring·i·ness (spríŋi:nis) *n.* the state or quality of being springy

spring·like (spríŋlaik) *adj.* having the qualities of or associated with spring ‖ resembling a spring or its action

spring lock a lock which fastens automatically with a spring bolt

Springs (spriŋz) a market town (pop. 153,974) of S. central Transvaal, South Africa, in Witwatersrand: gold and coal mines

spring·tail (spríŋteil) *n.* a member of *Collembola,* an order of primitive, wingless arthropods, which leap by suddenly straightening the penultimate segment of their bodies

spring tide a tide, with a range greater than that of ordinary tides, occurring a day or two after the new and full moon in each month (cf. NEAP TIDE)

spring·tide (spríŋtaid) *n.* (*rhet.*) springtime

spring·time (spríŋtaim) *n.* the season of spring ‖ (*rhet.*) the early stage of something, having the qualities associated with this season, e.g. new life, strong growth etc.

spring washer (*engin.*) a washer constructed of spiral coils, used to absorb vibrations which might otherwise loosen a nut

spring·y (spríŋi:) *comp.* **spring·i·er** *superl.* **spring·i·est** *adj.* resilient esp. under pressure, e.g. of feet etc. ‖ having many springs

sprin·kle (spríŋk'l) 1. *v. pres. part.* **sprin·kling** *past* and *past part.* **sprin·kled** *v.t.* to scatter in separate drops or particles, *to sprinkle water on clothes for ironing* ‖ to cover with drops or particles, *to sprinkle a floor with sand* ‖ to place (esp. small quantities of something) at wide intervals ‖ (with 'with') to vary or intersperse (e.g. talk or a text), *his book is sprinkled with anecdotes* ‖ *v.i.* to scatter or fly about in small drops or particles ‖ to rain lightly 2. *n.* the act or result of sprinkling [late M.E.]

sprinkler system a system of pipes designed to sprinkle water e.g. on a lawn, or on flying dust ‖ a fire protection device consisting of a system of pipes carrying water or some other extinguishing fluid. The pipes are designed to discharge automatically under the effect of the heat of fire

sprin·kling (spríŋkliŋ) *n.* a small quantity or number distributed here and there ‖ a small quantity falling, or made to fall, in little drops or scatterings

sprint (sprint) 1. *v.i.* to run for a short distance at the greatest speed of which one is capable ‖ *v.t.* to traverse in this way 2. *n.* a run of this kind, e.g. at the end of a distance race ‖ a short-distance race ‖ a horse race under one mile ‖ a short period of intensive activity [early Scand.]

Sprint *n.* (*mil.*) a high-acceleration, U.S. nuclear surface-to-air guided missile formerly deployed as part of the Safeguard ballistic missile system

sprint car (*sports*) a medium-size car with a large-car engine run in dirt track races

sprit (sprit) *n.* a short pole set from the mast to the further and upper corner of a sail for extending and raising it ‖ a bowsprit [O.E. *sprēot,* a spear or pole]

sprite (sprait) *n.* a fairy, an elf [fr. O.F. *esprit* or *esperit,* spirit]

sprit·sail (spríts'l) *n.* a sail extended by a sprit

sprock·et (sprókit) *n.* a tooth on a wheel's rim, engaging with the links of a chain ‖ a sprocket wheel ‖ a triangular piece of wood fastened to the upper surface of a rafter to change the angle of the eaves [etym. doubtful]

sprocket wheel a wheel with sprockets on it, such as that which engages with the chain of a bicycle

sprout (spraut) 1. *v.i.* (of a plant, shrub etc.) to put out young growth, *after the rain the trees sprouted* ‖ (of a person) to begin to be noticeably tall ‖ to germinate ‖ *v.t.* to grow (something new), *the tree sprouted leaves* ‖ to let (e.g. a moustache) grow ‖ to support (something that could be likened to a sprout), *every roof now sprouts an antenna* 2. *n.* a shoot on a plant ‖ (*pl.*) Brussels sprouts ‖ a new growth from a bud, seed etc. [O.E. *sprūtan*]

sprouting broccoli *Brassica oleracea italica,* fam. *Cruciferae,* a cauliflower bearing florets at the ends of branches which are cut for food while still tight and purplish or green

Spru·ance (sprú:əns), Raymond Ames (1886–1969), the youngest full admiral (at age 57) in U.S. naval history and probably the greatest U.S. naval tactician in the 2nd world war. As commander of a U.S. Navy task force, he secured the U.S. victory at Midway (1942)

spruce (spru:s) 1. *adj.* very neat, clean, tidy ‖ (of dress and appearance) trim 2. *v.t. pres. part.* **spruc·ing** *past* and *past part.* **spruced** (with 'up') to make very neat, tidy or trim ‖ *v.i.* (with 'up') to make oneself neat and trim [altered fr. *Pruce,* Prussia in the phrase *spruce leather*]

spruce *n.* a member of *Picea,* fam. *Pinaceae,* a genus of quick-growing conifers, with the branches close together and forming a conical head ‖ their light but strong wood [altered fr. *Pruce,* Prussia]

spruce beer a beverage made by fermenting with yeast a mixture of water, spruce leaves, spruce twigs and sugar

sprue (spru:) *n.* a channel or hole through which molten metal etc. is poured into a mold ‖ the waste metal filling this hole [etym. doubtful]

sprue *n.* a chronic disease of the digestive system occurring chiefly in visitors to certain tropical or subtropical areas. It is manifested by diarrhea, loss of weight, appetite and energy, and changes in the tongue and skin [fr. Du. *spruw*]

sprung alt. *past* and the *past part.* of SPRING

sprung rhythm a poetic rhythm (*HOPKINS) with origins traceable to Old English verse and nursery rhymes. Each metrical foot consists of a single stress, which can stand either alone or be placed before a number of unstressed syllables. Usually the feet contain from one to four syllables. They are assumed to be equal in strength and length, their seeming inequality being compensated by pause or emphasis. Scansion runs without break from beginning to end of the stanza [invented by G. M. HOPKINS]

spry (sprai) *comp.* **spry·er, spri·er** *superl.* **spry·est, spri·est** *adj.* (esp. of old people) quick in movement and in thought [etym. doubtful]

spud (spʌd) 1. *n.* a spade with a small blade, or sometimes with prongs, used for digging up big-rooted weeds ‖ (*pop.*) a potato 2. *v.t. pres. part.* **spud·ding** *past* and *past part.* **spud·ded** to dig up with a spud [prob. fr. O.N.]

spume (spju:m) 1. *n.* a mass of bubbles formed from a liquid 2. *v. pres. part.* **spum·ing** *past* and *past part.* **spumed** (esp. with 'out') to foam or discharge bubbles ‖ *v.t.* (esp. with 'out') to discharge (something) like foam [fr. O.F. *espume* or L. *spuma,* foam]

spu·mes·cence (spju:més'ns) *n.* the state or quality of being spumous

spu·mes·cent (spju:més'nt) *adj.* spumous

spu·mous (spjú:məs) *adj.* of, like or covered with spume

spum·y (spjú:mi:) *comp.* **spum·i·er** *superl.* **spum·i·est** *adj.* spumous

spun *past* and *past part.* of SPIN

spun glass fiber glass

spunk (spʌŋk) *n.* (*pop.*) spirited courage ‖ punk [etym. doubtful]

spunk·i·ly (spʌŋkili:) *adv.* (*pop.*) in a spunky manner

spunk·i·ness (spʌŋki:nis) *n.* the state or quality of being spunky

spunk·y (spʌŋki:) *comp.* **spunk·i·er** *superl.* **spunk·i·est** *adj.* (*pop.*) courageous, having spirit

spun silk yarn or cloth made from waste silk sometimes mixed with cotton

spun yarn (*naut.*) a line or rope made of two or more twisted rope yarns

spur (spə:r) 1. *n.* a device sometimes worn on the heel of a riding boot, with a point or spiked wheel (rowel) for pressing into a horse's flanks to force its pace ‖ a projection bearing some resemblance to this, e.g. a process on the legs of a cock ‖ a ridge projecting from a mountain ‖ the largest thrust of a tree ‖ a wall connecting a rampart with an interior work ‖ a climbing iron ‖ (*bot.*) a tubelike structure formed by the extension of a petal or sepal, e.g. in larkspur ‖ a metal device fastened to the leg of a gamecock for fighting ‖ a mental stimulus which results in a greater effort being made, *the spur of ambition* ‖ a spur track **on the spur of the moment** impulsively, without previous thought or plans **to win one's spurs** (*rhet.*) to secure recognition of one's work 2. *v. pres. part.* **spur·ring** *past* and *past part.* **spurred** *v.t.* to use a spur on (a horse) ‖ to furnish with spurs ‖ to cause to make a great effort, *ambition spurred him on* ‖ *v.i.* to spur a horse [O.E. *spora, spura*]

spurge (spə:rdʒ) *n.* a member of *Euphorbia,* fam. *Euphorbiaceae,* a genus of some 1,600 species of plants or bushes of tropical or temperate regions, yielding a bitter, milky juice. The flowers are very small, with one male and several females within a cup-shaped involucre [fr. O.F. *espurge*]

spur gear a wheel with teeth parallel to the axle

spurge laurel a member of *Daphne,* fam. *Thymelaeaceae,* a genus of Eurasian shrubs bearing yellow flowers before leafing

spu·ri·ous (spjúəri:əs) *adj.* having the appearance of being genuine, but without being so ‖ (*biol.*) like in appearance but morphologically or pathologically false ‖ (*law*) illegitimate, bastard [fr. L. *spurius*]

spurn (spə:rn) *v.t.* to reject with contempt [O.E. *spurnan*]

spur·ri·er (spé:ri:ər, spʌri:ər) *n.* a person who makes spurs

Spurs, Battle of the a battle (1302) in which a Flemish army defeated the French army of Philippe IV ‖ a battle (1513) in which an army under Henry VIII of England and the Emperor Maximilian I defeated the army of Louis XII of France

spurt, spirt (spə:rt) 1. *v.i.* (of a fluid) to shoot out suddenly in a jet, but not in great volume ‖ (of a person) to make a sudden, violent effort, esp. in a race ‖ *v.t.* to cause to rush out suddenly in a jet 2. *n.* a sudden shooting out of liquid in a jet ‖ a sudden short burst of activity or energy [etym. doubtful]

spur track a railroad track, or branch line, over which there is only irregular traffic

spur wheel a spur gear

sput·nik (spútnik) *n.* the first of the artificial satellites put in orbit by the U.S.S.R. [Russ.]

sput·ter (spʌtər) 1. *v.i.* to splutter ‖ *v.t.* to splutter ‖ (*phys.*) to deposit a very thin film of metal on (a surface) 2. *n.* a sputtering ‖ the sound of sputtering ‖ rapid, confused speech [imit.]

spu·tum (spjú:təm) *pl.* **spu·ta** (spjú:tə), **spu·tums** *n.* material expelled from the respiratory passages by clearing the throat, or by coughing [L.=spit]

spy (spai) *pl.* **spies** *n.* a person instructed to act secretly in gathering information, by observation or otherwise, about the actions, circumstances and intentions of an enemy, a potential enemy or rival, or a criminal, *a police spy* ‖ someone who keeps secret, close watch on others [fr. O.F. *espie*]

spy *pres. part.* **spy·ing** *past* and *past part.* **spied**

CONCISE PRONUNCIATION KEY: (**a**) æ, c*a*t; ɑ, c*a*r; ɔ f*aw*n; ei, sn*a*ke. (**e**) e, h*e*n; i:, sh*ee*p; iə, d*ee*r; ɛə, b*ea*r. (**i**) i, f*i*sh; ai, t*i*ger; ə:, b*i*rd. (**o**) o, *o*x; au, c*ow*; ou, g*oa*t; u, p*oo*r; ɔi, r*oy*al. (**u**) ʌ, d*u*ck; u, b*u*ll; u:, g*oo*se; ə, b*a*cillus; ju:, c*u*be. x, lo*ch*; θ, *th*ink; ð, *b*other; z, *Z*en; ʒ, cor*s*age. dʒ, sava*g*e; ŋ, ora*n*gutang; j, *y*ak; ʃ, *fi*sh; tʃ, fe*tch*; 'l, rabb*le*; 'n, redd*en*. Complete pronunciation key appears inside front cover.

v.t. to see, catch sight of ‖ (with 'out') to make a secret investigation of, *to spy out the terrain* ‖ (with 'on') to watch the activities in the manner of a spy, *to spy on one's neighbors* ‖ *v.i.* to act as a spy [fr. O.F. *espier*]

spy·glass (spáiglæs, spáiglɑs) *n.* a portable terrestrial telescope

sq. square

squab (skwɒb) **1.** *adj.* fat and dumpy ‖ unfledged **2.** *n.* a short, fat person ‖ an unfledged pigeon ‖ a thick cushion [etym. doubtful]

squab·ble (skwɒb'l) **1.** *v. pres. part.* **squab·bling** *past* and *past part.* **squab·bled** *v.i.* to engage in a noisy but not very serious argument or quarrel ‖ *v.t.* (*printing*) to disarrange (type that has been set) **2.** *n.* a noisy but not serious quarrel or argument [imit.]

squab·by (skwɒbi:) *comp.* **squab·bi·er** *superl.* **squab·bi·est** *adj.* short and fat, squab

squad (skwɒd) *n.* a small number of men organized to act together in work or in a military maneuver ‖ a number of men organized to act together, e.g. an athletic team [fr. F. *escouade*]

squad car a police patrol car equipped with radio communication

squad·ron (skwɒdrən) *n.* an air force unit between group and flight ‖ a unit of cavalry or of mechanized troops, tanks etc. ‖ a unit of battleships, varying in size and composition [fr. Ital. *squadrone*]

squadron leader an officer in the British Royal Air Force ranking below a wing commander and above a flight lieutenant

squal·id (skwɒlid) *adj.* repellently filthy, esp. because of neglect, *a squalid slum* ‖ wretched and often morally degrading, *squalid poverty* [fr. L. *squalidus*]

squall (skwɔl) **1.** *v.i.* (esp. of babies or young children) to cry loudly and discordantly ‖ to blow in a squall ‖ *v.t.* to utter in this way **2.** *n.* a sudden high wind, esp. when accompanied by rain, snow, hail etc. ‖ a noisy bout of temper, tearful screaming etc. **squal·ly** *adj.* characterized by squalls ‖ stormy [prob. imit.]

squal·or (skwɒlər) *n.* the state or quality of being squalid [L. fr. *squalere*, to be dry, rough, dirty]

squa·ma (skwéimə) *pl.* **squa·mae** (skwéimi:) *n.* (*biol.*) a scale, or feather or bony structure resembling a scale [L.=scale]

squa·mate (skwéimeit) *adj.* scaly, covered with scales [fr. L. *squamatus*]

squa·ma·tion (skwəméiʃən) *n.* the condition of being squamate ‖ arrangement of scales [fr. SQUAMA]

squa·mo·sal (skwəmóus'l) **1.** *n.* a membrane bone forming part of the posterior sidewall of the skull of many vertebrates **2.** *adj.* of this membrane bone ‖ squamous

squa·mose (skwéimous) *adj.* squamous

squa·mous (skwéimous) *adj.* covered with scales ‖ like scales ‖ (*anat.*) of the thin upper anterior portion of the temporal bone [fr. L. *squamosus*]

squan·der (skwɒndər) *v.t.* to use up unwisely and to no useful purpose, *to squander wealth* [etym. doubtful]

square (skwɛər) *pres. part.* **squar·ing** *past* and *past part.* **squared** *v.t.* to make square ‖ to cause to be at right angles ‖ to check for evenness or straightness ‖ to bring near the form of a right angle, *square your shoulders* ‖ to cause to conform, make consistent ‖ (esp. with 'off') to mark out in squares ‖ to bring into a state of even balance, *to square accounts* ‖ to pay (a bill) ‖ (*pop.*) to bribe ‖ (*math.*) to multiply (a number or quantity) by itself ‖ (*golf* etc.) to make the score in (a match) equal ‖ *v.i.* (with 'with') to agree or conform exactly, *his version does not square with theirs* ‖ (*golf* etc.) to even scores **to square the circle** to find a square equal in area to a given circle (an impossible geometrical calculation) ‖ to try to do the impossible **to square up** to move up (to someone) in a fighting posture ‖ to pay debts or bills [fr. O.F. *esquarrer*]

square 1. *adj.* having the shape of a square ‖ being at right angles or at a right angle ‖ broad in relation to height, *a square build* ‖ straight rather than curved, *a square jaw* ‖ unequivocal, *a square statement* ‖ leaving no balance ‖ in perfect adjustment, arranged in good order ‖ converted from linear to area measurement, *a square inch* ‖ being of a specified length in each of two directions at right angles, *10 meters square* ‖ (*naut.*) at right angles to the keel and mast **all square** having scored the same num-

ber of points in a game or completed a bargain of equal value to both parties **2.** *adv.* frankly, honestly, *he came square out with the facts* ‖ directly, *square in the middle of the town* ‖ so as to be in a square form, *fold the tea towels square* [fr. O.F. *esquarre*]

square *n.* a plane figure having four equal rectilinear sides, each adjacent pair forming a right angle ‖ anything approximating to this shape ‖ an instrument for determining and testing right angles ‖ a number which is the product of another number multiplied by itself, *9 is the square of 3* ‖ an open space surrounded by houses, esp. at the intersection of several streets, roughly square in shape and often laid out ornamentally ‖ (*hist.*) a body of troops drawn up in the form of a rectangle ‖ the unopened flower of the cotton plant and the bracts which enclose it ‖ (*pop.*) a person who is ignorant of the latest in slang, styles, fads etc. [fr. O.F. *esquire, esquare*]

square bracket (esp. *Br.*) one of a pair of punctuation marks [ ] very often used in texts to enclose either direct quotation or matter supplementary or extraneous to the text, as in U[nited] N[ations]

square dance a dance typically for four couples in which the dancers arrange themselves in a given form, e.g. a square, as in a quadrille

square deal (*pop.*) a transaction or treatment that is fair and honest

square knot a knot comprising opposite loops, each enclosing the parallel sides of the other

square leg (*cricket*) a position along a direction at right angles to the pitch and to the left of a right-handed batsman or right of one who is left-handed ‖ the fielder who has this position

square meal a satisfying meal

square measure a system of units of area (*MEASURES AND WEIGHTS)

square one the starting point

square out (*football*) a forward-pass play in which the receiver makes a short right angle after his initial run down the field

square piano an early oblong form of piano, like a box in shape, strung horizontally

square-rigged (skwɛ́ərríg'd) *adj.* of a sailing vessel the chief sails of which extend by horizontal yards suspended from the middle (cf. FORE-AND-AFT)

square root (*math.*) a quantity which, multiplied by itself, is equal to a given number, *3 is the square root of 9*

square sail (*naut.*) a rectangular sail set on a yard slung across the vessel

square shooter (*pop.*) a person who can be relied upon to be fair and honest

squar·rose (skwǽrous, skwɔ́rous) *adj.* (*biol.*) rough-surfaced with scales or processes ‖ (of leaves) stiff and crowded together [fr. L. *squarrosus*, scurfy, scabby]

squash (skwɒʃ, skwɔʃ) *n.* a member of *Cucurbita*, fam. *Cucurbitaceae*, a genus of gourd plants grown for their fruit. This is eaten baked, boiled or mashed as a vegetable, or fed to livestock ‖ one of these fruits [abbr. of Narragansett *asquutasquash*]

squash 1. *v.t.* to press into a shapeless state ‖ (with 'in') to force by pressure into too small a space, *we might squash five people into the back seat* ‖ (*pop.*) to suppress, *to squash a rebellion* ‖ (*pop.*) to reduce (a person) to silence by making a remark which belittles him or to which there is no possible answer ‖ *v.i.* to become pressed into a shapeless state ‖ (with 'into') to push and make oneself small enough to enter, *she squashed into the crowded train* **2.** *n.* (*Br.*) a beverage partly composed of fruit juice ‖ a closely packed crowd ‖ a game for two or four players played in a four-walled court with a special racket and soft ball. The ball is made to rebound off the front wall against any of the others. It is in play so long as it hits the front wall above the line drawn on this and does not hit the floor ‖ a squashing or the fact of being squashed ‖ the sound made by a soft body which collapses into a shapeless mass when it hits a hard surface **3.** *adv.* with the sound of a squash ‖ so as to squash [fr. O.F. *esquasser, esquacer*]

squash·i·ly (skwɒ́ʃili:, skwɔ́ʃili:) *adv.* in a squashy way

squash·i·ness (skwɒ́ʃi:nis, skwɔ́ʃi:nis) *n.* the state or quality of being squashy

squash racquets, squash rackets the game of squash, developed from the game of racquets

squash·y (skwɒ́ʃi:, skwɔ́ʃi:) *comp.* **squash·i·er** *superl.* **squash·i·est** *adj.* easily squashed ‖ looking squashed ‖ mushy

squat (skwɒt) **1.** *v. pres. part.* **squat·ting** *past* and *past part.* **squat·ted** *v.i.* to lower the body into a sitting posture, or sustain this posture, supporting it by the thigh muscles only ‖ (of animals) to keep as close to the ground as possible so as to escape observation ‖ to settle on land or in premises without any legal right to do so ‖ to settle on public land under government regulation in order to get a title to it ‖ *v.t. refl.* to cause (oneself) to assume a squatting position **2.** *adj.* short and thick ‖ being in a squatting position **3.** *n.* the posture of squatting [fr. O.F. *esquatir, esquater*, to beat or press down]

squat·ter (skwɒ́tər) *n.* a settler occupying government land in order to acquire legal title to it ‖ a person who occupies (esp. premises) without legal title ‖ (*Austral.*) a large-scale sheep farmer ‖ (*Austral.*) someone occupying an area of grazing land as a crown tenant

squat·ty (skwɒ́ti:) *comp.* **squat·ti·er** *superl.* **squat·ti·est** *adj.* dumpy

squaw (skwɔ) *n.* a North American Indian woman or wife [Narragansett *squaws*, Massachusetts *squa*, woman]

squawk (skwɔk) **1.** *v.i.* (esp. of birds) to utter a short, harsh, loud cry or cries, usually expressing angry complaint **2.** *n.* the sound of squawking ‖ *Nycticorax nycticorax hoactli*, a North American heron [imit.]

squawk standby (*mil.*) a code meaning *Switch identification friend or foe master control to 'standby' position*. Cf STOP SQUAWK

squeak (skwi:k) **1.** *v.i.* (of mice etc.) to utter a squeak or squeaks ‖ to make a sound like this, *the door squeaked on its hinges* ‖ (with 'past', 'by', 'through', 'into' etc.) to get by with a narrow margin, *he squeaked past with an inch to spare* ‖ (*pop.*) to tell the secrets one knows under fear of punishment ‖ *v.t.* to utter with a squeak **2.** *n.* a high-pitched, short cry of little volume *NARROW SQUEAK **squéak·i·ly** *adv.* **squéak·i·ness** *n.* **squeak·y** *comp.* **squeak·i·er** *superl.* **squeak·i·est** *adj.* squeaking [imit.]

squeal (skwi:l) **1.** *n.* a prolonged, very shrill cry, uttered under intense emotional stress or excitement, fear etc. **2.** *v.i.* to utter this cry ‖ (*pop.*) to become an informer [imit.]

squeam·ish (skwí:miʃ) *adj.* affected with nausea ‖ a little too easily disgusted or shocked ‖ excessively scrupulous [var. of older *squaymes, squemes, squeamous, squeamish*]

squee·gee (skwí:dʒi:) **1.** *n.* a strip of rubber mounted transversely at the end of a long handle, like a blade, used to sweep a surface clear of water ‖ (*photog.*) a rubber roller used to press a print flat on a mount **2.** *v.t. pres. part.* **squee·gee·ing** *past* and *past part.* **squee·geed** to sweep, smooth out etc. with a squeegee [etym. doubtful]

squeeze (skwi:z) **1.** *v. pres. part.* **squeez·ing** *past* and *past part.* **squeezed** *v.t.* to exert pressure on, esp. with opposite pressures, *to squeeze someone's hand* ‖ to force into a place by pressing, *she squeezed an extra shirt into his suitcase* ‖ to cause (people) to occupy less space than is comfortable, *we squeezed 20 people into our tiny room* ‖ to provide time or space for (something or someone) that cannot easily be fitted in, *the doctor squeezed him in before a patient who arrived late* ‖ to press (a fruit) so as to expel the juice ‖ to force (the juice) out of a fruit by pressing ‖ to exert financial or other pressure on (a person) in order to make him act in a certain way ‖ to get by force or unfair means ‖ to take an impression of (something) by pressing between waxed or wetted sheets of paper ‖ (*bridge*) to make (a player) unguard a suit as a result of discarding ‖ to hug ‖ *v.i.* to exert pressure (esp. two opposite pressures) ‖ to force one's way by compressing oneself, *he squeezed through the narrow gap* **2.** *n.* a squeezing or being squeezed ‖ a hug ‖ (*pop.*) enforced payment, or the force used to secure payment, *to put the squeeze on somebody* ‖ (*politics*) a financial policy designed to reduce the volume of personal or corporate expenditure ‖ a small quantity of something (e.g. juice) obtained by pressing ‖ (*bridge*) a technique of play which forces an opponent to give up a valuable card ‖ a papier mâché or wax mold [perh. an intensive of obs. *quease*, to press]

squelch (skweltʃ) **1.** *v.i.* to make a sucking sound with one's boots or shoes as one walks through mud, wet snow etc. or as one walks in wet boots or shoes ‖ *v.t.* to tread heavily on (mud, wet snow etc.) and make this sound ‖ to crush with a very firm refusal or rebuke etc. **2.** *n.* the sucking sound made when one walks over soft wet ground or in wet boots etc. ‖ a silencing remark [imit.]

squib (skwib) *n.* a small firework that burns with a hissing noise before exploding ‖ a witty attack in writing or speech **a damp squib** (*Br.*) such an attack which falls flat [prob. imit.]

squid (skwid) *pl.* **squid, squids** *n.* a member of various genera of marine cephalopod mollusks having a long, tapered body, two caudal fins, ten arms and an internal shell. Squids range greatly in size, are widely distributed and are used for food and as fish bait [etym. doubtful]

SQUID (*electr. acronym*) for superconducting quantum interference device, a superconductor ring connecting two or several junctions used in measuring small electric currents and magnetic fields

squig·gle (skwíg'l) 1. *v.i. pres. part.* **squig·gling** *past* and *past part.* **squig·gled** to writhe and squirm ‖ to progress in a confined area by making writhing, squirming movements 2. *n.* a mark resembling the shape of a squiggling worm [imit. or fr. SQUIRM+WRIGGLE]

squill (skwil) *n. Urginea maritima*, fam. *Liliaceae*, a bulbous plant found in the Mediterranean area. The bulb of the white variety is used as a diuretic and heart stimulant, and that of the red variety as a raticide [fr. L. *squilla* fr. Gk]

squinch (skwintʃ) *n.* an arch across the internal angle of a square tower, serving to support an octagonal spire etc. [fr. earlier *scunch* fr. O.F.]

squint (skwint) 1. *v.i.* to be crosseyed ‖ to look out of the corner of the eye ‖ to look through almost closed eyelids ‖ *v.t.* to narrow (one's eyes), e.g. in a look of suspicion 2. *n.* strabismus, the condition causing squinting ‖ a look out of the corner of the eye ‖ (*pop.*) a rapid glance, *to have a squint at something* ‖ a hole in the wall or pillar of a church giving an oblique view of the altar 3. *adj.* (of the eyes) affected with strabismus ‖ (of a look) out of the corner of the eye, *oblique* [shortened fr. ASQUINT]

squire (skwáiər) 1. *n.* (in England) a title of respect for a country gentleman, esp. the principal, local, resident landowner ‖ (*hist.*) the wellborn personal attendant of a knight 2. *v. pres. part.* **squir·ing** *past* and *past part.* **squired** to accompany (a girl), esp. to a dance ‖ (*hist.*) to be squire to [fr. O.F. *esquier*]

squire·ar·chy (skwáiərɑrki:) *pl.* **squire·ar·chies** *n.* (esp. *Br. hist.*) rule by the landed gentry or the landed gentry themselves, esp. with respect to their political influence

squirm (skwəːrm) 1. *v.i.* to contort the body in little writhing movements ‖ (with 'along') to proceed in this manner ‖ to have feelings of shame and discomfort 2. *n.* the act of squirming ‖ (*naut.*) a twist in a rope **squirm·y** *comp.* **squirm·i·er** *superl.* **squirm·i·est** *adj.* [prob. imit.]

squir·rel (skwə́ːrəl, skwʌ́rəl, esp. *Br.* skwírəl) *n.* a widely distributed rodent mammal of fam. *Sciuridae*, esp. *Sciurus vulgaris*, the red squirrel, and *S. carolinensis*, the gray squirrel. They live in trees, have lithe bodies, strong hind limbs and bushy tails. They feed mainly on nuts and seeds, and make stores of food. Their average size is around 10-12 ins, excluding the tail (*GROUND SQUIRREL, *FLYING SQUIRREL) [fr. A.F. *esquirel*, O.F. *esquireul* fr. L. fr. Gk]

squirt (skwəːrt) 1. *v.t.* to shoot a thin stream of (fluid) from a small orifice, *the pipe squirted water* ‖ to wet with a liquid or cover or hit with a fluid shot in this way, *the pipe squirted him as he passed* ‖ *v.i.* to be forced out in this way, *the beer squirted from the barrel* ‖ to eject liquid in a thin stream from a small orifice, *the barrel squirted in his face* 2. *n.* the act or an instance of squirting ‖ a thin stream of fluid forced out under pressure ‖ a device for squirting out a liquid ‖ (*pop.*) a pretentious boy or man whom one considers insignificant [prob. imit.]

squirting cucumber *Ecballium elaterium*, fam. *Cucurbitaceae*, a Mediterranean plant. When ripe, the long fruit ejects its seeds mixed in watery fluid from one end

SRAM (*mil. acronym*) for short-range, solid-propellant, air-to-surface attack missile

Sri Lanka, formerly Ceylon, an independent state (area 25,332 sq. miles, pop. 12,240,000) in S. Asia, an island in the Indian Ocean. Capital: Colombo. Race: 74% Sinhalese, and minorities of Tamils and Tamil-speaking Muslims or Moors. Languages: Sinhalese (official) and Tamil. Religion: 78% Hinayana Buddhist, 18% Hindu, smaller Christian and Moslem minori-

ties. The land is 20% forest. The north is flat, with a swampy coast. The south is mountainous (highest point Mt Pidurutalagala, 8,297 ft). The climate is tropical with southwest monsoons in summer and northeast monsoons in winter. Rainfall: 25-50 ins in the north and east, 75-200 ins in the center and southwest. Average temperatures (F.): 80° in the lowlands (with little seasonal variation), 54° (Jan.) and 62° (May) in the highlands. Livestock: cattle, water buffaloes, goats. Agricultural products: rice, tea, coconuts, rubber. Mineral resources: graphite, iron. Exports: tea, rubber, coconuts. Imports: rice, textiles, petroleum products, machinery, vehicles, sugar. University of Ceylon (1942) and two other universities. Monetary unit: rupee (100 cents). HISTORY. The Sinhalese migrated from S. India to Ceylon about the 5th c. B.C. Ceylon became the center of Buddhist civilization (3rd c. B.C.). Arabs introduced Mohammedanism (8th c. A.D.) and controlled trade until the arrival of the Portuguese (1505). The Dutch superseded the Portuguese (1638) but were overthrown by the British (1796). Ceylon was annexed to the East India Co. (1796-1802), became a British Crown Colony (1802) and an independent member of the Commonwealth (1948). In 1972 it was renamed Sri Lanka (beautiful island). Conflict between the majority Sinhalese, who controlled the government after independence and the Tamils, who had held most civil service and professional positions under the British, turned increasingly violent after 1983. Militant Tamils demanded a separate Tamil state in the north and east, where Tamils predominate. The continuing conflict disrupted the country's economy, and efforts to end the violence by granting the Tamils greater autonomy made little progress

Srin·a·gar (srínəgɑ́r) the summer capital (pop. 531,094) of Jammu and Kashmir (*KASHMIR), on both sides of the Jhelum in the Vale of Kashmir. Handicraft products: carpets, silver, copperware. Industry: textiles

sRNA transfer (*physiol.*) a ribonucleic acid that combines with some amino acids and messenger RNA in protein synthesis *also* (soluble) RNA *Cf* MESSENGER RNA

SR-71 (*mil.*) U.S. strategic reconnaissance plane (succeeding U-2) for long-range (3,000-mi) high-altitude (80,000 feet) flight, with speed of Mach 3; operative in 1981

SS-8 *GECKO

SS-18 U.S.S.R. ICBM, capable of delivering ten warheads

SS-15 *SCROOGE

SS-5 *GAMMON, KELT

SS-4 *GANEF, KITCHEN

SS-14 *SCAPEGOAT

SSN-18 U.S.S.R. submarine-launched, liquid-propellant, ballistic missile with a 7,500-km range; operational since 1975

SSN-4 (*mil.*) U.S.S.R. surface-to-surface and surface-to-air missile

SS-9 *GASKIN

SS-19 (*mil.*) U.S.S.R. intercontinental MIRV missile

SSN-X-17 (*mil.*) U.S.S.R. submarine-launched, solid-propellant ballistic missile with postboost vehicle, MIRV capability; operational in mid-1970s

SSPE (*med. abbr.*) for subacute sclerosis panencephalitis, a fatal brain disorder caused by dormant measles virus

SS-7 (*mil.*) *GRAIL, KERRY

SS-17 (*mil.*) U.S.S.R. missile with a 5-mi range

SS-6 (*mil.*) *GAINFUL, KINGFISH

SS-16 (*mil.*) U.S.S.R. ICBM that the U.S.S.R. agreed not to deploy during the life of the SALT I treaty

SST (*abbr.*) for supersonic transport

SS-10 (*mil.*) U.S.S.R. low-level air-defense weapon

SS-20 (*mil.*) U.S.S.R. 2 stage, solid-fuel ballistic missile launched from a tracked transport, in any of three versions: 1, a 1.5 megaton bomb with range of 3,500 mi., 2, a 50-kiloton warhead with range of 4,500, 3, with three individually targeted warheads

SS-22 (*mil.*) U.S.S.R. strategic solid-fuel, nuclear missile under development with 5,000-mi range

St common nouns, proper names and place-names beginning thus are listed at 'Saint'. (*The saints themselves are listed at 'John', 'Peter' etc.*)

stab (stæb) 1. *v. pres. part.* **stab·bing** *past* and

past part. **stabbed** *v.t.* to wound by piercing with a knife or other pointed weapon held in the hand ‖ to thrust (a knife etc.) in a specified way, direction etc. ‖ to inflict sharp emotional pain on ‖ *v.i.* to make a thrust or wound with or as if with a dagger, knife etc. 2. *n.* a thrust made with or as if with a pointed weapon ‖ a wound inflicted in this way ‖ (*pop.*, usually with 'at') an attempt to do something, *a stab at finding the answer* ‖ a sudden sensation of pain, anguish, envy etc. **a stab in the back** a treacherous attack **a stab in the dark** a random guess [of Scot. origin]

stab·al·loy (stǽbælɔi) *n.* (*mil.*) a metal alloy made from high-density depleted uranium with titanium and molybdenum for use in kinetic energy penetrators for armor-piercing munitions

Sta·bat Ma·ter (stɑ́bɑtmɑ́tər) a 13th-c. Latin hymn describing the sorrows of the mother of Christ at the Crucifixion ‖ a musical setting of this hymn [L. *stabat mater dolorosa*, the mother stood sorrowing (the opening words)]

Stabex export stabilization scheme created by the 1975 Rome Convention and signed by the Common Market and the 46 developing countries, to compensate a developing country when its export earnings in 18 specific commodities for one year fall below its average earnings of the previous five years, with funds contributed by Common Market members

sta·bile 1. (stéibil, *Br.* esp. stéibail) *adj.* stationary ‖ not fluctuating ‖ (*chem.*) resisting decomposition 2. (stéibi:l, *Br.* esp. stéibail) *n.* an abstract sculpture e.g. of metal (*CALDER, cf. MOBILE), none of the parts being articulated [fr. L. *stabilis*]

sta·bil·i·ty (stəbíliti:) *pl.* **sta·bil·i·ties** *n.* the quality or state of being stable ‖ a vow, made by certain monks, to remain in the same monastery for life [M.E. *stablete* fr. O.F. *stableté, estableté*]

stability analysis (*economics*) study of economic equilibrium between supply and demand

sta·bi·li·za·tion (steibəlizéiʃən) *n.* a stabilizing or being stabilized

sta·bi·lize (stéibəlaiz) *pres. part.* **sta·bi·liz·ing** *past* and *past part.* **sta·bi·lized** *v.t.* to render stable ‖ to prevent from changing, *to stabilize the cost of living* ‖ to equip (a vessel, aircraft etc.) with a stabilizer **sta·bi·liz·er** *n.* something that stabilizes, esp. a gyroscopic device to maintain steadiness in a vessel at sea [fr. F. *stabiliser* fr. L. *stabilis*]

sta·ble (stéib'l) 1. *n.* (often *pl.*) a building in which horses are housed, or a similar building for cattle ‖ a group of horses kept in such a building ‖ a group of racehorses belonging to a particular owner ‖ an establishment for the training of racehorses, or the owners and personnel of such an establishment 2. *v.t. pres. part.* **sta·bling** *past* and *past part.* **sta·bled** to put or keep (a horse etc.) in a stable [O.F. *estable*]

stable *adj.* remaining or able to remain unchanged in form, structure, character etc. under conditions tending to cause such change ‖ able to return to its original condition or recover its equilibrium after being slightly displaced ‖ permanent, enduring ‖ firm of purpose ‖ not easily thrown off balance ‖ (*chem.*) not readily decomposing or changing [O.F. *stable, estable*]

sta·ble·boy (stéib'lbɔi) *n.* a boy who works in a stable

sta·ble·man (stéib'lmən) *pl.* **sta·ble·men** (stéib'lmən) *n.* a man who works in a stable

sta·bling (stéibliŋ) *n.* accommodation for keeping and tending horses ‖ buildings used for this

Sta·broek (stɑ́bruːk) the original Dutch name for Georgetown, Guyana

stac·ca·to (stəkɑ́tou) 1. *adj.* (*mus.*, of a note) cut short and sharply detached from the other notes ‖ (*mus.*, of a passage) consisting of such notes (cf. LEGATO) 2. *adv.* in a staccato manner 3. *pl.* **stac·ca·tos, stac·ca·ti** (stəkɑ́ti:) *n.* a staccato manner of playing ‖ a series of abrupt disconnected sounds, *she spoke in a rapid staccato* [Ital.]

stack (staek) 1. *n.* a man-made pile, usually conical or rectangular, of hay, straw etc., frequently capped with a thatch ‖ a more or less orderly pile of things, *a stack of dishes* ‖ a pile of poker chips, sold to or won by a player ‖ (*pl.*) a structure filled with bookshelves separated by narrow aisles ‖ (*pl.*) the part of a library consist-

CONCISE PRONUNCIATION KEY: **(a)** æ, cat; ɑ, car; ɔ fawn; ei, snake. **(e)** e, hen; iː, sheep; iə, deer; ɛə, bear. **(i)** i, fish; ai, tiger; əː, bird.
(o) o, ox; au, cow; ou, goat; u, poor; ɔi, royal. **(u)** ʌ, duck; u, bull; uː, goose; ə, bacillus; juː, cube. x, loch; θ, think; ð, bother; z, Zen; ʒ, corsage;
dʒ, savage; ŋ, orangutang; j, yak; ʃ, fish; tʃ, fetch; 'l, rabble; 'n, redden. Complete pronunciation key appears inside front cover.

ing of such bookshelves ‖ (*Br.*) a measure of volume for fuel (wood or coal) equaling 108 cu. ft ‖ a tall vertical pipe or chimney, e.g. on a ship ‖ a chimney stack ‖ (*pop.*, often *pl.*) a large quantity, *stacks of money* ‖ (*mil.*) three rifles standing upright and leaning against each other with their butt ends resting on the ground 2. *v.t.* to make a stack of ‖ to load with stacks of something ‖ *v.i.* (often with 'up') to form a stack to **stack the cards** to cheat by arranging the cards so that they will be dealt in a certain way ‖ to prearrange a situation unfairly or dishonestly so that it will work to one's advantage [O.N. *stakkr*]

stacked heel a shoe heel built by laminating slices of leather

stack·yard (stǽkjɑrd) *n.* the area near farm buildings where the hay, straw, etc. is stacked

stad·dle (stǽd'l) *n.* a young forest tree, esp. one left to grow when others around it are felled ‖ the base or supporting framework of a stack [O.E. *stathol*, foundation, tree trunk]

stadholder *STADTHOLDER

sta·di·a (stéidi:ə) *n.* a stadia rod ‖ a method of surveying involving the use of a stadia rod [etym. doubtful]

stadia alt. *pl.* of STADIUM

stadia rod (*surveying*) a graduated rod used, with a theodolite or other instrument having a telescope and cross hairs, to measure distances

sta·di·um (stéidi:əm) *pl.* **sta·di·ums** *n.* an athletic field surrounded wholly or in part by a tiered structure seating spectators, usually having no roof ‖ (*Gk hist.*, *pl.* **sta·di·a**, stéidi:ə) a unit of length, usually about 200 yds long, or a running track of this length, usually semicircular with tiered seats for spectators ‖ (*pl.* **sta·di·a**, stéidi:ə) a stage in development, esp. the period between molts of an insect [L. fr. Gk *stadion*]

stadt·hold·er, stad·hold·er (stǽthouldər) *n.* (*hist.*) a governor or viceroy of a province or town in the Netherlands ‖ (*hist.*) the chief magistrate in the United Provinces [Du. *stadthouder* fr. *stad*, a place+*houder*, holder]

Staël (stɑl), Madame de (Anne Louise Germaine Necker, baronne de Staël-Holstein, 1766-1817), French woman of letters, who held one of the most brilliant political and intellectual salons of her time. Her most famous work was 'De l'Allemagne' (1810). She lived mainly in exile because of her opposition to Napoleon I

Staël, Nicolas de (1914-55), French painter born in Russia. His freely geometric abstractions, in rich colors and textures, derive remotely from nature

staff (stæf, stɑf) 1. *pl.* **staffs, staves** (steivz) *n.* a stick, pole etc. used as support in walking or climbing, or as a weapon ‖ a rod carried as a symbol of authority or of pastoral care ‖ (*mil.*, *pl.* **staffs**) a body of officers subordinate to the commanding officer and responsible to him for the administration and planning of his command ‖ (*pl.* **staffs**) a body of people working for a chief authority ‖ (*pl.* **staffs**) the personnel of an organization, *the school staff* ‖ a tall pole supporting a flag ‖ (*surveying*) a stick used in measuring altitudes ‖ (*mus.*) a set of five horizontal lines on or between which symbols of notes are written or printed, pitch being indicated by the position of the symbol (the top line representing the highest pitch) 2. *adj.* of or relating to a staff of people 3. *v.t.* to furnish with a staff of people [O.E. *stæf*]

staff *n.* a building material consisting of a mixture of cement, plaster of paris etc., used esp. in exterior work on temporary structures [etym. doubtful]

Staf·fa (stǽfə) an uninhabited islet of the Inner Hebrides, Scotland, comprised of basaltic pillars and caves (*FINGAL'S CAVE)

Staf·ford (stǽfərd), Henry, 2nd duke of Buckingham (c. 1454-83), English nobleman. He helped to place Richard III on the throne, but later revolted unsuccessfully and was beheaded

Staf·ford·shire (stǽfərdʃiər) (*abbr.* Staffs.) a county (area 1,153 sq. miles, pop. 994,000) of W. central England. County town: Stafford (pop. 54,900). University of Keele (1950)

staff sergeant a noncommissioned officer ranking just above a sergeant in the U.S. Army or the Marine Corps

stag (stæg) 1. *n.* the adult male of certain deer,

esp. of the red deer and other members of genus *Cervus* (cf. HIND) ‖ a male animal castrated when nearly mature ‖ a young gamecock before its first molt ‖ (*Br.*, *stock exchange*) someone who applies for shares before their issue, in the hope that he can sell them at a premium when the issue is made ‖ (*pop.*) a man who attends a social gathering unaccompanied by a woman 2. *adj.* (*pop.*) for men only, *a stag party* 3. *v.i. pres. part.* **stag·ging** *past* and *past part.* **stagged** (*Br.*) to act as a stag on the stock exchange 4. *adv.* (*pop.*) as a stag (unaccompanied man), *to go stag* [prob. fr. O.E. *stagga*]

stag beetle any of several large beetles of fam. *Lucanidae*, esp. *Lucanus cervulus*, the males of which have long branched mandibles resembling antlers

stage (steidʒ) 1. *n.* a large, raised platform on which plays etc. are performed before an audience ‖ the entire part of a theater that lies behind the proscenium ‖ (*rhet.*) the scene of an event ‖ a platform for landing passengers and goods from a vessel ‖ a building scaffold ‖ a platform for holding the objects to be observed through a microscope ‖ a tier of shelves for potted plants, esp. in a greenhouse ‖ a stopping place in a journey ‖ a point, period or level in a progressive change or development ‖ a section of a regularly traveled route ‖ the distance between two stopping places as a division of a journey, *to travel by easy stages* ‖ (*geol.*) a division of stratified rocks, corresponding to an age and ranking below series ‖ a section of a rocket containing a rocket engine or engines. It is usually detached and jettisoned when its propellant is used up ‖ a stagecoach **the stage** drama or the theater as a profession **to go on the stage** to become an actor or actress 2. *v. pres. part.* **stag·ing** *past* and *past part.* **staged** *v.t.* to put (a play) on the stage or organize (a similar entertainment) ‖ to conceive and carry out (something) in a surprising, dramatic way, *to stage a comeback* ‖ *v.i.* (of a play) to lend itself to theatrical performance, *the play stages well* [fr. O.F. *estage*]

stage·coach (stéidʒkoutʃ) *n.* (*hist.*) a horse-drawn coach carrying passengers and goods and running regularly over a set route divided into stages

stage·craft (stéidʒkræft, stéidʒkrɑft) *n.* the art of writing, acting or producing a play

stage direction a notation in the text of a play directing the action, movement etc. of the players

stage door the door by which players, stage personnel etc. enter and leave a theater

stage fright nervous tension or fear sometimes experienced by a person about to perform or speak in public

stage·hand (stéidʒhænd) *n.* a person employed to move scenery and stage properties

stage-man·age (stéidʒmænidʒ) *pres. part.* **stage-man·ag·ing** *past* and *past part.* **stage-man·aged** *v.t.* to act as stage manager of (a production) ‖ to rig (something apparently taking its proper course, e.g. a trial, committee meeting etc.) so as to produce a certain outcome or effect

stage manager the person responsible for the technical efficiency (curtains, stage, scenery, properties etc.) of a stage production (cf. HOUSE MANAGER)

stage-struck (stéidʒstrʌk) *adj.* fascinated with the stage, esp. passionately set on becoming an actor or actress

stage whisper any loud whisper that is (usually by intention) audible to others than the person addressed

stagey *STAGY

stag·fla·tion (stægfléiʃən) *n.* (*economics*) period of economic stagnation with substantial increases in prices —**stagflationary** *adj.* Cf SLUMPINFLATION

stag·ger (stǽgər) 1. *v.i.* to walk with uncertain, uneven steps, continually veering in direction and keeping a precarious balance ‖ *v.t.* to cause to reel under a blow ‖ to shock or astonish as if with a blow ‖ to arrange (things) in oblique or zigzag fashion, e.g. so as not to interrupt a view ‖ (*aeron.*) to set (a wing) so that its forward edge projects beyond the forward edge of another wing ‖ to arrange (holidays, periods of activity, attendance etc.) so that different groups of people are away, active, present etc. at different times, *staff lunch hours have been staggered* 2. *n.* a staggering movement ‖ a zigzag or oblique arrangement ‖ (*aeron.*) the staggering of a wing, or resulting distance by which a forward edge

projects beyond another ‖ (*pl.*) a disease of domestic animals, esp. horses, affecting the central nervous system and causing a staggering gait [altered fr. dial. *stacker*, to reel fr. O.N. *stakra*]

staggered hours system of staff assignments beginning and ending at various hours to avoid overcrowding of facilities Cf FLEXTIME

stag·ing (stéidʒiŋ) *n.* the act or manner of putting on a play on the stage ‖ scaffolding ‖ (*hist.*) travel by stagecoach or the running of a stagecoach as a business ‖ in-flight separation of the first stage of a missile with more than one propulsion stage

staging post (*mil.*) troop assembly area for a military operation *also* staging area

stag·nan·cy (stǽgnənsi:) *n.* the quality or state of being stagnant

stag·nant (stǽgnənt) *adj.* (of a fluid or a body of water) not in motion or flowing ‖ foul from lack of motion ‖ dull through lack of variety of activity [fr. L. *stagnans* (*stagnantis*)]

stag·nate (stǽgneit) *pres. part.* **stag·nat·ing** *past* and *past part.* **stag·nat·ed** *v.i.* (of a liquid or gas) to be motionless or cease to flow ‖ to become foul because of lack of motion ‖ to become dull, e.g. by staying too long in the same place **stag·na·tion** *n.* a stagnating or being stagnant [fr. L. *stagnare* (*stagnatus*)]

stag party a social gathering for men only

stag·y, stage·y (stéidʒi:) *comp.* **stag·i·er** *superl.* **stag·i·est** *adj.* showily exaggerated, e.g. in dress, manner or speech

staid (steid) *adj.* set in steady habits, well balanced and rather dull [var. of *stayed*, *past part.* of STAY]

stain (stein) 1. *v.t.* to make an unwanted spot on the surface of, *ink stained the cloth* ‖ to color by using a pigment which soaks in, *to stain a section for microscope examination* ‖ to spoil, taint (a reputation etc.) ‖ *v.i.* to become stained in any of these ways, *this material stains easily* 2. *n.* the colored area resulting from staining ‖ the material with which one stains, esp. in staining wood or sections to be examined through the microscope ‖ a moral taint etc. [fr. O.F. *desteindre*, to cause to lose color]

stained glass glass given a color by the presence of a metal or metallic oxide in its composition, or by having a pigment burned into its surface. It is used for decorative windows, esp. in churches. The earliest extant stained glass dates from the 11th c. (Augsburg)

Stai·ner (stéinər), Sir John (1840-1901), English composer and organist. He wrote much church music and is best known for his oratorio 'The Crucifixion' (1887)

stain·less (stéinlis) *adj.* not blemished ‖ not susceptible to discoloration

stainless steel steel that is highly resistant to stain or rust because its principal alloying constituent is chromium (12% to 20%)

stair (stɛər) *n.* a constructed step or one of a set of such steps by which one can ascend or descend from one level or floor to another, esp. indoors ‖ (*pl.*) such a set of steps [O.E. *stæger*]

stair·case (stɛərkeis) *n.* a flight of stairs together with its supporting and protecting structures ‖ the part of a building occupied by this

stair rod a rod of wood, metal etc. serving to hold a stair carpet in place where it turns upward from one tread to the next

stair·way (stɛərwei) *n.* a flight or several flights of stairs

stair·well (stɛərwel) *n.* the vertical shaft enclosing the stairs in a building

stake (steik) 1. *n.* a length of esp. wood, pointed at one end so that it can be driven into the ground and used as a marker, support etc. ‖ (*hist.*) the post to which a person was bound for burning to death ‖ a share or interest in something jointly owned, or in something affecting many, *a stake in the country's welfare* ‖ money deposited as a wager ‖ (*pl.*) money competed for, e.g. in a horse race ‖ a horse race etc. in which a prize is offered ‖ (*hist.*) a grubstake **at stake** being risked, *he has a lot at stake in this venture* **the stake** (*hist.*) execution by burning 2. *v.t. pres. part.* **stak·ing** *past* and *past part.* **staked** to support, protect, mark out, secure etc. with a stake or stakes ‖ to wager (money etc.) on the success or failure of an event ‖ (*pop.*) to back (someone or something) financially in hope of future profit ‖ to assert (a claim) (*hist.*) to grubstake [O.E. *staca*]

Staked Plain *LLANO ESTACADO

stake·hold·er (stéikhouldər) *n.* someone with

CONCISE PRONUNCIATION KEY: (**a**) æ, *cat*; ɑ, *car*; ɔ *fawn*; ei, *snake*. (**e**) e, *hen*; i:, *sheep*; iə, *deer*; ɛə, *bear*. (**i**) i, *fish*; ai, *tiger*; ə:, *bird*. (**o**) o, *ox*; au, *cow*; ou, *goat*; u, *poor*; ɔi, *royal*. (**u**) ʌ, *duck*; u, *bull*; u:, *goose*; ə, *bacillus*; ju:, *cube*. x, *loch*; θ, *think*; ð, *bother*; z, *Zen*; ʒ, *corsage*; dʒ, *savage*; ŋ, *orangutang*; j, *yak*; ʃ, *fish*; tʃ, *fetch*; 'l, *rabble*; 'n, *redden*. Complete pronunciation key appears inside front cover.

whom money stakes are deposited until it is known who has won the wager

Sta·kha·nov·ism (stəkǽnəvizəm) n. (Russ. hist.) a collective effort at increasing production by a simplification and reorganization of methods of work, the initiative coming from the workers themselves, and special privileges and bonuses being accorded for superior performance. The term is associated particularly with a movement of the mid-1930s [after Aleksei G. Stakhanov (b. 1906), Russ. miner of the Donbas]

sta·lac·tite (stəlǽktait, stǽlæktait) n. a deposit of calcium carbonate resembling an icicle, formed cumulatively when water containing calcium bicarbonate has dripped very slowly from the roof of a limestone cave **stal·ac·tit·ic** (stælæktítik) adj. [fr. Mod. L. stalactites fr. Gk stalaktos, dropping, dripping]

sta·lag·mite (stəlǽgmait, stǽləgmait) n. a deposit of calcium carbonate somewhat like an inverted stalactite, standing on the floor of a limestone cave. It is formed cumulatively when water containing calcium bicarbonate has dripped from the roof **stal·ag·mit·ic** (stæləgmítik) adj. [fr. Mod. L. stalagmites fr. Gk stalagma, drop, drip]

stale (steil) **l.** adj. (of food or drink) impaired in texture, taste etc. through age || (of a smell) suggesting the presence of something impaired in this way || (of an atmosphere) no longer fresh || (of bread) being a day or more old || (of information, a joke etc.) having lost novelty and interest through being already well known || (of an athlete etc.) in a deteriorated condition through too much or too little activity || (law, esp. of a claim) impaired in force through having been allowed to be dormant too long **2.** v. pres. part. **stal·ing** past and past part. **staled** v.i. to become stale || v.t. to make stale [M.E., etym. doubtful]

stale 1. n. the urine of horses, cattle etc. **2.** v.i. pres. part. **stal·ing** past and past part. **staled** (of horses, cattle etc.) to urinate [etym. doubtful]

stale·mate (stéilmeit) **1.** n. (chess) a position in which one player not in check cannot move without putting his king in check. It results in a draw || a set of circumstances in which no progress can be made, a stalemate in negotiations **2.** v.t. pres. part. **stale·mat·ing** past and past part. **stale·mat·ed** to bring into the position of stalemate [fr. obs. stale fr. A.F.+MATE (checkmate)]

Sta·lin (stálin) (Joseph Vissarionovich Dzhugashvili, 1879-1953), Russian Communist statesman. The son of a Georgian shoemaker, he studied for the priesthood, but became a Marxist and was expelled (1899) from his seminary. He became a leading member of the Bolshevik party and, after several periods of imprisonment, joined the Soviet cabinet as people's commissar for nationalities (1917). He was elected general secretary of the central committee of the party (1922) and, after Lenin's death (1924), established himself as the virtual ruler of the U.S.S.R., ousting opponents and potential rivals in a series of purges in the 1930s. He departed from Lenin's economic policy (1928) and forced through a program of agricultural collectivization, liquidating the kulaks and attempting rapid industrialization through five-year plans. Army reforms were carried out, and a police state was set up, dominated by the OGPU. He formed a nonaggression pact with Nazi Germany (1939). When Germany attacked the U.S.S.R. (1941) he assumed full military and political leadership. He took part in the conferences at Tehran (1943), Yalta (1945) and Potsdam (1945). He retained most of his offices until his death. His rule was denounced officially in the U.S.S.R. from 1956 onwards

Sta·lin·a·bad (stálinəbad) *DYUSHAMBE
Sta·lin·grad (stálingræd) *VOLGOGRAD
Sta·li·no (stalí:nou) *DONETSK
Sta·lin·o·grod (stəlinougróud) *KATOWICE
Stalin Peak *COMMUNISM, MT
Sta·linsk (stálinsk) *NOVOKUZNETSK

stalk (stɔk) n. the main stem of a herbaceous plant || a slender supporting or connecting part, e.g. (biol.) a pedicel, peduncle or petiole [M.E. stalke, etym. doubtful]

stalk 1. v.i. to walk stiffly, as wading birds do || to walk with exaggerated haughtiness, usually in anger || to pursue e.g. deer in such a way as not to be seen, heard or scented by them || (rhet.) to progress in an ominous, silent manner, plague stalked through the streets || v.t. to pursue (deer etc.) by stalking || (rhet.) to move through

in an ominous, silent manner, famine stalked the land **2.** n. a stiff gait || the act of stalking deer etc. [M.E. stalke fr. O.E.]

stalk·ing-horse (stɔ́kiŋhɔrs) n. a real or dummy horse used as cover by a hunter || something used as a mask to conceal one's real intentions etc. || (politics) a candidate put forward to cause division in the opposition or to conceal someone else's candidacy

stalk·y (stɔ́ki:) comp. **stalk·i·er** superl. **stalk·i·est** adj. long and slender, like a stalk || having stalks

stall (stɔl) **1.** n. a compartment in a barn or stable, housing one animal || a booth or table used elsewhere than in a store for displaying goods on sale (e.g. in a market, at a charity bazaar etc.) || a fixed seat in the choir of a church used by a member of the clergy, or one used by a member of the choir || (Br.) any of the theater seats in the rows nearest to the stage (Br., pl.) the occupants of these seats || a cover to protect a sore finger, toe etc. || (aeron.) the condition resulting from stalling, marked by loss of altitude and failure of the controls to respond normally **2.** v.t. to put or keep (an animal) in a stall || to cause (an engine) to stop because of overloading or insufficient fuel || to cause (a motor vehicle) to stop, by stopping its engine in this way || to cause (an aircraft) to lose the forward speed necessary to maintain its altitude and respond to the controls || to cause to stick fast, e.g. in mud or snow || v.i. of (an engine or vehicle) to stop by being stalled || to stick fast, e.g. in mud or snow || (of an aircraft) to become stalled [O.E. steall]

stall 1. v.i. (pop.) to talk or act evasively in the hope of delaying something or putting someone off || v.t. (pop., esp. with 'off') to get rid of or delay by evasion, stall off the insurance man **2.** n. (pop.) a trick used to get out of making a decision, giving a straight answer etc. [A.F. estal, estale, decoy bird]

stall-feed (stɔ́lfi:d) pres. part. **stall-feed·ing** past and past part. **stall-fed** (stɔ́lfed) v.t. to fatten (an animal) by keeping it in its stall and feeding it well

stal·lion (stǽljən) n. an uncastrated male horse, esp. one kept for breeding purposes [O.F. estalon]

stal·wart (stɔ́lwərt) **1.** adj. (rhet.) unshaken in determination or loyalty by risks or difficulties || (rhet., esp. of a man) of strong, sturdy build **2.** n. (rhet.) a stalwart person || (rhet.) a zealous supporter of a cause, esp. a political one [fr. obs. stalworth fr. O.E. stœlwierthe]

sta·men (stéimən) n. the male organ of a flower, consisting of a filament bearing an anther containing pollen [L.=thread]

Stam·ford Bridge, Battle of (stǽmfərd) a battle fought (Sept. 25, 1066) in Yorkshire, England, in which Harold II of England defeated an invasion by his brother Tostig and Harald III of Norway

stam·i·na (stǽminə) n. capacity for resisting fatigue or disease [L. pl. of stamen, thread]

stam·i·nal (stǽmin'l) adj. (bot.) of or having a stamen or stamens || of, relating to or having stamina [fr. L. stamen (staminis), thread and STAMINA]

stam·i·nate (stǽminit) adj. having or producing stamens || having stamens but no pistils [fr. L. staminatus, consisting of threads]

stam·i·node (stǽminoud) n. a staminodium

stam·i·no·di·um (stæminóudiəm) pl. **stam·i·no·di·a** (stæminóudiə) n. a rudimentary, imperfect or sterile stamen [Mod. L. fr. L. stamen (staminis), a thread]

stam·mer (stǽmər) **1.** v.i. to speak with difficulty, repeating sounds and syllables and making frequent pauses in which no sound can be made || v.t. (often with 'out') to utter in this way, to stammer out an excuse **2.** n. the affliction or habit of stammering [O.E. stamerian]

stamp (stæmp) **1.** v.t. to make (a mark) by pressure, to stamp a design in clay || to print or affix a mark by pressure on, to stamp a dish with a design || to affix postage or revenue stamps to (an envelope, document etc.) || to bring (one's foot or feet) down heavily, to stamp one's foot with impatience || to bring one's foot down heavily on, to stamp the floor || to mark out, identify, his tastes stamp him as a reactionary || to affect so deeply as to change permanently, stamped by his experiences as a prisoner || (with 'out') to crush, put an end to, extinguish etc. by or as if by a heavy downward pressure of the foot, to stamp out a cigarette, to stamp out a rebellion, to stamp out malaria || to crush (ore

etc.) into powder || v.i. to bring the feet or a foot down heavily **2.** n. the act of stamping, esp. with the foot || a device used to impress a mark || the mark made by such a device, the document bears the regimental stamp || an official mark, seal etc. set on goods or documents as proof that duty or taxes have been paid, or that other legal obligations have been fulfilled || a postage stamp || a machine or machine part used to crush ore etc. || a distinguishing quality or sign, he has the stamp of a soldier about him [M.E. stampen fr. Gmc]

Stamp Act (hist.) a British act of parliament (1765) extending the stamp duty on various documents to the colonies. It aroused much hostility in America, and was repealed (1766)

stam·pede (stæmpí:d) **1.** n. a sudden flight or rush of a number of frightened animals || an impulsive concerted rush, a stampede for the doors || any spontaneous mass action, a stampede for reform of tax laws **2.** v. pres. part. **stam·ped·ing** past and past part. **stam·ped·ed** v.i. to move or take part in a stampede || v.t. to cause to stampede [fr. Span. estampida, a crash]

stamping ground (pop.) a favorite place of resort

stamp mill a mill in which ore is crushed to powder

stance (stæns) n. a way of standing, esp. the way one places one's feet in certain sports, e.g. fencing and golf [F. fr. Ital. stanza, station, stopping place]

stanch (stantʃ, stɔntʃ) adj. staunch

stanch (stantʃ, stɔntʃ) v.t. to prevent or stop the flow of (blood) from a wound || to treat (a wound) so that the blood ceases to flow from it [fr. O.F. estanchier]

stan·chion (stǽnʃən, stánʃən) **1.** n. an upright bar, post etc. used as a support, esp. for a roof, deck etc. || a yoke consisting of two linked uprights for confining cattle in a stall **2.** v.t. to provide or secure with a stanchion [O.F. estanchon, estançon]

stand (stænd) **1.** v. pres. part. **stand·ing** past and past part. **stood** (stud) v.i. to be or remain in a position in which the body is motionless and more or less vertical, supported by one or both feet || to rise to such a position, will volunteers please stand || to be or remain erect and supported on its base, the house still stood after the earthquake || to be of a specified height, he stands six feet || to remain in the same position or place, let the dough stand for an hour before baking it || to be or remain in a specified position, condition etc., stand at attention, stand aloof || to maintain a position, resolve etc., stand firm, how does he stand on this question? || to cease walking, halt, stand where you are || to be in a certain place, his house stands at the corner || to have a certain position or be at a certain point on a scale, the temperature stands at 25°C || to remain unchanged, the dividend stands at 5% || (with infin. 'to gain', 'to lose' etc.) to be in a position to gain, lose etc., he stands to win a fortune on this race || (Br., with 'for') to be a political candidate, he is standing for the council || to remain valid or effective, old as they are, these rules still stand || (naut.) to move in a specified direction or in a specified course, they stood into harbor || v.t. to place in an erect position, he stood it on end || to place in a certain position, stand the table in the corner || to support without deformation, it will stand firing up to 1,300° || to undergo, to stand trial || to endure, she cannot stand noise || (pop.) to meet the expense of (e.g. a drink) when treating **to stand a chance** to have a possibility of succeeding, winning etc., he doesn't stand a chance against the others **to stand by** to be a passive spectator || to be present and ready to take action, stand by in case of trouble || (naut.) to be prepared to operate, stand by the lifeboat || to back up with support || to adhere to (a promise etc.) **to stand down** to withdraw (from a competition or an official position) || to leave the witness stand **to stand for** to represent, the symbol % stands for percent || (pop.) to tolerate, he won't stand for such nonsense || to advocate, to stand for free trade **to stand off** to remain at a distance || to keep (someone or something) at a distance || (Br.) to suspend for a time from employment || (naut.) to stand out **to stand on** (or upon) to insist on the observing or respecting of, to stand on ceremony || (naut., only with 'on') to keep on the same course **to stand one's ground** to maintain one's position against opposition **to stand out** to be prominent, attract special at-

tention ‖ to be persistent, *he stands out for his rights* ‖ (*naut.*) to hold a course away from shore **to stand over** to be postponed, *payment can stand over until next month* ‖ to supervise (someone) very closely in some activity, esp. disagreeably closely **to stand to** to refuse to contemplate changes **to stand to** (*mil.*) to take up action positions at, or positions for inspection at **to stand up** to rise into, or be in, a standing posture ‖ to prove valid or durable **to stand up for** to defend against opposition or from censure **to stand up to** to resist successfully, *to stand up to an ordeal* ‖ to face with courage, *you must stand up to him* **2.** *n.* a stopping of motion or progress ‖ (*mil.*) an action fought on the defensive ‖ (*fig.*) a position, maintained with regard to some issue, *to take a stand in favor of something* ‖ a place where one stands or is placed ‖ a piece of furniture for holding something specified, *umbrella stand, music stand* ‖ a raised structure used to accommodate spectators, members of a band etc. ‖ a temporary stall for exhibiting wares to be sold or looked at (e.g. at a fair or beside a road) ‖ a standing growth esp. of trees, *a stand of white pines* ‖ a place where a touring theatrical or other company gives a performance ‖ the stop made by such a company, *a one-night stand* ‖ a place where public vehicles, taxis etc. are parked while waiting for passengers ‖ a witness stand **to make a stand** to express one's support for a position or opinion and make no concessions ‖ to fight a defensive battle, *they fled instead of making a stand* [O.E. *standan*]
stand·a·lone (stǽndəloun) *adj.* of equipment that stands alone, i.e., not on a desk or other furniture
stand·ard (stǽndərd) **1.** *n.* a model to be followed or imitated, established by custom and consent ‖ a degree of quality, level of achievement etc. regarded as desirable and necessary for some purpose, *his performance was not up to our standards* ‖ an established unit of weight or other measurement, *standard of length* ‖ the legally established proportion of pure gold or silver in a coin ‖ the basis of value in a monetary system, *gold standard* (*heraldry*) the long, tapering flag of a king, lord, city etc. ‖ (*mil.*) the flag of a cavalry regiment ‖ a vertical supporting pillar, post etc. ‖ (*bot.*) a vexillum ‖ a shrub or tree grafted on one upright stem, not dwarfed or espaliered ‖ (*Br.*) one of the classes in a primary school **2.** *adj.* accepted as a model to be followed or imitated ‖ meeting the required standard ‖ regarded as having authoritative quality, *the standard work on the subject* ‖ of the ordinary type, without extra or unusual features, *the standard model of a washing machine* ‖ (*bot.*) of a shrub or tree grafted on one upright stem [O.F. *estendard*]
Standard (MR) *n.* (*mil.*) solid-fuel surface-to-air missile weighing 1,200 lbs, with 12-mi range, and radar detection
Standard Arm (*mil.*) an air-launched antiradiation missile (AGM-78) designed to home on and destroy radar emitters
stand·ard-bear·er (stǽndərdbɛərər) *n.* a soldier etc. carrying a standard (flag) ‖ (*rhet.*) a leader or representative of a movement, political party etc.
Stan·dard·bred (stǽndərdbred) *n.* a trotting horse of an American breed used in harness racing
standard industrial classification U.S. Government method of classifying business and public establishments according to their primary activity *also* SIC codes
stand·ard·i·za·tion (stændərdizéiʃən) *n.* a standardizing or being standardized
stand·ard·ize (stǽndərdaiz) *pres. part.* **stand·ard·iz·ing** *past* and *past part.* **stand·ard·ized** *v.t.* to make conform to a standard, *to standardize educational methods* ‖ to test against a standard
Standard Metropolitan Statistical Area geographic region designated by U.S. Government for allocation of grants, etc.
Standard Missile (*mil.*) a shipboard, surface-to-surface or surface-to-air missile [RIM 66; RIM 67 (extended range)] with a solid-propellant rocket engine, equipped with nonnuclear warhead and semiactive or passive homing
standard of living the level of material well-being, esp. of a community, nation etc.
Standard Oil Companies major units of the U.S. oil industry incorporated (1870) in Ohio by John D. Rockefeller, who became the first president. As a result of U.S. antitrust legislation,

the organization was broken up (1911) into more than 30 companies, including Standard Oil Company (New Jersey), Socony Mobil Oil Company, the Standard Oil Company of California, and the Standard Oil Company (Indiana)
Standards, National Bureau of the chief U.S. government agency established (1901) to conduct basic research in physics, chemistry, metallurgy, and engineering sciences. It is responsible for maintaining and developing standards of measurement for the U.S.A.
standard time the time in a country or locality, usually established by legislation or local custom, expressed in relation to a selected meridian
stand·by (stǽndbai) **1.** *n.* someone who or something that can be relied on in an emergency **2.** *adj.* ready to utilize time or space that may become available due to cancellations by others
stand·ee (stændíː) *n.* (*pop.*) a person standing in standing room, *this bus takes 25 standees*
stand·in (stǽndin) *n.* someone who takes up the position of a film actor until the cameras are ready ‖ any person who is a substitute
stand·ing (stǽndiŋ) *n.* reputation or status, esp. when high, *a man of standing* ‖ duration, *a feud of long standing* ‖ (*law*) qualification to initiate a law suit, esp. a class action suit **2.** *adj.* upright ‖ established, *a standing joke* ‖ permanent, not occasional, changing or temporary, *a standing arrangement* ‖ (of crops) not yet cut ‖ (of water) stagnant ‖ done from an erect position, *a standing jump* [STAND]
standing army a permanent army of regular soldiers
standing committee a permanent committee, esp. of a legislative body
standing-on-nines carry *HIGH-SPEED CARRY
standing order a standard procedural instruction constantly in force, *regimental standing orders* ‖ (*pl.*) standard rules of parliamentary procedure ‖ (*Br.*) a banker's order for the regular payment of a fixed amount on behalf of a customer
standing room space to stand ‖ accommodation available for standing when all seats in a theater, bus etc. are taken
standing wave a single-frequency mode of vibration of a body or physical system (e.g. an organ pipe or vibrating string) in which the amplitude varies from point to point, being constantly zero at certain points
Stan·dish (stǽndiʃ), Miles (or Myles, c. 1584-1656), American colonist born in England, the military leader of Plymouth Colony
stand-off bomb (*mil.*) a pilotless homing miniaircraft with a 100-mi range, launched from a bomber, capable of carrying a nuclear warhead
stand-off half (stǽndɔf, stǽndɒf) (*rugby*) the halfback having a position between the scrum half and the three-quarter backs, during a scrum
stand-off·ish (stændɔ́fiʃ, stændɒ́fiʃ) *adj.* reserved, aloof
stand-out (stǽndaut) *n.* a person or thing of conspicuous excellence
stand-pat (stǽndpæt) *adj.* (*pop.*) opposing change, conservative **stánd·pát·ter** *n.* (*pop.*) a conservative person
stand-pipe (stǽndpaip) *n.* a vertical pipe or tank in which water is stored at a certain level, esp. in order to secure uniform pressure in a water-supply system
stand-point (stǽndpɔint) *n.* a point of view from which something is considered or judged
stand-still (stǽndstil) *n.* a ceasing of movement or activity
stand-up (stǽndʌp) *adj.* done or taken while standing, *a stand-up lunch* ‖ (of a fight) characterized by hard hitting, without any attempts to disengage ‖ (of a collar) stiffened so as to stay upright ‖ (of a comedian) performing a monologue alone on stage without the help of a straight man or props or decor
Stan·ford Research Institute (stǽnfərd) (*abbr.* SRI) an organization founded (1946) under the auspices of Stanford University, Calif., as a nonprofit establishment providing specialized research services under contract to business, industry, foundations, and the U.S. government
Stanford University (Leland Stanford Junior University), a private U.S. institution of higher learning founded (1885) near Palo Alto, Calif.,

by Senator Leland Stanford (1824-93) and his wife Jane Lathrop (1825-1905) as a memorial to their son. The campus covers about 9,000 acres. The Hoover Institution of War, Revolution and Peace, founded during the 1st world war by Herbert Hoover, houses more than one million documents dealing with the 1st and 2nd world wars, 20th-c. revolutionary movements, and international relations
Stan·hope (stǽnəp), Philip Dormer *CHESTERFIELD, 4th earl of
Stanhope, Lady Hester Lucy (1776-1839), British traveler. She settled (1814) among the Druses in Syria, adopted a religion which combined elements of Islam and Christianity, and was venerated as a prophetess by the Beduin tribes
Stanhope, James, 1st Earl Stanhope (1673-1721), English statesman. A Whig, he was in charge of foreign affairs (1714-17, 1718-21) and was first lord of the treasury (1717-18)
Stan·is·laus I Leszczyński (stǽnislɔs) (1677-1766), king of Poland (1704-9, 1733-5) and duke of Lorraine (1736-66). He gained the throne as a result of Charles XII of Sweden's victories in the Northern War, but went into exile when Charles was defeated (1709). His election as king (1733) precipitated the War of the Polish Succession. He was defeated and, although he retained the title of king, was forced to give up his royal power. In exile in France, he became a patron of science and the arts
Stanislaus II Augustus (1732-98), last king of Poland (1764-95). He gained the throne through the influence of his mistress, Catherine II of Russia. The country remained under Russian influence throughout his reign, and was gradually reduced in size by the partitions of Poland, disappearing altogether in 1795
Stan·i·slav·sky (stænislávski:), Konstantin (Konstantin Sergeyevich Alekseyev, 1863-1938), Russian theatrical producer. A founder of the Moscow Art Theater (1898), he developed a new approach to acting and production based on realism, ensemble acting and the actor's complete identification with his character
stank alt. *past* of STINK
Stan·ley (stǽnli:), Edward George Geoffrey Smith *DERBY, 14th earl of
Stanley, Sir Henry Morton (1841-1904), British explorer. He found Livingstone near Lake Tanganyika (1871) and explored equatorial Africa (1874-7). He founded the Congo Free State (1879) in the service of King Leopold II of the Belgians
Stanley, Wendell Meredith (1904-71), U.S. biochemist and co-winner (with John H. Northrop and James B. Sumner) of the 1946 Nobel prize in chemistry, for preparation of enzymes and virus proteins in a pure form
Stanley Falls a series of waterfalls (dropping about 200 ft in 60 miles) in the upper Congo River above Kisangani, offering enormous hydroelectric potential
Stanley Pool an expanded section of the middle Congo River. Ports: Kinshasa, Brazzaville
Stanley v. Georgia a landmark decision (1969) of the U.S. Supreme Court, which ruled that to make private possession of obscene material a crime was unconstitutional
Stan·ley·ville (stǽnli:vil) *KISANGANI
stan·na·ry (stǽnəri:) *pl.* **stan·na·ries** *n.* (*Br.*) a tin mine or tin works **the Stannaries** (*Br. hist.*) a tin-mining district of Devon and Cornwall under the jurisdiction of special courts [fr. M.L. *stannaria*]
stan·nate (stǽneit) *n.* a salt of a stannic acid
stan·nic (stǽnik) *adj.* of, relating to or containing tin, esp. of a compound in which tin has a valence of 4 [fr. L.L. *stannum*, tin]
stan·nite (stǽnait) *n.* a natural sulfide of tin, copper and iron having a gray to black metallic luster [fr. L.L. *stannum*, tin]
stan·nous (stǽnəs) *adj.* of, relating to or containing tin, esp. of a compound in which tin has a valence of 2 [fr. L.L. *stannum*, tin]
stannous fluoride [SnF_2] (*chem.*) a fluoride compound used in toothpaste
Stan·ton (stǽntən), Edwin McMasters (1814-69), U.S. lawyer and secretary of war (1862-8) under Abraham Lincoln and Andrew Johnson. When President Johnson attempted to remove him from office for his harsh reconstruction measures, Stanton claimed protection under the Tenure of Office Act. He finally resigned after President Johnson survived impeachment by the Senate

Stanton, Elizabeth Cady (1815-1902), U.S. leader of women's rights. With Lucretia Mott she organized (1848) in New York the first U.S. women's rights convention, drafted a women's bill of rights, and drew up the first formal demand in the U.S.A. for women's suffrage

stan·za (stǽnzə) *n.* a group of lines of verse forming a structural division of a poem, usually in a recurring metrical pattern **stan·za·ic** (stænzéiik) *adj.* [Ital.=room, stanza]

sta·pe·dec·to·my (steipdéktəmi:) (*med.*) surgical removal (and replacement) of the stapes, innermost of three middle-ear bones —**stape-dectomized** *adj.*

stapedes alt. *pl.* of STAPES

sta·pe·di·al (stəpi:di:əl) *adj.* of the stapes ‖ near the stapes [fr. Mod. L. *stupedius* fr. *stapes* (*stapedis*), stapes]

sta·pes (stéipi:z) *pl.* **sta·pes,** **sta·pe·des** (stéipi:di:z) *n.* the innermost of the three bones of the middle ear [Mod. L. fr. M. L. =stirrup]

staph·y·lo·coc·cic (stæfələkóksik) *adj.* relating to or caused by a staphylococcus

staph·y·lo·coc·cus (stæfələkókəs) *pl.* **staph·y·lo·coc·ci** (stæfələkóksai) *n.* a member of *Staphylococcus,* fam. *Micrococcaceae,* a genus of nonmotile bacteria living on the skin and mucous membranes, that are gram-positive and cause inflammation [Mod. L. *Staphylococcus* fr. Gk *staphulē,* bunch of grapes+*kokkos,* berry]

sta·ple (stéip'l) **1.** *n.* the principal commodity produced, grown or sold in a particular place, *coffee is the staple of the country* ‖ a chief ingredient or constituent, *potatoes are the staple of their diet* ‖ a commodity for which the demand is constant and which is regularly kept in stock, e.g. flour, sugar and salt ‖ a raw material ‖ fiber of wool, cotton etc. with reference to its length or quality **the Staple** (*Eng. hist.*) a place royally appointed as a market for certain English goods intended for export in the 14th and 15th cc. ‖ (*hist.*) the merchant group having exclusive purchase rights at these markets **2.** *adj.* of, relating to or having the nature of a staple (commodity) **3.** *v.t. pres. part.* **sta·pling** *past and past part.* **sta·pled** to grade (wool, cotton etc.) according to the quality of its fiber [O.F. *estaple,* emporium]

staple 1. *n.* a U-shaped metal bar with pointed ends, designed to be driven into a post or wall to form a holder for a hook etc. ‖ a small piece of wire in the form of a square bracket, used to fasten sheets of paper etc. together by pushing both ends through the sheets and bending them back so that they cannot slip out **2.** *v.t. pres. part.* **sta·pling** *past and past part.* **sta·pled** to fasten with a staple or staples [O.E. *stapol,* post]

Staple Act a British act of parliament (1663) under which all trade, whether English or foreign, to English colonies had to be shipped from an English port

sta·pler (stéiplər) *n.* a person whose job is grading wool

stapler *n.* a hand-operated device for stapling together sheets of paper etc.

star (star) **1.** *n.* any of a vast number of hot, usually luminous celestial bodies, consisting of matter comprising most of the known elements in varying percentages in a highly ionized state, and found distributed in galaxies throughout the known universe ‖ a conventional symbol for such a body, often having five projecting points or several lines radiating from a central point ‖ this as a sign of excellence, rank etc. ‖ a mark thought of as resembling this, e.g. a white mark on a horse's forehead ‖ a person preeminent in some activity, esp. in the entertainment world or in sports, *stars of screen and stage* ‖ a leading performer in a play, film etc. ‖ an asterisk ‖ (*pl.*) heavenly bodies supposed to exert an influence on a person's life **to see stars** (*pop.*) to see bright points of light as a result of a blow on the head **2.** *v. pres. part.* **star·ring** *past and past part.* **starred** *v.i.* to be the most prominent person in a collective activity ‖ to be the star in a film, play etc. ‖ *v.t.* to furnish or mark with the symbol of a star or with an asterisk ‖ to introduce or publicize (an actor or actress) as a star [O.E. *steorra*]

—In the Milky Way galaxy alone it is estimated that there are about 200 billion stars. Stars are classified and catalogued according to size (*DWARF STAR, *GIANT STAR), temperature and spectrum, positions and motions, luminosity (*MAGNITUDE) and other special characteristics (e.g. periodic or sudden variations in brightness or spectrum, *VARIABLE STAR, *DOU-

BLE STAR). While magnitudes, densities and diameters vary widely, the masses of stars are limited: almost all star masses measured vary between one-tenth and 10 times the mass of our sun. The principal energy-producing reaction is thought to be the same for most stars: the thermonuclear conversion of hydrogen to helium (*CARBON CYCLE)

star anise *Illicium verum,* fam. *Magnoliaceae,* a small tree native to E. Asia, cultivated in China ‖ the dried fruit of this tree, used as a spice

star aniseed the dried fruit of the star anise, used as a spice

star apple a tree of genus *Chrysophyllum,* fam. *Sapotaceae,* esp. *C. cainito,* a tropical American evergreen bearing an apple-shaped purplish edible fruit, whose carpels in section present a starlike figure ‖ this fruit

star·board (stárbərd) **1.** *n.* the side of a ship or aircraft that is on the right of someone aboard facing forward (opp. PORT) **2.** *v.t.* to turn or put (the helm) over to starboard [O.E. *stēorbord*]

starch (startʃ) **1.** *n.* a white granular polysaccharide ($C_6H_{10}O_5$)n, synthesized by green plants and stored by them as a food reserve, and which upon hydrolysis yields an indeterminate number of dextrose molecules. Starch is obtained industrially from corn and potatoes, is an important foodstuff, and is used also as an adhesive in the paper and textile industries, in laundering and in pharmacy and medicine ‖ starchy foods ‖ stiffness of manner **2.** *v.t.* to stiffen (cloth etc.) with starch [M.E. *sterche* fr. O.E. fr. *stearc,* stiff]

Star Chamber (*Eng. hist.*) a court which developed (14th and 15th cc.) out of the king's council, and was used by the Tudors as a tribunal to deal with powerful nobles. The court was used by James I and Charles I as a tool of arbitrary government, and became notorious for summary procedure, torture and extortion. It was abolished (1641) by the Long Parliament

starch·i·ness (stártʃi:nis) *n.* the quality or state of being starchy

starch·y (stártʃi:) *comp.* **starch·i·er** *superl.* **starch·i·est** *adj.* of or like starch ‖ containing starch ‖ stiff and unbending in manner or attitude ‖ stiffened with starch

star·dom (stárdəm) *n.* the status of being a star in the entertainment or sports world

star·dust (stárdʌst) *n.* a great number of small stars in the night sky, appearing to the observer like a scattering of dust ‖ a mood of dreamy or romantic enchantment

stare (stɛər) **1.** *v. pres. part.* **star·ing** *past and past part.* **stared** *v.i.* to look fixedly with wide eyes, *to stare in amazement* ‖ to be vividly conspicuous, *the staring white houses of Greece* ‖ to have a blank, unseeing look, *staring factory windows* ‖ *v.t.* to affect (a person) in a specified way by a stare, *she stared him into silence* **to stare (someone) down** to meet the stare of (someone) by staring back at him till he looks away **to stare (someone) in the face** to be seen by (someone) to be obvious or inevitable, *ruin stared him in the face* **to stare (someone) up and down** to stare at (someone), as if inspecting him, in a rude manner **2.** *n.* a fixed gaze [O.E. *starian*]

Star·fight·er *n.* (*mil.*) a U.S. supersonic, single-engine, turbojet (F-104) with a nuclear and nonnuclear weapon capable of carrying 450 lbs. It is used by non-U.S. nations as a prime air interceptor; manufactured by Lockheed

star·fish (stárfiʃ) *pl.* **star·fish·es, star·fish** *n.* a member of *Asteroidea,* a class of echinoderms possessing five radially symmetric arms, and a mouth on the under surface of a central disk. The under surface of the arms bears rows of tube feet by which the animal crawls and grasps its prey

star·gaze (stárgeiz) *pres. part.* **star·gaz·ing** *past and past part.* **star·gazed** *v.i.* to contemplate the stars ‖ to be lost in abstract contemplation [back-formation fr. older *stargazer,* astrologer or astronomer]

stark (stark) **1.** *adj.* bare, bleak, *a stark landscape* ‖ sheer, utter, *stark lunacy* **2.** *adv.* absolutely, *stark mad* [O.E. *stearc,* hard, unyielding]

stark-nak·ed (stárknéikid) *adj.* completely naked [older *start-naked* fr. obs. *start,* tail of an animal+NAKED]

star·let (stárlit) *n.* (*pop.*) a young film actress who is being prepared for a career as a star

Star·lift·er (stárliftə:r) *n.* (*mil.*) a large cargo transport (C-141) powered by four turbofan engines, capable of intercontinental range with

heavy payloads and airdrops

star·light (stárlait) *n.* the light emitted by the stars

star·like (stárlaik) *adj.* resembling a star in brilliance or in having the shape of a conventional star symbol

star·ling (stárling) *n.* a bird of genus *Sturnus,* fam. *Sturnidae,* esp. *S. vulgaris,* a very active, gregarious bird, about 8 ins long, with a short tail, sharp-pointed bill, and dark brown or black iridescent plumage. Starlings live near human habitations in Europe, the U.S.A., Australia and New Zealand ‖ any bird of fam. *Sturnidae* [O.E. *stærlinc*]

starling *n.* a protective structure of piles around the piers of a bridge [perh. corrup. of obs. *staddling* fr. O.E. *stathol,* foundation]

star·lit (stárlit) *adj.* illuminated by the light from stars

star-of-Beth·le·hem (stárəvbéθlihem) *pl.* **stars-of-Beth·le·hem, star-of-Beth·le·hem** *n.* a plant of genus *Ornithogalum,* fam. *Liliaceae,* esp. *O. umbellatum,* an Old World plant now also found in the eastern U.S.A., having small, greenish, star-shaped blossoms

Star of David a six-pointed star consisting of two equilateral triangles, a symbol of Judaism and of the Republic of Israel [trans. Heb. *mogēn dovid,* shield of David]

star·quake (stárkweik) *n.* (*astron.*) a major eruption or change in the shape, size, energy output, etc., in a celestial body

starred (stard) *adj.* marked with stars ‖ influenced by the stars

starred form (*linguistics*) a form marked to indicate a historical reconstruction or deviation from the normal use of a term

star route a surface route in the U.S. postal service not accessible by railroad or steamship. Before rural free delivery was established, private contracts were made with bonded bidders to carry the mail over these routes. A Second Assistant Postmaster General was indicted during President Garfield's administration for fraudulently increasing the compensation of star-route contractors, but was cleared of such charges by President Arthur's administration. The scandal led to civil service reform

star·ry (stári:) *comp.* **star·ri·er** *superl.* **star·ri·est** *adj.* full of stars ‖ shining like stars ‖ coming from the stars

star·ry-eyed (stári:aid) *adj.* bemused with enchantment or wonder ‖ filled with or characterized by foolish, blindly enthusiastic idealism

STARS (acronym) proposed solar thermal aerostat research station, a rigid, spherical envelope up to one mile in diameter, designed to collect solar energy sufficient to supply some to earth and to modify weather, esp. fog dispersal

Stars and Bars (*Am. hist.*) the original flag of the Confederate States of America, consisting of three bars of red, white, red, and in the upper left-hand corner a blue field containing seven stars representing the seven states that had seceded at the time that the flag was adopted

Stars and Stripes the flag of the U.S.A., consisting of 13 horizontal stripes alternately red (7) and white (6), and 50 white stars (one for each state) on a blue field in the upper left-hand corner

star sapphire a sapphire that, when cut with a convex surface and polished, exhibits asterism

star shell (*mil.*) an explosive shell which upon bursting releases a shower of brilliant lights and is used esp. for signaling

star·span·gled (stárspæng'ld) *adj.* scattered or dusted with stars

Star-Spangled Banner the flag of the U.S.A. ‖ the name of the national anthem of the U.S.A., from a poem by Francis Scott Key

start (start) **1.** *v.t.* to cause (something) to come into existence, operation or activity, *who started that rumor?, start the car, they started the meeting with cocktails* ‖ to experience the first stage of (something) for the first time or after a period of not experiencing it, *he started life in poverty, she started feeling sick just after dessert* ‖ to perform or do the first stages of (an action, course etc.) for the first time or after a period of not performing or doing it, *to start reading a book* ‖ to cause (someone) to become engaged in a specified course of action or to experience something for the first time, *start him learning Latin next year, to start a baby on solid food* ‖ to establish, *to start a millinery shop*

‖ to drive (an animal) from its lair, nest, hiding place etc. ‖ to cause (nails, mechanical parts etc.) to loosen and become displaced ‖ to give the signal for the beginning of (a race) ‖ to give (runners in a race) the signal to run ‖ *v.i.* to come into existence, operation or activity, *the party starts at 9:00, the train started with a jolt* ‖ (of a person, vehicle, ship etc.) to set forth on a journey ‖ to spring up or out suddenly from or as if from shock ‖ (of mechanical parts etc.) to become displaced or loosened, *some timbers in the hull have started* ‖ (of the eyes) to bulge out or seem to bulge out, as an effect of shock etc. **to start in** to begin the preliminary work of an undertaking **to start off** to begin a program, undertaking etc. ‖ (of a program, undertaking etc.) to start, *the evening started off badly* **to start out** to start a journey or a course of action etc., *she started out to make a cake but it ended up as fudge* **to start up** to begin to function, *the Japanese course starts up next week* ‖ to give a little jump in fear ‖ to cause to begin to function, *to start up a generator* **2.** *n.* the starting of an action, journey, race or course of events ‖ an opportunity, advantage etc. assisting the starting of something, *a rich uncle gave him a start in life* ‖ a position in advance of others in a race etc. ‖ the point where a race etc. starts ‖ a nervous jerk or jump due to surprise or shock **stárt·er** *n.* someone who gives the signal for the start of a race ‖ a person or animal that starts in a race ‖ the self-starter of a motor [O.E. *styrtan*, to leap]

starting gate (*horse racing*) a barrier behind which the horses line up for a race. The barrier lifts automatically when the starting bell is rung

starting post a post at the starting point of a race

starting price the final odds offered on a horse before a race

star·tle (stárt'l) *v. pres. part.* **star·tling** *past* and *past part.* **star·tled** *v.t.* to cause to jump in alarm or surprise ‖ *v.i.* to become alarmed **stár·tling** [O.E. *steartlian*, to kick, struggle]

star·va·tion (starvéiʃən) *n.* a starving or being starved

starve (starv) *pres. part.* **starv·ing** *past* and *past part.* **starved** *v.i.* to die for lack of food ‖ to suffer acutely from lack of food ‖ (*pop.*) to feel very hungry ‖ (with 'for') to suffer from mental or spiritual deprivation, *starving for affection* ‖ *v.t.* to cause to die of hunger ‖ to deprive of food ‖ to compel by depriving of food, *starve the city into submission* ‖ (with 'for' or 'of') to cause to suffer from mental or spiritual privation, *starved for affection* **stárve·ling** *n.* (*rhet.*) a badly under-nourished person or animal [O.E. *steorfan*, to die]

stash (stæʃ) *v.t.* (*pop.*) to hide or put (something) away for future use [prob. a blend of STORE+CACHE]

sta·sis (stéisis, stǽsis) *pl.* **sta·ses** (stéisi:z, stǽsi:z) *n.* a stoppage or slowing of the normal flow of fluids or semifluids in a bodily organ or vessel, esp. a slowing of e.g. circulating blood or of movement of the intestines [Mod. L. fr. Gk *stasis*, a standing still]

stat·cou·lomb (stǽtkú:lɒm) *n.* (*phys.*) a unit of charge in the cgs system of electrostatic units, equal to 33×10^{-10} coulomb [fr. ELECTRO-STATIC+COULOMB]

state (steit) **1.** *n.* a form or mode of being, a condition, *what is the state of your health?* ‖ such a condition with respect to the mind or emotions, or to growth or development, *a state of great happiness, the larval state* ‖ a condition of emotional agitation, *to work oneself up into a state* ‖ a self-governing political community occupying its own territory ‖ a partly autonomous member of a political federation, *the 50th state of the U.S.A.* ‖ luxury and splendor, *to live in state* ‖ (*chem., phys.*) the condition of aggregation or arrangement of matter, *the gaseous state* (cf. PHASE) ‖ the condition of a physical system separate from all other conditions of that system and specified by definite quantities of energy, entropy, momentum etc. **State** the political organism as an abstract concept, *Church and State* **the States** (*pop.*) the U.S.A. **to lie in state** (of a dead person, esp. a public figure) to be laid in a draped coffin in a public place so that mourners can pay the last respects **2.** *adj.* pertaining to a state ‖ involving or calling for some display of ceremony, *a state occasion* **3.** *v.t. pres. part.* **stat·ing** *past* and *past part.* **stat·ed** *v.t.* to utter (a fact, opinion, principle etc.) or put it in

writing etc., esp. in a way that is formal [fr. ESTATE and fr. L. *status*]

State attorney a legal officer appointed to represent a state in the courts

state bank a bank owned, chartered or controlled by a government **State bank** a bank chartered by a state of the U.S.A. and operating under its laws

state capitalism an economic system under which the State owns a very large part of the means of production

state chicken (*mil.*) in air intercept, a code meaning *I am at a fuel state requiring recovery, tanker service, or diversion to an airfield*

state-craft (stéitkræft, stéitkrɑft) *n.* the art of managing state affairs

stat·ed (stéitid) *adj.* fixed, declared, *the stated price* ‖ officially recognized ‖ explicitly announced, *his stated opinion*

State Department the department of the executive branch of the U.S. government in charge of foreign relations

state·house (stéithaus) *pl.* **state·hous·es** (stéithauziz) *n.* a state capitol

state lamb (*mil.*) in air intercept, a code meaning *I do not have enough fuel for an intercept plus reserve required for carrier recovery.*

state·less (stéitlis) *adj.* being without a registered or recognized nationality or citizenship

state·li·ness (stéitli:nis) *n.* the quality of being stately

state·ly (stéitli:) *comp.* **state·li·er** *superl.* **state·li·est** *adj.* of dignified and impressive appearance or manner

state·ment (stéitmənt) *n.* the act of stating in speech, writing etc. ‖ that which is stated ‖ (*mus.*) the stating of a theme or the theme itself ‖ a financial accounting sheet setting out liabilities and assets

Stat·en Island (stǽt'n) an island (area 57 sq. miles) in New York harbor, part of New York City (*RICHMOND, New York)

Staten Island (*Span.* Isla de los Estados) an island (c. 45 miles long) of Argentina, off the eastern tip of Tierra del Fuego

state of grace (*theol.*) the condition of being in receipt of divine favor

state of nature (*theol.*) the normal moral condition of man

state of the art the highest level of technology in a field at any given time —**state-of-the-art** *adj.*

state-registered nurse (*Br.*, *abbr.* S.R.N.) a nurse who is fully qualified, having passed the national examination

state·room (stéitru:m, stéitrum) *n.* a private cabin on a ship ‖ a private room on a train

State's attorney a State attorney

States General the bicameral legislative body in the Netherlands ‖ (*hist.*) the assembly of the three estates (clergy, nobles and commons) in the Netherlands (15th c.-1796) or in France (14th c.-1789) [trans. of F. *Etats Généraux*]

states·man (stéitsmən) *pl.* **states·men** (stéitsmən) *n.* a person having a large degree of responsibility in the government of a state ‖ such a person when characterized by wisdom and broadmindedness **státes·man·like** *adj.* characteristic of a wise statesman **státes·man·ly** *adj.* **státes·man·ship** *n.*

state socialism a theory that equalization of income and opportunity should be achieved through legislation by the existing state power, rather than through revolution

states' rights rights allowed (i.e. not denied) by the U.S. Constitution to individual states, as opposed to those vested in the federal government. A strong states' rights doctrine was expounded (1861–5) by the Confederate states. Any conflict between state and federal authority is settled by the supreme court of the U.S.A.

state tiger (*mil.*) in air intercept, a code meaning *I have sufficient fuel to complete my mission as assigned.*

stat·ic (stǽtik) **1.** *adj.* having no motion relative to the earth ‖ being in equilibrium while subject to two or more forces ‖ not changing, *static economy* **2.** *n.* atmospherics **stát·i·cal** *adj.* of statics [fr. Mod. L. *staticus*, acting by weight only fr. Gk *statikos*, causing to stand]

static electricity the charge possessed by stationary electric particles

static friction the force resisting the starting of sliding friction (cf. DYNAMIC FRICTION)

stat·ics (stǽtiks) *n.* a branch of science dealing with the relations among the forces that produce equilibrium

sta·tion (stéiʃən) **1.** *n.* a place where someone or something stands, either habitually or for a specified time, *the policeman took up his station near the door* ‖ a building, post etc. where a body of people work together, *a police station* ‖ a place along a route where trains or buses stop to take on or discharge passengers, merchandise etc. ‖ the building or buildings connected with this place ‖ an installation for the transmission and/or receipt of radio or television communication ‖ (*Austral.*) a sheep or cattle run with its buildings ‖ a place or region to which a ship, fleet etc. is assigned ‖ a position on a ship assigned to each member of the crew in case of emergency or battle ‖ rank, status in society ‖ (*biol.*) the characteristic habitat of a plant or animal **2.** *v.t.* to assign a position or post to [F.]

sta·tion·ar·y (stéiʃəneri:) *adj.* not moving ‖ not changing, *the temperature is stationary* ‖ not migratory or itinerant [fr. L. *stationarius*, having a fixed station]

stationary state (*phys.*) a stable or metastable quantum state associated with a wave (*QUANTUM THEORY), an integral number of whose wavelengths may be accommodated by the dimensions of the system

stationary wave (*phys.*) a standing wave

sta·tion·er (stéiʃənər) *n.* a seller of writing materials **sta·tion·er·y** (stéiʃəneri:) *n.* writing materials, esp. writing paper and envelopes [fr. L. *stationarius*, a tradesman with a fixed shop (not itinerant)]

sta·tion·mas·ter (stéiʃənmæstər, stéiʃənmɑstər) *n.* the official in charge of a railroad station

Stations of the Cross a series of 14 symbols, pictures or bas-reliefs, recalling episodes of the Passion of Jesus Christ, before which special devotions are performed, usually in a church

station wagon a car having a door at the rear end, and one row or two rows of rear seats which can be folded or removed to make room for extra luggage, equipment etc.

stat·ism (stéitizəm) *n.* economic control and planning by a highly centralized state government

stat·ist (stéitist) *n.* a statistician [fr. L. *status*, state]

stat·ist (stéitist) **1.** *n.* an advocate of statism **2.** *adj.* advocating statism

sta·tis·tic (stətístik) *n.* a statistical item [back-formation fr. STATISTICS]

sta·tis·ti·cal (stətístik'l) *adj.* of, concerning, based on or consisting of statistics [fr. older *statistic* fr. G. *statistisch* fr. Mod. L. *statisticus*]

statistical mechanics the study and description of physicochemical phenomena from the point of view of the statistical behavior of large ensembles of parts comprising a system, or of their mechanical motions (*KINETIC THEORY, *MAXWELL-BOLTZMAN DISTRIBUTION)

stat·is·ti·cian (stætistíʃən) *n.* an expert in collecting, compiling and interpreting statistics [fr. obs. *statistic*, statistics]

sta·tis·tics (stətístiks) *n.* the collection and study of numerical data, esp. as a branch of mathematics in which deductions are made on the assumption that the relationships between a sufficient sample of numerical data are characteristic of those between all such data ‖ (*pl.*) these data [pl. of obs. *statistic*, statistics fr. G. *statistik* fr. Mod. L. *statisticus* adj., of the state, statistical]

Sta·ti·us (stéiʃi:əs) Latin epic poet (c. 40-c. 96), author of the 'Thebaid' and the 'Achilleid'

stat·o·cyst (stǽtəsist) *n.* a vesicle containing a statolith, found in certain invertebrates. It functions as an organ of equilibrium [fr. Gk *statos*, stationary+CYST]

stat·o·lith (stǽtəliθ) *n.* the body contained in a statocyst. It is composed mainly of calcium carbonate ‖ a similar body in a fish or amphibian ‖ (*bot.*) a solid body in the cytoplasm, e.g. a starch grain, thought to be responsible for variations in orientation of an organ or part [fr. Gk *statos*, stationary+*lithos*, stone]

sta·tor (stéitər) *n.* the fixed part of an electrical machine, within which or around which the rotor revolves [L. fr. *stare*, to stand]

stat·o·scope (stǽtəskoup) *n.* an aneroid barometer for recording small variations in atmospheric pressure ‖ an instrument which registers small changes in the rise and fall of an aircraft [fr. Gk *statos*, stationary+*skopein*, to observe]

stat·u·ar·y (stǽtʃu:eri:) **1.** *n.* statues collectively ‖ the art of making statues **2.** *adj.* of or relating to statues or the making of statues ‖ (of a mate-

CONCISE PRONUNCIATION KEY: **(a)** æ, *cat*; ɑ, *car*; ɔ *fawn*; ei, *snake*. **(e)** e, *hen*; i:, *sheep*; iə, *deer*; ɛə, *bear*. **(i)** i, *fish*; ai, *tiger*; ə:, *bird*. **(o)** o, *ox*; au, *cow*; ou, *goat*; u, *poor*; ɔi, *royal*. **(u)** ʌ, *duck*; u, *bull*; u:, *goose*; ə, *bacillus*; ju:, *cube*. x, *loch*; θ, *think*; ð, *bother*; z, *Zen*; ʒ, *corsage*; dʒ, *savage*; ŋ, *orangutang*; j, *yak*; ʃ, *fish*; tʃ, *fetch*; 'l, *rabble*; 'n, *redden*. Complete pronunciation key appears inside front cover.

rial) suitable for making statues [fr. L. *statuarius* adj.]

stat·ue (stǽtʃuː) *n.* a three-dimensional representation of a person or animal, carved in stone, wood etc., or cast in bronze or plaster, or modeled in some plastic material [F. fr. L. *statua* fr. *stare* (*status*), to stand]

Statue of Liberty a bronze figure (almost 150 ft high) of a woman holding up a torch, on Liberty Island in New York harbor, designed by Bartholdi. It was completely refurbished for the celebration of its centennial in 1986

stat·u·esque (stætʃuːésk) *adj.* (esp. of a woman) strikingly tall and well proportioned ‖ having the stateliness and grace associated with statues

stat·u·ette (stætʃuːét) *n.* a very small statue [F.]

stat·ure (stǽtʃər) *n.* the height of a person ‖ moral or intellectual worth, esp. when impressively high [O.F.]

sta·tus (stéitəs, stǽtəs) *n.* position, rank or social standing ‖ prestige, *to confer status on someone* ‖ the legal position of a person, *marital status, the status of an alien* [L.]

status quo (kwou) *n.* the existing state of affairs [L.=state in which]

stat·ut·a·ble (stǽtʃutəbˈl) *adj.* statutory

stat·ute (stǽtʃuːt) *n.* a law passed by a legislative body and formally placed on record in a written or printed form ‖ the written or printed record of this law ‖ an ordinance of some chartered body, corporation etc. [F. *statut*]

statute book the written or printed record of the statutes of a state or nation

statute law the written law to be used in given circumstances as established by legislative acts (cf. COMMON LAW, cf. EQUITY)

statute mile a mile (1,760 yds) as a fixed unit of distance in the U.S.A. and Great Britain

statute of limitations (*law*) a statute stipulating a period of time after the elapsing of which civil or criminal proceedings cannot be undertaken in cases of specified kinds

Statute of Westminster *WESTMINSTER, STATUTE OF

stat·u·to·ry (stǽtʃutɔriː, stǽtʃutouriː) *adj.* of or relating to or having the nature of a statute or statutes ‖ conforming to a statute ‖ established by statute ‖ (of an offense) declared by statute to be an offense and therefore legally punishable

statutory rape sexual intercourse with a girl below the age of consent (even when she is willing)

staunch (stɔntʃ, stɑntʃ) *v.t.* to stanch

staunch *adj.* firmly loyal, *a staunch friend* ‖ (esp. of a ship) watertight ‖ strongly made [fr. O.F. *estanche*, watertight]

Sta·vang·er (stəvángər) a port (pop. 52,000) in S.W. Norway. Industries: fishing, shipbuilding, metallurgy, mechanical engineering. Romanesque-Gothic cathedral (12th-13th cc.)

stave (steiv) 1. *n.* one of the strips of wood set edge to edge to form the sides of a barrel, tub etc. ‖ (*mus.*) a staff ‖ the rung of a ladder ‖ a stanza of a poem or song 2. *v. pres. part.* **stav·ing** *past* and *past part.* **staved,** (esp. *naut.*) **stove** (stouv) *v.t.* (esp. with 'in') to break a hole in (a boat, cask etc.) ‖ to supply with staves *v.i.* (e.g. of a boat) to become stove in **to stave off** to keep at a distance, ward off, *to stave off a disaster* [fr. STAVES, alt. pl. of STAFF]

staves alt. *pl.* of STAFF

Stav·ro·pol (stávrəpʌl) (called Voroshilovsk 1935-43) a city (pop. 271,000) in the R.S.F.S.R., U.S.S.R., in the N. Caucasus: food processing, mechanical engineering, natural gas extraction

stay (stei) 1. *v.i.* to be in the same place or condition over a period, rather than change place or condition, *to stay indoors, stay calm* ‖ to reside for a while, *to stay at a hotel* ‖ to stop, halt, *stay where you are* ‖ to wait, *won't you stay till he comes?* ‖ to go on without flagging, *the favorite is staying well* ‖ *v.t.* (*rhet.*) to prevent or slow the progress of ‖ to postpone ‖ to appease (hunger, thirst etc.) temporarily ‖ to be in the same place or condition during (a period of time) ‖ (esp. with 'out') to be in the same place or condition until the end of, *he decided to stay the month out* ‖ to have unflagging endurance in (a race, course etc.) 2. *n.* a remaining in one place or residing, *a stay of one week* ‖ (*law*) a postponement, *a stay of execution* [A.F. *estaier*]

stay 1. *v.t.* to support, prop up 2. *n.* a prop, buttress etc. ‖ someone who or something that provides support and aid ‖ a strip of stiffening

material used in corsets, shirt collars etc. ‖ (*pl., old-fash.*) a corset [O.F. *estayer*]

stay 1. *n.* (*naut.*) a strong rope or cable supporting a mast or spar **in stays** (of a ship) tacking **to miss stays** (of a ship) to fail to make a tack 2. *v.t.* (*naut.*) to support or secure by means of stays ‖ (*naut.*) to put (a ship) on the other tack ‖ *v.i.* to tack [O.E. *stæg*]

stay-at-home (stéiəthɔum) 1. *n.* a person who prefers remaining in or near his own home to traveling around 2. *adj.* of, designating or characteristic of such a person

stay·be·hind (stéibiːhaind) *n.* (*mil.*) agent, or group of agents established in a given country to be activated in the event of overrun by hostile forces or other circumstances under which normal access would be denied —**staybehind force** *n.*

staying power stamina

stay-in strike a strike in which employees stay at their place of work but refuse to perform their duties

stay·sail (stéisˈl, stéiseil) *n.* (*naut.*) a sail spread on a stay

stead (sted) *n.* (in phrases) **in someone's** (or **something's**) **stead** in someone's (or something's) place as a substitute **to stand (someone) in good stead** to be of service to (someone), esp. in a difficulty [O.E *stede*]

stead·fast (stédfæst, stédfɑst, stédfəst) *adj.* adhering firmly and faithfully to a principle, cause etc. ‖ firm, unchanging, fixed, *a steadfast gaze* [O.E. *stedefæst*]

stead·i·ly (stédiliː) *adv.* in a steady manner

stead·i·ness (stédiːnis) *n.* the quality or state of being steady

stead·y (stédiː) 1. *comp.* **stead·i·er** *superl.* **stead·i·est** *adj.* not changing, constant, regular, *a steady speed* ‖ maintaining an unchanging position, posture or quality ‖ well balanced and serious, not frivolous ‖ (of a ship) keeping almost upright or keeping to the same course ‖ not easily excited or upset ‖ not given to sudden changes of behavior etc. **to go steady** (*pop.*) to go out regularly with the same person of the opposite sex, and only with that person ‖ (*pop.*, of two persons of the opposite sex) to go out together in this way 2. *v. pres. part.* **stead·y·ing** *past* and *past part.* **stead·ied** *v.t.* to make steady ‖ *v.i.* to become steady [prob. fr. STEAD]

steady state theory (*meteor.*) hypothesis that the universe had no beginning but was formed and continues to grow through the spontaneous creation of hydrogen, replenishing matter from all that is destroyed Cf BIG BANG THEORY

steak (steik) *n.* a beefsteak ‖ any thick slice of meat or fish [O.N. *steik*]

steak Diane a sirloin steak pounded thin, cooked in sherry and cognac

steal (stiːl) 1. *v. pres. part.* **steal·ing** *past* **stole** (stoul) *past part.* **sto·len** (stóulən) *v.t.* to take (something not rightfully belonging to one) without its owner's consent, esp. secretly ‖ to obtain without asking permission, *to steal a kiss* ‖ to secure, accomplish etc. without being seen, *she stole a glance at him* ‖ (*games*) to secure (a point, run etc.) by surprising the opponents' defense ‖ (*baseball*) to gain (another base) without the help of a hit or error ‖ *v.i.* to engage in stealing to go, come etc. without being noticed, *he stole silently away* ‖ (*baseball*) to get to a base without the help of a hit or error **to steal a march on** to get an advantage over by craftiness 2. *n.* (*Am.*=*Br.* snip) something bought or for sale at an unexpectedly low price, a real bargain ‖ (*baseball*) the act of stealing a base ‖ an instance of this [O.E. *stelan*]

stealth (stelθ) *n.* a way of taking action designed to escape notice, *they came upon him by stealth* [M.E. *stalthe, stelthe* fr. *stelan*, to steal]

Stealth (*mil.*) an aircraft coated with radar-absorbent material making it virtually invisible to radar. It was announced August 1980 *also* **stealthy aircraft**

stealth·i·ly (stélθiliː) *adv.* in a stealthy way

stealth·i·ness (stélθiːnis) *n.* the quality or state of being stealthy

stealth·y (stélθiː) *comp.* **stealth·i·er** *superl.* **stealth·i·est** *adj.* characterized by stealth

steam (stiːm) *n.* the invisible vapor into which water is converted when it boils ‖ the cloud of water droplets formed by the partial condensation of this vapor as it is cooled ‖ (*pop.*) energy, drive **to let (or blow) off steam** to get rid of surplus energy by activity or of emotional tension by expressing oneself strongly [O.E. *stēam*]

steam *v.i.* to emit steam or vapor ‖ to be converted into steam ‖ to escape into the air as steam, esp. as a cloud of steam ‖ to move as the result of propulsion by steam, *the train steamed out of the station* ‖ (of a surface) to become covered with condensed vapor ‖ *v.t.* to subject to the action of steam, in cooking, cleaning etc. ‖ to emit (steam or vapor) [O.E. *stēman, stȳman*]

steam·boat (stíːmbout) *n.* a steamship

steam boiler a boiler in which water is converted into steam

steam box the steam chest of a steam engine

steam chest a chamber where steam is stored before it enters the cylinder of a steam engine

steam coal hard coal used esp. for steam boilers

steam engine an engine, esp. a locomotive, driven by steam pressure

—The invention of the coal-burning steam engine revolutionized industrial production in the 18th c. and opened the way to the development of mechanized transport by rail and sea. The modern steam engine, using high-pressure superheated steam, remains a major source of electrical power and means of marine propulsion, though oil has replaced coal as the fuel in many installations and the reciprocating engine has given way to the steam turbine

steam·er (stíːmər) *n.* something driven by steam, e.g. a steamship or a steam engine ‖ a container, esp. a cooking utensil, in which things are steamed

steamer chair a deck chair

steam fitter a person who installs and repairs steam pipes and similar equipment

steam generator jumpers *SPONGES

steam hammer a forging hammer worked by steam power

steam·i·ly (stíːmiliː) *adv.* in a steamy manner

steam·i·ness (stíːmiːnis) *n.* the quality or state of being steamy

steam navvy (*Br.*) a steam shovel

steam·roll·er (stíːmroulər) 1. *n.* a steam-driven vehicle with a very heavy roller used for flattening freshly laid road surfaces ‖ (*pop.*) a person who or force that ruthlessly overrides any opposition 2. *v.t.* to flatten with a steamroller ‖ to impose (a policy, idea etc.) by overriding all opposition ‖ to force (a group etc.) to accept or approve a policy etc. ‖ *v.i.* to move ahead in the manner of a steamroller

steam·ship (stíːmʃip) *n.* a ship driven by steam

steam shovel (*Am.*=*Br.* steam navvy) a large, steam-operated digging machine

steam·y (stíːmiː) *comp.* **steam·i·er** *superl.* **steam·i·est** *adj.* full of steam ‖ giving off steam ‖ of or like steam ‖ covered with steam

steamy (*golf*) a short shot or putt that goes beyond the hole

ste·ar·ic (stiːǽrik, stíərik) *adj.* of, relating to, like or obtained from stearin ‖ of or relating to stearic acid [fr. F. *stéarique* fr. Gk *stear*, fat, tallow]

stearic acid a white, crystalline fatty acid, $CH_3(CH_2)_{16}COOH$, obtained esp. by saponification from animal and hard vegetable fats, and used in making candles, soap etc.

ste·a·rin (stíːərin) *n.* an ester of glycerol and stearic acid, found in many vegetable and animal fats **ste·a·rine** (stíːərːn) *n.* the solid part of a fat (cf. OLEIN) [F. *stéarine* fr. Gk *stear*, fat, tallow]

ste·a·tite (stíːətait) *n.* a gray-green or brown talc ‖ a porcelain made mainly from this, and used for insulators **ste·a·tit·ic** (stiːətítik) *adj.* [fr. L. *steatitis* fr. Gk fr. *stear*, tallow]

steed (stiːd) *n.* (*rhet.*) a horse, esp. one full of mettle and ridden in battle [O.E. *stēda*, stallion]

steel (stiːl) 1. *n.* any of numerous alloys of iron and 0.1–1.5% carbon in the form of iron carbide (esp. cementite), often with other metals (e.g. chromium, manganese, nickel etc.) alloyed to impart special physical properties. Steel can be cast, rolled, drawn etc. In the solid state it is hard and possesses great tensile strength. It is used in construction work, in cutting tools, in wire cables etc. It is formed by reducing the carbon content of cast iron, or by the diffusion of carbon into wrought iron ‖ a rod of steel with a rough surface, for sharpening knives ‖ (*rhet.*) a sword ‖ firm resolution, *a man of steel* ‖ a narrow, thin piece of steel used for stiffening, e.g. in a corset 2. *v.t.* to make (esp. oneself) resolute, *he steeled himself to undergo the pain* 3. *adj.*

---

made of, pertaining to, or like steel ‖ having the color of steel [O.E. *stýle*]

Steele (stiːl), Sir Richard (1672-1729), English man of letters, born in Dublin. He is best known for his essays in 'The Tatler' and 'The Spectator', the periodicals he edited, and largely wrote, in collaboration with Addison. He also wrote several comedies

steel engraving the process of engraving a design in steel ‖ an impression taken from the steel plate

steel·i·ness (stíːliːnis) *n.* the quality or state of being steely

steel wool a material made of intricately meshed fine steel shavings used for cleaning metal surfaces and smoothing wood surfaces

steel·work (stíːlwəːrk) *n.* the steel part of a construction ‖ articles in steel

steel·work·er (stíːlwəːrkər) *n.* someone employed in manufacturing steel

steel·works (stíːlwəːrks) *pl.* **steelworks** *n.*, *sing.* or *pl.* a plant where steel in manufactured

steel·y (stíːliː) *comp.* **steel·i·er** *superl.* **steel·i·est** *adj.* made of steel ‖ having great strength and hardness ‖ severe, cold and penetrating, *a steely stare* ‖ of the gray-blue color of tempered steel

Steel·yard (stíːljərd, stíːjərd) *(Eng. hist.)* the headquarters (13th c.-1597) in London of the Hanseatic League

steel·yard (stíːljərd, stíːjərd) *n.* a horizontal bar with its pivot near one end, having a short arm from which an object to be weighed is suspended, and a long graduated arm along which a counterweight is moved to produce equilibrium and give a reading from the graduations. Known masses suspended from the free end of the long arm enable greater loads to be weighed [fr. STEEL+YARD, (*obs.*) a rod]

Steen (stein), Jan (1626-79), Dutch painter. He specialized in domestic and tavern scenes

steen·bok (stíːnbɒk, stéinbɒk) *n.* a member of *Raphicerus*, a genus of small antelopes of E. and S. Africa, esp. *R. campestris* [Du. fr. *steen*, stone+*bok*, buck (male goat)]

steep (stiːp) **1.** *adj.* making a large angle, approaching 90° with the horizontal, *a steep hillside* ‖ (*pop.*, of a demand, price etc.) excessive ‖ (of an account, tale etc.) exaggerated or incredible **2.** *n.* a steep slope, esp. of a hill [O.E. *stēap*, high]

steep **1.** *v.t.* to soak (something) thoroughly in a liquid ‖ to cause (tea etc.) to infuse ‖ (often *fig.*) to immerse, saturate ‖ *v.i.* to soak in a liquid to infuse **2.** *n.* a steeping or being steeped ‖ the liquid in which something is steeped [M.E. *stepe*, *stipa*]

steep·en (stíːpən) *v.t.* to make (a slope etc.) steeper ‖ *v.i.* to become steeper

stee·ple (stíːpʼl) *n.* a church tower together with a spire ‖ a spire [O.E. *stýpel*, *stēpel*]

stee·ple·chase (stíːpʼltʃeis) *n.* a horse race with jumps, either across country or on a special course ‖ a cross-country foot race with obstacles **stée·ple·chas·er** *n.* a horse or rider, or a runner, in a steeplechase [orig.=a cross-country race towards a church steeple]

stee·ple·jack (stíːpʼldʒæk) *n.* a man who professionally repairs or paints lofty structures, e.g. spires or tall chimneys

Steer (stiər), Philip Wilson (1860-1942), English landscape painter. He was greatly influenced by the French Impressionists

steer (stiər) *n.* a young castrated bull [O.E. *stēor*]

steer **1.** *v.t.* to direct the course of, *to steer a ship*, *to steer the conversation around to a certain topic* ‖ to direct (a course) ‖ *v.i.* to direct the course of a ship, car etc. ‖ to respond to such directing, *this car steers easily* **to steer clear of** to avoid **2.** *n.* (*pop.*) a friendly hint or suggestion [O.E. *stīeran*]

steer·age (stíəridʒ) *n.* the part of some passenger ships allotted to passengers paying the smallest fare, and providing the barest accommodation ‖ the effectiveness of the helm in steering a ship

steer·age·way (stíəridʒwei) *n.* (*naut.*) a forward speed sufficient to enable a ship to answer the helm

steering committee a committee in a legislative or other body concerned with controlling the order of business

steering wheel the wheel which controls the direction of a vehicle or vessel

steers·man (stíərzmən) *pl.* **steers·men** (stíərzmən) *n.* (*naut.*) a helmsman

steeve (stiːv) **1.** *v.t. pres. part.* **steev·ing** *past*

and *past part.* **steeved** to stow (cargo) in the hold of a ship **2.** *n.* a long spar used for stowing cargo [F. *estiver*]

steeve **1.** *v. pres. part.* **steev·ing** *past* and *past part.* **steeved** *v.i.* (of a bowsprit) to have an upward angle from the horizontal ‖ *v.t.* to cause (a bowsprit) to have such an angle **2.** *n.* this angle [etym. doubtful]

Stef·an's law (stéfænz) (*phys.*) the statement that the total amount of thermal radiation emitted per second per square centimeter of a black body is proportional to the fourth power of the body's absolute temperature [after Josef Stefan (1835–93), Austrian physicist]

Stef·fens (stéfænz), (Joseph) Lincoln I (18661936), U.S. journalist, political philosopher, and leader in the muckraker movement. His articles, collected in 'The Shame of the Cities' (1904), reveal with wit and irony the shortcomings of the Horatio Alger success story. His visit (1919) to Petrograd occasioned his remark, 'I have been over into the future, and it works'

steg·o·saur (stégəsɔr) *n.* a member of *Stegosaurus*, suborder *Stegosauria*, a genus of large herbivorous dinosaurs of the Upper Jurassic of North America, esp. *S. ungulatus*, which had a small head and rows of bony plates projecting up from the backbone [fr. Mod. L. *Stegosaurus* fr. Gk *stegos*, roof+*sauros*, lizard]

Stei·chen (stáikən), Edward (1879-1973), U.S. photographer. During the 1st world war he helped to introduce aerial photography

Stein (stain), Gertrude (1874-1946), American writer who lived chiefly in Paris from 1903. Her best-known book is 'The Autobiography of Alice B. Toklas' (1933). Her prose style was marked by syntactical experiment, and she had some influence on American writers of the 1920s

Stein (ʃtain), Baron Heinrich Friedrich Karl von and zum (1757-1813), Prussian statesman. As Prussian prime minister (1807-9) he abolished serfdom, made military service obligatory for all classes, and rearranged financial and administrative affairs. He was instrumental in forming the final coalition against Napoleon

stein (stain) *n.* an earthenware beer mug, usually with an attached lid ‖ the quantity of beer held in this [G., prob. fr. *steingut*, stoneware]

Stein·beck (stáinbek), John Ernst (1902-68), American novelist whose works include 'Of Mice and Men' (1937), 'The Grapes of Wrath' (1939), 'Cannery Row' (1945), 'East of Eden' (1952; film, 1955), 'The Winter of Our Discontent' (1961), and 'Travels with Charley' (1962). He won the Nobel prize for literature (1962)

stein·bock (stáinbɒk) *n.* an ibex [G.=wild goat]

steinbock *n.* a steenbok

Stei·ner (stáinər, ʃtáinər), Rudolf (1861-1925), German teacher and philosopher, born in Austria. He founded anthroposophy, a system of thought which attempted to deduce the nature of the world from the nature of humanity. His system of education is followed in a number of schools named after him

Stein·metz (stáinmets), Charles Proteus (1865-1923), American engineer and inventor, born in Germany. His work in electricity did much to advance the progress of applied industrial chemistry. The magnetic arc lamp was one of his many inventions

Stein·way (stáinwei), Henry (Heinrich Engelhard Steinweg, 1797-1871), German-U.S. piano manufacturer. who completed the first Steinway piano in New York City in the 1820s

ste·le (stíːliː, stiːl) *n.* an upright inscribed slab or pillar serving as a monument, grave marker etc. ‖ (*bot.*) the central cylinder of vascular tissue in the roots and stems of plants, surrounding the pith and consisting of the xylem, phloem and pericycle, and enclosed in turn by the cortex [fr. Gk *stēlē*]

stel·lar (stélər) *adj.* of or relating to a star ‖ like or having the nature of a star ‖ made of stars ‖ principal, *a stellar role* [fr. L.L. *stellaris* fr. L. *stella*, star]

stellar guidance (*mil.*) a system in which a guided missile may follow a predetermined course with reference primarily to the relative position of certain preselected celestial bodies

stellar wind (*meteor.*) charged particles (plasma) emitted from the corona of stars Cf SOLAR WIND

stel·late (stéleit) *adj.* shaped like a conventional star ‖ (of leaves, cells, ganglia etc.) coming out from a center in rays or points **stél·lat·ed** *adj.* [fr. L. *stellatus*, covered with stars]

Stel·len·bosch (stélənbuʃ) an agricultural market (pop. 18,000) in S.W. Cape Province, South Africa, founded in 1681. Afrikaans University (1916)

stel·li·form (stéliform) *adj.* having the shape of a star [fr. Mod. L. *stelliformis* fr. L. *stella*, star]

stel·lite (stélait) *n.* (*metall.*) any of several alloys composed mainly of cobalt with a smaller proportion of chromium, sometimes with other metals. Stellite is used in making surgical instruments, cutting tools etc. [*Stellite*, a trademark]

stel·lu·lar (stéljulər) *adj.* shaped like a small conventional star ‖ radiating like a star [fr. L.L. *stellula* dim. of *stella*, star]

stem (stem) **1.** *n.* the roughly cylindrical main aerial axis of a tree or plant which serves as its support and as the channel for conveying plant foods from the roots to the leaves, fruits etc. ‖ the slender connection between a flower, fruit or leaf and the branch, main stem or twig ‖ the shaft projecting from a watch, having a knob at the end for winding the spring ‖ the slender rod or tube supporting a wineglass or other vessel on its base ‖ the tube of a tobacco pipe ‖ the thick stroke of a printed or written letter ‖ (*mus.*) the vertical line extending up or down from the rounded part of a note ‖ (*gram.*) the part of a word which remains unchanged by inflectional additions ‖ the chief line of descent of a family ‖ (*naut.*) the vertical piece of iron or timber at the bow of a ship, to which the sides are fastened ‖ (*naut.*) the bow **from stem to stern** from one end to the other **2.** *v. pres. part.* **stem·ming** *past* and *past part.* **stemmed** *v.t.* to remove the stem of ‖ (of a ship or navigator) to make headway against (a current, tide etc.) ‖ (*rhet.*) to make progress against (a difficulty etc.) ‖ *v.i.* to be derived, *his reckless stems from vanity* [O.E. *stefn*, *stemn*]

stem **1.** *v. pres. part.* **stem·ming** *past* and *past part.* **stemmed** *v.t.* to dam up (a stream etc.) ‖ to hold back, *to stem an attack* ‖ *v.i.* (*skiing*) to slow down or stop by forcing outward the heel of one ski (single stemming) or both skis (double stemming) **2.** *n.* (*skiing*) an act of stemming [O.N. *stemma*]

stem-wind·ing (stémwaindiŋ) *adj.* very good; stirring; firstrate —**stem-winder** *n.*

sten (sten) *n.* a Sten gun

stench (stentʃ) *n.* a powerful, offensive smell [O.E. *stenc*]

sten·cil (sténsəl) **1.** *n.* a thin sheet of metal, waxed paper etc., perforated with lettering or a design which is reproduced on a paper or fabric, on which the sheet is laid, when ink or paint is forced through the apertures ‖ the pattern or lettering so produced **2.** *v.t. pres. part.* **sten·cil·ing**, esp. *Br.* **sten·cil·ling** *past* and *past part.* **sten·ciled** esp. *Br.* **sten·cilled** to make (an impression) from a stencil ‖ to make an impression on (a paper or fabric) using a stencil [older *stanesile* prob. fr. M.E. *stansel* v., to ornament with varied colors]

Sten·dhal (stɛːdæl) (Marie Henri Beyle, 1783-1842), French writer. His deep psychological insight and the irony underlying his romanticism put him far in advance of his time, and his two greatest novels, 'le Rouge et le Noir' (1830) and 'la Chartreuse de Parme' (1839), became famous only long after his death. Each of these novels revolves around the unsuccessful struggle of a sensitive, intelligent young man to make a career or find happiness in the bigoted, reactionary society of the period following Napoleon's downfall. Stendhal also wrote short stories, accounts of travels and several autobiographical studies

Sten gun a British small, light submachine gun [fr. the initials of Sheppard and Turpin, its inventors+ENGLAND]

ste·nog·ra·pher (stənɔgrəfər) *n.* a person employed, e.g. in an office, to take down and transcribe shorthand [STENOGRAPHY]

sten·o·graph·ic (stɛnəgræfik) *adj.* of or relating to stenography ‖ written in shorthand **sten·o·gráph·i·cal** *adj.*

ste·nog·ra·phy (stənɔgrəfi) *n.* the process or skill of making and transcribing shorthand notes [fr. Gk *stenos*, narrow+*graphia*, writing]

sten·o·type (sténətaip) *n.* a letter or letter combination that represents a phonogram in stenotypy ‖ a machine that reproduces such symbols

sten·o·typ·y (sténətaipiː) *n.* a type of shorthand using ordinary letters to represent sounds,

CONCISE PRONUNCIATION KEY: **(a)** æ, c*a*t; ɑ, c*a*r; ɔ f*aw*n; ei, sn*a*ke. **(e)** e, h*e*n; iː, sh*ee*p; iə, d*ee*r; ɛə, b*ea*r. **(i)** i, f*i*sh; ai, t*i*ger; əː, b*i*rd. **(o)** o, *o*x; au, c*ow*; ou, g*oa*t; u, p*oo*r; ɔi, r*oy*al. **(u)** ʌ, d*u*ck; u, b*u*ll; uː, g*oo*se; ə, b*a*cillus; juː, c*u*be. x, lo*ch*; θ, *th*ink; ð, bo*th*er; z, *Z*en; ʒ, corsa*g*e; dʒ, sava*g*e; ŋ, ora*ng*utang; j, *y*ak; ʃ, *f*ish; tʃ, fe*tch*; 'l, rabb*le*; 'n, redd*en*. Complete pronunciation key appears inside front cover.

words and phrases [fr. Gk *stenos*, narrow+*tupē*, impression]

sten·tor (sténtɔr) *n.* a member of *Stentor*, a genus of trumpet-shaped protozoans, often brightly colored [Mod. L., after *Stentor*, Gk herald in the Iliad who had a powerful voice]

sten·to·ri·an (stentɔ́riːən, stentóuriːən) *adj.* (of the voice, spoken sounds etc.) very loud [after *Stentor*, Gk herald in the Iliad who had a powerful voice]

step- (step) *prefix* a combining element used with kinship terms to specify degree of affinity as a result of parental remarriage [O.E. *stēop-*]

step (step) *n.* a single movement made by lifting up one foot and setting it down in a different position ‖ the distance covered by such a movement ‖ a manner of moving on foot, *a heavy step* ‖ a mark or sound made by the foot in walking etc. ‖ one of a series of movements in dancing ‖ a set sequence of movements in dancing ‖ (*pl.*) a course followed in walking, *to retrace one's steps* ‖ pace, esp. in marching ‖ something on which the foot is placed in ascending or descending ‖ one unit in a flight of stairs or (*pl.*) a flight of esp. outdoor stairs or a series of these ‖ the rung of a ladder ‖ (*Br., pl.*) a stepladder ‖ a very short distance, *a step away* ‖ a degree in a scale, *to go up a step in someone's estimation* ‖ one of a series of stages in a process, activity etc. ‖ (*mus.*) a degree of the staff or scale ‖ (*mus.*) the interval between two such consecutive degrees ‖ (*naut.*) the socket holding a mast ‖ (of a quarry or mine) a shelf or ledge cut in the vertical surface ‖ (*mech.*) the lower bearing on which a vertical shaft rotates **in step** synchronizing the movements of one's feet with those of others with whom one is walking, marching or dancing **out of step** not in step **step by step** gradually **to keep step** to stay in step **to take steps** to begin to do what is necessary in order to achieve a certain purpose [O.E. *stœpe*, *stepi*]

step *pres. part.* **step·ping** *past* and *past part.* **stepped** *v.i.* to move by performing a step or steps, *please step forward* ‖ to execute a step with the foot ‖ to put or press the foot on something specified, *to step on someone's foot* ‖ (*pop.*) to walk a little way, *step down to the drug store* ‖ to enter into a position, condition etc. as if with a step, *to step into a fortune* ‖ *v.t.* to take (a stride etc.), *step three paces* ‖ to execute the steps of (a dance) ‖ (*naut.*) to fit (a mast) into its socket ‖ to provide with steps **to step down** to give up a position of authority, retire ‖ to decrease the voltage of (an electric current) using a transformer **to step in** to intervene **to step off** to pace (a distance) **to step on it** (*pop.*) to hurry **to step out** to begin to walk faster ‖ to go out to have a good time ‖ to leave a room, house etc. for a short time ‖ (*Br.*) to pace (a distance) **to step up** to increase, *to step up production* ‖ to increase the voltage of (an electric current) using a transformer [O.E. *stepan*, *stœpan*]

step·broth·er (stépbrʌðər) *n.* one's stepparent's son by a former marriage

step-by-step (stépbaistép) *adj.* gradual

step-by-step diplomacy the techniques of the Nixon-Ford administrations' efforts from 1973 to 1975 to settle the Arab-Israeli conflict

step·child (stéptʃaild) *pl.* **step·chil·dren** (stéptʃildrin) *n.* the child of one's husband or wife by a former marriage [O.E. *stēopcild*]

step·daugh·ter (stépdɔːtər) *n.* a female stepchild [O.E. *stēopdohtor*]

step-down (stépdaun) *n.* a decrease in amount, size, power, importance etc.

step·fa·ther (stépfɑðər) *n.* a male stepparent [O.E. *stēopfœder*]

Ste·phen (stíːvən) (c. 1097-1154), king of England (1135-54). Ignoring the oath he had sworn to his uncle Henry I that he would support the claim of Henry's daughter Matilda to the English throne, he invaded England on Henry's death (1135) and had himself proclaimed king. Matilda waged a civil war (1139-53) against him, in the course of which Stephen was imprisoned for six months (1141). The war ended when Stephen recognized Matilda's son Henry (later Henry II) as his heir

Stephen I, St (c. 969-1038), duke (997-1001) and first king (1001-38) of Hungary. He introduced Christianity into his kingdom, and is the patron saint of Hungary. Feast: Sept. 2

Stephen, St (*d.* c. 35 A.D.). the first Christian martyr, whose death by stoning prepared the eyewitness Saul (later St Paul) for his conversion. Feast: Dec. 26

Stephen Harding, St (*d.* 1134), English monastic reformer. As abbot of Cîteaux (c. 1109–c. 1134) he did much to strengthen the newly formed Cistercian order. Feast: Apr. 17

Ste·phens (stíːvənz), Alexander Hamilton (1812-83), vice-president of the Confederate States during the Civil War. As a champion of states' rights and civil liberty, he opposed the grant of extraconstitutional war powers to President Jefferson Davis. He urged (1864) the unconditional discharge of Federal prisoners in the South

Ste·phen·son (stíːvənsən), George (1781-1848), British engineer. He constructed the first successful steam locomotive (1814) and built the Stockton and Darlington line (1825), the first British passenger railroad. His 'Rocket' won an open competition for locomotives (1829), covering 12 miles in 53 minutes. He and his son Robert (1803-59) engineered many of the earliest railroads, in Britain and abroad

step·lad·der (stéplædər) *n.* a folding ladder having broad flat steps and a frame hinged to the back

step·moth·er (stépmʌðər) *n.* a female stepparent [O.E. *stēopmōdor*]

step·par·ent (stéppɛərənt, stéppærənt) *n.* the husband or wife of one's mother or father by a remarriage

steppe (step) *n.* a vast, treeless, usually level plain in S.E. Europe or Asia [fr. Russ. *stepi*]

step·ping-stone (stépiŋstoun) *n.* a stone, usually one of a series, projecting above the water of a stream, firmly placed in a marsh etc., enabling a crossing to be made by stepping from one stone to the next ‖ a means of advancement

step·sis·ter (stépsistər) *n.* one's stepparent's daughter by a former marriage

step·son (stépsʌn) *n.* a male stepchild [O.E. *stēopsunu*]

step-up (stépʌp) *n.* an increase in amount, size, power, importance etc.

ste·ra·di·an (stəréidiːən) *n.* unit solid angle, being the solid angle subtended at the center of a sphere by an area of its surface equal to the square of the radius [fr. Gk *stereos*, solid+RADIAN]

ster·co·ra·ceous (stəːrkəréiʃəs) *adj.* of, relating to or containing dung [fr. L. *stercus* (*stercoris*), dung]

ster·e·o (stériːou, stíəriːou) **1.** *n.* (*printing*) a stereotype ‖ a stereoscopic method, effect or system, e.g. a stereoscopic photograph or a stereophonic sound system **2.** *adj.* of or relating to space ‖ stereoscopic ‖ stereophonic [by shortening]

ster·e·o·bate (stériːəbeit, stíəriːəbeit) *n.* (*archit.*) a solid foundation of a building, pillar etc. as visible above ground [F. or L.]

ster·e·o·chem·is·try (stèriːoukémistriː, stìəriːoukémistriː) *n.* the study of the space arrangement of the atoms in a molecule and their effect on chemical properties [fr. Gk *stereos*, solid+CHEMISTRY]

ster·e·o·gram (stériːəgræm, stíəriːəgræm) *n.* a stereographic diagram or stereograph [fr. Gk *stereos*, solid+*gramma*, a letter]

ster·e·o·graph (stériːəgræf, stíəriːəgræf, stériːəgrɑːf, stíəriːəgrɑːf) *n.* a design or picture viewed stereoscopically, or made to represent solid figures in three dimensions **ster·e·og·ra·phy** (stèriːógrəfiː, stìəriːógrəfiː) *n.* the technique of drawing solid bodies on a plane surface ‖ stereoscopic photography [fr. Gk *stereos*, solid+*graphos*, written]

ster·e·o·i·so·mer·ic (stèriːouaisəmérik, stìəriːouaisəmérik) *adj.* of, pertaining to or exhibiting stereoisomerism

ster·e·o·i·som·er·ism (stèriːouaisómərizəm, stìəriːouaisómərizəm) *n.* isomerism which results from different space arrangements of atoms in molecules of the same composition and structural formula (*STRUCTURAL ISOMERISM, cf. OPTICAL ISOMERISM, cf. GEOMETRICAL ISOMERISM) [fr. Gk *stereos*, solid+ISOMERISM]

ster·e·ol·o·gy (stèriːólədʒiː, stìəriːólədʒiː) *n.* the study of three-dimensional objects seen in two dimensions, e.g., in brain studies —**stereological** *adj.* —**stereologically** *adv.*

ster·e·o·met·ric (stèriːəmétrik, stìəriːəmétrik) *adj.* of or produced by stereometry **ster·e·o·mét·ri·cal** *adj.* **ster·e·o·mét·ri·cal·ly** *adv.*

ster·e·om·e·try (stèriːómitriː, stìəriːómitriː) *n.* the science of determining the volumes of solid figures [fr. Gk *stereos*, solid+*-metria*, measurement]

ster·e·o·phon·ic (stèriːəfónik, stìəriːəfónik) *adj.*

of sounds which appear to have their sources distributed in space, even when they are emitted by e.g. two loudspeakers [fr. Gk *stereos*, solid+*phōnē*, voice]

ster·e·op·ti·con (stèriːóptikɒn, stìəriːóptikɒn) *n.* a pair of projectors used in conjunction so that one view seems to dissolve while the next forms [Mod. L. fr. Gk *stereos*, solid+*optikos*, optic]

ster·e·o·scope (stériːəskoup, stíəriːəskoup) *n.* a device by which each of two photographs, taken from slightly different angles, is viewed by one eye only, giving the impression of a three-dimensional view **ster·e·o·scop·ic** (stèriːəskópik, stìəriːəskópik), **ster·e·o·scóp·i·cal** *adjs* **ster·e·o·scóp·i·cal·ly** *adv.* **ster·e·os·co·py** (stèriːóskəpiː, stìəriːóskəpiː) *n.* [fr. Gk *stereos*, solid+*skopein*, to observe]

ster·e·o·tape (stériːəteip) *n.* magnetic tape that records sound stereophonically —**stereotape** *adj.*

ster·e·o·tax·is (stèriːətǽksis) *n.* (*med.*) three-dimensional location of a point in the nervous system from coordinates guiding an electrode or needle —**stereotaxic** *adj.* —**stereotaxically** *adv.*

ster·e·o·type (stériːətaip, stíəriːətaip) **1.** *n.* a plate providing a solid printing surface cast from a mold taken from a body of movable type ‖ a rigidly conventional expression, idea, character etc. **2.** *v.t. pres. part.* **ster·e·o·typ·ing** *past* and *past part.* **ster·e·o·typed** to make (a plate) from movable type ‖ to print (an impression) from a stereotype **stér·e·o·typed** *adj.* lacking originality [F. *stéréotype*]

ster·e·o·typ·y (stériːətaipiː, stíəriːətaipiː) *n.* (*printing*) the process of making, and printing from, stereotype plates ‖ (*med.*) frequent, almost mechanical, repetition of the same action or formulas of speech, as in some cases of schizophrenia [F. *stéréotypie*]

ster·ic (stérik) *adj.* pertaining to the spatial arrangement of atoms [fr. Gk *stereos*, solid]

ste·rig·ma (stərígmə) *pl.* **ste·rig·ma·ta** (stərígmətə), **ste·rig·mas** *n.* a filament (esp. growing from the basidium of some fungi) from the top of which conidia are produced [Mod. L.]

ster·ile (stérəl, *Br.* esp. stérail) *adj.* lacking the ability to produce offspring ‖ lacking the ability to bear fruit, spores etc. ‖ (of land) unproductive ‖ (*bacteriol.*) free from living microorganisms ‖ lacking in inspiration, ideas etc., *a sterile writer* ‖ leading to no conclusion, *a sterile argument* [fr. L. *sterilis*]

ste·ril·i·ty (stəríliti:) *n.* the state or quality of being sterile [fr. L. *sterilitas*]

ster·i·li·za·tion (stèrəlizéiʃən) *n.* a sterilizing or being sterilized

ster·i·lize (stérəlaiz) *pres. part.* **ster·i·liz·ing** *past* and *past part.* **ster·i·lized** *v.t.* to render incapable of producing offspring ‖ to cause (soil) to become unfruitful by the deliberate use of a herbicide, or as the result of natural exhaustion of fertility ‖ to rid (instruments, surgical dressings etc.) of living microorganisms [fr. STERILE]

ster·let (stɔ́ːrlit) *n. Acipenser ruthenus*, fam. *Acipenseridae*, a small variety of sturgeon prized for its flavor and its caviar [fr. Russ. *sterlyadi*]

ster·ling (stɔ́ːrliŋ) **1.** *n.* the legal currency of England ‖ the legal currency (1707) of Great Britain ‖ (*hist.*) the English silver penny ‖ sterling silver ‖ articles made from sterling silver **2.** *adj.* of or relating to British sterling ‖ calculated in terms of British sterling ‖ (of silver) having an accepted standard of purity, usually 925 parts of silver alloyed with 75 parts of copper ‖ made of sterling silver ‖ of excellent quality, *sterling character* [prob. O.E. perh. fr. supposed *steorling*, coin with a star (some Norman coins bore a star)]

stern (stɔːrn) *adj.* severe, *stern discipline* ‖ uncompromising, *a stern judge* ‖ cold and forbidding in appearance, *a stern landscape, a stern face* ‖ (*rhet.*) determined, *stern resolve* [O.E. *styrne*]

stern *n.* the rear end of a ship [prob. fr. O.N. *stjörn*, steering]

sterna alt. *pl.* of STERNUM

ster·nal (stɔ́ːrn'l) *adj.* of, relating to or situated near the sternum

stern chase (*naut.*) a chase in which the pursuing vessel follows in the wake of the vessel being pursued

stern drive (*motorboating*) motor with an inboard engine on an outboard drive *also* inboard-outboard

Sterne (stə:rn), Laurence (1713-68), British writer, born in Ireland. His works include 'The Life and Opinions of Tristram Shandy, Gentleman' (1759-67) and 'A Sentimental Journey through France and Italy' (1768). These are an extraordinary mixture of prurience, robustness and sentimentality. Their sentimental element is a part of the 18th-c. cult of sensibility. The enormous rambling structure is all Sterne's own

stern·fore·most (stə́:rnfɔ́rmọust, stə́:rnfóurmọust) adv. (of a ship) with the stern foremost

stern·most (stə́:rnmọust) adj. farthest astern

stern·post (stə́:rnpọust) n. (naut.) a post, usually now of metal, joining the keel to the stern deck and usually having the rudder attached

stern sheets (naut.) the space between the stern of an open boat and the thwart nearest to it

stern·son (stə́:rnsən) n. (naut.) the end of a keelson to which the sternpost is fastened

ster·num (stə́:rnəm) pl. **ster·nums, ster·na** (stə́:rnə) n. the broad vertical bone to which the ribs are attached in front [Mod. L. fr. Gk sternon, chest]

stern·way (stə́:rnwẹi) n. (naut.) progress stern foremost

ster·oid (stérɔid) n. (chem.) any of a class of compounds having a complex structure like the sterols, and that usually includes the sterols and numerous naturally occurring compounds, e.g. vitamin D, certain hormones and glucosides [fr. STEROL+Gk eidos, form]

ster·ol (stéroul, stérɔl) n. (chem.) any of a large class of complex alcohols, some of which (e.g. cholesterol, ergosterol) are highly active physiologically. They are characterized by a complex four-ring molecular system [fr. CHOLESTEROL, ERGOSTEROL]

ster·tor (stə́:rtər) n. (med.) the act of making a heavy sound like snoring while breathing, or an instance of this **ster·tor·ous** (stə́:rtərəs) adj. [Mod. L. fr. stertere, to snore]

Ste·sich·o·rus (stesíkərəs) (6th c. B.C.), Greek poet, author of choral lyrics on epic subjects. Only fragments survive

stet (stet) 1. n. the word used as an indication to a printer that an instruction to delete is to be ignored. (Dots are also put under the matter concerned.) 2. v.t. pres. part. **stet·ting** past and past part. **stet·ted** to write 'stet' against [L.=let it stand]

steth·o·scope (stéθəskọup) n. (med.) an instrument which, placed on the thorax, conveys amplified sounds of the heartbeat or lung action, through earphones, to a doctor examining a patient **steth·o·scop·ic** (steθəskópik), **steth·o·scóp·i·cal** adj. **steth·o·scóp·i·cal·ly** adv. **ste·thos·co·py** (steθóskəpi): n. [F. stéthoscope fr. Gk stethos, chest+skopein, to observe]

Stet·son (stétsən) n. a wide-brimmed felt hat with a high crown, worn esp. by cowboys [Trademark, after John Batterson Stetson (1830-1906), U.S. hat manufacturer]

Stet·tin (ʃtetí:n) *SZCZECIN

Stet·tin·i·us (stətíni:əs), Edward Reilly, Jr (1900-49), U.S. industrialist and statesman. He strongly influenced the formation of the United Nations, and served (1945-9) as the first U.S. delegate to that body

Steuart *STUART

Steu·ben (stú:bən, stjú:bən, ʃtɔ́iben), Frederick William Augustus, Baron von (1730-94), Prussian officer who trained American soldiers during the Revolutionary War. His Regulations for the Order and Discipline of the Troops of the United States (1779) served until 1812 as the official U.S. military manual

Ste·van Du·šan (stévəndú:ʃən) (c. 1308-55), king (1331-46) and czar (1346-55) of Serbia. He subjugated Albania, Thessaly, Epirus and all of Macedonia except Salonica, and dominated much of the Byzantine Empire. He died while marching on Constantinople

Stevan Ne·man·ja (nimánja) (1114-1200), ruler of Serbia (1168-96). He founded the first effective Serbian state, which was ruled by his descendants until 1371

ste·ve·dore (stí:vədɔr, stí:vədour) n. a man employed to store goods in a ship's hold, or to unload such goods [fr. Span. estivador fr. estivar, to stow cargo]

Ste·vens (stí:vənz), Alfred (1817-75), British sculptor, painter and draftsman best known for his equestrian statue of Wellington in St Paul's Cathedral

Stevens, John (1749-1838), U.S. inventor of marine and rail conveyances. His petition to Congress secured the Patent Law of 1790, the basis for the present U.S. patent system. He was the first to use steam power for screw propulsion in navigation. His 'Phoenix' made (1807) the first voyage of a steamboat in ocean waters. He introduced (1811) the world's first steam-ferry service. He obtained (1815) the first U.S. charter for a railway ever granted, and designed (1825) the first U.S. steam locomotive

Stevens, Thaddeus (1792-1868), U.S. politician. A Whig (1849-53) and then a Republican (1859-68) member of the House of Representatives from Pennsylvania, he became chairman of the House Ways and Means committee in 1861 and was instrumental in developing Reconstruction policy. At odds with Pres. Andrew Johnson over the Reconstruction issue, he was unable to get his own rigid schedule passed, but he did establish one of political and legal equality for blacks. He served as a House prosecutor during the impeachment trial of Pres. Johnson (1868)

Stevens, Wallace (1879-1955), American poet. His themes are the related ones of the relativity (and sensuousness) of sense perception, the nature of art and the order it creates, the relations of subject and object, the problem of belief, the possibility of the meeting of minds in art. All this is expressed in colorful, whimsical, light-toned verse, full of neologisms, words borrowed from other languages, and curious turns of phrase. His ideas are well expressed in his earliest work 'Harmonium' (1923). Other works include 'Ideas of Order' (1936), 'The Man with the Blue Guitar' (1937), 'Transport to Summer' (1947)

Ste·ven·son (stí:vənsən), Adlai Ewing (1900-65), U.S. political leader, twice defeated (1952, 1956) as Democratic contender for the U.S. presidency by Dwight D. Eisenhower. He became (1961) U.S. Ambassador to the United Nations

Stevenson, Robert (1772-1850), Scottish engineer, famous as a builder of lighthouses

Stevenson, Robert Louis (1850-94), British novelist, essayist and poet. Among his novels are 'Kidnapped' (1886), 'The Strange Case of Dr Jekyll and Mr Hyde' (1886) and 'The Master of Ballantrae' (1889). Some of his essays were collected in 'Virginibus Puerisque' (1881) and he also wrote travel accounts, e.g. 'Travels with a Donkey in the Cévennes' (1879). He was a meticulous craftsman and a rare storyteller. His adventure story 'Treasure Island' (1883) is one of the immortal children's books, and 'A Child's Garden of Verses' (1885) remains a classic

stew (stu:, stju:) 1. v.t. to cook slowly and for a long time in a relatively small amount of liquid in a closed vessel, just below boiling point ‖ v.i. to be cooked in this way ‖ (of a person) to feel as if being slowly cooked because of heat or lack of oxygen ‖ (pop.) to fret, to be anxious, to stew about the weather to stew in one's own juice to suffer the consequences of one's actions 2. n. stewed meat and vegetables or a dish of this ‖ (pop.) a condition of anxious turmoil, to be in a stew [O.F. estuver]

stew·ard (stú:ərd, stjú:ərd) 1. n. a ship's officer in charge of stores and arrangements about meals ‖ a male attendant who looks after the personal needs of passengers aboard ship ‖ an employee on an airplane, train etc. in charge of preparing and serving meals etc. (Br.) someone who shows people to their seats and maintains order at a public meeting, dance, public performance etc. ‖ someone who is responsible for the conduct of a race, athletic meet etc. ‖ a manager, acting for the owner, of a large landed estate, its mansion, tenants etc. ‖ an official responsible for provisioning a club, college etc. 2. v.t. to act as a steward for **stéw·ard·ess** n. a woman steward, e.g. on an airplane (Am.= Br. air hostess) or one who attends female passengers on a ship **stéw·ard·ship** n. [O.E. stiweard]

Stew·art (stú:ərt, stjú:ərt), Potter (1915-85), U.S. Supreme Court associate justice (1956-81). A judge of the 6th circuit U.S. Court of Appeals, he was appointed to the Supreme Court by Pres. Dwight Eisenhower. He was a moderate and often responsible for casting the 'swing vote' when the court was split. He wrote the majority opinion in 'Elkins v. United States' (1960), concerning illegally obtained evidence; 'Katz v. United States' (1967), prohibiting unauthorized wiretaps; and 'Jones v. Alfred H. Mayer Co.'

(1968) and 'Hills v. Gautreaux' (1976), both civil rights cases

Stewart, Robert, Viscount Castlereagh *CASTLEREAGH

Stewart *STUART

Stewart, Dugald (1753-1828), British moral philosopher. He expounded the philosophy of Reid, i.e. a belief in the existence of the external world and in the application of common sense to philosophical problems. His principal work is 'Elements of the Philosophy of the Human Mind' (3 vols, 1792-1827)

Stewart Island an island (area 670 sq. miles, pop. 500) south of South Island, New Zealand: fish, granite

stew·pan (stú:pæn, stjú:pæn) n. a pan with a lid, used for stewing

S-3 (mil.) *VIKING

stib·ine (stíbi:n, stíbain) n. a poisonous, gaseous compound, SbH₃, of antimony and hydrogen [STIBIUM]

stib·i·um (stíbi:əm) n. antimony [L.]

stib·nite (stíbnait) n. a mineral, Sb₂S₃, occurring in prismatic crystals and providing one of the main sources of antimony [STIBINE]

stick (stik) 1. n. a piece of wood cut or broken from a tree ‖ such a piece of wood shaped and smoothed for a particular use, e.g. a walking stick, a drumstick ‖ something resembling a thin, shaped piece of wood, a stick of sealing wax ‖ a number of bombs released from an aircraft to explode at regularly spaced points along a straight line ‖ (naut.) a mast ‖ (sports) any of the various implements used to propel a ball etc., e.g. a hockey stick ‖ (aeron.) a vertical lever by which certain controls are operated ‖ (printing) a composing stick ‖ (printing) type which, when set, occupies 2 ins of one column, esp. in a newspaper ‖ a piece or part of something, not a stick of furniture remained ‖ (pop., with 'the') a beating ‖ (pop.) a stiff, formal person, a dull old stick the sticks (pop.) the remote countryside, backwoods 2. v.t. to furnish (a plant) with sticks as climbing supports [O.E. sticca]

stick pres. part. **stick·ing** past and past part. **stuck** (stʌk) v.t. to cause to adhere, to stick a stamp on an envelope ‖ to paste or otherwise fasten (a notice, poster etc.) to a board, wall etc. for public attention ‖ (with 'in', 'into' or 'through') to thrust (a pointed object) so as to penetrate or pierce something or someone, she stuck a pin into the cloth ‖ to penetrate or pierce with a pointed thing or things, to stick a pincushion with pins ‖ to place (various objects) here and there, to stick knickknacks all over a room ‖ to put casually, he stuck the letter in his pocket ‖ (pop.) to force to do an unpleasant chore or to pay a bill, by some kind of ruse, they stuck him for the entire dinner ‖ v.i. to become embedded in something by means of a sharp point ‖ to adhere ‖ to become fixed, the car stuck in the mud ‖ to become or remain motionless, the car stuck on the hill ‖ to continue one's efforts in spite of a desire to let them slack off, he never sticks to anything for very long ‖ to scruple, draw the line, he sticks at nothing ‖ to remain, he stuck close to my heels ‖ (with 'out', 'up', 'down' etc.) to protrude to stick by to remain loyal to to stick out to be insistent and not give in ‖ to endure to stick up to commit armed robbery upon to stick up for to support in argument, take the part of **stíck·er** n. someone who pastes up notices ‖ someone whose job is to sever the jugular vein of an animal in a slaughterhouse ‖ an adhesive label ‖ a rod connecting two reciprocating levers of an organ ‖ a person, racehorse etc. showing powers of endurance ‖ (pop.) a puzzling problem [O.E. stician]

stick·com·mand·er (stíkəmændər) n. (mil.) individual who is in charge of parachutists from the time they enter an aircraft until the time of their exit

stick·i·ly (stíkili) adv. in a sticky way

stick·i·ness (stíki:nis) n. the state or quality of being sticky

sticking plaster adhesive tape used to cover wounds

stick insect any of various insects of Phasmatidae and related families of suborder Phasmatodea, having a long, thin, sticklike body

stick lac the natural lac that covers small twigs and lac insects, used in dyes, polishes etc.

stick·le (stík'l) pres. part. **stick·ling**, past and past part. **stick·led** v.i. to be obstinate about a trifling matter ‖ (with 'at') to refrain from action because of scruples, to stickle at signing a petition [M.E. stightle fr. O.E. stihtan, to rule, set in order]

stick·le·back (stík'lbæk) *n.* any of various small scaleless fishes of fam. *Gasterosteidae* found in both fresh and salt water and having sharp spines in front of the dorsal fin. The male builds the nest and guards it during the breeding season [fr. O.E. *sticel*, a prick]

stick·ler (stíklər) *n.* a person who exaggerates the importance and insists on the observance of regulations etc. ‖ (*pop.*) a puzzling problem, question etc.

stick·pin (stíkpin) *n.* an ornamental pin worn in a necktie

stick shift (*automobile*) a manually operated gearshift mechanism on the floor or steering column of a motor vehicle

stick·up (stíkʌp) *n.* an armed robbery

stick·y (stíki:) *comp.* **stick·i·er** *superl.* **stick·i·est** *adj.* tending to stick ‖ covered with something adhesive or gummy, *sticky fingers* ‖ (*cricket*, of a wicket) having a yielding surface after rain ‖ (*pop.*) difficult, *a sticky problem* ‖ apt to be hard to please or persuade ‖ (of climate) very humid

Stieg·litz (stí:glits), Alfred (1864-1946), U.S. photographer whose photographic prints, notably the portrait of Georgia O'Keeffe and the 'Equivalents', were the first to be displayed in U.S. museums

stiff (stif) 1. *adj.* resistant to bending or change of shape, *stiff bristles* ‖ (of muscles, joints etc.) sore and lacking in suppleness ‖ (of a semifluid substance) resisting the relative motion of its parts, *a stiff paste* ‖ (of machinery) hard to move ‖ resolute and unyielding ‖ lacking ease or grace ‖ formidable, *stiff competition* ‖ difficult, *a stiff examination* ‖ (of winds, currents) blowing or moving with strong, steady force ‖ (*pop.*) of high alcoholic content, *a stiff drink* ‖ (*pop.*, of prices) very high ‖ (*pop.*) severe, harsh, *a stiff fine* 2. *n.* (*pop.*) a person, *he's a lucky stiff* ‖ (*pop.*) a corpse 3. *adv.* exceedingly, *scared stiff* **stiff·en** *v.t.* to make stiff ‖ *v.i.* to become stiff [O.E. *stíf*]

stiff-necked (stífnekt) *adj.* (*rhet.*) obstinate in an arrogant way

sti·fle (stáifəl) *pres. part.* **sti·fling** *past and past.* **sti·fled** *v.t.* to keep (someone) from breathing by preventing the access of enough air ‖ to repress, *to stifle a yawn* ‖ to suppress, *to stifle a revolt* ‖ to silence, *the noise of the machine stifled his cries* ‖ *v.i.* to die or become stifled [M.E. *stufle, stuffle* cf. O.F. *estouffer*, to smother]

stifle *n.* the joint between the femur and tibia in the hind leg of a horse, dog and some other quadrupeds, corresponding to the knee in man [origin unknown]

sti·fling (stáifliŋ) *adj.* almost unbearably hot and stuffy

Stif·ter (ʃtíftər), Adalbert (1805-68), Austrian novelist. 'Der Nachsommer' (1857) and 'Witiko' (1865-7) were his best-known works, characterized by poetic realism. His 'Studien' (6 vols, 1844-50) is a collection of tales of the Bohemian forest

stig·ma (stígmə) *pl.* **stig·ma·ta** (stígmətə), **stig·mas** *n.* (*bot.*) that part of the pistil or gynoecium which receives the pollen ‖ (*zool.*) a body in some algae and protozoans that is sensitive to red light ‖ (*zool.*) an arthropod spiracle ‖ (*zool.*) the aperture of the trachea of insects ‖ (*zool.*) a colored wing spot of certain butterflies and other insects ‖ a mark of social disgrace, *the stigma attached to going bankrupt* **stig·ma·ta** *pl. n.* marks appearing on the body, sometimes accompanied by bleeding, which resemble the wounds of the crucified Christ [L. fr. Gk *stigma*, a prick]

stig·mat·ic (stigmætik) 1. *adj.* of or relating to a social stigma ‖ of or relating to stigmata ‖ (*phys.*) anastigmatic 2. *n.* someone who has stigmata [fr. M.L. *stigmaticus*]

stig·ma·tism (stígmətizəm) *n.* (*optics*) the condition of coming to a true focal point [prob. fr. Gk *stigmatismos*]

stig·ma·ti·za·tion (stigmətizéifən) *n.* a stigmatizing or being stigmatized

stig·ma·tize (stígmətaiz) *pres. part.* **stig·ma·tiz·ing** *past and past part.* **stig·ma·tized** *v.t.* to attach a label of disgrace to, *he stigmatized it as an act of cowardice* ‖ to mark with stigmata [M.L. *stigmatizare*]

Stijl, De (dəstáil) a Dutch movement advocating the synthesis of art and architecture, originated in 1917 by Theo van Doesburg and based on the neoplasticism of Mondrian. It stressed the exclusive use of horizontal and vertical lines and of primary colors. It influenced the Bauhaus

stil·bite (stílbait) *n.* a crystalline hydrous silicate of aluminum, calcium and sodium [F. fr. Gk *stilbein*, to shine]

stile (stail) *n.* an arrangement of steps on either side of a fence, for people to climb over. It eliminates the need for people to open a gate and so reduces the risk of cattle etc. escaping

stile *n.* one of the vertical boards in the frame of a paneled door etc. [perh. fr. Du. *stijl*, doorpost]

sti·let·to (stilétou) *pl.* **sti·let·tos, sti·let·toes** *n.* a small, thin dagger ‖ a pointed tool used to pierce holes in leather or cloth [Ital. dim. of *stilo*, dagger]

stiletto heel a very thin high heel on a woman's shoe

Stil·i·cho (stílikou), Flavius (c. 360-408), Roman general. As guardian of Honorius and regent of the Western Roman Empire (395-408), he fought several battles against the Visigoths under Alaric. He was arrested on the orders of Honorius, and executed for high treason after he had been accused of collusion with Alaric

Still (stil), Andrew Taylor (1828-1917), U.S. physician who founded (1892) at Kirksville, Mo., the first American School of Osteopathy

still (stil) *n.* an apparatus used for distilling alcoholic liquors or preparing distilled water

still 1. *adj.* having no motion, *still water* ‖ (of a beverage) not effervescing, *still cider* ‖ making or having no sound, *still night* 2. *n.* complete silence, *the still of the night* ‖ a static photograph, esp. one taken from a motion picture and used in publicity 3. *adv.* at a given time just as before it, *he was still expecting to be asked, I am still wondering what to do, they will still be here tomorrow* ‖ even now (even then), *I still don't (didn't) understand* ‖ (with comp.) even, *this is still hotter* ‖ without sound or movement, *sit still* ‖ (used intensively) yet, *still another example* 4. *conj.* nevertheless [O.E. *stille*]

still *v.t.* to quiet, *to still one's fears* ‖ to make silent, to satisfy or appease (a desire etc.) ‖ *v.i.* (*rhet.*) to become motionless or silent, the *music stilled and they began to chatter* [O.E. *stillan*]

still·age (stílidʒ) *n.* a stand on which e.g. a cask is placed to keep it off the ground

still bank nonmechanical bank with slot for inserting coins

still·birth (stílbə:rθ) *n.* the birth of a dead fetus

still·born (stílbɔrn) *adj.* dead when born

still life *pl.* **still lifes, still lives** a painting or photograph of inanimate objects ‖ painting or photography of such objects, as a genre

still·room (stílru:m, stílrum) *n.* (*Br.*) a room in a large house in which preserves, liqueurs etc. are kept

still·son wrench (stílsən) a wrench with an adjustable, milled jaw loosely bolted to a fixed milled jaw in such a way that pressure on the handle tightens the grip of the jaws. It is used for gripping and turning round objects (pipes etc.)

stilt (stilt) *n.* one of a pair of long poles, each of which has a footrest at some distance from its lower end, used to elevate the wearer and permit him to walk with long strides ‖ one of a number of posts on which a house is supported to raise it above ground or water level ‖ (*pottery*) a support which holds a pot above a shelf or sagger base in a kiln, so that the glaze will not unite with shelf or sagger ‖ a member of *Himantopus* or of *Cladorhynchus*, genera of long-legged, three-toed, limicoline birds inhabiting marshy places **stilt·ed** *adj.* raised on or supported by stilts ‖ (of speech, manner, style etc.) stiff and artificial ‖ (*archit.*) supported by vertical masonry set on the imposts of an arch [M.E.]

Stil·ton cheese (stílten) a rich cow's milk cheese made in Leicestershire, England [fr. *Stilton*, England, where it was first sold]

Stil·well (stílwel, stílwəl), Joseph Warren ('Vinegar Joe') (1883-1946), U.S. general, commander of U.S. Army forces in the China-Burma-India (CBI) theater during the 2nd world war. He fought vigorously but unsuccessfully to preserve the Burma Road supply line and to persuade China to break the Japanese blockade. A U.S. proposal that he be given command of all Chinese forces was rejected by the Chiang Kai-shek regime, which forced his recall

Stim·son (stímsən), Henry Lewis (1867-1950), U.S. lawyer and political leader. Appointed special commissioner to Nicaragua (then occupied by U.S. Marines) by President Calvin Coolidge, he arranged (1927) an armistice between President Adolfo Díaz and rebel leader José María Moncada, under which the U.S.A. would supervise the 1928 elections. As governor general of the Philippine Is, he strove to convert them into 'self-governing possessions or colonies whose citizens did not participate in our citizenship'. As Secretary of State (1929-33) under President Herbert Hoover, he set forth, in the wake of Japanese aggression in Manchuria, the Stimson Doctrine, whereby the U.S. government would not formally recognize any situation, treaty, or agreement violating U.S. treaty rights or the Pact of Paris. As secretary of war under President Franklin Roosevelt, he helped to expand the U.S. Army during the 2nd world war, and as chief atomic policy adviser to President Harry Truman, he recommended the bombing of Hiroshima and Nagasaki and later justified this on humanitarian grounds

stim·u·lant (stímjulənt) *n.* something which stimulates ‖ a drug or other agent which temporarily increases the activity of an organ or some vital process [fr. L. *stimulans* (*stimulantis*) fr. *stimulare*, to goad]

stim·u·late (stímjuleit) *pres. part.* **stim·u·lat·ing** *past and past part.* **stim·u·lat·ed** *v.t.* to rouse (a person), e.g. to greater effort ‖ to act as a spur to (intelligence, application etc.) ‖ to arouse (appetite) ‖ (*med.*) to activate the functioning of (an organ) ‖ *v.i.* to act as a stimulant [fr. L. *stimulare* (*stimulatus*)]

stim·u·la·tion (stimjuléifən) *n.* a stimulating or being stimulated [fr. L. *stimulatio* (*stimulationis*)]

stim·u·la·tive (stímjuleitiv) 1. *adj.* tending to stimulate 2. *n.* something which stimulates

stim·u·lose (stímjulous) *adj.* (*bot.*) having stinging hairs or cells [fr. Mod. L. *stimulosus*]

stim·u·lus (stímjuləs) *pl.* **stim·u·li** (stímjulai) *n.* something (e.g. an environmental change) that stimulates physiological activity ‖ something that acts as a spur to mental processes [L.=goad]

sting (stiŋ) 1. *v. pres. part.* **sting·ing** *past and past part.* **stung** (stʌŋ) *v.t.* to wound with a sting, esp. so as to produce a swelling or inflammation on the skin ‖ to affect with pain like that caused by a sting, *stung by sleet and wind* ‖ (*fig.*) to goad, *he was stung into action* ‖ to cause emotional pain to, *to be stung by a remark* ‖ (*pop.*) to overcharge or extract money from, *he stung me for ten dollars* ‖ *v.i.* to cause or feel the pain of a sting, *stinging icy water, his face stung in the wind* 2. *n.* the wound or pain caused by a stinger ‖ a sudden, sharp pain like that caused by a stinger ‖ a stinger ‖ something which causes an emotional pain ‖ the act of stinging ‖ stinging quality or capacity, *the sting of his words* ‖ (*slang*) a successful confidence game; a rigged chance to fleece someone; a simulated criminal operation set up to entrap criminals [O.E. *stingan*]

sting·er (stíŋər) *n.* a small sharp organ in some animals and plants, able to pierce the skin of a victim and often to inject poison or an irritant from a connected gland, thus causing pain or paralysis ‖ (*pop.*) a painful blow or remark ‖ a cocktail made of brandy and liqueur

Stinger *n.* (*mil.*) an 11-lb, shoulder-fired, artillery missile weapon with infrared homing; manufactured by General Dynamics Co.

stin·gi·ly (stíndʒili:) *adv.* in a stingy manner

stin·gi·ness (stíndʒi:nis) *n.* the state or quality of being stingy

stinging cell a nematocyst

stinging nettle a plant of fam. *Urticaceae*, esp. *Urtica dioica*, a perennial stinging weed of Eurasia and North America

sting·ray (stíŋrei) *n.* a member of fam. *Dasyatidae*, rays having sharp spines near the end of their whiplike tail which are capable of inflicting great pain

stin·gy (stíndʒi:) *comp.* **stin·gi·er** *superl.* **stin·gi·est** *adj.* refusing, or being extremely unwilling to give any more than a very small amount ‖ meager, inadequate, *a stingy helping of meat*

stink (stiŋk) 1. *v. pres. part.* **stink·ing** *past* **stank** (stæŋk), **stunk** (stʌŋk) *past part.* **stunk** *v.i.* to emit a strong and very unpleasant smell ‖ to offend one's moral sense extremely, *the deal stinks of corruption* ‖ (*pop.*) to be very low in quality, *his performance stank* ‖ *v.t.* (esp. with 'up') to cause to stink **to stink out** to drive out with an offensive smell **2.** *n.* a strong, foul smell **to make** (or **raise** or **cause**) **a stink** to cause trouble, esp. in public over something offensive or supposedly offensive [O.E. *stincan*]

stink bomb a small bomb which emits an evil smell when made to explode

stink·bug (stíŋkbʌg) *n.* any of several insects, esp. of fam. *Pentatomidae*, which emit a foul smell

stink·horn (stíŋkhɔrn) *n.* any of several foul-smelling fungi of the order *Phallales*

stink·ing (stíŋkiŋ) **1.** *adj.* foul-smelling || (*pop.*) very objectionable **2.** *adv.* (*pop.*) to an extreme degree, *stinking rich*

stink·pot (stíŋkpɒt) *n.* (*hist.*) a pot of burning sulfur hurled on the deck of an enemy vessel

stint (stint) **1.** *v.t.* to be parsimonious with (something), *don't stint the paint* || to limit (someone) parsimoniously or with frugality, *they stint themselves to buy books* || *v.i.* to be sparing in giving **2.** *n.* limitation, *he gives without stint* || an allotment or period of work, *he has done his stint for today, he did his stint in the army* [O.E. *styntan*, to blunt]

stipe (staip) *n.* (*biol.*) a short stalk, stem or stemlike support, e.g. the stem-bearing pileus in agaric fungi, the stalk of seaweeds etc. [F.]

sti·pel (stáip'l) *n.* (*bot.*) the stipule of a leaflet [Mod. L. *stipella* dim. of *stipula*, a stalk]

sti·pend (stáipend) *n.* a fixed, usually moderate sum of money paid, e.g. to a clergyman, at regular intervals for services rendered [O.F. *stipende, stipendie* fr. L.]

sti·pen·da·ry magistrate (staipéndəri:) (*Br.*) a paid magistrate who is a qualified lawyer and who exercises duties similar to those of a justice of the peace

sti·pen·di·a·ry (staipéndi:eri:) **1.** *adj.* working for, or receiving, a stipend || (of services) paid for by a stipend **2.** *pl.* **sti·pen·di·a·ries** *n.* (*Br.*) a stipendiary magistrate [fr. L. *stipendiarius*]

sti·pes (stáipi:z) *pl.* **stip·i·tes** (stípiti:z) *n.* (*zool.*) a stemlike part, esp. the second segment of a maxilla in insects and crustaceans [L.]

stip·ple (stip'l) **1.** *v.t. pres. part.* **stip·pling** *past* and *past part.* **stip·pled** to cover with dots (in drawing, engraving, painting etc.) in order to shade or make gradations of tone **2.** *n.* this method of work || the effect produced in this work || a thin layer of paint applied over another color, allowing the ground color to show through in many places [Du. *stippelen* fr. *stippen*, to speckle]

stip·u·late (stípjuleit) *pres. part.* **stip·u·lat·ing** *past* and *past part.* **stip·u·lat·ed** *v.t.* to state as a condition for reaching an agreement || to specify, *to stipulate a date* || *v.i.* (with 'for') to state a demand or requirement, *we stipulated for the use of marble* [fr. L. *stipulari* (*stipulatus*)]

stip·u·late (stípjulit) *adj.* having stipules [fr. Mod. L. *stipulatus*]

stip·u·la·tion (stipjuléiʃən) *n.* a stipulating || something stipulated [L. *stipulatio* (*stipulationis*)]

stip·u·la·tor (stípjuleitər) *n.* someone who stipulates [L.]

stip·ule (stípju:l) *n.* one of two leaflike or membranous processes developed at the base of a leaf, sometimes modified into a tendril or spine [F.]

stir (stə:r) **1.** *v. pres. part.* **stir·ring** *past* and *past part.* **stirred** *v.t.* to give relative motion to the parts of (a fluid or semifluid), usually by moving an implement through it with a continued rotary motion in order to make the composition homogeneous || to cause (something added) to form a uniform mixture with that to which it is added, *to stir pigment into paint* || (esp. with 'up') to cause to rise by stirring or as if by stirring, *his slow stirred up some mud, to stir up trouble* || to cause to move, esp. to change the position of very slightly, *the breeze stirred the leaves* || to cause to act, feel or think, *the news stirred him to action, to stir the imagination* || to arouse strong emotions of an idealistic kind in || *v.i.* to begin to move, *nobody stirred before daybreak* || to move a little, *he stirred slightly in his sleep* || to move, *he did not stir while you were gone* || to be able to be stirred, *the glaze does not stir easily* || to begin to develop, *discontent is stirring among the farmers* **2.** *n.* the act of stirring || a slight movement among things, persons etc., *a stir in the audience* || a state of excitement, *he created a stir by his behavior* [O.E. *styrian*]

Stir·ling (stə́:rliŋ) a county (area 451 sq. miles, pop. 195,000) in central Scotland || its county town (pop. 38,638), with a medieval castle, res-

idence of many Scottish monarchs (12th c.-1603)

stir·ring (stə́:riŋ) *adj.* arousing strong emotions of an idealistic kind

stir·rup (stírəp, stə́:rəp) *n.* a footrest for a horseman, usually a loop of iron, suspended by a strap from the saddle || a clamp or support having a similar U-shape [O.E. *stīgrāp*]

stirrup bone the stapes

stirrup cup a drink handed as a farewell gesture to a mounted horseman before he rides away

stirrup iron the iron part of a riding stirrup

stirrup leather the adjustable leather strap of a stirrup

stirrup pump a small hand pump with a stirrup support and a short hose attached. The pump is placed e.g. in a bucket of water and is used to put out small fires

stish·o·vite [SiO₂] (stíʃəvait) a dense polymorph of quartz created under pressure believed of extraterrestrial origin; named for S. M. Stishov, Russian mineralogist. It was discovered by Edward Ching Te-Cha and others in 1962

stitch (stitʃ) **1.** *n.* one in-and-out passage of a thread through a fabric in sewing or embroidering || the piece or loop of thread left in the material by this action || one turn of the wool etc. around the needle or hook in knitting, crocheting etc. || the resulting loop in the knitted or crocheted fabric || a particular style of making such loops in sewing, embroidering, knitting or crocheting || (*pop.*, always neg., or quasi-neg.) a bit, the least bit, *he hasn't done a stitch of work, hardly a stitch of clothing on* || one in-and-out passage of a needle threaded with catgut, wire etc. used by a surgeon in closing a wound || one of the loops of catgut, wire etc. so made || a sudden sharp pain in the side **in stitches** in helpless laughter **2.** *v.t.* (often with 'up') to fasten, repair, make or ornament with stitches || to staple (folded printed sheets) for binding || *v.i.* to sew [O.E. *stice*]

sto·a (stóuə) *pl.* **sto·ae** (stóui:), **sto·as** *n.* (*archit.*) an ancient Greek portico [Gk]

stoat (stout) *pl.* **stoats, stoat** *n.* the European ermine, esp. in its brown, summer coat [etym. doubtful]

sto·chas·tic (stəkǽstik) *adj.* pertaining to chance or conjecture || (*math.*) random [fr. Gk *stochastikos* fr. *stochazesthai*, to aim at a target, guess]

stochastic process (*math.*) in probability theory a system involving time parameters used to define a process utilizing random variables, e.g., of the economy, ecosystem, etc. *also* random process

stock (stɒk) **1.** *n.* an accumulation of things which is maintained as a constant source of supply, esp. as the basis of a storekeeper's or manufacturer's business || an accumulation of goods for future use, *a stock of provisions* || ancestors, family || a group of animals or plants having the same line of descent || a major racial division of mankind || a group of related languages || shares of corporate capital or their certificates of ownership || the material necessary for running an enterprise, e.g. the tractors, tools, hen houses etc. of a farm || livestock || the raw material from which a manufactured article, e.g. paper, is made || the fixed base or holding part of a tool, weapon, anchor etc. || the wooden part of a rifle by which the barrel is held || the butt of a whip || the estimation in which a thing or person is held, *his stock has gone up* || (*pl., naut.*) a wooden framework supporting the hull of a ship being built or repaired on land || (*pl., hist.*) a wooden frame with holes for confining the ankles (and sometimes the wrists) of a wrongdoer sentenced to be exposed in this way to public view and ridicule || liquid in which bones, meat, fish or vegetables have been simmered, used as a basis for soups, sauces etc. || a theatrical stock company || the plays presented by a stock company || a piece of cotton or silk material worn over the chest with a stiff white collar by some priests and clergymen || (*hist.*) a wide cravat wrapped twice around the neck and looped in front in a loose knot || a similar cravat worn as part of a riding outfit || a member of *Matthiola*, fam. *Cruciferae*, a genus of plants bearing fragrant, four-petaled flowers on long stalks || (*zool.*) a colony of zooids connected to form a compound organism || a hive of bees || the stem of a tree or bush into which a graft is inserted || a plant from which cuttings are prepared || the trunk of a tree or stem of a plant **in stock** manufactured and available for

purchase **off the stocks** (of a ship) launched || completed **on the stocks** (of a ship) being built || in progress, *he has two novels on the stocks* **out of stock** not available for purchase because current stocks are exhausted **to take stock** to check the number, condition etc. of what is in supply || to make an inspection so as to assess resources etc. **2.** *v.t.* to furnish with a stock, *he stocked his shop with canned foods* || to have and be able to supply, *he does not stock that kind of food* || to furnish (a tool, weapon etc.) with a stock || to furnish (a farm) with stock || to accumulate a supply of || *v.i.* (esp. with 'up') to take in stocks esp. of manufactured goods **3.** *adj.* always maintained in stock || pertaining to the recording or handling of a stock, *stock clerk* || (of an argument, answer etc.) usually used, not original || relating to a theatrical stock company || (of an animal) used to breed a strain || (of a farm) devoted to breeding [O.E. *stoc, stocc*]

stock·ade (stokéid) **1.** *n.* a fortification consisting of a fence of posts set firmly and close together || any strong enclosure fenced by posts in this way **2.** *v.t. pres. part.* **stock·ad·ing** *past* and *past part.* **stock·ad·ed** to furnish with a stockade [F. *estacade* fr. Span.]

stock·brok·er (stókbroukər) *n.* someone who deals in stocks and shares **stock·brok·er·age** (stókbroukərid3) *n.* stockbroking **stóck·brok·ing** *n.* the business of a stockbroker

stock·car (stókkɑr) *n.* (*rail.*) a car for transporting livestock

stock car a standard make of car with a supercharged engine used for racing in competition with similar cars

stock company a company the capital of which is subscribed by, or owned by, stockholders or shareholders || a permanent company of repertory actors usually having its own theater

stock exchange a place where stocks are bought and sold || a regulated association of stockbrokers for the business of buying and selling stocks

stock·fish (stókfiʃ) *pl.* **stock·fish, stock·fish·es** *n.* a fish cured in the open air without salt [prob. fr. Du. *stokvisch*]

Stock·hau·sen (stókhauz'n), Karlheinz (1928-), German composer, a leading exponent of serial music

stock·hold·er (stókhouldər) *n.* a person who owns stock (shares of corporate capital)

Stock·holm (stókhoum) the capital (pop. 1,512,200 with agglom. 1,145,000) and commercial and industrial center of Sweden, on a cluster of islands and peninsulas where Lake Mälar joins the Baltic. Industries: iron and steel, mechanical and electrical engineering, chemicals, oil refining, metalwork, textiles, printing and publishing. The old city (13th-c. churches, 18th-c. royal palace) is on the central islands, surrounded by modern quarters cut by canals and gardens. University (1877), national museums. Stockholm was founded in the 13th c. and became the capital in the 17th c.

stock·i·ly (stókili:) *adv.* in a stocky manner

stock·i·ness (stóki:nis) *n.* the state or quality of being stocky

stock·i·net, stock·i·nette (stɒkinét) *n.* a machine-knitted cotton fabric with some elasticity, used esp. for underwear

stock·ing (stókiŋ) *n.* a close-fitting covering for the foot and leg knit in nylon, silk, wool, cotton or other fiber **in one's stocking feet** wearing stockings, but no shoes

stocking cap a long knitted cap tapering at the end and finished off with a pom-pom

stocking mask a nylon stocking worn over the face to conceal identity, e.g., for use in a robbery

stock-in-trade (stókintréid) *n.* the goods, equipment etc. of a shop or business

stock·ist (stókist) *n.* (*Br.*) someone who keeps a supply of specified goods for sale

stock·job·ber (stókd3ɒbər) *n.* a stockbroker, esp. an unscrupulous one || (*Br.*) someone who acts as an intermediary between a broker selling and a broker buying. He often speculates by buying on the rise

stock·man (stókmən) *pl.* **stock·men** (stókmən) *n.* a man who owns or raises livestock || (stókmæn) a man who keeps records of stock or gives out supplies, e.g. in a warehouse || (*Br.* and *Austral.*) someone who herds livestock, esp. sheep or cattle

stock market a stock exchange || the buying and selling of stocks and shares

stock·pile (stókpail) **1.** *n.* a reserve, esp. of essential matériel accumulated for use when the normal sources of supply are cut off **2.** *v. pres. part.* **stock·pil·ing** *past* and *past part.* **stock·piled** *v.t.* to accumulate a stockpile of ‖ *v.i.* to accumulate a stockpile

Stock·port (stókpɔrt, stókpourt) a port and county borough (pop. 136,496) in Cheshire and Lancashire, England, on the Mersey: cotton textiles, metalware, machinery

stock·pot (stókpɒt) *n.* a pot in which stock (e.g. for soup) is prepared and kept

stock raising the breeding and raising of livestock

stock saddle a cowboy's saddle with a high pommel and horn for the lariat

stock-still (stókstíl) *adj.* completely motionless

stock·tak·ing (stókteikiŋ) *n.* the periodic checking and valuing of a business's stock

stock·whip (stókhwip, stókwip) *n.* (*Br.*) a short-handled whip with a long lash, used by stockmen in herding cattle

stock·y (stóki:) *comp.* **stock·i·er** *superl.* **stock·i·est** *adj.* short, sturdy and thickly built ‖ (of plants) having sturdy, thick stems

stock·yard (stókjɑrd) *n.* a place where livestock, esp. cattle and hogs, are penned, usually prior to slaughter or shipment

Stod·dert (stódərt), Benjamin (1751-1813), the first U.S. secretary of the navy (1798-1801). He expanded the navy from a complement of three frigates to a total of more than 50 vessels

stodge (stɒdʒ) **1.** *v.t. pres. part.* **stodg·ing** *past* and *past part.* **stodged** to cram with food, facts etc. ‖ *v.i.* to eat to excess **2.** *n.* (*pop.*) dull, heavy, filling food **stódg·i·ly** *adv.* in a stodgy way **stodg·i·ness** *n.* the state or quality of being stodgy **stódg·y** *comp.* **stodg·i·er** *superl.* **stódg·i·est** *adj.* (of food) heavy and filling ‖ dull, tedious, *a stodgy person* [etym. doubtful]

sto·gie, sto·gy (stóugi:) *pl.* **sto·gies** *n.* a thin, cylindrical cigar with a strong flavor

sto·ic (stóuik) **1.** *n.* a person who endures hardship and adversity with fortitude **Sto·ic** an adherent of Stoicism **2.** *adj.* able to bear hardship and adversity with fortitude, or manifesting this ability, *stoic calm* **Sto·ic** of or relating to the Stoics and their doctrines **stó·i·cal** *adj.* **sto·i·cism** (stóuisizəm) *n.* stoical behavior **Sto·i·cism** the philosophical doctrine of the Stoics. As first conceived by Zeno, Stoicism was a metaphysical system which stressed the correspondence between man and nature as a whole. Wisdom was held to consist in the knowledge of the whole, but to pursue it man had to hold his passions in check. In later Stoicism, represented by Seneca, Epictetus and Marcus Aurelius, the emphasis shifted to the ethical aspect: a Stoic was taught to endure hardship and adversity with fortitude [fr. L. *stoicus* fr. Gk fr. *stoa*, porch (from which Zeno taught)]

stoi·chi·om·e·try (stɔikaiómitri:) *n.* the study of the laws of chemical combination by weight and volume [fr. Gk *stoicheion*, element+*metron*, measure]

stoke (stouk) *pres. part.* **stok·ing** *past* and *past part.* **stoked** *v.t.* to look after (a fire, furnace etc.) by adding fresh fuel and spreading it around, regulating the air supply etc. ‖ to add fuel to (a fire, furnace etc.) ‖ *v.i.* to be a stoker [backformation fr. STOKER]

stoke·hold (stóukhould) *n.* (*naut.*) the hold containing the furnaces, where the ship's stokers work

stoke·hole (stóukhoul) *n.* the mouth of a furnace, into which fuel is fed ‖ the place in front of a furnace where the stoker or stokers stand [fr. and partly trans. of Du. *stookgat*]

Stoke-on-Trent (stóukɒntrént, stóukɒntrént) a county borough (pop. 257,800) in N. Staffordshire, England, center of the English pottery industry. Other industries: coal mining, brickmaking

stok·er (stóukər) *n.* a man who feeds and tends a fire, furnace etc. ‖ a device which automatically feeds a furnace etc. [Du.]

Stokes' law (stouks) (*phys.*) a law stating that a small sphere falling through a viscous medium acquires a uniform velocity given by

$$\frac{2}{9} \cdot \frac{r^2 g}{\eta} \cdot (d_1 - d_2)$$

where r is its radius, g the acceleration due to gravity, η the coefficient of viscosity, d_1 and d_2 the densities of the sphere and the medium respectively ‖ (*phys.*) a law stating that the frequency of luminescence excited by radiation cannot be in excess of the luminescence of the

radiation which excites it [after Sir George Stokes (1819–1903), Br. physicist]

STOL (*aerospace acronym*) short takeoff and landing —**stolport** *n.* the airfield *Cf* CTOL, VTOL, V/STOL

stole (stoul) *n.* a long, wide length of material, fur etc. worn by women, draped over the shoulders ‖ (*eccles.*) a long, narrow length of silk worn by bishops and priests around the neck and hanging in front from the shoulders ‖ (*hist.*) the outer robe of a Roman matron [fr. L. *stola* fr. Gk]

stole *past* of STEAL

stolen *past part.* of STEAL

stol·id (stólid) *adj.* difficult to arouse, either emotionally or mentally [fr. L. *stolidus*]

sto·lid·i·ty (stolíditi:) *n.* the state or quality of being stolid [fr. L. *stoliditas*]

sto·lon (stóulən) *n.* (*bot.*) a trailing stem, either above or below ground, which roots at intervals along its length to develop new plants ‖ (*zool.*) a creeping growth which gives rise to new individuals or colonies, e.g. coral [fr. L. *stolo* (*stolonis*), sucker of a plant]

Sto·ly·pin (stɒlí:pin), PiotrArkadevich (1863-1911), Russian statesman. As minister of the interior and prime minister (1906-11), he sought to suppress the revolutionary movement by mass exiles and executions. His agrarian reforms (1906) created a landowning kulak class, and freed labor for industry

sto·ma (stóumə) *pl.* **sto·ma·ta** (stóumətə), **sto·mas** *n.* (*bot.*) a minute epidermal pore on a leaf through which gaseous exchange takes place, together with the two bean-shaped guard cells which surround it ‖ (*zool.*) a mouth or mouthlike orifice, esp. an ingestive opening in lower animals [Mod. L. fr. Gk *stoma* (*stomatos*), mouth]

stom·ach (stámək) **1.** *n.* an enlarged portion of the alimentary canal of a vertebrate between the esophagus and the small intestine. It has a strong muscular wall which contracts rhythmically, thoroughly grinding and mixing food, and a lining that contains glands which secrete digestive enzymes ‖ any of the separate parts of such an organ, e.g. in ruminants ‖ a digestive cavity, e.g. in invertebrates ‖ the soft part of the body which contains the stomach ‖ (*rhet.*) appetite, liking, to *have no stomach for (something)* **2.** *v.t.* to find palatable or digestible, *to be unable to stomach rich food* ‖ to accept without revulsion or protest, *nobody could stomach such insolence* [O.F. *estomac*, *stomaque* fr. L. fr. Gk]

stom·ach·ache (stáməkeik) *n.* a pain in the stomach or in the area of the body surrounding the stomach

stom·ach·er (stáməkər) *n.* (*hist.*) a woman's ornamental garment worn in the 15th–17th cc. under or over a laced bodice and covering the breast and abdomen, ending downwards in a point

sto·mach·ic (stəmǽkik) **1.** *adj.* of or pertaining to the stomach ‖ aiding the digestive processes **2.** *n.* a medicine for aiding digestion [fr. L. *stomachicus* fr. Gk]

stomach pump a type of suction pump used to withdraw the contents of the stomach, esp. when these include a poison

stomach tooth (*pop.*) either of the first canine teeth in the lower jaw, the appearance of which is often accompanied by stomach disorders

stomata alt. *pl.* of STOMA

stom·a·tal (stómət'l, stóumət'l) *adj.* of, relating to, or being a stoma [fr. Gk *stoma* (*stomatos*), mouth]

sto·mat·ic (stoumǽtik) *adj.* relating to or being a stoma [fr. Mod. L. *stomaticus* fr. Gk]

stom·a·ti·tis (stɒmətáitis, stoumətáiitis) *n.* inflammation of the inside of the mouth [Mod. L. fr. Gk *stoma* (*stomatos*), mouth+*-itis*, inflammation]

sto·ma·tol·o·gy (stoumətólədʒi:) *n.* the branch of medicine dealing with the mouth and its diseases [fr. Gk *stoma* (*stomatos*), mouth+*logos*, discourse]

sto·mo·dae·um, sto·mo·de·um (stoumədí:əm) *pl.* **sto·mo·dae·a, sto·mo·de·a** (stoumədí:ə), **sto·mo·dae·ums, sto·mo·de·ums** *n.* the anterior ectoderm-lined portion of the alimentary canal [Mod. L. fr. Gk *stoma*, mouth+*hodaios*, on the way]

stomp (stomp) **1.** *v.t.* to bring (one's feet) down heavily ‖ to bring one's feet heavily down on, *stomping the platform impatiently* ‖ *v.i.* to put one's feet down heavily, *to stomp up and down in a rage* ‖ to dance a stomp **2.** *n.* a jazz dance

involving heavy stamping, or the music for this

Stone (stoun), Harlan Fiske (1872-1946), U.S. Supreme Court associate justice (1925-41) and chief justice (1941-6). He was dean of Columbia Law School (1910-23) and U.S. attorney general (1924-5) before being appointed to the Court by Pres. Calvin Coolidge. He was esp. concerned with individual liberty and social justice. As an associate justice he wrote the majority opinion in such cases as 'United States v. Classic' (1941) and 'United States v. Darby Lumber Co.' (1941). As chief justice he spoke for the Court in 'Ex parte Quirin' (1942), 'Hirabayashi v. United States' (1943), 'In re Yamachita' (1946) and 'Girouard v. United States' (1946)

Stone, Lucy Blackwell (1818-93), U.S. social reformer and lecturer. She campaigned (1848) throughout Canada and the U.S.A. against slavery. She helped to organize (1869) the American Woman's Suffrage Association, and served (1869-72) as its first president

stone (stoun) **1.** *n.* rock (an aggregate of particles) ‖ a piece of rock, esp. larger than a grain or particle but smaller than a boulder ‖ a piece of rock shaped and used for a particular purpose, e.g. a grindstone, a tombstone ‖ a small piece of an ornamental and rare mineral, cut and polished to show its color or refraction and reflection of light to the best advantage (*med.*) a calculus ‖ something hard, and usually rounded, e.g. the hard case of the kernel in a drupaceous fruit or the seed in some other fruits ‖ a piece of prepared limestone upon which a lithographic design is drawn ‖ (*pl.* **stone**) a British unit of weight equal to 14 lbs avoirdupois ‖ (*printing*) the smooth, flat surface upon which type is imposed ‖ (*backgammon*) a playing piece **a stone's throw** a short distance **to leave no stone unturned** to use every possible means to achieve a purpose **2.** *v.t. pres. part.* **ston·ing** *past* and *past part.* **stoned** to throw stones at ‖ to take the stones out of (fruit) ‖ to pave or face with stone **3.** *adj.* made of stone or of a hard substance resembling stone [O.E. *stān*]

Stone Age the earliest prehistoric period, when stone implements and weapons were used (preceding the Bronze Age). It is divided into the Eolithic, Paleolithic, Mesolithic and Neolithic periods

stone-broke (stóunbróuk) *adj.* completely without funds

stone cell a sclereid

stone·chat (stóuntʃæt) *n. Saxicola torquata,* a European songbird. The male has a predominantly black head, wings and tail, with a white collar and white upper tail coverts

stone-cold (stóunkóuld) *adj.* very cold

stone·crop (stóunkrɒp) *n.* a member of *Sedum*, fam. *Crassulaceae,* esp. *S. acre,* a European creeping evergreen plant having pungent leaves and yellow flowers [O.E. *stāncrop* fr. *stān*, stone+*crop*, a sprout]

stone·cut·ter (stóunkʌtər) *n.* someone who cuts and shapes stone ‖ a machine which does this

stone-deaf (stóundéf) *adj.* completely deaf

stone fly a member of *Plecoptera,* an order of insects whose aquatic, carnivorous larvae are used as bait in trout fishing

stone fruit a drupe

Stone·henge (stóunhendʒ) the remains of a large group of standing stones on Salisbury Plain, England, probably erected between 1800 B.C. and 1400 B.C. When complete, Stonehenge consisted of two concentric circles of tooled stones, surrounding two concentric horseshoe-shaped groups, the whole surrounded by a circular ditch 300 ft in diameter. The uprights of the outer circle were connected by lintels, the fitting of which required great technical skill. There are many theories about the purpose of Stonehenge, emphasis being placed on the marking of sunrise and sunset at particular points of the calendar by the alignment of the stones. It seems to have been a sanctuary for the worship of the sun, perhaps also an observatory. The monument is surrounded by Bronze Age barrows, and may well have been connected with burial ceremonies

stone marten *Martes foina,* a S. European and Asian marten with a white mark on its breast and throat ‖ its fur

stone-ma·son (stóunmeis'n) *n.* a mason who builds or works stone

Stones River, Battle of (stóunz) a major Civil War engagement (Dec. 31, 1862 – Jan. 2, 1863)

in central Tennessee, part of a Union campaign to split the Confederate forces into three parts. U.S. troops led by Gen. William Rosecrans routed Confederate forces under Gen. Braxton Bragg and captured Murfreesboro, a city (pop. 13,000) nine miles to the south. Both sides suffered heavy losses

stone·wall (stóunwól) v.i. (cricket, of a batsman) to play defensive strokes only and not attempt to score

stonewalling v. pres. part. (slang or colloq.) **1.** obstructing or permanently stopping something, e.g., an investigation, a vote **2.** refusing to move from a position —**stonewall** v.

stone·ware (stóunwęạr) n. a nonporous, well-vitrified pottery made of high-fired siliceous clay or a mixture of clay and crushed flint

stone·work (stóunwę:rk) n. stone construction ‖ the part of a construction that is made of stone

ston·i·ly (stóunili:) adv. in a stony way

ston·i·ness (stóuni:nis) n. the state or quality of being stony

ston·y (stóuni:) comp. **ston·i·er** superl. **ston·i·est** adj. containing many stones, stony ground ‖ as hard as stone ‖ lacking pity, stony hearts ‖ without human warmth, a stony silence, stony glance

ston·y-broke (stóuni:bróuk) adj. (Br.) stone-broke

stood past and past part. OF STAND

stooge (stu:dʒ) **1.** n. someone who acts as a butt for a comedian ‖ (pop.) a stool pigeon (informer) ‖ any underling with no say of his own **2.** v.i. pres. part. **stooging** past and past part. **stooged** to act as a stooge [origin unknown]

stook (stuk, stu:k) **1.** n. (Br.) a shock of sheaves **2.** v.t. (Br.) to pile (sheaves of grain) in this way [M.E. stouk prob. fr. M.L.G. stúke]

stool (stu:l) **1.** n. a backless and armless seat ‖ a footstool ‖ a decoy bird ‖ the stump of a tree, or a group of stumps capable of putting out new shoots ‖ one of these shoots ‖ the evacuation of waste matter from the bowels ‖ the waste matter so evacuated ‖ (pop.) a stool pigeon **2.** v.i. to send up shoots from a root or stump [O.E. stól, seat]

stool pigeon a pigeon used as a decoy ‖ (pop.) a person who informs to the police

stoop (stu:p) n. a small porch at the entrance of a house

stoop 1. v.i. to bend the body forward and downward, he stooped to write in the dust ‖ to walk or stand habitually with the head, neck and shoulders bent forward and downward ‖ (of a bird of prey) to fly or drop swiftly downwards ‖ to lower one's dignity or moral standards, to stoop to spying ‖ v.t. to bend (part of the body) forward and downward **2.** n. a stooping ‖ a posture in which the head, neck and shoulders are permanently bent forward and downward ‖ the swoop of a bird towards its prey [O.E. stúpian]

stoop *STOUP

stop (stɒp) **1.** v. pres. part. **stopping** past and past part. **stopped** v.t. to discontinue, cease (doing something), to stop running ‖ to cause to cease to move or to act, he stopped his car at the crossroads, she stopped him in the middle of his speech ‖ to prevent from moving or acting, he won't stop me from going ‖ to cut off, withhold, to stop supplies ‖ (often with 'up') to fill (a hole, crack etc.) in order to prevent passage through or into it, or to prevent it from becoming larger ‖ (often with 'up') to close, obstruct (a passageway, opening etc.), leaves stopped up the drain ‖ to close, plug (a body orifice), to stop one's ears ‖ (securities) to buy or sell at a specified price should the market reach such a price ‖ (Br.) to fill (a tooth) in order to arrest decay ‖ to instruct one's bank to withhold payment of (a check etc.) ‖ (pop.) to receive (a blow), he stopped a fast one ‖ (bridge) to constitute a stop for (a suit) ‖ (mus.) to alter the vibrating length of (the string of a violin etc.) by the pressure of a finger ‖ (mus.) to close one or more finger holes of (a wind instrument) in order to produce a particular note ‖ (mus.) to produce (a note) thus ‖ v.i. to cease to do something ‖ to cease operating ‖ to come to an end ‖ to leave off, discontinue an activity, journey etc. permanently or temporarily ‖ (often with 'up') to become obstructed ‖ (Br.) to stay, to stop at home **to stop down** (photog.) to narrow the opening of (a lens) by means of a diaphragm **to stop off** to make a brief stay at a place while on a journey **to stop out** to cover part or parts of (a surface to be printed) with a substance which prevents printing **2.** n. a stopping or being stopped, to put a stop to something ‖ a place

where a bus, streetcar etc. picks up or deposits passengers ‖ (Br.) a punctuation mark in printing or writing indicating a pause, esp. a full stop ‖ a stopper (plug) ‖ (Br., bridge) a stopper ‖ (mus.) the act of closing a finger hole of a wind instrument to alter the pitch of its tone, or the finger hole itself, or a key closing it ‖ (mus.) the act of pressing a string of a stringed instrument in order to alter the pitch, or the place on the string where this pressure is applied ‖ (mus.) a set of organ pipes of like tone and quality ‖ (mus.) a device for admitting, or preventing the access of, air to such a set of pipes ‖ (phon.) a consonant formed by completely stopping the outgoing breath, e.g. with the lips, tongue or velum ‖ (photog.) the aperture of a lens camera ‖ the depression between and in front of the eyes that is present in most dogs, where the nose ends and the forehead begins [O.E. stoppian]

stop·cock (stópkɒk) n. a device for permitting or preventing the flow of a fluid through a pipe

stope (stoup) n. (mining) the underground excavation formed as layers of ore are mined [perh. rel. to STEP]

stop·gap (stópgæp) n. a person or thing serving as a substitute or temporary expedient

stop·light (stóplait) n. a traffic signal ‖ a red light on the back of a motor vehicle which goes on when the brake pedal is pressed

stop·out (stópaut) n. one who interrupts an education for a short period

stop·o·ver (stópouvər) n. a short stop at a place breaking a journey

stop·page (stópidʒ) n. a stopping or being stopped

stop·per (stópər) **1.** n. a plug or other device which closes an opening, e.g. of a decanter ‖ (naut.) a rope or other means of checking the run of a cable etc. ‖ (bridge, Am.=Br. stop) a card or group of cards in a suit which prevents an opponent from scoring **2.** v.t. to close or fit with a stopper

stop press (Br.) a late news bulletin added to a newspaper after it has been put on the machines ready for printing **stóp-press** adj. done or inserted while a printing press is stopped during its run

stop squawk (mil.) in air intercept, a code meaning Turn identification friend or foe master control to 'off.' Cf SQUAWK STANDBY

stop·watch (stópwɒtʃ) n. a watch with a dial reading up to fractions of a second. It can be started and stopped by a control and is used in timing races etc.

stor·age (stóridʒ, stóuridʒ) n. a storing or being stored ‖ space for storing ‖ the charge for storing

storage battery a storage cell

storage cell a device for storing electricity as chemical energy. It is charged by passing an electric current between two plates (electrodes) in an ionizing liquid (the electrolyte.) This current causes chemical changes in the electrolyte and plates. When electrical energy is required the plates are joined via an electrical circuit and the stored chemical energy is released as electrical energy until the charges have been completely reversed, the storage cell then being discharged

stor·age-ring (stóridʒriŋ) n. (nuclear phys.) a circular tract on which a beam of accelerated particles moves to collide with a beam moving in a counter direction, for the creation of new particles

sto·rax (stóræks, stóuræks) n. a resin obtained from the bark of Liquidambar orientalis, fam. Hamamelidaceae, an Asiatic tree, used as an expectorant (*FRIAR'S BALSAM) and in perfumery ‖ a sweet-smelling resin obtained from various trees of genus Styrax, esp. S. officinalis [L. fr. Gk sturax]

store (stɔr, stour) n. a number of things, or an amount of something, put aside for future use, a store of food ‖ a place where a store of something is kept, ammunition store ‖ a room, set of rooms or building where retail sale is carried on ‖ any shop ‖ (pl.) supplies kept for use when needed, ship's stores **in store** kept for future use ‖ in waiting, a surprise in store for them **to set store by** to value greatly [M.E. stor fr. O.F. estor, storing]

store pres. part. **storing** past and past part. **stored** v.t. to accumulate and keep for future use ‖ (esp. passive) to furnish or supply ‖ to put into storage ‖ to provide storage room for ‖ v.i. to bear storing, some foods won't store [M.E. storen fr. O.F.]

store·house (stórhaus, stóurhaus) pl. **store·hous·es** (stórhauziz, stóurhauziz) n. a place where things are stored ‖ a rich source, a storehouse of information

store·keep·er (stórki:pər, stóurki:pər) n. a person who is in charge of stores ‖ someone who owns and manages a store

store·room (stórru:m, stóurru:m, stórrum, stóurrum) n. a room in which goods are stored

store·ship (stórʃip, stóurʃip) n. (naut.) a ship which carries supplies

sto·ry, sto·rey, pl. **sto·ries, sto·reys** n. one of the floor-to-ceiling portions of a building above ground level ‖ (collect.) all the rooms on the same level of a building [prob. same word as STORY (oral or written account)]

storey *STORY (portion of a building)

sto·ried (stóri:d, stóuri:d) adj. (rhet.) celebrated in legend or history ‖ (rhet.) decorated with legendary or historical scenes

storied, storeyed adj. (in compounds, of a building) having a specified number of stories, two-storied

stork (stɔrk) pl. **storks, stork** n. a member of Ciconiidae, a family of large Old World wading birds with a long bill and long legs, related to the herons [O.E. storc]

Storm, Theodor (1817-88), German lyric poet and novelist, known esp. for his story 'Immensee' (1852)

storm (stɔrm) **1.** n. a very strong wind (64–72 m.p.h. on the Beaufort scale) ‖ a heavy fall of rain, snow, hail or sleet ‖ any violent atmospheric disturbance in the air, e.g. a thunderstorm ‖ a cloud of dust or sand driven by the wind ‖ a thick fall of missiles ‖ a violent access of passion, esp. of jealousy or rage ‖ any domestic commotion or public agitation, a storm in parliament ‖ a loud and vigorous expression, a storm of protests ‖ (mil.) an attack in force on a fortified place, to take by storm **2.** v.i. to rain, snow, hail etc. ‖ with violence to be in a passion of rage ‖ to rush angrily and violently, to storm out of the house ‖ v.t. to capture or attempt to capture by attack, to storm a citadel [O.E.]

storm·bound (stórmbaund) adj. unable to proceed because of a storm

storm cellar a cyclone cellar

storm center, Br. **storm centre** the center of an atmospheric storm ‖ the center or focus of a disturbance

storm cone (Br.) a cone-shaped device hoisted as a signal that a storm is imminent

storm door an additional door placed outside an entrance door for protection against winter weather

storm·i·ly (stó:rmili) adv. in a stormy way

storm·i·ness (stórmi:nis) n. the state or quality of being stormy

storm petrel Hydrobates pelagicus, fam. Hydrobatidae, a small (6 ins) black petrel, having white wing and tail markings and frequenting the coasts of the N. Atlantic and Mediterranean. It is popularly thought to presage storms

storm surge (meteor.) a large rise of the water level during a gale

storm window an additional window placed outside a regular one for protection against winter weather

storm·y (stórmi:) comp. **storm·i·er** superl. **storm·i·est** adj. having the characteristics of a storm ‖ characterized by storms ‖ characterized by violence or passion, a stormy meeting

stormy petrel a storm petrel ‖ a person regarded as a herald of trouble, strife or violence or someone who delights in such trouble etc.

Sto·ry (stóri:, stóuri:), Joseph (1779-1845), U.S. jurist and associate justice (1812-45) of the U.S. Supreme Court. The decisions he wrote include 'Martin v. Hunter's Lessee' (1816), which assured Supreme Court supremacy over State courts in all civil cases involving the U.S. constitution and laws. He wrote several concurring opinions in support of John Marshall. He usually dissented from the opinions of the Taney court

sto·ry (stóri:, stóuri:) pl. **sto·ries** n. an oral or written account of a real or imagined event or events, the story of one's life, adventure stories ‖ the plot of a literary work ‖ a news item in a newspaper ‖ a particular, esp. a biased, account of an event etc. ‖ an amusing anecdote ‖ a rumor circulating ‖ (pop.) a lie [A.F. estoire]

sto·ry·book (stóri:buk, stóuri:buk) **1.** n. a book consisting of a story or stories for children **2.**

adj. tenderly romantic and idealistic, *a story book romance*

sto·ry·tell·er (stóri:telər, stóuri:telər) *n.* someone who writes or tells stories ‖ (*pop.*) a liar

Stoss (ʃtɔs), Veit (c. 1440-1533), German sculptor and wood-carver, known esp. for his altarpiece at Krakow

sto·tin·ka (stoutínkə) *n.* unit of currency in Bulgaria, equal to 1/100th lev

stoup, stoop (stu:p) *n.* (*Roman Catholicism*) a basin for holy water ‖ (*hist.*) a large drinking mug or bowl or its contents [O.N. *staup*]

stout (staut) *adj.* having a heavy and rotund body ‖ strong, *stout timbers* ‖ brave, *a stout fellow* ‖ (*rhet.*) resolute, firm, *stout resistance* [O.F. *estout*, brave fr. Gmc]

stout *n.* a dark brown beer, brewed from black malt in the grist and strongly flavored with hops [prob.=*stout beer, stout ale* fr. (obs.) stout *adj.*, having body]

stout·heart·ed (stáuthártid) *adj.* (*rhet.*) courageous

stove (stouv) *n.* a largely enclosed apparatus in which fuel is burned to provide heat for comfort or cooking ‖ any heated chamber, used e.g. for drying manufactured articles [prob. M.L.G. or M.Du.=a heated room]

stove alt. *past* and *past part.* OF STAVE

stove·pipe (stóuvpaip) *n.* an iron or steel tube conveying the gaseous products of combustion from a stove to a flue or to the open air ‖ a stovepipe hat

stovepipe hat a man's tall silk hat

stow (stou) *v.t.* to pack away in an enclosed space, *to stow books in a cupboard* ‖ to fill (a hold etc.) with cargo ‖ to hold, have enough space for, *the attic will stow all the apples you grow* ‖ (*naut.*) to furl **to stow away** to store (something) where it will not be in the way ‖ to hide on board a ship, train etc. in order to travel without paying the fare [fr. older *stow*, a place, fr. O.E. *stōw*]

stow·age (stóuidʒ) *n.* a stowing or being stowed ‖ the manner of being stowed ‖ the goods stowed ‖ storage capacity

stow·a·way (stóuəwei) *n.* a person who hides on board a ship, train etc. in order to avoid paying the fare

Stowe (stou), Harriet Elizabeth Beecher (1811-96), American writer, who wrote 'Uncle Tom's Cabin' (1852), an antislavery novel which had great political influence

S.T.P. (*phys.*) standard temperature and pressure, i.e. normal temperature and pressure (*N.T.P.*) ‖ (*abbr.*) for a psychedelic drug named for the serenity, tranquility, and peace it purports to bring about

stra·bis·mal (strəbízməl) *adj.* of or relating to strabismus

stra·bis·mic (strəbízmik) *adj.* strabismal **stra·bís·mi·cal** *adj.*

stra·bis·mus (strəbízməs) *n.* (*med.*) a disorder of vision in which both eyes cannot be focused on the same spot at the same time [Mod. L. fr. Gk]

Stra·chey (stréitʃi:), Giles Lytton (1880-1932), English author, known for his ironic biographies 'Eminent Victorians' (1918) and 'Queen Victoria' (1921). His 'Landmarks in French Literature' (1912) is a minor classic of literary criticism

strad·dle (stréd'l) **1.** *v. pres. part.* **strad·dling** *past* and *past part.* **strad·dled** *v.i.* to walk, or stand, with the legs wide apart ‖ to sprawl ‖ to sit on a fence, wall etc. with one leg on either side of it ‖ (*pop.*) to favor or seem to favor both sides of an issue ‖ *v.t.* to stand over or sit on (something) with one leg on either side of it ‖ to spread (the legs) wide apart ‖ (*pop.*) to be or seem to be in favor of both sides of (an issue) ‖ (*gunnery*) to put down shots beyond and short of (a target) **2.** *n.* the act or position of straddling ‖ (*stock exchange*) an option enabling the holder to deliver or call for a certain number of shares at a certain price within a certain time [rel. to STRIDE]

Stra·del·la (strədélə), Allessandro (1645-82), Italian composer. His work included operas, cantatas, oratorios and motets

Stra·di·va·ri (strɑdiːváriː, strædivéari:) a famous family of Italian violin makers of Cremona. The most famous is Antonio (1644-1737). He produced at least 1,116 instruments, many of which are still in existence

strad·i·var·i·us (strædivéari:əs) *n.* a violin made by the Stradivari family, esp. by Antonio Stradivari

strafe (streif, *Br.* esp. strɑf) **1.** *v.t. pres. part.*

straf·ing *past* and *past part.* **strafed** to sweep (e.g. a ground area) with machine-gun fire, esp. from low-flying aircraft **2.** *n.* such an attack [fr. G. *Gott strafe England*, God punish England (a 1st World War phrase)]

Straf·ford (stræfərd), Thomas Wentworth, 1st earl of (1593-1641), English statesman entrusted by Charles I with the task of bringing the north of England (1629-33) and Ireland (1633-40) into subjugation. The ruthless methods he employed led to his impeachment. The Long Parliament brought in a bill of attainder. Strafford was executed with the king's consent, the royal authority being thus greatly diminished

strag·gle (stræg'l) *pres. part.* **strag·gling** *past* and *past part.* **strag·gled** *v.i.* to lag behind, or stray away from, the main body, esp. from a line of march ‖ to grow or be untidily separated from the rest **strág·gly** *comp.* **strag·gli·er** *superl.* **strag·gli·est** *adj.* [etym. doubtful]

straight (streit) **1.** *adj.* having an unchanging direction, like a thread pulled tight between two points on a plane surface ‖ of something approximately thus, *a straight back* ‖ showing no deviation from the vertical or horizontal ‖ (of character) honest, trustworthy ‖ frank, esp. acknowledging unpleasant truths, *a straight answer* ‖ tidy and in proper order, *put the room straight* ‖ correctly stated or understood, *let's get the facts straight* ‖ unmixed, *it was straight farce* ‖ (of alcoholic liquor) undiluted ‖ (of hair) not curly ‖ (of racing tips) coming direct from a supposedly reliable source ‖ (of actors and parts in plays) portraying individuals and not types (cf. CHARACTER) ‖ (of an engine) having its cylinders arranged in line ‖ (of a cricket bat) held (for play) at right angles to the ground ‖ (*slang*) of one who is conventional, e.g., esp. not homosexual, a drug user, or a hippie **2.** *adv.* in a straight line ‖ vertically and/or horizontally, not at an angle ‖ in a morally upright way ‖ directly, unequivocally **3.** *n.* a straight part of something, esp. the final stretch of a racetrack between the last bend and the winning post ‖ (*poker*) a sequence of five cards not all of one suit [M.E. *streght, straght*, originally an adjectival use of the past part. of *strecchen*, to stretch]

straight and narrow (with 'to keep to the' or 'to follow the') a morally and legally irreproachable way of living or behaving [adaptation of Matthew vii, 14]

straight angle an angle of 180°

straight-arm (stréitɑrm) *v.t.* (esp. *football*) to ward off (a would-be tackler) by keeping an arm extended straight from the shoulder and by placing the palm of the hand anywhere on the tackler's body

straight·a·way (stréitəwei) **1.** *adj.* extending in a straight course ahead **2.** *n.* the straight part of a racecourse **3.** *adv.* immediately, at once

straight·bred (stréitbred) *adj.* (of animals) having the blood of only one single breed or strain (*CROSSBRED*)

straight-cut (stréitkʌt) *adj.* (of tobacco prepared for smoking) cut lengthwise from the leaf

straight-edge (stréitedʒ) *n.* a length of metal or wood etc. having a straight edge, used in carpentry, metalwork etc. to rule a straight line or to check the straightness of something

straight·en (stréit'n) *v.t.* to make straight ‖ *v.i.* to become straight

straight-faced (stréitféist) *adj.* betraying no facial sign of amusement

straight fight (*Br.*, *politics*) an election contest between the candidates of two parties only

straight flush (*poker*) a hand consisting of five cards in sequence and of the same suit

straight·for·ward (streitfɔ́rwərd) **1.** *adj.* honest and direct without hiding anything, frank ‖ presenting no hidden difficulties ‖ clear-cut, unequivocal **2.** *adv.* straight ahead ‖ in a straightforward way **straight·for·wards** *adv.*

straightjacket *STRAITJACKET*

straightlaced *STRAITLACED*

straight man (*Am.*=*Br.* feed) an actor who supplies a comedian with cue lines for jokes

straight-out (stréitaut) *adj.* (*pop.*) straightforward, frank **straight out** *adv.* frankly, directly

straight razor (*Am.*=*Br.* cutthroat) a razor with a rigid blade, the case of which forms a handle when the razor is in use

straight ticket a ballot cast for all the candidates of a single party (cf. SPLIT TICKET)

straight·way (stréitwei) *adv.* (*rhet.*) straightaway

strain (strein) *n.* a group of organisms possessing a particular physiological quality (e.g. high mortality in microorganisms, good wool yield in sheep or strong scent in roses) though lacking clear structural distinctions from related forms ‖ (*rhet.*) a line of descendants, *the royal strain* ‖ an inherited but not dominant quality ‖ a persistent trait of character, *a strain of selfishness* [O.E. *strēon, strīon*]

strain **1.** *v.t.* to exert such a force on (a body) that it ceases to be elastic and is damaged or suffers injury, *to strain a muscle* ‖ to injure by overuse or misuse, *to strain one's eyes* ‖ to force (oneself) to the utmost, *she strained herself to finish in time* ‖ to injure (oneself) either mentally or physically by too much effort, *she strained herself getting the work finished in time* ‖ to cause mental tension in ‖ to make excessive demands on, *to strain a person's generosity* ‖ to subject (a relationship) to a considerable degree of tension ‖ (esp. past participle) to introduce such tension into (an atmosphere) ‖ to force from words (a meaning not intended by the author or speaker) ‖ to change the dimensions of (an elastic body) by the application of external force ‖ to force (a body) to its elastic limit ‖ to pass (a liquid) through a filter or sieve ‖ to remove (solid particles) from a liquid by filtering ‖ *v.i.* to make or exert great physical or mental effort ‖ to be subjected to great physical or mental stress ‖ to filter or sieve **to strain at** to try to move (e.g. a stone) or pull etc. on (e.g. a rope) with a great effort **to strain one's ears** to listen very carefully, esp. for something barely audible **2.** *n.* a straining or being strained ‖ a deformation of an elastic body under an applied force (*HOOKE'S LAW*, cf. STRESS) ‖ the resistance offered by an elastic body to the straining force ‖ a straining force which exceeds the elastic limit of a body ‖ mental tension causing distress ‖ injury or damage caused by straining ‖ a great demand imposing hardship, *a strain on one's resources* ‖ the tenor or tone of something written or uttered, *to speak in lofty strains* ‖ a tune or part of one ‖ (esp. *pl.*) sounds, esp. heard from a distance [M.E. *streyne* fr. O.F.]

strain·er (stréinor) *n.* a sieve or filter

straining piece a short, thick timber which takes the strain of joists or rafters

strait (streit) *n.* (often *pl.*) a narrow stretch of water between two land masses ‖ (often *pl.*) severely restricting difficulties, *financial straits* [M.E. *streit*, O.F. *estreit*]

straitened circumstances lack of money, poverty (usually in connection with someone not used to this condition)

strait·jack·et, straight·jack·et (stréitdʒækit) *n.* a garment of very strong material used to bind the arms against the body and so restrain the movements of a violent, usually insane, person who could harm himself or others

strait·laced, straight·laced (stréitleist) *adj.* exceedingly strict about matters of propriety, often in conjunction with an apparently joyless observance of religion

Straits Question (streits) (*hist.*) an international dispute over the right of passage through the Dardanelles and the Bosporus. By the Treaty of Unkiar Skelessi (1833), the Turks undertook to close the Straits to foreign warships, except those of Russia. A new international agreement (1841) closed the Straits to all foreign warships in peacetime. This remained in force until 1923, when the Straits were demilitarized by the Treaty of Lausanne. They were again militarized by Turkey after an international convention (1936), but were reopened to Allied shipping in 1945 (*EASTERN QUESTION*)

Straits Settlements a former British colony in the Malay Peninsula, comprising Malacca, Penang, Singapore and dependencies, established (1826) by the British East India Company. It became a Crown colony (1867) and was dissolved (1946)

strait waistcoat (*Br.*) a straitjacket

strake (streik) *n.* (*naut.*) an unbroken line of planks or plates running along the side of a vessel from stem to stern [O.E. *streccan*, stretch]

stra·mo·ni·um (strəmóuni:əm) *n.* the thorn apple ‖ the dried leaf of a thorn apple, used esp. in the treatment of asthma

strand (strænd) **1.** *n.* (*rhet.* and *Ir.*) the shore of a body of water (esp. of a sea or lake) **2.** *v.t.* to drive onto the shore ‖ to run (a boat) aground ‖ to cause (someone) to find himself accidentally and unwillingly held up on a journey or left suddenly somewhere without resources, *the fog stranded passengers at the airport* (esp. *pass.*) to leave ashore when the tide goes out or water level sinks, *the whale was stranded* [O.E.]

strand 1. *n.* any of the threads, strings, wires etc. which, when twisted together, form a rope, cord, cable etc. ‖ a tress or single long hair ‖ a single string of beads or pearls etc. **2.** *v.t.* to form (e.g. a rope) from strands ‖ to insert strands into (e.g. cloth) ‖ to break one or more of the strands of (a rope) ‖ *v.i.* (of a rope) to break one or more of its strands [etym. doubtful]

Strang (stræŋ), James Jesse (1813-56), U.S. Mormon leader. He established (1847) at Beaver Is. in Lake Michigan a colony for Mormons unwilling to accept the leadership of Brigham Young. His despotic rule led to his assassination

strange (streindʒ) *adj.* not within one's previous experience, *the town was strange to him* ‖ not expected, *a strange result* ‖ unusual, outlandish, *strange clothes* ‖ (*rhet.*) not accustomed, *to be strange to desert life* ‖ odd, unaccountable, *strange behavior* ‖ arousing wonder or astonishment, *strange shapes* [O.F. *estrange*]

strangeness number (*particle phys.*) a quantum number (0, a negative or positive integral) representing an unexplained delay in interactions between elementary particles —**strange particle** *n.* —**symbol S**

stran·ger (streíndʒər) *n.* a person who has not been in a place before, a newcomer, *a stranger to the town* ‖ a person who is not known to one ‖ (*rhet.*) a person who has had no experience of some specified thing, *a stranger to fear* ‖ (*law*) a person who is not a party to an agreement, title etc. ‖ (*Br., parliament*) a person not a member of the British House of Commons [fr. O.F. *estrangier*]

stran·gle (stræŋg'l) *pres. part.* **stran·gling** *past* and *past part.* **stran·gled** *v.t.* to kill by compressing the windpipe and so preventing breathing ‖ to make breathing very difficult for ‖ to crowd out (a plant) so that it cannot develop ‖ to suppress (e.g. criticism) ‖ *v.i.* to be strangled [O.F. *estrangler*]

stran·gle·hold (stræŋg'lhould) *n.* an illegal hold in wrestling which prevents free breathing ‖ any force or influence which prevents freedom of action

stran·gles (stræŋg'lz) *n.* an infectious catarrh of horses and other equines, caused by a bacterium

stran·gu·late (stræŋgjuleit) *pres. part.* **stran·gu·lat·ing** *past* and *past part.* **stran·gu·lat·ed** *v.t.* to stop the circulation of fluid or blood supply in (a tissue), e.g. in hernia ‖ *v.i.* to become constricted in this way **stran·gu·la·tion** *n.* the action or process of strangling ‖ the state of being strangled ‖ the state of being strangulated [fr. L. *strangulare* (*strangulatus*), to choke]

stran·gu·ry (stræŋgjuri:) *pl.* **stran·gu·ries** *n.* a disease causing the urine to be passed painfully and in drops ‖ slow and painful urination [fr. L. *stranguria*]

strap (stræp) **1.** *n.* a long strip of leather etc. of uniform width, and usually pierced with holes for the insertion of the pin of a buckle, used to fasten or bind ‖ a strip of metal used similarly ‖ a razor strop ‖ a shoulder strap ‖ a leather loop fastened to the top of a boot to help in pulling it on ‖ a similar loop suspended from the ceiling of public vehicles for a standing passenger to hold as a support **2.** *v.t. pres. part.* **strap·ping** *past* and *past part.* **strapped** to fasten or bind with a strap ‖ to beat with a leather strap ‖ to strop (a razor) [dial. var. of STROP]

strap·hang·er (stræphæŋər) *n.* (*pop.*) a standing passenger who clings for support to one of the straps suspended for this purpose in a public vehicle

strap·pa·do (strəpéidou, strəpádou) **1.** *n.* (*hist.*) a torture consisting of hoisting the victim on a rope by his wrists (usually tied behind his back) and then allowing him to drop part of the way to the ground ‖ the apparatus for inflicting this torture **2.** *v.t.* to torture in this way [fr. F. *strapade*, *estrapade* fr. Ital.]

strap·per (stræpər) *n.* (*pop.*) someone very big and strong in build

strap·ping (stræpiŋ) *adj.* (*pop.*) very big and strong in build

strap·work (stræpwəːrk) *n.* an ornamental design (inlaid, cut into stone etc.) resembling endless, intertwined straps, in regular geometrical pattern

Stras·bourg (stræzbuːr, strɑ́sbəːrg) a port and industrial center (pop. 248,712) in Bas-Rhin, E. France, on the Ill River, near the Rhine. Industries: metallurgy, food and drink processing, woodworking, chemicals, oil refining. Cathedral (12th-16th cc.), palaces (18th c.), churches, half-timbered houses. University (1621)

Strasbourg, Oath of an oath of alliance sworn (842) by Louis the German and Charles the Bald, in revolt against Lothair I. The Romance text of the oath is the earliest known specimen of French in its oldest form

strass (stræs) *n.* a glass of high lead content used in making artificial gems [G. after Joseph *Strasser*, a German jeweler]

strata alt. *pl.* of STRATUM

strat·a·gem (strǽtədʒəm) *n.* a subtle piece of planning designed to trick or gain an end ‖ a ruse, esp. (*hist.*) one to deceive the enemy in warfare [F. *stratagème* fr. L.]

stra·tal (stréit'l, strǽt'l, strɑ́t'l) *adj.* of or relating to a stratum or strata

stra·te·gic (strətí:dʒik) *adj.* of or relating to strategy ‖ of material needed for war but not available in sufficient quantity in the country needing it **stra·té·gi·cal** *adj.* **stra·té·gi·cal·ly** *adv.* **stra·té·gics** *n.* the science of strategy [fr. Gk *stratēgikos*]

strategic capability (*mil.*) the capacity to destroy an enemy under specified circumstances

strat·e·gist (strǽtidʒist) *n.* a person skilled in strategy [F. *stratégiste*]

strat·e·gy (strǽtidʒi:) *pl.* **strat·e·gies** *n.* the science and art of conducting a military campaign in its large-scale and long-term aspects (cf. TACTICS) ‖ an instance of the application of this ‖ skill in using stratagems ‖ the use of such skill in achieving a purpose [F. *stratégie* fr. Gk]

Strat·ford de Red·cliffe (strǽtfərddərédklif), 1st Viscount *CANNING, Stratford

Strat·ford-u·pon-A·von (strǽtfərdəpənéivən, strǽtfərdəpɒnéivən) a town (pop. 20,100) in Warwickshire, England, Shakespeare's birthplace: annual Shakespeare festival

Strath·clyde (stræθkláid) (*hist.*) a British kingdom in S.W. Scotland and N.W. England (c. 7th-10th cc.)

Strath·co·na and Mount Royal (stræθkóunə), Donald Alexander Smith, 1st Baron (1820-1914), Canadian statesman. He was largely responsible for the success of the Canadian Pacific Railway. He donated several million dollars to educational, religious, and financial institutions

Strath·more (stræθmɔ́r, stræθmóur) a fertile, populous valley (100 miles long, 5-10 miles wide) in E. Scotland on the southeast side of the Grampians, where the Highlands end

strath·spey (stræθspéi) *n.* a Scottish dance of slower tempo than the reel ‖ the music for this dance [after *Strathspey*, in Scotland]

strati *pl.* of STRATUS

stra·tic·u·late (strətíkjulit) *adj.* (*geol.*) having thin parallel strata [fr. Mod. L. *straticulum* fr. L. *stratum*, layer]

strat·i·fi·ca·tion (strætifikéiʃən) *n.* (*geol.*) the formation of strata ‖ (*geol.*) the condition of being stratified ‖ (*geol.*) the manner in which something is stratified ‖ arrangement in strata [fr. M.L. *stratificatio* (*stratificationis*) fr. *stratificare*, to stratify]

stratificational grammar (*linguistics*) a form of grammar conceiving of language as a series of levels linked by certain rules: developed by S. M. Lamb

stratified charge engine a dual-fed internal combustion engine in which one richer fuel sparks the engine and a less concentrated fuel sustains the motion

strat·i·form (strǽtifɔrm) *adj.* having a stratified formation ‖ having the form of a stratus

strat·i·fy (strǽtifai) *pres. part.* **strat·i·fy·ing** *past* and *past part.* **strat·i·fied** *v.t.* to arrange or form in strata ‖ *v.i.* to become arranged in strata

stra·tig·ra·phy (strətígrəfi:) *n.* the branch of geology dealing with the study of stratified rocks, in order to trace the historical changes in the geography of the earth [fr. L. *stratum*, something spread or laid down+ Gk *-graphia*, writing]

stra·to·cu·mu·lus (streitoukjú:mjuləs, strætoukjú:mjuləs) *n.* a cloud formation having the appearance of dark mounds piled on top of one another. Clouds in this formation are usually seen in the northern hemisphere in winter and do not bring rain

Strat·o·for·tress (strætoufɔ́rtrəs) *n.* (*mil.*) an all-weather, intercontinental, strategic heavy bomber (B-52), powered by eight turbojet engines, with range extended by in-flight refueling

Strat·o·freight·er (strǽtoufreitəːr) *n.* (*mil.*) a strategic aerial tanker-freighter (KC-97), powered by four reciprocating engines, equipped for in-flight refueling of bombers and fighters

strat·o·pause (strǽtoupɔz) *n.* the level separating the stratosphere and mesosphere, occurring between 18 miles and 30 miles. It is the level at which the temperature begins to increase rapidly with altitude

strat·o·scope (strǽtouskoup) *n.* an astronomical telescope to take celestial photographs sent to earth, carried by a balloon

strat·o·sphere (strǽtəsfjər) *n.* a division of the earth's atmosphere extending about 30 miles (depending upon season, latitude and weather conditions in the troposphere) from the tropopause. In the stratosphere the temperature changes only little with increasing altitude. Because of its low moisture content and the absence of large convection currents the stratosphere is an excellent region for air travel (*STRATOPAUSE) [fr. STRATUM+ATMOSPHERE]

Strat·o·tank·er (strǽtoutænkər) *n.* (*mil.*) a multipurpose aerial tanker-transport (KC-135) powered by four turbojet engines, equipped for high-speed, high-altitude refueling of bombers and fighters

strat·o·vol·ca·no (strætouvɒlkéinou) *n.* (*geol.*) a volcano made up of alternating layers of lava flows, volcanic ash, and cinders *also* composite volcano

stra·tum (stréitəm, strǽtəm, strɑ́təm) *pl.* **stra·ta** (stréitə, strǽtə, strɑ́tə), **stra·tums** *n.* a roughly horizontal layer of homogeneous material with its surfaces parallel to those of layers of material of different kinds on either side ‖ (*biol.*) a thin layer of tissue ‖ (*geol.*) a layer of rock composed of one material, e.g. shale or limestone, lying between rock beds of other materials ‖ a level or division, *social stratum* [L. *something spread or laid down*]

stra·tus (stréitəs, strǽtəs) *pl.* **stra·ti** (stréitai, strǽtai) *n.* an unbroken sheet of low-altitude clouds [fr. L. *sternere* (*stratus*), to spread out]

Strauss (straus, G. ʃtraus), Johann (1825-99), Austrian composer. He is best known for his waltzes, esp. 'The Blue Danube' (1866). He also wrote popular operettas, 'Die Fledermaus' (1873) being the most successful. Johann was one of three sons of Johann the Elder (1804-49), himself a master of the waltz

Strauss, Richard (1864-1949), German composer. He is known chiefly for his symphonic poems and operas but his output includes works for string orchestra, horn concerti, songs and ballet music. His early compositions are symphonic poems, of which the best known are 'Don Juan' (1889), 'Death and Transfiguration' (1890), 'Till Eulenspiegel' (1895) and 'A Hero's Life' (1889). His operas begin with 'Salome' (1905), a setting of Oscar Wilde's play. Most of his other operas, which include 'Elektra' (1908), 'Der Rosenkavalier' (1909-11), 'Ariadne auf Naxos' (1912) and 'Arabella' (1933), have librettos by Hugo von Hofmannsthal

Stra·vin·sky (strəvínski:), Igor (1882-1971), Russian composer, naturalized French (1934), then American (1945). His first success was with the music for the ballet 'The Fire Bird' (1910). His collaboration with Diaghilev led to 'Petrouchka' (1911) and 'The Rite of Spring' (1913). The early works, scored for enormous orchestras, were strongly Russian in character and show the influence of Rimsky-Korsakov, his teacher, yet they were so novel and disturbing that there was a riot at the first performance of 'The Rite of Spring'. Stravinsky then went through a neoclassical period, modified in the 1930s, when he employed small forces and compact forms. He was a rhythmic and harmonic innovator and almost without exception kept to tonality, though in some later works he used a serialist technique allied to twelve-tone music. Stravinsky was perhaps one of the most penetrating intelligences ever applied to music, yet this analytic search has produced the most 'primitive' or rhythmically exciting music of the century. Other works of his include 'Oedipus Rex' (1926-7), 'Symphony of Psalms' (1930), 'Persephone' (1934) and 'The Rake's Progress' (1951), an opera in neo-Mozartian style

straw (strɔ) **1.** *n.* the stems of any of several cereals after cutting and threshing. Straw is used esp. for bedding in stables and for thatch-

CONCISE PRONUNCIATION KEY: **(a)** æ, c*a*t; ɑ, c*a*r; ɔ f*aw*n; ei, sn*a*ke. **(e)** e, h*e*n; iː, sh*ee*p; iə, d*ee*r; ɛə, b*ea*r. **(i)** i, f*i*sh; ai, t*i*ger; əː, b*i*rd. **(o)** o, *o*x; au, c*ow*; ou, g*oa*t; u, p*oo*r; ɔi, r*oy*al. **(u)** ʌ, d*u*ck; u, b*u*ll; uː, g*oo*se; ə, b*a*cillus; juː, c*u*be. x, lo*ch*; θ, *th*ink; ð, *b*o*th*er; z, *Z*en; ʒ, corsa*g*e; dʒ, sava*g*e; ŋ, orangutan*g*; j, *y*ak; ʃ, *f*ish; tʃ, fe*tch*; 'l, rabb*le*; 'n, redd*en*. Complete pronunciation key appears inside front cover.

ing, stuffing and insulating etc. ‖ one of these stems ‖ a tube of plastic or paper used for drawing liquids into the mouth ‖ used to indicate something of little or no worth, *she doesn't care a straw what happens* **a straw in the wind** a small sign indicative of some coming event, an omen **the last straw** the very last in a series of humiliations, misfortunes, blows of fate etc., after which nothing seems possible or bearable **to catch** (or **clutch** or **grasp**) **at a straw** to make use of anything, however small, that might possibly be of help in a desperate situation **2.** *adj.* made of straw, *straw matting* ‖ resembling straw, straw-colored [O.E. *strēaw*]

straw·ber·ry (stróːberi, stróːbəri) *pl.* **straw·ber·ries** *n.* a member of *Fragaria*, fam. *Rosaceae*, a genus of plants widely cultivated for their edible, juicy, sweet, red fruit ‖ the fruit of any of these plants ‖ the vivid pinkish red of this fruit [O.E. *strēawberige, strēowberige*]

strawberry blonde a woman who has reddish blonde hair and a fair complexion

strawberry jar a ceramic plantholder resembling a strawberry, with openings on the sides through which additional plants may be grown

strawberry tree *ARBUTUS

straw·board (stróːbɔrd, stróːbɔuərd) *n.* coarse cardboard made of straw pulp and used in making boxes, in bookbinding etc.

straw man a man of straw

straw vote an unofficial poll taken by letters of inquiry, group questioning etc. in order e.g. to determine the chances of a candidate

stray (strei) **1.** *v.i.* (with 'from') to leave a proper place or course, *they strayed from the path and were soon lost* ‖ (*rhet.*) to deviate morally ‖ to move lingeringly and absently, *her hand strayed over its fur* ‖ (*rhet.*) to roam **2.** *n.* something (esp. a domestic animal) which has strayed ‖ (*pl., radio*) static electrical effects which disturb reception **3.** *adj.* having strayed, *a stray dog* ‖ out of place, *stray hairs* ‖ random, *stray shots were heard* [var. of older *astray* v., *estray* v., fr. O.F. *estraier*]

streak (striːk) **1.** *n.* a linear, usually irregular, mark differing in color and/or texture from the background it appears on ‖ a trace, *a streak of cruelty* ‖ a sudden temporary manifestation, *a streak of good luck, a streak of genius* ‖ the color shown when a mineral is scratched (for identification) ‖ (of lightning) a flash **2.** *v.t.* to mark with a streak or streaks ‖ *v.i.* to become streaky ‖ (*pop.*) to move very fast [O.E. *strica*]

streak·er (stríːkər) *n.* one who runs nude in public, usu. in a sprint or slightly longer run for the purpose of attracting attention in order to make some sort of statement, or for diversion — **streak** *v.* —**streaking** *n.*

streak·i·ly (stríːkili) *adv.* in a streaky manner

streak·i·ness (stríːkiːnis) *n.* the state or quality of being streaky

streak·ing (stríːkiŋ) *n.* hair-coloring style in which some strands are bleached —**streaked** *adj.*

streak·y (stríːkiː) *comp.* **streak·i·er** *superl.* **streak·i·est** *adj.* marked with streaks ‖ occurring in streaks

stream (striːm) **1.** *n.* a small body of fresh water flowing either permanently or seasonally in a channel on or under the earth ‖ a quantity of something fluid in motion, *a stream of sand trickled out* ‖ a continuous procession of people or animals moving in one direction ‖ a linked succession of events, *the stream of history* ‖ a continuous emission, *a stream of words* ‖ the flow or current of a fluid ‖ the direction of this flow ‖ a swift oceanic current, e.g. the Gulf Stream ‖ (*Br. education*) a group (of pupils) who have been classed according to academic performance, *C-stream students* **2.** *v.i.* to flow in, or as if in, a stream, *the rain streamed down* ‖ to emit fluid in a stream, *her eyes were streaming* ‖ to be moved and esp. extended by, or as if by, a stream or current, *the flag streamed in the wind* ‖ (of many people or things) to move in one direction, *workmen streamed from the factory* ‖ (of something static, e.g. a road) to appear to have a fast current because of one's own speed of moving along or beside it ‖ *v.t.* to emit (fluid) in a stream, *her eyes streamed tears* ‖ to cause (e.g. a flag) to move and extend as if carried by a stream or current ‖ (*naut.*) to throw (the anchor buoy) overboard before casting anchor ‖ (*mining*) to wash (a surface) with a stream of water in order to see if it contains ore ‖ (*Br. education*) to class (pupils) into streams according to their academic performance **strēam·er** *n.* a long,

narrow piece of fabric attached at one end and put to stream out in the wind ‖ a festive decoration for a room made of a long thin ribbon of colored paper ‖ (*pl.*) the aurora borealis ‖ a banner headline [O.E. *strēam*]

stream·let (stríːmlit) *n.* a small stream (body of fresh water)

stream·line (stríːmlain) **1.** *n.* a direction of smooth flow within a liquid or gas past a solid body or a line drawn to indicate this ‖ the contour given to a solid body so that it can move through a fluid with the minimum resistance **2.** *v.t. pres. part.* **stream·lin·ing** *past* and *past part.* **stream·lined** to shape (a solid body) in this way ‖ to render more efficient by modernizing, *the new director soon streamlined the business* **stréam·lined** *adj.* shaped so as to be able to move through a fluid with minimum resistance ‖ planned in such a way that progress is made as easy and rapid as possible ‖ modernized and speeded up

streamline flow a manner of flow such that continuous streamlines can be drawn through the whole length of the course

stream of consciousness (*psychol.*) individual conscious experience regarded as continuously moving forward in time in an uneven flow. In creative writing the interior monologue makes use of this to reveal character and comment on life [originated by William JAMES]

street (striːt) *n.* a road in a town or village, usually hard-surfaced and provided with drainage and artificial lighting and having buildings on one or both sides ‖ this road together with the houses etc. abutting it ‖ (*collect.*) the people who live or work in the houses etc. of this road, *the whole street knew about it* [O. E. *strēt*]

street book (*trading*) a daily record kept by futures commission merchants and clearing members showing details of each futures transaction

street·car (stríːtkɑr) *n.* (*Am.=Br.* tram) a passenger car for public transport running on rails laid in the street or roadway and driven by electric current from a conduit or from overhead wires

street-cor·ner conservative (stríːtkɔrnər) one who calls him- or herself a conservative, without understanding the term

street-lev·el propulsion (stríːtlevəl) the force of opinions held by uninformed and unorganized masses of people

street·light (stríːtlait) *n.* one of a series of lamps, each mounted on a lamppost, placed at intervals along a street or road

street people those who are habitually active in or present on the street or parks, e.g., hippies, hustlers, and, esp. in ethnic or ghetto neighborhoods, usu. older people who spend their day and early evening hours seated in chairs on the sidewalk or before their doors or watching from their windows

street·scape (stríːtskeip) *n.* an urban landscape or view of a street or streets

street theater short plays or pantomime, usu. antiestablishment, presented on the street or in a park, usu. by a volunteer company *also* GUERILLA THEATER

street·walk·er (stríːtwɔkər) *n.* a prostitute who solicits in the street

street·wise (stríːtwaiz) *adj.* aware of the mores of street people and skilled in dealing with them *syn* streetsmart

street·work·er (stríːtwɜrkər) *n.* social worker active with neighborhood youth

strength (streŋθ) *n.* capacity to exert force ‖ ability to resist attack ‖ capacity to resist strain, stress etc. ‖ physical, emotional or mental resources ‖ the potency of a drug or beverage ‖ the effectiveness of something in stimulating the senses or influencing the mind ‖ (*mil.*) fighting capacity, reckoned in numbers and equipment (of arguments, legal cases etc.) soundness ‖ (*commerce*) the tendency of prices on the stock exchange or in the commodity market etc. to remain high **on the strength of** relying on **strength·en** *v.t.* to make stronger ‖ *v.i.* to become stronger [O.E. *strengthu*]

stren·u·ous (strénjuːəs) *adj.* involving a great effort, *strenuous attempts* ‖ requiring a great effort, *a strenuous occupation* [fr. L. *strenuus*, vigorous]

strep·to·coc·cal (streptəkɔ́kl) *adj.* of or caused by streptococci

strep·to·coc·cic (streptəkɔ́ksik) *adj.* streptococcal

strep·to·coc·cus (streptəkɔ́kəs) *pl.* **strep·to·coc·ci** (streptəkɔ́ksai) *n.* a member of *Strepto-*

coccus, a genus of nonmotile, gram-positive bacteria, usually occurring in chains of coccoid cells. Many produce infections (e.g. erysipelas, impetigo) in man [Mod. L. fr. Gk *streptos*, twisted+*kokkos*, berry]

strep·to·my·cin (streptoumáisin) *n.* an antibiotic produced by the South American soil fungus *Streptomyces griseus* and used in the treatment of various bacterial infections (e.g. tuberculosis) [fr. Gk *streptos*, twisted+*mukēs*, fungus]

strep·to·ni·grin (streptounáigrin) [$C_{25}H_{22}N_4O_8$] *n.* (*pharm.*) toxic antibiotic used in cancer treatment

Stre·se·mann (ʃtréizəmɑn), Gustav (1878-1929), German liberal statesman. As foreign minister (1923-9), he signed the Locarno Pact (1925) and the Kellogg-Briand Pact (1928). Nobel peace prize (1926)

stress (stres) **1.** *n.* (*phys.*) the state of an elastic body under conditions of strain expressed quantitatively as force applied per unit area (*HOOKE'S LAW) ‖ a state in which a strong demand is made on the nervous system ‖ special emphasis given to something ‖ the relative intensity with which a syllable is uttered ‖ a strong syllable (*mus., prosody*) accent **2.** *v.t.* to give emphasis to ‖ to accent, *stress the first syllable* ‖ to impart mechanical stress to, *prestressed concrete* [prob. a form of DISTRESS n.]

stretch (stretʃ) **1.** *v.t.* to pull or otherwise exert force on (an elastic body), causing it to assume its full potential dimensions or dimensions greater than those it has when not thus pulled etc. ‖ to pull or spread out fully ‖ to cause (something) to occupy a given amount of space or given distance, *stretch the wires across the valley* ‖ to strain (a tendon) ‖ to make (something) permanently larger by exerting forces beyond the elastic limit, *to stretch a shoe* ‖ (often with 'out') to cause (a limb etc.) to reach out to full length, *to stretch one's arms* ‖ (*refl.*, often with 'out on') to cause (oneself) to lie full length ‖ (*refl.*) to ease (oneself) from a cramped or curled position by straightening the body ‖ to make (food etc.) appear to go further ‖ to try to make (the law, the truth etc.) go beyond their proper limits ‖ to lay (someone) flat ‖ (*pop.*) to knock (someone) flat ‖ to cause (e.g. the intelligence or imagination) to exceed previous limits **2.** *v.i.* (of an elastic body) to become enlarged in length and/or breadth ‖ to become permanently enlarged ‖ to be able to endure strain, *will your generosity stretch that far?* ‖ to ease oneself from a cramped or curled position by straightening the body ‖ to occupy a given amount of time or space, *the war stretched over four years* ‖ (often with 'out') to lie full length ‖ to become stretched or capable of being stretched ‖ to reach out, esp. one's hand, *can you stretch for it?* **to stretch a point** to make a special concession ‖ to go beyond what is justified, e.g. in reaching a conclusion, interpreting a text etc. **to stretch one's legs** to take a short walk **2.** *n.* a stretching or being stretched ‖ capacity for being stretched ‖ the extent to which something can be stretched without damage ‖ a length or area, *a stretch of rope, a stretch of grass* ‖ a continuous period, *a stretch in the army* ‖ (*pop.*) a period of imprisonment ‖ a short walk for relaxation or mild exercise ‖ a usually straight section of racetrack **strétch·er** *n.* a length of canvas etc. stretched between parallel poles and used for carrying, esp. the sick or dead in a prone position ‖ a brick or stone laid lengthwise, parallel to the face of the wall of which it forms part ‖ any of various frames upon which cloth, canvas etc. is stretched or shaped ‖ (*rowing*) a crosspiece against which a rower can brace his feet [O.E. *streccan*]

stretch·er-bear·er (strétʃərbɛərər) *n.* a person carrying one end of a stretcher

stretch-out (strétʃaut) *n.* (*pop.*) a reorganization within an industry which results in more work being done by the same number of employees for little or no additional pay

stretch receptor a muscle end sensitive to stretch, e.g., in the lung *also* muscle spindle

stretch·y (strétʃi) *comp.* **stretch·i·er** *superl.* **stretch·i·est** *adj.* elastic ‖ apt to stretch too far

stret·to (strétou) *pl.* **stret·ti** (stréti:), **stret·tos** *n.* (*mus.*) a direction that the pace of a piece of music should quicken ‖ (*mus.*) a term used of the overlapping of entries in fugal compositions. The second voice enters with the subject before the first voice has finished uttering it [Ital.]

CONCISE PRONUNCIATION KEY: **(a)** æ, cat; ɑ, car; ɔ fawn; ei, snake. **(e)** e, hen; iː, sheep; iə, deer; ɛə, bear. **(i)** i, fish; ai, tiger; əː, bird. **(o)** o, ox; au, cow; ou, goat; u, poor; ɔi, royal. **(u)** ʌ, duck; u, bull; uː, goose; ə, bacillus; juː, cube. x, loch; θ, think; ð, bother; z, Zen; ʒ, corsage; dʒ, savage; ŋ, orangutang; j, yak; ʃ, fish; tʃ, fetch; 'l, rabble; 'n, redden. Complete pronunciation key appears inside front cover.

strew (stru:) *pres. part.* **strew·ing** *past* **strewed** *past part.* **strewed, strewn** (stru:n) *v.t.* to scatter in separate particles or drops over a surface, *to strew sand* || to drop or throw about in a disorderly way || to cover (a surface) in this way, *the ground was strewn with leaves* [O.E. streowian, streawian, strewian]

strewn field a location where tektites (small meteorites) have fallen

stri·a (stráiə) *pl.* **stri·ae** (stráii:) *n.* a narrow groove || one of the thin, parallel bands of color marking some rocks, shells etc. || (*archit.*) a fillet, esp. one separating the flutes of a column || a stripe or line distinguished from its surroundings by color, relief or texture etc. [L.]

stri·ate 1. (stráieit) *v.t. pres. part.* **stri·at·ing** *past* and *past part.* **stri·at·ed** to mark with or as if with striae **2.** (stráiit) *adj.* marked with parallel striae **strí·at·ed** *adj.* [fr. L. striare (striatus), to groove]

striated muscle contractile tissue with marked transverse striations, forming the skeletal muscle of the vertebrate body (cf. SMOOTH MUSCLE, cf. CARDIAC MUSCLE, cf. SKELETAL MUSCLE)

stri·a·tion (straiéiʃən) *n.* the condition of being striated || the way striae are arranged || a stria

strick·en (stríkən) *alt. past part.* OF STRIKE || *adj.* afflicted by some overwhelming disaster, grief, disease etc. || (*rhet.*, of a hunted animal) wounded || (in compounds) suddenly possessed by a specified emotion etc., *panic-stricken, terror-stricken* || (of a measure) having its contents leveled with a strickle [alt. *past part.* of STRIKE]

strick·le (stríkl) **1.** *n.* an instrument for removing surplus grain from a measure above the level of the rim || a straightedge of stone or roughened steel used to sharpen the curved blade of a scythe etc. || a template with a beveled edge used to shape a mold in a foundry **2.** *v.t. pres. part.* **strick·ling** *past* and *past part.* **strick·led** to shape with a strickle [O.E. stricel]

strict (strikt) *adj.* rigorous and often severe in imposing discipline, *a strict schoolmaster* || adhering rigorously to rules or standards, *a strict teetotaler* || requiring unswerving obedience, *strict rules* || precise, exact, rigorously adhered to, *strict tempo* || (*bot.*, of stems etc.) not drooping **strict·ly** *adv.* **strictly speaking** according to the rules when interpreted without latitude, *strictly speaking I should not be here* || literally, in every respect corresponding with the facts, *it's not, strictly speaking, true* [fr. L. stringere (strictus), to draw or bind tight]

stric·ture (stríktʃər) *n.* an adverse criticism || (*med.*) an abnormal contraction of a duct or channel of the body, esp. of the male urethra [fr. L. strictura, contraction]

stride (straid) **1.** *v. pres. part.* **strid·ing** *past* **strode** (stroud) *past part.* **strid·den** (strídn) *v.i.* to walk with long steps || *v.t.* to pass over (e.g. a ditch) in one step || to go over, through, along, up and down etc. with long steps, *to stride the deck* **2.** *n.* a long walking step || the distance covered by such a step || a striding gait || (*pl.*) rapid advances, *strides to recovery* **to hit one's stride** (*Am.=Br.* **to get into one's stride**) to become adjusted so that one works or plays with full efficiency **to take in one's stride** to do (something), or adjust oneself to (something) easily or without fuss [O.E. strīdan]

stri·dence (stráidns) *n.* stridency

stri·den·cy (stráidnsi:) *n.* the state or quality of being strident

stri·dent (stráidnt) *adj.* (of a sound) loud, grating and harsh [fr. L. stridens (stridentis) fr. stridere, to creak]

stride piano jazz form of piano playing in which the right hand plays the melody while the left hand plays a chord or a note at a higher octave

strid·u·lant (strídʒulənt) *adj.* stridulating || stridulous

strid·u·late (strídʒuleit) *pres. part.* **strid·u·lat·ing** *past* and *past part.* **strid·u·lat·ed** *v.i.* (of cicadas, grasshoppers etc.) to make a shrill, strident sound by rubbing together certain hard parts of the body **strid·u·la·tion** *n.* [fr. Mod. L. stridulare (stridulatus)]

strid·u·lous (strídʒuləs) *adj.* making a shrill chirping sound [fr. L. stridulus]

stri·é (stri:jéi) *n.* a cloth that has irregular stripes or streaks of similar color in the background, producing a mottled effect

strife (straif) *n.* a condition of enmity often arising out of rivalry || (*rhet.*) a prolonged struggle for power or superiority || discord, *domestic strife* [O.F. estrif]

stri·ga (stráigə) *pl.* **stri·gae** (stráigi:), **stri·gas** *n.* (*bot.*, esp. *pl.*) a stiff bristle [L.]

strig·il (strídʒəl) *n.* (*Gk* and *Rom. hist.*) a scraper for removing sweat from the skin || one of a group of curved or undulating flutings adorning esp. Roman architecture || (*zool.*) a comblike mechanism, situated on the junction of the tibia and the tarsum on the first legs of bees and other insects, and used for cleaning the antennae [fr. L. strigilis]

stri·gose (stráigous) *adj.* (*bot.*) having strigae || (*biol.*) marked by small furrows [fr. Mod. L. strigosus fr. striga, a furrow]

strike (straik) **1.** *v. pres. part.* **strik·ing** *past* **struck** (strʌk) *past part.* **struck, strick·en** (stríkən) *v.t.* to deal (someone) a blow || to deliver (a blow) || to hit (e.g. a ball) || to collide forcibly with || (with 'together') to cause to collide or come into contact forcibly, *she struck their heads together* || to touch (e.g. keys), esp. so as to produce a musical note or sound || to touch e.g. keys so as to produce (a musical note or sound), *to strike a chord* || (of a clock) to chime (the hour) || to cause (a match) to ignite by friction || to remove with a sharp blow (*rhet.*, of disaster, illness, death) to come suddenly and esp. violently upon, *the plague struck the town yesterday* || (esp. used passively with 'down') to afflict suddenly and violently (of lightning) to damage or destroy || (*rhet.*) to wound or affect the feelings of, *the news struck him to the quick* || to make (a medal) by stamping || (of sound) to become audible to || (of light) to fall on and illuminate brightly, *the sun struck the weathercock* || to make an impression or impact on, *they were struck by its speed* || (of an idea or thought) to occur suddenly to || to seem to (someone), *it strikes me as impossible* || to make a discovery of (e.g. oil) || to produce (sparks) to assume (an attitude or pose) to arrive at (a bargain, balance, average etc.) || to level off (a measure of grain) with a strickle || to cause (a plant) to take root || to lower, take down (sails, tents, flags etc.) || to vacate the site of (a camp) || to hook (a fish) by a sudden sharp pull || to dismantle (theater scenery) || (with 'on') to arrive at (a solution) || to come across unexpectedly, *he struck the main road* || to come up against, *they struck various difficulties* || to cause (someone) to become blind, dumb etc. || (*naut.*, with 'down') to lower (cargo) into the hold || to harpoon (a whale) || (of a snake) to sink the fangs into || to cease (work) in order to put pressure on an employer || (*mil.*) to attack (an enemy or target) || (with 'out') to cancel or erase || *v.i.* to deal a blow or blows || to attack || to proceed in a specified direction, *he struck south* || to chime, *one o'clock struck* || (of a match) to become ignited || (of a fish) to grab at the bait || (of a snake) to sink or try to sink its fangs into its prey || (of a ship) to run aground || (*naut.*) to lower the flag, esp. as a sign of surrender || (*geol.*) to extend in a certain direction || (of a plant) to take root || (of a seed) to germinate || (with 'for') to go in the direction of || to stop working in order to put pressure on an employer **to strike home** (of a punch, blow etc.) to be very effective || (of a remark) to produce a very pronounced effect **to strike off** to sever || to remove (the name of) someone from a register and thus debar him of specified privileges **to strike out** (baseball) to be put out as a result of three strikes || (baseball) to put (a batter) out by pitching three strikes **to strike out** for to begin to swim or row vigorously in the direction of **to strike out on one's own** to start a new enterprise alone **to strike up** to begin to make music, *the band struck up* || to begin to play (something), *the band struck up a waltz* || to begin (a friendship, a conversation) with someone met casually **2.** *n.* a blow || a ceasing to work in order to put pressure on an employer || the number of coins minted or medals struck at one time || a fish's bite at the bait || the discovery of a deposit of oil etc. || a strickle || (*geol.*) the horizontal direction of a stratum || (baseball) a pitched ball which is struck at but missed, or which is fairly delivered but not struck at, or which is hit but not caught, or which is, on a third strike, hit as a foul tip caught by the catcher, or which is, on a third strike, bunted foul || (*bowling*) the act of knocking down all the pins with the first bowl || the score made in this way [O.E. strican]

strike·break·er (stráikbreikər) *n.* a person engaged to do a striker's work || someone who supplies workers to an employer during a strike

strike·break·ing (stráikbreikiŋ) *n.* the breaking up of a workers' strike

strike cruiser (*mil.*) warship designed to operate with carrier strike forces or surface action groups

strike·out (stráikaut) *n.* (baseball) the out made by a batter when he has been charged with three strikes

strike pay an allowance paid out by a trade union to those on official strike

strik·er (stráikər) *n.* a person who strikes || a worker on strike || something that strikes, e.g. the hammer in a chiming clock || an enlisted man in the army employed as orderly to an officer

strik·ing (stráikiŋ) *adj.* remarkable, impressive, attracting attention || on strike || of or relating to a device that strikes

Strind·berg (stríndbə:rg, strínbə:rg, strínbærjə), August (1849-1912), Swedish writer best known for his plays. He also wrote poems, short stories, two volumes of autobiography, and novels, of which the best-known is 'The Red Room' (1879). He inaugurated a new movement in European drama with the dramatic naturalism of his two best-known plays, 'The Father' (1887) and 'Miss Julie' (1888). There are mystical, symbolic and supernatural elements in the later plays, of which the best-known are 'The Dance of Death' (1901) and 'The Ghost Sonata' (1907). Themes of social satire and criticism and of sexual and class conflict occur throughout his writings, which are also colored by his own conceptions of psychology

string (striŋ) **1.** *n.* a thin length of twisted fiber, thinner than cord, used for tying etc. || a length of e.g. silk or twine on which e.g. beads or fish can be threaded || a length of tape etc. used for tying or fastening || (*pl.*) the cords pulled to actuate a puppet || a natural fiber, e.g. that along one edge of a bean pod || a row of beads or other objects threaded on or as if on a string, *a string of onions* || a number of things of any kind arranged or ranging one behind the other, *a string of cars, a string of events* || a number of things linked or tied together, *a string of sausages, a string of mules* || several homogeneous business concerns owned by one person or company, *a string of hotels* || a length of wire, gut etc. which produces sound when under tension and when made to vibrate by striking, plucking or bowing || (*pl.*) the stringed instruments of an orchestra collectively || (*pl.*) the players of these instruments || a bowstring || the horses from one racing stable || a group of players rated according to ability || (*archit.*) a stringcourse || that part of the side of a stair supporting the treads and risers || (*billiards*) a balkline || (*billiards*) the score or device used to record this || (*pop.*) a condition attached to something || a source that can be used to promote the interests of someone **to have two strings to one's bow** to have two alternative courses of action at one's disposal **to pull strings** to exert one's personal influence, or ask someone else to do this for one **2.** *v. pres. part.* **string·ing** *past* and *past part.* **strung** (strʌŋ) *v.t.* to furnish with a string or strings || (*archery*) to fit a bowstring to (a bow) || to thread on a string || to fasten with a string || to remove the stringy fibers from, *to string beans* || to connect or put in an unbroken series, *to string ideas together* || (with 'out') to arrange in a long line || to cause (something) to extend along a given distance, *string the wire around the room* || *v.i.* (*billiards*) to determine the order of playing by causing the cue ball to rebound off the foot cushion and stop as close to the head cushion (or sometimes to the head string) as possible || to string fibers || to stretch out in a long line **to string (someone) along** (*pop.*) to fool (someone) **to string along with** to stay with, follow or go along with (someone), esp. rather long-sufferingly **to string out** to prolong to **to string up** (*pop.*) to hang (execute) || to bring into a state of nervous tension [O.E. streng]

string bean (*Am.=Br.* runner bean) a bean of which the unripe pod is eaten as food, the fiber down the side of the pod having first been removed

string·board (stríŋbɔrd, stríŋbourd) *n.* (*archit.*) a facing used to cover the ends of the steps in a staircase

string·course (stríŋkɔrs, stríŋkours) *n.* (*archit.*) a projecting horizontal band stretching around the outside of a building

stringed (striŋd) *adj.* (of musical instruments) having strings

strin·gen·cy (stríndʒənsi:) *pl.* **strin·gen·cies** *n.* the state or quality, or an instance, of being stringent

strin·gen·do (strindʒéndou) *n.* (*mus.*) a direction to play at an accelerating speed [Ital.]

strin·gent (stríndʒənt) *adj.* strict, rigid, *stringent rules* ‖ tight, limiting, *stringent financial conditions* ‖ (of reasoning) convincing, closely argued [fr. L. *stringens* (*stringentis*) fr. *stringere*, to draw tight]

strin·ger (stríŋər) *n.* a long horizontal member of a structural framework, e.g. for supporting the floorboards of a building or the sections of a bridge ‖ (*aeron.*) a longitudinal member used for strengthening a fuselage or wing in certain types of aircraft ‖ a railroad tie

string·i·ness (stríŋi:nis) *n.* the state or quality of being stringy

string-piece (stríŋpi:s) *n.* a long heavy piece of timber laid horizontally and used to support and strengthen various sorts of framework

string tie a necktie made of a very narrow width of material and usually tied in a bow

string·y (stríŋi:) *comp.* **string·i·er** *superl.* **string·i·est** *adj.* consisting of fibers or strings ‖ like a string, long and thin ‖ (of meat) fibrous, tough ‖ (of liquid) viscid ‖ (of people) thin and wiry or scrawny

strip (strip) *pres. part.* **strip·ping** *past* and *past part.* **stripped** *v.t.* to remove (clothing) ‖ to remove the clothing of (someone) ‖ to remove (a covering), *to strip the bark from a tree* ‖ to deprive (something) of its covering, *to strip a tree of its bark* ‖ to deprive (someone) of a possession etc. ‖ to take (a possession etc.) from someone ‖ to divest (a person) of medals, decorations, honors etc. ‖ to remove (medals, decorations, honors etc.) from someone ‖ to remove or pull back the bedclothes from (a bed) ‖ to remove or pull back (the bedclothes) from a bed ‖ to squeeze the last drop of milk from (a cow) ‖ to dismantle (a gun) ‖ to pluck the old hair from (a rough-coated dog) ‖ to break the thread of (a screw) or the teeth of (a cog) ‖ to empty (e.g. a room) of furniture etc. ‖ to remove (furniture etc.) from a room ‖ to make (something) bare by taking away removable parts ‖ to take away (removable parts) from something ‖ (*pop.*) to make (an automobile) lighter, for extra speed, by removing nonessential parts ‖ to remove the central rib from (tobacco leaves) ‖ to pick the cured leaves from the stalks of (tobacco) ‖ to tear off ‖ *v.i.* to undress ‖ to come off in strips **to strip down** to prepare (a surface) for painting etc. by cleaning off old paint etc. ‖ to take to pieces (an engine) in order to clean and service it [M.E. *stripe, strepe, strupe*, O.E. *strīpan, strȳpan*, to plunder]

strip *n.* a long narrow piece of more or less uniform width, *a strip of land* ‖ a comic strip ‖ an airstrip ‖ (*Br.*) a trough in which ores are washed and separated **to tear a strip off** (*Br.*, *pop.*) to rebuke (someone) very severely [prob. M.L.G. *strippe*]

strip cartoon (*Br.*) a comic strip

strip chart graph presented on a long, continuous strip, e.g., a patient's fever chart

strip city an urban area connecting two separate cities, e.g., between New York and Newark

strip cropping the planting of separate crops in contiguous strips along the contours of hillsides to combat erosion

stripe (straip) *n.* a stroke or lash with a whip ‖ (*rhet.*) the mark left on the body by such a stroke or lash [prob. fr. L.G. or Du.]

stripe 1. *n.* a long narrow band usually of uniform width, distinguished by color or texture from its surroundings ‖ a short band or one of a number sewn on a uniform to denote rank, service, good conduct etc. ‖ a particular kind of character, opinion etc., *scholars of a different stripe* 2. *v.t. pres. part.* **strip·ing** *past* and *past part.* **striped** to mark with a stripe or stripes **striped** (straipt, stráipid) *adj.* [prob. fr. M.L.G. or Du. *strīpe*]

striped bass *Roccus saxatilis*, fam. *Serranidae*, a game and food fish having longitudinal black stripes and ranging from 20 lbs to (rarely) 100 lbs in weight

striped muishond *Ictonyx striata*, a ferretlike muishond

strip farming the allotment of land to individual farmers in separated strips so that good and bad land may be fairly distributed ‖ strip cropping

strip lighting the lighting of a room with one or more tubular, fluorescent lamps

strip·ling (striplıŋ) *n.* (*rhet.*) a youth

strip mining process of stripping the land of its surface rock and soil to make available underlying mineral deposits

strip-tease (stríptı:z) *n.* a theatrical or cabaret act in which a person removes his/her clothes in front of the audience item by item usually to music

strip·y (stráipi:) *comp.* **strip·i·er** *superl.* **strip·i·est** *adj.* marked with stripes

strive (straiv) *pres. part.* **striv·ing** *past* **strove** (strouv) *past part.* **striv·en** (strívən) *v.i.* to make great efforts, *to strive to convince someone* ‖ (with 'towards') to struggle or endeavor to attain some end ‖ (with 'with') to vie or contend [M.E. *striven*]

strobil *STROBILE

strob·i·la·ceous (strɒbəléiʃəs) *adj.* relating to a strobilus ‖ resembling a strobilus ‖ having strobili

strob·ile, strob·il (stróbəl) *n.* a strobilus [F.]

strob·i·lus (stróbələs) *pl.* **strob·i·li** (stróbəlai) *n.* (*bot.*) a conelike aggregation of sporophylls, e.g. in club mosses ‖ a flower of imbricated scales, e.g. in hops ‖ the cone of a gymnosperm [L.]

stro·bo·scope (stróubəskoup, strɒbəskoup) *n.* (*phys.*) a device by which small differences of frequency between two simple periodic or simple oscillatory motions can be measured, depending on the principle that if they are viewed together, they will appear to coincide at regular intervals of time which can be measured. Thus if there are *n* coincidences per second, the difference in frequency is *n* **stro·bo·scop·ic** (stroubəskɒpik, strɒbəskɒpik), **stro·bo·scop·i·cal** *adjs.* [fr. Gk *strobos*, a twisting or whirling around+*skopein*, to observe]

strode *past* of STRIDE

Stroess·ner (strésnər), Alfredo (1912-   ), Paraguayan general and dictator (1954-   ). He had himself reelected president for the sixth time in 1983

stroke (strouk) 1. *n.* a blow ‖ (in various ball games) the act of striking the ball ‖ an attempt to strike the ball ‖ a sudden manifestation (of e.g. genius, luck etc.) ‖ the sound of a bell or a striking clock ‖ a heartbeat ‖ an attack of apoplexy ‖ a single, combined movement of the limbs propelling a swimmer through the water ‖ a stylized set of such movements, e.g. breaststroke or crawl ‖ a single movement of a piston or similar thing ‖ the distance covered in this movement ‖ a single movement of the hand in painting, drawing, writing etc. ‖ a single mark made by a brush, pencil, pen etc. ‖ (in negative constructions) a minimum of work, *not a stroke was done* ‖ a movement made in keeping time ‖ an oblique or vertical line used in printing, esp. to divide alternatives, as in 'and/or' ‖ (*rowing*) the oarsman who sits nearest the stern of the boat and sets the pace ‖ the position he occupies ‖ (*rowing*) a single pull on the oar ‖ style of rowing in respect to length, speed and frequency of these pulls 2. *v.t. pres. part.* **strok·ing** *past* and *past part.* **stroked** to be stroke for (a crew or boat) ‖ to draw the horizontal line across the upright in (the letter t) [M.E. *strōk* prob. fr. O.E.]

stroke 1. *v.t. pres. part.* **strok·ing** *past* and *past part.* **stroked** to pass esp. the hand gently over once or repeatedly, esp. in the same single direction ‖ to strip the last drop of milk from (a cow) 2. *n.* a stroking movement [O.E. *strācian*]

stroll (stroul) 1. *v.i.* to walk leisurely ‖ *v.t.* to walk leisurely along or through, *strolling the boulevard* 2. *n.* a short leisurely walk **stróll·er** *n.* (*Am.*=*Br.* pushchair) a light wheeled chair for pushing a young child out in ‖ someone out for a stroll [etym. doubtful]

strolling player (*old-fash.*) one of a band of actors, acting on improvised stages etc. and going from place to place off the established theater circuits

stro·ma (stróumə) *pl.* **stro·ma·ta** (stróumətə) *n.* (*anat.*) the connective tissue binding and supporting an organ ‖ the transparent, filmy framework of some cells ‖ the soft, vascular framework in the meshes of which the ovarian follicles are embedded ‖ the protoplasmic body of a plastid [L.=bed covering fr. Gk]

stro·mat·o·lite (stroumǽtəlait) *n.* (*geol.*) fossil of blue-green, self-forming algae found in sedimentary layers of rock *also* callenia —**stro·matolitic** *adj.*

Strom·bo·li (strómbɔli:) the northern-most island (area 5 sq. miles, pop. 100) of the Lipari Is, Italy. It is an active volcano (3,040 ft), but is inhabited: Malmsey, capers

strong (strɔŋ) 1. *adj.* having great physical strength ‖ performed with great physical strength ‖ able to resist considerable force ‖ morally powerful ‖ intellectually powerful ‖ (of appearance) indicative of strength of character ‖ (of personality, character) making an impact, tending to dominate or control ‖ especially proficient or well informed, *strong in history* ‖ powerful because of esp. physical resources (e.g. numbers, wealth, supplies), *a strong contingent of men, a strong economy* ‖ having the force of a specified number, *a contingent 100 strong* ‖ (of a course of action) efficacious but extreme, *strong measures* ‖ firmly grounded, *strong faith, a strong suspicion* ‖ exerting great effect on one of the senses, *strong light* ‖ (of things affecting the sense of smell) unpleasantly powerful ‖ loyal and enthusiastic, *strong supporters* ‖ (of language, words etc.) forceful sometimes to the point of abuse ‖ intense in degree or quality, *strong devotion, strong colors* ‖ concentrated or having a high content of some specified or understood ingredient, *strong tobacco, strong coffee* ‖ having a high alcohol content ‖ unaffected by alcohol, *a strong head* ‖ not squeamish, *a strong stomach* ‖ marked, *a strong resemblance* ‖ (of wind) blowing forcefully ‖ (of lenses) having a high magnifying power ‖ (*chem.*, of an acid or base) ionizing to a high degree in solution ‖ (*gram.*, in Germanic languages) designating a verb that changes its tense by an internal vowel variation (e.g. 'sing, sang, sung') ‖ (*commerce*) characterized by stable or rising prices 2. *adv.* in a strong way, *at 80 he's still going strong* [O.E. *strang, strong*]

strong-arm (strɔŋɑrm) 1. *adj.* (*pop.*) using physical force, often without warrant 2. *v.t.* (*pop.*) to use physical force upon

Strong·bow (strɔŋbou), Richard *PEMBROKE, 2nd earl of

strong·box (strɔŋbɒks) *n.* a small safe or chest for money and valuables

strong force (*nuclear phys.*) short (10^{-23}) elemental force in mesons and baryons that holds protons and neutrons together in the atomic nucleus, and that when released provides nuclear power *also* strong interaction

strong·hold (strɔŋhould) *n.* a fortress ‖ a center of support for a cause or faction, *a stronghold of Catholicism*

strong man a man e.g. in a circus who performs feats of muscular strength ‖ (*pop.*) a dictator

strong-mind·ed (strɔŋmáindid) *adj.* having firm and independent convictions ‖ able to resist temptation, resolute

strong·room (strɔŋru:m, strɔŋrum) *n.* a special fireproof and burglarproof room for storing money or valuables

stron·gyl (strɒndʒil) *n.* a strongyle

stron·gyle (strɒndʒil, strɒndʒail) *n.* any of various roundworms of fam. *Strongylus* parasitic in the digestive tract and tissues of horses and causing extreme debility [fr. Mod. L. *strongylus* fr. Gk *strongulos*, round]

stron·gy·lo·sis (strɒndʒəlóusis) *n.* infestation by strongyles [Mod. L.]

stron·ti·a (strónʃi:ə) *n.* strontium oxide [Mod. L.]

stron·ti·an (strónʃi:ən, strónti:ən) *n.* strontium [after *Strontian*, Argyllshire, Scotland, where it was first discovered]

stron·ti·an·ite (strónʃi:ənait, strónti:ənait) *n.* strontium carbonate, $SrCO_3$, found in various natural forms

stron·ti·um (strónʃi:əm, strónti:əm) *n.* a metallic element (symbol Sr, at. no. 38, at. mass 87.63), chemically similar to calcium. Its compounds, which give a crimson flame coloration, are used in fireworks, and its oxide is used in sugar refining. Its radioactive isotope, strontium 90, released by the explosion of a hydrogen bomb, is dangerous to health [fr. STRONTIA]

strontium 90 (*nuclear phys.*) radioisotope with a half-life of 28 yrs, created by reactor-fusion, used in radiation therapy, atomic batteries, and measuring devices *also* radiostrontium

strontium oxide SrO, an oxide, esp. the crystalline monoxide, of strontium, resembling lime

strop (strop) 1. *n.* a leather strip on which a razor can be sharpened 2. *v.t. pres. part.* **strop·ping** *past* and *past part.* **stropped** to sharpen with a strop [O.E.]

stro·phan·thin-K (strəfǽnθinkéi) *n.* a bitter,

poisonous glycoside obtained from the seeds and bark of *Strophanthus kombé*, an E. African vine. It is used as a heart stimulant and as an arrow poison [fr. Mod. L. fr. Gk *strophos*, a twisted cord+*anthos*, flower]

stro·phe (stróufi:) the lines sung by the chorus as it moved from right to left in an ancient Greek choral drama ‖ the stanza answered by the antistrophe in a Pindaric ode ‖ a stanza, esp. one of the divisions of an ode **stroph·ic** (strófik) *adj.* [Gk *strophē*, a turning]

stro·phoid (stróufoid) *n.* (*math.*) a curve in a plane that is made by a point moving on variable line *A* and passing through point *B*, where *A* to *B* is equal to the *B* intercept value

strove *past* of STRIVE

struck *past* and alt. *past part.* of STRIKE

struck jury (*law*) a jury of 12 members specially selected from an original panel of 48 special jurymen by various processes of elimination

struc·tur·al (strʌ́ktʃərəl) *adj.* of or relating to structure

structural engineering the branch of civil engineering dealing with the design and building of dams, bridges and other large structures

structural formula a chemical formula consisting of an arrangement of chemical symbols (e.g. lines for bonds, dots for nonbonding valence electrons and the usual abbreviations for the chemical elements) showing two-dimensionally the arrangement of atoms in a molecule (cf. EMPIRICAL FORMULA, cf. MOLECULAR FORMULA)

struc·tur·al-func·tion·al theory (strʌ́ktʃərəl-fʌ́ŋkʃənəl) the basis for analysis of a system deduced from analysis of intended and unintended effects in a smaller similar system *also* structural functionalism

struc·tur·al·ism (strʌ́ktʃərəlizm) *n.* a school of thought common to several of the human sciences (psychology, ethnology etc.) tending to define phenomena as elements of organized totalities that can be formulated in mathematical terms

structural isomerism isomerism in which the atoms are linked in different ways in each form (cf. STEREOISOMERISM, cf. OPTICAL ISOMERISM)

struc·tur·al·ly (strʌ́ktʃərəli:) *adv.* with regard to structure

structural reform (*agriculture*) process of improving elements of an agricultural industry by changing farm size, skills, and access

structural steel steel prepared in various shapes for use in the construction of bridges, buildings etc.

struc·ture (strʌ́ktʃər) 1. *n.* something (e.g. a building or an organism) made of parts fitted or joined together ‖ the essential supporting portion of this (e.g. the framework of steel girders supporting a building) ‖ the way in which constituent parts are fitted or joined together, or arranged to give something its peculiar nature or character, *plant structure, the structure of society* 2. *v.t. pres. part.* **struc·tur·ing** *past* and *past part.* **struc·tured** to give a structure to [fr. L. *structura* fr. *struere* (*structus*), to build]

struc·tur·ism (strʌ́ktə·rizəm) *n.* art form that has three dimensions of sculpture, uses color of painting, emphasizes basic geometric forms — **structurist** *n.*

struc·tur·iz·a·tion (strʌktə·rəzéiʃən) *n.* process of organizing any complex intellectual material into a cohesive form — **structurize** *v.*

strug·gle (strʌ́g'l) 1. *v.i. pres. part.* **strug·gling** *past* and *past part.* **strug·gled** to make strenuous efforts, *to struggle to survive* ‖ to move the limbs or body violently to free oneself, *he struggled out of the car* ‖ (with 'with' or 'against') to contend physically with someone, or mentally with a problem etc. ‖ to make one's way with difficulty, *to struggle to the end of a book* 2. *n.* the act of struggling ‖ a great effort ‖ a strenuous contending with someone or something [etym. doubtful]

strum (strʌm) 1. *v. pres. part.* **strum·ming** *past* and *past part.* **strummed** *v.i.* to play a stringed musical instrument casually or without ability ‖ *v.t.* to play (a tune, or an instrument) in this way 2. *n.* the act or sound of strumming [imit.]

stru·ma (strú:mə) *pl.* **stru·mae** (strú:mi:) *n.* (*bot.*) a cushionlike swelling on a plant organ, e.g. a moss capsule ‖ (*med.*) a goiter [L. = a scrofulous tumor]

stru·mose (strú:mous) *adj.* (*bot.*) having a struma [fr. L. *strumosus*]

strum·pet (strʌ́mpit) *n.* (*old-fash., rhet.*) a prostitute

strung *past* and *past part.* of STRING

strung out *adj.* (*slang or colloq.*) 1. addicted to a drug 2. debilitated from drug use

strut (strʌt) 1. *v.i. pres. part.* **strut·ting** *past* and *past part.* **strut·ted** to walk esp. slowly, stiffly and with head erect, with an air of self-importance 2. *n.* the characteristic walk of cocks, peacocks etc. or of a self-important person [O.E. *strūtian* (meaning obscure)]

strut 1. *n.* a piece or member of wood, metal etc. designed to resist stress 2. *v.t. pres. part.* **strut·ting** *past* and *past part.* **strut·ted** to support with struts ‖ to fit struts to [etym. doubtful]

stru·thi·ous (strú:θi:əs) *adj.* of or relating to flightless birds, e.g. ostriches [fr. L. *struthio*, ostrich fr. Gk]

Stru·ve (ʃtrú:və), Friedrich Georg Wilhelm von (1793-1864), German-Russian astronomer born in Germany, noted for his discovery and study of double stars. His son Otto Wilhelm (1819-1905) discovered about 500 double stars and a satellite of Uranus. A grandson of Otto Wilhelm, Otto Struve (1897-1963), born in Russia, naturalized American (1927), was an outstanding U.S. astronomer, who discovered the existence of interstellar gas

strych·nine (stríknin, stríkni:n, stríknain) *n.* a highly poisonous crystalline alkaloid, $C_{21}H_{22}N_2O_2$, obtained from nux vomica. It is used in minute doses as a stimulant [F. fr. L. fr. Gk]

Stu·art, Stew·art, Steu·art (stú:ərt, stjú:ərt) a member of the Scottish dynasty which ruled Scotland (1371-1714) and England (1603-49, 1660-1714). Their claim to the English throne derived from the marriage of James IV of Scotland and Margaret Tudor, daughter of Henry VII of England. Their great-grandson ruled Scotland as James VI and England as James I. After the deposition (1688) of James II and the death without surviving issue of his daughters Mary II and Anne, the British throne passed to the house of Hanover. Thereafter the Jacobites upheld without success the claims of James Francis Edward Stuart, Charles Edward Stuart and Henry Stuart

Stuart, Charles Edward (1720-88), known as the 'Young Chevalier', 'Bonnie Prince Charlie' and the 'Young Pretender', son of James Francis Edward Stuart, 'the Old Pretender'. The center of Jacobite hopes for the restoration of the Stuart monarchy in Britain, he led (1745) the rebellion known as 'the 45' in favor of his father's claim to the throne, but was defeated at the Battle of Culloden (1746) by the army of George I

Stuart, Gilbert (1755-1828), American portrait painter, most famous for his portraits of George Washington

Stuart, Henry *DARNLEY

Stuart, Henry Benedict Maria Clement (1725-1807), Cardinal York, younger brother of Charles Edward Stuart, the last Jacobite pretender to the British throne

Stuart, James, 1st earl of Murray *MURRAY

Stuart, James Ewell Brown ('Jeb') (1833-64), Confederate cavalry commander in the American Civil War noted for his daring raids

Stuart, James Francis Edward (1688-1766), known as the 'Old Pretender', son of James II. The Jacobite claimant to the English throne after his father's death (1701), he made several unsuccessful attempts to incite rebellion in Scotland (1708, 1715, 1719, 1745)

Stuart, John *BUTE, 3rd earl of

Stuart, Mary *MARY QUEEN OF SCOTS

stub (stʌb) 1. *n.* a stump of a tree ‖ the short piece left when a pencil, crayon, candle etc. is almost all used ‖ the butt of a cigarette ‖ the counterfoil of a check, a ticket or receipt etc. 2. *v.t. pres. part.* **stub·bing** *past* and *past part.* **stubbed** to pull up (a stump) by the roots ‖ to clear (land) of stumps, roots etc. ‖ to strike and hurt (a toe) against a hard obstacle ‖ (with 'up') to dig or pull up (weeds) ‖ (often with 'out') to put out (a cigarette) by crushing the lit end [O.E.]

stub axle the axle of a single wheel, one end being attached by a swivel pin to the framework or chassis, allowing the wheel to be steered

stub·bi·ness (stʌ́bi:nis) *n.* the state or quality of being stubby

stub·ble (stʌ́b'l) *n.* the short stalk of wheat, barley etc. left standing in the field after reaping ‖

a rough, short growth, e.g. of beard **stub·bly** *adj.* [O.F. *estuble, stuble*]

stub·born (stʌ́bərn) *adj.* (of people) inflexibly declining to change a chosen position, line of behavior, opinion etc., esp. when this attitude is unreasonable ‖ hard to get rid of, not responding to treatment, *a stubborn stain, a stubborn illness* ‖ (of animals) refusing obedience, difficult to handle ‖ (of wood or stone) hard to work ‖ (of problems etc.) hard to work out [etym. doubtful]

Stubbs (stʌbz), George (1724-1806), English painter. He is best known for his paintings of horses

Stubbs, William (1825-1901), British historian and bishop. He is best known for his 'Constitutional History of England' (1874-8) and his learned editions of medieval chronicles

stub·by (stʌ́bi:) *comp.* **stub·bi·er** *superl.* **stub·bi·est** *adj.* short and thick, *stubby fingers*

stuc·co (stʌ́kou) 1. *n.* fine plaster used for covering interior walls and ceilings and for molding decorative work on them ‖ a mixture of cement, sand and lime applied to outside walls to form a hard covering ‖ work done in stucco 2. *v.t.* to cover with stucco [Ital.]

stuck *past* and *past part.* of STICK **to be stuck with** to be unable to free oneself of (a bore, an unpleasant job etc.)

stuck-up (stʌ́kʌp) *adj.* (*pop.*) assuming an unwarranted attitude of superiority

stud (stʌd) 1. *n.* a collection of horses kept for breeding, racing etc. ‖ the place where these horses are kept ‖ any male animal kept for breeding ‖ a studhorse **at** (or **in**) **stud** for breeding 2. *adj.* of or pertaining to a stud ‖ kept for breeding [O.E. *stōd*]

stud 1. *n.* a short, thick nail or rivet with a large head often made in ornamental shapes and used mainly for decoration ‖ a shirt fastening consisting of a detached button, sometimes ornamental, joined by a short shank to a broader base ‖ a short, thick stump of leather or metal nailed to the bottom of a boot to give a better grip ‖ a crosspiece in a link of chain cable ‖ a post to which the laths of a partition are nailed ‖ a dowel, pin or spindle in a mechanism, e.g. a lathe or watch ‖ the stub of a tree ‖ a stud bolt 2. *v.t. pres. part.* **stud·ding** *past* and *past part.* **stud·ded** to furnish with studs ‖ to set objects thickly on or as if on, *the piano was studded with ornaments* [O.E. *studu, stuthu*]

stud bolt a threaded bolt furnished with a nut

stud·book (stʌ́dbuk) *n.* an official register of pedigrees of horses and other purebred animals

stud·ding sail (stʌ́diŋseil, *naut.* stʌ́ns'l) (*naut.*) a light sail set at the side of a square sail in fair winds [etym. doubtful]

Stu·de·ba·ker (stú:dəbeikər, stjú:dəbeikər), Clement (1831-1901), U.S. wagon manufacturer. He founded (1868) with his brother John (1833-1917) the Studebaker Brothers Manufacturing Company, one of the world's largest producers of wagons and carriages. In the early 20th c. they began the manufacture of electric and gasoline automobiles

stu·dent (stú:d'nt, stjú:d'nt) *n.* a person who attends a university, college or school for study ‖ anyone making a serious study of a subject [Late M.E. *studiant, studient* fr. O.F. *estudiant*]

Student Nonviolent Coordinating Committee *SNCC

student power the influence of a student body in school administration

Students for a Democratic Society (*abbr.* SDS), a loosely organized U.S. political movement of the extreme left. It was founded (1962) and led campus demonstrations against U.S. policies during the 1960s and early 1970s. Its most militant members, the Weathermen, carried out violent attacks against the U.S. capitalist and police systems

student union 1. student activity group on a college campus 2. the headquarters of such a group

stud farm a place where horses are bred

stud·horse (stʌ́dhɔrs) *n.* a stallion kept chiefly for breeding

stud·ied (stʌ́di:d) *adj.* thought-out, *a well studied plot* ‖ premeditated, calculated, *studied rudeness*

stu·di·o (stú:di:ou, stjú:di:ou) *pl.* **stu·di·os** *n.* the workroom of an artist, musician, photographer etc. ‖ a place from which radio or television programs are transmitted ‖ a building or group of buildings in which movies are made [Ital.]

studio couch an upholstered couch, usually with loose bolsters for the back. It converts into a bed, typically by means of a sliding bed frame stored away under the seat

stu·di·ous (stú:di:əs, stjú:di:əs) *adj.* devoted or given to study ‖ carefully meditated, painstaking, *a studious effort to appear unbiased* [fr. L. *studiosus*]

stud poker (*cards*) a variety of poker in which each player is dealt certain of his cards face up

stud·y (stʌdi:) *pl.* **stud·ies** *n.* the acquiring of knowledge, esp. from books, *a life devoted to study* ‖ a close and prolonged process of observation, inquiry and thought, *Darwin made a study of certain finches* ‖ the subject thus inquired or thought about ‖ (*pl.*) institutional education, *to stop one's studies* ‖ a preliminary painting or drawing for a work of art or a comparable painting or drawing made as an exercise ‖ (*mus.*) a composition designed to give practice in a technique ‖ a literary work in which some theme or subject is explored, *'Macbeth' is a study of evil* ‖ an actor with respect to his capacity for learning a part, *a slow study* ‖ the learning of a part in a play ‖ something that can be scrutinized as though it were a book or a picture, *his face was a study* ‖ a room set apart for studying in [O.F. *estudie*]

study *pres. part.* **stud·y·ing** *past* and *past part.* **stud·ied** *v.t.* to seek knowledge of by study ‖ to observe very closely ‖ to pay careful attention to, *to study one's answer* ‖ to memorize (a part in a play) ‖ *v.i.* to be a student ‖ to apply the mind in order to get knowledge [O.F. *estudier*]

study hall a period for students to do homework in ‖ a room used for school students to study in

stuff (stʌf) *n.* the material of which something is made ‖ material or things used for some purpose, *the plumber went to collect his stuff* ‖ cloth, esp. woolen cloth ‖ the essence or basic quality of some esp. abstract thing, *the stuff of freedom* ‖ personal belongings, *leave your stuff in the hall* ‖ some thing or things not specified but usually identifiable from the context, *we eat a lot of stuff from our own garden, the publishers have produced a lot of new stuff this year* ‖ worthless ideas, opinions, writings etc. **to do one's stuff** (*pop.*) to do what one can be relied upon to do, esp. when this excites admiration **to know one's stuff** (*pop.*) to have thorough knowledge of a particular field [M.E. *stoffe, stof*, O.F. *estoffe*]

stuff *v.t.* to force (something or things) into a limited space by pressure, *to stuff onions into a jar* ‖ (with 'with') to fill (a limited space) with something or with things, *to stuff a jar with onions* ‖ to fill (a cushion, mattress etc.) with padding ‖ (of a padding) to distend (something) ‖ (*taxidermy*) to fill the skin of (a dead animal, bird, fish etc.) in order to restore its natural shape ‖ (*toymaking*) to give (e.g. a rag doll) a naturalistic shape by distending it fully ‖ to put a bill, circular etc. in (an envelope) for dispatching ‖ to put (a bill, circular etc.) into an envelope for dispatching ‖ (*cookery*) to fill (something to be eaten) with esp. a savory mixture ‖ to gorge (food) ‖ to fill with food, to give too much to eat to ‖ (*refl.*) to eat too much, to gorge ‖ to plug or stop up (e.g. a crack) ‖ (with 'up') to block, stop up (nasal passages) etc. ‖ to cram (something) esp. hastily and surreptitiously, *they stuffed the body under the bed* ‖ (with 'with') to fill or clutter (the mind) ‖ to force or cram (e.g. facts or notions) into the mind ‖ to put fraudulent votes into (a ballot box) ‖ to treat (leather) with oil, tallow etc. to soften and preserve it ‖ *v.i.* to eat too much, gorge oneself [O.F. *estoffer* or etym. doubtful]

stuff and nonsense worthless opinions, ideas, words etc.

stuffed shirt (*pop.*) a person, often pompous and self-satisfied, who is set in his ways and ideas

stuff·i·ly (stʌfili:) *adv.* in a stuffy manner

stuff·i·ness (stʌfi:nis) *n.* the state or quality of being stuffy

stuff·ing (stʌfiŋ) *n.* the material with which something is stuffed ‖ a preparation, esp. savory, used for filling food ‖ the act or process of someone who stuffs ‖ the result of this process **to knock the stuffing out of (someone)** to knock (someone) around until he has no fight left in him, or to shock (someone) into such a condition

stuffing box a container which holds packing firmly against a moving mechanical part, e.g. a piston rod, to prevent leakage of steam etc. along the part

stuffing drum a closed container in which leather is impregnated with softeners (oil, tallow) under heat and pressure

stuff shot (*basketball*) basket throw made from above the basket *also* dunk shot

stuff·y (stʌfi:) *comp.* **stuff·i·er** *superl.* **stuff·i·est** *adj.* close and ill-ventilated and usually hot ‖ (of the nasal passages) congested ‖ (*pop.*) prim ‖ (*pop.*) pompous and dull

stul·ti·fi·ca·tion (stʌltifikéiʃən) *n.* a stultifying or being stultified

stul·ti·fy (stʌltifai) *pres. part.* **stul·ti·fy·ing** *past* and *past part.* **stul·ti·fied** *v.t.* to render futile or useless ‖ to cause to be ridiculous ‖ (*law*) to declare (someone) to be of unsound mind and therefore not legally responsible [fr. L.L. *stultificare*, to make foolish]

stum (stʌm) *n.* unfermented grape juice [Du. *stom, must*]

stum·ble (stʌmb'l) 1. *v.i. pres. part.* **stum·bling** *past* and *past part.* **stum·bled** to have a partial fall or to lurch forward as a result of missing one's footing or hitting one's foot against an obstacle, *to stumble downstairs* ‖ (esp. of people) to progress unsteadily or lurchingly, *to stumble along the road* ‖ to hesitate and make a mistake or mistakes in speaking, reading aloud or playing a musical instrument etc. ‖ (*rhet.*) to err (with 'on', 'upon') to find, come upon by accident or chance 2. *n.* the act of stumbling ‖ a slip (mistake) [M.E. *stomble*, stumble]

stumbling block (*fig.*) an obstacle esp. to the understanding

stump (stʌmp) 1. *n.* a short piece of the trunk of a felled or fallen tree projecting from the ground ‖ the stalk of esp. a cabbage or related plant when the leaves have been removed ‖ the remaining part of an amputated limb or organ ‖ a rudimentary limb or vestigial organ ‖ a wooden leg ‖ the stub of a pencil or cigarette or check ‖ the part of a broken, ground down or badly decayed tooth remaining in the gum ‖ a heavy, clumsy step ‖ the sound of such a step ‖ (*cricket*) one of the three wooden sticks forming the uprights of a wicket ‖ a place where a political speech is made **to draw stumps** (*cricket*) to pull up the stumps to show play is discontinued or a game over **to go on the stump** to go around the country canvassing for political election 2. *v.i.* to walk stiffly and heavily ‖ to make speeches in a political cause ‖ *v.t.* to remove stumps from (land) ‖ (*cricket*) to cause (a batsman not in his crease) to be out, by knocking a bail or the bails off, holding the ball in the hand which does this ‖ to tour (a district) canvassing for political election ‖ (*pop.*) to baffle **to stump up** (*Br.*) to pay up money ‖ (*Br.*) to pay (a sum of money) [late M.E. *stompe*]

stump 1. *n.* (*Br.*) paper, soft leather or india rubber rolled or shaped into a cylinder and used to blur or soften lines drawn in pencil or crayon 2. *v.t.* to blur, shade, soften or treat (a line, drawing etc.) with a stump [perh. fr. F. *estompe*]

stump·i·ness (stʌmpi:nis) *n.* the state or quality of being stumpy

stump·y (stʌmpi:) *comp.* **stump·i·er** *superl.* **stump·i·est** *adj.* (of people) stocky, thickset ‖ (of things) short and thick, *a stumpy tail*

stun (stʌn) 1. *v.t. pres. part.* **stun·ning** *past* and *past part.* **stunned** (of a person) to render unconscious or semiconscious, esp. by a blow on the head, *to stun an ox* ‖ (of a blow) to render unconscious or semiconscious, *the blow stunned the ox* ‖ to cause (someone) to be mentally or emotionally numbed, esp. suddenly 2. *n.* the act or effect of stunning ‖ the condition of being stunned [fr. O. F. *estoner*, to astonish]

stung *past* and *past part.* of STING

stun gas an antiriot gas that incapacitates by causing disorientation

stun gun antiriot gun that fires sand, bird shot, and similar nondeadly missiles *Cf* BATON GUN

stunk alt. *past* and *past part.* of STINK

stun·ning (stʌniŋ) *adj.* (*pop.*) very attractive ‖ that stuns, *a stunning blow* ‖ profoundly shocks, *stunning news* ‖ causing admiring astonishment, *stunning workmanship*

stun·sail, stun·s'l (stʌns'l) *n.* a studding sail

stunt (stʌnt) *v.t.* to check the growth or development of ‖ to check (growth or development) [O.E.=foolish]

stunt 1. *n.* something done to show off skill or daring or ingenuity, for publicity, to attract custom etc. 2. *v.i.* to do stunts [etym. doubtful]

stunt man a man who doubles professionally for an actor when it is necessary for the part for dangerous feats to be performed

stu·pa (stú:pə) *n.* a domed monumental shrine to the Buddha [Skr. *stūpa*]

stu·pe·fa·cient (stu:piféiʃənt, stju:piféiʃənt) 1. *adj.* causing profound drowsiness or stupor 2. *n.* a medicine or narcotic causing either of these conditions [fr. L. *stupefaciens* (*stupefacientis*) fr. *stupefacere*, to make stupid]

stu·pe·fac·tion (stu:piféækʃən, stjupiféækʃən) *n.* utter astonishment ‖ a state of profound drowsiness or stupor [F. *stupéfaction*]

stu·pe·fy (stú:pifai, stjú:pifai) *pres. part.* **stu·pe·fy·ing** *past* and *past part.* **stu·pe·fied** *v.t.* to put into a state of profound lethargy ‖ to make dull-witted or stupid ‖ to cause utter consternation in [F. *stupéfier*]

stu·pen·dous (stu:péndəs, stju:péndəs) *adj.* amazing, esp. because of size or intensity, *a stupendous effort* [fr. L. *stupendus* gerundive of *stupere*, to be struck senseless, or be amazed at]

stu·pid (stú:pid, stjú:pid) 1. *adj.* (of persons) lacking intelligence ‖ (of actions) resulting from lack of intelligence ‖ (of persons or animals) foolish in speech or behavior ‖ in a state of stupor 2. *n.* a stupid person [fr. L. *stupidus*]

stu·pid·i·ty (stu:píditi:, stju:píditi:) *pl.* **stu·pid·i·ties** *n.* the quality or condition of being stupid ‖ a stupid act, remark etc. [fr. L. *stupiditas*]

stu·por (stú:pər, stjú:pər) *n.* a state of drowsiness or profound lethargy caused by drink, drugs etc. ‖ mental apathy often resulting from severe shock **stu·por·ous** *adj.* [L.]

stur·di·ly (stə́rdili:) *adv.* in a sturdy way

stur·di·ness (stə́rdi:nis) *n.* the state or quality of being sturdy

stur·dy (stə́rdi:) 1. *comp.* **stur·di·er** *superl.* **stur·di·est** *adj.* strongly built ‖ healthy and hardy, *a sturdy plant* ‖ resolute, *a sturdy fighter* 2. *n.* gid [O.F. *estourdi*, stunned, dazed, reckless, violent]

Stur·geon (stə́rdʒən), William (1783-1850), British scientist. He constructed the first useful electromagnet (1823), and devised the moving coil galvanometer (1836)

stur·geon (stə́rdʒən) *n.* a member of *Acipenser*, fam. *Acipenseridae*, a genus of ganoid fishes widely distributed in fresh and salt waters of the northern temperate regions, and highly valued for their roe, which is made into caviar, and for their flesh, esp. when smoked (*ISINGLASS) [A. F. *sturgeon, esturgeoun*]

Sturluson, Snorri *SNORRI STURLUSON

Sturm und Drang (ʃtúrmuntdráŋ) a late 18th-c. German literary movement in reaction to the Enlightenment, foreshadowing Romanticism. The main representatives were Goethe and Schiller as young men and Herder [G.=storm and stress]

stut·ter (stʌ́tər) 1. *v.i.* to keep repeating sounds or syllables in an effort to speak, usually as the result of nervous tension ‖ *v.t.* to speak in this way 2. *n.* an act or instance of stuttering ‖ the affliction of having to stutter [M.E. *stutten*]

Stutt·gart (stútgɑrt, ʃtútgɑrt) the capital (pop. 584,600) of Baden-Württemberg, West Germany: mechanical engineering, precision and optical instruments, automobiles, textiles chemicals, furniture, printing and publishing. University

Stuy·ve·sant (stáivəsənt), Peter (1592-1672), Dutch colonial administrator. As governor general of New Netherland (1647-64), he ruled autocratically but efficiently. He was forced to cede the colony to the English (1664)

sty (stai) 1. *pl.* **sties** *n.* a pigsty 2. *v.t. pres. part.* **sty·ing** *past* and *past part.* **stied** to keep in a sty [O.E. *stī*]

sty, stye *pl.* **sties, styes** *n.* a small, inflamed swelling at the base of an eyelash [etym. doubtful]

Styg·i·an (stídʒi:ən) *adj.* of or pertaining to the River Styx ‖ (*rhet.*) utterly black, *Stygian gloom* [fr. L. *Stygius* fr. Gk]

style (stail) 1. *n.* the distinguishing way in which something is done, said, written, made, executed etc. ‖ the distinctive character of a particular school or type of music, painting, architecture or writing etc., or of the work of a particular person ‖ the way in which literary or musical content is expressed ‖ manner or tone assumed in speech or oratory ‖ sort, *a new style of lampshade* ‖ (*pop.*) preferred type, *not my style of film* ‖ the fashion, pattern and cut of clothing ‖ a person's full title ‖ correct mode of address, *what is the correct style for addressing a dean?* ‖ (without article) a mode of living or way of acting judged elegant or distinguished ‖ (*hist.*) a writing instrument for use on wax tablets ‖ the conventions followed by a printer or publisher in using capital letters, hyphens, certain spellings etc. ‖ (*bot.*) the slender stalklike portion of the pistil connecting the stigma to the ovary ‖ (*zool.*) an abdominal bristlelike process on male insects 2. *v.t. pres. part.* **styl·ing** *past and past part.* **styled** to give (someone) his proper designation ‖ to fashion (e.g. clothes or furniture) according to the current mode ‖ to cause to accord with a customary style [O.F. *style, stile* fr. L.]

sty·let (stáilit) *n.* a surgeon's probe ‖ a stiletto ‖ (*zool.*) a style ‖ a graver [F. fr. Ital.]

styl·ish (stáiliʃ) *adj.* in current fashion, esp. when this is fine or elegant ‖ showing marked elegance in dress, bearing, execution of a movement etc.

styl·ist (stáilist) *n.* a writer who cultivates a fine literary style ‖ an athlete or game player with good style ‖ a person who creates or advises on style in any commercial enterprise **sty·lís·tic, sty·lís·ti·cal** *adjs.* of or relating to style, esp. literary style **sty·lís·ti·cal·ly** *adv.*

stylistics *n.* (*linguistics*) study and art of the selection of language characteristics created by a situation, esp. a literary situation *Cf* FIRTHIAN

sty·lite (stáilait) *n.* one of a class of solitary ascetics who lived on platforms on top of pillars or columns in the 5th c., esp. in Syria

styl·ize (stáilaiz) *v.t. pres. part.* **styl·iz·ing** *past and past part.* **styl·ized** to use convention for calculated aesthetic effect in the rendering of (a subject) [fr. STYLE]

sty·lo·bate (stáiləbeit) *n.* (*archit.*) a length of raised, flat-topped stonework supporting a row of columns [fr. L. *stylobata* fr. Gk]

sty·loid (stáiloid) *adj.* (*anat.*) of any of several long slender processes, esp. of the long, thin projection from the temporal bone of man [fr. Mod. L. *styloides* fr. Gk]

sty·lom·e·try (stailómətri:) *n.* (*stylistics*) study of the development of a work by analysis (usu. with computers) of the number of parts of speech, imagery, thoughts, and similar factors

sty·lus (stáiləs) *pl.* **sty·li** (stáilai), **sty·lus·es** *n.* a pointed instrument for writing on waxed surfaces or for making carbon copies ‖ a needle point, often of sapphire or diamond, for cutting recordings or playing records ‖ (*zool.*) a style ‖ (*bot.*) a style ‖ the gnomon on a sundial ‖ an ancient instrument used for writing on parchment or papyrus ‖ a device for punching dots in preparing Braille [L.]

sty·mie (stáimi:) 1. *n.* (esp. *golf*) a lie of a player's ball on a green which prevents his opponent from making the shot he wants to make 2. *v.t. pres. part.* **sty·mie·ing** *past and past part.* **sty·mied** to impede (one's opponent) thus ‖ to impede or hinder [etym. doubtful]

Stym·pha·lis (stimféilis) a lake of Arcadia where Hercules killed the iron-beaked birds (*HERACLES)

styp·tic (stíptik) 1. *adj.* having an astringent effect ‖ tending to check bleeding 2. *n.* a styptic substance [fr. L.L. *stypticus*]

sty·rax (stáireks) *n.* a member of *Styrax*, fam. *Styracaceae*, a genus of shrubs and trees found in Java and Thailand, some of which yield benzoin ‖ a balm yielded by some species, storax

sty·rene (stáiri:n) *n.* liquid hydrocarbon $C_6H_5CH{=}CH_2$ obtained esp. from ethylbenzene and serving as the raw material for many plastics [fr. L. *styrax, styrax*]

Styr·i·a (stíri:ə) (G. *Steiermark*) a province (area 6,326 sq. miles, pop. 1,191,400) of S.E. Austria. Capital: Graz

Sty·ron (stáirən), William (1924-), U.S. writer, whose novel 'The Confessions of Nat Turner' (1967) won the Pulitzer Prize (1968). Other novels include 'Lie Down in Darkness' (1951), 'The Long March' (1956), 'Set This House on Fire' (1960) and 'Sophie's Choice' (1979). Some of his essays are collected in 'This Quiet Dust' (1982)

Styx (stiks) (*Gk mythol.*) one of the principal rivers of Hades across which Charon ferried the souls of the dead

su·a·bil·i·ty (su:əbíliti:) *n.* the state or quality of being suable

su·a·ble (sú:əb'l) *adj.* capable of being or liable to be sued in court

Suá·rez (swárez), Francisco de (1548-1617),

Spanish Jesuit theologian. His most notable work was in political philosophy and international law, the 'De legibus ac Deo legislatore' (1612). He rejected the doctrine of the divine right of kings in 'Defensio fidei catholicae' (1613), and vested political authority in the sovereign people, this authority being ultimately from God. He placed spiritual authority above temporal authority

sua·sion (swéiʒən) *n.* (*rhet.*) persuasion, *moral suasion* [fr. L. *suasio (suasionis)*]

suave (swɑv) *adj.* bland, smooth and unctuous (when applied to people, suggesting also superficiality or lack of sincerity) **suáv·i·ty** *pl.* **suav·i·ties** *n.* the state or quality of being suave ‖ (*pl.*) delights, pleasures and amenities, *the suavities of civilized living* [F.]

sub (sʌb) 1. *n.* (*pop.*) an abbreviation for various words beginning 'sub-', e.g. submarine, substitute 2. *v.i. pres. part.* **sub·bing** *past and past part.* **subbed** (*pop.*) to be a substitute for another

sub- (sʌb) *prefix* under (e.g. subterranean) ‖ lower than or inferior to (e.g. sublieutenant) ‖ to a lesser degree than, not completely (e.g. subarctic) a smaller division or less important part (e.g. subarea) ‖ (*chem.*) with less than the normal amount of a specified substance (e.g. subalkaline) ‖ (*chem.*) basic [L. *sub*, under, close to, up to, towards]

sub·ac·id (sʌbǽsid) *adj.* slightly acid to the taste ‖ (of remarks) rather sarcastic ‖ (*chem.*) having less than the normal amount of acid [fr. L. *subacidus*]

sub·a·cute (sʌbəkjú:t) *adj.* (*med.*) between acute and chronic

sub·a·gent (sʌbéidʒənt) *n.* an agent's agent

sub·al·pine (sʌbǽlpain) *adj.* of or relating to the lower slopes of the Alps ‖ of or relating to the higher upland slopes of mountains just below the tree line [fr. L. *subalpinus*]

sub·al·tern (slvbɔ́ltə:rn, *Br.* sʌbɔltən) 1. *n.* (*Br., mil.*) a commissioned officer below the rank of captain ‖ a person holding a subordinate position ‖ (*logic*) a subaltern proposition 2. *adj.* subordinate ‖ (*logic*) particular, with reference to a related universal [fr. L.L. *subalternus*]

sub·ant·arc·tic (sʌbæntɑ́rktik, sʌbæntɑ́rtik) *adj.* of, relating to or designating a region near or just north of the Antarctic Circle

sub·a·quat·ic (sʌbəkwǽtik, sʌbəkwɔ́tik) *adj.* (*biol.*) partly aquatic ‖ (*bot.*) of or relating to plants growing under water

sub·a·que·ous (sʌbéikwi:əs) *adj.* existing under the surface of water, esp. of the sea ‖ (*geol.*) formed under the water ‖ (of equipment etc.) made to be used under the water

sub·arc·tic (sʌbɑ́rktik, sʌbɑ́rtik) *adj.* of, relating to or designating a region near or just south of the Arctic Circle

sub·a·tom·ic (sʌbətɔ́mik) *adj.* (*phys.*) of, relating to, or being any of the particles smaller than an atom

sub·ax·il·la·ry (sʌbǽksələri) *adj.* (*bot.*) situated beneath an axil

sub·base·ment (sʌ́bbeismənt) *n.* a basement or story, or a series of these, located beneath the true basement of a building

sub-Carpathian Russia *TRANSCARPATHIA

sub·class (sʌ́bklæs, sʌ́bklɑs) *n.* (*taxonomy*) the primary division of a class, esp. that between a class and an order

sub·cla·vi·an (sʌbkléivi:ən) 1. *adj.* under the clavicle 2. *n.* the subclavian artery, vein or muscle [fr. Mod. L. *subclavius*]

sub·clin·i·cal (sʌbklínik'l) *adj.* (*med.*) of an illness before it has manifested itself

sub·com·mit·tee (sʌ́bkəmiti:) *n.* a small committee formed from a larger one, appointed usually to consider or deal with some particular aspect of the latter's work

sub·com·pact (sʌbkómpækt) *n.* an automobile smaller than a compact car *Cf* INTERMEDIATE

sub·con·scious (sʌbkónʃəs) 1. *adj.* (of memories, emotions etc.) not normally admitted to consciousness, or apparently forgotten 2. *n.* the sum of such mental activity. The content of the subconscious may emerge into consciousness through dreams, psychotherapy etc.

sub·con·ti·nent (sʌbkóntinənt) *n.* a very large landmass smaller than those usually called continents, e.g. Greenland ‖ a very large landmass forming part of a continent and having a certain geographical or political independence, e.g. India

sub·con·tract 1. (sʌbkóntrækt) *n.* a contract to do a specified part of the work for which some-

one else has made a prime contract 2. (sʌbkəntrækt) *v.t.* to put out (part of the work for which one has contracted) as a subcontract **sub·con·trác·tor** *n.*

sub·cor·ti·cal (sʌbkɔ́rtik'l) *adj.* situated beneath a cortex, esp. the cerebral cortex ‖ (of insects) living and feeding under the bark of a tree

sub·cos·tal (sʌbkɔ́stəl, sʌbkústəl) 1. *adj.* (*anat.*) situated below a rib 2. *n.* (*anat.*) a subcostal part [fr. Mod. L. *subcostalis*]

sub·cul·ture (sʌ́bkʌltʃər) *n.* a religious, economic or regional etc. group identified by shared patterns of behavior which differ from those of the surrounding culture

sub·cu·ta·ne·ous (sʌbkju:téini:əs) *adj.* used, introduced, situated or occurring beneath the skin ‖ (of parasites) living beneath the skin of the host [L.L. *subcutaneus*]

sub·dea·con (sʌbdí:kən) *n.* (*Roman Catholic and Orthodox Church*) a priest in holy orders, below a deacon ‖ (*Anglican Church*) the epistoler, who may be either a priest or a layman [A.F., O.F. *soudiakene, subdiacne*]

sub·del·e·ga·tion (sʌbdeləgéiʃən) *n.* transference of one's responsibility and authority as a delegate to another person —**subdelegate** *n.* —**subdelegate** *v.*

sub·di·ac·o·nate (sʌbdaiǽkənit) *n.* the office or rank of a subdeacon

sub·di·vide (sʌbdiváid, sʌ́bdivaid) *pres. part.* **sub·di·vid·ing** *past and past part.* **sub·di·vid·ed** *v.t.* to divide again (a part resulting from a previous division) ‖ to divide up (a piece of land) into lots for selling ‖ *v.i.* to become subdivided [fr. L.L. *subdividere*]

sub·di·vi·sion (sʌbdiviʒən) *n.* one of the parts resulting when something is subdivided ‖ a subdividing or being subdivided ‖ a piece of land resulting from this [fr. L.L. *subdivisio (subdivisionis)*]

sub·dom·i·nant (sʌbdóminənt) *n.* (*mus.*) the fourth degree in a major or minor scale, immediately below the dominant, or fifth

sub·duc·tion (sʌbdʌ́kʃən) *n.* process of moving under a base, e.g., a tectonic plate from the earth's crust —**subduct** *v.*

sub·due (səbdú:, səbdjú:) *pres. part.* **sub·du·ing** *past and past part.* **sub·dued** *v.t.* to control, discipline or bring into subjection ‖ to make (sound, color etc.) less intense ‖ to reduce the vivacity of (someone's, one's own, spirits) [late M.E. *sodewe, subdewe*]

sub·ed·it (sʌbédit) *v.t.* to act as subeditor of

sub·ed·i·tor (sʌbéditər) *n.* an assistant editor ‖ (*Br.*) someone who prepares copy for the editor's or publisher's approval

sub·em·ploy·ment (sʌbemplɔ́imənt) *n.* part-time or full-time employment at subsistence level *Cf* UNDEREMPLOYMENT

su·ber·ic acid (su:bérik) a crystalline acid $HOOC(CH_2)_6COOH$ obtained from alkaline hydrolysis of suberin or by oxidation of cork, castor oil etc. with nitric acid

su·ber·in (sú:bərin) *n.* a complex mixture of fatty substances which constitute the basic part of the cell walls of cork and yields suberic acid among other acid products [F. *subérine*]

su·ber·i·za·tion (su:bərizéiʃən) *n.* (*bot.*) the conversion of the cell walls of plants into corklike tissue, impervious to water, through infiltration with suberin

su·ber·ize (sú:bəraiz) *pres. part.* **su·ber·iz·ing** *past and past part.* **su·ber·ized** *v.t.* (*bot.*) to cause the suberization of [fr. L. *suber*, cork, cork oak]

su·ber·ose (sú:bərous) *adj.* being, or having the physical properties of, cork [fr. Mod. L. *suberosus* fr. *suber*, cork]

su·ber·ous (sú:bərəs) *adj.* suberose

sub·fam·i·ly (sʌ́bfæmili:, sʌ́bfæmli:) *pl.* **sub·fam·i·lies** *n.* (*taxonomy*) the category between genus and family

sub·fusc (sʌbfʌ́sk) 1. *adj.* drab 2. *n.* (*Br.*, in some universities) dark clothes worn on formal occasions

sub·ge·nus (sʌbdʒí:nəs) *pl.* **sub·gen·er·a** (sʌbdʒénərə) *n.* (*taxonomy*) the category between genus and species

sub·gla·cial (sʌbgléiʃəl) *adj.* of, relating to, or formed in or by the bottom of a glacier

sub·head (sʌ́bhed) *n.* a subheading **súb·head·ing** *n.* the title or heading of part of a chapter, essay etc. ‖ a subordinate heading of a title, e.g. of a newspaper article

sub·hu·man (sʌbhjú:mən) *adj.* less than hu-

CONCISE PRONUNCIATION KEY: (a) æ, c*a*t; ɑ, c*a*r; ɔ f*aw*n; ei, sn*a*ke. (e) e, h*e*n; i:, sh*ee*p; iə, d*ee*r; ɛə, b*ea*r. (i) i, f*i*sh; ai, t*i*ger; ə:, b*i*rd. (o) o, *o*x; au, c*ow*; ou, g*oa*t; u, p*oo*r; ɔi, r*oy*al. (u) ʌ, d*u*ck; u, b*u*ll; u:, g*oo*se; ə, b*a*cillus; ju:, c*u*be. x, lo*ch*; θ, *th*ink; ð, bo*th*er; z, *Z*en; ʒ, corsa*g*e; dʒ, sava*g*e; ŋ, ora*n*gutang; j, *y*ak; ʃ, *f*ish; tʃ, fet*ch*; 'l, rabb*le*; 'n, redd*en*. Complete pronunciation key appears inside front cover.

man, esp. failing to reach standards expected by or of humans ‖ unfit or unsuitable for humans, *subhuman conditions* ‖ (of taxonomic classifications) excluding man

sub·in·dex (sʌ́bindeks) pl. **sub·in·dex·es, sub·in·di·ces** (sʌ́bindisiːz) n. (*math.*) an inferior index, written on the right of the symbol

sub·ja·cent (sʌbdʒéisənt) adj. underlying, *subjacent causes* ‖ situated lower down, *subjacent levels* [fr. L. *subjacens (subjacentis)* fr. *subjacere*]

sub·ject (səbdʒékt) v.t. (with 'to') to cause to submit ‖ (with 'to') to cause to undergo, *to subject a person to cross-examination* ‖ (with 'to') to expose or lay open, *to subject someone to ridicule* [O.F. *subjecter, subgetter* or L. *subjectare*]

sub·ject (sʌ́bdʒikt) adj. (esp. with 'to') owing allegiance, *subject to the crown* ‖ under external government or rule, *a subject nation* ‖ (with 'to') apt to suffer frequently, prone, *subject to fits* ‖ (with 'to') exposed, *subject to typhoons* ‖ falling under the control or authority of someone ‖ (with 'to') depending, conditional, *subject to approval* [O.F. *suget, subject*]

subject (sʌ́bdʒikt) n. a member of a state in relation to his government, or owing allegiance to a sovereign or other ruler, or any member of a state except the sovereign himself ‖ something constituting or chosen as a matter for thought, discussion, action or study etc. ‖ that which is pictured or represented by an artist, sculptor, photographer etc. ‖ the theme, argument or matter of a literary composition ‖ one of the branches of learning taught in a school, college etc. ‖ someone or something experimented on ‖ a body used for anatomical demonstration or dissection ‖ a person suffering from a specified physical or mental complaint, *an asthma subject* ‖ (*gram.*) the noun, or its equivalent, governing a verb (cf. OBJECT) ‖ (*logic*) the term of a proposition about which something is stated ‖ (*philos.*) the thinking mind as opposed to the object thought about ‖ (*philos.*) a substance as distinct from its attributes ‖ (*mus.*) a group of notes forming the basis of esp. a formal composition, e.g. a fugue or sonata, usually prominently stated and repeated or developed [O.F. *suget, soget, subject* fr. L.]

sub·jec·tion (səbdʒékʃən) n. a subjecting or being subjected [O.F.]

sub·jec·tive (səbdʒéktiv) adj. seen from the point of view of the thinking subject and conditioned by his personal characteristics (opp. OBJECTIVE), *subjective opinion, a subjective poem* ‖ (*gram.*) nominative ‖ (*philos.*) determined by the thinking subject as opposed to universally accepted reality (*OBJECTIVE) **sub·jec·tiv·ism** n. (*philos.*) an idealist system which admits no other reality than that of the thinking subject **sub·jec·tiv·i·ty** n. [fr. L. L. *subjectivus*]

subject matter the matter, theme or argument of something written, often as opposed to the way in which it is treated or expressed ‖ (*law*) a matter in dispute

sub·join (sʌ́bdʒɔin) v.t. to add (something) to the end of something stated or written [fr. obs. F. *subjoindre* fr. L.]

sub ju·di·ce (sʌ́bdʒúːdisiː, subjúːdiki:) (*law*) before the judge or court, i.e. not decided [L.]

sub·ju·gate (sʌ́bdʒugeit) pres. part. **sub·ju·gat·ing** past and past part. **sub·ju·gat·ed** v.t. to conquer and hold in subjection [fr. L. *subjugare (subjugatus)*]

sub·ju·ga·tion (sʌbdʒugéiʃən) n. a subjugating or being subjugated [fr. L.L. *subjugatio (subjugationis)*]

sub·junc·tive (səbdʒʌ́ŋktiv) 1. adj. (*gram.*) of or relating to a verbal mood denoting possibility, probability, desire etc. rather than actual fact (cf. INDICATIVE, cf. IMPERATIVE) 2. n. a verb in this mood ‖ the subjunctive mood [fr. L.L. *subjunctivus*]

sub·kil·o·ton weapon (sʌ́bkílətʌn) (*mil.*) less than 1 kiloton, having the effect of less than 1,000 tons of TNT, e.g., of a nuclear weapon *Cf* KILOTON WEAPON

sub·lan·guage (sʌ́blæŋgwidʒ) n. (*linguistics*) the language of a subculture (e.g., dialect) or special group (e.g., jargon) within a culture

sub·lease 1. (sʌ́bliːs) n. the lease granted by a tenant to a subtenant of part or all of a property 2. (sʌbliːs) v.t. pres. part. **sub·leas·ing** past and past part. **sub·leased** to grant a sublease on ‖ to receive or hold a sublease on

sub·let 1. (sʌ́blét) v.t. pres. part. **sub·let·ting** past and past part. **sub·let** to rent out part or all

of (a property rented or leased from the owner) 2. (sʌ́blet, sʌblét) n. a property obtained by or available for subletting

sub·lieu·ten·ant (sʌblu:ténənt, *Br.* sʌblefténənt) n. (*Br.*) a Royal Navy officer ranking immediately below a lieutenant

sub·li·mate (sʌ́blimeit) 1. v.t. pres. part. **sub·li·mat·ing** past and past part. **sub·li·mat·ed** to purify (a solid) by heating it under such a pressure that it sublimes and then cooling the vapor until it passes directly into the solid state ‖ (*psychol.*) to redirect (a primitive impulse) towards a higher aim more compatible with civilized man's tastes and aspirations ‖ v.i. to become sublimated 2. n. a substance obtained by sublimating [fr. L. *sublimare (sublimatus)*]

sub·li·ma·tion (sʌbləméiʃən) n. a sublimating or being sublimated ‖ the process of sublimating ‖ a product of sublimating [F. or fr. L.L. *sublimatio (sublimationis)*]

Sublimaze *FENTANYL

sub·lime (səbláim) 1. adj. arousing the sensation of awe, esp. by reason of perfection, nobility etc. ‖ lofty, exalted ‖ outstanding with respect to spiritual, moral or intellectual qualities ‖ (*anat.*, of muscles) lying near the surface 2. n. **the sublime** that which is sublime, sublime quality [fr. L. *sublimis*]

sublime pres. part. **sub·lim·ing** past and past part. **sub·limed** v.i. to pass directly from the solid to the vapor state, usually by the action of heat ‖ v.t. to cause to undergo this process, sometimes in both directions, e.g. in the purification of certain chemicals such as iodine, naphthalene etc. [O.F. *sublimer*, to make sublime]

sub·lim·i·nal (sʌblímin'l) adj. not rising above the threshold of consciousness (cf. SUPRALIMINAL) ‖ (esp. of advertising) designed to act on the mind at a subconscious level [SUB-+L. *limen (liminis)*, threshold]

sub·lim·i·ty (səblímiti:) n. the state or quality of being sublime [fr. L. *sublimitas*]

sub·lu·nar (sʌblúːnər) adj. sublunary

sub·lu·na·ry (sʌblúːnəri:) adj. (*astron.*) situated or existing beneath the moon [fr. Mod. L. *sublunaris*]

sub·lux·a·tion (sʌbləkséiʃən) n. an incomplete or partial dislocation (as of two vertebrae squarely situated atop one another) —**sublux** v. —**subluxed** adj.

sub·ma·chine gun (sʌbməʃíːn) a light machine gun designed to be fired from the shoulder or waist

sub·mar·gin·al (sʌbmárdʒin'l) adj. below the minimum necessary for e.g. economic exploitation or for living a normal life, *a submarginal salary* ‖ (*biol.*) placed nearly at the margin

sub·ma·rine (sʌ́bməriːn, sʌbməríːn) 1. adj. existing, operating etc. under water, esp. the sea 2. n. a vessel, esp. a warship, designed to operate submerged ‖ (*surfing*) board too small for proper use

submarine launched ballistic missile (*mil.*) missile capable of being launched underwater, e.g., Polaris, Poseidon, Trident etc. **SLBM**

submarine rocket (*mil.*) submarine-launched, surface-to-surface rocket (UUM-44A), primarily antisubmarine, with nuclear depth charge or homing torpedo payload, and a 50-mi range *acronym* subroc

sub·max·il·la (sʌbmæksílə) pl. **sub·max·il·lae** (sʌbmæksíli:) **sub·max·il·las** n. the lower jaw or jawbone, esp. the mandible of man **sub·max·il·lar·y** (sʌbmæksələri:, *Br.* esp. sʌbmæksíləri) adj. [Mod. L.]

submaxillary gland either of the two salivary glands located on each side of the lower jaw

sub·me·di·ant (sʌbmíːdi:ənt) n. (*mus.*) the sixth degree of the major or minor scale halfway between the subdominant and upper tonic

sub·merge (səbmə́rdʒ) pres. part. **sub·merg·ing** past and past part. **sub·merged** v.t. to place beneath or as if beneath the surface of a liquid, *the river submerged large tracts of land, submerged in debt* ‖ v.i. to plunge beneath the surface of the water etc. ‖ to become as though covered by water **sub·mér·gence** n. [fr. L. *submergere*]

sub·merse (səbmə́rs) pres. part. **sub·mers·ing** past and past part. **sub·mersed** v.t. to submerge **sub·mérsed** adj. (*bot.*) growing entirely under water **sub·mers·i·ble** (səbmə́rsəb'l) adj. capable of being submerged and of operating under water [fr. L. *submergere (submersus)*]

sub·mer·sion (səbmə́rʒən, səbmə́rʃən) n. a

submerging or being submerged [fr. L. *submersio (submersionis)*]

sub·mi·cro·scop·ic (sʌbmaikrəskópik) adj. of things too small to be seen through an ordinary, light microscope

sub·mil·li·me·ter (sʌbmílləmi:tər) adj. of less than one mm in size

sub·min·i·a·ture (sʌbmíni:ətʃə:r) adj. smaller than miniature, e.g., microcircuits on small silicon chips *also* microminiature

sub·mis·sion (səbmíʃən) n. the act of submitting ‖ the state of being willing to submit ‖ something offered for consideration ‖ (*law*) an agreement in which parties undertake to abide by a decision or obey an authority ‖ (*law*) the act of referring a matter to arbitration [fr. O.F. or fr. L. *submissio (submissionis)*]

sub·mis·sive (səbmísiv) adj. willing to submit, humbly obedient [fr. L. *submittere (submissus)*, to submit]

sub·mit (səbmít) pres. part. **sub·mit·ting** past and past part. **sub·mit·ted** v.t. to cause to undergo ‖ to offer (oneself) of one's free will, *to submit oneself to an ordeal* ‖ to offer for consideration, examination, a decision etc., *to submit a case for judgment* ‖ to offer as an opinion, *I submit that there is another point of view* ‖ v.i. to cease to offer resistance ‖ to defer to another's wishes, opinions etc. [fr. L. *submittere*]

sub·mul·ti·ple (sʌbmʌ́ltəp'l) n. a number or quantity exactly dividing another number or quantity [fr. L.L. *submultiplus*]

sub·nor·mal (sʌbnɔ́rməl) 1. adj. below, lower than, less than or smaller than normal ‖ having less than normal intelligence 2. n. a person of subnormal intelligence **sub·nor·mál·i·ty** n.

sub·nu·clear (sʌbnúːkli:ə:r) adj. of particles of the nucleus of the atom

sub·nu·cle·on (sʌbnúːkli:ɒn) n. hypothetical portion of a nuclear particle

sub·or·der (sʌ́bɔrdər) n. (*taxonomy*) the category between an order and a family

sub·or·di·nate 1. (səbɔ́rd'nit) adj. inferior in order, rank, importance etc., *a subordinate officer* ‖ (with 'to') subject, subsidiary or subservient, *subordinate to one's superiors* 2. (səbɔ́rd'nit) n. a person working under someone else or inferior in the official hierarchy 3. (səbɔ́rd'neit) v.t. pres. part. **sub·or·di·nat·ing** past and past part. **sub·or·di·nat·ed** to treat or consider as of secondary importance, *you must subordinate your private interests* ‖ (with 'to') to make subject or subservient, *to subordinate personal profit to the good of the community* [fr. M.L. *subordinare (subordinatus)*]

subordinate clause (*gram.*) a clause dependent upon another clause and not itself a formal sentence (cf. MAIN CLAUSE)

subordinate conjunction (*gram.*) a conjunction used to introduce a subordinate clause

sub·or·di·na·tion (səbɔrd'néiʃən) n. a subordinating or being subordinated [fr. L.L. *subordinatio (subordinationis)*]

sub·or·di·na·tive (səbɔ́rd'neitiv) adj. (*gram.*) containing or introducing a subordinate clause ‖ involving subordination

sub·orn (səbɔ́rn) v.t. to incite (a person), usually by bribery, to commit perjury or other unlawful acts ‖ to obtain (e.g. evidence) by bribery or other corrupt means [fr. L. *subornare*]

sub·or·na·tion (sʌbɔrnéiʃən) n. the act of suborning, esp. the crime of inciting someone to commit perjury ‖ the testimony thus procured [fr. L. *subordinatio (subordinationis)*]

Su·bo·ti·ca (su:bótitsə) a market town (pop. 75,000) in Vojvodina, Yugoslavia, near the Hungarian frontier: metallurgy, food processing

sub·phy·lum (sʌ́bfailəm) pl. **sub·phy·la** (sʌ́bfailə) n. (*taxonomy*) the main division of a phylum

sub·plot (sʌ́bplɒt) n. a secondary plot in a play, novel, film etc.

sub·poe·na (səpíːnə) 1. n. (*law*) a written order commanding a person to appear in a court of justice under penalty 2. v.t. pres. part. **sub·poe·na·ing** past and past part. **sub·poe·naed** (*law*) to serve with such an order [L.=under a penalty]

sub·pro·fes·sion·al (sʌbprouféʃənəl) n. paraprofessional

sub·re·gion (sʌ́brí:dʒən) n. one of the principal divisions of a region, e.g. for administration or with regard to distribution of animals or plants **sub·ré·gion·al** adj.

sub·rep·tion (səbrépʃən) n. (*eccles. law*) the obtaining of a dispensation by concealing the truth **sub·rep·ti·tious** (sʌbreptíʃəs) adj. [fr. L. subreptio (subreptionis)]

subroc (mil. acronym) for submarine rocket

sub·ro·ga·tion (sʌbrəgéiʃən) n. (law) the substitution of one party for another as creditor so that the new creditor succeeds to the first creditor's rights in law and equity [fr. L. subrogatio (subrogationis)]

sub·sat·el·lite (sʌbsǽtəlait) n. a satellite launched by an orbiting satellite

sub·scribe (səbskráib) pres. part. **sub·scrib·ing** past and past part. **sub·scribed** v.t. to contribute or agree to contribute, to subscribe large sums to charity ‖ to write (one's name) at the foot of a document ‖ to add one's signature to (a document, letter to the press etc.), esp. to do this so as to show agreement or solidarity ‖ (of a bookseller or publisher) to take prepublication orders for (new books etc.) ‖ v.i. to make a subscription ‖ to promise a subscription to **subscribe to** to take in regularly (a periodical, newspaper etc.) ‖ to express agreement with ‖ to sign one's name, esp. to an official document [fr. L. subscribere, to write underneath]

sub·script (sʌ́bskript) **1.** adj. of, relating to, or being a character printed or written directly below another character, e.g. the cedilla under the letter 'c' in 'Besançon', or below and to the side of it, e.g. the '2' in H₂O (cf. SUPERSCRIPT) **2.** n. a subscript sign, letter etc., e.g. a mathematical subindex [fr. L. subscribere (subscriptus), to write underneath]

sub·scrip·tion (səbskrípʃən) n. the act of subscribing ‖ a sum subscribed ‖ the amount raised through subscribed sums ‖ matter subscribed at the end of a document ‖ a signifying of assent or the assent itself, subscription to the doctrine of infallibility ‖ a method of selling a new publication by giving a price concession to those who order before publication ‖ (Br.) membership fees paid at regular intervals to a club, society etc. ‖ the prepayment made to secure future issues of e.g. a periodical [fr. L. subscriptio (subscriptionis)]

sub·sec·tion (sʌ́bsekʃən) n. a subdivision of a section ‖ a subordinate part

sub·se·quence (sʌ́bsikwəns) n. the act or state of being subsequent ‖ that which is subsequent

sub·se·quent (sʌ́bsikwənt) adj. following (in time or order), later **subsequent to** following [F. subséquent or fr. L. subsequens (subsequentis)]

sub·serve (səbsə́rv) pres. part. **sub·serv·ing** past and past part. **sub·served** v.t. to serve as a means of promoting, to subserve one's ends [fr. L. subservire]

sub·serv·i·ence (səbsə́rviːəns) n. the state or quality of being subservient ‖ subservient behavior

sub·serv·i·en·cy (səbsə́rviːənsi:) pl. **sub·serv·i·en·cies** n. subservience

sub·serv·i·ent (səbsə́rviːənt) adj. servile, obsequious ‖ useful as a means or instrument [fr. L. subserviens (subservientis) fr. subservire, to serve below]

sub·shell (sʌ́bʃel) n. (nuclear phys.) a segment of an electron's orbit

sub·side (səbsáid) pres. part. **sub·sid·ing** past and past part. **sub·sid·ed** v.i. (of ground, a building etc.) to sink in level or settle down into a lower position ‖ (of water) to return to a normal level, the flood soon subsided ‖ (of the sea) to fall into a calmer state ‖ (of a storm, excitement, fever etc.) to abate ‖ to sink down exhaustedly, to subside into a chair [fr. L. subsidere]

sub·sid·ence (səbsáid'ns, sʌ́bsidəns) n. the act or process of subsiding [fr. L. subsidentia]

sub·sid·i·ar·y (səbsídi:eri:) **1.** adj. auxiliary, supplementary, to serve in a subsidiary capacity ‖ (of a company) controlled by another company which owns a majority of its shares ‖ pertaining to or of the nature of a subsidy, a subsidiary payment **2.** pl. **sub·sid·i·ar·ies** n. an assistant ‖ a subsidiary company [fr. L. subsidiarius]

sub·si·dize (sʌ́bsidaiz) pres. part. **sub·si·diz·ing** past and past part. **sub·si·dized** v.t. to pay a subsidy to ‖ to aid with public money

sub·si·dy (sʌ́bsidi:) pl. **sub·si·dies** n. a nonreturnable grant of money to an individual, group or subsection of the economy, by the state or by a public or private body, to secure some beneficial result, e.g. to help out of financial difficulty, to lower prices, to encourage development etc. ‖ (Br. hist.) money granted to the

sovereign by parliament to meet special needs [A.F. subsidie]

sub·sist (səbsíst) v.i. to keep oneself alive esp. on means that provide only the barest necessities, to subsist on a pension ‖ to exist or continue to exist, specimens still subsist in the forests of Peru ‖ (philos.) to be logically true and sound [fr. L. subsistere, to stand still, stand firm, cease]

sub·sist·ence (səbsístəns) n. a means of providing oneself with the necessities of life, esp. the bare necessities ‖ (philos.) real existence ‖ (philos.) the quality of being logically true and sound [fr. L.L. subsistentia]

subsistence agriculture farming that produces all or almost all the necessities for a farm family, e.g., in low-income countries also subsistence farming

subsistence economy an economy not based on money and in which there is little or no buying and selling, though there may be bartering

subsistence farming a primitive system of farming, in which each farm provides only for the needs of the individual farm family and makes no surplus to sell

sub·soil (sʌ́bsɔil) n. the layer of material immediately beneath the soil, in process of being broken up through the agency of water, plant roots, worms etc., but as yet not enriched by humus or by the products of soil bacteria (cf. TOPSOIL)

sub·son·ic (sʌbsɔ́nik) adj. pertaining to speeds less than that of sound (opp. SUPERSONIC)

sub·spe·cies (sʌ́bspi:ʃi:z) pl. **sub·spe·cies** n. (taxonomy) the category below a species [Mod. L.]

sub·stance (sʌ́bstəns) n. the matter, stuff, material of which a thing is made ‖ the main content, the substance of an argument ‖ (philos.) the essential, underlying reality of something, in which accidents, qualities, attributes and phenomena inhere ‖ solidity, correspondence with reality, there is no substance in his beliefs ‖ (rhet.) wealth, a man of substance ‖ the quality in cloth etc. that makes for durability **in substance** essentially, details apart [fr. L.L. fr. L.]

sub·stand·ard (sʌbstǽndərd) adj. falling short of a legally required or generally accepted standard

sub·stan·tial (səbstǽnʃəl) adj. having real existence, not imaginary ‖ firmly based, a substantial argument ‖ relatively great in size, value or importance, a substantial income, substantial agreement ‖ (of meals) large and filling ‖ (of food or drink) very nutritive ‖ strong, made to last, substantial toys ‖ well-off, financially sound ‖ (philos.) of the nature of substance [fr. L.L. substantialis]

sub·stan·tial·ism (səbstǽnʃəlizəm) n. (philos.) the doctrine that there are substantial realities underlying phenomena

sub·stan·ti·al·i·ty (səbstǽnʃiːǽliti:) n. the quality or state of being substantial ‖ solidity ‖ genuineness [fr. L.L. substantialitas]

sub·stan·tial·ly (səbstǽnʃəli:) adv. in a substantial manner ‖ essentially, to a large degree

sub·stan·ti·ate (səbstǽnʃiːeit) pres. part. **sub·stan·ti·at·ing** past and past part. **sub·stan·ti·at·ed** v.t. to establish, prove or make good (a statement, claim, charge etc.) **sub·stan·ti·a·tion** n. [fr. Mod. L. substantiare (substantiatus) fr. substantia, substance]

sub·stan·ti·val (sʌbstəntáivəl) adj. (gram.) of, relating to or having the nature of a substantive **sub·stan·ti·val·ly** adv.

sub·stan·tive (sʌ́bstəntiv) **1.** adj. (gram.) expressing existence, the substantive verb (i.e. 'to be') ‖ (gram.) of or used as a substantive ‖ having a separate and independent existence, not inferred, derived etc. ‖ (of dyes) not requiring a mordant ‖ (mil., of a person) appointed definitely to a specified rank ‖ (mil., of a rank) definite (as distinct from 'acting', 'temporary' etc.) ‖ (law) of or pertaining to the rules of right administered by a court, as distinguished from the forms of procedure **2.** n. (gram.) a noun or group of words used as the grammatical equivalent of a noun [O.F. fr. L.L.]

sub·state (sʌ́bsteit) n. a region within a state but less than a state, established for administration, e.g., West Berlin

sub·sta·tion (sʌ́bsteiʃən) n. a subsidiary or branch station

sub·sti·tute (sʌ́bstitu:t, sʌ́bstitju:t) **1.** n. a person or thing taking the place of another person or thing **2.** v. pres. part. **sub·sti·tut·ing** past and past part. **sub·sti·tut·ed** v.t. to put in the place

of another person or thing, to substitute nylon for cotton ‖ v.i. to take the place of another person or thing, he is substituting for his brother **sub·sti·tu·tion** n. **sub·sti·tu·tion·al**, **sub·sti·tu·tive**, adjs. [fr. L. substituere (substitutus), to set up]

sub·strate (sʌ́bstreit) n. a substratum ‖ (biochem.) a substance acted upon, e.g. by an enzyme [fr. Mod. L. substratum]

sub·strat·o·sphere (sʌbstrǽtəsfiər) n. the part of the atmosphere just below the stratosphere

sub·stra·tum (sʌbstréitəm, sʌbstrǽtəm, sʌbstrútəm) pl. **sub·stra·ta** (sʌbstréitə, sʌbstrǽtə, sʌbstrútə), **sub·stra·tums** n. a layer underneath, esp. constituting a supporting layer for that which is above it, e.g. the subsoil under surface soil, or an element of truth in a rumor which deforms the truth [Mod. L. fr. substernere, to spread underneath]

sub·struc·ture (sʌ́bstrʌktʃər) n. the part of a building which serves as the foundation ‖ the earth track prepared to support the ties and rails of a railroad

sub·sume (səbsú:m) pres. part. **sub·sum·ing** past and past part. **sub·sumed** v.t. (logic) to include under a category or principle ‖ to include in a larger schema, class etc. [fr. Mod. L. subsumere]

sub·sump·tion (səbsʌ́mpʃən) n. a subsuming or being subsumed ‖ something subsumed [fr. Mod. L. subsumptio (subsumptionis) fr. subsumere, to subsume]

sub·tem·per·ate (sʌbtémpərit) adj. of or pertaining to the colder regions of the temperate zones

sub·ten·an·cy (sʌbténənsi:) n. the holding of a property as subtenant

sub·ten·ant (sʌbténənt) n. a person who rents a house, flat etc. from a tenant

sub·tend (səbténd) v.t. (geom.) to lie opposite to, the arc of a circle subtends an angle at the center ‖ (bot.) to surround so as to enclose [fr. L. subtendere fr. sub, under+tendere, to stretch]

sub·ter·fuge (sʌ́btərfju:dʒ) n. the use of stratagems as a means of avoiding or evading ‖ a deceptive stratagem enabling one to get out of a situation etc. [fr. L. subterfugium fr. subterfugere, to flee secretly]

sub·ter·ra·ne·an (sʌbtəréini:ən) adj. situated, existing, operating or functioning underground [fr. L. subterraneus]

sub·ther·a·peu·tic (sʌbθɛərəpjú:tik) adj. of a preventive drug dosage esp. in the feed of chickens and other animals

sub·til·i·sin (sʌbtíləsən) (biochem.) an enzyme involved in breaking down proteins produced by a soil bacillus

sub·til·i·za·tion (sʌtlizéiʃən) n. a subtilizing or being subtilized [fr. M.L. subtilizatio (subtilizationis)]

sub·til·ize (sʌtlaiz) pres. part. **sub·til·iz·ing** past and past part. **sub·til·ized** v.t. to make subtle ‖ v.i. to use subtlety [fr. M.L. subtilizare fr. subtilis, subtle]

sub·ti·tle (sʌ́btait'l) **1.** n. a subsidiary title to a book ‖ (esp. pl.) words projected on the screen to explain the action in a silent movie or translate the dialogue of a foreign movie **2.** v.t. pres. part. **sub·ti·tling** past and past part. **sub·ti·tled** to give a subtitle or subtitles to

sub·tle (sʌ́t'l) adj. hard to grasp, difficult to define or distinguish, elusive, a subtle distinction ‖ making fine distinctions, acute, a subtle mind ‖ ingenious, cunning, clever, a subtle argument ‖ working insidiously, secretly or imperceptibly, a subtle technique of extracting money [O.F. soutil, sotil, sutil]

sub·tle·ty (sʌ́tlti:) pl. **sub·tle·ties** n. the quality or state of being subtle, esp. the making of fine distinctions ‖ a subtle distinction [O.F. sutilte, soutilte]

sub·tly (sʌ́tli:) adv. in a subtle manner

sub·ton·ic (sʌbtɔ́nik) n. (mus.) the seventh degree of a major or minor scale

sub·to·pi·a (sʌbtóupi:ə) (Br., ironic) a paradise consisting of endless suburbia ‖ an expanse of suburbs, esp. small houses, over the countryside [SUB+UTOPIA]

sub·tract (səbtrǽkt) v.t. (esp. with 'from') to take away (a number or quantity) from another number or quantity ‖ v.i. (with 'from') to cause an unwelcome lessening, does it subtract from your enjoyment? ‖ (math.) to do subtraction or a subtraction [fr. L. subtrahere (subtractus)]

sub·trac·tion (səbtrǽkʃən) n. (math.) the act or process of subtracting [fr. L.L. subtractio (subtractionis)]

sub·trac·tive (səbtrǽktiv) adj. involving subtraction ‖ that is to be subtracted ‖ tending to subtract [fr. M.L. *subtractivus*]

sub·tra·hend (sʌ́btrəhend) *n.* (*math.*) the number to be subtracted (from the minuend) [fr. L. *subtrahendus*]

sub·trop·ic (sʌbtrópik) *adj.* subtropical

sub·trop·i·cal (sʌbtrópi'l) *adj.* almost tropical ‖ of or pertaining to regions near the Tropics ‖ (of a plant) needing a subtropical climate

subtropical climate a warm climate which, unlike the tropical climate, has distinct seasons. Two types are distinguished: dry subtropical (or Mediterranean climate), characterized by long dry summers and usually found on the west side of continents, and wet subtropical, with higher rainfall and wet summers, found on the east of continents

sub·trop·ics (sʌbtrópiks) *pl. n.* subtropical regions

su·bu·late (sú:bjulit) *adj.* (*biol.*, esp. of leaves) narrow and tapering from the base to a fine point [fr. Mod. L. *subulatus* fr. *subula*, awl]

sub·urb (sʌ́bə:rb) *n.* one of the residential or industrial districts on the edge of a big town or city **sub·ur·ban** *adj.* pertaining to the suburbs ‖ having the qualities considered characteristic of the suburbs ‖ having the qualities considered characteristic of the people who live in the suburbs, e.g. dreariness, narrowness of outlook, conformity etc. [O.F. *suburbe*]

sub·ur·ban·i·za·tion (sʌbə:rbənəzéiʃən) *n.* creation of suburbs —**suburbanize** *v.*

sub·ur·bi·a (səbə́:rbi:ə) *n.* the suburbs of a city and their inhabitants

sub·ven·tion (səbvénʃən) *n.* a grant of money from a government, charitable foundation etc. to further some undertaking [O.F. *subvencion, subvention*]

sub·ver·sion (səbvə́:rʒən, səbvə́:rʃən) *n.* a subverting or being subverted [O.F. fr. L.L. *subversio (subversionis)*]

sub·ver·sive (səbvə́:rsiv) **1.** *adj* tending to subvert **2.** *n.* a subversive person [fr. L. *subvertere (subversus)*, to subvert]

sub·vert (səbvə́:rt) *v.t.* to cause the downfall or ruin of (e.g. the government of a country) ‖ to corrupt (a person) by undermining his faith or morals etc. [O.F. *subvertir*]

sub·vi·ral (sʌbváir'l) *adj.* of a part of a virus

sub·way (sʌ́bwei) *n.* an underground passage or tunnel for pedestrians, esp. under a street or railroad ‖ an underground conduit for gas mains, water supply, telephone wires etc. ‖ (*Am.=Br.* underground) a city railroad system running entirely or mainly in tunnels under the ground

suc·ceed (səksí:d) *v.i.* to be successful, to have success, to attain a desired end ‖ to be the successor, *to succeed to a throne* ‖ to ensue, to follow (in order or time), *a long peace succeeded* ‖ *v.t.* to take the place previously occupied by, to be the successor to, *he succeeded his father as head of the firm* ‖ to come after, to follow in order or time, *night succeeds day* ‖ to succeed **to** to inherit [O.F. *succeder* or fr. L. *succedere*]

suc·cess (səksés) *n.* the accomplishment of what is desired or aimed at, achievement, *military success, academic success* ‖ attainment of wealth, fame, prosperity etc. ‖ a person who or thing which succeeds **suc·céss·ful** *adj.* [fr. L. *succedere (successus)*]

suc·ces·sion (səkséʃən) *n.* a following in order, *shots in rapid succession* ‖ a series of things in order, *a succession of disasters* ‖ the act or right of following one's predecessor in a post, position or title ‖ the order in which persons succeed each other (to thrones, titles etc.) ‖ a geological, ecological or seasonal sequence of species ‖ the process of development of plant communities **in succession** one after another **in succession to** as successor of **suc·cés·sion·al** *adj.* [fr. L. *successio (successionis)*]

suc·ces·sive (səksésiv) *adj.* following one immediately after another, consecutive, *six successive victories* [fr. M.L. *successivus*]

suc·ces·sor (səksésər) *n.* a person or thing that succeeds another [O.F. *successour* fr. L.]

suc·cinct (səksíŋkt) *adj.* clearly expressed in few words [fr. L. *succingere (succinctus)*, to gird up]

suc·cin·ic acid (səksínik) white, crystalline acid (CH₂COOH)₂ used in the preparation of dyes, lacquers etc. [fr. F. *succinique*]

suc·cor, *Br.* **suc·cour** (sʌ́kər) **1.** *v.t.* (*rhet.*) to relieve the difficulty or distress of, *to succor the homeless* **2.** *n.* (*rhet.*) help given in time of need [O.F. *socorre, sucurre, secourre*]

suc·cor·ance (sʌ́kərəns) *n.* the need for sustaining care —**succorant** *adj.*

suc·co·tash (sʌ́kətæʃ) *n.* a side dish consisting of lima beans and corn kernels cooked together [Narragansett *msiquatash*, fragments]

suc·cu·bus (sʌ́kjubəs) *pl.* **suc·cu·bi** (sʌ́kjubai) *n.* a demon in female form supposed to have sexual intercourse with men in their sleep (cf. INCUBUS) [M.L.]

suc·cu·lence (sʌ́kjuləns) *n.* the state or quality of being succulent

suc·cu·len·cy (sʌ́kjulənsi:) *n.* succulence

suc·cu·lent (sʌ́kjulənt) **1.** *adj.* juicy ‖ (*bot.*) having tissues full of juice or sap **2.** *n.* a plant with fleshy leaves or fleshy stems or both [fr. L. *succulentus*]

suc·cumb (səkʌ́m) *v.i.* (with 'to') to yield to superior strength, *to succumb to a temptation* ‖ to cease to offer resistance ‖ (*rhet.*) to die [O.F. *succomber*]

suc·cur·sal (səké:rs'l) **1.** *adj.* (esp. *eccles.*) subsidiary, auxiliary, *succursal chapels* **2.** *n.* a succursal institution [fr. F. *succursale*]

suc·cus·sion (səkʌ́ʃən) *n.* the action or condition of shaking violently ‖ (*med.*) a method of diagnosing if fluid is present in a body cavity, esp. the thorax, by shaking the body [fr. L. *succussio (succussionis)*]

such (sʌtʃ) **1.** *adj.* of a kind previously or about to be mentioned or implied, *such people are dangerous, such action as may be necessary* ‖ so great, I *cannot afford such a price* ‖ of the same quality as something just mentioned (used to avoid the repetition of one word twice in a sentence), *never accept a thing as factual unless you can prove it such* ‖ of a degree or quantity stated or implicit, *such luxury is unfamiliar to me* ‖ similar, comparable, *is there such a book in English?* ‖ poor, inconspicuous, slight of its kind, *the crowd, such as it was, soon dispersed* **2.** *pron.* (with 'as') those people who, *such as heard the news came* ‖ the same as something just mentioned (used to avoid repetition of one word twice in a sentence), *never call a man a thief till you can prove him such* ‖ that part of something just stated or about to be stated, *the turkey, such of it as remained, fed the unexpected visitors* ‖ this thing, these circumstances etc., *if such is the case we will go* ‖ this or that kind of person or thing, *such is my considered opinion* **3.** *adv.* this or that degree of, *such bad spelling is intolerable* [O.E. *swelc, swilc, swylc*]

such and such (with 'a' or 'an') not specifically designated, *they went to such and such a place*

such·like (sʌ́tʃlaik) **1.** *adj.* of a similar kind, *he plays tennis and squash and such-like games* **2.** *pron.* persons or things of a similar kind

Su·chow (sú:dʒou) (or **Tungshan**) a communications center (pop. 700,000) in N.W. Kiangsu. China, on the Grand Canal: textiles (esp. silk)

Suchow *KIUCHAN

suck (sʌk) **1.** *v.t.* to draw (liquid) into the mouth by producing a partial vacuum as a result of contracting the muscles of the lips, tongue and cheeks ‖ to draw (air) into the lungs by inflating them ‖ to draw up (moisture etc.) by or as if by suction, *roots suck water from the earth* ‖ to draw liquid from (e.g. an orange) by the action of the tongue, lips and cheeks ‖ to hold (e.g. the thumb) in the mouth ‖ to allow (e.g. candy) to dissolve slowly in the mouth ‖ *v.i.* to draw something by or as if by producing a vacuum ‖ to draw milk from a breast or udder or bottle with the mouth ‖ to make the sound of sucking ‖ (of waves, with 'at') to cause erosion by their action ‖ (of a defective water pump) to draw up air instead of water **to suck in** (or **down**) (of quicksand or a whirlpool) to swallow up, engulf **to suck up** to absorb by capillarity ‖ to cause (a liquid) to rise by making the pressure above it less than atmospheric pressure **to suck up to** (esp. *Br.*, *pop.*) to toady to (someone) in order to gain favor **2.** *n.* the act of sucking ‖ the sound of sucking **súck·er** *n.* someone who, or something which, sucks ‖ (*zool.*) an organ used to suck blood or to assist in attachment (e.g. on a fly's foot etc.) ‖ (*bot.*) a shoot from a root or the underground part of a stem ‖ (*pop.*) someone who is easily taken in and gotten the better of ‖ (*pop.*) a lollipop [O.E. *sūcan*]

suck·le (sʌ́k'l) *pres. part.* **suck·ling** *past* and *past part.* **suck·led** *v.t.* (of mammals) to give (the newly born) milk from the teat

Suck·ling (sʌ́kliŋ), Sir John (1609-42), English Cavalier lyric poet

suck·ling (sʌ́kliŋ) *n.* an infant or a young animal still getting milk from the teat

Su·cre (sú:kre), Antonio José de (1795-1830), South American revolutionist. He helped Bolívar in the revolt of the Spanish-American colonies and was the first president of Bolivia (1826-8)

Sucre the constitutional capital (pop. 63,259) of Bolivia (*LA PAZ) on the central plateau at 9,331 ft. Spanish cathedral (17th c.). University (1624). Founded by the Spanish in 1538, Sucre was the first city in South America to revolt against Spain (1809)

su·cre (sú:kre) *n.* the monetary unit of Ecuador, or a coin of this amount

su·crose (sú:krous) *n.* a sweet, crystalline, dextrorotatory sugar, C₁₂H₂₂O₁₁, which occurs widely in the fluids of plants and upon hydrolysis yields a molecule of dextrose and one of fructose

suc·tion (sʌ́kʃən) **1.** *n.* the process of raising a fluid by reducing the pressure above it and so causing it to be forced upwards by the atmospheric pressure beneath it ‖ the act of causing one body to adhere to another by making the pressure between them less than the external atmospheric pressure **2.** *adj.* causing suction ‖ operating by suction [O.F.]

suction pump a pump which operates by causing a partial vacuum in a tube immersed in a fluid, by raising a close-fitting piston in the tube (cf. FORCE PUMP)

suction stop (*phon.*) a click

suc·to·ri·al (sʌktóri:əl, sʌktóuri:əl) *adj.* (*zool.*, of organs) adapted for sucking, either for feeding or for adhering ‖ (*zool.*) having such organs ‖ (*zool.*) of or relating to *Suctoria*, subphylum *Ciliophora*, a class of protozoans which suck up food through specialized tentacles [fr. Mod. L. *suctorius* fr. *sugere (suctus)*, to suck]

Su·dan (su:dǽn) a republic (area 967,000 sq. miles, pop. 19,900,000) in N.E. Africa. Capital: Khartoum. People: mainly Arab-Nubian in the north, Nilotic (Dinka, Nuer, Shilluk, Bari) and Azande in the south. Languages: Arabic (official), African languages, English. Religion: 54% Moslem (north), 20% local African (south), 2% Christian. Universities: Khartoum (1956), Khartoum branch of Cairo University (1955), Islamic University (1965). The land is 3% arable, 10% pasture and grazing and 18% forest. It is mainly a plateau (1,000–3,000 ft), with mountains in the west (the Marra, rising to 10,130 ft), the south (to 10,456 ft), and near the Red Sea coast (to 9,000 ft). The south is mainly rain forest (White Nile valley) and savanna, the center semidesert except close to the Nile, and the north desert. South of Khartoum, between the White and the Blue Nile, is the fertile Gezira plain, the economic heart of the country. Average temperatures (F.) at Khartoum: Jan. 70°, July 80°. Extremes: 40°-115°. Rainfall: Khartoum 6 ins, S. White Nile valley 37 ins, southwest 43 ins. Livestock: cattle, sheep, goats, camels, donkeys, horses. Agricultural products: cotton, peanuts, sesame, dates, hides and skins, melon seeds, oil cake, durra, pulses, seed oil, castor seed, beans, wheat, corn, citrus and tropical fruits. Forestry products: gum arabic (95% of world supply), railroad ties. Mineral resources (largely unexploited): gold, iron, copper, manganese, white mica, vermiculites, salt, chromite, quartz and marble. Manufactures and industries: cement, food processing, rolling stock. Exports: cotton, gum arabic, peanuts, sesame, cottonseed, durra, oil cake, camels, hides and skins, cattle, sheep. Imports: cotton goods, machinery, metals, petroleum products, sugar, vehicles, tea, textiles, fertilizers, jute sacks. wheat flour, coffee, tires. cigarettes and tobacco. Port: Port Sudan. Monetary unit: Sudanese pound (100 piasters). HISTORY. The north of the Sudan formed the ancient country of Nubia, which was colonized by Egypt (2nd millennium B.C.). It was converted to Coptic Christianity (6th c. A.D.), but became part of Islam when conquered by the Arabs (15th c.). It was overrun (1820-2) by Mohammed Ali of Egypt. In Egyptian service, Baker and Gordon completed the conquest of the south and began to suppress the slave trade. The Mahdi led a revolt (1883-5), but his power was broken (1898) by an Anglo-Egyptian force under Kitchener. The Sudan was under an Anglo-Egyptian condominium (1899-1953), after which it was self-governing until Jan. 1, 1956, when it became an independent republic. It joined the Arab League and the U.N. (1956). A coup d'état

---

(1958) was followed by the establishment of military rule (1958-64). Parliamentary government was reestablished (1965). A revolt of the South against northern domination erupted (1962). A new army coup d'état (1969) introduced a degree of Arab socialism, and renamed the country the Sudan Democratic Republic. A certain autonomy was granted (1972) to the south. Civil war erupted again (1983) when the southern region was divided into three provinces and strict Islamic law was imposed throughout the country. Gen. Gaafar al Nimiery, in power since 1969 except for a brief period in 1971, was overthrown (1985) after nationwide riots protesting his imposition of economic austerity measures demanded by the U.S.A. and the International Monetary Fund. A transition government tried to improve the economy and to end foreign support for the southern rebels by attempting to improve relations with Libya and Ethiopia

Sudan an imprecisely delineated geographical region of Africa generally considered to include northern and central Chad, northern and central Sudan, and Eritrea || the name given by the Arab invaders of N. Africa to the belt of sahel country south of the Sahara from the Atlantic to the Red Sea

Su·da·nese (suːdʼníːz, suːdʼníːs) 1. adj. of or relating to the Sudan or its people 2. pl. **Su·da·nese** n. a native or inhabitant of the Sadan

Su·dan·ic (suːdǽnik) 1. adj. Sudanese 2. n. a large group of languages spoken in an area of west and central Africa from S. Sudan to Senegal (*AFRICAN LANGUAGES)

Sudanic civilization a civilization, based on divine kingship and an elaborate bureaucracy, which flourished in west and central Africa from the 4th c. onward. The most famous Sudanic states were Ghana, Kanem, Songhai and Hausa. They were converted to Islam in the Middle Ages and fell into decay at various dates between the 16th and 19th cc.

su·dar·i·um (suːdéəriəm) pl. **su·dar·i·a** (suːdéəriə) n. a veronica (cloth) [L.]

su·da·to·ri·um (suːdətóːriəm, suːdətóuriəm) pl. **su·da·to·ri·a** (suːdətóːriə, suːdətóuriə) n. (esp. Rom. hist.) the heated room in which sweat baths are taken [L.]

Sud·bur·y (sʌdbəriː, sʌdbəriː) a town (pop. 91,829) in central Ontario, Canada, center of a mining area producing nickel. University (1957)

sudd (sʌd) n. vegetable matter consisting mainly of papyrus stems and a type of aquatic grass (Vossia procera), floating on and congesting parts of the upper White Nile [Arab.=an obstructing]

sud·den (sʌdʼn) 1. adj. of a change or event which occurs without noticeable preparation, a sudden fall of temperature || unexpected, a sudden bend in the road 2. n. (only in the phrase) **all of a sudden** suddenly, unexpectedly [A.F. sodein, sudein]

sudden infant death syndrome (med.) unexpected infant (1 to 4 months) mortality that occurs during sleep, the cause of which is presently unknown abbr. SIDS also crib death, sleep apnea syndrome

Su·der·mann (zúːdərmɑn), Hermann (1857-1928), German dramatist and author of novels and short stories. These last include 'The Excursion to Tilsit' (1917). His play 'Heimat' (1893) was translated into English as 'Magda' (1896)

Su·de·ten·land (suːdéitʼnlænd, zuːdéitʼnlɑnt) the northern border region of Czechoslovakia, along the Erzgebirge and the Sudeten Mtns. It had a largely German-speaking population and was annexed (1938) by Hitler. It was returned (1945) to Czechoslovakia and most of the German population was expelled

Su·de·ten Mountains (suːdéitʼn, zuːdéitʼn) a mountain system separating Silesia, Poland from Bohemia, Czechoslovakia. Highest peak: Schneekoppe (5,259 ft)

su·dor·if·er·ous (suːdəríːfərəs) adj. (of glands) producing or carrying sweat [fr. Mod. L. sudoriferus]

su·dor·if·ic (suːdəríːfik) 1. adj. inducing sweat 2. n. a sweat-producing drug [fr. Mod. L. sudorificus]

Su·dra (súːdrə) n. a Hindu of the fourth and lowest of the chief castes, comprising manual workers (*BRAHMIN, *KSHATRIYA, *VAISYA) [fr. Skr. sūdra]

suds (sʌdz) pl. n. frothy, soapy water or the froth itself **súds·y** comp. **suds·i·er** superl. **suds·i·est** adj. frothy [etym. doubtful]

Sue (sy), Eugène (1804-57), French novelist, author of 'les Mystères de Paris' (1842-3) and 'le Juif errant' (1844-5)

sue (suː) pres. part. **su·ing** past and past part. **sued** v.t. to bring a legal action against, to sue someone for damages || (law) to carry (an action) through to decision || (law) to appeal to (a court) || v.i. (law) to bring an action with a view to securing redress || (rhet.) to make a petition or entreaty, to sue for mercy [A.F. suer, siwer]

suede, Br. esp. **suéde** (sweid) n. leather having the flesh side napped by buffing. It is used for shoes, gloves etc. [F. Suède, Sweden in gants de suède, Swedish gloves]

sued·et·ta (sweidétə) n. synthetic suede

Su-11 *MAIDEN

su·et (súːit) n. the hard fat surrounding the kidneys and loins of cattle and sheep, used in cooking or in making tallow [dim. of A.F. sue, seu fr. L. sebum, tallow]

Sue·to·ni·us (switóuniəs) (Gaius Suetonius Tranquillus, c. 69–c. 140), Roman historian, author of the 'De vita Caesarum', historical biographies of the Roman emperors from Julius Caesar to Domitian

Su·ez (suːéz, Br. súːiz) a port (pop. 368,000) in Egypt at the head of the Gulf of Suez (the northwestern arm of the Red Sea) and entrance to the Suez Canal: oil refining, fertilizers

Suez Canal a ship canal (100 miles long) in E. Egypt linking, by way of several lakes and without any locks, the Red Sea (Gulf of Suez) with the Mediterranean at Port Said. It enables vessels to sail between Europe and the East without rounding Africa (almost halving the distance between London and Bombay, for example). The canal was planned and built (1854-69) by de Lesseps with French and Egyptian capital. On Disraeli's initiative, Britain bought a major interest in the company controlling the canal (1875). It was nationalized (1956) by Egypt, and the resultant military intervention by Britain, France and Israel was stopped by the U.N. The canal, which had been blocked by Egypt, was reopened (1957) but was again blocked (June 1967) after the third Arab-Israeli war. It remained closed for eight years. Plans were announced to widen and deepen the canal (1975)

suf·fer (sʌfər) v.t. to be made to bear, to suffer punishment, suffer discomfort || to be the victim of, to suffer loss || to put up with, to suffer fools gladly || to be subjected to, to suffer damage in transport || (old-fash.) to allow || v.i. to experience pain or injury || to experience loss, damage, deterioration etc., carpets suffer from damp [A.F. suffrir]

suf·fer·ance (sʌfərəns) n. tacit consent **on sufferance** under conditions of being permitted but not welcomed [O.F. suffrance, soffrance]

suf·fer·ing (sʌfəriŋ) n. mental or physical pain || the bearing of pain, distress, loss, damage etc.

suf·fice (səfáis) pres. part. **suf·fic·ing** past and part. **suf·ficed** v.i. to be enough || v.t. to be enough for [fr. O.F. suffire (suffis)]

suf·fi·cien·cy (səfíʃənsiː) pl. **suf·fi·cien·cies** n. an adequate amount || the state or quality of being sufficient [fr. L. sufficientia]

suf·fi·cient (səfíʃənt) adj. enough, as much as is needed [O.F.]

suf·fix (sʌfiks) n. a sound, syllable or syllables added to the end of a word or to a word base to change its meaning or give it grammatical function or to form a new word (e.g. '-ly', '-ness', '-ed' etc.) || (math.) a subindex 2. (sʌfiks, səfíks) v.t. to add as a suffix [fr. Mod. L. suffixum fr. suffigere, to fasten on beneath]

suf·fo·cate (sʌfəkeit) pres. part. **suf·fo·cat·ing** past and past part. **suf·fo·cat·ed** v.t. to kill by stopping respiration || to hinder the respiration of || to oppress, smother || v.i. to die by being suffocated || to have too little air to breathe [fr. L. suffocare (suffocatus), to choke]

suf·fo·ca·tion (sʌfəkéiʃən) n. a suffocating or being suffocated [fr. L. suffocatio (suffocationis)]

Suffolk (sʌfək), Thomas Howard, 1st earl of (1561-1626), lord chamberlain of England (1603-14), lord high treasurer (1614-18). He was removed from office when found guilty of embezzlement

Suffolk a county (area 1,482 sq. miles, pop. 588,400) in E. central England. It is divided administratively into East Suffolk (area 871 sq.

miles, pop. 343,000, county town: Ipswich) and West Suffolk (area 611 sq. miles, pop. 130,000, county town: Bury St Edmunds)

Suffolk Resolves resolutions adopted (1774) by the colonial assembly of Massachusetts which declared the Intolerable Acts void and recommended the establishment of a colonial militia

suf·fra·gan (sʌfrəgən) 1. n. a bishop who has no cathedral of his own, but serves as assistant to the bishop of a diocese 2. adj. of such an assistant bishop [O.E.]

suf·frage (sʌfridʒ) n. the right to vote in political elections || (esp. pl.) a vote of assent **suf·fra·gette** (sʌfrədʒét) n. a female agitator for women's suffrage **súf·fra·gist** n. an advocate of extension of political suffrage, esp. to women [O.F.]

suf·fuse (səfjúːz) pres. part. **suf·fus·ing** past and past part. **suf·fused** v.t. to spread or cover completely, to permeate with light, a liquid, a color etc. [fr. L. suffundere (suffusus)]

suf·fu·sion (səfjúːʒən) n. a suffusing or being suffused || something that suffuses, esp. a flush or a blush [fr. L. suffusio (suffusionis)]

Su·fi (súːfiː) 1. n. an adherent of Sufism 2. adj. relating to Sufism or to Sufis **Sú·fism** n. a system of mainly heterodox, mystical groups within Islam. Developing in Persia and Iraq (9th–13th cc.) Sufism advocated asceticism and meditation as a means of achieving rapturous union with the Divine: among the dervish orders certain forms of dancing were used to induce ecstasy. It also encouraged the worship of saints, and it formed communities and orders, both practices being quite against orthodox teaching. The work of al-Ghazzali (1058–1111, *GHAZZALI) caused Sufism to be accepted in orthodox circles, however, and it then reinvigorated an Islam too much governed by arid scholasticism **Su·fís·tic** adj. [Arab. çûfî, man of wool]

Su-15 *FLAGON

sug·ar (ʃúgər) 1. n. sucrose, esp. in the white crystallized form obtained chiefly by processing the juice expressed from sugarcane or from sliced sugar beets, and refining and evaporating it. Sugar is an important flavoring and preservative for other foods || one of a class of simple carbohydrates soluble in water (e.g. fructose, maltose, sucrose, glucose) including oligosaccharides and monosaccharides, that vary widely in sweetness || a spoonful or lump of sugar 2. v.t. to sweeten with sugar || to sprinkle with sugar || (esp. Br.) to make (something unpleasant) more agreeable by flattery, cajolery etc. || v.i. to form sugar || to become granular like sugar **to sugar off** to finish the boiling down of maple syrup until it is thick enough to crystallize **to sugar the pill** to make something unpleasant acceptable [O.F. çucre fr. M.L. fr. Arab.]

Sugar Act of 1764 a British act of Parliament passed to raise revenue and offset colonial administrative costs. It gave customs officials more power, freed them from damage suits in colonial courts, and elaborated the bonds, bills of lading, and other papers used in colonial commerce in order to prevent fraud. It lowered the duty on foreign molasses, but this duty was henceforth to be collected (the contraband trade having being tolerated until then). It thus directly threatened the rum trade, which depended on molasses

sugar almond (Br.) a Jordan almond

sugar beet a beet having white roots grown for its sugar. After the root is crushed and the sugar extracted, the residue is used as fodder and as a fertilizer. The leaves are converted into silage

Sugar Bowl New Orleans stadium where postseason college football games have been played since 1935

sug·ar·cane (ʃúgərkein) n. Saccharum officinarum, a species of tall, coarse perennial grass (8–20 ft in height), having jointed stems and a terminal flower cluster. It is one of the chief sources of sugar

sug·ar·coat (ʃúgərkout) v.t. to coat something with sugar || to make (something difficult or unpleasant) seem easier or more attractive than it really is || to conceal (something unpalatable) under a pleasing surface **súg·ar·coat·ed** adj. **súg·ar·coat·ing** n.

sugar daddy (pop.) an elderly man who provides luxuries for the young woman he keeps as mistress

sug·ar·house (ʃúgərhaus) pl. **sug·ar·hous·es** (ʃúgərhauziz) n. a building where sugar is processed, esp. where maple sugar and maple syrup are made

sug·ar·i·ness (ʃúgərinis) n. the state or quality of being sugary

sug·ar·loaf (ʃúgərlouf) pl. **sug·ar·loaves** (ʃúgərlouvz) n. a conical mass of refined sugar ‖ a hill or mountain shaped like a sugarloaf **sug·ar·loaf** adj. shaped like a cone of sugar

sugar maple any of various North American maples, esp. Acer saccharum, from whose sap maple syrup and maple sugar are made. Sugar maples are also highly valued for their hardwood

sug·ar·y (ʃúgəri:) adj. of or containing sugar ‖ very sweet ‖ granular, like refined sugar ‖ sentimental and cloying ‖ (of a person's manner, voice etc.) excessively and usually insincerely sweet

Su·ger (syʒer) (c. 1081-1151), French cleric and statesman, abbot of Saint-Denis. He was the chief minister of Louis VI and Louis VII, and was regent of France (1147-9) during Louis VII's absence on crusade. He wrote a life of Louis VI

sug·gest (səgdʒést, sədʒést) v.t. to put forward for consideration, to suggest an alternative route ‖ to make one think of, bring to mind, esp. by free association, the symphony suggests a sunrise ‖ to propose (someone or something) as a possibility ‖ to intimate ‖ to serve as an inspiration for, prompt the doing of, a drama suggested by Harlem race riots [fr. L. suggerere (suggestus), to bring under]

sug·gest·i·bil·i·ty (səgdʒéstəbíliti:, sədʒéstəbíliti:) n. the state or quality of being suggestible

sug·gest·i·ble (səgdʒéstəb'l, sədʒéstəb'l) adj. (of a person) readily able to be influenced by suggestion, esp. hypnotic suggestion ‖ being mentally susceptible to the influence and opinions of persons other than oneself ‖ able to be suggested

sug·ges·tion (səgdʒéstʃən, sədʒéstʃən) n. a suggesting or being suggested ‖ that which is suggested ‖ a partly formed idea which, if developed, would be the basis of a judgment ‖ a very slight amount, a suggestion of mockery in his tone ‖ the process whereby one thought leads to another, a part evokes a whole etc. ‖ (psychol.) a mental process which results in the acceptance of beliefs arising from a source considered expert or authoritative. The technique of advertising often rests on it ‖ hypnosis [O.F. suggestioun fr. L.]

sug·ges·tive (səgdʒéstiv, sədʒéstiv) adj. stimulating ideas, emotions etc. ‖ tending to suggest something indecent

Su·har·to (su:hártou) (1921-), Indonesian general and statesman. When President Sukarno was deprived (1967) of his presidential powers Suharto had them temporarily ascribed (Mar. 1967) to himself, and set about rebuilding the economy. He adopted a peaceful policy toward Malaysia, and sought to counter the influence of Communist China. He was reelected in 1973, 1978, and 1983

Suhl (zu:l) a district (area 1,492 sq. miles, pop. 575,000) of East Germany (*THURINGIA)

Sui (swi:) a dynasty which ruled China (590-618). Under it the Chinese empire was greatly extended

su·i·cid·al (su:isáid'l) adj. having an inclination towards suicide ‖ involving or leading to suicide ‖ involving esp. willful destruction of one's own interests, career etc.

su·i·cide (sú:isaid) n. the act of killing oneself intentionally ‖ an action for which one is responsible and which damages one's career or reputation irreparably, political suicide [fr. Mod. L. suicidum fr. sui, of oneself + caedere, to kill]

suicide n. a person who intentionally takes his own life, or attempts to do so [Mod. L. suicida fr. sui, of oneself + caedere, to kill]

suicide connection technique for reversing rotation of a large electric motor (from full speed ahead to reverse) by so wiring the field and armature circuits to make it a generator, feeding energy to field coils to negate stored magnetism quickly

suicide seat seat next to the driver of a motor vehicle

suicide squad (football) team group that defends the player kicking off

su·i·cid·ol·o·gy (su:isaidɔ́lədʒi:) n. the study of suicides —**suicidologist** n.

suit (su:t) 1. n. a jacket and pants of the same material, sometimes with a vest as well ‖ a jacket and skirt of the same material ‖ the act of suing in a court of law ‖ an action taken to a court of law ‖ an act of petitioning or requesting ‖ (old-fash.) courtship, to press one's suit ‖ one of the four sets of cards (clubs, diamonds, spades, hearts) in a deck ‖ (naut.) a set of sails ‖ (hist.) a set of armor ‖ an outfit adapted to a particular activity or circumstance, a space suit ‖ a bathing suit **to follow suit** (cards) to play a card of the suit led ‖ to follow an example, watch what he does and follow suit 2. v.t. to meet the needs or wishes of, be convenient for, would it suit you to come tomorrow? ‖ to fit in with, that suits my plans ‖ (esp. used passively) to fit for, he isn't suited for salesmanship ‖ to look well on, green suits you ‖ to be good for the health of, the climate does not suit her **to suit oneself** to satisfy one's own needs, convenience or wishes [A.F. siute]

suit·a·bil·i·ty (su:təbíliti:) n. the quality of being suitable

suit·a·ble (sú:təb'l) adj. meeting the requirements of a situation, purpose etc. ‖ unobjectionable as regards propriety **súit·a·bly** adv.

suit·case (sú:tkeis) n. a flat, rectangular container, with a hinged lid and a handle, used for carrying clothes etc. on a journey

suite (swi:t) n. a set of matching furniture ‖ a set of rooms, e.g. in a hotel ‖ a retinue, personal staff ‖ (mus.) an instrumental composition consisting of a set of movements, esp. (hist.) consisting of an allemande, courante, saraband, gigue, sometimes with additions, in related keys [F.]

suit·ing (sú:tiŋ) n. cloth of which men's and women's suits are made

suit·or (sú:tər) n. (law) a petitioner or plaintiff in a lawsuit ‖ a petitioner ‖ (old-fash.) a man who courts a woman with a view to marriage [A.F. seutor, suitour]

Sui·yüan (swí:jyán) a former province of N. China, part of Inner Mongolia since 1954

Su·kar·na·pu·ra (su:kɑrnəpúərə) *DJAJAPURA

Su·kar·no (su:kárnou), Achmed (1901-70), Indonesian statesman, first president of Indonesia (1945-67). He assumed dictatorial powers (1960) and became head of state for life (1963), but was forced to give up power in 1967

Su·khu·mi (sú:xumi:) the capital (pop. 114,000) of the Abkhazian A.S.S.R., U.S.S.R., a port and resort on the E. Black Sea

su·ki·ya·ki (su:ki:jáki:, ski:jáki:) n. a Japanese dish of thin slices of meat fried with bean sprouts, mushrooms, onions and other vegetables, served with soy sauce [Jap.]

Suk·koth (súkout, súkəs) n. a Jewish harvest festival commemorating the temporary shelter granted the Jews in the wilderness. It lasts 7–9 days, beginning the 15th of Tishri (cf. JEWISH CALENDAR) [Heb. Sukkôth, pl. of sukkāh, a thicket, arbor]

Suk·kur (súkkur) a town (pop. 158,876) in N. Sind, Pakistan, on the Indus, at the center of a great irrigation system (the Sukku and Lloyd barrage, 1928-32)

Su·lai·man Range (sulaimán) a mountain range 250 miles long in Pakistan, west of the middle Indus (Takht-i-Sulaiman, 11,100 ft)

Su·la·we·si (su:ləwéisi:) (Celebes) a mountainous fertile island (area 72,976 sq. miles, pop. 9,263,700) in the Greater Sundas, since 1950 one of the ten provinces of Indonesia. Chief town: Makassar. Products: rice, coffee, tobacco, cocoa, copra, nickel. The Dutch occupied the Makassar area in the south in the 17th c. but did not pacify all the tribes of the island, mainly Malay, until the early 20th c. (*INDONESIA)

sul·cate (sálkeit) adj. (biol.) grooved, furrowed **súl·cat·ed** adj. [fr. L. sulcare (sulcatus), to furrow]

sul·cus (sálkəs) pl. **sul·ci** (sálsai) n. a groove, furrow, esp. (anat.) a shallow furrow or fissure on the surface of the brain separating one convolution from another [L.]

Su·lei·man I (sʊ:leimán) 'the Magnificent' (1494-1566), Ottoman sultan (1520-66). He expanded the Ottoman Empire to its greatest extent, capturing Belgrade (1521) and Rhodes (1522) and unsuccessfully besieging Vienna (1529). He defeated the Hungarians at Mohacs (1526) and annexed Hungary (1540). His fleet dominated the Mediterranean and he conquered the Red Sea coast of Arabia. He was a great legislator and patron of the arts, and built many famous mosques

sul·fa·di·a·zine, sul·pha·di·a·zine (sʌlfədáizi:n) n. $C_{10}H_{10}N_4O_2S$, a sulfa drug

sul·fa drug (sálfə) any of a class of therapeutic agents that are sulfonamides, chemically related to sulfanilamide. These bacteriostatic drugs are particularly effective against diseases caused by streptococci, pneumococci and meningococci. The most prominent of these drugs are, in addition to sulfanilamide: sulfapyridine, sulfathiazole and sulfadiazine

sul·fa·nil·a·mide, sul·pha·nil·a·mide (sʌlfəníləmaid) n. $H_2NC_6H_4SO_2NH_2$, the parent compound of most of the sulfa drugs

sul·fa·pyr·i·dine, sul·pha·pyr·i·dine (sʌlfəpíərədi:n) n. $C_{11}H_{11}N_3O_2S$, a sulfa drug

sul·fate, sul·phate (sálfeit) 1. n. a salt or ester of sulfuric acid 2. v.t. pres. part. **sul·fat·ing, sul·phat·ing** past and past part. **sul·fat·ed, sul·phat·ed** to treat with a sulfate, or sulfuric acid ‖ (elec.) to form a whitish deposit of lead sulfate on (the plates of a battery) ‖ v.i. to become sulfated

sul·fa·thi·a·zole, sul·pha·thi·a·zole (sʌlfəθáiəzoul) n. $C_9H_9N_3O_3S_2$, a sulfa drug

sul·fide, sul·phide (sálfaid) n. a binary compound of sulfur with another element ‖ a compound of sulfur with an organic radical

sul·fin·py·ra·zone [$C_{23}H_{20}N_2O_3S$] (sʌlfinpáirəzoun) n. (pharm.) drug that stimulates excretion of uric acid, used in treatment of gout and heart infarction; marketed as Anturane

sul·fite, sul·phite (sálfait) n. a salt or ester of sulfurous acid **sul·fit·ic, sul·phit·ic** (sálfítik) adj.

sul·fon·a·mide, sul·phon·a·mide (sʌlfónəmaid) n. any of the compounds of the group SO_2NH_2 or of its derivatives, many of which are used in destroying harmful bacteria. The first sulfonamide, known as 'M and B' (1933) was used in treating pneumonia. More recent members of the group are used to treat infections of the intestinal, urinary and respiratory tracts

sul·fo·nate, sul·pho·nate (sálfəneit) 1. n. a salt or ester of a sulfonic acid 2. v.t. pres. part. **sul·fo·nat·ing, sul·pho·nat·ing** past and past part. **sul·fo·nat·ed, sul·pho·nat·ed** to convert into a sulfonic acid, salt or halide

sul·fo·na·tion, sul·pho·na·tion (sʌlfənéiʃən) n. the process of sulfonating

sul·fone, sul·phone (sálfoun) n. any of a group of organic compounds containing the radical SO_2 in which the sulfur atom is linked doubly with carbon in various combinations ‖ a product of sulfur compound oxidation used in treatment of leprosy

sul·fon·ic acid, sul·phon·ic acid (sʌlfónik) any of several acids that contain the SO_3H group and are derived from sulfuric acid by the replacement of an OH group

sul·fo·nyl, sul·pho·nyl (sálfənil) n. the bivalent radical SO_2 occurring in sulfones, sulfonic acids etc.

sul·fo·nyl·u·re·a (sʌlfəniljurí:ə) n. (pharm.) any of a number of drugs that lessen blood sugar by increasing secretion of endogenous insulin, used in treating diabetes

sul·fur, sul·phur (sálfər) 1. n. a multivalent nonmetallic element (symbol S, at. no. 16, at. mass 32,064) found in crystalline or amorphous form. It occurs abundantly and widely in nature, in the free state and combined as sulfides and sulfates. It is used in the making of sulfuric acid, vulcanizing rubber, gunpowder, matches, dyes, fungicides, insecticides and in medicines [L. sulphur, sulfur]

sul·fu·rate, sul·phu·rate (sálfjureit) pres. part. **sul·fu·rat·ing, sul·phu·rat·ing** past and past part. **sul·fu·rat·ed, sul·phu·rat·ed** v.t. to sulfurize **sul·fu·ra·tion, sul·phu·ra·tion** n.

sul·fur-bot·tom, sul·phur-bot·tom (sálfərbɒtəm) n. the blue whale

sulfur dioxide, sulphur dioxide the stable oxide of sulfur, SO_2. It is gaseous at ordinary atmospheric pressure, with a choking and penetrating smell, but is easily liquefied by pressure. It is used in making sulfuric acid, as a reducing and bleaching agent in refining, as a preservative, as an insecticide, as a disinfectant, in refrigerating circuits etc.

sul·fu·re·ous, sul·phu·re·ous (sʌlfjúəri:əs) adj. of, consisting of, or like sulfur ‖ sulfur yellow in color ‖ having the qualities of sulfur when burning

sul·fu·ret·ed hydrogen, sul·phu·ret·ted hydrogen, sul·fu·ret·ted hydrogen (sálfjuretid) hydrogen sulfide

sul·fu·ric, sul·phu·ric (sʌlfjúərik) adj. of, relating to, or containing sulfur

---

sulfuric acid, sulphuric acid the dibasic acid H_2SO_4, a dense, oily, colorless liquid (oil of vitriol) which very readily dissolves and ionizes in water, with the evolution of much heat. It is used extensively in the chemical industry, in oil refining, and in manufacturing fertilizers, detergents, explosives, dyes, rayon etc.

sul·fu·rize, sul·phu·rize (sʌ́lfjuraiz) *pres. part.* **sul·fu·riz·ing, sul·phu·riz·ing** *past and past part.* **sul·fu·rized, sul·phu·rized** *v.t.* to combine or impregnate with sulfur ‖ to fumigate or bleach with sulfur dioxide fumes

sul·fur·ous, sul·phur·ous (sʌlfjúərəs, sʌ́lfərəs) *adj.* of, pertaining to or containing sulfur

sulfurous acid, sulphurous acid an unstable, weak acid, H_2SO_3, known in its aqueous solution, that is a good reducing and bleaching agent

sulfur trioxide, sulphur trioxide the oxide SO_3, which readily combines with water to form sulfuric acid

sul·fur·y, sul·phur·y (sʌ́lfəri:) *adj.* of, relating to or resembling sulfur

sul·in·dac [$C_{20}H_{17}FO_3S$] (sʌ́lindɑk) *n.* (*pharm.*) analgesic anti-inflammatory drug used in treating arthritis; marketed as Clinoril

sulk (sʌlk) **1.** *v.i.* to make one's resentment or vexation felt by others by not talking to them, not cooperating etc. **2.** *n.* the state of sulking, *in a sulk* ‖ (*pl.*) a fit of sulking **súlk·i·ly** *adv.* **súlk·i·ness** *n.* the state of being sulky **súlk·y 1.** *comp.* **súlk·i·er** *superl.* **súlk·i·est** *adj.* sulking or inclined to sulk ‖ suggesting sulkiness **2.** *pl.* **súlk·ies** *n.* a light two-wheeled cart having one seat and no body, esp. used for trotting races [origin unknown]

Sul·la (sʌ́lə), Lucius Cornelius (138 B.C.–78 B.C.), Roman soldier and statesman. Consul in 88 B.C., he defeated (85 B.C.) Mithridates VI of Pontus, overthrew his political opponents at Rome, and was made dictator with extraordinary powers. He proscribed his enemies and reinstated the power of the senate, establishing a moderately aristocratic constitution. This pattern of autocratic rule, followed by other military commanders, eventually overthrew the Roman republic

sul·lage (sʌ́lidʒ) *n.* a deposit of mud ‖ refuse or sewage ‖ molten metal scoria [origin unknown]

sul·len (sʌ́lən) *adj.* gloomy, ill-humored and unsociable, *a sullen mood* ‖ dull, heavy, *a sullen sky, sullen tones* ‖ sluggish, *a sullen pace* [M.E. *soleine* fr. O.F. *solain*, alone fr. L.]

Sul·li·van (sʌ́livən), Sir Arthur Seymour (1842–1900), English composer. The combination of W. S. Gilbert's witty and topical words and Sullivan's music gave the theater 'H.M.S. Pinafore' (1878), 'The Pirates of Penzance' (1880), 'The Mikado' (1885), 'The Gondoliers' (1889) and other highly skillful light operas. Sullivan was also the composer of sacred cantatas, anthems and hymn tunes which are still sung

Sullivan, Harry Stack (1892–1949), U.S. psychiatrist. Rejecting Sigmund Freud's libidinal theory of personality development, he believed that the development of human peculiarities was governed by interpersonal phenomena

Sullivan, Louis Henri (1856–1924), American architect. His functional approach to design made for organic unity in his steel-frame commercial buildings. His work was of great importance in the evolution of American architecture

Sul·ly (syli:), Maximilien de Béthune, baron de Rosny, duc de (1560–1641), French statesman. A Protestant, he served under the future Henri IV in the Wars of Religion, becoming that king's minister (1598–1610). He proved a brilliant administrator, restoring the country's finances, encouraging agriculture and industry, and building roads and canals

Sul·ly (sʌ́li:), Thomas (1783–1872), U.S. portrait painter. His works include 'Washington Crossing the Delaware' (1818) and portraits of the Marquis de Lafayette (1824–5) and of Queen Victoria (1837)

sul·ly (sʌ́li:) *pres. part.* **sul·ly·ing** *past and past part.* **sul·lied** *v.t.* to soil (a reputation etc.) [prob. fr. F. *souiller*, to soil]

sul·phur *SULFUR (and for other derived words beginning 'sulph-' *SULF-)

sul·tan (sʌ́ltən) *n.* a Moslem ruler, esp. a former emperor of Turkey [F. fr. Arab.]

sul·tan·a (sʌltɑ́nə, sʌltɑ́nə) *n.* the wife of a sultan or any female member of his family ‖ a small, seedless yellow grape grown esp. in the Mediterranean area, e.g. at Izmir, used to make a white wine or dried (*RAISIN) for use in cakes, puddings etc. ‖ this raisin ‖ a member of *Porphyrio*, a genus of purple gallinules [Ital.]

sul·tan·ate (sʌ́ltəneit, sʌ́ltənit) *n.* the rank, office or reign of a sultan ‖ the territory governed by a sultan

sul·tan·ship (sʌ́ltənʃip) *n.* the rank, office or reign of a sultan

sul·tri·ly (sʌ́ltrili) *adv.* in a sultry manner

sul·tri·ness (sʌ́ltri:nis) *n.* the state or quality of being sultry

sul·try (sʌ́ltri:) *comp.* **sul·tri·er** *superl.* **sul·tri·est** *adj.* (of weather) hot and oppressive ‖ (of people) passionately sensual [fr. obs. *sulter* v., perh. fr. obs. *swulter*, var. of SWELTER]

Su·lu Archipelago (súːluː) a group of 870 islands (area 1,087 sq. miles, pop. 317,876) in the Philippines, southwest of Mindanao. Largest island: Jolo. Chief town and port: Jolo (pop. 18,000). Religion: 95% Moslem. Products: rice, coconuts, fruit, fish, pearls, lumber. A sultanate established in the 16th c., it resisted Spanish domination. It came under U.S. control (1899). It became (1940) part of the Commonwealth of the Philippines

Sulu Sea a part of the Pacific between the Philippine Is and Sabah

sum (sʌm) **1.** *n.* an amount of money either specified or indefinite, *he paid a big sum for it* ‖ the whole amount of something ‖ gist, summary ‖ the result obtained by adding ‖ numbers to be added together ‖ (*pop.*) a problem in arithmetic **in sum** in short **2.** *v.t. pres. part.* **sum·ming** *past and past part.* **summed** (often with 'up') to add together **to sum up** to gather together the important parts of (a speech, lecture etc.) in a brief statement ‖ to arrive at a considered opinion concerning the character, qualities etc. of (a person) [O.F. *summe, somme* fr. L. *summus*, highest]

su·mac, su·mach (ʃúːmæk, súːmæk) *n.* any of various members of *Rhus*, fam. *Anacardiaceae*, a genus of shrubs native to warm and temperate regions, having simple or pinnate leaves ‖ a shrub of this genus ‖ a substance used in tanning and dyeing made from the dried and powdered leaves of certain of these shrubs ‖ the wood of one of these shrubs (*POISON SUMAC) [O.F. or M.L. fr. Arab. *summāq*].

Su·ma·tra (sumɑ́trə) an island (area 166,789 sq. miles, pop. 28,016,160) of the Greater Sundas, Indonesia. Chief town: Palembang. A volcanic range (Kerintji, 12,467 ft) runs along the west coast. The east is an alluvial plain, largely rain forest. At present undeveloped, Sumatra has great economic potential. Products: rice, spices, tobacco, coffee, palm kernels, lumber, petroleum, coal, tin, gold. HISTORY. Sumatra was the center of a Hindu empire (8th c.). Arab traders visited the island (13th c.) and, after a period of Javanese rule, Sumatra adopted Islam as its religion (late 16th c.). The Portuguese began to trade with Sumatra (early 16th c.) but were driven out by the Dutch, whose position was challenged in turn by the English. The Dutch gained control of the whole island, subjugating the last native state in 1905. It became part of Indonesia (1945)

Sum·ba (súːmbə) an island (area 4,305 sq. miles, pop. 182,000) in the Lesser Sundas, Indonesia. Chief town and port: Waingapoe (pop. 3,000). Products: sandalwood (now largely depleted), horses, cattle, cereals, tobacco, copra, coffee

Sum·ba·wa (su:mbɑ́wə) an island (area 5,693 sq. miles, pop. 320,000) of the Lesser Sundas, Indonesia. Chief town and port: Raba (pop. 7,000). Products: cattle and horses, cereals, tobacco, cotton, copra, coffee

Su·mer (súːmər) an ancient region in S. Mesopotamia. Its non-Semitic people developed a flourishing civilization by c. 3500 B.C. They were masters of metalworking and pottery, and developed a cuneiform system of writing. Sumer became merged (c. 2200 B.C.) with Babylonia

Su·me·ri·an (sumíəri:ən, suméri:ən) **1.** *adj.* of, relating to or characteristic of Sumer ‖ of, relating to, or characteristic of the people of Sumer **2.** *n.* an inhabitant of Sumer ‖ the ancient language of Sumer, surviving in cuneiform inscriptions. It seems to be related to no other language, either living or dead

sum·ma·ri·ly (səméri·li, sʌ́məri·li) *adv.* in a summary way

sum·ma·rist (sʌ́mərist) *n.* a person who makes a summary

sum·ma·ri·za·tion (sʌ̀mərizéiʃən) *n.* a summarizing or being summarized

sum·ma·rize (sʌ́məraiz) *pres. part.* **sum·ma·riz·ing** *past and past part.* **sum·ma·rized** *v.t.* to sum up, make a summary of, *to summarize an argument* ‖ to be a summary of

sum·ma·ry (sʌ́məri:) *adj.* giving the essentials briefly, summarizing, *a summary report* ‖ done quickly without formality, *summary punishment* ‖ of or using procedure which omits much of the formality required by common law, *summary courts* (opp. PLENARY) ‖ marked by less than proper consideration, *summary treatment* [fr. L. *summarius*]

sum·ma·ry *pl.* **sum·ma·ries** *n.* a short statement of the essential points of a matter [fr. L. *summarium*]

summary court-martial a military court for offenses less serious than those warranting a special court-martial, with one commissioned officer presiding who can impose only certain limited fines or punishments

sum·ma·tion (səméiʃən) *n.* the act of adding ‖ an aggregate ‖ a cumulation, esp. (*biol.*) of small stimuli which together are able to induce a nerve impulse ‖ a final summing up **sum·ma·tion·al** *adj.* [fr. Mod. L. *summatio* (*summationis*) fr. *summare*, to sum]

sum·mer (sʌ́mər) **1.** *n.* the warmest season of the year, when a region faces the sun most directly (from the June solstice to the September equinox in the northern hemisphere or from the December solstice to the March equinox in the southern hemisphere) **2.** *adj.* of summer ‖ done in the summer **3.** *v.i.* to pass the summer ‖ *v.t.* to provide (sheep, cattle etc.) with pasture during the summer [O.E. *sumor*]

summer *n.* a large, horizontal beam carrying a dead load in building, esp. a main beam supporting girders or the joists of a floor ‖ a stone or wooden lintel of a door or window [A.F. *sumer, somer*]

Sum·mer·all (sʌ́mərɔl), Charles Pelot (1867–1955), U.S. general. As commander of U.S. forces in France during the 1st world war, he proved the value of coordinating artillery action with infantry operations

sum·mer·house (sʌ́mərhaus) *pl.* **sum·mer·hous·es** (sʌ́mərhauziz) *n.* a lightly constructed, covered building in a garden or park, for shade in summer

summer lightning heat lightning

summersault *SOMERSAULT

summer solstice the time when the sun reaches the June solstice for the northern hemisphere or the December solstice for the southern hemisphere

summer squash any of a number of small squashes grown in the summer. They are eaten when not quite ripe, before the seeds and rind become hard

summer stock plays put on during the summer season by a repertory company in a resort or small town

sum·mer·time (sʌ́mərtaim) *n.* the summer season

sum·mer·y (sʌ́məri:) *adj.* of, relating to, or like summer

sum·ming-up (sʌ́miŋʌp) *pl.* **sum·mings-up** *n.* a summary

sum·mit (sʌ́mit) *n.* the highest point, esp. of hills and mountains ‖ the top, the highest point e.g. of ambitions or achievements ‖ a conference held by heads of state [O.F. *sommette, somete* dim. of *some, sum*, sum]

summit diplomacy personal, face-to-face negotiation between heads of state, of the world's leading countries —**summit conference** *n.*

summit meeting a summit (conference)

sum·mon (sʌ́mən) *v.t.* to order to appear ‖ to cite (a jury) ‖ to cite (an accused person or witness) to appear in court ‖ to call a meeting of (e.g. a committee) ‖ to call upon for support for some action, *to summon all one's strength* ‖ to adjure, *he summoned them to surrender* [fr. O.F. *somondre*, to warn]

sum·mons (sʌ́mənz) **1.** *pl.* **sum·mons·es** *n.* a request or order to appear, attend, perform some action etc., esp. (*law*) an official written order to appear in court ‖ a signal which summons **2.** *v.t.* to serve with a summons [O.F. *sumunse, somounse*]

Sum·ner (sʌ́mnər), Charles (1811–74), American statesman, a leader of the antislavery movement

Sumner, James Batcheller (1887–1955), U.S. biochemist and co-winner (with J. H. Northrop

CONCISE PRONUNCIATION KEY: **(a)** æ, c*a*t; ɑ, c*a*r; ɔ f*aw*n; ei, sn*a*ke. **(e)** e, h*e*n; iː, sh*ee*p; iə, d*ee*r; ɛə, b*ea*r. **(i)** i, f*i*sh; ai, t*i*ger; əː, b*i*rd. **(o)** o, *o*x; au, c*ow*; ou, g*oa*t; u, p*oo*r; ɔi, r*oy*al. **(u)** ʌ, d*u*ck; u, b*u*ll; uː, g*oo*se; ə, b*a*cillus; juː, c*u*be. x, lo*ch*; θ, *th*ink; ð, *b*o*th*er; z, *Z*en; ʒ, corsa*g*e; dʒ, sava*g*e; ŋ, ora*ng*utang; j, *y*ak; ʃ, *f*ish; tʃ, fe*tch*; 'l, rabb*le*; 'n, redd*en*. Complete pronunciation key appears inside front cover.

and W. M. Stanley) of the 1946 Nobel prize in chemistry, for research in enzymes

Sumner, William Graham (1840-1910), U.S. sociologist and economist. Advocating an extreme laissez-faire policy, he opposed any government measures which interfered with the natural intercourse of trade

sump (sʌmp) n. an oil container at the base of the crankcase of an internal-combustion engine ‖ a drainage pit ‖ a cesspool [M.L.G. sump or M.Du. somp, sump or fr. G. sumpt, swamp]

sump·tion (sʌmpʃən) n. (logic) a major premiss

sump·tu·ar·y (sʌmptʃuːɛriː) adj. pertaining to or controlling expenditure [fr. L. sumptuarius]

sumptuary law a law limiting private expenditure, esp. (hist.) on religious or moral grounds

sump·tu·ous (sʌmptʃuːəs) adj. of very great splendor ‖ lavish, luxurious [O.F. somptueux, sumptueux]

Sumter *FORT SUMTER

sun (sʌn) 1. n. the central controlling body of the solar system, lying at the principal focus of all the planetary orbits. In the galactic frame of reference, the sun is a typical dwarf yellow star located in a spiral arm near the outer edge of the Milky Way ‖ the light or heat received from the sun ‖ any heavenly body that is the center of a solar system ‖ (rhet.) a source of splendor **a place in the sun** an opportunity to expand and thrive **under the sun** in the world 2. v. pres. part. **sun·ning** past and past part. **sunned** v.t. to expose to direct radiation from the sun ‖ v.i. to sit or lie in direct sunlight [O.E. sunne]
—The sun is a spherical body (diameter 865,400 miles) of mass 4.39×10^{27} tons (being 3.33×10^5 times more massive than the earth and 740 times more massive than the sum of the masses of the nine planets it controls) and density 1.44 times that of water. Its composition, spectroscopically determined (*FRAUNHOFER LINES), is approx. 90% hydrogen and approx. 10% helium, with small amounts of all the other known elements. Its structure includes a core whose center is at a temperature of 15 million degrees C. and at a pressure of billions of atmospheres: under such conditions matter is limited to an extremely dense gaseous state. The solar interior is surrounded by the photosphere. The extremely extended atmosphere of the sun consists of two regions: the chromosphere and the corona.
The energy of the sun is derived from the thermonuclear conversion of hydrogen into helium, which is thought to occur continuously in the extreme conditions found in the solar interior. This energy (in the form of heat and electromagnetic radiation) forces its way to the solar surface, the solar integrity being maintained by an oppositely directed intense gravitation (28 times greater at the surface of the sun than at the earth's surface). Only a small fraction of the total solar energy output (2.40×10^{14} horsepower distributed over its surface) reaches the earth, but it is responsible directly or indirectly for innumerable energy-requiring processes (e.g. growth of all plant and animal life, the winds, the production of power from natural fuels etc.) (*SUNSPOT CYCLE)

sun arc a sun lamp

sun·bath (sʌnbæθ, sʌnbɑːθ) n. a period of exposure of the body to the sun or to a sun lamp

sun·bathe (sʌnbeɪð) pres. part. **sun·bath·ing** past and past part. **sun·bathed** v.i. to take a sunbath

sun·beam (sʌnbiːm) n. a ray of sunlight

sun bear Helarctos malayanus (or Ursus malayanus), fam. Ursidae, a small, mainly black bear with a short, fine coat, inhabiting the forests of the Malay Peninsula and islands east of Borneo

Sun·belt (sʌnbelt) n. the area of the southern U.S. from Virginia to California

sun·bird (sʌnbəːrd) n. any of a number of small songbirds of fam. Nectariniidae, with brilliant glossy plumage, resembling hummingbirds. They are found in Africa, S. Asia, Australia and the East Indies

sun·bon·net (sʌnbɒnit) n. a bonnet for women and girls with a front brim to shade the face and a back flap to shield the neck from the sun

sun·burn (sʌnbəːrn) 1. n. reddening and blistering with consequent peeling of the skin through too sudden and too long exposure to the sun ‖ tanning of the skin through exposure to the sun 2. v. pres. part. **sun·burn·ing** past and past part. **sun·burned, sun·burnt** (sʌnbəːrnt) v.t. to

cause to be bronzed or blistered by the sun ‖ v.i. to become bronzed or blistered by exposure to the sun

sun·dae (sʌndeɪ) n. a portion of ice cream served with sauce, fruit, nuts, whipped cream etc. [etym. doubtful]

Sun·da Islands (sʌndə) a group of mountainous, volcanic islands in the Malay Archipelago, divided into the Greater and the Lesser Sundas. The Greater Sundas consist of Java, Sumatra, Borneo, Sulawesi and adjacent islands. The Lesser Sundas (Nusa Tenggara) comprise the chain running from Bali to Timor

sun dance a ceremonial dance of North and South American Indians in honor of the sun at the summer solstice

Sun·dar·bans (sʌndərbənz) a region (about 6,000 sq. miles) of swampy islets formed by the Ganges delta in Bengal, India and Bangladesh

Sun·day (sʌndiː, sʌndeɪ) n. the first day of the week, the Christian sabbath **a month of Sundays** a very long time [O.E. sunnandœg, day of the sun]

Sunday best one's best clothes, kept esp. for wearing on Sundays

Sunday school a voluntary school held usually in a parish on Sunday for the religious instruction of children ‖ the teachers and pupils of such a school

sun·der (sʌndər) v.t. (rhet.) to break or tear apart ‖ (rhet.) to keep apart ‖ v.i. (rhet.) to break apart, to separate **in sunder** (rhet.) asunder [Late O.E. syndrian, sundrian]

Sun·der·land (sʌndərlənd), Robert Spencer, 2nd earl of (1640-1702), English statesman. An opportunist, he was in the pay of Louis XIV while also intriguing to put William of Orange on the English throne

Sunderland a port and county borough (pop. 196,152) in Durham, England: coal mining, shipbuilding, mechanical engineering

sun·dew (sʌnduː, sʌndjuː) n. a member of Drosera, fam. Droseraceae, a genus of low-growing perennial insectivorous plants, with a rosette of broad, hairy leaves, found in swamps and other damp places

sun·di·al (sʌndaɪəl) n. a device which during hours of sunlight indicates the time by a shadow cast by a stationary arm (gnomon) on a dial marked in hours. The shadow is cast at different points of the dial because of changes in the position of the earth in relation to the sun

sun disk (archaeol.) a winged disk, symbol of Ra and other ancient Middle Eastern sun gods

sun dog a parhelion ‖ a small halo on the parhelic circle

sun·down (sʌndaun) n. the part of day when the sun is setting

sun·dries (sʌndriːz) pl. n. miscellaneous items, esp. items individually of small importance

sun·dry (sʌndriː) adj. various ‖ miscellaneous, sundry items [O.E. syndrig, separate]

sun·fast (sʌnfæst, sʌnfɑːst) adj. not fading when exposed to sunlight

sun·fish (sʌnfiʃ) pl. **sun·fish, sun·fish·es** n. any of several related forms of saltwater fishes of genus Ranzania ‖ any of several American freshwater fishes of fam. Centrarchidae, usually brilliantly colored

sun·flow·er (sʌnflauər) n. a member of Helianthus, fam. Compositae, a genus of tall-growing plants, esp. H. annuus, with large, often very large, yellow-rayed flowers which turn to face the sun. They are cultivated esp. for the oil extracted from the seeds

Sung (suŋ) a Chinese dynasty (960-1279) under whose rule Chinese culture was in one of its most creative periods

sung past part. of SING

Sun·ga·ri (suŋgɑrɪ) the chief river (800 miles long) of Manchuria, China, rising near the North Korean border and flowing north, by way of a large lake (Sungari Reservoir) below Yungki, the head of navigation, to the Amur. It is frozen Nov.-Apr.

sun·glass·es (sʌnglæsiz, sʌnglɑːsiz) pl. n. spectacles with lenses which are tinted to protect the eyes from glare

sun·god (sʌngɒd) n. a god, e.g. Mithras, identified with the sun

Su-9 *FISHPOT

Su-19 *FENCER

sunk past and alt. past part. of SINK

sunk·en (sʌŋkən) alt. past part. of SINK ‖ adj. below the surrounding level, a sunken garden ‖ lying at the bottom of an ocean, river etc., a

sunken ship ‖ appearing as if hollow, sunken cheeks

sun·lamp (sʌnlæmp) n. an electric lamp which produces ultraviolet radiation used as a substitute for sunlight for therapeutic purposes, or for acquiring a suntan at home

sun lamp a large lamp reflecting light by a parabolic mirror, used on film sets

sun·light (sʌnlaɪt) n. the light emanating from the sun

sun·lit (sʌnlit) adj. shining in the light of the sun

sunn (sʌn) n. sunn hemp [Urdu, Hindi, san]

Sun·na, Sun·nah (sunə) n. the official tradition of the sayings and deeds of Mohammed held in reverence by most Moslems as supplementary to the Koran [Arab.= way, manner of life]

sunn hemp Crotalaria iuncea, fam. Papilionaceae, a plant with yellow flowers, grown in the East Indies ‖ the hemplike fiber of this plant, lighter and stronger than jute, and used for ropes, bags etc.

Sun·ni (suniː) n. a Sunnite [Arab. sunnī, lawful]

sun·ni·ly (sʌnili) adv. in a sunny manner

sun·ni·ness (sʌniːnis) n. the state or quality of being sunny

Sun·nite (sunait) n. one of the great majority of Moslems who accept the full Sunna

sun·ny (sʌniː) comp. **sun·ni·er** superl. **sun·ni·est** adj. made bright or warm by the sun ‖ cheerful, a sunny disposition

sun parlor, Br. **sun parlour** a room or large porch having glass walls to keep the wind out and let the sunshine in

sun porch a sun parlor

sun-pumped laser (sʌnpʌmpt) crystal laser utilizing solar energy concentrated by a parabolic mirror for pumping into a laser

sun·rise (sʌnraiz) n. the appearance of the sun above the horizon in the morning ‖ the time when this happens

sun·room (sʌnruːm, sʌnrum) n. a sun parlor

sun·set (sʌnset) n. the disappearance of the sun below the horizon at the end of the day ‖ the time when this happens ‖ the visually impressive effects of light, clouds etc. which accompany the disappearance of the sun

sunset laws legislation providing for lifetime limitation on new government agencies, established to curb growth of a bureaucratic establishment

sun·shade (sʌnʃeid) n. a parasol ‖ an awning

sun·shine (sʌnʃain) n. the light received directly from the sun ‖ the shining of the sun ‖ cheerfulness ‖ a cause of cheerfulness **sun·shin·y** adj.
—The three main components of sunshine are: visible radiation or light, ultraviolet radiation, which is a germicidal agent and producer of vitamin D, and infrared radiation, which is a heat-producing element forming half of all solar radiation reaching the earth's surface

sun·spot (sʌnspɒt) n. a dark area on the sun consisting of a gray region surrounding a darker central one. Sunspots occur singly and in groups (often pairs), are transient, appear to move steadily, vary widely in size, and are associated with strong magnetic fields (*SUNSPOT CYCLE)

sunspot cycle the roughly periodic variation in the number of sunspots, reaching a maximum, on an average, every 11 years, and accompanied by a reversal of magnetic polarity for the spots in the northern and southern hemispheres, which has not yet been satisfactorily explained. Sunspots are only one form of solar activity (*SOLAR FLARE, *SOLAR PROMINENCE)

sun·stone (sʌnstoun) n. aventurine feldspar

sun·stroke (sʌnstrouk) n. heatstroke brought about by excessive exposure to the heat of the sun

sun·tan (sʌntæn) 1. n. a tan color of the skin acquired by exposure to the sun or to a sunlamp 2. v.i. pres. part. **sun·tan·ning** past and past part. **sun·tanned** to acquire such a tan

sun·up (sʌnʌp) n. sunrise

Sun Yat-sen (sunjɑːtsén) (1866-1925), Chinese revolutionary. He united all the Chinese revolutionary parties under the Kuomintang (1911) and was appointed provisional president of the republic (1911-12) after the fall of the Manchus

sup (sʌp) 1. v.t. pres. part. **sup·ping** past and past part. **supped** (old-fash.) to drink in small mouthfuls 2. n. (old-fash.) a small mouthful of liquid [O.E. sūpan]

sup pres. part. **sup·ping** past and past part. **sup-**

ped *v.i.* to have supper [O.F. *soper, super, souper*]

su·per (súːpər) 1. *n.* (*theater*) a supernumerary actor ‖ (*pop.* and *commerce*) a product of extra quality, size etc. ‖ (*bookbinding*) mull ‖ (*pop.*) a superintendent ‖ a removable upper story of a beehive, where the bees store honey 2. *v.t.* (*bookbinding*) to reinforce (books) with mull 3. *adj.* (*pop.*) of high quality [L. *super*, above]

super- (súːpər) *prefix* over, above (as in 'superstructure') ‖ higher in rank or position (as in 'supervisor') ‖ greater in quality, amount or degree (as in 'superabundance') ‖ surpassing all or most others of its kind (as in 'superbomber') ‖ extra, additional (as in 'supertax') ‖ (*biol.*) constituting a category more inclusive than is usual (as in 'superfamily') ‖ (*chem.*) having an unusually large amount of a specified ingredient (as in 'superphosphate') [fr. L. *super* adv. and prep., above, on top of, beyond etc.]

su·per·a·ble (súːpərəbˈl) *adj.* surmountable, conquerable [fr. L. *superabilis*]

su·per·a·bound (suːpərəbáund) *v.i.* to be very or too abundant [fr. L.L. *superabundare*]

su·per·a·bun·dance (suːpərəbʌ́ndəns) *n.* the quality or state of being superabundant ‖ an excess [fr. L.L. *superabundantia*]

su·per·a·bun·dant (suːpərəbʌ́ndənt) *adj.* abounding in great or too great quantity [fr. L.L. *superabundans* (*superabundantis*), to superabound]

su·per·ac·ti·nide series (suːpəræktənaid) *n.* hypothetical heavy elements 122 to 153

su·per·add (suːpərǽd) *v.t.* to add (something) to something that has already been added to [fr. L. *superaddere*]

su·per·al·loy (súːpərælɔi) *n.* a metal alloy with the capacity to resist high stresses, temperatures, etc.

su·per·an·nu·ate (suːpərǽnjuːeit) *v. pres. part.* **su·per·an·nu·at·ing** *past* and *past part.* **su·per·an·nu·at·ed** *v.t.* to cause to retire on pension, esp. because of old age ‖ *v.i.* to become retired, esp. because of old age [back-formation fr. SUPERANNUATED]

su·per·an·nu·at·ed (suːpərǽnjuːeitid) *adj.* out-of-date ‖ disqualified from work, usually on a pension, esp. because of old age [fr. Mod. L. *superannuatus*]

su·per·an·nu·a·tion (suːpərænjuːéiʃən) *n.* a superannuating or being superannuated ‖ a pension received by a superannuated person [fr. SUPERANNUATE or SUPERANNUATED]

su·perb (supə́ːrb) *adj.* of the highest quality ‖ magnificent to behold ‖ majestic in size, proportions etc. [fr. L. *superbus*, proud]

Super Bowl annual championship game of winners of American and National Football Leagues; played in January since 1967

su·per·cal·en·der (suːpərkǽləndər) 1. *n.* a calender consisting of highly polished rollers which impart a smooth, glazed finish to paper etc. 2. *v.t.* to process with a supercalender

su·per·car·go (súːpərkɑrgou) *pl.* **su·per·cargos, su·per·cargoes** *n.* an officer in a merchant ship in charge of cargo and all commercial affairs [alt. of earlier *supracargo* fr. Span. *sobrecargo*]

su·per·charge (súːpərtʃɑrdʒ) *pres. part.* **su·per·charg·ing** *past* and *past part.* **su·per·charged** *v.t.* to force air and/or fuel under pressure into (an internal-combustion engine) to increase its power **súːpər·charg·er** *n.* a mechanism (e.g. a pump or compressor) used to supply an internal-combustion engine with a greater volume of air than is possible at ambient pressures. It is used on most aircraft engines, for high-performance automotive engines etc.

su·per·cil·i·ary (suːpərsíliːeriː) *adj.* of, relating to, or in the region of the eyebrow [fr. Mod. L. *superciliaris* fr. *supercilium*, eyebrow]

su·per·cil·i·ous (suːpərsíliːəs) *adj.* showing patronizing disdain [fr. L. *superciliosus* fr. *supercilium*, eyebrow]

su·per·class (súːpərklæs, súːpərklɑs) *n.* (*taxonomy*) a classification ranking between a phylum and a class

su·per·clus·ter (súːpərklʌstər) *n.* (*astron.*) a large group of galaxies

su·per·con·duc·tiv·i·ty (suːpərkɒndʌktíviːti:) *n.* (*phys.*) the property in certain metals (lead, tin, vanadium etc.) and alloys of losing virtually all electrical resistance when cooled below a transition temperature near absolute zero. Practical use of this phenomenon is made esp. in

magnetic-computer memory stores **su·per·con·duc·tor** *n.*

supercontinent *PROTOCONTINENT

su·per·cool (súːpərkuːl) *v.t.* (*chem.*) to bring to a temperature below the normal transition point for a change of state without this change occurring

supercountry *SUPERPOWER

su·per·cur·rent (súːpərkʌrənt) *n.* (*electr.*) electrical current running without resistance, as through a metal at or near absolute zero

su·per·dense (súːpərdens) *adj.* (*astron.*) extremely compacted, e.g., a quasar, a black hole

su·per·e·go (súːpəriːgou, súːpəregou) *n.* (*psychoanal.*) the idealized image that a person builds up of himself in response to authority and social pressures. Fundamentally unconscious, it rises to consciousness on critical occasions and serves as a kind of policeman of the personality

su·per·e·ro·ga·tion (suːpərerəgéiʃən) *n.* the act or process of doing more than is required by duty or obligation ‖ an instance of this **works of supererogation** (*Roman Catholicism*) the good deeds done, e.g. by saints, over and above those required by God [fr. L.L. *supererogatio* (*supererogationis*)]

su·per·e·rog·a·to·ry (suːpərerɒ́gətɔri:, suːpərerɒ́gətouri) *adj.* of, relating to, or characterized by supererogation ‖ performed to a degree beyond what is required or promised ‖ (*loosely*) superfluous [fr. M.L. *supererogatorius*]

su·per·fam·i·ly (súːpərfæməli:, súːpərfæmli:) *n.* (*taxonomy*) a classification ranking above a family and regarded as being equivalent to a suborder

su·per·fec·ta (súːpərfektə) *n.* (*wagering*) a wager in which the first four finishers in a race must be selected in proper order *Cf* PERFECTA, TRIFECTA

su·per·fec·un·da·tion (suːpərfekəndéiʃən, suːpərfiːkəndéiʃən) *n.* the successive fertilization of two or more ova during the same ovulation period

su·per·fe·ta·tion, Br. also **su·per·foe·ta·tion** (suːpərfitéiʃən) *n.* (*biol.*) the successive fertilization of two or more ova of different ovulations in the same uterus, occurring normally in some viviparous fishes ‖ (*bot.*) the fertilization of an ovule by more than one type of pollen [Mod. L. *superfetatio*]

su·per·fi·cial (suːpərfíʃəl) *adj.* of or relating to a surface ‖ not penetrating further than the surface, *superficial cuts* ‖ apparent rather than real, *a superficial resemblance* ‖ without depth of mind, feeling or imagination ‖ (of a unit of measure) square **su·per·fi·ci·al·i·ty** (suːpərfiʃiː-plíti:) *n.* **su·per·fi·cial·ly** *adv.* [fr. L. *superficialis*]

su·per·fi·cies (suːpərfíʃiːz, suːpərfíʃiːiz) *pl.* **su·per·fi·cies** *n.* a surface [L. fr. *super*, above+*facies*, the face]

su·per·fine (suːpərfáin) *adj.* extremely fine

su·per·flu·i·ty (suːpərflúːiti:) *pl.* **su·per·flu·i·ties** *n.* the quality or state of being superfluous ‖ a copious oversupply ‖ (*esp. pl.*) something superfluous [O.F. *superfluite*]

su·per·flu·ous (supə́ːrfluːəs) *adj.* being more than is needed, *superfluous words* ‖ not needed, unnecessary, *a superfluous remark* [fr. L. *superfluus*]

superfoetation *SUPERFETATION

su·per·grade (súːpərgreid) *n.* U.S. Government employment status higher than the highest basic status

su·per·heat 1. (suːpərhíːt) *v.t.* (*chem.*) to bring to a temperature above the normal transition point for a change of state without this change occurring, esp. to heat above boiling point without boiling taking place ‖ to heat (esp. a vapor) not in contact with its liquid to keep it free from suspended liquid droplets, *superheated steam* 2. (suːpərhíːt) *n.* the amount of extra heat imparted to a vapor in superheating **su·per·heat·er** *n.* an apparatus for superheating steam

su·per·heav·y (súːpərhevi:) *adj.* (*phys.*) of elements with a mass greater than known elements, sometimes prefixed by eka-, e.g., eka-hafnium

su·per·het·er·o·dyne (suːpərhétərədain) 1. *adj.* (*radio*) of a widely employed system of radio reception in which the heterodyne principle is used to produce a modulated beat signal of intermediate frequency. Substitution of the intermediate carrier signal for a radio frequency carrier signal permits more efficient amplifica-

tion and precise tuning of the amplifier circuit to the locally produced beat frequency, the system resulting in a sensitive and selective radio receiver 2. *n.* (*radio*) such a receiver [fr. SUPERSONIC+HETERODYNE]

su·per·high·way (suːpərháiwei) *n.* an expressway, freeway, turnpike or other main road for high-speed driving

su·per·hu·man (suːpərhjúːmən) *adj.* beyond normal human capacity or power, *superhuman strength* ‖ supernatural, *superhuman intervention* [fr. M.L. *superhumanus*]

su·per·im·pose (suːpərimpóuz) *pres. part.* **su·per·im·pos·ing** *past* and *past part.* **su·per·im·posed** *v.t.* to lay (one thing) on or upon another, *to superimpose speech on recorded music* **su·per·im·po·si·tion** (suːpərimpəzíʃən) *n.* a superimposing or being superimposed

su·per·in·cum·bent (suːpərinkʌ́mbənt) *adj.* lying on something else ‖ (of pressure) exerted from above [fr. L. *superincumbens* (*superincumbentis*) fr. *superincumbere*, to lie on]

su·per·in·tend (suːpərinténd) *v.t.* to direct the execution of (e.g. a job of work) ‖ to have charge of (a group of people) [fr. eccles. L. *superintendere*]

su·per·in·tend·ence (suːpərinténdəns) *n.* the act or function of superintending **su·per·in·ténd·en·cy** *n.* the office, rank or jurisdiction of a superintendent ‖ superintendence [fr. M.L. *superintendentia*]

su·per·in·tend·ent (suːpərinténdənt) *n.* a person who superintends ‖ the head of a police department ‖ the custodian of a building ‖ (*Br.*) a police officer ranking just above an inspector [eccles. L. *superintendens* (*superintendentis*) fr. *superintendere*]

su·pe·ri·or (supíəriːər) 1. *adj.* high or higher in position, rank, status etc. ‖ better in quality, worth, ability etc. ‖ greater in value, amount, power etc. ‖ showing that one thinks oneself better than others, *a superior smile* ‖ (*astron.*) farther from the sun than the earth, *a superior planet* ‖ (*bot.*) growing or arising from another part or organ ‖ (*anat.*) situated above a like part or organ, or above the normal position ‖ (*printing*, of a character) placed above the line of type, e.g. '3' in 'a³' 2. *n.* a person who is superior in rank or authority ‖ a person who controls a religious community ‖ (*printing*) a superior character **su·pe·ri·or·i·ty** (supiəriːɔ́riti:, supiəriːɒ́riti:) *n.* [O.F.]

superiority complex a neurotic condition resulting from subconscious belief in one's superiority to others

Superior, Lake the most northwesterly of the Great Lakes of North America, and one of the world's largest sheets of fresh water (area 31,820 sq. miles, maximum depth 1,180 ft). It is bounded by the U.S.A. and Canada and is joined to Lakes Michigan and Huron by the St Mary River. Part of the St Lawrence Seaway system, it carries a large volume of grain and iron ore shipments. Main ports: Port Arthur and Thunder Bay, Ontario, and Duluth, Minnesota

su·per·jet (súːpərdʒet) *n.* a supersonic jet aircraft

su·per·la·tive (supə́ːrlətiv) 1. *adj.* of the highest quality, kind, degree etc. ‖ excessive ‖ (*gram.*) expressing the highest degree of comparison of the quality indicated by the adjective or adverb (usually shown in English by the addition of '-est' or by the use of 'most' with the positive form) 2. *n.* the highest degree of something ‖ someone or something superlative ‖ (*gram.*) the superlative degree of comparison ‖ (*gram.*) a word or form in this degree (esp. *pl.*) ‖ highly exaggerated language [O.F. *superlatif*]

su·per·lu·na·ry (suːpərlúːnəri:) *adj.* situated above the moon [fr. SUPER-+ L. *luna*, moon]

su·per·man (súːpərmæn) *pl.* **su·per·men** (súːpərmen) *n.* an idealized man, regarded by Nietzsche as the next stage in the evolution of man: a being with greatly superior physical and mental qualities ‖ (*loosely*) a person who possesses greatly developed physical or mental qualities

su·per·mar·ket (súːpərmɑrkit) *n.* a large self-service food and household goods store, the articles being arranged in open-shelf display

su·per·mi·ni·com·put·er (súːpərminiːkʌmpjúːtər) *n.* (*computer*) processing unit with a 32-bit capacity

su·per·mol·e·cule (súːpərmɒləkjuːl) *n.* (*phys.*) a molecule composed of more than one molecule, e.g., anomalous water, a polymer, a protein —

CONCISE PRONUNCIATION KEY: **(a)** æ, c*a*t; ɑ, c*a*r; ɔ f*aw*n; ei, sn*a*ke. **(e)** e, h*e*n; iː, sh*ee*p; iə, d*ee*r; ɛə, b*ea*r. **(i)** i, f*i*sh; ai, t*i*ger; əː, b*i*rd. **(o)** o, *o*x; au, c*ow*; ou, g*oa*t; u, p*oo*r; ɔi, r*oy*al. **(u)** ʌ, d*u*ck; u, b*u*ll; uː, g*oo*se; ə, b*a*cillus; juː, c*u*be. x, lo*ch*; θ, *th*ink; ð, b*o*ther; z, *Z*en; ʒ, cor*s*age; dʒ, sava*ge*; ŋ, ora*ng*utang; j, *y*ak; ʃ, *f*ish; tʃ, *f*etch; 'l, ra*bble*; 'n, re*dden*. Complete pronunciation key appears inside front cover.

supermolecular *adj.* —**supramolecular** *adj.*

su·per·mul·ti·plet (súːpərmʌltəplet) *n.* (*nuclear phys.*) a group consisting of smaller groups of nuclear particles

su·per·nal (supéːrn'l) *adj.* (*rhet.*) pertaining to a celestial realm [O.F.]

su·per·na·tant (suːpərnéit'nt) *adj.* floating on the surface (e.g. of a clear liquid above a precipitate) [fr. L. *supernatans* (*supernatantis*) fr. *supernatare*, to float]

su·per·nat·u·ral (suːpərnætʃərəl) 1. *adj.* not able to be explained in terms of the known laws which govern the material universe, *a supernatural phenomenon* 2. *n.* (with 'the') that realm of experience which is inexplicable in terms of the known laws of nature ‖ a supernatural ‖ being, force etc. **su·per·nat·u·ral·ism** *n.* the quality or state of being supernatural belief in the supernatural **su·per·nat·u·ral·ist** *n.* **su·per·nat·u·ral·is·tic** *adj.* **su·per·nat·u·ral·ize** *v.t. pres. part.* **su·per·nat·u·ral·iz·ing** *past* and *past part.* **su·per·nat·u·ral·ized** to make supernatural ‖ to treat as supernatural [fr. M.L. *supernaturalis*]

su·per·no·va (suːpərnóuvə) *n.* (*astron.*) a nova with the brightness of many millions of suns, occurring very rarely ‖ a star that has exhausted its nuclear fuel, collapsed into a superdense state, and exploded with a final burst of enormous energy, releasing in one second an energy equivalent to that released by the sun in 60 years [Mod. L. fr. *super-*, above+NOVA]

su·per·nuke (súːpərnuːk) *n.* (*slang*) a technical adviser in a nuclear energy plant

su·per·nu·mer·a·ry (suːpərnúːmərəriː, suːpərnjúːmərəri) 1. *adj.* above the prescribed number, extra ‖ superfluous 2. *pl.* **su·per·nu·mer·ar·ies** *n.* a supernumerary person or thing ‖ a person employed for use as need directs rather than for regular service ‖ (*theater*) an actor having a small part, e.g. in a crowd scene [fr. L.L. *supernumerarius*]

su·per·or·der (suːpərórdər) *n.* (*taxonomy*) a classification ranking between an order and a class or subclass

su·per·o·vu·late (súːpəróvjuːleit) *v.* to produce more eggs at one time than is normal —**super·ovulation** *n.*

su·per·phos·phate (suːpərfósfeit) *n.* any of various commercial phosphate fertilizers obtained by acidulating ground, insoluble phosphate rock

su·per·plas·tic (súːpərplæstik) *adj.* of the ability to change form easily under heat or other treatment —**superplasticity** *n.*

su·per·pose (suːpərpóuz) *pres. part.* **su·per·pos·ing** *past* and *past part.* **su·per·posed** *v.t.* to place over, or upon, something else ‖ (*geom.*) to place (a figure) over another so that like parts of each coincide [F. *superposer*]

su·per·po·si·tion (suːpərpəzíʃən) *n.* a superposing or being superposed (*PRINCIPLE OF SUPERPOSITION*) [F.]

su·per·po·tent (súːpərpóutənt) *adj.* having excessive power

su·per·pow·er (súːpərpauər) *n.* a nation which, by reason of its economic, political and military strength, influences the polices of less powerful nations

Super Sabre (*mil.*) a supersonic, single-engine, turbojet, tactical fighter/bomber (F-100), capable of employing nuclear and nonnuclear weapons

sup·er·sat·u·rate (suːpərsætʃəreit) *pres. part.* **su·per·sat·u·rat·ing** *past* and *past part.* **su·per·sat·u·rat·ed** *v.t.* (*chem.*) to produce a solution of (something) or to produce (a solution) having a higher concentration of solute than at saturation, e.g. by the heating and slow undisturbed cooling or very rapid cooling of a saturated solution **sup·er·sat·u·ra·tion** *n.*

su·per·scribe (súːpərskraib, suːpərskráib) *pres. part.* **su·per·scrib·ing** *past* and *past part.* **su·per·scribed** *v.t.* to write (something) upon, put (an inscription) on or over something ‖ to write an inscription on the top or surface or outside of (something) [fr. L.L. *superscribere*]

su·per·script (súːpərskript) *adj.* of, relating to, or being a character printed or written directly above, or above and to the side of another character, e.g. the acute accent on the final 'a' of 'Paraná' or the '3' in 'p³' (cf. SUBSCRIPT) 2. *n.* a superscript character [fr. L. *superscriptus*]

su·per·scrip·tion (suːpərskrípʃən) *n.* the act of superscribing ‖ that which is superscribed ‖

(*pharm.*) the Latin word 'recipe' or its symbol ℞ on a prescription [fr. L.L. *superscriptio* (*superscriptionis*)]

su·per·sede (suːpərsíːd) *pres. part.* **su·per·sed·ing** *past* and *past part.* **su·per·sed·ed** *v.t.* to outmode and take the place of, *buses superseded streetcars* ‖ to take the position, office etc. of, *to supersede someone as treasurer* ‖ to replace, to *supersede a written test by an oral* **su·per·se·dure** (suːpərsíːdʒər) *n.* supersession, esp. the superseding of an old or inferior queen bee by a better one [O.F. *superseder*]

su·per·sen·si·ble (suːpərsénsəb'l) *adj.* beyond the grasp of the senses **su·per·sen·si·bly** *adv.*

su·per·sen·so·ry (suːpərsénsəri) *adj.* supersensible

su·per·sen·su·al (suːpərsénʃuːəl) *adj.* supersensible

su·per·ses·sion (suːpərséʃən) *n.* a superseding or being superseded [fr. M. L. *supersessio* (*supersessionis*)]

super set (*weight lifting*) exercises for a set of muscles, followed by exercises for an opposing set of muscles

super ship a large cargo ship capable of sailing around South America

su·per·son·ic (suːpərsónik) *adj.* of waves of greater frequency than those to which the human ear responds (above about 20,000 cycles per second, esp. in electronics) ‖ of motion faster than the speed of sound waves in air (above about 738 m.p.h.) ‖ moving at this speed **su·per·són·ics** *n.* the science dealing with supersonic phenomena (*SONIC, *SUBSONIC)

su·per·star (súːpərstɑr) *n.* 1. (*astron.*) a celestial body, emitting great energy, e.g., quasar 2. a widely known personality of superior talent in the entertainment field or, by extension, in another field —**superstardom** *n.*

su·per·sta·tion (súːpərsteiʃən) *n.* a television station with national satellite connections

su·per·sti·tion (suːpərstíʃən) *n.* a belief or beliefs justified neither by reason nor evidence nor by any religious canon [O.F.]

su·per·sti·tious (suːpərstíʃəs) *adj.* of or relating to superstition ‖ manifesting superstition [O.F. *superstitieux*]

su·per·stra·tum (súːpərstreitəm, súːpərstrætəm, súːpərstrɑːtəm) *pl.* **su·per·stra·ta** (súːpərstreitə, súːpərstrætə, súːpərstrɑːtə), **su·per·stra·tums** *n.* a stratum overlying another

su·per·struc·ture (súːpərstrʌktʃər) *n.* a structure built upon another structure ‖ (*archit.*) the entire building above the main supporting level ‖ (*naut.*) the structure of a ship above the main deck

su·per·tax (súːpərtæks) *n.* (*Br. hist.*) tax at above the normal rate, on income over a certain level, replaced by surtax

su·per·ton·ic (suːpərtónik) *n.* (*mus.*) the second degree of the major or minor scale, next above the tonic

su·per·vene (suːpərvíːn) *pres. part.* **su·per·ven·ing** *past* and *past part.* **su·per·vened** *v.i.* to happen unexpectedly and in a way which has the effect of preventing or radically changing some planned course of action ‖ to follow closely after some event or set of circumstances [fr. L. *supervenire*]

su·per·ve·ni·ent (suːpərvíːnjənt) *adj.* supervening as something added, *supervenient grace* [fr. L. *superveniens* (*supervenientis*) fr. *supervenire*, to supervene]

su·per·ven·tion (suːpərvénʃən) *n.* the act or process of supervening ‖ a supervening event [fr. L.L. *superventio* (*superventionis*)]

Su·per·vielle (syparvjel), Jules (1884–1960), French poet. He was born in Montevideo and lived in Uruguay for many years. His most famous poems are 'Gravitations' (1925), 'Naissances' (1951) and 'le Corps tragique' (1959). He also wrote short stories and plays

su·per·vise (súːpərvaiz) *pres. part.* **su·per·vis·ing** *past* and *past part.* **su·per·vised** *v.t.* to superintend (work or the person doing it) [fr. M.L. *supervidere* (*supervisus*)]

su·per·vi·sion (suːpərvíʒən) *n.* a supervising or being supervised [fr. M.L. *supervisio* (*supervisionis*)]

su·per·vi·sor (súːpərvaizər) *n.* a person who supervises ‖ (*education*) a person in some school systems who supervises teachers in planning, method etc. or in the teaching of special courses

su·per·vi·so·ry *adj.* of or relating to supervision, supervisory duties [M.L.]

su·pi·nate (súːpineit) *pres. part.* **su·pi·nat·ing** *past* and *past part.* **su·pi·nat·ed** *v.t.* to turn (a

hand or hand and arm) so that the palm is upward (cf. PRONATE) [fr. L. *supinare* (*supinatus*), to lay backward]

su·pi·na·tion (suːpinéiʃən) *n.* a supinating or being supinated ‖ the position resulting from this [fr. L. *supinatio* (*supinationis*)]

su·pi·na·tor (súːpineitər) *n.* a muscle in the forearm which causes supination [Mod. L. fr. *supinare*, supinate]

su·pine (suːpáin) 1. *adj.* lying flat on the back (opp. PRONE) ‖ (of a hand) with the palm upward or away from the body ‖ listless through laziness or indifference or both 2. *n.* (*Latin gram.*) a verbal noun formed from the past participle and having only two forms, accusative and ablative [fr. L. *supinus*]

sup·per (sʌ́pər) *n.* a light meal taken in the evening ‖ the evening meal eaten by those who have dinner at midday [O.F. *soper, super, souper*]

sup·plant (səplænt, səplʌnt) *v.t.* to supersede (another) esp. by force, cunning etc. ‖ to take the place of, *why should tea supplant coffee as a national drink?* [O. F. *supplanter*]

sup·ple (sʌ́p'l) 1. *adj.* easily bent, *a supple bow of yew* ‖ (of the body, limbs etc.) able to bend without effort, *supple fingers* ‖ (of a person or his mind) readily changing to meet new situations 2. *pres. part.* **sup·pling** *past* and *past part.* **sup·pled** *v.t.* to make supple [O.F. fr. L. *supplex*, bending under]

sup·ple·ly (sʌ́p'liː) *adv.* in a supple manner

sup·ple·ment 1. (sʌ́pləmənt) *n.* something added ‖ a section added to a book etc., or a separate volume, giving additional information etc. ‖ a separate section issued with a newspaper containing feature articles etc. ‖ (*math.*) the amount to be added to a given angle or arc to make 180° or a semicircle 2. *v.t.* to add to, *to supplement one's pay* ‖ to supply a deficiency in **sup·ple·men·tal** (sʌpləmént'l), **sup·ple·men·ta·ry** *adjs.* [fr. L. *supplementum*]

supplementary angles two angles whose sum is 180°

sup·ple·men·ta·tion (sʌpləmentéiʃən) *n.* the act or process of supplementing ‖ an instance of supplementing

sup·pli·ant (sʌ́pliːənt) 1. *adj.* (*rhet.*) asking humbly ‖ (*rhet.*) expressing supplication, *a suppliant prayer* 2. *n.* (*rhet.*) a person who supplicates [F.]

sup·pli·cant (sʌ́plikənt) 1. *n.* a suppliant 2. *adj.* supplicating [fr. L. *supplicans* fr. *supplicare*, to supplicate]

sup·pli·cate (sʌ́plikeit) *pres. part.* **sup·pli·cat·ing** *past* and *past part.* **sup·pli·cat·ed** *v.t.* to ask for in humble petition ‖ to entreat (God, a person) for something ‖ *v.i.* to make humble entreaty [fr. L. *supplicare* (*supplicatus*)]

sup·pli·ca·tion (sʌplikéiʃən) *n.* the act or process of supplicating ‖ a humble request, prayer etc. [O.F.]

sup·pli·ca·to·ry (sʌ́plikətɔri, sʌ́plikətɔuri) *adj.* supplicating [fr. M.L. *supplicatorius*]

sup·pli·er (səpláiər) *n.* someone who, or something which, supplies

sup·ply (səplái) 1. *v. pres. part.* **sup·ply·ing** *past* and *past part.* **sup·plied** *v.t.* to give (something needed or wanted), *to supply necessary tools* ‖ to fill the needs of, *to supply a town with electricity* ‖ to satisfy (a need), *to supply proof* ‖ to furnish (something that was missing), *to supply a deficiency* ‖ to serve as a substitute for (a clergyman), or occupy (his church or pulpit) for him ‖ *v.i.* to act as substitute for a clergyman 2. *pl.* **sup·plies** *n.* the act of supplying ‖ (often *pl.*) stock or stores available for use ‖ (*pl.*) stores for the armed forces ‖ (*pl.*) money granted for the expenses of a government ‖ (*econ.*) the amount or quantity of goods available on the market for purchase ‖ a clergyman who temporarily fills another clergyman's place [fr. O.F. *sopleer, soupleer*]

sup·ply (sʌ́pli) *adv.* supplely

sup·ply-side (sʌpláisaid) *n.* (*economics*) approach to solution of economic problems with emphasis on increasing (or decreasing) the total supply of products, e.g., to reduce (or increase) prices

sup·ply teacher (səplái) (*Br.*) a teacher unassigned to a particular school but available to fill a temporary vacancy

sup·port (səpórt) 1. *v.t.* to carry the weight of ‖ to prevent from falling, sinking etc., *to support a roof by struts* ‖ to be actively in favor of, *to support a cause* ‖ to assist or strengthen morally, *she supported him in his struggle* ‖ to be or provide an argument in favor of or additional evidence for, *this supports his theory* ‖ to bear, endure, *to support extremes of climate* ‖ to bear the cost of providing for, *to support a family* ‖ to give assistance to (troops already engaged) ‖ to act with (a principal actor or actors) in a secondary role ‖ to second (a resolution in committee) ‖ (*heraldry*, only in passive) to flank as supporter **2.** *n.* a supporting or being supported ‖ someone who or something which supports ‖ a means of sustenance **sup·pórt·a·ble** *adj.* **sup·pórt·er** *n.* a person who supports a cause, team etc. ‖ a partisan ‖ (*heraldry*) one of a pair of figures standing beside or supporting the shield **sup·port·ive** (səpórtiv, səpóurtiv) *adj.* providing support [fr. O.F. or F. *supporter*]

support hose stockings with elastic threads

support level (*securities*) a price level at which customers customarily enter the market to buy

sup·pos·a·ble (səpóuzəb'l) *adj.* able to be supposed

sup·pose (səpóuz) *pres. part.* **sup·pos·ing** *past* and *past part.* **sup·posed** *v.t.* to think likely, *I suppose he may come today* ‖ to presume, believe without firm cause, *I supposed him to be away from home* ‖ to admit as a possibility or probability, *I suppose you know what to do* ‖ (used in the imperative) to imagine (something) so as to consider an effect, *suppose you miss your train*, or as the basis, or illustration, of an argument, *suppose this grain of sand to be the universe* ‖ (of a theory etc.) to postulate, presuppose ‖ (used in passive) to expect, require, as being desired, *I'm supposed to tell you about it* **sup·posed** (səpóuzd, səpóuzid) *adj.* thought, but not known, to be true, *his supposed death by drowning* ‖ imagined, *supposed profits* **sup·pos·ed·ly** (səpóuzidli:) *adv.* **sup·pos·ing** *conj.* on the supposition that, in the event that [O.F. *supposer*]

sup·po·si·tion (sʌpəzíʃən) *n.* the act of supposing ‖ that which is supposed ‖ **sup·po·si·tion·al** *adj.* [O.F.]

sup·pos·i·to·ry (səpózitɔri:, səpózitouri:) *pl.* **sup·pos·i·to·ries** *n.* a cylinder, cone or oval made of cacao butter etc. which is inserted into the rectum or vagina, where it dissolves and releases the medicament it contains [fr. L.L. *suppositorium*]

sup·press (səprés) *v.t.* to subdue, put down by force, *to suppress a revolt* ‖ to withhold (facts etc.) ‖ to hold back, *to suppress laughter* ‖ to prevent the publication or revelation of ‖ to check the flow of, stop ‖ to dismiss from the conscious mind [fr. L. *supprimere* (*suppressus*)]

sup·pres·sion (səpréʃən) *n.* a suppressing or being suppressed ‖ the conscious dismissing of an unacceptable idea, desire, painful memory etc. from the mind (cf. REPRESSION) [fr. L. *suppressio* (*suppressionis*)]

sup·pu·rate (sʌ́pjureit) *pres. part.* **sup·pu·rat·ing** *past* and *past part.* **sup·pu·rat·ed** *v.i.* to discharge pus [fr. L. *suppurare* (*suppuratus*)]

sup·pu·ra·tion (sʌpjuréiʃən) *n.* the formation or discharging of pus

sup·pu·ra·tive (sʌ́pjureitiv) *adj.* characterized by suppuration [fr. Mod. L. *suppurativus*]

su·pra·cel·lu·lar (sú:prəséljuːlə:r) *adj.* having more than a single cell

su·pra·lap·sar·i·an (su:prəlæpséari:ən) **1.** *n.* a believer in the Calvinist doctrine that predestination preceded man's creation and fall (cf. INFRALAPSARIAN) **2.** *adj.* of or relating to this doctrine or to someone holding it **su·pra·lap·sár·i·an·ism** *n.* [fr. Mod. L. *supralapsarius*]

su·pra·lim·i·nal (su:prəlímin'l) *adj.* conscious, rising above the threshold of consciousness (cf. SUBLIMINAL) [fr. L. *supra*, above, over + *limen* (*liminis*), threshold]

su·pra·re·nal (su:prərí:n'l) **1.** *adj.* adrenal **2.** *n.* an adrenal gland [fr. Mod. L. *suprarenalis*]

suprarenal gland an adrenal gland

su·pra·ther·mal ion detector (sú:prəθə:rm'l) a device for recording information about ions on lunar surfaces

su·prem·a·cy (suprémasi:) *n.* the quality or state of being supreme ‖ the position of being superior to all others in something, *naval supremacy*

Supremacy, Act of (*Eng. hist.*) an act of parliament (1559) proclaiming the sovereign supreme head of the Church of England

su·preme (suprí:m) *adj.* being the highest authority ‖ highest in quality ‖ highest in degree [fr. L. *supremus* superl. of *superus*, that is above]

Supreme Being God

Supreme Court the highest judicial body in the

U.S.A., consisting of nine members appointed for life by the President with the Senate's approval ‖ its equivalent in some other countries ‖ the highest judicial body in some states of the U.S.A.

Supreme Court of Judicature the high court system of England and Wales, established by acts of parliament (1873, 1875), which incorporates several former courts. It includes the Court of Appeal and the High Court of Justice, which has divisions of Chancery, King's Bench, probate, divorce and admiralty

supreme sacrifice the sacrifice of one's life, esp. as an act of heroism

Supreme Soviet the highest legislative body of the U.S.S.R., consisting of two elected chambers of equal status, the Soviet of the Union and the Soviet of Nationalities (1,443 members in all). It appoints the presidium of the Supreme Soviet, which acts as the supreme authority between sessions, and the Council of Ministers, the highest executive and administrative body

su·pre·mo (səprí:mou) *n.* (*Br.*) **1.** person in charge **2.** the head of an organization

Suppression of Communism Act in Republic of South Africa, law restricting the speech, writing, or gathering of nonwhites

suq *SOUK

Sur (suər) *TYRE

su·ra (súərə) *n.* any of the sections or chapters in the Koran [Arab. *sūrah*, step]

Su·ra·ba·ya, Soe·ra·ba·ya (suərəbújə) a port (pop. 2,289,000) in N. Java, Indonesia, at the west end of Madura Strait. Industries: mechanical and electrical engineering, chemicals, oil refining, textiles. University

su·rah (súərə) *n.* soft twilled silk or rayon used in clothing [perh. after SURAT in India]

Su·ra·kar·ta, Soe·ra·kar·ta (suərəkúrtə) a commercial center (pop. 368,000) in central S. Java, Indonesia. Industries: textiles, food processing, machinery

su·ral (súərəl) *adj.* (*anat.*) of or relating to the calf of the leg [fr. Mod. L. *suralis* fr. *sura*, calf of the leg]

Su·rat (sú:rət, suræt) a port (pop. 471,656) in Gujarat, India, on the Tapti near its mouth: silk and cotton textiles, brocades, carpets, inlaid work

sur·charge (sə́:rtʃɑrdʒ) **1.** *v.t. pres. part.* **sur·charg·ing** *past* and *past part.* **sur·charged** *v.t.* to overcharge (a person or an amount) ‖ to overprint (a stamp) with a surcharge ‖ to overload ‖ to overfill ‖ (*law*) to make as an additional charge, *to surcharge legal fees involved in collecting an account* **2.** *n.* a charge or tax over and above what is standard ‖ an overprint on a stamp (esp. to change its value), or the stamp bearing this ‖ (*Br.*) a charge made for delivering an unstamped or understamped letter etc. ‖ an additional burden ‖ (*law*) a surcharging ‖ (*law*) a statement showing this [O.F. *surcharger*]

sur·cin·gle (sə́:rsing'l) *n.* a belt passing under a horse's belly to keep its blanket or pack in place [O.F. *surcengle*]

sur·coat (sə́:rkout) *n.* (*hist.*) a loose tunic worn over armor ‖ (*hist.*) a long or short fitted robe worn in the late Middle Ages by men and women [O.F. *surcot, sorcot, sircot*]

surd (sə:rd) **1.** *adj.* (*math.*, of a quantity) irrational ‖ (*phon.*) voiceless **2.** *n.* an irrational number ‖ a voiceless speech sound (opp. SONANT) [fr. L. *surdus*, deaf, trans. Gk *alogos*, without reason]

sure (ʃuər) **1.** *adj.* accepted as the truth, *a sure sign of rain* ‖ accepting something as true, *I am sure it will rain* ‖ that can be relied upon, *a sure friend, a sure winner, a sure profit* ‖ safe, *to make a rope sure* **2.** *adv.* (*pop.*) certainly **for sure** certainly, *we leave tomorrow for sure* **sure enough** just as expected or promised, *we cleaned the spark plugs and sure enough it started* **to be sure** certainly ‖ admittedly ‖ **to make sure** to make certain [O.F. *sure, seure*]

sure·fire (ʃúərfaiər) *adj.* that can be relied on to be successful, do as is expected etc.

sure·foot·ed (ʃúərfútid) *adj.* placing the feet with certainty in difficult terrain

sure·ly (ʃúərli:) *adv.* in a sure manner ‖ without a doubt

sure·ty (ʃúəriti:, ʃúərti:) *pl.* **sure·ties** *n.* the condition of being sure ‖ a person who makes himself a guarantor for another's actions ‖ something pledged as security **to stand surety** to pledge a sum of money for a person's appearance in court or for his payment of a debt [O.F. *surte, seurte*]

surf (sə:rf) **1.** *n.* the foam of waves breaking on the shore ‖ the swell of the sea breaking on the shore **2.** *v.i.* to ride a wave to shore on a surfboard [etym. doubtful]

sur·face (sə́:rfis) **1.** *n.* the two-dimensional boundary of a material body, having zero or constant or variable curvature, *the surface of the earth* ‖ (*geom.*) that which has length and breadth but no depth ‖ the outward aspect of something, *a mere surface of sophistication* ‖ (*aeron.*) an airfoil **on the surface** so far as the eye can judge **2.** *v. pres. part.* **sur·fac·ing** *past* and *past part.* **sur·faced** *v.t.* to smooth the surface of, to polish ‖ to bring (e.g. a submarine) to the surface of the water ‖ *v.i.* to come to the surface of the water ‖ (*mining*) to work at or near the surface **3.** *adj.* of or at the surface ‖ (*mining*) working at or near the surface ‖ superficial [F.]

sur·face-ac·tive (sə́:rfisæktiv) *adj.* of or pertaining to a substance that modifies the behavior of a liquid at its surfaces and interfaces (but not in the interior of the liquid), usually by changing the surface tension or interfacial tension of the liquid

sur·face-ef·fect ship (sə́:rfisifɛkt) an air-cushion vehicle that operates over water; e.g., a Hovercraft *Cf* GROUND-EFFECT MACHINE

surface plate (*mech.*) a steel plate used as a standard of flatness in precision work

surface structure (*linguistics*) in transformational grammar, the sentence structure expressed phonetically *Cf* DEEP STRUCTURE

surface tension a condition of (usually) liquid surfaces that causes liquids to tend to assume shapes of minimum surface and is the result of unbalanced intermolecular forces acting near the surfaces. It may be treated quantitatively as if the surface of a liquid were a thin elastic membrane under tension (*CAPILLARITY)

sur·face-to-air-missile (sə́:rfistu:ɜərmís'l) *n.* (*mil.*) an earth-launched guided missile with an airborne target *acronym* SAM

surface-to-air missile envelope (*mil.*) the air space within the kill capabilities of a surface-to-air missile system

sur·fac·tant (sə:rfǽktənt) *n.* (*chem.*) **1.** a substance that facilitates the spreading of another substance, e.g., a detergent *also* surface-active agent **2.** an oil-water compound for application on skin or hair

surf and turf seafood and beef, e.g., in a restaurant, lobster and steak

surf·board (sə́:rfbɔrd, sə:rfbourd) *n.* a long narrow board used in riding in to shore on the surf

surf·boat (sə́:rfbout) *n.* a boat specially adapted to travel through the surf

sur·feit (sə́:rfit) **1.** *n.* an oversupply, excess, *a surfeit of apples* ‖ overindulgence in eating and drinking ‖ the feeling resulting from this **2.** *v.t.* to oversupply, *to surfeit a market* ‖ to overfeed ‖ to satiate [A.F., O.F. *sorfait*]

surfer's knot (*surfing*) a friction bump at knee or instep characteristic of active surfers

surf roof a removable ceiling panel in a motor vehicle

surge (sə:rdʒ) **1.** *v. pres. part.* **surg·ing** *past* and *past part.* **surged** *v.i.* (of the sea) to heave and swell in great force and agitation ‖ to move through, or as if through, heavy seas, *a surging ship, surging crowds, surging emotions* ‖ (*naut.*, of a rope or chain) to slip around the windlass etc. with a jerk ‖ (*elec.*, of current) to make a sudden short rise followed by a drop ‖ *v.t.* (*naut.*) to slip (a rope or chain) around the windlass etc. **2.** *n.* the heaving of waves ‖ a great billow ‖ a sudden access of interest, enthusiasm, pity etc. ‖ (*naut.*) the tapered part of a windlass etc. on which the rope or chain slips ‖ (*naut.*) the slipping movement of the rope or chain ‖ (*elec.*) a sudden abnormal rise of current followed by a drop [fr. L. *surgere*, to rise]

sur·geon (sə́:rdʒən) *n.* a medical practitioner who performs surgery ‖ a surgeonfish [A.F. *surgien*, O.F. *cirurgien*]

sur·geon·fish (sə́:rdʒənfiʃ) *pl.* **sur·geon·fish, surgeon·fish·es** *n.* any of various fishes of fam. *Teuthidae*, having one or more movable lance-shaped spines on each side of the end of the tail

surgeon's knot a reef knot in which the first loop has two turns, used esp. in tying ligatures and surgical stitches

sur·ger·y (sə́:rdʒəri:) *pl.* **sur·ger·ies** *n.* the work of a surgeon in operating manually or instrumentally upon injuries, defects etc. ‖ the branch

---

CONCISE PRONUNCIATION KEY: **(a)** æ, c*a*t; ɑ, c*a*r; ɔ f*aw*n; ei, sn*a*ke. **(e)** e, h*e*n; i:, sh*ee*p; iə, d*ee*r; ɛə, b*ea*r. **(i)** i, f*i*sh; ai, t*i*ger; ə:, b*i*rd. **(o)** o, *o*x; au, c*ow*; ou, g*oa*t; u, p*oo*r; ɔi, r*oy*al. **(u)** ʌ, d*u*ck; u, b*u*ll; u:, g*oo*se; ə, b*a*cillus; ju:, c*u*be. x, lo*ch*; θ, *th*ink; ð, bo*th*er; z, *Z*en; ʒ, cor*s*age. dʒ, sava*g*e; ŋ, ora*n*gutang; j, *y*ak; ʃ, fi*sh*; tʃ, fe*tch*; 'l, rabb*le*; 'n, redd*en*. Complete pronunciation key appears inside front cover.

of medicine dealing with this ‖ the operating theater of a surgeon or hospital ‖ (Br.) a doctor's, dentist's or veterinary surgeon's consulting room or dispensary [fr. O.F. *surgerie*]

sur·gi·cal (só:rdʒik'l) *adj.* of or relating to surgeons or surgery ‖ used in surgery ‖ resulting from surgery

su·ri·cate (súərikeit) *n. Suricata tetradactyla*, fam. *Viverridae*, a four-toed gray and black S. African mammal related to the mongoose [F. *surikate* fr. Afrik. prob. fr. native name]

Su·ri·name (suərənæm) (formerly Dutch or Netherlands Guiana) a republic (area 55,143 sq. miles, pop. 377,000) in N.E. South America. Capital: Paramaribo. People: 30% mulatto, 37% Asian Indian, 15% Indonesian, 10% Bush Negro, 1% Indian, 1% European, 1% Chinese. Religion: 20% Moslem, 20% Hindu, 20% Protestant, 16% Roman Catholic, 1% Confucian. Languages: Dutch (official), English, local patois. The land is mainly forest (gum and dyewoods, tropical hardwoods). Under 3% is cultivated. Hills in the center and south rise to 4,200 ft. Average temperature (F.): 75°-85°. Rainfall: over 100 ins along the coast, lower inland. Agricultural products (coastal belt only): rice, sugarcane, cocoa, coffee, corn, rum, tropical fruits. Forestry products: balata rubber, railroad ties, fuel, lumber. Mineral resources: bauxite. Exports: bauxite, lumber and plywood, rice, fruit. Imports: machinery, fuels and oil, textiles, food, vehicles. Monetary unit: Suriname guilder. HISTORY. Suriname was colonized by the English (17th c.) and was captured by the Dutch (1667). The colony was developed by slave labor (18th c.). It was again held by Britain (1799-1802 and 1804-14). Indian and Javanese laborers immigrated (19th c.). Suriname was integrated into the Netherlands (1922), gained self-government (1955) and full independence as a parliamentary republic (1975). The government was overthrown (1980) and a national military council assumed power

Su·ri·na·me (suərinámə) a river (c. 300 miles long) in N. Suriname, flowing into the Atlantic at Paramaribo

sur·li·ly (só:rlili) *adv.* in a surly manner

sur·li·ness (só:rli:nis) *n.* the state or quality of being surly

sur·ly (só:rli:) *comp.* **sur·li·er** *superl.* **sur·li·est** *adj.* uncivil, bad-tempered [earlier *sirly*, masterful fr. SIR]

sur·mise 1. (sərmáiz, só:rmaiz) *n.* a supposition based on very slight evidence 2. (sərmáiz) *v. pres. part.* **sur·mis·ing** *past* and *past part.* **surmised** *v.t.* to guess ‖ *v.i.* to make a guess, suppose [O. F. *surmise*, accusation]

sur·mount (sə:rmáunt) *v.t.* to overcome, *to surmount a difficulty* ‖ to place on the top of ‖ to climb over ‖ to surpass in height ‖ to lie at the top of [A.F., O.F. *surmunter*]

sur·name (só:rneim) 1. *n.* a family name ‖ (*hist.*) a name attached to a person, e.g. by reason of his occupation or place of birth or residence, later developing into such a family name 2. *v.t. pres. part.* **sur·nam·ing** *past* and *past part.* **surnamed** (*hist.*) to give a surname to [after A.F., O.F. *surnum, sornom*]

sur·pass (sərpǽs, sərpás) *v.t.* to excel ‖ to exceed, *to surpass all expectations* **sur·páss·ing** *adj.* [F. *surpasser*]

sur·plice (só:rplis) *n.* (*eccles.*) a white, loose, linen vestment having wide sleeves, worn by officiating clergy and choristers [A.F. *surpliz*, O.F. *sourpeliz*]

sur·plus (só:rplʌs, só:rpləs) 1. *n.* excess in receipts over expenditure, *budget surplus* ‖ something left over and not required, *a surplus of stock* 2. *adj.* in excess of requirements, *surplus stock* [A.F., O.F.]

sur·plus·age (só:rplʌsidʒ) *n.* surplus ‖ unnecessary words, esp. (*law*) superfluous matter in a plea or indictment [fr. M.L. *surplusagium*]

surplus value (in Marxist theory) the difference between the value of a worker's labor and the wages paid him by his employer

sur·prise (sərpráiz) 1. *n.* the emotion excited by something, e.g. an act or event, totally unexpected ‖ the cause of this emotion **to take by surprise** to come upon suddenly or unexpectedly ‖ to catch unprepared ‖ to astonish ‖ to capture by a sudden, unexpected attack 2. *v.t. pres. part.* **sur·pris·ing** *past* and *past part.* **surprised** to cause to experience unexpected emotion, *his generosity surprised me* ‖ to catch, come upon or attack suddenly and unexpectedly, *to surprise a thief, to surprise an enemy* ‖ to cause to feel sudden, unexpected disapproval, *his be-*

---

havior surprised me ‖ to bring (something) to light by some sudden, unexpected action, *to surprise a secret out of someone* **sur·prís·ing** *adj.* [fr. A.F., O.F. *surprise*, past part. of *surprendre*]

sur·re·al·ism (sərí:əlizəm) *n.* a movement in art and literature originated in Paris (1924) by Breton. Formulated at a time when psychoanalysis was gaining ground, surrealism aimed to liberate into the creative act the image-forming powers of the unconscious and so transcend reality as it is conceived by the day-to-day intelligence. Surrealism emerged out of dada, and it claimed writers, including de Quincey, Rimbaud and Lautréamont, as its precursors. It found direction and method in Breton's manifestos and his development of automatism, and it was furthered in the writings esp. of Eluard, Aragon and Prévert. Painters inspired by de Chirico portrayed unconscious or dream images. Masson, Ernst, Arp and Miró developed abstract forms symbolizing unconscious thought, Duchamp produced objects with symbolic significance, and Picabia, Chagall, Picasso and Giacometti all participated in surrealist exhibitions. Dali and Buñuel produced a surrealist film, 'Le Chien Andalou' (1928). Surrealism, which also became philosophical and political, ceased to be a formal group or school, but has been influential as a liberating force. Surrealist elements can be recognized in much contemporary art **sur·ré·al·ist** 1. *n.* a painter, writer etc. who practices surrealism 2. *adj.* of, relating to, practicing or characterized by surrealism **sur·re·al·ís·tic** *adj.* [fr. F. *surréalisme*]

sur·re·but·tal (sə:ribʌ́t'l, sʌribʌ́t'l) *n.* (*law*) a surrebutter [fr. O.F. *sur*, over+ REBUTTAL]

sur·re·but·ter (sə:ribʌ́tər, sʌribʌ́tər) *n.* (*law*) a plaintiff's reply to a defendant's rebutter

sur·re·join·der (sə:ridʒóindər, sʌridʒóindər) *n.* (*law*) a plaintiff's reply to a defendant's rejoinder

sur·ren·der (səréndər) 1. *v.t.* to give up (something) to someone or something, esp. under compulsion, *to surrender one's watch to a robber, to surrender one's army to the enemy* ‖ to give (oneself) up to e.g. emotion ‖ to sign away one's rights under (an insurance policy) in return for an agreed sum ‖ *v.i.* to acknowledge defeat and by so doing put oneself into the power of an adversary, *the Germans surrendered to the Allies* **to surrender to bail** (Br.) to appear in court in discharge of bail 2. *n.* the act of surrendering ‖ the giving up of an insurance policy by the owner in return for a cash payment **in surrender** as an indication that defeat is accepted [A.F.]

sur·rep·ti·tious (sə:rəptíʃəs, sʌrəptíʃəs) *adj.* secretive, stealthy ‖ acting in a secretive, stealthy way ‖ obtained in a secretive, stealthy way [fr. L. *surrepticius*]

Sur·rey (só:ri:, sʌ́ri:), Henry Howard, earl of (c. 1517-47), English poet. With Wyatt, he introduced into English verse French and Italian forms. He employed the first English blank verse in his translation 'Certain Bokes of Virgiles Aenaeis' (1557)

Surrey a county (area 722 sq. miles, pop. 995,800) in S.E. England. County town: Kingston-upon-Thames

sur·rey (só:ri:, sʌ́ri:) a late 19th-c. fourwheeled, two-seated carriage [after SURREY in England]

sur·ro·gate 1. (só:rəgeit, sʌ́rəgeit) *v.t. pres. part.* **sur·ro·gat·ing** and *past part.* **sur·ro·gat·ed** to appoint as a substitute for oneself or another 2. (só:rəgit, sʌ́rəgit) *n.* a substitute, esp. (*Church of England*) a deputy for a bishop or chancellor ‖ (in certain states of the U.S.A.) a judicial officer who presides over the probate of wills and testaments, settlement of estates etc. [fr. L. *surrogare* (*surrogatus*), to elect in place of another]

surrogate mother a woman who bears a child for the convenience of another woman, conceiving such child by artificial insemination

sur·round (səráund) 1. *v.t.* to encircle, *the ocean surrounds the land* ‖ to cause to become encircled, *to surround a house with trees* ‖ to cut off (a military unit etc.) by enclosing with troops ‖ to form the entourage or setting of, *surrounded by sycophants, surrounded by luxury* 2. *n.* (Br.) a floor covering between carpet and wall or any border or edging of a particular material **sur·róund·ing** 1. *adj.* which surrounds 2. *n.* (*pl.*) environment ‖ environs [O.F. *suronder, souronder*, to overflow]

---

sur·tax (só:rtæks) 1. *n.* an extra tax, esp. a graduated tax on income above a certain sum in addition to the basic tax 2. *v.t.* to levy such an extra tax on [F. fr. *surtaxe*]

Sur·tees (só:rti:z), Robert Smith (1803-64), English novelist. He created Jorrocks, a sporting grocer who appears in 'Jorrocks' Jaunts and Jollities' (1838) and 'Handley Cross' (1843). Hunting life provides much of the rollicking humor and satire

sur·veil·lance (sərvéiləns) *n.* a close watch, esp. one kept over a prisoner ‖ supervisor, e.g. of a prison [F. fr. *surveiller*, to supervise]

sur·veil·lant (sərvéilənt) *n.* a person who keeps a close watch over another ‖ a supervisor, e.g. of a prison [fr. F. *surveiller*, to supervise]

sur·veille (sərvéil) *v.* to keep under observation

sur·vey 1. (sərvéi) *v.t.* to measure the extent, contours etc. of (a land area) with a view to making an accurate and detailed map ‖ to examine (a building) in detail in order to discover any defects in its structure etc. ‖ to examine the whole extent of (something), noting details, *they sadly surveyed the scene before them* ‖ to consider (a problem, state of affairs etc.) in general and in detail, *the last chapters survey the closing years of her reign* 2. (só:rvei) *n.* a general inspection ‖ a careful examination, as a whole and in detail ‖ the process of surveying an area of land ‖ an area that has been surveyed ‖ a department or group of people engaged in such work ‖ the result of surveying in the form of a map, report etc. [A.F. *surveier*, to look over]

sur·vey·or (sərvéiər) *n.* a person whose profession is surveying land etc. ‖ a customs official who ascertains the amount, value etc. of imported goods ‖ a person who inspects, e.g. a building, in detail for the purpose of ascertaining its value, condition etc. ‖ (Br.) an official inspector of weights and measures etc. [A.F., O.F. *surveour, surveiour*]

surveyor's chain a Gunter's chain

sur·vey·or·ship (sərvéiərʃip) *n.* the office of surveyor

surveyor's level an instrument consisting of a revolving telescope fitted with a spirit level, used for testing horizontality

sur·viv·al (sərváivəl) *n.* the act, state or fact of surviving ‖ something that survives, e.g. a custom, belief etc.

survival of the fittest *NATURAL SELECTION

sur·vive (sərváiv) *pres. part.* **sur·viv·ing** *past* and *past part.* **survived** *v.t.* to live or exist longer than, *to survive one's husband* ‖ to continue to live or exist in spite of (an experience, condition etc.), *to survive an earthquake* ‖ *v.i.* to continue to live or exist **sur·ví·vor** *n.* a person who or thing which survives **sur·ví·vor·ship** *n.* (*law*) the right of any survivor of a small group sharing a joint inheritance or other property interest to take the share of any member of the group who dies [A.F. *survivre*]

survivor *n.* one who will not accept defeat

Su·sa (sú:sə) an ancient city of Persia in the lower Karun basin. It was the capital of Elam (c. 4000 B.C.) and was the residence of the Achaemenid kings of Persia: remains of the palace

Susa *SOUSSE

Su·šak (sú:ʃak) *RIJEKA

sus·cep·ti·bil·i·ty (səseptəbíliti) *pl.* **sus·cep·ti·bil·i·ties** *n.* the state or quality of being susceptible ‖ (*pl.*) sensibilities ‖ the quality of being liable or exposed or prone, *susceptibility to attack* ‖ (*elec.*) the ratio of the intensity of magnetization of a substance to the strength of the magnetizing force [SUSCEPTIBLE]

sus·cep·ti·ble (səséptəb'l) *adj.* affected or influenced particularly easily ‖ (Br.) easily offended ‖ responding easily to the attractions of women **susceptible of** admitting, allowing, *susceptible of proof* **susceptible to** liable to, *susceptible to disease* ‖ able to be influenced by, *susceptible to flattery* **sus·cép·ti·bly** *adv.* [fr. M.L. *susceptibilis*]

sus·cep·tive (səséptiv) *adj.* emotionally susceptible [fr. M.L. *susceptivus*]

Su-7B *SUKHPI

Su-17 *FITTER

su·shi (sú:ʃi:) *n.* Japanese dish of raw fish served in thin slices

Su·si·an (sú:ziən) *n.* a native or inhabitant of Susa ‖ the Iranian language spoken in Elam [fr. L. *Susiani*, inhabitants of Susa or of Susiana province of the ancient Persian empire, roughly coextensive with Elam]

---

sus·pect 1. (səspékt) *v.t.* to believe (someone) guilty of something to his discredit without conclusive proof ‖ to form a notion of (someone) not necessarily based on fact, *we suspect he is a genius* ‖ to presume (something) to be not what it seems, *to suspect a picture of being a fake* ‖ to mistrust, *to suspect a generalization on principle* ‖ *v.i.* to be suspicious **2.** (sÁspekt) *adj.* suspected **3.** (sÁspekt) *n.* someone suspected, esp. of a crime [fr. L. *suspicere* (*suspectus*), to look up to, admire, mistrust]

sus·pend (səspénd) *v.t.* to attach to some elevated point without support from below, *to suspend a lamp from the ceiling* ‖ to hold floating on or in a fluid, or as if on or in a fluid, *a pall of smoke was suspended over the city* ‖ to debar, usually for a time, from the exercise of an office or function or the enjoyment of a privilege ‖ to hold or keep undetermined, *to suspend judgment* ‖ (*Am.=Br.* rusticate) to send (a student) away for a time from a university or college as punishment [O.F. *suspendre, sospendre*]

suspended animation temporary cessation of normal physical functions

sus·pend·er (səspéndər) *n.* (*pl., Am.=Br.* braces) shoulder supports for keeping trousers up ‖ (*Br.*) a garter (elastic device for keeping a sock or stocking up)

suspender belt (*Br.*) a garter belt

sus·pense (səspéns) *n.* the state of anxious expectancy or uncertainty that usually develops while waiting for a decision, outcome etc. ‖ (in drama, fiction and the movies) an effect of intense and prolonged expectancy ‖ (*law*) temporary suspension of a right etc. **to keep** (or **hold**) **in suspense** to keep in a state of uncertainty or indecision [O.F. *suspens, suspense, delay*]

suspense account (*bookkeeping*) an account for temporary entries before they are assigned to their proper places

sus·pen·sion (səspénʃən) *n.* a suspending or being suspended ‖ the method by which something is suspended ‖ the device by which something is suspended ‖ an imposed temporary withdrawal of a right or privilege ‖ the stoppage of payment of debts because of financial failure ‖ (*mus.*) the holding over and merging of a note or notes of a chord with the chord that follows, or a note or notes thus held and merged ‖ (*phys., chem.*) a two-phase system in which a finely divided solid is dispersed in a solid, liquid or gas [fr. L.L. *suspensio* (*suspensionis*)]

suspension bridge a bridge suspended from cables which pass over supporting towers and are firmly anchored at each end

sus·pen·sor (səspénsər) *n.* a suspensory ‖ (*bot.*) a mass of cells serving to force the developing plant embryo into contact with the food supply of the megaspore [M.L.]

sus·pen·so·ry (səspénsəri) **1.** *adj.* serving to suspend, *a suspensory muscle* ‖ leaving undetermined or incomplete for the time being **2.** *pl.* **sus·pen·so·ries** *n.* a suspensory muscle, bandage etc. [fr. L. *suspendere* (*suspensus*), to suspend]

sus·pi·cion (səspíʃən) *n.* the act or an instance of suspecting ‖ the state of mind of one who suspects ‖ the merest inkling, *he hadn't a suspicion of the truth* ‖ a barely noticeable amount, *a suspicion of garlic* **above suspicion** not to be suspected because held in such high reputation **on suspicion** because of being suspected **under suspicion** suspected [A.F. *suspecioun*]

sus·pi·cious (səspíʃəs) *adj.* suspecting or having a tendency to suspect ‖ arousing suspicion ‖ showing suspicion [O.F. *suspecious, suspicious*]

sus·pi·ra·tion (sʌspəréiʃən) *n.* (*rhet.*) a profound sigh [fr. L. *suspiratio* (*suspirationis*)]

sus·pire (səspáiər) *pres. part.* **sus·pir·ing** *past and past part.* **sus·pired** *v.i.* esp. with 'for') to sigh profoundly, esp. with longing [fr. L. *suspirare*, to breathe out]

Sus·que·han·na (sʌskwəhǽnə) a river (444 miles long) flowing from the Catskill Mtns, New York State, through E. Pennsylvania and N.E. Maryland to the Chesapeake Bay. A second headstream, the West Branch (200 miles long) flows from the Alleghenies through central Pennsylvania before joining the main stream

Sus·sex (sÁsiks) a county (area 1,457 sq. miles, pop. 1,278,000) in S. England. University (1959, at Brighton). Sussex is divided administratively into East Sussex (area 829 sq. miles, pop. 652,900, county town: Lewes) and West Sussex (area 628 sq. miles, pop. 625,100, county

town: Chichester) ‖ (*hist.*) the kingdom of the South Saxons, founded in the late 5th c. It became part of Wessex (825)

'Sussex' a French unarmed cross-Channel ship which was sunk (1916) by the Germans during the 1st world war. The casualties included several Americans, and the action led to a deterioration in U.S.-German relations

sus·tain (səstéin) *v.t.* to prevent from falling, collapsing or giving way, esp. for a time, *to sustain tension* ‖ to keep going, *to sustain a conversation* ‖ to provide with nourishment etc. ‖ to support, bear (a weight etc.) ‖ to endure (criticism etc.) ‖ to support the validity or truth of ‖ to experience (a loss or injury) ‖ to act (a role) [A. F., O.F. *sustenir, soustenir*]

sustained yield *adj.* of a requirement that trees cut down in a forest area be replaced by new plantings to ensure future lumber supplies — **sustained yield** *n.*

sus·tain·ment (səstéinmənt) *n.* a sustaining or being sustained

sus·te·nance (sÁstənəns) *n.* nourishment ‖ a means of livelihood ‖ a sustaining or being sustained [fr. A.F. *sustenance*, O. F. *sostenance*]

sus·ten·ta·tion (sʌstentéiʃən) *n.* a sustaining or being sustained, maintenance ‖ sustenance [A.F., O.F. *sustentacion*]

Su·su (súːsuː) *pl.* **Su·su, Su·sus** *n.* a member of a W. African people living in the Sudan, Guinea and N. Sierra Leone ‖ this people ‖ the Mande language of this people

Su·ther·land (sÁðərlənd), Graham (1903-80), British artist. He is best-known for his war paintings of desolate landscapes, his portraits (including Maugham and Churchill), his 'Crucifixion' in St Matthew's Church, Northampton, England, and his tapestry of 'Christ in Majesty' at Coventry Cathedral, England

Sutherland a county (area 2,028 sq. miles, pop. 13,000) of northernmost Scotland. County town: Dornoch (pop. 900)

Sut·lej (sÁtlidʒ) a tributary (900 miles long) of the Indus flowing from S.W. Tibet through the Punjab, forming part of the India-Pakistan border. It joins the Chenab, forming the Panjnad, 50 miles above the junction with the Indus

sut·ler (sÁtlər) *n.* (*hist.*) a person who followed an army for the purpose of selling provisions [M. Du. *soeteler* fr. *soetelen*, to do menial work]

su·tra (súːtrə) *n.* (*Brahminism*) an aphorism or a collection of short rules ‖ (*Buddhism*) one of the narrative scriptures, esp. the dialogues of the Buddha ‖ (*Jainism*) any of various scriptures, esp. one recounting the life of the founder of Jainism [Skr. *sūtra*, a thread]

sut·tee (sʌtíː, sÁtiː) *n.* the act or custom by which a Hindu widow willingly immolates herself on her husband's funeral pyre. Suttee has been a statutory offense since 1829 ‖ a Hindu widow committing this act **sut·tee·ism** *n.* [Skr. *satī*, a virtuous wife]

Sut·ter (sÁtər), John Augustus (1803-80), U.S. frontiersman. He founded (1839) New Helvetia in the Sacramento Valley of California. It became a large, rich colony and the nucleus of the 1849 gold rush after gold was first discovered at his farm, 'Sutter's Mill', by his partner

Sutton Hoo (sÁt'nhúː) the site in Suffolk, England, of a burial mound (c. 650) of an Anglo-Saxon warrior, probably a king. It was remarkable for the fine cloisonné jewelry and the ornamental gold and silver goods from many parts of W. Europe, esp. from Scandinavia, which it contained

su·tu·ral (súːtʃərəl) *adj.* of, relating to or near a suture [F. or fr. Mod. L. *suturalis*]

su·ture (súːtʃər) **1.** *n.* (*anat.*) a line of union between bones, esp. in the skull ‖ (*surg.*) the stitching up of a wound ‖ the thread or wire used in this operation ‖ a line or seam along which two things or parts have been united ‖ (*bot.*) a line of dehiscence ‖ (*zool.*) a line of juncture between two structures, e.g. the cusps of bivalve mollusks **2.** *v.t. pres. part.* **su·tur·ing** *past and past part.* **su·tured** to stitch (a wound) [F.]

Su·va (súːvə) the chief port and capital (pop. 66,018) of Fiji, on Viti Levu

Su·vo·rov (suːvɔ́rəf), Aleksandr Vasilyevich (1729-1800), Russian field marshal. He distinguished himself in the Russo-Turkish Wars of 1768-74 and 1787-92, crushed Kosciusko's rebellion in Poland (1794), and led the Austrian and Russian forces in Italy (1798-9)

Su·wan·nee (swɔ́ni, swɔ́niː, swɔ́ni, swɔ́niː) a river (240 miles long) rising in S.W. Georgia

and flowing to the Gulf of Mexico. Its name was used by Stephen Foster in his popular ballad, 'Old Folks at Home' or 'Swanee River'

su·ze·rain (súːzərein) *n.* (*hist.*) a feudal overlord ‖ a state with political control over another [F.]

su·ze·rain·ty (súːzəreinti:) *n.* the position or power of a suzerain [F. *suzeraineté*]

Sval·bard (svÁlbɑr) (Spitsbergen) a mountainous, partly ice-covered archipelago (land area 24,295 sq. miles, pop. 3,600, mainly Russian) in the Arctic Ocean, belonging to Norway. Main islands: Vestspitsbergen (area 15,000 sq. miles), Nordaustlandet, Barentsöya, Edgeöya (*Eng.* West Spitsbergen, Northeast Land, Barents Is. and Edge I.). Highest point: 5,445 ft, on Vestspitsbergen. Products: coal, furs. There is oil on Vestspitsbergen

S-val·ue (ésvælju:) *n.* (*nuclear phys.*) increase in value of nuclear fuel after 1% burn up *Cf* R-VALUE

Sve·a·land (svéiələnd) *SWEDEN

svelte (svelt, sfelt) *adj.* slender, graceful [F.]

Sverd·lovsk (sveərdlɔ́fsk) (formerly Ekaterinburg) a communications center (pop. 1,211,000) in the R.S.F.S.R., U.S.S.R., in the E. Urals. Industries: iron and steel, heavy machinery, chemicals, food processing. University, two cathedrals (18th c.), opera house. Czar Nicholas II and his family were shot here in 1918 by the Bolsheviks

Sve·vo (zvévɔ), Italo (Ettore Schmitz, 1861-1928), Italian novelist. He is best known for 'La coscienza di Zeno' (1923, trans. 'The Confessions of Zeno', 1930). James Joyce did much to make him widely known

SW, S.W. Southwest, southwestern

swab (swɒb) **1.** *n.* a floor mop, esp. one used for cleaning the decks of a ship ‖ a twist of cotton etc. attached to a thin stick and used for treating a wound, cleaning out the mouth, nose etc. ‖ a specimen collected on such a twist for examination ‖ (*pop.*) an unpleasant or contemptible man or boy **2.** *v.t. pres. part.* **swab·bing** *past and past part.* **swabbed** to clean (e.g. a deck) with a swab ‖ to medicate or clean with a swab [fr. Du. *zwabber* fr. *zwabben*, to splash, sway]

Swa·bi·a (swéibiːə) German medieval duchy, seat of the Hohenstaufens in the 12th and 13th cc. Today it is a part of S.W. Bavaria

Swa·bi·an (swéibiːən) **1.** *n.* a native or inhabitant of Swabia ‖ the High German dialect of the Swabians **2.** *adj.* of or relating to Swabia, its people, language etc.

swad·dle (swɒd'l) *pres. part.* **swad·dling** *past and past part.* **swad·dled** *v.t.* to wrap (a baby) in swaddling clothes [M.E. *swathel-* fr. *swathelbond*, swaddling clothes]

swaddling clothes (esp. *hist.*) narrow bands of cloth wrapped around newborn and young infants to prevent free movement of the limbs

swag (swæg) **1.** *n.* (*pop.*) booty stolen by thieves ‖ (*pop.*) any ill-gotten gains ‖ (*Austral.*) a bundle carried by a miner, itinerant laborer etc. ‖ a festoon used as an ornamental motive ‖ a hanging fold of material ‖ a large hanging cluster of flowers **2.** *v.i. pres. part.* **swag·ging** *past and past part.* **swagged** (*Austral.*) to travel with a swag [prob. fr. O.N.]

swage (sweidʒ) **1.** *n.* a smith's die for working metal cold by hammering **2.** *v.t. pres. part.* **swag·ing** *past and past part.* **swaged** to shape with a swage [O.F. *souage, souaige*]

swage block a heavy block of iron with grooves or perforations, used for shaping metals by hammering

swag·ger (swǽgər) **1.** *v.i.* to walk in a way that betrays great conceit **2.** *n.* a swaggering gait [SWAG v.]

swagger stick a short light cane or stick carried in the hand by army officers

swag·ging (swǽgiŋ) *n.* appropriation of government property —**swag** *n.* —**swag** *v.*

swag·man (swǽgmən) *pl.* **swag·men** (swǽgmən) *n.* (*Austral.*) a worker traveling the countryside with a swag

Swa·hi·li (swɑhíːli:) *pl.* **Swa·hi·li, Swa·hi·lis** *n.* a member of a Bantu-speaking people living in and near Zanzibar ‖ this people ‖ a Bantu language spoken by them and used as a lingua franca in parts of E. Africa

swain (swein) *n.* (*old-fash.*) a male suitor [O.N. *sveinn*, boy, attendant]

swale (sweil) *n.* a marshy depression in a stretch of land [perh. fr. older *swale*, shade, a shady place, prob. of Scand. origin]

swal·low (swɒlou) *n.* a member of *Hirundini-*

dae, a family of small (7 ins) migratory birds, flying with great speed and occurring in almost all parts of the world [O.E. *swealwe*]

swallow 1. *v.t.* to cause (food, drink etc.) to pass down the throat and into the stomach ‖ (often with 'up') to engulf, envelop, *swallowed up by the shadows* ‖ to accept (e.g. a statement) without testing it for truth, *he swallowed the tale without hesitation* ‖ to accept (an insult etc.) in a submissive way ‖ to hold back (pride, tears, laughter etc.) ‖ to retract (e.g. words said) ‖ *v.i.* to take food etc. through the throat into the stomach ‖ to make the throat movement characteristic of this, esp. under stress of emotion **2.** *n.* the act of swallowing ‖ the amount swallowed in one gulp ‖ (*naut.*) an aperture in a block through which the rope reeves [O.E. *swelgan*]

swallow dive (*Br.*) a swan dive

swal·low·tail (swóloutẹil) *n.* a deeply forked tail ‖ a butterfly with such a tail ‖ any of several hummingbirds ‖ a swallow-tailed kite ‖ (*naut.*) a double-pointed pennant ‖ a tailcoat

swal·low-tailed kite (swóloutẹild) *Elanoides forficatus,* fam. *Accipitridae,* a kite of central and southern U.S.A., white with black wings, black back and black forked tail

swam *past* of SWIM

swa·mi (swámi:) *pl.* **swa·mies** *n.* a title of respect for a Hindu religious teacher [Hindī *swāmī,* master, prince, fr. Skr. *svāmin*]

Swam·mer·dam (svámərdam), Jan (1637-80), Dutch naturalist who founded the science of entomology. He was a pioneer in the use of the microscope, and is said to be the first to have observed red blood corpuscles

swamp (swɒmp) **1.** *n.* spongy ground largely covered by standing water of little depth **2.** *v.t.* to fill (a boat) with water ‖ (*loosely*) to make very wet ‖ to submerge under too many or too great demands, *swamped with orders* ‖ to overwhelm, *swamped by a crowd of admirers* ‖ *v.i.* to become submerged and sink **swámp·y** *comp.* **swamp·i·er** *superl.* **swamp·i·est** *adj.* [prob. fr. Du. *zwamp,* sponge]

Swan (swɒn), Sir Joseph Wilson (1828-1914), British physicist, electrician and inventor. He invented the photographic dry plate and bromide paper. He also devised a form of incandescent electric lamp and an electric safety lamp for miners

swan (swɒn) *n.* any of various large, stately, usually white, long-necked aquatic birds of fam. *Anatidae,* esp. *Cygnus olor.* They occur wild in many parts of the world, and are kept semidomesticated in ponds, lakes etc. In the wild state they migrate south each winter in V-shaped flocks [O.E. *swan, swon*]

swan dive (*Am.=Br.* swallow dive) a forward dive in which the arms are spread sideways until the swimmer is about to enter the water

swank (swæŋk) **1.** *n.* (*pop.*) ostentatious display, e.g. in manner, dress or speech **2.** *v.i.* (*pop.*) to show off arrogantly **3.** *adj.* (*pop.*) swanky **swánk·y** *comp.* **swank·i·er** *superl.* **swank·i·est** *adj.* (*pop.*) ostentatious, showy ‖ elegant, stylish [etym. doubtful]

swan·ner·y (swɒnəri) *pl.* **swan·ner·ies** *n.* a place where swans are bred or kept

swans·down (swɒnzdaun) *n.* the down of the swan, used for powder puffs, dress trimmings etc. ‖ a soft cotton flannel having a nap on the right side, used for making infants' apparel etc.

Swan·sea (swɒnzi:, swɒnsi:) a port (pop. 186,199) in Glamorganshire, S.E. Wales. Industries: metallurgy, shipbuilding, mechanical engineering. University College (1920), part of the University of Wales

swan song (in legend) the beautiful song of a dying swan ‖ a final pronouncement, or act, esp. the last work of a writer or musician

swan-up·ping (swɒnʌpiŋ) *n.* the process or practice of nicking young swans on the beak as a mark of ownership ‖ an annual English ceremony on the Thames in which swans belonging to the Crown or some corporation are so marked

swap maternity (*insurance*) provision in group health-insurance plans providing immediate maternity benefits to a newly covered woman out terminating coverage on a pregnancy in progress upon termination of a woman's coverage *Cf* FLAT MATERNITY, SWITCH AND FLAT MATERNITY

SWAPO (*acronym*) for South-West Africa Peoples Organization, native political and military movement in Namibia

swap, swop (swɒp) *pres. part.* **swap·ping, swop·ping** *past* and *past part.* **swapped, swopped 1.** *v.t.* (*pop.*) to exchange by barter **2.** *n.* (*pop.*) the act of bartering ‖ (*pop.*) something bartered [M.E. *swappen,* to strike, prob. imit.]

sward (swɔrd) *n.* (*rhet.*) an expanse of grass-covered soil [O.E. *sweard,* a skin]

swarm (swɔrm) **1.** *n.* a large number of honeybees emigrating from a hive with their queen to establish a new colony ‖ a colony of honeybees settled in a hive ‖ any great moving throng, *a swarm of pilgrims, a swarm of mosquitoes* ‖ (*biol.*) a collection of single-celled independent organisms, esp. zoospores **2.** *v.i.* (of bees) to emigrate in a body from a hive to form a new colony ‖ to move around in large numbers, *sightseers swarmed over the park* ‖ (of a place) to be crowded ‖ (*biol.,* e.g. of zoospores from a sporangium) to escape in a swarm with a characteristic oscillating movement [O.E. *swearm*]

swarm *v.i.* (esp. with 'up') to climb by gripping alternately with the hands and legs ‖ *v.t.* to climb up (a pole etc.) in this manner [etym. doubtful]

swarm cell a swarm spore

swarm spore (*biol.*) any of various motile sexual or asexual spores, e.g. a zoospore

swart (swɔrt) *adj.* (*rhet.*) swarthy [O.E. *sweart*]

swarth·i·ness (swɔrði:nis) *n.* the state or quality of being swarthy

swarth·y (swɔrði:, swɔrθi:) *comp.* **swarth·i·er** *superl.* **swarth·i·est** *adj.* dark-colored, *a swarthy complexion* [var. of SWART]

swash (swɒʃ, swɒʃ) *adj.* (*printing,* of capital letters) having ornamental strokes at top and bottom [prob. derived fr. obs. *aswash, aslant*]

swash 1. *v.i.* (of liquid) to move with a splash ‖ to act in a blustering, arrogant way ‖ *v.t.* to cause (water etc.) to splash about **2.** *n.* a body of water splashing forcefully against something ‖ the sound or motion of swashing water [imit.]

swash·buck·ler (swɒʃbʌklər, swɒʃbʌklər) *n.* (*hist.*) a swaggering, blustering, fighting man out for romantic adventure **swásh·buck·ling** *adj.* characterized by swagger and bluster

swas·ti·ka (swɒstikə) *n.* an ancient symbol or ornament in the form of a Greek cross having the ends of the arms bent to form right angles arranged clockwise or counterclockwise. The clockwise swastika was adopted (1933) as the emblem of the National Socialist German Workers' Party

swat, swot (swɒt) **1.** *v.t. pres part.* **swat·ting, swot·ting** *past* and *past part.* **swat·ted, swot·ted** to hit with a quick sharp blow, *to swat a fly* **2.** *n.* a quick sharp blow [variant of SQUAT]

SWAT 1. (*acronym*) Special Weapons and Tactics Team **2.** (*mil. acronym*) for Sidewinder (which see) angle tracking

swatch (swɒtʃ) *n.* a sample piece of fabric, leather etc. [etym. doubtful]

swath (swɒθ, swɔθ) *n.* a line of grass or grain after it has been scythed or reaped ‖ the width of the path so cut [O.E. *sweth, swathu,* track]

swathe (sweið, swɒð) **1.** *v.t. pres. part.* **swath·ing** *past* and *past part.* **swathed** to wrap, bind etc. with a swathe or swathes, *swathed in bandages* ‖ to enwrap deeply, so as partially to obscure, *swathed in furs, hills swathed in mist* **2.** *n.* a wrapping or bandage [O.E. *swarthian*]

Swa·tow (swátáu) a port and industrial center (pop. 280,400) in Kwangtung, China, at the mouth of the Han on the South China Sea

sway (swei) **1.** *v.i.* to swing rhythmically from side to side from or as if from a fixed base ‖ to go forward while moving in this way, *to sway down the road* ‖ to incline to one side as a result of some force, e.g. wind, *the bus swayed to the right* ‖ to fluctuate in one's attitude or opinions ‖ *v.t.* to cause to swing from side to side ‖ to cause to incline to one side as a result of some force ‖ to change the opinions of by eloquence, demagogy etc., *to sway a crowd in one's favor* ‖ to exert an influence upon ‖ (*naut.,* esp. with 'up') to hoist (a mast etc.) **2.** *n.* a swaying or being swayed ‖ control, *to hold sway* [prob. fr. L.G. *swājen,* to be moved hither and thither by the wind]

sway·back (swéibæk) *n.* (esp. of horses) a hollow sagging of the back **sway·backed** *adj.*

swayed (sweid) *adj.* swaybacked

Swa·zi (swázi:) *pl.* **Swa·zi, Swa·zis** *n.* a member of a Bantu people inhabiting Swaziland ‖ this people ‖ the language spoken by this people

Swa·zi·land (swázi:lænd) (Ngwane) a state (area 6,704 sq. miles, pop. 601,200) in S.E. Africa, a member of the Commonwealth and of

the U.N. Capital: Mbabane (pop. 29,875). People: 96% Swazi (Bantu), small European and mulatto minorities. Languages: Swazi, English. Religion: mainly local African, 30% Christian. The land is 6% cultivated. It lies on the east side of the S. African plateau, descending from the rugged, forested High Veld (over 5,000 ft), through a mixed farming and ranching region (averaging 3,000 ft), to a low, fertile plateau (1,000 ft), with hills (2,000 ft) along the Mozambique border. Average temperatures (F.): (Jan.) 60° in the west, 70° in the east, (July) 50° in the west, 60° in the east. Rainfall: 55 ins (west), 26 ins (east). Livestock: cattle, goats. Agricultural products: cotton, tobacco, corn, sugar, bananas, lumber, pineapples, rice, tomatoes, peanuts, beans, sweet potatoes. Mineral resources: asbestos, iron ore, tin, barytes, gold, silver, coal, beryl, diaspore, pyrophyllite, kaolin and alunite. Manufacturing industries (food processing, forestry products) are being developed. Exports: asbestos, sugar, cattle, seed cotton, rice, gum, lumber, hides and skins, citrus fruit, canned pineapples, tobacco. Monetary unit: lilangeni (100 cents). HISTORY. The Swazis migrated south to Swaziland (mid-18th c.) and came into conflict with the Zulus. Britain intervened to stop tribal warfare (1840s) and made Swaziland a protectorate of the Transvaal (1894). Its administration was transferred to the governor of the Transvaal (1903) and to a high commissioner (1907). It acquired internal self-government (1967) King Sobhuza II, who ruled 1921-82, and was succeeded by his son Makhosetive, whose mother became queen regent (1983)

swear (sweər) **1.** *v. pres. part.* **swear·ing** *past* **swore** (swɔr, swour) *past part.* **sworn** (swɔrn, swourn) *v.i.* to make a solemn oath ‖ to use sacred words irreverently ‖ (*loosely*) to use obscene language ‖ *v.t.* to affirm by solemn oath ‖ to take (an oath) to declare forcefully to be true, *he swore he didn't know the man* ‖ to promise solemnly, *she swore not to be late* ‖ (*law*) to administer an oath to ‖ to bind by solemn oath **to swear by** to have or express complete confidence in, *he swears by that firm* **to swear in** to induct into office by administering an oath **to swear off** to pledge oneself to renounce, *to swear off smoking* **to swear to** (in negative or interrogative constructions) to be positively sure of, *I couldn't swear to the color of his hair* **2.** *n.* a swearword ‖ a spell of swearing [O.E. *swerian*]

swear·word (swéərwə:rd) *n.* a blasphemous or obscene word

sweat (swet) *n.* the usually colorless saline fluid secreted by the sweat glands ‖ a sweating or being sweated, esp. sweating induced by a sudorific ‖ moisture exuded from, and forming beadlike drops on, a surface ‖ exercise, esp. a hard gallop, given a horse to make it sweat ‖ hard work ‖ the fermentation that occurs during the aging of tobacco ‖ a state of anxiety, impatience etc., *in a sweat to learn the results* [M.E. *swet, swete*]

sweat *v.i.* to excrete moisture through the openings of the sweat glands ‖ (of green plants, cheese etc.) to exude moisture in the form of beadlike drops ‖ (of rocks, glass etc.) to collect surface moisture from the air by condensation ‖ (of tobacco leaves) to ferment ‖ (of hides) to become putrid ‖ to toil laboriously, *to sweat to get a job done* ‖ *v.t.* to cause to excrete sweat from the skin, *to sweat a horse* (with 'away', 'off', 'out' etc.) to get rid of by excreting sweat, *to sweat out a fever* ‖ to make wet with sweat, *to sweat one's socks* ‖ to exact an unjustly large amount of labor from (employees etc.) at low wages and under bad conditions ‖ to ferment (e.g. tobacco leaves) ‖ to putrefy (e.g. hides) ‖ to heat (a metal) in order to extract a fusible component ‖ to join (a metal) to another metal by partial melting ‖ to cause (melted solder) to run between two contiguous surfaces in order to join them **to sweat blood** to slave away at some task ‖ to be in a fearful state of apprehension, anxiety etc. [O.E. *swǣtan*]

sweat·band (swétbænd) *n.* a leather band inside a hat serving to prevent sweat from the brow from seeping through and damaging the exterior of the hat

sweat·er (swétər) *n.* a knitted garment, with or without sleeves, for the upper part of the body. It can be in pullover or jacket style

sweat gland a tubular gland that excretes sweat through a duct connecting with a minute pore on the surface of the skin. In man these

---

glands are distributed in nearly all parts of the skin

sweat·i·ly (swétili:) *adv.* in a sweaty manner

sweat·i·ness (swéti:nis) *n.* the state or quality of being sweaty

sweat pants loose cotton jersey pants with a thick nap on the inner side, close-fitting cuffs, and a drawstring at the waist. They are worn esp. by athletes before and after exercising

sweat shirt a long-sleeved pullover of cotton jersey having a thick nap on the inner side, worn esp. by athletes before and after exercising

sweat-shop (swétʃɒp) *n.* a small factory where workers work long hours for low wages under unwholesome conditions

sweat suit an athlete's sweat pants and sweat shirt

sweat·y (swéti:) *comp.* **sweat·i·er** *superl.* **sweat·i·est** *adj.* running with sweat || smelling of sweat || causing sweat

Swede (swi:d) *n.* a native or inhabitant of Sweden [fr. M.L.G. or M. Du.]

swede (swi:d) *n.* (*Br.*) a rutabaga

Swe·den (swí:d'n) a kingdom (area 173,620 sq. miles, pop. 8,327,500) of N.W. Europe (Scandinavia). People and language: Swedish, small Lapp and Finnish minorities. Religion: 95% Evangelical Lutheran (established Church), small Nonconformist, Roman Catholic and Jewish minorities. The land is 9% cultivated, 2% pasture, 50% forest and 9% lakes. Sweden is divided into three geographical regions: Norrland (the northern 60%, incl. Lapland, mountainous except for a narrow coastal plain), Svealand (the central lake plain), and Götaland (the fertile southern plateau and plain, incl. Scania, the chief agricultural district, in the far south). The chief mountain range is the Kjölen, along the Norwegian border, highest in the north (Kebnekaise, 6,963 ft), and cut by many lakes, from which rivers flow to the Gulf of Bothnia. Average temperatures (F.) in Feb. and July: Stockholm 26° and 62°, Gothenburg 30° and 62°, Lapland 5° and 54°. Snow lasts an average of 47 days in Scania, 190 days in Lapland. Rainfall: N. Norrland under 20 ins, Stockholm 23 ins, W. Svealand 35 ins. Livestock: cattle, hogs, horses, sheep, reindeer, poultry. Agricultural products: cereals, vegetables, sugar beets, potatoes, hay, dairy products, furs. Forestry products: lumber, pulpwood, fuel, pitch, tar. Mineral resources: iron ore, silver, lead, copper, zinc, manganese, arsenic, sulfur, coal, uranium. Industries: mining, pig iron, steel and steel products, fishing, pulp and paper, chemicals, electrical and electronic machinery, aluminum, textiles, agricultural machinery, shipbuilding, porcelain, glass, vehicles, aircraft, hydroelectricity, tobacco, furniture, matches, armaments, cutlery, rayon, plastics, tourism, cement, bricks. Exports: machinery, raw materials, manufactures, pulp and paper, transport equipment, metals, wood, cork, iron and steel, hydroelectricity (to Denmark by submarine cable). Imports: machinery, raw materials, manufactures, oil and fuels, foodstuffs and livestock, transport equipment, chemicals. Ports: Stockholm, Gothenburg (ice-free). Stockholm and Gothenburg are connected by the Göta canal (360 miles). Sweden has rail access to Narvik and Murmansk. Universities: Uppsala (1477), Lund (1668), Gothenburg (1889), Stockholm (1877). Monetary unit: krona (100 öre). HISTORY. The inhabitants of Sweden, probably of Germanic origin, established trading links with the rest of Europe in the Iron Age. The chief tribes were the Svear in central Sweden and the Goths in the south. They took part in Viking raids (8th-10th cc.), esp. those toward Russia. Christianity was introduced (9th c.) by St Ansgar, but did not spread widely until the reign (1150-60) of Eric IX. Finland was conquered and Christianized (mid-12th c.). Many Swedish towns gained wealth and power under the influence of the Hanseatic League (13th c.). Stockholm emerged as the capital (mid-13th c.). Margaret, elected queen of Sweden in 1389, united the kingdom with Denmark and Norway by the Union of Kalmar (1397). Denmark proved unable to impose its rule on Sweden, and after many rebellions, Sweden broke away (1523) under Gustavus I. He established his rule over the whole country except the south, which remained under Danish rule, encouraged industry and trade, organized an army and navy, and made Lutheranism the state religion. His successor, Eric XIV, continued the

struggle with Denmark and conquered Estonia (1561). Sweden was briefly united with Poland under Sigismund III before he was deposed (1599). Gustavus II and his minister Oxenstièrna made Sweden a dominant European power and leader of the Protestant cause in the Thirty Years' War, at the end of which Sweden gained Pomerania and Bremen (1648). Denmark was forced to cede the south of Sweden (1660). Under Charles XII, Sweden was involved in the Northern War (1700-21), in which, despite early victories, it lost all its German and Baltic territories except Finland. Sweden abandoned its ambition of dominating the Baltic, the nobility increased its power at the expense of the monarchy, and the cultural revival (which included the work of Celsius, Swedenborg and Linnaeus) ensued (18th c.). Gustavus III restored royal authority (1771-92). Under Charles XIII Sweden was involved in the Napoleonic Wars, in which it lost Finland (1809), but this was compensated by a union with Norway (1814). Bernadotte succeeded to the throne (1818) as Charles XIV. The 19th c. saw the growth of parliamentary government and of industrialization. Hostility toward Norway grew, and the two countries were separated (1905). During the long reign (1907-50) of Gustavus V, Sweden remained neutral in both world wars. Socialist governments carried out much social legislation. Sweden joined the U.N. (1946) and maintained its strictly neutral foreign policy. A new constitution was adopted (1975). Charles XVI Gustav became king (1973) on the death of Gustav VI Adolf. Prime Minister Olof Palme was assassinated (1986)

Swe·den·borg (swí:d'nbɒrg), Emmanuel (1688-1772), Swedish scientist and mystical thinker. He wrote on algebra, mining, metallurgy, physiology and psychology. He interpreted his mystical revelations of the spiritual world in 'Arcana coelestia' (1749-56)

Swe·den·bor·gi·an (swi:d'nbɔ́rdʒi:ən) **1.** *adj.* of a member of a Protestant sect, the Church of the New Jerusalem, founded (1788) by Robert Hindmarsh, a London printer, and based on Swedenborg's doctrines **2.** *n.* a member of this sect

Swed·ish (swí:diʃ) **1.** *adj.* of or relating to the country, language or inhabitants of Sweden **2.** *n.* the N. Germanic language spoken in Sweden and a section of Finland **the Swedish** the Swedish people
—The Swedish language is spoken by about 6,500,000 persons in Sweden and by the coastal population of a section of Finland. It is also spoken on most of the islands of the Baltic, including some off the coast of Estonia. It is spoken as a second language by many Finns. Swedish forms with Danish an E. Norse group. Runic inscriptions in Sweden date from the 5th c. The oldest manuscripts date from c. 1250

Swedish syndrome a psychological bonding between captors and usu. political captives, resulting from the absolute dependence of the latter

sweep (swi:p) **1.** *v. pres. part.* **sweep·ing** *past and past part.* **swept** (swept) *v.i.* (of news, disease, emotion etc.) to spread rapidly || to move with proud or dignified grace, *she swept off the stage* || (of a long dress or train) to trail with a rustling sound || to move so that a long dress or train trails with a rustling sound || to extend in a wide or long curve, *the hills sweep down to the sea* || to move in a wide curve || to use a broom or something resembling a broom in cleaning, clearing etc. || *v.t.* to pass swiftly across, along, over or through, *plague swept the country* || to have a large arc of fire command over, or to fire over, *the guns swept the landing beach* || to move or remove with a continuous pushing force, *he swept the litter off his desk with his hand* || to clean of dust, debris etc. by using a broom or brush or something resembling this || to make (a path, way etc.) with or as if with a broom || to direct the gaze over in a wide arc, *he swept the valley with his binoculars* || to drag (e.g. the bottom of a river) || to cause to move lightly over, *she swept her fingers over the strings* || to touch lightly in passing over (e.g. the keys or strings of a musical instrument) **2.** *n.* the action or an act of sweeping || someone whose work is sweeping, esp. a chimney sweep || a long sweeping line or contour, *the sweep of a skirt* || a long sweeping movement, *the sweep of an oar, the sweep of a scythe* || the range of extent of a sweeping movement, *within the sweep of the telescope* || a wide

expanse, *a sweep of meadow* || (*mil.*) a reconnaissance, attack etc. ranging over a specific area || a device consisting of a pole pivoted to an upright, used to draw up a bucket of well water || the sail of a windmill || (*naut.*) a long pole used to propel a barge || a length of cable used in dragging for obstructions, e.g. mines, in the sea || (*pop.*) a sweepstake **swéep·er** *n.* [etym. doubtful]

sweep·ing (swí:piŋ) **1.** *n.* the action of a sweeper || (*pl.*) things swept up, refuse **2.** *adj.* on a very large scale, *a sweeping victory* || too comprehensive to allow of distinctions, *a sweeping statement* || moving in a wide curve or having the shape of a wide curve, *a sweeping gesture*

sweep net a large seine let down from a boat in a wide curve and then hauled ashore

sweep·stake (swí:psteik) *n.* a horse race in which the total stakes put up by competitors go to the winner || a method of gambling on a race in which the money put on by those taking part is shared among those who draw the horses running first, second and third **swéep·stakes** *n.* a sweepstake

sweet (swi:t) **1.** *adj.* having the characteristic taste of sugar || containing sugar || pleasing to the senses, *a sweet sound* || not salted or salty, *sweet butter* || (of milk) not sour || (of wine) retaining some of its natural sugar || (of soil) good for growing crops, not acid || smooth-running, *a sweet engine* || showing kindness or the desire to please, *that is very sweet of you* || characterized by gentleness, kindliness etc., *a sweet nature* || (*jazz*) characterized by suavity of rhythm, harmonies and tempo, not improvised **2.** *n.* (*pl.*) sweet edible things || (*Br.*) the dessert course of a meal || (*Br.*) a piece of candy || (*pl.*, *rhet.*) pleasures, delights, *the sweets of victory* || (*rhet.*, in addressing someone) a beloved person **sweet on** (*old-fash.*) in love with, or beginning to be in love with, someone [O.E. *swēte*]

sweet basil *BASIL

sweet·bread (swí:tbred) *n.* the pancreas or thymus gland of a calf or other young animal prepared as a cooked dish

sweet·bri·er, sweet·bri·ar (swí:tbraiər) *n.* eglantine

sweet cicely *Myrrhis odorata*, fam. *Umbelliferae*, a white-flowered European aromatic herb || any of several North American plants of genus *Osmorhiza*

sweet cider *CIDER (nonalcoholic)

sweet corn any of several varieties of corn grown for the table

sweet·en (swí:t'n) **1.** *v.t.* to make sweet to the taste, e.g. by adding sugar || to make more agreeable to hear or to smell || to put into a kinder mood || (*rhet.*) to make more attractive or more enjoyable || to make (soil) less acid by applying lime || to neutralize (an acid) by means of an alkali || to divest (e.g. seawater) of salt || *v.i.* to become sweet **sweet·en·ing** (swí:t'niŋ, swí:tniŋ) *n.* that which sweetens || the act or process of making sweet

sweet flag calamus (*Acorus calamus*)

sweet gale *Myrica gale*, fam. *Myricaceae*, a bog shrub of the north temperate zone having bitter-tasting, fragrant leaves

sweet·heart (swí:thɑrt) *n.* a girl or woman in relation to the boy or man in love with her, or a boy or man in relation to the girl or woman in love with him || a term of endearment

sweet·meat (swí:tmi:t) *n.* (esp. *pl.*) a piece of confectionery

sweet pea *Lathyrus odoratus*, fam. *Papilionaceae*, an ornamental climbing plant having pinnate leaves and large, sweetly scented, blue, purple, red, pink, salmon or white flowers

sweet pepper any of certain plants of genus *Capsicum*, bearing a pepper of large size and mild flavor || the fruit itself

sweet potato *Ipomoea batatas*, fam. *Convolvulaceae*, a trailing vine grown in warm regions for its sweet tubers || the tuber, cooked and eaten as a vegetable

sweet-scent·ed (swí:tsɛntid) *adj.* having a sweet scent

sweet·sop (swí:tsɒp) *n. Annona squamosa*, fam. *Annonaceae*, a tropical American tree bearing sweet cone-shaped fruit || the fruit itself

sweet-tem·pered (swí:ttémpərd) *adj.* possessing a loving, equable, patient disposition

sweet tooth fondness for sweet foods

sweet william *Dianthus barbatus*, fam. *Caryophyllaceae*, a biennial plant having bracteate heads of brightly colored flowers

Swein (svein) 'Forkbeard' (c. 960-1014), king of

Denmark (986-1014). He led a series of raids on England (1002-14) and exacted large sums as Danegeld from Ethelred II. His son Cnut succeeded (1016) to the English throne

swell (swel) **1.** *v. pres. part.* **swell·ing** *past* **swelled** *past part.* **swol·len** (swóul'n), **swelled** *v.i.* to increase in volume, esp. as a result of internal pressure, *the boil began to swell* ‖ to increase in number, degree, quantity etc., *the population has swollen to over a million* ‖ (of sound and of some musical instruments) to become louder ‖ (esp. of a body of water) to rise above the normal level, *the river is swelling* ‖ to curve outward or upward, *the cask swells in the middle* ‖ to seem to be puffed up (with conceit, pride etc.) ‖ (*rhet.*, of the heart) to become charged with emotion, *her heart swelled with grief* ‖ *v.t.* to cause (a body of water) to rise above the normal level ‖ to cause to increase in volume, size etc. ‖ to affect with pride etc. **2.** *n.* the act of swelling ‖ the state or quality of being swollen, *the swell of a belly, the swell of a pot* ‖ (*mus.*) an increase followed by a decrease in loudness ‖ (*mus.*) the symbol (<>) indicating this ‖ a device in some harpsichords for regulating volume ‖ a swell box ‖ (of the sea, or other large body of water) a succession of long, unbroken waves ‖ a rounded elevation, esp. on the floor of the sea ‖ (*pop.*) a person of high social standing **3.** *adj.* (*pop.*) excellent, marvelous etc., *a swell party* [O.E. *swellan*]

swell box a compartment in an organ containing the reeds or a set of pipes and fitted with shutters that open or close in order to regulate the volume

swell·ing (swéliŋ) *n.* an increase or being increased in size, volume etc. ‖ a swollen part of something, esp. an abnormal bodily protuberance or distension

swel·ter (swéltər) **1.** *v.i.* to be oppressively hot **2.** *n.* a sweltering condition ‖ oppressive heat **swél·ter·ing** *adj.* sweltry **swél·try** *comp.* **swel·tri·er** *superl.* **swel·tri·est** *adj.* oppressively hot [O.E. *sweltan*, to die]

swept *past* and *past part.* of SWEEP

swept·back (swéptbæk) *adj.* (of aircraft wings) set so that the leading edge is at an obtuse angle with the fuselage ‖ (of an aircraft) having such wings

swerve (swə:rv) **1.** *v. pres. part.* **swerv·ing** *past* and *past part.* **swerved** *v.i.* to change direction suddenly, *he swerved in order to avoid a collision* ‖ (of a ball) to curve in flight ‖ to deviate from an acceptable or right course of conduct, action etc. ‖ *v.t.* to cause to change direction, curve in flight, or deviate from an acceptable or right course of conduct etc. **2.** *n.* the act of swerving ‖ a sudden change of direction ‖ a curve in flight of a ball [O.E. *sweorfan*, to scour]

Swift (swift), Gustavus Franklin (1839-1903), U.S. merchant who founded (1885) Swift and Company, the first corporation to develop international markets for American beef. He was the first to ship dressed beef from Chicago to the east coast, to sponsor the creation of a refrigerator car, and to develop beef by-products (incl. margarine, soap, glue and fertilizer)

Swift, Jonathan (1667-1745), Irish satirist. He was dean of St Patrick's Cathedral, Dublin. 'Gulliver's Travels' (1726) is a universal satire, with the particular themes of courtly life, politics, academicism and mankind in general, but the public took it as fiction, and it has become a children's classic. His other works include 'A Tale of a Tub' (1704), a brilliant satire on the history of the Christian religion, 'The Battle of the Books' (1704), and the pathetic 'Journal to Stella'. In his own time Swift was an active though embittered politician, and his 'Drapier's Letters' (1724) had an immediate and decisive political effect. Swift's genius is flawed by a basic horror of human life: a horror that tends to impart a sense of terror and disequilibrium to his greatest works, as in 'The Modest Proposal' (1729) or the conclusion of 'Gulliver's Travels'

swift (swift) **1.** *adj.* moving or capable of moving with great speed, or characterized by great speed, *a swift horse, a swift gallop* ‖ rapid, made or done without hesitation, *a swift reply* **2.** *n.* any of numerous small birds of fam. *Apodidae*, resembling swallows but having narrower wings and shorter tails, esp. *Apus apus* ‖ a member of *Sceloporus*, a genus of fast-running lizards ‖ an adjustable reel for winding yarn,

silk etc. ‖ one of the cylinders in a carding machine [O.E.]

Swift and Company *SWIFT, Gustavus Franklin

swig (swig) **1.** *v. pres. part.* **swig·ging** *past* and *past part.* **swigged** *v.t.* (*pop.*) to drink in large gulps ‖ *v.i.* (*pop.*) to drink large gulps or quantities **2.** *n.* (*pop.*) a drink taken in a long steady gulp or series of gulps [origin unknown]

swill (swil) **1.** *v.t.* (esp. with 'down' or 'out') to pour quantities of water in, on or over, so as to flush out ‖ to wash roughly, *to swill one's body under the pump* ‖ to cause (some liquid) to lap around inside a vessel by rotating it ‖ to drink greedily, *to swill beer* ‖ *v.i.* to drink something greedily **2.** *n.* hogs' liquid food ‖ garbage ‖ (*pop.*) a swig [O.E. *swillan, swilian*, to wash]

swim (swim) **1.** *v. pres. part.* **swim·ming** *past* **swam** (swæm) *past part.* **swum** (swʌm) *v.i.* to move through or under the surface of water by movements of the limbs, strokes of fins, flippers, tail etc. ‖ to move as if through water ‖ to be immersed in or surrounded by a liquid, or as if so immersed or surrounded, *swimming in chocolate sauce* ‖ to appear to whirl around one, *the room swam as I stood there* ‖ (of the head) to experience dizziness ‖ *v.t.* to cross by propelling oneself through water, *to swim a stream* ‖ to use (a specified stroke) for such propelling ‖ to force to swim, *to swim a mule across a pond* ‖ to compete in (a race for swimmers) **to swim against the stream** to go counter to the majority in one's ideas, policies etc. **2.** *n.* an act or a period of swimming ‖ a state of dizziness ‖ that part of a river etc. in which fish abound **in the swim** following currently fashionable modes [O.E. *swimman*]

swim bladder an air-filled bladder in fish, developed as a diverticulum of the alimentary canal, which makes swimming at varying depths possible

swim·mer·et (swiməret) *n.* (*zool.*) one of the small paired abdominal appendages of some crustaceans either for use in swimming or for carrying eggs

swimming (swímiŋ) **1.** *n.* the act or sport of swimming **2.** *adj.* used in, involving, or adapted to swimming ‖ overflowing with or as if with water, *swimming eyes* ‖ afflicted with dizziness, *a swimming head*

swim·ming·ly (swímiŋli) *adv.* going along rapidly and easily with no hitches, *everything went swimmingly*

Swin·burne (swínbərn), Algernon Charles (1837-1909), English poet and critic. Swinburne's early verse, esp. 'Poems and Ballads' (1866), burst upon a Victorian public, used to Tennyson's melodies and didacticism, with the force of beating rhythm, contrived alliteration, an unconcealed pagan hedonism, an element of perversion, and an excess of imagery. His best poems have survived moral disapproval, and as a critic he led the way to a revaluation of the Jacobean dramatists

swin·dle (swínd'l) **1.** *v. pres. part.* **swin·dling** *past* and *past part.* **swin·dled** *v.t.* to trick (a victim) ‖ to get (e.g. money) by fraud or trickery ‖ *v.i.* to get money etc. by fraud or trickery **2.** *n.* the act or process or an instance of swindling [back-formation fr. SWINDLER]

swin·dler (swíndlər) *n.* a person who practices swindling [fr. G. *schwindler*, a fantastic schemer]

swine (swain) *pl.* **swine** *n.* a hog

swine fever (*Br.*) hog cholera

swine flu (swainflu:) a strain of influenza—an infectious disease of the respiratory tract—caused by the influenza virus similar to that that caused the worldwide epidemic in 1918-9, first researched by virologist Richard Slope in 1928. In 1976, fearful of another epidemic, U.S. health officials sponsored mass inoculation of the American public. Serious side effects in some recipients, however, suspended the vaccination program after a few months

swine·herd (swáinhə:rd) *n.* (*rhet.*) a person who tends swine

swing (swiŋ) **1.** *v. pres. part.* **swing·ing** *past* and *past part.* **swung** (swʌŋ) *v.i.* (of an object suspended from an overhead support) to sway freely to and fro, *a pendulum swings* ‖ to turn on or as if on a hinge, pivot etc., *she swung around on her heel* ‖ to move in a curved path, *he swung around the bend in the road* ‖ to go back and forth in a swing or hammock ‖ to turn as if in a certain direction, *opinion swung in his favor* ‖ to move along in a rhythmic, swaying motion, *to swing down a road* ‖ (*pop.*) to be executed by

hanging ‖ to dance to swing music ‖ to use a sweeping arm movement in hitting or aiming at someone or something, *he swung at the man, but missed* ‖ (*naut.*, of a ship) to turn with the wind or tide while riding a single anchor ‖ to get oneself to a point or from point to point by grasping a fixed support and pulling, or by leaping from one fixed support to another, *to swing aboard a bus, to swing through the trees* ‖ *v.t.* to cause (something grasped) to move through the air with a sweeping motion, *to swing a bat* ‖ to cause (something suspended) to move back and forth, *to swing a censer* ‖ to cause (a person) to go back and forth in a swing or hammock ‖ to cause to turn on or as if on an axis, *to swing someone around to one's point of view* ‖ to cause to hang, *to swing a hammock* ‖ to convey (a suspended object) from one point to another, e.g. with a crane ‖ to exert an influence on in a way showing bias, *to swing a jury* ‖ (*pop.*) to manage (something) satisfactorily, *will he be able to swing the job?* ‖ to play (music) in the style of swing **2.** *n.* the arc or length of arc of a swinging object, *the swing of a pendulum* ‖ the act or an instance of swinging, *give it a swing* ‖ the manner of swinging, *with a steady swing* ‖ the rhythmic beat of poetry or music ‖ a seat suspended by ropes from a fixed support, in which one can swing to and fro ‖ the act of moving thus, *my turn for a swing* ‖ a free, easy motion, esp. in marching or walking ‖ the force behind a swinging or throwing motion ‖ (*commerce*) a shift markedly upwards or downwards in the price of stocks or in the trend of some business activity ‖ the course or development of some activity ‖ freedom of action, *let him have full swing in the management* ‖ the characteristic style of jazz music, esp. after 1935, depending on a distribution of accent that produces a lively but relaxed effect, the basic material being continuously taken up in free solo variations **in full swing** operating with full vigor [O.E. *swingan*]

swing bridge a type of drawbridge that can turn about a vertical axis to permit vessels to pass

swing-by (swíŋbai) *n.* (*aerospace*) **1.** the passing of celestial body by a spacecraft, usu. taking advantage of its gravitational force **2.** orbital deviation caused by gravitational pull, making possible a change in course of a passing body **3.** used attributively, the use of such force

swinge·ing (swíndʒiŋ) *adj.* (*Br.*, *pop.*, e.g. of a fine or judicial sentence) enormous [O.E. *swengan*, to make swing]

swing·er (swíŋə:r) *n.* (*slang*) **1.** one who has many sexual partners **2.** one who is up-to-date in modern fashions and activities **3.** one who is active on the contemporary social scene — **swing** *v.* —**swinging** *n.*

swin·gle (swíŋ'l) *n.* a wooden instrument for beating and cleaning flax ‖ the swipple of a flail [M. Du. *swinghel*]

swingle *pres. part.* **swin·gling** *past* and *past part.* **swin·gled** *v.t.* to clean (flax) by beating with a swingle [M. Du. *swinghelen*]

swin·gle·tree (swíŋ'ltri:) *n.* a whiffletree

swing shift a shift normally from 4 p.m to midnight in a factory which operates 24 hours a day ‖ the workers working this shift

swing-wing (swíŋwiŋ) *n.* (*aerospace*) an aircraft in which retractable wings can be adjusted for various speeds, retreating toward the fuselage to minimize wind resistance —**swing wing** *n.* the wing itself —**swing-wing** *adj.*

swin·ish (swáiniʃ) *adj.* of, like or fit for swine

swipe (swaip) **1.** *v. pres. part.* **swip·ing** *past* and *past part.* **swiped** *v.i.* to make a powerful swinging blow, *to swipe at a ball* ‖ *v.t.* (*pop.*) to steal ‖ to hit with a swinging blow **2.** *n.* a powerful blow [var. of SWEEP]

swip·ple (swíp'l) *n.* that part of a flail that strikes the grain in threshing

swirl (swə:rl) **1.** *v.i.* (esp. of water) to move in eddies and whirls ‖ (of birds etc.) to move fast in a circular course ‖ (of the head) to have a whirling, dizzy sensation ‖ *v.t.* to cause to whirl **2.** *n.* a whirling movement ‖ an act or instance of swirling ‖ a swirling mass of water etc. ‖ a twist, curl, *a swirl of lace* [etym. doubtful]

swish (swiʃ) **1.** *v.i.* to cut through the air, e.g. with a whip, causing a sharp hissing or whistling sound ‖ (esp. of silk garments) to rustle ‖ *v.t.* to cause (e.g. a whip) to swish **2.** *n.* the sharp, hissing sound of a whip etc. cutting through the air, or the rustling sound of esp. silk garments brushing against the ground ‖ a movement accompanying the sound of swish-

---

CONCISE PRONUNCIATION KEY: **(a)** æ, c*a*t; ɑ, c*a*r; ɔ f*aw*n; ei, sn*a*ke. **(e)** e, h*e*n; i:, sh*ee*p; iə, d*ee*r; ɛə, b*ea*r. **(i)** i, f*i*sh; ai, t*i*ger; ə:, b*i*rd. **(o)** o, *o*x; au, c*ow*; ou, g*oa*t; u, p*oo*r; ɔi, r*oy*al. **(u)** ʌ, d*u*ck; u, b*u*ll; u:, g*oo*se; ə, b*a*cillus; ju:, c*u*be. x, lo*ch*; θ, *th*ink; ð, bo*th*er; z, *Z*en; ʒ, corsa*g*e; dʒ, sava*g*e; ŋ, ora*ng*utang; j, *y*ak; ʃ, *fi*sh; tʃ, fe*tch*; 'l, rabb*le*; 'n, redd*en*. Complete pronunciation key appears inside front cover.

ing, *the swish of a lion's tail* **swish·y** *adj.* [imit.]

Swiss (swis) **1.** *adj.* of or relating to Switzerland or to a native or inhabitant of Switzerland **2.** *n.* a native or inhabitant of Switzerland

Swiss chard (tʃard) *n. Beta vulgaris cicla,* a variety of beet having large, yellow-green leaves and thick, juicy stalks, both of which are eaten cooked or in salads [older *card* fr. F. *carde,* edible leafstalk of the artichoke]

Swiss cheese a hard, pale yellow cheese originating in Switzerland. Large holes form in it as it ripens

Swiss Guard (*hist.*) a member of any of various companies of Swiss mercenary soldiers ‖ a member of the papal guard of the Vatican

switch (switʃ) **1.** *n.* a device for diverting a train from one line to another ‖ a device for diverting an electric current from one wire to another, or for making or breaking an electric circuit ‖ the act of switching ‖ a thin, flexible stick, twig etc. ‖ a quick, lashing blow with a stick, twig etc. ‖ a tress of hair which a woman can add to her own to enhance her hairdo ‖ a wiry tuft of hairs at the end of the tail of some animals, e.g. a cow ‖ a complete change, *a switch in one's political opinions* **2.** *v.t.* to divert (something) to, or as if to, another track ‖ to beat with, or as if with, a switch ‖ to move with a jerk, *the horse switched its tail* ‖ *v.i.* to move from, or as if from, one set of railroad tracks to another **to switch on** (**off**) to turn on (off) by using an electric switch ‖ to start up (turn off) a radio or television set [prob. L.G.]

switch and flat maternity (*insurance*) provision in a group health-insurance plan providing maternity benefits to female employees only as dependents, i.e., when their husbands are covered, thereby denying maternity benefits to single women *Cf* FLAT MATERNITY, SWAP MATERNITY

switch·back (switʃbæk) *n.* a zigzag railroad or road on a steep hill or mountain face ‖ (*Br.*) a roller coaster

switch·blade (switʃbleid) *n.* a switchblade knife

switchblade knife a pocket knife with a spring-operated blade that is released by pressure on a button on the handle

switch·board (switʃbɔrd, switʃbourd) *n.* (*elec.*) a board or panel fitted with switches which control a number of electrical circuits, *a telephone switchboard*

switched-on (switʃdón) *adj.* (*slang*) in contact with events; alert to what is happening

switch foot (*surfing*) surfer who is comfortable on either foot

switch-hit·ter (switʃhítər) *n.* (*baseball*) a player who can bat either right-handed or left-handed

switch horn (*mil.*) in naval mine warfare, a switch in a mine operated by a projecting spike *Cf* HORN

switch·man (switʃmən) *pl.* **switch·men** (switʃmən) *n.* a person who operates railroad switches

switch sale the unethical sale of a more expensive item by a store that advertised a bargain in order to attract customers *also* bait-and-switch, bait-and-switch sale —**switch selling** *n.* the practice

Swith·in, Swith·un (swíðin), St (*d.* 862), bishop of Winchester (852-62). Tradition has it that when his body was removed from its original burial place to Winchester Cathedral (July 15, 971), the saint expressed his disapproval by causing a 40-day rainfall. The superstition thus arose in Britain that rain on July 15 means rain for the next 40 days

Switz·er·land (switsərlənd) a federal republic (area 15,941 sq. miles, pop. 6,384,300) of W. central Europe. Capital: Bern. Largest town: Zurich. Languages: German (72%), French (20%), Italian (6%), Romansh (1%, mainly in Graubünden). Religion: 53% Protestant, 46% Roman Catholic, small Old Catholic and Jewish minorities. The land is 6% arable, 46% meadow and pasture, 24% forest. The Bernese, Pennine, Lepontine and Rhaetian Alps, cut by deep valleys, cover the southern 60% of the country. Highest peak: Matterhorn, 14,780 ft. The Jura, on the French border, rise to over 5,000 ft. The rest of the country is a hilly plateau (1,000-3,000 ft), with several large lakes. Average temperatures (F.) in Jan. and July: Basel 32° and 66°, Davos 19° and 54°, St Gotthard 18° and 46°. Rainfall: Valais valley under 25 ins, upper Rhine valley 50 ins, northeastern

mountains 96 ins. Livestock: cattle, hogs, sheep, poultry. Agricultural products: cereals, dairy products, fruit, vegetables, potatoes, sugar beets, wine, tobacco. Mineral resources: salt, coal, manganese, graphite, iron ore, lignite, marble, gneiss, granite. Industries: food processing, brewing, textiles, iron and steel, machinery, metals, scientific instruments, watches and clocks, aluminum, tourism, musical instruments, hydroelectricity, rolling stock, forestry, woodwork, pottery, jewelry, chemicals, tobacco, footwear, building materials. Exports: machinery, instruments, watches and clocks, chemicals, silk goods. cotton goods, cheese, iron and steel goods, embroidery, chocolate. Imports: machinery, iron and steel, vehicles, chemicals, coal and coke, cotton, wool, wheat. River port: Basle. There are seven universities, the oldest being Basle (1460), Lausanne (1537) and Geneva (1559). Monetary unit: Swiss franc (100 rappen or centimes). HISTORY. The region was inhabited by the Helvetii, a Celtic tribe, when it was conquered (58 B.C.) by the Romans. It was overrun by the Alemanni, the Burgundians and the Franks (5th-6th cc. A.D.). It was Christianized (7th-8th cc.). It was divided (9th c.) between Swabia and Burgundy, but was reunited (1032) as part of the Holy Roman Empire. By the 13th c. it had become split into a number of feudal principalities, many of them dominated by the houses of Hapsburg and Savoy. To meet the threat of Hapsburg domination the cantons of Schwyz, Unterwalden and Uri formed a defensive league (1291), defeated an Austrian army (1315), and were joined by Lucerne (1332), Zurich (1351), Glarus and Zug (1352) and Bern (1353). This Swiss Confederation defeated Charles the Bold of Burgundy and Emperor Maximilian I, and was recognized as independent (1499). More cantons joined the confederation, raising the number to 13 by 1513. After being defeated by the French (1515) in the Italian Wars, the cantons adopted a policy of permanent neutrality (1516), though many Swiss mercenaries continued to serve other countries. The Reformation, preached by Zwingli and Calvin, was widely adopted by the urban areas (16th c.), which were intermittently at war with the rural cantons until 1712. Swiss independence was formally recognized by the Treaties of Westphalia (1648). Switzerland lost political importance (18th c.) but prospered as a financial and intellectual center. The French established the Helvetic Republic (1798-1803), but Napoleon reestablished the confederation of cantons. The Congress of Vienna (1814-15) guaranteed Swiss independence and neutrality. After a short civil war (1847) between radicals and the Sonderbund, a new constitution made Switzerland a federal state (1848). Industry and communications were developed (late 19th c.). Switzerland gained importance as the headquarters of various international organizations (11% of the population are non-Swiss) and as an international financial center. It remained neutral in both world wars and after World War II it concentrated on maintaining its neutrality, improving education and welfare programs and developing its economy into one of the world's richest

swiv·el (swívəl) **1.** *n.* a mechanical device consisting of a pivot mounted in a ring so that the two parts of the device can revolve independently **2.** *v.i. pres. part.* **swiv·el·ing,** *esp. Br.* **swiv·el·ling** *past* and *past part.* **swiv·eled,** *esp. Br.* **swiv·elled** to turn on or as if on a swivel [rel. to O.E. *swifan,* to move in a sweeping course]

swivel chair a chair having one pillar support which screws into a base so that the height of the seat can be altered and the user can swing around on it to face in any direction

swiz·zle stick (swíz'l) a thin rod, with or without prongs, for stirring drinks

swollen alt. *past part.* of SWELL

swoon (swu:n) **1.** *v.i.* (*rhet.*) to faint **2.** *n.* (*rhet.*) the action of fainting [M.E. *swounen* prob. fr. O.E. *geswogen,* unconscious]

swoop (swu:p) **1.** *v.i.* (esp. of birds) to descend swiftly and suddenly, often in a wide, sweeping arc ‖ (esp. with 'down') to make a sudden attack, esp. from a great distance **2.** *n.* a swooping movement ‖ a sudden attack **at one fell swoop** by a single act of attack or a single effort [O.E. *swāpan,* to sweep]

swop *SWAP

sword (sɔrd, sourd) *n.* a weapon having a long,

thin cutting blade fitted into a hilt which incorporates a guard **to cross swords** to disagree, argue violently [O.E. *sweord*]

sword dance a folk dance involving the use of swords ‖ a dance, esp. a solo dance, performed around swords laid on the ground

sword·fish (sɔrdfiʃ, sourdfiʃ) *pl.* **sword·fish,** **sword·fish·es** *n. Xiphias gladius,* fam. *Iphiidae,* an enormous (200–600 lbs) game and food fish found in the Mediterranean and the Atlantic, having a long, rigid, swordlike upper jaw

sword grass any of several grasses or sedges of which the leaves have sharp or toothed edges

sword·play (sɔrdplei, sourdplei) *n.* the art of fencing with the saber etc.

swords·man (sɔrdzmən, sourdzmən) *pl.* **swords·men** (sɔrdzmən, sourdzmən) *n.* a man skilled in fencing with the saber etc.

sword stick a hollow walking stick in which a sword blade is concealed

swore *past* of SWEAR

sworn (sworn, sworun) *past part.* of SWEAR‖ *adj.* bound by oath or as if by oath, *sworn enemies*

swot *SWAT

swum *past part.* of SWIM

swung *past* and *past part.* of SWING

syb·a·rite (síbərait) *n.* a person inordinately attached to comfort, pleasure and luxury **syb·a·rit·ic** (sibəritik), **syb·a·rit·i·cal** *adjs.* **syb·a·rit·ism** (síbəritizəm) *n.* [fr. L. *Sybarita* fr. Gk fr. *Sybaris,* an ancient Greek town in S. Italy famous as a center of luxury]

syc·a·more (síkəmor, síkəmour) *n. Platanus occidentalis,* a large, spreading plane tree of eastern and northern U.S.A. ‖ *Acer pseudoplatanus,* a genus of Eurasian maple trees, having striking yellow flowers. Sycamores are widely planted as shade trees ‖ the wood of either of these trees [O.F. *sicamor, sichamor* fr. L. fr. Gk]

sycamore fig *Ficus sycomorus,* fam. *Moraceae,* a genus of sycamore trees of Egypt and Asia Minor, having sweet, edible fruit resembling a fig

sy·co·ni·um (sikóuni:əm) *pl.* **sy·co·ni·a** (sikóuni:ə) *n.* a multiple fruit developed from many flowers enclosed in a fleshy receptacle, e.g. the fig [Mod. L. fr. Gk *sukon,* fig]

syc·o·phan·cy (síkəfənsi:) *n.* servile flattery [fr. L. *sycophantia* fr. Gk]

syc·o·phant (síkəfənt) *n.* a person who habitually uses flattery to gain personal advantage **syc·o·phan·tic** (sikəfǽntik) *adj.* [fr. L. *sycophanta* fr. Gk]

sy·co·sis (sikóusis) *pl.* **sy·co·ses** (sikóusi:z) *n.* an infection of the scalp or shaved area of the face [Mod. L. fr. Gk *sukōsis* fr. *sukon,* fig]

Sydney, Algernon *SIDNEY, ALGERNON

Syd·ney (sídni:) the chief city and port (pop. 3,231,700) of Australia, capital of New South Wales on Port Jackson, an inlet (½–1½ miles wide, 8 miles long) of the Pacific. Industries: textiles, food processing, foundries, automobiles, machinery, plastics, oil refining. Port Jackson is crossed by a single-span arch bridge (1932). Sydney University (1850) and University of New South Wales (1958)

sy·e·nite (sáiənait) *n.* an igneous rock, chiefly of orthoclase, with hornblende and other minerals **sy·e·nit·ic** (saiənítik) *adj.* [F. *syénite* fr. L. fr. Gk]

sy·li (sí:li:) *n.* unit of currency in Guinea, equal to 100 cauries

syl·la·bary (síləbɛri:) *pl.* **syl·la·bar·ies** *n.* a set or table or system of written characters representing syllables rather than individual sounds [fr. Mod. L. *syllabarium* fr. *syllaba,* syllable]

syl·lab·ic (silǽbik) **1.** *adj.* relating to a syllable or syllables ‖ of a consonant which by itself forms a syllable without a vowel sound (e.g. the '1' in 'battle') ‖ pronounced distinctly with stress on each syllable ‖ of a verse form arranged according to syllables per line rather than according to rhythm or accent **2.** *n.* (*phon.*) a vocal speech sound capable by itself of forming a syllable **syl·lab·i·cal·ly** *adv.* [fr. Mod. L. *syllabicus* fr. Gk]

syl·lab·i·cate (silǽbikeit) *pres. part.* **syl·lab·i·cat·ing** *past* and *past part.* **syl·lab·i·cat·ed** *v.t.* to syllabify [fr. SYLLABICATION]

syl·lab·i·ca·tion (silæbikéiʃən) *n.* syllabification [fr. M.L. *syllabicatio (syllabicationis)* fr. *syllabicare,* to form into syllables]

syl·lab·i·fi·ca·tion (siləbifikéiʃən) *n.* formation of or division into syllables, or the method of such division [fr. M.L. *syllabificare* fr. *syllaba,* syllable]

CONCISE PRONUNCIATION KEY: **(a)** æ, c**a**t; ɑ, c**a**r; ɔ f**aw**n; ei, sn**a**ke. **(e)** e, h**e**n; i:, sh**ee**p; iə, d**ee**r; ɛə, b**ea**r. **(i)** i, f**i**sh; ai, t**i**ger; ə:, b**i**rd. **(o)** o, **o**x; au, c**ow**; ou, g**oa**t; oi, p**oor**; ɔi, r**oy**al. **(u)** ʌ, d**u**ck; u, b**u**ll; u:, g**oo**se; ə, b**a**cillus; ju:, c**u**be. x, lo**ch**; θ, **th**ink; ð, bo**th**er; z, **Z**en; ʒ, corsa**g**e; dʒ, sava**g**e; ŋ, ora**ng**utang; j, **y**ak; ʃ, **f**ish; tʃ, **f**etch; 'l, rabb**l**e; 'n, redd**e**n. Complete pronunciation key appears inside front cover.

syl·lab·i·fy (silébifai) *pres. part.* **syl·lab·i·fy·ing** *past* and *past part.* **syl·lab·i·fied** *v.t.* to form or divide into syllables [fr. L. *syllaba*, syllable]

syl·la·bize (síləbaiz) *pres. part.* **syl·la·biz·ing** *past* and *past part.* **syl·la·bized** *v.t.* to syllabify [fr. M.L. *syllabizare* fr. Gk]

syl·la·ble (síləb'l) *n.* a word or part of a word pronounced with a single sounding of the voice. It is usually composed of one vowel sound of great sonority and one or more consonants of less sonority ‖ the letter or letters (or symbols) written to represent a spoken syllable ‖ the least bit, *not a syllable of truth in it* [A.F. *sillable* fr. L. fr. Gk]

syllabub *SILLABUB

syl·la·bus (síləbəs) *pl.* **syl·la·bus·es, syl·la·bi** (síləbai) *n.* a brief outline of the ground to be covered in a course of lessons, lectures etc. [Mod. L. fr. Gk]

syl·lep·sis (silépsis) *pl.* **syl·lep·ses** (silépsi:z) *n.* (*gram.*) the application of one word to govern or modify two others in different senses though it agrees grammatically with only one of them **syl·lep·tic** (siléptik) *adj.* [L. fr. Gk *sullēpsis*, a putting together]

syl·lo·gism (síləd3izəm) *n.* a logically consistent argument consisting of two propositions (major and minor premises), and a conclusion deduced from them ‖ a branch of logic concerned with syllogisms **syl·lo·gis·tic, syl·lo·gís·ti·cal** *adjs.* [O.F. *sillogisme* or fr. L. fr. Gk]

syl·lo·gize (síləd3aiz) *pres. part.* **syl·lo·giz·ing** *past* and *past part.* **syl·lo·gized** *v.i.* to reason by syllogism ‖ *v.t.* to put (an argument) into syllogistic form [O.F. *silogiser, sillogiser* or fr. M.L.]

sylph (silf) *n.* (in the Paracelsian system) a spirit inhabiting the air, mortal and soulless, and generally female ‖ a slender, graceful woman or girl [fr. M.L. *sylphes pl. n.*, G. *sylphen*]

sylph·id (sílfid) *n.* a young or small sylph [F. *sylphide*]

Sylt (zilt) *SCHLESWIG-HOLSTEIN

syl·van, sil·van (sílvən) *adj.* of, relating to, characteristic of or situated in a wood ‖ wooded [fr. F. *sylvain* or fr. L. *silvanus, sylvanus*]

syl·van·ite (sílvənait) *n.* an ore of gold or silver combined with tellurium [after TRANSYLVANIA, place of earliest discovery]

Syl·ves·ter I, Sil·ves·ter I (silvéstər), St (*d.* 335), pope (314-35). Feast: Dec. 31

Sylvester II (c. 940-1003), pope (999-1003). He was a distinguished teacher and was the first French pope

sylviculture *SILVICULTURE

syl·vine (sílvin) *n.* sylvite

syl·vite (sílvait) *n.* a mineral, KCl, consisting of natural potassium chloride, found in colorless cubes or masses. It is an important source of potassium [fr. Mod. L. *sal digestivus sylvii* (old name)]

Symbionese Liberation Army terrorist anti-establishment organization, founded in California (1971), noted for kidnapping Patricia Hearst (1974) *abbr.* **SLA**

sym·bi·ont (símbaiɔnt, símbi:ɒnt) *n.* (*biol.*) an organism living in symbiosis [prob. fr. G. fr. Gk *sumbiountos* fr. *sumbioun*, to live together]

sym·bi·o·sis (simbaióusis, simbi:óusis) *n.* (*biol.*) the intimate association of two dissimilar organisms from which each organism benefits [Mod. L. fr. Gk *sumbiōsis*, a living together]

sym·bi·o·tic (simbaiótik, simbi:ótik) *adj.* of or characterized by symbiosis **sym·bi·ót·i·cal·ly** *adv.* [fr. Gk *sumbiōtikos*]

sym·bol (símb'l) *n.* a sign or object accepted as recalling, typifying or representing a thing, quality or idea ‖ a character, mark or sign standing for some process, idea, quality etc., e.g. as used in science, mathematics and music ‖ (*psychoanal.*) an act or object that represents a repressed unconscious drive, memory etc. **sym·bol·ic** (simbólik), **sym·ból·i·cal** *adjs.* **sym·ból·i·cal·ly** *adv.* [fr. L.L. *symbolum* fr. Gk]

symbolic logic a method of reasoning which operates with symbols rather than words

symbolic racism covert racism made legal by tokenism

sym·bol·ism (símb'lizəm) *n.* representation by symbols ‖ a system of symbols symbolic meaning **Sym·bol·ism** the theories and practices of the Symbolists
—Symbolism came into being in the literature of Europe in the late 19th and early 20th cc. in reaction to naturalism and realism. Complex and deliberately planned, a Symbolist work

was to express perfectly an intention on the part of the artist and create in the mind of the reader the exact equivalent. Mallarmé defined it as the recovering for poetry of the power of music, which communicated more subtly and precisely than any language could. Hence Symbolist poetry made use of the nonliteral, figurative powers of language: tone, association and metaphor. It became an art of elaborate structure, developing an image or network of images which caused the dislocation of normal syntax. Though this 'pure' symbolism is peculiar to Mallarmé and Valéry, it was prefigured by Laforgue and others and there are elements of it in such diverse writers as Hopkins, Eliot, Proust and Joyce. In music Symbolism is typified by Debussy, in drama by Maeterlinck, and its impact is felt in many Impressionist paintings

sym·bol·ist (símb'list) *n.* a person who uses symbols ‖ a writer or artist who uses symbolism **Sym·bol·ist** (*theol.*) a person who denies transubstantiation and regards the Eucharist as symbolic ‖ an exponent of Symbolism in literature, art or music

sym·bol·ize (símb'laiz) *pres. part.* **sym·bol·iz·ing** *past* and *past part.* **sym·bol·ized** *v.t.* to be a symbol of ‖ to represent by a symbol or symbols ‖ *v.i.* to use symbols [fr. F. *symboliser*]

sym·met·ric (simétrik) *adj.* symmetrical

sym·met·ri·cal (simétrik'l) *adj.* exhibiting symmetry

sym·me·trize (símitraiz) *pres. part.* **sym·me·triz·ing** *past* and *past part.* **sym·me·trized** *v.t.* to make symmetrical [fr. F. *symétriser*]

sym·me·try (símitri:) *pl.* **sym·me·tries** *n.* the quality of possessing exactly corresponding parts on either side of an axis (thus a circle has symmetry about any chosen diameter) ‖ a formal correspondence between two sets of mathematical symbols ‖ (*loosely*) the quality of being well balanced or well proportioned ‖ (*biol.*) regularity in form or similarity of structure [F. or fr. L.L. *symmetria* fr. Gk]

sym·mog·ra·phy (simógrəfi:) *n.* art form of linear thread design, e.g., string craft, nail craft

sym·pa·thet·ic (simpəθétik) *adj.* of, relating to or possessing sympathy ‖ exactly fitting in with one's mood or attitude ‖ favorably disposed, sympathetic towards contemporary design ‖ (*physiol.*) of or relating to the sympathetic nervous system ‖ (*phys.*, of vibrations, sound etc.) caused by vibrations from a neighboring body ‖ (*literary criticism*) likable, attractive to the reader **sym·pa·thét·i·cal·ly** *adv.* [fr. Mod. L. *sympatheticus* fr. Gk]

sympathetic nervous system the part of the autonomic nervous system which has motor nerve fibers originating in the cervical, thoracic and lumbar regions of the spinal cord and that generally depresses glandular secretion, decreases muscle tone and induces blood-vessel contraction (cf. PARASYMPATHETIC NERVOUS SYSTEM)

sympathetic strike a strike in which workers not themselves involved in an industrial dispute go on strike to demonstrate their solidarity with those directly concerned

sym·pa·thize (símpəθaiz) *pres. part.* **sym·pa·thiz·ing** *past* and *past part.* **sym·pa·thized** *v.i.* to feel or communicate sympathy ‖ (esp. with 'with') to feel or express compassion for the sufferings, sorrows etc. of others ‖ to be in intellectual agreement ‖ (with 'with') to be favorably disposed [F. *sympathiser*]

sym·pa·tho·lyt·ic (simpəθoulítək) *adj.* (*chem.*) antagonistic to the sympathetic nervous system —**sympatholytic** *n.*

sym·pa·thy (símpəθi:) *pl.* **sym·pa·thies** *n.* a sharing in the emotions of others, esp. the sharing of grief, pain etc. ‖ a feeling for the ills, difficulties etc. of others ‖ a mutual liking resulting from an affinity of feeling ‖ (*physiol.*) the relation between bodily parts or organs whereby a disorder, pain etc. in one part or organ induces a similar effect in another **to be in sympathy with** to be favorably disposed towards (a cause, opinion etc.) ‖ to identify oneself with the opinion of (someone) [fr. L.L. *sympathia* fr. Gk]

sympathy strike a sympathetic strike

sym·pat·ric (simpǽtrək) *adj.* (*envir.*) occupying an area in common with another species

sym·pet·al·ous (simpét'ləs) *adj.* (*bot.*) having a tubular corolla formed by the union of a number of petals (opp. POLYPETALOUS) [fr. Gk *sun*, with+PETALOUS]

sym·phon·ic (simfónik) *adj.* of, relating to, or

having the form or nature of a symphony ‖ of or relating to harmony of sound

symphonic poem a term introduced by Liszt to describe an orchestral work of symphonic dimensions which interprets something nonmusical, e.g. a legend

sym·pho·ny (símfəni:) *pl.* **sym·pho·nies** *n.* (*mus.*) an extended musical composition in sonata form for full orchestra ‖ a symphony orchestra [O.F. *simphonie* fr. L. fr. Gk]

symphony orchestra a large orchestra which performs symphonies and other large-scale orchestral works

sym·phy·sis (símfisis) *pl.* **sym·phy·ses** (símfisi:z) *n.* (*anat., zool.*) the union of certain bones, e.g. the halves of the lower jaw meeting at the chin ‖ the union of bones by fibrocartilage without a synovial membrane [Mod. L. fr. Gk *sumphusis*, a growing together]

sym·po·di·al (simpóudi:əl) *adj.* of, designating or characterized by a sympodium

sym·po·di·um (simpóudi:əm) *pl.* **sym·po·di·a** (simpóudi:ə) *n.* (*bot.*) a system of branches in which the main axis stops growing and the process of elongation is carried on by lateral branches [Mod. L. fr. Gk *sun*, with+*podion*, a little foot]

sym·po·si·um (simpóuzi:əm) *pl.* **sym·po·si·a** (simpóuzi:ə), **sym·po·si·ums** *n.* a group discussion or a collection of published articles on a single theme ‖ a set of spoken or written contributions to a discussion of a single subject ‖ (*ancient Greece*) a banquet followed by drinking, music and intellectual discussion [L. fr. Gk *sun*, with+*potēs*, a drinker]

symp·tom (símptəm) *n.* a condition in the body or in its behavior, noted by the patient, suggesting the presence of injury or disease (cf. SIGN)

symp·to·mat·ic (simptəmǽtik) *adj.* of or relating to symptoms ‖ constituting a symptom ‖ in accordance with symptoms **symp·to·mát·i·cal·ly** *adv.* [F. *symptomatique*]

symp·tom·a·tol·o·gy (simptəmətólədʒi:) *n.* the branch of medicine dealing with the symptoms of disease [fr. Mod. L. *symptomatologia*]

syn- (sin) *prefix* with, together with, at the same time, by means of [Gk *sun*, with]

synaeresis *SYNERESIS

synaesthesia *SYNESTHESIA

syn·a·gog·i·cal (sinəgódʒik'l) *adj.* of a synagogue

syn·a·gogue (sínəgɔg, sínəgɒg) *n.* a Jewish community meeting for religious observances or instruction ‖ the building or assembly place used by Jewish communities for this [O.F. *sinagoge* or fr. L.L. fr. Gk]

syn·a·loe·pha, syn·a·le·pha (sinəlí:fə) *n.* (*gram.*) the blending of two syllables into one, esp. by suppressing the final vowel of the first, e.g. 'th' unknown' for 'the unknown' [L.L. fr. Gk fr. *sunaleiphein*, to coalesce, melt together]

syn·an·thro·py (sinǽnθroupi:) *n.* of the ecology in which human beings exist —**synanthropic** *adj.*

syn·apse (sinǽps, sínæps) *n.* (*physiol.*) the region at which a nervous impulse passes from one nerve cell to another, formed by the contact of processes of the two cells and responsible for the selection and propagation of nerve impulses characteristic of developed central nervous systems (*ACETYLCHOLINE) [fr. Gk *sunapsis*, junction]

syn·ap·sis (sinǽpsis) *pl.* **syn·ap·ses** (sinǽpsi:z) *n.* (*biol.*) the process characteristic of the prophase of the first meiotic division in which the chromosomes, without prior splitting, join in pairs, corresponding chromosomes from each parent being associated ‖ synapse [Mod. L. fr. Gk *sunapsis*, junction]

syn·ap·to·ne·mal (sinǽptoní:məl) *n.* (*genetics*) ribbon-shaped structures in pairing of chromosomes, believed to take part in the genetic process *also* synaptinemal complex

syn·ar·thro·sis (sinɑrθróusis) *pl.* **syn·ar·thro·ses** (sinɑrθróusi:z) *n.* (*anat.*) a joining of bones by a fibrous tissue which does not permit movement between them [Mod. L. fr. Gk *sunarthrōsis*, a linking together]

syn·carp (sínkɑrp) *n.* (*bot.*) a multiple fleshy fruit **syn·cár·pous** *adj.* (*bot.*) possessing carpels joined in a compound ovary (e.g. in the tulip) ‖ referring to a syncarp [fr. SYN-+Gk *karpos*, fruit]

synch·ing (sínkiŋ) *n.* synchronization of an on-stage entertainer's lip movements to a tape played off-stage *also* lip-synching —**lip-synch** *v.* —**synch** *v.*

CONCISE PRONUNCIATION KEY: (a) æ, c*a*t; ɑ, c*a*r; ɔ f*aw*n; ei, sn*a*ke. **(e)** e, h*e*n; i:, sh*ee*p; iə, d*ee*r; ɛə, b*ea*r. **(i)** i, f*i*sh; ai, t*i*ger; ə:, b*i*rd. **(o)** o, *o*x; au, c*ow*; ou, g*oa*t; u, p*oo*r; ɔi, r*oy*al. **(u)** ʌ, d*u*ck; u, b*u*ll; u:, g*oo*se; ə, b*a*cillus; ju:, c*u*be. x, l*o*ch; θ, *th*ink; ð, bo*th*er; z, *Z*en; ʒ, corsa*g*e; dʒ, sava*g*e; ŋ, ora*n*gutang; j, *y*ak; ʃ, *fi*sh; tʃ, fe*tch*; 'l, rabb*le*; 'n, redd*en*. Complete pronunciation key appears inside front cover.

syn·chro·cy·clo·tron (siŋkrousáiklətrɒn) *n.* (*phys.*) a device similar to a cyclotron but having an alternating electric field whose frequency may be adjusted to compensate relativistic mass changes. The synchrocyclotron produces particles having energies in the range 10^5–10^7 eV [fr. *synchro-*, synchronous, synchronized+CYCLOTRON]

syn·chro·mesh (síŋkrəmeʃ) *n.* an arrangement of gears which synchronizes the driving and driven parts before they engage, eliminating shock and noise when the engagement is made [fr. *synchro-*, synchronous, synchronized+MESH]

syn·chron·ic (siŋkrónik, sinkrónik) *adj.* synchronous ‖ (*linguistics*) of or describing the structure of a language at one particular time (opp. DIACHRONIC) [fr. L.L. *synchronus*]

syn·chro·nism (síŋkrənizəm) *n.* the fact or quality of being synchronous ‖ the chronological arrangement of contemporary events, trends, leading figures etc. in different parts of the world or in different aspects of history ‖ a table setting this out [fr. Mod. L. *synchronismus* fr. Gk]

syn·chro·nis·tic (siŋkrənístik) *adj.* synchronous

syn·chro·ni·za·tion (siŋkrənizéiʃən) *n.* a synchronizing or being synchronized

syn·chro·nize (síŋkrənaiz) *pres. part.* **syn·chro·niz·ing** *past* and *past part.* **syn·chro·nized** *v.i.* to occur at the same time ‖ to proceed at the same rate ‖ *v.t.* to cause to occur at the same time or to proceed at the same time ‖ to regulate so as to agree in time, *to synchronize watches* ‖ to put (events) at the same date or time ‖ (*movies*) to adjust (sounds) with the action ‖ to adjust (the shutter of a camera) so that the flashbulb goes off when the shutter opens [fr. Mod. L. *synchronismus* fr. Gk *sunchronizein* fr. *sunchronos*, contemporary]

synchronized swimming sport in which competitors perform gymnastic maneuvers, ballet, circular swimming, underwater somersaults *also* water ballet

syn·chro·nous (síŋkrənəs) *adj.* existing or occurring at the same time ‖ exactly coinciding in time, rate etc. ‖ (*phys.*) having the same phase and period [fr. L.L. *synchronus* fr. Gk]

synchronous orbit (*aerospace*) path of a communications relay station satellite that is traveling at the same speed as the earth, the satellite thus appearing to remain over one point on earth —**synchronous satellite** *n.*

syn·chro·tron (síŋkrətrɒn) *n.* (*phys.*) any of several particle accelerators utilizing some combination of frequency modulated alternating electric fields (as in the synchrocyclotron) for accelerating the particles and using specially designed focusing magnetic fields (as in the betatron) for maintaining stable orbits. Synchrotrons can be used to accelerate positively charged or negatively charged particles and produce particles with energies in the range 10^{10}–10^{12} eV [fr. *synchro-*, synchronous, synchronized+Gk *-tron*, instrument]

synchrotron radiation (*phys.*) radiation emitted by celestial bodies conceived as orbiting in and accelerated by a magnetic field similar to a vast synchrotron

syn·clas·tic (sinklǽstik) *adj.* (of a surface, e.g. the surface of a sphere) having the same curvature in all directions around any given point (opp. ANTICLASTIC) [fr. SYN-+Gk *klastos*, broken]

syn·cli·nal (sinkláin'l) *adj.* (*geol.*) of strata which dip towards a common point or line (opp. ANTICLINAL) **sýn·cline** *n.* (*geol.*) such an arrangement of strata (opp. ANTICLINE) [fr. Gk *sun*, syn+*klinein*, to incline together]

Syncom *n.* any of several U.S. communications relay satellite placed in synchronous equatorial orbit

syn·co·pate (síŋkəpeit, sínkəpeit) *pres. part.* **syn·co·pat·ing** *past* and *past part.* **syn·co·pat·ed** *v.t.* to shorten (a word) by syncope ‖ (*mus.*) to shift the regular accent in (a composition) to a normally unaccented beat **syn·co·pá·tion** (siŋkəpéiʃən) *n.* a syncopating or being syncopated ‖ (*gram.*) syncope ‖ syncopated rhythm [fr. L.L. *syncopare* (*syncopatus*), to affect with syncope]

syn·co·pe (síŋkəpi:, sínkəpi:) *n.* (*gram.*) the shortening of a word by dropping sounds or syllables from the middle of it ‖ loss of consciousness due to a sudden transient failure of blood

supply to the brain [fr. L.L. fr. Gk fr. *sun*, together+*koptein*, to cut off, cut short]

syn·cret·ic (siŋkrétik, sinkrétik) *adj.* syncretistic

syn·cre·tism (síŋkrətizəm, sínkrətizəm) *n.* attempted reconciliation of conflicting or opposite beliefs, e.g. in philosophy or religion, esp. uncritically ‖ the development of a religion by the subsuming of older forms ‖ perception in which incompatible elements are fused, e.g., in dreams ‖ (*gram.*) the fusion into one of two or more differently inflected grammatical forms of a word **sýn·cre·tist** *n.* **syn·cre·tís·tic** *adj.* of or relating to syncretism or to a syncretist [fr. Mod. L. *syncretismus* fr. Gk]

syn·cre·tize (síŋkritaiz, sínkritaiz) *pres. part.* **syn·cre·tiz·ing** *past* and *past part.* **syn·cre·tized** *v.t.* to unite or attempt to unite (conflicting tenets), esp. without critical understanding ‖ *v.i.* to become fused or united ‖ to practice syncretism [fr. Mod. L. *syncretizare* fr. Gk]

syn·dac·tyl, syn·dac·tyle (sindǽktil) **1.** *adj.* (of some birds and some mammals) having two or more digits wholly or partly united **2.** *n.* a bird or mammal having syndactyl digits **syn·dác·tyl·ism** *n.* [fr. SYN-+Gk *daktulos*, finger]

syn·des·mo·sis (sindesmóusis) *pl.* **syn·des·mo·ses** (sindesmóusi:z) *n.* (*anat.*) an articulation of joints in which the bones are united by a ligament **syn·des·mot·ic** (sindesmótik) *adj.* [Mod. L. fr. Gk *sundesmos*, ligament]

syn·det·ic (sindétik) *adj.* (*gram.*) serving to connect [fr. Gk *sundetikos* fr. *sundein*, to bind together]

syn·dic (síndik) *n.* an official, esp. one who manages the business matters of a university or other corporation **sýn·di·cal** *adj.* [fr. F. fr. L.L. fr. Gk]

syn·di·cal·ism (síndik'lizəm) *n.* a political and economic theory advocating the use of general strikes and force by the workers to enable them to overthrow parliamentary government and establish a dictatorship of the proletariat, in which the means of production would be controlled by the trade unions. The theory, allied to anarchism, originated in France in the 19th c. **sýn·di·cal·ist** *adj.* and *n.* [fr. F. *syndicalisme*]

syn·di·cate 1. (síndikit) *n.* a body of syndics ‖ a group of persons or firms authorized jointly to promote some common interest ‖ a chain of newspapers ‖ an organization selling feature stories, cartoons etc. to several newspapers or magazines for simultaneous publication **2.** (síndikeit) *v. pres. part.* **syn·di·cat·ing** *past* and *past part.* **syn·di·cat·ed** *v.t.* to join together to form a syndicate ‖ *v.t.* to control as or form into a syndicate ‖ to sell (feature stories etc.) to several newspapers or magazines for simultaneous publication **syn·di·cá·tion** *n.* [fr. F. *syndicat* fr. M.L.]

syn·drome (síndroum) *n.* a group of disease symptoms commonly found in association with one another ‖ a number of disparate things regarded as an associated group [Mod. L. fr. Gk *sundromē*, a running together]

syn·ec·do·che (sinékdəki:) *n.* the rhetorical device by which the part is taken for the whole ('so much a head' instead of 'so much per person'), the whole for the part, the genus for the species, the species for the genus, the matter for the thing made of it etc. [L.L. fr. Gk *sunekdochē*, a receiving together]

syn·ec·tics (sinéktiks) *n.* method of stating and solving problems through analogy by brain storming, utilizing persons of diverse backgrounds —**synectic** *adj.* —**synectically** *adv.*

syn·er·e·sis, syn·aer·e·sis (sinírəsis, sinérisis) *n.* (*prosody*) the contraction of two like vowels into a single syllable, esp. so as to form a diphthong (opp. DIAERESIS) ‖ syni*zesis* [Mod. L. fr. Gk *sunairesis*, a talking together]

syn·erg·a·my (siné:rgəmi:) *n.* group marriage —**synergamous** *adj.*

syn·er·get·ic (sinərdʒétik) *adj.* synergic [fr. Gk *sunergētikos* fr. *sunergein*, to work with, cooperate]

syn·er·gic (siné:rdʒik) *adj.* of or characterized by synergy [fr. Mod. L. *synergicus* fr. Gk]

syn·er·gism (sínərdʒizəm) *n.* (*theol.*) the doctrine that divine grace and human activity cooperate in the work of regeneration ‖ (esp. of drugs) the combined action of two or more which have a greater total effect than the sum of their individual effects **sýn·er·gist** *n.* (*theol.*) a person who holds the doctrine of synergism ‖ (*med.*) a muscle, organ or drug acting in syn-

ergy with another or others **syn·er·gis·tic** *adj.* (*theol.*) of or relating to synergism ‖ (*med.*) able to act in synergism [fr. Mod. L. *synergismus* fr. Gk]

syn·er·gy (sínərdʒi:) *pl.* **syn·er·gies** *n.* (*med.*) the working together of two or more muscles, organs or drugs [fr. Mod. L. *synergia*, joint work fr. Gk]

syn·e·sis (sínisis) *n.* (*gram.*) a construction which conforms to the general sense rather than to syntax (e.g. use of a plural verb with a collective singular noun) [Mod. L. fr. Gk *sunesis*, understanding]

syn·es·the·sia, syn·aes·the·sia (sinisθí:ʒi:ə, sinisθí:ʒə) *n.* (*psychol.*) the spontaneous association of sensations of different kinds, e.g. the suggestion of a certain color by certain sounds [Mod. L. fr. Gk *sun*, with+*aisthēsia*, sensation]

syn·fuel (sínfju:l) *n.* synthetic fuel

syn·gam·ic (singǽmik, singæmik) *adj.* of or characteristic of syngamy

syn·ga·my (síŋgəmi:) *n.* (*biol.*) sexual: reproduction by the fusion of gametes [fr. SYN-+Gk *gamos*, marriage]

Synge (siŋ), John Millington (1871-1909), Irish playwright. His works include 'Riders to the Sea' (1905), 'The Playboy of the Western World' (1907) and 'Deirdre of the Sorrows' (1910). In these plays he makes use of the vigorous and vivid dialect of the fishermen and peasants of W. Ireland

syn·ge·ne·ic (sindʒəní:ik) *adj.* (*genetics*) of a similar or identical genotype Cf ALLOGENEIC

syn·gen·e·sis (sindʒénisis) *n.* (*biol.*) derivation of the zygote in sexual reproduction from both the paternal and the maternal substance ‖ (*geol.*) the formation of sediments in place **syn·ge·net·ic** (sindʒənétik) *adj.* [Mod. L.]

syn·graph (síŋgræf) *n.* a written agreement signed by all parties involved

syn·i·ze·sis (sinizí:sis) *n.* the contraction of two syllables into a single syllable by the pronunciation of two adjacent vowels as though they were a single vowel [L.L. fr. Gk *sunizēsis*, collapse]

syn·met·al (sínmet'l) *n.* synthetic nonmetallic material that conducts electricity

syn·od (sínəd) *n.* (*eccles.*) a consultative council of clergy ‖ a Presbyterian ecclesiastical court which acts as an administrative body intermediate between the General Assembly and the presbyteries ‖ a council [fr. L.L. *synodus* fr. Gk]

syn·od·al (sínəd'l) *adj.* of, relating to, or constituting a synod [fr. L.L. *synodalis*]

syn·od·ic (sinódik) *adj.* synodical **syn·ód·i·cal** *adj.* synodal ‖ (*astron.*) of or relating to conjunction, exp. of the interval between two successive conjunctions of the same bodies [fr. L.L. *synodicus* fr. Gk]

syn·oe·cism (siní:sizəm) *n.* a joining together of villages or small towns to form one administrative complex, e.g. a Greek city-state ‖ (*bot.*) the state of being synoicous [fr. Gk *sunoikismos*, wedlock, act of combining into one city-state]

syn·oi·cous (siní:kəs) *adj.* (*bot.*) having stamens and pistils in the same flower or on the same flower head or, in certain mosses, having archegonia and antheridia in the same involucre or on the same receptacle [Gk *sunoikos*, dwelling together]

syn·o·nym (sínənim) *n.* a word having the same meaning as another word in the same language in one or more of its senses, *'car'* and *'automobile'* are synonyms (opp. ANTONYM) ‖ a metonym ‖ (*biol.*) a rejected taxonomic name **syn·o·ným·ic** *adj.* **syn·o·nym·i·ty** (sinənímiti:) *n.* **syn·on·y·mous** (sinónəməs) *adj.* [fr. L.L. *synonymum*, *synonymor* fr. Gk *sunōnumos* fr. *sun*, together+*onum*, name]

syn·on·y·my (sinónəmi:) *pl.* **syn·on·y·mies** *n.* the quality or fact of being synonymous ‖ a collection of synonyms ‖ the study of synonyms [fr. L.L. *synonymia* fr. Gk]

syn·op·sis (sinópsis) *pl.* **syn·op·ses** (sinópsi:z) *n.* an outline, summary [L.L. fr. Gk *sunopsis*, a general view]

syn·op·tic (sinóptik) **1.** *adj.* providing a general summary **Syn·op·tic** of or relating to the first three books (Matthew, Mark, Luke) of the New Testament, which agree frequently in subject, order and language **2.** *n.* one of the Synoptic Gospels **syn·óp·ti·cal** *adj.* **syn·óp·ti·cal·ly** *adv.* [fr. Mod. L. *synopticus* fr. Gk]

synoptic (*meteor.*) of data collected at many points simultaneously to present overview of weather conditions

synoptic chart a meteorological map presenting data and analyses which describe weather conditions over a large area at a given moment in time

Syn·op·tist (sinóptist) n. an author of one of the Synoptic Gospels

syn·o·vi·a (sinóuvi:ə) n. the fluid produced by the transparent internal lining membrane of joints, acting as a lubricant **syn·ó·vi·al** adj. of or secreting synovia **syn·o·vi·tis** (sinəváitis) n. inflammation in a synovial membrane [Mod. L.]

syn·tac·tic (sintǽktik) adj. syntactical **syn·tác·ti·cal** adj. of or relating to syntax or in accordance with the rules of syntax [fr. Mod. L. syntacticus fr. Gk]

syn·tax (síntæks) n. the arrangement of words in a sentence showing their constructional relationship ‖ the branch of grammar concerned with this [fr. F. syntaxe fr. L.L. fr. Gk]

syn·thase (sínθeis) n. (biochem.) any synthetic enzyme used in catalysis

syn·the·sis (sínθisis) pl. **syn·the·ses** (sínθisi:z) n. (logic) a method of demonstration which consists in reasoning from self-evident propositions, laws or principles to arrive by a series of deductions at what one seeks to establish ‖ an exposition assembling the various parts into a whole, a historical synthesis ‖ (chem.) the formation of a compound from elements or simpler compounds **sýn·the·sist** n. **sýn·the·size** (sínθisaiz) v.t. pres. part. **syn·the·siz·ing** past and past part. **syn·the·sized** to form into a whole by synthesis ‖ (chem.) to produce (e.g. an organic compound) by synthesis [L. fr. Gk sunthesis, a putting together, composition]

syn·the·tase (sínθəteis) n. (biochem.) a catalytic enzyme that causes the formation of nucleoside monophosphate or diphosphate from nucleoside triphosphate also ligase

syn·the·siz·er (sínθəsaizər) n. (electr.) a device that creates complex entities of simple sound or frequency elements e.g., a voice synthesizer in a computer

syn·thet·ic (sinθétik) 1. adj. relating to or involving synthesis produced by synthesis ‖ artificial, man-made, synthetic fibers ‖ using inflections or affixes to express syntactical relationships 2. n. a synthetic product, e.g. nylon **syn·thét·i·cal·ly** adv. [fr. F. synthétique or Mod. L. syntheticus fr. Gk]

synthetic foam a strong, pressure-resistant plastic containing air cells to reduce weight in packing

synthetic fur fun fur (which see)

syn·the·tize (sínθitaiz) pres. part. **syn·the·tiz·ing** past and past part. **syn·the·tized** v.t. to synthesize

syph·i·lis (sífəlis) n. a chronic, often congenital venereal disease, caused by the spirochete Treponema pallidum. If untreated the disease may result in the degeneration of many organs and tissues of the body **syph·i·lit·ic** (sifəlítik) n. and adj. [Mod. L. after 'Syphilis sive Morbus Gallicus', a poem by Girolamo Fracastoro (1483–1553)]

sy·phon, si·phon (sáifən) n. a bottle holding a tube fitted at the top with a valve which when opened allows the carbonated water in the bottle to be ejected [fr. L. sipho (siphonis), tube, pipe fr. Gk]

Syr·a·cuse (sírəkju:s) a city (pop. 170,105) in central New York State: chemicals, car parts, electrical appliances, mechanical engineering. University (1870)

Syr·a·cuse (Ital. Siracusa) a port (pop. 89,000) in S.E. Sicily: Greek theater (5th c. B.C.) and temples, Roman amphitheater. Castle (13th c.), baroque cathedral (17th-18th cc.), palaces. Syracuse was founded as a Greek colony (8th c. B.C.), defeated an attack by Athens (415-413 B.C.) and was sacked (212 B.C.) by the Romans

Syr-Dar·ya (si:rdárjə) (ancient Jaxartes) a river (1,370 miles long, navigable along its middle course) formed in the Ferghana Valley by streams from the Tien Shan and Altai Mtns, and flowing north through Uzbekistan, Tadzhikistan and Kazakhstan, U.S.S.R., to the Aral Sea

Syr·i·a (síri:ə) a republic (area 71,210 sq. miles, pop. 8,979,000) in W. Asia. Capital: Damascus. People: 90% Arab, small Turkish, Turkoman, Kurdish, Circassian, Armenian and other minorities. Language: Arabic, minority languages. Religion: 72% Sunnites, 11% Shi'ites, 2% Druze, 3% Greek Orthodox, 2% Armenian Orthodox, 2% Roman Catholic, smaller Christian sects, some Jews. The population is 10% nomadic (Beduins). The land is 30% arable, 34% pasture and grazing, and 2% forest. It is largely a plateau (1,000-3,000 ft), with the Ansariyeh Mtns (rising to 5,194 ft) near the northwest coast, the Anti-Lebanon Mtns (*HERMON) on the Lebanon border, Gebel Druse (5,900 ft) in the south, and isolated massifs in the center. The Euphrates basin (1,000-3,000 ft) crosses the northeast. East of the Anti-Lebanon Mtns, the Syrian Desert covers the south. The north is semiarid grassland (livestock, dry cereal culture). Average temperatures (F.) for Jan. and July: Latakia 56° and 81°, Palmyra 46° and 110°, E. Euphrates valley 43° and 90°. Rainfall: Aleppo 15 ins, Damascus 9 ins, coast 20-40 ins, desert under 5 ins. Livestock: sheep, goats, cattle, donkeys, mules, camels. Agricultural products: wheat, rice, other cereals, sugar beets, pulses, fruit, olives, tomatoes, figs, cotton, tobacco, almonds, dairy products. Mineral resources: asphalt, natural gas, bitumen, basalt, building stone, salt. Industries: food processing, soap, cement, tobacco, tanning, textiles, glass, footwear, metalware, wine. Exports: cotton, cereals, silk fabrics, wool, cottonseed, lentils, sheep. Imports: iron and steel, machinery, fuel and oils, silk, wool, wood, vehicles, chemicals. Chief port: Latakia. Universities: Damascus (1924) and Aleppo (1961). Monetary unit: Syrian pound (100 piasters). HISTORY. Situated on trade routes between the Mediterranean and Mesopotamia, Syria was settled (3rd millennium B.C.) by Semitic Amorites. Canaanites settled on the coast (2nd millennium B.C.) and the Aramaeans established their capital at Damascus (11th c. B.C.). Parts of Syria were overrun by the Egyptians and the Hittites (18th-10th cc. B.C.), the Assyrians (8th c. B.C.), the Babylonians or Chaldeans (7th c. B.C.) and the Persians (6th c. B.C.). Control passed (333 B.C.) to Alexander the Great, and after his death (323 B.C.) to the Seleucids, under whom Hellenistic culture was introduced. Syria was conquered (63 B.C.) by the Romans under Pompey. It flourished under Roman rule and the south of the country saw the rise of Christianity. Syria passed to the Byzantine Empire (395 A.D.) and was fully converted to Christianity, but was overrun (633-6) by the Arabs and was gradually converted to Islam. Damascus prospered as the capital of the Umayyad caliphate (651-750), but Syria declined when the Abbasids moved the caliphate to Baghdad. The Seljuk Turks and the Mamelukes repelled the Crusades (11th-13th cc.), and the Ottoman Turks established their rule (1516). Syria was invaded by the French (1799), and by the Egyptians (1832) under Ibrahim Pasha, who ruled as governor (1833-9). Arab nationalism began in Lebanon and Syria about the turn of the century, and separatist movements against the Turks were encouraged by Britain and France during the 1st world war. With Lebanon, Syria became a French mandate (1920). The French put down a rebellion (1925-7) with severity. Syria was occupied (1941) by the British and the Free French, and was declared independent (Jan. 1, 1944), but sporadic fighting continued between French and Syrian forces until 1945. Syria joined the Arab League and the U.N. (1945). After a series of coups d'état, Syria joined the United Arab Republic (1958), but seceded (1961). After further revolts, it sought closer links with the United Arab Republic (1963). A further military coup took place in 1966. Syria joined (1971) the Union of Arab Republics (with Egypt and Lebanon). Syria lost territory on the Golan Heights to Israel during wars (1967, 1973). Syrian troops occupied most of Lebanon (1976) in an effort to end civil war in that country. A military coup (1970) brought Gen. Hafiz al-Assad to power. He was elected president by public referendum (1971) and reelected (1978, 1985)

Syr·i·ac (síri:æk) 1. adj. of, relating to or written in Syriac 2. n. Aramaic ‖ a form of Aramaic spoken by Eastern Christian communities ‖ the liturgical language used by some Eastern Christian Churches (cf. PESHITTA, cf. NESTORIAN CHURCH)

Syr·i·an (síri:ən) 1. n. a native or inhabitant of Syria ‖ a member of a Syrian Church 2. adj. of or relating to Syria, its peoples, language, culture etc. ‖ of, relating to or being one of the Eastern Churches using Syriac liturgies, e.g. the Nestorian-Church

Syrian Desert (Arab. Hamad) a desert region covering most of S. Syria and S.W. Iraq, and adjoining regions of Jordan and Saudi Arabia

sy·rin·ga (siríngə) n. a member of Philadelphus, fam. Saxifragaceae, a genus of shrubs of temperate regions having strong-scented white flowers [Mod. L. fr. Gk surinx (suringos), shepherd's pipe]

sy·ringe (siríndʒ, síríndʒ) 1. n. a piston-fitted hand cylinder, or a rubber bulb with a nozzle, into which a liquid is sucked and then ejected in a stream for cleansing, spraying or injecting 2. v.t. pres. part. **sy·ring·ing** past and past part. **sy·ringed** to inject, cleanse etc. with a syringe [fr. M.L. siringa, syrynga]

sy·rin·ge·al (siríndʒi:əl) adj. of or relating to the syrinx

syr·inx (síriŋks) pl. **sy·rin·ges** (siríndʒi:z), **syr·inx·es** n. a panpipe ‖ the vocal organ of birds [L. fr. Gk surinx, a pipe]

Syro- (sírou) combining form Syrian and ‖ Syriac and

Sy·ros (sáirɒs) (or Syra) an island (area 31 sq. miles, pop. 18,642) of the N. Cyclades, containing their chief port, Hermoupolis (pop. 14,000)

syr·up, sir·up (sírəp, sə́:rəp) n. a thick liquid consisting of a concentrated solution of sugar and water ‖ such a thick liquid with flavoring or some medicinal substance added, cough syrup ‖ evaporated juice of sugarcane before crystallization of the sugar, in the process of manufacturing cane sugar ‖ cloying sentimentality **sýr·up·y, sír·up·y** adj. [O. F. sirop, cyrop]

sys·tal·tic (sistǽltik, sistóltik) adj. (physiol., of the heart) characterized by regular contraction and dilatation [fr. L.L. systalticus fr. Gk]

sys·tem (sístəm) n. an orderly, interconnected, complex arrangement of parts, the nervous system ‖ a set of principles linked to form a coherent doctrine, a philosophical system ‖ a method of organization, administration or procedure ‖ (geol.) a major division of rocks, formed during a period or era, the Devonian system ‖ (astron.) a group of orbiting heavenly bodies moving about a central body ‖ (biol.) a group of bodily organs having the same or similar structure and which act as a unit in performing a vital bodily function, the circulatory system ‖ (biol.) a method of classification ‖ a set of units permitting the basic measurements to be clearly and simply stated, the metric system ‖ calculated orderliness, to work with system [fr. L.L. systema fr. Gk]

system approach a mathematical approach to the study of the components of a system to define how the system will behave under various circumstances Cf SYSTEMS ANALYSIS

sys·tem·at·ic (sistəmǽtik) adj. constituting a system, a systematic philosophy ‖ working in accordance with a system, methodical ‖ relating to classification in biology **sys·tem·át·i·cal·ly** adv. **sys·tem·at·ics** n. the science of classification [fr. L.L. systematicus fr. late Gk]

sys·tem·a·tist (sístəmətist) n. a taxonomist

sys·tem·a·ti·za·tion (sistəmətizéiʃən) n. a systematizing or being systematized

sys·tem·a·tize (sístəmətaiz) pres. part. **sys·tem·a·tiz·ing** past and past part. **sys·tem·a·tized** v.t. to make into a system

sys·tem·ic (sistémik) adj. of or relating to a system, esp. (physiol.) of or relating to the entire bodily system

sys·tem·i·za·tion (sistəmizéiʃən) n. systematization

sys·tem·ize (sístəmaiz) pres. part. **sys·tem·iz·ing** past and past part. **sys·tem·ized** v.t. to systematize

system levels a set of criteria used to analyze political systems, their efficiency, benefits, problems, etc.

systems analysis the study of an activity to determine objectives and how to accomplish them most efficiently, e.g., procedures for collecting, manipulating, and evaluating computer data to improve control over an operation —**systems analyst** n.

systems engineering a technique of management theory involving rationalistic models of business organizations, based on the interrelation of components and on the input and output of the total system under consideration

sys·to·le (sístəli:) n. (physiol.) the regular contraction of an organ (e.g. the heart or an artery) by which the blood is driven forward (opp. DIAS-

TOLE) **sys·tol·ic** (sistólik) *adj.* [Mod. L. fr. Gk *sustolē*, contraction]

syz·y·gy (sízidʒi:) *pl.* **syz·y·gies** *n.* (*astron.*) a point of conjunction or opposition of a planet, esp. the moon, with the sun [fr. L.L. *syzygia* fr. Gk]

Szcze·cin (ʃtʃetsíːn) (*G.* Stettin) a port and naval base (pop. 381,000) in Poland on the Oder near its mouth, with shipbuilding, machinery, paper, chemical and metallurgical industries.

It includes a free port. Churches (12th and 14th cc.)

Sze·chwan (sʌtʃwán) a province (pop. 90,000,000) of western and central China, around the middle Yang-tze-kiang. Capital: Chengtu. It is the largest and most populous province, at the heart of which lies the Red Basin, a rich agricultural region with extensive mineral resources

Sze·ged (séged) a town (pop. 175,700) in S. Hun-

gary on the Tisza. Industries: textiles, food processing. University

Szek·ler (séklər) *n.* the Transylvanian branch of the Magyar people ‖ their dialect of Hungarian, written in its own runic alphabet

Sze·ming (súːmíŋ) *AMOY

Szent-Györ·gyi (sentdjɔ́ardji:), Albert von Nagyrapolt (1893-   ), Hungarian biochemist. He isolated vitamin C and prepared it in bulk from Hungarian paprika (Nobel prize, 1937)

CONCISE PRONUNCIATION KEY: (**a**) æ, c*a*t; ɑ, c*ar*; ɔ f*aw*n; ei, sn*a*ke. (**e**) e, h*e*n; iː, sh*ee*p; iə, d*ee*r; ɛə, b*ea*r. (**i**) i, f*i*sh; ai, t*i*ger; əː, b*i*rd. (**o**) o, *o*x; au, c*ow*; ou, g*oa*t; u, p*oor*; ɔi, r*oy*al. (**u**) ʌ, d*u*ck; u, b*u*ll; uː, g*oo*se; ə, b*a*cill*u*s; juː, c*u*be. x, lo*ch*; θ, *th*ink; ð, bo*ther*; z, *Z*en; ʒ, corsa*g*e; dʒ, sava*g*e; ŋ, ora*ng*uta*ng*; j, *y*ak; ʃ, *f*ish; tʃ, fe*tch*; ʼl, rabb*le*; ʼn, redd*en*.   Complete pronunciation key appears inside front cover.

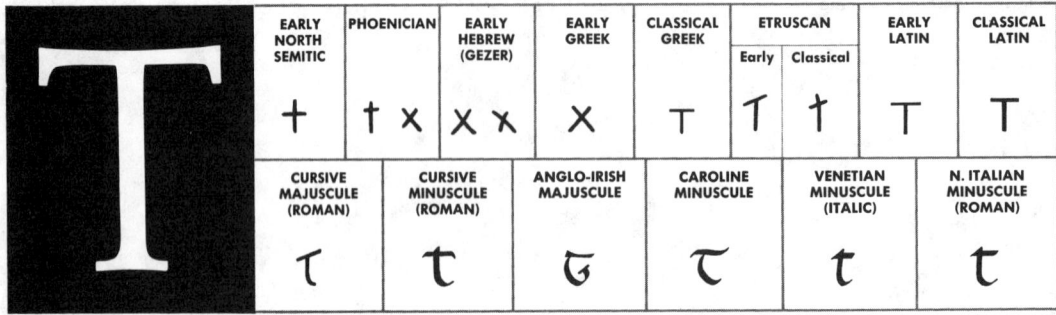

EARLY NORTH SEMITIC	PHOENICIAN	EARLY HEBREW (GEZER)	EARLY GREEK	CLASSICAL GREEK	ETRUSCAN		EARLY LATIN	CLASSICAL LATIN
					Early	Classical		
T	†X	XX	X	T	T	†	T	T

CURSIVE MAJUSCULE (ROMAN)	CURSIVE MINUSCULE (ROMAN)	ANGLO-IRISH MAJUSCULE	CAROLINE MINUSCULE	VENETIAN MINUSCULE (ITALIC)	N. ITALIAN MINUSCULE (ROMAN)
T	τ	Ᏻ	τ	t	t

Development of the letter T, beginning with the early North Semitic letter. Evolution of both the majuscule, or capital, letter T and the minuscule, or lowercase, letter t are shown.

T,t (ti:) the twentieth letter of the English alphabet **to a T** exactly
T (*electr. symbol*) for **1.** tera (10^{12}) **2.** (*symbol*) for testa, high-frequency current with moderate voltage
TA (*abbr.*) for **1.** teaching assistant **2.** (*abbr.*) for transactional analysis
Taal (tɑl) (with 'the') Afrikaans [Du.=language, speech]
tab (tæb) *n.* a small loop or flap attached to or forming an extension of something, having a special use or ornamental value, e.g. the lettered projection of a filing card or a point of lace or other trimming ‖ an unpaid bill, *pick up the tab*, or the price that has to be paid for something, *what will the tab be?* ‖ (*Br., mil.*) a collar mark denoting the rank of a staff officer **to keep tab** (or **tabs**) **on** (*Br.* **to keep tab of**) to keep a check on [etym. doubtful]
tab·a·nid (tǽbənid) *n.* a member of *Tabanidae*, a family of flies comprising the horseflies etc., whose females suck blood [fr. L. *tabanus*, gadfly]
tab·ard (tǽbərd) *n.* (*hist.*) a tunic worn by a knight over his armor and emblazoned with his arms ‖ a herald's cloak emblazoned with his sovereign's arms [O.F. *tabart, tabar*]
Ta·bas·co (təbǽskou, tɑbɑ́sko) a gulf state (area 9,783 sq. miles, pop. 1,101,300) of S.E. Mexico, covered by lagoons, swamps, and dense forests (Tabasco means 'damp earth'). Capital: Villahermosa (pop. 34,000). Main agricultural products: bananas, cocoa, coffee, rice, sugarcane, corn and tropical fruits. Forest products: valuable fine woods and dyewoods. Potential oil wealth
ta·bas·co (təbǽskou) *n.* a pungent sauce made from the fruit of the capsicum [after *Tabasco*, a river and state in Mexico]
tab·by (tǽbi:) *pl.* **tab·bies** *n.* a cat with brownish-gray fur marked with dark, wavy stripes ‖ a female cat (opp. TOM) ‖ (*old-fash.*) a sour scandalmongering woman, esp. if she is unmarried [etym. doubtful]
tab·er·nac·le (tǽbərnæk'l) *n.* (*eccles.*) an ornamental repository for the pyx or consecrated elements ‖ (*archit.*) a niche or recess having a canopy ‖ a Nonconformist place of worship ‖ (*naut.*) a socket or hinged post enabling the mast of a vessel to be lowered in order to pass under a low bridge **the Tabernacle** the portable sanctuary containing the Ark of the Covenant serving as a place of worship for the Jews in their wanderings in the desert when they came out of Egypt [O.F.]
tabernacle work (*archit.*) pierced tracery or other carved ornamental work, e.g. over niches, choir stalls etc. in churches

ta·bes (téibi:z) *pl.* **ta·bes** *n.* (*med.*) the process of wasting that sometimes accompanies a chronic disease, e.g. tuberculosis ‖ (*med.*) tabes dorsalis [L.= a wasting away]
tabes dor·sa·lis (dɔrséilis) (*med.*) a form of syphilis marked by wasting, lack of coordination of movement and disturbances of digestive and sensory organs
ta·bet·ic (təbétik) **1.** *adj.* of, resembling, or having tabes dorsalis **2.** *n.* a person having tabes dorsalis [fr. L. *tabes*, a wasting away]
ta·bla (tǽblə) *n.* Indian tuned drum, usu. in a pair, of two sizes
ta·ble (téib'l) **1.** *n.* a piece of furniture having a flat, horizontal, usually smooth surface of wood or other material. It is supported by legs or a pedestal or pedestals, and is used to sit at for meals, for working, for playing games etc. ‖ a group of people sitting around this, esp. for eating ‖ a flat, often movable part of a machine tool on which material to be worked is fastened ‖ a stringcourse ‖ a tableland ‖ the upper flat facet of a gem (cf. CULET) ‖ (*anat.*) the internal or external layer of the bony tissue of the skull ‖ (*backgammon*) one of the two leaves of the board or either half of a leaf ‖ an orderly arrangement of facts set out for easy reference, *a table of contents* ‖ an arrangement of numerical values etc. in vertical columns, *logarithmic tables* **to keep** (or **set**) **a good** (**poor** etc.) **table** to serve good (poor etc.) food at one's table **to turn the tables on** (someone) to put (someone) who had the advantage over one at a disadvantage **under the table** into a state of unconsciousness or near unconsciousness, *to drink someone under the table* **2.** *v.t. pres. part.* **ta·bling** *past* and *past part.* **ta·bled** (*Br.*) to put forward (a proposal etc.) for consideration by an assembly ‖ to postpone a decision on (e.g. a proposal) indefinitely ‖ to tabulate ‖ (*naut.*) to reinforce the edge of (a sail) by making a wide hem [O.E. *tabule, tabele*]
tab·leau (tǽblou, tæblóu) *pl.* **tab·leaus, tableaux** (tǽblouz, tæblóuz) *n.* a group of people so posed (e.g. in a pageant) as to seem to the beholder to have a significant unity [F.]
ta·bleau vi·vant (tǽblouviːvã) *pl.* **ta·bleaux vivants** (tǽblouviːvã) *n.* a static, wordless representation of a scene, esp. a historical scene, famous picture etc. by one or more persons [F.]
ta·ble·cloth (téib'lklɔθ, téib'lklɒθ) *pl.* **ta·blecloths** (téib'lklɔθs, téib'lklɒθs, téib'lklɔðz, téib'lklɒðz) *n.* a cloth used to cover a dining table
ta·ble-cut (téib'lkʌt) *adj.* (of a gem) cut with a flat upper surface larger than the culet, with facets linking the table to the girdle

ta·ble d'hôte (tɑbldout) *n.* a fixed list of dishes for a fixed price, in a restaurant etc. (cf. A LA CARTE) [F.=the host's table]
ta·ble·land (téib'llænd) *n.* (*geol.*) a plateau
table linen tablecloths, napkins etc.
Table Mountain a flat-topped mountain (3,550 ft) rising steeply above Cape Town, South Africa
table rapping spirit rapping
ta·ble·spoon (téib'lspuːn) *n.* a large spoon used for serving food from a dish to a plate. It holds about four teaspoonfuls ‖ a tablespoonful **ta·ble·spoon·ful** (téib'lspuːnful) *pl.* **ta·ble·spoon·fuls** *n.* as much as a tablespoon will hold
tab·let (tǽblit) *n.* a flat piece of stone or metal inscribed as a memorial ‖ a medical pastille ‖ a pad of writing paper ‖ a small flat block of soap, chocolate etc. ‖ (*hist.*) a small thin, flat piece of clay, wax etc. used to write on a table-cut gem [O.F. *tablete*]
table talk informal conversation, e.g. at a dinner table, esp. such discursive matter in published form
table tennis a game distantly related to tennis, played usually indoors on a table with round wooden bats and a small plastic ball
table turning spirit rapping
ta·ble·ware (téib'lwɛər) *n.* dishes, plates, glasses, cutlery etc. used in setting a table and for serving food and drink
tab·loid (tǽblɔid) *n.* a small-format, heavily illustrated newspaper featuring news items of a sensational nature ‖ any publication adopting a similar format or size of page [*Tabloid*, a trademark applied to certain chemicals used in concentrated form in pharmacy and medicine]
ta·boo, ta·bu (təbúː) **1.** *n.* the prohibition of certain contacts, words, actions etc. on religious grounds among many primitive peoples ‖ the state or quality of being thus prohibited ‖ anything which is prohibited by tradition or social usage **2.** *adj.* placed under taboo ‖ forbidden on grounds of tradition or social usage **3.** *v.t.* to place under taboo ‖ to condemn as not proper because of convention etc. [Tongan *tabu*]
ta·bor (téibər) *n.* (*hist.*) a small drum played with the hand by a musician to accompany his own playing of a threeholed pipe [O.F. *tabur, tabour* fr. Pers.]
Ta·bo·ra (təbɔ́rə, tabóurə) a commercial center and rail junction (pop. 67,392) in W. Tanganyika, Tanzania
tab·o·ret, tab·ou·ret (tǽbərit) *n.* a low stool [fr. F. *tabouret*, small drum]
Ta·bor, Mount (téibər) a domelike hill (929 ft) near Nazareth, traditionally regarded as the mountain of the Transfiguration
tabouret *TABORET

Ta·briz (tɑbríːz) the chief city (pop. 598,576) of Azerbaijan, Iran, a trade center: dried fruit, rugs, silks. University

tabu *TABOO

tab·u·la (tǽbjulə) *pl.* **tab·u·lae** (tǽbjuliː) *n.* one of the transverse septa of various corals and hydroids [L.=table]

tab·u·lar (tǽbjulər) *adj.* set out in the form of a table, *a tabular statement* ‖ used in setting out such a table ‖ computed from a table ‖ having a flat, tablelike surface, laminated ‖ composed of broad, flat crystals, *a tabular mineral* ‖ (of a crystal) having a flat parallel base and top [fr. L. *tabularis*]

tab·u·la ra·sa (tǽbjulərásə) *pl.* **tab·u·lae ra·sae** (tǽbjuliːrásiː) the human mind thought of as being a perfect blank at birth, before it begins to receive impressions ‖ a clean sweep, complete obliteration (e.g. of awkward or painful memories) [L. =cleaned tablet]

tab·u·late (tǽbjuleit) **1.** *v.t. pres. part.* **tab·u·lat·ing** *past* and *past part.* **tab·u·lated** to arrange in tabular form **2.** *adj.* having tabulae ‖ (of rocks, crystals etc.) having a flat, tablelike surface **tab·u·lá·tion** *n.* **táb·u·la·tor** *n.* an arrangement of stops for the carriage of a typewriter so that columns of figures etc. can be set out in vertical lines ‖ an office worker who makes tabulations ‖ a business machine for tabulating data [fr. L.L. *tabulari* (*tabulatus*)]

tac·a·ma·hac (tǽkəməhæk) *n.* a pungent oleoresin obtained from any of several tropical trees of the genera *Protium* (esp. *P. heptaphyllum* and *P. altissimum*) and *Bursera*, used as incense and in ointments ‖ the resin exuded by the North American balsam poplar [fr. obs. Span. *tacamahaca*, fr. Aztec]

tacan (*mil.* acronym) for tactical air navigation, an ultrahigh frequency electronic air navigation system that provides a single continuous indication of bearing and distance (slant range) to the tacan station

Ta·ca·ri·gua, Lake (tɑkɑrí:gwɑ) *VALENCIA, LAKE

tach (tæk) *n.* short for tachometer, a rotation speed-measuring device

tach·e·om·e·ter (tækiːómitər) *n.* a tachymeter [F. *tachéomètre*]

tach·i·na fly (tǽkinə) any of numerous dark gray or black dipterous flies of fam. *Tachinidae*, whose larvae are parasitic in caterpillars and other harmful insects

tachism (French, *tâche*, 'spot, blot') abstract painting utilizing improvised techniques, e.g., splattering, dribbling, pouring, as works of Jackson Pollock *also* tachist *adj, n. Cf* ACTION PAINTING

tach·isme (tǽʃizəm) *n.* *ABSTRACT EXPRESSIONISM [F.]

ta·chom·e·ter (tækómitər) *n.* an instrument for measuring the speed of rotation of a revolving shaft etc. **ta·chóm·e·try** *n.* [fr. Gk *tachos*, speed+METER]

tach·y·car·di·a (tækikárdi:ə) *n.* (*med.*) an abnormally fast heartbeat [fr. Gk *tachus*, swift+*kardia*, heart]

tach·y·lyte (tǽkilait) *n.* a black, glassy form of basalt **tach·y·lyt·ic** (tækəlítik) *adj.* [G. *tachylit* fr. Gk *tachus*, swift+*lutos*, soluble]

ta·chym·e·ter (tækímitər) *n.* (*survey.*) an instrument used to locate distant points quickly ‖ an instrument for measuring speed [fr. Gk *tachus*, swift+METER]

tach·y·on (tǽkiːɒn) *n.* (*particle phys.*) hypothetical elementary particle characterized by speed greater than light, with energy decreasing in proportion to speed, named by American physicist Gerald Feinberg (1933–) based on Einstein's theories

tac·it (tǽsit) *adj.* existing or implied but not stated, *tacit agreement* ‖ (*law*) arising by operation of law [fr. L. *tacere* (*tacitus*), to be silent]

tac·i·turn (tǽsitəːrn) *adj.* not given to saying much [fr. L. *taciturnus*]

tac·i·tur·ni·ty (tæsitə́ːrniti:) *n.* the state or quality of being taciturn [M.F. *taciturnité* or fr. L.]

Tac·i·tus (tǽsitəs), Marcus Claudius (c. 200-76), Roman emperor (275-6). An austere and honest ruler, he was assassinated after a reign of 10 months

Tacitus, Publius Cornelius (c. 55–c. 120), Roman historian. His works include 'Dialogue on Orators' (c. 79-81), 'Agricola' (c. 98), 'Germania' (c. 98) and two fragments of longer histories: the 'Histories' (104-10, covering the years 68-70) and the 'Annals' (115-17, covering most of the years 14-68). His style is exceedingly terse and polished

tack (tæk) **1.** *n.* a short, sharp nail having a broad, usually flat, head ‖ a long stitch, esp. a basting stitch ‖ a stitch used to hold down a pleat etc. temporarily ‖ (*naut.*) a rope used to fasten the corner of any of certain sails ‖ the corner so fastened ‖ the direction in which a vessel sails as the result of the position of her sails and helm ‖ the act of changing this direction by shifting the sails and helm ‖ the distance sailed after such a change and before the course is altered ‖ an act of tacking ‖ a course of action, *to try a new tack* **2.** *v.t.* to fasten with a tack or tacks ‖ to baste (stitch temporarily) ‖ to hold down (a pleat etc.) temporarily by a stitch ‖ to append as an addition, *to tack a postscript on a letter* ‖ (*naut.*) to change the course of (a ship or boat) when sailing against the wind by putting the helm over and shifting the sails ‖ to navigate (a sailing ship or boat) by a series of tacks ‖ *v.i.* (*naut.*) to change the direction of a sailing ship or boat ‖ (*naut.*, of a sailing ship or boat) to change direction by making a tack ‖ to change one's course of action [fr. O.F. *tache*, fibula, large nail]

tack·i·ness (tǽkiːnis) *n.* the state or quality of being tacky

tack·le (tǽk'l) **1.** *n.* (*naut.*) a ship's rigging ‖ a mechanism for lifting weights by ropes and pulleys ‖ equipment, *fishing tackle* ‖ (*football* and *rugby*) the act of tackling an opponent ‖ an instance of this ‖ (*football*) either of two players between the guard and the end on either side of the line of scrimmage ‖ the harness for a horse **2.** *v. pres. part.* **tack·ling** *past* and *past part.* **tack·led** *v.t.* to come to grips with, esp. in order to subdue, *to tackle an opponent* ‖ (*pop.*) to apply oneself to (a problem or a hard piece of work) ‖ (often with 'up') to harness (a horse) ‖ (*football* and *rugby*) to seize and stop or pull down (an opposing player with the ball) ‖ (*soccer*) to intercept or obstruct (an opponent with the ball) ‖ *v.i.* (*football* and *rugby*) to seize and stop or pull down an opponent with the ball ‖ (*soccer*) to intercept or obstruct an opponent with the ball [M.L.G., L.G. *takel*]

tack·y (tǽki:) *comp.* **tack·i·er** *superl.* **tack·i·est** *adj.* (of glue, paint etc.) not quite set and still sticky to the touch [fr. older *tack* n., adhesiveness]

tacky *comp.* **tack·i·er** *superl.* **tack·i·est** *adj.* (*pop.*) shabby, dowdy [etym. doubtful]

tac·log group (tǽklɒg) (*mil.*) representatives designated by army troop commanders to assist Navy control officers aboard control ships in the ship-to-shore movements of troops, equipment, and supplies

Ta·co·ma (təkóumə) a port (pop. 158,501) in the state of Washington, on Puget Sound: wood and metallurgical industries, food processing

Ta·con·ic (təkɒ́nik) *adj.* (*geol.*) of a North American mountain-making episode during the late Ordovician period [fr. *Taconic Mtns* in northeastern U.S.A.]

tact (tækt) *n.* an understanding of how to avoid giving offense and of how to keep or win goodwill **tact·ful** (tǽktfəl) *adj.* [fr. L. *tactus*, touch]

tac·tic (tǽktik) *n.* tactics ‖ a detail of tactics [fr. Mod. L. *tactica* fr. Gk]

tactic *adj.* of, relating to, or showing biological taxis [fr. Mod. L. *tacticus* fr. Gk]

tac·ti·cal (tǽktik'l) *adj.* of or pertaining to tactics ‖ (of a plan of action etc.) astutely thought out so as to advance a purpose or gain an advantage ‖ (*mil.*) of relatively short-range U.S. and U.S.S.R. nuclear weapons stationed in Europe [fr. Gk *taktikos*]

tactical warning (*mil.*) **1.** a notification that the enemy has initiated hostilities **2.** in satellite and missile surveillance, a notification to operational command centers that a specific threat is occurring

tactical weapon (*mil.*) weapon used in the battlefield

tac·ti·cian (tæktíʃən) *n.* a person with a sound knowledge of tactics ‖ a person who maneuvers cleverly in any situation

tac·tics (tǽktiks) *n.* (construed as *sing.*) the science and art of using a fighting force to the best advantage having regard to the immediate situation of combat (cf. STRATEGY) ‖ (construed as *pl.*) carefully worked-out steps taken to achieve a purpose [TACTIC]

tac·tile (tǽktəl, tǽktail) *adj.* of, relating to or perceived by the sense of touch ‖ (*physiol.*) of capsular corpuscles in the skin and some mucous membranes believed to constitute special organs of touch **tac·til·i·ty** (tæktíliti:) *n.* [fr. L. *tactilis*, tangible]

tact·less (tǽktlis) *adj.* lacking tact

tac·tu·al (tǽktʃuːəl) *adj.* of or relating to the sense or the organs of touch [fr. L. *tactus*, touch]

Tadjikistan *TADZHIKISTAN

tad·pole (tǽdpoul) *n.* the tailed, legless, aquatic larva of the frog, toad or certain other amphibians after emerging from the egg and while still possessing external or internal gills [M.E. *tāde*, *tadde*, toad +*poll*, head]

Ta·dzhik (tádʒik) *n.* a member of a people of old Iranian stock scattered among the populations of Afghanistan and Turkestan

Ta·dzhik·i·stan (tadʒikistán) (or Tadjikistan) a constituent republic (area 55,240 sq. miles, pop. 3,801,000) of the U.S.S.R., in central Asia. Capital: Dyushambe. Religion: mainly Moslem. The country is mountainous, rising to the Pamirs in the east. Resources (largely unexploited): brown coal, lead, zinc, oil, uranium, arsenic. Industries: agriculture (cattle and sheep raising, fruit, cotton, cereals), engineering, food processing, hydroelectricity, cotton and silk textiles. It became a constituent republic in 1929

Tae·gu (táiguː) a city (pop. 1,311,078) in central South Korea, the market for a cereal and tobacco-growing region: textiles, foodstuffs

Tae·jon (táidʒɒn) a rail center (pop. 506,703) in S.E. South Korea: railroad stock, silk, leather

tae·ni·a, te·ni·a (tíːniːə) *n.* (*archit.*, Doric order) a band separating the frieze from the architrave ‖ (*anat.*) a ribbonlike band of muscle or nerve tissue ‖ (*zool.*) the tapeworm [L. fr. Gk *tainia*, ribbon]

taf·fe·ta (tǽfitə) *n.* a thin, rather stiff glossy fabric of natural or artificial silk [O.F. *taffetas*, *taphetas* fr. Pers.]

taff·rail (tǽfreil) *n.* (*naut.*) the rail around the stern of a ship [fr. Du. *tafereel*, a panel]

taf·fy (tǽfi:) *n.* candy made by boiling down brown sugar or molasses, then pulling it until it is supple and light in color [etym. doubtful]

ta·fi·a (tǽfiːə) *n.* a variety of inferior rum distilled from sugarcane juice [Creole F. or Malay]

Taft (tæft), Robert Alphonso (1889-1953), U.S. political leader. As U.S. senator (1938-53) from Ohio, he led opposition to President Franklin Roosevelt's New Deal and vigorously fought U.S. participation in the United Nations Organization, the European Recovery Program, and the Atlantic Pact. He drafted (1947) the Taft-Hartley Labor Act. He lost (1952) the Republican presidential nomination to Dwight D. Eisenhower

Taft, William Howard (1857-1930), 27th president (1909-13) of the U.S.A., a Republican. As the first civil governor (1900-4) of the Philippine Is, he improved U.S.-Filipino relations. He worked closely with President Theodore Roosevelt as his secretary of war (1904-8), and succeeded him. As president he continued Roosevelt's policy of dollar diplomacy in Latin America, introduced (1910) the postal savings bank and (1912) the parcel-post system, and created (1911) the Department of Labor. He was nevertheless criticized by progressives for his conservatism. He served (1921-30) as chief justice of the Supreme Court

Taft-Hartley Labor Act (Labor-Management Relations Act) a U.S. Congressional act (1947) sponsored by Senator Robert A. Taft and Representative Fred A. Hartley, which was passed over President Harry Truman's veto. It declared that the union or the employer must, before ending a collective-bargaining agreement, notify the other party and a government mediation service. It authorized the government to obtain an 80-day injunction against any strike that endangered national health or safety. Other provisions prohibited jurisdictional strikes and secondary boycotts, denied protection to workers on wildcat strikes, and outlawed the closed shop. It bound unions to file evidence with the U.S. Department of Labor that their union officers were not Communists before they could use the facilities of the National Labor Relations Board

tag (tæg) **1.** *n.* a label of plastic, metal etc. for fastening to something for identification, classification etc. ‖ the hard tip on each end of a shoelace to facilitate insertion through eyelets ‖ the tip of the tail of an animal, esp. of a fox ‖ a cliché or hackneyed quotation ‖ a lock of dirty, matted sheep's wool ‖ a hanging, tattered bit of cloth **2.** *v. pres. part.* **tag·ging** *past* and *past part.* **tagged** *v.t.* to attach a tag to ‖ (with 'on') to

TUV

attach as an addition, esp. rather clumsily and awkwardly, *to tag a few notes on to a new edition* ‖ to rid (a sheep) of tags ‖ (*pop.*) to follow closely and with persistence ‖ *v.i.* (with 'along') to join up temporarily with someone else, esp. without previous arrangement or invitation ‖ to drag oneself (itself) along a little to the rear [etym. doubtful]

tag 1. *n.* a children's game in which a player (called 'it') chases other players until he manages to touch one, who in turn becomes 'it' **2.** *v.t. pres. part.* **tag·ging** *past* and *past part.* **tagged** to touch (a player) in this game ‖ (*baseball*) to hit (the ball) with the bat **to tag out** (*baseball*) to put out (a runner) by touching him with the ball [etym. doubtful]

Ta·ga·log (təgáloɡ) *pl.* **Ta·ga·log, Ta·ga·logs** *n.* a people of central Luzon in the Philippines ‖ a member of this people ‖ an Austronesian language of this people that is the official national language of the Republic of the Philippines

Ta·gan·rog (tágɒnrɒɡ) a port (pop. 277,000) in the R.S.F.S.R., U.S.S.R., on the Sea of Azov: iron and steel, machinery, leather, food processing

tag day (*Am.=Br.* flag day) a day on which small emblems are permitted to be sold on the streets by volunteers in aid of charity

tag end the very last part of something, *the tag end of the day* ‖ (*pl.*) bits or fragments

tag·ma (tǽɡmə) *pl.* **tag·ma·ta** (tǽɡmətə) *n.* a body segment of an arthropod, e.g. the thorax of an insect or a compound body section formed by the embryonic fusion of two or more somites, e.g. the cephalothorax of a spider [Mod. L. fr. Gk *tagma*, arrangement]

tag·meme (tǽɡmiːm) *n.* (*linguistics*) in tagmemic grammar, a unit of arrangement at a substitution point or a correlation shot (including the class of words found or to be substituted at that point), any part of a sentence where other words could be substituted within the same structure

tagmemic grammar (*linguistics*) theory of grammar involving concept of a tagmeme to convey formal and functional information developed by American grammarian K. L. Pike (1930–) *Cf* EMICETIC

tag·mene (tǽɡmiːn) *n.* (*linguistics*) the smallest meaningful unit of grammatical form —**tag·mentist** *n.*

Ta·gore (təɡɔ́r), Rabindranath (1861-1941), Indian author. He wrote in Bengali, but translated much of his work into English. 'Gitanjali' is his best-known work. His 'Collected Poems and Plays' appeared in 1936

tag sale sale of personal property from one's home or immediately outside one's home *also* garage sale, yard sale

Ta·gus (téiɡəs) (*Span.* Tajo, *Port.* Tejo) the longest river (566 miles) of Iberia, flowing from E. New Castile, Spain, across Estremadura and central Portugal to a wide estuary at Lisbon, navigable only in W. Portugal

Ta·hi·ti (təhíːti) the main island (area 402 sq. miles, pop. 95,604) of French Polynesia, in the Society Is. Chief town: Papeete. People: mainly mixed Polynesian-European, 10% Chinese. Highest point: 7,339 ft. Industries: agriculture (taro, breadfruit, yams, coconuts, vanilla), fishing, tourism

Ta·hi·tian (təhíːʃən) **1.** *adj.* pertaining to Tahiti, its inhabitants, language etc. **2.** *n.* a native or inhabitant of Tahiti, esp. one of the native Polynesian people ‖ the Polynesian language of Tahiti

Tai *THAI

tai chi or **tai chi chuan** (tai dʒi: tʃuːɑn) *n.* Chinese system of calisthenics, self-defense, and mediation that produces bodily flexibility and peace of mind

Tai·chung (táidʒúŋ) a commercial center (pop. 330,000) in W. Taiwan

Ta·if (táːf) the summer capital (pop. 30,000) of Hejaz, Saudi Arabia, 50 miles east of Mecca, a resort (on the edge of an oasis) at 5,200 ft

tai·ga (táiɡə) *n.* the coniferous forests of Siberia separating the tundra from the steppe [Russ.]

Taigeytos *TAYGETUS MOUNTAINS

tail (teil) **1.** *n.* the part of the body posterior to the anus in many vertebrates, *peacock's tail*, or this as a caudal appendage in prolongation of the vertebral column, *monkey's tail* ‖ something resembling this in form or position, e.g. the long bright trail behind a comet or meteor ‖ the last part of something, *the tail of a procession* ‖ (also *pl.*) the reverse side of a coin ‖ (*cricket*) the weaker members of the team ‖ the unit at the

rear of an aircraft combining horizontal and vertical stabilizing surfaces with movable surfaces for controlling flight direction ‖ the bottom of a printed page ‖ the part of a man's coat which hangs at the back ‖ (*pl.*) a tailcoat ‖ (*pl.*) full evening dress ‖ (*mus.*) the stem of a written note ‖ the string of paper weights or rags which stabilize a kite ‖ a long braid or switch of hair ‖ the rear end of a vehicle or implement, e.g. a cart or plow **to turn tail** to cease facing someone or something because of fear **with the tail between the legs** in a defeated or dejected way **2.** *v.t.* to remove the ends or stalks from, *to tail gooseberries* ‖ to furnish with a tail, *to tail a kite* ‖ (*pop.*) to follow (someone) so as to observe his actions ‖ to form the tail of (e.g. a procession) ‖ to add on at the end, esp. with excessive length, *to tail on strings of dependent clauses* ‖ (esp. with 'in' or 'into') to fasten the end of (a beam, brick etc.) into a wall etc. ‖ *v.i.* (with 'along' or 'behind') to tag along behind someone or something ‖ (with 'off' or 'away') to subside, *her voice tailed off* ‖ (with 'off') to become gradually poorer in quality towards the end ‖ (with 'out' or 'away') to spread out so as to form a straggling line ‖ (of a timber, brick etc., with 'in' or 'into') to be fastened by an end into a wall etc. **to tail aground** (*naut.*) to ground stern first [O.E. *tægel*]

tail 1. *n.* (*law*) the state or condition of entailment **2.** *adj.* (*law*) limited as to tenure [A.F. *taylé, tailé* fr. O.F. *taillier*, to cut, shape]

tail·board (téilbɔrd, téilbourd) a tail gate

tail·coat (téilkout) *n.* a man's coat, worn on formal occasions, having a long, divided skirt at the back

tail end the concluding part of anything

tail gate the hinged or sliding board or platform at the rear of a van, station wagon etc., which can be raised or lowered to facilitate loading and unloading ‖ the lower gate of a canal lock

tail·gate (téilgeit) *v. pres. part.* **tail·gat·ing** *past* and *past part.* **tail·gat·ed** *v.i.* to drive dangerously close behind another vehicle ‖ *v.t.* to drive dangerously close behind (another vehicle)

tail·ing (téiliŋ) *n.* (*pl.*) the refuse material separated out in processing, e.g. in milling, mining etc. ‖ (*archit.*) of a projecting stone or brick) the part embedded in the wall

tail lamp a taillight

taille (taij) *n.* (*F. hist.*) a feudal tax levied on commoners under the ancient regime [F.]

tail·light (téilait) *n.* a red warning light at the back of a vehicle

tai·lor (téilər) **1.** *n.* a person whose occupation is making men's and women's coats, suits etc. **2.** *v.i.* to work as a tailor ‖ *v.t.* to make (garments) to measure ‖ to fashion to suit a particular need, *the play was tailored for a special audience* ‖ to style (women's garments) with the trim, simple lines characteristic of men's clothes [O.F. *tailleor, tailleur*]

tai·lor·bird (téilərbəːrd) *n.* any of several varieties of Asiatic and African birds of fam. *Sylviidae*, esp. *Orthotomus sutorius*, that sew leaves together to support and hide their nests

tai·lor·made (téilərméid) *adj.* made and fitted by a tailor, *a tailor-made suit* ‖ fashioned specially for the occasion or conditions

tail·piece (téilpiːs) *n.* a part forming the end of something ‖ an ornamental design at the end of a chapter or page of a book ‖ the triangular block to which the strings of a violin etc. are fastened ‖ a short beam or rafter tailed in a wall and supported by a header

tail plane the horizontal surfaces of an aircraft tail, including the elevator and stabilizer

tail·race (téilreis) *n.* the part of a millrace just beyond the millwheel ‖ a channel in which the tailings from treated ore are floated away

tail skid a device on an aircraft to take the weight at the rear end of the fuselage when the aircraft is at rest or taxiing

tail·spin (téilspin) *n.* a spiral dive, nose-foremost, by an aircraft

tail·stock (téilstɒk) *n.* the movable head of a lathe

tail·wa·ter (téilwɑtər) *n.* (*envir.*) water immediately downstream from a structure, e.g., a dam, hydroelectric plant

tail wind a wind blowing in the same general direction as the course of an aircraft or a boat in motion

Tai·myr Peninsula, Tay·myr Peninsula (taimíːr) the northernmost part of Siberia, U.S.S.R., on the central Arctic coast, inhabited by nomads. Products: uranium, cobalt, nickel, lead

Tai·nan (táinán) a port (pop. 474,835) of S.W. Taiwan, formerly the capital: ironworks, food processing

Taine (ten), Hippolyte Adolphe (1828-93), French critic and historian. He applied theories of determinism to literary criticism, aesthetics and psychology. His best-known work is 'Origines de la France contemporaine' (1875-93). He wrote a lively and unorthodox 'Histoire de la littérature anglaise' (1864-72)

Tai·no (táinou) *n.* an Amerind of the Arawak group living at the time of discovery in Puerto Rico, Haiti and E. Cuba. They were decimated by the Spanish conquistadores

taint (teint) **1.** *v.t.* to cause to rot, putrefy, *tainted meat* ‖ to corrupt morally ‖ to cause to be slightly spoiled by some undesirable quality, *tainted with suspicion* **2.** *n.* a trace of infection or corruption [fr. ATTAINT]

Tai·pei (taipéi) the capital (pop. 2,238,840 of economic center of Taiwan, near the northern coast. Industries: metalworking, food processing, glass, chemicals. University

Tai·ping Rebellion (táipíŋ) a rebellion in China (1850-65), led by Hung Hsiu-ch'uan, which attempted to overthrow the Manchu government. The rising was suppressed with the aid of American and British troops under Gordon, leaving China bankrupt and chaotic

Tai·ta·o Peninsula (taitáɔ) a peninsula on the southwest coast of Chile, north of the Gulf of Peñas

Tai·wan (táiwán) (Formosa) a republic (area 13,890 sq. miles, pop. 19,157,407) in E. Asia. It is a Pacific island, 90 miles off S.E. China. It includes the Pescadores (Penghu) Islands, and 13 scattered offshore islands, incl. Quemoy and Matsu. Capital: Taipei. People: 98% Chinese, with Japanese and aboriginal minorities. Language: Chinese (Amoy dialect). Japanese is widely spoken. The land is 50% forest and 24% arable. The mud flats and sandbanks of the west coast give way to lowlands, while on the east coast steep cliffs rise to the densely wooded peaks of the Taitung and Chungyang Mtns (highest point 14,000 ft). The monsoons bring up to 290 ins of rain to the northern and southern tips but only 40–60 ins in the west. There are frequent typhoons. Average temperatures (F.): 50°-60° in winter, 80°-90° in summer. Pigs are raised. Taiwan is the world's chief source of camphor. Timber: hardwoods, pine. Minerals: silver, copper, coal, oil. Industries: flour milling, sugar refining, tobacco. Exports: camphor, sugar, bananas and pineapples, coal, tea, rice, gold. Other products: sweet potatoes, tobacco. Imports: vegetables, iron, opium, textiles. Ports: Kaohsiung, Keelung. National Taiwan university. Monetary unit: new Taiwan yuan. HISTORY. Chinese immigrants settled the island extensively (15th-17th cc.) and Spanish, Dutch and Portuguese traders visited it (16th and 17th cc.). China annexed the island (1683). It was ceded to Japan (1895) and restored to China (1945). Chiang Kai-shek retreated to the island after his expulsion from the mainland by the Communists (1949) and controls it as president of the National Republic of China. The People's Republic of China considers Taiwan as one of its 22 provinces and the Communists are determined to 'liberate' the island. The Kuomintang government and the U.S.A. signed a pact (1954) under which the U.S.A agreed to protect the republic. After its expulsion from the mainland, the Taiwan government continued to represent China, a founding member, at the U.N., until it was unseated in 1971. In 1975 Chiang Kai-Shek died and vice-president Yen Chia-kan took office as president, although leadership of the Kuomintang passed to Chiang's son Chiang Ching-Kuo. In 1978 the U.S.A. unilaterally terminated its security pact with Taiwan, and U.S.-Taiwan relations have continued to be ambiguous

Tai·yuan (táijyán) (formerly Yangku) the capital (pop. 1,020,000) of Shansi, N. China. Industries: iron and steel, heavy engineering, textiles. Institute of Technology

Ta·ja·mul·co, Ta·ju·mul·co (tɑhɑmúːlkɔ, tɑhuːmúːlkɔ) a volcanic mountain (13,816 ft) in W. Guatemala. It is the highest point in Central America

Taj Ma·hal (tázˈməhál, tádʒˈməhál) the magnificent white marble mausoleum built (c. 1632–c. 1643) in Agra, Uttar Pradesh, India, by the Mogul emperor Shah Jahan in memory of his favorite wife Mumtaz Mahal. It is in a garden with pools and fountains. The sun filters restfully into the building through fretted marble screens

Tajumulco *TAJAMULCO

ta·ka (táks) *n.* currency unit of Bangladesh since 1977 *abbr.*, Tk

Ta·ka·ma·tsu (takɑmɑtsu:) a port (pop. 228,000) of N. Shikoku, Japan, on the Inland Sea. Industries: textiles, lacquerware. Ruins of Takamatsu castle (built 1588), gardens

Ta·kao (tákáou) *KAOHSIUNG

take (teik) 1. *v. pres. part.* **tak·ing** *past* **took** (tuk) *past part.* **tak·en** (téikən) *v.t.* to get possession of by using force or superior strength, *the army took the town* ‖ to capture, *the thief was taken by the police* ‖ (*cards*) to win (a trick) or capture (an opponent's card) ‖ (*chess*) to put out of play, *bishop takes pawn* ‖ (*cricket*) to cause (a wicket) to fall ‖ to put the hand on or in so as to give or receive guidance, *take my hand while we cross the road* ‖ to guide (somebody) in this way, *to take a child by the hand* ‖ to grip, grasp or seize etc. with the fingers, hands, arms, teeth or an instrument ‖ to surprise, attack, catch or overcome, esp. suddenly, *we took them unawares* ‖ (with 'with', in passive constructions) to have as a sudden illness or indisposition, *to be taken with a violent pain* ‖ (with 'with', in passive constructions) to captivate, charm, *she was taken with the house on sight* ‖ to eat, drink or receive into the body in some other way, *to take snuff, take sedatives* ‖ to expose oneself to the benefits of (the air and the sun) ‖ to enter into a relationship with (someone), *to take a lover, to take pupils* ‖ to steal or remove without right, *who has taken the dictionary from the library?* ‖ to assume (office, control etc.) ‖ to hire or rent, *to take a house by the sea* ‖ to pay for (something) to be regularly delivered, *the family takes one newspaper and two pints of milk daily* ‖ to bind oneself by (e.g. an oath, vow) ‖ to win in competition, *to take third place in a race* ‖ to proceed along, *we took a different road home* ‖ to select, *take any example you wish* ‖ to make use of, *he took every opportunity to insult us* ‖ to make use of as a means of transport, *to take a bus across Paris* ‖ to convey or cause to go, *the blue bus takes you past the door, that road takes you a longer way around* ‖ to write down (notes, dictation) ‖ to write down esp. as a record, *to take someone's measurements* ‖ to read as a measurement *to take someone's temperature, take soundings* ‖ to require, *it took two men to lift the bed* ‖ to need with respect to size, *to take size 11 shoes* ‖ to derive (nourishment, comfort, satisfaction etc.) ‖ to provide room for, *the car takes six people comfortably* ‖ to photograph ‖ to allow oneself to be given, *don't take lifts from strangers* ‖ to supervise (e.g. a rehearsal) ‖ to give a lesson to (a class) ‖ (esp. *Br.*) to give as a lesson, *to take French with seven-year-olds* ‖ to study or have as a course of study, *to take French at the university* ‖ to allow oneself to adopt (a specified attitude), *to take a serious view of a situation* ‖ to decide to have or be in the process of having (something) for one's pleasure or benefit, *to take exercise, take a holiday* ‖ to conduct (someone or something) somewhere in one's company, *to take a dog for a walk* ‖ to carry (something) to someone, *take the eggs to your grandmother* ‖ (with 'with') to carry (something) and keep it, *take it with you* ‖ to keep (something) for a specified time or purpose, *take the book to read in bed* ‖ to remove, *to take a bone from a hungry dog* ‖ to subtract, *take 13 from 20* ‖ to capture the attention of, *it takes the eye* ‖ to react to, *to take news badly* ‖ to react well to (punishment, criticism, a joke etc.) ‖ to occupy (a chair, a place in line etc.) ‖ (*gram.*) to be constructed with, *a transitive verb takes a direct object* ‖ *v.i.* to get or gain possession ‖ (of an inoculation) to be effective ‖ (of a graft, cutting etc.) ‖ to begin to thrive ‖ to be liked by an audience, *the play did not take well in the provinces* ‖ to be a subject of a specified quality or sort for photography, *she never takes well* ‖ (with 'from') to detract, *it takes from her enjoyment* **to take aback** to cause to feel a small unpleasant shock of surprise **to take away** to carry off in one's possession ‖ to subtract **to take down** to lower ‖ to pull down piece by piece (e.g. a building) ‖ to make a written record of **to take for** to identify (someone) wrongly as someone or something, *what do you take me for?* ‖ (*pop.*) to cheat (a person), *he took me for $5* **to take in** to receive into one's home for money, *to take in lodgers* ‖ out of kindness, *to take in stray cats* ‖ to undertake to do at home, *to take in washing* ‖ to carry inside ‖ to make narrower or smaller, esp. by sewing, *to take in a*

skirt ‖ to furl (a sail) ‖ to deceive, *he was taken in by their apparent kindness* ‖ to seize the meaning of, *we could hardly take in what was being said* ‖ to include in a visit, *we took in the Louvre on our weekend in Paris* **to take it** to submit to criticism, ridicule etc. with composure **to take it easy** to rest, work less hard **to take it hard** to be intensely hurt emotionally **to take it lying down** to be submissive **to take it on the chin** to endure punishment, suffering etc. bravely **to take it out of (someone)** to make (someone) exhausted **to take it out on (someone)** to vent one's bad temper etc. on (someone) **to take off** to remove (clothes etc.) ‖ to begin to move, esp. of an aircraft as it becomes airborne ‖ to deduct ‖ (*pop.*) to mimic ‖ to conduct away (also used reflexively) **to take on** to agree to do, *to take on a job* ‖ to accept a fight or contest with ‖ to engage (an employee) ‖ (*pop.*) to express sorrow or vexation with a painful display of emotion ‖ to assume (e.g. a quality) **to take out** to remove ‖ to acquire (insurance, a patent, a license) by making the necessary payment ‖ to pay the first installment of (a subscription) ‖ (*pop.*) to escort to places of entertainment etc. ‖ (*bridge*) to counter a call by (one's partner) in a suit by bidding higher in a different suit **to take over** to assume responsibility for (e.g. a debt, lease) ‖ to assume control of ‖ to relieve someone of a responsibility by assuming it **to take to** to develop a fondness or aptitude for ‖ to betake oneself to, begin to walk etc. in, on etc. ‖ to develop the habit of using, *to take to a cane* **to take up** to pick up ‖ to make shorter, esp. by sewing ‖ to absorb ‖ to adopt as a pastime or pursuit ‖ to resume, to pursue further, *to take up a story* ‖ to challenge on a matter of argument, *I'll take you up on that point* ‖ to occupy (time) ‖ to make a protégé of (someone) ‖ to subscribe to (a loan etc.) **to take upon oneself** to begin (to do something) without invitation, instruction or prompting **to take up with** (*pop.*) to become friendly with **2.** *n.* the act of taking ‖ an amount taken or received in payment ‖ the act of capturing an animal or the number of animals caught at one time ‖ the portion of one scene in the making of a film that is photographed at one time ‖ an instance of photographing this [O.E. *tacan*]

take·a·way (téikəwei) *n.* **1.** *GIVEBACK **2.** (*Br.*) takeout

take-home pay pay after all deductions (income tax, social security etc.) have been made

taken *past part.* of TAKE

take·off (téikɔf, téikpf) *n.* the act of leaving the ground, e.g. in jumping or in beginning a flight in an aircraft ‖ the point at which this takes place ‖ the act of mimicking someone or something, esp. in order to ridicule

take·out (téikaut) *adj.* of food prepared to be eaten off-premises

take·o·ver (téikɔuvər) *n.* the assuming of control, ownership or management of e.g. a corporation, or an instance of this

tak·ing (téikiŋ) **1.** *adj.* attractive, *very taking ways* **2.** *n.* (*pl.*) money received for the sale of goods, tickets etc.

Ta·kla Ma·kan (táklɑmɑkán) a sandy desert (area 125,000 sq. miles) in the Tarim Basin, Sinkiang, China, between the Kunlun and Tien Shan. Chief oases: Yarkand, Khotan

Takoradi *SEKONDI-TAKORADI

tal·a·poin (tǽləpɔin) *n. Cercopithecus talapoin*, fam. *Cercopithecidae*, a small, white and olive-colored W. African monkey [Port. *talapão*, Buddhist monk]

Tal·bot (tǽlbət), William Henry Fox (1800–77), English scientist. He developed an early system of photography (1839), independently of Daguerre

talc (tælk) *n.* a basic silicate of magnesium, $Mg_3Si_4O_{10}(OH)_2$, occurring in nature and having a soapy feel (varieties are soapstone and French chalk), used as a solid lubricant, toilet powder etc. ‖ (*pop.*) talcum powder ‖ mica, or a thin sheet of it [F. fr. M.L. fr. Arab. fr. Pers.]

tal·cum (tǽlkəm) *n.* talc [M.L.]

talcum powder powdered talc, usually perfumed, used as a powder for the body

tale (teil) *n.* an account of a real or imagined event ‖ a piece of gossip ‖ a lie **to tell tales** to make known things which another person would prefer kept secret, and which do not concern the teller [O.E. *talu*=Du. *taal*, speech]

tale·bear·er (téilbɛərər) *n.* someone who reports privately out of malice or officiousness, esp. to someone in authority, the doings of a third per-

son likely to meet with disapproval or punishment

tale·bear·ing (téilbɛəriŋ) *n.* the activity of a talebearer

tal·ent (tǽlənt) *n.* innate mental or artistic aptitude (as opposed to acquired ability) less than genius, *his work shows talent* ‖ (*hist.*) any of several units of weight or money of account used in Greece, Syria, Palestine and Babylon **tál·ent·ed** *adj.* having talent [O.E. fr. L. fr. Gk *talanton*, pair of scales, unit of weight or money]

ta·ler, tha·ler (tálər) *pl.* **ta·ler, tha·ler** *n.* (*hist.*) any of various large silver coins used in certain German states from the 15th to the late 19th cc. [G.]

ta·les (téili:z) *pl.* **ta·les** *n.* (*law, pl.*) persons summoned from among bystanders for jury service in order to make up the full number ‖ (*law*) the writ summoning such jurors to attend **to pray a tales** to plead that a jury be completed in number [L., pl. of *talis*, such]

ta·les·man (téili:zmən, téilzmən) *pl.* **ta·les·men** (téili:zmən, téilzmən) *n.* a person summoned to serve on a jury in order to complete its number

tale·tell·er (téiltɛlər) *n.* a talebearer ‖ someone who tells stories

Ta·lien (dáljén) (*Jap.* Dairen) the northernmost year-round port of China, in S.W. Liaoning (Manchuria), with Lushun forming the agglomeration of Luta (pop. 1,508,000). Industries: heavy and precision engineering, shipbuilding, food processing (esp. soybeans), textiles, chemicals, building materials. A former treaty port, it was modernized (1899) as the terminus of the Trans-Siberian railroad. It was the capital of Kwantung (1905–45), when the territory was leased to the Japanese

Tal·i·e·sin (tæli:ésin) (late 6th c.) Welsh bard, the author of about a dozen heroic odes or lays in 'The Book of Taliesin'

tal·i·pes (tǽlipi:z) *n.* (*med.*) clubfoot [Mod. L. fr. *talus*, ankle+*pes*, foot]

tal·i·pot (tǽləpɔt) *n. Corypha umbroculifera*, fam. *Palmae*, the lofty fan palm (60–100 ft) of Ceylon, the Malabar Coast and the Philippines. The fanlike leaves are used for umbrellas, fans and, cut into strips, as a substitute for writing paper ‖ a starch obtained from this tree [fr. Sinhalese *talapata*]

tal·is·man (tǽlizmən, tǽlismən) *n.* an object, esp. a figure carved or cut at a time regarded as astrologically favorable, supposed to have magical protective qualities **tal·is·man·ic** (tælizmǽnik, tælismǽnik), **tal·is·mán·i·cal** *adj.* [fr. Span. fr. Ital. fr. Gk]

talk (tɔk) **1.** *v.i.* to express ideas, thoughts etc. in speech ‖ to chatter idly to gossip ‖ to hold consultation ‖ to convey ideas by manual signs ‖ to make sounds resembling those of speech ‖ *v.t.* to express in speech, *to talk sense* ‖ to make use of in speaking, *to talk French* ‖ to bring into a specified condition by talking, *to talk oneself hoarse, talk someone into agreement* ‖ to discuss, *to talk business* ‖ to talk about one's prowess in (something) without matching one's words with one's performance, *he talks a good game of tennis* **to talk (someone) around** to persuade by talking **to talk at** to say something critical of (a person) in his hearing, to a third person **to talk back** to answer rudely or impertinently **to talk big** to boast **to talk down** to reduce (a person) to silence by speaking loudly **to talk down to** to talk patronizingly to **to talk of** to take as a topic of conversation **to talk out** (*Br.*) to prevent a vote from being taken in parliament on (a bill) by speaking until the closure is moved **to talk (someone) over** to persuade (a person) to change his mind by talking to him **to talk (something) over** to discuss (a subject) at length and in detail **to talk (someone) round** (*Br.*) to persuade by talking **to talk shop** to talk about one's occupation, to the exclusion of matters of more general interest **2.** *n.* the act of talking ‖ a speech ‖ a formal conference ‖ gossip ‖ idle chatter ‖ empty phrases ‖ the subject of conversation, *the talk of the town* [M.E. *talkien*, *talken*]

talk·a·tive (tɔ́kətiv) *adj.* inclined to talk

talk·ie (tɔ́ki) *n.* (*pop.*) an early film equipped with a sound track

talk·ing-to (tɔ́kiŋtu:) *n.* a carefully argued rebuke at some length

talk show (*broadcasting*) a program in which celebrities or other persons discuss or are interviewed on subjects of interest

tall (tɔl) *adj.* above average height, *he is tall for his age* ‖ of a specified height, *four feet tall* ‖ (of things) rising high in the air, *a tall oak* ‖ (*pop.*) difficult to believe, exaggerated, *a tall story* ‖ (of a drink) served in a long, narrow glass ‖ (*pop.*, of talk) high-flown ‖ (*pop.*) great or large in amount, *a tall price* ‖ (*pop.*) formidable, *a tall order* [etym. doubtful]

tal·lage (tǽlidჳ) *n.* (*hist.*) a feudal fee paid by a tenant to his lord ‖ (*hist.*) a feudal due levied by a lord, esp. one levied arbitrarily by Norman kings on their demesne lands and royal boroughs [O. F. *taillage*]

Tal·la·has·see (tæləhǽsi:) the capital (pop. 81,548) of Florida

tall·boy (tɔ́lbɔi) *n.* a high chest of drawers composed of two sections, one on top of the other

Tall·chief (tɔ́ltʃi:f), Maria (1925-), U.S. ballet dancer, notable as prima ballerina in the New York City ballet for her dancing in e.g. 'The Firebird', 'Orpheus', and 'Nutcracker'

Tal·ley·rand-Pé·ri·gord (tælrǽpeiri:gɔr), Charles Maurice de, prince of Benevento (1754-1838), French diplomat. As bishop of Autun, Talleyrand supported the cause of the French Revolution, and resigned his see (1791). He was minister of foreign affairs (1797-1807), surviving the political changes of Directory, Consulate and Empire. He began (1808) to intrigue against Napoleon, and supported (1814) the Bourbon restoration. He represented France with great skill at the Congress of Vienna (1815), and helped Louis-Philippe to overthrow the Bourbon monarchy (1830), after which he was ambassador in London (1830-5). He claimed in his 'Mémoires' (published 1891-2) that his frequent changes of policy were dictated by the interests of France, but he has often been considered a mere opportunist

Tal·linn (tǽlin) (formerly Revel, Reval) the capital (pop. 430,000) and chief port of Estonia, U.S.S.R., on the Gulf of Finland. Industries: shipbuilding, woodworking, metalworking, textiles, food processing. Castle (14th c.), Gothic churches (13th-15th cc.) and town hall (14th c.), baroque palace (18th c.)

Tal·lis (tǽlis), Thomas (c. 1515-85), English composer. His skill is shown as much in his simple motets (still sung as anthems) as in his stupendous 'Spem in alium' for 40 voices, i.e. 8 five-part choirs. He was the father of English choral church music

tal·lith (tális) *n.* a scarf worn during prayer by orthodox Jewish males over the age of 13 [Rabbinical Heb. *ṭallith* fr. *ṭalal*, to cover]

tal·low (tǽlou) *n.* a mixture of hard animal fats obtained by rendering esp. beef or mutton fat. It is composed of glycerides, and is used in making candles, soap etc. ‖ any of various fats resembling this obtained from plants **tál·low·y** *adj.* [M.E. *talz, talgh* prob. fr. M.L.G.]

tal·ly (tǽli:) **1.** *pl.* **tal·lies** *n.* (*hist.*) a piece of wood in which notches were cut as a method of recording number. When it was used as a record of payment, the stick was split across the notches, each party to the transaction keeping one of the matching sections ‖ a recorded score or recorded count of objects ‖ something complementary to or completing something else ‖ an identifying tag or label ‖ a card for recording a bridge player's score **2.** *v. pres. part.* **tal·ly·ing** *past* and *past part.* **tal·lied** *v.t.* (often with 'up') to count, *to tally up the election returns* ‖ to furnish (e.g. a bale of goods) with a tag or label ‖ to record (e.g. a number) on or as if on a tally ‖ *v.i.* to match or be consistent, *their stories did not tally* [fr. L. *talea*, stick]

tal·ly·ho (tǽli:hóu) **1.** *n.* and *interj.* the cry of a huntsman upon sighting a fox **2.** *v.i.* to make this cry [prob. alt. of F. *taïaut, tayaut*, used in hunting deer]

Tal·mud (tálmud, tǽlmud) *n.* the body of oral Jewish law, comprising the Mishnah and the Gemara, additional to the Torah, compiled (6th c.) in Babylonia **Tal·múd·ic, Tal·múd·i·cal** *adjs.* **Tál·mud·ist** *n.* [Heb. *talmūdh*, instruction]

tal·on (tǽlən) *n.* a pointed, curved claw, esp. the claw of a bird of prey ‖ the back heel of a molar tooth ‖ the projection of the bolt of a lock which the key bears on in turning ‖ the stock of cards left after dealing in certain games, e.g. solitaire ‖ (*archit.*) an ogee molding [O.F.]

Talos (mil.) a 7,000-lb shipborne, surface-to-air missile (RIM-8) with solidpropellant rocket ramjet engine, with a speed of Mach 3.25, a 50-mi range, nuclear or nonnuclear warhead capability, and command, beam-rider homing guidance

ta·lus (téiləs) *pl.* **ta·lus·es, ta·li** (téilai) *n.* (*anat.*) the astragalus, which, with the tibia and fibula, forms the ankle joint ‖ (*anat.*) the entire ankle ‖ (*zool.*, esp. of birds and insects) a part corresponding to the ankle [L.]

talus *n.* (*fortification*) the slope of a wall which tapers or is built against an inclined bank ‖ (*geol.*) a slope of fragments of rock formed by the weathering of a cliff face ‖ (*geol.*) a mass of rock debris at the foot of a cliff [F.]

tam (tæm) *n.* a tam-o'-shanter

tam·a·ble, tame·a·ble (téiməb'l) *adj.* able to be tamed

Ta·ma·le (tæmáli:) the main commercial center (pop. 120,000) and airport of N. Ghana. Cotton ginning

ta·ma·le (təmáli:) *n.* a Mexican dish consisting of ground meat seasoned with chile pepper and rolled in cornmeal pastry, wrapped in corn husks and steamed [Span. *tamal*, pl. *tamales*]

ta·man·du·a (təmǽndu:ə) *n. Tamandua tetradactyla*, fam. *Myrmecophagidae*, a Central and South American tree-dwelling anteater having a long, prehensile tail [Port. fr. Tupi]

tam·a·rack (tǽməræk) *n.* any of several North American larches, esp. *Larix larieina*, fam. *Pinaceae* ‖ the wood of this tree [etym. doubtful]

tam·a·rin (tǽmərin) *n.* a member of *Leontocebus*, fam. *Callithricidae*, a genus of small South American marmosets, having silky fur and long, canine teeth [F. fr. Carib.]

tam·a·rind (tǽmərind) *n. Tamarindus indica*, fam. *Papilionaceae*, a widely cultivated tropical tree having hard yellowish wood used in work done on the lathe ‖ its fruit, the acid pulp of which is used in cooking and as a laxative drink [fr. Arab. *tamr-hindi*, date of India]

tam·a·risk (tǽmərisk) *n.* a member of *Tamarix*, fam. *Tamaricaceae*, a genus of evergreen shrubs (16–20 ft), having feathery clusters of pink or white flowers and small leaves [fr. L. *tamariscus* fr. Arab. *tamir*, a date]

Ta·ma·tave (tamatáv) the chief port (pop. 59,100) of Madagascar, linked to Antananarino by rail: meat packing

Ta·mau·li·pas (tɑmaulí:pɑs) a northern state (area 30,822 sq. miles, pop. 1,968,800) of Mexico. The land ranges from the sparsely inhabited sandy coast to the wooded mountains and fertile plains of the interior. Capital: Ciudad Victoria (pop. 62,551). Agriculture: sugar, cereals, tobacco, cotton, fruit and coffee. Other important industries: stock raising and mining (primarily copper). Important cities: Tampico, Nuevo Laredo, Matamoros

Ta·ma·yo (tamájɔ), Franz (1880-1956), Bolivian poet and defender of the Indians. He was elected president in 1935, but the Army refused to allow him to take office

Tamayo, Rufino (1899-), Mexican painter. Influenced by cubism and esp. by Picasso, he paints richly colored expressionist compositions of figures, animals and birds, incorporating elements of Mexican folklore

tam·ba·la *pl.*, **-la** *or* **-las** (tambálə) *n.* currency unit of Malawai, equal to 1/100 kwacha

tam·bour (tǽmbuər) **1.** *n.* (*mus.*) a drum ‖ a person playing a drum ‖ a frame consisting of two closely fitting hoops between which a fabric is stretched when it is being embroidered ‖ the embroidery made on such a frame ‖ (*archit.*) one of the cylindrical courses of a column ‖ (*archit.*) the circular wall supporting a dome etc. ‖ the sloping buttress or projection in a court tennis or fives court for deflecting the ball **2.** *v.t.* to embroider, using a tambour ‖ *v.i.* to work this type of embroidery [F. fr. Ital. fr. Arab. fr. Pers.]

tam·bou·rine (tæmbərí:n) *n.* a small drum consisting of a wooden hoop with skin or parchment stretched across it at one end and loose metal disks set around the circumference. It is rattled and struck with the hand or knuckles [fr. F. *tambourin* dim. of *tambour*, drum]

tame (teim) **1.** *adj.* (of animals) domesticated ‖ (of undomesticated animals) unafraid of man ‖ lacking liveliness, mild and dull ‖ (of plants or land) cultivated **2.** *v.t. pres. part.* **tam·ing** *past* and *past part.* **tamed** to make tame ‖ to bring under control, make submissive [O.E. *tam*]

tameable *TAMABLE

Tam·er·lane (tǽmərlein) *TIMUR

Tam·il (tǽməl) *pl.* **Tam·il, Tam·ils** *n.* a member of a Dravidian people living in S. India and N. Ceylon ‖ the Dravidian language of the Tamils ‖ the script used in writing this language

Ta·mil Na·du (tǽməlnádu:) (formerly Madras) a state (area 50,331 sq. miles, pop. 48,297,456)

on the Coromandel Coast of India, sloping down from the Eastern Ghats. Crops (mainly under irrigation): cereals, peanuts, coffee, tea, cotton. Minerals (largely unexploited): iron ore, bauxite, gypsum ‖ its capital (pop. 1,729,000), a port (artificial harbor) and commercial center. Industries: textiles, tanning, pottery, dyemaking. University (1857)

Tam·ma·ny (tǽməni:) a political organization founded in Manhattan, New York, after the Revolutionary War. It exercised great influence over the Democratic party in New York. It became notorious for corruption in the 19th c., notably (1865-71) when, under Tweed, it gained control of New York and defrauded it of many millions of dollars. The organization declined in the 1930s. The name comes from a 17th-c. Delaware Indian chief, Tamanend

Tammany Hall Tammany ‖ the Tammany headquarters

tam-o'-shan·ter (tæməʃǽntər) *n.* a woolen cap having a close-fitting headband and flat, round, very full crown, usually decorated with a pompon [after the hero of Burns's poem 'Tam o' Shanter']

tam·ox·i·fen [$C_{26}H_{29}NO$] (tæmóksifen) *n.* (*pharm.*) nonsteroidal drug used to counter estrogenic properties, tested on animals; marketed as Nolvade

tamp (tæmp) *v.t.* (*mining*) to pack (a drill hole) with clay, sand etc. above the charge, to obtain a full directed blast ‖ to ram down (the charge) in a drill hole ‖ to pack down tightly (e.g. tobacco in a pipe) [perh. back-formation fr. *tampin* var. of TAMPION]

Tam·pa (tǽmpə) a port and resort (pop. 271,523) in central W. Florida: tobacco and chemical industries, food processing, shipbuilding. University (1931)

tam·per (tǽmpər) *v.i.* (only in) **to tamper with** to bribe or intimidate, *to tamper with a witness* ‖ to meddle with, so as to alter for the worse, *do not tamper with old traditions* [var. of TEMPER]

Tam·pe·re (támpere) an industrial and commercial center (pop. 165,807) in S.W. Finland: textile, chemical, wood and metal industries

Tam·pi·co (tæmpí:kou, tampí:kɔ) a sea and river port (pop. 123,000) in central E. Mexico near the chief oil fields: oil refining, chemicals

Tampico Incident a U.S.-Mexican incident (1914) in Tampico, Mexico. When some of Admiral Henry Mayo's sailors were arrested without warrant, he demanded an immediate apology from the Mexican government. The latter's failure to acquiesce led to the U.S. naval occupation of the port of Veracruz

tam·pi·on (tæmpí:ən) *n.* a plug or canvas cover for the muzzle of a gun to keep out dirt and damp ‖ a plug for the end of an organ pipe [fr. F. *tampon*]

tam·pon (tǽmpon) **1.** *n.* a plug of cotton etc. put into an orifice or wound in order to stop bleeding or to absorb secretions **2.** *v.t.* to plug with a tampon [F.]

tam·tam (tǽmtæm) *n.* a tom-tom ‖ a large diskshaped gong [Hindi]

tan (tæn) **1.** *n.* the bark of oak or other trees containing tannic acid, used in tanning hides ‖ any tanning substance ‖ a color of the skin acquired by exposure to the sun and wind ‖ a light brown color **2.** *comp.* **tan·ner** *superl.* **tan·nest** *adj.* of or for tan or tanning ‖ light brown [F., prob. of Celtic origin]

tan *pres. part.* **tan·ning** *past* and *past part.* **tanned** *v.t.* to convert (hide) into leather. Heavy and medium-weight hides are usually treated with vegetable tanning agents and lighter hides and skins with liquors containing chromium salts ‖ to treat (nets, sails etc.) with a hardening mixture of oak bark etc. ‖ to make brown by exposure to the sun or wind ‖ (*pop.*) to thrash (someone) severely ‖ *v.i.* to become brown by exposure to the sun etc. **to tan (someone's) hide** to thrash (someone) severely [O.E. *tannian* fr. M.L.]

tan *abbr.* of TANGENT

Ta·na (tánɑ) a river (500 miles long) rising in the Aberdare Mtns, Kenya, and curving northeast and south to the Indian Ocean

Tana a marshy lake (area 1,100 sq. miles) in N. Ethiopia, south of Gondar, considered as the main source of the Blue Nile

tan·a·ger (tǽnədჳer) *n.* any of various North and South American passerine birds of fam. *Thraupidae*. They are 6–8 ins long and the males are brilliantly colored (*SCARLET TANAGER) [fr. Mod. L. *Tanagra* fr. Tupi]

CONCISE PRONUNCIATION KEY: **(a)** æ, c*a*t; ɑ, c*a*r; ɔ f*aw*n; ei, sn*a*ke. **(e)** e, h*e*n; i:, sh*ee*p; iə, d*ee*r; ɛə, b*ea*r. **(i)** i, f*i*sh; ai, t*i*ger; ə:, b*i*rd. **(o)** o, *o*x; au, c*ow*; ou, g*oa*t; u, p*oo*r; ɔi, r*oy*al. **(u)** ʌ, d*u*ck; u, b*u*ll; u:, g*oo*se; ə, b*a*cillus; ju:, c*u*be. x, lo*ch*; θ, *th*ink; ð, bo*th*er; z, *Z*en; ჳ, cor*s*age; dჳ, sava*g*e; ŋ, ora*ng*utang; j, *y*ak; ʃ, *fi*sh; tʃ, fet*ch*; 'l, rabb*le*; 'n, redd*en*. Complete pronunciation key appears inside front cover.

Tan·a·gra (tǽnəgrə) an ancient town of Boeotia famous for the delicate terra-cotta figurines discovered in ancient tombs

Ta·na·na·rive *ANTANANARIVO

tan·bark (tǽnbɑrk) n. a bark used in tanning or (when spent) as a covering for a circus ring, racetrack etc.

Tan·cred (tǽŋkrid) (d. 1112), Norman, Sicilian prince, one of the leaders of the 1st Crusade. He took part in the capture of Jerusalem (1099) and was prince of Galilee (1099-1112) and prince of Antioch (1111-12)

tan·dem (tǽndəm) **1.** n. a bicycle with two seats, one behind the other ‖ a carriage drawn by two horses harnessed one behind the other ‖ the team of horses so harnessed **2.** adv. one behind another [L.= at length (of time)]

Ta·ney (tóni:), Roger Brooke (1777-1864), U.S. lawyer and jurist. As attorney general (1831-3) under President Andrew Jackson, he opposed renewing the charter of the Bank of the United States and was chiefly responsible for Jackson's veto of the renewal. As secretary of the treasury (1833-5) under Jackson, he removed all federal funds from the bank. He was appointed (1836) chief justice of the Supreme Court where he wrote, notably, the Dred Scott decision

T'ang (tæŋ) a Chinese dynasty (618-906) during which internal organization and diplomacy were extensively developed. Peace and prosperity were accompanied by great achievements in the arts

tang (tæŋ) **1.** n. a sharp taste or smell ‖ a characteristic quality ‖ (with 'of') a trace, a tang of autumn in the air ‖ a projecting piece, e.g. the shank of a chisel or knife, which joins the blade of the tool to the haft ‖ a surgeonfish ‖ a projecting finger rest on the handle of a scissors **2.** v.t. to furnish (a knife etc.) with a tang [O.N. tange, point]

tang n. any of several coarse seaweeds, esp. of the genus Fucus, fam. Fucaceae [of Scand. origin]

Tan·ga (tǽŋgə) a port and rail terminus (pop. 21,000) in N.E. Tanganyika, Tanzania

Tan·gan·yi·ka *TANZANIA

Tanganyika a long narrow lake (area 12,700 sq. miles), part of the Great Rift Valley, separating Burundi and Tanzania from the Democratic Republic of the Congo and Zambia

Tan·ge (tǽŋge), Kenzo (1913-), Japanese architect. His works integrate Japanese architectural traditions with modern needs, materials and functional concepts. His buildings include Kagawa Prefectural Office (1955-8)

tan·gen·cy (tǽndʒənsi:) n. the quality or state of being tangent

tan·gent (tǽndʒənt) **1.** n. a line or plane which meets a curve or curved surface at a single point without intersecting it, even if further extended ‖ (math., abbr. tan) a measure of the magnitude of an angle expressed as the constant ratio of the opposite to the adjacent side (not the hypotenuse) of the angle in a right-angled triangle **to go** (or **fly**) **off on** (or **at**) **a tangent** to change abruptly from the subject under consideration **2.** adj. touching without intersecting **tan·gen·tial** (tændʒénʃəl) adj. of, relating to or of the nature of a tangent [fr. L. tangens (tangentis) fr. tangere, to touch]

tangential motion (astron.) the motion through space of a star, corrected for distance, i.e. its velocity component perpendicular to the observer (cf. PROPER MOTION)

tan·ge·rine (tændʒərí:n) n. a variety of mandarin orange grown in the U.S.A. and southern Africa [fr. F. Tanger, Tangier]

tan·gi·bil·i·ty (tændʒəbíliti:) n. the state or quality of being tangible

tan·gi·ble (tǽndʒəb'l) adj. able to be perceived by the sense of touch ‖ objective, definite, tangible proof of crime ‖ (law) being a corporeal item able to be valued, tangible assets **tán·gi·bly** adv. [fr. L. tangibilis fr. tangere, to touch]

Tan·gier (tændʒíər) (F. Tanger, Arab. Tanja) a port of entry (pop. 187,894) and former free port in Morocco on the Strait of Gibraltar. Ceded to Britain by Portugal (1662), abandoned to the Moors (1684), it became an international zone (1924), was under Spain (1939-45) and again had its international status restored (1945), finally becoming part of Morocco (1956) as a free zone. It was fully integrated (1962) into the country

tan·gle (tǽŋg'l) **1.** n. an interweaving of fibers or of stems, branches etc. so caught up and confused as to be almost inextricable, a tangle of undergrowth ‖ a state of confusion, his business affairs are in a tangle ‖ a device, consisting of a bar to which are attached pieces of rope etc., used for sweeping over the sea bottom in order to entangle and catch delicate sea animals **2.** v. pres. part. **tan·gling** past and past part. **tangled** v.t. to form into a tangle ‖ to catch in or as if in a net ‖ v.i. to become tangled **to tangle with** (pop.) to become involved in an argument or a fight with (someone) **tán·gly** comp. **gli·er** superl. **tan·gli·est** adj. [prob. var. of older tagle, of Scand. origin]

tan·go (tǽŋgou) **1.** n. a ballroom dance of Argentinian provenance ‖ the music for this dance **2.** v.i. to dance the tango [Span.]

tan·gram (tǽŋgrəm) n. a square Chinese puzzle in seven pieces, from which many figures can be made [etym. doubtful]

Tang·shan (tɑ́ŋʃɑn) a coal-mining center (pop. 800,000) in N.E. Hopei, China: steel, glass, cement

Tan·guy (tɑ́gi:), Yves (1900-55), American painter born in France. An adherent of surrealism, he created works in which vast, realistic settings are filled with dreamlike images

tang·y (tǽŋi:) comp. **tang·i·er** superl. **tang·i·est** adj. having a tang

Tan·jore (tændʒɔ́r, tændʒóur) (or Thanjavur) a former princely capital (pop. 140,547) in E. Madras, India, on the River Cauvery. Handicrafts: silks, carpets, inlaid metalwork. Hindu temple (11th c.)

tank (tæŋk) **1.** n. a large container for liquids or gases ‖ (mil.) a tracked vehicle, armor-plated and carrying a gun and automatic weapons, capable of rapid movement over difficult country **2.** v.t. to put, process or store in a tank [fr. Port. tanque, pond. The military vehicle was so named during production (1915) as a security measure]

tan·ka (tǽŋkə) n. a Japanese verse form consisting of five lines, the first and third of which have five syllables and the others seven [Jap.]

tank·age (tǽŋkidʒ) n. the act of putting into tanks ‖ the capacity or contents of a tank ‖ the charge for storage in tanks ‖ the dried animal residues of slaughterhouses used as a fertilizer or coarse feed

tank·ard (tǽŋkərd) n. a large beer mug or other drinking vessel with a handle, sometimes having a lid [M.E.]

tank car a truck or railroad car used for transporting liquids or gases in a tank or tanks

tank·er (tǽŋkər) n. a ship built to carry liquids, esp. mineral oil in bulk ‖ a heavy road or rail vehicle which is essentially a large tank on wheels, for transporting gasoline, milk, wine etc.

tank suit a one-piece swim suit with shoulder straps

tank top informal outer shirt with wide shoulder straps

tan·nage (tǽnidʒ) n. the act, process or result of tanning hides to make leather

Tan·nen·berg, Battle of (tǽnənbə:rg) a battle (1410) in E. Prussia in which Ladislaus II of Poland defeated the Teutonic Knights, stopping their advance eastward ‖ a battle (Aug. 26-30, 1914) in which a German army under Hindenburg and Ludendorff heavily defeated a Russian army and took over 100,000 prisoners. With the ensuing German victory at the Masurian Lakes (Sept. 6-15, 1914), Russia's invasion of Germany was totally crushed

tan·ner (tǽnər) n. a craftsman who tans hides to make leather [TAN V.]

tanner n. (Br., pop.) the former sixpenny bit, a coin of the value of six pennies that ceased to be minted when the British money was decimalized (1971) [etym. doubtful]

tan·ner·y (tǽnəri:) pl. **tan·ner·ies** n. a place where hides are tanned ‖ tannage

tan·nic (tǽnik) adj. of, relating to, derived from or resembling tan or tannin

tannic acid tannin

tan·nin (tǽnin) n. any of various astringent, complex phenolic substances, obtained from barks, woods, leaves, roots and fruits of plants and variously used in tanning, medicine, dyeing, ink manufacture etc. [F. tanin fr. tan, tan]

tan·rec (tǽnrek) n. a tenrec

tan·sy (tǽnzi:) pl. **tan·sies** n. a member of Tanacetum, fam. Compositae, a genus of herbaceous, strong-smelling plants, esp. T. vulgare, having yellow flowers and bitter leaves [O.F. tanesie fr. M.L. fr. Gk athanasia, immortality]

Tan·ta (tɑ́ntə) a town (pop. 285,000) in the Nile delta, Egypt, site of annual fairs and Moslem festivals

tan·ta·li·za·tion (tæntˈlizéiʃən) n. a tantalizing or being tantalized

tan·ta·lize (tǽntˈlaiz) pres. part. **tan·ta·liz·ing** past and past part. **tan·ta·lized** v.t. to tease by arousing expectations that are repeatedly disappointed [after TANTALUS]

tan·ta·lum (tǽntˈləm) n. a metallic element (symbol Ta, at. no. 73, at. mass 180.948) that is very unreactive and has a high melting point. It is used in heat resistant and corrosion-resistant alloys and in surgical instruments. The carbide is used as an abrasive and in tools [Mod. L. after TANTALUS (because of the difficulties resulting from its unreactiveness)]

Tan·ta·lus (tǽntˈləs) (mythol.) a king of Lydia, who served the flesh of his son Pelops to the gods at a banquet. He was punished in Hades with eternal thirst and hunger: he had to stand up to his neck in water which disappeared when he tried to drink, and under branches of fruit which constantly eluded his grasp

tan·ta·mount (tǽntəmaunt) adj. (with 'to') equivalent in effect or value, the tax was tantamount to robbery [fr. A.F. tant amunter, to amount to as much]

Tan·tra (tɑ́ntrə) n. any of several Hindu religious writings (8th–13th cc.) of a kind which opposed the religious and social sanctions of Brahmanism **Tán·trism** n. a form of Mahayana Buddhism which arose in N. India and incorporated the teachings of the Hindu Tantras and traditional mystical beliefs. It encourages theurgic practices in the attainment of enlightenment [Skr.=loom, warp, system]

tan·trum (tǽntrəm) n. a fit of bad temper indulged in before another person or persons [origin unknown]

Tan·za·ni·a (tænzéini:ə, tænzɑní:ə) a republic (area 364,900 sq. miles, pop. 19,112,000) and member of the Commonwealth in E. Africa, formed (Apr. 27, 1964) by the union of Tanganyika and Zanzibar, with Julius Nyerere as its first president (1961-85). A 1977 constitution calls for a president, vice-president, and national assembly. Zanzibar has controlled its own internal affairs since 1965. The breakup of the East African Community, a growing trade deficit, and a costly invasion of Uganda in 1979 to help overthrow Idi Amin all contributed to a 30% decline in per capita income between 1978 and 1984. A secessionist movement on Zanzibar led to the resignation of Zanzibar President Aboud Jumbe, and his successor, Ali Hassan Mwinyi, became president of Tanzania in 1985 (*TANGANYIKA, *ZANZIBAR)

Tao·ism (táuizəm, dáuizəm) n. a Chinese religion founded (6th c. B.C.) by Lao-tzu. Classic Taoism is based on the concept of Tao, the universal force harmonizing nature. To achieve harmony, man should identify himself with the basic spirit of nature by contemplation. This philosophic Taoism, influenced by Buddhism and Confucianism, evolved (c. 5th c.) into a pantheistic religion of hero worship and magical and mystical rites, with monastic orders. Taoism has about 30 million adherents in China

Ta·or·mi·na (tɑɔrmí:nə) a resort (pop. 10,085) in E. Sicily at the foot of Etna: Greek theater (restored)

T'ao Yuan-ming (táujwúnmíŋ) (c. 365-427), Chinese poet, who wrote in praise of the simple life

tap (tæp) n. a device which controls the flow of a fluid from or through a pipe or from a container ‖ a tool for cutting the thread of an internal screw ‖ (elec.) a point where a connection can be made in a circuit **on tap** available when required ‖ on draft [O.E. tæppa]

tap 1. v. pres. part. **tap·ping** past and past part. **tapped** v.t. to cause (something) to rap on something else, to tap a stick on a table ‖ to strike lightly with a rapping sound, to tap a table with a stick ‖ (with 'out') to type or keyboard (literary copy) ‖ (esp. with 'out') to produce by light little raps, to tap out a message on a wall ‖ to reinforce the heel or toe of (a shoe) with a thickness of leather or metal ‖ v.i. to make a light impact or series of little raps on something, to tap impatiently with one's fingers ‖ to walk lightly, making clicking sounds with the heels **2.** n. a light rap or blow ‖ the sound of this ‖ a leather or metal reinforcement of the sole or heel of a shoe [O.F. taper]

tap pres. part. **tap·ping** past and past part. **tapped** v.t. to furnish (a cask etc.) with a tap ‖

to permit (liquid) to flow from a cask, tree etc. by opening a hole or vent ‖ to open a hole in (a cask, tree etc.) so that liquid can flow out ‖ to draw off a fluid from (an abscess etc.) ‖ to make a connection with (a service pipe or cable) ‖ to connect a listening device to (an electric wire, cable etc.) in order to intercept telephonic etc. communications ‖ to steal (electricity) by connecting up with another circuit ‖ to make a female screw thread on (a nut) ‖ to draw on (resources) [O. E. *tœppian*]

ta·pa (tápə) *n.* the bark of the paper mulberry ‖ a rough cloth made in Polynesia from the pounded bark of the paper mulberry and other plants. It is decorated and used for ceremonial clothing, house decoration etc. [Polynesian]

Ta·pa·jós (tɑpɑʒɔ́s) (or **Tapajóz**) a navigable tributary (500 miles long) of the Amazon in central Brazil

tap dance an exhibition dance in which the rhythm of the music is tapped out by the feet of the dancer, who wears specially made shoes **tap-dance** (tǽpdæns) *pres. part.* **tap-danc·ing** *past* and *past part.* **tap-danced** *v.i.* to perform a tap dance

tape (teip) 1. *n.* a narrow strip of cotton, silk, rayon etc. used in dressmaking, for tying bundles etc. ‖ a narrow roll of thin adhesive paper or plastic ‖ a long, narrow flexible strip of metal used by surveyors for measuring ‖ a narrow roll of paper on which a teleprinter prints a message ‖ a narrow band of plastic covered with magnetic oxide on which tape recordings are made ‖ (*pop.*) a tape recording ‖ (*bookbinding*) one of the bands to which the signatures are sewn and which help to attach the sewn pages to the cover ‖ a length of narrow material stretched breast-high across the finishing line of a race track ‖ a tape measure 2. *v.t. pres. part.* **tap·ing** *past* and *past part.* **taped** to furnish with tape ‖ to fasten with tape ‖ to record on magnetic tape ‖ to join the sections of (a book) with tape [perh. fr. O.E. *tœppan*]

tape deck device for recording and playing magnetic tapes (or tape cassettes) of words, music, or other sounds *also* tape player

tape eraser *BULK ERASER

tape measure a tape or strip of strong fabric or flexible metal, marked in inches, feet, meters etc., used for measuring

tape music electronic music recorded on magnetic tape for commercial distribution

ta·per (téipər) 1. *n.* (*hist.*) a small, slender wax candle ‖ a long, wax-covered wick used for lighting candles etc. ‖ a gradual narrowing 2. *v.i.* to narrow gradually *v.t.* to make gradually narrower **to taper off** to become gradually less in number, amount etc. 3. *adj.* regularly narrowing down to a point, *a chair with taper legs* [O.E. *tapur, tapor, taper*]

tape-re·cord (téiprikɔrd) *v.t.* to record on a magnetic tape [back-formation fr. TAPE RECORDING]

tape recorder a magnetic recorder using magnetic tape

tape recording the act of recording on magnetic tape (*MAGNETIC RECORDER*) ‖ the recording produced

tap·es·tried (tǽpistri:d) *adj.* covered with or as if with tapestry ‖ worked in tapestry

tap·es·try (tǽpistri:) *pl.* **tap·es·tries** *n.* a heavy, hand-worked fabric with pictures or designs formed by threads inserted over and under the warp according to the requirements of color (not worked from selvage to selvage as in weaving) and used for hangings, chair seats etc. ‖ a machine-made fabric imitating this [O.F. *tapisserie*]

ta·pe·tum (təpí:təm) *pl.* **ta·pe·ta** (təpí:tə) *n.* (*biol.*) any of various membranous layers of the retina or choroid of the eye, esp. a reflecting layer in the choroid of nocturnal animals ‖ (*bot.*) the special nutritive layer investing the sporogenous tissue of a sporangium [L.L.=carpet]

tape·worm (téipwərm) *n.* a member of *Cestoda*, a subclass of long, ribbonshaped parasitic worms which as adults infest the intestines of man and other vertebrates and, in the larval stage, infest great numbers of vertebrates and invertebrates

tap·i·o·ca (tæpi:óukə) *n.* cassava starch processed into grains, flakes etc. and used in milk puddings, for thickening soups etc. and commercially as a size or adhesive [fr. Tupi-Guarani *tipioca*]

ta·pir (téipər) *pl.* **ta·pir, ta·pirs** *n.* any of several nonruminant, chiefly nocturnal ungulates of fam. *Tapiridae*, native to South and Central America, Malaya and Sumatra. They are about 3 ft tall, are clumsily and heavily built, and have four front and three hind toes, a short but flexible proboscis, and a brownish, almost hairless body [fr. Tupi *tapira* or *tapura*]

tap·pet (tǽpit) *n.* (*mach.*) an arm or lever moved by a cam etc. to cause intermittent motion, as in the valve gear of an internal-combustion engine etc.

tap·room (tǽpru:m, tǽprum) *n.* a bar where esp. beer is kept on tap

tap·root (tǽpru:t, tǽprut) *n.* a primary root growing vertically downward and giving off small subsidiary roots in succession

taps (tæps) *pl. n.* (*mil.*) lights-out sounded by a bugle ‖ the bugle call sounded at a military funeral [prob. alt. of obs. *taptoo, tattoo*]

Tap·ti (túpti:) a river (436 miles long) of Madhya Pradesh and Gujarat, India, flowing from the central Satpura Range to the Arabian Sea

tar (tar) 1. *n.* a thick, black or dark brown viscous liquid obtained by the destructive distillation of wood, coal etc. It is used in road making, to preserve wood and iron, and as the source of many dyes, antiseptics etc. 2. *v.t. pres. part.* **tar·ring** *past* and *past part.* **tarred** to cover with tar ‖ to attach a moral stigma to **tarred with the same brush** (or **stick**) having the same faults or having committed the same misdemeanors **to tar and feather** to cover (a person) with tar and feathers as a punishment or humiliation [O.E. *teru, teoru*]

tar *n.* (*pop.*) a sailor [shortened fr. TARPAULIN]

Tar·a (tɛ́rə) a low hill in County Meath, Ireland, the seat of Irish kings from prehistoric times to the 6th c. St Patrick preached here

Tar·a·na·ki (tæranáki) a region (area 3,750 sq. miles, pop. 103,000) of W. North Island, New Zealand: dairy products, lumber. Chief town: New Plymouth (pop. 31,000)

tar·an·tel·la (tærəntélə) *n.* a whirling S. Italian folk dance in 6/8 time for couples with tambourines ‖ the music for this dance [Ital., dim. of *Taranto*, Italy]

Ta·ran·to (tɑránto) (ancient Tarentum) a port and naval base (pop. 243,800) in Apulia, Italy, on the Gulf of Taranto, which separates the heel and the toe of Italy: shipbuilding, engineering, textiles, chemicals, fishing

ta·ran·tu·la (tərǽntʃulə) *n.* any of various hairy, big spiders of fam. *Theraphosidae*, found in hot countries. The bite of the tarantula is painful but not dangerous to man ‖ *Lycosa tarantula*, fam. *Lycosidae*, a very large brown European spider [M.L. after *Taranto*, Italy]

Ta·ra·wa Island (tərɑ́wə, tǽrəwə) an atoll (area 7.7 sq. miles) of the Gilbert Is in the western central Pacific. Occupied (1941) by the Japanese during the 2nd world war, it was recaptured (1943) by the U.S. Marines

ta·rax·a·cum (tərǽksəkəm) *n.* the dried rhizome and roots of the dandelion used medicinally [M.L. fr. Arab.]

Tar Baby policy action undertaken by President Richard M. Nixon of nonsupport for colonial powers in Africa, verbal encouragement to emerging African nations, and continuation of good relations with Rhodesia (now Zimbabwe) and Republic of South Africa

Tar·be·la (tɑrbélə) the site of a great dam project, on the Indus in Pakistan, northwest of Rawalpindi (*INDUS*)

Tar·bell (tárbel, tárbəl), Ida Minerva (1857-1944), U.S. journalist, known for 'muckraking' exposés of political and corporate corruption, and biographer, notably of Abraham Lincoln

tar·boosh (tɑrbú:ʃ) *n.* a brimless red felt cap resembling a fez, worn alone or as part of a turban by Moslem men in E. Mediterranean countries [Arab. *tarbūsh*]

tar·di·grade (tárdigreid) *n.* a member of *Tardigrada*, a division of *Arthropoda*, comprising minute, aquatic, spiderlike animals having four pairs of legs and no mouth appendages [F. or fr. L. *tardigradus*, walking slowly]

tar·di·ly (tárdili:) *adv.* in a tardy manner

tar·di·ness (tárdi:nis) *n.* the quality or state of being tardy

tar·dy (tárdi:) *comp.* **tar·di·er** *superl.* **tar·di·est** *adj.* coming late, *a tardy apology* ‖ happening later than is desirable or expected, *a tardy departure* [F. *tardif*]

tare (tɛər) 1. *n.* the weight of the container or vehicle in which goods are packed and weighed, deducted from the gross weight in order to arrive at the net weight ‖ this deduction 2. *v.t. pres. part.* **tar·ing** *past* and *past part.* **tared** to ascertain the weight of (a container, vehicle etc.) or to allow for this [F. fr. Arab. *tarhah*, that which is thrown away]

tare *n.* any of several vetches, esp. *Vicia sativa*, fam. *Papilionaceae* ‖ the seed of any of these ‖ (*pl., Bible*) choking weeds [etym. doubtful]

tar·get (tárgit) *n.* a circular straw mat having a canvas cover painted with five concentric circles, shot at in archery ‖ a sheet of cardboard or thin wood, similarly marked, aimed at in rifle shooting etc. ‖ the score made in target shooting ‖ any object at which a missile is aimed ‖ an object of attack, criticism etc. ‖ an end which it is hoped to reach by an effort, or any planning objective, *his target was the saving of $1000* ‖ (of an X-ray tube) the metallic surface upon which the stream of cathode rays is focused ‖ a small railroad switch signal ‖ (*surveying*) a sliding sight on a leveling staff ‖ (*hist.*) a small, round shield [dim. of *targe*, a shield]

target language (*computer*) the language into which the language of a program is to be translated for the ongoing operation *also Cf* SOURCE LANGUAGE

tar·get·a·ble (tárgətəb'l) *adj.* capable of being hit or accomplished —**on target** in the right direction; correct

target marketing (*business*) strategy or strategies designed for a single market segment

Tar·gum (tárgəm) *pl.* **Tar·gums, Tar·gu·mim** (tɑrgumí:m) *n.* an Aramaic translation or paraphrase of part of the Old Testament [fr. Chaldean *targūm*]

tar·iff (tǽrif) *n.* a scale of duties imposed by a government on goods imported or exported ‖ the duty imposed ‖ any scale of rates or charges, e.g. for accommodation in a hotel [fr. Ital. *tariffa* fr. Arab.]

Ta·ri·ja (tɑrí:hɑ) a city and the commercial center (pop. 24,000, altitude 6,400 ft) of S. Bolivia

Ta·rim (tɑrí:m) a river (1,250 miles long) rising (as the Khotan) in the Kunlun and curving in a marshy course through S. Sinkiang-Uighor, China, to end in a sink ‖ its basin (350,000 sq. miles), enclosed by the Kunlun, Pamirs and Tien Shan

Tar·king·ton (tárkiŋtən), (Newton) Booth (1869-1946), U.S. novelist and playwright. His novels, notably 'Seventeen' (1916) and 'The Magnificent Ambersons' (1918) explore the adolescent and adult life of the middle class in midwest towns

tar·la·tan (tárlətən) *n.* a thin muslin, stiffened with size and used esp. as a dress material [F. *tarlatane* prob. of Indian origin]

tar·mac (tármæk) *n.* the hard, level surface of a road, airfield runway etc. [short for *tarmacadam* fr. TAR+MACADAM]

Tarn (tɑrn) a department (area 2,231 sq. miles, pop. 338,000) of S. France (*LANGUEDOC). Chief town: Albi (pop. 49,456)

tarn (tɑrn) *n.* a small lake surrounded by mountains [M.E. *terne* fr. O.N.]

Tarn-et-Ga·ronne (tærneigærɔn) a department (area 1,440 sq. miles, pop. 183,300) of S. France (*GUYENNE, *LANGUEDOC). Chief town: Montauban (pop. 50,420)

tar·nish (tárniʃ) 1. *v.t.* to dull the brightness of (a metallic surface) by covering it with a film of sulfide, oxide etc. ‖ to sully ‖ *v.i.* to become tarnished 2. *n.* the condition of being tarnished ‖ the film causing this ‖ (of honor or reputation) the condition of being sullied [fr. F. *ternir* (*terniss-*)]

ta·ro (tárou) *n. Colocasia esculenta*, fam. *Araceoe*, a plant grown throughout the tropics for its starchy, edible rhizome ‖ this rhizome [native Polynesian name]

ta·rot (tárou) *n.* one of a set of playing cards first used in Italy in the 14th c. The figured cards are used in fortune-telling and as trumps in the game played with the entire set ‖ the game played [F. fr. Ital., origin unknown]

tar·pan (tárpæn) *n.* a small grayish-brown wild horse of central Asia [Tatar]

tar·pau·lin (tɑrpɔ́lin, tárpəlin) *n.* waterproof canvas or a sheet of this [etym. doubtful]

tar·pon (tárpən) *pl.* **tar·pon, tar·pons** *n. Tarpon atlanticus* or *Megalops atlanticus*, a large (up to 200 lbs) marine game fish common in the Gulf of Mexico off the coast of Florida [etym. doubtful]

Tar·quin·i·us Pris·cus (tɑrkwíni:əspərískəs), Lucius, fifth king of Rome (616-579 B.C.)

Tarquinius Su·per·bus (supé:rbəs), Lucius, seventh and last king of Rome (534-510 B.C.), expelled by Brutus (*LUCRETIA)

tar·ra·gon (tǽrəgən, tǽrəgɒn) *n. Artemisia dracunculus,* fam. *Compositae,* a European perennial wormwood, grown for its aromatic leaves [fr. Span. *taragona* fr. Arab. fr. Gk]

Tar·ra·go·na (tærəgóunə) a province (area 2,505 sq. miles, pop. 516,078) of E. Spain (*CATALONIA) ‖ its capital (pop. 138,705), a walled port. Roman walls, aqueduct, theater etc., Romanesque-Gothic cathedral (12th-13th cc.)

tar·ry (tári:) *comp.* **tar·ri·er** *superl.* **tar·ri·est** *adj.* covered with tar or resembling tar

tar·ry (tǽri:) *pres. part.* **tar·ry·ing** *past and past part.* **tar·ried** *v.i.* (*rhet.*) to linger behind, delay [origin unknown]

tar·sal (túrs'l) **1.** *adj.* of or relating to the tarsus ‖ being or relating to the tarsi of the eyelids **2.** *n.* a tarsal bone or plate [fr. Mod. L. *tarsalis* fr. *tarsus, tarsus*]

tar sands oil-rich sands, principally in Canada

tar·si·a (túrsi:ə) *n.* intarsia [Ital.]

tar·si·er (túrsi:ər) *n.* any of several members of *Tarsius,* fam. *Tarsiidae,* a genus of nocturnal, arboreal mammals of the East Indies, related to the lemurs, and having elongated tarsal bones in the hands and feet. Of a grayish-brown color, they are about the size of a squirrel, and have large ears, large eyes and a long tufted tail [F. fr. *tarse, tarsus*]

Tar·sus (túrsəs) a trade center (pop. 102,186) in S.W. central Turkey. In ancient times it was the capital of Cilicia. It prospered under Roman rule and was the birthplace of St Paul

tar·sus (túrsəs) *pl.* **tar·si** (túrsai) *n.* (*anat.*) the ankle ‖ (*anat.*) the small bones supporting the ankle ‖ the shank of a bird's leg ‖ the end segment of an insect's or crustacean's leg ‖ a plate of fibrous connective tissue serving to support the eyelid [Mod. L. fr. Gk *tarsos,* the flat part of the foot or rim of the eyelid]

tart (turt) *n.* a piece of baked pastry containing jam, fruit etc. ‖ (*Br.*) fruit covered with pastry and baked [O.F. *tarte*]

tart *adj.* having an acid taste ‖ (*fig.*) sharp, cutting, *a tart reply* [O.E. *teart*]

tart *n.* a girl or woman of loose morals, esp. a prostitute [shortened fr. SWEETHEART]

tar·tan (túrt'n) *n.* a closely woven woolen fabric, cross-barred with stripes in various widths and colors which form distinctive patterns. The fabric is used mainly by the Highlanders of Scotland, almost every clan having its own individual pattern ‖ any such pattern [etym. doubtful]

tartan *n.* a single-masted Mediterranean vessel, carrying a large lateen sail and a jib [F. *tartane* fr. Ital. perh. fr. Arab.]

tar·tar (túrtər) *n.* a brownish-red deposit, chiefly of acid potassium tartrate, found in the juice of grapes and deposited in wine barrels (*CREAM OF TARTAR) ‖ a deposit on the teeth consisting mainly of calcium phosphate [O.F. *tartre,* perh. of Arab. origin]

Tar·tar (túrtər) Tatar

Tartar (*mil.*) a 1,500-lb shipborne, surface-to-air missile (RIM-24) with solid-propellant rocket engine, 10-mi range, semiactive radar direction, and a nonnuclear warhead capability

Tartar A.S.S.R. Tatar A.S.S.R.

Tar·tar·e·an (tartéəri:ən) *adj.* of or relating to Tartarus

tartar emetic a poisonous crystalline salt, $2K(SbO)C_4H_4O_6 \cdot H_2O$, used in medicine and as a mordant in dyeing

tar·tar·ic (tartǽrik) *adj.* of, relating to, containing or derived from tartar or tartaric acid

tartaric acid $HOOC(CHOH)_2 \cdot COOH$, an acid, having four stereoisomeric forms, occurring widely in plants and used in dyeing, calico printing, in making effervescent laxatives etc.

Tar·ta·rus (túrtərəs) (*Gk mythol.*) a region of the underworld where the wicked were punished, and the place where Zeus confined the Titans

Tar·ta·ry (túrtəri:) Tatary

tart·let (túrtlit) *n.* a small pastry tart

tar·trate (túrtreit) *n.* a salt or ester of tartaric acid [F.]

Tar·tu (túrtu:) (G. *Dorpat, Russ.* formerly *Yurev*) a city (pop. 104,000) of E. Estonia, U.S.S.R. Industries: mechanical engineering, wood and food processing. University (1632 and 1802)

tart up or **tart** *v.* (*Br.*) to dress up or overadorn

Tar·zan (túrzən, túrzæn) a fictional character created by Edgar Rice Burroughs and popularized in many movies. Tarzan was the child of parents who died in the African jungle. He was brought up by an ape, became immensely strong and agile and the friend of all the jungle creatures, and had fabulous adventures

Ta·shi La·ma (túʃi:lúmə) *LAMA

Tash·kent (taʃként) the capital (pop. 1,779,000) of Uzbekistan, U.S.S.R., an ancient oasis trading city, now economic and cultural center of Soviet central Asia. Industries: heavy machinery, cotton textiles, food processing, paper, chemicals. Arab mausoleum (9th c.). University

TASI (*acronym*) for time assignment speech interpolation, a technique for using intervals of silence on transatlantic telephone cables to transmit information, involving complex switching, enabling a doubling of capacity

task (tæsk, task) **1.** *n.* a definite amount of work set or undertaken ‖ any piece of work that has to be done **to take to task** to blame or censure for neglecting to do a task or for committing a fault **2.** *v.t.* (*rhet.*) to burden with a task [O.N.F. *tasque*]

task force (*mil.*) a temporary grouping of men or units under one commander, formed for carrying out a special mission ‖ a group of people formed temporarily to solve a particular problem

task·mas·ter (tǽskmæstər, túskmastər) *n.* (esp. in phrase) **a hard taskmaster** a person who demands hard work from others, and who is difficult to satisfy

Tas·man (tǽzmən), Abel Janszoon (c. 1603-59), Dutch navigator. Under the patronage of Van Diemen, he led an expedition (1642-3) which discovered Tasmania and New Zealand, and visited some of the islands of Tonga and Fiji. On a later expedition he explored the north coast of Australia (1644)

Tas·ma·ni·a (tæzméini:ə) an island (area 24,450 sq. miles) and state (area, including the Macquarie Is, 26,215 sq. miles, pop. 414,000) of Australia, 268 miles off the southeast coast, between the Indian Ocean and the Tasman Sea. Capital: Hobart. Chief port: Launceston. It is mountainous (Ben Lomond, 5,160 ft) and largely forested. Exports: metals, newsprint, lumber, fruit, wool, cereals, dairy produce. State university (1890). Tasmania was discovered (1642) by Tasman, and called Van Diemen's Land until 1855

Tas·ma·ni·an (tæzméini:ən) **1.** *n.* a native or inhabitant of Tasmania, esp. one of the extinct aborigines ‖ any of various languages of the Tasmanian aborigines **2.** *adj.* pertaining to Tasmania or its inhabitants

Tasmanian devil *Sarcophilus Harrisii,* a fierce, carnivorous, burrowing marsupial of Tasmania. It is about the size of a large cat and has a black coat and white chest markings

Tasmanian wolf *Thylacinus cynocephalus,* fam. *Dasyuridae,* a carnivorous doglike marsupial of Tasmania. It is about 40 ins long and has a smooth grayish-brown coat striped with black towards the back

Tasman Sea the part of the Pacific between Australia and New Zealand

tas·sel (tǽs'l) **1.** *n.* a tuft of threads or cords fastened at one end to form a pendant ornament ‖ a tuft of loose threads, occurring as the inflorescence of some plants (e.g. corn) **2.** *v. pres. part.* **tas·sel·ing,** esp. *Br.* **tas·sel·ling** *past and past part.* **tas·seled,** esp. *Br.* **tas·selled** *v.i.* (often with 'out') to put forth tassels ‖ *v.t.* to furnish with or as if with tassels [O.F. *tasel, tassel,* a clasp]

tas·ses (tǽsiz) *pl. n.* (*hist.,* of armor) a series of overlapping metal plates suspended from the waist to form a short skirt for protecting the thighs [fr. F. *tassette,* a small pocket or pouch]

tas·sets (tǽsits) *pl. n.* tasses [fr. F. *tassette,* a small pocket or pouch]

Tas·so (túsɔ), Torquato (1544-95), Italian epic poet. His 'Aminta' (1573) is a lyrical and pastoral drama. His masterpiece, 'Jerusalem Delivered' (1581), is an epic celebrating the 1st Crusade. He inspired many poets, esp. Spenser and Byron

taste (teist) *n.* the sense which perceives and distinguishes between salt, bitter, sour and sweet substances through the stimulation of the taste buds in the mouth by a solution of the substance in the saliva ‖ the flavor detected through this sense ‖ the sensation resulting from this stimulation ‖ a tasting ‖ a small amount of a substance examined for its taste ‖ discernment where beauty is concerned ‖ a brief experiencing of something, *a taste of night life* ‖ a liking, predilection, *a taste for adventure* **in good** (**poor, bad** etc.) **taste** pleasing (not pleasing) aesthetically, morally etc. **to leave a nasty taste in the mouth** to make one feel slightly disgusted in the aftermath by what seemed momentarily enjoyable [O.F. *tast*]

taste *pres. part.* **tast·ing** *past and past part.* **tast·ed** *v.t.* to examine (a substance) for its taste by putting some in one's mouth ‖ to distinguish the taste of, *you could taste the rum in the cake* ‖ to experience, *to taste the rigors of an Arctic winter* ‖ to eat or drink a small amount of ‖ (esp. *hist.*) to sample (food or drink prepared for another) to discover if it is poisoned ‖ *v.i.* to have the sense of taste ‖ to have a specified flavor, *the ice cream tasted of rum* [O.F. *taster*]

taste bud a cluster of cells at the base of the papillae of the tongue constituting the sense organ of taste

taste·ful (téistfəl) *adj.* being in or showing good taste

taste·less (téistlis) *adj.* failing to excite the sensation of taste ‖ lacking artistic taste ‖ being in bad taste

tast·er (téistər) *n.* a person who tests quality by tasting ‖ any of several devices used by tasters ‖ (esp. *hist.*) a person who tastes food or drink prepared for another to discover if poison is present ‖ an instrument for taking a sample of butter or cheese [A.F. *tastour*]

tast·i·ly (téistili:) *adv.* in a tasty way

tast·i·ness (téisti:nis) *n.* the state or quality of being tasty

tast·y (téisti:) *comp.* **tast·i·er** *superl.* **tast·i·est** *adj.* having a very pleasant taste

tat (tæt) *n.* *TIT FOR TAT

tat *pres. part.* **tat·ting** *past and past part.* **tat·ted** *v.i.* to do tatting ‖ *v.t.* to make by tatting [etym. doubtful]

TAT (*psych.*) thematic apperception test (which see)

Ta·tar (tútər) **1.** *n.* (*hist.*) a member of the Mongolian horde which overran Asia and part of Europe in the Middle Ages (*MONGOL) ‖ a member of a people of Turkish origin, chiefly Moslem, living in the U.S.S.R. They number 5 million and are divided into three groups: Kazan or Volga Tatars, living mainly in the Volga region and the Urals, Siberian Tatars, living in scattered groups in W. Siberia, and Crimean Tatars. These last lived in the Crimea until 1945, formerly a Tatar autonomous republic, when they were all deported to Uzbekistan and Kazakhstan for alleged collaboration with the Germans. They have not since been rehabilitated **2.** *adj.* of Tatary or the Tatars ‖ of the language of the Tatars [Pers. *Tātār*]

Tatar A.S.S.R. an autonomous republic (area 26,200 sq. miles, pop. 3,453,000) of the R.S.F.S.R., U.S.S.R., on the middle Volga. Capital: Kazan. People: Tatar

Ta·ta·ry (tútəri:) (*hist.*) the area ruled by the Tatars

Ta·tra Mountains (tútrə) a pair of rugged massifs: the High Tatra (summit: 8,737 ft), on the Polish-Czechoslovakian frontier, and the Low Tatra, entirely in Czechoslovakia, containing the highest peaks of the Carpathians

tat·ter (tǽtər) *n.* a torn piece of fabric, paper etc., usually hanging loosely ‖ (*pl.*) ragged clothing, *dressed in tatters* [of Scand. origin]

tatter *v.t.* to tear into shreds, make ragged ‖ *v.i.* to become ragged [prob. back-formation fr. TATTERED]

tat·tered (tǽtərd) *adj.* in tatters ‖ wearing torn, ragged clothing

tat·ter·de·mal·ion (tætərdəméiljən) *n.* a person clothed in rags [TATTER+*demalion,* origin unknown]

tat·ting (tǽtiŋ) *n.* narrow lace made by knotting each loop of thread, using a small shuttle ‖ the act or process of making this lace [origin unknown]

tat·tle (tǽt'l) **1.** *v.i. pres. part.* **tat·tling** *past and past part.* **tat·tled** to engage in idle talk ‖ to tell other people's secrets **2.** *n.* idle talk, gossip **tat·tler** (*old-fash.*) a gossip [imit.]

tat·tle·tale (tǽt'lteil) *n.* a talebearer

tat·too (tætú:), esp. *Br.* tatú:) *pl.* **tat·toos** *n.* a signal sounded on a drum or bugle to call troops to quarters ‖ a rapid succession of light taps, *the rain beat a tattoo on the roof* ‖ (*mil.*) an outdoor entertainment given at night, consisting of military exercises accompanied by music [earlier *taptoo* fr. Du. *tap toe,* shut the tap (a signal for closing bars)]

tattoo 1. *v.t.* to mark (the skin) with a permanent pattern by puncturing it and inserting a pigment ‖ to make (patterns) in this way 2. *n.* the marks thus made [fr. Polynesian *tatau*]

tat·ty (tǽti:) *comp.* **tat·ti·er** *superl.* **tat·ti·est** *adj.* of an inferior sort or quality or in an inferior condition, shabby [perh. rel. to O.E. *tætteca*, rag, tatter]

tau (tau) *n.* the 19th letter (T, τ = t) of the Greek alphabet

taught *past* and *past part.* of TEACH

tau meson *K MESON

taunt (tɔnt) *adj.* (*naut.*, of a mast) very tall [etym. doubtful]

taunt 1. *v.t.* to jeer at ‖ to accuse (someone) in a jeering way of some contemptible crime or failing (e.g. cowardice) ‖ to provoke by a taunt 2. *n.* a jibe, a jeering accusation [etym. doubtful]

Tau·nus Mountains (táunus) a wooded range (rising to 2,886 ft) on the E. Rhine plateau in Hesse, West Germany: tourism

taupe (toup) *n.* a soft, brownish-gray color

Tau·po (táupou) the largest lake (area 238 sq. miles) in New Zealand, in central North Island

tau·rine (tóri:n) *n.* a crystalline compound, $H_2NCH_2CH_2HSO_3$, occurring esp. in the muscle juices of invertebrates etc. [fr. L. *taurus*, bull (because it was first found in the bile of an ox)]

taurine *adj.* of or relating to a bull [fr. L. *taurinus*]

tau·rom·a·chy (tɔrómǝki:) *n.* the art or practice of bullfighting [Span. *tauromaquia*]

Tau·rus (tóras) a northern constellation ‖ the second sign of the zodiac, represented as a bull [L.=bull]

Taurus Mountains (*Turk.* Toros) a mountain chain of central S.W. Turkey running parallel to the Mediterranean coast, with several peaks over 11,000 ft. Chief pass: the Cilician Gates, above Tarsus

Taus·sig (tóusig), Frank William (1859-1940), U.S. economist. His 'Wages and Capital' (1896) and 'International Trade' (1927) modernized the classical school of economics as formulated by John Stuart Mill. He helped to draft the tariff and commercial policy clauses of the Treaty of Versailles (1919)

taut (tɔt) *adj.* (of a rope, wire, muscle etc.) under longitudinal tension, *a taut string* ‖ tense, *taut nerves* ‖ (esp. *naut.*) trim and tidy **taut·en** *v.t.* to make taut ‖ *v.i.* to become taut [M.E. *toght*]

tau·tog (tɔtɔ́g, tɔtóg) *n. Tautoga onitis*, fam. *Labridae*, an edible marine fish of the Atlantic coast of the U.S.A. [fr. Algonquian *tautauog* pl. of *tautau*, a blackfish]

tau·to·log·i·cal (tɔt'lódʒik'l) *adj.* of, relating to or using tautology

tau·tol·o·gism (tɔtólǝdʒizǝm) *n.* the use or an instance of tautology

tau·tol·o·gist (tɔtólǝdʒist) *n.* a person who uses tautology

tau·tol·o·gize (tɔtólǝdʒaiz) *pres. part.* **tau·tol·o·giz·ing** *past* and *past part.* **tau·tol·o·gized** *v.i.* to use tautology

tau·tol·o·gy (tɔtólǝdʒi:) *pl.* **tau·tol·o·gies** *n.* the useless repetition of an identical meaning in different terms ‖ an example of this [fr. L.L. *tautologia* fr. Gk]

tau·to·mer (tótǝmǝr) *n.* one form of a tautomeric compound

tau·to·mer·ic (tɔtǝmérik) *adj.* of, relating to or characterized by tautomerism

tau·tom·er·ism (tɔtómǝrizǝm) *n.* (*chem.*) the existence of two isomers in a mixture in stable equilibrium, this equilibrium being preserved by their interconvertibility [fr. Gk *to auto*, the same+*meros*, a part]

tav·ern (tǽvǝrn) *n.* (*old-fash.*) an inn or bar [O.F. *taverne*]

Tav·er·ner (tǽvǝrnǝr), John (c. 1495-1545), English composer of church music (masses, motets etc.). He also wrote songs and madrigals

taw (tɔ) *n.* the large, usually glass, marble which a marble player shoots with ‖ the mark from which a marble is played ‖ one of the games played with marbles [etym. doubtful]

taw *v.t.* to convert (a skin) into leather by treating it with alum, salt etc. [O.E. *tawian*, to make]

taw·dri·ly (tɔ́drili:) *adv.* in a tawdry manner

taw·dri·ness (tɔ́dri:nis) *n.* the state or quality of being tawdry

taw·dry (tɔ́dri:) *comp.* **taw·dri·er** *superl.* **taw·dri·est** *adj.* showy but of very poor quality [after the old *St Audrey's* fair at Ely, England]

taw·ni·ness (tóni:nis) *n.* the quality of being tawny

taw·ny (tóni:) *comp.* **taw·ni·er** *superl.* **taw·ni·est** *adj.* of a light reddish-yellow brown color [A.F. *taune*, O.F. *tané* fr. *tan*, tan]

tax (tæks) 1. *n.* a charge on a person's income or property, *direct tax* or on the price of goods sold, *indirect tax* made by a government to collect revenue ‖ a heavy demand made upon one's strength, patience etc. 2. *v.t.* to impose a tax on (a person) or upon (goods) ‖ to make a heavy demand on, *his persistence taxed my patience* ‖ to accuse in a challenging way, *to tax someone with being idle* ‖ (*law*) to fix the amount of (costs etc.) **tax·a·bil·i·ty** *n.* **tax·a·ble** *adj.* [O.F. *taxer*]

tax·a·tion (tækséiʃǝn) *n.* the imposition of a tax ‖ the system by which taxes are imposed ‖ the revenue obtained by imposing taxes

tax-based income policy *TIP

tax-de·ferred income (tæksdifǝ́:rd) cash received by an investor on which tax is not presently payable, but which may have to be paid at a later date, e.g., deduction for depreciation

tax-ex·empt (tæksigzempt) *adj.* of dividends distributed to shareholders after taxes have been paid by the corporation ‖ exempt from tax

tax exile one who leaves a country to avoid paying taxes

tax farmer (*hist.*, esp. in France) someone who bought from the government the right to collect taxes

tax-free (tæksfrí:) *adj.* tax-exempt

tax haven a country that has a low rate of or no business, income, or inheritance taxes

tax·i (tǽksi:) 1. *n.* an automobile carrying passengers for a charge 2. *v. pres. part.* **tax·i·ing**, **tax·y·ing** *past* and *past part.* **tax·ied** *v.i.* to ride in a taxi ‖ (of an aircraft) to move over the surface of the ground or water e.g. in parking or in taking off ‖ *v.t.* to transport by or as if by taxi ‖ to cause (an aircraft) to taxi [short for TAXIMETER]

tax·i·cab (tǽksi:kæb) *n.* a taxi

taxi dancer a girl employed in a dance hall to dance with patrons for a fee

tax·i·der·mal (tæksidǝ́:rmǝl) *adj.* of or pertaining to taxidermy

tax·i·der·mic (tæksidǝ́:rmik) *adj.* taxidermal

tax·i·der·mist (tæksidǝ́:rmist) *n.* a person skilled in taxidermy

tax·i·der·my (tæksidǝ́:rmi:) *n.* the art of preparing and mounting the skins of animals to give a lifelike effect [fr. Gk *taxis*, arrangement+*derma*, skin]

Tax·il·a (tæksílǝ) an ancient city near Peshawar, Pakistan, where excavations have revealed extensive remains of civilizations which flourished from the 7th c. B.C. to the 7th c. A.D. and numerous Gandharan sculptures showing strong Hellenistic influences

tax·i·me·ter (tǽksi:mi:tǝr) *n.* a device fitted to a taxi which registers the distance traveled and the fare due [F. *taximètre* fr. *taxe*, a tariff+*mètre*, a meter]

tax·is (tǽksis) *pl.* **tax·es** (tǽksi:z) *n.* (*biol.*) the movement (sometimes orientation) of a small mobile organism towards the source of a stimulus (positive taxis), or away from it (negative taxis) (cf. KINESIS, cf. TROPISM) ‖ (*med.*) manual pressure used to adjust displaced organs ‖ (*Gk hist.*) an army subunit of varying size [Gk=arrangement]

taxi squad 1. (*sports*) a group of professional football players who practice with a team but are not eligible to play 2. (*politics*) a group of political partisans who drive voters to the polls

tax loss 1. of a business loss used to offset federal income tax 2. (*Br.*) lossmaker

tax·o·di·um (tæksóudi:ǝm) *n.* a member of *Taxodium*, fam. *Taxodiaceae*, a genus of deciduous conifers common in North American swamps. The hard red wood of some species is used for roof shingles [Mod. L. fr. *taxus*, yew]

tax·o·nom·ic (tæksǝnómik) *adj.* of or pertaining to taxonomy **tax·o·nóm·i·cal** *adj.* **tax·o·nóm·i·cal·ly** *adv.*

tax·on·o·my (tæksónǝmi:) *n.* the science of classification ‖ the principles and method of classification of living organisms into phyla, species etc. [fr. F. *taxonomie* fr. Gk]

tax·pay·er (tǽkspeiǝr) *n.* a person who pays or is liable to pay a tax

tax selling (*securities*) sales made near the end of the year to establish gains or losses in order to minimize income taxes

tax shelter an investment that enables the taxpayer to have substantial deductions from income tax, e.g., for depletion, depreciation — **tax-sheltered** *adj.*

Tay (tei) the longest river (120 miles) of Scotland, rising in W. Perth and flowing southeast through its estuary, the Firth of Tay, to the North Sea. Ports: Dundee, Perth. The lake Loch Tay (15 miles long, up to 1 mile wide) lies on its upper course

Tay·ge·tus Mountains (teiídʒitǝs) (*Gk* Taigeytos) a range (summit 7,904 ft) of the S. central Peloponnesus, Greece

Tay·lor (téilǝr), Edward (c. 1645-1729), American Puritan minister and poet. His 'Poetical Works' (published 1939), characterized by elaborate images of heaven and hell, are in the metaphysical tradition

Taylor, Jeremy (1613-67), English bishop and writer. He is known for his sermons and for his 'Holy Living' (1650) and 'Holy Dying' (1651)

Taylor, Maxwell Davenport (1901-), U.S. general. During the 2nd world war he helped to organize (1942) the U.S. Army's first airborne units and commanded them in the invasions of North Africa, Sicily, and Italy. He served (1955-9) as chief of staff of the U.S. Army and (1962-4) as chairman of the Joint Chiefs of Staff. He was Ambassador (1964-5) to the Republic of Vietnam

Taylor, Zachary (1784-1850), 12th president (1849-50) of the U.S.A., a Whig. His election was due to his successful command of a U.S. force in the Mexican War (1846-8). He died before he could implement his policies: the exclusion of slavery from newly acquired lands and opposition to what became the Compromise of 1850

Taymyr Peninsula *TAIMYR PENINSULA

Tay-Sachs disease (téisæks) *n.* (*med.*) an inherited (esp. among Jews) neurological disease of infants leading to brain degeneration, blindness, paralysis, and death by age 2; named for British physician Warren Tay and American neurologist Bernard P. Sachs

Tbi·li·si (tpílisi) (formerly Tiflis) the capital (pop. 1,066,000) of Georgia, U.S.S.R., on the Kura, an ancient trading center. Industries: mechanical engineering, textiles (esp. silk), food processing, wood, tourism. Byzantine cathedral (6th c.), churches, hot springs, university

T-Bond (tí:bond) *n.* U.S. treasury bond; T-Bond futures market is the purchase and sale of government bonds for future delivery

TCE (*abbr.*) for trichlorethylene chloroformate diphogene, a toxic waste substance with a safe level of 2-4 parts per billion. It was used as poison gas in World War I

T cell *n.* (*cytol.*) a lymph antibody freely circulating in blood that attaches to and destroys viruses, fungi, and certain bacterial infections, and rejects foreign tissue and tumors *also* T lymphocyte *Cf* B CELL

Tchai·kov·sky (tʃaikɔ́fski:), Piotr Ilyich (1840-93), Russian composer. His symphonies, e.g. No. 4 (1877) and No. 6, the 'Pathetic' (1893), and his piano and violin concertos express the lonely, romantic and striving aspects of Tchaikovsky. His 'light' music, esp. the ballet music, shows an immense melodic and rhythmical fertility. He also wrote songs and operas

TDR (*abbr.*) for transferable development rights, a device that enables the owner of a property to transfer the privilege of construction to another property owner suitably situated

te (ti:) *n.* (*Br., mus.*) ti

tea (ti:) *n. Thea sinensis* or *Camellia sinensis*, fam. *Theaceae*, a shrub cultivated from antiquity in China, and now grown in Japan, India, Ceylon etc. ‖ its dried and prepared leaves, used to make a beverage ‖ this beverage ‖ any of a number of plants used like tea ‖ a beverage made like tea by infusion ‖ a light meal towards late afternoon ‖ a social gathering at which tea is served ‖ (*Br.*) high tea [prob. fr. Du. *thee* fr. Malay fr. Chin.]

—Tea is a hardy evergreen bush, having whitish, mildly fragrant flowers. The fruit is a capsule containing three hard-shelled nuts. Most commercial propagation is from seed. Cultivation is in plantations, often terraces. The plants thrive best in protected, well-drained, near-tropical localities. The leaves can be picked two or three years after the seeds have been planted, and the shrub may yield for 25 to 50 years. There are three main types of tea:

CONCISE PRONUNCIATION KEY: (a) æ, c*a*t; ɑ, c*a*r; ɔ f*aw*n; ei, sn*a*ke. (e) e, h*e*n; i:, sh*ee*p; iǝ, d*ee*r; ɛǝ, b*ea*r. (i) i, f*i*sh; ai, t*i*ger; ǝ:, b*i*rd. (o) o, *o*x; au, c*ow*; ou, g*oa*t; u, p*oo*r; ɔi, r*oy*al. (u) ʌ, d*u*ck; u, b*u*ll; u:, g*oo*se; ǝ, *a*bacillus; ju:, c*u*be. x, lo*ch*; θ, *th*ink; ð, *b*o*th*er; z, *Z*en; ʒ, corsa*g*e; dʒ, sava*g*e; ŋ, ora*n*gutang; j, *y*ak; ʃ, *f*ish; tʃ, fe*tch*; 'l, rabb*le*; 'n, redde*n*. Complete pronunciation key appears inside front cover.

green, oolong and black. Green tea is unfermented, its leaves being put immediately into firing machines. Oolong tea is partially fermented and black tea is fermented for 12 to 24 hrs. The leading tea-producing country is India, though it began to be cultivated there as late as 1836

Tea Act a British act of parliament (1773) which repealed all the Townshend acts except that which placed a tax on tea imported into the American colonies. It led to the Boston Tea Party

tea bag a cloth or filter paper bag holding enough tea for one serving, for infusion in boiling water

tea ball a small perforated metal ball-shaped container used esp. for making an individual cup of tea

tea break (*Br.*) a short rest period during the working day, equivalent to U.S. coffee break

tea cart a tea wagon

tea ceremony a semireligious social custom of Zen origin introduced into Japan from China in the 15th c. It is marked by extreme refinement of gesture

teach (ti:tʃ) *pres. part.* **teach·ing** *past and past part.* **taught** (tɔt) *v.t.* to give instruction to, to train, *to teach a class of nurses* ‖ to give to another (knowledge or skill which one has oneself), *to teach someone how to drive* ‖ to give instruction in for a living, *he teaches the violin* ‖ to cause to understand, *that will teach him not to interfere* ‖ *v.i.* to be a teacher **to teach school** to be a schoolteacher **téach·a·ble** *adj.* capable of being taught **téach·er** *n.* a person who teaches, esp. for a living **téach·ing** *n.* the act of someone who teaches ‖ the profession of a teacher ‖ (often *pl.*) something that is taught, *the teachings of religion* [O.E. *tǽcean*]

teach-in (ti:tʃin) *n.* long, often unauthorized, meeting, debate, or lecture on a controversial issue

teaching hospital a large hospital to which a medical school is attached

teaching machine (*education*) device to provide instruction, esp. one programmed to ask questions and respond to answers on a one-to-one basis

tea·cup (tí:kʌp) *n.* a cup for drinking esp. tea **a storm in a teacup** much fuss and excitement about something of small importance

tea·cup·ful (tí:kʌpful) *pl.* **tea·cup·fuls** *n.* as much as a teacup can hold

tea·house (tí:haus) *pl.* **tea·hous·es** (tí:hauziz) *n.* a place where tea is served in the Orient

teak (ti:k) *n. Tectona grandis*, fam. *Verbenaceae*, a large East Indian tree now also grown in W. Africa and tropical America for its wood ‖ this hard, close-grained wood, used esp. for shipbuilding and furniture [Port. *teca* fr. Malayalam]

tea·ket·tle (tí:ketʼl) *n.* a utensil having a lid, spout and handle, used to boil water in

teal (ti:l) *pl.* **teal, teals** *n.* a member of *Anas*, fam. *Anatidae*, a genus of small freshwater ducks of Europe and North America, esp. the green-winged *A. carolinensis* [M.E. *tele*]

tea leaf *pl.* **tea leaves** a leaf of tea, esp. after it has infused

team (ti:m) 1. *n.* two or more draft animals harnessed together ‖ two or more draft animals and the vehicle they draw ‖ a single draft animal and the vehicle it draws ‖ a number of people working together on a common task ‖ a group forming one side in a game 2. *v.i.* (often with 'up') to join in a common task, *the farmers teamed up to get the crops in* ‖ *v.t.* to cause to work in a team ‖ to haul with a team [O.E. *tēam*]

team foul (*sports*) one of the maximum personal fouls allowed at the beginning of a basketball game before free throws are given to the opposing team

team handball (*sports*) a soccerlike game of two seven-player teams involving a large ball that is thrown, dribbled, and caught

team·ster (tí:mstər) *n.* the driver of a team of animals ‖ a person who drives a truck for a living

team teaching (*education*) instruction by a group of teachers for a small group of students, directed by a leading teacher, usu. under an open plan (which see) usu. associated with a special project

team·work (tí:mwɜrk) *n.* the quality whereby individuals unselfishly subordinate their own part to the general effort of the group with whom they are working or playing

tea·pot (tí:pɒt) *n.* a pot in which tea is brewed and which has a spout for pouring out the brew **a tempest in a teapot** a storm in a teacup (*TEACUP)

'Teapot Dome' Scandal *OIL RESERVES SCANDAL

tear (tiər) 1. *n.* a drop of the saline fluid secreted by the lachrymal gland and serving normally to moisten, lubricate and cleanse the eye ‖ (*pl.*) drops of this secretion that overflow the eyelids and stream down the face when certain strong emotions, e.g. sadness, pity, joy or great amusement, are aroused, or when the eye is irritated by dust, soap etc. ‖ (*pl.*) the visible expression of grief ‖ something resembling a tear, e.g. a defect in glass caused by a bit of vitrified clay **in tears** weeping 2. *v.i.* (of the eyes) to fill with tears [O.E. *tēar*]

tear (tɛər) 1. *v. pres. part.* **tear·ing** *past* **tore** (tɔr) *past part.* **torn** (tɔrn) *v.t.* to break the fiber of (a fabric, paper etc.) by exerting a strong pull, *to tear a piece of cloth* ‖ to make (e.g. a hole) in this way ‖ to remove by making an opening in this way, *to tear a letter from its envelope* ‖ to injure by lacerating, *the teeth of the saw tore his leg* ‖ to subject to intense or conflicting emotions, *she was torn as to what she ought to do* ‖ to divide into opposing groups, *the nation was torn by dissension* ‖ *v.i.* to give way under a strong pull, *the paper tore when the parcel fell* ‖ (*pop.*) to move rapidly, *he tore down the road* ‖ **to tear at** to pull wildly at, *he tore at the rope which bound him* ‖ **to tear down** to pull down violently ‖ to demolish ‖ to denigrate **to tear into** to attack critically or physically with wild violence **to tear oneself away** to overcome a strong desire to stay by an effort of will **to tear to pieces** to criticize devastatingly **to tear up** to destroy by tearing into pieces ‖ to cause to cease to be operative, *to tear up a treaty* 2. *n.* the act of tearing ‖ the line of break resulting from tearing [O.E. *teran*]

tear bomb (tiər) a bomb containing tear gas

tear·drop (tíərdrɒp) *n.* a tear ‖ a pendant gem on an earring or necklace shaped like a tear

tear·ful (tíərfəl) *adj.* shedding tears ‖ accompanied by tears ‖ causing tears

tear gas (tiər) any one of several substances, used in the form of vapor or smoke, that irritate the eyes and often cause chemical burns on the skin. Tear gas is used mainly for dispersing crowds

tear·ing (tɛəriŋ) *adj.* violent, *a tearing rage*

tear·jerk·er (tíərdʒɜrkər) *n.* a sentimental story, play etc. with a sad ending

tea·room (tí:ru:m, tí:rum) *n.* a restaurant serving light meals

tea rose any of various half-hardy hybrid shrub roses derived mainly from *Rosa odorata*, a Chinese rose, the flowers of which have a scent resembling tea

tear sheet (tɛər) a part of a publication torn out and sent to the advertiser etc. whom it concerns, as evidence that his copy was duly printed

Teas·dale (tí:zdeil), Sara (1884-1933), U.S. poet. Her works include 'Sonnets to Duse and Other Poems' (1907) and 'Love Songs' (1917)

tease (ti:z) 1. *v. pres. part.* **teas·ing** *past and past part.* **teased** *v.t.* to annoy (a person or animal) by making him or it the victim of irritating remarks or actions repeated time and time again ‖ to attempt to do this ‖ (esp. of children) to importune persistently, *they teased their father for more candies* ‖ to separate or pull apart the fibers of (wool, flax etc.) by using a comb or tease ‖ to raise a nap on (cloth) with a teasel ‖ *v.i.* to indulge in teasing 2. *n.* a teasing or being teased ‖ a person who teases [O.E. *tǽsan*, to tear or pull to pieces]

tea·sel, tea·zel (tí:zʼl) *n.* a member of *Dipsacus*, fam. *Dipsacaceae*, a genus of thistlelike plants, esp. *D. fullonum*, having a prickly stem and hooked bracts surrounding the flower heads ‖ this flower head when dried, used to separate the surface fibers of a fabric and raise a nap ‖ a wire device used in place of this [O.E. *tǽsel*, *tǽsl*]

tea·spoon (tí:spu:n) *n.* a small spoon for stirring tea etc. and for eating certain foods ‖ a teaspoonful **tea·spoon·ful** (tí:spu:nful) *pl.* **tea·spoon·fuls** *n.* as much as a teaspoon will hold

teat (ti:t) *n.* the protrusion of a mammal's breast or udder through which milk is drawn ‖ (*Br.*) a rubber nipple through which milk can be sucked from a nursing bottle [O. F. *tete*]

tea towel (*Br.*) a dish towel

tea tree *Lycium afrum*, fam. *Solanaceae*, an African spiny shrub bearing solitary purple flowers ‖ any of various members of *Leptospermum* or *Melaleuca*, genera of Australian shrubs or trees

tea wagon a small table on casters or wheels used to transport food etc. within a room or building

teazel *TEASEL

Teb·el·ized (tebélaizd) *adj.* application of a finish to fabrics that resists creasing and crushing and recovers from wrinkling; trademark of Tootal, Broadhurst & Lee Company, Ltd.

tech·ne·ti·um (tekní:ʃiːəm) *n.* a very rare radioactive metallic element (symbol Tc, at. no. 43, mass of isotope of longest known half-life 97) [Mod. L. fr. Gk *technētos*, artificial]

tech·nic (téknik) 1. *adj. (rare)* technical 2. *n.* (*pl., rare*) technique ‖ (*pl.*) technology **téch·ni·cal** *adj.* pertaining to the mechanical, industrial or applied sciences of, used in or pertaining to a particular science, art, skill etc., *technical terms* ‖ showing technique, *technical skill* ‖ pertaining to the law as this is stated, *a technical right* ‖ arising from mechanical causes, *a technical difficulty* **tech·ni·cál·i·ty** *pl.* **tech·ni·cal·i·ties** *n.* the use of technical terms ‖ a detail of no particular importance arising merely from the way in which a regulation etc. is worded ‖ the state or quality of being technical ‖ a point of detail etc. in a given science or skill which only a specialist would be aware of [fr. Gk *technikos* fr. *techne*, an art]

technical knockout (*boxing*) a knockout occurring when the referee rules that a boxer is unable to continue fighting because of injury

technical sergeant a non-commissioned officer in the air force ranking above a staff sergeant and below a master sergeant

tech·ni·cian (tekníʃən) *n.* a person skilled in the technical details and techniques of a subject ‖ a painter, musician etc. whose mastery of the technique of his art may or may not serve the quality of his expression [TECHNIC]

Tech·ni·col·or (téknikʌlər) *n.* a color process used in making some movies [Trademark]

tech·nique (tekní:k) *n.* the entire body of procedures and methods of a science, art or craft ‖ skill in these procedures and methods ‖ (*loosely*) a way of achieving a purpose, *a technique for getting money out of the country* [F.]

tech·noc·ra·cy (teknókrəsi) *pl.* **tech·noc·ra·cies** *n.* government by technical experts **tech·no·crat** (téknəkræt) *n.* **tech·no·crát·ic** *adj.* [fr. Gk *technē*, art + -*kratia*, rule]

tech·no·log·ic (teknəlódʒik) *adj.* technological **tech·no·log·i·cal** (teknəlódʒikʼl) *adj.* of, relating to or characterized by technology ‖ due to developments in technology

tech·nol·o·gist (teknólədʒist) *n.* someone who specializes in some branch of technology [fr. TECHNOLOGY]

tech·nol·o·gize (teknólədʒaiz) *v.* to change by introducing new technology

tech·nol·o·gy (teknólədʒi:) *pl.* **tech·nol·o·gies** *n.* the science of technical processes in a wide, though related, field of knowledge. Thus industrial technology embraces the chemical, mechanical and physical sciences as these are applied in industrial processes ‖ technical terminology [fr. Gk *technologia*, systematic treatment]

technology transfer transfer of technical knowledge generated and developed in one place to another in order to achieve some practical end

tech·nop·o·lis (teknópələs) *n.* a large community in which technology plays a dominant role —**technopolitan** *adj.*

tech·no·struc·ture (téknəstrʌktʃər) *n.* **1.** in a society, the personnel, equipment, and facilities for high-technology industry **2.** the hierarchy of technology management

techy *TETCHY

tec·ton·ic (tektónik) *adj.* of or relating to tectonics

tec·tón·ics *n.* the art and science of constructing buildings ‖ a branch of geology dealing with land structure, esp. folding and faulting [fr. L.L. *tectonicus* fr. Gk fr. *tektōn*, builder]

tec·tri·ces (téktrisi:z) *pl. n.* the coverts of a bird [L.]

Te·cum·seh (tikámsə) (c. 1768-1813), chief of the Shawnee Indians. He sided with the British in the War of 1812

ted (ted) *pres. part.* **ted·ding** *past and past part.* **ted·ded** *v.t.* to turn over and spread (grass) to dry in the air **téd·der** n. [M.E., akin to O.N. *tethja*, to manure]

Ted·der (tédər), Arthur William, 1st Baron Tedder (1890-1967), marshal of the Royal Air Force. As commander of the Allied air forces in the Middle East (1941-3), he helped to drive the German army from N. Africa. He was deputy supreme commander of the Allied invasion of Europe (1944-5)

teddy bear a child's stuffed toy bear [after Theodore (*Teddy*) Roosevelt]

Te De·um (ti:dí:əm, teidéium) n. an ancient Latin hymn beginning 'Te Deum laudamus' ('We praise Thee, O God') sung at Matins ‖ a special thanksgiving service in which this hymn is sung ‖ the musical setting for this hymn [L.]

te·di·ous (tí:di:əs) adj. boring, causing psychological fatigue, usually because of needless repetition and lengthiness [fr. L.L. *taediosus*]

te·di·um (tí:di:əm) n. the state or quality of being tedious [fr. L. *taedium*]

Ted·lar (tédlər) n. trademark for insulation using alternating layers of aluminum, nylon, and nylon net used to retain heat in a space vehicle

tee (ti:) n. the letter T, t in the alphabet ‖ anything shaped like a T **to a tee, to a T** exactly

tee 1. n. (*golf*) the area from which a person drives at the beginning of a hole ‖ (*golf*) a wooden or plastic peg, or conical elevation of earth etc., on which the ball is placed for driving 2. v.t. pres. part. **tee·ing** past and past part. **teed** (*golf*, often with 'up') to place (the ball) on a tee ‖ to tee off ‖ (*golf*) to drive [etym. doubtful]

teed-off (tí:dɔf) adj. (*colloq.*) angry; irritated

teem (ti:m) v.i. (of rain etc.) to come down in torrents ‖ v.t. to pour (molten metal) into a mold [M.E. *tēmen* fr. O.N. *tœma*, to empty]

teem v.i. to be full, *the river teems with fish* ‖ to pullulate, *ideas teemed in his mind* [O.E. *tīeman*, to produce]

-teen suffix used to form cardinal numbers from thirteen through nineteen

teen-age (tí:neidʒ) adj. of or relating to teenagers or to adolescence

teen-ag·er (tí:neidʒər) n. a person in his teens

teens (ti:nz) pl. n. the years 13–19 in a person's life

tee·ny (tí:ni:) comp. **tee·ni·er** superl. **tee·ni·est** adj. (*pop.*) very small [var. of TINY]

teen·y·bop·per (tí:ni:bɒpə:r) n. (*slang or colloq.*) (pejorative) a teenager devoted to adolescent fads in dress, rock 'n' roll music, star worship Cf GROUPIES

teepee *TEPEE

Tees (ti:z) a river (70 miles long) rising in Cumberland, N. England. It forms the Yorkshire-Durham border as far as the North Sea

tee·ter (tí:tər) 1. v.i. to move along in a wobbly manner ‖ to show doubt, indecision etc. ‖ (of children) to seesaw 2. n. the act of teetering

tee·ter-tot·ter (tí:tərtɒtər) 1. n. a seesaw 2. v.i. to play on a seesaw

teeth pl. of TOOTH

teethe (ti:ð) pres. part. **teeth·ing** past and past part. **teethed** v.i. to develop teeth [M.E. prob. representing supposed O.E. *tēthan* fr. *tōth*, tooth]

teething ring a bone, rubber or plastic ring on which a teething infant can bite

tee·to·tal (ti:tóut'l) adj. of or pertaining to complete abstinence from alcoholic drinks ‖ completely abstaining from alcoholic drinks ‖ (*pop.*) complete, *a teetotal failure* **tee·tó·tal·ism** n. **tee·tó·tal·er**, esp. Br. **tee·tó·tal·ler** n. a person who never drinks alcohol

teff (tef) n. *Eragrostis abyssinica*, fam. *Gramineae*, an African cereal grass, the grain of which yields a fine, white flour

Tef·lon (téflɒn) n. (*chem.*) trade name of the Du Pont Corp. for its tetrafluoroethylene polymer fiber, Teflon is chemical-resistant, does not absorb moisture, and is the most nonwettable fiber known

teg (teg) n. (*Br.*) a sheep in its second year [perh. of Scand. origin]

Te·ge·a (ti:dʒí:ə) an ancient Greek city in S.E. Arcadia: ruins of the temple of Athene

teg·men (tégmən) pl. **teg·mi·na** (tégminə) n. (*biol.*) the covering of an organ or part of a living organism, esp. the integument, e.g. endopleura **teg·men·tal** (tegmént'l) adj. [L. fr. *tegere*, to cover]

Teg·ner (teŋnéir), Esaias (1782-1846), Swedish

poet. His most famous work is 'Frithjof's Saga' (1825), based on an Old Icelandic saga

Te·gu·ci·gal·pa (tegu:si:gálpə) the capital (pop: 316,800) and commercial center of Honduras, on the S. central plateau. Industries: textiles, food processing. Spanish cathedral (18th c.). National university and theater

teg·u·lar (tégjulər) adj. (*archit.*) made of, resembling or pertaining to tiles [fr. L. *tegula*, a tile]

teg·u·ment (tégjumənt) n. (*biol.*) an integument **teg·u·men·tal** (tegjumént'l), **teg·u·men·ta·ry** adjs [fr. L. *tegumentum* fr. *tegere*, to cover]

Teh·ran, Te·he·ran (teərǽn, teərán) the capital (pop. 3,774,000) of Iran, near the S. Elburz foothills. Industries: metallurgy, mechanical engineering, textiles, glass, tobacco, chemicals. Palace (18th c.). National university (1935), museums. Founded in the 12th c., Tehran became the capital in 1788

Tehran Conference the meeting (Nov. 28–Dec. 1, 1943) of Stalin, Roosevelt and Churchill, at which plans for an Allied invasion of France were coordinated with a Russian offensive against Germany

Te·huan·te·pec, Gulf of (təwántəpek) a wide-mouthed gulf bounded by the states of Chiapas and Oaxaca in S.E. Mexico

Tehuantepec, Isthmus of an isthmus (130 miles wide) between the Bay of Campeche and the Gulf of Tehuantepec in S. Mexico

T-80 tank (*mil.*) U.S.S.R. tank with an automatic loading, 125-mm gun, laser rangefinder, and night-vision equipment

Teil·hard de Char·din (teijærdəʃærdɛ̃), Pierre (1881-1955), French Jesuit priest, paleontologist, theologian and philosopher. In his principal work 'The Phenomenon of Man' (1938-40) he attempts to unfold the mystery of the evolution of man and to correlate religious experience with the findings of natural science

Teil·hard·i·an (ti:lhárdi:ən) adj. of the social evolutionary theories formulated by French theologian Pierre Teilhard de Chardin (1881–1955)

tek·tite (téktait) n. a rounded glassy body, probably of meteoritic origin, found in several parts of the world [fr. Gk *tēktos*, molten]

telaesthesia *TELESTHESIA

tel·a·mon (téləmɒn) pl. **tel·a·mo·nes** (teləmóuni:z) n. (*archit.*) a male figure used as a supporting pillar or column (cf. CARYATID) [L. fr. Gk *telamōn*, bearer]

tel·au·to·gram (telɔ́tɔgræm) n. the image transmitted by telautograph [TELAUTOGRAPH+Gk *gramma*, a letter]

tel·au·to·graph (telɔ́tɔgræf, telɔ́tɔgrəf) n. a telegraph which transmits facsimile half-tone images by a reception process of electrolysis or of scanning with a modulated light beam [fr. Gk *tēle*, far off+ AUTOGRAPH]

Tel A·viv (téləví:v) the main industrial center (pop. with Jaffa 334,900) of Israel, on the Mediterranean. Industries: metallurgy, textiles, chemicals, leatherwork, diamond cutting, food processing, printing and publishing. University. Ashdod replaced Tel Aviv-Jaffa as a port (1965)

tele- (téli) prefix far off, covering a distance ‖ television [fr. Gk *tēle-* fr. *tēle*, far off]

tel·e·cast (télikæst, télikəst) 1. pres. part. **tel·e·cast·ing** past and past part. **tel·e·cast, tel·e·cast·ed** v.t. and i. to televise 2. n. a television broadcast [TELE-+ BROADCAST]

tel·e·com·mu·ni·ca·tion (telikəmju:nikéiʃən) n. any process of communication over a considerable distance (by telegraph, telephone, radio etc.) ‖ (pl.) the science that deals with these processes

tel·e·con·fer·ence (télikɒnfrəns) n. a conference held telecommunicationally

tel·e·di·ag·no·sis (telədaiəgnóusəs) n. (*med.*) diagnosis of an illness through closed-circuit electronic equipment, principally television, e.g., to shipboard or a region without medical facilities

tel·e·du (télidu:) n. *Mydaus meliceps*, fam. *Viverridae*, a small carnivorous mammal of Java and Sumatra which ejects a stinking fluid when alarmed [Malay]

tel·e·fac·sim·i·le (teləfæksíməli:) n. technique for transmitting letters, photographs, and other graphic material over telephone lines *also* facsimile transmission

tel·e·gram (téligræm) n. a message transmitted, or received, by telegraphy [fr. TELE+Gk *gramma*, a letter]

tel·e·graph (téligræf, téligrɑf) 1. n. a method of transmitting messages over long distances by sending electrical impulses along a conducting wire or, in wireless telegraphy, in the form of electromagnetic waves. The timing of the impulses transmitted is controlled according to an agreed system, e.g. the Morse code, and the impulses received are deciphered by the same code ‖ a telegram 2. v.t. to send (a message) by telegraphy ‖ to send a message to by telegraphy ‖ v.i. to send a telegram **tel·e·graph·ic** (téligræfik) adj. **tel·e·gráph·i·cal·ly** adv. **te·leg·ra·phy** (təlégrəfi) n. the act or process of sending by telegraph [F. *télégraphe* fr. Gk *tēle*, far off+*graphos*, written]

Telegu *TELUGU

tel·e·ki·ne·sis (telikiní:sis, telikainí:sis) n. the movement of a body without any apparent physical agency (as reported in psychic research) **tel·e·ki·net·ic** (telikinétik) adj. [fr. TELE-+Gk *kinēsis*, motion]

tel·e·mail (télomeil) n. subscription network with video display terminals that provides instant communication with subscribers and nonsubscribers via Western Union Telex and Mailgram

Tel·e·mann (téləmɑn), Georg Philipp (1681-1767), German composer. He wrote 600 overtures, 40 operas, over 160 church services and many sonatas and suites

tel·e·mark (téləmɑrk) n. (*skiing*) a swinging turn, the ski on the outer curve being advanced and then turned gradually inward [after *Telemark*, a region in S. Norway]

tel·e·me·chan·ics (teləməkæniks) pl. n. the science of controlling the moving parts of a machine by remote control

te·lem·e·ter (təlémitər, téləmi:tər) 1. n. an apparatus for recording physical changes which occur at a distance 2. v.t. to transmit (data) from a distant source, e.g. a spacecraft, to a receiving station for recording **tel·e·met·ric** (teləmétrik) adj. **te·lém·e·try** n.

tel·en·ce·phal·ic (telənsəfælik) adj. of the telencephalon

tel·en·ceph·a·lon (telenséfəlɒn) n. (*anat.*) the cerebral hemispheres of a vertebrate's forebrain [Mod. L. fr. Gk *telos*, end+ ENCEPHALON]

tel·e·o·log·ic (teli:əlódʒik, ti:li:əlódʒik) adj. of or relating to teleology **te·le·o·lóg·i·cal** adj.

tel·e·ol·o·gist (teli:ólədʒist, ti:li:ólədʒist) n. someone who subscribes to teleology

tel·e·ol·o·gy (teli:ólədʒi:, ti:li:ólədʒi:) n. the doctrine of final causes, esp. that natural and historic processes are determined not only by causality but also by their ultimate purposes, e.g. attainment of the kingdom of heaven, human welfare etc. [fr. Mod. L. *teleologia* fr. Gk *telos*, end+ *logos*, word]

tel·e·on·o·my (teli:ónəmi:) n. government policy dominated by a single purpose or project

tel·e·op·er·a·tor (teli:ópəreitə:r) n. mechanical device that is operated from a distance Cf AUGMENTOR

tel·e·o·saur (téli:əsɔr, ti:li:əsɔr) n. a member of *Teleosaurus*, fam. *Teleosauridae*, a genus of extinct crocodiles, whose fossils occur in the Jurassic strata [fr. Mod. L. *Teleosaurus* fr. Gk *teleos*, end+*sauros*, lizard]

tel·e·ost (téli:ɒst, ti:li:ɒst) 1. n. a member of *Teleostei*, a class or subclass of true bony fishes, incl. the majority of all present-day fishes 2. adj. of or belonging to the teleosts **tel·e·os·te·an** (teli:ósti:ən, ti:li:ósti:ən) n. and adj. [fr. Gk *teleos*, complete+*osteon*, bone]

tel·e·path·ic (teləpǽθik) adj. of or communicated through telepathy **tel·e·páth·i·cal·ly** adv.

te·lep·a·thist (təlépəθist) n. a believer in telepathy ‖ a supposed possessor of telepathic power

te·lep·a·thy (təlépəθi:) n. communication, apparently without the use of sight, sound etc., between the minds of different persons [fr. TELE-+Gk *pathos*, suffering]

tel·e·phone (téləfoun) 1. n. a device for converting sounds into electrical impulses, transmitting these through a conducting wire and reconverting them into sounds at the receiving end of the wire. The transmitter is usually a carbon microphone. The receiver is an iron diaphragm which vibrates as the impulses affect an electromagnet, between the poles of which the impulses pass around a solenoid 2. v. pres. part. **tel·e·phon·ing** past and past part. **tel·e·phoned** v.t. to transmit (a message) by means of a telephone ‖ to speak to on the telephone. esp. to initiate a call to ‖ v.i. to use the telephone

tel·e·phon·ic (tɛləfónik) *adj.* of or relating to the telephone ‖ transmitted by telephone **tel·e·phón·i·cal·ly** *adv.* [fr. Gk *tele*, far off+*phone*, sound]

telephone book a book containing the names, addresses and telephone numbers of telephone subscribers

telephone diplomacy the practice of conducting international negotiations by telephone *Cf* HOT LINE

telephone directory a telephone book

te·leph·o·ny (təléfəni:) *n.* the system of transmitting and receiving sounds by telephone [fr. Gk *tēle*, far off+*-phonia*, sounding]

tel·e·pho·to (tɛləfóutou) *adj.* of a narrow-angle lens system of long focal length which gives a magnified image of a distant object, used esp. in cameras [abbr. of TELEPHOTOGRAPHIC]

tel·e·pho·to·graph (tɛləfóutəgræf, tɛləfóutəgrɒf) *n.* a photograph taken with a telephoto lens [fr. Gk *tēle*, far off+PHOTOGRAPH or back-formation fr. TELEPHOTOGRAPHIC]

tel·e·pho·to·graph·ic (tɛləfóutəgræfik) *adj.* of or relating to telephotography [fr. Gk *tēle*, far off+PHOTOGRAPHIC]

tel·e·pho·tog·ra·phy (tɛləfətógrəfi:) *n.* phototelegraphy (transmission of photographs by telegraphy) ‖ the photographing of distant objects using a telephoto lens [TELEPHOTOGRAPH]

tel·e·print·er (téləprintər) *n.* a teletypewriter

tel·e·pro·cess·ing (tɛləprósesiŋ) *n.* (*computer*) processing systems that use data from remote points

tel·e·promptor (téləprɒmptər) *n.* a prompting device for a speaker or actor on television

tel·e·ran (téləræn) *n.* (*air traffic control acronym*) for television-radar navigation, a navigational system that employs television and radar to locate and guide in-flight aircraft

tel·e·scope (téliskoup) 1. *n.* an optical device that focuses light (*OBJECTIVE) from distant objects so that the image formed may be observed (*EYEPIECE). Telescopes are usually tubular in form and vary in size from easily portable to very large instruments mounted so that they can be focused and turned on several axes by means of electric motors and fine gears. They are classified according to function (*TERRESTRIAL TELESCOPE, *ASTRONOMICAL TELESCOPE) or according to the nature of the objective (*REFLECTING TELESCOPE, *REFRACTING TELESCOPE) 2. *v.* *pres. part.* **tel·e·scop·ing** *past* and *past part.* **tel·e·scoped** *v.t.* to cause to close up in such a way that the parts are thrust one into another like sections of a hand telescope, *the collision telescoped four coaches of the train* ‖ to shorten (a plan, speech, form of organization etc.) by condensing the important parts and omitting the less important ‖ *v.i.* to close up like a hand telescope **tel·e·scop·ic** (tɛliskópik) *adj.* **tel·e·scóp·i·cal·ly** *adv.* **te·les·co·py** (təléskəpi:) *n.* the science of the construction and use of telescopes [fr. Ital. *telescopio* or Mod. L. *telescopium* fr. Gk *teleskopos*, far-seeing fr. *tēle*, far off+*skopein*, to observe]

tel·es·the·sia, tel·aes·the·sia (tɛlesθí:ʒə) *n.* perception of a distant object or event which cannot be due to any of the normal senses receiving a stimulus **tel·es·thet·ic, tel·aes·thet·ic** (tɛlesθétik) *adj.* [Mod. L. fr. Gk *tēle*, far off+*aisthēsis*, perception]

tel·e·thon (téleθɒn) *n.* an hours-long television program designed to promote a cause or raise funds for a charity

Tel·e·type (télitaip) *n.* a teletypewriter ‖ a message sent by this [Trademark]

tel·e·type·writ·er (tɛlitáipraitər, télitaipraitər) *n.* a device, similar to a typewriter, by which electrical impulses are transmitted telegraphically by a keyboard, and typed by an attachment to the receiving apparatus

tel·e·vise (téləvaiz) *pres. part.* **tel·e·vis·ing** *past* and *past. part.* **tel·e·vised** *v.t.* and *i.* to broadcast by television

tel·e·vi·sion (téliviʒən) *n.* the transmission of visual images by means of electromagnetic waves. The television camera scans the field of view and activates a photoelectric cell, the impulses from which, propagated as electromagnetic waves, cause the electron beam of a cathode-ray tube in the receiver (television set) to scan the viewing screen in steps identical with those of the scanning camera, thus reproducing the field of view on the screen ‖ a television receiving set

television diplomacy the use of television to affect public opinion in international relations

Tel·ex (téleks) *n.* (*acronym*) for teleprinter and exchange, a system for communication by teletypewriters wire-connected through automatic exchanges —**telex** *n.* the message; *v.* to send messages by Telex

telfer *TELPHER

Tel·ford (télfərd), Thomas (1757-1834), Scottish engineer, famous for the roads, bridges, canals, docks, harbors and buildings which he constructed. They include the London-to-Holyhead road, the Menai Strait suspension bridge and the Caledonian Canal

Tell (tel), Wilhelm (early 14th c.), legendary Swiss hero who, refusing to do homage to a symbol of the German emperor, was sentenced to shoot an apple from his son's head, using bow and arrow. He did it successfully. He is looked on as a hero of the Swiss struggle for independence, and is the subject of a drama by Schiller and an opera by Rossini

tell (tel) *pres. part.* **tell·ing** *past* and *past part.* **told** (tould) *v.t.* to make (something) known esp. by saying or writing it, *to tell the facts* ‖ to give an account of (something) esp. by saying or writing it, esp. in a detailed and orderly manner, *to tell a story* ‖ to inform (someone) of something ‖ to supply information about ‖ to command, order (someone) to do something ‖ to reveal by gestures, glances, change of color etc. ‖ to divulge ‖ to decide, choose, *she can't tell which is best* ‖ to discern, differentiate, *she could not tell him by his voice, it is difficult to tell them apart* ‖ *v.i.* (with 'of') to give a description, account, report etc. ‖ (with 'of') to give or be an indication ‖ to be a determining factor, *the boxer's experience told in his favor* ‖ (*pop.*) to make known something which ought to be kept secret **to tell off** to count off a number of (persons) from a larger total, e.g. so as to assign a task to them ‖ (*pop.*) to rebuke **to tell on** to make a demand on, produce strain or fatigue in, *the pace began to tell on them* ‖ (*pop.*) to report the misdeeds of [O.E. *tellan*]

Tell-el-A·mar·na (télélámá:rnə) an ancient city of upper Egypt in the Nile valley with impressive remains of the palace of Amenhotep IV. Many cuneiform tablets have been recovered from its archives

Tel·ler (télər), Edward (1908-), Hungarian-U.S. physicist. His research into the development, application, and control of nuclear energy made possible (1952) the first successful U.S. hydrogen bomb explosion

tell·er (télər) *n.* a person who tells a story etc. ‖ a bank employee who receives or pays out money ‖ a person who counts the votes cast e.g. in a legislative assembly

Teller Amendment a U.S. amendment (1898) to the declaration of war against Spain. It was sponsored by Senator Henry Moore Teller (1830-1914). It pledged the U.S.A. to the creation of an independent Cuba

tell·ing (téliŋ) *adj.* effective, impressive, *a telling argument* ‖ making a big demand, *a telling climb*

tell·tale (téltɛil) 1. *n.* a person who informs, esp. about the small misdeeds of others ‖ any of many mechanical devices serving to record or warn, esp. (*naut.*) a device attached to a ship's steering wheel showing the position of the tiller or rudder 2. *adj.* revealing, *a telltale blush*

tel·lu·ri·an (telúəri:ən) 1. *adj.* of, pertaining to, or characteristic of the earth 2. *n.* (*rhet.*) an inhabitant of the earth [fr. L. *tellus* (*telluris*), the earth]

tel·lu·ric (telúərik) *adj.* of or pertaining to the earth [fr. L. *tellus* (*telluris*), the earth]

telluric *adj.* of or containing tellurium, esp. tellurium of high valence [TELLURIUM]

tel·lu·ride (téljuraid) *n.* a compound of tellurium with one other element or radical, esp. one more highly electropositive

tel·lu·rite (téljurait) a mineral, TeO_2, found as small yellow or white crystals in the earth's crust ‖ a salt of tellurous acid

tel·lu·ri·um (telúəri:əm) *n.* a semimetallic chemical element (symbol Te, at. no. 52, at. mass 127.60) occurring in a white brittle crystalline form and a brown-to-black amorphous form. It resembles sulfur in its chemical behavior. It is used chiefly as a secondary vulcanizing agent in heavy-duty rubbers. It is also used as an alloying element with lead and in steels **tél·lu·rized** *adj.* combined with tellurium **tél·lu·rous** *adj.* of or containing tellurium, esp. tellurium of low valence [Mod. L. fr. *tellus* (*telluris*), the earth]

Tel·lus (téləs) (*Rom. mythol.*) the goddess of the earth

tel·o·dy·nam·ic (tɛloudainæmik) *adj.* of or pertaining to the transmission of machine power to a distant place, esp. by means of ropes, pulleys etc. [fr. Gk *tēle*, far off+ DYNAMIC]

tel·o·phase (téləfeiz) *n.* (*biol.*) the fourth and final stage of mitosis and meiosis, during which the chromosome material disperses, forming two new nuclei. Cytoplasmic division follows (*PROPHASE, *METAPHASE, *ANAPHASE) [fr. Gk *telos*, end+PHASE]

Te·los (tí:lɒs) (*Gk* Tilos) an island (area 25 sq. miles, pop. 1,100) of the Dodecanese, Greece

Tel·pak (télpæk) *n.* a Bell System service that leases wide-band communication channels

tel·pher, tel·fer (télfər) *n.* a container or passenger car slung from an overhead cable and propelled by electric power **tél·pher·age, tél·fer·age** *n.* a system of conveyance using telphers [fr. Gk *tēle*, far off+*pherein*, to bear]

tel·son (télsən) *n.* (*zool.*) the unpaired terminal abdominal segment of many arthropods, e.g. the middle lobe of a lobster's tail [Gk=limit]

Tel·star (télstɑr) *n.* (*communications*) a transatlantic communication satellite, launched in 1962

Tel·u·gu, Tel·e·gu (téləgu:) *pl.* **Tel·u·gu, Tel·u·gus, Tel·e·gu, Tel·e·gus** 1. *n.* a Dravidian people living in Andhra Pradesh, India ‖ a member of this people ‖ their Dravidian language 2. *adj.* of Telugu or the Telugus

Te·ma (téimə) a deepwater port in S.E. Ghana, opened in 1962

Tem·bi (témbi:) *TEMPE, VALE OF

tem·blor (témblər) *n.* an earthquake [Span.]

Tem·bu·land (témbu:lænd) *TRANSKEIAN TERRITORIES

tem·er·ar·i·ous (tɛmərɛ́əri:əs) *adj.* (*rhet.*) taking no account of probable consequences, reckless [fr. L. *temerarius*]

te·mer·i·ty (təmériti:) *n.* recklessness [fr. L. *temeritas*]

Tem·ne (témni:) *n.* a people of central and E. Sierra Leone ‖ a member of this people ‖ the language of this people

tem·peh (témpei) *n.* a high-protein Asian food or condiment prepared by fermenting soybeans with a mold fungus

tem·per (témpər) 1. *v.t.* to bring (glass, steel etc.) to a desired state of consistency, hardness etc. by heating and then cooling rapidly ‖ to bring (clay) to a desired consistency by adding water and kneading ‖ to prepare (pigment) for use by adding oil ‖ to make less harsh, *to temper justice with mercy* ‖ (*mus.*) to modify the pitch of (an instrument, note or chord) to a temperament ‖ *v.i.* to be or become tempered 2. *n.* the state of a metal, alloy, clay etc. as regards its hardness, consistency etc. ‖ anger, *a fit of temper* or the tendency to become angry, *she has a temper* ‖ the emotional state of a person or community, *in a good temper* **to get** (or **fly**) **into a temper** to become suddenly angry **to keep** (**lose**) **one's temper** to control (fail to control) the impulse to be angry [O.E. *temprian* fr. L. *temperare* and O.F. *temprer*]

tem·per·a (témpərə) *n.* a method of painting pictures using pigments suspended in an albuminous or colloidal substance (e.g. white of egg) [Ital.]

tem·per·a·ment (témprəmənt) *n.* the characteristic physiological and emotional state of an individual, which tends to condition his responses to the various situations of life, *a gloomy temperament* ‖ hypersensitivity common in artists, actors, musicians etc. and frequently displayed in fits of temper ‖ (*mus.*) the method or act of adjusting the relationship between the fragments of successive semitones on the piano, organ and other fixed-pitch instruments, or the system of relationships adopted (*EQUAL TEMPERAMENT, *MEANTONE TEMPERAMENT) **tem·per·a·men·tal** (tɛmpəmént'l) *adj.* (of a person) liable to rapid and intense changes of mood [fr. L. *temperamentum*, proper mixing]

tem·per·ance (témpərəns) *n.* the quality or state of being temperate ‖ the virtue which moderates desires and passions (*CARDINAL VIRTUES) ‖ moderation in eating and drinking, esp. in drinking alcoholic drinks ‖ total abstinence from alcoholic drinks [A.F. *temperaunce*]

tem·per·ate (témpərit) *adj.* moderate, avoiding both of two extremes ‖ (of climate) never very hot or very cold ‖ of the regions between the Tropic of Cancer and the Arctic Circle or between the Tropic of Capricorn and the Antarctic

---

CONCISE PRONUNCIATION KEY: **(a)** æ, c*a*t; ɑ, c*a*r; ɔ f*aw*n; ei, sn*a*ke. **(e)** e, h*e*n; i:, sh*ee*p; iə, d*ee*r; ɛə, b*ea*r. **(i)** i, f*i*sh; ai, t*i*ger; ə:, b*i*rd. **(o)** o, *o*x; au, c*ow*; ou, g*oa*t; u, p*oo*r; ɔi, r*oy*al. **(u)** ʌ, d*u*ck; u, b*u*ll; u:, g*oo*se; ə, b*a*cillus; ju:, c*u*be. x, lo*ch*; θ, *th*ink; ð, bo*th*er; z, *Z*en; ʒ, corsa*g*e; dʒ, sava*g*e; ŋ, ora*ng*utan*g*; j, *y*ak; ʃ, *f*ish; tʃ, fe*tch*; 'l, rabb*le*; 'n, redd*en*. Complete pronunciation key appears inside front cover.

Circle ‖ (*mus.*) tempered (esp. to equal temperament) [fr. L. *temperare (temperatus),* to mix in due proportions]

tem·per·a·ture (témprətʃər) *n.* (*phys.*) a quantitative measure of the tendency of heat to flow in a given direction using one of a number of arbitrary scales based on an observable phenomenon, such as the volume change of mercury ‖ the internal heat of the body, *his temperature was above normal* ‖ the excess of this above normal (98.4°F. or 98.6°F.) [fr. L. *temperatura*]

temperature-humidity index *COMFORT INDEX

tem·pered (témpərd) *adj.* (used in combination) having a specified disposition, *bad-tempered, even-tempered* ‖ modified by the admixture of another quality or substance, *justice tempered with mercy* ‖ (*mus.*) tuned to temperament ‖ (of a metal) brought to the proper degree of hardness or elasticity

tem·pest (témpist) *n.* a very violent wind, esp. when accompanied by hail, heavy rain or snow ‖ a very violent upsurge or expression of emotion [O.F. *tempeste*]

tem·pes·tu·ous (tempéstʃuːəs) *adj.* of or marked by raging storms or gales ‖ violent, turbulent [fr. L. *tempestuosus*]

Tem·pe, Vale of (témpi:) (*Gk* Tembi) a narrow wooded valley (5 miles long) in N.E. Thessaly, Greece, between Mt Ossa and Mt Olympus, opening on to the Gulf of Salonica

Tem·plar (témplər) *n.* (*hist.*) a Knight Templar ‖ (*Br.*) a barrister having chambers in the Temple, London [O.F. *templier* after the Temple in Jerusalem, near which the Templars had their headquarters]

tem·plate, tem·plet (témplit) *n.* a pattern, usually of thin sheet metal or wood, used when cutting, shaping etc. ‖ a block of wood or metal inserted in a wall to distribute vertical pressures ‖ (*genetics*) a macro-molecule (DNA or RNA) on which an enzyme creates a complementary strand [etym. doubtful]

Temple (témp'l), Sir William (1628-99), English diplomat and author. He negotiated an alliance with the Netherlands and Sweden (1668) and the marriage of the future William III and Mary II (*OSBORNE)

Temple, William (1881-1944), archbishop of Canterbury (1942-4). His works include 'Readings in St John's Gospel' (1939-40), 'Nature, Man and God' (1934) and 'Christianity and the Social Order' (1942). He exercised powerful leadership in reform movements within the Anglican Church, and in the formation of the World Council of Churches

tem·ple (témp'l) *n.* a device in a loom for keeping the cloth stretched transversely [F.]

temple *n.* (esp. in ancient Greece, Rome or Egypt) a building used for the worship of a god **Temple** (*hist.*) one of three successive religious buildings of the Jews in ancient Jerusalem **The Temple** the Inner Temple and Middle Temple of the Inns of Court [O.E. *tempel, templ* fr. L. *templum* and O.F. *temple*]

temple *n.* either of the flat portions of the head between the ear and the forehead [O.F.]

Temple of Jerusalem Solomon's temple to God, built by Phoenician craftsmen. It had a unifying influence in Judaism as it was its only center of sacrificial worship. The fortunes of Judaism were involved in its destruction in 586 B.C. and reconstruction in 516 B.C. A third Temple built by Herod c. 20 B.C., still standing in the time of Christ, was destroyed in 70 A.D. The site is now occupied by the Moslem shrines of the Dome of the Rock and the Mosque of Omar

templet *TEMPLATE

tem·po (témpou) *pl.* **tem·pi** (témpi:), **tem·pos** *n.* (*mus.*) the speed at which a piece of music is played or is meant to be played ‖ rate of movement or of some activity (e.g. at which a play is performed) [Ital.]

tem·po·ral (témpərəl) *adj.* of or situated near a temple or the temples of the head [fr. L. *temporalis* fr. *tempora,* the temples of the head]

temporal *adj.* concerned with life on earth, in contrast to life after death (opp. SPIRITUAL) ‖ of or relating to secular, worldly matters (cf. ECCLESIASTICAL) ‖ of or relating to life in time (cf. ETERNAL) ‖ of time (cf. SPATIAL) ‖ (*gram.*) expressing time or tense ‖ (*Br.*) of peers of the realm as distinguished from archbishops or bishops in the House of Lords, *Lords temporal* **tém·po·ral·ism** *n.* (*philos.*) a doctrine stressing the ultimate reality of time **tém·po·ral·ist** *n.* **tém·po·ral·is·tic** *adj.* [fr. L. L. *temporalis*]

tem·po·ral·i·ty (tempəræliti) *pl.* **tem·po·ral·i·ties** *n.* secular property, esp. (*pl.*) the revenues of a church or an ecclesiastic [fr. L. *temporalitas*]

tem·po·rar·i·ly (tempərɛ́rili:) *adv.* for a time only [TEMPORARY]

tem·po·rar·i·ness (tempərɛri:nis) *n.* the state or quality of being temporary

tem·po·rar·y (témpəreri:) *adj.* lasting, or intended to last, only for a short time [fr. L. *temporarius*]

tem·po·ri·za·tion (tempərizéiʃən) *n.* the practice or act of temporizing

tem·po·rize (témpəraiz) *pres. part.* **tem·po·riz·ing** *past* and *past part.* **tem·po·rized** *v.i.* to act so as to gain time in a difficult situation, esp. by making a policy of avoiding decisions or of agreeing only to what does not commit one very far ‖ (with 'with') to come to terms [F. *temporiser*]

tempt (tempt) *v.t.* to try to persuade (someone) to do something, esp. something which will involve him in a sinful or wrongful act ‖ to be attractive, enticing etc. to, *the publicity tempts me* ‖ (*rhet.*) to run the risk of provoking, *to tempt fate* [O.F. and A.F. *tempter*]

temp·ta·tion (temptéiʃən) *n.* a tempting or being tempted ‖ something which tempts [O.F. *temptaciun, tentation*]

tempt·er (témptər) *n.* someone who tempts **tempt·ress** (témptris) *n.* a woman who tempts [M.E. *temptour*]

Te·mu·co (temúːkɔ) a city and trade center (pop. 150,560) in S. central Chile: grains, fruit, lumber

ten (ten) 1. *adj.* being one more than nine (*NUMBER TABLE) 2. *n.* twice five ‖ the cardinal number representing this (10, X) ‖ 10 o'clock ‖ a playing card marked with 10 spots ‖ (*pl.*) in mathematical calculations, the column of figures two places to the left of the decimal point [O.E. *tien, tēn*]

ten·a·bil·i·ty (tenəbíliti:) *n.* the state or quality of being tenable

ten·a·ble (ténəb'l) *adj.* able to be held, *the office is tenable for one year* ‖ able to be held against attack ‖ able to be maintained, *an opinion no longer tenable* [F]

ten·ace (téneis) *n.* (*cards*) a combination in one hand of the best and third-best cards of a suit, the second-best card being held by an opponent [fr. Span. *tenaza,* pincers]

te·na·cious (tənéiʃəs) *adj.* holding fast, *a tenacious grasp* ‖ firmly held, *tenacious beliefs* ‖ adhesive ‖ retentive, *a tenacious memory* ‖ persistent, *a tenacious tenor* [fr. L. *tenax (tenacis)*]

te·nac·i·ty (tənǽsiti:) *n.* the state or quality of being tenacious ‖ (*phys.*) tensile strength [fr. L. *tenacitas*]

te·nac·u·lum (tinǽkjuləm) *pl.* **te·nac·u·la** (tinǽkjulə), **te·nac·u·lums** *n.* a surgical instrument with a sharp hook for picking up arteries etc. in the course of an operation [L.=holder]

te·nail, te·naille (tinéil) *n.* (*fortification*) a low outwork between two bastions in the main defense ditch [F. *tenaille,* pincers]

ten·an·cy (ténənsi:) *pl.* **ten·an·cies** *n.* tenure as tenant ‖ property held by a tenant

ten·ant (ténənt) 1. *n.* someone paying rent to the owner for the use of land or a building ‖ (*law*) someone holding real estate by any kind of right 2. *v.t.* (esp. *past part.*) to occupy as a tenant **tén·ant·a·ble** *adj.* fit to be occupied by a tenant [O.F.]

tenant farmer a farmer cultivating land owned by another and paying a rent in money or produce

ten·ant·ry (ténəntri:) *pl.* **ten·ant·ries** *n.* tenants collectively ‖ the state or condition of being a tenant

Te·nas·ser·im (tənǽsərim) the southernmost coastal region of Burma: rubber plantations, rice

tench (tenʃ) *pl.* **tench, tench·es** *n. Tinca tinca,* fam. *Cyprinidae,* a teleostean fish (10–12 ins) inhabiting European and Asiatic lakes and rivers. The flesh is coarse and insipid [O.F. *tenche*]

Ten Commandments *DECALOGUE

tend (tend) *v.t.* to take care of, look after (people, animals, machines etc.) ‖ (*naut.*) to stand by (a cable) in order to prevent fouling ‖ *v.i.* (pop., with 'to') to give attention, *you tend to the baby* [shortened fr. ATTEND]

tend *v.i.* to have a prevailing direction, *the wind is tending to the south* ‖ to be prone to act or think in a certain way, *he tends to drive too fast* ‖ to lead or be directed towards a condition or

result, *a political situation tending towards anarchy* [F. *tendre*]

ten·den·cy (téndənsi:) *pl.* **ten·den·cies** *n.* the quality of tending towards something or of tending to do something [fr. M.L. *tendentia*]

ten·den·tious, ten·den·cious (tendénʃəs) *adj.* (of thought, writing etc.) having deliberate bias [as it fr. M.L. *tendentia,* tendency, after G. *tendenziōs*]

ten·der (téndər) *n.* someone who tends ‖ a small vessel used to transport passengers, goods, fuel etc. from or to a larger ship ‖ a small vessel for passing communications between shore and a larger ship ‖ a vehicle attached to a locomotive, carrying its fuel and water supply

tender 1. *v.t.* to offer (services etc.), offer for acceptance, *to tender one's resignation* ‖ (*law*) to offer (money or services) to meet an obligation and avoid prosecution ‖ *v.i.* (often with 'for') to put in a competitive estimate for work to be done 2. *n.* an offer of a formal nature, esp. a competitive offer for a contract for work to be done ‖ (*law*) an offer of money or services made to meet an obligation and avoid prosecution ‖ *LEGAL TENDER [A. F. *tender,* F. *tendre*]

tender *adj.* easily damaged, *a tender plant* ‖ (of food) easily chewed ‖ sore to the touch, *tender gums* ‖ sensitive to emotional pain ‖ young and readily impressionable, *of a tender age* ‖ quick to feel compassion or affection etc. ‖ expressing or resulting from such emotions, *a tender smile* ‖ (of a subject of talk) apt or able to cause emotional pain [O.F. *tendre*]

ten·der·foot (téndərfut) *pl.* **ten·der·foots** *n.* a newcomer to a place or situation ‖ a Scout or Girl Scout in the beginners' group

ten·der·heart·ed (téndərhúrtid) *adj.* easily aroused to pity, sorrow etc.

ten·der·ize (téndəraiz) *v.t. pres. part.* **ten·der·iz·ing** *past* and *past part.* **ten·der·ized** to subject (meat) to a process or machine which makes it tender

ten·der·loin (téndərlɔin) *n.* the most tender undercut of the loin of pork or beef

ten·der·om·e·ter (tendə:rómətə:r) *n.* a device for testing the maturity and tenderness of vegetables and fruit

ten·di·nous (téndinəs) *adj.* of or like a tendon or tendons ‖ consisting of tendons [fr. F. *tendineux* fr. Mod. L.]

ten·don (téndən) *n.* a strong band of connective tissue joining a muscle to some other part [fr. M.L. *tendo (tendonis, tendinis)*]

ten·dril (téndrəl) *n.* a leafless organ in climbing plants, resembling a thin coil of wire and serving as a means of attachment to a support [perh. fr. L. *tendere,* F. *tendre*]

Ten·e·brae (ténəbri:) *pl. n.* (*Roman Catholicism*) Matins and Lauds during the last three days of Holy Week, at which the candles are progressively extinguished [L.=shadows]

ten·e·bres·cence (tenəbrésəns) *n.* process of darkening by exposure to X-rays, cathode rays, heat, or some forms of light

ten·e·brous (ténəbrəs) *adj.* (*rhet.*) mysterious, full of obscurities ‖ (*rhet.*) dark, gloomy [O.F. *tenebrus* fr. L.]

Tène, La (læten) a locality of Neuchâtel, Switzerland which has given its name to the civilization of the second Iron Age, the Gallic period preceding the Roman occupation. Archaeological finds at La Tène include remains of vehicles and harness, weapons and many tools

ten·e·ment (ténəmənt) *n.* (*law*) any kind of permanent property, e.g. land or titles or rents, held by one person ‖ a tenement house ‖ an apartment in a tenement house [A.F. fr. M.L. *tenementum,* a holding]

tenement house a building divided into rented apartments, esp. in the poor, crowded, squalid section of a city

Ten·e·rife (tenərí:f) the largest island (area 795 sq. miles, pop. 473,971) of the Canary Is, Spain. Capital: Santa Cruz de Tenerife. Highest point: 12,192 ft (an active volcano). Exports: wine, oranges and bananas, market produce

te·nes·mus (tinézməs) *n.* (*med.*) a continual desire to evacuate the bowels and bladder, characterized by painful straining without effect [M.L. fr. Gk]

ten·et (ténit, *Br.* also tí:net) *n.* a principle, belief or doctrine held by a person or a group [L.=he holds]

Teng H'saio-ping (Deng Xiaoping) (duŋʃi:áupin) (1904-), Chinese Communist revolutionary and political leader. An early Communist leader, he became China's vice-premier (1952) and then Communist party general secretary

CONCISE PRONUNCIATION KEY: **(a)** æ, c*a*t; ɑ, c*a*r; ɔ f*aw*n; ei, sn*a*ke. **(e)** e, h*e*n; i:, sh*ee*p; iə, d*ee*r; ɛə, b*ea*r. **(i)** i, f*i*sh; ai, t*i*ger; ə:, b*i*rd. **(o)** o, *o*x; au, c*ow*; ou, g*oa*t; u, p*oo*r; ɔi, r*oy*al. **(u)** ʌ, d*u*ck; u, b*u*ll; u:, g*oo*se; ə, *a*bacillus; ju:, c*u*be. x, lo*ch*; θ, *th*ink; ð, bo*th*er; z, *Z*en; ʒ, corsa*g*e; dʒ, sava*g*e; ŋ, orangutan*g*; j, *y*ak; ʃ, *fi*sh; tʃ, fe*tch*; 'l, rabb*le*; 'n, redd*en*. Complete pronunciation key appears inside front cover.

(1956). He was purged during the Cultural Revolution and again in 1976 but was reinstated (1977) and as the party's senior vice-chairman became China's most powerful leader. In 1982, Teng was named chairman of the newly created Central Advisory Commission after resigning as party vice-chairman. He remained the most influential member of the Politburo and chairman of the party's Military Commission. He sought more foreign participation in Chinese enterprise and attempted to reform China's economy

tenia *TAENIA

Ten·iers (ténjərz), David (1610-90), Flemish painter, son of David Teniers the Elder (1582-1649). The son, the more famous of the two, is noted esp. for his genre scenes of peasant life

Tenn. Tennessee

Ten·nent (ténənt), Gilbert (1703-64), Presbyterian leader of the Great Awakening religious revival. While a minister in New Brunswick, N.J. (from 1726) he was influenced by Theodore Frelinghuysen, who taught that religion should be a matter of the heart as well as the mind. Tennent traveled on evangelistic missions (1740-1) and a sermon he preached (1740) contributed to the breach between New Side (pro-revival) and Old Side (traditionalist) Presbyterians. Later he modified his views and was influential in reuniting the Presbyterians (1758)

Ten·nes·see (tenəsí:) (abbr. Tenn.) a state (area 42,244 sq. miles, pop. 4,651,000) of the southeast central U.S.A. Capital: Nashville. Chief city: Memphis. Its rolling uplands lie between the Appalachians in the east and the Mississippi valley in the west. Agriculture: cotton, tobacco, corn, fodder crops, dairy and beef cattle. Resources: coal, zinc (leading state producer), phosphates, copper, building stone. Industries: chemicals (esp. synthetic fibers), metal refining and products, food processing, textiles. State university (1794) at Knoxville. Tennessee was ceded (1783) by Britain to the U.S.A. It became (1796) the 16th state

Tennessee the chief tributary (652 miles long) of the Ohio River, rising near Knoxville, Tennessee, and flowing first south, then north, through Alabama, Tennessee and S.W. Kentucky (*TENNESSEE VALLEY AUTHORITY)

Tennessee Valley Authority (abbr. T.V.A.) a federal agency of the U.S.A. founded in 1933 for developing the resources of the natural economic unit formed by the Tennessee valley states: Tennessee, Kentucky, Mississippi, Alabama, North Carolina, Georgia and Virginia. Its chief duties are flood control, maintenance of navigation, provision of electric power, afforestation and development and production of fertilizers and munitions

ten·nis (ténis) n. lawn tennis ‖ court tennis [M.E. tenetz prob. fr. A.F. tenetz=F. tenez, take, catch]

Tennis-Court Oath (F. hist., Serment du Jeu de Paume) the oath taken (June 20, 1789) by the third estate that they would not separate until they had given France a constitution. The king having closed the assembly's usual meeting place, the deputies had assembled in a nearby tennis court

tennis elbow pain and inflammation of the elbow, caused by violent or suddenly frequent use of certain muscles in a twisting movement of the hand

ten·nist (ténist) n. tennis player

Ten·ny·son (ténis'n), Alfred, Lord (1809-92), English poet. His collections 'Poems Chiefly Lyrical' (1832) and 'Poems' (2 vols, 1842) established his reputation. In 1850 he published 'In Memoriam', a series of lyric elegies in which his art reaches full expression. His later work never consistently reached these heights, although there were occasional lyric triumphs, e.g. 'Ode on the Death of the Duke of Wellington' (1852), 'Maud' (1855), and 'The Idylls of the King' (1859). He had a very fine ear for the melody and movement of verse

Te·noch·ti·tlán (tenoutʃtitlán) the capital of the Aztecs, today Mexico City. Founded c. 1325, it was an impressive city of canals and floating gardens, with more than 300 temples and 146 shrines. The principal temple (teocali) stood on the site of the present cathedral. The city was destroyed by the Spaniards in 1521

ten·on (ténən) 1. n. the end of a piece of wood shaped to fit into a corresponding mortise in a second piece 2. v.t. to shape to fit into a mortise ‖ to join (two pieces of wood) with a mortise ‖ to

join (two pieces of wood) with a mortise and tenon [F.]

ten·or (ténər) 1. n. the general, little varying course or overall direction, the even tenor of events ‖ the general drift of spoken or written remarks etc. ‖ (law) intent or purpose ‖ (law) an exact copy ‖ (mus.) a male voice between baritone and alto, ranging approx. from one octave below middle C to one octave above it ‖ someone who sings with this voice ‖ a musical part written for such a singer ‖ the lowest bell of a peal used for change ringing 2. adj. (mus.) of or relating to a tenor ‖ (of an instrument in a family of instruments) having approx. the range of a tenor voice, a tenor saxophone [O.F.]

Te·nos (tí:nɒs) (Gk Tinos) an island (area 79 sq. miles, pop. 10,000) of the N. Cyclades, Greece

ten·pence (ténpəns) n. (Br., hist.) the sum of ten pennies

ten·pin (ténpin) n. a pin used in tenpins ‖ (pl., construed as sing.) a game of American origin, in which a large heavy ball is bowled along a long wooden alley at 10 pins set up in a triangular pattern

ten·rec (ténrek) n. any of several small insectivorous mammals of fam. Tenrecidae native to Madagascar, esp. Tenrec ecaudatus, a common tailless species [fr. Malagasy tàndraka]

tense (tens) 1. adj. showing or undergoing emotional strain ‖ characterized by or causing emotional stress ‖ stretched tight ‖ (phon.) spoken with tensed muscles esp. of the tongue 2. v. pres. part. **tens·ing** past and past part. **tensed** v.t. to make tense ‖ v.i. (often with 'up') to be or become tense [fr. L. tendere (tensus), to stretch]

tense n. (gram.) any of the forms of a verb expressing the time of the action or the state of being, present tense, future perfect tense ‖ (gram.) a set of forms for the various persons for a given time, recite the present tense of 'amare' [O.F. tens, time]

ten·si·bil·i·ty (tensəbíliti:) n. the state or quality of being tensible

ten·si·ble (ténsəb'l) adj. able to be extended or stretched [fr. L. tendere (tensus), to stretch]

ten·sile (ténsəl, esp. Br. ténsail) adj. able to be extended in length ‖ pertaining to tension [fr. Mod. L. tensilis fr. tendere (tensus), to stretch]

tensile strength (phys.) the maximum force of tension to which a material can respond without breaking

ten·sil·i·ty (tensíliti:) n. the state or quality of being tensile

ten·si·om·e·try (tensi:ómətri:) n. (phys.) the study of tensile strength —**tensiometric** adj.

ten·sion (ténʃən) n. a tensing or being tensed ‖ a force tending to cause extension of a body, or the force tending to restore the shape of an extended elastic object ‖ the force tending to minimize the surface of a fluid (*SURFACE TENSION) ‖ the state of a conductor carrying an electric current ‖ a state of emotional stress ‖ a state of repressed hostility ‖ the dynamic relationship between parts of a work of art set off one against another **tén·sion·al** adj. [prob. F. fr. L.L. tensio (tensionis)]

tension lag platform floating structure moored by steel pipe tether at deepwater sea bottom that resists natural weather forces; developed by Conoco abbr. TLP

ten·sor (ténsər) n. (anat.) a muscle which stretches or tightens ‖ (math.) a magnitude by which components of a system may be transformed linearly and of which the notion of vector is a special case [Mod. L. fr. tendere (tensus), to stretch]

tent (tent) 1. n. a shelter made of canvas, skins etc., supported by a pole or poles and secured by ropes 2. v.i. to live in a tent ‖ to equip with a tent or tents ‖ to lodge in a tent or tents [O.F. tente]

tent 1. n. (med.) a roll of absorbent material used to keep a wound open 2. v.t. (med.) to keep open with a tent [F. tente, a probe (surgical instrument)]

ten·ta·cle (téntək'l) n. a slender flexible organ on the head of many invertebrate animals, used for feeding, exploration, prehension or attachment ‖ a hairlike outgrowth on the leaves of some insectivorous plants (e.g. sundew) ‖ something that seems to reach out and have a grasp hard to evade, the tentacles of the law **ten·tac·u·lar** (tentǽkjulər), **ten·tac·u·late** (tentǽkjulit) adjs [fr. Mod. L. tentaculum fr. tentare, to touch]

ten·ta·tive (téntətiv) adj. provisional, subject to modification if unsatisfactory, a tentative ar-

rangement ‖ hesitating, a tentative smile [fr. M.L. tentativus]

ten·ter (téntər) n. a frame for stretching cloth to keep its shape when drying [etym. doubtful]

ten·ter·hook (téntərhuk) n. a hook used to hold cloth on a tenter **on tenterhooks** in a state of acutely anxious expectancy

tenth (tenθ) 1. adj. being number ten in a series ‖ being one of the ten equal parts of anything 2. n. the person or thing next after the ninth ‖ one of ten equal parts of anything (1/10) ‖ the tenth day of a month 3. adv. in the tenth place ‖ (followed by a superlative) except nine, the tenth biggest [O.E. tēotha]

Tenth Amendment (1791) final amendment in the Bill of Rights of the U.S. Constitution. It provides that powers not delegated to the federal government by the Constitution nor prohibited to the states are reserved to the states or to the people. The amendment was intended to prevent the new national government from usurping the authority of the states. Although the reserved powers are not enumerated in the amendment, they have been understood to include internal matters such as local government, education and regulation of intrastate commerce, labor and business, as well as family concerns such as marriage, divorce and inheritance. Although today the 10th Amendment is not seen as limiting the authority of the federal government, it was cited to curtail powers of Congress in such landmark Supreme Court cases as Hammer v. Dagenhart (1918) and Schecter Poultry Corporation v. United States (1935)

tent stitch a diagonal stitch used in embroidery

tent-trail·er (ténttreilər) n. a flat trailer drawn by a motor vehicle carrying a deployable canvas ceiling and sides that can provide tent shelter

ten·u·is (ténju:is) pl. **ten·u·es** (ténju:i:z) n. (phon.) a voiceless stop (e.g. k, p, t) [L.=thin, narrow]

ten·u·i·ty (tenú:iti:, tenjú:iti:) n. slenderness ‖ (of air or a fluid) thinness, lack of density ‖ (fig.) poverty, meagerness [fr. L. tenuitas]

ten·u·ous (ténju:əs) adj. flimsy, thin, a tenuous web ‖ (of air, fluid) not dense ‖ so subtle as to be only vaguely apprehensible, a tenuous distinction [fr. L. tenuis, thin]

ten·ure (ténjər) n. the act, manner or right of holding office or property, esp. real estate ‖ the period of holding this [A.F., O.F.]

Tenure of Office Act a U.S. Congressional act (1867) sponsored by Congressmen who opposed the policies of President Andrew Johnson. It denied the president authority to dismiss any official whose appointment had been confirmed by the Senate, unless the Senate approved the dismissal. Johnson's subsequent removal of Secretary of War Edwin Stanton led to the president's trial for impeachment. In 1926 the Supreme Court ruled the act unconstitutional

te·nu·to (tenú:tou, tənjú:tou) 1. adj. (mus.) sustained to its full time value 2. adv. to be sustained in this way (opp. STACCATO) [Ital.=held]

Ten Years' War the war fought (1866-78) in Cuba in the east between the Spanish authorities and the guerrillas (mambises) led by Carlos Manuel de Céspedes. Spanish domination continued

Ten·zing Norkay (ténziŋ) (c. 1913-86), the Sherpa who, with Sir Edmund Hillary, climbed Mount Everest for the first time (May 29, 1953)

Te·o·a·mox·tli (teiouamóstli:) the ancient chronicle of the Toltecs, written (pictographically) by the patriarch Hueman, who led the Toltecs south from California. The book is now in the Historische Kunstmuseum, Vienna

te·o·nan·a·catl (ti:ounánəcætl) n. any of several American mushrooms (e.g., Psilocybe) that is hallucinogenic when ingested

Te·o·ti·hua·can (teiouti:wakán) a religious center of a pre-Toltec and Toltec civilization (300 B.C.-900 A.D.) on a site 34 miles northeast of Mexico City. With a population of 250,000 at its zenith, and with an area larger than that of Athens or Rome, it was the largest city in pre-Columbian America, and was America's first real urban center. Among its monuments are the pyramids of the sun (216 ft. high) and the moon, built between the 1st and 2nd cc. A.D. (In the absence of the wheel, domestic animals and metal tools, they required the labor of 10,000 men for 20 years.) Their purpose was religious and scientific, a temple on the top of the larger

---

pyramid serving as an observatory. The temple of Quetzalcóatl is adorned with alternating figures of Quetzalcóatl and Tlaloc

te·pa [C₆H₁₂N₃OP] (tí:pə) n. (chem.) a compound related to ethylenimine, used as an insecticide, in flame-proofing textiles, and in the treatment of some forms of cancer

te·pee, tee·pee (tí:pi:) n. a conical tent made esp. of skins stretched over a framework of poles, used by North American Indians [fr. Siouan or Dakota *típi*]

tep·id (tépid) adj. slightly warm ‖ unenthusiastic, without warmth, *a tepid reception* **te·pid·i·ty** (tepíditi:) n. the state or quality of being tepid [fr. L. *tepidus*]

te·qui·la (tikí:lə) n. a fiery Mexican drink distilled from several species of agave, esp. *Agave tequilana* ‖ this plant [Span.]

ter- (tər) prefix three ‖ (chem.) having three atoms, radicals etc. [L.]

tera- combining form meaning a trillion

ter·a·bit (téərəbit) n. (computer) one million million bits (binary digits) of information Cf GIGABIT, KILOBIT, MEGABIT

ter·a·to·gen (tərétədʒən) n. (med.) an agent that causes fetal malformation during the first three months of pregnancy, e.g., rubella —**ter·atogenesis** n. production of such malformations —**teratogenic** adj. —**teratogenicity** the tendency to cause such malformation

ter·a·toid (térətɔid) adj. (biol.) abnormally formed [fr. Gk *teras* (*terat-*), monster]

ter·a·tol·o·gy (tərətólədʒi:) n. (biol.) the study of malformations and monstrosities [fr. Gk *teras* (*teratos*), monster+*logos*, discourse]

ter·bi·um (tə́:rbiəm) n. (chem.) a usually trivalent and rarely tetravalent rare-earth element (symbol Tb, at. no. 65, at. mass 158.924) [Mod. L. after *Ytterby*, Sweden]

Ter Borch, Ter·borch (tərbɔ́rʃ), Gerard (1617-81), Dutch painter. He excelled in portraits and in genre painting. His interiors faithfully reflect the life of the rich burgher class of his day

ter·bu·ta·line [C₁₂H₁₉NO₃] (terbjú:təli:n) n. (pharm.) bronchodilator used to relieve acute bronchospasm in pulmonary disease; marketed as Brethine and Bricanyl

terce (tə:rs) n. (eccles.) the third of the canonical hours (9 a.m.) ‖ the office for this [O.F.]

ter·cel (tə́:rsl) n. a tiercel

terce·let (tə́:rslit) n. a tiercel

ter·cen·te·nar·y (tə:rséntəneri: təːrsenténəri:) 1. pl. **ter·cen·te·nar·ies** n. a 300th anniversary ‖ a period of 300 years 2. adj. of a 300-year period [fr. L. *ter*, three times+CENTENARY]

ter·cen·ten·ni·al (tə:rsenténi:əl) 1. n. a tercentenary 2. adj. tercentenary

ter·cet (tə́:rsit) n. (prosody) three successive lines, e.g. a stanza esp. in terza rima or a triplet [F. fr. Ital.]

-tere combining form meaning a chromosome filament in the process of cell division in the formation of germ cells

ter·e·binth (térəbinθ) n. *Pistacia terebinthus*, fam. *Anacaraiaceae*, a small European tree yielding a kind of turpentine [fr. L. *terebinthus* fr. Gk]

ter·e·bin·thine (terəbínθin, terəbínθain) adj. of turpentine [fr. L. *terebinthinus*]

te·re·bra (tərí:brə) pl. **te·re·bras, te·re·brae** (tərí:bri:) n. an ovipositor modified for boring in certain hymenopterans [L.=borer]

te·re·do (tərí:dou) pl. **te·re·dos, te·re·di·nes** (tərí:d'ni:z) n. a shipworm [L. fr. Gk *teredon*, a boring worm]

Ter·ence (térəns) Latin dramatist (c. 190-159 B.C.), author of six surviving plays based on Greek comedies: the 'Andria', 'Hecyra', 'Heautontimorumenos', 'Eunuchus', 'Phormio' and 'Adelphi'. They are polished and humanitarian, and have more psychological interest than the comedies of Plautus

Te·re·sa (tərí:sə, teréisə), **Mother** (1910-), Albanian nun, known for her humanitarian work in the slums of Calcutta, India. She began as a teacher in the Calcutta school run by her order but in 1946 received permission to leave the convent and establish a home for the dying poor. She also founded an orphanage and in 1950 established a new Roman Catholic order of sisters, the Missionaries of Charity. The order now comprises 700 women who work with the very poor on five continents. She received the Nobel peace prize (1979)

Teresa (Theresa) of Avila St (1515-82), Spanish reformer of the Carmelite order, and Doctor of the Church. She founded 17 houses for

nuns and, with St John of the Cross, nearly as many houses for monks. Her writings, which are among the greatest in Christian mysticism, include 'The Way of Perfection' (c. 1565). Feast: Oct. 15

Teresa (Theresa) of Li·sieux (li:zjə:), St (1873-97), French Carmelite nun, also known as St Teresa of the Child Jesus and the Little Flower of Jesus. She wrote 'The Story of a Soul' (1897), her spiritual autobiography. Feast: Oct. 3

te·rete (tərí:t) adj. (biol.) cylindrical, usually tapering at the ends [fr. L. *teres* (*teretis*), round]

ter·gal (tə:rg'l) adj. (zool.) of the tergum, dorsal [fr. L. *tergum*, the back]

ter·gi·ver·sate (tə:rdʒivərseit) pres. part. **ter·gi·ver·sat·ing** past and past part. **ter·gi·ver·sat·ed** v.i. to practice tergiversation [fr. L. *tergiversari* (*tergiversatus*), to turn one's back]

ter·gi·ver·sa·tion (tə:rdʒivərséiʃən) n. change of principles or allegiance, esp. involving a desertion ‖ avoidance of decisions or firm action by roundabout ways [fr. L. *tergiversatio* (*tergiversationis*)]

ter·gum (tə́:rgəm) pl. **ter·ga** (tə́:rgə) n. (zool.) the back [L.]

ter·i·ya·ki (teri:jáki:) n. Japanese dish of steak, fish, chicken, or shellfish with garlic, and/or ginger and then broiled or grilled over charcoal

term (tə:rm) 1. n. a period of time, measured between its beginning and end, *a term of 10 years, term of office* ‖ a subdivision of the academic year ‖ (law) one of the periods of the year during which the courts are in session ‖ the end of a period, *to come to its term* ‖ (law) an estate the enjoyment of which is fixed to end on a certain date ‖ (law) the period for which an estate is granted ‖ one of a set of words having exact limited meanings in cetrain uses, *a technical term* ‖ one of the words peculiar to certain meanings to a particular subject, *a medical term* ‖ (math.) each of the quantities composing a ratio, a sum, or an algebraic expression ‖ (math.) the numerator or denominator of a fraction ‖ (logic) a word or phrase which is the subject or predicate of a proposition ‖ the normal time for the end of pregnancy, *born before term* ‖ (pl.) requirements as to conditions, price etc., *terms of surrender, terms of an agreement* ‖ (pl.) language of a specified sort, *vague terms* ‖ (archit.) an armless statue the lower part of which ends in a pedestal **in terms of** as expressed by, *it is not to be considered in terms of money* **on good (bad) terms with** having good (bad) personal relations with **to bring (someone) to terms** to persuade (someone) to enter into an agreement **to come to terms** to arrive at an agreement 2. v.t. to name or define by a term [F. *terme*]

ter·ma·gant (tə́:rməgənt) n. a woman who is a terrible scold [early M.E. *tervagant*, a character in the mystery plays]

Ter·man (tə́:rmən), Lewis Madison (1877-1956), U.S. psychologist, best known for his application of intelligence tests to school-children. His chief contribution was the Stanford Revision of the Binet-Simon Intelligence Tests (1916, 1937)

ter·mi·na·bil·i·ty (tə:rminəbíliti:) n. the state or quality of being terminable

ter·mi·na·ble (tə́:rminəb'l) adj. (of an agreement) able to be terminated [fr. (obs.) *terminen*, to terminate]

ter·mi·nal (tə́:rmin'l) 1. adj. of or forming the end ‖ occurring each term, *terminal examinations* ‖ (of a disease) considered likely to be fatal ‖ (bot.) growing at the end of a branch or stem ‖ ending a series, *terminal joints* ‖ of or relating to a terminus 2. n. an end, extremity ‖ a terminus (end of route, station, town or building) ‖ a device at the end of an electric wire etc. for facilitating connections ‖ (archit.) a carving, ornament etc. at the end of a pillar, column etc. ‖ (computer) the instrument, usu. a keyboard, enabling data to enter or leave a system [fr. L. *terminalis*]

ter·mi·nate (tə́:rmineit) pres. part. **ter·mi·nat·ing** past and past part. **ter·mi·nat·ed** v.t. to bring to an end, to close, *to terminate an agreement* ‖ v.i. to come to an end [fr. L. *terminare* (*terminatus*)]

ter·mi·na·tion (tə:rmineíʃən) n. a terminating or being terminated ‖ the end of something in space or time, *at the termination of the examination* ‖ (gram.) the final sound, letters or syllable of a word [fr. L. *terminatio* (*terminationis*)]

ter·mi·na·tive (tə́:rmineitiv) adj. tending to terminate

ter·mi·na·tor (tə́:rmineitər) n. someone or something that terminates ‖ (astron.) the line dividing the light from the dark part of the moon or a planet [L.L.]

terminer *OYER AND TERMINER

ter·mi·no·log·i·cal (tə:rmin'lódʒik'l) adj. having to do with terminology

ter·mi·nol·o·gy (tə:rminólədʒi:) pl. **ter·mi·nol·o·gies** n. the terms proper to an art, science, profession etc. [fr. L. *terminus*, term+*logos*, discourse]

ter·mi·nus (tə́:rminəs) pl. **ter·mi·ni** (tə́:rminai), **ter·mi·nus·es** n. either end of a rail, air or bus route ‖ the station, buildings, town etc. at such an end ‖ (archit.) a term [L.=end, limit, boundary]

ter·mi·tar·i·um (tə:rmitéəriəm) pl. **ter·mi·tar·i·a** (tə:rmitéəriə) n. an elaborate, chambered earth mound, often 10–12 ft high, built as a nest by a termite colony [L.]

ter·mite (tə́:rmait) n. a member of *Isoptera*, an order of very small, white, soft-bodied, social insects living esp. in the tropics. Each colony has a large, winged king and queen, with multitudes of wingless, sterile workers and soldiers. The many species do very great damage to wood [fr. L. *termes* (*termitis*), woodeating worm]

term·or (tə́:rmər) n. (law) someone who holds land etc. for a term of years, or for life [A.F. *termer*]

terms of reference (Br.) instructions given to define the limits within which an inquiry, report etc. must be kept and up to which it must go

terms of trade the ratio between prices of two trading countries, a factor in the balance of payments of each one

tern (tə:rn) n. a member of various genera of *Laridae*, esp. *Sterna*, a genus of slender, gull-like sea birds, 9–21 ins in length. They have sharply pointed bills which they point downwards while diving. The tail is deeply forked. Most terns are pearly-white with black caps. They are found in many parts of the world, esp. along the North Atlantic coasts [of Norse origin]

tern n. something consisting of a set of three, e.g. three numbers drawn to win a big lottery prize [F. *terne*]

ter·na·ry (tə́:rnəri:) adj. consisting of three ‖ arranged in groups of three ‖ third in a series ‖ (chem.) containing three different parts, e.g. elements, atoms or components ‖ (metall.) of an alloy of three elements ‖ (math.) having three variables ‖ of a scale of numbers using three as the base [fr. L.L. *ternarius*]

ternary alloy an alloy of iron, silicon, and aluminum with high magnetic properties

ternary form (mus.) a form in which a movement consists of three sections, the third being a repetition or near-repetition of the first

ter·nate (tə́:rneit) adj. being or arranged in a group of three ‖ (bot.) having three leaflets

ter·pene (tə́:rpi:n) n. (chem.) one of a series of isomeric hydrocarbons, C₁₀H₁₆, obtained by distillation from certain plants, esp. conifers. They include pinene (in oil of turpentine) and limonene (in citrus oils) ‖ any of a large class of hydrocarbons (C₅H₈), that are generally regarded as constituted from a linking up of branched fragments containing five carbon atoms and that are found in plants, esp. as constituents of resins or essential oils (*ISOPRENE) [fr. obs. *terpentin* fr. TURPENTINE]

Terp·sich·o·re (tə:rpsíkəri:) (Gk mythol.) the Muse of dancing

terp·si·cho·re·an (tə:rpsikərí:ən) adj. (rhet.) of or pertaining to dancing [TERPSICHORE]

Ter·ra (térrɑ), Gabriel (1873-1942), Uruguayan jurist, politician, and president of the Republic (1931-8). In 1933 he suspended congress, dissolved the council of administration which served as a check on the power of the executive, and abolished the constitution. In 1934 he promulgated a new constitution, but ruled largely by decree

ter·ra pl. **-rae** (térə) n. (astron.) surface area of the moon as distinguished from its *marias*, or seas

ter·race (térəs) n. a raised level cut into the side of a hill ‖ a level space, often paved, adjoining a house etc. and used e.g. for sitting in the sun or enjoying a view ‖ (geol.) a raised bench ‖ a row of houses joined together ‖ a row of houses built on a raised level or on the side of a hill [F. *terrasse*]

terrace v.t. pres. part. **ter·rac·ing** past and past

part. **ter·raced** to form into a terrace or terraces ‖ to add a terrace to [TERRACE *n.* or *F. terrasser*]

terrace house (*Br.*) a town house (which see)

ter·ra-cot·ta (terəkótə) 1. *n.* hard, brownish-red pottery (of which statues etc. are made) fired unglazed ‖ a statue made of this ‖ the brownish-red color of terra-cotta 2. *adj.* brownish-red ‖ made of terra-cotta [Ital.=baked earth]

ter·ra fir·ma (térəfə́:rmə) *n.* the solid land we walk securely on (as opposed to water or space) [L.=firm land]

ter·rain (teréin) *n.* a stretch of land with respect to its features or condition considered from a particular (e.g. tactical) point of view ‖ (*geol.*) a terrane [F.]

ter·rane (teréin) *n.* (*geol.*) a rock formation or series of formations [TERRAIN]

ter·ra·pin (térəpin) *n.* a freshwater, edible turtle of fam. *Testudinidae* found mainly in North America [of Algonquian origin]

ter·raz·zo (terǽzou, terázou, terǽtsou, terátsou) *n.* a flooring consisting of broken bits of marble or stone set in cement and rubbed to a high polish [Ital.=terrace, balcony]

terre·plein (térəplein) *n.* (*fortification*) the platform of a rampart behind the parapet, where the guns are mounted [F.]

ter·res·tri·al (teréstri:əl) 1. *adj.* earthly (opp. CELESTIAL) ‖ of the earth, *terrestrial motion* ‖ consisting of land, not water ‖ (*zool.*) living on land ‖ (*bot.*) growing on land 2. *n.* an inhabitant of the earth [fr. L. *terrestris*]

terrestrial magnetism the weak, natural magnetic field of the earth as a whole. Its origin is unknown. It would result at points external to the earth's surface if there were a short bar magnet at the center of the earth, with its south pole pointing to the north magnetic pole of the earth. The intensity and direction of this field varies irregularly over the surface of the earth, both diurnally and over long periods of time, the variations being attributed to the source within the earth and the electric currents in the atmosphere, in space, and flowing between the earth and space (*MAGNETIC MERIDIAN, *DIP, *SUNSPOT CYCLE, *MAGNETIC STORM, *DECLINATION)

terrestrial telescope a refracting telescope with an erecting lens system, used for viewing terrestrial objects

ter·ret (térit) *n.* a ring on a harness pad through which the driving reins pass [O.F. *toret, touret* dim. of *tor, tour,* tour]

ter·ri·ble (térəb'l) *adj.* arousing terror ‖ (*pop.*) excessive, hard to bear, *terrible heat* ‖ (*pop.*) very bad, *a terrible reception* **ter·ri·bly** *adv.* very ‖ in a terrible manner [F.]

ter·ric·o·lous (teríkələs) *adj.* (*biol.*) living in or on the earth [fr. L. *terricola,* earth dweller]

ter·ri·er (téri:ər) *n.* any of various small, exceedingly active dogs which dig into the burrow of the creature they are hunting. There are many breeds, mainly short-haired or rough-haired [F. (*chien*) *terrier*]

Terrier *n.* (*mil.*) a 3,000-lb surface-to-air missile (RIM-2) with solid-fuel rocket engine, equipped with beam-rider homing guidance and a nuclear or nonnuclear warhead capability

ter·rif·ic (terífik) *adj.* (*pop.*) extreme, very great, very large, or in any way extraordinary, *terrific haste, a terrific success* ‖ (*pop.*) very good indeed, *a terrific welcome* **ter·rif·i·cal·ly** *adv.* [fr. L. *terrificus* fr. *terrere,* to frighten]

ter·ri·fy (térifai) *pres. part.* **ter·ri·fy·ing** *past and past part.* **ter·ri·fied** *v.t.* to fill with terror [fr. L. *terrificare*]

ter·rig·e·nous (terídʒənəs) *adj.* (esp. of an ocean floor) produced by erosion from the earth [fr. L. *terrigenus,* born of earth]

ter·ri·to·ri·al (teritó:ri:əl, teritóuri:əl) 1. *adj.* of territory or a territory, *territorial possessions* ‖ of or limited to a specific territory, *territorial waters* 2. *n.* (*Br.*) a member of the Territorial Army [fr. L.L. *territorialis*]

Territorial Army (*Br.*) a standing, reserve army organized in 1908 on a county basis. It was disbanded (Jan. 1968) on grounds of economy

territorial imperative (*zool.*) possible innate characteristic of animals to define and regard areas as their own; title of book by American writer Robert Ardrey (1908–)

ter·ri·to·ry (téritə:ri, téritouri) *pl.* **ter·ri·to·ries** *n.* the area ruled by a sovereign or other authority ‖ (*games*) either half of the playing area (e.g. in hockey) with respect to its defense by a team

‖ (*zool.*) an area defended by a male bird or mammal as breeding and feeding ground ‖ a region depending on a foreign government but having some degree of autonomy, *overseas territories* ‖ (*U.S., Canadian* and *Austral. hist.*) an area not admitted to full rights as a state or province ‖ an administrative division ‖ an area allotted to a traveling salesman etc. to cover ‖ a very large tract of country ‖ a sphere or field of scholarship etc. [fr. L. *territorium*]

ter·ror (térər) *n.* great fear ‖ a person or thing that causes great fear ‖ (*pop.*) a person who is a dreadful nuisance **the Terror** the period of the French Revolution from the fall of the Girondists (June 2, 1793) to the fall of Robespierre (July 27, 1794), dominated by the Committee of Public Safety. Its mass executions were intended to galvanize national resistance in the face of foreign invasion [O. F. *terreur*]

ter·ror·ism (térərizəm) *n.* the policy of using acts inspiring terror as a method of ruling or of conducting political opposition [F. *terrorisme*]

ter·ror·ist (térərist) *n.* a person who favors or practices terrorism [F. *terroriste*]

ter·ror·ize (térəraiz) *pres. part.* **ter·ror·iz·ing** *past and past part.* **ter·ror·ized** *v.t.* to fill with terror ‖ to dominate by inducing terror

ter·ry (téri:) *pl.* **ter·ries** *n.* one of the uncut loops forming the pile of a pile fabric ‖ terry cloth [origin unknown]

terry cloth a cotton pile fabric made of uncut loops, used e.g. for toweling

terse (tə:rs) *adj.* concise, succinct [fr. L. *tergere* (*tersus*), to wipe]

ter·tial (tə́:rʃəl) 1. *adj.* (*zool.*) of the flight feathers of a bird's wing 2. *n.* a tertial feather [fr. L. *tertius,* third]

ter·tian (tə́:rʃən) 1. *adj.* (*med.,* of a fever) occurring every 48 hours 2. *n.* (*med.*) a tertian fever [M.E. *fever terciane* or *terciane*]

ter·ti·ar·y (tə́:rʃi:eri:, tə́:rʃəri:) 1. *adj.* third in order or rank ‖ (*chem.*) characterized by replacement in the third degree or by a carbon atom united by three bonds to other members ‖ (*eccles.*) of a monastic third (lay) order **Ter·ti·ar·y** of the period of geological time before the Quaternary, marked by the dominance of mammals and by the formation of high mountains such as the Alps and Himalayas (*GEOLOGICAL TIME) 2. *pl.* **ter·ti·ar·ies** *n.* a tertial feather ‖ (*eccles.*) a member of a monastic third order **the Tertiary** the Tertiary period or system of rocks [fr. L. *tertiarius*]

tertiary care (*med.*) services provided by highly specialized providers, e.g., neurologists, neurosurgeons, thoracic surgeons, intensive care units

tertiary education (*Br.*) education beyond the secondary level, universities, and technical training

tertiary treatment (*envir.*) cleaning of waste water that goes beyond the second or biological state, to remove nutrients, e.g., phosphorous, nitrogen, and most suspended solids

Ter·tul·li·an (tə:rtʎli:ən) (Quintus Septimius Florens Tertullianus, c. 160-c. 220), theologian and apologist, born in Carthage. One of the first Christian theologians to write in Latin, he gave the Western Church its terminology. In his 'De praescriptione haereticorum' (197-8) he championed orthodox Trinitarianism and Christology. He was later (c. 210) an influential adherent of Montanism

Ter·uell (terwél) a province (area 5,720 sq. miles, pop. 150,900) of E. Spain (*ARAGON) ‖ its capital (pop. 19,000)

ter·va·lent (tə:rvéilənt) *adj.* (*chem.*) having three valences (cf. TRIVALENT) [fr. L. *ter,* thrice+*valens* (*valentis*) fr. *valere,* to be strong]

ter·za ri·ma (tə́:rtsəri:mə) *n.* a verse form consisting of hendecasyllable tercets, rhyming aba, bcb, cdc and so on. It was used by Dante in the 'Divine Comedy' [Ital.=third rhyme]

TESL (*education abbr.*) for teaching English as a second language *Cf* TFL

Tes·la (téslə), Nikola (1856-1943), Croatian-American electrician and inventor who made practical the use of alternating current. He emigrated to the U.S.A. (1884) and worked briefly for Thomas Edison. His demonstration (1888) of how a magnetic field could be made to rotate by supplying two coils at right angles with alternating current of different phases led to his patenting of the alternating-current motor and its sale to George Westinghouse, who made it the basis for the Westinghouse power system. Tesla also did noteworthy research on

high-voltage electricity, transformers, telephone and telegraph systems, and plants for wireless power transmission

tes·la (téslə) *n.* a unit of magnetic flue density in the mks system equal to one weber per sq meter; named for Austrian-born electrician Nikola Tesla (1856–1943) *abbr.* T

tes·se·late, tes·sel·late (tésəleit) *pres. part.* **tes·se·lat·ing, tes·sel·lat·ing** *past and past part.* **tes·se·lat·ed, tes·sel·lat·ed** *v.t.* to form into mosaic ‖ to decorate with mosaic **tés·se·lat·ed, tés·sel·lat·ed** *adj.* made into a mosaic ‖ reticulate **tes·se·lá·tion, tes·sel·lá·tion** *n.* [fr. M.L. *tessellare* (*tessellatus*) fr. L. *tessella,* tessera]

tes·ser·a (tésərə) *pl.* **tes·ser·ae** (tésəri:) *n.* a small usually square piece of marble, glass etc. used in mosaic **tés·ser·al** *adj.* [L. fr. Gk]

test (test) 1. *n.* an examination of the nature or value of anything ‖ the method used in making such an examination ‖ a standard by which a thing's qualities are tried ‖ a set of problems, questions etc. by which a person's knowledge, abilities, aptitudes or character are assessed ‖ a set of circumstances, occurring naturally or deliberately contrived, in which the nature or qualities of a person or thing are revealed, *the race was an endurance test for both driver and car* ‖ (*chem.*) a method or reaction for identifying a substance ‖ the reagent used for this ‖ (*Br., hist.*) a cupel (cup) ‖ (*Br.*) such a cup and its support, which form the hearth of a reverberatory furnace 2. *v.t.* to submit to a test ‖ (*chem.*) to examine by means of a reagent or reagents [O.F. *test,* pot]

test *n.* (*zool.*) the external shell or hard covering of many invertebrates [fr. L. *testa,* tile, pot]

tes·ta (téstə) *pl.* **tes·tae** (tésti:), **tes·ta** *n.* (*bot.*) the outer coat of a seed [L.]

tes·ta·ceous (testéiʃəs) *adj.* of or of the nature of a shell or shells ‖ having a shell ‖ (*biol.*) of the reddish-brown color of unglazed earthenware [fr. L. *testaceus,* consisting of shell, brick or tile]

Test Act (*Br. hist.*) any of several acts of parliament, in force 1672-1828, requiring a person holding office under the Crown to take oaths of allegiance and supremacy, renounce belief in transubstantiation etc.

tes·ta·cy (téstəsi:) *n.* (*law*) the state of being testate

tes·ta·ment (téstəmənt) *n.* (*law*) a will ‖ (*Bible*) a solemn covenant, esp. the covenant between God and man, *Old Testament* **Tes·ta·ment** a copy of the New Testament books of the Bible [fr. L. *testamentum,* will]

tes·ta·men·ta·ry (testəméntəri:) *adj.* (*law*) of a will or its administration ‖ (*law*) bequeathed by will ‖ (*law*) in accordance with a will [fr. L. *testamentarius*]

tes·tate (téstit) 1. *adj.* (*law*) having left a legally valid will 2. *n.* (*law*) a deceased person who left such a will [fr. L. *testari* (*testatus*), to testify]

tes·ta·tor (téstéitər, testéitər) *n.* (*law*) a testate [A.F. *testatour*]

tes·ta·trix (testéitriks) *pl.* **tes·ta·tri·ces** (testéitrisi:z) *n.* (*law*) a female testator [L.L.]

test ban an international agreement not to hold atmospheric tests of nuclear weapons

test case (*law*) a matter submitted for a legal decision in order that a general principle may be established which will govern similar matters

test drive a short trial run of a motor vehicle, esp. in order to determine whether to purchase it —**test-drive** *v.*

tes·ter (téstər) *n.* the frame on which the canopy of a four-poster bed rests, or the canopy and frame together ‖ a baldacain over an altar or pulpit [fr. O.F.]

tes·ti·cle (téstik'l) *n.* one of the two male gonads, the site of production both of male gametes (spermatozoa) and of the male sex hormone (*TESTOSTERONE). In most mammals the testicles are formed inside the developing embryo and descend into the scrotum before the attainment of sexual maturity (*ENDOCRINE GLAND) [fr. L. *testiculus*]

tes·tic·u·late (testíkjulit) *adj.* (*bot.,* of some orchids) having two tubercles shaped like testicles [fr. L.L. *testiculatus*]

tes·ti·fy (téstifai) *pres. part.* **tes·ti·fy·ing** *past and past part.* **tes·ti·fied** *v.i.* to bear witness ‖ (*law*) to give evidence ‖ to be evidence ‖ *v.t.* to be evidence of, *his look testified his guilt* ‖ to affirm, esp. under oath [fr. L.L. or M.L. *testificare*]

tes·ti·ly (téstili:) *adv.* in a testy manner

tes·ti·mo·ni·al (tẹstəmóuni:əl) **1.** *n.* a written statement concerning the character of a person or value of a thing ‖ a gift made to show corporate appreciation of services rendered by an individual **2.** *adj.* pertaining to or constituting a testimonial or testimony [O.F.]

tes·ti·mo·ny (téstəmouni:) *pl.* **tes·ti·mo·nies** *n.* evidence ‖ something which is evidence ‖ (*law*) an oral or written statement made under oath, esp. by a witness in a legal proceeding [fr. L. *testimonium*]

tes·ti·ness (tésti:nis) *n.* the state or quality of being testy

tes·tis (téstis) *pl.* **tes·tes** (tésti:z) *n.* a testicle [L.]

test match (*cricket*) one of a short series of international cricket matches

tes·tos·ter·one (testóstəroun) *n.* a male sex hormone produced by the testicles that promotes the development of the genital glands and male secondary sexual characteristics, as well as having an influence on the overall growth and vigor of the organism [TESTIS+STEROL]

test pilot a pilot employed to fly and test new aircraft, esp. prototypes

Tes·tra Ben·a·zine [C₁₉H₂₇NO₃] (téstrəbénəzi:n) *n.* (*pharm.*) trademark for tranquilizer drug used in treating depression and psychoses

test tube (*chem.*) a glass tube, closed at one end, used in making chemical tests

test-tube baby (test tju:b) **1.** embryo resulting from an egg that is removed from the mother's ovary, fertilized in a test tube with the father's sperm, then inserted into the mother's uterus for term of pregnancy **2.** a baby conceived by this process *Cf* EMBRYO TRANSFER

tes·tu·di·nal (testú:d'n'l, testjú:d'n'l) *adj.* (*zool.*) of or like a tortoise or tortoiseshell **tes·tu·di·nar·i·ous** (testu:d'néəri:əs, testju:d'néəri:əs) *adj.* [fr. L. *testudo* (*testudinis*), tortoise]

tes·tu·di·nate (testú:d'nit, testjú:d'nit) **1.** *n.* a member of *Testudinata* (or *Chelonia*), an order of reptiles comprising turtles and tortoises. Their vertebrae, ribs and dermal bones are fused with a bony box having horny scales **2.** *adj.* of or relating to such a reptile [fr. L.L. *testudinatus*]

tes·tu·do (testú:dou, testjú:dou) *pl.* **tes·tu·dos, tes·tu·di·nes** (testú:d'ni:z, testjú:d'ni:z) *n.* (*Rom. hist.*) a formation of soldiers with their shields held over their heads in close order, used to screen other troops, or to attack the walls of a building or town under siege [L.=tortoise, tortoiseshell]

tes·ty (tésti:) *comp.* **tes·ti·er** *superl.* **tes·ti·est** *adj.* irritable, given to petty fits of ill temper [A.F. *testif*]

te·tan·ic (tətǽnik) *adj.* of, producing or tending to produce tetanus ‖ of, producing or tending to produce tetany [fr. L. *tetanicus* fr. Gk]

tet·a·nus (tét'nəs) *n.* a disease, marked by painful, tonic spasms of the voluntary muscles esp. of the jaw, caused by the bacterial infection of wounds, esp. by bacteria in mud or dust. The disease does not readily answer to treatment, but may be prevented by inoculation ‖ (*physiol.*) a muscular contraction of long duration due to rapid, successive stimuli [L. fr. Gk *tetanos*, spasm]

tet·a·ny (tét'ni:) *n.* (*med.*) a disorder characterized by periodic tonic spasms of the involuntary muscles, caused by deficiency of calcium in the blood due to malfunction of the parathyroid glands [fr. F. *tétanie*, periodic tetanus]

tetch·y, tech·y (tétʃi:) *comp.* **tetch·i·er, tech·i·er** *superl.* **tetch·i·est, tech·i·est** *adj.* irritable, peevish [etym. doubtful]

tête-à-tête (téitətéit, tétətét) **1.** *adv.* between two people, privately **2.** *adj.* confidential, private **3.** *pl.* **tête-à-têtes** *n.* a private conversation between two people [F.]

tête-bêche (tétbéʃ) *adj.* (*philately*, of a pair of stamps) printed so that one stamp is inverted in relation to the other [F. *n.*=pair of inverted stamps fr. *tête*, head+*bêche* fr. obs. *bechevet*, double bed-head]

teth·er (téðər) **1.** *n.* a rope, chain etc. preventing an animal from moving away from a restricted locality **at the end of one's tether** having borne as much as one can bear ‖ at the end of one's financial resources **2.** *v.t.* to attach a tether to [prob. fr. O.N. *tjöthr*]

Tetouan *TETUAN

tetra- (tétrə) *prefix* four, consisting of four ‖ (*chem.*) having four atoms, radicals etc. [Gk fr. *tettares, tettara*, four]

tet·ra·ba·sic (tẹtrəbéisik) *adj.* (*chem.*) of an acid containing four hydrogen atoms replaceable by basic atoms or radicals

tet·ra·chord (tétrəkɔrd) *n.* (*mus.*) a diatonic series of four notes with an interval of a perfect fourth between the first and last notes, the basic unit of ancient Greek music **tet·ra·chor·dal** *adj.* [fr. Gk *tetrachordon*, a musical instrument fr. *tetra-*, four+*chorde*, string]

tet·rad (tétræd) *n.* a set of four ‖ (*chem.*) a tetravalent element, atom or radical ‖ (*biol.*) a group of four cells produced by the successive divisions of a mother cell ‖ (*biol.*) a temporary grouping of chromosomes by fours formed by the first meiotic division [fr. Gk *tetras* (*tetrad-*), group of four]

tet·ra·dac·tyl (tẹtrədǽktəl) **1.** *adj.* (of an animal) having four digits **2.** *n.* a tetradactyl animal

tet·ra·dy·na·mous (tẹtrədáinəməs) *adj.* (*bot.*) having four long stamens and two shorter ones, e.g. in *Cruciferae* [fr. Mod. L. *tetradynamia* fr. Gk *tetra-*, four+*dunamis*, power]

tet·ra·eth·yl lead (tẹtrəéθəl) a heavy, colorless, poisonous liquid, Pb(C₂H₅)₄, added to gasoline to prevent knocking in an internal-combustion engine

tet·ra·gon (tétrəgɒn) *n.* (*geom.*) a four-angled plane figure **te·trag·o·nal** (tetrǽgən'l) *adj.* (*geom.*) having four angles ‖ of a crystal system in which there are three axes at right angles, the two lateral axes being equal [fr. Gk *tetragonon*]

Tet·ra·gram·ma·ton (tẹtrəgrǽmətɒn) *n.* the word composed of four letters which is the Hebrew name for Jehovah (written JHVH, IHVH, JHWH, YHVH, YHWH, considered too sacred to pronounce) [Gk fr. *tetragrammatos* adj., having four letters]

tet·ra·he·dral (tẹtrəhí:drəl) *adj.* of, pertaining to or like a tetrahedron [fr. late Gk *tetraëdros*]

tet·ra·he·drite (tẹtrəhí:drait) *n.* a gray mineral, (CuFe)₁₂B₄S₁₃, usually consisting of tetrahedral crystals, worked esp. for the silver and copper which it often contains [G. *tetraëdrit*]

tet·ra·he·dron (tẹtrəhí:drən) *pl.* **tet·ra·he·drons, tet·ra·he·dra** (tẹtrəhí:drə) *n.* (*geom.*) a solid figure with four faces, esp. four triangular faces [fr. late Gk *tetraedron*]

tet·ra·hy·dro·can·nab·i·nol [C₂₁H₃₀O₂] (tẹtrəhaidroukanǽbinɔl) *n.* (*chem.*) **1.** a phenol derived from hemp resin that provides the chief intoxicant in marijuana **2.** a synthetic preparation with the same qualities *abbr.* THC

tet·ra·hy·dro·zo·line [C₁₃H₁₆N₂] (tẹtrəhaidrózouli:n) *n.* (*pharm.*) a nasal decongestant; marketed as Tyzine and Visine

tet·ra·hy·men·a (tẹtrəháimenə) *n.* (*biol.*) a ciliate protozoan commonly used in biochemical (esp. genetic) research

te·tral·o·gy (tetrǽlədʒi:) *pl.* **te·tral·o·gies** *n.* a series of four connected dramatic works, esp. three ancient Greek tragedies followed by a satyric play given at the festival of Dionysus [fr. Gk *tetralogia*]

te·tram·er·al (tetrǽmərəl) *adj.* tetramerous

te·tram·er·ous (tetrǽmərəs) *adj.* (*bot.*) arranged in sets of four ‖ (*zool.*) having four joints in each tarsus [fr. Mod. L. *tetramerus* fr. Gk]

te·tram·e·ter (tetrǽmitər) *n.* (*prosody*) a line of four feet [fr. L. *tetrametrus* fr. Gk]

tet·ra·ploid (tétrəplɔid) **1.** *adj.* having or being four times the haploid number of chromosomes **2.** *n.* a tetraploid organism [TETRA-+-*ploid* fr. DIPLOID and HAPLOID]

tet·ra·pod (tétrəpɒd) **1.** *adj.* having four feet or four limbs **2.** *n.* a four-footed animal, esp. one of the higher vertebrates [fr. Mod. L. *tetrapodus* fr. Gk]

tet·rap·ter·ous (tetrǽptərəs) *adj.* (*biol.*) having four wings [Mod. L. *tetrapterus*]

tet·ra·py·rrole or **tetrapyrrol** (tetrəpáiroul) *n.* (*chem.*) a group of compounds with four pyrole rings connected in a ring, e.g., in chlorophyll, or in a chain, e.g., phycobilins

te·trarch (tí:trɑrk, tétrɑrk) *n.* (*hist.*) a governor of the fourth part of a province of the Roman Empire **té·trarch·ate** *n.* the office of a tetrarch [fr. L.L. *tetrarcha*, L. *tetrarches* fr. Gk]

te·trar·chy (tí:trɑrki: tétrɑrki:) *pl.* **te·trar·chies** *n.* the area governed by a tetrarch ‖ the jurisdiction of a tetrarch [fr. L. L. *tetrarchia*]

tet·ra·spore (tétrəspɔr, tétrəspour) *n.* (*bot.*) a group of four asexual nonmotile spores produced by the sporangium of certain algae

tet·ra·stich (tétrəstik) *n.* a poem or stanza of four lines [fr. L. *tetrastichon* fr. Gk]

te·tras·ti·chous (tetrǽstikəs) *adj.* (*bot.*, e.g. of the flowers on some spikes) arranged in four rows [L.L. *tetrastichus*, of four rows]

tet·ra·syl·lab·ic (tẹtrəsilǽbik) *adj.* having four syllables [TETRASYLLABLE]

tet·ra·syl·la·ble (tétrəsiləb'l) *n.* a four-syllable word

tet·ra·va·lent (tẹtrəvéilənt) *adj.* (*chem.*) having a valence of four (cf. QUADRIVALENT) [fr. Gk *tetra-*, four+L. *valens* (*valentis*) fr. *valere*, to be strong]

tet·rode (tétroud) *n.* (*elec.*) a four-electrode electron tube containing an anode, a cathode, a control grid and a screen grid [TETRA-+Gk *hodos*, way]

te·trox·ide (tetróksaid) *n.* an oxide containing four oxygen atoms

Te·tuan (tetwán) (F. Tetouan) a city (pop. 137,080) in N. Morocco: food processing, tobacco

Tet·zel (tétsəl), Johann (c. 1465-1519), German Dominican monk. His preaching on indulgences provoked Luther to publish his Wittenberg theses (1517)

Teu·co *BERMEJO

Teu·to·bur·ger Wald, Battle of (tɔitoubuɑrgɔrvúlt) a battle (9 A.D.) in Westphalia, Germany, in which a group of German tribes annihilated a Roman army, ending Rome's attempts to conquer Germany

Teu·ton (tú:t'n, tjú:t'n) *n.* a member of the Teutonic people, esp. a German ‖ (*hist.*) a member of an ancient German tribe which invaded Gaul and was wiped out by Marius at Aix-en-Provence (102 B.C.) [fr. L. *Teutones, Teutoni* pl. ns.]

Teu·ton·ic (tu:tónik, tju:tónik) *adj.* pertaining to the peoples of N. Europe who speak a Germanic language, esp. the Germans ‖ (*hist.*) pertaining to the ancient Teutons [fr. L. *Teutonicus*]

Teutonic Knight a member of a military and religious order founded at Acre (1190-1) by German merchant crusaders during the third Crusade, to care for the sick. It became (1198) an order of knights, confined to Germans of noble birth, and increasingly military. The Teutonic Knights embarked (1229) on a crusade against Prussia, which they ruled during the 13th and 14th cc. The order was secularized in 1525, suppressed by Napoleon in 1809, and revived in Austria in 1840. It became a mendicant order in 1929. A Protestant branch, the bailiwick of Utrecht, exists as a corporation of noblemen

Tew·fik Pasha (tú:fik, tjú:fik) (Mohammed Tewfik, 1852-92), khedive of Egypt (1879-92), son of Ismail Pasha. He was ruler in little more than name, the real power being exercised by Britain and France during his reign

Tewkes·bur·y, Battle of (tú:ksbəri:, tjú:ksbəri:, tú:ksbɛri:, tjú:ksbɛri:) a battle (1471) in which Edward IV of England defeated Henry VI and Margaret of Anjou during the Wars of the Roses

Tex. Texas

Tex·as (téksəs) (*abbr.* Tex.) a state (area 267,399 sq. miles, pop. 15,280,000) of the southwest U.S.A., on the Gulf of Mexico. Capital: Austin. Chief cities: Houston, Dallas. It is largely a plain, with a wide flat coastal belt and semiarid mountains and plateaus in the extreme west. Agriculture: cotton, sorghums, beef cattle, pecans (first state producer of all these), cereals (incl. rice), vegetables, citrus fruits, dairy and poultry products. Resources: oil and natural gas (first state producer), salt, sulfur, limestone. Industries: chemicals, oil refining, food processing, transport equipment, machinery. State university (1883) at Austin. Texas was explored (16th and 17th cc.) by the Spanish, and was part of Mexico (1821-36). It became an independent republic (1836) and the 28th state of the U.S.A. (1845)

Texas citrus mite a red spider (*Eutetrarychus banksi*) that attacks leaves of citrus trees

'Texas v. White' a ruling (1869) of the U.S. Supreme Court after the Civil War. Invoking the Constitution, the Court declared that secession from the Union was inadmissible, as the United States was 'an indissoluble Union of indissoluble states'

Tex·co·co de Mo·ra (teskɔ́kɔðemɔ́rɑ) a town in central Mexico, in the state of Mexico. Originally it was the city-state of the kingdom of the Chichimecas, whose most famous monarch was Netzahualcoyotl

text (tekst) *n.* the sustained narrative, train of thought or argument etc. in a written or printed

CONCISE PRONUNCIATION KEY: **(a)** æ, c*a*t; ɑ, c*a*r; ɔ f*aw*n; ei, sn*a*ke. **(e)** e, h*e*n; i:, sh*ee*p; iə, d*ee*r; ɛə, b*ea*r. **(i)** i, f*i*sh; ai, t*i*ger; ə:, b*i*rd. **(o)** o, *o*x; au, c*ow*; ou, g*oa*t; u, p*oo*r; ɔi, r*oy*al. **(u)** ʌ, d*u*ck; u, b*u*ll; u:, g*oo*se; ə, b*a*cillus; ju:, c*u*be. x, lo*ch*; θ, *th*ink; ð, bo*th*er; z, *Z*en; ʒ, corsa*g*e; dʒ, sava*g*e; ŋ, ora*ng*utang; j, *y*ak; ʃ, *fi*sh; tʃ, *fe*tch; 'l, rabb*le*; 'n, redd*en*. Complete pronunciation key appears inside front cover.

work, as distinguished from footnotes, commentaries etc. ‖ the subject matter of a speech etc., esp. as written down ‖ a short extract from the Scriptures, often used as the theme of a sermon ‖ an author's original writing, as compared with e.g. a translation of it ‖ a particular version of a writing, *the First Folio text* ‖ the wording used in something written, engraved etc. ‖ (*mus.*) a printed score ‖ (*mus.*) the words of a song, libretto etc. or the words of a poem etc. set to music ‖ a textbook [F. *texte*]

text·book (tékstbuk) *n.* a book written and published for use by students as a basis for their studies

text hand a large style of handwriting (from the custom of writing the text in a larger hand than the notes etc.)

tex·tile (tékstil, tékstail, tékstəl) 1. *adj.* woven ‖ suitable for weaving ‖ pertaining to weaving 2. *n.* a woven fabric ‖ a fiber suitable for weaving [fr. L. *textilis*, woven and *textile opus*, woven fabric]

textile finishing the final treatment of a fabric, after it has been woven, dyed or printed, designed to give it special qualities (impermeability etc.), esp. surface qualities of glossiness (*CALENDERING), fleeciness etc.

textile printing a process of imprinting colored patterns on a fabric by means of a roller or press, in contrast to interweaving or dyeing

tex·tu·al (tékstʃuːəl) *adj.* pertaining to a literary text, *textual criticism* ‖ contained in the text, *textual errors* [O.F. *textuel*]

textual criticism the close study and analysis of a literary text, esp. to determine the best reading ‖ a method of literary criticism based on close study of the text itself rather than on sources, biography etc.

tex·tu·al·ly (tékstʃuːəli) *adv.* as regards the text ‖ verbatim

tex·ture (tékstʃər) *n.* the distinctive character of a textile fabric which results from the quality of its threads and the way these are woven ‖ the parts of a whole thought of as woven like a textile fabric ‖ the structure of a rock, tissue etc. ‖ (*arts*) the quality produced by the arrangement, treatment or handling of a medium, material etc., *the rich texture of the orchestration* [fr. L. *textura*, a weaving]

T-50 *n.* (*mil.*) Chinese main battle tank, with 85-mm guns

T-55 *n.* (*mil.*) U.S.S.R. main battle tank, with 100-mm gun, eight machine guns; considered obsolescent

TFL (*education abbr.*) for teaching English as a foreign language *Cf* TESL

TG (*linguistics abbr.*) for 1. transformational generative 2. transformational grammar

T-group (tíːgruːp) *n.* (*psych.*) short for training group, a form of psychotherapy depending on the process of feedback from interactions within the group in a psychologically unthreatening environment *Cf* ENCOUNTER GROUP, SENSITIVITY TRAINING

-th *suffix* used to denote a state or condition, as in 'warmth' [part O. Gmc., part O.E. or O.N.]

-th *suffix* used to indicate ordinal numbers after three, as in 'fourth' [fr. O.E. *-pa*, *-pe* or *-opa*, *-ope*]

Th (*chem.*) thorium

Thack·er·ay (θækəri:), William Makepeace (1811-83), English novelist. He wrote the 'History of Henry Esmond' (1852), 'Vanity Fair' (1847-8), 'Pendennis' (1848-50), 'The Newcomes' (1853-5), 'The Virginians' (1857-9) and books of lectures and essays. Like his near contemporary Dickens, Thackeray was a popular writer, working for the enlarged reading public of his day and esp. for serial publication. Both authors were humorists, sentimentalists and social satirists. But instead of writing about the lower classes and social abuses, Thackeray satirized romantic sentimentality and the snobbishness and futility of upper-class life

Thad·dae·us (θædiːəs), St *JUDE, St

Thai·land (táilænd) (formerly Siam) a kingdom (area 198,250 sq. miles, pop. 52,700,000) in S.E. Asia. Capital: Bangkok. People: 94% Thai, with Chinese, Malay, and smaller Cambodian, Annamese, Shan and Burmese minorities. Language: Thai, some Chinese and English. Religion: 90% Hinayana Buddhism, 4% Moslem, with small Confucianist and Christian minorities. 60% of the land is forest. 16% is cultivated in the central basin and 7% elsewhere. The central alluvial plain (under 150 ft) of the Chao Phraya is surrounded by mountains, highest in the northwest (Doi Inthanon 8,514

ft). N. Thailand, between the Salween and the Mekong, is a region of deep valleys (1,000 ft) and mountain ranges (5,000-8,000 ft) covered with hardwood forest, running north-south. The east is a shallow, sparsely populated sandstone basin. Mountains running the length of the southern peninsula (rain forest) rise to 3,000 ft. Average temperatures (F.): Bangkok 77° (Dec.) and 86° (Apr.). Rainfall: north and center 50 ins, Chao Phraya delta 40-50 ins, Bangkok 77 ins, eastern basin 15 ins, Isthmus of Kra 130 ins. Livestock: water buffaloes, cattle, hogs, horses, elephants. Agricultural products: rice, corn, sugarcane, copra, peanuts, cotton, kenaf, tobacco, sesame, coconuts, beans, rubber, fruit. Forestry products: teak and other hardwoods, gurjun, charcoal. Mineral resources (mainly in the peninsula): tin, lead, coal, copper, lignite, wolfram, antimony, manganese, iron ore, fluorite, gypsum, silver, gold, tungsten, semiprecious stones, salt. Industries: textiles, paper, cement, sugar refining, fishing, furniture, tourism. Exports: rice, rubber, corn, tin, tapioca, jute, teak. Imports: manufactures, machinery, fuels and oil, chemicals, foodstuffs. Chief port: Bangkok. There are six universities, the oldest being Chulalongkorn, Bangkok (1917). Monetary unit: baht (100 satang). HISTORY. Asian tribes settled in Thailand (c. 1st c. A.D.). Thais from the mountains of Yunnan moved down into the valley and set up several independent kingdoms. The country came under the influence of the Khmer kingdom (c. 10th c.), but asserted its independence (14th c.) under a new line of kings with their capital at Ayudhya. Wars followed with the Burmese and the Cambodians until the 19th c. The Portuguese began trading with Thailand (1511) and were replaced by the British, the Dutch and the French (17th c.). A coup d'état (1688) largely cut Siam off from foreign influence. Ayudhya was destroyed (1767) by the Burmese, and the capital was moved to Bangkok (late 18th c.) by the founder of the present ruling dynasty. Thailand was again opened to Western influence (mid-19th c.) and many Western reforms were introduced. France forced Thailand to surrender its claims to Cambodia (1867) and Laos (1893). Kedah, Kelantan, Trengganu and Perlis were ceded to Britain (1909). Thailand joined the Allies (1917) in the 1st world war. A coup d'état (1932) resulted in a constitutional monarchy. After attempting to seize back the regions it had lost to French Indochina, Thailand was invaded by the Japanese (1941-4). It joined the U.N. (1946) and SEATO (1954). A coup d'état (1951) restored the 1932 constitution. Britain, Australia and the U.S.A. contributed to Thailand's defense against Communist infiltration from Laos (1960s)

Thai, Tai (tai) *pl.* **Thais, Thai, Tais, Tai** *n.* a native or inhabitant of Thailand or a descendant of a native or inhabitant of Thailand ‖ the language of Thailand ‖ a race of people living in parts of Thailand, Laos, North Vietnam, S. China and Burma ‖ a group of languages usually considered as belonging to the Sino-Tibetan language group

thal·a·men·ceph·a·lon (θæləmenséfələn) *n.* the diencephalon [fr. Gk *thalamos*, thalamus + ENCEPHALON]

thal·a·mus (θæləməs) *pl.* **thal·a·mi** (θæləmai) *n.* the receptacle of a flower ‖ the larger portion of the diencephalon (*BRAIN) that is a major sensory coordinating area, sending sensory impulses to the cerebral cortex [L.]

thal·as·se·mi·a (θæləsíːmiːə) *n.* (*med.*) a congenital form of anemia, esp. among Mediterranean peoples, due to impaired synthesis of a polypeptide chain —**thalassemic** *adj.*

tha·las·sic (θəlǽsik) *adj.* of or relating to the sea ‖ of or relating to bays, gulfs and small bodies of water or inland seas [F. *thalassique* fr. Gk]

tha·las·so chemistry (θəlǽsou) chemistry of sea water

tha·las·so·pho·bi·a (θəlǽsəfóubiːə) *n.* abnormal fear of the sea —**thalassophobe** *n.* —**thalassophobic** *adj.*

tha·las·so·ther·a·py (θəlǽsəθérəpi:) *n.* treatment of illness by sea voyages —**thalassotherapeutic** *adj.*

thaler *TALER

Tha·les (θéili:z) (c. 640–c. 547 B.C.), philosopher of Miletus, one of the Seven Sages of Greece. He was also renowned as a mathematician, statesman and astronomer. He predicted the total eclipse of the sun which occurred on May 25,

585 B.C. He believed that water was the origin of the world

Tha·li·a (θəláiə, θéili:ə) (*Gk mythol.*) the Muse of comedy ‖ one of the three Graces, patroness of festivities

tha·lid·o·mide [$C_{13}H_{10}N_2O_4$] (θəlídəmaid) *n.* (*pharm.*) a sedative and hypnotic drug that was found to be responsible for malformed offspring when used during pregnancy —**thalidomide embryopathy** *n.* the malformation

thal·lic (θælik) *adj.* of, relating to or containing thallium, esp. of compounds in which it is trivalent

thal·li·um (θæli:əm) *n.* a bluish-white, usually monovalent but sometimes trivalent, metallic element (symbol Tl, at. no. 81, at. mass 204.37), resembling soft lead. Thallium compounds are very poisonous and are used esp. in pesticides [fr. Gk *thallos*, green shoot (because of the bright green line of the thallium spectrum)]

thal·loid (θæloid) *adj.* (*bot.*) of, resembling or consisting of a thallus

thal·lo·phyte (θæləfait) *n.* a member of *Thallophyta*, a primary division or subkingdom of the plant kingdom including algae, fungi and bacteria (cf. EMBRYOPHYTE) [fr. Mod. L. *Thallophyta* pl. n. fr. Gk *thallos*, green shoot + *phuton*, plant]

thal·lous (θæləs) *adj.* of or relating to thallium, esp. of compounds in which the element is monovalent

thal·lus (θæləs) *pl.* **thal·li** (θælai), **thal·lus·es** *n.* the plant body of a thallophyte that does not possess any organs or tissues homologous with those of higher plants but is composed of parts performing the same functions as the root, stem, leaves and vascular system of higher plants. There is wide variation in size and form of thalli, from microscopic one-celled plants to complex treelike marine algae [L. fr. Gk *thallos*, green shoot]

thal·weg (tálveg, tálveik) *n.* the principle of law widely adopted in the Americas to establish the exact territorial limit where a border runs along a river. The limit is taken as the deepest point of the river, as against the principle adopted in Europe of taking the midpoint [G., fr. *Thal*, valley + *weg*, way]

Thames (temz) a river (209 miles long) rising in the Cotswolds, S. England, and flowing east to the North Sea, navigable by large ships to London

Thames, Battle of the an engagement (1813) on the Thames River near Chatham, Ont., during the War of 1812. A U.S. force commanded by Gen. William H. Harrison defeated the British and their Indian supporters. The victory restored U.S. supremacy in the Northwest

than (ðæn, *unstressed* ðən) 1. *conj.* used after a comparative adjective or adverb to connect the first to the second part of a comparison, *he runs faster than you*, *we finished sooner than we expected* ‖ used to express difference of kind, manner etc., *nothing other than a two-year contract would satisfy him* ‖ when, *hardly were the words uttered than he began to regret them* 2. *prep.* (only in phrases) **than whom, than which** compared to whom, compared to which, *than which there is nothing better* [O.E. *thanne*, *thonne*, *thænne*]

than·age (θéinidʒ) *n.* the land held by a thane ‖ the tenure of this land ‖ the office of a thane

thane, thegn (θein) *n.* (*Eng. hist.*) a freeman (in Anglo-Saxon England) holding land in return for military service to a noble [O.E. *thegen*, *thegn*, *thēn*]

thank (θæŋk) 1. *v.t.* to express gratitude to ‖ to hold responsible for, *we can thank him for our loss* **to have oneself to thank** to be oneself to blame for one's loss, failure etc., *if you get into trouble you'll have only yourself to thank* [O.E. *thancian*, *thoncian*]

thank·ful (θæŋkful) *adj.* feeling or expressing gratitude [fr. obs. *thank*, thanks]

thank·less (θæŋklis) *adj.* (of a person) ungrateful ‖ (of a task or occupation) unproductive, unprofitable, unrewarding [fr. obs. *thank*, thanks]

thank offering something offered as an expression of gratitude, esp. to God

thanks (θæŋks) *pl. n.* gratitude or an expression of gratitude ‖ a formula usually without a following verb for expressing gratitude, *thanks for telling me* ‖ grace before or after a meal, *to return thanks* **thanks to** owing to ‖ with the help of **no** (esp. *Br. small*) **thanks to** without any help from ‖ in spite of [O.E. *thanc*, *thonc*]

---

thanks·giv·ing (θæŋksgívíŋ) *n.* the act of expressing thanks, esp. to God **Thanksgiving** *n.* Thanksgiving Day

Thanksgiving Day a day, the fourth Thursday in November, set apart in the U.S.A. for recalling the goodness of God in blessing the Pilgrims with their first good harvest (1621) and, by association, for thanking God for all his bounty ‖ (in Canada) the second Monday in October, similarly kept as a national holiday

Thant (tɑnt, θɑnt), U (1909-74), Burmese diplomat, secretary-general of the U.N. (1962-72)

Thar (tɑr) (or Indian Desert) a sandy desert (about 100,000 sq. miles) in Rajasthan, India, and West Pakistan

Tha·sos (θéisɒs) a wooded, mountainous Greek island (area 152 sq. miles, pop. 15,000) off the Macedonian coast: olives, wine, marble

that (ðæt) 1. *pl.* **those** (ðouz) *adj.* designating the person to whom or thing to which attention is drawn, *he will like that one, take that road* ‖ designating one of two things which are compared or contrasted, *this hat is cheaper than that one* ‖ designating the person or thing further away than another, *she can reach this shelf but not that one* ‖ designating some well-known person or thing not described, *oh, that laugh of his!* 2. *pl.* those *pron.* (demonstrative) the person or thing indicated or understood, *that will be enough, those who agree are in the majority* ‖ the thing farther away, *she can reach this but not that* ‖ one of two things which are compared or contrasted, *this is cheaper than that* ‖ (relative, used in restrictive clauses, or often omitted) who, whom or which, *the play that we saw together* or when, *the day that he was born* 3. *adv.* (pop.) to such a degree, *he isn't that blind and is sure to notice* ‖ to an extent previously designated or about to be designated, *you shouldn't spend that much* 4. *conj.* introducing a noun clause, *she saw that he was ill* ‖ introducing a causal clause, *he regrets that he was too ill to come* ‖ (rhet.) introducing a clause expressing purpose, *she did it that he might go free* ‖ introducing a clause expressing a result, *he drove so fast that he had an accident* ‖ (rhet.) introducing an elliptical sentence expressing surprise, indignation, a wish etc., *would that the end might never come!* **at that** even so, what is more ‖ at that point **in that** because, insofar as, *he was right in that the name had not changed, but...* **that is, that is to say** used to introduce a further explanation of something previously stated, explained, discussed etc. **that's that** that's settled, finished [O.E. *þæt*]

thatch (θætʃ) 1. *v.t.* to cover with thatch 2. *n.* a covering, esp. for a roof, made of straw, reeds, leaves, rushes etc. ‖ this material [O.E. *theccan, theccean*]

Thatch·er (θǽtʃər), Margaret Hilda (1925-   ), Britain's first woman prime minister (1979-   ). A member of the House of Commons from 1959, she became secretary of state for education and science when the Conservatives returned to power (1970). She replaced Edward Heath as Conservative party leader (1975) and when her party won a decisive victory in a general election (1979) she became the first woman prime minister in European history. Her popularity eroded (1981) when cuts in government spending and strict control of the money supply contributed to Britain's worst recession since the 1930s. The Falkland Islands War (1982), which restored British sovereignty in the Falklands through military force to expel Argentina, was extremely popular. Her government was reelected (1983), winning a substantial majority in Parliament. Her decision to allow British-based U.S. jets to attack Libya and her stand opposing economic sanctions against South Africa caused controversy in 1986

Thau·mas (θɔ́məs) (*Gk mythol.*) father of the Harpies

thau·ma·turge (θɔ́mətə:rdʒ) *n.* someone who works or supposedly works miracles **thau·ma·túr·gic, thau·ma·tur·gi·cal** *adjs* [fr. M.L. *thaumaturgus* fr. Gk]

thau·ma·tur·gy (θɔ́mətə:rdʒi:) *n.* the working of miracles or supposed miracles [fr. Gk *thaumatourgia*]

thaw (θɔ) 1. *v.i.* (esp. of ice, snow or frozen food) to become liquid or soft due to the temperature rising above freezing point ‖ (of weather) to become warm enough to melt ice or snow ‖ to become less hard, less numb, less icy etc. as a result of being warmed ‖ to become more friendly, less stiff in manner ‖ *v.t.* to cause to thaw ‖ to cause to become more friendly 2. *n.* a

thawing ‖ (of weather) warmth which will cause a thaw ‖ a becoming less stiff in manner [O.E. *þawian*]

THC *TETRAHYDROCANNABINOL

the (ðə *before consonants*, ði: *before vowels and when used emphatically*) 1. *adj.* the definite article used to denote a person or thing or persons or things being spoken of or already mentioned, *the paint is dry* ‖ used to denote that which is present, near at hand etc., *the soup is good* ‖ used before the names of things which are unique or designated or identified by a title, *the Irrawaddy, the Prince of Wales* ‖ used emphatically to denote best, best-known, most valued etc., *he is the best composer for me* ‖ (equivalent to a possessive pronoun) used of something belonging to a person already mentioned, *take her by the elbow* or of someone in an understood family relationship, *how are the children?* ‖ (commerce) for every, per, each, *potatoes at 2 dollars the sack* ‖ used to denote the particular person or thing or particular kind out of many, identified by a modifier, *the next house, the man who lives there, the car of the year, the duty to vote, the spoken word* ‖ used to denote a person, animal etc. considered generically, *the rose is my favorite flower* ‖ preceding an adjective used substantivally, *the young, the occult* 2. *adv.* (used before a comparative adjective or adverb) to that extent, in that degree, *it is the more precious because of its association* ‖ **the... the** to what extent... to that extent, *the sooner the better* [O.E. *se* masc. nom. (with 'th-' from other genders and cases)]

the·an·throp·ic (θi:ənθrópik) *adj.* being both God and man **the·an·thro·pism** (θi:ǽnθrəpìzəm) *n.* the theological doctrine of the union of divine and human nature in the incarnate Christ ‖ the attributing of human characteristics to the divine ‖ belief in a theanthropic being [fr. eccles. Gk *theanthrōpos* fr. *theos, god+anthrōpos, man*]

the·ar·chy (θí:ɑrki:) *pl.* **the·ar·chies** *n.* a political system under which men are governed by God or gods ‖ a class or body of ruling gods [fr. eccles. Gk *thearchia* fr. *theos, god+-archia, a ruling*]

theater of cruelty dramatic art form designed to convey sense of suffering and evil by creating a nonverbal atmosphere and utilizing various shock techniques, originated in the 1930s by French surrealist actor and writer Antonin Artaud (1896-1948), who saw such drama as a ceremonial act of purgation

theater of fact dramatic presentations based on current events, often utilizing involved personalities and actual public statements and words from the news

theater of involvement dramatic presentations designed to shock and upset middle-class standards and so to create social change

theater of panic (*Fr., théâtre panique*) theater characterized by a contrasting blend of rustic vitality (Pan), tragedy and fun, refinement and bad taste; coined by Fernando Arrabal (1932-)

theater of protest dramatic presentations, e.g., street theater, designed to influence public opinion in favor of social change

theater of the absurd dramatic presentations that depict the absurdity of the human condition in an incomprehensible universe by abandoning realistic form and utilizing fantastic or other eccentric means

theater of the mind dramatic presentations designed to simulate a psychedelic milieu, e.g., with flashing lights, hallucinogenic background

theater of the streets *STREET THEATER

the·a·ter, the·a·tre (θíatər) *n.* a building or open space where dramatic performances are given, furnished with a stage for the actors and seats for the audience ‖ dramatic art, *it makes good theater* ‖ the written dramatic literature of a country, period or person, *the theater of Elizabethan England* ‖ a place where dramatic events occur, *a theater of war* ‖ a room furnished with a demonstration bench and tiers of seats, used for teaching and demonstrating ‖ (Br.) an operating theater [fr. L. *theatrum* fr. Gk]

the·a·ter·go·er, the·a·tre·go·er (θíatərgouər) *n.* a person who attends the theater frequently

the·at·ri·cal (θi:ǽtrik'l) *adj.* of or pertaining to the theater, *a theatrical entertainment* ‖ suggesting the theater, *theatrical gestures* **the·at·ri·cal·ism, the·at·ri·cál·i·ty** *ns* **the·at·ri·cals** *pl. n.* dramatic performances (esp. amateur and private) [fr. L.L. *theatricus* fr. Gk]

the·at·rics (θi:ǽtriks) *n.* theatrical performances ‖ theatrical behavior or effects [fr. L.L. *theatricus*, of the theater, fr. Gk]

Thebes (θi:bz) an ancient city of Upper Egypt on the Nile, the site of two modern villages, Luxor and Karnak. It was the capital of the Middle Kingdom. Restored by the Ptolemies and the Romans, it was destroyed by an earthquake (27 B.C.). Principal ruins: tombs of the Kings (in the Valley of the Kings, across the Nile from Luxor and Karnak) and several temples of Ammon, esp. the Great Temple (begun in the 12th dynasty) at Karnak

Thebes (modern Thiva, pop. 15,899) an ancient city of Boeotia which became for a short period (mid-4th c. B.C.) the leading power in Greece, under Epaminondas

the·ca (θí:kə) *pl.* **the·cae** (θí:si:) *n.* (bot.) a spore case, sac or capsule ‖ (anat., zool.) a structure serving as a protective covering for an organ or for a whole organism, e.g. the spinal cord, follicle or pupa [L. fr. Gk *thēkē*, a case]

thee (ði:) *pron.* objective case of THOU [O.E. *thec, theh*, accusative of *thu, thū*, thou and *the*, dative of *thu, thū*]

theft (θeft) *n.* the act of stealing something ‖ an instance of this

thegn *THANE

the·ine (θí:i:n, θí:ain) *n.* (chem.) caffeine [fr. Mod. L. *thea*, tea]

their (ðɛər) *possessive adj.* of, belonging to or done by them [fr. O.N. *theira, theirra* genitive pl. of demonstrative *sā, sū*, that, the]

theirs (ðɛərz) *possessive pron.* that or those belonging to them, *the fault is theirs* [THEIR]

the·ism (θí:izəm) *n.* the belief in a god or gods, esp. belief in the one God who created and rules the universe (cf. ATHEISM, cf. DEISM) [fr. Gk *theos*, god]

the·ist (θí:ist) *n.* someone who believes in theism **the·ís·tic** *adj.* [fr. Gk *theos*, god]

them (ðem) *pron.* objective case of THEY, *we caught them* [M.E. *theim, theym* fr. O.N. *theim*]

the·mat·ic (θi:mǽtik) *adj.* of or constituting a theme **the·mát·i·cal·ly** *adv.* [fr. Gk *thematikos*]

thematic apperception test (*psych.*) projective psychological test in which the subject describes or otherwise responds to a series of black-and-white pictures, developed by American psychometrist Henry Murray (1892-   ) *abbr.* TAT

theme (θi:m) *n.* the matter with which a speech, essay etc. is chiefly concerned ‖ (gram.) a stem ‖ (mus.) a structurally important element of a composition developed, repeated, inverted etc. ‖ an entire musical passage on which variations are based ‖ a short composition set by a schoolteacher ‖ a signature tune [M.E. *teme* fr. O.F.]

theme song a recurrent song in a musical, movie etc. ‖ a signature tune

The·mis (θí:mis) (*Gk mythol.*) the goddess of justice or law

The·mis·to·cles (θi:místəkli:z) (c. 525-c. 460 B.C.), Athenian statesman and general. As leader of the democratic party during the Persian Wars he determined the strategy which led to the decisive Greek naval victory at Salamis (480 B.C.) and the retreat of Xerxes I. Accused of treason and corruption, he was ostracized (c. 471 B.C.) and fled to Persia, where he was well received by Artaxerxes I

them·selves (ðəmsélvz) *pl. pron.* refl. form of THEY, *they hurt themselves* ‖ emphatic form of THEY, *they themselves escaped unhurt*

then (ðen) 1. *adv.* at that time, *he was not there then* ‖ at the time immediately following, *he shut the door and then locked it* ‖ at another time, *if you are going to be in this neighborhood I will see you then* ‖ next in sequence, order etc., *first come the girls and then the boys* ‖ in addition, *and then there's the problem of finding capable nurses* ‖ consequently, as a logical result, *if you didn't bring it then you must be very forgetful* 2. *adj.* being at an understood past time, *the then headmaster ordered these books* 3. *n.* that time, *since then I have not seen him* [O.E. *thanne, thænne, thonne*]

then and there at once, immediately

the·nar (θí:nɑr) 1. *n.* the palm of the hand or the sole of the foot ‖ the muscular ball at the base of the thumb 2. *adj.* of a thenar [Mod. L. fr. Gk]

thence (ðens) *adv.* (rhet.) from that place or that time ‖ for that reason ‖ (rhet.) from that source [M.E. *thennes, thannes* fr. earlier *thenne*]

thence·forth (ðénsfɔ́rθ, ðénsfóurθ) *adv.* from that time onward

thence·for·ward (ðénsfɔ́rwərd) *adv.* thenceforth

thence·for·wards (ðénsfɔ́rwərdz) *adv.* thenceforth

the·o·bro·mine (θi:əbróumi:n) *n.* (*chem.*) a bitter crystalline alkaloid, resembling caffeine, contained in cacao beans, and to a less extent in kola nuts and tea, used as a heart stimulant and diuretic [fr. Mod. L. *Theobroma*, a genus of trees including cacao fr. Gk *theos*, god + *broma*, food]

the·o·cen·tric (θi:əséntrik) *adj.* centered in God [fr. Gk *theos*, god + *kentrikos*, in or at the center]

the·oc·ra·cy (θi:ókrəsi:) *pl.* **the·oc·ra·cies** *n.* government by priests or men claiming to know the will of God ‖ a state thus governed [fr. Gk *theokratia*]

the·oc·ra·sy (θi:ókrəsi:) *n.* a mixing of several gods in one in the minds of worshipers ‖ the identification of one god with another in worship ‖ an act of union of the soul with the supreme spirit resulting from contemplation [fr. Gk *theokrasia*]

the·o·crat (θí:əkræt) *n.* a ruler in a theocracy ‖ someone who advocates theocracy [THEOCRATIC]

the·o·crat·ic (θi:əkrǽtik) *adj.* of or pertaining to a theocracy [fr. Gk *theokratia*, theocracy]

The·oc·ri·tus (θi:ókritəs) (3rd-2nd cc. B.C.), Greek poet born at Syracuse, author of the 'Idylls'. He was the first to write bucolic poems

the·od·i·cy (θi:ódisi:) *pl.* **the·od·i·cies** *n.* vindication of the justice and goodness of God in spite of the existence of evil in the world ‖ natural theology [fr. F. *'Théodicée'*, a work by Leibniz fr. Gk *theos*, god + *dikē*, justice]

the·od·o·lite (θi:ód'lait) *n.* an instrument used by surveyors to measure vertical and horizontal angles, consisting of a small telescope moving along a graduated scale [origin unknown]

The·o·do·ra (θi:ədɔ́rə, θi:ədóurə) (c. 508-48), Byzantine empress (527-48), consort of Justinian I, over whom she exercised great influence

The·od·o·ric (θi:ódərik) 'the Great' (c. 454-526), king of the Ostrogoths (c. 474-526). Encouraged by the Byzantine emperor Zeno, he invaded Italy (488) and defeated (489-93) Odoacer, the Gothic king. He had Odoacer murdered (493). He took the title 'king of Italy', and he ruled well, preserving Roman laws and institutions, repairing roads and public buildings, and showing toleration toward the Roman Catholic Church

The·o·do·si·us I (θi:ədóuʃi:əs, θi:ədóuʃəs) 'the Great' (c. 346-95), Roman emperor (379-95). He was appointed by Gratian to rule the eastern part of the empire after the death of Valens. He also administered the western part in the name of Valentinian II after the death (388) of Maximus. A Christian, he established Catholicism as the official religion (380), condemned both Arianism and paganism, and convened the Council of Constantinople (381). On his death, the division of the Roman Empire became final, Arcadius inheriting the east and Honorius the west

Theodosius II (401-50), Byzantine emperor (408-50), son of Arcadius. He was forced to pay increasing amounts of tribute to the Huns under Attila. The Council of Ephesus (431) was held during his reign, and the Codex Theodosianus, a summary of imperial legislation since Constantine I, was compiled (438)

the·o·gon·ic (θi:əgónik) *adj.* of or relating to theogony

the·og·o·ny (θi:ógəni:) *pl.* **the·og·o·nies** *n.* the origin, generation or descent of the gods, as told in myths [fr. Gk *theogonia*]

the·o·lo·gian (θi:əlóudʒən) *n.* a person who is learned in theology [F. *théologien*]

the·o·log·i·cal (θi:əlódʒik'l) *adj.* of or relating to theology

theological virtues the three virtues: faith, hope and charity

the·ol·o·gize (θi:ólədʒaiz) *pres. part.* **the·ol·o·giz·ing** *past and past part.* **the·ol·o·gized** *v.i.* to write or speculate about theology ‖ *v.t.* to treat from the point of view of theology, to fit into a theological scheme [fr. M.L. *theologizare* and prob. THEOLOGY]

the·ol·o·gy (θi:ólədʒi:) *pl.* **the·ol·o·gies** *n.* the science which studies God and all that relates to him, including religion and morals. Christian theology has many branches, e.g. ascetical (dealing with training in virtue), dogmatic (the

formulation of doctrine), moral (the behavior of man in the light of his final destiny), mystical (contemplation of union with God), natural (in which God is known by the light of human reason alone), pastoral (dealing with the care of souls) and positive (dealing with revealed truth) ‖ a particular system of religious teaching and practice [F. *théologie* fr. L. fr. Gk]

the·om·a·chy (θi:óməki:) *pl.* **the·om·a·chies** *n.* war or a battle among the gods [fr. Gk *theomachia*]

the·o·mor·phic (θi:əmɔ́rfik) *adj.* made in the image of a deity [fr. Gk *theomorphos*]

the·oph·a·ny (θi:ófəni:) *pl.* **the·oph·a·nies** *n.* the appearance of God or a deity in a form visible to man [fr. L.L. *theophania* fr. Gk]

The·oph·i·lus (θi:ófələs), St (2nd c.), bishop of Antioch, a Father of the Christian Church, author of the 'Apologia'. Feast: Dec. 20

The·o·phras·tus (θi:əfrǽstəs) (c. 372–c. 287 B.C.), Greek philosopher. He succeeded Aristotle as head of the Lyceum. He wrote scientific and philosophical treatises, but is best known for 'Characters', a collection of vivid sketches depicting various ethical types. The book was widely imitated by later writers

the·or·bo (θi:ɔ́rbou) *n.* (*hist.*) a musical instrument, a lute with a double neck to accommodate extra bass strings, played esp. in the 17th c. [fr. F. *théorbe*, *téorbe* fr. Ital.]

the·o·rem (θí:ərəm, θíərəm) *n.* (*math.*) a statement susceptible of logical proof when certain facts are accepted as true ‖ (*math.*) an expression of a rule or relationship in terms of a formula or symbols, *binomial theorem* [F. *théoréme* or fr. L.L. *theorema* fr. Gk]

the·o·ret·ic (θi:ərétik) *adj.* theoretical [fr. L. L. *theoreticus* fr. Gk]

the·o·ret·i·cal (θi:ərétik'l) *adj.* based on theory, not on factual knowledge ‖ of, pertaining to or being theory ‖ tending to theorize **the·o·re·ti·cian** (θi:ərétiʃən) *n.* a theorist [fr. L.L. *theoreticus* fr. Gk]

the·o·ret·ics (θi:ərétiks) *pl.* *n.* the speculative parts of a science or art [THEORETIC]

the·o·rist (θí:ərist) *n.* someone who theorizes [THEORY]

the·o·rize (θí:əraiz) *pres. part.* **the·o·riz·ing** *past and past part.* **the·o·rized** *v.i.* to engage in constructing a theory or theories ‖ *v.t.* to construct a theory or theories about

the·o·ry (θí:əri:, θíəri:) *pl.* **the·o·ries** *n.* an organized body of ideas as to the truth of something, usually derived from the study of a number of facts relating to it, but sometimes entirely a result of exercising the speculative imagination ‖ knowledge of a science or art derived from such study and speculation (cf. PRACTICE) ‖ a general body of assumptions and principles, *the theory of democracy* ‖ a group of mathematical theorems presenting a comprehensive and systematic view of a subject, *the theory of probability* ‖ a conjecture, *have you any theory as to who could have done it?* [fr. L.L. *theoria* fr. Gk]

theory of games the application of mathematical logic to the strategy, tactical moves and fluctuating odds of situations involving conflict and where several lines of action are possible for the opponents, e.g. in competitive business and in war

theory of knowledge *EPISTEMOLOGY

theory of numbers number theory

Theory Z (*business*) management technique in which employees are enlisted to assume responsibility for greater productivity and in meeting problems, usu. in order to meet or surpass competition

the·o·soph·ic (θi:əsófik) *adj.* of or relating to theosophy **the·o·sóph·i·cal** (θi:əsófik'l) *adj.*

the·os·o·phist (θi:ósəfist) *n.* a believer in theosophy **The·os·o·phist** an adherent of Theosophy [fr. M.L. *theosophus* fr. late Gk]

the·os·o·phy (θi:ósəfi:) *n.* any philosophical and religious system based on intuitive knowledge of the divine

The·os·o·phy a system of thought and practice derived from esp. Buddhist and Brahminical religious mysticism by Madame Blavatsky in 1875 in the U.S.A., and propagated by the Theosophical Society which she founded. It claims to be a synthesis of those elements in all religions which result from divine revelation, and to enable its followers to establish personal communion with God [fr. M.L. *theosophia* fr. late Gk]

The·ra (θíərə) *SANTORIN

ther·a·peu·tic (θerəpjú:tik) *adj.* curative **ther-**

a·péu·ti·cal *adj.* [fr. Mod. L. *therapeuticus* fr. Gk]

therapeutic community (*psych.*) a social organization within a structured therapeutic setting, integrating responsibility between patients and staff, overcoming patient dependency, that is esp. effective in rehabilitating drug addicts and alcoholics

therapeutic index (*pharm.*) a measure of drug effectiveness based on the ratio of the largest dose producing no side effects to the lowest dose therapeutically effective

ther·a·peu·tics (θerəpjú:tiks) *n.* the branch of medical practice concerned with curing or treating diseases, injuries etc. ‖ L. L. *therapeutica* adj. fr. Gk *therapeutikē* (*technē*), (the art of) healing]

ther·a·pist (θérəpist) *n.* someone skilled in a particular therapy, *an occupational therapist*

ther·a·py (θérəpi:) *n.* the treating of the physically or mentally ill by therapeutic means [fr. Mod. L. *therapia* fr. Gk]

Ther·a·va·da (θerəvádə) *BUDDHISM

there (ðɛər) 1. *adv.* in or at that place, *she saw him there* ‖ to or towards that place, *he went there yesterday* ‖ then, at that point, *there he interrupted* ‖ in those circumstances, *there was his chance of escape* ‖ right now, *there goes the bell* 2. *pron.* used as an introductory word in impersonal constructions, esp. when the verb has no complement, *there were only two left* 3. *n.* that place, *from there they went south* 4. *interj.* used to express confirmation, *there, I told you so!* or comfort, *there, you will soon be better* or triumph, *there, it's finished* [O.E. *thǽr*, *thēr*]

there·at (ðɛərǽt) *adv.* (*archaic*) on account of that ‖ (*archaic*) at that place or time

there·a·bout (ðɛ́ərəbaut) *adv.* thereabouts

there·a·bouts (ðɛ́ərəbauts) *adv.* near that place ‖ near to that number, amount etc., *ten pounds or thereabouts* [O.E. *thǽr*, *abūtan*]

there·af·ter (ðɛərǽftər, ðɛəráftər) *adv.* after that time or place [O.E. *thǽrǽfter*]

there·by (ðɛərbái) *adv.* thus, by this or that means **thereby hangs a tale** there is an interesting story in this connection [O.E. *thǽrbī*]

there·fore (ðɛ́ərfɔr, ðɛ́ərfour) *adv.* for that reason [M.E. *thǽrfore*, *therefore*]

there·from (ðɛərfrʌ́m, ðɛərfróm) *adv.* (*rhet.*) from that, from it [M.E.]

there·in (ðɛərín) *adv.* (*legal contexts*) in that thing, place etc. ‖ (*rhet.*) in that respect, *we don't know all the facts and therein lies our difficulty* [O.E. *thǽrin*]

there·in·af·ter (ðɛərinǽftər, ðɛərináftər) *adv.* (*legal contexts*) later in the same document

there·in·be·fore (ðɛərinbifór, ðɛərinbifóur) *adv.* (*legal contexts*) earlier in the same document

there·of (ðɛərʌ́v, ðɛəróv) *adv.* (*legal contexts*) of the place, thing, event etc. just mentioned [O.E. *thǽr of*]

there·on (ðɛərón, ðɛərón) *adv.* (*rhet.*) on that thing just mentioned ‖ (*rhet.*) thereupon [O.E. *thǽron*]

Theresa *TERESA

there·to (ðɛərtú:) *adv.* (*legal contexts*) to it, to that, *the condition applying thereto* [O.E. *thǽr tō*, *thǽrtō*]

there·un·der (ðɛərʌ́ndər) *adv.* (*legal contexts*) under that heading or under the conditions just set out ‖ (*rhet.*) under that thing, place etc. just specified [O.E. *thǽrunder*]

there·u·pon (ðɛ́ərəpón, ðɛ́ərəpón) *adv.* immediately after that ‖ (*legal contexts*) as a result of that [M.E. *ther upon*, *ther up on*]

there·with (ðɛərwiθ, ðɛərwið) *adv.* (*archaic*) immediately after that ‖ (*archaic*) with this, that or it ‖ (*archaic*) in addition to that

ther·i·an·throp·ic (θíəri:ænθrópik) *adj.* (e.g. of a sphinx or a mermaid) half human and half animal ‖ relating to belief in or worship of such beings [fr. Gk *thērion*, beast + *anthrōpos*, man]

ther·i·o·mor·phic (θíəri:əmɔ́rfik) *adj.* (esp. of a god) having the form of an animal [fr. Gk *thērion*, beast + *morphē*, shape]

therm (θə:rm) *n.* any of several practical units of heat energy, e.g. one equal to 100,000 British thermal units [fr. Gk *thermos*, hot, *thermē*, heat]

ther·mal (θə́:rməl) *adj.* pertaining to heat, *thermal capacity* or to a source of heat, *thermal spring* or to something caused by heat, *thermal dissociation* [fr. Gk *thermē*, heat]

thermal breeder (*nuclear phys.*) atomic power plant using slow neutrons, producing small amounts of fissionable material fuel as a by-product *also* thermal reactor

thermal capacity (*phys.*) heat capacity

thermal conductivity (*phys.*) ability to conduct heat ‖ (of a substance) the amount of heat transmitted across a cube of unit volume in unit time when the temperature difference between the faces of the cube is 1° C. (cf. ELECTRICAL CONDUCTIVITY)

thermal diffusion (*phys.*) the separation of the heavy from the light components of a fluid mixture under the influence of a temperature gradient

thermal energy analyzer device used to pinpoint nitrosome concentrations in chemicals; developed by Thermo Electron Corp. *abbr.* TEA

thermal neutron (*phys.*) a neutron of low energy, emitted in the disintegration of some radioactive nuclei, e.g. U²³⁵

thermal pollution (*envir.*) industrial disposal of heated liquid into rivers or other natural waters, causing undesirable ecosystemic changes *also* heat pollution

thermal volt *KELVIN

ther·mic (θέːrmik) *adj.* thermal [fr. Gk *thermē*, heat]

Ther·mi·dor (θέːrmidɔr, termi:dɔr) *n.* (*F. hist.*) the 11th month of the French Revolutionary calendar ‖ the coup d'etat of 9 Thermidor (July 27, 1794) in which Robespierre and his supporters were overthrown and the Terror was ended [F. fr. Gk *thermē*, heat+*dōron*, gift]

therm·i·on (θέːrmiən) *n.* (*phys.*) an ion produced by heating a substance (usually to incandescence) **therm·i·on·ic** (θəːrmaiónik) *adj.* of or operating by means of thermions [fr. Gk *thermos*, hot, *thermē*, heat+ION]

thermionic tube (*electr.*) device that emits electrons from a hot metal cathode, e.g., electron gun in a cathode-ray tube, precursor of the transistor

ther·mis·tor (θəːrmístər) *n.* an electrical resistor whose resistance is a known, rapidly varying function of temperature. Thermistors are made usually of rare-earth and certain other metallic oxides, and are used esp. as thermometers and in katharometers [fr. THERMAL+RESISTOR]

therm·it (θέːrmit) *n.* thermite

therm·ite (θέːrmait) *n.* a mixture of aluminum powder and a metallic oxide (usually iron oxide), which yields molten iron, alumina and large quantities of heat when ignited by a magnesium fuse. It is used in welding and in incendiary bombs [fr. *Thermit*, a trademark]

thermo- (θέːrmou) *prefix* heat ‖ thermoelectric [Gk fr. *thermos*, hot, *thermē*, heat]

ther·mo·chem·is·try (θəːrmoukémistri) *n.* the study of the heat relations in chemical changes

ther·mo·cou·ple (θέːrmoukʌp'l) *n.* (*phys.*) a device, consisting of two dissimilar metallic conductors in contact, that produces an electrical current whose magnitude depends on the temperature of the junction. It is used to measure temperature and in thermopiles (*SEEBECK EFFECT)

ther·mo·dy·nam·ic (θəːrmoudainǽmik) *adj.* pertaining to thermodynamics **ther·mo·dy·nám·ics** *n.* the branch of physics dealing with the relation between heat and other forms of energy (*LAW OF THERMODYNAMICS)

ther·mo·e·lec·tric (θəːrmouiléktrik) *adj.* of or relating to thermoelectricity **ther·mo·e·léc·tri·cal** *adj.*

thermoelectric effects *JOULE EFFECT, *PELTIER EFFECT, *SEEBECK EFFECT, *THOMSON EFFECT

ther·mo·e·lec·tric·i·ty (θəːrmouilektrísiti:, θəːrmouːlektrísiti:) *n.* electrical energy produced by the action of heat, e.g. in the Seebeck and other thermoelectric effects

ther·mo·form (θέːrməfɔrm) *n.* process of molding plastics (for packaging) by using heat — **thermoform** *v.* — **thermoformable** *adj.*

ther·mo·gen·e·sis (θəːrmoudʒénisis) *n.* (*biol.*) the production of heat by the oxidation of foodstuffs in the body, or by other physical or chemical changes within the body

ther·mo·ge·net·ic (θəːrmoudʒənétik) *adj.* of thermogenesis [fr. Gk *thermē*, heat+GENETIC]

ther·mo·gen·ic (θəːrmoudʒénik) *adj.* of or relating to thermogenesis [fr. THERMO-+ Gk -*genēs*, born of]

ther·mo·graph (θέːrməgræf, θέːrməgrɑf) *n.* a recording thermometer, used chiefly by meteorologists

ther·mog·ra·phy (θərmógrəfi:) *n.* 1. raised-printing process in which resin dusts are used to raise lettering, imitating copperplate engraving 2. (*med.*) technique of body-heat measurement used for early detection of cancer cells, which tend to have an elevated temperature 3. technique for measuring temperatures of distant surfaces — **thermogram** *n.* the product — **thermograph** *n.* the apparatus — **thermograph** *v.*

ther·mo·gra·vim·e·try (θəːrməgrəvímətri:) *n.* the measurement of changes in weight due to temperature change — **thermogravimetric** *adj.*

ther·mo·la·bile (θəːrmouléibil) *adj.* (*biochem.*) unstable, i.e. losing its characteristic properties, when heated (opp. THERMOSTABLE)

ther·mom·e·ter (θərmómitər) *n.* any of several types of instrument used to measure temperature on any of several temperature scales **ther·mo·met·ric** (θəːr-məmétrik), **ther·mo·mét·ri·cal** *adjs.* **ther·mom·e·try** (θərmómitri:) *n.* (*THERMISTOR, *RESISTANCE THERMOMETER, *THERMOCOUPLE, *PYROMETER, *GAS THERMOMETER) [fr. Gk *thermē*, heat, *thermos*, hot +*metron*, measure]

ther·mo·nu·cle·ar (θəːrmounúːkliːər, θəːr-mounjúːkliːər) *adj.* relating to nuclear fusion

ther·mo·phil (θέːrməfil) 1. *n.* a thermophile 2. *adj.* thermophile **ther·mo·phile** (θέːrməfail) 1. *n.* (*biol.*, e.g. of certain bacteria) an organism which thrives at relatively high temperatures (e.g. 50–55° C.) 2. *adj.* (*Br.*) of or relating to a thermophile [THERMO-+Gk *philos*, dear, loving]

ther·mo·phys·i·cal *adj.* of the physical properties of materials at various temperatures

ther·mo·pile (θέːrməpail) *n.* an instrument, consisting of a number of thermocouples arranged in series, used for measuring incident radiant energy by the heating effect it produces, or as a portable generator of electric current (*SOLAR BATTERY)

ther·mo·plas·tic (θəːrmouplǽstik) 1. *adj.* becoming soft or plastic when heated and rigid again when cool 2. *n.* a thermoplastic substance, e.g. polystyrene

Ther·mop·y·lae (θərmópəli:) a passage (wider now than in ancient times) between the Oeta Mtns and the marshy shore of Thessaly, Greece, 9 miles southeast of Lamia. Leonidas and 300 Spartans fought a rearguard action here to the death (480 B.C.) to delay the Persian army of Xerxes I during the Persian War

Ther·mos (θέːrməs) *n.* a doublewalled vessel used to keep substances at a temperature other than that of the surroundings. The space between the walls is evacuated to prevent heat transfer by conduction and convection, and the walls are silvered to reduce radiation [Trademark]

Thermos bottle a Thermos

ther·mo·set·ting (θəːrmousétiŋ) *adj.* of plastics and resins, which when once heated and compressed, resist further heat treatment

Thermos flask (esp. *Br.*) a Thermos

ther·mo·sol (θέːrməsɔl) *n.* process for dyeing synthetic fibers by utilizing heat for dispersal and penetration of dyestuffs

ther·mo·sphere (θέːrməsfiər) *n.* (*meteor.*) the region of the earth's atmosphere above the mesosphere about 50 mi. from the surface, including exosphere and part of ionosphere, at which temperature increases with height —**thermospheric** *adj. Cf* MESOSPHERE

ther·mo·sta·ble (θəːrmousteéib'l) *adj.* (*biochem.*) not losing its characteristic properties when heated (opp. THERMOLABILE)

ther·mo·stat (θέːrməstæt) *n.* a device used to maintain a constant temperature by cutting off the heat supply when this temperature is reached and restoring it when the temperature begins to fall as a result of cooling **ther·mo·stát·ic** *adj.* **ther·mo·stát·i·cal·ly** *adv.* [fr. THERMO-+Gk *statos*, standing]

ther·mo·tax·is (θəːrmoutǽksis) *n.* (*biol.*) a reaction, esp. a locomotor reaction, of an organism to heat stimuli ‖ the regulation of body temperature [Mod. L. fr. Gk *thermē*, heat+*taxis*, arrangement]

ther·mo·trop·ic (θəːrmoutrópik) *adj.* of or showing thermotropism [fr. THERMO-+Gk *tropos*, a turning]

ther·mot·ro·pism (θəːrmótrəpizəm) *n.* (*bot.*) a tropism in plants in response to heat stimuli

the·sau·rus (θisɔ́rəs) *pl.* **the·sau·ri** (θisɔ́rai), **the·sau·rus·es** *n.* a useful literary collection or selection, esp. a book of synonyms and antonyms [L. fr. Gk *thēsauros*, treasure]

these *pl.* of THIS

The·se·us (θíːsiːəs, θíːsjuːs) (*Gk mythol.*) hero and king of Athens. He is associated with Heracles and his campaign against the Amazons. Helped by Ariadne, daughter of King Minos, he killed the Minotaur in the labyrinth of Crete. He married Ariadne, but deserted her in Naxos

the·sis (θíːsis) *pl.* **the·ses** (θíːsiːz) *n.* a proposition ‖ a reasoned argument, esp. in a written dissertation on a theme connected with the specialty by a candidate for any of certain academic degrees ‖ (*logic*) an affirmation (cf. ANTITHESIS, cf. HYPOTHESIS) ‖ (*prosody*) the unaccented part of a metrical foot (opp. ARSIS) [Gk =a placing]

Thes·pi·an (θéspiən) 1. *adj.* of dramatic art ‖ of Thespis 2. *n.* (*rhet.*) an actor ‖ (*hist.*) a native or inhabitant of Thespiae, a town of ancient Greece [after THESPIS]

Thes·pis (θéspis) (6th c. B.C.) Greek poet who won a prize for tragedy at Athens (534 B.C.). He is considered the founder of Greek tragedy

Thes·sa·lo·ni·ans, Epistles to the (θesəlóuniːənz) the 13th and 14th books of the New Testament, almost certainly written (c. 51) by St Paul to the Church at Thessaloniki. They condemn false ideas that the second coming of Christ is at hand

Thes·sa·lo·ni·ki (θesəlóunikai) *SALONICA

Thes·sa·ly (θésəli:) a region of N. Greece consisting of plains surrounded by mountains: Ossa and Pelion on the Aegean coast (east), Olympus (north), Pindus (west), Oeta (south). It includes the Vale of Tempe. It was famous in antiquity for its cavalry. It was conquered by Macedon (4th c. B.C.) and became part of the Roman Empire (146 B.C.), of Turkey (1393) and of Greece (1881)

the·ta (θéitə, θíːtə) *n.* the eighth letter (θ, θ=th) of the Greek alphabet [Gk *thēta*]

theta pinch quick-pulsed compression of a magnetic field around ionized gas (plasma), used to control fusion

theta wave (*physiol.*) a brain wave pattern of 4 to 8 Hz with voltage greater than in alpha waves, which occurs in many brain regions, esp. the hippocampus *Cf* ALPHA WAVE, DELTA WAVE

the·ur·gic (θiːəːrdʒik) *adj.* of or relating to theurgy **the·ur·gi·cal** *adj.*

the·ur·gist (θíːəːrdʒist) *n.* a person who practices theurgy

the·ur·gy (θíːəːrdʒiː) *n.* divine intervention in nature or in human affairs, e.g. in a miracle ‖ the power possessed by a human being to secure or prevent such divine action, esp. the magical power which certain Neoplatonists believed might be acquired by long training, self-purification and esoteric learning and practices [fr. L. *theurgia*, fr. Gk]

thew (θjuː) *n.* (*rhet.*, esp. *pl.*) muscle, strength [fr. O.E. *thēaw*, custom]

they (ðei) *pron.*, *3rd person pl.*, *nominative case* two or more persons, animals or things already mentioned ‖ (*pop.*) people or a group of people generally, *they say it will be a hard winter* [M.E. *thei* fr. O.N. *their*]

they'd (ðeid) *contr.* of THEY HAD, THEY WOULD

they'll (ðeil) *contr.* of THEY WILL, THEY SHALL

they're (ðɛər, ðéiər) *contr.* of THEY ARE

they've (ðeiv) *contr.* of THEY HAVE

thi·a·min (θáiəmin) *n.* thiamine

thi·a·mine (θáiəmiːn, θáiəmin) *n.* vitamin B₁ (*DIET), the antineuritic member of the vitamin B complex [fr. Gk *theion*, sulfur+AMINE]

thi·a·zine (θáiəziːn) *n.* any of a class of compounds having a ring comprised of an atom of sulfur, an atom of nitrogen and four atoms of carbon ‖ a derivative of one of these compounds [fr. Gk *theion*, sulfur+AZINE]

thi·a·zole (θáiəzoul) *n.* a colorless liquid, C₃H₃NS, resembling pyridine ‖ any of its derivatives, used in dyes [fr. Gk *theion*, sulfur+AZOLE]

thick (θik) 1. *adj.* of relatively great depth from one surface to its opposite surface ‖ large in diameter, *a thick log* ‖ broad, *a thick line* ‖ dense, closely massed together, *thick underbrush* ‖ (of the atmosphere in a room) stuffy ‖ viscous, *a thick syrup* ‖ measured between opposite surfaces, *three inches thick* ‖ (of speech) hoarse and indistinct because the words are run together ‖ (of regional or foreign accent) strongly marked ‖ (*pop.*) slow to understand ‖ (*pop.*) intimately friendly **a bit thick** (*Br.*, *pop.*) unreasonable, *he thought it a bit thick that he was not allowed to speak* 2. *adv.* thickly ‖ in close succession, *the questions came thick on one another* **to lay it on thick** to exaggerate ‖ to flatter grossly 3. *n.* the most intense, crowded part, *the thick of the fray*

through thick and thin through all circumstances, favorable and unfavorable **thick·en** *v.t.* to make thick, *to thicken a sauce* ‖ *v.i.* to become thick or thicker, *the fog has thickened* ‖ to become more involved, *the plot thickens* **thick·en·ing** *n.* the act of making or becoming thick ‖ an ingredient, e.g. flour, used to thicken ‖ the part where something becomes thicker [O.E. *thicce*]

thick·et (θíkit) *n.* a thick growth of small trees and undergrowth [O.E. *thiccet*]

thick film (*electr.*) a multimolecular film of ink used to cover and insulate circuit wiring

thick·head (θíkhed) *n.* (*pop.*) a stupid person **thíck·héad·ed** *adj.*

thick·ness (θíknis) *n.* the state or quality of being thick ‖ the smallest of the three linear dimensions (cf. LENGTH, cf. WIDTH) [O.E. *thicness*]

thick·set (θiksét) *adj.* (of a person) short, but strong and compact in build ‖ planted or set close together

thick-skinned (θikskínd) *adj.* having a thick skin ‖ insensitive to insults, criticisms, reproaches etc.

thick-wit·ted (θikwítid) *adj.* stupid, slow to understand

thief (θi:f) *pl.* **thieves** (θi:vz) *n.* a person who steals [O.E. *theof*]

Thiers (tjɛr), Adolphe (1797-1877) French statesman and historian. A moderate liberal, he helped to bring about the revolution of 1830. He was prime minister in 1836 and 1840, but later became an opponent of the July Monarchy. His opposition to Napoleon III's coup d'état (1851) sent him into temporary exile. Thiers warned of the disastrous consequences of war with Prussia (1870). After the Franco-Prussian War he negotiated peace, suppressed the Commune and became president of France (1871-3). He is the author of 'History of the French Revolution' and 'History of the Consulate and the Empire'

Thiès (tjes) a commercial center (pop. 69,000) in W. Senegal, on the lower Niger: aluminum phosphates

thieve (θi:v) *pres. part.* **thiev·ing** *past* and *past part.* **thieved** *v.t.* to take by theft ‖ *v.i.* to practice theft **thiev·er·y** *n.* theft [O. E. *theofian*]

thiev·ish (θí:viʃ) *adj.* characteristic of, or like, a thief

thigh (θai) *n.* the part of the human leg between the hip and the knee ‖ the corresponding part in the leg of a bird or quadruped ‖ the third section of the leg of an insect [O.E. *theoh*]

thigh·bone (θáiboun) *n.* the bone of the leg extending from the hip to the knee. In man it is the longest and largest bone

thill (θil) *n.* the shaft of a cart or wagon, esp. one of a pair between which a draft animal is hitched [origin unknown]

thim·ble (θímb'l) *n.* a cap of metal etc. worn on the fingertip in sewing so that the needle can be pushed through a fabric without hurting the finger ‖ a short metal tube or sleeve ‖ (*naut.*) an iron ring with a grooved rim around which a rope is spliced to prevent it from chafing [O.E. *thymel*, thumbstall]

thim·ble·ber·ry (θímb'lberi:) *pl.* **thim·ble·ber·ries** *n.* any of several American blackberries or raspberries bearing soft fruits shaped like sewing thimbles

thim·ble·ful (θímb'lful) *pl.* **thim·ble·fuls** *n.* a very small quantity of a liquid, generally alcoholic liquor

thim·ble·rig (θímb'lrig) 1. *n.* a swindling game in which the operator has three thimble-shaped cups and a pea. He passes the cups over the pea and the victim bets that the pea will be found under a particular cup 2. *v.t. pres. part.* **thim·ble·rig·ging** *past* and *past part.* **thim·ble·rigged** to cheat or swindle by this game **thim·ble·rig·ger** *n.* someone who operates the game

thin (θin) 1. *adj. comp.* **thin·ner** *superl.* **thin·nest** having little extent between opposite surfaces, *a thin sheet of paper* ‖ small in diameter, *a thin rope* ‖ (of a person or animal) of slender build, or noticeably lacking fat ‖ not closely massed together, *his hair is thin on top* ‖ of little density, *a thin oil, a thin mist* ‖ of little strength or substance, *a thin voice, thin tea, a thin plot* ‖ lacking plausibility or persuasion, *a thin excuse* ‖ (*photog.*) not contrasty, lacking density **a thin time** a time of hardship or great discomfort, tedium, trouble etc. 2. *adv.* thinly, *spread the butter thin* [O.E. *thynne*]

thin *pres. part.* **thin·ning** *past* and *past part.*

thinned *v.t.* to make thin ‖ (esp. with 'out') to reduce in number or mass ‖ *v.i.* to become thin, or thinner [O.E. *thynnian*]

thine (ðain) 1. *possessive pron.* that or those belonging to thee 2. *possessive adj.* (used in place of 'thy' before a noun beginning with a vowel or mute 'h'), *thine honor* [O.E. *thin*]

thin-film solar cells (θinfilm) (*electr.*) inexpensive solar cells consisting of a thin, flexible metal or plastic material in which a thin film of a semiconductor material has been evaporated, used as a power source in spacecraft

thing (θiŋ) *n.* that which consists of matter, a body, or object, esp. that which is no more than matter, i.e. not a living person or animal ‖ used in reference to a person, esp. in often condescending expressions of affection, pity etc., *she's a sweet thing, he's a wicked old thing* ‖ an action, *what would be the best thing to do next?* ‖ something not specifically named, *what's that thing he's carrying?* ‖ (*colloq.*) a uniquely personal activity, *he's doing his thing* ‖ something uttered or thought, *the president said some good things in his speech* ‖ (*pl.*) affairs or concerns, *the things of the mind* ‖ (*pl.*) belongings, clothes, utensils etc., *he left his things at the station* ‖ (*pl.*) circumstances in general, *things will get better* **a thing** (in negative expressions) anything, *he wouldn't do a thing to help us* **a thing or two** (with 'know' or 'tell') facts derived from thorough familiarity with a subject, *he knows a thing or two about economics* **first thing** at the earliest possible moment, *do it first thing in the morning* **to make a good thing of** to profit financially by **to see things** to have hallucinations **the thing** that which is appropriate or correct, *the thing to do in that case is rush to the hospital* ‖ that which is polite, *it is hardly the thing to leave an invitation unanswered* ‖ that which is fashionable, *stripes are the thing this season* [O.E.]

thing·um·a·bob (θíŋəməbɒb) *n.* a thingumajig

thing·um·a·jig (θíŋəmədʒig) *n.* (*pop.*) a substitute used when one doesn't know, or has momentarily forgotten, the proper name of something or (*Br.*) someone

think (θiŋk) *pres. part.* **think·ing** *past* and *past part.* **thought** (θɔt) *v.i.* to engage in the process of arranging ideas in a pattern of relationships or of adding new ideas soon to be related to such a pattern ‖ to turn something over in the mind, e.g. to consider advantages and disadvantages ‖ (with 'of') to have a specified opinion, *he doesn't think much of that play* ‖ (with 'of') to have consideration or concern, *think of your family first* ‖ (with 'of') to make provision, *you must think of the future* ‖ (with 'of' or 'about') to have in mind as a provisional plan, *we're thinking of going to the beach* ‖ to consider as a possible candidate, *we are thinking of John for that position* ‖ to remember, *can you think of his name?* ‖ *v.t.* to conceive in the mind, *to think strange thoughts* ‖ to have as a firm conviction, *I think she is lying* ‖ to have as a tentative opinion, *I think she might refuse* ‖ to work out by reasoning, *I can't think how the story will end* ‖ to determine by reflection, *I can't think what is best to do* ‖ to bring to a specified condition by mental activity, *to think oneself into a state of depression* ‖ (with 'to' + infinitive) to remember, or have the idea of doing etc. (something) when one could reasonably be expected to have it, *he didn't think to lock the door* ‖ to be obsessed with the idea of, *he thinks and dreams flying* **to think aloud** to speak one's ideas as they occur **to think better of** to change (e.g. an opinion or decision) on further reflection, *he was going to tell us the story but thought better of it* ‖ **to think nothing of** to take for granted (what would seem odd, hard etc., to others), *he thinks nothing of walking 20 miles a day* **to think out** (or **through**) to examine carefully (a problem) so as to reach a conclusion **to think over** to consider or reconsider, ponder at length **to think twice** to reflect with special care before taking action **to think up** to make up (a plan, answer etc.) in the mind [O.E. *thencan, thencean*]

think·a·ble (θíŋkəb'l) *adj.* able to be thought ‖ able to be entertained as an idea or possibility

think·ing (θíŋkiŋ) 1. *n.* the mental process of one who thinks ‖ an opinion or judgment, *to my thinking they will be outmoded in four years* ‖ a body of thought, *modern thinking* 2. that thinks or can think

think tank an institution or group involved in researching and solving difficult, interdisci-

plinary problems, the solutions to which often affect public policy *also* think factory

thin-lay·er chromatography (θinléiər) (*chem.*) an accurate, rapid process of color photography in which the absorbent medium is a thin layer of silica gel, aluminum, or cellulose on a glass plate *abbr.* TLC —**thin-layer chromatographic** *adj.* Cf GAS-LIQUID CHROMATOGRAPHY

thin·ner (θínər) 1. *adj.* more thin 2. *n.* a liquid used to make something (e.g. paint or printing ink) more thin

thin-skinned (θínskínd) *adj.* having a thin skin ‖ unusually sensitive to criticism

thi·o acid (θáiou) an acid in which sulfur wholly or partly replaces oxygen [fr. Gk *theion*, sulfur]

thi·o·al·de·hyde (θaiouǽldəhaid) *n.* an aldehyde in which oxygen is replaced by sulfur

thi·o·ben·da·zol [C₁₀H₇N₃S] (θaioubéndəzɒl) *n.* (*pharm.*) a drug used to treat fungus or roundworm infection

thi·o·cy·a·nate (θaiousáiəneit) *n.* a salt or ester of thiocyanic acid

thi·o·cy·an·ic acid (θaiousaiǽnik) a strong-smelling, unstable liquid acid, HSCN or HNCS, obtained by distilling a thiocyanate salt with dilute sulfuric acid

Thi·o·kol (θáiɒkɒl) *n.* (*chem.*) any of a number of rubberlike polymers (RSXN), where R is a divalent organic radical and X varies usually between 2 and 4. They are very resistant to the swelling effect of oils [Trademark]

thi·on·ic (θaiónik) *adj.* relating to or containing sulfur [fr. Gk *theion*, sulfur]

Thi·o·nine (θáiəni:n, θáiənin) *n.* a violet dye, C₁₂H₉N₃S, used in microscopy to stain objects [Trademark]

thi·o·rid·a·zine [C₂₁H₂₆N₂S₂HCl] (thaiourídəzi:n) *n.* (*pharm.*) a phenothiazine tranquilizer and antidepressant used in treating schizophrenia; marketed as Mellaril

thi·o·sul·fate, thi·o·sul·phate (θaiousʌlfeit) *n.* a salt or ester of thiosulfuric acid, used in photography, dyeing etc.

thi·o·sul·fu·ric acid, thi·o·sul·phu·ric acid (θaiousʌlfjúərik) an unstable acid, H₂S₂O₃, derived from sulfuric acid. It exists in solution or in the form of salts and esters

thi·o·u·re·a (θaioujurí:ə) *n.* a crystalline substance, CS(NH₂)₂, used in organic syntheses [Mod. L. fr. Gk *theion*, sulfur +*ouron*, urine]

third (θə:rd) 1. *adj.* being number three in a series (*NUMBER TABLE) ‖ next after the second in importance, quality, rank etc. ‖ being one of the three equal parts of anything ‖ of or pertaining to the gear immediately above second in a vehicle 2. *n.* the person or thing next after the second ‖ one of three equal parts of anything (1/3) ‖ (*Br.*) a grading in the third class of an examination ‖ a third prize in a race or other contest ‖ the gear immediately above second in a vehicle ‖ the third day of a month ‖ (*mus.*) the note three steps above or below a given note in a diatonic scale, inclusive of both notes ‖ (*mus.*) the interval between these notes ‖ (*mus.*) a combination of these notes 3. *adv.* in the third place ‖ (followed by a superlative) except two, *third biggest* [O.E. *thridda, thridde*]

Third Amendment (1791) part of the Bill of Rights in the U.S. Constitution that requires permission of the owner for the peacetime quartering of soldiers in a private home; in wartime the matter must be resolved 'in a manner to be prescribed by law.' Arising from the American colonists' resentment over the housing of British soldiers, the amendment is not relevant in modern times, nor has it ever been the subject of a judicial decision. The amendment's underlying principle remains significant, however, because of its implication that civilian authority has precedence over that of the military

third base (*baseball*) the base to be touched third by a base runner ‖ the player placed here

third-class (θə́:rdklǽs, θə́:rdklás) 1. *adj.* of or relating to a class, grade etc. below second 2. *adv.* at third-class rate, in third-class accommodation

third degree a severe, sometimes brutal, questioning of a criminal suspect to try to force a confession ‖ (*freemasonry*) a mastermason

third-degree burn a burn in which the skin is destroyed through the depth of the derma and possibly into the underlying tissues. It may be accompanied by shock

third estate the commons, as distinguished

from the nobles and clergy, in a States General or parliament

Third International the Comintern

third man (*cricket*) a fielder, or his position, further from the wicket than point and in the same straight line

third market (*securities*) the over-the-counter market *Cf* FOURTH MARKET

third order a body of Christian lay men and women either living in the world and affiliated to a religious order as seculars or living in community as regulars

third party (*law*) a person other than the two principals involved in a case

third person (*gram.*) the person or thing spoken of, as distinguished from the person speaking and the person spoken to

third-rate (θə́:rdréit) *adj.* of poor quality, *a third-rate hotel*

Third Reich the Nazi regime in Germany (1933-45). The First Reich was the Holy Roman Empire (962-1806) and the Second was the German Empire (1871-1918)

third-stream (θə́:rdstrí:m) *adj.* of music combining jazz and classical music

Third World the countries in which economic development still has far to go, and which belong neither to the group of industrial states having a liberal economy nor to the socialist-type group of states

thirst (θə:rst) *n.* a desire for drink ‖ any keen desire, *a thirst for knowledge* [O.E. *thurst*]

thirst *v.i.* to feel thirsty ‖ (*rhet.*) to have a keen desire, *thirsting for revenge* [O.E. *thyrstan*]

thirst·i·ly (θə́:rstili:) *adv.* in a thirsty manner

thirst·i·ness (θə́:rsti:nis) *n.* the state or quality of being thirsty

thirst·y (θə́:rsti:) *comp.* **thirst·i·er** *superl.* **thirst·i·est** *adj.* feeling thirst ‖ dry, *thirsty soil* ‖ (*rhet.*) having a strong desire, *thirsty for adventure* [O.E. *thurstig, thyrstig*]

thir·teen (θə́:rtí:n) 1. *adj.* being one more than 12 (*NUMBER TABLE) 2. *n.* ten plus three ‖ the cardinal number representing this (13, XIII) [O.E. *thrēotīene, thrēotēne*]

Thirteen Colonies, the (*Am. hist.*) the colonies of British North America which adopted (1776) the Declaration of Independence, and became the original United States. They were Connecticut, Delaware, Georgia, Maryland, Massachusetts, New Hampshire, New Jersey, New York, North Carolina, Pennsylvania, Rhode Island, South Carolina and Virginia

thir·teenth (θə́:rtí:nθ) 1. *adj.* being number 13 in a series (*NUMBER TABLE) ‖ being one of the 13 equal parts of anything 2. *n.* the person or thing next after the 12th ‖ one of 13 equal parts of anything (1/13) ‖ the 13th day of a month [O.E. *thrīetēotha, thrēotēotha*]

Thirteenth Amendment (1865) an amendment to the U.S. Constitution providing that 'neither slavery nor involuntary servitude' will exist in the United States and giving Congress the power to enforce this article by legislation. The amendment was the first unconditional constitutional action against the institution of slavery and the first of four amendments (others are the 14th, 15th and 24th) protecting the equal status of black Americans. Recent Supreme Court decisions have interpreted the amendment to include prohibition of racial discrimination in the disposal of property, in the making and enforcement of contracts, and in private employment

thir·ti·eth (θə́:rti:iθ) 1. *adj.* being number 30 in a series (*NUMBER TABLE) ‖ being one of the 30 equal parts of anything 2. *n.* the person or thing next after the 29th ‖ one of 30 equal parts of anything (1/30) ‖ the 30th day of a month [O.E. *thrītigotha*]

thir·ty (θə́:rti:) 1. *adj.* being 10 more than 20 (*NUMBER TABLE) 2. *pl.* **thir·ties** *n.* three times 10 ‖ the cardinal number representing this (30, XXX) ‖ **the thirties** (of temperature, a person's age, a century etc.) the span 30-9 [O.E. *thrītig*]

Thirty-nine Articles the statements of belief to which Anglican clergymen give general assent at their ordination. They broadly define the doctrinal position of the Church of England in terms of the Reformation controversies. They were ratified by Convocation (1571)

30-pull *n.* (*football*) a play in which the quarterback spins and fakes a pass to the fullback but throws the ball to a linesman

thir·ty-sec·ond note (θə́:rti:sékənd) *n.* (*mus.* *Am.=Br.* demisemiquaver) a note equal to half a sixteenth note

Thirty Years' War a series of political and religious wars (1618-48) caused mainly by the political rivalry between Catholic and Protestant princes in Germany and the interest of foreign powers in German affairs. The chief phases of the war were: (a) The BOHEMIAN WAR (1618-23), in which a Protestant revolt in Bohemia was crushed by the Catholic League at the White Mountain (1620) and Spain conquered the Palatinate (1621-3). (b) The DANISH WAR (1624-9), in which Christian IV of Denmark was defeated by the Hapsburgs (1626) and signed the Treaty of Lübeck (1629). (c) The SWEDISH WAR (1630-5), in which Gustavus II of Sweden invaded Germany (1630) and defeated the Hapsburg army at Breitenfeld (1631). The Hapsburg victory of Nordlingen (1634) was followed by the Treaty of Prague (1635). (d) The FRENCH WAR (1635-48), in which France under Richelieu entered the war against the Hapsburgs, winning the victories of Rocroi (1643) and Lens (1648). The Thirty Years' War, which devastated Germany and increased French power at the expense of Spain, was ended by the Treaties of Westphalia (1648)

this (ðis) 1. *pl.* **these** (ði:z) *adj.* of that which is here (compared with that which is there), or near (in space or time), or just mentioned 2. *pl.* **these** *pron.* the person or thing here, or near (in space or time), or just mentioned 3. *adv.* to this extent or degree, *this long* [O.E. *thes* masc., *thēos* fem., *this* neut.]

this·tle (θísəl) *n.* any of several genera of tall, prickly plants of fam. *Compositae*, esp. of genera *Carduus, Circium* and *Onopordon*. Many are troublesome weeds [O. E. *thistil*]

this·tle·down (θísəldaun) *n.* the pappus attached to the seeds of a thistle, by which they are carried by the wind

this·tly (θísli:) *adj.* full of thistles

thith·er (θíðər,ðíðər) 1. *adv.* (*rhet.*) to or towards that place 2. *adj.* (*rhet.*) on the more distant side, *the thither shore of the lake* [O.E. *thider*]

Thi·va (θí:va) *THEBES

thix·ot·ro·py (θiksótrəpi:) *n.* the property exhibited by certain gels of becoming liquefied on being shaken, stirred etc. and of settling into a gel again when left standing [fr. Gk *thixis*, action of touching+*tropos*, turning]

tho, tho' (ðou) *conj., adv.* (*pop.*) though

thole (θoul) *n.* one of two pegs in the gunwale of a boat used as an oarlock [O.E. *thol, tholl*]

tho·lei·ite (θóuləait) *n.* (*geol.*) a basalt generated in the upper mantle of the earth's crust under the oceans —**tholeiitic** *adj.* containing tholeiite

thole·pin (θoulpin) *n.* a thole

Thom·as (tómas), St, one of the 12 Apostles. He doubted the Resurrection until he saw and touched the wounds of Christ. According to tradition he went to India as a missionary (*CHRISTIANS OF ST THOMAS). Feast: Dec. 21

Thomas Becket, St *BECKET

Thomas, Christians of St *CHRISTIANS OF ST THOMAS

Thomas, Dylan (1914-53), British poet, born in Wales. His books include '18 Poems' (1934) and 'Twenty-five Poems' (1936), in which the symbolism owes much to Freud and to the Bible, but where much is also highly personal and obscure, and 'Deaths and Entrances' (1946) on which his greatness ultimately rests: a handful of passionate lyrics, with love and death, childhood and the beauty of the world for their themes, and a diction, imagery and metrical skill which make many of them memorable. He also published various prose works among which are the 10 autobiographical stories, 'Portrait of the Artist as a Young Dog' (1940), and the radio script 'Under Milk Wood' (a poetic play, 1954). He also made a reputation as a reader of poetry, his own and others

Thomas, George Henry (1816-70), U.S. Union general during the Civil War. His stand at the Battle of Chattanooga (1863) saved the Union army from complete rout. He defeated (1864) Gen. J. B. Hood at Nashville

Thomas à Kem·pis (kémpis) (c. 1379-1471), German monk, author of devotional works. He is generally supposed to have written 'The Imitation of Christ'. He lived most of his adult life in the Augustinian convent of Mount St Agnes near Zwolle (Netherlands)

Thomas A·qui·nas (əkwáinəs), St (c. 1225-74), Italian theologian and scholastic philosopher. He is the author of 'Summa contra Gentiles' (1259-64), a defense of Christianity in the light of the attacks made by Averroes and his followers in their interpretations of Aristotle, and 'Summa Theologica' (1267-73), his greatest work, which he intended to be a sum of all learning. He also wrote several commentaries on Aristotle, who greatly influenced his thinking. The teachings of St Thomas have had an enormous influence on the Roman Catholic Church and have been officially declared the basis of theological studies

Thomas More, St *MORE

Tho·mism (tóumizəm) *n.* the philosophy and theology of Thomas Aquinas. Thomism distinguishes sharply between faith and reason: while reason cannot establish doctrines, which are a matter of faith, it can show that they are not contrary to reason **Thó·mist** *adj.* and *n.* **Tho·mis·tic** *adj.*

Thomp·son (tómpsən), Sir Benjamin (Count von Rumford, 1753-1814), British-U.S. scientist. His 'Enquiry Concerning the Source of Heat Which is Excited by Friction', a study which he presented (1798) to the British Royal Society, defined heat as a mode of motion rather than a material substance

Thompson, Francis (1859-1907), British poet. He is best known for his long mystical poem 'The Hound of Heaven' (included in 'Poems', 1893)

Thompson, Sir John Sparrow David (1844-94), Canadian statesman. His term as minister of justice in the Sir John Macdonald administration was marked by his masterly exposition of the government position on the execution (1885) of Louis Riel and the Jesuit Estates Act (1885). He became (1892) prime minister of Canada

Thompson submachine gun (*abbr.* tommy gun) a light automatic weapon with a pistol grip, which may be fired from the shoulder or hip [after John Taliaferro *Thompson* (1860–1940), American general, one of its two inventors]

Thom·son (tómsən), Elihu (1853-1937), U.S. electrical engineer and inventor. He demonstrated (1875) the transmission of signals without wires

Thomson, Sir George Paget (1892-1975), British physicist, son of Sir J. J. Thomson. He is known for his work on the diffraction of electrons by crystals. Nobel prize (1937)

Thomson, James (1700-48), British poet, born in Scotland. He is best known for 'The Seasons' (1726-30), four long meditative and descriptive poems which foreshadowed the Romantics' interest in nature

Thomson, Sir Joseph John (1856-1940), British physicist. He discovered the electron (1897) and added to the development of the electrical theory of atomic structure. Nobel prize (1906)

Thomson, Virgil (1896-), U.S. composer and critic. He created two operas, 'Four Saints in Three Acts' (1928) and 'The Mother of Us All' (1947), and wrote songs, piano sonatas, a cello concerto, stage and film music etc.

Thomson, William *KELVIN

Thomson effect (*phys.*) the redistribution of the temperature differential along an otherwise homogenous conductor due to the passage of a current [after William *Thomson*, Lord Kelvin]

thong (θɒŋ, θɔŋ) *n.* a leather strip used for fastening e.g. heavy boots ‖ the leather lash of a whip [O.E. *thwang, thwong*]

Thor (θɔr) (*Norse mythol.*) the god of thunder, the son of Odin. He was represented as being armed with a remarkable hammer, which returned to his hand after he had thrown it. Thursday is named after Thor

tho·rac·ic (θɔræsik, θouræsik) *adj.* of, in or near the thorax or of, in or near the vertebra between the lumbar and cervical vertebrae [fr. Mod. L. *thoracicus* fr. Gk]

thoracic duct the trunk of the system of lymphatic vessels emptying into the subclavian vein and receiving lymph and intestinal fluids from the abdomen, lower limbs and the entire left side of the body

thoracic gland (*entomology*) the gland in some insects that controls moulting *also* prothoracic gland

tho·rax (θɔ́ræks, θóuræks) *pl.* **tho·rax·es, tho·ra·ces** (θɔ́urəsi:z) *n.* that part of the body in higher vertebrates which contains the heart and lungs and a number of structures passing between the neck and the abdomen. It is supported by the ribs and sternum. Movement of these and the diaphragm causes a partial vacuum within the thorax, as a result of

---

CONCISE PRONUNCIATION KEY: **(a)** æ, c*a*t; ɑ, c*a*r; ɔ f*aw*n; ei, sn*a*ke. **(e)** e, h*e*n; i:, sh*ee*p; iə, d*ee*r; ɛə, b*ea*r. **(i)** i, f*i*sh; ai, t*i*ger; ə:, b*i*rd. **(o)** o, *o*x; au, c*ow*; ou, g*oa*t; u, p*oo*r; ɔi, r*oy*al. **(u)** ʌ, d*u*ck; u, b*u*ll; u:, g*oo*se; ə, b*a*cillus; ju:, c*u*be. x, lo*ch*; θ, *th*ink; ð, bo*th*er; z, Z*e*n; ʒ, corsa*g*e; dʒ, sava*g*e; ŋ, ora*ng*utang; j, *y*ak; ʃ, *fi*sh; tʃ, fe*tch*; 'l, rabb*le*; 'n, redd*en*. Complete pronunciation key appears inside front cover.

which air is drawn into the lungs (*RESPIRATION) ‖ the body region behind the head in insects and some other animals [L. fr. Gk *thōrax*, the chest]

Tho·reau (θɔróu), Henry David (1817-62), American naturalist and writer. He is best known for 'Walden' (1854), an account of his experiment in living alone at Walden Pond, near Concord, Massachusetts, to observe the life of the woods. Thoreau was a friend of Emerson and the transcendentalists. A powerful social critic, he was disturbed by the trend of Western civilization toward a fully industrial urban society dominated by the profit motive. His essay 'On the Duty of Civil Disobedience' (1849) has inspired such men as Gandhi

tho·ri·a (θɔ́ri:ə, θóuri:ə) *n.* thorium oxide, ThO₂, a white powder

tho·rite (θɔ́rait, θóurait) *n.* the naturally occurring silicate of thorium, ThSiO₄ [Swed. *thorit*]

tho·ri·um (θɔ́ri:əm, θóuri:əm) *n.* a heavy, radioactive metallic chemical element (symbol Th, at. no. 90, at. mass 232.038). Its compounds occur in the minerals monazite and thorite, and its oxide is used for coating incandescent mantles [Mod. L. after THOR]

Thorn (θɔrn) *THORUN

thorn (θɔrn) *n.* the woody part of a leaf or stem modified to a stiff, sharp point ‖ a hawthorn or other plant or tree bearing thorns ‖ the wood of any of these ‖ any of various sharply pointed protuberances on an animal, e.g. on a sea urchin ‖ a source of sharp irritation ‖ (in Old English and Old Norse) the name of the runic symbol for the 'th' sounds e.g. in 'thin' and 'this' **a thorn in one's side** a continual or frequent cause of annoyance or trouble [O.E.]

thorn apple a member of *Datura,* fam. *Solanaceae,* a genus of plants, shrubs etc. bearing prickly fruit and large trumpet-shaped flowers, esp. the jimson weed ‖ the fruit of the hawthorn

Thorn·dike (θɔ́rndaik), Edward Lee (1874-1949), U.S. educator and psychologist. He developed a method of testing and measuring intelligence and learning ability

Thorn·hill (θɔ́rnhil), Sir James (c. 1676-1734), English baroque painter. He is best known for decorative works, e.g. the dome at St Paul's Cathedral, London and the Painted Hall of the Royal Naval College, Greenwich

thorn·i·ness (θɔ́rni:nis) *n.* the quality or state of being thorny

Thorn·ton (θɔ́rntən), William (1759-1828), U.S. architect. He designed most of the central portion of the Capitol exterior at Washington, D.C., and many Washington residences

thorn·y (θɔ́rni:) *comp.* **thorn·i·er** *superl.* **thorn·i·est** *adj.* full of thorns or spines ‖ beset with difficulties or controversy, *a thorny question*

thor·ough (θə́:rou, θʌ́rou) *adj.* proceeding or done with great care or attention to detail, completeness etc., *a thorough worker, thorough knowledge* ‖ complete in all respects, *a thorough gentleman* [Later O.E. *thuruh*]

thorough bass (*mus.*) continuo

thor·ough·bred (θə́:rəbred, θʌ́rəbred) **1.** *adj.* of or pertaining to any horse, dog etc. of pure breed **Thor·ough·bred** of or pertaining to a Thoroughbred **2.** *n.* any horse, dog etc. of pure breed **Thoroughbred** an English breed of horse, raced or used for hunting or riding, bred from English mares crossed with Arab stallions

thor·ough·fare (θə́:rəfεər, θʌ́rəfεər) *n.* a road or passage available to traffic and not closed at either end, esp. a main highway

thor·ough·go·ing (θə́:rəgouiŋ, θʌ́rəgouiŋ) *adj.* very thorough

Thorpe (θɔrp), James Francis 'Jim' (1888-1953), U.S. athlete, selected by sportswriters as the greatest athlete of the first half of the 20th century. Of American Indian, Irish and French descent, he competed in track and field, lacrosse, baseball and football (All-American 1911, 1912), at Carlisle (Pa.) Indian School. In the 1912 Olympic Games he won the decathlon and pentathlon, setting records in both events, but he was stripped of his gold medals (1913) when it was learned that he had earned money playing baseball. He played professional football (from 1915) and professional baseball (1913-9). He became a charter member (1963) of the Pro Football Hall of Fame, and in 1982 the Olympic Committee voted to restore his gold medals

those *pl.* of THAT

Thoth (θouθ, tout) (*Egyptian mythol.*) the god of wisdom and magic, identified with the Greek Hermes. He is the inventor of speech and writing, the arts and sciences. He is usually represented as having the body of a man and the head of an ibis

thou (ðau) (objective THEE, possessive THY or THINE) 2nd *pers. sing. personal pron.* now almost only used in prayer to God [O.E. *thu, thū*]

thou (ðau) *n.* (*pop.*) a thousand

though (ðou) **1.** *conj.* used to introduce a statement of fact or a possibility which might prevent a second statement from being true but does not in fact do so (drawing attention to the opposition involved in the two statements), *he is still active though very old* **as though** as if, *he spoke as though he meant it* **2.** *adv.* nevertheless, *the ground was muddy, it was a good game though* [of Scand. origin]

thought (θɔt) *n.* the action or process of thinking ‖ the capacity to think ‖ an idea or pattern of ideas ‖ the patterns of ideas characteristic of a period, a person, social group or field of activity, *modern thought, political thought* ‖ consideration, *don't give it a moment's thought* ‖ intention, *he once had the thought of selling the house* ‖ meditation, *engrossed in thought* [O.E. *thoht*]

thought *past* and *past part.* of THINK

thought·ful (θɔ́tfəl) *adj.* absorbed in the process of thinking, *you look very thoughtful* ‖ characterized by or resulting from a long or careful process of thought, *a thoughtful speech* ‖ showing consideration for others, *a thoughtful act*

thought·less (θɔ́tlis) *adj.* said or done without having given thought to a probable result ‖ showing lack of consideration for others

thou·sand (θáusənd) **1.** *n.* 10 times 100 (*NUMBER TABLE) ‖ the cardinal number representing this (1,000, M) ‖ (*pl.*) in mathematical calculations, the column of figures four places to the left of the decimal point **thousands of** a great many **2.** *adj.* being 10 times 100 **thou·sandth** (θáuzəndθ) **1.** *adj.* being number 1,000 in a series (*NUMBER TABLE) ‖ being one of the 1,000 equal parts of anything **2.** *n.* the person or thing next after the 999th ‖ one of 1,000 equal parts of anything (1/1,000) [O.E. *thūsend*]

Thousand Days' War a civil war fought (1899-1902) in Colombia between conservative and liberal forces. It resulted in 100,000 deaths, and this left Colombia unable to resist (1903) the U.S.-backed, secession of Panama

Thrace (θreis) (*Gk Thraki*) the southeastern part of the Balkan peninsula shared by Greece, Turkey and Bulgaria since 1878. Historically the region has varied greatly in extent. Its coast was settled by the Greeks (8th-1st cc. B.C.). The rest of the region remained independent until conquered by Persia (512-479 B.C.), Macedon (342-281 and 211-196 B.C.), and Rome (46 A.D.). The Ottoman Turks took Adrianople (1361) and Constantinople (1453) and the region became part of the Ottoman Empire

Thra·cian (θréiʃən) **1.** *adj.* pertaining to Thrace, its people, culture etc. **2.** a native or inhabitant of Thrace ‖ (*hist.*) an Indo-European language spoken by the early inhabitants of Thrace

thraldom *THRALLDOM

thrall (θrɔl) *n.* (*hist.*) a slave or person held in bondage **to hold in thrall** (*rhet.*) to enchant, enthrall [O.E. *thrǣl*]

thrall·dom, thral·dom (θrɔ́ldəm) *n.* (*hist.*) the condition of a thrall ‖ (*rhet.*) servitude

thrash (θræʃ) **1.** *v.t.* to strike repeatedly with a cane or whip ‖ to thresh (wheat etc.) ‖ to defeat soundly ‖ *v.i.* to move the limbs or body violently ‖ (*naut.*) to sail against contrary winds **to thrash over** (or **out**) to discuss (a matter) in detail in order to discover the truth or a solution **2.** *n.* the act of thrashing ‖ a leg movement used by swimmers in the crawl and backstroke [O.E. *therscan*]

thrash·er (θrǽʃər) *n.* any of several American songbirds of fam. *Mimidae* [perh. fr. Br. dial. *thrasher, thresher,* thrush]

thread (θred) **1.** *n.* a fine cord made by twisting two or more strands of cotton, silk etc. together, used in sewing ‖ such cords collectively ‖ any of the fibers used in weaving a material ‖ a natural or manufactured threadlike filament ‖ that which gives continuity to, or is continuous in, an argument, speech, story etc. ‖ the spiral grooves of a screw, bolt etc. **2.** *v.t.* to pass a thread through the eye of (a needle) ‖ to put (beads etc.) together by passing a thread

through each ‖ to furnish (e.g. a screw or tube) with a thread ‖ to feed film into (a movie camera or projector) ‖ to interweave with or as if with threads, *hair threaded with silver* ‖ to make (a way) between a number of obstacles, or in a maze of streets, by changes of direction ‖ *v.i.* (esp. with 'through') to make a way [O.E. *thrǣd*]

thread·bare (θrédbεər) *adj.* of a fabric from which the nap has been worn away ‖ wearing shabby clothes ‖ (of an argument, expressed opinion, joke etc.) so familiar as to have lost its interest ‖ (of an excuse, plot etc.) obviously inadequate

thread·worm (θrédwərm) *n.* a threadlike nematode, esp. one infesting the human rectum

thread·y (θrédi:) *comp.* **thread·i·er** *superl.* **thread·i·est** *adj.* of or resembling a thread ‖ (of the pulse) thin and feeble (of the voice) weak

threat (θret) *n.* a statement or other indication of intention to hurt, punish, destroy etc. ‖ an indication that an undesirable event or catastrophe may occur, *a threat of rain, a threat to party unity* [O.E. *thrēat*]

threat·en (θrét'n) *v.t.* to utter or otherwise indicate a threat to (someone) ‖ to promise (something harmful, evil etc.) as a threat ‖ to indicate the approach of (something unpleasant, harmful etc.), *the clouds threaten rain* [O.E. *thrēatnian*]

threatened species (*biol.*) a species that might become endangered within a short period of time *Cf* ENDANGERED SPECIES

three (θri:) **1.** *adj.* being one more than two (*NUMBER TABLE) **2.** *n.* two plus one ‖ the cardinal number representing this (3, III) ‖ three o'clock ‖ a playing card (domino etc.) marked with three symbols (spots etc.) [O.E. *thrī, thrīo, thrēo*]

three-base hit (*baseball*) a triple

three-color process (*printing*) a color-printing process in which three inks of different primary colors are superimposed in separate printings, sometimes with a fourth printing, in black

three-cor·nered (θrí:kɔrnərd) *adj.* having three corners or angles ‖ (of a contest) having three contestants, each competing with the other two, *a three-cornered election fight*

three-di·men·sion·al (θrí:diménʃən'l) *adj.* (*abbr.* 3-D) having, or appearing to have, length, breadth and depth in space ‖ (*math.*) able to be represented by reference to three axes at right angles to one another

three·fold (θrí:fould) **1.** *adj.* triple **2.** *adv.* to three times as much or as many ‖ by three times [O.E. *thrīfeald, thrȳfeald*]

Three Mile Island 1. site near Harrisburg, PA, of 1979 nuclear accident **2.** by extension, prototype of risk of nuclear energy

three-mile limit (*internat. law*) the strip of coastal waters three miles wide over which a state has national sovereignty

three·pence (θrépəns, θrʌ́pəns, θrí pəns) *n.* (*Br.*) a value, expressed in terms of money, equal to that of three pence (*Br., hist.*) a threepenny bit

three·pen·ny (θrépəni:, θrʌ́pəni:, θrípəni:) *adj.* (*Br.*) costing or worth threepence

threepenny bit (*Br., hist.*) a coin worth three pennies. It ceased to be minted when the British currency was decimalized (1971)

three-phase (θrí:feiz) *adj.* (*elec.*) of, relating to, or operating by a combination of three circuits actuated by superimposed electromotive currents that differ in phase by 120°.

three-piece (θrí:pi:s) **1.** *adj.* made or consisting of three pieces, e.g. a costume of separate coat, skirt and jacket **2.** *n.* such a costume

three-ply (θrí:plai) *adj.* having three strands, layers etc.

three-quar·ter (θrí:kwɔrtər) *n.* (*rugby*) a back whose position lies between that of halfback and fullback

three-quarter *adj.* of or relating to three quarters of the full length or size

three-quarter binding a book binding in which the spine and corners are covered in one material and the sides in another, the material on the spine extending over one third of the width of the sides (cf. FULL BINDING, cf. HALF BINDING, cf. QUARTER BINDING)

three-quar·ter-bound (θrí:kwɔrtərbaund) *adj.* (of a book) having a threequarter binding

Three Rivers *TROIS RIVIÈRES

three·score (θrí:skɔr, θrí:skóur) *adj.* sixty, three times twenty

three·some (θrí:səm) *n.* a group of three persons

‖ (*golf*) a game in which three players compete

Three-Tier Agreement (θrí:tíər) an arms limitation proposal advanced by the U.S. at the Geneva SALT talks in May 1977, including a treaty limiting strategic weapons for eight years, a protocol limiting certain other weapons for three years, and a statement of principles for future arms reduction

thre·node (θrí:noud, θrénoud) *n.* a threnody

thre·no·di·al (θrinóudiəl) *adj.* threnodic

thre·nod·ic (θrinódik) *adj.* of or like a threnody

thren·o·dist (θrénədist) *n.* a singer or composer of threnodies

thren·o·dy (θrénədi:) *pl.* **thren·o·dies** *n.* (*rhet.*) a song of lamentation, esp. a funeral song, dirge [fr. Gk *thrēnōdía*]

thresh (θreʃ, *Br.* also θræʃ) *v.t.* to separate the grain from the ear of (wheat etc.) *v.i.* to thresh grain ‖ to toss about, thrash **to thresh out** to go over (a problem) repeatedly until it is clarified and solved **thrésh·er** *n.* a threshing machine [O.E. *threscan, therscan*]

thresher shark *Alopias vulpinus*, fam. *Lamnidae*, a large, long-tailed shark measuring up to 20 ft in length, found in all oceans. It is an excellent game fish, but not highly regarded as food

threshing machine a power-driven machine for threshing out grain

thresh·old (θréʃhould, θréʃould) *n.* the plank or stone at the bottom of a doorway ‖ a beginning, *the threshold of a career* ‖ the point at which a stimulus of increasing strength is first perceived or produces its specific response, *auditory threshold* [O.E. *therscold, therscwold*]

threw *past* of THROW

thrice (θrais) *adv.* (*rhet.*) three times [M.E. *thries,* three times]

thrift (θrift) *n.* the practice of avoiding wasteful or avoidable expenditure ‖ a member of *Armeria*, fam. *Plumbaginaceae*, a genus of low-growing plants, esp. *A. maritima*, bearing pink or white flowers and found in coastal and mountainous regions of the north temperate zone [O.N.]

thrift·i·ly (θríftili:) *adv.* in a thrifty manner

thrift·i·ness (θrífti:nis) *n.* the quality or state of being thrifty

thrift shop 1. a shop that sells secondhand merchandise contributed to a charity **2.** by extension a shop dealing in secondhand merchandise

thrift·y (θrífti:) *comp.* **thrift·i·er** *superl.* **thrift·i·est** *adj.* practicing thrift ‖ (esp. of plants and animals) thriving, growing well

thrill (θril) **1.** *v.t.* to cause tense emotional excitement (of joy, horror etc.) in ‖ *v.i.* to feel tense emotional excitement **2.** *n.* a moment of excitement or intense emotion ‖ (*med.*) an unnatural vibration in the respiratory or circulatory systems

thrill·er *n.* a fictional work designed to thrill the audience or reader [M.E.]

thrips (θrips) *n.* a member of *Thrips,* fam. *Thripidae,* a genus of minute hemipterons having thin, fringed wings and sucking mouthparts. They feed mainly on plant juices and are regarded as pests [L. fr. Gk *thrips,* woodworm]

thrive (θraiv) *pres. part.* **thriv·ing** *past* **throve** (θrouv), **thrived** *past part.* **thrived, thriv·en** (θrívən) *v.i.* to grow and function well ‖ to have good health ‖ to do well financially [M.E. fr. O.N.]

throat (θrout) *n.* the front part of the neck ‖ the upper part of the passage leading from the mouth to the stomach and lungs and including the larynx, pharynx, trachea and esophagus ‖ a narrow passage, esp. one serving as an entrance **to cut one's own throat** to act to one's own disadvantage **to ram something down somebody's throat** to compel someone to listen to something he does not want to hear **to stick in one's throat** to fail to be uttered through pressure of emotion [O.E. *throte, throtul*]

throat·i·ly (θróuti:li:) *adv.* in a throaty manner

throat·i·ness (θróuti:nis) *n.* the state or quality of being throaty

throat·y (θróuti:) *comp.* **throat·i·er** *superl.* **throat·i·est** *adj.* (of a sound) produced chiefly in the throat ‖ (of the voice) rather deep and rough, as though coming from low down in the throat ‖ (of an animal) having a large, loose-skinned throat

throb (θrob) **1.** *v.i. pres. part.* **throb·bing** *past and past part.* **throbbed** to vibrate ‖ (of the pulse etc.) to beat strongly ‖ to show emotional

excitement **2.** *n.* a pulsation of low frequency but large amplitude, esp. of the heart or arteries ‖ the sound produced by throbbing, *the throb of the drums* [M.E. perh. imit.]

throe (θrou) *n.* (*rhet.*) a spasm of pain or anguish ‖ (*pl.*) a painful struggle, esp. of childbirth or of death [M.E. *throw, throwe* prob. fr. O.E. *thrāwu,* pain]

throm·bin (θrómbin) *n.* (*biochem.*) an enzyme which enables fibrinogen to form fibrin, causing blood clots (*PROTHROMBIN) [fr. Gk *thrómbos,* a clot of blood]

throm·bo·gen (θrómbədʒin) *n.* prothrombin [fr. Gk *thrómbos,* a clot of blood, lump+-*genēs,* born of]

throm·bo·sis (θrombóusis) *n.* the formation of a clot inside a blood vessel, esp. in the coronary or cerebral arteries [Mod. L. fr. Gk *thrombosis,* curdling]

throm·bus (θrómbəs) *pl.* **throm·bi** (θrómbai) *n.* a fibrinous clot formed in a blood vessel, which remains where it formed (cf. EMBOLUS) [Mod. L. fr. Gk *thrómbos,* a clot of blood]

throne (θroun) **1.** *n.* a chair (usually decorated with carving, inlaid woods or jewels etc.) reserved for the use of a sovereign, bishop etc. when he is exercising his authority, and placed on a dais in order to symbolize this authority ‖ sovereignty ‖ the sovereign ruler ‖ a raised seat for a painter's model ‖ (*pl.*) an order of angels (*ANGEL) **2.** *v.t. pres. part.* **thron·ing** *past and past part.* **throned** to place on a throne ‖ to vest with the powers of sovereignty [O.F. *trone* fr. L. fr. Gk]

throng (θrɔŋ, θrɒŋ) **1.** *n.* a great many people assembled together, esp. crowded together ‖ a great number of things crowded together, *a throng of ants* **2.** *v.i.* to move in a throng or assemble so as to form a throng ‖ *v.t.* to occupy (a space) by crowding into it [M.E. *thrang, throng* prob. shortened fr. O.E. *gethrang,* a crowd]

thros·tle (θrós'l) *n.* a song thrush ‖ (*Br.*) a worsted spinning frame [O.E. *throstle*]

throt·tle (θrót'l) **1.** *v.t. pres. part.* **throt·tling** *past and past part.* **throt·tled** to choke ‖ to reduce the supply of steam, air, gasoline etc. in (an engine) and so reduce its rate of working **2.** *n.* a valve which regulates the supply of gasoline vapor and air to an engine ‖ the hand lever or foot pedal controlling this valve [perh. dim. of THROAT]

throttle valve a throttle

through (θru:) **1.** *prep.* from one end to the other end of, *to walk through a room* ‖ in one side and out the other side of, *to climb through a window* ‖ from the beginning to the end of, during, *to sleep through the night* ‖ in the state of being or having finished, esp. successfully, *to be through one's finals* ‖ among, *the news spread through the crowd* ‖ by way of, *we came through Rome* ‖ by means of, *he got the job through her influence* ‖ by reason of, *they stopped through fear of reprisal* ‖ (with a preceding specified time) up to and including, *Monday through Friday* **2.** *adv.* in one side and out the other ‖ from end to end ‖ from the beginning to the end ‖ all the way, *this train goes through to Chicago* ‖ to a conclusion, *to see a thing through* ‖ completely, *wet through* **3.** *adj.* not involving a change of e.g. train, *a through ticket* ‖ not involving a passenger in a change, *a through train* ‖ at the end of one's abilities or resources, *he's through as a tennis player* ‖ finished, *are you through with that book?* ‖ allowing free passage, *no through way* ‖ having no further dealings, *he's through with her forever* [O.E. *thurh*]

through and through utterly, *he is a scholar through and through*

through·out (θru:áut) **1.** *adv.* continuously, from beginning to end of a distance or period of time **2.** *prep.* in or during every part of

through·put (θrú:put) *n.* (*computer*) the total product of all facets of a unit's operations

throughway *THRUWAY

throve *alt. past* of THRIVE

throw (θrou) **1.** *v. pres. part.* **throw·ing** *past* **threw** (θru:) *past part.* **thrown** (θroun) *v.t.* to cause suddenly to move through the air by a muscular effort and fling of the arm ‖ to propel through the air, *the hose throws a 20-foot jet* ‖ to cause to fall to the floor or ground ‖ to cause to move rapidly, *he threw his reserves into the battle* ‖ to project, *that lamp throws a poor light* ‖ (with 'on') to put hurriedly, *he threw a log on the fire, throw some clothes on the boy* ‖ to construct (something) quickly, *to throw a bridge across a river* ‖ to cause a sudden change in the circum-

stances of, *he was thrown out of work* ‖ to shed, *the horse threw a shoe, a snake throws its skin* ‖ (of animals) to give birth to ‖ (*card games*) to play or discard ‖ to cast (dice) ‖ to make a (specified cast) at dice ‖ (*pop.*) to lose (a contest) by choice ‖ (*pop.*) to give (a party) ‖ to twist strands of (silk) into thread ‖ to shape on a potter's wheel ‖ to activate (the lever) of a machine, engine etc. or (the switch) of an electric circuit etc. ‖ to cause (the blame) to fall on someone or something ‖ to place (an obstacle) in the way of someone ‖ to put (an automobile etc.) into a specified gear ‖ *v.i.* to cast or hurl something **to throw away** to discard as of no value ‖ to be wasteful of ‖ to fail to use (a chance) **to throw back** to reflect (light, heat etc.) ‖ to cause to fall back ‖ to revert to ancestral type **to throw in** to add as an extra, esp. without charge ‖ to interject (e.g. a remark) ‖ to engage (the clutch of a motorcar etc.) **to throw in one's lot with** to choose (one party or group) and accept its fate **to throw off** to elude (a pursuer) ‖ to cast off ‖ to emit ‖ to write or say in a casual manner ‖ to cause (hounds) to lose the scent ‖ to mislead, *his air of innocence threw them off* **to throw oneself at** to try to win the friendship or love of in too blatant a fashion **to throw oneself into** to become wholeheartedly engaged in **to throw oneself on** (or **upon**) to abandon oneself to (e.g. the mercy of someone) **to throw open** to open suddenly and completely ‖ to permit unrestricted access to ‖ **to throw out** to remove forcibly from a place ‖ to dismiss ‖ to reject ‖ to throw away ‖ to utter (e.g. a suggestion) ‖ to disengage (a clutch) ‖ (*baseball*) to put out (a runner) by throwing the ball to a baseman ‖ to upset the calculations of, disconcert ‖ to cause to stand out **to throw over** to have no more to do with ‖ to abandon **to throw together** to construct or make hastily and carelessly **to throw up** to vomit ‖ to construct very quickly ‖ to abandon (a job etc.) ‖ to remind someone uncharitably of (something) as a reproach or criticism **2.** *n.* the action of one who throws ‖ an instance of throwing ‖ the distance something is or can be thrown, *a throw of 100 yards* ‖ a cast of dice or the number cast ‖ (*geol.*) the vertical displacement of strata due to faulting ‖ (*pottery*) a period of using the wheel ‖ (*pottery*) one complete movement of the hands up the wall of a pot in throwing ‖ a light spread for a bed etc. ‖ (*mach.*) the motion of a moving part, e.g. a cam, or the extent of its motion ‖ (*wrestling*) the act of throwing an opponent or a particular method of doing this [O.E. *thráwan*]

throw·a·way (θróuəwei) *n.* a handbill

throwaway *adj.* **1.** designed to be discarded after use **2.** (*theater*) of dialogue delivered so to be hardly heard

throwaway children children (usu. ages 1–13 yrs) whose parents do not want them at home

throw·back (θróubæk) *n.* a reversion to ancestral type ‖ an instance of this ‖ someone or something exhibiting this

throw·off (θróuɔf, θróuɒf) *n.* (*printing*) a device that stops impression but allows the press to keep running

throw·ster (θroustər) *n.* a person who throws silk

throw·weight (θróuweit) *n.* (*mil.*) a measure of the warhead-carrying capacity of an ICBM

thru (θru:) *prep., adv.* and *adj.* (*pop.*) through

thrum (θrʌm) **1.** *n.* the loose fringe on a loom when the web has been cut ‖ one of the warp threads of which this consists ‖ a thread of a tassel ‖ (*pl.*) waste yarn ‖ (*naut.,* esp. *pl.*) short pieces of rope or spun yarn used e.g. to wrap around rigging to prevent chafing **2.** *v.t. pres. part.* **thrum·ming** *past and past part.* **thrummed** to cover with thrum ‖ (*naut.*) to sew thrums on (a sail) [O.E.=ligament]

thrum 1. *v. pres. part.* **thrum·ming** *past and past part.* **thrummed** *v.i.* to make a drumming sound with the fingers ‖ to play idly on a stringed instrument ‖ *v.t.* to drum on (something) with the fingers ‖ to play idly on (a stringed instrument) **2.** *n.* the act or sound of thrumming [imit.]

thrum-eyed (θrʌmaid) *adj.* (of a flower, esp. of fam. *Primulaceae*) having a short style and long stamens extending to the mouth of the tubular corolla (cf. PIN-EYED)

thrush (θrʌʃ) *n.* any of various small or medium-sized songbirds of fam. *Turdidae* incl. the song thrush and the American robin [O.E. *thrȳsce*]

thrush *n.* a disease of the mouth and throat caused by infection with a fungus. It appears in the form of slightly raised white patches on the membranes of the mouth, tongue and throat, and occurs esp. in emaciated children ‖ a suppurative and inflammatory disease of the frog of a horse's hoof [origin unknown]

thrust (θrʌst) **1.** *v. pres. part.* **thrust·ing** *past* and *past part.* **thrust** *v.t.* to push suddenly and with force, *he thrust his weight against the crowd* ‖ to cause (a weapon or sharp body) to pierce, *he thrust the dagger into his side* ‖ to force (a person) into a situation against his own or someone else's wishes ‖ to impose, *the obligation was thrust upon him* ‖ to interpose (a question etc.), esp. aggressively ‖ to force (a way) by pushing ‖ to extend (a limb, branch etc.) in some direction or into some place ‖ *v.i.* to make a sudden push ‖ to force one's way, *he thrust through the crowd* ‖ to make a stab ‖ (*rhet.*) to surge powerfully upwards or press outwards, *a great oak thrusting upwards towards the sky* **2.** *n.* a sudden violent push, e.g. with a pointed weapon ‖ the strong pressure of one part of a structure against another, e.g. of an arch on its abutments ‖ the driving force exerted through a propeller shaft, e.g. in an airplane ‖ the forward reaction to the jet exhaust of an engine ‖ (*geol.*) an almost horizontal fault [M.E. *thrusten, thrysten*]

thrust chamber (*aerospace*) the area in a propulsion rocket in which force accumulates before ejection, e.g., the reaction chamber

thrust·er or **thrust·or** (θrʌ́stə:r) *n.* (*eng.*) **1.** an engine including motor hydraulic pump and piston that produces a thrust by expelling a jet of gas, fluid, or particles **2.** (initial capitals) trade name for a device used to apply force to a brake

thrust stage (*theater*) stage sometimes including an extending runway in which audience surrounds the performing area on three sides

thru·way, through·way (θrú:wei) *n.* an expressway

Thu·cyd·i·des (θu:sídidi:z)(c. 460–c. 395 B.C.), Athenian historian. The failure of an expedition led by him during the Peloponnesian War led to his exile (424-404 B.C.). His 'History of the Peloponnesian War' (to 411 B.C.) is an impartial, concise and scientific work which sets him among the greatest ancient historians

thud (θʌd) **1.** *v.i. pres. part.* **thud·ding** *past* and *past part.* **thud·ded** to fall with or make a dull heavy sound **2.** *n.* a dull sound of short duration caused by an impact without vibration [prob. imit.]

thug (θʌg) *n.* any person who uses violence or brutality, esp. a criminal **Thug** (*hist.*) a member of an Indian religious organization of murderers and robbers (c. 13th–19th cc.) put down (1828–35) by the British under Bentinck [Hindi *ṭhai*, swindler]

thug·gee (θʌ́gi:) *n.* (*hist.*) the practice of murder and robbery by the Thugs of India [Hindi *ṭhagi*]

Thu·le (θú:li:) the name given by the Greeks and Romans to an island (Iceland, Norway, or most probably one of the Shetlands) which was the most northerly part of the then known world

Thule a former trading center in N.W. Greenland, now a U.S. strategic base

thu·li·um (θú:li:əm) *n.* a chemical element (symbol Tm, at. no. 69, at. mass 168.934) belonging to the rare-earth group [Mod. L. fr. THULE]

thumb (θʌm) **1.** *n.* the short thick digit of the hand which is opposable to the fingers and is also distinguished from them by having only two phalanges ‖ the part of a glove or mitten which covers this digit ‖ the corresponding digit in an animal **all thumbs** clumsy in handling something **under someone's thumb** completely dominated by someone **2.** *v.t.* to handle or manipulate with the thumb, *to thumb the pages of a book* ‖ to try to stop (a driver or his car) in order to get a ride ‖ to make (one's way) by this method **to thumb a ride, thumb a lift** to hitchhike **to thumb through** to turn over the pages of (a book etc.) in a quick reading or search [O.E. *thuma*]

thumb index an index in which the initial letters or titles are made visible by grooves or tabs **thúmb-in·dex** *v.t.* to supply with a thumb index

thumb·nail (θʌ́mneil) **1·** *n.* the nail of the thumb **2.** *adj.* very small or concise, *a thumbnail sketch*

thumb piano *MBIRA

thumb·print (θʌ́mprint) *n.* an impression made by the inside top joint of the thumb

thumb·screw (θʌ́mskru:) *n.* a screw with a flattened head that may be turned with the thumb and finger ‖ (*hist.*) an instrument of torture in which the thumb was crushed

thumbs-down (θʌ́mzdáun) *n.* a signal of rejection or disapproval

thumb·stall (θʌ́mstɔl) *n.* a leather sheath worn to protect the thumb ‖ a rubber device worn on the thumb, e.g. to help one in sorting mail

thumbs-up (θʌ́mzʌ́p) *n.* a signal of acceptance or approval **thumbs up!** good luck!

thumb·tack (θʌ́mtæk) *n.* (*Am.=Br.* drawing pin) a tack or pin with a round, flat head, used esp. for fastening paper to a drawing board or bulletin board

thump (θʌmp) **1.** *v.t.* to strike with a thump ‖ to defeat heavily ‖ (with 'out') to play (a tune) in a loud, unmusical way, esp. on the piano ‖ *v.i.* to deliver thumps ‖ to fall with a thump ‖ to make the noise of a thump or thumps, *his heart thumped in his chest* **2.** *n.* a dull, heavy blow, or the sound of it **thump·ing** *adj.* (*pop.*) very big, *a thumping price* [imit.]

thun·der (θʌ́ndər) **1.** *n.* the sound accompanying an atmospheric electrical discharge (i.e. lightning) due to the explosive expansion of suddenly heated air ‖ loud sounds compared with this, *the thunder of horses' hoofs* ‖ vehement rhetoric **to steal someone's thunder** to use the ideas, arguments etc. of someone before he can use and get credit for them himself **2.** *v.i.* (*impers.*) to produce the sound of thunder ‖ to produce a very loud sound ‖ to utter violent denunciations ‖ *v.t.* to utter in a thundering voice [O.E. *thunor*]

Thunder Bay, a city (pop. 112,486) and port in Ontario, Canada, on Lake Superior. Formerly Fort William, it handles enormous outgoing shipments of grain, newsprint and furs and incoming freights of coal

thun·der·bolt (θʌ́ndərboult) *n.* a single, intense discharge of electricity, accompanied by the sound of thunder ‖ an imaginary missile hurled to earth when a great clap of thunder bursts ‖ a conventional representation of this ‖ something or someone destructive or violent

Thunderbolt II *n.* (*mil.*) a twin-engine, subsonic, turbofan, STOL tactical fighter/bomber (A-110), equipped with a 30-mm cannon, capable of employing a variety of air-to-surface launched weapons in the close air support role, and is supplemented by air refueling; manufactured by Fairchild and Republic

Thunderchief *n.* (*mil.*) a supersonic, single-engine, turbojet-powered tactical, all-weather fighter (F-105), capable of delivering nuclear or nonnuclear weapons and rockets, equipped with the Sidewinder weapon and an in-flight refueling capacity

thun·der·clap (θʌ́ndərklæp) *n.* a loud crash of thunder ‖ anything that is profoundly shocking because of its suddenness, violence etc.

thun·der·cloud (θʌ́ndərklaud) *n.* a dense cloud of water drops which, by coalescing, have acquired electric charges equal to, and likely to exceed, their capacities

thun·der·head (θʌ́ndərhed) *n.* a round mass of cumulus cloud with shining white edges that often appears before a thunderstorm

thun·der·ing (θʌ́ndəriŋ) *adj.* that thunders ‖ (*pop.*) extremely big or impressive, *a thundering lie*

thun·der·ous (θʌ́ndərəs) *adj.* like thunder, esp. in its loudness

thun·der·show·er (θʌ́ndərʃauər) *n.* a rain shower accompanied by thunder and lightning

thun·der·storm (θʌ́ndərstɔrm) *n.* a storm of rain and wind accompanied by lightning and thunder

thun·der·strick·en (θʌ́ndərstrikən) *adj.* thunderstruck

thun·der·struck (θʌ́ndərstrʌk) *adj.* temporarily deprived of the power to speak or think by a sudden access of emotion, esp. astonishment

thun·der·y (θʌ́ndəri·) *adj.* thundering or threatening to thunder

Thur. Thursday

Thur·ber (θə́:rbər), James (1894-1961), U.S. humorist and cartoonist, author of 'The Owl in the Attic' (1931), 'Thurber Country' (1953) etc.

Thur·gau (tú:rgau) a German-speaking, largely Protestant canton (area 397 sq. miles, pop. 183,795) of N. Switzerland, on Lake Constance. Capital: Frauenfeld (pop. 11,000)

Thü·ring·er Wald (týriŋərvɔlt) a wooded mountain range (rising to 3,225 ft) on the southwest border of East Germany, with scattered industries (glassmaking, light engineering)

Thu·rin·gi·a (θuríndʒi:ə) (G. Thüringen) a former state of East Germany in the central German highland, now included in the districts of Suhl, Erfurt and Gera. (Other centers: Weimar, Eisenach.) The wooded Harz Mtns in the north, and Thüringer Wald in the south, descend to the fertile Thuringian basin on the upper Saale. Agriculture: cereals, root vegetables, market produce, fruit, flowers, wine. Industries: engineering, light manufacturing. An old tribal land conquered by the Franks (6th–8th cc.), it passed (14th c.) to the ruling house of Saxony and split into several duchies, which joined the German Empire (1871) and were united in 1920

Thur·mond (θə́:rmənd), (James) Strom (1902-), U.S. political leader, Senator (South Carolina). He ran (1948) as the presidential candidate for the States' Rights Democratic party ('Dixiecrats'), comprising Southerners who bolted the Democratic party in opposition to President Harry Truman's civil rights program. Elected to the Senate as a Democrat in 1954, he became a Republican in 1964; chairman of the Judiciary Committee from 1981

Thurs. Thursday

thu·ri·ble (θúərəb'l) *n.* a censer [fr. L. *thuribulum*]

thu·ri·fer (θúərəfər) *n.* an acolyte who carries and swings a censer [Mod. L. fr. *thus* (*thuris*), incense + -*fer*, bearing]

Thu·rin·gi·an (θuríindʒi:ən) *adj.* of or relating to Thuringia

Thurs·day (θə́:rzdi:, θə́:rzdei) *n.* the fifth day of the week [O.E. *Thunres-dæg, thursdæg, thuresdæg*, Thor's day]

thus (ðʌs) *adv.* in this way, *do it thus* ‖ for this reason, *he was not there and thus you could not have seen him* ‖ to this extent or degree, *thus far* ‖ as an example of what immediately precedes [O.E.]

Thut·mo·se I (θʌtmóusə) (d. c. 1508 B.C.), Egyptian pharaoh (c. 1525–c. 1508 B.C.) of the 18th dynasty. He conquered Nubia as far as the third cataract of the Nile and Syria as far as the Euphrates

Thutmose III (d. c. 1436 B.C.), Egyptian pharaoh (c. 1490–c. 1436 B.C.) of the 18th dynasty, son of Thutmose I. He ruled jointly until c. 1469 B.C. with his wife and half sister Hatshepsut. He firmly established Egyptian rule in Syria and built up an empire stretching to the Euphrates

thwack (θwæk) **1.** *v.t.* to whack **2.** *n.* a flat heavy blow [prob. imit.]

thwart (θwɔrt) **1.** *v.t.* to prevent (a plan) from being carried out ‖ to prevent (someone) from carrying out a plan **2.** *adj.* transverse **3.** *adv.* transversely **4.** *n.* (*naut.*) an oarsman's seat at right angles to the length of the boat [Early M.E. *thwert* fr. O.N. *thvert*, transverse]

thy (ðai) *possessive adj.* (THINE before an initial vowel and in the absolute) of or pertaining to or done by thee [Early M.E. *thī*]

Thy·es·tes (θaiésti:z) *ATREUS

thyme (taim) *n.* a member of *Thymus*, fam. *Labiatae*, a genus of plants found chiefly in Mediterranean regions. They are low aromatic shrubs with tiny leaves and small bilabiate purple flowers. Oil used in thymol is obtained from the foliage. *T. vulgaris*, the common garden thyme, is used for seasoning in cooking [fr. F. *thym* fr. L. fr. Gk]

thy·mine (θáimi:n) *n.* a crystalline pyrimidine base ($C_5H_6N_2O_2$) obtained by hydrolysis from deoxyribonucleic acid [fr. G. *thymin*]

thy·mol (θáimɔl) *n.* an aromatic phenol, $CH_3C_6H_3(C_3H_7)OH$, derived from the natural oil of thyme and used as an antiseptic

thy·mus (θáiməs) *n.* a ductless glandular structure of undetermined function behind the breastbone, which degenerates with the onset of puberty [Mod. L. fr. Gk]

thy·ra·tron (θáirətrɔn) *n.* (*electr.*) a triode filled with argon, neon, helium, or other gas, in which ionization takes place when sufficient positive swing of the negative grid potential exists and the anode and grid potentials lose control *abbr.* TN

thy·ris·tor (θairístə:r) *n.* (*electr.*) solid-state switching device, similar to a thyratron, for semiconductors to convert alternating current in one or two directions controlled by an elec-

CONCISE PRONUNCIATION KEY: **(a)** æ, c*a*t; ɑ, c*a*r; ɔ, f*aw*n; ei, sn*a*ke. **(e)** e, h*e*n; i:, sh*ee*p; iə, d*ee*r; ɛə, b*ea*r. **(i)** i, f*i*sh; ai, t*i*ger; ə:, b*i*rd. **(o)** o, *o*x; au, c*ow*; ou, g*oa*t; u, p*oo*r; ɔi, r*oy*al. **(u)** ʌ, d*u*ck; u, b*u*ll; u:, g*oo*se; ə, b*a*cillus; ju:, c*u*be. x, lo*ch*; θ, *th*ink; ð, *b*o*th*er; z, *Z*en; ʒ, cor*s*age; dʒ, sa*v*age; ŋ, ora*n*gutang; j, *y*ak; ʃ, *fi*sh; tʃ, fe*tch*; 'l, rabb*le*; 'n, redd*en*. Complete pronunciation key appears inside front cover.

trode, e.g., a silicon-controlled rectifier, gate turn-off switch

thyrocalcitonin *CALCITONIN

thy·roid (θáirɔid) 1. *n.* an endocrine gland of many vertebrates in the pharyngeal area secreting thyroxine, which principally increases the rate of oxidative reactions in metabolism, thus greatly influencing growth and development ‖ thyroid extract 2. *adj.* of or pertaining to the thyroid [fr. Gk *thureoeidēs*, shield-shaped]

thyroid cartilage a large cartilage in the larynx

thy·rox·in (θairóksin) *n.* thyroxine

thy·rox·ine (θairóksi:n, θairóksin) *n.* (*biochem.*) a hormone secreted by the thyroid that stimulates the rate of metabolism of the entire organism

thyr·sus (θə́:rsəs) *pl.* **thyr·si** (θə́:rsai) *n.* a long shaft or spear, tipped with a pine cone and wrapped with vine leaves or ivy carried by Dionysus, the satyrs etc. ‖ (*bot.*) an inflorescence in which the main axis is racemose and the secondary axes are cymose (e.g. in the lilac) [L. fr. Gk]

thy·sa·nu·ran (θaisənúərən, θaisənjúərən) 1. *adj.* of *Thysanura*, an order of wingless insects having bristle-like caudal appendages 2. *n.* a member of this order **thy·sa·nú·rous** *adj.* [fr. Mod. L. fr. Gk *thusanos*, tassel+*oura*, a tail]

thy·self (ðaisélf) *pron.* reflexive or emphatic form of THOU

ti, *Br.* also **te** (ti:) *n.* (*mus.*) the seventh note of any diatonic scale in movable-do solmization

ti (ti:) *n.* any of many varieties of Asiatic and Pacific woody plants of genus *Cordyline*, fam. *Liliaceae* [Tahitian, Marquesan, Samoan and Maori]

Ti·a·hua·na·co (tj:awanákou, tjəwanákou) the center in W. Bolivia of a pre-Inca civilization which dominated Peru and Bolivia. The stone structures at Tiahuanaco are particularly fine. Construction began prior to 600 A.D., and additional building took place c. 1100

ti·ar·a (ti:ǽrə, ti:úrə) *n.* a coronet of usually precious metal and precious stones worn by women ‖ the triple crown worn by the pope ‖ (*hist.*) a headdress worn by ancient Persians [L. fr. Gk]

Tib·bu (tíbu:) *pl.* **Tib·bus, Tib·bu** *n.* a Negroid people living in the Tibesti Mtns area of Central Africa ‖ a member of this people

Ti·ber (táibər) (*Ital.* Tevere) a river 244 miles long, rising in the Apennines in Tuscany and flowing through Umbria and Latium to the Tyrrhenian Sea, navigable by small boats 30 miles past Rome

Ti·be·ri·as (taibíəri:əs) a town (pop. 26,000) of N. Israel on the Sea of Galilee (or Sea of Tiberias)

Ti·be·ri·us (taibíəri:əs) (Tiberius Julius Caesar Augustus, 42 B.C.–37 A.D.), second Roman emperor (14–37), adopted son of Augustus. He won military distinction in many parts of Europe, and was an efficient if austere and unpopular emperor. After 26 A.D. he lived in seclusion on Capri

Ti·bes·ti Mtns (tibésti:) a range in N. Chad, the highest part (Emi Koussi, 11,204 ft) of the central Saharan mountain system

Ti·bet (tibét) an autonomous region (area 470,000 sq. miles, pop. 1,750,000) of China. Capital: Lhasa. Language: Tibetan. Religion: Lamaism. Tibet consists largely of a plateau (averaging 13,000 ft) between the Himalayas and the Kunlun Mtns. In the south are the forested valleys of the Sutlej and Tsangpo (Brahmaputra). Livestock: yaks, goats, sheep, camels. Agriculture (barley, fruit, vegetables) is confined to the Tsangpo valley. Minerals: salt, gold, uranium, iron, coal. Manufactures: cloth, carpets, leather. A modern road (1957) links Tibet with the rest of China. HISTORY. Tibet emerged as an independent kingdom in the 7th c. It came under the influence of the Chinese T'ang dynasty and Buddhism was introduced from India (8th c.). It was conquered by the Mongols under Kublai Khan (13th c.), and by the Chinese Manchu dynasty (1720). With British encouragement, Tibet declared its independence from China (1913). It was invaded by China (1950) and a Communist administration was set up. A revolt broke out (1959) against Communist rule, and the Dalai Lama took refuge in India. The Panchen Lama took over as head of government (1959-64). In 1965, Tibet became an autonomous region of China and since 1980 has been ruled by the head of the Tibetan Communist party. In 1980, Tibetan pil-

grims were once again allowed to visit holy sites and Tibetan language and culture were no longer suppressed. In 1985 tourists were allowed to pass between Tibet and Nepal

Ti·bet·an (tibét'n) 1. *n.* a member of the native race of Tibet. Tibetans are mixed in the west and south with Indian peoples and in the east with Chinese ‖ a native or inhabitant of Tibet ‖ the Tibeto-Burman language of the Tibetans 2. *adj.* of or relating to Tibet, its people, language, culture etc.

Ti·bet·o-Bur·man (tibétoubə́:rmən) 1. *n.* a family of languages including Tibetan and Burmese ‖ a member of a people speaking a Tibeto-Burman language 2. *adj.* of or relating to any of these languages or peoples

Ti·bet·o-Bur·mese (tibétoubə́:rmí:z, tibétoubə:rmí:s) *n.* and *adj.* Tibeto-Burman

tib·i·a (tíbi:ə) *pl.* **tib·i·ae** (tíbi:i:), **tib·i·as** *n.* the inner and usually larger of the two bones between the knee and ankle of the vertebrate leg ‖ the fourth joint (from the base) of the leg of an insect [L.]

tib·i·al (tíbi:əl) *adj.* of the tibia [fr. L. *tibialis*]

Ti·bul·lus (tibλ́əs) (c. 50–19 B.C.), Roman lyric poet. He wrote elegies on love and nature

tic (tik) *n.* a sudden or recurrent twitch usually of the facial muscles [etym. doubtful]

ti·cal (təkál, tíkəl) *n.* (*pop. abbr.* tic) the baht, the basic monetary unit of Thailand [Thai fr. Malay *tikal*, a monetary unit]

tic dou·lou·reux (ti:kdu:lu:rə́:) *n.* trigeminal neuralgia [F.=painful tic]

ti·car·cil·lin [$C_{15}H_{16}N_2O_6S_2$] (taicɑrsílin) *n.* (*pharm.*) semisynthetic penicillin used in septicemia and in respiratory, genito-urinary, skin, and soft tissue infections; marketed as Ticar

Ti·ci·no (titʃí:nou) an Italian-speaking Catholic canton (area 1,088 sq. miles, pop. 265,899) in S. Switzerland. Capital: Bellinzona (pop. 12,000)

tick (tik) 1. *n.* one of the light sounds made by the escapement of a clock etc. ‖ any similar noise ‖ (*Br.*, *pop.*) a short interval of time ‖ a small distinguishing mark usually signifying agreement and used e.g. by someone checking for correctness 2. *v.i.* to make the sound of a tick or of a series of ticks ‖ *v.t.* to mark with a tick ‖ (with 'off' or 'out') to register or announce with a ticking sound ‖ (*Br.*, *pop.*, with 'off') to rebuke **to tick along** to move forward, go by or progress at an even, reasonably satisfactory rate **to tick over** (*Br.*, of an engine) to idle ‖ (*Br.*) to keep on working smoothly on minimum effort [prob. imit.]

tick *n.* any of various arachnids of the superfamily *Ixododae*, related to mites but larger than these. An adult tick has an oval nonsegmented body with a movable head through which it draws blood from man and other animals after burrowing under the skin. Ticks transmit various infectious diseases, e.g. Rocky Mountain spotted fever ‖ any of various parasitic dipterous insects, e.g. the sheep ked [M.E. *teke*, *tyke* prob. fr. O.E.]

tick *n.* a case or covering containing feathers, hair etc., used to form a mattress, pillow etc. ‖ ticking [fr. L. *teca*, *theca* fr. Gk]

tick *n.* (*Br.*, *pop.*) credit, *to buy on tick* ‖ (*securities*) a change in price up or down [shortened fr. TICKET]

tick·er (tíkər) *n.* a telegraphic instrument that prints news, stock quotations etc. on a paper ribbon

ticker tape the paper ribbon used in a ticker

tick·et (tíkit) 1. *n.* a tag (label) showing the price, material etc. of an article ‖ a piece of paper or cardboard authorizing the bearer to use a specified service, *a train ticket* or to be admitted to a concert, meeting, theater etc. ‖ a document serving as a license, *captain's ticket* ‖ the candidates of a particular political party ‖ the principles and program of a political party ‖ (*pop.*) a means of getting something desirable, *a car is the ticket to happiness* ‖ a notice issued to someone who has violated a traffic regulation 2. *v.t.* to attach a ticket to ‖ to provide a ticket for [F. *étiquette*]

ticket inspector (*Br.*) the conductor on a train

ticket-of-leave man (*Br. hist.*) a convict released from prison but required to report regularly to the police and behave well

tick·ing (tíkiŋ) *n.* a strong heavy cotton material of which mattress or pillow covers are made

tick·le (tík'l) 1. *v.t. pres. part.* **tick·ling** past and past part. **tick·led** *v.t.* to touch (someone, or a part of the body) where the nerve ends are numerous and sensitive, and by so doing to

cause laughter, spasmodic movement etc. ‖ to capture (trout etc.) with bare hands ‖ to excite agreeably ‖ *v.i.* to have a tingling sensation **to tickle (someone) pink** (or **to death**) to make (someone) very pleased indeed or amuse (someone) intensely 2. *n.* a tickling or being tickled ‖ a tickling sensation **tick·lish** (tíkliʃ) *adj.* sensitive to tickling ‖ needing very careful handling, difficult, *a ticklish situation* ‖ sensitive, touchy, *he is ticklish on points of protocol* [etym. doubtful]

Tick·nor (tíknər, tíknɔr), William Davis (1810-64), U.S. publisher, the first to pay foreign authors for rights in their works. He became (1832) a founder of Ticknor and Fields, a firm which published the works of famous contemporaries

tick off *v.* (*colloq.*) to make irate

tick-tack (tíktæk) *n.* (*Br.*) a code of signaling with hands and arms used by men employed at a race track by bookmakers to keep them informed about the trends in the betting

tick-tack-toe (tíktæktóu) *n.* (*Am.*=*Br.* naughts-and-crosses) a game of skill in which two players take turns marking Xs and Os, respectively, on a nine-spaced figure formed by two pairs of parallel lines intersecting at right angles. The first to complete a diagonal or row with his marks is the winner

tick·y-tack·y (tíki:tǽki:) *adj.* (*slang or colloq.*) undistinguished, shoddy —**ticky-tack** *n.*

Ti·con·der·o·ga, Fort (taikɔndəróugə) a British fort in N.E. New York, captured (1775) during the Revolutionary War by American troops under Benedict Arnold and Ethan Allen

tid·al (táid'l) *adj.* pertaining to, due to or affected by the tides

tidal barrage a barrier in a watercourse which utilizes the natural movements of the tide, usually to generate electricity (*TIDAL POWER STATION)

tidal dock a dock within which the depth of water varies with the tides, i.e. is at the same level as the water outside it

tidal power station a construction by means of which the inrush and outrush of seawater, during the flow and ebb of the tides, into and out of an enclosed reservoir, operate turbines which generate electricity

tidal wave an unusually large wave or very high water, esp. one caused by an earthquake ‖ a sudden spread of intense emotion throughout a community or some other reaction on a big scale, e.g. as manifest in a very large majority vote

tid·bit (tídbit) *n.* a dainty or delicate morsel of food ‖ an interesting bit of information, gossip etc.

tid·dly-wink (tídli:wiŋk) *n.* a piece used in tiddlywinks **tíd·dly-winks** *pl. n.* a game in which small disks are flicked by the downward and backward slipping pressure of a larger disk into a small container [origin unknown]

tide (taid) 1. *n.* the alternate rising and falling of the seas, usually twice a day, in response to the gravitational attractions of the moon and sun ‖ (in compounds only) a period of time, esp. the season of one of the great Christian festivals, *Christmas-tide* ‖ something thought of as ebbing and flowing like the tide, *the tide of public opinion* 2. *v. pres. part.* **tid·ing** past and past part. **tid·ed** *v.i.* (*naut.*) to use the tide in entering or leaving an estuary, harbor etc. ‖ to flow like the tide ‖ *v.t.* to carry with the tide **to tide over** to see (someone) safely through a temporary difficulty [O.E. *tīd*, time]

tide·land (táidlænd) *n.* land that is exposed at low tide and covered at high tide

tide rip rough water caused by opposing tides or currents

tide·wa·ter (táidwɔtər, táidwɔtər) *n.* the water that overflows a land surface at flood tide ‖ low coastal land affected by the tide

tide·way (táidwei) *n.* the channel, part of a river etc. in which tidal currents flow

ti·di·ly (táidili:) *adv.* in a tidy manner

ti·di·ness (táidi:nis) *n.* the state or quality of being tidy

ti·dings (táidiŋz) *pl. n.* (*rhet.*) news [O.E. *tidung*, an event]

ti·dy (táidi:) 1. *comp.* **ti·di·er** *superl.* **ti·di·est** *adj.* in place, in order, *tidy hair* ‖ in the habit of arranging things in their proper places, *a tidy housekeeper* ‖ (*pop.*) substantial, large, *a tidy sum* 2. *v.t. pres. part.* **ti·dy·ing** past and past part. **ti·died** (esp. with 'up') to make tidy, *to tidy up a room* 3. *n. pl.* **ti·dies** a lace or other cover

CONCISE PRONUNCIATION KEY: **(a)** æ, c*a*t; ɑ, c*a*r; ɔ f*aw*n; ei, sn*a*ke. **(e)** e, h*e*n; i:, sh*ee*p; iə, d*ee*r; ɛə, b*ea*r. **(i)** i, f*i*sh; ai, t*i*ger; ə:, b*i*rd. **(o)** o, *o*x; au, c*ow*; ou, g*oa*t; u, p*oo*r; ɔi, r*oy*al. **(u)** ʌ, d*u*ck; u, b*u*ll; u:, g*oo*se; ə, b*a*cillus; ju:, c*u*be. x, lo*ch*; θ, *th*ink; ð, bo*th*er; z, *Z*en; ʒ, cor*s*age; dʒ, sa*v*age; ŋ, ora*ng*utang; j, *y*ak; ʃ, *f*ish; tʃ, fe*tch*; 'l, rabb*le*; 'n, redd*en*. Complete pronunciation key appears inside front cover.

for the arms or headrest of a chair etc. to protect it from dirt or wear [M.E. fr. *tīd*, tide]

tie (tai) **1.** *v. pres. part.* **ty·ing** *past* and *past part.* **tied** *v.t.* to secure (a cord etc.) by a knot or bow ‖ to make (a knot or bow) in a cord etc. ‖ to prevent from moving by means of a knotted cord etc. ‖ to fasten together or connect firmly ‖ to prevent the freedom of action of, *tied to one's bed by illness* ‖ to be equal with in a competition ‖ (*mus.*) to join (notes) by a line ‖ to put under some conditional relationship, *the house is tied to the job* ‖ *v.i.* to be closed or fastened by means of a tie ‖ to be equal in a competition, *they tied for third place* **to tie down** to fasten down (e.g. a hatch) ‖ to commit (e.g. capital) so as to leave one without freedom of action **to tie in** to link (an additional part) with a whole ‖ to arrange so as to be coordinated and not to conflict with something else, *tie in your holiday plans with theirs* ‖ to be in agreement, *the statements do not tie in* **to tie up** to fasten (someone or something) by tying ‖ to restrict the freedom of, esp. to cause to be so busy that invitations or engagements cannot be accepted ‖ to cause to be not readily available, *capital tied up in property* ‖ to fasten (a boat) by a hawser **2.** *n.* a cord, string etc. used for tying something ‖ something which restricts freedom of movement, e.g. a beam holding together a structure ‖ something which restricts personal freedom ‖ a linking force between two or more things, *religious ties* ‖ a competition or election that ends in a draw ‖ (*mus.*) a curved line indicating notes of the same pitch which are to have their time values run together and not be sounded separately ‖ (*Am.=Br.* sleeper) a beam of wood resting in loose stones (to allow for small lateral movement), to the surface of which are fastened the steel rails of a railroad track ‖ a necktie [O.E. *tigan*]

tie·back (táibæk) *n.* a strip of material used for tying back a curtain ‖ (*pl.*) curtains with tiebacks

tie beam a horizontal beam holding rafters in position ‖ any beam serving as a tie

Tieck (ti:k), Ludwig (1773-1853), German Romantic poet, dramatist and novelist. One of his most successful books was 'Volksmärchen von Peter Lebrecht' (1795-6, 3 vols) a collection of fairy tales, poetry and satiric dramas. He was also a literary scholar, critic and translator

tied cottage (*Br.*) a cottage which a farm worker can live in only so long as he is employed by its owner

tied house (*Br.*) a public house whose manager is free to sell the beer etc. only of the brewer to whom the place belongs (cf. FREE HOUSE)

tie-dye (táidai) *v.* to create designs in fabrics by knotting them before immersion in a dye so that some areas are not colored —**tie-dyed** *adj.* *Cf* BANDHIA

Tien Shan (tjénʃán) a mountain range running along the Kirghizia-China border through central Sinkiang-Uighur, with several peaks over 15,000 ft (summit: 23,260 ft, in the center), and caravan passes over 12,000 ft. Three glaciers around the central peaks are 48, 44 and 31 miles long

Tien·tsin (tjéntsín) a port (pop. 4,250,000) in Hopei, N. China, on the Grand Canal, commercial center of the N. China plain. Industries: metallurgy, chemicals, textiles, food processing. University (1919). A treaty signed here (1858) opened China to European trade. The city was governed by an international commission (1900-7) after the Boxer Rebellion

Tie·po·lo (tjépɔlɔ), Giovanni Battista (1696-1770), Italian painter. The influence of Veronese is seen in his frescoes, with their splendid figures in elaborate colorful costume seen from a characteristically low viewpoint against a cloudless bright sky. He decorated numerous palaces in Würzburg and in Madrid. He is also known as a draftsman and etcher

tier (tiər) **1.** *n.* one of two or more parallel rows of seats at different levels, e.g. in a Greek theater ‖ one of any comparable series of rows, e.g. of shelves in a greenhouse or layers of a wedding cake **2.** *v.t.* to pile or arrange in tiers [fr. older *tire* fr. F. *tire* fr. *tirer*, to elongate]

tierce (tiərs) *n.* (*fencing*) the third position for guard, parry or thrust ‖ (*heraldry*) a field of three differently colored parts ‖ (*hist.*) a liquid measure, a third of a pipe or 42 gallons ‖ (*hist.*) a cask holding this amount ‖ (*eccles.*) terce ‖ (*card games*, təːrs) a sequence of three cards of the same suit [O.F.]

tier·cel (tiərs'l) *n.* the male of certain hawks, e.g. the peregrine [O.F. *tercel*]

Tier·ra del Fue·go (tjérraðelfwégɔ) a mountainous, sparsely inhabited archipelago (area 27,595 sq. miles) at the southern tip of South America. The eastern half plus Staten Is. (area 8,095 sq. miles) belongs to Argentina, the western half (area 19,500 sq. miles) to Chile. Industries: sheep farming, fishing, trapping, petroleum extraction ‖ the main island (area 18,530 sq. miles) of this archipelago

Tier·ra y Li·ber·tad (tjérrai:li:bertáð) the Mexican crusade against oppression led by Emiliano Zapata [Span.=land and liberty]

tie-up (táiʌp) *n.* a close connection, *is there any tie-up between the firms?* ‖ a cessation of movement or action, e.g. a traffic jam

tiff (tif) **1.** *n.* an emotional mood of mild anger or indignation ‖ a slight quarrel **2.** *v.i.* to be in a tiff ‖ (with 'with') to quarrel slightly [origin unknown]

Tif·fa·ny (tífəni:), Charles Lewis 1812-1902), U.S. merchant. He founded the jewelry firm of Tiffany and Company, New York City. He introduced (1851) the English standard of sterling silver into the U.S.A.

Tiffany, Lewis Comfort (1848-1923), U.S. artist. He established the interior decorating firm known as Tiffany Studios in New York, which specialized in iridescent and Art Nouveau glass work

Tif·lis (tíflis) *TBILISI

ti·ger (táigər) *pl.* **ti·gers, ti·ger** *n. Felis tigris*, fam. *Felidae*, a large (8-10 ft long), ferocious, carnivorous mammal native to Asia. It has an orange-fawn coat irregularly crossed with black stripes, a white belly and no mane ‖ any of several related animals, e.g. the American jaguar and the S. African leopard ‖ a fiercely aggressive person in a position of authority ‖ (*Br., hist.*) a groom standing at the back of a light vehicle driven by his master [O.F. *tigre*]

tiger beetle any of several voracious carnivorous beetles of fam. *Cicindelidae* with striped or spotted wing cases

ti·ger-flow·er (táigərflʌuər) *n.* a member of *Tigridia*, fam. *Iridaceae*, a genus of tropical American bulbous plants with brilliant yellow, purple, white or orange flowers

Tiger II *n.* (*mil.*) aircraft (F-5E) carrying two 30-mm guns, missiles, etc.; made by Northrop for export

tiger lily *Lilium tigrinum*, fam. *Liliaceae*, a lily native to China, widely cultivated for its black-spotted, pendent, orange flowers

tiger moth any of various richly colored, long-winged moths of fam. *Arctiidae*

tight (tait) **1.** *adj.* closely packed, *a tight arrangement* ‖ allowing too little freedom of movement, *a tight coat* ‖ rigidly set, *a tight smile* ‖ (esp. in compounds) so constructed that air, water etc. cannot pass through, *an airtight can, watertight shoes* ‖ (of money) hard to borrow, at high interest rates ‖ (of a commodity) in short supply ‖ (of a market) characterized by scarcity ‖ strict, *tight control* ‖ (*pop.*) drunk ‖ (*pop.*) stingy ‖ (of a contest) in which the opponents are evenly matched, *a tight game* ‖ (of a situation) difficult or dangerous to deal with ‖ (*printing*, of a page) too full of matter ‖ (*printing*, of setting) characterized by having very little space between words **2.** *adv.* in a tight way **to sit tight** to avoid action and bide one's time **tight·en** *v.t.* to make tight ‖ *v.i.* to become tight [of Scand. origin]

tight end (*football*) an offensive end who places himself within two yds of the tackle

tight·fist·ed (táitfístid) *adj.* loath to part with money

tight-lipped (táitlípt) *adj.* making a strong effort of the will so as to surmount a difficulty and esp. so as not to betray emotion ‖ giving no secrets away

tight·rope (táitroup) *n.* a tautly stretched rope or wire, some height above the ground, on which an acrobat performs

tights (taits) *pl. n.* a skintight garment covering the body usually from the waist down

tight·wad (táitwɒd) *n.* a tightfisted person

Tig·lath-pi·le·ser I (tíglæθpailí:zər) (*d.* 1078 B.C.), king of Assyria (c.1116–1078 B.C.). A great soldier, he conquered Armenia, Cappadocia and Lebanon

Tiglath-pileser III (*d.* 728 B.C.), king of Assyria (746-728 B.C.), having usurped the throne. He conquered N. Syria

ti·gress (táigris) *n.* a female tiger ‖ a fiercetempered woman

Ti·gris (táigris) one of the two great rivers of Mesopotamia. It flows 1,150 miles from the mountains of E. Turkey through Iraq (navigable to Baghdad), joining the Euphrates to form the Shatt-al-Arab. Its middle course is liable to flood disastrously

Tih·wa (tí:wə) *URUMCHI

Ti·jua·na (ti:hwánɑ, tị:əwánə) a town (pop. 461,257) in N.W. Mexico near the U.S. border. Industries: tourism, gambling

Ti·kal (ti:kál) the largest of the ancient Mayan cities, in N. Guatemala, noted for the number of its monuments, pyramids and temples and the quality of its wood carvings

tik·chung (tiktʃú:ŋ) *n.* silver currency of Bhutan *Cf* NGULTRUM

tike *TYKE

Til·burg (tílbəːrg) a town (pop. 153,117) in North Brabant, Netherlands: textiles, railroad cars etc.

til·bur·y (tílbəri:, tílbəri:) *pl.* **til·bur·ies** *n.* (*hist.*) a light, springy, two-wheeled open carriage for two persons [after a 19th-c. British coach builder]

til·de (tíldə) *n.* a sign (˜) placed e.g. over the letter 'n' in Spanish to denote that it is pronounced as a palatal nasal sound (nj), e.g. in 'señor' ‖ this sign used in Portuguese to denote nasalization of a vowel [Span.]

Til·den (tíldən), Samuel Jones (1814-86), U.S. statesman. A leading New York Democrat, he played an important role in the destruction of the Tweed Ring. He ran as the Democratic presidential nominee in the disputed 1876 election, in which a new Electoral Commission voted in favor of the Republican candidate (*COMPROMISE OF 1877)

tile (tail) **1.** *pl.* **tiles, tile** *n.* a thin, usually rectangular piece of fired, unglazed clay, sometimes ogee-shaped when used on roofs or walls ‖ a square or shaped piece of fired clay or other material (e.g. vinyl) used for flooring ‖ a similar piece of porcelain or other glazed ware, used ornamentally ‖ an earthenware or concrete drainpipe ‖ a small flat piece of baked earthenware used in covering vessels in which metals are fused ‖ tiling **2.** *v.t. pres. part.* **til·ing** *past* and *past part.* **tiled** to cover with tiles **til·ing** *n.* the process of covering with tiles ‖ tiles collectively ‖ a surface covered with tiles [O.E. *tigule, tigele*]

till (til) *n.* (*geol.*) boulder clay [origin unknown]

till *n.* a money drawer or tray, e.g. in a bank ‖ a cash register ‖ the money contained in any of these [origin unknown]

till 1. *prep.* up to the time of, *he waited till 10 p.m.* **2.** *conj.* up to the time when, until, *wait till he comes* [Old Northumbrian *til* fr. O.N.]

till *v.t.* (*rhet.*) to work (the soil) for cultivation **till·age** *n.* the tilling of the soil ‖ land that has been tilled ‖ the crops on such land [O.E. *tilian*, to strive]

til·ler (tílər) *n.* (*naut.*) the lever arm by means of which the rudder is turned [O.F. *telier, tellier*]

tiller 1. *n.* one of the side shoots of a plant, esp. of grasses and cereals, sprouting from the base of the axils of the lower leaves ‖ a sapling or young tree, esp. a shoot sprouting from the stump of a felled tree **2.** *v.i.* to put forth tillers [prob. fr. O.E. *telgor*]

Til·ley (tíli:), Sir Samuel Leonard (1818-96), Canadian statesman. As minister of finance (1878-85) in the 2nd Sir John Alexander Macdonald administration, he introduced (1878) the protective tariff plan which became the basis of Canadian financial policy

Til·lich (tílix), Paul Johannes (1886-1965), U.S. theologian. He incorporated depth psychology into Christian doctrine, postulating that faith is 'ultimate concern', that God is the 'ground of being' or 'being-itself', and that man should strive for 'new being', rather than salvation

Til·ly (tíli:), Johann Tserklaes, count of (1559-1632), general of the Catholic League during the Thirty Years' War, in which he won the battles of the White Mountain (1620), Magdeburg (1631) and Breitenfeld (1631). He was defeated (1632) by Gustavus II of Sweden, and mortally wounded

Tilos *TELOS

Til·sit (tílzit) *SOVETSK

Tilsit, Treaty of a treaty signed July 1807, by France, Russia and Prussia. Part of Prussia became the Grand Duchy of Warsaw, part went to Russia and part to Saxony. The Prussian army was limited to 42,000 men. The Confederation of the Rhine was recognized

tilt (tilt) 1. *v.i.* to slant from the horizontal or the vertical ‖ (*hist.*) to joust ‖ *v.t.* to cause to slant from the horizontal or the vertical ‖ (*hist.*) to poise (a lance) for a thrust ‖ (*hist.*) to charge (one's opponent) in a tilt ‖ to hammer or forge (metal) with a tilt hammer 2. *n.* a tilting or being tilted ‖ (*hist.*) a joust ‖ a tilt hammer **at full tilt** at full speed [M.E. *tilten* fr. O.E. *tealt*, shaky]

tilt *n.* a covering, esp. of canvas, stretched on a frame and mounted over a wagon, a market stall, or a boat etc. [M.E. *tild* perh. influenced by 'tent']

tilth (tilθ) *n.* (*rhet.*) cultivation of the soil ‖ (*rhet.*) cultivated land [O.E. *tilth, tilthe* fr. *tilian*, to till]

tilt hammer a heavy hammer used in forging which is tilted up and then allowed to drop

tilt wheel (*automobile*) steering wheel of a motor vehicle capable of angle adjustment by the driver

tilt·yard (tíltjɑrd) *n.* (*hist.*) a place used for tilts and tournaments

tim·bal, tym·bal (tímb'l) *n.* (*hist.*) a kettledrum [F. *timbale*]

tim·bale (tímb'l, tēbɑl) *n.* a dish of creamed chicken, lobster or fish etc., seasoned and cooked in a pastry mold [F.]

tim·ber (tímbər) 1. *n.* trees yielding wood suitable for construction ‖ timberland ‖ (*Br.*) lumber (wood for construction) ‖ a thick piece of wood forming, or ready to form, part of a structure, *roof timbers* ‖ (*naut.*) one of the curved beams of wood forming the ribs of a ship 2. *interj.* a shouted warning that a tree is falling

timber *v.t.* to cover, supply, support etc. with timbers [O.E. *timbran* and *timbrian*]

tim·bered (tímbərd) *adj.* made of or furnished with timbers ‖ covered with growing timber [O.E.]

tim·ber·head (tímbərhed) *n.* (*naut.*) the upper end of a ship's timber, esp. such a timber used as a bollard

timber hitch a looped knot in a rope used in tying a rope to a spar or log

tim·ber·ing (tímbəriŋ) *n.* a construction, esp. the support network of a mineshaft, made of timbers

tim·ber·land (tímbərlænd) *n.* an expanse of trees, esp. of trees used for lumber

tim·ber·line (tímbərlɑin) *n.* the tree line

timber wolf *Canis lupus lycaon*, a large brownish-gray wolf of northern North America, now largely extinct

tim·bre (tǽmbər, tēbr) *n.* the quality of a musical sound, depending on what overtones are present and their respective amplitudes [F.]

tim·brel (tímbrəl) *n.* an ancient tambourine [dim. of M.E. *timbre*, kettledrum fr. O.F.]

Tim·buk·tu, Tim·buc·too (tɪmbʌktú) (F. Tombouctou) an ancient caravan trading center (pop. 20,483) in central Mali near the Niger on the edge of the Sahara. It flourished in the 14th-16th cc. as a center of Moslem culture and commerce

Tim·by (tímbi), Theodore Ruggles (1819-1909), U.S. inventor of the revolving turret (1843), which was the main feature of the Civil War armored vessel the 'Merrimack'

time (tɑim) 1. *n.* the physical quantity measured by clocks. In classical physics time was regarded as extending infinitely into the past and future and was considered independent of the events which defined it. This implied that the simultaneity of events was absolute, i.e. independent of the situation of the observer. The special theory and general theory of relativity radically changed this concept of time, linking it to the position and relative motion of the clock and its observer ‖ finite duration as distinguished from infinity ‖ earthly duration as distinguished from eternity ‖ a duration, *it lasted a long time* ‖ a point in progress, *at that time he was away from home* ‖ (often *pl.*) a period of history with reference to a region, person etc., *the time of Persia's supremacy* ‖ (esp. *pl.*) a period of history having certain characteristics, customs etc., *in biblical times* ‖ a specific period of a year, *harvest time*, or of a day, *dinner time* ‖ a period of duration available for certain action to be taken, *I will do it if I have the time* ‖ a period during which certain action is taken, *he served his time in the navy* ‖ the point or period appropriate to the beginning, performance or ending of a course of action, *it is time we went, it's time to make a change* ‖ a favorable period, *now is the time to buy* ‖ (*mus.*) the duration of a note or pause ‖ (*mus.*) the rhythm of a

composition in terms of the grouping of beats into bars of equal duration, indicated by the time signature ‖ (*mus.*) the tempo at which a composition is to be performed or is performed ‖ (esp. *pl.*) general conditions, *exciting times* ‖ a period characterized by a general condition or event, *a time of struggle* ‖ a period or occasion with reference to a personal reaction to it, *to have a good time* ‖ rate of speed in driving, marching, working etc. ‖ the period worked or to be worked by an employee ‖ rate of pay, esp. reckoned by the hour, *time and a half for overtime* ‖ lifetime ‖ the end of life, *his time had come* ‖ (*Br.*) closing time in a public house as fixed by law, '*Time, gentlemen, please*' ‖ end of play in a game or match formally declared by the umpire, referee etc. ‖ a period of imprisonment ‖ a term of apprenticeship ‖ the usual, allotted or shortest period during which something is done, *what is the cooking time for a boiled egg?* ‖ a repeated occasion, recurrence of the same thing, *that's the third time you've told me* ‖ (*pl.*) following a number and used with a comparative adjective or adverb to indicate magnitude, *five times higher* **against time** before a certain time and with barely enough time for what must be done **ahead of time** before the required, proper or expected moment **all the time** during all the specified period ‖ continuously ‖ very often, *he says it all the time* **at a time** in one operation, *it does six pairs at a time* **at the same time** occurring at the same point in the progress of time ‖ nevertheless, though it is so, *I like it but at the same time it frightens me* **at times** sometimes **behind time** late, in arrears **behind the times** old-fashioned, not up-to-date **for the time being** for the present, provisionally **from time to time** occasionally **in time** before a specified point in the progress of time has passed, *were you in time for the train?* ‖ after the passage of sufficient time, *we will find out in time* ‖ in the right tempo **in good time** with an ample margin of time, *he got there in good time for his train* ‖ as a happy end to a period of waiting, *and in good time they were married* **in no time** very quickly, *he did it in no time* **many a time** on many occasions **on time** at the appointed hour, on schedule ‖ (*pop.*) on the installment plan **out of time** (*mus.*) failing to sound notes at the same time as others in a choir, orchestra etc. or to keep step in marching **to gain time** to play for time, delay action until a more favorable time ‖ (of a timepiece) to go too fast **to pass the time of day** to stop for a little chat **to take one's time** to take all the time one needs to do something ‖ to be slow doing something 2. *v.t. pres. part.* **tim·ing** *past* and *past part.* **timed** to cause to occur at a particular point in the progress of time, *he timed his arrival for nightfall* ‖ to measure the duration of ‖ to adjust the performance of (something) so that it occupies a particular portion of time, *he timed his speech to last 20 minutes* ‖ to set the rhythm or tempo of 3. *adj.* having to do with time ‖ regulated to open, explode etc. at a given time ‖ payable at a future date ‖ having to do with payment of goods over a period of time [O.E. *tima*]

time after time repeatedly

time and again repeatedly

time and motion study a study of the time taken, and the energy used, in doing work, with a view to securing greater efficiency and establishing standards

time and time again repeatedly, esp. tiresomely often

time bomb a bomb fitted with a clockwork device which detonates it at a predetermined time

time card a card recording the time of arrival at and departure from one's place of work

time clock a clock which records on a card the time of arrival and departure of an employee

timed capsule (*pharm.*) encapsulated drug that is effective at a time later than ingestion *also* spansule

time dilation (*phys.*) the slowing of time in a speeding object as its velocity increases relative to another moving body, as hypothesized in the theory of relativity

time-ef·fec·tive (tǽimifektiv) *adj.* sufficiently rewarding to warrant the time spent

time exposure exposure of a film for a fixed time, usually more than half a second ‖ a photograph taken in this way

time frame a period of time

time fuse a fuse so contrived that it will burn

for a known time before detonating an explosive

time-hon·ored, *Br.* **time-hon·oured** (tɑimpnərd) *adj.* having the authority that goes with long custom

time·keep·er (tɑimkiːpər) *n.* (*Br.*) a clock or watch, esp. with regard to its efficiency, *a good timekeeper* ‖ someone whose job is to observe and record the time or duration of a game, race etc., e.g. of a round in a boxing match ‖ someone who records the hours worked by employees

time lag a period of time which passes before a cause produces its effect ‖ a delay

time·less (tɑimlis) *adj.* not limited by time ‖ unaffected by the passing of time

time·li·ness (tɑimliːnis) *n.* the state or quality of being timely

time·ly (tɑimliː) *comp.* **time·li·er** *superl.* **time·li·est** *adj.* at a very suitable time, opportune

time out a pause in work or other activity ‖ (*football, basketball* etc.) any time requested, e.g. to make substitutions, discuss strategy etc., during play and not counted in the playing time

time·piece (tɑimpiːs) *n.* any instrument used for measuring time

time reversal (*phys.*) the principle that a sequence of operations will occur in reverse order if the time sequence is reversed

times (tɑimz) *prep.* multiplied by

time-sav·ing (tɑimsɑiviŋ) *adj.* enabling work etc. to be done in less time

time-serv·er (tɑimsərvər) *n.* a person who adapts his actions to please someone in authority instead of acting according to his convictions **time-serv·ing** *adj.*

time sharing 1. (*computer*) arrangement for use of equipment on an hourly basis 2. (*real estate*) purchase of a property for use at a specified time only, e.g., for vacations

time signal a broadcast to announce the exact time of day so that clocks and watches can be synchronized

time signature a sign denoting the tempo of a piece of music, placed after the key signature. It is usually a fraction, the denominator of which indicates the kind of note taken as the unit, the numerator indicating the number of these to a bar

time·ta·ble (tɑimteibʹl) *n.* a tabulated list of the times at which certain events or activities are required to occur, or the order of occurrence ‖ a schedule of arrival and departure times of regular services of buses, trains, aircraft etc.

time-test·ed (tɑimtestəd) *adj.* not disproved over a long period

time trial (*sports*) a competition in which the recorded time is used as the basis of judging the winner

time·work (tɑimwərk) *n.* work paid for by the day or by the hour (cf. PIECEWORK)

time-worn (tɑimwɔrn) *adj.* hackneyed ‖ showing signs of wear because of age

time zone any of the 24 zones, each approx. 15° of longitude in width, into which the globe is divided successively from the Greenwich meridian, for maintaining a regular sequence of time changes, each 1 hour earlier than in the zone immediately east of it

tim·id (tímid) *adj.* very sensitive to real or imagined causes of fear ‖ lacking self-confidence [fr. L. *timidus*]

ti·mid·i·ty (timíditiː) *n.* the state or quality of being timid [fr. L. *timiditas*]

tim·ing (tɑimiŋ) *n.* the regulation of the speed of e.g. an engine or a theatrical production so as to give the most effective result

Ti·mi·şoa·ra (tɪmiːʃwɑrɑ) a communications center (pop. 288,237) in Banat, W. Rumania. Industries: textiles, food processing. Castle (16th c.). University (1945)

Ti·mor (tíːmɔr) a mountainous island (area 13,071 sq. miles) of the Lesser Sundas, part of Indonesia. The Indonesian province East Nusa Tenggara occupies the western half with its capital at Kupang (pop. 7,000). People: Malay-Papuan, with small Negrito (interior) and Chinese minorities. Religion: Christian and Moslem. The north is savanna, while the center and south are largely covered with rain forest. Highest point: 9,678 ft, in the east. Exports: sandalwood, copra, trepang, some coffee, meat and fish. HISTORY. The island was visited by the Portuguese (16th c.), but their control over it was challenged after 1613 by the Dutch. Timor was partitioned between them (1859). After Japanese occupation of the island (1942-5), Dutch

Timor became part of Indonesia. Divided between Portuguese Timor (E half) and Ambeno (W half) until the Portuguese left in 1975, Timor now consists of two provinces, West and East, with Kupang and Dili as respective provincial capitals. An independence movement, Fretelin, was suppressed by Indonesia following the Portuguese departure and East Timor was formally incorporated as Indonesia's 27th province in 1976

tim·o·rous (tímərəs) *adj.* timid, easily frightened ‖ indicating or marked by timidity, *a timorous voice* [O.F. *temeros, temerous*]

Timor Sea the part of the Indian Ocean between N. Australia and Timor

Tim·o·thy (tíməθi:), St (*d. c.* 97), first bishop of Ephesus, companion and helper of St Paul. Feast: Jan. 24

tim·o·thy (tíməθi:) *n. Phleum pratense*, a long, spiked European grass introduced into North America and grown chiefly for hay [prob. after *Timothy* Hanson, who introduced it c. 1720 into the U.S.A.]

Timothy and Titus, Epistles to the 15th, 16th and 17th books of the New Testament, three encyclical letters of doubtful authorship, written in the late 1st c. or early 2nd c., warning against heresies. They are known as the Pastoral Epistles

timothy grass timothy

tim·pa·ni, tym·pa·ni (tímpəni:) *pl. n.* a set of two or more kettledrums played by one man in an orchestra or band **timpanist** *TYMPANIST [Ital., pl. of *timpano*, kettledrum]

Tim·rod (tímrɒd), Henry (1828-67), U.S. poet, known as the 'laureate of the Confederacy'. His works include 'The Cotton Boll' and 'Ethnogenesis'

Ti·mur (timúər) (Tamerlane, c. 1336-1405), Mongol conqueror. Having gained the throne of Samarkand, he tried to reunite the empire of Genghis Khan, conquering the Tatars (1392) and the Turks (1402). He died during an invasion of China

tin (tin) **1.** *n.* a lustrous, silvery metallic element (symbol Sn, at. no. 50, at. mass 118.70) which is soft, malleable, ductile and resistant to the chemical action of air and water at ordinary temperatures ‖ (*Br.*) a can (container for preserving foodstuffs) ‖ tinplate **2.** *v.t. pres. part.* **tin·ning** *past* and *past part.* **tinned** to coat with tin ‖ (*Br.*) to can (preserve by packing in an airtight can) **3.** *adj.* made of tin [O.E.]
—Tin occurs mainly as the oxide, cassiterite, the principal sources being Malaya, Indonesia, Bolivia and the Congo. It is extracted by reducing the concentrated ore with carbon at 1,200–1,300° C. Refined tin is used in the manufacture of tinplate and as an alloy in solder, bronze, Babbitt metal etc. Lesser uses include the manufacture of tinfoil and of collapsible tubes for packaging

tin·a·mou (tínəmu:) *n.* any of various members of *Tinamidae*, a family of South American birds which resemble partridges. They are heavily built and measure from 9–15 ins long. Their eggs have a curious metallic luster [F. fr. Galibi (Carib) *tinamu*]

Tin·ber·gen (tínbɛərgən), Jan (1903-69), Dutch economist, who shared the first Nobel prize for economics (1969) with Ragnar Frisch. He won the award for constructing econometric systems—developing and using mathematical models to analyze and structure economic behavior. His books include 'Shaping the World Economy' (1962) and 'Development Planning' (1967)

Tinbergen, Nikolaas (1907-), Dutch zoologist and ethologist, who shared the Nobel prize for physiology or medicine (1973) with Konrad Lorenz and Karl von Frisch. A pioneer in the study of animal behavior under natural conditions, Tinbergen analyzed specific stimuli that elicit specific responses in animals. His works include 'The Study of Instinct' (1951), 'Social Behavior in Animals' (1953), 'The Herring Gull's World' (1960) and 'Animal Behavior' (1965)

tin·cal (tíŋkʼl) *n.* a crude, commercial, hydrated borax [Malay *tingkal*]

Tin·che·brai, Battle of (tɛ̃ʃbrei) a battle in Normandy (1106) in which Henry I of England defeated his brother Robert II of Normandy

tinc·to·ri·al (tiŋktóri:əl, tiŋktóuri:əl) *adj.* pertaining to color, esp. that of a dye [fr. L. *tinctorius*]

tinc·ture (tíŋktʃər) **1.** *n.* a solution, usually in alcohol, of a medicinal substance, *tincture of* iodine ‖ a slight coloration ‖ an imbued quality, *a tincture of liberalism* ‖ (*heraldry*) any of the colors, metals or furs used in emblazoning **2.** *v.t. pres. part.* **tinc·tur·ing** *past* and *past part.* **tinc·tured** to add a trace of color to ‖ to imbue slightly with a specified quality [fr. L. *tinctura* a dyeing]

Tindal, Tindale *TYNDALE

tin·der (tíndər) *n.* a dry substance with a low ignition temperature, readily ignited by a spark [O.E. *tynder, tyndre*]

tin·der·box (tíndərbɒks) *n.* (*hist.*) a small metal box containing charred linen as tinder and equipped with a flint and steel for making a spark

tine (tain) *n.* one of the thin, pointed parts of an antler, fork, harrow etc. [O.E. *tind*]

tin·e·a (tíni:ə) *n.* (*med.*) any of several fungus skin infections, esp. ringworm [L.=worm, moth]

tin·foil (tínfɔil) *n.* an alloy of lead and tin or aluminum beaten into thin sheets and used for wrapping

ting (tiŋ) **1.** *n.* a light ringing sound produced by a single tap e.g. on a small bell **2.** *v.i.* to make this sound ‖ *v.t.* to cause to make this sound [imit.]

tinge (tindʒ) **1.** *v.t. pres. part.* **tinge·ing, ting·ing** *past* and *past part.* **tinged** to impart a little color or flavor to ‖ to impart a certain slight quality to, *thanks tinged with envy* **2.** *n.* the color, flavor, quality etc. imparted [fr. L. *tingere*, to stain]

tin·gle (tíŋgʼl) **1.** *v. pres. part.* **tin·gling** *past* and *past part.* **tin·gled** *v.i.* to have a sensation as if the skin were being gently pricked or stung at innumerable points ‖ *v.t.* to cause to have this sensation **2.** *n.* this sensation [var. of TINKLE]

ti·ni·ly (táinili) *adv.* in a tiny way

ti·ni·ness (táini:nis) *n.* the state or quality of being tiny

tink·er (tíŋkər) **1.** *n.* an itinerant tinsmith who mends metal kitchen utensils ‖ (in Ireland and Scotland) a gipsy or wandering beggar **2.** *v.t.* to mend (metal utensils) ‖ *v.i.* to make an amateurish attempt to repair or adjust something [M.E. *tinkere*]

tin·kle (tíŋkʼl) **1.** *v. pres. part.* **tin·kling** *past* and *past part.* **tin·kled** *v.i.* to make a succession of light metallic tings ‖ *v.t.* to cause to make these sounds **2.** *n.* a tinkling sound [prob. frequentative of older *tink*, to emit a metallic sound]

tin·man (tínmən) *pl.* **tin·men** (tínmen) *n.* a tinsmith

tin·ni·ly (tínili:) *adv.* in a tinny manner

tin·ni·ness (tíni:nis) *n.* the quality or state of being tinny

tin·ni·tus (tináitəs) *n.* a ringing sound in the ears not caused by any external stimulation [L. fr. *tinnire*, to tinkle]

tin·ny (tíni:) *comp.* **tin·ni·er** *superl.* **tin·ni·est** *adj.* of or containing tin ‖ like tin, esp. in sound, taste or material

Tinos *TENOS

Tin Pan Alley the commercial world of popular music publishers and composers

tin·plate (tínpleit) *n.* thin sheet steel or iron coated with tin **tín·plate** *pres. part.* **tin·plat·ing** *past* and *past part.* **tin·plat·ed** *v.t.* to coat with tin

tin·pot (tínpɒt) *adj.* (*pop.*) poor in conception, execution or quality

tin pyrites stannite

tin·sel (tínsəl) **1.** *n.* tin, brass or an alloy with a bright luster, beaten into very thin sheets and used in thin strips, threads etc. to give glittering decorative effects ‖ that which is brilliant but worthless **2.** *adj.* made of, or adorned with, tinsel ‖ superficially brilliant but worthless **3.** *v.t. pres. part.* **tin·sel·ing,** esp. *Br.* **tin·sel·ling** *past* and *past part.* **tin·seled,** esp. *Br.* **tin·selled** to adorn with or as if with tinsel **tín·sel·ly** *adj.* [fr. O. F. *estincelle*]

tin·smith (tínsmiθ) *n.* someone who works tin

tin·stone (tínstoun) *n.* cassiterite

tint (tint) **1.** *n.* a color containing some white (*COLOR, cf. SHADE) ‖ any lighter or darker hue of the same color ‖ a small quantity of one color present in another ‖ any slight modifying element in something ‖ (*engraving*) an effect of shadow or texture produced by a series of close parallel lines ‖ (*printing*) a background of light color, e.g. one on which a halftone block can be printed ‖ a hair dye **2.** *v.t.* to furnish with a tint [prob. fr. earlier *tinct*, perh. influenced by Ital. *tinta*]

tin·tin·nab·u·la·tion (tintinæbjuléifən) *n.* the ringing, jingling or tinkling sound of bells [fr. L. *tintinnabulum*, bell]

Tin·to·ret·to (tintərétou) (Jacopo Robusti, 1518-94), Venetian painter. He painted a vast number of magnificently conceived works, full of a sense of drama and very rich in color. They are executed with an impressionistic brushwork, unconventional and even violent contrasts of perspective, and with extreme contrasts of light and shade. The Scuola di S. Rocco in Venice was entirely decorated by him, with scenes from the life of the Virgin, the life of Christ, and Christ's Passion

tin·type (tíntaip) *n.* a positive photograph made directly on an iron plate that has been coated with a sensitized film

tin·ware (tínwɛər) *n.* articles made of tinplate

ti·ny (táini:) *comp.* **ti·ni·er** *superl.* **ti·ni·est** *adj.* exceedingly small [etym. doubtful]

tip (tip) **1.** *v.t. pres. part.* **tip·ping** *past* and *past part.* **tipped** (*baseball, cricket*) to strike (the ball) lightly with a glancing blow **2.** *n.* a light, glancing stroke [origin unknown]

tip 1. *n.* the pointed or tapering end of a long slim object ‖ a small object attached to the end of something thin, e.g. the ferrule of an umbrella, the filter of a cigarette etc. ‖ a thin brush of camel's hair etc. used for laying gold leaf in bookbinding **2.** *v.t. pres. part.* **tip·ping** *past* and *past part.* **tipped** to furnish with a tip ‖ to form the tip of [origin unknown]

tip 1. *v. pres. part.* **tip·ping** *past* and *past part.* **tipped** *v.t.* to cause to incline ‖ (often with 'over') to cause to overturn ‖ (*Br.*) to empty by tilting ‖ to raise slightly or touch (one's hat) in deference ‖ *v.i.* to become inclined ‖ (often with 'over') to become overturned **2.** *n.* a tipping or being tipped ‖ (*Br.*) a tipple (place where trucks are emptied) ‖ (*Br.*) a place where something is tipped, *a rubbish tip* [origin unknown]

tip 1. *v.t. pres. part.* **tip·ping** *past* and *past part.* **tipped**, often with 'off' to impart information to, or give useful advance warning of, in a confidential manner ‖ to forecast (something) as a winner or likely to bring in money ‖ to give a small gift of money to, esp. in recognition of services rendered **2.** *n.* a suggestion, or piece of information, privately given, esp. the probable winner of a race etc., or the best way to do something ‖ a small gift of money, esp. in recognition of services rendered [etym. doubtful]

TIP (acronym) for tax-based income policy, a system of rewarding price and wage stability and penalizing wage increases

tip·cart (típkɑrt) *n.* a vehicle with a body so pivoted that its contents may be tipped out

tip lorry *pl.* **tip lorries** (*Br.*) a dump truck

tip·off (típɒf, típɔf) *n.* a useful warning or hint conveyed privately

Tip·pe·ca·noe, Battle of (tipikənú:) an engagement (1811) in Indiana, in which William Henry Harrison led U.S. troops to victory against an Indian force headed by Tecumseh

Tip·per·ar·y (tipərɛ́əri:) an inland county (area 1,643 sq. miles, pop. 123,565) of the Irish Republic (*MUNSTER). County seat: Clonmel (pop. 11,622)

tip·pet (típit) *n.* (*hist.*) a long hanging piece of material attached to a sleeve, hood or cape ‖ (*hist.*) a short cape, esp. of fur, having loose, dangling ends ‖ an ecclesiastical vestment [origin unknown]

Tip·pett (típit), Michael Kemp (1905-), English composer. He first became known with his oratorio 'A Child of our Time' (1941), written on a political theme. He has also written operas, orchestral and chamber music, and songs

tip·ple (típʼl) **1.** *v. pres. part.* **tip·pling** *past* and *past part.* **tip·pled** *v.i.* to tend to be a drunkard ‖ *v.t.* to drink (intoxicating liquor) in small quantities at a time but persistently **2.** *n.* (*rhet.*) an alcoholic drink [rel. to Norw. dial. *tipla*, to drip slowly]

tipple *n.* (*Am.=Br.* tip) a place where loaded trucks etc. are emptied ‖ the place where tipping from wagons etc. is done

tip·si·ly (típsili:) *adv.* in a tipsy way

tip·si·ness (típsi:nis) *n.* the state or quality of being tipsy

tip·staff (típstæf, típstɑf) *n.* a lawcourt official [contr. of 'tipped staff' from his former badge of office]

tip·ster (típstər) *n.* a person who supplies racing tips or other information, usually for a fee

tip·sy (típsi:) *comp.* **tip·si·er** *superl.* **tip·si·est** *adj.* somewhat intoxicated ‖ not steady, shaky [perh. fr. TIP V. (to cause to incline)]

CONCISE PRONUNCIATION KEY: **(a)** æ, c*a*t; ɑ, c*a*r; ɔ f*aw*n; ei, sn*a*ke. **(e)** e, h*e*n; i:, sh*ee*p; iə, d*ee*r; ɛə, b*ea*r. **(i)** i, f*i*sh; ai, t*i*ger; ə:, b*i*rd. **(o)** o, *o*x; au, c*ow*; ou, g*oa*t; u, p*oo*r; ɔi, r*oy*al. **(u)** ʌ, d*u*ck; u, b*u*ll; u:, g*oo*se; ə, b*a*cillus; ju:, c*u*be. x, lo*ch*; θ, *th*ink; ð, bo*th*er; z, *Z*en; ʒ, corsa*g*e; dʒ, sava*g*e; ŋ, ora*n*gutang; j, *y*ak; ʃ, *fi*sh; tʃ, fe*tch*; ʼl, rabb*le*; ʼn, redd*en*. Complete pronunciation key appears inside front cover.

tip·toe (típtou) 1. *adv.* on the tips of one's toes 2. *v.i.* to proceed on the tips of one's toes 3. *n.* (in the phrase) **on tiptoe** on the tips of one's toes ‖ in a state of alert expectancy

tip-top (típtóp) 1. *adj.* (*pop.*) of the highest quality 2. *n.* the highest point or part ‖ the best of all

Ti·pu Sa·hib, Tip·poo Sa·hib (tí:pu:sáhib) (c. 1751-99), sultan of Mysore (1782-99), son of Hyder Ali. He continued (1782-4, 1790-9) his father's wars against the British

ti·rade (tairéid) *n.* a long, rhetorical harangue or written passage full of vehement criticism or invective [F. fr. Ital.]

Ti·ra·den·tes (ti:rudénti:s) (né Joaquim José de Silva Xavier, 1748-92), leader of a Brazilian independence movement centered in a conspiracy (1789) in the state of Minas Gerais. He was executed and his rebellion aborted by the Portuguese authorities. He was considered a national hero after Brazil became independent (1822)

Ti·ra·na (ti:rána) the capital (pop. 175,000) of Albania, 18 miles east of Durres at the foot of the central mountains. Industries: textiles, lignite mining. University (1957)

tire (tair) *pres. part.* **tir·ing** *past* and *past part.* **tired** *v.t.* to use up the strength of ‖ to use up the patience or interest of ‖ *v.i.* to lose strength by exertion etc. ‖ to lose patience or interest **to tire of** to lose patience or interest in **to tire out** to make very tired [O.E. *tīoran, tēorian*]

tire 1. *n.* a band of elastic steel etc. around the rim of e.g. a wagon wheel, holding its sections together or reducing rolling friction ‖ (*Am.=Br.* tyre) a solid rubber band, or a rubber casing making an airtight fit with a wheel rim (the whole being treated as a tube and filled with air, no inner tube being used), or a heavy rubber casing to contain an inner tube filled with air, placed around the wheel of a vehicle to absorb shock 2. *v.t. pres. part.* **tir·ing** *past* and *past part.* **tired** to fit with a tire [perh. short for M.E. *atir*, attire]

tired (táiərd) *adj.* weary ‖ hackneyed, *a tired joke* **tired of** having endured as much as one is willing to stand of (something)

tire·less (táiərlis) *adj.* seemingly incapable of becoming tired

Ti·re·si·as (tairí:si:əs) (*Gk mythol.:*) a blind prophet of Thebes mentioned frequently in Greek literature, esp. in connection with the family of Oedipus

tire·some (táiərsəm) *adj.* tending to exhaust one's patience

Ti·ro·le·an (tiróuli:ən) *adj.* Tirolese

Ti·ro·lese (tirəlí:z, tirəlí:s) 1. *adj.* pertaining to the Tirol or its people 2. *n.* a native of the Tirol

Tir·ol, Tyr·ol (tírəl, tiróul) an alpine province (area 4,884 sq. miles, pop. 586,297) of W. Austria. Capital: Innsbruck ‖ (*hist.*) a former province of Austria, divided (1919) between Austria (modern Tirol) and Italy (Trentino-Alto Adige)

TIROS (*meteor. acronym*) for television infrared observation satellite, a satellite with infrared cameras used to obtain and transmit weather information, esp. about clouds, ice floes

Tir·pitz (tírpits), Alfred von (1849-1930), German admiral. After being state secretary of the navy (1896) and minister of state for Prussia (1898), he became lord high admiral (1911). He organized and planned the submarine blockade of the British Isles (1915-16)

Tir·so de Mo·li·na (tí:rsɔðemɔlí:na) (Gabriel Tellez, c. 1571-1648), Spanish dramatist. 'El burlador de Sevilla' established the popular Don Juan theme in drama

Ti·ru·chi·ra·pal·li (tirutʃirəpáli:, tirutʃirápəli:) (formerly Trichinopoly) a town (pop. 307,400) in Madras, India, at the head of the Cauvery delta. Industries: railroad engineering, silk textiles, cigars, goldwork

Tir·yns (tírinz) an ancient Achaean city in Argolis, Greece, near modern Nauplia: remains of palaces (c. 1600-900 B.C.)

Tisa (River) *TISZA

tis·sue (tíʃu:, *Br.* tíʃju:) *n.* (*biol.*) an aggregate of like cells and intercellular material, of which animal and plant organs are composed ‖ a thin, semitransparent woven fabric ‖ an intricately interwoven group of ideas etc., *a tissue of lies* ‖ a piece of tissue paper [O.F. *tissu*]

tissue committee (*med.*) a committee that evaluates surgery performed in a hospital on the basis of the extent of agreement among the pre-operative, postoperative, and pathological diagnoses, and on the acceptability of the procedures undertaken for the diagnosis —**tissue review** *n.* the review and evaluation

tissue culture the process or technique of growing tissues in an artificial medium ‖ a culture of tissue

tissue paper very thin, soft, translucent paper used in gift wrapping etc.

tissue typing (*med.*) technique for analyzing and selecting human tissues for compatibility on a transplant

tis·su·lar (tíʃələ:r) *adj.* of organic tissue

Ti·sza (tísɒ), István (1861-1918), Hungarian statesman, son of Kálmán Tisza. As prime minister (1903-5, 1913-17), he sought to make Magyar influence dominant in Austria-Hungary, esp. over the Serbs

Tisza, Kálmán (1830-1902), Hungarian statesman, prime minister (1875-90). He rehabilitated Hungary financially and politically, and introduced compulsory education

Tisza (*Serb.* and *Russ.* Tisa) the chief tributary (610 miles long) of the Danube, flowing from the Carpathians in the S.W. Ukraine, U.S.S.R., across E. Hungary and N.E. Yugoslavia

tit (tit) *n.* a titmouse [prob. onomatopoeic]

tit *n.* (*pop.*, not in polite usage) a woman's breast or the nipple of this [O.E. *titt*]

Ti·tan (táit'n) (*mythol.*) any of the 12 children of Heaven and Earth, ancient gods of Greece, probably of the pre-Hellenic population. They were Oceanus, Coeus, Crius, Hyperion, Iapetus, Cronus, Theia, Rhea, Themis, Mnemosyne, Phoebe, Tethys. They were crushed by their descendants, the Olympian gods, led by Zeus

Ti·tan·ic (taitǽnik) *adj.* of or like the Titans **ti·tan·ic** having great size or strength ‖ calling for very great effort [fr. Gk *Titanikos*]

ti·tan·ite (táit'nait) *n.* a silicate of calcium and titanium, CaTiSiO$_5$ [G. *titanit*]

ti·ta·ni·um (taitéini:əm) *n.* a silvery-gray metallic element (symbol Ti, at. no. 22, at. mass 47.90) resembling iron. It is widely distributed as compounds but difficult to extract. It is often added to various steel alloys and used as a structural material in jet engines, missiles etc. because of its heat-resistant qualities [fr. Gk *Titanes*, the Titans]

titanium dioxide the compound TiO$_2$, occurring naturally in various crystalline forms (e.g. rutile, anatase). It is used commercially in the form of a white amorphous powder as a pigment or to improve the covering or light-reflecting properties of paints, plastics, rubber etc. Certain of the crystalline forms are valued as gems

Titan II *n.* (*mil.*) a liquid-propellant, two-stage, rocket-powered ICBM (LGM-25C) that is guided to its target by an all-inertial guidance and control system. It is equipped with a nuclear warhead and deployed in underground silos

tit·bit (títbit) *n.* a tidbit

Titch·e·ner (títʃənər), Edward Bradford (1867-1927), English-U.S. experimental and systematic psychologist and head of the structural school. His chief contribution is the encyclopedic handbook 'Experimental Psychology' (1901-5)

ti·ter, esp. *Br.* **ti·tre** (táitər) *n.* the concentration of a substance in a solution as determined by titration [F. *titre*]

tit for tat a blow delivered in return for a blow ‖ a reply in kind

tithe (taið) *n.* a tenth part of agricultural produce etc. paid as tax or as an offering, esp. (*hist.*) such a tax levied to support a church [early M.E. *tigthe, tigethe*]

tithe *pres. part.* **tith·ing** *past* and *past part.* **tithed** *v.t.* (*hist.*) to subject to a tithe [O.E. *teogothian*]

tith·ing (táiðiŋ) *n.* the act of levying or collecting a tithe ‖ (*Eng. hist.*) an administrative division of 10 householders (*FRANKPLEDGE) [O.E. *tēothung*]

Ti·tian (tíʃən) (Tiziano Vecelli) (c. 1490-1576), Venetian painter. His most famous works include 'The Assumption of the Virgin' (1518, in Venice), 'Sacred and Profane Love' (1510-12, in Rome), 'Holy Family with Adoring Shepherd' and 'Noli me tangere' (both c. 1516 and both in the National Gallery, London), and many noble portraits. Besides the great religious masterpieces he also painted classical figures and historical scenes. He communicated directly through paint, and his color sense and mastery of light as a unifying factor allowed him to infringe the classical rules of composition with safety. His dynamic compositions, asymmetrical, rising and receding, helped to establish the canons of baroque art. His portraits were the first in European art which by painterly means fixed a personality, as distinct from merely recording a set of features by draftsmanship

ti·tian (tíʃən) *adj.* of a reddish-brown color [after Titian, who often painted hair this color]

Ti·ti·ca·ca (ti:ti:káka) a navigable lake (area 3,500 sq. miles) in Bolivia and Peru, in the Andes at 12,500 ft

tit·il·late (tít'leit) *pres. part.* **tit·il·lat·ing** *past* and *past part.* **tit·il·lat·ed** *v.t.* to stimulate pleasantly by or as if by tickling [fr. L. *titillare* (*titillatus*), to tickle]

tit·i·vate, tit·i·vate (títiveit) *pres. part.* **tit·i·vat·ing, tit·i·vat·ing** *past* and *past part.* **tit·i·vat·ed, tit·i·vat·ed** *v.t.* to make (esp. oneself) smart or neat in appearance **tit·i·vá·tion, tit·i·vá·tion** *n.* [earlier *tiddivate* fr. TIDY]

tit·lark (títlɑrk) *n.* the pipit

ti·tle (táit'l) 1. *n.* a word, phrase or sentence used to designate a book, chapter, poem etc., thus distinguishing it from others and often indicating the nature of its contents ‖ a similar indication for a painting, statue etc. ‖ a title page ‖ a division of a law book, statute etc. ‖ the form of words at the beginning of a legal document or statute, indicating its nature ‖ a word or phrase attached, usually as a prefix, to the name of a person in order to denote his office, social dignity or status, esp. a status of nobility ‖ an epithet ‖ a ground for a claim, *he has lost all title to our esteem* ‖ (*law*) the legal right to the ownership of property, or the evidence of this right ‖ (*Anglican Communion*) a source of income and fixed sphere of work required of a candidate for ordination ‖ (*Roman Catholicism*) a parish or church, esp. in or near Rome, in the charge of a cardinal ‖ (*sports*) that which affords recognition as the best athlete, team etc. in a particular sport, *world heavyweight title* 2. *v.t. pres. part.* **ti·tling** *past* and *past part.* **ti·tled** to furnish with a title **ti·tled** *adj.* having a title of nobility [O.F.]

title deed a deed containing the evidence of someone's legal ownership

title page a page at the beginning of a book, treatise etc. giving the name of the book, its author and its publisher etc.

title role the character in a play etc. after whom the play is titled

ti·tling (táitliŋ) *n.* the act of impressing a title on a book or the title thus impressed ‖ (*printing*) type used for display

tit·mouse (títmaus) *pl.* **tit·mice** (títmais) *n.* any of various small (4–6 ins), short-billed birds of fam. *Paridae*. They generally roam in mixed bands, and nest in holes in summer [M.E. *titmose*]

Ti·to (tí:tou) (Josip Broz, 1892-1980), Yugoslav statesman and marshal. He led the Communist guerrilla resistance against the German Occupation of Yugoslavia (1941-5), and became (1945) the head of state of the federal people's republic. At first dominated by the U.S.S.R., he broke with the Cominform (1948) and established his own version of communism in Yugoslavia. He was elected president in 1953 and president for life in 1974. He adopted a foreign policy independent of the Soviet bloc, maintaining sound relations with East European socialist states as well as with Western and nonaligned nations

ti·trate (táitreit) *pres. part.* **ti·trat·ing** *past* and *past part.* **ti·trat·ed** *v.t.* to subject to titration ‖ *v.i.* to perform titration **ti·trá·tion** *n.* an analytical procedure for the determination of reactive capacity, usually of a solution. It consists of adding a reagent in small portions of known volume (e.g. from a burette) to a known volume or mass of a solution or substance until a desired end point (e.g. a color change in an indicator or in the reactants) indicating a known degree of reaction is obtained. It is widely used in quantitative analysis [fr. F. *titrer* fr. *titre*, title]

titre *TITER

tit·ter (títər) 1. *v.i.* to laugh in a halfhearted or half-suppressed way, often suggesting affectation or nervousness 2. *n.* such a laugh [imit.]

tittivate *TITIVATE

tit·tle (tít'l) *n.* (only in) **not one jot or tittle** absolutely none at all [M.E. *titel, titil*, a small mark over a letter or word]

---

tit·tle-tat·tle (títˈltætˈl) 1. *n.* idle gossip 2. *v.i. pres. part.* **tit·tle-tat·tling** *past* and *past part.* **tit·tle-tat·tled** to engage in idle gossip

tit·tup (títˈəp) *pres. part.* **tit·tup·ing**, esp. *Br.* **tit·tup·ping** *past* and *past part.*, esp. *Br.* **tit·tupped** *v.i.* to prance and caper along in a way designed to attract attention || (of a horse) to gallop or canter easily **tít·tup·py** *adj.* inclined to tittup || wobbly [prob. imit.]

tit·u·ba·tion (títˈjubéiʃən) *n.* an unsteady, staggering gait, esp. caused by certain nervous disorders

tit·u·lar (títˈjulər) 1. *adj.* being as specified in title only, *titular head of state* || of or relating to a title, *titular privileges* || (of a bishop or abbot) holding his title from a defunct administration 2. *n.* a person having the title of an office, esp. without its duties or obligations || (*Roman Catholicism*) the person or thing after which a church is named [fr. L. *titulus*, title]

Ti·tus (táitəs) (*New Testament*) the convert and assistant to whom St Paul addressed one of the Pastoral Epistles

Titus (Titus Flavius Sabinus Vespasianus, c. 40-81), Roman emperor (79-81), son of Vespasian. He succeeded his father as Roman commander in the war against the Jews and sacked Jerusalem (70). He was a popular emperor and helped the victims of the eruption of Vesuvius (79), which destroyed Pompeii and Herculaneum, and those of the great fire at Rome (80)

tiz·zy (tízi) *pl.* **tiz·zies** *n.* (*pop.*) a state of foolish excitement or temporary emotional disturbance [origin unknown]

Tlá·loc (tlálóuk), the Otomí god of rain (and hence among the highest in the pantheon)

Tlax·ca·la (tlæskálə) the smallest state (area 1,555 sq. miles, pop: 556,597) in Mexico, with the highest density (183 persons per sq. mile) among the states. It lies at a mean altitude of 7,000 ft on the central plateau. Capital: Tlaxcala (pop. 35,384). Agriculture (cereals) and handicrafts (weaving) are the main occupations. After being conquered (1519) it was Hernán Cortés' principal ally in the conquest of Mexico (1519-21), its loyalty to Spain bringing it many privileges and relative prosperity. It contains the oldest church (1521) in the Americas

Tlem·cen (tlemsén) an ancient commercial center (pop. 115,054) in N.W. Algeria. Mosques (11th and 14th cc.)

Tlin·git (tlíŋgit) *pl.* **Tlin·git, Tlin·gits** *n.* a group of Indian peoples of the southeastern coast of Alaska. They have declined from about 10,000 (18th c.) to about 4,000 || a member of one of this group of peoples || their language

TLP (*astron. abbr.*) for transient lunar phenomena

T lymphocyte (*cytol.*) T cell (which see)

TM (*abbr.*) for Transcendental Meditation

tme·sis (tmíːsis) *pl.* **tme·ses** (tmíːsiːz) *n.* the interposition of one or more words between the parts of a compound word, e.g. 'what man soever' for 'whatsoever man' [L. fr. Gk *tmēsis*, a cutting]

TM-65 (*mil.*) U.S.S.R. main tank with turbojet aircraft engine mounted on a turnable truck used to expel chemicals with engine exhaust

TNT *TRINITROTOLUENE

TNT equivalent (*mil.*) a measure of the energy release, esp. from the detonation of a nuclear weapon, in terms of the amount of TNT that would release the same amount of energy when exploded

to (tuː, *unstressed* tə) 1. *prep.* in the direction of, *to the left* || used to indicate someone or something reached, *he ran to his father's arms* || used to indicate position or contact, *perpendicular to the base, his hands to the wall* || into a condition of, *ground to powder* || used to indicate a result, *they fought to a standstill, to our surprise they arrived on time* || for the purpose of, *they came to our aid* || used to indicate the object of a right or claim, *pretensions to learning* || in accompaniment with, *marching to the band* || with respect to, *subject to criticism* || used to indicate degree or extent, *stirred to the depths* || in conformity with, *made to his specifications* || in comparison with, *the score was 6 to 4* || used to indicate possession or attribution, *the key to the door* || used to indicate attachment, *he held to his opinion* || (in time expressions) used to indicate the period before the hour, *5 to 7* || until, *from 2 to 6* || constituting, *4 quarts to a gallon* || introducing the subject of a toast, *here's to your health* || used after a verb to indicate the receiver of the

action, *give the book to her* || used to define the scope of an adjective, *it looks easy to me* or a noun, *a threat to society* || used as a sign of the verbal noun, *no objection to his coming* || as a sign of the infinitive, *he wants to go* || used elliptically for the infinitive, *don't work harder than you have to* 2. *adv.* fixed or fastened, *the window was fast to* || to consciousness, *he came to after 5 minutes* || (*naut.*) close to the wind [O.E. *tō*]

toad (toud) *n.* a member of *Bufonidae*, a family of small, tailless, leaping amphibians with a warty skin having poison glands. They are terrestrial except when breeding, and feed primarily on insects || a contemptible, repulsive person [O.E. *tādige*, origin unknown]

toad·flax (tóudflæks) *n.* a European and North American perennial plant, *Linaria vulgaris*, with small yellow or orange flowers

toad spit cuckoo spit

toad·stool (tóudstuːl) *n.* a fungus with an umbrella-shaped pileus || (*pop.*) a poisonous mushroom

toad·y (tóudi) 1. *pl.* **toad·ies** *n.* someone who grossly and servilely flatters people from whom he hopes to get advantages 2. *v.i. pres. part.* **toad·y·ing** *past* and *past part.* **toad·ied** (with 'to') to behave in this way (toward someone) **tóad·y·ism** *n.* [fr. older *toadeater*, charlatan's assistant, toady]

to and fro in one direction and then in the opposite one, repeatedly

toast (toust) 1. *v.t.* to brown the surface of by exposure to heat || to make hot or very hot || to propose or drink a toast to || *v.i.* to become toasted or as if toasted || to drink a toast 2. *n.* bread browned by exposure to heat and served hot or cold with butter etc. || a drink in honor of a person or thing || a proposal to drink to someone or something || the person or thing drunk to || someone who is the subject of public admiration [O.F. *toster*, to roast or grill]

toasting fork a long-handled fork for toasting bread etc. over a fire

toast·mas·ter (tóustmæstər, tóustmɑstər) *n.* a person appointed to propose toasts, introduce speakers etc., e.g. at a banquet

to·bac·co (təbǽkou) *n.* a member of *Nicotiana*, fam. *Solanaceae*, a genus of plants with large ovate leaves and white or pink flowers, native to tropical America but now cultivated in many parts of the world || the dried and cured leaves of *N. tabacum* smoked, chewed or used as snuff || manufactured products made from these leaves (*NICOTINE) [Span. *tabaco* fr. Carib]

to·bac·co·nist (təbǽkənist) *n.* a retailer in tobacco

To·bey (tóubiː), Mark (1890-1976), American painter. His works, which have a close relation to abstract expressionism, reveal the influence of Oriental calligraphy

To·bi·as (təbáiəs) (*Bible*) the son of Tobit in the book Tobit

To·bit (tóubit) a book included in the Roman Catholic canon but placed in the Apocrypha in the King James Version, telling the story of Tobit, a devout Jew. It is a story of family life and filial devotion

to·bog·gan (təbógən) 1. *n.* a long, narrow sled of flat boards which curve upward at the front, used for coasting downhill or for travel or transport on ice or snow 2. *v.i.* to ride on a toboggan || to fall rapidly in value [Canadian F. *tabagan* fr. Algonquian]

to·bra·my·cin [C₁₈H₃₇N₅O₉] (toubrəmáisin) *n.* (*pharm.*) antibiotic used against pseudomonic aeruginosa, *E coli*, klebsiella, staphylococcus, etc.; marketed as Nebcin

To·bruk (tóubruk) a port (pop. 58,869) in E. Libya, the scene of much fighting (Jan. 1941-Nov. 1942) in the 2nd world war. It was evacuated by the Germans after the Battle of Alamein

To·by (tóubi) *pl.* **To·bies** *n.* a jug or mug for beer or ale in the shape of a heavy old man with a three-cornered hat [fr. *Toby*, dim. of Tobias]

To·can·tins (tɔkɑntíːns) a river (1,700 miles long) in Brazil flowing from the central highlands to the Amazon delta below Belém

toc·ca·ta (təkátə) *n.* (*mus.*) a fast single movement for a keyboard instrument originally designed to exhibit a performer's technique. The term is also used for other compositions, not necessarily of a single movement [Ital.]

To·char·i·an, To·khar·i·an (toukǽriːən) 1. *n.* a member of a people of European origin living in central Asia (1st millennium A.D.) || their Indo-European language 2. *adj.* of this people or their language

Tocque·ville (tóukvil, tɔkvíːl), Charles Alexis Henri Clérel de (1805-59), French liberal statesman and political writer. His 'Democracy in America' (1835) is a penetrating study of American society and politics and an indirect lesson to nations striving for democracy. His 'The Ancien Régime and the Revolution' (1856) stressed the continuity of prerevolutionary trends in the French Revolution

toc·sin (tóksin) *n.* a warning bell || the ringing of a warning bell || something thought of as a signal of disaster [F.]

to·day (tədéi) 1. *adv.* in or during this present day || in the present time, nowadays 2. *n.* the present time or period [O.E. *tō dæg*]

tod·dle (tódˈl) 1. *v.i. pres. part.* **tod·dling** *past* and *past part.* **tod·dled** (esp. of a small child) to walk with short, uncertain steps 2. *n.* a toddling **tód·dler** *n.* a child beginning to learn to walk [origin obscure]

tod·dy (tódi) *pl.* **tod·dies** *n.* sap obtained from several E. Indian palms || a drink consisting of whiskey, brandy etc., mixed with hot water, sugar and spices [Hind. *tārī* fr. *tār*, palm tree]

Tod·le·ben, Tot·le·ben (tóutleibən), Franz Eduard Ivanovich (1818-84), Russian general. He distinguished himself in the Crimean War by his brilliant defense of Sevastopol (1854-5)

to-do (tədúː) *n.* a fuss, commotion

to·dy (tóudi) *pl.* **to·dies** *n.* a member of *Todus*, fam. *Todidae*, a genus of small West Indian insectivorous birds, allied to the kingfisher [fr. F. *todier*]

toe (tou) 1. *n.* any of the five digits of the human foot || any of the digits of an animal's foot || the forepart of the foot (opp. HEEL) || that part of a shoe, sock or other foot covering which covers the forepart of the foot || anything suggesting a toe in location, shape etc., e.g. the forepart of the hitting surface of a golf club **on one's toes** alert **to step on someone's toes** to offend someone, esp. by stealing his prerogatives 2. *v.t. pres. part.* **toe·ing** *past* and *past part.* **toed** to equip (a stocking etc.) with a toe || to drive (a nail) in slantwise for greater security || (*golf*) to hit (the ball) with the toe of the club [O.E. *tā*]

toe cap an extra piece of leather which covers the toe of a shoe or boot

toed (toud) *adj.* (in compounds) furnished with a specified number or kind of toes || (of a nail) driven in slantwise || (of wood) held firmly by nails driven in slantwise

toe·hold (tóuhould) *n.* a niche, crevice etc. just large enough to support the toes in climbing || a means of access, *the inheritance gave him a toehold in society* || a hold in which a wrestler wrenches his opponent's foot

toe-in (tóuin) *n.* an adjustment of the front wheels of a car so that they make a slight angle with one another, being closer together at the front than at the back. This reduces the wear and makes steering more accurate

toe·nail (tóuneil) *n.* the nail growing on a toe || a nail driven in obliquely

toe pick (*ice skating*) a short serration of front of the skate blade *also* toe rake

toff (tof) *n.* (*Br., pop.*) a man who by dress and manner shows himself to be of superior social status [perh. fr. TUFT, tassel]

tof·fee, tof·fy (tófi:, tófi) *pl.* **tof·fees, tof·fies** *n.* a hard or chewy candy made by boiling sugar with butter, sometimes mixed with nuts etc. [origin unknown]

tog (tog) 1. *n.* (*pl., pop.*) clothes, *football togs* 2. *v.t. pres. part.* **tog·ging** *past* and *past part.* **togged** (*Br., pop.*, with 'up' or 'out') to dress for some special occasion, activity etc. [prob. fr. cant *togeman, togman* fr. L. *toga*, cloak]

to·ga (tóugə) *n.* (*hist.*) a man's loose outer garment hanging from a shoulder, worn in public by a Roman citizen || a similar garment worn e.g. by Africans **to·gaed** (tóugəd) *adj.* wearing a toga [L.]

to·geth·er (təgéðər) *adv.* in or into contact or union, *the pages are stuck together* || in or into the same place, group etc., *put them all together so that you can find them again* || at the same time, *the two things happened together* || with each other || in succession, *it rained for days together* || in a body, *all the workers together* || into agreement, *try to bring the two firms together* || by combined action, *together they pushed the stalled car* **together with** including, with in addition, *the house together with its grounds* **to get together** to meet in order to engage in a joint activity **to go together** to accompany one another || to be sweethearts, *they have been going together for 2 years* || to

---

harmonize, *these colors don't go together* **to hang together** to be consistent, be logical, *his story doesn't hang together* **to·geth·er·ness** *n.* (*pop.*) warm fellowship [O.E. *togœdere, tŏgadore*]

together *adj.* (*colloq.*) **1.** in control **2.** well organized or integrated *get yourself together*

tog·gle (tóg'l) **1.** *n.* a wooden or metal pin or bolt passed through a loop, staple, eye of a rope etc., esp. as a fastening ‖ a toggle joint or a device having one **2.** *v.t. pres. part.* **tog·gling** *past* and *past part.* **tog·gled** to fasten with, or fit with, a toggle [etym. doubtful]

toggle joint two rods or plates joined together at their ends and at an angle by a hinge, enabling the direction of the resistance to an applied force to be varied

toggle switch the common electric light switch, in which pressure on the lever operates a toggle joint

To·go (tóugou) a republic (area 19,000 sq. miles, pop. 2,872,000) in W. Africa. Capital and port: Lomé. People: Ewe and other groups in the south, smaller Negro and Hamitic groups in the north. Language: French, African languages. Religion: 75% local African, 20% Christian, 5% Moslem. The land is 41% cultivated and 9% forest. Behind the coastal lagoons and swampy plain it rises to an undulating plateau (largely savanna in the north and south, deciduous forest in the center), crossed diagonally by the Togo Mtns (rising to 3,346 ft). Average temperatures (F.): north of the Togo Mtns 72°-92°, south of them 70°-85°. Rainfall: north 45 ins, Togo Mtns 60 ins, south 30 ins. Livestock: goats, cattle, sheep, hogs. Agricultural products: corn, yams, cassava, plantains, peanuts, coffee, cocoa, palm oil and kernels, copra, cotton, manioc, millet, sorghum, rice, meat, hides and skins. Fish is plentiful. Minerals: phosphates, bauxite, iron. Exports: cocoa, coffee, palm kernels, copra, cotton. Imports: cotton cloth, machinery, vehicles, oil, wines and spirits, sugar, cement. Monetary unit: franc CFA. Togo was created an independent republic (Apr. 27, 1960) from the former French Togoland. Sylvanus Olympio served as the first president until his assassination in 1963. A second coup in 1967 forced his successor, Nicolas Grunitzy, to flee the country and established Gnassingbe Eyadema as military chief. Eyadema founded the Togolese People's Assembly, Togo's only political party, in 1969, and appointed a civilian cabinet. A new constitution established in 1979 in a directly elected legislature and Eyadema was elected to a second 7-year term as president

To·go·land (tóugoulænd) a former German protectorate in W. Africa, on the Gulf of Guinea. The area was settled by the Ewe people from the Niger (12th c. onwards). The Portuguese began trading in slaves (15th c.) and the French established trading posts (17th c.). The Germans united the area (1880s) as a protectorate, recognized by France (1897) and Britain (1899). Britain occupied the western third and France the rest (1914), and this partition was confirmed (1922) in the League of Nations mandates of British Togoland and French Togoland. These became U.N. trusteeships (1946). After an election (1956), British Togoland joined Ghana (1957). French Togoland became an autonomous republic (1956) and became fully independent (Apr. 27, 1960) as Togo

toil (tɔil) *n.* long, hard effort ‖ (*rhet.*) a task performed with such effort [A.F.=dispute]

toil *v.i.* to work very hard and for a long time ‖ to move slowly and with great effort, *to toil up a hill* [A.F. *toiler,* to strive]

toi·let (tóilit) *n.* the process of dressing, washing, shaving, making up the face, doing one's hair etc. ‖ (*rhet.*) all the clothes and accessories which a woman dressed with style is wearing, *an elaborate toilet* ‖ a lavatory ‖ a plumbing fixture for receiving human urine and feces, consisting of a hopper into which water is released usually by a system of weights and plungers, and a device for flushing away the contents of the hopper ‖ the room containing this fixture [F. *toilette,* dim. of *toile,* cloth]

toi·let·ries (tóilitri:z) *pl. n.* articles used in making one's toilet, e.g. soap

toilet water a scented liquid containing alcohol, used after washing or bathing

toils (tɔilz) *pl. n.* circumstances from which it is difficult to escape, entanglements, *in the toils of the moneylender* [O.F. *teile, toile,* a cloth, a net]

toil·some (tóilsəm) *adj.* laborious

toil·worn (tóilwɔrn) *adj.* worn out by toil ‖ showing signs of being so worn, *toilworn features*

To·jo (toudʒou), Hideki (1884-1948), Japanese general. As Japanese premier (1941-4), he attacked Pearl Harbor and led operations against the Allies, and was executed as a war criminal

toka unit of currency in Bangladesh

to·ka·mak (tóukəmæk) (*nuclear phys.*) a doughnut-shaped endless-tube device in which ionized gas (plasma) is contained by magnetic fields, used in attempts to produce thermonuclear fusion *Cf* STELLARATOR

To·kay (toukéi) *n.* a sweet, golden Hungarian dessert wine [after *Tokaj* in Hungary]

To·ke·lau Islands (tóukəláu) a group of three atolls (area 4 sq. miles, pop. 1,554) in the central Pacific (Polynesia), formerly part of the Gilbert and Ellice Is colony but administered by New Zealand since 1926

to·ken (tóukən) **1.** *n.* an act or object serving as a symbol or evidence of something, *accept this book as a token of our friendship* ‖ a keepsake ‖ a disk (usually metal) exchangeable under some systems for goods, transportation etc. ‖ (*Br.*) a paper voucher, *a book token* **by the same token** on the same grounds, following from this **in token of** as evidence of **2.** *adj.* serving as a token ‖ merely symbolic, *they put up a token resistance* [O.E. *tācn, tæcen*]

to·ken·ism (tóukənizəm) *n.* policy or practice of fulfilling legal and/or moral obligations by a nominal conformity, e.g., in hiring practices as by hiring a single black person —**tokenistic** *adj.*

token payment a small sum paid as evidence that the total debt is acknowledged

token strike (*Br.*) a labor strike which lasts only a few hours

Tokharian *TOCHARIAN

To·ku·ga·wa (tóku:gɑwə) a family of shoguns founded by Ieyasu, which controlled Japan (1603-1867)

To·ku·shi·ma (tɔku:ʃi:mɑ) a port (pop. 171,000) in N.E. Shikoku, Japan: cotton textiles, mechanical engineering

To·kyo (tóuki:ou, tóukjou) the capital (pop. 11,634,927) and the financial and commercial center of Japan, a port on Tokyo Bay (area approx. 600 sq. miles), on central E. Honshu. Industries: mechanical engineering, chemicals, textiles, food processing, light manufacturing printing and publishing. Built on a river plain and cut by canals, it centers on the imperial palace (19th c.) and park, surrounded by moats. The city was rebuilt in Occidental style after an earthquake (1923) and heavy bombing (1945). Principal cultural institutions: university (1877), imperial museums, National Diet library, Kabuki theater. Tokyo was founded in 1456. It became a provincial capital in 1590 and the imperial capital in 1868

Tokyo Round the seventh of the major multilateral trade negotiations held under the auspices of GATT in Geneva in October 1973, placing special emphasis on the export needs of developing countries, and discussions on nontariff barriers to trade, trade in agricultural goods, and trade protectionism

Tol·bert (tóulbərt), William Richard (1913-80), president of Liberia (1971-80). He was killed during a military coup

told *past* and *past part.* of TELL **all told** in total

To·le·do (təlí:dou) a port and rail center (pop. 354,635) in Ohio, on Lake Erie: glass, mechanical engineering, automobiles, coal shipment. University (1872)

To·le·do (təlí:dou, toléðɔ) a province (area 5,919 sq. miles, pop. 471,806) of central Spain (*NEW CASTILE) ‖ its capital (pop. 51,400), also the historic capital of New Castile. Visigothic-Moorish-Spanish city walls, medieval bridges, alcazar (16th-c. fortress, restored after near destruction in 1936), Gothic cathedral (13th-15th cc.) and churches. Conquered by the Romans in 192 B.C., Toledo became a Church center very early, and later (534-712) became the capital of Visigothic Spain. It remained important under the Moslems and, after reconquest (1085) by Castile, was the Castilian capital until 1560. Its sword blades have been famous since Roman times

tol·er·a·ble (tólərəb'l) *adj.* able to be tolerated ‖ adequate or fairly good, *a tolerable knowledge of French* **tól·er·a·bly** *adv.* [F. *tolérable*]

tol·er·ance (tólərəns) *n.* readiness to allow others to believe or act as they judge best ‖ (*biol.*) the ability of an organism to survive in difficult conditions (of heat, cold, drought etc.) ‖ (*mech.*) the permissible error in size etc. of a machine part or manufactured article, *a tolerance of a thousandth of an inch* ‖ (*med.*) the natural or developed ability to take in drugs etc. without suffering harmful effects ‖ (*coinage*) remedy [F. *tolérance*]

tol·er·ant (tólərənt) *adj.* willing to tolerate the beliefs, way of living etc. of others ‖ (*med.*) of or having a tolerance F. *tolérant*

tol·er·ate (tóləreit) *pres. part.* **tol·er·at·ing** *past* and *past part.* **tol·er·at·ed** *v.t.* to support (pain) with fortitude (a nuisance) with forbearance ‖ to permit, *you should not tolerate such rudeness* ‖ to respect (the conduct, opinions, beliefs etc. of others) without sitting in judgment on them ‖ (*med.*) to be able to take (a drug etc.) without suffering harmful effects [fr. F. *tolérer*]

tol·er·a·tion (tɒləréiʃən) *n.* the act of tolerating something ‖ freedom to practice a particular religious cult without incurring civil disabilities [F. *tolération*]

Toleration, Act of (*Eng. hist.*) an act of parliament (1689) granting limited religious freedom to Protestant dissenters

Toleration Act of 1649 (Maryland's Act Concerning Religion), a pioneer act passed by the assembly of Maryland which granted freedom of conscience to all Christian denominations

Tol·kien (tóulki:n, tólki:n), John Ronald Reuel (1892-1973), British writer and medievalist. His best-known works include 'The Hobbit' (1937), the trilogy 'The Lord of the Rings' (1954-5), and 'The Silmarillion' (1977)

toll (toul) *n.* a tax or charge levied on those who use a particular service (e.g. a bridge, road etc.) ‖ (*rhet.*) a cost in life or limb or in suffering, damage etc., *the war took a terrible toll of the youth of the nation* [O.E.]

toll 1. *v.t.* to ring (a bell) with strokes separated by long, equal intervals, usually as a solemn signal of death, disaster etc. ‖ *v.i.* (of a bell) to sound thus **2.** *n.* a tolling ‖ the sound made thus [perh. fr. M.E. *tollen,* to pull, prob. fr. O.E.]

toll bar an obstruction on a road, bridge etc. where a toll must be paid

toll·booth (tóulbu:θ) *n.* a booth where tolls are paid

toll bridge a bridge at which a toll is charged for passage

toll-free number (tóulfrí:) a Bell System telephone number preceded by 800 permitting calls to be made from certain areas and charged at wholesale rate to the receiver of the calls

toll·gate (tóulgeit) *n.* a gate on a road, bridge etc. where a toll is to be paid

toll·house (tóulhaus) *pl.* **toll·hous·es** (tóulhauziz) *n.* a booth etc. where a toll is taken ‖ a tollkeeper's house

toll·keep·er (tóulki:pər) *n.* (*Br.*) a person who collects tolls

Tol·man (tóulmən), Richard Chace (1881-1948), U.S. physical chemist and physicist. His major contributions were in chemical kinetics, statistical mechanics, relativity and relativistic cosmology

tol·met·in [$C_{15}H_{15}NO_3$] (tóulmetin) *n.* (*pharm.*) nonsteroidal anti-inflammatory drug used in treating rheumatoid arthritis; marketed as Tolectin

Tol·pud·dle Martyrs (tólpʌd'l) a group of six farm workers sentenced (1834) to transportation for seven years for having formed a trade-union branch at the village of Tolpuddle, Dorset, England. The affair showed the hostility of the Whig government to the growing trade-union movement, and led to the dissolution of the Grand National Consolidated Trades Union

Tol·stoy (tóulstɔi, tólstɔi), Alexy Nikolayevich (1882-1945), Russian novelist. His best-known work was 'Peter the Great' (1929-34, Eng. trans. 1936), a fictionalized biography

Tolstoy, Count Leo (Lev) Nikolayevich (1828-1910), Russian novelist and moral philosopher. He came of a rich and noble family. Toward the end of his life he rejected the institutions of society, including personal property and the state itself, together with corrupted art, in a kind of saintly anarchism. Before this crisis he had written his two masterpieces: 'War and Peace' (1864-9) and 'Anna Karenina' (1875-7). Few novelists can approach Tolstoy either in scope (the whole movement of European soci-

CONCISE PRONUNCIATION KEY: **(a)** æ, c*a*t; ɑ, c*a*r; ɔ f*aw*n; ei, sn*a*ke. **(e)** e, h*e*n; i:, sh*ee*p; iə, d*ee*r; ɛə, b*ea*r. **(i)** i, f*i*sh; ai, t*i*ger; ə:, b*i*rd. **(o)** o, *o*x; au, c*ow*; ou, g*oa*t; u, p*oo*r; ɔi, r*oy*al. **(u)** ʌ, d*u*ck; u, b*u*ll; u:, g*oo*se; ə, b*a*cill*u*s; ju:, c*u*be. x, lo*ch*; θ, *th*ink; ð, bo*th*er; z, *Z*en; ʒ, corsa*g*e. dʒ, sava*g*e; ŋ, orangutan*g*; j, *y*ak; ʃ, *f*ish; tʃ, fe*tch*; 'l, rabb*le*; 'n, redd*en*. Complete pronunciation key appears inside front cover.

ety, the nature and conduct of a continental war) or in the depth of his analysis of man as a social being

Tol·tec (tóltek) n. (hist.) a member of a Nahuatlan people who flourished in Mexico (c. 7th–12th cc.). The Toltecs smelted metal, built massive pyramids and practiced sun worship and human sacrifice. Their culture was assimilated by the Aztecs **Tól·tec·an** adj. [Span. tolteca]

to·lu (təlú) n. balsam of Tolu [Span. tolú after Santiago de Tolú, in Colombia]

tol·u·ene (tólju:i:n) n. a colorless liquid hydrocarbon, $C_6H_5CH_3$, distilled esp. from coal tar and used in the manufacture of dyes, drugs and trinitrotoluene [fr. tolu, balsam of Tolu+Gk -ēnē, fem. patronymic suffix]

to·lu·i·dene (təlú:idi:n) n. an isomeric amine, $CH_3C_6H_4NH_2$, derived from toluene and used in the manufacture of dyes

tol·u·ol (tólju:oul) n. toluene, esp. when referring to commercial grades [fr. tolu, balsam of Tolu+ALCOHOL]

tom (tom) n. the male of some animals, esp. the cat [dim. of Thomas]

Tom (slang) (pejorative) a black person who humbles himself to white people or advocates a white position in a black-white controversy; from the character in Uncle Tom's Cabin, by Harriet Beecher Stowe also Uncle Tom —**Tom** v. —**Tomism, Uncle Tomism** n. the response or practice

tom·a·hawk (tómǝhɔk) n. a light ax used by North American Indians [of Algonquian origin]

Tomahawk n. (mil.) a pilotless, turbojet, solid-fuel missile (BGM-109), 18 ft. long, weighing 3,200 lbs, fired from a submarine, with nuclear capability and a 1,200-mi range

tom·al·ley (tómæli:) n. a fatty substance (often called liver) in the North American lobster, considered a delicacy [prob. fr. Carib]

to·ma·to (tərnéitou, təmátou) pl. **to·ma·toes** n. Lycopersicon esculentum, fam. Solanaceae, a trailing herbaceous annual originating in South America and widely cultivated for its fruit ‖ this fruit, red or yellow when ripe, fleshy, juicy and rich in vitamins, eaten fresh, cooked, or canned, and also processed into juice [Span. tomate fr. Nahuatl tomatl]

tomb (tu:m) n. a burial chamber ‖ a stone construction within or under which a person lies buried [Early M.E. toumbe, tumbe fr. A.F. tumbe, O.F. tombe]

tom·bac, tom·bak (tómbæk) n. an alloy of copper and zinc used for cheap jewelry etc. [F. fr. Malay tambága, copper]

tom·bo·la (tombóulǝ) n. ‖ (Br.) bingo ‖ (Br.) a lottery, esp. one organized for charity [F. or Ital. fr. tombolare, tumble]

Tom·bouc·tou (tombu:ktú:) *TIMBUKTU

tom·boy (tómbɔi) n. a girl who likes boyish sports and activities

tomb·stone (tú:mstoun) n. a gravestone

tom·cat (tómkæt) n. a male cat

Tomcat n. (mil.) a twin-turbofan, dual-crew, supersonic, long-range interceptor (F-14) designed to operate from aircraft carriers, with air-to-air and air-to-ground missiles and conventional ordnance

Tom, Dick and Harry (tom, dik, hæri:) (often preceded by 'any' or 'every') anybody or everybody, people of no particular importance

tome (toum) n. a book, esp. one that is large, heavy and scholarly [F. fr. L. fr. Gk]

to·men·tose (təméntous) adj. covered with short woolly hairs [fr. Mod. L. tomentosus fr. L. tomentum, stuffing for cushions]

to·men·tum (təméntəm) pl. **to·men·ta** (təméntə) n. (bot.) a close covering or felting of downy, cottony or woolly hairs on leaves or stems ‖ (anat.) the mass of wool-like blood vessels comprising the inner surface of the pia mater [Mod. L. fr. L.=cushion stuffing]

tom·fool (tomfú:l) 1. n. a silly fool, esp. someone who acts with stupid thoughtlessness 2. adj. silly, senseless 3. v.i. to play the tomfool **tom·fool·er·y** (tómfú:ləri:) pl. **tom·fool·er·ies** n. silly behavior

tom·my (tómi:) pl. **tom·mies** n. (Br.) a rod used e.g. to give purchase on a socket wrench [fr. Tommy, nickname for Thomas]

tommy pl. **tommies** n. (Br.) a private in the army ‖ any British soldier [fr. Thomas Atkins, made-up name on model army forms showing soldiers how to fill them in]

tommy gun a Thompson submachine gun ‖ a similar automatic weapon

tom·my·rot (tómi:rɔt) n. utter nonsense

to·mog·ra·phy (toumógrəfi:) n. (med.) system of X-rays that photographs a body layer by layer through movement of the apparatus also body-section radiography, laminography, planigraphy, sectional radiography

to·mor·row (təmórou) 1. n. the day following today 2. adv. on or during the day following today [M.E. fr. to morgen, to morwen]

tom·pi·on (tómpi:ən) n. a tampion

Tomp·kins (tómpkənz), Daniel D. (1774-1825), U.S. vice-president under James Monroe (1817-25). His vice-presidency was marked by a long controversy over charges that he had mishandled funds while serving as governor of New York (1807-17)

Tomsk (tomsk) a city (pop. 439,000) in the R.S.F.S.R., U.S.S.R., in W. Siberia: engineering, chemical and wood industries and nuclear research. University (1888)

tom·tit (tómtít) n. (Br.) Parus caeruleus, the blue tit ‖ one of various small birds, e.t. a nuthatch

tom·tom (tómtɒm) n. an Oriental or African drum with a small head, played with the hands or sticks [Hind. tam-tam, imit.]

ton (tʌn) n. a register ton ‖ a unit of volume for a ship's cargo, usually equal to 40 cu. ft ‖ a unit of volume for measuring the displacement of a ship equal to 35 cu. ft ‖ a European measure of capacity for lumber, usually equal to 40 cu. ft ‖ any of various units of weight, e.g. for wheat, lime, plaster, gravel, stone etc. ‖ (pop., esp. pl.) a great deal, tons of money (*LONG TON, *SHORT TON, *METRIC TON) [O.E. tunne]

ton n. (Br.) 1. a century 2. a score of 100% 3. a speed of 100 mph 4. (cricket) 100 runs

ton·al (tóun'l) adj. pertaining to tone or to tonality ‖ (mus.) having the internal intervals of a musical phrase modified when it is repeated at an interval on grounds of key (instead of being exactly reproduced), a tonal fugue **to·nál·i·ty** pl.

to·nal·i·ties n. (mus.) the quality of having key (cf. ATONALITY) ‖ (painting) the color relationships in a painting [fr. M.L. tonalis]

Tone (toun), Theobald Wolfe (1763-98), Irish revolutionary. He negotiated with the French for an invasion of Ireland to assist the Irish rebels, but was captured by the English and convicted of treason. He committed suicide

tone (toun) 1. n. the quality of a sound, the mellow tone of a cello ‖ (mus.) a pure sound which is vibrating as a whole with its minimum frequency (the fundamental note) ‖ (mus.) an interval of two semitones ‖ (mus.) any of the eight Gregorian modes used in singing the Psalms ‖ (mus.) a note ‖ an inflection or modulation of the voice denoting an emotion etc., a cross tone of voice ‖ a way of speaking or writing which denotes the person's sentiments, purpose etc., the tone of a letter ‖ (painting) the general effect of a painting in relation to its color, light and shade ‖ (of color) degree of luminosity ‖ (linguistics) the musical pitch of a sound, word etc. ‖ (linguistics) a rising, falling or other pitch by which words are distinguished, e.g. in ancient Greek or in Pekingese Chinese ‖ (photog.) the color or shade of a print ‖ (physiol.) the proper condition of organs or tissues for healthy functioning ‖ the general moral or social condition of a city, community etc. 2. v. pres. part. **ton·ing** past and past part. **toned** v.t. to give a certain tone of color or sound to ‖ (photog.) to change the silver color of (a print) into a colored image ‖ v.i. to be harmonious ‖ (photog., of a print) to change in color through a chemical reaction **to tone down** to reduce the loudness, pitch, contrast, luminosity etc. of ‖ to reduce (demands) or soften (remarks etc.) ‖ to become reduced or modified thus **to tone up** to impart tone to (muscles, the system etc.) [O.E. ton]

tone color, Br. tone colour (mus.) timbre

toned (tound) adj. (of paper) slightly off-white ‖ characterizing a tone language

tone-deaf (tóundéf) adj. unable to distinguish differences of pitch in music

tone language a language, e.g. Pekingese Chinese, in which variations in tones are utilized to distinguish words of different meanings which ordinarily would sound alike

tone·less (tóunlis) adj. without any expressive quality, a toneless voice

tone poem an orchestral composition, usually in one movement, based on a literary theme and tending to evoke images

to·net·ic (tounétik) adj. (linguistics) of or relating to tones ‖ of or relating to tone languages

to·nét·ics n. (linguistics) the study of tones

tong (tɔŋ, tɒŋ) n. a Chinese secret society in the U.S.A., Singapore etc., esp. one involved in vice or racketeering [Chin. t'ang, meeting place]

Ton·ga (tóngə) (or Friendly Islands) an independent sovereign state (land area 270 sq. miles, pop. 104,000) in the S. Pacific (Polynesia), consisting of some 150 volcanic and coral islands. The three main groups (north-south) are Vava'u, Ha'apai and Tongatapu. Capital and chief port: Nukualofa (pop. 20,357), on Tongatapu, the main island. People: Polynesian. Language: Tongan. Religion: mainly Methodist. Highest point: 3,380 ft. Average temperatures (F.): 70°-80°. Rainfall: Vava'u 110 ins, Tongatapu 70 ins. Exports: copra, bananas, watermelons, pineapples. Other products: cereals, vegetables, fish. Imports: textiles, processed foods, hardware, fuels, tobacco. Monetary unit: Tongan pound. HISTORY. The islands were peopled by Polynesians from Samoa when discovered (1616) by the Dutch. They were explored (1773, 1777) by Cook, and named the Friendly Islands. A successful Wesleyan mission was established (1826). Tonga became a constitutional monarchy (1862) and a British protectorate (1900). It became independent (June 4, 1970), and a member of the Commonwealth. King Taufa'ahau Tupou IV succeeded his mother, Queen Salote, in 1965

ton·ga (tóngə) n. a light, horse-drawn, two-wheeled carriage used in India [Hind. tāngā]

Tong·hak (tóngək) a syncretist religion founded (1859) in Korea, based on Shamanism, Confucianism and Buddhism, with a ritual based on Roman Catholic usage. It has about 2,000,000 adherents

tongs (tɔŋz, tɒŋz) pl. n. (sometimes construed as sing.) an implement constructed of two rods, often with clawed working ends, pivoted together at or near the handle end, used to grasp and lift (coal lumps in a hearth etc.) [O.E. tang, tange]

tongue (tʌŋ) 1. n. a mobile, extensible structure of muscles of most vertebrates which is attached to the floor of the mouth and to the hyoid bone. It is an important organ of taste, ingestion of food and, in man, of articulation in speech ‖ a similar organ, e.g. a lingula or radula, found in various invertebrates ‖ an animal's tongue prepared for the table ‖ manner of speech with regard to the way something is said or what is said, a smooth tongue, a lying tongue ‖ a language or dialect, a foreign tongue ‖ the leather flap under the laces of a shoe ‖ a projecting part of a piece of wood, as in matchboard, for fitting into a groove ‖ the clapper of a bell ‖ the pin of a buckle ‖ a tapering rail forming part of a railroad switch ‖ a long, thin promontory of land or inlet of water ‖ a vibrating part in the reed of some wind instruments **on the tip of one's tongue** one's immediate intention (to say something specified), it was on the tip of my tongue to ask the same question ‖ almost, but not quite, remembered, his name is on the tip of my tongue **to find one's tongue** to be able to speak again after shock or embarrassment **to give tongue** (of hounds) to bay, esp. when in sight of game **to hold one's tongue** to remain silent 2. v. pres. part. **tongu·ing** past and past part. **tongued** v.i. (mus.) to use tonguing ‖ to project like a tongue ‖ v.t. (mus.) to play by tonguing ‖ to cut a tongue on (a piece of wood etc.) ‖ to fit together by means of a tongue-and-groove joint [O.E. tunge]

tongue-and-groove joint (tʌ́ŋəngrú:v) a joint in which a tongue on the edge of one board fits into a groove on the edge of another

tongue in cheek adv. with irony or insincerity

tongue-lash·ing (tʌ́ŋlæʃiŋ) n. a very severe reproof

tongue-tie (tʌ́ŋtai) n. the inability to move the tongue normally, owing to excessive shortness of the frenum **tóngue-tied** adj. suffering from this disability ‖ speechless through shyness etc.

tongue twister a word or phrase which is difficult to pronounce because of similarity of sounds, alliteration etc.

tongu·ing (tʌ́ŋiŋ) n. (mus.) the use of the tongue on a wind instrument to obtain a rapid staccato effect or to modulate the intonation

ton·ic (tónik) 1. adj. inducing tonicity ‖ (med.) characterized by prolonged muscular contraction, tonic spasm ‖ mentally or morally invigorating ‖ (mus.) pertaining to or based on a keynote ‖ relating to tone in painting or photography ‖ (phon.) stressed ‖ (linguistics) tonetic 2.

n. an invigorating medicine, meant to tone up the system ‖ anything which has a similar effect on the nerves or mind ‖ (*mus.*) the keynote of the scale ‖ (*phon.*) an accented syllable [fr. Gk *tonikos*]

tonic accent stress placed on a syllable, esp. by raising the pitch

to·nic·i·ty (tounísiti:) *n.* (*physiol.*) a normal healthy elasticity in the tissues or muscles

tonic sol-fa (*mus.*) an English system of notation for a diatonic scale based not on fixed pitch but on tonality or relation to the keynote. The notes are named *do* (keynote), *re, mi, fa, sol, la, ti.* The system is used to train singers in sight-reading (*SOLMIZATION)

to·night (tənáit) 1. *adv.* on or during the present night, *you are tired tonight* ‖ on the coming night of the present day, *I'll see you tonight* 2. *n.* the night that has begun but not ended ‖ the coming night, *tonight is the play's first night* [O.E. *tō niht*]

to·nite (tóunait) *n.* a high explosive prepared from guncotton [fr. L. *tonare*, to thunder]

ton·ka bean (tóŋkə) any of various members of *Dipteryx*, fam. *Leguminosae*, a South American plant, esp. *D. odorata* ‖ the pleasant-smelling seed of *D. odorata*, containing coumarin, and used in perfumes and as flavoring for tobacco etc.

Ton·kin (tónkín) (*hist.*) the former name of the northern provinces of Vietnam, established (1883) as a protectorate by the French. It was administered (1887-1945) as part of French Indochina, became (1945) a province of the independent republic of Vietnam, and then formed (1954) the northern and central region of North Vietnam

Tonkin Gulf resolution an authorization requested (1964) by U.S. President Lyndon B. Johnson of Congress, following the alleged attack by North Vietnamese warships on U.S. Navy vessels in international waters in the Gulf of Tonkin. The resolution gave Congressional support for 'all necessary action to protect our armed forces and to assist nations covered by the SEATO treaty'. In effect this was a blank check for the president, as Congress had not declared war. The resolution was repealed (Jan. 12, 1971)

Ton·le-Sap (tónleisáp) a lake (area 1,000-2,500 sq. miles, depending on season, esp. on the effect of the S.W. monsoon) in W. Cambodia: fisheries

ton·nage, tun·nage (tánid3) *n.* the carrying capacity of a vessel measured in tons ‖ the total carrying capacity of a fleet, esp. of a merchant fleet ‖ a duty based on the cargo capacity of a vessel ‖ a charge per ton on cargo carried on canals or in ports

to·nom·e·ter (tounómitər) *n.* (*mus.*) an instrument, esp. a tuning fork, for determining pitch ‖ (*med.*) an instrument for measuring pressure (e.g. blood pressure) or tension (e.g. of the eyeball) ‖ an instrument for measuring vapor pressure **to·no·met·ric** (tounəmétrik) *adj.* **to·nóm·e·try** *n.* [fr. Gk *tonos*, stretching, pitch+METER]

ton·sil (tónsəl) *n.* one of a pair of lymphatic organs situated on either side of the throat at the entrance to the pharynx [fr. L. *tonsillae* pl. n.]

ton·sil·lar (tónsələr) *adj.* of, pertaining to or affected by the tonsils [fr. M.L. or Mod. L. *tonsillaris*]

ton·sil·lec·to·my (tɒnsəléktəmi:) *pl.* **ton·sil·lec·to·mies** *n.* removal of the tonsils by surgery [fr. L. *tonsillae*, tonsils +Gk -*ektomē*, a cutting out]

ton·sil·li·tis (tɒnsəláitis) *n.* inflammation of the tonsils [Mod. L. fr. L. *tonsillae*, tonsils]

ton·sil·lot·o·my (tónsəlótəmi:) *pl.* **ton·sil·lot·o·mies** *n.* incision of a tonsil [fr. L, *tonsillae*, tonsils+Gk -*tome*-, a cutting]

ton·so·ri·al (tɒnsóri:əl, tɒnsóuri:əl) *adj.* (esp. *jocular*) of or relating to barbers or their trade [fr. L. *tonsorius*]

ton·sure (tónʃər) 1. *n.* the shaving of the head or of a portion of the head on admission to the priesthood or to some monastic orders ‖ the part of the head left bare by such shaving 2. *v.t. pres. part.* **ton·sur·ing** *past* and *past part.* **ton·sured** to shave the head or crown of [F. or fr. L. *tonsura*]

ton·tine (tontí:n) *n.* an annuity system in which the share of a subscriber who dies is divided among the surviving subscribers until ultimately the whole income is enjoyed by the last survivor ‖ the share of each subscriber [after

Lorenzo *Tonti* (c. 1630–c. 1695), Italian banker who originated the system]

Ton·ton Ma·coute (tɔ̃tɔ̃mæku:t) *DUVALIER

to·nus (tóunəs) *n.* (*physiol.*) tonicity [L. fr. Gk *tonos*]

too (tu:) *adv.* excessively, more than is sufficient, necessary or desirable, *the cup is too big* ‖ (intensively) very, *you are too kind* ‖ also, *they are coming tomorrow and I hope you will come too* ‖ to a regrettable degree, *it's too bad* [stressed form of TO]

took *past* of TAKE

tool (tu:l) 1. *n.* anything which, held in the hand or hands, assists a person to do manual work ‖ the working part of a machine ‖ a machine tool ‖ anything used in the performance of nonmanual work, *a dictionary is a useful tool for a translator* ‖ a person who is made use of by another, e.g. for committing a crime ‖ (*bookbinding*) a hand stamp used to impress a letter or design on the cover of a book 2. *v.t.* to shape with a tool ‖ to impress letters or designs on (a book cover) with a tool ‖ (often with 'up') to equip (a factory etc.) with tools, machines etc. ‖ *v.i.* to use a tool or tools [O.E. *tōl*]

tool·bar (tú:lbɑr) *n.* a bar at the rear of a tractor to which different implements (harrow, roller etc.) can be attached

tool·box (tú:lbɒks) *n.* a box for tools ‖ a box in which the cutting tool of a planing or other machine is clamped

tool·ing (tú:liŋ) *n.* decorative work or designs done with a tool ‖ the set of tools used in a factory

tool·mak·er (tú:lmeikər) *n.* a machinist who makes and repairs the tools, instruments etc. used in a machine shop

toon (tu:n) *n. Cedrela toona,* fam. *Meliaceae,* a large East Indian and Australian tree yielding a reddish wood used esp. for cabinetmaking, and whose flowers yield a dye ‖ the wood of this tree [Hind. *tun, tün,* Skr. *tunna*]

toot (tu:t) 1. *v.t.* to cause (a horn etc.) to produce a short sharp note ‖ to blow a short note on (a horn or trumpet) ‖ *v.i.* to sound a short note on a whistle, horn or trumpet 2. *n.* such a sound [prob. imit.]

tooth (tu:θ) 1. *pl.* **teeth** (ti:θ) *n.* one of the hard, bonelike processes set in the jaws of most vertebrates and some invertebrates, used in man for masticating food and in forming speech sounds, and in animals for tearing, grinding and holding food, and for defense (cf. CANINE TOOTH, cf. INCISOR, cf. MOLAR). An adult human normally has 32 teeth, each one rooted in a socket in the jaw, developing around a central bundle of nerves and coated with a hard white enamel ‖ a toothlike projection e.g. on the edge of a leaf or the rim of a cogwheel **armed to the teeth** very heavily armed **in the teeth of** facing, fully exposed to, *in the teeth of the wind* ‖ in direct opposition to, in spite of, *in the teeth of the hostile critics* **to get one's teeth into** (something) to begin to cope effectively with (a difficulty) or to begin to grasp or master (something) **to put teeth into** to provide (esp. a law) with effective means of enforcement **to set one's teeth** to bring the upper and lower teeth tightly together ‖ to adopt a determined attitude, show oneself ready to suffer or endure or master **to show one's teeth** to put on a threatening attitude 2. *v.t.* to furnish with teeth ‖ *v.i.* to interlock as cogged wheels [O.E. *tōth*]

tooth·ache (tú:θeik) *n.* a pain in or near the nerve of a tooth

tooth and nail with all one's energy and every resource (in a fight, argument etc.)

tooth·brush (tú:θbrʌʃ) *n.* a small brush for cleaning the teeth

tooth·comb (tú:θkoum) *n.* (*Br.*) a comb with very close-set teeth **to go through something with a fine-tooth comb** (*Br.* **with a toothcomb**) to search or examine something with minute care

toothed (tu:θt) *adj.* having teeth ‖ (in compounds) having a specified number or kind of teeth, *saber-toothed tiger*

toothed whale one of the two main divisions of whales, constituting the suborder *Odontoceti,* e.g. the sperm whale

tooth·ing (tú:θiŋ) *n.* (generally *pl.*) alternate gaps and projections left at the end of a brick or stone wall to allow bonding in a later extension

tooth·less (tú:θlis) *adj.* having no teeth

tooth·paste (tú:θpeist) *n.* a paste dentifrice

tooth·pick (tú:θpik) *n.* a small pointed stick of wood, metal or plastic for removing fragments of food lodged in or between the teeth

tooth powder a powdered dentifrice

tooth·some (tú:θsəm) *adj.* (*old-fash.*) with an appetizing taste, tasty

tooth·wort (tú:θwə:rt, tú:θwɔrt) *n. Lathraea squamaria,* fam. *Orobanchaceae,* a herbaceous parasite on the hazel and beech with creeping rhizomes covered with broad fleshy scales ‖ a member of *Dentaria,* fam. *Cruciferae,* a genus of perennial creeping plants cultivated for their big white, rose or purple flowers

tooth·y (tú:θi:) *comp.* **tooth·i·er** *superl.* **tooth·i·est** *adj.* having large teeth or showing lots of teeth, *a toothy grin*

too·tle (tú:t'l) 1. *v. pres. part.* **too·tling** *past* and *past part.* **too·tled** *v.i.* to make fluty noises, esp. on a musical instrument 2. *n.* the act or sound of tootling [frequentative of TOOT]

top (tɒp) 1. *n.* the highest peak of something, *the top of the hill* ‖ the highest or best attainable position, rank, status, degree, pitch etc., *there is room at the top in his profession, at the top of one's voice* ‖ a cover, esp. a lid ‖ the upper part of a garment ‖ (*chem.*) the most volatile part of a mixture ‖ (*naut.*) a small platform near the top of a lower mast to which are fastened the shrouds of the topmast ‖ the part of a plant (esp. one with an edible root) that grows above the ground ‖ (*Br.*) high (the highest-ratio gear of a vehicle) ‖ the folding roof of a car or baby carriage **on top** successful **on top of** in addition to **on top of the world** in a state of great elation **over the top** over the front of a trench in order to attack ‖ above a specified goal or limit 2. *v.t. pres. part.* **top·ping** *past* and *past part.* **topped** to be higher or more than, *he tops his companions by six inches* ‖ to go over the top of ‖ to constitute the top of ‖ to do better than, *he topped his previous performance* ‖ to be at the top of ‖ to furnish with a top ‖ (*Br.,* with 'up') to add fresh liquid to so as to bring the contents to a higher level, *let me top up your glass* ‖ to remove the top or tops of, *top the bean plants* ‖ (*naut.*) to tilt (a yard) so that one end is higher than the other ‖ (*chem.*) to remove the most volatile parts from ‖ (*games*) to hit (a ball) above the center **to top off** to finish by adding a final touch 3. *adj.* on or at the top, *the top sheet* ‖ highest, *top prices* ‖ in the greatest degree, *top priority* ‖ (*pop.*) first in some understood scale, *top performance* [O.E.]

top *n.* a toy shaped to spin on its tapered point [O.E.]

to·paz (tóupæz) *n.* a mineral, $Al_2SiO_4(F,OH)_2$, consisting of a compound of aluminum and silica. It may be transparent, white, pale blue, pale green or yellow. Topazes are used mainly as gem stones, the yellow topaz being the most precious ‖ either of two large, brilliant South American hummingbirds, *Topaza pella* and *T. pyra* [M.E. fr. O.F. *topaze, topace* fr. L. fr. Gk]

to·paz·o·lite (toupǽzəlait) *n.* a yellow or greenish variety of garnet, esp. andradite

top boot a high boot reaching to just below the knee, worn by jockeys, hunters etc.

top·coat (tópkout) *n.* an overcoat ‖ a final coat of paint etc.

top dog (*pop.*) a person who is recognized as boss, esp. after having to fight for power

top dollar (*colloq.*) the highest possible price *ant.* bottom dollar

top drawer (esp. in the phrase) **out of the top drawer** (*Br., pop.*) born to the high social position actually occupied

top·dress (tópdres) *v.t.* to apply a topdressing to (cf. SIDE-DRESS) **tóp·dress·ing** *n.* a dressing of fertilizer spread on the surface of a field or garden

tope (toup) *n.* a dome-shaped Buddhist shrine [Hindi *tōp* prob. fr. Skr. *stūpa*]

tope (toup) *v. pres. part.* **top·ing** *past* and *past part.* **toped** *v.i.* (*rhet.*) to drink alcohol frequently and heavily [origin unknown]

to·pee, to·pi (tóupi:) *n.* a pith helmet, worn for protection against the sun [Hind. *topī*]

To·pe·ka (təpí:kə) the capital (pop. 115,266) of Kansas: meat packing, mechanical engineering, flour milling. University (1944)

Topeka (Free State) Constitution a constitution drafted (1854) by antislavery elements in the territory of Kansas. Opposing the proslavery territorial government, it outlawed slavery in Kansas, but nevertheless prohibited all blacks from entering the state. It was finally passed (1856) by Congress after bitter debate.

Kansas joined the Union as a free state only in 1861, however

top·flight (tópfláit) *adj.* (*pop.*) of the highest rank, ability etc.

top·gal·lant (təgǽlənt, tɒpgǽlənt) **1.** *adj.* (*naut.*, of a mast or sail) above the topmast and below the royal mast ‖ (of weather) allowing top gallant sails to be set **2.** *n.* a topgallant mast or sail

top-ham·per (tóphæmpər) *n.* (*naut.*) all the weight carried on or above a ship's deck, including masts, rigging, bridge etc. ‖ needlessly encumbering matter, e.g. superfluous possessions

top hat a man's tall cylindrical hat that is black or gray in color and usually made of silk. It is worn on certain formal occasions or as part of certain civilian uniforms

top-heav·i·ness (tóphevi:nis) *n.* the quality or state of being top-heavy

top-heav·y (tóphevi:) *adj.* unstable because the center of mass is high above the base ‖ (of an organization) having an unstable structure due to too great a concentration of highly paid top personnel ‖ overcapitalized

to·phus (tóufəs) *pl.* **to·phi** (tóufai) *n.* tufa ‖ (*med.*) a hard crystalline deposit in the tissues of sufferers from gout, causing great pain [L.=sandy stone]

topi *TOPEE

to·pi·ar·y (tóupi:əri:) **1.** *adj.* relating to the art of clipping or training shrubs, trees, hedges etc., into ornamental shapes **2.** *n.* bushes clipped thus ‖ the art of clipping bushes thus [fr. L. *topiarius*, of or relating to ornamental gardening]

top·ic (tópik) *n.* a subject of discussion, argument or writing **tóp·i·cal** *adj.* dealing with or referring to what is happening currently ‖ arranged by topics ‖ (*med.*) local, affecting or applied to a particular part of the body, *topical application* [fr. L. *topica* fr. Gk]

top·knot (tópnɒt) *n.* an arrangement of hair gathered into a knot high on the head, esp. arranged with flowers or ribbons ‖ a little crest of feathers ‖ a little tuft of hair on the top of the head ‖ *Zeugopterus punctatus*, an edible European flatfish with a tapering filament on its head

top·less (tóplǝs) *adj.* without covering the breasts *topless dancing*

top·mast (tópmæst, tópmǝst) *n.* the section of mast immediately above the lower mast and below the topgallant

top·most (tópmǝust) *adj.* highest

top·notch (tópnɒtʃ) *adj.* (*pop.*) first-rate, of the highest skill or quality

top-o-cen·tric (tɒpǝséntrik) *adj.* of perception from a specific point on earth

to·pog·ra·pher (tǝpógrǝfǝr) *n.* a specialist in topography

top·o·graph·ic (tɒpǝgrǽfik) *adj.* topographical (of or relating to topography)

top·o·graph·i·cal (tɒpǝgrǽfik'l) *adj.* of or relating to topography ‖ relating to the representation or mention of a locality in a poem, painting etc.

to·pog·ra·phy (tǝpógrǝfi:) *pl.* **to·pog·ra·phies** *n.* a description of all the surface features, natural and artificial, of a particular region ‖ all such surface features of a region ‖ the science of drawing maps and/or diagrams which represent these features ‖ topographic surveying [fr. L.L. *topographia* fr. Gk]

top·o·log·i·cal (tɒpǝlódʒik'l) *adj.* of properties that do not change in structure or form

topological equivalent an object similar to another in that it could be a copy of the other made on a stretched elastic plate

to·pol·o·gy (tǝpólǝdʒi:) *n.* (*math.*) the study of the properties of a geometrical figure that are unaffected when it is subjected to any continuous transformation or deformation [fr. Gk *topos*, place + *logos*, word]

to·pon·y·my (tǝpónǝmi:) *n.* the study, esp. etymological, of place-names [fr. Gk *topos*, a place+*onoma*, a name]

top·per (tópǝr) *n.* (*pop.*) a top hat

top·ple (tóp'l) *pres. part.* **top·pling** *past* and *past part.* **top·pled** *v.i.* to cease to be stable on a base and fall ‖ to be, or seem to be, on the point of falling over because of top-heaviness ‖ *v.t.* to cause to topple ‖ to cause to fall from a position of power or privilege

tops (tɒps) **1.** *adj.* (*pop.*) first-rate in quality, performance etc. **2.** *n.* **the tops** a person or thing one heartily approves of

TOPS (acronym) for **1.** (*aerospace*) thermoelectric outer planet spacecraft, used in exploration of planets **2.** teletype optical projection system, a system for plotting radar data received by teletype on the projection of a target with a grease pencil *Cf* DOPS, POPS

top·sail (tóps'l, tópseil) *n.* (in a square-rigged ship) the square sail immediately above the mainsail or course (sometimes divided into the upper and lower topsails) ‖ (in a fore-and-aft-rigged ship) the sail above or on the gaff

topsail schooner a two-masted schooner with a square topsail or topsails on the foremast

top sawyer the man who works in the upper position when using a saw in a sawpit ‖ (*Br.*, *pop.*) the dominating person in an activity or situation

top secret (of military or governmental documentary information) of the highest category of secrecy **tóp·sé·cret** *adj.*

top sergeant (*pop.*) a first sergeant

top·side (tópsaid) **1.** *n.* (*naut.*, esp. in *pl.*) the side of a ship above the waterline ‖ (*Br.*) a cut of beef, the outer part of a round of beef, cut from the middle of a hind leg **2.** *adv.* (*naut.*) on deck **tóp·sides** *adv.*

top·soil (tópsɒil) *n.* the upper few inches of the soil in which worms, beneficial bacteria and naturally accumulating humus are to be found (cf. SUBSOIL)

top·sy-tur·vi·ly (tópsi:tǝ́:rvili:) *adv.* in a topsy-turvy manner

top·sy-tur·vi·ness (tópsi:tǝ́:rvi:nis) *n.* the state or quality of being topsy-turvy

top·sy-tur·vy (tópsi:tǝ́:rvi:) **1.** *adv.* upside down ‖ in or into a disorderly or muddled state **2.** *adj.* in this condition [prob. fr. TOP +earlier *terve*, to turn, turn over or overturn]

toque (touk) *n.* a woman's close-fitting hat usually with no brim ‖ (*hist.*) a man's hat of the 16th c., with a small narrow brim and pleated fullness on top, decorated with a plume ‖ *Macaca sinica*, a small brown or reddish-brown macaque [F.]

tor (tɔr) *n.* a steep rocky hill or an outcrop of rock, standing up steeply from its surroundings [O.E.]

To·rah, To·ra (tórǝ, tóurǝ) *n.* the Hebrew name for the Mosaic Law (Pentateuch) ‖ the scroll of the Pentateuch used liturgically in a synagogue [Heb.]

torc *TORQUE (necklace)

torch (tɔrtʃ) *n.* a portable light made of resinous wood or tow impregnated with e.g. tallow to make it inflammable ‖ (*Br.*) a flashlight ‖ (*Roman Catholicism*) a candle in a tall candlestick with no foot or base, carried esp. by some of the servers at Benediction ‖ a very hot flame device, e.g. an oxyacetylene lamp for welding ‖ (*rhet.*) a source of enlightenment, *the torch of learning* **to carry a** (or **the**) **torch for** (*pop.*) to be in love with (esp. someone who doesn't reciprocate) [O.F. *torche*]

torch·bear·er (tórtʃbɛǝrǝr) *n.* a person who carries a flaming torch ‖ (*rhet.*) a person who hands on knowledge, enlightenment etc.

torch·light (tórtʃlait) **1.** *n.* the light of a torch or torches **2.** *adj.* of, pertaining to or done by torchlight

tor·chon lace (tórʃɒn) a coarse single-thread bobbin or machine-made lace [F. *torchon*, duster, dishcloth]

torch singer a person who sings torch songs

torch song a popular song of sentimental character, usually about unrequited love [fr. the phrase *to carry a torch for someone* (*TORCH)]

torch·wood (tórtʃwud) *n.* a member of *Amyris*, fam. *Rutaceae*, a genus of tropical American shrubs and trees the wood of which is resinous and burns very readily

Tor·de·sil·las, Treaty of (tǝrdeisí:ljǝs) an agreement (1494) between Spain and Portugal, dividing the non-Christian world into two zones of influence, the division passing 370 leagues west of the Cape Verde Islands. This gave the New World to Spain, except for part of Brazil, which fell within Portugal's share. Portugal was also to have Africa and India (*LONDON, TREATY OF (1604))

tore (tǝr) *n.* (*archit.* and *geom.*) a torus

tore *past of TEAR

tor·e·a·dor (tóri:ǝdɔr) *n.* (not used by Spaniards) a bullfighter (*TORERO) [Span.]

to·re·ro (tǝréro) *n.* a bullfighter [Span.]

tor·ic (tórik, tórik) *adj.* of or shaped like a torus

toric lens a lens of which one surface has different curvatures in its two main meridians, and is used for correcting astigmatic vision

to·ri·i (tóri:i:, tóuri:i:) *pl.* **to·ri·i** *n.* a gateway to a Shinto shrine, consisting of two uprights supporting an upward-curving lintel with a straight crosspiece below it [Jap.]

tor·ment (tórment) *n.* great and usually protracted pain of mind or body ‖ a source or cause of this [O.F. *tourment*]

tor·ment (tǝrmént) *v.t.* to cause torment to ‖ to vex, worry or annoy excessively [O.F. *tourmenter, tormenter*]

tor·men·til (tórmǝntǝl) *n. Potentilla tormentilla*, fam. *Rosaceae*, a yellow-flowered, low-growing Eurasian plant, the astringent root of which is used esp. in dyeing and in tanning [F. *tormentille*]

tor·men·tor (tǝrméntǝr) *n.* someone who torments ‖ (*theater*) either of the flats or curtains projecting into the wings on each side of the stage ‖ (*movies*) a covered screen on a set for absorbing echoes [O.F. *tormenteour*]

torn *past part.* of TEAR

tor·na·do (tɔrnéidou) *pl.* **tor·na·does, tor·na·dos** *n.* a violent, whirling wind accompanied by a funnel-shaped cloud, small in diameter and appearing to grow down from dark cumulonimbus clouds. Tornadoes of this kind, which are terribly destructive, occur most frequently in the central Mississippi valley. Their average width is 300-400 yds. Their paths may extend up to 50 miles and their speeds vary between 10 and 50 m.p.h. The wind speed in the vortex has been estimated as between 100 and 500 m.p.h., but in the very center, because of centrifugal effects, there is an area of near calm ‖ a violent storm consisting of a squall accompanying a thunderstorm, sudden in origin and short in duration, occurring in W. Africa. With this kind of tornado, which is caused by the meeting of warm, damp, monsoon air with dry air from the Sahara, there is usually torrential rain. The front of such a tornado can extend up to 200 miles [perh. fr. Span. *tronada*, thunderstorm]

Tornado *n.* U.S.S.R. mechanized infantry combat vehicle armed with 25-millimeter automatic gun and 7.2-millimeter machine guns

to·roid (tórɒid, tóurɒid) **1.** *n.* the surface generated by the rotation of a plane closed curve about an axis lying in its plane which does not intersect it **2.** *adj.* of or pertaining to a toroid **tor·rói·dal** *adj.*

To·ron·to (tǝróntou) the second largest city (pop. 599,217, with agglom. 2,137,395) in Canada and capital of Ontario, a port on Lake Ontario. Industries: mechanical and electrical engineering, automobiles, shipbuilding, textiles, food processing, publishing, banking. University (1827)

Toronto, University of a Canadian educational institution founded (1827) in Toronto. It blends the English college system with the U.S. faculty system

to·rose (tórous, tóurous) *adj.* (*zool.*) knobbed ‖ (*bot.*, of a stem etc.) swollen or bulging here and there [fr. L. *torosus*, brawny]

To·ros Mountains (tɒrós) *TAURUS MOUNTAINS

tor·pe·do (tɔrpí:dou) **1.** *pl.* **tor·pe·does** *n.* a long, self-propelled, cigar-shaped missile, charged with an explosive warhead and fired underwater or from an aircraft to blow up ships ‖ (*rail.*) a detonator, fastened to the top of a rail, which explodes when a locomotive goes over it, warning the crew of impending danger ‖ an explosive cartridge lowered into an oil well to clear it ‖ (*zool.*) the electric ray ‖ a small firework which when thrown against a hard surface explodes loudly ‖ a large sandwich on a long roll, usu. of cheese, cold cuts, and condiments **2.** *v.t.* to destroy or attack with a torpedo ‖ to clear (an oil well or its shaft) with a torpedo [L.— stiffness, numbness, the electric ray]

torpedo net a heavy steel net suspended in the water, e.g. across a harbor entrance, to protect warships from attack by torpedoes

torpedo tube a tube from which a warship fires torpedoes

tor·pid (tórpid) *adj.* having ceased to move or feel for a period, e.g. in hibernation ‖ lethargic **tor·pid·i·ty** *n.* [fr. L. *torpidus*]

tor·por (tórpǝr) *n.* suspended animation ‖ a state of mental inactivity ‖ mental or spiritual listlessness or apathy **tor·pór·ific** *adj.* [L.]

tor·quate (tórkweit) *adj.* (*zool.*) collared, having a ring of distinctive color around the neck [fr. L. *torquatus*, wearing a necklace]

torque (tork) *n.* (*phys.*) the agency that produces or tends to produce torsion: a vector quantity defined as the product of the tangential force and the perpendicular distance from

---

CONCISE PRONUNCIATION KEY: **(a)** æ, c*a*t; ɑ, c*a*r; ɔ, f*aw*n; ei, sn*a*ke. **(e)** e, h*e*n; i:, sh*ee*p; iǝ, d*ee*r; ɛǝ, b*ea*r. **(i)** i, f*i*sh; ai, t*i*ger; ǝ:, b*i*rd. **(o)** o, *o*x; au, c*ow*; ou, g*oa*t; u, p*oo*r; ɔi, r*oy*al. **(u)** ʌ, d*u*ck; u, b*u*ll; u:, g*oo*se; ǝ, *ba*cillus; ju:, c*u*be. x, lo*ch*; θ, *th*ink; ð, *b*o*th*er; z, *Z*en; ʒ, cor*s*age; dʒ, sa*v*age; ŋ, oranguta*ng*; j, *y*ak; ʃ, *f*ish; tʃ, fe*tch*; 'l, rabb*le*; 'n, redd*en*. Complete pronunciation key appears inside front cover.

the line of action of the force of the axis of rotation ‖ (*Br.* also **torc**, *hist.*) a necklace of twisted metal, esp. gold, worn e.g. by the ancient Celts [fr. L. *torques*, a twisted necklace]

torque arm a rod running from the axle housing to the torque tube in an automobile etc. for taking up the torque reactions of driving and braking

torque converter a hydraulic device for providing the torque required at the driven shaft by transmitting and multiplying the torque from the driving shaft

Tor·que·ma·da (tɔrkimáða, tɔrkemáða) Tomás de) (1420-98), Spanish inquisitor-general notorious for his cruelty (*INQUISITION). He was largely responsible for the expulsion of the Jews from Spain (1492)

torque·me·ter (tɔ́rkmiːtər) *n.* an instrument that measures torque

torque tube a hollow tube surrounding the propeller shaft of an automotive vehicle designed to take up the torque reactions of braking and driving

torr (tɔr) *n.* a unit of pressure equal to the pressure of 1 mm. of mercury at standard temperature and gravity [after TORRICELLI]

tor·re·fac·tion (tɔrifǽkʃən, tɔrifǽkʃən) *n.* a torrefying or being torrefied

tor·re·fy, tor·ri·fy (tɔ́rifai, tɔ́rifai) *pres. part.* **tor·re·fy·ing, tor·ri·fy·ing** *past* and *past part.* **tor·re·fied, tor·ri·fied** *v.t.* to dry up or parch with heat (esp. drugs and ores, so that they may be powdered) [F. *torréfier*]

Tor·rens (tɔ́reən, tɔ́renz) a salt lake (area approx. 2,500 sq. miles) in E. South Australia, 25 ft below sea level. In the dry season it becomes a salt marsh

tor·rent (tɔ́rənt, tɔ́rənt) *n.* a violently rushing stream ‖ a great downpour of rain or great flow of a fluid ‖ a flood of violent language, tears etc. **tor·ren·tial** (tərénʃəl) *adj.* [F. fr. L. fr. *torrere*, to burn, boil, rush]

Tor·re·ón (tɔ́reón) a commercial center (pop. 262,744) in N.E. Mexico: cotton textiles, metallurgy

Tor·res Strait (tɔ́ris) the shallow strait (average width: 90 miles) separating Queensland, Australia and New Guinea, containing many shoals and reefs

Tor·res Ve·dras (tɔ́risvéidrəs) (*hist.*) three lines of fortification built by Wellington to defend Lisbon against the French (1810-11)

Tor·ri·cel·li (tɔritʃéli:), Evangelista (1608-47), Italian mathematician and physicist. He discovered the principle of the mercury barometer (1643) and showed that Aristotle was in error in stating that a vacuum is an impossibility. He also improved the microscope and the telescope

Tor·ri·cel·li·an vacuum (tɔritʃéliːən) the near-vacuum above the mercury in a barometer. This space contains mercury vapor of vapor pressure not greater than 0.004 mm.

tor·rid (tɔ́rid, tɔ́rid) *adj.* (of land areas) very hot and dry or exposed to great heat ‖ of the zone between the Tropic of Cancer and the Tropic of Capricorn, where the sun is vertically overhead at some point of the year [fr. L. *toridus*]

torrify *TORREFY

Tor·ri·gia·no (tɔrri:dʒáno), Pietro (1472-1522), Florentine sculptor. He was invited to England, where his main work is Henry VII's tomb in Westminster Abbey

Tor·ri·jos (tɔrri:hos), Omar (1929-81), Panamanian general, and president (1968-81) following a coup d'état which ousted President Arnulfo Arias. He survived (1969) a conspiracy by National Guard officers and José Pinilla to remove him and remained a powerful political figure until his death in a plane crash in 1981. He and U.S. President Jimmy Carter negotiated the Panama Canal treaties of 1978

tor·sade (tɔrsád) *n.* (*cosmetology*) small hairpiece of coils or curls used in creating a hairstyle

tor·sel (tɔ́rs'l) *n.* a piece of iron or wood or stone in a wall, on which the end of a floor joist rests [fr. O.F. *tassel*, a bit of stone or wood to stop a hole]

tor·si·bil·i·ty (tɔrsəbíliti) *n.* the ability to resist torsion

tor·sion (tɔ́rʃən) *n.* the act of turning one end of an object about a longitudinal axis while the other is fixed or turned in the opposite direction ‖ the state of being so twisted ‖ the force tending to restore an elastic object so twisted ‖ (*math.*) the rate of change of the curvature with arc length **tor·sion·al** *adj.* [F. fr. L.L.]

torsion balance (*phys.*) an instrument that can measure small forces by allowing them to twist a calibrated fiber measuring the deflection by means of a mirror fixed to the fiber and a lamp and scale

torsion bar a rod in an automobile etc. that restricts sideways movement of the rear axle relative to the frame

tor·so (tɔ́rsou) *pl.* **tor·sos** *n.* the trunk of the human body ‖ a carved, modeled, painted or drawn representation of this, whether as a complete work of art, or as a fragment, or as part of a complete figure [Ital.=stump]

Tor·stens·son (tɔ́rstensən), Lennart, count of Ortala (1603-51), Swedish general. He led the Swedish invasion of Germany (1641-6) during the Thirty Years' War, distinguishing himself at Breitenfeld (1642)

tort (tɔrt) *n.* (*law*) a breach of duty, other than a breach of contract, for which the offender will be subject to legal responsibility [O.F.]

tor·ti·col·lis (tɔrtikólis) *n.* (*med.*) a persistent muscular spasm which causes the head and neck to be held at an unnatural angle [Mod. L. fr. *tortus*, twisted + *collum*, neck]

tor·til·la (tɔrti:ə) *n.* a pancake, made of corn flour, cooked on a hot iron plate or stone, and eaten in Mexico as the equivalent of bread ‖ an omelet originating in Spain and containing potatoes and onions [Span dim. of *torta*, a cake]

tor·tious (tɔ́rʃəs) *adj.* (*law*) of or involving a tort

tor·toise (tɔ́rtəs) *n.* any terrestrial species of turtle, esp. of genera *Testudo* and *Gopherus* [fr. L.L. *tortuca*]

tortoise beetle a member of *Chrysomelidae*, a family of tortoise-shaped beetles whose larvae feed on leaves

tor·toise·shell (tɔ́rtəsʃel) **1.** *n.* the material forming the shell of the turtle, esp. the semi-transparent material forming the carapace of the hawksbill turtle. It is of a rich mottled reddish or golden brown color and can be molded when heat is applied to it. It is used for inlaying and for making combs and small decorative boxes etc. **2.** *adj.* made of tortoiseshell ‖ colored like tortoiseshell

tortoiseshell butterfly a member of *Nymphalis*, fam. *Nymphalidae*, a genus of widely distributed butterflies with wings patterned like tortoiseshell

Tor·to·la (tɔrtóulə) the largest island (area 24 sq. miles, pop. 6,800) of the Virgin Is and chief island of the British group, in the Leeward Is, West Indies. Capital: Road Town (pop. 2,000), a port of entry

Tor·tu·ga, La (latɔrtú:gə) an island (area 85 sq. miles) in the Caribbean Sea off the north central coast of Venezuela. It became (early 17th c.) the chief pirate stronghold in the West Indies

tor·tu·os·i·ty (tɔrtʃu:ósiti) *pl.* **tor·tu·os·i·ties** *n.* the state or quality of being tortuous ‖ an instance or example of this [fr. L. *tortuositas*]

tor·tu·ous (tɔ́rtʃu:əs) *adj.* having many twists and turns ‖ not open, frank or straightforward ‖ hard to follow because involved [A.F.]

tor·ture (tɔ́rtʃər) **1.** intense pain or suffering of body or mind ‖ the infliction of such pain or suffering. Physical torture was once employed on a worldwide scale as part of the ordinary process of judicial procedure ‖ a method of inflicting intense pain or suffering ‖ a cause of such pain or suffering **2.** *v.t. pres. part.* **tor·tur·ing** *past* and *past part.* **tor·tured** to subject to torture ‖ to misuse (words) so as to distort their meaning ‖ to wrench out of shape [F. fr. L.]

tor·tur·ous (tɔ́rtʃərəs) *adj.* causing torture ‖ accompanied by torture [A.F.=O. F. *torturens*, *tortureux* fr. L. *tortura*, torture]

To·run (tɔ́ru:nj) (G. Thorn) a port (pop. 170,000) in N. central Poland on the Vistula. Industries: chemicals, food processing. University (1945)

to·rus (tɔ́rəs, tóurəs) *pl.* **to·ri** (tɔ́rai, tóurai) *n.* (*archit.*) a semicircular molding, esp. at the base of a column ‖ (*bot.*) a receptacle of a flower ‖ (*bot.*) a swollen stalk bearing flowers ‖ (*bot.*) a thickened membrane between plant cells ‖ (*anat.*) any smooth, rounded, esp. bony projection on a part of the body ‖ (*geom.*) a surface or solid generated by the revolution of a circle about an axis in its plane which does not intersect it [L.]

To·ry (tɔ́ri:), Geoffroy (c. 1480-1533), French typographer, engraver and writer. He was influential in introducing Roman type into France as well as in standardizing spelling, punctua-

tion and the use of accent marks. In 1530 he became the king's printer

To·ry (tɔ́ri:, tóuri) **1.** *pl.* **To·ries** *n.* (*Am. hist.*) a person who opposed the breach with Britain in the Revolutionary War (1775-83) ‖ (*Br.*) a member or supporter of the Conservative party ‖ (*Ir. hist.*) any of the dispossessed Irish outlaws (17th c.) who plundered and killed English settlers ‖ (*Eng. hist.*) a member of the political group who opposed (1679) Whig attempts to exclude the future James II from the succession to the throne. After 1688, most Tories supported the Anglican Church and the hereditary right to the throne. Briefly in power (1710-14) under Harley and Bolingbroke, they were discredited for their Jacobite leanings, and were out of office until the accession (1760) of George III, when many of them joined the 'king's friends'. The French Revolution brought many Whigs to support the Tories in the defense of the landed classes, and made the party more reactionary. The Tory party was ousted (1830) by the Whigs, and was remodeled in the 1830s by Peel to form the Conservative party **2.** *adj.* of, being or holding the beliefs of a Tory **To·ry·ism** *n.* [Anglicized spelling of Ir. Gael. assumed *tōraidhe, tōraighe*, pursuer]

Tos·ca·ni·ni (tɔskəni:ni:), Arturo (1867-1957), Italian conductor, considered one of the greatest of his time. He began his conducting career when he stepped in at short notice and conducted Verdi's 'Aida' without a score (1886). By 1898 he had become chief conductor at La Scala, Milan. He served with the Metropolitan Opera, New York (1908-15) and was principal conductor of the New York Philharmonic (1928-36) before the NBC Symphony was created for him (1937). He led this group until his retirement (1954). Known for his fidelity to composers' scores, he was also noted for his ability to elicit virtuoso performances from his musicians

tosh (tɔʃ) *n.* stupid nonsense [origin unknown]

toss (tɔs, tɒs) **1.** *v.t.* to throw casually or without force, esp. over a short distance ‖ (of horned animals) to throw up into the air with the horns ‖ (of a horse etc.) to unseat (its rider) ‖ (*Br.*) to flip (a pancake) ‖ to cause to move up and down or to and fro jerkily or restlessly, *waves tossed the boat* ‖ to allow to move in this way, *the flowers tossed their heads in the wind* ‖ to flick (a coin) into the air and let it fall heads or tails, as a method of letting fate decide whether the course of action previously agreed on if the coin falls heads is to be put into operation or that agreed on if it falls tails ‖ to agree with (someone) to let a matter be settled in this way, *I'll toss you for who goes first* ‖ to jerk (the head) quickly upwards and backwards, esp. in people as a willful gesture of defiance and in horses as a sign of restiveness ‖ to mix (food) gently so as to coat e.g. with a dressing, *to toss a salad, to toss carrots in butter* ‖ to put (clothes) on carelessly and hurriedly ‖ (with 'down') to swallow quickly, esp. in a single draft ‖ to turn (hay) over with a pitchfork in order to dry it ‖ *v.i.* to move violently, jerkily and restlessly or as if restlessly up and down or to and fro, *the clothes on the line tossed in the wind* ‖ (of people unable to sleep properly) to roll around restlessly in bed ‖ to flip a coin **to toss aside** to reject casually or summarily **to toss for it** to decide between alternatives by flipping a coin **to toss off** to swallow (a drink) in a single draft ‖ to compose without apparent effort, *to toss off a sonnet* ‖ to enumerate casually, *to toss off a few names* **to toss out of** to leave with a flounce **to toss up** to flip a coin in order to decide between two alternatives **2.** *n.* a tossing or being tossed or an instance of being tossed ‖ a toss-up **to argue the toss** (*Br.*) to continue to object or argue etc. after a decision has been given in a dispute etc. **to take a toss** to be thrown by a horse [origin unknown]

toss-up (tɔ́sʌp, tɒ́sʌp) *n.* an even chance or a matter in which an even chance is involved, *it's a toss-up whether or not he'll come* ‖ the tossing of a coin

Tos·tig (tɔ́stig) (d. 1066), earl of Northumbria, son of Earl Godwin. With Harald III of Norway, he invaded England (1066) and was defeated and killed at Stamford Bridge by the army of his brother Harold II

tot (tɔt) *n.* a toddler ‖ (esp. *Br.*) a small measure of drink, esp. of spirits, *a tot of rum* [etym. doubtful]

tot *pres. part.* **tot·ting** *past* and *past part.* **tot·ted** *v.t.* (with 'up') to add up ‖ *v.i.* (with 'up') to total

CONCISE PRONUNCIATION KEY: **(a)** æ, c*a*t; ɑ, c*ar*; ɔ f*aw*n; ei, sn*a*ke. **(e)** e, h*e*n; i:, sh*ee*p; iə, d*eer*; ɛə, b*ear*. **(i)** i, f*i*sh; ai, t*i*ger; ə:, b*ir*d. **(o)** o, *o*x; au, c*ow*; ou, g*oa*t; u, p*oor*; ɔi, r*oy*al. **(u)** ʌ, d*u*ck; u, b*u*ll; u:, g*oo*se; ə, b*a*cill*u*s; ju:, c*u*be. x, lo*ch*; θ, *th*ink; ð, bo*th*er; z, *Z*en; ʒ, corsa*g*e; dʒ, sava*g*e; ŋ, orangutan*g*; j, *y*ak; ʃ, *fi*sh; tʃ, fe*tch*; 'l, rabb*le*; 'n, redd*en*. Complete pronunciation key appears inside front cover.

to·tal (tóut'l) 1. *adj.* entire, constituting the whole, *the total sum* ‖ utter, complete, *a total failure* 2. *n.* the sum of a number of items ‖ a total wreck 3. *v. pres. part.* **to·tal·ing** esp. *Br.* **to·tal·ling** *past and past part.* **to·taled,** esp. *Br.* **to·talled** *v.t.* to calculate the total of ‖ to amount to as a total, *the damages totaled $50* ‖ (*slang or colloq.*) to wreck a motor vehicle beyond repair ‖ *v.i.* (with 'up') to begin to be considerable in amount, number etc., *incidental expenses soon total up* ‖ (with 'up to') to add up to, amount to, *the bill totals up to $100* [F.]

total eclipse an eclipse in which a celestial body is wholly obscured

to·tal·i·tar·i·an (toutælitéəri:ən) *adj.* of a form of government or state in which the lives and actions of every individual, and every enterprise, are controlled by a dictator or dictatorial caucus **to·tal·i·tár·i·an·ism** *n.*

to·tal·i·ty (toutǽliti:) *pl.* **to·tal·i·ties** *n.* the condition of being total ‖ a whole ‖ (*astron.*) the phase during which an eclipse is total [fr. M.L. *totalitas*]

to·tal·i·za·tor (tóut'lizeitər) *n.* a parimutuel machine

to·tal·ize (tóut'laiz) *pres. part.* **to·tal·iz·ing** *past and past part.* **to·tal·ized** *v.t.* to combine into a total **tó·tal·iz·er** *n.* a totalizator

to·tal·i·zer, totalisator, tote (tóut'laizə:r) *n.* device that lists sums bet on each horse race and the odds on each competitor

to·tal·ly (tóut'li:) *adv.* completely

total war war in which the whole population of a country is involved, and to which all its resources are devoted, waged against the whole population and resources of the enemy, civilian as well as military

tote (tout) 1. *pres. part.* **tot·ing** *past and past part.* **tot·ed** *v.t.* (*pop.*) to carry, esp. in the arms or on the back, *to tote a gun* 2. *n.* (*pop.*) a carrying ‖ (*pop.*) something carried [etym. doubtful] **tote** *n.* a pari-mutuel machine

to·tem (tóutəm) *n.* something, esp. an animal, which members of a totem group have as their sign. In many cases the members believe it shares some sort of kinship with them, e.g. descent from a common ancestor. Animals make the most common totems, but parts of animals, plants, objects, abstract qualities and colors can also serve ‖ a fabricated, esp. a carved, image of this [fr. Ojibwa or some kindred Algonquian language]

totem group a group of people united by their relationship to a common totem

to·tem·ic (toutémik) *adj.* of, like or relating to a totem ‖ having the nature of a totem ‖ characterized by totemism

to·tem·ism (tóutəmizəm) *n.* religious beliefs and practices based on totems ‖ social organization by totem groups

to·tem·ist (tóutəmist) *n.* a person who practices totemism ‖ a specialist in the study of totemism **to·tem·ís·tic** *adj.*

totem pole (only of Indians of N.W. America) a column of cedarwood carved with totemic symbols

To·ti·la (tɒtílə) (d. 552), last king of the Ostrogoths (541-52). After conquering central and S. Italy, Sicily, Corsica and Sardinia he was defeated and killed by Narses

to·ti·pal·mate (toutəpǽlmit) *adj.* (of certain swimming birds) having the four toes completely joined by a web **to·ti·pal·ma·tion** (toutəpælméiʃən) *n.*

Totleben *TODLEBEN

tot lot a small recreation area for children

tot·ter (tɒ́tər) 1. *v.i.* to walk, or stand shakily, as if about to overbalance ‖ to be so weak as to be about to lose authority, power etc. 2. *n.* an unsteady gait **tót·ter·y** *adj.* [perh. fr. Norse]

tou·can (tú:kən) *n.* any of various members of *Ramphastidae,* a family of tropical American birds having a lightly constructed, brilliantly colored bill about 8 ins long, roughly as long as the body itself. They feed on fruit, seeds, insects etc. The plumage is yellow, black and red [F. fr. Port. fr. Tupi]

touch (tʌtʃ) 1. *v.t.* to perceive, experience or explore the nature of (something) by e.g. putting a finger into or onto it, i.e. by letting the nerve ends in and under the skin register its presence and nature, *do not touch the poison cactus* ‖ to be or become so close to (something) that there is no intervening space, *the wheels of the car touched the curb* ‖ to seem to do this, *the sun touched the horizon* ‖ to exert very slight force on, *touch the ball with your cue* ‖ to go as high or as low or as far as, *the temperature touched 40°* ‖ to operate (an electric switch etc.) ‖ (in negative constructions) to compare in quality with, *she can't touch him as a pianist* ‖ (in negative or interrogative constructions) to interfere with or disarrange, *don't touch the papers on my desk* ‖ (in negative or interrogative constructions) to injure slightly, *he was hardly touched by the fall* ‖ to get possession of, *you can't touch trust money* ‖ to do physical harm to, esp. by violence, *don't you dare touch that child* ‖ to relate to, *anything touching that subject interests me* ‖ to begin to deal with, *we didn't touch the last item on the agenda* ‖ (in negative or interrogative constructions) to eat a bite of or consume a drop of, *he did not touch his lunch* ‖ to arouse a tender or sympathetic response in, *the story touched us all* ‖ (in negative or interrogative constructions) to cause pain or anger in, *her husband's rages no longer touch her* ‖ (*pop.*) to obtain a loan, subscription or gift of money from, *he touched us for 50 dollars* ‖ (in negative or interrogative constructions) to be efficacious in removing, curing or dealing with, *water won't touch that stain* ‖ (*hist.*) to test (gold etc.) by a touchstone ‖ to mark (metal) with an official stamp after it has been tested ‖ to press (the keys) of or pluck or bow (the strings) of a musical instrument in order to make it sound ‖ to cause (a musical instrument) to sound by pressing its keys or plucking or bowing its strings ‖ to cause (a chord) to sound ‖ (in negative or interrogative constructions) to leave a mark or impression on, *his years in prison appear not to have touched him* ‖ (*geom.*) to be tangential to ‖ to misappropriate or use without right, *he would never have touched your bicycle* ‖ (of a ship) to touch at ‖ (*hist.,* of English or French sovereigns) to lay the hand on (a scrofulous person) in order to cure him ‖ (in negative constructions) to concern oneself with, handle, *don't touch the project* ‖ to put the fingers briefly to (the hat or forelock) as a polite salutation ‖ (in negative or interrogative constructions) to make use of, *she never touches the typewriter now* ‖ to apply (something) lightly and briefly to something else, *touch a match to the fire* ‖ to apply something lightly and briefly to, *he just touched the horse with the whip* ‖ *v.i.* (of two or more things) to be or become so close to one another that there is no intervening space ‖ (*math.*) to be tangential **to touch at** (of a ship) to call at (a port) **to touch down** (of an aircraft) to land ‖ (*rugby*) to score a try by touching the ground with the ball behind the opponents' goal line **to touch in** to draw or paint in (a detail) very lightly **to touch off** to start off, get going, *to touch off a revolution* ‖ to ignite or cause to explode ‖ to describe briefly with pleasing subtlety **to touch on** (or **upon**) to relate to, pertain to ‖ to make brief reference to ‖ to verge on **to touch up** to work on (e.g. a painting) by adding some corrective strokes to treat (a photograph) so that it will reproduce well ‖ to rouse with or as if with a flick of the whip 2. *n.* a touching or being touched ‖ the manner of playing the keys or strings of a musical instrument or of tapping the keys of a keyboard machine, usually in relation to lightness or heaviness ‖ the manner in which the keys of an instrument or machine respond to being touched ‖ a distinctive manner, trait, quality etc., *the touch of a master* ‖ the well-contrived introduction of a detail for special effect, *his referring to the social aspect of the problem was a clever touch* ‖ a gentle stroke, tap etc. ‖ a small quantity, *a touch of red* ‖ a slight degree, *he fired a touch too high* ‖ (of a disease or illness) a mild attack, *a touch of lumbago* ‖ a light mark made with a brush, pen or pencil ‖ (*physiol.*) the sense by which nerve ends in and under the skin give the perception that something is in contact with the skin ‖ the sensation conveyed by this sense, *she revels in the touch of fur* ‖ (*change ringing*) a set of changes amounting to less than a full peal ‖ (*pop.*) the act of borrowing money or getting a subscription or money gift out of someone ‖ (*pop.*) the person the money is obtained from, *an easy touch* ‖ (*pop.*) the money obtained ‖ (*hist.*) the act of testing the quality of gold and silver by rubbing it on a touchstone ‖ the official stamp or mark put upon gold or silver to show that it has been tested ‖ the stamp or punch used ‖ (*fencing*) a hit that scores a point ‖ (*rugby* and *soccer*) the area outside the touchlines, *to kick the ball into touch* **in** (**out of**) **touch** in (not in) communication by correspondence, radio etc. or informed (not in-formed) about events etc. **to lose touch** to fail to maintain communication or keep oneself informed [O.F. *tochier, tuchier*]

Touch-A-Mat·ic (tʌtʃəmǽtik) *n.* Bell System telephone automatic dialer that remembers and dials up to 31 numbers at the touch of a button

touch and go a highly precarious situation which could prove disastrous, *it was touch and go whether he would survive*

touch·back (tʌ́tʃbæk) *n.* (*football*) a grounding of the ball behind one's own goal line, when the ball has been passed over the goal line by an opponent (cf. SAFETY)

touch·down (tʌ́tʃdaun) *n.* (*football*) a play in which a player grounds the ball on or past the opponent's goal line, or the score so made (6 points) ‖ (*rugby*) the scoring of a try (3 points) ‖ the moment when the landing gear of an aircraft touches the ground as it comes in to land

tou·ché (tu:ʃéi) 1. *interj.* (*fencing*) used to to acknowledge a touch ‖ used to acknowledge that one has been scored off by a clever remark etc. 2. *n.* (*fencing*) a touch [F.]

touched (tʌtʃt) *adj.* moved by feelings of pity or gratitude ‖ showing slight traces of esp. some color, *the sky in the west was touched with pink* ‖ (*pop.*) slightly crazy

touch football a form of football in which tackling is replaced by touching

touch·i·ly (tʌ́tʃili:) *adv.* in a touchy manner

touch·i·ness (tʌ́tʃi:nis) *n.* the quality or state of being touchy

touch·ing (tʌ́tʃiŋ) 1. *adj.* arousing tender or grateful feeling 2. *prep.* (*rhet.*) concerning

touch·line (tʌ́tʃlain) *n.* either of two lines marking the side limits of the playing field in various games (hockey, rugby and soccer etc.)

touch paper paper impregnated with potassium nitrate, used as a slow-burning fuse in fireworks etc.

touch·stone (tʌ́tʃstoun) *n.* a black flintlike stone, e.g. jasper or schist, formerly used in assaying gold or silver ‖ a criterion or test of quality, ability etc.

Touch-Tone telephone (tʌ́tʃtoun) touch-button telephone that produce tones to control automatic dialing; trademark of the Bell System

touch-type (tʌ́tʃtaip) *pres. part.* **touch-typ·ing** *past and past part.* **touch-typed** *v.i.* to type on a typewriter without needing to look at the keys

touch·wood (tʌ́tʃwʊd) *n.* punk

touch·y (tʌ́tʃi:) *comp.* **touch·i·er** *superl.* **touch·i·est** *adj.* apt to be easily offended ‖ apt to cause offense, *a touchy subject*

Tou·cou·leur (tu:ku:lə́:r) *n.* a Moslem people of W. Africa, esp. the Senegal River valley

Toug·gourt (tu:gú:rt) an oasis trading center (pop. 84,000) in E. Algeria in the N. Sahara

tough (tʌf) 1. *adj.* hard to break but not necessarily hard to bend ‖ (of food) difficult to cut, bite into or chew (opp. TENDER) ‖ strong, difficult to tear or wear through, *a tough fabric* ‖ able to resist disease, endure hardship etc., *a tough constitution* ‖ difficult to get the better of, *a tough bargainer* ‖ challenging because difficult to do or perform, *a tough job* ‖ requiring endurance, *a tough fight* ‖ hard to bear, harsh, *tough sanctions* ‖ (of people) apt to be aggressive and lawless ‖ (of districts) frequented by such people and therefore hard to supervise and potentially dangerous ‖ hard to impress or win around, *a tough audience* ‖ hard to learn, understand, solve etc., *a tough problem* **to get tough with** to change one's attitude and begin to be aggressive towards 2. *n.* someone, esp. a man or boy, apt to be aggressive and lawless 3. *adv.* **to act tough** (*pop.*) to behave in a menacing, aggressive manner, esp. as a bluff **tóugh·en** *v.t.* to make tough or tougher ‖ *v.i.* to become tough or tougher [O.E. *tōh*]

Tou·lon (tu:lɔ́:) a port (pop. 180,508) and naval base in Var, France, 42 miles east of Marseilles. Industries: shipbuilding, engineering, chemicals

Tou·louse (tu:lu:z) the chief town (pop. 371,143) of Haute-Garonne, France, and historical capital of Languedoc, on the Garonne. Industries: metalworking, textiles, paper, chemicals and fertilizers, aircraft. Gothic cathedral (12th-13th cc.), Romanesque (11th c.) and Gothic churches, mansions in pink brick (16th c.), neoclassical town hall (18th c.). University (1230)

Tou·louse-Lau·trec (tu:lu:zloutrek), Henri de (1864-1901), French painter and lithographer.

CONCISE PRONUNCIATION KEY: **(a)** æ, c*a*t; ɑ, c*a*r; ɔ, f*aw*n; ei, sn*a*ke. **(e)** e, h*e*n; i:, sh*ee*p; iə, d*ee*r; ɛə, b*ea*r. **(i)** i, f*i*sh; ai, t*i*ger; ə:, b*i*rd. **(o)** o, *o*x; au, c*ow*; ou, g*oa*t; u, p*oo*r; ɔi, r*oy*al. **(u)** ʌ, d*u*ck; u, b*u*ll; u:, g*oo*se; ə, b*a*cillus; ju:, c*u*be. x, lo*ch*; θ, *th*ink; ð, bo*th*er; z, *Z*en; ʒ, cor*s*age; dʒ, sava*ge*; ŋ, orangutan*g*; j, *y*ak; ʃ, *fi*sh; tʃ, fe*tch*; 'l, rabb*le*; 'n, redd*en*. Complete pronunciation key appears inside front cover.

Much of his work, which included many brilliant poster designs, was a sardonic comment on the life of the Parisian demimonde

tou·pee (tu:péi) *n.* (*hist.*) a topknot of hair usually forming the crowning feature of an 18th-c. wig ‖ (*hist.*) an 18th-c. wig with such a topknot ‖ a small wig or a patch of false hair used to hide baldness [prob. fr. F. *toupet*, a tuft of hair]

tour (tuər) 1. *n.* a journey made for sightseeing, business or education, ending at the place from which one started out ‖ a walk around a garden, house etc. for purposes of inspection ‖ a series of performances by a theatrical or similar company in a succession of theaters ‖ a tour of duty 2. *v.i.* to make a tour, be on tour ‖ *v.t.* to make a tour through or of ‖ to present (a play etc.) in a circuit of theaters [F.]

tou·ra·co (túərəkou) *n.* a member of *Turacus*, fam. *Musophagidae*, a genus of African birds (1–2 ft long) having brilliant red wing feathers which yield turacin [F. fr. a W. African name]

Tou·raine (tu:ren) a former province of France in the S. Paris basin, comprising most of Indre-et-Loire and small parts of Loir-et-Cher and Indre. It consists largely of wooded plateaus and fertile valleys, with famous châteaus, esp. along the Loire. Industries: agriculture (wine, fruit, market produce), tourism. Historic capital: Tours. Formed in Merovingian times as the countship of Tours, it passed to Anjou (11th c.) and England before the French crown annexed it (1259). It was a duchy-apanage until 1584

Tou·rane (tu:réin) *DA NANG

Tour·coing (tur:kwɛ̃) a textile-manufacturing town (pop. 102,543) in Nord, France, near the Belgian frontier

tour de force (túərdəfórs, túərdəfóurs) *pl.* **tours de force** (túərdəfórs, túərdəfóurs) *n.* a feat of strength or skill [F.]

tour·ism (túərizəm) *n.* the practice of touring for pleasure ‖ the industry of attracting tourists and catering to them

tour·ist (túərist) *n.* a person visiting or staying at a place on holiday ‖ tourist class

tourist class a type of accommodation on ocean liners etc. cheaper and less comfortable than first or second class but more comfortable than steerage

tourist trap (pejorative) a site designed to attract tourists, esp. for the purpose of exploiting them

tour·ma·line, tur·ma·line (túərməlin) *n.* any of several complex silicates, containing boron, the crystals of which polarize light and exhibit pyroelectric and piezoelectric properties. Some varieties are cut as gems [F. fr. Sinhalese]

Tour·nai (tu:rnei) a town (pop. 67,291) in Hainault, Belgium, on the Scheldt. Romanesque-Gothic cathedral (12th-13th cc.)

tour·na·ment (túərnəmənt, tó:rnəmənt) *n.* (*hist.*) a contest in which mounted knights in armor fought with blunted weapons ‖ (*hist.*) a meeting for knights to practice their sports and exercises ‖ a meeting at which a number of individual competitors or teams of competitors compete for championship in some particular game by a series of elimination contests, *a chess tournament* [O.F. *torneiement, tornoiement*]

Tour·neur (tó:rnər), Cyril (c. 1575-1626), English playwright. His reputation rests on two tragedies, 'The Revenger's Tragedy' (1607) and 'The Atheist's Tragedy' (1611)

tour·ney (túərni, tó:rni:) 1. *pl.* **tour·neys** *n.* a tournament 2. *v.i.* to contend in a tournament [M. E. fr. O.F. *tornei, torneier*]

tour·ni·quet (tó:rnikit, túərnikit) *n.* a bandage or cloth for temporarily stopping bleeding or for arresting the circulation of the blood by compression. It is twisted tightly around a limb, finger or toe above the wound, sting etc. by threading a stick or other similar thing through the cloth and winding it around [F. fr. *tourner*, to turn]

tour of duty a period spent doing military or administrative duty, esp. in a foreign country

Tours (tu:r) the chief town (pop. 132,209) of Indre-et-Loire, France, historic capital of Touraine, on the Loire. Gothic cathedral (13th-16th cc.), medieval and Renaissance quarters

tou·sle (táuz'l) 1. *v.t. pres. part.* **tou·sling** *past* and *past part.* **tou·sled** to make (hair, bedclothes, garments etc.) wildly untidy and out of place, esp. by rough handling 2. *n.* the state of being tousled ‖ a tousled mass (of hair etc.) [frequentative of M.E. *tusen*, to handle roughly]

Tous·saint   Lou·ver·ture (tu:sɛ́:lu:vertyr) (1743-1803), Haitian general and statesman. An African slave, he joined the slave revolt against the French (1791) and made himself the ruler of Haiti (1801), but was taken prisoner and died in France

tout (taut) 1. *v.i.* (*pop.*, often with 'for') to solicit custom with often annoying persistence, or appeal to individuals for votes, donations etc. ‖ (esp. *Br.*) to watch racehorses in training so as to get information for betting ‖ *v.t.* to hawk (something) with annoying persistence ‖ to get information on (racehorses) for betting purposes 2. *n.* a person who touts [M.E. *tuten*]

tow (tou) 1. *n.* coarse and broken fibers removed from flax, hemp or jute during scutching or hackling and used for twine etc. [perh. rel. to O.N. *tō*, uncleaned flax or wool]

TOW (*mil. acronym*) for tube-launched, optically tracked, wire-guided antitank-missile weapon system (BGM-71A), with a 23-mi range; manufactured by Hughes Aircraft Co.

tow 1. *v.t.* to pull along with a rope or hawser 2. *n.* a towing or being towed ‖ a towline ‖ something towed **in tow** attached by a rope and pulled along ‖ in or under one's care, guidance etc. [O.E. *togian*]

to·wage (tóuidʒ) *n.* a towing or being towed ‖ the fee for being towed

to·ward (tɔrd, tourd, təwórd) *prep.* in the direction of, *walk toward the sea* ‖ with regard to, in relation to, *to feel angry toward someone* ‖ for the purpose of helping, augmenting or making possible etc., *the money will go toward a holiday* ‖ (of time) approaching, near, *toward midnight* ‖ facing, *the handle toward my hand* [O.E. *tōweard*]

to·wards (tɔrdz, tourdz, təwórdz) *prep.* toward [O.E. *tōweardes*]

tow·a·way zone (tóuəwei zoun) *n.* zone from which illegally parked vehicles may be towed away by the police

tow·boat (tóubout) *n.* a tugboat with squared bows

tow car (*Am.*=*Br.* breakdown lorry) a tow truck

tow·el (táuəl) 1. *n.* a piece of absorbent material used to dry something **to throw in the towel** to admit defeat or failure 2. *v. pres. part.* **tow·el·ing**, esp. *Br.* **tow·el·ling** *past* and *past part.* **tow·eled**, esp. *Br.* **tow·elled** *v.t.* to dry or rub down with a towel ‖ *v.i.* to use a towel **tow·el·ing**, esp. *Br.*, **tów·el·ling** *n.* the absorbent material of which towels are made [O.F. *toaille*]

towel horse a rack for drying or airing towels on

tow·er (táuər) 1. *n.* a tall structure, high in proportion to its lateral dimensions, either standing independently or forming part of another edifice. Towers may be used e.g. as reservoirs, for hanging bells, or may contain rooms, usually one above the other. When used e.g. for transmission or observation, they are very often mere skeleton steel frameworks ‖ a tower and its surrounding edifices used as a fortress or prison ‖ a vertical structure, not necessarily particularly tall, through which gases or liquids are passed to be cooled or purified etc. 2. *v.i.* to rise high in the air ‖ (of birds of prey) to soar high in the air in order to be able to swoop on prey ‖ (of wounded game birds) to rise vertically in the air before falling ‖ (with 'above' or 'over') to be extremely tall, esp. to rise to dominating height **tów·er·ing** *adj.* very high, esp. from the point of view of someone looking up from below ‖ (of emotions) very intense, *a towering rage* [O.E. *torr* fr. L. *turris*]

Tower Hill rising ground on the north bank of the Thames by the Tower of London, once a place of execution

Tower of Babel a tower intended to reach heaven but which stopped short when God caused the builders to speak a multitude of different languages (Genesis xi, 1-9)

Tower of London a group of buildings east of the City of London on the north bank of the Thames. The central keep was begun in 1078. For centuries the Tower was the main state prison. Today it is a historical museum containing the Crown jewels, a collection of armor, and other historical objects

tower of strength a person who provides in valuable encouragement and practical support

tow·head (tóuhed) *n.* a person who has a head of very light blond hair ‖ such a head of hair **tow·head·ed** *adj.*

tow·hee (təhwí:, tawi:) *n.* the North American chewink [imit.]

tow·line (tóulain) *n.* a rope etc. used for towing

town (taun) *n.* a place consisting of an agglomeration of houses, shops and other buildings, bigger than a village but usually smaller than a city. Most towns have paved roads, street lighting and public systems of drainage, water supply, power supply and transport and an organized local government. The inhabitants are mostly engaged in trade, industry or administration ‖ the people who live in this place, *the whole town was discussing the news* ‖ the way of life of such people, *to prefer the town to the country* ‖ a municipal corporation, simpler than a city, having powers of rural administration ‖ (*pop.*) a city ‖ (without article) a particular town clearly understood from the context, *to be out of town* ‖ (without article) the business or shopping center of a town, *to go into town* ‖ (*Br.*, without article and always with 'in' or 'up to') the capital, *to go up to town* (i.e. to go to London) ‖ a piece of ground having a great many prairie dog burrows ‖ a piece of ground having many penguin nests **on the town** seeking the pleasures of town, esp. its night life **to go to town** (*pop.*) to do something (made clear by the context) very intensely, often to the point of excess, *the organist went to town in the last movement* **to go to town on** (*pop.*) to work on (something) fast and efficiently, esp. in short bursts [O.E. *tūn*]

town clerk (*Am.*) an official who keeps a town's records and writes up its official proceedings ‖ (*Br.*) an official, usually a lawyer, appointed to administer a town's affairs and act as secretary to the town council

town council (*Br.*) the elected administrative body of a town **town councillor** a member of such a body

town crier (esp. *hist.*) a town official who makes public announcements by word of mouth

town hall the main public building of a town, used for transacting official business etc.

town house a single-family house that is attached to a similar house on one side *Cf* TERRACE HOUSE

town meeting a general meeting of the taxpaying inhabitants of a town

town·scape (táunskeip) *n.* overall view of an urban area involving plan, lighting, street surfaces, etc.; coined by Camillo Sette (1920–   )

towns·folk (táunzfouk) *n.* townspeople

Town·shend (táunzend), Charles, 2nd viscount ('Turnip Townshend', 1674-1738), English statesman and agriculturist. After an active life in politics, he resigned (1730) over disagreements with his brother-in-law, Sir Robert Walpole. He made experiments in four-course crop rotation and the cultivation of turnips which are important in the history of agriculture

Townshend, Charles (1725-67), British statesman, grandson of the 2nd Viscount Townshend. As chancellor of the exchequer (1766-7) he promoted the Townshend Acts (1767), a series of measures taxing the American colonies, notably by imposing duties on glass, lead, paints, paper and tea. The duties aroused bitter opposition, and all except the one on tea were repealed (1770). They helped to precipitate the Revolutionary War

town·ship (táunʃip) *n.* (*U.S.A., Canada*) a division of a county with some administrative powers ‖ (*public land surveying*) a district containing 36 sq. miles [O.E. *tūnscipe*]

towns·man (táunzmən) *pl.* **towns·men** (táunzmən) *n.* (esp. *Br.*) a person who lives in a town, esp. a man born and bred in a town

towns·peo·ple (táunzpi:p'l) *n.* the inhabitants of a town

Towns·ville (táunzvil) a port (pop. 59,000) in Queensland, Australia

tow·path (tóupæθ, tóupɑθ) *pl.* **tow·paths** (tóupæðz, tóupɑðz, tóupæθs, tóupɑθs) *n.* a path, esp. along a canal, used by men or animals for towing boats

tow·rope (tóuroup) *n.* a rope used for towing

tow truck (*Am.*=*Br.* breakdown lorry) a truck for towing disabled cars or cars immobilized by snow etc.

tox·ae·mi·a *TOXEMIA

toxaemia of pregnancy *TOXEMIA OF PREGNANCY

tox·e·mi·a, tox·ae·mi·a (tɒksí:mi:ə) *n.* the presence in the blood of poisonous substances usually of bacterial origin [Mod. L.]

toxemia of pregnancy a condition of unknown origin, peculiar to pregnant women, characterized by hypertension, visual disturbances, and the presence of albumin in the urine etc.

tox·ic (tóksik) *adj.* of or pertaining to or caused by poison, *a toxic symptom* ‖ poisonous, *toxic gas* [fr. M.L. *toxicus*, poisoned]

tox·i·cant (tóksikənt) 1. *adj.* poisonous 2. *n.* a pest control which kills by poisoning (as distinct from one which repels) [fr. M.L. *toxicans* (*toxicantis*) fr. *toxicare*, to poison]

tox·ic·i·ty (tɔksísiti:) *n.* the state, quality or degree of being poisonous

tox·i·co·log·i·cal (tɔksikəlódʒik'l) *adj.* of or pertaining to toxicology

tox·i·col·o·gy (tɔksikóledʒi:) *n.* the study of poisons [F. *toxicologie*]

tox·i·co·sis (tɔksikóusis) *pl.* **tox·i·co·ses** (tɔksikóusi:z) *n.* a diseased condition caused by a poison [Mod. L.]

toxic shock syndrome (*med.*) vaginal infection (*bacterium staphylococcus aureus*) sometimes fatal, characterized by drop in blood pressure, kidney malfunction, vomiting, and diarrhea. It is associated with use of tampons *abbr.* TSS

tox·in (tóksin) *n.* any of several intensely poisonous substances produced by certain bacteria

tox·oid (tóksɔid) *n.* a toxin rendered nonpoisonous, capable of inducing the formation of powerful antibodies. Toxoids are used in immunization e.g. against diphtheria

tox·oph·i·lite (tɔksófəlait) 1. *n.* a person skilled in archery 2. *adj.* relating to archers or archery

tox·óph·i·ly *n.* the sport of archery ‖ love of archery [fr. *Toxophilus*, a book by Ascham fr. Gk *toxon*, bow + *-philos*, loving]

toy (tɔi) 1. *n.* a child's plaything 2. *adj.* made as a toy, *toy soldiers* ‖ of or like a toy ‖ (of some breeds of animal, esp. dogs) bred so as to be very small, *a toy bull terrier* 3. *v.i.* (with 'with') to give something not very serious consideration, *to toy with an idea* ‖ (with 'with') to make half-hearted attempts at eating something because one has no appetite, *to toy with one's food* [origin unknown]

To·ya·ma (tɔjɑmɑ) a commercial center (pop. 305,000) in central W. Honshu, Japan: pharmaceuticals, aluminum, textiles

Toyn·bee (tɔinbi:), Arnold (1852-83), British economist and social reformer. His most important work is 'Lectures on the Industrial Revolution of the 18th Century in England' (1884)

Toynbee, Arnold Joseph (1889-1975), British historian, nephew of Arnold Toynbee. His 'A Study of History' (1934-54) is an attempt to analyze history in terms of the growth and decline of civilizations. His thesis is that a civilization's survival depends on its ability to respond successfully to challenges, both spiritual and material

To·yo·ha·shi (tɔjɔhɑʃi:) an industrial town (pop. 215,000) in central E. Honshu, Japan: textiles, metallurgy, food processing

TQC (*acronym*) for total quality control, system for building "perfection" into all aspects of manufacturing and business administration, with zero allowable defects, developed in Japan 1970's

tra·be·at·ed (tréibi:eitid) *adj.* (*archit.*) constructed with horizontal beams, not arched **tra·be·a·tion** *n.* (*archit.*) an entablature [fr. L. *trabs* (*trabis*), a beam]

tra·bec·u·la (trəbékjulə) *pl.* **tra·bec·u·lae** (trəbékjuli:), **tra·bec·u·las** *n.* (*anat.*) a row of cells bridging a cavity, e.g. a cartilage ‖ (*bot.*) a row of sterile cells extending across the sporangium of a pteridophyte **tra·béc·u·lar** *adj.* [L. dim. of *trabs*, a beam]

Trab·zon (trɑbzón) *TREBIZOND

trace (treis) *n.* (esp. *pl.*) a sign (e.g. a footprint, or slime) left by something moving over a surface ‖ an indication left behind, *there was no trace of his having been there* ‖ a survival from the past, vestige, *that great empire left few traces* ‖ a very small amount, the merest indication, *no trace of embarrassment* ‖ (*phys.*) the bright spot on the screen of a cathode ray tube, or the path it follows ‖ (*psychol.*) a neural or mental change resulting from the learning process ‖ the marking made by certain instruments, e.g. a seismograph ‖ something traced or drawn [F.]

trace *pres. part.* **trac·ing** *past* and *past part.* **traced** *v.t.* to follow (a path, track etc.) ‖ to follow the traces of ‖ to follow back the course or line of, *to trace a river to its source* ‖ to follow back the history or development of, *to trace one's ancestry* ‖ to discern (esp. by touch) by following the outlines of ‖ to discover by inquiry, investigation etc. (esp. something lost etc.), *to*

trace a missing person ‖ to mark out (a sketch, plan etc.) ‖ to copy (esp. an outline drawing) by marking the lines on a transparent paper etc. laid over the original ‖ (of a machine) to record (e.g. heartbeats) in linear form ‖ to write, form (characters or outlines) laboriously ‖ *v.i.* (of e.g. a family) to have a traceable history, go back in time [O.F. *tracier*]

trace *n.* one of the two side straps, chains etc. by which a horse etc. pulls a vehicle. It is attached at one end to the animal's collar and at the other to the whiffletree **to kick over the traces** to cease to accept authority, restraints etc. and act as one pleases [M.E. *traice, trais* fr. O.F.]

trace element a chemical element involved in the physiological processes of plants and animals, essential to them although present only in very small quantities (e.g. copper, iodine etc.)

trace element micronutrients chemicals required in minute quantities for healthy animal or plant life

trac·er (tréisər) *n.* a bullet or shell which reveals its trajectory by illuminating it, usually with a phosphorescent light ‖ a device for tracing designs ‖ a substance (e.g. an element, atom or compound) that is introduced into a biological, chemical or physical process and can be followed along its path by its radioactivity, unusual isotopic mass, color etc. ‖ a person who traces missing articles, esp. in transportation services ‖ the official form sent out to expedite the tracing of a missing article

Tracer *n.* (*mil.*) a twin-reciprocating engine, airborne radar platform (E–1) designed to operate from aircraft carriers for the detection and interception control of airborne targets

tracers *n.* (*med.*) conditions or diseases chosen for inclusion in programs that seek to assess the quality of medical care as representative of the quality of care given generally

trac·er·y (tréisəri:) *pl.* **trac·er·ies** *n.* graceful and decorative interlacing of lines, esp. open stonework in the head of Gothic windows or vaulting, or natural phenomena (e.g. frost flowers on windowpanes) recalling these

tra·che·a (tréiki:ə) *pl.* **tra·che·ae** (tréiki:i:), **tra·che·as** *n.* (in vertebrates) a tube through which air passes to and from the lungs, extending from the larynx to the lungs. In man it is about 4 ins long and about 1 in. in diameter ‖ (in insects and other arthropods) an air tube of the respiratory system ‖ (*bot.*) a xylem element or series of elements resembling an animal trachea (*VESSEL) **trá·che·al** *adj.* [M.L.]

tra·che·id (tréiki:id) *pl.* **tra·che·ids, tra·che·ides** (trəkí:idi:z) *n.* an elongate, tapering firm-walled cell characteristic of the xylem. When mature it lacks protoplasm. Variously modified, it serves in water conduction, storage and support (*VESSEL) [fr. M.L. *trachea*, trachea]

tra·che·o·phyte (tréiki:əfait) *n.* a member of *Tracheophyta*, a phylum of *Embryophyta*, including green plants with a vascular support and water-transport system. The phylum includes lycopsids, pteropsids, psilopsids and sphenopsids [fr. Mod. L. *Tracheophyta* fr. M.L. *trachea*, trachea + Gk *phuton*, plant]

tra·che·ot·o·my (treiki:ótəmi:) *pl.* **tra·che·ot·o·mies** *n.* a surgical incision of the trachea [fr. TRACHEA + Gk *-tomē*, a cutting]

tra·cho·ma (trəkóumə) *n.* a chronic contagious disease of the eye, with roughening of the inner surface of the lids, often causing blindness if not treated. It is common in many tropical countries **tra·chom·a·tous** (trəkómətəs) *adj.* [Mod. L. fr. Gk *trachōma*, roughness]

trac·ing (tréisiŋ) *n.* the act of someone who traces ‖ the copy of a design, map, drawing etc. traced on transparent paper or cloth ‖ a record made by a cardiograph, seismograph etc.

track (træk) 1. *n.* a path worn by the passage of men or animals ‖ a narrow, unpaved road ‖ something, e.g. the ruts left by wheels, the scent of an animal or the wake of a ship, which shows that a person or thing has passed ‖ (*Br.*, *education*) system of grouping students according to intelligence, ability, or aptitude ‖ (*pl.*) footprints ‖ the course followed by something, *the track of a meteor* ‖ any of various prepared courses (e.g. of grass or cinder) on which athletic contests or races are held ‖ the width between a pair of wheels on a vehicle ‖ one of the jointed metal caterpillar treads of e.g. a tank ‖ the road with rails and ties on which a train or similar thing runs **in one's tracks** just where one is, *to stop in one's tracks* **on the right**

(wrong) track pursuing the line of investigation likely (unlikely) to lead to the solution **on the track of** actively and successfully occupied in finding or pursuing (a person, solution or thing) **to cover** (or **cover up**) **one's tracks** deliberately to conceal what one has been doing or leave no evidence of where one has been **to follow in someone's tracks** to mirror in one's own career the earlier career of someone else **to keep** (**lose**) **track of** to keep (fail to keep) an up-to-date record of (e.g. expenses) ‖ to have (no longer to have) up-to-date information, news etc. about (e.g. friends or current events) **to make tracks** to take one's leave **to make tracks for** to go, esp. make a departure, hurriedly and purposefully toward 2. *v.t.* to hunt or pursue by following the tracks of ‖ to follow the course of (someone or something) by the traces left behind ‖ to keep up with (something) on its course, *to track an airplane with a searchlight* ‖ (with 'down') to follow the traces of and find ‖ (*Am.=Br.* tread) to bring (e.g. mud) on the feet into a room etc. and leave marks where one walks ‖ to equip with caterpillar treads ‖ *v.i.* to have a specified width between a pair of wheels or runners, *this car tracks 4 ft* ‖ (of wheels) to be in alignment ‖ to leave tracks all over a surface ‖ (*movies*, of the camera) to move toward or away from a static subject or along beside a moving subject while photographing it **track·age** (trækidʒ) *n.* rails of railroad track ‖ (of a railroad company) the right to use the tracks of another company ‖ the charge for this right [O.F. *trac, traq*]

tracker action the mechanical action joining the pipes and keyboards in older types of organ

track event an athletic contest, carried out on a track prepared for racing (cf. FIELD EVENT)

track·lay·er (træklei̯ər) *n.* (*Am.=Br.* plate-layer) someone who places or maintains railroad tracks

track·man (trækmən) *pl.* **track·men** (trækmən) *n.* (*Am.=Br.* linesman) someone who checks railroad tracks for safety

track record (*colloq.*) any record of successes or failures

track suit warm-up suit used by athletes

track telling (*mil.*) communication between command and operations during and after surveillance Cf BACK TELL

tract (trækt) *n.* a short pamphlet or treatise, usually on a religious or political subject, intended for distribution or propaganda purposes [M.E. *tracte* fr. L.]

tract *n.* a wide expanse of land etc. without precise boundaries ‖ (*anat.*) a structure through or along which something passes, *respiratory tract* ‖ (*anat.*) a bundle of nerve fibers having the same origin, termination and function ‖ (*eccles.*) verses of Scripture sung or recited at Mass before the reading of the Gospel, at special times, e.g. Lent, requiems etc. [fr. L. *trahere* (*tractus*), to draw]

trac·ta·bil·i·ty (træktəbíliti:) *n.* the quality or state of being tractable

trac·ta·ble (træktəb'l) *adj.* (of persons or animals) easily handled or controlled, pliant ‖ (of materials) malleable, easily worked **trác·ta·bly** *adv.* [fr. L. *tractabilis*]

Trac·tar·i·an (træktéəri:ən) 1. *adj.* pertaining to the Oxford movement 2. *n.* a founder or supporter of the Oxford movement **Trac·tár·i·an·ism** *n.* the Oxford movement [after the 'Tracts for the Times' published 1833–41 by the Oxford movement]

trac·tate (trækteit) *n.* a treatise [fr. L. *tractatus*, a handling]

tract house a house similar in style to all others in a development area

trac·tile (træktəl, *Br.* træktail) *adj.* that can be physically drawn out in length [fr. L. *trahere* (*tractus*), to draw]

trac·tion (trækʃən) *n.* the act of hauling, or power used in hauling, a vehicle ‖ pulling force ‖ the force of adhesive friction exerted by a body on the surface on which it moves ‖ a pulling force exerted, esp. on a limb containing a fractured bone, by an apparatus consisting of weights and pulleys ‖ the state of tension created by this force, *three months in traction* **trác·tion·al** *adj.* [fr. M.L. *tractio* (*tractionis*)]

traction engine a steam or diesel engine used for hauling heavy vehicles on roads or over difficult terrain

trac·tive (træktiv) *adj.* used for pulling or hauling

---

trac·tor (trǽktər) n. a vehicle, either wheeled or fitted with tank tracks, used for hauling or propelling, esp. on farms, or as a source of power, e.g. for threshing machines ‖ a truck with a driver's cab and no body, used for hauling a large trailer or trailers etc. ‖ a traction engine ‖ an airplane with a propeller or propellers forward of the main supporting surfaces ‖ (med.) an instrument used to exert traction [Mod. L. fr. trahere (tractus), to draw]

trac·tor·cade (trǽktərkeid) n. an organized demonstration by farmers driving their tractors to the site of protest (U.S., 1977–1978)

trade (treid) 1. n. the business of distribution, selling and exchange ‖ any branch of such business, the grocery trade ‖ persons engaged in a field of commerce ‖ a deal, a purchase and sale ‖ an exchange ‖ a craft (cf. PROFESSION, OCCUPATION) ‖ (pl.) trade winds 2. v. pres. part. trading past and past part. trad·ed v.i. to engage in trade, buy and sell as a business ‖ to have business dealings (with someone) ‖ to make an exchange (with someone) ‖ to be a customer (at a specified store) ‖ v.t. to exchange or barter, they traded rum for gold dust to trade in to hand over (a discarded article) as part payment for its replacement, to trade in an old car for a new one to trade on to take unfair advantage of [M.L.G. trade, a track]

Trade Agreements Act a U.S. Congressional act (1934) of President Franklin Roosevelt's New Deal. It created reciprocal trade treaties with several foreign countries, to encourage foreign trade

trade cycle (Br.) business cycle

trade discount a deduction from the retail price of goods made by the manufacturer in favor of the retailer

Trade Expansion Act a U.S. Congressional act (1962) under the John Kennedy administration. It empowered the President to cut tariffs, to give him leverage if needed in getting tariff concessions from Europe and so meet the competition of the European Common Market

trade gap the amount by which a country's imports have exceeded its exports over a period

trade-in (tréidɪn) n. an article taken by a dealer from a purchaser as part payment for some other article, usually of the same kind

trade·mark (tréidmɑrk) 1. n. the name or distinctive symbol or device attached to goods for sale, and usually legally registered, as a warrant of their production by a particular firm or individual 2. v.t. to affix a trademark to ‖ to register (a symbol etc.) as a trademark

trade name the name by which an article is known to the trade that deals in it ‖ the name under which a firm does business ‖ a name used as a trademark, esp. one that is registered and legally protected

trade-off (tréidɔf) n. 1. in decision-making, selecting the choice from analysis of advantages and disadvantages of two or more alternatives 2. an offset in a bargain —trade off v.

trade price the price at which goods are sold between members of the same trade, or by wholesale dealers or manufacturers to retailers

trad·er (tréidər) n. a person engaged in some form of commerce ‖ a ship chartered for carrying goods for trade

trade school a secondary school specializing in courses in skilled trades

trades·folk (tréidzfouk) n. (old-fash.) tradespeople

trades·man (tréidzmən) pl. trades·men (tréidzmən) n. a storekeeper ‖ (Br., mil.) a soldier with special technical qualifications, e.g. a radio operator, who receives pay over and above that due to his military rank

trades·peo·ple (tréidzpiːpʼl) n. people engaged in trade

trades union a trade union

Trades Union Congress (abbr. T.U.C.) the central body representing all British trade unions affiliated to it, founded 1868

trades unionism trade unionism

trades unionist trade unionist

trade union a labor union ‖ (hist.) a voluntary association of wage earners in any craft or trade organized to protect their interests, i.e. wages, conditions and hours of work etc., against the employers **trade unionism** the system or principles of collective bargaining through trade unions **trade unionist** a member of a trade union

trade wind a wind blowing from the tropical high-pressure belts toward the equatorial region of low pressure, from the northeast in the northern hemisphere and southeast in the southern hemisphere. In many areas trade winds blow with regularity throughout the year, though there are variations with season and location [fr. naut. phrase to blow trade, to blow a regular course]

trading post the station of a trader or trading company established in a remote undeveloped region for purposes of trade with the local population

trading stamp a paper stamp handed by a tradesman to a customer making a purchase. Devised to encourage business, trading stamps represent a small percentage of the value of each purchase and can be redeemed for merchandise or cash

tra·di·tion (trədíʃən) n. a cultural continuity transmitted in the form of social attitudes, beliefs, principles and conventions of behavior etc. deriving from past experience and helping to shape the present ‖ a convention established by constant practice ‖ a belief, legend etc. based on oral report, usually accepted as historically true though not verifiable ‖ the transmitting of cultural continuity, beliefs, legends etc. ‖ a religious law or teaching, or a body of these, held to have been received originally by oral transmission. In the Jewish religion these are the laws given to Moses on Sinai and later embodied in the Mishnah. In the Christian religion they are a body of extra-biblical teachings handed down orally within the Christian community. In the Moslem religion they are an account of the sayings and doings of Mohammed later embodied in the Sunna **tra·dí·tion·al** adj. **tra·dí·tion·al·ism** n. exaggerated respect for tradition ‖ fundamentalism **tra·dí·tion·al·ist** n. **tra·dí·tion·al·is·tic** adj. **tra·dí·tion·al·ly** adv. [O.F. tradicion, a handing over]

trad·i·tor (trǽditər) pl. **trad·i·to·res** (trǽditɔ́riːz, trǽditóuriːz) n. (hist.) a traitor or informer among early Christians at the time of the Roman persecutions [L.]

tra·duce (trədúːs, trədjúːs) pres. part. **tra·duc·ing** past and past part. **tra·duced** v.t. to speak evil of or misrepresent [fr. L. traducere, to lead across, lead along as a spectacle, bring into disgrace]

tra·du·cian·ism (trədúːʃənɪzəm, trədjúːʃənɪzəm) n. (theol.) the doctrine that the soul of a child, with its attribute of original sin, derives from its parents at the moment of conception [fr. L.L. traducianus fr. tradux (traducis), a propagated shoot]

Tra·fal·gar, Battle of (trəfǽlgər) a decisive sea battle (Oct. 21, 1805) off S.W. Spain. The British fleet under Nelson broke the line of the French and Spanish fleets, capturing 20 vessels. The battle established British naval supremacy in the Napoleonic Wars and forced Napoleon to abandon his plan of invading Britain. Nelson was killed in the battle

traf·fic (trǽfik) n. the passage to and fro of people and esp. of vehicles on a road or street, or of ships, aircraft etc. on their routes ‖ the volume of passengers or freight carried, e.g. by a particular transport company, within a given period ‖ the passage of calls, signals etc. through a communications system or the volume of calls, signals etc. passed ‖ illicit or shady business dealings ‖ (rhet.) exchange by barter or by buying and selling ‖ (rhet.) any dealings, e.g. intellectual ones, involving exchange [F. trafique]

traffic pres. part. **traf·fick·ing** past and past part. **traf·ficked** v.i. to conduct traffic, esp. illicit traffic (in a commodity) [fr. O.F. trafiquer]

traffic circle (Am.=Br. roundabout) a round plot of ground at the intersection of crossroads, around which all traffic must go in the direction indicated

traffic light a system of colored lights, usually automatically controlled, at road crossings or points of traffic concentration, to regulate traffic

trag·a·canth (trǽgəkænθ) n. a member of Astragalus, fam. Papilionaceae, a genus of low perennial shrubs native to S.E. Europe and W. Asia (Iran) ‖ the gum which exudes from this shrub, used esp. in preparing pills, emulsions and creams and as an adhesive [F. tragacante fr. L. fr. Gk]

tra·ge·di·an (trədʒíːdiːən) n. an actor specializing in tragic roles ‖ an author of tragedies [prob. fr. O.F. tragediane]

tra·ge·di·enne (trədʒiːdiːén) n. an actress specializing in tragic roles [F. tragédienne]

trag·e·dy (trǽdʒidi) pl. **trag·e·dies** n. a drama portraying the conflict between the individual human will and fate or necessity, traditionally depicting a hero or heroine transcending, or succumbing to, a series of catastrophic events ‖ the theoretical principles of this kind of drama ‖ a calamity, an event causing distress, sadness, anguish, shock etc. in varying degrees ‖ tragic quality [O.F. tragedie fr. L. fr. Gk]
—Aristotle, basing his theory on the practice of the great Athenian tragedians, said that tragedy should move the reader or spectator to pity and terror, performing a catharsis, or purification by purging, of the emotions. The tragic hero evoked sympathy for his greatness of character but alienated it also—and caused his own downfall—by some personal flaw, esp. arrogant pride (*HUBRIS). Later writers on tragedy also tend to concentrate on these two features: the spectator's involvement—part identification, part repudiation—in the nature of the central figure, and the conflict and final balance of emotion which the greatest tragedy calls forth. It is curiously allied to the greatest comedy: there is the same complexity in the hero (e.g. Molière's Alceste in 'le Misanthrope', though in comedy the spectator feels a smaller degree of involvement in his fate. But in both comedy and tragedy the spectator is finally reconciled to the hero's fate. The degree to which the dramatist can invoke sympathy and understanding, the bitterness of the fate which overtakes the hero, and yet the ultimate rightness of the result: these three produce the most serious, the most painful, the most inward, and yet the most liberating moments in literature

trag·ic (trǽdʒik) adj. causing grief, disappointment or horror and shock, a tragic accident ‖ appropriate to, or pertaining to, tragic drama ‖ expressing tragedy, a tragic expression **trág·i·cal·ly** adv. [fr. L. tragicus]

trag·i·com·e·dy (trǽdʒikɔ́midi) pl. **trag·i·com·e·dies** n. a drama in which the currents of tragedy and comedy are (usually ironically) blended ‖ an event or situation in which the elements of tragedy and comedy are intermixed [F. tragicomédie fr. L. fr. Gk]

trag·i·com·ic (trǽdʒikɔ́mik) adj. having the nature of tragicomedy [fr. tragi- (combining form of 'tragic')+COMIC]

trag·o·pan (trǽgəpæn) n. a member of Tragopan, a genus of brilliantly colored Asiatic pheasants, having the back and breast covered with white or buff ocelli. The male has two brightly colored wattles and a pair of fleshy erectile horns on its head [L.=a fabulous Ethiopian bird fr. Gk tragos, goat+PAN the God)]

Tra·herne (trəhɔ́ːrn), Thomas (1637–74), English mystical writer. His poems were not published till 1903 and his prose work, 'Centuries of Meditations', till 1908. The latter were written to provide instruction in 'the way of felicity'

trail (treil) 1. v.t. to pull (something) along behind one, esp. over the ground or another surface ‖ to pursue (a person) by following up information about his movements ‖ to hunt (an animal) by following its tracks ‖ to trace the whereabouts of by esp. long investigation, they trailed the stolen jewels to an alley in Rome ‖ to shadow, keep secret watch on (someone) ‖ to allow to hang loosely or float behind one, to trail one's fingers in the water ‖ (mil.) to carry (e.g. a rifle) at the trail arms ‖ to lag behind (another or others) e.g. in a race ‖ to leave traces of (something), to trail sand all over the floor ‖ v.i. to hang down or float loosely ‖ to walk or progress slowly because of weariness or unwillingness ‖ (with 'behind') to fail to keep up with others ‖ (of a plant) to grow to a considerable length along the ground or over a surface ‖ to leave haphazard tracks or traces, she could see where the water had trailed all over the clean floor to trail off (of a sound) to dwindle gradually into silence, her voice trailed off to trail one's coat to try to provoke a calculated reaction in someone 2. n. the track or traces left by the passage of an animal or person ‖ a blazed or trodden path through a wild region ‖ something left behind by or following in the wake of a moving object, the car raised a trail of dust ‖ a long, thin wisp, trails of smoke were coming from the factories ‖ (Br., mil.) a horizontal position for carrying a rifle in the right hand, with the right arm fully extended downward, at the trail ‖ the part of the stock of a towed field gun which rests on the ground when the gun is unlimbered and put into action [prob. fr. O.N.F. *trailler*]

trail arms (*mil.*) a position in drilling in which the rifle is held in the right hand with the butt end raised just above the ground and the muzzle inclined forward

trail bike a lightweight motorcycle designed for rough terrain

trail·blaz·er (tréiblẹizər) *n*. the first person to mark out a path for others to follow ‖ a pioneer in some enterprise

trail·er (tréilər) *n*. someone who or something which trails ‖ a short extract from a new film exhibited as advance publicity ‖ a wheeled vehicle designed to be towed by a car or truck, esp. (*Am.= Br.* caravan) one containing sleeping quarters and arrangements for cooking and eating

trailer park area licensed to permit the parking of recreational vehicles, i.e., campers and trailers, and usu. providing water and electricity *also* trailer camp, trailer court

trailing arbutus *Epigaea repens,* fam. *Ericaceae,* a creeping, evergreen plant, having fragrant pink and white flowers and oblong, hairy leaves. It blossoms in early spring mainly in the northeastern U.S.A.

trailing edge (*aeron.*) the rear edge of an airfoil (cf. LEADING EDGE)

train (trein) *n*. a line of railroad cars coupled together with or without the engine that draws them ‖ (*old-fash.*) a retinue, body of habitual followers ‖ a series of persons or things following or linked to one another, *a mule train, train of events* ‖ (*mil., hist.*) a group of men, vehicles and animals carrying supplies, ammunition etc. at the rear of an army ‖ an elongation of a robe or the skirt of a woman's dress made to trail along the ground or to be carried ‖ a bird's long tail, esp. a peacock's ‖ a line of inflammable material, usually gunpowder, laid over a distance to an explosive charge, for safe firing of the charge ‖ a series of connected wheels or parts in machinery, for transmitting or modifying motion, esp. in a watch or clock ‖ a series of physical oscillations, *a train of sound waves* ‖ an orderly linked sequence, *a train of thought, train of reactions* **in the train of** following (something) as a result, *the tornado brought havoc in its train* **to set in train** to cause (events) to happen which will lead to other desired effects [F. *traîne* fem. and *train* masc.]

train *v.t.* to cause (a person or animal) to respond to discipline and instruction ‖ to make (a person or animal) efficient in some activity by instruction and repeated practice ‖ to make (a plant) grow in a desired direction by pruning and tying it ‖ (with 'on') to direct (a gun, camera etc.) ‖ *v.i.* to make one's own body more efficient by exercise and diet, or one's intelligence and memory by application ‖ to go by rail [M.E. O.F. *traïner, trahiner*]

train·band (tréinbænd) *n*. a 16th-c., 17th-c. or 18th-c. militia [shortened fr. trained band]

train·bear·er (tréinbẹrər) *n*. a person appointed to carry the train of another's robe or gown on ceremonial occasions

train·ee (treiní:) *n*. a person undergoing training ‖ someone undergoing military training

train·ee·ship (treiní:ʃip) *n*. the period of status of being a trainee

train·er (tréinər) *n*. a person who trains, esp. someone who trains athletes, horses etc. for racing or sport, or someone who trains circus animals ‖ a machine used in training

train·ing (tréiniŋ) *n*. preparatory discipline for participants in athletics etc. ‖ the instructing and directing of such participants ‖ instruction and practice in a particular skill, *first-aid training* **in training** undergoing a course of instruction or direction ‖ at full pitch of physical condition and expertise for sport or athletics **out of training** not at the pitch of physical fitness and expertise needed for sport or athletics

training ship a ship for training boys in seamanship ‖ a ship equipped to train men for the merchant marine or the navy

train·man (tréinmən) *pl.* **train·men** (tréinmən) *n*. a subordinate member of a train crew

train oil whale oil

traipse, *Br.* also **trapes** (treips) 1. *v.i. pres. part.* **traips·ing,** *Br.* also **trapes·ing** *past* and *past part.* **traipsed,** *Br.* also **trapesed** to trudge for a long distance without a fixed route, *we traipsed all over town looking for a room* 2. *n*. a long, tiring walk [earlier *trapass* prob. fr. O.F. *trapasser,* to pass beyond]

trait (treit, esp. *Br.* trei) *n*. a distinguishing characteristic, quality or feature [F.]

trai·tor (tréitər) *n*. a person who betrays a trust or acts against a sworn loyalty, esp. someone guilty of the crime of treason [O.F. *traitre*]

trai·tor·ous (tréitərəs) *adj.* characteristic of or having the character of a traitor ‖ having the nature of treason

trai·tress (tréitris) *n*. a female traitor [O.F. *traitresse*]

Tra·jan (tréidʒən) (Marcus Ulpius Trajanus, 53–117), Roman emperor (98–117). His conquest of Dacia (c. 106) is commemorated in the sculptures of Trajan's Column in Rome. His military and civil administration was firm and efficient

tra·jec·to·ry (trədʒéktəri:) *pl.* **tra·jec·to·ries** *n*. the path of a body in space, esp. of a projectile ‖ (*geom.*) a curve or surface cutting at a constant angle a system of curves or surfaces [fr. M.L. *trajectorius*]

tram (træm) *n*. (*Br.*) a streetcar ‖ a four-wheeled wagon running on rails for transporting coal from the face to the loading base in a mine [prob.=L.G. *traam,* a beam]

tram *n*. yarn made of lightly twisted silk strands, used esp. for the weft of the best velvets and silks [F. *trame*]

tram·car (trǽmkɑr) *n*. (*Br.*) a streetcar

tram·line (trǽmlạin) *n*. (*Br.*) a route served by streetcars ‖ (*Br., pl.*) the rails on which a streetcar runs ‖ (*pl., Br., pop.*) a pair of parallel lines bounding the sides of a lawn-tennis court, of which the inner marks the boundary of the singles court

tram·mel (trǽməl) 1. *n*. a net used for fowling or fishing, esp. a triple dragnet made with three layers of different sized mesh ‖ a shackle used to teach a horse to amble ‖ an adjustable pothook set in the chimney of an open fireplace ‖ (*pl.*) impediments to free movement or action, *the trammels of legal procedure* ‖ (*mech.*) an instrument for drawing ellipses ‖ a gauge for aligning or adjusting machine parts ‖ (*pl.,* often with 'pair of') a beam compass 2. *v.t. pres. part.* **tram·mel·ing,** esp. *Br.* **tram·mel·ling** *past* and *past part.* **tram·meled,** esp. *Br.* **tram·melled** to catch in a trammel ‖ to hamper, prevent the free play of [O.F. *tramail*]

tra·mon·tane (trəmóntein) *n*. the cold, dry, northerly wind in Italy and the Mediterranean blowing from the Alps [fr. Ital. *tramontana,* north wind]

tramp (træmp) 1. *v.i.* to march or walk with a heavy tread ‖ to travel on foot or go for long walks, *to spend a week tramping across the hills* ‖ *v.t.* to trample ‖ to make (one's way or a specified distance) by tramping ‖ to walk purposefully across, down, over etc., esp. wearily or reluctantly, *to tramp the streets looking for work* 2. *n*. the sound of heavy footsteps ‖ a cargo boat not traveling on a regular line but picking up cargo wherever it offers ‖ a long walk usually for pleasure ‖ a person without work and with no fixed home who tramps the country living by begging and sometimes by casual labor ‖ a woman of loose morals [M.E. *trampen*]

tram·ple (trǽmp'l) 1. *v. pres. part.* **tram·pling** *past* and *past part.* **tram·pled** *v.t.* to crush or pack down by treading on, *to trample grapes* ‖ (with 'out') to extinguish (a fire) by stamping it out with one's feet ‖ to bring (e.g. mud) on the feet somewhere where it is not wanted, *to trample mud into a carpet* ‖ *v.i.* to tread heavily ‖ (with 'on', 'upon' or 'over') to tread heavily and crush, bruise, injure or spoil something, *to trample over flowerbeds* 2. *n*. the sound of trampling [M.E. *trampelen* frequentative of *trampen,* to tramp]

tram·po·lin (trǽmpəlin) *n*. a trampoline

tram·po·line (trǽmpəlin) *n*. a large canvas sheet stretched in a frame by springs, providing a platform of extreme elasticity for acrobats, tumblers, clowns etc. or for exercising on [Span. *trampolin* fr. Ital. *trampoli,* stilts]

tram·way (trǽmwẹi) *n*. (*Br.*) the rails along which streetcars run

trance (træns, trɑns) *n*. a state of insensibility to external surroundings with partial, but unconscious, retention of function. It may be either self-induced or brought on by hypnosis ‖ a state of profound abstraction due to intense concentration of mind, as in religious contemplation, which may be accompanied by ecstasy, exaltation or (sometimes) hallucination [O.F. *transe*]

tran·dem (trǽndəm) *n*. (*surfing*) a surfboard holding three surfers

tran·quil (trǽŋkwil) *adj.* free from agitation or perturbation, peaceful [fr. L. *tranquillus*]

tran·quil·ite (trǽŋkwilait) *n*. compound of titanium, iron, and magnesium found in rock recovered from the moon's Sea of Tranquility

tran·quil·i·za·tion, tran·quil·li·za·tion (træŋkwilizéiʃən) *n*. a tranquilizing or being tranquilized

tran·quil·ize, tran·quil·lize (trǽŋkwilaiz) *pres. part.* **tran·quil·iz·ing, tran·quil·liz·ing** *past* and *past part.* **tran·quil·ized, tran·quil·lized** *v.t.* to make tranquil ‖ (*med.*) to reduce tension in by drugs **tran·quil·iz·er, tran·quil·liz·er** (trǽŋkwilaizər) *n*. something that tranquilizes, esp. a sedative drug

tran·quil·li·ty, tran·quil·i·ty (træŋkwíliti:) *n*. the stage or quality of being tranquil [O.F. *tranquillité*]

trans- (trænz, træns) *prefix* on or to the other side of, beyond, over, across ‖ from one state to another, as in 'transliterate'

trans·act (trænsǽkt, trænzǽkt) *v.t.* to perform, carry through (e.g. a business affair) ‖ *v.i.* to conduct business [fr. L. *transigere (transactus),* to carry through, accomplish]

trans·ac·ti·nide series (trænsǽktənaid) hypothetical elements following element 103 (lawrencium) in the periodic table *Cf* SUPERACTINIDE SERIES

trans·ac·tion (trænsǽkʃən, trænzǽkʃən) *n*. the performance or management of business etc. ‖ something transacted, a business deal ‖ (*pl.*) records, esp. published, of the proceedings of a learned society [fr. L. *transactio (transactionis)*]

trans·ac·tion·al analysis (trænsǽkʃənəl) (*psych.*) a form of group therapy based on three positions or roles (child, adult, parent), and six types of transactions (work, intimacy, etc.) carried on as 'games' in which subjects alternately assumes roles in order to provide verbal outlets for undesired responses; developed by American psychologist Eric Berne (1910–1970) *abbr.* TA

trans·ac·tor (trænsǽktər, trænzǽktər) *n*. a person who transacts

Trans A·lai (trænsəlái, trænzəlái) a mountain range extending west from the Chinese border between Kirghizia and Tadzhikistan, U.S.S.R. (Lenin, 23,386 ft)

Trans-Alaska Pipeline (trænzəlǽskə) an oil pipeline that runs from Prudhoe Bay, an arm of the Arctic Ocean, to Valdez, an ice-free port on the Gulf of Alaska, a distance of 800 miles. The 48-inch-diameter pipeline can carry over 2 million barrels of crude oil per day from Alaska's North Slope fields. The pipeline, built by a consortium of 8 oil companies, was completed in 1977 at a cost of nearly $8 billion, making it the costliest private construction project in history

trans·al·pine (trænsǽlpain, trænzǽlpain) *adj.* on the north side of the Alps (cf. CISALPINE) [fr. L. *transalpinus,* across the Alps (i.e. from Italy)]

Transalpine Gaul *GAUL

trans·am·i·na·tion (trænsæmənéiʃən) *n*. (*biochem.*) change of amino acids from one molecule to another, promoted by an enzyme —**trans·aminase** or **aminotransferase** *n*. the enzyme

trans·at·lan·tic (trænsətlǽntik, trænzətlǽntik) *adj.* on the other side of the Atlantic Ocean, esp. from the European point of view ‖ crossing or extending across the Atlantic Ocean ‖ pertaining to, characteristic of or coming from the region or people on the other side of the Atlantic, *transatlantic cultural influences*

trans·bus (trǽnsbʌs) *n*. bus designed to accommodate the handicapped, esp. in urban transit

Trans·cau·ca·sia (trænskɔkéiʒə, trænzkɔkéiʒə) a region of the U.S.S.R. south of the Caucasus comprising the Armenian, Azerbaijan and Georgian Soviet Socialist Republics. Products: oil, manganese, tea, citrus fruits and wine. A Transcaucasian republic existed until 1936, when it was split up into its present divisions

tran·scend (trænsénd) *v.t.* to be or go beyond the limits or powers of, *to transcend belief* ‖ to surpass, excel, *it transcended all our hopes* ‖ (*philos., theol.,* of God or a god) to be above, separate from or independent of (experience, the material universe) [fr. L. *transcendere*]

tran·scend·ence (trænséndəns) *n*. the fact, state or act of being transcendent **tran·scénd·en·cy** *n*. [fr. M.L. *transcendentia*]

tran·scend·ent (trænséndənt) *adj.* beyond normal limits, surpassing, *of transcendent beauty* ‖ being outside or going beyond the limits of pos-

CONCISE PRONUNCIATION KEY: (**a**) æ, c*a*t; ɑ, c*a*r; ɔ f*aw*n; ei, sn*a*ke. (**e**) e, h*e*n; i:, sh*ee*p; iə, d*ee*r; ɛə, b*ea*r. (**i**) i, f*i*sh; ai, t*i*ger; ə:, b*i*rd. (**o**) o, *o*x; au, c*ow*; ou, g*oa*t; u, p*oo*r; ɔi, r*oy*al. (**u**) ʌ, d*u*ck; u, b*u*ll; u:, g*oo*se; ə, bacill*u*s; ju:, c*u*be. x, lo*ch*; θ, *th*ink; ð, bo*th*er; z, *Z*en; ʒ, corsa*g*e; dʒ, sava*g*e; ŋ, orangutan*g*; j, *y*ak; ʃ, *f*ish; tʃ, fe*tch*; 'l, rabb*le*; 'n, redd*en*. Complete pronunciation key appears inside front cover.

sible human experience ‖ (in Kant) going beyond the limits of possible knowledge (cf. TRANSCENDENTAL) ‖ being above and independent of the limitations of the material universe (cf. IMMANENT) [fr. L. *transcendens* (*transcendentis*) fr. *transcendere*, to transcend]

tran·scen·den·tal (trænsendént'l) *adj.* belonging to pure reason, prior to all experience and a necessary condition of that experience, *according to Kant space and time are transcendental concepts* (cf. TRANSCENDENT) **tran·scen·dén·tal·ism** *n.* any philosophical system which attributes *a priori* reality to what exists outside the bounds of human experience ‖ an American philosophical school represented by Emerson and characterized by a certain pantheistic mysticism **tran·scen·dén·tal·ist** *n.* [fr. M.L. *transcendentalis*]

transcendental meditation a meditation technique in which mind is released from tension through use of a mantra, creating a feeling of calm and spiritual well-being *abbr.* TM

trans·con·ti·nen·tal (trænskɒntinént'l, trænzkɒntinént'l) *adj.* extending or going across a continent

tran·scribe (trænskráib) *pres. part.* **tran·scrib·ing** *past* and *past part.* **tran·scribed** *v.t.* to copy out in manuscript or type (notes, shorthand etc.) ‖ to arrange or adapt (a piece of music) for an instrument, voice etc. other than that for which it was originally written ‖ (*radio*) to record (material) for broadcast at a later time ‖ (*genetics*) to carry a message from DNA to RNA through the synthesis of an enzyme ‖ *v.i.* to make a transcription [fr. L. *transcribere*]

tran·script (trænskript) *n.* a copy written or typed [O.F. *transcrit*]

transcriptase *REVERSE TRANSCRIPTASE

tran·scrip·tion (trænskrípʃən) *n.* something transcribed ‖ a transcribing or being transcribed [F.]

trans·duce (trænsdú:s) *v.* (*biol.*) to cause the transfer of molecules between microorganisms by means of a viral agent

trans·duc·er (trænsdú:sər, trænzdú:sər, trænsdjú:sər, trænzdjú:sər) *n.* (*phys.*) a device for transferring power, generated in one system, to another system, in the same or another form ‖ (*biol.*) a virus that causes a change in the genetic character of a microorganism through action of nucleic acid [fr. L. *transducere*, to lead across]

trans·earth (trænsə:rθ) *adj.* (*astronautics*) of the path of a spacecraft between the earth and a celestial body

tran·sect 1. (trænsekt) *n.* (*bot.*) a line or strip of vegetation chosen for study **2.** (trænsékt) *v.t.* to cut across **tran·séc·tion** *n.* [fr. L. *trans, across+secare* (*sectus*), to cut]

tran·sept (trænsept) *n.* either of the two transverse wings of a cruciform church built at right angles to the nave ‖ the entire transverse section crossing between nave and choir in a cruciform church **tran·sép·tal** *adj.* [fr. M.L. or Mod. L. *transseptum* fr. *trans*, across+*septum*, hedge]

trans·fer 1. (trænsfə́:r, trænzfə́:r, trænsfər, trænzfər) *v. pres. part.* **trans·fer·ring** *past* and *past part.* **trans·ferred** *v.t.* to move from one place or position to another, *the manager was transferred to a different branch* ‖ to redirect from one person or object to another, *to transfer one's affection to someone else* ‖ to pass legal ownership or control of to another person, *he transferred the shares to a nephew* ‖ (*sports*) to trade (a professional player) to another club etc. ‖ (*arts*) to convey (a design etc.) from one surface to another, esp. by transfer paper to a lithograph stone ‖ *v.i.* to get out of one bus, train etc. and into another so as to continue a journey ‖ to change one's work or position, esp. within an organization, *he transferred from sales to advertising* **2.** (trænsfər, trænzfər) *n.* a transferring or being transferred ‖ something or someone transferred ‖ a design on paper etc. which can be transferred to another surface ‖ (*law*) an act of conveyance of property from one person to another or the deed drawn up for it ‖ a ticket entitling the bearer to change from one bus or streetcar to another within a specified period **trans·fer·ence** (trænsfərəns, trænzfərəns, trænsfə́:rəns, trænzfə́:rəns) *n.* a transferring or being transferred ‖ (*psychoanal.*) the transfer of desires or sentiments, esp. those retained in the unconscious from childhood, to another object, e.g. the redirection of a girl's feelings for her father to a male figure usually much older than herself [fr. L. *transferre*, to carry across]

transfer cell (*botany*) the cell in a plant that exchanges dissolved substances with the outside environment

trans·fer·en·tial (trænsfərénʃəl, trænzfərénʃəl) *adj.* of or relating to transference or to a transfer

transfer factor (*med.*) the immunity protein stored in white blood cells that recognizes a disease and prevents its recurrence; discovered by American biochemist H. Sherwood Lawrence (1916–)

transfer paper a specially prepared coated paper that allows a design on it to be transferred to another surface. Some papers need moisture for this, some need heat, some need pressure

transfer payments public funds distributed to persons for a special purpose in accordance to a legal formula, e.g., social security, unemployment compensation, veterans' benefits

transfer RNA (*genetics*) a form of RNA that combines with amino acids and messenger RNA to cause remaining amino acids to combine in a certain sequence in protein synthesis *abbr.* tRNA *Cf* MESSENGER RNA, RIBOSOMAL RNA

trans·fig·u·ra·tion (trænsfigjuréiʃən, trænzfigjuréiʃən, trænsfigjuréiʃən, trænzfigjuréiʃən) *n.* a transfiguring or being transfigured **the Transfiguration** the change in Christ's appearance described in Matthew xvii and celebrated by the Christian Church on Aug. 6 [fr. L. *transfiguratio* (*transfigurationis*)]

trans·fig·ure (trænsfígjər, trænzfígjər) *pres. part.* **trans·fig·ur·ing** *past* and *past part.* **trans·fig·ured** *v.t.* to change the appearance of in a very great degree, usually in a pleasing way, *the architect had transfigured the old barns, joy transfigured her face* [fr. L. *transfigurare*, to change the shape of]

trans·fix (trænsfíks, trænzfíks) *v.t.* to impale upon or pierce with a pointed instrument ‖ to pierce through or to make as if paralyzed by a strong emotion etc., *transfixed with horror* **trans·fíx·ion** *n.* [fr. L. *transfigere* (*transfixus*), to fix through]

trans·form (trænsfórm, trænzfórm) *v.t.* to change the form or appearance of, esp. (with 'into') to metamorphose ‖ to change the character or nature of radically ‖ (*phys.*) to change (energy) from one kind to another ‖ (*elec.*) to change (an electric current) into one of different voltage [fr. L. *transformare*]

trans·for·ma·tion (trænsfərméiʃən, trænzfərméiʃən) *n.* a transforming or being transformed ‖ (*old-fash.*) false hair worn to supplement a woman's natural hair, or as a wig ‖ (*genetics*) the taking up of free DNA to acquire genetic properties ‖ (*computer*) the change in composition or structure of data without any change in values or meanings [fr. L.L. *transformatio* (*transformationis*)]

trans·for·ma·tion·al grammar (trænsfərméiʃən'l) a generative grammar with a transformational component, i.e. a section of rules for the transformation and transposition of elements of a sentence to make a different sentence

transformation scene (*pantomime*) an elaborate scene in which the actors and scenery gradually change their appearance in full view of the audience for the lavish finale

trans·form·er (trænsfórmər, trænzfórmər) *n.* (*elec.*) a device for converting a varying current from one voltage to another. In a step-up transformer the low-voltage current is passed through a primary coil of a few thick turns, wound on an iron core. An alternating magnetic field is thus created, and this produces, by mutual induction, a high-voltage current in a secondary coil consisting of a large number of turns of thin wire, the ratio of the voltages being roughly equal to that of the number of turns in the two coils. A step-down transformer operates in the reverse sense

transform fault (*geol.*) a crack in the earth's crust in a steplike pattern that is believed to indicate direction of plate movements

trans·fuse (trænsfjú:z, trænzfjú:z) *pres. part.* **trans·fus·ing** *past* and *past part.* **trans·fused** *v.t.* to communicate (a quality) to, *to transfuse one's enthusiasm into a class* ‖ to permeate, *his enthusiasm transfused the class* ‖ to transfer (blood) from one person into the vein of another or from one animal into another ‖ to inject (a saline solution) into a vein ‖ to subject (a patient) to a transfusion [fr. L. *transfundere* (*transfusus*), to pour across]

trans·fu·sion (trænsfjú:ʒən, trænzfjú:ʒən) *n.* a transfusing, esp. of fluids (blood, plasma, solu-

tions containing various foods, minerals or drugs) into the veins of a patient [fr. L. *transfusio* (*transfusionis*)]

trans·gress (trænsgrés, trænzgrés) *v.t.* to break (a rule, law etc.) ‖ to go beyond (a limit etc.) ‖ *v.i.* (*rhet.*) to sin [F. *transgresser*]

trans·gres·sion (trænsgréʃən, trænzgréʃən) *n.* a sin ‖ a transgressing [F.]

trans·gres·sor (trænsgrésər, trænzgrésər) *n.* a person who transgresses

tran·ship (trænʃíp) *pres. part.* **tran·ship·ping** *past* and *past part.* **tran·shipped** *v.t.* and *i.* to transship **tran·shíp·ment** *n.*

trans·hu·mance (trænshjú:məns, trænzhjú:məns) *n.* the seasonal transfer of livestock to mountain or lowland pastures [F.]

tran·sience (trénʃəns, trénʒəns) *n.* the state or quality of being transient **trán·sien·cy** *n.*

tran·sient (trénʃənt, trénzənt) **1.** *adj.* brief, short-lived, impermanent ‖ staying for only a short time, esp. of hotel guests **2.** *n.* a person who stays in a hotel etc. for only a short time ‖ a person who has no fixed abode or employment and who wanders about looking for temporary work [fr. L. *transiens* (*transientis*) fr. *transire*, to go across]

trans·il·lu·mi·nate (trænsilú:mineit, trænzilú:mineit) *pres. part.* **trans·il·lu·mi·nat·ing** *past* and *past part.* **trans·il·lu·mi·nat·ed** *v.t.* (*med.*) to pass a strong light through (tissue or an organ) for examination

tran·sis·tor (trænzístər) *n.* any of several types of device incorporating an arrangement of semiconductor material (esp. germanium with controlled low concentrations of arsenic, indium, antimony etc.) and suitable contacts capable of performing many of the functions of thermionic and photoemissive tubes (such as power, voltage or current amplification) with low power requirements and large saving of space ‖ a radio set using transistors instead of tubes [TRANSFER+RESISTOR]

trans·it (trænsit, trænzit) **1.** *n.* a moving or being moved across, over, or from one place to another ‖ the movement of one heavenly body across the disk of a larger one, or its apparent movement across a meridian ‖ a transit instrument ‖ the transport or conveyance of goods or persons from one place to another **in transit** in the process of being moved ‖ (*aerospace*) navigation satellite that utilizes the Doppler effect for fixing position of ships and aircraft **2.** *v.t.* (*astron.*) to move across the disk of (a larger heavenly body) ‖ (*astron.*) to cross (a meridian) ‖ to turn (a telescope etc.) about its horizonal transverse axis ‖ *v.i.* to make a transit [fr. L. *transire* (*transitus*), to go across]

transit compass a variety of theodolite used to measure horizontal angles

transit instrument an instrument furnished with a rotating telescope and a circular scale, used to observe the transit of a heavenly body across a meridian ‖ a transit compass

tran·si·tion (trænzíʃən, trænsíʃən, *Br.* trænsíʃən) *n.* a change or passage from one place, action, mood, topic etc. to another ‖ a development that forms part of an ordered progression, *a transition from limited autonomy to full independence* ‖ (*mus.*) a passage which joins two others more important than itself ‖ (*mus.*) a sudden change of key not effected by modulation ‖ (*genetics*) a mutation in RNA or DNA in which a purine or a pyrimidine base is substituted for another **tran·si·tion·al** *adj.* [fr. L. *transitio* (*transitionis*)]

transition point (*phys.*) the temperature at which two physical states of the same substance are in equilibrium ‖ (*loosely*) the temperature at which a substance changes its physical state

transition temperature (*phys.*) a transition point

tran·si·tive (trænsitiv, trænzitiv) **1.** *adj.* (*gram.*, of certain verbs) expressing an action directed toward or performed on some person or thing (*DIRECT OBJECT) **2.** *n.* a verb or construction which is transitive [fr. L.L. *transitivus*]

tran·si·to·ri·ly (trænsitɔ́rili:, trænzitɔ́rili:, trænsitɔuríli:, trænzitɔuríli:) *adv.* in a transitory manner

tran·si·to·ri·ness (trænsitɔ́ri:nis, trænzitɔ́ri:nis, trænsitɔuri:nis, trænzitɔuri:nis) *n.* the state or quality of being transitory

tran·si·to·ry (trænsitɔ́ri:, trænzitɔ́ri:, trænsitɔuri:, trænzitɔuri:) *adj.* passing, temporary, not lasting [O.F. *transitoire*]

Trans·jor·dan (trænsdʒɔ́rd'n, trænzdʒɔ́rd'n) the former name of the Hashimite Kingdom of Jordan (*JORDAN)

CONCISE PRONUNCIATION KEY: **(a)** æ, c*a*t; ɑ, c*a*r; ɔ f*aw*n; ei, sn*a*ke. **(e)** e, h*e*n; i:, sh*ee*p; iə, d*ee*r; ɛə, b*ea*r. **(i)** i, f*i*sh; ai, t*i*ger; ə:, b*i*rd. **(o)** o, *o*x; au, c*ow*; ou, g*oa*t; u, p*oo*r; ɔi, r*oy*al. **(u)** ʌ, d*u*ck; u, b*u*ll; u:, g*oo*se; ə, b*a*cillus; ju:, c*u*be. x, lo*ch*; θ, *th*ink; ð, bo*th*er; z, *Z*en; ʒ, cor*s*age; dʒ, sava*ge*; ŋ, orangutan*g*; j, *y*ak; ʃ, *fish*; tʃ, fe*tch*; 'l, rabb*le*; 'n, redd*en*. Complete pronunciation key appears inside front cover.

Trans·kei (trænskai) *n.* enclave nation in the Republic of South Africa whose 'independence' since October 15, 1976 has been largely unrecognized by other nations. It is the home of the Xhosa people

Trans·kei·an Territories (trænskéiən, trænzkéiən) an African reserve (area 16,554 sq. miles, pop. 2,238,000), mainly pasture and grazing land, in N.E. Cape Province, South Africa. It comprises Transkei and Tembuland (inhabited by Kaffirs), Griqualand East (inhabited by people of mixed Bushman and Hottentot origin) and Pondoland (inhabited by a Bantu people related to the Zulus). Capital: Umtata (pop. 7,000)

trans·late (trænzléit, trænsléit) *pres. part.* **trans·lat·ing** *past* and *past part.* **trans·lat·ed** *v.t.* to put (a word, text or language) into another language retaining the sense || to put in different words of the same language, esp. in order to make clearer, *to translate scientific language for the layman* || to convert into another form, *to translate words into deeds* || (*eccles.*) to transfer (a bishop) to another see || to retransmit (a telegraphic message) || (*phys.*) to subject (a body) to simple displacement, without any other mode of motion || to convey (someone) straight to heaven or paradise without death's intervention || (*genetics*) to form an amino acid molecule from codon material provided by messenger RNA || *v.i.* to make a translation or translations || to be able to be translated [prob. fr. L. *transferre* (*translatus*)]

trans·la·tion (trænzléiʃən, trænsléiʃən) *n.* a translating or being translated || something translated, either the original or the new version || (*phys.*) motion by displacement only **trans·la·tion·al** *adj.* [O.F. or fr. L. *translatio* (*translationis*)]

trans·la·tor (trænzléitər, trænsléitər, trænzleitər, trænsleitər) *n.* a person who makes linguistic translations [O.F. or L.]

trans·lit·er·ate (trænzlítəreit, trænslítəreit) *pres. part.* **trans·lit·er·at·ing** *past* and *past part.* **trans·lit·er·at·ed** *v.t.* to replace (letters of one alphabet) by letters of another with the same phonetic sounds || to write (a word or words) in the letters of another alphabet **trans·lit·er·a·tion** *n.* [fr. L. *trans*, across+*littera*, letter]

trans·lo·cate (trænzlóukeit, trænslóukeit) *pres. part.* **trans·lo·cat·ing** *past* and *past part.* **trans·lo·cat·ed** *v.t.* to cause to change location, esp. to transfer (dissolved food materials) from one position in a plant body to another **trans·lo·ca·tion** *n.* the passage of food material in solution inside the body of a plant || the transfer of part of a chromosome to another part of the same chromosome or to a different chromosome

trans·lu·cence (trænzlú:sns, trænslú:sns) *n.* the state or quality of being translucent **trans·lú·cen·cy** *n.*

trans·lu·cent (trænzlú:snt, trænslú:snt) *adj.* of a medium through which light passes, but in such a way that a clear image cannot be formed of the object viewed through it (cf. TRANSPARENT, cf. OPAQUE) [fr. *translucens* (*translucentis*) fr. *translucere*, to shine through]

trans·lu·cid (trænzlú:sid, trænslú:sid) *adj.* translucent [fr. L. *translucidus*]

trans·lu·nar (trænslú:nə:r) *adj.* (*astronautics*) of the travel of a spacecraft from earth toward the moon

trans·mem·brane (trænsmémbrein) *adj.* of the transfer from one side of a membrane to another

trans·mi·grant (trænzmáigrənt, trænsmáigrənt) *n.* a person passing through a country on his way to a new country in which he is to settle

trans·mi·grate (trænzmáigreit, trænsmáigreit) *pres. part.* **trans·mi·grat·ing** *past* and *past part.* **trans·mi·grat·ed** *v.i.* to migrate from one place or country to another || (of the soul) to pass at death from one body to another [fr. L. *transmigrare* (*transmigratus*)]

trans·mi·gra·tion (trænzmaigréiʃən, trænsmaigréiʃən) *n.* the act or an instance of transmigrating || the transmigration of souls [fr. L.L. *transmigratio* (*transmigrationis*)]

transmigration of souls the passing of individual souls at death into new bodies or different forms of life

trans·mi·gra·to·ry (trænzmáigrətɔri:, trænsmáigrətɔri:, trænzmáigrətɔuri:, trænsmáigrətɔuri:) *adj.* of transmigration || tending to or in the habit of transmigrating

trans·mis·si·bil·i·ty (trænzmisəbíliti:, trænsmisəbíliti:) *n.* the state or quality of being transmissible

trans·mis·si·ble (trænzmísəb'l, trænsmísəb'l) *adj.* able to be transmitted [fr. L. *transmittere* (*transmissus*)]

trans·mis·sion (trænzmíʃən, trænsmíʃən) *n.* a transmitting or being transmitted || something transmitted, esp. a radio or television program || the passage of radio waves in the space between the transmitting and receiving stations || the mechanism (e.g. clutch, gearbox, transmission shaft) by which power is transmitted from the engine to the axle of a car etc. [fr. L. *transmissio* (*transmissionis*)]

transmission electron microscope microscope that illuminates an image by transmitted electrons passing through the specimen

trans·mit (trænzmít, trænsmít) *pres. part.* **trans·mit·ting** *past* and *past part.* **trans·mit·ted** *v.t.* to send, or cause or permit to pass, from one place or person to another || to be a medium for, or serve to communicate (light, heat, sound etc.) || to communicate || to pass on to others by inheritance or heredity || to pass on (an infection or disease) to a person, animal or organism || to convey (drive) from one mechanical part to another || to send (a signal) by radio waves or over a wire || *v.i.* to send out a signal by radio waves or over a wire **trans·mít·ter** *n.* a person who or thing which transmits [fr. L. *transmittere*, to send across]

trans·mog·ri·fy (trænzmógrifai, trænsmógrifai) *v.t.pres. part.* **trans·mog·ri·fy·ing** *past* and *past part.* **trans·mog·ri·fied** to change or alter utterly in form or appearance, esp. with grotesque or humorous effect [origin unknown]

trans·mut·a·bil·i·ty (trænzmju:təbíliti:, trænsmju:təbíliti:) *n.* the state or quality of being transmutable

trans·mut·a·ble (trænzmju:təb'l, trænsmju:təb'l) *adj.* capable of being transmuted **trans·mút·a·bly** *adv.* [fr. M.L. *transmutabilis*]

trans·mu·ta·tion (trænzmju:téiʃən, trænsmju:téiʃən) *n.* a transmuting or being transmuted || (*chem.*) the change of one element into another || (*biol.*) the change of one species into another [fr. L.L. *transmutatio* (*transmutationis*)]

trans·mute (trænzmjú:t, trænsmjú:t) *pres. part.* **trans·mut·ing** *past* and *past part.* **trans·mut·ed** *v.t.* to cause to change in form, nature or substance || *v.i.* to be transmuted [fr. L. *transmutare*, to change]

tran·som (trænsəm) *n.* a lintel || a horizontal bar in a window (cf. MULLION) || between the top of a door and a window directly over it || a window above the lintel of esp. a door || the horizontal bar of a cross or a gallows || any of various horizonal beams, esp. one supporting the afterdeck of a vessel [M.E. *traunsum* prob. fr. L. *transtrum*, crossbeam]

tran·son·ic (trænsónik) *adj.* (*aeron.*) of, relating to or moving at a speed close to the speed of sound

trans·pa·cif·ic (trænspəsífik, trænzpəsífik) *adj.* on the other side of the Pacific Ocean || crossing the Pacific Ocean

trans·par·en·cy (trænspéərənsi:, trænzpéərənsi:, trænspéərənsi:, trænzpéərənsi:) *pl.* **trans·par·en·cies** *n.* the state or quality of being transparent || something transparent, esp. a color photograph, picture or design imprinted on a thin transparent piece of film, glass etc. and viewed by transmitted light [fr. M.L. *transparentia*]

tran·spar·ent (trænspéərənt, trænzpéərənt, trænspærənt, trænzpærənt) *adj.* of a medium through which light can travel with minimal scattering, so that objects can be viewed clearly through it (cf. TRANSLUCENT, cf. OPAQUE) || easy to detect or perceive, *a transparent lie* || of a medium through which radiation of any sort can travel without deformation [fr. M.L. *transparens* (*transparentis*) fr. *transparere*, to appear through]

trans·pierce (trænspíərs, trænzpíərs) *v.t. pres. part.* **trans·pierc·ing** *past* and *past part.* **trans·pierced** to pierce through [F. *transpercer*]

tran·spi·ra·tion (trænspəréiʃən) *n.* the giving off of water vapor through the pores or stomata || the passage of gas through a capillary tube or porous substance because of pressure or temperature differences [fr. M.L. or Mod. L. *transpiratio* (*transpirationis*)]

tran·spire (trænspáiər) *pres. part.* **tran·spir·ing** *past* and *past part.* **tran·spired** *v.i.* to become known or apparent || (*pop.*) to come about, happen, *it transpired that he could come*

after all || to emit a gas or liquid through tissues or pores, e.g. (of plants) to give off watery vapor || to be emitted as a gas or liquid || *v.t.* to give off (water vapor, perspiration) through pores or stomata [F. *transpirer*]

trans·plant 1. (trænsplǽnt, trænzplǽnt, trænsplǽnt, trænzplʌ́nt) *v.t.* to remove and plant in another place || to settle (people or animals) in another area || (*surgery*) to graft (living tissue or an organ) from one part of the body to another or from one person to another || *v.i.* to bear being transplanted **2.** (trænsplǽnt, trænzplǽnt, trænsplǽnt, trænzplʌ́nt) *n.* a transplanting || something transplanted, e.g. body tissue **trans·plan·tá·tion** *n.* [fr. L.L. *transplantare*]

trans·plan·tate (trænsplǽntət) *n.* (*med.*) tissue that has been used in a transplant

tran·spon·der (trænspóndə:r) *n.* device capable of receiving a signal and responding immediately, e.g., in a satellite

trans·port 1. (trænspórt, trænzpórt, trænspóurt, trænzpóurt) *v.t.* to carry (goods, people or animals) from one place to another || (*hist.*) to ship (a convict) to a penal colony overseas || to cause (a person) to be carried away with strong emotion **2.** (trǽnsport, trǽnzport, trǽnspourt, trǽnzpourt) *n.* the act or process of transporting || a vessel or vehicle, esp. a ship or large aircraft, used to transport || (*hist.*) a convict sentenced to be transported || the state of being very strongly moved by an emotion, *in a transport of rage* || (*computer*) the mechanism that carries disk, tape, or paper past the sensing and recording heads **trans·por·ta·tion** *n.* a transporting or being transported || a means of transporting || the cost of transporting || (*hist.*) the punishment of shipping a convict to a penal colony [fr. F. *transporter*]

Transportation, U.S. Department of (*abbr.* DOT) a cabinet-level department of the U.S. government. Established in 1966, it is headed by the secretary of transportation. Major divisions are U.S. Coast Guard, Federal Aviation Administration, Federal Highway Administration, Federal Railroad Administration, Urban Mass Transportation Administration, Maritime Administration, St. Lawrence Seaway Development Corp. and National Highway Traffic Safety Administration

transporter bridge a bridge with a high span from which a movable platform is suspended on which loads can be conveyed across a navigable waterway without disturbing shipping

trans·pose (trænspóuz, trænzpóuz) *pres. part.* **trans·pos·ing** *past* and *past part.* **trans·posed** *v.t.* to cause (two things) to change places, each being made to occupy the position previously occupied by the other (esp. words in a sentence, sentences in a paragraph etc.) || (*algebra*) to move (a term) from one side to the other of an equation sign (involving a change of sign) || to write or play (a musical composition) in a key other than the original || *v.i.* to write or play music in a key other than the original || to admit of transposing [F. *transposer*]

transposing instrument a musical instrument, e.g. the clarinet, that sounds at a fixed interval above or below the note written

trans·po·si·tion (trænspəzíʃən, trænzpəzíʃən) *n.* a transposing or being transposed || something transposed [prob. F. or fr. M.L. *transpositio* (*transpositionis*) fr. L. *transponere*, to place across]

trans·sex·u·al (trænsékʃu:əl) *n.* a person of one sex who undergoes surgery to modify his or her sex organs to become physically like the opposite sex, commonly because of psychological identity with the other sex —**transsexual** *adj.* —**transsexualism** *n.*

trans·ship (trænsʃíp, trænzʃíp) *pres. part.* **trans·ship·ping** *past* and *past part.* **trans·shipped** *v.t.* to transfer (men or cargo) from one ship or vehicle to another || *v.i.* to leave one ship or vehicle and board another **trans·shíp·ment** *n.*

Trans-Si·be·ri·an Railroad (trænssaibíəri:ən, trænzsaibíəri:ən) the world's longest railroad, in the U.S.S.R., from Chelyabinsk in the Urals to Vladivostok on the Pacific (4,388 miles). Built 1891-1915, it greatly speeded up the colonization of Siberia and the development of industrially important mineral deposits (*KUZNETZ, *KARAGANDA)

tran·sub·stan·ti·ate (trænsəbstǽnʃi:eit) *pres. part.* **tran·sub·stan·ti·at·ing** *past* and *past part.* **tran·sub·stan·ti·at·ed** *v.t.* to change from one substance to another || (*Roman Catholicism*) to effect transubstantiation in (the sacramental elements) **tran·sub·stan·ti·a·tion** n. (Roman Catholicism) the doctrine that the sacramental elements of bread and wine, when consecrated in the Mass, are changed into the body and blood of the risen Christ (cf. CONSUBSTANTIA-TION, cf. IMPANATION) [fr. M.L. transubstantiare (transubstantiatus)]

tran·su·date (trǽnsudeit) n. a fluid which has passed through a membrane or other permeable substance [fr. Mod. L. transudare (transudatus), to transude]

tran·su·da·tion (trænsudéiʃən) n. a transuding or being transuded ‖ a transudate [F. transudation]

tran·sude (trænsúːd) pres. part. **tran·sud·ing** past and past part. **tran·sud·ed** v.i. to pass through a membrane or other permeable substance ‖ v.t. to cause to pass through a membrane etc., to exude [F. transuder]

trans·u·ran·ic (trænsjurǽnik, trænzjurǽnik) adj. pertaining to the artificial, radioactive elements having atomic numbers greater than that of uranium (92) (*PERIODIC TABLE)

Trans·vaal, the (trǽnzval, trǽnsval) the northern province (area 109,621 sq. miles, pop. 8,351,000) of South Africa. Capital: Pretoria. Chief city: Johannesburg. It is largely wild (3,000–6,000 ft), sloping down from the Drakensberg Mtns to the Vaal and Limpopo Rivers. Agriculture: stock raising, corn and other cereals, potatoes, citrus fruits. Resources: gold (leading world producer), coal, diamonds, copper, tin, asbestos, chrome. Industries: metallurgy, iron and steel, electrical products, chemicals, textiles, food processing, engineering. There are three universities: Witwatersrand, Pretoria and Potchefstroom. HISTORY. The indigenous Matabele were defeated (1836-8) by Boers of the Great Trek, and an independent Boer republic was established (1856). It was annexed by Britain (1877) but rebelled successfully (1881). The discovery (1886) of gold at Witwatersrand brought many new immigrants, known as Uitlanders, to the Transvaal. After the Boer War (1899-1902), the Transvaal became a British colony (1902). It joined the Union of South Africa (1910)

trans·ver·sal (trænzvɔ́ːrsl, trænsvɔ́ːrsl) 1. adj. transverse 2. n. (geom.) a straight line intersecting other lines [fr. M.L. transversalis]

trans·verse 1. (trænzvɔ́ːrs, trænsvɔ́ːrs, trǽnzvəːrs, trǽnsvəːrs) adj. crossing from side to side or lying across or crosswise 2. (trænzvɔ́ːrs, trænsvɔ́ːrs) v.t. pres. part. **trans·vers·ing** past and past part. **trans·versed** to lie across or pass across 3. (trænzvɔ́ːrs, trænsvɔ́ːrs, trǽnzvəːrs, trǽnsvəːrs) n. something transverse, esp. a muscle which is transverse to other parts of the body [fr. L. transvertere (transversus), to turn across]

transverse wave a wave (e.g. a water wave or an electromagnetic wave) in which the vibrating element (e.g. the particles of the medium or field vector) oscillates in a direction perpendicular to the direction of propagation of the wave

trans·ves·tism (trænzvéstizəm, trænsvéstizəm) n. (psychol.) the practice of dressing in the clothes of the opposite sex as a form of sexual inversion [fr. G. transvestismus]

trans·ves·tite (trænzvéstait, trænsvéstait) n. (psychol.) someone who practices transvestism [G. transvestit]

Tran·syl·va·ni·a (trænsilvéiniə) the northwestern region of Rumania, a fertile, wooded plateau surrounded north, east and south by the Carpathians: cereals, fruit, cattle raising. Natural gas and lignite are exploited. Chief town: Cluj

Tran·syl·va·ni·an Alps (trænsilvéiniən) the southern range of the Carpathians in S.W. Rumania between Transylvania and Walachia. Highest point: Negoi (8,346 ft)

tran·yl·cy·pro·mine [C₉H₁₁N] (trænilsaipróumiːn) n. (pharm.) a monoamine oxidase inhibitor used as an antidepressant; marketed as Parnate

trap (træp) 1. n. a man-made device into which an animal may enter unawares, or be driven or lured, and in which it is captured and sometimes killed ‖ something devised to put an unsuspecting person in a situation which is to his disadvantage and from which it is hard or impossible for him to escape ‖ any hidden hazard, a linguistic trap ‖ a device, e.g. a water-filled bend, in a pipe, to prevent noxious gases from passing (e.g. in the outflow pipe of a sink,

toilet etc.) ‖ a light, horse-drawn, two or four-wheeled passenger vehicle, the body of which is supported on springs ‖ (sports) a compartment or other device from which e.g. a racing greyhound or clay pigeons can be suddenly released ‖ (golf) a bunker ‖ a trapdoor ‖ (mus., pl.) the percussion instruments of a dance band 2. v. pres. part. **trap·ping** past and past part. **trapped** v.t. to catch in a trap or as if in a trap ‖ to furnish with a trap, to trap a pipe ‖ to prevent (a gas, liquid etc.) from passing or proceeding further ‖ v.i. to set traps for game [O.E. treppe, træppe]

trap n. (geol.) any of various dark igneous rocks, e.g. basalt, which have a structure resembling a flight of steps [Swed. trapp]

trap·door (trǽpdɔ́r, trǽpdóur) n. a small, sliding, lifting or hinged door in a floor, roof or ceiling

trapdoor spider a member of Ctenizidae, a family of large spiders living in warm, dry climates, which construct subterranean dwellings lined with silk and closed by a hinged door. The spider sits behind this and waits for prey

tra·peze (trəpíːz) n. a short horizontal bar suspended by two parallel ropes or wires, used by gymnasts and acrobats [F. trapèze]

tra·pe·zi·um (trəpíːziəm) pl. **tra·pe·zi·ums**, **tra·pe·zi·a** (trəpíːziə) n. (Am.=Br. trapezoid) a quadrilateral having no two sides parallel ‖ (Br.=Am. trapezoid) a quadrilateral with two sides parallel ‖ (anat.) a small bone of the wrist near the base of the thumb [Mod. L. fr. Gk]

tra·pe·zi·us (trəpíːziəs) n. one of a pair of large, flat triangular muscles of the back serving to rotate the scapula [Mod. L. trapezius]

tra·pe·zo·he·dron (trəpiːzouhíːdrən, træpizouhíːdrən) pl. **tra·pe·zo·he·drons, tra·pe·zo·he·dra** (trəpiːzouhíːdrə, træpizouhíːdrə) n. a solid figure, the faces of which are trapezoids [Mod. L. fr. trapezium+Gk hedra, a seat]

trap·e·zoid (trǽpizɔid) 1. n. (Am.=Br. trapezium) an irregular four-sided figure ‖ (Br.=Am. trapezium) a quadrilateral having no two sides parallel ‖ (anat.) a small bone of the wrist near the base of the index finger 2. adj. of, or in the form of, a trapezoid **trap·e·zói·dal** adj. [Mod. L. fr. Gk]

trap·per (trǽpər) n. a person who traps wild animals, esp. for their furs

trap·pings (trǽpiŋz) pl. n. ornamental equipment or embellishments, esp. those associated with an official position ‖ a horse's ornamented cloth covering, caparison

Trap·pist (trǽpist) 1. adj. of or pertaining to the austere reform of the Cistercian order carried out (c. 1664) by de Rancé, on the principles of strict seclusion from the world, silence and liturgical worship for seven hours daily 2. n. a Cistercian monk under the Trappist rule [fr. F. trappiste after La Trappe, an abbey in Normandy where the reform began]

traps (træps) pl. n. (Br., pop.) personal effects [prob. fr. TRAPPINGS]

trap·shoot·ing (trǽpʃuːtiŋ) n. the sport of shooting at clay pigeons catapulted into the air from traps

trash (træʃ) 1. n. shoddily made articles ‖ rubbish ‖ meaningless talk or writing, nonsense ‖ worthless books etc. ‖ (without article) people considered as of no account ‖ loppings off trees, hedges etc. ‖ bagasse 2. v.t. to lop (trees) ‖ to strip the outer leaves from (immature sugarcane) [origin unknown] ‖ (slang) to turn something into trash by vandalism, spoilation, or (figuratively) disparagement

trash·i·ly (trǽʃili) adv. in a trashy manner

trash·i·ness (trǽʃiːnis) n. the state or quality of being trashy

trash·y (trǽʃi) comp. **trash·i·er** superl. **trash·i·est** adj. of or like trash (shoddily made articles, nonsense)

Tras·i·mene (trǽzəmiːn) (Ital. Trasimeno) a lake (area 50 sq. miles) near Perugia in the Central Apennines, Italy, the scene of Hannibal's ambush of the Roman consul Flaminius (217 B.C.)

Trasop (acronym) for investment tax credit employee stock ownership plan, from the Technical Corrections Act of 1979

trass (træs) n. (geol.) a volcanic rock rich in fragments of pumice, used in making hydraulic cement [Du. tras]

trau·ma (tráumə, trɔ́mə) pl. **trau·ma·ta** (tráumətə, trɔ́mətə), **trau·mas** n. a physical wound or injury ‖ a violent emotional blow, esp. one which has a lasting psychic effect ‖ a neu-

rotic condition resulting from physical or emotional injury [Gk]

trau·mat·ic (trəmǽtik) adj. concerning, producing or resulting from trauma [fr. L.L. traumaticus fr. Gk]

trau·ma·tism (tráumətizəm, trɔ́mətizəm) n. the neurotic condition caused by a trauma ‖ a trauma [fr. Gk trauma (traumatos), a wound]

tra·vail (trəvéil, trǽveil) 1. n. (rhet.) the pains of childbirth ‖ (rhet.) any intense mental or physical pain or laborious work 2. v.i. (rhet.) to suffer the pains of childbirth (rhet.) to work hard or painfully [O.F.]

Trav·an·core (trǽvənkɔr) a former princely state in S. India, included since 1956 in Kerala. Chief town: Trivandrum

trav·el (trǽvəl) 1. v. pres. part. **trav·el·ing**, esp. Br. **trav·el·ling** past and past part. **trav·eled**, esp. Br. **trav·elled** v.i. to make a journey, esp. one of considerable length ‖ to make journeys abroad ‖ to proceed in a given direction or pass from one point to another, the pain traveled down his arm ‖ to be transmitted, sound waves will not travel through a vacuum ‖ to seem to move or journey, thoughts travel fast, her glance traveled over the crowd ‖ (sometimes with 'in') to work as a traveling salesman, to travel in encyclopedias ‖ to bear transporting, some wines will not travel ‖ (of a piece of machinery) to move in a set path ‖ v.t. to journey over or through (a region etc.) ‖ to cover (a distance) ‖ (of a traveling salesman) to have (a region) as the territory to be covered **to travel light** to travel with the minimum of baggage 2. n. the act or process of traveling ‖ the movement of a piece of machinery in a set path or the extent of this, the piston has a travel of nine inches ‖ (also pl.) journeys, esp. those made abroad ‖ a branch of literature describing such journeys ‖ the number of people or vehicles traveling on a route, traffic [var. of TRAVAIL]

trav·el·a·tor or **trav·el·la·tor** (trǽvəleit'r) n. a moving walkway, e.g., in some airports

trav·eled, esp. Br. **trav·elled** (trǽv'ld) adj. having experience of traveling, a much traveled man ‖ used by travelers, a much traveled route ‖ (geol.) erratic

trav·el·er, esp. Br. **trav·el·ler** (trǽvələr) n. a person who travels ‖ (Br.) a commercial traveler ‖ a piece of machinery, e.g. a type of crane, constructed to slide laterally along a support ‖ (naut.) an iron ring that slides up and down a rope or spar

trav·el·er's check, Br. **trav·el·ler's cheque** a check, purchased from a banking concern, which can be cashed when presented at any of the bank's correspondents anywhere, or can be used for purchases

trav·el·er's·joy, esp. Br. **trav·el·ler's·joy** (trǽvələrdzɔ́i) n. Clematis vitalba, the wild clematis

trav·el·er's·tree, esp. Br. **trav·el·ler's·tree** (trǽvələrtríː) n. Ravenala madagascariensis, fam. Musaceae, a subtropical or tropical tree having leaf petioles which contain a clear, watery, drinkable sap

traveling salesman (Am.=Br. commercial traveller) a manufacturer's representative who goes from retailer to retailer to secure orders

trav·e·lo·gue, trav·e·log (trǽvəlɔg, trǽvəlog) n. a documentary film describing a foreign country ‖ a lecture on a journey, illustrated by slides etc.

trav·erse (trǽvəːrs) 1. n. the action or instance of traversing ‖ something which lies or goes across, e.g. a section of a road, cut in diagonals up a steep hillside ‖ a bar, line etc. placed across something ‖ a sideways course, e.g. of a climber negotiating an obstacle to upward movement ‖ a place where it is necessary to follow such a course ‖ a zigzag course followed, e.g. by a ship at sea or by a skier ‖ a survey made in a series of legs, the end of one being the start of the next ‖ one of the legs of such a survey ‖ a curtain divided vertically and running on a rail, wire etc. as part of stage scenery ‖ (geom.) a transversal line ‖ (mach.) the sideways movement of a part ‖ (mach.) a device for imparting this movement ‖ the horizontal sweep of a gun ‖ (law) the formal denial of an allegation etc. ‖ (manège) the movement of a horse forward and sideways, with the head turned to one side and the tail to the other ‖ (fencing) the act of traversing 2. adj. transverse [O.F. travers, travers, traverse]

tra·verse (trəvɔ́ːrs, trǽvəːrs) pres. part. **tra·vers·ing** past and past part. **tra·versed** v.t. to move across or through ‖ to move back and forth along ‖ to extend across ‖ to turn (a gun) and direct it on its target ‖ to make a survey of by means of a traverse ‖ (*law*) to deny the truth of (an allegation etc.) ‖ (*law*) to deny or take issue upon (an indictment) ‖ *v.i.* to go across, along, up and down etc. ‖ to pivot laterally ‖ (*climbing, skiing, survey.* etc.) to make a traverse ‖ (*manège*) to execute a traverse ‖ (*fencing*) to slide one's blade toward the opponent's hilt while applying pressure to his blade [O.F. *traverser*]

trav·er·tin (trǽvɜrtin) *n.* travertine

trav·er·tine (trǽvɜrti:n) *n.* a buff-colored porous mineral, formed in streams and esp. hot springs by the deposition of calcium carbonate. It hardens on exposure to the air and is used as a building stone in warm climates, esp. Italy [Ital. *travertino*]

trav·es·ty (trǽvisti:) 1. *pl.* **trav·es·ties** *n.* a grotesque or crude imitation intended to make a thing imitated appear ridiculous ‖ a ridiculously inferior imitation 2. *v.t. pres. part.* **trav·es·ty·ing** *past* and *past part.* **trav·es·tied** to make a travesty of [F. *travesti*, disguised]

Trav·is (trǽvɜs), William B. (1809-36), U.S. lawyer and soldier, a hero of the Texas Revolution. He participated in the capture of San Antonio (1835) and led the defense against Mexican siege (Feb. 23–March 6, 1836) of the Alamo, where he died

trawl (trɔl) 1. *n.* a large, wide-mouthed bag net which is dragged along the bottom of the sea for fish by a boat ‖ a trot (for fishing) 2. *v.i.* to fish with a trawl ‖ *v.t.* to catch (fish) with a trawl **trawl·er** *n.* a boat used to catch fish by using trawl nets [etym. doubtful]

tray (trei) *n.* a flat piece of wood, metal, plastic etc., usually rimmed, for carrying or holding small, light objects ‖ the contents of a tray ‖ a shallow lidless compartment in a traveling trunk etc. [O.E. *trīg*]

treach·er·ous (trétʃɜrəs) *adj.* of the character or actions of a traitor ‖ unreliable, full of hazards, *treacherous ice* [O.F. *trecheros*]

treach·er·y (trétʃɜri:) *pl.* **treach·er·ies** *n.* disloyalty, perfidy ‖ treason ‖ an act of disloyalty or treason [O.F. *tricherie, trecherie* fr. *tricher*, to cheat]

trea·cle (trí:k'l) *n.* (*Br.*) molasses **trea·cly** *adj.* thick and sticky [M.E. *tryacle, triacle*]

tread (tred) 1. *v. pres. part.* **tread·ing** *past* **trod** (trod) *past part.* **trod·den** (tród'n), **trod** *v.i.* to move on foot, to walk, *to tread lightly across the room* ‖ to set the foot down, *to tread on a cigarette stub, tread in a puddle* ‖ to put down the foot so as to exert pressure, *to tread on the accelerator* ‖ (of a male bird) to copulate ‖ to proceed, *tread cautiously in your dealings with him* ‖ *v.t.* to beat down or wear away by walking on, *to tread a path, to tread a hole in a carpet* ‖ to pack down by pressing with a foot or feet, *to tread soil around newly planted seedlings* ‖ to crush with the foot or feet, *to tread grapes* ‖ (*rhet.*) to walk on, *to tread dry land* ‖ (of a male bird) to copulate with (a female bird) ‖ (*Br.*) to track (mud etc.) **to tread down** to oppress ‖ to wear down **to tread on** (*Br.*) to dismiss (a suggestion, idea) summarily **to tread on someone's toes** to offend someone esp. by usurping his prerogatives **to tread water** to keep oneself upright and one's head above water level in water where one is out of one's depth, by moving one's feet up and down with treading movements 2. *n.* the action, sound or way of treading, *we heard his tread on the stairs, a heavy tread* ‖ the horizontal part of a step in a staircase (cf. RISER) ‖ the width of this from front to back ‖ a piece of e.g. rubber put on a step to protect the step from becoming worn ‖ the undersurface of a shoe or the thickened, scored face of a tire which makes contact with the ground ‖ a chalaza of a bird's egg [O.E. *tredan*]

trea·dle (tréd'l) 1. *n.* a foot-operated lever on a machine etc. 2. *v.i. pres. part.* **trea·dling** *past* and *past part.* **trea·dled** to operate a treadle [O.E. fr. *tredan*]

tread·mill (trédmɪl) *n.* (*hist.*) a mill worked by people constantly treading on steps set in the circumference of the great mill wheel. The work was formerly a punishment for prisoners ‖ a mill driven by an animal treading on an endless belt ‖ any wearyingly monotonous activity

trea·son (trí:z'n) *n.* an attempt to overthrow by illegal means the government to which a person owes allegiance ‖ the act or attempted act of working for the enemies of the state ‖ (*Br.*) an attempt to kill or injure the sovereign ‖ betrayal

of trust, disloyalty (to a cause, friend etc.) **trea·son·a·ble, trea·son·ous** *adjs.* [F. *tresun*]

treas·ure (tréʒɜr) 1. *n.* anything very valuable ‖ (*hist.*) a store of money, jewels etc. ‖ a person whom one thinks of as being of rare excellence 2. *v.t. pres. part.* **treas·ur·ing** *past* and *past part.* **treas·ured** to value highly ‖ to keep in the memory with special pleasure, *to treasure someone's words* [O.F. *tresor*]

treas·ur·er (tréʒɜrɜr) *n.* an official in charge of the finances of a government, society etc. ‖ a governmental officer in charge of the receipt, care and paying out of public money [A.F. *tresorer*]

treasure trove money, jewels etc., of unknown ownership, found hidden [A.F. *tresor trové*]

treas·ur·y (tréʒɜri:) *pl.* **treas·ur·ies** *n.* a building used to store money, valuables etc. ‖ (esp. in book titles) a collection of things prized, *a treasury of poetry* ‖ the funds of a society, corporation, state etc. **Treas·ur·y** a government department responsible for the public revenue and expenditure or the buildings in which the business of this department is transacted [O.F. *tresorie*]

treasury bill a government obligation bearing no interest but issued at a discount and payable at par when it matures (usually in 90 days)

treasury bond a government promissory note, valid for not more than six years and bearing a fixed rate of interest

treasury note a currency note issued by the U.S. Treasury Department ‖ (*Br., hist.*) a £1 or 10-shilling currency note issued by the Treasury 1914–28

Treasury, U.S. Department of the a cabinet-level department of the U.S. government that oversees the nation's finances. Established in 1789, its first secretary was Alexander Hamilton. The secretary of the treasury ranks second in the president's cabinet, is the president's chief adviser on fiscal affairs, and is required by law to report to Congress each year on the government's fiscal operations and its financial condition. The secretary must also manage the public debt and conduct financial dealings with other nations. Operating bureaus of the Treasury Department include Comptroller of the Currency, U.S. Customs Service, Bureau of Engraving and Printing, Internal Revenue Service, U.S. Mint, Bureau of Alcohol, Tobacco and Firearms, and the Secret Service

Treasury Bench (*Br.*) the front bench occupied by British government ministers in the House of Commons

treat (tri:t) 1. *v.t.* to behave toward (someone or something), *I don't like the way he treats his dog* ‖ to regard in a specified way, *to treat something as a joke* ‖ to pay for the food, drink or entertainment etc. of (another person) ‖ to give medical attention to (a patient) ‖ to try to cure or alleviate (a disease) ‖ to subject to chemical action ‖ to cover or coat with some preparation ‖ (sometimes with 'of') to expound or be an exposition of (something) in words or writing, *the book treats two main topics* ‖ *v.i.* (sometimes with 'with') to negotiate ‖ to pay for another's food, drink or entertainment etc. ‖ (with 'of') to offer an exposition or discussion 2. *n.* something that gives special delight, pleasure or satisfaction ‖ one's turn to pay for the food, drinks or entertainment of another or others [O.F. *tretier, traitier*]

treat-and-re·lease (trí:tændrilí:s) *n.* hospital policy of providing only emergency out-patient treatment and refusing to admit patients when a hospital has few available beds

trea·tise (trí:tis) *n.* a written study of a particular subject, dealt with systematically and thoroughly [A.F. *tretiz*]

treat·ment (trí:tmənt) *n.* the act or a method or manner of treating someone or something ‖ medical or surgical care ‖ an instance of this ‖ a detailed outline of the plot of a proposed screenplay or television script

trea·ty (trí:ti:) *pl.* **trea·ties** *n.* a formal, signed and ratified agreement between states [A.F. *treté*]

treaty port (*hist.*) a port opened by treaty to foreign trade, esp. in 19th-c. China

Treb·i·zond (trébizond) (*Turk.* Trabzon) a port (pop. 107,412 of Turkey on the Black Sea. Founded as a Greek colony (8th c. B.C.) on the trade route from central Europe to Asia, it became famous as the center of an empire founded (1204) by the Comnenus family. It fell (1461) to the Turks. Byzantine churches

tre·ble (tréb'l) 1. *adj.* three times as much, as many or as great ‖ consisting of or existing in three parts ‖ (*mus.*, of a voice or instrument) singing or playing the upper part in musical harmony ‖ (*mus.*) of or for a soprano, esp. (*Br.*) a boy soprano, or of the upper part in instrumental music ‖ high-pitched 2. *n.* the highest singing voice ‖ (*Br.*) a boy soprano or boy soprano voice ‖ the upper part of a musical composition ‖ an instrument playing this part ‖ (*old-fash.*) a highpitched voice or sound ‖ (*change ringing*) the highest bell of a ring [O.F.]

treble *pres. part.* **tre·bling** *past* and *past part.* **tre·bled** *v.t.* to make three times as much, as many or as great ‖ *v.i.* to become three times as much, as many or as great

treble clef (*mus.*) the symbol (𝄞) placing G above middle C on the second line of the staff from the bottom. Parts for high-pitched instruments and voices and right-hand piano parts are written in the treble clef

treble staff *pl.* **treble staves** (*mus.*) the staff carrying the treble clef

tre·cen·to (tretʃéntou) *n.* the 14th c. in Italy with respect to its art, architecture etc. [Ital. short for *mil trecento*, 1300]

tre·de·cil·lion (treidisíljən) *n.* *NUMBER TABLE [fr. L. *tres*, three+DECILLION]

tree (tri:) 1. *n.* any tall, perennial, woody plant usually with a single elongated stem (trunk) and having a head of branches and foliage, or foliage only ‖ anything resembling this, or thought of as resembling this, esp. as having branches spreading from a single stem, *family tree* ‖ (in compounds) part of a structure or implement, *axletree* ‖ a shoe tree ‖ (*chem.*) a tree-shaped mass of crystals **the Tree** the cross on which Christ died **up a tree** in a tight or difficult situation ‖ (*computer*) a directed graph in which each node has one or more predecessors (parents), used in logic 2. *v.t.* to chase up a tree ‖ to stretch (a shoe) on a shoe tree ‖ to place in a difficult situation [O.E. *trēow*]

tree bark a rippled or wavy effect caused by bias tensions that sometimes appears on a bonded fabric when it is stretched horizontally

tree creeper *Certhia familiaris*, fam. *Certhiidae*, a small brown and buff European bird with a silvery underside. It climbs trees spirally searching for food in the bark ‖ *Certhia familiaris americana*, also called 'brown creeper'

tree diagram (*linguistics*) in transformational grammar, a diagram of components as branches of the sentence structure

tree fern a member of *Cyatheaceae* or *Marattiaceae*, families of tropical treelike ferns

tree frog any of various arboreal frogs of fam. *Polypedatidae*. They have adhesive suckers on the toes

tree line the limit above which trees do not grow on mountains or in high latitudes

tree·nail, tre·nail (trí:neil) *n.* a wooden peg which swells in its hole when moistened and is used to fasten timbers together, esp. in shipbuilding

tree of heaven a member of *Ailanthus*, fam. *Simaroubaceae*, a genus of ornamental trees grown esp. for shade

tree toad a tree frog

tree·top (trí:top) *n.* the top branches of a tree

tre·foil (trí:fɔil) *n.* a clover ‖ (*archit.*) an ornament with three lobes or cusps in window tracery etc. [A.F. *trifoil*]

Treitsch·ke (tráitʃkə), Heinrich von (1834-96), German historian. His strongly nationalist views had a considerable influence on Germany in the 20th c. His main work was his 'History of Germany in the Nineteenth Century' (1874-94)

trek (trek) 1. *v.i. pres. part.* **trek·king** *past* and *past part.* **trekked** (*hist.*) to travel by ox wagon ‖ to make a long, hard or tedious journey 2. *n.* (*hist.*) a long journey by ox wagon or a stage on the journey ‖ a long, hard or tedious journey or leg of a journey (*GREAT TREK) [Afrik. fr. Du. *trekken*]

trel·lis (trélis) 1. *n.* a flat, light frame consisting of wooden or metal latticelike strips crossing one another in various patterns, used as a screen or for plants to climb on 2. *v.t.* to furnish with a trellis ‖ to train on a trellis [O.F. *treliz, trelis, trelice*]

trel·lis-work (tréliswɜːrk) *n.* latticework of wooden or metal strips

trem·a·tode (trémətoud) *n.* a member of *Trematoda*, a class of *Platyhelminthes*, including flukes and parasitic flatworms. Most of these

---

CONCISE PRONUNCIATION KEY: (a) æ, cat; ɑ, car; ɔ fawn; ei, snake. **(e)** e, hen; i:, sheep; iə, deer; ɛə, bear. **(i)** i, fish; ai, tiger; ə:, bird. **(o)** o, ox; au, cow; ou, goat; u, poor; ɔi, royal. **(u)** ʌ, duck; u, bull; u:, goose; ə, bacillus; ju:, cube. x, loch; θ, think; ð, bother; z, Zen; ʒ, corsage; dʒ, savage; ŋ, orangutang; j, yak; ʃ, fish; tʃ, fetch; 'l, rabble; 'n, redden. Complete pronunciation key appears inside front cover.

move by muscular action and have organs of attachment consisting of suckers and hooks. The life history of some trematodes (e.g. liver fluke) is completed in two hosts [fr. Mod. L. *Trematoda* fr. Gk fr. *trēma (trēmatos)*, hole]

trem·blant (trémblənt) *adj.* constructed with springs to create a vibrating motion, e.g., in jewelry

trem·ble (trémb'l) 1. *v.i. pres. part.* **trem·bling** *past* and *past part.* **trem·bled** to shake involuntarily from fear, excitement etc. ‖ to vibrate with light, rapid movements 2. *n.* a trembling or fit of trembling **trém·bler** *n.* (elec.) the automatic vibrator which makes and breaks an electric circuit, e.g. in a type of electric bell ‖ any of various birds of genera *Cinclocerthia* and *Rhamphocinclus*, fam. *Mimidae*, found in the West Indies **trém·bles** *pl. n.* the poisoning of livestock, esp. cattle, by an alcohol present in *Eupatorium rugosum* and some other plants. It can be fatal **trém·bly** *comp.* **trem·bli·er** *superl.* **trem·bli·est** *adj.* trembling, shaky [O.F. *trembler*]

tre·men·dous (triméndəs) *adj.* enormous ‖ arousing awe or wonder because of extreme size, power, majesty etc. [fr. L. *tremendus*]

trem·o·lan·do (tremǝlǽndou) *adv.* (mus.) with a tremolo effect [Ital.]

trem·o·lant (trémǝlǝnt) 1. *adj.* (esp. of certain organ pipes) having a vibrating note 2. *n.* an organ pipe whose notes have a vibrating quality ‖ a device in a musical instrument which causes a note to have vibrating quality

trem·o·lite (trémǝlait) *n.* a calcium magnesium silicate [after *Tremola*, in Switzerland, where it was discovered]

trem·o·lo (trémǝlou) *pl.* **trem·o·los** *n.* the quick repetition of a single note on a stringed instrument produced by rapid bowing up and down ‖ the quick alternation between two notes on an instrument ‖ an organ stop which produces a vibrating effect ‖ a rapid variation of pitch in the singing voice, esp. as a fault [Ital.]

trem·or (trémǝr) *n.* a trembling, e.g. in poplar leaves ‖ a vibration such as accompanies an earthquake ‖ a quavering sound in speaking ‖ an involuntary quivering of the limbs etc. from weakness, disease or age ‖ a shudder such as marks the onset of fever ‖ a state of tremulous excitement [O.F. *tremor, tremour*]

trem·u·lant (trémjulənt) 1. *adj.* tremulous 2. *n.* (mus.) a tremolo (organ stop) [fr. L. *tremulans (tremulantis)* fr. *tremulare*, to tremble]

trem·u·lous (trémjuləs) *adj.* trembling ‖ apprehensive ‖ betraying apprehension ‖ quivering, e.g. with excitement [fr. L. *tremulus*]

trenail *TREENAIL

trench (trentʃ) *n.* a long, narrow and usually deep hollow cut in the ground ‖ (mil.) such a hollow with parapets formed of the earth dug out of it, often strengthened with sandbags, for protecting soldiers from enemy fire [O.F. *trenche*]

trench *v.t.* to dig (ground) in order to make a trench ‖ to dig (ground) in successive trenches so that the soil well below the surface is brought to the top ‖ *v.i.* to dig a trench or trenches ‖ (with 'on' or 'upon') to encroach [O.F. *trenchier*]

trench·an·cy (tréntʃənsi:) *n.* the state or quality of being trenchant

trench·ant (tréntʃənt) *adj.* keen and effective, vigorous, *trenchant measures* ‖ penetrating, incisive, *trenchant criticisms* ‖ (biol.) adapted for cutting [O.F.]

trench coat a thick, usually lined, double-breasted, belted, waterproof coat having deep pockets and sleeves with buckled straps on them

trench·er (tréntʃər) *n.* (hist.) a wooden board on which meat used to be carved [A.F. *trenchour*]

trench·er·man (tréntʃərmən) *pl.* **trench·er·men** (tréntʃərmən) *n.* (rhet.) used with the epithets 'good', 'stout' etc.) a hearty eater

trench fever an intermittent fever, thought to be transmitted by body lice. It affected soldiers living for long periods in the trenches in the 1st world war

trench foot a condition of the feet characterized by chilblains, swelling and sharp pain, sometimes leading to gangrene, caused by prolonged standing under cold, wet conditions

trench mortar a light mortar which lobs a small bomb or grenade from a trench

trench mouth Vincent's infection

trend (trend) 1. *n.* a tendency, general direction, *the trend of public opinion* ‖ a dominant movement revealed by a statistical process, *decen-*

nial price trends 2. *v.i.* to have a tendency or general direction [O.E. *trendan*]

tren·dy (tréndi:) *adj.* (slang or colloq.) fashion-following — **trendily** *adv.* — **trendiness** *n.* — **trendsetter** *n.* — **trendsetting** *adj.*

Treng·ga·nu (trengǽnu:) a state (area 5,027 sq. miles, pop. 542,280) of Malaysia in E. Malaya. Capital: Kuala Trengganu (pop. 29,000). Transferred (1909) from Siam to Britain, it joined the Federation of Malaya (1948)

Trent (trent) a river (170 miles long, navigable for 95) flowing from N. Staffordshire, England, to the Humber

Trent *TRENTO

Trent Affair an Anglo-U.S. incident (1861) during the Civil War. The U.S. warship 'San Jacinto' detained the British vessel 'Trent' and seized two Confederate commissioners on board. Great Britain, outraged by this violation of its neutrality, deliberated a declaration of war against the Union. War was averted (1862) when the U.S.A. disavowed the act and released the Confederate prisoners

Trent, Council of the 19th ecumenical council, held at Trento (1545-7, 1551-2, 1562-3). Certain Catholic doctrines were freshly formulated in the spirit of the Counter-Reformation, in an attempt to strengthen the Roman Catholic Church doctrinally and administratively against Protestantism

trente-et-qua·rante (trɑnteikærɑnt) *n.* rouge et noir [F.]

Tren·ti·no-Al·to A·di·ge (trentí:nɔáltɔádi:dʒe) an autonomous region (area 5,256 sq. miles, pop. 876,249) of Italy in the Alps, comprised of the semiautonomous provinces of Alto Adige or South Tirol (language: 65% German, 32% Italian, 3% Ladin) and Trentino (Italian-speaking). Alternating capitals: Bolzano (G. Bozen), Trento. Industries: cattle-raising, fruit, tourism. HISTORY. The whole area was given to Austria (1815), but Trentino passed to Italy (1866). Austria attempted to Germanize Alto Adige, provoking the Irredentist movement, but this and Trentino were given to Italy (1919), and Austrian agitation increased. Despite a large degree of automony granted in 1947, the problem continued to cause tension between Italy and Austria

Tren·to (tréntɔ) a communications center (pop. 91,767) and capital (alternating with Bolzano) of Trentino-Alto Adige, Italy, in Trentino on the River Adige. Byzantine cathedral (13th-14th cc.) (*TRENT, COUNCIL OF)

Tren·ton (tréntən) the capital city (pop. 92,124) of New Jersey, on the Delaware: textiles, mechanical engineering, light manufacturing. Washington crossed the Delaware near Trenton and decisively defeated the British here (1776)

Trenton and Princeton, Battles of the first engagements (1776-7) of the American Revolution won by Gen. George Washington in the open field. American forces under Washington crossed the Delaware River and surprised and captured (1776) 918 Hessians around Trenton, N.J. The patriots, avoiding a British relief force led by Cornwallis, then struck at Princeton. The battles greatly raised American morale

tre·pan (tripǽn) 1. *n.* a tool used in boring shafts etc. ‖ a trephine 2. *v.t. pres. part.* **tre·pan·ning** *past* and *past part.* **tre·panned** to cut out or bore with such a tool ‖ to trephine [fr. M.L. *trepanum* fr. Gk]

tre·pang (tripǽŋ) *n.* any of several holothurians, dried and smoked for use in soup in China [Malay *tripang*]

tre·phine (trifí:n) 1. *n.* a small cylindrical saw used in surgery for removing circular disks of bone from the skull 2. *v. pres. part.* **tre·phin·ing** *past* and *past part.* **tre·phined** *v.t.* to operate on with a trephine ‖ *v.i.* to perform this operation [older *trafine* fr. L. *tres fines*, three ends]

trep·i·da·tion (trepidéiʃən) *n.* a state of fear, excitement or apprehension [fr. L. *trepidatio (trepidationis)* fr. *trepidare*, to tremble]

tres·pass (tréspəs) 1. *n.* a trespassing ‖ (Bible) a sin ‖ (law) an actionable wrong against another's person, property or rights, or an action for damages arising from this 2. *v.i.* to enter someone's property unlawfully ‖ to encroach or make an undue claim, *to trespass on someone's hospitality* ‖ (Bible) to sin ‖ (law) to commit a trespass [O.F. fr. *trespasser*]

Tres Pun·tas, Cape (trespú:ntəs) a cape in S. Argentina, at the south entrance to the Gulf of San Jorge

tress (tres) *n.* (rhet.) a lock of hair ‖ (pl., rhet.) a woman's hair, esp. when long and loose [O.F. *tresce*]

tres·sure (tréʃər) *n.* (heraldry) a narrow orle

tres·tle (trés'l) *n.* a pair of hinged or jointed splayed legs used as one of two or more supports on which planks, a tabletop etc. are laid ‖ a braced framework of wood or metal for carrying a road or railroad over a gully or other depression [O.F. *trestel*]

tres·tle-tree (trés'ltri:) *n.* (naut.) one of a pair of horizontal fore-and-aft timbers on a mast supporting the crosstrees, topmast etc.

tret·i·noin (trétinɔin) *n.* vitamin A medication used to cause light peeling of the skin in treating acne

Trèves (trev) *TRIER

Tre·vi·so (treví:zɔ) a walled town (pop. 75,000) in Veneto, Italy: Romanesque-Renaissance cathedral, 13th-c. palaces, churches

Trev·i·thick (trévəθik, trəví:θik), Richard (1771-1833), British engineer. He invented the high-pressure steam engine (1800)

trews (tru:z) *pl. n.* the close-fitting tartan pants worn by certain Scottish regiments [Ir. Gael. *trius*]

trey (trei) *n.* a playing card, die or domino having three spots [A.F., O.F. *trei, treis*]

tri- (trai) *prefix* three, consisting of three ‖ three times or into three ‖ occurring every three ‖ (chem.) having three atoms, radicals etc. [Gk]

tri·a·ble (tráiəb'l) *adj.* (law) that can be tried

tri·ac·id (traiǽsid) 1. *n.* (chem.) an acid having three acid hydrogen atoms 2. *adj.* (chem.) capable of combining with three molecules of a monoacid or one of a triacid ‖ (chem., of acid salts) containing three replaceable hydrogen atoms

tri·ad (tráiæd) *n.* a group of three ‖ (chem.) an element, atom or radical with a valence of three ‖ (mus.) a chord of three notes, esp. a common chord ‖ a Welsh literary form consisting of short prose aphorisms grouped in threes [F. *triade* fr. L. fr. Gk]

triad *n.* (computer) research tool that permits work on microcomputer full development system (FDS) and target system used in minicomputer research

triad concept (mil.) U.S. defense strategy based on fixed intercontinental missiles, submarine-launched missiles, and bombers

Triad 1 U.S. three-part strategic defense system based on submarine-launched missiles, MX land-based missiles, and bombers

tri·age (trí:ɑʒ) *n.* (med.) 1. the sorting or screening of patients seeking hospital care, to determine which service (e.g., medical, surgical, or nonphysician) is initially required and with what priority 2. originally, the sorting of battle or disaster casualties for those requiring immediate help, those who can wait, and those beyond help

tri·al (tráiəl) 1. *n.* a test or testing by examination or experiment ‖ (loosely) a trying out ‖ a test of character, powers of endurance etc. ‖ a hardship ‖ a person who or thing which is a source of annoyance or trouble ‖ the state or fact of being proved by suffering or endurance, *hour of trial* ‖ a judicial examination of inquiry and determination of a cause in a court of law **on trial** in the state of being tested for a period ‖ in the midst of judicial examination by a court ‖ provisionally accepted, that is to be rejected or sent back if not satisfactory 2. *adj.* relating to, serving as or used as a trial, *a trial period* [A.F. *trial, tried*]

trial and error the process of finding the solution to a problem by making random tests instead of by applying first principles

trial balance a comparison of the totals on the credit and debit side of a record of accounts at a given date

trial balloon a project, statement etc. tentatively advanced in order to test public reaction

trial jury a petty jury

trial run an initial testing of something (e.g. a mechanism or a play) under normal working conditions

tri·am·cin·o·lone [$C_{21}H_{27}FO_6$] (traiæmsínǝloun) *n.* (pharm.) a corti-drug used in treating psoriasis and other allergies marketed as Aristocort, Kenacort, and Kenalog

tri·an·gle (tráiæŋg'l) *n.* (geom.) a plane figure bounded by three straight lines ‖ part of a spherical surface bounded by three arcs of great circles ‖ anything of this shape, or any three things which, if joined by straight lines, would result in this shape being formed ‖ a set square ‖

CONCISE PRONUNCIATION KEY: **(a)** æ, c*a*t; ɑ, c*a*r; ɔ, f*aw*n; ei, sn*a*ke. **(e)** e, h*e*n; i:, sh*ee*p; iə, d*ee*r; ɛə, b*ea*r. **(i)** i, f*i*sh; ai, t*i*ger; əː, b*i*rd. **(o)** o, *o*x; au, c*ow*; ou, g*oa*t; u, p*oo*r; ɔi, r*oy*al. **(u)** ʌ, d*u*ck; u, b*u*ll; u:, g*oo*se; ə, b*a*cillus; ju:, c*u*be. x, lo*ch*; θ, *th*ink; ð, bo*th*er; z, *Z*en; ʒ, corsa*g*e; dʒ, sava*g*e; ŋ, orangutan*g*; j, *y*ak; ʃ, *f*ish; tʃ, fe*tch*; 'l, rabb*le*; 'n, redd*en*. Complete pronunciation key appears inside front cover.

(*mus.*) a percussion instrument consisting of a triangular steel rod with one angle open. It emits a clear note when struck with another steel rod ‖ a person who plays this instrument in a band or orchestra ‖ a group of three people involved in some situation, esp. an eternal triangle ‖ this situation [F. or fr. L. *triangulum*]

triangle of forces the polygon law of vectors applied to three vectors. It was discovered by Stevinus

tri·an·gu·lar (traiǽŋgjulər) *adj.* of or shaped like a triangle ‖ involving three things, parts, persons etc. ‖ (e.g. of a prism) having a triangle for its base **tri·an·gu·lár·i·ty** *n.* [fr. L.L. *triangularis*]

tri·an·gu·late (traiǽŋgjuleit) 1. *v.t. pres. part.* **tri·an·gu·lat·ing** *past* and *past part.* **tri·an·gu·lat·ed** to make triangular ‖ to divide into triangles ‖ (*survey.*) to measure or map (a region) by dividing it into triangles, working from a fixed base 2. *adj.* consisting of or marked with triangles **tri·an·gu·lá·tion** *n.*

Tri·a·non (tri:æn5) either of two small palaces in the park of Versailles, France. The Grand Trianon was built (1687) by J. H. Mansart for Louis XIV. The Petit Trianon was built (1762-8) by J. A. Gabriel for Louis XV

Tri·as (tráiæs) *adj.* (*geol.*) Triassic **the Trias** the Triassic [L.L. fr. Gk *trias*, three]

Tri·as·sic (traiǽsik) *adj.* of or relating to the earliest period or system of the Mesozoic era, marked by the dominance of reptiles and the appearance of gymnosperm plants (*GEOLOGICAL TIME) **the Triassic** the Triassic period or system of rocks [fr. TRIAS]

tri·ath·lon (traiǽθlon) *n.* competitive sporting event for women including 100-meter sprint, shotput, and high jump, sometimes including trap-shooting and fly-casting

tri·at·ic stay (traiǽtik) (*naut.*) a rope attached at one end to the foremast and at the other to the mainmast and used for hoisting boats etc. [etym. doubtful]

tri·a·tom·ic (traiətómik) *adj.* of a molecule having three atoms ‖ of a molecule having three replaceable atoms or radicals

trib·al (tráib'l) *adj.* of, relating to, or like a tribe or tribes ‖ organized by tribes, *a tribal society* **tríb·al·ism** *n.* organization by tribes ‖ strong feeling for the tribe

tri·ba·sic (traibéisik) *adj.* (*chem.*) of an acid containing three hydrogen atoms replaceable by basic atoms or radicals, e.g. phosphoric acid [fr. Gk *tri*-, three+BASIC]

tribe (traib) *n.* a human community developed by an association of, and interbreeding between, a number of families, opposed in principle to crossbreeding with other communities, and preserving its own customs, beliefs and organization ‖ (*Gk. hist.*) a phyle ‖ (*Rom. hist.*) one of the three original divisions of the Roman people or one of the 35 divisions into which these were later subdivided ‖ a subdivision in some taxonomic classifications between genus and order or genus and family ‖ (*pop.*) a number of people associated by family relationship or by common interests etc, *a dislike for journalists as a tribe* [M.E. *tribu* fr. O.F.]

Tri·bec·a (traibéka) *n.* area in Manhattan between Canal and Barclay Sts., west of Church St., where lofts have been converted into artists' studios

tribes·man (tráibzmən) *pl.* **tribes·men** (tráibzmən) *n.* a member of a tribe

tri·bol·o·gy (traibóladʒi) *n.* the science of lubrication [fr. Gk. *tribein*, to rub+*logos*, discourse]

tri·brach (tráibræk) *n.* a metrical foot of three short syllables [fr. L. *tribrachys* fr. Gk]

trib·u·la·tion (tribjuléiʃən) *n.* suffering caused by adversity ‖ an instance of this ‖ a cause of such suffering or distress [O.F.]

tri·bu·nal (traibjú:n'l) *n.* a group of persons empowered to decide a specific issue according to the law, arbitrate in a dispute etc. ‖ a bench or seat for judges, magistrates etc. [L.]

trib·u·nate (tríbjunit) *n.* (*hist.*) the office or function of a tribune ‖ (*hist.*) the term of office of a tribune [fr. L. *tribunatus*]

trib·une (tríbju:n) *n.* (*Rom. hist.*) an official originally elected to protect plebeians' rights against the patricians ‖ (*Rom. hist.*) an officer who had two months a year in command of a legion **tríb·une·ship** *n.* tribunate [fr. L. *tribunus*, head of a tribe]

tribune *n.* a dais for speakers confronting an assembly ‖ (in a basilica) the bishop's throne ‖

the apselike structure containing this [F. fr. Ital.]

trib·u·tar·y (tríbjuteri:) 1. *pl.* **trib·u·tar·ies** *n.* a stream flowing into a larger stream or a lake 2. *adj.* contributory ‖ in the nature of tribute ‖ paying tribute, as an acknowledgment of subjection [fr. L. *tributarius*]

trib·ute (tríbju:t) *n.* a payment in money or kind exacted from a city or state by a more powerful state, by right of conquest or in return for protection ‖ the obligation or liability to make such a payment ‖ (*loosely*) any forced payment ‖ a grateful, affectionate or admiring acknowledgment made to a person ‖ a gift or offering expressing admiration, gratitude or affection [fr. L. *tributum*]

trice (trais) 1. *v.t. pres. part.* **tric·ing** *past* and *past part.* **triced** (*naut.*, with 'up') to haul up and secure (a sail) 2. *n.* (only in) **in a trice** in an instant [M.Du. *trīsen*, Du. *trijsen*]

tri·ceps (tráiseps) *pl.* **tri·cep·ses** (tráisepsiz), **tri·ceps** *n.* a muscle with three points of origin, esp. the muscle situated at the back of the upper arm [Mod. L. fr. *triceps*, triple-headed]

tri·cha·tro·phi·a (traikætətróufi:ə) *n.* hair brittleness due to atrophy of hair bulbs

tri·chi·a·sis (trikáiəsis) *n.* (*med.*) the turning inward of the eyelashes so that they rub against the eye [Mod. L. fr. Gk fr. *thrix* (*trichos*), hair]

tri·chi·na (trikáinə) *pl.* **tri·chi·nae** (trikáini:), **tri·chi·nas** *n. Trichinella spiralis*, fam. *Trichinellidae*, a hairlike, parasitic nematode infesting the intestine and (in larval form) the muscle or muscle fibers esp. of hogs. Eating insufficiently cooked pork from a hog infested with trichinae can communicate trichinosis to man **trich·i·nized** (tríkinaizd) *adj.* infested with trichinae [Mod. L. fr. Gk *trichinos* adj., of hair]

trich·i·ni·a·sis (trikináiəsis) *n.* trichinosis

Trich·i·nop·o·ly (trikinópəli:) *TIRUCHIRAPALLI

trich·i·no·sis (trikinóusis) *n.* a disease, characterized by fever, diarrhea and muscular pains, caused by infestation with trichinae [Mod. L.]

trich·i·nous (tríkinəs) *adj.* infested with trichinae ‖ relating to trichinae or trichinosis

tri·chlor·fon [C₄H₈Cl₃O₄P] (traiklórfɒn) *n.* (*organic chem.*) a compound used as an agricultural insecticide and vermicide

tri·chlo·ride (traiklóraid, traiklóuraid) *n.* a compound having three atoms of chlorine in combination with an element or radical

tri·chlor·o·phe·nol [C₆H₂Cl₃OH] (traiklɔrəfí:nɔl) *n.* (*chem.*) a toxic bactericide and fungicide used as a defoliant *syn.* 2,4,6-T

trich·o·cyst (tríkəsist) *n.* a hairlike process in the ectoderm of certain ciliate protozoans, thought to serve as an organ of attachment [fr. Gk *thrix* (*trichos*), hair+ *kustis*, sac]

trich·oid (tríkəid) *adj.* like hair, capillary [fr. Gk *trichoeidēs* fr. *thrix* (*trichos*), hair]

tri·cho·lo·gi·a (traikəlóudʒi:ə) *n.* the plucking out of one's hair

tri·chol·o·gy (trikóladʒi:) *n.* the study of hair and its diseases **tri·chól·o·gist** *n.* [fr. Gk *thrix* (*trichos*), hair+*logos*, discourse]

tri·chome (tráikoum, tríkoum) *n.* (*bot.*) an outgrowth from the epidermis of a plant, e.g. a hair, scale etc. ‖ a filamentous thallus ‖ a hair tuft on a myrmecophilous insect [fr. Gk *trichōma*, growth of hair]

tri·chot·o·mous (traikótəməs) *adj.* divided into three parts ‖ dividing into three parts

tri·chot·o·my (traikótəmi:) *n.* a division into three parts [fr. Gk *tricha*, in three+-*tomē*, a cutting]

tri·chro·ic (traikróuik) *adj.* exhibiting trichroism

tri·chro·ism (traikróuizəm) *n.* the property in some crystals of showing different colors when viewed from three different points

tri·chro·mat·ic (traikrəmǽtik) *adj.* of, pertaining to, having or using three colors

tri·chro·ma·tism (traikróumətizəm) *n.* the quality of state of being trichromatic

trick (trik) 1. *n.* an act or action designed to deceive ‖ a dextrous feat intended to puzzle or cause wondering admiration, *a conjuring trick* ‖ a practical joke ‖ an act of mischief or meanness ‖ an inexplicable process, *by some trick of memory* ‖ a knack, *to learn the trick of flipping a pancake* ‖ a mannerism or habitual peculiarity, *she had a trick of half closing her eyes* ‖ (*cards*) the cards played and taken in one round ‖ (*cards*) a scoring unit ‖ (*naut.*) a turn at the helm usually lasting two hours **the tricks of the trade** the special techniques that consti-

tute the expertise of an experienced craftsman **to do the trick** to produce the desired effect **up to tricks** resorting to mischievous or deceptive behavior 2. *adj.* of or relating to or intended as a trick 3. *v.t.* to deceive by a trick ‖ (esp. with 'out of') to defraud, cheat, *tricked out of his winnings* **to trick out** (or **up**) to dress in finery ‖ to put pretty things on, deck **trick·er·y** *n.* [O.N.F. *trique*]

trick·i·ly (tríkili:) *adv.* in a tricky manner

trick·i·ness (tríki:nis) *n.* the state or quality of being tricky

trick·le (trík'l) 1. *v. pres. part.* **trick·ling** *past* and *past part.* **trickled** *v.i.* (of a liquid) barely to flow, to come in a succession of drops ‖ (of an object) to emit or have dripping over it a thin stream of liquid, *the cave roof trickled with moisture* ‖ to come or go as if in a thin, intermittent stream, *news came trickling in, the guests trickled away* ‖ to move very slowly and as if hesitantly ‖ *v.t.* to give forth or cause to flow in a thin stream or in drops 2. *n.* a series of drops, a thin stream, or something compared to this, *a trickle of information* [M.E. *triklen*]

trickle *v.t.* (*golf*) to cause (a ball) to move forward very slowly as if creeping forward ‖ *v.i.* (of a golf ball) to move in this way [prob. fr. E. Anglian var. of TRUCKLE]

trick·ster (tríkstər) *n.* a person who plays dishonest tricks

trick·y (tríki:) *comp.* **trick·i·er** *superl.* **trick·i·est** *adj.* difficult to understand or deal with, calling for careful handling, *a tricky situation* ‖ deft, adroit, *some tricky driving*

tri·clin·ic (traiklínik) *adj.* (of a crystal) having or characterized by three unequal axes which are obliquely inclined

tri·col·or, *Br.* **tri·col·our** (tráikʌlər, *Br.* tríkələ) 1. *adj.* having three colors 2. *n.* a three-colored flag, esp. the French flag of three vertical colors (blue, white, red) [fr. L.L. *tricolor* and F. *tricolore*]

tri·con (tráikɒn) *n.* a navigation system in which three ground stations send radio signals arranged so that pulses arrive at the same time from different distances

tri·corn (tráikɔrn) *n.* a cocked hat

tri·cot (trí:kou) *n.* a warp-knitted run-resistant fabric used in underwear etc. ‖ a soft ribbed fabric of wool or wool blend used in dresses etc. [F. fr. *tricoter*, to knit]

tri·cus·pid (traikʌ́spid) 1. *adj.* (e.g. of a tooth) having three cusps ‖ of or relating to the tricuspid valve 2. *n.* the tricuspid valve ‖ a tricuspid tooth **tri·cus·pi·date** (traikʌ́spideit) *adj.* [fr. L. *tricuspis* (*tricuspidis*)]

tricuspid valve a valve in the heart of higher vertebrates that consists of three triangular overlapping flaps permitting the flow of blood in a single direction, from the right auricle to the right ventricle

tri·cy·cle (tráisik'l) 1. *n.* a light vehicle like a bicycle, but having a pair of wheels arranged side by side behind a single front wheel 2. *v.i. pres. part.* **tri·cy·cling** *past* and *past part.* **tri·cy·cled** to ride a tricycle [F.]

tri·dent (tráid'nt) 1. *n.* a fish spear with three prongs, esp. as associated with Neptune and Britannia, who are portrayed carrying one as a scepter ‖ a three-pronged spear used in gladiatorial fights 2. *adj.* having three prongs **tri·dént·al** *adj.* [fr. L. *tridens* (*tridentis*)]

Trident *n.* (*mil.*) the sea-based strategic weapons system consisting of the nuclear-powered Trident submarine and Trident ballistic missiles; manufactured by Lockheed as part of the CONUS support complex designed to replace Polaris and Poseidon in 1982 *Cf* TRIAD

Trident I *n.* (*mil.*) a three-stage, solid-propellant ballistic missile (UGM-96) capable of being launched from a Trident submarine, sized to permit backfit into Poseidon submarines, equipped with advanced guidance and MIRV nuclear warheads

Trident II *n.* (*mil.*) a solid-propellant 18,700-lb ballistic missile (UGM-93A) with 4,500 nautical mi range, capable of being launched from a Trident submarine, larger than and replacing the Trident I, Poseidon, and Polaris

Tri·den·tine (traidénti:n) *adj.* of or relating to the Council of Trent [fr. M.L. *Tridentinus* fr. *Tridentum*, Trent]

tri·duc·tor (traidʌ́ktər) *n.* a device utilizing iron-core transformers and capacitators to increase power line frequency

triecious *TRIOECIOUS

tried (traid) *past* and *past part.* of TRY *adj.* proved, tested reliable

---

tri·en·ni·al (traiéni:əl) **1.** *adj.* happening every three years || lasting three years **2.** *n.* an event that occurs every three years || a third anniversary [fr. L. *triennium*, a period of three years]

tri·en·ni·um (traiéni:əm) *pl.* **tri·en·ni·ums, tri·en·ni·a** (traiéni:ə) *n.* a period of three years [L.]

Trier (tríər) (F. Trèves) a communications center (pop. 100,338) and wine market in Rhineland-Palatinate, West Germany, on the Moselle. Roman ruins, Romanesque cathedral (4th-12th cc.)

tri·er (tráiər) *n.* a person or animal who tries hard (makes great efforts) || a person who tests something || an implement used in testing something, *a seed trier*

Tri·este (tri:ést) a port (pop. 265,500) in Friuli-Venezia Giulia, Italy, at the head of the Adriatic. Industries: shipbuilding, mechanical engineering, oil refining. It includes a free port. Cathedral (12th-14th cc.). Under the Hapsburgs from 1382, it prospered in the 18th and 19th cc. and became a great trading, shipping and financial center. It became Italian in 1920. From 1945 the Trieste region was divided into two zones, under British-American and Yugoslav military administrations. In 1954, the northern zone, with a mainly Italian population and including the city, went to Italy, and the southern zone (N.W. Istria) became Yugoslav. University (1924)

tri·fec·ta (traiféktə) *n.* (*horse racing*) method of betting in which the winner must select the first three finishers of a race in proper order to win *also* triple *Cf* PERFECTA, QUINIELA

tri·fid (tráifid) *adj.* (*biol.*) divided, or partially cleft, into three lobes [fr. L. *trifidus*]

tri·fle (tráifəl) *n.* a valueless, insignificant fact or thing || a small amount of money, *it cost a mere trifle* || a dessert made of sponge cake, cream, fruit etc. || a common type of pewter used in small utensils || (*pl.*) utensils made from this **a trifle** (used adverbially) a little, *a trifle too old for the part* [M.E. *trufle*]

trifle *pres. part.* **tri·fling** *past* and *past part.* **tri·fled** *v.i.* (with 'with') to talk or act lightly or insincerely, *to trifle with someone's affections* || *v.t.* (with 'away') to pass (time) idly or wastefully || to spend (money) frivolously **not to be trifled with** to be treated with proper respect

tri·fling *adj.* slight, insignificant [O.F. *truffler, truiffler*]

tri·flu·o·per·a·zine [C₂₁H₂₄F₃N₃S] (traiflu:oupérəzin) *n.* (*pharm.*) a tranquilizer used in treating severe anxiety and some forms of mental illness; marketed as Stelazine

tri·flu·ra·lin [C₁₃H₁₆F₃N₃O₄] (traiflú:rəlin) *n.* (*organic chem.*) a weed killer used to protect cotton, beans, and vegetables

tri·fo·li·ate (traifóuli:it) *adj.* (*bot.*) having three leaves growing from the same point || trifoliolate **tri·fo·li·at·ed** (traifóuli:eitid) *adj.* [fr. Gk *tri-*, three+L. *foliatus* fr. *folium*, leaf]

tri·fo·li·o·late (traifóuli:əleit) *adj.* (*bot.*) having three leaflets growing from the same point [fr. Gk *tri-*, three+Mod. L. *foliolum* dim. of *folium*, leaf]

tri·fo·ri·um (traifóri:əm, traifóuri:əm) *pl.* **tri·fo·ri·a** (traifóri:ə, traifóuri:ə) *n.* (*archit.*) a gallery or arcade in the wall above the arches of the nave and sometimes those of the choir of a church [M.L.]

tri·form (tráifɔrm) *adj.* existing in three forms || formed in three parts [fr. L. *triformis*]

tri·func·tion·al (traifʌŋkʃən'l) *adj.* (*chem.*) of a compound containing a molecule with three highly reactive sites capable of combining with other molecules, e.g., in polymerization

trig (trig) *adj.* (*old-fash.*) trim and neat in appearance [O.N. *tryggr*]

trig 1. *n.* trigonometry **2.** *adj.* trigonometrical [by shortening]

Tri·ga·ran·te (tri:garánte) the name (=Three Guarantees) given to the Mexican army formed (1821) by Iturbide and to the Plan of Iguala which it proclaimed. It guaranteed for Mexico independence from Spain, the Catholic religion as the sole religion, and racial equality in that anyone could hold office

tri·gem·i·nal (traidʒémin'l) **1.** *adj.* (*anat.*) relating to a trigeminal nerve **2.** *n.* (*anat.*) a trigeminal nerve [fr. L. *trigeminus*, born three together]

trigeminal nerve either nerve of the fifth pair of cranial nerves

trigeminal neuralgia neuralgia affecting the trigeminal nerves, characterized by painful muscular spasms

trig·ger (trígər) **1.** *n.* the steel catch which is pulled to fire a firearm, or similar catch used to actuate some other mechanism **quick on the trigger** apt to shoot (or take other action) imprudently quickly **2.** *v.t.* (sometimes with 'off') to start, get going, esp. to be the immediate, relatively unimportant cause of (some event or series of events) || to release the trigger of (a gun etc.) [earlier *tricker* fr. Du. *trekker* fr. *trekken*, to pull]

trig·ger·fish (trígərfiʃ) *pl.* **trig·ger·fish, trig·ger·fish·es** *n.* a member of *Balistidae*, a family of fish inhabiting warm seas, having up to three sturdy erectile spines on the anterior dorsal fin. There are both edible and poisonous varieties

trig·ger·hap·py (trígərhæpi:) *adj.* too ready to take action by shooting

trigger price a minimum fair price for imported goods. Products sold below this price 'trigger' an immediate investigation of presumed 'dumping'

trig list (*mil.*) a list published by some Army units that includes essential survey-point information for triangulation in determining position

tri·glyph (tráiglif) *n.* (*archit.*) a tablet with three vertical grooves projecting from a Doric frieze and alternating with the metopes **tri·glyph·ic** *adj.* [fr. L. *triglyphus* fr. Gk]

tri·gon (tráigon) *n.* a triangle || an ancient triangular Oriental harp with four strings || (*astrology*) one of the groups of three signs of the zodiac 120° distant from each other into which the zodiac is divided || the cutting edge of an upper molar [fr. L. *trigonum* fr. Gk]

trig·o·nal (trígən'l) *adj.* triangular, esp. in section || (*math.*) of a system of trilinear coordinates || (of a crystal) characterized by a vertical axis of threefold symmetry [fr. L. *trigonalis*]

trig·o·no·met·ric (trigənəmétrik) *adj.* of, relating to or done by trigonometry **trig·o·no·met·ri·cal** *adj.*

trig·o·nom·e·try (trigənómitri:) *n.* the branch of mathematics concerned with the sides and angles of triangles, their measurement and the relations between them [fr. Mod. L. *trigonometria* fr. Gk *trigōnon*, triangle+*-metria*, measurement]

tri·graph (tráigræf, tráigraf) *n.* (*phon.*) a combination of three letters which represent one sound [fr. Gk *tri-*, three+*graphē*, writing]

tri·he·dral (traihí:drəl) *adj.* of or relating to a trihedron

tri·he·dron (traihí:drən) *pl.* **tri·he·drons, tri·he·dra** (traihí:drə) *n.* a figure formed by three plane surfaces meeting at a point [Mod. L. fr. Gk *tri-* three+*hedra*, a seat]

tri·jet (tráidʒet) *n.* a vehicle powered by three jet engines —**trijet** *adj.*

tri·ju·gate (traidʒú:git, tráidʒugeit) *adj.* (*bot.*, of a leaf) having three pairs of leaflets [fr. L. *trijugus*, threefold]

tri·lat·er·al (trailætərəl) **1.** *adj.* having three sides || involving three parties **2.** *n.* a figure having three sides, triangle [fr. L. *trilaterus*]

tri·lat·er·al·ism (trailætərəlizəm) *n.* the relationship based on economic and military cooperation among the U.S., Western Europe, and Japan in the 1970s (in contrast to the unilateralism of the Nixon-Kissinger era)

tril·by (trílbi:) *pl.* **tril·bies** *n.* (*Br.*) a fedora [worn in the stage version (1895) of G. du Maurier's novel *Trilby*]

tri·lin·e·ar (trailíni:ər) *adj.* consisting of, involving or enclosed by three lines [fr. TRI-+L. *linearis*, linear]

tri·lin·gual (trailíŋgwəl) *adj.* knowing and able to use three languages || consisting of or expressed in three languages [fr. L. *trilinguis*]

tri·lit·er·al (trailítərəl) **1.** *adj.* consisting of three letters, esp. three consonants **2.** *n.* a triliteral root or word [fr. TRI-+L. *littera*, a letter]

trill 1. *n.* a musical ornament consisting of the alternation of a note and the note a whole step or half step above it || a similar sound, e.g. the warble of a bird || (*phon.*) a quick vibration of the tongue or uvula, e.g. in pronouncing the 'r' of some languages || (*phon.*) the sound made || (*phon.*) the letter or word pronounced in this way **2.** *v.t.* to sing, say or produce (a sound) with a trill || *v.i.* to make trills with the voice [fr. Ital. *trillare*]

Tril·ling (trílin), Lionel (1905-75), U.S. critic and author. His socio-psychological essays include 'The Liberal Imagination' (1950), 'The Opposing Self' (1955), and 'A Gathering of Fugitives' (1956). His novel 'The Middle of the Journey' (1947) explores the moral and political

structure of the U.S.A. during the 1930s and 1940s

tril·lion (tríljən) *n.* *NUMBER TABLE **tríl·lionth** *n.* and *adj.* [F.]

tri·lo·bate (trailóubeit) *adj.* (*bot.*) having three lobes

tri·lo·bite (tráiləbait) *n.* a member of the class or subclass *Trilobita*, extinct aquatic arthropods found widely in Paleozoic deposits. The body is divided into three lobes. The central lobe bears biramous appendages [fr. Mod. L. *Trilobites* fr. Gk *tri-*, three+*lobos*, lobe]

tril·o·gy (trílədʒi:) *pl.* **tril·o·gies** *n.* (*Gk drama*) a group of three tragedies each complete in itself but each connected in subject with the other two. The three plays of such a group were performed in succession in Athens at the festival of Dionysus || any set of three novels, musical compositions etc. so related [fr. Gk *trilogia*]

trim (trim) **1.** *v. pres. part.* **trim·ming** *past* and *past part.* **trimmed** *v.t.* to cut away unnecessary or unwanted parts from, *to trim a moustache, to trim meat of fat* || to shorten by cutting, *to trim one's nails* || (often with 'up') to make tidy || to decorate (e.g. a garment) with ornamental additions || (*bookbinding*) to guillotine folded sheets || to clean and cut (the wick of a lamp) || (*carpentry*) to shape and smooth || (*naut.*) to adjust the cargo, ballast etc. of (a ship) to make her float on an even keel || (*aeron.*) to adjust for up-and-down or horizontal movement || (*naut.*) to adjust (the sails or a sail) according to the direction of the wind || to decorate (a shop window) with goods || (*pop.*) to thrash soundly || *v.i.* to adjust one's opinion to fall in with the party in power or the majority || (*naut.*, of a vessel) to assume a position in the water on an even keel **2.** *n.* a state of proper fitness for work or action, *in fighting trim* || (*naut.*) the position of a ship or boat etc. in the water with respect to balance fore-and-aft || (*aeron.*) the angle of flight of an aircraft with respect to balance fore-and-aft || a light haircut || (*bookbinding*) the amount to be cut away from folded sheets at the edges || material cut away in order to trim something || a decorative addition to e.g. a garment || the interior furnishings of a car || the lighter woodwork used in the finishing of a building, esp. the frames around windows and doors || (*Am.*=*Br.* window dressing) the displaying of goods attractively in a shop window **3.** *comp.* **trim·mer** *superl.* **trim·mest** *adj.* neat, compact || in good order, well arranged and well cared for, *trim lawns* [O.E. *trymian, trymman*, to put in order]

tri·mar·an (tráiməræn) *n.* a pleasure sailboat with three parallel hulls *Cf* CATAMARAN

trim·er·ous (trímərəs) *adj.* (*bot.*, of flowers) composed of three similar parts || (*zool.*) possessing or seeming to possess three joints in each tarsus [Mod. L. *trimerus*]

trim·e·ter (trímitər) **1.** *n.* a line of verse consisting of three metrical feet **2.** *adj.* having three metrical feet **tri·met·ri·cal** (traimétrik'l) *adj.* [fr. L. *trimetrus* fr. Gk]

tri·meth·o·prim [C₁₄H₁₈N₄O₃] (traiméθəprim) *n.* (*pharm.*) synthetic antibacterial drug; marketed as Proloprim

trimetrogen (*photography*) *FAN CAMERAS

tri·mip·ra·mine (traimíprəmi:n) *n.* (*pharm.*) antidepressant, sedative drug; marketed as Surmontil

trim·mer (trímər) *n.* a person who or thing which trims, used in various manufacturing processes || a person who changes his political beliefs or fluctuates between one political party and another out of self-interest || a person who stores coal or cargo in a ship so as to keep her correct balance || (*pl.*) shears for clipping etc. || a transverse beam holding the ends of joists truncated so as to leave a well for a staircase or passage for a chimney etc. || a person responsible for window displays in a shop

trim·ming (trímiŋ) *n.* the act of trimming || ornamental material sewn on to clothes || (*pl., pop.*) the usual garnishes (esp. supplementary dishes) that accompany roast meat || (*pl.*) things trimmed away || (*pop.*) a sound thrashing

tri·morph (tráimɔrf) *n.* any of the three crystalline forms of a trimorphic substance [back-formation fr. TRIMORPHISM]

tri·mor·phic (traimɔ́rfik) *adj.* exhibiting trimorphism

tri·mor·phism (traimɔ́rfizəm) *n.* (*zool.*) the existence of one species in three different forms || (*bot.*) the existence of three different forms (of leaves, flowers etc.) upon specimens of the same species || (*crystall.*) the property in certain substances of crystallizing in three different forms [fr. Gk *trimorphos* fr. *tri-*, three+*morphē*, form]

tri·mor·phous (traimórfəs) *adj.* trimorphic

tri·nal (tráin'l) *adj.* triple [fr. L.L. *trinalis*]

tri·na·ry (tráinəri:) *adj.* triple [fr. L.L. *trinarius*]

Trin·co·ma·lee (triŋkouməlí:) a port (pop. 44,000) in N.E. Sri Lanka

trine (train) 1. *adj.* triple || (*astrology*) favorable 2. *n.* (*astrology*) the aspect of two signs of the zodiac 120° apart, considered as favorable || a set of three **the Trine** the Trinity [O.F.]

trine immersion a form of baptism in which the person being baptized is immersed three times, in the names of the Trinity

Trin·i·dad and To·ba·go (trínidæd, təbéigou) a state in the lesser Antilles off the Orinoco estuary, composed of Trinidad (area 1,980 sq. miles, pop. 1,168,000) and Tobago (area 116 sq. miles) islands. Capital: Port-of-Spain. People: mainly African and East Indian, with mulatto, European, and Chinese minorities. The islands are mountainous and wooded. Main industries: oil extraction and refining, asphalt (both on Trinidad), agriculture (copra, cacao, sugar, fruit and vegetables, livestock raising), tourism. HISTORY. Inhabited by Arawak and Carib Indians, Trinidad was sighted by Columbus (1498). Trinidad was settled by the Spanish from 1532, but remained subject to raids by the Dutch and French until ceded to Britain (1802). Possession of Tobago was disputed between the Dutch and French (17th-18th cc.), and the island was ceded to Britain (1814). Trinidad and Tobago were amalgamated (1888). Jointly they became a member of the Federation of the West Indies (1958-62) and an independent state within the Commonwealth (Aug. 31, 1962), and a member of the Organization of American States (1967). Despite a prosperous tourist industry, unemployment remains high. The economic advantage held by the white minorities has increased black militancy, which erupted (1970) into widespread violence

Trinidad asphalt a natural asphalt found in a pitch lake in Trinidad

Trin·i·tar·i·an (trinitéəri:ən) 1. *adj.* of or relating to the Roman Catholic order of the Holy Trinity formally founded in Rome (1198), having as its principal purpose the ransoming of Christians held captive by the Moslems. Today the order is devoted mainly to teaching and nursing || of or relating to the Trinity || of or relating to the doctrine of the Trinity or to the adherents of this doctrine 2. *n.* a member of the Order of the Holy Trinity || someone who adheres to the doctrine of the Trinity **Trin·i·tar·i·an·ism** *n.* the doctrine of the Trinity || adherence to this doctrine [16th-c. L. *trinitarius*]

tri·ni·tro·tol·u·ene (trainaitroutólju:i:n) *n.* (*abbr.* TNT) a flammable toxic derivative of toluene ($C_7H_5N_3O_6$) obtained by the nitration of toluene. Though moderately stable to heat and friction, it is a powerful explosive used for shells, bombs etc., either alone or in conjunction with other explosive or stabilizing substances (e.g. cordite) [fr. TRI-+Gk *nitron*, niter+TOLUENE]

tri·ni·tro·tol·u·ol (trainaitroutólju:ɔl, trainaitroutólju:ɒl) *n.* trinitrotoluene

trin·i·ty (tríniti) *n. pl.* **trin·i·ties** *n.* a group of three **the Trin·i·ty** (*Christian theology*) the union in one Godhead of three persons: Father, Son and Holy Ghost [O.F. *trinite*]

Trinity Brethren members of Trinity House

Trinity House a corporation, providing navigational aids (pilots, lighthouses, buoys etc.) in British coastal waters, founded by Henry VIII in 1514

trin·ket (tríŋkit) *n.* a small ornament worn on the dress or person || a small ornamental object [origin unknown]

tri·no·mi·al (trainóumi:əl) 1. *adj.* (*math.*) consisting of three terms || (*taxonomy*) of a name comprising three terms (genus, species and subspecies) 2. *n.* (*math.*) a trinomial expression || (*biol.*) a trinomial name [fr. TRI-+BINOMIAL]

trin·o·scope (trínəskoup) *n.* a color-television projection system utilizing three color-filtered picture tubes

tri·o (trí:ou) *pl.* **tri·os** *n.* a group of three, *a trio of friends* || a musical composition written for three performers || the performers of such a piece || the middle section of a minuet (or march or scherzo written in minuet form) [Ital.]

tri·ode (tráioud) *n.* a thermionic vacuum tube, possessing three electrodes: anode, cathode and control grid [fr. TRI-+ELECTRODE]

tri·oe·cious, tri·e·cious (traií:ʃəs) *adj.* (*bot.*) having staminate, pistillate and hermaphrodite flowers on different plants of the same species [fr. Mod. L. *Triœcia* fr. Gk *tri-*, three+*oikos*, house]

tri·o·let (tráiəlit) *n.* an eight-lined stanza rhyming a b a a a b a b, the first line being repeated at the 4th and 7th and the second line at the 8th [F.]

tri·ox·ide (tráiɒksaid) *n.* an oxide containing three oxygen atoms

trip (trip) 1. *v. pres. part.* **trip·ping** *past* and *past part.* **tripped** *v.i.* (often with 'up') to lose one's balance by e.g. catching one's toe on something || (often with 'up') to make a mistake, blunder || to make a mistake in speaking, *to trip over a word* || (*rhet.*) to move with light, rapid steps or (of a meter) as if with such steps || (*horology*, of the tooth of an escape wheel) to run past the pallet without locking || to become actuated by the operating of a switch || *v.t.* (often with 'up') to cause (someone) to lose his balance by e.g. impeding the movement of his feet || (often with 'up') to cause to make a mistake || to expose (someone) as having told a lie by e.g. asking him a catch question || (*naut.*) to raise (an anchor) so that it hangs clear of the bottom || (*naut.*) to tilt (a yard or topmast) preparatory to lowering it || to operate (a switch or other mechanism) by releasing a catch 2. *n.* a tripping up || a short journey over a set route, *regular trips between the islands* || a journey || (*Br.*) a group outing, excursion || (*mech.*) the action of tripping || (*naut.*) a tack to windward || (*slang or colloq.*) a hallucinatory experience induced by a psychedelic drug, esp. LSD; by extension, an intensely interesting experience or hobby [O.F. *treper*, *triper*, *tripper*]

tri·par·tite (traipártait) *adj.* divided into or having three parts || (*biol.*) divided into three parts extending nearly to the base, *a tripartite leaf* || of an action or agreement made by three persons or groups [fr. L. *tripartitus*]

tripe (traip) *n.* part of the first or second stomach of a ruminant used for food || (*pop.*) worthless matter, e.g. poor entertainment or foolish talk [O.F. *tripe*, *trippe*]

trip-ham·mer (tríphæmər) *n.* a heavy power hammer operated by the tripping action of a cam or lever

tri·phen·yl·meth·ane (traifen'lméθein) *n.* a crystalline hydrocarbon, CH(C_6H_5)$_3$, used as a base in synthetic dyes

triph·thong (trífθəŋ, trífθɒŋ) *n.* a combination of three vowel sounds together in a single utterance of the voice [fr. TRI-+DIPHTHONG]

tri·pin·nate (traipíneit) *adj.* (*bot.*) trebly pinnate **tri·pín·nat·ed** *adj.*

tri·ple (tríp'l) 1. *adj.* having three parts || repeated three times || three times as much, as many or as great || (of musical time) having three beats to the bar 2. *n.* (*baseball*) a hit which enables the batter to reach third base || a group of three || an amount three times as much, as many or as great || (*pl., change ringing*) a peal rung on seven bells || combining form meaning sets with ordered elements, e.g., sextriple [F. or fr. L. *triplus*]

triple *pres. part.* **tri·pling** *past* and *past part.* **tri·pled** *v.t.* to make three times as much, as many or as great || *v.i.* to become three times as much, as many or as great [fr. M. L. *triplare*]

Triple Alliance an alliance (1668) of England, the Netherlands and Sweden against France || an alliance (1717) of Britain, the Netherlands and France against Spain || an alliance (1865) of Argentina, Brazil and Uruguay against Paraguay || an alliance (1882) of Germany, Austria and Italy against France and Russia, which survived until 1915

Triple Alliance, War of the the conflict (1865-70) that pitted Paraguay against the combined forces of Argentina, Brazil and Uruguay. Paraguay suffered enormous losses (305,000 out of a population of 525,000, incl. all but 28,000 of its menfolk)

triple blind a research method, esp. for evaluating drugs in which subjects, those carrying out the experiment, and those analyzing the data, are unaware of the treatment used *Cf* DOUBLE BLIND

Triple Entente an informal alliance (c. 1907-17) between Great Britain, France and Russia, in opposition to the Triple Alliance of 1882

tri·ple-ex·pan·sion (tríp'likspǽnʃən) *adj.* of an engine in which the steam expands successively in three cylinders at different, decreasing pressures while working the same crankshaft

triple jump (*sports*) a track-and-field event combining a hop, a step, and a jump in succession

triple play (*baseball*) a play by which three players are put out

triple point (*phys.*) the temperature and pressure at which three phases of a substance (i.e. solid, liquid, vapor) can exist in equilibrium

triple sheer a tightly woven, opaque, flat-surfaced cloth that appears to be almost sheer

trip·let (tríplit) *n.* a set of three || one of a set of three offspring born at one birth || three rhyming lines of verse as a stanza or subunit of a sonnet etc. || (*mus.*) three notes equal in value performed in the place of the two or four etc. which the key signature would suggest as normal || (*pl., naut.*) three links of chain between cable and anchor ring || (*chem.*) a state in which two unpaired electrons are present || (*navigation*) a system for determining position utilizing signals from three stations || (*optics*) a trifocal lens

triple time (*mus.*) a time with three beats to the bar

tri·plex (tráipleks) *adj.* triple, esp. having three constituent parts [L.]

trip·li·cate 1. (tríplikit) *adj.* made in three identical copies || of one of these copies 2. (tríplikit) *n.* one of three such copies **in triplicate** in three identical copies 3. (tríplikit) *v.t. pres. part.* **trip·li·cat·ing** *past* and *past part.* **trip·li·cat·ed** to reproduce so as to have three identical copies **trip·li·ca·tion** *n.* [fr. L. *triplicare* (*triplicatus*), to treble]

tri·plic·i·ty (triplísiti) *pl.* **tri·plic·i·ties** *n.* the state or quality of being triple || a group of three || (*astrology*) a trigon [fr. L.L. *triplicitas* (*triplicitatis*)]

trip·lo·blas·tic (triploublǽstik) *adj.* having three primary germ layers

trip·loid (tríploid) 1. *adj.* having or being three times the haploid number of chromosomes 2. *n.* a triploid organism (Cf. TETRAPLOID) [TRI-+-ploid fr. DIPLOID and HAPLOID]

tri·ply (trípli:) *adv.* in a triple degree or amount

tri·pod (tráipɒd) *n.* a seat, table, stool etc. having three legs || a stand with three legs for setting up a camera, theodolite etc. || a cauldron etc. resting on three legs || (*Gk hist.*) the altar at Delphi from which the priestess delivered her oracles **trip·o·dal** (trípəd'l), **tri·pod·ic** (traipódik) *adjs* [fr. L. *tripus* (*tripodis*) fr. Gk]

Trip·o·li (trípəli:) a port (pop. 551,477) and former capital of Libya, in W. Tripolitania, an ancient trading center. Industries: light manufacturing, food processing

Tripoli a port (pop. 175,000) and agricultural market in N. Lebanon. Industries: oil refining, tanning, soap making, spinning

Tri·pol·i·ta·ni·a (tripolitéini:ə) the northwestern province (area 110,000 sq. miles, pop. 800,000) of Libya, extending from the Mediterranean into the Sahara. Chief town: Tripoli. It was taken by the Turks (1551). Italy conquered it (1912), colonized it, and held it until the 2nd world war. Products: olives, cereals, fruit, cattle, oil

Tri·pol·i·tan War (tripólitən) a U.S. war (1803) initiated by President Thomas Jefferson against the Barbary pirates of North Africa. He sent a naval force to Tripoli and so put an end to the harassing of U.S. ships in that area

tri·pos (tráipɒs) *n.* (*Cambridge University*) the final examination for the honors degree || an honours course [prob. fr. L. *tripus*, tripod]

trip·per (trípər) *n.* (*Br.*) a person visiting a holiday or pleasure resort || (*Br.*) a person going on a group excursion || a mechanical device that trips something

trip·ping (trípiŋ) *adj.* moving or as if moving with a light and nimble step, *a tripping rhythm* || (*heraldry*) passant

trip·tych, trip·tich (tríptik) *n.* a painting or carving on three adjacent and usually hinged panels. The lateral panels are usually half the width of the central one and made to fold across it [fr. TRI-+DIPTYCH]

Tri·pu·ra (tripúərə) a former princely state (area 4,036 sq. miles, pop. 1,699,000) in the hilly jungle region between Assam and Bangladesh, forming a territory of India. Capital:

CONCISE PRONUNCIATION KEY: **(a)** æ, c*a*t; ɑ, c*a*r; ɔ f*aw*n; ei, sn*a*ke. **(e)** e, h*e*n; i:, sh*ee*p; iə, d*ee*r; ɛə, b*ea*r. **(i)** i, f*i*sh; ai, t*i*ger; əː, b*i*rd. **(o)** o, *o*x; au, c*ow*; ou, g*oa*t; u, p*oo*r; ɔi, r*oy*al. **(u)** ʌ, d*u*ck; u, b*u*ll; uː, g*oo*se; ə, b*a*cillus; juː, c*u*be. x, lo*ch*; θ, *th*ink; ð, bo*th*er; z, *Z*en; ʒ, cor*s*age; dʒ, sava*g*e; ŋ, ora*ng*utang; j, *y*ak; ʃ, *fish*; tʃ, fe*tch*; 'l, rabb*l*e; 'n, redd*en*. Complete pronunciation key appears inside front cover.

Agartala (pop. 59,625). Products: rice, tea, tobacco, jute

tri·que·tra (traikwíːtrə) *n.* a triangular ornament constructed of three intersecting loops or lobes [L.]

tri·que·trous (traikwíːtrəs) *adj.* triangular ‖ (*bot.*) of a stem which has three sharp angles on its surface [fr. L. *triquetrus*]

tri·reme (tráiriːm) *n.* an ancient Roman or Greek galley with three banks of oars [fr. L. *triremis*]

tri·sect (traisékt) *v.t.* to divide into three equal parts **tri·sec·tion, tri·sec·tor** *ns.* [fr. TRI-+L. *secare* (*sectus*), to cut]

tris·kele (tráiskiːl) *n.* a triskelion

tris·kel·i·on (triskéliːɒn) *n.* a figure or device whose central part bears three bent legs or branches radiating outwards [fr. Gk *tri-*, three+*skelos*, a leg]

tris·mus (trízməs) *n.* lockjaw [Mod. L. fr. Gk *trismos*, a scream, a grinding or rasping]

tri·so·mic (traisóumik) *adj.* (*genetics*, of a nucleus or organism) triploid, having one chromosome present in triplicate and the others in duplicate [fr. *Gk tri-*, three+*sōma*, body]

Trist (trist), Nicholas Philip (1800-74), U.S. diplomat who negotiated (1848) the Treaty of Guadalupe Hidalgo, ending the Mexican War

Tris·tan (trístæn, trístɑn, trístən) the hero of a medieval legend, the oldest known version of which comes from Scotland, though the most familiar version is of 12th-c. French origin re-modeled on Celtic material. Tristan (or Tristram), accompanying Iseult (or Isolde) to Cornwall from Brittany for her marriage with King Mark, accidentally drinks with her a magic love potion. It binds them inextricably together in a love which ultimately brings about both their deaths. The story has been retold in English by Malory, Matthew Arnold and Swinburne and in German by Gottfried von Strassburg, whose version was used by Wagner in his opera (1865)

Tris·tan da Cu·nha (trístəndəkúːnjə) a group of four small islands in the S. Atlantic, forming a dependency (pop. 300) of St Helena. Only Tristan (a volcano 6,750 ft high, with a habitable plateau of 12 sq. miles) is inhabited. Products: potatoes, fruit, livestock, fish. The islands were discovered by the Portuguese (1506), were settled from 1810, and were annexed by Britain (1816). The inhabitants were evacuated to Britain after volcanic eruptions (1961) but most of them returned to the island (1963). Some of these emigrated to Britain (1966)

tris·tich·ous (trístikəs) *adj.* arranged in three rows, esp. (*bot.*) three vertical rows [Late Gk *tristichos*]

Tris·tram (trístrəm) *TRISTAN

tri·sul·fide, tri·sul·phide (traisʌlfaid) *n.* (*chem.*) a compound consisting of three atoms of sulfur combined with either an element or a radical

tri·syl·lab·ic (traisilǽbik) *adj.* having three syllables **tri·syl·lab·i·cal·ly** *adv.*

tri·syl·la·ble (tráisiləbˈl) *n.* a word of three syllables

trite (trait) *adj.* stale through too frequent repetition, and boringly obvious [fr. L. *terere* (*tritus*), to rub]

tri·ter·pene [C₃₀H₄₈C₅H₈₆] ` (traitéːrpiːn) *n.* (*chem.*) a group of hydrocarbons related to terpene that occurs in plants and volatile oils

trit·i·um (trítiːəm, tríʃəm) *n.* a radioactive isotope of hydrogen (at. mass 3, symbol H³, ³H or T) having a half-life of 12.5 years [Mod. L. fr. Gk *tritos*, third]

Tri·ton (tráitˈn) (*Gk mythol.*) the sea god, son of Poseidon and Amphitrite ‖ (*Gk mythol.*) any of a race of inferior sea gods having a fish's tail but the head and torso of a man

tri·ton (tráitˈn) *n.* (*zool.*) any of various gastropod mollusks, esp. of fam. *Cymatiidae*, measuring up to 1 ft in length. They have a rough, wrinkly conical shell and are found in tropical seas [after TRITON (sea god)]

triton *n.* (*chem.*) the nucleus of the tritium atom [Gk neuter of *tritos*, third]

trit·u·ra·ble (trítʃərəbˈl) *adj.* that can be triturated

trit·u·rate (trítʃəreit) **1.** *v.t.* *pres. part.* **trit·u·rat·ing** *past* and *past part.* **trit·u·rat·ed** to grind to fine powder, esp. under a liquid **2.** *n.* (*pharm.*) a triturated preparation **trit·u·ra·tion, trít·u·ra·tor** *ns.* [fr. L.L. *triturare* (*trituratus*)]

tri·umph (tráiəmf) *n.* a complete and thoroughly decisive victory ‖ the feeling of pride and joy associated with the winning of such a victory ‖ (*Rom. hist.*) a pageant in which a victori-

ous general, on his return to Rome, paraded through the city and displayed his prisoners and spoils of war [O.F. *triumphe, triomphe*]

triumph *v.i.* to exult in victory ‖ (with 'over') to boast at the expense of the vanquished ‖ (with 'over') to get the better of after a hard struggle, *to triumph over one's difficulties* ‖ (*Rom. hist.*) to celebrate a military triumph [O.F. *triumpher*]

tri·um·phal (traiʌmfəl) *adj.* pertaining to or commemorating a triumph [fr. L. *triumphalis*]

tri·um·phal·ism (traiʌmfəlizəm) *n.* belief that a particular set of dogma is universal and eternal —**triumphalist** *n.*

tri·um·phant (traiʌmfənt) *adj.* victorious ‖ exultant [fr. L. *triumphans* (*triumphantis*) fr. *triumphare*, to triumph]

tri·um·vir (traiʌmvər) *pl.* **tri·um·virs, tri·um·vi·ri** (traiʌmvərai) *n.* (*Rom. hist.*) a magistrate jointly charged with two colleagues to administer a branch of government **tri·úm·vi·ral** *adj.* [L.]

tri·um·vi·rate (traiʌmvərit) *n.* (*Rom. hist.*) government by triumvirs, or the term of office of a triumvir ‖ any group of three men in authority [fr. L. *triumviratus*] —The word is esp. applied to the political association of Pompey, Julius Caesar and Crassus (60 B.C.) to seize power (the 1st Triumvirate) and to that of Mark Antony, Octavius and Lepidus (43 B.C.) after the murder of Caesar (the 2nd Triumvirate)

tri·une (tráijuːn) *adj.* three in one, the *triune God* **tri·ú·ni·ty** *n.* [fr. TRI-+L. *unus*, one]

tri·va·lent (traivéilənt) *adj.* (*chem.*) having a valence of three (cf. TERVALENT) [fr. TRI-+L. *valens* (*valentis*) fr. *valere*, to be strong]

Tri·van·drum (trivǽndrəm) the capital (pop. 409,672) of Kerala, India. Industries: rubber, fisheries, textiles, pharmaceuticals. Crafts: wood and ivory carving. University of Kerala (1937)

triv·et (trívit) *n.* a three-legged iron stand or a bracket hooking on to a grate to put a kettle etc. on by the fire ‖ a metal plate mounted on three short legs to hold a hot dish in order to protect the top of a table [M.E. *trefet* prob. fr. L. *tripes* (*tripedis*), three-footed]

triv·i·a (trívi:ə) *pl. n.* insignificant, unimportant matters or things [L.]

triv·i·al (trívi:əl) *adj.* of very little importance or value, trifling [fr. L. *trivialis*, of a place where three ways meet]

triv·i·al·i·ty (trivi:ǽliti) *pl.* **triv·i·al·i·ties** *n.* the state or quality of being trivial ‖ a trifle (a valueless, insignificant fact or thing) [fr. L. *trivialitas*]

trivial name (*biol.*) the Latin species name, following the genus name and agreeing with it grammatically ‖ the vernacular name for an organism or chemical substance (as compared with its scientific name)

triv·i·um (trívi:əm) *pl.* **triv·i·a** (trívi:ə) *n.* (in medieval education) grammar, rhetoric and logic, the elementary division of the seven liberal arts (*QUADRIVIUM), being the required studies for the bachelor's degree [L.=a place where three roads meet]

tRNA (*genetics abbr.*) for transfer RNA (which see)

Tro·ad (tróuæd) the region in northwestern Asia Minor which surrounded ancient Troy

troat (trout) *v.i.* to make the cry of a buck in rut [prob. fr. O.F. *trout*, a cry to urge on hounds etc.]

tro·car (tróukər) *n.* a triangular surgical instrument used to pierce body cavities in order to withdraw fluid [fr. F. *troquart, trois-quarts* fr. *trois*, three+*carre*, side]

tro·cha·ic (troukéiik) **1.** *adj.* of or made up of trochees **2.** *n.* (*pl.*) a trochaic foot or verse [F. *trochaique* or fr. L. *trochaicus* fr. Gk]

tro·chan·ter (troukǽntər) *n.* a bony prominence serving for the attachment of muscles located on the upper part of the femur in many vertebrates including man ‖ the second segment from the base of the leg of an insect [F. fr. Gk *trechein*, to run]

tro·chee (tróukiː) *n.* a prosodic foot consisting of a long or stressed syllable followed by a short or unstressed one [fr. L. *trochaeus* fr. Gk *trochaios* (*pous*), running (foot)]

troch·i·lus (trókələs) *pl.* **troch·i·li** (trókəlai) *n.* *Trochilus polytmus*, a Jamaican long-tailed hummingbird ‖ the North American humming-bird ‖ the crocodile bird ‖ any of several European warblers [L. fr. Gk *trochilos*, a runner]

troch·le·a (tróklíːə) *n.* (*anat.*) a bone structure resembling a pulley, e.g. the surface of the

inner condyle of the humerus, with which the ulna articulates **troch·le·ar** *adj.* of or connected with a trochlea [L.=pulley]

trochlear muscle the superior oblique muscle of the eye, which controls its downward and lateral motion

trochlear nerve either one of the fourth pair of cranial nerves, which are motor nerves for trochlear muscles

tro·choid (tróukɔid) **1.** *adj.* (*anat.*, of a joint) rotating on a longitudinal axis ‖ (*geom.*) of a curve generated by a point in the plane of one curve rolling on another **2.** *n.* (*anat.*) a trochoid joint ‖ (*geom.*) a trochoidal curve **tro·chói·dal** *adj.* [fr. Gk *trochoeidēs*, wheel-like]

troch·o·phore (trókəfɔr, trókəfour) *n.* (*zool.*) the free-swimming ciliated larval stage of many annelid worms, mollusks, rotifers and other aquatic invertebrates [fr. Gk *trochos*, wheel+*-phoros*, bearing]

trod *past* and *alt. past part.* of TREAD

trodden *alt. past part.* of TREAD

trog·lo·dyte (tróglədait) *n.* a prehistoric cave dweller ‖ a person who lives in a house built in the living rock ‖ an anthropoid ape **trog·lo·dyt·ic** (tróglədítik), **trog·lo·dýt·i·cal** *adjs.* [fr. L. *troglodyta* fr. Gk]

troi·ka (tróikə) *n.* a Russian carriage drawn by three horses abreast ‖ such a team of horses ‖ a group of three, esp. of rulers [Russ.]

Trois-Ri·vières (trwæːri·vjer) (*Eng.* Three Rivers) a port (pop. 50,466) in Quebec, Canada, on the St Lawrence, founded in 1634

Tro·jan (tróudʒən) **1.** *adj.* of ancient Troy, its people or culture **2.** *n.* a native of ancient Troy **to work like a Trojan** to work intensely hard [fr. L. *Troianus*]

Trojan War (*Gk mythol.*) the 10-year siege of Troy by the Greeks, provoked by Paris' abduction of Helen, wife of Menelaus of Sparta. Agamemnon attacked Troy with an army which included Achilles, Patroclus, Odysseus, Nestor and two warriors called Ajax. The Trojans under Hector kept up their resistance until they were tricked (despite the warnings of Cassandra and Laocoön) into hauling inside the walls a huge wooden horse which the Greeks had apparently abandoned, but which in fact was full of Greek soldiers who, once inside, were able to sack the city. The story of the war, which is thought to reflect a real siege of Troy c. 1200 B.C., is the subject of Homer's 'Iliad'. It has been the greatest single pagan influence on later art, being a repository of allusion, metaphor and situation

troll **1.** *v.t.* to sing (a song) in a loud, jolly, carefree way ‖ to fish in (a lake etc.), or to fish for, by drawing a line with a spoon attached behind a boat ‖ *v.i.* to fish in this way ‖ to sing away loudly and merrily **2.** *n.* the act of trolling ‖ the spoon or spoon and line used in trolling ‖ (*Br.*) the reel of a fishing rod [etym. doubtful]

troll *n.* (*Scand. mythol.*) one of the supernatural beings, formerly thought of as giants, but later as dwarfs, inhabiting caves, hills etc. [O.N.]

trol·ley, trol·ly (tróliː) *pl.* **trol·leys, trol·lies** *n.* (*Br.*) a small, low, four-wheeled vehicle used for transporting goods ‖ (*Br.*, *rail.*) a handcar ‖ a grooved wheel, at the end of a pole, running along an overhead wire from which electric power is conducted to the motor of a vehicle ‖ a wheeled basket or carriage etc. that runs suspended from an overhead track ‖ a trolleybus ‖ a streetcar ‖ (*Br.*) a tea wagon [etym. doubtful]

trol·ley·bus (tróliːbʌs) *n.* an electric bus powered from overhead wires but running on tires (not on a laid track)

trolley car a streetcar

trol·lop (tróləp) *n.* a slattern [etym. doubtful]

Trol·lope (tróləp), Anthony (1815-82), English novelist. His most successful novels center in the imaginary cathedral town of Barchester and portray clerical life and provincial society with realism, a touch of satire, and neat character drawing. They include 'The Warden' (1855), 'Barchester Towers' (1857), 'Doctor Thorne' (1858) and 'The Last Chronicle of Barset' (1867)

trolly *TROLLEY

trom·bone (trombóun) *n.* (*mus.*) a brass wind instrument consisting of a metal U-shaped tube bent twice upon itself and ending in a trumpet-shaped mouth, with a slide for controlling the length of vibrating column of air, or (rarely) valves, like a trumpet ‖ (*mus.*) an organ stop having a comparable tone **trom·bón·ist** *n.* [fr. Ital. fr. *tromba*, trumpet]

trom·mel (trómǝl) n. (mining) a revolving sieve used for sizing crushed ore or rock [G.=drum]

tro·mom·e·ter (troumómitǝr) n. an instrument for detecting and recording slight earth tremors [fr. Gk tromos, trembling+METER]

Tromp (tromp), Maarten Harpertszoon (1597-1653), Dutch admiral. His victory over a Spanish fleet (1639) marked the end of Spain's naval power. He won control (Nov. 1652) of the English Channel from England in the 1st Dutch War, but was twice defeated in 1653 and killed in the final battle

trompe (tromp) n. an apparatus for producing a blast in a forge or furnace by means of a column of water descending in a tube to suck air down [F.]

trompe l'œil (trómplói, trͻpleͮ) n. (painting) an illusory effect of reality produced e.g. by shading and perspective [F.=trick the eye]

Trom·sö (trómsou) a fishing port (pop. 46,454) in N. Norway: polar research stations

Trond·heim (trónheim) a port (pop. 135,100) and former capital (pre-14th c.) of Norway, on the central west coast. Industries: fishing, shipbuilding, mechanical engineering, hydroelectricity. Gothic cathedral (12th-13th cc.)

troop (tru:p) 1. n. (pl.) soldiers, armed forces ‖ a body of soldiers, esp. a unit of cavalry under a captain, a unit of artillery within a battery or a unit of armored vehicles ‖ a scout unit ‖ a lot of people, troops of summer visitors ‖ a herd or flock 2. v.i. (often with 'off') to go in groups or crowds, they went trooping off to the movies ‖ to go in a more or less orderly file, they trooped into the canteen [O.F. trope, F. troupe]

troop carrier an armored vehicle for cross-country transport of infantry ‖ an aircraft for carrying troops with their equipment to an operational zone

troop·er (trú:pǝr) n. a cavalry soldier with the rank of private ‖ a private in a state police, esp. one using a motorcycle ‖ a mounted policeman ‖ (Br.) a troopship

Trooping the Color a ceremonial mounting of the guard on the British sovereign's official birthday, in the presence of the sovereign, the regimental colors being carried along the ranks of the Brigade of Guards

troop·ship (trú:pʃip) n. a ship for transporting troops

tro·pae·o·lin, tro·pe·o·lin (troupí:ǝlin) n. any of various orange and orange-yellow azo dyes, some of which are used for staining in biological work [TROPAEOLUM]

tro·pae·o·lum (troupí:ǝlǝm) n. a member of Tropaeolum, fam. Tropaeolaceae, a genus of mainly climbing, flowering plants native to South America, esp. T. majus, the nasturtium [Mod. L. dim. of Gk tropaion, trophy]

trope (troup) n. (rhet.) a word or expression used figuratively ‖ a medieval liturgical interpolation, melodic or textual [fr. L. tropus fr. Gk]

tropeolin *TROPAEOLIN

troph·ic (trófik) adj. relating to nutrition, trophic ulcers [fr. Gk trophikos fr. trophē, nourishment]

troph·o·blast (trófǝblæst) n. (embry.) a specialized ectodermic layer on the outside of the blastula in many mammal embryos. It is believed to attach the egg to the wall of the uterus and to supply food to the embryo **troph·o·blas·tic** adj. [fr. Gk trophē, nourishment+blastos, germ]

troph·o·plasm (trófǝplæzǝm) n. the nutritive or vegetative part of a cell (cf. IDIOPLASM, cf. KINOPLASM) [fr. Gk trophē, nourishment+PLASM]

tro·phy (tróufi:) pl. **tro·phies** n. a silver cup or other object won in a sporting contest ‖ a mounted hunting memorial, e.g. a fox's mask ‖ any object cherished as a memento of a success won ‖ (in ancient Greece and Rome) a memorial consisting of armor, weapons etc. taken from an enemy and set up in honor of a god ‖ an architectural or decorative motif grouping a shield, spear, plumed helmet, standard etc. [F. trophée fr. L. fr. Gk]

trop·ic (trópik) 1. n. either of two parallels of latitude on the globe passing through the most northerly and southerly points on the earth's surface (approx. 23½° N. and S.) at which the sun can be vertically overhead at noon (*TROPIC OF CANCER, *TROPIC OF CAPRICORN) ‖ either of the two corresponding circles of the celestial sphere which the sun just reaches at the point of its greatest declination **the Tropics** the region between the Tropics of Cancer and Capricorn 2. adj. pertaining to the Tropics **trop·i·cal** adj. of

or as if of the Tropics ‖ of or like a trope [fr. L. tropicus fr. Gk]

tropical climate a climatic regime characterized by high temperatures (minimum average 64° F.) and heavy rainfall (yearly minimum about 60 ins) throughout the year, except on the tropical margins, where there is a distinct dry season

tropical fish any of various exotic fish kept in aquariums

tropical year a solar year

tropic bird a member of Phaëthon, fam. Phaëthontidae, a genus of tropical seabirds. They have white plumage with black markings, and the central pair of tail feathers is greatly elongated

Tropic of Cancer the parallel of latitude 23½° north of the equator (*TORRID)

Tropic of Capricorn the parallel of latitude 23½° south of the equator (*TORRID)

tro·pism (tróupizǝm) n. the involuntary movement or orientation toward (positive tropism) or away from (negative tropism) a source of stimulus, e.g. a response of plants to light (*TAXIS) [fr. Gk tropos, a turning]

tro·po·col·la·gen (trópǝkólǝdʒǝn) n. (biochem.) a fundamental precursor of connective tissue (bone and cartilage of animals) containing similar elongated molecules

trop·o·log·i·cal (trͻpǝlódʒik'l) adj. of or involving tropology

tro·pol·o·gy (trǝpólǝdʒi:) pl. **tro·pol·o·gies** n. the use of metaphors in speaking or writing ‖ figurative exegesis of the Bible, stressing moral meaning ‖ a collection of tropes or a treatise on figurative language [fr. L.L. tropologia fr. Gk]

trop·o·pause (trópǝpͻz) n. the level separating the troposphere and the stratosphere, occurring at an altitude of 5-10 miles [fr. tropos, a turning+PAUSE]

trop·o·phyte (trópǝfait) n. a plant which is mesophytic in summer and xerophytic in winter [fr. Gk tropos, a turning+phuton, a plant]

trop·o·sphere (trópǝsfiǝr) n. a division of the earth's atmosphere extending from ground level to altitudes ranging 5-10 miles (depending on season and where it is measured on the earth). It is the region in which the temperature declines rapidly with altitude and which contains most of the moisture in the atmosphere, and is therefore the region where convection currents (winds) and clouds are found (*TROPOPAUSE) [fr. Gk tropos, a turning+SPHERE]

tropospheric scatter 1. the scatter propagation of radio waves by a result of irregularities in the physical properties of the troposphere 2. an over-the-horizon ground-to-ground multichannel radio system that utilizes the reflective properties of the troposphere

Tros·sachs, the (trósæks) a romantic wooded mountain valley in Perth, Scotland

trot (trot) n. a setline ‖ one of the short attached lines

trot pres. part. **trot·ting** past and past part. **trot·ted** v.i. (of a horse etc.) to move at a steady pace, the action of the feet being in diagonal pairs and the rhythm duple (not quadruple) ‖ (of bipeds) to move at a pace between walking and running ‖ v.t. to make (a horse) trot ‖ to go (a specified distance) at this gait **to trot out** (pop.) to produce or introduce (an often repeated joke, superior knowledge etc.) for admiration or consideration or approval [O.F. troter]

trot n. the action of trotting ‖ the sound of a horse trotting ‖ (pop.) a crib (translation used by students) [F.]

Trot n. (slang) a Trotskyist; one who subscribes to the socialist doctrine of Leon Trotsky (1879–1940)

troth (trǝθ, trouθ) n. (rhet.) one's plighted word **to plight one's troth** (rhet.) to pledge one's loyalty in betrothal [O.E. trēowth, truth]

trot·line (trótlain) n. a setline

Trot·sky (trótski:), Leon (Lev Davidovich Bronstein, 1879-1940), Russian revolutionist. Returning to Russia (1917) after long periods of imprisonment and exile, he played a leading part in bringing the Bolsheviks to power. He was minister of war (1918-25), but, after Lenin's death (1924), came into conflict with Stalin's policy of abandoning the aim of world revolution. He was exiled from the U.S.S.R. (1929) and was murdered in Mexico (possibly at the instigation of Stalin)

Trot·sky·ist (trótski:ist) 1. n. a follower of Trotsky, believing like him in the necessity for

armed revolution in every country 2. adj. of or pertaining to Trotsky or his ideas or followers

Trot·sky·ite (trótski:ait) 1. n. a Trotskyist 2. adj. Trotskyist

trot·ter (trótǝr) n. a horse bred and trained for trotting races ‖ the foot of a pig or other animal, esp. as food

trotting race a form of horse racing. Specially bred horses race at a trot, pulling a sulky on which the driver sits

trou·ba·dour (trú:bǝdͻr, trú:bǝdour, trú:bǝduǝr) n. one of a class of poets and poetmusicians, often of noble birth or knightly rank, and sometimes itinerant, living in S. France, N. Spain and Italy in the 11th, 12th and 13th cc. (cf. TROUVÈRE). They wrote mainly in the langue d'oc, on courtly love and deeds of chivalry, and are responsible for many set forms of verse (*BERTRAN DE BORN) ‖ a strolling minstrel [F. fr. Prov.]

trou·ble (trʌb'l) 1. v. pres. part. **trou·bling** past and past part. **trou·bled** v.t. to cause to worry or grieve ‖ to disturb mentally ‖ to afflict, troubled by rheumatism ‖ to put to inconvenience ‖ to make turbid ‖ v.i. to put oneself to some inconvenience, don't trouble to fetch it 2. n. worry ‖ misfortune ‖ a difficult situation ‖ a person or thing that causes difficulty ‖ effort, pains, he takes trouble with his work ‖ (pop.) that which is wrong, the trouble with you is that you don't try ‖ (pl.) social disturbances ‖ a physical weakness or ailment not specifically named, stomach trouble **to take trouble** to exert oneself and be painstaking [O.F. troubler]

troubled waters a situation involving difficulties for somebody which someone not concerned may be tempted to turn to his own profit

trou·ble·mak·er (trʌb'lmeikǝr) n. a person who sets up discord between others

trou·ble·shoot·er (trʌb'lʃu:tǝr) n. a person employed to locate faults in power circuits etc. ‖ a mediator in social disputes ‖ an expert at detecting and dissolving an obstruction to business, political or military affairs

trou·ble·some (trʌb'lsǝm) adj. giving trouble

trou·blous (trʌbləs) adj. (rhet.) disturbed or disturbing [O.F. troubleus]

trough (trͻf, trof) n. a long open receptacle for animal food etc. ‖ a similar receptacle for washing ore, kneading dough etc. ‖ a depression, esp. between ocean waves ‖ (meteorol.) a long, narrow area of low atmospheric pressure between areas of higher pressure ‖ a water conduit, esp. a rainwater gutter under the eaves of a roof ‖ the low point in a business cycle ‖ (statistics) the low point in a curve between higher points ‖ (geol.) a valley that is longer than it is wide [O.E. trog]

trounce (trauns) pres. part. **trounc·ing** past and past part. **trounced** v.t. to defeat overwhelmingly [etym. doubtful]

troupe (tru:p) n. a company of entertainers, acrobats etc. **troup·er** n. a member of a troupe, esp. one on tour **a real trouper** a person who can be relied on to show team spirit in all circumstances [F. = a troop]

trou·sers (tráuzǝrz) pl. n. an outer garment (often called a 'pair of trousers') extending from the waist to the ankles and divided so that the wearer's legs are separately covered ‖ (Br.) a boy's short pants [older trouse perh. fr. Ir. Gael. triubhas]

trouser suit (Br.) a pantsuit

trous·seau (trú:sou) pl. **trous·seaux** (tru:sóu, trú:souz), **trous·seaus** n. a bride's personal clothing, together with the linen etc. for the household [F.]

trout (traut) pl. **trout, trouts** n. any of several food and game fishes of fam. Salmonidae, esp. genera Salmo and Salvelinus, closely related to, but smaller than, the salmon. Most are freshwater species [O.E. truht]

trou·vère (trú:vɛǝr) n. one of a class of poets living in N. France (cf. TROUBADOUR) in the 11th-14th cc., writing in the langue d'oïl, and famous esp. for their chansons de geste and chivalric romances, those drawn from the Arthurian legend (*CHRÉTIEN DE TROYES) [O.F.]

trove (trouv) *TREASURE TROVE

tro·ver (tróuvǝr) n. (law) a gaining possession of goods by finding and keeping ‖ an action in common law to recover the value of goods stolen or wrongfully detained [O.F. trover, to find]

trow·el (tráuǝl) 1. n. a short, flat-bladed tool for spreading mortar etc. ‖ a scoop for lifting or planting plants, bulbs etc. **to lay it on with a trowel** to praise, flatter, apologize etc. fulsomely 2. v.t. pres. part. **trow·el·ing**, esp. Br.

trow·el·ling *past* and *past part.* **trow·eled**, esp. *Br.* **trow·elled** to spread, smooth, shape etc. with a trowel [M.E. *truel* fr. O.F. *truele*]

Troy (troi) an ancient city (*TROJAN WAR) near the western entrance to the Dardanelles, in modern Turkey. Excavations, begun (1871) by Schliemann, revealed nine successive cities on the site, dating from Neolithic to Roman times

troy *adj.* in or by troy weight

Troyes (trwæ) the chief town (pop. 72,167) in Aube, France, and historic capital of Champagne, on the upper Seine, center of the hosiery industry. Gothic cathedral (13th-14th cc.), churches (12th-16th cc.)

Troyes, Treaty of an agreement (1420) between Henry V of England and Charles VI of France during the Hundred Years' War. Henry was to marry Charles's daughter and was to succeed to the French throne after Charles's death. The treaty was repudiated (1429) by Charles VII

troy weight a system of weight units used esp. for precious metals (*MEASURES AND WEIGHTS) [after TROYES, France, where it was first used]

tru·an·cy (trú:ənsi:) *pl.* **tru·an·cies** *n.* an act or instance of playing truant ‖ the state of being truant

tru·ant (trú:ənt) **1.** *n.* a pupil who stays away from school without permission ‖ anyone who absents himself from work or duty without good reason **to play truant** to absent oneself in this manner **2.** *adj.* of or pertaining to a truant ‖ (*rhet.*) idle, wandering, *truant thoughts* [O.F. = beggar, prob. fr. Celt.]

truce (tru:s) *n.* a temporary peace arranged between enemies or opponents [M.E. *trewes, triewes* pl. of *trewe, triewe*, truth to a promise]

tru·cial (trú:ʃəl) *adj.* denoting or relating to any of the Trucial States, or their rulers, or to the coast of the Persian Gulf where the Trucial States are situated [fr. TRUCE]

Trucial States or **Trucial Oman** *UNITED ARAB EMIRATES

truck (trʌk) **1.** *n.* commodities suitable for exchange, barter or sale in small quantities ‖ barter as a practice ‖ vegetables raised to sell ‖ (*pop.*) dealings, *she won't have any truck with him* ‖ odds and ends of little value ‖ (*Br. hist.*) goods supplied in lieu of money wages, a method of payment suppressed by the Truck Acts of the 19th c. **2.** *v.t.* to exchange, barter or trade ‖ (*Br. hist.*) to pay on the truck system ‖ *v.i.* to exchange or barter goods [O.F. *troquer*, to exchange]

truck 1. *n.* a strong, usually four-wheeled vehicle used for road transport of heavy loads ‖ a wheeled vehicle, often with a flat top, for moving loads e.g. in a warehouse ‖ (*Br., rail.*) an open freight car ‖ (*rail.*) a revolving undercarriage on wheels ‖ (*naut.*) a wooden disk at a masthead, with holes for fastening halyards ‖ a handcart for moving loads on a railroad platform etc. ‖ shelved framework mounted on wheels **2.** *v.t.* to transport in or on a truck [prob. fr. L. *trochus*, a hoop]

truck·age (trʌkidʒ) *n.* transportation by truck ‖ the charge for this

truck·er (trʌkər) *n.* a truck farmer

trucker *n.* a person in the business of transporting goods by truck ‖ a truck driver

truck farm a market garden **truck farmer** a market gardener

truck·le (trʌk'l) *pres. part* **truck·ling** *past* and *past part.* **truck·led** *v.i.* (with 'to') to cringe, be servile [A.F. *trocle*, a pulley]

truckle bed a low bed mounted on small wheels that can be stowed away easily under a higher bed

truc·u·lent (trʌkjulənt) *adj.* (of a person or behavior) sharply self-assertive ‖ (of criticisms etc.) harsh and scathing [fr. L. *truculentus*, wild, fierce]

Tru·deau (tru:dóu), Pierre Elliot (1921-), Canadian statesman. He was appointed minister of justice and attorney-general of Canada (Apr. 1967), succeeded Lester Pearson as leader of the Liberal party and was elected prime minister (Apr. 1968). He invoked (1970) emergency police powers to counter the terrorist acts of the separatist Front de Libération du Québec. His party lost its majority in parliament in 1972 and Trudeau formed a coalition with the New Democratic Party. Although the Liberals regained a parliamentary majority in 1974, they were defeated in May 1979, and Trudeau resigned as prime minister. He was returned to office in Feb. 1980 and oversaw the rewriting of

the federal constitution, which became law in 1982. Trudeau resigned as prime minister in June 1984

trudge (trʌdʒ) **1.** *v. pres. part.* **trudg·ing** *past* and *past part.* **trudged** *v.i.* to walk doggedly under fatiguing conditions ‖ *v.t.* to cover (a distance) in this way **2.** *n.* a long walk in such conditions [etym. doubtful]

trudg·en, trudg·eon (trʌdʒən) *n.* the trudgen stroke

trudgen stroke a stroke in swimming combining a scissors kick and alternate overarm movement [after John *Trudgen*, 19th-c. English swimmer]

true (tru:) **1.** *adj.* in agreement with fact ‖ faithful to another or others, or to a cause or allegiance, *a true friend, true to his principles* ‖ rightful, *the true heir* ‖ genuine, sincere, *a true Christian* ‖ accurate, correct, *true to a thousandth of an inch* ‖ correctly and accurately shaped, fitted, placed etc., *these boards are not true* ‖ properly so called, *true statesmanship, the whale is a true mammal* **to come true** to turn out in reality as desired, expected or prophesied **2.** *adv.* accurately, *to aim true* ‖ (*biol.*) in conformity with the characteristics of the stock, *to breed true* **3.** *v.t. pres. part.* **true·ing, tru·ing** *past* and *past part.* **trued** (often with 'up') to make accurate, straight, level etc. or adjust so as to conform to a standard **4.** *n.* **in** (**out of**) **true** correctly (not correctly) aligned or adjusted [O.E. *trēowe*]

true bill a legal indictment found by a grand jury to be justified by the evidence

true-blue (trú:blú:) *adj.* utterly loyal ‖ (*Br.*) staunchly Conservative in politics

true·bred (trú:bréd) *adj.* of unmixed breed, purebred

true north the direction determined by the geographic north pole of the earth (cf. MAGNETIC NORTH)

truf·fle (trʌfəl) *n.* the very dark brown, edible fruiting body of *Tuber*, a genus of fungi (class Ascomycetes) growing underground in parts of Europe. Truffles are esteemed as a delicacy [prob. fr. O.F. *trufe, truffe*]

trug (trʌg) *n.* (*Br.*) a rounded oblong shallow basket of wood strips or plastic, with a handle, for garden produce [perh. var. of TROUGH]

tru·ism (trú:izəm) *n.* a statement the truth of which is self-evident

Tru·ji·llo (tru:hí:jou) a coastal city and commercial center (pop. 240,322) in N.W. Peru. The ruins of the pre-Incan city of Chan-Chan lie four miles to the east

Tru·ji·llo Mo·li·na (tru:hí:jəmolí:na), Rafael Leonidas (1891-1961), president of the Dominican Republic (1930-8, 1942-52). His absolute dictatorship achieved some economic progress but aroused widespread opposition. He was assassinated

tru·ly (trú:li:) *adv.* truthfully, in accordance with the truth ‖ (*intensive*) utterly, really, *a truly lamentable performance* ‖ accurately, *foundations laid truly* **yours truly** a formal ending for an impersonal letter, followed by the signature [O.E. *trēowlíce*]

Tru·man (trú:mən), Harry S (1884-1972), 33rd president (1945-53) of the U.S.A., a Democrat, who succeeded on the death of President Franklin Roosevelt. After Germany's surrender (1945) he attended the Potsdam Conference, and ordered the dropping of the atomic bomb on Japan. He unified (1947) the army, navy, and air force under the U.S. Department of Defense. In the cold war which followed the 2nd world war he formulated the Truman Doctrine. Military and economic aid was given to Greece and Turkey to counter Soviet influence in that area. The policy of resisting Soviet expansion was strengthened by the Marshall Plan and the Point Four Program. Plagued by the Republican-controlled 80th Congress (1946-8), Truman had difficulty in implementing his Fair Deal. He promoted the formation (1949) of NATO. He ordered (1950) U.S. troops to the defense of South Korea, placing them under the aegis of the United Nations but assuming the leadership of the Allied cause in the Korean War. His administration was marked by the 'Red Scare' of the early 1950s

Truman Doctrine a U.S. foreign policy doctrine (1947) formulated by President Harry S Truman, which declared that 'whenever aggression, direct or indirect, threatened the peace and security of the United States, action would be taken to stop that aggression'. The

doctrine was applied esp. in Greece and Turkey

Trum·bull (trʌmb'l), Jonathan (1710-85), American political leader and governor (1769-84) of the colony of Connecticut. During the Revolutionary War he was a chief counselor of George Washington

trump (trʌmp) **1.** *n.* (*card games*) any card of a suit designated as having temporarily a higher rank than the other suits ‖ (*pl.*) this suit of cards ‖ (*pop.*) a person who gives one great help in a crisis **to turn up trumps** (*Br.*, of a person) to show an excellent side to one's character, esp. by giving help in some crisis **2.** *v.t.* to take (a card) with a trump card, play a trump card on ‖ *v.i.* to play a card from the trump suit **to trump up** to concoct fraudulently (an excuse, charge etc.) [alt. fr. TRIUMPH]

trump card a trump ‖ an ultimate course of action which one believes cannot fail

trump·er·y (trʌmpəri) **1.** *pl.* **trump·er·ies** *n.* worthless articles ‖ nonsense **2.** *adj.* worthless, paltry (though often showy) [F. *tromperie*, deceit]

trum·pet (trʌmpit) **1.** *n.* (*mus.*) a wind instrument fashioned from a long metal tube, with a small cup-shaped mouthpiece and a wide, curved, funnel-shaped free end. The type used in the orchestra and in dance bands has three valves ‖ something resembling this in shape, *an ear trumpet* ‖ an organ stop with a tone like a trumpet's ‖ the sound made by a trumpet ‖ a similar sound, esp. that of an elephant **to blow one's own trumpet** to praise oneself to others **2.** *v.t.* to announce by, or as if by, sounding a trumpet ‖ *v.i.* to play the trumpet ‖ to make a sound like that of a trumpet [F. *trompette*]

trumpet creeper *Campsis radicans,* fam. *Bignoniaceae,* a North American creeper having large, red, trumpet-shaped flowers

trum·pet·er (trʌmpitər) *n.* a person who plays a trumpet ‖ a soldier, herald etc. who signals on a trumpet ‖ a trumpeter swan ‖ a member of *Psophia,* fam. *Psophidae,* esp. *P. crepitans,* a long-legged, long-necked South American bird with a loud cry ‖ a member of *Latris,* fam. *Latrididae,* esp. *L. lineata,* a food fish of New Zealand and Australia ‖ any of various other fishes that make a trumpetlike sound when taken from the water ‖ a pigeon of an Asiatic breed with a crested crown and feathered feet

trumpeter swan *Olor buccinator,* a North American wild swan

Trum·pler (trʌmplər), Robert Julius (1886-1956), Swiss-U.S. astronomer, noted for his research into galactic star clusters, observational tests of relativity theory, and the study of Mars

trun·cate (trʌnkeit) **1.** *v.t. pres. part.* **trun·cat·ing** *past* and *past part.* **trun·cat·ed** to shorten by cutting off the top or end ‖ (*crystall.*) to replace (an angle, edge, corner) by a plane, esp. a plane inclined equally to adjacent faces **2.** *adj.* (*biol.*) ending as though cut off at the tip **trún·cat·ed** *adj.* [fr. L. *truncare* (*truncatus*)]

trun·ca·tion (trʌnkéiʃən) *n.* a truncating or being truncated ‖ (*banking*) a system of storing customers' cancelled checks in lieu of returning them with monthly statements [fr. L.L. *truncatio* (*truncationis*)]

trun·cheon (trʌntʃən) *n.* a policeman's nightstick [O.F. *tronchon*]

trun·dle (trʌnd'l) **1.** *n.* a small wheel or roller ‖ the act of trundling ‖ a lantern pinion or one of its bars ‖ a mechanism for transmitting motion in an organ-stop action **2.** *v. pres. part.* **trundling** *past* and *past part.* **trun·dled** *v.t.* to cause (esp. a heavy, awkward object) to roll along ‖ *v.i.* to roll awkwardly on or as if on wheels [O.E. *trendel*, a circle, ring]

trundle bed a truckle bed

trunk (trʌnk) **1.** *n.* the main stem of a tree, excluding branches and roots ‖ the human or animal body excluding the head and limbs ‖ a proboscis, esp. of an elephant ‖ the thorax of an insect ‖ the main stem of a blood vessel or nerve ‖ a trunk line ‖ (*archit.*) the central shaft of a column ‖ a large piece of heavy luggage with a hinged lid, used for transporting a quantity of clothes etc. on a journey ‖ the covered luggage container of an automobile ‖ a perforated box for keeping fish alive in after they have been caught ‖ the pipe piston of a trunk engine ‖ (*naut.*) the part of a cabin rising above deck level, or the superstructure above the hatches ‖ (*naut.*) a watertight housing for a centerboard or rudder ‖ (*pl.*) a man's bathing suit ‖ (*pl.*) light shorts worn for sports **2.** *adj.* of a main line in a rail, road, telephone etc. system [O.F. *tronc*]

trunk call a long-distance telephone call

trunk engine a steam engine having a pipe piston (trunk), wide enough for one end of the connecting rod to be attached to the crank and the other to pass through the trunk and be pivoted to the piston ‖ an engine with a trunk piston to the open end of which the connecting rod is pivoted. Most internal-combustion engines are of this type

trunk hose (*hist.*) short, puffed-out breeches reaching halfway down the thigh, worn esp. in the late 16th c.

trunk line the main telephone connection between exchanges at a considerable distance from one another ‖ a main line in a rail or other transport system

trun·nion (trʌ́njən) *n.* (*mech.*) a cylindrical pivot around which a piece may turn ‖ each of the two fixed projecting gudgeons on the side of a cannon which rest on the carriage and allow movement in the vertical plane [fr. F. *trognon*, stump]

truss (trʌs) *n.* a padded belt or other device used to support a hernia ‖ a supporting framework e.g. for a bridge, roof etc. ‖ (*Br.*) a bundle of hay or straw of standard weight ‖ (*archit.*) a projection of stone, wood etc. like a large corbel, to support a structure ‖ (*naut.*) a heavy iron fitting for securing the lower yards to the mast, esp. a ring around the lower mast with a pivot attachment to a lower yard at the center ‖ a compact terminal flower or fruit cluster [F. *trousse*]

truss *v.t.* to tie up by binding fast ‖ to secure the limbs of (a chicken etc.) ‖ to skewers in preparation for cooking ‖ to support with a truss or trusses [fr. F. *trousser*]

trust (trʌst) *n.* confidence in a person or thing because of the qualities one perceives or seems to perceive in him or it ‖ the person in whom or thing in which one has confidence ‖ acceptance of something as true or reliable without being able to verify it, *on trust* ‖ a responsibility, charge or duty involving the confidence of others, *a position of trust* ‖ a person or thing committed to one as a charge, duty etc. ‖ faith in the future ‖ the responsibility resulting from having others' confidence placed in one, *he considered his office a sacred trust* ‖ (*law*) an equitable right or interest in a property held by one person on behalf of another ‖ the property so administered ‖ a body of trustees ‖ an association of companies organized for defeating competition, obliging the shareholders in each to transfer their stock to a central committee and to surrender voting rights while retaining rights to profit shares [O.N. *traust*]

trust *v.t.* to have faith or trust in, *she trusts him implicitly* ‖ to rely on (someone) to do something or permit (someone) to use something in the proper way ‖ to believe, *if one can trust the report in the papers* ‖ to confide (someone or something) to a person's responsible care ‖ to commit someone or something to the responsible care of (a person) *v.i.* to have faith, *to trust in God* ‖ (with 'to') to resign hopefully one's chances of success, *to trust to luck* [O.N. *treysta*]

trust company any corporation formed in order to function as a trustee ‖ a bank formed under state laws for handling trusts as well as performing ordinary bank duties except the issuing of bank notes

trus·tee (trʌstíː) *n.* a person legally invested with property rights in the interests of another ‖ each of a body of people, often elected, managing the affairs of an institution ‖ a country responsible for a trust territory ‖ a garnishee

trustee process the process of attachment by garnishment

trus·tee·ship (trʌstíːʃip) *n.* a position as a trustee ‖ the work of a trustee ‖ the administrative control exerted by a country over a trust territory placed under its authority

trust·ful (trʌ́stfəl) *adj.* ready to trust, not suspicious

trust fund a fund established (esp. by testament) for the benefit of a person or institution under provisions over which the beneficiary has no control and which a trustee has the duty of applying

trust·i·ly (trʌ́stili:) *adv.* in a trusty manner

trust·i·ness (trʌ́sti:nis) *n.* the quality of being trusty

trust·ing (trʌ́stiŋ) *adj.* disposed to trust

trust territory a non-self-governing territory placed under the authority of the United Nations or a deputed authority by the U.N. Trusteeship Council. Such a territory may be a former mandate under the League of Nations, a territory taken from an ex-enemy state after the 2nd world war, or one placed under such authority by the state responsible for its government

trust·wor·thi·ly (trʌ́stwə:rðili:) *adv.* in a trustworthy manner

trust·wor·thi·ness (trʌ́stwə:rði:nis) *n.* the quality of being trustworthy

trust·wor·thy (trʌ́stwə:rði:) *adj.* deserving trust

trust·y (trʌ́sti:) **1.** *adj. comp.* **trust·i·er** *superl.* **trust·i·est** (*rhet.*) trustworthy **2.** *pl.* **trust·ies** *n.* a convict who is considered trustworthy and who is given special privileges

Truth (truːθ), Sojourner (1797–1883), U.S. preacher, abolitionist and feminist. Born a slave and named Isabella Baumfree, she ran away (1827) and settled in New York City, where she joined a religious cult. Disillusioned, she broke with it (1843) and adopted the name Sojourner Truth as a symbol of her spiritual mission. She campaigned for black emancipation and women's suffrage, becoming the leading black woman orator. After the U.S. Civil War she helped in the resettlement of emancipated slaves and continued her work on behalf of women and blacks

truth (truːθ) *pl.* **truths** (truːðz, truːθs) *n.* the state or quality of being true ‖ something which is true ‖ accuracy, sincerity, integrity, *he argued thus in all truth* ‖ agreement with fact, *how can you test the truth of what he says?*

truth·ful *adj.* telling the truth ‖ habitually telling the truth ‖ (of a story, account, evidence etc.) true [O.E. *trīewth*, *trȳwth*, *trēowth*]

truth-in-lend·ing (trúːθinléndiŋ) *n.* (*banking*) 1968 requirement that full disclosure of credit terms be made to consumers

Truth Squad a team of propagandists devoted to denying (false) statements made by the opposition, esp. regarding controversial political issues

truth table (*computer*) a compilation of switching function to follow a logical path in which the all configurations of input and output are presented, showing the truth or falsity of each configuration; used as the basis for a logical integrated circuit

try (trai) **1.** *v. pres. part.* **try·ing** *past* and *past part.* **tried** *v.t.* to attempt to do, *he tried skiing but never liked it* ‖ to test the operation of, *try the brakes* ‖ to test experimentally, *try twice the quantity* ‖ to submit (someone) to judicial inquiry ‖ to submit (a case) to judicial examination ‖ to bore, irritate ‖ to fatigue ‖ to strain (the eyes, someone's patience etc.) ‖ to attempt to open (a door, window etc.) in order to see if it is fastened ‖ to submit (something) to a testing experience ‖ *v.i.* (often with 'to' or 'and' and a coordinate verb) to make an effort to do something, *try and be patient* ‖ to make an experiment **to try it on** (*Br.*) to see how far one can go in some attempt to deceive or wheedle, well knowing there is little chance of succeeding **to try on** to put (a garment) on to test it for fit or see if one likes it **to try one's hand** to see if one has an aptitude for something by attempting it **to try out** to use in order to test the efficiency or quality of ‖ to test the ability of (someone) to perform a given job etc. ‖ to render down (blubber or fat) **to try out for** to submit oneself to a test or audition in order to gain a place e.g. on a team or in the cast of a play **2.** *pl.* **tries** *n.* an effort ‖ (*rugby*) a score of 3 points made by touching down the ball in the opponents' in-goal, entitling the scoring side to attempt to convert the try into a goal [O.F. *trier*]

try·ing (tráiiŋ) *adj.* causing impatience and annoyance ‖ causing worry or affliction

try·ma (tráimə) *n.* (*bot.*) a nutlike drupe, e.g. the fruit of the walnut, in which the epicarp and mesocarp separate, the hard two-valved endocarp [Mod. L. fr. Gk *truma*, *trumē*, a hole]

Try·on (tráiən), William (1729–88), British colonial governor. As governor (1765–71) of North Carolina, he suppressed colonial agitation against British taxation and refused the colonial assembly permission to meet. As governor (1771–80) of New York, he vigorously supported the Loyalist cause

try-on (tráiɒn, tráiɔn) *n.* (*Br.*, *pop.*) an attempt to deceive or get something not likely to be given etc., without expecting to succeed

try·out (tráiaut) *n.* a practical test of efficiency ‖ an opportunity to demonstrate qualifications, e.g. for a role in a play etc. ‖ a performance or series of performances of a play before its official opening, to test the reaction of the audience, make improvements etc.

tryp·a·no·some (trípənəsoum) *n.* a member of *Trypanosoma*, fam. *Trypanosomatidae*, a genus of parasitic infusorian flagellate protozoans which live in the blood of man and other vertebrates and are the cause of sleeping sickness and other serious diseases [Mod. L. fr. Gk *trupanon*, borer + *soma*, body]

tryp·a·no·so·mi·a·sis (tripənousoumáiəsis) *n.* any disease caused by a trypanosome, esp. sleeping sickness

tryp·sin (trípsin) *n.* a pancreatic enzyme, splitting proteins into amino acids **tryp·tic** (tríptik) *adj.* of or relating to trypsin [perh. fr. Gk *truein*, to rub down, digest]

tryp·sin·i·za·tion (tripsinəzéiʃən) *n.* (*physiol.*) the process of digestion

tryp·to·phan (tríptəfæn) *n.* a crystalline amino acid, $(C_8H_6N)CH_2CH(NH_2)COOH$, resulting e.g. from tryptic digestion, and necessary in the nutrition of humans and animals [fr. TRYPTIC + Gk *phainein*, to appear]

tryp·to·phane (tríptəfein) *n.* tryptophan

try·sail (tráis'l) *n.* (*naut.*) a small triangular sail bent to a gaff and hoisted on a small mast behind a lower mast, esp. as a storm sail

try square an instrument having a flat metal blade at right angles to the handle, used for measuring right angles

tryst (trist, traist) *n.* (*rhet.*) an agreement between lovers to meet at a certain time and place ‖ (*rhet.*) that meeting [fr. M.E. *triste*, trust]

Tsam·kong (tsámkɔ́ŋ) a port (pop. 269,000) in S. Kwangtung, China, on Kwangchow Bay, under extensive development since 1955

Tsang·po (tsáŋpɔ́) *BRAHMAPUTRA

tsar *CZAR

tsarina *CZARINA

tset·se, tzet·ze (tsétsi:, tsí:tsi:) *n.* the tsetse fly [Tswana (Bantu language of Botswana)]

tsetse fly, tzetze fly a member of *Glossina*, fam. *Glossinidae*, a genus of central and S. African bloodsucking flies which transmit sleeping sickness and other diseases to man and cause a highly fatal disease in domestic animals, esp. cattle and horses

T-72 *n.* (*mil.*) U.S.S.R. tank with 120-mm smooth-bore gun, panoramic day-night sight, and infrared searchlight or laser range finder

T-shirt (tíːʃəːrt) *n.* a collarless, short-sleeved, pullover shirt, usually in cotton

Tshom·be (tʃɔ́mbei), Moise (1919–69), Congolese statesman. He led his province of Katanga in secession from the Congo (1960–3), and was prime minister of the provisional government of the Congo (1964–5). He was condemned to death (Mar. 1967) in absentia by a Kinshasa military tribunal. An airplane in which he was flying (July 1967) to the Balearic Is was forced down in Algeria, where he died in captivity, untried

Tsi·nan (dʒíːnán) the ancient capital (pop. 867,379) of Shantung, China, a canal port near the Hwang-ho. Industries: textiles, food processing, mechanical engineering, light manufactures

Tsing·hai (tʃíŋhái) a province (area 278,300 sq. miles, pop. 3,897,706) of N.W. China. Capital: Sining (pop. 72,000)

Tsing Hai (tʃíŋhái) (*Mongol* Koko Nor) a shallow lake (area 2,300 sq. miles) with no outlet, in N.E. Tsinghai, China, at 10,500 ft

Tsing·tao (tsíntáu, tʃíndáu) a port and industrial center (pop. 1,500,000) in E. Shantung, China. Industries: textiles, food processing, paper, building materials, railroad stock. University (1926)

Tsing·yuan (tʃíŋjyán) *PAOTING

Tsinling Shan *CHINLING SHAN

Tsi·tsi·har (tsí:tsi:hɑr) *LUNGKIANG

T-64 *n.* (*mil.*) U.S.S.R. tank, similar to T-62, with missile firing capacity

T-62 *n.* (*mil.*) U.S.S.R. tank with 115-mm main gun, with telescopic device, produced since 1964

T square a drawing instrument shaped like a T for drawing parallel lines or used to support a set square

TSS (*abbr.*) for toxic shock syndrome

tsu·nam·i (tsuːnámiː) *n.* a large destructive sea wave generated by an earthquake or volcanic eruption

---

CONCISE PRONUNCIATION KEY: **(a)** æ, c*a*t; ɑ, c*ar*; ɔ, f*aw*n; ei, sn*a*ke. **(e)** e, h*e*n; i:, sh*ee*p; iə, d*ee*r; ɛə, b*ea*r. **(i)** i, f*i*sh; ai, t*i*ger; ə:, b*ir*d. **(o)** o, *o*x; au, c*ow*; ou, g*oa*t; u, p*oo*r; ɔi, r*oy*al. **(u)** ʌ, d*u*ck; u, b*u*ll; u:, g*oo*se; ə, b*a*cillus; ju:, c*u*be. x, lo*ch*; θ, *th*ink; ð, bo*th*er; z, *Z*en; ʒ, corsa*g*e; dʒ, sava*g*e; ŋ, ora*n*guta*n*g; j, *y*ak; ʃ, *f*ish; tʃ, fe*tch*; 'l, rab*ble*; 'n, red*den*. Complete pronunciation key appears inside front cover.

Tsu·shi·ma Islands (tsú:ʃi:mɑ) two islands (area 269 sq. miles, pop. 59,000) of Japan, between Kyushu and Korea: fishing. They are separate only at high tide

TTBT (*abbr.*) for Threshold Test Ban Treaty, signed by the U.S. and the U.S.S.R. on July 3, 1974, prohibiting underground nuclear tests in excess of 150 kiloton limit

T-time (tí:taim) *n.* (*aerospace*) the take-off or firing time

Tu·a·mo·tu Archipelago (tu:əmóutu:) (F. Tuamotu) a coral archipelago (area 330 sq. miles, pop. 8,537) comprising some 60 atolls and islets, in French Polynesia. Main islands: Rangiroa, Fakarava. Religion: mainly Roman Catholic. Exports: copra, phosphates, mother-of-pearl

Tua·reg (twáreg) *n.* a member of a nomadic Berber people of the central and Western Sahara, Hamitic in speech and Moslem in religion. The men wear indigo-dyed veils over the lower part of the face, while the women go unveiled

tu·a·ta·ra (tu:ətá:rə) *n. Sphenodon punctatum*, a reptile (about two and a half feet in length) found only in little islands off the New Zealand coast

tub (tʌb) 1. *n.* an open circular wooden vessel with a flat bottom, made of staves held together by hoops ‖ a similar vessel of metal, plastic etc. ‖ (*mining*) a bucket used for carrying ore etc. ‖ a boat used for practice rowing ‖ a tub and its contents or the contents of a tub, esp. this as a measure, *a tub of butter* ‖ (*pop.*) a slow or clumsy ship ‖ (*pop.*) a bathtub ‖ (*old-fash.*) the act of taking a bath 2. *v. pres. part.* **tub·bing** *past* and *past part.* **tubbed** *v.t.* to wash in a tub ‖ to put or plant in a tub ‖ to train (a rower) in a tub ‖ *v.i.* (*old-fash.*) to take a bath ‖ to practice rowing in a tub [late M.E. *tubbe*]

tu·ba (tú:bə, tjú:bə) *n.* one of several low-pitched musical instruments, having valves and a cupped mouthpiece. The largest often encircle the body of the musician. The bass tuba is normally the lowest bass brass instrument in an orchestra ‖ a powerful organ stop of 8-ft pitch ‖ *pl.* **tu·bae** (tú:bi:, tjú:bi:) (*Rom. hist.*) a straight bronze war trumpet [L. = a trumpet]

tu·bal (tú:b'l, tjú:b'l) *adj.* like or of a tube, esp. a Fallopian tube

tu·bate (tú:beit, tjú:beit) *adj.* having or forming a tube

tub·by (tʌ́bi:) *comp.* **tub·bi·er** *superl.* **tub·bi·est** *adj.* (esp. of a person) very fat and usually short ‖ tub-shaped

tube (tu:b, tju:b) 1. *n.* a long, narrow, hollow cylinder for holding or passing liquids, gases etc. ‖ a small, flexible cylinder with a screw cap for holding toothpaste, mustard etc. ‖ a thin, hollow channel in a plant or animal, *bronchial tubes* ‖ (*Br.*) the subway ‖ a tunnel for motor or rail traffic ‖ an electron tube ‖ (with "the") (*slang*) television 2. *v.t. pres. part.* **tub·ing** *past* and *past part.* **tubed** to provide with tubes ‖ to enclose in tubes [F.]

tu·ber (tú:bər, tjú:bər) *n.* a modified underground stem (e.g. the potato), shortened, thickened and fleshy, with buds which may become new plants (cf. TUBEROUS ROOT) ‖ (*anat.*) a swelling ‖ a member of *Tuber*, a genus of underground fungi (*TRUFFLE) [fr. L. *tuber* dim. of *tuba* = swelling]

tu·ber·cle (tú:bə·rk'l, tjú:bə·rk'l) *n.* (*anat., zool.*) a small, round elevation, esp. of a bone ‖ (*med.*) a nodular lesion, esp. of a tuberculous infection ‖ (*bot.*) a small swelling or nodule, esp. one on the roots of leguminous plants ‖ a rib knob articulating with the transverse process of a vertebra ‖ a prominence marking the nuclei of various nerves of the central nervous system [fr. L. *tuberculum* dim. of *tuber* = a swelling]

tubercle bacillus *Mycobacterium tuberculosis*, the microorganism causing tuberculosis

tu·ber·cu·lar (tubé:rkjulər, tjubé:rkjulər) *adj.* of, having or like tubercles ‖ tuberculous [fr. L. *tuberculum*, tubercle]

tu·ber·cu·late (tubé:rkjuleit, tjubé:rkjuleit) *adj.* (*bot.*) having tubercles **tu·bér·cu·lat·ed** *adj.* **tu·ber·cu·lá·tion** *n.* [fr. Mod. L. *tuberculatus* fr. *tuberculum*, tubercle]

tu·ber·cu·lin (tu:bé:rkjulin, tjubé:rkjulin) *n.* an extract of tuberculosis bacilli used in diagnosing tuberculosis [fr. L. *tuberculum*, tubercle]

tuberculin test a diagnostic test of tuberculosis: the presence of past or present infection is indicated by the appearance of inflammation at the site of a subcutaneous injection of tuberculin

tu·ber·cu·lo·sis (tubə:rkjulóusis, tjubə:rkjulóusis) *n.* a highly variable infectious disease of man and some other vertebrates caused by the

tubercle bacillus. The disease may be acute or chronic and generally attacks the respiratory tract, although any tissue may be affected. The symptoms (fever, loss of weight etc.) are caused by the toxins produced by the infecting organism, which also cause the formation of characteristic nodes consisting of a packed mass of cells and disintegration products surrounding a knot of dead tissue [Mod. L. fr. *tuberculum*, tubercle]

tu·ber·cu·lous (tubé:rkjuləs, tjubé:rkjuləs) *adj.* having or pertaining to tuberculosis ‖ tubercular

tu·be·rose (tú:bərǫuz, tjú:bərǫuz) *n. Polianthes tuberosa,* fam. *Amaryllidaceae,* a bulbous, low-growing plant, bearing fragrant white, lilylike flowers [fr. Mod. L. *tuberosa* fr. *tuberosus,* knobby]

tu·ber·ose (tú:bərous, tjú:bərous) *adj.* tuberous

tu·ber·os·i·ty (tu:bərósiti:, tjuːbərósiti:) *pl.* **tu·ber·os·i·ties** *n.* a rounded eminence, e.g. on a bone for the attachment of a muscle or tendon [F. *tubérosité*]

tu·ber·ous (tú:bərəs, tjú:bərəs) *adj.* (*bot.*) of, like, having or being a tuber or tubers ‖ reproducing by tubers [F. *tubéreux*]

tuberous root a thick root, e.g. the dahlia, like a tuber but bearing no buds to scale leaves

tu·bic·o·lous (tubíkələs, tjubíkələs) *adj.* (e.g. of certain annelids) living in a self-made tube ‖ (of certain spiders) weaving a tubelike web [fr. L. *tubus,* a rube + *colere,* to dwell]

tub·ing (tú:biŋ, tjú:biŋ) *n.* tubes collectively ‖ a set of tubes ‖ a piece of tube ‖ material for tubes

Tü·bin·gen (týbiŋən) a town (pop. 67,800) in Baden-Württemberg, West Germany, on the Neckar. University (1477)

Tub·man (tʌ́bmən), Harriet (c. 1820-1913), U.S. black abolitionist leader. A Maryland slave, she escaped (1849) to Philadelphia. She returned to the South almost every year, leading over 300 slaves to freedom in the North

Tubman, William Vacanarat Shadrach (1895-1971), Liberian statesman, president of Liberia (1944-71)

tub-thump·er (tʌ́bθʌmpər) *n.* someone who is often guilty of tub-thumping

tub-thump·ing (tʌ́bθʌmpiŋ) *n.* the use of ranting, extravagant language in speeches, sermons etc.

tu·bu·lar (tú:bjulər, tjú:bjulər) *adj.* of, shaped like, made of or provided with a tube or tubes ‖ sounding like air passing through tubes [fr. L. *tubulus*]

tu·bule (tú:bju:l, tjú:bju:l) *n.* a small tube or (esp. *anat.*) tubular structure [fr. L. *tubulus*]

Tu·ca·pel (tu:kɑpél) a Spanish fort in Arauco, Chile, site of a battle (1554) between the Spaniards under Valdivia and the Indians under Lautaro, in which Valdivia was killed

tuck (tʌk) 1. *v.t.* to push (something) into a little space, pocket etc., or under something, where it will be neatly held or conveniently hidden ‖ to thrust the edges of (a sheet, napkin, shirt etc.) in or under something which will keep it secured ‖ to make tucks in (a garment or fabric) ‖ to draw up in, or as if in, a folded manner, *to tuck one's legs under a chair* ‖ (with 'up') to push up or back into folds so as to hold in position, *tuck your sleeves up* ‖ (with 'in') to cover (a person) with bedclothes, *tuck the baby in* ‖ *v.i.* to make tucks ‖ to be disposed of by tucking, *the ends tuck in under the mattress* **to tuck in** (*Br., pop.*) to eat with a hearty appetite 2. *n.* the act or an instance of tucking ‖ a fold sewn into a garment so as to shorten it or take it in, or for decoration ‖ (*naut.*) the after part of the hull where the bottom planks meet ‖ (*Br., pop.*) candy, cookies etc. for children **túck·er** 1. *v.t.* (*pop.*, often with 'out') to exhaust 2. *n.* best bib and tucker one's smartest set of clothes [O.E. *tūcian*]

tuck-in (tʌ́kin) *n.* (*Br., pop.*) a big meal eaten with appetite

tuck-point (tʌ́kpɔint) *v.t.* to finish (brickwork or stonework) with projecting lines of putty or fine lime mortar

tuck-shop (tʌ́kʃɒp) *n.* (*Br.*) a shop at a school, selling eatables, esp. candy

Tuc·son (tú:sɒn) an agricultural market town (pop. 330,537) in S. Arizona. Industries: food processing, electronic engineering, tourism. Spanish mission church (18th c.). University (1891)

Tu·cu·mán (tu:ku:mán) a city (pop. 366,392) in N. Argentina at the foot of the Andes, founded

in 1565. Industries: food processing (esp. sugar), railroad stock. University (1914)

Tucumán, Declaration of the declaration of Argentina's independence from Spain, signed (July 9, 1816) in the name of the United Provinces of La Plata at the Constituent General Congress held in Tucumán

Tu·dor (tú:dər, tjú:dər) 1. *n.* a member of the dynasty ruling England 1485-1603 (Henry VII, Henry VIII, Edward VI, Mary I, Elizabeth I) 2. *adj.* of or relating to a Tudor or his times ‖ (*archit.*) of the late perpendicular Gothic style, marked by a characteristic flattened arch, shallow moldings, and much wall paneling

Tues. Tuesday

Tues·day (tú:zdi:, tjú:zdi:, tú:zdei, tjú:zdei) *n.* the third day of the week [O.E. *Tīwes dæg,* Tīw's day after Tīw, god of war]

tu·fa (tú:fə, tjú:fə) *n.* a soft porous rock (calcium carbonate) formed as a deposit around springs ‖ **tuff tu·fa·ceous** (tu:féiʃəs, tju:féiʃəs) *adj.* [Ital. *tufo, tufa,* a kind of porous stone]

tuff (tʌf) *n.* a rock formed of compacted volcanic fragments of varied composition **tuff·a·ceous** (tʌféiʃəs) *adj.* [fr. F. *tufe, tuffe, tuf* fr. Ital.]

tuft (tʌft) 1. *n.* a bunch or cluster of feathers, hairs etc. growing together at the base ‖ a small clump of plants or trees ‖ a beard on the tip of a man's chin ‖ (*hist.*) a gold tassel worn by titled undergraduates at Oxford and Cambridge ‖ a buttonlike cluster of loops serving to finish off the threads drawn tightly through a mattress or quilt to secure the padding, or a covered button serving this purpose 2. *v.t.* to arrange in tufts ‖ to provide with a tuft, esp. to pass tufts of thread through depressions in (mattresses etc.) to hold the stuffing in place ‖ *v.i.* to grow in or take the form of tufts **tuft·ed** *adj.* (of birds) having a crest ‖ (of plants) growing in tufts ‖ (of plants) bearing flowers in dense clusters **túft·y** *comp.* **tuft·i·er** *superl.* **tuft·i·est** *adj.* [perh. fr. O. F. *touffe*]

tug (tʌg) 1. *v. pres. part.* **tug·ging** *past* and *past part.* **tugged** *v.t.* to pull with force, *to tug a heavy cart* ‖ to make a sudden vigorous pull at ‖ (*shipping*) to pull by means of a tugboat, *to tug a liner out of port* ‖ *v.i.* to use force or violence in pulling 2. *n.* a strong, violent pull ‖ a pulling force ‖ a struggle, esp. a struggle between conflicting emotions, desires etc. ‖ the trace of a harness ‖ a tugboat [M.E. *toggen* fr. O.E. *tēon,* to draw, pull, tug]

tug·boat (tʌ́gbǫut) *n.* a small powerful steamer for towing e.g. larger ships, logs etc.

tu·ghrik (tú:gri:k) *n.* the basic monetary unit of the Mongolian People's Republic ‖ a note or coin of the value of one tughrik [Mongol *dughurik,* a round thing, a wheel]

tug-of-war (tʌ́gəvwɔ́r) *pl.* **tugs-of-war** *n.* a contest in which a team of men at one end of a rope tries to pull a team at the other end of the rope across a line between them ‖ a close, hard struggle between two parties etc.

Tug·well (tʌ́gwəl), Rexford Guy (1891-1979), the last U.S. governor of Puerto Rico (1941-6), sent by Pres. Franklin Roosevelt to prepare the island for conversion to commonwealth status. Part of Roosevelt's 'brain trust' group of advisers, he served as assistant and under-secretary of agriculture, where he headed the Rural Resettlement Administration, which sought to relocate farmers to more productive land. He also served as director of the University of Chicago's Institute of Planning (1946-52)

tui (tú:i:) *n. Prosthemadera novaeseelandiae,* a New Zealand glossy black honey eater with white markings [Maori]

Tui·le·ries (twi:ləri:) a former royal palace in Paris, begun in 1564 and destroyed (1871) by the Commune. Its vast formal gardens are now a public park

tu·i·tion (tu:íʃən, tju:íʃən) *n.* the price charged for instruction ‖ teaching **tu·i·tion·al, tu·i·tion·ar·y** *adjs* [A.F. fr. L. *tuitio,* guard, guardianship]

Tu·la (tú:lə) a city (pop. 521,000) in the R.S.F.S.R., U.S.S.R., in the Moscow basin. Industries: iron and steel, mechanical engineering, metalworking. Medieval kremlin

Tu·la (tú:lə) a town (pop. 2,000) in central Mexico, 45 miles north of Mexico City. It is the site of the impressive ruins of what is believed to have been the capital of the Toltec kingdom, founded in 677 and destroyed by the Chichimecas in 1116

tu·la·re·mi·a (tu:ləri:mí:ə) *n.* an infectious disease of rodents, some domestic animals and man. It is caused by a bacterium and is trans-

---

CONCISE PRONUNCIATION KEY: (a) æ, c*a*t; ɑ, c*a*r; ɔ f*aw*n; ei, sn*a*ke. **(e)** e, h*e*n; i:, sh*ee*p; iə, d*ee*r; ɛə, b*ea*r. **(i)** i, f*i*sh; ai, t*i*ger; ə:, b*i*rd. **(o)** o, *o*x; au, c*ow*; ou, g*oa*t; u, p*oo*r; ɔi, r*oy*al. **(u)** ʌ, d*u*ck; u, b*u*ll; u:, g*oo*se; ə, b*a*cillus; ju:, c*u*be. x, lo*ch*; θ, *th*ink; δ, bo*th*er; z, *Z*en; ʒ, cor*s*age; dʒ, sa*v*age; ŋ, orangutan*g*; j, *y*ak; ʃ, *f*ish; tʃ, fe*tch*; 'l, rabb*le*; 'n, redd*en*. Complete pronunciation key appears inside front cover.

mitted by the bite of bloodsucking insects, or (in man) by the handling of infected animals. It occurs chiefly in North America, Scandinavia and parts of Asia Minor. It causes an ulcer at the site bitten, with inflamed lymph glands and fever [Mod. L. after *Tulare* County, California + Gk *haima*, blood]

tu·lip (túː lip, tjúː lip) *n.* a member of *Tulipa*, fam. *Liliaceae*, a genus of bulbous herbaceous plants bearing a large, showy, bell-shaped flower on a single tall stem. About 50 species are known, and innumerable varieties of *T. gesneriana*, the garden tulip, have been developed. It was introduced into W. Europe from Turkey in the 16th c. ‖ the flower or the bulb of this plant [F. *tulipe* fr. Turk. fr. Pers.]

tulip tree *Liriodendron tulipifera*, fam. *Magnoliaceae*, a tall North American timber tree with flowers resembling the tulip. It yields a light, fine-grained white wood used for making furniture

tu·lip·wood (túː lipwu̞d, tjúː lipwu̞d) *n.* the wood of the tulip tree ‖ any of various colored or striped woods yielded by certain Brazilian and Australian trees

Tull (tʌl), Jethro (1674-1741), English agriculturist. The seed drill which he invented (c. 1701), and his advocacy of thorough tilling with plow and hoe, were important in the history of English agriculture

tulle (tuːl, tjuːl, tyl) *n.* a sheer, sometimes stiffened, machine-made net, of silk or nylon, used for veils, dresses etc. [after *Tulle*, a city in France]

Tul·sa (tʌ́lsə) a city (pop. 360,919) in N.E. Oklahoma, on the Arkansas River, center of a great oil field. Industries: oil refining, metallurgy, mechanical engineering, cotton textiles. University (1921)

Tul·si Das (túːlsiːdás) (c. 1532-1623), Indian poet. His poetry, devoted almost exclusively to the praise of Rama, includes the epic 'Ramacarit-manas' (1575)

tum·ble (tʌ́mbˈl) **1.** *v. pres. part.* **tum·bling** *past* and *past part.* **tum·bled** *v.i.* to fall to the ground through tripping up or losing one's balance or no longer having support ‖ to move hurriedly and without restraint, control or grace, *they came tumbling into the study* ‖ (with 'down') to fall into ruin ‖ to drop in price at a rapidly increasing pace ‖ to fall suddenly from power ‖ to toss or roll about ‖ (of words) to issue in a spate without proper control ‖ to perform feats of acrobatic agility such as handsprings and somersaults ‖ (*pop.*, with 'to') to understand something suddenly, or become aware of a situation ‖ *v.t.* to cause to fall ‖ to rumple, put in disorder by rough handling ‖ to spin (metal objects etc.) in a tumbling barrel **2.** *n.* a fall ‖ the state of being rumpled or disorderly, *in a tumble* ‖ a confused pile or litter, *a tumble of books and papers covered the desk* ‖ a handspring, somersault etc. [M.E. *tumbel* frequentative or dim. of O.E. *tumbian* to dance, to fall]

tum·ble·bug (tʌ́mbˈlbʌg) *n.* a dung beetle

tum·ble·down (tʌ́mbˈldau̞n) *adj.* dilapidated, beginning to fall into ruin

tumble home 1. *n.* a curving of the sides of a ship inwards above the point of greatest breadth **2.** *v.i.* (of the sides of a ship) to curve in this way

tum·bler (tʌ́mblər) *n.* an acrobat ‖ someone who tumbles ‖ an ordinary drinking glass without a foot or stem ‖ the quantity it holds ‖ a tumbling barrel ‖ a person who operates a tumbling barrel ‖ a domestic pigeon of a breed which somersaults in flight ‖ (*mach.*) a projecting piece on a revolving shaft or rockshaft, setting in motion another piece ‖ the movable part of a reversing or speed-changing gear ‖ a moving part of the mechanism of a lock that must be moved to a certain position (e.g. by a key) for the bolt to be thrown ‖ the part of the hammer in a gunlock on which the mainspring acts ‖ a roly-poly (weighted toy)

tum·ble·weed (tʌ́mbˈlwiːd) *n.* any of various plants that break away from their roots at maturity and are blown by the wind over the prairies, scattering seed

tumbling barrel a revolving box containing emery powder in which castings etc. are cleaned by friction ‖ a similar device in which plastics, leather, clothes etc. are whirled as part of a finishing process

tumbling bay a weir

tumbling box a tumbling barrel for small articles

tum·brel, tum·bril (tʌ́mbrəl) *n.* a heavy two-wheeled farm tipcart for carting manure etc. ‖ an open cart used in the French Revolution to carry victims to the guillotine [fr. M.L. *tumbrellum, tumberellum*, a ducking stool fr. O.F.]

tu·me·fac·tion (tuː mifǽkʃən, tjuː mifǽkʃən) *n.* a tumefying or being tumefied ‖ a swollen part

tu·me·fy (túː mifai, tjúː mifai) *pres. part.* **tume·fy·ing** *past* and *past part.* **tume·fied** *v.t.* to cause to swell, inflate ‖ *v.i.* to become swollen ‖ to become tumid [F. *tuméfier*]

tu·mes·cence (tu:mésˈns, tju:mésˈns) *n.* a swelling up or the state of swelling up ‖ a swollen part [TUMESCENT]

tu·mes·cent (tu:mésˈnt, tju:mésˈnt) *adj.* becoming swollen ‖ somewhat tumid [fr. L. *tumescens* (*tumescentis*) fr. *tumescere*, to swell up]

tu·mid (túː mid, tjúː mid) *adj.* swollen ‖ (of language) bombastic, inflated **tu·mid·i·ty** *n.* [fr. L. *tumidus*]

tum·my (tʌ́mi) *pl.* **tum·mies** *n.* (a child's word, or euphemism) the stomach or belly

tu·mor, Br. tu·mour (túː mər, tjúː mər) *n.* a body swelling, esp. an abnormal growth of tissue, either benign or malignant [L. *tumor* = a swelling]

tu·mor·gen·ic or **tum·or·i·gen·ic** (túː mərdʒénik) *adj.* (*med.*) causing or tending to cause tumors —**tumorigenesis** *n.* the creation of tumors

tu·mor·ous (túː mərəs, tjúː mərəs) *adj.* of, like or relating to a tumor ‖ having tumors or a tumor [fr. L. *tumorosus*]

tumour *TUMOR

Tu·muc-Hu·mac Mtns (tu:múː ku:mák) a range (2,000-3,000 ft) in N. Brazil, extending west to east along the boundary between Suriname and French Guiana on the north and Brazil on the south

tu·mult (túː məlt, tjúː məlt) *n.* an uproar made by a crowd of people, esp. when rioting ‖ any noisy and violent, usually confused, disturbance ‖ a confused and excited state of mind or of the emotions ‖ a jumble of objects, words etc. **tu·mul·tu·ous** (tu:mʌ́ltʃu:əs, tju:mʌ́ltʃu:əs) *adj.* [fr. L. *tumultus*]

tu·mu·lus (túː mjuləs, tjúː mjuləs) *pl.* **tu·mu·li** (túː mjulai, tjúː mjulai) *n.* an ancient burial mound [L. = a mound]

tun (tʌn) *n.* a large cask for beer, wine etc. ‖ a measure of liquid capacity (esp. one equivalent to 252 wine gallons) ‖ a brewer's fermenting vat [O.E. *tunne*]

tu·na (túː nə, tjúː nə) *n.* a member of *Thunnus*, fam. *Scombroidea*, a genus of large marine fishes, esp. *T. thynnus*, a highly prized game and food fish, living in shoals in temperate seas and sometimes growing up to 10 ft in length ‖ the flesh of this fish [Am. Span., perh. rel. to L. *tunnus, thunnus*, tunny]

tuna *n.* a member of *Opuntia*, a genus of prickly pears, esp. *O. tuna* of Central America and the West Indies ‖ the edible fruit of these plants [Span., of West Indian origin]

tun·a·ble laser (túː nəbˈl) a laser that can be adjusted to cover the light spectrum used in holography, plasma physics, and spectroscopy

Tuna War prohibition of tuna fishing by Peru for an area 200 mi off its coast (1972–1977), resulting in ship seizures and other incidents *Cf* COD WAR

tun·dra (tʌ́ndrə) *n.* an often flat, treeless plain largely covered with mosses and lichens, having a marshy soil with a permanently frozen subsoil, found in Arctic and subarctic regions [Russ.]

tune (tu:n, tju:n) **1.** *n.* a succession of notes so related that they constitute a musical structure, with a sequence and rhythm which are relatively simple, esp. the melody in the upper part of a simple composition ‖ correct musical pitch, *to sing out of tune* ‖ harmonious relationship, *in tune with current ideas* **to change one's tune** to adopt a radically different attitude towards something or someone **to the tune of** to the amount of **2.** *v. pres. part.* **tun·ing** *past* and *past part.* **tuned** *v.t.* to adjust (an instrument) to correct musical pitch ‖ (*radio*) to adjust (a circuit) with respect to resonant frequency ‖ (*radio*) to adjust (a receiving apparatus) to the wavelength of a particular transmitter ‖ to adjust (a motor) so that it runs perfectly ‖ *v.i.* (*radio*, with 'in') to adjust a radio receiver to the wavelength of a particular transmitter ‖ (of an orchestra, with 'up') to check instruments for pitch in readiness to play **túne·ful** *adj.* melodious ‖ full of catchy airs **tún·er** *n.* a person whose job is to tune pianos, organs etc. ‖ (*radio*) a res-

onant circuit, or more than one, in a receiving set [perh. var. of TONE]

tune out *v.* **1.** to cease watching a television broadcast or listening to radio broadcast by turning to another channel or turning off the receiver **2.** (*colloq.*) by extension, to refuse to notice

Tung·hai (túŋhái) *SINHAILEN

tung oil (tʌŋ) an oil extracted from the seeds of any of several Chinese trees of genus *Aleurites*, fam. *Euphorbiaceae*, esp. *A. fordii*, and used mainly in the manufacture of hard-drying paints, varnishes etc. [fr. Chin. *yu t'ung* fr. *yu*, oil + *t'ung*, name of the tree]

Tung·shan (túŋʃán) *SUCHOW

tung·sten (tʌ́ŋstən) *n.* a metallic element akin to chromium (symbol W, at. no. 74, at. mass 183.85) It has the highest melting point of all metals. It is used esp. in electric light filaments and for alloying steel **túng·stic** *adj.* [Swed. fr. *tung*, heavy + *sten*, stone]

Tung·ting Hu (túŋtíŋhúː) a lake (area 4,000 sq. miles in the rainy season) in N.E. Hunan, China, fed by many rivers, and connected by canal to the Yangtze, for which it serves as overflow during the summer rains

Tun·gus (tuŋgúːz) *pl.* **Tun·gus, Tun·gus·es** *n.* a member of a people of esp. Siberia speaking Tungusic languages. They number about 45,000. They are mainly reindeer herdsmen and fishermen, and practice Shamanism ‖ their Tungusic language **Tun·gu·sic 1.** *n.* a subfamily of Altaic languages of central and E. Siberia and Manchuria, including Manchu **2.** *adj.* of the Tungus people ‖ of Tungusic

Tun·gu·ska (tʌŋgúːskə) the name of three tributaries of the Yenisei in central Siberia, U.S.S.R.: the Lower Tunguska (2,550 miles long), rising north of L. Baikal, the Stony Tunguska (980 miles), further south, and the Upper Tunguska (another name for the Lower Angara)

tu·nic (túː nik, tjúː nik) *n.* (*hist.*) a loose, knee-length or longer, usually sleeveless, slip-on garment belted at the waist and worn by men and women in ancient Greece and Rome ‖ (*Br.*) a jumper (sleeveless slip-on garment) ‖ (esp. *Br.*) a short, close-fitting jacket worn e.g. by policemen ‖ a short garment worn by girls and women for dancing classes, sports etc. ‖ (*eccles.*) a tunicle ‖ a tunica [fr. L. *tunica*]

tu·ni·ca (túː nikə, tjúː nikə) *pl.* **tu·ni·cae** (túː niki:, tjúː niki:) *n.* (*anat., zool.*) a membrane or tissue encasing or covering an organ [Mod. L. = coat]

tu·ni·cate (túː nikit, tjúː nikit) **1.** *adj.* (*biol.*) covered with a tunica ‖ of or relating to a tunicate ‖ (*bot.*) having many concentric layers, e.g. a bulb ‖ (esp. of insects) having each joint buried in the preceding one **2.** *n.* any member of the subphylum *Urochorda*, degenerate sessile marine animals, the larvae of which show typical chordate features, but which lack most chordate characteristics in the adult form (e.g. the sea squirt) **tu·ni·cat·ed** (túː nikeitid, tjúː nikeitid) *adj.* [fr. L. *tunicatus*], to clothe with a tunic]

tu·ni·cle (túː nik'l, tjúː nik'l) *n.* (*eccles.*) a short vestment worn by a subdeacon over the alb at Mass ‖ a close-fitting vestment worn under the dalmatic by a bishop at pontifical Mass ‖ (*anat.*) a tunica [fr. L. *tunicula*, a little tunic]

TU-95 *TU-20

tuning fork a two-pronged steel instrument which gives a tone of constant pitch when struck, thus serving as a standard for tuning instruments or for indicating pitch to voices

Tu·nis (túː nis, tjúː nis) the capital (pop. 550,404), commercial center and (with its outport La Goulette) chief port of Tunisia, on the northeast coast. Industries: superphosphates and other chemical products, metallurgy, building materials, food processing, fishing, handicrafts. Great Mosque (8th-9th cc.), casbah (13th c.), medieval quarters

Tu·ni·sia (tu:níː ʒə, tu:níː ʃə) a republic (area 63,362 sq. miles, pop. 6,629,600) in N. Africa. Capital: Tunis. People: Arab (94%), with small European and Berber minorities. Language: Arabic, French, small Berber and Italian minorities. Religion: Sunni Moslem (state religion), 4% Roman Catholic, small Orthodox, Jewish and Protestant minorities. The land is 13% arable, 23% pasture and grazing, and 6% forest (cork, oak, pine). The wooded E. Atlas Mtns (highest peak 5,065 ft) cross the north, cut by wide, fertile plains (cereals), which with the eastern coastal zone (citrus fruit in the north, olives in the south) and Djerba constitute the

CONCISE PRONUNCIATION KEY: **(a)** æ, *cat*; ɑ, *car*; ɔ *fawn*; ei, *snake*. **(e)** e, *hen*; iː, *sheep*; iə, *deer*; ɛə, *bear*. **(i)** i, *fish*; ai, *tiger*; əː, *bird*. **(o)** o, *ox*; au, *cow*; ou, *goat*; u, *poor*; ɔi, *royal*. **(u)** ʌ, *duck*; u, *bull*; uː, *goose*; ə, *bacillus*; juː, *cube*. x, *loch*; θ, *think*; ð, *bother*; z, *Zen*; ʒ, *corsage*; dʒ, *savage*; ŋ, *orangutang*; j, *yak*; ʃ, *fish*; tʃ, *fetch*; 'l, *rabble*; 'n, *redden*. Complete pronunciation key appears inside front cover.

agricultural region. The center is dry steppe (livestock), merging with the Sahara in the south. Average temperatures (F.): Tunis 53° (Jan.), 79° (July). Rainfall: northern mountains over 24 ins, northeast and center 16-24 ins, Tunis 16 ins, Sfax 8 ins, Gafsa 4 ins. Livestock: sheep, goats, cattle, donkeys, camels, horses. Agricultural products: cereals, olives, citrus fruit, dates (Saharan oases), vines, esparto, tobacco, vegetables. Forestry products: lumber, cork. Minerals: phosphates, iron ore, lead and zinc, natural gas, silver. Manufactures and industries: textiles, carpets, leather goods, footwear, pottery, copperware, olive oil refining, wines and liquors, fishing, food processing, cement. Exports: olive oil, phosphates, wines, iron ore, fruit, wheat, lead, dates. Imports: foodstuffs, machinery, fuels and oil, iron and steel, textiles, clothing, vehicles, paper, chemicals. Main ports: Tunis, Bizerta. University (in Tunis). Monetary unit: Tunisian dinar (1,000 milliemes). HISTORY. Tunisia was colonized by the Phoenicians, who founded (c. 814 B.C.) the city of Carthage. This was destroyed (146 B.C.) by the Romans. The area was conquered by the Vandals (5th c. A.D.), became part of the Byzantine Empire (6th c.) and was conquered by the Arabs (7th c.). The native Berbers were converted to Islam. Tunisia became part of the Ottoman Empire (16th c.) and a center of Barbary pirates. The beys of Tunisia gained virtual independence, but were heavily in debt by the 19th c. and submitted to Italian and French intervention. Tunisia became a French protectorate (1881), though this was contested by Italy until the 2nd world war, when Tunisia was a center of the N. African campaign. A nationalist movement developed under Bourguiba, and Tunisia became independent (Sept. 1, 1955) and a republic (July 25, 1957) with Bourguiba as president. The country joined the United Nations (1956) and the Arab League (1958). Palestinian Liberation Organization headquarters moved to Tunis in 1982. In 1983, Tunisia, Algeria and Mauritania signed a cooperation treaty

tunnage *TONNAGE

tun·nel (tʌn'l) 1. n. a passageway of wide section cut through a hill or cliff side or under the ground, sea or a river, and made permanent with masonry, for a road or railroad to go through ‖ (*mining*) an underground gallery ‖ a passage dug underground by an animal ‖ a wind tunnel 2. v. *pres. part.* **tun·nel·ing**, esp. Br. **tun·nel·ling** *past and past part.* **tun·neled**, esp. Br. **tun·nelled** *v.t.* to pass through or under (something) with or as if with a tunnel ‖ *v.i.* to make or use a tunnel [O.F. *tonel*]

tunnel curl tube (*surfing*) the arch of an ocean wave just before it breaks

tunnel diode (*electr.*) a junction diode containing a thin depletion layer, permitting electrons to bypass a negative-resistant barrier, used for amplification at low levels, switching, and computer data storage *also* Esaki diode

tunnel vision 1. straight-ahead vision without periphery 2. (*colloq.*) by extension, narrow-mindedness

tun·ny (tʌni:) *pl.* **tun·nies** *n.* tuna [prob. fr. F. *thon* fr. Prov. or Ital. fr. L. fr. Gk]

TU-154A *n.* (*mil.*) NATO code name 'Careless,' U.S.S.R. transport aircraft with 87,630-lb capacity, 3,727-mi range, capable of carrying 120 passengers

TU-144 *n.* (*mil.*) U.S.S.R. transport with a speed of Mach 2.35, capable of carrying 140 passengers, competitive with Concorde

TU-134 *n.* (*mil.*) U.S.S.R. short-to-medium-range bomber with turbofan engines, 18,000-lb capacity, range of 500 mi.

tup (tʌp) 1. *n.* (Br.) a ram (male sheep) ‖ the striking face of a steam hammer ‖ any of various devices acting as hammers, e.g. a pile driver 2. v. *pres. part.* **tup·ping** *past and past part.* **tupped** *v.t.* (Br., of a ram) to cover (a ewe) ‖ *v.i.* (Br., of a ewe) to accept the ram [etym. doubtful]

Tú·pac A·ma·ru (tú:pʌkʌmáːru:) (d. 1579), Peruvian Inca who rebelled against Spanish rule and was executed by order of Francisco de Toledo (viceroy 1569-81, d. c. 1582)

Túpac Amaru (né José Gabriel Condorcanqui, 1742-81), Peruvian cacique and descendant of the Incas. He rebelled (1780) against Spanish rule. He was defeated (1781) by the forces under viceroy Agustín de Jáuregui y Aldecoa, and he and his family were tortured and executed

Tu·pa·ma·ros (tu:pəmárous) an extreme left-wing organization in Uruguay which is also known as the National Liberation Movement. It is named after Túpac Amaru and specializes in urban guerrilla warfare

tu·pe·lo gum (tú:pəlou, tjú:pəlou) *Nyssa aquatica*, fam. *Cornaceae*, a swamp tree of the southern U.S.A. ‖ its wood, used for cheap construction work and inexpensive furniture [Creek]

Tu·pi (tú:pi:) *pl.* **Tu·pi, Tu·pis** *n.* a member of a group of Tupi-Guaranian peoples inhabiting parts of Brazil, esp. the valleys of the Amazon ‖ their language, serving as a lingua franca in the Amazon valley **Tú·pi·an** *adj.* of or relating to the Tupi or other Tupi Guaranian peoples or the Tupi language

Tu·pi-Gua·ra·ni (tú:pi:gwɑrɑni:) *n.* a South American people living in an area extending from eastern Brazil to the Peruvian Andes, and from Guiana to Uruguay ‖ a member of this people ‖ Tupi-Guaranian **Tú·pi-Gua·rá·ni·an** 1. *adj.* of or relating to the Tupi-Guarani 2. *n.* a group of languages widely distributed in tropical South America and including Tupi and Guarani

tuppence *TWOPENCE

tuppenny *TWOPENNY

Tu·pun·ga·to (tu:pu:ŋgátɔ) a peak (22,300 ft) in the Andes Mtns on the Chile-Argentina border, about 40 miles northeast of Santiago, Chile

Tu·ra (tú:ra), Cosimo (c. 1430–c. 1498), Italian painter of Ferrara, much influenced by Mantegna

tu·ra·cin (túərəsin, tjúərəsin) *n.* a red pigment containing copper, obtained from the touraco

Tu·ra·ni·an (turéini:ən, tjuréini:ən) 1. *n.* the Ural-Altaic family of languages ‖ a member of any of the peoples who speak them 2. *adj.* of these languages or the people who speak them [fr. Pers. *Turān*, region north of the oxus]

tur·ban (tɔ́:rbən) *n.* a headdress, formed of a long piece of cloth wound around the head or sometimes around a cap, worn by men, esp. in eastern Mediterranean and southern Asian countries ‖ a hat for women resembling this **túr·baned** *adj.* [fr. Pers. *dulband, dōlband*]

tur·ba·ry (tɔ́:rbəri:) *pl.* **tur·ba·ries** *n.* a place where turf or peat is dug ‖ (Br. law) the right to dig turf on another person's land [A.F. *turberie* fr. O.F.]

tur·bel·lar·i·an (tə:rbəléəri:ən) *n.* a member of Turbellaria, a class of free-living, soft-bodied flatworms of the phylum *Platyhelminthes*, living in fresh or salt water or occasionally on land. Some are parasitic [fr. Mod. L. *Turbellaria* fr. L. *turbella*, a little crowd]

tur·bid (tɔ́:rbid) *adj.* having the sediment stirred up ‖ thick, dense, e.g. with smoke ‖ not clear, muddled in thought or feeling **tur·bid·i·ty** *n.* [fr. L. *turbidus*, disturbed]

tur·bid·im·e·ter (tə:rbədímətə:r) *n.* a device that measures the amount of suspended solids in a liquid

turbidity 1. haziness in the atmosphere due to pollution 2. murkiness in water due to suspended materials

tur·bi·nal (tɔ́:rbin'l) 1. *adj.* turbinate 2. *n.* a turbinate bone or cartilage

tur·bi·nate (tɔ́:rbinit) 1. *adj.* (*anat.*) of the thin, scroll-like, bony or cartilaginous plates on the walls of the nasal chambers ‖ (*zool.*, of a shell) rolled in sharply decreasing spiral whorls ‖ (*bot.*) shaped like a cone resting on its apex 2. *n.* a turbinate bone ‖ a turbinate shell **tur·bi·nat·ed** (tɔ́:rbineitid) *adj.* **tur·bi·na·tion** *n.* [fr. L. *turbinatus* fr. *turbo*, a whirlwind]

tur·bine (tɔ́:rbain, tɔ́:rbin) *n.* an engine, usually consisting of curved vanes on a central rotating spindle, actuated by the reaction, impulse, or both, of a current (water, steam or gas) subjected to pressure. Turbines are more economical, mechanically simpler, and at higher speed provide more regular rotation than reciprocating engines [F. fr. L. *turbo* (*turbinis*), a whirlwind]

tur·bo·car (tɔ́:rboukɑr) *n.* (*automobile*) fuel-efficient motor vehicle powered by a turbine engine

tur·bo·charg·er (tɔ́:rboutʃɑrdʒə:r) *n.* (*automobile*) a device for motor vehicles using exhaust gases to force the air-fuel mixture into cylinders, causing a bigger detonation than in normally aspirated motors

tur·bo·cop·ter (tɔ́:rboukɒptə:r) *n.* a helicopter deriving its power from gas turbine engines

tur·bo·e·lec·tric (tɔ́:rbouiléktrik) *adj.* of a turbine generator used as a power source

tur·bo·fan (tɔ́:rboufæn) *n.* (*aerospace*) gas turbine engine that shares its power with a multi-bladed propeller, used esp. for ventilation *also* ducted fan

turbojet a jet engine with air supplied by a turbine-driven compressor, the turbine being activated by exhaust gases

tur·bo·jet engine (tɔ́:rboudʒet) (*aeron.*) a jet engine having a compressor, driven by the power developed from a turbine, which supplies compressed air to the combustion chamber, and having a discharge nozzle directing heated air and gases rearward

tur·bo·prop (tɔ́:rbouprɒp) *n.* a jet engine having a turbine-driven propeller, usually with additional thrust from the expulsion of hot exhaust gases ‖ an aircraft powered by such an engine [short for *turbo-propeller engine*]

tur·bo·pump (tɔ́:rboupʌmp) *n.* a pump that is powered by a ram-air turbine and full or hydraulic pump, used for guided missiles and as emergency equipment for aircraft, e.g., in a nuclear rocket

tur·bo·shaft (tɔ́:rbouʃæft) *n.* a turbine engine used through a transmission system to power helicopter rotors, pumps, etc.

tur·bot (tɔ́:rbət) *pl.* **tur·bot, tur·bots** *n.* *Psetta maxima*, a European flatfish weighing up to 30 or 40 lbs, highly valued as food [O.F. *tourbout*]

tur·bo·train (tɔ́:rboutrein) *n.* turbine engine-powered train

tur·bu·lence (tɔ́:rbjuləns) *n.* the state or quality of being turbulent **túr·bu·len·cy** *n.*

tur·bu·lent (tɔ́:rbjulənt) *adj.* in a state of commotion or stormy agitation ‖ violent by nature and hard to control ‖ (*phys.*, of flow) erratic in velocity [fr. L. *turbulentus* fr. *turbare*, to disturb (*turba*, a crowd)]

tu·reen (turí:n, tjurí:n) *n.* a deep, covered dish for holding soup etc. [F. *terrine*]

Tu·renne (tyren), Henri de la Tour d'Auvergne, vicomte de (1611-75), French marshal. He displayed his genius for strategy in the Thirty Years' War, the wars of the Fronde, the War of Devolution and the 3rd Dutch War

turf (tɔ:rf) 1. *pl.* **turves**, **turfs** *n.* grass and the earth in which its matted roots are mingled ‖ a piece of this peat used as fuel ‖ (*pop.*) the grass-grown surface of a piece of land ‖ (with 'the') horseracing 2. *v.t.* to cover with turf **to turf out** (Br.) to throw out or away **túrf·y** *adj.* [O.E.]

Tur·fan (túrfán) a depression (about 5,000 sq. miles) in the Tarim basin, E. Sinkiang, China, south of the Tien Shan, containing the lowest point (425 ft below sea level) in Asia. An Indo-Persian civilization flourished here (c. 300 A.D.) ‖ an oasis trading town (pop. 20,000) at its northern edge: Buddhist temples, sculptures, Nestorian and Manichaean manuscripts

Tur·ge·nev (tə:rgéinjev), Ivan Sergeyevich (1818-83), Russian writer. His work was unpopular in official circles, partly because of his liberal Western tendencies. 'A Sportsman's Sketches' (1852), a collection of stories of peasant life, was an impassioned plea for the abolition of serfdom. His other works include the play 'A Month in the Country' (1850) and the novel 'Fathers and Sons' (1862). He influenced Chekhov and, through him, European literature as a whole

tur·ges·cence (tə:rdʒés'ns) *n.* the condition of being swollen ‖ a swelling ‖ (*rhet.*) bombast

tur·ges·cent (tə:rdʒés'nt) *adj.* becoming turgid or swollen [fr. L. *turgescens* (*turgescentis*) fr. *turgescere*, to swell up]

tur·gid (tɔ́:rdʒid) *adj.* unhealthily or abnormally swollen ‖ bombastic, inflated, *a turgid literary style* **tur·gid·i·ty** *n.* [fr. L. *turgidus* fr. *turgere*, to swell]

tur·gor (tɔ́:rgər) *n.* (esp. *bot.*) normal turgidity in living cells or tissues, esp. due to the taking up of fluid [L.L. fr. L. *turgere*, to swell]

Tur·got (tyrgou), Anne Robert Jacques, Baron de l'Aulne (1727-81), French economist, controller general of finances (1774-6). Influenced by the teachings of the physiocrats, he attempted a radical reform of the French economy, freeing trade, encouraging industry and attacking monopolies. The privileged classes rallied against him, and brought about his fall

Tu·rin (túərin, tjúərin, turín, tjurín) (*Ital.* Torino) an industrial center (pop. 1,143,263) in Piedmont, Italy, on the Po. Industries: automobiles, mechanical engineering, chemical industries, textiles, food processing, vermouth.

Cathedral (15th c.), palaces (12th-14th and 17th cc.), museums (celebrated Egyptian and Renaissance art collections), libraries, university (1404). Of pre-Roman origin, Turin was ruled by the house of Savoy (13th-18th cc.) and became the capital of the kingdom of Sardinia in 1720. It was the capital of Italy 1861-5

Tu·ring machine (tú:riŋ) (*computer*) a mathematical model of a computer with a potentially infinite storage capacity; named for A. M. Turing, English mathematician (1912–1954)

tu·ri·on (túəri:ən, tjúəri:ən) *n.* (*bot.*) a young, scaly shoot, e.g. as asparagus shoot, rising from a bud on an underground stem [F. fr. L. *turio* (*turionis*), shoot]

Turk (tə:rk) *n.* a native or inhabitant of Turkey, esp. one of the Moslem people of Turkey ‖ a member of any of numerous Asiatic peoples speaking a Turkic language

Tur·ke·stan (tə:rkistǽn, tə:kistán) a historical region of central Asia, now comprising W. Sinkiang-Uighur (China) and Kazakhstan, Kirghizia, Tadzhikistan, Uzbekistan and Turkmenistan (U.S.S.R.). It was chiefly under Persian and Chinese influence until conquered by the Arabs (8th c.). It was invaded by Genghis Khan (13th c.) and Timur (14th c.). Bukhara and Samarkand became centers of culture and trade. The east remained under Chinese control, and the west was annexed by Russia (1853-76)

Tur·key (tə́:rki:) a republic (area 301,302 sq. miles, pop. 49,155,000) in W. Asia and S.E. Europe. Capital: Ankara. Chief city: Istanbul. People: 84% Turks, 12% Kurds, 1% Arabs, small Circassian, Greek, Georgian, Armenian and Bulgarian minorities. Language: 90% Turkish, 6% Kurdish, minority languages. Religion: 98% Moslem, 1% Christian (mainly Greek Orthodox and Gregorian), small Jewish minority. The land is 32% arable, 37% pasture and 13% forest. Trakya or Thrace (European Turkey) is a rolling, cultivated plain with mountains on the north and south. Asian Turkey (Anatolia, Armenia and Kurdistan), except for coastal plains, is an elevated plateau (mainly 6,000–10,000 ft), crossed by many high ranges, esp. east of the Mediterranean, and cut by river valleys. Highest peaks: Buyak Agri or Ararat (16,946 ft), Suphan (13,697 ft). The plateau, partly cultivated (esp. in the west), is largely semidesert, with alpine pasture and evergreen forest on higher slopes and in the east. The Black Sea slopes are fertile. Average temperatures (F.) in Jan. and July: Istanbul 42° and 74°, central Black Sea coast 45° and 74°, Ankara 30° and 75°, Erzurum 15° and 66°, E. Syrian border 65° and 85°. Rainfall: Lake Tuz basin 1-8 ins, Istanbul 24 ins, central Black Sea coast 28 ins, E. Black Sea coast 92 ins, Ankara 13 ins, Erzurum 20 ins. Livestock: sheep, goats, cattle, donkeys, mules, horses, water buffalo, camels. Agricultural products: cotton, tobacco, cereals (esp. wheat), olives and olive oil, silk, dried fruits, dairy products, rice, hemp, flax, sugar beets, grapes, figs, citrus fruit, nuts, licorice root, almonds, mohair, skins and hides, furs, wool, gums, canary seed, linseed, sesame, vegetables, sultana raisins, opium. Forestry products: pine, fir, beech, cedar, oak. Mineral resources: coal, petroleum, iron ore, uranium, chrome, sulfur, copper, antimony, manganese, salt, tungsten, lignite. Manufactures and industries: mining, textiles, iron and steel, fishing, cement, paper and pulp, carpets, glass, pottery, hydroelectricity, tourism, silk, sugar, leather, chemicals, fertilizers, canned goods, wines and liquor, vegetable oils, soap, oil refining. Exports: tobacco, fruit and nuts, cotton, mohair, livestock, minerals, sugar, hides and skins. Imports: machinery, cereals, vehicles, oil and petroleum products, iron and steel, chemicals, fabrics and yarns, rubber, paper. Chief ports: Istanbul, Izmir. Universities: Istanbul (2), Ankara (2), Izmir and Erzurum. Monetary unit: Turkish pound or lira (100 piasters or kurus). HISTORY. (For early history *ASIA MINOR, *THRACE, *OTTOMAN EMPIRE.) The overthrow (1922) of the Ottoman Empire by Atatürk was followed by the Treaty of Lausanne (1923) and the proclamation of a republic (Oct. 29, 1923). Under Atatürk's dictatorial presidency (1923-38), many Western reforms were introduced and economic problems were tackled. Turkey joined he Balkan Entente (1934) but remained neutral in the 2nd world war until 1945, when it declared war on Germany and Japan. It joined the U.N. (1945), NATO (1952), the Bal-

kan Pact (1954) and the Central Treaty Organization (1955). The government was overthrown (1960) by a coup d'état, and a new constitution was introduced (1961). Greek and Turkish sections of the population on Cyprus erupted in fighting in 1964. In 1974, Cypriot President Makarios had been overthrown and Greece seemed about to annex the island, prompting Turkish troops to invade and occupy almost half of the island. U.S.-Turkey relations suffered from the continuing Turkish presence in Cyprus: in 1975 the U.S.A. cut off military aid to Turkey and Turkey promptly closed U.S. military bases in Turkey. Some bases were reopened following negotiations the following year. Aegean Sea oil exploration further exacerbated tensions between Greece and Turkey, and political and economic conditions in Turkey worsened as oil prices rose and terrorism became more of a problem. In 1980 the military took control of the government

tur·key (tə́:rki:) *pl.* **tur·keys** *n. Meleagris gallopavo*, fam. *Meleagrididae*, a large (up to 4 ft long and up to 35 lbs in weight) gallinaceous American bird domesticated in many parts of the world, raised mainly for its excellent flesh **to talk turkey** to be realistic in commercial bargaining, esp. by making proposals likely to be acceptable [short for TURKEYCOCK, applied in the 16th c. to the guinea fowl]

turkey (*slang*) 1. a failure; a flop 2. an inpatient whom a hospital believes does not need hospital admission, not usu. a malingerer

turkey buzzard *Cathartes aura*, fam. *Cathartidae*, a vulture of South and Central America and the southern U.S.A.

tur·key-cock (tə́:rki:kɒk) *n.* a male turkey

Tur·ki (tə́:rki:) 1. *adj.* of any of the central Asian Turkic languages ‖ of the peoples who speak these languages 2. *n.* these languages ‖ any of the peoples who speak them

Tur·kic (tə́:rkik) 1. *adj.* of or relating to a subfamily of the Altaic language group ‖ of or relating to any of the people who speak these languages ‖ (*loosely*) Turkish 2. *n.* the Turkic subfamily of languages

Turk·ish (tə́:rkiʃ) 1. *adj.* of Turkey or the Turks ‖ of the Turkic languages, esp. of Osmanli 2. *n.* the Turkic language of Turkey, esp. Osmanli

Turkish bath a bath in which a person is surrounded by hot steam and made to perspire heavily and is then given a massage and a cold shower ‖ the place where such a bath is given

Turkish delight a jellylike candy, cut in cubes and dusted with sugar

Turkish Empire the Ottoman Empire

Turkish tobacco a highly aromatic tobacco used chiefly in cigarettes, and grown esp. in Turkey and Greece

Turkish towel a towel made of terry cloth

Turk·man (tə́:rkmən) *pl.* **Turk·men** (tə́:rkmən) *n.* a native of Turkmenistan ‖ a Turkoman

Turk·men (tə́:rkmən) *n.* the Turkic language of the Turkomans, Turkoman

Turk·me·ni·an (tə:rkmí:ni:ən) *adj.* of or relating to Turkmenistan or its people

Turk·me·ni·stan (tə:rkmenistán, tə:rkmenistán) a constituent republic (area 188,400 sq. miles, pop. 2,759,000) of the U.S.S.R. in central Asia. Capital: Ashkhabad. The Kara Kum desert occupies most of the region. Agriculture (dependent on irrigation): cotton, cereals, fruit, vines, vegetables. Livestock: camels, goats, sheep (esp. for astrakhan fur). Resources: oil, coal, sulfur, salt, magnesium. Industries: chemical manufactures, cotton, light engineering, oil refining. Part of Turkestan, it was conquered by Russia (1869-95) and became a constituent republic in 1924

Tur·ko·man (tə́:rkəmən) *pl.* **Tur·ko·mans** *n.* a member of any of a group of chiefly Moslem Turkic tribes inhabiting Turkmenistan, Uzbekistan and Kazakhstan, U.S.S.R. ‖ the language of the Turkomans

Tur·ko·men (tə́:rkəmən) Turkmenistan

Turks and Cai·cos Islands (tə:rks, káikɒs) two groups of islands (land area 166 sq. miles, pop. 7,436), nine being inhabited, at the east end of the Bahamas, geographically part of the latter but forming a distinct British Crown Colony. Main islands: Grand Caicos, Cockburn Town. Capital: Grand Turk (pop. 2,300). People: Afro-West Indian and mullatto. Exports: salt, fish, conch shell, sisal. The islands were discovered by the Spanish (1512), came under British control (18th c.) and were administered as a dependency of Jamaica (1874-1959). They were part

of the Federation of the West Indies (1959-62) and became a Crown Colony

Tur·ku (túrku:) (*Swed.* Abo) a port (pop. 163,665) in S.W. Finland. Industries: shipbuilding, textiles, food processing. Cathedral, castle (both 13th c.). Finnish (1922) and Swedish (1919) universities

turmaline *TOURMALINE

tur·mer·ic (tə́:rmərik) *n. Curcuma longa*, fam. *Zingiberaceae*, a perennial low-growing East Indian plant ‖ its yellow rhizome, dried and powdered and used esp. in curry powder, for coloring foods, as a stimulant and as a chemical indicator of alkalis, which turn the color reddish brown ‖ an orange or reddish-brown dye obtained from the rhizome [etym. doubtful]

tur·moil (tə́:rmɔil) *n.* violent agitation or great confusion, *mental turmoil* [etym. doubtful]

turn (tə:rn) 1. *v.t.* to cause to move through an arc of a circle or about an axis or central point, *to turn a wheel* ‖ to cause to move in this way as part of a process of opening or shutting, *to turn a door handle* ‖ to perform (a cartwheel, somersault or handspring) ‖ to shape (something) on a lathe ‖ to trim superfluous clay from (a pot) on a potter's wheel ‖ to cause (a lathe) to work (*knitting*) to form (a heel) by increasing and decreasing ‖ (sometimes with 'over') to put the other side of (a page) uppermost in order to read or write on it ‖ to dig or plow (soil) so as to bring to the surface the parts formerly lying underneath ‖ (with 'out') to expel, drive out ‖ (with 'out') to cause (something) to come out of its mold, *to turn out a jelly* ‖ to unpick (a garment or part of a garment) and sew it together again wholly or partially inside out so that the worn side is hidden, *to turn a collar* ‖ (with 'up') to make (a folded collar) stand up ‖ to alter the course of (something), *he turned the conversation to more cheerful topics* ‖ to proceed around (a corner) ‖ to cause to go away, or to send away, *to turn someone from one's door* ‖ (with 'on') to direct, aim, *turn the hose on the fire* ‖ to cause to change opinion or attitude, *the speech turned the crowd in our favor* ‖ to get beyond (a certain age), *he has turned 40* ‖ (with 'into') to drive, cause to enter, *to turn sheep into a pen* ‖ to affect (a person) in a specified way, *prison turned him bitter* ‖ to twist (an ankle) ‖ to make sour, rancid, bad, curdled, *the heat turned the milk*, or to seem to cause curdling in, *it turns one's stomach* ‖ to form or construct neatly or gracefully, *to turn a phrase* ‖ (with 'to') to cause (the mind, attention, thoughts) to concentrate on ‖ to cause to change color, *frost turned the leaves early* ‖ to cause to take on a specified color, *cold turned their ears pink* ‖ to cause (something) to change the direction in which it is facing, *turn your chair to the table* ‖ (with 'down') to fold back the sheets of (a bed) to make it ready to occupy ‖ (*mil.*) to go around, *to turn the enemy's flank* ‖ (*cricket*) to cause (a ball) to break ‖ (with 'into') to paraphrase, translate or express in different words, *can you turn the text into good English?* ‖ (with 'into' or 'to') to cause to be regarded in a specified way, *he turned the play into a farce* ‖ *v.i.* to move through an arc of a circle or about an axis or central point, *the wheel turned slowly* ‖ to use a lathe ‖ to become altered in form, outlook, attitude etc., *the wine turned to vinegar*, *the man turned nasty, the leaf turned yellow* ‖ to change direction, *turn right here, they turned and ran* ‖ (of leaves) to change color ‖ to become sour or rancid ‖ to be dependent for its development on something specified, *the plot turns on a lost bracelet* ‖ (esp. with 'toss and') to move about restlessly in bed ‖ (of the wind) to change quarter ‖ (of the tide) to start to ebb or flow ‖ (of the mind) to become deranged ‖ (of the eye, gaze etc.) to look ‖ (with 'from') to glance aside ‖ (with 'from') to face about so as not to see something, *she turned from the sight* ‖ to seem to go in a certain direction, *his thoughts turned homeward* ‖ (of the stomach) to be upset ‖ (of the head) to seem to reel ‖ (with 'to') to take up something as a new interest, hobby etc., *to turn to gardening* ‖ (with 'to') to change in nature, *sorrow turned to joy* ‖ (*impers.*, of the weather) to change in character in a specified way, *it turned to rain* **not to know which way to turn** not to know how to start dealing with harassing circumstances **to turn against** to become hostile towards or prejudiced against someone or something one formerly liked ‖ to cause (someone) to become hostile or prejudiced in this way **to turn away** to change the direction in which one is going or looking, from horror etc. or from indifference ‖ to send away (someone seeking admittance, work etc.) unsatisfied **to turn back** to abandon progress and return by the way one has come ‖ to cause (someone or something) to do this ‖ **to turn down** to reject (an offer, application, person proposing marriage or a proposal of marriage) ‖ to lessen the output of heat, light or sound of (something) by manipulating controls ‖ to manipulate controls to lessen (sound, heat, brightness) ‖ (of the mouth or of eyes at the corners) to point downwards **to turn in** (of feet, toes, eyes) to point inwards, *his toes turn in* ‖ to submit, hand in, *to turn in a report* ‖ to relinquish, give up to an authority, *he turned in his revolver to the police* ‖ (*Br.*) to trade (e.g. a car) in ‖ (*pop.*) to go to bed to sleep **to turn into** to change form and become, *tadpoles turn into frogs* ‖ to change in character and become, *it turned into a nice day* ‖ to transform, *to turn ideas into deeds* **to turn loose** to put (esp. domestic animals) to roam free e.g. in a field ‖ to leave complete liberty to, *you can turn him loose in the library* **to turn low** to decrease the flow of (sound, light, heat) by operating a control ‖ to decrease the flow of sound, light, heat in (something) by operating a control **to turn off** to stop the flow of (water, gas, oil, electric current, or sound, light or heat) by operating a control ‖ to stop the flow of water, gas, oil, electric current etc. by operating (a tap or switch) **to turn on** to make a sudden unexpected attack on, *the dog turned on its master* ‖ to start (water, gas, oil, electric current, or sound, light or heat) flowing by operating a control ‖ to start the flow of water, gas, oil, electric current etc. by operating (a tap or switch) **to turn out** (of feet) to point outwards ‖ to cause to have a specified quality with respect to dress or appearance, *a well turned-out regiment* ‖ to cause to assemble or parade, *turn out the guard* ‖ to empty, esp. for searching, *to turn out one's pockets* ‖ to turn off (a light etc.) ‖ to produce, *the factory turns out 5,000 cars a week* ‖ (*Br.*) to clean (e.g. a room) thoroughly ‖ to prove to be, *it turned out a disaster* ‖ to leave one's home to assemble, *the whole town turned out to welcome them* or (*Br.*) to leave the house and face bad weather, *do we have to turn out on such a night?* ‖ (*pop.*) to get out of bed **to turn over** to transfer ownership or responsibility for, *he turned over the business to his son* ‖ to think about, consider the different aspects of (something), *to turn over a problem* ‖ to buy and then sell (a stock of goods) in the course of business ‖ to trade to the value of, *they turn over a small fortune each month* ‖ to read cursorily or glance at (the pages of a book) **to turn to** to apply to, call on, for help ‖ to consult for reference ‖ (*pop.*) to begin to work in earnest **to turn up** (of eyes, noses, mouths, toes or shoes) to point slightly upward (a dress etc.) at the hem ‖ to fold (a hem) and stitch it, esp. so as to shorten a garment ‖ to expose (a playing card) ‖ to bring to the surface by digging etc. ‖ to increase the output of heat, light or sound of (something) by manipulating controls ‖ to manipulate controls in order to increase (sound, heat, brightness) ‖ to arrive, esp. unexpectedly ‖ to be found after being missing ‖ to happen in an unplanned way, *something will turn up to get you out of the difficulty* **2.** *n.* a turning through an arc of a circle or about an axis or central point ‖ the act of taking or changing a direction, *to make a turn to the right* ‖ a bend or curve where a change of direction occurs ‖ a single coil ‖ a winding of rope or wire etc. around something ‖ a twisted condition ‖ one of alternating or successive opportunities or obligations, *my turn to start, your turn to pay* ‖ (*Br.*) an act in a variety show, circus etc. ‖ a small unpleasant shock, *it gave him a turn to hear her voice* ‖ a sudden attack of feeling unwell or ill ‖ (*mus.*) an ornament around a written note, consisting of the notes above and below the written note and played in the order E D C D where the written note is D ‖ (*mus.*) the symbol (∾) indicating this ‖ a deed of a specified character done to someone, *a good turn* ‖ a development in the progress of something, *a new turn of affairs* ‖ (*Br., stock exchange*) the mean between a stock-jobber's buying and selling price ‖ a short walk or drive, *a turn around the town* ‖ a period of duty or activity, *a turn at the helm* ‖ a specific period in which a person or group of people is at work ‖ (*mil.*) a drill maneuver in which marching troops change direction by turning through 90° (cf. WHEEL) so as to advance in ranks not files ‖ a bent (mental inclination), *to be of a scientific turn* ‖ a form thought of as molded, *the turn of her neck, an ugly turn*

of phrase ‖ (of a year or century) the period when the date changes **at every turn** constantly and in all directions, *held up at every turn* **by turns** in succession **in turn** in proper sequence **on the turn** (of the tide) about to begin ebbing or flowing ‖ (of milk, butter etc.) beginning to go sour, rancid or bad **out of turn** not in proper sequence ‖ tactlessly, without prudence, *I'm afraid I spoke out of turn* **to a turn** to just the right degree **to serve someone's turn** to suffice for someone's particular need **to take turns** to do something one after another in regular order **turn and turn about** in turn [O.E. *tyrnan* and *turnian* fr. L. *tornare*, to turn in a lathe, round off]

turn·a·round (tə́:rnəraund) *adj.* of the time required to complete an operation and begin the next one

turn·buck·le (tə́:rnbʌk'l) *n.* a tubular link commonly having a right-hand thread on one end and a left-hand thread on the other, used for tightening a rod or wire

turn·coat (tə́:rnkout) *n.* a renegade

turn·down (tə́:rndaun) *adj.* made to be worn folded downwards, or able to be worn in this way

Tur·ner (tə́:rnər), Joseph Mallord William (1775-1851), English landscape painter. At first he worked exclusively in watercolor, but later he worked in oil as well. He began as an emulator of Claude's calm, static, visionary landscapes bathed in clear liquid light, but evolved steadily toward another vision: of the broken light and prismatic colors of an atmosphere which partly revealed, partly concealed the accidents of an actual scene. After Turner's first trip to Italy (1819) his works became remarkable for their color and luminosity and the swirling movement of his brushwork. Rushing wind, tossing water, broken and reflected light, a world of reflections and movement, a rainbow of pure colors: such things characterize his later art. He incorporated the iron ships, the trains and bridges of the industrial age, but they seem as visionary and phantasmal as all else in his universe. As a firm adherent of the direct vision in the open air, and as a keen analyst of the effects of light, Turner led to the French Impressionists

Turner, Nat (1800-31), black leader of the Southampton slave insurrection (1831) in Virginia. He believed himself to be prompted by divine inspiration, and he and his band of 60 murdered 55 whites before being captured and convicted. The incident led to stricter slave codes

turn·er (tə́:rnər) *n.* a person who works a lathe **túrn·er·y** *pl.* **turn·er·ies** *n.* the craft of lathe work ‖ the products of a turner ‖ a turner's workshop

Turner's syndrome *n.* (*med.*) an inherited sex aberration in which only one sex chromosome (X) is included in the chromosomes, named for American physician Henry Herbert Turner (1892–) also gonadial dysgenesis

turn·ing (tə́:rniŋ) *n.* a point where a road turns or where it diverges from another ‖ the act of a person or thing making a turn ‖ the process of shaping things on a lathe, turnery ‖ (*pl.*) scraps that become detached from material turned

turning point a point in any process or situation at which a decisive change occurs

tur·nip (tə́:rnip) *n. Brassica rapa*, fam. *Cruciferae*, a rough hairy-leaved biennial plant with a large fleshy taproot ‖ the rutabaga ‖ the root of either plant, used for stock and human food [earlier *turnepe, turnep* rel. to O.E. *nǣp*, a turnip fr. L.]

turn·key (tə́:rnkȳ) *pl.* **turn·keys** *n.* (*hist.*) a prison warder having charge of the keys

turnkey *adj.* complete and ready for use

turn·off (tə́:rnɔf, tə́:rnɒf) *n.* a side road ‖ a ramp leading from an express highway

turn off *v.* (*slang*) **1.** to cause a lack of interest in **2.** to become disinterested *ant.* turn on —**turn-off** *n.* —**turn-off, turned-off** *adj.*

turn on *v.* (*slang*) **1.** to awaken a strong interest in, *she turns me on.* **2.** to become interested in *ant.* turn off —**turn-on, turned-on** *adj.* —**turn-on** *n.*

turn·out (tə́:rnaut) *n.* a turning out ‖ a gathering of people for a demonstration, parade, meeting etc. ‖ personal appearance as regards dress and equipment ‖ a coach or carriage with its horse or horses, harness and attendants ‖ a clearing out of drawers and cupboards etc., usually with a view to cleaning ‖ the output of a product over a specified period

turn·o·ver (tə́:rnouvər) *n.* the total money received by a business from sales over a specified period or for a particular transaction ‖ the cycle of purchase, sale and replacement of stock in a business ‖ the rate at which this process is completed ‖ the rate of production of a machine ‖ the movement of people or things into and out of an establishment, *the depot's turnover of recruits doubled* ‖ the number of workers leaving employment and being replaced within a given period ‖ the ratio of this number to the average labor force maintained ‖ a pie or pastry made by folding one half of the crust upon the other half to contain meat, fruit or jam ‖ something that is turned over, e.g. the flap on an envelope ‖ (*Br.*) a newspaper article in essay style given a prominent position ‖ (*sports*) an error or violation that causes loss of the ball

turn·pike (tə́:rnpaik) *n.* (*hist.*) a tollgate ‖ a fast highway on which a toll is levied ‖ (*loosely*) any main road [TURN+older *pike*, pickaxe. A turnpike was originally a spiked road barrier]

turn·plate (tə́:rnpleit) *n.* (*rail.*) a turntable

turn·stile (tə́:rnstail) *n.* a gate, with four arms set at right angles, revolving on a central post, allowing the passage of only one person at a time, and used at entrances to ball parks etc.

turn·ta·ble (tə́:rnteib'l) *n.* (*rail.*) a circular revolving platform for reversing engines ‖ the revolving disk which carries the record in a record player ‖ any revolving disk or platform like these, e.g. one used for theatrical scenery

turn·up (tə́:rnʌp) **1.** *n.* (*Br.*) a trouser cuff **2.** *adj.* made to be turned or folded upwards

tur·pen·tine (tə́:rpəntain) *n.* an essential oil, chiefly pinene, derived by distilling the oleoresin secreted by several coniferous trees, esp. the terebinth [older *terebentyne, terbentyne* fr. O.F. L.]

Tur·pin (tə́:rpin), Dick (1706-39), English highwayman who, according to legend, rode his horse Black Bess without a stop from London to York, in an effort to escape capture. He was hanged

tur·pi·tude (tə́:rpitu:d, tə́:rpitju:d) *n.* inherent wickedness ‖ a particular example of such wickedness [F.]

Tur·qui·no, Pico (tu:rkí:nɔ) *SIERRA MAESTRA

tur·quoise (tə́:rkwɔiz, tə́:rkɔiz) **1.** *n.* an opaque sky-blue or blue-green precious stone, consisting of basic aluminum phosphate colored by traces of copper. It occurs in rock deposits, esp. in Iran, Arizona and New Mexico ‖ this bluegreen color **2.** *adj.* of this blue-green color [M.E. *turkeis* fr. O.F. *turqueise*, Turkish (because it was first introduced into Europe from Turkey)]

tur·ret (tə́:rit, tʌ́rit) *n.* a small tower projecting from the wall or a corner of a larger structure ‖ a revolving armored covering for a gun on a fort, ship or tank or mounted on a heavily armored aircraft ‖ a holder for cutting tools etc. in a machine tool ‖ (*hist.*) a very tall square structure on wheels used for assaulting a fortified place **túr·ret·ed** *adj.* having a turret or turrets ‖ (of a shell) having whorls that form a high turretlike spiral [O.F. *torete, tourete*]

turret lathe (*Am.=Br.* capstan lathe) a lathe with cutting tools held in a special head

tur·ric·u·late (təríkjulit) *adj.* having a small turret or shaped like one

tur·tle (tə́:rt'l) **1.** *pl.* **tur·tles, tur·tle** *n.* a reptile of the order *Testudinata* (or *Chelonia*), including both marine and terrestrial species (*TORTOISE), but (esp. *Br.*) popularly limited to the marine genera. 'Turtle' properly designates all reptiles with a shell. Turtles are characterized by having soft scaly-skinned bodies, strong, horny-edged, toothless jaws and retractile heads, limbs and tails. The turtle's characteristic shell is a case of bone, covered by horny shields. In some marine species the shell is more leathery than horny. Turtles may be herbivorous and/or carnivorous. They lay eggs which they bury in sand and leave to hatch by the heat of the sun. Their size can vary from a few inches to several feet. Turtles are longer-lived than other animals ‖ (*loosely*) a tortoise esp. a small one **to turn turtle** to turn upside down or capsize **2.** *v.i. pres. part.* **tur·tling** *past* and *past part.* **tur·tled** to hunt for turtles [O.E. *turtla, turtle* fr. L. *turtur*, a turtledove]

tur·tle·dove (tə́:rt'ldʌv) *n. Streptopelia turtur*, a small variety (11 ins) of lightbrown dove found throughout temperate areas of Europe and Asia. It is known for its plaintive cooing and the affection it shows for its mate [fr. obs. *turtle* fr. O.E. *turtla, turtle* fr. L. *turtur*+DOVE]

tur·tle·neck (tə:rt'lnɛk) *n.* (*Am.=Br.* poloneck) a turnover collar fitting the neck closely, mainly used for sweaters, or a sweater having such a collar ‖ (*Br.*) a high, close-fitting collar on a knitted garment, worn not turned down, or a sweater with such a collar

turves alt. *pl.* of TURF

Tus·can (táskən) 1. *adj.* of or referring to Tuscany or its inhabitants ‖ of or relating to or resembling one of the classical orders of Roman architecture characterized by the angular plainness of its capitals 2. *n.* an inhabitant or native of Tuscany ‖ any of the dialects spoken in Tuscany, esp. the one accepted as standard literary Italian [F. fr. L.L. *Tuscanus*]

Tus·ca·ny (táskəni) (*Ital.* Toscana) a region (area 8,876 sq. miles, pop. 3,600,233) of N.W. central Italy. Chief towns: Florence, Leghorn. The mountains of the north and east, and the hills of the center, are cut by broad river valleys opening on to a wide marshy coastal plain. Industries: agriculture (vines, wheat and other cereals, sugarcane, olives), mining (lignite, iron, sulfur, marble), textiles, wine, tourism. Its small medieval states (Pisa, Siena etc.) were united in the 15th and 16th cc. under Florence, which became (1569) the capital of the grand duchy of Tuscany and was incorporated (1860) into Sardinia

Tus·ca·ro·ra (tʌskərórə, tʌskəróurə) *pl.* **Tus·ca·ro·ra, Tus·ca·ro·ras** *n.* an Iroquois Indian people originally of North Carolina. War (1711-13) with the white settlers forced them to join the Iroquois League as a sixth nation ‖ a member of this people. In the 1960s they numbered about 700, in Canada and New York ‖ their language

tush (tʌʃ) *n.* a long pointed tooth, esp. the canine tooth of a horse ‖ a small or dwarfed tusk in some Indian elephants [var. of TUSK]

tusk (tʌsk) 1. *n.* a long, sharp tooth, often curved, which projects beyond the closed mouth of certain animals (e.g. the elephant, wild boar and walrus) and is used for digging up food or for defense ‖ (*carpentry*) an additional, strengthening tenon below a principal tenon 2. *v.t.* to gore, tear up etc. with tusks ‖ to provide with tusks **túsk·er** *n.* an elephant or wild boar with strongly developed tusks [O.E. *tusc, tux*]

tus·sah (tásə) *n.* a strong, coarse, light-brown silk obtained from the undomesticated silkworm which is the larva of the moth *Antheraea paphia* (or *A. mylitta*) ‖ a fabric (e.g. shantung) made of this silk ‖ the silkworm producing this silk [Hindi and Urdu *tasar*]

Tus·saud (tysou') Marie (1760-1850), Swiss founder of the famous 'Madame Tussaud's' (təsódz) permanent exhibition in London of some 500 life-size wax models of historical and contemporary figures

tus·sive (tásiv) *adj.* (*med.*) pertaining to or caused by a cough [fr. L. *tussis*, a cough]

tus·sle (tás'l) 1. *v.i. pres. part.* **tus·sling** *past* and *past part.* **tus·sled** to struggle in fight, sport or controversy 2. *n.* a struggle, scuffle or controversy [prob. rel. to TOUSLE]

tus·sock (tásək) *n.* a thick bunch of grass or sedge forming a little hillock [prob. alt. fr. obs. *tusk*, a tuft]

tus·sore (tásɔr) *n.* (esp. *Br.*) tussah

tut (tʌt) *interj.* an exclamation of remonstrance, impatience etc.

Tut·ankh·a·men (tʊˌtaŋkámən) Egyptian king (1352-1343 B.C.) of the 18th dynasty. His tomb, discovered (1922) almost intact near Thebes, yielded furniture and other funerary objects of great splendor, throwing new light on the art and life of ancient Egypt

tu·te·lage (tú:'lidʒ, tjú:'lidʒ) *n.* guardianship, protection ‖ instruction ‖ the state of being under a guardian or tutor [fr. L. *tutela*, guardianship]

tu·te·lar (tú:'lər, tjú:'lər) *adj.* tutelary

tu·te·lar·y (tú:'lɛri, tjú:'lɛri) 1. *adj.* pertaining to a guardian or to guardianship ‖ serving as a guardian 2. *pl.* **tu·te·lar·ies** *n.* a tutelary deity or saint [fr. L. *tutelarius* fr. *tutela*, protection]

Tu·ti·co·rin (tʊˌtikɔrín) a port (pop. 124,000) in S. Madras, India: cotton spinning, salt, pearl fishing

tu·tor (tú:tər, tjú:tər) 1. *n.* a private teacher ‖ (in some American universities) a teacher below the rank of instructor ‖ (*Br.*) an official responsible in some universities and colleges for the studies and in others for the welfare of a number of students ‖ (*Br.*) a book of instructions, *a guitar tutor* 2. *v.t.* to teach privately or on an

individual basis ‖ *v.i.* to earn a living by private or individual teaching **tú·tor·age** *n.* [O.F.]

tu·to·ri·al (tu:tóri:əl, tju:tór:i:əl, tu:tóuri:əl, tju:tóuri:əl) 1. *n.* a session of personal instruction with a college tutor 2. *adj.* of a tutor or tutors

tu·tor·ship (tú:tərʃip, tjú:tərʃip) *n.* the position or duties of a tutor

tut·ti (tú:ti:) 1. *adj.* (*mus.*) for all voices or instruments 2. *n.* (*mus.*) a passage for chorus or orchestra without soloists [Ital. pl. of *tutto*, all]

tut·ti-frut·ti (tú:ti:frú:ti:) *n.* a confection or an ice cream dish containing mixed (usually candied) fruits [Ital.=all fruits]

tut·ty (táti:) *n.* an impure zinc oxide obtained from zinc-smelting furnace flues and used as a polishing powder [F. *tutie* fr. Arab.]

Tu·tu (tú:tu:), Desmond Mpilo (1931-), African Anglican clergyman, who received the Nobel peace prize (1984) for his efforts to end apartheid in South Africa. Ordained in 1960, he became Anglican dean of Johannesburg (1975-6), bishop of Lesotho (1976-8) and the first black general secretary of the South African Council of Churches (1979) before being elected the first black bishop of Johannesburg (1984-86). From 1986 he was archbishop of Cape Town. An advocate of nonviolence, he has called for outside economic pressure to force South Africa's white-dominated government to end apartheid

tu·tu (tú:tu:) *n.* a ballet dancer's very short skirt of gauze frills [F.]

Tu·tu·ola (tu:tu:óulə), Amos (1920-), Nigerian writer, who writes in English. His novels include 'The Palm-Wine Drinkard' (1952), 'Simbi and the Satyr of the Dark Jungle' (1955), 'Feather Woman of the Jungle' (1962), 'Ajaiyi and His Inherited Poverty' (1967) and 'The Witch Herbalist of the Remote Town' (1980)

TU-20 *n.* (*mil.*) NATO code name 'Bear,' U.S.S.R. maritime reconnaissance plane with range of 7,800 mi, ceiling of 41,000 ft, speed of 500 mph (805 km) equipped with radar scanner, streamlined blisters for refueling (Formerly TU-95)

TU-28 *n.* (*mil.*) NATO code name 'Fiddler,' U.S.S.R. twin-jet interceptor with range of 3,100 mi speed of 1,150 mph, ceiling of 65,620 ft.

Tu·va A.S.S.R. (tú:və) an autonomous republic (area 65,810 sq. miles, pop. 274,000) of the R.S.F.S.R., U.S.S.R., in S. Siberia bordering the Mongolian People's Republic. People: Turkic. Capital: Kyzyl (pop. 42,000)

Tu·va·lu (tu:vəlu:) (formerly Ellice Islands) an independent state (area 10 sq. mi, pop. 8,000) of the Commonwealth of Nations, comprising nine islands in the Pacific Ocean just south of Kiribati (formerly Gilbert Islands) and near the intersection of the equator and the international date line. Capital: Funafuti atoll. Industry: fishing. Remittances from Tuvaluans living abroad, foreign aid and the sale of postage stamps are important sources of income. A British protectorate (from 1892), part of the Gilbert and Ellice Islands Colony (from 1916) and a separate self-governing colony (from 1975), Tuvalu gained independence in 1978

tux·e·do (tʌksí:dou) *pl.* **tux·e·dos** *n.* a tailless, usually dark-colored, dress coat [after a country club at Tuxedo Park, N.Y.]

tu·yere (twi:jéər) *n.* a nozzle or pipe used to blow air with force into a blast furnace, forge etc. [F.=nozzle]

Tuz (tu:z) a salt lake (area 770 sq. miles) in central Anatolia, Turkey. In summer it becomes a salt marsh

TV television

TV dinner a packaged, precooked, usu. quick-frozen, dish, requiring only heating before serving

twad·dell (twódl) *n.* a hydrometer for measuring the specific gravity of liquids heavier than water [after W. Twaddell, its 19th-c. Scottish inventor]

twad·dle (twód'l) 1. *n.* silly, meaningless talk or writing 2. *v.i. pres. part.* **twad·dling** *past* and *past part.* **twad·dled** to talk or write foolishly [origin unknown]

Twain (twein), Mark (Samuel Langhorne Clemens, 1835-1910), American writer. His fame rests on his brilliant books based on the Mississippi River: 'The Adventures of Tom Sawyer' (1876) and 'The Adventures of Huckleberry Finn' (1883). The two great children's books, with 'The Tragedy of Pudd'nhead Wil-

son' (1894), are really an effective comment on Southern life, full of deft irony. His many other books, which vary in quality, include 'Life on the Mississippi' (1883), based on his adventures as a riverboat pilot, and 'Roughing It' (1872), drawn from his experiences as a young man in the Far West. He was a great storyteller. His powerful presence in his writing, and the relationship he establishes with his readers, have helped to make him perhaps the most widely read of all American authors

twain (twein) *adj.* and *n.* (*archaic*) two [O.E. *twēgen*]

twang (twæŋ) 1. *n.* the harsh, vibrating sound made by a string under tension when it is plucked ‖ a sharp, nasal quality in the speaking voice 2. *v.t.* to pluck (a stretched string) so that it makes this sound ‖ to play (an instrument or a tune) in this way ‖ to pronounce with a twang ‖ *v.i.* to make the sound of a taut, plucked string ‖ to speak with a twang [imit.]

tweak (twi:k) 1. *v.t.* to pinch and pull with a quick twisting jerk, *to tweak someone's nose* 2. *n.* a sharp pinch or pull [origin unknown]

Tweed (twi:d), 'Boss' William Marcy (1823-78), American politician. As head of Tammany, he gained effective control of New York (1865-71) and, with his corrupt subordinates, defrauded the city of many millions of dollars

Tweed a river (97 miles long) in S.E. Scotland, flowing from S. Peebles to the North Sea, forming part of the English border: salmon fishing

tweed (twi:d) *n.* a strong twilled woolen or wool and cotton cloth, originating in S. Scotland, usually woven with different colored yarns, and used esp. for suits and coats ‖ (*pl.*) clothes made from this material **twéed·y** *adj.* [a trade name originally based on a misreading of Scottish *tweel*, twill, and associations with R. *Tweed*]

Tweed Ring a corrupt political machine which controlled city government in New York in the latter 19th c., headed by William Marcy 'Boss' Tweed

tweet (twi:t) 1. *n.* the chirping note of a bird 2. *v.i.* to make this sound [imit.]

tweez·ers (twí:zərz) *pl. n.* a small two-pronged instrument used to pick up or grip small objects, pull out hairs etc. [fr. earlier *tweeze*, a case for small instruments fr. F. *étuys, étuis*, cases]

twelfth (twelfθ) 1. *adj.* being number 12 in a series (*NUMBER TABLE) ‖ being one of the 12 equal parts of anything 2. *n.* the person or thing next after the 11th ‖ one of 12 equal parts of anything (1/12) ‖ the 12th day of a month [O.E. *twelfta*]

Twelfth Amendment (1804) an amendment to the U.S. Constitution reforming the method by which the Electoral College elects the president and vice-president. Under Article II, Section 1 of the Constitution, each elector was to cast a single ballot for both offices, not specifying a preference as to which of the two candidates was for which of the two offices. The candidate receiving the most votes would become president and the runner-up vice-president. The unforeseen formation of political parties, however, resulted in the electors' choosing (1796) a president and vice-president from different parties. In the 1800 election party-pledged electors were chosen. The casting of two ballots for the same ticket resulted in a tie between presidential candidate Thomas Jefferson, who was chosen by the House of Representatives, and his running-mate, Aaron Burr. The situation led to a call for reform and to the 12th Amendment. The amendment specifies: 1) separate ballots for each office; 2) whoever has the most votes (if a majority) for each office will be elected to that office; 3) if a majority is lacking, the House of Representatives will vote for the president among the three leading candidates, and the Senate will elect the vice-president from between the two highest candidates; 4) no person legally ineligible to be president can be vice-president

Twelfth Day Epiphany, formerly marking the close of the Christmas festival

Twelfth Night the eve of Epiphany, kept as the last night of Christmas festivities

twelve (twelv) 1. *adj.* being one more than 11 (*NUMBER TABLE) 2. *n.* 10 plus two ‖ the cardinal number representing this (12, XII) ‖ 12 o'clock **the Twelve** the 12 Apostles [O.E. *twelf*]

twelve·mo (twélvmou) *adj.* and *n.* duodecimo

twelve·month (twélvmʌnθ) *n.* a year

twelve-note (twélvnout) *adj.* twelve-tone

Twelv·er (twélvər) *n.* a member of a Shi'ite sect which recognizes 12 Imams and awaits the reappearance of the last as the Mahdi on the Last Day. The beliefs of this sect have been the official religion of Persia since 1502

twelve-tone (twélvtoun) *adj.* (*mus.*) based on a system of composition developed esp. by Schönberg in which the 12 notes of the octave are treated as equal, i.e. as having relation only to one another (cf. KEY), all parts of a composition being constructed from these 12 separate tones in conformity with the series or row in which the composer has chosen to place them

Twelve Tribes of Israel, the *ISRAEL (Jacob)

twen·ti·eth (twénti:iθ) **1.** *adj.* being number 20 in a series (*NUMBER TABLE) || being one of the 20 equal parts of anything **2.** *n.* the person or thing next after the 19th || one of 20 equal parts of anything (1/20) || the 20th day of a month [O.E. *twentigotha*]

Twentieth Amendment (1933) an amendment to the U.S. Constitution providing for the orderly installation of the president, vice-president and members of Congress, shortening their 'lame duck' status, and clarifying the status of the president-elect and vice-president-elect with respect to presidential succession. The major provisions are: 1) the terms of the president and vice-president will end and new terms will begin on January 20 following an election, and members of Congress will end and begin their terms on January 3; 2) Congress will convene at least once a year, beginning on January 3 unless Congress selects another day; 3) if the president-elect dies, the vice-president-elect becomes president; or, if the president has not been chosen (under the Twelfth Amendment) or if the president-elect does not qualify, the vice-president-elect serves as president until the president-elect does qualify; or, if neither qualifies, Congress will declare how to appoint an acting president until a president or vice-president is qualified; 4) if Congress must choose a president or vice-president, Congress will also provide by law for the orderly succession to these offices in the event the designated person dies or is disqualified

twen·ty (twénti) **1.** *adj.* being one more than 19 (*NUMBER TABLE) **2.** *pl.* **twen·ties** *n.* twice 10 || the cardinal number representing this (20, XX) **the twenties** (of temperature, a person's age, a century etc.) the span 20 to 29 [O.E. *twentig*]

Twenty-fifth Amendment (1967) an amendment to the U.S. Constitution that provides procedures for fulfilling the duties of the presidency in the event of a president's death, resignation or removal as well as the prompt filling of a vice-presidential vacancy. The amendment's four provisions are: 1) in the event of removal, death or resignation of a president, the vice-president becomes president; 2) in the event of a vacancy in the vice-presidency, the president nominates a vice-president, who must be confirmed by a majority vote in both houses of Congress; 3) when a president declares an inability to serve in office, the president's duties will be assumed by the vice-president as acting president until the president declares his or her ability to resume them; 4) when the vice-president and either a majority of the heads of the executive departments or a specific congressionally determined body consider a president unable to fulfill his or her duties, the vice-president becomes acting president

Twenty-first Amendment (1933) an amendment to the U.S. Constitution that repeals the 18th Amendment, which prohibited the manufacture of and trafficking in intoxicating liquors. The 21st Amendment thus became the first amendment adopted to repeal another amendment

twen·ty-five (twénti:fáiv) *n.* (*rugby, hockey*) the line 25 yards in front of the goal line or the space between this line and the goal line

Twenty-fourth Amendment (1964) an amendment to the U.S. Constitution that bans the use of poll taxes in federal elections and gives Congress the power to enforce the amendment. It states that in any presidential or congressional election, no citizen can be denied, by the state or federal government, the right to vote because of failure to pay a poll tax or any other tax. Although only 5 states (Alabama, Arkansas, Mississippi, Texas and Virginia) required payment of a poll tax as a prerequisite to vote, an amendment was needed to eliminate the practice completely

Twenty-second Amendment (1951) an amendment to the U.S. Constitution that limits the presidential tenure to two terms of office. It further states that if a vice-president succeeds to the presidency with 2 years or less of the former president's remaining term, the new president may be elected to 2 more terms; otherwise the new president may be elected to only 1 more term. This amendment was proposed by a Republican Congress in reaction to the 4-term presidency of Franklin D. Roosevelt, who broke the 2-term tradition begun by George Washington

Twenty-sixth Amendment (1971) an amendment to the U.S. Constitution providing that citizens who are 18 years old or older may vote. This amendment is the 4th of the amendments to clarify voting rights (others are the 15th, 19th and 23rd). Its passage was occasioned by the massive protests in the 1960s by students and other young people against the Vietnam war and by their argument that 'if we're old enough to fight, we're old enough to vote.' The amendment reduced the voting age from 21 to 18

Twenty-third Amendment (1961) an amendment to the U.S. Constitution granting the right of citizens in the District of Columbia to vote in presidential elections, a right denied since 1802, when the district was established. The amendment states that the number of electors, appointed by the district government, for president and vice-president cannot exceed those of the least-populous state—or 3 votes in the electoral college

twice (twais) *adv.* two times || on two occasions || doubly **to think twice** to reflect carefully, hesitate out of prudence [O.E. *twiges*]

twice-laid (twáisléid) *adj.* made from strands of old rope or ends of rope

twid·dle (twíd'l) **1.** *v. pres. part.* **twid·dling** *past* and *past part.* **twid·dled** *v.t.* to twirl idly || *v.i.* to toy fussily, *to twiddle with the radio* **to twiddle one's thumbs** to have nothing better to do than turn one's thumbs around each other **2.** *n.* a slight twisting motion [prob. onomatopeic]

twig (twig) *n.* a small shoot from a branch of a tree, often one without leaves || a very small branch of a nerve or artery || a divining rod **twig·gy** *comp.* **twig·gi·er** *superl.* **twig·gi·est** *adj.* long and thin like a twig || full of twigs [Northern O.E. *twigge*]

twi·light (twáilait) **1.** *n.* the dim light between total darkness and sunrise, or esp. between sunset and darkness || the period when this light appears || any dim light || a period or range of existence just beyond the illumination of human knowledge || the period that follows full development, glory etc. **2.** *adj.* of, pertaining to, like or appearing at twilight [Late M.E. fr. *twi-*, *two*+*lēoht*, light]

twill (twil) **1.** *n.* a textile fabric patterned with diagonal lines, produced by passing the weft threads over one and under two (or more) warp threads || this pattern **2.** *v.t.* to weave so as to produce this pattern [O.E. *twili*]

twin (twin) **1.** *adj.* related as one of a pair of twins, *a twin sister* or (of ideas) as if one of a pair of twins || having identical characteristics with another thing and functioning as the complement to it, *twin propellers* || (*biol.*) occurring in pairs || (*crystall.*) formed by twinning **2.** *n.* either one of a pair of offspring produced in a single birth. Twins are conceived from the fertilization and subsequent splitting of a single ovum, *identical twins* or from separate ova, *fraternal twins* || a person or thing very closely resembling another || a compound crystal composed of crystals which have grown together in a relation of symmetry **the Twins** Gemini **3.** *v. pres. part.* **twin·ning** *past* and *past part.* **twinned** *v.i.* to give birth to twins || to be paired (with another) || (*crystall.*) to grow together in a relation of symmetry || *v.t.* to associate as a pair, *the projects are twinned in the chairman's plan* [O.E. *twinn*]

twin double (*wagering*) a contract in which the bettor must pick the winners of four consecutive events to win

twine (twain) **1.** *n.* strong cord composed of two or more strands of e.g. Manila hemp twisted together || a vine or plant stem which curves and twists || a coil, twist **2.** *v. pres. part.* **twin·ing** *past* and *past part.* **twined** *v.t.* to form (something) by twisting strands together || to twist (strands) so as to form something || to interweave flowers into (a garland) || to cause to wind around and clasp someone or something || to interlace, *she twined her fingers in his* || *v.i.* to

coil || to grow in coils, wind so as to clasp a branch etc. || to be winding in form, *the road twines through narrow valleys* [O.E. *twīn*]

twinge (twindʒ) **1.** *v. pres. part.* **twing·ing** *past* and *past part.* **twinged** *v.t.* to affect with a sudden sharp pain || *v.i.* to be affected in this way **2.** *n.* a sudden sharp physical pain || a stab of mental pain [O.E. *twengan*, etym. doubtful]

twink (twink) **1.** *v.i.* to wink or blink || to twinkle **2.** *n.* (*pop.*) an instant, *in a twink* [Late M.E. *twinken*]

twin·kle (twíŋk'l) **1.** *v. pres. part.* **twin·kling** *past* and *past part.* **twin·kled** *v.i.* (e.g. of the stars viewed through the earth's atmosphere) to emit intermittent gleams of light in rapid succession || (of the eyes) to sparkle with fun, malice etc. || *v.t.* to emit (light) in intermittent gleams in rapid succession **2.** *n.* a twinkling **twin·kling** *n.* a quick sparkling or flashing, esp. of a star or of eyes || an instant, *in a twinkling* [O.E. *twinclian*]

twin-screw (twínskrú:) *adj.* (of a ship) having two screw propellers, twisted in opposite directions

twirl (twə:rl) **1.** *v.t.* to cause to rotate rapidly, esp. with the fingers || to whirl with a flourish, *to twirl drumsticks* || to twiddle || to twist so as to curl (esp. moustache ends) || *v.i.* to rotate rapidly || (with 'around') to turn around with a very quick movement **2.** *n.* a rapid rotation || a curl, esp. a curling flourish made with the pen [etym. doubtful]

twist (twist) **1.** *v.t.* to alter the shape of (an object) by applying equal, parallel but oppositely directed forces || to cause to rotate || to cause to spiral || to distort or warp || to cause (two or more threads, strands etc.) to wind around one another, e.g. in making a rope || to make (e.g. a rope) by this action || to wrench so as to cause to be out of shape or place, *to twist an ankle* || (*games*) to cause (a ball) to move with a rotary or spinning motion || to distort the meaning of, *to twist someone's words* || to contort (the facial muscles) || (*Br., pop.*) to cheat (someone) || *v.i.* to turn, or be distorted, about an axis || to change direction sharply and repeatedly || to writhe, squirm, *he twisted free of the rope which tied him* **2.** *n.* a twisting or being twisted || a personal tendency, esp. an eccentric one, thought of as deforming the personality || an unexpected development in a situation or story || a deliberate distortion or perversion of meaning || a bad wrench, *he gave his ankle a twist* || a loaf of bread made in a twisted form || tobacco leaves twisted into a roll || strong cotton or silk yarn made by twisting, *a twist of silk* || (*phys.*) a torque || (of rifling) the degree of slope of the grooves || (*games*) spin imparted to a ball || (*Br.*) a spiral of paper serving as a packet or carrier, e.g. for groceries || a type of front or back dive **twist·er** *n.* (*pop.*) a tornado or cyclone || (*games*) a ball that twists || a baffling problem etc. **twist·y** *comp.* **twist·i·er** *superl.* **twist·i·est** *adj.* having many twists and turns, *a twisty path* || not straightforward, dishonest, *a twisty politician* [M.E.]

twis·tor (twístər) *n.* (*computer*) a storage device utilizing a helical magnetic wire enwrapped by a nonmagnetic wire to send the signals

twit (twit) *pres. part.* **twit·ting** *past* and *past part.* **twit·ted** *v.t.* to tease, mock, esp. in order to comment on some fault or weakness [O.E. *ætwītan*]

twitch (twitʃ) **1.** *v.i.* to move involuntarily with slight spasmodic jerks || (with 'at') to make a light, jerking pull or pulls || *v.t.* to pull with a light jerk or jerks || to move (a body part) nervously and jerkily **2.** *n.* a sudden involuntary jerk or contraction, e.g. of a muscle || a quick light pull or tug || a device for restraining a horse, e.g. during an operation. It consists of a loop of cord or leather fastened around its lip or muzzle and tightened with an attached stick [O.E. *twiccian*]

twitch grass couch grass

twit·ter (twítər) **1.** *v.i.* (of small birds) to utter a succession of thin chirps || (of people) to be in a flurry and make agitated little noises or say silly things || to tremble and be very agitated, *twittering with fear* || *v.t.* to express in an agitated manner **2.** *n.* the succession of chirping sounds made by birds || a state of nervous agitation in people **twit·ter·y** *adj.* [M.E. *twiteren*, imit.]

two (tu:) **1.** *adj.* being one more than one (*NUMBER TABLE) **2.** *n.* one plus one || the cardinal number representing this (2, II) || two o'clock || a playing card (domino etc.) marked with two symbols (spots etc.) **in two** into two parts **or two** (with 'a' + singular noun) used as an imprecise plural, *they walked a mile or two* **to put two and two together** to guess correctly from separate incomplete pieces of information [O.E. *twā, tū*]

two-base hit (*baseball*) a double

two-bit (tú:bit) *adj.* (*pop.*) cheap, worthless ‖ petty, of little importance [=worth two bits (*BIT*)]

two-by-four (tú:bəfɔr, tú:bəfour) **1.** *adj.* (*pop.*) small, petty, of little importance ‖ (*pop.*) cramped, narrow **2.** *n.* a piece of lumber of cross-section two inches by four inches

two-edged (tú:éd3d) *adj.* having two cutting edges ‖ ambiguous, esp. able to be understood as a compliment or the reverse

two-faced (tú:feist) *adj.* having two surfaces ‖ hypocritically deceitful **two-fac-ed-ly** (tú:feis-idli:) *adv.*

two-fist-ed (tú:fistid) *adj.* virile, vigorous

two-fold (tú:fould) **1.** *adj.* dual **2.** *adv.* two times as much or as many ‖ by two times [M.E. fr. older *twifold*]

two-hand-ed (tú:hǽndid) *adj.* needing two hands for use, used with both hands, *a two-handed sword* ‖ ambidextrous ‖ (of a card game) for two people ‖ needing two people to operate (e.g. a saw)

two-man rule (tú:mǽn) **1.** (*mil.*) system prohibiting individual access to nuclear weapons and their components by requiring the presence of at least two authorized persons, each capable of detecting incorrect or unauthorized procedures with respect to the task to be performed **2.** (*Br. education*) system of schooling with a common program from ages 11 to 13 or 14 and an upper school with selective training thereafter *also* two-man concept, two-man policy

two-mast-er (tú:mǽstər, tú:mástər) *n.* a sailing ship having two masts

two-pence, tup-pence (tʌpəns) *n.* (*hist.*) the sum of two British pennies before decimalization (1971)

two-pen-ny, tup-pen-ny (tʌpni:) *adj.* worth or costing twopence

two-pen-ny-half-pen-ny (tʌpni:héipni:) *adj.* (*Br.*) unimportant, worthless

two-piece (tú:pi:s) *adj.* (of a garment) consisting of two separate matching pieces

two-ply (tú:plai) *adj.* (of wood) having two layers ‖ (of wool, wire etc.) having two strands ‖ woven double, *a two-ply carpet*

Two Sicilies, Kingdom of the *SICILIES, KINGDOM OF THE TWO*

two-some (tú:səm) *n.* (*golf*) a game or match between two players ‖ (*pop.*) a couple, two people together

two-step (tú:step) *n.* a ballroom dance in 2/4 time ‖ a piece of music for this

two-time (tú:taim) *pres part.* **two-tim-ing** *past* and *past part.* **two-timed** *v.t.* (*pop.*) to deceive (a mistress, lover, wife or husband) with someone else ‖ (*pop.*) to double-cross (someone)

two-way (tú:wei) *adj.* moving or permitting movement, transmission etc. in each of two directions ‖ (*math.*) varying in two ways ‖ (*mech.*), of a cock or valve) arranged to permit the flow to be in either of two channels ‖ mutual ‖ involving two persons or groups

-ty *suffix* indicating a state or quality, as in 'enmity' [M.E. *-tie, -tee, -te* fr. O.F. *-te*, earlier *-tet* (*-ted*) fr. L. *-itas*]

-ty *suffix* indicating a multiple of ten, as in 'forty' [O.E. *-tig*]

ty-coon (taikú:n) *n.* a business magnate, powerful financier [fr. Jap. *taikun*, great prince fr. Chin.]

Ty-dings-Mc-Duf-fie Independence Act (táidiŋzməkdʌfi:) a U.S. Congressional act (1934) under President Franklin Roosevelt's administration. It granted independence to the Philippines after a ten-year probationary period, which was interrupted by the 2nd world war. In 1946 the Philippines achieved an independent commonwealth status

Tye (tai), Christopher (c. 1500-73), English composer. His style influenced the church music of the Elizabethan composers

tying *pres. part.* of TIE

tyke, tike (taik) *n.* a mongrel dog ‖ a mischievous child ‖ (*Br.*) a rascal [O.N. *tík*, bitch]

Ty-ler, John (1790-1862), 10th president (1841-5) of the U.S.A., following the death of President William Harrison. He was a Whig, and was the first vice-president to assume the presidency. His opposition to many Whig poli-

cies and his staunch states' rights policy aroused the vigorous opposition of his cabinet which resigned (1841) in block, except for secretary of state Daniel Webster, who remained to complete negotiations on the Webster-Ashburton Treaty (1843). President Tyler advanced the annexation of Texas

Tyler, Wat *PEASANTS' REVOLT*

ty-lo-sin [$C_{45}H_{77}NO_{17}$] (táiləsin) *n.* (*pharm.*) an antibiotic derived from an actinomycete, used as a food additive and in veterinary medicine; marketed as Tylan

tymbal *TIMBAL*

tym-pan (tímpən) *n.* a frame across which paper, cloth or parchment is stretched for equalizing the type pressure of a hand printing press ‖ a membranous part of an apparatus which functions like the eardrum ‖ (*archit.*) a tympanum [fr. L. *tympanum*, drum or O.F. *tympan, timpan*, drum]

tympani *TIMPANI*

tym-pan-ic (timpǽnik) *adj.* of or like a drum ‖ of the tympanum or eardrum [fr. TYMPANUM]

tympanic bone the bone which supports the eardrum and partly encloses the tympanum in a mammal's skull

tympanic membrane the eardrum

tym-pa-nist, tim-pa-nist (tímpənist) *n.* a musician who plays the timpani [fr. L. *tympanista* fr. Gk]

tym-pa-ni-tes (timpənáiti:z) *n.* (*med.*) a swelling of the abdomen caused by accumulation of gas or air, esp. in the intestine **tym-pa-nít-ic** (timpənítik) *adj.* [fr. Gk *tumpanitēs*, of a drum]

tym-pa-num (tímpənəm) *pl.* **tym-pa-na** (tímpənə), **tym-pa-nums** *n.* the eardrum ‖ the middle ear ‖ a drum ‖ the diaphragm of a telephone ‖ (*archit.*) the triangular recessed face of a pediment, or triangular space in a door between the lintel and the arch [L.=drum fr. Gk]

Tyn-dale, Tin-dal, Tin-dale (tínd'l), William (c. 1494-1536), English Protestant reformer. Forced into exile in 1524, he made a translation of the Bible into English of exceptional literary quality. He was burned as a heretic

Tyn-dall (tínd'l), John (1820-93), British physicist, noted for his work on the conductivity of heat by gases, on the audibility of sound, and on the qualities of atmospheric light

Tyne (tain) a river (30 miles long) flowing across E. Northumberland, England, to the North Sea, navigable to Newcastle

Tyn-wald, Tyne-wald (tínwɔld, tínwəld) the legislature of the Isle of Man

typ-al (táip'l) *adj.* of or serving as a type

type (taip) **1.** *n.* a kind or sort, *music of a type we enjoy* ‖ (*biol.*) the individual regarded as most fully exemplifying the characteristics of a genus etc. and which gives its name to that genus etc. ‖ (*biol.*) the sum of the characteristics of a large number of individuals, used in arriving at a classification and providing the norm against which variants are assessed and classified ‖ the combination of characteristics in a breed of animal that make it suitable for a specific use, *dairy type* ‖ a person, thing or event regarded as symbolic, esp. (*Bible*) one prefiguring the antitype that was to follow ‖ a piece of esp. metal having on its upper surface a character in relief which when inked and brought under pressure against paper leaves an impression of the character ‖ such pieces collectively, *is the book in type yet?* ‖ the design and size of the impressions printed from such pieces, *what type is the book printed in?* ‖ the central device on either side of a medal or coin etc. **2.** *v. pres. part.* **typ-ing** *past* and *past part.* **typed** *v.t.* to write (matter) using a typewriter ‖ to classify according to type ‖ to prefigure as a type ‖ to cast (an actor) over and over in the same kind of role until he becomes identified in the mind of the public with it ‖ *v.i.* to use a typewriter [fr. F. *type* or L. *typus* fr. Gk *tupos*, impression]

type-face (táipfeis) *n.* (*printing*) a face (surface or set of characters)

type-found-er (táipfaundər) *n.* someone who makes printers' type for setting by hand

type-found-ry (táipfaundri:) *pl.* **type-found-ries** *n.* a factory or workshop where type is made by a typefounder

type genus (*biol.*) the genus regarded as most typical of a family and which gives the family its name

type-high (táiphái) *adj.* having the same height as printing type (0.9186 in. in English-speaking countries)

type metal the alloy used esp. to cast printers' type and plates. It consists mainly of lead, with antimony, tin and sometimes copper

type-script (táipskript) *n.* a piece of typewritten matter

type-set (táipset) *v.t. pres. part.* **type-set-ting** *past* and *past part.* **type-set** (*printing*) to set in type, compose **type-set-ter** *n.* a compositor ‖ a machine for setting type

type species (*biol.*) the species regarded as most typical of a genus and which gives the genus its name

type specimen (*biol.*) an individual plant or animal serving as the type of a species or a smaller group ‖ (*printing*) a printed sample of a font or series of types displayed to show content, form and capacities

type-write (táiprait) *pres. part.* **type-writ-ing** *past* **type-wrote** (táiprout) *past part.* **type-writ-ten** (táiprit'n) *v.t.* to write (something) with a typewriter ‖ *v.i.* to use a typewriter [back-formation fr. TYPEWRITER]

type-writ-er (táipraitər) *n.* a machine operated by a keyboard which causes metal characters to strike paper through an inked ribbon and so leave an impression on the paper

type-writ-ing (táipraitiŋ) *n.* the act or process of using a typewriter ‖ typewriter work

type-writ-ten (táiprit'n) *adj.* typed on a typewriter [fr. older *typewrite*, to type]

ty-phoid (táifoid) **1.** *n.* typhoid fever **2.** *adj.* of or relating to typhus ‖ of or relating to typhoid fever [fr. TYPHUS]

typhoid fever an acute infectious disease caused by a bacterium in impure food or water, producing a prolonged, debilitating fever and diarrhea

Typhon *n.* (*mil.*) Navy surface-to-air missile with a short range and nuclear capability

ty-phoon (taifú:n) *n.* a violent cyclone in the China Sea and around the Philippines occurring most frequently in late summer and early autumn [fr. Chin. dial. *tai fung*, big wind]

Typhoon *n.* (*mil.*) NATO term for U.S.S.R. 30,000-ton, nuclear-powered submarine with an estimated speed of 45 knots. Diving capability of 4,000 ft, and carrying 20 ballistic missiles, it was first launched in 1980

ty-phous (táifəs) *adj.* of or of the nature of typhus

ty-phus (táifəs) *n.* any of several human infectious diseases conveyed by the bite of lice, fleas and other biting arthropods whose cells are inhabited by rickettsiae. The louse-borne variety occurs in explosive epidemics, often as a result of wars, earthquakes and other disasters which cause large numbers of people to be herded together in insanitary conditions. The other varieties are endemic in parts of Asia, Africa and America. Symptoms include a rash, high fever lasting about a fortnight, with vomiting, prostration, delirium and sometimes pneumonia [Mod. L. fr. Gk *tuphos*, stupor]

typ-ic (típik) *adj.* (*biol.*) of or conforming to a type [F. *typique* fr. L. fr. Gk]

typ-i-cal (típik'l) *adj.* characteristic of an individual, *one of his typical scathing remarks* ‖ characteristic of a class, *a typical sample of what we produce* ‖ (*biol.*) displaying the essential characteristics of a group ‖ relating to a symbolic type or types, *typical interpretations are characteristic of medieval criticism* [fr. M.L. *typicalis*]

typ-i-fi-ca-tion (tipifikéiʃən) *n.* a typifying or being typified ‖ something which typifies

typ-i-fy (típifai) *pres. part.* **typ-i-fy-ing** *past* and *past part.* **typ-i-fied** *v.t.* to be the representative symbol of, *the dove typifies peace* ‖ to embody the essential characteristics of, *love of the poor and oppressed typified the man* ‖ (*biol.*) to be the type of (a genus, species etc.)

typ-ist (táipist) *n.* a person who operates a typewriter, esp. for a living

ty-pog-ra-pher (taipógrəfər) *n.* someone who lays out copy and sees to all the elements of printing design [fr. M.L. *typographus*, printer]

ty-po-graph-ic (taipəgrǽfik) *adj.* typographical **ty-po-graph-i-cal** *adj.* of or relating to typography ‖ of or relating to printing by letterpress **ty-po-graph-i-cal-ly** *adv.*

ty-pog-ra-phy (taipógrəfi:) *n.* the art and practice of the typographer ‖ printed matter with respect to the way in which it is set out [F. *typographie*]

ty-pol-o-gy (taipólədʒi:) *n.* the doctrine or study of symbols or types, esp. those of Scripture ‖ a study based on the comparison or classification

CONCISE PRONUNCIATION KEY: (a) æ, c*a*t; ɑ, c*a*r; ɔ f*aw*n; ei, sn*a*ke. **(e)** e, h*e*n; i:, sh*ee*p; iə, d*ee*r; ɛə, b*ea*r. **(i)** i, f*i*sh; ai, t*i*ger; ə:, b*i*rd. **(o)** o, *o*x; au, c*ow*; ou, g*oa*t; u, p*oo*r; ɔi, r*oy*al. **(u)** ʌ, d*u*ck; u, b*u*ll; u:, g*oo*se; ə, b*a*cill*u*s; ju:, c*u*be. x, lo*ch*; θ, *th*ink; ð, bo*th*er; z, *Z*en; ʒ, corsa*g*e; dʒ, sava*g*e; ŋ, ora*ng*utang; j, *y*ak; ʃ, *fi*sh; tʃ, fet*ch*; 'l, rabb*le*; 'n, redde*n*. Complete pronunciation key appears inside front cover.

of types, e.g. of social groups, of archaeological remains etc. [fr. Gk *tupos*, type+*logos*, discourse]

ty·ran·nic (tirǽnik) *adj.* tyrannical **ty·rán·ni·cal** *adj.* acting like or characteristic of a tyrant, esp. unjustly severe in the use of power or authority **ty·rán·ni·cal·ly** *adv.* [fr. L. *tyrannicus* fr. Gk]

ty·ran·ni·cide (tirǽnisaid) *n.* someone who kills a tyrant ‖ the act of killing a tyrant [F. fr. L. *tyrannicida* (1st definition) and *tyrannicidium* (2nd definition) fr. *tyrannus*, tyrant+*caedere*, to kill]

tyr·an·nize (tirənaiz) *pres. part.* **tyr·an·niz·ing** *past* and *past part.* **tyr·an·nized** *v.i.* to behave like a tyrant ‖ *v.t.* to treat tyrannically [F. *tyranniser*]

tyr·an·no·saur (tirǽnəsɔr) *n. Tyrannosaurus rex*, an enormous two-footed carnivorous dinosaur of the Upper Cretaceous in North America [Mod. L. *tyrannosaurus*]

tyr·an·nous (tírənəs) *adj.* characterized by tyranny [fr. L. *tyrannus*, tyrant]

tyr·an·ny (tírəni:) *pl.* **tyr·an·nies** *n.* despotic rule ‖ the unjust and cruel exercise of power of any sort ‖ a tyrannical act [O.F. *tyrannie* fr. L. fr. Gk]

ty·rant (táirənt) *n.* an oppressive or cruel ruler or master, a despot ‖ someone behaving like a despot ‖ (*Gk hist.*) an arbitrary and absolute ruler who took power by force [O.F. fr. L. fr. Gk]

Tyre (taiər) an ancient seaport (modern Sur, Lebanon, pop. 14,000) of Phoenicia, which flourished (12th-8th cc. B.C.) as a trading center, esp. for the export of Tyrian purple dye and silk

tyre (taiər) **1.** *n.* (*Br.*) a tire (solid rubber tube or casing) **2.** *v.t. pres. part.* **tyr·ing** *past* and *past part.* **tyred** (*Br.*) to fit with a tire

Tyr·i·an purple (tíri:ən) a crimson or purple dye prepared by the ancient Greeks and Romans from the glands of various gastropod mollusks and used in the robes of emperors, nobles etc. (*TYRE) ‖ a strong purplish red

ty·ro (táirou) *pl.* **ty·ros** *n.* a beginner, someone learning a craft etc. [L. *tiro*, a newly enlisted soldier]

Tyrol *TIROL

Ty·rone (tiróun) an inland county (area 1,261 sq. miles, pop. 139,073) of Northern Ireland. County town: Omagh (pop. 8,000)

Tyr·rhe·ni·an Sea (tirí:ni:ən) the part of the Mediterranean between the Italian mainland and Corsica, Sardinia and Sicily

Tyr·tae·us (təːrtí:əs) (7th c. B.C.), Greek poet, leader of the Spartans in one of their wars against Messenia. A few fragments survive of his patriotic and war songs, said to have been sung by Spartans on the march

Tyu·men (tju:mén) a communications center (pop. 378,000) in the R.S.F.S.R.. U.S.S.R., on a tributary of the Irtysh, the oldest (1586) Russian town in Siberia: shipbuilding, wood industries

tzar *CZAR

Tza·ra (tsára), Tristan (1896-1963), Rumanian poet. As editor of the magazine 'Dada' (1916-20) he was a pioneer of surrealism (*DADA)

tzarina *CZARINA

Tze·po (dzépɔ) (formerly Poshan) a coal-mining center (pop. 184,000) in central Shantung Province, China

tzetze *TSETSE

tzi·gane (tsigán) *n.* a gypsy, esp. a Hungarian gypsy [F. fr. Hung.]

CONCISE PRONUNCIATION KEY: **(a)** æ, c*a*t; ɑ, c*a*r; ɔ f*a*wn; ei, sn*a*ke. **(e)** e, h*e*n; i:, sh*ee*p; iə, d*ee*r; ɛə, b*ea*r. **(i)** i, f*i*sh; ai, t*i*ger; əː, b*i*rd. **(o)** o, *o*x; au, c*ow*; ou, g*oa*t; u, p*oo*r; ɔi, r*oy*al. **(u)** ʌ, d*u*ck; u:, b*u*ll; u:, g*oo*se; ə, b*a*cillus; ju:, c*u*be. x, lo*ch*; θ, *th*ink; ð, bo*th*er; z, *Z*en; ʒ, corsa*g*e; dʒ, sava*g*e; ŋ, ora*ng*utang; j, *y*ak; ʃ, *f*ish; tʃ, fe*tch*; 'l, rabb*le*; 'n, redd*en*. Complete pronunciation key appears inside front cover.

				CLASSICAL GREEK	ETRUSCAN		EARLY LATIN	MODERN ROMAN
					Early	Classical		
U				Υ	Υ	V	V	U

CURSIVE MAJUSCULE (ROMAN)	CURSIVE MINUSCULE (ROMAN)	ANGLO-IRISH MAJUSCULE	CAROLINE MINUSCULE	VENETIAN MINUSCULE (ITALIC)	N. ITALIAN MINUSCULE (ROMAN)
u	y	u	u	u	u

A. C. SYLVESTER, CAMBRIDGE, ENGLAND

Development of the letter U, beginning with the classical Greek letter. Evolution of both the majuscule, or capital, letter U and the minuscule, or lowercase, letter u are shown.

U, u (ju:) the 21st letter of the English alphabet

U (ju:) *adj.* upper-class *ant.* non-U

U·ban·gi (ju:bǽŋgi:) (*F.* Oubangui) a tributary (660 miles long, navigable by steamer for 350) of the Congo, rising in N.E. Zaïre and forming part of the country's frontiers with the Central African Republic and the Republic of the Congo

U·ban·gi-Sha·ri (ju:bǽngi:ʃári:) **CENTRAL AFRICAN REPUBLIC

U·be (ú:bi:) a port (pop. 160,000) in S.W. Honshu, Japan: coal mines, textile and chemical industries

U·bi·co (u:bí:kou), Jorge (1878-1946), Guatemalan general and president (1931-44), who made liberal concessions to U.S. enterprises and twice changed the constitution in order to prolong his term of office. He was overthrown by a popular movement

u·biq·ui·none (ju:bəkwínoun) *n.* (*chem.*) a yellow compound that carries electrons through filaments in the cell's energy supply system *also* coenzyme

u·biq·ui·tous (ju:bíkwitəs) *adj.* present everywhere, esp. present everywhere at the same time [fr. Mod. L. *ubiquitarius* fr. L. *ubique*, everywhere]

u·biq·ui·ty (ju:bíkwiti) *n.* the state of being everywhere at the same time [fr. Mod. L. *ubiquitas* fr. L. *ubique*, everywhere]

U-boat (jú:bout) *n.* a German submarine [fr. G. *U-boot*, short for *Unterseeboot*, undersea boat]

U·ca·ya·li (u:kəjáli:) the chief tributary (1,200 miles long, navigable for 600) of the Amazon, in E. and N. Peru

Uc·cel·lo (u:tʃélou, *Ital.* u:ttʃellɔ), Paolo (1397-1475), Florentine painter, important in the history of painting for his intensive study of linear perspective and foreshortening. He is esp. famous for his three paintings of 'The Battle of San Romano, 1432' (1456-60) in the Uffizi, Florence, the National Gallery, London and the Louvre, Paris

u·dal (jú:d'l) *n.* an ancient system of land tenure which survives in Orkney and the Shetlands [O.N. *ōthal*]

U·dall (jú:d'l), Nicholas (1505-56), English playwright. He is best known for his posthumous 'Ralph Roister Doister' (c. 1577), a 'comic interlude' based on classical models, e.g. Plautus and Terence, and generally considered to be the first complete English comedy

ud·der (ʌ́dər) *n.* in cattle etc. the pendulous baggy organ containing two or more mammary glands, each having one teat or nipple [O.E. *ūder*]

U·di·ne (ú:di:ne) a city (pop. 103,600) in Friuli-Venezia Giulia, Italy, at the foot of the Alps. Castle (11th c.), Romanesque cathedral, 15th-c. town hall

Ud·murt A.S.S.R. (údmʌərt) an autonomous republic (area 16,250 sq. miles, pop. 1,516,000) of the E. European R.S.F.S.R., U.S.S.R. People: Finnic. Capital: Izhevsk

u·dom·e·ter (ju:dómitər) *n.* a rain gauge **u·do·met·ric** (ju:dəmétrik) *adj.* [fr. F. *udomètre*]

Ue·le (wélei) a headstream (700 miles long) of the Ubangi, crossing northeastern Zaïre

U·fa (u:fá) the capital (pop. 1,009,000) of the Bashkirian A.S.S.R., U.S.S.R., in the W. Urals: engineering, oil refining, lumber, food processing, metallurgy

Uf·fi·zi (u:fí:tsi:) **FLORENCE

UFO, U.F.O. unidentified flying object

u·fol·o·gy (ju:fólədʒi:) *n.* the study of unidentified flying objects (UFOs) —**ufological** *adj.* —**ufologist** *n.*

U·gan·da (ju:gǽndə) a republic (area 93,981 sq. miles, pop. 13,651,000), comprised of 18 administrative districts, and a member of the British Commonwealth, in E. central Africa. Capital: Kampala. People: about half belong to Bantu groups, while non-African minorities include Indians (1%), Europeans and Arabs. Language: English (official), Luganda, Swahili, local and minority languages. Religion: mainly traditional African, with Christian (20%) and Moslem minorities. The country is 8% forest, and predominantly agricultural. It is a plateau (3,000-5,000 ft), mainly savanna, between the Great Rift Valley and Lake Victoria, with high massifs (**RUWENZORI, **ELGON) on the southwestern and eastern borders, and with many lakes and rivers. Average temperatures (F.) in Kampala 69° (July), 74° (Jan.). Rainfall: Kampala 46 ins, interior under 40 ins. Livestock: cattle, goats, sheep. Agricultural products: cotton, coffee, tea, tobacco, peanuts, corn, castor-oil plant seeds, sisal, sugar, millet, plantains, beans, sweet potatoes. Mineral resources: copper, cobalt, limestone, phosphates, tungsten, tin, beryl. Industries: fishing, lumber (hardwoods), hydroelectricity, fertilizers, cement, chemicals, bicycles. Exports: cotton, coffee, copper, tea, animal foodstuffs, hides and skins, peanuts, electricity. Imports: machinery, textiles, clothing, metals, vehicles, rubber, gasoline. University College of the University of East Africa at Kampala (1939). Monetary unit: shilling (100 cents). HISTORY. Various tribes migrated to Uganda before the 18th c., forming clans in the northeast and kingdoms in the southwest, notably that of Buganda. Arab slave and ivory traders reached Uganda from Zanzibar (mid-19th c.). The first European to reach it

was Speke (1862). Baker discovered Lake Albert (1864) and Stanley explored Buganda (1875). Britain proclaimed a protectorate over Buganda (1894), extended (1896) to most of the rest of Uganda. Executive and legislative councils were established (1921), and Uganda became an independent member of the Commonwealth (Oct. 9, 1962). The constitution proclaiming the republic, and the creation of a unitary state in place of the federal state, was approved (Sept. 8, 1968). President Obote was overthrown (Jan. 25, 1971) by an army coup d'état. Gen. Amin formed a new government, which rapidly took the shape of a dictatorship. Amin's erratic and ruthless behavior alienated many other countries and led to his overthrow in April 1979 by exiled Tanzanian-supported Ugandan troops. Political conditions continued unstable and in May 1980 new President Binaisa was deposed by a military commission. Obote returned from exile and was elected president but he was overthrown in July 1985. New President Lt. Gen. Tito Okello promised an early return to civilian rule

U·ga·rit (u:gərí:t) an ancient city excavated at Ras-Shamra, near Latakia, N. Syria. It flourished as a cultural and trading center (4th millennium-2nd millennium B.C.). Excavations yielded cuneiform tablets of the 14th c. B.C.

ugh (ʌg, ʌx, ux) *interj.* used to express disgust or extreme repugnance

ug·li·fi·ca·tion (ʌglifikéiʃən) *n.* an uglifying or being uglified

ug·li·fy (ʌ́glifai) *pres. part.* **ug·li·fy·ing** *past* and *past part.* **ug·li·fied** *v.t.* to make ugly

ug·li·ness (ʌ́gli:nis) *n.* the state or quality of being ugly

ug·ly (ʌ́gli:) *comp.* **ug·li·er** *superl.* **ug·li·est** *adj.* unpleasant to look at, unsightly ‖ morally offensive ‖ (*pop.*) surly, quarrelsome, *an ugly mood* ‖ fraught with danger, *an ugly situation* [O.N. *uggligr*, to be dreaded]

ugly American an American abroad who is unappreciative of the native culture: from the 1955 book, *The Ugly American*, by Eugene Burdick (1918–1965) and William Lederer (1912–)

ugly duckling someone who after an unpromising start turns out to have fine qualities or personal beauty [fr. a story by Hans ANDERSEN]

UGM-84A (*mil.*) **HARPOON
UGM-96 (*mil.*) **TRIDENT I
UGM-73A (*mil.*) **POSEIDON
UGM-27 (*mil.*) **POLARIS

U·gri·an (ú:gri:ən, jú:gri:ən) **1.** *n.* a member of the eastern division of the Finno-Ugrian peoples **2.** *adj.* of or relating to the Ugrians ‖ Ugric

CONCISE PRONUNCIATION KEY: **(a)** æ, c*a*t; a, c*a*r; ɔ f*aw*n; ei, sn*a*ke. **(e)** e, h*e*n; i:, sh*ee*p; iə, d*ee*r; ɛə, b*ea*r. **(i)** i, f*i*sh; ai, t*i*ger; ə:, b*i*rd. **(o)** o, *o*x; au, c*ow*; ou, g*oa*t; u, p*oo*r; ɔi, r*oy*al. **(u)** ʌ, d*u*ck; u, b*u*ll; u:, g*oo*se; ə, b*a*cillus; ju:, c*u*be. x, lo*ch*; θ, *th*ink; ð, bo*th*er; z, *Z*en; ʒ, corsa*g*e; dʒ, sava*g*e; ŋ, orangutа*ng*; j, *y*ak; ʃ, fi*sh*; tʃ, fe*tch*; 'l, rabb*le*; 'n, redd*en*. Complete pronunciation key appears inside front cover.

U·gric (úːgrik, júːgrik) *adj.* of, relating to or characteristic of the Finno-Ugric languages of the Ugrians

UH-1 (*mil.*) *IROQUOIS

Uh·land (úːlɑnt), Johann Ludwig (1787-1862), German Romantic poet, playwright and essayist, famous mainly for his ballads and patriotic songs

Ui·ghur (wíːguər) *n.* a member of a Turkic people found primarily in the Tarim Basin ‖ their Turkic language

Uit·land·er (éitlændər) *n.* (*hist.*) a foreign immigrant, esp. a British one, in the Transvaal and the Orange Free State as referred to by the Boers before the Boer War (1899–1902) [Afrik. fr. *uit*, out + *land*, land]

Uj·jain (úːdʒain) a Hindu holy city (pop. 203,278) in N.W. Madhya Pradesh, India. Industries: textiles. Temples

u·kase (juːkéiz, júːkeis) *n.* an edict, esp. an edict of czarist Russia having the force of law [Russ *ukazŭ*, edict]

ukelele *UKULELE

U·kraine (juːkréin) an E. European constituent republic (area 231,990 sq. miles, pop. 49,757,000) of the U.S.S.R., occupying most of the southwest and consisting mainly of fertile steppe. Capital: Kiev. Other centers: Kharkov, Donetsk, Odessa. People: 77% Ukrainian, 17% Russian, Polish and other minorities. Agriculture: wheat, corn (25% of Soviet grain production), sugar beets (50% of Soviet production), sunflower seed, cotton, flax, vegetables, fruit, tobacco, cattle, hogs, sheep. Resources: coal (36% of Soviet production), iron ore, oil, salt, fish. Industries: mining (esp. coal, iron, manganese), iron and steel, chemical and mechanical engineering, food processing, textiles. HISTORY. The Ukraine was divided between Russia and Austria (18th c.), was briefly independent (1917-20), and became a constituent republic of the U.S.S.R. (1923). It joined the United Nations (1945)

U·krain·i·an (juːkréiniən) **1.** *adj.* of or relating to the Ukraine, its people or language **2.** *n.* a native or inhabitant of the Ukraine ‖ the Slavic language of the Ukrainians

u·ku·le·le, u·ke·le·le (juːkəléiliː) *n.* a small four-stringed musical instrument resembling the guitar [Hawaiian]

U·lad·is·laus I (juːlædislɔs) (*Hung.* Ulászló) king of Hungary *LADISLAUS III king of Poland

Uladislaus II king of Hungary *LADISLAUS II, king of Bohemia

U·lagh Muz·tagh (uːláːmuːstáː) *KUNLUN

u·la·ma, u·le·ma, u·la·mas, u·le·ma, u·le·mas (úːləmə) *pl.* **u·la·ma, u·la·mas, u·le·ma, u·le·mas** *n.* the body of professional theologians and legalists of Islam. The ulama provides the teachers and leaders of worship in the mosques, as there is no ordained priesthood within Islam ‖ a member of an ulama [fr. Arab. *'ulamā* pl. of *'alim*, learned]

U·lan Ba·tor (úːlɑnbátɔr) (formerly Urga) the capital (pop. 457,000) of the Mongolian People's Republic, at the northern edge of the Gobi Desert, formerly a lamasery and caravan station, now a rail and industrial center (meat packing, tanning, felt and fur industries). University

U·lan U·de (úːlɑnuːdéi) the capital (pop. 310,000) of the Buriat A.S.S.R., R.S.F.S.R., U.S.S.R.: railroad stock, building materials, textiles, food processing, glass

U·lász·ló (uːláʒlou) kings of Hungary *LADISLAUS III, king of Poland, *LADISLAUS II, king of Bohemia

Ul·bricht (úːlbrixt), Walter (1893–1973), East German political leader. He joined the communist party (1918) when it was established and was a member of the German Reichstag (1928-33) but left Germany when Hitler came to power. He worked with the Republicans during the Spanish Civil War and the Russians during the 2nd world war. Ulbricht became East Germany's deputy prime minister (1949) and secretary of the Socialist Unity (Communist) party (1950). His harsh regime led to open rebellion (1953) and to a stream of refugees to West Germany until the Berlin Wall was built (1961). During the last decade of Ulbricht's regime, his economic reforms resulted in East Germany's attaining the Communist world's highest standard of living. He resigned as party secretary (1971) but remained chairman of the Council of State until his death

ul·cer (ʌlsər) *n.* an inflamed discontinuity in the skin or mucous membranes of the body. It may be due to injury, infection or the action of corrosive fluids (*PEPTIC ULCER) ‖ (*rhet.*) a source or condition of corruption [fr. L. *ulcus* (*ulceris*), a sore]

ul·cer·ate (ʌlsəreit) *pres. part.* **ul·cer·at·ing** *past and past part.* **ul·cer·at·ed** *v.t.* to make ulcerous ‖ *v.i.* to become ulcerous [fr. L. *ulcerare* (*ulceratus*)]

ul·cer·a·tion (ʌlsəréiʃən) *n.* a becoming ulcerated or state of being ulcerated ‖ an ulcer or several ulcers in a group [fr. L. *ulceratio* (*ulcerationis*)]

ul·cer·a·tive (ʌlsərətiv, ʌlsəreitiv) *adj.* of, relating to, characterized by or causing an ulcer or ulcers [fr. M.L. *ulcerativus*]

ul·cer·ous (ʌlsərəs) *adj.* having an ulcer or ulcers ‖ having the nature of an ulcer [fr. L. *ulcerosus*]

U·le·å·borg (úːleouborj) *OULU

ulema *ULAMA

Ul·fi·las (úlfilæs) *WULFILA

ul·lage (ʌlidʒ) *n.* the amount by which a barrel or similar vessel falls short of being full ‖ loss of contents by evaporation, oozing etc. [A.F. *ulliage*]

Ulls·wa·ter (ʌlzwɒtər, ʌlzwɒtər) a lake (8 miles long) in Cumberland and Westmorland, England (*LAKE DISTRICT)

Ulm (ulm) a town (pop. 93,800) in Baden-Württemberg, West Germany, on the Danube. Gothic cathedral (14th c.-19th c.)

Ulm, Battle of, a battle (Oct. 20, 1805) in which the Austrian army surrendered to Napoleon early in the Napoleonic Wars

ul·na (ʌlnə) *pl.* **ul·nae** (ʌlniː), **ul·nas** *n.* the inner of the two bones of the forearm of man or corresponding part of the forelimb of vertebrates higher than fishes **úl·nar** *adj.* [L. = elbow]

u·lot·ri·chous (juːlótrikəs) *adj.* (*anthrop.*) belonging to a race having crisp, crinkled hair [fr. Mod. L. *ulotrichi* fr. Gk *oulos*, crisp + *thrix* (*trichos*), hair]

Ul·ster (ʌlstər) the northernmost province (area 3,094 sq. miles, pop. 226,037) of Ireland, comprising Cavan, Donegal and Monaghan counties ‖ (*hist.*) an ancient kingdom of N. Ireland, now comprising modern Ulster and Northern Ireland ‖ (*pop.*) Northern Ireland

ul·ster (ʌlstər) *n.* a long loose overcoat, often belted [after ULSTER, Ireland, where such coats were originally made]

ul·te·ri·or (ʌltíəriːər) *adj.* further, more distant ‖ beyond what is evident or professed, *ulterior motives* [L. comp. adj. = further]

ul·ti·mate (ʌltəmit) **1.** *adj.* farthest away in space or time ‖ eventual, *their ultimate victory is not in question* ‖ final, *the ultimate test* ‖ that cannot be analyzed, separated out etc. in any greater detail, *in the ultimate analysis* **2.** *n.* that which is ultimate [fr. L.L. *ultimare* (*ultimatus*), to come to an end]

ultimate frisbee team field game with 7 competitors on each side, with objective of placing frisbee across opponent's goal line

ul·tim·a·tist (ʌltəméitist) *n.* an uncompromising extremist —**ultimatism** *n.* —**ultimatistic** *adj.*

ul·ti·ma·tum (ʌltəméitəm, ʌltəmátəm) *pl.* **ul·ti·ma·tums, ul·ti·ma·ta** (ʌltəméitə, ʌltəmátə) *n.* the final terms offered or demanded by one of the parties in diplomatic negotiations, the rejection of which usually leads to complete rupture, or war [fr. L.L. neut. of *ultimatus*, ultimate]

ul·ti·mo (ʌltəmou) *adv.* (*commerce*, abbr. **ult.**, **ulto.**) in the month preceding the present one [L. *ultimo* (*mense*), in the last (month)]

ul·tra (ʌltrə) **1.** *adj.* extreme, sometimes to the point of being fanatical **2.** *n.* an extremist [L. = beyond]

ultra- *prefix* beyond, as in 'ultraviolet' ‖ to an extreme degree, as in 'ultramodernism' ‖ beyond the range of, as in 'ultramicroscopic' [fr. L. *ultra*, beyond]

ul·tra·cen·tri·fuge (ʌltrəséntrifjuːdʒ) *n.* a high-speed centrifuge for effecting the sedimentation of submicroscopic particles

ul·tra·fax (ʌltrəfæks) *n.* (*electr.*) trademark of RCA Corporation incorporating television, radio, facsimile, and film recording

ul·tra·fiche (ʌltrəfiːʃ) *n.* (*optics*) a microfilm of documents reduced for filing to 1/90 or less normal size —**ultrafiche** *adj.*

ul·tra·ís·mo (uːltraíːsmɔ) *n.* a literary movement created (1919) by Spanish and Spanish-American poets, notably Jorge Luis Borges and Eugenio Montes. The movement called for a total renewal of the spirit and technique of poetry. Its poems are characterized by vivid images and striking metaphors [Span.]

ul·tra·ma·rine (ʌltrəməríːn) **1.** *n.* a vivid blue pigment originally obtained by reducing lapis lazuli to powder ‖ a blue pigment prepared by heating a mixture of soda ash, sulfur, charcoal etc. It is used in paints, printing inks etc. ‖ the blue color of this pigment **2.** *adj.* ultramarine-colored [fr. M.L. *ultramarinus* fr. L. *ultra*, beyond + *mare*, sea (because lapis lazuli came from beyond the sea)]

ul·tra·mi·cro·scope (ʌltrəmáikrəskoup) *n.* a microscope employing a beam of intense light projected through the sample perpendicularly to the axis of the objective, permitting the observation of submicroscopic, colloidal particles by the light they scatter against a dark field **ul·tra·mi·cro·scop·ic** (ʌltrəmáikrəskópik) *adj.*

ul·tra·mi·cro·tome (ʌltrəmáikrətoum) *n.* (*electr.*) a device designed to cut very thin tissue sections for use in an electron microscope —**ultramicrotomy** *n.*

ul·tra·mon·tane (ʌltrəmóntein) **1.** *adj.* of the principles or practices of ultramontanism **2.** *n.* an advocate of ultramontanism [fr. M.L. *ultramontanus* fr. *ultra*, beyond + *mons* (*montis*), mountain]

ul·tra·mon·ta·nism (ʌltrəmóntənizəm) *n.* (*hist.*) the advocacy, within the Roman Catholic Church, of the increase of papal authority, as opposed to such theories as Gallicanism. It was firmly established by the declaration of papal infallibility (1870) **ul·tra·món·ta·nist** *n.* [F. *ultramontanisme*]

ul·tra·mun·dane (ʌltrəmʌndein, ʌltrəmʌndéin) *adj.* being beyond the limits of the known universe [fr. L.L. *ultramundanus* fr. *ultra*, beyond + *mundus*, the world]

ul·tra·son·ic (ʌltrəsónik) *adj.* supersonic **ul·tra·són·ics** *n.* supersonics [fr. L. *ultra*, beyond + *sonus*, sound]

ultrasonic bonding technique of bonding metals by utilizing ultrasonic vibration, mechanical pressure, and a wiping motion *Cf* ULTRASONIC SOLDERING, ULTRASONIC WELDING

ultrasonic cleaning technique creating ultrasonic waves in a liquid in which objects are washed

ultrasonic coagulation technique using ultrasonic waves to bond small particles into larger ones

ultrasonic holography technique for reproducing an interior or exterior three-dimensional image of a solid through the interference pattern of ultrasonic waves *Cf* HOLOGRAPHY

ultrasonics *n.* (*acoustics*) study of source waves beyond the range of human hearing (20 kHz) used for nondestructive testing of metals, medical examination of a fetus, and, in very high intensity, for scaling boilers and in dentist's drilling —**ultrasonic** *adj.* —**ultrasonically** *adv.*

ultrasonic scanner (*med.*) device that utilizes echoes from ultrasonic waves for body tissue diagnosis *Cf* ULTRASONOGRAPH

ultrasonic sealing technique for sealing plastic packages by heat, utilizing the pressure of ultrasonic vibrations

ultrasonic soldering technique utilizing heat and high-frequency vibrations for creating bubbles in soldering, avoiding the use of a flue to remove oxide films on metal *Cf* ULTRASONIC BONDING, ULTRASONIC WELDING

ultrasonic stroboscope device utilizing an ultrasonic beam to interrupt a light beam

ultrasonic therapy (*med.*) therapeutic use of ultrasonic (0.7 to 1.0 MHz) pulse converted to heat *also* ultrasound diathermy

ultrasonic welding technique that utilizes ultrasonic waves to bond metal without heat *Cf* ULTRASONIC BONDING, ULTRASONIC WELDING

ul·tra·son·o·graph (ʌltrəsónəgræf) *n.* (*acoustics*) diagnostic device utilizing ultrasonic (15–20 MHz) waves to penetrate tissue *Cf* ULTRASONIC SCANNER —**ultrasonogram** *n.* the resulting record —**ultrasonography** *n.* the use —**ultrasonologist** *n.* the user —**ultrasound diagnosis** *n.*

ul·tra·sound (ʌltrəsaund) *n.* produce of ultrasonic waves, widely used in diathermy, medical diagnosis, cleaning, etc.

Ul·tra·suede (ʌltrəsweid) *n.* trademark for washable, suedelike fabric that is 60% polyester and 40% nonpolyurethane

ul·tra·vi·o·let (ʌltrəváiəlit) **1.** *adj.* (*abbr.* UV) relating to, producing or using ultraviolet radiation **2.** *n.* ultraviolet radiation

CONCISE PRONUNCIATION KEY: **(a)** æ, c*a*t; ɑ, c*a*r; ɔ, f*aw*n; ei, sn*a*ke. **(e)** e, h*e*n; iː, sh*ee*p; iə, d*ee*r; ɛə, b*ea*r. **(i)** i, f*i*sh; ai, t*i*ger; əː, b*i*rd. **(o)** o, *o*x; au, c*ow*; ou, g*oa*t; u, p*oo*r; ɔi, r*oy*al. **(u)** ʌ, d*u*ck; u, b*u*ll; uː, g*oo*se; ə, b*a*cillus; juː, c*u*be. x, lo*ch*; θ, *th*ink; ð, bo*th*er; z, *Z*en; ʒ, corsa*g*e; dʒ, sava*g*e; ŋ, orangutan*g*; j, *y*ak; ʃ, *f*ish; tʃ, fe*tch*; 'l, rabb*le*; 'n, redd*en*. Complete pronunciation key appears inside front cover.

ultraviolet imagery (*electromagnetics*) imagery produced from the sensing of ultraviolet radiations reflected from a surface

ultraviolet microscope a microscope that employs ultraviolet light to stimulate fluorescence in the sample

ultraviolet radiation electromagnetic waves of wavelength between the violet end of the visible band and X rays (3,800 Å–100 Å). It is present in sunlight and has an important role as a photochemical agent in certain life processes (*FLUORESCENCE, *VITAMIN D, *SPECTROSCOPY)

ul·u·late (júːljuleit, Áljuleit) *pres. part.* **ul·u·lat·ing** *past* and *past part.* **ul·u·lat·ed** *v.i.* (*rhet.*) to howl ‖ (*rhet.*) to wail and lament **ul·u·lá·tion** *n.* [fr. L. *ululare* (*ululatus*), imit.]

Ul·ya·novsk (uljánɔfsk) (formerly Simbirsk) a city (pop. 485,000) in the R.S.F.S.R., U.S.S.R., on the middle Volga: engineering, wood industries, food processing

U·lys·ses (juːlísiːz) Latin name for Odysseus

U·may·yad (uːmáijæd) a member of a Moslem caliphate which ruled Islam (661-750). The Umayyads also ruled in Spain (756-1031)

um·bel (Ámbʼl) *n.* an inflorescence in which all the pedicels arise from the top of the main stem and form a flat or rounded cluster ‖ an arrangement of parts resembling this [fr. L. *umbella*, parasol]

um·bel·late (Ámbəleit, Ámbəlit) *adj.* having, consisting of, resembling or forming an umbel or umbels **úm·bel·lat·ed** *adj.* [fr. Mod. L. *umbellatus*]

um·bel·lif·er·ous (ʌmbəlífərəs) *adj.* having an umbel or umbels [fr. UMBEL+L. *ferre*, to bear]

um·ber (Ámbər) **1.** *n.* a dark brown earth rich in manganese and ferric oxides and used as a permanent pigment (cf BURNT UMBER, cf RAW UMBER) **2.** *adj.* of the color of umber [fr. F. (*terre d'*) *ombre* or Ital. (*terra di*) *ombra*, (earth of) shade]

Um·ber·to I (umbértou) (1844-1900), king of Italy (1878-1900)

Umberto II (1904-83), last king of Italy (1946). On the abdication of his father, Victor Emmanuel III, he was made king, but a month later a referendum established a republic, and he went into exile

um·bil·i·cal (Ambílikʼl) *adj.* of or relating to the navel [fr. M.L. *umbilicalis*]

umbilical cord a cordlike structure joining the fetus to the placenta of the mother ‖ the cable connecting an outside astronaut or aquanaut to his or her ship ‖ a power supply line to a rocket or spacecraft preceding takeoff

um·bil·i·cate (Ambílikeit, Ambílikit) *adj.* shaped like a navel, having a central depression ‖ (of some spiral shells) having an open umbilicus [fr. L. *umbilicatus*]

um·bil·i·cus (Ambílikəs, Ambiláikəs) *pl.* **um·bil·i·ci** (Ambílisai, Ambəláisai) *n.* the navel ‖ the hilum of a seed ‖ the basal depression of certain spiral shells [L.]

um·bo (Ámbou) *pl.* **um·bo·nes** (Ambóuniːz), **um·bos** *n.* the boss of a shield ‖ (*anat.*) the rounded elevation in the tympanic membrane of the ear ‖ the swollen point of a cone scale of a pine tree ‖ the rounded elevation above the hinge of a bivalve shell **um·bo·nal** (Ámbənʼl), **um·bo·nate** (Ámbəneit) *adjs* [L.=boss of a shield]

um·bra (Ámbrə) *pl.* **um·brae** (Ámbriː) *n.* the shadow from which all light from a given source is excluded by an object, e.g. a planet, esp. by the earth or moon in an eclipse (cf PENUMBRA) ‖ the darker central part of a sunspot [L.=shade]

um·brage (Ámbridʒ) *n.* resentment **to take (give) umbrage** to feel (cause to feel) pique [O.F. fr. L. *umbra*, shadow]

um·bra·geous (Ambréidʒəs) *adj.* (*rhet.*) shady ‖ (*rhet.*) quick to feel suspicious and resentful [F. *ombrageux*]

um·brel·la (Ambrélə) *n.* a portable device which, when opened, is used to keep rain off a person or to protect him from the sun, or in some Asian and African countries serves as a symbol of dignity. It consists of a circular canopy of cotton, silk etc. stretched across collapsible steel ribs radiating from a center pole, the end of the pole forming a handle ‖ a larger version of this used to provide shade ‖ a protective force of fighter aircraft ‖ the contractile dome-shaped disk of a jellyfish, serving as a swimming organ [fr. Ital. *ombrella*, sunshade]

umbrella 1. *adj.* of a general covering of many things, groups, or subjects *an umbrella organi-*

zation **2.** (*business*) a contract or protective arrangement covering many or all risks

umbrella bird a member of *Cephalopterus*, fam. *Cotingidae*, a genus of South and Central American birds allied to the crow, remarkable for their crest of blueblack feathers rising from the head and curving forward over the beak

umbrella pine *Sciadopitys verticillata*, fam. *Pinaceae*, a Japanese evergreen tree having needle-shaped leaves in whorls like umbrellas, and a flat-domed crown

umbrella tree *Magnolia tripetala*, a North American magnolia having thin, oval leaves clustered at the ends of the branches ‖ any of various trees having leaves shaped or arranged in an umbrellalike fashion

Um·bri·a (Ámbriːə) a mountainous region (area 3,377 sq. miles, pop. 802,400) of central Italy, cut by the upper Tiber. Chief town: Perugia. Industries: agriculture (olives, vines), livestock raising (cattle, hogs), metalworking

Um·bri·an (Ámbriːən) **1.** *adj.* of, relating to or characteristic of the province of Umbria or the people inhabiting Umbria ‖ of, relating to or characteristic of the Italian language of ancient Umbria **2.** *n.* a native or inhabitant of Umbria ‖ the Italic language of ancient Umbria

Umbrian school the school of painting (15th-16th cc.) which included Perugino

u·mi·ak (úːmiːæk) *n.* an open Eskimo boat made by stretching skins over a wooden frame, paddled esp. by women and children [Eskimo]

um·laut (úmlaut) *n.* a vowel modification caused by assimilation to a vowel or semivowel (now generally lost) in the following syllable ‖ a vowel resulting from such assimilation ‖ a mark (¨) placed over the affected vowel, esp. in modern German [G. fr. *um*, about+*laut*, sound]

um·pir·age (Ámpaiəridʒ) *n.* the authority or position of an umpire ‖ an instance of umpiring

um·pire (Ámpaiər) **1.** *n.* someone chosen to enforce the rules of play and decide disputes in certain games, e.g. cricket or baseball (cf REFEREE) ‖ an arbitrator ‖ (*law*) a third person appointed to make a decision in a disagreement between arbitrators **2.** *v. pres. part.* **um·pir·ing** *past* and *past part.* **um·pired** *v.i.* to act as umpire ‖ *v.t.* to act as umpire in or of [older *a numpire* taken as *an umpire* fr. O.F. *nonper*, uneven (i.e. a third party)]

ump·teen (Ámptíːn) *adj.* (*pop.*) very many [facetious extension of words in *-teen*]

ump·ti·eth (Ámptiːəθ) *adj.* numberless

Um·ta·li (uːmtáliː) an agricultural and goldmining center (pop. 30,000) in Zimbabwe near the Mozambique border, linked by rail with the coast

U.N., UN *UNITED NATIONS

un- (ʌn) *prefix* not, lack of, opposite, as in 'unemployment' [O.E. *un-*]

un- *prefix* added to verbs to indicate a reversal of the action of the verb, as in 'untie' ‖ added to nouns to indicate a release from the state expressed by the noun, as in 'undress' [O.E. *un-*, *on*]

un·a·ble (Anéibʼl) *adj.* not able

un·a·bridged (Anəbrídzd) *adj.* not abridged

un·ac·com·pa·nied (Anəkámpəniːd) *adj.* not accompanied ‖ (*mus.*) with no accompaniment

un·ac·com·plished (Anəkámplіʃt) *adj.* not finished or achieved ‖ having no accomplishments

un·ac·count·a·ble (Anəkáuntəbʼl) *adj.* inexplicable ‖ not accountable, not responsible **un·ac·cóunt·a·bly** *adv.*

un·ac·count·ed for (Anəkáuntid) unexplained, not accounted for

un·ac·cus·tomed (Anəkástəmd) *adj.* unusual ‖ (with 'to') not accustomed, *unaccustomed to this sort of thing*

un·a·dopt·ed (Anədóptid) *adj.* (*Br.*, of roads) not made up or maintained by the local authority

un·ad·vised (Anædváizd) *adj.* ill-considered, rash ‖ without advice **un·ad·vis·ed·ly** (Anædváizdli) *adv.*

un·af·fect·ed (Anəféktid) *adj.* without affectation ‖ not affected or influenced

un·al·ien·a·ble (Anéiljənəbʼl, Anéiliːənəbʼl) *adj.* inalienable

U·na·mu·no (uːnəmúːnou), Miguel de (1864-1936), Spanish philosopher and essayist. In 'The Tragic Sense of Life in Men and in Peoples' (1913) he made a profound and highly individualistic analysis of modern man

u·na·nim·i·ty (juːnənímiti) *n.* the state or quality of being unanimous [fr. O.F. *unanimite*]

u·nan·i·mous (juːnǽnəməs) *adj.* being of one mind, being in complete agreement ‖ arrived at

with complete agreement, *a unanimous decision*

un·an·swer·a·ble (ʌnǽnsərəbʼl) *adj.* that cannot be refuted or answered

un·ap·proach·a·ble (Anəpróutʃəbʼl) *adj.* not able to be approached ‖ unrivaled

un·armed (Anáːrmd) *adj.* having no weapons ‖ (of plants or animals) having no scales, claws, spines etc.

u·na·ry (júːnəriː) *adj.* made up of only one component *also* monadic

un·as·sum·ing (Anəsúːmiŋ) *adj.* modest, not pretentious

un·at·tached (Anətǽtʃt) *adj.* not attached ‖ not belonging to a particular group, organization etc. ‖ (*old-fash.*) not married or engaged

un·at·tend·ed (Anəténdid) *adj.* alone, not accompanied ‖ not looked after, not attended to

un·a·vail·ing (Anəvéiliŋ) *adj.* having no useful effect

un·a·void·a·ble (Anəvɔ́idəbʼl) *adj.* inevitable, not avoidable **un·a·vóid·a·bly** *adv.*

un·a·ware (Anəwéər) **1.** *adj.* not aware **2.** *adv.* unawares

un·a·wares (Anəwéərz) *adv.* by surprise, *we caught him unawares* ‖ unintentionally, without noticing

un·bal·anced (Anbǽlənst) *adj.* lacking balance ‖ mentally unstable ‖ (*accounting*) not balanced

un·beat·en (Anbíːtʼn) *adj.* not defeated ‖ (*rhet.*) untrodden, *unbeaten paths* ‖ not whipped

un·be·com·ing (Anbikámiŋ) *adj.* not becoming, *unbecoming clothes* ‖ unseemly, not decent

un·be·known (Anbinóun) **1.** *adj.* unknown **2.** *adv.* **unbeknown to** without the knowledge of, unknown to

un·be·lief (Anbilíːf) *n.* disbelief, incredulity ‖ lack of belief, esp. of religious belief

un·be·liev·a·ble (Anbilíːvəbʼl) *adj.* true but astounding ‖ unacceptable as being true

un·be·liev·er (Anbilíːvər) *n.* someone who questions the truth of something ‖ a person who has no belief in matters of religion

un·be·liev·ing (Anbilíːviŋ) *adj.* incredulous ‖ not believing

un·bend (Anbénd) *pres. part.* **un·bend·ing** *past* and *past part.* **un·bent** *v.t.* to make straight ‖ (*naut.*) to unfasten (sails, ropes etc.) ‖ *v.i.* to become straight ‖ to become less distant or less stiff in manner

un·bend·ing (Anbéndiŋ) *adj.* inflexible in decision ‖ stiff and distant in manner

unbent *past* and *past part.* OF UNBEND

un·bid·den (Anbídʼn) *adj.* not invited ‖ not commanded

un·bind (Anbáind) *pres. part.* **un·bind·ing** *past* and *past part.* **un·bound** (Anbáund) *v.t.* to untie, unfasten ‖ to remove restraints or restrictions from ‖ to undo the binding of (a book) [O.E. *unbindan*]

un·blessed (Anblést) *adj.* without something considered a blessing, *a house unblessed with modern comforts* ‖ unholy, wicked

un·blush·ing (Anbláʃiŋ) *adj.* shameless ‖ not blushing

un·born (Anbɔ́rn) *adj.* not yet born ‖ not brought into being

un·bos·om (Anbúːzəm, Anbúːzəm) *v.t.* to reveal (one's feelings, thoughts etc.) ‖ *v.i.* to reveal one's feelings, thoughts etc. **to unbosom oneself** to relieve (oneself) of the strain of hidden feelings, thoughts etc. by revealing them

un·bound (Anbáund) *past* and *past part.* of UNBIND ‖ *adj.* not bound ‖ (of a book) not having a binding

un·bound·ed (Anbáundid) *adj.* without restraint, *unbounded joy* ‖ without limits in extent, quantity etc.

un·bowed (Anbáud) *adj.* (*rhet.*) undefeated ‖ not bowed

un·bri·dled (Anbráidʼld) *adj.* unrestrained ‖ having no bridle on

un·bro·ken (Anbróukən) *adj.* intact, whole ‖ not disordered, *despite the casualties their ranks remained unbroken* ‖ uninterrupted ‖ (of a horse) not broken in

un·bun·dle (Anbándʼl) *v.* to separate the elements of combined cost price, etc., from a package figure

un·bur·den (Anbɔ́ːrdʼn) *v.t.* to remove a burden from ‖ to relieve (oneself, one's conscience or one's mind) of worry or anxiety ‖ to rid oneself of the burden of (guilt, remorse etc.) e.g. by confiding in someone

un·called-for (Ankɔ́ldfɔr) *adj.* unnecessary ‖ impertinent, *an uncalled-for remark*

CONCISE PRONUNCIATION KEY: **(a)** æ, c*a*t; ɑ, c*a*r; ɔ f*aw*n; ei, sn*a*ke. **(e)** e, h*e*n; iː, sh*ee*p; iə, d*ee*r; ɛə, b*ea*r. **(i)** i, f*i*sh; ai, t*i*ger; əː, b*i*rd. **(o)** o, *o*x; au, c*ow*; ou, g*oa*t; u, p*oo*r; ɔi, r*oy*al. **(u)** ʌ, d*u*ck; u, b*u*ll; uː, g*oo*se; ə, b*a*cillus; juː, c*u*be. x, lo*ch*; θ, *th*ink; ð, bo*th*er; z, *Z*en; ʒ, corsa*g*e; dʒ, sava*g*e; ŋ, orangutan*g*; j, *y*ak; ʃ, *fi*sh; tʃ, fe*tch*; ʼl, rabb*le*; ʼn, redd*en*. Complete pronunciation key appears inside front cover.

un·can·ni·ly (ʌnkǽnili:) *adv.* in an uncanny way or to an uncanny degree

un·can·ni·ness (ʌnkǽni:nis) *n.* the quality of being uncanny

un·can·ny (ʌnkǽni:) *comp.* **un·can·ni·er** *superl.* **un·can·ni·est** *adj.* inspiring feelings of apprehension ‖ almost superhuman, *uncanny powers of observation*

un·cap (ʌnkǽp) *v.* to uncover; to reveal

un·cer·e·mo·ni·ous (ʌnserəmóuni:əs) *adj.* brusque, curt, abrupt ‖ without ceremony or formality

un·cer·tain (ʌnsə́:rt'n) *adj.* not certainly known ‖ not having certain knowledge ‖ not certain to occur ‖ not reliable variable

un·cer·tain·ty (ʌnsə́:rt'nti:) *pl.* **un·cer·tain·ties** *n.* the quality or state of being uncertain ‖ something uncertain

uncertainty principle a principle, derived by Heisenberg as a logical consequence of quantum mechanics, according to which it is impossible to specify simultaneously the values of position and momentum or energy and time for a particle in a quantized system. The more precisely one of these quantities is known the less precise becomes our knowledge of the other

un·chris·tian (ʌnkrístʃən) *adj.* not of the Christian religion ‖ not befitting a Christian ‖ not according to principles of Christian behavior

un·ci·al (ʌnʃi:əl, ʌnʃl) 1. *adj.* of, relating to, or written in, the rounded unlinked letters used esp. in Greek and Latin manuscripts 300–900 A.D. 2. *n.* an uncial letter ‖ a manuscript written in uncials [fr. L. *uncialis*, of an inch fr. *uncia*, twelfth part (of a pound or foot)]

un·ci·form (ʌnsifɔrm) 1. *adj.* of a bone in the distal row of the wrist, on the same side as the ulna ‖ of a hook-shaped process on the unciform bone or a similar process on the ethmoid bone 2. *n.* an unciform bone [fr. L. *uncus*, a hook]

un·ci·nate (ʌnsinit, ʌnsineit) *adj.* (*biol.*) hooked [fr. L. *uncinatus* fr. *uncinus*, a hook-shaped part]

un·cir·cum·cised (ʌnsə́:rkəmsaizd) *adj.* not circumcised ‖ (*Bible*) heathen ‖ (*Bible*) gentile, not Jewish

unclad *alt. past* and *past part.* of UNCLOTHE

un·clasp (ʌnklǽsp, ʌnklásp) *v.t.* to loosen or release the clasp of ‖ to release from a clasp ‖ *v.i.* to loosen a grasp or grip

un·cle (ʌŋk'l) *n.* the brother of one's mother or father ‖ the husband of one's aunt ‖ (*pop.*) a cry meaning 'Stop, I've had enough!' [A.F.]

un·clean (ʌnklí:n) *adj.* morally impure ‖ ceremonially impure ‖ not clean, dirty

Uncle Sam (*pop.*) the government of the U.S.A. personified ‖ (*pop.*) the U.S.A. as a nation [prob. a jocular expansion of U.S.]

Uncle Tom *n.* a servile black person, esp. in relation to white people, from *Uncle Tom's Cabin*, by Harriet Beecher Stowe —**Uncle Tom** *adj.* —**Uncle Tomish** *adj.* —**Uncle Tomism** *n.*

un·cloak (ʌnklóuk) *v.t.* to remove a cloak from ‖ to expose (a plot etc. or a criminal) ‖ *v.i.* to take off a cloak

un·clothe (ʌnklóuð) *pres. part.* **un·cloth·ing** *past* and *past part.* **un·clothed**, **un·clad** (ʌnklǽd) *v.t.* to undress (someone)

un·com·fort·a·ble (ʌnkʌ́mfərtəb'l) *adj.* causing discomfort ‖ feeling discomfort ‖ uneasy **un·com·fort·a·bly** *adv.*

un·com·mit·ted (ʌnkəmítid) *adj.* not committed ‖ not bound to do something

un·com·mon (ʌnkɔ́mən) *adj.* unusual

un·com·mu·ni·ca·tive (ʌnkəmjú:nikətiv, ʌnkəmjú:nikeitiv) *adj.* reticent, disinclined to talk or to give information

un·com·pro·mis·ing (ʌnkɔ́mprəmaiziŋ) *adj.* making no concessions in negotiation, bargaining etc. ‖ free of compromise, *uncompromising integrity*

un·con·cern (ʌnkənsə́:rn) *n.* lack of concern, indifference

un·con·cerned (ʌnkənsə́:rnd) *adj.* not troubled, worried etc. ‖ not concerned, *unconcerned with the merits or demerits of the case* **un·con·cern·ed·ly** (ʌnkənsə́:rnidli:) *adv.*

un·con·di·tion·al (ʌnkəndíʃən'l) *adj.* absolute, without any qualifying conditions

un·con·di·tioned (ʌnkəndíʃənd) *adj.* (*psychol.*) not conditioned ‖ (*philos.*) absolute, not subject to conditions

un·con·form·i·ty (ʌnkənfɔ́rmiti:) *pl.* **un·con·form·i·ties** *n.* (*geol.*) a rock formation in which the strata are not arranged in the order in which they were formed, usually because inter- mediate strata were completely eroded before the later strata were formed

un·con·scion·a·ble (ʌnkɔ́nʃənəb'l) *adj.* unscrupulous, unaffected by conscience ‖ immoderate, inordinate **un·con·scion·a·bly** *adv.*

un·con·scious (ʌnkɔ́nʃəs) 1. *adj.* not endowed with consciousness ‖ temporarily without consciousness ‖ (with 'of') not conscious ‖ not intended, *an unconscious insult* ‖ of or relating to the unconscious 2. *n.* the area of mental activity which escapes mental awareness. It contains images, ideas etc. which have been repressed, but which emerge in dreams, pathological states etc., and may motivate behavior

un·con·scious·ness (ʌnkɔ́nʃəsnis) *n.* lack of consciousness

un·con·sti·tu·tion·al (ʌnkɔnstitú:ʃən'l, ʌnkɔnstitjú:ʃən'l) *adj.* not in accordance with the constitution **un·con·sti·tu·tion·al·i·ty** *n.*

un·cor·rect·a·ble (ʌnkəréktəb'l) *adj.* not capable of being corrected —**uncorrectably** *adv.*

un·count·ed (ʌnkáuntid) *adj.* not counted ‖ innumerable

un·cou·ple (ʌnkʌ́p'l) *pres. part.* **un·cou·pling** *past* and *past part.* **un·cou·pled** *v.t.* to disconnect ‖ to set (hounds) free from a leash

un·couth (ʌnkú:θ) *adj.* (of a person or his manners, bearing etc.) awkward, rough ‖ (of style, language etc.) not polished [O.E. *uncūth*, unknown]

un·cov·er (ʌnkʌ́vər) *v.t.* to remove the cover or covering from ‖ to reveal, disclose ‖ *v.i.* (old-fash.) to take one's hat off one's head

un·cov·ered (ʌnkʌ́vərd) *adj.* without a cover or covering ‖ not covered by insurance etc. ‖ wearing no protection against the rain, wind or cold, esp. bareheaded

un·crowned (ʌnkráund) *adj.* reigning but not having gone through the coronation rite, *Edward VIII was uncrowned king of England*

unc·tion (ʌ́ŋkʃən) *n.* an anointing with oil as an act of religious significance ‖ the oil used ‖ an anointing with an ointment etc. for healing purposes ‖ religious fervor ‖ effusiveness in speech or manner [fr. L. *unctio* (*unctionis*)]

unc·tu·ous (ʌ́ŋktʃu:əs) *adj.* (esp. of speech or manner) effusive ‖ made of or containing oil or fat ‖ (of soil) soft and rich ‖ (of clay) plastic [fr. M.L. *unctuosus*, greasy]

un·cut (ʌnkʌ́t) *adj.* not cut ‖ (of a gem) not cut to shape ‖ (of a book) not having the pages trimmed ‖ (of a play etc.) not abridged

un·daunt·ed (ʌndɔ́ntid) *adj.* fearless, not daunted

un·de·ceive (ʌndisí:v) *pres. part.* **un·de·ceiv·ing** *past* and *past part.* **un·de·ceived** *v.t.* to free from false beliefs, ideas or impressions

un·de·cid·ed (ʌndisáidid) *adj.* that is not decided ‖ not having reached a decision

un·de·cil·lion (ʌndisíljən) *n.* *NUMBER TABLE [fr. L. *undecim*, eleven+MILLION]

un·dee, un·dé, un·dée (ʌndei) *adj.* (heraldry) wavy [O.F. *unde* fr. L. *unda*, wave]

un·de·mon·stra·tive (ʌndəmɔ́nstrətiv) *adj.* not showing one's feelings

un·de·ni·a·ble (ʌndináiəb'l) *adj.* indisputable, certain, that cannot be denied **un·de·ni·a·bly** *adv.*

un·der (ʌ́ndər) 1. *prep.* in, at, or to a position lower than, *to put felt under a carpet* ‖ in a position lower than the surface of, *under the ground* ‖ covered by, *under heavy blankets* ‖ lower in amount, quality, rank etc. than, *under average in weight* ‖ according to, *under the terms of the new contract* ‖ taking into account, *under the circumstances* ‖ indicated or represented by, *under a new name* ‖ suffering the action or effect of, *under ether* ‖ concealed by, sheltered by, *under a false name, under cover of darkness* ‖ within the designation of, *classify the entry under 'music'* ‖ bound by, *under an oath of secrecy* ‖ subject to (a specified penalty, threat etc.), *under pain of dismissal* ‖ subject to the guidance, authority, instruction etc. of, *Raphael studied under Perugino* ‖ during the reign of, *the monasteries were destroyed under Henry VIII* ‖ (of a piece of ground) planted or sown with, *under clover* 2. *adv.* in or to a lower position, beneath ‖ in or to a position of subordination, subjection etc. ‖ so as to be covered, concealed etc. ‖ less than the required amount etc. ‖ less than a certain age, weight, length etc., *forbidden to children of 10 and under* 3. *adj.* located or moving at a lower position than something or on the lower surface of something ‖ lower in amount, degree etc. ‖ lower in authority, rank etc. [O.E.]

under- *prefix* in, at, to or from a lower position ‖ in a subordinate position, as in 'understudy' ‖ to a degree, amount etc. considered below standard [M.E.]

un·der·a·chiev·er (ʌndərətʃí:vər) *n.* one who performs below his or her capacity —**underachieve** *v.* —**underachievement** *n.*

un·der·act (ʌndərǽkt) *v.t.* to act (a part) with less than full dramatic feeling ‖ *v.i.* to perform with less than full dramatic feeling

un·der·age (ʌndəréidʒ) *adj.* below the legal or required age

un·der·arm (ʌndərɑrm) 1. *adj.* performed with the arm swinging below the level of the shoulder 2. *adv.* with an underarm movement 3. *n.* the armpit

un·der·bid (ʌndərbíd) 1. *v.t. pres. part.* **un·der·bid·ding** *past* and *past part.* **un·der·bid** to bid less than (a competing bidder) ‖ (cards) to bid less on (a hand) than its strength warrants 2. *n.* an instance of underbidding

un·der·brush (ʌndərbrʌ́ʃ) *n.* undergrowth

un·der·car·riage (ʌndərkæridʒ) *n.* the landing gear of an aircraft ‖ a supporting framework

un·der·char·ac·ter·i·za·tion (ʌndərkærəktə:rəzéiʃən) *n.* insufficient development of the characters in a play, novel, or story

un·der·charge 1. (ʌndərtʃɑrdʒ) *v.t. pres. part.* **un·der·charg·ing** *past* and *past part.* **un·der·charged** to charge (someone) too little ‖ to charge (goods) at a lower price than is usual or permissible ‖ to load (a gun) with an insufficient charge 2. (ʌndərtʃɑrdʒ) *n.* an instance of undercharging for goods or the amount of this

un·der·class (ʌndərklæs) *n.* those on a lower economic, social, or educational level than those of the middle class

un·der·class·man (ʌndərklǽsmən, ʌndərklásmən) *pl.* **un·der·class·men** (ʌndərklǽsmən, ʌndərklásmən) *n.* a freshman or sophomore

un·der·clothes (ʌndərklouðz, ʌndərklouz) *pl. n.* clothes worn next to the body, under the outer garments

un·der·cloth·ing (ʌndərklouðiŋ) *n.* underclothes

un·der·coat (ʌndərkout) *n.* (of longhaired animals) a growth of hair under and partly concealed by the main growth of hair ‖ a layer of paint etc. applied as base for a top coat

undercoating *n.* (*motor vehicle*) a rustproofing placed on the under surface of a chassis —**undercoat** *v.*

un·der·cov·er (ʌndərkʌ́vər, ʌndərkʌ́vər) *adj.* acting or carried out secretly

un·der·croft (ʌndərkrɔ́ft, ʌndərkrɔft) *n.* a crypt [fr. UNDER+obs. *croft*, crypt fr. L.]

un·der·cur·rent (ʌndərkə.rənt, ʌndərkʌrənt) *n.* a current below the upper surface of water or air ‖ an underlying tendency running counter to openly expressed opinion or feeling

un·der·cut 1. (ʌndərkʌ́t) *v.t. pres. part.* **un·der·cut·ting** *past* and *past part.* **un·der·cut** to cut away from the undersurface of ‖ to make an undercut in (a tree) ‖ to undersell ‖ to work for lower wages than ‖ (golf, tennis etc.) to hit (the ball) so as to give it backspin 2. (ʌndərkʌt) *n.* an underhand stroke, e.g. in tennis, to impart backspin ‖ a notch cut in a tree below the level of the major cut, on the side where the tree is to fall ‖ (*Br.*) a joint of meat cut from the lower side of a sirloin ‖ a cut made below or beneath another cut 3. (ʌndərkʌt) *adj.* cut away so as to stand out in relief

un·der·de·vel·oped (ʌndərdivéləpt) *adj.* less developed than is normal ‖ (*photog.*) not developed enough to give a good image ‖ (of a country or region) not industrially or economically reaching the level that could be reached if the necessary capital, technicians etc. were available

un·der·do (ʌndərdú:) *pres. part.* **un·der·do·ing** *past* **un·der·did** (ʌndərdíd) *past part.* **un·der·done** (ʌndərdʌ́n) *v.t.* to cook (meat) very lightly ‖ to cook (food) for insufficient time

un·der·dog (ʌndərdɔg, ʌndərdɔg) *n.* someone who gets the worst of a struggle ‖ a victim of social injustice

un·der·done (ʌndərdʌ́n) *past part.* of UNDERDO ‖ *adj.* (of meat) very lightly cooked, rare ‖ (of food) insufficiently cooked

un·der·em·ploy·ment (ʌndərimplɔ́imənt) *n.* 1. employment that does not utilize one's best skills 2. part-time employment *Cf* SUBEMPLOYMENT

un·der·es·ti·mate 1. (ʌndəréstəmeit) *v.t. pres. part.* **un·der·es·ti·mat·ing** *past* and *past part.* **un·der·es·ti·mat·ed** to rate (something or someone) below true worth ‖ to quote too low a

CONCISE PRONUNCIATION KEY: **(a)** æ, c*a*t; ɑ, c*ar*; ɔ f*aw*n; ei, sn*a*ke. **(e)** e, h*e*n; i:, sh*ee*p; iə, d*eer*; ɛə, b*ear*. **(i)** i, f*i*sh; ai, t*i*ger; ə:, b*i*rd. **(o)** ɔ, *o*x; au, c*ow*; ou, g*oa*t; u, p*oor*; ɔi, r*oy*al. **(u)** ʌ, d*u*ck; u, b*u*ll; u:, g*oo*se; ə, b*a*cillus; ju:, c*u*be. x, lo*ch*; θ, *th*ink; ð, bo*th*er; z, *Z*en; ʒ, corsa*g*e; dʒ, sava*g*e; ŋ, oranguta*ng*; j, *y*ak; ʃ, *f*ish; tʃ, fe*tch*; 'l, rabb*le*; 'n, redd*en*. Complete pronunciation key appears inside front cover.

figure in giving an estimate for **2.** (ʌndəréstəmit) *n.* too low a rating or estimate **un·der·es·ti·ma·tion** *n.*

un·der·ex·pose (ʌndərikspóuz) *pres. part.* **un·der·ex·pos·ing** *past and past part.* **un·der·ex·posed** *v.t.* (*photog.*) to expose (*film*) for too short a time **un·der·ex·po·sure** (ʌndərikspóuʒər) *n.*

un·der·feed (ʌndərfí:d) *pres. part.* **un·der·feed·ing** *past and past part.* **un·der·fed** (ʌndərféd) *v.t.* to give insufficient food to || to stoke (a fire) from below

un·der·foot (ʌndərfút) *adv.* under the foot or feet || (*pop.*) in the way

un·der·gar·ment (ʌndərgɑrmənt) *n.* a garment, e.g. a petticoat, meant to be worn under another garment

un·der·glaze (ʌndərgleiz) **1.** *adj.* (*ceramics*) applied before glazing **2.** *n.* a pigment for application before glazing

un·der·go (ʌndərgóu) *pres. part.* **un·der·go·ing** *past* **un·der·went** (ʌndərwént) *past part.* **un·der·gone** (ʌndərgɔn, ʌndərgón) *v.t.* to endure, experience

un·der·grad·u·ate (ʌndərgrǽdʒu:it) **1.** *n.* a university student who has not yet obtained his first (or bachelor's) degree **2.** *adj.* of, for or consisting of undergraduates || having the status of an undergraduate

un·der·ground 1. (ʌndərgraund) *adj.* being below the surface of the ground || not public, secret **2.** *n.* (ʌndərgraund) (*Br.=Am.* subway) an underground railroad **the underground** a secret resistance movement, esp. in an occupied or totalitarian country **3.** (ʌndərgráund) *adv.* beneath the earth's surface || in or into hiding

underground railroad a city railroad running in tunnels under a city **Underground Railroad** (*Am. hist.*) a chain of sympathizers who provided a system of escape before the Civil War for slaves who ran away from the South to the free states and Canada

underground railway an underground railroad

un·der·grown (ʌndərgróun, ʌndərgroun) *adj.* not grown to full or normal size or development

un·der·growth (ʌndərgrouθ) *n.* shrubs, saplings etc. growing on the forest floor

un·der·hand (ʌndərhǽnd) **1.** *adj.* deceitful, sly || performed with the hand below the level of the shoulder **2.** *adv.* in an underhand manner || with an underhand arm action

un·der·hand·ed (ʌndərhǽndid) *adj.* secret, sly || shorthanded

un·der·hung (ʌndərhʌ́ŋ) *adj.* (of the lower jaw) projecting beyond the upper jaw || having such a jaw || resting and moving on a track or rail underneath, not suspended

un·der·kill (ʌndərkil) *n.* **1.** use of force inadequate to accomplish the task **2.** by extension, use of restraint in the exercise of power

un·der·laid (ʌndərléid) *past and past part.* of UNDERLAY || *adj.* laid underneath || supported or strengthened by having something laid underneath

underlain *past part.* of UNDERLIE

un·der·lay 1. (ʌndərléi) *v. pres. part.* **un·der·lay·ing** *past and past part.* **un·der·laid** (ʌndərléid) *v.t.* to lay under, to support or line with something placed underneath || to adjust with an underlay || *v.i.* (*Br., mining*, of a vein) to incline from the vertical **2.** (ʌndərlei) *n.* something laid under, esp. a varying thickness of paper placed under type to raise it to the right level for printing || (*Br., mining*) an inclination of a vein from the vertical

underlay *past* of UNDERLIE

un·der·lie (ʌndərlái) *v. pres. part.* **un·der·ly·ing** *past* **un·der·lay** (ʌndərléi) *past part.* **un·der·lain** (ʌndərléin) *v.t.* to lie or be under || to be the basis or foundation of || to lie hidden under (external appearances) || (*finance*, of a right, security etc.) to be prior to (another right etc.) || (*Br., mining*) to underlay

un·der·line 1. (ʌndərláin, ʌndərlain) *v.t. pres. part.* **un·der·lin·ing** *past and past part.* **un·der·lined** to draw a line under (e.g. a word) esp. for emphasis || to emphasize **2.** (ʌndərlain) *n.* a line drawn underneath a printed or written word

un·der·ling (ʌndərliŋ) *n.* (used contemptuously) a subordinate

un·der·lip (ʌndərlip) *n.* the lower lip

un·der·ly·ing (ʌndərláiiŋ) *adj.* lying or placed underneath || being at the basis but not immediately obvious

underlying structure *DEEP STRUCTURE

un·der·mine (ʌndərmáin) *pres. part.* **un·der·min·ing** *past and past part.* **un·der·mined** *v.t.*

to dig under so as to cause a fall || (of water) to wash away the foundations of || (*fig.*) to weaken or injure by crafty, indirect methods || to weaken or ruin gradually, *drugs undermined his health*

un·der·most (ʌndərmoust) **1.** *adj.* lowest in position, rank etc. **2.** *adv.* lowest

un·der·neath (ʌndərní:θ) **1.** *adv.* beneath, below **2.** *prep.* beneath, below **3.** *adj.* lower, under **4.** *n.* the bottom surface

un·der·nour·ished (ʌndərnó:riʃt, ʌndərnʌ́riʃt) *adj.* not provided with enough food

un·der·nour·ish·ment (ʌndərní:riʃmənt, ʌndərnʌ́riʃmənt) *n.* lack of adequate food

un·der·oc·cu·pied (ʌndərɔ́kju:paid) *adj.* of not utilizing space, skill, or a facility to its capacity

underpaid *past and past part.* of UNDERPAY

un·der·pants (ʌndərpænts) *pl. n.* an undergarment covering the lower torso and sometimes the upper thigh, with a separate division for each leg

un·der·pass (ʌndərpæs, ʌndərpɒs) *n.* a tunnel or passageway for traffic or pedestrians or both, passing under a railroad or highway

un·der·pay (ʌndərpéi) *pres. part.* **un·der·pay·ing** *past and past part.* **un·der·paid** (ʌndərpéid) *v.t.* to pay less than is just or adequate

un·der·pin (ʌndərpín) *pres. part.* **un·der·pin·ning** *past and past part.* **under·pinned** *v.t.* to support by placing masonry, woodwork etc. underneath **un·der·pin·ning** *n.* materials or a structure that gives support e.g. for a wall

un·der·play (ʌndərpléi) *v.t.* to play (a role) in an intentionally restrained manner || to fail to give (a role) its full dramatic emphasis || to minimize the importance of || (*cards*) to play (one's hand) for less than its full value

un·der·plot (ʌndərplɒt) *n.* a subordinate plot in a story, play etc.

un·der·pop·u·la·tion (ʌndərpɒpju:léiʃən) *n.* a state of having less population than would be acceptable, esp. with consideration of available resources

un·der·priv·i·leged (ʌndərprívəlidʒd, ʌndərprívlidʒd) *adj.* living under social and economic conditions below an acceptable level

un·der·pro·duc·tion (ʌndərprədʌ́kʃən) *n.* the production of an amount that is too small to satisfy demand, less than the norm, or less than full capacity

un·der·proof (ʌndərprú:f) *adj.* lower in alcohol content than proof spirit

un·der·rate (ʌndərréit) *pres. part.* **un·der·rat·ing** *past and past part.* **un·der·rat·ed** *v.t.* to attribute less than full worth or importance to

un·der·score (ʌndərskɔ́r, ʌndərskóur) *pres. part.* **un·der·scor·ing** *past and past part.* **un·der·scored** *v.t.* to underline

un·der·sea 1. (ʌndərsi:) *adj.* being, happening, or meant for use below the surface of the sea **2.** (ʌndərsi:) *adv.* under the sea

un·der·seas (ʌndərsi:z) *adv.* undersea

un·der·sec·re·tar·y (ʌndərsékriteri:) *pl.* **un·der·sec·re·tar·ies** *n.* an assistant secretary, esp. in a department of state

un·der·sell (ʌndərsél) *pres. part.* **un·der·sell·ing** *past and past part.* **un·der·sold** (ʌndərsóuld) *v.t.* to sell at a lower price than || to sell at a price lower than the value of

un·der·set (ʌndərset) *n.* an underlying vein of ore || an undercurrent

un·der·shap·er (ʌndərʃeipər) *n.* women's elastic undergarment

un·der·shirt (ʌndərʃə:rt) *n.* (*Am.=Br.* vest) an undergarment covering the upper part of the body

un·der·shoot (ʌndərʃu:t, ʌndərʃú:t) *pres. part.* **un·der·shoot·ing** *past and past part.* **un·der·shot** (ʌndərʃɒt, ʌndərʃót) *v.t.* to shoot or fire short of (the target) || (of an aircraft) to fail to get onto (the runway or flight deck) in coming into land || *v.i.* to shoot or fire short of the target

un·der·shorts (ʌndərʃɔrts) *pl. n.* underpants

un·der·shot (ʌndərʃɒt) *adj.* (of the lower jaw) underhung || (of a wheel) driven by water passing beneath it

un·der·side (ʌndərsaid) *n.* the underneath, the side or surface facing downwards

un·der·signed 1. (ʌndərsáind) *adj.* signed below || whose name is signed below **2.** (ʌndərsaind) *n.* (with 'the') the person or persons having signed below

un·der·size (ʌndərsáiz) *adj.* undersized

un·der·sized (ʌndərsáizd) *adj.* smaller than average or normal

un·der·skirt (ʌndərskə:rt) *n.* a skirt worn under another skirt, esp. a waistlength petticoat

un·der·slung (ʌndərslʌŋ) *adj.* (of a chassis) with the frame slung below the axles

undersold *past part.* of UNDERSELL

un·der·stand (ʌndərstǽnd) *pres. part.* **un·der·stand·ing** *past and past part.* **un·der·stood** (ʌndərstúd) *v.t.* to seize the meaning of || to be thoroughly acquainted with, expert in the use or practice of, *to understand machinery* || (*philos.*) to form a reasoned judgment concerning (something) || to possess a passive knowledge of (a language) || to appreciate and sympathize with || to gather, infer, *what do you understand will happen?* || to interpret, attribute a specified meaning to, *I understand the message to mean they aren't coming* || to accept as a fact, believe, *I understand that I shall be repaid* || (used in the passive) to supply mentally (a word, idea etc.) || *v.i.* to have the power of seizing meanings, forming reasoned judgments etc. || to feel and show sympathy, tolerance etc. [O.E. *understandan*, to stand under]

un·der·stand·ing (ʌndərstǽndiŋ) **1.** *n.* the ability to understand || the act of one who understands || (*philos.*) the power to form reasoned judgments || an informal agreement that is only morally binding || a resolution of differences **2.** *adj.* feeling and showing sympathy, tolerance etc.

un·der·state (ʌndərstéit) *pres. part.* **un·der·stat·ing** *past and past part.* **under·stat·ed** *v.t.* to represent as being less or less important etc. than is in fact the case, often as a trick of style for effect **un·der·state·ment** *n.*

un·der·steer (ʌndərstíər) *v.* (*motor vehicle*) to turn a vehicle less than intended

un·der·stood (ʌndərstúd) *past and past part.* of UNDERSTAND || *adj.* agreed upon || (esp. *gram.*) implied, not specified

un·der·stud·y (ʌndərstʌdi:) **1.** *pl.* **un·der·stud·ies** *n.* an actor who learns another actor's part in order to be able to replace him if necessary **2.** *v. pres. part.* **un·der·stud·y·ing** *past and past part.* **un·der·stud·ied** *v.t.* to be the understudy of || to study (someone else's part) || *v.i.* to be an understudy

un·der·surface (ʌndərsə́rfis) *n.* the surface lying underneath

un·der·take (ʌndərtéik) *pres. part.* **un·der·tak·ing** *past* **un·der·took** (ʌndərtúk) *past part.* **un·der·tak·en** (ʌndərtéikən) *v.t.* to embark on, *to undertake a journey* || to assume responsibility for (something) || to promise (to do something)

un·der·tak·er *n.* a person whose trade is preparing the dead for burial and managing funerals **un·der·ták·ing** *n.* something undertaken, e.g. a heavy task || a promise, esp. one required by law || (ʌndərtéikiŋ) the business of an undertaker

un·der·tone (ʌndərtoun) *n.* a low sound || a barely audible tone of voice || a subdued color, esp. one which softens or transmutes another

undertook *past* of UNDERTAKE

un·der·tow (ʌndərtou) *n.* the undercurrent pulling strongly seaward or parallel with the coastline when waves are breaking on the shore

un·der·trick (ʌndərtrik) *n.* (*bridge*) a trick falling short of contract

un·der·val·u·a·tion (ʌndərvælju:éiʃən) *n.* an undervaluing || a valuation that is too low

un·der·val·ue (ʌndərvǽlju:) *pres. part.* **un·der·val·u·ing** *past and past part.* **un·der·val·ued** *v.t.* to set too low a value on || to underestimate

un·der·wa·ter (ʌndərwɔtər, ʌndərwɒtər) **1.** *adj.* placed, growing, happening etc. under water || used or to be used under water below a ship's waterline **2.** *adv.* under the water

underwater hockey form of stick hockey played underwater by skin divers in a deep swimming pool

un·der·wear (ʌndərwɛər) *n.* underclothes

un·der·weight 1. (ʌndərwéit) *adj.* weighing less than the weight normal for an age or height || weighing less than the legally required weight **2.** (ʌndərweit) *n.* the condition of weighing less than is normal or legally required

underwent *past* of UNDERGO

un·der·whelm (ʌndərwélm) *v.* to fail to impress —**underwhelming** *adj. ant.* overwhelm

un·der·wing (ʌndərwiŋ) *n.* one of the posterior wings of some insects, esp. moths

un·der·wood (ʌndərwud) *n.* undergrowth

Underwood Tariff Act a U.S. Congressional act (1913) introduced by Representative Oscar Wilder Underwood (1862-1929). It drastically

---

reduced tariff schedules and transferred many articles to the free list. It provided for free trade between the Philippine Is and the U.S.A. Its enforcement was interrupted (1914) by the outbreak of the 1st world war

un·der·world (ʌ́ndərwə:rld) *n.* (*rhet.*) the home of departed spirits ‖ the criminal section of society

un·der·write (ʌ́ndərrait, ʌndərráit) *pres. part.* **un·der·writ·ing** *past* **un·der·wrote** (ʌ́ndərrout, ʌndərróut) *past part.* **un·der·writ·ten** (ʌ́ndərrít'n, ʌndərrít'n) *v.t.* to execute (an insurance policy, esp. a marine policy) ‖ to undertake to meet the financial losses of ‖ to purchase (an issue of bonds etc.) on a fixed date and at a fixed price ‖ to guaran ᴄe the purchase of (stocks, bonds etc.) issued for public subscription ‖ to affix one's signature to (an insurance policy) thereby assuming liability in case of specified loss or damage ‖ to assume liability to the sum of ‖ *v.i.* to be an underwriter in the insurance business **ún·der·writ·er** *n.*

un·de·sign·ing (ʌndizáiniŋ) *adj.* having no hidden, self-seeking purpose

un·de·sir·a·ble (ʌndizáiərəb'l) 1. *adj.* objectionable ‖ not wanted, not to be encouraged 2. *n.* an objectionable person

un·did *past of* UNDO

un·dies (ʌ́ndi:z) *pl. n.* (*pop.*) women's or children's underclothes

un·dine (ʌndi:n, ʌndí:n) *n.* a female water sprite who, according to some legends, could acquire a soul if she married a mortal and had a child [fr. Gk fr. Mod. L. *Undina* fr. L. *unda*, wave]

un·di·rect·ed (ʌndiréktid, ʌndairéktid) *adj.* not directed ‖ (e.g. of a letter) not addressed

un·do (ʌndú:) *pres. part.* **un·do·ing** *past* **un·did** (ʌndíd) *past part.* **un·done** (ʌndʌ́n) *v.t.* to open by untying etc. ‖ to unfasten (a button, garment etc.) ‖ to destroy (what has been done or accomplished) ‖ (*rhet.*) to bring to ruin or destruction **un·do·ing** *n.* the act of unfastening ‖ (*rhet.*) a bringing to ruin or destruction ‖ (*rhet.*) a cause of this ‖ the destruction of something done or accomplished **un·dóne** *adj.* unfastened ‖ (*rhet.*) brought to ruin [O.E. *undón*]

un·dock (ʌndɔ́k) *v.* (*aerospace*) to disconnect or uncouple from another spacecraft

undone *adj.* not done

un·doubt·ed (ʌndáutid) *adj.* not doubted or disputed, regarded as certain **un·dóubt·ed·ly** *adv.* certainly

UNDP (*abbr.*) for United Nations Development Program, agency to assist in technical training and technology transfer to developing nations

un·draw (ʌndrɔ́) *pres. part.* **un·draw·ing** *past* **un·drew** (ʌndrú:) *past part.* **un·drawn** (ʌndrɔ́n) *v.t.* to draw or pull back or aside (e.g. a curtain)

un·dreamed (ʌndrí:md) *adj.* (usually with 'of') beyond what one would have thought to be possible, *splendors undreamed of*

un·dreamt (ʌndrémt) *adj.* undreamed

un·dress 1. (ʌndrés) *v.t.* to take off the clothes of ‖ *v.i.* to take off one's clothes 2. (ʌndrés) *n.* comfortable, informal dress ‖ ordinary clothes as opposed to uniform ‖ a state of being only partly dressed 3. (ʌndres) *adj.* of or relating to informal clothes, esp. uniform

un·dressed (ʌndrést) *adj.* not dressed ‖ without a dressing

undrew *past of* UNDRAW

UNDRO (*acronym*) for United Nations Disaster Relief Organization

Und·set (únset), Sigrid (1882-1949), Norwegian novelist. Her best-known work is the trilogy 'Kristin Lavransdatter' (1920-2), the story of a woman's life in medieval Norway

un·due (ʌndjú:, ʌndjú:) *adj.* excessive, beyond what is expected or required ‖ improper, inappropriate

undue influence (*law*) influence over another person which prevents him from exercising his own will

un·du·lant (ʌ́ndʒulənt, ʌ́ndjulənt) *adj.* wavelike in form or movement

undulant fever a disease caused by bacteria of the genus *Brucella*, fam. *Brucellaceae*, contracted by human beings, esp. from infected milk or dairy products. It is characterized by remittent fever and general exhaustion, and can last for months

un·du·late (ʌ́ndʒuleit, ʌ́ndjuleit) *pres. part,* **un·du·lat·ing** *past and past part.* **un·du·lat·ed** *v.i.* to have a wavelike motion or form ‖ *v.t.* to cause to move in a wavy, sinuous manner ‖ to give a wavelike form to **un·du·lat·ed** *adj.* having a wavelike surface, edge or marking **un·du·lá-**

tion *n.* a wavelike motion ‖ a wavy form ‖ a pulsation ‖ (*phys.*) wave motion or a wave or vibration **un·du·la·to·ry** (ʌ́ndʒulətɔ:ri:, ʌ́ndjulətɔri:, ʌ́ndʒulətɔuri:, ʌ́ndjulətɔuri:) *adj.* [fr. L. *undulatus* fr. *unda*, a wave]

undulatory theory *WAVE THEORY

un·du·ly (ʌndú:li:, ʌndjú:li:) *adv.* excessively

un·dy·ing (ʌndáiiŋ) *adj.* (of fame, devotion etc.) perpetual

un·earned (ʌ:rnd) *adj.* undeserved ‖ derived from investments etc., *unearned income*

unearned increment an increase of value of land etc. due to increased demand, rather than to any labor or expenditure by the owner

un·earth (ʌnə́:rθ) *v.t.* to dig up ‖ to bring to light, *to unearth new facts*

un·earth·li·ness (ʌnə́:rθli:nis) *n.* the state or quality of being unearthly

un·earth·ly (ʌnə́:rθli:) *adj.* not belonging to the earth ‖ celestial, supernatural ‖ (*pop.*) preposterous, *an unearthly time to get up*

un·eas·i·ly (ʌní:zili:) *adv.* in an uneasy manner

un·eas·i·ness (ʌní:zi:nis) *n.* the state or quality of being uneasy

un·eas·y (ʌní:zi:) *comp.* **un·eas·i·er** *superl.* **un·eas·i·est** *adj.* uncomfortable, restless ‖ disturbed, troubled, *he fell into an uneasy sleep* ‖ anxious, rather frightened ‖ ill at ease

un·em·ploy·a·ble (ʌnimplɔ́iəb'l) 1. *adj.* not employable, esp. not fit for paid employment, because of age, physical incapacity etc. 2. *n.* a person not fit for paid employment

un·em·ployed (ʌnimplɔ́id) 1. *adj.* not in paid employment ‖ not being used ‖ not invested 2. *n.* (only in) **the unemployed** that part of the working population not in paid employment

un·em·ploy·ment (ʌnimplɔ́imənt) *n.* the state of being unable to secure paid employment ‖ lack of employment

unemployment benefit a weekly sum paid from public funds to an unemployed worker under a state security scheme ‖ a payment by a trade union or by an employer to an employee unable to work

unemployment compensation unemployment benefit paid under state laws

un·en·closed (ʌninklóuzd) *adj.* not fenced in ‖ (of nuns) not restricted to the convent

un·e·qual (ʌní:kwəl) *adj.* not of the same dimensions, *unequal lengths* ‖ not uniform in quality, degree etc., *unequal abilities, unequal vibrations* ‖ (esp. with 'to') not fit or adequate, *unequal to hard work*

un·e·qualed, esp. *Br.* **un·e·qualled** (ʌní:kwəld) *adj.* without equal, *unequaled beauty*

un·e·quiv·o·cal (ʌnikwívək'l) *adj.* admitting of no doubt or question as to meaning or intention, not ambiguous

un·err·ing (ʌnə́:riŋ, ʌnériŋ) *adj.* certain, sure ‖ free from error

UNESCO (ju:néskou) *UNITED NATIONS EDUCATIONAL, SCIENTIFIC AND CULTURAL ORGANIZATION

un·es·sen·tial (ʌnisénʃəl) 1. *adj.* not of basic importance 2. *n.* something not of basic importance

un·e·ven (ʌní:vən) *adj.* not smooth, *an uneven road surface* ‖ not of the same size, length or quantity, *uneven rates of pay* ‖ not of the same quality or capacity, *uneven competitors* ‖ not consistently good or bad, *uneven progress* ‖ (of numbers) odd

un·ex·am·pled (ʌnigzǽmp'ld, ʌnigzámp'ld) *adj.* without precedent

un·ex·cep·tion·a·ble (ʌniksépʃənəb'l) *adj.* beyond the reach of criticism, above reproach **un·ex·cép·tion·a·bly** *adv.*

un·ex·cep·tion·al (ʌniksépʃən'l) *adj.* not exceptional, ordinary ‖ unexceptionable ‖ not admitting of any exception

un·fail·ing (ʌnféiliŋ) *adj.* not failing ‖ inexhaustible ‖ certain, reliable

un·fair (ʌnféər) *adj.* not just ‖ not according to business ethics, *unfair practices*

un·faith·ful (ʌnféiθfəl) *adj.* failing one's trust, disloyal ‖ adulterous ‖ not accurate

un·fa·mil·iar (ʌnfəmíljər) *adj.* not well known, strange ‖ (with 'with') having little or no experience, *unfamiliar with firearms* **un·fa·mil·i·ar·i·ty** (ʌnfəmili:ǽriti) *n.*

un·fa·vor·a·ble, *Br.* **un·fa·vour·a·ble** (ʌnféivərəb'l) *adj.* not favorable, adverse, *unfavorable criticisms* ‖ (*rhet.*, of the wind) contrary

Unfederated Malay States *MALAYA

un·feel·ing (ʌnfí:liŋ) *adj.* unsympathetic, hardhearted ‖ without feeling

un·fin·ished (ʌnfíniʃt) *adj.* not finished, incomplete ‖ rough, unpolished ‖ (of woolen cloth) not bleached or dyed etc. after weaving

un·fit (ʌnfít) 1. *adj.* not fit, not suitable ‖ not fitted, not suitably adapted for a given purpose ‖ not well, in poor physical condition 2. *v.t. pres. part.* **un·fit·ting** *past and past part.* **un·fit·ted** to render unsuitable

un·fix (ʌnfíks) *v.t.* to undo the fixing of, disengage ‖ to unsettle ‖ (*chem.*) to make (a compound) soluble

un·flap·pa·ble (ʌnflǽpəb'l) *adj.* (*colloq.*) not easily ruffled **—unflappability** *n.* **—unflappably** *adv. ant.* flappable

un·fledged (ʌnflédʒd) *adj.* not fledged ‖ immature, undeveloped ‖ (of an arrow) not having vanes

un·flinch·ing (ʌnflíntʃiŋ) *adj.* resolute, not wavering

un·fold (ʌnfóuld) *v.t.* to open from its folds ‖ to cause to reveal itself gradually to the vision or mind ‖ *v.i.* to open out ‖ to reveal itself gradually to the vision or mind [O.E. *unfealdan*]

un·formed (ʌnfɔ́rmd) *adj.* not having a definite shape or structure ‖ immature

un·for·tu·nate (ʌnfɔ́rtʃənit) 1. *adj.* not favored by chance, fortune etc., unlucky ‖ much to be regretted, *an unfortunate incident* 2. *n.* an unfortunate person

un·found·ed (ʌnfáundid) *adj.* having no foundation of reason or fact

un·friend·li·ness (ʌnfréndli:nis) *n.* the state or quality of being unfriendly

un·friend·ly (ʌnfréndli:) 1. *adj.* (of relations between people) not friendly ‖ (of people, nations, animals etc.) hostile ‖ (*rhet.*) unfavorable, *a regime unfriendly towards artists* 2. *adv.* in an unfriendly manner

un·frock (ʌnfrɔ́k) *v.t.* to deprive (a priest) of his priest's orders

un·fruit·ful (ʌnfrú:tfəl) *adj.* not producing offspring ‖ not bearing fruit ‖ (of soil) bad for producing crops ‖ unprofitable

un·furl (ʌnfə́:rl) *v.t.* to unfold, to loose from a state of being furled ‖ *v.i.* to become unfurled

un·gain·li·ness (ʌngéinli:nis) *n.* the state or quality of being ungainly

un·gain·ly (ʌngéinli:) *adj.* clumsy, awkward [M.E. *ungeinliche* fr. *ungein*, perilous fr. *un-*, not+ O.N. *gegn*, ready]

Un·ga·ret·ti (u:ŋgarétti:), Giuseppe (1888-1970), Italian poet, author of 'Allegria' (1931), 'Sentimento del Tempore' (1933), 'Il Dolore' (1947), 'La Terra Promessa' (1950), 'Un grido e paesaggi' (1952)

Un·ga·va Bay (ʌŋgéivə) a large inlet (200 miles long, 160 miles wide at the mouth) between the northern tip of Labrador and the Ungava Peninsula, Canada

Ungava Peninsula a hilly, lake-studded peninsula (400 miles long, 350 miles wide) between the Hudson Bay and Ungava Bay, Quebec, Canada

un·god·li·ness (ʌngɔ́dli:nis) *n.* the state or quality of being ungodly

un·god·ly (ʌngɔ́dli:) *adj.* wicked ‖ (*pop.*) unreasonable, *what an ungodly hour to call*

un·gov·ern·a·ble (ʌngʌ́vərnəb'l) *adj.* that will not submit to control

un·gra·cious (ʌngréiʃəs) *adj.* lacking courtesy or good manners ‖ not attractive

un·gram·mat·i·cal (ʌngrəmǽtik'l) *adj.* not according to the rules of grammar

un·grate·ful (ʌngréitfəl) *adj.* without gratitude ‖ of an unpleasant nature, *ungrateful chores*

un·gual (ʌ́ŋgwəl) 1. *adj.* of, relating to or resemble a claw, nail or hoof 2. *n.* a claw, nail or hoof [fr. L. *unguis*, claw, nail]

un·guard (ʌngárd) *v.t.* to expose to attack ‖ (*bridge*) to expose (a high card) to the risk of loss by discarding a lower card **un·gúard·ed** *adj.* without a guard ‖ marked by lack of caution, *an unguarded moment*

un·guent (ʌ́ŋgwənt) *n.* an ointment [fr. L. *unguens* (*unguentis*) fr. *unguere*, to anoint]

un·guic·u·late (ʌŋgwíkjulit) *adj.* (*zool.*, of mammals) having claws or nails as distinct from hoofs ‖ (*bot.*) having an unguis 2. *n.* a mammal having claws or nails **un·guíc·u·lat·ed** *adj.* [fr. L. *unguiculus* dim. of *unguis*, nail, claw]

un·guis (ʌ́ŋgwis) *pl.* **un·gues** (ʌ́ŋgwi:z) *n.* (*zool.*, of vertebrates) a claw, nail or hoof ‖ (*zool.*) the chitinous hook on the foot of an insect ‖ (*bot.*) a clawshaped petal base [L.]

un·gu·la (ʌ́ŋgjulə) *pl.* **un·gu·lae** (ʌ́ŋgjuli:) *n.* an ungual **ún·gu·lar** *adj.* [L.=a hoof]

CONCISE PRONUNCIATION KEY: **(a)** æ, c*a*t; ɑ, c*a*r; ɔ f*aw*n; ei, sn*a*ke. **(e)** e, h*e*n; i:, sh*ee*p; iə, d*ee*r; ɛə, b*ea*r. **(i)** i, f*i*sh; ai, t*i*ger; ə:, b*i*rd. **(o)** o, *o*x; au, c*ow*; ou, g*oa*t; u, p*oo*r; ɔi, r*oy*al. **(u)** ʌ, d*u*ck; u, b*u*ll; u:, g*oo*se; ə, b*a*cillus; ju:, c*u*be. x, lo*ch*; θ, *th*ink; ð, bo*th*er; z, *Z*en; ʒ, corsa*g*e; dʒ, sava*g*e; ŋ, orangutan*g*; j, *y*ak; ʃ, *fish*; tʃ, fe*tch*; 'l, rabb*le*; 'n, redd*en*. Complete pronunciation key appears inside front cover.

un·gu·late (ʌ́ŋgjulit) **1.** *adj.* hoofed ‖ of or relating to hoofed mammals **2.** *n.* a hoofed mammal [fr. L. *ungulatus* fr. *ungula,* hoof]

un·hal·lowed (ʌnhǽloud) *adj.* not consecrated, *unhallowed ground* ‖ wicked, impious

un·hap·pi·ness (ʌnhǽpi:nis) *n.* the state or quality of being unhappy

un·hap·py (ʌnhǽpi:) *comp.* **un·hap·pi·er** *superl.* **un·hap·pi·est** *adj.* sad, in low spirits ‖ unlucky, *it was an unhappy day for me when they met* ‖ not appropriate, *an unhappy combination of colors*

un·har·ness (ʌnhárnis) *v.t.* to remove the harness from ‖ to liberate (e.g. a source of energy)

un·health·i·ness (ʌnhélθi:nis) *n.* the state or quality of being unhealthy

un·health·y (ʌnhélθi:) *comp.* **un·health·i·er** *superl.* **un·health·i·est** *adj.* not in good health ‖ not evincing good health, *an unhealthy complexion* ‖ not conducive to good health, *an unhealthy diet* ‖ not sound morally ‖ (*pop.*) risky

un·heard (ʌnhə́:rd)*adj.* not heard ‖ not given a hearing

un·heard-of (ʌnhə́:rdǫv, ʌnhə́:rdʌv) *adj.* never met with until now, unprecedented

un·hinge (ʌnhíndʒ) *pres. part.* **un·hing·ing** *past* and *past part.* **un·hinged** *v.t.* to remove from its hinges ‖ to upset the balance of (the mind)

un·ho·ly (ʌnhóuli:) *comp.* **un·ho·li·er** *superl.* **un·ho·li·est** *adj.* not holy, impious ‖ used intensively) very bad, *an unholy mess*

un·hook (ʌnhúk) *v.t.* to unfasten the hook or hooks of ‖ to remove from a hook

un·hoped-for (ʌnhóuptfǫr) *adj.* not expected

un·horse (ʌnhórs) *pres. part.* **un·hors·ing** *past* and *past part.* **un·horsed** *v.t.* to throw from a horse ‖ to take a horse away from (a vehicle)

uni- (júːni:) *combining form* having or consisting of one only, as in 'uniparous' [L. *unus,* one]

U·ni·ate, U·ni·at (júːni:æt) *n.* a member of an Eastern Christian church which acknowledges the pope's supremacy but preserves its own rites, liturgy and canon law, and has its own patriarch [Russ. *uniyatu* fr. *uniya,* a union fr. L. *unus,* one]

u·ni·ax·i·al (juːni:ǽksi:əl) *adj.* (esp. of a crystal) having only one optic axis ‖ (*biol.*) monaxial

u·ni·cam·er·al (juːnikǽmərəl) *adj.* (of a parliament etc.) having only one chamber [fr. UNI+L. *camera,* chamber]

UNICEF the agency established (1946) by the United Nations General Assembly for dealing with malnutrition, diseases etc. of children all over the world [*United Nations International Children's Emergency Fund*]

u·ni·cel·lu·lar (juːniséljulər) *adj.* (*biol.*) consisting of only one cell

u·ni·corn (júːnikǫrn) *n.* a legendary animal generally depicted as having the head and body of a horse, the hind legs of a stag, the tail of a lion, and having a long tapering horn growing from the middle of its forehead. In the Middle Ages the unicorn was a symbol of strength and virginity. Its powdered horn would safeguard one from poison, and sweeten the foulest or most bitter waters ‖ a representation of this animal, e.g. in heraldry or as a supporter of the royal arms in Britain or Scotland [A.F., O.F. *unicorne* or fr. L. *unicornis* fr. *unus, one*+*cornu,* horn]

u·ni·cy·cle (júːnisaik'l) *n.* a singlewheeled, pedal-propelled vehicle used esp. by clowns or other entertainers

unidentified flying object (*abbr.* UFO, U.F.O.) a flying saucer or other mysterious, apparently man-made thing seen flying through the air

u·ni·fi·a·ble (júːnifǎiəb'l) *adj.* that can be unified

u·ni·fi·ca·tion (juːnifikéiʃən) *n.* a unifying or being unified

u·ni·fied tax (júːnifaid) *n.* (*Br.*) progressive individual tax (replacing income tax and surtax), established in 1973

u·ni·fo·li·ate (juːnifóuli:it) *adj.* (*bot.*) having only one leaf ‖ unifoliolate

u·ni·fo·li·o·late (juːnifóuli:əleit) *adj.* (*bot.*) compound in structure but having only one leaflet

u·ni·form (júːnifǫrm) **1.** *adj.* being the same in form, character, degree etc. without variation, *a rod of uniform thickness* ‖ conforming to a rule, pattern or norm ‖ consistent throughout a state, country etc. **uniform with** having the same form, appearance etc. as **2.** *n.* a costume worn by all of a certain

category (prisoners, airline stewardesses etc.)

ú·ni·formed (ʌníːfǫrmd) *adj.* wearing a uniform [F. *uniforme* or fr. L. *uniformis*]

u·ni·form·i·ty (juːnifórmiti) *n.* the state or quality of being uniform [F. *uniformité* or fr. L. *uniformitas*]

Uniformity, Act of (*Eng. hist.*) any of four acts of parliament (1549, 1552, 1559, 1662) prescribing the use of the Book of Common Prayer in the services of the Church of England

u·ni·fy (júːnifai) *pres. part.* **u·ni·fy·ing** *past* and *past part.* **u·ni·fied** *v.t.* to make one ‖ *v.i.* to become one [fr. M.L. *unificare*]

u·ni·lat·er·al (juːnəlǽtərəl) *adj.* done or undertaken etc. by one side or party only, *unilateral disarmament* ‖ (*biol.*) arranged or produced on one side only ‖ (*med.*) affecting only one side of the body, *unilateral paralysis* ‖ (*law*) binding or affecting one party only ‖ (*sociology*) indicating or tracing descent through either the maternal or paternal line only (cf. BILATERAL) ‖ (*phon.*) pronounced with the breath passing along one side of the tongue only [fr. Mod. L. *unilateralis*]

un·im·peach·a·ble (ʌnimpíːtʃəb'l) *adj.* not open to question, beyond reproach

un·im·proved (ʌnimprúːvd) *adj.* (of land) not improved, e.g. not cultivated, built upon etc. ‖ not bred selectively ‖ (of a road) not paved

un·ion (júːnjən) *n.* a uniting or being united ‖ something united ‖ a combination (esp. of qualities), *the union of strength and beauty* ‖ unity, harmony ‖ a marriage ‖ a grouping of states, political groups etc. for some specific purpose ‖ an emblem symbolizing the unification of states, sovereignties etc., used esp. on the upper inner corner of a national flag ‖ this part of the flag ‖ (*Eng. hist.*) a 19th-c. governmental unit comprising two or more parishes united for administration of poor relief ‖ a device for joining parts together, esp. a kind of joint for coupling pipes ‖ a trade union **the Union** the United States of America ‖ (*Am. hist.*) the 23 Northern states which opposed the Confederate states in the Civil War (1861-5). They were: Maine, New Hampshire, Vermont, Massachusetts, Rhode Island, Connecticut, New York, New Jersey, Delaware, Maryland, Pennsylvania, Ohio, Michigan, Indiana, Kentucky, Illinois, Wisconsin, Minnesota, Iowa, Missouri, Kansas, Oregon and California [F.]

Union, Act of the Act (1707) unifying Scotland and England in the United Kingdom of Great Britain under a single government, each retaining its own legal system and national Church. Scotland thus recognized the Hanoverian succession, and acquired a share of English trade

Union Islands the Tokelau Islands

un·ion·ism (júːnjənizəm) *n.* the tradeunion movement **Un·ion·ism** (*Am. hist.*) loyalty to the Union during the Civil War

un·ion·ist (júːnjənist) *n.* a member of a trade union ‖ a supporter of trade unionism **Un·ion·ist** (*Am. hist.*) a supporter of the Union during the Civil War

un·ion·i·za·tion (juːnjənizéiʃən) *n.* a unionizing or being unionized

un·ion·ize (júːnjənaiz) *pres. part.* **un·ion·iz·ing** *past* and *past part.* **un·ion·ized** *v.t.* to organize into a trade union or unions ‖ to cause to conform with the rules etc. of a trade union

Union Jack the national flag of the United Kingdom, combining the crosses of St George, St Andrew and St Patrick ‖ any flag consisting only of a national union

Union League of America, the a U.S. organization of clubs formed in the North (1862) by Ohio Republicans to inspire 'uncompromising and unconditional loyalty to the Union' and to revitalize the enervated Republican party. At its peak of influence after the Civil War, it worked in the cause of Negro enfranchisement, seeking the resultant vote for the Republican party. Membership came to consist mainly of blacks, directed by white politicians who introduced elaborate secret ceremonies with a politico-mystical tenor. As a result of discord between blacks and whites, it rapidly declined after 1869, while giving rise to reactionary movements, notably the Ku Klux Klan

Union of South Africa *SOUTH AFRICA

Union of Soviet Socialist Republics (U.S.S.R.) a federal republic (area 8,650,000 sq. miles, pop. 277,930,000) in E. Europe and Northern and Central Asia. Capital: Moscow. It consists of 15 constituent republics, each inhabited by a major national group: the Russian

Soviet Federal Socialist Republic (R.S.F.S.R.), Ukraine, Kazakhstan, Uzbekistan, Byelorussia, Georgia, Azerbaijan, Moldavia, Lithuania, Kirghizia, Tadzhikstan, Latvia, Armenia, Turkmenistan and Estonia. (For physical geography see separate entries.) These constituent republics include a number of national autonomous republics and autonomous regions. People: 77% Slavic (incl. 55% Russian, 18% Ukrainian, 4% Byelorussian), with Baltic, Armenian, Jewish and various Caucasian, Turkic, Iranian and Mongol minorities. Religion (the majority profess none): 24% Russian Orthodox, 11% Moslem (esp. Central Asia and Caucasia), 2% Protestant (esp. Latvia and Estonia), 2% Roman Catholic (esp. Lithuania and W. Ukraine), 1% Armenian, 1% Jewish, small Buddhist minority (esp. Buriat and Kalmyk A.S.S.R.s). The land is 32% forest, 20% pasture, 18% arable or cultivated. Average temperatures (F.): Kaliningrad 25° (Jan.) and 64° (July), Lvov 25°-66°, Riga 25°-64°, Leningrad 18°-64°, Archangel 9°-59°, Moscow 12°-64°, Kiev 21°-67°, Batumi 43°-73°, Tbilisi 20°-75°, Samarkand 32°-77°, Sverdlovsk 3°-63°, Irkutsk −6°-63°, Dikson (Yenisei estuary) −13°-41°, Vladivostok 5°-65°, Delen (Bering Strait) −10°-41°, Verkhoyansk (E. Siberia) −58°-60°. Rainfall: Kaliningrad 28 ins, Riga 24 ins, Leningrad 21 ins, Archangel 19 ins, Moscow 25 ins, Batumi 95 ins, Baku 10 ins, Samarkand 13 ins, Sverdlovsk 18 ins, Irkutsk 15 ins, Vladivostok 15 ins, Verkhoyansk 4 ins. Livestock: cattle, sheep, hogs, goats, horses. Agricultural products: cereals (esp. Ukraine, Central European R.S.F.S.R., W. Siberia, N. Kazakhstan, Urals, Volga region, N. Caucasus), cotton, sugar beets, potatoes, vegetables, meat, wool, dairy produce, fruit, tea, flax, hemp, sunflower seed, beans, furs, lumber, fish. Mineral resources: coal, petroleum, iron ore, copper, titanium, manganese, chromites, lead, zinc, bauxite, gold, uranium, asbestos, mica, phosphates, wolframite and molybdenite, potash and deposits of most other minerals. Manufactures and industries: mining, iron and steel, oil refining, aluminum, chemicals and fertilizers, textiles, machinery, vehicles, locomotives, tractors, hydroelectricity, lumber, paper, woodwork and furniture, atomic energy, footwear, clocks and watches, armaments, aircraft, foodstuffs, radio and television sets, refrigerators, sewing machines, bicycles, rubber, sugar, soap, cement, bricks. The world's longest pipeline links the Ural-Volga oil fields with Poland, East Germany, Czechoslovakia and Hungary. Exports: fuels and raw materials including grain (47%), machinery and equipment (10%), consumer goods (9%). Imports: fuels and raw materials (29%), machinery and equipment (35%), consumer goods (24%). Main ports: Leningrad, Archangel, Murmansk, Odessa, Baku, Vladivostok, Riga, Tallinn. There is an extensive network of canals. There are about 750 institutes for higher education, the oldest universities being Vilnius (1578), Tartu (1632) and Moscow (1755). Monetary unit: ruble (100 kopeks). HISTORY. (For previous history *RUSSIA) The Bolsheviks having seized power (Nov. 7, 1917) under Lenin, the country was faced with a civil war (1918-21), in which anti-Communist forces unsuccessfully opposed the new regime, and a war with Poland (1920), in which Pilsudski unsuccessfully invaded the Ukraine. Lenin regained control (1921), but in the face of a severe economic crisis was forced to modify his Marxian socialist policy as a temporary concession to capitalism (1921-8). The U.S.S.R. was officially established (1922), and the 1924 constitution, based upon public ownership of the land and of the means of production, put legislative power in the hands of the soviets, under the leadership of the Supreme Soviet. After Lenin's death (1924), a struggle for leadership developed, notably between Trotsky and Stalin, resulting in the victory of Stalin. Lenin's economic policy was abandoned in favor of the first five-year plan (1928), under which heavy industry was greatly expanded and a collectivization of agriculture was carried out. Opposition from kulaks and private tradesmen was ruthlessly stamped out. State control over culture and education was increased, and a series of political purges was carried out (1930s) by the secret police. The U.S.S.R. signed (1939) a mutual nonaggression pact with Germany, and shared in the annexation of Poland (1939). Estonia, Latvia and Lithuania were annexed (1939), and Bessarabia and N. Bukovina were occupied (1940). The U.S.S.R. invaded Finland (1939) and annexed the Karelian Isthmus (1940). Germany invaded the U.S.S.R. (1941) and besieged Leningrad, but was repulsed from Moscow. The German attack on Stalingrad (1942-3) was one of the decisive battles of the 2nd world war. The Russian counteroffensive (1943-5) drove the Germans back through E. Europe, reaching Berlin (1945). The U.S.S.R. declared war on Japan (1945) and rapidly conquered much of Manchuria and Korea. It took part in the conferences at Tehran (1943), Yalta (1945) and Potsdam (1945), joined the U.N. (1945) and emerged as a major world power. The Russian policy of Communist expansion, abandoned officially (1943) with the dissolution of the Comintern, was resumed (1947) with the establishment of the Cominform. Nonaggression and mutual assistance pacts were made with the neighboring countries of E. Europe, which now became people's republics. Relations between the U.S.S.R. and the West deteriorated in the cold war, and worsened further with the outbreak of the Korean War (1950-3). After Stalin's death (1953), the regime showed more liberal tendencies. The post of prime minister was held by Malenkov (1953-5), Bulganin (1955-8), Khrushchev (1958-64) and Kosygin (1964-80). Soviet economic planning placed more emphasis on consumer goods, in a seven-year plan (1959-65) which was incorporated (1960) in a 20-year plan. Khrushchev's government found increasing difficulty in increasing agricultural output at the desired rate. The U.S.S.R. launched the first artificial satellite into space (1957), sent the first rocket to the moon (1959), sent the first man into space (1961), landed the first probe on the moon (1966) and landed the first probe on Venus (1967). Tension with the West was maintained over the question of German reunification, the building of the Berlin wall (1961), the Cuba crisis (1962) and the war in Vietnam (1964-75). Ideological disagreements with China appeared (1959), and the rift widened progressively, involving other Communist countries. Relations with European socialist countries were marked by difficulties with Rumania and, esp., by the intervention (1968) of Warsaw Pact troops in Czechoslovakia to end the liberalization of the regime. Khrushchev was ousted from power in 1964 by a group led by Leonid Brezhnev, who pursued a policy of détente with the West. In 1982 leadership passed to Yuri Andropov, who died two years later, and then to Konstantin Chernenko, who died in 1985. Mikhail Gorbachev assumed power in 1985

Union Pacific Railroad the first transcontinental railroad in the U.S.A., chartered (1862) by Congress. The Union Pacific joined (1869) the Central Pacific near Ogden, Utah, and a golden spike marks the juncture. The railroad was involved in the Crédit Mobilier of America scandal. Greatly expanded under the direction of Edward H. Harriman, it lost (1904-13) its monopolistic control through the action of the U.S. Supreme Court

union shop an establishment where workers are employed even if they do not belong to a trade union, provided they become members within a specified time (*CLOSED SHOP)

union suit long underwear with the shirt and drawers cut as a single garment

u·nip·ar·ous (ju:nípərəs) *adj.* producing one egg or offspring at a birth ‖ (*bot.*) having a cymose inflorescence with only one axis at each branching [fr. Mod. L. *uniparus* fr. *unus*, one+*parere*, to bear]

u·ni·po·lar (ju:nəpóulər) *adj.* (*biol.*, of a nerve cell) having one process only ‖ (*elec.*) having or acting by one magnetic or electrical pole

u·ni·pol·i·tics (ju:nipplátiks) *n.* concept of a global authority to protect humankind, offered at the World Habitat Conference, Canada, 1972

u·nique (ju:ní:k) *adj.* being the only one of its kind ‖ not like anything else of its kind, incomparable ‖ (*loosely*) rare, unusual [F.]

unique species (*envir.*) species of special scientific, local, or national interest

u·ni·sex (jú:niseks) *adj.* **1.** suitable for both men and women, e.g., clothes, hairstyles **2.** indistinguishable as to sex —**unisex** *n.* the trend Cf INTERSEX, UNISEXUAL

u·ni·sex·u·al (ju:nísékʃu:əl) *adj.* of one sex only, esp. (*zool.*) male only or female only, not hermaphroditic ‖ (*bot.*) diclinous

u·ni·son (jú:niz'n, jú:nis'n) *n.* coincidence in pitch of two or more notes, voices etc. **in unison** with identity of note and pitch ‖ in complete agreement [O.F. or fr. L.L. *unisonus*]

u·nit (jú:nit) *n.* a fixed quantity adopted as a standard of measurement for other quantities of the same kind, *the centimeter is a unit of length* ‖ a single thing, person or group that is a distinguishable element of a larger whole, *the family is the basic unit of society* ‖ (*math.*) the element which divides every other of a set of elements ‖ (*pl.*) in mathematical calculations, the column of figures immediately to the left of the decimal point ‖ any subdivision (regiment, battalion etc.) of an army whose strength is laid down by regulations ‖ an element of furniture manufactured in such a way that it can be fitted with others like it, or with complementary elements, to form an ensemble (bookcase, kitchen cabinet etc.) [fr. L. *unus*, one]

U·ni·tar·i·an (ju:nitéəri:ən) **1.** *n.* a member of a Protestant denomination believing in the unity of God as opposed to the doctrine of the Trinity. The Unitarian denomination developed in Poland and Transylvania (late 16th c.) and in England and North America (17th-18th cc.) and has come to be undogmatic, advocating tolerance and stressing reason as a guide to belief **2.** *adj.* of or relating to the Unitarians **U·ni·tár·i·an·ism** *n.*

Unitarian Universalist Association *UNIVERSALIST CHURCH

u·ni·ta·rio (u:ni:tári:ɔ) *n.* (*Argentinian hist.*) a supporter of strong central government in a close federation of the provinces. The conflict between unitarios and federalistas was the cause of civil war in Argentina in the 19th c. [Span.]

u·ni·tar·y (jú:niteri:) *adj.* of or relating to a unit or units ‖ having the character of a unit ‖ based on or characterized by unity

unit car a freight train that operates with little or no uncoupling, usu. in a shuttle run

unit character (*biol.*) a trait dependent on a single gene, inherited according to Mendel's laws

u·nite (ju:náit) *pres. part.* **u·nit·ing** *past* and *past part.* **u·nit·ed** *v.t.* to bring together so as to make one ‖ to have or show (qualities etc.) in common ‖ to bring together in common cause ‖ to cause to become attached ‖ to bring together by a legal or moral bond ‖ *v.i.* to become one or as if one ‖ to cooperate ‖ to become combined **u·nit·ed** *adj.* made one, brought together ‖ resulting from being brought together or made one, *a united effort* ‖ getting on together well, harmonious, *a united staff*

United Arab Emirates (formerly Trucial States) seven Arab sheikhdoms (total area approx. 32,000 sq. miles, pop. 1,121,800) on the Persian Gulf coast of Arabia between Qatar and the Musandam peninsula (formerly known as the Pirate Coast): Abu Dhabi, Dubai, Sharjah and Kalba, Ajman, Umm al Qaiwain, Ras al Khaimah, Fujairah. Capital, chief town and port: Abu Dhabi (pop. 243,000), in Abu Dhabi. The land is flat desert, except for mountains on the east (Gulf of Oman) coast, rising to 4,000 ft. Main export: petroleum (esp. from Abu Dhabi). Other products: fish, vegetables, dates, pearls. Monetary unit: the Bahrain dinar in Abu Dhabi, elsewhere the Saudi rial (100 paise). HISTORY. The sheikhdoms, Moslem since the 7th c., entered into a series of treaties with Britain (1820, 1853 and 1892), suppressing piracy and slavery and establishing British protection. Independence was declared in Dec. 1971. A flood of foreign workers came into the country because of the oil boom; almost half the population is South Asian. The native Arabs are nearly all Moslems. Authority remains with the seven hereditary sheiks, who choose a president from among themselves. Since 1971 Zaid bin Sultan al-Nahayan of Abu Dhabi has been president

United Arab Republic a union (1958-61) of Egypt and Syria. Yemen entered (Feb. 1958) into a Federal Union with the United Arab Republic. Syria seceded (1961) and the union was dissolved, but Egypt maintained the name as its official title until 1971. Attempts were made to revive the union with the addition of Iraq (1963), and to form a common market with Iraq, Kuwait and Jordan (1964)

United Church of Canada a Protestant denomination formed (1925) by the union of the Methodist, Congregationalist, and Presbyterian Churches in Canada

United Church of Christ a U.S. Protestant denomination formed (1957) by the union of the Congregational Christian Churches and the Evangelical and Reformed Church

United Fruit Company a U.S. corporation formed (1899) in New Jersey that soon monopolized the cultivation, transportation, and marketing of bananas in the West Indies and Central America. It came to dominate the communications and transportation facilities in Central America and became deeply involved in Caribbean politics

United Kingdom of Great Britain and Northern Ireland *GREAT BRITAIN

United Nations (*abbr.* U.N., UN) an international organization to maintain world peace and security and to promote economic, social and cultural cooperation among nations, set up (1945) as a successor to the League of Nations. Its charter was signed by 50 nations and there are now more than 150 members meeting annually in the General Assembly. Problems of world peace are dealt with by the Security Council, and the U.N.'s main judicial organ is the International Court of Justice. The U.N.'s specialized agencies include the Food and Agriculture Organization, the General Agreement on Tariffs and Trade, the International Atomic Energy Agency, the International Civil Aviation Organization, the International Finance Corporation, the International Labor Organization, the International Monetary Fund, the International Telecommunication Union, the United Nations Educational, Scientific and Cultural Organization, the Universal Postal Union, the World Bank, the World Health Organization and the World Meteorological Organization. Headquarters: New York

United Nations Children's Fund *UNICEF

United Nations Educational, Scientific and Cultural Organization (*abbr.* UNESCO) an agency of the U.N. set up in 1946 to contribute to peace and security by promoting international collaboration in education, science and culture

United Provinces the name given to the independent republic of the Netherlands (1648-1795)

United States Air Force Academy a military institution in Colorado Springs, Colo., authorized (1958) by Congress to train cadets to be U.S. Air Force officers

United States Coast Guard Academy an institution established (1876) in New London, Conn., to train officers for the U.S. Coast Guard

United States Information Agency (*abbr.* USIA) an agency of the U.S. government, established (1953) to promote, through communications media, a better understanding abroad of the U.S.A. and its foreign policies. Its best-known activity is the Voice of America radio program, which transmits information overseas in more than 36 languages

United States Marine Corps an armed service (originally within the U.S. Naval Department) established (1798) by Act of Congress. It is trained for integrated land-sea-air action. In 1834 the president was authorized to order marines to duty with the army. Since its creation it has made over 300 landings on foreign shores

United States Merchant Marine Academy an institution established (1936) at Kings Point, N.Y., to train officers for the U.S. Merchant Marine

United States Military Academy an institution established (1802) at West Point, N.Y., to train cadets to be U.S. Army officers

United States Naval Academy an institution for training U.S. Navy officers founded (1845) at Annapolis, Md.

United States of America (*abbr.* U.S.A., USA) a federal republic (area 13,618,770 sq. miles, pop. 231,534,000) in North America, incl. Hawaii and Alaska. Capital: Washington. Largest city: New York. Overseas territories: Puerto Rico, Virgin Is, American Samoa, Guam, Wake and Midway. The U.S.A. also controls the Trust Territory of the Pacific Islands (the Caroline Is, Marshall Is and Marianas Is). People: white, Afro-American and mulatto, small American Indian, Japanese, Chinese, Southeast Asian and Filipino minorities. Language: English, minority and immigrant languages. Religion: 51% Protestant (30 principal denominations), 22% Roman Catholic, 3% Jewish, 2% Orthodox. The land (excluding

CONCISE PRONUNCIATION KEY: (**a**) æ, c*a*t; ɑ, c*a*r; ɔ f*a*wn; ei, sn*a*ke. (**e**) e, h*e*n; i:, sh*ee*p; iə, d*ee*r; ɛə, b*ea*r. (**i**) i, f*i*sh; ai, t*i*ger; ə:, b*i*rd. (**o**) o, *o*x; au, c*ow*; ou, g*oa*t; u, p*oo*r; ɔi, r*oy*al. (**u**) ʌ, d*u*ck; u, b*u*ll; u:, g*oo*se; ə, b*a*cillus; ju:, c*u*be. x, lo*ch*; θ, *th*ink; ð, bo*th*er; z, *Z*en; ʒ, cor*s*age; dʒ, sa*v*age; ŋ, oranguta*ng*; j, *y*ak; ʃ, *fish*; tʃ, fe*tch*; 'l, rabb*le*; 'n, redd*en*. Complete pronunciation key appears inside front cover.

Hawaii and Alaska) is 25% forest, 36% pasture and 24% arable. Main industrial zone: the Great Lakes-North Atlantic coast region. The Atlantic coast is greatly indented. The cultivated (increasingly industrialized) coastal plain, narrow between Maine and Cape Cod, widens toward the Gulf of Mexico to merge with the lower Mississippi basin and E. Texas plains. Behind it the wooded Appalachian system stretches from New England to central Alabama, incl. wide fertile valleys between New York State and Tennessee, and poor, eroded hills in Kentucky and West Virginia. The Mississippi-Missouri basin (cereals, cotton, petroleum) stretches from the Gulf of Mexico to the Great Lakes, broken only by the Ozarks and by the lower Canadian Shield around Lake Superior. West of it to the Rockies (Mt Elbert, 14,431 ft) lie the Great Plains (cereals, grazing land), rising to 5,000 ft in the west. Between the Rockies (*ROCKY MTNS) and the Cascade (Mt Rainier, 14,410 ft) and Sierra Nevada (Mt Whitney, 14,495 ft) ranges lies an arid plateau region (mining, cattle raising, cereals) divided into the Columbia and Colorado plateaus and the Great Basin, with a large desert in S. Nevada, S.E. California and W. Arizona. Fertile valleys in Washington, most of Oregon, and central California and desert valleys elsewhere separate the Cascades and Sierra Nevada from the wooded coast ranges (1,000-5,000 ft). The Pacific coast has few harbors. Average temperatures (F.) in Jan. and July: New York City 32°-75°, Chicago 26°-74°, Nashville 39°-79°, New Orleans 54°-80°, Denver 30°-71°, S.W. Arizona 55°-91°, Los Angeles 52°-71°, Seattle 39°-63°. Rainfall: New York City 42 ins, Chicago 33 ins, Nashville 47 ins, New Orleans 60 ins, Denver 14 ins, Arizona desert 3 ins, Los Angeles 15 ins, Seattle 32 ins. Livestock: cattle, hogs, sheep, horses, mules, poultry. Agricultural products: corn, cotton, hay, wheat, soybeans, tobacco, rice, oats and other cereals, potatoes, sugar beets, beans, cottonseed, sugarcane, sweet potatoes, apples, peaches, pears, citrus fruit, linseed, peanuts, meat, dairy products and market produce. Forestry products: Douglas fir, yellow pine, hardwood, resin, turpentine. It is the world's fourth producer of fish. Mineral resources: copper (leading world producer), iron ore (2nd world producer), coal and anthracite (2nd world producer), petroleum (leading world producer), uranium, silver, lead, zinc, bauxite, gold, natural gas, gypsum, chromite, molybdenum, phosphates, sulfur, salt. Manufactures and industries: iron and steel, mining, heavy engineering, hydroelectricity, food processing, textiles, vehicles, flour milling, meat packing, chemicals, locomotives and rolling stock, aircraft, electrical machinery, metallurgy, leather, tires, atomic energy, precision and optical instruments, tobacco, clothing, furniture, paper and pulp, printing, light manufactures, ships, aluminum, plastics, armaments, electronics. Exports: machinery, chemicals, wheat, vehicles, metals, textiles, foodstuffs, aircraft, tobacco, oil, coal, wood, pulp and paper, rubber, oilseeds and oils, raw cotton, radio and television sets, fruit, meat, military equipment, vegetables, iron and steel. Imports: oil, machinery and vehicles, metals, coffee, textiles, wood and paper, cane sugar, iron and steel, iron ore, meat, fish, rubber, chemicals, fruit, whiskey and other liquor, raw wool, diamonds, animals, cocoa. There are over 300 universities, the oldest being Harvard (1636). Chief ports: New York City, Philadelphia, Baltimore, New Orleans, San Francisco. Main fishing ports: Boston, Portland (Maine), Monterey, Los Angeles. Monetary unit: U.S. dollar (100 cents). HISTORY. The North American continent is thought to have been discovered (c. 1000 A.D.) by Vikings under Leif Ericson, but the existence of the New World was not known for certain in Europe until the voyage (1492) of Columbus. There were probably about 1,500,000 American Indians at this time in what is now the U.S.A. Spain began to colonize Florida (1565) and extended its control over much of Texas and the West. France explored from the Great Lakes, down the Mississippi, to Louisiana. After Sir Walter Raleigh had failed in his attempt to found a colony in Virginia (1584-9), the first permanent English settlement in North America was established there (1607) by a chartered company. Effective colonization in New England began when the Pilgrim Fathers settled at Plymouth (1620).

Maine and New Hampshire were settled (1622) by a chartered company. The Puritans of Massachusetts founded Connecticut (1635) and Rhode Island (1636). The Dutch founded a colony along the Hudson and the Delaware (1620s), which was conquered by the English (1664), together with a former Swedish colony which had been founded on the Delaware (1638) and taken by the Dutch (1655). Maryland was founded by English Roman Catholics (1634). The Carolinas were settled (1670) by a company chartered by Charles II. New Jersey was detached (1664) from the former Dutch colony now renamed New York, and was colonized by Quakers (1670s). Quakers also founded Pennsylvania (1682), granted by Charles II to Penn, who also received Delaware (1682). Georgia was founded (1733) as an English military post against French and Spanish rivalry and as a refuge for imprisoned debtors. Most of these Thirteen Colonies eventually passed to royal control. The colonies attracted increasing numbers of settlers from Europe, many of them fleeing from religious or political persecution, until by 1775 the population was over two and a half million. The economy was based on agriculture, notably in the Southern states, where tobacco and cotton plantations were worked by imported African slaves. The Indians were driven back westward. Colonial and maritime rivalry with France led to King William's War (1689-97), Queen Anne's War (1701-13), King George's War (1745-8) and the French and Indian War (1754-63). The colonies increased their powers of self-government during these wars, and the British triumph in the Treaty of Paris (1763), by removing the French and Indian threat, lessened the colonies' dependence on Britain. British attempts to prevent westward migration (1763), to tax the colonies in accordance with mercantilist theory and to enforce the Navigation Acts caused widespread resentment. The Stamp Act was withdrawn (1766) but an attempt to allow the British East India Company a tax exemption to dispose of a tea surplus on the American market provoked the Boston Tea Party (1773). Britain retaliated with the Intolerable Acts (1774). The Revolutionary War broke out (1775-83), and the Thirteen Colonies adopted the Declaration of Independence (July 4, 1776). The colonies united as the U.S.A. under the Articles of Confederation (1781), superseded by the U.S. Constitution (1789), which gave the federal government greatly increased powers. Washington, the leader of the American colonies during the war, became the first president of the U.S.A. (1789-97) under the Constitution. Out of the disagreement between Hamilton and Jefferson as to states' rights arose a two-party system. In foreign policy, the Federalists tended to be pro-English and the Antifederalists pro-French. During Jefferson's administration (1801-9), the Louisiana Purchase (1803) greatly increased U.S. territory. As the frontier was pushed back westwards, the U.S.A. came into conflict with the British in the north, and the Spanish in the south. The invention (1793) of the cotton gin rapidly made cotton the dominant crop in the South, and encouraged the spread of plantations and slave labor. Maritime rivalry with Britain led to the War of 1812, after which the U.S.A. recognized Canada as a British possession, and obtained full access to the northwest. During Monroe's administration (1817-25), Florida was bought from Spain (1819), and the Monroe Doctrine was proclaimed (1823). As more settlers moved west and southwest, and new states were set up, a sharp division arose between states in which slavery was legal and those in which it was not. The issue was postponed by the Missouri Compromise (1820-1). The frontier made its mark on U.S. democracy during the presidency (1829-37) of Jackson, under whom the Democratic party took shape, the spoils system was developed and the nullification issue was raised. As a result of Jackson's financial measures, Van Buren had to face an economic crisis during his administration (1837-41). As the Industrial Revolution made its influence felt, communications and industry were developed. By the 1840s, the population had risen to 17,000,000. Settlement in Texas led the U.S.A. to annex it (1845), provoking the Mexican War (1846-8). The U.S.A. gained new territory by the settlement (1846) of the Oregon Question, the Treaty of Guadalupe Hidalgo (1848) and the Gadsden Purchase (1854). The

California gold rush (1849) raised the question of whether California should be a slave or free-soil state. The attempt to settle this by the Compromise of 1850 created more bitterness, which was increased by the Kansas-Nebraska Act (1854) and the Dred Scott Decision (1857). After Lincoln's election as president (1860) the Civil War broke out (1861-5). The Emancipation Proclamation abolished slavery (1863) and the war ended in victory for the North. In the Reconstruction period which followed, war damage in the South was slowly repaired and industrialization begun. Mineral wealth was exploited, industrial progress continued rapidly in the North and, at a time when speculation and business combinations were unchecked by legislation, vast fortunes were made by Rockefeller, Carnegie and Morgan among others. Labor began to organize. The West was fully opened up for mining, cattle ranching and grain production. The Indians were virtually confined to reservations. Settlement rapidly followed the building of railroads across the continent. Alaska was bought from Russia (1867), Hawaii was annexed (1898) and, after the Spanish-American War (1898), American influence was extended to Puerto Rico, Cuba and the Philippines. With the opening (1914) of the Panama Canal, the U.S.A. had become a major world power, with a population of 92,000,000. After McKinley's assassination, Theodore Roosevelt held the presidency (1901-9), attacking trusts and encouraging the conservation of national resources. Under his successor, Taft, the Republican party was weakened by the secession of the Progressive party, and Woodrow Wilson, a Democrat, became president (1913-21). This administration established the Federal Reserve System (1913) and carried out social reform. Wilson attempted to keep the U.S.A. neutral in the 1st world war, but the German use of unrestricted submarine warfare brought the U.S.A. into the war on the side of the Allies (1917). Wilson took a leading part in peace negotiations (1918) and in setting up the League of Nations, but the Senate refused to ratify the treaty. Apart from promoting the Kellogg-Briand Pact (1928), the U.S.A. adopted an isolationist foreign policy. Prohibition was in force (1919-33). National prosperity rapidly increased in a speculative boom during the administrations of Harding (1921-3) and Coolidge (1923-9). Hoover's administration (1929-33) faced the ensuing economic depression without great success. F. D. Roosevelt's New Deal was more successful. U.S. isolationism came to an end with Roosevelt's good-neighbor policy toward Latin America. When the 2nd world war broke out, the U.S.A. remained neutral, but supplied lend-lease help to Britain (1941). After the Japanese attack on Pearl Harbor (1941), the U.S.A. declared war on the Axis (1941). Industry was organized for war production and a huge war effort was made. The U.S.A. developed the atomic bomb, and used it on Japan, bringing the war to a close (1945). The U.S.A. took a leading part in the organization of the U.N. (1945), supplied aid to Europe under the Marshall Plan (1948-52) and, as the cold war developed, proposed the formation of NATO (1949). Truman's administration (1945-53) brought in a program of social reform. The U.S.A. gave massive support to South Korea in the Korean War (1950-3). McCarthy went to extreme lengths to root out communist sympathizers in government office. The presidency passed to the Republicans under Eisenhower (1953-61). His administration saw the end of the Korean War and the formation (1954) of SEATO. Under the guidance of Dulles, the U.S.A. built up a defense system capable of meeting any aggression by immediate retaliation. Technological rivalry with the U.S.S.R. gave rise to competition in the exploration of space, and the U.S.A. launched its first artificial satellite (1958). Alaska and Hawaii became states of the U.S.A. (1959). The question of civil rights for blacks flared up and became the major domestic issue during Kennedy's presidency (1961-3). His prestige suffered from U.S. collusion in the abortive attempt by Cuban exiles to oust Castro by a landing at the Bay of Pigs (Apr. 1961). The presence of Soviet missiles on Cuba brought (Oct. 1962) the U.S.A. and the U.S.S.R. to the brink of war before Khrushchev backed down. Following Kennedy's assassination (Nov. 1963), the presidency passed to Vice-President

Lyndon B. Johnson, who gradually increased U.S. military support for South Vietnam, without achieving the military victory he sought. He intervened (Apr. 1965) in the Dominican Republic, reviving Latin American distrust of U.S. motives. Despite his unprecedented success in legislation, esp. in the field of civil rights and in his 'unconditional war on poverty', he decided (Apr. 1968) not to seek reelection. The eight-year Democratic run was ended by the election of Republican Richard Nixon, whose platform was based on an end to the war, the return to law and order, and the control of inflation. The first manned circumnavigation of the moon (Dec. 1968) and the first landing of a man (Neil Armstrong) on the moon (July 1969) enhanced U.S. prestige, somewhat offset by unprecedented disaffection in the U.S. academic community and esp. among youth over the continuing war and domestic racism. U.S. and South Vietnamese forces were sent (Apr. 1970) into Cambodia in search of North Vietnam's sanctuaries, and the operation aroused massive protest at home. U.S. land forces were withdrawn (by July 1, 1970) from Cambodia. President Nixon paid official visits (1972) to China and to the U.S.S.R. The Watergate crisis (1973-4) resulted in the resignations of several high government officials and culminated in the threat of impeachment and subsequent resignation of Pres. Nixon in Aug. 1974. Gerald Ford, who had replaced Spiro Agnew as vice president, served as president until 1977, when Democrat Jimmy Carter assumed office. Pres. Carter was instrumental in negotiating an Egyptian-Israeli peace treaty and the Panama Canal treaty; he also dealt with oil shortages, high inflation rates, and international crises caused by the Soviet invasion of Afghanistan and the taking of U.S. embassy personnel as hostages by Iranian students. The 1980 elections provided a landslide victory for Republican challenger Ronald Reagan, who survived an assassination attempt in 1981 and a serious recession early in his administration. A very large federal budget deficit continued to be a problem but unemployment and inflation rates dropped and Reagan was reelected in 1984 over opponent Walter Mondale. Civil strife in Central America, the growing budget deficit, tax reform, and long-term defense planning, esp. of the 'star wars' program, were among the chief issues of Reagan's second term

United States Steel Corporation steel producer. Incorporated (1901) by J.P. Morgan and Company, it became the first billion-dollar corporation in the U.S.A. It represented an early example of the domination of industry by investment bankers

United States Trust Territory of the Pacific former Japanese-mandated islands (area 700 sq. miles, pop. 91,000) of the Caroline, Marshall, and Mariana groups, administered by the U.S.A. as a Trusteeship for the United Nations. The area contains 2,141 atolls and islands (only 96 are inhabited). Administrative center: Saipan (pop. 6,700), Mariana Is

United States v. Roth (rɔθ, rɒθ) a landmark decision (1957) of the U.S. Supreme Court which confirmed that 'obscenity is not within the area of constitutionally protected speech or press'

'United States v. See·ger' (síːgər) a landmark decision (1965) of the U.S. Supreme Court, which held that it was not necessary to believe in a 'Supreme Being' in order to register as a conscientious objector

'United States v. Welsh' a landmark decision (1970) of the U.S. Supreme Court which extended the rights guaranteed by the 'U.S. v. Seeger' decision (1965). It held that exemption from military service could be solely on moral and ethical grounds, provided only that the dissentients' conscience 'would give them no rest or peace if they allowed themselves to become a part of an instrument of war'

unit factor (*biol.*) a gene on which a unit character depends

u·nit·hold·er (júːnithouldəːr) *n.* (*Br.*) (*securities*) a stockholder

u·ni·tive (júːnitiv) *adj.* having unity ‖ tending to unite

unit magnetic pole a unit of magnetic pole strength equal to the strength of a magnetic pole that would exert a force of 1 dyne on an identical pole 1 centimeter away

unit train a train that provides pickup from sender and delivery to consumer

unit trust (*securities*) a share in an inflexible portfolio of securities, (especially bonds not to be sold) deposited with a trustee until underlying securities mature or the trust is dissolved; designed to lower trust-management fees

u·ni·ty (júːniti) *pl.* **u·ni·ties** *n.* the state of being one, singleness ‖ the state of being made one, unification ‖ a whole made up of separate elements ‖ full agreement, harmony ‖ (*math.*) the numeral or unit 1 ‖ (*math.*) any quantity considered as a unit or 1 ‖ continuity of purpose, action etc. ‖ an arrangement of parts capable of producing a concentrated total effect in an artistic work, or the effect so produced ‖ any of the three principles laid down by Aristotle (and observed esp. in French classical drama) affirming that the action must occur within 24 hours, in one place and with no comic relief or subplot, so as to produce the desired heightening and concentration [F. *unité*]

u·ni·va·lent (juːnivéilənt) *adj.* (*biol.*) of a single, unpaired chromosome separating in the first meiotic division ‖ (*chem.*) having one valence (cf. MONOVALENT) [fr. UNI- + L. *valens* (*valentis*) fr. *valere*, to be strong]

u·ni·valve (júːnivælv) **1.** *adj.* (of a shell) having only one valve ‖ (of a mollusk) having such a shell **2.** *n.* a mollusk having a univalve shell ‖ this shell

u·ni·ver·sal (juːnivə́ːrsˈl) **1.** *adj.* general, for everything or everybody, *a universal remedy* ‖ involving all of a kind, e.g. everybody concerned or present, *by universal request* ‖ of widest scope, *a universal genius* ‖ present everywhere ‖ (of a machine tool) able to perform all the operations on a piece without being taken down and set up again ‖ (*logic*) of every member of a class (opp. PARTICULAR) **2.** *n.* (*philos.*) a general proposition, concept or idea [O.F. *universel* or fr. L. *universalis*]

universal coupling a universal joint

U·ni·ver·sal·ism (juːnivéːrslˈizəm) *n.* the theological doctrine that ultimately all men will be saved by God's grace **U·ni·vér·sal·ist** *n.*

Universalist Church a liberal Protestant denomination of the U.S.A. and Canada, founded (late 18th c.) in the U.S.A. Under the leadership of Hosea Ballou, it established colleges, seminaries, and newspapers. Its basic tenet posits that the love and goodness of God assure triumph over all evil. In 1960 its members numbered over 70,000, in about 400 churches. In 1961 it merged with the American Unitarian Association to form the Unitarian Universalist Association

u·ni·ver·sal·i·ty (juːnivərsǽliti) *n.* the state or quality of being universal [F *universalité* or fr. L.L. *universalitas*]

u·ni·ver·sal·ize (juːnivéːrsəlaiz) *pres. part.* **u·ni·ver·sal·iz·ing** *past* and *past part.* **u·ni·ver·sal·ized** *v.t.* to make universal

universal joint a joint or coupling allowing freedom of movement in all directions

u·ni·ver·sal·ly (juːnivéːrsəli) *adv.* in a universal manner, in every instance or in every part or place

Universal Postal Union (*abbr.* U.P.U.) an international organization regulating postage agreements between countries. Founded in 1874, it became (1947) a specialized agency of the U.N.

universal product code a 10-digit code based on ratio of printed bars to adjacent space, affixed to a package and readable electronically or by laser beam. It is used by retail stores for inventory control and checkout *abbr.* UPC

universal suffrage suffrage for all adult citizens except the insane, aliens and criminals

u·ni·verse (júːnivəːrs) *n.* the cosmos ‖ the earth and its inhabitants ‖ one's environment or field of interest regarded as a distinct world [F. *univers*]

U·ni·ver·si·dad de Bue·nos Ai·res (uːniːvẹrsi-ðáð̌ðebwénɔsáires) the leading university of Argentina, founded in 1821

U·ni·ver·si·dad de Chi·le (uːniːvẹrsiːðáððetʃíːle) the leading university of Chile, founded (1737) in Santiago and reorganized by Andrés Bello

U·ni·ver·si·dad de Cór·do·ba (uːniːvẹrsiːðáð̌ðekórðoba) the oldest university (1621) in Argentina

U·ni·ver·si·dad Na·cio·nal Au·tón·o·ma de Mé·xi·co (uːniːvẹrsiːðáðnɑθjonálautónɔmaðeméhiːkɔ) (*abbr.* UNAM) the second oldest university in the Americas, founded (1551) in Mexico City. Its university city was built by President Miguel Alemán. Its buildings, esp.

the Central Library, are famous for their murals

U·ni·ver·si·dad de San Cris·tó·bal de Hua·man·ga (uːniːvẹrsíːdáð̌ðesánkriːstɔ́balðewamángɑ) a Peruvian university in Ayacucho. In opening (1960) its doors to Quechua Indians, it became the first Latin American university to offer higher education in an Indian language

U·ni·ver·si·dad de San Mar·cos (uːniːvẹrsi-ð̌áðð̌esánmárkɔs) the oldest surviving university in the Americas, founded (1551) in Lima, Peru

U·ni·ver·si·da·de do Bra·sil (uːniːvẹrsiːdáðedɔbrazíːl) the first university in Brazil, founded (1920) in Rio de Janeiro by the federal government as a prototype for twenty others

u·ni·ver·si·ty (juːnivéːrsiti) *pl.* **u·ni·ver·si·ties** *n.* a group of faculties providing higher education and empowered to grant academic degrees ‖ the teachers and the persons taught in such an institution ‖ the buildings and grounds of such an institution [A.F. *université*]
—All universities can trace their spiritual origin (and many their actual origin) to the 'studia generalia' of the Middle Ages, centers of study licensed and privileged by secular or ecclesiastical authority, open to students of all classes and nationalities. The earliest universities (apart from the 10th-c. medical school of Salerno) were in Paris, Bologna, Oxford and Cambridge

university extension the making available by a university of its lecturers and the running of courses of instruction, for the benefit of people who are not members of that university

University of Puerto Rico the leading university of Puerto Rico, at Río Piedras outside San Juan, with other campuses at San Juan, Mayagüez and Humacao

un·kempt (ʌnkémpt) *adj.* (of hair) uncombed ‖ very untidy because of neglect, *an unkempt garden* [fr. UN-+older *kempt* fr. *kemb*, to comb]

Un·ki·ar Ske·les·si, Treaty of (uŋkjárskelesíː) a treaty (1833) between Russia and Turkey, closing the Dardanelles to foreign warships except those of Russia

un·kind (ʌnkáind) *adj.* not kind ‖ (of climate or weather) harsh **un·kínd·ly** *adv.*

un·kind·ly (ʌnkáindliː) *adj.* unkind [M.E.]

un·known (ʌnnóun) **1.** *adj.* not known **2.** *n.* an unknown quantity

unknown quantity (*math.*) an undetermined quantity figuring in a mathematical formulation and usually designated by a symbol, e.g. 'x' or 'y'

un·lead·ed (ʌnlédid) *adj.* (*printing*) without leads between the lines, set solid ‖ of a gasoline containing no lead

un·learn (ʌnléːrn) *pres. part.* **un·learn·ing** *past* and *past part.* **un·learned, un·learnt** (ʌnléːrnt) *v.t.* to rid one's mind of (something already learned)

un·learn·ed (ʌnléːrnid, ʌnléːrnd) *adj.* possessing no learning ‖ characterized by a lack of learning *unlearned speech* ‖ not acquired by study ‖ known without being learned

un·leash (ʌnlíːʃ) *v.t.* to release from, or as if from, a leash

un·leav·ened (ʌnlévənd) *adj.* made without leaven

un·less (ʌnlés) **1.** *conj.* if... not, *we have met before, unless I am mistaken* ‖ except when, except that, *unless he is hungry he will not touch it* **2.** *prep.* except, *nothing, unless rain, could prevent us from coming* [fr. on+less, 'on' assimilated to ,un-,]

un·let·tered (ʌnlétərd) *adj.* lacking education ‖ illiterate

un·like (ʌnláik) **1.** *adj.* not alike, dissimilar **2.** *prep.* not like, *such behavior is unlike him* [M.E. *unliche, unlike*]

un·like·li·hood (ʌnláikliːhud) *n.* improbability ‖ something improbable

un·like·li·ness (ʌnláikliːnis) *n.* improbability

un·like·ly (ʌnláikliː) **1.** *adj.* improbable, not likely ‖ unpromising, not likely to succeed **2.** *adv.* improbably

un·lim·ber (ʌnlímbər) *v.t.* to make (a gun) ready for action by detaching the limber

un·lim·it·ed (ʌnlímitid) *adj.* without limits ‖ boundless, vast

un·linked (ʌnlínkt) *adj.* (*genetics*) of a different linkage group

un·list·ed (ʌnlístid) *adj.* not listed ‖ (of securities) not listed among the ones admitted for trading on the stock market

CONCISE PRONUNCIATION KEY: **(a)** æ, c*a*t; ɑ, c*a*r; ɔ f*aw*n; ei, sn*a*ke. **(e)** e, h*e*n; iː, sh*ee*p; iə, d*ee*r; ɛə, b*ea*r. **(i)** i, f*i*sh; ai, t*i*ger; əː, b*i*rd. **(o)** o, *o*x; au, c*ow*; ou, g*oa*t; u, p*oo*r; ɔi, r*oy*al. **(u)** ʌ, d*u*ck; u, b*u*ll; uː, g*oo*se; ə, b*a*cillus; juː, c*u*be. x, lo*ch*; θ, *th*ink; ð, bo*th*er; z, *Z*en; ʒ, corsa*g*e; dʒ, sava*g*e; ŋ, ora*ng*utan*g*; j, *y*ak; ʃ, *fish*; tʃ, fe*tch*; 'l, rabb*le*; 'n, redd*en*. Complete pronunciation key appears inside front cover.

unlisted number a telephone number not recorded in the published directory and not available from Information; (*Br.*) exdirectory number

un·load (ʌnlóud) *v.t.* to remove the goods from (a vehicle, vessel etc.) ‖ to remove (a cargo, load etc.) ‖ to remove the burden from ‖ to remove the charge from (a gun) ‖ (*pop.*) to sell (stock holdings etc.) in quantity and at a low price ‖ *v.i.* to discharge something, esp. a cargo

un·lock (ʌnlók) *v.t.* to open the lock of (a door) ‖ to free (a lock) with a key ‖ to tell the secrets of, *to unlock one's heart* ‖ (*rhet.*) to solve, *to unlock a mystery* ‖ *v.i.* to become unlocked

un·looked-for (ʌnlúkt-fɔr) *adj.* not anticipated, not expected

un·loose (ʌnlúːs) *pres. part.* **un·loos·ing** *past and past part.* **un·loosed** *v.t.* to loosen ‖ to set free

un·loos·en (ʌnlúːs'n) *v.t.* to unloose

un·love·ly (ʌnlʌ́vli:) *adj.* unsightly

un·luck·i·ly (ʌnlʌ́kili:) *adv.* in an unlucky way, by a misfortune

un·luck·i·ness (ʌnlʌ́kinis) *n.* the state or quality of being unlucky

un·luck·y (ʌnlʌ́ki:) *comp.* **un·luck·i·er** *superl.* **un·luck·i·est** *adj.* not lucky ‖ (*rhet.*) ill-omened

un·make (ʌnméik) *pres. part.* **un·mak·ing** *past and past part.* **un·made** (ʌnméid) *v.t.* to ruin, destroy ‖ to depose from a position of authority, rank etc.

un·man (ʌnmǽn) *pres. part.* **un·man·ning** *past and past part.* **un·manned** *v.t.* to deprive of manly qualities **un·manned** *adj.* lacking a crew of men, *guns left unmanned*

un·man·ner·li·ness (ʌnmǽnərlinis) *n.* the state or quality of being unmannerly

un·man·ner·ly (ʌnmǽnərli:) *adj.* impolite

un·mask (ʌnmǽsk, ʌnmáːsk) *v.t.* to remove the mask from ‖ to expose the true nature or identity of, *to unmask a criminal* ‖ *v.i.* to take off one's mask

un·mean·ing (ʌnmíːniŋ) *adj.* without meaning

un·men·tion·a·ble (ʌnménʃənəb'l) *adj.* not fit to be mentioned, esp. because indecent

un·mis·tak·a·ble (ʌnmistéikəb'l) *adj.* that cannot be mistaken, clear, obvious **un·mis·ták·a·bly** *adv.*

un·mit·i·gat·ed (ʌnmítigeitid) *adj.* not lessened in intensity etc., *unmitigated grief* ‖ absolute, unqualified, *an unmitigated ass*

un·mor·al (ʌnmɔ́rəl, ʌnmɔ́rəl) *adj.* amoral

un·nat·u·ral (ʌnnǽtʃərəl) *adj.* not natural ‖ lacking or counter to behavior, feelings etc. that are considered natural or normal

un·nec·es·sar·y (ʌnnésiseri:) *adj.* not necessary, needless

un·nerve (ʌnnɔ́ːrv) *pres. part.* **un·nerv·ing** *past and past part.* **un·nerved** *v.t.* to destroy the self-control of, cause to be nervous

un·num·bered (ʌnnʌ́mbərd) *adj.* (*rhet.*) innumerable ‖ bearing no number

un·oc·cu·pied (ʌnɔ́kupaid) *adj.* empty, not occupied ‖ without occupation, idle ‖ not occupied by troops

un·or·gan·ized (ʌnɔ́rgənaizd) *adj.* not organized ‖ not having organic structure ‖ not belonging to a trade union

un·pack (ʌnpǽk) *v.t.* to remove from its packaging ‖ to empty (a trunk, case etc.) of its contents ‖ *v.i.* to unpack a trunk, case etc.

un·par·al·leled (ʌnpǽrəleld) *adj.* having no equal

un·par·lia·men·ta·ry (ʌnpɑrləméntəri:) *adj.* not in accordance with parliamentary practice

un·per·son (ʌnpɔ́ːrsən) *n.* an individual the memory of whom has been erased from all records and who is otherwise not recognized (based on practice in U.S.S.R., 1936–1938); coined by English author George Orwell

un·pick (ʌnpík) *adj.* to remove stitches from (sewing, knitting etc.), *to unpick a seam*

un·pleas·ant (ʌnpléz'nt) *adj.* disagreeable, not pleasant **un·pléas·ant·ness** *n.* the quality or state of being unpleasant ‖ an unpleasant situation etc., esp. a quarrel

un·plumbed (ʌnplʌ́md) *adj.* not fully investigated

un·polled (ʌnpóuld) *adj.* (of a vote) not cast ‖ not included in a poll

un·pop·u·lar (ʌnpópjulər) *adj.* not popular, viewed with disfavor by the majority

un·prac·ticed, *Br.* **un·prac·tised** (ʌnprǽktist) *adj.* not skilled

un·prec·e·dent·ed (ʌnprésidəntid) *adj.* without precedent

un·pre·pared (ʌnpripéərd) *adj.* not worked out ahead ‖ not ready ‖ not emotionally adjusted in advance, esp. for a shock

un·prin·ci·pled (ʌnprínsəpəld) *adj.* without moral principles

un·print·a·ble (ʌnpríntəb'l) *adj.* not suitable for printing (because blasphemous, obscene, slanderous etc.)

un·pro·fes·sion·al (ʌnprəféʃən'l) *adj.* not professional ‖ not in accordance with professional etiquette

un·qual·i·fied (ʌnkwólifaid) *adj.* lacking the necessary qualifications ‖ without reservation, *unqualified praise*

un·quan·ti·fi·a·ble (ʌnkwɒntəfáiəb'l) *adj.* not capable of being measured

un·ques·tion·a·ble (ʌnkwéstʃənəb'l) *adj.* not open to question **un·qués·tion·a·bly** *adv.*

un·quote (ʌnkwóut) *pres. part.* **un·quot·ing** *past and past part.* **un·quot·ed** (used in the imperative, esp. in dictating) to close a quotation

un·rav·el (ʌnrǽvəl) *pres. part.* **un·rav·el·ing**, esp. *Br.* **un·rav·el·ling** *past and past part.* **un·rav·elled** *v.t.* to untangle ‖ to undo (a knitted garment) ‖ to solve (a complex problem) ‖ *v.i.* to become unraveled

un·read (ʌnréd) *adj.* not well-read

un·read·a·ble (ʌnríːdəb'l) *adj.* too turgid, dull, precious etc. to be read with pleasure ‖ illegible

un·read·y (ʌnrédi:) *adj.* not ready ‖ slow to learn, *an unready pupil*

un·re·al (ʌnríəl) *adj.* not real ‖ existing only in the mind

un·re·al·i·ty (ʌnriːǽliti:) *pl.* **un·re·al·i·ties** *n.* the state or quality of being unreal ‖ something unreal

un·rea·son (ʌnríːz'n) *n.* absence of reason

un·rea·son·a·ble (ʌnríːz'nəb'l) *adj.* not reasonable ‖ beyond the bounds of reason, immoderate **un·réa·son·a·bly** *adv.*

un·rea·son·ing (ʌnríːz'niŋ) *adj.* not reasoning ‖ not controlled by reason

un·reeve (ʌnríːv) *pres. part.* **un·reev·ing** *past and past part.* **un·rove** (ʌnróuv), **un·reeved** *v.t.* (*naut.*) to withdraw (a rope) from a block or other opening

un·re·gen·er·ate (ʌnridʒénərit) *adj.* not made spiritually regenerate ‖ persisting obstinately in an opinion or outlook, *an unregenerate philistine* **un·re·gen·er·at·ed** (ʌnridʒénəreitid) *adj.* unregenerate

un·re·lent·ing (ʌnriléntiŋ) *adj.* not weakening in determination ‖ not becoming compassionate ‖ not slackening in intensity, speed etc.

un·re·mit·ting (ʌnrimítiŋ) *adj.* persevering ‖ kept up without interruption

un·re·served (ʌnrizɔ́ːrvd) *adj.* unqualified, without modification, *unreserved praise* ‖ frank in speech or behavior **un·re·serv·ed·ly** (ʌnrizɔ́ːrvidli:) *adv.*

un·rest (ʌnrést) *n.* restlessness, uneasiness ‖ collective discontent

un·re·strained (ʌnristréind) *adj.* not reticent or reserved ‖ not kept in check

un·rip (ʌnríp) *pres. part.* **un·rip·ping** *past and past part.* **un·ripped** *v.t.* and *v.i.* to rip open

un·ripe (ʌnráip) *adj.* (of fruit etc.) not ripe

un·ri·valed, esp. *Br.* **un·ri·valled** (ʌnráivəld) *adj.* without a rival or equal

un·roll (ʌnróul) *v.t.* to open from a rolled position ‖ to unfold to the view ‖ *v.i.* to become unrolled

un·round (ʌnráund) *v.t.* to pronounce (a normally rounded vowel) without rounding the lips ‖ to make (the lips) not rounded, e.g. in pronouncing a normally rounded vowel

unrove alt. *past* and *past part.* of UNREEVE

un·ruf·fled (ʌnrʌ́fəld) *adj.* not ruffled emotionally serene

un·ru·li·ness (ʌnrúːli:nis) *n.* the state or quality of being unruly

un·ru·ly (ʌnrúːli:) *comp.* **un·ru·li·er** *superl.* **un·ru·li·est** *adj.* refusing to submit to rule, undisciplined and causing trouble

un·sad·dle (ʌnsǽd'l) *pres. part.* **un·sad·dling** *past and past part.* **un·sad·dled** *v.t.* to remove the saddle from ‖ to throw from the saddle

un·said (ʌnséd) *past* and *past part.* of UNSAY ‖ *adj.* thought but not uttered, kept suppressed in the mind ‖ *UNSAY

un·sat·u·rat·ed (ʌnsǽtʃəreitid) *adj.* not saturated ‖ (*chem.*, of a compound, esp. of carbon) containing double or triple bonds and hence capable of forming other compounds by addition ‖ (*chem.*, of a solution) capable of absorbing

or dissolving further solute at a given temperature and pressure

un·sa·vor·y, *Br.* **un·sa·vour·y** (ʌnséivəri:) *adj.* unpleasant in taste or smell ‖ tasteless, insipid ‖ morally offensive, disgusting

un·say (ʌnséi) *pres. part.* **un·say·ing** *past and past part.* **un·said** (ʌnséd) *v.t.* to withdraw (what one has said)

un·scathed (ʌnskéiðd) *adj.* without being physically or morally hurt

un·sci·en·tif·ic (ʌnsaiəntifík) *adj.* not in accordance with scientific method ‖ not acting from knowledge of scientific method

un·scram·ble (ʌnskrǽmb'l) *pres. part.* **un·scram·bling** *past and past part.* **un·scram·bled** *v.t.* to put (a scrambled message) into clear form

un·screw (ʌnskrúː) *v.t.* to remove or loosen (a screw, lid etc.) by turning ‖ to remove a screw-on lid from ‖ to remove the screws from ‖ *v.i.* to admit of unscrewing ‖ to become unscrewed

un·scru·pu·lous (ʌnskrúːpjuləs) *adj.* unprincipled ‖ dishonest

un·seal (ʌnsíːl) *v.i.* to break the seal on or undo the sealing of ‖ to end the imposed constraint on, open, *drink unsealed his lips*

un·sea·son·a·ble (ʌnsíːzənəb'l) *adj.* not usual for the time of year, *unseasonable weather* ‖ (*rhet.*) badly timed, inopportune, *an unseasonable remark*

un·seat (ʌnsíːt) *v.t.* to throw or remove from a seat, esp. from the saddle ‖ to remove from office, e.g. from a seat in Parliament

un·seem·ly (ʌnsíːmli:) **1.** *adj.* not seemly, indecorous, unbecoming **2.** *adv.* in an unseemly way

un·seen (ʌnsíːn) **1.** *adj.* not seen ‖ not able to be seen ‖ (*Br.*, of a passage set for translation) sight **2.** *n.* (*Br.*) a sight translation

un·set·tle (ʌnsét'l) *pres. part.* **un·set·tling** *past and past part.* **un·set·tled** *v.t.* to cause to be no longer stable ‖ to cause to be no longer sure or determined ‖ to cause to lose one's mental or emotional composure ‖ to cause (the stomach) to be slightly upset **un·sét·tled** *adj.* (of an account) not paid ‖ not stable ‖ not orderly ‖ not decided ‖ not populated or cultivated ‖ not settled in one place ‖ not legally disposed of, *unsettled property* ‖ (of weather) changeable ‖ mentally or emotionally discomposed

un·ship (ʌnʃíp) *pres. part.* **un·ship·ping** *past and past part.* **un·shipped** *v.t.* (*naut.*) to unload (cargo etc.) from a ship ‖ (*naut.*) to remove (e.g. oars or the mast) from position

un·sight·ly (ʌnsáitli:) *adj.* unpleasant to see

un·skilled (ʌnskíld) *adj.* not skilled ‖ not requiring skill

un·skill·ful, esp. *Br.* **un·skil·ful** (ʌnskílfəl) *adj.* not skillful ‖ betraying lack of skill

un·sling (ʌnslíŋ) *pres. part.* **un·sling·ing** *past and past part.* **un·slung** (ʌnslʌ́ŋ) *v.t.* to take from a slung position ‖ (*naut.*) to remove from slings

un·so·cia·bil·i·ty (ʌnsouʃəbíliti:) *n.* the state or quality of being unsociable

un·so·cia·ble (ʌnsóuʃəb'l) *adj.* not sociable, by nature solitary, shunning society ‖ not conducive to sociability **un·só·cia·bly** *adv.*

un·so·cial (ʌnsóuʃəl) *adj.* not willingly associating with others ‖ antisocial

un·sound (ʌnsáund) *adj.* not physically, mentally or morally sound ‖ (esp. of market produce) not in good condition ‖ open to logical attack ‖ (of a thing) liable to collapse, *an unsound chair* ‖ (of sleep) uneasy, fitful

un·spar·ing (ʌnspéəriŋ) *adj.* without reserve in giving, striving etc. ‖ without mercy

un·speak·a·ble (ʌnspíːkəb'l) *adj.* indescribably bad ‖ inexpressibly delightful **un·spéak·a·bly** *adv.*

un·sta·ble (ʌnstéib'l) *adj.* in a condition which may very easily change or be changed ‖ not to be depended on ‖ characterized by emotional instability (*chem.*) readily decomposing

un·stead·y (ʌnstédi:) *comp.* **un·stead·i·er** *superl.* **un·stead·i·est** *adj.* not firm or firmly under control ‖ emotionally changeable ‖ lacking regularity, *an unsteady pulse*

un·stop (ʌnstóp) *pres. part.* **un·stopping** *past and past part.* **un·stopped** *v.t.* to take the stopper from ‖ to free from obstruction

un·strik·a·ble (ʌnstráikəb'l) *adj.* of a job on which a strike is illegal

un·string (ʌnstríŋ) *pres. part.* **un·string·ing** *past and past part.* **un·strung** (ʌnstrʌ́ŋ) *v.t.* to loosen or remove the strings of (a violin etc.) ‖ to take (beads etc.) from a string ‖ (esp. in passive) to cause (a person or his nerves) to become disordered

un·strung (ʌnstrʌŋ) *adj.* having the strings removed or loosened || emotionally distressed

un·stud·ied (ʌnstʌdi:d) *adj.* unaffected, not artificial

un·sub·stan·tial (ˌʌnsəbstænʃəl) *adj.* not having material substance || not very solid || having no real basis of fact

un·sung (ʌnsʌŋ) *adj.* not sung || not praised in verse or song, not given recognition, *unsung heroes*

un·sus·pect·ed (ʌnsəspéktid) *adj.* not suspected || not known or thought to exist

un·taught (ʌntɔ́t) *adj.* without formal education || not learned from teachers

un·teach (ʌntí:tʃ) *pres. part.* **un·teach·ing** *past and past part.* **un·taught** (ʌntɔ́t) *v.t.* to cause (someone) to forget something learned || to teach the opposite of (something previously taught)

Un·ter·mensch (úntərmenʃ) *pl.* **-en** (*German*) an alleged lower species or type of human being *ant.* Übermensch

Un·ter·wal·den (úntərvɑldən) a German-speaking and mainly Catholic canton in central Switzerland. It is divided into Nidwalden (area 106 sq. miles, pop. 28,617) and Obwalden (area 189 sq. miles, pop. 25,865). It formed (1291) part of the original league with Schwyz and Uri which was the nucleus of the Swiss Confederation

un·thank·ful (ʌnθǽŋkfəl) *adj.* not thankful || not pleasant and not appreciated, *an unthankful task*

un·think·a·ble (ʌnθíŋkəb'l) *adj.* so extraordinary as not to be conceivable to the mind || out of the question, not to be considered as a possibility

un·think·ing (ʌnθíŋkiŋ) *adj.* thoughtless or showing lack of thought || lacking the power of thought

un·ti·dy (ʌntáidi:) *adj.* not neat or orderly in dress, appearance, habit etc. || not kept in proper order, *untidy account books*

un·tie (ʌntái) *pres. part.* **un·ty·ing, un·tie·ing** *past and past part.* **un·tied** *v.t.* to undo (something tied, fastened or knotted) || *v.i.* (of something tied, fastened or knotted) to become undone

un·til (ʌntíl) **1.** *prep.* till, to the time of, *we waited until nightfall* (in negative constructions) before (some specified time), *don't come until after dark* **2.** *conj.* to the time when || to the degree, place or point that, *he pleaded until he got it* || (in negative constructions) before, *he didn't come until the show began* [M.E. *untill* fr. O.N.]

un·time·li·ness (ʌntáimli:nis) *n.* the state or quality of being untimely

un·time·ly (ʌntáimli:) **1.** *adj. comp.* **un·time·li·er** *superl.* **un·time·li·est** done or occurring before the proper time, premature || inopportune **2.** *adv.* too soon || inopportunely

un·to (ʌ́ntu:) *prep.* (*rhet.* or *archaic*) to, *render unto Caesar...* || (*rhet.* or *archaic*) till, until, *unto this day*

un·told (ʌntóuld) *adj.* not told || too much or too many to count or measure

un·touch·a·ble (ʌntʌ́tʃəb'l) **1.** *adj.* not to be touched || immune from criticism or attack **2.** *n.* a member of a large group in India belonging to the lowest caste or regarded as having no caste, and formerly excluded from the social and religious privileges of Hinduism. The persecution of untouchables was made illegal by the Indian constituent assembly (1949) and the Pakistan constituent assembly (1950)

un·to·ward (ʌntɔ́rd, ʌntóurd, ʌntəwɔ́rd) *adj.* fractious, difficult to manage || not favorable or lucky, *untoward circumstances* || unseemly

un·trav·eled, esp. *Br.* **un·trav·elled** (ʌntrǽvəld) *adj.* (of a road etc.) not used by travelers || (of a person) not having traveled much

un·tried (ʌntráid) *adj.* not tested, inexperienced || not tried in court

un·true (ʌntrú:) *adj.* not true, false || (*rhet.*) unfaithful or disloyal || not perfectly flat, level etc., not forming a perfect right angle etc. **un·trú·ly** *adv.*

un·truth (ʌntrú:θ) *pl.* **un·truths** (ʌntrú:θs, ʌntrú:ðz) *n.* lack of truthfulness or a falsehood

un·truth·ful (ʌntrú:θfəl) *adj.* untrue, false || inclined to tell lies

un·tu·tored (ʌntú:tərd, ʌntjú:tərd) *adj.* untaught, owing nothing to formal instruction

un·used (ʌnjú:zd) *adj.* not currently in use || never having been used || (ʌnjú:st) (with 'to') unaccustomed

un·u·su·al (ʌnjú:ʒuəl) *adj.* rare, different from others || being of or showing a greater or stronger degree than usual, *to work with unusual speed*

un·ut·ter·a·ble (ʌnʌ́tərəb'l) *adj.* inexpressibly delightful || unspeakably horrid

un·var·nished (ʌnvɑ́rniʃt) *adj.* not varnished || plain, unembellished, *the unvarnished truth*

Un·ver·dor·ben (únferdɔrbən), Otto (1806-73), German chemist who was the first to prepare aniline (1826)

un·voice (ʌnvóis) *pres. part.* **un·voic·ing** *past and past part.* **un·voiced** *v.t.* (*phon.*) to pronounce without voicing

un·voiced (ʌnvóist) *adj.* not expressed, not spoken || (*phon.*) not voiced

un·wea·ried (ʌnwíəri:d) *adj.* doggedly persistent in effort || showing dogged persistence

un·wept (ʌnwépt) *adj.* (*rhet.*, of tears) not shed || (*rhet.*) not wept for

un·whole·some (ʌnhóulsəm) *adj.* not wholesome, not conducive to physical or mental health || morally harmful

un·wield·i·ly (ʌnwí:ldli:) *adv.* in an unwieldy way

un·wield·i·ness (ʌnwí:ldi:nis) *n.* the state or quality of being unwieldy

un·wield·y (ʌnwí:ldi:) *comp.* **un·wield·i·er** *superl.* **un·wield·i·est** *adj.* difficult to handle or manage because of bulk or size || clumsy, ungainly

un·wil·ling (ʌnwíliŋ) *adj.* not willing, reluctant || done, said etc. reluctantly

un·wind (ʌnwáind) *pres. part.* **un·wind·ing** *past and past part.* **un·wound** (ʌnwáund) *v.t.* to undo, unroll (what is wound) || (*rhet.*) to sort out or straighten (something muddled or involved) || *v.i.* to become unwound

un·wise (ʌnwáiz) *adj.* ill-considered || foolish

un·wit·ting (ʌnwítiŋ) *adj.* unaware, not knowing || not intentional [O.E. *unwitende*]

un·wont·ed (ʌnwɔ́ntid, ʌnwóuntid, ʌnwʌ́ntid) *adj.* unaccustomed || uncommon, rarely met with

un·world·li·ness (ʌnwə́:rldli:nis) *n.* the state or quality of being unworldly

un·world·ly (ʌnwə́:rldli:) *comp.* **un·world·li·er** *superl.* **un·world·li·est** *adj.* not concerned with worldly matters || not of this world, spiritual

un·wor·thi·ly (ʌnwə́:rðili:) *adv.* in an unworthy manner

un·wor·thi·ness (ʌnwə́:rði:nis) *n.* the state or quality of being unworthy

un·wor·thy (ʌnwə́:rði:) *comp.* **un·wor·thi·er** *superl.* **un·wor·thi·est** *adj.* falling short of what is required, lamentably below standard || (esp. with 'of') not deserving || mean, contemptible

unwound *past and past part.* of UNWIND

un·writ·ten (ʌnrít'n) *adj.* not written || (of laws) not included in the statutes but based on long custom or strong general feeling || not written on

up (ʌp) **1.** *adv.* from a lower towards a higher location || towards a greater degree of intensity, *warming up* || towards a higher rank or social condition || to a higher amount, value, degree etc., *the property has gone up since he bought it* || from an earlier to a later period, *from youth up* || from below the horizon || (*Br.*) to the capital || in the direction thought of as higher, *going up north* || in or to a standing position || out of bed || in reserve, *to lay up stores* || into view, consideration, action etc. || into a state of excitement, *don't get worked up* || (*baseball*) to a turn at bat, *who is coming up next?* || so as to be even with in space, time, condition etc., *keeping up with the neighbors* || (*naut.*) towards the point from which the wind blows || (*sports, games*) ahead of an opponent with respect to points, strokes etc. (*sports, games*) for each side, *the score is 2 up* || (in combination with verbs) used as an intensive, *burn up, eat up, dry up* || (used in combination with verbs without effecting a change in meaning), *to light up one's pipe* **2.** *prep.* to, toward or at a higher point on or in, *climb up the stairs* || to or towards a higher condition in or on, *up the social scale* || at a point farther along, *she lives up the road* || toward the source of (a river) **up to** as far as (a designated part or point), *up to her knees in mud* || as much as, *the elevator will hold up to three people* || until, *up to this time* **3.** *adj.* directed toward a position that is higher or that is thought of as higher || in a higher position or condition showing above the ground, *the corn is up* || above the horizon, *the moon is up* || advanced in amount, degree etc. || in a standing position || out of bed || (e.g. of the wind) in an active or agitated state || in an inner

or elevated part of a country or territory || (*Br.*) resident at a university etc. || at an end, *our time is up* || happening, being planned etc. || (*baseball*) at bat || (*sports, games*) ahead of one's opponent **it's all up with** there is no hope for **up against** faced with, confronted with, *up against a difficult problem* **up against it** in difficulty **up and doing** actively busy **up for** before court for (trial) || being considered for (an office etc.) **up on** (or **in**) informed about, *she is always well up on the latest fashions* **up to** doing, *what are they up to?* || equal to (a task etc.) || incumbent upon || dependent on the decision or action of || well aware of, *she's up to his tricks* **4.** *n.* (in the phrase) **on the up and up** getting better and better or more and more successful || straightforward, honest **ups and downs** periods of good and bad fortune **5.** *v. pres. part.* **up·ping** *past and past part.* **upped** *v.i.* (with 'and' and a verb) to take decisive action with regard to some specified matter, *she upped and slapped him on the cheek* || *v.t.* (*Br.*) to collect together (swans) for their annual marking (cf. SWAN-UPPING) || to increase, *to up taxes* || to bet more than || to move to a higher position, *to up sails* **to up with** to raise (the arm, a weapon etc.), esp. in a threatening way, *he upped with an ax* [O.E. *up, uppe*]

up- (ʌp) the combining form of UP [O.E.]

up-an·chor (ʌ́pæŋkər) *v.i.* (*naut.*) to draw up the anchor before getting under way

up-and-com·ing (ʌ́pənkʌ́miŋ) *adj.* able and energetic and on the way to being successful

up-and-down (ʌ́pəndáun) *adj.* rising and falling alternately

U·pan·i·shads (u:pǽniʃædz, u:pʌ́niʃədz) the main body of the sacred writings of Hinduism. There are over 100 separate books, most of them consisting of a mixture of stories, dialogues, aphorisms and allegorizings of ideas from the Vedas. The books were written c. 600—c. 300 B.C. Their most characteristic doctrine is that of monism [Skr.=secret teachings]

u·pas (jú:pəs) *n. Antiaris toxicaria,* fam. *Moraceae,* a tall evergreen tree of S.E. Asia yielding a latex used in concocting an arrow poison || this poison [fr. Malay *ūpas,* poison (*pōhun ūpas,* poison tree)]

up·beat (ʌ́pbi:t) *n.* (*mus.*) the beat before the main accented note, or the conductor's gesture indicating this

up·bow (ʌ́pbou) *n.* (in playing a bowed instrument) a stroke from the tip to the heel of the bow (cf. DOWN-BOW)

up·braid (ʌpbréid) *v.t.* to scold, reproach [O.E. *upbregdan*]

up·bring·ing (ʌ́pbriŋiŋ) *n.* the process of training and education in childhood and youth

up·cast (ʌ́pkæst, ʌ́pkɑst) **1.** *adj.* directed or inclined upwards, *upcast eyes* **2.** *n.* (*mining*) a shaft provided for the upward passage of air || (*mining*) the material cast up in digging

up·con·vert·er (ʌpkənvə́:rtər) *n.* (*electr.*) **1.** device that converts radiant energy to another form, e.g., using a laser beam to produce a three-dimensional image **2.** an amplifier that converts input frequency to a greater output frequency —**upconvert** *v.t.*

up·coun·try 1. (ʌ́pkʌntri:) *adj.* of, relating to or situated in the interior of a country or region **2.** (ʌ́pkʌntri) *n.* the interior of a country or region **3.** (ʌpkʌ́ntri) *adv.* in or toward the interior of a country or region

up·date (ʌpdéit) *pres. part.* **up·dat·ing** *past and past part.* **up·dat·ed** *v.t.* to bring (e.g. matter in a book) up to date by adding or correcting

Up·dike (ʌ́pdaik), John (1932-), U.S. writer of short stories, notably 'Same Door' (1959), and of novels, notably 'Rabbit, Run' (1961), 'The Centaur' (1962), 'Couples' (1968), 'Bech: A Book' (1970), 'A Month of Sundays' (1975), 'Rabbit is Rich' (1981, Pulitzer Prize), 'Bech is Back' (1982) and 'The Witches of Eastwick' (1984)

up·draft (ʌ́pdræft) **1.** *adj.* (of a kiln) in which the heated air passes upward, to an outlet at the top **2.** *n.* an upward movement of air or other gas

up·end (ʌpénd) *v.t.* to set on end or as if on end || *v.i.* to rise on end

up·field (ʌpfí:ld) *n.* (*football*) area toward the goal post —**upfield** *adj.* —**upfield** *adv.*

up·front (ʌpfrʌ́nt) *adj.* **1.** paid in advance **2.** straightforward and honest

up·grade 1. (ʌ́pgreid) *n.* a rising slope **on the upgrade** improving || increasing **2.** (ʌ́pgréid) *adv.* uphill **3.** (ʌ́pgreid) *v.t. pres. part.* **up·grad-**

CONCISE PRONUNCIATION KEY: **(a)** æ, c*a*t; ɑ, c*a*r; ɔ f*aw*n; ei, sn*a*ke. **(e)** e, h*e*n; i:, sh*ee*p; iə, d*ee*r; ɛə, b*ea*r. **(i)** i, f*i*sh; ai, t*i*ger; ə:, b*i*rd. **(o)** o, *o*x; au, c*ow*; ou, g*oa*t; u, p*oo*r; ɔi, r*oy*al. **(u)** ʌ, d*u*ck; u, b*u*ll; u:, g*oo*se; ə, b*a*cill*u*s; ju:, c*u*be. x, lo*ch*; θ, *th*ink; ð, *b*o*th*er; z, *Z*en; ʒ, cor*s*age; dʒ, sava*g*e; ŋ, ora*n*gutang; j, *y*ak; ʃ, fi*sh*; tʃ, fet*ch*; 'l, rabb*le*; 'n, redd*en*. Complete pronunciation key appears inside front cover.

ing *past* and *past part.* **up·grad·ed** to promote, advance to a higher grade ‖ (*commerce*) to raise the quality of (a product)

up·heav·al (ʌphí:vəl) *n.* an upheaving or a being upheaved, esp. by volcanic action ‖ a violent social commotion

up·heave (ʌphí:v) *pres. part.* **up·heav·ing** *past* and *past part.* **up·heaved** *v.t.* (esp. *geol.*) to lift up with violent effort or force ‖ *v.i.* to rise upward with great force

upheld *past* and *past part.* of UPHOLD

up·hill 1. (ʌphíl) *adv.* in an ascending direction **2.** (ʌphíl) *adj.* ascending ‖ (of a task, struggle etc.) slow and difficult

up·hold (ʌphóuld) *pres. part.* **up·hold·ing** *past* and *past part.* **up·held** *v.t.* to maintain or support morally or spiritually ‖ to give physical support to ‖ to confirm, decide in favor of, *the court upheld his claim* ‖ to lift up to a higher position, *with arms upheld*

up·hol·ster (ʌphóulstər, əpóulstər) *v.t.* to provide (furniture) with padding, springs, textile covering etc. [backformation fr. UPHOLSTERER or UPHOLSTERY]

up·hol·ster·er (ʌphóulstərər, əpóulstərər) *n.* a person whose trade is upholstery [fr. earlier *upholdster* fr. M.E. *upholder*, auctioneer, tradesman]

up·hol·ster·y (ʌphóulstəri:, əpóulstəri:) *n.* the craft and trade of upholstering ‖ the materials used in upholstering [fr. earlier *upholdster*]

up·keep (ʌpkí:p) *n.* the maintenance of buildings, roads, equipment etc. ‖ the cost of such maintenance ‖ the state of a building etc. with regard to such maintenance, *in good upkeep*

up·land (ʌplənd, ʌplænd) **1.** *n.* the area of land high above sea level **2.** *adj.* situated on high land ‖ living or growing on high ground

up·lift 1. (ʌplíft) *v.t.* to sing out, utter loudly, *voices uplifted in praise* ‖ to give spiritual or moral encouragement to ‖ (*geol.*) to push up (part of the earth's surface) above the surrounding land **2.** (ʌplíft) *n.* (*Br.*, *pop.*) morally elevating talk of a vaguely benevolent nature ‖ spiritual encouragement ‖ (*geol.*) the raising of a part of the earth's surface above the surrounding land ‖ (*geol.*) the mass raised

up·man·ship (ʌpmənʃip) *n.* the practice of scoring an advantage in status *syn.* one-upmanship

up·most (ʌpmoust) *adj.* uppermost

up·on (əpɔ́n, əpón) *prep.* on ‖ up and on

up·per (ʌpər) **1.** *adj.* higher in position or place, *an upper story* ‖ (of notes, voices etc.) higher in pitch ‖ higher in status, *the upper classes* ‖ farther north or higher up or farther from the sea, *the upper Amazon* ‖ pertaining to or being the northern part of an area, *upper Manhattan* ‖ (*geol.*, of strata) nearer the surface of the earth **Upper** (*geol.*, of a division of a period etc.) later, more recent, *Upper Cambrian* **2.** *n.* the part of a shoe or boot above the sole ‖ (*pop.*) an upper berth **on one's uppers** in dire need, penniless or almost so ‖ (*slang* or *colloq.*) a stimulant drug, esp. amphetamine

Upper Austria (*G.* Oberösterreich) a province (area 4,625 sq. miles, pop. 1,132,000) of N. Austria. Capital: Linz

Upper Canada (*hist.*) a province of Canada (1791-1840) which was predominantly English in population. It was equivalent to the southern part of modern Ontario

up·per·case 1. *n.* (*printing*, abbr. u.c.) capital letters **2.** *adj.* (of a letter) capital (cf. LOWERCASE)

upper class the class of people generally considered to rank above the middle class. The usual criteria are wealth, cultivation and ancestry **úp·per·cláss** *adj.*

upper crust (*pop.*) the best or most prominent of a social class, esp. the upper class

up·per·cut 1. (ʌpərkʌt) *n.* a blow delivered at close quarters from below to the point of the chin, with the arm bent at the elbow **2.** (ʌpərkʌt) *v.* *pres. part.* **up·per·cut·ting** *past* and *past part.* **up·per·cut** *v.t.* to hit with such a blow ‖ *v.i.* to deliver such a blow

upper house the higher chamber in a legislative body having two chambers (cf. LOWER HOUSE)

up·per·most (ʌpərmoust) **1.** *adj.* highest in place, rank, power, position etc., *the uppermost layers* ‖ being in the most prominent position, *the uppermost thoughts in his mind* **2.** *adv.* in or into the highest position ‖ in or into the most prominent position

Upper Volta *BURKINA FASO

up·ping (ʌpiŋ) *n.* *SWAN-UPPING

up·pish (ʌpiʃ) *adj.* (*pop.*) uppity

up·pi·ty (ʌpiti:) *adj.* (*pop.*) aggressively conceited, arrogant

Upp·sa·la (ʌpsalə) a city (pop. 146,192) in E. central Sweden. Gothic cathedral (13th-15th cc.). University (1477) and library with fine collection of manuscripts

up·raise (ʌpréiz) *pres. part.* **up·rais·ing** *past* and *past part.* **up·raised** *v.t.* to lift up, *with upraised eyebrows*

up·rak·en (u:prɑkən) *n.* (*karate*) an inverted fist with the roof of the middle finger forming the contact point

up·rate (ʌpréit) *v.* to improve on a rating scale

up·right (ʌprɑit) **1.** *adj.* being in a vertical or erect position ‖ morally honorable ‖ greater in height than in width **2.** *adv.* in a vertical position **3.** *n.* a vertical support for a structure, e.g. a stake ‖ (*pl.*) a goalpost on e.g. a football field ‖ an upright piano [O.E. *upriht*, *uppriht*]

upright piano a piano with vertical strings (cf. GRAND PIANO)

up·ris·ing (ʌprɑiziŋ) *n.* an insurrection

up·roar (ʌprɔr, ʌprɔur) *n.* a noisy tumult **up·roar·i·ous** (ʌprɔ́ri:əs, ʌpróuri:əs) *adj.* very noisy, usually as a result of, or provoking, convulsive laughter [fr. Du. *oproer*. confusion]

up·root (ʌprú:t, ʌprút) *v.t.* to tear up by the roots ‖ to remove from a settled residence or occupation ‖ to eradicate

up·rush (ʌprʌʃ) *n.* a powerful upward movement ‖ a sudden rising of emotion, *an uprush of pity*

up·set 1. (ʌpset) *n.* an upsetting or being upset ‖ a slight physical ailment ‖ an emotional disturbance ‖ a totally unexpected defeat, e.g. in an athletic contest ‖ (*mech.*) that part of a bar etc. that is upset ‖ (*mech.*) a tool used in upsetting **2.** *v.* (ʌpsét) *pres. part.* **up·set·ting** *past* and *past part.* **up·set** *v.t.* to tip over or capsize ‖ to cause physical or mental distress to ‖ to disarrange, cause confusion in, *to upset plans* ‖ (*mech.*) to shorten or thicken (a bar of heated metal) by hammering the end ‖ to defeat unexpectedly, e.g. in an athletic contest ‖ *v.i.* to be tipped over, capsize **3.** (ʌpsét) *adj.* emotionally or physically distressed

upset price the fixed minimum price for property put up for auction

up·shot (ʌpʃɒt) *n.* outcome, final result

up·side down (ʌpsɑid) in an inverted position or condition, with the top part underneath ‖ in great disorder, *thieves left the place upside down* **to turn upside down** to reduce (e.g. a room) to a state of great disorder, e.g. in searching for a lost article **úp·side-dówn** *adj.* in an inverted position, with the top part underneath [M.E. *up so doun*, up as if down]

up·si·lon (jú:psəlɒn, ʌpsəlɒn, *Br.* esp. ju:psáilən) *n.* the 20th letter (Υ, υ=y, u) of the Greek alphabet

up·stage (ʌpstéidʒ) **1.** *adv.* toward the back of the stage, away from the footlights **2.** *adj.* of or relating to the rear part of the stage ‖ (*pop.*) affecting superiority, distant and condescending **3.** *v.t.* *pres. part.* **up·stag·ing** *past* and *past part.* **up·staged** to treat with condescension and superiority ‖ to put (a fellow actor) at a disadvantage by maneuvering to keep him in an upstage position

up·stairs (ʌpstéərz) **1.** *adv.* on or towards an upper floor of a house etc. **2.** *adj.* of or relating to an upper floor ‖ situated above the ground floor **3.** *n.* that part of a house etc. that is above the ground floor

up·stand·ing (ʌpstændiŋ) *adj.* (of a youth or man) independent in spirit and morally upright ‖ standing up straight

up·start (ʌpstɑrt) *n.* a person who has risen swiftly from a humble position to wealth or power, and presumes on it by arrogant behavior

up·state (ʌpstéit) **1.** *adj.* of or from that part of a state outside some large city, esp. to the north **2.** *n.* an upstate region, esp. northern New York State **úp·stát·er** *n.*

up·stream (ʌpstrí:m) **1.** *adv.* in a direction towards the source of a stream **2.** *adj.* located or directed upstream

up·stroke (ʌpstrouk) *n.* an upward stroke of the pen in writing

up·swing (ʌpswiŋ) *n.* the upward arc of a swinging movement ‖ an upward trend, improvement

up·take (ʌptéik) *n.* a ventilating shaft ‖ a pipe for carrying gases and smoke from a furnace

etc. to a chimney **quick (slow) on** (*Br.* **in**) **the uptake** quick (slow) in understanding

up·thrust (ʌpθrʌst) *n.* (*geol.*) an upheaval of part of the earth's crust, commonly occurring with faulting

up·tick (ʌptik) *n.* (*securities*) a small price rise

up·tight (ʌptáit) *adj.* (*pop.*) not relaxed, showing nervous tension ‖ (*pop.*) rigidly conservative, *uptight about the race problem*

up·time (ʌptaim) *n.* time in which equipment is in operation *Cf* DOWNTIME

up-to-date (ʌptədéit) *adj.* including all information available up to the present moment‖(of a person) informed about current events ‖ currently fashionable ‖ dealt with up to the present, *all my correspondence is up-to-date* ‖ (of a person) having left nothing undone, *he is up-to-date as regards his cataloguing*

up-to-the-min·ute (ʌptu:ðəmínit) *adj.* (*pop.*) including or taking into account the latest information, *an up-to-the-minute weather report* ‖ in the very latest style

up·town (ʌptáun) **1.** *adv.* in or toward the upper residential area of a city, esp. that removed from the main business section **2.** *adj.* belonging to, or situated in, this area **3.** *n.* this area

up·turn 1. (ʌptə́:rn) *v.t.* to turn over, *to upturn a boat* ‖ to direct upward, *upturned eyes* **2.** (ʌptə:rn) *n.* an upward trend

up·val·ue (ʌpvǽlju:) *v.* to revalue upward — **upvaluation** *n.* *Cf* DEVALUE

up·ward (ʌpwərd) **1.** *adv.* to or toward a higher position ‖ toward the head, *from the waist upward* ‖ toward a higher rank, degree, price etc. ‖ toward a higher or better condition ‖ turned toward the sky, *palms upward* ‖ indefinitely more, *50 francs and upward* ‖ toward or into later life, *from boyhood upward* ‖ toward the top of the paper, *a stroke made with the pen traveling upward* **upward** (or **upwards**) **of** more than ‖ rather less than **2.** *adj.* directed or moving toward or situated in a higher position ‖ showing improvement, *an upward trend* [O.E. *upweard*]

upward mobility 1. the condition in which persons of lower economic and social status may rise to higher levels **2.** that movement upward —**upwardly mobile** *adj.* ant. downward mobility

up·wards (ʌpwərdz) *adv.* upward

up·well·ing (ʌpweliŋ) *n.* (*biol.*) movement of nutrient life from the bottom of the sea toward the surface

Ur (ə:r, uər) an ancient city of Chaldaea in Babylonia, the original home of Abraham. It had developed a flourishing civilization by c. 3500 B.C., and had extended its power over Sumer, Akkad, Elam and N. Mesopotamia by the 2nd millennium B.C. It was destroyed (c. 2009 B.C.) by the Elamites and Amorites, although its ziggurat remained

Ur- (*prefix*) meaning original; original form, e.g., Ur-text, Ur-instrument, Ur-racialism

U·ra·bá, Gulf of (u:rabá) a bay on the northwest coast of Colombia, the inner section of the Gulf of Darien

uraemia *UREMIA

u·rae·us (juərí:əs) *pl.* **u·rae·i** (juərí:ai) *n.* a representation of the sacred asp on the headdress of ancient Egyptian divinities and rulers, symbolizing supreme power [Mod. L. fr. Gk *ouraios*, trans. of Egyptian word for 'cobra']

U·ral (júərəl) a river (1,580 miles long) in the R.S.F.S.R. and Kazakhstan, U.S.S.R., flowing from the S. Urals to the Caspian, navigable by steamer to Orenburg: sturgeon fisheries

U·ral-Al·ta·ic (júərəlæltéiik) **1.** *adj.* pertaining to the Ural and Altai mountain regions ‖ belonging to a large group of languages of N. Europe and Asia, including the Uralic and Altaic families ‖ of the people speaking these languages **2.** *n.* this group of languages

U·ra·li·an (juəréili:ən) *adj.* Uralic

U·ral·ic (jurǽlik) **1.** *adj.* of a family of languages, with two main subfamilies: Finno-Ugric, which includes Hungarian, Finnish and a number of languages spoken by small groups in Russia, and Samoyed, spoken by less than 20,000 people, mostly nomads in the N.W. Russian tundra **2.** *n.* this family of languages

U·rals (júərəlz) a chain of mountains (highest peak 6,184 ft) in the U.S.S.R., running from the Arctic Ocean nearly to the Aral Sea, generally considered to form the boundary between Europe and Asia. The central area, rich in minerals (coal, oil, iron ore, manganese, platinum, nickel, gold etc.), has become a leading industrial center: iron and steel, other metal products, nitrates, heavy machinery. Chief city: Magnitogorsk

u·ra·nal·y·sis (juərənǽlisis) *n.* urinalysis

U·ra·ni·a (juəréiniə) the Muse of astronomy ‖ an epithet of Aphrodite

u·ran·ic (juərǽnik) *adj.* of, relating to or containing uranium, esp. in its higher valence

u·ran·i·nite (juərǽnənait) *n.* a mineral, UO₂, consisting largely of an oxide of uranium, and containing thorium, certain rare-earth metals and lead. When heated it often yields a gas consisting chiefly of helium (*PITCHBLENDE)

u·ra·ni·um (juəréiniəm) *n.* a radioactive white metallic element of the chromium group (symbol U, at. no. 92, at. mass 238.03), the heaviest of the elements found in nature, occurring in combination in pitchblende and certain other minerals. Natural uranium consists of the isotopes U238 (which can be converted into plutonium) 99.28%, U235 0.71%, and U234 in a minute amount. U235 and plutonium are used as a source of atomic energy [Mod. L. fr. *Uranus*, the planet]

uranium dioxide (*chem.*) toxic, flammable, radioactive crystals derived from uranium trioxide by heating in ceramic glazing and packing nuclear fuel rods *symbol* UO₂

uranium trioxide [UO₃] (*chem.*) an orange-colored radioactive compound used in ceramics, pigments, and in the uranium refining process, used for coloring ceramics *syn.* orange oxide, uranium oxide

u·ra·nous (júərənəs) *adj.* of, relating to, or containing uranium, esp. in its lower valence

U·ra·nus (júərənəs, juəréinəs) (*Rom. mythol.*) the god of the heavens, father of Saturn ‖ the seventh planet from the sun (mean orbital diameter=1.783 billion miles) and the third largest in the solar system (mass approx. 14.63 times that of Earth), having a linear diameter of 32,320 miles. Uranus revolves around the sun with a sidereal period of 84 earth years and rotates on its own axis with a period of 10.1 hrs. Its physical condition and atmosphere resemble that of Jupiter, Saturn and Neptune. It has five known satellites. Voyager 2 spacecraft visited Uranus in Jan. 1986

u·ra·ra·te (ju:rɑrɑtei) *n.* (*judo*) a rear throw

urb (ə:rb) *n.* an urban area

Ur·bain (yrbɛ̃), Georges (1872-1938), French chemist known for his studies of rare earths

ur·ban (ə́:rbən) *adj.* of, relating to, belonging to or characteristic of a city or town or of people living in a city or town (opp. RURAL) [fr. L. *urbanus*, of the city]

ur·bane (ə:rbéin) *adj.* having the sophisticated manners or polish associated with life in urban society [F. *urbain*]

urban enterprise zones program of tax incentives for small businesses to locate in rundown areas and so provide local employment, proposed in 1980 by Congressman Jack Kemp and Robert Garcia

urban guerrilla a revolutionary who conducts guerrilla tactics in a metropolitan area

Ur·ban II (ə́:rbən) (c. 1042-99), pope (1088-99). He proclaimed the 1st Crusade

ur·ban·i·ty (ə:rbǽniti:) *pl.* **ur·ban·i·ties** *n.* the quality of being urbane ‖ polished manners ‖ (*pl.*) sophisticated remarks [F. *urbanité*]

ur·ban·i·za·tion (ə:rbənizéiʃən) *n.* an urbanizing or being urbanized

ur·ban·ize (ə́:rbənaiz) *pres. part.* **ur·ban·iz·ing** *past* and *past part.* **ur·ban·ized** *v.t.* to render (a rural area) more urban by adding features characteristic of city life

ur·ban·oid (ə́:rbənɔid) *adj.* similar to a city

ur·ban·ol·o·gy (ə:rbənɔ́lədʒi:) *n.* the study of cities and their social and economic problems — **urbanologist** *n.*

urban renewal 1. a program to replace city slums with habitable for usable buildings **2.** rehabilitation (and rebuilding) of a decaying urban area with or without government aid

urban sprawl the erratic growth of a city

Urban VI (Bartolomeo Prignano, 1318-89), pope (1378-89). His election provoked the Great Schism

Ur·bi·no (u:rbí:nɔ) an agricultural market (pop. 16,296) in the N. Marches, Italy: ducal palace (mainly 15th c.), Renaissance churches. University (1564)

ur·ce·o·late (ə́:rsi:əlit, ə́:rsi:əleit) *adj.* (*bot.*) urn-shaped [fr. Mod. L. *urceolatus* fr. *urceolus* dim. of *urceus*, pitcher]

ur·chin (ə́:rtʃin) *n.* a mischievous young boy ‖ a sea urchin [var. of older *hurcheon* fr. O.N.F. *herichon*, a hedgehog]

Ur·du (úərdu:, ə́:rdu:) *n.* an Indic language of India and the official literary language of Pakistan. It is closely related to Hindi but is usually written in Persian script and shows a strong Persian influence [Hind. *urdū*=camp, fr. Turki]

-ure *sufix* indicating act, process or result, as in 'exposure', or function or office, as in 'prefecture' [fr. F. *-ure* and L. *-ura*]

u·re·a (jurí:ə, júəri:ə) *n.* a soluble crystalline compound, CO(NH₂)₂, formed in the body of man and other mammals by the decomposition of protein. It is passed into the urine by the kidneys. Urea is also present in small quantities in blood, perspiration and other body fluids. Synthesized urea is used in fertilizers etc. [Mod. L. fr. F. *urée* fr. Gk]

urea-formaldehyde resin a thermosetting resin produced by condensing urea with formaldehyde and used in plastics, adhesives and finishes

u·re·di·o·spore (jurí:di:əspɔr, jurí:di:əspour) *n.* (*bot.*) one of the reddish summer spores borne on the sporophore of rust fungi [alt. fr. UREDOSPORE]

u·re·do·spore (jurí:dəspɔr, jurí:dəspour) *n.* a urediospore [fr. L. *uredo*, blight + SPORE]

u·re·mi·a, u·rae·mi·a (juərí:miə) *n.* a serious toxic condition caused by an accumulation in the blood of waste products normally eliminated in the urine. It is characterized by violent headache, vomiting and, in its acute form, by convulsions and coma [Mod. L.]

u·re·o·tel·ic (ju:ri:ətélik) or **u·re·o·co·tel·ic** *adj.* of the excretion of urea containing nitrogen, e.g., in mammals —**ureotelism** *n.*

u·re·ter (jurí:tər) *n.* one of the paired ducts which convey urine from the kidneys to the bladder in man or other mammals or from the cloaca in lower vertebrates [Med. L. fr. Gk]

u·re·thra (jurí:θrə) *pl.* **u·re·thras, u·re·thrae** (juərí:θri:) *n.* the canal which in most mammals discharges urine from the bladder, and in the male serves also as the genital duct **u·ré·thral** *adj.* [L.L. fr. Gk]

U·rey (júəri:), Harold Clayton (1893-1981), American chemist. He is known for his work on the various methods of separating uranium isotopes. Nobel prize (1934)

Ur·fa (uərfá) (*anc.* Edessa) a commercial center (pop. 147,488) in S. Turkey. The rise of its theological school (4th-5th cc.), refuting the heresies of Manes and Arius, made it a religious center in the Byzantine Empire. Under Arab rule from 639, it was occupied by the Crusaders from 1098 to 1144 when it fell to the Turks

Ur·fé (yrfei), Honoré d', marquis de Valbromey, comte de Châteauneuf (1567-1625), French author of the pastoral romance 'l'Astrée' (1607-19), which influenced French taste until the mid-17th c.

Ur·ga (ú:rgə) *ULAN BATOR

urge (ə:rdʒ) **1.** *v. pres. part.* **urg·ing** *past* and *past part.* **urged** *v.t.* to compel to go in a specified direction ‖ to attempt earnestly to persuade or encourage ‖ to bring (a need) to notice or to advocate (an action) in a persistent way, *to urge reform* ‖ to force to greater speed ‖ *v.i.* to make earnest recommendations, entreaties etc. **2.** *n.* the act or process of urging ‖ a strong, instinctive desire, *an urge to travel* [fr. L. *urgere*, to press, drive]

ur·gen·cy (ə́:rdʒənsi:) *pl.* **ur·gen·cies** *n.* the state or quality of being urgent

ur·gent (ə́:rdʒənt) *adj.* requiring immediate attention, of pressing importance importunate, *urgent entreaties* [F.]

U·ri (úəri:) a German-speaking, mainly Catholic canton (area 415 sq. miles, pop. 33,883) in central Switzerland. With Schwyz and Unterwalden it formed the 13th-c. league which was the nucleus of the Swiss Confederation

U·ri·bu·ru (u:ri:bú:ru:), José Evaristo (1831-1914), Argentinian politician and president of the Republic (1895-8), and interim president (1903)

Uriburu, José Félix (1868-1933), Argentinian general and provisional president of the Republic (1930-2), after leading a military coup d'état against President Hipólito Yrigoyen. His administration (dominated mainly by the rich and conservative classes) ruled by decree

u·ric (júərik) *adj.* of or relating to urine, occurring in or derived from urine [F. *urique*]

uric acid a white, odorless, tasteless, nearly insoluble, dibasic acid, C₅H₄N₄O₃. It is found in small quantities in the urine of man and other

mammals and is the chief constituent in the excrement of birds, reptiles and invertebrates

u·ri·nal (júərin'l) *n.* a fixture into which men or boys urinate ‖ a building, room or enclosure containing one or more of these ‖ a receptacle into which a bedridden male can pass urine [O.F.]

u·ri·nal·y·sis (juərinǽlisis) *pl.* **u·ri·nal·y·ses** (juərinǽlisi:z) *n.* a chemical analysis of the urine [Mod. L.]

u·ri·nar·y (júərineri:) **1.** *adj.* of or relating to urine ‖ of or relating to, or occurring in, the organs concerned with the formation and discharge of urine **2.** *pl.* **u·ri·nar·ies** *n.* a urinal (fixture or building) [fr. L. *urina*, urine]

urinary system a system in man and most mammals consisting essentially of the kidneys, ureters, bladder and urethra

u·ri·nate (júərineit) *pres. part.* **u·ri·nat·ing** *past* and *past part.* **u·ri·nat·ed** *v.i.* to discharge urine [fr. M.L. *urinare* (*urinatus*)]

u·ri·na·tion (juərinéiʃən) *n.* the act or process of urinating

u·rine (júərin) *n.* in mammals, a fluid formed in the kidneys and excreted through the urinary organs [O.F.]

u·ri·nif·er·ous (juərinífərəs) *adj.* (*anat.*) conveying urine

u·ri·nous (júərinəs) *adj.* of, pertaining to, resembling or containing urine

Uris (júərəs), Leon (1924-), U.S. novelist and screenwriter. He achieved fame with his massive adventure novels that placed fictional protagonists in semifactual historical contexts such as the founding of the state of Israel ('Exodus,' 1959; film, 1961), the Berlin airlift ('Armaggedon,' 1964), the Cuban missile crisis ('Topaz,' 1967; film, 1969) and the Easter Rising in Ireland ('Trinity,' 1976). Earlier novels included 'Battle Cry' (1953) and 'Mila 18' (1960). He has also written screenplays, such as 'Gunfight at the OK Corral' (1957)

Ur·mi·a (úərmi:ə) *REZAYEH

urn (ə:rn) *n.* a closed metal vessel fitted with a tap and sometimes equipped with a heating device, used for making and dispensing a large supply of tea, coffee etc. ‖ a vase or jar with a pedestal, esp. as used in ancient times for preserving the ashes of the dead after cremation [fr. L. *urna*]

uro- (júərou) *combining form* urine, urination [fr. Gk *ouron*, urine]

uro- *combining form* tail [fr. Gk *oura*, tail]

u·ro·chord (júərəkɔrd) *n.* (*zool.*) the notochord of larval ascidians and some adult tunicates

u·ro·gen·i·tal (juəroudʒénit'l) *adj.* relating to the urinary and genital organs

u·ro·ki·nase (ju:roukáineis) *n.* (*biochem.*) kidney-produced enzyme that increases fibrinolytic activity and is used to disintegrate blood clots

u·ro·log·ic (juərəlɔ́dʒik) *adj.* urological

u·ro·log·i·cal (juərəlɔ́dʒik'l) *adj.* of or relating to urology

u·rol·o·gist (juərɔ́lədʒist) *n.* a specialist in urology

u·rol·o·gy (juərɔ́lədʒi:) *n.* a branch of medicine dealing with the urogenital tract in the male and the urinary tract of the female

u·ro·pod (júərəpɔd) *n.* any of the abdominal appendages of a crustacean, esp. either of the flat appendages of the last abdominal segment of the lobster [fr. URO-+Gk *pous* (*podos*), a foot]

u·ro·pyg·i·al (juərəpídʒi:əl) *adj.* of or relating to the uropygium

u·ro·pyg·i·um (juərəpídʒi:əm) *n.* that part of the termination of a bird's body that supports the tail feathers [M.L. fr. Gk]

Ur·quhart (ə́:rkərt), Sir Thomas (1611-60), Scottish translator of three books of Rabelais (1653, 1693)

Ur·qui·za (u:rkí:sɑ), Justo José de (1801-70), Argentinian general and caudillo, and victor over Rosas at Monte Caseros (1852). He served (1852-4) as director of the confederation and (1854-60) as president. During the civil war which followed his forces were defeated (1861) by Mitre at Pavón. While governor of Entre Ríos he was assassinated

Ur·sa Ma·jor (ə́:rsəméidʒər) the most conspicuous constellation of the northern hemisphere. It contains the seven bright stars called the Big Dipper

Ur·sa Mi·nor (ə́:rsəmáinər) the northern constellation which contains the polestar

ur·sine (ə́:rsain) *adj.* of, relating to or characteristic of a bear ‖ resembling a bear [fr. L. *ursinus*]

CONCISE PRONUNCIATION KEY: **(a)** æ, c*a*t; ɑ, c*a*r; ɔ f*aw*n; ei, sn*a*ke. **(e)** e, h*e*n; i:, sh*ee*p; iə, d*ee*r; ɛə, b*ea*r. **(i)** i, f*i*sh; ai, t*i*ger; ə:, b*i*rd. **(o)** o, *o*x; au, c*ow*; ou, g*oa*t; u, p*oo*r; ɔi, r*oy*al. **(u)** ʌ, d*u*ck; u, b*u*ll; u:, g*oo*se; ə, b*a*cill*u*s; ju:, c*u*be. x, lo*ch*; θ, *th*ink; ð, *b*o*th*er; z, *Z*en; ʒ, cor*s*age; dʒ, sava*g*e; ŋ, ora*ng*utang; j, *y*ak; ʃ, *f*ish; tʃ, *f*etch; 'l, rabb*le*; 'n, red*d*en. Complete pronunciation key appears inside front cover.

Ur·su·la (ə́:rsulə, ə́:rsjulə), St (c. 4th c.), British princess martyred by the Huns at Cologne, together with other virgins numbering, according to medieval legend, 11,000. Feast: Oct. 21

Ur·su·line (ə́:rsulain, ə́:rsjulain, ə́:rsulin, ə́:rsjulin) *n.* a member of a teaching and nursing order of nuns, founded 1535 at Brescia [after St URSULA]

ur·ti·car·i·a (ə:rtikéəri:ə) *n.* hives [Mod. L. fr. *urtica*, a nettle]

ur·ti·ca·ri·a·gen·ic (ə:rtikεəri:ədʒénik) *adj.* (*med.*) causing a temporary nettle rash, welts, or hives on the skin —**urtica** *n.* a wheal on the skin —**urticant** *n.* a substance causing a skin wheal —**urticaria** *n.* the allergic disorder — **urticate** *v.*

U·ru·guay (júərugwai, u:ru:gwái) a republic (area 72,172 sq. miles, pop. 2,967,000) on the southeast coast of South America. Capital: Montevideo. People: mostly of European stock, some mestizos. Language: Spanish. Religion: mainly Roman Catholic. The land is 66% pasture and grazing, 12% cultivated, and 3% forest. It is mainly a rolling, grassland plain, crossed by two chains of hills, and rising to tablelands (2,000 ft) on the Brazilian border. Average temperatures (F.) in Montevideo: Jan. 72°, July 50°. Rainfall: 38 ins along the Río de la Plata, 50 ins in the north. Livestock: sheep, cattle, horses, hogs. Agricultural products: wheat, rice, other cereals, linseed, sunflower seed, peanuts, cotton, sugar beets, sugarcane, fruit, wine. Mineral resources: gold, copper. Manufactures and industries: meat packing, oil refining, cement, steel, aluminum, textiles, chemicals, engineering, wool processing, hydroelectricity. Exports: wool, meat, leather and hides, combed wool, wheat flour, linseed and linseed oil. Imports: machinery, vehicles, fuels and oil, lumber, raw cotton. University at Montevideo (1949). Monetary unit: peso (100 centésimos). HISTORY. Uruguay was inhabited by Indian tribes when the Río de la Plata was explored (1516) by a Spanish expedition. Settlements were established by the Spanish (1624) and the Portuguese (1680). The Spanish drove the Portuguese out (18th c.). After a military revolt (1810-20) led by Artigas against Spanish rule, the Portuguese annexed Uruguay to Brazil (1820) but it again revolted (1825) and joined Argentina in war against Brazil. After British intervention, Uruguay was recognized as an independent republic (1828). It was weakened by civil war (1836-52), sporadic rebellions and war against Paraguay (1865-70). Great economic progress was made in the early 20th c. President Batlle y Ordóñez introduced (1903-7, 1911-15) a New Deal of radical social reform and dominated Uruguayan politics until his death in 1929. The vacuum he left, and the Depression of the early 1930s, allowed Gabriel Terra to establish (1933-8) a dictatorship. Despite fissions, Batlle's Colorado party retained power until it was ousted in the elections of 1958 by the opposition Blanco (Nationalist) party. During that time Uruguay developed its welfare state, joined (Feb. 15, 1945) the Allies in the 2nd world war, and became (1945) a member of the U.N. The presidency was replaced (1951) by a succession of Swiss-style National Councils, composed of six members drawn from the majority party and three from the minority, and operating by majority vote. Four members of the majority party took turns as the nation's nominal president. After the inauguration (1965) of Washington Beltrán, the Blanco party leader, inflation was such (38% in 1965) that a referendum was held in the 1966 elections. The executive council was scrapped and Uruguay, in a new constitution, reverted to government by a single chief executive. Gen. Oscar Gestido was elected president. On his death (1967), he was succeeded by Vice-President Jorge Pacheco Areco. Growing inflation (135% in 1967) fanned economic and political discontent, symbolized in the activities of the Tupamaros, who engage in daring, well planned robbery and kidnapping which earn popular sympathy by their exposure of corruption. Despite this, Uruguay's democratic stability and noninvolvement in Latin American rivalries have made it the natural choice of locale for several Western Hemisphere diplomatic conferences. At Punta del Este the Alliance for Progress was launched (1961), and Montevideo became (1961) the headquarters of the Latin American Free Trade Association (LAFTA). Strikes and urban terrorism dis-

rupted political life in the mid-1960s, and between 1973-6 elected government officials were ousted by the military. Civil rights violations became widespread and thousands of political dissenters were jailed. Following elections in 1984, Julio Sanguinetti took office as president

Uruguay a river (980 miles long, navigable most of its length) flowing from S.E. Brazil to the Río de la Plata, forming the borders of S. Brazil and Uruguay with Argentina

U·rum·chi (u:rú:mtʃi:) (*Chin.* Tihwa) the walled capital (pop. 275,000) of Sinkiang-Uighur, W. China, an oasis trading center: iron and steel, textiles, chemical industries

u·rus (júərəs) *n. Bos primigenus*, fam. *Bovidae*, an extinct wild ox thought to be the ancestor of domestic cattle [L.]

U.S., US *UNITED STATES OF AMERICA

us (ʌs) *pron., objective case of* WE, *send it to us, he gave us a lecture* [O.E. *ūs*]

U.S.A., USA *UNITED STATES OF AMERICA

us·a·bil·i·ty (ju:zəbiliti:) *n.* the quality or state of being usable

us·a·ble, use·a·ble (jú:zəb'l) *adj.* fit to be used

U.S.A.F. United States Air Force

us·age (jú:sidʒ, jú:zidʒ) *n.* the way in which someone or something is used or treated, or an instance of this ‖ long established use or custom ‖ the way of using language in speech or writing, or an instance of this, *a usage borrowed from the french* [O.F.]

us·ance (jú:zəns) *n.* (*commerce*) the time allowed (not counting a period of grace) for payment of bills of exchange [O.F.]

use *pres. part.* **us·ing** *past* and *past part.* **used** *v.t.* to make (something) perform its function for a specified or understood end, *they used bulldozers to clear the forest, use your intelligence* ‖ to deal with, *he considers himself unfairly used* ‖ (often with 'up') to consume completely, *they use half a ton of coal every week* ‖ (old-fash.) to smoke or chew (tobacco) or to take (narcotics) habitually ‖ to exploit for some end, esp. a selfish one ‖ (in the passive (ju:st) with 'to') to accustom, *he was used to her way of working* ‖ *v.i.* (in the past (ju:st) with an infinitive) to be accustomed, *I used to see a lot of him* [O.F. *user*]

use (ju:s) *n.* the act, state or custom of using or being used ‖ the power to use, *to lose the use of an eye* ‖ a way of using, *to put to an unaccustomed use* ‖ usefulness, *what use is there in attempting to do it?* ‖ the right, permission or privilege to use, *the firm gave us the use of its name* ‖ the opportunity to use ‖ function, the purpose for which something is used ‖ custom, habit, practice ‖ (*law*) the enjoyment of the benefits deriving from property either by the occupier or by someone to whom it is delegated under a trust ‖ (*eccles.*) a body of ritual, *the Sarum use* **in use** being used **to have no use for** to have no need of ‖ to dislike strongly ‖ to be impatient with **to make use of** to use ‖ to turn to advantage **to put to use** to find a use for **to turn** (or **put**) **to good use** to do something useful with (something or someone) [O.F. *us*]

useable *USABLE

used (ju:zd) *adj.* secondhand, *a used-car market* **used up** fully consumed

use·ful (jú:s·fəl). *adj.* likely to be of some practical value, *useful advice*

use·less (jú:slis) *adj.* of no practical value ‖ (of a person) rendering no service whatsoever

us·er (jú:zər) *n.* (*law*) the enjoyment of a right of use, esp. a presumptive right arising from long-continued use [prob. fr. F. *user*, to use]

Usher *USSHER

ush·er (ʌ́ʃər) **1.** *n.* someone who escorts people to seats, e.g. in a church, theater etc. ‖ (esp. *Br.*) an official whose function is to walk ahead of a person or persons of rank ‖ (*Br. hist.*) an assistant teacher in a private school **2.** *v.t.* to conduct to a seat or into someone's presence ‖ *v.i.* to act as an usher **to usher in** to mark the beginning of, *a series of reforms ushered in the new regime*

ush·er·ette (ʌʃərét) *n.* a woman employed to show people to seats in a cinema, theater etc. [A.F. *usser*, O.F. *ussier, uissier* var. of *huissier*]

Us·hua·ia (u:swája) an Argentine town (pop. 10,998) at the southern tip of Tierra del Fuego, the most southerly agglomeration in the world

Üs·küb (uskúb) *SKOPJE

Üs·ku·dar (úsku:dar) Turkish name for Scutari (*ISTANBUL)

Us·pa·lla·ta Pass (u:spajáta) (or La Cumbre) a

pass in the Andes Mtns between Mendoza, Argentina, and Santiago, Chile

Ussh·er, Ush·er (ʌ́ʃər), James (1581-1656), Irish bishop and scholar. His 'Annales Veteris et Novi Testamenti' (1650-4), ascribing the creation of the world to 4004 B.C., was for long the basis of biblical chronology

U.S.S.R. *UNION OF SOVIET SOCIALIST REPUBLICS

Us·turt Plateau (ú:sturt) a rocky desert (area 92,000 sq. miles) in the southern R.S.F.S.R. and Uzbekistan, U.S.S.R., between the Caspian and Aral Seas

u·su·al (jú:ʒu:əl, jú:ʒwəl) *adj.* normal in practice **as usual** in his or its habitual way, *as usual he overate* **u·su·al·ly** *adv.* on most occasions, customarily [O.F. or fr. L. *usualis*]

u·su·fruct (jú:sufrʌkt, jú:zufrʌkt) *n.* (*law*) the right to use and enjoy the profits of another person's property, without diminishing, impairing or wasting the substance of it [fr. L.L. *usufructus* fr. *usus*, use + *fructus*, fruit]

u·su·fruc·tu·ar·y (ju:zufrʌ́ktʃu:eri:) **1.** *adj.* of or relating to the right of usufruct **2.** *pl.* **u·su·fruc·tu·ar·ies** *n.* someone who enjoys the right of usufruct [fr. L.L. *usufructuarius*]

U·sum·bu·ra (u:sumbúra) *BUJUMBURA

u·su·rer (jú:ʒərər) *n.* someone who lends money at interest, esp. at exorbitant interest [A.F.]

u·su·ri·ous (ju:ʒúəri:əs) *adj.* practicing usury involving usury, *usurious transactions*

u·surp (ju:sə́:rp, ju:zə́:rp) *v.t.* to seize and hold (a position, function, prerogative) rightly belonging to another ‖ *v.i.* (with 'on' or 'upon') to encroach upon a right, privilege, office etc. **u·sur·pá·tion** *n.* [O.F. *usurper*]

u·su·ry (jú:ʒəri:) *n.* the practice of lending money at interest, esp. at an exorbitant or illegal rate of interest [A.F. *usurie* fr. M.L. *usuria*]

U·tah (jú:tɔ, jú:tɑ) (*abbr.* Ut.) a state (area 84,916 sq. miles, pop. 1,554,000) of the western U.S.A. in the Great Basin and the Rocky Mtns. Capital: Salt Lake City. Agriculture: beef cattle, dairy and poultry products, sheep, wheat and fodder crops (dependent upon irrigation). Resources: copper, gold, oil, coal, iron ore, uranium, lead, silver, zinc and salt. Industries: metal and oil refining, food processing. State university (1850) at Salt Lake City. Utah was settled by Mormons (1847) and was ceded (1848) by Mexico to the U.S.A. After the Mormons, under their president Wilford Woodruff (1807-98), agreed (1890) to abandon polygamy, Utah was admitted (1896) into the Union as the 45th state

U·ta·ma·ro (u:tamarɔ) (1753-1806), Japanese master of the colored woodcut. The freshness of his vision, the precision yet freedom of his compositional devices and his unconventionality of theme had some influence on French Impressionist painting

Ute (ju:t, jú:ti) *pl.* **Ute, Utes** *n.* a group of Shoshonean peoples of Colorado, Utah and New Mexico ‖ a member of any of these peoples ‖ their language

u·ten·sil (ju:ténsəl) *n.* any of various vessels or devices used in a kitchen, e.g. a cooking pot or eggbeater ‖ any of various tools used by artisans, farmers etc. ‖ a vessel, ornament etc. used in church services [O.F. *utensile*]

u·ter·ine (jú:tərain, jú:tərin) *adj.* of, relating to or situated in the uterus ‖ having the same mother but a different father, *uterine brothers* [O.F. *uterin, uterine* or fr. L.L. *uterinus*]

u·ter·us (jú:tərəs) *pl.* **u·ter·i** (jú:tərai) *n.* the organ in female mammals in which the embryo (fetus) develops and is nourished before birth ‖ an enlarged portion of the oviduct of various vertebrate and invertebrate animals, e.g. monotremes, modified into a place where the young or eggs can develop [L.]

U Thant *THANT, U

U·ther Pen·drag·on (jú:θərpendrǽgən) king of the Britons in the Arthurian legend, father of King Arthur

U·ti·ca (jú:tikə) a manufacturing city and port of entry (pop. 75,632) in central New York, within an agricultural and dairying region. Manufactures: textiles, firearms, machinery, beds. Utica College (1946)

u·tile (jú:t'l) *adj.* practical, useful (as opposed to purely ornamental or aesthetic) [F.]

u·til·i·tar·i·an (ju:tʃilitéəri:ən) **1.** *adj.* of or relating to utility ‖ stressing utility (as opposed to beauty) ‖ of or relating to utilitarianism ‖ advocating utilitarianism **2.** *n.* a supporter of the doctrine of utilitarianism

u·til·i·tar·i·an·ism (ju:tʃilitéəri:ənizəm) *n.* the

CONCISE PRONUNCIATION KEY: **(a)** æ, c**a**t; ɑ, c**a**r; ɔ, f**aw**n; ei, sn**a**ke. **(e)** e, h**e**n; i:, sh**ee**p; iə, d**ee**r; εə, b**ea**r. **(i)** i, f**i**sh; ai, t**i**ger; ə:, b**i**rd. **(o)** o, **o**x; au, c**ow**; ou, g**oa**t; u, p**oo**r; ɔi, r**oy**al. **(u)** ʌ, d**u**ck; u, b**u**ll; u:, g**oo**se; ə, b**a**cill**u**s; ju:, c**u**be. x, lo**ch**; θ, **th**ink; δ, **b**o**th**er; z, **Z**en; ʒ, cor**s**age; dʒ, sava**g**e; ŋ, ora**n**gutang; j, **y**ak; ʃ, **fi**sh; tʃ, fe**tch**; 'l, rabb**le**; 'n, redde**n**. Complete pronunciation key appears inside front cover.

doctrine, expounded by Jeremy Bentham, that the moral and political rightness of an action is determined by its utility, defined as its contribution to the greatest good of the greatest number

u·til·i·ty (ju:tíliti:) *pl.* **u·til·i·ties** *n.* the quality or state of being useful ‖ (*econ.*) the ability to satisfy human wants ‖ a public utility ‖ a service provided by one of these ‖ (*pl.*) stock shares in public utility companies [O.F. *utilite*]

utility player (*sports*) a team member capable of playing several different positions

u·ti·liz·a·ble (jú:t'ḷaizəb'l) *adj.* able to be utilized

u·ti·li·za·tion (ju:tilizéiʃən) *n.* a utilizing or being utilize'd

u·ti·lize (jú:t'laiz) *pres. part.* **u·ti·liz·ing** *past* and *past part.* **u·ti·lized** *v.t.* to make use of [fr. F. *utiliser*]

u·ti pos·si·de·tis (jú:taipɒsidí:tis) a principle of international law, widely applied in treaties in the Americas, whereby at the end of a war belligerents' territorial rights are determined according to the territory they occupy or control

ut·most (Λtmoust) **1.** *adj.* of the greatest degree, *one's utmost efforts* ‖ situated at the most remote point **2.** *n.* the best of one's ability or power, *to do one's utmost* ‖ the highest attainable point or degree [O.E. *ūtemest*, double superl. of *ūt*, out]

U·to-Az·tec·an (ju:touǽztekən) *n.* an American Indian linguistic group of the western U.S.A., including the Shoshonean, Piman and Nahuatlan families ‖ a member of a people speaking a Uto-Aztecan language

u·to·pi·a (ju:tóupi:ə) *n.* any imaginary political and social system in which relationships between individuals and the State are perfectly adjusted **u·to·pi·an 1.** *adj.* ideal but impractical **2.** *n.* someone who believes in the immediate perfectibility of human society by the application of some idealistic scheme **u·tó·pi·an·ism** *n.* [Mod. L. fr. Gk *ou*, not + *topos*, place (after 'Utopia' by Sir Thomas More (1516), describing an island in which such conditions existed)]

U·trecht (jú:trekt, jú:trext) a province (area 535 sq. miles, pop. 922,800) of the central Netherlands ‖ its capital (pop. 264,000). Industries:

metalwork, mechanical and chemical engineering, textiles, ceramics. Gothic cathedral (14th c.) and churches, moat, canals. University (1636)

Utrecht, Peace of a series of treaties (1713) concluding the War of the Spanish Succession. Philip V kept Spain and abandoned his claims to the French throne and Emperor Charles VI obtained Milan, Naples, Sardinia and the Spanish Netherlands. Britain gained Gibraltar, Minorca, Newfoundland and Acadia, as well as the monopoly of the slave trade with Spanish America. French expansion was halted, and Louis XIV recognized the Protestant succession in Britain

u·tri·cle (jú:trik'l) *n.* the pouchlike part of the labyrinth of the ear into which the semicircular canals open ‖ (*anar.*) any of several other pouchlike parts ‖ an air cell or bladder in some aquatic plants [fr. F. *utricule* or L. *utriculus*]

u·tric·u·lar (ju:tríkjulər) *adj.* of or relating to a utricle ‖ containing or resembling a utricle [fr. L. *utriculus*, small bag]

U·tril·lo (ytri:jou), Maurice (1883-1955), French painter. He is best known for his Paris street scenes

Ut·tar Pra·desh (ụtərprədéʃ) a state (area 113,410 sq. miles, pop. 94,775,000) of India bordering Tibet and Nepal, consisting largely of the Ganges-Jumna basin. Capital: Lucknow. Largest town: Kanpur. Industries: intensive agriculture (rice, other cereals, cotton, sugarcane, pulses), textiles, chemicals, paper, food processing

ut·ter (Λtər) *v.t.* tụ express vocally, esp. in speech ‖ to emit (sounds) as if speaking ‖ to fabricate and put into circulation (false coins etc.) [fr. M.Du. *uteren*, to speak, make known, drive away and fr. OUT]

utter *adj.* with no qualification whatsoever, *utter ruin* [O.E. *ūtera, ūttera* comp. *Of ūt*, out]

ut·ter·ance (Λtərəns) *n.* the act, power or manner of expressing vocally ‖ something uttered ‖ (*rhet.*) power of speech, *to be robbed of utterance* **to give utterance to** to express verbally [fr. UTTER v.]

ut·ter·ly (Λtərli:) *adv.* fully [fr. UTTER adj.]

ut·ter·most (Λtərmoust) *adj.* and *n.* (used as an intensive) utmost

U-2 Incident an international incident (1960) precipitated when the Soviet Union shot down a

U.S. U-2 high-altitude intelligence plane. The U.N. Security Council refused to censure the U.S.A. The pilot was sentenced in the Soviet Union to ten years' imprisonment for espionage, but was exchanged (1962) for two Soviet Union spies who had been imprisoned in the U.S.A.

UUM-44A (*mil.*) *SUBMARINE ROCKET

u·ve·a (jú:vi:ə) *n.* (*anat.*, of the eye) the posterior pigmented layer of the iris ‖ (*anat.*, of the eye) the iris, choroid and ciliary body, taken collectively [M.L. fr. L. *uva*, a grape]

U·vi·con (jú:vəkɒn) *n.* a special television camera that includes an ultraviolet-sensitive cathode-ray tube, an electron accelerator, and other features

u·vu·la (jú:vjulə) *pl.* **u·vu·las, u·vu·lae** (jú:vjuli:) *n.* a fleshy conical body suspended from the soft palate over the back of the tongue [M.L. dim. of *uva*, a grape]

u·vu·lar (jú:vjulər) **1.** *adj.* of or pertaining to the uvula ‖ (*phon.*) pronounced with the aid of the uvula **2.** *n.* (*phon.*) a uvular sound [fr. Mod. L. *uvularis*]

Ux·mal (u:zmál) a town in Mexico, in N. Yucatán. Built in stone, c. 1000 A.D., it was an important center of Mayan civilization

ux·o·ri·ous (Λksóri:əs, Λksóuri:əs, Λgzóri:əs, Λgzóuri:əs) *adj.* excessively fond of one's wife ‖ showing such excessive fondness [fr. L. *uxorius*]

U·yu·ni, Sa·lar de (suláröeu:jú:ni:) a salt marsh (90 miles long, 75 miles wide) in S.W. Bolivia, near the Chilean border

Uz·bek, Uz·beg (uzbek) *n.* a Turkic people of Turkestan ‖ a member of this people ‖ their Turkic language

Uz·bek·i·stan (úzbekistæn, úzbekistɑn) a constituent republic (area 173,546 sq. miles, pop. 15,391,000) of the U.S.S.R. in central Asia. Capital: Tashkent. It is a plateau, mainly desert in the west, rising to high mountains in the east. Agriculture: cereals on the highest plains, sheep breeding in the desert regions, with cotton (third largest world producer), fruit and silk dependent on intensive irrigation. Resources: coal, oil, copper, building materials. Industries: mining, oil refining, iron and steel, mineral fertilizers, cotton. Part of Turkestan, Uzbekistan was conquered by Russia (1865-76), and became a constituent republic in 1925

CONCISE PRONUNCIATION KEY: (a) æ, cat; ɑ, car; ɔ fawn; ei, snake. **(e)** e, hen; i:, sheep; iə, deer; ɛə, bear. **(i)** i, fish; ai, tiger; ə:, bird. **(o)** ɒ, ox; au, cow; ou, goat; u, poor; ɔi, royal. **(u)** Λ, duck; u, bull; u:, goose; ə, bacillus; ju:, cube. x, loch; θ, think; ð, bother; z, Zen; ʒ, corsage; dʒ, savage; ŋ, orangutang; j, yak; ʃ, fish; tʃ, fetch; 'l, rabble; 'n, redden. Complete pronunciation key appears inside front cover.

				CLASSICAL GREEK	ETRUSCAN		EARLY LATIN	CLASSICAL LATIN
					Early	Classical		
				Y	Y	V	V	V
	ROMAN UNCIAL	ANGLO-IRISH MAJUSCULE	CAROLINE MINUSCULE		MODERN ITALIC		MODERN ROMAN	
	V	U	U		v		V	

A. C. SYLVESTER, CAMBRIDGE, ENGLAND

Development of the letter V, beginning with the classical Greek letter. Evolution of both the majuscule, or capital, letter V and the minuscule, or lowercase, letter v are shown.

V, v (vi:) the 22nd letter of the English alphabet ‖ the roman numeral for 5

Va. Virginia

Vaal (vɑl) a river (700 miles long) rising in the High Veld, Transvaal, South Africa, and forming the Transvaal-Orange Free State border. It joins the Orange River near Kimberley. Its dams furnish vast irrigation systems

va·can·cy (véikənsi:) *pl.* **va·can·cies** *n.* the state of being vacant ‖ an empty place or space ‖ a room in a hotel etc. available for occupation ‖ a post in employment which is not occupied ‖ vacuity of mind [fr. M.L. *vacantia*]

va·cant (véikənt) *adj.* empty, not filled ‖ (of a post or seat etc.) unoccupied ‖ untenanted ‖ not mentally active ‖ showing empty-headedness, *a vacant grin* ‖ (*law*, of land) unused or unoccupied ‖ (*law*) having no claimant [O.F.]

vacant possession (*Br.*, *law*) availability for immediate occupation

va·cate (veikéit, véikeit) *pres. part.* **va·cat·ing** *past* and *past part.* **va·cat·ed** *v.t.* to go away and leave unoccupied, *to vacate a house* ‖ to make vacant (a position or occupation) ‖ (*law*) to annul, to make void [fr. *vacare* (*vacatus*), to be empty]

va·ca·tion (veikéiʃən, vəkéiʃən) **1.** *n.* a holiday ‖ a fixed and regular period of holiday (esp. in courts of law and universities) ‖ the act of going away and leaving a place or position empty **on vacation** away from work, school etc. for a period of leisure **2.** *v.i.* to take a vacation **va·cá·tion·er, va·cá·tion·ist** *ns* a holidaymaker [O.F.]

vac·ci·nal (væksin'l) *adj.* of vaccine or vaccination

vac·ci·nate (væksineit) *pres. part.* **vac·ci·nat·ing** *past* and *past part.* **vac·ci·nat·ed** *v.t.* to inoculate with a vaccine **vac·ci·ná·tion** *n.* a vaccinating or the practice of vaccinating

vac·cine (væksi:n, væksí:n) **1.** *n.* a preparation consisting of the living viruses of cowpox, used in vaccination ‖ a preparation of microorganisms, either dead, or virulent and living, or attenuated and living, that are administered so as to produce (or increase) immunity to a particular disease **2.** *adj.* of or pertaining to vaccinia or vaccination [fr. L. *vaccinus* fr. *vacca*, a cow]

vac·cin·i·a (væksíni:ə) *n.* (*med.*) cowpox (esp. when produced by inoculation) [Mod. L.]

vac·il·late (væsəleit) *pres. part.* **vac·il·lat·ing** *past* and *past part.* **vac·il·lat·ed** *v.i.* to change repeatedly from one opinion or intention to another ‖ to sway to and fro **vac·il·lá·tion** *n.* **vac·il·la·to·ry** (væsələtɔri:, væsələtouri:) *adj.* [fr. L. *vacillare* (*vacillatus*), to waver]

va·cu·i·ty (vækjú:iti:) *pl.* **va·cu·i·ties** *n.* the state or quality of being vacuous ‖ something pointless [fr. L. *vacuitas*]

vac·u·o·late (vækju:ouleit) *adj.* vacuolated **vác·u·o·lat·ed** *adj.* containing vacuoles

vac·u·ole (vækju:oul) *n.* (*biol.*) a minute cavity in cell protoplasm containing air, sap or partly digested food ‖ a small cavity in organic tissue [F.]

vac·u·ous (vækju:əs) *adj.* having or showing a lack of understanding or intelligence or serious purpose ‖ emptied of content (e.g. of air or gas) [fr. L. *vacuus*, empty]

vac·u·um (vækju:əm, vækju:m) **1.** *pl.* **vac·u·ums, vac·u·a** (vækju:ə) *n.* a part of space in which no matter exists ‖ a space largely exhausted of air ‖ space containing air or gas at a pressure below that of the atmosphere ‖ (*pl.* **vacuums**) a void, *her departure left a vacuum* ‖ (*pl.* **vacuums**) a vacuum cleaner **2.** *v.t.* to clean with a vacuum cleaner [L. neut. of *vacuus*, empty]

—Aristotle insisted that a vacuum was an impossibility, using this argument to explain the cohesion of a solid, and this dogma persisted for 2,000 years. Galileo, Torricelli, Otto von Guericke, Pascal and Boyle showed that it was possible to create a close approximation to a vacuum, the only limitation being the vapor emitted by the container. The possibility of a perfect-vacuum in nature is now not excluded

vacuum bottle a Thermos

vacuum brake a continuous series of brakes applied to the wheels of a train etc. when a brake rod, held in position by a bellows exhausted of air, is released by admitting air to the bellows. The brakes are released when an air pump again exhausts the bellows

vacuum cleaner a machine which removes dirt and dust from carpets etc. by the suction produced by a motordriven air pump

vacuum flask (*Br.*) a Thermos

va·cu·um-packed (vækju:əmpækt, vækju:mpækt) *adj.* packed in a can, jar etc. from which most of the air has been removed before it was sealed

vacuum pump an air pump which exhausts the air from a container ‖ a pulsometer

vacuum tube an electron tube containing an almost perfect vacuum

va·de me·cum (véidi:mí:kəm, vádi:mí:kəm) *n.* a handbook or manual [L.=go with me]

vag·a·bond (vægəbɒnd) **1.** *adj.* wandering, not settled in a fixed home ‖ characteristic of a wandering way of life **2.** *n.* a person who wanders around from place to place rather than settle down in one place or to one job ‖ a tramp **vag·a·bond·age** (vægəbɒndidʒ) *n.* [O.F. or fr. L. *vagabundus*]

va·gar·y (véigəri:, vəgéəri:) *pl.* **va·gar·ies** *n.* an irrational idea, passing fancy ‖ an odd or irrational action [prob. fr. L. *vagari*, to wander]

V-agent (ví:eidʒənt) *n.* a toxic chemical nerve gas, e.g., Vx, GB

va·gi·na (vədʒáinə) *pl.* **va·gi·nae** (vədʒáini:), **va·gi·nas** *n.* a sheath or sheathlike tube, esp. the canal leading from the uterus to the vulva in female mammals ‖ (*bot.*) the expanded sheathlike portion of a leaf base **vag·i·nal** (vədʒain'l, vædʒin'l) *adj.* [L.=sheath]

vaginal ring (*med.*) intrauterine contraceptive device that releases hormones over a three-year period, approved for use in Western Europe

vag·i·nate (vædʒineit) *adj.* having or in the form of a sheath or vagina [fr. Mod. L. *vaginatus*]

va·gran·cy (véigrənsi:) *n.* vagabondage ‖ the offense of being a vagrant

va·grant (véigrənt) **1.** *adj.* wandering, esp. having no settled home ‖ living the life of a tramp ‖ random, stray, *vagrant thoughts* ‖ of or characteristic of a vagrant ‖ (of plants) growing in a straggly way **2.** *n.* someone who has no settled home, a vagabond ‖ (*law*) a tramp, beggar, prostitute etc. whose way of life makes him or her liable to arrest [M.E. *vagraunt, vagaraunt* perh. fr. A.F.]

vague (veig) *adj.* not clearly grasped in the mind, *vague ideas* ‖ not precise in expression, *vague language* ‖ not firmly determined, *vague plans* ‖ hazy, not clearly perceived, *a vague figure in the background* ‖ (of a person) not clearly formulating or expressing ideas [F.]

va·gus nerve (véigəs) (*anat.*) either one of the tenth pair of cranial nerves arising from the medulla

vain (vein) *adj.* thinking too highly of one's appearance, attainments etc. ‖ failing to produce the desired result, *a vain attempt to escape* ‖ empty, *vain boasts* **in vain** without success ‖ to no purpose **to take someone's name in vain** to speak about someone without proper respect [O.F.]

vain·glo·ri·ous (veinglóri:əs, veinglóuri:əs) *adj.* full of vainglory ‖ boastful

vain·glo·ry (veinglóri:, veinglóuri:) *n.* excessive show of vanity ‖ extreme conceit [fr. M.L. *vana gloria*]

vair (vɛər) *n.* (*hist.*) the fur of a squirrel used for lining and trimming clothes in the 13th and 14th cc. ‖ (*heraldry*) a fur represented by rows of small bell-shaped figures of two alternate tinctures, usually azure and argent [O.F. *vair, veir*]

Vai·she·shi·ka, Vai·se·si·ka (vaiʃéiʃikə, vaiʃeʃí:kə) *n.* a system of Hindu philosophy involving an atomic theory of cosmology, founded c. 500 B.C. [Skr.]

CONCISE PRONUNCIATION KEY: **(a)** æ, c*a*t; ɑ, c*a*r; ɔ f*aw*n; ei, sn*a*ke. **(e)** e, h*e*n; i:, sh*ee*p; iə, d*ee*r; ɛə, b*ea*r. **(i)** i, f*i*sh; ai, t*i*ger; ə:, b*i*rd. **(o)** o, *o*x; au, c*ow*; ou, g*oa*t; u, p*oo*r; ɔi, r*oy*al. **(u)** ʌ, d*u*ck; u, b*u*ll; u:, g*oo*se; ə, b*a*cillus; ju:, c*u*be. x, lo*ch*; θ, *th*ink; ð, bo*th*er; z, *Z*en; ʒ, corsa*g*e; dʒ, sava*g*e; ŋ, ora*n*gutang; j, *y*ak; ʃ, *f*ish; tʃ, fe*tch*; 'l, rabb*le*; 'n, redd*en*. Complete pronunciation key appears inside front cover.

Vaish·na·va, Vais·na·va (váiʃnəvə) *n.* a worshipper of Vishnu **Váish·na·vism, Váis·na·vism** *ns*

Vais·ya (váisjə, váiʃə) *n.* a Hindu of the third of the four chief castes, comprising farmers and merchants (*BRAHMIN, *SUDRA, *KSHATRIYA) [Skr.=peasant]

Va·la·don (vælædɔ̃), Marie-Clémentine, called Suzanne (1867-1938), French painter, mother of Utrillo

Va·lais (vælei) a mainly French-speaking and Catholic canton (area 2,026 sq. miles, pop. 218,707) of S.W. Switzerland. Capital: Sion (pop. 16,000)

val·ance (væləns, véiləns) *n.* a length of curtain hung decoratively across the top of a window ‖ a length of cloth draped along the sides and bottom of a bed, or under a shelf etc. [prob. fr. O.F.]

Val·dai Hills (vɑldái) a range of hills (rising to 1,050 ft) between Moscow and Leningrad, U.S.S.R., forming the Volga-Dnieper watershed

Val-de-Marne (vældəmɑrn) a department (area 94 sq. miles, pop. 1,215,700) of N. central France, southeast of Paris (*ILE-DE-FRANCE). Chief town: Créteil (pop. 31,000)

Val·di·via (vɑldí:vjɑ), Pedro de (c. 1500-54), Spanish conquistador. At the head of 150 Spaniards he conquered Chile and founded Santiago (1541), Valdivia (1552) etc. He died at Tucapel in a battle with the Araucanian Indians under Lautaro

Valdivia the chief town (pop. 103,600) of S. Chile, founded in 1552

Val-d'Oise (vældwæz) a department (area 482 sq. miles, pop. 840,900) of N. central France, north of Paris (*ILE-DE-FRANCE). Chief town: Pontoise (pop. 14,000)

vale (veil) *n.* (*rhet.*, and in place names) valley [O.F. *val*]

val·e·dic·tion (vælidíkʃən) *n.* a farewell [fr. L. *valedicere* (*valedictus*), to say farewell]

val·e·dic·to·ri·an (vælidiktóri:ən, vælidiktóuri:ən) *n.* a student, usually the one with the highest marks, who delivers a valedictory

val·e·dic·to·ry (vælidíktəri:) **1.** *adj.* spoken or done as a valediction **2.** *pl.* **val·e·dic·to·ries** *n.* a parting speech, a farewell oration, esp. at graduation in high schools, universities etc. [fr. L. *valedicere* (*valedictus*), to say farewell]

va·lence (véiləns) *n.* the combining power of an element or radical, which may be defined as the number of atoms of hydrogen (or its equivalent) that one atom of the element or one radical will combine with or displace. The Latin prefixes (uni-, bi-, ter-, quadri- etc.) are preferred when indicating the number of valences exhibited and the Greek ones (mono-, di-, tri-, tetra- etc.) are preferred for the specific valence of an atom or radical (*OXIDATION STATE) [fr. L. *valentia*, vigor, capacity]

Va·len·cia (vɑlénsjɑ), Guillermo (1873-1943), Colombian poet, politician, orator and diplomat. He wrote 'Ritos' (1898) and 'Catay' (1928)

Valencia, Guillermo León (1909-71), Colombian politician and president (1962-6), son of the poet Guillermo Valencia

Va·len·ci·a (vɑlénʃi:ə, vɑlénsi:ə, vɑlénθi:ɑ) a region of S. Spain on the Mediterranean, forming Castellón, Valencia, and Alicante provinces. The coastal plain, much of it intensely irrigated, rises to mountains in the east. Agricultural products: citrus fruits, olives, vines, vegetables, rice, silk. Industries: textiles, food processing, chemicals, tourism. Historic capital: Valencia. Colonized by Greeks and Carthaginians before the Romans, it was conquered from the Moors (1238) by Aragon

Valencia a province (area 4,150 sq. miles, pop. 3,487,200) of E. Spain ‖ its capital (pop. 750,994), also the historic capital of the region of Valencia, a port. Industries: ceramics, food processing, automobile assembly, mechanical engineering, plastics, steel. Gothic cathedral (restored 18th c.), fortifications, public buildings (15th c.) and baroque churches. University (1500)

Valencia a city (pop. 455,000) in N. Venezuela, founded in 1555: textiles, food processing, tanning

Va·len·ci·a, Lake (vɑlénʃi:ə, vɑlénsjɑ) or Tacarigua, a lake (area 125 sq. miles) in N. Venezuela, southwest of Caracas

Va·len·ci·ennes (vælɑ̃sjen) *n.* a fine bobbin lace of wide net and very clear pattern, the net background and the pattern being made from the same threads [after *valenciennes*, a city in N. France]

va·len·cy (véilənsi:) *pl.* **va·len·cies** *n.*, (esp. *Br.*) valence [fr. L. *valentia*, vigor, capacity]

Va·lens (véilənz) (c. 328-78), Roman emperor (364-78). The younger brother of Valentinian I, he was appointed to rule the eastern part of the empire

Val·en·tine (væləntain), St, bishop of Terni in Umbria, martyred c. 273. Feast: Feb. 14

val·en·tine (væləntain) *n.* a sweetheart chosen on St Valentine's Day (Feb. 14), the day when birds were believed to begin mating ‖ a sentimental or satiric letter or greeting card sent to someone of the opposite sex on this day [O.F.]

Val·en·tin·i·an I (væləntíni:ən) (321-75), Roman emperor (364-75). He ruled the western part of the empire and appointed his brother Valens to rule the east

Valentinian II (c. 371-92), Roman emperor (375-92). He ruled jointly with his half brother Gratian

Valentinian III (419-55), Roman emperor (425-55). He was driven by the Vandals from Africa

Val·en·ti·no (vælɑntí:nou), Rudolph (Rodolpho d'Antonguolla, 1895-1926), U.S. movie star, the screen's first 'Latin lover'. His roles in 'The Four Horsemen of the Apocalypse', 'The Sheik', 'Blood and Sand', and 'Monsieur Beaucaire' made him the idol of millions of women

Valera *DE VALERA

Va·le·ri·an (vəlíəri:ən) (Publius Licinius Valerianus, c. 190–c. 260), Roman emperor (253-60). He left the government in the hands of his son Gallienus, while he led the army against the Goths and the Persians. He was captured (260) by the Persians, and died in captivity

va·le·ri·an (vəlíəri:ən) *n.* any species of *valeriana*, fam. *valerianaceae*, a genus of herbaceous plants with clusters of small, strong-smelling, pink or white flowers. The rhizomes and roots of *v. officinalis* yield a carminative and antispasmodic preparation [fr. O.F. *valeriane* or M.L. *valeriana*]

Va·le·ri·us Flac·cus (vəlíəri:əsflǽkəs), Gaius (*d.* c. 90 A.D.), Latin epic poet, author of the 'Argonautica'

Va·le·ri·us Max·i·mus (vəlíəri:əs mǽksəməs) (early 1st c. A.D.), Roman historian, author of an unreliable historical work in nine volumes dedicated to Tiberius

Va·lé·ry (vælɛiri:), Paul Ambroise (1871-1945), French poet and critic. He was strongly influenced by Mallarmé, and his poetry is in many ways a continuation of Mallarmé's work. It is extremely deliberate, though striving toward the status of magic or music, syntactically original, oblique, and calculatingly metaphorical. With Valéry art became so much a matter of deliberation that not surprisingly it became hard for him to write at all, and much of his art is 'about' the process of creating art. His poem 'le Cimetière marin' (1922) rises to a moment of anguished directness, and awareness of the quality of being alive, and of being dead. His criticism sums up a whole French tradition of writing about the nature of art, and the relationships between the art-object, the artist and the world of experience

val·et (vælit, vælei, væléi) **1.** *n.* a personal manservant ‖ a hotel attendant who looks after the clothes of patrons **2.** *v.t.* to act as valet to [F.]

Valetta *VALLETTA

val·e·tu·di·nar·i·an (vælitu:d'néəri:ən, vælitju:d'néəri:ən) **1.** *n.* an invalid, esp. one who is morbidly interested in or anxious about his state of health **2.** *adj.* relating to or characteristic of a valetudinarian **val·e·tu·di·nár·i·an·ism** *n.* **va·le·tu·di·nar·y** (vælitú:d'nɛri:, vælitjú:d'nɛri:) *adj.* [fr. L. *valetudinarius* fr. *valetudo* (*valetudinis*), state of health]

val·gus (vælgəs) *n.* (*med.*) a position of abnormal outward turn of a joint or joints (cf. VARUS) [L.=bandy-legged]

Val·hal·la (vælhælə) (*Norse mythol.*) the hall of the heroes into which Odin receives those who have fallen bravely in battle

val·iance (væljəns) *n.* (*rhet.*) bravery **vál·ian·cy** *n.* (*rhet.*) valiance [A.F. or Fr. O.F. *vaillance*]

val·iant (væljənt) *adj.* (*rhet.*) stouthearted, brave, heroic [fr. O.F. *vaillant, vaillant*]

val·id (vælid) *adj.* seen to be in agreement with the facts or to be logically sound, *valid arguments* ‖ (*law*) in conformity with the law, and therefore binding ‖ based on sound principle, *a valid method* [fr. F. *valide* or L. *validus*, strong]

val·i·date (vælideit) *pres. part.* **val·i·dat·ing** *past* and *past part.* **val·i·dat·ed** *v.t.* to make valid or binding ‖ to confirm the validity of [fr. M.L. *validare* (*validatus*)]

val·i·da·tion (vælidéiʃən) *n.* a making or being made valid

va·lid·i·ty (vəliditi:) *pl.* **va·lid·i·ties** *n.* the state, fact or quality of being valid legally or in argument [fr. L.L. *validitas*]

val·in·o·my·cin (vælinəmáisin) *n.* an antibiotic that makes cell walls permeable to ions of some chemicals (e.g., potassium), useful in ion transport experiments

va·lise (vəlí:s, vəlí:z) *n.* a small traveling case ‖ (*Br.*) an officer's bedding roll [F. fr. Ital.]

Val·kyr·ie (vælkíəri:, vælkíəri:) *n.* (*Norse mythol.*) one of the virgin goddesses, riding in the air over the field of battle, who escort to valhalla the heroes who fall

Va·lla·do·lid (vɑljɑðɔlí:ð) a province (area 2,922 sq. miles, pop. 489,636) of N. central Spain (*OLD CASTILE, *LEON) ‖ its capital (pop. 297,255). Industries: mechanical engineering, automobile assembly, aluminum, chemicals. Cathedral (16th c.), Gothic and baroque churches. University

Valladolid (Mexico) *MORELIA

Val·lan·di·gham (vəlǽndigəm), Clement Laird (1820-71), U.S. politician, advocate of states' rights. He was banished (1863) behind Confederate lines for voicing pro-Southern sympathies. Upon his return (1864) into national politics he was leader of the Knights of the Golden Circle, a copperhead secret society

Va·lle (váje), José Cecilio del (1780-1834), Honduran writer and leader in the struggle for Central American independence. He drafted the declaration (1821) proclaiming it

val·lec·u·la (vəlékjulə) *pl.* **val·lec·u·lae** (vəlékjuli:) *n.* (*anat.*, *bot.*) a groove or furrow **val·léc·u·lar, val·lec·u·late** (vəlékjuleit) *adjs* [L.L. var. of L. *vallicula* dim. of *valles* (*vallis*), valley]

Val·le d'A·o·sta (válledɑ́ostɑ) an autonomous region (area 1,260 sq. miles, pop. 114,591) of N.W. Italy in the Alps, bordering France and Switzerland. Capital: Aosta. Language: French dialect. Agriculture: cereals, wine, fruit, livestock. Resources: coal, iron ore, copper, hydroelectricity. It became a duchy (1238) and was allied to Savoy until 1814, when it was made part of the kingdom of Sardinia

Va·lle-In·clán (váljei:ŋklún), Ramón María Del (1869-1936), Spanish poet, novelist and dramatist. His best-known work is perhaps 'Sonatas' (1902-5), four novels with a Don Juan-type hero

Val·le·jo (vajého), César (1895-1938), Peruvian poet and novelist, spokesman for the underprivileged, esp. the Andean Indian, and champion of social reform. His works include the poems 'Heraldos negros' (1918) and the novels 'Trilce' (1922) and 'El tungsteno' (1931)

Val·let·ta, Va·let·ta (vəléta) the capital (pop. 14,042) and chief port of Malta, founded (1566) by the Knights Hospitalers. University (1769). Dockyards

val·ley (væli:) *pl.* **val·leys** *n.* a long depression in the earth's surface resulting either from its folding or from erosion by a river or glacier ‖ (*archit.*) the internal angle at the junction of two roof slopes ‖ any dip or hollow ‖ the land drained or watered by a great river system [O.F. *valee, vallee*]

Valley Forge the winter quarters (1777-8) near Philadelphia of Washington and his army of 11,000 during a critical period of the Revolutionary War. About 3,000 died of cold, malnutrition and sickness

vallonia *VALONIA

Val·my, Battle of (vælmi:) the first battle (Sept. 20, 1792) of the French Revolutionary Wars. The Prussian army was repulsed by the French, and forced to withdraw beyond the Rhine

Va·lois (vælwæ) the royal house of France (1328-1589), a younger branch of the Capetian line. It was succeeded by the Bourbons

Va·lo·na (vəlóunɑ) *VLONA

va·lo·ni·a, val·lo·ni·a (vəlóuni:ə) *n.* large dried acorn cups of *Quercus aegilops*, the valonia oak of S.W. Europe and Asia Minor, used in tanning, dyeing and making ink [Ital. *vallonía, vallonéa* fr. Mod. Gk]

val·or, Br. val·our (vælər) *n.* (*rhet.*) personal courage, esp. in battle [O.F.]

val·or·i·za·tion (vælərizéiʃən) *n.* an attempt, usually by a government, to fix or stabilize artificially the price of an article **val·or·ize** (væləraiz) *pres. part.* **val·or·iz·ing** *past* and *past*

CONCISE PRONUNCIATION KEY: **(a)** æ, c*a*t; ɑ, c*a*r; ɔ f*aw*n; ei, sn*a*ke. **(e)** e, h*e*n; i:, sh*ee*p; iə, d*ee*r; ɛə, b*ea*r. **(i)** i, f*i*sh; ai, t*i*ger; ə:, b*i*rd. **(o)** o, *o*x; au, c*ow*; ou, g*oa*t; u, p*oo*r; ɔi, r*oy*al. **(u)** ʌ, d*u*ck; u, b*u*ll; u:, g*oo*se; ə, b*a*cillus; ju:, c*u*be. x, lo*ch*; θ, *th*ink; ð, bo*th*er; z, *Z*en; ʒ, cor*s*age; dʒ, sava*ge*; ŋ, ora*n*gutan*g*; j, *y*ak; ʃ, *fi*sh; tʃ, fe*tch*; 'l, rabb*le*; 'n, redd*en*. Complete pronunciation key appears inside front cover.

part. **val·or·ized** v.t. to determine and stabilize the price of (an article) [fr. VALOR, (obs.) value]

val·or·ous (vǽlərəs) adj. (rhet., of people) courageous ‖ (rhet., of actions) showing valor [fr. O.F. valeureux]

valour *VALOR

Val·pa·rai·so (vælpəráizou) the chief port (pop. 249,000) of Chile and of W. South America. Industries: oil refining, food processing, light manufactures, chemical products. University (1949), Catholic University (1929)

val·pro·ic acid [C₈H₁₆O₂] (vælpróuik) (pharm.) a carboxylic derivative used as an anticonvulsive, marketed as Depakene

val·u·a·ble (vǽlju:əb'l, vǽljub'l) 1. adj. of great value, a valuable property ‖ very useful, his help was most valuable 2. n. (pl.) precious possessions, small personal objects of value such as jewelry etc. **vál·u·a·bly** adv.

val·u·a·tion (vælju:éiʃən) n. an estimation of a thing's worth, esp. by a professional appraiser ‖ the value, cost or price estimated ‖ a personal view of one's own or somebody else's character or merits [O.F. valuacion]

val·u·a·tor (vǽlju:eitər) n. an appraiser

val·ue (vǽlju:) 1. n. the measure of how strongly something is desired for its physical or moral beauty, usefulness, rarity etc., esp. expressed in terms of the effort, money etc. one is willing to expend in acquiring, retaining possession of, or preserving it ‖ a principle, quality etc. that arouses such desire, moral values ‖ fair return, to get good value for one's money ‖ purchasing power, the value of the pound ‖ the monetary equivalent of something, property to the value of $5,000 ‖ (math.) the amount represented by an expression or symbol ‖ (mus.) the duration of a tone as indicated by its note ‖ (phon.) the quality of a sound ‖ (painting) the relationship between the parts of a painting in terms of light and shade ‖ the importance or rank accorded to a playing card, chessman etc. 2. v.t. pres. part. **val·u·ing** past and past part. **val·ued** to estimate the value of, he valued the property at $10,000 ‖ to regard as having a high value, to value someone's friendship **vál·u·er** n. (Br.) an appraiser [O.F. fem. of valu past part. of valoir, to be worth]

value added by manufacture (business) value measure derived by subtracting the cost of materials from the value of shipments. abbr. VAM. Cf VALUE-ADDED TAX

value-added tax (business) a tax based on the value added at each stage of production from raw-material processing to consumer. It is designed to fall ultimately on the consumer. abbr. VAT. Cf VALUE ADDED BY MANUFACTURE

va·lu·ta (vəlú:tə) n. the exchange value of a currency in terms of another currency [Ital.= value]

val·vate (vǽlveit) adj. like a valve ‖ (bot.) of, or having, petals or sepals which meet at their edges but do not overlap ‖ (bot.) opening as if by valves, e.g. of anthers which release pollen, or of fruits which release seeds by means of valve-like structures [fr. L. valvatus, having folding doors]

valve (vælv) n. any of innumerable natural or man-made devices which control the direction or volume of flow of a fluid or (Br.=Am. tube) of electricity ‖ (bot.) the lidlike structure of certain anthers ‖ (bot.) one of the segments into which a capsule dehisces ‖ (zool.) one of the separate parts of the shell of a diatom or of any of certain mollusks ‖ (mus., of the trumpet etc.) a device for varying the tube length to alter the pitch of a tone [fr. L. valva, leaf of a door]

valve chest the steam chest of a steam engine

val·vu·lar (vǽlvjulər) adj. of or relating to a valve or valves, esp. the cardiac valves, valvular disease

val·vule (vǽlvju:l) n. a small valve [F.]

vamp (væmp) 1. n. the upper part of a boot or shoe in front of the ankle seam ‖ (mus.) an improvised accompaniment or introduction or fill-in between verses 2. v.t. to repair the vamp of (a boot or shoe) ‖ to patch ‖ (mus.) to improvise (an accompaniment, introduction etc.) ‖ v.i. (mus.) to improvise an accompaniment etc. [O.F. avanpié fr. avant, before+pié, foot]

vamp 1. n. a woman who uses her physical allure to attract and exploit men ‖ an actress who plays the part of such a woman 2. v.t. to attract and exploit (a man) by playing the vamp ‖ v.i. to act the vamp [shortened fr. VAMPIRE]

vam·pire (vǽmpaiər) n. (in popular superstition) a ghost or evil spirit which leaves a grave at night to suck the blood of people asleep ‖ a person who exploits others ruthlessly ‖ a vampire bat ‖ a stage trapdoor used in theaters to effect sudden disappearances [F. fr. Magyar vampir fr. Slavic]

vampire bat a member of Desmodus or of Diphylla, fam. Desmodontidae, genera of South and Central American bats which live on the fresh blood of animals and are often carriers of disease ‖ any of several large South and Central American bats once reputed to suck blood, but which actually feed on insects

vam·pir·ism (vǽmpaiərizəm) n. belief in vampires ‖ the habits or actions of vampires

Van (vɑn) a salt lake (area 1,450 sq. miles) in E. Turkey (Armenia)

van (væn) n. the leading section of an army, fleet, or procession ‖ the people who take the lead in some movement [shortened fr. VANGUARD]

van n. a large covered vehicle for carrying furniture and other goods by road ‖ (Br.) a small covered truck, e.g. for delivery of groceries, parcels etc. ‖ (Br., rail.) a baggage car [shortened fr. CARAVAN]

van n. a shovel for dressing ores ‖ (rhet.) a bird's wing [var. of FAN]

va·na·di·um (vənéidi:əm) n. (chem.) a malleable, white metallic element (symbol V, at. no. 23, at. mass 50.942) occurring in a few rare minerals. It is used in alloying, esp. to make a very hard steel, and in the form of vanadic acid, HVO₃, as a catalyst in oxidizing aniline (using sodium chlorate as the oxidizer) [Mod. L. fr. O.N. Vanadis, a Scandinavian goddess]

Van Al·len radiation belt (vænǽlən) either of two layers of intense ionizing radiation that surround the earth in its outer atmosphere, ranging from approx. 1,500 to approx. 12,000 miles above its surface. They have particles charged with high energies [after James A. van Allen (b. 1914), U.S. physicist]

Van·brugh (vǽnbrə), Sir John (1664-1726), English playwright and architect. His plays, notably 'The Relapse' (1697) and 'The Provok'd Wife' (1697), are comedies of manners. His country mansions, e.g. Castle Howard and Blenheim Palace, are in an impressive baroque style

Van Bur·en (vænbjúərən), Martin (1782-1862), eighth president (1837-41) of the U.S.A., a Democrat. He organized the Albany Regency. He served as secretary of state (1829-31) and as vice-president (1832-6) under President Andrew Jackson. As president he responded to the economic crisis of 1837 by endorsing a federal Treasury independent of the nation's banking and financial system, ultimately established in 1840 by an act of Congress. Later he became (1840) the Democratic presidential candidate and (1848) candidate of the Freesoil party, and was both times defeated

van·co·my·cin (vænkəmáisin) n. (pharm.) antibiotic used to combat gram-positive staphylococcic infections; marketed as Vancocin

Van·cou·ver (vænkú:vər), George (1758-98), English navigator and explorer. After mapping the coasts of Australia and New Zealand (1791) he made a thorough survey of the northwest coast of America (1792-4)

Vancouver the chief Pacific port (pop. 414,281, with agglom. 1,169,831) of Canada, in British Columbia, on the Inside Passage and the Fraser River. Industries: oil refining, sawmilling, pulp and paper, food processing, shipbuilding. University of British Columbia (1915)

Vancouver Island a mountainous, wooded island (area 13,408 sq. miles, pop. 437,802) off S.W. Canada, part of British Columbia. Chief town: Victoria. Products: lumber, coal

Van·dal (vænd'l) n. a member of an E. Germanic tribe originally from the southern shores of the Baltic. They overran Gaul and Spain (406-29) and N.W. Africa (429-42), sacked Rome (455) and commanded the Mediterranean until their kingdom was overthrown (534) by Belisarius **vandal** someone who wantonly or ignorantly destroys or disfigures natural or human works of beauty **ván·dal·ism** n. wanton destruction or spoiling of what should be preserved [fr. L. vandalus]

Van de Graaff generator (vændəgræf) (phys.) a device for separating electrostatic charges by a continuous process, thus building up extremely high electrostatic potential (e.g. up to 15 million volts). It is used to accelerate the charged particles of the atom (e.g. protons) to high energies [after R. van de Graaff (1901-67), U.S. physicist]

Van·der·bilt (vǽndərbilt), Cornelius (1794-1877), U.S. railroad magnate. He gained control (1867) of the New York Central Railroad and connected (1873) Chicago with New York by rail. He donated $1 million to found Vanderbilt University in Nashville, Tenn.

van der Goes (vændərgouz), Hugo (c. 1440-82), Flemish painter. Only one authenticated painting of his has survived, a triptych of the Adoration in the Uffizi gallery at Florence, other attributions being based on this

van der Helst (vændərhelst), Bartholomaeus (c. 1611-70), Dutch painter. He was a masterly draftsman and is esp. known for his collective portraits

van der Waals equation (vændərwɔlz) (phys.) an equation of state for gases and vapors that is related to the ideal gas law but which takes into account the actual volume of the gas molecules and the effect of intermolecular attractions between them. It is written

$$\left(P + \frac{a}{V_2}\right)(V - b) = nRT$$

(where P = pressure, V = volume, T = temperature on the Kelvin scale, R = the gas constant, n = the number of moles and a and b are constants which depend on the gas). It describes the behavior of gases over a considerably wider range of pressure than the ideal gas law [after Johannes D. van der Waals (d. 1923), Du. physicist]

van der Wey·den (vændərváid'n), Roger (c. 1400-64), Flemish painter. His religious works, e.g. 'The Descent from the Cross' (c. 1435) in the Prado, Madrid, show a deep spirituality combined with great dramatic power, and a profound understanding of human suffering. He also painted fine portraits

Van De·van·ter (vændəvæntər), Willis (1859-1941), associate justice of the U.S. Supreme Court (1911-37). He practiced law before becoming (1890) chief justice of the Wyoming Supreme Court. He served (1903-10) on the U.S. Circuit Court until appointed to the U.S. Supreme Court by Pres. William Howard Taft. A conservative, he was one of the Court majority that struck down much of Pres. Franklin D. Roosevelt's New Deal legislation

van de Vel·de (vændəveld), Adriaen (1636-72), Dutch painter. He specialized in landscapes and animal paintings

van de Velde, Henry (1863-1957), Belgian architect and decorator. From an early art nouveau style, he developed theories of pure form and functional aesthetics which influenced the development of modern design, esp. in Germany

van de Velde, Willem (1633-1707), Dutch painter, brother of Adriaen. He painted at the courts of Charles II and James II of England and excelled in seascapes and naval battles

Van Die·men (vændí:mən), Anton (1593-1645), Dutch colonial administrator. An expedition sent by him to Australia discovered (1642) Van Diemen's Land, now Tasmania

van Don·gen (vændɔ́ŋgən), Kees (1877-1968), French painter of Dutch origin. He was one of the early protagonists of Fauvism but is best known for his later society portraits

Vandyke beard a neatly trimmed, pointed beard

Van·dyke, van Dyck (vændáik), Sir Anthony (1599-1641), Flemish painter. After six years in Italy (1621-7) he became, jointly with Rubens, court painter at Antwerp. His technique owes much to Rubens' swift, very sensitive painting. From about 1630 to his death he lived mainly in London. He is famous for his portraits, esp. those of the patricians and courtiers of Caroline England. He was one of the first society painters: his subjects are made to represent an ideal of arrogant refinement

vane (vein) n. a broad, thin, often curved surface fastened to a pivoted or rotating body. Vanes are used under a current of air or water to make a pivoted body (e.g. a weather vane, sail of a windmill etc.) rotate, or to drive a body forward or to give a bomb etc. a steady direction ‖ the barbs of a feather ‖ (archery) a feather on an arrow shaft ‖ (surveying) a movable disk on a surveying staff which can be brought into line with the telescope ‖ one of the sights on a compass etc. [var. of older *fane* fr. O.E. *fana*, a flag]

Vä·nern (vénərn) a lake (area 2,141 sq. miles) in S.W. Sweden

van Eyck (vænáik), Jan (*d.* 1441), the founder with his brother Hubert (*d. c.* 1426; some art historians have doubted that Hubert existed) of the Flemish school of painting. Their work survives in an altarpiece, 'The Adoration of the Lamb' in the church of St Bavon, at Ghent (inaugurated 1432), in other religious paintings, and in portraits. The van Eycks mark the moment in N. Europe when medieval art is left behind and 'modern' modeling, perspective and lighting based on close observation take its place

vang (væŋ) *n.* (*naut.*) either of the two guy ropes extending from the top of the gaff to the deck [var. of O.E. *fang*]

van Gogh (vænxóx, *Eng.* vængóu), Vincent (1853-90), Dutch Postimpressionist painter, one of the first expressionists. His early work, inspired by Millet's paintings and by religious missionary zeal, portrayed Dutch peasant life in dark, somber colors. In 1886 he went to live in France. In Paris, where he came in contact with the Impressionists, and esp. when he moved to Provence, he began to use pure, bright color, and his brush strokes themselves, in their very shapes and rhythms, convey the pressure of a joyous perception of life, of growth, goodness and love, as well as agonized premonitions of madness and death. His paintings convey the reality of landscapes, still life and people, transfigured by his intensity of feeling about them. His painting career was concentrated in some ten years of feverish work. His last years were spent in asylums, and finally he shot himself

van Goy·en (vængóijən), Jan Josephszoon (1596-1656), Dutch painter. He is noted for his landscapes and seascapes

van·guard (vǽngard) *n.* the soldiers who march at the front of an army, or this section of an army ‖ the forefront of a movement [fr. O.F. *avangarde*]

va·nil·la (vənílə) *n.* a member of *vanilla*, fam. *Orchidaceae*, a genus of climbing, epiphytic orchids, native to tropical America and the West Indies ‖ a food and tobacco flavoring extracted from the pods of *V. planifolia* (now synthesized on a large scale) [fr. early Span. *vainilla*, little sheath]

van·ish (vǽniʃ) *v.i.* to become no longer able to be seen or felt, *he vanished in the mist, the pain suddenly vanished* ‖ to pass out of existence, *all hope of recovery finally vanished* ‖ (*math.*, of a number or quantity) to become zero [aphetic fr. O.F. *evanir* (*evaniss-*)]

vanishing cream a cosmetic cream, used as a foundation, which is absorbed by the skin

vanishing point the point at which receding parallels, drawn in perspective, would meet

van·i·ty (vǽniti) *pl.* **van·i·ties** *n.* the fact or quality of being vain ‖ something of no real worth ‖ a source of self-satisfaction ‖ a vanity case ‖ a dressing table [O.F. *vanite*]

vanity case a small case fitted with lipstick, compact, mirror etc.

vanity plate a motor vehicle license plate carrying a word, name, and/or numbers selected by the owner

vanity surgery (*med.*) cosmetic surgery

van·ner (vǽnər) *n.* a machine with a wide shaking rubber belt used for dressing ores ‖ a man who separates ore with a van

van Os·ta·de (vænóstədə), Adriaen (1610-85), Dutch painter and etcher, pupil of Franz Hals. He painted scenes of village life and tranquil Dutch exteriors

van Ostade, Isaac (1621-49), brother and pupil of Adriaen van Ostade, known for his brilliant wintry landscapes

van·quish (vǽŋkwiʃ, vǽnkwiʃ) *v.t.* (*rhet.*) to overcome in battle or conflict, to conquer ‖ (*rhet.*) to overcome (a feeling) [M.E. fr. O.F. *vencus* past part. and *venquis* past tense of *veintre*, to conquer]

van·tage (vǽntidʒ, vántidʒ) *n.* a condition or position conferring superiority ‖ (*Br.*, tennis) advantage [fr. A.F., var. of O.F. *avantage*]

vantage point a place or condition particularly favorable for viewing or understanding something

Va·nu·atu (vanu:átu:) formerly New Hebrides, an island republic, part of a volcanic archipelago (total area 5,700 sq. miles, pop. 112,596, incl. some 3,000 Europeans) in the S.W. Pacific

(Melanesia). Main islands: Espiritu Santo, Malekula, Epi, Efate. Capital: Vila (pop. 14,000, on Efate). Main exports: copra, cocoa. The islands were visited by the Portuguese (1606), the French (1768) and the British (1774). They were placed under an Anglo-French naval commission (1887), and were administered (1906-80) as an Anglo-French condominium until independence on July 30, 1980

vap·id (vǽpid) *adj.* lacking zest or interest **va·pid·i·ty**, *n.* [fr. L. *vapidus*, savorless]

va·por, *Br.* **va·pour** (véipər) 1. *n.* (*chem.* and *phys.*) a substance in a gaseous state but below its critical temperature, and so liquefiable by pressure alone ‖ a liquid, esp. water, dispersed and suspended in the air in the form of very small drops ‖ a combination of vaporized matter and air, e.g. the explosive mixture in an internal-combustion engine ‖ (*pl., old-fash.*) nervous depression 2. *v.t.* to emit as vapor ‖ to reduce to vapor ‖ *v.i.* to rise as vapor [A.F.]

vapor density, *Br.* **vapour density** the density of a vapor or gas by comparison with that of some standard (e.g. hydrogen)

va·por·if·ic (veipərífik) *adj.* vaporous [fr. Mod. L. *vaporificus*]

va·por·i·za·tion (veipərizéiʃən) *n.* a vaporizing or being vaporized

va·por·ize (véipəraiz) *pres. part.* **va·por·iz·ing** *past and past part.* **va·por·ized** *v.t.* to change into vapor ‖ *v.i.* to be changed into vapor

va·por·iz·er (véipəraizər) *n.* a device for converting a liquid into a vapor or fine droplets, usually by the application of heat or by spraying (cf. ATOMIZER)

va·por·ous (véipərəs) *adj.* forming vapor ‖ giving off vapor ‖ like vapor

vapor plumes emissions of visible droplets in fine gas

vapor pressure, *Br.* **vapour pressure** the pressure exerted by the vapor of a substance

vapour *VAPOR

va·que·ro (vakéərou) *n.* a Spanish-American or southwest U.S. cowboy [Span.]

Var (vær) a department (area 2,333 sq. miles, pop. 626,100) of S. France (*PROVENCE). Chief towns: Draguignan, Toulon

var·ac·tor or **varactor diode** (værǽktə:r) *n.* (*electr.*) a semiconductor diode on which the capacitance varies with the voltage applied, used as a tuning element in amplifier and oscillator circuits

Va·ra·na·si (vərənázi:) (or Banaras, *Eng.* Benares) a trade center (pop. 583,856) in S.E. Uttar Pradesh, India, on the Ganges. It is a holy city to Hindus, Buddhists and Jains, receiving a million pilgrims annually. Handicrafts and manufactures: silks, shawls, brocades, brass, jewelry, textiles, chemicals. There are some 1,500 temples. Mosque of Aurangzeb (1669), observatory (1693), Hindu university (1916)

Va·ran·gi·an (vərǽndʒiːən) *n.* (*hist.*) one of the viking warriors who raided the Baltic coast, founded states in Russia (9th c.), and attacked Constantinople (10th c.). The Russ, a Varangian tribe, gave their name to Russia

Var·dha·ma·na (vərdhəméinə) *JAINISM

var·ec, var·ech (vǽrek) *n.* kelp [F. *varech*]

Va·re·la (baréla), Juan Cruz (1794-1839), Argentinian neoclassical poet

Va·rèse (varéz), Edgar (1883-1965), U.S. composer (born French). His experiments in sonority (incl. the use of electronic instruments) were 30 years ahead of his time. He was a pupil of Roussel, d'Indy and Widor

Var·gas (várgəs), Getúlio Dornelles (1883-1954), Brazilian politician and dictator (1930-45, 1951-4), following a coup d'état. He established (1937) a corporative state, the Estado Novo, modeled after Salazar's Portugal. He was ousted (1945) by the military but was nevertheless reelected (1950) by the masses. Pressure by the military again forced his resignation (1954). He committed suicide in the same year

var·i·a·bil·i·ty (vɛəri:əbíliti:) *n.* the state or quality of being variable ‖ a tendency to vary

var·i·a·ble (vɛ́əriːəb'l) 1. *adj.* apt to change, *variable winds* ‖ able to be changed ‖ (*biol.*, of a structure, species, function etc.) not true to type ‖ (*math.*) characteristic of a quantity which may have different values 2. *n.* something variable ‖ (*pl.*) the latitudes between the trade-wind zones ‖ (*math.*) a term representing a quantity which may have any value, or any of the values within certain limits ‖ (*math.*) a symbol for such a quantity (cf. CONSTANT) [O.F.]

variable annuity a contract in which annual payments fluctuate with the return on stocks or other income sources that change with economic conditions

variable condenser (*elec.*) a condenser of which the capacity can readily be varied

variable geometry aircraft (*aeronautics*) a retractable wing that can be adjusted inflight for speed changes. *also* variable sweep wing, swing wing

variable levy a formula applied to agricultural imports providing a rise in tariff levies as international prices drop

variable rate mortgage (*banking*) a mortgage in which the interest is adjusted periodically in accordance with prevailing interest rates

variable star a star displaying varying magnitude either cyclically or without any discernible period (*CEPHEID, *NOVA, *DOUBLE STAR)

variable time fuze, esp. *Br.* **variable time fuse** a proximity fuze

var·i·a·bly (vɛ́əri:əbli) *adv.* in a variable manner

var·i·ance (vɛ́əri:əns) *n.* a sharp disagreement or difference of opinion ‖ a variation, difference, change, *a marked variance in temperature* ‖ (*law*) a difference or disagreement between two documents, statements etc. which should agree **at variance** in disagreement, *at variance with the known facts* ‖ antagonistic, at loggerheads, *husband and wife were often at variance* [O.F.]

var·i·ant (vɛ́əri:ənt) 1. *adj.* differing and alternative, *variant spellings of 'Shakespeare'* 2. *n.* one of two or more alternatives of a form, reading, spelling etc. [O.F.]

var·i·a·tion (vɛəri:éiʃən) *n.* change as a process, condition or fact ‖ departure from a standard or norm, or an instance of this ‖ the measure of this departure, the extent to which a thing varies ‖ (*mus.*) one of a number of repetitions of a theme in a variety of elaborate, developed or disguised forms ‖ (*biol.*) the structural or functional difference between closely related individuals within a species ‖ (*astron.*) a change in the normal movement of a heavenly body, esp. in the orbit of a planet ‖ (*phys.*) *DECLINATION **var·i·a·tion·al** *adj.* [O.F.]

var·i·cel·la (værisélə) *n.* (*med.*) chicken pox **var·i·cél·loid** *adj.* resembling chicken pox [Mod. L. dim. of *variola*]

varices *pl.* of VARIX

var·i·co·cele (værikousi:l) *n.* (*med.*) a swelling formed by varicose veins of the spermatic cord in the scrotum [Mod. L. fr. L. *varix*, an enlarged vein+Gk *kēlē*, tumor]

var·i·col·ored, *Br.* **var·i·col·oured** (vɛ́ərikʌlərd) *adj.* having various colors [fr. L. *varius*, varied+COLORED]

var·i·cose (værikous) *adj.* swollen, distended, esp. of veins (*VARIX) ‖ of or having varicose veins **var·i·co·sis, var·i·cos·i·ty** (værikósiti:) *ns* the condition of being varicose [fr. L. *varicosus* fr. *varix*, an enlarged vein]

var·ied (vɛ́əri:d) *adj.* of different kinds, not all the same ‖ variegated ‖ varying

var·i·e·gate (vɛ́ərigeit, vɛ́əri:əgeit) *pres. part.* **var·i·e·gat·ing** *past and past part.* **var·i·e·gat·ed** *v.t.* to supply with various colors ‖ to diversify, to give variety to **vár·i·e·gat·ed** *adj.* (*bot.*) dappled or streaked with various colors ‖ varied, full of variety **var·i·e·gá·tion** *n.* [fr. L. *variegare* (*variegatus*), to make varied]

var·i·e·tal (vəráiit'l) *adj.* of or pertaining to a variety ‖ constituting a variety (as opposed to an individual or species)

va·ri·e·ty (vəráiiti:) *pl.* **va·ri·e·ties** *n.* the state or quality of not being always or everywhere the same ‖ a number or collection of things differing in character, *a variety of reasons* ‖ (*biol.*) a group having certain qualities in common which distinguish it from a larger class to which it belongs, and which may or may not be inherited, *a variety of strawberry noted for its late fruiting* ‖ one of a number of different forms or kinds of the same thing, *a thousand varieties of selfishness* ‖ entertainment as given in variety shows [F. *variété* or fr. L. *varietas*, diversity]

variety show a presentation of different forms of light entertainment (e.g. acrobatics, conjuring, dancing, singing etc.)

var·i·form (vɛ́ərifɔrm) *adj.* having various forms

va·ri·o·la (vəráiələ) *n.* smallpox **va·ri·o·lar** *adj.* [M.L. fr. L. *varius*, varied]

var·i·ole (vɛ́ərioul) *n.* (*biol.*) a small shallow

pitlike depression resembling a pockmark ‖ a spherule of a variolite [M.L. *variola*, pustule]

var·i·o·lite (vέǝri:ǝlait) *n.* (*geol.*) a spherulitic basalt the surface of which resembles pockmarked skin **var·i·o·lit·ic** (vɛǝri:ǝlítik) *adj.* of or like variolite ‖ pockmarked [fr. M.L. *variola*]

va·ri·o·lous (vǝráiǝlǝs) *adj.* of, resembling or having variola

var·i·om·e·ter (vɛǝri:ómitǝr) *n.* (*radio*) a variable inductance of two coils connected in series, one inside the other, the inner coil rotating [fr. L. *varius*, various+METER]

var·i·o·rum edition (vɛǝri:ɔ́rǝm, vɛǝri:óurǝm) an edition containing textual variants with notes by various commentators [L.=of various (persons)]

var·i·ous (vέǝri:ǝs) *adj.* of different kinds, *various crops* ‖ characterized by variety, *his reasons are many and various* ‖ (*loosely*) several [fr. L. *varius*, diverse]

var·ix (vέǝriks) *pl.* **var·i·ces** (vέǝrisi:z) *n.* (*med.*) a permanent abnormal swelling of a vein, artery or lymph vessel ‖ a vein, artery or lymph vessel swollen thus ‖ a ridge on the whorl of some univalves [L.]

var·let (várlit) *n.* a medieval page ‖ (*hist.*) a knight's attendant training to become a squire ‖ (*archaic*) a knave [O.F.]

var·mint (vármint) *n.* (*pop.*) an animal classed as vermin ‖ (*pop.*) a lowdown, troublesome pest of a person

Var·na (várnǝ) (called Stalin 1949-56) the chief port (pop. 124,000) of Bulgaria. Industries: mechanical engineering, shipbuilding. University (1920)

var·nish (várniʃ) **1.** *n.* a liquid solution of resin, prepared in spirits or oil, applied to wood and metal surfaces to give a hard glossy transparent coating ‖ the gloss or shine of any polished surface, natural or man-made ‖ a superficial polish of manners and outward behavior **2.** *v.t.* to put a coat of varnish on ‖ to improve superficially, *to varnish a reputation* [fr. O.F. *vernis*]

Var·ro (vǽrou), Marcus Terentius (116-27 B.C.), Roman scholar. Of his many works, only his treatise on agriculture and parts of 'De lingua latina' survive

var·si·ty (vársiti:) *pl.* **var·si·ties** *n.* (*Br.*, *pop.*) university ‖ (*sports*) a team that represents a university, college, school or club, in a game [shortened fr. 18th-c. pronunciation of UNIVERSITY]

var·us (vέǝrǝs, vǽrǝs) *n.* (*med.*) a position of abnormal inward turn of a joint or joints (cf. VALGUS) [L.=knockkneed]

varve dating (vɑrv) (*archaeology*) use of sequence of sedimentary layers formed by melting ice as a means of establishing the time of an archeological deposit

var·y (vέǝri:) *pres. part.* **var·y·ing** *past* and *past part.* **var·ied** *v.t.* to introduce variety into ‖ *v.i.* to undergo change, *the temperature varies greatly* ‖ to differ, *opinions on the matter vary* ‖ (with 'from') to deviate from e.g. a standard, *this varies from the normal practice* ‖ (*biol.*) to display variation **to vary as** to change in value, amount or quality in direct or indirect proportion to [fr. O.F. *varier*]

VAS (*meteor. acronym*) for visible-infrared spin, a scan radiometer sonde sensor that provides three-dimensional analysis of weather conditions; produced for NASA by Hughes Aircraft Co.

Va·sa (vázǝ) a royal dynasty which ruled in Sweden (1523-1654) and in Poland (1587-1668)

Va·sa·ri (vazári:), Giorgio (1511-74), Italian artist and architect, chiefly famous for his book 'Lives of the Most Eminent Painters, Sculptors and Architects' (1550, 2nd enlarged edition 1568), known as Vasari's 'Lives'

Vasco da Gama *GAMA, VASCO DA

Vas·con·ce·los (vɑskɔnsélɔs), José (1882-1959), Mexican educator, philosopher, writer and politician. As director (1920-4) of the National University of Mexico and minister of education in Obregón's administration, he constructed schools and raised the literacy level. As teacher and philosopher he led the movement which asserted the uniqueness of Latin American culture as a product of a particular racial mixture in a particular physical setting. He lost the presidential election (1929) to Calles and went into exile. His autobiographical work 'Ulises Criollo' (trans. 'Mexican Ulysses') is in four volumes (1935-9). Other works are 'La Raza cósmica' (1925) and 'Indología' (1927)

vas·cu·lar (vǽskjulǝr) *adj.* of, consisting of or containing vessels or ducts adapted for the transmission or circulation of blood, sap etc. [fr. Mod. L. *vascularis* fr. *vasculum*, small vessel]

vascular bundle a group of special plant cells, consisting of vessels and sieve tubes, often in association with parenchyma and sclerenchyma, which may be separated by a band of cambial cells forming a strand of the vascular system

vascular cylinder (*bot.*) the stele

vas·cu·lar·i·ty (vǽskjulǽriti:) *n.* the quality or state of being vascular

vascular ray (*bot.*) a ribbonlike band of parenchyma cells stretching radially through tissues of the vascular cylinder from the xylem to the phloem, serving to store synthesized food material

vascular system the system of a body made up of vascular tissue and, in humans, comprising the heart, arteries, veins etc.

vascular tissue (*bot.*) tissue involved mainly in fluid transport, esp. the tissue of plants including xylem and phloem, through which the sap flows

vas·cu·li·tus (vǽskju:láitis) *n.* (*med.*) inflammation of a vessel, esp. blood, lymph

vas de·fe·rens (vǽsdéfǝrǝnz) *pl.* **va·sa de·fe·ren·ti·a** (véisǝdefǝrénʃi:ǝ) *n.* (*anat.*) the duct that carries sperm from the testicle to the ejaculatory duct of the penis [Mod. L.=the vessel which carries down]

vase (veis, veiz, vaz) *n.* a glass, pottery or metal vessel used as a container for cut flowers or as an ornament [F.]

vas·e·line (vǽsǝli:n, vǽsǝli:n) *n.* petrolatum [fr. vaseline, a trademark, fr. G. *wasser*, water+Gk *elaion*, oil]

va·si·form (véisifɔrm, véizifɔrm) *adj.* shaped like a hollow tube or vase ‖ consisting of a duct [fr. Mod. L. *vasiformis*]

va·so·ac·tive (veizouǽktǝv) *adj.* (*med.*) affecting the expansion or contraction of blood vessels —**vasoactivity** *n.*

vas·o·con·stric·tor (vǽsoukǝnstríktǝr) **1.** *adj.* (*physiol.*) causing constriction of a blood vessel **2.** *n.* a nerve or drug causing such constriction [fr. L. *vas*, vessel+CONSTRICTOR]

vas·o·di·la·tor (vǽsoudailéitǝr, vǽsoudiléitǝr) **1.** *adj.* (*physiol.*) causing dilatation of a blood vessel **2.** *n.* a nerve or drug causing such dilatation [fr. L. *vas*, vessel+DILATOR]

vas·o·mo·tor (vǽsoumóutǝr) *adj.* (*physiol.*) pertaining to the nerves or nerve centers which control the size of the blood vessels, e.g. sympathetic and parasympathetic nerves [fr. L. *vas*, vessel+MOTOR]

vas·sal (vǽs'l) **1.** *n.* (*hist.*) a feudal tenant who vowed obedience to his lord and in return held land under him ‖ (*hist.*) a servant, bondman, slave **2.** *adj.* (*hist.*) of or relating to a vassal ‖ (*rhet.*) subject, *vassal states* [O.F. fr. M.L. fr. Celt.]

vas·sal·age (vǽsǝlidʒ) *n.* (*hist.*) the state of being a vassal ‖ (*rhet.*) servitude, esp. political servitude [O.F.]

Vas·sar College (vǽsǝr) a U.S. private educational institution formerly for women only, now coeducational. It was founded (1861) by Matthew Vassar (1792-1868) near Poughkeepsie, N.Y., as Vassar Female College, and renamed (1867)

vast (vǽst, vast) *adj.* immensely large in area ‖ very great, *a vast improvement* [fr. L. *vastus*, immense]

Väs·ter·ås (vɛ̀stǝróus) a city (pop. 118,100) in Sweden on Lake Mälar. Gothic cathedral (13th c.)

vat (vǽt) **1.** *n.* a large open tub, tank etc., used usually to hold liquids in bulk or in which to dye or steep **2.** *v.t. pres. part.* **vat·ting** *past* and *past part.* **vat·ted** to place or treat in a vat [var. of FAT fr. O.E. *fæt*]

VAT (*abbr.*) for value-added tax

vat dye a dye of a large class rendered soluble in alkalis by reducing them to leuco compounds, and becoming insoluble again by oxidation after fabrics have been steeped in the solution in a vat (e.g. indigo)

Vat·i·can (vǽtikǝn) the pope's palace on the Vatican hill in Rome. Its many buildings, of different dates and styles, begun in 1277 but mainly mid-15th-late 16th cc., include the Sistine Chapel (1473-81, *MICHELANGELO), the Nicholas V chapel decorated by Fra Angelico (1477), great rooms decorated by Raphael (1508-17), galleries of painting, sculpture and archaeology, and the library of about 67,000 manuscripts and half a million books

Vatican City the only surviving Papal State (area 108 acres, pop. 1,000) surrounding the Vatican in Rome, recognized as an independent state by the Lateran Treaty (1929). It has full sovereign rights and powers (army, police force, currency, diplomatic service etc.), under the sovereignty of the pope. It contains the Basilica of St Peter (1506-1629)

Vatican Council the 20th ecumenical council, held in Rome (1869-70), which affirmed papal infallibility (1870) ‖ the 21st ecumenical council, held in Rome (1962-5). It discussed liturgical reform and Christian unity

Vät·tern (vétǝrn) a lake (area 733 sq. miles) in S. Sweden, linked to Lake Vänern and hence to the Baltic by the Göta Canal

Vau·ban (voubã), Sébastien Le Prestre, seigneur de (1633-1707), French military engineer. He fortified France's frontiers, strengthening over 300 old fortresses and building 33 new ones. He developed a devastating siege method based on a system of parallel trenches, and conducted 53 sieges

Vau·cluse (vouklyz) a department in S.E. France (area 1,381 sq. miles, pop. 390,400) (*PROVENCE, *COMTAT-VENAISSIN). Chief town: Avignon

Vaud (vou) a French-speaking, largely Protestant canton (area 1,256 sq. miles, pop. 528,747) of W. Switzerland. Capital: Lausanne

vaud·e·ville (vódǝvil, vóudǝvil, vɔ́dvil, vóudvil) *n.* music-hall variety entertainment [fr. L. *vadere*, to go+*virer* to turn]

Vau·dreuil de Ca·va·gnal (voudrǝ:jdǝkævænjǽl), Pierre François de Rigaud, marquis de (1698-1778), the last governor (1755-60) of New France. In 1760 he surrendered all French Canada to the British

Vaughan (vɔn), Henry (1622-95), Welsh metaphysical poet. His output was small and has more of Herbert's quiet simplicity than of Donne's energy and complexity in it. His collections include 'Silex scintillans' (1650) and 'Thalia rediviva' (1678)

Vaughan Wil·liams (vɔnwíljǝmz), Ralph (1872-1958), British composer. His work springs from his interest in the traditional folk music of Britain, and esp. its characteristic modes, which give his music its tonality. He wrote 9 symphonies, operas, much choral music, orchestral works, hymns, songs and chamber music. He was also a scholar and an arranger of genius, and was active in the publication of much English folk music and the republishing of much English church music

vault (vɔlt) **1.** *v.i.* to project oneself through the air, often over an object or barrier, esp. using one's hands or a pole as a lever to provide the necessary impetus ‖ *v.t.* to project oneself over in this way, *to vault a gate* **2.** *n.* a leap or jump made with the help of the hands or a pole ‖ *POLE VAULT [fr. O.F. *vouter* fr. *voute*, vault]

vault 1. *n.* (*archit.*) an arched construction in masonry forming a roof or decorating or supporting the true roof ‖ a usually arched room, usually underground, esp. a cellar or burial chamber ‖ the fireproof, burglarproof room of a bank ‖ (*rhet.*) a vaultlike space or covering, the *vault of heaven* ‖ (*anat.*) the arched roof of a cavity **2.** *v.t.* to cover with a vault or arched roof structure ‖ to construct as a vault, *a vaulted roof* ‖ *v.i.* to curve in the shape of a vault **vault·ing** *n.* (*archit.*) vaulted work ‖ the art of building vaults [Late M.E. *voute* fr. O.F. *voute, vaulte, vaute*]

vaulting horse a wooden horse or frame used for agility exercises in gymnastics

vaunt (vɔnt, vant) **1.** *v.t.* (*rhet.*) to boast of, to brag about ‖ *v.i.* (*rhet.*) to boast, to brag **2.** *n.* (*rhet.*) a boast [O.F. *vanter*]

Vau·que·lin (vouklɛ̃), Louis Nicolas (1763-1829), French chemist who discovered chromium (1798) and many compounds of beryllium

Vau·ve·nargues (vouvǝnɛrg), Luc de Clapiers, marquis de (1715-47), French writer and moralist best known for his 'Introduction à la connaissance de l'esprit humaine' (1746), characterized by a confident optimism in the human heart and its passions

vav·a·sor, vav·a·sour (vǽvǝsɔr, vǽvǝsour) *n.* a feudal lord of intermediary rank having vassals under him but holding his land under a superior lord or knight [O.F. *vavasour, vavassour* or M.L. *vavassor*]

vav·a·so·ry (vǽvǝsɔri:, vǽvǝsouri:) *pl.* **vav·a·so·ries** *n.* (*hist.*) the lands held by a vavasor ‖ tenure of land by a vavasor

vavasour *VAVASOR

Váz·quez (váskes), Horacio (1860-1936), Dominican general and president of the Republic (1902-3, 1924-30), his second term dating from the departure of the U.S. Marines

Váz·quez de Co·ro·na·do (váθkeθðekɔrɔnáðɔ), Juan (c. 1523-65), Spanish colonial administrator, son of the conquistador Francisco Vázquez de Coronado (1510-50). He was Spain's first governor (adelantado) in that country

V-beam radar (ví:bi:m) (*electr. mil.*) a system for measuring height, distance, and bearing of a target, using two beams of radar, one vertical, the other inclined

VC (*abbr.*) for Vietcong, term for the Communist and insurgent forces in South Vietnam during Vietnam War, 1965–1975

veal (vi:l) *n.* calf's flesh as food [A.F. *vel*, O.F. *veel, veal*]

Veb·len (véblən), Thorstein (1857-1929), U.S. economist and social scientist. He was one of the first to analyze the psychological bases of social institutions. His two most important works are 'The Theory of the Leisure Class' (1899) and 'The Theory of Business Enterprise' (1904)

vec·tor (véktər) *n.* (*math.*) a quantity that is specified by magnitude, direction and sense, that may be represented in some reference systems by an orientated arrowed line segment whose length is a simple function of the magnitude. The displacement, acceleration or velocity of a particle, or the force on a body, are examples of vectors (cf. SCALAR) ‖ (*biol.*) an agent that transmits a pathogen from one organism to another either mechanically as a carrier (e.g. the housefly for typhoid) or biologically, with a role in a life cycle (e.g. the mosquito for the malaria parasite) **vec·to·ri·al** (vektóri:əl, vektúri:əl) *adj.* [L.=carrier]

vector *v.* (*aeronautics*) to direct

vector meson (*particle phys.*) a class of unstable elementary particles (including omega, phi, and rho mesons) with a mass of more than 1,200 million electron volts

vector quantity a vector

vectors, law of *POLYGON LAW OF VECTORS

Ve·da (véidə) any of the four books of the ancient Hindu scripture [fr. Skr. *vēda*, knowledge, sacred book]

Ve·dan·ta (vədántə, vədǽntə) *n.* the orthodox Hindu school of philosophy concerned chiefly with the latter part of the Vedas [Skr. *vēdánta*]

Vedanta Society the Ramakrishna Mission

Ve·dan·tic (vədántik, vədǽntik) *adj.* of or relating to Vedanta

Ve·dan·tism (vədántizəm, vədǽntizəm) *n.* the philosophy of Vedanta

Ve·dan·tist (vədántist, vədǽntist) 1. *n.* someone who professes vedantism 2. *adj.* Vedantic

V. E. Day May 8, 1945, the date of the Allied victory in Europe in the 2nd world war

Ved·da, Ved·dah (védə) *n.* a member of an aboriginal people living in the forests of Ceylon. They are hunters and cave dwellers and practice ancestor worship

ve·dette (vidét) *n.* (*navy*) a small armed vessel used for scouting or escorting ‖ (*mil., hist.*) a mounted sentry in the advance of an army for observing enemy activities [F. fr. Ital.]

Ve·dic (véidik) 1. *n.* the Indic language of the Vedas, Vedic Sanskrit 2. *adj.* of or relating to the Vedas, the language in which they are written etc.

ve·du·tis·ta (veidu:tísta) *n.* (*Italian, veduta,* 'view') cityscape artist, e.g., Piranesi, Panini

veer (viər) 1. *v.i.* (of the wind) to change direction clockwise (opp. BACK) ‖ (of a ship) to turn with the head away from the direction of the wind ‖ to turn gradually or change direction, *then the road veers to the right* ‖ (esp. of a mental attitude, opinion etc.) to change in direction *v.t.* (*naut.*) to change the course of (a vessel) away from the direction of the wind 2. *n.* a change of direction [fr. F. *virer*, to turn]

veer *v.t.* (*naut.*, usually with 'out') to let out (a rope, chain etc.) [M.Du. *vieren*]

veer·y (víəri:) *pl.* **veer·ies** *n. Hylocichla fuscescens*, a very small tawny thrush of E. North America [perh. imit.]

Ve·ga (véigə) the brightest star in the constellation Lyra

Vega, Lope de *LOPE DE VEGA

veg·an (védʒn) *n.* a vegetarian who eats no dairy products. **—veganism** *n.*

veg·e·ta·ble (védʒitəb'l, védʒtəb'l) 1. *n.* a plant (as distinguished from an animal or mineral), esp. an edible plant or an edible part of a plant (e.g. cabbage, lettuce, bean, potato etc.) ‖ a human being who is nonfunctional, either figuratively or literally 2. *adj.* pertaining to, having the nature of, or made from, a plant [O.F.]

vegetable butter any vegetable oil which is solid at ordinary temperatures, e.g. cacao butter

vegetable ivory the endosperm of the ivory nut. It has the appearance of ivory, takes a high polish, and is used esp. for buttons

vegetable marrow the large, tender fruit of *Cucurbita pepo*, fam. *Cucurbitaceae*, cultivated and eaten as a vegetable. It is one of several varieties of summer squash

veg·e·tal (védʒit'l) *adj.* of or relating to vegetation ‖ consisting of or extracted from vegetables ‖ of or relating to growth (e.g. in plants) [fr. L. *vegetare*]

veg·e·tar·i·an (vedʒitéəri:ən) 1. *n.* a person who abstains from eating meat, either keeping strictly to a vegetable and fruit diet, or also eating eggs, milk and butter 2. *adj.* relating to vegetarians or vegetarianism ‖ consisting of vegetables **veg·e·tár·i·an·ism** *n.*

veg·e·tate (védʒiteit) *pres. part.* **veg·e·tat·ing** *past* and *past part.* **veg·e·tat·ed** *v.i.* to grow in the manner of a plant ‖ to live an inactive life without much intellectual stimulus or physical exertion [fr. L. *vegetare* (*vegetatus*), to enliven]

veg·e·ta·tion (vedʒitéifən) *n.* plant life in general, with respect to geographical variation or scenery ‖ the act or process of vegetating ‖ (*med.*) a morbid bodily plantlike or spongelike growth [fr. L.L. and M.L. *vegetatio* (*vegetationis*)]

veg·e·ta·tive (védʒiteitiv) *adj.* of or concerned with vegetation ‖ of growth in plants, as opposed to the reproductive period ‖ having the power to stimulate growth in plants ‖ (*biol.*) of reproduction by bud formation, or by other asexual methods in plants or animals ‖ of a life lived without intellectual stimulus or physical exertion [fr. M.L. *vegetativus*]

veg out (vedʒ) *v.* (*slang*) to become a vegetable

ve·he·mence (ví:əmans) *n.* the state or quality of being vehement **vé·he·men·cy** *n.* vehemence [fr. late O.F. or fr. L. *vehementia*]

ve·he·ment (ví:əmənt) *adj.* violent ‖ showing or arousing intense feeling [fr. O.F. or fr. L. *vehemens* (*vehementis*), violent]

ve·hi·cle (ví:ik'l) *n.* any kind of contrivance, on wheels or runners, used to carry people or goods from one place to another over land (e.g. a carriage, bicycle, sleigh etc.) ‖ a means of transmission, *matter is the vehicle of energy* ‖ a fluid used as a medium for a suspension of a pigment ‖ a substance with which the active agent of a medicine is compounded ‖ any person or thing used as a medium to convey ideas, emotions etc., *a newspaper is a powerful propaganda vehicle* [fr. F. *véhicule* or L. *vehiculum*]

ve·hic·u·lar (vi:híkjulər) *adj.* of or for vehicles ‖ serving as a vehicle [fr. L.L. *vehicularis*]

veil (veil) 1. *n.* a piece of light material draped over the face, worn esp. by many oriental women for modesty and protection from sun and dust ‖ a piece of transparent material used as a hat trimming, sometimes covering the eyes or face ‖ the headdress of a nun, usually covering the head and shoulders ‖ a cover or curtain to hide or protect something (e.g. a veil on a statue or plaque) ‖ a covering ‖ (*fig.*) a cloak, disguise, mask etc., *interference under the veil of friendship* ‖ the calyptra of a moss ‖ a veil **to take the veil** to become a nun 2. *v.t.* to cover or hide with a veil, *mist veiled the valley* ‖ to conceal, disguise etc., *to veil one's intentions* **véil·ing** *n.* material used for veils ‖ an act or instance of covering with a veil or as if with a veil ‖ a veil [A.F. and O.N.F. *veile* and *veil*]

veiling luminance the phenomenon of diffusion of light by water

vein (vein) *n.* one of the tubular vessels with moderately thin walls that carry blood in a steady stream from the capillaries to the heart in vertebrates. The pressure of the blood in the veins is low and because of this they are equipped on the inner walls with cuplike valves to keep the blood from flowing back ‖ (*geol.*) a fissure in rock filled with ore (in most cases deposited there by water) ‖ (*geol.*) a mineral deposit ‖ a specified attitude or mood expressed in speech or writing, *in a jocular vein* ‖ a streak

or stripe in wood, marble etc. of a different shade or color or texture from the rest ‖ (*biol.*) a rib in a leaf or insect's wing **veined** *adj.* having veins ‖ marked with veins **véin·ing** *n.* a pattern of veins, e.g. in marble [O.F. *veine*]

ve·la·men (vəléimən) *pl.* **ve·lam·i·na** (vəlǽminə) *n.* (*anat.*) a membrane, esp. one covering parts of the brain ‖ (*bot.*) a specialized moisture-absorbing tissue at the apex of the aerial roots of epiphytic orchids [L.=a covering]

ve·lar (ví:lər) *adj.* of a velum, esp. of the soft palate of the mouth ‖ (*phon.*, of a sound) formed with the back of the tongue against the soft palate [fr. L. *velaris* fr. *velum*, a sail]

Ve·las·co I·bar·ra (vəláskɔi:bárra), José María (1893-1979), five times (1934-5, 1944-7, 1952-6, 1960-1, 1968-72) the elected president of Ecuador. A demagogue without party or program, he was three times deposed as a result of political and economic chaos and his unpopular austerity measures. He resigned (1970) for the fourth time, but the military persuaded him to accept dictatorial powers. He shut down the universities, dissolved Congress, and ranged himself against the Supreme Court. He was overthrown (1972) by an army coup d'état and replaced by Brig. Gen. Guillermo Rodriguez Lara

ve·late (ví:lit, ví:leit) *adj.* (*biol.*) having a veil or velum [fr. L. *velum* or fr. L. *velare* (*velatus*), to cover]

Ve·laz·quez (vəlǽskiz, veláθkeθ), Diego Rodriguez de Silva y (1599-1660), Spanish painter. Philip IV was his patron and many of his finest portraits were of the royal family and the court, including dwarfs and jesters. Velazquez was early influenced by Caravaggio's 'realism' and chiaroscuro. A whole range of paintings is devoted to Spanish domestic life, in subtle color schemes of warm brown, gray and cream. They are pictures of acceptance, dignity and harmony. In contrast with them are the court portraits, where cardinal red and royal purple take the place of brown sackcloth, and the character of the noble sitter is rendered with sometimes terrifying perception. The speed and economy of Velazquez's brushwork, and his ability to capture surface and light with techniques which seem to disappear on close inspection, made him a powerful influence on French Impressionism

Ve·láz·quez de Cué·llar (veláθkeθðekwéjar), Diego de (1465-1524), Spanish conquistador. With Pánfilo de Narváez he led (1511) an expedition to Cuba and by 1514 the island was conquered. As Cuba's first governor (1514-21, 1523-4), he founded (1514) Santiago and (1519) Havana. He organized four expeditions to Mexico

Vel·cro (vélkrou) *n.* trade name for fabric created with hooked surface to adhere to other fabrics, sometimes in lieu of fasteners

veld, veldt (velt) *n.* open grassland in S. Africa, esp. the flat, treeless country of the Transvaal plateau [Du. *veld*, a field]

vel·le·i·ty (velí:iti:) *pl.* **vel·le·i·ties** *n.* a weak desire or resolution, esp. one so weak that it does not lead to action [fr. F. *velléité* or M.L. *velleitas*]

Vel·lore (velɔ́r, velóur) an agricultural center (pop. 114,000) in N. Madras, India: temple (14th c.), fortress (17th c.)

vel·lum (véləm) *n.* a fine parchment made from specially treated calfskin etc. and used for writing on or for binding books ‖ a manuscript written on this [O.F. *velin*]

vellum paper imitation vellum, esp. for letter writing

ve·loc·im·e·ter (vi:lousímətə:r) *n.* a device that uses the Doppler effect and its echo to measure sound velocity in water, e.g., sound, machinery

ve·loc·i·pede (vəlósəpi:d) *n.* (*hist.*) an early form of bicycle or tricycle propelled by thrusts of the feet against pedals [fr. F. *vélocipède*]

ve·loc·i·ty (vəlósiti:) *pl.* **ve·loc·i·ties** *n.* rate of motion ‖ (*phys.*) the time rate of change of a displacement vector, being a vector parallel to the displacement vector ‖ (*chem.*) the rate of disappearance of the reactants or of the appearance of products in a chemical reaction [fr. F. *vélocité* or fr. L. *velocitas*]

velocity of escape *ESCAPE VELOCITY

velocity ratio the ratio of the displacement of any part of a machine to that of the driving part in the same time

vel·o·drome (véladroum) *n.* a building or sta-

CONCISE PRONUNCIATION KEY: (a) æ, c*a*t; ɑ, c*a*r; ɔ f*aw*n; ei, sn*a*ke. **(e)** e, h*e*n; i:, sh*ee*p; iə, d*ee*r; ɛə, b*ea*r. **(i)** i, f*i*sh; ai, t*i*ger; ə:, b*i*rd. **(o)** o, *o*x; au, c*ow*; ou, g*oa*t; u, p*oo*r; ɔi, r*oy*al. **(u)** ʌ, d*u*ck; u, b*u*ll; u:, g*oo*se; ə, b*a*cill*u*s; ju:, c*u*be. x, lo*ch*; θ, *th*ink; ð, bo*th*er; z, *Z*en; ʒ, cor*s*age. d*ʒ*, sava*ge*; ŋ, ora*ng*utan*g*; j, *y*ak; ʃ, *fi*sh; tʃ, fe*tch*; 'l, rabb*le*; 'n, redd*en*. Complete pronunciation key appears inside front cover.

dium with a specially designed track for cycle racing [F. *vélodrome*]

ve·lour, ve·lours (vəlúər) pl. **ve·lours** (vəlúərz) n. a velvetlike woven fabric ‖ a fur felt used for hats [F.+velvet]

ve·lum (víːləm) pl. **ve·la** (víːlə) n. (biol.) a membrane, esp. the soft palate of the mouth [L.=sail, covering]

ve·lu·ti·nous (vəlúːtʼnəs) adj. (biol.) velvety, covered with very fine, short, upright hairs [fr. Mod. L. *velutiniis* fr. M.L. *velutum*, velvet]

vel·vet (vélvít) 1. n. a closely woven fabric, esp. one wholly or partly of silk, with a short, soft nap or pile on one side ‖ something resembling this, e.g. in softness ‖ the furry skin covering the growing antlers of deer 2. adj. made of or covered with velvet ‖ like velvet [fr. M.L. *velvetum*]

vel·vet·een (vélvitíːn) n. cotton material woven with a short pile

vel·vet·y (vélvitiː) adj. soft and smooth to the touch, the palate or the ear etc.

ve·nal (víːnʼl) adj. mercenary, esp. open to bribery and corruption ‖ involving mercenary motives or corruption [fr. L. *venalis*]

ve·nal·i·ty (viːnǽliti:) n. the state or quality of being venal [fr. F. *vénalité* or L. L. *venalitas*]

ve·na·tion (viːnéiʃən, vənéiʃən) n. the system or arrangement of veins on leaves and insects' wings [fr. L. *vena*, vein]

vend (vend) v.t. (esp. law) to sell, offer for sale

vend·ee (vendíː) n. (law) the person to whom an object is sold [fr. F. *vendre* or L. *vendere*, to sell]

Ven·dée (vādei) a department (area 2,690 sq. miles, pop. 450,600) in W. France (*POITOU). Chief town: La Roche-sur-Yon (pop. 48,053). The Vendée was the center of a royalist uprising (1793-6) against the 1st French republic

Ven·dô·miaire (vādeimjɔ̃ːr) n. (F. hist.) the 1st month of the French Revolutionary calendar ‖ the Paris royalist insurrection of 13 Vendémiaire (Oct. 5, 1795), crushed by Barras and Napoleon with a 'whiff of grapeshot'

ven·det·ta (vendétə) n. a blood feud, laying an obligation of honor on the members of a family to take revenge upon the killer or injurer of one of them, or upon a member of his family, thus instigating a chain of vengeance from generation to generation [Ital.]

vending machine an automatic coin-operated machine from which goods (candies, cigarettes etc.) can be obtained

ven·dor (véndər, vendɔ́r) n. a person who sells, esp. one who hawks his goods in a public place

ve·neer (vəníər) 1. v.t. to cover (a surface of wood) with a thin coating of a finer wood ‖ to bond together (layers of wood) to form plywood 2. n. a thin layer of fine wood laid over the surface of a cheaper wood and used in cabinetmaking ‖ any of the thin layers bonded together to form plywood ‖ any refined outer covering concealing a coarse structure ‖ a superficial show, *a veneer of charm* **ve·neer·ing** (vəníəriŋ) n. a thin layer of material for plywood etc. ‖ the process of applying a veneer to wood [fr. G. *furnieren* fr. F.]

venepuncture *VENIPUNCTURE

ven·er·a·bil·i·ty (venərəbíliti:) n. the state or quality of being venerable

ven·er·a·ble (vénərəbʼl) adj. deserving or evoking profound respect and veneration on account of age, probity, intellectual power, or (of objects and places) historical or religious associations ‖ (*Anglican Communion*) used as a courtesy title of an archdeacon ‖ (*Roman Catholicism*) used as a title given to those judged to have attained the first of three degrees of sanctity (cf. BLESSED, cf. SAINT) **vén·er·a·bly** adv. [fr. L. *venerabilis*]

ven·er·ate (vénəreit) pres. part. **ven·er·at·ing** past and past part. **ven·er·at·ed** v.t. to regard with the deepest respect or reverence ‖ to worship as holy **ven·er·a·tion, vén·er·a·tor** ns [fr. L. *venerari* (*veneratus*), to worship]

ve·ne·re·al (vəníəriːəl) adj. (of disease) contracted by sexual intercourse (*GONORRHEA, *SYPHILIS) ‖ having or relating to venereal disease ‖ (*rhet.*) of or relating to sexual activity [fr. L. *venereus* fr. *Venus* (*veneris*), goddess of love]

ven·er·y (vénəri:) n. (hist.) the sport of hunting with hounds [O.F. *venerie*]

venery n. (rhet.) the practice or pursuit of sexual pleasure [fr. L. *Venus* (*Veneris*), the goddess of love]

Ve·ne·tian (vəníːʃən) 1. n. a native or inhabitant of Venice 2. adj. of or relating to Venice

Venetian blind a window covering constructed of thin horizontal slats of wood, plastic etc. held together by vertical tapes in such a way that they can be turned, lowered or raised to admit or exclude light

Venetian glass decorative glassware made at Murano in the Venice lagoon (since the 13th c.)

Venetian School a school of painters in Venice in the 15th and 16th cc. including notably the Bellini brothers, Carpaccio, Giorgione, Titian, Tintoretto and Veronese

Ve·ne·to (vénətɔ) a region (area 9,858 sq. miles, pop. 4,355,049) of N.E. Italy in the Dolomites and the N. Italian plain. Chief towns: Venice, Verona. Agriculture: (30% irrigated) cereals, sugar beets, fruit, vines, silk. Industries: sugar refining, oil refining, metallurgy, textiles. It formed part of Lombardy-Venetia (1815-66)

Ven·e·zue·la (venəzwéilə) a republic (area 352,143 sq. miles, pop. 17,993,000) in N. South America. Capital: Caracas. People: 70% mestizo, 20% European stock, small Indian, African and mulatto minorities. Language: Spanish. Religion: Roman Catholic. The land is 3% arable, 16% pasture and 20% forest. In the West, separated by the Maracaibo basin (the country's great oil field) are the northernmost chains of the Andes, the Sierra de Perija on the Colombian border and the Sierra de Merida (to 16,000 ft) extended in the coast ranges. The lengthwise valley, which divides the latter (and in which Caracas lies), is the chief agricultural region. The lower Andean slopes and, progressively, the savanna lowlands (traditionally grazing land) of the Orinoco basin are also cultivated. The southeast is occupied by the largely unexplored Guiana highlands (rain forest), rising to 8,260 ft. Venezuela includes 72 islands in the Caribbean. Average temperatures (F.): Caracas 69°, coast and interior 80°. Rainfall: coast and coast ranges 20-40 ins, interior 40-80 ins (rainy season: Apr.-Dec.). Livestock: cattle, hogs. Agricultural products: coffee, corn, rice, cotton, cocoa, sugarcane, wheat, tobacco, beans, sisal, rubber, divi-divi, copaiba, vanilla, dairy products, potatoes, bananas. Mineral resources: petroleum (second world producer), iron ore, coal, gold, natural gas, diamonds, manganese, phosphate, sulfur, nickel, salt, asbestos, copper. Manufactures and industries: petroleum products, steel, foodstuffs, textiles, cement, tires, clothing, footwear, lumber, leather, hydroelectricity, fishing. Exports: petroleum and petroleum products, iron ore, coffee, cocoa. Imports: chemicals, machinery, manufactured goods, vehicles, foodstuffs, metals. Chief ports: La Guaira (for Caracas), Maracaibo. Universities: Caracas (3), Mérida, Maracaibo, Carabobo, Oriente. Monetary unit: bolívar (100 centimos). HISTORY. Columbus discovered the mouth of the Orinoco (1498), and Ojeda and Vespucci explored the coast (1499). Despite attacks by the native Carib Indians, Spanish settlements were made (1520s). Emperor Charles V leased the colony to a German merchant family until 1546. The coast formed part of the Spanish Main and was a center of piracy and smuggling (16th and 17th cc.). Venezuela was joined to the Spanish viceroyalty of New Granada (*COLOMBIA), revolted (1810) under Miranda and declared itself independent (July 5, 1811). Fighting continued until Bolívar incorporated Venezuela in Greater Colombia (1819). It became a separate state (1830). A boundary dispute with British Guiana (1895-6) provoked considerable tension between Britain and the U.S.A. Venezuela's political history has been punctuated by civil wars, revolts and military coups. The state was almost bankrupt in the late 19th c. but the exploitation of oil helped to restore solvency (early 20th c.) and the bolívar had become (late 1960s) South America's most stable currency. Modern Venezuela may be said to date from 1936, following the death (1935) of the patriarchal dictator Juan Vicente Gómez. The military junta under Rómulo Betancourt (1945-7) was followed by the first constitutionally elected president, Rómulo Gallegos (1948). A military coup d'état overthrew his government and installed the dictatorship (1953-8) of Marcos Pérez Jiménez. In the elections of 1958, Betancourt, founder of the Democratic Action (AD) party, was constitutionally elected. He supported friendly U.S.-Venezuelan relations and American investments and he implemented moderate agrarian

reform and industrial development. The elections of 1963 were won by his AD lieutenant Raúl Leoni, who continued his programs. As a result of three fissions in the AD, the party lost the elections of 1968 to the Social Christian party (COPEI) under Rafael Caldera. Succeeding elections put Carlos Andrés Pérez (AD), Louis Herrera Campíns (COPEI), and Jaime Lusinchi (AD) into the presidency

Venezuela, Gulf of a gulf in N.W. Venezuela, between the Guajira peninsula in Colombia and the Paraguaná peninsula in Venezuela

Ven·e·zue·lan (venəzwéilən) 1. n. a native or inhabitant of Venezuela 2. adj. of or relating to Venezuela

venge·ance (véndʒəns) n. damage or harm done to another in retaliation for damage or harm to oneself or an associate **with a vengeance** intensively, to a degree much greater than might be expected, *he has cleaned up the organization with a vengeance* [O.F.]

venge·ful (véndʒfəl) adj. disposed to acts of vengeance ‖ vindictive [fr. older *venge*, to avenge]

ve·nial (víːnjəl, víːniːəl) adj. pardonable, *a venial offense* ‖ (*Roman Catholicism*, of a sin) minor in gravity or committed heedlessly (cf. MORTAL) **ve·nial·i·ty** (viːnjǽliti:, viːniːǽliti:) n. [O.F. or fr. L. *venialis*]

Ven·ice (vénis) (*Ital.* Venezia) a port (pop. 360,300) in Veneto, Italy, built on islands (cut by over 100 canals and linked by some 400 bridges) in a lagoon of the Adriatic. Industries (confined to the suburbs): oil refining, metallurgical and chemical industries, shipbuilding, glass and jewelry manufacture. The Grand Canal, lined with palaces (mainly 15th c.) and crossed by the Rialto bridge (1590), divides the city. The eastern, older part centers on San Marco Basilica (Byzantine, 11th c.) and the Doges' Palace (Gothic, 14th-15th cc.). There are Gothic, Renaissance and baroque churches, a university (1868), and museums (works of the Venetian School etc.). The town grew during the barbarian and Lombard invasions of Italy, and was united (697) under one leader, the doge. It became an independent republic, gained control of the Adriatic, and prospered under a merchant aristocracy. Venice used the Crusades to extend its trade through the Levant and into the Black Sea, defeating (1380) Genoa, its main commercial rival. By the mid-15th c. it had conquered the Dalmatian coast, Euboea, Crete and Cyprus, as well as a wide area of N.E. Italy, but its prosperity suffered from Turkish competition (late 15th c.) in the eastern Mediterranean, and the discovery (end of the 16th c.) of the Cape route to India. Venice remained important for its schools of painting (15th and 16th cc.) and music (17th and 18th cc.). After the Napoleonic Wars, Venice was placed (1815) under Austrian rule, which a revolution (1848) failed to shake off. Venice joined Italy (1866) after the Seven Weeks' War

ven·i·punc·ture, ven·e·punc·ture (víːnəpʌŋktʃər, vénəpʌŋktʃər) n. (med.) insertion of a hollow needle into a vein, either to take a blood test or to give an injection [fr. L. *vena*, vein+PUNCTURE]

ven·i·son (vénis,n, véniz,n, Br. vénzən) n. the flesh of deer as food [A.F. and O.F.]

Ve·ni·zé·los (venəzéiləs), Eleuthérios (1864-1936), Greek politician, prime minister (1910-15, 1917-20, 1924, 1928-32). Born on the island of Crete, he worked for the union of Crete with Greece, a union proclaimed in 1905 but not realized until 1913. He went to Greece (1909) and became the Liberal party leader, then prime minister (1910). During the Bakan Wars (1912-13) he helped defeat the Turks and almost doubled Greece's territory. He favored Britain and France in the 1st world war and resigned as prime minister (1915) because Greece's pro-German King Constantine advocated continuing neutrality. He returned to Athens (1917) as prime minister on the abdication of Constantine. Greece then entered the war on the Allied side. Venizélos acquired considerable territory for Greece, principally at Turkey's expense, following the war. He fled Greece (1935) after being implicated in an anti-monarchist revolt and died in exile in Paris

ven·om (vénəm) n. the poisonous fluid secreted by certain snakes, spiders, insects etc. and transmitted by bite or sting ‖ spite, malice, in character, speech or behavior [A.F. and O.F. *venim*, var. of *venin*]

ven·om·ous (vénəməs) *adj.* poisonous, containing venom ‖ malicious, spiteful ‖ having a poison gland or glands [O.F. *venimeux*]

ve·nose (vi:nous) *adj.* (*bot.*) venous

ve·nos·i·ty (ví:nɒsiti:) *n.* the state or quality of being venous or venose

ve·nous (ví:nəs) *adj.* (*physiol.*) of a vein or veins ‖ (*bot.*) having veins ‖ (*physiol.*, of blood) being carried in the veins back to the heart after circulating in the body [fr. L. *venosus*]

vent (vent) **1.** *n.* a small aperture designed to provide an outlet from a confined space or an inlet into it, e.g. the bunghole of a barrel ‖ a channel of release e.g. for energy etc. ‖ the anus, esp. the anal aperture of lower vertebrates **2.** *v.t.* to make an aperture in ‖ to relieve (one's feelings) in words or actions, *to vent one's anger on someone* [fr. F. *vent*, wind and F. *évent*, a vent]

vent *n.* a tailored slit, esp. one in the back of a coat [var. of older *fent* fr. F. *fente*, slit]

ven·ter (véntər) *n.* (*bot.*) the swollen base of an archegonium ‖ (*zool.*, of vertebrates) the abdomen ‖ a protuberance, e.g. of muscle, on that concavity in a bone ‖ (*law*) the womb ‖ (*law*) a wife as the mother of a man's children [A.F. *ventre*, *venter* or L. *venter*, womb]

ven·ti·late (véntəleit) *pres. part.* **ven·ti·lat·ing** *past* and *past part.* **ven·ti·lat·ed** *v.t.* to cause the passage of air into or through ‖ to expose to the air so as to freshen ‖ to furnish with an opening for the escape of air, gas etc. ‖ to give full and free expression to (a grievance, controversy etc.) [fr. L. *ventilare* (*ventilatus*), to fan]

ven·ti·la·tion (ventəléiʃən) *n.* a ventilating or being ventilated ‖ a system for ensuring the circulation of fresh air in a room, building or other confined space [fr. L. *ventilatio* (*ventilationis*)]

ven·ti·la·tor (véntəleitər) *n.* a contrivance for ensuring the free passage of air in an enclosed space

ven·tral (véntrəl) *adj.* (*anat.*) of or relating to the lower or abdominal surfaces, in human anatomy sometimes anterior (opp. DORSAL) ‖ (*bot.*) of or relating to the lower surface [F. or fr. L. *ventralis*]

ven·tri·cle (véntrik'l) *n.* a cavity or chamber of the body, esp. in the heart ‖ the main contractile chamber or either of the two chambers connecting the auricles and the arteries ‖ a cavity in the brain's system of communicating cavities [F. *ventricule* or fr. L. *ventriculus*]

ven·tri·cose (véntrikous) *adj.* (*biol.*) swelling out in the middle or to one side [fr. Mod. L. *ventricosus*]

ven·tric·u·lar (ventríkjulər) *adj.* of or like a ventricle ‖ abdominal [L. *ventriculus*]

ven·tri·lo·qui·al (ventrəlóukwi:əl) *adj.* of, belonging to, or using ventriloquism

ven·tril·o·quism (ventríləkwizəm) *n.* utterance which makes hearers think that the sound comes from a source other than the actual speaker

ven·tril·o·quist (ventríləkwist) *n.* someone who practices the art of ventriloquism, esp. an entertainer **ven·tril·o·quis·tic** *adj.*

ven·tril·o·quize (ventríləkwaiz) *pres. part.* **ven·tril·o·quiz·ing** *past* and *past part.* **ven·tril·o·quized** *v.i.* to act as a ventriloquist ‖ *v.t.* to utter (sounds) as a ventriloquist

ven·tril·o·quy (ventríləkwi:) *n.* ventriloquism [fr. M.L. or Mod. L. *ventriloquium*]

Ven·tris (véntris), Michael George Francis (1922-56), British architect. He deciphered (1953) the Linear B script of Minoan civilization, showing it to be an early form of Greek

ven·ture (véntʃər) **1.** *n.* something involving a risk which one decides to attempt **at a venture** as a guess, without real calculation **2.** *v. pres. part.* **ven·tur·ing** *past* and *past part.* **ven·tured** *v.t.* to risk, dare ‖ to venture an opinion ‖ *v.i.* to take a risk **vén·ture·some** *adj.* [fr. older *aventure*, adventure]

Ven·tu·ri (ventú:ri:) *n.* a Venturi meter

Venturi meter a device to determine fluid flow, e.g. in a pipeline, or in measuring airspeed, that measures the pressure drop at a constriction in a tube [after G. B. *Venturi* (1746–1822), Ital. physicist]

Venturi tube a Venturi meter

ven·tur·ous (véntʃərəs) *adj.* prepared to face danger, take risks etc. ‖ attended with risk or danger [aphetic var. of ADVENTUROUS]

ven·ue (vénju:, vénu:) *n.* the scene or area of an action, esp. of a crime ‖ (*law*) the area within which the original proceedings in a trial are held, and the jury is gathered **to change the venue** (*law*) to remove the legal proceedings

from the area where originally brought (so as to avoid prejudice, riot etc. or for the convenience of the parties or witnesses) ‖ (*Br.*) an appointed meeting place, point of assembly [O.F.=a coming]

Ve·nus (ví:nəs) (*Rom. mythol.*) the goddess of beauty and love, identified with the Greek Aphrodite ‖ the second planet from the sun (mean orbital diameter=67 million miles), roughly comparable to the earth in mass and size (mass=4.81 x 10^{21} tons, diameter=7,550 miles). Venus revolves around the sun with a sidereal period of 224.7 earth days and appears to have a rotation period of 117 earth days (the planet's atmosphere turning with an independent retrograde motion in only 4 earth days). Its atmosphere, containing a yellowish cloud blanket, is composed of carbon dioxide with 4% nitrogen, 0.5% oxygen and traces of water vapor. Temperature in the ground is about 890°F. and pressure about 90 atmospheres. Pioneer Venus I has been orbiting the planet since 1978, and other spacecraft observations have been made by U.S. Mariner and Soviet Venera landers

Venus probe *n.* (*aerospace*) 1978 mission to explore Venus, made by U.S. Pioneer and Mariner and U.S.S.R. Venera

Ve·nus's-flow·er-bas·ket (ví:nəsəsfláuərbæskit, ví:nəsəsfláuərbɑskit) *n.* a member of *Euplectella*, a glass sponge inhabiting deep waters off the Philippines. The dried skeletons, made of lacy siliceous spicules, are of great beauty

Ve·nus's-fly·trap (ví:nəsəsfláitræp) *n. Dionaea muscipula*, fam. *Droseraceae*, an insectivorous plant native to North and South Carolina

Venus's looking-glass a plant of the genus *Specularia*, esp. *S. speculum-veneris*

ve·ra·cious (vəréiʃəs) *adj.* truthful, speaking the truth as a matter of course ‖ true, accurate [fr. L. *verax* (*veracis*), truthful]

ve·rac·i·ty (vərǽsiti:) *pl.* **ve·rac·i·ties** *n.* the quality of telling the truth ‖ the quality of being true ‖ something true [F. *véracité* or M.L. *veracitas*]

Ver·a·cruz (verəkrú:z) a central gulf state (area 27,759 sq. miles, pop. 5,091,000) of Mexico. Capital: Jalapa (pop. 72,000). The land varies from the tropical lowlands of its 50-mile coastline to the central plateau region of the interior, cut into rich forested valleys. Its wealth is based on commerce (over 40 rivers cross the state), agriculture (cotton, sugar, rum, pineapples, tobacco, cacao, vanilla, and various fruits), and manufacturing (cotton and other textiles). Under a massive reclamation project (1950s) three dams were built to provide hydroelectric power, and modern farm methods were introduced. There are important archaeological remains

Veracruz a port (pop. 340,500) in E. Mexico. Industries: food and tobacco processing, tanning. Colonial fortresses and church. Founded (1519) by Cortes, the city prospered as the chief link between New Spain and Cádiz, though vulnerable to piracy. It was captured by the French in 1838, by the Americans under Winfield Scott in 1847, by the French in 1861, and by a U.S. force under Admiral Mayo in 1914, when President Wilson intervened to prevent foreign supplies from reaching Gen. Victoriano Huerta during the Mexican revolution

Ver·a Cruz (vérəkrú:z) the original name given to Brazil by the Portuguese

ve·ran·da, ve·ran·dah (vərǽndə) *n.* an open, roofed portico or gallery extending along a side of a house [fr. Port. *varanda* fr. Hind.] .

verb (və:rb) *n.* (*gram.*) any of a class of words expressing an action performed or state suffered or experienced by a subject [O.F. *verbe* or fr. L. *verbum*, word, verb]

ver·bal (vá:rb'l) *adj.* relating to or consisting of words, *verbal dexterity* ‖ oral, spoken, not written, *a verbal message* ‖ (of translation) literal, word for word ‖ (*gram.*) relating to or derived from a verb ‖ (*gram.*) used to form verbs **vér·bal·ism** *n.* a verbal expression ‖ the use of words which sound well but have little content in reality, or an instance of this [O.F. or fr. L. *verbalis*, consisting of words]

ver·bal·ize (vá:rb'laiz) *pres. part.* **ver·bal·iz·ing** *past* and *past part.* **ver·bal·ized** *v.i.* to be verbose ‖ *v.t.* to express in words ‖ to convert (another part of speech) into the form of a verb [F. *verbaliser*]

ver·bal·ly (vá:rb'li:) *adv.* in words, esp. in spoken words

verbal noun a noun derived from a verb and having some of the characteristics of a verb. In English it is either a noun ending in '-ing' or an infinitive (e.g. 'reading' in 'reading is fun', or 'to read' in 'to read is fun')

ver·bas·cum (vərbǽskəm) *n.* mullein [L.]

ver·ba·tim (vərbéitim) **1.** *adv.* word for word, exactly as spoken or written **2.** *adj.* copied exactly from the original word-for-word [M.L.]

ver·be·na (vərbí:nə) *n.* a member of *Verbena*, fam. *Verbenaceae*, a genus of plants mainly of tropical America. Several varieties are widely cultivated as garden plants for their showy, sweet-smelling flowers (*VERVAIN) [M.L. and Mod. L.]

ver·bi·age (vá:rbi:idʒ) *n.* the use of more words than are needed [F.]

verb·i·cide (və:rbəsaid) *n.* inflation of word meanings with use of large-scale modifiers and avoidance in precision, e.g., excessive use of 'very,' 'really,' 'unbelievable,' etc.

ver·bose (vərbóus) *adj.* employing or containing more words than are necessary [fr. L. *verbosus*]

ver·bos·i·ty (vərbósiti:) *n.* the state or quality of being verbose [F. *verbosité* or fr. postclassical L. *verbositas*]

Ver·cin·get·o·rix (və:rsindʒétəriks) (d. 46 B.C.), Gallic chieftain. He was the leader of an unsuccessful Gallic revolt (52 B.C.) against the Romans under Caesar. He graced Caesar's triumph in Rome and was then put to death

Ver·da·guer (verdɑgér), Mosen Jacinto (1845-1902), Catalan poet. One of his most intensely patriotic epics, 'La Atlántida' (1877), was set to music, in part, by Falla

ver·dan·cy (vá:rd'nsi:) *n.* the state or quality of being verdant

ver·dant (vá:rd'nt) *adj.* (esp. of vegetation) very green or fresh ‖ (*rhet.*) immature, inexperienced, *verdant youth* [prob. fr. VERDURE]

Ver·di (véərdi:), Giuseppi Fortunino Francesco (1813-1901), Italian composer. 'Nabucodonosor' (1842) was his first popular opera but he reached his peak with 'Rigoletto' (1851), 'Il Trovatore' (1853) and 'La Traviata' (1853). In his last period, ushered in by 'Aïda' (1871), Verdi forsook melodrama and his noblest operas, e.g. 'Otello' (1887), and his comic opera 'Falstaff' (1893), contain few set arias. The seamless vocal line is intensely dramatic and expressive. His whole gift issued in sounds uniquely adapted to the open-throated Italian voice, expressing through this, with orchestral and dramatic genius, a passionate involvement in human conflicts. In addition to the operas Verdi wrote a dramatic 'Requiem' (1874)

ver·dict (vá:rdikt) *n.* (*law*) the decision of a jury after hearing evidence in a case of civil or criminal law ‖ a considered judgment after examination of evidence [A. F. *verdit*]

ver·di·gris (vá:rdigris, vá:rdigri:s) *n.* a green or greenish-blue crystalline substance formed on copper, brass or bronze, consisting of basic copper carbonate or copper sulfate or both ‖ a green or greenish-blue poisonous substance obtained from treating copper with acetic acid and used as a pigment [A.F. and O.F. *vert de Grece*, *vert-de-gris*, green of Greece]

Ver·dun (verdœ̃, ve:rdʌn) a town (pop. 23,621) in Meuse department, France, on the Meuse. Romanesque-Gothic cathedral (11th-13th cc.). In the 1st world war, Pétain held it against a massive German offensive in a battle (Feb. 21-Dec. 15, 1916) in which more than a million men were killed

Verdun, Treaty of a treaty (843) among the three sons of Emperor Louis I, dividing up Charlemagne's empire. Louis II 'the German' received the eastern part, Charles II 'the Bald' the western part and Lothair I the center and the Imperial crown

ver·dure (vá:rdʒər) *n.* the greenness of fresh vegetation ‖ green vegetation [O.F.]

Ve·ree·ni·ging (fərí:niɡiŋ) a coal-mining center (pop. 79,000) in Transvaal, South Africa, on the Vaal. The treaty ending the Boer War was signed here (1902)

verge (və:rdʒ) *pres. part.* **verg·ing** *past* and *past part.* **verged** *v.i.* to tend towards a certain direction, *the road verges eastward, his policies verge increasingly to the Left* [fr. L. *vergere*, to bend, turn]

verge 1. *n.* a border, edge ‖ the imaginary line at which a new condition or action starts, *on the verge of madness, on the verge of jumping* ‖ the grass border of a road, flower bed, path etc. ‖ a rod or staff carried before a dignitary as a symbol of authority ‖ (*archit.*) the shaft of a column ‖ (*archit.*) an edge of tiling projecting over a gable ‖ (*horology*) the spindle of a watch balance ‖ (*Br. hist.*) the 12-mile area around the king's court delimited as subject to the Lord High Steward's jurisdiction **2.** *v.i. pres. part.* **verg·ing** *past* and *past part.* **verged** (with 'on') to come near to being something specified, *this remark verges on libel* [O.F.]

Ver·gennes (vəˈrʒen), Charles Gravier, comte de (1717-87), French statesman. As foreign minister (1774-86) he supported the American colonies in their revolt against British rule

verg·er (vəˈrdʒər) *n.* a church official who directs the congregation to their seats in a church, and has the general care of the church's interior ‖ (*Br.*) a beadle employed to carry a verge before certain dignitaries [prob. fr. A.F.]

Vergilian *VIRGILIAN

Ver·gil, Vir·gil (vəˈrdʒil), Polydore (c. 1475-1555), English historian and humanist, born in Italy. Under the patronage of Henry VII he wrote 'Historiae Anglicae libri XXVI' (1534), a history of England based on a critical study of documents and much used by later writers

Vergil (Publius Vergilius Maro) *VIRGIL

Ver·gniaud (vernjou), Pierre Victurnien (1753-93), French revolutionist. He was a leader of the Girondists, and one of the greatest orators of the French Revolution

Ver·hae·ren (vereiren), Emile (1855-1916), Belgian lyric poet writing in French. He belonged to the Symbolist school

ver·i·fi·a·ble (vérifaiəb'l) *adj.* able to be verified

ver·i·fi·ca·tion (verifikéiʃən) *n.* a verifying or being verified [O.F. *verificacion*]

ver·i·fy (vérifai) *pres. part.* **ver·i·fy·ing** *past* and *past part.* **ver·i·fied** *v.t.* to confirm, or test, the truth or accuracy of ‖ to cause the truth of (something) to be perceived (usually in passive constructions) ‖ (*law*) to affirm, at the end of a pleading, the truth of (matters alleged in the pleading) ‖ (*law*) to substantiate by proofs [fr. O.F. *verifier*]

ver·i·ly (vérili) *adv.* (*archaic*) in truth

ver·i·si·mil·i·tude (verisimílitu:d, verisimílitju:d) *n.* the quality, in a work of the imagination, of seeming to be true, either by reference to the external world of reality or by reference solely to the artist's canons of truth for his imagined world ‖ an apparent truth [fr. L. *verisimilitudo*]

ve·ris·mo (veirí:zmou) *n.* use of ordinary material in the arts in preference to classic or historic material, esp. in opera —**verist** *adj.* — **verist** *n.* —**veristic** *adj.*

Ve·rís·si·mo (verí:si:mɔ), Erico Lopes (1905-75), Brazilian novelist, author of 'Gato prêto em campo de neve' (1941) and 'O senhor embaixador' (1965)

ver·i·ta·ble (véritəb'l) *adj.* real, genuine, authentic (often loosely and merely as an intensive), *a veritable mountain of a man* **vér·i·ta·bly** *adv.* [fr. O.F. and A.F.]

ver·i·ty (vériti:) *pl.* **ver·i·ties** *n.* truth ‖ a basic truth of religion or ethics etc. [A.F. and O.F. *verite, veritet*]

ver·juice (vəˈrdʒu:s) *n.* the sour juice extracted from unripe fruit (esp. grapes and crab apples), formerly used in cooking [O.F. *verjus*]

Ver·kho·yansk (vəˈrkoujænsk, *Russ.* verxʌjánsk) a mining town (pop. 10,000) in the Yakut A.S.S.R., U.S.S.R., in E. Siberia, reputed to have the lowest recorded temperature (-94°F.) in the northern hemisphere

ver·kramp·te (fɛərkrámptə) *n.* (narrow-minded ones) member of right-wing faction of the Republic of South Africa's National Party

Ver·laine (verlen), Paul (1844-96), French poet. He is generally considered a Symbolist, but he was rather a lyric poet with an intensely refined musical and rhythmic sense. His poems are highly sophisticated, yet cultivate a simplicity akin to folk poetry. His verse attracted French composers, especially Fauré, and the combination of Verlaine's and Fauré's gifts is exquisite

ver·lig·tes (fɛərlíxtes) *n.* (enlightened ones) liberal faction of the Republic of South Africa's National Party

Ver·meer (vərmíər) (Jan Vermeer van Delft, 1632-75), Dutch painter. Only 40 of his pictures are known. His favorite subjects are interiors and domestic scenes, where, often, the calm, silent figure of a woman is surrounded by a softly diffused light that echoes from surface to surface. Vermeer's subtle composition, his exceptional handling of light and his cool, delicate colors place him among the greatest of the Dutch masters

ver·meil (vóːrmeil, vóːrməl) *n.* silver gilt ‖ a transparent varnish used to give a luster to gilt [A.F. and O.F.]

ver·mi·cel·li (vəˌrmiséli:, vəˌrmitʃéli:) *n.* very thin threads or tubes of rolled and dried pasta used esp. to give substance to soups [Ital.=little worms]

ver·mi·cide (vóːrmisaid) *n.* (*med.*) a chemical compound used for destroying intestinal worms [fr. L. *vermis*, worm+*caedere*, to kill]

ver·mic·u·lar (vəˈrmíkjulər) *adj.* wormlike in appearance or movement ‖ marked with wavy lines like worm tracks ‖ caused by worms [fr. M.L. *vermicularis*]

ver·mic·u·late (vəˈrmíkjuleit) *adj.* decorated with coiling, wormlike patterns **ver·mic·u·lat·ed** *adj.* vermiculate [fr. L. *vermiculari* (*vermiculatus*)]

ver·mic·u·la·tion (vəˌrmíkjuléiʃən) *n.* motion like that of a worm ‖ the state of being worm-eaten ‖ decoration, e.g. in stonework, resembling a tight coiling pattern of worm tracks [fr. L. *vermiculatio* (*vermiculationis*)]

ver·mic·u·lite (vəˈrmíkjulait) *n.* a silicate mineral of the mica family which expands greatly on heating and yields a lightweight product used as a heat and sound insulator and as a mulch in seedbeds [fr. L. *vermiculari*, to be wormy]

ver·mi·form (vóːrmifɔrm) *adj.* in the shape of a worm [fr. M.L. *vermiformis*]

vermiform appendix *APPENDIX

ver·mi·fuge (vóːrmifju:dʒ) **1.** *adj.* intended to eliminate intestinal worms **2.** *n.* a vermifuge medicine [F. or fr. Mod. L. *vermifugus*]

ver·mil·ion, ver·mil·lion (vərmíljən) **1.** *n.* mercuric sulfide, HgS, used as a pigment ‖ the brilliant red color produced by this pigment **2.** *adj.* of this color [A.F. and O.F. *vermeillon*]

ver·min (vóːrmin) *n.* (*collect.*) animals (e.g. rats), insects (e.g. lice) or certain birds (e.g. jays) harmful to crops, plants, human health or hygiene ‖ people thought of as resembling such creatures [A.F. and O.F. *vermin, vermine*]

ver·min·ous (vóːrminəs) *adj.* infested with lice, rats, or other vermin ‖ of or consisting of vermin ‖ caused or carried by vermin [fr. L. *verminosus*]

Ver·mont (vərmónt) (*abbr.* Vt.) a state (area 9,609 sq. miles, pop. 516,000) in the northeast U.S.A., in New England, crossed by the Green Mtns. Capital: Montpelier. Agriculture: maple sugar, dairy and poultry farming, hay and fodder crops. Resources: timber, asbestos, granite, marble. Industries: forest products, food processing, machinery and machine tools, tourism. State university (1791) at Burlington. Vermont was explored by the French (17th c.) and settled (18th c.) by the English. It declared itself an independent republic (1777) and became (1791) the 14th state of the U.S.A.

ver·mouth (vərmú:θ) *n.* a liquor used chiefly as an appetizer. It is produced from a blend of white wine with aromatic herbs (French vermouth) and sometimes sweetening (Italian vermouth) [F. fr. G. *wermuth*, wormwood]

ver·nac·u·lar (vərnǽkjulər) **1.** *adj.* of, using, or relating to the speech of a region or ethnic group (not one introduced from outside, not a dead language of learning) **2.** *n.* the indigenous language or dialect of a region [fr. L. *vernaculus*, domestic]

ver·nal (vóːrn'l) *adj.* belonging to, occurring in or associated with, the season of spring ‖ *EQUINOX [fr. L. *vernalis*]

ver·nal·i·za·tion (vəˌrn'lizéiʃən) *n.* the act or process of vernalizing

ver·nal·ize (vóːrn'laiz) *pres. part.* **ver·nal·iz·ing** *past* and *past part.* **ver·nal·ized** *v.t.* to induce the premature flowering and fruiting of (a plant) by artificial treatment of the seed or bulb, e.g. by exposure to moisture at low temperature in darkness, so that the plant embryo completes part of its development independently of its rate of growth [VERNAL]

ver·na·tion (vərnéiʃən) *n.* (*bot.*) the arrangement of leaves within a bud [fr. Mod. L. *vernatio* (*vernationis*) fr. *vernare*, to flourish]

Verne (vəˈrn, *F.* vern), Jules (1828-1905), French novelist. His classic science-fiction novels include 'Five Weeks in a Balloon' (1863), 'Twenty Thousand Leagues under the Sea' (1870), and 'Around the World in 80 Days'

(1873), and anticipate many later inventions. He also wrote romances equally popular with children, e.g. 'Michael Strogoff' (1876)

Ver·net (verne), Claude Joseph (1714-89), French painter of seascapes and battles. His son Carle (1758-1835) painted horses and battles. Carle's son Horace (1789-1863) also painted battles, notably for Louis-Philippe

ver·ni·er (vóːrni:ər) *n.* a small auxiliary scale made to slide along the main, fixed scale of an instrument to enable smaller intervals of the main scale to be measured ‖ a small auxiliary device used with a main device to obtain finer adjustment, e.g. a small-capacity variable condenser connected in parallel with a main condenser [after Pierre *Vernier* (1580–1637), F. mathematician]

vernier rocket (*aerospace*) an auxiliary rocket used for fine adjustments in speed or direction

Ver·non (vóːrnən), Edward (1684-1757), British admiral. Commanding an expedition against the Spanish West Indies colonists, he sacked (1739) Portobelo (Porto Bello). He was called 'Old Grog', from his wearing of grogram clothing. He diluted his seamen's rum ration to reduce drunkenness, and the drink came to be known as 'grog', from his nickname. Mt Vernon, George Washington's half brother's estate, is named after him

Ve·ro·na (vəróunə) an agricultural market (pop. 118,600) in Veneto, Italy, on the Adige. Industries: food processing, fertilizers, paper. Roman amphitheater, Romanesque churches, Romanesque-Gothic cathedral (12th-16th cc.), Renaissance piazzas and palaces

Ver·o·nal (véran'l) *n.* barbital [trademark fr. G.]

Ve·ro·ne·se (verɔnéze) (Paolo Cagliari, 1528-88), Italian painter of the Venetian school. Apart from frescoes, his masterpieces are huge and magnificent pageant paintings often treating religious subjects, e.g. 'The Marriage of Cana' (1563) and 'The Feast of Levi' (1573). Many of his paintings are crowded with graceful courtly figures, sumptuously dressed and dignified in gesture, and very often seen from a viewpoint low down which emphasizes their grandeur

Ve·ron·i·ca (vərónikə), St, a woman who, according to tradition, met Jesus on his way to Calvary and wiped the sweat and blood from his face with a piece of white linen. The imprint of his face was miraculously preserved on it. The act is commemorated in the devotions of the Stations of the Cross. Feast: July 12

veronica *n.* speedwell

veronica *n.* a bullfighter's pass with the cape to swing the charging bull to the side of his body as he stands without moving his feet [Span.]

vé·ron·ique (veirouní:k) *adj.* of a dish garnished with grapes

Ver·ra·za·no (verəzánou, *Ital.* verratsúnɔ), Giovanni da (c. 1480–c. 1527), Italian explorer. Commissioned by François I of France, he sailed along the North American coast from North Carolina to Maine, penetrated the Hudson estuary, and reached Newfoundland

Ver·roc·chio (verókjɔ), Andrea del (1435-88), Florentine sculptor, painter and goldsmith. His most famous surviving work is the equestrian statue in bronze of Bartolommeo Colleoni at Venice

ver·ru·ca (verú:kə) *pl.* **ver·ru·cae** (verú:si:) *n.* a wart ‖ (*biol.*) a wartlike elevation or projection on a plant or animal [L.=wart]

ver·ru·cose (verú:kous) *adj.* covered with verrucae [fr. L. *verrucosus*]

ver·ru·cous (verú:kəs) *adj.* of, like or pertaining to a wart [fr. L. *verruca*]

Ver·sailles (versaij) the chief town (pop. 94,145) of Yvelines, France, 12 miles southwest of Paris. The palace of Versailles, long the model of royal and princely magnificence throughout Europe, was built (1661-86) for Louis XIV, as residence, court, and seat of government, chiefly by Le Vau and Jules Mansart, in French classical style. In the park, laid out by Le Nôtre, are the Great Trianon (1687), and the Little Trianon (1762) and other separate buildings

Versailles, Treaty of the treaty (June 28, 1919) between Germany and the Allies at the end of the 1st world war. Its most notable features were the establishment of the League of Nations and its penal treatment of Germany. Germany was forced to pay heavy reparations and to yield Alsace-Lorraine to France as well as other possessions to Poland, Belgium, Denmark and Japan. Danzig was to be a free city, the Saar was to be occupied by the French for 15 years and the Rhineland by the Allies for the same period. Germany renounced its overseas colonies, which were placed under League of Nations mandate. The U.S. Senate refused to ratify the treaty and many of its armament clauses remained a dead letter

ver·sant (vớːrsənt) n. (geog.) the slope of the side of a range of hills or mountains ‖ the general inclination of mountainous country [F.]

ver·sa·tile (vớːrsəťl, Br. vớːrsətail) adj. possessing various skills ‖ easily adapted to different activities ‖ (zool.) capable of turning forward or backward or up and down ‖ (of an anther) swinging freely [F. or fr. L. versatilis]

ver·sa·til·i·ty (vəːrsətíliti:) n. the state or quality of being versatile [F. versatilité]

verse (vəːrs) n. poetry, esp. metrical poetry ‖ a stanza of a poem ‖ (in classical prosody) one metrical line ‖ the solo part of a song having a chorus ‖ a numbered section of a chapter in the Bible [O.E. fers fr. L.]

versed (vəːrst) adj. (with 'in') skilled or knowledgeable from study, experience etc., a man versed in the arts of navigation [fr. L. versari (versatus), to be experienced]

versed sine the remainder after subtracting the cosine of an angle from unity

ver·si·cle (vớːrsiˈk'l) n. a short verse, esp. as said or sung by the priest liturgically and followed by a response from the congregation [fr. L. versiculus]

ver·si·fi·ca·tion (vəːrsifikéiʃən) n. a versifying ‖ metrical structure ‖ a metrical version of something [fr. L. versificatio (versificationis)]

ver·si·fy (vớːrsifai) pres. part. **ver·si·fy·ing** past and past part. **ver·si·fied** v.t. to turn into verse ‖ v.i. to compose verses [O.F. versifier]

ver·sion (vớːrʒən, vớːrʃən) n. a passage or work translated from one language into another ‖ an account or description of something from a particular point of view ‖ one stage in the evolution of a developing form, she preferred the first version of the portrait to the final one ‖ (med.) the manual turning of a fetus in the uterus [F. or fr. L. versio (versionis)]

ver·so (vớːrsou) pl. **ver·sos** n. the lefthand page of a book or folded sheet ‖ (printing) the back of a leaf (opp. RECTO) ‖ the reverse side of a coin, medal etc. [fr. L. verso (folio), on the left (leaf)]

verst (vəːrst) n. a Russian measure of length equal to 3,500 feet (1,067 meters) [fr. Russ. versta]

ver·sus (vớːrsəs) prep. (law, sports, abbr. v. or vs.) against, opposed to ‖ as contrasted with, town v. country [L.]

ver·te·bra (vớːrtəbrə) pl. **ver·te·brae** (vớːrtəbri:), **ver·te·bras** n. one of the bony or cartilaginous segments composing the spinal column of a vertebrate, consisting of a cylindrical mass of bone with a dorsal arch arising from it enclosing the spinal cord. Vertebrae are jointed to each other, and in higher vertebrates bear various appendages by which the spinal column is strengthened and attached to muscles and other bones, e.g. ribs [L.=joint]

ver·te·bral (vớːrtəbrəl) adj. of or referring to a vertebra, the vertebrae or the spinal column ‖ having, or composed of, vertebrae [fr. M.L. or Mod. L. vertebralis]

ver·te·brate (vớːrtəbrit, vớːrtəbreit) 1. adj. having a spinal column, furnished with a jointed backbone 2. n. (zool.) a member of Vertebrata, a subphylum of animals including all those with a segmented spinal column, together with a few primitive forms in which the backbone is represented by a persistent notochord [fr. L. vertebratus, jointed]

ver·te·bra·tion (vəːrtəbréiʃən) n. the formation of or division into vertebrae or similar segments [VERTEBRA]

ver·tex (vớːrteks) pl. **ver·tex·es**, **ver·ti·ces** (vớːrtisi:z) n. the top, highest point ‖ (geom.) the point opposite a base ‖ (geom.) the meeting point of an axis and a curve ‖ (astron.) the zenith ‖ (anat.) the apex of the skull [L.=whirl, whirlpool]

ver·ti·cal (vớːrtiˈk'l) 1. adj. having a direction in line with the earth's center, perpendicular ‖ of or at the highest point or zenith ‖ (anat.) of or at the crown of the head ‖ (econ.) of an organization combining every stage of the production and distribution of manufactured goods 2. n. a perpendicular line, plane or circle [F. or fr. L.L. verticalis]

vertical angle (astron.) an angle measured ver-

tically upwards or downwards from the horizon ‖ a vertically opposite angle

vertical circle an azimuth circle

vertical grouping placement of children of ages 5–7 into a familylike group in which older children help teach the younger, e.g., in kibbutzim

ver·ti·cal·i·ty (vəːrtikǽliti:) n. the state or quality of being vertical

ver·ti·cal·ly (vớːrtikli:) adv. in a vertical manner ‖ straight up and down or straight overhead

vertically opposite angle (math.) either of the two opposed angles resulting from the intersection of two lines or planes

vertical thinking problem-solving technique involving overcoming obstacles in the path chosen, said to be characteristic of 'convergers.' Cf LATERAL THINKING

vertices alt. pl. of VERTEX

ver·ti·cil (vớːrtisil) n. (bot.) a set of similar parts, e.g. leaves or flowers, radiating from the same point on an axis, a whorl **ver·ti·cil·late** (vəːrtísilit, vəːrtisíleit) adj. **ver·tic·il·la·tion** n. [fr. L. verticillus, a whorl]

ver·tig·i·nous (vəːrtídʒinəs) adj. of or having vertigo ‖ causing vertigo [fr. L. vertiginosus, someone suffering from giddiness]

ver·ti·go (vớːrtigou) n. (med.) a sensation of whirling caused e.g. by heights, in which one tends to lose one's equilibrium. The sensation is also associated with certain diseases [L.]

ver·ti·port (vớːrtəpɔrt) n. pad for takeoff and landing of VTOLs. also VTOL port. Cf STOLPORT

vertu *VIRTU

ver·vain (vớːrvein) n. a verbena, esp. the European Verbena officinalis [A.F. and O.F. verveine]

verve (vəːrv) n. vivacity, liveliness, energy, esp. in conversation, works of imagination etc. [F.]

ver·vet (vớːrvit) n. Cercopithecus pygerythrus, the S. and E. African guenon, a small monkey with black chin, hands and feet [F.]

Ver·woerd (fərvúərd), Hendrik Frensch (1901-66), South African statesman, Nationalist prime minister of South Africa (1958-66). He pursued a policy of apartheid. He was assassinated

Ve·ry (víəri:), Frank Washington (1852-1927), U.S. astronomer and physicist. He estimated the temperature of the moon's surface, studied the radiation of the firefly, showed that the white nebulae are galaxies, and verified the presence of oxygen and hydrogen in the atmosphere of Mars

ver·y (véri:) 1. comp. **ver·i·er** superl. **ver·i·est** adj. same, precise, the very man we want to see ‖ actual, caught in the very act ‖ complete, absolute, that's the very opposite of what I said ‖ (used as an intensive) even, they tax the very air you breathe 2. adv. (used as an intensifier) absolutely, that is the very same one ‖ in a high degree, extremely, a very steep cliff [A.F. verrey, verai, O.F. verai, vrai]

Ve·ry light (víəri:, véri:) a flare fired from a pistol as a signal [after Edward W. Very (1852–1910), U.S. naval officer]

Ve·sa·li·us (viséiliəs), Andreas (1514-64), Flemish anatomist who questioned the medical doctrines of Aristotle and Galen, which had held sway for centuries, and whose 'De humani corporis fabrica' (1543) formed the basis from which modern research was developed

Ve·sey (víːzi:), Denmark (1767-1822), leader of a U.S. slave revolt (1822). Born in Africa, he purchased his freedom from a slave-ship captain (1800) with $600 won in a lottery. He plotted a slave uprising in Charleston, S.C. (1822), but was executed along with 34 other blacks when the plot was discovered

ve·si·ca (vəsáikə) pl. **ve·si·cae** (vəsáisit:) n. (anat.) a bladder **ves·i·cal** (vésəkəl) adj. [L.]

ves·i·cant (vésikənt) 1. adj. producing or tending to produce blisters 2. n. a drug etc. that produces blisters [fr. Mod. L. vesicans (vesicantis)]

ves·i·ca pis·cis (vésikəpísis, vésikəpískis) n. an upright, pointed oval, often used in Christian art to surround a sacred figure

ves·i·cate (vésikeit) pres. part. **ves·i·cat·ing** past and past part. **ves·i·cat·ed** v.t. to raise a blister or blisters on ‖ v.i. to become blistered [fr. Mod. L. vesicare]

ves·i·ca·to·ry (vésikətɔːri:, vésikətouri:) 1. pl. **ves·i·ca·to·ries** n. a vesicant 2. adj. vesicant [fr. M.L. or early Mod. L. vesicatorius]

ves·i·cle (vésiˈk'l) n. (bot.) a globular swelling containing air ‖ (zool.) a small globular or bladderlike air space in tissue ‖ (zool.) a small cavity or sac, usually containing fluid ‖ (geol.) a small cavity in a mineral or rock [fr. F. vésicule or L. vesicula]

ve·sic·u·lar (vəsíkjulər) adj. covered with vesicles ‖ resembling a vesicle in form or structure [fr. early Mod. L. vesicularis]

ve·sic·u·late (vəsíkjuleit) adj. vesicular **ve·sic·u·lat·ed** adj. vesiculate [fr. Mod. L. vesiculatus]

Ves·pa·si·an (vespéiʒən, vespéiʒi:ən) (Titus Flavius Sabinus Vespasianus, 9-79), Roman emperor (69-79). Commander in the war against the Jews, he was proclaimed emperor by his troops and overthrew Vitellius. He reestablished the economic and political stability of the empire after the civil wars of 68-9

Ves·per (véspər) the evening star (Venus)

ves·per·al (véspərəl) n. (eccles.) a book of prayers and music used at vespers ‖ a covering for the white linen altar cloths when no service is being held [fr. L.L. vesperalis]

ves·pers (véspərz) pl. n. (eccles.) the sixth of the seven canonical hours, marked in a monastic community by an act of worship ‖ a public act of worship at this hour, evensong ‖ *SICILIAN VESPERS [O.F. vespres]

ves·per·tine (véspərtain) adj. of, occurring, or active in the evening, e.g. of the opening of a flower or the flying of an insect [fr. L. vespertinus]

ves·pi·ar·y (véspi:ɛri:) pl. **ves·pi·ar·ies** n. a nest of social wasps [irreg. fr. L. vespa, wasp, after 'apiary']

ves·pid (véspid) 1. n. (zool.) a member of the insect family Vespidae, which includes wasps, hornets etc. 2. adj. of these insects [fr. Mod. L. Vespidae fr. vespa, wasp]

ves·pine (véspain) adj. of or pertaining to a wasp or wasps [fr. L. vespa, wasp]

Ves·puc·ci (vespúːtʃi:), Amerigo (1454-1512), Italian navigator. He made two journeys to the New World, for Spain (1499-1500) and for Portugal (1501-2), exploring the northeast coast of South America. His account of these discoveries spread over Europe, and a German cartographer named the American continent after him

ves·sel (vés'l) n. a container for liquids ‖ a boat or ship (excluding boats propelled by oars or poles and excluding small sailboats) ‖ (biol.) a tube or canal through which a fluid can pass ‖ (bot.) a continuous tube formed by the superposition of numerous specially adapted tracheids, that serves in water conduction [O.F.]

vest (vest) v.t. (usually of a priest) to clothe with a ceremonial garment ‖ to grant authority, property, rights or privileges to (someone) ‖ (with 'in') to put (a right or privilege) in the control of someone ‖ v.i. to put on robes or vestments ‖ (of a right etc.) to be vested [fr. O.F. vestir]

vest n. a man's short, close-fitting, sleeveless garment covering the chest and belly, worn over the trouser top and under the jacket ‖ (Br.) an undershirt [fr. F. veste]

Ves·ta (véstə) (Rom. mythol.) goddess of the hearth, identified with the Greek Hestia. Her temple in Rome was served by six priestesses, the Vestal virgins, vowed to chastity

vested interest a personal interest or right to derive or share a benefit, protected by law, custom etc. ‖ (pl.) persons who derive or stand to derive financial benefit or power from a situation, esp. who derive benefits which they are unwilling to forgo even if these benefits conflict with public welfare or social morality

ves·tib·u·lar (vestíbjulər) adj. of or like a vestibule

ves·ti·bule (véstibju:l) n. an enclosed space between the outer and inner door or doors of a building, through which one must pass in order to enter the building proper ‖ (Gk and Rom. hist.) an enclosed or partially enclosed courtyard before the entrance of a house etc. ‖ the partly enclosed porch of a church etc. ‖ (anat., zool.) a cavity which forms an entrance to another cavity ‖ the enclosed entrance to a railroad car on a passenger train or the covered passage between two cars [fr. L. vestibulum, entrance hall]

ves·tige (véstidʒ) n. faintly visible or otherwise discernible evidence of the former presence or existence of something which is no longer

vestiture present ‖ (usually in negative constructions) a very small amount, *not a vestige of truth in his statement* ‖ (*biol.*) a small degenerate or imperfectly developed structure, e.g. the vermiform appendix, which may have been complete and functional in some ancestor **ves·tig·i·al** (vestídʒiəl) *adj.* [F. fr. L. *vestigium*, footprint, trace]

ves·ti·ture (véstitʃər) *n.* (*zool.*) a natural body covering, e.g. of feathers, hairs, scales etc. [fr. M.L. *vestitura*]

vest·ment (véstmənt) *n.* (*eccles.*) a liturgical garment worn by a priest, deacon, acolyte etc. during an act of worship ‖ a ceremonial robe [A.F. and O.F. *vestement*]

ves·try (véstri:) *pl.* **ves·tries** *n.* a sacristy, a room in a church used to contain the vestments and sacred vessels, the official records etc. The clergy and the choir robe and disrobe in it, and it serves as the official office of the parish ‖ (*Anglican* and *Episcopal Churches*) a body of church members which administers the secular affairs of the parish [prob. fr. A.F. *vestrie, vesterie*]

ves·try·man (véstri:mən) *pl.* **ves·try·men** (véstri:mən) *n.* a member of a vestry

ves·ture (véstʃər) *n.* (*archaic*) garments collectively ‖ (*law*) everything that grows on a piece of land except trees [A.F. and O.F.]

ve·su·vi·an·ite (vəsú:vi:ənait) *n.* a brown or green double silicate of aluminum and calcium, colored by traces of iron, first found in the ejections of Vesuvius

Ve·su·vi·us (vəsú:vi:əs) an active volcano (4,000 ft) 5 miles southeast of Naples, Italy. Its first known eruption (79 A.D.) destroyed the towns of Pompeii and Herculaneum at its foot

vet (vet) **1.** *n.* (*pop.*) a veterinarian **2.** *v.t.* *pres. part.* **vet·ting** *past and past part.* **vet·ted** (*pop.*) to make a veterinary examination of or give treatment to (an animal) ‖ (*Br., pop.*) to examine and check, esp. for accuracy

vet. a veteran

vetch (vetʃ) *n.* a member of *Vicia*, fam. *Papilionaceae*, a genus of scrambling annual or perennial plants, found in many parts of the world. Some species are cultivated as fodder plants [O.N.F. *veche, vecche*]

vetch·ling (vétʃliŋ) *n.* a member of *Lathyrus*, fam. *Papilionaceae*, a genus of small plants closely allied to vetch

vet·er·an (vétərən, vétrən) **1.** *adj.* of or pertaining to long service or experience in some form of activity, esp. in soldiering **2.** *n.* (*abbr.* vet.) someone who has had long service or experience in some form of activity, esp. in soldiering ‖ an ex-serviceman qualified to receive benefits according to status [fr. early Mod. F. or fr. L. *veteranus* fr. *vetus* (*veteris*), old]

Veterans Day an annual U.S. holiday held every Nov. 11th, originally (1919) celebrated as Armistice Day to commemorate the end of the 1st World war. President Dwight Eisenhower changed (1954) its name and dedicated it to the sacrifices made by all U.S. servicemen

Veterans of Foreign Wars (*abbr.* V.F.W.) a U.S. organization created (1899) at Columbus, Ohio, by veterans of the Spanish-American War, and chartered (1936) by Congress to promote the welfare of all veterans

vet·er·i·nar·i·an (vetərinéəri:ən, vetrinéəri:ən) *n.* (*Am.=Br.* veterinary surgeon) a person who practices veterinary medicine or surgery [fr. L. *veterinarius*]

vet·er·i·nar·y (vétərineri:, vétrineri:) **1.** *adj.* of the science of treating and preventing diseases of animals, esp. of domestic animals **2.** *pl.* **vet·er·i·nar·ies** *n.* a veterinarian [fr. L. *veterinus*, of or pertaining to (draft) cattle]

veterinary surgeon (*Br.*) a veterinarian

vet·i·ver (vétivər) *n. Andropogon zizamoides,* cuscus [fr. F. *vétyver* fr. Tamil *vettvēru*]

ve·to (ví:tou) **1.** *n. pl.* **ve·toes** a right, vested by law in a person or constitutional body, to declare inoperative a decision made by others ‖ the exercise of this right ‖ a veto message **2.** *v.t.* to refuse consent to by using the right of veto ‖ (*pop.*) to forbid flatly [L.=I forbid]

veto message a document in which the executive power sets out its reasons for not approving a proposed law

vex (veks) *v.t.* to annoy (someone) [O.F. *vexer*]

vex·a·tion (vekséiʃən) *n.* a vexing or being vexed ‖ something which annoys one **vex·a·tious** *adj.* causing vexation ‖ (*law,* of actions) instituted without real grounds and meant to

cause trouble or annoyance [O.F. or fr. L. *vexatio* (*vexationis*)]

vexed question a matter about which people have argued, or do argue, hotly

vex·il·lar·y (véksəleri:) **1.** *adj.* of a standard or ensign **2.** *n.* (*Rom. hist.*) one of a class of veteran soldiers ‖ a standard-bearer [fr. L. *vexillarius*, standard-bearer]

vex·il·late (véksəleit) *adj.* having a vexillum or vexilla

vex·il·lol·o·gy (veksəlóledʒi:) *n.* the study of flags, their design and manufacture **—vexillologic** *adj.* **—vexillological** *adj.* **—vexillologist** *n.*

vex·il·lum (veksíləm) *pl.* **vex·il·la** (veksilə) *n.* (*Rom. hist.*) a square flag carried by a Roman standard-bearer ‖ (*Rom. hist.*) a body of troops under one banner ‖ (*bot.*) the large upper petal of a papilionaceous flower ‖ the vane of a feather ‖ (*eccles.*) a linen or silk pennant or flag partly wound around a bishop's staff [L.]

Vé·ze·lay (veizəlei) a town (pop. 500) in Yonne, France, where St Bernard preached (1146) the 2nd Crusade. Romanesque-Gothic abbey (11th-12th cc.)

VFW-Fokker F-28 *n.* 85-seat passenger jet with range of 1,000 nautical mi.

vi·a (váiə, ví:ə) *prep.* by way or means of, *he went to Rome via Paris* [L.]

vi·a·bil·i·ty (vaiəbíliti:) *n.* the state or quality of being viable [F. *viabilité*]

vi·a·ble (váiəb'l) *adj.* (of a fetus) able to maintain an independent life ‖ (of seeds etc.) capable of growth and development ‖ (of a state) economically, politically or socially able to be independent ‖ (of ideas, propositions, theories) sound, workable if translated into action [F.=able to live]

vi·a·duct (váiədʌkt) *n.* a bridge supported by many pillared arches, over which road or rail transport can pass [fr. L. *via*, a way (after 'aqueduct')]

vi·al (váiəl) *n.* a small cylindrical container of glass etc., used to contain liquids [M.E. *viole, fiole*]

vi·and (váiənd) *n.* (usually *pl., rhet.*) food [A.F., O.F. *viande*]

vi·at·i·cum (vaiætikəm) *pl.* **vi·at·i·cums, vi·at·i·ca** (vaiætikə) *n.* (*eccles.*) the Eucharist administered to a dying person ‖ (*Rom. hist.*) provisions or money granted to an envoy about to make a journey [L.=traveling money]

Viau (vjou), Théophile de (1590-1626), French poet, author of the tragedy 'Pyrame et Thisbé' (1617) and of the scurrilous satire 'le Parnasse satyrique' (1622)

vibes or **vibrations** (vaibs) *n.* **1.** an aura or spirit emanating from a person or situation. **2.** an instinctive sense of the nature of a person or a situation

Viborg *VYBORG

vi·brac·u·lar (vaibrǽkjulər) *adj.* of or like vibracula ‖ having vibracula

vi·brac·u·loid (vaibrǽkjuloid) *adj.* of or like a vibraculum or vibracula

vi·brac·u·lum (vaibrǽkjuləm) *pl.* **vi·brac·u·la** (vaibrǽkjulə) *n.* (*zool.*) one of the threads by which bryozoans lash the water so as to bring food within reach, or in order to defend themselves [Mod. L. fr. L. *vibrare*, to shake]

vi·bra·harp or **vi·bra·phone** (váibrəharp, váibrəfoun) *n.* a percussion instrument containing electrically operated valves **—vibraharpist** *n.* **—vibraphonist** *n.*

vi·bran·cy (váibrənsi:) *n.* the state or quality of being vibrant

vi·brant (váibrənt) *adj.* vibrating ‖ full of life and energy ‖ (of sound) resonant [fr. L. *vibrans* (*vibraniis*) fr. *vibrare*, to vibrate]

vi·bra·phone (váibrəfoun) *n.* a percussion instrument like a xylophone but having electrically operated resonators under the bars which give a vibrating effect

vi·brate (váibreit) *pres. part.* **vi·brat·ing** *past and past part.* **vi·brat·ed** *v.i.* to move to and fro with simple periodic motion ‖ (of sounds) to seem to quiver ‖ to respond sympathetically ‖ *v.t.* to cause to vibrate [fr. L. *vibrare* (*vibratus*), to shake]

vi·bra·tile (váibrət'l, váibrətail) *adj.* able to vibrate or be vibrated ‖ of, like, or characterized by vibration **vi·bra·til·i·ty** (vaibrətíliti:) *n.* [fr. Mod. L. *vibratilis* fr. L., *vibrare* (*vibratus*), to vibrate]

vi·bra·tion (vaibréiʃən) *n.* a vibrating or being vibrated ‖ (*phys.*) the simple periodic to-and-fro motion of a body etc., e.g. the vibrating string of

a violin ‖ a single instance of this [fr. L. *vibratio* (*vibrationis*)]

vibration syndrome *n.* (*med.*) Raynaud's Phenomenon

vi·bra·tive (váibrətiv) *adj.* vibratory

vi·bra·to (vibrátou) *n.* (*mus.*) an effect produced by rapid changes in the loudness of a single note [Ital.]

vi·bra·tor (váibreitər) *n.* a device which vibrates or causes vibration

vi·bra·to·ry (váibrətɔ:ri:, váibrətouri:) *adj.* of, like, or consisting of vibration causing vibration ‖ vibrating or capable of vibrating ‖ vibrant

vi·bris·sa (vaibrísə) *pl.* **vi·bris·sae** (vaibrísi:) *n.* (*zool.*) one of the stiff facial hairs in some mammals often serving as a tactile organ, esp. near the mouth, e.g. a cat's whisker ‖ one of the stiff feathers near the beak or around the eye of a bird ‖ one of a pair of bristles near the upper angles of the mouth cavity in some dipterans ‖ a hair in the nostril [L. *vibrissae* pl. fr. *vibrare*, to vibrate]

vi·bro·graph (váibrəgræf, váibrəgraf) *n.* an instrument used to measure and record vibrations

vi·bron·ic (vaibrónik) *adj.* of electronic vibrations

Vi·bro·sis (vaibróusis) *n.* trade name by Conoco for vibrators used to create seismic signals for geological exploration

vi·bur·num (vaibɜ:rnəm) *n.* a member of *Viburnum,* fam. *Caprifoliaceae,* a genus of shrubs and small trees native to northern temperate and subtropical regions, including *V. lantana,* the wayfaring tree, and *V. opulus,* the guelder rose. Many species are cultivated for their ornamental white or pink flowers [L.=the wayfaring tree]

vic·ar (víkər) *n.* (*Br.*) the priest in charge of a parish in which formerly all or the greater part of the tithes were paid to another recipient and the vicar received a stipend (cf. RECTOR) ‖ (*Roman Catholicism*) a priest acting as the representative of another ‖ (*Episcopal Church*) a priest in charge of a church dependent on a larger church ‖ a representative, *the pope is called 'the Vicar of Christ'* [A.F. *vicare, vicaire* fr. L. *vicarius,* substitute]

vic·ar·age (víkəridʒ) *n.* the residence of a vicar ‖ his benefice

vicar apostolic *pl.* **vicars apostolic** (*Roman Catholicism*) a titular bishop acting as the papal delegate in administering a missionary area

vic·ar·gen·er·al (víkərdʒénərəl) *pl.* **vic·ars·gen·er·al** (*Church of England*) a lay legal official assisting a bishop or archbishop ‖ a representative of a bishop in matters of jurisdiction in a diocese

vi·car·i·al (vaikéəri:əl, vikéəri:əl) *adj.* of or pertaining to a vicar or to his office ‖ delegated [fr. L. *vicarius*]

vi·car·i·ous (vaikéəri:əs, vikéəri:əs) *adj.* acting, or done, on behalf of someone else or in his place, *vicarious suffering* ‖ of someone else's experiences which one shares imaginatively, *vicarious pleasure* ‖ (*physiol.*) of the performing by one organ of the function normally performed by another organ [fr. L. *vicarius*]

vice (vais) *n.* a habitual disposition to choose evil ‖ an evil practice ‖ (in animals) a fault, e.g. (in a horse) tossing back the head [A.F., O.F.]

vice *VISE

vi·ce (váisi:) *prep.* (*rhet.*) in place of [L.]

vice- (vais) *prefix* someone acting in the place of someone else

vice admiral a naval officer ranking above a rear admiral and below an admiral **vice admiralty**

vice-chan·cel·lor (váistʃǽnsələr, váistʃǽnsələr) *n.* the assistant to a chancellor, esp. the administrative head of a university, acting for the chancellor **vice-chan·cel·lor·ship** *n.*

vice-con·sul (váiskónsəl) *n.* a consular representative appointed to serve where the duties are too light to warrant the appointment of a consul ‖ an assistant to a consul general **vice-cón·su·late** *n.*

vice-ge·ren·cy (vaisdʒíerənsi:) *pl.* **vice-ge·ren·cies** *n.* the office or jurisdiction of a vicegerent

vice-ge·rent (vaisdʒíerənt) *n.* someone appointed to act for a superior, esp. a ruler [fr. M.L. *vicegerens* (*vicegerentis*)]

vi·cen·ni·al (vaiséni:əl) *adj.* occurring at intervals of 20 years ‖ lasting for 20 years [fr. L.L. *vicennium,* period of 20 years]

Vi·cen·te (vi:sénti:), Gil (c. 1465-1536), Portuguese dramatist. His 44 plays, some of which are written in Portuguese and some in Spanish, include religious dramas ('Trilogia de las Barcas') and comedies ('Don Duardos'). He was also a goldsmith

Vi·cen·za (vi:tʃénza) a city (pop. 117,571) in Veneto, Italy. Gothic cathedral (13th c.), many buildings designed by Palladio, notably the Teatro Olimpico (1580-5)

vice-pres·i·den·cy (váisprézidənsi:) *n.* the office or term of office of a vicepresident

vice-pres·i·dent (váisprézidənt) *n.* someone empowered to act for, or in the absence of, a president ‖ someone serving as a president's assistant, e.g. in a corporation **vice-pres·i·dén·tial** *adj.*

vice-re·gal (váisrí:g'l) *adj.* pertaining to a viceroy

vice-re·gent (váisrí:dʒənt) *n.* the assistant or deputy of a regent

vice·roy (váisrɔi) *n.* a man appointed by a sovereign to rule in his stead over one of his dominions ‖ *Limenitis archippus*, a red and black American butterfly [F. *viceroi*]

vi·ce ver·sa (váisivə́·rsə, váisvə́·rsə) *adv.* similarly when the terms are reversed, *green enhances yellow and vice versa* [L.]

Vi·chy (vi:ʃi:) a spa (pop. 32,117) in Allier, central France. It was the seat of Pétain's government of France (1940-4)

vic·i·nage (vísinidʒ) *n.* (*rhet.*) a neighboring area, vicinity [fr. O.F. *visenage, voisinage*]

vic·i·nal (vísin'l) *adj.* (*rhet.*) of a locality, local, *a vicinal road* ‖ (*crystall.*) of a subordinate facet [fr. L. *vicinalis*]

vi·cin·i·ty (visíniti:) *pl.* **vi·cin·i·ties** *n.* the immediate neighborhood **in the vicinity of** close to, *accidents in the vicinity of 10,000 a year* [fr. L. *vicinitas* fr. *vicinus*, neighbor]

vi·cious (víʃəs) *adj.* characterized by vice given over to vice, *a vicious neighborhood* ‖ seeking to injure, *a vicious kick* ‖ (esp. of a horse) having a vice or vices ‖ spiteful, vindictive ‖ faulty, not valid, *a vicious argument* [A.F. or fr. L. *vitiosus* fr. *vitium*, vice]

vicious circle a course of action in which the result achieved defeats the purpose of the act, e.g. making a wage demand because of the cost of living when to secure the demand raises the cost of living ‖ a combination of problems or disorders which aggravate one another, *a vicious circle of poverty-ignorance-poverty* ‖ (*logic*) a faulty reasoning which consists of drawing a conclusion from a proposition which itself assumes the conclusion ‖ (*economics*) in currency markets, events leading to the decline in the value of a currency

vi·cis·si·tude (visísitu:d, visísitju:d) *n.* (esp. *pl.*) a change in fortune or in a situation, esp. for the worse **vi·cis·si·tú·di·nous** *adj.* [O.F. and F. or fr. L. *vicissitudo*]

Vick·er·y (víkəri:), Howard Leroy (1892-1946), U.S. admiral. During the 2nd world war he directed a shipbuilding program which produced over 5,500 oceangoing ships, greatly contributing to the Allied victory

Vicks·burg Campaign (víksbə:rg) a Civil War campaign (1862-3) launched by U.S. Gen. Ulysses S. Grant to gain control of the section of the Mississippi River, between Port Hudson, La., and Vicksburg, Miss., still held by the Confederates. After an initial failure, Grant captured many Confederate-held towns, including Vicksburg after a six months' siege. The Union subsequently held full control of the Mississippi River

Vi·co (ví:kɔ), Giambattista (1668-1744), Italian philosopher and historian. He was the first to write history in terms of the rise and fall of human societies and to make use of myths, legends, poetry and the study of linguistics as historical evidence. His philosophical work 'The New Science' (1725) has had a wide influence

vic·tim (víktim) *n.* a person or thing made to suffer by a cause which is stated or implied, *a victim of circumstances* ‖ (*hist.*) a living creature offered up as a sacrifice ‖ someone who is cheated or made a dupe **vic·tim·i·za·tion** *n.* **vic·tim·ize** *pres. part.* **vic·tim·iz·ing** *past* and *past part.* **vic·tim·ized** *v.t.* to cause to be a victim [fr. L. *victima*]

vic·tim·less crime (víktimləs) an illegal act that hurts no one but the person who commits it, e.g., drug taking

vic·tim·ol·ogy (vɪktəmóːlədʒi:) *n.* the study of victims of crimes and their behavior, esp. that leading to their becoming victims —**victimologist** *n.*

vic·tor (víktər) *n.* the winner of a contest [A.F. or L. fr. *vincere* (*victus*), to overcome]

Vic·tor Em·man·u·el I (víktərimǽnju:əl) (*Ital.* Vittorio Emanuele) (1759-1824), king of Sardinia (1802-21). A reactionary, he abdicated (1821) rather than accede to demands for a constitution

Victor Emmanuel II (1820-78), last king of Sardinia (1849-61) and first king of Italy (1861-78), son of Charles Albert. With the aid of Cavour, he carried out many liberal reforms, and obtained French support in driving the Austrians from northern Italy (1859)

Victor Emmanuel III (1869-1947), king of Italy (1900-46). After the defeat and death of Mussolini, with whose policies he had concurred, he was forced to abdicate (1946). Italy became a republic one month later

Vic·to·ri·a (viktɔ́ri:ə, viktóuri:ə) (1819-1901), queen of Great Britain (1837-1901) and empress of India (1876-1901), niece of William IV. Her accession marked the end of the connection between the British and Hanoverian thrones. Victoria took an active interest in the policy of her ministers, and was soundly advised and supported by her husband, Albert of Saxe-Coburg Gotha. Her relations with Melbourne, Peel and Disraeli were excellent but she was not on good terms with Palmerston and Gladstone. Her conscientious approach to her duties did much to raise the reputation of the monarchy. Her long retirement after Albert's death was unpopular, but the diamond jubilee of her reign was celebrated (1897) with universal enthusiasm. Victoria's reign saw the rapid industrialization of Britain, and a vast growth of national wealth, reflected in the imperialism of the late 19th c.

Vic·to·ri·a (vi:ktɔ́rja), Manuel Félix Fernández (called Guadelupe, 1786-1843), Mexican soldier, politician, and the first federalist president of Mexico (1824-9), following the overthrow of Iturbide. He introduced (1824) the first liberal constitution ,

Vic·to·ri·a (viktɔ́ri:ə, viktóuri:ə) a state (area 87,884 sq. miles, pop. 3,907,900) at the southeast tip of Australia. Capital: Melbourne. The Great Dividing Range occupies the east and center. The northwest is semiarid. Agriculture: wheat, oats, barley, hay, potatoes, fruit and vines, sheep and cattle farming, dairying. Resources: timber, lignite, antimony, silver, tin, hydroelectric power. Industries: food processing, agricultural machinery, textiles, chemicals, iron and steel. University of Melbourne (1853), Monash University (1958), Latrobe University (1967)

Victoria the capital (pop. 64,379) of British Columbia, Canada, a port on S.E. Vancouver I.: fishing, tourism. University (1961)

Victoria *HONG KONG

Victoria a lake (area 26,828 sq. miles, altitude 3,720 ft) in Kenya, Tanzania and Uganda. Its outlet is the White Nile. It was discovered (1858) by Speke, and explored (1875) by Stanley

Vic·to·ri·a (viktɔ́ri:ə, viktóuri:ə, vi:ktɔ́ri:ɑ), Tomás Luis de (Tommaso Ludovico da Vittoria, c. 1540-1611), Spanish composer. He was a contemporary of Palestrina, and worked in Rome for much of his life. He was a master of polyphonic church music (masses, motets, psalms, hymns)

vic·to·ri·a (viktɔ́ri:ə, viktóuri:ə) *n.* (*hist.*) a four-wheeled horse-drawn carriage, with a low seat for two persons, a raised seat for the driver, and a folding top ‖ *Victoria regia*, the royal or giant water lily of the Amazon [after Queen VICTORIA]

Victoria Cross (*abbr.* V.C.) the highest British award for valor, instituted (1856) by Queen Victoria during the Crimean War

Victoria Falls a waterfall (5,580 ft wide, 350-400 ft high), broken by islands into four parts, in the Zambezi on the Zimbabwe-Zambia border: hydroelectricity. The falls were discovered by Livingstone (1855)

Victoria Island an island (area 82,000 sq. miles, pop. about 612, Eskimos) in the Arctic Ocean, forming part of the Northwest Territories of Canada

Vic·to·ri·an (viktɔ́ri:ən, viktóuri:ən) **1.** *n.* some-

one living during, or born in, the reign of Queen Victoria (1837-1901) **2.** *adj.* characteristic of, or pertaining to, the British way of life during the reign of Queen Victoria ‖ having stiff or prim habits of thought and manner **vic·tó·ri·an·ism** *n.*

Vic·tor·i·an·a (viktɔ:ri:ǽnə) *n.* **1.** artifacts of the Victorian era **2.** a collection of such artifacts

Victoria Ny·an·za (naiǽnzə) the former name of Lake Victoria

Vic·to·ri·o (viktóuri:ou) (1825-80), American Apache Indian chief and military leader. After leading sporadic raids during the 1870s, he broke out of the San Carlos reservation (1879) and led the Warm Springs Apache to the Black Mountains, where he held off U.S. and Mexican troops for 15 months by using strategically placed encampments to limit the enemy attackers to a number comparable to his own 35 to 50 warriors. Surprised by the Mexicans at Tres Castillos, on the Plains of Chihuahua, he fought until his ammunition gave out, then killed himself

vic·to·ri·ous (viktɔ́ri:əs, viktóuri:əs) *adj.* having won a victory ‖ of or pertaining to victory [A.F. or fr. L. *victoriosus*]

vic·to·ry (víktəri:) *pl.* **vic·to·ries** *n.* the winning of a contest, esp. final success in battle or war ‖ a military engagement fought and won ‖ a contest won [A.F. and O.F. *victorie*]

vict·ual (vít'l) *n.* (*pl., old-fash.*) food and, more rarely, other provisions [A.F. and O.F. *vitaile, vitaille*]

victual *pres. part.* **vict·ual·ing**, esp. *Br.* **vict·ual·ling** *past* and *past part.* **vict·ualed**, esp. *Br.*, **vict·ualled** *v.t.* to provision (e.g. a ship) ‖ *v.i.* to take on provisions [fr. A.F. and O.F. *vitailler*]

vict·ual·ler, vict·ual·er (vít'lər) *n.* (*Br.*) a publican holding a license to sell food and alcoholic drinks on his premises ‖ a provisioning ship ‖ (*hist.*) a person who provisioned an army or navy [A.F. and O.F. *vitailler, vitaillier*]

vi·cu·ña, vi·cu·gna (vikú:nə, vikjú:nə, vikú:njə) *n. Lama vicugna*, a mammal of the Andes related to the llama and alpaca, but smaller. Its coat produces very soft, highly valued wool ‖ this wool ‖ a cloth woven from this wool [Span. fr. Quechuan]

Vi·dal (vidál), Gore (1925-), U.S. author, known for his cynical humor and literary eclecticism. His first 3 novels, 'Williwaw' (1946), 'The City and the Pillar' (1948) and 'The Judgment of Paris' (1952), were critical successes, but he gained wider fame with his Hollywood spoof 'Myra Breckinridge' (1968) and with such later works as 'Burr' (1973), '1876' (1976), 'Creation' (1981) and 'Lincoln' (1984). He also wrote 2 successful plays, 'Visit to a Small Planet' (1957) and 'The Best Man' (1960; film, 1964), and published collections of literary and political essays including 'The Second American Revolution' (1982)

vi·dar·a·bine ($C_5H_5N_5$) (vaidárəbi:n) *n.* (*pharm.*) an antiviral ointment used to treat inflammation of the cornea and the conjunctiva; marketed as Vira-A. *also* adenine, arabinoside

vi·de (váidi:) *v. imper.* (*abbr.* v.) see (directing a reader to some other page or passage in a book etc.) [L. *imper. sing.* of *videre*, to see]

vi·de·li·cet (vidéliset) *adv.* (*abbr.* viz.) that is to say, namely [L. fr. *videre licet*, it is permitted to see]

vid·e·o (vídi:ou) **1.** *n.* the visual element of television (cf. AUDIO) ‖ television **2.** *adj.* of or pertaining to television

video cassette or **video cartridge** a videotape encased in a cartridge that can be played on a video cassette recorder

video cassette recorder device for recording a television program from a television set for later playback. *abbr.* VCR

vid·e·o·disc (vídi:oudisk) *n.* a plastic disc containing a television recording

vid·e·o·ize (vídi:ouaiz) *v.* to adapt for television

vid·e·o·phone or **vid·e·o·tel·e·phone** (vídi:oufoun) *n.* a telephone that transmits a view of the speaker. *also* viewphone. *Cf* PICTUREPHONE

vid·e·o·play·er (vídi:oupleijər) *n.* a device attached to a television set, that can record and replay a television program

video tape a magnetic tape used to record a television program or part of a program to be broadcast at a later time

vid·e·o·tex (vídi:outeks) *n.* system of information retrieval through home television sets

vid·i·con (vídəkɒn) *n.* (*electr.*) camera tube ca-

---

pable of receiving photoconduction that is scanned by electrons to transmit images

vie (vai) *pres. part.* **vy·ing** *past* and *past part.* **vied** *v.i.* to compete, *they vied for first place* [aphetic fr. O.F. *envier*, to increase the stake]

Vied·ma, Lake (vjédmɑ) a lake (53 miles long) north of Lake Argentino, in S. central Argentina

Vi·en·na (vi:énə) (G. Wien) the capital (pop. 1,515,666) and economic center of Austria, on a branch of the Danube, constituting a province (area 250 sq. miles). Industries: machinery, metalworking, food processing, textiles, light manufactures. The ancient and medieval site, now circled by the 'Ring' boulevard, remains the center of the city. The principal monuments, apart from the Gothic cathedral (14th c.), are of the 18th and 19th cc. Examples of Viennese baroque architecture include Belvedere and Schönbrunn palaces, the winter palace and Karlskirche. Main cultural institutions: opera (Staatsoper, 1861), theater (Burgtheater), university (1365), national library, museums (celebrated Renaissance and baroque collections). A Celtic settlement and Roman garrison town, it became (1278) the residence of the Hapsburgs. It withstood sieges by the Turks in 1529 and 1683. At the end of the Napoleonic Wars it was the political center of Europe and was a flourishing cultural center (18th-19th cc.)

Vienna, Congress of the conference (1814-15) of European powers at the end of the Napoleonic Wars. Statesmen present included Metternich, Castlereagh and Talleyrand. By the Treaty of Vienna (June 8, 1815), Austria lost Belgium to Holland, but gained interests in Italy. Prussia gained territory notably along the Rhine. Russia gained Finland from Sweden, and much of Poland. Denmark lost Norway to Sweden. Great Britain gained many colonies, notably Cape Colony, Heligoland and Malta. The German Confederation was set up. France, by the Second Treaty of Paris (Nov. 20, 1815), was deprived of her imperial conquests, and made to pay a war indemnity

Vienne (vjen) a department (area 2,711 sq. miles, pop. 357,400) in W. central France (*POITOU, *TOURAINE). Chief town: Poitiers

Vienne, Council of an ecumenical council (1311-12) at which the Knights Templars were suppressed at the instigation of Philippe IV of France

Vienne (Haute-) *HAUTE-VIENNE

Vi·en·nese (vi:əni:s, vi:əní:z) **1.** *adj.* of or pertaining to Vienna **2.** *n.* a native or inhabitant of Vienna

Vien·tiane (vjəntján) the administrative capital (pop. 176,637) and commercial center of Laos, a port on the Mekong River (cf. LUANG PRABANG)

Vie·ques (vjékes) (or Crab Island) a fertile island and municipality (area 51 sq. miles, pop. 7,000), ten miles east of Puerto Rico. The U.S. Navy leases the east half of the island from Puerto Rico

Vier·wald·stät·ter See (fíərvɑltʃtetərzéi) *LUCERNE

Vi·et·cong (vi:étkɒ́ŋ, vjɛtkɒ́ŋ, vi:étkɒŋ) **1.** *n.* the name given by their adversaries to the National Liberation Front, the Communist-led political and military organization operating against the U.S.-supported South Vietnamese government ‖ a member of this organization **2.** *adj.* of or pertaining to this organization [short for Vietnamese *Viet Nam Cong Sam*, Vietnamese Communist]

Vi·et·minh (vjetmín, vi:etmín, vi:étmin) *HÔ CHIMINH

Vi·et·nam·ese (vjɛtnəmí:z, vi:ɛtnəmí:z, vjɛtnəmí:s, vi:ɛtnəmí:s) *pl.* **Vi·et·nam·ese 1.** *adj.* of or pertaining to Vietnam ‖ of or pertaining to the language of Vietnam **2.** *n.* a native or inhabitant of Vietnam ‖ the language of Vietnam

Vietnam, Socialist Republic of, a country in S.E. Asia, bordered by the South China Sea (S), Gulf of Tonkin (E), People's Republic of China (N), Laos (W), and Cambodia (SW) (area: 127,242 sq. miles, pop. 55,503,000). Capital: Hanoi. People: Vietnamese, highland tribes, some Chinese. Language: Vietnamese, minority languages. Religion: mainly Buddhist and Taoist, with animist minorities. Mountains, mainly wooded and cut by deep river valleys, cover most of the country. Highest peak: Fan Si Pan (11,191 ft). The coast is largely muddy. Average temperatures (F.) in Hanoi: (Jan.) 63°,

(June) 80°. Rainfall: 70-100 ins. Agricultural products: rice, sugarcane, rubber, peanuts, copra, corn, cotton, tea, vegetables, coffee, tobacco, castor oil, shellac, silk, fruit. Minerals: coal, apatite, gold, phosphates, salt, tin, chromite, iron, zinc, tungsten, antimony, manganese. Industries: steel, building materials, textiles, hydroelectricity, fishing, food processing and brewing, paper. Exports: minerals, rice, rubber, salt, tea, cinnamon, bamboo, hardwoods, manufactures, foodstuffs. Ports: Haiphong, Da Nang, Ho Chi Minh City. University: Hanoi. Monetary unit: dong (10 hao, 100 xu). HISTORY. After Chinese rule for more than 1,000 years, Vietnam achieved independence 939 A.D. The conflict between the Vietnamese monarchy and Catholic missionaries from Europe (18th c.) allowed the French to conquer the region (1858-83). It was administered first as Annam, Chochin-China, and Tonkin, and later (after 1887) as part of French Indochina. After the Japanese occupation (1940-5), Vietnamese nationalists declared the country an independent republic (1945). Despite war (1946-54) the French were unable to regain control and ended with French defeat at Dien Bien Phu (1954). A Geneva conference (1954) divided the country at the 17th parallel into North and South Vietnam. Under the presidency of Ho Chi Minh, guerrilla troops from North Vietnam began in 1958 to invade South Vietnam and fierce fighting developed, gradually involving the U.S.A. The U.S.A. steadily increased its military commitment in South Vietnam to a high (July 1969) of 550,000. Yet North Vietnam's Tet offensive (Feb. 1968), though costly to the North, disabused the American people of the hope of a military solution to the conflict. Discouraged by the growing anti-war movement at home, Johnson decided (Apr. 1968) not to seek reelection. Richard Nixon's electoral promise to end the war was based on three premises: success in the peace negotiations in Paris initiated by Johnson, success in the 'Vietnamization' program of steadily turning the military operations over to the South Vietnamese themselves, and a de-escalation of North Vietnamese and Viet Cong operations in South Vietnam. On Apr. 30, 1970, President Nixon announced an attack on the North's sanctuaries and arms stockpiles in Cambodia, by U.S. and South Vietnamese forces. The invasion was limited to 21.7 miles and U.S. forces were withdrawn by July 1, 1970. South Vietnamese forces remained in Cambodia and retained the support of U.S. air power. A new North Vietnamese offensive was launched (1972) in South Vietnam. U.S. troops were finally withdrawn in 1973 and two years later the South Vietnam government, under Nguyen Van Thieu, collapsed. The country was officially reunited on July 2, 1976, and has since developed closer ties with the Soviet Union, joining COMECON in 1978. Also in 1978, Vietnam invaded neighboring Cambodia (Kampuchea), managing the 1979 overthrow of the ruling regime and establishing a pro-Vietnamese government in its place. A guerrilla war continued between the two forces, however. China, allied with Cambodia, briefly invaded Vietnam in Feb. 1979

Vi·et·nam syndrome (vi:etnám) (*psych.*) sense of guilt and other complexes over the Vietnam war inhibiting similar overt foreign involvement by U.S.

view (vju:) **1.** *n.* what one can see from where one is, *a truck blocked the view* ‖ a wide spread of country as seen from a commanding position, *fine views to north and west* ‖ a painting or photograph of a scene ‖ visual inspection, *they asked for a view of the house and grounds*, esp. an inspection by a jury of the scene of a crime ‖ range of vision, *she disappeared from view* ‖ a mental survey, *a critical view of postwar literature* ‖ an opinion or set of opinions, *differing views* **in full view** completely visible **in view of** in sight of ‖ having regard to, considering **on view** displayed for public inspection **to have in view** to have as a possible option, opportunity, employment etc. ‖ to keep in mind the possibility of, *we must have in view the danger of a surprise attack* **with a view to** in order to arrive at or secure **2.** *v.t.* to inspect, *permission to view the house* ‖ to regard attentively ‖ to consider, take up a mental attitude towards, *he views the situation with alarm* **view·er** *n.* member of a television audience ‖ a device for looking at color slides [A. F. *veiwe, viewe*]

view·find·er (vjú:faɪndər) *n.* (*photog.*) a camera attachment which shows in miniature the field of view

view·phone (vjú:foun) *n.* videophone

view·point (vjú:pɔɪnt) *n.* a point of view

vig·il (vídʒəl) *n.* the act of remaining awake at night, esp. in order to keep watch, or to pray ‖ the period of such wakefulness ‖ (*eccles.*) the eve of a festival, esp. when observed as a fast ‖ (*pl.*) evening prayers [A.F. and O.F. *vigile*]

vig·i·lance (vídʒələns) *n.* watchfulness, a being on the alert, esp. in order to guard against possible harm or error [F. or fr. L. *vigilantia*]

vigilance committee a group of citizens who agree voluntarily to watch for any infringement of a law or of their rights and privileges, esp. with a view to taking the law into their own hands where the law appears to be ineffective. Such groups were formed in U.S. frontier communities, esp. mining towns, to maintain law and order until a regularly constituted government force could be created (*VIGILANTE)

vig·i·lant (vídʒələnt) *adj.* of someone who is tirelessly on the alert [F. or fr. L. *vigilans* (*vigilantis*)]

vig·i·lan·te (vídʒəlǽnti:) *n.* a member of a vigilance committee [Span.]

vi·gin·til·lion (vaɪdʒɪntíljən) *n.* *NUMBER TABLE [fr. L. *viginti*, twenty+MILLION]

vi·gnette (vinjét) **1.** *n.* a portrait (engraving, photograph etc.) of head and shoulders which shades off into the background ‖ an ornament, esp. of vine leaves and tendrils to decorate a chapter head or chapter end of a book or the title page or half title ‖ a flourish around a capital letter in a manuscript or on a title page ‖ a brief but clear verbal description, esp. of a person **2.** *v.t.* *pres. part.* **vi·gnet·ting** *past* and *past part.* **vi·gnet·ted** to make a vignette portrait of ‖ to shade off the background of (a portrait) [F.]

Vi·gno·la (vi:njólɑ), Giacomo Barozzi da (1507-73), Italian architect. He built many fine churches and palaces, esp. in Rome, and is famous for his 'Treatise on the Five Orders of Architecture' (1562)

Vi·gny (vi:nji:), Alfred de (1797-1863), French poet. His romanticism was of a stoical and elevated sort which sets larger-than-life figures face-to-face with an impressive destiny. Besides lyric poetry ('Poèmes antiques et modernes', 1826 and 'les Destinées', 1864) he wrote novels, including 'Cinq-Mars' (1826) and dramas, including 'Chatterton' (1835)

Vi·go (ví:gou) a port (pop. 230,611) in Galicia, Spain: sardine fishing, canning

vig·or *Br.* **vig·our** (vígər) *n.* physical or intellectual power ‖ vitality, strength **in vigor** (*law*) in force or enforceable [A. F., O.F. *vigor*]

vig·or·ous (vígərəs) *adj.* of, having, calling for or done with vigor [A.F., O.F.]

vigour *VIGOR

Vi·i·pu·ri (ví:puəri:) *VYBORG

Vi·ja·ya·wa·da (vɪdʒəjəwáːdə) (formerly Bezwada) a rail center (pop. 317,258) in Andhra Pradesh, India, on the Kistna, headquarters of the Kistna canal system. Industries: steel, chemicals. Hindu and Buddhist shrines

vi·king (váikiŋ) *n.* (*hist.*) one of the Scandinavian warriors who raided (8th–10th cc.) the coasts of Europe, the British Isles, Iceland and Greenland. One group, the Varangians, pillaged the Baltic, settled in Russia (9th c.) and reached Constantinople (10th c.). Others harried the north coast of Europe (9th c.), sacking Paris (845 and 856) and giving their name to Norsemen or Northmen to Normandy. In England (9th and 10th cc.), where they were known as the Danes, they settled in the Danelaw, took the English throne (11th c.) and built up a vast empire under Cnut. Other vikings, under such leaders as Eric the Red and Leif Ericson, reached Greenland and are thought to have landed in North America (c. 1000) [fr. O.N. *víkingr* perh. fr. O.N. *vík*, creek, inlet]

Viking *n.* (*mil.*) a twin-turbofan-engine, multi-crew aircraft (S-3) capable of operating from aircraft carriers

Viking I *n.* U.S. rocket to Mars, touched down July 20, 1976

vi·la·yet (vi:lájet) *n.* a Turkish province or main administrative division [Turk. fr. Arab.]

Vil·ca·bam·ba (vi:lkɑbámbɑ) the last great capital of the Incas, located by 16th-c. chronicles in the southern Peruvian Andes. For about 40 years after the Conquest (1530), some 4,000 Indians continued to resist the Spaniards from their last redoubt, which they embellished with palaces, temples, fountains, gardens and courtyards. After the Spaniards killed (1572) the last Inca ruler, Vilcabamba was apparently abandoned and became the 'lost city of the Incas'. An expedition (1959-64) discovered (1964) 6-10 sq. miles of ruins, on three succeeding plateaus between 4,500 ft and 12,000 ft, to the northwest of Machu Picchu

vile (vail) *comp.* **vil·er** *superl.* **vil·est** *adj.* morally hateful ‖ foul, *a vile stench* [A.F. and O.F. *vil*]

vil·i·fi·ca·tion (vɪlifikéiʃən) *n.* a vilifying or being vilified

vil·i·fy (vɪlifai) *pres. part.* **vil·i·fy·ing** *past* and *past part.* **vil·i·fied** *v.t.* to impute scandalous behavior to, say abusive things about [fr. L.L. *vilificare*]

vil·i·pend (vɪləpend) *v.t. (rhet.)* to speak of with contempt [O.F. *vilipender* or fr. L. *vilipendere*]

Vil·la (víːja), Francisco ('Pancho', né Doroteo Arango, 1887-1923), Mexican bandit and revolutionist, and one of the most popular figures of the Mexican Revolution. His contribution in the initial stage of 1910-11 helped to overthrow Porfirio Díaz and secure the presidency for Francisco Madero. When Madero was overthrown (1913) by Victoriano Huerta, Villa joined the opposing constitutionalist forces of Venustiano Carranza. At the head of his cavalry, Los Dorados, he gained control of N. Mexico and was instrumental in forcing (1914) Huerta's resignation. Breaking with Carranza, he and Emiliano Zapata occupied (1914-15) Mexico City. Angered by U.S. President Wilson's recognition of Carranza, his followers attacked (1917) Columbus, N.M. It is not known if Villa took part, but he was held responsible. He was unsuccessfully pursued for 11 months (1916-17) by a U.S. punitive expedition led by Gen. Pershing. He was assassinated at Parral (Chihuahua). His life is retold in numerous stories and songs

vil·la (víːlə) *n.* a holiday house, esp. by the sea or in mountains ‖ a country house, esp. an imposing one ‖ (*Br.*) a small suburban house with its own garden ‖ (*Rom. hist.*) a luxurious residence, usually with extensive grounds and often with an agricultural estate attached [L. and Ital.]

Vi·lla Cis·ne·ros (víːjaθiːsnérɔs, víːjasiːsnérɔs) *SPANISH SAHARA

vil·lage (vɪlidʒ) *n.* the houses and other buildings of a community of between about a hundred and a few thousand people ‖ the community occupying a village **vil·lag·er** *n.* someone who lives and works in a village [O.F.]

vil·lag·i·za·tion (vɪlədʒəzéiʃən) *n.* placing land rights in the hands of the village. *ant.* nationalization

vil·lain (vɪlən) *n.* someone guilty or capable of vile deeds or wickedness ‖ the character in a play or novel opposed to the hero and motivating much of the action ‖ *VILLEIN **vil·lain·ous** *adj.* [A.F. and O.F. *vilein, villain*]

vil·lain·y (vɪləni) *pl.* **vil·lain·ies** *n.* villainous conduct ‖ a villainous act ‖ the state or quality of being villainous [A.F. and O.F. *vilenie, vileinie, vilanie*]

Vil·la-Lo·bos (víːlələbɔs), Heitor (1887-1959), prolific Brazilian composer. His compositions (instrumental, chamber, vocal, operatic and symphonic) include many which echo or exploit African and Indian themes in local Brazilian music

vil·la·nelle (vɪlənél) *n.* a poem of five tercets and a final quatrain with two rhymes [F. fr. Ital.]

Vil·lard (vilár, vilárd), Henry (1835-1900), U.S. journalist and financier, of German origin. He reported the Lincoln-Douglas debates (1858), the discovery (1859-60) of gold in Colorado, and some of the major engagements of the Civil War. He purchased (1881) and combined the 'New York Evening Post' and the weekly 'Nation', and organized (1890) the Edison General Electric Company

Vi·lla-ro·el (víːjərɔ́el), Gualberto (1908-46), Bolivian army officer and dictator (1943-6). He was assassinated

Vi·llar·ri·ca (vɪjarrɪ́ka) an industrial city (pop. 35,000) in S. central Paraguay: sugar refineries, distilleries, sawmills, flour mills, brick and tile works

-ville (*colloq.*) combining form usu. used with an adjective to indicate the character of a thing or place, e.g., *dullsville, weirdsville*

Vi·lle·da Mo·ra·les (víːjéðamɔráles), Ramón (1909-71), Honduran liberal politician and president of the Republic (1957-63). He was deposed by the army

Ville·har·douin (viːlærdwɛ̃), Geoffroi de (c. 1150–c. 1213), French chronicler, author of 'La Conquête de Constantinople' (c. 1212), a main source for the history of the 4th Crusade, in which he took part

vil·lein, vil·lain (vɪlən) *n.* (*hist.*) a workman bound in service to his feudal lord or to a feudal estate [A.F. *villein, villain*]

vil·lein·age (vɪlənidʒ) *n.* the status of a villein ‖ a villein's tenure [A.F. *vilenage, villenage*]

Ville·neuve (viːlnəːv), Pierre Charles Jean Baptiste Sylvestre de (1763-1806), French admiral. He was defeated by Nelson at Trafalgar (1805) and committed suicide

Vil·liers (vɪlərz, vɪljərz), George, dukes of Buckingham *BUCKINGHAM

vil·li·form (vɪlifɔrm) *adj.* resembling villi (*VILLUS) ‖ set densely together like the pile of velvet

Vil·lon (viːjɔ̃), François (1431–c. 1465), French poet. His name was probably François de Montcorbier, but he took the name of his patron, Guillaume de Villon. His 'Petit testament' (c. 1456), 'Grand testament' (1461) and 'Epitaphe Villon' ('Ballade des Pendus', 1462-3) show him as at once sardonic and humane, earthy and impassioned

Villon (viːjɔ̃), Jacques (Gaston Duchamp, 1875-1956), French cubist painter and engraver. His works, comprising still lifes, landscapes and figure studies, combine cubism and representation of nature, suggesting a continuation of the researches of Cézanne

vil·lose (vɪlous) *adj.* villous

vil·los·i·ty (vɪlɔ́siti:) *n.* the state of being villous ‖ a villus ‖ a coating of villi

vil·lous (vɪləs) *adj.* of, like, or covered with, villi

vil·lus (vɪləs) *pl.* **vil·li** (vɪlai) *n.* one of the minute vascular processes on the inner lining of the small intestine. They project into the lumen and help the absorption of digested food ‖ one of the processes on the chorion through which nourishment passes to the embryo [L.=tuft of hair]

Vil·ni·us (vɪlni:əs) (*Russ.* Vilna, *Pol.* Wilno) the capital (pop. 492,000) of Lithuania, U.S.S.R. Industries: mechanical engineering, food processing, textiles, woodworking, light manufactures. University (1578)

Vil·yu·i (vɪljuːiː, vɪljuːí) (Viljny) a tributary (1,500 miles long, navigable for 750) of the Lena in central Siberia, U.S.S.R.

vim (vim) *n.* vigor, energy [L. acc. of *vis*, strength]

Vi·my Ridge, Battle of (viːmiː) the site of a very costly Allied attack (1917) on a German position, mainly by Canadian troops, during the 1st world war

vi·na (víːnə) *n.* an Indian musical instrument, usually with four strings, with a fingerboard of bamboo, and two gourd resonators [Skr. and Hindi *vīnā*]

vi·na·ceous (vainéiʃəs) *adj.* wine-colored [fr. L. *vinaceus*]

Vi·ña del Mar (víːnjaðelmár) a residential suburb and seaside resort (pop. 262,100) of Valparaíso, Chile

vin·ai·grette (vɪnəgrét) *n.* an ornamental vessel containing aromatic vinegar or smelling salts etc. ‖ a vinaigrette sauce [F. fr. *vinaigre*, vinegar]

vinaigrette sauce a sauce of chopped parsley, shallots etc., in vinegar and oil, served cold with artichokes, asparagus, cold meat, fish etc.

vi·nasse (vinǽs) *n.* the liquor remaining when alcoholic liquor is fermented and distilled, used as a source of potassium carbonate [F.]

vin·blas·tine (C₄₆H₅₈O₉N₄) (vɪnblǽsti:n) *n.* (*pharm.*) an alkaloid drug used in treating leukemia and lymphoma; marketed as Velban. *also* vincaleukoblastine

Vin·cent de Paul (vínsəntdəpɔ́l, vɛ̃sɑ̃dəpɔ́l), St (c. 1581-1660), French priest. He worked to help foundlings, galley slaves, war wounded and all sick and suffering, and to send out missionaries. He founded the Lazarists (1625) and the Sisters of Charity (1633). Feast: July 19

Vin·cent of Beau·vais (vɛ̃sɑ̃vbouvei) (c. 1190–c. 1264), French friar. He wrote most of the 'Speculum majus' (c. 1244), an encyclopedia summarizing the knowledge of his time

Vin·cent's infection (vínsənts) infection of the respiratory tract and the mouth, marked by painful ulceration, esp. of the mucous membranes [after Jean H. *Vincent* (d. 1950), F. bacteriologist]

Vinci, Leonardo da *LEONARDO DA VINCI

vin·cris·tine (C₄₆H₅₆N₄O) (vɪnkrísti:n) *n.* (*pharm.*) an anticarcinogenic made from the Madagascar periwinkle; marketed as Oncovin

vin·cu·lum (víŋkjuləm) *pl.* **vin·cu·lums, vin·cu·la** (víŋkjulə) *n.* (*math.*) a line drawn above two or more terms to indicate that these are to be treated as a unit ‖ (*anat.*) a ligament [L.]

Vin·dhya Range (víndjə) a range of hills (mainly 1,500-2,000 ft) crossing India from Gujarat to Bihar, forming the Ganges-Narbada watershed

vin·di·cate (víndikeit) *pres. part.* **vin·di·cat·ing** *past* and *past part.* **vin·di·cat·ed** *v.t.* to prove the truth or virtue of, after this has been questioned or denied [fr. L. *vindicare (vindicatus*, to claim]

vin·di·ca·tion (vindikéiʃən) *n.* a vindicating or being vindicated ‖ a fact which vindicates [O.F. or fr. L. *vindicatio (vindicationis*)]

vin·di·ca·to·ry (víndiketɔri:, víndikətɔ́uri:) *adj.* serving to vindicate ‖ (*law*) punitive, *vindicatory legislation*

vin·dic·tive (vindíktiv) *adj.* having the motive of revenge [fr. L. *vindicta*, revenge]

vine (vain) *n.* a member of *Vitis*, fam. *Vitaceae*, a genus of slender, woody, climbing plants, with alternate, palmate-veined leaves, esp. *V. vinifera*, the grapevine, cultivated in Mediterranean-type climates since very early civilizations ‖ any plant having a long, slender, flexible stem that supports itself by creeping along the ground or by climbing over some object [O.F. *vine, vigne*]

vin·e·gar (vínigər) *n.* a liquid containing up to 6% acetic acid, obtained by the oxidation of the ethyl alcohol in wine, beer etc. by bacteria, and used as a preservative in pickling and as a condiment **vín·e·gar·y** *adj.* [O.F. *vynegre, vinaigre*]

vin·er·y (váinəri:) *pl.* **vin·er·ies** *n.* a greenhouse in which vines are cultivated for dessert grapes [fr. M.L. *vinarium*]

vine·yard (vínjərd) *n.* a plot of land where grapevines are growing

vingt-et-un (vɛ̃teiœ̃) *n.* blackjack

vin·i·fy (vínəfai) *v.* to ferment grape juice into wine

vi·nos·i·ty (vainɔ́siti:) *n.* the state or quality of being vinous [fr. L. *vinositas*, the flavor of wine]

vi·nous (váinəs) *adj.* pertaining to, caused by, made from or addicted to wine [fr. L. *vinosus*]

Vin·son (vínsən), Frederick Moore (1890-1953), U.S. lawyer, Congressman, and chief justice (1946-53) of the U.S. Supreme Court. As secretary of the treasury (1945-6) under President Harry Truman, he helped to establish the International Monetary Fund. As chief justice he believed in a broad interpretation of federal governmental powers, as is shown in his dissenting opinion in 'Youngstown Sheet and Tube Co. v. Sawyer' (1952), in which he supported President Wilson's seizure of the steel industry. In 'Shelley v. Kraemer' (1948) he upheld the rights of racial minorities under the equal protection clause of the 14th amendment

vin·tage (víntidʒ) **1.** *n.* the picking and pressing of grapes for wine ‖ the season for this ‖ the yield of wine or grapes gathered in a particular season or district ‖ a wine of a particular year, *a prewar vintage* **2.** *adj.* venerable, having an excellence that has survived the passing of time, *a vintage car* ‖ not in style any more, outmoded [A.F. altered fr. *vindage, vendage*]

vintage wine a wine of superior quality of a particular year and place put aside for full maturing

vintage year a year productive of vintage wines ‖ a year productive of some specified thing of good quality in good numbers

vint·ner (víntnər) *n.* a wine merchant [alteration of older *vinter*, A.F. fr. L. *vinum*, vine]

vi·nyl (váin'l) *n.* the monovalent, unsaturated group CH₂= CH derived from ethylene ‖ a polymer of a vinyl compound ‖ a resin, plastic or synthetic fiber made from a vinyl compound [fr. L. *vinum*, wine]

vi·nyl·i·dene (vainílidi:n) *n.* the divalent, unsaturated group CH₂=C, the polymerized compounds of which form useful resins [fr. VINYL]

vi·ol (váiəl) *n.* a medieval stringed instrument

CONCISE PRONUNCIATION KEY: (a) æ, c*a*t; ɑ, c*a*r; ɔ f*aw*n; ei, sn*a*ke. **(e)** e, h*e*n; i:, sh*ee*p; iə, d*ee*r; ɛə, b*ea*r. **(i)** i, f*i*sh; ai, t*i*ger; ə:, b*i*rd. **(o)** o, *o*x; au, c*ow*; ou, g*oa*t; u, p*oo*r; ɔi, r*oy*al. **(u)** ʌ, d*u*ck; u, b*u*ll; u:, g*oo*se; ə, b*a*cillus; ju:, c*u*be. x, lo*ch*; θ, *th*ink; ð, bo*th*er; z, *Z*en; ʒ, corsa*g*e; dʒ, sava*g*e; ŋ, ora*ng*utang; j, *y*ak; ʃ, *fi*sh; tʃ, fe*tch*; 'l, rabb*le*; 'n, redd*e*n. Complete pronunciation key appears inside front cover.

made chiefly in treble, tenor and bass sizes, having frets, and bowed in a style differing from that used for the violin, viola etc., to which they gave place at about the end of the 17th c. [fr. A.F., O.F. *viele, vielle* altered after F. *viole*]

vi·o·la (vi:óulǝ) *n.* a stringed instrument larger than a violin, tuned one-fifth lower than a violin, and having a range of more than three octaves above C below middle C ‖ a member of the orchestra who plays this instrument [Ital. and Span.]

vi·o·la (váiǝlǝ, vaióulǝ) *n.* a member of *Viola*, fam. *Violaceae*, a genus of lowgrowing plants bearing large, solitary flowers of various colors (cf. PANSY, cf. VIOLET). About 400 species are known ‖ a hybrid derived from the garden pansy [L.=a violet]

vi·o·la·ceous (vaiǝléiʃǝs) *adj.* of violet color ‖ belonging to fam. *Violaceae*, the violet family [fr. L. *violaceus*, violet-colored]

vi·o·la da gam·ba (vi:óulǝdǝgámbǝ, vi:óulǝdǝgámbǝ) *n.* a bass instrument of the viol family, having a range roughly equal to that of the cello. It remained in use as a solo instrument until the late 18th c. [Ital.+leg viol]

vi·o·la d'a·mo·re (vi:óulǝdǝmórei, vi:óulǝdǝmóurei) *n.* a stringed instrument related to the viols, but without frets. When one of the seven main strings is bowed a sympathetic resonance is set up in the under string of a secondary set [Ital.=viol of love]

vi·o·late (váiǝleit) *pres. part.* **vi·o·lat·ing** *past and past part.* **vi·o·lat·ed** *v.t.* to break (a promise, law, principle etc.) by forceful opposition to it ‖ to rape ‖ to fail conspicuously to show respect for, *to violate a person's privacy* ‖ to desecrate (something sacred) [fr. L. *violare* (*violatus*)]

vi·o·la·tion (vaiǝléiʃǝn) *n.* a violating or being violated [O.F. *violacion* or fr. L. *violatio* (*violationis*)]

vi·o·la·tor (váiǝleitǝr) *n.* a person who violates

vi·o·lence (váiǝlǝns) *n.* use of physical force so as to damage or injure ‖ intense natural force or energy ‖ an abusive use of force ‖ passion, fury ‖ distortion of meaning ‖ desecration **to do violence to** to offend, outrage, *to do violence to someone's sense of justice* [A.F. and O.F.]

vi·o·lent (váiǝlǝnt) *adj.* characterized by the exercise or production of very great force, *a violent storm* ‖ markedly intense, *violent colors* ‖ furious, *violent language* ‖ caused by violence ‖ tending to pervert meaning [O.F. or fr. L. *violentus*]

vi·o·let (váiǝlit) **1.** *n.* a small-flowered plant of the genus *Viola*, esp. the fragrant *V. odorata* ‖ the bluish-purple color of the flowers of *V. odorata* ‖ a pigment, fabric etc. of the color of these flowers ‖ any of various similar plants of different genera **2.** *adj.* having a violet color [dim. of O.F. *viole*]

vi·o·lin (vaiǝlín) *n.* a four-stringed treble musical instrument played with a bow and having a compass of three and a half octaves or more above G below middle C ‖ the member of an orchestra who plays this instrument, *first violin* [fr. Ital. *violino*]

vi·o·lin·ist (vaiǝlínist) *n.* a violin player [fr. Ital. *violinista*]

Viol·let-le-Duc (vjɔleilǝdyk), Eugene Emmanuel (1814-79), French architect. He led the Gothic revival, and his two dictionaries of medieval architecture and furniture are standard works. He also restored many medieval buildings and monuments, including Notre-Dame de Paris and Carcassonne

vi·o·lon·cel·lo (vaiǝlǝntʃélou) *n.* a cello [Ital.]

VIP (vi:aipí:) *n.* a person of eminence or importance, esp. a high government official [very important person]

VIP (*computer abbr.*) for variable information processing, an extensive general information storage system used by Naval Ordnance Laboratory

vi·per (váipǝr) *n.* an adder ‖ (*rhet.*) a person who behaves with great malice, or who shows rank ingratitude **vi·per·ous** (váipǝrǝs) *adj.* of, relating to or characteristic of a viper or vipers ‖ (*rhet*) malicious [O.F. *vipere, vipre* or fr. L. *vipera*, snake]

viper's bugloss *n. Echium vulgare*, fam. *Boraginaceae*, a rough hairy biennial, with short dense cymose inflorescences of flowers, pink in bud and bright blue in bloom

Vi·ra·co·cha (vi:rǝkóutʃǝ) the Inca creator god and god of rain. He dwelt in Lake Titicaca. The name was given (16th c.) by the ancient Peruvians and Chileans to the Spanish conquistadores

vi·ra·go (virágou) *pl.* **vi·ra·goes, vi·ra·gos** *n.* a shrewish, noisy woman, esp. one who is big and strong [L.=manlike woman]

vir·e·lay (vírǝlei) *n.* a Provençal verse form of short lines, either composed in stanzas each of which have two rhymes only, the last rhyme in a stanza becoming the main rhyme of the succeeding stanza, or else composed entirely on two rhymes, lines 1 and 2 ending alternate stanzas and closing the poem together but reversed in order [O.F. *virelai*]

vir·e·o (víri:ou) *pl.* **vir·e·os** *n.* any of various small New World insectivorous birds of fam. *vireonidae*, having gray or olive-green plumage

vi·res·cence (virés̩ns, vairés̩ns) *n.* (*bot.*) greenness, esp. abnormal greenness in a petal usually colored otherwise

vi·res·cent (virés̩nt, vairés̩nt) *adj.* turning green ‖ greenish [fr. L. *virescens* (*virescentis*) fr. *virescere*, to become green]

vir·gate (vɔ́:rgit, vɔ́:rgeit) *adj.* (*bot.*) long, straight and slim as a rod ‖ (*bot.*) having many twigs [fr. L. *virgatus*]

Vir·gil·i·an (vǝrdʒíli:ǝn) *adj.* in the style of Virgil [fr. L. *Vergilianus*]

Vir·gil, Ver·gil (vɔ́:rdʒǝl), (Publius Vergilius Maro, 70-19 B.C.), Latin poet. Patronized by Maecenas and Augustus, he was able to devote his entire life to poetry. The 'Eclogues' (43-37 B.C.), a collection of pastoral poems, and the 'Georgics' (37-30 B.C.), a series of didactic poems on the art of farming, established him as the foremost poet of his age. The remaining 11 years of his life were devoted to the composition of 'Aeneid', his masterpiece. In this epic he employed Homeric hexameters to glorify the legendary past of Rome. Throughout the Latin Middle Ages Virgil was looked upon as the model of the poet, and widely imitated. Dante takes him as his guide in the first two books of the 'Divine Comedy'

vir·gin (vɔ́:rdʒin) **1.** *n.* a person who has not had sexual intercourse, esp. a girl or woman ‖ (in the early Christian Church) a chaste woman or girl noted for her piety and faith and so accorded a special place in the community **the Virgin** *MARY, THE VIRGIN ‖ (*astron.*) the constellation Virgo **2.** *adj.* of or being a virgin ‖ not yet cultivated or otherwise brought into use, *virgin forest* ‖ (of elements) occurring uncombined in the earth's crust, *virgin sulfur* ‖ (of metals) obtained by simple smelting of an ore ‖ (of oils) obtained from the first pressing of a fruit or nut [A.F. and O.F. *virgine*]

vir·gin·al (vɔ́:rdʒin'l) *n.* a small keyboard musical instrument in a frame without legs, of the 16th and 17th cc. The strings are plucked, as in a harpsichord [prob. O.F. or fr. L. *virginalis*]

virginal *adj.* of or appropriate to a virgin [O.F. or fr. L. *virginalis*]

virgin birth (*theol.*) the doctrine that Jesus was born to a virgin mother, Mary. According to Christian theology Jesus was begotten by the Holy Ghost ‖ (*zool.*) parthenogenesis

Vir·gin·ia (vǝrdʒínjǝ) (*abbr.* Va.) a state (area 40,815 sq. miles, pop. 5,550,000) on the southern Atlantic coast of the U.S.A. Capital: Richmond. It is largely a hilly plateau extending from the Appalachians to the coastal plain. Agriculture: tobacco, cereals, peanuts, apples, dairying, poultry, beef cattle. Resources: coal, building materials, lead, zinc. Industries: chemicals, tobacco products, textiles, shipbuilding, food processing. State university (1819) at Charlottesville. Virginia, named after Elizabeth I, 'the Virgin Queen', was the first permanent English settlement in North America (1607). It was one of the Thirteen Colonies, and became (1788) the 10th state of the U.S.A.

Virginia and Kentucky Resolutions three resolutions passed by state legislatures during the administration of President John Adams. The first (1798) was authored by James Madison and the other two (1798, 1799) by Vice-President Thomas Jefferson. They advocated the repeal of the Alien and Sedition Acts (1798) and held that the Federal government possessed only limited and delegated powers. Jefferson further contended that the states, and not the national government, should be the arbiter of whether the latter had exceeded its mandate. This authority to determine the constitutionality of federal laws eventually passed to the U.S. Supreme Court. The resolutions

were invoked (1860) by the seceding Southern states

Virginia Company *LONDON COMPANY

Virginia creeper *Parthenocissus quinquefolia*, fam. *Vitaceae*, a vine which climbs by attaching tendrils to its host

Virginia deer *Odocoileus virginianus*, the most abundant North American deer, also called white-tailed deer because its long tail has a white underside

Virginia Plan a plan proposed by the Virginia delegation at the Constitutional Convention of 1787. It advocated the creation of strong national government rather than the strengthening of the confederation of states, and it provided for a federal judiciary and a power of amendment to be lodged outside the legislature. The plan was opposed by the less populous states because its distribution of the legislative seats favored the more populous states

Virginia reel a spirited American country dance in which couples form a long set opposite one another and execute lively steps in a pattern including a reel, to the music of a fiddle

Virginia, University of a U.S. educational institution founded (1819) near Charlottesville, Va., by Thomas Jefferson

Virginia, West *WEST VIRGINIA

Virgin Islands a cluster of small islands in the Leeward group, West Indies, divided between the British Virgin Islands and the Virgin Islands of the U.S.A. Population: mainly Afro-West Indian and mulatto. The islands were discovered (1493) by Columbus, and were settled (17th c.) by England and Denmark

Virgin Islands, British a British colony (land area 59 sq. miles, pop. 10,030) occupying the 36 eastern islands (11 inhabited) of the Virgin Is. Capital: Road Town (pop. 2,000) on Tortola Is. Industries: truck farming, fruit, fishing. The islands were taken by English pirates (1666) and were administered (1871-1956) as part of the Leeward Is colony

Virgin Islands of the United States an overseas territory (land area 133 sq. miles, pop. 95,591) of the U.S.A. occupying the 52 western islands (3 inhabited) of the Virgin Is. Main islands: St Thomas (area 32 sq. miles) and St Croix (area 82 sq. miles). Capital: Charlotte Amalie on St Thomas. Industries: agriculture (cattle raising, sugarcane, truck farming), fuel bunkering, rum, fishing, tourism. The islands were bought from Denmark by the U.S.A. (1917)

vir·gin·i·ty (vǝrdʒíniti:) *n.* the state or quality of being a virgin [A.F. and O.F. *virginite*]

vir·gin·i·um (vǝrdʒíni:ǝm) *n.* the old name for francium [Mod. L. after the state of VIRGINIA]

Virgin Mary *MARY, THE VIRGIN

Vir·go (vɔ́:rgou) an equatorial constellation ‖ the sixth sign of the zodiac

vir·gu·late (vɔ́:rgjulit, vɔ́:rgjuleit) *adj.* (*bot.*) rod-shaped [fr. L. *virgulatus* fr. *virgula* dim. of *virga*, rod]

vir·i·des·cence (viridés'ns) *n.* greenishness

vir·i·des·cent (viridés'nt) *adj.* greenish [fr. L.L. *viridescens* (*viridescentis*) fr. *viridescere*, to become green]

vir·id·i·an (viridi:ǝn) *n.* a deep green pigment with blue overtones [fr. L. *viridis*]

vir·id·i·ty (viríditi:) *n.* greenness, e.g. of the color of young leaves ‖ (*rhet.*) freshness, innocence [fr. L. *viriditas*]

vir·ile (víral, *Br.* vírail) *adj.* having in marked degree the characteristics of a man as a male being ‖ capable of procreating ‖ forceful and vigorous as befits a man [O.F. *viril* or fr. L. *virilis*]

vir·il·i·ty (viríliti:) *n.* the state or quality of being virile [fr. F. *virilité* or L. *virilitas*]

vir·i·on (váiri:ɒn) *n.* (*genetics*) a complete infective viral particle made up of RNA in a protein shell that controls the form of viral replicating. *Cf* INTERFERON

vi·rol·o·gy (vairólǝdʒi:) *n.* the study of viruses [fr. Mod. L. *virus*, virus+Gk *logos*, discourse]

virtual literacy the capacity to understand the world

virtual memory (*computer*) a peripheral look ahead, look behind notational memory. *also* virtual storage

virtual process (*quantum mech.*) a process used in creating a hypothetical model, where a real model is not realizable

virtual storage (*computer*) virtual memory (which see)

virtuous cycle (*economics*) proposed procedure that a government would set in motion auto-

---

CONCISE PRONUNCIATION KEY: **(a)** æ, c*a*t; ɑ, c*a*r; ɔ, f*aw*n; ei, sn*a*ke; **(e)** e, h*e*n; i:, sh*ee*p; iǝ, d*ee*r; ɛǝ, b*ea*r. **(i)** i, f*i*sh; ai, t*i*ger; ǝ:, b*i*rd. **(o)** o, *o*x; au, c*ow*; ou, g*oa*t; u, p*oo*r; ɔi, r*oy*al. **(u)** ʌ, d*u*ck; u, b*u*ll; u:, g*oo*se; ǝ, b*a*cillus; ju:, c*u*be. x, lo*ch*; θ, *th*ink; ð, bo*th*er; z, *Z*en; ʒ, corsa*g*e; dʒ, sava*g*e; ŋ, ora*ng*utang; j, *y*ak; ʃ, *fi*sh; tʃ, fe*tch*; 'l, rabb*le*; 'n, redd*en*. Complete pronunciation key appears inside front cover.

matically to prevent currency devaluation, e.g., increase in interest rates, price stabilization, import restriction. *Cf* VICIOUS CYCLE

vir·tu, ver·tu (vərtú:) *n.* a liking for, or knowledge of, curios, antiques etc. curios, antiques etc. collectively [Ital. *virtù*]

vir·tu·al (vớ:rtʃuəl) *adj.* being something specified in essence or effect though not in name [fr. M.L. *virtualis*]

virtual focus the point from which light appears to diverge but does not in fact do so, or the point to which convergent rays are directed but which they do not reach

virtual image an image formed of virtual foci

vir·tu·al·i·ty (vờ:rtʃu:æliti:) *n.* the state or quality of being virtual

vir·tu·al·ly (vớ:rtʃuəli:) *adv.* almost entirely

vir·tue (vớ:rtʃu:) *n.* a quality held to be of great moral value (*CARDINAL VIRTUES, *THEOLOGICAL VIRTUES) ‖ moral excellence, goodness ‖ female chastity ‖ (of a remedy) power to do good ‖ (*pl.*) an order of angels (*ANGEL) **by** (or **in**) **virtue of** on the strength or authority of, *he was able to do it by virtue of his office* [A.F., O.F. *vertu*]

vir·tu·os·i·ty (vờ:rtʃu:ósiti:) *n.* great technical ability in a fine art, esp. in the playing of a musical instrument

vir·tu·o·so (vờ:rtʃu:óusou) *pl.* **vir·tu·o·sos, vir·tu·o·si** (vờ:rtʃu:óusi:) *n.* someone very highly skilled in the technique of a fine art, esp. in the playing of a musical instrument [Ital.=skilled, learned]

vir·tu·ous (vớ:rtʃuəs) *adj.* showing or having moral virtue ‖ chaste [A.F. and O.F. *vertuous*]

vir·u·lence (vírulens) *n.* the quality of being virulent **vir·u·len·cy** *n.* virulence [fr. L. *virulentia*]

vir·u·lent (vírulənt, vírjulənt) *adj.* (of a disease) characterized by severity, rapidity of course and malignancy ‖ (of a microorganism) extremely toxic or poisonous ‖ malignant, bitterly hostile, *virulent enmity* [fr. L. *virulentus,* poisonous]

vi·rus (váirəs) *pl.* **vi·rus·es** *n.* a submicroscopic entity consisting principally of nucleoprotein and able to pass through bacteria-retaining filters. Viruses have many characteristics of living organisms (e.g. they are capable of growth and multiplication in living cells) and are recognized by their toxic or pathogenic effects in plants and animal cells (e.g. they are the agents which cause mumps, rabies or mosaic) [L.=a slimy liquid]

vi·sa (ví:zə) 1. *n.* an official endorsement of a passport denoting that the owner has permission either to enter or cross a particular country 2. *v.t.* to endorse (a passport) in this way [F.]

vis·age (vízidʒ) *n.* (*rhet.*) the face [A.F. and O.F.]

vis·a·giste (vi:zaʒí:st) *n.* a makeup artist

Vi·sa·kha·pat·nam (visákapátnəm) (formerly Vizagapatam) a port (pop. 352,504) in N. Andhra Pradesh, India: shipbuilding

vis·à·vis (vi:zəví:) 1. *n.* face to face, *they talked vis à vis* 2. *n.* the person facing one 3. *prep.* as compared with ‖ with respect to ‖ facing [F.]

Vi·sa·yas (visáiəz) the central group of islands in the Philippines: Panay, Samar, Leyte, Negros, Bohol, Masbate, and about 480 adjacent smaller islands

viscacha *VIZCACHA

vis·cer·a (vísərə) *pl. n.* the bodily organs occupying the great cavities, esp. the stomach, intestines etc. which occupy the trunk [L.=inner organs]

vis·cer·al (vísərəl) *adj.* of, like, or felt in the viscera [fr. M.L. *visceralis*]

vis·cid (vísid) *adj.* viscous ‖ (of leaves) covered with a sticky substance **vis·cíd·i·ty** *n.* [fr. L.L. *viscidus*]

vis·cin (vísin) *n.* a sticky substance, $C_{10}H_{24}O_4$, obtained from various plants, esp. from mistletoe berries [F.]

Vis·con·ti (vi:skónti:) the ruling family of Milan (1277-1447)

vis·cose (vískous) *n.* a thick, brownish liquid prepared by the interaction of cellulose with sodium hydroxide and carbon disulfide. The liquid, which is largely a solution of cellulose xanthate, is forced through small holes into a solution (*CUPRAMMONIUM SOLUTION) which decomposes the xanthate and gives threads of cellulose (viscose rayon). The liquid is also used for the manufacture of cellulose film from which transparent wrappings are made [fr. L. *viscosus,* viscous]

vis·cos·i·ty (viskósiti:) *pl.* **vis·cos·i·ties** *n.* the quality or property of a fluid that causes it to resist flow (*VISCOSITY, COEFFICIENT OF) [O.E. *viscosite* or fr. M.L. *viscositas*]

viscosity, coefficient of the ratio in a fluid flow of the shearing stress to the rate of shear strain. With increasing temperature the coefficient falls for a liquid (e.g. molasses) and rises for a gas (e.g. steam)

vis·count (váikaunt) *n.* a British peer of lower rank than an earl but of higher rank than a baron ‖ the courtesy title of the eldest son of an earl before he succeeds to the title **vís·count·cy** *n.* the rank of a viscount [A.F. *vescounte, viscounte,* O.F. *visconte, viconte*]

vis·count·ess (váikauntis) *n.* the wife of a viscount, or sometimes the title held in the holder's own right

vis·count·y (váikaunti:) *pl.* **vis·count·ies** *n.* a viscountcy ‖ (*hist.*) the land or jurisdiction of a viscount

vis·cous (vískəs) *adj.* having viscosity ‖ (of leaves) viscid ‖ sticky, slow-flowing [A.F. *viscous* or fr. L. *viscosus*]

vise, *Br.* **vice** (vais) *n.* a tool by which an object being worked is gripped between two jaws, which are brought together by a screw [O.F. *vis*]

Vi·shin·sky, Vy·shin·sky (viʃínski:), Andrei Yanuarievich (1883-1954), Russian diplomat. As foreign minister (1949-53) and as the chief U.S.S.R. delegate to the U.N. he attacked Western rearmament policy

Vish·nu (víʃnu:) one of the chief gods of Hinduism. Originally a member of the pantheon worshipped in the Vedic hymns, he came to be identified with the divine principle of grace. Brahma (the creator), Vishnu (the preserver) and Siva (the dissolver) form the threefold manifestation of divine activity. Vishnu is believed to have been incarnated on nine occasions in order to save the world. The last of these incarnations (avatars) was as Krishna, and there is to be a tenth, as Kalkin, whose coming will herald the end of the world as we know it

vis·i·bil·i·ty (vizəbíliti:) *n.* the fact or state of being visible ‖ range of vision, esp. with respect to weather conditions (mist, fog etc.) [fr. L.L. *visibilitas*]

vis·i·ble (vízəb'l) *adj.* able to be seen ‖ apparent to the mind, *without visible means of support* **vís·i·bly** *adv.* [O.F. or fr. L. *visibilis*]

vis·i·ble-in·fra·red spin-scan radiometer (vízəb'línfrəred) device that takes pictures during day or night by sensing reflected sunlight or surface heat radiation

visible spectrum the part of the electromagnetic spectrum that may be perceived by the human eye. It extends from a wavelength of almost 3800Å (violet light) to almost 7600Å (red light)

Vis·i·goth (vízigoθ) *n.* a member of the western division of the Goths, who, under their leader Alaric, invaded Italy and sacked Rome (410). They established a kingdom covering most of S. Gaul and Spain (5th c.), but they lost Gaul to Clovis (507), while the Spanish kingdom survived until the Moorish conquest (711)

vi·sion (víʒən) 1. *n.* the act of seeing or the ability to see, *range of vision* ‖ a picture formed in the mind, *visions of future greatness* ‖ imaginative foresight, *a man of vision* ‖ a supernatural apparition ‖ something seen, esp. something very beautiful 2. *v.t.* to see as if in a vision **ví·sion·al** *adj.* **ví·sion·ar·y** 1. *pl.* **ví·sion·ar·ies** *n.* someone who imagines how things should be and pays little regard to how they actually are or are likely in fact to be 2. *adj.* conjured up in the imagination without being related to facts ‖ inclined to be a visionary ‖ of the nature of a vision [A.F. *visiun, visioun,* O.F. *vision* or fr. L. *visio* (*visionis*)]

—Vision occurs when light, entering the eye and focused on the retina, causes chemical changes in the cells of the retina. Impulses travel from these cells by way of the optic nerve to the brain, where they are interpreted in the conscious mind. The brain is therefore an active partner with the eye, and its misinterpretation can result in an optical illusion. Thus judgments of color and of the speed of a moving object may easily be subject to error

vi·sion-mix (víʒənmiks) *v.* (*cinematography*) to integrate current shots or stills with motion pictures or video pictures

vis·it (vízit) 1. *v.t.* to go or come to see (someone) socially, often for a short vacation, *to visit relatives* ‖ to inspect as a sightseer, *to visit a* monument ‖ to inspect with authority, *an archdeacon visits the parishes of a diocese* ‖ to call on in charity, *to visit the sick* ‖ to pay a professional call on, *to visit a patient* ‖ to call on for professional advice, *to visit one's doctor* ‖ to go to (a holy place) as an act of devotion ‖ (*Bible*) to bless, comfort (someone) ‖ (*Bible,* with 'on' or 'upon') to take vengeance for (sin) ‖ (*Bible*) to avenge sin on (a person) ‖ (*rhet.,* with 'with') to afflict with injury or trouble ‖ to migrate for part of the year to ‖ *v.i.* to make a visit 2. *n.* a visiting or being visited ‖ a period of time spent in visiting ‖ (*naut.*) the boarding of a neutral state by an officer of a state at war, for reasons of search [O.F. *visiter* or fr. L. *visitare,* to go to see]

vis·i·tant (vízitənt) *n.* a migratory bird coming to a district for a certain time ‖ a fantastic visitor, *visitants from Mars* ‖ a phantom **Vis·i·tant** a member of the order of Sisters of the visitation [F. or fr. L. *visitans* (*visitantis*) fr. *visitare,* to visit]

vis·i·ta·tion (vizitéiʃən) *n.* an official visit for inspection, e.g. by an archdeacon ‖ an instance of affliction or of blessing regarded as divine punishment or reward ‖ (*zool.*) an abnormal invasion of a district by animals, *a visitation of rats* ‖ (*naut.*) a visit **the Vis·i·ta·tion,** the visit of the virgin Mary to S. Elizabeth (Luke i, 39) ‖ the feast commemorating this (July 2) [A.F. *visitacioun* or fr. L. *visitatio* (*visitationis*)]

Visitation, Sisters of the a contemplative order of nuns (Visitants) founded (1610) by St Francis of Sales for the care of the sick

vis·i·ta·to·ri·al (vizitətóri:əl, vizitətóuri:əl) *adj.* of or pertaining to visitation ‖ having the power of inspection

visiting card (*Br.*) a calling card

vis·i·tor (vízitər) *n.* someone who makes a visit [A.F. *visitour,* O.F. *visiteor, visiteur*]

vis·i·to·ri·al (vizitóri:əl, vizitóuri:əl) *adj.* visitatorial

vi·sor, vi·zor (váizər) *n.* (*armor*) a movable, perforated part of a helmet, covering the face but permitting sight and speech through the perforations ‖ the peak of a cap, shielding the eyes from direct sunlight ‖ any of various similar devices used to shade the eyes, e.g. one on a car windshield [A.F. *viser* fr. F. *vis,* face]

VISTA *VOLUNTEERS IN SERVICE TO AMERICA

vis·ta (vístə) *n.* a view extending into the distance but bounded, e.g. by headlands or rows of trees ‖ a mental view into the distant past or future [Ital.]

Vis·tu·la (vístʃu:lə) (*Pol.* Wisla) the chief river (680 miles long) of Poland, flowing from the Carpathians to the Baltic, navigable to Torun

vis·u·al (víʒu:əl) *adj.* of, pertaining to, or used in, seeing ‖ obtained by or arising from seeing, *visual proof* ‖ relying on sight, *visual control* ‖ visible ‖ of or producing a mental image ‖ (*optics*) optical [O.F. or fr. L.L. *visualis*]

visual aids devices to assist understanding or memory by displaying what is to be understood or memorized in a visible form (picture, chart etc.)

visual instrument a keyboard device that projects colored visual patterns on a screen, often to accompany music

vis·u·al·i·za·tion (viʒu:əlizéiʃən) *n.* a visualizing or being visualized ‖ a mental picture

vis·u·al·ize (víʒú:əlaiz) *pres. part.* **vis·u·al·iz·ing** *past and past part.* **vis·u·al·ized** *v.t.* to form a mental picture of

visual pollution the unsightly products of industry, advertisements, waste disposal, graffiti, etc.

visual purple rhodopsin

vi·tal (váit'l) 1. *adj.* of, concerned with or necessary to life ‖ full of life ‖ essential, *of vital importance* 2. *n.* (*pl.*) those parts of the body without which life cannot continue (e.g. the heart or brain, in contrast to a limb) [O.F. or fr. L. *vitalis*]

vi·tal·ism (váit'lizəm) *n.* the doctrine that life has its origin elsewhere than in physical or chemical causation (opp. MECHANISM) **vi·tal·ist** *n.* **vi·tal·ís·tic** *adj.* [F. *vitalisme*]

vi·tal·i·ty (vaitǽliti:) *pl.* **vi·tal·i·ties** *n.* the quality of being alive, esp. the strength of this quality, *his vitality was lowered by his long illness* ‖ animation, energy, liveliness [fr. L. *vitalitas*]

vi·tal·ize (váit'laiz) *pres. part.* **vi·tal·iz·ing** *past and past part.* **vi·tal·ized** *v.t.* to give energy or vigor to, to animate

vital signs (*med.*) basic diagnostic elements, e.g., pulse rate, respiratory rate, body temperature, blood pressure

vital statistics a record of births, marriages and deaths ‖ (*pop.*, of a woman) measurements around the bosom, the waist and the hips

vi·ta·min (váitəmin) *n.* any of a number of organic chemical substances, present in various foods and essential in very small quantities (less than 25 mg. per day) to health (*DIET) [fr. L. *vita*, life+AMINE]

vi·ta·mi·za·tion (váitəməzéiʃən) *n.* process of taking or giving vitamins —**vitamize** *v.*

vi·tel·lar·i·um (viteléəri:əm) *pl.* **vi·tel·lar·i·a** (viteléəri:ə) *n.* a yolk gland [Mod. L. fr. *vitellus*]

vi·tel·lin (vitélin, vaitélin) *n.* a protein in the yolk of an egg [fr. L. *vitellus*, the yolk of an egg]

vi·tel·line (vitélin, vaitélin) *adj.* of the yolk of an egg ‖ of the color of an egg yolk [fr. M.L. *vitellinus*]

vitelline duct (*med.*) in an embryo, the part of the yolk sac that opens into the midgut or the lower portion of the future ileum. *also* umbilical duct, yolk stalk

vitelline membrane the transparent membrane surrounding an egg yolk

Vi·tel·li·us (vitéli:əs), Aulus (15-69), Roman emperor (69). Commander of the legions on the Rhine, he was proclaimed emperor by his troops but was defeated by Vespasian later in the year

vi·tel·lus (vitéləs, vaitéləs) *pl.* **vi·tel·lus·es** (*embry.*) the yolk of an egg [L.]

Vi·ter·bo (vitérbou) an agricultural market (pop. 58,618) in Latium, Italy. Romanesque-Gothic cathedral (12th-16th cc.), Romanesque and Gothic churches, papal palace (13th c.), Farnese palace (15th c.)

vi·ti·ate (víʃi:eit) *pres. part.* **vi·ti·at·ing** *past* and *past part.* **vi·ti·at·ed** *v.t.* to spoil, make defective, lessen the quality of ‖ to corrupt (morals or taste) ‖ (*law*) to invalidate or make wholly or partly ineffective **vi·ti·a·tion, ví·ti·a·tor** *ns* [fr. L. *vitiare* (*vitiatus*)]

vit·i·cul·ture (vítikʌltʃər, váitikʌltʃər) *n.* the science of growing grapes ‖ the cultivation of grapevines [fr. L. *vitis*, VINE+CULTURE]

Vi·ti Le·vu (ví:ti:lévu:) *FIJI

Vit·im (vítəm) a tributary (1,190 miles long) of the Lena in southern Siberia, U.S.S.R., rising east of Lake Baikal

Vi·to·ri·a (vitóri:ə, vitóuri:ə) the capital (pop. 175,000) of Álava, Spain: Gothic cathedral (14th c.). Wellington defeated the French here (1813)

vit·re·ous (vítri:əs) *adj.* of, pertaining to or made of glass ‖ like glass, glassy [fr. L. *vitreus* fr. *vitrum*, glass]

vitreous body vitreous humor

vitreous electricity positive electricity generated by rubbing glass with silk

vitreous humor, *Br.* **vitreous humour** (*anat.*) the transparent jellylike content of the back chamber of the eyeball

vi·tres·cence (vitrés'ns) *n.* the state of becoming or being vitreous

vi·tres·cent (vitrés'nt) *adj.* tending to become glass [fr. L. *vitrum*, glass]

vit·ri·fac·tion (vitrifǽkʃən) *n.* vitrification

vit·ri·fi·a·ble (vítrifaiəb'l) *adj* capable of being vitrified

vit·ri·fi·ca·tion (vitrifikéiʃən) *n.* a vitrifying or being vitrified ‖ something vitrified [fr. M.L. or Mod. L. *vitrificatio* (*vitrificationis*)]

vit·ri·form (vítriform) *adj.* having the form or appearance of glass

vit·ri·fy (vítrifai) *pres. part.* **vit·ri·fy·ing** *past* and *past part.* **vit·ri·fied** *v.i.* to become glass or glasslike ‖ *v.t.* to change into glass or a glasslike substance by heat and fusion [fr. F. *vitrifier* or M.L. *vitrificare*]

vit·ri·ol (vitri:əl) *n.* any of several metallic sulfates, esp. sulfate of iron ‖ oil of vitriol ‖ savage criticism or invective [O.F. or fr. M.L. *vitriolum*]

vit·ri·ol·ic (vitri:ólik) *adj.* of, like or made from vitriol ‖ (of criticism or invective) savage [F. *vitriolique*]

Vi·tru·vi·us (vitrú:vi:əs) (Marcus Vitruvius Pollio, 1st c. B.C.), Roman architect, author of the celebrated treatise 'De architectura', based on earlier Greek works and his own experience. It had great influence on the Renaissance

vit·ta (víta) *pl.* **vit·tae** (víti:), **vit·tas** *n.* (*Rom. hist.*) a headband, fillet or garland ‖ (*eccles.*) the lappet of a miter ‖ (*bot.*) one of the oil receptacles in the pericarp of plants of fam. *Umbelliferae* ‖ (*zool.*) a band or stripe of color ‖ (*zool.*) a longitudinal ridge in diatoms **vit·tate** (víteit) *adj.* [L.]

vi·tu·per·ate (vitú:pəreit, vaitú:pəreit, vitjú:pəreit, vaitjú:pəreit) *pres. part.* **vi·tu·per·at·ing** *past* and *past part.* **vi·tu·per·at·ed** *v.t.* to hurl abuse at [fr. L. *vituperare* (*vituperatus*)]

vi·tu·per·a·tion (vitju:pəréiʃen, vaitju:pəréiʃen, vitjú:pəréiʃen, vaitjú:pəréiʃen) *n.* the act of vituperating ‖ wordy and vehement abuse [O.F. or fr. L. *vituperatio* (*vituperationis*), blaming]

vi·tu·per·a·tive (vitú:pərətiv, vaitú:pərətiv, vitjú:pərətiv, vaitjú:pərətiv) *adj.* characterized by or having the nature of vituperation [fr. L. *vituperativus* or fr. VITUPERATE]

Vi·tus (váitəs), St, Sicilian martyr (c. 303) of the Diocletian persecution, one of the saints invoked for the cure of convulsive disorders (*CHOREA). Feast: June 15

vi·va·ce (vivátʃei) *adv.* (*mus.*) in a lively, brisk manner [Ital.]

vi·va·cious (vivéiʃəs, vaivéiʃəs) *adj.* full of life, high-spirited, animated [fr. L. *vivax* (*vivacis*), tenacious of life]

vi·vac·i·ty (vivǽsiti:, vaivǽsiti:) *n.* the state or quality of being vivacious ‖ mental liveliness [O.F. *vivacite* or fr. L. *vivacitas*]

Vi·val·di (viváldi:), Antonio (c. 1675-1741), Italian composer of suites and concertos, mainly for strings, e.g. 'The Four Seasons'. He also wrote church music and over 40 operas, and was a violin virtuoso

vi·var·i·um (vaivéəri:əm) *pl.* **vi·var·i·a** (vaivéəri:ə), **vi·var·i·ums** *n.* a glass tank or enclosure for keeping animals or plants as nearly as possible in their natural state, esp. for observation [L.]

vi·va vo·ce (váivəvóusi:) **1.** *adv.* by word of mouth, orally **2.** *adj.* oral, *a viva voce examination* [M.L.=with the living voice]

vi·ver·rine (vivérin, váivərain) *adj.* of or relating to *Viverridae*, a family of small, catlike, carnivorous mammals that includes the civet [fr. Mod. L. *viverrinus*]

Vi·ves (ví:ves), Juan Luis (1492-1540), Spanish humanist philosopher and educationalist. His 'De anima et vita' (1538) was one of the first works on psychology

viv·id (vivid) *adj.* providing a very strong stimulus to the eye, *vivid colors* or to the imagination or memory, *a vivid recollection* [fr. L. *vividus*]

viv·i·fi·ca·tion (vivifikéiʃən) *n.* a vivifying or being vivified [fr. L. *vivificatio* (*vivificationis*)]

viv·i·fy (vívifai) *pres. part.* **viv·i·fy·ing** *past* and *past part.* **viv·i·fied** *v.t.* to enliven, animate [fr. F. *vivifier*]

viv·i·par·i·ty (vivəpǽriti:) *n.* the state or quality of being viviparous

vi·vip·a·rous (vivípərəs, vaivípərəs) *adj.* (*zool.*) bringing forth young alive (cf. OVIPAROUS) ‖ (*bot.*) producing bulbs or seeds that germinate while still attached to the parent plant **vi·vip·a·ry** *n.* reproduction by means of shoots and bulbils [fr. L. *viviparus*]

viv·i·sect (vivisékt, vívisekt) *v.t.* to perform vivisection on ‖ *v.i.* to practice vivisection [back-formation fr. VIVISECTION]

viv·i·sec·tion (vivisékʃən) *n.* the performance of scientific experiments involving surgical operation on living animals for the furtherance of medical or other research **viv·i·sec·tion·al** *adj.* **viv·i·sec·tion·ist** *n.* someone who approves of or practices vivisection **vív·i·sec·tor** *n.* someone who vivisects [fr. L. *vivus*, alive+*sectio* (*sectionis*), a cutting]

vix·en (víksən) *n.* a she-fox ‖ a badtempered, spiteful or quarrelsome woman **víx·en·ish** *adj.* [Late M.E. *fixen* fr. O.E.]

vi·yel·la (vaijélə) *n.* twill-weave cloth of 50% cotton, 50% wool, designed to look like all-wool flannel

viz. *VIDELICET

Vi·za·ga·pat·am (vizəgəpátəm) *VISAKHAPAT-NAM

viz·ca·cha, vis·ca·cha (vizkátʃə) *n.* a member of *Lagostomus*, a genus of South American burrowing rodents, resembling the chinchilla, but larger (about 2 ft long) [Span. fr. Quechuan]

Viz·ca·ya (viskája) a province (area 836 sq. miles, pop. 1,181,401) in N. Spain. Capital: Bilbao (*BASQUE PROVINCES)

vi·zier, vi·zir (vizíər, víziər) *n.* a highranking government official in Moslem countries [fr. Turk. *vezir* fr. Arab.]

vizor *VISOR

V.J. Day Sept. 2, 1945, the date of the victory over Japan and the end of the 2nd world war

Vlach (vlax) *n.* a member of a people living in parts of S.E. Europe who speak a Rumanian dialect [Bulg. and Serbian]

Vlad·i·mir (vlǽdəmiər), St (c. 955-1015), prince of Kiev, grandson of St Olga. He accepted Christianity (c. 989) and established the Greek Orthodox faith in Kiev. Feast: July 15

Vladimir a town (pop. 296,000) in the R.S.F.S.R., U.S.S.R., in the Moscow industrial region. Industries: mechanical engineering, textiles and food processing. 12th-c. cathedrals, churches. Vladimir was the capital of Russia (c. 1150-1238)

Vladimir II Mo·nom·a·chus (mounómakəs) (1053-1125), grand duke of Kiev (1113-25). He was the author of a humane code of laws

Vla·di·vos·tok (vlædivóstok) the chief Pacific port (pop. 550,000) of the U.S.S.R., in S.E. Siberia, terminus of the Trans-Siberian Railroad, and a naval base. Industries: shipbuilding, engineering and food processing. University

Vla·minck (vlæmɛ̃k), Maurice de (1876-1958), French painter of the Fauve school, best known for his landscapes

Vlis·sing·en (vlísiŋən) *FLUSHING

Vlo·na, Vlo·në (vlóunə) (or Vlorë, *Ital.* Valona) a port and naval base (pop. 55,500) in S.W. Albania

Vl·ta·va (vʌltavə) *MOLDAU

vo·ca·ble (vóukəb'l) *n.* a word, esp. one regarded phonologically (i.e. with regard to its sound rather than to its meaning) [F. or fr. L. *vocabulum*]

vo·cab·u·lar·y (voukǽbjuləri:) *pl.* **vo·cab·u·lar·ies** *n.* a list of words, usually arranged alphabetically and defined, explained or translated ‖ the range of language, the stock of words at a person's command, or used in a particular work, branch of a subject, language etc. [fr. M.L. *vocabularius*]

vo·cal (vóuk'l) **1.** *adj.* of or pertaining to the voice, *vocal organs* ‖ made or uttered by the voice, spoken or sung composed for the voice ‖ having a voice ‖ inclined to express oneself or one's opinions freely ‖ (*phon.*) voiced ‖ vocalic **2.** *n.* (*phon.*) a voiced sound ‖ what the singer sings in a popular song [fr. L. *vocalis*]

vocal cords elastic folds of membrane inside the larynx which vibrate to produce voice sounds

vo·cal·ic (voukǽlik) *adj.* of or containing vowel sounds ‖ being a vowel, or functioning as one

vo·cal·ism (vóuk'lizəm) *n.* the use of the voice in speech or song ‖ the art of singing a vowel system

vo·cal·ist (vóuk'list) *n.* a singer

vo·cal·i·ty (voukǽliti:) *n.* the quality of having voice ‖ the quality of being vocal

vo·cal·ize (vóuk'laiz) *pres. part.* **vo·cal·iz·ing** *past* and *past part.* **vo·cal·ized** *v.t.* to form or utter with the voice, esp. to sing ‖ to insert the vowel marks in (Hebrew or Arabic texts) ‖ (*phon.*) to voice ‖ (*phon.*) to change into or use as a vowel ‖ *v.i.* to utter sounds, esp. to sing or exercise the voice with runs of vowel sounds ‖ (*phon.*) to be changed into a vowel

vo·cal·ly (vóuk'li:) *adv.* in a vocal manner by singing ‖ in regard to vowels

vo·ca·tion (voukéiʃən) *n.* a conviction that one is called by God to do a particular kind of work, that one is fitted for it and has a duty to do it ‖ the work about which one has this conviction ‖ any trade, profession or occupation (cf. AVOCATION) **vo·cá·tion·al** *adj.* [O.F. or fr. L. *vocatio* (*vocationis*)]

voc·a·tive (vókətiv) **1.** *adj.* (*gram.*, in certain inflected languages) of the case used in addressing a person or thing directly **2.** *n.* the vocative case ‖ a word in the vocative case [O.F. *vocatif*, *vocative* or fr. L. *vocativus*]

vo·cif·er·ance (vousífərəns) *n.* the quality of being vociferous

vo·cif·er·ant (vousífərənt) *adj.* vociferous [fr. L. *vociferans* (*vociferantis*)]

vo·cif·er·ate (vousífəreit) *pres. part.* **vo·cif·er·at·ing** *past* and *past part.* **vo·cif·er·at·ed** *v.t.* to utter in a loud voice ‖ *v.i.* to shout or cry out in a loud voice [fr. L. *vociferari* (*vociferatus*)]

vo·cif·er·a·tion (vousífəréiʃən) *n.* a vociferating, clamor [O.F. *vociferacion* or fr. L. *vociferatio* (*vociferationis*)]

vo·cif·er·ous (vousífərəs) *adj.* noisily clamorous, making an outcry [fr. L. *vociferari*, to cry out]

CONCISE PRONUNCIATION KEY: (**a**) æ, c*a*t; ɑ, c*a*r; ɔ f*aw*n; ei, sn*a*ke. (**e**) e, h*e*n; i:, sh*ee*p; iə, d*ee*r; ɛə, b*ea*r. (**i**) i, f*i*sh; ai, t*i*ger; ə:, b*i*rd. (**o**) ɔ, *o*x; au, c*ow*; ou, g*oa*t; u, p*oo*r; ɔi, r*oy*al. (**u**) ʌ, d*u*ck; u, b*u*ll; u:, g*oo*se; ə, b*a*cillus; ju:, c*u*be. x, lo*ch*; θ, *th*ink; ð, bo*th*er; z, *Z*en; ʒ, corsa*ge*; dʒ, sava*ge*; ŋ, ora*ng*utang; j, *y*ak; ʃ, *fi*sh; tʃ, fe*tch*; 'l, rabb*le*; 'n, redd*en*. Complete pronunciation key appears inside front cover.

vodas 1. (*acronym*) for voice-operated switching device to cut out singing, used to improve communications in oceanic radio telephone by suppressing echoes 2. an echo-suppressing device that automatically switches a subscriber's line on to a transmitting station

vod·ka (vódkə) *n.* liquor with a high percentage of alcohol, distilled from rye, wheat or potatoes etc. [Russ.]

Vo·gel (fóug'l), Hermann Karl (1841-1907), German astronomer who discovered spectroscopic binaries

Vo·gels·berg (fóugəlsberx, vóugəlzbə:rg) *HESSEN

vogue (voug) *n.* a prevalent or current fashion popularity or a period of popularity **in vogue** in fashion [F.=rowing fr. Ital.]

Vo·gul (vóug'l) *n.* a member of an Asiatic people now chiefly located in the N. Urals ‖ their Finno-Ugric language

voice (vɔis) 1. *n.* the sound uttered from the mouth, esp. from the human mouth in speaking or singing etc. ‖ the faculty or power of human utterance ‖ the vocal organs, *he strained his voice* ‖ expression, utterance, *to give voice to one's misgivings* ‖ a vote or opinion ‖ the medium by which something is expressed or represented, *the voice of party policy* ‖ (*phon.*) a sound uttered when the breath vibrates the vocal cords, producing a resonance absent in breath alone ‖ (*gram.*) one of the verb forms which express the relation of subject to action in a sentence, *active voice, passive voice* ‖ (*mus.*, in harmony or counterpoint) one of the threads running through a composition, esp. a fugue **in voice** in good condition for talking or singing **to have a voice in** to have the right to express an opinion about (a matter) **to raise one's voice** to give expression to one's disapproval or disagreement **with one voice** unanimously 2. *v.t. pres. part.* **voic·ing** *past* and *past part.* **voiced** to express, give utterance to, *he voiced the general feeling of the meeting* ‖ (*mus.*) to regulate the tones of (an organ pipe or wind instrument under construction) ‖ (*phon.*) to give voice to [A.F, *voiz, voice,* O.F. *voiz, vois*]

voice box the larynx

voiced (vɔist) *adj.* having a specified kind of voice, *a loud-voiced man* ‖ uttered with the vocal cords vibrating, *'b'* and *'v'* are voiced consonants

voice·less (vɔislis) *adj.* having no voice ‖ (*phon.*, e.g. of 'k', 'p' and 't') not voiced ‖ (*rhet.*) having no vote

voice multiplexing technique for compressing two to four voices into a single channel for simultaneous transmission

Voice of America *UNITED STATES INFORMATION AGENCY

voice-o·ver (vɔisouvər) *n.* the voice of an unseen narrator in a television or motion picture

voice·print (vɔisprint) *n.* a distinctive spectographic pattern of a person's voice, developed by Dr. Lawrence G. Kersla —**voiceprinter** *n.* —**voiceprinting** *n.*

voice recognition unit (*computer*) a peripheral computer device that responds to spoken words

voice response (*computer*) a device that stores sounds and plays them back on signal, e.g., bank records that are voiced when authorized signal is presented

voice synthesizer (*computer*) a computer programmed to simulate speech in response to queries or signals. *also* speech synthesizer

voice warning system device that issues prerecorded vocal warnings under conditions that warrant them, e.g., failure of an aircraft operational system

void (vɔid) 1. *adj.* containing nothing ‖ (of an office or position) vacant, unfilled ‖ (*law*) invalid, null ‖ (with 'of') lacking, without, *void of good taste* 2. *n.* an empty space, vacuum ‖ a feeling of emptiness or great loss ‖ (*archit.*) an opening left in a wall etc., e.g. for a window [A.F., O.F. *voide*]

void *v.t.* (*law*) to annul, to invalidate ‖ to discharge (the contents of something) **void·a·ble** *adj.* [partly fr. A.F. and O.F. *voider, vuider,* partly an aphetic form of AVOID]

void·ance (vɔid'ns) *n.* (*eccles.*, of a benefice) the state of being vacant ‖ the act of voiding [A.F. *voidaunce,* O.F. *vuidance*]

void·ed (vɔidid) *adj.* made void ‖ having an opening ‖ (*heraldry*, of a charge or bearing) hav-

ing the central part cut away so as to show the field

voile (vɔil) *n.* a thin, semi-transparent dress material in cotton, wool or silk [F.= veil]

Voi·ture (vwætyr), Vincent (1579-1648), French poet. He was an original member of the Académie, and one of the most distinguished wits of the Rambouillet salon

voix ce·leste (vwáseilést) *n.* an organ stop of 8-foot pitch with a soft, tremulous effect, produced by the combination of two pipes to each note, tuned with a slight interval [F.=heavenly voice]

Voj·vo·di·na, Voi·vo·di·na (vɔ́ivədi:nɑ) an autonomous province (area 8,407 sq. miles, pop. 1,935,115) of Serbia, Yugoslavia. Capital: Novi Sad. Hungarian from the 11th c., it was devastated under Turkish rule (16th c.), passed to the Hapsburgs (1699) and to Yugoslavia (1918)

vol. volume

vo·lant (vóulənt) *adj.* flying, able to fly ‖ (*heraldry*) represented in flying posture [F.]

Vol·a·pük (vóuləpyk, vóuləpyk) *n.* an artificial international language derived mostly from German, English and Latin, invented (1879) by Johann M. Schleyer (1831-1912), a German priest [fr. *vol,* world (alteration of Eng. 'world')+*a,* connecting vowel+*pük,* speech (alteration of Eng. 'speak')]

vo·lar (vóulər) *adj.* (*anat.*) of the palm of the hand or of the sole of the foot [fr. L. *vola*]

volar (*abbr.*) for volunteer army (which see)

vol·a·tile (vólət'l, *Br.* vólətail) *adj.* evaporating quickly and easily at ordinary temperature ‖ changeable, fickle, *volatile behavior* **vol·a·til·i·ty** (vɔlətíliti:) *n.* [O.F. and F. *volatil, volatile* or fr. L. *volatilis*]

volatile oil an essential oil

volatile storage (*computer*) storage where data are lost when power is turned off

vol·a·til·i·za·tion (vɔlətilizéifən) *n.* a volatilizing or being volatilized

vol·a·til·ize (vólət'laiz) *pres. part.* **vol·a·til·iz·ing** *past* and *past part.* **vol·a·til·ized** *v.t.* to cause to evaporate ‖ *v.i.* to evaporate

vol-au-vent (vɔulouvɑ̃) *n.* a baked casing of puff pastry with a filling of meat, chicken or fish etc. [F.]

vol·can·ic (vɔlkǽnik) *adj.* of, like, or produced by, a volcano **vol·cán·i·cal·ly** *adv.* [F. *volcanique* fr. Ital.]

volcanic glass glass formed naturally by molten lava which has cooled too rapidly to crystallize

vol·can·ic·i·ty (vɔlkənísiti:) *n.* the state or quality of being volcanic [F. *volcanicité*]

vol·can·ism (vólkənizəm) *n.* volcanic power or activity [F. *volcanisme*]

vol·can·ist (vólkənist) *n.* a person who specializes in volcanos [fr. VOLCANO or F. *volcaniste*]

vol·can·ize (vólkənaiz) *pres. part.* **vol·can·iz·ing** *past* and *past part.* **vol·can·ized** *v.t.* to treat with, or subject to, volcanic heat [fr. F. *volcaniser*]

vol·ca·no (vɔlkéinou) *pl.* **vol·ca·noes, vol·ca·nos** *n.* a rift or vent in the earth's crust through which molten material from the depths of the earth is erupted at the surface as flows of lava or clouds of gas and ashes. Characteristically a conical hill is formed, but the appearance of a volcano may vary with such factors as the fluidity of the lava, position of the orifices etc. Active volcanoes include Cotopaxi, Mauna Loa, Vesuvius, Etna and Stromboli. Among those dormant are Pelée and Popocatepetl. Believed extinct are Aconcagua, Kilimanjaro, Orizaba and Fujiyama [Ital. *volcano, vulcano*]

vol·ca·no·gen·ic (vɔlkænoudʒénik) *adj.* created by a volcano

vol·ca·nol·o·gist or **vulcanologist** (vɔlkənólədʒist) *n.* an expert on volcanic phenomena

vol·can·ol·o·gy (vɔlkənólədʒi:) *n.* the science of volcanic phenomena [VOLCANO + Gk *logos,* discourse]

vole (voul) *n.* a member of *Microtus,* fam. *Cricetidae,* a genus of rodents widely distributed in the northern hemisphere. They are closely related to the lemmings and muskrats and resemble rats and mice physically [orig. *vole mouse* fr. Norw. *vollmus* fr. *voll,* field+*mus,* mouse]

vol·et (vóli) *n.* a wing or panel of a triptych [F.=shutter]

Vol·ga (vólgə) a river (2,300 miles long) in the western R.S.F.S.R., the longest in Europe, flowing from the Valdai Hills east to Kazan, then south to a great delta on the Caspian, navigable past Rybinsk. Though frozen five months a year

in the north, it is the country's chief waterway (linked by canal to the Baltic, the White Sea, the Don and Moscow). It drains 530,000 sq. miles. Hydroelectricity

Vol·go·grad (vólgəgræd) (Stalingrad 1925-61, previously Tsaritsyn), a communications and industrial center (pop. 929,000) in the R.S.F.S.R., U.S.S.R., on the lower Volga and the Volga-Don canal: metallurgical industries, metalworking, heavy machinery, hydroelectricity, oil refining, sawmilling, food processing. It was the scene of a heavy German defeat (Sept. 1942–Feb. 1943) which was one of the turning points of the 2nd world war. The town was completely destroyed

vol·i·tant (vólitənt) *adj.* (*rhet.*) flying or capable of flying [fr. L. *volitans* (*volitantis*) fr. *volitare,* to fly about]

vol·i·ta·tion (vɔlitéifən) *n.* (*rhet.*) flight [fr. M.L. *volitatio* (*volitationis*)]

vo·li·tion (voulíʃən) *n.* the exercise of one's will ‖ the ability to use one's will **vo·li·tion·al** *adj.* [F.]

vol·ley (vóli:) 1. *pl.* **vol·leys** *n.* (of a firearm etc.) a discharge of many missiles at the same time ‖ the missiles thus discharged ‖ a loud, rapid outburst of noise, oaths, cheers etc. ‖ (*cricket*) a full toss ‖ (*tennis*) the flight of a ball in play before it bounces ‖ (*tennis*) a return of the ball before it bounces, or a series of returns of this kind 2. *v. pres. part.* **vol·ley·ing** *past* and *past part.* **vol·leyed, vol·lied** *v.t.* to discharge, return, bowl, throw etc. in a volley ‖ *v.i.* to make a volley [fr. F. *volée*]

vol·ley·ball (vóli:bɔl) *n.* a game played by volleying a large inflated ball between players' hands over a net 8 ft high. Teams are six to a side. The court measures 60 ft × 30 ft maximum

Vo·los, Bo·los (vóulɔs) a port (pop. 49,000) in E. Thessaly, Greece, at the head of the gulf of the same name (the ancient Gulf of Pagasae)

Vol·sci (vólski:, vólsi:) *n.* an ancient people of pre-Roman Italy living in Latium **Vol·sci·an** (vólski:ən, vólfən) 1. *n.* one of the Volsci 2. *adj.* of the Volsci [L.]

Vol·stead Act (vólsted) a law passed by the U.S. Congress (1919) defining alcoholic liquor and providing for the enforcement of Prohibition [after Andrew Joseph *Volstead* (1860-1947), U.S. legislator, who promoted the law]

Vol·sun·ga Saga (vólsuŋə) an Icelandic saga of a family of heroic warriors, descended from Volsung (or Walsung), grandson of Odin, chief of the gods. Volsung's son Siegfried (or Sigurd, or Sigemund) is the hero of the 'Nibelungenlied' and of Wagner's romanticized operatic cycle 'The Ring'

volt (voult) *n.* the practical unit of electromotive force, being the force necessary to transmit 1 ampere of current against 1 ohm resistance [after Alessandro VOLTA]

volt, volte (vɔlt, voult) *n.* (*manège*) the gait of a horse moving sideways in a circle ‖ (*fencing*) a sudden movement or leap back to avoid a thrust [F. *volte* fr. Ital.]

Vol·ta (vóltə), Count Alessandro (1745-1872), Italian physicist. He developed a theory of current electricity, devised the voltaic pile, the electrophorus and electroscope, and hydrolyzed water. The volt is named after him.

Vol·ta (vóultə) a river system of W. Africa whose main streams, the Black Volta (540 miles long), flowing from western Burkina Faso (formerly Upper Volta) and forming the northwest frontier of Ghana, and the White Volta (450 miles long), flowing from central Burkina Faso, join in central Ghana to form the Volta proper (250 miles long), which continues across Ghana to a delta east of Accra. The smaller Red Volta, rising between the Black and White, joins the latter in N.E. Ghana. The system is navigable only between rapids but supports a vast hydroelectric scheme in Ghana

volt·age (vóultidʒ) *n.* potential difference, expressed in volts

vol·ta·ic (vɔltéiik) *adj.* pertaining to electricity produced by chemical action or by surface contact and friction [after Alessandro VOLTA]

voltaic cell a primary cell

Vol·taire (voultéər, vɔlter) (François Marie Arouet, 1694-1778), French man of letters, historian and philosopher. His plays include 'Zaïre' (1732) and 'Mérope' (1743). His prose tales, notably 'Zadig' (1747) and 'Candide' (1759), were vehicles for social and political satire. His philosophical work, e.g. 'Lettres philosophiques' (1734) and 'Essai sur les mœurs et l'esprit des nations' (1756), influenced European thought for generations. His historical work 'Le siècle de Louis XIV' (1751) is readable and reasonably accurate. Voltaire has been accepted as one of the world's great men partly because of the force of his personality. Endowed with enormous wit, he was the foremost propagandist for the leading ideas of the 18th c.: free inquiry, the dignity of man, equality (despite his own aristocratic attitudes) and freedom of conscience. It has been said that he fostered not a revolutionary proletariat but an ungovernable middle class

vol·tam·e·ter (vɒltǽmitər) n. an instrument for measuring the amount of an electric current by the gas generated or by the amount of metal (usually copper or silver) deposited by electrolysis

volt·am·me·ter (vóultæmmi:tər) n. an instrument for indicating the range or ranges of volts and amperes

volt·am·pere (vóultæmpiər) n. an electrical unit equal to the product of 1 volt and 1 ampere which for direct current is equivalent to 1 watt

Vol·ta Re·don·da (vóltərəðóndə) a city (pop. 147,261) in E. Brazil, near Rio de Janeiro. It is the largest iron and steel center in Latin America

volte *VOLT

volte-face (vɒltfás) n. a sudden, total change of opinion, line of conduct etc. [F.]

volt·me·ter (vóultmi:tər) n. (elec.) an instrument used to measure potential difference (in volts or millivolts). It is similar in structure to an ammeter, but has a high resistance in series, little current passing through the instrument

vol·u·bil·i·ty (vɒljubíliti:) n. the quality or state of being voluble [fr. F. volubilité or fr. L. volubilitas]

vol·u·ble (vóljub'l) adj. characterized by or producing an unhesitating flow of words || (bot.) twisting, twining **vól·u·bly** adv. [F. or fr. L. volubilis]

vol·ume (vólju:m, vóljum) n. the amount of space occupied by, or contained in, something measured by the number of cubes each with an edge 1 unit long that it can contain, or measured in any other standard manner appropriate to the shape (sphere, cone etc.) concerned || an amount, quantity etc., the volume of turnover || (mus.) loudness or fullness of sound || a bound assemblage of printed sheets, forming a book or one of several separately bound parts of a book || (archit., sculpture) a defined mass || (hist.) a roll or scroll (of papyrus etc.) **to speak volumes for** to be abundant evidence of, it speaks volumes for his kindness of heart [O.F. volum, volume]

vo·lu·me·ter (volú:mitər, voljú:mitər) n. an instrument for measuring the volumes of gases, liquids and solids [VOLUME+METER]

vol·u·met·ric (vɒljumétrik) adj. of or pertaining to the measurement of volume, esp. pertaining to a system of quantitative chemical analysis based on measurements of concentrations by volume (cf. GRAVIMETRIC) **vol·u·mét·ri·cal** adj. **vol·u·mét·ri·cal·ly** adv. [VOLUME+METRIC]

vo·lu·mi·nos·i·ty (vəlju:minósiti:) n. the state or quality of being voluminous

vo·lu·mi·nous (vəlú:minəs) adj. (of a work) consisting of many volumes || (of a writer) producing many books || writing or speaking at length, a voluminous critic || written or spoken at great length, voluminous correspondence || of great size, bulky || loose, ample, voluminous folds of drapery [fr. L.L. voluminosus, full of folds]

vol·un·tar·i·ly (vólənterili:, vɒləntéərili:) adv. in a voluntary manner

vol·un·tar·i·ness (vólənteri:nis) n. the state or quality of being voluntary

vol·un·tar·y (vɒləntéri:) 1. adj. acting, made or done freely, not under constraint or compulsion, a voluntary contribution || brought about, established or supported by voluntary action || (of body parts or movements) controlled by or subject to the will, a voluntary muscle || able to act of one's own free will, having free will, man is a voluntary agent || (law) done or made by consent without consideration in the form of money or services 2. pl. **vol·un·tar·ies** n. an organ solo, esp. one played in church before, during or after a service || the music written for this [fr. O.F. voluntaire, volontaire or fr. L. voluntarius]

vol·un·teer (vɒləntíər) 1. n. a person who undertakes some task or service of his own free will, esp. one who chooses to serve in the armed forces || (law) a person to whom a voluntary transfer of property is made 2. adj. voluntary ||

made up of volunteers, a volunteer army || (of crops) self-sown 3. v.i. to offer oneself willingly, esp. for service in the armed forces || v.t. to offer willingly (one's services, a remark, an explanation etc.) [fr. F. volontaire]

volunteer army an army made up of volunteers, without resort to a draft. abbr. volar

Volunteers in Service to America (abbr. VISTA), a U.S. government agency introduced (1964) by President Lyndon Johnson under the Economic Opportunity Act. Akin to a domestic Peace Corps, it provided for men and women to serve as teachers and social workers among American Indians, migratory workers, the mentally ill, and other disadvantaged groups

Volunteers of America a religious and philanthropic organization, akin to the Salvation Army, founded in 1896

vo·lup·tu·ar·y (vəlÁptʃuːəri:) 1. pl. **vo·lup·tu·ar·ies** n. someone who loves sensual pleasures inordinately (cf. ASCETIC) 2. adj. of, concerned with, or given up to, sensual pleasure [fr. L. voluptuarius, postclassical form of voluptarius fr. voluptas, pleasure]

vo·lup·tu·ous (vəlÁptʃuːəs) adj. full of sensual delight || enjoying sensual pleasures to the full || suggesting sensual pleasure [fr. O.F. voluptueux or L. voluptuosus]

vo·lute (vəlú:t) 1. n. (archit.) a spiral scroll used esp. to decorate Ionic, Corinthian and Composite capitals || a spiralshaped form || (zool.) a member of Voluta, a genus of chiefly tropical gastropods with a spiral shell || a volution of a spiral shell 2. adj. having a spiral shape **vo·lút·ed** adj. twisted spirally || (archit.) ornamented with volutes [fr. L. voluta or fr. F.]

vo·lu·tion (vəlú:ʃən) n. a revolving or rolling movement || a spiral || a whorl of a spiral shell [fr. L. volere (volutus), to roll]

vol·va (vólvə) n. (bot.) the cup-shaped membranous structure around the base of the stem of some mushrooms (e.g. agarics and stinkhorns), or enveloping the sporophore [L. fr. volvere, to roll]

vo·mer (vóumər) n. (anat.) the small thin bone which in man and most vertebrates forms part of the separation of the nostrils [L.=plowshare]

vom·it (vómit) v.t. to throw up from the stomach through the mouth || (rhet.) to pour out violently or in quantity, to vomit obscenities || v.i. to throw up the contents of the stomach through the mouth [fr. L. vomere (vomitus) or fr. vomitare (frequentative of vomere)]

vomit n. that which is vomited || the act of vomiting [A.F. vomit, vomite, O.F. vomite or fr. L. vomitus]

vom·i·tive (vómitiv) adj. vomitory [F. vomitif, vomitive]

vom·i·to·ry (vómitəri:, vómitouri:) adj. of or pertaining to vomiting || inducing vomiting [fr. L. vomitorius]

vomitory pl **vom·i·to·ries** n. (Rom. hist.) one of the passages for entrance and exit in a theater or amphitheater [fr. L. vomitorium]

Von·ne·gut (vánəgət), Kurt, Jr. (1922-), U.S. writer. One of the country's most popular authors from the 1960s, he combines science fiction, social satire and black comedy in his novels, which include 'Player Piano' (1951), 'Cat's Cradle' (1963), 'Slaughterhouse-Five' (1969; film, 1972), 'Breakfast of Champions' (1973), 'Slapstick' (1976), 'Jailbird' (1979) and 'Galápagos' (1985). His play, 'Happy Birthday, Wanda June', was successfully produced in 1971

voo·doo (vú:du:) 1. pl. **voo·doos** n. an Animist religion accompanied by black magic. It was originally African, and is still practiced by some Creoles and Afro-West Indians in the West Indies (esp. Haiti) and southern U.S.A. || a sorcerer skilled in this || the spell cast by such a sorcerer || a person or thing bringing bad luck 2. v.t. to bewitch with voodoo **vóo·doo·ism, vóo·doo·ist** ns [Dahomey vodu]

Voodoo n. (mil.) a supersonic, twin-engine turbojet (F-101B) carrying both nuclear and nonnuclear air-to-air missiles

vor (acronym) for very-high-frequency omni ranges, an air navigational radio aid that uses phase comparison of a ground-transmitted signal to determine bearing

vo·ra·cious (vəréiʃəs, vouréiʃəs, vouréiʃəs) adj. greedy for food, gluttonous, a voracious eater || characterized by insatiable eagerness, a voracious reader [fr. L. vorax (voracis)]

vo·rac·i·ty (vərǽsiti:, vɔrǽsiti:, vourǽsiti:) n.

the state or quality of being voracious [F. voracité or fr. L. voracitas]

Vor·arl·berg (fórrurlberx) the western-most province (area 1,005 sq. miles, pop. 226,000) of Austria. Capital: Bregenz (21,000)

vor·lage (fórlagə) n. (skiing) a forward leaning position with skis flat on the ground

Vo·ro·nezh (vArónəʃ) an industrial center (pop. 820,000) in the S.W. European R.S.F.S.R., U.S.S.R., the market for the black earth region. Industries: synthetic rubber, food processing, agricultural and nuclear engineering. University (1918)

Vo·ro·shi·lov (vɔrʌʃí:lʌf), Kliment Yefremovich (1881-1969), Russian general and statesman. He was defense minister (1925-40), helped to organize the defense of Leningrad (1941-3) and was president in the U.S.S.R. (1953-60)

Vo·ro·shi·lov·grad (vɔrʌʃí:lʌfgrat) (formerly Lugansk) a city (pop. 474,000) of the Ukraine, U.S.S.R., in the Donbas: railroad engineering, metallurgy, coal mining

Vo·ro·shi·lovsk (vɔrʌʃí:lʌfsk) *STAVROPOL

Vor·ster (fórstər), Balthazar Johannes (1915-83), South African Nationalist statesman, minister of justice (1961-6), prime minister (1966-78), and president (1978-79)

vortac (acronym) for very-high-frequency omnirange tacan, an air navigation system in heavily trafficked air routes, utilizing civilian-operated facilities for guidance and military tacan for distance

vor·tex (vórteks) pl. **vor·ti·ces** (vórtisi:z), **vor·tex·es** n. a mass of whirling fluid, esp. a whirlpool || a whirlwind || (phys.) a volume of matter the particles of which rotate rapidly around an axis || a social situation thought of as tending to engulf **vor·ti·cal** (vórtik'l) adj. [L. vortex (vorticis)]

vor·ti·cel·la (vɔrtisélə) pl. **vor·ti·cel·lae** (vɔrtiséli:), **vor·ti·cel·las** n. (biol.) a member of Vorticella, a genus of unicellular protozoans having a bell-shaped, ciliated body, the protoplasm being extended as a stalk which can be spirally contracted. They usually inhabit fresh water, attached to plants [Mod. L. dim. fr. vortex (vorticis)]

vor·ti·cism (vórtisizəm) n. an English art movement related to cubism and futurism, dating from 1912, founded by Wyndham Lewis **vór·ti·cist** n. [fr. L. vortex (vorticis)]

Vos (vous), Cornelis de (1585-1651), Flemish painter, esp. of portraits

Vosges (vouʒ) a wooded mountain range (Ballon de Guebwiller, 4,672 ft) in N.E. France, rising from the Rhine plain parallel with the Black Forest: dairy farming, forestry, hydro-electricity, textiles, wine, paper

Vosges a department (area 2,303 sq. miles, pop. 398,000) of N.E. France in the Vosges Mtns (*LORRAINE). Chief town: Épinal (pop. 42,810)

vo·ta·ress (vóutəris) n. a woman votary

vo·ta·ry (vóutəri:) pl. **vo·ta·ries** n. (hist.) someone who devoted himself to the service and worship of a pagan god || (rhet.) a devotee [fr. L. vovere (votus), to vow]

vote (vout) n. a formal expression of opinion, or of a decision to elect someone or to pass a law or resolution, usually signified in response to a proposal by voice, gesture or ballot || an opinion expressed by a majority, a vote of censure || the act of voting || votes collectively, the vote was 18,000 || the collective votes of a group or party, the Irish vote || the right to vote || (Br.) money granted for a specific purpose, the army vote [fr. L. votum, a vow]

vote pres. part. **vot·ing** past and past part. **vot·ed** v.i. to use one's vote || v.t. to decide, accept or establish etc. by a vote || to grant (e.g. a sum of money) by vote || to declare by general consent, the picnic was voted a success || (pop.) to suggest, I vote we stop for lunch **to vote down** to defeat by a vote **to vote in** to elect or establish by a vote **to vote out** to defeat (and esp. so remove from office) by a vote [fr. L. vovere (votus), to vow]

vote of confidence (Br.) a vote demanded for a proposed bill or measure which the government considers essential to its policy and is prepared to resign over

voting booth (Am.=Br. polling booth) a partitioned-off compartment set up temporarily at the polls to allow privacy in voting

vo·tive (vóutiv) adj. offered, consecrated etc. in fulfillment of a vow or promise [fr. L. votivus]

votive Mass (Roman Catholicism) a mass celebrated in place of that appointed for the day, e.g. one for a private intention

vouch (vautʃ) *v.i.* (with 'for') to be guaranteed ‖ *v.t.* to testify, *she vouched that he was with her at the time* ‖ (*law*) to summon (a person) into court to give warranty of title [A.F. and O.F. *vocher, voucher*]

vouch·er (váutʃər) *n.* (*law*) a document, receipt etc. certifying that a sum of money has been paid or that accounts are correct ‖ (*law*) the calling to court of a person to give warranty of title ‖ (*Br., commerce*) a coupon that entitles a buyer or customer to goods at reduced prices, or to articles given away by a manufacturer to stimulate sales. ‖ (*Br.*) a coupon serving in lieu of cash payment, *a luncheon voucher* [A.F. *voiicher*]

vouch·safe (vautʃséif) *pres. part.* **vouch·saf·ing** *past* and *past part.* **vouch·safed** *v.t.* to condescend to grant, to give as a favor

Vou·et (vu:ei), Simon (1590-1649), French painter. He worked as court painter for Louis XIII on the decoration of the Louvre and the Luxembourg palaces, in the baroque style

vous·soir (vu:swár) *n.* one of the wedge-shaped stones forming an arch or vault [O.F. *vausoir, vaussoir*]

vow (vau) *n.* a solemn promise or pledge, esp. one made to a deity **to take vows** to join a religious community [A.F. *vu, vou, vo*]

vow *v.t.* to promise solemnly, esp. to God, *to vow obedience* ‖ to resolve emphatically ‖ *v.i.* to make a vow [fr. O.F. *vouer, vower*]

vow·el (váuəl) *n.* a voiced speech sound where the breath is not stopped (cf. CONSONANT) ‖ a letter in the alphabet representing a vowel sound (a, e, i, o, u) **vów·el·ize** *pres. part.* **vow·el·iz·ing** *past* and *past part.* **vow·el·ized** *v.t.* to insert the vowel points or signs in (e.g. a Hebrew text) [O.F. *vouel*]

vowel point a mark above, below or attached to a consonant to indicate the vowels, e.g. in Hebrew

vox an·gel·i·ca (vóksændʒélikə) *n.* an organ stop of 8-foot pitch producing a delicate tone [L. = angelic voice]

vox hu·ma·na (vókshju:mánə) *n.* an organ stop of 8-foot pitch producing a sound akin to the human voice [L.=human voice]

voy·age (vóiidʒ) *n.* a long journey, esp. by sea [M.E. *veage, vayage, voiage* fr. O.F., A.F.]

voyage *pres. part.* **voy·ag·ing** *past* and *past part.* **voy·aged** *v.i.* to make or go on a voyage ‖ *v.t.* to travel over (a distance) on a voyage [fr. F. *voyager*]

Voyager I *n.* U.S. spacecraft launched in 1977 to explore Jupiter

Voyager II *n.* spacecraft launched in 1977 to explore Saturn

vo·ya·geur (vóiidʒər) *n.* a man employed by Canadian fur companies to carry goods and passengers mainly by boat between remote trading posts in the Hudson Bay territory [F.]

vo·yeur (vwajé:r, vɔijé:r) *n.* someone who finds sexual pleasure in looking at sex acts, genital organs etc. **vo·yéur·ism** *n.* [F.]

Voy·sey (vóisi:), Charles Francis Annesley (1857-1941), British architect whose work strongly influenced art nouveau. He designed town and country houses with attention to the logical and tasteful fulfillment of living requirements

VP (*abbr.*) for verb phrase.

VP, V.P. Vice-President

vs. versus

VSO (*abbr.*) for liquor, *very superior old*, 12–17 yrs old

VSOP (*abbr.*) for liquor, *very superior old pale*, 18–25 yrs old

V/STOL (*abbr.*) for vertical short take-off and landing, an aircraft that only requires a short runway. *Cf* CTOL, Q/STOL, STOL, VTOL

Vt. Vermont

VTOL (*abbr.*) for vertical take-off and landing aircraft capable of vertical ascent

VTOLport *See* VERTIPORT

Vuil·lard (vwi:jær), Édouard (1868-1940), French painter, known esp. for his quiet domestic scenes

Vul·can (válkən) (*Rom. mythol.*) *HEPHAESTUS

vul·ca·nist (válkənist) *n.* one who believes that volcanoes exist on the moon. *Cf* HOT MOONER

vul·can·ite (válkənait) *n.* ebonite

vul·can·i·za·tion (válkənizéiʃən) *n.* the act or process of vulcanizing

vul·can·ize (válkənaiz) *pres. part.* **vul·can·iz·ing** *past* and *past part.* **vul·can·ized** *v.t.* to treat (rubber) with sulfur at a high temperature so as to increase its strength and elasticity ‖ *v.i.* to undergo this process [fr. VULCAN]

vul·can·ol·o·gy (válkənólədʒi:) *n.* volcanology [fr. VULCAN+Gk *logos*, discourse]

Vulcan Phalanx (*mil.*) an Army sixbarrelled, 20-mm rotary-fired artillery gun that provides low-altitude air defense

vul·gar (válgər) *adj.* indecent, *a vulgar joke* ‖ offensive to one's finer feelings, *a vulgar display of riches* ‖ of or characteristic of the common people, *a vulgar superstition* ‖ normally accepted, most common, *take the word in its vulgar connotation* ‖ (of speech) vernacular [fr. L. *vulgaris* fr. *vulgus*, the common people]

vulgar fraction (*math.*) a common fraction

vul·gar·i·an (válgéəriən) *n.* a vulgar person, esp. a rich person of low tastes and manners

vul·gar·ism (válgərizəm) *n.* a word, phrase or expression considered vulgar ‖ vulgarity

vul·gar·i·ty (válgǽriti:) *pl.* **vul·gar·i·ties** *n.* the state or quality of being vulgar ‖ a vulgar act, habit etc. [fr. L. *vulgaritas*]

vul·gar·i·za·tion (válgərizéiʃən) *n.* a vulgarizing or being vulgarized

vul·gar·ize (válgəraiz) *pres. part.* **vul·gar·iz·ing** *past* and *past part.* **vul·gar·ized** *v.t.* to popularize ‖ to make coarse

vulgar Latin a form of Latin spoken by the people of ancient Rome (as distinguished from classical Latin). It is the chief source of the Romance languages

Vul·gate (válgit, válgeit) the Latin version of the Scriptures made largely by St Jerome directly from Hebrew, and in use in the Roman Catholic Church. The Council of Trent chose it (recension of 1592) as the authentic text to which reference must be made in matters of theology

vul·ner·a·bil·i·ty (válnərəbíliti:) *n.* the state or quality of being vulnerable

vul·ner·a·ble (válnərəb'l) *adj.* open to attack, hurt or injury, *a vulnerable position* ‖ capable of being hurt or wounded (either because insufficiently protected or because sensitive and tender) ‖ (*bridge*, of the side that has won one game) liable to greater penalties than the opponents **vúl·ner·a·bly** *adv.* [fr. L.L. *vulnerabilis*]

vul·ner·ar·y (válnəreri:). **1.** *adj.* used in healing, *a vulnerary herb* **2.** *pl.* **vul·ner·ar·ies** *n.* a plant, ointment, drug etc. for healing wounds [fr. L. *vulnerarius*]

vul·pine (válpain) *adj.* of or like a fox ‖ crafty, cunning [fr. L. *vulpinus*]

vul·ture (váltʃər) *n.* one of a group of large birds of prey of tropical and temperate regions, characterized by a strong elongated ripping beak and a featherless neck and head. They often feed on carrion. Examples include the griffon vulture, the turkey buzzard, the lammergeyer and the condor ‖ a rapacious person [A.F. *vultur* and *voutre*, O.F. *voltour, voutour* or L. *vultur* or fr. L. *vulturius*]

vul·tur·ine (váltʃərain) *adj.* of or like a vulture [fr. L. *vulturinus*]

vul·tur·ous (váltʃərəs) *adj.* like a vulture

vul·va (válvə) *n.* (*anat.*) the orifice or external parts of the female genitals **vúl·var, vúl·vate** *adjs* [L.]

VVSOP (*abbr.*) for liquor, *very, very superior old pale liquor*, 25–40 yrs old

VX (*mil.*) symbol for a very lethal secret nerve gas believed to be ethyl. S-diementhylamino-ethyl methylphosphonothiolate; responsible for death of 6,000 sheep in Utah, March 1960. *Cf* BZ, CS, GB

Vyat·ka (vjátkɑ) *KIROV

Vy·borg, Vi·borg (ví:bɔrg) (*Finn.* Viipuri) a lumber port (pop. 65,000) in the northwestern R.S.F.S.R., U.S.S.R., near the Finnish border, blocked by ice four months a year. Swedish castle (1293), town hall (15th c.)

vying *pres. part.* of VIE

Vyshinsky *VISHINSKY

	EARLY NORTH SEMITIC	PHOENICIAN	EARLY HEBREW (GEZER)	EARLY GREEK	ETRUSCAN		EARLY LATIN	CLASSICAL LATIN
					Early	Classical		
W	Y	Ч	ЧУ	Ч	Ꝑ	7	7	W

		MODERN ITALIC	MODERN ROMAN
← SEE LETTERS F, V, AND U →		W	W

Development of the letter W, beginning with the early North Semitic letter. Evolution of both the majuscule, or capital, letter W and the minuscule, or lowercase, letter w are shown.

A. C. SYLVESTER, CAMBRIDGE, ENGLAND

W, w (dʌb'lju:) the 23rd letter of the English alphabet

W, W. West, Western

Wa (wæ) *n.* a tribal people living in the mountains of N.E. Burma and Yunnan, China ‖ a member of this people ‖ their Mon-Khmer language

Waal, Arm of the (vɑl) the southern branch of the Rhine delta

Waals (vɑls), Johannes Diderik Van der (1837-1923), Dutch physicist who worked on molecular forces of attraction. He derived the equation expressing the pressure, volume and temperature relations for a substance in both the gaseous and liquid states. Nobel prize (1910)

WAAM program *n.* U.S. 3-weapon tactical anti-tank defense, including Cyclops, cruise-type missile; ERAM, extended range anti-armor mines; and WASP, multiple miniature missiles

Wa·bash (wɔ́bæʃ) a river (475 miles long) rising in W. Ohio, flowing southwesterly across Indiana to form the S. Indiana-Illinois boundary, and emptying into the Ohio River in S.W. Indiana

wack·e (wǽkə) *n.* (geol.) a chiefly dark gray rock, like sandstone, produced by decomposition of igneous rock [G.]

wack·y (wǽki:) *comp.* **wack·i·er** *superl.* **wack·i·est** *adj.* (pop.) crazy, absurdly silly [etym. doubtful]

wad (wɒd) **1.** *n.* a handy, compact lump of soft material (paper, cotton wool, rag etc.), esp. when used to stop an opening or to stuff between things to keep them apart ‖ (pop.) a roll, esp. of paper money ‖ (pop.) a great deal of money ‖ a felt disk used to keep powder and shot in position in a cartridge **2.** *v.t. pres. part.* **wadding** *past* and *past part.* **wadded** to stuff, pack, plug or stop with a wad or wads ‖ to pad or line with soft material ‖ to press into a wad [etym. doubtful]

wad·cut·ter (wɑ́dkʌtər) *n.* (shooting) a flat-topped target bullet

Wad·den·zee (vɑ́d'nzei) part of the North Sea between the Frisian Is and the Dutch mainland, forming the inlet to the Ijsselmeer

wad·ding (wɒdiŋ) *n.* (collect.) wads (lumps of soft material) ‖ the material used in making wads or for packing fragile objects, lining garments, stuffing cushions etc.

Wad·ding·ton, Mt (wɒ́diŋtən) the highest point (13,260 ft) in British Columbia, Canada, in the Coast Range

wad·dle (wɒd'l) **1.** *v.i. pres. part.* **wad·dling** *past* and *past part.* **wad·dled** to walk like a duck with short, ungainly steps and the body moving slightly from side to side **2.** *n.* such a gait [rel. to WADE]

Wade (weid), Benjamin Franklin (1800-78), U.S. Senator (1851-69) from Ohio. With Representative Henry W. Davis he drafted the Wade-Davis bill and, when President Lincoln rejected it by pocket veto, they wrote the Wade-Davis Manifesto (1864) attacking Lincoln. As president pro tempore (1865) of the Senate and therefore next in line for the presidency, Wade vigorously sought the impeachment of President Andrew Johnson

wade (weid) **1.** *v. pres. part.* **wad·ing** *past* and *past part.* **wad·ed** *v.i.* to walk through some depth of water, mud, snow or sand etc. ‖ *v.t.* to cross (a stream etc.) on foot **to wade in** to make an energetic start **to wade into** to attack (someone) or set to work on (something) vigorously **to wade through** to get through with effort and difficulty, e.g. to read (a difficult or verbose book) with perseverance **2.** *n.* an act of wading **wad·er** *n.* a wading bird ‖ (pl.) thigh-high or waist-high waterproof boots or pants and boots for wading, worn by anglers etc. [O.E. wadan, to go, wade]

Wade-Davis Bill a U.S. Congressional bill (1864) of the Civil War, initiated by Senator Benjamin F. Wade and Representative Henry W. Davis, who held that reconstruction of the Southern states was a matter for the legislature, and not for the executive branch of the government. It was rejected by President Abraham Lincoln by pocket veto

Wa·di Hal·fa (wɑ́di:hɑ́lfə) a port (pop. 10,000) in the N. Sudan on the Nile, whose original site is flooded by the Aswan High Dam reservoir

wa·di, wa·dy (wɑ́di:) *pl.* **wa·dis, wa·dies** *n.* (in N. Africa and S.W. Asia) a riverbed through which water flows only in the rainy reason [Arab. wādī]

wading bird a long-legged bird (e.g. a stork or heron) which wades in shallow water after food

Wad Me·da·ni (wɑ́dmédɑni:) an agricultural market (pop. 57,000) in the central Sudan on the lower Blue Nile

wa·fer (wéifər) **1.** *n.* a very thin, crisp cake, e.g. as eaten with ice cream ‖ a thin, papery disk of unleavened bread consecrated in the Eucharist ‖ a disk of red gummed paper or dried paste stuck on documents instead of a seal ‖ (electr.) a thin polished piece of semiconductor crystal material, usu. silicon, on which circuits are fabricated, etched, or printed **2.** *v.t.* to seal or fasten with a wafer ‖ (agriculture) to compress agricultural products, e.g., alfalfa, into cookie-size cakes [M.E. wafre fr. A.F. fr. M.L.G.]

waf·fle (wɒfəl) *n.* a soft, crisp batter cake baked on a waffle iron [fr. Du. wafel, wafer]

waffle 1. *n.* (Br., pop.) imprecise verbosity **2.** *v.i. pres. part.* **waf·fling** *past* and *past part.* **waf·fled** (Br., pop.) to talk or write verbosely and imprecisely [origin unknown]

waffle iron a utensil with studded, sometimes folding pans in which batter is baked to make a waffle

waft (wɒft, wæft) **1.** *v.t.* to carry (e.g. a small boat, balloon, feathers, seeds, sounds, scents etc.) gently across water by wave or wind, or through the air ‖ *v.i.* to move floating or as if floating on water or in the air **2.** *n.* a puff, whiff, gentle gust or breath (of scent, wind, smoke etc.) ‖ (naut.) a usually knotted flag or pennant used e.g. as a signal ‖ (rhet.) a wafting motion [back-formation fr. older wafter, a convoy prob. fr. Du. or L.G. wachter, a guard]

wag (wæg) **1.** *v. pres. part.* **wag·ging** *past* and *past part.* **wagged** *v.t.* to shake quickly to and fro or up and down a number of times ‖ *v.i.* to move in this way ‖ (pop., of the tongue) to move busily in idle chattering **2.** *n.* an instance of wagging [M.E. wagge fr. O.E. wagian, to shake, oscillate]

wag *n.* someone with a reputation for making witticisms [prob. fr. WAG v.]

wage (weidʒ) *n.* a reward received by nonprofessional workers, usually in the form of a weekly payment of an agreed sum (cf. SALARY, calculated either according to the hours worked (including overtime) or according to the work done (piecework) ‖ (econ., pl.) the share of the total product of industry that goes to labor ‖ (archaic, usually pl. construed as sing.) reward, the wages of sin is death [A.F.]

wage *pres. part.* **wag·ing** *past* and *past part.* **waged** *v.t.* to engage in, carry on (a war, conflict, campaign) [O.N.F. wagier, to pledge]

wage differential an agreed ratio or sum by which a skilled worker's wages are to exceed an unskilled worker's wages

wage drift tendency of wages to move upward from an agreed-upon base

wage-push inflation (weidʒpuʃ) the rise in prices induced by increased wages. *Cf* DEMAND-PULL INFLATION

wa·ger (wéidʒər) **1.** *n.* something, esp. money, staked on the outcome of an uncertain event ‖ an act of wagering ‖ something on which such an act is made **2.** *v.t.* to stake (money etc.) on the outcome of an uncertain event [A.F. wageure fr. wager, to wage]

wag·ger·y (wǽgəri:) *pl.* **wag·ger·ies** *n.* waggish humor or an instance of this

wag·gish (wǽgiʃ) *adj.* involving practical joking or witticisms ‖ of or like a wag (joker)

wag·gle (wǽg'l) **1.** *v. pres. part.* **wag·gling** *past* and *past part.* **wag·gled** *v.i.* to wag frequently and rapidly ‖ to move with quick little undula-

---

CONCISE PRONUNCIATION KEY: **(a)** æ, cat; ɑ, car; ɔ fawn; ei, snake. **(e)** e, hen; i:, sheep; iə, deer; ɛə, bear. **(i)** i, fish; ai, tiger; əː, bird. **(o)** o, ox; au, cow; ou, goat; u, poor; ɔi, royal. **(u)** ʌ, duck; u, bull; u:, goose; ə, bacillus; juː, cube. x, loch; θ, think; ð, bother; z, Zen; ʒ, corsage; dʒ, savage; ŋ, orangutang; j, yak; ʃ, fish; tʃ, fetch; 'l, rabble; 'n, redden. Complete pronunciation key appears inside front cover.

tions ‖ *v.t.* to cause to waggle ‖ (*golf*) to swing (a club) over a ball as a preparation for the stroke proper **2.** *n.* a short rapid wag or undulating movement ‖ (*golf*) a waggling **wág·gly** *adj.* swaying, unsteady, twisting [WAG]

waggon *WAGON

waggonette *WAGONETTE

Wag·ner (vágnər), Wilhelm Richard (1813-83), German operatic composer. Apart from an early symphony (1832), a few marches and songs, and 'Siegfried Idyll' (1870), his fame rests on his operas. The earlier ones, culminating in 'Tannhäuser' (1843-4) and 'Lohengrin' (1846-8), were followed by his masterpiece, the great 'Ring' cycle (*NIBELUNGENLIED): 'Das Rheingold' (1869), 'Die Walküre' (1870), 'Siegfried' (1876) and 'Götterdämmerung' (1874). In most of his operas, including 'Die Meistersinger von Nürnberg' (1862-7) and 'Parsifal' (1877-82) he used Teutonic legend and history to serve a very personal mixture of feelings: a romantic association between love and death, a fusion between the erotic and the mystical, an ideal of heroism and nationalism. He believed strongly that opera must be a unified work of art; he wrote his own librettos and supervised every detail of production to achieve a carefully calculated impact on the beholder. His operas are structurally indivisible units. He used leitmotifs to identify his characters, or to allude to symbolic themes, and these leitmotifs could be transformed, blended, or carried on from one work to another. The whole structure and procedure of his operas, esp. his continuous but varied melodic line and his orchestration and characteristic harmony, were new in European music. Through Mahler, Berg and Schönberg, Wagner leads to 20th-c. music

Wagner Act (wǽgnər) a law passed (1935) by the U.S. Congress setting up the National Labor Relations Board, and affirming the right of employees to organize themselves in trade unions and to bargain collectively

wag·on, *Br.* also **wag·gon** (wǽgən) *n.* a four-wheeled vehicle for transporting heavy loads ‖ a dinner wagon ‖ a patrol wagon ‖ (*Br.*) an open railroad car ‖ **on (off) the wagon** (*pop.*) no longer (again) drinking alcoholic beverages **wág·on·er**, *Br.* also **wág·gon·er** *n.* the driver of a wagon [Du. *wagen*]

wag·on·ette, *Br.* also **wag·gon·ette** (wǽgənét) *n.* (*hist.*) a four-wheeled, horse-drawn pleasure carriage (open or with a removable cover) with facing seats along each side, behind a transverse seat

wa·gon-lit (vægóli:, wǽgənli:) *pl.* **wa·gons-lits** (vægóli:, wǽgənzli:z) *n.* (in Europe) a railroad sleeping car divided into individual compartments ‖ one such compartment [F.]

Wa·gram, Battle of (vágrəm) a battle fought (July 6, 1809) northeast of Vienna in which Napoleon defeated Austria during the Napoleonic Wars

wag·tail (wǽgteil) *n.* any of several small, slim, mainly European birds of fam. *Motacillidae*, related to the pipits. They jerk their long tails up and down when they are running or perching ‖ any of various similar American and Australian birds

Wah·ha·bi, Wa·ha·bi (wəhábi:) *n.* a member of a puritanical sect of Islam founded (c. 1744) by Muhammad ibn Abd-el-Wahhab (1703–92) in Nejd, Saudi Arabia. The Wahhabis conquered Arabia (1803), were beaten by the Ottoman Turks (1819) and acquired political power under King ibn Saud (early 20th c.) **Wah·há·bism, Wa·há·bism** *n.*

wa·hi·ne (wəhí:ni:) *n.* (*surfing*) a woman surfer, from a Polynesian word for woman

wa·hoo (wáhu:) *pl.* **wa·hoos** *n.* a North American shrub of fam. *Celastraceae*, esp. *Euonymus atropurpureus*, bearing purple capsules and scarlet seeds [Am. Indian *úhawhu*, cork elm]

waif (weif) *n.* a stray, helpless person, esp. an abandoned or neglected child ‖ a stray animal ‖ (*law*) any ownerless property found by chance [A.F., O.F. *gaif*, prob. of Scand. origin]

Wai·ka·to (waikátou) the longest river (220 miles) of New Zealand, flowing from Lake Taupo across N. North Island to the Pacific

wail (weil) **1.** *n.* a long drawn-out cry of pain or grief ‖ the act of making such cries ‖ a sound like such a cry, *the wail of the sirens* **2.** *v.i.* to utter a wail ‖ (*pop.*) to complain, esp. with self-pity [prob. O.N. *vei*, woe]

Wailing Wall a wall in Jerusalem, reputed to contain some of the stones from Solomon's Temple. Jews traditionally bewail at it the destruction (70 A.D.) of the Temple by the Romans

wain (wein) *n.* (*archaic*) a four-wheeled large farm wagon **the Wain** the Big Dipper, the seven bright stars in Ursa Major [O.E. *wægen*, *wæn*, wheeled vehicle]

wain·scot (wéinskət, wéinskɒt) **1.** *n.* wooden paneling or boarding covering the walls of a room, esp. the lower part of them ‖ (*Br. hist.*) fine-quality oak imported for this ‖ the lower part of the walls of a room when they are finished in some other material than is used for the rest **2.** *v.t. pres. part.* **wain·scot·ing**, esp. *Br.* **wain·scot·ting** *past* and *past part.* **wain·scot·ed**, esp. *Br.* **wain·scot·ted** to panel (a room etc.) with wainscot **wáin·scot·ing**, esp. *Br.* **wáin·scot·ting** *n.* wainscot or the material used for it [fr. M.L.G. *wagenschot* prob. fr. *wagen*, a wagon]

wain·wright (wéinrait), Jonathan Mayhew (1883-1953), U.S. general. He commanded (1942) the unsuccessful defense of Bataan and Corregidor and underwent torture in a Japanese prison camp (1942-5) in Manchuria. He was awarded the Congressional Medal of Honor

wain·wright (wéinrait) *n.* a craftsman who makes and repairs wagons

waist (weist) *n.* the narrow part of the human body between ribs and hips ‖ that part of a garment which covers the waist ‖ (*old-fash.*) the bodice or upper part of a woman's dress ‖ (*old-fash.*) a blouse ‖ the waistline ‖ the narrow part of the abdomen of some insects, e.g. the wasp ‖ (*naut.*) the middle part of a ship between quarterdeck and forecastle ‖ the narrow middle part of an object, *the waist of a violin* [M.E. *wast* prob. rel. to O.E. *weaxan*, to grow]

waist·band (wéistbænd) *n.* a band or belt around the waist attached to a garment, e.g. the top part of a skirt, trousers etc. or the lower part of a jacket, blouse etc., often serving to keep the garment in position

waist·cloth (wéistklɔθ, wéistklɒθ) *pl.* **waist·cloths** (wéistklɔðz, wéistklɒðz, wéistklɔθs, wéistklɒθs) *n.* a loincloth

waist·coat (wéskət, wéistkout) *n.* (*Br.*) a vest (man's garment worn over the trouser top and under the jacket)

waist·line (wéistlain) *n.* the waist of the human body, considered with respect to position or size ‖ the line at which the bodice and skirt of a dress meet

wait (weit) **1.** *v.i.* (often with 'for') to remain in a place or in a state of inactivity, indecision, delay or anticipation because of some event expected to happen or a person expected to arrive etc. ‖ to be in readiness, *your dinner is waiting for you* ‖ to be set aside for later action, to remain undone for the time being, *that decision can't wait* ‖ to act as a waiter ‖ *v.t.* to await, **wait for,** *to wait one's opportunity* ‖ to delay, *to wait dinner for someone* **to wait on** to attend or serve (someone), esp. at table **to wait out** to endure something distressing, e.g. a storm or a setback, hoping that it will change for the better or stop **to wait up** (with 'for') to refrain from going to bed at one's normal bedtime in expectation of someone's arrival or of news etc. **2.** *n.* an act or period of waiting, *a long wait at the station* ‖ (*pl.*, esp. *Br.*) street singers of Christmas carols **to lie in wait** to be on the watch, in hiding, ready to make an attack etc. [early M.E. *waite, waiten* fr. A.F., O.N.F. *waitier* fr. O.H.G.]

Wai·tan·gi Day (waitǽŋi:) New Zealand's national day, Feb. 6, a public holiday

Waitangi, Treaty of a treaty (1840) between Britain and the Maori chiefs of New Zealand, by which the Maoris ceded all rights and powers of sovereignty to the British monarch while retaining all territorial rights, in return for British protection

Waite (weit), Morrison Remick (1816-88), U.S. jurist, Chief Justice (1874-88) of the U.S. Supreme Court. He represented the U.S.A. as prosecutor in the Alabama Arbitration. As Chief Justice he broadly interpreted the 'due process' clause of the 14th amendment in favor of private businesses, a position maintained by the Court until the 1930s

wait·er (wéitər) *n.* a man employed to serve food or drink, esp. one who waits on tables in a restaurant ‖ a salver or tray for dishes etc.

wait·ing (wéitiŋ) **1.** *adj.* that waits ‖ of or for a wait ‖ that is in attendance **2.** *n.* the act of someone who waits **in waiting** in attendance (e.g. on

a king or queen) ‖ (*Br., mil.*) next in turn for some duty etc.

waiting game a deliberate reserving of action so as to allow a situation to develop, in the hope of having better opportunities later on

waiting room a room provided for those who have to wait, esp. for a train or to see a doctor, dentist etc.

wait·ress (wéitris) *n.* a woman or girl who waits on tables in a restaurant etc.

waive (weiv) *pres. part.* **waiv·ing** *past* and *past part.* **waived** *v.t.* to agree to forgo or prefer not to insist on (a claim, right or privilege) **wáiv·er** *n.* (*law*) the act of waiving or giving up some established claim, right or privilege ‖ a document, or clause in an agreement, making this effective [fr. A.F. *weyver*, to allow to become a waif]

Wa·ka·ya·ma (wákajáma) a port (pop. 285,000) in S.E. Honshu, Japan: cotton textiles, woodworking

wake (weik) *pres. part.* **wak·ing** *past* **woke** (wouk), **waked** *past part.* **waked, wok·en** (wóukən) *v.i.* (often with 'up') to become conscious after sleep or after being in a semiconscious state ‖ (often with 'up') to return to alertness, pay attention again ‖ to become imaginatively aware of something, *he woke to the beauty of his surroundings* ‖ (among the Irish) to hold a wake ‖ *v.t.* (often with 'up') to rouse (someone) from sleep ‖ to rouse, revive, *the music wakes sad memories* ‖ (often with 'to') to cause to become aware of something, *he woke his audience to the need for concerted action* ‖ (among the Irish) to hold a wake over [O.E. *wæcnan*, to arise, be born and *wacian*, to wake, watch]

wake *n.* (among the Irish) a vigil over a corpse before burial, often accompanied by drinking and festivity ‖ (*Br., hist.*) a parish festival held annually in commemoration of the patron saint of the church ‖ (*pl.*, in some parts of England) an annual holiday [M.E. prob. representative of supposed O.E. *wacu*, and partly a new formation of WAKE v.]

wake *n.* the track in the water behind a moving ship, or something thought of as like this **in the wake of** behind, following in the tracks of, *traders came in the wake of explorers and missionaries* [fr. O.N. *vaku, vök*, hole, opening in ice]

wake·ful (wéikfəl) *adj.* watchful, alert ‖ unable to sleep ‖ marked by lack of sleep

Wake Island (weik) an atoll comprising three islets (area 3 sq. miles, pop. 150) in the N. Pacific between the Marianas and Hawaii, annexed by the U.S.A. (1900) and used as a calling place for transpacific aircraft. It was occupied (1941-5) by the Japanese

Wake·field (wéikfi:ld), Edward Gibbon (1796-1862), British colonial statesman. He contributed to the drawing up of the Durham Report (1839) and promoted the colonization of New Zealand

wak·en (wéikən) *v.t.* to rouse from sleep or lethargy ‖ to stir into awareness, activity etc. ‖ to cause to realize or remember ‖ *v.i.* to become awake [O.E. *wæcnan*]

wake-surf·ing (wéiksə:rfiŋ) *n.* surfing behind a motor boat

wak·ing (wéikiŋ) *adj.* marked by a condition of wakefulness, *waking hours*

Waks·man (wáksmən), Selman Abraham (1888-1973), U.S. microbiologist who received the 1952 Nobel prize in physiology and medicine for his discovery of streptomycin and its value in treating tuberculosis

Wa·la·chi·a, Wal·la·chi·a (wɒléiki:ə) the southern region of Rumania, consisting largely of the fertile plain (wheat, corn) of the lower Danube basin. Chief towns: Bucharest, Ploesti. Historically, it was comprised of Oltenia, or Lesser Walachia, in the west and Muntenia, or Greater Walachia, in the east. There are rich oil fields in the north, in the foothills of the S. Carpathians. It united with Moldavia to form Rumania (1859)

Wa·la·chi·an, Wal·la·chi·an (wɒléiki:ən) **1.** *adj.* of Walachia, its people or language **2.** *n.* the Rumanian language of the Walachians ‖ a native or inhabitant of Walachia ‖ a Vlach

Wal·bur·ga (wɒlbéːrgə, valbúərgə), St (c. 710–c. 779), English abbess. Feast: Feb. 25

Wal·che·ren (wálxərən) a former island (area 82 sq. miles) at the mouth of the Scheldt in Zeeland, Netherlands, now attached to the mainland. Chief towns: Flushing, Middelburg

---

Wal·deck-Rous·seau (vældekru:sou), Pierre Marie René (1846-1904), French statesman. During his term of office (1899-1902) as prime minister, a law was passed (1901) which suppressed some secular powers of the Church and resulted in the separation (1905) of Church and State in France

Wal·den·ses (wɔldénsi:z) pl. n. the members of a reforming Christian sect founded (c. 1175) by Peter Waldo (Pierre Waldo, c. 1140-c. 1217), French religious reformer. He preached in the valleys of Dauphiné, Provence and Piedmont. He taught from the Scriptures in the vernacular and was vowed to poverty and simplicity. The Waldenses were excommunicated (1184) and suffered persecution (16th c.) and were not officially tolerated until 1848 **Wal·den·si·an** (wɔldénsi:ən, wɔldénʃən) adj. [M.L.]

Wal·den·ström's   **mac·ro·glo·bu·lin·e·me·a** (váldenstremz mækrəglɒbju:liní:mi:ə) n. (med.) disease of proteins in antibodies that fight infection, resulting in excess production of plasma cells and lymphocytes; discovered in 1914 by Dr. Jan G. Waldenstrom, Swedish physician

Wald·heim (válthaim), Kurt (1918-), Austrian statesman, foreign minister (1968-70), Secretary-General of the United Nations (1972-81). Controversy over his having been in Hitler's army during World War II and his possible involvement in sending Jews to their deaths marked his successful campaign for election as president of Austria (1986)

Wald·see·mül·ler (váltzeimylər), Martin (c. 1475-c.1521), German geographer. He gave to the American continent the first name of his friend Amerigo Vespucci, on the grounds that Vespucci was the first to call America a 'new world'

wale (weil) 1. n. a weal on the skin left by a whip, cane etc. ‖ a ridge on the surface of cloth, e.g. in corduroy ‖ (naut., esp. pl.) one of the extra thick planks in the sides of a wooden ship ‖ a wooden or steel brace on a row of piles on a dam or trench ‖ (basketry) a strong band formed by weaving three or four rods one after the other into a single course 2. v.t. pres. part. **wal·ing** past and past part. **waled** to mark (the flesh) with a wale or wales ‖ to supply with a wale or wales [O.E. walu]

Wales (weilz) a country (area, including Monmouthshire, 8,016 sq. miles, pop. 2,790,462) in the west of Great Britain. It is a division of the United Kingdom. Chief town: Cardiff. Language: English, Welsh (1% Welsh only, 25% bilingual). The land is 12% arable, 6% forest, largely pasture and grazing. Wales forms a rugged massif, partly covered with forest and moorland, with a lowland fringe widest along the English border and south coast. The massif is largely between 600 and 2,000 ft, rocky in the north and coal-bearing (esp. anthracite) in the south. It is highest in the northwest, rising to 3,560 ft (Snowdon). Average temperatures (F.): 42° (Jan.) and 60° (July). Rainfall: less than 50 ins in the lowlands, 50-80 ins in the moorland massif, well over 80 ins in the mountains. Chief ports: Cardiff, Swansea, Newport. The University of Wales is made up of colleges in Aberystwyth (1872), Bangor (1884), Cardiff (1883) and Swansea (1920). HISTORY. Wales is thought to have been originally inhabited by Iberians and to have been overrun (c. 6th c. B.C.) by Celts. The Romans conquered the north and south (1st c. A.D.), but had little influence on most of the country. After the Roman withdrawal (early 5th c.), the Celts of Wales maintained their independence against the Anglo-Saxon invaders of England, challenging the authority of Offa of Mercia (8th c.). Wales was converted to Christianity (c. 6th c.) by Celtic missionaries, notably St David. William I of England, unable to subdue Wales, appointed earls to control the Welsh marches. The Welsh, notably under Llewelyn ap Iorwerth and Llewelyn ap Gruffydd, successfully opposed English attempts to invade until the late 13th c., when Edward I conquered the country, his son, the future Edward II, becoming prince of Wales (1301).. Revolts against English rule continued, notably (1400-9) under Owen Glendower. The Tudors, a Welsh dynasty, fought in the Wars of the Roses as representatives of the Lancastrian claim, and one of them ascended (1485) the English throne as Henry VII. Under Henry VIII, Wales and the marches were brought into a legal union with England (1534-6). (For subsequent history *ENGLAND, *GREAT BRITAIN)

Walesa (vawénsə), Lech (1943-) Polish labor leader, chairman of the Solidarity labor organization (1980-2), winner of the Nobel peace prize (1983). An electrician, he was leader of his factory's strike coordination committee and was named chairman of Solidarity soon after the government granted the right to form independent trade unions. He was jailed after martial law was imposed (1981) and was released when Solidarity was dissolved by the government (1982). He continued to work for labor's rights

walk (wɔk) 1. v.i. to move in such a way that the legs support the body, one foot (in two-legged creatures) or two feet (in four-legged creatures) being always on the ground (cf. RUN) ‖ to travel on foot ‖ (of a ghost) to show itself ‖ (baseball) to advance to first base as a result of having been pitched four balls ‖ (basketball) to foul by moving more than two steps with the ball without either passing or dribbling ‖ v.t. to pass over, through etc. by walking, to walk the Lake District ‖ to cause to walk, he walked his horse through the village ‖ to walk beside and push (a bicycle or motorcycle) ‖ to accompany on foot, I'll walk you home ‖ (baseball) to advance (a batter) to first base by pitching four balls ‖ (basketball) to foul by advancing more than two steps with (the ball) without either passing or dribbling **to walk away from** to outdistance (one's opponents or rivals) easily ‖ to emerge from (an accident) without serious injury **to walk away with** to win (something) by a large margin ‖ to steal ‖ (of an actor, singer etc.) to win far the most attention and applause from the audience in (a show) **to walk off** to leave, esp. without saying good-bye ‖ to rid oneself of (e.g. excess fat) by walking ‖ to measure (a distance, boundary etc.) by walking **to walk off with** to win (something) by a large margin ‖ to steal ‖ (of an actor, singer etc.) to win by far the most attention and applause from the audience in (a show) **to walk out** to leave, esp. in such a way as to show disapproval, disappointment etc. ‖ to go on strike **to walk out on** to abandon or desert without warning **to walk over** (or **all over**) to show complete disregard for the rights, wishes etc. of (someone) ‖ (pop.) to defeat (one's opponent) overwhelmingly **to walk over the course** (of a horse) to be the only competitor in a race and win it by going over (the course) at a walk **to walk (someone) off his feet** to tire (someone) out by making him walk a long way **to walk the streets** to walk aimlessly in the streets ‖ to be a prostitute 2. n. the act of walking ‖ the route taken when walking ‖ a route pleasant to walk over ‖ a path designed to be walked along ‖ a stroll taken or journey made on foot for pleasure or exercise ‖ a distance walked ‖ a manner of walking ‖ a slow pace, to go at a walk ‖ (Br.) the circuit taken by a hawker etc. ‖ (athletics) a race in which one walks over the course ‖ (baseball) an advance to first base as a result of four balls ‖ a sheepwalk ‖ a ropewalk ‖ (Br.) a section of forest under the charge of a keeper ‖ (in the West Indies) a plantation of trees [O.E. wealcan, to roll, toss and wealcian, to muffle up, curl]

walk·a·way (wɔ́kəwei) n. an easily won contest

Walk·er (wɔ́kər), David (1785-1830), U.S. black leader, one of the first militants to protest against the repression of blacks. His pamphlet 'Walker's Appeal in four articles together with a preamble to the Colored Citizens of the World, but in particular and very expressly to those of the United States of America' was an argument against slavery. He himself had the status of a free man

Walker, Francis Amasa (1840-97), U.S. economist and statistician, known for his theories on wages and profits in 'The Wages Question' (1876) and for his advocacy of international bimetallism

Walker, Robert John (1801-69), U.S. statesman. As secretary of the treasury (1845-9) under President James Polk, he made it independent of the U.S. banking and financial system, and he helped to improve Anglo-U.S. relations by the Walker Tariff (1846), a revenue as opposed to a protective tariff. He served (1857) as governor of Kansas during the critical period when proslavery and antislavery forces vied for supremacy

Walker, William (1824-60), U.S. adventurer. Leading a small band of filibusters, he seized (1856) Nicaragua and proclaimed himself president. He planned to establish slave labor to

develop the economy, build a canal that would attract world trade, and create a military empire of Central American states. He was deposed (1857) largely through the efforts of Cornelius Vanderbilt. After a final seizure of Nicaragua (1860) he was executed by a British firing squad in Honduras

walk·ie-talk·ie, walk·y-talk·y (wɔ́ki:tɔ́ki:) n. a portable battery-operated radio transmitter and receiver used out of doors and when on the move over short distances

walking catfish a catfish (Clarias batrachas) capable of moving about on dry land

walking papers (Am.=Br. marching orders) dismissal from employment

walking stick a stick carried when walking, often as a support **walk·ing·stick** (wɔ́:kiŋstik) n. a stick insect

walk-off (wɔ́kɔf) n. 1. a departure marking the end of an incident 2. a desire not to be associated with a person or event; a walkout

walk of life calling, profession ‖ social status

walk-on (wɔ́kɔn, wɔ́kɒn) n. (theater, movies etc.) a minor role that involves only a brief appearance, usually without spoken lines ‖ the actor who plays this

walk-out (wɔ́kaut) n. a strike ‖ the act of leaving as a sign of disapproval etc.

walk-o·ver (wɔ́kouvər) n. a horse race in which the only starter has merely to walk over the course in order to win ‖ an easy win

walk-up (wɔ́kʌp) n. an apartment house without an elevator ‖ an apartment above the ground floor in such a building

walk-up adj. open to the street for doing business without customers having to enter a building, esp. of a bank

walk·way (wɔ́kwei) n. a passage for walking

Walkyrie *VALKYRIE

walky-talky *WALKIE-TALKIE

wall (wɔl) n. a usually vertical structure, esp. in masonry, large in surface area as compared with thickness, built to enclose, support, divide, protect, retain etc. ‖ the surface of such a structure, hang it up on the wall ‖ something which resembles a man-made wall, a wall of mountains, esp. with regard to surface, paintings on the walls of a cave ‖ the upright part of the structure of a hollow vessel, the wall of a pot ‖ (anat., biol.) a layer of structural material bounding an organ, cavity, cell etc. ‖ something seen as a barrier to understanding or social intercourse, a wall of silence **to drive** (or **push**) **to the wall** to force (someone) into a desperate or difficult position **to go to the wall** to experience defeat ‖ to fail in business **to have one's back to the wall** to be hard pressed, be in a very difficult situation **with one's back to the wall** in a desperate or very difficult situation [O.E.]

wall v.t. to furnish with a wall (with 'in') to enclose within a wall ‖ (with 'up') to shut with a wall ‖ (with 'off') to divide, separate etc. with a wall [O.E. weallan]

wal·la·by (wɔ́ləbi:) pl. **wal·la·bies** n. any of several small kangaroos of Macropus and related genera [native Austral. wolabá]

Wal·lace (wɔ́lis), Alfred Russel (1823-1913), British naturalist. He spent many years in South America and the East Indies. He developed, independently, a theory of evolution similar to Darwin's. The theories were published simultaneously in 1858

Wallace, George Corley (1919-), U.S. politician and 5-time governor of Alabama, a conservative Democrat. The champion of states' rights and 'segregation forever', he polled 13.5% of the popular vote as 3rd party candidate in the 1968 presidential election. With 46 electoral votes, he almost put the election into the House of Representatives. He was a candidate (1972) for the Democratic presidential nomination. An attempt on his life (1972) left him as a paraplegic. He retired from public life (1986), citing ill health

Wallace, Henry Agard (1888-1965), American politician, Democratic vice-president of the U.S.A. (1941-5). He founded the Progressive party (1948)

Wallace, Lewis (1827-1905), U.S. general, politician and author of three historical romances: 'The Fair God' (1873), a tale of the Mexican conquest; 'Ben Hur' (1880), a story of the coming of Christ, made into a successful play and two motion pictures; and 'Prince of India' (1893), a narrative concerning the Wandering Jew and the Byzantine empire

Wallace, Sir Richard (1818-90), British art collector and philanthropist. His collection of pictures (esp. French 18th-c.), sculpture and furniture, bequeathed to Britain (1897), forms the national Wallace Collection, London

Wallace, Sir William (c. 1272-1305), Scottish patriot. He led the resistance to Edward I, whom he defeated at Stirling (1297). He was routed at Falkirk (1298), betrayed (1305) and executed in London

Wal·lace·ism (wáləsizəm) *n.* a principle supporting states rights and espousing anti-integration policies; from George C. Wallace, former governor of Alabama

Wallachia *WALACHIA

Wallachian *WALACHIAN

wall·board (wɔ́lbɔrd, wɔ́lbourd) *n.* a large sheet of boarding made from wood pulp, gypsum etc. and used to line walls or ceilings

wall cloud eyewall (*meteor.*) the high wall surrounding the eye of a hurricane

Wal·len·stein (válenʃtain, wɔ́lenstain), Albrecht Wenzel Eusebius von, duke of Friedland and Mecklenburg, prince of Sagan (1583-1634), German soldier and statesman. He commanded the Hapsburg armies in the Thirty Years' War, winning many victories until his defeat at Lützen (1632). He was assassinated on the orders of Ferdinand II

Wal·ler (wɔ́lər, wɔ́lər), Edmund (1606-87), English poet and politician. He is remembered esp. for two poems, 'Go, Lovely Rose' and 'On a Girdle'

wal·let (wɔ́lit, wɔ́lit) *n.* a pocketbook or small flat, folding case for carrying papers, paper money etc. || (*hist.*) a beggar's or pilgrim's bag in which he carried his provisions [origin unknown]

wall·eye (wɔ́lai) *pl.* **wall·eyes** *n.* an eye in which the iris is streaked or whitish or different from the other eye, or which has a divergent squint || opaqueness and whiteness of the cornea of the eye due to injury or disease [back-formation fr. *walleyed*]

Walleye *n.* (*mil.*) U.S. air-to-surface glide bomb (AGM-62X A) for the stand-off destruction of large, semihard targets, incorporating a contrast tracking television system for guidance

wall·eyed (wɔ́laid) *adj.* having walleye || having glaring eyes [Late M.E. *wawileghed*, O.N. *vagleygr*]

walleyed pike *Stizostedion vitreum,* fam. *Percidae,* a large pike perch of North America valued as a food and game fish

wall·flow·er (wɔ́lflauər) *n.* a perennial plant of genus *Cheiranthus,* fam. *Cruciferae,* esp. *C. cheiri,* native to S. Europe and widely cultivated for its fragrant yellow, brown, red or purplish flowers || (*pop.*) a girl sitting out at a dance because she has not been asked to dance

wall game a kind of football played only at Eton College, England

Wal·lis (wɔ́lis, wɔ́lis), John (1616-1703), English mathematician, one of the founders of the Royal Society. He was the first to deal mathematically with the concept of infinity, and his 'Arithmetica Infinitorum' (1657) paved the way for the development of the calculus and of the binomial theorem

Wallis and Futuna two groups of volcanic and coral islands (area 119 sq. miles, pop. 9,192) in the Pacific between Fiji and Samoa, forming an overseas territory of France. It is ruled by native kings. People: Polynesian. Main islands: Futuna, Uvea. The islands became a French protectorate (1842) and an overseas territory (1961) of France

Wal·loon (wɔlú:n) 1. *n.* a member of the French-speaking population of Belgium occupying the southern part of the country (cf. FLEMING) || the French dialect of the Walloons 2. *adj.* of the Walloons or their French dialect [F. *Wallon* fr. Gmc]

wal·lop (wɔ́ləp) 1. *v.t.* (*pop.*) to hit hard || (*pop.*) to thrash || (*pop.*) to defeat soundly 2. *n.* (*pop.*) a heavy blow **wal·lop·ing** 1. *adj.* (*pop.*) huge, thumping, whopping 2. *n.* (*pop.*) a severe thrashing [M.E. *walopen,* to gallop fr. O.N.F.]

wal·low (wɔ́lou) 1. *v.i.* (esp. of some animals) to roll about with pleasure (e.g. in mud) || (of a ship) to roll in rough water || to revel with self-indulgence (e.g. in sentiment or luxury) 2. *n.* a mudhole or other place where animals (esp. buffaloes and hippopotamuses) wallow [O.E. *wealwian*]

wall·pa·per (wɔ́lpeipər) 1. *n.* paper, usually decorative, for covering the walls of a room 2. *v.t.* to cover with such paper

wallpaper music (*Br.*) piped background music in a public place

Wall Street the stock exchange and money market of the U.S.A. [after a street in Manhattan, New York City]

wall-to-wall (wɔ́ltu:wɔ́l) *adj.* completely covering a floor

wal·nut (wɔ́lnʌt, wɔ́lnət) *n.* a member of *Juglans,* fam. *Juglandaceae,* a genus of tall-growing trees of temperate regions || the edible fruit (a two-lobed seed in a shell, enclosed by a husk) of these trees || the wood of these trees, esp. of the black walnut, which takes a high polish and is used in cabinetmaking, for gunstocks etc. [O.E. *walhhnutu*]

Wal·pole (wɔ́lpoul, wɔ́lpoul), Horace, 4th earl of Orford (1717-97), English man of letters. He is famous for his Gothic novel. 'The Castle of Otranto' (1765) and for his 3,000 letters. He was one of the men responsible for the growing pre-Romantic taste for the Gothic, as a reaction to 18th–c. classicism in the arts

Walpole, Sir Robert, 1st earl of Orford (1676-1745), English statesman. As first lord of the treasury and chancellor of the exchequer, he led the Whig administration (1721-42) and was effectively prime minister. His encouragement of trade and his cautious domestic policy did much to increase national wealth and to strengthen the Hanoverian dynasty. He reduced the national debt, land tax and customs duties. He avoided involving Britain in war, until he was forced to participate in the War of Jenkins' Ear (1739-41) and the War of the Austrian Succession (1740-8). He helped to establish the collective responsibility of prime minister and cabinet to parliament

Wal·pur·gis Night (valpúərgis) the night of April 30/May 1, when a witches' sabbath (particularly associated with the Brocken peak in the Harz Mtns.) was said to take place. St Walburga was accidentally connected with this ancient superstition (her bodily remains were transferred from her monastery to Eichstätt in Germany on May 1)

wal·rus (wɔ́lrəs, wɔ́lrəs) *n.* either of two species of Arctic, marine, seal-like, carnivorous mammals of fam. *Odobenidae: Odobenus rosmarus,* which inhabits the N.W. Atlantic Arctic, and *O. divergens,* which inhabits the Bering Sea and the Siberian and Alaskan coasts. Males weigh up to 2,000 lbs and are up to 12 ft long; females are smaller. Walruses are hunted for their blubber (which yields an excellent oil), skins (leather) and canine tusks (ivory) [prob. fr. Du. *walrus, walros*]

Wal·sall (wɔ́lsɔl) a county borough (pop. 178,900) in Staffordshire, England: coal mining, tanning, mechanical engineering

Walsh (wɔlʃ), Thomas James (1859-1933), U.S. lawyer and senator (1912-33) from Montana. He prosecuted with vigor the investigations into the oil reserves scandals of the Harding administration. He helped write the 18th and 19th amendments to the Constitution

Wal·sing·ham (wɔ́lsiŋəm), Sir Francis (c. 1530-90), English statesman. He was secretary of state (1573-90) to Elizabeth I

Wal·ter (wɔ́ltər), Hubert (*d.* 1205), English prelate and statesman, archbishop of Canterbury (1193-1205). As chief justiciar of England (1193-8), he was the effective ruler when Richard I was at the Crusades. He was chancellor (1199-1205) under King John

Wal·ther von der Vo·gel·wei·de (váltərfonderfóugəlvaidə) (c. 1170-1230), German lyric poet. After service at the court of Vienna he became a minnesinger. His love poetry and his treatment of social and political themes in verse and maxims make him the most celebrated of the German medieval lyric poets

Wal·ton (wɔ́ltən), Izaak (1593-1683), English writer. 'The Compleat Angler' (1653, enlarged in 1655 and subsequently) is his most popular work. He also wrote lives of John Donne (1640), Richard Hooker (1665), George Herbert (1670) and others

Walton, Sir William (1902-83), British composer. His works include 'Façade', a suite for 'declamation' and chamber orchestra (1923, 1926), 'Sinfonia Concertante for piano and orchestra' (1929), the cantata 'Belshazzar's Feast' (1931) and 'Symphony' (1935)

waltz (wɔlts) 1. *n.* a smooth, graceful dance in triple time to a flowing melody || the music for this dance || a composition in this rhythm 2. *v.i.* to dance a waltz || *v.t.* to dance a waltz with to

waltz off with to win (a race, prize etc.) with great ease [fr. G. *walzer*]

waltzing Matilda (*Austral.*) traveling on foot carrying a pack [prob. fr. WALTZ (*slang*), to carry + *matilda,* a tramp's roll]

Wal·vis Bay (wɔ́lvis) an enclave (area 374 sq. miles, pop. 25,000) of Cape Province, South Africa, on the coast of Namibia, administered as part of the latter territory || the deep-water port which gives it its importance: whaling, refueling

wam·pum (wɔ́mpəm, wɔ́mpəm) *n.* beads made of shells strung together and used by North American Indians as money or ornaments [shortened fr. *wampumpeag* fr. Narragansett *wampompeag* fr. *wampan,* white + *api,* string + -*ag,* pl. suffix]

wan (wɔn) *comp.* **wan·ner** *superl.* **wan·nest** *adj.* (of a person's complexion) unhealthily pale || (of the light or stars etc.) barely perceptible || (of a smile) faint, feeble [O.E. *wann,* dark]

Wan·a·ma·ker (wɔ́nəmeikər), John (1838-1922), U.S. merchant who established (1869) John Wanamaker and Company, one of the first large department stores in the U.S.A. He was a pioneer in the use of advertising

Wan·chu·an (wántʃyán) *CHANGKIAKOW

wand (wɔnd) *n.* a slender stick or rod, esp. one carried by a fairy, magician, conjurer etc. || a wooden or metal staff carried as a symbol of authority || (*archery*) a slat 6 ft by 2 ins used as a target, placed at 100 yds for men, 60 yds for women [O.N. *vøndr*]

wan·der (wɔ́ndər) *v.i.* (of a person) to travel or move around with no set route or goal || (often with 'off') to stray away without set purpose from one's home, companions etc. || (of the mind or a person) to be confused, incoherent or delirious || to digress, *to wander from the subject* || (of a river, road etc.) to follow an intricate course **wan·der·ing** *n.* a leisurely traveling around || (*pl.*) leisurely journeys || (*pl.*) incoherent speech or thoughts [O.E. *wandrian*]

Wandering Jew a Jew who, according to a legend first recorded in the 13th c., insulted Christ on the way to Calvary and was condemned to wander from place to place knowing no rest until the Day of Judgment

wan·der·lust (wɔ́ndərlʌst) *n.* a strong desire to travel, esp. an obsessive desire to get away from a settled way of living [G.]

wan·der·oo (wɔndəru:) *pl.* **wan·der·oos** *n.* *Presbytis senex,* fam. *Colobidae,* a purple-faced langur of eastern Asia || *Macaca silenus,* a black macaque of India having a tufted tail and a gray ruff [Sinhalese *wanderu,* monkey]

wane (wein) 1. *v.i.* pres. part. **wan·ing** past and past part. **waned** (of the moon) to diminish in size and brilliance after being at the full (cf. WAX) || (of the tide) to ebb || to decline or decrease in power, strength, importance, reputation, influence etc. 2. *n.* the act or process of waning || the period from the full moon to the new moon **on the wane** on the decline [O.E. *wanian*]

Wang·a·nu·i (wɔŋənú:i) a port (pop. 37,000) in Wellington, North Island, New Zealand

wan·gle (wǽŋg'l) 1. *v.t.* pres. part. **wan·gling** past and past part. **wan·gled** (*pop.*) to get by cunning, *to wangle a free ticket* || (*pop.*) to falsify, *to wangle the accounts* 2. *n.* (*pop.*) a wangling [etym. doubtful]

Wan·kel engine (váŋkəl) *n.* (*motor vehicle*) a small, light, rotary engine that utilizes a rounded triangular rotor-piston and that has only two major moving parts. It was named for Felix Wankel, German engineer. *also* epitrochoidal engine

want (wɔnt, wɔnt) *n.* the state or fact of having too little of something desirable or needed || an insufficiency through personal failing, *a want of tact* || need, *in want of a haircut* || privation because of poverty, *freedom from want* || (*pl.*) desires, requirements, *a man of few wants* [fr. O.N. *vant* neut. of *vanr,* lacking, wanting]

want *v.t.* (with the infinitive) to wish fervently, *they want to go to America* || to wish for, *I want some coffee* || (esp. *Br.*) to need, *the house wants a cleaning* || to possess less than the usual or required amount of, *he wants the stamina of a long-distance runner* || to wish to see or speak to (someone), *your father wants you* || (*esp.* with 'for') to suffer need, *he never wanted for affection as a child* **to want for nothing** to have everything one needs (even though poor, or because rich) [O.N. *vanta*]

want ad a classified advertisement (esp. in a newspaper) for employment or an employee etc.

CONCISE PRONUNCIATION KEY: **(a)** æ, c*a*t; ɑ, c*ar*; ɔ f*aw*n; ei, sn*a*ke. **(e)** e, h*e*n; i:, sh*ee*p; iə, d*ee*r; ɛə, b*ear*. **(i)** i, f*i*sh; ai, t*i*ger; ə:, b*ir*d. **(o)** o, *o*x; au, c*ow*; ou, g*oa*t; u, p*oor*; ɔi, r*oy*al. **(u)** ʌ, d*u*ck; u, b*u*ll; u:, g*oo*se; ə, b*a*cillus; ju:, c*u*be. x, lo*ch*; θ, *th*ink; ð, bo*th*er; z, *Z*en; ʒ, cor*s*age; dʒ, sava*ge*; ŋ, orangutan*g*; j, *y*ak; ʃ, *fi*sh; tʃ, fe*tch*; 'l, rabb*le*; 'n, redd*en.* Complete pronunciation key appears inside front cover.

want·ed (wɔ́ntid, wɔ́ntid) *adj.* being searched for so as to be brought to trial

want·ing (wɔ́ntiŋ, wɔ́ntiŋ) **1.** *adj.* not present when it should be, *mustard was wanting in the salad* ‖ deficient, *wanting in initiative* **2.** *prep.* without, short of, *a watch wanting only its spring*

wan·ton (wɔ́ntən) **1.** *adj.* lewd, licentious, *wanton thoughts* ‖ showing utter lack of moderation or justification, *wanton destruction* ‖ luxuriant, uncontrolled, *roses in wanton profusion* ‖ (*rhet.*) sportive, playful, *in wanton mood* **2.** *n.* (*old-fash.*) a sexually promiscuous woman [M.E. *wantowen* fr. O.E. *wan-*, wanting + *togen*, past part. of *tēon*, to discipline]

wap·en·take (wǽpənteik, wɔ́pənteik) *n.* (*hist.*) a division corresponding to the hundred in certain English shires [fr. O.N. *vápnatak*, weapon-taking fr. the showing of weapons as a form of voting]

wap·i·ti (wɔ́piti:) *pl.* **wap·i·ti, wap·i·tis** *n. Cervus canadensis,* fam. *Cervidae,* a North American elk related to, but larger than, the European and Asian red deer [fr. Am. Ind. name]

war (wɔr) **1.** *n.* armed conflict between nations, tribes or other groups or an instance of this, *civil war, a war of conquest, the wars of religion* ‖ a concerted effort to put down, reduce or exterminate *a war on locusts* ‖ a state of hostility without resort to arms, *the cold war* ‖ the theory of conducting a war *at war* engaged in a war **to declare war** to declare officially that a state of war exists **to go to war** to enter into a war **2.** *v.i. pres. part.* **war·ring** *past* and *past part.* **warred** to be at war ‖ to engage in an effort to reduce or exterminate something [O.N.F. *werre* fr. O.H.G.]

Wa·ran·gal (wʌ́rəŋg'l) a town (pop. 156,000) in N. Andhra Pradesh, India: cotton spinning, carpets

War·beck (wɔ́rbek), Perkin (c. 1474-99), Flemish pretender to the English throne who led an unsuccessful rising against Henry VII (1497)

War between the States the American Civil War (*CIVIL WAR, AMERICAN)

war·ble (wɔ́rb'l) **1.** *v. pres. part.* **war·bling** *past* and *past part.* **war·bled** *v.i.* (of birds) to sing with long trills ‖ to produce a continuous trilling sound ‖ *v.t.* to sing (a song) thus **2.** *n.* the sound, or act, of warbling [O.F. *werbler, werbloier*]

warble *n.* a small tumor or swelling produced on the back of cattle, deer etc. by the larva of a botfly or a warble fly ‖ the larva of a warble fly [etym. doubtful]

warble fly any of various dipterous flies of fam. *Oestridae,* the larvae of which live under the skin of certain animals (cattle, deer, rabbits etc.)

war·bler (wɔ́rblər) *n.* any of various small, vividly marked North American songbirds of fam. *Parulidae* ‖ any of various small Old World songbirds of fam. *Sylviidae,* related to the thrushes [fr. WARBLE *n.*]

war·bon·net (wɔ́rbɒnit) *n.* a headdress worn by certain Plains Indians consisting of a band with a long extension of eagle feathers attached to it at the back

war correspondent a journalist reporting news from a war zone

war cry *pl.* **war cries** (*hist.*) a name or phrase shouted by soldiers when charging, to encourage each other or to intimidate the enemy ‖ a party slogan, catchword

Ward (wɔrd), Lester Frank (1841-1913), U.S. sociologist, a founder of systematic American sociology. He postulated a 'sociocracy', a society which could be scientifically planned, and he emphasized the need for the study of function rather than of structure

ward (wɔrd) *v.t.* (with 'off') to turn aside (a blow) ‖ (with 'off') to avert (a danger) [O.E. *weardian*]

ward *n.* a person, esp. a minor, under the care of a court or a legal guardian ‖ the state of being under the care of a court or guardian, *a child in ward* ‖ the guardianship of a person in this state ‖ an administrative district in a borough or city, esp. an electoral district ‖ a division of a prison or hospital ‖ a large room containing several beds or a set of such rooms in a hospital, *a children's ward* ‖ the inner court of a castle ‖ one of the projections in a lock case that resists the turning of a key other than the right one ‖ one of the corresponding key notches [O.E. *weard,* a watching]

-ward *suffix* toward a specified point, position, area etc., as in 'northward', 'skyward' [O.E. *-weard*]

ward·en (wɔ́rd'n) *n.* an official having special supervisory duties and who sees that regulations or laws are observed, *game warden, air-raid warden* ‖ (*eccles.*) a churchwarden ‖ the official in charge of a prison ‖ (*Br.*) the title of the principal of some colleges or other institutions

wárd·en·cy, wárd·en·ship *ns* [fr. O.F. *wardein*]

ward·er (wɔ́rdər) *n.* (*Br.*) a prison guard **wárd·ress** *n.* (*Br.*) a woman warder [A. F. *wardour*]

ward·robe (wɔ́rdroub) *n.* a tall piece of furniture to keep clothes in, usually fitted with racks, hangers, shelves etc. ‖ a person's clothes ‖ (*theater*) a room where costumes are kept ‖ (in titles) the department of a royal household in charge of the royal clothes, jewels etc. [A.F. *warderobe*]

ward·room (wɔ́rdru:m, wɔ́rdrʌm) *n.* the living quarters, esp. the mess, for the officers of a warship ‖ a ship's officers collectively

-wards *suffix* -ward [O.E. *-weardes* fr. *-weard,* toward + *-es,* gen. ending]

ward·ship (wɔ́rdʃip) *n.* guardianship

ware (weər) *n.* (*pl.*) goods for sale ‖ (in compounds) manufactured articles, *silverware, ironware* ‖ pottery classified according to its nature, *earthenware* or provenance, *Chelsea ware* [O.E. *waru,* merchandise]

ware *v.t.* (imperative only, esp. in hunting) to beware of, avoid [O.E. *warian,* fr. *wær* adj., cautious]

ware·house (wéərhɑus) **1.** *pl.* **ware·hous·es** (wéərhɑuziz) *n.* a building, or room in a building, where goods are stored ‖ a repository for furniture etc. ‖ a customs storehouse where dutiable goods are kept until duty is paid **2.** *v.t. pres. part.* **ware·hous·ing** *past* and *past. part.* **ware·housed** to put (goods etc.) in a warehouse for safekeeping ‖ to put (goods etc.) in a warehouse under bond

war·fare (wɔ́rfeər) *n.* a state of war ‖ (*fig.*) strife

war game a training exercise for military staffs carried out without the participation of troops

war·head (wɔ́rhed) *n.* the explosive head of a missile (detached when not needed)

Warhol (wɔ́rhɒl), Andy (1931-) U.S. artist, founder of the Pop-Art movement of the 1960s. He was known for his paintings of enlarged comic strip and mass media images, the latter usually repeated across and up and down the canvas. He pioneered a unique silk-screening process to produce such images as Popeye, Superman, Coca Cola cans, Campbell's soup cans, and the face of Elizabeth Taylor (1964). He also made some experimental films, including 'Sleep' (1963), 'Empire' (1964) and 'The Chelsea Girls' (1966)

war·horse (wɔ́rhɔrs) *n.* a cavalry officer's mount ‖ a veteran soldier or old political campaigner

war·i·ly (wéərili:) *adv.* in a wary manner

war·i·ness (wéəri:nis) *n.* the state or quality of being wary

war·like (wɔ́rlaik) *adj.* favoring or inclined to favor war or strife ‖ (*mil.*) of, relating to or for war ‖ (*rhet.*) befitting a soldier

Warlock (wɔ́rlɒk), Peter (Philip Heseltine, 1894-1930), British composer. His work was slight but filled with grace, wit and energy. His songs (many in the Elizabethan style) and his 'Capriol' suite for strings (1926) are best known

war·lock (wɔ́rlɒk) *n.* a man who practices witchcraft, sorcery etc. [O.E. *wærloga,* traitor, enemy, devil]

war·lord (wɔ́rlɔrd) *n.* a military commander who has seized effective power over the civilians of an area

warm (wɔrm) **1.** *adj.* having roughly the same temperature as the human body, *warm water* ‖ serving to keep the body at this temperature, *warm clothes* ‖ emitting heat, esp. in a comforting degree, *a warm fire* ‖ (of a person) slightly overheated, esp. after strenuous work or exercise ‖ affectionate, *warm friends* ‖ very cordial, *a warm welcome* ‖ emotionally excited, esp. slightly angry ‖ (of color) in the range yellow through orange to red ‖ (of an animal's scent or trail) fresh, strong ‖ (of a player in a game involving a search for a hidden object) near to the object being looked for ‖ (*pop.*) not very pleasant, *he left when things began to get warm* **2.** *v.i.* (often with 'up') to become warm ‖ *v.t.* (often with 'up') to make warm ‖ to fill with

pleasant emotions, *the crackling of the fire warmed her heart* **to warm over** to reheat (cooked food) **to warm up** to make or become more animated ‖ (*sports*) to exercise before going into a game, race etc. ‖ to reheat (cooked food) [O.E. *wearm*]

warm-blood·ed (wɔ́rmblʌ́did) *adj.* (of a bird or mammal) having a constant blood temperature considerably above that of the surrounding medium

warm front (*meteor.*) the edge of a warm air mass advancing against a colder air mass

warm-heart·ed (wɔ́rmhɑ́rtid) *adj.* affectionate, readily sympathetic etc.

warming pan a closed brass or copper pan to hold hot embers, with a long handle, formerly used to warm beds

war·mon·ger (wɔ́rmʌ̀ŋgər, wɔ́rmɒ̀ŋgər) *n.* a person who advocates war, esp. under the guise of patriotism

warmth (wɔrmθ) *n.* the state or quality of being warm [M.E. *wermthe* prob. fr. O.E.]

warm-up (wɔ́rmʌ̀p) *n.* an act or period of exercising before a game, race etc.

warn (wɔrn) *v.t.* to draw the attention of (someone) to the probable results of an act, or to an impending danger ‖ to inform beforehand, *he warned them that he intended to leave in two weeks* ‖ to rebuke (someone) mildly for misbehavior, breaking a rule etc., *this time I'm just warning you* ‖ *v.i.* to give warning **to warn off the course** (*Br.*) to prohibit (a jockey) from riding or (an owner) from running a horse in races **to warn off the premises** to order or advise (someone) to refrain from trespassing ‖ to order (someone) to leave the premises **wárn·ing 1.** *adj.* that warns **2.** *n.* the act of someone who warns ‖ the fact of being warned ‖ something which warns [O.E. *warenian, wearnian*]

warning path or **warning track** (*baseball*) a cleared area near the outside fence designed to alert an outfielder that he is approaching an obstacle

War of 1812 a war (1812-15) between Britain and the U.S.A. It arose from American resentment at the trade embargo imposed by France in the Continental System and by Britain in the orders-in-council of 1807 and 1809 during the Napoleonic Wars. Other causes were the British claim to search American ships for British deserters, and Anglo-American rivalry in the American northwest. During the war an American invasion of Canada failed (1812), a British force sacked Washington (1814), and several sea battles failed to produce a decisive result. New England remained hostile to the war. The war was settled by an agreement that both sides should give up territory captured, and appoint a commission to settle the Canadian boundary. After the signing of the treaty (Dec. 24, 1814) the British were defeated at New Orleans (Jan. 8, 1815). The war strengthened American nationalism and encouraged the growth of American industry

War of American Independence *REVOLUTIONARY WAR

War of Independence the Revolutionary war

war of nerves warfare designed to undermine the morale of the enemy, esp. by psychological means

War of Secession the American Civil War

War on Poverty *OFFICE OF ECONOMIC OPPORTUNITY

War on Poverty a series of long- and short-range plans designed to help the U.S. poor, proposed by President Lyndon Johnson (1964)

warp (wɔrp) *n.* the lengthwise threads in a fabric or on a loom, crossed by the weft or woof ‖ a twist or distortion in wood, esp. due to improper drying ‖ the state or fact of being so distorted ‖ a twist or distortion in the mind or character often resulting in perverse or irrational behavior ‖ (*naut.*) a towline attached to a fixed object, e.g. an anchor, and used for hauling a boat toward the object ‖ sediment deposited by water [O.E. *wearp*]

warp *v.t.* to cause (wood) to become twisted ‖ to cause (the mind, character etc.) to become as though twisted ‖ to give a false account or interpretation of ‖ to arrange (yarn etc.) so as to form a warp ‖ (*naut.*) to haul (a ship) with a warp ‖ to let water flood (land) so as to leave a deposit of warp ‖ to choke (a passage) with warp ‖ *v.i.* to become twisted or distorted ‖ to warp a ship ‖ (of a ship) to be warped ‖ to wind the yarn off bobbins in order to form the warp [O.E. *weorpan,* to throw]

CONCISE PRONUNCIATION KEY: **(a)** æ, c*a*t; ɑ, c*a*r; ɔ f*a*wn; ei, sn*a*ke. **(e)** e, h*e*n; i:, sh*ee*p; iə, d*ee*r; ɛə, b*ea*r. **(i)** i, f*i*sh; ai, t*i*ger; ə:, b*i*rd. **(o)** o, *o*x; au, c*ow*; ou, g*oa*t; u, p*oo*r; ɔi, r*oy*al. **(u)** ʌ, d*u*ck; u, b*u*ll; u:, g*oo*se; ə, b*a*cillus; ju:, c*u*be. x, lo*ch*; θ, *th*ink; ð, bo*th*er; z, *Z*en; ʒ, corsa*g*e; dʒ, sava*g*e; ŋ, orangutan*g*; j, *y*ak; ʃ, *fi*sh; tʃ, fe*tch*; 'l, rabb*le*; 'n, redd*en*. Complete pronunciation key appears inside front cover.

war paint paint applied to the face and body esp. by American Indians preparing to make war

war·path (wórpæθ, wórpɑθ) *pl.* **war·paths** (wórpæðz, wórpɑðz, wórpæθs, wórpɑθs) *n.* the route taken by North American Indians when moving to attack an enemy **on the warpath** bearing down to punish, on the lookout for offenders

warp beam (*weaving*) a roller in a loom, on which the warp threads are wound

war·plane (wórplein) *n.* an airplane used for warfare

war·rant (wórənt, wórənt) *n.* legal authorization || moral justification || a document authorizing the arrest of a person, the search of premises etc. || a voucher authorizing the payment of a sum of money, *a pension warrant* || the authorizing certificate of rank granted to a warrant officer || a royal or official authorization or license || (*Br.*) a receipt for goods stored in a warehouse [O.F. *warant, warand*]

warrant *v.t.* to justify, *the circumstances warrant these measures* || to guarantee, *warranted 22-carat gold* || (*law*) to secure the title of (e.g. an estate) **wár·rant·a·ble** *adj.* **wár·rant·a·bly** *adv.* **war·ran·tee** (wɔrəntí:, wɔrəntí:) *n.* (*law*) the person to whom a warranty is made **wár·rant·er, wár·rant·or** *ns* (*law*) someone who gives a warrant or warranty [O.F. *warantir*]

warrant officer an officer in the armed forces, between a commissioned officer and a noncommissioned officer in rank

warrantor *WARRANTER

war·ran·ty (wórəntí:, wórəntí:) *pl.* **war·ran·ties** *n.* (*law*) an assurance given by the seller that the thing sold is exactly as represented in the sale agreement || (*insurance*) an undertaking by the person insured that a statement of risk is a true statement, or that a condition of the contract as stated has been or will be exactly fulfilled || a justification or authorization || a guarantee [fr. A.F. *warantie*]

War·rau (wəráu) *pl.* **War·rau, War·raus** *n.* a South American Indian people chiefly inhabiting the delta of the Orinoco River, but also scattered along the coasts of Guyana and Suriname || a member of this people || their language

War·ren (wórən, wórən), Earl (1891-1974), U.S. jurist, chief justice (1953-69) of the U.S. Supreme Court. A defender of civil liberties against government encroachment, his notable decisions include 'Brown v. Board of Education of Topeka, Kansas' (1954). In the economic realm he supported federal anti-trust laws

Warren, Robert Penn (1905-), U.S. novelist, poet and critic. His novels include 'At Heaven's Gate' (1943), 'All the King's Men' (1946, Pulitzer prize), 'Band of Angels' (1955) and 'A Place to Come To' (1977). Two of his poetry collections also won Pulitzer Prizes: 'Promises' (1957) and 'Now and Then' (1979). He had a distinguished teaching career at several universities, notably Louisiana State (1934-42) and Yale (1950-6, 1961-73). He was named the U.S.A.'s first poet laureate (1986)

war·ren (wórən, wórən) *n.* a piece of uncultivated ground containing many rabbit burrows || the rabbits inhabiting this area || a cramped and overcrowded district, tenement house etc. || any network of narrow roads or passages [fr. A.F. *warenne*]

Warren Commission (1963-4) committee charged with the investigation of the assassination of Pres. John F. Kennedy. Pres. Lyndon B. Johnson chose Chief Justice Earl Warren as chairman and Senators Richard Russell and John Sherman Cooper, Representatives Hale Boggs and Gerald R. Ford, Allen Dulles and John J. McCloy as members. In Sept. 1964, when the committee issued its findings, its conclusion that no conspiracy existed became a controversial issue

war·ri·or (wóri:ər, wórjər, wóri:ər, wórjər) *n.* (*rhet.* and *hist.*) a man experienced in warfare || a fighting man in a tribe [A.F. *werreieor*]

War·saw (wórsɔ) (*Pol.* Warszawa) the capital and economic center (pop. 1,611,600) of Poland, on the middle Vistula. Industries: iron and steel, motor vehicles, mechanical and electrical engineering, printing and publishing, light manufactures. The central old city, on the high left bank, was restored to its 18th-c. appearance after the 2nd world war. Principal monuments: Gothic cathedral (14th c.), 15th-c. and 17th-c. churches, 18th-c. neoclassical palaces (now government buildings). Modern quarters, with the Soviet-style Palace of Culture, stadium etc., surround it on both banks. Main cultural institutions: university (1818), national libraries, academies and museums, celebrated national theaters. Warsaw became the capital in the 16th c. It was conquered by the Swedes (1655-6, 1702-5), the Russians (1794, 1813, 1831), the French (1806) and the Germans (1915-18). In the 2nd world war, it was bombarded by the Germans (1939), the Jewish ghetto was exterminated (1943) by Nazi troops, and a revolt by the Polish underground was put down (1944). The city was systematically destroyed and 600,000 people were killed

Warsaw, Grand Duchy of a state (1807-15) formed by Napoleon, including most of the land gained by Prussia in the partitions of Poland

Warsaw Pact a treaty (1955) of defense and mutual assistance signed by Albania, Bulgaria, Czechoslovakia, East Germany, Hungary, Poland, Rumania and the U.S.S.R. in response to the formation of NATO. Albania withdrew (1968) when Czechoslovakia was invaded

war·ship (wórʃip) *n.* a heavily armed ship used in naval combat

wart (wort) *n.* a small hard excrescence on the skin, esp. of the hands or face, resulting from abnormal proliferation of the papillae || (*bot.*) a small protuberance or lump on the surface of plants [O.E. *wearte*]

War·ta (várta) the chief tributary (474 miles long, navigable for 250) of the Oder, flowing north and west through W. Poland

wart·hog (wórthɔg, wórthog) *n.* a member of *Phacochoerus*, fam. *Suidae*, a genus of large-headed wild hogs of N.E. and S. Africa having warty excrescences on the face and large protruding tusks

war·time (wórtaim) *n.* the period during which a war is being fought

wart·y (wórti:) *comp.* **wart·i·er** *superl.* **wart·i·est** *adj.* having warts or lumps like warts || resembling a wart

War·wick (wórik, wórik), John Dudley, earl of, and duke of Northumberland (c. 1502-53), English soldier and conspirator. He was executed after having persuaded Edward VI to alter the succession in favor of his daughter-in-law, Lady Jane Grey

Warwick, Richard Neville, earl of, 'the King-maker' (1428-71), English nobleman who fought for the Yorkists in the Wars of the Roses, securing the throne (1461) for Edward IV, but restoring (1470-1) the Lancastrian Henry VI. He was killed in battle (1471) at Barnet when Edward IV regained the throne

War·wick·shire (wórikʃiər, wórikʃiər) (*abbr.* Warwick) a county (area 976 sq. miles, pop. 473,620) in central England. County town: Warwick. University of Warwick, near Coventry (1965)

war·y (wéəri:) *comp.* **war·i·er** *superl.* **war·i·est** *adj.* on one's guard, on the lookout for danger, trickery etc.

was *past* (1st and 3rd person sing.) of BE

Wash. Washington

wash (woʃ, woʃ) **1.** *v.t.* to make (clothes etc.) clean with soap and water || to remove (dirt, stains etc.) from clothes etc. by soaping and scrubbing these in water || to cleanse (esp. the face and hands) with soap and water || to be suitable as a washing agent for, *this powder will not wash woolens* || (*chem.*) to pass (a gas) through a liquid in order to remove soluble elements || (*chem.*) to pass distilled water through (a precipitate in a filter) || to pass water through or over (earth etc.) in order to separate ore etc. || to sift (ore etc.) by the action of water || (of the sea, a river, waves etc.) to flow over, against or past, *the waves washed the decks, heavy seas washed the lighthouse* || to make (a gulley etc.) by the action of water || to sweep along or away in a rush of water, *several crates were washed overboard* || to purify (the soul) || to brush a thin coat of color on in a continuous movement with a fully charged brush || to cover (a metal) with a thin coat of gold, silver etc. || (esp. of a cat) to cleanse (the body or fur) by licking a paw and rubbing its body or fur repeatedly with the wet paw || *v.i.* to cleanse oneself, one's hands, face etc. with soap and water || to clean clothes etc. by soaping, rubbing etc. in water || to bear or stand up to the operation of being laundered || to serve as a cleansing agent || (*Br., pop.*, in negative constructions) to bear investigation, *that excuse won't wash* || (of water) to move with a gentle, splashing sound || to be eroded by the action of rain, a river etc. || (*stock exchange*) to make a wash sale **to wash away** to remove or be removed by washing or by a rush of water **to wash down** to clean with quantities of water || to follow (food, a pill etc.) with a drink of water or other liquid **to wash off** to remove or be removed by washing **to wash one's hands of** to disclaim responsibility for || to refuse to have anything more to do with **to wash out** to wash (clothes etc.) || to remove (stains etc.) by soaping and rubbing in water || (of a stain) to be removed by washing **to wash up** (*Br.*) to wash the dishes and cutlery after a meal **2.** *n.* the action or process of washing || a quantity of linen, clothes etc. washed or waiting to be washed || an eddy or swirl of agitated water, esp. that made by a ship, or the sound of this debris (soil, mud etc.) accumulated and deposited by the tide, running rivers etc. || soil yielding gold or other precious metals or gems under washing || kitchen slops and waste scraps given to hogs || any thin, tasteless beverage (e.g. weak tea), or something compared with this, e.g. vapid speech or writing || a liquid used for a thin coat of color, esp. watercolor, applied in a continuous movement with a fully charged brush || a wash drawing || a thin coat of gold, silver etc. laid on something || the disturbance behind the passing of an aircraft or its propeller || (*stock exchange*) a wash sale [O.E. *wœscan*]

wash·a·ble (wóʃəb'l, wóʃəb'l) *adj.* capable of being washed without fading, shrinking etc. || soluble in water

wash·ba·sin (wóʃbeisin, wóʃbeisin) *n.* a shallow bowl for washing the hands and face, or this as a bathroom fixture

wash·board (wóʃbɔrd, wóʃbourd, wóʃbɔrd, wóʃbourd) *n.* a wooden board having a ribbed section of metal or glass set into it for scrubbing clothes || (*naut.*) a plank fixed along the gunwale or lower deck port to keep out the sea

wash·bowl (wóʃboul, wóʃboul) *n.* a washbasin

wash·cloth (wóʃklɔθ, wóʃklɔθ, wóʃklɔθ, wóʃklɔθ) *pl.* **wash·cloths** (wóʃklɔðz, wóʃklɔðz, wóʃklɔðz, wóʃklɔðz, wóʃklɔðs, wóʃklɔðs) *n.* a cloth for washing oneself

wash drawing a drawing done mainly in washes of ink or watercolor

washed-out (wóʃtáut, wóʃtáut) *adj.* faded in color || (*pop.*) tired out, played out

washed-up (wóʃtʌ́p, wóʃtʌ́p) *adj.* (*pop.*, of a person) done for, that is to be accounted a failure || (*pop.*, of a thing, e.g. a marriage) come to grief

wash·er (wóʃər, wóʃər) *n.* a flat ring or perforated disk of leather, rubber, metal etc. used to tighten a joint, screw etc. || a machine for washing something (e.g. clothes) || an apparatus in which gases are washed

wash·er·wom·an (wóʃərwumen, wóʃərwumən) *pl.* **wash·er·wom·en** (wóʃərwimin, wóʃərwimin) *n.* a woman who earns her living by washing clothes

wash·e·te·ri·a (waʃətíəri:ə) *n.* (*Br.*) **1.** a self-service laundry **2.** a self-service car wash

wash·house (wóʃhaus, wóʃhaus) *pl.* **wash·hous·es** (wóʃhauziz, wóʃhauziz) *n.* an outbuilding used as a laundry

wash·i·ness (wóʃi:nis, wóʃi:nis) *n.* the state or quality of being washy

wash·ing (wóʃiŋ, wóʃiŋ) *n.* the act of a person who or thing which washes || clothes, linen etc. washed or to be washed, esp. at one time || (*pl.*) the metal etc. obtained by washing ore etc.

washing machine a power-driven machine for washing clothes, linen etc.

washing soda crystalline sodium carbonate

Wash·ing·ton (wóʃiŋtən, wóʃiŋtən), Booker Taliaferro (1856-1915), American educator, author and black leader

Washington, George (1732-99), first president (1789-97) of the U.S.A. under the Constitution, called the 'Father of His Country'. He gained military experience in the French and Indian War (1754-63) and as a Virginian landowner, was a leader of the opposition to British colonial policy. With the outbreak of the Revolutionary War, he was appointed (1775) commander-in-chief of the Continental army. After his victory at Yorktown (1781), he presided over the Federal Constitutional Convention of 1787 and was largely responsible for its adoption of the U.S. Constitution. Unanimously elected president, he established a nonpartisan government which was respected at home and abroad. His Federalist policy, however, and his neutrality policy in the French Revolutionary Wars aroused the opposition of the Jeffersonians,

CONCISE PRONUNCIATION KEY: (a) æ, c*a*t; ɑ, c*a*r; ɔ f*aw*n; ei, sn*a*ke. **(e)** e, h*e*n; i:, sh*ee*p; iə, d*ee*r; εə, b*ea*r. **(i)** i, f*i*sh; ai, t*i*ger; ə:, b*i*rd. **(o)** o, *o*x; au, c*ow*; ou, g*oa*t; u, p*oo*r; ɔi, r*oy*al. **(u)** ʌ, d*u*ck; u, b*u*ll; u:, g*oo*se; ə, b*a*cillus; ju:, c*u*be. x, lo*ch*; θ, *th*ink; ð, bo*th*er; z, *Z*en; ʒ, corsa*g*e; dʒ, sava*g*e; ŋ, orangutan*g*; j, *y*ak; ʃ, *fi*sh; tʃ, fet*ch*; 'l, rabb*le*; 'n, redd*en*. Complete pronunciation key appears inside front cover.

which led to the organization of the Republican party (later the Democratic party)

Washington (abbr. Wash.) a state (area 68,192 sq. miles, pop. 4,245,000) in the northwest U.S.A. Capital: Olympia. Chief city: Seattle. The Cascade and Coast ranges cross the west. The east is an elevated plateau cut by the Columbia. Agriculture: fruit (esp. apples), vegetables, flower bulbs, wheat and other cereals, dairying. Resources: timber, building materials, uranium, lead and zinc. Industries: wood, pulp, paper, aircraft, shipbuilding, metal products, food processing, fishing. State university (1861) at Seattle. The coast was explored (late 18th c.) by the British, and the area was occupied jointly (1818-46) by Britain and the U.S.A. Washington became (1889) the 42nd state of the U.S.A.

Washington 2000 plan 1960-1980 development program for Washington, D.C., including renewal of surrounding communities

Washington, D.C. the capital (pop. 637,651) of the U.S.A., constituting the District of Columbia. The center was built on a radial plan (1793). The government buildings (White House, Capitol, Supreme Court etc.) are mainly neoclassical in style. Principal cultural institutions: National Gallery of Art, Smithsonian Institution (natural history museum), Library of Congress, Georgetown University (Catholic, 1815), George Washington University (1821), Howard University

Washington Conference (1921-2), an international meeting called by U.S. President Warren G. Harding in Washington, D.C., to negotiate a naval arms limitation program and reduce naval rivalries among the five powers. The U.S.A., Great Britain, Japan, France, Italy, China, Belgium, the Netherlands, and Portugal attended. The U.S.S.R. was excluded. In a Five-Power Treaty, the Conference agreed to limit the total capital ship tonnage of Great Britain, the U.S.A., and Japan to a ratio of 5:5:3 respectively and of France and Italy to 1.67 each. The conference produced the Four-Power Pact and an agreement to respect the military status quo in the territories and possessions of the powers in the North Pacific between Singapore and Pearl Harbor. It improved Japanese-American relations for a decade, and enhanced China's position by reaffirming the open door policy

wash·ing·to·ni·a (wɔʃɪŋtóuni:ə, wɒʃɪŋtóuni:ə) n. the sequoia [after George WASHINGTON]

Washington, Mount the highest peak (6,288 ft) in the White Mountains, New Hampshire, a part of the Appalachians

Washington's Birthday Feb. 22, a legal holiday in the majority of the states of the U.S.A. [after George WASHINGTON - (b. Feb. 22, 1732)]

Washington, Treaties of international agreements (1921-2) drawn up at the Washington Conference, namely the Four-Power Pact, the Naval Limitation Treaty, and the Nine-Power Treaty

Washington, Treaty of an international treaty (1871) drawn up in Washington, D.C., by an Anglo-U.S. commission. It provided notably for international arbitration in Geneva of the 'Alabama' incident. It improved relations among Great Britain, Canada and the U.S.A.

washing-up bowl (Br.) a dishpan

wash·leath·er (wɔʃleðər, wɒʃleðər) n. (Br.) a piece of soft sheepskin leather used for cleaning cars, windows etc. ‖ this leather

wash·out (wɔʃaut, wɒʃaut) n. the washing away of earth in the bed of a road, railroad etc. by a rainstorm, flood etc. ‖ the place where earth has been washed away ‖ (pop.) someone or something which is a complete failure

wash·rag (wɔʃræg, wɒʃræg) n. a cloth for washing oneself

wash·room (wɔʃru:m, wɔʃrum, wɒʃru:m, wɒʃrum) n. a lavatory in a public building, store, restaurant etc.

wash sale (stock exchange) a pretended sale of securities to make the market appear active

wash·stand (wɔʃstænd, wɒʃstænd) n. a piece of furniture designed to hold a washbasin and toilet requisites

Wash, the a bay of the North Sea between the coasts of Lincolnshire and N. Norfolk, England

wash·tub (wɔʃtʌb, wɒʃtʌb) n. a tub in which clothes are washed

wash·y (wɔʃi:, wɒʃi:) comp. **wash·i·er** superl. **wash·i·est** adj. weak and watery, washy soup ‖

(of style, emotions etc.) feeble and diffuse, washy sentiments ‖ (of color) too pale

was·n't (wɒzənt, wʌzənt) contr. of WAS NOT

wasp (wɒsp) n. any of numerous winged hymenopterous insects of many different families, esp. fam. Vespidae. They are universally distributed and include both social and solitary forms. The wasp is characterized by its well-developed wings, slender body (the abdomen of which is attached to the thorax by a narrow stalk) and its biting mouthparts. The sting of the female and worker wasps is mortal or paralyzing to other insects, spiders etc., and very painful to man **wasp·ish** adj. maliciously critical or apt to be so **wasp·y** comp. **wasp·i·er** superl. **wasp·i·est** adj. waspish ‖ full of wasps [O.E. wœfs, wœps, wœsp]

WASP or **Wasp** (acronym) for white Anglo-Saxon Protestant, esp a descendant of early settlers in U.S. —**Waspish** adj. —**Waspishness** n. —**Waspdom** n. the milieu

was·sail (wɒsəl, wóseil, wǽsəl, wǽseil, wɒséil) 1. n. (Eng. hist.) the toast offered when presenting a person with a cup of spiced wine or ale at a festivity, or the drink itself ‖ (Eng hist.) festivity with heavy drinking 2. v.t. (Eng. hist.) to drink to the health of ‖ v.i. (Eng. hist.) to drink a wassail [M.E. wœs hail fr. O.N. ves heill rel. to O.E. weshál=be in good health, be fortunate]

Was·ser·mann test (wásərmən) (med.) a test used to diagnose certain infectious diseases, esp. syphilis [after A. von Wassermann (1866-1925), G. bacteriologist].

Wast (vast), Hugo (Gustavo Martínez Zuviría, 1883-1962), Argentinian novelist. His novels depict rural life and tradition, notably 'Flor de Durazno' (1922),'Valle negro' (1918), and 'Desierto de piedra' (1925)

wast·age (wéistidʒ) n. loss by use, decay etc. ‖ the quantity or amount so lost ‖ avoidable loss due to wastefulness

waste (weist) 1. n. expenditure of goods, materials etc. without proportionate result, a waste of fuel, a waste of time ‖ needless and excessive consumption ‖ deterioration or decay by use, misuse or lack of use ‖ useless or damaged material produced during or left over from a manufacturing process ‖ a region naturally barren and desolate, or made so by man ‖ remnants of cotton fiber rejected during the process of manufacturing textiles and used to wipe machinery, absorb oil etc. ‖ superfluous matter, e.g. garbage, rubbish, ashes, human or animal excrement ‖ (geog.) the material resulting from land erosion, e.g. disintegrated rock, carried by streams to the sea **to go to waste** to be wasted, to become spoiled and useless 2. adj. (of land) desolate, uncultivated, or made barren by natural catastrophe or man ‖ (of land) not able to be cultivated ‖ of or pertaining to refuse, waste matter ‖ serving to hold or convey refuse, a waste bin ‖ discarded as useless or in excess of requirements **to lay waste to** ravage [A.F. wast]

waste pres. part. **wast·ing** past and past part. **wast·ed** v.t. to consume or spend to no purpose, or excessively, to waste effort ‖ to enfeeble and emaciate ‖ (rhet.) to lay waste, to devastate **to waste away** to be in process of being used up ‖ to destroy ‖ to dwindle in health and vitality [A.F. waster]

waste·bas·ket (wéistbæskit, wéistbɑskit) n. a receptacle for wastepaper

waste·ful (wéistfəl) adj. (of a person) spending money, or using materials extravagantly ‖ showing such extravagance, wasteful spending **wasteful of** causing the waste etc.

waste·land (wéistlænd) n. a tract of desolate, uncultivated country ‖ a devastated area ‖ a period in life or history thought of as spiritually barren

waste·pa·per (wéistpeipər) n. paper thrown away as being no longer useful

wastepaper basket a wastebasket

waste pipe a pipe connecting with a sewer etc. to carry away bath water, sink water etc.

waste products refuse produced during or left over from a manufacturing process ‖ material, e.g. feces, excreted from a living human or animal body

wast·er (wéistər) n. a ruinously extravagant, self-centered person without moral strength

wast·rel (wéistrəl) n. (old-fash.) a waster

watch (wɒtʃ) n. a small portable timepiece worked by a coiled spring, and designed to be worn on the wrist or carried in a pocket etc. ‖ (naut.) a period of time (usually 4 hours) during which part of a ship's company is required to be

on duty ‖ (naut.) that part of a ship's company on duty for a specified period ‖ (naut.) a sailor's period of duty ‖ a person or group of persons on duty, esp. at night, for purposes of guarding, protecting etc. ‖ (hist.) a guard, esp. a watchman or watchmen patrolling the streets at night ‖ (hist.) a division of the night (into three watches by the Jews and four watches by the Romans) **on the watch** on the lookout **to keep watch** to keep awake and alert for purposes of observing, discovering etc. ‖ (with 'over') to do this for the purpose of protecting or guarding [O.E. wœcce]

watch v.t. to observe (someone or something) attentively, to watch someone's reaction ‖ to be a spectator at, to watch a play on television ‖ to look after, to watch sheep ‖ to take a professional or private interest in, to watch a patient's progress ‖ to be careful about, pay attention to, watch your manners ‖ (Br.) to sit in on the trial of (a case) on behalf of a client who may be indirectly concerned ‖ v.i. to be closely observant, to watch while an experiment is being performed ‖ to stay awake, esp. at night, in order to attend a sick person, guard a prisoner etc. ‖ to be a spectator (as distinct from a participant) ‖ (with 'for') to keep a lookout, watch for the postman **to watch one's step** to act cautiously, proceed with care **to watch out** to keep a lookout ‖ to be careful **to watch over** to keep protective watch over (esp. a sick person) [fr. stem of O.E. wacian, to wake]

watch·case (wɒtʃkeis) n. the metal case enclosing the mechanism of a watch

Watch Committee (Br.) a special body of a county or borough council dealing with police discipline and matters of public order

watch crystal a cover of glass or plastic protecting the face of a watch

watch·dog (wɒtʃdɔg, wɒtʃdɒg) n. a dog kept to guard property

Watchdog Committee n. 1. originally, a Congressional Intelligence Oversight Board created to oversee activities of CIA by Executive Officers 2. by extension, any oversight committee

watch fire a fire lighted at night in a camp

watch·ful (wɒtʃfəl) adj. keenly observant or vigilant

watch glass (Br.) a crystal (cover of glass or plastic over the face of a watch)

watching brief (Br.) the brief of a barrister who watches a case for an indirectly concerned client

watch·mak·er (wɒtʃmeikər) n. a person who makes or repairs watches

watch·mak·ing (wɒtʃmeikiŋ) n. the business of making or repairing watches

watch·man (wɒtʃmən) pl. **watch·men** (wɒtʃmən) n. a guard, esp. of a large building at night

watch night a religious service lasting until after midnight on New Year's Eve (a practice begun by the Methodists in the 18th c.)

watch·tow·er (wɒtʃtauər) n. an observation tower from which a guard keeps lookout

watch·word (wɒtʃwə:rd) n. a motto or slogan, esp. one used as a rallying cry

wa·ter (wɔtər, wɒtər) 1. n. the transparent, colorless liquid, H_2O, which falls from the sky as rain, issues from the ground in springs, and composes three-quarters of the earth's surface in the form of seas, rivers, lakes etc. ‖ a body of this liquid ‖ this liquid with reference to its level (*HIGH WATER, *LOW WATER) ‖ the depth of this liquid, esp. with reference to displacement, the boat draws 6 ft of water ‖ a solution of some substance in this liquid, ammonia water ‖ any of various bodily fluids or secretions, e.g. tears, saliva, urine, amniotic fluid ‖ a shiny, wavy pattern imparted to some fabrics, e.g. silk, or some metals ‖ (pl.) natural mineral water ‖ (jewelry) the luster or transparency of a diamond or a pearl ‖ (commerce) nominal capital created by the issue of shares without a corresponding increase of paid-up capital or assets **by water** by ship or boat **in deep water** in great difficulties **in smooth water** in the state of no longer having difficulties **of the first water** (of a diamond or pearl) of first quality ‖ (of a person in a specified category) of the finest quality, a pianist of the first water **on** (or **upon**) **the water** (of a person) on a ship at sea ‖ (of a ship) at sea **to keep one's head above water** to manage to stay out of esp. financial difficulties, but only with a great struggle **to make one's mouth water** to excite a strong desire in one by looking or smelling appetizing **to make water** to urinate ‖

(of a ship or boat) to leak or ship water **to take** (or **take in**) **water** (of a ship or boat) to leak or ship water **to throw** (or **dash** or **pour**) **cold water on** to take a discouraging attitude towards (a plan etc.) **2.** *v.i.* (of the eyes) to run or fill with tears ‖ (of the mouth) to fill with saliva ‖ (esp. of a ship) to take on a supply of water ‖ (of animals) to drink water, *the cattle water at the creek* ‖ *v.t.* to soak or wet with water, *to water a garden* ‖ to give water to (an animal) to drink, *have the horses been watered?* ‖ to furnish (e.g. an army or a ship) with a supply of water ‖ to dilute by adding water to ‖ (*commerce*) to dilute (stock) by issuing shares uncovered by any increase of assets ‖ to impart a shiny, wavy pattern to (a fabric) by calendering ‖ (of a river etc.) to supply water to (land) ‖ to sprinkle (a road etc.) with water in order to lay dust **to water down** to dilute with or as if with water ‖ to make (criticism) less forceful by adding remarks intended to mollify [O.E. *wæter*] —Pure water is odorless, tasteless, transparent (although bluish in bulk) and relatively incompressible. It has a high specific heat and poor electrical conductivity. Under standard pressure it freezes (with slight expansion) to ice at 0°C, and boils at 100°C giving steam. The density is a maximum at 4°C, where it is taken as exactly 1 gm/cm³. Water has the chemical composition H_2O, ionizing as $H_2O = H^+ + OH^-$. It is neutral, a good ionizing agent and a good solvent

water bear a tardigrade

water bed a bed whose mattress is a vinyl bag filled with water, sometimes temperature controlled

water beetle any of numerous aquatic beetles, esp. of fam. *Dytiscidae*, having fringed hind legs that function like oars

water bird a swimming or wading bird

water biscuit a thin hard biscuit usually made of flour and water

water boatman *pl.* **water boatmen** a hemipteran insect of fam. *Notonectidae*, living in still water. They move about the surface of the water upside down, and are also good swimmers, propelling themselves with their long, thin, hairy hind legs

wa·ter·buck (wɔ́tərbʌk, wótərbʌk) *n.* any of various antelopes that live close to rivers and swim with ease, esp. either of two species of *kobus* of E. Africa [Du. *waterbok*]

water buffalo *pl.* **water buffalo, water buffaloes** *Bubalus bubalis* (or *Bos bubalis*), fam. *Bovidae*, the common domesticated Indian buffalo, used in most of the warm countries of Asia as a draft and milch animal

water butt a large open barrel for catching and storing rainwater

water cannon a large hose, usu. mounted on a truck, used to discharge pressurized water for riot control

water cart (*Br.*) a watering cart

water clock (*hist.*) a device for measuring time by the flow of a certain quantity of water

water closet (*abbr.* W.C.) a toilet (plumbing fixture) or the room containing it

wa·ter·col·or, *Br.* **wa·ter·col·our** (wɔ́tərkʌlər, wótərkʌlər) *n.* paint in solid or semisolid form for which water, rather than oil, is the solvent ‖ a picture executed with this paint ‖ the art of painting with this paint **wá·ter·col·or·ist,** *Br.* **wá·ter·col·our·ist** *n.*

wa·ter·cool (wɔ́tərkuːl, wótərkuːl) *v.t.* to cool (e.g. an engine) by means of circulating water

water cooler a device for dispensing cold drinking water in some public place

wa·ter·course (wɔ́tərkɔrs, wɔ́tərkɔʊrs, wótərkɔrs, wótərkɔʊrs) *n.* a stream of water, e.g. a river or brook ‖ the bed of such a stream, whether this flows permanently or seasonally ‖ a natural or artificial channel (e.g. a canal) for carrying water

wa·ter·craft (wɔ́tərkræft, wɔ́tərkrɑft, wótərkræft, wótərkrɑft) *n.* ships, boats etc. collectively ‖ skill in managing boats etc.

wa·ter·cress (wɔ́tərkres, wótərkres) *n. Nasturtium officinale*, fam. *Cruciferae*, a perennial cress living in running streams. Its pungent leaves are eaten as salad, cooked in soup etc.

wa·ter·fall (wɔ́tərfɔl, wótərfɔl) *n.* a steep or perpendicular descent of a stream or river

water flea any of various small, active aquatic crustaceans of genera *Cyclops* and *Daphnia*

wa·ter·flood (wɔ́tərflʌd) *n.* a process for pumping steam or water into a seemingly depleted oil well to force out residual oil. —**waterflood** *v.*

Wa·ter·ford (wɔ́tərfərd, wótərfərd) a southern county (area 710 sq. miles, pop. 77,315) of Munster province, Irish Republic ‖ its county seat (pop. 31,968), a port

wa·ter·fowl (wɔ́tərfaul, wótərfaul) *pl.* **wa·ter·fowl** *n.* any bird that frequents rivers and lakes, esp. a swimming bird ‖ (*pl.*) swimming game birds

water fowling the hunting of water fowl — **water fowl** *v.* —**water fowler** *n.*

wa·ter·front (wɔ́tərfrʌnt, wótərfrʌnt) *n.* the land or land and buildings or a section of a town abutting on a body of water

water gage, *Br.* **water gauge** an instrument attached to a steam boiler etc. for indicating the height of water inside ‖ water pressure expressed as a height in inches

water gap a pass in mountains with a stream running through it

water gas a mixture of carbon monoxide and hydrogen, obtained by passing steam over or through glowing coke kept at a high temperature by intermittent blasts of hot air. It is used chiefly as a source of hydrogen and in the manufacture of liquid fuels

water gate a floodgate for controlling the flow of water ‖ a gate giving access from a property to a river etc.

water gauge *WATER GAGE

water glass a tube or box with a glass bottom for examining objects under water ‖ (*chem.*) a viscous solution of sodium or potassium silicate, used for preserving eggs and in the manufacture of soaps and detergents, and in industry as a protective cement

water hammer the loud thumping noise in a water pipe caused by an air pocket interrupting the flow of water or by the entrance of water into a steam pipe

water hen the European moorhen ‖ the American coot ‖ any of several Australian birds of the genus *Tribonyx*

water hole a cavity or depression where water gathers, esp. a pool in a dry river bed ‖ a hole in the surface of ice

water hyacinth *Eichhornia crassipes*, fam. *Pontederiaceae*, a tropical floating aquatic plant troublesome as a river weed, esp. in Florida

water ice a dessert of frozen water, sweetened and flavored with fruit juice

wa·ter·i·ness (wɔ́təriːnis, wótəriːnis) *n.* the state or quality of being watery

watering can a metal or plastic container having a spout with (usually) a perforated nozzle, for watering plants

watering cart (*Am.*=*Br.* water cart) a tank on wheels carrying water or for sprinkling roads etc.

watering place a place where animals resort to drink ‖ a place where water can be obtained ‖ (*old-fash.*) a resort for swimming, boating etc. ‖ (*old-fash.*) a resort having mineral springs

water jacket a casing, through which water is circulated, surrounding a piece of machinery, esp. in the cooling system of many internal-combustion engines

water jump a water obstacle for a horse or runner in a steeplechase

water level the surface level of a body of water ‖ the waterline of a ship ‖ an instrument for showing the level of a body of water

water lily *pl.* **water lilies** any of several aquatic plants of fam. *Nymphaeaceae*, having large floating leaves and white or brightly colored (esp. yellow) flowers, found in warm and tropical fresh water

wa·ter·line (wɔ́tərlain, wótərlain) *n.* any of various lines on a ship up to which she may be submerged in the water, esp. when fully loaded (*PLIMSOLL LINE) ‖ (*papermaking*) a linear watermark ‖ the surface level of a body of water ‖ the mark left e.g. on a building by water which has subsided

wa·ter·logged (wɔ́tərlɔgd, wɔ́tərlɒgd, wótərlɔgd, wótərlɒgd) *adj.* (of ground) soaked with water, saturated ‖ (of a ship or boat) so full of water that she hardly floats and can barely be managed ‖ (of wood) so saturated with water that it has lost its buoyancy

Wa·ter·loo, Battle of (wɔtərlúː, wɒtərlúː) the final action (June 18, 1815) of the Napoleonic Wars, fought near the Belgian village of Waterloo. Napoleon was defeated by the British and Prussian armies under Wellington and Blücher

water main the main pipe in a water supply system

wa·ter·man (wɔ́tərmən, wótərmən) *pl.* **wa·ter·men** (wɔ́tərmən, wótərmən) *n.* a boatman, esp. one who makes a living by hiring out boats

wa·ter·mark (wɔ́tərmɑrk, wótərmɑrk) **1.** *n.* a mark showing the level to which water has risen or is expected to rise ‖ a faint translucent design impressed on certain kinds of paper at the moment of manufacture and visible only against the light, serving as a trademark or indication of type, size, category etc., and important in philately for the classification of stamps **2.** *v.t.* to stamp (paper) with a watermark ‖ to impress (a certain design) as a watermark

water meadow a meadow that is flooded at certain seasons

wa·ter·mel·on (wɔ́tərmɛlən, wótərmɛlən) *n. Citrullus vulgaris,* fam. *Cucurbitaceae,* a trailing vine native to tropical Africa but widely cultivated, esp. in warm climates ‖ its large round or elongated fruit, having a green or white rind and a pink, red or yellow, edible, very juicy, sweet pulp

water mill a mill powered by water

water moccasin *Agkistrodon piscivorus*, a pit viper of esp. the southern U.S.A. It is semi-aquatic and lives mainly in marshes and ditches

water nymph (*Gk* and *Rom. mythol.*) a goddess, e.g. a naiad, who lives in—or (in some cases) presides over—a body of water

water of constitution (*chem.*) water combined in a molecule in such a way that it cannot be expelled without destroying the unity of the entire molecule

water of crystallization (*chem.*) water of hydration found in many crystallized substances

water of hydration (*chem.*) water combined with some substance to form a hydrate. It can be expelled without fundamentally altering the composition of the substance

water on the brain hydrocephalus

water on the knee inflamed material exuded from the blood cells in the area of the knee joint following an injury to this part

water ouzel a member of *Cinclus*, fam. *Cinclidae*, a genus of birds related to the thrushes. They are able to walk on the bottom of streams in search of food

Water Pik a trademarked device designed to clean teeth by directing forceful streams of water onto and between teeth. *also* water toothpick, water pulse

water polo a game played in water by two teams of seven swimmers who pass a ball resembling a soccer ball to each other and try to throw it into the opponents' goal

wa·ter·pow·er (wɔ́tərpauər, wótərpauər) *n.* the energy of moving water converted into mechanical energy

wa·ter·proof (wɔ́tərpruːf, wótərpruːf) **1.** *adj.* that will not let water in or through **2.** *n.* (*Br.*) a waterproof garment, esp. a raincoat **3.** *v.t.* to make waterproof (e.g. by applying a silicone to a fabric)

water rail *Rallus aquaticus,* a European rail that lives in marshes

water rat a member of *Arvicola,* a genus of large aquatic voles ‖ a muskrat

water rate the charge for supply of water filtered, purified and piped to the consumer

wa·ter·re·pel·lent (wɔ́tərripɛlənt, wótərripɛlənt) *adj.* having a finish that minimizes absorption of water

water sail a sail set below a lower studding sail and close to the water, used when the breeze is extremely slight

water scorpion any of numerous aquatic insects of fam. *Nepidae,* having a long breathing tube extending from the abdomen

water seal a body of water in the bend of a pipe to prevent the passage of gas

wa·ter·shed (wɔ́tərʃɛd, wótərʃɛd) *n.* a ridge, or other line of separation, between two river systems or drainage areas ‖ the catchment area of a river system

wa·ter·side (wɔ́tərsaid, wótərsaid) **1.** *n.* the land on the edge of a river, lake or sea **2.** *adj.* of or on the waterside ‖ living or employed on the waterside

wa·ter·ski (wɔ́tərskiː, wótərskiː) *v.i.* to skim across water on short, broad skis (water skis) while being towed by a motorboat

water snake a member of *Natrix,* a genus of harmless freshwater snakes widely distributed in eastern U.S.A.

wa·ter·sol·u·ble (wɔ́tərsɒljuːbˈl, wótərsɒljuːbˈl) *adj.* (esp. of certain vitamins) soluble in water

CONCISE PRONUNCIATION KEY: **(a)** æ, c*a*t; ɑ, c*a*r; ɔ f*aw*n; ei, sn*a*ke. **(e)** e, h*e*n; iː, sh*ee*p; iə, d*ee*r; ɛə, b*ea*r. **(i)** i, f*i*sh; ai, t*i*ger; əː, b*i*rd. **(o)** o, *o*x; au, c*ow*; ou, g*oa*t; u, p*oo*r; ɔi, r*oy*al. **(u)** ʌ, d*u*ck; u, b*u*ll; uː, g*oo*se; ə, b*a*cill*u*s; juː, c*u*be. x, lo*ch*; θ, *th*ink; δ, *b*o*th*er; z, *Z*en; ʒ, corsa*g*e; dʒ, sava*g*e; ŋ, orangutan*g*; j, *y*ak; ʃ, *f*i*sh*; tʃ, *f*e*tch*; 'l, rabb*le*; 'n, redd*en*. Complete pronunciation key appears inside front cover.

water spider *Argyroneta aquatica*, a European aquatic spider that spins a balloon-shaped web beneath the surface of the water

wa·ter·spout (wɔ́tərspaut, wótərspaut) *n.* a pipe etc. for clearing water off a roof ‖ a column or spout of mist, spray and water caused by the meeting of a funnel-shaped cloud (extending from a heavy cumulonimbus cloud) and a mass of spray thrown up from the sea by a whirling wind. Waterspouts are most common in tropical or subtropical regions

water sprite a water nymph

water suit (*mil.*) a g-suit in which water is used in the interlining, automatically approximating the required hydrostatic pressure-gradient under G forces. *Cf* PRESSURE SUIT

water supply a system of storing water in reservoirs and piping it for use in houses, factories etc. ‖ the water thus stored

water table (*archit.*) a projecting, horizontal ledge set along the side of a wall for throwing off rainwater ‖ the surface below which the ground is saturated with water ‖ a gutter at the side of a road to take away water

wa·ter·tight (wɔ́tərtait, wótərtait) *adj.* constructed so as to be impermeable to water ‖ not liable to doubt, thoroughly sound, *a watertight alibi*, *a watertight project*

watertight compartment one of the compartments in a large ship, equipped with watertight doors or partitions which enable it to be sealed off completely in case of an emergency

water tower an elevated tank or reservoir into which water is pumped, thus furnishing a steady pressure to the system it feeds ‖ a fire-fighting apparatus capable of projecting water at a considerable height

water vapor, *Br.* **water vapour** water in the vapor state and below the critical temperature for water, in the earth's atmosphere (cf. STEAM)

wa·ter·way (wɔ́tərwei, wótərwei) *n.* a navigable channel, esp. a dredged river or canal ‖ a wooden channel hollowed out of thick planks along the edge of a ship's deck to drain away water into the scuppers ‖ a traffic route by water

wa·ter·wheel (wɔ́tərhwi:l, wɔ́tərwi:l, wótərhwi:l, wótərwi:l) *n.* a wheel rotated by the flow of water and used to work machinery, esp. in a mill ‖ a contrivance for raising water in buckets worked by a wheel

water wings inflated supports for a person learning to swim

wa·ter·works (wɔ́tərwə:rks, wótərwə:rks) *pl. n.* (usually construed as *sing.*) a system of reservoirs, mains, pumping stations etc. for the conservation and distribution of a water supply

wa·ter·y (wɔ́təri:, wótəri:) *adj.* containing too much water, overdiluted, *watery soup* ‖ soggy, *watery cabbage* ‖ soaked in or running with liquid, moist, *watery eyes* ‖ suggesting rain, rainy looking, *a watery sky* ‖ (of color) washy, *a watery green* ‖ (of blisters, pustules etc.) exuding a liquid resembling water

Wat·kin Mtns (wótkin) mountains in S.E. Greenland containing the highest peak (12,200 ft) in the country

Wat·lings Island (wótliŋz) *SAN SALVADOR

WATS (*acronym*) for Wide Area Telecommunication Service (which see)

Wat·son (wótsən), James Dewey (1928-), U.S. biologist. He researched into the molecular structure of deoxyribonucleic acid (DNA). In 1962 he shared the Nobel prize for physiology or medicine

Watson, John Broadus (1878-1958), American psychologist. He originated the school of psychology known as behaviorism

Wat·son-Watt (wótsənwót), Sir Robert Alexander (1892-1973), Scottish physicist. His proposals for locating aircraft by radio-pulse echo detection led to the development of radar

Watt (wot), James (1736-1819), Scottish engineer who made (1765) fundamental improvements to the Newcomen steam engine, leading to the widespread use of steam power in mines, factories etc. In partnership with Matthew Boulton, Watt built many engines at their foundry in Birmingham. The unit of power is named after him

watt (wot) *n.* the mks unit of power, equal to 1 joule/sec (1/746 horsepower) [after James WATT]

watt·age (wótidʒ) *n.* amount of electrical power expressed in watts

Wat·teau (vætou, wótou, wɒtóu), Jean Antoine (1684-1721), French painter. His work expresses the 18th-c. ideal of courtly grace and elegance beneath which one discerns a keen intelligence and an underlying melancholy. His favorite scenes are leafy parks in which satin-clad aristocrats pay court in a shimmer of approaching twilight, and of country festivals in which burly peasants and robust working people wear the costumes and masks of the commedia dell' arte. Watteau was a superb draftsman (e.g. his chalk studies) and colorist

Wat·ter·son (wótərs'n), Henry (1840-1921), U.S. journalist and newspaper editor. With Walter N. Haldeman he became (1868) founding-editor of the Louisville Courier-Journal, one of the South's most influential newspapers. He was largely responsible for the nomination of Samuel J. Tilden as the Democratic candidate in the 1876 presidential election

watt-hour (wótauər) *n.* a unit of energy equivalent to the power of one watt operating for one hour, and equivalent to 3,600 joules

wat·tle (wót'l) 1. *n.* a framework of interwoven sticks and twigs used to make walls, fences and roofs ‖ (*sing.* or *pl.*) rods and twigs so used, esp. to support a thatched roof ‖ any of various trees and shrubs of the genus *Acacia* ‖ wattle bark 2. *v.t. pres. part.* **wat·tling** *past* and *past part.* **wat·tled** to weave (twigs etc.) into wattle ‖ to make (walls etc.) of wattle ‖ to use (fence posts etc.) to make a barrier by interweaving flexible twigs and branches [O.E. *watul*]

wattle *n.* a wrinkled, usually brightly colored flap of skin hanging from the throat of some birds, e.g. the turkey, and some reptiles ‖ a barbel of a fish [origin unknown]

wattle bark the bark obtained from various Australian acacias and used in tanning

watt·me·ter (wótmi:tər) *n.* an instrument for measuring electrical power, esp. in watts

Watts (wots), Isaac (1674-1748), English hymn writer

Wa·tut·si (wɑtú:tsi:) *pl.* **Wa·tut·si, Wa·tut·sis** *n.* a tribe of tall, cattle-raising people inhabiting Burundi and Rwanda ‖ a member of this tribe

Waugh (wɔ), Evelyn (1903-66), British novelist. Hilarious satirical early novels include 'Decline and Fall' (1929) and 'Vile Bodies' (1930). Later works include 'Brideshead Revisited' (1944) and the war trilogy 'Men at Arms' (1952), 'Officers and Gentlemen' (1955) and 'Unconditional Surrender' (1961), brought together in 'The Sword of Honour'

wave (weiv) 1. *n.* (*phys.*) an energy-bearing, self-propagating disturbance in a medium or in space, that may be in the form of an elastic displacement of the particles of the medium, or of a cyclical change in its temperature or pressure, or a variation in the electric, magnetic or electric potential field of space ‖ a wave form ‖ a forward-moving swell on the surface of a liquid (e.g. of the ocean). The particles that make it up have an oscillatory motion, perpendicular to the direction of its motion. Its size depends on its cause, e.g. the friction between the water and the wind ‖ something which has the shape of a wave, e.g. an undulation in hair or in a rippling flag ‖ a gesture of the hand or arm in a sweeping movement ‖ a sudden temporary surge of strong feeling, *a wave of disgust* ‖ a natural or social phenomenon resulting in a sudden increase, *a crime wave* ‖ a movement having the impetus of an ocean wave, e.g. an advance of soldiers or a great influx of migrating people or animals ‖ (*pl.*, *rhet.*) the ocean 2. *v. pres. part.* **wav·ing** *past* and *past part.* **waved** *v.t.* to cause to move to and fro with a motion resembling that of a wave, *to wave a handkerchief* ‖ to make a threatening gesture with, *he waved his fist in my face* ‖ to call, order, express etc. with a waving motion of the hand or arm, *to wave good-bye* ‖ to give the form of waves to, *to wave one's hair* ‖ *v.i.* to move to and fro or up and down with the motion of a wave ‖ to have the form of a wave or waves, *her hair waves naturally* ‖ to make a signal of farewell, welcome etc. by moving something to and fro etc. with a wavelike motion **to wave aside** to dismiss (objections etc.) airily [O.E. *wafian*]

wave band a range of radio frequencies within which a radio or television transmission is permitted

wave cloud a lens-shaped cloud indicating a high point in air motion, an important phenomenon in glider aeronautics

wave equation the fundamental equation of wave mechanics. It is a partial differential equation whose physically admissible solutions (wave functions) describe states in which the system may exist. These states possess certain characteristic values of energy and angular momentum (*QUANTUM NUMBER). The square of the modulus of the wave function is proportional to the probability that the particle may be found in a given region at any given time when it is in a state represented by that wave function

wave form (*phys.*) a curve that represents graphically the state of a wave-propagating medium at an instant in time or the condition at a single point in the medium during the passage of a disturbance. Wave forms are usually constructed on rectangular coordinates whose ordinates represent the values of the propagated variation, corresponding to distance or time of propagation on the other axis

wave front (*phys.*) the surface comprising at some given moment the positions just reached by the waves proceeding from a given source ‖ a surface that is the locus of all points of a wave producing equal distortion in a wave-propagating medium

wave function (*phys.*, *abbr.* Q, ψ) a solution of the wave equation (*ORBITAL)

wave guide (*phys.*) a hollow metal conductor or cylindrical dielectric through which electromagnetic waves of length approx. 1 cm. (radar and television range) are transmitted with low energy loss by radiation and attenuation

wave·length (wéivleŋθ) *n.* (*phys.*, symbol λ) the distance, measured parallel to the path of propagation of a wave, between any point and the next successive point in phase at the same instant (e.g. the distance between successive points of maximum or minimum amplitude on the wave form)

wave·let (wéivlit) *n.* a tiny wave, a ripple ‖ (*phys.*) an elementary wave considered as a point source of a continuing disturbance

Wa·vell (wéivəl), Archibald Percival, 1st Earl Wavell (1883-1950), British field marshal. As commander in chief of the Middle East (1939-41) he distinguished himself in N. Africa. He was commander in chief in India (1941-3) and viceroy of India (1943-7)

wave mechanics a branch of quantum mechanics which represents the state of a physical system by means of an equation (*WAVE EQUATION) that attributes to the particle a wave character (*WAVE-PARTICLE DUALITY). This equation may be solved to provide meaningful values which accord with the wave character of the particle (*QUANTUM NUMBER), for the energy, momentum and position (e.g. an electron moving in the potential field of a nucleus). Such solutions are of an essentially statistical character, giving the probability that the particle will be in a given region at a given time rather than giving definite positions etc. Although wave-mechanics procedures lead in principle to exact solutions for any physical problem, they are of such great mathematical complexity that in practice only the simplest (2-body) systems (e.g. the hydrogen atom) can at present be solved exactly

wave motion (*phys.*) the motion of the particles of a medium in mechanically propagated waves (e.g. in water waves or sound waves)

wave number (*phys.*, used only of electromagnetic waves) the number of waves per centimeter of radiation of a given wavelength, being the reciprocal of the wavelength in centimeters (cf. FREQUENCY, cf. PERIOD)

wave-particle duality the concept in modern physics that associates a wavelength with a material particle, or a momentum of energy with a wave, in order to explain certain phenomena. Thus, electrons may be diffracted as if they were waves of wavelength λ = h/mv, where h is the Planck constant, m is the mass and v the velocity of the electron. Similarly electromagnetic radiation may behave as a beam of particles (e.g. photons in photoemission). It is found that electrons, photons, neutrons etc. have the properties of both waves and particles, and it may be appropriate to employ either wave mechanics or particle mechanics in their study

wa·ver (wéivər) 1. *v.i.* to hesitate between a choice of opinions or courses of action, *she wavered between going and staying* ‖ to begin to give way, to falter, *his confidence wavered under cross-examination* ‖ to move about unsteadily, *a wavering flame* ‖ (of the voice or a glance) to be unsteady **2.** *n.* a wavering [M.E. *waveren* fr. *waven*, to wave]

wave theory a theory in physics that light is transmitted by a wave motion (cf. CORPUSCULAR THEORY, *WAVE MECHANICS)

wave train (*phys.*) a uniform periodic wave of finite duration

wav·i·ly (wéivili:) *adv.* in a wavy manner

wav·i·ness (wéivi:nis) *n.* the state or quality of being wavy

wav·y (wéivi:) *comp.* **wav·i·er** *superl.* **wav·i·est** *adj.* (of a line or surface) having a form consisting of a succession of many little waves ‖ moving back and forth in a wavelike way, *fields of wavy corn*

wax (wæks) **1.** *n.* any of numerous mixtures that differ from fats in being harder and less greasy and that are principally constituted from higher fatty acids in the form of esters, e.g. beeswax, carnauba wax ‖ cerumen ‖ any of various natural or synthetic substances resembling wax in physical or chemical properties or both, e.g. paraffin wax ‖ a resinous preparation used by shoemakers for rubbing thread ‖ sealing wax **2.** *v.t.* to apply wax to [O.E. *weax*]

wax *v.i.* (esp. of the moon) to increase in size and brilliance until full ‖ (*rhet.*) to grow, to become (as specified), *to wax eloquent* [O.E. *weaxan*]

wax bean any of various kidney beans having long, yellow edible pods

wax·ber·ry (wǽksberi) *pl.* **wax·ber·ries** *n.* the waxy fruit of the wax myrtle ‖ the snowberry

wax·bill (wǽksbil) *n.* a member of *Estrilda*, fam. *Ploceidae*, a genus of small seed-eating birds, having bright bills resembling red, pink or white sealing wax, commonly kept as cage birds

waxed paper paper coated with white wax to make it waterproof and greaseproof

wax·en (wǽksən) *adj.* resembling wax ‖ covered with wax ‖ made of wax

wax·i·ness (wǽksi:nis) *n.* the state or quality of being waxy

wax insect any of various wax-secreting scale insects of fam. *Coccidae*, esp. *Ericerus pe-la*, a Chinese variety

wax myrtle any of various shrubs or trees of fam. *Myricideae*, esp. *Myrica cerifera*, a shrub of eastern North America having aromatic foliage and small hard berries coated with a grayish-white wax that is used for making candles

wax palm *Ceroxylon andicolum*, a South American palm, the stem of which secretes a resinous wax ‖ the carnauba

wax paper paper coated with white wax to make it waterproof and greaseproof

wax·wing (wǽkswin) *n.* a member of *Bombycilla*, fam. *Bombycillidae*, a genus of American and European passerine birds having a showy crest, brown, velvety plumage and secondary quills with tips resembling scarlet sealing wax

wax·work (wǽkswə:rk) *n.* a figure modeled in wax, usually representing a famous or notorious person, living or dead ‖ (*pl.*) an exhibition of such wax figures (*TUSSAUD)

wax·y (wǽksi:) *comp.* **wax·i·er** *superl.* **wax·i·est** *adj.* made of or resembling wax ‖ covered with or as if with wax ‖ (of tissue) affected with amyloid degeneration

way (wei) *n.* the course taken, or to be taken, in getting from one place to another, or the ground traveled over in taking such a course, *the way to the beach is rocky, clear the way* ‖ the distance to be moved through in going from one place to another, *a long way to Rome* ‖ direction of movement, *come this way* ‖ (with 'in') an aspect, respect, *in some ways you are mistaken* ‖ a characteristic trait of behavior, *winning ways* ‖ (with 'with') the ability to please, *a way with girls* ‖ (with 'with') the ability to handle or manipulate, *a way with motors* ‖ the procedures etc. involved in an activity, *the way to tie a reef knot* ‖ (*naut.*) the motion or rate of progress of a vessel through water ‖ (*naut., pl.*) the wooden structure over which a ship moves when being launched ‖ (*pl.*) the parallel guides on the bed of a machine, e.g. a lathe, along which a carriage moves ‖ (*pop.*) one's physical, mental, moral or economic condition, *in a poor way* ‖ (*pop.*) a district, area, *down our way* **by the way** along or near the side of the road ‖ incidentally **by way of** by a route passing through, *to Hong Kong by way of the Suez Canal* ‖ (followed by a gerund) in the state of, *she is by way of being a fine actress* **each way** (*Br.*, of a bet) laid for a win or a place **in a way** despite certain reservations, *I*

like the work in a way **in the family way** (*old-fash.*) pregnant **in the way of** in the course of **once in a way** (*Br.*) occasionally **on the** (or **its**) **way** in transit, *the package is on the way* ‖ in the course of the journey, *it happened on the way to Quebec* **out of harm's way** stored away safely **the way of the world** the way people do behave (rather than the way they should behave) **to come one's way** to come into one's experience or possession **to feel one's way** to proceed with great caution **to gather way** (*naut.*) to increase in speed from being stationary, or nearly so, until the engines or sails control movement **to give way** to yield ‖ to break, collapse **to go one's own way** to act independently **to go on one's way** to resume a journey **to go out of one's way** to put oneself to some trouble, *he went out of his way to amuse the children* **to have it both ways** to benefit by each of two contrary possibilities **to have** (or **get**) **one's way** to do (or be allowed to do) what one wishes **to know one's way around** to be experienced enough to be able to protect one's interests or achieve one's purposes in circumstances where the ignorant would find it hard to do so **to lead the way** to go first and lead others **to make one's own way** to prosper by one's own resources **to make one's way** to advance, esp. in a leisurely manner **to pave the way for** to take the preliminary actions which will cause or permit (something) to happen **to pay its way** (esp. of a business) to be self-supporting **to pay one's way** to meet one's own expenses **to see one's way clear** to feel that one can and should do something, *I can't see my way clear to taking that trip* **to stand in the way of** to be an obstacle to **under way** (*naut.*, of a ship or boat) making headway ‖ making progress [O.E. *weg*]

way *adv.* to a great degree, *way too deep* ‖ at a great distance, *way over there* [apheptic var. of AWAY]

way·bill (wéibil) *n.* a document containing information as to the nature of a shipment of goods in transit and instructions for delivery

way·far·er (wéifɛərər) *n.* (*rhet.*) a traveler, esp. on foot

way·far·ing (wéifɛərin) *adj.* (*rhet.*) traveling, esp. on foot

wayfaring tree *Viburnum lantana*, fam. *Caprifoliaceae*, a Eurasian shrub related to the guelder rose, and bearing dense white flowers and black berries. It is frequently found growing along the roadside ‖ *V. alnifolium*, a North American shrub

way·lay (weiléi) *pres. part.* **way·lay·ing** *past and past part.* **way·laid** (weiléid) *v.t.* to wait for and attack in order to rob etc. ‖ to catch (someone) on his way somewhere in order to engage him in conversation

Wayne (wein), Anthony (1745-96), American general. He distinguished himself by his courage and daring tactics in the Revolutionary War

way-out (wéiaut) *adj.* (*slang*) **1.** extreme **2.** unreal. *syn.* far-out

-ways *suffix* used to indicate direction, manner etc., as in 'sideways' [orig. gen. of WAY *n.*]

ways and means methods by which money can be raised or made available

way·side (wéisaid) **1.** *n.* the side of a road etc. **2.** *adj.* situated on, at or near the side of a road etc.

way station (*Am.=Br.* halt) a minor stopping place without a siding or facilities for handling goods other than passengers' luggage

way train a local train

way·ward (wéiwərd) *adj.* willfully turning away from what is right and proper, and heedless of the counsel of others, or showing willfulness and heedlessness [shortened fr. older *awayward*]

wayz·goose (wéizgu:s) *n.* the annual festivity (esp. an outing) of the employees in a printing establishment [etym. doubtful]

Wa·zir·i·stan (wəzjəristán) a mountainous, arid, border region of Pakistan, inhabited by unsubdued nomadic Pathan tribes, and disputed by Afghanistan

we (wi:) *pron.*, 1st person *pl.*, nominative case oneself and others, as named by oneself ‖ (used formally, esp. by a sovereign, an author or a judge) I [O.E. *we, wē*]

weak (wi:k) *adj.* having little physical strength, *too weak to climb higher* ‖ lacking force, a *weak blow* ‖ lacking resist only small strains, a *weak link* ‖ low in intensity, *weak sight* ‖ having a desired quality in only a slight degree, a *weak*

joke, *weak tea* ‖ morally feeble, *weak will* ‖ ineffective in the use of authority, a *weak government* ‖ lacking logical or persuasive force, a *weak argument* ‖ deficient in mental power, a *weak mind* ‖ having or showing a lack of knowledge or skill, *weak in history*, a *weak set of answers* ‖ (of bodily organs) liable to collapse or not performing well, a *weak bladder* ‖ (*gram.*) of a verb which is inflected by adding a suffix to the stem, not by an internal vowel change ‖ (*gram.*) of Germanic nouns and adjectives inflected by the addition of a suffix formerly belonging to a stem in -n ‖ (*prosody*, of a verse ending) not stressed ‖ (*commerce*) tending toward lower prices, a *weak market* ‖ (*chem.*, of an acid or base) only slightly ionized in solution

weak·en *v.t.* to make weak ‖ *v.i.* to become weak [O.N. *veikr*]

weak·fish (wí:kfiʃ) *pl.* **weak·fish, weak·fish·es** *n.* a member of *Cynoscion*, fam. *Sciaenidae*, a genus of North American marine food fishes, esp. *C. regalis*

weak force (*particle phys.*) a force with a hypothetical quantum of W particle, that governs the interactions of neutrinos, modifies the forces of gravity and electromagnetism, and causes radioactive decay. **also** weak interaction. *Cf* STRONG FORCE

weak-kneed (wí:kní:d) *adj.* lacking moral resolution

weak·ling (wí:klin) *n.* a physically weak person or animal ‖ a person without strength of character

weak·ly (wí:kli) **1.** *comp.* **weak·li·er** *superl.* **weak·li·est** *adj.* delicate in health, lacking a strong constitution **2.** *adv.* in a weak manner

weak-mind·ed (wí:kmáindid) *adj.* lacking in resolution ‖ foolish ‖ indicating foolishness or lack of resolution

weak·ness (wí:knis) *n.* the state of being weak ‖ a defect ‖ a self-indulgent fondness, a *weakness for olives*

weal (wi:l) *n.* (*rhet.*) well-being [O.E. *wela*, wealth]

weal *n.* the stinging, red mark on the skin left by the lash of a whip etc. [var. of WALE]

Weald (wi:ld) a region of open country, formerly forested, lying between the chalk hills of the North and South Downs in Kent, Sussex, Surrey and Hampshire, England

wealth (welθ) *n.* abundant worldly possessions ‖ an abundance of possessions or an abundance of anything, a *wealth of illustrations* ‖ (*econ.*) the natural resources of a country, whether or not exploited ‖ (*econ.*) the products of the economic activity of a nation ‖ (*econ.*) anything which can be exchanged for money or barter **wealth·i·ly** *adv.* **wealth·i·ness** *n.* **wealth·y** *comp.* **wealth·i·er** *superl.* **wealth·i·est** *adj.* having an abundance of worldly possessions ‖ characterized by abundance [M.E. *welthe* perh. rel. to WEAL]

wean (wi:n) *v.t.* to train (an infant or young animal that has been suckled) to accept food other than its mother's milk ‖ (with 'from') to induce (a person) to give up (undesirable associates or habits etc.) [O.E. *wenian*, to accustom]

weap·on (wépən) *n.* any instrument used for fighting ‖ (*zool.*) any part used in attacking, fighting or defending, esp. the spur of a gamecock ‖ any means of attack or defense, e.g. tears, strike action, irony [O.E. *wæpen*]

wear (weər) **1.** *v. pres. part.* **wear·ing** *past* **wore** (wɔr) *past part.* **worn** (wɔrn) *v.t.* to have (garments, ornaments) on the body, *to wear a coat, to wear a necklace* ‖ to have on one's person habitually, *to wear spectacles, to wear a beard* ‖ to arrange (one's hair, clothes etc.) in a specified way, *to wear one's hair short* ‖ to have (an expression) on the face, *to wear a smile* ‖ to diminish or impair by prolonged use, abrasion etc. ‖ to bring to a specified state by use, *to wear one's shirt to tatters* ‖ to make by scraping, rubbing, using etc., *to wear a hole in the carpet* ‖ (*naut.*, of a ship or boat) to fly (her flag) ‖ *v.i.* to diminish or deteriorate through use, friction etc. ‖ to resist damage or loss of quality by use etc., *material which wears well* ‖ to come to a specified state, *their hopes were thin* **to wear down** to make or become worn ‖ to diminish the resistance of (a person) by nagging ‖ to exhaust (a person) **to wear off** to diminish gradually, *the effects of the ether wore off* **to wear on** (of a specified period) to undergo the passage of time, *the day wore on* **to wear out** to make or become unfit for further use as a result of being worn ‖ to exhaust (a person) **2.** *n.* a wearing by friction, abrasion etc. or being so worn ‖ damage due to

CONCISE PRONUNCIATION KEY: **(a)** æ, c*a*t; ɑ, c*a*r; ɔ, f*a*wn; ei, sn*a*ke. **(e)** e, h*e*n; i:, sh*ee*p; iə, d*ee*r; ɛə, b*ea*r. **(i)** i, f*i*sh; ai, t*i*ger; ə:, b*i*rd. **(o)** o, *o*x; au, c*ow*; ou, g*oa*t; u, p*oo*r; ɔi, r*oy*al. **(u)** ʌ, d*u*ck; u, b*u*ll; u:, g*oo*se; ə, b*a*cillus; ju:, c*u*be. x, lo*ch*; θ, *th*ink; ð, bo*th*er; z, *Z*en; ʒ, cor*s*age; dʒ, sava*g*e; ŋ, ora*ng*utan*g*; j, *y*ak; ʃ, *fi*sh; tʃ, fe*tch*; 'l, rabb*l*e; 'n, redd*en.* Complete pronunciation key appears inside front cover.

use ‖ the amount of such damage ‖ the ability to resist damage due to use ‖ (*commerce*) garments, ornaments etc. worn on the body, *beach wear* [O.E. *werian*]

wear *v.t.* (*naut.*) to bring (a ship) about by putting up the helm ‖ *v.i.* (*naut.*, of a ship) to come about by turning the stern to the wind [etym. doubtful]

wear·a·ble (wéɔrəb'l) *adj.* suitable for wearing ‖ able to be worn

wear and tear loss of quality due to use over a passage of time

wea·ri·ly (wíɔrili:) *adv.* in a weary manner

wea·ri·ness (wíɔri:nis) *n.* the state or quality of being weary

wear·ing (wéɔriŋ) *adj.* of or pertaining to clothing, *wearing apparel* ‖ very tiring, *a wearing day*

wea·ri·some (wíɔri:səm) *adj.* causing physical or mental fatigue ‖ causing boredom

wea·ry (wíɔri:) 1. *comp.* **wea·ri·er** *superl.* **wea·ri·est** *adj.* tired and dispirited ‖ at the end of one's patience ‖ causing or showing tiredness or dispiritedness, *weary work, a weary sigh* ‖ (with 'of') bored or tired, *weary of studying* 2. *v. pres. part.* **wea·ry·ing** *past* and *past part.* **wea·ried** *v.t.* to cause to be weary ‖ *v.i.* to become weary [O.E. *wērig*]

wea·sel (wí:z'l) 1. *n.* a member of *Mustela*, fam. *Mustelidae*, a genus of small carnivorous mammals, native to almost all temperate and cold regions of the northern hemisphere. The weasel has a slender body, flattened head, long neck and short legs ‖ the fur or pelt of such an animal ‖ a tracked (land or amphibious) motor vehicle capable of going over snow or ice, traversing rivers etc. 2. *v.i.* (*pop.*, esp. with 'out') to get out of a bad situation, evade an obligation etc. in a cunning, equivocal manner [O.E. *wesule*]

weath·er (wéðər) 1. *n.* the atmospheric conditions (heat, cold, wetness, dryness, clearness, cloudiness etc.) prevailing at a given place and time ‖ adverse atmospheric conditions, e.g. rain, sleet etc., *the weather kept us in* to **make good (bad) weather** (*naut.*, of a vessel) to behave well (badly) in bad weather to **make heavy weather of** (*Br.*) to exaggerate the difficulty of (some task one is busy with) **under the weather** feeling slightly ill 2. *v.t.* to expose (e.g. wood, stone) to changing atmospheric conditions ‖ to discolor, disintegrate, wear away etc. by such exposure, *the stone facing was badly weathered* ‖ to pass safely through a storm, a dangerous or difficult time etc., *to weather a crisis* ‖ (*naut.*) to get to the windward of (a cape etc.) ‖ to slope (e.g. a roof) so that it will shed rain ‖ *v.i.* to resist the bad effects of weather, *the paint has weathered well* ‖ to undergo some change, e.g. discoloration or disintegration due to exposure to the weather 3. *adj.* (*naut.*) windward, *the weather beam* to **keep one's weather eye open** to be on the lookout [O.E. *weder*]

weath·er-beat·en (wéðərbi:t'n) *adj.* showing permanent signs of exposure to weather ‖ roughened, hardened, sunburned etc., *a weather-beaten face*

weath·er·board (wéðərbɔːrd, wéðərbourd) 1. *n.* a board adapted to shedding water easily by overlapping the one beneath ‖ (*naut.*) the windward side of a ship 2. *v.t.* to equip with weatherboards **weath·er·board·ing** *n.* weatherboards collectively

weath·er·bound (wéðərbaund) *adj.* (esp. of a ship) delayed or kept back by bad weather

weath·er·cock (wéðərkɒk) *n.* a flat device often shaped like a cock and free to pivot in the wind so as to show wind direction ‖ a person whose opinions and line of conduct change rapidly, according to what is fashionable or likely to be advantageous

weather gauge (*naut.*) the position of a sailing boat on the windward side of another, giving her an advantage in handling to **get the weather gauge of someone** to get an advantage over someone

weath·er·glass (wéðərglæs, wéðərglɑs) *n.* a barometer

weath·er·ing (wéðəriŋ) *n.* the action of the weather over a long period on the appearance of exposed objects, esp. (*geol.*) the erosive effects of weather on the earth's crust

weath·er·ly (wéðərli:) *adj.* (*naut.*) exerting so much lateral pressure (on the water) as to make little leeway

weath·er·man (wéðərmæn) *pl.* **weath·er·men** (wéðərmen) *n.* a person who forecasts or reports on weather conditions

Weatherman *n.* member of the militant underground radical splinter group of Students for a Democratic Society. Weathermen (and Weatherwomen) advocated revolution and practiced frequent demonstrations most actively in the early 1970s. The group was named for a line in Bob Dylan's 'Subterranean Homesick Blues,' *You don't need a weatherman / to know which way the wind blows*

weather map a map showing the state of the weather conditions at a given time, and over an extended area, by indicating the temperatures, wind directions and wind forces, areas of low and high pressures etc.

weath·er·om·e·ter (wéðərómətə:r) *n.* (*meteor.*) an all-purpose machine that can simulate in a few days the cumulative effects of years of heavy dew, rain, sunlight, and thermal shock

weath·er·proof (wéðərpru:f) 1. *adj.* able to resist exposure to the weather without suffering serious damage 2. *v.t.* to treat (a material) so as to make it thus

weather strip a strip of material used to cover cracks, joints etc. so as to exclude rain or drafts

weather stripping a weather strip

weather vane a vane pivoted so that it turns in the direction of the wind

weave (wi:v) 1. *v. pres. part.* **weav·ing** *past* **wove** (wouv) *past part.* **wo·ven** (wóuvən), **wove** *v.t.* to form (thread etc.) into a fabric by interlacing (the weft and warp) ‖ to make (a fabric) thus ‖ to make something by interlacing (rushes etc.) ‖ to make (something) thus ‖ to connect (a number of details, facts, ideas etc.) into a narrative, theory etc. ‖ to construct (a narrative, plot, scheme etc.) thus ‖ to direct in a winding course, *to weave one's way through a crowd* ‖ *v.i.* to engage in weaving ‖ to move this way and that in order to avoid obstacles, *to weave through traffic* 2. *n.* a manner or style of weaving, *a close weave* **weav·er** *n.* a person who weaves, esp. for a living ‖ a weaverbird ‖ (*basketball, lacrosse*) a series of movements in the form of an 8 involving several players to confuse opponents [O.E. *wefan*]

weav·er·bird (wí:vərbə:rd) *n.* any of various members of *Ploceidae*, a family of Asiatic, East Indian and African birds resembling finches. Their elaborate nests are woven of grasses, reeds etc. and very often hang from the branches of trees

web (web) 1. *n.* a piece of cloth in the process of being woven on a loom or just taken off the loom ‖ the fine network of threads spun by a spider or some other insects, e.g. the silkworm ‖ something intended to create mystery, entangle etc., *a web of conspiracy* ‖ (*biol.*) a tissue or membrane ‖ (*zool.*) a membrane uniting the digits of certain aquatic birds, frogs etc. ‖ (*zool.*) the vane of a feather ‖ a thin flat piece connecting the more solid parts in a girder etc. ‖ the arm of a crank ‖ a large reel of paper used on a rotary press, esp. in printing newspapers 2. *v.t. pres. part.* **web·bing** *past* and *past part.* **webbed** to cover or join with or as if with a web ‖ to snare with or as if with a web [O.E. *webb*]

Webb (web), Sidney James, 1st Baron Passfield (1859-1947), English social historian and Fabian socialist. He and his wife Beatrice (1858-1943) helped to found the London School of Economics (1895) and published the minority report of the Poor Law Commission (1909), 'History of Trade Unionism' (1894), 'English Local Government' (1906-29), and 'Soviet Communism: a New Civilization' (1935)

webbed (webd) *adj.* (e.g. of the feet of certain water birds) having the toes connected by a web or membrane

Web·be She·be·li (wébeiʃibéili:) a river (700 miles long) flowing from south central Ethiopia across S. Somalia to the Juba

web·bing (wébiŋ) *n.* a strong, woven fabric in the form of a narrow strip used for straps, upholstery tapes etc. ‖ (*Br., mil.*) a soldier's belt and equipment made mainly of hemp or jute fiber

We·ber (véibər), Carl Maria Friedrich Ernst von (1786-1828), German composer. His three operatic masterpieces are 'Der Freischütz' (1821), 'Euryanthe' (1823) and 'Oberon' (1826)

Weber, Max (1864-1920), German sociologist and economist. He was the first to view sociology as an empirical science. In 'The Protestant Ethic and the Spirit of Capitalism' (trans. 1930), he advanced the theory that there is a connection between Protestantism, esp. Calvinism, and the development of capitalism

Weber, Wilhelm Eduard (1804-91), German physicist who rationalized the system of electrical units by relating them to mass, length and time, and carried out many researches in electricity and magnetism

we·ber (véibər, wébər) *n.* the mks unit of magnetic flux equal to 10^8 maxwells [after Wilhelm E. WEBER]

We·bern (véibərn), Anton von (1883-1945), Austrian composer. He was a pupil of Schönberg (1904-8), and moved from early atonality to a later music in which there is no relation to tonal structure at all. His works include 'Five Pieces for Orchestra' (1911), songs, cantatas and string quartets

web-foot (wébfut) *pl.* **web-feet** (wébfiːt) *n.* (*zool.*) a foot having digits joined by webs **web-foot·ed** *adj.* having digits joined thus

Web·ster (wébstər), Daniel (1782-1852), American statesman, orator and lawyer. He supported nullification and the supremacy of the Union, and became a leader of the Whig party. He defended (1819) his alma mater in the Dartmouth College case, and the Bank of the U.S.A. in 'McCulloch v. Maryland'

Webster, John (c. 1580-c. 1625), English Jacobean dramatist. His tragedies 'The White Devil' (1612) and 'The Duchess of Malfi' (1623) are remarkable for their intense passion and their poetry

Webster, Noah (1758-1843), American lexicographer. His 'Compendious Dictionary of the English Language' (1806) preceded his crowning work, 'An American Dictionary of the English Language' (1828), revisions and abridgments of which have appeared from c. 1850 to the present day

Webster-Ashburton Treaty an Anglo-U.S. treaty (1842) negotiated in Washington, D.C., by Daniel Webster, the U.S. Secretary of State, and Lord Ashburton, the British representative. It settled the boundary dispute of the northeastern U.S.A. by granting over 7,000 sq. miles to the U.S.A. and opening to free navigation several waterways to both countries. It also settled the disputed U.S.-Canadian border along the Great Lakes. It was a precedent for peaceful settlement of disputes between Great Britain and the U.S.A.

Webster-Hayne Debate (hein), a debate (1830) between U.S. Senators Robert Hayne, a states' rights Southerner, and Daniel Webster, the defender of the supremacy of the Union

we'd (wi:d) *contr.* of WE HAD, WE SHOULD, WE WOULD

wed (wed) *pres. part.* **wed·ding** *past* and *past part.* **wed·ded** *v.t.* to marry ‖ to unite, *to wed charm and efficiency* ‖ *v.i.* to get married **wed·ded** *adj.* married ‖ of marriage [O.E. *weddian*, to pledge]

Wed. Wednesday

wed·ding (wédiŋ) *n.* the ceremony of marriage with its accompanying festivities ‖ (used in combinations) the anniversary of a marriage or the celebration of this, *silver wedding* [O.E. *weddung*]

We·de·kind (véidəkint), Frank (1864-1918), German dramatist. His plays were sharply critical of the bourgeoisie

we·deln (véid'ln) *n.* (*skiing*; German *wedeln*, 'to wag a tail'). a quick, short, rhythmic, fluid, parallel swiveling, by moving the rear of the skis sidewise —**wedel** *v.*

wedge (wedʒ) 1. *n.* a piece of wood or metal, thick at one end and narrowing down to a thin edge at the other, used for splitting wood, rock etc., for forcing something open, or for fixing into a crack to keep something in place etc. ‖ something shaped like a wedge, *a wedge of cake* ‖ an arrangement of troops, tanks etc. moving in the form of a wedge ‖ a formation of flying geese etc. ‖ a stroke resembling a wedge in cuneiform characters ‖ a golf club used for lofting **the thin end of the wedge** (*Br.*) a seemingly trifling demand etc. which sooner or later entails larger concession 2. *v.t. pres. part.* **wedg·ing** *past* and *past part.* **wedged** (with 'in', 'up' etc.) to fix tightly with a wedge or wedges ‖ to split open, force apart etc. by driving in a wedge ‖ to drive (an object) into a narrow area where it is held fast ‖ to cram into a small space, *wedged into the bus like sardines* [O.E. *wecg*]

wedge *pres. part.* **wedg·ing** *past* and *past part.* **wedged** *v.t.* to make (potter's clay) homogeneous and free of air bubbles by cutting it into wedges and slamming one wedge on top of another [origin unknown]

CONCISE PRONUNCIATION KEY: **(a)** æ, c*a*t; ɑ, c*a*r; ɔ f*aw*n; ei, sn*a*ke. **(e)** e, h*e*n; iː, sh*ee*p; iə, d*ee*r; ɛə, b*ea*r; **(i)** i, f*i*sh; ai, t*i*ger; əː, b*i*rd. **(o)** o, *o*x; au, c*ow*; ou, g*oa*t; u, p*oo*r; ɔi, r*oy*al. **(u)** ʌ, d*u*ck; u, b*u*ll; uː, g*oo*se; ə, bacill*u*s; juː, c*u*be. x, lo*ch*; θ, *th*ink; ð, bo*th*er; z, *Z*en; ʒ, cor*s*age; dʒ, sava*g*e; ŋ, ora*ng*utang; j, *y*ak; ʃ, *fish*; tʃ, fe*tch*; 'l, rabb*le*; 'n, redd*en*. Complete pronunciation key appears inside front cover.

Wedg·wood (wédʒwụd), Josiah (1730-95), English potter. He applied artistic standards to utilitarian objects (using Flaxman, among others, for his designs) and perfected the soft porcelain which bears his name

wed·lock (wédlɒk) *n*. (*rhet*.) the state of being married **born in (out of) wedlock** having parents legally (not legally) married [O.E. *wedlāc*]

Wednes·day (wénzdi:, wénzdẹi) *n*. the fourth day of the week [O.E. *Wōdnes dœg*, day of Woden]

wee (wi:) *comp*. **we·er** (wi:ər) *superl*. **we·est** (wí:əst) *adj*. very small [M.E. *we, wei*]

weed (wi:d) 1. *n*. any plant growing where it is not desired, esp. a wild plant growing in ground that is under cultivation ‖ seaweed ‖ a weak animal considered unfit for breeding (*old-fash*.) ‖ tobacco, esp. a cigarette or cigar 2. *v.t.* to remove weeds from ‖ to remove (weeds) esp. by pulling or forking up ‖ (with 'out') to get rid of undesirable elements ‖ *v.i.* to remove weeds **wéed·i·ness** *n*. the state or quality of being weedy **wéed·y** *comp*. **weed·i·er** *superl*. **weed·i·est** *adj*. full of weeds ‖ of, relating to or consisting of weeds ‖ thin and lanky, *a weedy youth* [O.E. *wēod*]

weeds (wi:dz) *pl. n*. mourning clothes ‖ (*archaic*) clothes [M.E. *wede* fr. O.E. *wǣd, wǣde*]

week (wi:k) *n*. a period of seven days, beginning (in the Christian calendar) with Sunday ‖ this period containing a specified holiday, *Easter week* ‖ the working days or hours of a seven-day period, *a 40-hour week* ‖ seven days before or after a specified day, *last Monday week, next Tuesday week* **a week of Sundays** a very long time **week after week** every week over a long period **week by week** each week **week in, week out** week after week without respite [O.E. *wice*]

week·day (wí:kdẹi) *n*. any day of the week except the sabbath

week·end (wí:kẹnd) 1. *n*. the end of the week, esp. the period from Friday night or Saturday until Monday morning 2. *adj*. of or on a weekend 3. *v.i.* to pass the weekend

week·end-use zone (wí:kẹndju:s) recreation area one to three hrs travel time from an urban center

week·ly (wí:kli:) 1. *adj*. happening, produced, done every week, *a weekly newspaper* ‖ lasting or continuing for a week ‖ reckoned by the week, *weekly pay* 2. *adv*. every week ‖ once a week ‖ by the week 3. *pl*. **week·lies** *n*. a publication produced every week

Weelkes (wi:lks), Thomas (c. 1575-1623), English composer, esp. of madrigals and anthems

weep (wi:p) *pres. part*. **weep·ing** *past* and *past part*. **wept** (wept) *v.i.* to shed tears, esp. in grief ‖ (with 'for') to mourn ‖ to exude or let fall water or some watery fluid ‖ *v.t.* (*rhet*.) to lament or cry for ‖ to shed (tears) ‖ to exude (a watery fluid) ‖ to bring to a specified condition by weeping, *to weep oneself to sleep* **wéep·er** *n*. someone who weeps ‖ a statue of a mourning figure found in some funerary sculptures ‖ a capuchin monkey **wéep·ing** *adj*. that weeps ‖ oozing moisture ‖ (of some trees) having slender, drooping branches [O.E. *wēpan*]

wee·ver (wí:vər) *n*. any of various members of *Trachinidae*, a family of edible marine fishes having a spinose head, upward-looking eyes and sharp, poisonous dorsal fins capable of causing serious wounds [O.F. *wivre*, serpent, dragon]

wee·vil (wí:vəl) *n*. any of various members of *Rhynchophora*, a group of small beetles widely distributed in Europe, Asia and North America, having a long head prolonged into a snout. The larvae of most of these do great damage to fruit, nuts, grain etc. [O.E. *wifel*]

weft (weft) *n*. (*weaving*) the thread crossing and woven into the warp to make the web [O.E. *wefta, weft*]

weigh (wei) *v.t.* to determine the weight of ‖ to hold (an object) in the hand in order to estimate its weight ‖ to consider the importance, relative truth or advantage of, *to weigh evidence* ‖ (*naut*.) to hoist or lift (an anchor) ‖ (esp. with 'out') to serve out (a quantity of something) by weight ‖ *v.i.* to have a certain weight, *it weighs 30 lbs* ‖ (with 'on' or 'upon') to be a burden, *the problem weighed on his mind* ‖ (often with 'with') to have importance, *his argument does not weigh with me* ‖ (*naut*.) to hoist anchor **to weigh down** to burden, cause to stoop or bend under a load ‖ to bring under emotional stress,

weighed down by grief **to weigh in** to weigh (a boxer, jockey etc.) before a contest or race in order to verify his weight ‖ to be so weighed ‖ to take strong physical action, or attack verbally, in order to deal with a situation etc. ‖ to have oneself and one's luggage etc. weighed before an airplane flight **to weigh one's words** to consider well the full implication of a statement before making it **to weigh out** to weigh (a jockey) after a race ‖ (of a jockey) to be weighed after a race [O.E. *wegan*, to carry]

weigh·beam (wéibi:m) *n*. a big steelyard

weigh·bridge (wéibrɪdʒ) *n*. a scale, at road-surface level, onto which vehicles etc. can be driven to be weighed

weight (weit) 1. *n*. the force acting on a body in a gravitational field, equal to the product of its mass and the acceleration of the body produced by the field. Strictly speaking, the value for the acceleration due to gravity depends upon position in the gravitational field and thus weight depends on where it is measured. However, since the value of the acceleration due to gravity is approximately equal (9.8 m/sec²) everywhere on the surface of the earth, and exactly the same when measured at different times but in the same place, this factor is often neglected. The value of the mass (with mass units) is often used instead, to mean the force (weight) on an object of given mass measured at the surface of the earth ‖ a known mass of metal used for comparing other weights ‖ a unit of mass or weight ‖ a system of units of weight, *Troy weight* ‖ the amount something or someone weighs ‖ a mass of metal used in a grandfather clock etc. to drive the mechanism ‖ an amount of matter, *can the floor support such a weight of furniture?* ‖ importance, *a matter of great weight to discuss* ‖ preponderance, *the weight of evidence is in his favor* ‖ (*sports*) a heavy metal ball that is put ‖ one of the various categories by which boxers and wrestlers are classified ‖ (*horse racing*) a number of pounds weight which a horse must carry in a handicap race ‖ (*statistics*) the importance of a value, usually related to its frequency ‖ (of clothing) heaviness or lightness according to season, *winter weight* ‖ the rhythm and stress value of sounds and syllables in verse **to carry weight** to be given serious consideration in the making of a decision, *his argument will carry weight* **to pull one's weight** to do one's share of work 2. *v.t.* to add weight to ‖ to lay a specified stress on, *to weight an argument unfairly* ‖ to add size etc. to (paper or a textile) ‖ to assign a weight to (a horse in a handicap race) ‖ (*statistics*) to give a value to (some item in a frequency distribution) [O.E. *wiht*]

weight·less (wéitlis) *adj*. apparently without gravitational pull ‖ having little or no weight **wéight·less·ness**

weight-lift·ing (wéitliftɪŋ) *n*. a sport in which weights attached to a long bar are lifted competitively according to prescribed rules, or as an exercise

weight-watch·er (wéitwɒtʃər) *n*. 1. one who diets to lose weight 2. Weight-Watcher, member of Weight-Watchers, Inc., a group organized to assist those who wish to lose weight; trademark

weight·y (wéiti:) *comp*. **weight·i·er** *superl*. **weight·i·est** *adj*. heavy, *a weighty load* ‖ burdensome, oppressive ‖ (*rhet*.) important, worthy of consideration, *weighty matters*

Wei-hai-wei (wéiháiwéi) (or Weihai) a port (pop. 222,000) near the tip of the Shantung peninsula, N.E. China: textiles, fishing. It was leased to Britain as a naval base (1898-1930)

Weill (vail), Kurt (1900-50), German-American composer. He is best known for his collaborations with Brecht on the satirical operas 'Aufstieg und Fall der Stadt Mahogonny' (1927) and 'Die Dreigroschenoper' (1929). He was eminent in America as a composer of musical comedies, e.g. 'One Touch of Venus' (1943). He also wrote a musical version of Elmer Rice's 'Street Scene' (1947)

Wei-mar (váimar) a town (pop. 63,326) in Thuringia, East Germany. Under Grand Duke Charles Augustus (1775-1828) it was one of Germany's leading cultural centers and was the home of Goethe, Schiller, Herder and Wieland. The republican constitution under which Germany was governed (1919-33) was drawn up and adopted here

Weir (wiər), Robert Walter (1803-89), U.S. portrait and landscape painter. His 'The Embarkation of the Pilgrims' hangs in the rotunda of the Capitol in Washington, D.C.

weir (wiər) *n*. an obstruction built across a river to raise the water level or to divert the flow of water ‖ a row of stakes set in a stream, river etc. to catch fish [O.E. *wer*]

weird (wiərd) *adj*. uncanny, supernatural ‖ (*pop*.) queer, odd, *a weird notion* [O.E. *wyrd*]

weird·o (wíərdou) *n*. (*slang*) a queer person

Weis·mann (váismǝn), August (1834-1914), German biologist. He demonstrated that acquired characteristics are not inherited by the progeny

Weiz·mann (váitsmǝn), Chaim (1874-1952), Israeli statesman and scientist. A leading Zionist, he was largely responsible for the Balfour Declaration (1917). He was the first president of Israel (1949-52)

Welch *WELSH (relating to Wales)

welch *WELSH (of bookmakers)

wel·come (wélkǝm) 1. *v.t. pres. part*. **wel·com·ing** *past* and *past part*. **wel·comed** to receive or greet (a person) with signs of pleasure ‖ to be glad about, *to welcome someone's return* ‖ to receive gladly, *to welcome suggestions* 2. *n*. a welcoming or being welcomed ‖ a manner of welcoming, *a hearty welcome* 3. *adj*. giving pleasure or received gladly, *welcome news, a welcome guest* ‖ permitted gladly, *you are welcome to use my car* 4. *interj*. a conventional expression of pleasure in greeting a guest or visitor [O.E. *wilcuma*, a welcome guest]

Weld (weld), Theodore Dwight (1803-95), U.S. abolitionist leader. He was editor (1836-40) of the American Anti-Slavery Society's newspaper, 'The Emancipator.' He led the national campaign to petition Congress against slavery, and wrote 'American Slavery As it Is' (1839), which influenced Harriet Beecher Stowe and many others

weld (weld) 1. *v.t.* to unite (metal surfaces) by heating the parts to be joined sufficiently for them to melt and mix before cooling (usually with an oxyacetylene or oxyhydrogen flame) ‖ to unite (surfaces) by softening them with heat and then hammering them together (as in wrought-iron work) ‖ to cause to become a unified whole, *he welded their stories into a single coherent account* ‖ *v.i.* to become welded 2. *n*. a welding or being welded ‖ a welded joint [altered fr. WELL, (obs.) to boil]

Welf (welf) *n*. a member of the German Guelph family

wel·fare (wélfɛǝr) *n*. the state of being healthy, happy and free from want ‖ organized work to promote this state in the members of a community who need to be helped [M.E. fr. *welfaren*, to fare well]

welfare mother a woman with dependent children, usu. with no husband, receiving government support via welfare benefits

welfare state a state based on the principle that the welfare of every individual is the collective responsibility of the community (cf. LAISSEZ-FAIRE)

welfare work *WELFARE (organized work)

well (wel) 1. *comp*. **bet·ter** (bétǝr) *superl*. **best** (best) *adv*. in a manner which gives satisfaction, *to work well* or which others would approve, *he treats his staff well but they still complain* ‖ proficiently, *to speak Urdu well* ‖ thoroughly, *soak the roots well* ‖ fully, quite, *well up to the knees in mud* ‖ by a large amount, *well over 50* ‖ very likely, *it may well be true* ‖ properly, correctly, *he can't very well refuse* ‖ intimately, *I know him well* ‖ satisfactorily from a material point of view, *do the boys eat well at school?* ‖ more than moderately or merely adequately, *do the brothers get on well?* ‖ easily, *he can well spare the money* **as well** also ‖ in the circumstances, *you might as well agree* **as well as** in addition to **to do well** to succeed materially **to do well to** to be wise to, *he would do well to see a dentist* 2. *adj*. in good health ‖ satisfactory, *is all well with him?* ‖ pleasing, *they look well against that wall* **very well** expressing agreement, approval etc. 3. *inten*. expressing surprise, resignation, satisfaction etc., *well! I never expected to see you here* [O.E. *wel, well*]

well *n*. a deep hole, usually cylindrical in shape and lined with bricks, stone etc., dug into the earth to such a depth as to reach a supply of water ‖ a shaft sunk into the earth to obtain oil, gas etc. ‖ the space running vertically through the floors of a building and containing the stairs or elevator ‖ any of various small cylindrical receptacles for holding a liquid, e.g. the reservoir of a fountain pen ‖ a spring of water, or a pool fed by a spring ‖ (*Br., pl.*, used esp. in place names) a place having mineral springs ‖ a

CONCISE PRONUNCIATION KEY: **(a)** æ, c*a*t; ɑ, c*a*r; ɔ f*aw*n; ei, sn*a*ke. **(e)** e, h*e*n; i:, sh*ee*p; iǝ, d*ee*r; ɛǝ, b*ea*r. **(i)** i, f*i*sh; ai, t*i*ger; ǝ:, b*i*rd. **(o)** o, *o*x; au, c*ow*; ou, g*oa*t; u, p*oo*r; ɔi, r*oy*al. **(u)** ʌ, d*u*ck; u, b*u*ll; u:, g*oo*se; ǝ, b*a*cillus; ju:, c*u*be. x, lo*ch*; θ, *th*ink; ð, bo*th*er; z, *Z*en; ʒ, corsa*g*e; dʒ, sava*g*e; ŋ, ora*n*gutang; j, *y*ak; ʃ, *f*ish; tʃ, fe*tch*; 'l, rabb*le*; 'n, redd*en*. Complete pronunciation key appears inside front cover.

rich source of supply, *a well of knowledge* ‖ (*naut.*) the enclosure containing and protecting the pumps of a vessel ‖ a compartment, having a perforated bottom, in the hold of a fishing boat, where the catch can be kept alive ‖ a space in the body of a vehicle designed to hold luggage ‖ (*Br.*) the space in a law court reserved for counsel [Anglian form of O.E. *wielle* and fr. *weallan*, to boil]

well *v.i.* (of a liquid or tears) to rise up and pour out copiously, *oil welled from the ground* ‖ to seem to rise up and pour forth copiously, *anger welled in his heart* [O.E. *wiellan*, to make boil]

we'll (wi:l) *contr.* of WE SHALL, WE WILL

well-ad·vised (wéladváizd) *adj.* sensible, wise

Wel·land Ship Canal (wéland) a ship waterway (28 miles long) opened by the Canadian government (1932), connecting Lakes Erie and Ontario, in S.E. Ontario. It has eight locks and a minimum depth of 25 ft

well-ap·point·ed (wéləpóintid) *adj.* well-furnished

well-bal·anced (wélbǽlənst) *adj.* (of a person) possessing a fortunate mixture of character traits ‖ (of a diet, meal etc.) composed of different foodstuffs in the right nutritive proportions

well-be·ing (wélbíːiŋ) *n.* the state of being healthy, happy and free from want

well-born (wélbórn) *adj.* born of a socially privileged family

well-bred (wélbréd) *adj.* educated for polite society, or displaying such education ‖ of good stock, *a well-bred terrier*

well-built (wélbílt) *adj.* (of a person) having pleasing proportions

well-dis·posed (wéldispóuzd) *adj.* feeling kindly or sympathetic

well-done (wéldʌ́n) *adj.* performed or executed well ‖ (esp. of meat) thoroughly cooked

Wel·ler (wélər), Thomas Huckle (1915-), U.S. physician and parasitologist who shared (with J.F. Enders and F.C. Robbins) the 1954 Nobel prize in physiology and medicine, for cultivation of the poliomyelitis viruses in tissue culture

Welles (welz), (George) Orson (1915-85) U.S. actor and director, principally known for his radio adaptation of 'The War of the Worlds' (1938) and the Academy Award-winning movie 'Citizen Kane' (1941), based on the life of William Randolph Hearst. He cofounded the Mercury Theatre on radio in 1937 on which the presentation of 'The War of the Worlds' created panic nationwide when some listeners thought the invasion from outer space was real. Other films include 'The Magnificent Ambersons' (1942), 'The Lady from Shanghai' (1948), 'Touch of Evil' (1958) and 'Chimes at Midnight' (1966)

Welles Gideon (1802-78), U.S. secretary of the navy (1861-9) under Presidents Abraham Lincoln and Andrew Johnson in the first Republican cabinet. He increased over sevenfold the number of ships and over sixfold the number of officers and seamen. He stressed the value of blockade against the Confederacy and supported the development of ironclads. He returned (1868) to the Democratic party

Welles, Sumner (1892-1961), U.S. diplomat. An expert in Latin American affairs, he was appointed (1922) commissioner to the Dominican Republic and was entrusted with the evacuation of U.S. troops from that country. He also served in Honduras and Cuba, and was undersecretary of state (1937-42)

Welles·ley (wélzli:), Richard Colley, Marquis Wellesley (1760-1842), British administrator. As governor general of India (1797-1805) he extended and strengthened British rule, and crushed the revolt of Tipu Sahib

Wellesley College a U.S. private educational institution for women in Wellesley, Mass., chartered (1870) as Wellesley Female Seminary

well-fa·vored, *Br.* **well-fa·voured** (wélféivərd) *adj.* (*rhet.*, of women) attractive in appearance

well-found (wélfáund) *adj.* furnished and equipped, *a well-found ship*

well-found·ed (wélfáundid) *adj.* firmly based on fact

well-groomed (wélgrúːmd) *adj.* (of a person) impeccable in dress and appearance ‖ (of a horse etc.) well tended

well-ground·ed (wélgráundid) *adj.* well-founded ‖ well instructed in the initial stages or fundamental principles of some discipline

well-han·dled (wélhǽnd'ld) *adj.* adroitly managed ‖ much handled, *well-handled stock*

well-head (wélhed) *n.* the top of a well shaft, or the structure built over it ‖ the source of a spring or stream

well-heeled (wélhíːld) *adj.* (*pop.*) quite wealthy

Wel·ling·ton (wéliŋtən), Arthur Wellesley, 1st duke of (1769-1852), British soldier and statesman, prime minister (1828-30). He distinguished himself in the Indian army (1797-1805), and commanded the British army in the Peninsular War (1808-14) and at Waterloo (1815), gaining the nickname 'the Iron Duke'. He attended the Congress of Vienna (1815). He became (1819) a member of the reactionary Tory cabinet. As prime minister (1828-30), he was persuaded to repeal the Test and Corporation Acts and to pass the Catholic Emancipation Act, but became unpopular for his opposition to parliamentary reform

Wellington a region (area 10,870 sq. miles, pop. 495,000) at the south end of North Island, New Zealand: dairy products, lumber, sheep. Chief town: Wellington

Wellington the capital (pop. 343,982), of New Zealand, a port at the south end of North Island. Industries: woolen textiles, meat packing, motor vehicle assembly. University (1897), National Art Gallery, national library

wel·ling·ton (wéliŋtən) *n.* a knee-length rubber boot [after the Duke of WELLINGTON]

wel·ling·to·ni·a (wèliŋtóuni:ə) *n.* (*Br.*, *pop.*) a sequoia [after the Duke of WELLINGTON]

well-in·ten·tioned (wélinténʃənd) *adj.* having or showing good intentions, but often misguided

well-knit (wélnít) *adj.* compact, *a well-knit frame* ‖ well-constructed, *a well-knit essay*

well-known (wélnóun) *adj.* widely known ‖ intimately known

well-mean·ing (wélmíːniŋ) *adj.* well-intentioned

well-meant (wélmént) *adj.* well-intentioned

well-nigh (wélnái) *adv.* (*rhet.*) almost

well-off (wélóf, wélóf) *adj.* well-to-do ‖ (with 'for') well provided

well-pre·served (wélprizə́:rvd) *adj.* (of an elderly person) carrying his or her age noticeably well

well-read (wélréd) *adj.* having read a great deal

Wells (welz), Henry (1805-78), U.S. pioneer expressman. He founded (1852, with William Fargo) Wells, Fargo & Company, an express firm which served the growing West

Wells, Herbert George (1866-1946), English author. Certain of his works, e.g. 'The Time Machine' (1895), 'The Invisible Man' (1897), 'The Shape of Things to Come' (1933), explore the effect of modern science and technology on men's lives and thought. His humorous, often satirical novels of realistic contemporary life include 'Kipps' (1908), 'Tono Bungay' (1909), 'The History of Mr Polly' (1910), 'Mr Britling Sees It Through' (1916). He also wrote many short stories and a popular 'Outline of History' (1920)

well-spo·ken (wélspóukən) *adj.* having a pleasant speaking voice and accent ‖ (*old-fash.*) courteous in speech

well-spring (wélspriŋ) *n.* (*rhet.*) a source of supply or inspiration etc.

well-thought-of (wélθɔ́ːtʌv, wélθɔ́ːtɒv) *adj.* of good reputation, esteemed highly

well-timed (wéltáimd) *adj.* arranged to occur at just the right moment, *a well-timed remark*

well-to-do (wéltədú:) *adj.* having a comfortably large income

well-wish·er (wélwiʃər) *n.* someone who wishes well to someone or something

well-worn (wélwɔ́rn, wélwóurn) *adj.* so often used as to be ineffective, *well-worn excuses*

wels (welz) *n.* a variety of large (up to 200-lbs) catfish

Wels·bach (vélsbɑx), Carl Auer, Baron von (1858-1929), Austrian chemist who used rare earths in constructing incandescent gas mantles (1886)

Wel·ser (vélsər) a German banking family from Augsburg, known from the 14th c. The company it formed set itself up (1509) in the Canaries and later in Santo Domingo. Between 1528 and 1546 it was authorized by Charles V to colonize Venezuela as a hereditary fief

Welsh (welʃ) **1.** *adj.* of or relating to Wales, its inhabitants or their language (the old spelling 'Welch' is preferred in some names, *Royal Welch Fusiliers*) **2.** *n.* the Brythonic Celtic language spoken in Wales **the Welsh** the people of Wales [O.E. *Welisc*, *Wælisc*] —Welsh was the language spoken in Britain before the coming of the Romans, and it survived and developed in the comparative isolation of Wales until the later Middle Ages. It is still spoken and written (with some difference between the spoken and literary languages) by a quarter of the Welsh population, and is taught in Welsh schools and colleges. A literary tradition has persisted

welsh, welch (welʃ, weltʃ) *v.i.* (of bookmakers) to leave the race track secretly and fail to pay winning bets ‖ to swindle by failing to pay one's debts [origin unknown]

Welsh corgi a cattle dog of a breed having short legs, an elongated body and a foxlike muzzle. Two distinct varieties (the Cardiganshire and the Pembrokeshire) are bred [Welsh *corgi* fr. *cor*, dwarf+*ci*, dog]

Welsh rabbit a dish consisting of seasoned cheese, melted and poured over toast

Welsh rarebit Welsh rabbit

Welsh terrier a terrier of a wire-haired black and tan breed (about 15 ins in height) resembling, though smaller than, an Airedale

welt (welt) **1.** *n.* a narrow strip of leather sometimes stitched between the upper of a shoe or boot and the sole ‖ an inflamed ridge raised on the skin by the lash of a whip etc. ‖ a narrow strip of material sewn along the edge or over the seam etc. of a garment as a trimming or reinforcement **2.** *v.t.* to provide (e.g. a shoe or boot) with a welt [origin unknown]

Welt·an·schau·ung (véltanʃauuŋ) *n.* a general view of life ‖ a cosmological philosophy [G.]

wel·ter (wéltər) **1.** *v.i.* to wallow **2.** *n.* turmoil, *a welter of blood and destruction* [M.Du. *welteren* or M.L.G. *weltern*]

welter 1. *adj.* (*horse racing*) of or relating to a race in which welterweights are carried **2.** *n.* (*pop.*) a welterweight [origin unknown]

wel·ter·weight (wéltərweit) *n.* (*horse racing*) a heavyweight rider ‖ (*horse racing*) a weight of 28 lbs sometimes carried as a handicap ‖ a professional or amateur boxer whose weight does not exceed 147 lbs

Welt·po·li·tik (véltpoulití:k) *n.* participation in international affairs, world politics [G.]

Welty (wélti:), Eudora (1909-) U.S. writer whose novels and stories usually depicted life in the South, esp. Mississippi. She won the Pulitzer Prize for 'The Optimist's Daughter' (1972). Other works include the novels 'The Robber Bridegroom' (1942), 'Delta Wedding' (1946), 'The Ponder Heart' (1954) and 'Losing Battles' (1970); short stories collected in 'The Golden Apples' (1949), 'The Bride of the Innisfallen' (1955), 'A Sweet Devouring' (1969) and 'The Collected Stories of Eudora Welty' (1980). Her autobiography 'One Writer's Beginnings' was published in 1984

wen (wen) *n.* a rune corresponding to the Old English and early Middle English to 'w' in the modern English alphabet [O.E.]

wen *n.* a cyst filled with sebaceous matter, generally located on the scalp [O.E. *wenn*]

Wen·ces·las (wénsislɔs), St (*Czech* Václav, *G.* Wenzel, c. 907-29), duke of Bohemia (921-9) and patron saint of Czechoslovakia. Feast: Sept. 28

Wenceslas IV (1361-1419), king of Bohemia and uncrowned Emperor (1378-1419), son of Emperor Charles IV. He failed to impose his authority on the Czechs and Germans. The Hussites defenestrated (1419) his Catholic counselors

wench (wentʃ) *n.* (*jocular*) a young woman [O.E. *wencel*, a child]

Wen·chow (wʌ́ndʒóu) (or Yungkia) a port (pop. 325,000) in Chekiang, E. China, founded in the 4th c. It was opened to international trade in 1876

Wend (wend) *n.* a member of a Slavic people of Saxony and East Prussia [fr. G. *Wende*, *Winde*]

wend (wend) *v.t.* (only in the phrase) **to wend one's way** to go unhurriedly along one's path [O.E. *wendan*, to turn]

Wend·ish (wéndiʃ) **1.** *adj.* of or relating to the Wends or to their West Slavic language **2.** *n.* the West Slavic language of the Wends

went *past* of GO

wen·tle·trap (wént'ltræp) *n.* any of various spirally coiled, usually white, mollusk shells much

CONCISE PRONUNCIATION KEY: (**a**) æ, c*a*t; ɑ, c*a*r; ɔ f*aw*n; ei, sn*a*ke. (**e**) e, h*e*n; i:, sh*ee*p; iə, d*ee*r; ɛə, b*ea*r. (**i**) i, f*i*sh; ai, t*i*ger; ə:, b*i*rd. (**o**) o, *o*x; au, c*ow*; ou, g*oa*t; u, p*oo*r; ɔi, r*oy*al. (**u**) ʌ, d*u*ck; u, b*u*ll; u:, g*oo*se; ə, b*a*cillus; ju:, c*u*be. x, lo*ch*; θ, *th*ink; ð, bo*th*er; z, *Z*en; ʒ, corsa*g*e; dʒ, sava*g*e; ŋ, ora*ng*utang; j, *y*ak; ʃ, *fi*sh; tʃ, fe*tch*; 'l, rabb*le*; 'n, redd*en*. Complete pronunciation key appears inside front cover.

sought after by collectors ‖ any of various mollusks of fam. *Epitoniidae*, having this sort of shell [Du. *wenteltrap*, a spiral staircase]

Went·worth (wéntwə:rθ), Thomas *STRAFFORD

wept *past* and *past part.* of WEEP

were (wə:r) *pl.* and *2nd pers. sing. past indicative* and *past subjunctive* of BE

we're (wiər) *contr.* of WE ARE

weren't (wə:rnt, wə́:rənt) *contr.* of WERE NOT

were·wolf (wə́:rwulf, wíərwulf, wéərwulf) *pl.* **were·wolves** (wə́:rwulvz, wíərwulvz, wéərwulvz) *n.* (in superstitious belief) a human being changed, or capable of changing, into a wolf [O.E. *werewulf*]

wer·geld (wə́:rgeld) *n.* (*hist.*) the money value set on a man, based on his rank, possessions etc., and exacted as a fine in cases of serious crime in Anglo-Saxon and Germanic law [fr. O.E. *wer*, man and *geld*, yield, payment]

Wer·ner (véərnər), Alfred (1866-1919), Swiss chemist who formulated the coordination theory of valence. Nobel prize (1913)

We·ser (véizər) a navigable river (300 miles long) flowing from Hesse through lower Saxony, West Germany, to the Baltic. Chief port: Bremen

Wes·ley (wésli:, wézli:), Charles (1707-88), English Methodist and writer of hymns, brother of John Wesley. His son, Samuel (1766-1837), and grandson, Samuel Sebastian (1810-76), were both distinguished organists and composers

Wesley, John (1703-91), English Anglican clergyman, evangelist, founder of Methodism, and writer of hymns. He rode yearly on horseback through Britain, preaching in the open air and organizing Methodist Societies. He inaugurated lay preachers and he ordained Dr Thomas Coke (1760) for evangelism in America

Wes·ley·an (wésli:ən, wézli:ən) **1.** *adj.* of or relating to the Methodist denomination founded by John Wesley **2.** *n.* a member of this denomination, a Wesleyan Methodist **Wés·ley·an·ism** *n.*

Wes·sex (wésiks) (*Eng. hist.*) an AngloSaxon kingdom, settled in the late 5th c., and originally centered on the upper Thames valley. It expanded in S. and W. England and became (early 9th c.) the dominant English kingdom. Under Alfred it resisted the Danes, and under Edward the Elder extended its power over the Danelaw (10th c.). The successors of these kings became the English royal house

West (west), Benjamin (1738-1820), Anglo-American painter. He excelled in historical subjects, e.g. 'The Death of General Wolfe' (1771), and portraits, and succeeded Reynolds as president of the Royal Academy (1792-1805, 1807-20)

west (west) **1.** *adv.* toward the west **2.** *n.* (usually with 'the') one of the four cardinal points of the compass (*abbr.* W., *COMPASS POINT) ‖ the direction of the setting sun at the equinox **the West** the western part of a country, esp. the states of the U.S.A. west of the Mississippi ‖ western Europe and America as opposed to the communist countries of eastern Europe and Asia **3.** *adj.* of, belonging to or situated toward the west ‖ facing west ‖ (of winds) blowing from the west [O.E.]

Wes·tar satellite (wéstar) Western Union's communication satellite for transmission of facsimile material, including color TV pictures

West Bengal *BENGAL

West Berlin *BERLIN

west by north N. 78° 45′ W., one point north of due west (*abbr.* W. b. N., W. by N., *COMPASS POINT)

west by south S. 78° 45′ W., one point south of due west (*abbr.* W. b. S., W. by S., *COMPASS POINT)

West End the western part of London, containing the smart shopping, entertainment and residential districts

west·er (wéstər) *v.i.* (*rhet.*, esp. of the sun) to move towards the west

west·er·ly (wéstərli:) **1.** *adj.* and *adv.* in or toward the west ‖ (of winds) from the west **2.** *pl.* **west·er·lies** *n.* a wind blowing from the west

west·ern (wéstərn) *adj.* situated, facing, coming from or moving toward the west **Western 1.** *adj.* of or relating to the West **2.** *n.* a story, film etc. of life in the West of the U.S.A. during the 2nd half of the 19th c. [O.E. *westerne*]

Western Australia the western state (area 975,920 sq. miles, pop. 1,673,200) of Australia. Capital: Perth. It is largely an arid, gently

undulating plateau with vast desert areas in the interior. Population is concentrated in the southwest. Agriculture: cattle and sheep ranching, and (southwest) cereals, fruit, dairying. Resources: gold, some coal, asbestos, iron ore and other minerals, timber. Industries: agricultural processing, forestry. University of Western Australia (1912) near Perth

Western Bug a river (470 miles long) flowing from the W. Ukraine, U.S.S.R., forming part of the Soviet-Polish border, and across E. Poland to the Vistula

Western Church that part of the Catholic Church which continued to recognize the Roman pope after the schism of the 9th c. ‖ (*loosely*) the Christian Churches of Western Europe and America (*ORTHODOX EASTERN CHURCH, *ROMAN CATHOLIC CHURCH)

Western Empire the Western Roman Empire

West·ern·er (wéstərnər) *n.* a native or inhabitant of the West, esp. of the Western part of the U.S.A.

Western Ghats *GHATS

western hemisphere the part of the earth west of the Atlantic Ocean, comprising North and South America

Western Isles the Hebrides

west·ern·ize (wéstərnaiz) *pres. part.* **west·ern·iz·ing** *past* and *past part.* **west·ern·ized** *v.t.* to cause to become Western in outlook, dress, character etc.

west·ern·most (wéstərnmoust) *adj.* furthest west

Western Nigeria *NIGERIA

Western Roman Empire the western part of the Roman Empire after the Byzantine Empire had separated from it (395)

Western saddle a stock saddle

Western Sahara (formerly Spanish Sahara) an area (area 102,680 sq. miles) on the N.W. African coast, with important fisheries. Chief port: Villa Cisneros (pop. 2,000). Livestock: camels, sheep, goats. Spanish settlement began in the 15th c. The area was taken under Spanish protection (1884) and became a Spanish province (1958). After discovery of high-grade phosphate in Western Sahara (1963), Morocco and Mauritania pressured Spain to relinquish the area; Algeria and later Libya backed a pro-independence group called the Polisario Front. The World Court ruled (1975) that Western Sahara should be given self-determination. Morocco sent 350,000 civilians into the area and Spain withdrew (1976, ceding the northern two thirds to Morocco and the remainder to Mauritania. Mauritania signed a treaty with Polisario renouncing its claims (1979) and Morocco annexed the entire area. Refusing to negotiate directly with the Polisario, Morocco built a fortified wall around the northwestern corner of Western Sahara, which contained most of the population and mineral resources as well as the coastal fisheries. Drought drove many nomadic Saharans into towns behind the wall, where Moroccan investment and settlement, designed to gain local support, caused an economic boom. Libya halted aid to the Polisario when it signed a treaty of union with Morocco (1984)

West Frisian Islands *FRISIAN ISLANDS

West Germany *GERMANY, FEDERAL REPUBLIC OF

West Indian 1. *n.* a native or inhabitant of the West Indies **2.** *adj.* of or relating to the West Indies

West Indies an archipelago of E. North America, divided into the Bahamas, in the Atlantic, and the Antilles, which curve east, south, and west from Florida to western Venezuela, separating the Atlantic from the Caribbean. The islands are mainly wooded, mountainous, and of volcanic origin, with some small coral atolls. The economy is everywhere based upon tropical agriculture. HISTORY. Columbus landed in the Bahamas (1492) and discovered many of the larger islands (1492-1504). The English settled Bermuda (1609), Barbados (1627) and the Bahamas (1629). Curaçao was settled by the Dutch (1634) and Guadeloupe and Martinique by the French (1635). England took Jamaica from Spain (1655), Dominica (1783), Grenada (1783), St Lucia (1803) and Tobago (1814) from France, and Trinidad (1802) from Spain. The Dominican Republic and Haiti became independent in the 19th c. After the Spanish-American War (1898), Puerto Rico and Cuba came under American control. Sugar-growing, based on slavery, prospered in the late 17th c. and 18th c., but declined in the 19th c. The Vir-

gin Islands were purchased by the U.S.A. from Denmark (1917). A trend toward self-government in the 20th c. culminated in the independence of most of the islands

West Indies, Federation of the a federation (1958-62) of Caribbean islands within the Commonwealth, comprising Jamaica, Barbados, Trinidad and the colonies of the Windward Islands and of the Leeward Islands. It was dissolved after the withdrawal of Jamaica and Trinidad

west·ing (wéstiŋ) *n.* (*naut.*) a sailing towards the west ‖ (*naut.*) the distance thus sailed

West·ing·house (wéstiŋhaus), George (1846-1914), American engineer. He invented (1869) the automatic compressedair brake used on railroads

West·land (wéstlənd) a region (area 6,010 sq. miles, pop. 25,000) of S.W. South Island, New Zealand. Industries: mining (coal, gold), lumber, tourism. Chief town: Greymouth (pop. 9,000)

West·ma·cott (wéstməkɔt), Sir Richard (1775-1856), British sculptor. His best-known work is probably 'Achilles' in Hyde Park, London, the memorial to Wellington (1822)

West·meath (westmí:ð) a northern county (area 681 sq. miles, pop. 61,300) in Leinster province, Irish Republic. County seat: Mullingar (pop. 6,000)

West·min·ster Abbey (wéstminstər) the ancient church in Westminster, London, developed from a Benedictine monastery (1050-65) and rebuilt in the 13th to 15th cc. Henry VII's chapel dates from 1503-19. The Abbey has been the coronation church of almost all English monarchs since William I and until 1760 most of them were also buried there. It is also the burial place of many distinguished citizens

Westminster Assembly an assembly of divines and some laity summoned (1643-9) by the Long Parliament to advise on ways of bringing the Church of England into line with Calvinist theology

Westminster, City of a borough (pop. 214,000) of London, site of the Houses of Parliament

Westminster Confession the Calvinist creed drawn up (1646) by the Westminster Assembly. It was adopted officially by the Church of Scotland and forms the basis of Congregationalism

Westminster, Palace of the neo-Gothic parliament building designed by Sir Charles Barry and built (1840-67) on the site of the old royal palace, of which the Hall (1097-9) remains

Westminster, Statute of the statute (1931) under which the full independence of the Dominions of the British Empire was recognized, including their responsibility for foreign affairs ‖ any of three statutes promulgated (1275, 1285 and 1290) during the reign of Edward II, establishing many of the bases of English law

West·more·land (wéstmɔrlənd, westmóurlənd), William Childs (1914-), U.S. general, commander (1964-8) of U.S. forces in Vietnam. His over-optimistic reports from the field contributed to the growing disillusionment at home among wide sections of the nation

West·mor·land (wéstmərlənd) a former county of N.W. England, now part of Cumbria

west-north·west (wéstnɔrθwést) **1.** *adv.* towards west-northwest **2.** *n.* N. 67° 30′ W., a compass point midway between west and northwest (*abbr.* W.N.W., *COMPASS POINT) **3.** *adj.* of or situated towards west-northwest ‖ (of winds) blowing from west-northwest

Wes·ton cell (wéstən) (*elec.*) a cadmium-mercury primary cell, used as giving a standard, uniform emf [after its inventor Edward *Weston* (1850-1936), Anglo-American manufacturer]

West·pha·li·a (westféiljə, westféili:ə) *NORTH RHINE-WESTPHALIA

Westphalia, Treaties of treaties signed (Oct. 24, 1648) by the Holy Roman Empire, France, Sweden, and the Protestant states of the Empire, ending the Thirty Years' War. The Holy Roman Empire was greatly weakened by the recognition of the German states. France gained Alsace, and emerged as the dominant power in Europe. Sweden gained the western part of Pomerania. Switzerland and the United Netherlands were recognized as independent. Religious toleration was extended to the Calvinists

West Point a military post on the Hudson River in New York State, site of the U.S. Military Academy (1802)

CONCISE PRONUNCIATION KEY: **(a)** æ, *c*at; ɑ, *c*ar; ɔ, *f*awn; ei, sn*a*ke. **(e)** e, h*e*n; i:, sh*ee*p; iə, d*ee*r; ɛə, b*ear*; ai, t*i*ger; ə:, b*i*rd. **(o)** o, *o*x; au, *c*ow; ou, g*oa*t; u, p*oo*r; ɔi, r*oy*al. **(u)** ʌ, d*u*ck; u, b*u*ll; u:, g*oo*se; ə, b*a*cillus; ju:, *cu*be. x, lo*ch*; θ, *th*ink; ð, *b*other; z, *Z*en; ʒ, corsa*g*e; dʒ, sava*g*e; ŋ, ora*n*gutang; j, *y*ak; ʃ, *fish*; tʃ, fe*tch*; 'l, rab*b*le; 'n, red*d*en. Complete pronunciation key appears inside front cover.

West·pol·i·tik (wɛstpólitik) *n.* Communist nations' policy of maintaining trade relations with the West. *Cf* OSTPOLITIK.

West Quod·dy Head (kwɒ́di:) a cape off S.E. Maine, the easternmost point of continental U.S.A.

West Saxon (*hist.*) a native of the kingdom of Wessex ‖ (*hist.*) the dialect spoken in Wessex, the main literary dialect of Anglo-Saxon

west-south·west (wéstsauθwést) 1. *adv.* towards west-southwest 2. *n.* S. 67° 30′ W., a compass point midway between west and southwest (*abbr.* W.S.W., *COMPASS POINT) 3. *adj.* of or situated towards west-southwest ‖ (of winds) blowing from west-southwest

West Virginia (*abbr.* W.Va.) a state (area 24,282 sq. miles, pop. 1,948,000) in the central eastern U.S.A. Capital: Charleston. It is crossed by the Appalachians in the east, and the remainder is an elevated hilly plateau. Agriculture: beef cattle, dairying, poultry, fruit (esp. apples, peaches), corn. Resources: coal (first state producer), oil and natural gas, building materials. Industries: chemicals, iron and steel, metal products, glass and pottery. State university (1867) at Morgantown. West Virginia split (1861) from Virginia during the Civil War, and became (1863) the 35th state of the U.S.A.

west·ward (wéstwərd) 1. *adv.* and *adj.* towards the west 2. *n.* the westward direction or part **wést·wards** *adv.*

wet (wɛt) *comp.* **wet·ter** *superl.* **wet·test** *adj.* imbued with, covered with or soaked in water or some other liquid ‖ characterized by much rain, *a wet climate* ‖ (of paint, ink etc.) not yet dried ‖ (of a baby) having urinated in his diaper ‖ (*naut.*, of a boat) apt to ship water over the bows or sides ‖ involving the use of water or some other liquid, *a wet process* ‖ preserved in a liquid ‖ permitting or favoring the sale of alcoholic liquors, *a wet state* [O.E. *wǣt*]

wet *pres. part.* **wet·ting** *past* and *past part.* **wet**, **wet·ted** *v.t.* to make wet ‖ to urinate in or on ‖ *v.i.* to become wet to wet down to damp with water or some other liquid [O.E. *wǣtan*]

wet *n.* water or some other liquid substance ‖ (with 'the') rain, rainy weather, *don't go out in the wet* ‖ someone in favor of the sale of alcoholic liquors [partly O.E. *wǣt, wǣta*, partly fr. WET adj.]

wet-and-dry-bulb thermometer (*phys.*) two similar thermometers mounted side by side, the bulb of one being kept wet and therefore cooled by evaporation. The difference between the two thermometer readings can be used to determine the relative humidity of the air

wet blanket a person who discourages fun or conversation by his sober mood

weth·er (wéðər) *n.* a castrated male sheep [O.E.]

wet lab entrance and egress compartment in an artificial underwater habitat

wet·look (wétluk) *n.* a shiny finish on fabric created by a urethane coating

wet nurse a nurse who suckles another woman's baby **wét-nurse** *pres. part.* **wet-nurs·ing** *past* and *past part.* **wet-nursed** *v.t.* to be a wet nurse to ‖ to pamper

we've (wi:v) *contr.* of WE HAVE

Wex·ford (wéksfərd) a southeastern county (area 908 sq. miles, pop. 86,351) of Leinster province, Irish Republic. County seat: Wexford (pop. 11,849)

Weyden *VAN DER WEYDEN

Wey·gand (veigã), Maxime (1867-1965), French general. Foch's chief of staff (1914-23), and army chief of staff (1930), Weygand was appointed French supreme commander (May 1940). He was Pétain's delegate-general in N. Africa (1940-1) but was relieved of his post and was imprisoned by the Germans (1942-5)

WF (*abbr.*) for 'withdrawn failing', a grade given to a failing student who withdraws from a course. *Cf* WP.

whack (hwæk, wæk) 1. *v.t.* to strike, esp. with a resounding blow ‖ (Br., *pop.*) to defeat 2. *n.* a resounding blow ‖ the sound of such a blow **out of whack** not in proper working order or condition **to take** (or **have**) **a whack at** to attempt **whacked** *adj.* (Br., *pop.*) tired out [prob. imit.]

whack·ing (hwǽkiŋ, wǽkiŋ) 1. *adj.* (*pop.*) very large, *a whacking success* 2. *adv.* (*pop.*) extremely, *a whacking big elephant*

whack·y (hwǽki:, wǽki:) *comp.* **whack·i·er** *superl.* **whack·i·est** *adj.* (*pop.*) wacky

whale (hweil, weil) 1. *n.* a member of any of

many species of immense, fishlike marine mammals of the order *Cetacea*. They measure up to 100 ft in length and can weigh as much as 150 tons. Whales are hunted for their flesh, for the oil extracted from their blubber, for their very elastic whalebone, and for ambergris and spermaceti. Whales form two groups: toothed whales and whalebone whales **a whale of a** (*pop.*) exceptionally good in quality, *a whale of a game* ‖ (*pop.*) very large, *a whale of a difference* 2. *v.i. pres. part.* **whal·ing** *past* and *past part.* **whaled** to hunt whales [O.E. *hwæl*]

whale *pres. part.* **whal·ing** *past* and *past part.* **whaled** *v.t.* (*pop.*) to beat (a person, animal etc.) severely, *he whaled his dog for chasing sheep* ‖ (*pop.*) to defeat thoroughly [origin unknown]

whale·boat (hwéilbout, wéilbout) *n.* (*hist.*) a long narrow rowboat pointed at both ends and used in whaling

whale·bone (hwéilboun, wéilboun) *n.* a horny substance growing in fringed plates in the palate of whalebone whales. It is exploited for use as a stiffening e.g. in corsets

whalebone whale one of the two main divisions of whales, constituting the suborder *Mysticeti* and including the rorqual, humpback, right whale etc.

whale oil a true fat, obtained from whales, consisting almost entirely of one molecule of glycerol in combination with three of fatty acids. By a process in which molecules of hydrogen are added to molecules of fatty matter in the presence of a nickel catalyst, whale oil is converted into high-grade soapmaking material and an edible fat used in the manufacture of margarine and other cooking fats (cf. SPERM OIL)

whal·er (hwéilər, wéilər) *n.* a boat used in hunting whales ‖ a person who hunts whales

wham (hwæm, wæm) 1. *v. pres. part.* **wham·ming** *past* and *past part.* **whammed** *v.t.* to hit, propel etc. with a hard blow, *he whammed the ball 250 yards down the fairway* ‖ *v.i.* to make a loud, heavy impact, *his car whammed into the tree* 2. *n.* this noisy impact [imit.]

wham·my (wǽmi:) *n.* (*colloq.*) a shocking or lethal blow

whang (hwæŋ, wæŋ) 1. *n.* a blow that makes a loud noise 2. *v.i.* to make this noise ‖ to make a very energetic attack, *he whanged into him* ‖ *v.t.* to hit with a whang [imit.]

wharf (hwɔrf, wɔrf) 1. *pl.* **wharves**, (hwɔrvz, wɔrvz), **wharfs** *n.* a landing stage to which barges and ships can be moored for loading and unloading 2. *v.t.* to moor (a ship) beside a wharf ‖ to place (goods) on a wharf **whárf·age** *n.* the fee for using a wharf ‖ accommodation at a wharf [Late O.E. *hwearf*]

wharf·in·ger (hwɔ́rfindʒər, wɔ́rfindʒər) *n.* the owner or manager of a wharf [apparently altered fr. earlier *wharfager* fr. WHARFAGE]

Whar·ton (hwɔ́rt'n, wɔ́rt'n), Edith (1862-1937), American writer. Her works include the novels 'Ethan Frome' (1911) and 'The Age of Innocence' (1920). She also wrote many short stories.

what (hwɒt, hwʌt, wɒt, wʌt, *unstressed* hwət, wət) 1. *pron.* used interrogatively, requiring something to be identified, *what is the time?*, (often used also elliptically) *did what?* ‖ that which, *he heard what I said* ‖ how much, *he told me what it would cost* **no matter what** despite anything that **to have what it takes** (*pop.*) to have the necessary qualities, *he has what it takes to make an officer* **what about** an expression used to introduce a suggestion, *what about having dinner together?* ‖ what is the state of affairs regarding, *what about your homework?* **what for?** for what reason or purpose? **what have you** et cetera **what if** what is (or will be or would be) the result if, *what if he can't come after all?* **what's what** the true state of affairs ‖ good quality, *he knows what's what in wines* 2. *adj.* used interrogatively, referring to the nature, identity etc. of a person or thing, *what kind of person is he?* ‖ whatever, *invent what stories you will* ‖ (in exclamations) how great, ridiculous etc., *what a pity!* 3. *adv.* to what extent, to what degree, *what do you care?* ‖ used to introduce 'with' in phrases suggesting 'because of', *what with the noise and the dogs we could hardly listen* ‖ (in exclamations) used as an intensive, *what cold weather!* 4. *interj.* an exclamation of surprise, anger etc., *what! he really jumped?* [O.E. *hwæt*]

what·ev·er (hwɒtévər, hwʌtévər, hwətévər, wɒtévər, wʌtévər, wətévər) 1. *pron.* anything that, *eat whatever you like* ‖ no matter what, *I'll*

do it, *whatever he says* ‖ used as an intensive form of the interrogative 'what', usually expressing astonishment, surprise etc., *whatever are you doing?* ‖ something of the sort, *he has a cottage, shack or whatever* 2. *adj.* all the, *they gave him whatever clothes he possesses* ‖ (in negative constructions) at all, *he has no clothes whatever*

Whatman-number *SOILING INDEX

what·not (hwɒ́tnɒt, hwʌ́tnɒt, wɒ́tnɒt, wʌ́tnɒt) *n.* a piece of furniture standing on legs and consisting of a set of open shelves, one above another, for displaying or storing away miscellaneous objects ‖ any of various other miscellaneous items, *pockets full of string, worms and whatnot* ‖ something of that sort, *use a rope or chain or whatnot*

what·so·ev·er (hwɒtsouévər, hwʌtsouévər, wɒtsouévər, wʌtsouévər) *pron.* and *adj.* whatever

wheal (hwi:l, wi:l) *n.* a weal [misspelled form of WEAL]

wheat (hwi:t, wi:t) *n.* any of various grasses of the genus *Triticum* cultivated widely in temperate regions, esp. *T. aestivum*, an annual cereal grass ‖ the grain yielded from these, which is processed into flour or meal and used as the major breadstuff in temperate areas and for animal feeding [O.E. *hwǣte*]

wheat·ear (hwí:tiər, wí:tiər) *n. Oenanthe oenanthe*, a small bluish-gray, black and white passerine bird of N. Europe, Asia and Alaska, related to the stonechat [older *wheatears*=white ass]

wheat·en (hwí:t'n, wí:t'n) *adj.* of or made of wheat or wheat flour ‖ of the fawn or pale yellow color of wheat [O.E. *hwǣten*]

wheat germ the embryo of the wheat seed rich in vitamins, esp. vitamin E, and linoleic acid oil

wheat·meal (hwí:tmi:l, wí:tmi:l) *n.* (Br.) the pure meal of wheat, the whole berry being ground (*WHOLE WHEAT) [O.E. *hwǣtemelu*]

Wheat·on (hwí:t'n, wí:t'n), Henry (1785-1848), U.S. jurist and diplomat. His works include 'Elements of International Law' (1836) and 'A History of the Law of Nations' (1845)

Wheat·stone (hwí:tstoun, wí:tstoun, *Br.* esp. hwí:tstən, wí:tstən), Sir Charles (1802-75), British physicist. With William Cooke, he patented a successful electric telegraph. He also invented the concertina

Wheatstone bridge a device for comparing and measuring electrical resistances. It consists of two parallel branches of conductors containing the resistances to be compared and a device (usually a galvanometer) to indicate the voltage or current flowing in each branch [after Sir Charles WHEATSTONE]

whee·dle (hwí:d'l, wí:d'l) *pres. part.* **whee·dling** *past* and *past part.* **whee·dled** *v.t.* to persuade by flattery, coaxing etc., *she wheedled him into giving her a new coat* ‖ to obtain in this way, *she wheedled a new coat out of him* [origin unknown]

wheel (hwi:l, wi:l) 1. *n.* a circular device, thin in relation to its face area, usually able to rotate about a central axle or pivot, with a durable but elastic rim or with regular teeth cut on the rim, and for lightness often supported by spokes joined to the hub instead of being left solid. The invention of the wheel enabled loads to be transported with relative ease, rolling friction being always much less than sliding friction. The use of cogged wheels also enabled power to be transmitted, e.g. in a clockwork mechanism, and to be varied at will (*GEAR) ‖ something resembling this device in shape, movement etc., e.g. a roulette wheel ‖ a large wheel formerly used as an instrument of torture ‖ the control of a car, ship etc., *the ship's captain had the wheel* ‖ a cycle of events, *the wheel has come full circle* ‖ a circular motion e.g. of marching soldiers, warships in line etc. turning around a pivot point ‖ (*pl.*) the functioning of something likened to a wheel mechanism, *the wheels of government* **to put one's shoulder to the wheel** to begin to use one's energies with determination in accomplishing some purpose or task **to take the wheel** to assume control of a ship, car etc. 2. *v.i.* to turn around on or as if on an axis, *he wheeled around when he heard her voice* ‖ to move on or as if on wheels ‖ to turn in a circular motion ‖ to change one's course of action, opinion etc. ‖ (*mil.*) to execute a wheel ‖ *v.t.* to cause to move on wheels ‖ to carry on wheels ‖ to wheel a vehicle ‖ to walk beside and push (a bicycle or motorcycle) ‖ to drive (a car, truck etc.) ‖ to cause to revolve or rotate || (*mil.*) to cause to execute a wheel [O.E. *hweogol, hwēol*]

wheel and axle a wheel fixed to an axle of smaller diameter, arranged so that a rope unwinds and winds on each respectively, the effort being applied to the wheel rope and the load hauled by the axle rope. A mechanical advantage is thus derived from the difference in turning moments

wheel animal a rotifer

wheel animalcule a rotifer

wheel·bar·row (hwí:lbærou, wí:lbærou) *n.* a shallow vehicle with one wheel in front and two legs and handles at the back, pushed by hand to transport earth, bricks etc.

wheel·base (hwí:lbeis, wí:lbeis) *n.* the distance between a vehicle's front and back axles

wheel·chair (hwí:ltʃɛər, wí:ltʃɛər) *n.* a chair on wheels in which an invalid can propel himself along, or be pushed by someone else

Whee·ler (hwí:lər, wí:lər) *n.* Benjamin Ide (1854-1927), U.S. classical scholar, philologist, and president (1899-1919) of the University of California during the period of its greatest development

wheel·er (hwí:lər, wí:lər) *n.* a wheelhorse || (used in hyphenated compounds) a vehicle having a specified number of wheels, *a two-wheeler*

wheel·er-deal·er (wí:lərdí:lər) *n.* a shrewd negotiator, businessperson, politician, or operator who specializes in fast purchases and sales —**wheeler-dealer** *adj.* —**wheeler-dealing** *v.*

wheel·horse (hwí:lhɔrs, wí:lhɔrs) *pl.* **wheel·hors·es** *n.* the horse or one of the horses nearest to the wheels of a vehicle (cf. LEADER) || (*pop.*) a hardworking and effective employee of an enterprise

wheel·house (hwí:lhaus, wí:lhaus) *pl.* **wheel·hous·es** (hwí:lhauziz, wí:lhauziz) *n.* the structure on a ship containing the wheel and navigating equipment

wheel·ie (wí:li:) *n.* (*sports*) a stunt of momentarily standing a vehicle, esp. a motorcycle, on its back wheel or wheels

wheel lock an obsolete type of gunlock in which the charge was ignited by sparks from a wheel spinning against a flint

Whee·lock (hwí:lɒk, wí:lɒk), Eleazar (1711-79), U.S. educator, founder (1770) and first president of Dartmouth College

wheel·race (hwí:lreis, wí:lreis) *n.* the place in a millrace where the mill wheel is set

wheel·wright (hwí:lrait, wí:lrait) *n.* someone who makes and repairs wheels, carts etc.

wheeze (hwi:z, wi:z) **1.** *v.i. pres. part.* **wheez·ing** *past* and *past part.* **wheezed** to breathe with difficulty, making a whistling sound || *v.t.* to utter wheezily **2.** *n.* a wheezing sound **whéez·i·ly** *adv.* **whéez·i·ness** *n.* **whéez·i·er** *comp.* **whéez·i·est** *superl.* **wheez·y** *adj.* [prob. O.N. *hvœsa*, to hiss]

whelk (hwelk, welk) *n.* a member of *Buccinum* and other genera of carnivorous gastropod mollusks, fam. *Buccinidae* and related families, esp. *B. undatum* of the Atlantic coasts, esteemed as food in Europe [O.E. *wioloc, weoloc*]

whelp (hwelp, welp) **1.** *n.* a young lion, tiger, bear, wolf etc. || a puppy || a naughty, insupportable child or youth || a tooth on a sprocket wheel || (*naut.*, esp. *pl.*) one of the ribs or ridges on the barrel of a capstan or windlass **2.** *v.t.* (of animals) to give birth to || *v.i.* (of animals) to give birth [O.E. *hwelp*]

when (hwen, wen) **1.** *adv.* at what time, *when does the train leave?* || on which occasion, *when did you last eat?* **2.** *conj.* at, during or after the time that, *that was when we missed you most, stop the machine when the whistle is blown* || every time that, *she gets a rash when she eats strawberries* || in view of the fact that, *why does he live like a miser when he is so rich?* || if, in the event that, *when three balls are missed the player is out* **3.** *pron.* what or which time, *when is the contract effective from?, when will you wait until?* **4.** *n.* the time of an event or an action, *I can't remember the when or the why of it* [O.E. *hwanne, hwonne, hwenne*]

whence (hwens, wens) **1.** *adv.* (*rhet.*) from where || (*rhet.*) from what source or origin **2.** *conj.* (*rhet.*) from what place or source [M.E. *whannes, whennes* fr. *whanne* fr. O.E. *hwanone*]

when·ev·er (hwenévər, wenévər) *adv.* and *conj.* at whatever time, as often as, *come whenever you like* || (used emphatically) when, *whenever will you grow up?*

when·so·ev·er (hwɛnsouévər, wɛnsouévər) *adv.* and *conj.* (*rhet.*, used emphatically) at whatever time

where (hwɛər, wɛər) **1.** *adv.* in or at what place, *where are you?* || to or toward what place, *where are you going?* || in what respect, *where does this argument break down?* || in what circumstances, *without friends where are you?* || from what place or source, *where do you get your money?* **2.** *conj.* in or at what or which place, *they have gone where the police can't get them* || to or toward the place to which, *I'll drive you where you're going* || in the or a case, situation, respect in which, *where some are weak and old others must shoulder the load* || insofar as, *there can be no problem where you are concerned* **3.** *n.* a place, esp. a place in which something is or occurs, *I only know it happened, but not the where or how* [O.E. *hwǣr, hwār*]

where·a·bouts (hwéərəbauts, wéərəbauts) **1.** *adv.* (used interrogatively) near or at what place, *whereabouts is your home?* **2.** *conj.* in what place, *tell us roughly whereabouts you put them* **3.** *n.* the place where someone or something is, *he's hiding his whereabouts*

where·as (hwɛəréz, wɛəréz) *conj.* while on the contrary, *some praise him, whereas others condemn him* || (in legal documents) since, considering that

where·at (hwɛəræt, wɛəræt) **1.** *adv.* (*archaic*) at which, at what **2.** *conj.* (*archaic*) upon which event

where·by (hwɛərbái, wɛərbái) **1.** *adv.* by which, *the ruse whereby they succeeded* **2.** *conj.* by which

where·fore (hwéərfɔr, hwéərfour, wéərfɔr, wéərfour) **1.** *adv.* (*rhet.*) why, for what reason or purpose **2.** *conj.* (*rhet.*) for which reason **3.** *n.* (esp. *pl.*) the reason, *the whys and the wherefores*

where·in (hwɛərín, wɛərín) **1.** *adv.* (*rhet.*) in which place || in what respect, *wherein did they transgress?* || (*rhet.*) in which, *armor wherein he trusted* **2.** *conj.* in what or in which

where·of (hwɛərʌ́v, hwɛərɒ́v, wɛərʌ́v, wɛərɒ́v) *adv.* and *conj.* (*rhet.*) of which, of what or of whom

where·on (hwɛərɒ́n, hwɛərɔ́n, wɛərɒ́n, wɛərɔ́n) **1.** *conj.* (*rhet.*) on what, on which **2.** *adv.* (*archaic*) on what?

where·so·ev·er (hwɛərsouévər, wɛərsouévər) *adv.* and *conj.* (*archaic*, emphatic for) wherever || (*archaic*) in or to whatever place

where·to (hwɛərtú:, wɛərtú:) *adv.* (*archaic*) to what place, purpose etc. || (*archaic*) to which

where·up·on (hwɛərəpɒ́n, hwɛərəpɔ́n, wɛərəpɒ́n, wɛərəpɔ́n) **1.** *conj.* (*rhet.*) after which, in consequence of which, *we disagreed, whereupon he left me* **2.** *adv.* upon which

wher·ev·er (hwɛərévər, wɛərévər) **1.** *conj.* at, in or to whatever place, *wherever you go you will find people much the same* **2.** *adv.* (used to express astonishment or incredulity) where, *wherever are you taking me?* || in any circumstance in which, *wherever it is possible*

where·with (hwɛərwíθ, hwɛərwíð, wɛərwíθ, wɛərwíð) *adv.* (*rhet.*) with which, *the means wherewith to travel* || (*archaic*) with what?

where·with·al (hwéərwiðəl, wéərwiðəl) *n.* the means, what is necessary, *how can he do that if he lacks the wherewithal?*

wher·ry (hwéri:, wéri:) *pl.* **wher·ries** *n.* a light shallow rowboat, pointed at both ends, used for carrying passengers and freight on rivers || a large lighter or barge used in Great Britain to transport freight **whér·ry·man** *pl.* **wher·ry·men** *n.* (*Br.*) someone who works on a wherry [origin unknown]

whet (hwet, wet) **1.** *v.t. pres. part.* **whet·ting** *past* and *past part.* **whet·ted** to sharpen by rubbing against a whetstone etc. || to stimulate, arouse, *to whet one's appetite* **2.** *n.* (*rhet.*) something that whets, *a whet to the appetite* [O.E. *hwettan*]

wheth·er (hwéðər, wéðər) *conj.* (followed by 'or', 'or whether') introducing the first of two or more possibilities, *I wonder whether it will rain or snow, I wonder whether it will rain or whether it will be fine* || (introducing an indirect question) if, *he asked me whether I would sing* || either, *we'll take the next offer, whether good or bad* [O.E. *hwœther, hwether*]

whet·stone (hwétstoun, wétstoun) *n.* a stone used for sharpening the blades of cutting tools [O.E. *hwetstān*]

whey (hwei, wei) *n.* the watery part of milk left when curds have formed and separated [O.E. *hwœg, hweg*]

which (hwitʃ, witʃ) **1.** *pron.* what one or ones of several things, persons etc. pointed out, denoted, described etc., *which do you prefer?* || whichever one or ones, *you may select which you like* || used as a relative in a subordinate clause representing a noun or noun phrase in the principal sentence, *he read the book which you lent him* || (used as a connective) a fact that, *he left—which in itself isn't important—abruptly* **2.** *adj.* what one or ones, *which road should I take?* || whatever, *run which way you will, you won't escape* || used as an introductory word, modifying a noun, and referring to an antecedent noun, clause etc., *he is studying economics, which knowledge is very important today* [O.E. *hwelc, hwilc, hwylc*]

which·ev·er (hwitʃévər, witʃévər) **1.** *pron.* any one or ones of several, *buy whichever is cheapest* **2.** *adj.* no matter which, *it's a nuisance whichever way you look at it*

which·so·ev·er (hwitʃsouévər, witʃsouévər) *pron.* and *adj.* (*archaic*, emphatic form of) whichever

whid·ah, whyd·ah (hwídə, wídə) *n.* the widow bird [alt. fr. *widow bird* after *Whidah* (now Ouidah), a town in Benin]

whiff (hwif, wif) **1.** *n.* a small volume of smoke, air etc., esp. one having a smell, suddenly expelled || the smell of this, *a whiff of perfume* || an inhalation of tobacco smoke, odor etc. **2.** *v.t.* to emit a small amount of (smoke, scent etc.) || *v.i.* to blow lightly [imit.]

whif·fle (hwífəl, wífəl) **1.** *v. pres. part.* **whif·fling** *past* and *past part.* **whif·fled** *v.i.* (of the wind) to blow in little gusts || to make a light whistling sound || (*Am.*) to change one's mind frequently || *v.t.* to blow, drive etc. with or as if with a gust of wind **2.** *n.* the act or a sound of whiffling [WHIFF]

whif·fle-ball (hwífəlbɔl) *n.* (*sports*) a plastic ball with openings to increase air resistance, used for golf, softball, or baseball practice

whif·fle-tree (hwífəltri:, wífəltri:) *n.* the pivoted crossbar of a cart, or of a plow or other implement, to which a horse's traces are fastened

Whig (hwig, wig) **1.** *n.* (*Scot. hist.*) someone supporting the Covenanters' cause (17th c.) || (*Eng. hist.*) someone belonging to the political group, led by Shaftesbury, which opposed (1679) the succession of the future James II on account of his Catholic sympathies. The Whigs were among the organizers of the Glorious Revolution (1688–9), and ruled Britain (1714–60), notably in the ministry (1721–42) of Walpole. They were again briefly in power (1782) under Rockingham, but were ousted by the Tories until 1830. They secured the passage of the Reform Act (1832) and other measures of reform. By 1868 the Whig party had merged with the new Liberal party || (*Am. hist.*) a colonist who supported the Revolutionary War (1775–83) || (*Am. hist.*) a member of the party which opposed (1834–56) the Democratic party. It was succeeded by the Republican party **2.** *adj.* of, being or holding the beliefs of a Whig **Whíg·ger·y** *n.* **Whíg·gish** *adj.* of or like Whigs or their doctrines **Whíg·gism** *n.* the doctrines and principles of Whigs, esp. of English Whigs [etym. doubtful]

while (hwail, wail) **1.** *n.* a period of time, *he stayed only for a short while once in a while* on infrequent occasions, *he comes once in a while* **the while** (*old-fash.*) during that time, *he kept his eyes on her the while* **2.** *v.t. pres. part.* **whil·ing** *past* and *past part.* **whiled** (with 'away') to make (time) pass pleasantly in order esp. to escape boredom, *she whiled away the hours of waiting by looking at the shops* [O.E. *hwil*, time]

while *conj.* during the time that, *she saw him only twice while he was staying there* || at the same time that, *he came to the door while I was ringing the bell* || although, *while we don't agree we continue to be friends* [O.E. *hwile*]

whilst (hwailst, wailst) *conj.* (esp. *Br.*) while

whim (hwim, wim) *n.* a freakish pattern of ideas and their associated emotions as a motive of action || (*mining*) a device for hoisting ore or water, with extending arms to which a horse or horses may be tied to do the turning [fr. older *whim-wham*, a trinket, origin unknown]

whim·brel (hwímbrəl, wímbrəl) *n. Numenius phaeopus*, a small European curlew [prob. imit.]

whim·per (hwímpər, wímpər) **1.** *v.i.* to utter feeble little cries of fear or complaint or discontent continued over a period almost nonstop || *v.t.* to utter whimperingly 2. *n.* a whimpering sound [imit.]

whimsey *WHIMSY

whim·si·cal (hwímzik'l, wímzik'l) *adj.* full of whims ‖ subject to whims **whim·si·cal·i·ty** (hwìmzikǽliti:, wìmzikǽliti:) *pl.* **whim·si·cal·i-ties** *n.*

whim·sy, whim·sey (hwímzi:, wímzi:) *n.* feeble or sentimental fancy, esp. as a degenerate element in a work of art

whin (hwin, win) *n.* gorse [prob. of Scand. origin]

whin (hwin, win) *n.* whinstone [origin unknown]

whin·chat (hwíntʃæt, wíntʃæt) *n. Saxicola rubetra*, a small European songbird

whine (hwain, wain) 1. *v. pres. part.* **whin·ing** *past* and *past part.* **whined** *v.i.* to cry in or utter a high-pitched, long drawn-out, plaintive sound ‖ to complain in a querulous or childish way ‖ *v.t.* to utter whiningly 2. *n.* a whining sound ‖ a complaint, esp. one that causes mild contempt [O.E. *hwīnan*]

whin·ny (hwíni:, wíni:) 1. *v. pres. part.* **whin·ny·ing** *past* and *past part.* **whin·nied** *v.i.* (of a horse) to neigh, esp. in a soft, gentle way ‖ *v.t.* to express by whinnying 2. *pl.* **whin·nies** *n.* a whinnying sound [imit.]

whin·stone (hwínstoun, wínstoun) *n.* any of various hard, dark, esp. basaltic rocks

whin·y (hwáini:, wáini:) *comp.* **whin·i·er** *superl.* **whin·i·est** *adj.* of, characterized by or given to whining

whip (hwip, wip) *n.* a lash with a handle used for driving a horse or urging one on, or for punishing ‖ something resembling a whip, e.g. a flexible rod ‖ a whipping or thrashing motion ‖ the sail arm of a windmill ‖ a light dessert made with whipped ingredients ‖ a hoisting apparatus consisting of a single rope and pulley ‖ a hunt official responsible for whipping in the hounds ‖ (*politics*) an official appointed to maintain party discipline and esp. to enforce attendance in Congress etc. ‖ a written notice sent around by this official in the House of Commons requesting members' attendance [partly fr. WHIP v. partly M.L.G., L.G. *wippe, wip*, quick movement]

whip *pres. part.* **whip·ping** *past* and *past part.* **whipped** *v.t.* to strike with a lash, rod etc. ‖ to beat to a froth, *to whip cream* ‖ to strike stingingly, *rain whipped our faces* ‖ to move, take, jerk etc. quickly, *he whipped the knife out of her hand* ‖ (pop.) to defeat by a good margin ‖ to fish (a river etc.) with a rod and line, casting with a whiplike action ‖ to bind (a rope etc.) with cord or twine to prevent fraying ‖ to wrap (a cord, twine etc.) around something, e.g. a handle ‖ to oversew (a seam) ‖ (esp. *naut.*) to hoist by rope and pulley ‖ *v.i.* to move quickly, to dart, *he whipped across the road* ‖ to flap with the noise made by the lash of a whip, *the flags whipped in the breeze* ‖ (*fishing*) to cast with a whiplike action **to whip in** to force (hounds) to form a close pack at a hunt ‖ to gather together (members of a political party) for a particular occasion **to whip out** to take out (something) with a sudden, quick movement, *he whipped out his pistol* **to whip up** to arouse, esp. by oratory or forceful persuasion, *to whip up enthusiasm* ‖ (pop.) to improvise (e.g. a meal) hurriedly [rel. to M.L.G., L.G. or Du. *wippen*, to swing]

whip·cord (hwípkɔrd, wípkɔrd) 1. *n.* tightly twisted cord, esp. that used for making whips ‖ a durable corded fabric, used for coats, riding breeches etc., made from worsted yarns 2. *adj.* tough, strong, and tightly knit, like the cord of a whip

whip hand control, position of advantage, *to have the whip hand over a person* [lit. = the hand used for holding the whip when driving a carriage]

whip·lash (hwíplæʃ, wíplæʃ) *n.* the lash of a whip ‖ a whiplash injury

whiplash injury a neck injury, common in automobile accidents, suffered when the head jerks suddenly backward or forward

whip·per-in (hwípərin, wípərin) *pl.* **whip·pers-in** *n.* a hunt official who whips in the hounds ‖ (*politics*) a party whip

whip·per·snap·per (hwípərsnæpər, wípərsnæp-ər) *n.* a young, esp. undersized boy who behaves with more self-importance than is proper [prob. an extension of obs. 'whip snapper', a cracker of whips]

whip·pet (hwípit, wípit) *n.* a dog of a fast-run-

ning breed resembling a small greyhound and used in coursing

whip·ping (hwípiŋ, wípiŋ) *n.* the act of someone who whips ‖ a beating or flogging ‖ stitching used in overcasting ‖ twine etc. used for whipping or binding, or the binding itself

whipping boy (*hist.*) a boy who shared a prince's education and was whipped in his stead for the prince's faults ‖ a person made to bear the blame which should fall on others

whipping post (*hist.*) a post to which a person was tied for a public whipping

Whip·ple (hwíp'l, wíp'l), George Hoyt (1878-1976), U.S. pathologist and educator, co-winner (with George R.Minot and William P. Murphy) of the 1934 Nobel prize in physiology and medicine for discovering that liver is essential to blood formation and is curative in the treatment of pernicious anemia

whip·ple·tree (hwípəltri:, wípəltri:) *n.* a whiffletree [perh. rel. to WHIP]

whip·poor·will (hwípɔrwil, wípɔrwil, hwípɔr-wíl, wípərwíl) *n. Caprimulgus vociferus*, a North American goatsucker active at night, when it repeats its call over and over [imit. of its cry]

whip·round (hwípraund, wípraund) *n.* (*Br.*) a collection or appeal for contributions, esp. towards a collective gift or to help someone in an emergency

whip·saw (hwípsɔ, wípsɔ) *n.* a long, narrow saw blade with its ends fixed in an elastic metal frame

whir, whirr (hwəːr, wəːr) 1. *v.i. pres. part.* **whir·ring, whirr·ing** *past* and *past part.* **whir-red** to move, esp. through the air, with a sound resembling that of a bird's wings in rapid flight 2. *n.* the sound itself [prob. of Scand. origin]

whirl (hwəːrl, wəːrl) 1. *v.i.* to revolve rapidly, *an unknown mass whirling through space* or seem to do so, *his brain was whirling* ‖ to rush with a great commotion, *to come whirling into a room* ‖ *v.t.* to cause to whirl 2. *n.* the act of whirling ‖ a whirling motion ‖ something that whirls ‖ a feeling of giddiness or confusion ‖ a continuous series of hectic activities, *a whirl of parties* [O.N. *hvirfla*]

whirl·i·gig (hwə́ːrligig, wə́ːrligig) *n.* (*Br.*) a pinwheel (child's toy)

whirligig beetle any of various members of *Gyrinidae*, a family of beetles which whirl on the surface of ponds, lakes etc.

whirling dervish *DERVISH

whirl·pool (hwə́ːrlpu:l, wə́ːrlpu:l) *n.* a circular eddy or current in a river or the sea caused by the shape of the channel, the effect of wind on tides, or by the meeting of currents

whirl·wind (hwə́ːrlwind, wə́ːrlwind) *n.* a rotating windstorm produced by a column of air moving rapidly in an upward spiral course and moving progressively over the surface of land or water

whirr *WHIR

whisk (hwisk, wisk) 1. *n.* an instrument for beating eggs, cream etc. ‖ a hairlike appendage, e.g. on the tail of some insects ‖ a quick, light movement 2. *v.t.* to beat (eggs, cream etc.) into a froth ‖ to transport with speed, *he whisked them off to the station in his car* ‖ to remove (something) with a quick, light motion, *she whisked the crumbs from the table* ‖ *v.i.* to move quickly **to whisk away** to remove (something) with a swift motion ‖ to go darting off [prob. fr. O.N.]

whisk broom a small, short-handled broom used esp. to brush clothes

whisk·er (hwískər, wískər) *n.* one of the long stiff bristles growing at either side of the mouth of some animals ‖ (*pl.*) the hairs growing in a beard or down the side of a man's cheeks ‖ (*naut.*) either of two spars extending on each side of the bowsprit for spreading the guys of the jibboom **whisk·ered, whisk·er·y** *adjs.* [WHISK v.]

whiskers *n.* (*chem.*) a monocrystalline fiber composite, used for reinforcing cement, resin, and silver amalgam

whis·key, Br. whis·ky (hwíski:, wíski:) *pl.* **whis·keys, whis·kies** *n.* a strong alcoholic liquor distilled from various grains (esp. malted barley, rye, wheat, corn) or from potatoes. 'Whisky' is (*Br.*) the preferred spelling for Scotch, 'whiskey' for Irish or bourbon ‖ a drink of whiskey [shortened fr. *usquebaugh* fr. Ir. Gael. *uisgebeatha*, water of life]

Whiskey insurrection an uprising (1794) of farmers in W. Pennsylvania against the U.S. government's efforts to enforce an excise tax on

distilled liquors. About 500 armed men burned down the home of the regional inspector and others tarred and feathered revenue officers. The uprising was suppressed without violence after President George Washington dispatched 13,000 troops to Pennsylvania. The Federalists considered that federal authority had triumphed over local defiance, but antifederalist feelings persisted in the region long afterwards

whis·per (hwíspər, wíspər) 1. *v.i.* to speak quietly without vibrating the vocal cords, esp. so as to be heard only by the person addressed ‖ to rustle, to make a soft sibilant sound, *the leaves whispered in the breeze* ‖ *v.t.* to utter in a whisper ‖ to mention secretly, spread as a rumor 2. *n.* a low soft utterance ‖ a soft sibilant sound ‖ a rumor [O.E. *hwisprian*]

whispering campaign a deliberate and systematic attempt to besmear someone (esp. in political contests) by spreading vicious rumors

whist (hwist, wist) *n.* a card game for four players paired as partners, each player having 13 cards. The game has many variations, and contract bridge was developed from it [earlier *whisk* prob. fr. whisking the cards from the table]

whis·tle (hwís'l, wís'l) 1. *v. pres. part.* **whis·tling** *past* and *past part.* **whis·tled** *v.i.* to make a shrill, piping sound by forcing the breath through pursed lips, or through a special instrument ‖ (of a bird) to make a sound resembling this ‖ to produce such a sound, esp. by swift movement, *the wind whistled through the trees* ‖ *v.t.* to utter by whistling ‖ to give an order to by whistling **to whistle for** to ask for or wish for in vain 2. *n.* a small instrument of wood, metal etc. blown to produce a shrill, piping sound ‖ a device used as a signal etc. through which air or steam is forced to produce a loud, piercing sound, *a factory whistle* ‖ the sound produced by either of these ‖ the sound produced when the breath is forced through pursed lips ‖ the piercing note of a bird ‖ something resembling this, *the whistle of bullets* ‖ an act of whistling **to wet one's whistle** (old-fash.) to take a drink, esp. a drink, of beer or liquor

whis·tler *n.* someone who or something that whistles ‖ any of various Australian and Polynesian birds related to the shrikes, having a whistling call ‖ *Marmota caligata*, a large marmot of North America ‖ a horse with the heaves [O.E. *hwistlan*]

whistle blower one who informs authorities of malfeasance in government or business

Whis·tler (hwíslər, wíslər), James Abbott McNeill (1834-1903), American painter and etcher. In his portraits and genre paintings he concentrated on subtle composition and refined color harmony

whis·tle-stop (hwís'lstɒp, wís'lstɒp) 1. *n.* an insignificant station where a train stops only by prearrangement or at a signal ‖ a brief stop at a small station in order that a political candidate on tour may stop to make a speech 2. *v.i. pres. part.* **whis·tle-stop·ping** *past* and *past part.* **whis·tle-stopped** (of a political candidate) to stop at whistle-stops in order to make speeches

Whit (hwit, wit) *adj.* of or relating to Pentecost (Whitsuntide)

whit (hwit, wit) *n.* the smallest possible amount, *not one whit the wiser* [O.E. *wiht*, a person]

Whit·by, synod of (hwítbi:, wítbi:) a meeting summoned at Whitby, N.E. England (664) by King Oswy of Northumbria to decide between Roman and Celtic ecclesiastical usages. The decision in favor of the Roman usage determined that the English Church was to be linked with continental Christendom (*WILFRID)

White (hwait, wait), Byron Raymond (1917-) U.S. associate justice of the Supreme Court (1962-). He played professional football (1938-9), was a Rhodes scholar (1939-40) and, after serving in the Navy, took his law degree at Yale. He was appointed to the Court by Pres. John F. Kennedy. Relatively conservative, he wrote the majority opinion in 'Duncan v. Louisiana' (1968), 'Williams v. Florida' (1970) and 'Taylor v. Louisiana' (1975), all concerning jury selection and trials. He also spoke for the Court in 'Washington v. Davis' (1976) and 'Columbus Board of Education v. Penick' (1979)

White, Edward Douglass, Jr. (1845-1921) U.S. Supreme Court associate justice (1894-1911) and chief justice (1911-21). A U.S. senator

(1890-94) he was appointed to the Court by Pres. Grover Cleveland. He wrote the majority opinion in 'Standard Oil Co. v. United States' (1911), which established the definition of a trust, and 'United States v. American Tobacco Co.' (1911). He spoke for the Court in 'Brushaber v. Union Pacific Railroad' (1916), which upheld the income tax; 'Guinn v. United States' (1915), which abolished the 'grandfather clause' in voting laws; and 'Selective Draft Law Cases' (1918)

White Gilbert (1720-93), English naturalist, author of 'The Natural History and Antiquities of Selborne' (1789)

White, Patrick (1912-) Australian writer, Nobel prize for literature (1973), born in England. His novels, usually of a search for truth, love and reality, include 'Happy Valley' (1939), 'The Tree of Man' (1955), 'Voss' (1957), 'Riders in the Chariot' (1961) and 'The Twyborn Affair' (1980). Short stories are collected in 'The Cockatoo' (1974) and poems in 'Thirteen Poems' (1929) and 'The Ploughman and Other Poems' (1935). He wrote 'Four Plays' (1965) and his autobiography 'Flaws in the Glass' (1982)

White a river (690 miles long) rising in the mountains of N.W. Arkansas, bending north into Missouri and returning southeast across Arkansas into the Mississippi River on the east boundary of Arkansas

white (hwait, wait) 1. *adj.* of the color sensation stimulated by a combination of all the wavelengths of visible light, or resulting from combinations of certain pairs of wavelengths, being the color of e.g. milk ‖ (of hair) gray or silver ‖ (of hair) very pale yellow ‖ (of wines) very pale yellow ‖ free from sin, pure ‖ pale, *white with terror* ‖ of or relating to the Caucasian division of mankind ‖ covered with snow ‖ blank, not printed upon, *leave the rest of the page white* ‖ (of silver and other metals) unburnished ‖ (of the members of a religious order) wearing white **to bleed (someone) white** to get money from (someone) until there is no more to be had 2. *n.* a white pigment, fabric etc. ‖ a member of the Caucasian division of mankind ‖ the white part of something ‖ the albuminous matter surrounding the yolk of an egg ‖ the white part of the eye surrounding the cornea ‖ any of various breeds or species of white hog, white horse, white butterfly etc. ‖ (*printing*) a blank space between words or lines ‖ (*archery*) the outermost ring of a target ‖ (*archery*) the shot that hits this ring ‖ (*board games*) the light-colored men or pieces, or the player having these ‖ (*pl., pop.*) leukorrhea [O.E. *hwīt*]

White Alice *ALICE

white ant a termite

white arsenic (*chem.*) an intensely poisonous arsenious oxide, As_2O_3

white·bait (hwáitbeit, wáitbeit) *n.* the young of various fishes used as food, esp. the young of any of various European herrings, or of the sprat

white·beam (hwáitbi:m, wáitbi:m) *n. Sorbus aria* (or *Pyrus aria*), fam. *Rosaceae*, a European ornamental tree bearing white flowers and red fruits

white bear polar bear

white blood cell a leucocyte

white book a book bound in white, containing an official government report or reports (in certain countries)

white bread light-colored bread made from refined wheat flour

white·cap (hwáitkæp, wáitkæp) *n.* the foam on the crest of a wave ‖ the male of the European redstart

white·col·lar (hwáitkɔ́lər, wáitkɔ́lər) *adj.* of, relating to or designating the salaried section of the working population (e.g. teachers, civil servants) whose duties call for the wearing of neat, conventional clothes

white corpuscle a leukocyte

white currant a shrub of genus *Ribes*, bearing white, edible berries ‖ its fruit

white damp a poisonous gas occurring in mines, formed by incomplete combustion of coal and composed mainly of carbon monoxide

whited sepulcher, *Br.* **whited sepulchre** a hypocrite, a corrupt person who makes a show of righteousness (Matthew xxiii, 27)

white dwarf (*astron.*) a whitish star of approximately the same size as the sun but with a greater density

white elephant a rare, pale-colored elephant of India, Ceylon, Thailand and Burma ‖ (*pop.*) any unwanted possession, esp. a property that is troublesome or expensive to keep

white ensign a white flag with the union in the upper quarter, flown by British warships and a few other, privileged vessels

white feather a symbol of cowardice (a white feather in a gamecock's tail supposedly being a sign of degeneracy)

White·field (hwáitfi:ld, wáitfi:ld, hwítfi:ld, wítfi:ld), George (1714-70), English Methodist preacher. He was associated with the Wesleys in the early days of Methodism, but separated from them (c. 1741) when he adopted Calvinistic views. He became chaplain to the Countess of Huntingdon's Connexion. He preached widely in North America

white·fish (hwáitfiʃ, wáitfiʃ) *pl.* **white·fish, white·fish·es** *n.* (*Br.*) any of various food fishes having white, dry flesh, e.g. cod, sole, whiting ‖ a member of *Coregonus*, fam. *Salmonidae*, a genus of food fishes resembling the salmon or trout and inhabiting freshwater lakes etc. of North America, Europe and Asia

white flag (*mil.*) a flag or white piece of cloth generally recognized as a signal of truce, or as a token of surrender or of some peaceful intention

White Friar a Carmelite friar

white frost hoarfrost

white gold gold alloyed usually with nickel and sometimes with zinc, tin or copper

White·hall (hwáithɔl, wáithɔl) a London street in which there are many government offices ‖ the British government, esp. in its administrative capacity

White·head (hwáithed, wáithed), Alfred North (1861-1947), British mathematician and philosopher. With Bertrand Russell he wrote 'Principia Mathematica' (1910-13), in which the fundamental propositions of logic and mathematics are derived from a few basic assumptions. In 'Concept of Nature' (1920) and 'Principle of Relativity' (1922) he developed an alternative to Einstein in physics, and in 'Process and Reality' (1927-9) a 'philosophy of organism'. Opposing positive and antireligious science, he sought to establish a modern philosophy which would take account of religious experience as well as of 20th-c. physics and sociology

white heat the temperature at which a body emits the whole range of wavelengths of the visible spectrum ‖ a state of extreme emotion or febrile activity

White·horse (hwáithɔrs, wáithɔrs) the capital (pop. 14,814) of Yukon Territory, Canada, on the upper Yukon River, a distributing and communications center

white horses waves crested with foam

white-hot (hwáithɔt, wáithɔt) *adj.* at white heat ‖ very excited, angry etc. ‖ working at intense pressure of activity

White House the official residence of the U.S. president, in Washington. It was built in the late 18th c. ‖ the executive government of the U.S.A.

white knight champion of a good cause

white lead basic lead carbonate, $2(PbCO_3)\cdot Pb(OH)_2$, used on account of its good covering power as a pigment

white lie a lie told for unmalicious reasons and therefore regarded as excusable

White·locke (hwítlɔk, wítlɔk), John (1757-1835), British general who led (1807) the unsuccessful British attack on Buenos Aires. He surrendered (July 6, 1807) to Liniers

white magic magic used in the service of good

white matter (*anat.*) the light-colored neural tissue, esp. of the central nervous system, mainly composed of cell processes (cf. GRAY MATTER)

white metal any of various tin-based alloys, used for bearings, castings etc. ‖ any of various lead-based alloys

White Monk a Cistercian monk

White Mountain, Battle of the a battle (Nov. 8, 1620) during the Thirty Years' War. The forces of the Catholic League, under Tilly, overwhelmed the Bavarian army, ending the Bavarian revolt and suppressing Protestantism in Bavaria

White Mountains a range in N. New Hampshire, part of the Appalachians: Mt Washington, 6,288 ft

whit·en (hwáit'n, wáit'n) *v.t.* to make white ‖ *v.i.* to become white

White Nile the main headstream (2,200 miles long) of the Nile (cf. BLUE NILE). It emerges from Lake Victoria at Ripon Falls and flows north through Lake Kyoga and the Murchison Falls into Lake Albert, then through N.W. Uganda and (as the Bahr-el-Jebel) into the Sudan, becoming the Bahr-el-Abiad ('white river'). It joins the Blue Nile at Khartoum. Its most distant source (the chief affluent of Lake Victoria) is the River Kagera (430 miles long) rising in W. Uganda

whit·en·ing (hwáit'niŋ, wáit'niŋ) *n.* whiting (powdered chalk) ‖ the act or process of making or becoming white

white noise (*acoustics*) nondescript, undefinable static sound used to mask annoying or distracting sound. *also* white sound

white oak *Quercus alba* a large, slow-maturing oak of the eastern U.S.A., yielding a hard wood ‖ this wood

white paper (esp. *Br.*) an informative government report issued on a matter which has received official investigation (cf. BLUE BOOK)

white pepper a powdered condiment obtained by grinding the husked seeds of the peppercorn

white pine *Pinus strobus*, a tall, graceful pine of eastern North America yielding a soft, light-colored wood of great commercial value ‖ this wood

white room *CLEAN ROOM

White Russia Byelorussia

white sauce a sauce made by blending butter and flour with milk, cream or stock

White Sea a gulf (area 36,000 sq. miles) of the Barents Sea on the northern coast of the U.S.S.R., in Europe. It receives the Northern Dvina and Onega Rivers. It is connected to the Baltic via Lakes Ladoga and Onega. Ice is a menace to shipping in winter. Chief port: Archangel

white slave a female held against her will and transported esp. from one state or country to another for purposes of prostitution **white slavery** such prostitution

white·smith (hwáitsmiθ, wáitsmiθ) 1. *n.* a tinsmith ‖ a finisher of metal goods 2. *v.i.* to work as a whitesmith

white sound (*acoustics*) white noise (which see).

white spirit (esp. *pl.*) a mixture of petroleum hydrocarbons, boiling at less than 200°C., used as a solvent and in paints and varnishes

white·throat (hwáitθrout, wáitθrout) *n. Sylvia communis*, an Old World warbler ‖ *Zonotrichia albicollis*, a common brown North American sparrow

white vitriol hydrated zinc sulfate, $ZnSO_4\cdot 7H_4O$

white·wash (hwáitwɔʃ, wáitwɔʃ, hwáitwpʃ, wáitwpʃ) 1. *n.* a liquid mixture of powdered lime or chalk and water, used for whitening walls, ceilings etc. ‖ an act or instance of covering up someone's faults, defects of character etc. ‖ (esp. *Br.*, law) the act or instance of clearing a bankrupt ‖ (*pop.*) a total defeat in a game (i.e. when the loser fails to score) 2. *v.t.* to cover with whitewash ‖ to gloss over or cover up (a person's faults etc.) ‖ (esp. *Br.*, law) to clear (a bankrupt) of liabilities ‖ (*pop.*) to prevent (an opponent) from scoring in a game

white whale *Delphinapterus leucas*, a beluga

whit·ey (hwáiti:) *n.* (*slang*) perjorative term for a white person, esp. as representative of white society

Whit·gift (hwítgift, wítgift), John (c. 1530-1604), English churchman. As archbishop of Canterbury (1583-1604) he attempted to carry out Elizabeth I's policy of establishing religious uniformity

whith·er (hwiðər, wiðər) 1. *adv.* (*rhet.*) to what place, where ‖ (*rhet.*) to what condition, result etc. 2. *conj.* to what place [O.E. *hwider*]

whith·er·so·ev·er (hwiðərsouévər, wiðərsoévər) *adv.* (*archaic*) to whatever place

whit·ing (hwáitiŋ, wáitiŋ) *n.* a finely powdered chalk (calcium carbonate), used in whitewash, putty, paint, polish etc.

whiting *n. Merlangus merlangus*, fam. *Gadidae*, an edible European marine fish ‖ *Merluccius bilinearis*, a common North American hake, important as a food fish ‖ any of various members of *Menticirrhus*, fam. *Sciaenidae*, a genus of North American marine food fishes

whit·ish (hwáitiʃ, wáitiʃ) *adj.* somewhat white

Whitlam (hwítləm, wítləm) (Edward) Gough (1916-) Australian statesman, prime minister (1972-5). He joined the Australian Labor Party (ALP) in 1945, climbing the ranks to the leadership position in 1967. The ALP won the election of 1972, putting Whitlam into the prime ministership. He attempted to make Australia independent of the larger world powers and fought for equal rights, but the failing worldwide economy intervened and his dismissal (1975) by the governor-general was endorsed by a subsequent election. He retired from leadership of the ALP in 1977

Whit·ley Council (hwítli:, wítli:) one of a number of joint boards of employers and workers, for negotiating wages and conditions of service, set up since 1917 in Great Britain in various industries, the civil service and local government [after J. H. *Whitley* (1866-1935), Br. politician]

Whit·lock (hwítlɒk, wítlɒk), Brand (1869-1934), U.S. diplomat and writer. As U.S. minister (1913-22, later ambassador) to Belgium during the German invasion, he saved many innocent Belgians from death at the hands of the German military

whit·low (hwítlou, wítlou) *n.* an infection of the pulp of the finger, esp. near the nail [M.E. *whitflaw, whitflow* perh.=white flaw]

Whit·man (hwítmən, wítmən), Walt (1819-92), American poet. His rhapsodic verse has virtually neither rhyme nor meter, but abounds in oratorical rhythms inspired esp. by Old Testament prophetic writings. His subject matter is his own expansive ego celebrating the democratic society and the wide horizons of developing America. There is an impressiveness in his invocations of America's multiplicity, and warm human feeling in his outgoing sympathy. 'Leaves of Grass' (1855, and several later editions) is his best-known collection

Whit·ney (hwítni:, wítni:), Eli (1765-1825), American inventor and manufacturer. He invented (1783) a mechanical cotton gin and developed the use of machine tools in producing small arms

Whitney, Josiah Dwight (1819-96), American geologist. He surveyed many parts of the U.S.A. and studied their mineral resources

Whitney, William Collins (1841-1904), U.S. lawyer, financier and (1885-9) secretary of the navy under President Grover Cleveland, providing the U.S.A. with an up-to-date naval force

Whitney, Mount the highest peak (14,495 ft) of the Sierra Nevada, California

Whit·sun (hwíts'n, wíts'n) 1. *adj.* of or relating to Whitsuntide 2. *n.* Whitsuntide

Whit·sun·day (hwítsʌ́ndi:, wítsʌ́ndi:, hwítsʌ́ndei, wítsʌ́ndei) *n.* the seventh Sunday after Easter Sunday, commemorating Pentecost [O.E. *Hwíta Sunnandæg,* White Sunday]

Whit·sun·tide (hwítsəntaid, wítsəntaid) *n.* the feast of Pentecost ‖ the holiday period at this time

Whit·ti·er (hwíti:ər, wíti:ər), John Greenleaf (1807-92), American Quaker poet and abolitionist. His most famous poem is 'Snow-Bound' (1866)

Whit·tle (hwít'l, wít'l), Sir Frank (1907-), British engineer. He invented the modern aircraft jet engine, the prototype of which made its first successful flight in 1941

whit·tle (hwít'l, wít'l) *pres. part.* **whit·tling** *past* and *past part.* **whit·tled** *v.t.* to slice pieces from (wood) with a knife ‖ to form (an object) by this method ‖ (*fig.*) to thin down, to reduce bit by bit ‖ *v.i.* to whittle wood **to whittle away** to take away by many small reductions **to whittle down** to reduce drastically by many small reductions [M.E. *thwitel* fr. O.E. *thwitan,* to cut, to pare]

whiz, whizz (hwiz, wiz) 1. *v. pres. part.* **whiz·zing, whizz·ing** *past* and *past part.* **whizzed** *v.i.* (of objects moving through the air at great speed) to make a whirring or hissing sound ‖ *v.t.* to cause to move with such a sound 2. *n.* this sound [imit.]

whiz·zer (hwízə:r) *n.* (*wrestling*) arm lock trapping one's arm against the opponent's body from a position beside the opponent

whiz kid (colloq.) a youth of prodigious intelligence

who (hu:) *pron.* what or which person or persons, *who is that woman?* ‖ which person or persons, *I didn't see who it was* ‖ that, the or a person or persons, *he likes women who dress well* [O.E. *hwā*]

whoa (hwou, wou) *interj.* a command to a horse to stop

who·dun·it (hu:dʌ́nit) *n.* (*pop.*) a detective story, or a play or film based on a detective story [coined from the jocular ungrammatical phrase 'who done it?']

who·ev·er (hu:évər) *pron.* whatever person, *whoever said that is a liar* ‖ (expressing surprise or puzzlement) who, *whoever said a thing like that?*

whole (houl) 1. *adj.* not lacking any part, with no part excepted, *the whole truth* ‖ entire, undivided, *the snake swallowed the rat whole* ‖ containing all its natural components, *whole meal* ‖ not diseased or injured ‖ not broken or damaged ‖ having both parents in common, *whole sister* 2. *n.* something which lacks none of its parts ‖ all that there is of something, *throughout the whole of history* **as a whole** taken altogether, *as a whole the piece isn't bad* **on the whole** everything being considered, *on the whole I agree with him*

whole-bod·y scanner (hóulbɒdi:) (*med.*) device that X-rays the internal tissue of the body and records electronically on a cathode-ray image or prints out instead of on X-ray film. *Cf* CAT SCAN

whole gale a wind having a speed 55-63 m.p.h.

whole-heart·ed (hóulhártid) *adj.* with complete willingness and sincerity

whole meal meal or flour made from the whole grain of wheat

whole milk milk with none of its constituents taken away

whole note (*mus., Am. =Br.* semibreve) a note (symbol ○) equal in duration to two half notes

whole number any number that is not a fraction

whole plate (*Br.*) a photographic plate or film of the size 6 ½ x 8 ½ ins

whole·sale (hóulseil) 1. *n.* the sale of goods in relatively large quantities to be retailed by others (opp. RETAIL) 2. *adj.* of or engaged in buying or selling in this way ‖ sold in this way ‖ on a large scale, indiscriminate, *wholesale slaughter* 3. *adv.* in a wholesale manner 4. *v. pres. part.* **whole·sal·ing** *past* and *past part.* **whole·saled** *v.i.* to be engaged in wholesale selling ‖ to be sold wholesale ‖ *v.t.* to sell (goods) wholesale

whole·some (hóulsəm) *adj.* good for the health, *wholesome food* ‖ healthy, *a wholesome climate* ‖ morally sound, *wholesome advice* [O.E. *hálsum*]

whole step a whole tone

whole tone (*mus.*) an interval consisting of two semitones

whole-tone scale a scale progressing only in whole tones, and hence outside the major and minor systems of ordinary diatonic notation. There are two such scales, one starting on C, the other on C♯

whole wheat *adj.* made of the pure meat of wheat, the whole grain being ground

whol·ly (hóulli:, hóuli:) *adv.* entirely, totally ‖ solely, exclusively [M.E. *holliche, iholliche*]

whom (hu:m) *pron.* the objective case of WHO

whoop (hu:p, hwu:p, wu:p) 1. *n.* a loud cry of joy or excitement ‖ the loud gasping breath taken after a fit of coughing (esp. in whooping cough) ‖ the hoot of an owl ‖ a war cry 2. *v.i.* to utter a loud cry of joy or excitement ‖ to gasp loudly in catching one's breath after a fit of coughing (esp. in whooping cough) ‖ (of an owl) to hoot ‖ *v.t.* to utter with a whoop ‖ (*pop.*) to increase, raise, *to whoop prices* [imit.]

whooping cough, *Br.* also **hooping cough** an infectious bacterial disease esp. prevalent among children, characterized by frequent coughs which are followed by a loud, convulsive intake of breath and often by vomiting

whooping crane *Grus americana,* a North American crane, now almost extinct, known for its mournful whooping cry

whop (hwɒp, wɒp) 1. *n.* (*pop.*) a heavy thud ‖ (*pop.*) a heavy blow 2. *v.t. pres. part.* **whop·ping** *past* and *past part.* **whopped** (*pop.*) to strike with a heavy blow **whóp·per** *n.* (*pop.*) anything uncommonly large of its kind ‖ (*pop.*) a shamelessly blatant big lie **whóp·ping** *adj.* (*pop.*) huge [origin unknown]

whore (hɔr, hour) 1. *n.* a woman who engages in promiscuous sexual intercourse for money 2. *v.i. pres. part.* **whor·ing** *past* and *past part.* **whored** (*rhet.*) to be a whore ‖ (*rhet.*) to fornicate with whores [O.E. *hóre*]

Whorf·i·an hypothesis (hwórfi:ən) (*linguistics*) theory that language determines perception of the world; by Benjamin Lee Whorf, American anthropologist (1941-)

whorl (hwɔrl, wɔrl, hwə:rl, wə:rl) *n.* one of the spiral turns of a univalve shell ‖ a decorative motive resembling this ‖ a circle of flowers or parts of a flower (calyx, corolla etc.) or leaves arising from a node ‖ a small pulley on a spindle in spinning or weaving machinery **whorled** *adj.* [M.E. *wharwyl, whorwhil* prob. variants of WHIRL]

whor·tle·ber·ry (hwɔ́:rt'lberi:, wɔ́:rt'lberi:) *pl.* **whor·tle·ber·ries** *n.* a bilberry or blueberry ‖ a huckleberry

whose (hu:z) *pron.* the possessive case of WHO and, usually, of WHICH (used before a noun as a possessive adjective or absolutely as an interrogative) [M.E. *hwōs* fr. O.E. *hwœs*]

who·so (hú:sou) *pron.* (*archaic*) whoever [M.E. *hwa swa*]

who·so·ev·er (hu:souévər) *pron.* (esp. in legal documents and formal declarations) whoever [M.E. fr. WHOSO+EVER]

why (hwai, wai) 1. *adv.* for what reason, *why were you late?* ‖ with what intention, *why bother?* ‖ on account of which, for which, *I see no reason why you should despair* 2. *n.* the reason, the explanation 3. *interj.* an exclamation expressing surprise, protest, reflection etc. [O.E. *hwī, hwȳ* instrumental case of *hwæt,* what]

whydah *WHIDAH

wic·ca (wíkə) *n.* witchcraft —**wiccan** *adj.*

Wich·i·ta (wítʃitɔ) the chief city (pop. 279,835) of Kansas, a rail center and market on the Arkansas river: meat packing, oil refining, aircraft, food processing

wick (wik) *n.* a piece or bundle of twisted fiber, cord or tape that by capillary action supplies a lamp or candle flame with oil or melted grease ‖ (*med.*) a strip of gauze placed in a wound to drain away fluids [O.E. *wēoce, wēoc*]

wick·ed (wíkid) *adj.* not good morally, violating the rules of morality ‖ malicious, *a wicked tongue* ‖ (*pop.*) trying, unpleasant, troublesome etc., *a wicked winter, a wicked smell, a wicked blight on the tomatoes* ‖ (esp. of a horse) vicious ‖ mischievous, roguish, *a wicked grin* [M.E. fr. *wikke,* evil]

wick·er (wíkər) 1. *n.* twigs or osiers plaited to make baskets, chairs, mats etc. 2. *adj.* consisting of, or made of, wicker [of Scand. origin]

wick·er·work (wíkərwə:rk) *n.* objects made of wicker ‖ the craft of making such objects

wick·et (wíkit) *n.* a small door or gate, esp. one close beside or contained in a larger one ‖ a small window or opening, e.g. at a ticket office ‖ a small gate used to regulate a flow of water (e.g. in a waterwheel), or for emptying the chamber of a canal lock ‖ (*croquet*) one of a series of small metal arches through which the ball is hit ‖ (*cricket*) either of two sets of three stumps crowned by two bails (one set at either end of the pitch) ‖ (*cricket*) the playing space between these two sets, esp. as regards its condition, *a fast wicket* ‖ (*cricket*) an inning of one batsman, *a match won by 10 wickets* ‖ (*cricket*) a period during which a pair stay together batting, *a first-wicket stand* **to keep wicket** (*cricket*) to be wicketkeeper [A.F. *wiket,* etym. doubtful]

wick·et·keep·er (wíkitki:pər) *n.* (*cricket*) the padded and gloved player who fields immediately behind the batsman's wicket, primarily to prevent byes and to catch or stump the batsman

wick·ing (wíkiŋ) *n.* the loosely woven cotton cord or tape used in a lamp or candle wick

wick·i·up (wíki:ʌp) *n.* a cone-shaped hut covered with reeds, grass etc. and used by nomadic Indians in dry regions of the west and southwest U.S.A. [fr. Algonquian]

Wick·low (wíklou) an eastern county (area 782 sq. miles, pop. 87,209) of Leinster province, Irish Republic. County seat: Wicklow (pop. 3,200)

Wicklow Mountains a range in Leinster, S.E. Irish Republic: Lugnaquilla, 3,039 ft

wid·der·shins (wídərʃinz) *adv.* in a counterclockwise direction, esp. thus regarded as unlucky, *to walk widdershins around a billiard table* [fr. M.L.G. *weddersinnes* fr. M.H.G. *wider,* against + *sin,* direction]

wide (waid) 1. *adj.* of relatively large extent from side to side, not narrow, *a wide road, a wide river* ‖ reaching over a vast area, *the wide world* ‖ relatively far apart, *at wide intervals* ‖ of a specified extent from side to side, *a table 2 feet wide* ‖ great in extent, *wide publicity, wide reading* ‖ roomy, loose, *wide sleeves* ‖ fully open, *wide eyes* ‖ (*fig.*, with 'of') far removed from, *wide of the truth* ‖ (*agric.*) containing a relatively small amount of protein compared with fats and carbohydrates, *a wide feed ration* ‖ (*finance,* of prices) fluctuating greatly between the highest and lowest levels ‖ (*phon.*) lax ‖ of considerable scope, *a wide selection of goods* ‖ (*Br., pop.*) sharp-witted but dishonest, *a wide boy* **wide of the mark** far from the point, purpose or truth, *a solution wide of the mark* **2.** *adv.* fully, as much as possible, *the door is wide open* ‖ far from the mark, aim, truth etc., *the remark went wide* **3.** *n.* (*cricket*) a wide ball [O.E. *wīd*]

wide-an·gle (wáidæng'l) *adj.* (of a camera lens) having or covering a wider field of view than an ordinary lens

Wide Area Telecommunications Service a Bell System service that lets contracting customers make or receive calls or transmit data within selected service areas at a fixed monthly rate, in lieu of individual call billing. (*acronym*) WATS

wide-a·wake (wáidəwéik) *adj.* fully awake, with one's eyes wide open ‖ alert, keen

wide ball (*cricket*) a ball judged by the umpire to be beyond the batsman's reach and counting one run to the batting side

wid·en (wáid'n) *v.t.* to make wide or wider ‖ *v.i.* to become wide or wider

wide-o·pen (wáidóupən) *adj.* lax in regulating or prohibiting the sale of alcoholic drinks, tolerating or allowing gambling, vice etc. ‖ open wide ‖ offering unlimited opportunity

wide receiver (*football*) pass receiver stationed at one side of the field

wide·spread (wáidspréd) *adj.* extended over a wide area, *widespread snowstorms* ‖ widely circulated, *widespread rumors*

widg·eon, wig·eon (wídʒən) *n.* any of numerous members of *Mareca,* a genus of freshwater ducks, esp. *M. penelope,* an Old World duck, *M. americana,* the American widgeon and *M. sibilatrix,* of southern South America [etym. doubtful]

Wi·dor (vi:dɔr), Charles Marie Jean Albert (1844-1937), French composer and organist. He was esp. famous for the organ compositions which he called symphonies

wid·ow (wídou) **1.** *n.* a woman who has not married again after her husband's death **2.** *v.t.* to make into a widow [O.E. *widewe, widuwe, wuduwe*]

widow bird any of numerous African weaverbirds, often kept as cage birds. During the breeding season, the males develop drooping tail feathers up to 1 ft in length

wid·ow·er (wídouər) *n.* a man who has not married again after his wife's death

wid·ow·hood (wídouhud) *n.* the state or period of time of being a widow

widow's peak a point formed by the roots of the hair in the center of the forehead

widow's weeds the heavy black mourning apparel, esp. the black veils, worn in many countries by a widow for a certain period [M.E. *wede* fr. O.E. *wǣd,* a garment]

width (widθ) *n.* measurement, distance or extent from side to side, *three feet in width* ‖ a piece of cloth etc. measured and cut, *a width of chintz* [17th-c. coinage]

Wie·de·mann-Franz law (ví:dəmɑnfrɑnts) (*phys.*) a law stating that the ratio of the electrical and thermal conductivities of a metal is proportional to the absolute temperature [after G. H. *Wiedemann* (1826–99) and K. *Franz* (1827–1902), G. physicists]

Wie·land (ví:lɑnt), Christoph Martin (1733-1831), German poet and author. His masterpiece 'Oberon' (1780), a romantic epic, exerted a powerful influence on German literature

wield (wi:ld) *v.t.* to use, exert (power, influence, authority etc.) ‖ to hold and use with the hands, *to wield a sledgehammer* **wield·y** *adj.* nicely balanced for handling, although weighty [fr. O.E. *wealdan* and *wyldan*]

Wie·licz·ka (vjelí:tʃka) a town (pop. 12,000) in Poland near Krakow: salt mining (since the 11th c.)

wie·ner (wí:nər) *n.* (*pop.*) a frankfurter [fr. G. *wienerwurst,* sausage of Vienna]

wie·ner schnit·zel (ví:nərʃnítsəl) *n.* a breaded veal cutlet [G.=Vienna cutlet]

Wies·ba·den (ví:sbɑd'n) the capital (pop. 272,600) of Hesse, West Germany, a commercial center and spa at the foot of the Taunus Mtns: film making, publishing, chemical and pharmaceutical works. It was the capital (1806-66) of the duchy of Nassau

wife (waif) *pl.* **wives** (waivz) *n.* the female partner in a marriage [O.E. *wīf*]

wife·ly (wáifli:) *adj.* of, like or befitting a wife [O.E. *wīflic*]

wig (wig) *n.* an artificial head covering of hair, worn e.g. as part of the official costume of a liveried servant or for ornamentation or for disguise [shortened fr. PERIWIG]

wig·an (wígən) *n.* a coarse canvaslike fabric used as a stiffening in tailoring [after *Wigan,* Lancashire]

wigeon *WIDGEON

wigged (wigd) *adj.* wearing a wig

wig·ging (wígiŋ) *n.* (esp. *Br., pop.*) a severe reprimand or scolding [fr. older *wig,* a wigging]

wig·gle (wíg'l) **1.** *v. pres. part.* **wig·gling** *past* and *past part.* **wig·gled** *v.t.* to cause to move in a small, rapid, to-and-fro, side-to-side or up-and-down movement ‖ *v.i.* to move in this way **2.** *n.* a wiggling movement [rel. to or fr. L.G. or M.L.G. *wiggelen*]

Wig·gles·worth (wíg'lzwə:rθ), Michael (1631-1705), American colonial Calvinistic clergyman, physician and poet. His best known work is 'The Day of Doom; or a Poetical Description of the Great and Last Judgment' (1662), which was used as a catechism for children

Wight, Isle of (wait) (*abbr.* I.O.W.) an island (area 147 sq. miles, pop. 95,000) in the English Channel, forming part of Hamshire. Administrative center: Newport (pop. 19,000). Chief port: Cowes. Industries: agriculture (wheat, fruit and vegetables, sheep), cement, tourism

wig·let (wíglət) *n.* a woman's hairpiece used to shape, lengthen, heighten, or frame a hairstyle

Wig·town (wígtən) a former county (area 485 sq. miles) of S.W. Scotland

wig·wag (wígwæg) **1.** *v. pres. part.* **wig·wag·ging** *past* and *past part.* **wig·wagged** *v.t.* to cause to move to and fro with considerable displacement ‖ *v.i.* to move in this way ‖ to signal by waving flags **2.** *n.* the act or art of wigwagging ‖ a wigwagged message

wig·wam (wígwɒm) *n.* a rounded or oval cabin or hut having a framework of poles, covered with hides, bark etc., used as a dwelling by North American Indians in the area of the Great Lakes and eastward [fr. Algonquian]

Wil·ber·force (wílbərfɔrs), William (1759-1833), British politician and evangelical, social reformer whose efforts resulted in the abolition of the slave trade (1807) and of slavery (1833) in the British Empire

Wil·bye (wílbi:), John (1574-1638), English composer noted esp. for his madrigals

wild (waild) **1.** *adj.* (of plants) propagated and growing without man's intervention ‖ (of animals) uncontrolled by man (opp. TAME, DOMESTICATED) ‖ (of a region) uninhabited and uncultivated by man ‖ uncivilized ‖ unrestrained by caution or convention ‖ fantastic, *wild fancies* ‖ (of the eyes or looks) suggesting near-madness ‖ out of control, *wild laughter* ‖ completely undisciplined, *a wild gang of boys* ‖ (of dress or appearance) peculiar in a fantastic way, *wild garb* ‖ (*pop.*) very angry ‖ (*pop.*) very enthusiastic ‖ irrational, *a wild guess* ‖ (*cards*) of a card which can be substituted for whatever card its player chooses **2.** *adv.* in a wild way **to run wild** to be uncontrolled **3.** *n.* **the wild** nature unspoiled by man **the wilds** great tracts of wild country [O.E. *wilde*]

wild and woolly disorderly and lacking in discipline or polish

wild boar *Sus scrofa,* *BOAR

wild·cat (wáildkæt) **1.** *n. Felis sylvestris,* a European cat larger than the domesticated cat, and with a shorter tail. It was notorious for its fierceness, but is now largely extinct ‖ *Felis ocreata* or *F. caffra,* an undomesticated cat of Africa and S.W. Asia ‖ (*pop.* **wildcat**) any of several other species of small undomesticated cat, e.g. lynx, ocelot ‖ a wildcat petroleum or gas well **2.** *adj.* risky, not to be relied upon, *a wildcat scheme* ‖ (of a petroleum or gas well) drilled in an area where there is no clear evidence that oil exists **3.** *v.i. pres. part.* **wild·cat·ting** *past* and *past part.* **wild·cat·ted** *v.t.* to drill a wildcat well

wildcat bank a bank which, before the National Bank Act of 1863-4, issued notes in excess of its assets

wildcat strike a strike in which the strikers act without the authority of their trade union

Wilde (waild), Oscar (1856-1900), Irish writer, playwright and wit. His fame now rests on the witty nonsense of the plays, esp. 'The Importance of Being Earnest' (1895). He also wrote in an aesthetic, mannered style, e.g. the novel

'The Picture of Dorian Grey,' (1884). He wrote a long poem, 'The Ballad of Reading Gaol' (1898), out of the experience of being imprisoned

wil·de·beest (wíldəbi:st) *n.* the gnu [Afrik.]

Wil·der (wáildər), Thornton (1897-1975), American writer. His works include the novel 'The Bridge of San Luis Rey' (1927) and the plays 'Our Town' (1938) and 'The Skin of Our Teeth' (1942) and 'Theophilus North' (1973)

wil·der·ness (wíldərnis) *n.* an uninhabited and uncultivated region ‖ a part of a large garden made to look as if it were independent of the gardener's mind or work [fr. O.E. *wildēor, wildedēor,* wild deer or *wildēoren,* wild]

wild·fire (wáildfaiər) *n.* (*hist.*) a highly combustible material hurled onto the deck of an enemy vessel in naval warfare **to spread like wildfire** (of rumor, plague etc.) to spread exceedingly fast

wild·fowl (wáildfaul) *pl.* **wild·fowl, wild·fowls** *n.* a game bird, esp. a game waterfowl **wild·fowl·ing** *n.* the sport of hunting such birds

wild goose any species of undomesticated goose, usually migratory from and to the Arctic

wild-goose chase a futile search, esp. one deliberately instigated

wild·ing (wáildiŋ) *n.* a plant sown by natural agencies, esp. a fruit tree ‖ the fruit of such a tree

wild·life (wáildlaif) *n.* animals living in the wild state

wild oat any of several noncultivated members of *Avena,* fam. *Gramineae,* esp. *A. fatua* of Europe **to sow one's wild oats** to indulge in pleasures and escapades (esp. amorous) in one's youth

wild rice *Zizania aquatica,* an aquatic perennial grass of North America, yielding edible grain ‖ *Z. latifolia,* a similar grass of Asia

wild-track (wáildtræk) *adj.* in filming, of an off-track sound, music, or commentary not connected with the story line

wild-wa·ter (wáildwɔtər) *n.* (*envir.*) a stream or river with strong turbulence or current; white water

Wild West the western states of the U.S.A. in the early days of their settlement, when there was no rule of law

wile (wail) **1.** *n.* an artful method of persuasion ‖ a trick using guile so as to deceive or snare **2.** *v.t. pres. part.* **wil·ing** *past* and *past part.* **wiled** to subject to blandishments or to guile **to wile away** to while away [M.E. *wil,* prob. of Scand. origin]

Wil·frid (wílfrid), St (634–c. 709), Anglo-Saxon Benedictine monk, bishop of York. He was influential in winning the victory for the Roman usage in the English Church (*WHITBY, SYNOD OF). Feast: Oct. 12

wilful *WILLFUL

Wil·helm I (vílhelm, wílhelm) (1797-1888), king of Prussia (1861-88), emperor of Germany (1871-88), second son of Frederick William III of Prussia. His plan to reorganize the army, in collaboration with van Roon, roused parliamentary opposition, and led to the appointment (1861) of Bismarck as prime minister. Wilhelm was proclaimed (1871) first Emperor of the Reich, and his reign saw the rise of Germany as a world power. Although often in disagreement with Bismarck, Wilhelm usually followed the latter's policy. Two attempts on Wilhelm's life (1878) were used by Bismarck as an excuse for antisocialist legislation

Wilhelm II (the 'Kaiser') (1859-1941), German emperor and king of Prussia (1888-1918), grandson of Wilhelm I of Germany. He succeeded his father Frederick III (1888) and forced Bismarck to resign (1890). He was the dominating force in the government from then on, trying to forestall socialism in Germany, and to pursue a weltpolitik abroad. His naval, commercial and colonial aspirations (*BAGHDAD RAILWAY) drove Great Britain into the Entente Cordiale with France. His impetuousness, and the alliances he created, contributed largely to the 1st world war. After the war, naval mutiny and civilian revolt led to his flight to Holland (Nov. 10, 1918), where he died in exile

Wil·hel·mi·na (wilhelmí:nə, wiləmí:nə) (1880-1962), queen of the Netherlands (1890-1948). She abdicated in favor of her daughter, Juliana

Wilhelmina a mountain range rising to 4,200 ft in central Surinam

CONCISE PRONUNCIATION KEY: (a) æ, c*a*t; ɑ, c*ar*; ɔ f*aw*n; ei, sn*a*ke. **(e)** e, h*e*n; i:, sh*ee*p; iə, d*ee*r; εə, b*ea*r. **(i)** i, f*i*sh; ai, t*i*ger; ə:, b*ir*d. **(o)** ɔ, *o*x; au, c*ow*; ou, g*oa*t; u, p*oo*r; ɔi, r*oy*al. **(u)** ʌ, d*u*ck; u, b*u*ll; u:, g*oo*se; ə, b*a*cill*u*s; ju:, c*u*be. x, lo*ch*; θ, *th*ink; δ, *b*o*th*er; z, *Z*en; ʒ, cor*s*age; dʒ, *s*ava*ge*; ŋ, ora*n*guta*ng*; j, *y*ak; ʃ, *f*i*sh*; tʃ, fe*tch*; 'l, rab*b*le; 'n, re*dd*en. Complete pronunciation key appears inside front cover.

Wil·helms·ha·ven (vílhelmshɑfən) a port, resort and naval base (pop. 101,000) in N. Lower Saxony, West Germany: shipbuilding, textiles, engineering

wil·i·ly (wáilili:) adv. in a wily way

wil·i·ness (wáili:nis) n. the quality of being wily

Wilkes (wilks), Charles (1798-1877), American naval officer and explorer. He commanded (1838-42) a scientific and exploratory expedition to the South Seas which visited New South Wales, Samoa, Fiji and Hawaii. He crossed the Antarctic Circle to sail along the ice front between 150° and 70° S. and established that Antarctica is a continent

Wilkes, John (1727-97), British radical politician. Outlawed for his scurrilous attacks on the government, he was repeatedly elected to parliament despite ministerial attempts to exclude him. He became a popular champion of parliamentary reform and of the cause of the American colonies in the Revolutionary War

Wil·kins (wílkinz), Sir George Hubert (1888-1958), Australian explorer. He made many expeditions to the Arctic as well as to Antarctica, and carried out pioneer flights in these regions to further exploration

Wil·kin·son (wílkinsən), James (1757-1825), U.S. general. As governor (1805-6) of the Louisiana Territory, he became involved in the schemes of Aaron Burr. Fearing public exposure, he informed President Thomas Jefferson of Burr's plot to disrupt the Union and served as the chief prosecution witness at Burr's trial. He was cleared (1811) of complicity

Wilkinson, John (1728-1808), English ironmaster who built and managed ironworks for large-scale production. The accuracy of his machine for boring cylinders (1774) contributed to the success of Watt's steam engine

will (wil) 1. n. the faculty of determining one's actions || the act or action of willing || something willed, an intention, command or request || moral strength or energy || determination, *the will to win* || disposition towards others, *ill will* || (*law*) a written statement of how one wishes one's property to be dealt with after one's death || the legal document containing this statement **against one's will** contrary to one's own wish **at will** as and when one pleases || (of property) held during the owner's good pleasure || (of a tenant) who may be turned out at any time **of one's own free will, of one's own will** voluntarily, completely without coercion **with a will** heartily, energetically 2. v.t. to dispose of (property) by a will || to ordain by the force of authority, law etc. || to determine by choice, *the separation was willed, not forced* || to dominate so as to control the actions of (someone), e.g. by hypnotic suggestion || v.i. to exercise the will [Ó.E. *willa*]

will *past* **would** (wud) auxiliary v. used to express futurity, usually implying determination, volition, necessity, obligation or acquiescence || used to express habit, *she will cry for hours at a time* || used to express ability or sufficiency, *this will be a suitable gift* || used to express probability, *this will be his reasoning* || used to express command, *everyone will meet here* || v.i. to wish, *try as they will they don't succeed* || v.t. to wish, choose, *do what you will* (cf. SHALL, cf. SHOULD, cf. WOULD) [O.E. *wyllan*]

Wil·laert (vílɑrt), Adrian (c. 1480-1562), Flemish composer, working chiefly at St Mark's, Venice. He wrote great double choir motets for antiphonal singing, Masses and madrigals

wil·let (wílit) n. *Catoptrophorus semipalmatus*, a large North American sandpiper, allied to the snipe [imit. of its call]

will·ful, wil·ful (wílfəl) adj. by intention, not accidental, *willful damage* || acting according to one's own desire, regardless of the dictates of others or of reason **will·ful·ly** adv.

William emperors of Germany *WILHELM

Wil·liam I (wíljəm) 'the Conqueror' (c. 1027-87), king of England (1066-87), son of Robert I of Normandy. As duke of Normandy (1035-87), he defeated (1054 and 1058) Henri I of France, and conquered Maine (1063). Claiming that Edward the Confessor had promised him (1051) the English throne, and that the promise had been renewed (1064) by Harold of Wessex, he invaded England (1066), defeating and killing Harold at Hastings. He imposed his rule on England by ravaging wide areas and distributing estates to his followers. He appointed (1070) Lanfranc archbishop of Canterbury and ordered Domesday Book to be drawn up (1086).

He dealt firmly with risings (1070-1, 1075 and 1082) and spent the end of his reign fighting in France

William II 'Rufus' (c. 1056-1100), king of England (1087-1100), son of William I. Sporadically at war with his elder brother Robert, duke of Normandy, he resorted to financial extortion. He appointed Anselm archbishop of Canterbury (1093) and their quarrel (1095-7) began the rift between Church and State. William was killed by an arrow while hunting in the New Forest

William III (1650-1702), king of England, Scotland and Ireland (1689-1702), son of William II of Orange. As stadtholder of the Netherlands (1672-1702) he emerged as the leader of European resistance to Louis XIV's aggression, defending the Netherlands against French invasions (1672-8), and marrying (1677) Mary, the Protestant daughter of the future James II of England. Invited by a group of political leaders to intervene in England (1688), he invaded and, after James II had fled to France, was proclaimed (1689) joint sovereign with his wife, Mary II. He brought England into the Grand Alliance (1689) against Louis XIV, defeated an invasion of Ireland by James II in a decisive victory at the Boyne (1690), gained favorable terms at Ryswick (1697), and renewed the anti-French alliance in the War of the Spanish Succession (1701-14)

William IV (1765-1837), king of Great Britain (1830-7), son of George III. His threat to create sufficient Whig peers to secure the passage of the Reform Bill of 1832 persuaded the Lords to agree to the measure

William I 'the Silent' (1533-84), prince of Orange, stadtholder of Holland, Zeeland and Utrecht (1555-84). He led the struggle of the northern provinces of the Netherlands for independence from Spanish rule. He was assassinated

William II (1626-50), prince of Orange, stadtholder of the Netherlands (1647-50). In the hope of extending his territory to the whole of the Low Countries he tried to renew the struggle with Spain after the Treaties of Westphalia

William III prince of Orange *WILLIAM III, king of England

William I (1772-1843), first king of the Netherlands and grand duke of Luxembourg (1815-40). The Congress of Vienna (1815) gave him the throne of what is now Belgium, the Netherlands and Luxembourg, but his autocratic attempts to impose Dutch supremacy caused Belgium to break away (1830). In the face of growing discontent he abdicated

William II 'the Lion' (1143-1214), king of Scotland (1165-1214). He formed an alliance with France (1168) but was captured by Henry II of England and forced to recognize English overlordship (1174). He bought political independence from Richard I of England (1189)

William and Mary, College of a state liberal arts university at Williamsburg, Va., founded by James Blair and chartered (1693) by King William and Queen Mary. The second oldest university in the U.S.A., it was the first to establish a law school

William Augustus *CUMBERLAND

William of Malmes·bur·y (mámzbəri) (d. c. 1143), English monk and historian. His 'Gesta regum Anglorum' and 'Historia novella' are authorities for Anglo-Norman history

William of Oc·cam (ókəm) (c. 1285–c. 1349), English nominalist philosopher. He was a Franciscan of independent thought, critical of Scholasticism and of the temporal power of the papacy. He opened the way for the Reformation by distinguishing between faith and reason. He was one of the first Christian thinkers to advocate the separation of Church and State

William of Tyre (c. 1130–c. 1185), archbishop of Tyre (1175–c. 1185), and historian of the Crusades to 1184

William of Wyke·ham (wíkəm) (1324-1404), English bishop and statesman. He was lord chancellor (1367-71 and 1389-91). He founded New College, Oxford (1379) and Winchester College at Winchester (1382)

Wil·liams (wíljəmz), Eric (1911-81), Trinidadian politician, leader of the People's National Movement, and prime minister (1962-81) of Trinidad and Tobago. He led his nation to independence (1962) from Britain and thereafter pursued a moderate policy opposed (1970) by black militants

Williams, Sir George (1821-1905), British philanthropist and founder (1844) of the Young Men's Christian Association (Y.M.C.A.)

Williams, Roger (c. 1603-83), colonial American clergyman who founded (1636) Providence (Rhode Island), which served as a refuge from religious persecution. He secured (1644) for his colony a grant from Parliament of absolute liberty of conscience, confirmed (1663) by royal charter

Williams, Tennessee (1914-83), American playwright, whose works convey the sexual tensions and suppressed violence of his characters, often in the idiom of his native South. His prodigious output of plays includes 'The Glass Menagerie' (1945), 'A Streetcar Named Desire' (1947), 'Cat on a Hot Tin Roof' (1955) 'Sweet Bird of Youth' (1959; film, 1961), and 'The Night of the Iguana' (1961; film, 1964). He also wrote film scripts, short stories, verse and novels, notably 'The Roman Spring of Mrs. Stone' (1950; film, 1961)

Williams, William Carlos (1883-1963), American poet. His long poem 'Paterson' appeared in five volumes (1946-1958)

Wil·li·brord (wílibrɔrd), St (658-739), Northumbrian missionary. He evangelized Friesland. Feast: Nov. 7

wil·lies, the (wíli:z) pl. n. (pop.) a mood of being jumpy, nervous and ill-at-ease

will·ing (wíliŋ) adj. working, helping etc. readily || done, given etc. readily || favorably disposed (to do something) || of the power of the will

Will·kie (wílki:), Wendell Lewis (1892-1944), U.S. industrialist and political leader. He ran as the Republican candidate against President Franklin D. Roosevelt in the 1940 presidential race, supporting Roosevelt's foreign policy program but vigorously attacking his New Deal. He was defeated, but polled the largest popular vote (22 million) ever received by a defeated candidate up to that time

will-o'-the-wisp (wíləðəwisp) n. a small volume of marsh gas emitted by the rotting vegetable matter in a marsh and oxidizing rapidly enough to emit light as it moves above the marsh || an objective which is beyond attainment or in some way illusory [older *Will with the wisp* (wisp=torch of burning hay or straw)]

Wil·lough·by (wíləbi:), Sir Hugh (d. 1554), English explorer. He died in an attempt to discover the Northeast Passage

wil·low (wílou) 1. n. a member of *Salix*, fam. *Salicaceae*, a genus of trees or shrubs, comprising 300 species, mainly of north temperate and arctic regions, usually growing near surface water. They bear catkins and have tough, pliable shoots and branches (*OSIER) || the wood of such a tree || (*Br., rhet.*) a cricket bat made of this wood || a machine used to beat, pick and cleanse raw wool etc. 2. v.t. to deal with (raw wool etc.) using this machine [O.E. *welig*]

willow herb a member of *Epilobium*, fam. *Onagraceae*, esp. *E. angustifolium*, a perennial plant with a purple racemose inflorescence, common on burnt and waste ground, esp. in temperate regions

willow pattern a usually blue chinoiserie china design featuring a willow and a little bridge, originating in Nanking and introduced into England c. 1780

wil·low·y (wíloui:) adj. slender and graceful || abounding in willows

will·pow·er (wílpauər) n. the power of controlling one's actions and emotions by an effort of the will

Will·stät·ter (vílʃtɛtər), Richard (1872-1942), German chemist, awarded the Nobel prize (1915) for his investigation of plant pigments

Wil·lugh·by (wíləbi:), Francis (1635-72), English naturalist. He worked on a systematic classification of birds and fishes, and traveled on the Continent with John Ray, collecting material for his 'Ornithologia' (1676)

wil·ly-nil·ly (wíli:níli:) adv. whatever the will of the person involved may be [fr. older *will I, nill I*, if I wish, if I do not wish]

Wil·ming·ton (wílmiŋtən) the largest city and port of entry (pop. 70,195) in Delaware: shipyards, tanneries, manufactures (rubber goods, iron and steel, textiles, leather, machinery, chemicals). It is the seat of DuPont Industries

Wil·mot Proviso (wílmət) an amendment initiated by U.S. Representative David Wilmot (1814-68) to a congressional bill, twice defeated (1846, 1847). It called for the prohibition of slavery and involuntary servitude in the terri-

---

CONCISE PRONUNCIATION KEY: (**a**) æ, c**a**t; ɑ, c**a**r; ɔ f**aw**n; ei, sn**a**ke. (**e**) e, h**e**n; i:, sh**ee**p; iə, d**ee**r; ɛə, b**ea**r. (**i**) i, f**i**sh; ai, t**i**ger; ə:, b**i**rd. (**o**) o, **o**x; au, c**ow**; ou, g**oa**t; u, p**oo**r; ɔi, r**oy**al. (**u**) ʌ, d**u**ck; u, b**u**ll; u:, g**oo**se; ə, b**a**cillus; ju:, c**u**be. x, lo**ch**; θ, **th**ink; ð, bo**th**er; z, **Z**en; ʒ, corsa**g**e; dʒ, sava**g**e; ŋ, orangutan**g**; j, **y**ak; ʃ, **f**ish; tʃ, **f**etch; 'l, rabb**le**; 'n, redd**en**. Complete pronunciation key appears inside front cover.

tory newly acquired from Mexico. The Wilmot Proviso polarized the conflict between abolitionists and the advocates of slavery. This tension was relieved only by the Compromise of 1850

Wil·son (wílsən), Charles Thompson Rees (1869-1961), Scottish physicist. He invented the Wilson cloud chamber (*CLOUD CHAMBER). Nobel prize (1927)

Wilson, Edmund (1895-1972), American literary critic and writer. 'Axel's Castle' (1931), an analysis of symbolism, is the best known of his books of criticism. 'Memoirs of Hecate County' (1946) is a collection of satirical stories and sketches

Wilson, Henry Lane (1857-1932), U.S. ambassador to Mexico during the Mexican Revolution (1910-21). An opponent of President Francisco Madero's regime, he entered a claim for damages sustained by U.S. citizens as a result of the revolutionary turmoil and urged U.S. President William H. Taft to intervene against Madero's government. He gave active support to Victoriano Huerta's takeover, and was believed to have colluded in the assassination (1913) of Madero and Vice-president Pino Suárez. During the interim before the inauguration of U.S. President Woodrow Wilson, he resigned his ambassadorial post

Wilson, James (1742-98), U.S. jurist. He was largely responsible for writing into the Constitution the principle that sovereignty resides in the people. He was made (1790) the first professor of law at what became the University of Pennsylvania

Wilson, James Harold (1916-   ), British Labour statesman. He led the Labour party to victory in the 1964 general election, and was prime minister (1964-70, 1974-6). He was knighted (1976) upon his retirement as prime minister and Labour party leader

Wilson, Richard (1714-82), English painter. He painted actual English and Italian scenes and typical 18th-c. idealized landscapes. His feeling for the spirit of the countryside, its forms, colors and atmosphere, was important in the development of landscape art

Wilson, Thomas Woodrow (1856-1924), 28th president (1913-21) of the U.S.A., a Democrat. He served (1902-10) as the first nonclerical president of Princeton University. A division in Republican ranks helped to elect him president. His administration lowered tariffs, established (1913) the Federal Reserve System, created (1914) the Federal Trade Commission, and secured (1914) passage of the Clayton Anti-Trust Act. The 17th, 18th, and 19th amendments were implemented during his administration. The general disorder prevailing in Mexico during the Revolution induced him to send (1914) U.S. Marines to Veracruz and (1915) Gen. John Pershing across the border to pacify Pancho Villa. He dispatched U.S. marines to Haiti (1915), the Dominican Republic (1916), and Cuba (1917). He favored neutrality early in the 1st world war, but later led the U.S.A. to declare war (1917) on Germany. He proposed (1918) the Fourteen Points as a possible basis of peace, and attended (1919) the peace conference in Paris. The Treaty of Versailles failed to fulfill his hopes, and though he was instrumental in establishing the League of Nations, the U.S. Senate refused to ratify U.S. membership in it

Wilson cloud chamber *CLOUD CHAMBER

Wilson, Mount a mountain (5,710 ft) in S.W. California, site of an observatory (1904)

Wilson's disease (*med.*) an inherited abnormality in copper metabolism affecting the liver and nervous system; named for S. A. K. Wilson, U.S. neurosurgeon. *also* hepatolenticular degeneration

wilt (wilt) 1. *v.i.* (of plants) to become limp due to a deficiency of water ‖ to lose strength or freshness ‖ *v.t.* to cause to wilt 2. *n.* the act of wilting or state of being wilted ‖ (*bot.*) a disease characterized by the drying out of terminal shoots, branches etc., or this drying-out condition [perh. alt. of older *welk*, to fade]

Wil·ton (wíltən) *n.* a carpet with the loops cut to form a soft, elastic pile, commonly patterned with designs suggesting Oriental design [after *Wilton*, England, where it was originally made, and still is]

Wilt·shire (wíltʃiər) (*abbr.* Wilts.) a county (area 1,345 sq. miles, pop. 513,800) of S.W. England. County town: Salisbury. Administrative center: Trowbridge (pop. 15,000)

wil·y (wáili:) *comp.* **wil·i·er** *superl.* **wil·i·est** *adj.* full of wiles, cunning

wim·ble (wímb'l) 1. *n.* a boring tool, e.g. a gimlet ‖ a tool for twisting rope 2. *v.t. pres. part.* **wim·bling** *past* and *past part.* **wim·bled** to twist (rope) with a wimble [A.F. fr. M.L.G.]

wimp (wimp) *n.* (*colloq.*) one who is unimportant, overly solicitous, or out-of-touch

wim·ple (wímp'l) 1. *n.* a covering for the head and neck and the sides of the face, worn by women in medieval times and still worn by many orders of nuns 2. *v.t. pres. part.* **wimpling** *past* and *past part.* **wim·pled** to clothe with a wimple ‖ to cause to ripple ‖ *v.i.* to fall in folds [O.E. *wimpel*]

win (win) 1. *v. pres. part.* **win·ning** *past* and *past part.* **won** (wʌn) *v.i.* to come first in a contest ‖ to achieve a victory ‖ (sometimes with 'out') to triumph, prevail ‖ (with 'through' etc.) to succeed, after a struggle, in reaching a certain state or place ‖ *v.t.* to achieve victory in (a fight, argument, contest etc.) ‖ to obtain by effort, *to win recognition, to win land back from the sea* ‖ to gain (the affection, esteem etc.) of another or others ‖ (often with 'over') to persuade (another) to accept one's point of view, cause etc. ‖ (*mining*) to extract (a mineral) from the surrounding rocks ‖ to extract (a metal) from its ore 2. *n.* a victory in a contest ‖ money etc. won, e.g. on a race [O.E. *winnan*]

wince (wins) 1. *v.i. pres. part.* **winc·ing** *past* and *past part.* **winced** to draw suddenly back slightly and become more rigid, from pain or as if from pain 2. *n.* a wincing [A.F.]

wince *n.* (*Br.*) a winch (reel over which a textile laps) [var. of WINCH]

winch (wintʃ) 1. *n.* a large wheel turned by a handle or motor and having attached to its axle a cable or chain, by means of which a load may be raised or lowered ‖ the crank of a revolving part of a machine ‖ a reel over which a textile laps, enabling the textile to be dipped into either of two vats 2. *v.t.* to haul with or as if with a winch [O.E. *wince*]

Win·ches·ter (wíntʃistər, wíntʃestər) a town (pop. 31,100) in Hampshire, England. Norman and Gothic cathedral (11th-14th cc.), boys' school (Winchester College, 1382)

Winchester *n.* an early type of breech-loading rifle, supplied automatically with fresh cartridges from a magazine [after O.F. *Winchester*, U.S. inventor]

Winck·el·mann (víŋkəlmɑn), Johann Joachim (1717-68), German archaeologist. His 'History of Ancient Art' (1764) marked the beginning of the academic study of classic art

wind (waind) 1. *v. pres. part.* **wind·ing** *past* and *past part.* **wound** (waund) *v.i.* to go or move in a curved path, esp. in one which is sinuous or spiral ‖ to move in this way so as to encircle ‖ *v.t.* to cause to wind ‖ to make (one's or its way) in a winding course ‖ to cause to encircle, *he wound a bandage around his arm* ‖ to cause to assume an elliptical or round shape, or to coil ‖ (often with 'up') to tighten the spring of by turning the screw or handle of (a clock, watch etc.) ‖ (often with 'up') to hoist by means of a winch etc. **to wind up** to conclude, *he wound up with a quotation* ‖ to bring (some activity) to a stop and regulate its affairs, *to wind up a business* ‖ to come to an end, stop ‖ to arrive at a specified condition or place, *they'll wind up in jail* 2. *n.* a winding or an instance of this ‖ a bend in a sinuous course [O.E. *windan*]

wind (wind) 1. *n.* a large body of air in rapid natural motion, its speed often being expressed (*BEAUFORT SCALE) in terms of the force it exerts on an obstacle to its motion. Its direction is that from which it comes, *a west wind* ‖ air set locally in motion, *he felt the wind it made as it rushed past him* ‖ air made to vibrate and thus produce sound, e.g. in the pipe or tube of a musical instrument ‖ (*mus., collect.*) the wind instruments (brass and woodwind) of an orchestra ‖ (*mus., pl.*) the players of such instruments ‖ breath, air drawn into or expelled from the lungs ‖ the ability to breathe air into the lungs ‖ (*boxing*) the solar plexus ‖ gas produced in the stomach and intestinal tract during digestion ‖ words spoken or written which have little significance **before the wind** (*naut.*) with the wind astern **close to** (or **near**) **the wind** (*naut.*) with the wind almost directly on the bow ‖ very close to indecency, or close to breaking the law **in the teeth of the wind, in the wind's eye** (*naut.*) with the wind directly on the bow of the boat **in the wind** in preparation or about to occur **off the wind** (*naut.*) with the wind on

either quarter **on the wind** (*naut.*) with the wind on either bow **to break wind** to release intestinal gases **to cast** (or **fling** or **throw**) **to the wind** (or **winds**) to reject on sudden impulse, *to cast one's scruples to the winds* **to get** (or **have**) **the wind up** (*Br.*) to become (or be) frightened **to get wind of** to have scent or sound of (a hunter etc.) brought by a wind ‖ to receive information about (something secret) **to put the wind up someone** (*Br.*) to frighten someone **to see how the wind blows** to find out the state of affairs in order to judge what is likely to happen **to take the wind out of someone's sails** (*naut.*) to sail to the windward of a sailing vessel ‖ to frustrate someone, e.g. by saying what he was about to say, giving the reasons he was about to give etc. 2. *v.t.* to cause to breathe with difficulty, either by exertion or by a blow to the diaphragm ‖ to receive the scent of ‖ to allow to recover breath by giving a rest to (a horse etc.) ‖ (waind, wind) *pres. part.* **wind·ing** *past* and *past part.* **wind·ed, wound** (waund) to sound (a horn or a note) [O.E.]

wind·age (wíndidʒ) *n.* the effect of the wind in deflecting a projectile, or the amount of this ‖ the allowance for this ‖ the difference in diameter between a bore of a firearm and the projectile ‖ the surface of e.g. a ship which is exposed to the wind

wind·bag (wíndbæg) *n.* a person who talks a great deal but who says nothing of importance ‖ a bag containing compressed air, e.g. in bagpipes

wind·blown (wíndbloun) *adj.* blown or as if blown by the wind ‖ (of trees) having a permanently twisted shape because of strong prevailing winds

wind·borne (wíndbɔrn, wíndbourn) *adj.* carried along by the wind

wind·break (wíndbreik) *n.* a row of trees or other means of providing shelter from the wind

wind·break·er (wíndbreikər) *n.* (*Am.*=*Br.* windcheater) an outer garment of leather or other wind-resistant material, gathered at the wrists and waist ‖ a windbreak

wind-bro·ken (wíndbroukən) *adj.* (of a horse) having the heaves

wind·cheat·er (wíndtʃi:tər) *n.* (*Br.*) a windbreaker (outer garment)

wind-chill factor (wíndtʃil) 1. the effect of wind velocity in raising or lowering discomfort caused by the temperature 2. an estimate of the effect of temperature and wind on people. *Cf* COMFORT INDEX, THI

wind cone a wind sock

wind down *v.* to bring to an end gradually

wind·er (wáindər) *n.* a device for winding, esp. the stem of a watch ‖ one of the steps in a spiral staircase

Win·der·mere (wíndərmiər) the largest English lake (10 miles long, up to 1 mile wide), in Lancashire and Westmorland, in the Lake District

wind·fall (wíndfɔl) *n.* a fruit blown off a tree by the wind ‖ something of value received unexpectedly, without any effort of one's own to secure it ‖ a tree blown down by the wind, or a piece of ground where trees have been blown down

windfall *adj.* of unexpected income or profit, esp. as the result of new laws —**windfall** *adj.*

wind-flow·er (wíndflauər) *n.* the anemone

wind·gall (wíndgɔl) *n.* a soft tumor on a horse's fetlock **wind-galled** *adj.*

wind gap a narrow pass in a mountain ridge, without a river in it

wind gauge an anemometer ‖ an instrument for measuring the supply of wind in an organ bellows

Wind·hoek (vínthuk) the capital (pop. 36,051) of Namibia, in a pastoral and mining region

wind·hov·er (wíndhʌvər, wíndhɒvər) *n.* (esp. *Br.*) a kestrel

wind·i·ly (wíndili:) *adv.* in a windy manner

wind·i·ness (wíndi:nis) *n.* the state or quality of being windy

wind·ing (wáindiŋ) 1. *n.* the act of someone or something that winds ‖ one complete turn of something which is wound ‖ the way in which something (e.g. a coil) is wound, *a shunt winding* ‖ the act of blowing a horn 2. *adj.* which winds ‖ discursive, rambling

winding drum a power-driven cylinder around which hoisting tackle is wound

winding engine an engine used for hoisting

winding frame a machine which winds yarn or thread

CONCISE PRONUNCIATION KEY: **(a)** æ, c*a*t; ɑ, c*a*r; ɔ f*aw*n; ei, sn*a*ke. **(e)** e, h*e*n; i:, sh*ee*p; iə, d*ee*r; ɛə, b*ea*r. **(i)** i, f*i*sh; ai, t*i*ger; ə:, b*i*rd. **(o)** o, *o*x; au, c*ow*; ou, g*oa*t; u, p*oo*r; ɔi, r*oy*al. **(u)** ʌ, d*u*ck; u, b*u*ll; u:, g*oo*se; ə, b*a*cillus; ju:, c*u*be. x, lo*ch*; θ, *th*ink; ð, bo*th*er; z, *Z*en; ʒ, cor*s*age; dʒ, sava*g*e; ŋ, orangutan*g*; j, *y*ak; ʃ, *f*ish; tʃ, fe*tch*; 'l, rabb*le*; 'n, redd*en*. Complete pronunciation key appears inside front cover.

winding sheet a shroud (long sheet)

wind instrument a musical instrument which produces sound by the vibration of air in a pipe or tube (the bassoon, clarinet, oboe, flute, saxophone etc. are woodwinds; the horn, trombone, trumpet, tuba etc. are brass winds)

Win·disch·gräts (víndiʃgrɛts), Alfred, Fürst zu (1787-1862), Austrian field marshal. He put down revolutions in Austria and Bohemia (1848)

wind·jam·mer (wínddʒæmər) n. (hist.) a large, fast merchant sailing vessel, esp. one fully rigged

wind·lass (wíndləs) n. a machine consisting of an axle around which a cable or chain is wound when a large wheel is turned, used for hauling and hoisting [altered after older *windle*, to wind, fr. M.E. *windas*, a windlass fr. O.N.]

wind loading provision for stress created by the wind on a high structure

wind·mill (wíndmɪl) n. a mill worked by sails turned by the wind, esp. to grind grain ‖ a pinwheel **to tilt at windmills** to expend energy in overcoming imaginary obstacles or opponents

win·dow (wíndou) n. an opening in the wall of a room, building etc. permitting light to enter, usually fitted with glass in a frame of wood or metal which may be partly slid, or turned on hinges, to permit air to pass ‖ a sash, casement etc. designed to fit such an opening ‖ the space directly behind such an opening used for displaying goods in a store case. ‖ a window pane ‖ an opening resembling a window, e.g. that in a window envelope ‖ (*meteor.*) area on earth not closed to extraterrestrial observation by absorption of electromagnetic radiation of most wavelengths ‖ (*meteor.*) a time slot in cycles of celestial bodies when an atmospheric penetration is advantageous ‖ a period when an opening appears, e.g., when a nation's defenses are down ‖ (*mil.*) an area on enemy's defense through which a missile or spacecraft can pass advantageously ‖ (*electr.*) wavelength through which electromagnetic observation is advantageous [M.E. *windoge* fr. O.N.]

window box a box resting on or outside a window sill in which plants can be cultivated ‖ a hollow within the sides of a sash window frame containing a heavy weight on the end of a sash cord to balance the weight of the sash

window dressing the displaying of goods in a store window ‖ the presenting of facts in such a way that a more favorable judgment is made than they warrant

window envelope an envelope with an aperture through which the address written on the contents shows

win·dow·pane (wíndoupein) n. a sheet of glass forming part of a window

window screen a wooden frame fitted with fine wire mesh or cotton netting for use on open doors and windows to keep insects out

window seat a seat, often forming the lid of a chest, built into a window bay

win·dow-shop (wíndouʃɒp) pres. part. **window-shop·ping** past and past part. **window-shopped** v.i. to look at goods displayed in store windows without going inside to buy

win·dow·sill (wíndousɪl) n. the sill of a window

wind·pipe (wíndpaip) n. the trachea

wind-pol·li·nat·ed (wíndpɒlineitid) adj. (*bot.*) fertilized by pollen carried on the wind

wind pump a pump activated by the force of the wind turning a vaned propeller wheel

wind rose (*meteor.*) diagram designed to show distribution of wind directions at a specified time and place, sometimes with speed groupings

wind·row (wíndrou) 1. n. a row of cut grass, wheat etc. raked up to dry in the wind ‖ a line of dust, leaves etc. piled up by the wind ‖ a trench in which sugar canes are laid to root 2. v.t. to arrange in a windrow

wind·sail (wíndseil) n. a canvas funnel or tube for ventilating the lower decks of a ship

wind scale a numerical scale measuring the velocity of wind (*BEAUFORT SCALE)

wind·screen (wíndskriːn) n. (*Br.*) a windshield

wind·shield (wíndʃiːld, wínʃiːld) n. (*Am.=Br.* windscreen) a sheet of glass in the front of a car or other vehicle to protect the driver and other occupants from wind, dust etc.

wind sleeve a wind sock

wind sock a fabric bag, with the shape of a cone and open at both ends, erected on a tall pole to indicate wind direction. It is distended by the

wind pressure through it, and is used esp. on airfields

Wind·sor (wínzər) the name adopted (1917) by the British royal house. Elizabeth II announced (1960) that her descendants, except those entitled to the title of prince or princess, will take the surname Mountbatten-Windsor

Windsor a town (pop. 27,000) in Berkshire, England, on the Thames, site of Windsor Castle (14th c., much restored, a royal residence, with a celebrated collection of paintings and drawings) and of Eton College

Windsor a port (pop. 192,083) in Ontario, Canada, across the Detroit River from Detroit: automobiles, chemical industries, metalworking

Windsor chair a plain wooden chair with or without arms, having a hoop-shaped back filled in with upright spindles. It has turned legs which are slightly raked, and a saddle seat

Windsor, duke of the title conferred (1936) on Edward VIII of Great Britain and Northern Ireland after his abdication

wind·storm (wíndstɔrm) n. a storm characterized by violent winds and occasionally accompanied by rain

wind·surf·ing (wíndsəːrfɪŋ) n. (*surfing*) employment of a specially designed surfboard with an independently swiveling mast, using the body as a stabilizing force

wind·swept (wíndswɛpt) adj. frequently raked by strong winds

wind tunnel a tunnel-like structure through which air can be forced at any required speed in order to test its effect on scale models of aircraft

wind·up (wáindʌp) n. the act of winding up or ending ‖ the last item bringing an entertainment or activity to a close ‖ (*baseball*) a swing of the arm before pitching

wind·ward (wíndwərd) 1. n. the direction from which a wind blows (opp. LEEWARD) 2. adj. in this direction ‖ of that side of a vessel etc. on which the wind blows 3. adv. towards the source of the wind

Windward Islands the name of two island groups, one in the West Indies, the other (Iles du Vent) in French Polynesia (*SOCIETY ISLANDS). The West Indian group forms the southern chain of the Lesser Antilles. It consists of Barbados, Dominica, Grenada, the Grenadines, St Lucia and St Vincent, and the French island of Martinique

wind·y (wíndi:) comp. **wind·i·er** superl. **wind·i·est** adj. exposed to frequent winds, *a windy corner* ‖ accompanied or characterized by wind, *one windy night* ‖ afflicted with stomach or intestinal gas ‖ wordy and without much significance, *a windy speech* ‖ (*Br., pop.*) frightened

wine (wain) 1. n. a drink made of the fermented juice of grapes ‖ a beverage prepared from fermented plant or fruit juice, *rhubarb wine* ‖ (*med.*) a solution of a drug in wine, *quinine wine* ‖ the dark, reddish-purple color of red wine 2. v.t. pres. part. **win·ing** past and past part. **wined** to entertain with wine, *to wine and dine someone* [O.E. *wīn* fr. L.]

—Red wine derives its color from the skins of dark-skinned grapes, which are left in the juice for some days while it ferments before the fruit is put through the press. White wine (often pale yellow) is made from the juice of light-skinned grapes, the fruit being put through the press as soon as it is picked. The alcoholic content of wine varies according to the kind of grape and the conditions of ripening etc. The flavor (*BOUQUET) is due to the esters and ethers present. Fermentation is largely completed in vats or casks, though for some white wines it may continue after bottling, giving a sparkling wine

wine cellar a cellar for storing wine

wine gallon *GALLON

wine·glass (wáinglæs, wáinglɑs) n. a small glass, usually with a slender stem and a foot, used for drinking wine, different shapes and sizes being customarily used for different types of wine

wine-grow·er (wáingrouər) n. someone who grows grapes for making wine

wine gum (*Br.*) a gumdrop

wine palm any of various palms whose sap is used to make palm wine

wine·press (wáinprɛs) n. a vat or machine in which the juice is extracted from grapes for wine making

wine·skin (wáinskɪn) n. a skin, usually of a goat, sewed into a bag in which wine can be carried

wing (wɪŋ) 1. n. one of the specialized appendages used by a bird, bat, insect etc. in flying ‖ such an appendage in a flightless bird, e.g. the ostrich ‖ one of the structures, on either side of the fuselage of an aircraft, which support the machine in the air ‖ a section of a building projecting from the central section ‖ a division of an army or a fleet to the right or left of the central division ‖ a faction within an organization or political party ‖ (*soccer, hockey* etc.) a position in the forward line furthest from the center, or the player occupying it ‖ something resembling a wing in form, function or position, e.g. a lateral expansion on many fruits and seeds which serves in wind dispersal, or the cartilage of the nose forming the nostrils etc. ‖ (*Br.*) a fender of a motor vehicle ‖ a subunit of an air force ‖ a side-piece fitting into the back of an easy chair as a head support or draft excluder ‖ (*theater, pl.*) the area just offstage right or left ‖ (*theater*) a piece of stage scenery, esp. a flat, which masks this area ‖ (*pl.*) insignia of proficiency worn by air force personnel ‖ one of the two lateral petals of a papilionaceous flower **on the wing** in flight **to clip someone's wings** to restrict someone's freedom of action **to lend wings to** (*rhet.*) to increase the speed of, *fear lent wings to his flight* **to take under one's wing** to assume a measure of protection for (someone), esp. by promoting his interests **to take wing** to fly away **under the wing of** in the state of having one's interests looked after by 2. v.i. to fly ‖ v.t. to equip with wings ‖ to wound in the wing [M.E. *wenge, wengen, wenges* fr. O.N.]

Win·gate (wíngeit, wíngeit), Orde Charles (1903-44), British army officer. As commander of the British and Chindit forces in Burma (1942-3) he developed the art of jungle guerrilla warfare

wing back formation (*football*) an attacking formation in which a back is immediately behind the end

wing case an elytron in insects

wing chair an easy chair the back of which has projecting sidepieces providing shelter from drafts and also a head support

wing commander an officer in the Royal Air Force ranking below a group captain and above a squadron leader

wing covert one of the small feathers lying over the flight feathers of a bird's wing

winged (wɪŋd, esp. *rhet.* wɪŋid) adj. having wings ‖ wounded in the wing

wing nut a butterfly nut

wing·spread (wíŋsprɛd) n. the distance between the tips of the fully spread wings of a bird ‖ the distance from wing tip to wing tip of an aircraft

wink (wɪŋk) 1. v.i. to close an eye and then at once open it, esp. as a gesture or signal conveying a message or suggesting mutual understanding ‖ to blink ‖ (of a source of light) to shine momentarily or intermittently ‖ v.t. to cause (an eye or eyelid) to wink ‖ to cause (a source of light) to wink, esp. as a signal **to wink at** to communicate with by winking ‖ to tolerate (what ought strictly not to be) and pretend not to have seen or known 2. n. an act of winking ‖ an instant of sleep, *forty winks* ‖ the message conveyed by a wink ‖ a short or intermittent gleam ‖ a very short time **not to sleep a wink** to get no sleep at all **to tip someone the wink** (esp. *Br.*) to give a hint or useful warning to someone [O.E. *wincian*]

win·kle (wíŋk'l) 1. n. periwinkle 2. v.t. pres. part. **win·kling** past and past part. **win·kled** (with 'out') to extract (something or someone) from a hiding place or strong defensive position [shortened fr. PERIWINKLE]

win·ner (wínər) n. someone who or something that wins ‖ (*pop.*) something extremely well done, made, thought out etc. ‖ (*pop.*) someone of first-rate ability

win·ning (wíniŋ) 1. adj. securing victory or gaining a contest ‖ attractive, *a winning smile* 2. n. a securing of victory ‖ (*pl.*) money won from gambling, contests etc.

winning gallery (*court tennis*) the netted opening below the side penthouse and furthest from the dedans

winning opening (*court tennis*) the dedans, the grille, or the winning gallery

Win·ni·peg (wínəpeg) the capital (pop. 564,473) of Manitoba, Canada, the country's largest grain market. Main industries: flour milling, meat packing, textiles and clothing. University of Manitoba (1877)

Winnipeg a lake (area 9,460 sq. miles) in Manitoba, Canada: fisheries

Win·ni·peg·o·sis (wɪ̩nəpegóusis) a lake (area 2,086 sq. miles) in Manitoba and Saskatchewan, Canada

win·now (wínou) *v.t.* to blow (grain) free of chaff ‖ to blow away (chaff) from grain ‖ to treat as though separating chaff from grain, *they winnowed the candidates down from 60 to 10* [O.E. *windwian* fr. *wind* n., wind]

win·some (wínsəm) *adj.* charming, attractive, winning in manner [O.E. *wynsum*, pleasant]

Win·ston-Sa·lem (wínstənséiləm) a tobacco-industry center (pop. 131,885) in North Carolina

win·ter (wíntər) 1. *n.* the season of the year in latitudes outside the Tropics when the warmth due to the sun's radiation is least (due to the inclination of the earth's axis as it moves in its orbit around the sun), i.e. the months of December, January and February in northern temperate latitudes, and of June, July and August in southern temperate latitudes 2. *adj.* of, for or adapted to the winter ‖ sown in winter (not in spring), *winter oats* 3. *v.i.* to live during the months of winter ‖ *v.t.* to maintain during the winter, *they winter the cattle in the lower valley* [O.E.]

winter aconite *Eranthis hyemalis*, fam. *Ranunculaceae*, a poisonous perennial herb of S.E. Europe and Asia with small yellow flowers appearing early in spring

winter book (*wagering*) handicapper's appraisal of odds for the following season

winter bud a dormant bud of a woody plant, protected by hard scales during the winter

winter cherry *Physalis alkekengi*, fam. *Solanaceae*, an Old World plant ‖ its small orange ornamental fruit

winter garden a conservatory, often built on to and accessible from a house, suitable for half-hardy plants

win·ter·green (wíntərgrɪ̩:n) *n.* a member of *Pyrola*, fam. *Pyrolaceae*, esp. *P. minor*, a genus of evergreen, low-growing shrubs of north temperate and arctic regions ‖ a member of *Gaultheria*, fam. *Ericaceae*, esp. *G. procumbens*, a North American plant from which an oil, used as an embrocation and in ointments and as a flavoring, is distilled ‖ this oil ‖ its flavor

Win·ter·hal·ter (vínterhɑltər), Franz Xaver (1805-73), German portrait painter. He was Queen Victoria's court painter of portraits

win·ter·ize (wínterɑiz) *pres. part.* **win·ter·iz·ing** *past* and *past part.* **win·ter·ized** *v.t.* to prepare (a house, automobile etc.) for the freezing conditions of winter

win·ter·kill (wínterkɪl) *v.t.* to kill (plants) by exposure to winter ‖ *v.i.* (of plants) to die by exposure to winter

winter quarters accommodation for the winter, e.g. for traveling circuses, geographical expeditions or (*hist.*) campaigning troops

winter solstice the time when the sun reaches the December solstice for the northern hemisphere or the June solstice for the southern hemisphere

Win·ter·thur (víntərtu:r) an industrial center (pop. 87,900) in Zurich canton, Switzerland, manufacturing rolling stock and locomotives

win·ter·time (wíntərtɑim) *n.* the winter season

Win·throp (wínθrəp), John (1588-1649), Colonial governor (1630-4, 1637-40, 1642-4, 1646-9) of Massachusetts and founder (1630) of the settlement that became Boston. As governor he ruled autocratically, and he established the Puritan ethic in Massachusetts social life

win·tri·ly (wíntrili) *adv.* in a wintry manner

win·tri·ness (wíntri:nis) *n.* the state or quality of being wintry

win·try (wíntri) *comp.* **win·tri·er** *superl.* **win·tri·est** *adj.* of or like winter ‖ quite unfriendly, chilling

winze (wínz) *n.* (*mining*) a shaft connecting different levels in a mine, used either for ventilation or communication [etym. doubtful]

wipe (waip) 1. *v. pres. part.* **wip·ing** *past* and *past part.* **wiped** *v.t.* to rub with a cloth etc. so as to free from surface moisture, dust etc. ‖ to clean by rubbing, *wipe your boots on the mat* ‖ to move one's hand over (a surface, e.g. one's brow) as if rubbing or cleaning ‖ (*plumbing*) to cover (a joint) smoothly with solder or soft lead ‖ *v.i.* to dry dishes etc. **to wipe away** (or **off**) to remove by wiping **to wipe out** to pay off (a debt) ‖ to destroy (e.g. a pocket of troops) ‖ to clean out or

remove by wiping **to wipe the floor with** (*pop.*) to defeat overwhelmingly and easily **to wipe up** to dry the dishes etc. 2. *n.* a wiping ‖ (*mach.*) a wiper **wip·er** *n.* someone who or something that wipes, esp. a device for sweeping rain from the windshield of an automobile etc. ‖ (*mach.*) a cam ‖ (*cinematography*) a technique in which one scene appears to push another off the screen [O.E. *wipian*]

wipe-out (wáipaut) *n.* 1. (*colloq.*) a complete destruction 2. (*surfing*) an accidental fall —**wipe out** *v.*

wire (wáiər) 1. *n.* metal drawn out into a threadlike form of uniform diameter ‖ a length of this ‖ fencing or netting made of this ‖ a suspended length of this on which acrobats perform, or one strung high between the winning posts of a race track ‖ barbed wire ‖ a telegram ‖ the telegraphic system, *send flowers by wire* ‖ (*papermaking*) the mesh on which wet paper is drained ‖ a snare for rabbits ‖ (*pl.*) the lines by which a puppet is controlled **to pull wires** to use influence to secure some favor or advantage **under the wire** just ahead of the deadline, at the last possible moment 2. *v. pres. part.* **wir·ing** *past* and *past part.* **wired** *v.t.* to furnish with a wire or wires ‖ to bind or fasten with wire ‖ to provide with an electric circuit, *to wire a house* ‖ to snare (an animal) using a noose of wire ‖ to telegraph ‖ (*croquet*) to place (a ball) behind a wicket in a way which prevents a successful shot ‖ *v.i.* to send a telegram [O.E. *wīr*]

wire cloth fabric woven from wire used e.g. for filters

wire cutter a tool with a very strong cutting edge, operated like scissors, used to cut wire

wire-draw (wáiərdrɔ) *pres. part.* **wire-draw·ing** *past* **wire-drew** (wáiərdru:) *past part.* **wire-drawn** (wáiərdrɔn) *v.t.* to draw (metal) into wire

wire gauge a gauge for measuring the diameter of wire or the thickness of sheet metal ‖ a system by which wire or sheet metal is graded according to size, or a size within such a system

wire gauze fine wire woven to make an open gauzy material, for strainers etc.

wire-hair (wáiərhɛər) *n.* a fox terrier with a short, stiff, curly coat

wire-haired (wáiərhɛərd) *adj.* (of a terrier) having short, stiff, curly hair

wire house (*securities*) a commission house with branch offices connected by electronic communications

wire·less (wáiərlis) 1. *adj.* (esp. *Br.*) of or relating to radiotelephony, radiotelegraphy, or radio 2. *n.* a method of communication by electromagnetic waves (often beamed) ‖ (esp. *Br.*) radio 3. *v.t.* and *i.* (esp. *Br.*) to radio

wire netting openwork material, made of woven wire, used for caging, fencing etc.

wire-pull·ing (wáiərpulɪŋ) *n.* the using of influence to secure favors etc.

wire recorder a magnetic recorder using a magnetized wire

wire rope a rope made by twisting a number of lengths of wire together

wire service a news agency which distributes copy to its subscribers by teletype

wire-sonde (wáiərsɒnd) *n.* (*meteor.*) device for gathering meteorological data, transmitted from a balloon to ground

wire-tap (wáiərtæp) 1. *v. pres. part.* **wire-tap·ping** *past* and *past part.* **wire-tapped** *v.i.* to listen clandestinely to telephone conversations by secretly making a connection with the telephone wire in use ‖ *v.t.* to listen to in this way ‖ to obtain (information etc.) in this way 2. *n.* this technique or an instance of it

wire-work (wáiərwə:rk) *n.* netting, gauze etc. constructed of wire

wire-worm (wáiərwə:rm) *n.* the larva of any of several insects destructive to the roots of plants, esp. the larva of click beetles, which may live for several years in the soil before metamorphosing into the imago ‖ a millepede

wire-wrap construction (wáiəræp) (*computer*) a method of constructing integrated circuits in which wires are used to connect two points with junctions and terminals; created by wrapping wire around those stakes without wiring

wir·i·ness (wáiəri:nis) *n.* the state or quality of being wiry

wir·ing (wáiərɪŋ) *n.* the arrangement of electric circuits in a building, a machine, electrical equipment etc.

wir·y (wáiəri:) *comp.* **wir·i·er** *superl.* **wir·i·est** *adj.* made of wire ‖ strong and flexible ‖ (of persons) lean and sinewy ‖ (of hair) stiff

Wis. Wisconsin

Wisc. Wisconsin

Wis·con·sin (wiskónsin) (*abbr.* Wis., Wisc.) a state (area 56,164 sq. miles, pop. 4,765,000) in the N. Central U.S.A., on the Great Lakes. Capital: Madison. Chief city: Milwaukee. It is an undulating plain, with an upland region in the north and west. Agriculture: dairy products (first state producer of milk and butter), hay, corn and fodder crops, vegetables, fruit. Resources: iron ore, building materials. Industries: machinery, metal products, paper, food processing. State university (1849) at Madison. Wisconsin was explored by the French (late 17th c.), was ceded to Britain (1763), became part of the Northwest Territory (1783) and became (1848) the 30th state of the U.S.A.

Wisconsin, University of a U.S. coeducational institution chartered (1848) at Madison, Wis. with undergraduate and graduate curricula at campuses in Madison and other cities

Wis·dom (wízdəm) a book included in the Roman Catholic canon but placed in the Apocrypha in the King James Version, containing sayings traditionally attributed to Solomon

wis·dom (wízdəm) *n.* the quality of being wise ‖ intelligence drawing on experience and governed by prudence ‖ a store of knowledge ‖ such knowledge converted into teaching, *the wisdom of the East* [O.E. *wīsdōm*]

wisdom tooth the back tooth on either side of both jaws in man, usually developing at 18–20 years of age

Wise (waiz), Henry Alexander (1806-76), U.S. politician and Confederate general in the Civil War. As governor of Virginia (1856-60), he signed the death warrant of John Brown

Wise, Isaac Mayer (1819-1900), U.S. rabbi, founder of Reform Judaism in the U.S.A.

Wise, John (1652-1725), American colonial clergyman of Massachusetts. Opposing Increase Mather and Cotton Mather, he championed church democracy in his influential 'The Churches Quarrel Espoused' (1710) and 'A Vindication of the Government of New England Churches' (1717)

wise (waiz) *adj.* having the ability to make a right decision or judgment by applying intelligent thought to a wide range of experience and knowledge, with prudence ‖ (of a decision, judgment or action) resulting from the use of this ability, *a wise choice* ‖ possessing great knowledge and intelligence ‖ (*pop.*) crafty, cunning ‖ (*pop.*) cocky, self-important **to be** (or **get**) **wise to** to be (or become) fully aware of **to put someone wise to** to inform someone about [O.E. *wīs*]

wise *n.* (*rhet.*, except as a suffix) way, manner **in no wise** (*rhet.*) not at all [O.E. *wīse*]

-wise *suffix* denoting manner, position, direction as in 'lengthwise' ‖ (*pop.*) with regard to, as in 'salarywise he has no complaints'

wise·a·cre (wáizeikər) *n.* a man who foolishly pretends to great knowledge [fr. Du. *wijsseggher* fr. O.H.G. *wizago*, a prophet]

wise·crack (wáizkræk) 1. *n.* a smart or flippant remark 2. *v.i.* to make such remarks

Wise·man (wáizmən), Nicholas Patrick Stephen (1802-65), British cardinal. He was the first Roman Catholic archbishop of Westminster (1850-65)

wi·sent (wízənt) *n. Bison bonasus*, fam. *Bovidae*, a European bison thought to be the ancestor of the American bison or buffalo [fr. G. fr. O.H.G. *wisunt*]

wish (wíʃ) 1. *v.t.* to have a feeling of unfulfilled satisfaction with respect to something or someone, *I wish I had a new car, I wish I knew more about him* ‖ to feel or express good or ill will or a specified wish, greeting or invocation (to or for someone), *I wish him no harm, he wished them every happiness* ‖ to require, *I wish you to do it* ‖ to foist off, *he wished the job on me* ‖ *v.i.* (with 'for') to hope, long to make a silent wish 2. *n.* a desire felt or expressed ‖ something wished for ‖ a request ‖ (*pl.*) greetings, *best wishes* [O.E. *wȳscan*]

Wish·art (wíʃɑrt, wíʃərt), George (c. 1513-46), Scottish religious reformer. His Protestant teaching (1544-6) converted Knox. He was burned as a heretic

wish·bone (wíʃboun) *n.* the forked bone between the neck and breast in birds. (A dried wishbone is pulled by two people, who silently wish while pulling, until it snaps. A popular superstition holds that the person pulling the longer piece will have his wish fulfilled ‖ (*football*) a variation of the T formation in which fullbacks are close to the scrimmage line and the halfbacks farther back

wish·ful (wíʃfəl) *adj.* having or manifesting a wish

wishful thinking thinking founded on desire and not on the facts

wish·y-wash·y (wíʃi:wɔʃi:, wíʃi:wɒʃi:) *adj.* weak, thin, watery ‖ (of a person) feeble and indecisive in character

Wis·la (víːslə) *VISTULA

wisp (wisp) *n.* a small bunch, *a wisp of hair* ‖ a small amount or mere trace of something, *a wisp of smoke* **wisp·y** *comp.* **wisp·i·er** *superl.* **wisp·i·est** *adj.* [origin unknown]

wist *past* and *past part.* of archaic WIT

Wis·ter (wístər), Owen (1860-1938), U.S. writer, best known for his 'The Virginian' (1902), a novel dealing with Wyoming cowboys

wis·te·ri·a, wis·tar·i·a (wístéəri:ə) *n.* a member of *Wisteria* (*Wistaria*), fam. *Papilionaceae*, a genus of chiefly Asiatic climbing shrubs cultivated for their sweet-scented pendulous racemes of white, blue, mauve or pink flowers [after Casper *Wistar*, U.S. physician]

wist·ful (wístfəl) *adj.* desiring a little sadly what it is not possible or easy to obtain, or revealing this state, *a wistful look* ‖ in a vague mood of unformulated melancholy or frustrated desire [prob. fr. older *wistly* adv., intently]

wit (wit) *n.* the association of apparently unrelated ideas in an unexpected, clever way, esp. with an effect of brilliance provoking laughter ‖ the ability to make such association ‖ a person with this ability ‖ intelligence, *shrewd native wit* ‖ (*pl.*) mental balance, *he must have lost his wits* **at one's wits' end** mentally in despair, **baffled out of one's wits** distracted, not thinking intelligently **to have** (or **keep**) **one's wits about one** to be mentally alert **to live by one's wits** to pick up a living as best one can, sometimes by trading on other people [O.E. *witt*, knowledge]

wit *pres. part.* **wit·ing, wit·ting** *past* wist, wiste (wist) *past part.* **wist** *v.t.* and *i.* (*archaic*) to know **to wit** (*rhet.*) namely [O.E. *witan*]

wit·an (wít'n) *pl. n.* (*hist.*) the members of the witenagemot [O.E. *pl.* of *Wita*, councilor, wise man]

witch (witʃ) 1. *n.* a woman practicing sorcery usually with the aid, or through the medium, of an evil spirit ‖ (*pop.*) an ugly old woman 2. *v.t.* (*rhet.*) to cast a spell on ‖ to bewitch [O.E. *wicce*]

witch ball (*hist.*) a hollow glass ball hung up in houses in the 18th c. to keep witches away

witch·craft (wítʃkræft, wítʃkrɑft) *n.* sorcery as practiced by a witch or witches [O.E. *wiececræft*]

—In medieval times witches were believed to be in league with Satan, from whom they received supernatural powers, to be guilty of the most hideous vices, including sexual intercourse with demons, and to be responsible for plagues, diseases of men and cattle, infanticide and the murder of their enemies. Persecution was authorized by Church and State, the most important ecclesiastical directive being Pope Innocent VII's bull 'Summis desiderantes' (1484). The use of torture to extract confessions provided what was taken to be convincing evidence of guilt, and these confessions confirmed the superstitions of the ignorant. At times witch-hunting became a mania and the climax came in England and Scotland, and in America, in the 17th c. Great numbers of people were cruelly put to death, commonly by burning. The next century brought a more skeptical attitude

witch doctor a medicine man among primitive peoples

witch elm *WYCH ELM

witch·er·y (wítʃəri:) *pl.* **witch·er·ies** *n.* witchcraft ‖ fascination

witches' sabbath a midnight assembly of witches, at which the powers of evil are supposed to be present, when black rites are celebrated and orgies held (*WALPURGIS NIGHT)

witch hazel, wych hazel a member of *Hamamelis*, fam. *Hamamelidaceae*, a genus of trees or shrubs which flower in late autumn after the leaves have fallen, esp. *H. virginica*, native to North America ‖ an alcoholic solution of a substance extracted from the bark of *H. virginiana* and used as a medicinal lotion

witch-hunt (wítʃhʌnt) *n.* (*hist.*) a pursuing and persecution of people accused of witchcraft ‖ a persecution of individuals belonging to an organization or community whose views are repugnant to those in authority **witch-hunt·ing** *n.*

wit·e·na·ge·mot, wit·e·na·ge·mote (wít'nəgəmóut, wít'nægəmóut) *n.* (*hist.*) an assembly of nobles, ecclesiastics and officials in Anglo-Saxon England, meeting irregularly to advise the king [O.E. fr. *witena*, gen. pl. of *wita*, wise man+*gemōt*, a gathering]

with (wið, wiθ) *prep.* used to indicate that two or more persons or things are together, near each other, in agreement, harmony etc., *red with blue* ‖ in the company of, *stay with your parents* ‖ accompanied by ‖ used to indicate someone spoken to, *he had a word with John* ‖ used to indicate the object of attention, sentiment etc., *she is pleased with her new dress* ‖ by means of, *to pay with a check* ‖ used to indicate the presence of, *crowded with people* ‖ among, *he lives with pygmies* ‖ possessing, characterized by, *a man with a wooden leg* ‖ by reason of having, because of, *in bed with a fever* ‖ having, *don't eat with your mouth open* ‖ in regard to, concerning, *what do you want with me?* ‖ used to indicate the object of a command, *off with his head!* ‖ in opposition to, *he fought with his friends* ‖ in the functioning of, *what's the matter with the television?* ‖ in the care or possession of, *leave the keys with the caretaker* ‖ at the same time as, *he gets up with the sun* ‖ at the time of, *with the ebbing tide his hopes dwindled* ‖ in the same direction as, *sail with the wind* ‖ in proportion to, *his avarice increased with his wealth* ‖ used to indicate the object of a comparison, *he is not on a level with the other competitors* ‖ used to indicate manner, *he walked with difficulty* ‖ plus, *these chairs, with the ones at the table, will be enough* ‖ including, *it's $20 with tax* ‖ as competently as, *he can swear with any of them* ‖ so as to be separated from, *he dispensed with their services* ‖ in spite of, *with all his faults he is a good man* ‖ used to indicate understanding or agreement, *are you with me?* ‖ used to indicate the object of a charge, threat etc., *menaced with eviction* **with this** (or **with that**) thereupon, after this (after that) [O.E.]

with·al (wiðɔ́l, wiθɔ́l) *adv.* (*rhet.*) moreover, besides ‖ (*rhet.*) nevertheless

with·draw (wiðdrɔ́, wiθdrɔ́) *pres. part.* **with·draw·ing,** *past* **with·drew** (wiðdrúː, wiθdrúː) *past part.* **with·drawn** (wiðdrɔ́n, wiθdrɔ́n) *v.t.* to take away, remove, *to withdraw an application* ‖ to take back, to retract, *to withdraw an offer* ‖ to draw back, *to withdraw one's hand* ‖ *v.i.* to leave, retire, *they withdrew to an inner room* **with·dráw·al** *n.* a withdrawing **with·dráwn** *adj.* reserved, shy [fr. O.E. *with-*, away, back+DRAW]

withe (wiθ) *n.* a tough flexible thin branch, esp. of willow or osier, used as a band for tying up bundles, e.g. of firewood [O.E. *withthe*]

with·er (wíðər) *v.i.* (of plants) to dry up and die for lack of moisture or because of extreme cold or heat, generally losing color ‖ to become lean and wrinkled ‖ (often with 'away') to lose vigor, *the opposition withered away* ‖ *v.t.* to cause to wither ‖ to reduce to silence, *she withered him with her sarcastic remarks* [prob. var. of WEATHER v.]

with·er·ite (wíðərait) *n.* (*mineral.*) a native barium carbonate, BaCO₃, found in white or gray crystals, also in columnar or granular masses [after W. *Withering*, English physician]

with·ers (wíðərz) *pl. n.* the ridge between the shoulder blades of a horse (and some other animals) [etym. doubtful]

with·er·shins (wíðərʃinz) *adv.* widdershins

With·er·spoon (wíðərspuːn), John (1723-94), Scottish-American Presbyterian minister, signer of the Declaration of Independence. His 'Ecclesiastical Characteristics' (1753) upheld dogmatic orthodoxy against the ministers who espoused humanism. He was appointed (1768) president of what became Princeton University

with·hold (wiðhóuld, wiθhóuld) *pres. part.* **with·hold·ing** *past* and *past part.* **with·held** (wiðhéld, wiθhéld) *v.t.* to hold back, refuse to give, *to withhold consent* [fr. O.E. *with-*, away, back+HOLD]

withholding tax the percentage of someone's income deducted at source by the employer and paid to the government in part payment of income tax

with·in (wiðín, wiθín) 1. *prep.* not beyond the limits of, *within sight* ‖ in the scope of, *within his capacity* ‖ inside, *safe within walls* ‖ (in expressions of time) in the course of, *within his lifetime* 2. *adv.* inside, indoors, *inquire within, seen from within* ‖ in the mind or conscience, *look within and consider your motives* [Late O.E. *withinnan*]

with·out (wiðáut, wiθáut) 1. *prep.* not having, *he came without any money* ‖ free from, *without worry* ‖ (followed by the pres. part.) refraining from, avoiding, *without making any noise* ‖ in need of, *without a job* ‖ devoid of, *without initiative* **it goes without saying** it is self-evident 2. *adv.* outside, outdoors, *seen from without* **to do** (or **go**) **without** to accept (or endure) a lack or deprivation (of some understood thing) [Late O.E. *withūtan*]

without prejudice (*law*) a caveat denoting that what is said or written must not impair an understood preexistent right or claim

with·stand (wiðstǽnd, wiθstǽnd) *pres. part.* **with·stand·ing** *past* and *past part.* **with·stood** (wiðstúd, wiθstúd) *v.t.* to stand up against, to resist, *to withstand a siege, to withstand criticism* [O.E. *withstandan*]

with·y (wíði:, wíθi:) *pl.* **with·ies** *n.* a withe

wit·less (wítlis) *adj.* foolish

wit·ness (wítnis) 1. *n.* a person who has observed a certain event, *the unwilling witness of a quarrel* ‖ a person who testifies to this observation, esp. in a court of law, and esp. under oath ‖ a person who testifies to the genuineness of a signature on a document by signing his own name to the document ‖ an authentication of a fact, testimony ‖ public affirmation of the truths of a religious faith ‖ something taken as evidence, *the embers were a witness of recent occupation* **to bear witness** to declare, on the strength of personal observation, that something is true ‖ to affirm the truths of a religious faith **Witness** a Jehovah's Witness 2. *v.t.* to observe (an event) ‖ to sign as a witness ‖ *v.i.* (esp. with 'to') to give as evidence, *this gift witnesses to his generosity* ‖ to bear witness [O.E. *witnes*, knowledge, testimony]

wit·ness-box (wítnisbɒks) *n.* (*Br.*) a witness stand

witness stand (*Am.*=*Br.* witness-box) an enclosure set aside for witnesses in a court of law

Wit·te (vítə), Count Sergei Yulievich (1849-1915), Russian statesman. As minister of finance, commerce and industry (1892-1903) he introduced the gold standard. He opened up Siberia by the Trans-Siberian Railroad. He was prime minister (1905-6)

wit·ted (wítid) *adj.* (in compounds) having wits of a specified quality, *slow-witted, dull-witted*

Wit·tels·bach (vítəlsbɒx) a German princely house which ruled in Bavaria and the Rhine Palatinate from the 12th c. to 1918

Wit·ten·berg (vítənberk) a town (pop. 52,500) in Halle, East Germany, on the middle Elbe. Luther nailed up (Oct. 31, 1517) his 95 theses here

Wit·te·veen Facility (vítəviːn) an International Monetary Fund emergency pool of $10 billion. It was authorized in 1977 to be used for loans to countries with serious debts

Witt·gen·stein (vítgənʃtain), Ludwig Joseph Johann (1889-1951), Austrian philosopher, author of 'Tractatus Logico-Philosophicus' (1921). His researches bore on the philosophy of psychology and mathematics, and were very influential in logical positivism

wit·ti·cism (wítisizəm) *n.* a witty remark

wit·ti·ly (wítili:) *adv.* in a witty way

wit·ti·ness (wítinis) *n.* the quality of being witty

wit·ting (wítiŋ) *adj.* deliberate, intentional, *witting deception* ‖ conscious, *a witting accomplice* **wit·ting·ly** *adv.*

wit·ty (wíti:) *comp.* **wit·ti·er** *superl.* **wit·ti·est** *adj.* possessing or manifesting wit [O.E. *witig, wittig*]

Wit·wa·ters·rand (witwɔ́tərzrænd, witwɒ́tərzrænd) a district of gold-bearing hills, the main world source of gold, in the Transvaal, South Africa. Chief town: Johannesburg. University (1921)

Witz (vits), Konrad (15th c.) Swabian painter. His masterpiece was the Heilspiegel altar (1435), surviving in fragments. He painted in a very realistic style, and shows strong Flemish influence

wivern *WYVERN

wives *pl.* of WIFE

wiz·ard (wízərd) *n.* a sorcerer, magician ‖ a person who seems to perform magic, *a financial*

---

wizard wiz·ard·ry n. [M.E. *wysard* fr. *wys, wis, wise*]

wiz·ened (wízənd) *adj.* having a dried-up or shriveled appearance [fr. older *wizen* fr. O.E. *wisnian*, to become dry]

Wla·dy·slaw (vladíslaf) kings of Poland *LADISLAUS

woad (woud) n. *Isatis tinctoria*, fam. *Cruciferae*, a European biennial plant which yields a dark blue dye ‖ this dye, esp. as used by the ancient Britons as a body coloring [O.E. *wād*]

wob·ble (wób'l) 1. *v. pres. part.* **wob·bling** *past* and *past part.* **wob·bled** *v.i.* to be unsteady on its or one's legs ‖ (of a top etc.) to move unsteadily from side to side while revolving ‖ to change repeatedly from one opinion or intention to another ‖ (of jelly etc.) to shake ‖ (of the voice or a sound) to quaver *v.t.* to cause to wobble 2. *n.* a wobbling movement or gait ‖ an instance of indecision or vacillation ‖ (of the voice or a sound) a quaver **wób·bly** *comp.* **wob·bli·er** *superl.* **wob·bli·est** *adj.* [of Gmc origin]

wob·bu·la·tor (wóbjuleitər) n. an instrument for testing radios, consisting of a device varying the carrier frequency rapidly [WOBBLE+MODULATOR]

Wo·dan, Wo·den (wóud'n) (*Anglo-Saxon mythol.*) the chief god, associated with Odin

Wode·house (wúdhaus), Pelham Grenville (1881-1975), English novelist, creator of a hilarious, coherent world. Among his best-known works are 'Leave it to Psmith' (1923), 'The Inimitable Jeeves' (1924), and 'Bertie Wooster Sees It Through' (1955)

Woden *WODAN

woe (wou) 1. *n.* (*rhet.*) sorrow, grief ‖ (*pl., rhet.*) troubles, afflictions, calamities 2. *interj.* (*rhet.*) alas [O.E. *wā, wǣ* interj., a cry of pain]

woe·be·gone (wóubigɔn, wóubigɒn) *adj.* sorrowful in appearance, dismal [WOE+older *begone* (past part.), beset]

woe·ful (wóufəl) *adj.* (*rhet.*) full of woe ‖ deplorable, *a woeful lack of tact*

wok (wɒk) n. bowllike traditional Chinese cooking pot

woke alt. *past* of WAKE

woken alt. *past part.* of WAKE

wold (would) n. (*Br.*) a tract of open, uncultivated country ‖ (*Br.*) an open, rolling hilly region including cultivated land [O.E. *wald, weald*, forest]

Wolf (vɔlf), Hugo (1860-1903), Austrian composer. He composed nearly 300 songs and brought the tradition of the German lied to the greatest pitch of refinement

wolf (wulf) 1. *pl.* **wolves** (wulvz) *n.* a member of *Canis*, a genus of large (about 27 ins. from shoulder to ground), fierce, doglike, carnivorous mammals, of Europe, Asia and North America, which hunt in small groups and prey on deer, caribou etc., though they subsist mainly on rabbits, though *C. lupus*, the gray or timber wolf, having coarse yellowish or brown fur, a straight bushy tail and erect pointed ears, was formerly very common throughout the northern hemisphere, but has been exterminated in most inhabited areas ‖ (*pop.*) a man who tries to pick up women and seduce them ‖ (*mus.*) a discordant sound sometimes heard in certain keys on organs tuned in meantone temperament ‖ (*mus.*) harshness due to unintended vibrations in some bowed instruments **a wolf in sheep's clothing** a person whose evil intentions are masked by a friendly manner **to cry wolf** to raise false alarms **to keep the wolf from the door** to avert hunger or poverty 2. *v.t.* to eat greedily and quickly, *to wolf one's dinner* [O.E. *wulf*]

wolf call whistled approval by a man of a girl's appearance as she passes in the street, as a sign of sexual attraction

wolf cub (*Br.*) a cub scout

Wolfe (wulf), James (1727-59), British general. He commanded the British attack (1759) on the French positions at Quebec during the French and Indian War and won the decisive victory of the Heights of Abraham, but was killed in the battle

Wolfe, Thomas Clayton (1900-38), American author. 'Look Homeward, Angel' (1929) and its sequel 'Of Time and the River' (1935) are largely autobiographical

Wolff·i·an body (wúlfi:ən) the mesonephros

wolf·hound (wúlfhaund) n. a very large dog used originally for hunting wolves (*BORZOI, *IRISH WOLFHOUND)

wolf·ish (wúlfiʃ) *adj.* of or like a wolf

wolf·ram (wúlfrəm) n. tungsten wolframite [G., etym. doubtful]

wolf·ram·ite (wúlfrəmait) n. ferrous tungstate, (Fe, Mn)WO₄, usually brownish or grayish-black, found in monoclinic crystals and granular or columnar masses [G. *wolframit*]

Wolf·ram von E·schen·bach (vɔlfrɑmfənéʃənbɑx) (c. 1170–c. 1220), German minnesinger. He is known esp. for 'Parzival', his only complete work

wolfs·bane (wúlfsbein) n. *Aconitum lycoctonum*, a variety of aconite ‖ winter aconite

wolf whistle a wolf call made by whistling. Traditionally it is a two-part sound, the second repeating the first and then sliding to a lower note

Wol·las·ton (wúləstən), William Hyde (1766-1828), English physicist and chemist. He devised the camera lucida, a goniometer for use in crystallography, and the collimator, and was the first to draw platinum wire

Wo·lof (wóulɒf) n. a people of the western Sudan near the mouth of the Senegal and Gambia Rivers ‖ a member of this people ‖ their language

Wols (vɔls), (Alfred Otto Wolfgang Schülze, 1913-51), German painter, living in France from 1932. Working in a manner parallel to that of abstract expressionism, and inspired by Klee, he painted small, nonobjective works of somber mood in a delicate, calligraphic style

Wolse·ley (wúlzli:), Garnet Joseph, 1st Viscount Wolseley (1833-1913), British field marshal. His most noted campaigns were in Ashanti (1814) and in Egypt (1882 and 1884-5). As commander in chief he began to modernize the British army (1895-1900)

Wol·sey (wúlzi:), Thomas (c. 1475-1530), English cardinal and statesman, archbishop of York (1514-30), lord chancellor of England (1515-29). He gained rapid promotion after the accession (1509) of Henry VIII and dominated the young king's foreign and domestic policy. He negotiated (1514) peace with France and a marriage between Henry's sister and Louis XII but, on the accession (1520) of the Emperor Charles V, Wolsey aligned England with the Empire against France. His policy ruined the royal finances, and his failure to obtain papal consent to Henry's divorce from Catherine of Aragon led to his arrest for treason (1530). He died on the way to stand trial

wolverene *WOLVERINE

Wol·ver·hamp·ton (wúlvərhæmptən) a county borough (pop. 150,000) in Staffordshire, England, in the Black Country: metalworking, chemical industries

wol·ver·ine, wol·ver·ene (wúlvəri:n) n. *Gulo luscus*, fam. *Mustelidae*, a carnivorous North American mammal about 3 ft. in length, having thick blackish fur and a pale forehead ‖ *Gulo gulo*, the glutton of N. Asian and European forests [dim. of WOLF]

wolves *pl.* of WOLF

wom·an (wúmən) 1. *pl.* **wom·en** (wímən) *n.* an adult female human being ‖ (without article) the female sex, women in general ‖ (with 'old') a rather fussy and effeminate man **the woman** womanly feeling, womanliness, *the woman in her was roused* 2. *adj.* female, *a woman doctor* [O.F. *wīfmann* fr. *wīf*, a female+*mann*, human being]

wom·an·hood (wúmənhud) n. the condition of being a woman ‖ women in general

wom·an·ish (wúməniʃ) *adj.* characteristic of a woman ‖ (of boys or men) not showing proper manly characteristics

wom·an·kind (wúmənkaind) n. women in general, the female sex

wom·an·li·ness (wúmənli:nis) n. the quality of being womanly

wom·an·ly (wúmənli:) *adj.* having the characteristics or qualities proper to a woman

womb (wu:m) n. the mammalian uterus ‖ (*fig.*) a place of origin and early development, *the womb of prehistory* [O.E. *wamb, womb*]

wom·bat (wómbæt) n. a member of *Phascolomys*, fam. *Vombatidae*, a genus of burrowing, nocturnal marsupial mammals native to Australia and Tasmania. They are about 3 ft. long, with coarse, bristly grayish fur ‖ the fur of the wombat [indigenous Australian name]

women *pl.* of WOMAN

wom·en·folk (wímənfouk) n. (*old-fash.*) the women of a family, village etc.

Women's Institute an organization founded in Canada (1897) and in Britain (1915) to enable women in rural areas to meet and work together in craft and cultural activities. It is now worldwide

Women's Lib *WOMEN'S LIBERATION

Women's Liberation (*abbr.* Women's Lib) the name given to the aggregate of organizations committed to redressing the inferior status of women. The movement has been effective esp. since 1970

women's liberation (sometimes initial capitals) feminist movement for equality of the sexes, including the elimination of formal and informal social and business restraints on women —**women's liberationist** n.

women's rights the position of political and economic legal equality with men claimed for women

won (wɒn) n. the basic monetary unit of North Korea ‖ a unit of currency of South Korea ‖ a coin or note of the value of one won [Korean]

won *past* and *past part.* of WIN

won·der (wándər) n. (without article) a state of astonished admiration, *lost in wonder at the display* ‖ a fact or circumstance causing surprise, *it was a wonder she came at all* ‖ (*pl.*) wonderfully good things, *the holiday did wonders for us all* ‖ a person whose skill or efficiency compels great admiration ‖ *SEVEN WONDERS OF THE WORLD* **it is no** (or **small**) **wonder that, no** (or **small**) **wonder...** it is not surprising that [O.E. *wundor*]

wonder *v.i.* to feel wonder ‖ to ask oneself questions ‖ *v.t.* to feel curiosity about, *he wondered what she would do next* ‖ to be in a state of perplexity about, *I wonder whether it is true* [O.E. *wundrian*]

won·der·ful (wándərfəl) *adj.* arousing wonder ‖ unusually good, *wonderful weather* [O.E. *wunderfull*]

won·der·land (wándərlænd) n. fairyland, an imaginary realm of magic and marvels

won·der·ment (wándərmənt) n. the feeling of wonder

won·der·struck (wándərstrʌk) *adj.* overcome with surprise, admiration or amazement

won·drous (wándrəs) *adj.* (*rhet.*) wonderful [alteration of older *wonders* adj.]

won·ky (wɒ́ŋki:) *comp.* **won·ki·er** *superl.* **won·ki·est** *adj.* (*Br., pop.*) loose, unsteady, wobbly ‖ (*Br., pop.*) amiss [etym. doubtful]

Won·san (wɔ́:nsɑn) an ice-free port and rail center (pop. 275,000) in North Korea on the Sea of Japan: rolling stock, shipbuilding, oil refining

wont (wount) 1. *adj.* (*rhet.*, used predicatively, with 'to') accustomed, *as he was wont to say* 2. *n.* (*rhet.*) custom, habit, *as is his wont* [O.E. *gewunod* past. part. of *gewunian*, to dwell, be accustomed]

won't (wount) *contr.* of WILL NOT

wont·ed (wóuntid, wɔ́ntid) *attrib. adj.* (*rhet.*) customary, usual, *with her wonted charm*

woo (wu:) *v.t.* (*old-fash.*, of a man) to court, seek in marriage ‖ to be assiduously attentive in seeking to win (something or someone), *to woo someone's favor* ‖ *v.i.* (*old-fash.*) to court a woman [O.E. *wōgian*]

Wood (wud), Christopher (1901-30), British painter. His work, including many Cornish and Breton scenes and landscapes, shows a refined color sense

Wood, Grant (1891-1942), U.S. painter. His 'American scene' canvases show the people and landscapes of the rural Midwest in a stern, stylized fashion, notably his 'American Gothic' and 'Daughters of Revolution'

Wood, Leonard (1860-1927), U.S. general, commander of the Rough Riders in Cuba during the U.S. occupation (1899-1902). As military governor of Cuba, he helped to eradicate yellow fever from the island

wood (wud) 1. *n.* the hard fibrous substance comprising the largest part of the stems and branches of trees and shrubs. It is predominantly xylem and phloem, intersected in many species with vascular rays (*LIGNOCELLULOSE, *HARDWOOD, *SOFTWOOD) ‖ this prepared for use in construction ‖ (*also pl.*) a collection of growing trees, larger than a thicket but smaller than a forest ‖ one of the large wooden balls used in the game of bowls ‖ (*golf*) a club with a wooden head ‖ (*mus.*) woodwind ‖ firewood **out of the woods** (*Am.=Br.* out of the wood) out of danger or difficulty **the wood** a keg, barrel etc. as distinguished from a bottle, *matured in the wood* 2. *adj.* made of wood ‖ used for working on or holding wood ‖ living or growing in the woods [O.E. *widu, wiodu, wudu*]

wood alcohol, wood spirit methanol

CONCISE PRONUNCIATION KEY: **(a)** æ, c*a*t; ɑ, c*a*r; ɔ f*aw*n; ei, sn*a*ke. **(e)** e, h*e*n; i:, sh*ee*p; iə, d*ee*r; ɛə, b*ea*r. **(i)** i, f*i*sh; ai, t*i*ger; ə:, b*i*rd. **(o)** o, *o*x; au, c*ow*; ou, g*oa*t; u, p*oo*r; ɔi, r*oy*al. **(u)** ʌ, d*u*ck; u, b*u*ll; u:, g*oo*se; ə, b*a*cillus; ju:, c*u*be. x, lo*ch*; θ, *th*ink; ð, bo*th*er; z, *Z*en; ʒ, cor*s*age; dʒ, sava*g*e; ŋ, orangutan*g*; j, *y*ak; ʃ, *fi*sh; tʃ, fe*tch*; 'l, rabb*le*; 'n, redd*en*. Complete pronunciation key appears inside front cover.

wood anemone *Anemone nemorosa*, the wild anemone of Europe ‖ *Anemone quinquefolia*, the wild anemone of North America

wood·bin (wúdbin) *n.* a box or bin for holding firewood

wood·bind (wúdbaind) *n.* woodbine

wood·bine (wúdbain) *n. Lonicera periclymenum*, the wild honeysuckle of Europe ‖ Virginia creeper [O.E. *wudubinde*]

wood block a solid block of wood, used e.g. for paving ‖ a relief die for printing from, cut esp. in boxwood

wood·chat (wúdtʃæt) *n.* any of several Asiatic birds of fam. *Turdidae*. The males are mostly blue with vivid red markings ‖ a S. European bird of fam. *Laniidae* [etym. doubtful]

wood·chuck (wúdtʃʌk) *n. Marmota monax*, fam. *Sciuridae*, a thickset North American marmot [fr. a North American Indian name]

wood·cock (wúdkɒk) *pl.* **wood·cocks, wood·cock** *n. Scolopax rusticola*, a small brown game bird of Europe and Asia ‖ *Philohela minor*, a related bird of North America [O.E. *wuducoc, wudecoc*]

wood·craft (wúdkræft, wúdkrɒft) *n.* skill in hunting and trapping and in maintaining oneself in woods and forests

wood·cut (wúdkʌt) *n.* a design cut on wood, usually along the grain (cf. WOOD ENGRAVING), to be printed from by letterpress ‖ a print from such a block ‖ the art or technique of cutting such designs

wood·cut·ter (wúdkʌtər) *n.* a person who fells trees or cuts the lumber on the site where the trees grew

wood·ed (wúdid) *adj.* covered with growing trees

wood·en (wúd'n) *adj.* made of wood ‖ as if made of wood, lifeless, expressionless, *a wooden stare* ‖ stiff, clumsy, *wooden gestures*

wood engraving a design engraved on wood, esp. across the grain (cf. WOODCUT), to be printed from by letterpress ‖ a print from such a block ‖ the art or technique of cutting such designs

wood·en-head·ed (wúd'nhedid) *adj.* stupid, obtuse

Wood·hull (wúdhʌl), Victoria (née Claflin, 1838-1927), U.S. journalist and lecturer. She founded (1870) with her sister Tennessee Claflin (1845-1923) a sensational weekly which championed the cause of women's suffrage. In 1872 she was nominated by the radical People's party as U.S. presidential candidate

wood hyacinth *Scilla nonscripta*, a European plant bearing a raceme of nodding, blue, bell-shaped flowers

wood·land (wúdlənd) 1. *n.* land largely given over to woods 2. *adj.* living or growing in woodland

wood lark *Lullula arborea*, a European species of lark

wood louse *pl.* **wood lice** a terrestrial isopod crustacean of suborder *Oniscoidea*, found under stones or bark, in damp moss etc.

wood·man (wúdmən) *pl.* **wood·men** (wúdmən) *n.* (esp. *Br.*) a woodsman

wood nymph (*Gk mythol.*) a dryad ‖ (*Gk mythol.*) a hamadryad ‖ a member of *Euthisanotia*, a genus of brilliantly colored moths ‖ a member of *Thalurania*, a genus of South American hummingbirds

wood·peck·er (wúdpekər) *n.* a member of any of several genera (e.g. *Picus, Dendrolopus*) of fam. *Picidae*, almost universally distributed. They are chisel-billed, wood-boring birds, strong in flight and having remarkably long tongues, and short stiff tails. These act as props when the birds are climbing tree trunks, which they drill into with their very hard bills in search of insects. They nest in holes in trees

wood pigeon the European ringdove ‖ *Columba fasciata*, the band-tailed pigeon of western North America

wood·pile (wúdpail) *n.* a pile of wood, esp. firewood

wood pulp the fiber of wood pulped to make paper, rayon etc.

wood·ruff (wúdrəf) *n.* a member of *Asperula*, fam. *Rubiaceae*, a genus of low-growing European woodland plants. The dried leaves of *A. odorata* were formerly used for scenting clothes and as a moth deterrent. *A. tinctoria* yields a dye from its roots usable in place of madder

wood·shed (wúdʃed) *n.* a shed used esp. for preparing and storing firewood

woods·man (wúdzmən) *pl.* **woods·men** (wúdzmən) *n.* a woodcutter or forester ‖ someone who has great knowledge of woodland life

wood sorrel *Oxalis acetosella*, fam. *Oxalidaceae*, a low-growing perennial woodland plant of Europe, Asia and North America with creeping rhizomes, trifoliate leaves, and acid sap in its leaves

woods·y (wúdzi:) *comp.* **woods·i·er** *superl.* **woods·i·est** *adj.* (esp. of smells) of or suggesting the woods

wood tar tar obtained from distilled wood

wood thrush *Hylocichla mustelina*, a North American thrush with a brown head and back and a white breast marked with large spots. It has a loud, clear song

wood tick a member of *Ixodoidea*, a tick whose young cling to bushes and fasten onto the bodies of passing animals

wood turning the art or process of shaping wood on a lathe

wood·wax·en (wúdwæksən) *n. Genista tinctoria*, fam. *Fabaceae*, a yellow-flowered Eurasian shrub, originally the source of a yellow dye [O.E. *wuduweaxe*]

wood·wind (wúdwind) *n.* the section of the orchestra comprising instruments made originally (and still generally) of wood and either blown directly (e.g. the flute) or with a reed (e.g. the oboe). The saxophone, though metal, is classed as woodwind since it is played like a woodwind and not like a brass instrument ‖ an instrument of this group

wood·work (wúdwə:rk) *n.* objects made of wood, esp. parts of a building or interior fittings made of wood

wood·work·ing (wúdwə:rkiŋ) 1. *n.* the art or activity of working wood 2. *adj.* of, pertaining to or used for working wood

wood·worm (wúdwə:rm) *n.* the larva of *Anobium punctatum*, fam. *Anobiidae*, the common furniture beetle, which lays its small, oval, white eggs in cracks in wood. The larvae burrow into and through the wood. They molt at intervals, pupate, and the adult beetle emerges in spring, leaving clearly visible exit holes. The life cycle may take one year or several years to complete

wood·y (wúdi:) *comp.* **wood·i·er** *superl.* **wood·i·est** *adj.* abounding in woods, well-wooded ‖ consisting of or like wood ‖ (of a plant) making woody stems etc.

woof (wuf, wu:f) *n.* the weft [O.E. ōwef]

wool (wul) *n.* the fibrous, usually crisped, growth on the skin of certain animals, esp. the sheep. When shorn off, cleansed and spun into yarn, it is used for knitting or weaving a soft, warm fabric ‖ this yarn ‖ (*biol.*) any fibrous growth resembling wool **to pull the wool over someone's eyes** to deceive someone as to the true facts [O.E. *wull*] —The fibers of wool are made of keratin, a scleroprotein, and have rough, scaly cuticles, which hook into one another when the fibers are spun into yarn. The yarn is full of air cells, making woolen textiles bad conductors of heat and thus suitable for wear in cold seasons or latitudes. The yarn made from fibers of long staple is called worsted

wool clip the annual crop of wool

wooled (wúld) *adj.* (in hyphenated compounds) having wool of a specified length or quality, *fine-wooled*

wool·en, esp. *Br.* **wool·len** (wúlən) 1. *adj.* made of wool 2. *n.* a fabric made of wool ‖ (*pl.*) woolen goods [O.E. *wullen*]

Woolf (wulf), Virginia (1882-1941), English novelist and critic. Her novels include 'Mrs. Dalloway' (1925), 'To the Lighthouse' (1927) and 'The Waves' (1931). Influenced by Proust and Joyce, she experimented in ways of making the novel seem more true to life by discarding plot and by allowing a character to emerge from the vision he forms out of his impressions of the life around him, with all its complexity and incoherence. She uses the interior monologue in the attempt to render sensitivity directly (*STREAM OF CONSCIOUSNESS). She was extremely eloquent, and her genius lies perhaps even more in her heightened language and arresting phrases than in her experiments with technique. In her criticism she justly rescued many minor figures from oblivion

wool fat wool grease

wool·gath·er·ing (wúlgæðəriŋ) 1. *n.* the pursuit of stray thoughts when one should be concentrating 2. *adj.* indulging in such stray thoughts

[fr. wandering about gathering wool left by sheep on wire, hedges etc.]

wool grease a fatlike, wax coating on the surface of the fibers of sheep's wool, used in dressing leathers and furs, in making printing inks, and as a source of lanolin

wool·grow·er (wúlgrouər) *n.* (*Br.*) someone who breeds sheep to produce wool

wooliness *WOOLLINESS

woollen *WOOLEN

Wool·ley (wúli:), Sir Charles Leonard (1880-1960), British archaeologist who excavated Ur (1927)

wool·li·ness, wool·i·ness (wúli:nis) *n.* the quality of being woolly

wool·ly, wool·y (wúli:) 1. *comp.* **wool·li·er, wool·i·er** *superl.* **wool·li·est, wool·i·est** *adj.* of or like wool ‖ covered with wool ‖ lacking clearness of definition ‖ (*pop.*) not thinking clearly ‖ showing lack of mental clarity 2. *pl.* **wool·lies, wool·ies** *n.* a woolen undergarment, esp. a long one

woolly bear any of the hairy larvae of the moths of fam. *Arctiidae*

Wool·man (wúlmən), John (1720-72), American Quaker leader, one of the first spokesmen for the abolition of slavery

wool·pack (wúlpæk) *n.* a cover into which fleeces are packed for transport ‖ a bale of wool ‖ a fleecy-looking cumulus cloud rising from a flat base [M.E.]

wool·sack (wúlsæk) *n.* (*Br.*) a large square cushion stuffed with wool on which the lord chancellor sits in the House of Lords **the woolsack** (*Br.*) the office of lord chancellor [M.E.]

wool stapler a dealer in wool, esp. one who sorts by staple before selling to manufacturers

Wool·worth (wúlwə:rθ), Frank Winfield (1852-1919), U.S. merchant. He established (1879) at Lancaster, Pa., his first successful five-and-ten-cent store, and incorporated (1911) the F.W. Woolworth Company. He had the Woolworth Building in New York City built (1913). It was then the highest building (792 ft) in the world. At the time of his death he owned more than 1,000 stores

wooly *WOOLLY

Woo·mer·a (wú:merə) a site, in central South Australia, of a weapons testing range (established 1947)

wooz·y (wú:zi:, wú:zi) *comp.* **wooz·i·er** *superl.* **wooz·i·est** *adj.* (*pop.*) confused or muddled as the result of a blow, too much alcohol etc. ‖ (*pop.*) physically weak, *to feel woozy after an operation*

Worces·ter (wústər) the county town (pop. 74,247) of Worcestershire, England, on the Severn, famous for its fine porcelain. Gothic cathedral (mainly 13th-14th cc.)

Worcester a manufacturing town (pop. 372,940) in central Massachusetts: mechanical engineering, metalworking, textiles, printing

Worces·ter·shire (wústərʃiər) (*abbr.* Worcs.) a W. Midland county (area 699 sq. miles, pop. 569,000) of England. County town: Worcester

word (wə:rd) 1. *n.* a speech sound or combination of sounds having meaning and used as a basic unit of language and human communication ‖ the written or printed symbol of one of these basic units of language ‖ (*pl.*) things said, *his words went unheeded* ‖ (*pl.*, used without an article) a dispute, *they had words on the matter* ‖ information, a message, *word came that he was still alive* ‖ a promise, an assurance, *he was as good as his word, you have my word for it* ‖ (*pl.*) promises of performance as opposed to actual performance (cf. DEED) ‖ a command, an order, *to give the word to attack* ‖ a password, watchword ‖ (*pl.*) the text (as distinct from the music) of a song, opera etc. ‖ (*pl.*) the text spoken by an actor **the Word** (*Christian theol.*) God incarnate in Jesus Christ ‖ (*Christian theol.*) the Bible as the revelation of God ‖ (*Christian theol.*) the gospel message **a good word** a recommendation, *he said a good word on your behalf* **a man (woman) of few words** a man (woman) apt to be silent rather than talkative **a word in season** a piece of well-timed advice **a word of advice** a piece of advice **a word to the wise** admonishment offered to someone intelligent enough to act on it **by word of mouth** orally rather than in writing **his (her) word is law** what he (she) says is obeyed without argument **in a (or one) word** to sum up briefly **in so many words** in a frank, blunt manner leaving no room for doubt **in words of one syllable** in simple, forthright language **the last word** the final decision || the last thing said, esp. in a dispute || the most up-to-date model, example etc., *the last word in sports cars* **to have a word with someone** to have a short talk with someone, esp. about some business matter || to admonish someone mildly, *he had a word with them about their continual lateness* **to put in a word (or a good word) for** to use one's influence in order to recommend someone or something **to take someone at his word** to believe that someone means what he says, esp. when he makes some attractive offer **to take someone's word for it** to believe that what a person says is true without verifying it **2.** *v.t.* to phrase, put into words, *he worded the protest very strongly* [O.E.]

word blindness alexia

word for word in exactly the same words || (of translating) done taking each word in turn instead of finding equivalents for wholes **word-for-wórd** *adj.*

word·i·ly (wə́:rdili:) *adv.* in a wordy way

word·i·ness (wə́:rdi:nis) *n.* the quality of being wordy

word·ing (wə́:rdiŋ) *n.* a putting into words || the words used

word·less (wə́:rdlis) *adj.* not expressed or capable of being expressed in words || having or able to find no words with which to express oneself

word of command (*Br.*) the exclamatory word or phrase giving an order, esp. to soldiers being drilled

word of honor, *Br.* **word of honour** an assurance staking one's honor that one is telling the truth

word order the arrangement of words in a phrase, clause or sentence

word-paint·ing (wə́:rdpeintiŋ) *n.* vivid or picturesque description in words

word-per·fect (wə́:rdpə́:rfikt) *adj.* in the condition of having committed (a speech, part in a play, poem etc.) accurately to memory

word-play (wə́:rdplei) *n.* verbal wit, esp. punning || an instance of this

word processing work-saving system of recording, storing, and retrieving typewritten data utilizing correctible magnetic tape or other storage facility, often with visual presentation on a screen —**word processor** *n.* the machine used

Words·worth (wə́:rdzwə̀:rθ), Dorothy (1771-1855), sister of William. She was a firm supporter and helpful critic of her brother. Her own place in literature is ensured by her 'Journals', published posthumously (1897)

Wordsworth, William (1770-1850), English poet. The 'Lyrical Ballads' (1798 and 1800), written jointly with Coleridge, are usually taken as the inauguration of English Romantic poetry. Wordsworth wrote most of the lyrics, 'Lines Written above Tintern Abbey' and other famous poems in this collection as well as the preface (1800 edition), in which he expounded his theories of poetry. In 1807 he published 'Poems in Two Volumes', containing 'The Happy Warrior', 'Ode to Duty' and the 'Immortality' ode. His later work could be said to be undistinguished (his long autobiographical poem 'The Prelude', published in 1850, was in fact a revision of a version written many years earlier), but his genius often shone in a sonnet or an unexpected couplet.

One important aspect of Wordsworth's poetry and of his whole intellectual position is that he linked literary changes to intellectual changes generally. His feeling for external nature, his reflections on his own mysterious apprehensions of the 'otherness' of the universe and on his relations with it (did he create what he saw, or did he receive admonitions from some kind of universal spirit?): these led him to question the whole nature of perception, and with Coleridge to move away from the 18th-c. intellectual traditions inspired by Locke. The theorizing found expression as immediate and troubling perceptions which touch the reader still.

He was important also for his personal history. He is the supreme example of that band of writers who welcomed the French Revolution as the great forward step toward social justice and human perfection. 'The Prelude' records (along with much else) the failure of his hopes, the despair to which it brought him, and his return to health and balance.

Wordsworth is the preeminent rather than the representative Romantic: at his best he relates in language of mysterious simplicity the traffic of the individual soul with the whole

framework of nature, the lasting force of childhood experience and, in adult life, 'the heavy and the weary weight of all this unintelligible world'. The verse of his great period seems to offer a way to acceptance, belonging and celebration which is entirely his own

word·y (wə́:rdi:) *comp.* **word·i·er** *superl.* **word·i·est** using many or too many words, *a wordy style* || using words, *wordy exchange*

wore past of WEAR

work (wə:rk) *n.* physical or mental activity undertaken to achieve a purpose (cf. PLAY) and involving the expenditure of effort || the end or purpose for which one expends such effort, *he made the abolition of slavery his life's work* || what one can achieve by such effort in a specified amount of time, *checking the entries will be a week's work* || (*pl.*) the output of a writer, artist, composer etc., *the works of Shakespeare* || any one item of this output, *'Measure for Measure' is a hard work to understand* || literary, artistic or musical output of a specified kind, *Goethe's scientific work* || what one does in order to earn money, *his work takes him abroad a lot* || all the activities proper to a specified person or kind of person, *a mother's work is never done* || toil involved in activities which one undertakes to do or which have to be done, *her sick mother made a lot of extra work* || the visible effect of natural happenings resulting in change, *the tree's bent form is the work of wind and rain* || a large engineering structure, e.g. a bridge || (*phys.*) a transference of energy measured by the product of a force and the component of the displacement of the point of application of the force parallel to the force. Work has the dimensions of energy || (*pl.*) a factory or industrial plant, *the works will shut completely during August* || (*pl.*) a fortified structure || (*pl.*) the moving parts of a mechanical device || the piece being cut, ground etc. in a machine tool etc. || (*pl., theol.*) good deeds (as contrasted with faith) || an example of the use of some skill or faculty, *thorough detective work* || needlework, embroidery etc. done for pleasure, *after dinner she got out her work* **out of work** unemployed because one is sick or cannot find work **to have one's work (or all one's work) cut out** to have as much as one can possibly cope with (to do something) **to make short (or quick) work of** to deal with or dispose of very quickly and effortlessly **to make work** to invent unnecessary tasks to do || to be the cause of extra work for someone **to set (or get) to work on** to begin (*a large task*) [O.E. *weorc*]

work *pres. part.* **work·ing** *past* and *past part.* **worked,** (*archaic* and *technical*) **wrought** (rɔt) *v.i.* to engage in activity designed to achieve a particular purpose (cf. PLAY) and requiring an expenditure of considerable effort, *he worked fast to move the furniture out in time* || to earn one's living, *she's too young to work and is still in school* || to be effective, have the desired or intended effect, *I'm afraid your plan won't work, did the medicine work?* || to be an employee of a specified sort, *he works in the printing business* || to get into a specified condition or position by movement, *the knot worked loose, his shirt worked up his back* || (of yeast or a liquid) to ferment || to show emotion, esp. distress, by muscular twitches or nervous movements of the limbs, *you could tell by the way his face worked that it was bad news, her hands were working in her lap as she talked* || (of a ship's timbers) to strain, esp. in a heavy sea || to move or sink very slowly, *the foundations show signs of working* || to proceed or make progress in some action or task, *it would be easier to work backwards* || to progress with difficulty, *he worked slowly along the ledge* || to apply oneself with effort, esp. to one's studies, *to work at one's scales* || (with 'on') to use wiles or persuasion, *work on your father until he agrees* || (of an artist) to use specified materials or techniques, *she works in oils, he works in blank verse occasionally* || (with 'out') to come to a satisfactory conclusion, *things will work out if you will just be patient* || *v.t.* to cause to labor, *he works his men too hard* || to bring about by labor or as if by labor, *to work a miracle* || to extract a mineral from (a mine etc.) || to cause (a specified material) to be transformed by one's efforts, *to work wood, work the clay into a cylinder*, esp. to manipulate (iron) by heating and hammering || to make (one's way) or cause (oneself) to advance by slow stages and with effort, *he worked his way along the ledge, he worked himself up to be head of the firm* || (with 'up', 'into' or 'up into') to excite or stimu-

late the emotions of, *she worked herself into a panic* || to sew or make by needlework, *to work a sampler* || to pay for (one's passage) in a ship by providing some service of equivalent value to the fare || to pay for (oneself or one's way) by doing a paid job or jobs or by some service, *to work one's way through college* || (with 'off') to repay (a debt) over a period by payments or services to the creditor at intervals || to solve (an equation) || to have (a region etc.) as one's sphere of operations, *he works the East Coast* || to cause to operate, *to work a pump* || to bring (oneself or an object) into or out of a specified condition by slow and esp. laborious effort, *he worked himself out of his fetters* || (with 'in' or 'into') to insert gradually by pressure or other careful manipulation, *to work a knife into a crack* || (with 'in') to mix or blend, esp. by stirring, *work the oil into the mixture drop by drop* || (with 'off') to get rid of by expending energy, *to work off surplus weight* || (with 'off') to find an outlet for (rage, excess energy etc.), *to work off one's bad temper on someone* || (with 'out') to find (a solution or compromise) or solve (a problem) by an effort of the mind or will, *you must work it out among yourselves* || (pop., with 'it') to contrive, *try to work it so that you get some extra leave* || (with 'up') to perfect the performance of by practice, *she will have to work up the last movement before the concert* **to work one's fingers to the bone** to exhaust oneself, esp. in menial tasks, often without receiving any gratitude **to work to death** to overwork || to use too often, *to work a phrase to death* **wórk·a·ble** *adj.* that can be worked or worked on || that will work, practicable [O.E. *wyrcan, wircan*]

work·a·day (wə́:rkədei) *adj.* dull and commonplace [M.E. *werkeday* fr. O.N.]

work·a·hol·ic (wə:rkəhɔ́lək) *n.* **1.** one addicted to work **2.** by extension, one who works excessively —**workaholism** *n.*

work·bag (wə́:rkbæg) *n.* a bag for sewing materials

work·bas·ket (wə́:rkbæskit, wə́:rkbɑskit) *n.* a basket for sewing materials

work·bench (wə́:rkbentʃ) *n.* a strong table on which manual or machine work is done

work·book (wə́:rkbʊk) *n.* a pupil's exercise book with printed problems etc. and space for answers || a book of instructions for procedure and operation || a book in which is recorded work accomplished or planned

work·box (wə́:rkbɔks) *n.* a box of materials or equipment, esp. for sewing

work·day (wə́:rkdei) *n.* a day on which work is carried on as usual, not a Sunday or holiday || the period of work on such a day, esp. the number of hours making up an accepted day for which a worker is entitled to full pay, *an eight-hour workday*

worked up agitated, emotionally upset or tense

work·er (wə́:rkər) *n.* a person who works || an employee || a member of the working class || a person who works hard || a neuter individual or sexually undeveloped female of certain social insects (bee, ant etc.)

work ethic belief that productive physical or mental labor is a prime virtue

work·fare (wə́:rkfɛər) *n.* government program that requires welfare recipients able to work to accept training or suitable public service work

work·horse (wə́:rkhɔrs) *n.* a horse used to perform hard work, e.g. plowing, hauling etc. || a steady, hard-working person

work·house (wə́:rkhaus) *pl.* **work·hous·es** (wə́:rkhauziz) *n.* (*Br. hist.*) a public institution to shelter homeless and poor people in return for work || a place of correction for petty offenders, e.g. drunkards or vagrants

work-in (wə́:rkin) *n.* a protest demonstration in which employees (or students) report to work but refuse to carry on the work

work·ing (wə́:rkiŋ) **1.** *adj.* engaging in manual labor or production, *the working class* || sufficient or adequate to allow work to be done or for a desired end to be achieved, *a working knowledge of German* || accurate enough to work by, *a working rule* || capable of being operated, *a working model* **2.** *n.* (*pl.*) excavations made in mining etc.

working assets (*accounting*) noncapital assets available for running a business

working capital funds which can be used in meeting expenses, as distinct from the fixed capital represented by buildings, site values etc. || current assets less current liabilities

CONCISE PRONUNCIATION KEY: **(a)** æ, c*a*t; ɑ, c*a*r; ɔ f*aw*n; ei, sn*a*ke. **(e)** e, h*e*n; i:, sh*ee*p; iə, d*ee*r; ɛə, b*ea*r. **(i)** i, f*i*sh; ai, t*i*ger; ə:, b*i*rd. **(o)** o, *o*x; au, c*ow*; ou, g*oa*t; u, p*oo*r; ɔi, r*oy*al. **(u)** ʌ, d*u*ck; u, b*u*ll; u:, g*oo*se; ə, *ba*cillus; ju:, c*u*be. x, lo*ch*; θ, *th*ink; ð, bo*th*er; z, *Z*en; ʒ, corsa*g*e; dʒ, sava*g*e; ŋ, orangutan*g*; j, *y*ak; ʃ, *fi*sh; tʃ, fe*tch*; ˈl, rabb*le*; ˈn, redd*en*. Complete pronunciation key appears inside front cover.

working class the social and economic class of people who work for wages, esp. the industrial workers

working day a workday

working drawing a scale drawing guiding builders, engineers etc. in their work

work·ing·man (wə́:rkiŋmæn) *pl.* **work·ing·men** (wə́:rkiŋmen) *n.* a man of the working class

working papers legal papers which a minor under some legally fixed age must have before he is allowed to work

working party (*Br.*) a committee appointed to investigate and report on a social or industrial problem ‖ (*mil.*) a body of men detailed for some special job

work·man (wə́:rkmən) *pl.* **work·men** (wə́:rk-mən) *n.* a workingman ‖ a workingman with respect to the quality of his work ‖ a skilled laborer or craftsman **wórk·man·like** *adj.* befitting a skilled workman ‖ thoroughly practical or well made **wórk·man·ship** *n.* the skill shown in a finished craft product or work of art

workmen's compensation compensation for accident or disease arising out of a workman's employment, which in certain countries the employer must pay by law

work of art a production of an artist, esp. in painting, sculpture etc. ‖ (*loosely*) anything very well made or performed

work·out (wə́:rkaut) *n.* a training session for a boxer, athlete etc.

work·peo·ple (wə́:rkpi:p'l) *pl. n.* (*Br.*) working men and women

work·room (wə́:rkru:m, wə́:rkrum) *n.* a room set apart for esp. manual work

work-rule action (wə́:rkrú:l) job slowdown action by strict application of regulations; (*Br.*) work-to-rule action

works council a committee formed by the management among the employees of a factory or plant, to consider problems of industrial relations, production etc.

work sheet a prepared document recording work done or to be done in a plant ‖ an accountant's trial statement sheet

work·shop (wə́:rkʃɒp) *n.* a room or building in which productive work or manufacture on a small scale is carried out ‖ an intensive seminar in some subject of study

work-shy (wə́:rkʃai) *adj.* lazy

Works Progress Administration (*abbr.* WPA), an independent agency established (1935) by executive order of President Franklin D. Roosevelt to employ persons on relief on useful projects. Headed (1935-8) by Harry Hopkins, it sponsored a large-scale construction program and many cultural projects, notably the Federal Theater Project. It employed 8.5 million persons and appropriated almost $11 billion from the federal government. An unfavorable Senate committee report (1939), as well as increasing employment, resulted in the reduction of its appropriations and (1943) in its dissolution

work study (*management*) system techniques utilizing analysis of ways of performing tasks, time studies, and creating standards, formerly part of time and motion studies

work·ta·ble (wə́:rktęib'l) *n.* a table having a surface on which work can be done and usually having drawers, e.g. for sewing materials

work-to-rule (wə́:rktu:rú:l) *n.* (*Br.*) labor demonstration applying strict interpretation to work rules, thus hampering production; (*U.S.*) work-rule action

world (wə:rld) **1.** *n.* the planet earth ‖ the universe ‖ the earth together with its inhabitants ‖ a distinct part of the universe or of the earth, *the Old World* ‖ human society, *the world lives in fear of nuclear warfare* ‖ a recognized part or period of human society, *the business world, the ancient world* ‖ any domain of existence, activity etc., *the animal world* ‖ everything other than oneself ‖ the totality of things, events etc. of which one has personal experience, *his world is rather limited* ‖ a great amount, *there is a world of difference between them* ‖ life on this earth, *he has departed from this world* ‖ secular rather than religious affairs ‖ a star or planet **for all the world** exactly, *it sounded for all the world as if he meant it* ‖ **for the world** for any consideration whatever, *I wouldn't hurt him for the world* **in the world** an intensive used with 'how', 'when', 'where', 'who' or 'why', *how in the world can they get there on time?* **out of this world** superb **to bring into the world** to give

birth to ‖ **to come into the world** to be born **world without end** (*rhet.* and *eccles.*) forever [O.E. *weorold, worold*]

World Alliance of Y.M.C.A's **YOUNG MEN'S CHRISTIAN ASSOCIATION

World Bank the International Bank for Reconstruction and Development founded at the Bretton Woods Conference (1944) by the Western powers and provided by them with assets (in bullion and currency), on the basis of which member nations and private firms if repayment is guaranteed by a member, may obtain credit for approved development and reconstruction enterprises without drawing upon national reserves. By the mid-1980s there were nearly 150 member nations. The World Bank is affiliated with the U.N. Headquarters: Washington

world-class (wə:rldklæs) *adj.* of a caliber suitable for international recognition, e.g., world-class tennis player

World Council of Churches an organization of the majority of Protestant and Orthodox Churches, constituted in 1948, enabling practical cooperation and common study to take place among its members. It sprang from the International Missionary Council (founded 1921), the Life and Work Movement (founded 1925) and the Faith and Order Movement (founded 1927). Its activities have been watched by the Roman Catholic Church with sympathetic interest. Headquarters: Geneva

World Federation of Trade Unions an international body representing the trade unions of the world, constituted in 1945, but confined since 1949 to the trade union federations with communist sympathies. Headquarters: Prague

World Food Conference 1974 conference sponsored by the United Nations, held in Rome, creating a 36-nation World Food Council and another meeting establishing the International Fund for Agricultural Development

World Health Organization an international body set up in 1948 under the aegis of the United Nations, though constitutionally independent. Its function is to direct and correlate efforts to overcome disease by technical assistance, research and education: in particular to combat diseases endemic in primitive or underdeveloped countries. Headquarters: Geneva

world line (*astron.*) space-time paths of photons emitted by the stars

world·li·ness (wə́:rldli:nis) *n.* the state or quality of being worldly

world·ling (wə́:rldliŋ) *n.* (*rhet.*) someone who is worldly-minded

world·ly (wə́:rldli:) *comp.* **world·li·er** *superl.* **world·li·est** *adj.* pertaining to the material world or its existence ‖ devoted to this life and its practical concerns and enjoyments rather than to spiritual concerns

world·ly-mind·ed (wə́:rldli:máindid) *adj.* intent on worldly interests or material success

world·ly-wise (wə́:rldli:wáiz) *adj.* experienced in the ways of the world and therefore cautious or prudent

World Meteorological Organization (*abbr.* W.M.O.) an agency of the U.N., set up in 1951 to promote international cooperation in meteorology

world power a state having sufficient economic and esp. military power to influence world politics

World Series a series of autumn games between champions of the two major U.S. baseball leagues to decide the national championship

World war, 1st the war (1914-18) between the Allies and the Central Powers. Its basic causes lay in the political, economic and colonial rivalries of the great powers, stretching back into the late 19th c. The rise of Pan-Slavism, with Russian encouragement, presented a grave threat to the stability of Austria-Hungary. The Franco-Prussian War had left France aggrieved by the loss of Alsace-Lorraine. The imperialism of the late 19th c., backed by an armaments race based on the rapid growth of heavy industry, esp. in Germany, added to international tension. Finally, the spread of secret diplomacy and the formation of the Triple Alliance and the Triple Entente made it inevitable that when war began it would rapidly involve many countries. The Moroccan crises (1905, 1911) brought France and Germany to the brink of war, and Austria's annexation of Bosnia-Herzegovina (1908) created another international crisis. The Balkan Wars (1912-13) were a further manifestation of the unrest in S.E. Europe. The assassination

(June 28, 1914) of Archduke Franz Ferdinand at Sarajevo precipitated the 1st world war.

Austria, under the guidance of Berchtold, issued an unacceptable ultimatum to Serbia and declared war (July 28, 1914). Russia mobilized in support of Serbia (July 29). Germany declared war on Russia (Aug. 1) and on France (Aug. 3). Germany, applying the Schlieffen plan, immediately invaded Belgium. This violation of Belgian neutrality led Britain to declare war on Germany (Aug. 4). Austria declared war on Russia (Aug. 6). Germany and Austria were joined by Turkey (Oct. 30, 1914) and Bulgaria (Oct. 5, 1915). The Allies were joined, among others, by Japan (Aug. 23, 1914), Italy (May 23, 1915) and the U.S.A. (Apr. 6, 1917).

The Germans advanced rapidly through Belgium and Luxembourg into N.E. France, forcing the French and a British expeditionary force to fall back toward Paris, with much hard fighting. The German failure to give sufficient weight to the right wing, as well as faults of communication between their armies and their high command, enabled Joffre to counterattack at the Marne (Sept. 6-13, 1914), driving the Germans back to the Aisne. Both sides, each trying to outflank the other, advanced toward the Channel ports, and the Allies stemmed the German advance at Ypres (Oct. 14-Nov. 13, 1914). Both sides dug in, and the line of battle became stabilized between Flanders and the Swiss border. It remained almost stationary here for the next three years, despite repeated attempts by each side to dislodge the other from its trenches and gain ground. The German use of poison gas at the 2nd Battle of Ypres (Apr. 22-May 2, 1915), the massive German onslaught at Verdun (Feb. 21-Dec. 15, 1916) and the British use of tanks at the Somme (July-Oct. 1916) all failed to break the stalemate in spite of over 2,000,000 casualties.

Meanwhile the Russian attack on E. Prussia was decisively crushed by the Germans at Tannenberg and the Masurian Lakes (Aug.26-Sept. 15,1914). By the end of 1915, the Germans had forced the Russians out of most of Poland. Repeated heavy defeats sapped Russian morale, the czar abdicated (Mar. 15, 1917), and the Bolshevik revolution was followed by armistice negotiations (Dec. 1917). By the time the Treaty of Brest-Litovsk was signed (Mar. 3, 1918), the Germans had overrun the Ukraine. In S. Europe, an Allied expedition to Gallipoli (Apr. 1915-Jan. 1916), with the aim of attacking Turkey and opening the Straits to help Russia, was a failure.

Italy, renouncing the Triple Alliance, remained neutral at the start of the war and then joined the Allies (May 1915). Italian and Austrian forces faced each other in stalemate in N. Italy until the Italians were routed (Oct. 24-Nov. 12, 1917). They counterattacked successfully, however, a year later. Serbia repulsed three Austrian attempts at invasion (Aug. 12-Dec. 15, 1914) but succumbed to a concerted German, Austrian and Bulgarian onslaught (Oct.-Nov. 1915). An Allied expedition to Salonica in support of Serbia was halted by the Bulgarians (Oct. 1915), but Bulgaria was forced to sue for an armistice (Sept. 1918). Russia attacked Turkey in the Caucasus (1914) and British troops advanced from the Persian Gulf north through Mesopotamia (1914-18). A Turkish attack on the Suez Canal was repulsed (Feb. 1915), and British, Australian and New Zealand troops defeated the Turks in Palestine and Iraq (1917-18). German colonies in Africa and the Pacific, and at Kiaochow, were captured by the Allies. Rumania was occupied (1917) by the Central Powers.

At sea, the main battle was fought at Jutland (May 31, 1916), after which the German surface fleet remained in harbor for the rest of the war. The German use of unrestricted submarine warfare, in an attempt to starve Britain, had the effect of bringing the U.S.A. into the war (Apr. 6, 1917).

The arrival of the U.S. troops in Europe counterbalanced the arrival of more German troops liberated by Russia's withdrawal from the war. The Allies, now with a unified command under Foch, were able to halt renewed German offensives in N.E. France (Mar. 21-July 17, 1918) and to push back the German line toward the Belgian frontier. After Bulgaria had fallen to the Allies (Sept. 29, 1918), followed by Turkey (Oct. 30, 1918) and Austria (Nov. 3, 1918), Ger-

CONCISE PRONUNCIATION KEY; **(a)** æ, c**a**t; ɑ, c**a**r; ɔ f**aw**n; ei, sn**a**ke. **(e)** e, h**e**n; i:, sh**ee**p; iə, d**ee**r; ɛə, b**ea**r. **(i)** i, f**i**sh; ai, t**i**ger; ə:, b**i**rd. **(o)** o, **o**x; au, c**ow**; ou, g**oa**t; u, p**oo**r; ɔi, r**oy**al. **(u)** ʌ, d**u**ck; u, b**u**ll; u:, g**oo**se; ə, b**a**cillus; ju:, c**u**be. x, lo**ch**; θ, **th**ink; ð, bo**th**er; z, **Z**en; ʒ, cor**s**age; dʒ, sava**g**e; ŋ, orangutan**g**; j, **y**ak; ʃ, **fi**sh; tʃ, fe**tch**; 'l, rabb**le**; 'n, redd**en**. Complete pronunciation key appears inside front cover.

man morale collapsed. In the face of naval mutiny and republican revolts, Wilhelm II fled to Holland (Nov. 10, 1918) and an armistice was signed (Nov. 11, 1918) at Compiègne.

The war was ended by a series of treaties, including the Treaty of Versailles (June 28, 1919), the Treaty of St Germain (Sept. 10, 1919) and the Treaty of Lausanne (1923). The war had cost about 8,700,000 lives, including about 3,350,000 on the side of the Central Powers, and 1,390,000 French, 1,700,000 Russians, 780,000 British and 120,000 Americans. The 1st world war saw the development of trench warfare and submarine warfare, increased mechanization (esp. the use of tanks), and the use of aircraft, first for observation and later also for bombing. Out of the war settlement came the establishment of the League of Nations. But tensions were also created which were to give rise to the 2nd world war 20 years later

World war, 2nd the war (1939-45) between the Allies and the Axis. Its origins lay in German resentment at the terms of the Treaty of Versailles (1919), the economic crisis of 1929-30 which favored the rise to power of Fascist dictators, the failure of the League of Nations to gain international acceptance for disarmament, and the policy of colonial conquest adopted by Germany, Italy and Japan as a means of acquiring raw materials and markets. Germany, prepared for military conquest by Hitler, remilitarized the Rhineland (1936) in violation of the Locarno Pact. The League of Nations failed to react firmly either to this or to the conquest (1935-6) of Ethiopia by Italy under Mussolini. The Spanish Civil War (1936-9), in which German and Italian intervention assured the victory of Franco, served as a proving ground for new techniques of warfare. Britain and France, unprepared for war, remained passive when Germany annexed Austria (Mar. 1938), and they continued their policy of appeasement in the Munich Agreement (Sept. 1938), sacrificing the Sudetenland to Germany. The German seizure of the whole of Czechoslovakia (Mar. 1939) and the Italian seizure of Albania (Apr. 1939) put an end to appeasement. Germany signed a military alliance with Italy (May 1939) and a nonaggression pact with the U.S.S.R. (Aug. 1939). After manufacturing incidents over the status of Danzig and the Polish Corridor, Germany invaded Poland (Sept. 1, 1939). Britain and France declared war on Germany (Sept. 3, 1939).

Poland succumbed rapidly to the German 'Blitzkrieg' (lightning war), a technique of massive concerted ground and air attack. The U.S.S.R. joined with Germany in partitioning Poland and then crushed Finland (1939-40). The British and French armies remained immobile throughout the winter, relying on the Maginot line. Germany invaded Denmark (Apr. 9, 1940), which fell immediately, and Norway, which was conquered by June 9, 1940. The Netherlands were overrun (May 10-14, 1940), as well as Belgium (May 10-28, 1940) and Luxembourg (May 10, 1940). The Maginot line was turned by the Germans at Sedan (May 13, 1940). A rapid German advance through N.E. France trapped the Allied forces on the coast at Dunkerque, whence they were evacuated to Britain (May 26–June 4, 1940). Italy declared war in support of Germany (June 10, 1940). The French armies under Weygand were unable to stop the German advance on Paris (June 14, 1940). France signed an armistice (June 22, 1940) with Germany, providing for German occupation of the north of the country. The Vichy government under Pétain was set up, while de Gaulle continued the struggle from London.

Britain, under the leadership of Churchill, defeated the German attempt to bomb it into submission in the Battle of Britain (Aug. 15, 1940–May 1941) and escaped invasion. In N. Africa, Italy invaded British Somaliland (Aug. 1940) and attempted to invade Egypt from Libya (Sept. 1940), but was checked by British forces. The British and Italian navies fought for control of the Mediterranean (1940-1), while German submarines attempted to cut off Britain's Atlantic supply routes. Greece repelled an Italian invasion from Albania (Oct. 1940–Mar. 1941), but fell to a German and Bulgarian attack (Apr. 1941) which also crushed Yugoslavia (Apr. 1941) and Crete (May 1941). The Allies conquered Italian East Africa (Dec.

1940–May 1941), Iraq (May 1941) and Syria (July 1941). Germany, with Finnish, Hungarian and Rumanian support, attacked the U.S.S.R (June 22, 1941) on a wide front and conquered most of European Russia by the winter of 1941, but halted west of Moscow. The U.S.A., while remaining neutral, agreed (1941) to supply lend-lease aid to Britain and the U.S.S.R. Churchill and Roosevelt drafted the Atlantic Charter (Aug. 1941). The U.S.A. was brought into the war (Dec. 8, 1941) by the Japanese attack on Pearl Harbor (Dec. 7, 1941). The Japanese rapidly overran the Philippines, Hong Kong, Malaya, Singapore, Burma, Indonesia and many of the Pacific islands, and were not checked by Allied naval and air victories until June 1942.

The war began to turn in the Allies' favor when the Axis forces under Rommel, sweeping back across N. Africa to Egypt, were routed by Montgomery's forces at Alamein (Oct. 1942). The U.S.A. landed troops in Algeria (Nov. 8, 1942) and, with British and Free French support, drove the Axis out of N. Africa by May 12, 1943. The Allies conquered Sicily (July-Aug. 1943) and advanced north up the mainland of Italy, which surrendered (Sept. 8, 1943), though German forces continued fighting in Italy. Meanwhile, the Russians, having successfully withstood a massive German offensive against Stalingrad (Sept. 1942-Feb. 1943), launched a counteroffensive which drove the Germans out of the U.S.S.R. by Aug. 1944. Underground movements in many German-occupied countries carried on successful guerrilla warfare and sabotage of German installations. The Poles rose in Warsaw (Aug. 1944). Allied counteroffensives gathered strength in New Guinea, the Pacific Is and Burma (1943-4).

The Allies had conferred together at Casablanca (Jan. 14-26, 1943), Quebec (Aug. 11-24, 1943) and Tehran (Nov. 28–Dec. 2, 1943), and had drawn up plans for the liberation of France. Under the command of Eisenhower, they invaded Normandy (June 6, 1944) and Provence (Aug. 15, 1944), and after much hard fighting drove the Germans out of France, liberating Paris on Aug. 25, 1944. Meanwhile the Russian offensive forced the surrender of Bulgaria (Sept. 11, 1944), Rumania (Sept. 12, 1944) and Finland (Sept. 19, 1944). Germany, fighting a rearguard action on all fronts, began to use rockets against Britain. The British landed in Greece (Oct. 1944), Belgrade was liberated by the Russians and the forces of Tito (Oct. 20, 1944) and the Germans withdrew from the Balkans. The Russians advanced through Poland, took E. Prussia and Czechoslovakia (Jan. 1945) and Vienna (Apr. 12, 1945), and overran E. Germany. The Allies crossed the Rhine (Mar. 7, 1945) and met Russian forces in Saxony (Apr. 25, 1945). As the Russians took Berlin (May 2, 1945), Hitler's suicide was reported. A German government formed by Doenitz surrendered unconditionally (May 7, 1945).

Meanwhile the British drove the Japanese from Burma (Feb. 1944–July 1945) and reestablished a supply route to China, which, by early 1945, had regained most of the territory lost to the Japanese. The Americans gradually expelled the Japanese from the scattered Pacific Is, the Philippines (1944-5), Okinawa (Apr. 1945) and Borneo (Aug. 1945). The U.S.S.R., having promised its support against Japan at Yalta (Feb. 4-12, 1945), invaded Manchuria. The U.S.A. dropped the first atomic bomb on Hiroshima (Aug. 6, 1945) and another on Nagasaki (Aug. 9, 1945), and Japan surrendered (Aug. 14, 1945).

The war, which cost more than 36 million lives, was the most destructive and widespread in history. Germany lost about 6 million lives, the U.S.S.R. about 17 million, Poland about 5,800,000, Yugoslavia about 1,600,000, Japan about 2 million, Italy about 450,000, Rumania about 460,000, France 570,000, the U.S.A. 400,000, Britain 400,000, Hungary about 430,000 and the Netherlands about 210,000. Millions were left homeless. Nazi Germany had attempted racial extermination, esp. of the Jews (of whom 6 million died), and had practiced atrocities in its concentration camps on a vast scale. Both the Allies and the Axis had increased their destructive power, culminating in the atomic bomb. After the war there emerged a new balance of power between the U.S.S.R., whose influence now spread through-

out Eastern Europe, and the U.S.A. Germany was divided into zones of occupation, leading to the deeper division between East and West Germany and preventing the signing of a full peace treaty with Germany. Europe as a whole slowly recovered from economic exhaustion. The United Nations organization was set up (1945).

Peace treaties were signed between the Allies and Italy, Rumania, Bulgaria, Hungary and Finland in Paris (Feb. 1947), between the Allies (except for the U.S.S.R.) and Japan in San Francisco (Sept. 1951) and between the U.S.S.R. and Japan (1956), and between the Allies and Austria (May 1955), establishing Austrian independence

world-wea·ry (wő:rldwiəri:) *adj.* tired of the world and its activities, esp. as the result of pursuing one's own pleasure

world·wide (wő:rldwáid) *adj.* pertaining or extending to all parts of the world

worm (wə:rm) **1.** *n.* an earthworm ‖ any of various elongated creeping animals with soft, often segmented bodies, e.g. the blindworm ‖ a similar creature parasitical on a mammal's tissues or intestines, e.g. a tapeworm ‖ (*loosely*) any of certain larvae resembling these ‖ (*pl.*) a disorder due to the presence of parasitic worms in the intestines etc. ‖ (*rhet.*) a mean, groveling or contemptible person ‖ the thread of a screw ‖ the shaft on which a spiral groove is cut ‖ a short revolving screw whose threads engage with a worm wheel ‖ something helical, e.g. a spiral pipe ‖ the spiral tube of a still in which vapor is cooled ‖ (*zool.*) the lytta **2.** *v.t.* to work (oneself or one's way) in a winding or insidious manner, *he wormed his way into her confidence* ‖ to elicit (information etc.) by devious ways, *to worm a secret out of someone* ‖ to cut the lytta of (a dog) ‖ to purge of intestinal worms ‖ (*naut.*) to wind fine rope or yarn around (a cable etc.) in order to fill in the spaces between the strands ‖ *v.i.* to move like a worm ‖ to look for worms for bait ‖ (with 'in' or 'into') to insinuate oneself by artful means [O.E. *wyrm*]

worm·cast (wő:rmkæst, wő:rmkɑst) *n.* a tube-shaped mass of earth voided by an earthworm and left on the surface of the ground

worm-eat·en (wő:rmi:t'n) *adj.* eaten into by worms, full of wormholes ‖ old-fashioned, worn out, *worm-eaten notions*

worm gear a gear consisting of a worm wheel engaging with a worm (short revolving screw) ‖ a worm wheel

worm·hole (wő:rmhoul) *n.* a hole made in soil by an earthworm ‖ a hole made in wood, fruit etc. by a worm or larva

Worms (vɔrms) a river port (pop. 74,200) in Rhineland-Palatinate, West Germany, on the Rhine. Romanesque cathedral (12th-13th cc.). Many Imperial diets were held here

Worms, Concordat of an agreement (1122) between Pope Calixtus II and Emperor Henry V, settling the Investiture Controversy. The Empire conceded to the papacy the exclusive right to invest bishops and abbots, but retained the right to prevent undesirable appointments

Worms, Diet of an assembly of the Holy Roman Empire at which Luther defended (1521) his doctrines before Charles V

worm wheel a toothed wheel that engages with the threads of a worm (short revolving screw)

worm·wood (wő:rmwud) *n. Artemisia absinthium*, fam. *Compositae*, an aromatic perennial woody plant of Europe and Asia yielding an oil used in making absinthe ‖ any plant of genus *Artemisia* ‖ (*rhet.*) bitterness, esp. bitter mortification [O.E. *wermod*]

worm·y (wő:rmi:) *comp.* **worm·i·er** *superl.* **worm·i·est** *adj.* full of worms ‖ burrowed by worms or larvae ‖ like a worm

worn *past part.* of WEAR

worn-out (wő:rnáut) *adj.* made useless by wear, *worn-out shoes* ‖ exhausted, tired out

worried *past* and *past part.* of WORRY

wor·ri·er (wő:ri:ər, wÁri:ər) *n.* someone given to worrying

wor·ri·ment (wő:ri:mənt, wÁri:mənt) *n.* (*rhet.*) anxiety, irritation ‖ (*rhet.*) a source of worry

wor·ri·some (wő:ri:səm, wÁri:səm) *adj.* causing worry ‖ easily and frequently worried

wor·ry (wő:ri:) **1.** *v. pres. part.* **wor·ry·ing** *past* and *past part.* **wor·ried** *v.t.* (esp. of a dog or wild carnivorous animal) to seize with the teeth and shake in order to kill or injure ‖ (esp. of a dog) to harass or tease by chasing, snapping at etc. ‖ to cause to feel disturbed or depressed, esp. through fear regarding some event, outcome etc. ‖ to give petty annoyance to, esp. by making continual demands upon the attention ‖ *v.i.* to feel a nagging fear about something, *to worry about one's health* ‖ (with 'along') to manage to meet one's day-to-day expenses by persistent effort ‖ (with 'through') to get to the end of a difficult piece of work or some hardship etc. by persistent effort **2.** *pl.* **wor·ries** *n.* a worrying or being worried ‖ an instance of this ‖ something that causes worry [O.E. *wyrgan*, to strangle]

worse (wə:rs) **1.** *adj.* bad in greater degree, *worse weather than usual* ‖ in a less good state of health, condition etc. **2.** *adv.* more badly, *he behaved even worse than usual* **3.** *n.* something worse or a worse state, *worse was to follow* **wórs·en** *v.t.* to make worse ‖ *v.i.* to become worse [O.E. *wiersa, wyrsa*]

wor·ship (wə́:rʃip) **1.** *n.* reverence, homage or honor paid to God ‖ ceremonies or services expressing such reverence, *public worship* ‖ an utterly devoted admiration for a person **Your (His) Worship** (esp. *Br.*) a courtesy title used to (or of) certain magistrates, officials etc. **2.** *v. pres. part.* **wor·ship·ing**, esp. *Br.* **wor·ship·ping** *past* and *past part.* **wor·shiped**, esp. *Br.* **wor·shipped** *v.t.* to pay religious devotion to, *to worship God* ‖ to idolize, adore, *he worships every hair on her head* ‖ *v.i.* to be full of adoration ‖ to take part in religious ceremonies **wór·ship·er**, esp. *Br.* **wór·ship·per** *n.* someone who worships **wór·ship·ful** *adj.* (esp. *Br.*, usually in formal titles) worthy, esteemed ‖ offering worship, adoring [O.E. *weorthscipe*]

worst (wə:rst) **1.** *adj.* most bad **2.** *adv.* most badly **3.** *n.* that which is worst, the worst part or state, *the worst of the journey is over* **at worst, at the worst** even on the least favorable reckoning **if worst comes to worst** (*Am.*=*Br.* **if the worst comes to the worst**) if the worst happens **to get the worst of it** to be defeated **4.** *v.t.* to defeat, esp. in argument [O.E. *wierresta, wyrresta, wyrsta, wersta*]

wor·sted (wústid, wə́:rstid) **1.** *n.* woolen yarn spun from long-fibered wool ‖ fabric made of such yarn **2.** *adj.* made of worsted fabric [after *Worsted*, former spelling of *Worstead* in Norfolk, England]

wort (wə:rt, wort) *n.* (only in plant names) a plant, esp. a herbaceous one, e.g. glasswort [O.E. *wyrt*, root, plant]

wort *n.* a sweet infusion of malt or other grain unfermented or in process of fermentation [O.E. *wyrt*, herb, root]

worth (wə:rθ) **1.** *n.* the amount of money etc. to which something is regarded as being equivalent, i.e. its monetary or material value ‖ the degree of excellence, importance etc. of someone or something as an indication of the degree to which he or it should be regarded as admirable, important, useful etc., *do not underestimate his worth, her poems are of little worth compared with her novels* ‖ the amount of something that may be purchased for a specified sum, *ten cents worth of nails* ‖ a person's material wealth, *what would you estimate his worth at?* **2.** *prep.* of the material worth of, *it is worth a great deal of money* ‖ deserving, *not worth consideration* ‖ rich to the extent of, *he died worth thousands* **for all one is worth** with all the energy, power etc. one possesses **for what it is worth** without any guarantee as to accuracy, truthfulness etc. [O.E. *weorth*]

wor·thi·ly (wə́:rðili:) *adv.* in a worthy way **wor·thi·ness** (wə́:rðinis) *n.* the quality of being worthy

worth·less (wə́:rθlis) *adj.* of no worth

worth·while (wə́:rθhwáil, wə́:rθwáil) *adj.* meriting the time, effort etc. involved, *was the excursion worthwhile?*

wor·thy (wə́:rði:) **1.** *comp.* **wor·thi·er** *superl.* **wor·thi·est** *adj.* having worth, *a worthy cause* ‖ respectable, *a worthy couple* ‖ (with 'of') deserving, *behavior worthy of punishment* ‖ (often with 'of') of a worth regarded as adequate, *a worthy opponent, an opponent worthy of him* **2.** *pl.* **wor·thies** *n.* a person of worth or eminence [M.E. *wurthi, worthy*]

Wouk (wouk), Herman (1915–), U.S. novelist, author of 'The Caine Mutiny' (1951), 'Marjorie Morningstar' (1955), 'Youngblood Hawke' (1962), 'The Winds of War' (1971) and 'War and Remembrance' (1978)

would (wud) *past* of WILL ‖ *auxiliary v.* used to express condition, *she would go if you would* ‖ used to express the future in indirect speech, *he said he would come* ‖ used in polite request, *would you please get me my hat?* ‖ (*rhet.*) used to express a wish, *would she were here!* ‖ used to

express doubt, *it would appear to be the case* (cf. WILL. cf. SHOULD) [M.E.]

would-be (wúdbi:) *adj.* desiring to be or self-styled, *a would-be orator*

would·n't (wúd'nt) *contr.* of WOULD NOT

wound (wu:nd) *n.* an injury to living tissues, esp. as the result of violence ‖ an injury to the feelings [O.E. *wund*]

wound *v.t.* to cause a wound or wounds in ‖ to hurt the feelings of ‖ *v.i.* to inflict a wound or wounds ‖ to hurt someone's feelings [O.E. *wundian*]

wound (waund) *past* and *past part.* of WIND, to go in a curved path ‖ alt. *past* and *past part.* of WIND, to sound (a horn etc.)

Wounded Knee Creek the site in South Dakota of an atrocity committed (1890) by the U.S. 7th Cavalry against a band of 350 men, women and children of the Minneconjon Sioux. More than half the Indians were massacred. The Plains Indians never again offered serious armed resistance to the white invaders

wound·wort (wú:ndwə:rt, wú:ndwort) *n.* a member of *Stachys*, fam. *Labiatae*, a genus of widely distributed annual or perennial low-growing plants with a tubular calyx and lipped corolla, formerly used for healing ‖ any of certain other plants that have been so used

Wou·wer·man (váuvərmən), Philips (1619-68), Dutch painter. He specialized in battle scenes, hunting scenes and seascapes

wove *past* and alt. *past part.* of WEAVE

woven alt. *past part.* of WEAVE

wove paper paper with a uniform, unlined surface, given to it by manipulation with a woven wire screen (cf. LAID PAPER)

WP (*abbr.*) for 'withdrawn passing,' a grade given to a passing student who withdraws from a course. *Cf* WF

W particle (*particle phys.*) hypothetical elementary particle believed to be the quantum of the weak force in nuclear interactions. *also* intermediate boson

wrack (ræk) *n.* seaweed thrown on shore by the tide, used e.g. as manure [M.Du. *wrak* or M.L.G. *wrack, wrak*, wreck]

wrack *n.* (esp. in phrase) **wrack and ruin** disaster, destruction, *he let the property go to wrack and ruin* [O.E. *wræc*, retribution]

wraith (reiθ) *n.* an apparition of a person, seen just before or just after his death ‖ a specter [Scot., etym. doubtful]

wran·gle (ræŋg'l) **1.** *v. pres. part.* **wran·gling** *past* and *past part.* **wran·gled** *v.i.* to quarrel noisily ‖ to argue ‖ *v.t.* (*western U.S.A.*) to herd or round up (horses or cattle) **2.** *n.* a noisy or angry quarrel or argument **wrán·gler** *n.* someone who wrangles ‖ (*Cambridge University*) a person winning first-class honors in the mathematical tripos [M.E. *wranglen* rel. to L.G. *wrangeln*, M.H.G. *rangeln*]

wrap (ræp) **1.** *v. pres. part.* **wrap·ping** *past* and *past part.* **wrapped** *v.t.* (often with 'up') to cover or enclose, *to wrap oneself up in a blanket, a landscape wrapped in mist* ‖ to conceal, *an affair wrapped in mystery* ‖ to arrange or fold as a covering, *wrap a scarf around your neck* ‖ (often with 'up') to make a parcel of ‖ *v.i.* (with 'around' etc.) to twine, *ivy wrapping round a tree trunk* ‖ to be arranged around something as a drapery, *a sari wraps several times around the waist* ‖ (with 'up') to put on extra clothes against the cold **wrapped up in** engrossed in ‖ very devoted to **2.** *n.* something, esp. a rug, shawl or extra garment, used to wrap oneself in **wráp·per** *n.* a paper wrapping enclosing a newspaper, periodical etc. for mailing ‖ a book jacket ‖ anything that wraps ‖ a person whose job is wrapping ‖ a dressing gown ‖ the tobacco leaf that covers a cigar **wráp·ping** *n.* anything with which something or someone is wrapped [etym. doubtful]

wrap·a·round (ræpəraund) *adj.* **1.** allembracing **2.** a flexible material used to wrap around an object **3.** a note, bond, or sale that leaves existing debts, leases, and agreements intact, e.g., in the purchase or sale of a property **4.** a type of skirt that wraps around the hips and ties at the waist

wraparound annuity a variable annuity to which a volatile investment (e.g., stocks, money market) has been added

wrasse (ræs) *n.* a member of *Labridue*, a family of brilliantly colored marine fish with spiny fins and prominent thick lips, found in warm seas [Cornish *wrach*]

wrath (ræθ, rɑθ, *Br.* esp. rɔθ) *n.* intense anger or indignation [O.E. *wræththu*]

Wrath, Cape the northwestern tip of Scotland, in Sutherland

wrath·ful (ræθfəl, rɑ́θfəl, *Br.* esp. rɔ́θfəl) *adj.* intensely angry ‖ arising from or characterized by wrath

wreak (ri:k) *v.t.* (*rhet.*) to give full play or effort to (one's anger etc.) ‖ (*rhet.*) to inflict (vengeance, harm etc.) [O.E. *wrecan*]

wreath (ri:θ) *pl.* **wreaths** (riðz, ri:θs) *n.* a circular band of flowers, leaves etc. for laying on a grave or memorial or used to decorate a door or window etc. or (*hist.*) to honor a victor ‖ something resembling this in shape, *a wreath of smoke* ‖ a representation in stone, metal or wood of a circular band of flowers, leaves etc. [O.E. *writha* fr. *writhan* v., to writhe]

wreathe (ri:ð) *pres. part.* **wreath·ing** *past* and *past part.* **wreathed** *v.t.* to form (flowers etc.) into a wreath ‖ to wind so as to form a wreath, *the snake wreathed itself around a branch* ‖ to encircle, *smoke wreathed the housetop* ‖ (with 'in', *passive*) to arrange the expression of, esp. so as to form smiles, *a face wreathed in smiles* ‖ *v.i.* to move in coils [fr. M.E. *wrethen past part.* of *writhen*, to writhe and fr. WREATH]

wreck (rek) **1.** *n.* the destruction or disablement esp. of a ship ‖ the ruins of a wrecked ship ‖ what is left of a building, vehicle etc., after destruction ‖ a person wasted by mental or physical sickness ‖ a spoiling or confounding, *the wreck of one's hopes* ‖ goods cast up by the sea from sunken ships **2.** *v.t.* to cause the wreck of, destroy, ruin ‖ *v.i.* to suffer wreck **wréck·age** *n.* the remains of a wrecked ship, vehicle, building etc. ‖ fragments of any wrecked structure **wréck·er** *n.* a person who wrecks or ruins ‖ a person who contrives the wreck of ships, e.g. by false signals, in order to plunder them ‖ (*Am.*=*Br.* housebreaker) someone whose business is demolishing buildings and disposing of the building materials ‖ a tow truck ‖ a person employed to recover wrecked ships or cargoes [A.F. *wrec, wrech*]

Wren (ren), Sir Christopher (1632-1723), English architect. He designed St Paul's Cathedral (1675-1711), over 50 other churches in London, and secular buildings such as the Sheldonian Theater at Oxford (1660s) and a wing of Hampton Court Palace (1690s). He had great mathematical and engineering skill, and used the classical orders with great imagination

wren (ren) *n.* any of many small singing birds of fam. *Troglodytidae* of tropical and temperate regions, e.g. *Troglodytes troglodytes*, a very small, dark-brown European bird with a short, erect tail, or *T. Troglodytes hiemalis*, its northern U.S. and Canadian representatative (the winter wren)

wrench (rentʃ) **1.** *v.t.* to pull or twist violently, *to wrench a door open* ‖ to injure or hurt by twisting violently, *to wrench one's arm* ‖ *v.i.* to twist or turn violently **2.** *n.* a violent twist, often combined with a sharp pull ‖ an injury caused by this ‖ an emotional pain, esp. from parting ‖ a tool with adjustable jaws for gripping and turning nuts or bolts etc. ‖ (*Am.*=*Br.* spanner) a tool for tightening nuts etc. (cf. MONKEY WRENCH) [O.E. *wrencan*, to twist]

wrest (rest) *v.t.* to obtain by using strength or violence or by great effort, *to wrest a living from the soil* ‖ to pull or force with a violent twist ‖ to arrive at (a meaning or interpretation) by distortion [O.E. *wræstan*]

wrest block the wooden plank in a piano in which the wrest pins are set

wres·tle (rés'l) **1.** *v. pres. part.* **wres·tling** *past* and *past part.* **wres·tled** *v.i.* to struggle with an opponent by grappling and trying to throw or trip him ‖ (of two opponents) to engage in such a struggle ‖ to struggle, *to wrestle with one's accounts* ‖ *v.t.* to struggle with (an opponent) by grappling with him and trying to throw or trip him ‖ (*western U.S.A.*) to throw (esp. a calf) for branding **2.** *n.* a wrestling bout ‖ a hard struggle **wrés·tler** *n.* **wrés·tling** *n.* a sport under any of various codes of rules, in which unarmed opponents grapple and try to throw each other [O.E. fr. *wræstan*, to wrest]

wrest pin one of the pins on a piano or harp around which are wound the ends of the strings, and by which the strings are tightened or slackened in tuning

wretch (retʃ) *n.* a person in great misfortune ‖ a contemptible or wicked person **wretch·ed** (rétʃid) *adj.* miserably sad ‖ of exceedingly poor quality, construction etc. ‖ contemptible ‖ causing or characterized by misery, *they live under wretched conditions* ‖ causing inconvenience,

CONCISE PRONUNCIATION KEY: **(a)** æ, c*a*t; ɑ, c*a*r; ɔ f*aw*n; ei, sn*a*ke. **(e)** e, h*e*n; i:, sh*ee*p; iə, d*ee*r; ɛə, b*ea*r. **(i)** i, f*i*sh; ai, t*i*ger; ə:, b*i*rd. **(o)** o, *o*x; au, c*ow*; ou, g*oa*t; u, p*oo*r; ɔi, r*oy*al. **(u)** ʌ, d*u*ck; u, b*u*ll; u:, g*oo*se; ə, b*a*cillus; ju:, c*u*be. x, lo*ch*; θ, *th*ink; ð, bo*th*er; z, *Z*en; ʒ, cor*s*age; dʒ, sava*g*e; ŋ, oranguta*ng*; j, *y*ak; ʃ, *f*ish; tʃ, fe*tch*; 'l, rabb*le*; 'n, redd*en*. Complete pronunciation key appears inside front cover.

discomfort, boredom etc. [O.E. *wrecca, wrœcca*, an outcast]

wrig·gle (ríg'l) 1. *v. pres. part.* **wrig·gling** *past and past part.* **wrig·gled** *v.i.* to twist and turn with short abrupt movements like those of a worm ‖ to move along in this way ‖ to act in an evasive, shifty way ‖ *v.t.* to cause to twist and turn with short abrupt movements ‖ to bring into a specified position or condition by twisting and turning abruptly, *to wriggle oneself free* 2. *n.* a wriggling movement [M.L.G. *wriggeln*]

Wright (rait), Frank Lloyd (1869-1959), American architect, creator of 'organic architecture', a mode of construction in which buildings are in close compositional relationship to their natural surroundings. His 'prairie style' houses, which he began constructing in 1902, are characterized by long, low horizontal lines and functional interiors: kitchen, living and dining areas forming an unbroken whole. His work includes the Guggenheim Museum, New York (1945-59)

Wright, Joseph (1734-97), English painter, known as Wright of Derby, famous for his candlelit studies, e.g. 'The Air Pump' (1768) and 'The Alchymist' (1771), and lunar landscapes

Wright, Orville (1871-1948) and his brother Wilbur (1867-1912), American aircraft engineers. They built the first stable and controllable heavier-than-air machine, which made its first flight (852 ft) at Kitty Hawk, North Carolina, in 1903

Wright, Richard (1908-60), U.S. black novelist. His 'Uncle Tom's Children' (1938) and 'Native Son' (1940) depict injustice against the blacks in the U.S.A.

wring (riŋ) 1. *v. pres. part.* **wring·ing** *past and past part.* **wrung** (rʌŋ) *v.t.* to squeeze and twist (wet clothes etc.), esp. so as to force out the moisture ‖ to force out (water etc.) by squeezing and twisting ‖ to twist forcibly ‖ to extort by mental or bodily coercion, *to wring a confession from someone* ‖ to squeeze, clasp or press, esp. with emotion, *to wring someone's hand* ‖ (*rhet.*) to pain, distress, *the sight wrung my heart* 2. *n.* a squeezing or twisting **wring·er** *n.* a machine for pressing water out of clothes **wring·ing** *adj.* (*Br.*) wringing wet [O.E. *wringan*]

wringing wet so wet that water can be squeezed out

wrin·kle (ríŋk'l) 1. *n.* a small furrow or ridge caused by a fold in a flexible surface, e.g. one formed in the skin as a mark of age, or one that disfigures cloth or a garment ‖ (*pop.*) a clever hint or suggestion about how to do something ‖ (*pop.*) a novel technique 2. *v. pres. part.* **wrinkling** *past and past part.* **wrin·kled** *v.t.* to produce wrinkles in, *to wrinkle one's forehead* ‖ *v.i.* to acquire wrinkles or a wrinkle **wrín·kled**, **wrín·kly** *adjs* [etym. doubtful]

wrist (rist) *n.* the joint between the hand and the arm ‖ the corresponding part in an animal ‖ the part of a garment covering the wrist [O.E.]

wrist·band (rístbænd) *n.* the part of the sleeve (esp. of a shirt) which covers the wrist

wrist·let (rístlit) *n.* a band around the wrist, esp. one incorporated in a glove or sleeve etc. for warmth

wristlet watch (*Br.*) a wristwatch

wrist·lock (rístlɒk) *n.* a twisting grip on the wrist used in wrestling to throw an opponent or make him helpless

wrist pin (*mech.*) a metal pin linking a piston and connecting rod

wrist·watch (rístwɒtʃ) *n.* a small watch worn on a strap or bracelet around the wrist

wrist wrestling arm wrestling with opponents, interlocking thumbs as the pressure point

writ (rit) *n.* a written command issued in the name of a sovereign, state, court of law etc. ‖ (*Br.*) a document issued by the crown, summoning one of the lords spiritual or temporal to attend Parliament or instructing a sheriff to hold an election of a member or members of parliament [O.E.=something written]

writ of cer·ti·o·ra·ri (sə:rʃi:ərérəai) a writ issuing from a superior court calling up the record of a proceeding in an inferior court for review [L. *certiorari*, to be informed or certified, pass. infin. of *certiorare*, to inform, from the use of *certiorari* in the L. original]

write (rait) *pres. part.* **writ·ing** *past* (rout) *past part.* **writ·ten** (rít'n) *v.i.* to form letters, figures or other significant symbols, esp. on paper, using a pencil, pen, brush etc. ‖ to compose books or other literary matter ‖ to write a letter (personal communication), *to*

write to somebody ‖ to produce the letters of the alphabet etc. on paper etc., *this pen writes well* ‖ *v.t.* to form (letters, figures, symbols etc.) on a surface ‖ to set down (language, information etc.) in letters, words or symbols, *write your name and address here* ‖ to cover or fill in with writing, *to write three pages, to write a check* ‖ to compose (a book, poem etc.) as an author ‖ to send a letter to, *he wrote them last week* ‖ to communicate or state in writing or in print, *he wrote them the latest news* ‖ to underwrite ‖ to draw up in legal form ‖ to show clearly, mark, stamp, *despair was written on every face* **to write down** to put in writing, record ‖ to describe, criticize or judge in a disparaging way, *she wrote him down as a nonentity* ‖ to reduce the nominal value of (stocks, goods etc.) **to write off** to compose rapidly and easily ‖ to record the cancellation of, *to write off a debt* ‖ to send away by mail, *to write off for a catalog* ‖ to dismiss from consideration **to write out** to write in full (esp. something public or official) ‖ to put in writing ‖ to exhaust (oneself) as a writer **to write up** to review or describe in writing, esp. favorably, in a newspaper etc. ‖ to record (an experiment etc.) in writing ‖ to expand (notes) into a piece of writing ‖ (*accounting*) to put down an excessive value for (an asset) **writ·er** *n.* someone who writes, esp. a professional author of books ‖ someone who writes insurance ‖ (*Br.*) a clerk, esp. in the navy or a government office [O.E. *wrītan*, to scratch, score, cut]

writer's cramp a painful spasmodic cramp of the finger muscles caused by writing for too long a time

write-up (ráitʌp) *n.* (*pop.*) an article in the press, esp. a favorable critical notice ‖ an unjustified increase in the assets on the books of a corporation

writhe (raið) 1. *v. pres. part.* **writh·ing** *past and past part.* **writhed** *v.i.* to twist, roll or turn about, esp. in pain ‖ to have a sensation of mental suffering, *to writhe with shame* ‖ *v.t.* to twist or contort (one's body or a part of it), esp. in pain or embarrassment 2. *n.* a writhing [O.E. *wrīthan*, to twist]

writ·ing (ráitiŋ) *n.* the act of someone who writes ‖ handwriting ‖ anything written, e.g. a literary composition, book, article, inscription etc. ‖ the occupation of a writer or author ‖ written form, *evidence in writing* ‖ style in literary composition, *sloppy ideas and shoddy writing* **the writing on the wall** a warning of doom to come (Daniel v)

written *past part.* of WRITE

Wro·claw (vrɔ́tslaf) (G. Breslau) a communications center (pop. 584,500) in Silesia, Poland, on the Oder. Industries: metalworking, chemical industries, textiles, heavy engineering. Gothic cathedral (14th c.), town hall and churches. University (1702)

wrong (rɒŋ) 1. *adj.* not in accordance with moral standards, not morally right ‖ not correct or accurate, false, *the wrong answer* ‖ mistaken, *you are wrong in thinking him intelligent* ‖ not suitable or proper, *they chose the wrong time to drop in* ‖ amiss, out of order, *what is wrong with the pump?* ‖ being other than the one it was expected to be, identified as or intended to be etc., *to take the wrong road* ‖ (of one side of a fabric) designed to be placed or worn downward or inward so as not to be seen 2. *n.* that which is morally wrong, *to choose between right and wrong* ‖ an act of injustice ‖ (*law*) an invading of the rights of someone **in the wrong** mistaken ‖ morally responsible for an offense **to put (someone) in the wrong** to make (someone) appear to be the offender, affix blame to (someone) 3. *adv.* incorrectly **to get (someone) wrong** to misunderstand the meaning or motives of (someone) **to go wrong** to take the wrong direction, road etc. ‖ to start on a course of wrongdoing or immoral behavior ‖ (of a mechanism, plan etc.) to get out of order, break down 4. *v.t.* to treat unfairly or judge unjustly ‖ (*old-fash.*) to seduce (a woman) [O.E. *wrang, wrong*, curved or crooked in form, direction etc.]

wrong·do·er (rɔ́ŋdú:ər) *n.* someone who acts in a way contrary to law or moral order

wrong·do·ing (rɔ́ŋdú:iŋ) *n.* crime ‖ sin

wrong·ful (rɔ́ŋfəl) *adj.* not fair, not just ‖ not lawful

wrong·head·ed (rɔ́ŋhédid) *adj.* obstinately and perversely clinging to something mistaken or inaccurate

wrote *past* of WRITE

wroth (rɔθ, roθ, *Br.* esp. rouθ) *adj.* (*rhet.*) angry, wrathful [O.E. *wrāth*]

wrought (rɔt) alt. *past* and *past part.* of WORK ‖ *adj.* worked, made, formed, fashioned ‖ (of metals) hammered and beaten into shape

wrought iron a very pure form of commercial iron, having a very small carbon content. It is tough, malleable, ductile and easily welded

wrought-up (rɔ́tʌp) *adj.* nervously excited, agitated

wrung *past* and *past part.* of WRING

wry (rai) *comp.* **wri·er** *superl.* **wri·est** *adj.* (of the neck or features) distorted, turned abnormally to one side ‖ (of features) distorted for a moment to express distaste, irony or bitterness ‖ (of a smile) made with such a distortion ‖ (of humor, remarks etc.) neatly turned, but bitter or ironic [O.E. *wrīgian* v., to turn]

wry·neck (ráinɛk) *n. Jynx torquilla*, a gray-brown European woodpecker which has a characteristic habit of stretching and twisting its neck ‖ any woodpecker of genus *Jynx* ‖ torticollis

Wu·chang (wú:tʃǽŋ) *WUHAN

Wu·han (wú:hán) the capital (pop. 2,226,000) of Hupei, China, the head of oceangoing shipping on the Yangtzekiang, at its confluence with the Han. It consists of the former cities of Hankow (the commercial center and former international city, with textile industries), Hanyang (the industrial center: iron and steel, mechanical engineering, chemicals) and Wuchang (the old walled capital). University (1905)

Wu·hsien (wú:ʃjén) (or Soochow) a port (pop. 700,000) in Kiangsu, China, on the Grand Canal, celebrated for its canals, bridges and medieval buildings. Industries: textiles, food processing, handicrafts (jade, lace)

Wu·hu (wú:hú:) a river port and rice market (pop. 250,000) on the Yangtzekiang in Anhwei, China: cotton textiles

Wul·fi·la (wúlfələ) (or Ulfilas, c. 311-83), Gothic bishop. He spread Arian Christianity among the Goths, and in his translation of the New Testament left the only surviving Gothic texts

Wundt (vunt), Wilhelm (1832-1920), German psychologist and philosopher, founder of experimental psychology, author of 'Elements of Physiological Psychology' (1873-4)

Wup·per·tal (vúpərtal) an industrial center (pop. 401,609) in central North Rhine-Westphalia, West Germany: textiles, chemical industries, pharmaceuticals, mechanical engineering, paper

Württemberg *BADEN-WÜRTTEMBERG

Würz·burg (výrtsbʊrk) a river port (pop. 112,500) and agricultural market in Bavaria, West Germany, on the Main, with engineering industries. Castle (13th-16th cc.), Romanesque-Gothic cathedral (12th c.), churches (8th-18th cc.), all damaged in the 2nd world war. University (1582)

Wu·sih (wú:ʃí:) a rail and industrial center (pop. 650,000) in Kiangsu, China: textiles, food processing, engineering, chemicals

Wu·tsin (wú:dʒín) (Changchow) a trading center (pop. 297,000) in S. Kiangsu, China on the Grand Canal

W. Va. West Virginia

WWW (*meteor. abbr.*) for World Weather Watch, a global weather service established by World Meteorological Organization in 1967

Wy·an·dotte (wáiəndɒt) *n.* a chicken of an American breed, usually white laced with black [after a North American Indian tribe]

Wy·att (wáiət), James (1746-1813), English architect, an early exponent of neo-Gothic

Wyatt, Sir Thomas (c. 1503-42), English poet and statesman. His sonnets, probably written in prison, were the first written in English. They were based on Petrarch so far as the form went, but used the rhythm of the speaking voice to counterpoint the 'correct' pattern. His voice was direct and frank in a courtly or mannered period

wych elm, **witch elm** (wítʃélm) *n. Ulmus glabra*, a Eurasian elm common in the British Isles ‖ the wood of this tree [var. of WITCH (as in 'witch hazel']

Wych·er·ley (wítʃərli:), William (c. 1640-1716), English playwright. His work was typical of the Restoration drama in its cynical acceptance of an amoral society, its surprising verbal coarseness, and its fondness for plots based on amorous intrigues. Best known are 'The Country-Wife' (1675) and 'The Plain-Dealer' (1677)

wych hazel the wych elm ‖ *WITCH HAZEL

CONCISE PRONUNCIATION KEY: **(a)** æ, c*a*t; ɑ, c*a*r; ɔ f*aw*n; ei, sn*a*ke. **(e)** e, h*e*n; i:, sh*ee*p; iə, d*ee*r; ɛə, b*ea*r. **(i)** i, f*i*sh; ai, t*i*ger; ə:, b*i*rd. **(o)** o, *o*x; au, c*ow*; ou, g*oa*t; u, p*oo*r; ɔi, r*oy*al. **(u)** ʌ, d*u*ck; u, b*u*ll; u:, g*oo*se; ə, b*a*cillus; ju:, c*u*be. x, lo*ch*; θ, *th*ink; ð, bo*th*er; z, *Z*en; ʒ, corsa*g*e; dʒ, sava*g*e; ŋ, orangutan*g*; j, *y*ak; ʃ, *f*ish; tʃ, fe*tch*; 'l, rabb*le*; 'n, redd*en*. Complete pronunciation key appears inside front cover.

Wyc·lif, Wyc·liffe (wíklif), John (c. 1320-84), English religious reformer. He and his followers translated the entire Bible into English. With the protection of his patron, John of Gaunt, he attacked many ecclesiastical abuses and doctrines, proclaimed that salvation depends upon predestination and grace rather than on membership of a visible Church, and insisted on the right of all men to have access to the Scriptures in the vernacular. His denial of transubstantiation was condemned (1381) as heretical. His followers were known as Lollards

Wyc·liff·ite (wíklifait) *n.* a Lollard

Wy·eth (wáiəθ), Andrew Newell (1917-), U.S. realist painter. His subjects are from Maine and Pennsylvania

Wy·lie (wáili:), Elinor (née Hoyt, 1885-1928), U.S. poet and novelist. Her verse shows the influence of the 17th-c. metaphysicals and includes 'Nets to Catch the Wind' (1921), 'Black Amour' (1923) and 'Trivial Breath' (1928). Her novels include 'Jennifer Lorn' (1923), 'The Orphan Angel' (1926) and 'Mr. Hodge and Mr. Hazard' (1928)

Wyo. Wyoming

Wy·o·ming (waióumiŋ) (*abbr.* Wyo.) a state (area 97,914 sq. miles, pop. 502,000) in the W. central U.S.A. Capital: Cheyenne. The Rocky Mtns lie in the west and south, and the east is mainly semiarid high plain. The Yellowstone National Park is in the northwest. Agriculture: cattle, sheep, hay, winter wheat, sugar beets (with much dependence on irrigation). Resources: oil, coal, uranium. Industries: oil refining, food processing. State university (1886) at Laramie. Most of Wyoming passed to the U.S.A. in the Louisiana Purchase (1803). It became (1890) the 44th state of the U.S.A. It was the first state of the U.S.A. to enfranchise women

Wys·pian·ski (vispjánski:), Stanislaw (1869-1907), Polish playwright and painter. His plays include 'The Wedding' (1901), 'Deliverance' (1903) and 'November Night' (1904)

Wyss (vi:s), Johann David (1743-1818), Swiss writer, author of the juvenile classic 'Swiss Family Robinson' (published 1812-27)

Wythe (wiθ), George (1726-1806), U.S. jurist and leader in Virginia's ratification of the U.S. Constitution. As professor of law (1779-90) at the College of William and Mary, he exerted a profound influence on the great men of his time, notably John Marshall, Thomas Jefferson and James Monroe

wy·vern (wáivər:n) *n.* (*heraldry*) a two-legged dragon with outspread wings and barbed tail [M.E. *wyver* fr. O.F. *wyvre*, var. of *vivre*, serpent]

CONCISE PRONUNCIATION KEY: **(a)** æ, c*a*t; ɑ, c*a*r; ɔ f*aw*n; ei, sn*a*ke. **(e)** e, h*e*n; i:, sh*ee*p; iə, d*ee*r; ɛə, b*ea*r. **(i)** i, f*i*sh; ai, t*i*ger; ə:, b*i*rd. **(o)** o, *o*x; au, c*ow*; ou, g*oa*t; u, p*oo*r; ɔi, r*oy*al. **(u)** ʌ, d*u*ck; u, b*u*ll; u:, g*oo*se; ə, b*a*cillus; ju:, c*u*be. x, lo*ch*; θ, *th*ink; ð, bo*th*er; z, *Z*en; ʒ, corsa*g*e; dʒ, sava*g*e; ŋ, ora*ng*utan*g*; j, *y*ak; ʃ, *fi*sh; tʃ, fe*tch*; 'l, rabb*le*; 'n, redd*en*. Complete pronunciation key appears inside front cover.

	CURSIVE MAJUSCULE (ROMAN)	CURSIVE MINUSCULE (ROMAN)	ANGLO-IRISH MAJUSCULE	CLASSICAL GREEK / CAROLINE MINUSCULE	EARLY LATIN / VENETIAN MINUSCULE (ITALIC)	CLASSICAL LATIN / N. ITALIAN MINUSCULE (ROMAN)

A. C. SYLVESTER, CAMBRIDGE, ENGLAND

Development of the letter X, beginning with the classical Greek letter. Evolution of both the majuscule, or capital, letter X and the minuscule, or lowercase, letter x are shown.

X, x (eks) the 24th letter of the English alphabet (sounded as 'z' when an initial letter) ‖ something shaped like this ‖ (*math.*) an unknown quantity or the symbol for this ‖ any unknown factor or quantity or unidentified person ‖ the Roman symbol for the number 10 ‖ **X** a symbol for Christ used in abbreviations, e.g. 'Xmas' for 'Christmas' [from the initial letter chi of Gk *Christos*, which looks like an English X]

X (eks) *adj.* motion picture rating for erotic films, admission to which persons under the age of 17 or 18 are not permitted. *Cf* G, PG, R

xan·thate (zǽnθeit) *n.* a salt or ester of a xanthic acid (ROCS·SH), esp. cellulose xanthate, used in the manufacture of viscose [fr. Gk *xanthos*, yellow]

xan·thic (zǽnθik) *adj.* (esp. *bot.*, of a flower) yellow [fr. Gk *xanthos*, yellow]

xan·thin (zǽnθin) *n.* (*chem.*) a yellow, non-water-soluble pigment found in yellow plants [fr. Gk *xanthos*, yellow]

xan·thine (zǽnθi:n) *n.* (*biochem.*) a crystalline compound, $C_5H_4N_4O_2$, found in blood, urine, muscle tissue and some plants [fr. Gk *xanthos*, yellow]

Xan·thip·pe (zæntípi:, zænθípi:) the wife of Socrates, a proverbial scold

xan·tho·ma (zænθóumə) *pl.* **xan·tho·mas, xan·tho·ma·ta** (zænθóumətə) *n.* a condition arising from a disorder of cholesterol metabolism, characterized by the forming of yellow patches on the skin [Mod. L. fr. Gk *xanthos*, yellow]

xan·tho·phyll (zǽnθəfil) *n.* $C_{40}H_{56}O_2$, the yellow pigment found in plastids and present in many plants **xan·tho·phýll·ic, xan·tho·phyll·ous** (zænθəfíləs, zænθəfələs) *adjs* [fr. Gk *xanthos*, yellow + *phullon*, leaf]

xan·thous (zǽnθəs) *adj.* (of a people) having yellowish, brown or red hair ‖ (of a people) having yellowish skin ‖ colored yellow [fr. Gk *xanthos*, yellow]

Xavier, St Francis *FRANCIS XAVIER

X-ax·is (éksæksis) *n.* (*mil.*) a horizontal axis in a system of rectangular coordinates, the line on which distances to the right or left (east or west) of the reference line are marked, especially on a map, chart, or graph

X chromosome *SEX CHROMOSOME

xe·bec (zí:bek) *n.* a small three-masted Mediterranean boat with triangular and square sails [earlier *chebec* fr. F.]

Xe·na·kis (zenáki:s), Yannis (1922-), Greek composer. He has applied the notion of probability to composition through the use of a computer where this has seemed useful. He was a pupil of Messiaen

xe·ni·a (zí:ni:ə) *n.* the appearance in seed, fruit or maternal tissues of characters belonging to the fertilizing plant or male parent [Mod. L. fr. Gk *xenia*, hospitality]

xe·no·bi·ol·o·gy (zenoubaióɫədʒi:) *n.* study of extraterrestrial living organisms. *syn.* exobiology

Xe·noc·ra·tes (zinɒ́krəti:z) (396-314 B.C.), Greek philosopher, a disciple of Plato, whose doctrine he tried to reconcile with that of Pythagoras

xe·nog·a·mous (zinɒ́gəməs) *adj.* of, pertaining to or characterized by xenogamy

xe·nog·a·my (zinɒ́gəmi:) *n.* (*bot.*) cross-fertilization [fr. Gk *xenos*, foreign + *gamos*, marriage]

xe·no·ge·ne·ic (zenoudʒəní:ik) *adj.* derived from another species —**xenogenesis** *n.*

xen·o·gen·e·sis (zenoudʒénisis) *n.* the supposed production of offspring completely unlike either parent [fr. Gk *xenos*, foreign + *genesis*, origin]

xe·no·graft (zénəgræft) *n.* tissue graft from a donor of a different specie. *also* heterograph —**xenoplastic** *adj. Cf* ALLOGRAFT, HOMOGRAFT

xe·nol·o·gy (zenɒ́lədʒi:) *n.* (*biol.*) study of the relationship between host and parasite

xen·o·mor·phic (zenoumɔ́rfik) *adj.* allotriomorphic [fr. Gk *xenos*, foreign + *morphē*, form]

xe·non (zí:nɒn, zénɒn) *n.* an inert gaseous element (symbol Xe, at. no. 54, at. mass 131.30), used to fill arc lamps, flash bulbs and electronic counters [fr. Gk neut. of *xenos*, strange]

xe·no·narc lamp (zénounɑrk) high-intensity lighting device used in motion picture projection, eye surgery, etc.

xenon lamp high-intensity lamp used in projectors and testing textile fading

Xe·noph·a·nes (zinɒ́fəni:z) (6th c. B.C.), Greek philosopher and poet, known for his monotheism

xen·o·phobe (zénəfoub) *n.* a person who shows xenophobia **xen·o·phó·bic** *adj.* [fr. Gk *xenos*, stranger, foreign + *phobos*, fear]

xen·o·pho·bi·a (zenəfóubi:ə) *n.* fear or dislike of strangers or foreigners [fr. Gk *xenos*, stranger, foreigner + *phobos*, fear]

Xen·o·phon (zénəfən, zénəfɒn) (c. 430–c. 355 B.C.), Greek general and writer. He was a disciple of Socrates, about whom he wrote the 'Memorabilia' and 'Apology'. In the 'Anabasis' he describes his part in Cyrus the Younger's expedition (401 B.C.) against Artaxerxes II and his command of the 10,000 Greek mercenaries. Exiled for 20 years from Athens for his Spartan sympathies, he wrote the 'Hellenica' (a history of Greece 411-362 B.C.), the 'Cyropaedia' (an idealized life of Cyrus the Great), and works on sport and politics

xe·ra·sia (zi:réiʒə) *n.* (*med.*) hair disease marked by dry hair and cessation of hair growth

xe·ric (zíərik) *adj.* (*bot.*, of an environment) having a low or deficient supply of moisture for plant life (cf. HYDRIC) ‖ tolerating or adapted to arid conditions [fr. Gk *xēros*, dry]

xe·rog·ra·phy (zirógrəfi:) *n.* a dry printing process in which a black mineral powder is deposited on, and adheres permanently to, those parts of a paper surface which are rendered sensitive by a photoelectric beam **xerox** *adj.* —**xerox** *n.* the copy —**xerox** *v.* to copy by xerography —Xerox trademark of the copiers of the Xerox Corporation [fr. Gk *xēros*, dry + *graphos*, written]

xe·roph·i·lous (zirófələs) *adj.* (*biol.*) adapted to or characteristic of an environment having a very limited water supply [fr. Gk *xēros*, dry + *-philos*, loving]

xe·roph·thal·mi·a (ziərɒfθǽlmi:ə) *n.* abnormal dryness of the eyeball due to a severe deficiency of vitamin A [fr. Gk *xēros*, dry + *ophthalmia*, eye disease]

xe·ro·phyte (zíərəfait) *n.* any plant growing in desert conditions or in an alkaline, acid, salt or dry soil **xe·ro·phyt·ic** (ziərəfítik) *adj.* [fr. Gk *xēros*, dry + *phuton*, plant]

xe·ro·ra·di·og·ra·phy (zíəroureidi:ógrəfi:) *n.* **1.** a process in which an electrostatic image is formed on a photoconductive medium by X-rays or gamma rays **2.** variation of mammography in which a Xerox plate is used instead of film to create an image —**xeroradiogram** *n.*

xe·rox (zíərɒks) *v.t.* to reproduce by xerography [fr. *Xerox*, a trademark]

Xerx·es I (zə́:rksi:z) 'the Great' (c. 519–c. 465 B.C.), king of Persia (c. 485 –c. 465 B.C.), son of Darius I. He invaded Greece, defeating the Spartans at Thermopylae (480 B.C.), but withdrew after the destruction of his fleet at Salamis (480 B.C.)

xi (zai, ksai, ksi:) *n.* the 14th letter (Ξ, ξ=x) of the Greek alphabet

Xin·gú (zingú:, ʃiŋgú:) a river (about 1,300 miles long) in Brazil rising in the N. Mato Grosso and flowing to the Amazon delta, navigable between rapids

xiph·i·ster·num (zifistə́:rnəm) *pl.* **xiph·i·ster·na** (zifistə́:rnə) *n.* (*anat., zool.*) the posterior segment of the sternum [fr. Gk *xiphos*, sword + STERNUM]

xiph·oid (zífoid) **1.** *adj.* (*anat.*) sword-shaped ‖ (*anat.*) of, relating to or being the xiphisternum **2.** *n.* the xiphisternum [fr. Mod. L. *xiphoides* fr. Gk]

xiphoid process the xiphisternum

xiph·o·su·ran (zifəsúərən) *adj.* (*zool.*) belonging to the arthropod order of *Xiphosura*, which comprises the king crabs [fr. Mod. L. fr. Gk *xiphos*, sword + *oura*, tail]

Xmas (krísməs) *n.* Christmas [fr. X (symbol for Christ)+-*mas* fr. CHRISTMAS]

XMGM-31A *PERSHING

XM-1 *n.* (*mil.*) Chrysler-built, 60-ton, turbine-engine tank replacing M-60

X ray an electromagnetic radiation in the wavelength range 0.1–100 Å produced when the inner satellite electrons of esp. heavy atoms that have been excited by collision with a stream of fast electrons (*X-RAY TUBE) return to their ground state, giving up, in the form of X rays, the energy previously imparted to them. X rays, being of high energy, have considerable ionizing and penetrating power, and are used for the internal examination of large cast-metal parts, visual diagnosis of many organic malfunctions, analysis of crystal structure (*X-RAY DIFFRACTION), treatment (*RADIOTHERAPY) of certain diseases etc. ‖ a photograph made by exposure to X rays [trans. of G. *X-strahl*, so named because its essential nature was not known]

X-ray (éksrei) **1.** *v.t.* to examine or treat with X rays **2.** *adj.* of or pertaining to X rays

X-ray astronomy the science of astronomy carried on by analysis of X-rays emitted by celestial bodies —**X-ray astronomer** *n.*

X-ray diffraction (*phys., chem.*) a method of determining crystal structure (i.e. symmetry, bond lengths and angles) based on the principle that X rays are diffracted by many crystals whose atomic dimensions are such as to allow them to act as natural diffraction gratings. If the wavelength of the X rays is known these dimensions may be determined

X-ray diffractometer device for measuring and recording X-ray diffraction patterns in powders or crystals to analyze their structure —**X-ray defraction** *n.*

X-ray nova (*meteor.*) an exploding star that emits X-rays

X-ray pulsar (*astron.*) a pulsar that emits X-rays

X-ray scanning process for scanning a solid material with X-rays to detect flaws

X-ray star or **X-ray source** (*meteor.*) a celestial body that emits X-rays

X-ray telescope (*meteor.*) a telescope mounted on a space vehicle or rocket, used in taking X-rays

X-ray tube (*phys.*) a vacuum tube in which a metal target emits X rays when bombarded by electrons from a thermionic cathode (the electron gun). The radiation emitted is characteristic of the potential drop across the tube, the temperature of the cathode and of the target material

xy·lan (záilən) *n.* a polysaccharide found in plant cell walls, esp. in wood, straw etc. [fr. Gk *xulon*, wood]

xy·lem (záiləm, záilem) *n.* a complex lignified plant tissue, comprising the woody portion of the vascular system in higher plants. It is a mixed tissue consisting of parenchymalike and fiberlike tracheids and vessels. Xylem acts as a support, conveys water and minerals, and often stores food (cf. PHLOEM, *WOOD) [fr. Gk *xulon*, wood]

xy·lene (záili:n) *n.* any of three isomeric, colorless, liquid hydrocarbons, $C_6H_4(CH_3)_2$, found in coal and wood tar and resembling toluene [fr. Gk *xulon*, wood]

xy·lo·graph (záiləgræf, záiləgrɑf) *n.* a wood engraving ‖ an impression from such an engraving [back-formation fr. XYLOGRAPHY]

xy·log·ra·phy (zailógrəfi:) *n.* the art of engraving in wood or of taking impressions from wood engravings [fr. F. *xylographie*]

xy·loph·a·gous (zailófəgəs) *adj.* (*biol.*, of certain mollusks, crustaceans and insects) boring into and feeding on wood [fr. Gk *xulon*, wood+*phagein*, to eat]

xy·lo·phone (záiləfoun) *n.* a percussion instrument consisting of a series of horizontal wooden bars arranged in graded length and tuned in a chromatic scale. It is played by striking the bars with small wooden hammers **xy·loph·on·ist** (zailófənist, záiləfounist) *n.* a person who plays the xylophone [fr. Gk *xulon*, wood+*phōnē*, voice, sound]

xy·lose (záilous) *n.* (*chem.*) a polysaccharide, $C_5H_{10}O_5$, found as a constituent of xylan [fr. Gk *xulon*, wood]

xy·lot·o·mous (zailótəməs) *adj.* (*zool.*, of certain insects) able to bore into or cut wood [fr. Gk *xulon*, wood+-*tomos* fr. *temnein*, to cut]

xyst (zist) *n.* a xystus

xys·tus (zístəs) *pl.* **xys·ti** (zístai) *n.* a long, roofed colonnade used for athletic training in ancient Greece in cold or wet weather [L. fr. Gk *xustos*, smooth]

XYY syndrome *n.* (*med.*) congenital male disorder (of an extra Y chromosome), hypothesized to be a factor in causing social inadequacy, aggressive behavior, and low intelligence

XYZ Affair a Franco-U.S. incident arising (1797) in Paris during negotiations to settle a dispute stemming from French depredations on U.S. commerce. The three U.S. agents, Charles C. Pinckney, Elbridge Gerry, and John Marshall, commissioned by President John Adams, were asked by the three agents acting on behalf of France, dubbed X, Y, and Z, to make a payment as a precondition of negotiations. The U.S. ministers refused, and the commission broke up. The affair, which roused feelings of outrage in the U.S.A. against France and brought the two countries to the brink of war until France climbed down, strengthened the Federalist position

---

CONCISE PRONUNCIATION KEY: **(a)** æ, c*a*t; ɑ, c*a*r; ɔ f*a*wn; ei, sn*a*ke. **(e)** e, h*e*n; i:, sh*ee*p; iə, d*ee*r; ɛə, b*ea*r. **(i)** i, f*i*sh; ai, t*i*ger; ə:, b*i*rd. **(o)** o, *o*x; au, c*ow*; ou, g*oa*t; u, p*oo*r; ɔi, r*o*yal. **(u)** ʌ, d*u*ck; u, b*u*ll; u:, g*oo*se; ə, b*a*cillus; ju:, c*u*be. x, lo*ch*; θ, *th*ink; ð, bo*th*er; z, *Z*en; ʒ, cor*s*age; dʒ, sava*g*e; ŋ, ora*n*gutang; j, *y*ak; ʃ, fi*sh*; tʃ, fet*ch*; 'l, rabb*le*; 'n, redd*en*. Complete pronunciation key appears inside front cover.

	EARLY NORTH SEMITIC	PHOENICIAN	EARLY HEBREW (GEZER)	EARLY GREEK	CLASSICAL GREEK	ETRUSCAN		EARLY LATIN	CLASSICAL LATIN
						Early	Classical		
Y	ʒ	ʒ	ʒʒ	I	I	I	I	IY	IY (i)

	CURSIVE MAJUSCULE (ROMAN)	CURSIVE MINUSCULE (ROMAN)				VENETIAN MINUSCULE (ITALIC)	MODERN ROMAN
	y	Y				y	y

A. C. SYLVESTER, CAMBRIDGE, ENGLAND

Development of the letter Y, beginning with the early North Semitic letter. Evolution of both the majuscule, or capital, letter Y and the minuscule, or lowercase, letter y are shown.

Y, y (wai) the 25th letter of the English alphabet ‖ something shaped like a Y ‖ (*algebra*) a second unknown quantity (x being the first), or the symbol for this

-y, -ey *suffix* denoting likeness, as in 'glassy', 'clayey' ‖ denoting characteristic quality, as in 'greeny', 'juicy'

-y *suffix* denoting state or quality, as in 'jealousy'

Ya·blo·noi (jáblənɔi) (Yablonovy) a range of mountains (1,000 miles long) in S.E. Siberia, U.S.S.R., forming the Arctic-Pacific watershed. Highest peak: 8,228 ft

yacht (jɒt) 1. *n.* any of various light, fast sailing or power-driven vessels, often luxuriously fitted, used for pleasure cruises, racing etc. 2. *v.i.* to race or cruise in a yacht **yácht·ing** *n.* the act or sport of racing or cruising in a yacht [fr. early Mod. Du. *jaghte* fr. *jaghtschip,* fast pirate ship]

yachts·man (jɒtsmən) *pl.* **yachts·men** (jɒtsmən) *n.* someone who owns or sails a yacht

YAG (*acronym*) for yttrium aluminum garnet, used in generating laser beams. *Cf* YIG

ya·hoo (jáhu:, jəhú:) *n.* a brutish lout [coined by SWIFT in 'Gulliver's Travels' (1726)]

Yah·weh, Yah·veh, Jah·weh, Jah·veh (jáwei, jávei) *n.* God, a transliteration of the Hebrew word which in the English Bible is written 'Jehovah'

yak (jæk) *n. Poephagus grunniens* (or *Bos grunniens),* a large, long-haired ruminant sharing some characteristics of both the bison and the ox, native to the mountainous region of central Asia and domesticated in Tibet and the foothills of the Himalayas. It has cylindrical horns curving outwards, and when wild may weigh up to 1,200 lbs [Tibetan *gyag*]

Ya·kut A.S.S.R. (jɑkú:t) an autonomous republic (area 1,197,760 sq. miles, pop. 152,000) in the R.S.F.S.R., U.S.S.R. (N.E. Siberia). Capital: Yakutsk

Ya·kutsk (jɑkú:tsk) the capital (pop. 82,000) of the Yakut A.S.S.R., U.S.S.R., a trading center on the Lena. University

ya·ku·za (jɑku:zɑ) *n.* membership in Yamaguchi, an organized criminal group (approximately 11,000 members) in Japan

Yale (jeil), Linus (1821-68), U.S. inventor of a compact pin-tumbler cylinder lock and of various improvements in lock mechanisms

Yale University a private university in New Haven, Connecticut, named after Elihu Yale (1648-1721), an early patron, and chartered in 1701. It consists of Yale College and other undergraduate schools for men and women, plus several graduate schools for men and women

Yalow (jálou), Rosalyn Sussman (1921-) U.S. physicist, co-winner of the Nobel prize for physiology or medicine (1977). She developed, with Solomon Berson, the radioimmunoassay (RIA) test to measure hormone, enzyme and protein amounts

Yal·ta Conference (jɔ́ltə, jɑ́ltə) a meeting (Feb. 4-11, 1945) at Yalta in the Crimea, U.S.S.R., between F. D. Roosevelt, Churchill and Stalin, at which the final defeat of Germany was planned. Germany was to be demilitarized and divided into four zones of occupation. The decision was taken to set up the U.N. and the frontiers of Poland were settled. Russian zones of influence in central and eastern Europe were established and the U.S.S.R. agreed to enter the war against Japan

Ya·lu (jálu:) a river (491 miles long, navigable for 420) flowing from S. Kirin, China (Manchuria) to the Yellow Sea, forming the border with North Korea: hydroelectricity

yam (jæm) *n.* the edible, starchy, tuberous root of certain plants of genus *Dioscorea,* fam. *Dioscoreaceae,* used as a staple food in tropical lowlands ‖ any plant of genus *Dioscorea* ‖ the sweet potato [Port. *inhame* or Span. *igname*]

Ya·ma·ga·ta (jɑmɑgɑtɑ), Prince Aritomo (1838-1922), Japanese soldier and statesman. As chief of the general staff during the Russo-Japanese War and as prime minister (1889-91 and 1898-1900) he ensured the rise of militarism in Japan

yam bean *Pachyrhizus erosus,* fam. *Papilionaceae,* a tropical perennial twining plant, cultivated for its edible turnip-like roots

yam·mer (jæmər) 1. *v.i.* to utter plaintive wailing or whimpering sounds ‖ to grumble and complain in a repetitious way ‖ to talk persistently and loudly 2. *n.* a yammering sound [alteration of M.E. *yomer* fr. O.E. *geōmrian* fr. *geōmor,* sorrowful]

Ya·na·on (jænæɔ̃, janáun) (or Yanam) a port (pop. 6,000) in the Godavari delta, India. The French held it 1763-1954

Yang *YIN AND YANG

Yang·chow (jǽntʃóu) *KIANGTU

Yang·ku (jǽŋký) *TAIYUAN

Yang·tze-kiang (jæntsi:kjǽŋ) the longest river (3,340 miles long, draining 750,000 sq. miles) and central artery of China, flowing south through gorges as deep as 13,000 ft from central Tibet to Yunnan, then north and east through the Red Basin and gorges in W. Szechwan across the central plain to a delta (where silt extends the coast by 20 yards a year) on the Pacific. It is navigable by steamer to Wuhan and by small vessels (hauled upstream at points) for half its length

Yank (jæŋk) *n.* (*pop.*) a Yankee

yank (jæŋk) 1. *v.t.* and *v.i.* (*pop.*) to pull with a jerk 2. *n.* (*pop.*) a sharp pull, a hard jerk [origin unknown]

Yan·kee (jǽŋki:) 1. *n.* an inhabitant of New England ‖ a native of any of the northern states of the U.S.A. ‖ a Union soldier in the American Civil War ‖ a citizen of the U.S.A. ‖ English as spoken by U.S. citizens, esp. in New England 2. *adj.* of or pertaining to Yankees [origin unknown]

Ya·oun·dé (jæu:ndei) the capital (pop. 450,000) of Cameroun, linked by rail with Douala

yap (jæp) 1. *v.i. pres. part.* **yap·ping** *past* and *past part.* **yapped** to bark snappishly ‖ (*pop.*) to talk in a scolding or complaining manner ‖ (*pop.*) to chatter 2. *n.* a sharp, shrill bark [imit.]

ya·pock, ya·pok (jəpók, jǽpək) *n. Chironectes minimus,* a small water opossum found in Central and South America, with webbed hind feet [after *Oyapok,* a river between Guiana and Brazil]

yapp (jæp) *n.* (*Br.*) divinity circuit binding [after *Yapp,* London bookseller for whom the style was first made (c. 1860)]

yar·bor·ough (járbə:rou, járbˌʌrou, *Br.* esp. járbrə) *n.* (*bridge*) a hand with no card above a nine [after Charles Anderson Worsley, 2nd Earl of *Yarborough* (d. 1897), who used to offer 1,000 to 1 against such a hand occurring]

yard (jɑrd) 1. *n.* a small open space completely or partly enclosed and adjoining a building ‖ an enclosure where a business or manufacture is carried on, *lumber yard* ‖ a space containing a complex system of railroad tracks (usually near a station) for shunting, assembling trains and parking passenger or freight cars ‖ a clearing in a forest where deer etc. gather in winter for feeding and protection **the Yard** Scotland Yard 2. *v.t.* to confine (cattle etc.) in a yard [O.E. *geard,* enclosure]

yard *n.* (*abbr.* yd) a unit of length equal to 3 ft (36 in) and equivalent to .9144 m. ‖ (*naut.*) a cylindrical spar tapering at the ends, slung from a mast to support and spread a sail [O.E. *gyrd,* gird, twig, stick]

yard·age (járdidʒ) *n.* the use of a yard for keeping cattle etc. at a railroad station ‖ the charge for such use [fr. YARD (small open space)]

yardage *n.* length, area or volume measured in linear, square or cubic yards [fr. YARD (unit of length)]

yard·arm (járdɑrm) *n.* (*naut.*) either half of a yard on a square-rigged vessel

yard goods piece goods (textiles sold to length, cut from the bolt)

yard·man (járdmən) *pl.* **yard·men** (járdmən) *n.* a man employed in a railroad or other yard ‖ a day laborer who does general outdoor work ‖ a man responsible for the building materials in a lumber yard

yard·mas·ter (járdmæstər, járdmɑstər) n. (rail.) a yard manager

yard sale *GARAGE SALE

yard·stick (járdstįk) n. a measuring stick a yard long, graduated in inches and feet ‖ a test of evaluation, standard of comparison, criterion

Yar·kand (jɑrkǽnd) (or Soche) an ancient oasis trading center (pop. 80,000) in S.W. Sinkiang-Uighur, China, in the Takla Makan: silk and wool weaving

yarn (jɑrn) 1. n. any spun thread (wool, flax, silk, cotton etc.) prepared for weaving, knitting, rope making etc. ‖ a long continuous strand of glass, paper, plastic, metal etc. ‖ a long, often exaggerated tale of adventure, esp. told by a seaman or traveler **to spin a yarn** to tell a long tale of untrue adventures ‖ to make up a long rambling excuse 2. v.i. to tell a yarn [O.E. gearn]

Ya·ro·slavl (jɑrʌsláv'l) a city (pop. 608,000) in the R.S.F.S.R., U.S.S.R., on the upper Volga. Industries: textiles, engineering, chemicals. Cathedral (1215). University

yar·row (jǽrou) n. Achillea millefolium, fam. Compositae, a strong-scented perennial plant of temperate regions, with a woody stem and terminal corymbs of close, white flowers [O.E. gearwe]

yash·mak (jaʃmák, jǽʃmæk) n. a double veil covering the face so that only the eyes are exposed, worn by some Moslem women in public [Arab. yashmaq]

yat·a·ghan (jǽtəgæn, jǽtəgən) n. a short Moslem sword with a double curved blade and no cross guard [Tui yátāghan]

Yates (jeits), Richard (1815-73), Civil War governor (1861-5) of Illinois. He aided the Union cause with large levies of troops and by curbing the powerful pro-Southern group in his state

yaup *YAWP

yaw (jɔ) 1. v.i. (of a ship or aircraft) to go off course 2. n. (of a ship or aircraft) a temporary deviation from course ‖ (of a missile) a wobble in flight [etym. doubtful]

Ya·wa·ta (jɑwɑta) a port (pop. 332,000) in N. Kyushu, Japan, part of the Kita-Kyushu conurbation

yawl (jɔl) n. a ship's jolly boat with four or six oars ‖ a two-masted, fore-and-aft-rigged sailboat, the mizzenmast (much smaller than the mainmast) being placed far aft ‖ a fishing boat with stem and stern alike and carrying one lugsail or more [fr. M.L.G. jolle or Du. jol]

yawn (jɔn) 1. v.i. to breathe in deeply, letting the mouth open wide, through sleepiness, weariness or boredom ‖ (rhet.) to open wide or stand wide open, a yawning chasm ‖ v.t. to say or express with a yawn, to yawn agreement 2. n. the act or an instance of yawning ‖ (colloq.) a bore [O.E. ginian, geonian]

yawp, yaup (jɔp) 1. v.i. to utter a loud, raucous cry ‖ (pop.) to talk continually and noisily 2. n. a loud, raucous cry [imit.]

yaws (jɔz) n. a contagious disease common in the Tropics, caused by a spirochete and usually acquired in childhood through bodily contact. Initially characterized by chronic raspberrylike skin ulcers, it may in later years cause severe bony or facial deformity [etym. doubtful]

Yazd (jezd) *YEZD

Y chromosome *SEX CHROMOSOME

ye (ji:) pron. (archaic and rhet.) you (originally nominative pl., later as sing., and still later as acc. sing. and pl.) [O.E. ge]

ye (ji:, ði:) def. art. (old method of printing) the [fr. confusion between O.E. letter þ and Roman y]

yea (jei) 1. adv. (archaic and rhet.) yes ‖ (archaic and rhet.) indeed ‖ (archaic and rhet.) moreover 2. n. (archaic) an expression of assent or agreement ‖ someone who votes in the affirmative [O.E. gēa, gē]

year (jiər) n. the period of time taken by the earth to complete one orbit around the sun, 365.2425 days ‖ a period of 12 lunar months ‖ a period of 365 days (366 in a leap year) forming the basic cycle of the Gregorian calendar ‖ one identifiable unit of such a calendar sequence, it happened in the year 1752 ‖ a period regarded as the major time unit in some way, though not corresponding with a calendar year, the academic year ends in June ‖ the period necessary for a planet to make one orbit around the sun ‖ a solar year ‖ a sidereal year ‖ a lunar year ‖ (pl.)

age, he is tall for his years **all year round** at all times during the year [O.E. gēar, gēr]

year·book (jíərbuk) n. a book published yearly giving information (esp. statistics) covering the past year's activities, events etc.

year·ling (jíarlin) 1. n. an animal more than one year old and less than two ‖ (racing) a colt which is a year old, dating from Jan. 1 of the year of foaling 2. adj. a year old

year·ly (jíərli:) 1. adj. occurring every year or once a year 2. adv. every year or once a year

yearn (jəːrn) v.i. (often with 'for') to be filled with longing ‖ (often with 'over') to feel tender compassion and affection **yéarn·ing** n. deep longing ‖ tender compassion and affection [O.E. giorna, geornan, giernan, to long for]

year of grace a year of the Christian era

year-round (jíərráund) adj. continuing throughout the year

yeast (ji:st) n. a substance found on the surface of fermenting sugary liquids containing ascomycetes of fam. Saccharomycetaceae, that multiply by budding and cause the fermentation of sugars, with the production of alcohol and carbon dioxide. Yeast is used esp. in brewing and in bread making ‖ any of various fungi that produce alcohol and carbon dioxide from sugar **yéast·y** adj. of or containing yeast ‖ exuberant, a yeasty performance ‖ foamy ‖ frivolous, trivial [O.E. gist]

Yeats (jeits), William Butler (1865-1939), Irish poet. His early poems (e.g. 'The Wind among the Reeds', 1899) sprang from late 19th-c. aestheticism, and were languorous and mannered. But they were distinguished from other verse of the period by their use of Irish mythology, and this sense of belonging to the culture of his native land remained with him and was always a strength. Two tendencies can be discovered in Yeats. The first was to elaborate a private mythology based on elements of spiritualism, classical lore, astrology and Eastern philosophy: this was mainly a source of symbols for his poetry, and produced the rich, oblique, rhetorical, sounding verse e.g. of 'Byzantium'. The second was a movement toward a naked direct utterance, sinewy yet musical, with the simplicity of folk poetry. In this mode he produced some of his most moving work, helped by his own sense of connection with the Irish nationalist cause. Yeats was also a playwright, writing some fine verse plays on Irish mythological subjects for the Abbey Theater, Dublin.

yegg (jeg) n. (pop.) a burglar, esp. a safebreaker [perh. fr. a surname]

yell (jel) 1. v.i. to utter a loud, inarticulate cry or shout, esp. in expression of emotion, pain or excitement ‖ v.t. to utter or express with such a cry or shout 2. n. an instance of yelling ‖ (sports) a rhythmic shout of encouragement to a competing team, consisting of a rhyme, sequence of syllables etc. [O.E. gellan, giellan]

yel·low (jélou) 1. adj. of the color sensation stimulated by the wavelengths of light in that portion of the spectrum between orange and green, being the color of e.g. ripe lemons ‖ (of members of the Mongolian race etc.) having a skin somewhat of this color ‖ (of paper, skin etc.) changed to this color, e.g. by old age or disease ‖ (pop.) cowardly ‖ (of a newspaper) full of sensationalism 2. n. a yellow color, pigment, fabric etc. ‖ the yolk of an egg ‖ (pl.) jaundice ‖ (pl.) any of several plant diseases characterized by yellowing of the foliage 3. v.t. to make yellow ‖ v.i. to become yellow [O.E. geolo, geolu]

yel·low·bird (jéloubəːrd) n. any of various North American goldfinches

yellow bunting the yellowhammer

yellow-dog contract an employment agreement by which a worker forgoes membership in a labor union during the period of his contract

yellow fever an acute infectious disease esp. of tropical areas, caused by a virus communicated to man by certain mosquitoes. It is characterized by fever, low pulse rate, black vomit and jaundice, and can be fatal

yel·low·ham·mer (jélouhæmər) n. Emberiza citrinella, a European finch. The male has a yellow head, neck and breast

yellow jack yellow fever ‖ a flag flown at the masthead to signal quarantine ‖ Caranx bartholomaei, fam. Carangidae, a golden and silvery edible fish of Florida and the West Indies

yellow jacket any of several varieties of bright yellow social wasps

Yel·low·knife (jélounaif) a gold-mining center (pop. 9,483) in the Northwest Territories, Canada, on Great Slave Lake

yellow ocher, Br. **yellow ochre** a pigment compounded of limonite with clay and silica ‖ an orange-yellow color

Yellow Pages the classified telephone directory

yellow pine any of several pines of North America, incl. Pinus echinata, P. rigida and the loblolly pine ‖ their wood

yellow rattle Rhinanthus crista-galli, fam. Scrophulariaceae, an annual plant of temperate regions. It is semiparasitic on grasses, bears yellow flowers, and has seed capsules in which winged seeds rattle when they are ripe

Yellow River *HWANG-HO

Yellow Sea (Chin. Hwang-hai) a gulf of the Pacific between China and Korea, so named because of the sediment brought to it by the Yangtze-kiang and Hwang-ho

yellow spot a yellowish area near the center of the retina, constituting the region where the vision is most perfect

Yel·low·stone (jéloustoun) a national park (area 3,458 sq. miles) in Wyoming, Montana and Idaho, in the Rockies, incl. peaks to 12,073 ft, and a celebrated volcanic region (geysers, hot springs)

Yellowstone a river (671 miles long) rising in Wyoming, flowing through Yellowstone National Park, crossing the Montana border and emptying into the Missouri River on the Montana-North Dakota boundary. Its valley is the spectacular Grand Canyon of the Yellowstone (2,000 ft wide, 1,200 ft deep)

yellow warbler Dendroica petechia, a small North American warbler. The male is bright yellow, streaked with brown underneath

yelp (jelp) 1. v.i. (esp. of a dog in fear, pain or great excitement) to make a sharp, high-pitched cry, or a series of such cries ‖ v.t. to utter with such a cry 2. n. such a cry [O.E. gielpan, to boast]

Yem·en (jémən) a republic (area 75,000 sq. miles, pop. 7,161,800) in S.W. Arabia. Capital: San'a. People: Arab, with Somali and other African admixture on the coast. Language: Arabic. Religion: Moslem. Behind the hot, humid coastal plain (Tihama) the land is mountainous, rising to a crest (highest point 12,336 ft) in the center, then sloping eastward to the Great Sandy Desert. The central plateau is the most fertile part of Arabia, supporting a large peasantry. Average temperatures (F.) in Jan. and July: coast 60° and 80°, central plateau 50° and 60°. Rainfall: coast under 5 ins, plateau 12 ins. Livestock: sheep, goats, cattle, mules, horses, donkeys, camels. Agricultural products: millet, wheat, other cereals, mocha coffee, qat, indigo, sesame, rice, cotton, grapes, dates, almonds, citrus and other fruit, tobacco. Mineral resources: salt. Exports: coffee, hides and skins, salt, qat. Chief port: Hodeida. Monetary unit: riyal. HISTORY. (For early history *ARABIA.) Yemen was converted to Islam (628) and was part of the Ottoman Empire (mid-16th.– mid-17th cc. and 1849-1918). Despite a treaty (1934) to settle the frontier with Aden Protectorate, border disputes continued. Yemen joined the Arab League (1945) and the U.N. (1947) and united in a Federal Union with the United Arab Republic (1958-61). The imam was overthrown (1962) and a republic was proclaimed. Fighting continued between republican tribes supported by the United Arab Republic and royalist tribes supported by Saudi Arabia. In support of its claim to sovereignty over the whole of southern Arabia, Yemen continued to attack the Federation of South Arabia and to incite subversion within it (1960s). A military coup d'état took place (Nov. 1967). An end to hostilities was negotiated (1970), the imam remaining in exile, but the constitution promulgated that same year was abrogated (1974) after a successful military coup led by Ibrahim al-Hamdi. Hamdi was assassinated (1977), as was his successor, but the country remained under military rule. Members of the Arab League began negotiations (1979) toward the eventual unification of the country with Yemen (Aden)

Yemen, People's Democratic Republic of (formerly People's Republic of South Yemen) a republic (area c. 60,000 sq. miles, pop. 1,998,000, *ARABIA) of S. Arabia, composing the former states making up the Federation of S. Arabia until independence (Nov. 1967): Aden, Audhali, Fadhli, Lahej, Lower Aulagi, Lower

Yafa'i, Wahidi, Beihan, Dhala, Aqrabi, Upper Aulaqi, Dathina, Haushabi, Sha'ib, Maflahi, Alawi together with the nonfederated states that were included in Aden Protectorate: Upper Yafai, Mausatta, Dhubi, Maflahi, Hadhrami, Quteibi, Alawi, Upper Aulaqi Sheikhdom, Quaiti, Kathiri, Mahri Sultanate of Quishn and Socotra, Birati, Mukalla. It also includes Perim and Kamaran, and claims the Kuria Muria Is. Capital: Aden. Products: subsistence crops, cotton, hides, skins, fish. The Minaean (1200-650 B.C.), Sabaean (930-115 B.C.) and Himyarite (115 B.C.–525 A.D.) civilizations dominated the area, which converted to Mohammedanism (mid-7th c.). Its trading and strategic potentialities were disputed by various European powers (16th-18th cc.). Local rulers entered into treaty relations with Britain (1839-1914). The Federation of South Arabia of six states was formed (1959) and extended (1959-63). Independence was achieved in Nov. 1967, and the name People's Republic of South Yemen was adopted. In 1970 the name was changed to People's Democratic Republic of Yemen. A 20-year treaty of friendship was signed (1979) with the U.S.S.R. Efforts to unite the two Yemens resulted in the drafting of a constitution for a unified state (1980) but relations remained tense, albeit slightly improved, between them

Yem·en·ite (jémənait) **1.** *n.* a native of Yemen **2.** *adj.* relating to Yemen or its inhabitants

yen (jen) *n.* (*pop.*) a persistent desire, *a yen to visit the East* [Chin.=opium]

yen *n.* the principal monetary unit of Japan, subdivided into 100 sen ‖ a coin or note representing this value [Jap. fr. Chin. *yüan*, round, dollar]

Ye·nan (jénán) (or Fushih) a town (pop. 50,000) in N. Shensi, China. It was the de facto political and military Communist capital (1935-47)

Ye·nan·gyaung (jénándʒáuŋ) an oil-field center (pop. 11,000) on the Irawaddy in central Burma

yen bond (*securities*) a bond payable in Japanese yen

Ye·ni·sei (jɛniséi) a river in central Siberia, U.S.S.R., rising near the Mongolian border and flowing 2,500 miles to the Arctic Ocean: hydro-electricity (Krasnoyarsk)

yen·ta (jénta) *n.* (*Yiddish*) a gossiping busybody, esp. a woman

Yen·tai (jéntái) *CHEEFOO

yeo·man (jóumən) *pl.* **yeo·men** (jóumən) *n.* a farmer who owns the freehold of his land ‖ (*hist.*) a freeholder of land above a certain value, entitled to serve on a jury and to rank next below an esquire when attached to a noble or royal family ‖ (*U.S. Navy*) a petty officer who does clerical work ‖ (*hist.*) a member of the yeomanry [M.E. *yeman*, *yoman* prob. shortened fr. *yongman*, young man]

yeoman of the guard (*Br.*) one of a bodyguard of 100 men, formed in 1485, allocated various duties attached to the sovereign

yeo·man·ry (jóumənri) *n.* (*Br. hist.*) a volunteer mounted armed force, formed in 1761 for home defense and absorbed (1907) in the Territorial Force ‖ yeomen collectively

yeoman service effective hard work contributed just when wanted or steadily over a period

yer·ba ma·té (jérbəmátei, jɑːrbəmátei) *MATÉ

Yerevan *EREVAN

yes (jes) **1.** *adv.* used to express agreement, consent, affirmation (opp. NO) ‖ used to express interest and as an invitation to say more **2.** *pl.* **yes·es, yes·ses** *n.* an act or instance of expressing agreement, consent or affirmation, esp. by saying 'yes' ‖ an affirmative reply or vote [O.E. *gēse, gīse*]

ye·shi·va (jeʃíːvə) *n.* a school for Talmudic study ‖ a Jewish day school which offers both secular and religious education [Heb.]

yes-man (jésmæn) *pl.* **yes-men** (jésmen) *n.* a subordinate who always agrees with his superior and expresses no opinions of his own, esp. as a method of self-advancement

yes·ter·day (jéstərdei, jéstərdi) **1.** *n.* the day which preceded today ‖ (*rhet.*) recent time **2.** *adv.* on or during yesterday ‖ (*rhet.*) at or during a recent time [O.E. *geostrandœg* fr. *geostran*, yesterday+*dœg*, day]

yes·ter·year (jéstərjiər) *n.* (*rhet.*) last year ‖ (*rhet.*) time not long ago [coined by D. G. ROSSETTI]

yet (jet) **1.** *adv.* up to and including the present time, *I have not seen him yet* ‖ as early as now, *don't go yet* ‖ at that time, *he was not yet mayor* ‖

at some future time, *we shall see him elected yet* ‖ before a specified time, *no one had yet been there until that voyage* ‖ still at present, *we must push on while there is yet light* ‖ in addition, *some want to go, some are willing to go, yet others prefer to stay* ‖ (with comparatives or after 'nor') even, *yet more important, it will not be finished next week, nor yet next year* **2.** *conj.* nevertheless, *he is rich, yet he is content* [O.E. *giet, gīeta*]

yet·i (jéti:) *n.* the abominable snowman [Tibetan]

yew (ju:) *n.* any of several evergreen, coniferous shrubs or trees of genus *Taxus*, fam. *Taxaceae*, of the north temperate zone, esp. *T. baccata* of Europe and Asia. It grows slowly and lives long, having a massive reddish-brown trunk, dark green lustrous needles and a scarlet aril enclosing the fruit. Yews are often a symbol of mourning ‖ the wood of a yew, used for making bows and for veneers [O.E. *īw, ēow*]

yé-yé (jéijei:) *n.* the French mod style in music and fashion, prominent in the 1960s —**yé-yé** *adj.*

Yezd (jezd) (or Yazd) a commercial center (pop. 135,978) in central Iran. Industries: cotton spinning, handicrafts (silk, wool, copperwork). It is a holy city for Zoroastrians

Yez·i·di (jézidi:) *n.* a member of a religious sect of Iraq and Syria of unknown origin. The religion is syncretistic and postulates belief in a Satan who, though formerly the author of evil, is now good and is the chief of the angelic hosts [origin unknown]

Ygg·dra·sil, Ygg·dra·sill (ígdrəsil) (*Norse mythol.*) a great ash tree binding together earth, heaven and hell with its roots and branches [O.N. fr. *Yggr*, Odin+*drasill*, horse]

Yid·dish (yídiʃ) **1.** *n.* a language, with origins perhaps as early as the 9th c., developed from the Middle High German (c. A.D. 1200–1350) spoken by Jews in Germany. In this were incorporated Hebrew words for religious customs, duties etc. Yiddish is written in the Hebrew alphabet, and shows a strong Slavic influence. As Jews migrated east and west it became the normal Jewish vernacular in Europe and America and the medium for a rich literature, still vigorous **2.** *adj.* of or in this language [fr. G. *jüdisch*, Jewish]

yield (ji:ld) **1.** *v.t.* to have as a product or result, *these trees will yield good lumber* ‖ to bring in as profit, interest, income etc., *an investment yielding 10%* ‖ to surrender (something), give (something) up, *to yield ground to one's opponents* ‖ to relinquish (the floor) to another speaker in a legislative assembly ‖ *v.i.* to be fruitful or profitable, *these fruit trees yield well* ‖ to admit the superiority of another, or admit defeat ‖ to give way to entreaty, pressure, argument etc. **to yield to no one** in to have as much of (a quality) as anyone else **2.** *n.* a yielding ‖ the amount yielded **yield·ing** *adj.* giving in or giving way to superior force ‖ readily submitting to another ‖ flexible, not rigid [O.E. *gieldan, geldan*, to pay]

yield point the point at which a body loses its elasticity so that deformation continues even though the body is not subjected to additional stress

YIG (*acronym*) for yttrium iron garnet, a synthetic iron-oxide crystal used in laser modulation as a sonic wave tuning filter. Cf YAG

Yin and Yang (jin, jæŋ) two forces through whose essences, according to Taoist cosmology, the universe was produced and cosmic harmony is maintained. Yin is dark, female and negative, and Yang is light, male and positive

Yip·pie (jípi:) *n.* a politically active radical group of hippies, from a member of the Youth International Party, prominent at Democratic Party National Convention in 1968

ylang-ylang *ILANG-ILANG

Y.M.C.A. *YOUNG MEN'S CHRISTIAN ASSOCIATION

yo·del (jóud'l) **1.** *v. pres. part.* **yo·del·ing**, esp. *Br.* **yo·del·ling** past and past part., esp. *Br.* **yo·delled** *v.i.* and *t.* to call or sing with repeated transitions to the falsetto (a custom of Swiss and Tyrolese mountaineers) **2.** *n.* a yodeled call or musical phrase or song **yó·del·er**, esp. *Br.* **yó·del·ler** *n.* [G. *jodeln*]

yo·ga (jóugə) *n.* a system of discipline and meditation widely practiced within Hinduism. The classic exposition is associated with the Sankhya school of philosophy, which maintains that enmeshed within the human organism is an eternally existent soul, and that complete control of the body can render the soul free from

physical interference. The use of yoga is also advocated by the monistic schools within Hinduism, as a means towards attaining enlightenment. The eight steps of yoga fall into three main groups (cf. the Noble Eightfold Path of Buddhism): (1) moral disciplines (against killing, lying, stealing, sexual impurity and possessiveness, and towards purity, contentment, austerity, study and God-centeredness) (2) physical disciplines (control over bodily posture, breathing and excitation of the senses) (3) stages of meditation (concentration, contemplation and ecstasy) [Hind., Skr.=union]

yogh (jouk, joux, joug) *n.* a Middle English symbol (ȝ) denoting a voiceless fricative or guttural, or a voiced palatal fricative [M.E., etym. doubtful]

yo·gi (jóugi:) *n.* someone who practices yoga [Hind. *yogī*]

yo·gurt, yo·ghurt, yo·ghourt (jóugərt) *n.* a milk product prepared by partial evaporation and then fermentation by the bacteria *Lactobacillus acidophilus* and *Streptococcus thermophilus* [Turk. *yōghurt*]

yoke (jouk) **1.** *n.* a wooden frame fitted across the necks of two oxen or other draft animals, for joining them together as they pull a plow or vehicle ‖ a pair of oxen so linked together ‖ a wooden bar shaped so that it rests across a person's shoulders for carrying balanced loads suspended at each end ‖ a crossbar, e.g. one from which a bell swings, or one by which a rudder is turned ‖ a coupling for pipes or for parts of a machine ‖ a shaped part of a garment at the shoulders or hips, to which gathered or pleated parts are sewn ‖ (*fig.*) a bond. esp. of marriage ‖ (*hist.*) an arch of spears under which the Romans made their beaten enemies pass in sign of submission **2.** *v.t. pres. part.* **yok·ing** past and past part. **yoked** to put under a yoke, join by a yoke ‖ to attach (e.g. an ox) to a cart etc. ‖ (*fig.*) to unite [O.E. *geoc*]

yo·kel (jóuk'l) *n.* a man from the country, esp. an old-fashioned one, as spoken of condescendingly by someone from a big city [etym. doubtful]

Yok·kai·chi (jɔkkaitʃi:) a port (pop. 200,000) in E. Honshu, Japan: textiles, rubber, porcelain

Yo·ko·ha·ma (joukəhámə) the chief seaport (pop. 2,694,600) of Japan, adjoining Tokyo. Industries: steel, automobiles, oil refining, chemicals, shipyards, mechanical engineering. Destroyed (1923) by earthquake, it was rebuilt in Western style

Yo·ko·su·ka (jɔkɔsukɑ, jəkɔ́skə, joukɔsuːkə) a port and naval base (pop. 421,000) in Honshu, Japan, at the entrance to Tokyo Bay

yolk (jouk) *n.* the yellow central part of the egg of a bird or reptile, containing proteins and serving as food for the developing embryo ‖ the material in any animal ovum that supplies food to the embryo [O.E. *geolca*, yellow part]

yolk *n.* an oily secretion found in the fleece of sheep [supposed O.E. *eowoca*]

yolk gland a gland (well developed in reptiles and birds) in connection with the reproductive system by which the ovum is furnished with a supply of food material

yolk·y (jóuki:) *adj.* of, like or containing egg yolk

Yom Kip·pur (jɔmkípər) *n.* the annual day of fasting and repentance ordained in the Mosaic Law and observed by Jews on the 10th day of Tishri (cf. JEWISH CALENDAR) [Heb. *yōm kippūr* fr. *yōm*, day+*kippūr*, atonement]

Yom Kippur War war initiated against Israel on Yom Kippur, October 6, 1973, by Egypt and Syria, and ended by the United Nations on October 24, 1973

yon (jɔn) *adj.* (*archaic and rhet.*) yonder [O.E. *geon*]

yon·der (jɔ́ndər) **1.** *adj.* (*old-fash.*) at a distance but visible, *yonder church tower* ‖ (*old-fash.*) more distant (opp. HITHER) **2.** *adv.* (*old-fash.*) at a somewhat distant yet visible place [M.E. *yonder, yender* fr. *yon*, yonder]

yo·ni (jóuni:) *n.* a symbol of the female genitals, venerated in Hindu worship [Skr.]

Yon·kers (jɔ́ŋkərz) a city and residential suburb (pop. 195,351) of New York City in S.E. New York

Yonne (jɔn) a department (area 2,892 sq. miles, pop. 313,800) in N.E. central France (*BURGUNDY, *ORLEANAIS). Chief town: Auxerre

yore (jɔr, jour) *n.* (only in the archaic phrase) **of yore** long ago, in former years [O.E. *geāra, geāro*]

Yo·ri·to·mo Mi·na·mo·to (jɔri:tɔmɔmi:nɑmɔtɔ) (c. 1147-99), Japanese soldier and the first shogun (1192-9). As a leader of the Minamoto clan, he defeated the rival Taira clan (1185) and established a centralized government at Kamakura

York (jɔrk), Edmund of Langley, duke of (1341-1402), son of Edward III of England. The title 'duke of York' was created to reward him for supporting Richard II against the Scots (1385)

York, Richard, duke of (1411-60), great-grandson of Edward III of England. He attempted unsuccessfully to claim the English throne during the Wars of the Roses, in the course of which he was killed. His son seized the throne as Edward IV

York the county town (pop. 100,000) of Yorkshire, England, a county borough. Industries: metalworking, railroad stock, chocolate. Gothic cathedral (12th-15th cc.), guildhall (15th c.), city walls (14th c.), castle (12th c.). University (1963). York was the military capital of Roman Britain, was the capital of Northumbria, and became the seat of an archbishop

York an English royal dynasty (1461-85) whose reigning members were Edward IV, Edward V and Richard III. Their rivalry with the house of Lancaster resulted in the Wars of the Roses (1455-85), and ended when the Lancastrian Henry VII united the two houses by marrying (1486) Elizabeth, daughter of Edward IV

york·er (jɔrkər) n. (cricket) a ball which pitches immediately in front of the batsman's bat [etym. doubtful]

York·ist (jɔrkist) n. (hist.) a descendant of Edmund of Langley, duke of York ‖ a member or adherent of the house of York in the Wars of the Roses

York·shire (jɔrkʃər) (abbr. Yorks.) former county (area 6,089 sq. miles) in N. England. It was divided (1974) into three counties: North, West and South Yorkshire

Yorkshire pudding a thin batter of plain flour, milk, water and salt, baked in an oven in meat dripping and eaten with roast beef

Yorkshire terrier a toy terrier of a shaggy variety, with long, silky, steel-blue or tan hair

York·town (jɔrktaun) a village (pop. 400) in S.E. Virginia, center of a national historical park. It was the scene of the surrender (1781) of the British forces under Cornwallis at the end of the Revolutionary War

Yo·ru·ba (jɔrubə, jóurubə) pl. **Yo·ru·ba, Yo·ru·bas** n. a member of a people of S.W. Nigeria, S. Togo and S.E. Dahomey numbering 5 million. Their historic kingdom dominated W. Africa until the 18th c. ‖ this people ‖ their language

Yo·sem·i·te Valley (jousémiti:) a famous valley (6 miles long, height 3,000–4,000 ft, floor c. 4,000 ft above sea level) in central California, in Yosemite National Park (area 1,182 sq. miles). It has spectacular U-shaped canyons with imposing summits

Yo·shi·da (jóuʃi:da), Shigeru (1878-1967), Japanese political leader and prime minister (1946-7, 1948-54)

you (ju:) pron., 2nd person sing. and pl., nominative and objective cases the person or persons to whom one is speaking, you are my friends, I overheard you ‖ (in generalizing) a person, one, you never know what may happen [O.E. ēow]

you'd (ju:d) contr. of YOU HAD, YOU WOULD

you'll (ju:l) contr. of YOU WILL, YOU SHALL

Young (jʌŋ), Arthur (1741-1820), British agricultural writer. His 'Travels in France during the years 1787-90' (1792) is a classic description of social and economic conditions in France on the eve of the French Revolution

Young, Brigham (1801-77), American Mormon leader. He led the westward migration of Mormons to Utah and founded Salt Lake City (1847)

Young, Edward (1683-1765), English poet. His 'Night Thoughts' ('The Complaint: or Nightthoughts', 1742-5) initiated the romantic taste for reflections on mortality

Young, Thomas (1773-1829), English physicist and doctor of medicine, whose experimental work on optical interference lent support to the wave theory of light. He put forward a theory of color vision, and independently of Champollion deciphered Egyptian hieroglyphics (*ROSETTA STONE)

Young, Whitney M., Jr. (1921-71) U.S. social worker, executive director (1961-71) of the National Urban League

young (jʌŋ) **1.** adj. in the early stages of development, a young child, a young country ‖ not far

advanced, the night is still young ‖ less advanced in years than another, young Mr. Brown (distinguishing him from his father) ‖ having the vigor, resilience etc. associated with those who are young, he is young for his years **2.** n. offspring **the young** young people **with young** (of an animal) pregnant [O.E. geong]

young·ber·ry (jʌ́ŋberi) pl. **young·ber·ries** n. a large, sweet, reddish-black berry which is the fruit of a hybrid between the blackberry and the dewberry, grown in the U.S.A. ‖ the bramble which yields it [after B. M. Young, U.S. fruit grower, who produced it (c. 1900)]

Young England *DISRAELI

young fustic the yellow dyewood of Cotinus coggygria, fam. Anacardiaceae, a European shrub yielding a substitute for fustic

Young Italy *MAZZINI

Young Men's Christian Association (Y.M.C.A.) an organization founded (1844) in London by Sir George Williams and others. Christian but nondoctrinal, nonsectarian and nonpolitical, it evolved (1855) into an international organization, the World Alliance of Y.M.C.A.s, with its headquarters at Geneva. The first Y.M.C.A. club in the Western Hemisphere was founded in Montreal, the second in Boston

Young Pretender *STUART, Charles Edward

Young's modulus (phys.) the constant ratio, for a given elastic substance, of the applied longitudinal stress to the change in length of unit length (symbol E)

young·ster (jʌ́ŋstər) n. a child or adolescent

Youngs·town (jʌ́ŋztaun) an industrial center (pop. 115,436) in N.E. Ohio: iron and steel, chemical industries, rubber, bricks

Young Turk a member of a reform movement within the Ottoman Empire (early 20th c.). The movement organized the revolt (1908) which deposed Abdul Hamid II (1909)

Young Women's Christian Association (Y.W.C.A.) an organization originated (1855-77) in England by Emma Robarts and Lady Kinnaird as a response to the ill-effects of the Industrial Revolution on the lives of young women, esp. in cities

your (juər, jɔr, jour, unstressed jər) poss. pronominal adj. of or belonging to you, your father ‖ used preceding certain titles in addressing the holder of the title, Your Majesty, Your Worship [O.E. ēower]

you're (juər) contr. of YOU ARE

yours (juərz, jɔrz, jourz) possessive pron. that or those belonging to you, this book is yours

your·self (juərsélf, jɔrsélf, joursélf, jərsélf) pl. **your·selves** pron. refl. form of YOU, you hurt yourself ‖ emphatic form of YOU, you do it yourself [M.E. your selfe, your selven]

youth (ju:θ) pl. **youths** (ju:ðz, ju:θs) n. the state or quality of being young ‖ the period from childhood to maturity ‖ a young man ‖ young people of both sexes ‖ an early stage of development [O.E. geoguth]

youth culture contemporary norms and lifestyle (dress, language, music) of young people. Cf COUNTER CULTURE

youth·ful (jú:θfəl) adj. of, pertaining to or befitting youth, youthful fashions ‖ young ‖ (geol.) of a land surface which has not yet suffered much erosion

youth hostel a building providing cheap overnight accommodation and often food for young travelers

youth·quake (jú:θkweik) n. major change brought about by the action of young people, e.g., China's Cultural Revolution

you've (ju:v) contr. of YOU HAVE

yowl (jaul) **1.** v.i. (esp. of an animal) to utter a long, loud, sad cry **2.** n. this cry [M.E. yoyele, youle]

yo-yo (jóujou) pl. **yo-yos, yo-yoes** n. a toy consisting of a double wooden disk, deeply grooved, which can be made to rise and fall on a string attached to its center and running in the groove ‖ (slang) a foolish person [fr. Yo-Yo, trademark]

Y·pi·ran·ga (i:pi:rǎ̃ŋgə) a river in Brazil, in the state of São Paolo. On its banks the regent Pedro uttered (Sept. 7, 1822) the 'cry of Ypiranga', proclaiming the independence of Brazil from Portugal

Y·po·á, Lake (i:pɔ́a) a lake (area c. 100 sq. miles) in S. Paraguay, navigable for small boats

Y·pres (i:pr) (Flem. Ieper) a town (pop. 34.400) in West Flanders, Belgium. Gothic cloth market (13th-14th cc.), cathedral (12th-15th cc.)

Ypres, Battle of a battle (Oct. 14–Nov. 13, 1914) of the 1st world war, ending in stalemate between the Germans and the Allies ‖ a battle (Apr. 22–May 2, 1915) of the 1st world war, in which an Allied advance was halted by the Germans, who used poison gas for the first time ‖ a battle (June 7–Nov. 6, 1917), also known as the Battle of Passchendaele, during the 1st world war, in which a British advance was achieved at a cost of 400,000 lives

Yp·si·lan·ti (ipsəlǽnti:), Alexander (1792-1828), Greek soldier and patriot. His revolt (1821) against the Turks in Moldavia marked the beginning of the Greek War of Independence

Ypsilanti, Demetrios (1793-1832), Greek soldier and patriot. The brother of Alexander, he played a prominent part in the Greek War of Independence

Y·ri·goy·en (i:ri:góien), Hipólito (1852-1933), Argentinian politician, leader of the Radicals (a reform group opposing conservative rule), and president of the Republic (1916-22, 1928-30). He was overthrown in a coup led by Gen. José F. Uriburu

yt·ter·bic (itə́rbik) adj. of or containing ytterbium

yt·ter·bi·um (itə́:rbi:əm) n. a rare-earth element (symbol Yb, at. no. 70, at. mass 173.04) [Mod. L. after Ytterby, Sweden]

yt·tri·a (ítri:ə) n. yttrium oxide, Y₂O₃ [Mod. L. after Ytterby, Sweden]

yt·tri·um (ítri:əm) n. a metallic element usually classed with the rare-earth metals (symbol Y, at. no. 39, at. mass 88.905) [Mod. L. fr. YTTRIA]

Yü·an (jyan) a Mongolian dynasty founded by Kublai Khan, which ruled China 1279-1368

yu·an (jyan) n. the former monetary unit of China (1914–49) ‖ the basic monetary unit of Taiwan ‖ a coin or note representing either of these

Yüan Shih-kai (jyánʃí:kái) (1859-1916), Chinese soldier and statesman, president of the Chinese republic (1912-16). He tried unsuccessfully to have himself proclaimed emperor

Yu·ca·tán (ju:kətǽn, ju:kətán) a low-lying peninsula (area 55,400 sq. miles), covered with rain forest, separating the Gulf of Mexico from the Caribbean. It comprises parts of Mexico, British Honduras and Guatemala. The northern half is one of the most important henequenraising regions in the world. The forests yield mahogany and other cabinet woods, vanilla, rubber, logwood and dyewood. The area was the center of Mayan civilization (100 B.C.–1200 A.D.) and of the Toltecs (1200-1450). Sites of magnificent ruins include Chichén Itzá

Yucatán a state (area 14,868 sq. miles, pop. 926,000) in Mexico, in the north of the Yucatán peninsula. Manufactures include rope, cordage, and coarse fabrics for sacking. Capital: Mérida (pop. 100,000), a commercial center and the center of the Yucatán henequen industry. It is also a tourist base for visiting many Mayan ruins

Yucatán Channel a strait (135 miles wide) between the west end of Cuba and the Yucatán peninsula, Mexico, connecting the Gulf of Mexico and the Caribbean Sea

yuc·ca (jʌ́kə) n. a member of Yucca, fam. Liliaceae, a genus of American plants with thin, rigid, lance-shaped leaves and a panicle of large white or violet flowers borne on an erect undivided stem. Fiber is extracted from the species grown in Mexico esp. from Y. baccata ‖ the flower of any of these plants [of Carib. origin]

Yu·go·sla·vi·a, Ju·go·sla·vi·a (ju:gousláɪvi:ə) a socialist federal republic (area 98,725 sq. miles, pop. 22,738,000) in S.E. Europe. Capital: Belgrade. Federated nationalities: Serbs (42%), Croats (23%), Slovenes (9%), Macedonians (5%), Montenegrins (3%). Other peoples: Albanians (4%), Magyars (3%), Turks (2%), small Bulgar, Czech, Slovak, Italian, Rumanian and other minorities. Language: Serbo-Croatian, Slovene and Macedonian dialects. Religion: 41% Orthodox, 32% Roman Catholic, 12% Moslem, 1% Protestant. The land is 33% arable, 26% pasture and 34% forest (esp. oak, fir, beech). Except for the fertile Danube-Sava basin in the northeast (Serbia), where population is concentrated, the country is rugged and mountainous. The Julian Alps (Triglav, 9,400 ft) and Karawanken Alps cross the north, the Dinaric Alps (5,900 ft north of Rijeka) run

---

along the west coast. The mountains in the interior rise to 8,800 ft near Skopje. Average temperatures (F.) in Belgrade: Jan. 32°, July 71°. Rainfall: south coast and center 60-85 ins, north coast and east 20-40 ins. Livestock: cattle, horses, sheep, hogs, goats, donkeys. Agricultural products: corn, wheat, barley, rye, sugar beets, tobacco, hemp, hay, sunflowers, potatoes, dairy products, apples, plums, pears, grapes, olives, walnuts. Mineral resources: coal, iron ore, copper, lead, bauxite, petroleum, zinc, gold, chrome, antimony, lignite, mercury, salt, manganese, barite, natural gas, magnesite, silver. Industries: iron and steel, oil refining, aluminum, mechanical engineering, heavy machinery, textiles, fertilizers, sulfuric acid, cement, sugar, wine, tourism, fishing, hydroelectricity, ships, paper, pulp, leather, bricks, tiles, soap. Exports: bauxite, lumber, pulp, cement, cattle, meat, lead, zinc, vegetables, fruit, tobacco, wine. Imports: machinery, vehicles, metals, coal, wheat, oil, fertilizers, textiles, chemicals, iron and steel, foodstuffs. Chief ports: Rijeka, Split, Dubrovnik, and Zadar on the Adriatic, Novi Sad and Belgrade on the Danube. Universities: Belgrade, Ljubljana, Sarajevo, Skopje, Zagreb. Monetary unit: dinar (100 paras). HISTORY. Yugoslavia was the name given (1929) to the kingdom formed (1918) by the union of Serbia, Bosnia-Herzegovina, Croatia, Macedonia, Montenegro and Slovenia. Such a union had been urged in the late l9th c. by the supporters of Pan-Slavism, and became possible when AustriaHungary collapsed in the lst world war. Alexander I, as regent (1918-21) and king (1921-34), failed to reconcile the various nationalities and was assassinated by Croat nationalists. The regency in the name of Peter II followed an increasingly pro-Axis policy until overthrown (1941) in a coup d'état. Yugoslavia was occupied 10 days later by the Germans. Among several guerrilla resistance

groups, a Communist group led by Tito received Allied support and controlled most of the country by the end of the 2nd world war. Yugoslavia was proclaimed a federal people's republic (1945) with Tito as head of state, and all means of production and natural resources were nationalized. It was a leading member of the Cominform until 1948, when it broke off relations with the U.S.S.R. Yugoslavia thereafter adopted an independent communist policy. The government was decentralized and collectivization of industry and agriculture was reduced. Yugoslavia's dispute with Italy over Trieste was settled (1954). Normal relations with the U.S.S.R. were resumed after 1955. The country was proclaimed a socialist federal republic (1963). The presidency became (1971) a collective presidency, with Tito at its head. After Tito's death (1980) his policies of nonalignment and decentralized economic management were continued. An austerity program was begun to reduce inflation and the country's large foreign debt

Yu·go·slav, Ju·go·slav (ju:gousláv, ju:gouslǽv) **1.** *n.* a native or inhabitant of Yugoslavia **2.** *adj.* of Yugoslavia or its people

Yu·go·sla·vi·an, Ju·go·sla·vi·an (ju:gousláv-i:ən) *n.* and *adj.* Yugoslav

Yu·go·sla·vic, Ju·go·sla·vic (ju:gouslávik, ju:gouslǽvik) *adj.* Yugoslav

Yu·ka·wa (ju:kɑwɑ), Hideki (1907-81), Japanese physicist. His theory of nuclear forces postulated (1935) the existence of mesons two years before they were first observed. Nobel prize (1949)

Yu·kon (jú:kɒn) a territory (area 207,076 sq. miles, pop. 21,600) in extreme N.W. Canada. Capital: Whitehorse (pop. 16,771). It is mountainous with a broad central plateau, mainly forest (unexploited) and grassland, with tundra in the north. Highest peak: Mt Logan (19,850

ft). Occupations: mining (silver, lead, zinc, gold), trapping. The Alaska Highway crosses the southwest. The Yukon became famous with the discovery (1896) of gold in the Klondike River area, and was constituted a Canadian territory (1898)

Yukon a river (2,000 miles long) flowing from the N.W. Yukon across Alaska to the Bering Sea

yule (ju:l) *n.* the festival or season of Christmas [O.E. *geōl, geōla*]

yule log a large log burned traditionally on an open fire on Christmas Eve

yule·tide (jú:ltaid) *n.* the Christmas season

Yun·gay (ju:ŋgái) a department and town (pop. 50,000) of Nuble province in central Chile, site of the victory (1839) of the Chileans under Manuel Bulnes over a Peru-Bolivian invasion force under Gen. Santa Cruz

Yung·ki (júŋkí:) (*Jap.* Kirin) a town (pop. 568,000) in Kirin; N.E. China, on the Sungari: wood and chemical industries, paper

Yung·kia (júŋdʒjá) *WENCHOW

Yung·ning (júŋníŋ) *NANNING

Yün·ho (júnhóu) *GRAND CANAL

Yun·nan (júnán) a province (area 123,539 sq. miles, pop. 32,553,817, one-third hill tribes) in S.W. China bordering Burma, Laos and North Vietnam. Capital: Kunming

Yun·nan·fu (júnánfú:) *KUNMING

yup·pie (jʌpi) *n.* a quasi-acronym for young urban professional, noted for devotion to upward economic mobility and for conspicuous consumption.

Yur·ev (jú:rjəf) *TARTU

Y·ve·lines (i:vli:n) a department (area 876 sq. miles, pop. 1,230,000) in N. central France, west of Paris (*ILE-DE-FRANCE). Chief town: Versailles

Y.W.C.A. *YOUNG WOMEN'S CHRISTIAN ASSOCIATION

CONCISE PRONUNCIATION KEY: **(a)** æ, c*a*t; ɑ, c*a*r; ɔ f*a*wn; ei, sn*a*ke. **(e)** e, h*e*n; i:, sh*ee*p; iə, d*ee*r; ɛə, b*ea*r. **(i)** i, f*i*sh; ai, t*i*ger; ə:, b*i*rd. **(o)** o, *o*x; au, c*o*w; ou, g*oa*t; u, p*oo*r; ɔi, r*o*yal. **(u)** ʌ, d*u*ck; u, b*u*ll; u:, g*oo*se; ə, b*a*cillus; ju:, c*u*be. x, lo*ch*; θ, *th*ink; ð, bo*th*er; z, *Z*en; ʒ, corsa*g*e; dʒ, sava*g*e; ŋ, ora*n*gutang; j, *y*ak; ʃ, fi*sh*; tʃ, fe*tch*; 'l, rabb*l*e; 'n, redde*n*. Complete pronunciation key appears inside front cover.

	EARLY NORTH SEMITIC	PHOENICIAN	EARLY HEBREW (GEZER)				CLASSICAL LATIN
Z	I	I	I				Z
	CURSIVE MAJUSCULE (ROMAN)	CURSIVE MINUSCULE (ROMAN)			VENETIAN MINUSCULE (ITALIC)	MODERN ROMAN	
	Z	z			Z	Z	

A. C. SYLVESTER, CAMBRIDGE, ENGLAND

Development of the letter Z, beginning with the early North Semitic letter. Evolution of both the majuscule, or capital, letter Z and the minuscule, or lowercase, letter z are shown.

Z, z (zi:, *Br.* zed) the last letter of the English alphabet

Zab·rze (záb3e) (*G.* Hindenburg) the chief coal-mining center (pop. 204,000) in Upper Silesia, Poland: iron and steel, chemicals

Za·ca·te·cas (sɑkatékɑs) a central plateau state (area 28,973 sq. miles, pop. 1,133,000) of Mexico. Its agricultural production (cereals, sugar and maguey) depends greatly on irrigation. Its 16th-c. mines (silver, gold, mercury, copper) are among the most famous in Mexico. Industries include the extraction of rubber from guayule and the making of sugar, rum, mescal, and various fabrics. There are many baroque churches of the colonial period

Zach·a·ri·as (zækəráiəs), St, Jewish priest of Jerusalem, father of John the Baptist. Feast: Nov. 5

Za·dar (zádɑr) (formerly Zara) a port (pop. 60,000) on the central Dalmatian coast, Yugoslavia. Romanesque cathedral (13th c.). It was Venetian (1409-1747), Austrian until 1920, and Italian until 1947

Zad·kine (zædki:n), Ossip (1890-1967), French cubist sculptor, born in Russia. He used complex abstract means in representing the human figure, notably voids or concave surfaces which suggest form (*CUBISM)

zaf·fer, zaf·fre (zæfər) *n.* an impure cobalt oxide used in enameling and as a blue pigment for painting on porcelain or glass [fr. Ital. *zaffera*]

Zag·a·zig (zægəzig) an agricultural market (pop. 200,800) in E. Egypt in the Nile delta. Ruins of the ancient city of Bubastis, a religious center (10th-4th cc. B.C.), are nearby

Za·greb (zágreb) the capital (pop. 768,700) of Croatia, Yugoslavia, on the Sava. Industries: metalworking, railroad stock, food processing, wood, plastics. Cathedral (13th-18th cc.), palace (14th c.). University (1874)

Zag·ros (zægrəs) a mountain system running from Lake Van, E. Turkey, through W. Iran to the Strait of Hormuz: Zardeh Kuh (14,921 ft)

zai·bat·su (zaibatsu:) *n.* the powerful Japanese financial establishment, from the Japanese word for 'wealth'

Za·ïre (zɑi:r) (formerly the Democratic Republic of the Congo) a republic (area 904,990 sq. miles, pop. 29,897,000) in central Africa. Capital: Kinshasa. Official language: French. Native languages: Kiswahili or Kingwana in the east, Tshiluba or Kiluba in the south, Lingala in the Congo basin, and Kikongo in the lower Congo. The land is 42% forest, 21% arable, 1% permanent pasture, and the rest savanna. The Congo basin forms a low-lying part (1,200–1,500 ft) of the African plateau. It is covered with dense tropical forest and marshes. In the east the land rises toward the Mitumba highlands (highest point 16,795 ft, on the Uganda border). In the southeast the plateau rises to 6,500 ft. The Congo basin has a hot, wet, equatorial climate. Average temperature: 78° F. (seasonal variation 4°). Rainfall: 60 ins in the north, 20 ins along the coast, 40 ins in the south. Livestock: goats, cattle. Agricultural products: coffee, cotton, rubber, tea, cocoa, palm oil, bananas. Mineral resources (Katanga): copper, diamonds, gold, silver, tin, cobalt, uranium, germanium, zinc, iron. Exports: copper, diamonds, palm oil, cobalt, cotton, rubber, coffee. Imports: machinery, manufactures, fuel oils, vehicles. Chief port: Matadi. Two pipelines link Matadi with Kinshasa. The Congo and its tributaries provide 8,500 miles of navigable waterway. Universities: Kinshasa (1954, Roman Catholic), Lubumbashi (1956, national). Monetary unit: zaïre (100 makuta). HISTORY. The Sudanic kingdom of Kongo was flourishing in the region of the Congo estuary when the Portuguese arrived (1482). Inhabited by the Bakongo, it was destroyed (late 17th c.) by contact with the Portuguese. Other Bantu peoples, the Balunda and the Baluba, founded (17th c.) a vast kingdom covering what is now S. Zaïre, W. Angola and Zambia. The Congo was explored by Stanley (1874-84). The Congo Free State was established under the personal rule of Leopold II of Belgium (1885), and was annexed to Belgium (1908). It was declared an independent republic (June 30, 1960) with Kasavubu as president. The U.N. intervened in subsequent civil strife which went on intermittently until the seccessionist province of Katanga was reintegrated into the State (1963). Rebel activity continued after the U.N. withdrawal (June 1964), but Belgian paratroopers intervened (Nov. 1964) to prevent further civilian massacres. Civil war continued under Tshombe's provisional government (1964-5). A coup d'état (Nov. 1965) overthrew Kasavubu. Gen. Mobutu became president. White mercenaries backed by police of Katangese origin occupied Bukavu (July 1967) and a second group of mercenaries, from Angola, infiltrated Katanga. Both groups were repulsed. The name Zaïre was adopted (Oct. 1971). Mobutu survived several coup attempts and plots to overthrow him, but opposition to him grew, esp. after Zaïre's involvement in Angola's civil war and the disclosure (1975) of Zaïre's bankruptcy. His regime was further threatened by Angola-based rebels who invaded (1977, 8) and had to be repelled by foreign troops. After 1977, Mobutu reversed his nationalization policy and agreed to submit Zaïre's economy to directives of the International Monetary Fund

za·ïre (zɑi:r) *n.* the basic monetary unit of Zaïre, divided into 100 makuta

Zaïre Republic formerly Democratic Republic of the Congo, earlier of the Belgium Congo — **Zairean** *n.* a native

Za·kyn·thos (zəkínθəs) (or Zante) a Greek island (area 156 sq. miles, pop. 35,000) in the Ionian Sea: vines, currants

Za·ma, Battle of (zéimə, zámɑ) a battle (202 B.C.) in N. Africa, in which Scipio Africanus defeated Hannibal, at the end of the 2nd Punic War

Zam·be·zi (zæmbí:zi:) a river (2,200 miles long, navigable over 1,700 miles in stretches between rapids) flowing from N. Zambia, forming the Zambian-Rhodesian border and crossing Mozambique to the Indian Ocean

Zam·bi·a (zémbi:ə) (formerly Northern Rhodesia) a republic (area 290,600 sq. miles, pop. 6,330,000) in central Africa. Capital: Lusaka. People: Bantu, 2% European, small Asian minority. Language: Bantu languages and English. Religion: mainly Animist, with large Christian and small Moslem minorities. The land is 5% cultivated. It is a plateau and is largely covered by savanna forest, with grassy plains and swamps around Lake Bangweulu and in the Kafue and Zambezi valleys. The copper belt, the chief source of wealth, lies along the Congo border. Average temperatures (F.): May-Sept. 60-80°, Sept.-Nov. 80°-90°, Nov.-Apr. 70°-80°. Rainfall: 20-30 ins in the Zambezi basin and Barotse plains, over 50 ins in the north and east. Livestock: cattle, sheep, goats. Agricultural products: corn, tobacco, kaffir corn, millet, cassava, peanuts, wheat, dairy produce, cotton, rice, pulses, coffee. Forest products: redwood (*Baikiaea plurifuga*), teak. Resources: copper, zinc, lead and vanadium, cobalt, manganese, gold, hydroelectricity. Industries: mining, fishing, food processing, metallurgy, copper smelting, furniture, cement. Exports: copper, tobacco, wood products, hides and skins. Imports: machinery, vehicles, food. There is railroad access to Lobito (Angola), Beira (Mozambique) and South Africa. University of Zambia (1966). Monetary unit: kwacha (100 ngwee). HISTORY. The country has yielded important evidence of prehistoric settlement. It is thought that an Iron Age people migrated to Zambia from E. Africa (1st millennium A.D.). The Bantu invaded from the 17th c. onwards, followed by Arabs from the north and Zulu and Basuto from the south (19th c.). After Portuguese expeditions across the country (late 18th and early 19th cc.), Livingstone traveled through Barotseland (1851) and discovered the Victoria Falls (1855). On the initiative of Rhodes, the British South Africa Company was chartered (1889) and by 1900 had extended its control over the whole country. The slave trade was stamped out. The country was unified (1911) as Northern Rhodesia and its administration assumed by the Crown (1924). It was a member of the Central African Federation (1953-63). Universal adult suffrage and internal self-government were introduced (1963). Kaunda was elected Northern Rhodesia's first prime minister (1964) and was its first president when it became an independent republic within the Commonwealth, under the name of Zambia (Oct. 24, 1964). Zambia joined the U.N. (1964). Relations with Southern Rhodesia were strained after the latter's white government unilaterally declared independence (1965) as Rhodesia, but improved from 1980 when black majority rule was achieved in the renamed Zimbabwe. A rail link from the Copperbelt through Tanzania to the sea was completed (1976) with China's help

Zam·bo·an·ga (sₐmbouáŋgₐ) a port (pop. 265,000) in S.W. Mindanao, Philippines

Za·men·hof (zéimₐnhɔf, zámₐnhɔf), Lazarus Ludovic (1859-1917), Polish linguist, an oculist by profession. He invented Esperanto

Za·mo·ra (zₐmɔ́rₐ) a province (area 4,097 sq. miles, pop. 224,369) in N.W. Spain (*LEON) ‖ its capital (pop. 39,000)

Zan·jón, Peace of (sₐnhɔ́n) an agreement (1878) between Spain and Cuba which ended the Ten Year War, or Great War (1868-78)

zan·shin (zₐnʃin) n. (*Japanese martial arts*) complete awareness

Zan·te (zźnti:) *ZAKYNTHOS

ZANU (*acronym*) for Zimbabwe African National Party

za·ny (zéini:) 1. *pl.* **za·nies** n. (*hist.*) a stage buffoon who mimicked the clown ‖ a person who acts like a buffoon 2. *comp.* **za·ni·er** *superl.* **za·ni·est** *adj.* ludicrous in a rather crazy way [F. *zani* fr. Ital. *zani, zanni*, a clown, orig. a familiar form of *Giovanni*, John]

Zan·zi·bar (zǽnzₐbɑr) a coralline island (area 640 sq. miles) in the Indian Ocean, 22 miles off Tanganyika ‖ a republic (area 1,020 sq. miles, pop. 475,655) consisting of Zanzibar and Pemba islands, forming part of Tanzania. Capital and port: Zanzibar. People: 80% African, 14% Arab, 6% Indian. Language: Swahili and other Bantu languages, Arabic, Gujarati, English. Religion: mainly Moslem, with minorities practicing Christianity or local African religions. The land is 51% cultivated. Zanzibar island is flat in the east and hilly (rising to 390 ft) in the west. Average temperature (Zanzibar): 80°. Rainfall: Zanzibar 58 ins, Pemba 80 ins. Exports: cloves (*PEMBA), clove oil, coconuts, copra, coconut oil, coir. Other products: rice, cassava, sweet potatoes, chilies, tobacco, corn, tropical fruit, soap, fish, jewelry, ivory and ebony ornaments. Imports: rice and other cereals, flour, textiles, gasoline, vehicles, tobacco. Monetary unit: Tanzanian shilling (100 cents). HISTORY. Arabs and Persians settled in Zanzibar from the 7th c. It was seized by the Portuguese (1503) and by the Arabs of Muscat and Oman (1698). A thriving trade in slaves and ivory developed, and the clove was introduced (early 19th c.). Zanzibar became independent (1856) and a British protectorate (1890). It gained independence (Dec. 10, 1963) within the Commonwealth. The sultan's government was overthrown by a coup d'état, and Zanzibar was declared a republic (Jan. 1964). It united (Apr. 27, 1964) with Tanganyika to form a republic which later took the name Tanzania

zap (zæp) 1. n. a sudden hit or other occurrence 2. v. to destroy suddenly 3. v. to apply electroshock therapy

Za·pa·ta (sₐpátₐ), Emiliano (c. 1883-1919), Mexican revolutionary leader. To the cry of 'Land and liberty' he led (1910) a revolt against President Porfirio Díaz which helped to install Francisco Madero in power. But he opposed Madero's agrarian program, and formulated his own agrarian proposals in the Plan of Ayala (1911). A champion of land redistribution, he continued his fight against Presidents Francisco Madero, Victoriano Huerta, and Venustiano Carranza. With Pancho Villa he occupied (1914-15) Mexico City three times. He was assassinated by an emissary of Carranza

za·pa·tis·mo (sₐpatí:smɔ) n. the Mexican agrarian reform movement of Emiliano Zapata. It become synonymous with agrarismo and later indianismo [Span.]

Za·po·lya (zápₐljₐ), John *JOHN I ZAPOLYA

Za·po·ro·zhe (zₐpₐrɔ́ʒₐ) (formerly Alexandrovsk) a city (pop. 760,000) in the S.E. Ukraine, U.S.S.R., on the Dnieper: iron and steel, aluminum, chemicals, agricultural machinery, automobiles

Za·ra (zárₐ, dzárₐ) *ZADAR

Za·ra·go·za (sₐrₐgɔ́sₐ), Ignacio (1829-62), Mexican general and politician. He routed (May 1862) the invading French forces at Puebla

Za·ra·go·za (θₐrₐgɔ́θₐ) *SARAGOSSA

Zar·a·thus·tra (zǽrₐθú:strₐ) the name of Zoroaster in the Avesta

zar·a·tite (zǽrₐtait) n. a hydrated carbonate of nickel, $NiCO_3 \cdot 2Ni(OH)_2 \cdot 4H_2O$, occurring in bright green aggregates [fr. Span. *zaratita*, after a Señor *Zarate*]

Za·ri·a (zári:ₐ) a market and rail center (pop. 224,000) in N. Nigeria, formerly a Hausa state. University (1962)

zeal (zi:l) n. persistent fervent devotion to a cause [M.E. *zele* fr. L. *zelus* fr. Gk *zēlos*]

Zea·land (zí:lₐnd) (*Dan.* Sjælland) Denmark's largest island (area 2,709 sq. miles), on which Copenhagen lies

zeal·ot (zélₐt) n. someone who acts for a cause with excessive zeal **Zealot** (*hist.*) a member of a Jewish sect which revolted against the Roman forces of occupation in Judea from 6 A.D. until the destruction of Jerusalem (70 A.D.) **zeal·ot·ry** n. behavior etc. characteristic of a zealot [fr. eccles. L. *zelotes* fr. Gk]

zeal·ous (zélₐs) adj. full of zeal, showing zeal [fr. M.L. *zelosus*]

ze·a·tin (zí:ₐtₐn) n. (*biochem.*) a substance with self-dividing properties that enables plants to grow, derived from sperm of maize

ze·bra (zí:brₐ) n. any of several swift-running equine mammals of S. and E. Africa, covered with alternating black (or brown) and white (or buff) stripes. They are rarely domesticated [Congolese]

zebra crossing (*Br.*) a broad band of alternate black and white stripes painted across a road, denoting that pedestrians have absolute priority over drivers

ze·bra·wood (zí:brₐwₐd) n. *Connarus guianensis*, fam. *Connaraceae*, a tree of tropical America and E. Africa, the striped hardwood of which is used in cabinetmaking ‖ any of several other trees or shrubs yielding similar wood ‖ the wood of any of these trees

ze·bu (zí:bju:, zí:bu:) n. *Bos indicus*, a bovine mammal, domesticated in the Malagasy Republic, India and the Far East for use as a draft animal. Zebus have a hump of fat on the shoulders. They tolerate heat well. They are often crossed with European breeds of cattle [fr. F. *zébu*]

Zeb·u·lun (zébjulₐn) Hebrew patriarch, son of Jacob ‖ the Israelite tribe of which he was the ancestor

Zech·a·ri·ah (zekₐráiₐ) a Minor Prophet (6th c. B.C.) of the Old Testament. Like Haggai, he urged the Jews to rebuild the Temple in Jerusalem ‖ the book of the Old Testament which contains his prophecies

zed (zed) n. (Br.) zee

zee (zi:) n. (*Am.*=*Br.* zed) the letter z

Zee·land (zí:lₐnd, zéilₐnt) the southwestern province (area 690 sq. miles, pop. 335,624) of the Netherlands. Capital: Middelburg

Zee·man effect (zéimₐn) (*phys.*) the splitting up of the lines in a line spectrum by a strong magnetic field, from which deductions can be made as to the atomic structure [after Pieter *Zeeman* (1865-1943), Du. physicist and Nobel prizewinner (1902) with LORENTZ]

ze·in (zí:in) n. a protein found in corn and used in the manufacture of textiles, plastics etc. [fr. *Zea*, the genus to which corn belongs]

Zeit·ge·ber (záitgeibₐːr) n. (*German*, usu. italics) a factor that affects the biological clock, e.g., light, temperature

zeit·geist (tsáitgaist) n. the dominant moral and intellectual character of a particular period [G.]

zel·ko·va (zélkₐvₐ) n. a Japanese tree similar to American elm, imported into the U.S.

zem·stvo (zémstvou) *pl.* **zem·stvos** n. (*Russ. hist.*) any of the provincial or district councils established (1864) by Alexander II. The zemstvos played an important part in the formation of a liberal intelligentsia. They were abolished (1917) by the Bolsheviks in favor of the soviets [Russ.]

Zen (zen) n. a school of Mahayana Buddhism traditionally founded in China (early 6th c.) by Bodhidharma and widespread in Japan since the 12th c. It teaches that enlightenment may be achieved by meditation and intuition, stimulated by the contemplation of beauty and simplicity [Jap.=religious meditation fr. Chin. *ch'an* fr. Skr. *jhāna* fr. Skr. *dhyāna*]

ze·na·na (zenánₐ) n. that part of a house in India or Persia which is reserved for the women [Hind. *zenāna, zanāna* fr. Pers.]

Zen Buddhism Zen **Zen Buddhist** an adherent of Zen

Zend (zend) n. the ancient Iranian language, allied to Sanskrit, in which the Avesta was written ‖ the Middle Persian translation of the Zoroastrian Avesta and commentary on it [Pers.=interpretation]

Zend-Avesta the Avesta

ze·ner diode (zí:nₐːr) (*electr.*) a silicon semiconductor that maintains fixed voltage in a circuit, for American physicist Clarence M. Zener

zener effect (*electr.*) the pronounced curvature in reverse voltage current characteristic of a diode

Zeng·er (zéŋₐr), John Peter (1697-1746), U.S. journalist. As publisher of the New York 'Weekly Journal', in which he attacked the colonial administration, he was imprisoned on libel charges. In a subsequent trial he was defended by Alexander Hamilton, who established that in cases of libel the truth was sufficient defense (and so advanced the cause of freedom of the press in America). Zenger was subsequently acquitted of all charges

ze·nith (zí:niθ, *Br.* esp. zéniθ) n. the point in the sky vertically above the observer (opp. NADIR) ‖ (*fig.*) the highest point, *at the zenith of his power* **ze·nith·al** adj. of, at or relating to the zenith ‖ (of a map) so drawn that the true directions from a central point are shown [O.F. *cenith, cenit* or M.L. *cenit*, fr. Arab.]

zenith distance (*astron.*) the angular distance of a heavenly body from the zenith

Zenj (zendʒ) a Moslem empire (10th-15th cc.), comprising various E. African coastal settlements. It was centered on Kilwa

Ze·no (zí:nou) (d. 491), Byzantine emperor (474-91). He was forced to recognize Odoacer's supremacy in Italy, but encouraged Theodoric to invade Italy and overthrow him. Zeno's reign was marked by frequent revolts

Zeno of Citium (c.334-c. 262 B.C.) Greek philosopher, founder of Stoicism, at Athens

Zeno of Elea (c. 490-c. 430 B.C.), Greek philosopher who supported the monism of his teacher Parmenides. He devised a number of arguments to prove the unreality of motion, the best known being the paradox of Achilles and the tortoise: Achilles can never overtake the tortoise, for when he reaches each successive starting point the tortoise is always further on

ze·o·lite (zí:ₐlait) n. one of a group of minerals with an open structure having channelways which can act as molecular sieves. They occur in certain volcanic rocks, and are hydrated aluminum silicates **ze·o·lit·ic** (zi:ₐlítik) adj. [fr. Swed. and G. *zeolit* fr. Gk *zein*, to boil]

Zeph·a·ni·ah (zefₐnáiₐ) a Minor Prophet (late 7th c. B.C.) of the Old Testament. He prophesied the doom of Judah and other nations ‖ the book of the Old Testament which contains his prophecies

zeph·yr (zéfₐr) n. (*rhet.*) a gentle breeze ‖ any lightweight fabric or yarn, or an article of clothing made from this [O.E. *zefferus* fr. L. *zephyrus* fr. Gk *zephuros*, the west wind]

Zep·pe·lin (zépₐlₐn) n. (*hist.*) a rigid, cigarshaped dirigible airship used for transatlantic voyages (from 1928) and, in the 1st world war, by the Germans for bombing raids [after Graf Ferdinand von *Zeppelin*, (1828-1917), G. aeronautical pioneer who designed and built such aircraft]

Zer·matt (tsermát) a resort (pop. 3,101) in Valais, Switzerland, below the Matterhorn at 5,315 ft

ze·ro (zíₐrou) 1. n. pl. **ze·ros, ze·roes** the numerical symbol 0 denoting absence of value (*NUMBER TABLE) ‖ the beginning of a numerical scale (of distance, time, temperature etc.) ‖ the temperature of pure melting ice under standard atmospheric pressure on the Centigrade and Réaumur scales ‖ *ABSOLUTE ZERO ‖ (*gunnery*) a sight setting which allows for elevation and wind deflection ‖ (*fig.*) the lowest point ‖ a nonentity 2. v.t. (with 'in') to adjust the sights of (a rifle) by calibrated firing under conditions of no wind ‖ to adjust (an instrument etc.) to a zero point, or to a point representing zero ‖ **to zero**

CONCISE PRONUNCIATION KEY: **(a)** æ, c*a*t; ɑ, c*a*r; ɔ f*aw*n; ei, sn*a*ke. **(e)** e, h*e*n; i:, sh*ee*p; iₐ, d*ee*r; ɛₐ, b*ea*r. **(i)** i, f*i*sh; ai, t*i*ger; ₐ:, b*i*rd. **(o)** o, *o*x; au, c*ow*; ou, g*oa*t; u, p*oo*r; ɔi, r*oy*al. **(u)** ʌ, d*u*ck; u, b*u*ll; u:, g*oo*se; ₐ, b*a*cillus; ju:, c*u*be. x, lo*ch*; θ, *th*ink; ð, bo*th*er; z, *Z*en; ʒ, corsa*ge*; dʒ, sava*ge*; ŋ, ora*ng*utan*g*; j, *y*ak; ʃ, *fi*sh; tʃ, fe*tch*; 'l, rabb*le*; 'n, redd*en*. Complete pronunciation key appears inside front cover.

in on to adjust fire on (a target) ‖ to move in close to ‖ to concentrate on **3.** *adj.* having the value of zero ‖ (*meteor.*) *ZERO VISIBILITY

ze·ro-based budgeting (zíəroubeisd) (*economics*) system of creating a budget without regard to previous budgets or present expenditures, in which each item must be justified for itself

zero bracket on U.S. income tax returns after 1978, amount of income on which no federal income tax is payable

zero hour the time at which a military operation (or other project) is planned to begin

zero norm *NIL NORM

ze·ro-or·der release (zíərouórdər) a perfect sustained-release timing mechanism in an encapsulated drug

zero point (*mil.*) the location of the center of a nuclear explosion at the instant of detonation

zero population growth conditions or program in which births and deaths are equalized. *abbr.* ZPG

ze·ro-sum (zíərousʌm) *adj.* meaningless

zero visibility (*meteor.*) visibility restricted to 50 ft vertically or 165 ft horizontally

zest (zest) *n.* a piquant, enhancing quality ‖ enthusiastic enjoyment, *to work with zest* ‖ a piece of lemon or orange peel added to a drink etc. to give flavor **zést·ful** *adj.* [F. *zeste*, a piece of orange or lemon peel]

ze·ta (zéitə, zí:tə) *n.* the sixth letter (Z, ζ=z) of the Greek alphabet

Zet·land (zétlənd) a county of Scotland (*SHETLAND ISLANDS)

zeu·glo·don (zú:glədɒn) *n.* a member of *Basilosaurus*, fam. *Basilosauridae*, a genus of Eocene or Miocene fossil cetacean mammals, related to the toothed whale and reaching 50–70 ft in length [Mod. L. fr. Gk *zeuglē*, loop of a yoke+*odous* (*odontos*), tooth]

zeug·ma (zú:gmə) *n.* a figure of speech in which one word is made to refer to two or more other words, but has to be differently understood in the different contexts, usually with a ludicrous effect, as in 'he took his time and the floor' [Gk=a yoke]

Zeus (zu:s) (*Gk mythol.*) the supreme god, identified with the Latin Jupiter. He was the son of Rhea and of Cronos, whom he overthrew. He symbolized nature and the elements and was regarded variously as the god of the earth and giver of fertility, the dispenser of good and evil, the giver of laws, the guardian of the hearth, property and liberty. His symbols were the eagle, the scepter and the thunderbolt, and his principal shrines were in Athens and Olympia

Zeux·is (zú:ksis) (5th-4th cc. B.C.), one of the most famous of ancient Greek painters

Zhda·nov (ʒdánəf) (formerly Mariupol), a port (pop. 467,000) in the Ukraine, U.S.S.R., on the Sea of Azov, serving the Donbas: iron and steel industries

Zhu·kov (ʒú:kəf), Georgi Konstantinovich (1896-1974), Russian marshal. He was victorious in the battles of Moscow (1941) and Leningrad (1943) and drove the Nazi armies back from the U.S.S.R. (1944-5). He was minister of defense (1955-7)

Zia ul-Haq (zí:əulhɒk), Muhammad (1924-   ) Pakistani statesman, president (1978-   ). He served as army chief of staff (1976-7) and chief martial law administrator (1977-8). He overthrew Pres. Zulfiqar Ali Bhutto (1977), who was later executed. As president Zia worked at Pakistani Islamicization and for better international relations, esp. with the U.S.A., China and India

zib·el·ine, zib·el·line (zíbəli:n, zíbəlain) *n.* sable fur ‖ a soft woolen fabric mixed with alpaca etc., having long silky hairs on the right side [fr. F. *zibeline* fr. Slav. *sobol*, sable]

zib·et, zib·eth (zíbit) *n.* Viverra zibetha, the Asiatic or Indian civet [fr. M.L. *zibethum* fr. Arab.]

Zieg·feld (zígfeld), Florenz (1869-1932), U.S. theatrical producer. He produced (1907) the 'Ziegfeld Follies', an annual revue noted for its spectacular staging, variety performances, and chorus of beautiful girls

zig·gu·rat (zígəræt) *n.* a lofty pyramidal tower of ancient Babylonia, with outside stairways and a shrine at the top [Assyrian *ziqquratu*, height, pinnacle]

zig·zag (zígzæg) **1.** *adj.* turning sharply left and right alternately as its course proceeds **2.** *n.* one of sudden turns in a road, course etc. ‖

such a road or course ‖ a design etc. having a zigzag form **3.** *adv.* in a zigzag path **4.** *v. pres. part.* **zig·zag·ging** *past* and *past part.* **zig·zagged** *v.i.* to be or take a zigzag course ‖ *v.t.* to make (one's way or its way) in a zigzag course [fr. F., origin unknown]

zik·ku·rat, zik·u·rat (zíkəræt) *n.* a ziggurat

zilch (ziltʃ) *n.* (*slang*) emphatically nothing — **zilch** *adj.*

Zimbabwe (zimbábwei) (formerly Rhodesia) a republic (area 150,333 sq. miles, pop. 8,376,000) in central Africa. Capital: Harare (formerly Salisbury). People: 96% Africans (mainly Matabele and Mashona), 3% European stock, small Asiatic and Colored minorities. Language: English, Bantu languages. Religion: mainly local African religions, with a Christian minority. A broad central plateau (averaging 4,000 ft, rising to over 5,000 ft in the northeast, mainly savanna woodland, forms the Zambezi-Limpopo watershed. Lowlands on either side fall to 2,000 ft along the Zambezi and along the southern border (under 1,000 ft in the southeast). Towards the Mozambique frontier rise the steep Inyanga and Melsetter massifs, culminating in Mt Inyangeni (8,250 ft). Average temperatures (F.): 65° on the plateau, with a mean Oct. maximum of 85° for the whole country. Rainfall: average 28 ins (from under 15 ins on the Limpopo Valley to over 40 ins along the Mozambique border). Livestock: cattle, sheep, goats, hogs. The land is 5% arable, 64% forest. Agricultural products: corn and tobacco, kaffir corn, vegetables, citrus fruits, beans, peanuts, sugar, rice, wheat, cotton, tea, dairy products. Resources: asbestos, gold, chrome ore, coal, tin, lithium, copper, timber (teak and mahogany). Manufactures and industries: mining, foodstuffs, textiles, iron and steel, clothing, cigarettes, electricity, metal products, oil refining. Exports: tobacco, cigarettes, minerals, hides, meat. Imports: metals, machinery, vehicles, textiles, food, fuel oils, paints, leather, rubber, chemicals, wines and spirits. There is railroad access to the ports of Beira and Maputo. University of Zimbabwe (1970). Monetary unit: Zimbabwe dollar (100 cents). HISTORY. The area was probably peopled by Bantu about the beginning of the Christian era. The Zimbabwe ruins (11th-15th cc.) give evidence of a high degree of political organization. The Matabele overran much of the area (early 19th c.). European interest in the region was stimulated by the discoveries (1850s) of Livingstone. Rhodes obtained from the Matabele chief a monopoly of the minerals in his kingdom (1888), and a British company was chartered (1889) to develop the region. Tribal warfare between the Matabele and the Mashona ended when their territories were united (1898) to form Southern Rhodesia. This became a self-governing British colony (1923) and was a member of the Central African Federation (1953-63). The Rhodesian government, led by Ian Smith, made a unilateral declaration of independence (Nov. 11, 1965) on the basis of white minority rule. Britain countered by an economic blockade and a comprehensive sanctions resolution was adopted (May 29, 1968) by the Security Council. Rhodesia became (1970) a republic, but black nationalists continued to seek greater representation in the government through the 1970s, despite considerable government repression. Smith negotiated an 'internal settlement' with black leaders (1978) and in 1979 elections the principle of universal suffrage was accepted. The country became Zimbabwe Rhodesia with Bishop Abel Muzorewa its first black prime minister. Guerrilla attacks on the government continued, however, as various rebel factions allied against it. An agreement was reached (1979) on a new constitution reducing the number of white-held seats in the parliament, and new elections were scheduled for 1980. The country was under direct British rule (Dec. 1979-April 1980) when it became independent Zimbabwe. Conflict continued, however, between blacks and whites and among various black factions, despite efforts by Prime Minister Robert Mugabe at conciliation and to improve the economy. In 1985 Mugabe announced plans to declare Zimbabwe a one-party state ‖ a group of ruins in W. Zimbabwe, probably of 11th-15th-c. Bantu origin: acropolis, temple, walls of granite monoliths. They were discovered in 1868

Zim·mer·mann Note (tsímərmʌn) a secret coded telegram addressed (Jan. 16, 1917) to the

German minister in Mexico by German Foreign Minister Arthur Zimmermann (1864-1940). With the object of reducing or nullifying U.S. intervention in Europe in the 1st world war by engaging U.S. strength in hostilities with Mexico and Japan, the Note offered Mexican President Venustiano Carranza an offensive and defensive alliance, and invited Mexico 'to reconquer her lost territory in Texas, New Mexico and Arizona' and to seek the immediate adherence of Japan. Intercepted and decoded by British Naval Intelligence, it was passed to President Woodrow Wilson who published it on Mar. 1, 1917. It convinced Americans of Germany's ill will toward them, and became one of the principal causes of the U.S. declaration of war against Germany five weeks later

zinc (ziŋk) **1.** *n.* a metallic element (symbol Zn, at. no. 30, at. mass 65.37), hard and resisting corrosion. It is used for coating sheet iron to prevent rust, in the manufacture of brass, in electric cells (because of its high solution-tension constant) and in making printing blocks **2.** *v.t. pres. part.* **zinc·ing, zinck·ing** *past* and *past part.* **zinced, zincked** to coat with zinc [fr. G. *zink*]

zinc blende naturally occurring zinc sulfide, ZnS

zinc carbonate a crystalline salt, $ZnCO_3$, occurring naturally as smithsonite, and known formerly (*Br.*) as hemimorphite

zinc·ic (zíŋkik) *adj.* of or containing zinc

zinckenite *ZINKENITE

zinck·y, zink·y, zinc·y (zíŋki:) *adj.* zincic

zin·co·graph (zíŋkəgræf, zíŋkəgrɑf) *n.* a printing block of zinc with an etched design ‖ a print taken from this [ZINCOGRAPHY]

zin·cog·ra·pher (ziŋkógrəfər) *n.* someone who practices zincography

zin·co·graph·ic (ziŋkəgræfik) *n.* of or relating to zincography **zin·co·gráph·i·cal** *adj.*

zin·cog·ra·phy (ziŋkógrəfi) *n.* the art or process of engraving on zinc or taking prints from such engravings [fr. Mod. L. *zincum*, zinc+Gk *graphos*, written]

zinc ointment an ointment containing zinc oxide, used to treat skin diseases

zinc·ous (zíŋkəs) *adj.* zincic

zinc oxide ZnO, an oxide used as a pigment and filler, in ointments etc. (*CALAMINE)

zinc silicate any of several silicates of zinc, including the basic variety, hemimorphite. It was known formerly (*Br.*) as smithsonite

zinc white zinc oxide used as a white pigment, e.g. in paint

zincy *ZINCKY

Zin·der (zíndər) a trading center (pop. 13,000) in S.E. Niger, terminus of a trans-Sahara motor route

zing (ziŋ) **1.** *n.* (*pop.*) zest, energy ‖ (*pop.*) a high-pitched humming noise **2.** *v.i.* (*pop.*) to make a high-pitched humming noise [*imit.*]

zing·er (zíŋə:r) *n.* (*slang*) a sharp witticism

zin·jan·thro·pus (zindʒænθrəpəs) *n.* a fossil hominid native to eastern Africa, believed extant 2 million B.C.

zin·ken·ite, zinck·en·ite (zíŋkənait) *n.* a double sulfide of antimony and lead, $PbSb_2S_4$, with a luster like steel [fr. G. *zinkenit* after J. K. L. *Zincken* (19th c.), G. mineralogist]

zinky *ZINCKY

zin·ni·a (zíni:ə) *n.* a member of *Zinnia*, fam. *Compositae*, a genus of half hardy annual plants, native to Mexico but widely cultivated. They bear showy, rayed flower heads [Mod. L. after J. G. Zinn (1727–59), G. botanist]

Zin·zen·dorf (tsíntsendɔrf), Nikolaus Ludwig, Graf von (1700-60), German religious leader. He established (1727) the Moravian Church, a revival of a Hussite protestant sect, and evangelized in Europe and the U.S.A. on behalf of it

Zi·on (záiən) a hill in Jerusalem on which the palace of King David was built, and later the Temple, taken as the religious, national and cultural center of the ancient Jews ‖ the Jewish people ‖ paradise, heaven ‖ a name often given to a Nonconformist chapel **Zi·on·ism** *n.* a worldwide political movement among Jews, begun (1897) by Theodor Herzl, to secure the reestablishing of a Jewish national home in Palestine. It triumphed with the setting up of Israel (1948) **Zí·on·ist** *n.* and *adj.* [O.E. fr. eccles. L. *Sion* fr. Heb.]

zip (zip) **1.** *n.* a short, sharp sound like that made by a bullet traveling through the air ‖ (*pop.*) vigor, snap ‖ (*Br.*) a zipper **2.** *v. pres. part.* **zip·ping** *past* and *past part.* **zipped** *v.i.* to go

---

CONCISE PRONUNCIATION KEY: **(a)** æ, c*a*t; ɑ, c*a*r; ɔ, f*aw*n; ei, sn*a*ke. **(e)** e, h*e*n; i:, sh*ee*p; iə, d*ee*r; ɛə, b*ea*r. **(i)** i, f*i*sh; ai, t*i*ger; ə:, b*i*rd. **(o)** o, *o*x; au, c*ow*; ou, g*oa*t; u, p*oo*r; ɔi, r*oy*al. **(u)** ʌ, d*u*ck; u, b*u*ll; u:, g*oo*se; ə, b*a*cillus; ju:, c*u*be. x, lo*ch*; θ, *th*ink; ð, b*o*ther; z, *Z*en; ʒ, corsa*g*e; dʒ, sava*g*e; ŋ, ora*ng*utang; j, *y*ak; ʃ, *fi*sh; tʃ, fe*tch*; 'l, rabb*le*; 'n, redd*en*. Complete pronunciation key appears inside front cover.

with the sound of a bullet flying through the air ‖ (*pop.*) to go very fast ‖ to be opened and closed with a zipper ‖ *v.t.* to fasten or unfasten with a zipper [imit.]

ZIP code U.S. postal-delivery zone number code of five digits used in the addressing of mail [Zone Improvement Program]; (*Br.*) postcode — **zip-code** *v.*

zip fastener (*Br.*) a zipper

zip·per (zípər) **1.** *n.* (*Am.=Br.* zip, zip fastener) a strip of interlocking metal or plastic teeth on tapes, used to fasten openings in garments, bags etc. **2.** *v.t.* and *i.* to fasten by means of a zipper [fr. *Zipper*, trademark]

zip·py (zípi:) *comp.* **zip·pi·er** *superl.* **zip·pi·est** *adj.* full of vigor

ZIPRA (*acronym*) for Peoples African Revolutionary Army led by Joshua Nkomo

zip top a package top removable by pulling a strip from the cover. Cf POP-TOP, RING-PULL

zir·cal·loy (zərkǽlɔi) *n.* (*metallurgy*) an alloy of zirconium and other metals with heat- and corrosion-resistant properties; used in nuclear reactors

zir·con (zə́:rkɒn) *n.* zirconium silicate, $ZrSiO_4$, a mineral found as tetragonal crystals of various colors. Some varieties (e.g. hyacinth) are cut into gems [fr. F. *zircone* fr. Ital. *giargone*]

zir·co·ni·a (zərkóuni:ə) *n.* zirconium dioxide, ZrO_2, a crystalline compound which has a very high melting point and is used as a refractory and in giving opacity to enamels [Mod. L.]

zir·co·ni·um (zə:rkóuni:əm) *n.* a metallic element (symbol Zr, at. no 40, at. mass 91.22). Zirconium compounds are used in the manufacture of ceramics and refractory materials, and the metal itself as a structural and container material in nuclear reactors [Mod. L.]

zith·er (zíθər) *n.* a musical instrument, esp. popular in Austria, consisting of 30 to 40 strings stretched over a flat sounding board, the strings being plucked with the fingers or with a plectrum. Some of the strings pass over a fret and are stopped with the left hand [G. fr. L. *cithara* fr. Gk *kithara*]

zi·zith (tsi:tsí:t, tsítsis) *pl. n.* the tassels at the corners of the tallith or of the outer garment worn by Orthodox Jewish males [Heb. *sīsīth*]

Žiž·ka (ʒíʃkə), Jan (*c.* 1370-1424), Bohemian soldier. He led the Hussite revolt (1420-4) against the Emperor Sigismund, winning several victories by unconventional military tactics

Zlin (zli:n) *GOTTWALDOV

zlo·ty (zlóti:) *pl.* **zlo·tys, zlo·ty** *n.* the basic Polish monetary unit ‖ a coin or note of the value of one zloty [Pol. *zloty*, golden]

zo·di·ac (zóudi:æk) *n.* an imaginary band on the celestial sphere of width 16°, bounded by two circles equidistant from the ecliptic, within which are contained the paths of the sun, principal planets and moon, and which is divided into 12 equal parts, each named after a constellation ‖ a figure showing the 12 parts with their symbols and emblems [O.F. *zodiaque* fr. L. *zodiacus* fr. Gk *zōidiakos* (*kuklos*), (circle) of signs]

zo·di·a·cal (zoudáiək'l) *adj.* pertaining to or within the zodiac [fr. L. *zodiacus*]

zodiacal light a triangular glow of light, seen in the Tropics, rising from the point of sunrise or sunset

Zof·fa·ny (zófəni:), Johann (1733-1810), British painter, of German parentage. He excelled in family groups and conversation pieces

Zog (zoug), (Ahmed Zogu, 1893-1961), president (1925-8) and king (1928-39) of Albania. He ruled despotically and was forced to flee when Italian forces invaded Albania (1939)

zois·ite (zɔ́isait) *n.* a double silicate of aluminum (or iron) and calcium [fr. G. *zoisit* after Baron *Zois* Von Edelstein (1747-1819), who discovered it]

Zo·la (zoulə), Émile (1840-1902), French novelist and leading exponent of naturalism. In his 20-volume 'Rougon-Macquart' series (1869-93) he traces the social and natural history of a family whose members are under the controlling power of heredity and environment. The best known of these novels are 'l'Assommoir' (1877), 'Germinal' (1885) and 'la Terre' (1887). A passionate social reformer, he played a courageous part in the defense of Dreyfus with his pamphlet 'J'accuse' (1898)

Zöll·ner illusion (tsœ́:lnər) the optical illusion produced by Zöllner's lines [after J. F. K. Zöllner (1834-82), G. physicist]

Zöllner's lines parallel lines, made by the series of short parallel lines ruled obliquely across them, to look as if they converge or diverge [after J. F. K. Zöllner]

Zoll·ver·ein (tsɔ́lfərain) a customs union of German states, formed (1834) under Prussian leadership. It encouraged German industrialization, and represented a political victory for Prussia over Austria, which was excluded from the union

Zom·ba (zómbə) the capital (pop. 15,705) of Malawi in the Shire Highlands. University of Malawi (1965)

zom·bi, zom·bie (zómbi:) *n.* a corpse revived by magic ‖ the snake deity of voodoo rites in Haiti and python deity in those of W. Africa ‖ (*pop.*) someone who looks macabre or who behaves as though half-dead **zóm·bi·ism** *n.* [of African origin]

zon·al (zóun'l) *adj.* of, resembling, constituting or consisting of a zone or zones [fr. Mod. L. *zonalis* fr. L. *zona*, zone]

zon·ate (zóuneit) *adj.* marked with zones ‖ (*bot.*) ringed, marked with bands of color **zón·at·ed** *adj.*

zo·na·tion (zounéiʃən) *n.* a zonate formation or structure ‖ the state of being zonal ‖ (*envir.*) formation of layers in soils, water, mountains, vegetations, etc., e.g., tree rings [ZONE]

zone (zoun) **1.** *n.* the area of the surface of a sphere bounded by two parallel planes which intersect the sphere ‖ one of the five climatic zones of the earth's surface (two polar circles, extending to 23°27' from the poles, two temperate zones, north and south between latitudes 23°27' and the polar circles, and the torrid zone, between latitudes 23°27' N. and 23°27' S.) ‖ (*biol.*) a region of characteristic fauna or flora ‖ (*biol.*) a belt or area to which species are limited ‖ an area or region of the body ‖ (*geol.*) a rock series of characteristic composition or fossils ‖ (*computer*) the channel on a tape, or position on a card, that designates the significance of the data ‖ an area within which a characteristic activity is carried on, *a fishing zone* or one set aside for a special purpose, *military zone* ‖ an area subject to a specific influence, *rain zone* ‖ an area within which one rate of postage is charged for parcels (parcel post zone), or a city district having its individual number (postal delivery zone) **2.** *v.t. pres. part.* **zon·ing** *past* and *past part.* **zoned** to mark off into zones ‖ to plan (a town) so that different sections are devoted to different purposes (residential, industrial etc.) [fr. L. *zona* fr. Gk *zōnē*, girdle]

zone (*computer*) the channel on a tape, or position on a card, that designates the significance of the data

zone refining (*metallurgy*) technique for purifying metals by passing a heat source past a metal so that impurities are concentrated at both ends. *also* zone melting

zoo (zu:) *n.* a place where live animals are kept in captivity for the public to see [ZOOLOGICAL GARDEN]

zo·o·chlo·rel·la (zouəklɔrélə) *pl.* **zo·o·chlo·rel·lae** (zouəklɔréli:) *n.* any of various symbiotic green algae of genus *Chlorella*, fam. *Chlorellaceae*, living in various animals, e.g. in hydra [Mod. L. fr. Gk *zōon*, animal+*Chlorella*, generic name]

zo·o·ge·o·graph·ic (zouədʒi:əgrǽfik) *adj.* of or pertaining to zoogeography **zo·o·ge·o·gráph·i·cal** *adj.*

zo·o·ge·og·ra·phy (zououdʒi:ógrəfi:) *n.* the scientific study of the geographical distribution of animals [fr. Gk *zōon*, animal+GEOGRAPHY]

zo·o·gle·a, zo·o·gloe·a (zouəglí:ə) *pl.* **zo·o·gle·as, zo·o·gloe·as, zo·o·gle·ae, zo·o·gloe·ae** (zouəglí:i:) *n.* a mass of bacteria embedded in a mucilaginous matrix formed when cell membranes absorb water and swell, frequently forming an iridescent film [fr. Gk *zōon*, animal+*gloios*, gummy substance]

zo·oid (zóuoid) *n.* a largely independent member of a compound animal organism, e.g. an individual in a coelenterate or polyzoan colony **zo·oi·dal** (zouóid'l) *adj.* [fr. Gk *zōon*, animal]

zo·o·log·ic (zouəlódʒik) *adj.* zoological

zo·o·log·i·cal (zouəlódʒik'l) *adj.* of or relating to zoology

zoological garden a zoo

zo·ol·o·gist (zouó*lə*dʒist) *n.* a specialist in zoology [fr. Mod. L. *zoologia*, zoology]

zo·ol·o·gy (zouó*lə*dʒi:) *n.* the branch of biology concerned with animal life and all its manifestations (cf. BOTANY) ‖ the animal life of a given region [fr. Gk *zōon*, animal+*logos*, discourse]

zoom (zu:m) **1.** *v.i.* (*aeron.*) to climb at a steep angle ‖ to make a loud humming or buzzing noise ‖ (of a motion picture or television image) to seem to approach or recede from the viewer rapidly ‖ *v.t.* to cause (an aircraft) to climb at a steep angle ‖ to cause (a motion picture or television image) to seem to approach or recede from the viewer **2.** *n.* a steep climb by a plane ‖ a loud, low hum or buzz ‖ a process by which a television or motion picture image is made to become quickly larger or smaller in the field of view [imit.]

zoom back (*optics*) camera-lens operation that makes the viewer seem to move rapidly away from a subject first seen from a relatively close viewpoint

zoom·er (zú:mər) *n.* (*optics*) camera with a zoom lens

zoom in (*optics*) camera-lens operation that makes the viewer seem to move rapidly toward a subject first seen at a greater distance, while remaining in constant focus. Cf ZOOM BACK

zoom lens a lens system used in motion picture and television cameras, in which the distance to the object being photographed may be changed rapidly while keeping the object in focus

zo·o·mor·phic (zouəmɔ́rfik) *adj.* representing a deity etc. in the form of an animal ‖ relating to or being a deity etc. represented in this way ‖ (of writing, art etc.) characterized by the use of animal forms **zo·o·mór·phism** *n.* [fr. *zoomorph*, a zoomorphic design or figure fr. Gk *zōon*, animal+*morphē*, shape]

zo·on (zóuon) *pl.* **zo·a** (zóuə) *n.* the product of a single egg (cf. ZOOID), whether an individual or a colony [Mod. L. fr. Gk *zōon*, animal]

zo·o·nos·es (zouənóusi:z) *n.* (*med.*) diseases and infections that naturally transmitted from vertebrate animals to human beings

zo·o·phyte (zóuəfait) *n.* an animal resembling a plant in appearance and/or growth **zo·o·phyt·ic** (zouəfítik), **zo·o·phýt·i·cal** *adj.* [Mod. L. *zoophyton* fr. Gk fr. *zōon*, animal+*phuton*, plant]

zo·o·spo·ran·gi·al (zououspərǽndʒi:əl) *adj.* of or relating to a zoosporangium

zo·o·spo·ran·gi·um (zououspərǽndʒi:əm) *pl.* **zo·o·spo·ran·gi·a** (zououspərǽndʒi:ə) *n.* (*bot.*) a sporangium in which zoospores develop [fr. Gk *zōon*, animal+SPORANGIUM]

zo·o·spore (zóuəspɔr, zóuəspour) *n.* a motile spore, e.g. a flagellated asexual spore of some fungi or an amoeboid or flagellated product of protozoan sexual or asexual reproduction [fr. Gk *zōon*, animal+SPORE]

Zo·que·an (sóukeiən) *pl.* **Zo·que·an, Zo·que·ans** *n.* a Mexican Indian people of E. Tabasco, Chiapas and Oaxaca ‖ a member of this people ‖ the Mixe-Zoque language stock

zo·ri (zouri:) *n.* a thonged Japanese sandal of any material

zo·ril (zóril, zóril) *n.* the striped muishond ‖ *Ictonyxfrenata*, a carnivorous mammal of N. Africa related to the striped muishond [fr. F. *zorille* fr. Span.]

zo·ril·la (zərílə) *n.* a zoril

Zo·ro·as·ter (zóurouæstər, zóurouæstər, zɔrouæstər, zourouæstər) (*c.* 660 –*c.* 583 B.C.), a prophet of ancient Persia. After seeing heavenly visions, he converted the king and court of Bactria to his faith. His sayings are collected in the Avesta. He instituted the caste of magus and founded a religion based on the belief that good and evil are absolutes. They are represented by the gods Ormazd and Ahriman who are engaged in constant warfare. The followers of Ormazd must strive for purity in thought, word and deed, based on a strict code of ethics. Man can attain perfection by individual choice of good. Zoroastrianism was the national religion of Persia and influential in the Near East until the rise of Islam (7th c.). The Parsees of India adhere to a form of this faith

Zo·ro·as·tri·an (zɔrouæstri:ən, zourouæstri:ən) **1.** *adj.* of or pertaining to Zoroaster or the religion of Zoroaster **2.** *n.* an adherent of the religion of Zoroaster **Zo·ro·às·tri·an·ism** *n.* [fr. L. *Zoroastres* fr. Gk fr. Zend *Zarathustra*]

Zor·ri·lla de San Mar·tín (sɔrríja:ðesánmartí:n), Juan (1855-1931), Uruguayan romantic poet, lawyer, and diplomat. His works include the national poem of Uruguay 'Tabaré' (1888), about a mestizo torn between his Indian and his Spanish heritage

Zor·ri·lla y del Mo·ral (θɔrrí:jai:ðelmɔrál), José (1817-93), Spanish poet. His romantic dramas include 'El zapatero y el rey' (1840-1) and Don Juan Tenorio' (1844)

Zos·i·mus (zósəməs, zóusəməs) (5th c. A.D.), Greek historian. He wrote a history of the Roman Empire from the late 3rd c. to 410

zos·ter (zòstər) n. (med.) shingles [L. fr. Gk zōstēr, girdle]

Zou·ave (zu:áv) n. a member of a French light infantry corps created (1831) in Algeria ‖ (hist.) a member of certain corps adopting the Zouave uniform, e.g. in the American Civil War, and in the Papal States (1860) [F. fr. Zouaoua, a Kabyle tribe of Algeria]

ZPG (abbr.) for 'zero population growth' (which see)

ZSU 57-2 n. (mil.) U.S.S.R. anti-aircraft missile carrier including two 57-mm guns

zuc·chet·to (zu:kétou) pl. **zuc·chet·tos** n. a skullcap worn by a Roman Catholic priest (black), bishop (purple), cardinal (red), or the pope (white) [fr. Ital. zucchetta fr. zucca, gourd, head]

zuc·chi·ni (zu:kí:ni:) pl. **zuc·chi·ni, zuc·chi·nis** n. a variety of summer squash with a dark green skin. It is like a cucumber in shape and is usually picked when less than 1 ft in length [Ital. pl. of zucchin, dim. of zucca, gourd]

Zug (tsu:x) a canton (area 93 sq. miles, pop. 75,930), German-speaking and mainly Catholic, in N. Switzerland ‖ its capital (pop. 20,000) on Lake Zug (area 15 sq. miles)

Zug·spit·ze (tsú:xʃpitsə) the highest peak (9,719 ft) in West Germany, in Bavaria on the Austrian frontier

Zui·der Zee (záidərzí:, záidərzéi) a former inlet (80 miles long) of the North Sea in the Netherlands. Part has been closed off by a dam and forms the IJsselmeer. Drainage has enabled nearly 550,000 acres to be reclaimed from the rest

Zu·lu (zú:lu:) 1. n. pl. **Zu·lu, Zu·lus** a member of an African nation living largely in N.E. Natal. The Zulus were a powerful military force in the early 19th c., esp. under their chief Dingaan, until defeated by the Boers (1838). Their kingdom was gradually divided and its components absorbed into the Transvaal (1888) and Natal (1897) ‖ the Bantu language of this people 2. adj. of the Zulus, their language or culture

zulu n. (angling) an artificial fly

Zu·lu·land (zú:lu:lænd) a region of native reserves (area 10,375 sq. miles) in N.E. Natal, South Africa, inhabited by the Zulus. Capital: Eshowe (pop. 3.000). Industries: cattle raising, cereals, mining (gold, coal, zircon)

zulu time (mil.) Greenwich mean time

Zu·már·ra·ga (θu:márraɡa), Juan de (c. 1468-1548), Spanish Franciscan monk, the first

bishop (1528-46) and archbishop (1546-8) of Mexico. He built the cathedral in Mexico City, introduced the printing press to the New World, and founded the college of Santa Cruz de Tlatelolco for the education of the Indians

Zu·ñi (zú:nji:, zú:ni:) n. a member of a North American Indian tribe in New Mexico ‖ their language, which constitutes a linguistic family **Zu·ñi·an** n. the Zuñi language family [Span fr. Am. Ind.]

Zup·pa in·gle·se (tsú:pa iŋléisi:) n. Italian sponge rum cake with custard cream and fruit

Zur·ba·rán (θu:rbarán), Francisco de (1598 – c. 1669), Spanish painter. His best works are characterized by clear, austere use of color and massive solid forms, in a splendid fusion of the mystical and the realistic

Zu·rich (zúərik) (G. Zürich) a German speaking, largely Protestant canton (area 665 sq. miles, pop. 1,122,839) in N. Switzerland, admitted to the Swiss Confederation in 1351 ‖ its capital, the largest town (pop. 379,600) in Switzerland, and the country's most important center of commerce, banking and industry (silk, cotton, machinery, paper, food), and a main cultural center of German Switzerland. It is on Lake Zurich (area 34 sq. miles). Churches in the old city include Grossmünster (11th-13th cc.), Fraumünster (12th c.) and St Peter's (13th c.). Town Hall (1698), university (1832), Federal Institute of Technology (1855)

Zwick·au (tsvíkau) an industrial center (pop. 123,475) in Saxony, East Germany: coal mining, mechanical engineering, textiles, chemicals

zwie·back (swí:bæk, zwí:bæk, swáibæk, zwáibæk) n. a rusk of toasted sweetened bread made with eggs [G. fr. zwie-, twice+backen, to bake]

Zwing·li (zwíŋli:, tsvíŋli:), Ulrich or Huldreich (1484-1531), Swiss religious reformer who rejected the papacy and attacked the authority of the priesthood, taking the Bible as the only rule of faith, with the object of restoring to the Church its former simplicity. He differed with Luther on the question of the real presence, holding that the communion was the commemoration of Christ's death, and not the repetition of the sacrifice

Zwing·li·an (zwíŋli:ən) 1. adj. pertaining to the doctrine of Zwingli 2. n. an adherent of this belief **Zwíng·li·an·ism** n.

zwit·ter·i·on (tsvítəraiən) n. an ion that bears both a positive and a negative charge, at differ-

ent positions **zwit·ter·i·on·ic** (tsvítəraiónik) adj. [G. fr. zwitter, hybrid+ion, ion]

Zwol·le (zwólə) the capital (pop. 78,585) of Overrijssel province, Netherlands: 15th-c. church, town hall

zy·ga·poph·y·sis (zaigəpófisis) pl. **zy·ga·poph·y·ses** (zaigəpófisi:z) n. (anat., zool.) one of the processes of a vertebra by which it articulates with adjacent vertebrae [Mod. L. fr. Gk zugon, yoke+apophusis, apophysis]

zy·go·dac·tyl (zaigoudǽktil) 1. adj. (of a bird) having two toes in the front of the foot and two behind 2. n. a bird (e.g. a parrot) having toes arranged in this way [fr. Gk zugon, yoke+DACTYL]

zy·go·ma (zaigóumə) pl. **zy·go·ma·ta** (zaigóumətə), **zy·go·mas** n. (anat., zool.) the bony arch of the cheek **zy·go·mat·ic** (zaigəmætik) adj. [Gk zugoma fr. zugon, yoke]

zy·go·mor·phic (zaigəmórfik) adj. (biol.) bilaterally symmetrical, divisible into similar parts in only one plane (cf. ACTINOMORPHIC) **zy·go·mór·phism** n. **zy·go·mór·phous** adj. [fr. Gk zugon, yoke+morphē, shape]

zy·go·sis (zaigóusis) pl. **zy·go·ses** (zaigóusi:z) n. (biol., esp. in compounds) a union of gametes, e.g. conjugation [Mod. L. fr. Gk zugōsis, a yoking]

zy·go·spore (záigəspɔr, záigəspour) n. a resting spore, formed by a conjugation of two similar reproductive cells, that eventually gives rise to a sporophyte generation (cf. OOSPORE) **zy·go·spor·ic** (zaigəspórik, zaigəspórik) adj. [fr. Gk zugon, yoke+SPORE]

zy·gote (záigout) n. a cell formed by the union of two gametes, e.g. the fertilized ovum **zy·got·ic** (zaigótik) adj. [fr. Gk zugōtos, yoked]

zy·mase (záimeis) n. an enzyme system found in yeast and other microorganisms, which is responsible for the fermentation of carbohydrates [fr. F. zymase fr. Gk zumē, leaven]

zy·mo·gen (záimədʒən) n. a substance capable of being transformed into a ferment, the precursor of an enzyme **zy·mo·gen·ic** (zaimədʒénik) adj. [fr. Gk zumē, leaven+-genēs, of a (specified) kind]

zy·mol·o·gy (zaimólədʒi:) n. the scientific study of fermentation [fr. Gk zumē, leaven ‖ logos, discourse]

zy·mo·sis (zaimóusis) pl. **zy·mo·ses** (zaimóusi:z) n. fermentation [fr. Gk zumōsis]

zy·mo·tic (zaimótik) adj. of, causing or caused by fermentation [fr. Gk zumōtikos]

zy·mur·gy (záimə:rdʒi:) n. the applied chemistry of fermentation processes [fr. Gk zumē, leaven+-ourgia, working]

ENCYCLOPEDIC
SUPPLEMENTS

FLAGS FROM WORLD HISTORY

CHARLEMAGNE

WILLIAM I (THE CONQUEROR) OF ENGLAND

PEASANTS' WAR (16TH-CENTURY GERMANY)

PETER I (THE GREAT) OF RUSSIA

HUDSON'S BAY COMPANY

JOSÉ DE SAN MARTIN

CHINA UNDER THE CH'ING DYNASTY
(19TH-CENTURY)

FLAG PROPOSED BY CECIL RHODES
FOR BRITISH AFRICA

FLAGS FROM AMERICAN HISTORY

VIKINGS

CHRISTOPHER COLUMBUS

HENRY HUDSON

BRITISH EXPLORERS AND SETTLERS
(FIRST UNION JACK)

FRENCH EXPLORERS AND SETTLERS
(17TH AND 18TH CENTURIES)

CONTINENTAL COLORS (1776)

FIRST STARS AND STRIPES (1777-95)

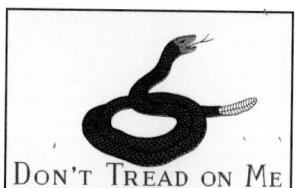

ESEK HOPKINS, FIRST COMMANDER IN
CHIEF OF THE CONTINENTAL NAVY

FIRST STAR-SPANGLED BANNER (1795-1818)

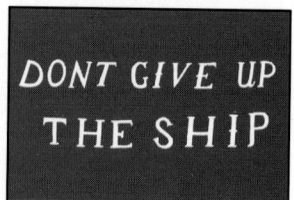

OLIVER HAZARD PERRY
(WAR OF 1812)

BEAR FLAG REPUBLIC (1846)

STARS AND BARS OF THE
CONFEDERACY (1861-63)

FORT SUMTER FLAG (1861)

FLAGS OF AFRICA

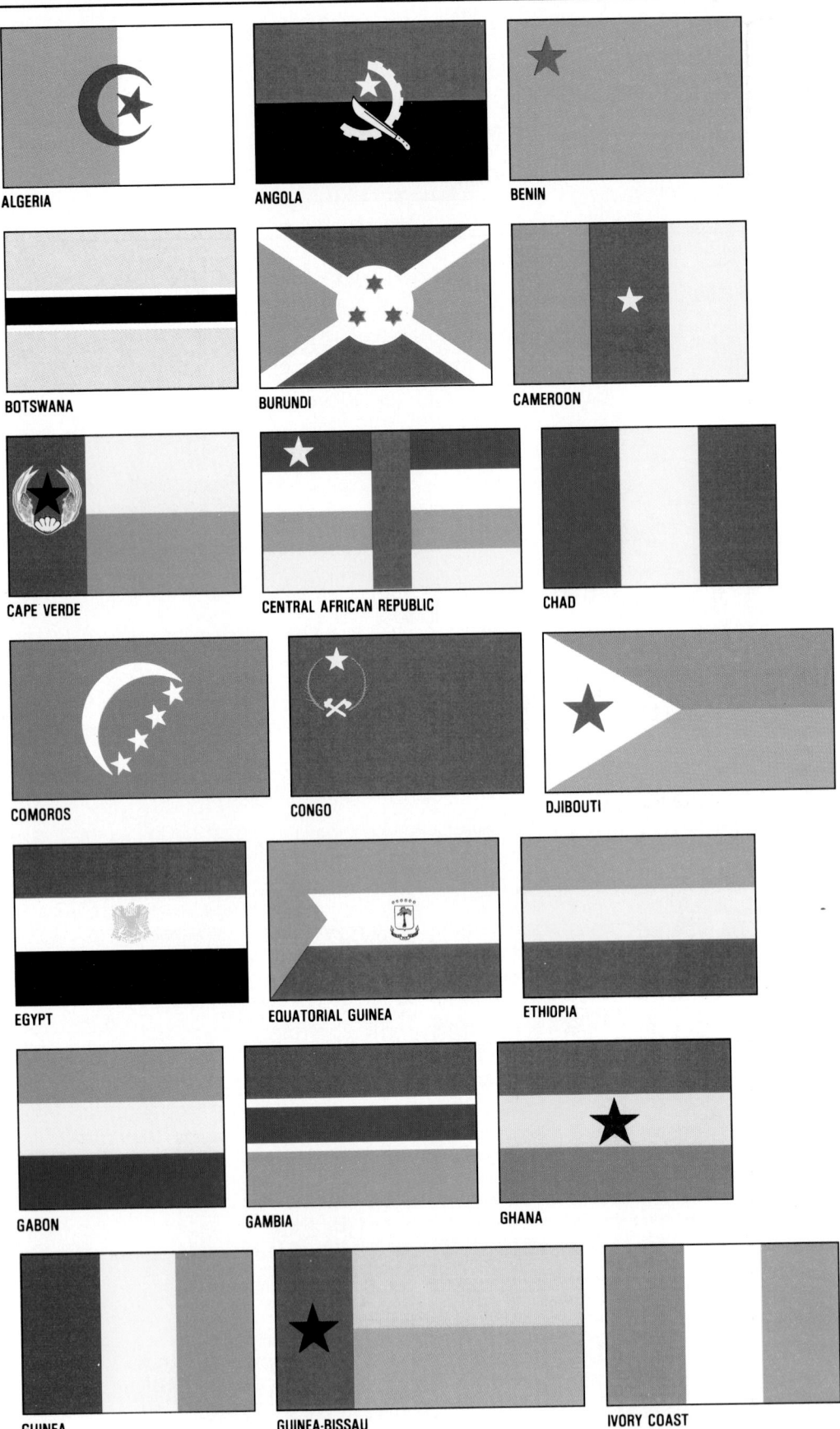

ALGERIA

ANGOLA

BENIN

BOTSWANA

BURUNDI

CAMEROON

CAPE VERDE

CENTRAL AFRICAN REPUBLIC

CHAD

COMOROS

CONGO

DJIBOUTI

EGYPT

EQUATORIAL GUINEA

ETHIOPIA

GABON

GAMBIA

GHANA

GUINEA

GUINEA-BISSAU

IVORY COAST

FLAGS OF AFRICA (continued)

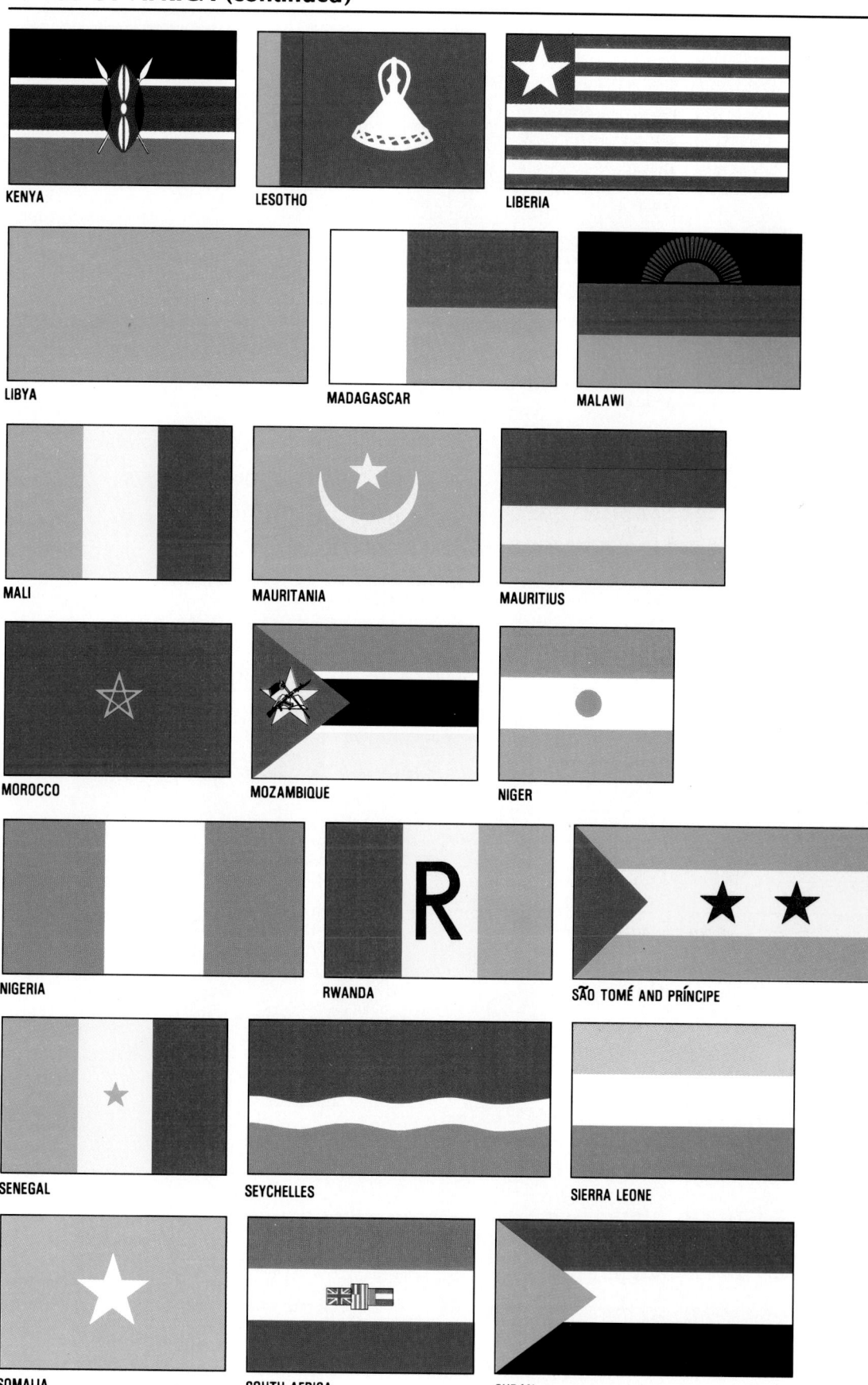

KENYA

LESOTHO

LIBERIA

LIBYA

MADAGASCAR

MALAWI

MALI

MAURITANIA

MAURITIUS

MOROCCO

MOZAMBIQUE

NIGER

NIGERIA

RWANDA

SÃO TOMÉ AND PRÍNCIPE

SENEGAL

SEYCHELLES

SIERRA LEONE

SOMALIA

SOUTH AFRICA

SUDAN

FLAGS OF AFRICA (continued)

SWAZILAND

TANZANIA

TOGO

TUNISIA

UGANDA

UPPER VOLTA

ZAIRE

ZAMBIA

ZIMBABWE

FLAGS OF ASIA

AFGHANISTAN

BAHRAIN

BANGLADESH

BHUTAN

BRUNEI

BURMA

CHINA, PEOPLE'S REPUBLIC OF

CHINA, REPUBLIC OF (TAIWAN)

CYPRUS

INDIA

INDONESIA

IRAN

FLAGS OF ASIA (continued)

IRAQ

ISRAEL

JAPAN

JORDAN

KAMPUCHEA

KOREA, NORTH

KOREA, SOUTH

KUWAIT

LAOS

LEBANON

MALAYSIA

MALDIVES

MONGOLIA

NEPAL

OMAN

PAKISTAN

PHILIPPINES

QATAR

SAUDI ARABIA

FLAGS OF ASIA (continued)

SINGAPORE

SRI LANKA

SYRIA

THAILAND

TURKEY

UNITED ARAB EMIRATES

VIETNAM

YEMEN (ADEN)

YEMEN (SANA)

FLAGS OF EUROPE

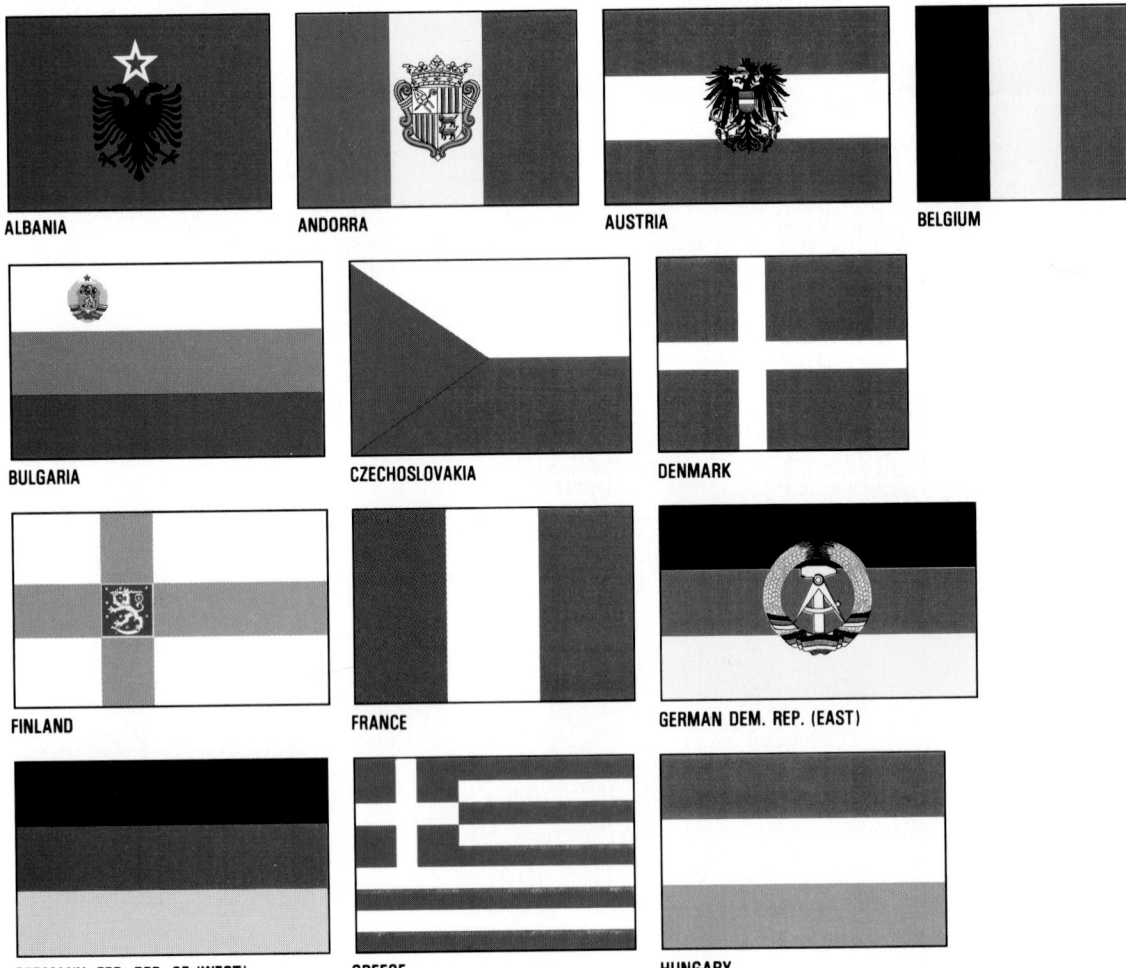

ALBANIA

ANDORRA

AUSTRIA

BELGIUM

BULGARIA

CZECHOSLOVAKIA

DENMARK

FINLAND

FRANCE

GERMAN DEM. REP. (EAST)

GERMANY, FED. REP. OF (WEST)

GREECE

HUNGARY

FLAGS OF EUROPE (continued)

ICELAND

IRELAND

ITALY

LIECHTENSTEIN

LUXEMBOURG

MALTA

MONACO

NETHERLANDS

NORWAY

POLAND

PORTUGAL

ROMANIA

SAN MARINO

SPAIN

SWEDEN

SWITZERLAND

UNION OF SOVIET SOCIALIST REPUBLICS

UNITED KINGDOM

VATICAN CITY

YUGOSLAVIA

FLAGS OF NORTH AMERICA

CANADA

MEXICO

UNITED STATES

FLAGS OF THE CARIBBEAN

ANTIGUA AND BARBUDA

BAHAMAS

BARBADOS

CUBA

DOMINICA

DOMINICAN REPUBLIC

GRENADA

HAITI

JAMAICA

SAINT KITTS-NEVIS

SAINT LUCIA

SAINT VINCENT AND THE GRENADINES

TRINIDAD AND TOBAGO

FLAGS OF CENTRAL AMERICA

BELIZE

COSTA RICA

EL SALVADOR

GUATEMALA

HONDURAS

NICARAGUA

PANAMA

FLAGS OF SOUTH AMERICA

ARGENTINA

BOLIVIA

BRAZIL

CHILE

COLOMBIA

ECUADOR

GUYANA

PARAGUAY

PERU

SURINAME

URUGUAY

VENEZUELA

FLAGS OF OCEANIA

AUSTRALIA

FIJI

KIRIBATI

NAURU

NEW ZEALAND

PAPUA NEW GUINEA

SOLOMON ISLANDS

TONGA

TUVALU

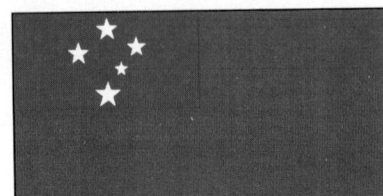

VANUATU

WESTERN SAMOA

FLAGS OF AUSTRALIA

NEW SOUTH WALES

NORFOLK ISLAND

NORTHERN TERRITORY

QUEENSLAND

SOUTH AUSTRALIA

TASMANIA

VICTORIA

WESTERN AUSTRALIA

FLAGS OF CANADA

ALBERTA

BRITISH COLUMBIA

MANITOBA

NEW BRUNSWICK

NEWFOUNDLAND

NORTHWEST TERRITORIES

NOVA SCOTIA

ONTARIO

PRINCE EDWARD ISLAND

QUEBEC

SASKATCHEWAN

YUKON TERRITORY

FLAGS OF THE UNITED STATES

ALABAMA

ALASKA

ARIZONA

ARKANSAS

CALIFORNIA

COLORADO

CONNECTICUT

DELAWARE

DISTRICT OF COLUMBIA

FLORIDA

GEORGIA

HAWAII

IDAHO

ILLINOIS

INDIANA

IOWA

KANSAS

KENTUCKY

LOUISIANA

MAINE

MARYLAND

MASSACHUSETTS

MICHIGAN

MINNESOTA

MISSISSIPPI

MISSOURI

MONTANA

FLAGS OF THE UNITED STATES (continued)

NEBRASKA

NEVADA

NEW HAMPSHIRE

NEW JERSEY

NEW MEXICO

NEW YORK

NORTH CAROLINA

NORTH DAKOTA

OHIO

OKLAHOMA

OREGON

PENNSYLVANIA

RHODE ISLAND

SOUTH CAROLINA

SOUTH DAKOTA

TENNESSEE

TEXAS

UTAH

VERMONT

VIRGINIA

WASHINGTON

WEST VIRGINIA

WISCONSIN

WYOMING

FLAGS OF THE U.S. GOVERNMENT

PRESIDENT

VICE-PRESIDENT

SECRETARY OF STATE

DEPT. OF THE TREASURY

SECRETARY OF DEFENSE

ATTORNEY GENERAL

DEPT. OF THE INTERIOR

DEPT. OF AGRICULTURE

SECRETARY OF COMMERCE

DEPT. OF LABOR

DEPT. OF TRANSPORTATION

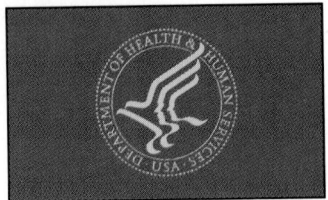

DEPT. OF HEALTH AND
HUMAN SERVICES

DEPT. OF HOUSING AND
URBAN DEVELOPMENT

DEPT. OF ENERGY

DEPT. OF EDUCATION

U.S. ARMY

U.S. MARINE CORPS

U.S. NAVY

U.S. AIR FORCE

U.S. COAST GUARD

JACK OF U.S. WARSHIPS

FLAGS OF UNITED STATES TERRITORIES

AMERICAN SAMOA

PALAU (BELAU)

GUAM

NORTHERN MARIANAS

MARSHALL ISLANDS

FEDERATED STATES OF MICRONESIA

PUERTO RICO

U.S. VIRGIN ISLANDS

FLAGS OF INTERNATIONAL ORGANIZATIONS

UNITED NATIONS

RED CROSS

RED CRESCENT

RED MAGEN DAVID

OLYMPICS

NATO

ORG. OF AMERICAN STATES

COMECON

ORG. OF AFRICAN UNITY

ARAB LEAGUE

INTERNATIONAL CODE FLAGS

INTERNATIONAL CODE PENNANTS

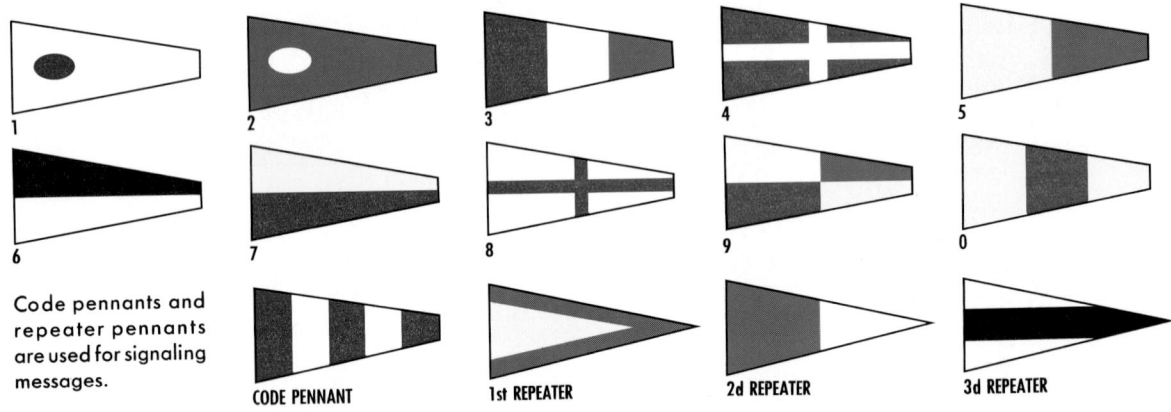

Code pennants and repeater pennants are used for signaling messages.

CODE PENNANT   1st REPEATER   2d REPEATER   3d REPEATER

WEATHER BUREAU FLAGS

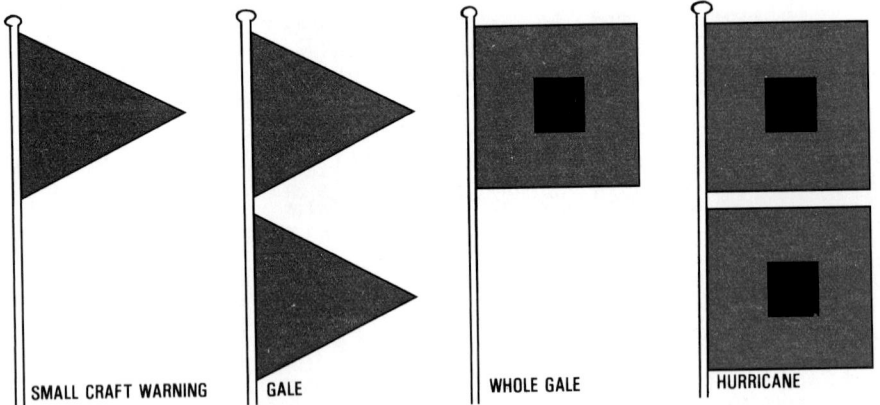

SMALL CRAFT WARNING   GALE   WHOLE GALE   HURRICANE

MONOCHROMATIC MESSAGE FLAGS

DEATH   DANGER   QUARANTINE   PROCEED   TRUCE   DISTRESS

DICTIONARY OF SYNONYMS AND ANTONYMS

A

abandon, abdicate, discontinue, relinquish, resign, surrender, vacate, desert, forsake, leave, quit. ANT.—defend, maintain, occupy, stay, support.

abase, degrade, disgrace, mock, shame. ANT.—dignify, elevate, honor, praise.

abate, assuage, decrease, diminish, lessen, lower, mitigate, moderate, reduce, suppress. ANT.—enlarge, increase, intensify, prolong, revive.

abbreviate, abridge, condense, contract, curtail, lessen, limit, reduce, shorten. ANT.—enlarge, expand, extend, lengthen.

abbreviation, abridgement, contraction, curtailment, reduction, shortening. ANT.—enlargement, expansion, extension.

abdicate, abandon, relinquish, renounce, resign, surrender, vacate; desert, forsake, leave, quit. ANT.—defend, maintain, retain, stay.

aberrant, abnormal, deviate, eccentric, peculiar, unnatural, unusual, variable. ANT.—normal, ordinary, regular, usual.

abet, aid, assist, encourage, help, incite, stimulate. ANT.—deter, discourage, hinder, oppose, resist.

abeyance, adjournment, inaction, reservation, suspension. ANT.—action, enforcement, renewal, revival.

abhor, despise, detest, dislike, execrate, hate, loathe. ANT.—admire, desire, esteem, like, relish.

ability, aptitude, aptness, capability, capacity, dexterity, efficiency, faculty, knowledge, power, skill, talent. ANT.—incapacity, incompetency, stupidity.

abnormal, aberrant, erratic, irregular, odd, unnatural, unusual. ANT.—normal, usual, standard.

abode, domicile, dwelling, habitation, house, home, quarters, residence.

abolish, end, eradicate, throw out; abrogate, annul, cancel, invalidate, nullify, revoke. ANT.—confirm, continue, establish, institute, legalize, restore.

abominable, detestable, foul, hateful, horrible, loathsome, odious, repugnant, revolting, vile. ANT.—agreeable, enjoyable, delightful, pleasant.

abominate, abhor, despise, detest, dislike, hate, loathe. ANT.—admire, approve, cherish, like, love.

abrupt, hasty, impetuous, precipitate, quick, sudden; blunt, brusque, curt, rude, short; craggy, precipitous, rugged, sharp, steep. ANT.—anticipated, expected; courteous, gradual, smooth.

absent, away, departed, missing; absent-minded, abstracted, distracted, preoccupied. ANT.—attending, here, present; attentive.

absolute, complete, entire, infinite, perfect, pure, total, ultimate, unconditional; arbitrary, autocratic, despotic, supreme, tyrannous, unrestricted. ANT.—accountable, conditional, contingent, dependent, limited.

absolve, acquit, clear, discharge, exonerate, pardon, release. ANT.—accuse, bind, blame, charge, convict, incriminate.

absorb, assimilate, consume, engulf, imbibe, incorporate, merge, swallow; engage, engross. ANT.—discharge, dispense, eject, emit, exude.

abstinence, abstention, continence, fasting, moderation, self-denial, self-restraint, sobriety, temperance. ANT.—excess, gluttony, greed, intemperance, self-indulgence.

abstract, detach, excerpt, remove, select, separate; appropriate, steal; abridge, summarize. ANT.—add, combine, insert, replace, return, unite.

abstracted, appropriated, drawn from, parted, removed, separated, stolen; abridged, summarized. ANT.—added, combined, replaced, returned, united.

absurd, foolish, inconsistent, irrational, ludicrous, nonsensical, preposterous, ridiculous, self-contradictory, senseless, unreasonable. ANT.—logical, rational, reasonable, sensible, sound.

abundant, bountiful, copious, lavish, opulent, plentiful, profuse, rich. ANT.—insufficient, rare, scant, scarce.

abuse, damage, desecrate, dishonor, disparage, insult, maltreat, molest, oppress, persecute, revile, upbraid. ANT.—approve, commend, laud, protect, respect, shield.

abuse, asperse, defame, disparage, harm, ill-use, malign, persecute, vilify; misuse. ANT.—cherish, favor, honor, praise, protect, respect, sustain.

academic, bookish, erudite, formal, learned, literary, pedantic, scholarly, theoretical. ANT.—common-sense, ignorant, practical, simple.

accede, agree, assent, consent. ANT.—dissent, protest, refuse.

accelerate, dispatch, expedite, facilitate, forward, hasten, hurry, push, quicken, rush, speed up. ANT.—block, hinder, impede, obstruct, resist, retard, slow.

accident, calamity, casualty, chance, diaster, happening, misfortune, mishap. ANT.—calculation, design, intention, plan, purpose.

accentuate, emphasize, exaggerate, heighten, intensify, stress, underline. ANT.—minimize, moderate, subdue.

acclaim, applaud, cheer, extol, honor, glorify, laud. ANT.—berate, dishonor, jear, revile.

accommodate, adapt, adjust, arrange, conform, harmonize, oblige, serve, supply. ANT.—embarrass, disarrange, obstruct, prevent.

accompany, attend, chaperon, conduct, convoy, escort, follow, join. ANT.—desert, leave.

accomplice, abettor, accessory, ally, assistant, associate, confederate. ANT.—adversary, enemy, opponent, rival.

accomplish, achieve, attain, complete, consummate, do, effect, execute, finish, fulfill, manage, perform. ANT.—block, defeat, fail, frustrate, spoil.

accord, agree, allow, assent, concede, grant, permit; agreement, acquiesment, harmony, reconciliation, unison. ANT.—contend, disallow, dispute, question; dissension, opposition, strife.

accost, address, approach, greet, solicit, speak to. ANT.—avoid, evade, pass by.

account, chronicle, description, detail, history, narrative, recital, computation, reckoning, record, statement.

accrue, accumulate, amass, collect, gather, grow, increase, store. ANT.—diminish, disperse, dissipate.

accumulate, accrue, amass, assemble, collect, gather, hoard, increase, pile, store. ANT.—diminish, disperse, dissipate, spend, waste.

accuse, blame, censure, charge, denounce, incriminate, indict. ANT.—absolve, acquit, exonerate, vindicate.

achieve, accomplish, do, effect, execute, fulfill, gain, realize, win. ANT.—abandon, fail, lose, miss.

achievement, deed, exploit, feat, performance; accomplishment, attainment, execution, realization, ANT.—neglect, omission; defeat, failure, misfortune.

acquaintance, cognizance, companionship, experience, familiarity, friendship, intimacy, knowledge. ANT.—ignorance, inexperience, unfamiliarity.

acquire, attain, collect, earn, get, obtain, procure, reach, secure, win. ANT.—fail, forego, lose, miss, surrender.

act, accomplishment, action, deed, do, doing, enact, execute, feat, operation, perform, transaction; decree, edict, law, statute. ANT.—abstain, cease, discontinue, stop.

action, achievement, activity, battle, deed, exploit, motion, movement, performance. ANT.—idleness, inactivity, inertia, repose.

active, operative, working; busy, industrious; agile, alert, brisk, energetic, lively, mobile, nimble, quick, sprightly. ANT.—dormant, inactive; idle, indolent, passive.

activity, action, agility, alertness, briskness, energy, enterprise, exercise, intensity, liveliness, motion, progress, quickness, rapidity. ANT.—dullness, idleness, inactivity, inertia.

actuality, certainty, fact, reality, truth; act, circumstance, deed, event, factual, incident, occurrence, sure. ANT.—delusion, fiction, supposition, theory, unreal.

adapt, accommodate, adjust, conform, modify, fit. ANT.—derange, misapply, misfit.

add, adjoin, affix, annex, append, attach, augment, increase. ANT.—deduct, detach, reduce, remove, subtract, withdraw.

address, accost, approach, greet, hail, salute, speak to. ANT.—avoid, ignore, pass by.

adequate, ample, capable, commensurate, enough, fitting, qualified, satisfactory, sufficient, suitable. ANT.—deficient, insufficient, lacking, scant.

adhere, attach, clasp, cleave, cling, fasten, grasp, grip; have, hold, keep, maintain, occupy, possess, retain, support; check, confine, accommodate, carry, contain. ANT.—leave, loosen, unfasten.

adjacent, abuting, adjoining, beside, bordering, close, near, next, neighboring. ANT.—away from, beyond, distant, disconnected, separate.

admire, appreciate, approve, esteem, praise, respect, venerate. ANT.—abhor, despise, detest, dislike, hate.

admissible, acceptable, allowable, justifiable, permissible, tolerable, suitable, warranted. ANT.—inadmissible, irrelevant, unacceptable, unsuitable.

admit, accept, acknowledge, agree, allow, assent, concede, confess, grant, open, permit, sanction. ANT.—debar, deny, dismiss, refuse, reject.

advance, accelerate, elevate, forward, further, improve, move, proceed, promote; allege, bring forward, offer, propose, propound; proceed, suggest. ANT.—halt, oppose, retard, return, retreat, withdraw.

advantage, gain, mastery, superiority, victory; benefit, help, profit. ANT.—detriment, handicap, harm, hindrance, restriction.

adverse, antagonistic, contrary, hostile, opposed, opposite; unfavorable. ANT.—favor, cooperate, assist, approve.

advice, admonish, counsel, instruct, recommend, suggest; inform, notify. ANT.—deceive, misdirect, misinform.

affect, alter, change, influence, modify, concern, interest, regard; impress, melt, move, soften, subdue, touch; adopt, assume, feign, pretend.

affection, attachment, friendliness, fondness, goodwill, kindness, love, tenderness. ANT.—animosity, antipathy, aversion, dislike, indifference, repugnance.

affirm, assert, aver, declare, maintain, state, swear, warrent. ANT.—contradict, demur, deny, dispute, oppose, nullify.

afraid, alarmed, cowardly, fearful, frightened, scared, timid, timorous. ANT.—assured, bold, brave, composed, courageous, valorous.

aggravate, heighten, increase, intensify, magnify, worsen; annoy, embitter, exasperate, irritate, provoke. ANT.—appease, improve, mitigate, soften, soothe.

aggregate, amount, collection, conglomeration, entirety, mass, sum, total, whole. ANT.—element, part, particular, unit.

agility, activity, briskness, energy, enterprise, intensity, liveliness, movement, quickness, rapidity, vigor. ANT.—dullness, idleness, inactivity, inertia.

agitate, arouse, disturb, excite, perturb, provoke, rouse, ruffle, shake, stir, trouble. ANT.—calm, ease, placate, soothe, quiet.

agony, ache, anguish, distress, misery, pain, suffering, trial, torment, torture, woe. ANT.—comfort, ease, happiness, health, mitigation, relief.

agree, accede, acquiesce, approve, assent, comply, concur, conform, consent. ANT.—contradict, differ, disagree, dispute, dissent.

agreeable, acceptable, amiable, gratifying, pleasant, pleasing, suitable, welcome, willing. ANT.—disagreeable, obnoxious, offensive, unpleasant.

aim, aspiration, design, end, endeavor, goal, intention, purpose. ANT.—aimlessness, carelessness, lack of purpose.

alarm, affright, apprehension, consternation, dismay, fear, signal, terror, warning. ANT.—assurance, calm, composure, peace, quiet, security, tranquility.

alien, adverse, contrasted, foreign, hostile, irrelevant, remote, strange, unlike. ANT.—akin, germane, relevant.

allege, affirm, aver, cite, claim, declare, maintain. ANT.—contradict, deny, dissent, refute, repudiate.

alleviate, abate, allay, diminish, extenuate, lighten, mitigate, relieve, soften, soothe. ANT.—aggravate, agitate, augment, increase, intensify, irritate.

alliance, association, coalition, combination, confederacy, federation, partnership, union; compact, marriage, treaty. ANT.—divorce, schism, secession, separation.

allot, apportion, dispense, distribute, divide, mete; allocate, assign, give, grant, measure. ANT.—confiscate, deny, keep, refuse, retain, withhold.

allow, empower, permit, sanction, tolerate; authorize, give, grant, yield; acknowledge, admit, concede. ANT.—deny, forbid, protest, refuse, resist.

allude, hint, imply, insinuate, intimate, refer, suggest. ANT.—declare, specify, state.

allure, attract, bewitch, captivate, charm, coax, entice, invite, seduce, tempt. ANT.—dissuade, discourage, repel, threaten.

ally, accessory, accomplice, assistant, associate, confederate. ANT.—adversary, enemy, opponent.

alone, deserted, desolate, isolated, lonely, secluded; unaccompanied, unaided; lone, only, single, solitary. ANT.—accompanied, attended, together.

also, besides, furthermore, in addition, likewise, moreover.

alternative, choice, elective, option, preference. ANT.—no choice, obligation, required.

always, ceaselessly, constantly, continually, eternally, ever, forever, perpetually. ANT.—never, occasionally, rarely, sometimes.

amalgamate, blend, coalesce, combine, consolidate, fuse, mingle, merge, unite. ANT.—separate, divide.

amateur, apprentice, beginner, learner, neophyte, nonprofessional, novice. ANT.—authority, expert, master, professional.

ambiguous, dubious, equivocal, indefinite, obscure, vague. ANT.—clear, explicit, lucid, unequivocal.

ambition, aspiration, desire, eagerness, end, goal, incentive. ANT.—contentment, indifference, laziness, resignation, satisfaction.

amend, better, change, correct, improve, reform, repair. ANT.—blemish, corrupt, debase, spoil.

amiable, agreeable, engaging, friendly, good-natured, gracious, pleasant. ANT.—disagreeable, hateful, ill-natured.

among, amid, amidst, between, interspersed, mingle, mixed. ANT.—apart, alone, separate.

amount, aggregate, collection, mass, number, quantity, sum, total, whole. ANT.—individual, part, particular.

ample, broad, extensive, great, large, spacious, wide; abundant, bountiful, complete, copious, full, generous, plentiful, profuse, rich, sufficient. ANT.—limited, small; insufficient, lacking, meager, sparse.

amplification, accrual, augmentation, dilation, enhancement, enlargement, expansion, extension, growth, heighten, increase, intensification, magnification, multiplication, raising. ANT.—contraction, condensation, curtailment, decrease, diminishing, reduction.

analogous, akin, alike, allied, comparable, correlative, correspondent, like, parallel, resemblance, similar. ANT.—different, dissimilar, divergent, incongruous.

anger, animosity, displeasure, exasperation, fury, indignation, ire, irritation, passion, petulance, rage, resentment, temper, vexation, wrath. ANT.—calmness, conciliation, forbearance, patience, peace, pleasantness, self-control.

angry, enraged, exasperated, furious, incensed, indignant, irate, irritated, maddened, provoked, wrathful. ANT.—calm, happy, placid, pleased, satisfied.

anguish, agony, affliction, distress, grief, misery, pain, sorrow, suffering, torment, torture. ANT.—comfort, joy, relief, solace.

animate, activate, encourage, enliven, inspire, rouse, quicken, vitalize. ANT.—deactivate, discourage, kill.

animosity, bitterness, dislike, enmity, grudge, hatred, hostility, malevolence, malice, rancor, spite. ANT.—esteem, friendliness, goodwill, love.

annihilate, abolish, annul, destroy, eliminate, eradicate, extinguish, nullify, obliterate. ANT.—activate, preserve, save.

announce, advertise, broadcast, declare, expound, make known, notify, proclaim, promulgate, publish, report, reveal, tell. ANT.—bury, conceal, refrain, stifle, suppress, withhold.

annoy, bother, chafe, disturb, harass, harry, irk, irritate, molest, pester, plague, tease, trouble, vex. ANT.—accommodate, aid, console, gratify, please, soothe.

answer, acknowledge, confute, defend, rebut, rejoin, reply, respond, retort. ANT.—argue, ask, inquire, question.

anticipation, apprehension, contemplation, expectation, foresight, foretaste, forethought, hope, preconception, presentiment. ANT.—doubt, dread, fear, surprise, wonder, worry.

antipathy, abhorrence, antagonism, aversion, detest, dislike, hatred, opposition, repugnance, repulsion. ANT.—admiration, approval, liking, regard, respect.

anxiety, anguish, apprehension, care, concern, disquiet, dread, fear, misgiving, solicitude, trouble, worry. ANT.—assurance, confidence, contentment, equanimity, nonchalance, peace.

apology, alibi, acknowledgement, confession, defense, excuse, explanation, justification, plea. ANT.—accusation, censure, complaint, denial, dissimulation.

appalling, alarming, awful, dire, dreadful, frightful, ghastly, hideous, horrible, horrid, repulsive, terrible. ANT.—assuring, beautiful, calming, enchanting, enjoyable, fascinating.

apparent, clear, evident, manifest, obvious, plain, self-evident, transport, unambiguous, unmistakable, visible. ANT.—ambiguous, dubious, hidden, indistinct, uncertain, unclear.

appeal, apply, ask, beg, beseech, call, entreat, plead, pray, request, supplicate. ANT.—deny, disclaim, refuse, recall, renounce.

appear, arise, arrive, emanate, emerge, issue, look, seem. ANT.—be, exist; disappear, vanish, withdraw.

appearance, advent, arrival, coming, air, aspect, demeanor, form, look, manner, mien; fashion, guise, pretense, semblance. ANT.—absence, departure, disappearance, leaving.

appease, allay, alleviate, assuage, calm, compose, conciliate, lull, mollify, pacify, placate, quell, quiet, relieve, satisfy, soothe. ANT.—aggravate, arouse, excite, incense, inflame, provoke.

appetite, hunger, relish, stomach, thirst, zest; craving, desire, inclination, liking, longing, passion, zest. ANT.—aversion, dislike, distaste, renunciation, repugnance, satiety.

appoint, assign, choose, command, designate, direct, name, ordain, select. ANT.—cancel, dismiss, remove, withdraw.

appreciate, admire, cherish, enjoy, esteem, prize, regard, value; apprehend, comprehend, realize, understand; improve, rise. ANT.—belittle, depreciate, disparage, misapprehend, misunderstand.

approach, accost, address, arrive, come near, greet, hail, speak to. ANT.—avoid, leave, depart.

appropriate, applicable, apt, becoming, fitting, particular, proper, suitable; assume, embezzle, loot, pilfer, plagiarize, plunder, purloin, steal. ANT.—contrary, improper, inappropriate; bestow, give, restore, return.

approval, approbation, assent, commendation, consent, endorsement, praise, sanction, support. ANT.—censure, reprimand, rejection, reproach.

approve, accept, appreicate, commend, like, praise; authorize, confirm, countenance, endorse, ratify, sanction, validate. ANT.—criticize, disapprove, disparage; condemn, nullify, reject.

aptness, ability, aptitude, capability, capacity, dexterity, knowledge, power, qualification, skill, talent. ANT.—inability, incapacity, incompetencey.

ardent, eager, enthusiastic, earnest, enthusiastic, fervent, fervid, glowing, impassioned, intense, keen, passionate, vehement, warm, zealous. ANT.—apathetic, indifferent.

ardor, devotion, eagerness, enthusiasm, fervor, passion, rapture, spirit. ANT.—apathy, disinterest, indifference, unconcern.

argue, debate, differ, discuss, dispute, plead, reason, wrangle; imply, indicate, prove, show. ANT.—agree, ignore, overlook, reject.

arraign, accuse, censure, charge, cite, incriminate, indict. ANT.—absolve, acquit, discharge, exonerate, release.

arraignment, accusation, charge, incrimination, indictment. ANT.—exculpation, exoneration, pardon.

arrange, adjust, array, assort, classify, dispose, group, organize, place; devise, organize, plan, prepare. ANT.—confuse, disarrange, disorder, disturb, scatter.

arrest, apprehend, check, delay, detain, halt, hinder, interrupt, obsruct, restrain, seize, stop, withhold. ANT.—activate, discharge, free, liberate, release.

arrive, appear, attain, come, emerge, land, reach, visit. ANT.—disappear, depart, exit, go, leave.

arrogant, disdainful, haughty, insolent, overbearing, proud. ANT.—humble, meek, servile.

artificial, affected, assumed, bogus, counterfeit, ersatz, fake, fictitious, sham, spurious, synthetic, unreal. ANT.—genuine, natural, real, true.

ascend, advance, climb, mount, progress, rise, scale, soar, tower. ANT.—decline, descend, fall, sink.

ask, appeal, beg, claim, entreat, invite, petition, request, solicit; inquire, interrogate, query, question. ANT.—answer, command, demand, dictate, insist, order, refuse, reply.

aspersion, abuse, defamation, desecration, dishonor, disparagement, insult, invective, outrage, profanation, reproach, reviling, upbraiding. ANT.—approval, commendation, plaudit, respect.

aspiration, aim, ambition, craving, desire, goal, hope, longing, objective. ANT.—contentment, indifference, laziness.

assault, assail, attack, bombard, charge, invade, onslaught, pound, rape, storm, strike. ANT.—defend, oppose, protect, surrender.

assemble, collect, combine, congregate, convene, gather, join, meet, muster, unite. ANT.—disperse, scatter.

assent, accept, acquiesce, agree, allow, approve, concede, concur, consent, ratify, recognize. ANT.—disapprove, reject.

assert, affirm, allege, claim, declare, express, insist, maintain, state. ANT.—contradict, deny, refute, reject.

assist, abet, aid, further, help, promote, serve, support, sustain. ANT.—hamper, hinder, impede, prevent.

assistant, abettor, accessory, accomplice, accessory, accomplice, ally, associate, confederate. ANT.—adversary, opponent, rival.

associate, affiliate, ally, attach, combine, confederate, conjoin, connect, couple, join, link, unite. ANT.—disrupt, divide, disassociate, estrange, part, separate.

assume, appropriate, arrogate, take, usurp; adopt, affect, pretend, simulate, wear; presume, suppose. ANT.—relinquish, concede, grant, surrender; doff, remove; demonstrate, prove.

assurance, arrogance, assuredness, boldness, certainty, confidence, conviction, courage, firmness, security, self-reliance; pledge, promise; assertion, declaration, statement. ANT.—humility, modesty, shyness, timidity, trepidation.

astonish, amaze, astound, frighten, perplex, startle, surprise. ANT.—bore, calm.

attach, adjoin, affix, annex, append, connect, fasten, join, stick, unite. ANT.—detach, disengage, remove, separate, sever, unfasten.

attachment, adherence, affection, affinity, bond, devotion, esteem, friendship, liking, regard. ANT.—alienation, aversion, enmity, estrangement, separation.

attack, aggression, assail, assault, criticism, denunciation, invade, offense, onslaught; convulsion, fit, paroxysm. ANT.—aid, defend, oppose, protect, resistance, surrender.

attain, accomplish, achieve, acquire, arrive, earn, effect, gain, get, master, obtain, procure, reach, secure, win. ANT.—abandon, desert, discard, fail, relinquish.

attempt, attack, effort, endeavor, essay, experiment, trial, undertaking. ANT.—inaction, laziness, neglect.

attend, accompany, care for, escort, follow, guard, protect, serve, tend, watch; be present, frequent. ANT.—abandon, absent, desert.

attention, alertness, circumspection, concentration, consideration, diligence, mindfulness, notice, observation, watchfulness; application, contemplation, reflection, study. ANT.—disregard, indifference, negligence.

attraction, affinity, allure, captivation, charm, fascination, magnation, pull. ANT.—rejection, repulsion.

attitude, disposition, standpoint, viewpoint; aspect, pose, position, posture, stance; stand.

attractive, alluring, captivating, charming, enchanting, engaging, enticing, inviting, magnetic, pleasing, seductive, winning. ANT.—forbidding, obnoxious, repellent, repulsive.

audacity, arrogance, boldness, effrontery, fearlessness, impudence, rashness, temerity. ANT.—circumspection, humility.

austere, cruel, harsh, exacting, rigid, severe, sharp, stern, unrelenting. ANT.—gentle, kind, meek, mild, gentility, humility, meekness, restraint.

authentic, genuine, pure, legitimate, true, verifiable; accurate, authortative, certain, correct, reliable, trustworthy. ANT.—counterfeit, disputed, erroneous, false, spurious.

authority, command, control, domination, dominion, force, justification, power, right, supremacy; authorization, license, permission, rule, sanction; importance, influence, prestige, weight. ANT.—impotence, incapacity, weakness; denial, prohibition.

auxiliary, aid, ally, ancillary, assisting, conducive, confederate, furthering, helping, instrumental, subsidiary. ANT.—competitive, obstructive, opposing, retarding.

available, accessible, obtainable, on hand, prepared, present, ready, usable. ANT.—inaccessible, unavailable.

average, fair, intermediate, mean, median, mediocre, medium, moderate, normal, ordinary, usual. ANT.—exceptional, extraordinary, outstanding, unusual.

aversion, abhorrence, antipathy, disgust, disinclination, dislike, distaste, dread, hatred, loathing, opposition, repugnance, repulsion, reluctance. ANT.—affection, attachment, devotion, enthusiasm, liking.

avoid, avert, dodge, escape, eschew, elude, evade, forbear, forestall, shun. ANT.—confront, encounter, meet, oppose, seek.

award, adjudge, allot, allow, bestow, honor, recognize, reward. ANT.—ignore, reject, withhold, withdraw.

aware, alert, apprised, cognizant, conscious, informed, mindful, observant, perceptive. ANT.—ignorant, oblivious, unaware.

away, abroad, absent, aside, departed, gone, distant. ANT.—close, here, present.

awful, appalling, dire, dreadful, frightful, gruesome, horrie, terrible; awe-inspiring, imposing, impressive, majestic, solemn. ANT.—attractive, pleasant, commonplace, lowly, vulgar.

awkward, bungling, clumsy, gauche, inept, maladroit, rough, ungraceful, unskillful. ANT.—adroit, graceful, skillful.

axiom, adage, aphorism, apothegn, byword, fundamental, maxim, principle, proposition, proverb, rule, saying, theorem, truism. ANT.—absurdity, paradox, sophism.

B

backward, regressive, retrogressive, retrograde, revisionary; dull, sluggish, stupid; disinclined, indisposed, loath, reluctant. ANT.—advanced, civilized, intelligent, progressive.

bad, base, deleterious, evil, immoral, noxious, pernicious, rotten, sinful, unsound, spurious, vile, villainous, wicked. ANT.—excellent, good, honorable, moral, right, virtuous.

balance, composure, equilibrium, harmony, poise, stability, steadiness, proportion, symmetry; excess, remainder, remains, residue. ANT.—fall, imbalance, instability, unsteadiness.

baleful, bad, base, deleterious, evil, harmful, immoral, noxious, pernicious, wicked. ANT.—excellent, good, honorable, moral.

banal, commonplace, fatuous, hackneyed, inane, insipid, ordinary, trite, vapid. ANT.—exciting, fresh, novel, original, striking.

banish, debar, deport, dismiss, eject, exclude, exile, expatriate, expel, ostracize, oust. ANT.—accept, admit, forgive, receive, repatriate.

barbarous, atrocious, barbaric, brutal, crude, cruel, inhuman, merciless, ruthless, savage, uncivilized, uncultured, uncouth. ANT.—civilized, cultured, humane, kind, polite, refined.

barren, desolate, empty, sterile, unproductive. ANT.—fecund, fertile, productive.

barrier, bar, blockade, bulwark, obstacle, obstruction, rampart. ANT.—admittance, entrance, opening, passage.

base, abject, contemptible, degraded, despicable, ignominious, inferior, low, mean, shameful, sordid, vile, vulgar. ANT.—esteemed, exalted, lofty, moral, noble, righteous, superior.

bashful, abashed, coy, diffident, embarrassed, modest, sheepish, shy, timid, timorous. ANT.—adventurous, daring, fearless, gregarious.

basic, essential, fundamental, indispensable, primary, principal, vital. ANT.—additional, extra, secondary.

batter, beat, belabor, bruise, demolish, dent, disfigure, mar, pound, pummel, smash, thrash. ANT.—cover, protect, secure, treat gently.

battle, combat, conflict, contest, fight, fray, skirmish, strife, struggle. ANT.—accord, agree, peace, truce.

bear, support, sustain, uphold; allow, endure, maintain, permit, suffer, tolerate; carry, convey, transport; produce, spawn, yield. ANT.—avoid, cast aside, dodge, evade, refuse, shun.

beat, batter, belabor, buffet, castigate, flog, hit, knock, pound, pummel, punch, strike, thrash; conquer, defeat, overpower, overthrow, rout, subdue, vanquish, whip; palpitate, pulsate, pulse, throb. ANT.—assist, help, defend, shield; fail, relinquish, surrender.

beautiful, attractive, beauteous, charming, comely, elegant, graceful, handsome, lovely, pretty. ANT.—foul, hideous, homely, repulsive, unsightly.

becoming, befitting, comely, decorous, decent, fitting, pleasing, proper, seemly, suitable, worthy. ANT.—unbecoming, displeasing, unseemly, unsuitable.

before, ahead, earlier, forward, prior, sooner. ANT.—after, afterward, behind, later.

beg, adjure, ask, beseech, crave, entreat, implore, importune, petition, pray, request, solicit, supplicate. ANT.—assist, bestow, cede, favor, give, grant.

begin, commence, enter, inaugurate, initiate, institute, open, originate, start. ANT.—complete, conclude, end, finish, terminate.

beginning, commencement, inauguration, inception, opening, origin, outset, source, start. ANT.—close, completion, conclusion, consummation, end, finish, termination.

behavior, action, attitude, bearing, breeding, carriage, conduct, deed, demeanor, deportment, disposition, manner, strategy, tactics.

belief, certitude, confidence, conviction, credence, faith, opinion, persuasion, reliance, trust. ANT.—denial, doubt, heresy, incredulity.

beloved, dear, esteemed, precious, valued; costly, expensive, valuable. ANT.—despised, unwanted; cheap.

below, beneath, lower, under, underneath. ANT.—above, aloft, over, overhead.

bend, bow, contract, crook, curve, deflect, divert, flex, incline, lean, stoop, turn, twist; influence, mold; submit, yield. ANT.—break, resist, stiffen, straighten.

beneficial, advantageous, good, helpful, profitable, salutary, useful, wholesome. ANT.—destructive, detrimental, harmful, injurious.

benefit, advantage, avail, behalf, blessing, favor, gain, good, interest, profit, service. ANT.—distress, handicap, injury, trouble.

benevolence, altruism, beneficence, charity, generosity, goodwill, humanity, kindness, liberality, magnanimity, munificence, philanthropy. ANT.—cruelty, ill-will, malevolence, selfishness, unkindness.

beyond, above, distant, far, farther, more, over superior, yonder. ANT.—close by, here, near.

bias, bent, disposition, inclination, leaning, partiality, penchant, predilection, predisposition, prejudice, proneness, propensity, slant, tendency. ANT.—equity, fairness, impartiality, justice.

big, bulky, colossal, enormous, extensive, giant, great, huge, hulking, immense, large, majestic, massive, monstrous, vast. ANT.—little, petite, slight, small, tiny.

bigoted, dogmatic, fanatical, hidebound, illiberal, intolerant, narrow-minded, opinionated, prejudiced. ANT.—liberal, open-minded, progressive, tolerant.

bind, attach, connect, engage, fasten, fetter, join, link, obligate, restrain, restrict, secure, tie. ANT.—free, loose, release, unfasten, untie.

bitter, acrid, biting, distasteful, pungent, sharp, sour, tart; galling, grievous, painful, poignant; cruel, fierce; acrimonious, caustic, harsh, sardonic, severe. ANT.—agreeable, pleasant, sweet.

blame, accuse, censure, condemn, implicate, rebuke, reprehend, reproach, reprove, upbraid. ANT.—absolve, acquit, exonerate; praise.

blank, bare, barren, empty, vacant, void. ANT.—filled, occupied.

bleak, bare, chilly, cold, desolate, dreamy, dismal, dull, gloomy. ANT.—cheerful, pleasant, warm, serene.

blemish, blot, mark, speck, stain; defect, disfigurement, disgrace, dishonor, fault, flaw, imperfection. ANT.—adornment, decoration, embellishment, perfection, purity.

blend, adjoin, amalgamate, coalesce, combine, commingle, conjoin, consolidate, fuse, merge, mingle, mix, unite. ANT.—decompose, disintegrate, separate.

blind, ignorant, oblivious, sightless, undiscerning, unmindful, unseeing; careless, headlong, heedless, obtuse, rash; stupid. ANT.—aware, calculated, discerning, farsighted, perceiving, sensible.

bliss, blessedness, blissfulness, ecstasy, gladness, happiness, joy, rapture. ANT.—grief, misery, pain, sadness, wretchedness.

block, bar, barricade, clog, close, stop; impede, hinder, obstruct. ANT.—clear, open; aid, assist, further, promote.

bluff, abrupt, blunt, bold, brusque, brazen, coarse, discourteous, frank, outspoken, uncivil. ANT.—civil, courteous, pleasant.

blunt, dull, edgeless, obtuse, pointless, stolid, thick-witted, unsharpened; abrupt, bluff, brusque, direct, impolite, outspoken, harsh, forthright, rough, unceremonious. ANT.—polished, polite, suave, subtle, tactful.

boast, bluster, brag, crow, exult, flaunt, flourish, glory, vaunt. ANT.—apologize, deprecate, minimize.

body, carcass, corpse, remains; form, frame, torso; bulk, mass; aggregate, association, company, group, society.

bold, adventurous, audacious, brave, courageous, daring, determined, fearless, intrepid; brazen, forward, impudent, insolent, rude; abrupt, conspicuous, prominent, striking. ANT.—bashful, cowardly, timid, retiring, shy.

bondage, captivity, confinement, imprisonment, serfdom, servitude, slavery. ANT.—freedom, liberation.

book, booklet, brochure, compendium, handbook, manual, pamphlet, textbook, tract, treatise, volume, work.

border, boundry, brink, edge, extremity, fringe, frontier, limit, margin, outskirts, rim, termination, trimming, verge. ANT.—center, core, inside, interior, mainland, region.

boredom, doldrums, dullness, ennui, lack of interest, tedium, weariness. ANT.—activity, excitement, motive, stimulus.

bother, annoy, disturb, harass, haunt, inconvenience, molest, perplex, pester, plague, tease, trouble, upset, worry. ANT.—gratify, please, relieve, soothe.

bottom, base, basis, foot, foundation, groundwork, lowest part. ANT.—apex, peak, summit, top, upper part.

bound, hop, jump, leap, ski; spring, vault; circumscribe, confine, curb, define, limit. ANT.—crawl, walk; enlarge extend.

bountiful, abundant, ample, copious, opulent, overflowing, plenteous, plentiful, profuse, rich. ANT.—deficient, insufficient, scant, scarce.

brag, bluster, boast, flaunt, flourish, vaunt. ANT.—debase, degrade, demean, denigrate.

brave, adventurous, bold, courageous, daring, fearless, hardy, heroic, intrepid, undaunted, valiant, valorous, venturesome. ANT.—cowardly, cringing, fearful, timid, weak.

break, burst, crack, crush, demolish, destroy, fracture, infringe, pound, rack, rend, rupture, sever, shatter, shiver, smash, split, squeeze; disobey, infringe, transgress, violate. ANT.—join, mend, repair, restore, unite.

breed, bear, beget, conceive, engender, generate, procreate, propagate, start; foster, nurture, raise, rear. ANT.—abort, kill, murder.

brief, concise, curt, laconic, pithy, short, succinct, terse; fleeting, momentary, passing, short-lived, transient. ANT.—extended, lengthy, long, prolonged, protracted.

bright, brilliant, clear, gleaming, lucid, luminous, lustrous, radiant, scintillating, shining, sunny, translucent; clever, intelligent, smart, witty. ANT.—dark, dull, gloomy, stupid.

bring, adduce, attract, bear, carry, cause, conduct, convey, draw, fetch, impart, induce, produce, transfer, transport, transmit. ANT.—abandon, leave, relinquish.

brisk, cool, fresh, refreshing, stimulating.

briskness, action, activity, agility, energy, enterprise, intensity, liveliness, quickness, rapidity, vigor. ANT.—dullness, idleness, inactivity.

brittle, breakable, crisp, crumbling, delicate, fragile, frail, tenuous. ANT.—durable, enduring, tough, strong, unbreakable.

broad, ample, comprehensive, extensive, large, sweeping, vast, wide; liberal, tolerant. ANT.—confined, conservative, narrow, restricted.

broken, crushed, destroyed, fractured, interrupted, reduced, ruptured, separated, shattered, smashed, wrecked. ANT.—repaired, united, whole.

brotherhood, brotherliness, fellowship, kindness, solidarity, unity; association, clan, fraternity, society. ANT.—acrimony, discord, opposition, strife.

brusque, hasty, precipitate, sudden, unannounced, unexpected; abrupt, blunt, curt, rude; harsh, precipitous, rough, rugged, steep. ANT.—anticipated, expected; courteous, gradual.

brutal, barbarous, bestial, brutish, carnal, coarse, cruel, ferocious, gross, inhuman, merciless, rough, rude, ruthless, savage. ANT.—civilized, courteous gentle, humane, kind.

build, construct, erect, establish, found, make, manufacture, put up, raise, rear. ANT.—demolish, destroy.

buoyant, effervescent, light, resilient; animated, blithe, cheerful, elated, lively, spirited, vivacious. ANT.—dejected, depressed, despondent, sullen.

burden, afflict, encumber, load, oppress, overload, trouble. ANT.—alleviate, console, ease, mitigate.

burn, blaze, char, consume, cremate, incinerate, ignite, scald, scorch, sear, singe. ANT.—extinguish, stifle, subdue, quench.

bury, conceal, cover, entomb, hide, immure, inhume, inter. ANT.—display, exhume, expose, reveal.

business, art, commerce, concern, duty, employment, engagement, enterprise, job, occupation, profession, pursuit, trade, vocation, work. ANT.—avocation, hobby.

busy, active, assiduous, diligent, hard-working, industrious, perseverant. ANT.—apathetic, indifferent, lethargic.

but, and, barely, besides, except, further, furthermore, however, just, moreover, nevertheless, notwithstanding, provided, save, still, though, unless, yet.

buy, acquire, bribe, get, negotiate, obtain, procure, purchase, secure. ANT.—market, sell, transfer, vend.

by, beside, near, next to; by means of, through, with; according to; from.

C

calamity, adversity, casualty, catastrophe, disaster, misfortune, mishap, ruin. ANT.—advantage, benefit, blessing, fortune.

calculate, calculation, compute, consider, count, enumerate, estimate, figure, reckon, value, weigh. ANT.—assume, conjecture, guess, miscalculate.

call, address, assemble, clamour, command, convoke, cry, demand, designate, exclaim, ejaculate, invite, name, phone, proclaim, rally, roar, scream, shout, shriek, summon, utter, yell.

callous, hard, impenitent, indifferent, indurate, insensible, insensitive, obdurate, tough, unfeeling, unsusceptible. ANT.—compassionate, sensitive, soft, tender.

calm, alleviate, appease, assuage, lull, pacify, placate, quell, quiet, relieve, satisy, soothe, tranquilize. ANT.—agitate, anger, arouse, incite, incense, inflame.

calm, collected, composed, cool, dispassionate, peaceful, placid, quiet, sedate, self-possessed, serene, still, tranquil, undisturbed, unperturbed. ANT.—agitated, angry, excited, violent.

calumny, aspersion, detraction, defamation, libel, lying, scandal, slander, vilification. ANT.—charity, commendation, defense, flattery, kindness, praise.

cancel, abolish, annul, delete, eliminate, erase, expunge, invalidate, nullify, obliterate, quash, repeal, rescind, revoke. ANT.—approve, confirm, enforce, ratify.

candid, frank, free, honest, ingenous, open, sincere, straightforward, truthful; fair, impartial, just, unbiased. ANT.—artful, insincere, scheming, sly.

candor, fairness, frankness, impartiality, openness, rectitude, responsibility, sincerity, truthfulness, uprightness. ANT.—artifice, cheating, deceit, dishonesty, fraud, guile, stratagem.

capability, ability, aptitude, aptness, capacity, dexterity, efficiency, faculty, qualification, skill, talent. ANT.—incapacity, incompetency, unreadiness.

capable, able, clever, competent, efficient, fitted, qualified, skillful, suitable. ANT.—inadequate, incapable, incompetent, unable, unfit.

capacity, ability, aptness, capability, power, skill, talent; content, expanse, magnitude, size, volume. ANT.—impotence, inability, incapacity.

capital, chief, excellent, essential, fine, first, important, leading, major, principal, paramount; assets, collateral, money, property. ANT.—secondary, unimportant; impecunious, poor, poverty.

capitulate, abandon, acquiesce, relinquish, renounce, submit, surrender, yield. ANT.—conquer, overcome, rout.

capricious, changeable, fickle, idiosyncratic, inconstant, unstable, variable, vacillating. ANT.—constant, dependable, stable, steady.

captivity, bondage, confinement, imprisonment, servitude, slavery, subjection. ANT.—freedom, independence, liberty.

capture, apprehend, arrest, catch, grasp, take, seize, snare, take, trap. ANT.—free, liberate, lose, release.

care, concern, trouble, solicitude, worry; attention, caution, regard, precaution, vigilance, wariness, watchfulness; charge, custody, guardianship, ward. ANT.—disregard, indifference, neglect.

career, avocation, business, calling, course, experience, line, occupation, profession, pursuit, sphere, vocation. ANT.—idleness, retirement.

careful, attentive, meticulous, prudent, scrupulous, thoughtful; cautious, circumspect, discreet, guarded, vigilant, wary, watchful. ANT.—careless, improvident, indifferent, lax, negligent.

careless, inattentive, indiscrete, reckless, thoughtless, unconcerned. ANT.—accurate, careful, meticulous.

caress, cuddle, embrace, fondle, hug, kiss, pamper, pet. ANT.—annoy, buffet, neglect, spurn, tease, vex.

caricature, burlesque, exaggeration, farce, imitation, mimicry, parody, ridicule. ANT.—accuracy, exactitude, reality, truth.

carnal, base, concupisent, corporeal, lascivious, lustful, sensual, voluptuous, worldly. ANT.—chaste, ethereal, intellectual, spiritual.

carping, captious, caviling, disparaging, fault-finding, hypercritical, pedantic. ANT.—appreciative, approving, commendatory, encouraging.

carriage, bearing, behavior, demeanor, deportment, disposition, manner, mien.

carry, bring, convey, move, remove, support, sustain, transmit, transport. ANT.—abandon, drop, leave.

cartel, combination, monopoly, pool, trust.

case, circumstance, condition, contingency, event, example, occurrence, situation.

caste, ancestry, blood, category, class, descent, grade, kind, lineage, order, race, rank.

casual, careless, chance, cursoary, haphazard, incidental, informal, nonchalant, offhand, random, relaxed, unconcerned, unpremediated. ANT.—expected, formal, intended, planned.

casualty, accident, adversity, calamity, disaster, misfortune, mishap. ANT.—design, intention, prosperity, purpose.

catastrophe, adversity, affliction, blow, calamity, casualty, cataclysm, disaster, mishap, misery, ruin. ANT.—benefit, blessing, happiness.

catch, apprehend, arrest, capture, clasp, grasp, grip, overtake, seize, snare, trap. ANT.—cast aside, liberate, lose, release, miss.

catching, communicable, contagious, infectious, pestilential, virulent. ANT.—healthful, hygienic, noncommunicable.

category, caste, class, denomination, division, genre, heading, kind; grade, order, rank, set.

catharsis, cleansing, purge, purification.

cause, agent, antecedent, determinant, inducement, motive, origin, originator, principle, reason, source; create, effect, evoke, incite, induce, occasion, originate, prompt. ANT.—consequence, development, effect, end, result.

caustic, acrid, bitter, biting, distasteful, pungent, sour, tart; acrimonious, harsh, sardonic, severe. ANT.—mellow, pleasant, sweet.

caution, care, heed, prudence, vigilance, wariness, watchfulness; admonish, counsel, injunction, warning. ANT.—abandon, carelessness, recklessness.

cautious, attentive, heedful, prudent, scrupulous, thoughtful; careful, circumspect, discreet, careless, vigilant, wary. ANT.—hasty, heedless, impetuous.

cease, abandon, desist, conclude, desist, discontinue, stop, terminate; relinquish, resign, surrender. ANT.—continue, initiate, persist, stay.

cede, assign, convey, delivery, grant, relinquish, surrender, transfer, yield. ANT.—gain, receive, win.

celebrate, commemorate, honor, keep, observe, solemnize; commend, extol, honor, laud, praise. ANT.—disregard, ignore, neglect, disgrace, dishonor, profane.

celebrated, distinguished, eminent, famous, glorious, illustrious, noted, renowned. ANT.—ignominious, unknown.

celebration, commemoration, festivity, glorification, observance.

celerity, alacrity, haste, quickness, rapidity, speed, swiftness. ANT.—slowness, sluggishness.

celestial, divine, ethereal, godlike, heavenly, holy, supernatural, transcendant. ANT.—earthly, infernal, mortal.

censure, blame, condemn, criticize, denounce, reproach, reprimand, rebuke, reproach, reprove, upbraid. ANT.—approve, commend, endorse, praise.

center, core, focus, heart, hug, middle, midpoint, midst, nucleus. ANT.—border, periphery, rim.

ceremony, form, formality, observance, parade, pomp, protocol, rite, ritual, solemnity.

certain, assured, definite, fixed, incontrovertible, indubitable, inevitable, positive, reliable, secure, sure, true, undeniable, unquestionable. ANT.—doubtful, false, probable, questionable.

certainty, assuredness, confidence, conviction, firmness, self-reliance, surety, statement.

certify, assure, attest, aver, declare, demonstrate, inform, prove, state, testify. ANT.—deny, disown, repudiate.

chagrin, confusion, dismay, humiliation, mortification, shame, vexation.

chain, course, progression, sequence, series, set, string, succession.

challenge, defiance, demand, invitation, question; obstacle, opportunity, trial.

chance, accident, calamity, casualty, contingency, disaster, fate, fortune, happen, luck, misfortune, mishap, occur, random, transpire. ANT.—aim, design, intention, purpose.

change, alteration, alternation, innovation, modification, mutation, revolution, substitution, transition, variation. ANT.—permanence, stability, uniformity.

change, exchange, substitute; alter, convert, modify, shift, transform, vary, veer. ANT.—retain; continue, preserve, stabilize.

changeable, fickle, inconstant, shifting, unstable, vacillating, variable, wavering. ANT.—constant, stable, steady.

chaos, anarchy, confusion, disorder, disorganization, jumble, muddle, shambles, snarl. ANT.—order, organization, system.

character, class, description, disposition, individuality, kind, nature, personality, reputation, repute, standing, temperament; mark, sign, symbol, type.

characteristic, attribute, feature, idiosyncracy, individuality, mark, peculiarity, property, singularity, quality, trait.

charge, accuse, arraign, ascribe, assess, attack, censure, exhort, incriminate, indict; tax. ANT.—absolve, acquit, exonerate.

charity, alms, altruism, benefaction, benevolence, bounty, generosity, humanity, kindness, liberality, magnanimity, philanthropy, tenderness. ANT.—inhumanity, malevolence, selfishness.

charlatan, cheat, faker, fraud, humbug, impostor, mountebank, pretender, quack.

charming, alluring, attractive, bewitching, captivating, delightful, enchanting, engaging, fascinating, irresistable, ravishing, winning. ANT.—offensive, repulsive, revolting.

chase, follow, hunt, persist, pursue, seek, stalk, track, trail. ANT.—avoid, elude, escape, flee, lose.

chaste, clean, clear, genuine, immaculate, pure, unadulaterated, uncontaminated; guiltless, innocent, sincere, uncorrupted, undefiled, virgin, virtuous. ANT.—foul, polluted, tainted; corrupt, defiled, lewd, wanton.

chasten, afflict, correct, discipline, humble, humiliate, subdue. ANT.—assist, cheer, comfort, encourage.

chastise, castigate, correct, discipline, punish, reprove, reprimand, strike, whip. ANT.—comfort, forgive, pardon.

cheap, inexpensive, low-priced, poor; beggarly, common, inferior, mean, petty, shabby, contemptible, despicable. ANT.—costly, dear, expensive, valuable, dignified, noble, worthy.

cheat, beguile, bilk, deceive, defraud, dupe, fool, hoax, hoodwink, outwit, swindle, trick, victimize.

check, analyze, audit, curb, examine, hinder, impede, inquire, interrogate, question, quiz, repress, restrain, review, scan, scrutinize, survey, view, watch. ANT.—disregard, hasten, neglect, omit.

cheer, comfort, console, encourage, gladden, solace, soothe, sympathize. ANT.—antagonize, depress, dishearten.

cheerful, buoyant, gay, happy, joyous, lighthearted, merry, sprightly. ANT.—dejected, gloomy, morose, sad, sullen.

cherish, appreciate, hold dear, prize, treasure, value; foster, nurture, protect, shelter. ANT.—abandon, dislike, disregard, neglect.

chicanery, deception, duplicity, fraud, intrigue, machination, subterfuge, trickery. ANT.—fair dealing, honesty.

chief, captain, chieftain, commander, head, leader, master, principal, ruler. ANT.—attendant, servant, subordinate.

chief, cardinal, essential, first, leading, main, paramount, predominant, pre-eminent, prime, supreme. ANT.—minor, secondary.

chivalrous, brave, courageous, courteous, gallant, generous, heroic, knightly, spirited, valiant, valorous. ANT.—cowardly, rude, unmannerly, timerous.

choice, alternative, determination, election, option, preference, selection, volition; excellent.

choose, cull, elect, opt, pick, select. ANT.—refuse, reject.

chronic, confirmed, constant, established, inveterate, rooted, settled. ANT.—occasional, temporary.

chronicle, account, description, history, narration, narrative, recital, record.

circuitous, crooked, devious, distorted, erratic, indirect, roundabout, swerving, tortuous, wandering, winding. ANT.—direct, straight.

circular, bulbous, chubby, curved, cylindrical, globular, plump, rotund, round, spherical.

circumspection, anxiety, care, concern, solicitude, worry; attention, caution, discreetness, heed, regard, vigilance, wariness. ANT.—audaciousness, disregard, indifference, negligence.

circumstance, condition, detail, event, fact, happening, incident, item, occurrence, particular, point, position, situation.

circumvent, balk, check, foil, forestall, frustrate, outwit, prevent, thwart. ANT.—aid, help.

cite, advance, affirm, allege, assign, claim, declare, maintain, mention, name, quote, summon. ANT.—deny, disprove, neglect, refute.

civil, affable, considerate, courteous, cultivated, gracious, polite, refined, urbane, well-mannered. ANT.—boorish, ill-mannered, rude.

civilization, breeding, cultivation, culture, education, enlightenment, illumination, polish, refinement. ANT.—ignorance, illiteracy, vulgarity.

claim, advance, affirm, allege, assert, aver, contend, declare, demand, express, maintain, state; defend, support, uphold. ANT.—contradict, deny, refute.

clamor, blare, cry, din, hubbub, hullabaloo, noise, outcry, racket, row, sound, tumult, uproar. ANT.—quiet, silence, stillness.

clandestine, concealed, covert, furtive, hidden, private, secret, stealthy, surreptitious. ANT.—conspicuous, exposed, known, open.

clarify, decipher, educate, explain, illustrate, interpret, make clear, purify, refine, resolve, unravel. ANT.—confuse, muddy, obscure.

clasp, adhere, clutch, grasp, grip, hold, have, keep, maintain, occupy, possess, retain, support.

class, caste, category, denomination, division, genus, group, kind; degree, grade, order, rank, set, standing; elegance, excellence.

classic, antique, clean-cut, elegant, first-rate, model, neat, pure, refined, simple, trim; Greek or Roman. ANT.—barbaric, baroque, mixed, modern.

clean, unadulterated, cleanse, mop, purify, scrub, spotless, stainless, sweep, wash. ANT.—dirty, soiled, stained.

clear, cloudless, fair, sunny; limpid, transparent; apparent, distinct, evident, intelligible, lucid, manifest, obvious, plain, perspicuous, unmistakable, vivid; open, unobstructed. ANT.—cloudy, overcast; ambiguous, obscure, vague.

clemency, charity, compassion, forgiveness, leniency, mercy, mildness, pity. ANT.—punishment, vengeance.

clever, able, adroit, dexterous, keen, quick, quick-witted, skillfull, talented, witty; bright, expert, ingenious, intelligent, sharp, smart. ANT.—awkward, clumsy, slow, unskilled; foolish, ignorant, stupid.

cleverness, comprehension, intellect, intelligence, perspicacity, sagacity, sense, understanding; fun, humor, irony, pleasantry, satire, wit.

climax, acme, apex, cosummation, culmination, height, peak, summit, vertex, zenith. ANT.—anticlimax, depth, floor.

climb, ascend, mount, rise, scale, soar. ANT.—descend, fall.

cloak, clothe, conceal, cover, disguise, hide, mask, protect, screen, shield, shroud, veil. ANT.—bare, expose, reveal, unveil.

clog, see close.

cloister, abbey, convent, hermitage, monastery, nunnery, priory; isolation, meditation, retirement, seclusion, solitude.

close, abutting, adjacent, adjoining, contiguous, immediate, impending, near, nearby, neighboring; confidential, devoted, intimate. ANT.—away, distant, faraway, removed.

close, bar, enclose, fence in, occlude, seal, shut; clog, obstruct, plug, stop; cease, complete, conclude, end, finish, terminate. ANT.—open, unlock; begin, commence, start.

clothes, apparel, array, attire, clothing, dress, garb, garments, raiment. ANT.—nakedness, nudity.

cloudy, dark, dim, indistinct, murky, obscure, shadowy. ANT.—bright, clear, distinct, sunny.

clumsy, awkward, cumbersome, inept, maladroit, ponderous, unwieldly, unskillful. ANT.—adroit, dexterous, skillful.

clutch; cling to, embrace, grapple, grasp, grip, seize. ANT.—free, release.

coalition, alliance, association, combination, confederacy, federation, league, partnership, union.

coarse, crude, harsh, impure, rough, unrefined; bawdy, gross, immodest, indelicate, inelegant, rude, unpolished, vulgar. ANT.—fine, refined, smooth; cultivated, cultured, dainty.

coax, cajole, entice, inveigle, invite, persuade, wheedle.

coerce, compel, constrain, drive, enforce, force, impel, oblige. ANT.—allure, convince, induce, persuade, prevent.

coercion, compulsion, constraint, force, pressure, violence. ANT.—persuasion.

cogent, convincing, effective, forcible, persuasive, potent, powerful, sound, strong, urgent. ANT.—ineffective, unconvincing, weak.

cognizance, acquaintance, awareness, information, knowing, knowledge, learning, perception, scholarship, understanding, wisdom. ANT.—ignorance.

cohesion, cementing, coagulation, coherence, concretion, consolidation, integration.

coincide, accord, agree, collude, concur, correspond, equal, harmonize, match, square, syncronize, tally. ANT.—differ, disagree, diverge.

cold, arctic, bleak, chilly, cool, freezing, frigid, frosty, frozen, icy, wintry; indifferent, passionless, reserved, stoical, unconcerned, unfeeling. ANT.—heated, hot, torrid; affectionate, passionate.

collapse, cave in, decline, decrease, diminish, drop, fail, faint, fall, fall down, sink, subside; stumble, topple, tumble.

colleague, ally, associate, collaborator, companion, comrade, confederate, consort, friend, mate, partner. ANT.—adversary, opponent, stranger.

collect, accumulate, amass, assemble, concentrate, congregate, consolidate, gather, gain, hoard, obtain, pile; reap, receive. ANT.—disperse, distribute, scatter.

collected, calm, composed, cool, placid, quiet, sedate, tranquil; unperturbed. ANT.—agitated, excited, perturbed.

collision, clash, conflict, encounter, fight, impact, meeting, shock, struggle; contention, controversy, discord, clashing, interference, opposition, variance. ANT.—agreement, concord, harmony.

colloquial, conversational, dialectal, familiar, informal.

collusion, cabal, combination, complicity, conspiracy, deceit, intrigue, machination, plot, treachery, treason.

color, complexion, dye, hue, paint, pigment, shade, stain, tincture, tinge, tint; blush, flush, redden.

colossal, elephantine, enormous, gargantuan, gigantic, huge, immense, large, mammoth, prodigious, tremendous. ANT.—little, small, tiny.

comatose, drowsy, faint, lethargic, stuporous, torpid, unconscious.

combat, battle, brawl, conflict, contest, duel, encounter, fight, skirmish, struggle; controversy, discord, opposition. ANT.—accord, peace, truce.

combination, alliance, association, coalition; confederacy, entente, federation, league, partnership, union; blend, mixture.

combine, accompany, adjoin, associate, attach, conjoin, connect, couple, join, link, unite; mix, blend.

combustion, burning, oxidation; disturbance, rioting, violence.

comely, beautiful, charming, elegant, fair, fine, graceful, handsome, lovely, pleasing, pretty. ANT.—homely, unattractive, unsightly.

comfort, aid, allay, alleviate, assist, cheer, console, encourage, gladden, relieve, solace, soothe, support, succor, sympathize. ANT.—antagonize, depress, dishearten, trouble.

comfortable, acceptable, agreeable, commodious, contented, cozy, gratifying, warm, pleasurable, protected, relaxed, restful, well-off. ANT.—miserable, wretched.

comical, amusing, diverting, droll, farcical, funny, humorous, laughable, ludicrous, ridiculous, witty. ANT.—serious, sober, solemn.

command, bidding, decree, dictate, direct, direction, injunction, instruction, mandate, order, requirement. ANT.—requisition; authority, control, govern, power, rule.

command, point, train; conduct, govern, guide, manage, regulate, rule; bid, direct, instruct, order. ANT.—countermand, distract, misdirect, misguide.

commemorate, celebrate, honor, memorialize, observe; solemnize. ANT.—disdain, dishonor, neglect.

commensurate, celebrate, honor, solemnize; commend, extol, glorify, praise. ANT.—overlook; disgrace, dishonor, profane.

commence, arise, begin, enter, establish, found, inaugurate, initiate, institute, introduce, open, originate, start. ANT.—cease, complete, finish, terminate.

commencement, beginning, inception, opening, outset, start. ANT.—completion, consummation, end, termination.

commend, appreciate, approve, praise; authorize, confirm, endorse, praise, ratify, sanction. ANT.—censure, criticize, condemn, rebuke.

comment, annotation, note, observation, remark, statement.

commerce, business, enterprise, industry, intercourse, trade, work.

commiseration, compassion, condolence, empathy. ANT.—coldness, indifference.

commission, appointment, authority, board, committee, delegation, duty, errand, function, power, warrant.

commit, perform, perpetrate; commend, consign, entrust, trust; bind, obligate, pledge. ANT.—fail, neglect, release, renounce; free, loose.

commodious, accommodating, appropriate, comfortable, convenient, expedient, favorable, roomy, timely, useful, suitable. ANT.—confined, inconvenient, troublesome, uncomfortable.

commodity, articles, assets, goods, materials, possessions, property, stock, wares.

common, habitual, frequent, mutual, ordinary, prevalent, public, usual; low, mean, vulgar. ANT.—aristocratic, extraordinary, scarce; noble, refined.

commotion, agitation, chaos, confusion, disarray, disorder, disturbance, ferment, tumult, turmoil. ANT.—calmness, order, peace, tranquility.

communicate, convey, disclose, divulge, impart, inform, promulgate, reveal, tell, transmit. ANT.—conceal, suppress, withhold.

communion, association, concord, fellowship, intercourse, sacrament, union. ANT.—alienation; contention, discord.

community, area, district, locality, neighborhood, region, section.

commute, exchange, interchange, reduce, substitute, travel.

compact, close, condensed, constricted, contracted, dense, firm, narrow, pressed, snug, stretched, tense, tight. ANT.—diffuse, loose, relaxed, slack.

compact, accordance, concord, concurrence, understanding, unison; agreement, bargain, contract, covenant, pact. ANT.—disagreement, dissension, variance.

companion, associate, colleague, comrade, consort, crony, fellow, friend, mate, partner. ANT.—adversary, enemy, stranger.

company, assembly, band, conclave, convention, party, throng, troop; association, fellowship, society, corporation. ANT.—dispersion, loneliness, seclusion, solitude.

comparable, akin, alike, allied, analogous, correlative, corresponding, like, parallel, similar. ANT.—dissimilar, divergent, incongruous, opposed.

compare, contrast, differentiate, discriminate, distinguish.

compassion, commiseration, kindness, mercy, pity, sympathy. ANT.—cruelty, inhumanity, ruthlessness, severity, tyranny.

compatible, accordant, agreeable, congruous, consonant, correspondent, harmonious. ANT.—

contradictory, incompatible, incongruous, inconsistent.

compel, coerce, constrain, drive, enforce, force, impel, oblige. ANT.—deter, hamper, impede, obstruct.

compensation, earnings, payment, recompense, return, reward, salary, stipend, wages. ANT.—forfeiture, loss, penalty.

competent, capable, efficient, fitted, proficient, qualified, skillful. ANT.—inadequate, incapable, incompetent, inept.

complain, deplore, grouch, grumble, lament, protest, remonstrate, repine, whine. ANT.—applaud, approve, praise, sanction.

complete, accomplish, achieve, conclude, consummate, end, finish, perfect, terminate; thorough, total, unbroken, undivided. ANT.—abandon, neglect, withdraw; deficient, lacking, unfinished.

complex, complicated, compound, intricate, involved, obscure. ANT.—apparent, plain, simple.

complexion, color, hue, pigment, shade, tincture, tinge, tint. ANT.—paleness, transparency.

compliant, humble, meek, modest, submissive, unassuming, unpretentious. ANT.—arrogant, boastful, haughty, ostentatious, proud, vain.

compliment, adulation, commendation, endorse, flattery, praise, tribute. ANT.—censure, criticism, denounce, reprehend.

comply, accede, acquiesce, agree, assent, consent; coincide, concur, conform, submit. ANT.—disagree, dissent, disobey, oppose.

comport, act, bear, behave, carry, conduct, operate.

compose, construct, create, fashion, formulate, forge, produce, shape; constitute, form; arrange, combine, organize; devise, frame, invent. ANT.—agitate, destroy, disfigure, dismantle.

composed, calm, collected, comfortable, imperturbable, peaceful, placid, quiet, sedate, tranquil. ANT.—agitated, excited, perturbed.

composer, author, creator, inventor, maker, originator.

composure, balance, calmness, equilibrium, poise, self-possession. ANT.—agitation, excitement, rage, turbulence.

compound, alloy, amalgamate, blend, combine, complex, complicated, composite, fraternize, join. ANT.—elemental, simple, single, unmixed.

comprehend, apprehend, conceive, discern, embrace, grasp, know, learn, perceive, realize, see, understand. ANT.—exclude, misapprehend, misinterpret, mistake, misunderstand.

comprehension, cognizance, discernment, insight, understanding. ANT.—ignorance, insensibility, misconception.

compress, condense, consolidate, constrict, crowd, reduce, squeeze. ANT.—expand, extend, increase, rarify, stretch, swell.

comprise, consist, contain, embody, embrace, encompass, hold, include, involve. ANT.—except, fall short, lack, reject.

compromise, accommodation, adjustment, agreement, arbitration, concession, conciliation. ANT.—controversy, disagreement, dispute, dissention.

compulsion, might, potency, power, strength, vigor; coercion, constraint, force, urgency. ANT.—feebleness, frailty, impotence, weakness; persuasion.

compute, calculate, count, enumerate, estimate, figure, reckon. ANT.—conjecture, guess, surmise.

comrade, associate, colleague, companion, consort, friend, partner. ANT.—adversary, stranger.

conceal, bury, camouflage, cover, disguise, hide, mask, screen, secrete, veil. ANT.—disclose, divulge, expose, lay bare, reveal, uncover.

concede, assent, acquiesce, permit, sanction, surrender; authorize, give, grant, relinquish yield; acknowledge, admit, allow. ANT.—object, protest, refuse, reject.

conceit, egotism, pride, self-glorification, vanity. ANT.—diffidence, humility, meekness, modesty.

conceive, become pregnant, concoct, design, devise, frame, imagine, visualize.

concentrated, close, compact, compressed, condensed, crowded, dense, thick. ANT.—diluted, dispersed, dissipated, sparse.

concept, conception, idea, notion, thought. ANT.—entity, matter, substance.

concern, affair, business; anxiety, care, solicitude, worry. ANT.—apathy, inconsequence, indifference, unconcern.

concise, brief, compact, condensed, crisp, incisive, pithy, succinct, terse. ANT.—lengthy, redundant, repetitive, verbose, wordy.

conclusion, close, completion, consummation, determination, termination; decision, deduction, inference, resolution, result. ANT.—beginning, commencement, inception, introduction, preamble, prelude, start.

concord, accordance, agreement, harmony, peace. ANT.—difference, disagreement, discord, dissension, variance.

concrete, actual, definite, firm, hard, material, particular, specific, solidified, tangible. ANT.—abstract, immaterial, intangible.

concur, agree, approve, assent, certify, comply, consent; coincide, conform, endorse. ANT.—argue, contradict, differ, disapprove, dispute, dissent, oppose, reject.

condemn, blame, censure, denounce, doom, reprehend, reproach, reprobate, reprove, upbraid; convict, sentence. ANT.—approve, commend, condone, forgive, praise; absolve, acquit, exonerate, pardon, set free.

condition, case, circumstance, situation, state; provision, requirement, specification, stipulation, term; make ready for work or use.

conditional, contingent, dependent, relying, subject, subordinate. ANT.—absolute, autonomous, independent.

condone, absolve, allow, disregard, excuse, forgive, overlook, pardon, remit. ANT.—condemn, forbid, punish.

conduct, action, attitude, bearing, behavior, carriage, demeanor, deportment, disposition, manner.

conduct, direct, govern, guide, lead, steer; manage, regulate, supervise.

confederate, abettor, accessory, accomplice, ally, assistant, associate, colleague, supporter. ANT.—adversary, enemy, opponent, opposition.

confederation, alliance, coalition, confederacy, entente, federation, league, union; compact, treaty. ANT.—schism, separation.

confer, converse, consult, deliberate, discuss, talk; bestow, donate, give, grant.

confess, acknowledge, admit, allow, avow, concede, disclose, divulge, own, reveal. ANT.—conceal, deny, disclaim, disguise, disown, repudiate, veil.

confidence, assurance, assuredness, boldness, certitude, conviction, self-possession, surety. ANT.—apprehension, diffidence.

confine, bind, bound, circumscribe, enclose, encompass, envelop, fence, imprison, limit, restrict. ANT.—develop, enlarge, expand, free, release, unfetter.

confirm, corroborate, substantiate, verify; assure, establish, settle; approve, fix, ratify, sanction; strengthen, validate. ANT.—annul, abrogate, cancel, destroy, shatter, void.

confiscate, appropriate, capture, commandeer, take; grip, seize. ANT.—give back, restore, return.

conflict, battle, combat, duel, encounter, fight, struggle; contention, discord, dissention, opposition, strife, variance, war. ANT.—concord, harmony, peace, repose, tranquility.

conform, adapt, adjust; assent, comply, submit. ANT.—dissent.

confront, combat, encounter, meet squarely, oppose. ANT.—agree, submit, support.

confuse, bewilder, complicate, confound, derange, disconcert, obscure, perplex, puzzle. ANT.—clarify, illumine, organize.

confusion, agitation, chaos, clutter, commotion, disarrangement, disarray, discomposure, disorder, ferment, jumble, pendemonium, stir, tumult, turmoil. ANT.—method, order, sense, system.

confute, confound, confuse, defect, dismay, disprove, refute. ANT.—affirm, confirm, endorse, prove, verify.

congruous, accordant, agreeing, compatible, consonant, correspondent, in harmony. ANT.—contradictory, discrepant, incongruous.

conjecture, guess, hypothesis, presumption, speculation, supposition, theory. ANT.—certainty, fact, proof, truth.

connect, adjoin, affiliate, affix, annex, append, attach, join, link, unite. ANT.—detach, disconnect, disengage, separate.

conquer, beat, checkmate, crush, defeat, humble, master, overcome, overthrow, prevail, quell, rout, subdue, subjugate, surmount, vanquish. ANT.—cede, forfeit, lose, retreat, succumb, surrender.

conquest, subjugation, triumph, victory. ANT.—defeat, failure.

conscientious, careful, exacting, honest, incorruptible, just, scrupulous, trusty, upright. ANT.—corrupt, dishonest, unjust.

conscious, apprised, aware, certain, cognizant, informed, mindful, percipient, sensible. ANT.—ignorant, insensible, oblivious, senseless, unaware.

consecrate, dedicate, exalt, extol, glorify, hallow, honor, revere, sanctify, venerate. ANT.—debase, degrade, dishonor.

consent, accede, acquiesce, agree, allow, assent, comply, concede, concur, conform, yield. ANT.—demur, disagree, dissent, prevent, protest, refuse.

consequence, effect, end, fruit, issue, outcome, product, sequel. ANT.—beginning, cause, commencement, origin, start.

conserve, maintain, preserve, save; retain; keep, guard, protect. ANT.—discard, reject; relinquish; neglect.

consider, contemplate, deliberate, examine, meditate, ponder, reflect, weigh; regard. ANT.—abandon, dismiss, forget, ignore, neglect, overlook.

considerate, cautious, charitable, kind, prudent; meditative, solicitous, sympathetic, unselfish. ANT.—harsh, impervious, inconsiderate, rash, repressive, scornful, thoughtless.

consideration, attention, care, mindfulness, watchfulness, reflection; pay, recompense, value. ANT.—disregard, failure, indifference, negligence, omission, oversight.

consign, commit, condemn, delegate, deliver, devote, send, ship. ANT.—hold, receive, retain.

consistent, accordant, agreeing, compatible, conforming, consonant, constant, equable, harmonious, regular, undeviating, uniform. ANT.—contradictory, discrepant, incongruous, inconsistent, varying.

console, cheer, comfort, ease, freshen, gladden, invigorate, soothe, support. ANT.—depress, grieve, wound.

consolidate, affiliate, amalgamate, blend, coalesce, combine, compact, compress, condense, conjoin, fuse, merge, solidify, unite. ANT.—disjoin, disperse, separate, sever, thin(out).

conspicuous, celebrated, clear, commanding, distinguished, manifest, noticeable, obvious, outstanding, plain, prominent, visible. ANT.—concealed, covered, hidden, obscure, unknown, unseen, secret.

conspiracy, cabal, collusion, combination, intrigue, plot, treachery.

constancy, faithfulness, fealty, fidelity, firmness, fixedness, loyalty, permanence, reliability, resolution, stability, steadiness. ANT.—capriciousness, disloyalty, faithlessness, fickleness, fluctuation, instability, vacillation.

constantly, always, continually, eternally, ever, evermore, forever, incessantly, perpetually, unceasingly. ANT—fitfully, never, occasionally, rarely, sometimes.

consternation, alarm, amazement, astonishment, dismay, fear, horror, panic, surprise, terror, wander. ANT.—calm, peacefulness, quietness, repose, tranquility.

constrain, compel, confine, drive, force, oblige, press, prevent, repress, restrain, urge. ANT.—ask, implore, plead, supplicate.

constrict, bind, compress, cramp, hamper, limit, shrink, squeeze, tighten. ANT.—expand, free, loosen, release, untie.

construct, build, compose, erect, fabricate, form, frame, make, produce. ANT.—demolish, destroy, dismantle, raze.

consult, confer, discuss, seek advisement.

consume, absorb, annihilate, assimilate, destroy, devour, engulf, exhaust, imbibe, squander, swallow, waste. ANT.—accumulate, collect, gather, hoard, store.

consummate, accomplish, achieve, close, complete, conclude, end, execute, finish, fulfill, perfect, terminate; absolute, best, excellent, supreme. ANT.—incomplete, second rate, unfinished.

contagious, catching, communicable, pestilential, spreading, virulent. ANT.—incommunicable.

contaminate, befoul, corrupt, debase, defile, deprave, infect, poison, pollute, soil, stain, taint, vitiate. ANT.—disinfect, purify.

contemplate, conceive, picture, meditate, muse, ponder, reflect, consider, study; intend, view. ANT.—discard, disregard, neglect, reject.

contemporary, coequal, coeval, coincident, contemporaneous, current, modern, new, simultaneous. ANT.—ancient, antiquated, bygone, old.

contempt, derision, detestation, disdain, disregard, disrespect, disparagement, mockery, scorn, slight, slur. ANT.—approbation, awe, endorsement, esteem, regard, respect.

contemptible, depraved, degenerate, despicable, low, mean, scurrilous, sordid, vile. ANT.—admirable, dignified, exalted, gracious, pleasing, respectable, worthy.

contend, battle, combat, compete, contest, cope, dispute, engage, fight, grapple, maintain, oppose, strain, struggle, vie. ANT.—cease, cede, desert, halt, stop, quit.

contention, altercation, animosity, battle, combat, conflict, duel, enmity, feud, fight, struggle; controversy, discord, opposition, quarrel, strife; variance. ANT.—amity, benevolence, concord, goodwill, harmony, kindness, regard, respect, sympathy.

contentment, acceptance, delight, ease, gladness, happiness, joy, satisfaction, serenity. ANT.—despair, discomfort, dissent, grief, misery, regret, sadness, sorrow.

contest, argue, contend, debate, dispute, fight, object, oppose; altercation, battle, conflict, engagement, feud, match, race. ANT.—agree, assent, relinquish; calm, repose, tranquility.

contingent, conditional, dependent, depending, relying, subject, subordinate. ANT.—autonomous, independent.

continual, ceaseless, constant, continuous, endless, incessant, invariable, perpetual, persistent, steady, unbroken, unceasing, uninterrupted, unremitting, unvarying. ANT.—checked, concluded, intermittent, interrupted, stopped.

continuance, continuation, duration, existence, extension, production, prolongation. ANT.—arrest, finish, hindrance, impediment, stoppage.

continue, advance, extend, maintain, proceed, persevere, persist, sustain. ANT.—arrest, check, complete, desist, end, finish, interrupt.

contract, abbreviate, abridge, condense, diminish, lessen, narrow, reduce, restrict, shorten, shrink; agreement, cartel, covenant, pledge, promise. ANT.—elongate, enlarge, expand, extend, lengthen.

contradict, correct, contravene, demur, disclaim, dispute, oppose, recall, recant, rectify, refute. ANT.—acquiesce, accept, approve, agree, confirm, sanction, seal, sign, verify, vouch.

contrary, adverse, antagonistic, opposed, opposite, conflicting, contradictory, counteractive, dissimilar, unlike. ANT.—agreeing, alike, correspondent, homogeneous, similar.

contrast, differentiate, discriminate, distinguish; antithesis, disparity, dissimilarity, divergence, incongruity, variation.

contravene, annul, contradict, defeat, hinder, interpose, nullify, obstruct, oppose, thwart, void. ANT.—agree, approve, assent, assist, concur, consent.

contribute, add(to), aid, assist, befriend, benefit, cooperate, donate, favor, furnish, help, share, subscribe, supply. ANT.—counteract, disapprove, harm, ignore, neglect, oppose, shun, withhold.

contrite, penitent, regretful, remorseful, repentant, sorrowful. ANT.—impenitent, obdurate, remorseless.

contrivance, apparatus, appliance, construction, design, device, invention, mechanism; plan, plot, ruse, scheme, trick.

contrive, arrange, design, devise, execute, form, frame, invent, make, plan, plot, project, scheme. ANT.—abolish demolish, disrupt, ruin, smash.

control, coerce, command, direct, dominate, guide, govern, hold, manage, regulate, rule, superintend; check, curb, prevent, repress, restrain. ANT.—abandon, forsake, ignore, relinquish, renounce, resign.

controversy, altercation, argument, bickering, contention, debate, disagreement, dispute, quarrel, squabble, wrangling. ANT.—agreement, concord, forbearance, harmony, peace, restraint.

convalesce, improve, rally, recover, recuperate, revive. ANT.—die, fail, falter, regress.

convene, assemble, collect, congregate, convoke gather, meet, muster. ANT.—adjourn, disperse, scatter.

convenient, accessible, adapted, appropriate, available, commodious, favorable, fitting, handy, opportune, suitable. ANT.—inaccessible, inconvenient, inexpedient, troublesome, unsuitable.

conventional, accepted, customary, formal, ordinary, orthodox, prevalent, social, stipulated, usual. ANT.—extraordinary, foreign, informal, irregular, strange, unconventional, unusual.

convergence, approach, assemblage, concourse, confluence, conjunction, focal point, meeting. ANT.—disjunction, divergence, division.

conversation, chat, colloquy, communication, communion, conference, dialogue, discourse, discussion, intercourse, interview, palaver, parley, talk.

converse, chat, communicate with, discuss, speak with; communion, conversation, discussion, intercourse, parley.

convert, adapt, alter, change, metamorphose, modify, resolve, shift, transfigure, transform, transmute, turn(from), veer. ANT.—retain; continue, keep, maintain, persist, preserve.

convey, bring, carry, communicate, impart, inform, transmit, transport. ANT.—hold, keep, preserve, retain.

convict, criminal, culprit, felon, malefactor, offender, transgressor; censure, condemn, doom, sentence. ANT.—absolve, acquit, exonerate, pardon.

convince, affect, clarify, coax, exhort, induce, influence, persuade, prevail upon, satisfy, sway, touch, win over. ANT.—deprecate, dissuade, warn.

convivial, cordial, festive, hospitable, jolly, merry, sociable. ANT.—dismal, severe, solemn, staid.

convoke, assemble, call, collect, convene, gather, muster, summon. ANT.—adjourn, disband, discharge, dismiss, disperse, dissolve, separate.

convolution, circumvolution, coil, curl, involution, sinuosity, twist, wave, winding line. ANT.—level surface, straight line, uncurved.

convoy, accompany, attend, chaperone, escort, go with, protect, support, watch over. ANT.—abandon, avoid, desert, ignore, leave, neglect, quit.

cool, apathetic, calm, distant, fresh, frigid, frosty, gelid, indifferent, shivery, unfeeling, unresponsive, wintry; freeze, harden, refrigerate. ANT.—feeling, glowing, responsive, sultry, sunny, warm-hearted.

cooperate, aid, approve, assist, combine, connive, encourage, endorse, forward, fraternize, help, perform, plan, promote, relieve, second, support. ANT.—delay, disturb, encumber, handicap, hinder, impede, prevent.

copious, abundant, ample, bountiful, exuberant, overflowing, plenteous, plentiful, profuse, rich, teeming. ANT.—deficient, meager, scant, scarce, sparse.

cordial, amicable, earnest, friendly, genial, gracious, hearty, kindly, pleasant, sincere, sociable, warm. ANT.—aloof, cool, hostile, indifferent, inhospitable, taciturn, unfriendly.

corporal, bodily, carnal, corporeal, in the flesh, physical, somatic; material. ANT.—immaterial, incorporeal, spiritual.

corpulent, beefy, fat, fleshy, obese, paunchy, plump, portly, rotund, stocky, stout, thickset. ANT.—gaunt, lean, slender, thin.

correct, accurate, exact, faultless, impeccable, precise, proper, right, true. ANT.—erroneous, inaccurate, incorrect, false, faulty, untrue, wrong.

correct, amend, mend, improve, rectify, reform, remedy, repair; chastise, discipline, punish, reprove. ANT.—aggravate, ignore, spoil; coddle, condone, pamper.

correlation, correspondence, likeness, reciprocation, similarity. ANT.—difference, disparagement, divergence, unlikeness.

corroborate, affirm, approve, assure, back, certify, confirm, endorse, sanction, support. ANT.—contradict, deny, disallow, disclaim, disprove, oppose, refute.

corrupt, base, contaminated, contemptible, corrupted, crooked, debased, demoralized, depraved, dishonest, impure, infected, lewd, low, perverted, profligate, putrid, rotten, spoiled, tainted, unprincipled, unscrupulous, unsound, venal, vitiated. ANT.—clean, decent, honorable, noble, pure, wholesome.

corruption, baseness, criminality, decay, degradation, depravity, graft, guiltiness, infamy, perversion, putrefaction, rottenness, swindling, vice, wickedness. ANT.—honesty, integrity, morality, soundness, uprightness.

counsel, acquaint, admonish, advise, apprise, guide, inform, instruct, recommend, suggest, warn. ANT.—conceal, misinform, mislead, withhold.

count, calculate, compute, enumerate, figure, number, reckon, score, total. ANT.—conjecture, estimate, guess, miscalculate.

counterfeit, artificial, bogus, dishonest, ersatz, fake, false, feigned, fictitious, forged, fraudulent, phony, sham, spurious, synthetic, unreal. ANT.—genuine, honest, natural, real, true.

couple, adjoin, attach, combine, conjoin, connect, copulate, join, link, unite; brace, pair, two. ANT.—detach, disconnect, disjoin, separate.

courage, boldness, bravery, chivalry, daring; dauntlessness, fearlessness, fortitude, gallantry, hardihood, heroism, intrepidity, mettle, prowess, spirit, valor. ANT.—cowardice, fear, pusillanimity, timidity, weakness.

courteous, affable, agreeable, civil, considerate, cultivated, genteel, mannerly, obliging, polished, polite, refined, suave, urbane, well-bred, well-mannered. ANT.—boorish, dictatorial, discourteous, impertinent, rude, uncivil, uncouth.

covenant, agreement, alliance, concord, understanding; bargain, compact, concordat, contract, pact, stipulation. ANT.—difference, disagreement, variance.

cover, cloak, clothe, conceal, curtain, disguise, envelop, guard, hide, mask, overlay, overspread, protect, screen, shield, veil; comprise, embody, embrace. ANT.—bare, divulge, expose, reveal, uncover, unveil.

covert, clandestine, concealed, disguised, furtive, hidden, secret, sly, underhand, unseen. ANT.—candid, conspicuous, evident, explicit, frank, open, overt, unconcealed, visible.

covetousness, avarice, craving, cupidity, desire, envy, greed, jealousy. ANT.—benevolence, generosity, liberality, munificence.

cowardly, afraid, chicken-hearted, effeminate, faint-hearted, not courageous, shy, sissy, spiritless, timid, timorous. ANT.—bold, brave, courageous, daring, dauntless.

crafty, calculating, cunning, deceitful, foxy, furtive, guileful, plotting, scheming, shrewd, stealthy, surreptitious, sly, tricky, underhand, wily. ANT.—candid, frank, ingenuous, open, sincere, undesigning.

crass, brutish, coarse, crude, insensitive, raw, rough, uncouth, unfinished, unpolished, unrefined. ANT.—finished, cultivated, polished, refined.

craving, appetite, desire, longing, passion, yearning. ANT.—disgust, distaste, repugnance.

crazy, crazed, delirious, demented, deranged, idiotic, imbecilic, insane, lunatic, mad, maniacal. ANT.—rational, reasonable, sane, sensible.

create, bring about, cause, design, engender, fashion, form, formulate, generate, invent, make, originate, produce; appoint, ordain. ANT.—annihilate, destroy; disband, terminate.

credible, believable, plausible, probable, reasonable, reliable, trustworthy. ANT.—improbable, incredible, unbelievable.

crest, acme, crown, head, peak, pinnacle, summit, top, plume, tuft; decoration, insignia. ANT.—base, bottom.

crime, atrocity, depravity, felony, immorality, infringement, injustice, misdeed, misdemeanor, offense, outrage, transgression, vice, wickedness, wrong. ANT.—benevolence, benignity, honor, innocence, morality, uprightness, virtue.

criminal, convict, culprit, delinquent, felon, malefactor, offender, transgressor; abominable, blamable, culpable, felonious, iniquitous, sinful, vicious, vile, wrong. ANT.—faultless, good, honest, innocent, just, legal, sinless, virtuous.

crisis, critical juncture, crucial point, emergency, exigency, strait, turning point. ANT.—calm, equilibrium, normality.

crisp, breakable, brittle, crumbling, fragile, frail, splintery; brisk, bracing, fresh, lively, sharp. ANT.—flexible, tough, unbreakable.

criterion, fact, gauge, law, measure, model, norm, opinion, principle, proof, rule, standard, test, touchstone. ANT.—chance, conjecture, guess, possibility, probability, supposition.

critical, discerning, discriminating, exact, fastidious, particular; captious, carping, caviling, censorious, disapproving, faultfinding; acute, crucial, decisive, momentous, pressing, urgent. ANT.—cursory, superficial; approving, commendatory, encouraging; insignificant, unimportant.

crooked, abased, adulterated, corrupt, criminal, deceitful, defiled, degraded, depraved, dishonest, fraudulent, lawbreaking, vitiated; angular, bent, bowed, curved, deformed, winding, wry, zig-zag. ANT.—honest, law-abiding, mortal, respectable, direct, regular, straight.

crowd, assembly, horde, masses, mob, multitude, populace, throng; compress, cramp, jostle, press, shove, squeeze, swarm.

crown, apex, chief, crest, head, peak, pinnacle, ridge, summit, top, vertex, vortex, zenith; coronet, tiara; decorate, glorify, honor. ANT.—base, bottom, foot, foundation.

cruel, barbarous, brutal, cold-blooded, ferocious, harsh, inhuman, merciless, pitiless, ruthless, savage, sadistic. ANT.—benevolent, charitable, passionate, considerate, gentle, humane, kind, merciful.

cull, choose, pick out, select, separate. ANT.—refuse, reject.

culmination, acme, apex, climax, conclusion, consummation, crown, end, height, peak, summit, termination, zenith. ANT.—base, beginning, inception.

culprit, criminal, delinquent, felon, malefactor, offender, sinner, transgressor, wrongdoer.

cultivate, civilize, develop, educate, farm, foster, grow, promote, pursue, raise, refine, tend, train, work. ANT.—depress, deteriorate.

culture, breeding, civilization, cultivation, development, education, enlightenment, knowledge, learning, propagation, refinement, scholarship. ANT.—boorishness, ignorance, illiteracy, pretension, stupidity, vulgarity.

cultured, cultivated, educated, enlightened, polished, refined, well-bred. ANT.—crude, ignorant, simple, uncouth.

cunning, calculating, crafty, devious, plotting, scheming, sly; artful, clever, skillful, tricky. ANT.—direct, honest; clumsy, dull, inept, stupid.

curb, bridle, check, constrain, control, hinder, hold back, inhibit, limit, repress, restrain, stop, suppress. ANT.—aid, encourage.

cure, antidote, healing, remedy, restorative.

curious, examining, inquiring, inquisitive, interesting, interrogative, meddling, prying, searching; odd, peculiar, queer, strange, unusual. ANT.—disinterested, dull, incurious, indifferent, unconcerned; common, ordinary.

cursory, careless, desultory, flimsy, frivolous, imperfect, shallow, slight, superficial. ANT.—complete, deep, meticulous, painstaking, perfect, profound, thorough.

curt, abrupt, unexpected, hasty, precipitate, sudden; blunt, brusque, rude; harsh, rough, sharp. ANT.—gradual, smooth; courteous.

curtail, abbreviate, abridge, condense, contract, diminish, lessen, limit, reduce, restrict, retrench, shorten. ANT.—elongate, enlarge, extend, lengthen, prolong.

custom, convention, fashion, habit, manner, mores, practice, precedent, rule, usage, wont. ANT.—departure, deviation, difference, divergence, irregularity.

cynical, contemptuous, distrustful, doubtful, pessimistic, petulant, satirical, testy. ANT.—believing, calm, good-natured, pleasant.

D

dainty, choice, delicate, elegant, exquisite, fastidious, fine, particular, pleasant, pleasing, pretty, pure, rare, refined, soft, sweet, tender. ANT.—coarse, harsh, inferior, repellent, unpleasant, vulgar.

dally, caress, coquet, dawdle, delay, flirt, fondle, idle, linger, philander, prolong, toy. ANT.—be attentive, hurry.

dam, bar, block, choke, clog, hamper, hinder, impede, obstruct, stop, suppress. ANT.—open, release, unblock.

damage, deface, harm, hurt, impair, injure, mar, spoil, wound; detriment, disadvantage, evil, injury, loss, misfortune, spoilation, wrong. ANT.—enhance, improve, mend, perfect, repair; advantage, award, benefit, favor, recompense, reward.

damn, anathematize, ban, banish, condemn, denounce, execrate, punish. ANT.—benefit, bless, exalt, favor, praise, promote.

danger, defenseless, exposure, hazard, insecurity, jeopardy, menace, peril, precariousness, risk. ANT.—carefulness, certainty, confidence, preservation, security, sureness.

daring, adventurous, audacious, bold, brave, chivalrous, courageous, defiant, enterprising, fearless, impudent, intrepid, obtrusive, stout-hearted. ANT.—cautious, chicken-hearted, cowardly, diffident, hesitating, modest, retiring, shy, timid.

dark, black, clouded, dim, gloomy, murky, obscure, opaque, overcast, shadowy; dusky; dismal, gloomy, mournful, somber, sorrowful; evil, sinister, sullen, wicked; hidden, mysterious, mystic, occult, secret. ANT.—bright, clear, distinct, illumined, brilliant, pleasant; apparent, transparent, visible.

daunt, appall, discourage, dishearten, dismay, frighten, intimidate, scare, terrify. ANT.—aid, animate, assist, embolden, encourage, help, stimulate, succor.

dazzle, amaze, astonish, astound, bewilder, blind, confound, daze, impress, overpower. ANT.—befog, dampen, darken.

dead, deceased, defunct, departed, extinct, gone, inanimate, lifeless, obsolete, perished, spiritless. ANT.—alive, animate, being, continuing, enduring, existent, existing, living.

deadly, destructful, destructive, mortal, noxious, poisonous, virulent. ANT.—animating, energizing, invigorating, preservative, stimulating, strengthening, wholesome.

deal, affair, agreement, conspiracy, racket, transaction; allocate, allot, apportion, barter, distribute, give, mete, share. ANT.—hold, keep, receive, retain.

dear, beloved, esteemed, precious, valued; costly, exorbitant, expensive, high-priced, scarce, valuable. ANT.—despised, unwanted, valueless, worthless; cheap, common, inexpensive, low-priced.

debase, abase, adulterate, contaminate, corrupt, defile, degrade, deprave, dishonor, humiliate, impair, lower, pervert, shame, taint, vitiate. ANT.—elevate, enhance, improve, lift, raise, vitalize.

debate, argue, contend, discuss; dispute, reason.

debauch, adulterate, contaminate, corrupt, debase, defile, degrade, pervert, pollute, seduce.

debris, detritus, litter, remains, rubbish, rubble, ruins, sediment, trash, wreckage.

debt, arrears, charge, debit, deficit, liability, obligation. ANT.—asset, excess, overage.

decay, decline, decompose, degenerate, dwindle, ebb, molder, putrefy, rot, spoil, wane, waste. ANT.—bloom, flourish, grow, increase, luxuriate, rise.

deceit, artifice, beguilement, cheat, chicanery, cunning, deceitfulness, deception, delusion, duplicity, falseness, fraud, guile, sham, treachery, trickery, wiliness. ANT.—authenticity, candor, honesty, openness, sincerity, truthfulness, uprightness.

deceive, be dishonest with, beguile, cheat, circumvent, defraud, delude, dupe, entrap, lie to, mislead, outwit, trick. ANT.—advise, aid, assure, be candid, be frank, be truthful, counsel, help, succor.

decent, adequate, becoming, befitting, decorous, fit, proper, respectable, seemly, suitable; chaste, modest. ANT.—inadequate, reprehensible, unsuitable; coarse, improper, indecent, lewd, obscene, vulgar.

deception, beguilement, chicanery, craft, cunning, deceit, deceitfulness, delusion, dishonesty, duplicity, equivocation, fabrication, falsehood, fraud, guile, prevarication, trickery, sham, wiliness. ANT.—candor, frankness, honesty, openness, simplicity, square-dealing, sincerity, truthfulness, veracity.

decide, adjudicate, conclude, determine, end, judge, resolve, settle, terminate. ANT.—defer, delay, postpone, procrastinate, suspend, vacillate, wait, waver.

decision, conclusion, determination, finding, judgment, outcome, resolution, result, verdict. ANT.—deferment, delay, indefiniteness, indetermination, postponement, procrastination.

declaration, affirmation, allegation, announcement, assertion, avowal, proclamation, profession, statement, utterance. ANT.—denial, retraction, silence.

decline, descent, slant, slope; decay, decrease, degenerate, depreciate, deteriorate, diminish, dwindle, ebb, fail, lessen, retrogress, sink, wane, weaken; refuse, reject. ANT.—incline; improve, increase; accept.

decompose, crumble, decay, disintegrate, disperse, grow, improve, increase, multiply.

decorate, adorn, beautify, bedeck, embellish, enrich, garnish, ornament, trim. ANT.—strip, uncover.

decorum, dignity, etiquette, form, propriety, sedateness, seemliness. ANT.—impropriety, indecency, license.

decoy, beguile, entice, entrap, lure, mislead, tempt. ANT.—guide, lead, reveal, show.

decrease, abate, contract, curtail, decline, deduct, diminish, dwindle, lessen, minimize, narrow, reduce, shorten, shrink, subtract, wane. ANT.—add, develop, dilate, enlarge, expand, extend, grow, increase, widen.

decree, adjudicate, arbitrate, command, decide, determine, dictate, direct, judge, ordain, prescribe, sentence; edict, judgment, law, order, ordinance, statute.

decry, belittle, censure, condemn, criticize, depreciate, derogate, discredit, disparage, lower, minimize. ANT.—acclaim, aggrandize, approve, commend, exalt, extol, magnify, praise.

dedicate, apportion, bless, consecrate, devote, enshrine, give, hallow, offer, set apart. ANT.—alienate, desecrate, misapply, misconvert, misuse.

deduce, assume, believe, conclude, deem, derive, infer, judge, presume, reason, suppose, think.

deed, accomplishment, achievement, act, action, commission, exploit, feat, performance, perpetration, transaction. ANT.—failure, omission.

deface, blemish, damage, deform, disfigure, harm, hurt, impair, mar, spoil. ANT.—enhance, mend, repair.

defeat, beat, checkmate, conquer, crush, foil, frustrate, humble, master, overcome, quell, rout, subdue, subjugate, surmount, triumph, vanquish, whip, win. ANT.—capitulate, cede, lose, retreat, surrender, yield.

defect, blemish, deficiency, drawback, error, failure, fault, flaw, impediment, imperfection, incompleteness. ANT.—advantage, completeness, excellence, faultlessness, perfection.

defend, cover, fortify, guard, insure, plead, protect, safeguard, save, screen, secure, shelter, shield; advocate, espouse, justify, maintain, uphold, vindicate. ANT.—abandon, abdicate, attack, desert, forsake, oppose, relinquish, renounce, resign, surrender.

defense, apology, bulwark, excuse, fortress, guard, justification, protection, refuge, safeguard, shelter, shield, vindication. ANT.—abandonment, betrayal, capitulation, desertion, surrender.

defer, adjourn, break up, delay, dissolve, hinder, postpone, procrastinate, prolong, protract, put off, restrain, retard, suspend. ANT.—accelerate, advance, expedite, forward, further, hasten, quicken, stimulated.

deficient, defective, imperfect, inadequate, incomplete, insufficient, lacking, scanty, scarce, short, wanting. ANT.—adequate, ample, perfect, satisfactory, sufficient.

defile, befoul, contaminate, corrupt, debauch, infect, seduce, soil, spoil, stain, sully, taint. ANT.—clean, cleanse, disinfect, glorify, purify, sanctify, wash.

define, ascertain, decide, describe, determine, elucidate, explain, fix, interpret, limit. ANT.—confuse, derange, distort, mix, tangle, twist.

definite, bounded, certain, circumscribed, clear, definitive, determined, exact, explicit, fixed, limited, positive, precise, specific. ANT.—confused, equivocal, indefinite, indistinct, unbounded, vague.

definition, commentary, description, determination, elucidation, explanation, exposition, interpretation, meaning, rendering, restriction, significance, specification, translation. ANT.—absurdity, confusion, nonsense, vagueness.

deflate, empty, exhaust, reduce; humble. ANT.—blow up, fill, inflate, raise; flatter, praise.

deflect, avert, deviate, diverge, divert, swerve, turn, twist. ANT.—hit, strike.

deform, contort, cripple, deface, disfigure, distort, impair, injure, spoil. ANT.—beautify, improve, perfect, repair.

deformed, crippled, disfigured, disjointed, distorted, malformed, misshapen, twisted, unseemly, unsightly. ANT.—graceful, shapely, symmetrical, regular, well-built, well-formed.

defraud, beguile, cheat, deceive, delude, deprive, dupe, fool, gull, hoodwink, inveigle, overreach, rob, swindle, trick. ANT.—assist, befriend, contribute, help, remunerate, requite, support.

defray, adjust, bear, clear, discharge, liquidate, meet, pay, satisfy, settle. ANT.—abjure, deny, disclaim, disown, embezzle, refuse, repudiate.

deft, adept, adroit, agile, assured, clever, dexterous, expert, handy, nimble, skillful. ANT.—awkward, clumsy, inept, maladroit, ungainly.

defy, attack, brave, challenge, dare, disobey, flout, obstruct, oppose, provoke, resist, slight, spurn, thwart. ANT.—accept, cooperate, obey, relent, yield.

degenerate, corrupt, debase, debauch, decay, decline, demoralize, depreciate, deteriorate, diminish, dwindle, sink, weaken, worsen. ANT.—ameliorate, ascend, improve, increase.

degradation, abasement, baseness, debasement, decline, degeneracy, disgrace, dishonor, dismissal, humiliation, meanness, removal, vice. ANT.—admiration, ascendancy, elevation, exaltation, honor, reward, superiority.

degrade, abase, abash, break, corrupt, crush, debase, demote, discredit, humble, humiliate, mortify, shame, subdue, vitiate. ANT.—elevate, exalt, honor, praise.

degree, class, distinction, division, extent, grade, honor, interval, mark, measure, order, qualification, quality, rank, space, stage, station, step, testimony. ANT.—size, space, mass, numbers.

dejection, depression, despair, despondency, discontent, gloom, heaviness, melancholy, pensiveness, sadness, sorrow. ANT.—cheer, delight, exhilaration, gaiety, hilarity, joy, merriment.

delay, defer, postpone, procrastinate; arrest, detain, hinder, impede, prolong, protract, retard, stay; dally, dawdle, linger, loiter, tarry. ANT.—dispatch, expedite, facilitate, hasten, precipitate, quicken.

delectable, agreeable, delightful, delicious, gratifying, luscious, palatable, pleasant, savory, sweet, tasty, toothsome. ANT.—acrid, distasteful, loathsome, nauseating, repulsive, unpalatable, unsavory.

deleterious, bad, baleful, base, damaging, deadly, destructive, evil, harmful, hurtful, immoral, iniquitous, noxious, pernicious, poisonous, sinful, unsound, unwholesome, villainous, wicked. ANT.—advantageous, healthful, helpful, honorable, moral, reputable, salutary.

deliberate, careful, cautious, considered, contemplated, designed, intentional, judged, pondered, prudent, reasoned, slow, studied, thoughtful, unhurried, weighed; consider, consult, contemplate, estimate, examine, heed, meditate, ponder, regard, reflect, study, weigh. ANT.—careless, hasty, imprudent, unintentional; discard, neglect, reject, spurn.

delicate, compassionate, dainty, fastidious, feeble, fine, fragile, frail, gentle, nice, refined, sensitive, sickly, slender, slight, soft, tender,

weak. ANT.—boisterous, coarse, depraved, indelicate, robust, rude, vulgar.

delicious, appetizing, choice, dainty, delectable, delightful, exquisite, gratifying, luscious, luxurious, palatable, pleasing, savory, sweet, tasteful. ANT.—acrid, coarse, disagreeable, distasteful, nauseous, unpalatable, unsavory.

delightful, agreeable, alluring, charming, enjoyable, glad, gratifying, inspiring, merry, pleasant, pleasing, pleasurable, satisfactory. ANT.—depressing, mournful, offensive, painful, wearisome.

delirium, aberration, dementia, frenzy, hallucination, insanity, lunacy, madness, mania, raving, wandering. ANT.—normality, reason, saneness, sanity, steadiness.

deliver, convey, give, hand over, impart, surrender, transfer, yield; announce, communicate, impart, proclaim, pronounce; discharge, emancipate, free, liberate, redeem, release, rescue, save. ANT.—confine, withhold; betray, capture, imprison, restrain, restrict.

delusion, chimera, deception, error, fallacy, fantasy, hallucination, illusion, mirage, misconception, phantom. ANT.—actuality, certainty, fact, materiality, reality, substance, truth.

demand, ask, beg, beseech, charge, crave, exact, implore, inquire, levy, order, request, require, seek, solicit, supplicate. ANT.—give, offer, present, reply, tender.

demeanor, air, appearance, attitude, bearing, behavior, conduct, manner. ANT.—misbehavior, unmannerliness.

demented, crazy, frenzied, insane, irrational, lunatic, maniacal. ANT.—lucid, normal, rational, reasonable, sane.

demise, alienation, conveyance, death, decease, end, transfer. ANT.—birth, non-alienation.

demolish, annihilate, destroy, devastate, dismantle, eradicate, exterminate, extinguish, level, obliterate, overturn, ravage, raze, ruin, wreck. ANT.—construct, embellish, improve, mend, restore, uphold.

demonstration, certainty, conclusion, consequence, corroboration, deduction, evidence, exhibition, explanation, exposition, induction, manifestation, presentation, proof, show, substantiation, verification. ANT.—concealment, confusion, distortion, falsification, misrepresentation.

demoralize, confuse, corrupt, disconcert, discourage, disorganize, incapacitate, pervert, undermine. ANT.—encourage, exalt, hearten, inspire, invigorate, organize.

demur, balk, delay, disapprove, dissent, falter, hesitate, object, pause, scruple, vacillate, waver. ANT.—accept, agree, assent, consent, decide, persevere, proceed.

demure, coy, decorous, diffident, modest, prim, prudish, sedate, shy, sober, staid. ANT.—impudent, indecorous, shameless, wanton.

denote, connote, express, imply, indicate, intend, mark, mean, signify, specify.

denounce, accuse, arraign, blame, censure, charge, condemn, curse, decry, indict, reprehend, reprimand, reproach, reprove, scold, upbraid. ANT.—applaud, commend, praise.

dense, close, compact, compressed, concentrated, crowded, impenetrable, thick; dull, obtuse, slow, solid, stupid, substantial. ANT.—dispersed, open, rare, scattered, sparse, thin; clever, quick.

deny, contradict, contravene, gainsay, oppose, refute; abjure, disavow, disclaim, disown, forbid, renounce; refuse, repudiate, withhold. ANT.—admit, affirm, agree, assert, concede, confirm.

depart, abandon, decamp, decease, desert, deviate, die, forsake, go, leave, quit, retire, set

out, vanish, vary, withdraw. ANT.—abide, dwell, linger, remain, stay, tarry.

dependable, certain, reliable, sure, trustworthy, trusty. ANT.—questionable, uncertain, unreliable, untrustworthy.

dependent, collateral, conditional, consequent, contingent, relative, reliant, relying, subject. ANT.—absolute, autonomous, categorical, independent, unconditional.

depict, characterize, delineate, describe, draw, illustrate, paint, picture, portray, sketch. ANT.—caricature, confound, confuse, distort.

deplete, diminish, drain, empty, exhaust, lessen, weaken. ANT.—augment, enlarge, fill, increase, strengthen.

deplore, be sorry (for), complain, cry (for), deprecate, fret, grieve, lament, mourn, wail, weep. ANT.—boast, cheer, delight, rejoice, revel.

deportment, air, bearing, behavior, carriage, comportment, conduct, demeanor, form, manner, mien, style.

deposit, hoard, lay down, leave, pledge, place, save, store; precipitate; sediment.

depravity, corruption, degeneracy, depravation, deterioration, immorality, sinfulness, wickedness. ANT.—honor, integrity, justice, morality, purity, virtue.

deprecate, condemn, deplore, disapprove, protest, regret. ANT.—approve, commend, endorse.

depreciate, decline, decrease, degenerate, deteriorate, diminish, dwindle, weaken; decry, denounce, despise, detract, disparage, underrate, undervalue. ANT.—increase, magnify, raise; approve, commend, extol, praise.

depress, abase, debase, degrade, deject, discourage, disgrace, dispirit, humble, humiliate, lower, sink. ANT.—cheer, comfort, encourage, praise, stimulate.

depression, despair, despondency, gloom, hopelessness, melancholy, misery, pessimism. ANT.—business boom; contentment, elation, hope, lightheartedness, optimism.

deprive, abridge, bereave, debar, depose, despoil, dispossess, divest, rob, separate, strip, take. ANT.—assist, confer, endow, enrich, repay, restore.

derelict, abandoned, neglected, wrecked; delinquent, negligent; bum, outcast, tramp, vagrant.

derision, contempt, disdain, disregard, disrespect, insult, irony, jeering, mockery, raillery, ridicule, sarcasm, scorn, slight, slur, sneering. ANT.—adulation, flattery, regard, respect, reference.

derivation, beginning, birth, cause, commencement, cradle, foundation, fountain, inception, nucleus, origin, rise, root, source, spring. ANT.—consequence, end, harvest, issue, outgrowth, termination.

derogatory, belittling, defamatory, deprecatory, disparaging, lessening. ANT.—favoring, helping, lauding, praising.

descent, debasement, degradation, decline; declivity, fall, slant, slope; ancestry, genesis, lineage, origin, pedigree. ANT.—ascension, ascent, climb, elevation, mountain, rise.

describe, characterize, define, delineate, depict, explain, express, illustrate, narrate, picture, portray, recite, recount, relate, represent. ANT.—caricature, confuse, deceive, distort, exaggerate, misrepresent.

desecrate, abuse, debase, defile, misuse, pervert, pollute, profane, secularize. ANT.—cleanse, consecrate, hallow, purify, sanctify.

desert, abandon, abdicate, abjure, forsake, leave, quit, relinquish, secede; surrender, vacate; wasteland, wilderness; due, merit, reward.

ANT.—continue, remain; garden, oasis, pasture; penalty, retribution.

deserve, be worthy of, earn, have right to, merit, win. ANT.—undeserving, unworthy of.

design, decoration, delineation, diagram, draft, drawing, object, outline, pattern, picture, plan, project, sketch; artfulness, contrivance, cunning, end, intention, purpose, scheme. ANT.—accident, chance; candor, sincerity.

designate, appoint, characterize, choose, denominate, denote, indicate, manifest, name, reveal, select, show, signify, specify. ANT.—conceal, divert, falsify.

designing, astute, crafty, cunning, scheming, sly, tricky, underhanded, unscrupulous. ANT.—candid, frank, honest, naïve, open.

desire, affection, ambition, appetite, ardor, aspiration, concupiscence, coveting, craving, eagerness, hungering, inclination, longing, wish, yearning, zeal. ANT.—abhorrence, aversion, detestation, distaste, repulsion.

desirable, acceptable, advisable, beneficial, delightful, enviable, judicious, pleasing, profitable, proper, valuable, wanted, worthy. ANT.—baneful, detrimental, harmful, injurious, noxious.

desist, abstain, arrest, bar, cease, check, discontinue, drop, end, halt, impede, obstruct, quit, relinquish, seal, stop, terminate. ANT.—continue, endure, proceed, retain, wait.

desolate, abandoned, alone, bare, bereaved, bleak, dejected, deserted, dismal, dreary, forgotten, forlorn, forsaken, inhospitable, lonely, miserable, secluded, solitary, uninhabited, unpeopled, waste, wild. ANT.—cultivated, enjoyable, fertile, inhabited, pleasant, teeming.

despair, dejection, depression, desperation, despondency, discouragement, gloom, hopelessness, pessimism, sadness. ANT.—anticipation, confidence, elation, faith, optimism.

desperate, audacious, bold, careless, critical, despondent, determined, extreme, foolhardy, frantic, furious, hopeless, irretrievable, mad, reckless, wild. ANT.—cautious, composed, confident, hopeful, peaceful, satisfied.

despicable, abject, base, contemptible, corrupt, cowardly, depraved, low, lying, malicious, nasty, pitiful, mean, scurrilous, shameless, sordid, vile, vulgar, worthless. ANT.—exalted, honorable, noble, praiseworthy, respectable.

despise, abhor, abominate, condemn, denounce, deride, detest, disdain, dislike, hold in contempt, loathe, scorn, spurn. ANT.—admire, applaud, cherish, commend, love.

despondent, dejected, depressed, despairing, disconsolate, disheartened, dispirited, doleful, low, melancholy, sad. ANT.—buoyant, ebullient, elated, happy, joyous.

despotic, absolute, arbitrary, arrogant, autocratic, cruel, tyrannical, tyrannous. ANT.—conditional, constitutional, limited.

destination, bourn, design, doom, end, fate, goal, intention, location, objective, point, port, purpose, terminus.

destiny, chance, conclusion, condition, decree, doom, end, fate, finality, fortune, judgment, lot, necessity, outcome, portion, predestination, predetermination. ANT.—choice, freedom, volition, will.

destitution, beggary, distress, indigence, lack, need, pauperism, penury, poverty, privation, want. ANT.—abundance, affluence, opulence, prosperity, security.

destroy, annihilate, consume, demolish, devastate, dismantle, dispel, eradicate, exterminate, extirpate, kill, obliterate, overthrow, ravage,

raze, ruin, slaughter, terminate. ANT.—construct, fabricate, invigorate, renew, strengthen.

destruction, abolishment, annihilation, cataclysm, demolition, desolation, devastation, downfall, eradication, extermination, extinction, extirpation, fall, havoc, obliteration, overthrow, subversion. ANT.—recovery, renewal, restitution, restoration, revival.

desultory, abnormal, cursory, discursive, erratic, flighty, irregular, loose, rambling, superficial, unsettled, wandering. ANT.—constant, firm, methodical, stable, unalterable.

detach, disconnect, disengage, disjoin, disunite, loosen, part, remove, separate, sever, unfasten, untie, withdraw. ANT.—adhere, bind, coalesce, link, merge.

detail, appoint, assign, describe, itemize, narrate, particularize, relate, report, tell; account, article, description, item, minutia, narrative, particular, portion, recital, specification, trifle. ANT.—conceal, reserve, stifle, suppress; entirety, whole.

detain, arrest, bar, check, confine, curb, delay, hinder, impede, keep, limit, prevent, repress, restrain, retain, retard, stay, stop, withhold. ANT.—free, hasten, liberate, release, precipitate.

detect, apprehend, ascertain, catch, determine, disclose, discover, espy, expose, ferret out, find, identify, perceive, uncover, unearth, unmask. ANT.—blunder, miss, omit, overlook, pass by.

deter, discourage, disincline, dissuade, frighten, hinder, prevent, stop, warn. ANT.—encourage, foster, promote, stimulate, urge.

deteriorate, atrophy, collapse, corrode, decay, decline, decompose, discolor, disintegrate, ebb, erode, mold, oxidize, recede, retrogress, rot, rust, wane, wear. ANT.—improve, refurbish, renew.

determine, affect, ascertain, bound, conclude, decide, define, end, find out, fix, influence, limit, resolve, restrict, settle, specify. ANT.—doubt, falter, hesitate, vacillate, waver.

determined, decided, firm, fixed, immovable, resolute, stable, stubborn, unalterable, unwavering, willful. ANT.—irresolute, fluctuating, uncertain, undecided, wavering.

detest, abhor, abominate, despise, dislike, execrate, hate, loathe. ANT.—admire, appreciate, cherish, love, respect.

detour, by-pass, deviation, digression, side road. ANT.—direct route, highway.

detraction, aspersion, backbiting, calumny, defamation, depreciation, derogation, diminution, disparagement, libel, slander, vilification. ANT.—admiration, commendation, praise, recommendation, respect.

detriment, bane, damage, deterioration, disadvantage, evil, harm, hurt, impairment, inconvenience, infliction, injury, loss, misfortune, wrong. ANT.—advantage, assistance, benefit, favor, gain, profit.

devastate, demolish, desolate, despoil, pillage, ruin, sack, strip, waste, wreck. ANT.—benefit, cultivate, enrich, preserve, restore.

develop, amplify, cultivate, disclose, disentangle, enlarge, evolve, exhibit, expand, extend, grow, mature, uncover, unfold, unravel. ANT.—compress, conceal, contract, hide, restrict.

development, disclosure, expansion, evolution, growth, improvement, maturing, progress, project, subdivision, unfolding. ANT.—compression, curtailment, decline, degeneration.

deviate, bend, deflect, depart from, digress, diverge, divert, shift, shunt, sidetrack, stray, swerve, wander. ANT.—continue, direct, persevere, persist, remain.

device, agent, channel, instrument, means, medium, vehicle; apparatus, artifice, contrivance, design, gadget, invention, machine; plan, ruse, scheme, stratagem. ANT.— hindrance, impediment, obstruction.

devious, circuitous, crooked, indirect, mazy, roundabout, swerving, tortuous, wandering, winding; crooked, cunning, tricky. ANT.—direct, straight; honest, straightforward.

devise, arrange, bequeath, concoct, contrive, invent, make, plan, prepare, will. ANT.—disarrange, fumble, muddle.

devoid, bare, destitute, empty, lacking, unendowed, unprovided, void, wanting, without. ANT.—abundant, complete, full, possessing, replete.

devolve, alienate, authorize, be handed down, commission, consign, depute, deliver, fall (upon).

devote, allot, apply, apportion, appropriate, assign, attend, consign, dedicate, study. ANT.—misappropriate, misuse, pervert, squander, waste.

devotion, adherence, ardor, consecration, dedication, devoutness, earnestness, fidelity, intensity, observance, piety, religiousness, sincerity, zeal. ANT.—alienation, apathy, aversion, indifference, neglect, unfaithfulness.

devour, bolt, consume, destroy, eat greedily, gobble, gorge, prey upon, swallow (up), waste. ANT.—disgorge, vomit.

devout, devotional, earnest, fervent, godly, holy, moral, pietistic, pious, religious, reverent, righteous, sacred, sincere, spiritual. ANT.—atheistic, impious, profane, secular, worldly.

dexterity, ability, adroitness, aptitude, aptness, art, capability, cleverness, deftness, facility, handiness, skill. ANT.—awkwardness, blundering, clumsiness, ineptitude.

diagram, blueprint, chart, drawing, map, outline, plan, sketch.

dialect, accent, idiom, jargon, patois, provincialism, vernacular. ANT.—official language, standard speech.

dictate, command, decree, direct, order, prescribe. ANT.—ask, beg, follow, obey, plead.

dictatorial, arbitrary, arrogant, dogmatic, domineering, haughty, imperious, overbearing, tyrannical. ANT.—acquiescent, docile, obsequious, submissive, subservient, passive.

diction, choice of words, enunciation, phraseology, pronunciation, vocal expression.

die, cease, decay, decease, decline, depart, expire, fade, languish, pass away, perish, recede, sink, vanish, wane, wither; mold, stamp. ANT.—begin, endure, flourish, grow, live, survive.

difference, deviation, discrepancy, disparity, dissimilarity, distinction, divergence, inequality, separation, variation, variety; disagreement, discord, dissension, estrangement. ANT.—congruity, similarity, uniformity; agreement, harmony.

different, contrary, differing, discordant, dissimilar, distinct, distinctive, divers, diverse, heterogeneous, incongruous, unlike, variant, various. ANT.—alike, congruous, harmonious, homogeneous, same.

differentiate, contrast, discriminate, distinguish, isolate, particularize, separate. ANT.—confound, confuse, group, mingle.

difficult, arduous, complex, complicated, demanding, enigmatical, hard, intricate, involved, laborious, obscure, perplexing, puzzling, rigid, toilsome, troublesome, trying, unmanageable, unyielding. ANT.—easy, facile, pleasant, simple, tranquil.

difficulty, annoyance, anxiety, argument, complication, contention, dilemma, discouragement, dispute, distress, embarrassment, entanglement, impediment, intricacy, obstacle, obstruction, oppression, perplexity, problem, trouble, worry. ANT.—comfort, facility, felicity, flexibility, pleasure, satisfaction.

diffident, bashful, hesitant, modest, shrinking, shy, timid. ANT.—bold, brash, brazen.

diffuse, copious, discursive, repetitive, tedious, tiresome, wordy. ANT.—abbreviated, brief, restricted.

diffusion, broadcasting, circulation, distribution, dispersion, spreading. ANT.—collection, restriction, suppression.

dignify, adorn, advance, award, decorate, elevate, ennoble, exalt, extol, glorify, honor, magnify, prefer, proclaim, promote, revere. ANT.—belittle, degrade, demean, humiliate, slander.

dignity, decency, decorum, eminence, grace, greatness, propriety, stateliness, station, worth. ANT.—degradation, lowliness.

digress, bend, deflect, depart, deviate, diverge, divert, ramble, sidetrack, stray, turn aside, wander. ANT.—continue, persevere, persist, preserve.

dilapidated, crumbling, decayed, depreciating, deteriorating, sagging. ANT.—rebuilt, renewed, restored.

dilate, broaden, distend, enlarge, expand, extend, increase, magnify, open, spread, stretch, swell, widen. ANT.—abridge, compress, contract, diminish, reduce.

dilemma, difficulty, fix, perplexity, plight, predicament, problem, quandary. ANT.—advantage, freedom, solution.

diligence, alertness, application, assiduity, attention, care, carefulness, earnestness, heed, industry, intensity, keenness, perseverance, quickness. ANT.—ennui, indolence, laziness, lethargy, slowness.

dilute, reduced, thin, watery, weak. ANT.—concentrated, rich, strong, thick.

dim, blurred, clouded, dull, faint, gloomy, indefinite, indistinct, misty, mysterious, obscure, shaded, shadowy. ANT.—bright, brilliant, clear, distinct.

dimension, amplitude, area, bulk, capacity, extent, magnitude, measurement, size.

diminish, abate, abridge, assuage, compress, contract, curtail, decrease, degrade, dwindle, impair, lessen, lower, minimize, moderate, reduce, shorten, shrink. ANT.—amplify, enlarge, increase, intensify, magnify.

din, clamor, clangor, clash, clatter, hubbub, noise, racket, row, tumult, uproar. ANT.—quiet, silence, stillness.

diplomatic, adroit, artful, courteous, discreet, judicious, politic, tactful. ANT.—blunt, gruff, rude, tactless.

direct, aim, point, train; conduct, control, demonstrate, explain, govern, guide, head, inform, instruct, lead, manage, order, regulate, supervise, teach, usher. ANT.—deceive, delude, misdirect, misguide.

direction, address, aim, course, end, goal, inclination, line, tendency, way; administration, government, leadership, management, superintendence; command, control, guidance, instruction, order.

dirty, dingy, discolored, filthy, foul, grimy, muddy, soiled, squalid; indecent, obscene, sordid; base, contemptible, despicable, low, mean, shabby. ANT.—clean, immaculate, spotless; pure, wholesome.

disability, decrepitude, defect, disqualification, feebleness, forfeiture, handicap, impotence, inability, inadequacy, incompetence, infirmity, powerlessness, unfitness, weakness. ANT.—ability, capability, capacity, power, strength.

disadvantage, block, check, detriment, difficulty, drawback, evil, harm, hindrance, hurt, prejudice, stumbling, block. ANT.—advantage, assistance, benefit, profit, utility.

disaffect, alienate, disdain, dislike, disorder, estrange.

disagree, argue, clash, combat, contend, differ, dispute, dissent, fight, oppose, quarrel, vary. ANT.—agree, coincide, concur, harmonize.

disappear, cease, depart, dissolve, evaporate, fade, melt, vanish, withdraw. ANT.—appear, materialize.

disappoint, baffle, betray, deceive, delude, fail, foil, frustrate, thwart, vex. ANT.—assist, befriend, please, support, relieve.

disapproval, blame, censure, condemnation, depreciation, disapprobation, dislike, disparagement, odium. ANT.—approval, sanction.

disaster, adversity, calamity, casualty, cataclysm, catastrophe, evil, misadventure, mischance, misfortune, mishap, tragedy. ANT.—advantage, fortune, privilege, prosperity.

disband, break up, demobilize, disperse, dissolve. ANT.—assemble, mobilize, unite.

disburse, expend, distribute, pay, settle, spend. ANT.—collect, deposit, receive, retain, save.

discard, abandon, cancel, discharge, dismiss, divorce, eliminate, reject, repudiate, scrap, shed. ANT.—adopt, embrace, keep, retain.

discern, descry, detect, discover, discriminate, distinguish, espy, know, observe, perceive, recognize, see, understand. ANT.—disregard, neglect, omit, overlook, slight.

discerning, acute, critical, discriminating, exacting, fastidious, particular, sharp-sighted, shrewd. ANT.—cursory, shallow, superficial, uncritical.

discernment, acumen, discrimination, insight, judgment, penetration, perspicuity. ANT.—obtuseness.

discharge, acquit, clear, dismiss, eject, emit, exile, expel, fire, free, oust, pay, perform, project, release, retire, settle, shoot. ANT.—load, hire, imprison, retain.

disciple, adherent, devotee, follower, votary.

discipline, control, order, regulation, restraint; drill, instruction, method, rule, training; chastisement, correction, punishment. ANT.—chaos, confusion, disorder, mutiny, turbulence.

disclaim, abandon, deny, disallow, disavow, disown, reject, renounce, repudiate, retract. ANT.—acknowledge, claim, own, recognize.

disclose, acknowledge, betray, concede, declare, discover, divulge, expose, grant, inform, reveal, show, tell, uncover, unfold, unmask, unveil, utter. ANT.—cloak, conceal, cover, deceive, withhold.

disconsolate, broken-hearted, cheerless, dejected, depressed, despondent, dismal, doleful, gloomy, inconsolable, lugubrious, melancholy, mournful, sad, sorrowful. ANT.—cheerful, glad, happy, joyous, merry.

discontent, disappointment, disillusionment, dissatisfaction, frustration, uneasiness, vexation. ANT.—content, peace, satisfaction.

discord, animosity, clash, confusion, contention, difference, disagreement, disharmony, dissension, dissonance, disturbance, harshness, quarreling, variance, wrangling. ANT.—agreement, amity, concord, harmony, peace.

discount, allowance, deduction, drawback, loss, rebate, reduction, refund. ANT.—increase, increment, premium, rise.

discourage, block, check, dampen, depress, deter, dishearten, dispirit, dissuade, hamper, hinder, impede, obstruct, oppose, prevent, resist, restrain, retard, thwart. ANT.—assist, encourage, expedite, facilitate, promote.

discourteous, abusive, blunt, boorish, disrespectful, forward, gruff, ill-mannered, impolite, impudent, insolent, rough, rude, surly, uncivil, ungracious, unmannerly, unpolished, vulgar. ANT.—civil, courteous, genteel, polished, polite.

discover, ascertain, contrive, descry, detect, discern, disclose, elicit, expose, find, find out, invent, learn, manifest, realize, reveal, uncover, unearth. ANT.—cover, hide, mask, screen, suppress.

discreet, attentive, careful, cautious, circumspect, considerate, discerning, discriminating, judicious, prudent, sensible, serious, thoughtful, watchful, wise. ANT.—indiscreet, injudicious, rash, thoughtless.

discrepancy, contrariety, difference, disagreement, inconsistency, variance. ANT.—accordance, agreement, concurrence, harmony.

discretion, carefulness, caution, circumspection, finesse, foresight, judgment, prudence, sagacity, thoughtfulness. ANT.—foolishness, imprudence, rashness, recklessness, thoughtlessness.

discrimination, acumen, acuteness, care, caution, circumspection, differentiation, discernment, distinction, foresight, forethought, heed, perception, perspicacity, prudence, sagacity, vigilance, wisdom. ANT.—carelessness, imprudence, negligence, rashness, senselessness.

discuss, analyze, argue, confer, consult, controvert, converse, debate, deliberate, dispute, examine, explain.

disdain, arrogance, contempt, contumely, derision, detestation, haughtiness, pride, scorn, scornfulness, superciliousness. ANT.—admiration, esteem, regard, respect, reverence.

disease, affliction, ailment, complaint, disorder, distemper, illness, infirmity, malady, plague, pestilence, sickness, unhealthiness, unsoundness. ANT.—health, healthiness, soundness, sturdiness, vigor.

disengage, clear, detach, disentangle, extricate, free, liberate, loose, loosen, release, separate, unravel, withdraw. ANT.—attach, bind, fasten, tighten, unite.

disfigure, blemish, damage, deface, deform, distort, injure, mar, mutilate, spoil. ANT.—adorn, decorate, repair, restore.

disgrace, abasement, baseness, disfavor, dishonor, disrepute, humiliation, infamy, ignominy, mortification, odium, opprobrium, reproach, scandal, shame. ANT.—dignity, exaltation, glory, honor, renown, respect.

disguise, camouflage, change, cloak, conceal, cover, dissemble, feign, hide, mask, masquerade, pretend, screen, secrete, shroud, suppress, veil, withhold. ANT.—bare, disclose, divulge, expose, reveal, uncover.

disgust, abhorrence, abomination, aversion, detestation, dislike, distaste, hatred, loathing, nausea, repugnance, resentment, revulsion. ANT.—admiration, approbation, esteem, respect, reverence.

dishonest, cheating, corrupt, corruptible, crooked, debased, deceitful, false, fraudulent, lying, perfidious, unsound, unscrupulous, untrue, untrustworthy, venal, vitiated. ANT.—honest, scrupulous, trustworthy.

dislike, abhorrence, antipathy, aversion, disaffection, disapproval, disinclination, distaste, hatred, loathing, repugnance, repulsion. ANT.—affection, attachment, devotion.

disloyal, apostate, disaffected, faithless, false, perfidious, subversive, traitorous, treacherous, treasonable, unfaithful, unpatriotic. ANT.—faithful, loyal, true, worthy.

dismal, bleak, cheerless, dark, depressing, dingy, direful, doleful, dolorous, dreadful, dreary, dull, funereal, gloomy, horrible, horrid, melancholy, sad, somber, sorrowful, unhappy. ANT.—bright, cheerful, joyous, pleasant.

dismantle, demolish, raze, strip, take apart, take down. ANT.—assemble, build, construct, raise.

dismay, alarm, anxiety, apprehension, awe, consternation, discouragement, dread, fear, fright, horror, misgiving, trepidation. ANT.—assurance, confidence, courage, intrepidity.

dismiss, banish, bounce, decline, depose, discard, discharge, exile, expel, fire, oust, remove, repel, repudiate, suspend. ANT.—accept, recall, retain.

disobey, defy, disregard, ignore, infringe, invade, rebel, resist, transgress, violate. ANT.—accept, obey, submit.

disorder, anarchy, bustle, chaos, confusion, disarrangement, disorganization, disturbance, illness, indisposition, irregularity, jumble, muddle, riot, sickness, tumult. ANT.—order, organization, system, vigor.

disorderly, chaotic, confused, disheveled, irregular, lawless, tumultuous, unrestrained, unruly. ANT.—calm, disciplined, law-abiding, neat, orderly.

disparage, asperse, belittle, decry, defame, deprecate, depreciate, derogate, discredit, dishonor, lower, minimize, traduce, underestimate, underrate, undervalue. ANT.—aggrandize, commend, exalt, magnify, praise, sanction.

dispatch, accelerate, conclude, expedite, hasten, kill, perform, send, speed, transmit. ANT.—hold, retain, slow.

dispel, banish, diffuse, dismiss, disperse, disseminate, dissipate, dissolve, rout, scatter, spread, strew. ANT.—accumulate, amass, assemble, collect, gather, increase.

dispense, administer, allocate, allot, apply, apportion, appropriate, assign, carry out, distribute, dole out, execute, mete, sell; excuse, exempt, release. ANT.—absorb, keep, retain, withhold.

disperse, diffuse, dispel, disseminate, dissipate, dissolve, distribute, fade, scatter, separate, sow, strew. ANT.—amass, assemble, collect, concentrate, gather.

displace, confuse, crowd out, depose, derange, disarrange, discharge, dislodge, dismiss, displant, dispossess, disturb, eject, jumble, mislay, misplace, mix, remove, shift, unseat, unsettle, uproot. ANT.—arrange, classify, group, sort.

display, exhibit expose, flaunt, open, parade, reveal, show, unfold; evince, manifest; array, demonstration, exhibition, flourish, layout, manifestation, ostentation, show. ANT.—conceal, cover, disguise, hide, suppress.

displease, anger, annoy, antagonize, bother, chagrin, disappoint, disgruntle, disgust, dissatisfy, disturb, exasperate, gall, harass, irritate, mortify, pester, pique, plague, provoke, tantalize, taunt, tease, trouble, vex, worry. ANT.—delight, gratify, pacify, propitiate, satisfy.

dispose, adapt, adjust, arrange, bestow, classify, conform, give, locate, order, place, regulate, settle. ANT.—conceal, disarrange, disorder, displace, retain.

disposition, bent, bias, character, inclination, leaning, make-up, nature, personality, proclivity, temper, temperament, tendency; adjustment, arrangement, control, disposal.

dispute, altercation, argument, contention, contest, controversy, debate, denial, difference, disagreement, discord, discussion, dissension, estrangement, feud, quarrel, questioning, squabble, variance. ANT.—agreement, concord, harmony, unison.

disqualify, bar, disable, disenfranchise, incapacitate, prohibit, remove from contention. ANT.—accept, fit, quality.

disregard, contemn, disobey, ignore, neglect, omit, overlook, skip, slight. ANT.—include, notice, regard.

disrespectful, contemptuous, derisive, discourteous, disparaging, flippant, impertinent, impious, impolite, insolent, insulting, irreverent, uncivil. ANT.—courteous, respectful.

dissatisfaction, disappointment, disapproval, discomfort, discontent, disgruntlement, dislike, displeasure, distaste, malcontentment, uneasiness. ANT.—contentment, gratification, happiness, recompense, satisfaction.

dissect, analyze, anatomize, cut up, examine. ANT.—assemble, synthesize.

dissent, censure, condemn, conflict, contend, differ, disagree, disapprove, disclaim, dispute, except, oppose, vary. ANT.—agree, commend, concur, endorse, sanction.

dissertation, commentary, composition, discourse, essay, homily, lecture, sermon, study, theme, thesis, tract.

dissipate, debauch, diffuse, disperse, lavish, scatter, spread, squander, waste. ANT.—absorb, accumulate, conserve, preserve, save.

dissolve, destroy, disappear, disintegrate, disorganize, divide, evanesce, evaporate, fade, render, thaw, vanish. ANT.—assemble, concentrate, unite.

distant, afar, apart, faint, far, indistinct, remove, removed, separated; aloof, cold, cool, haughty, indifferent, reserved, shy, stiff, unfriendly. ANT.—close, near, nigh, cordial, friendly, sympathetic, warm.

distasteful, disagreeable, disgusting, displeasing, loathsome, nauseating, objectionable, obnoxious, offensive, repellent, repugnant, repulsive, unpalatable, unsavory. ANT.—agreeable, delectable, pleasing, savory, welcome.

distend, blow up, dilate, expand, grow, inflate, stretch, swell, tumefy. ANT.—constrict, contract, narrow, shrink.

distinct, apparent, clear, definite, evident, exact, lucid, manifest, obvious, plain, precise, unmistakable, visible. ANT.—ambiguous, indefinite, obscure, unclear, vague.

distinction, attribute, characteristic, feature, peculiarity, property, quality, trait; acumen, acuteness, clearness, discernment, discrimination, elevation, eminence, judgment, note, rank, superiority. ANT.—amalgamation, combination; inferiority, mediocrity, sameness.

distinguished, brilliant, celebrated, conspicuous, eminent, extraordinary, famous, glorious, great, illustrious, noble, noted, prominent, renowned, well-known. ANT.—common, obscure, ordinary, unknown, unobtrusive.

distort, bend, contort, deface, deform, disfigure, falsify, gnarl, impair, mangle, misconstrue, misshape, pervert, slant. ANT.—align, balance, explain, straighten.

distract, bewilder, confound, confuse, daze, derange, disorder, embarrass, mislead, mystify, perplex. ANT.—allay, assure, mitigate, pacify, reassure.

distress, adversity, agony, anguish, calamity, catastrophe, danger, grief, hardship, misadventure, misery, misfortune, need, pain, perplexity, sorrow, suffering, torment, trouble, unhappiness, wretchedness. ANT.—comfort, joy, relief, satisfaction.

distribution, allotment, apportionment, arrangement, classification, deal, dispensation, disposal, division, dole, partition. ANT.—collection, hoard, maintenance, retention, storage.

distrust, disbelief, doubt, misgiving, mistrust, skepticism, suspicion, uncertainty. ANT.—belief, certainty, conviction, faith, trust.

disturb, agitate, annoy, arouse, bother, confuse, derange, disarrange, discompose, disconcert, disorder, displace, distress, interrupt, perplex, perturb, rouse, trouble, unbalance, unsettle, vex, worry. ANT.—compose, pacify, quiet, settle, soothe.

divergent, branching, contrary, deviating, differing, disagreeing, diverse, separating, varying. ANT.—convergent, identical, parallel, similar.

divest, bare, denude, deprive, disrobe, peel, strip, unclothe, uncover, undress. ANT.—clothe, cover, invest, restore (property).

diverse, contrary, different, dissimilar, distinct, divergent, diversified, heterogeneous, unlike, variant; divers, miscellaneous, numerous, several, sundry, various. ANT.—alike, identical, same, selfsame, similar.

divide, detach, disconnect, disengage, disjoin, dissolve, disunite, partition, separate, sever, split, sunder; allot, apportion, assign, dispense, distribute. ANT.—combine, convene, fasten, join, unite.

divine, celestial, consecrated, godlike, heavenly, holy, sacred, sanctified, spiritual, superhuman, supernatural, transcendent, venerable. ANT.—blasphemous, diabolical, impious, profane, wicked.

division, allotment, compartment, department, detachment, difference, discord, disunion, partition, portion, share. ANT.—concord, indivisibility, oneness, union, unity.

divulge, betray, communicate, describe, disclose, discover, expose, impart, inform, relate, reveal, show, tell, uncover, unveil. ANT.—cloak, conceal, disguise, hide, obscure.

do, accomplish, achieve, complete, conclude, consummate, effect, enact, execute, finish, fulfill, perform, terminate; carry on, conduct, discharge, transact; make, produce, work; commit, perpetrate. ANT.—evade, shirk.

docile, amenable, compliant, gentle, manageable, meek, mild, obedient, pliable, pliant, submissive, tame, tractable, yielding. ANT.—determined, mulish, obstinate, stubborn, unyielding.

doctrine, belief, conviction, creed, cult, dogma, faith, gospel, opinion, persuasion, precept, principle, propaganda, proposition, religion, rule, teaching, tenet, theory.

document, account, archive, certificate, chronicle, deed, manuscript, notation, paper, record, script, statement, writing.

dodge, avoid, elude, equivocate, escape, evade, quibble, side-step. ANT.—approach, confront, encounter, face, meet.

dogmatic, arrogant, authoritarian, dictatorial, doctrinaire, domineering, imperious, immovable, magisterial, opinionated, overbearing, peremptory, positive, unchangeable; authoritative, doctrinal. ANT.—fluctuating, indecisive, questioning, skeptical, vacillating.

dole, allot, apportion, dispense, distribute; allotment, alms, apportionment, benefit, distribution, division, gratuity, pittance, portion, share.

domestic, domesticated, gentle, household, internal, native, tame. ANT.—foreign, savage, untamed, wild.

domicile, abode, accommodations, apartment, dwelling, habitation, home, lodging, residence, quarters.

dominant, aggressive, authoritative, commanding, controlling, domineering, governing, imperative, imperious, lordly, predominant, prevailing, ruling. ANT.—humble, non-aggressive, obscure, retiring, subordinate.

dominion, ascendancy, authority, control, government, jurisdiction, sway; commonwealth, country, district, empire, region, territory. ANT.—bondage, dependency, inferiority, subjection, submission.

donation, benefaction, benefit, bequest, boon, bounty, charity, contribution, endowment, favor, gift, grant, gratuity, largess, present, provision, subscription. ANT.—deprivation, loss.

done, achieved, completed, concluded, consummated, ended, executed, finished, over, performed, solved. ANT.—inchoate, incomplete, partial, raw, unfinished.

dormant, inactive, inert, quiescent, sleeping, unconscious, unoccupied. ANT.—active, awake, industrious, occupied, working.

double, counterpart, duplicate, stand-in, twin, understudy; duplicate, enlarge, repeat; bipartite, coupled, dual, duplex, paired, twin, twofold. ANT.—lone, single, unique.

doubt, agnosticism, concern, disbelief, distrust, dubiousness, hesitancy, hesitation, incredulity, indecision, irresolution, misgiving, mistrust, perplexity, qualm, quandary, question, scruple, skepticism, suspense, suspicion, unbelief, uncertainty. ANT.—assurance, belief, certainty, conviction, faith.

doubt, hesitate, question, waver; distrust, mistrust, suspect. ANT.—believe, confide, rely upon, trust.

draft, delineate, draw, sketch; call up, conscript, impress; bill of exchange, check, letter of credit, money order; breeze, wind.

draw, drag, haul, pull, tow, tug; extract, remove, take out; unsheathe; allure, attract, entice, induce, lure; delineate, depict, sketch, trace; compose, draft, formulate, write; conclude, deduce, derive, infer; extend, lengthen, prolong, protract, stretch. ANT.—alienate, rebuff, reject, repel, repulse.

drawback, allowance, defect, detriment, discount, flaw, hindrance, injury, rebate. ANT.—advantage, benefit, extra, premium.

dread, alarm, anxiety, apprehension, awe, consternation, dismay, fear, fright, horror, misgiving, panic, terror, trepidation. ANT.—boldness, bravery, confidence, courage.

dreadful, appalling, awful, dire, fearful, formidable, frightful, ghastly, horrible, terrible. ANT.—beautiful, enchanting, enjoyable, lovely.

dream, chimera, conceit, deception, delusion, fallacy, fancy, fantasy, hallucination, illusion, imagination, nightmare, reverie. ANT.—actuality, materiality, reality, solidity, verity.

dreary, bleak, cheerless, dark, depressing, discouraging, disheartening, dismal, doleful, dull, funereal, gloomy, lonesome, melancholy, sad, somber, wearisome. ANT.—cheerful, joyous, lively, pleasant.

dress, apparel, appearance, array, attire, clothing, costume, drapery, frock, garb, garments, gown, habiliments, habit, raiment, robes, uniform, vestments, vesture. ANT.—bareness, disarray, nakedness, nudity.

drift, end, inference, intent, meaning, objective, purpose, result, scope, tendency, tenor; bearing, course, direction; advance, be carried, deviate (from course), float, heap up, move, wander.

drill, condition, discipline, exercise, instruction, lesson, practice, repetition, study, training; boring tool; bore, perforate, puncture. ANT.—idleness, repose, rest.

drive, coerce, compel, force, hammer, hurl, impel, incite, propel, push, thrust; actuate, conduct, control, direct, guide, move, steer, ride. ANT.—drag, tow, tug; discourage, hinder, repress.

drop, collapse, decline, decrease, descend, diminish, fall, plunge, sink, subside; stumble, topple, tumble, droop, extend downward, faint, hang; dribble, drip, trickle, percolate; abandon, dismiss, give up, relinquish; cease, stop, terminate. ANT.—rise, soar; flow, splash; continue, pursue.

drown, deluge, engulf, immerse, inundate, muffle, overflow, overpower, overwhelm, perish, plunge, sink, submerge, suffocate, swamp. ANT.—extricate, preserve, recover.

drug, anesthetic, biological compound, dope, extract, medicine, narcotic, pharmaceutical; anesthetize, desensitize, knock out, narcotize, sedate.

dry, arid, dehydrated, desiccated, drained, juiceless, moistless, parched, thirsty, watertight; barren, dull, jejune, prosy, stale, tedious, tiresome, uninteresting, vapid. ANT.—damp, moist; fresh, interesting, lively.

dubious, doubtful, equivocal, hesitant, problematical, questionable, reluctant, uncertain, unclear, unreliable, unsettled, unsure. ANT.—certain, definite, positive, sure.

dull, dense, doltish, half-witted, insipid, obtuse, senseless, slow, stolid, stupid, vapid, witless; blunt, obtuse; boring, commonplace, dismal, dreary, gloomy, monotonous, prosy, sad, tedious, uninteresting; insensate, unfeeling; dry, lifeless; dark, dim. ANT.—animated, intelligent, sharp; clear, interesting.

dumb, brainless, dense, dull, foolish, obtuse, senseless, stupid, witless; aphonic, mute, speechless, voiceless. ANT.—alert, bright, clever, discerning, intelligent; articulate, fluent, talkative, voluble.

duplicate, copy, counterpart, exemplar, facsimile, likeness, replica, reproduction, tracing, transcript, twin; copy, redo, repeat, reproduce, trace. ANT.—original, prototype.

duplicity, artifice, deceit, dishonesty, fraud, guile, hypocrisy, perfidy. ANT.—guilelessness, honesty, openness, simplicity.

durable, abiding, changeless, constant, continuing, enduring, fixed, hard, indestructible, lasting, permanent, remaining, strong, unchangeable. ANT.—ephemeral, temporary, transient, transitory, unstable.

duress, captivity, coercion, compulsion, confinement, constraint.

duty, accountability, allegiance, business, calling, charge, employment, function, obligation, office, province, responsibility, service, task. ANT.—betrayal, disloyalty, falsehood, inconstancy, irresponsibility.

dwelling, abode, accommodations, apartment, domicile, flat, habitat, habitation, hearth, home, house, quarters, residence, seat.

dwindle, abridge, contract, curtail, decline, decrease, diminish, drop, fade, fall, lessen, melt, narrow, reduce, shorten, shrink, wane. ANT.—augment, enlarge, expand, multiply, widen.

dye, color, imbue, infuse, pigment, stain, tinge, tint. ANT.—bleach, fade.

E

eager, ablaze, ambitious, anxious, ardent, athirst, avid, burning, desirous, earnest, enthusiastic, fervent, glowing, hot, impassioned, impatient, impetuous, importunate, intense, intent, keen, longing, solicitous, vehement, yearning, zealous. ANT.—apathetic, indifferent, phlegmatic, uninterested.

earn, achieve, acquire, attain, deserve, gain, get, make, merit, obtain, secure, win. ANT.—forfeit, lose.

earnest, ardent, candid, eager, fervent, frank, genuine, heartfelt, honest, open, resolute, serious, sincere, straightforward, true, truthful, unfeigned, upright, warm, zealous. ANT.—affected, capricious, dishonest, insincere, untruthful.

earnings, allowance, commission, emolument, income, interest, profits, remuneration, reward, salary, stipend, wages. ANT.—costs, expenses, losses.

earthly, base, carnal, earthy, global, material, mundane, profane, sordid, temporal, worldly. ANT.—heavenly, immaterial, incorporeal, spiritual.

ease, allay, alleviate, assuage, comfort, facilitate, lighten, mitigate, pacify, relieve, soothe; comfort, contentment, peace, quietude, repose, security, solace, tranquility; easiness, expertise, facility. ANT.—annoyance, discomfort, disquiet, turmoil, vexation; difficulty.

easy, comfortable, effortless, elementary, facile, light, relaxed, simple, unanxious, uncomplicated; flexible, manageable, pliant, smooth. ANT.—arduous, demanding, difficult, hard, laborious.

ebb, abate, decay, decline, dwindle, fall, lessen, recede, retire, retreat, sink, wane. ANT.—flow, improve, increase, revive, wax.

eccentric, aberrant, bizarre, curious, deviating, erratic, odd, outlandish, peculiar, quaint, queer, singular, strange, unusual, wayward. ANT.—common, conventional, familiar, normal, regular.

economical, circumspect, frugal, moderate, penurious, provident, reasonable, saving, sparing, thrifty, watchful. ANT.—extravagant, improvident, lavish, munificent, wasteful.

ecstasy, bliss, delight, ebullience, elation, exaltation, glee, glorification, joy, rapture, ravishment, transport. ANT.—depression, despair, doldrums, melancholy, pessimism.

eddy, reverse, spin, swirl, whirl; maelstrom, vortex, whirlpool. ANT.—calm, still.

edge, border, boundary, brim, brink, butt, circumference, extremity, fringe, margin, periphery, rim, ring, side, tip, verge; intensity, keenness, sharpness, sting. ANT.—center, extension, interior; bluntness, dullness.

edict, announcement, command, decree, law, mandate, manifesto, order, ordinance, proclamation, public notice, statute, writ.

edifice, building, establishment, house, skyscraper, structure.

edit, adapt, arrange, change, compile, compose, correct, rectify, reduce, revise, select, trim.

education, background, cultivation, culture, development, discipline, edification, enlightenment, instruction, knowledge, learning, scholarship, schooling, study, training. ANT.—ignorance, illiteracy.

eerie, curious, fantastic, grotesque, odd, peculiar, strange, supernatural, uncanny, weird. ANT.—natural, normal, usual.

efface, annul, blot, cancel, destroy, erase, expunge, obliterate, wipe. ANT.—confirm, keep, renew, retain, strengthen.

effect, achieve, accomplish, attain, complete, conclude, consummate, do, execute, finish, fulfill, perform, realize; completion, conclusion, consequence, consummation, issue, outcome, result. ANT.—abandon, defeat, fail, neglect, omit; beginning, cause, commencement, origin, source.

effective, adept, capable, competent, conducive, effectual, efficacious, efficient, fruitful, potent, productive, proficient, serviceable, talented, trenchant, useful. ANT.—fruitless, incompetent, ineffectual, inefficient, nonproductive.

effeminate, feminine, unmanly, unvirile, womanish. ANT.—manly, masculine, robust, virile.

effervescent, bubbling, buoyant, frothy, gay, gleeful, volatile. ANT.—flat, sedate, sober, staid.

efficiency, ability, adaptability, capability, capacity, competency, effectiveness, fitness, power, proficiency, suitability, thoroughness. ANT.—impotence, inability, inadequacy, incompetency, weakness.

effort, application, attempt, endeavor, energy, essay, exertion, trial, work; labor, pains, strain, strife, struggle, toil, trouble. ANT.—ease, failure, neglect.

egotistic, boastful, bombastic, conceited, egocentric, inflated, narcissistic, ostentatious, pretentious, pompous, self-centered, self-important, showy, vain. ANT.—deferent, humble, modest, reserved, unobtrusive.

eject, banish, cast out, discard, discharge, dislodge, dismiss, exile, expel, evict, oust, propel, remove. ANT.—accept, appoint, establish, settle, retain.

elaborate, gaudy, ostentatious, showy; complex, complicated, detailed, intricate, perfected, polished, refined. ANT.—common, ordinary, simple, unrefined, usual.

elapse, expire, glide, go away, intervene, lapse, pass, vanish. ANT.—remain, stand still, stay.

elastic, adaptable, compliant, ductile, extensible, flexible, limber, lithe, pliable, pliant, resilient, rubbery, springy, stretchable, supple, tractable. ANT.—brittle, rigid, stiff, tense, unbending.

elated, animated, delighted, ecstatic, exhilarated, exultant, gleeful, high-spirited. ANT.—depressed, downhearted, gloomy, low.

elect, call, choose, cull, decide on, judge, opt, ordain, pick, prefer, select. ANT.—cancel, recall, refuse, reject.

elegant, beautiful, courtly, elaborate, fair, fine, handsome, lovely, luxurious, opulent, polished, pretty, refined, rich, sophisticated, sumptuous. ANT.—common, repulsive, rustic, unrefined, vulgar.

elementary, basic, constituent, easy, elemental, fundamental, initial, primary, rudimentary; pure, simple, uncompounded, unmixed. ANT.—abstruse, advanced, complex, intricate; compounded, mixed.

elevate, advance, buoy, dignify, erect, exalt, glorify, heighten, hoist, honor, improve, lift, promote, raise, revere, uplift. ANT.—abase, condemn, deprecate, depreciate, depress.

elicit, bring forth, draw, educe, evoke, extort, extract, prompt, wrest. ANT.—repress, suppress.

eliminate, abolish, abrogate, banish, cancel, delete, discharge, dislodge, efface, eject, eradicate, erase, excise, exclude, expel, expunge,

expurgate, exterminate, extirpate, liquidate, obliterate, oust, proscribe, pluck, remove. ANT.—accept, admit, include, maintain, preserve.

elongate, extend, lengthen, prolong, protract, stretch. ANT.—contract, shrink, slacken, shorten.

elucidate, clarify, decipher, explain, expound, illuminate, illustrate, interpret. ANT.—becloud, confuse, darken, distract, obscure.

elude, avert, avoid, baffle, dodge, escape, eschew, evade, foil, frustrate, parry. ANT.—attract, confront, encounter, meet, solicit.

emanate, arise, come, emerge, flow, issue, originate, proceed, radiate, stem. ANT.—return, sink, withdraw.

emancipate, free, let go, liberate, release, set free. ANT.—confine, imprison, subjugate.

embarrass, abash, annoy, bewilder, bother, complicate, confound, confuse, discomfit, disconcert, distress, encumber, entangle, fluster, hamper, hinder, mortify, obstruct, perplex, plague, rattle, trouble, vex. ANT.—cheer, encourage, help, inspire, relieve.

embellish, adorn, beautify, deck, decorate, enrich, garnish, ornament, trim; exaggerate. ANT.—debase, defame, strip, obliterate; simplify.

embezzle, appropriate, cheat, defalcate, defraud, falsify, filch, forge, misapply, misappropriate, misuse, pilfer, plunder, purloin, rob, swindle. ANT.—balance, recompense, reimburse, return, satisfy.

emblem, brand, figure, image, representation, sign, symbol, token, trademark.

embody, codify, comprise, concentrate, contain, embrace, hold, include, incorporate, integrate, systematize. ANT.—discharge, disperse, disintegrate, exclude.

embrace, caress, clasp, encircle, hug; accept, adopt, espouse, receive, subscribe to, welcome; comprehend, comprise, contain, embody, include, incorporate. ANT.—exclude, reject, renounce, scorn, spurn.

emergency, casualty, crisis, dilemma, distress, exigency, juncture, pressure, quandary, strait, urgency. ANT.—conventionality, regularity, routine, stability, solution.

emigrate, abandon, depart, egress, escape, leave, migrate, move, part, quit. ANT.—dwell, remain, reside, stay.

eminent, celebrated, conspicuous, distinguished, elevated, exalted, famous, foremost, glorious, illustrious, noted, prominent, renowned, superior, supreme, well-known. ANT.—common, humble, insignificant, obscure, ordinary.

emit, breathe forth, discharge, eject, emanate, exhale, expel, express, hurl, issue, open, publish, report, shoot, spurt, utter, vent. ANT.—contain, retain, stop, suppress.

emotion, affection, feeling, impression, inspiration, mood, passion, presentiment, sensation, sensibility, sentiment. ANT.—apathy, dispassion, impassivity, indifference, insensibility.

empathy, affinity, appreciation, commiseration, compassion, insight, sensitivity, understanding. ANT.—insensitivity, unfeelingness.

emphatic, affecting, determined, effective, energetic, forceful, forcible, insistent, pointed, potent. ANT.—bashful, bland, modest, reserved, weak.

employment, business, calling, career, craft, engagement, job, occupation, profession, pursuit, service, vocation, work. ANT.—ennui, idleness, inactivity, laziness, leisure.

empty, bare, barren, destitute, devoid, foolish, hollow, hungry, meaningless, senseless, stupid,

unfilled, unfurnished, unoccupied, vacant, vacuous, void, worthless. ANT.—erudite, full, inhabited, occupied, replete.

enable, allow, authorize, empower, let, permit, sanction. ANT.—disallow, oppose, prevent.

enchant, bewitch, captivate, charm, enrapture, enthrall, entice, fascinate, ravish. ANT.—disenchant, disgust, offend, repel.

encompass, beset, circumscribe, encircle, enclose, enfold, envelop, environ, gird, hem in, invest, span, surround. ANT.—free, release, unwrap.

encounter, assailment, assault, attack, battle, clash, collision, combat, conflict, engagement, fight, invasion, meeting, onslaught, skirmish, struggle. ANT.—amity, avoidance, concord, consonance, harmony, retreat, union.

encourage, advise, animate, cheer, comfort, embolden, enliven, exhilarate, favor, hearten, impel, incite, inspire, inspirit, urge; foster, promote, sanction, stimulate, spur, support. ANT.—deject, deter, discourage, dispirit, dissuade.

encroach, attack, infract, infringe, intrude, invade, poach, transgress, trespass, violate. ANT.—abandon, avoid, evacuate, relinquish, shun.

encumbrance, burden, clog, drag, difficulty, drawback, hindrance, impediment, lien, load, mortgage, obstacle, weight. ANT.—advantage, assistance, incentive, stimulant.

end, aim, ambition, cessation, close, completion, conclusion, consequence, expiration, extremity, finish, goal, issue, limit, object, purpose, result, termination, terminus; cease, close, conclude, stop, terminate. ANT.—beginning, commencement, inception, introduction; inaugurate, institute, establish, start.

endanger, expose, hazard, imperil, jeopardize, peril, risk. ANT.—guard, protect, secure.

endeavor, aim, aspire, attempt, contend, contest, essay, exert, strive, try, undertake; labor, pains, strain, strife, struggle, toil.

endless, boundless, ceaseless, constant, continuous, eternal, everlasting, illimitable, immeasurable, imperishable, incessant, infinite, interminable, perpetual, unbounded, uninterrupted, unlimited. ANT.—bounded, finite, limited, transient, transitory.

endorse (also spelled indorse), assist, attest, authorize, back, confirm, corroborate, guarantee, ratify, recommend, sanction, secure, sign, subscribe, support, warrant. ANT.—admonish, censure, denounce, oppose, reject.

endowment, ability, attainment, benefaction, benefit, bequest, bounty, capacity, donation, empowerment, genius, gift, grant, gratuity, mentality, natural gift, provision, qualification, talent. ANT.—drawback, harm, injury, loss.

endurance, allowance, continuance, courage, diligence, firmness, forbearance, fortitude, long-suffering, patience, perseverance, persistence, resignation, resistance, stamina, strength, submission, tolerance. ANT.—faltering, succumbing, surrender, weakness.

enemy, adversary, antagonist, attacker, calumniator, competitor, defamer, defiler, falsifier, foe, opponent, predator, rival, slanderer, traducer, vilifier. ANT.—accomplice, ally, comrade, confederate, friend.

energetic, active, aggressive, animated, brisk, cogent, determined, diligent, dynamic, enterprising, forcible, industrious, lively, mighty, potent, powerful, spirited, strong, vigorous. ANT.—idle, lazy, listless, spiritless, vacillating.

energy, effectiveness, efficiency, force, might, potency, power, puissance, robustness, strength, vigor, vim, vitality, zeal. ANT.—apathy, frailty, impotence, indolence, weakness.

enervate, attenuate, daze, debilitate, enfeeble, impair, injure, paralyze, reduce, sap, soften, weaken, weary. ANT.—animate, buoy, energize, invigorate, strengthen.

enforce, coerce, compel, constrain, drive, exact, execute, exert, force, impel, necessitate, oblige, persuade, press, require, strain, urge. ANT.—dismiss, disregard, give up, leave, omit.

enfranchise, emancipate, empower, enable, free, license, release, right, qualify. ANT.—disenfranchise, disqualify, revoke (license).

engage, busy, employ, engross, enlist, hire; bind, commit, pledge; mesh (with gears). ANT.—dismiss, release; decline, refuse; disengage.

engagement, appointment; battle, combat, encounter; betrothal, bond, commitment, compact, consenting, espousal, pledge, plighting.

engender, breed, cause, create, excite, fashion, form, formulate, generate, incite, make, originate, procreate, produce, reproduce. ANT.—annihilate, demolish, destroy.

engross, absorb, assimilate, bewitch, captivate, consume, engulf, fascinate, monopolize, swallow up; busy, engage, occupy. ANT.—dissatisfy, neglect, repel.

engulf, absorb, assimilate, bury, consume, deluge, drown, entomb, fill up, inundate, overcome, overflow, overwhelm, sink, swallow up. ANT.—discharge, dispense, emit, expel.

enhance, advance, augment, elevate, heighten, increase, intensify, magnify, raise, swell. ANT.—assuage, degrade, diminish, reduce.

enigmatic, baffling, cryptic, inscrutable, mysterious, puzzling, vague. ANT.—clear, explicit, obvious, open, plain.

enjoyment, bliss, comfort, delight, ecstasy, exultation, gladness, gratification, happiness, hedonism, indulgence, joy, liking, pleasure, rapture, satisfaction. ANT.—dejection, discomfort, misery, sorrow, unhappiness.

enlarge, add, amplify, augment, broaden, dilate, distend, expand, extend, grow, heighten, increase, lengthen, magnify, protuberate, spread, swell, widen. ANT.—abbreviate, abridge, condense, contract, diminish.

enlighten, brighten, clarify, communicate, disclose, edify, educate, elucidate, illuminate, illumine, illustrate, inculcate, indoctrinate, irradiate. ANT.—confound, confuse, darken, obfuscate, obscure.

enlist, attract, engage, employ, enroll, enter, get, hire, incorporate, induce, interest, join, obtain, procure, register, reserve, retain. ANT.—check, constrain, demobilize, deter, hold back.

enliven, animate, arouse, brighten, cheer, encourage, excite, exhilarate, gladden, quicken, refresh, rouse, stimulate, vivify. ANT.—dampen, debilitate, exhaust, sadden, stultify.

enmity, abhorrence, acrimony, animosity, antagonism, antipathy, aversion, detestation, disgust, hatred, hostility, illwill, invidiousness, malevolence, malice, malignity, rancor, repugnance, spitefulness. ANT.—affection, cordiality, friendliness, good will, love.

ennui, boredom, languor, listlessness, surfeit, tedium. ANT.—buoyancy, enthusiasm, energy, vigor.

enough, adequate, ample, full, plenty, satisfactory, sufficient. ANT.—deficient, inadequate, lacking, scant.

enrage, anger, chafe, craze, exasperate, goad, incense, inflame, infuriate, irk, madden. ANT.—appease, conciliate, soften, soothe, pacify.

enrich, adorn, beautify, embellish; cultivate, fertilize, improve; endow. ANT.—deplete, impoverish, reduce, rob, take from.

enroll, enlist, enter, inscribe, join, list, record, register, subscribe. ANT.—cancel, deactivate, discard, reject.

ensue, follow; succeed, come next; result. ANT.—forsake; precede; cause.

enter, penetrate, pierce, perforate; enlist in, enroll, join, register; encroach, intrude; begin, introduce, start. ANT.—depart, exit, vacate, withdraw.

enterprise, achievement, activity, adventure, business, commerce, endeavor, engagement, project, undertaking, venture, work. ANT.—inaction, indolence, passivity, sloth.

entertainment, amusement, diversion, enjoyment, fun, game, merriment, party, pastime, play, pleasure, recreation, social event, sport. ANT.—boredom, ennui, labor, toil, work.

enthusiasm, ardor, devotion, eagerness, earnestness, excitement, fervency, fervor, inspiration, intensity, optimism, passion, vehemence, vigor, warmth, zeal. ANT.—apathy, calmness, ennui, indifference, lethargy, pessimism.

entice, allure, attract, beguile, captivate, charm, draw, enchant, ensnare, fascinate, inveigle, lure, prevail upon, seduce, tempt, wheedle. ANT.—alienate, disgust, reject, repel, repulse.

entire, all, complete, intact, integral, perfect, total, unabridged, unbroken, undivided, unimpaired, unscathed, whole. ANT.—defective, deficient, incomplete, partial.

entrance, door, doorway, entry, gate, gateway, ingress, inlet, opening, portal; admission, beginning, commencement, initiation. ANT.—egress, exit, outlet; departure, exclusion, rejection, withdrawal.

entreat, ask, beg, beseech, implore, importune, petition, plead, request, solicit, supplicate. ANT.—command, compel, demand, force, take.

envelop, blanket, conceal, cover, embrace, enclose, encompass, enfold, hide, surround, wrap. ANT.—open, reveal, uncover, unwrap.

envious, cautious, covetous, displeased, invidious, jealous, malicious, odious, resentful, suspicious. ANT.—benevolent, charitable, helpful, laudatory, pleased, well-disposed.

environment, background, conditions, location, neighborhood, setting, surroundings, vicinity.

envoy, agent, ambassador, commissioner, delegate, diplomat, messenger, nuncio, plenipotentiary, representative.

epicurean, fastidious, gastronomic, luxurious, particular, sensual, sybaritic, voluptuous. ANT.—ascetic, austere, puritanical, self-denying.

episode, affair, circumstance, event, happening, incident, issue, occurrence.

epistle, communication, dispatch, lesson, letter, message, missive, note, writing.

epitome, abridgment, abstract, compendium, condensation, digest, summary, syllabus, synopsis, synthesis; embodiment, essence, ideal example of. ANT.—augmentation, development, expansion, extension, increment.

equable, calm, constant, equal, even, regular, serene, steady, unchanging, uniform, unruffled. ANT.—changeable, fluctuating, spasmodic, variable.

equal, adequate, alike, commensurate, equable, equitable, equivalent, even, fair, identical, invariable, just, like, same, uniform, unvarying; compeer, match, parallel, peer, rival, tie. ANT.—different, disparate, disproportionate, dissimilar, unjust; inferior, subordinate.

equanimity, balance, calmness, composure, evenness, poise, serenity, self-control. ANT.—agitation, anxiety, disturbance, excitation, perturbation.

equipment, accouterments, apparatus, array, furnishings, gear, material, outfit, paraphernalia.

equitable, fair, honest, impartial, just, objective, reasonable, unbiased, unprejudiced. ANT.—biased, dishonorable, fraudulent, inequitable, partial.

equivalent, alike, commensurate, equal, identical, indistinguishable, interchangeable, like, reciprocal, same, synonomous, tantamount. ANT.—contrary, disparate, dissimilar, opposed, unequal.

eradicate, abolish, annihilate, destroy, eliminate, erase, expel, exterminate, extinguish, extirpate, kill, nullify, oust, remove, uproot. ANT.—establish, fortify, foster, propagate, secure.

erase, cancel, cross out, delete, efface, eliminate, expunge, obliterate, rub out; abolish, abrogate, annul, invalidate, nullify, quash, repeal, rescind, revoke. ANT.—confirm, enact, perpetuate.

erect, unbent, upright, straight, vertical; build, construct, raise. ANT.—bent, cringing, crooked, horizontal, recumbent; raze.

erode, abrade, corrode, destroy, deteriorate, eat, gnaw, rub, wear, weather.

erotic, carnal, concupiscent, erogenous, libidinous, lustful, passionate, sensual, sexual. ANT.—celibate, passionless, spiritual.

erratic, aberrant, capricious, changeable, desultory, flighty, fluctuating, odd, peculiar, strange, uncertain, unreliable, unruly, wandering. ANT.—dependable, methodical, regular, reliable, steady.

erroneous, fallacious, false, faulty, inaccurate, incorrect, mistaken, unprecise, untrue, wrong. ANT.—correct, right, true.

error, blunder, deviation, fall, fallacy, fault, inaccuracy, indiscretion, misapprehension, misconception, omission, oversight, slip, transgression. ANT.—accuracy, certitude, correction, precision, truth.

erudite, cultured, educated, enlightened, knowing, learned, scholarly. ANT.—ignorant, illiterate, uneducated, unlettered.

eruption, commotion, discharge, efflorescence, explosion, outbreak, outburst; rash.

escape, abscond, break, decamp, defect, flee, fly; avert, avoid, elude, evade, shun. ANT.—confront, face, invite, meet.

escort, accompany, attend, chaperon, conduct, convoy, guard, guide, lead, protect, safeguard, serve, tend, squire, usher, watch.

especially, chiefly, definitely, mainly, particularly, primarily, principally, specially, specifically.

essay, article, composition, disquisition, dissertation, thesis; attempt, effort, trial.

essential, basic, characteristic, fundamental, indispensable, inherent, intrinsic, key, necessary, requisite, vital. ANT.—auxiliary, expendable, extrinsic, optional, peripheral.

establish, authorize, form, found, institute, organize, raise, set up; confirm, fix, ordain, sanction, settle, strengthen; confirm, demonstrate, prove, substantiate, verify. ANT.—abolish, demolish, overthrow, unsettle, upset; controvert, disprove, scorn.

estate, belongings, commodities, domain, effects, goods, holdings, inheritance, land, merchandise, possessions, property, stock, wares, wealth. ANT.—destitution, poverty, privation, want.

esteem, admiration, appreciation, approbation, approval, commendation, deference, favor, honor, praise, regard, reverence, sanction, value, veneration; estimate, rate, reckon.

estimate, appraise, assess, assign, calculate, compute, count, evaluate, measure, rate, reckon, value, weigh. ANT.—disregard, guess.

estrangement, alienation, disaffection, removal, separation, withdrawal. ANT.—affinity, alliance, bond, coalition, union.

eternal, boundless, ceaseless, deathless, endless, enduring, immortal, imperishable, infinite, never-ending, perpetual, timeless, undying, unending. ANT.—ephemeral, finite, mortal, mutable, temporal, transient.

ethical, decent, good, honest, honorable, just, moral, principled, righteous, scrupulous, virtuous. ANT.—amoral, corrupt, dishonest, licentious, unethical.

eulogize, applaud, celebrate, commend, compliment, extol, laud, praise. ANT.—condemn, degrade, demean, scorn.

evacuate, abandon, clear, desert, emit, empty, expel, leave, purge, quit, relinquish, retreat, vacate. ANT.—charge, enter, fill, occupy, take over.

evade, avoid, shun; dodge, equivocate, quibble; conceal, deceive, trick. ANT.—confront, face; confess, declare, verify.

evaporate, disappear, disperse, dissolve, dry, evanesce, fade, vanish, vaporize. ANT.—appear, consolidate, crystallize.

evaluate, appraise, assess, calculate, estimate, judge, rate, value, weigh. ANT.—guess, hazard.

even, flat, flush, level, plane, smooth; equal, unbroken, uniform, unvarying; calm, peaceful. ANT.—jagged, rough; broken, irregular; agitated, troubled.

event, affair, circumstance, episode, happening, incident, issue, milestone, occurrence; consequence, end, outcome, result. ANT.—antecedent, cause, origin, start.

everlasting, ceaseless, deathless, endless, eternal, immortal, imperishable, incessant, infinite, interminable, perpetual, timeless, unceasing, undying. ANT.—ephemeral, finite, mortal, temporal, transient.

evict, debar, deprive, discard, dispossess, eject, exclude, expel, oust. ANT.—accept, admit, receive, welcome.

evidence, confirmation, corroboration, data, demonstration, documentation, facts, grounds, indication, premises, proof, testimony, verification. ANT.—contradiction, disproof, fallacy, invalidity, refutation.

evident, apparent, clear, conspicuous, discernible, distinct, incontrovertible, indisputable, indubitable, manifest, obvious, open, overt, patent, perceptible, plain, unmistakable, visible. ANT.—concealed, covert, hidden, obscure, questionable.

evil, baseness, calamity, contamination, corruption, crime, depravity, disaster, harm, ill, immorality, iniquity, malignity, mischief, misfortune, offense, profligacy, sin, transgression, ungodliness, vice, viciousness, wickedness, wrong; base, deleterious, immoral, noxious, pernicious, sinful, vicious, wicked. ANT.—goodness, innocence, purity, virtue; honorable, moral, reputable.

evince, demonstrate, disclose, display, evidence, exhibit, indicate, manifest, prove, show. ANT.—conceal, hide, repress, suppress.

evoke, arouse, educe, elicit, excite, provoke, rouse, stimulate, summon, waken. ANT.—quiet, repress, silence, squelch, stifle.

exact, accurate, correct, definite, distinct, literal, methodical, particular, precise, punctual, rigorous, scrupulous, specific, strict, true, undeviating, unequivocal; demand, extort, wrest.

ANT.—approximate, careless, erroneous, inaccurate, vague, variable; request.

exaggerate, amplify, embellish, embroider, enlarge, expand, heighten, magnify, overdo, overstate, stretch. ANT.—depreciate, lessen, minimize, reduce, understate.

exalt, advance, aggrandize, applaud, commend, consecrate, dignify, elevate, ennoble, erect, extol, glorify, hallow, honor, laud, magnify, praise, raise. ANT.—degrade, dishonor, humble, humiliate, scorn.

examination, analysis, audit, check-up, exploration, inquiry, inquisition, inspection, interrogation, investigation, probing, query, quest, questioning, quiz, research, scrutiny, search, test, trial, review. ANT.—disregard, inattention, negligence.

example, archetype, exemplification, ideal, illustration, instance, model, pattern, precedent, prototype, representation, sample, specimen, symbol, typical case.

exasperate, aggravate, annoy, chafe, enrage, exacerbate, frustrate, incense, inflame, infuriate, irritate, nettle, provoke, vex. ANT.—appease, calm, mitigate, palliate, soften.

exceed, eclipse, excel, outdo, outstrip, surmount, surpass, top, transcend. ANT.—fail, fall behind, lag, tarry.

excellent, admirable, commendable, eminent, estimable, exemplary, expert, favorable, honorable, meritorious, peerless, prime, proficient, superior, surpassing, valuable, worthy. ANT.—inferior, lesser, negligible, poor.

except, barring, but, excepting, excluding, exempting, omitting, rejecting, saving. ANT.—admitting, embracing, including.

exceptional, infrequent, occasional, unusual; choice, extraordinary, incomparable, marvelous, novel, precious, rare, remarkable, scarce, singular, uncommon, unique, unparalleled, unprecedented, wonderful. ANT.—customary, frequent, ordinary, usual; abundant, commonplace, numerous, worthless.

excerpt, abbreviation, citing, clipping, culling, extract, quote, selection.

excess, extravagance, immoderation, intemperance, lavishness, luxuriance, plenty, profusion, redundance, redundancy, superabundance, superfluity, surplus, waste. ANT.—dearth, deficiency, lack, paucity, want.

exchange, barter, change, convert, reciprocate, substitute, swap, switch, trade, transfer. ANT.—preserve, retain.

excite, activate, aggravate, agitate, arouse, awaken, disconcert, disquiet, disturb, goad, incense, incite, induce, inflame, irritate, kindle, perturb, provoke, rouse, stimulate, stir up, taunt, unsettle. ANT.—allay, calm, pacify, quiet, tranquilize.

exclaim, call out, clamor, cry, cry out, ejaculate, proclaim, shout, vociferate. ANT.—murmur, mutter, whisper.

exclude, ban, bar, blackball, boycott, debar, except, expel, obviate, omit, ostracize, prevent, prohibit, reject, shut out, veto. ANT.—accept, admit, include, incorporate, welcome.

excruciating, acute, agonizing, extreme, grueling, intense, overwhelming, painful, racking, rending, severe, tormenting. ANT.—comforting, mild, pleasing, soothing.

excursion, digression, divergence, episode, expedition, jaunt, journey, outing, travel, trip, tour, voyage.

excuse, absolve, acquit, exculpate, exempt, exonerate, forgive, free, pardon, release, remit; alibi, apology, defense, explanation, plea, pretext, vindication. ANT.—convict, prosecute, punish; accusation.

execrate, abhor, berate, condemn, curse, damn, objurgate, reprehend, revile. ANT.—applaud, commend, extol, laud, praise.

execute, accomplish, achieve, administer, attain, carry out, complete, consummate, do, effect, finish, fulfill, obtain, perfect, perform, realize; behead, electrocute, guillotine, hang. ANT.—abandon, fail, neglect, omit, shelve.

exempt, absolved, clear, excluded, excused, free, freed, liberated, privileged, released, unbound, unchecked, uncontrolled, undrafted, unrestricted. ANT.—answerable, bound, compelled, nonexempt, obliged.

exercise, act, action, activity, application, drill, employment, exertion, lesson, operation, performance, practice, task, training, use; calisthenics, gymnastics. ANT.—idleness, indolence, relaxation, repose, rest.

exertion, attempt, effort, endeavor, grind, labor, strain, struggle, toil, travail, trial. ANT.—idleness, inaction, laziness, lethargy.

exhausted, consumed, depleted, drained, empty, faint, fatigued, jaded, spent, tired, wasted, wearied, weary, worn. ANT.—fresh, hearty, invigorated, rested, restored.

exhibit, demonstrate, disclose, display, evince, expose, flaunt, manifest, parade, present, reveal, show. ANT.—conceal, cover, disguise, hide.

exhilarate, elate, enliven, inspirit, invigorate, rejoice, stimulate, thrill. ANT.—deject, depress, discourage, repress, sadden.

exigency, crisis, demand, difficulty, distress, emergency, need, strait, urgency, want. ANT.—normality, regularity.

exile, banishment, deportation, expatriation, expulsion, extradition, ostracism, proscription. ANT.—admittance, welcome.

existence, animation, being, life, liveliness, reality, spirit, vigor, vitality, vivacity. ANT.—death, demise, languor, lethargy.

exonerate, absolve, acquit, clear, discharge, except, exempt, free, justify, release, relieve, restore, vindicate. ANT.—accuse, blame, censure, condemn, indict.

exorbitant, excessive, extravagant, extreme, inordinate, over-priced, unreasonable. ANT.—below cost, fair, inexpensive, moderate, reasonable.

expand, advance, amplify, augment, develop, dilate, distend, enlarge, extend, grow, increase, magnify, mature, spread, stretch, swell, widen. ANT.—abbreviate, atrophy, contract, diminish, shrink, wane.

expansion, development, dilation, distention, elaboration, enlargement, unfolding, unraveling; evolution, growth, maturing, progress. ANT.—abbreviation, compression, curtailment.

expect, anticipate, await, contemplate, envision, foresee, hope, look for. ANT.—despair of, doubt, fear.

expedite, accelerate, advance, dispatch, facilitate, forward, hasten, hurry, push, quicken, rush, speed, urge. ANT.—hinder, impede, obstruct, retard, slow.

expedition, campaign, cruise, excursion, journey, mission, passage, pilgrimage, quest, safari, tour, travel, trek, trip, undertaking, voyage; alacrity, speed.

expel, banish, discharge, dismiss, evict, excommunicate, exile, ostracize, oust, proscribe, remove; dislodge, eject, eliminate, excrete, void. ANT.—accept, admit, include, invite; absorb, take in.

expense, charge, cost, disbursement, expenditure, outgo, outlay, payment, price, upkeep, value. ANT.—gain, income, profits, receipts, revenue.

expensive, costly, dear, high-priced. ANT.—cheap, inexpensive, worthless.

experience, adventure, encounter, episode, happening, incident, meeting, occurrence; feeling, sensation; background, knowledge, practice, sagacity, seasoning, testing, wisdom. ANT.—ignorance, inexperience, lack of knowledge.

experiment, assay, attempt, endeavor, examination, exercise, practice, research, test, trial, undertaking.

expert, able, accomplished, adept, adroit, apt, clever, competent, ingenious, masterful, practiced, proficient, skilled, skillful. ANT.—awkward, bungling, incompetent, inexpert, maladroit, unskillful.

expire, cease, decease, depart, die, disappear, end, pass away, perish, sink, vanish. ANT.—commence, live, survive.

explain, clarify, decipher, elucidate, expound, illustrate, interpret, manifest, resolve, solve, teach, unfold, unravel. ANT.—baffle, cloud, confuse, mystify, obscure.

explanation, clarification, deduction, defense, elucidation, explication, exposition, excuse, interpretation, justification, key, solution.

explicit, clear, comprehensible, definitive, determinate, distinct, evident, exact, express, intelligible, lucid, manifest, obvious, plain, positive, precise, specific. ANT.—ambiguous, equivocal, hazy, obscure, vague.

exploit, adventure, bold act, deed, feat; accomplishment, achievement, attainment, performance, realization; manipulate, take advantage of, use unfairly. ANT.—neglect, omission; defeat, failure.

exposed, agape, ajar, open, unclosed, uncovered, unlocked, unmasked, unveiled; clear, passable, unobstructed; accessible, public, unrestricted. ANT.—concealed, hidden, suppressed.

expound, analyze, clarify, construe, elucidate, explain, express, illuminate, illustrate, interpret, lecture, present, state, teach. ANT.—baffle, confuse, darken, obscure.

express, clear, definitive, explicit, lucid, manifest, positive, specific, unmistakable; fast, quick, rapid, speedy; affirm, assert, avow, claim, communicate, declare, denote, designate, dispatch, explain, forward, propound, recite, represent, say, send, signify, specify, state, tell, utter. ANT.—ambiguous, equivocal, implied, obscure, vague; slow; conceal, restrain, retain, suppress, withhold.

exquisite, appealing, attractive, charming, choice, dainty, delicate, elegant, excellent, fine, matchless, perfect, precious, rare, refined, select, splendid, superb, vintage; beautiful, debonair, handsome, pretty; acute, intense, sharp. ANT.—common, ordinary, unrefined, worthless; ugly; dull, mild.

extant, contemporary, enduring, existent, existing, lasting, surviving, undestroyed. ANT.—departed, destroyed, extinct, gone.

extemporaneous, ad lib, extemporary, informal, impromptu, improvised, informal, offhand, unplanned, unpremeditated, unprepared, unstudied. ANT.—designed, planned, premeditated, prepared, studied.

extend, add, amplify, augment, dilate, distend, enlarge, elongate, expand, lengthen, protract, spread, stretch; give, grant. ANT.—contract, decrease, loosen, reduce, shrink, slacken; take.

extensive, broad, expanded, sweeping, vast, wide. ANT.—confined, narrow, restricted.

extent, amount, compass, degree, expanse, length, magnitude, measure, range, reach, scope, size, stretch, volume.

exterior, cover, face, front, outside, shell, skin, surface. ANT.—core, inside, interior, internal (part).

exterminate, abolish, annihilate, banish, decimate, destroy, eradicate, expel, extirpate, kill, overthrow, uproot. ANT.—cherish, guard, maintain, preserve, protect.

external, exterior, extrinsic, foreign, outer, outside, superficial. ANT.—domestic, inside, internal, intrinsic, within.

extinguish, abate, abolish, annihilate, choke, destroy, eradicate, exterminate, extirpate, obscure, quench, suppress. ANT.—animate, ignite, kindle, light.

extol, celebrate, commend, eulogize, exalt, glorify, honor, laud, praise. ANT.—decry, disgrace, dishonor, profane.

extract, derive, distill, draw, educe, elicit, eradicate, evoke, extirpate, extort, obtain, pull, remove. ANT.—insert, instill, introduce.

extraneous, foreign, irrelevant, remote, strange, unconnected. ANT.—akin, germane, relevant.

extraordinary, egregious, exceptional, inordinate, marvelous, peculiar, phenomenal, rare, remarkable, singular, special, uncommon, unusual, unwonted, wonderful. ANT.—common, customary, ordinary, standard, usual.

extravagant, abundant, copious, excessive, extreme, exuberant, immoderate, improvident, inordinate, lavish, liberal, luxuriant, overflowing, plentiful, prodigal, profuse, wasteful. ANT.—economical, meager, parsimonious, penurious, sparse.

extreme, farthest, greatest, maximum, outermost, utmost; final, last, terminal, ultimate; extravagant, immoderate, intensive; fanatical, radical. ANT.— adjacent, near; calm, dispassionate; moderate.

extricate, affranchise, deliver, disengage, disentangle, free, let go, liberate, loose, ransom, release, rescue, unbind, unchain, unfasten, untie. ANT.—bind, chain, confine, incarcerate, restrain.

exuberant, abundant, copious, energetic, lavish, luxuriant, overflowing, profuse, prolific, rank, vigorous, wanton. ANT.—austere, barren, depleted, needy, sterile.

F

fabric, cloth, dry goods, material, organization, structure, stuff, substance, textile.

fabricate, arrange, build, compose, construct, counterfeit, devise, erect, fake, feign, forge, form, frame, invent, plan, prevaricate, produce, put together. ANT.—demolish, disrupt, ruin, shatter, wreck.

fabulous, amazing, astounding, exaggerated, extraordinary, false, feigned, fictitious, incredible, legendary, mythical, ridiculous, untrue. ANT.—common, credible, proven, usual, true.

facade, affectation, appearance, cover-up, false front, front, ornamentation, veneer. ANT.—base, character, sincerity.

face, appearance, countenance, features, mien, physiognomy, visage; assurance, audacity, boldness, confidence, effrontery, impertinence, impudence; brave, challenge, confront, dare, defy, meet, oppose, resist, venture; cover, exterior, front, outside, surface. ANT.—humility, timidity; shrink, retreat, withdraw; interior, rear.

facile, able, adroit, agreeable, apt, artful, clever, dexterous, easy, expert, flexible, proficient, skillful, smooth, tactful. ANT.—awkward, difficult, disagreeable, rude, tedious.

facilitate, allay, alleviate, assuage, ease, lighten, mitigate, relieve, soothe. ANT.—confound, distress, disturb.

facility, ability, adroitness, civility, cleverness, courtesy, dexterity, ease, expertness, proficiency, readiness, skillfulness. ANT.—awkwardness, difficulty, discourtesy, ineptitude.

facsimile, copy, duplicate, pattern, photograph, picture, replica, reproduction, transcript. ANT.—distinction, opposite, variation.

fact, actuality, certainty, evidence, reality, truth; act, circumstance, deed, detail, event, incident, item, occurrence, point. ANT.—fiction, supposition, theory, delusion, falsehood.

faction, block, cabal, circle, clique, combination, coterie, denomination, division, party, sect, wing. ANT.—conformity, entirety, homogeneity, unity.

factious, contentious, dissident, insubordinate, rebellious, recalcitrant, seditious. ANT.—cooperative, helpful, united.

factitious, artificial, bogus, counterfeit, fabricated, forced, phony, sham, spurious, synthetic, unnatural. ANT.—authentic, bona fide, genuine, natural, real.

factor, actor, agent, attorney, bailiff, commissioner, delegate, deputy, manager, proxy, representative, steward, vicar; constituent, element, part.

faculty, ability, aptitude, bent, capability, capacity, function, gift, knack, power, skill, talent. ANT.—impotence, inability, incapacity, incompetence, ineptness.

fade, bleach, blur, deteriorate, dim, disappear, dwindle, ebb, evanesce, pale, taper off, vanish, wane, wither. ANT.—darken, enhance, improve, recover, strengthen.

fail, abandon, abort, collapse, decline, default, defeat, desert, disappoint, drop, fade, flounder, leave, miscarry, neglect, omit, quit, wither. ANT.—accomplish, achieve, capture, deliver, recover.

faint, dim, faded, faltering, fatigued, feeble, inaudible, indistinct, irresolute, languid, listless, pale, powerless, thin, timid, weak, wearied, worn. ANT.—distinct, forceful, intrepid, strong, vigorous.

fair, bright, clear, dry, light, mild, pleasant, sunny; attractive, blond, comely, lovely; candid, decent, equitable, frank, honest, impartial, just, open, reasonable, unbiased; average, mediocre, passable. ANT.—foul, tempestuous, ugly, unattractive; devious, dishonorable, fraudulent, partial; excellent, first-rate, worst.

faith, assurance, conviction, credence, reliance, trust; belief, creed, doctrine, dogma, tenet; constancy, fidelity, loyalty, promise, word. ANT.—doubt, incredulity, mistrust, skepticism; infidelity.

faithful, attached, constant, dependable, devoted, firm, honorable, incorruptible, loyal, staunch, steadfast, true, unswerving, unwavering; accurate, reliable, trusty. ANT.—disloyal, false, fickle, treacherous, untrustworthy.

fall, abate, collapse, decline, decrease, descend, diminish, drop, ebb, lessen, plunge, sink, subside, weaken; stumble, topple, totter, tumble; droop, extend downward, hang. ANT.—arise, ascend, climb, reach, scale, soar.

fallacy, casuistry, delusion, equivocation, error, fantasy, illusion, misconception, mistake, sophistry, subterfuge, untruth. ANT.—certainty, fact, reality, truth, verity.

false, bogus, counterfeit, deceptive, dishonest, erroneous, fabricated, fallacious, illusory, incorrect, lying, mendacious, misleading, mock, pretended, sham, spurious, unreal, untrue.

ANT.—accurate, confirmed, substantiated, true, valid.

falter, delay, demur, doubt, flinch, fluctuate, hesitate, hobble, pause, reel, shrink, slip, stammer, stutter, totter, tremble, vacillate, weaken. ANT.— continue, endure, persevere, persist.

familiar, acquainted, cognizant, conversant, informed, intimate, knowing, versed, well-known; accessible, affable, amicable, approachable, casual, close, comfortable, courteous, easy, friendly, informal, sociable, unconstrained, unreserved; common, customary, usual; disrespectful, impudent. ANT.—constrained, distant, formal, reserved, unfamiliar.

famous, celebrated, distinguished, eminent, glorious, honorable, illustrious, noted, renowned, well-known. ANT.—ignominious, infamous, obscure, undistinguished, unknown.

fanatical, biased, bigoted, dogmatic, extreme, illiberal, intolerant, narrow-minded, obsessed, prejudiced, rabid, radical, unreasonable, zealous. ANT.—dispassionate, liberal, reasonable, tolerant.

fancy, conceit, conception, idea, imagination, notion; caprice, fantasy, vagary, whim; fondness, inclination; elaborate, ornamental, ornate. ANT.—actuality, reality; precision, stability; aversion; plain, unadorned.

fantastic, capricious, fanciful, far-fetched, imaginary, visionary, whimsical; bizarre, eccentric, odd, peculiar, quaint, strange, vague; amazing, wonderful. ANT.—fixed, precise, steady; common, ordinary, usual.

far, away, distant, remote, removed. ANT.—close, convenient, handy, near.

farcical, absurd, comic, droll, foolish, funny, hilarious, ludicrous, ridiculous. ANT.—sober, tragic.

far-sighted, clairvoyant, clear-sighted, foresighted, judicious, level-headed, prepared, prudent. ANT.—impractical, imprudent, injudicious, rash, unprepared.

fascinate, allure, beguile, bewitch, captivate, delight, enamor, enchant, enrapture, enthrall, entrance, ravish. ANT.—agitate, anger, disgust, repel, weary.

fashion, appearance, fashion, manner, mode, vague; cast, contrive, create, design, fabricate, form, make, manufacture, mold, sculpture, style.

fast, accelerated, brisk, expeditious, fleet, lively, quick, rapid, speedy, swift; constant, firm, inflexible, lasting, permanent, secure, solid, stable, steadfast, steady, tight, unswerving, unyielding; dissipated, dissolute, reckless, wild. ANT.—slow, sluggish; insecure, loose, unstable, unsteady; exemplary, upright, virtuous.

fasten, affix, anchor, attach, bind, connect, link, lock, secure, tie. ANT.—detach, loosen, open, release, untie.

fastidious, choosy, critical, finicky, fussy, meticulous, particular, squeamish. ANT.—gross, indifferent, tasteless, uncritical.

fat, beefy, corpulent, fleshy, obese, portly, rotund, stout, swollen, thickset, unctuous, unwieldy; luxuriant, rich, wealthy, well-to-do. ANT.—gaunt, lean, slender, slim, thin; indigent, penniless, poor.

fatal, deadly, lethal, mortal, murderous, pernicious. ANT.—animating, enlivening, invigorating, nourishing, vital.

fate, chance, consequence, fortune; destiny, doom, issue, lot, outcome, result; predestination, predetermination.

fatigue, debilitation, enervation, exhaustion, languor, lassitude, tiredness, weakness, weariness. ANT.—liveliness, rejuvenation, restoration, vigor, vivacity.

fault, blemish, defect, detriment, drawback, error, failure, flaw, foible, imperfection, misdeed, misdemeanor, mistake, omission, shortcoming, slip, weakness. ANT.—correctness, merit, perfection.

favorable, advantageous, assisting, auspicious, beneficial, conducive, helpful, propitious, salutary, useful. ANT.—detrimental, disadvantageous, harmful, hindering, opposed.

fear, alarm, apprehension, anxiety, cowardice, dismay, disquietude, dread, fright, horror, panic, phobia, scare, terror, timidity, trepidation; awe, reverence. ANT.—assurance, boldness, bravery, courage, fearlessness; nonchalance, unconcern.

feasible, achievable, attainable, practicable, practical, workable. ANT.—impractical, inconceivable, unrealistic, visionary.

feat, accomplishment, achievement, act, action, attainment, deed, execution, exercise, exploit, maneuver, operation, performance. ANT.—failure, inactivity, laziness, passivity, stagnation.

fee, account, bill, charge, compensation, cost, emolument, pay, payment, remuneration.

feeble, debilitated, decrepit, delicate, enervated, exhausted, faint, forceless, frail, impaired, infirm, languid, puny, sickly, weak. ANT.—forceful, hearty, lusty, stout, strong, vigorous.

feeling, consciousness, sensation, sense, sensitivity; affection, emotion, passion, sensibility, sentiment, sympathy, tenderness; conviction, impression, opinion. ANT.—anesthesia, unconsciousness; coldness, imperturbability, insensibility, stoicism; fact.

felicitate, compliment, congratulate, greet. ANT.—discourage, dismay, reject.

felonious, corrupt, criminal, depraved, evil, heinous, injurious, malicious, noxious, perfidious, perverse, vicious. ANT.—commendable, decent, honorable, meritorious, praiseworthy.

feminine, female, ladylike, maidenly, womanish, womanlike, womanly; delicate, soft, tender. ANT.—male, manly, mannish, masculine; hardy, strong, virile.

ferment, agitate, boil, bubble, concoct, embroil, excite, fret, heat, leaven, raise, roil, seethe, stir. ANT.—calm, cool, dampen, quiet, soothe.

ferocious, barbarous, brutal, brutish, cruel, fearsome, fierce, murderous, ravenous, vehement, violent, wild. ANT.—docile, gentle, harmless, manageable, tame.

fertile, abundant, bountiful, copious, exuberant, fecund, fruitful, luxuriant, plenteous, plentiful, productive, prolific, rich, teeming. ANT.—barren, childless, fruitless, sterile, unproductive.

fervent, animated, ardent, eager, enthusiastic, intense, passionate, zealous. ANT.—cool, grudging, hesitant, impassive, phlegmatic.

fetid, foul-smelling, malodorous, noisome, putrid, rank, repulsive, stinking. ANT.—aromatic, fragrant, perfumed, sweet-smelling.

feudal, dependent, downtrodden, enslaved, peasant, servile, subject, vassal. ANT.—aristocratic, free, independent.

fever, ardor, delirium, excitement, frenzy, heat, mania, temperature. ANT.—calmness, coolness.

fiasco, catastrophe, debacle, failure, miscarriage. ANT.—achievement, success, triumph, victory.

fickle, capricious, changeable, fanciful, fitful, inconstant, irresolute, restless, shifting, unreliable, unstable, variable, volatile, wavering, wayward. ANT.—constant, reliable, stable, steady, trustworthy.

fiction, allegory, creation, epic, fable, fabrication, falsehood, fancy, figment, imagination, invention, legend, myth, narrative, novel, parable, romance, story, tale. ANT.—fact, history, reality, truth, verity.

fidelity, adherence, allegiance, constancy, devotion, faithfulness, fealty, integrity, loyalty, obedience, steadfastness, support, zeal; accuracy, exactness, precision, truth. ANT.—disloyalty, faithlessness, inconstancy, perfidy, treachery.

fiendish, atrocious, cruel, demoniac, devilish, diabolical, infernal, inhuman, malicious, malignant. ANT.—angelic, benign, kindly.

fierce, angry, barbarous, brutal, dangerous, enraged, ferocious, fiery, passionate, savage, truculent, violent, wild. ANT.—docile, kind, peaceful, placid, tender.

fight, battle, box, brawl, combat, conflict, contend, contest, dispute, quarrel, scuffle, skirmish, squabble, strive, struggle, wrangle.

figment, fabrication, falsehood, fantasy, fiction, imagination, invention. ANT.—fact, reality, truth.

figure, allegory, amount, appearance, character, construction, design, emblem, form, metaphor, numeral, outline, picture, representation, shape, sum, symbol, type.

fill, fill up, occupy, pack, pervade; distend, feed, glut, gorge, load, permeate, sate, satiate, satisfy, saturate, stuff, swell. ANT.—deplete, drain, empty, exhaust, void.

filter, clarify, infiltrate, purify, refine, screen, separate, settle, strain.

final, concluding, conclusive, decisive, definitive, ending, extreme, last, terminal, ultimate. ANT.—first, inaugural, original, rudimentary, unending.

fine, admirable, attractive, choice, clarified, dainty, delicate, elegant, excellent, exquisite, keen, minute, nice, polished, pure, refined, sensitive, smooth, splendid, small, thin; ground, pulverized; amercement, charge, cost, forfeiture, penalty. ANT.—blunt, coarse, rough, unpolished, thick; amends, compensation, reward.

finish, accomplish, achieve, close, complete, conclude, consummate, end, execute, fulfill, get done, perfect, terminate; close, completion, end, termination, terminus. ANT.—begin, initiate, start; initiation, origin, source.

finite, bounded, circumscribed, determinate, limited, measurable, restricted, terminate. ANT.—endless, eternal, infinite, unbounded.

firm, constant, enduring, fixed, resolute, rugged, solid, stable, steadfast, steady, strong, tenacious, unfaltering, unyielding. ANT.—defective, disjointed, irresolute, wavering, weak.

first, beginning, chief, earliest, initial, leading, original, premier, primary, prime, primeval, primitive, pristine; chief, foremost. ANT.—hindmost, last, latest, least, subordinate.

fit, accommodate, adapt, adjust, conform, equip, prepare, suit; adapted, appropriate, becoming, befitting, competent, congruous, pertinent, prepared, proper, qualified, seemly. ANT.—disturb, misapply, misfit; awkward, inadequate, incongruous, unfit.

fitful, capricious, changeable, convulsive, desultory, fickle, inconstant, intermittent, restless, spasmodic, unstable, variable, whimsical. ANT.—constant, reliable, stable, steady, trustworthy, uniform.

fix, affix, attach, bind, fasten, link, place, plant, root, secure, set, stick, tie; define, determine, establish, limit, locate, prepare, set, settle; adjust, correct, mend, rectify, regulate, repair, restore. ANT.—displace, remove, unfasten; alter, change, disturb, modify; damage, mistreat.

flaccid, drooping, flabby, lax, limber, loose, soft, weak, yielding. ANT.—firm, strong, sturdy, tenacious, unyielding.

flagrant, atrocious, glaring, gross, infamous, monstrous, outrageous, rank, wicked. ANT.—mild, unrestrained.

flame, blaze, burn, flare, ignite, light. ANT.—extinguish, quench.

flashy, flamboyant, gaudy, garish, jazzy, meretricious, pretentious, showy. ANT.—simple, sober, subdued.

flat, even, flush, horizontal, level, plane; dull, insipid, stale, tasteless, vapid; dejected, depressed, heavy, low, spiritless. ANT.—hilly, irregular, mountainous, sloping; bubbling, exciting, frothy, savory; keen, spirited.

flatter, blandish, blarney, cajole, coax, court, entice, exalt, extol, fawn, laud, praise, soften, wheedle. ANT.—denounce, insult, mock, ridicule, spurn.

flaunt, blazon, brandish, expose, flash, flourish, parade, vaunt. ANT.—cloak, conceal, disguise, hide, retire.

flavor, essence, gusto, quality, relish, savor, soul, spirit, tang, taste, zest.

flawless, exact, immaculate, impeccable, perfect, pure, spotless, unblemished, unmarred, whole. ANT.—damaged, defective, flawed, imperfect, tainted.

fleeting, brief, ephemeral, evanescent, flitting, fugitive, momentary, passing, short, temporary, transient, transitory, vanishing. ANT.—constant, enduring, eternal, long-lived, perpetual.

flexible, bending, compliant, docile, ductile, elastic, limber, lithe, plastic, pliable, pliant, supple, tractable, yielding. ANT.—brittle, obstinate, rigid, stiff, unbending.

flicker, flare, fluctuate, flutter, glint, quiver, shimmer, waver. ANT.—glow, shine steadily.

flinch, cower, cringe, falter, recoil, retreat, run, shrink, wince, withdraw. ANT.—confront, face, hold out, sustain.

fling, cast, chuck, heave, pitch, throw, toss. ANT.—catch.

float, drift, fly, glide, hover, sail, skim, wave.

flourish, brandish, conquer, grow, increase, prosper, thrive, triumph, vaunt, wave, win. ANT.—collapse, decay, diminish, fade, weaken.

flow, circulate, course, float, glide, gush, move, pass, roll, run, spout, spurt, stream; emanate, issue, originate, proceed, progress, result; abound, be copious. ANT.—cease, cork, retard, stagnate, stop.

fluctuate, change, deflect, detour, deviate, digress, hesitate, oscillate, sway, swerve, teeter, totter, undulate, vacillate, vary, veer, vibrate, wander, waver. ANT.—adhere, decide, persist, remain, stick.

fluent, copious, easy, expert, flowing, liquid, moving, smooth, voluble. ANT.—hesitant, motionless, slow, sluggish, stammering.

flux, activity, change, discharge, flow, fluctuation, motion, mutation, transition. ANT.—constancy, fixity, inactivity, stability.

fly, ascend, flit, float, flutter, glide, hover, mount, rise, sail, skim, soar, wing; dart, rush, shoot, spring; abscond, decamp, escape, flee, run away. ANT.—descend, fall, plummet, sink; remain, stay.

focus, center, centrum, concentration, cynosure, limelight.

foe, adversary, antagonist, enemy, opponent, rival, vilifier. ANT.—assistant, comrade, friend, helper.

follow, come next, succeed; comply, conform, heed, obey, observe, practice; adopt, copy, imitate, mimic; accompany, attend; chase, pursue, trace, track, trail; ensue, result. ANT.—precede; guide, lead; avoid, elude, flee; cause.

follower, adherent, attendant, devotee, disciple, henchman, partisan, pupil, protege, pursuer, servant, successor, supporter, votary. ANT.—chief, head, leader, master; adversary, antagonist, objector, oppressor, scorner.

folly, absurdity, fatuity, foolishness, imbecility, imprudence, indiscretion, madness, misconduct, shallowness, silliness, simplicity, weak-mindedness, weakness. ANT.—cunning, discernment, judgment, prudence, reasonableness, wisdom.

fondle, caress, cuddle, indulge, neck, nuzzle, pet, stroke, toy. ANT.—disdain, reject.

fool, cheat, con, deceive, delude, dupe, hoodwink, trick; buffoon, clown, harlequin, jester; blockhead, dolt, dunce, idiot, imbecile, nincompoop, numbskull, oaf, simpleton. ANT.—genius, philosopher, sage, scholar.

foolish, absurd, asinine, brainless, crazy, fatuous, idiotic, imbecile, irrational, nonsensical, preposterous, ridiculous, senseless, silly, simple, witless. ANT.—astute, judicious, prudent, sagacious, wise.

forbearance, abstention, abstinence, fortitude, leniency, patience, self-denial, tolerance. ANT.—excess, haste, impatience, intolerance, self-indulgence, strictness.

force, energy, intensity, might, potency, power, strength, vigor; coercion, compulsion, constraint, duress, violence; aggregation, armament, army, battalion, body, company, division, navy, number, organization, regiment, troops; coerce, compel, constrain, drive, impel, incite, instigate, push, rush. ANT.—feebleness, frailty, impotence, weakness; persuasion; hamper, retard, suppress, thwart.

forego, see FORGO.

foreign, alien, distant, extraneous, far, remote, strange, unaccustomed, unknown, unnatural. ANT.—accustomed, familiar, indigenous, known.

forever, always, continually, endlessly, eternally, everlastingly, immortally, unremittingly. ANT.—briefly, fleetingly, shortly, temporarily.

forget, disregard, ignore, lose, neglect, omit, overlook, slight. ANT.—recall, recollect, remember, reminisce.

forgo (forego), abandon, abstain, desist, leave, quit, relinquish, renounce, resign, waive. ANT.—accomplish, execute, fulfill, perform, yield.

form, assemble, build, construct, create, design, erect, fashion, forge, make, mold, produce, shape; compose, constitute, make up; arrange, combine, organize, plan; devise, frame, invent; conformation, figure, formation, structure; ceremony, ritual, image, likeness. ANT.—destroy, disfigure, dismantle, misshape, wreck; amorphism, distortion, irregularity, shapelessness.

formal, ceremonial, ceremonious, decorous, exact, functional, methodical, orderly, precise, proper, punctilious, regular, ritualistic, solemn, stiff, systematic. ANT.—casual, easy, natural, unconstrained, unconventional.

former, antecedent, anterior, before, foregoing, preceding, previous, prior. ANT.—after, ensuing, latter, succeeding, subsequent.

formulate, devise, concoct, express, fabricate, frame. ANT.—fumble, guess, hazard.

forte, feature, genius, knack, skill, strong point, talent. ANT.—clumsiness, impotence, incompetence.

fortuitous, accidental, casual, chance, contingent, felicitous, fortunate, happy, incidental, lucky, propitious, random. ANT.—arranged, calculated, deliberate, plotted, unlucky.

fortunate, advantageous, auspicious, benign, encouraging, favored, felicitous, fortuitous, fortunate, happy, lucky, propitious, prosperous, satisfied, successful. ANT.—cheerless, condemned, crushed, ill-fated, persecuted.

fortune, accident, chance, destiny, end, fate, goal, luck; determination, judgment; inheritance, possession, property, riches, wealth. ANT.—catastrophe, downfall, hardship, misfortune, poverty.

forward, advance, aggrandize, bring forward, cultivate, elevate, encourage, expedite, favor, further, help, promote. ANT.—hinder, oppose, retard, retreat, withhold.

foul, dirty, fetid, filthy, grimy, muddy, polluted, putrid, soiled, squalid, tainted; indecent, nasty, obscene, offensive, vulgar; base, contemptible, corrupt, despicable, low, mean, pitiful, shabby. ANT.—clean, immaculate, neat, presentable; pure, unblemished, wholesome.

foundation, base, basis, bottom, endowment, establishment, footing, ground, groundwork, institution, origin, root, substructure, support, underpinning, understructure. ANT.—arch, crown, peak, superstructure, top.

fraction, bit, division, part, percentage, piece, portion, section, segment. ANT.—all, entirety, total, whole.

fracture, breach, break, crack, rent, rift, rupture, split. ANT.—conjugation, juncture, union.

fragile, breakable, brittle, delicate, feeble, frail, infirm, weak. ANT.—durable, enduring, hardy, strong, sturdy, tough.

frank, aboveboard, candid, direct, easy, familiar, free, honest, ingenuous, plain, sincere, straightforward. ANT.—cunning, deceptive, dishonest, hypocritical, insincere.

fraud, artifice, cheat, chicanery, deceit, deception, dishonesty, duplicity, forgery, guile, hoax, imposition, imposture, swindle, treachery, trick. ANT.—fairness, honesty, integrity, sincerity, truth.

free, autonomous, emancipated, exempt, freed, independent, liberated, unconfined, unconstrained, unencumbered, unfettered, unobstructed, unrestricted; clear, loose, open, unfastened, unobstructed; immune; careless, candid, easy, familiar, frank, open, unreserved; artless, bounteous, bountiful, generous, liberal, munificent; costless, gratis. ANT.—confined, restrained, restricted; blocked, clogged, impeded; subject; illiberal, parsimonious, stingy; costly, expensive, priceless.

freedom, deliverance, emancipation, exemption, familiarity, franchise, frankness, immunity, independence, liberation, liberty, license, openness, prerogative, privilege, right, unrestraint. ANT.—bondage, coercion, compulsion, constraint, servitude.

freight, burden, cargo, lading, load, shipment, transportation.

frenzy, agitation, delirium, derangement, excitement, fury, madness, mania, rage, wildness. ANT.—calmness, delight, sanity.

frequent, common, general, habitual, many, numerous, often, persistent, recurrent, recurring, regular, repeated, usual. ANT.—exceptional, infrequent, rare, scanty, sporadic.

fresh, modern, new, novel, recent, unused; additional, further; brisk, cool, hardy, healthy, natural, refreshing, vigorous, young; artless, green, inexperienced, natural, raw; bold, cheeky, flippant, impertinent. ANT.—decayed, faded, hackneyed, musty, stagnant; courteous, deferential, respectful.

fret, agitate, anger, annoy, chafe, corrode, disturb, fidget, gall, gnaw, worry. ANT.—calm, placate, please, soften, soothe.

friction, abrasion, attrition, erosion, frication, grating, rubbing, traction; conflict, disagreement, discord, disharmony. ANT.—lubrication, smoothness; accord, agreement, harmony, unity.

friend, companion, comrade, confidant, crony, intimate, pal; adherent, advocate, defender, patron, supporter; ally, associate, colleague. ANT.—adversary, enemy, stranger.

friendly, affable, affectionate, amicable, brotherly, companionable, cordial, genial, intimate, kindly, neighborly, propitious, sociable, solicitous, sympathetic. ANT.—antagonistic, cool, distant, hostile, reserved.

frighten, abash, affright, alarm, appall, astound, browbeat, daunt, discourage, dishearten, dismay, dispirit, hector, horrify, intimidate, scare, startle, terrify, terrorize, threaten. ANT.—embolden, gladden, inspire, reassure, soothe.

frigid, arctic, chilling, cool, ice-cold; dull, formal, inhibited, lifeless, passionless, reserved, rigid. ANT.—temperate, warm; amorous, fervid, responsive, uninhibited.

fringe, border, boundary, edge, edging, flounce, outskirts, perimeter, tassel, trimming. ANT.—center, core, heart, inside, interior.

front, anterior, facade, face, forepart, prow, van; bearing, brow, forehead, manner, mien. ANT.—astern, back, posterior, rear.

frown, disapprove, glare, glower, lower, scowl, sulk. ANT.—approve, beam, shine, smile.

frugal, conservative, economical, miserly, moderate, parsimonious, penurious, provident, saving, sparing, stingy, temperate, thrifty. ANT.—extravagant, intemperate, self-indulgent, wasteful.

fruitful, abundant, ample, bountiful, copious, exuberant, fecund, fertile, luxuriant, plenteous, productive, prolific, rich, teeming, yielding. ANT.—barren, fruitless, impotent, sterile, unproductive.

frustrate, baffle, balk, bar, circumvent, confound, counteract, defeat, disappoint, disconcert, foil, hinder, nullify, prevent, stop, thwart. ANT.—accomplish, facilitate, fulfill, further, promote.

fulfill, accomplish, complete, consummate, finish, realize, terminate; discharge, perform; comply, fill, meet, satisfy. ANT.—abandon, disappoint, fail, neglect, withdraw.

full, crammed, filled, glutted, gorged, packed, replete, sated, satiated, soaked, stocked, surfeited, swollen; ample, complete, copious, extensive, plentiful, sufficient, whole; baggy, flowing, loose, voluminous; circumstantial, detailed, exhaustive. ANT.—depleted, devoid, empty, vacant; insufficient, lacking, partial.

function, bailiwick, business, duty, job, office, position, role, task; do, moderate, officiate, operate, perform, preside, serve, work. ANT.—idleness, unemployment; ignore, malfunction, mismanage.

fundamental, basic, chief, elemental, essential, indispensable, intrinsic, primary, principal, radical. ANT.—auxiliary, dispensable, secondary, subordinate, superficial.

funny, absurd, amusing, bizarre, comical, diverting, droll, farcical, humorous, laughable, ludicrous, ridiculous, witty; curious, odd, queer. ANT.—melancholy, sad, serious, sober, solemn.

furious, angry, ferocious, fierce, frenzied, fuming, inflamed, infuriated, raging, turbulent, violent, wild. ANT.—calm, composed, peaceful, self-possessed, tranquil.

furnish, appoint, cater, endow, equip, fit, outfit, provide, purvey, supply; afford, give, produce, yield. ANT.—denude, despoil, divest, strip, withhold.

further, advance, aid, assist, expedite, promote, support. ANT.—check, delay, frustrate, hinder, impede.

furtive, clandestine, covert, secret, sly, stealthy, surreptitious. ANT.—aboveboard, forthright, open, overt.

futile, abortive, empty, fruitless, idle, ineffective, ineffectual, resultless, unsatisfying, useless, vain, valueless. ANT.—beneficial, conducive, efficient, profitable, useful.

G

gain, accretion, acquisition, advantage, behalf, benefit, emolument, favor, good, increase, increment, interest, net, profit; accomplish, achieve, acquire, attain, benefit, consummate, earn, effect, get, obtain, procure, profit, reach, realize, reap, secure, win. ANT.—decrease, handicap, loss; forfeit, lose, surrender.

galaxy, array, assemblage, bevy, cluster, collection, company, constellation, group.

gamble, bet, chance, hazard, play, risk, speculate, stake, wager. ANT.—insure, invest, plan, safeguard.

game, adventure, amusement, contest, diversion, entertainment, festivity, frolic, fun, gaiety, gambol, lark, match, merriment, merrymaking, pastime, play, recreation, sport; courageous, daring, disposed, favorable, sporting, valiant, willing. ANT.—business.

gamut, compass, extent, range, register, scope.

gap, abyss, aperture, breach, cavity, chasm, chink, cleft, crack, crevice, fissure, gulf, hiatus, hole, hollow, interstice, lacuna, opening, orifice, passage, space, vacancy, vacuity, void.

garble, corrupt, deface, distort, falsify, misquote, misrepresent, misstate, mix, muddle, mutilate, pervert, scramble. ANT.—clarify, communicate, correct, edit, unscramble.

garment, apparel, array, attire, clothes, clothing, drapery, dress, garb, habiliment, raiment, robe, vestment, vesture, wrap. ANT.—nakedness, nudity.

garner, accumulate, collect, deposit, harvest, hoard, husband, reserve, save, store.

garnish, adorn, array, beautify, bedeck, deck, decorate, embellish, enhance, enrich, furnish, grace, ornament, strew, trim. ANT.—debase, defame, expose, strip, uncover.

garrulous, babbling, bumptious, chattering, chatty, loquacious, prattling, prolix, talkative, verbose, wordy. ANT.—laconic, reticent, silent, taciturn, uncommunicative.

gather, accumulate, acquire, amass, assemble, collect, congregate, convene, convoke, group, meet, muster; compress, contract; cull, garner, glean, harvest, heap, pick, pile, reap; conclude, deduce, infer, judge. ANT.—disband, disperse, distribute, scatter, separate.

gaudy, cheap, flamboyant, flashy, garish, glaring, tasteless, tawdry, vulgar. ANT.—pale, refined, solemn, somber, tasteful.

gauge, calculation, caliber, criterion, diameter, evaluation, measure, norm, standard, template, thickness. ANT.—estimate, guess, hazard.

gaunt, attenuated, bony, emaciated, empty, flimsy, haggard, hollow, hungry, lank, lean, meager, scanty, scraggy, scrawny, shriveled, shrunken, skinny, slender, slight, slim, spare, thin, withered. ANT.—broad, bulky, fat, obese, portly.

gay, blithe, buoyant, cheerful, colorful, convivial, festive, frolicsome, glad, happy, hilarious, jolly, jovial, joyful, lighthearted, lively, merry, sprightly, vivacious, waggish. ANT.—depressed, glum, mournful, sad, sullen.

gaze, behold, discern, eye, gape, gawk, glance, look, peer, stare, survey, view, watch; examine, inspect, observe, regard. ANT.—avert, ignore, miss, overlook.

genealogy, ancestry, descent, lineage, parentage, pedigree, progeniture, stock.

general, all-embracing, common, commonplace, comprehensive, conventional, customary, everyday, extensive, familiar, frequent, generic, habitual, inclusive, indefinite, normal, ordinary, popular, prevailing, prevalent, regular, universal, usual, whole, widespread; indefinite, inexact, vague. ANT.—exceptional, rare, singular; definite, particular, specific.

generally, chiefly, commonly, mainly, ordinarily, principally, usually. ANT.—especially, occasionally, particularly, rarely, seldom.

generation, age, breed, creation, engendering, family, formation, procreation, production, reproduction; epoch, era, period, span, time. ANT.—breakdown, dissolution, obliteration, wreckage.

generic, characteristic, comprehensive, general, ideal, representative, typical. ANT.—individual, particular, peculiar, special.

generosity, altruism, beneficence, benevolence, bounty, bountifulness, charity, humanity, kindness, lavishness, liberality, magnanimity, munificence, nobleness, philanthropy. ANT.—cruelty, inhumanity, malevolence, selfishness, unkindness.

generous, beneficent, bountiful, forgiving, giving, high-minded, honorable, liberal, magnanimous, munificent, openhanded, open-hearted, unselfish, wholehearted. ANT.—covetous, greedy, miserly, selfish, stingy.

genial, affable, animated, brotherly, cheerful, congenial, convivial, cordial, fraternal, hospitable, pleasant, pleasing, warm-hearted, well-disposed. ANT.—doleful, inhospitable, moody, petulant, sullen.

genius, ability, acumen, aptitude, brains, brilliance, capacity, creativity, endowment, faculty, gift, inspiration, intellect, knack, leaning, perspicacity, propensity, sagacity, talent; intellectual, master, prodigy, wizard. ANT.—ineptitude, obtuseness, shallowness, stupidity; dolt, dullard, moron.

gentle, benign, calm, compliant, docile, genteel, meek, mild, moderate, pacific, peaceful, placid, relaxed, serene, soft, soothing, tame, temperate, tender, tractable. ANT.—fierce, harsh, rough, savage, violent.

genuine, actual, authentic, bona fide, exact, frank, honest, legitimate, natural, proven, real, sincere, tested, true, unadulterated, unaffected, unalloyed, unmixed, unquestionable, valid, veritable. ANT.—artificial, bogus, counterfeit, false, sham.

germ, beginning, first principal, origin, rudiment, source; bud, embryo, seed; spore; microbe, microorganism, pathogen. ANT.—conclusion, end, fruit, issue, outgrowth.

germane, allied, appropriate, apropos, cognate, fitting, pertinent, related, relevant. ANT.—inapplicable, irrelevant, unfitting, unrelated.

germinate, bud, develop, effloresce, evolve, grow, shoot, sprout, swell, vegetate. ANT.—die.

gesture, indication, motion, movement, portent, sign, signal, symbol.

get, achieve, acquire, arrive, attain, capture, comprehend, earn, gain, generate, grasp, learn, obtain, procure, propagate, reach, receive, secure, seize. ANT.—abnegate, forfeit, leave, renounce, surrender.

ghastly, ashen, cadaverous, dreadful, frightful, ghostly, grisly, hideous, horrible, pallid, revolting, shocking, terrifying. ANT.—attractive, captivating, healthy, pleasant, rosy.

ghost, apparition, banshee, fairy, goblin, haunt, image, phantom, shade, shadow, specter, spirit, sprite, spook, wraith. ANT.—essence, existence, fact, reality, substance.

giant, colossal, enormous, gigantic, huge, immense, monstrous, super, titanic, vast, whopping. ANT.—dwarf, infinitesimal, minute, stunted, tiny.

gift, alms, benefaction, bequest, bestowal, boon, bounty, charity, donation, endowment, favor, grant, gratuity, largess, legacy, munificence, present; provision, support; aptitude, faculty, genius, knack, talent. ANT.—deprivation, forfeiture, indemnity, loss; incapacity, ineptitude, stupidity.

gigantic, amazing, colossal, elephantine, enormous, extensive, gargantuan, great, huge, immense, mammoth, massive, monstrous, prodigious, stupendous, titanic, vast. ANT.—diminutive, insignificant, little, minute, tiny.

gimmick, adjunct, angle, contrivance, device, fraud, gadget, swindle, trick.

gird, arm, bind, clothe, encircle, endow, equip, fortify, furnish, girdle, invest, support, surround. ANT.—divest, loosen, release, strip, untie.

girth, boundary, cinch, circumference, corpulence, dimensions, measure, outline, perimeter.

gist, core, crux, drift, essence, import, meaning, pith, point, purpose, sense, significance, signification, substance, tenor, upshot.

give, bestow, bequeath, confer, contribute, convey, deliver, donate, furnish, grant, impart, present, provide, supply, yield. ANT.—deprive, keep, retain, seize, withdraw.

glad, blithesome, cheerful, cheering, content, delighted, exulting, gay, gratified, happy, jolly, joyful, joyous, lighthearted, merry, pleased, pleasing, vivacious. ANT.—dejected, depressed, dispirited, melancholy, sad.

glamour, allure, aura, bewitchment, charm, enchantment, fascination, magic, spell. ANT.—blandness, dullness, lackluster, obscurity.

glance, eye, gaze, look, scan, see; view, watch. ANT.—avert, hide, miss, overlook.

glare, beam, dazzle, flash, gleam, glimmer, glisten, glow, radiate, scintillate, sparkle, twinkle; frown, glower, scowl, stare.

glassy, bright, crystalline, glossy, lustrous, polished, silken, smooth, transparent, vitreous; dull-eyed, expressionless, limpid. ANT.—dim, lusterless, obscure, opaque, tarnished.

gleam, beam, blaze, flash, flicker, glare, glimmer, glance, glint, glisten, glitter, glow, radiate, ray, scintillate, shimmer, shine, sparkle, twinkle.

glib, articulate, diplomatic, facile, fluent, oily, polished, sleek; smooth, suave, urbane, vocal, voluble. ANT.—harsh, inarticulate, rough, rugged, stammering.

gloat, brag, boast, crow, exult, flaunt, rejoice, revel, triumph. ANT.—condole, commiserate, sympathize.

gloomy, cheerless, crestfallen, dejected, depressed, depressing, despondent, disconsolate, discontented, discouraged, dismal, dispirited, doleful, downcast, dull, funereal, glum, heavy, melancholy, miserable, moody, morose, oppressive, pessimistic, sad, somber, sorrowful, sullen, unhappy; clouded, dark, dim, dusky, shady. ANT.—cheerful, happy, joyous, merry, optimistic.

glorify, adore, applaud, bless, celebrate, consecrate, dignify, elevate, enshrine, enthrone, esteem, exaggerate, exalt, extol, hallow, honor, idolize, laud, magnify, prize, revere, sanctify, value, venerate. ANT.—abase, debase, degrade, dishonor, mock.

glorious, brilliant, celebrated, elevated, exalted, grand, high, lofty, magnificent, majestic, marvelous, noble, raised, resplendent, shining, splendid, sublime, supreme, wondrous. ANT.—atrocious, base, contemptible, ignoble, ridiculous.

glossy, elegant, glazed, lustrous, polished, refined, reflecting, shining, sleek, velvety; deceptive, showy, specious, superficial. ANT.—lusterless, rough, unpolished; genuine, honest, uncouth, unrefined.

glow, beam, blaze, burn, flame, flare, flash, flicker, glare, gleam, glimmer, glisten, glitter, light, radiate, scintillate, shimmer, shine, sparkle, twinkle. ANT.—die, fade.

glum, blue, dejected, dismal, dispirited, dour, gloomy, low, moody, morose, sulky, sullen. ANT.—amiable, buoyant, cheerful, joyous, merry.

glut, overfeed, overstock, oversupply; cloy, cram, deluge, flood, gorge, overeat, sate, satiate, satisfy, stuff, surfeit. ANT.—abstain, curb, deplete, empty, void.

glutinous, adhesive, cohesive, gluey, gummy, sticky, viscid, viscous. ANT.—clean, dry, glueless, powdery.

gnarled, contorted, knotted, knotty, rugged, twisted. ANT.—direct, plain, smooth, straight.

go, abandon, abscond, budge, decamp, depart, desert, disappear, exit, fade, flee, leave, move, pass, proceed, quit, recede, relinquish, retire, retreat, run, step, stir, travel, vanish, walk, withdraw. ANT.—arrive, come, enter, stay, stop.

goad, impel, pressure, prod, prompt, provoke, push, spur, urge. ANT.—deter, discourage, dissuade, restrain.

goal, aim, ambition, aspiration, desire, destination, end, hope, intention, object, objective; basket, end zone, finish line, target.

godly, consecrated, devotional, devout, divine, godlike, hallowed, immaculate, incorrupt, inviolate, pious, pure, religious, reverent, sacred, saintly, sinless, stainless. ANT.—corrupt, profane, sacrilegious, ungodly, wicked.

good, chaste, conscientious, exemplary, honest, incorrupt, moral, pure, reliable, reputable, righteous, sinless, upright, virtuous, worthy; admirable, commendable, excellent, genuine, precious, real, sound, valid; benevolent, gracious, humane, kind; agreeable, cheerful, friendly, genial, gratifying, health-giving, invigorating, pleasant; fair, honorable, immaculate, stainless, unspotted, untainted; auspicious, beneficial, favorable, profitable, propitious, serviceable, suitable, useful, valuable; able, capable, efficient, expert, proficient, skillful; adequate, ample, satisfactory, sufficient. ANT.—contemptible, evil, injurious, odious, vile.

goods, belongings, chattels, commodities, effects, freight, material, merchandise, property, stock, wares.

gorge, bolt, cram, fill, glut, gobble, sate, satiate, surfeit. ANT.—diet, fast, starve.

gorgeous, dazzling, glorious, grand, magnificent, majestic, resplendent, splendid, superb, surpassing. ANT.—common, homely, modest, plain, unpretentious.

govern, administer, command, conduct, control, curb, dictate, direct, dominate, guide, influence, lead, manage, mold, order, oversee, regulate, reign, restrain, rule, superintend, supervise. ANT.—acquiesce, assent, obey, submit, surrender.

graceful, beautiful, becoming, comely, congruous, dignified, easy, elegant, flowing, fluid, harmonious, lithe, nimble, pleasing, refined, smooth, supple, symmetrical, tasteful, trim, unaffected. ANT.—awkward, clumsy, gawky, ungainly, unrefined.

gracious, agreeable, amiable, beneficent, benevolent, compassionate, congenial, courteous, engaging, friendly, good-natured, hospitable, kind, merciful, mild, munificent, pleasing, tender. ANT.—acrimonious, churlish, disagreeable, ill-natured, surly.

grade, brand, category, denomination, genre, kind; order, rank, set, stage, step; hill, incline, slope. ANT.—sameness, uniformity; level, plane.

gradual, creeping, dawdling, delaying, deliberate, dull, inching, laggard, leisurely, progressive, sluggish, slow, step-by-step, tired, unintermittent. ANT.—abrupt, hasty, quick, rapid, swift.

graduate, end, finish, qualify; adapt, adjust, calibrate, measure, proportion, regulate.

graft, bud, scion, shoot, transplant; booty, bribe, corruption, favoritism, kickback, loot.

grandeur, augustness, dignity, greatness, loftiness, magnificence, majesty, pomp, splendor, stateliness. ANT.—humility, lowliness, simplicity.

grant, allocate, allot, apportion, appropriate, assign, bestow, confer, deal, dispense, distribute, divide, furnish, give, measure, mete, present, transfer; accede, agree, allow, comply, concede, concur, permit, yield; benefaction, endowment, gift, present, privilege, reward. ANT.—confiscate, damage, refuse, retain, withhold; oppose, reject, renounce; charge, decrement, deduction, forfeiture, loss.

graphic, clear, definite, detailed, distinct, explicit, forcible, illustrative, pictorial, powerful, striking, telling, vivid. ANT.—abstract, ambiguous, obscure, weak.

grapple, clasp, clinch, clutch, contend, hook, seize, struggle, wrestle; comprehend, understand, unite. ANT.—abandon, ignore, loose, release, surrender.

grasp, apprehend, arrest, capture, catch, clasp, clutch, grapple, grip, lay hold of, retain, seize, snare, trap; comprehend, discern, perceive, recognize, understand. ANT.—extricate, liberate, lose, release; misconstrue, misunderstand.

grate, abrade, creak, grind, pulverize, rasp, scrape, scratch; annoy, irritate, jar, vex. ANT.—comfort, placate, please, soothe.

grateful, appreciative, beholden, gratified, indebted, obliged, thankful; acceptable, agreeable, pleasing. ANT.—thankless, unappreciative; abusive, careless, rude.

gratification, comfort, consolation, contentment, delight, ease, enjoyment, fulfillment, happiness, indulgence, pleasure, relief, reward, satisfaction, self-indulgence, solace, succor. ANT.—affliction, discomfort, misery, sacrifice, submission, suffering.

gratis, free, freely, gratuitous. ANT.—costly.

gratuitous, free, groundless, spontaneous, unfounded, unprovoked, voluntary, wanton. ANT.—deserved, earned, merited, warranted.

grave, consequential, critical, heavy, important, momentous, serious, weighty; demure, dignified, earnest, intense, ponderous, sedate, sober, solemn, staid, thoughtful. ANT.—insignificant, trifling, trivial; airy, buoyant, frivolous, merry.

great, big, enormous, gigantic, huge, immense, large, vast; numerous, countless; celebrated,

eminent, famed, famous, illustrious, prominent, renowned; critical, important, momentous, serious, vital, weighty; august, dignified, elevated, exalted, glorious, grand, honorable, majestic, noble; excellent, fine, magnificent, splendid; brave, chivalrous, courageous, daring, fearless, heroic, intrepid, valiant. ANT.—diminutive, little, minute, small; common, obscure, ordinary, unknown; menial, paltry, servile, shameful.

greedy, acquisitive, avaricious, covetous, grasping, grudging, illiberal, mercenary, miserly, parsimonious, rapacious, selfish; devouring, gluttonous, ravenous, stingy, voracious. ANT.—charitable, generous, munificent, philanthropic, sharing; full, satisfied.

greet, accost, address, approach, hail, receive, salute, speak to, welcome. ANT.—avoid, ignore, pass by.

gregarious, affable, amicable, companionable, convivial, friendly, hospitable, neighborly, outgoing, sociable. ANT.—antisocial, disagreeable, hermitic, inhospitable, unsociable.

grief, adversity, affliction, anguish, bereavement, calamity, catastrophe, distress, heartache, lamentation, misery, mourning, pain, sadness, sorrow, trial, tribulation, woe. ANT.—comfort, exhilaration, gladness, happiness, joy.

grievance, affliction, burden, complaint, damage, detriment, grief, hardship, harm, injury, injustice, sorrow, trial, tribulation, wrong. ANT.—benefit, happiness, justice, right, victory.

grieve, bemoan, bewail, deplore, lament, mourn, regret, rue, sorrow, suffer, weep; afflict, distress, pain, try, wound. ANT.—celebrate, rejoice, revel; console, heal.

grim, austere, dour, forbidding, gloomy, glum, inflexible, morose, severe, sinister, stern, sullen, terrifying, threatening. ANT.—blithe, enlivening, pleasant, serene, wining.

grip, capture, clasp, clutch, grab, grasp, hold, seize, snare, trap. ANT.—drop, loosen, relax, release.

grit, courage, decision, endurance, fortitude, mettle, nerve, pluck, spirit; abrasive, gravel, sand. ANT.—cowardice, fear, timidity.

groan, complain, cry, growl, grumble, lament, moan, sigh, sob, wail. ANT.—applaud, cheer, laugh, rejoice, sing.

grope, attempt, finger, fumble, grapple, hesitate, search, try. ANT.—comprehend, perceive.

gross, aggregate, entire, total, whole; brutal, enormous, glaring, grievous, manifest, plain; coarse, crass, earthy, indelicate, lewd, obscene, repulsive; rough, rude, vulgar; big, bulky, corpulent, fat, fleshy, great, large, monstrous, obese, thick. ANT.—proper, refined; moral, purified, spiritual; appealing, comely, delicate.

grotesque, absurd, bizarre, fantastic, incongruous, misshapen, monstrous, odd, strange, unnatural. ANT.—average, customary, normal, typical, usual.

grouch, complain, grumble, lament, murmur, mutter, mope, protest, remonstrate, repine, sulk, whine. ANT.—applaud, approve, praise, rejoice.

ground, base, basis, bottom, foundation, groundwork, support, underpinning; assumption, postulate, premise, presumption, presupposition, principle; land, locality, property, region, territory; base, establish, fix, set, settle; educate, instruct, train. ANT.—derivative, superstructure, trimming; demolish, unsettle.

group, aggregation, assemblage, assembly, audience, band, brood, bunch, class, clique, cluster, collection, company, crowd, flock, herd, horde, lot, meeting, mob, order, pack, party, set, swarm, throng, troupe.

groveling, abject, begging, contemptible, debased, crawling, cringing, cowering, crouching, despicable, dishonorable, fawning, ignoble, ignominious, low, lowly, mean, menial, servile, sneaking, snivelling, sordid, vile, vulgar. ANT.—commanding, controlling, esteemed, exalted, righteous.

grow, advance, accumulate, amplify, augment, bud, burgeon, develop, dilate, distend, enlarge, expand, extend, germinate, increase, inflate, mature, puff, stretch, swell, thicken, tumefy; breed, cultivate, farm, nurture, plant, raise, sow. ANT.—atrophy, contract, decay, diminish, shrink, stagnate; destroy, kill.

growl, bemoan, complain, groan, grumble, howl, mumble, murmur, mutter, snarl. ANT.—hum, purr, sing.

growth, accretion, advancement, development, elaboration, expansion, extension, increase, unfolding, unraveling; evolution, maturing, multiplication, progress, proliferation. ANT.—abbreviation, compression, curtailment, decline, failure.

grudge, animosity, aversion, detestation, enmity, grievance, hatred, hostility, ill will, malevolence, malice, malignity, rancor, resentment, resistance, spite. ANT.—affection, kindness, love, sympathy, toleration.

gruff, abrupt, acrimonious, blunt, brusque, churlish, coarse, cross, curt, harsh, morose, rough, rude, short, snappish, snarling, sour, stern, surly, unceremonious, uncivil, unpolished. ANT.—affable, complaisant, gracious, polished, serene.

guarantee, security, surety, warranty; affirm, allege, assert, attest, certify, declare, endorse, insure, guard, support, testify, verify, vouch, warrant. ANT.—deny, disown, ignore, reject, renounce.

guard, conceal, cover, curtain, defend, disguise, envelop, fortify, hide, mask, preserve, protect, safeguard, screen, secure, shelter, shield, shroud, treasure, veil. ANT.—disregard, divulge, expose, neglect, reveal.

guess, assume, believe, conjecture, estimate, fancy, imagine, opine, reckon, speculate, suppose, surmise. ANT.—ascertain, calculate, know, measure.

guide, conduct, control, direct, govern, lead, manage, pilot, regulate, shepherd, steer, supervise. ANT.—abandon, misguide, mislead, neglect.

guile, artifice, beguilement, cheat, chicanery, cunning, deceit, deception, dishonesty, double-dealing, duplicity, fraud, hypocrisy, imposture, sham, slyness, subtlety, trick, wiliness. ANT.—candor, honesty, integrity, openness, sincerity, truthfulness.

guilty, blameworthy, censurable, corrupt, criminal, culpable, faulty, immoral, liable, sinful, stained, tarnished, wicked. ANT.—blameless, faultless, innocent, innocuous, spotless.

guise, air, appearance, aspect, behavior, clothing, custom, demeanor, dress, garb, look, manner, mien, pose, posture, practice, role, semblance.

gush, burst, flood, flow, issue, pour, rave, spout, spurt. ANT.—fade, stop, trickle, wane.

H

habit, addiction, continuation, custom, fashion, manner, method, mode, observance, practice, prevalence, routine, style, use, way, wont; clothes, dress, garb, raiment.

habitual, accustomed, common, customary, established, frequent, general, often, perpetual, persistent, recurrent, regular, usual. ANT.—exceptional, infrequent, rare, uncommon, unique.

hack, botch, break, chip, chop, cut, drudge, lacerate, mangle, mutilate, split, tear, toil.

haggard, careworn, debilitated, emaciated, exhausted, fretted, gaunt, hollow-eyed, wasted, weak, weary. ANT.—exuberant, forcible, powerful, robust, vigorous.

haggle, bargain, cavil, deal, dicker, patter, quibble, stickle, wrangle.

hail, acclaim, accost, address, applaud, approach, cheer, greet, herald, honor, salute, summon, welcome. ANT.—avoid, disregard, ignore, scorn, shun.

hale, chipper, healthy, hearty, lusty, robust, salubrious, salutary, sound, strong, vigorous, well, wholesome. ANT.—delicate, diseased, feeble, frail, infirm.

half-hearted, cool, dull, indifferent, perfunctory, unenthusiastic, uninterested. ANT.—ardent, enthusiastic, warm, wholehearted, zealous.

hall, atrium, auditorium, building, corridor, dormitory, edifice, entrance, headquarters; house, manor, mansion, passage, residence, vestibule.

hallow, aggrandize, bless, consecrate, dignify, elevate, ennoble, erect, exalt, extol, glorify, raise, reverse, sanctify, venerate. ANT.—debase, degrade, curse, dishonor, humble.

hallucination, aberration, chimera, delusion, fantasy, illusion, mirage, phantasm, vision. ANT.—existence, reality, truth.

halt, arrest, bar, cease, check, close, cork, desist, discontinue, doubt, end, falter, hesitate, hinder, impede, intermit, interrupt, linger, obstruct, pause, stop, suspend, terminate. ANT.—advance, persevere, proceed, promote, speed.

hamper, encumber, hinder, impede, obstruct, perplex, prevent, restrain, restrict, retard, shackle, thwart. ANT.—assist, ease, facilitate, promote, relieve.

handicap, burden, defect, disadvantage, drag, encumbrance, impediment, limitation, obstruction, penalty; allowance, odds. ANT.—advantage, asset, benefit, remuneration, reward.

handle, direct, feel, finger, manage, manipulate, negotiate, operate, ply, wield; cope.

handsome, attractive, beauteous, beautiful, charming, comely, elegant, fair, fine, good-looking, graceful, lovely, pretty, shapely; ample, generous, large, liberal. ANT.—foul, hideous, homely, repulsive; insignificant, mean, poor, small.

handy, able, accessible, adapted, adept, adroit, advantageous, appropriate, available, clever, commodious, convenient, dexterous, favorable, fitting, helpful, ready, resourceful, skilled, skillful, suitable, timely, useful. ANT.—awkward, inconvenient, inopportune, troublesome, unskilled.

hang, attach, dangle, depend, drape, droop, hover, lean, suspend, swing; execute, gibbet, lynch.

happen, accrue, arrive, bechance, befall, betide, chance, come, ensue, eventuate, follow, occur, result, supervene, take place, transpire.

happiness, beatitude, blessedness, bliss, contentment, delight, ecstasy, exultation, felicity, gladness, merriment, mirth, peace, pleasure, rapture, satisfaction, wellbeing. ANT.—adversity, catastrophe, despair, grief, misery.

happy, blessed, blissful, blithe, bright, buoyant, cheerful, contented, delighted, delightful, ecstatic, elated, exhilarated, favorable, fortunate, gay, glad, gratified, jocund, jovial, joyful, joyous, merry, mirthful, opportune, pleasing, propitious, prosperous, rapturous, spirited, successful, thrilled, vivacious. ANT.—depressed, distressed, gloomy, heartsick, morose.

harass, aggravate, agitate, anger, annoy, badger, bother, calumniate, chafe, deride, disturb, enrage, exasperate, harry, incense, inflame, infuriate, irritate, molest, nag, nettle, pester, plague, provoke, rouse, ruffle, tantalize, taunt, tease, torment, traduce, twit, vex, vilify, worry. ANT.—comfort, delight, encourage, gratify, soothe.

harbor, cherish, contain, cover, foster, guard, house, nurture, protect, shield. ANT.—banish, eject, exile, expel.

hard, compact, concrete, durable, firm, impenetrable, impervious, rigid, solid, stable, steady, strong; arduous, burdensome, difficult, laborious, onerous, toilsome, tough, troublesome; intricate, perplexing, puzzling; austere, cruel, demanding, exacting, grinding, harsh, pitiless, rigorous, severe, stern, strict, unfeeling, unforgiving, unrelenting. ANT.—elastic, flabby, fluid, plastic, pliable, soft; easy, effortless, facile; compassionate, gentle, tender.

harden, anneal, cool, ossify, petrify, solidify, stiffen, toughen; accustom, brace, confirm, discipline, fortify, habituate, inure, season, steel, train. ANT.—melt, soften, warm; coddle, indulge, pamper, spoil.

hardship, adversity, affliction, burden, calamity, catastrophe, disaster, distress, injustice, misery, misfortune, oppression, ordeal, privation, suffering, trial, tribulation, trouble. ANT.—alleviation, assistance, blessing, consolation, profit.

hardy, brave, courageous, enduring, fearless, intrepid, resistant, robust, tenacious, undaunted, unyielding, vigorous. ANT.—delicate, feeble, infirm, puny, weak.

harm, abuse, damage, deprivation, deterioration, detriment, evil, hurt, ill, impairment, infliction, injury, loss, mischief, misfortune, mishap, wrong. ANT.—advancement, benefit, boon, favor.

harmful, baneful, damaging, deleterious, detrimental, hurtful, injurious, mischievous, noxious, pernicious, prejudicial, ruinous. ANT.—advantageous, beneficial, healing, helpful, profitable.

harmless, blameless, dependable, faultless, incorrupt, innocuous, inoffensive, protected, pure, reliable, safe, secure, trustworthy, undefiled. ANT.—dangerous, hazardous, injurious, perilous, unsafe.

harmony, agreement, alliance, coincidence, concord, concurrence, consonance, unanimity, understanding, unison; adaptation, concordance, congruity, consistency; amity, agreeableness, compatibility, suitableness. ANT.—conflict, disagreement, discord, dissension, variance.

harsh, abusive, acrimonious, austere, bitter, blunt, brutal, caustic, coarse, cutting, exacting, grating, gruff, hard, harsh, heartless, jarring, overbearing, rigorous, rough, rugged, severe, stern, strict, stringent, uncivil, unfeeling. ANT.—courteous, gentle, melodious, mild, soft.

harvest, crop, fruit, proceeds, produce, product, reaping, result, return, store, yield; consequence, effect, outcome, result; acquire, gain, garner, gather, glean, reap. ANT.—lose, plant, sow, squander.

hassle, argument, brawl, controversy, disagreement, dispute, fight, melee, quarrel, scrap, wrangle. ANT.—agreement, harmony.

haste, acceleration, briskness, celerity, dispatch, expedition, fleetness, flurry, hurry, quickness, rapidity, rush, speed, swiftness, urgency, velocity; accelerate, expedite, hurry, precipitate,

press, quicken, urge. ANT.—delay, lingering, slowness, tarrying; decelerate, delay, procrastinate, retard.

hasten, accelerate, expedite, hurry, hustle, precipitate, quicken, race, run, rush, speed, spur. ANT.—delay, detain, prolong, retard, tarry.

hasty, brisk, cursory, fast, hurried, lively, precipitate, quick, rapid, rushing, speedy, swift; careless; excitable, foolhardy, impatient, imprudent, impulsive, indiscreet, irascible, rash, reckless, sharp, testy. ANT.—slow, sluggish; cautious, judicious, patient, thoughtful.

hate, abhor, abominate, despise, detest, dislike, execrate, loathe. ANT.—admire, cherish, like, love, revere.

hatred, abhorrence, acrimony, animosity, antipathy, aversion, bitterness, detestation, dislike, enmity, grudge, hostility, ill will, loathing, malevolence, malice, malignity, odium, rancor, repugnance. ANT.—admiration, affection, friendship, love, reverence.

haughty, arrogant, cavalier, contemptuous, disdainful, egotistical, overbearing, proud, supercilious, swaggering, vain. ANT.—ashamed, humble, lowly, meek, unpretentious.

haul, deliver, drag, draw, lug, pull, tow, trail, tug. ANT.—drive, impel, shove, thrust.

haunt, attend, frequent, return (to), visit; disturb, frighten, obsess, persecute, terrorize; follow, importune, resort.

hauteur, arrogance, contempt, disdain, haughtiness, loftiness, pomp, pride, sauciness, scorn, superciliousness. ANT.—condescension, humility, lowliness, plainness.

have, carry, control, get, hold, obtain, occupy, maintain, own, possess, seize, take. ANT.—abandon, lack, lose, need, surrender.

haven, anchorage, asylum, harbor, port, refuge, retreat, shelter.

hazard, casualty, chance, contingency, danger, gamble, jeopardy, peril, risk, uncertainty, venture. ANT.—certainty, immunity, protection, safety, security.

hazardous, critical, dangerous, fearful, insecure, menacing, perilous, precarious, risky, threatening, uncertain, unsafe. ANT.—assured, firm, protected, safe, secure.

hazy, ambiguous, cloudy, dim, foggy, gauzy, indefinite, indistinct, murky, nebulous, obscure, uncertain, unclear, undetermined, unsettled, vague, wavering. ANT.—clear, explicit, lucid, precise, specific.

head, boss, chief, commander, director, foreman, leader, manager, master, principal, ruler; acme, apex, crest, crown, culmination, peak, pinnacle, summit, top; crisis, culmination; capacity, instinct, mind, understanding. ANT.—follower, subordinate; base, bottom, foot; incapacity, incompetence.

heal, cure, fix, harmonize, knit, mend, reconcile, remedy, repair, restore, soothe. ANT.—break, damage, harm, injure.

healthy, bracing, hale, hearty, invigorating, lusty, robust, sound, strong, vigorous, virile, well; beneficial, harmless, healing, hygienic, nutritious, salubrious, salutary, sanitary, wholesome. ANT.—delicate, frail, infirm; injurious, insalubrious, noxious.

heap, accrue, accumulate, add, aggregate, amass, augment, bank, collect, enlarge, expand, gather, hoard, increase, load, stock, store, swell; bestow, cast, give. ANT.—diminish, disperse, dissipate, minimize, scatter.

hear, attend, audit, consider, harken, heed, judge, learn, listen, monitor, note, regard.

heart, center, core, essence, focus, kernel, middle, midpoint, midst, nub, nucleus, pith. ANT.—

border, exterior, outside, outskirts, periphery, rim.

heartache, affliction, anguish, distress, grief, heartbreak, lamentation, misery, misfortune, mourning, sadness, sorrow, trial, tribulation, woe. ANT.—blitheness, comfort, happiness, joy, solace.

heartbroken, abject, comfortless, desolate, disconsolate, discouraged, disheartened, distressed, forlorn, miserable, pitiable, wretched. ANT.—consoled, contented, fortunate, happy, joyful.

hearty, ardent, cheerful, cordial, enthusiastic, friendly, genial, glowing, gracious, sincere, sociable, warm; healthy, robust, sturdy, vigorous; earnest, genuine. ANT.—aloof, cool, reserved, taciturn; feeble, weak; deceptive, hypocritical, insincere.

heat, caloric, warmth, torridity; ardor, enthusiasm, excitement, fervency, fervor, fever, fire, impetuosity, intensity, passion, vehemence, zeal. ANT.—cold, frigidity, gelidity; apathy, lethargy, stoicism.

heathen, godless, heathenish, infidel, irreligious, pagan, paganic, unbelieving, unconverted. ANT.—believer, Christian, Jewish, Moslem.

heave, billow, bulge, elevate, hoist, lift, raise, rise, surge, swell, throw, toss, vomit. ANT.—ebb, lower, recede.

heavy, bulky, massive, ponderous, unwieldy, weighty; burdensome, cumbersome, grievous, onerous, oppressive, severe, troublesome, trying, vexatious; depressed, dull, gloomy, grave, sad, serious, sluggish. ANT.—inconsiderable, light; animated, brisk.

hectic, agitated, excited, feverish, flustered, nervous, restless, unsettling. ANT.—calm, cool, serene, unhurried.

heed, alertness, attachment, attention, care, caution, circumspection, consideration, devotion, mindfulness, notice, observance, vigilance, watchfulness; application, concentration, contemplation, reflection, study; attend, consider, contemplate, deliberate, examine, meditate, mind, notice, ponder, reflect, study, weigh; esteem, regard, respect. ANT.—apathy, indifference, omission; ignore, neglect, overlook.

height, acme, apex, culmination, peak, summit, zenith; altitude, loftiness; elevation; eminence, prominence, stature. ANT.—base, depth, floor, lowliness.

heighten, advance, amplify, augment, enhance, improve, increase, intensify, magnify, strengthen. ANT.—decrease, diminish, lessen, reduce, traduce.

heir, beneficiary, inheritor, legatee, scion, successor.

help, abet, aid, assist, benefit, cooperate, encourage, foster, nourish, succor, support, sustain, uphold; facilitate, further, improve, promote; alleviate, ameliorate, mitigate, relieve, remedy. ANT.—discourage, impede, thwart; arrest, counteract, hinder; afflict, injure.

herald, announce, declare, foretell, inform, introduce, precede, proclaim, publish. ANT.—silence, stifle, suppress.

herd, assemblage, drove, clock, gathering, group, horde, mob, multitude, school, throng.

hereditary, ancestral, congenital, constitutional, genetic, inherent, inherited, innate, patrimonial, transmitted. ANT.—acquired, bought, earned, won.

heretic, apostate, dissenter, nonconformist, nonjuror, renegade, schismatic, sectarian, sectary, secularist, separatist, traitor, unbeliever. ANT.—believer, loyalist.

hermetic, air-tight, sealed; cabalistic, emblematic, mysterious, occult. ANT.—clear, obvious, open, plain.

heroic, audacious, bold, brave, chivalrous, courageous, daring, dauntless, fearless, gallant, intrepid, majestic, noble, undaunted, valiant, valorous. ANT.—cowardly, cringing, fearful, spiritless, timid.

hesitate, defer, delay, demur, doubt, falter, fear, fluctuate, pause, question, scruple, stall, stammer, stutter, vacillate, wait, waver. ANT.—continue, decide, persevere, proceed, resolve, tackle.

heterogeneous, conglomerate, contrary, contrasted, different, discordant, dissimilar, mingled, mixed, nonhomogeneous, unlike, variant. ANT.—homogeneous, identical, same, uniform, unvarying.

hidden, abstruse, concealed, covert, esoteric, latent, masked, quiescent, recondite, secret, undeveloped, unrevealed, unseen. ANT.—conspicuous, evident, explicit, exposed, manifest, visible.

hide, bury, camouflage, cloak, conceal, cover, curtain, disguise, dissemble, mask, screen, secrete, sequester, shade, shield, shroud, suppress, veil, withhold. ANT.—disclose, divulge, exhibit, expose, reveal.

hideous, abhorrent, abominable, awful, disgusting, dreadful, frightful, ghastly, grim, grisly, horrible, loathsome, monstrous, nauseating, putrid, repellent, repulsive, revolting, shocking, terrifying, ugly. ANT.—alluring, captivating, delightful, soothing, splendid.

high, elevated, lofty, raised, tall, towering; eminent, exalted, noble; arrogant, boastful, bumptious, conceited, haughty, ostentatious, proud; costly, expensive; acute, intense, shrill, strident, strong; happy, intoxicated, merry. ANT.—short, stunted, tiny; base, low, mean; humble, meek; cheap, inexpensive; mild, weak; sober.

hilarious, blithe, gay, gleeful, jocund, jolly, joyful, lighthearted, merry, mirthful. ANT.—glum, morose, sad, somber.

hinder, block, check, encumber, hamper, impede, inhibit, interrupt, obstruct, postpone, prevent, resist, restrain, retard, stop, thwart. ANT.—assist, expedite, facilitate, hasten, promote.

hint, allusion, implication, intimation, inkling, innuendo, insinuation, reminder; allude (to), imply, insinuate, intimate, refer (to), suggest. ANT.—affirmation, declaration, statement; conceal, suppress, withhold.

hire, employ, engage, use; contract (for), lease, let, rent. ANT.—discard, discharge, reject; buy, purchase.

history, account, annals, archives, autobiography, biography, chronicle, description, detail, events, facts, log, lore, memoir, memorial, muniments, narration, narrative, recital, record, relation, report, saga, story; past. ANT.—fable, fiction, legend, myth, romance.

hit, batter, beat, knock, pound, pummel, punch, rap, slap, smite, strike; achieve, attain, contact, find, gain, reach, win.

hoard, accrue, accumulate, amass, collect, garner, gather, heap, increase, pile, save, stock, store, treasure. ANT.—diminish, disperse, dissipate, scatter, waste.

hoax, antic, artifice, canard, cheat, deception, delusion, device, fakery, fraud, guile, humbug, imposture, joke, ploy, ruse, spoof, stunt, subterfuge, swindle, trick, wile. ANT.—candor, honesty, openness, sincerity.

hobble, falter, limp, stagger, totter; bind, fetter, handicap, hold, impede, limit, restrain, shackle. ANT.—progress, speed, travel; aid, expedite, help, release.

hobby, amusement, avocation, diversion, enjoyment, fad, game, interest, pastime, recreation.

hold, adhere, clasp, clutch, grasp, grip; have, keep, maintain, occupy, own, possess, retain, support; check, confine, control, curb, detain, restrain; accommodate, carry, contain, receive, stow; affirm, attest, consider, judge, regard, think. ANT.—abandon, relinquish, renounce, surrender, vacate.

hole, abyss, aperture, cavity, chasm, excavation, fissure, gap, gulf, perforation, pit, rent; cave, den, holt, lair; opening, pore, void. ANT.—closure, imperforation.

hollow, empty, unfilled, vacant, void; artificial, faithless, false, hypocritical, insincere, superficial, transparent, vain; cavernous, concave, depressed, sunken. ANT.—full, solid, sound; genuine, sincere; convex, raised.

holy, angelic, blessed, consecrated, dedicated, devoted, devotional, devout, divine, godly, hallowed, immaculate, incorrupt, pious, pure, religious, reverent, righteous, sacred, saintly, spiritual, uncorrupt, virtuous. ANT.—diabolical, profane, sacrilegious, secular.

home, abode, domicile, dwelling, habitat, hearth, hearthstone, quarters, residence, seat; asylum, haven, refuge, retreat, sanctuary; birthplace, country, native land; heaven; family.

homely, common, ordinary, plain, unadorned, unattractive, uncomely; coarse, inelegant, rough, rude. ANT.—attractive, beautiful, fair, handsome, pretty; charming, dignified, polished, suave.

homogeneous, alike, consonant, harmonious, identical, same, similar, uniform. ANT.—heterogeneous, miscellaneous, mixed, unharmonious, variegated.

hone, file, grind, sharpen, strengthen, strop, whet. ANT.—make dull, roughen.

honest, candid, conscientious, fair, frank, genuine, honorable, ingenuous, just, principled, reliable, reputable, scrupulous, sincere, trustworthy, truthful, upright, unadulterated, unmixed. ANT.—deceitful, dishonest, fraudulent, lying, tricky; adulterated.

honesty, candor, fairness, faithfulness, frankness, honor, integrity, justice, openness, probity, rectitude, responsibility, self-respect, sincerity, trustworthiness, uprightness, veracity. ANT.—cheating, deceit, dishonesty, fraud, perfidy.

honor, admiration, adoration, adulation, commendation, deference, dignity, esteem, fame, glory, homage, praise, renown, respect, reverence, worship; confidence, faith, reliance, trust; admire, consider, esteem, heed, respect, revere, reverence, value, venerate; dignify, elevate, esteem. ANT.—contempt, derision, disgrace, reproach; abuse, despise, disdain, neglect, scorn.

honorary, commemorative, emeritus, gratuitous, titular. ANT.—complete, full, true.

hope, anticipation, aspiration, assurance, belief, desire, expectancy, expectation; confidence, faith, optimism, prospect, trust. ANT.—despair, despondency, fear, gloom, pessimism.

hopeless, abandoned, brokenhearted, condemned, dejected, despairing, futile, immitigable, inconsolable, incurable, irredeemable, irreparable, irretrievable, irrevocable, rash, reckless, ruined, useless. ANT.—cheering, encouraging, promising, reassuring, stimulating.

horde, army, assemblage, band, bevy, crew, crowd, crush, gang, host, masses, mob, multitude, pack, populace, press, rabble, swarm, throng, troop.

horizontal, even, flat, level, linear, parallel, plane, straight; prone, supine. ANT.—hilly, inclined, sloping; erect, upright, vertical.

horrible, appalling, atrocious, awful, dire, dreadful, fearful, frightful, ghastly, grim, heinous, hideous, horrid, repulsive, shocking, terrible. ANT.—beautiful, enchanting, enjoyable, fascinating, lovely.

horror, alarm, antipathy, apprehension, aversion, awe, consternation, disgust, dismay, dread, fear, foreboding, loathing, terror. ANT.—assurance, comfort, confidence, consolation, delight.

hospitable, companionable, convivial, cordial, friendly, kind, neighborly, receptive, sociable. ANT.—grudging, inhospitable, reserved, solitary, unsociable.

host, entertainer; innkeeper, landlord; army, legion; horde, multitude, throng. ANT.—boarder, caller, guest, patron, visitor.

hostile, adverse, antagonistic, antipathetic, belligerent, bitter, contrary, inimical, malevolent, opposed, rancorous, repugnant, unfriendly, warlike. ANT.—amicable, cordial, favorable, neutral, uncommitted.

hot, blazing, burning, flaming, heated, scalding, scorching, searing, torrid, warm; ardent, eager, excited, fervent, fervid, fiery, hot-blooded, impetuous, intense, passionate; peppery, pungent, spicy. ANT.—cold, cool, freezing; apathetic, frigid, impassive, indifferent, passionless, phlegmatic; bland, sweet.

however, albeit, although, but, nevertheless, notwithstanding, still, though, yet; whatever, whatsoever.

hug, caress, clasp, coddle, cuddle, embrace, enfold, fondle, hold, press, squeeze. ANT.—annoy, buffet, spurn.

huge, capacious, colossal, enormous, extensive, giant, gigantic, great, immense, monstrous, tremendous, vast. ANT.—diminutive, little, miniature, small, tiny.

humane, benevolent, benign, benignant, charitable, civilized, clement, compassionate, forbearing, forgiving, gracious, human, kind, lenient, merciful, sympathetic, tender, tolerant. ANT.—brutal, cruel, merciless, pitiless, unfeeling.

humble, compliant, lowly, meek, modest, plain, poor, simple, submissive, unassuming, unobtrusive, unostentatious, unpretentious; abase, abash, break, crush, debase, degrade, humiliate, mortify, shame, subdue. ANT.—arrogant, boastful, haughty, proud, vain; dignify, elevate, exalt, honor, praise.

humbug, cheat, counterfeit, deception, dodge, fake, falseness, feint, fraud, hoax, hypocrisy, imposition, pretense, sham, trick. ANT.—honesty, reality, truth, validity.

humdrum, boring, commonplace, dull, everyday, monotonous, ordinary, prosaic, routine, tedious, tiresome, usual. ANT.—exciting, lively, stimilating.

humiliation, abashment, chagrin, mortification; abasement, disgrace, dishonor, disrepute, ignominy, odium, opprobrium, scandal, shame; humbleness, meekness. ANT.—dignity, glory, honor, praise, renown.

humor, caprice, chaff, comicality, drollery, facetiousness, fancy, jesting, jocosity, jocularity, joke, waggery, whimsicality, wit; disposition, mood, temper; favor, indulge, pamper, pet, placate, please, satisfy, spoil. ANT.—depression, gloom, gravity, melancholy, sorrow; affront, enrage, exasperate, irritate, provoke.

hunch, feeling, impression, intuition, omen, premonition, presentiment, suspicion; hump, protuberance; chunk, lump.

hunger, appetite, craving, desire, eagerness, inclination, longing, passion, relish; starvation.

ANT.—disgust, distaste, renunciation, repugnance; satiety.

hungry, avid, covetous, famished, greedy, ravenous, starving, thirsting, voracious. ANT.—replete, sated, satisfied.

hunt, examination, exploration, inquiry, investigation, pursuit, quest, search; chase, ferret, investigate, probe, pursue, search, seek, stalk. ANT.—abandonment, cession, resignation; desert, forsake, quit, relinquish, surrender.

hurl, cast, dart, expel, explode, fling, impel, pitch, project, propel, release, shoot, spring, throw, thrust, toss. ANT.—draw, haul, hold, pull, retain.

hurry, accelerate, drive, expedite, force, hasten, impel, precipitate, press, quicken, rush, scurry, speed. ANT.—dawdle, delay, detain, hinder, impede, procrastinate, retard, stall, tarry.

hurt, abuse, affront, damage, deteriorate, disfigure, harm, impair, injure, insult, maltreat, mar, outrage, pain, spoil, victimize, wound, wrong. ANT.—ameliorate, benefit, compliment, help, preserve.

hush, calm, muffle, quiet, relieve, silence, stifle, still. ANT.—amplify, encourage, excite, incite.

hustle, accelerate, bustle, dash, drive, expedite, hasten, hurry, jostle, push, run, rush, scurry, spur. ANT.—dawdle, delay, procrastinate, slow, stall.

hybrid, crossbred, half-blooded, half-bred, mixed, mongrel, mutant. ANT.—pedigreed, purebred, thoroughbred, unmixed.

hygienic, healthy, salubrious, salutary, sanitary, sterile, uncontaminated, wholesome. ANT.—contagious, contaminated, diseased, foul, infectious, noxious, unsanitary.

hypnotic, influential, impelling, irresistible, lethargic, magnetic, mesmeric, narcotic, quieting, soporific. ANT.—disturbing, exciting, reviving, stimulating.

hypocritical, canting, deceiving, deceptive, deluding, dishonest, dishonorable, dissembling, dissimulating, double-dealing, false, feigning, pharisaical, pretending, pretentious, sanctimonious, specious, unctuous, unprincipled. ANT.—candid, honest, ingenuous, principled, sincere.

hypothesis, assumption, conjecture, inference, postulate, presumption, proposal, supposition, theory, thesis. ANT.—certainty, confirmation, demonstration, fact, proof.

I

icy, chilled, chilling, cold, frigid, frosty, frozen, polar; cool, distant, forbidding, unemotional. ANT.—fiery, hot, torrid, tropical; ardent, fervent, passionate.

idea, abstraction, belief, concept, conception, fancy, image, impression, notion, opinion, principle, scheme, theory, thought. ANT.—actuality, entity, matter, reality, substance.

ideal, fancied, illusory, imaginary, impractical, intellectual, metaphysical, psychical, psychological, spiritual, unreal, utopian, visionary; complete, exemplary, faultless, perfect, supreme. ANT.—actual, material, real; faulty, imperfect.

identical, alike, coalescent, coincident, duplicate, equal, equivalent, indistinguishable, same, synonymous, uniform. ANT.—contrary, disparate, dissimilar, distinct, opposite.

identify, analyze, catalog, characterize, classify, determine, distinguish, name, note, point out, recognize; brand, label, mark, tag. ANT.—confuse, misinterpret, misname, mistake, mix up.

idiomatic, colloquial, dialectal, peculiar, regional, special, standard, stylized, vernacular. ANT.—classic, cultured, standard.

idle, aimless, barren, dormant, futile, inactive, indolent, inert, lazy, pointless, shiftless, slothful, unemployed, unimportant, unoccupied, unprofitable, unused, useless, vain. ANT.—active, employed, fruitful, industrious, occupied.

idolize, adore, deify, glorify, revere, venerate, worship. ANT.—abase, defile, desecrate, hate, profane.

ignoble, abject, base, coarse, contemptible, debased, degenerate, degraded, depraved, despicable, dishonorable, groveling, ignominious, low, lowly, mean, menial, scandalous, scurrilous, servile, shameful, sordid, vile, vulgar, worthless; humble, low-born, plebeian, poor, untitled. ANT.—esteemed, exalted, honored, lofty, noble, righteous.

ignorant, dense, illiterate, obtuse, shallow, superficial, unacquainted, uncultivated, uneducated, uninformed, uninstructed, unknowing, unlearned, unlettered, untaught. ANT.—cultured, educated, erudite, literate, wise.

ignore, disregard, forget, neglect, omit, overlook, reject, shun, skip, slight, snub. ANT.—acknowledge, heed, notice, recognize, regard.

ill, afflicted, ailing, diseased, distempered, feeble, impaired, indisposed, infirm, morbid, sick, sickly, unhealthy, unwell; calamity, danger, distress, evil, hardship, misery, pain, sorrow, trouble, vexation. ANT.—healthy, robust, vigorous, well; favor, fortune, prosperity, welfare.

illegal, banned, contraband, criminal, dishonest, illegitimate, illicit, interdicted, outlawed, prohibited, proscribed, unauthorized, unlawful, unlicensed. ANT.—authorized, honest, judicial, lawful, legal, permissible.

illogical, fallacious, incoherent, inconsistent, specious, spurious, unreasoned, unsound, untenable. ANT.—logical, reasoned, sensible, sound.

illuminate, brighten, clarify, demonstrate, elucidate, enlighten, explain, illumine, illustrate, irradiate, lighten, reveal. ANT.—complicate, confuse, darken, obfuscate, obscure, puzzle.

illusion, apparition, chimera, deception, delusion, dream, fallacy, fancy, fantasy, hallucination, mirage, phantom, vision; fairy, ghost, ghoul, poltergeist, specter, sprite, sprite. ANT.—actuality, certainty, happening, reality, substance.

illustration, drawing, engraving, etching, image, likeness, painting, panorama, photograph, picture, portrait, portrayal, print, representation, scene, sketch, view; case, comparison, example, instance, specimen.

illustrious, acclaimed, celebrated, distinguished, eminent, famed, famous, great, prominent, renowned; critical, important, momentous, serious, vital, weighty; august, dignified, elevated, grand, majestic, noble; brilliant, excellent, fine, magnificent, superior, superlative. ANT.—diminutive, little, minute, small; common, humble, obscure, ordinary, unknown; menial, paltry.

imagination, conceit, concept, conception, creation, fancy, fantasy, idea, impression, mental image, notion. ANT.—actuality, existence, materiality, realism, substance.

imaginative, artistic, clever, creative, fanciful, inventive, mystical, original, poetical, talented, visionary. ANT.—dull, factual, literal, methodical, prosaic.

imagine, conceive, dream, envision, fancy, picture, pretend, visualize; apprehend, assume, believe, conjecture, guess, opine, presume, suppose, surmise, think.

imbecile, blockhead, buffoon, cretin, dolt, dunce, fool, halfwit, idiot, ignoramus, moron, nincompoop, numbskull, oaf, simpleton, witling. ANT.—genius, intellectual, philosopher, sage, scholar.

imbue, animate, color, impregnate, infuse, inspire, instill, penetrate, permeate, pervade, saturate, suffuse.

imitate, ape, caricature, copy, counterfeit, duplicate, falsify, follow, impersonate, mimic, mirror, mock, personate, parody, represent, reproduce, simulate, transcribe. ANT.—alter, distort, diverge, oppose, vary.

immanent, inborn, inherent, innate, internal, intrinsic, natural, subjective; universal (as God). ANT.—acquired, external, extrinsic, objective.

immaterial, inessential, insignificant, irrelevant, trifling, trivial, unimportant; disembodied, impalpable, impertinent, incorporeal, spiritual, unsubstantial. ANT.—essential, important, relevant; corporeal, material, substantial.

immature, callow, childish, crude, embryonic, green, juvenile, premature, raw, undeveloped, unready, unripe, untimely. ANT.—adult, aged, grown, mature, ripe.

immeasurable, abysmal, boundless, endless, eternal, illimitable, immense, infinite, interminable, measureless, unbounded, unfathomable, unlimited, vast. ANT.—bounded, circumscribed, finite, limited, measurable.

immediately, abruptly, at once, directly, forthwith, instantaneously, instantly, now, presently, promptly, right away, speedily, straightaway. ANT.—after a while, by and by, distantly, hereafter, later.

immemorial, ancient, dateless, early, immemorable, old, prehistoric, timeless. ANT.—memorable, new, recent, young.

immense, colossal, elephantine, enormous, gargantuan, gigantic, great, huge, large, mighty, monstrous, prodigious, stupendous, titanic, tremendous, vast. ANT.—diminutive, dwarfish, microscopic, minute, tiny.

immerse, bathe, dip, douse, dunk, engulf, flood, inundate, plunge, sink, submerge; absorb, engage, engross, involve, overwhelm. ANT.—elevate, recover, retrieve, uncover, uplift.

imminent, abeyant, approaching, brewing, coming, destined, impending, inevitable, menacing, near, nigh, ominous, overhanging, pressing, threatening. ANT.—afar, distant, improbable, remote, retreating.

immoderation, excess, exorbitance, extravagance, extremism, inordinateness, intemperance, profusion, superabundance, superfluity, surplus. ANT.—dearth, deficiency, moderation, paucity, restraint.

immoral, bad, corrupt, depraved, dissolute, evil, indecent, lecherous, licentious, loose, profligate, unprincipled, vicious, wicked. ANT.—chaste, high-minded, noble, pure, virtuous.

immortal, abiding, ceaseless, deathless, endless, eternal, everlasting, imperishable, infinite, permanent, perpetual, timeless, undying. ANT.—ephemeral, finite, mortal, temporal, transitory.

immovable, anchored, cemented, constant, firm, fixed, fused, immobile, obdurate, rooted, stable, steadfast. ANT.—mobile, movable, plastic, wavering, yielding.

immune, excused, exempt, free, freed, hardened to, not liable, resistant, unaffected by, unsusceptible; clear, loose, open, unfastened, unobstructed. ANT.—subject.

immunity, acquittal, clearance, discharge, dispensation, exculpation, exemption, exoneration, freedom, license, privilege, protection, release, respite. ANT.—condemnation, conviction, indictment, interdiction, sequestration.

immutable, abiding, ceaseless, constant, continual, enduring, faithful, fixed, invariant, permanent, perpetual, persistent, stable, unalterable, unchanging, unwavering. ANT.—fluctuating, mutable, vacillating, variable, wavering.

impair, adulterate, blemish, blight, corrode, corrupt, cripple, damage, deface, degrade, deteriorate, harm, hurt, injure, mar, spoil, taint, weaken. ANT.—ameliorate, benefit, enhance, mend, repair.

impart, bestow, communicate, confer, convey, disclose, divulge, enlighten, give, grant, inform, instruct, notify, relate, reveal, tell, transmit. ANT.—conceal, hide, puzzle, suppress, withhold.

impartial, disinterested, equitable, fair, honest, indifferent, just, neutral, nonpartisan, nonsectarian, reasonable, unbiased, unconcerned, unprejudiced. ANT.—biased, dishonorable, fraudulent, involved, partial.

impasse, bar, deadlock, end, limit, obstacle. ANT.—clearance, gain, opening, solution.

impatient, abrupt, brusque, eager, fidgety, fretful, fussy, impetuous, nervous, restless. ANT.—calm, controlled, forbearing, patient, tolerant.

impeccable, faultless, immaculate, incorrupt, innocent, perfect, spotless. ANT.—defective, imperfect, messy, stained, sullied.

impede, arrest, bar, block, check, clog, counteract, delay, encumber, frustrate, hamper, hinder, interrupt, obstruct, offset, oppose, prevent, repress, restrain, retard, stop, thwart. ANT.—advance, assist, further, help, promote.

impediment, barrier, block, difficulty, disability, encumbrance, hindrance, inhibition, obstacle, obstruction, restriction, wall, weakness. ANT.—aid, assistance, collaboration, help, support.

impel, actuate, coerce, compel, constrain, drive, force, goad, induce, influence, instigate, move, oblige, prod, push, stimulate, urge. ANT.—delay, prevent, repress, repulse, suppress.

impenetrable, compact, dense, firm, hard, impervious, rigid, solid; arduous, burdensome, difficult, onerous, tough; abstruse, esoteric, intricate, perplexing, puzzling; adamant, cruel, harsh, obtuse, rigorous, severe, stern, stolid, strict, unfeeling. ANT.—brittle, elastic, flabby, fluid, penetrable, plastic, soft; easy, effortless, facile, simple; clear, comprehensible, intelligible; gentle, lenient, tender.

imperative, absolute, commanding, compelling, compulsory, critical, essential, exigent, impelling, important, importunate, inescapable, inexorable, insistent, mandatory, necessary, obligatory, peremptory, pressing, required, requisite, unavoidable, urgent, vital. ANT.—insignificant, optional, petty, trivial, unimportant.

imperceptible, inappreciable, inconspicuous, indistinct, indistinguishable, insignificant, invisible, negligible, undiscernible, unseen. ANT.—apparent, evident, perceptible, striking, visible.

imperfection, blemish, defect, deficiency, drawback, error, failure, fault, flaw, frailty, inadequacy, infirmity, mistake, shortcoming, stain, transgression, wrong. ANT.—completeness, correctness, faultlessness, perfection, purity.

imperil, endanger, expose, hazard, jeopardize, risk, threaten, uncover. ANT.—defend, guard, safeguard, secure, shield.

impersonate, ape, copy, duplicate, feign, imitate, mimic, mock, personify, portray, represent, simulate. ANT.—alter, distort, diverge, invent.

impertinent, abusive, arrogant, audacious, bold, brazen, contemptuous, impudent, insolent, insulting, intrusive, meddling, offensive, officious, rude; absurd, inane, inapplicable,

irrelevant, trivial. ANT.—considerate, courteous, polite, respectful; important, momentous, pertinent, serious, significant.

impetuous, careless, fiery, hasty, heedless, impulsive, incautious, intractable, passionate, quick, rash, reckless, ungovernable, unruly. ANT.—cautious, composed, reasoning, retiring, tranquil.

impetus, force, impulse, incentive, momentum, motive, pressure, stimulus.

impinge, clash, collide, encroach, infringe, hit, strike, trespass, touch, violate. ANT.—avoid, defer, miss, pass, respect.

implant, embed, engraft, fix, graft, inculcate, infuse, insert, instill, plant, set in, sow. ANT.—eliminate, excise, remove, uproot.

implement, accomplish, achieve, do, effect, effectuate, execute, expedite, fulfill, perform, realize. ANT.—cancel, defer, hinder, restrict.

implicate, accuse, blame, censure, challenge, charge, cite, embroil, enfold, entangle, imply, impute, incriminate, inculpate, involve, link, rebuke, reproach, trap, upbraid. ANT.—absolve, acquit, defend, exonerate, support.

implicit, accepted, implied, inferred, known, presupposed, recognized, tacit, understood, unspoken. ANT.—declared, explicit, expressed, specific.

imply, connote, hint, infer, insinuate, involve, mean, signify, suggest. ANT.—assert, define, describe, express, state.

import, emphasis, importance, influence, significance, stress, value, weight; bring in, convey, imply, introduce, purport, signify, transport. ANT.—insignificance, triviality; export, send out, ship out.

important, appreciable, authoritative, consequential, critical, decisive, essential, grave, great, imposing, influential, leading, material, momentous, paramount, powerful, pressing, principal, prominent, relevant, serious, significant, substantial, urgent, weighty. ANT.—insignificant, irrelevant, petty, picayune, trivial.

imposing, arresting, august, commanding, eminent, grand, grandiose, high, illustrious, imperial, impressive, lofty, magnificent, majestic, noble, stately, striking, sublime, towering. ANT.—common, humble, insignificant, ordinary, undignified.

impractical, impracticable, inexpedient, unachievable, unattainable, unfeasible, unrealistic, unworkable, visionary. ANT.—feasible, possible, practical, reasonable, workable.

impressive, absorbing, affecting, arresting, awesome, commanding, considerable, deep, exciting, forcible, imposing, majestic, momentous, moving, notable, penetrating, profound, prominent, remarkable, stirring, striking, thrilling, touching, vital. ANT.—commonplace, ordinary, shallow, trivial, unimpressive.

imprison, cage, confine, constrain, detain, enclose, hold, impound, incarcerate, limit, lock up, restrain. ANT.—acquit, discharge, extricate, free, release.

impromptu, ad lib, extemporaneous, improvised, impulsive, offhand, spontaneous, unplanned, unrehearsed. ANT.—deliberate, planned, premeditated, prepared, rehearsed.

improper, discourteous, immodest, incorrect, indecent, indelicate, lewd, offensive, unbecoming, unsuitable, wrong. ANT.—considerate, correct, fitting, proper, seemly.

improve, advance, ameliorate, amend, better, correct, help, mend, purify, rectify, refine, reform, revise; gain, get better, progress. ANT.—corrupt, damage, debase, impair, vitiate; decline, worsen.

imprudent, careless, heedless, incautious, indiscreet, reckless, thoughtless, unforeseeing, unwise. ANT.—careful, cautious, circumspect, meticulous, prudent.

impudence, arrogance, audacity, boldness, crudity, discourtesy, disrespect, effrontery, impertinence, incivility, insolence, presumption, rudeness, sauciness. ANT.—courtesy, diffidence, gentility, politeness, respect.

impulsive, careless, excitable, fiery, foolhardy, forcible, hasty, headstrong, heedless, impatient, impetuous, imprudent, incautious, indiscreet, quick, rash, reckless, uninhibited. ANT.—cautious, heedful, prudent, reasoning, restrained.

impure, adulterated, contaminated, corrupt, corrupted, debased, defiled, depraved, foul, indecent, mingled, mixed, obscene, polluted, profligate, putrid, spoiled, smutty, tainted, unsound, venal, vitiated. ANT.—clean, immaculate, impeccable, pure, spotless.

impute, allege, ascribe, assign, attribute, blame, brand, charge, implicate, inculpate, indict, trace (to). ANT.—defend, endorse, exculpate, exonerate, vindicate.

inactive, dormant, idle, inanimate, indolent, inert, latent, lazy, motionless, passive, quiescent, resting, sedentary, torpid, unemployed, unoccupied. ANT.—active, dynamic, industrious, occupied, working.

inadequate, defective, deficient, incompetent, incomplete, insufficient, lacking, partial, scanty, short, unfit, wanting. ANT.—adequate, ample, enough, satisfactory, sufficient.

inadvertent, accidental, careless, chance, heedless, negligent, thoughtless, unconscious, unintentional, unobservant. ANT.—attentive, careful, intentional, planned.

inane, absurd, banal, foolish, frivolous, insipid, pointless, silly, trite, vapid. ANT.—expressive, important, meaningful, salient, significant.

inappropriate, discordant, improper, inapt, incongruous, infelicitous, tasteless, unfitted, unsuitable. ANT.—appropriate, apt, becoming, fitting, proper.

inaugurate, arise, begin, commence, found, initiate, install, institute, introduce, open, originate, start. ANT.—adjourn, close, complete, finish, terminate.

incentive, enticement, incitement, inducement, lure, motive, provocation, spur, stimulus.

inception, beginning, birth, commencement, founding, inauguration, initiation, opening, origin, onset, source, start. ANT.—close, completion, consummation, end, termination.

incessant, ceaseless, constant, continual, continuous, endless, everlasting, interminable, perennial, perpetual, persistent, unceasing, uninterrupted, unremitting. ANT.—interrupted, occasional, periodic, rare, sporadic.

incident, chance, episode, event, happening, occasion, occurrence, situation.

incidental, accidental, accessory, associated, casual, collateral, concomitant, contingent, fortuitous, minor, nonessential, occasional, secondary, subordinate, undesigned, unintended. ANT.—cardinal, elementary, essential, fundamental, vital.

incisive, brief, compact, concise, condensed, crisp, decisive, direct, pithy, succinct, summary, terse. ANT.—lengthy, prolix, verbose, wordy.

incite, actuate, animate, arouse, cause, encourage, enrage, excite, fire, foment, goad, impel, induce, inflame, instigate, prompt, provoke, rouse, stimulate, stir up, urge. ANT.—deter, pacify, quiet, restrain, soothe.

inclination, bending, gradient, incline, leaning, slope; affection, allurement, attachment, attraction, bent, bias, desire, disposition, fancy, liking, partiality, penchant, predilection, preference, prejudice, proneness, propensity, tendency. ANT.—apathy, aversion, distaste, nonchalance, repugnance.

include, accommodate, comprise, consist of, contain, embody, embrace, encompass, hold, incorporate, involve, surround, take in. ANT.—eliminate, exclude, omit, preclude, reject.

income, annuity, dividends, earnings, emolument, gain, interest, proceeds, profits, receipts, rents, revenue, salary, stipend, wages, winnings. ANT.—charge, cost, expense, loss, outgo.

incompetent, bungling, clumsy, floundering, heavy-handed, inadequate, incapable, ineffectual, inefficient, inept, inexpert, maladroit, stumbling, unable, unfit, unqualified, unskilled, unsuitable, untalented. ANT.—competent, deft, expert, proficient, skillful.

incongruous, conflicting, contradictory, contrary, disagreeing, discordant, discrepant, disparate, divergent, illogical, incompatible, inconsistent, inharmonious, irreconcilable, mismatched, paradoxical. ANT.—compatible, congruous, consistent, correspondent, harmonious, homologous.

inconsiderate, careless, selfish, tasteless, thoughtless, undiscerning, unfeeling, unsympathetic. ANT.—considerate, helpful, sensitive, sympathetic, thoughtful.

inconsistent, changeable, contrary, fluctuating, incompatible, inconsonant, inconstant, shifting, unstable, unsteady, unsuitable, vacillating, variable, varying, wavering. ANT.—constant, stable, steady, unchanging, uniform.

incorporate, amalgamate, blend, consolidate, embody, establish, form, merge, mix, unite. ANT.—disperse, dissolve, divide, remove, separate.

increase, accelerate, accrue, advance, amplify, augment, develop, dilate, distend, enhance, enlarge, expand, extend, grow, heighten, inflate, intensify, magnify, multiply, raise, spread, swell, wax. ANT.—atrophy, contract, decrease, diminish, reduce.

incredible, astonishing, fantastic, far-fetched, implausible, suspicious, unbelievable. ANT.—believable, credible, creditable, plausible, realistic.

increment, addition, enlargement, increase, raise. ANT.—decline, decrease, diminution, loss.

incriminate, accuse, arraign, blame, censure, charge, implicate, impute, indict, involve, link. ANT.—absolve, acquit, exonerate, release, vindicate.

inculcate, discipline, drill (into), imbue, impart, implant, impress, indoctrinate, instill, instruct, teach.

incumbent, binding, coercive, imperative, inescapable, necessary, peremptory, pressing, stringent, urgent; occupant, officeholder. ANT.—absolved, exempt, free, liberated, released.

indebted, appreciative, beholden, grateful, thankful; bound, liable, obligated, owing, unpaid. ANT.—thankless, unappreciative; cleared (up), settled (accounts), squared (with) paid.

indecent, coarse, dirty, disgusting, filthy, gross, immodest, immoral, improper, impure, indelicate, lewd, obscene, offensive, pornographic, shameless, smutty, unbecoming. ANT.—decent, modest, pure, refined, virtuous.

indefinite, ambiguous, confused, dim, equivocal, hazy, inconclusive, indeterminate, inexact, lax, loose, obscure, uncertain, unclear, undefined, unfixed, unlimited, unsettled. ANT.—absolute, certain, evident, positive, unquestionable.

independent, alone, autonomous, exempt, free, liberated, self-governing, self-reliant, self-sufficient, separate, single, sovereign, unallied, unconfined, uncontrolled, unrestrained, unrestricted; affluent, rich, wealthy; exclusive, irrespective. ANT.—contingent, dependent, enslaved, restricted, subordinate; poor; inclusive.

indicate, connote, denote, designate, differentiate, disclose, evidence, hint, imply, intimate, manifest, mark, point out, register, reveal, show, signal, signify, specify, testify. ANT.—conceal, distract, divert, falsify, mislead.

indication, designation, emblem, evidence, gesture, hint, implication, manifestation, mark, note, omen, portent, proof, sign, signal, suggestion, symbol, symptom, token.

indict, accuse, arraign, blame, censure, charge, impeach, incriminate. ANT.—absolve, acquit, exonerate, release, vindicate.

indifference, apathy, callousness, carelessness, coldness, detachment, disinterest, disinterestedness, impartiality, impassivity, inattention, insensibility, insouciance, insusceptibility, neutrality, nonchalance, supineness, unconcern. ANT.—affection, ardor, fervor, passion, vivacity.

indigence, dearth, destitution, distress, famine, hunger, insufficiency, misery, necessity, need, pauperism, penury, poverty, privation, starvation, tenuity, want. ANT.—abundance, affluence, plenty, riches, wealth.

indigenous, aboriginal, domestic, endemic, inborn, inherent, innate, native, natural. ANT.—alien, foreign, imported, introduced, naturalized.

indignation, acrimony, agitation, anger, animosity, annoyance, exasperation, fury, huff, irascibility, ire, passion, petulance, pique, rage, resentment, scorn, temper, virulence, wrath. ANT.—forbearance, equanimity, patience, self-control, tranquility.

indignity, abuse, affront, discourtesy, dishonor, disparagement, disrespect, embarrassment, humiliation, ignominy, insult, irreverence, mockery, offense, opprobrium, outrage, scurrility, slight, taunt, vituperation. ANT.—courtesy, dignity, homage, praise, reverence.

indirect, circuitous, crooked, distorted, erratic, implied, inferred, oblique, roundabout, swerving, tortuous, wandering, winding; crooked, cunning, devious, tricky. ANT.—direct, straight, unswerving; blunt, candid, explicit, straightforward.

indiscreet, foolhardy, foolish, heedless, imprudent, rash, reckless, thoughtless, unwise. ANT.—careful, discreet, prudent, sensible, wise.

indiscriminate, heterogeneous, mixed, promiscuous, uncritical, unwise. ANT.—chosen, critical, homogeneous, selective.

indispensable, basic, essential, expedient, fundamental, imperative, intrinsic, necessary, needed, prerequisite, required, requisite, vital. ANT.—dispensable, extrinsic, optional, peripheral, superfluous.

indistinct, abstruse, ambiguous, blurred, cloudy, confused, cryptic, darkened, dim, dusky, faint, hazy, indefinite, imperceptible, inaudible, indistinguishable, misty, mysterious, nebulous, obscure, shadowy, uncertain, unintelligible, vague. ANT.—clear, distinct, lucid, obvious, perceptible.

individual, characteristic, different, distinct, distinctive, idiosyncratic, marked, original, particular, peculiar, personal, separate, singular, special, specific, unique. ANT.—common, conventional, general, ordinary, universal.

indoctrinate, discipline, drill, imbue, initiate, instruct, teach, train. ANT.—confuse, misguide, mislead, neglect.

indolent, drowsy, dull, idle, inactive, ineffectual, inert, lackadaisical, languid, lazy, lethargic, listless, remiss, slack, slothful, sluggish, somnolent, soporific, supine, torpid. ANT.—active, alert, assiduous, diligent, industrious.

indomitable, firm, impregnable, insurmountable, invincible, invulnerable, unassailable, unconquerable, untameable, unyielding. ANT.—feeble, powerless, vulnerable, weak, yielding.

induce, actuate, bring about, cause, create, effect, encourage, evoke, impel, incite, influence, instigate, motivate, move, originate, persuade, prompt, spur, stimulate, urge. ANT.—discourage, dissuade, hamper, repel, repress.

induct, initiate, install, introduce, invest, lead into; conclude, generalized, infer. ANT.—expel, lead away, reject; end, withdraw.

industrious, active, assiduous, busy, diligent, hard-working, indefatigable, perseverant, persistent, sedulous, zealous. ANT.—inactive, indolent, lackadaisical, laggard, lethargic.

inebriated, drunk, drunken, high, intoxicated, tight, tipsy; exhilarated, heartened, refreshed, stimulated. ANT.—abstinent, sober, temperate; calm, unmoved.

ineffective, assailable, feeble, frail, futile, idle, impotent, inadequate, ineffectual, inefficacious, unavailing, unfruitful, unproductive, useless, vain, vulnerable, weak. ANT.—effective, efficacious, potent, powerful, successful.

inept, awkward, clumsy, foolish, fumbling, inappropriate, incapable, maladroit, unfit, unhandy, unproductive, unskillful. ANT.—able, adroit, apt, competent, skillful.

inert, dead, dilatory, dormant, idle, impassive, impotent, inactive, indolent, lazy, lifeless, phlegmatic, powerless, quiescent, slothful, sluggish, stolid, supine, torpid. ANT.—active, industrious, moving, operational, working.

inevitable, assured, avoidless, certain, definite, fated, imminent, indefeasible, indubitable, ineluctable, inescapable, necessary, positive, predestined, sure, unavoidable, undeniable, unquestionable. ANT.—avoidable, doubtful, indeterminate, questionable, uncertain.

inexhaustible, illimitable, indefatigable, infinite, limitless, never-ending, untiring, unwearied. ANT.—ending, finite, limited, short-lived, wearying.

inexpensive, cheap, low-priced, reasonable (in price); beggarly, common, inferior, mean, shabby. ANT.—costly, dear, expensive, high-priced; valuable.

infantile, babyish, childish, immature, juvenile, naïve, puerile, young. ANT.—adult, grown up, mature, of age.

infatuated, beguiled, captivated, charmed, deluded, enamored, enthralled, fascinated, foolish. ANT.—disgusted, disillusioned, fancy-free, prudent, sensible.

infection, communicability, contagion, contamination, disease, epidemic, germs, impurity, poison, pollution, vitiation.

infectious, catching, communicable, contagious, contaminating, defiling, epidemic, noxious, pestiferous, pestilential, polluting, sickening, virulent, vitiating. ANT.—antiseptic, harmless, healthful, hygienic, sanitary.

inference, answer, conclusion, consequence, corollary, deduction, derivation, illation, judgment, result, solution. ANT.—assumption, foreboding, foresight, preconception, presupposition.

inferior, deficient, inadequate, lesser, lower, minor, poorer, secondary, shoddy, subordinate, substandard. ANT.—better, first-class, foremost, prime, superior.

infinite, boundless, continual, continuing, countless, endless, eternal, everlasting, illimitable, immeasurable, incalculable, incomprehensible, inexhaustible, innumerable, interminable, perpetual, termless, timeless, unbounded, unlimited. ANT.—bounded, circumscribed, finite, limited, restricted.

infirm, ailing, debilitated, decrepit, doddering, drooping, enervated, enfeebled, exhausted, faint, feeble, forceless, frail, impaired, invalid, languid, powerless, sickly, spent, unhealthy, weak, worn. ANT.—forceful, hale, robust, sturdy, vigorous.

inflate, bloat, blow up, dilate, distend, elate, enlarge, exaggerate, expand, fill, pad, stuff. ANT.—compress, condense, deflate, shrink, trim.

inflexible, determined, dogged, firm, headstrong, immovable, inexorable, intractable, obdurate, obstinate, rigid, stiff, strict, stubborn, tenacious, uncompromising, unyielding. ANT.—compliant, elastic, flexible, pliable, yielding.

influence, absolutism, ascendancy, attraction, authority, character, command, control, credit, despotism, domination, effect, importance, leadership, magnetism, mastery, patronage, power, predominance, prerogative, pressure, prominence, reputation, rule, superiority, supremacy, sway, weight; actuate, act upon, affect, bias, carry weight, compel, control, counteract, direct, dominate, draw, drive, modify, move, outweigh, predominate, prejudice, pull, regulate, restrain, rouse, rule, spur. ANT.—impotence, inferiority, subjection, subserviency, weakness.

inform, acquaint, advise, apprise, edify, educate, enlighten, explain, impart, instruct, notify, relate, teach, tell, warn. ANT.—conceal, delude, distract, mislead.

informal, conventional, customary, easy, familiar, natural, offhand, regular, simple, unceremonious, unconstrained, unconventional, unofficial. ANT.—ceremonious, formal, official, perfunctory, rigid.

information, data, fact, instruction, intelligence, knowledge, learning, lore, news. ANT.—conjecture, guesswork, ignorance, rumor.

infrequent, irregular, isolated, occasional, odd, rare, scarce, sporadic, strange, unusual. ANT.—customary, frequent, ordinary, scheduled, usual.

infuse, animate, imbue, implant, inoculate, inspire, instill, permeate, steep.

ingenious, able, adroit, apt, bright, brilliant, capable, clever, competent, creative, deft, dexterous, endowed, expert, fertile, fresh, gifted, handy, imaginative, inventive, novel, original, productive, proficient, qualified, quick-witted, ready, resourceful, sagacious, sharp, skillful, talented. ANT.—bungling, clumsiness, fumbling, ineptitude, unqualified.

ingenuous, aboveboard, artless, candid, direct, fair, frank, free, guileless, honest, literal, natural, open, outspoken, plain, simple, sincere, straightforward, truthful, unaffected, undisguised, unsophisticated, unworldly. ANT.—artificial, cunning, deceptive, designing, scheming.

ingratitude, lack of response, thanklessness, unappreciation, unconcern, ungratefulness. ANT.—appreciation, gratefulness, gratitude, responsiveness, thankfulness.

ingredient, component, constituent, element, factor, material, part, substance.

inhabit, abide, dwell, establish residence, fill, live in, lodge, make home at, nestle, occupy, remain, rent, reside, room, settle, sojourn, stay, tenant. ANT.—abandon, exit, retreat, vacate, withdraw.

inherent, congenital, connatal, genetic, inborn, inbred, ingrained, inherent, inherited, innate, intrinsic, native, natural, real. ANT.—acquired, external, extraneous, extrinsic, supplemental.

inheritance, bequest, birthright, heritage, legacy, patrimony.

inhibit, arrest, bar, block, bridle, check, constrain, cramp, curb, disallow, discourage, hinder, hold back, impede, interdict, limit, obstruct, obtrude, oppose, prevent, prohibit, proscribe, repress, restrain, restrict, stop, sublimate, suppress, suspend, thwart. ANT.—aid, encourage, free, incite, liberate.

inhuman, barbarous, bestial, bloodthirsty, brutal, cold-blooded, cruel, diabolical, ferocious, fiendish, harsh, hateful, hellish, infernal, malevolent, malignant, pitiless, rancorous, remorseless, ruthless, savage, truculent, unfeeling, venomous. ANT.—benevolent, charitable, compassionate, humane, merciful.

iniquitous, baleful, base, criminal, degrading, deleterious, diabolical, dissolute, evil, fiendish, foul, immoral, infamous, infernal, lawless, nefarious, noxious, profligate, reprobate, shameful, sinful, transgressing, unjust, unprincipled, unrighteous, unsound, villainous, wicked. ANT.—exemplary, good, honorable, moral, reputable.

initial, antecedent, basic, beginning, earliest, elementary, first, fundamental, original, primary, prime, primeval, primitive, pristine, rudimentary; chief, foremost. ANT.—hindmost, last, latest; least, subordinate.

initiate, arise, begin, commence, enter, establish, inaugurate, indoctrinate, institute, introduce, invest, open, originate, start. ANT.—close, complete, finish, raze, terminate.

initiative, acceleration, action, drive, energy, enterprise, leadership, responsibility. ANT.—cowardice, lethargy, shyness, timidity.

injunction, bidding, canon, command, directive, law, mandate, order (of a judge), ordinance, regulation, rule.

injurious, damaging, defamatory, deleterious, destructive, detrimental, disadvantageous, harmful, hurtful, libelous, mischievous, pernicious, prejudicial, wrongful. ANT.—advantageous, beneficial, helpful, profitable, salutory.

injury, blemish, damage, detriment, disadvantage, grievance, harm, hurt, impairment, injustice, loss, mischief, prejudice, wound, wrong. ANT.—benefit, blessing, emolument, relief, remedy.

injustice, bias, encroachment, favoritism, grievance, illegality, inequality, inequity, infringement, injury, unfairness, violation, wrong. ANT.—equity, fairness, justice, lawfulness, righteousness.

inkling, clue, hint, idea, impression, indication, inference, innuendo, notice, suggestion, suspicion, tip.

innocent, artless, blameless, clean, exemplary, faultless, harmless, guiltless, impeccable, innocuous, irreproachable, lawful, pure, righteous, sinless, spotless, stainless, uninvolved, upright, virginal, virtuous. ANT.—corrupt, culpable, guilty, lascivious, sinful.

innocuous, gentle, harmless, inoffensive, insipid, mild, pallid, safe, undetrimental, uninjurious. ANT.—blighting, destructive, detrimental, injurious, pestilential.

innovation, addition, alteration, change, introduction, invention, modification, newness, novelty, remodeling, variation. ANT.—custom, habit, old (way), rut, tradition.

inquest, audit, examination, inquiry, inquisition, inspection, interrogation, investigation, probe, research, scrutiny.

inquire, examine, explore, hunt, interrogate, meddle, probe, pry, pursue, query, question, reconnoiter, research, scan, scout, scrutinize, search, seek, sift; ask, beg, claim, demand, entreat, invite, request, solicit. ANT.—abandon, neglect, shelve; answer, contradict, reply.

inquisitive, curious, inquiring, interrogative, intruding, intrusive, meddlesome, meddling, nosy, peeping, peering, prying, scrutinizing, searching, sniffing, snoopy. ANT.—apathetic, indifferent, lackadaisical, negligent, unconcerned.

insane, aberrant, crazy, daft, delirious, demented, deranged, fanatical, foolish, frenetic, frenzied, idiotic, imbecilic, incoherent, irrational, lunatic, mad, maniacal, manic, mentally ill, paranoiac, psychopathic, psychotic, rabid, raging, unbalanced, unsound. ANT.—lucid, rational, reasonable, sane, stable.

insecure, dangerous, endangered, exposed, hazardous, ill-protected, imperiled, precarious, rickety, risky, shaky, unguarded, unsafe, unstable; anxious, apprehensive, concerned, fearful, troubled, uncertain, worried. ANT.—safe, secure, fortified, strong; assured, certain, confident, serene.

insensitive, callous, cold, dull, hard, impenitent, indurate, insensible, obdurate, obtuse, phlegmatic, remote, thick-skinned, tough, unaffected, unemotional, unfeeling, unimpressionable, unresponsive. ANT.—compassionate, empathetic, responsive, sensitive, tender.

insertion, implantation, infusion, injection, inlay, inoculation, installation, interpolation, introduction. ANT.—extraction, removal, transfer, withdrawal.

insolent, abusive, arrogant, blustering, brazen, bumptious, contemptuous, contumelious, defiant, disdainful, disrespectful, domineering, haughty, imperious, impertinent, impudent, insulting, offensive, overbearing, presumptuous, rude, supercilious, swaggering, threatening, unmannerly. ANT.—considerate, courteous, humble, polite, respectful; abased, cowardly, groveling, parasitic, sniveling.

inspection, audit, checking, comparison, critique, examination, inquest, inquiry, inquisition, investigation, measuring, observation, overseeing, probing, review, scanning, scrutiny, study, supervision, survey.

inspiration, animation, arousal, enthusiasm, exaltation, fire, incitement, predilection, revelation, stimulation; fancy, hunch, impulse, notion, whim; incentive, influence, spur, stimulus; inhalation. ANT.—apathy, habitude, lethargy; aversion; exhalation.

insight, acumen, comprehension, discernment, intuition, introspection, judgment, keenness, penetration, perception, perspicacity, perspicuity, shrewdness, understanding. ANT.—confusion, ignorance, obtuseness, perplexity, shallowness.

insignificant, cheap, frivolous, inconsequential, meaningless, minute, paltry, petty, small, trifling, trivial, unimportant, valueless, worthless. ANT.—important, momentous, significant, valuable, weighty.

insinuate, connote, hint, imply, indicate, infer, ingratiate, intimate, involve, mean, purport, signify, suggest. ANT.—assert, express, state; conceal, disguise, suppress, veil.

insipid, bland, characterless, dull, flat, flavorless, inanimate, lifeless, mawkish, stale, tasteless, unimaginative, uninteresting, unsavory, vapid. ANT.—appetizing, exhilarating, racy, savory, tasty.

insistent, aggressive, clamorous, demanding, exigent, imperative, importunate, pressing, urgent. ANT.—acquiescent, agreeable, indifferent, lenient, tolerant.

instance, application, case, elucidation, example, exemplification, illustration, lesson, object, occurrence, point, sample, specimen, type.

instantaneous, abrupt, at once, direct, hasty, immediate, prompt, rapid, sudden, unexpected. ANT.—anticipated, delayed, gradual, late, slow.

instantly, abruptly, directly, forthwith, immediately, instantaneously, now, presently, promptly, straightaway, suddenly, urgently, without delay. ANT.—distantly, hereafter, in a while, later, sometime.

instinctive, accustomed, automatic, congenital, constitutional, fundamental, habitual, impulsive, inborn, ingrained, inherent, innate, intrinsic, involuntary, mechanical, natural, offhand, reflexive, regular, spontaneous, typical, usual. ANT.—acquired, deliberate, learned, meditated, voluntary, willed.

institute, begin, build, enact, erect, establish, fix, form, found, initiate, introduce, invent, invest, ordain, order, organize, originate, plan, raise, sanction, settle, start. ANT.—abolish, demolish, raze, terminate, unsettle.

instruct, admonish, advise, coach, command, convey, counsel, direct, discipline, drill, edify, educate, enlighten, exhort, expound, guide, impart, inculcate, indoctrinate, inform, instill, prime, promulgate, school, teach, train, tutor. ANT.—delude, falsify, misguide, misinform, misinterpret.

instrumental, accessory, assisting, auxiliary, conducive, contributory, expeditious, helpful, promoting, serviceable, serving, subsidiary. ANT.—detrimental, hindering, impeding, injurious, obstructive.

insubordination, contrariness, contumacy, defiance, disobedience, intractability, mutiny, perversity, rebellion, refractoriness, revolt, stubbornness. ANT.—loyalty, obedience, submission, tractability.

insufficient, bare, deficient, drained, imperfect, inadequate, incompetent, incomplete, lacking, limited, meager, rare, scant, scarce, short, slack, sparse ANT.— abundant, ample, copious, rich, sufficient.

insulate, alienate, cover, detach, disconnect, disengage, isolate, part, protect, quarantine, retire, seclude, segregate, separate, sequester, sunder, withdraw, wrap. ANT.—associate, connect, integrate, mingle, unite.

insult, abuse, acerbity, affront, derision, discourtesy, disrespect, gall, impudence, incivility, indignity, insolence, libel, mockery, offense, rudeness, scurrility, slight, slur, snub; abuse, affront, dishonor, injure, mock, offend, outrage, wrong. ANT.—apology, courtesy, homage, salutation; defer, praise, respect, revere.

integral, centralized, complete, consummate, constituent, definite, entire, one, perfect, uncut, unitary, whole. ANT.—divisional, fractional, indefinite, partial, segmental.

integration, alliance, amalgamation, blending, combination, consolidation, fusion, joining, merger, mingling, mixture, unification, union. ANT.—isolation, seclusion, segregation, separation.

integrity, candor, constancy, fairness, faithfulness, fidelity, frankness, honesty, honor, incorruptness, justice, loyalty, morality, openness, probity, purity, rectitude, responsibility, righteousness, sincerity, trustworthiness, uprightness, virtue; completeness, entirety, soundness, value, wholeness, worth. ANT.—deceit, fraud, infidelity, treason, turpitude; fragmentation, imperfection, loss, worthlessness.

intelligence, acumen, aptitude, astuteness, comprehension, discernment, grasp, insight, intellect, knowledge, mental ability, mind, penetration, perspicacity, reason, sense, understanding, wit; inside facts, secret information, secret report. ANT.—emotion, feeling, passion.

intelligent, alert, apt, astute, bright, brilliant, capable, clever, discerning, exceptional, keen, knowing, perceptive, quick, sensible, sharp, smart; enlightened, intellectual, knowledgeable, well-informed. ANT.—dull, insipid, obtuse, shallow, stupid.

intend, aim, contemplate, delineate, design, desire, destine, devise, hope, mean, outline, plan, plot, prepare, project, propose, purpose, scheme, sketch, try, want, wish.

intensity, acuteness, ardor, concentration, depth, eagerness, earnestness, emphasis, fervor, force, magnitude, might, potency, power, pressure, strain, strength, tension, toughness, vehemence, vigor. ANT.—feebleness, lassitude, lethargy, passivity, weakness.

intentional, aimed at, calculated, contemplated, deliberate, designed, determined, intended, meant, planned, premeditated, projected, purposed, studied, voluntary, willful. ANT.—accidental, fortuitous, haphazard, random, unforeseen.

intercept, ambush, appropriate, arrest, avert, block, catch, check, cut off, hinder, interpose, interrupt, obstruct, prevent, stop, take away, waylay. ANT.—aid, boost, forward, succor, uphold.

interest, advantage, appeal, attention, behalf, benefit, charm, claim, concern, curiosity, fascination, gain, inquisitiveness, portion, premium, profit, right, share, stake, title; absorb, amuse, appeal to, beguile, cheer, concern, delight, divert, enliven, entertain, enthrall, fascinate, gratify, hold attention, intrigue, occupy, please. ANT.—apathy, indifference, insolvency, loss; bore, displease, stupefy, tire, vex.

interfere, bar, block, clash, collide, conflict, delay, frustrate, hamper, hinder, impede, inconvenience, interpose, interrupt, intrude, meddle, mediate, obstruct, obtrude, oppose, stall, tamper, thwart. ANT.—abet, aid, clear, help, stand aside.

interior, heart, inmost, inner, inside, internal, inward, middle; bowels, core, enclosure, hinterlands, inland. ANT.—boundary, coast, exterior, external, periphery.

interminable, boundless, continuous, endless, eternal, everlasting, illimitable, immeasurable, incessant, infinite, limitless, permanent, tedious, unbounded, unlimited, vast. ANT.—bounded, confined, finite, intermittent, periodic.

intermittent, alternate, broken, cyclic, discontinuous, fitful, flickering, fluttering, infrequent, interrupted, occasional, periodic, recurrent, remittent, spasmodic. ANT.—constant, continual, incessant, perpetual, regular.

internal, domestic, enclosed, esoteric, ingrained, inherent, innate, inner, inside, interior, intrinsic, inward. ANT.—alien, external, foreign, outer, superficial.

interpose, inject, insert, intercalate, interject, interpolate, introduce; arbitrate, intercede, intercept, interfere, interrupt, intersperse, intervene,

intrude, meddle, mediate, negotiate, obtrude, sandwich, tamper. ANT.—extract, omit, withdraw; avoid, overlook, shun.

interpret, clarify, construe, decipher, decode, define, describe, disentangle, elucidate, explain, explicate, expound, illuminate, manifest, paraphrase, render, reveal, solve, translate, unfold, unravel. ANT.—confuse, distort, misconstrue, misinterpret, mystify.

interrogation, examination, inquiry, inquisition, interpellation, investigation, probe, query, test. ANT.—acknowledgement, answer, rejoinder, reply, response.

interrupt, arrest, adjourn, break, check, cut, defer, delay, disconnect, discontinue, disturb, divide, hinder, interfere, obstruct, postpone, sever, stay, stop, suspend. ANT.—continue, maintain, persist, prolong, sustain.

intervene, arbitrate, intercede, interpose, mediate, negotiate, step in; inject, insert, interfere, interject, interlope, introduce, intrude, meddle; divide, part, sever; befall, happen, occur. ANT.—ignore, stand aside; assist, help; assemble, convene.

intimate, affectionate, close, confidential, familiar, friendly, internal, loving, near, personal, private, secret, special, trusted. ANT.—ceremonious, cool, distant, formal, remote.

intimate, v. see insinuate.

intolerable, detestable, impossible, insufferable, insupportable, offensive, painful, unbearable, unendurable. ANT.—bearable, endurable, passable, satisfying, tolerable.

intolerant, biased, bigoted, discriminatory, dogmatic, fanatical, illiberal, narrow-minded, prejudiced, unfair, unyielding. ANT.—impartial, lenient, nondiscriminatory, open-minded, unbiased.

intrepid, adventurous, audacious, bold, brave, courageous, daring, dauntless, fearless, lionhearted, mighty, nervy, plucky, powerful, strong, unafraid, unflinching, unshrinking, valiant, valorous. ANT.—cowardly, cringing, fainthearted, flinching, timid, trembling.

intricate, complex, complicated, compound, confused, convoluted, difficult, disarranged, inextricable, involved, irregular, knotted, labyrinthine, mixed, perplexing, raveled, tangled. ANT.—arranged, clear, plain, simple, uncompounded.

intrigue, cabal, chicanery, collusion, complication, connivance, conspiracy, craft, cunning, design, double-dealing, duplicity, machination, maneuvering, plan, plot, scheme, secret, stratagem, trickery, wire-pulling.

intrinsic, congenital, essential, fundamental, genuine, honest, inborn, inbred, indigenous, ingrained, inherent, innate, native, natural, real, subjective, true. ANT.—external, extraneous, extrinsic, incidental, objective.

introduction, beginning, commencement, foreword, inception, initiation, interjection, interpolation, meeting, overture, preamble, preface, prelude, presentation, prologue, start. ANT.—conclusion, end, epilogue, finale, postlude.

intrusive, encroaching, infringing, inquisitive, interfering, invading, meddlesome, obtrusive, snooping, trespassing. ANT.—unintrusive, unobtrusive, retiring.

intuitive, emotional, guessing, heedless, impulsive, instinctive, involuntary, unreasoning, unreflective; discerning, insightful, knowing, perceptive. ANT.—calculated, meditated, planned, reasoned; obtuse.

invalidate, abolish, abrogate, annul, cancel, counteract, negate, neutralize, null, nullify, quash, recall, revoke, stop, void. ANT.—endorse, establish, promote, sustain, validate.

invaluable, dear, expensive, inestimable, precious, priceless, valuable. ANT.—cheap, nugatory, useless, worthless.

invasion, aggression, assault, attack, entrance, foray, incursion, ingress, ingression, inroad, intrusion, irruption, onslaught, outbreak, raid, take-over. ANT.—defense, evacuation, fortification, protection, safeguard.

invective, abuse, aspersion, blasphemy, censure, condemnation, contumely, defamation, denouncement, denunciation, deprecation, disapprobation, disapproval, disparagement, insult, obloquy, opprobrium, raillery, reprimand, reprehension, reproach, sarcasm, scurrility, upbraiding, vituperation. ANT.—approval, commendation, laudation, plaudit, sanction.

invent, coin, conceive, concoct, conjure, contrive, design, devise, draft, fabricate, fashion, form, frame, imagine, improvise, manufacture, originate, outline, plan, project, sketch, visualize; deceive, equivocate, fake, falsify, lie, misrepresent, misstate. ANT.—copy, imitate, reproduce; disabuse, disillusionize.

inventory, catalog, itemization, list, record, register, roll, roster, schedule, table; contents, stock, store, supply; examination, inspection, investigation.

investigation, catechism, discussion, examination, exploitation, exploration, inquiry, inquisition, interrogation, pursuit, query, quest, question, research, review, search, scrutiny. ANT.—disregard, inactivity, inattention, neglect, overlooking.

invincible, formidable, impregnable, incontestable, indomitable, inseparable, insuperable, insurmountable, invulnerable, irresistible, mighty, overpowering, resistless, sovereign, unassailable, unconquerable, unvanquishable, unyielding. ANT.—impotent, powerless, puny, vulnerable, weak.

invisible, evanescent, gaseous, imperceptible, indistinguishable, intangible, microscopic, occult, undiscernible, undisclosed, unreal, unseen, vaporous. ANT.—evident, perceptible, real, substantial, visible.

involve, comprehend, compromise, contain, cover, denote, embarrass, embroil, entail, entangle, envelop, enwrap, implicate, imply, include, incriminate, overwhelm, signify. ANT.—disconnect, disengage, extricate, separate, unravel.

irate, angry, enraged, ferocious, fierce, fuming, furious, incensed, infuriated, irritated, mad, nettled, piqued, provoked, rabid, raging, stormy, wrathful. ANT.—appeased, calm, pleased, quiet, restrained.

irk, annoy, bother, chafe, discompose, disturb, fret, inconvenience, irritate, perturb, pester, tease, trouble, upset, vex. ANT.—console, delight, gladden, please, soothe.

irony, banter, criticism, derision, mockery, paradox, quip, raillery, reproach, ridicule, sarcasm, satire, twist. ANT.—approval, courtesy, deference, esteem, respect.

irrational, absurd, crazed, crazy, daft, demented, fatuous, feeble-minded, foolish, inconsistent, injudicious, illogical, nonsensical, odd, preposterous, queer, ridiculous, self-contradictory, silly, strange, stupid, unreasonable, unsound, vacuous, weak-minded. ANT.—logical, lucid, rational, reasonable, sound.

irreconcilable, divergent, implacable, incompatible, incongruous, inconsequent, inexorable, quarrelsome, unappeasable. ANT.—appeasable, compatible, congruous, reconcilable, solvable.

irregularity, aberration, abnormality, anomaly, asymmetry, caprice, deviation, disorderliness, eccentricity, fitfulness, inordinateness, inconstancy, intermittency, tardiness, unruliness, variation. ANT.—method, order, regularity, stability, system.

irrelevant, alien, extraneous, foreign, immaterial, inapplicable, inapposite, inappropriate, inconsequent, remote, strange, unconnected, unessential, unrelated. ANT.—apt, fitting, germane, pertinent, relevant.

irremediable, beyond help, hopeless, incurable, irrecoverable, irreparable, irretrievable, irrevocable, useless. ANT.—curable, recoverable, reparable.

irresolute, doubting, drifting, fickle, fluctuating, half-hearted, hesitant, hesitating, ineffective, irresponsible, lukewarm, pliable, shaky, uncertain, undecided, undetermined, unsettled, unstable, unsteady, vacillating, volatile, wavering, wobbling; bending, fragile, frail, yielding. ANT.—enduring, potent, powerful, relentless, tenacious.

irresponsible, arbitrary, capricious, careless, faltering, flighty, fluctuating, foolish, giddy, heedless, immature, irresolute, purposeless, rash, reckless, thoughtless, unaccountable, unanswerable, unreliable, unstable, unsteady, wobbly. ANT.—accountable, dependable, reliable, steady, trustworthy.

irritable, cantankerous, captious, choleric, excitable, fidgety, fiery, fractious, fretful, hasty, hot, ill-tempered, irascible, peevish, petulant, querulous, sensitive, snappy, susceptible, testy, thin-skinned, touchy. ANT.—agreeable, calm, composed, serene, tranquil.

irritate, aggravate, agitate, anger, annoy, bother, chafe, disturb, enrage, exacerbate, exasperate, fluster, foment, harass, inconvenience, inflame, infuriate, irk, madden, pester, pique, provoke, ruffle, sting, taunt, tease, trouble, vex. ANT.—accommodate, console, gratify, moderate, pacify.

isolate, alienate, disconnect, dissociate, exclude, insulate, quarantine, retire, seclude, segregate, separate, sequester, withdraw. ANT.—associate, integrate, join, mingle, unite.

issue, aftermath, conclusion, consequence, culmination, denouement, effect, emanation, eventuality, finish, fruits, offspring, product, progeny, result, termination; event, incident; point, question, subject, topic; arise, emanate, emerge, emit, ensue, eventuate, exude, flow, originate, proceed, result, spew, spread, spring, start; publish; circulate money; abound, be copious. ANT.—contain, repress, retain, suppress.

itinerary, circuit, course, flight, guidebook, log, map, path, plan, record, route, travel plans, trip.

J

jam, block, bruise, cram, crowd, crush, force, impede, improvise (music), interfere, mass, pack, press, push, squeeze, tamp, wedge. ANT.—expand, free, diffuse, disperse, separate.

jargon, argot, babble, bosh, cant, dialect, gibberish, idiom, jive, lingo, patois, phraseology, shop talk, slang, trade talk, vernacular.

jealous, covetous, distrustful, doubtful, doubting, dubious, envious, invidious, jaundiced, mistrustful, resentful, suspicious; solicitous, vigilant, watchful. ANT.—content, indifferent, lenient, serene, trusting.

jeer, deride, fleer, flout, gibe, hoot, mock, ridicule, scoff, sneer, taunt. ANT.—compliment, flatter, honor, laud, praise.

jeopardize, chance, compromise, conjecture, dare, endanger, expose, hazard, imperil, menace, peril, risk, threaten, venture. ANT.—determine, guard, insure, protect, shield.

jest, banter, humor, joke, prank, quip, wisecrack, witticism.

jocular, comical, droll, facetious, funny, humorous, joking, merry, pleasant, sportive, waggish, witty. ANT.—dull, grave, morose, serious.

join, accompany, add, adjoin, affiliate, associate, attach, bind, cement, combine, conjoin, connect, consolidate, couple, enter, knit, link, marry, tie, unify, unite. ANT.—detach, disconnect, leave, sever, sunder.

joint, articulation, collaboration, combination, connection, cooperation, junction, juncture, link, meeting, union; dove-tail, dowel, hinge, mitre, mortise, pivot, seam, welding; associated, combined, shared, united. ANT.—separate, single.

jolly, blithe, cheerful, congenial, convivial, frolicsome, gay, happy, humorous, jocose, jocular, jocund, jovial, joyous, merry, playful, sprightly, vivacious, witty. ANT.—depressed, glum, melancholy, mournful, sullen.

journal, account, chart, daily register, daybook, diary, gazette, log, magazine, newspaper, periodical, publication, record, register.

journey, course, cruise, excursion, expedition, jaunt, passage, peregrination, pilgrimage, safari, tour, travel, trek, trip, voyage. ANT.—stay, stop.

joy, bliss, cheer, delight, ecstasy, elation, exultation, felicity, gaiety, gladness, glee, happiness, merriment, mirth, pleasure, rapture, transport. ANT.—affliction, depression, despair, grief, wretchedness.

judge, adjudicator, arbiter, arbitrator, censor, connoisseur, critic, custodian, guardian, interpreter, judiciary, magistrate, protector, referee, reviewer, umpire; decide, decree, determine; adjudicate, arbitrate, condemn, try, umpire; appreciate, consider, estimate, evaluate, measure, think.

judgment, award, decision, discernment, decree, discrimination, injunction, intellectuality, perspicacity, ruling, sagacity, sentence, understanding, wisdom. ANT.—arbitrariness, senselessness, stupidity, thoughtlessness, vacuity.

jumble, confuse, disarrange, mess, mingle, mix up, muddle, shuffle; agitation, chaos, commotion, confusion, disarrangement, disarray, disorder, ferment, stir, tumult, turmoil. ANT.—arrange, classify, file, rectify, systematize; certainty, order, peace, tranquility.

jump, bounce, bound, caper, hop, jerk, leap, pounce, skip, spring, start, twitch, vault.

just, blameless, candid, conscientious, earned, equitable, fair, honest, honorable, impartial, innocent, judicious, lawful, legal, legitimate, merited, precise, rightful, scrupulous, sincere, true, unbiased, upright. ANT.—corrupt, deceitful, dishonest, fraudulent, lying, villainous.

justice, equity, fairness, fair play, impartiality, justness, lawfulness, legality, propriety, reasonableness, rectitude, right, righteousness, uprightness. ANT.—corruption, dishonor, favoritism, inequity, unlawfulness.

justify, absolve, acquit, advocate, clear, defend, excuse, exonerate, extenuate, forgive, free, maintain, support, uphold, vindicate. ANT.—accuse, blame, convict, indict, stigmatize.

K

keen, acrid, acute, ardent, bitter, caustic, clever, cunning, cutting, discerning, fervid, incisive, intense, lively, penetrating, perspicacious, piercing, pointed, quick, sagacious, severe, sharp, shrewd, stinging, vivid, wily, witty, zealous. ANT.—apathetic, blunt, dull, lethargic, sluggish.

keep, conserve, continue, defend, guard, maintain, preserve, protect, save, secure, support, sustain, tend, uphold; confine, detail, hold, imprison, reserve, restrain, retain, suppress, withhold; adhere, execute, obey; celebrate, commemorate, honor, observe. ANT.—destroy, discard, reject; dismiss, release, relinquish; disobey, ignore; abandon, forsake.

kill, assassinate, annul, butcher, choke, decimate, delete, destroy, extinguish, immolate, massacre, murder, obliterate, slaughter, slay, smother, strangle, veto. ANT.—animate, protect, resuscitate, safeguard, vivify.

kin, clan, family, kindred, kinsfolk, kinsmen, kith, relatives, siblings, tribe.

kind, accommodating, affable, affectionate, amiable, beneficent, benevolent, benign, caring, charitable, compassionate, considerate, cordial, forbearing, gentle, good, gracious, humane, indulgent, kind-hearted, kindly, loving, merciful, obliging, sympathetic, tender, thoughtful; brand, breed, category, character, class, family, genus, ilk, offspring, order, progeny, race, relation, sort, species, stock, strain, type, variety. ANT.—cruel, inhuman, merciless, ruthless, vicious.

kindred, affinity, consanguinity, family, kin, kinsfolk, kinsmen, relations, relationship, relatives; allied, analogous, congenial, corresponding, empathetic, like, parallel, related, similar, sympathetic. ANT.—disconnection, foreigners, strangers; dissimilar, foreign, heterogeneous, unlike, unrelated.

kingdom, country, domain, dominion, empire, monarchy, nation, realm, rule, sovereignty.

kiss, buss, caress, cuddle, embrace, fondle, osculation, pax (kiss of peace), touch of the lips.

knack, ability, adeptness, adroitness, aptitude, cleverness, deftness, dexterity, expertness, facility, faculty, ingenuity, proficiency, readiness, skill, skillfulness, talent; device, trick. ANT.—awkwardness, clumsiness, incompetence, ineptitude.

knit, affiliate, bind, connect, crochet, interlace, intermingle, intertwine, join, link, loop, net, spin, tie, unite, weave, web. ANT.—divide, separate, unravel, untie.

knot, assemblage, bond, bunch, cluster, collection, complication, connection, difficulty, entanglement, gathering, intricacy, ligature, perplexity, protuberance, snarl, tangle, tie, tuft.

know, appreciate, apprehend, ascertain, cognize, comprehend, conceive, discern, distinguish, fathom, hold, interpret, perceive, recognize, remember, think, understand. ANT.—dispute, doubt, forget, misapprehend, misconstrue.

knowledge, acquaintance, apperception, apprehension, cognition, cognizance, comprehension, education, enlightenment, erudition, experience, familiarity, information, learning, light, lore, perception, recognition, scholarship, science, understanding, wisdom. ANT.—blindness, enigma, ignorance, illiteracy, stupidity.

L

labor, drudgery, effort, endeavor, exertion, industry, pains, painstaking, plodding, striving, struggle, task, toil, travail, work; childbirth. ANT.—idleness, inertia, lethargy, relaxation, sloth.

lack, dearth, deficiency, demerit, depletion, distress, failing, fault, inadequacy, insufficiency, neediness, privation, poverty, scantiness, scarcity, shortage; need, want. ANT.—abundance, excess, profusion, sufficiency, surplus.

lag, dally, dawdle, delay, fall behind, falter, idle, linger, loiter, plod, retard, saunter, slacken, stagger, tarry, trudge. ANT.—accelerate, bound, dash, hasten, hustle.

lame, crippled, defective, deformed, disabled, faltering, halt, hesitating, hobbling, impotent, limping, maimed; feeble, ineffective, unconvincing, unsatisfactory, weak. ANT.—agile, robust, vigorous; convincing, effective, forceful.

lament, anguish, bemoan, bewail, commiserate, cry, deplore, fret, grieve, mourn, regret, repine, rue, wail, weep, worry. ANT.—celebrate, cheer, delight in, exult, rejoice.

language, brogue, cant, dialect, diction, expression, idiom, jargon, lingo, linguistics, literature, patois, philology, phraseology, slang, speech, terminology, tongue, utterance, vernacular, vocabulary, voice, words.

languid, apathetic, debilitated, drooping, drowsy, dull, faint, feeble, flagging, heartless, irresolute, laggard, languorous, leisurely, lethargic, listless, pensive, pining, sickly, slack, slow, sluggish, torpid, weak, wearied. ANT.—animated, brisk, enthusiastic, spirited, vigorous.

lanky, bony, gangling, gaunt, lank, lean, narrow, overgrown, raw-boned, slim, spare, wiry. ANT.—brawny, burly, husky, portly, sturdy.

lapse, backsliding, blunder, boner, delay, error, fault, flaw, fumble, gap, indiscretion, misstep, mistake, omission, oversight, passing, sin, slip.

larceny, appropriation, burglary, embezzlement, peculation, pilfering, pillage, plunder, purloinment, robbery, shoplifting, theft. ANT.—compensation, recoupment, repayment, restoration, return.

large, abundant, ample, big, broad, bulky, capacious, colossal, commodious, copious, corpulent, enormous, extensive, gigantic, grand, great, huge, immense, magnificent, massive, mighty, monstrous, long, obese, plentiful, roomy, sizeable, towering, vast, wide. ANT.—infinitesimal, microscopic, minute, paltry, puny.

lash, abuse, beat, castigate, drive, flagellate, flail, goad, impel, press, pummel, scourge, spank, spur, strike, urge, whip; satirize, scold, rate.

last, closing, concluding, conclusive, crowning, extreme, final, finishing, hindmost, latest, least, supreme, terminal, ultimate, utmost. ANT.—commencing, first, foremost, leading, primary.

late, delayed, dilatory, lagging, overdue, slow, tardy; deceased, demised, departed; bygone, defunct, extinct, gone, lapsed; advanced, new, recent. ANT.—early, prompt, punctual, ready; alive, animated, living; aged, ancient, antique, old.

latent, allusive, concealed, dormant, hidden, implicit, implied, inactive, inherent, invisible, involved, lurking, passive, potential, quiescent, recondite, secret, undeveloped, unknown, unobserved, unperceived, unseen, vestigial. ANT.—apparent, conspicuous, known, prominent, unmistakable, visible.

latitude, breadth, compass, distance, extent, freedom, leeway, length, range, reach, room, scope, space, sweep, width; laxity.

laudable, admirable, commendable, creditable, deserving, dutiful, estimable, excellent, exemplary, honorable, ideal; meritorious, model, praiseworthy, righteous, worthy. ANT.—corrupt, damnable, degraded, iniquitous, odious.

laughable, absurd, amusing, asinine, bizarre, comic, comical, droll, eccentric, facetious, farcical, foolish, funny, jocose, ludicrous, quaint, ridiculous, waggish, whimsical. ANT.—depressive, funereal, melancholy, morbid, painful.

launch, begin, cast, commence, dart, dispatch, enlarge, expatiate, float, hurl, inaugurate, initiate, open, project, start, throw. ANT.—close, end, finish, land, splash down.

lavish, abundant, costly, dear, excessive, exhaustive, exorbitant, exuberant, generous, inordinate, liberal, luxuriant, prodigal, profligate, profuse, replete, superabundant, unrestrained, unstinted, wasteful; bestow, deluge, dissipate, expend, flood, glut, gorge, indulge, inundate, load, misuse, overload, overrun, scatter, spend, squander, waste, wear out. ANT.—deficient, inadequate, jejune, meager, scanty; conserve, curtail, economize, skimp, treasure.

law, act, canon, code, command, commandment, constitution, covenant, decree, edict, enactment, equity, formula, jurisprudence, justice, legality, legislation, mandate, order, ordinance, precept, principle, regulation, rule, statute. ANT.—felony, illegality, lawlessness, outlawry, transgression.

lawful, admitted, allowable, approved, authorized, canonical, conceded, constitutional, granted, judicial, legal, legislative, legitimate, licit, official, permissible, recognized, right, rightful, sanctioned, warranted. ANT.—arbitrary, criminal, illegal, prohibited, unauthorized.

lax, careless, depraved, derelict, desultory, flaccid, immoral, inaccurate, lawless, limp, neglectful, negligent, relaxed, remiss, unconscientious, undutiful, unobservant, unprincipled, vague, weak. ANT.—determined, faithful, honorable, meticulous, rigid, rigorous.

lay, common, earthly, mundane, noncleric, noncclesiastical, nonprofessional, popular, profane, secular, temporal, worldly; arrange, deposit, dispose, place, put, set. ANT.—professional, spiritual, unworldly; disarrange, disturb, misplace, remove.

lazy, idle, inactive, indolent, inert, lackadaisical, laggard, lethargic, negligent, shiftless, sleepy, slothful, sluggish, supine, torpid, weak, worn. ANT.—active, assiduous, diligent, industrious, persevering.

lead, conduct, direct, escort, guide, pilot, shepherd, steer; command, control, govern, manage, regulate, superintend, supervise; begin, open, pioneer, precede, start. ANT.—perform; acquiesce, comply, obey, submit; follow.

leader, captain, chief, chieftain, commander, conductor, director, guide, head, master, principal, ruler, superior, vanguard. ANT.—adherent, devotee, disciple, follower, henchman.

league, alliance, association, cartel, club, coalition, combination, confederacy, confederation, entente, federation, fraternity, partnership, pool, society, union.

leak, dribble, drip, escape, exude, filter, ooze, overflow, pass, percolate, seep, spill, trickle.

lean, bend, cant, career, crook, decline, deflect, deviate, dip, hang, heel, incline, list, sag, shelve, sidle, slant, slope, tend, tip; depend, rely, trust. ANT.—erect, raise, rise, straighten.

leap, bound, caper, dance, frisk, frolic, gambol, hop, jerk, jump, romp, skip, spring, start, trip, vault.

learn, acquire, ascertain, determine, discern, discover, gain, gather, hear, imbibe, master, memorize, read, receive, study, unearth.

learned, academic, accomplished, deep, discerning, educated, enlightened, erudite, informed, intelligent, knowing, lettered, literate, pedantic, penetrating, philosophic, profound, sagacious, scholarly, solid, sound, well-informed, wise. ANT.—dull, ignorant, illiterate, shallow, uncultured.

leave, absence, allowance, concession, consent, freedom, furlough, holiday, liberty, license, permission, vacation, withdrawal; abandon, allow, decamp, depart, desert, forsake, give up, go, let, permit, quit, relinquish, renounce, retire, vacate, withdraw. ANT.—confinement, hindrance, prohibition, restriction, taboo; abide, endure, persist, remain, tarry.

lecture, address, discourse, dissertation, homily, lesson, prelection, sermon, speech, talk; scold, upbraid.

legal, admitted, allowable, allowed, authorized, constitutional, correct, equitable, fair, lawful, legitimate, permissible, rightful, sanctioned, valid, warranted. ANT.—criminal, illegal, illicit, prohibited, unconstitutional.

legendary, fabulous, fanciful, fictitious, mythical, romantic, traditional. ANT.—actual, factual, historical, real, true.

legitimate, correct, genuine, justifiable, lawful, legal, logical, real, sanctioned, true, valid, warranted. ANT.—illegal, illegitimate, invalid.

leisure, calm, ease, peace, quiet, relaxation, repose, rest, tranquility; cessation, freedom, idleness, intermission, leave, liberty, pause, retirement, respite, sparetime, vacation. ANT.—agitation, commotion, disturbance, tumult; drudgery, duty, toil, travail, work.

lengthen, dilate, draw out, elongate, extend, increase, prolong, protract, stretch. ANT.—abbreviate, curtail, cut, shorten, speed.

lenient, assuaging, charitable, clement, compassionate, easy-going, forbearing, forgiving, gentle, humane, indulgent, kind, merciful, moderate, reasonable, tender, tolerant. ANT.—brutal, cruel, pitiless, tyrannical, unfeeling.

lessen, abate, abridge, contract, curtail, decrease, deduct, diminish, narrow, pare, reduce, shrink, shorten, subtract, trim. ANT.—amplify, enlarge, expand, increase, strengthen.

let, allow, authorize, bear, concede, empower, grant, permit, sanction, suffer, tolerate, warrant, yield; lease, rent. ANT.—defeat, halt, inhibit, obstruct, prevent.

lethargy, apathy, drowsiness, insensibility, languor, lassitude, listlessness, numbness, passivity, stupefaction, stupor, torpor. ANT.—activity, alertness, energy, liveliness, vitality.

level, balanced, equal, even, flat, flush, horizontal, plane, smooth, uniform; genuine, honest. ANT.—hilly, irregular, learning, lumpy, rugged; dishonest.

lewd, coarse, dirty, disgusting, filthy, gross, impure, indecent, lecherous, lustful, obscene, offensive, pornographic, prurient, smutty. ANT.—chaste, decent, modest, pure, refined.

liable, accountable, amenable, answerable, apt, bound, chargeable, exposed to, likely, responsible, subject to, susceptible. ANT.—absolved, exempt, free, immune, unlikely.

libel, asperse, damage, defame, detract, injure, lampoon, satirize, slander, vilify; aspersion, backbiting, calumny, defamation, slander, vilification. ANT.—defend, elevate, help, justify; applause, commendation, defense, flattery, praise.

liberal, ample, bountiful, broad-minded, extensive, extravagant, free, generous, large, lavish, leftist, lenient, magnanimous, munificent, noble-minded, prodigal, profuse, tolerant, unselfish. ANT.—confined, conservative, greedy, penurious, narrow, restricted.

liberate, absolve, acquit, clear, deliver, discharge, dismiss, emancipate, extricate, free, loose, pardon, ransom, redeem, release, rescue, save, set free, unchain, unshackle, untie. ANT.—confine, imprison, oppress, prohibit, restrict.

liberty, autonomy, emancipation, freedom, independence, liberation, self-government; allowance, dismissal, exemption, furlough, immunity, leisure, license, opportunity, permission, privilege, right. ANT.—bondage, captivity, imprisonment, oppression, slavery; confinement, constraint, detention, duress, obligation.

license, allow, approve, authorize, commission, endorse, permit, sanction, warrant; exemption, familiarity, freedom, immunity, independence, liberty, privilege. ANT.—ban, check, forbid, limit, withhold; bondage, compulsion, necessity, servitude.

lie, deceive, deviate, distort, equivocate, evade, exaggerate, falsify, fib, misinform, misrepresent, stretch; lie (down), recline, remain, repose, rest, stay. ANT.—be honest, declare (truth); arise, be upright, rise, sit, stand.

life, animation, being, buoyancy, essence, existence, liveliness, principle, spirit, vigor, vitality, vivacity; origin, source; duration, longevity, survival. ANT.—cessation, death, demise, inaction, languor.

lifeless, dead, deceased, defunct, demised, departed, dull, extinct, flat, gone, inactive, inanimate, insensible, spiritless, stagnant, unconscious. ANT.—alive, animate, brisk, living, vigorous, vital.

lift, boost, elevate, erect, exalt, heave, heighten, hoist, intensify, lift, raise, uplift; purloin, steal, take. ANT.—abase, depreciate, depress, destroy, lower; repay, return.

light, beam, blaze, brightness, brilliancy, dawn, flame, gleam, glow, illumination, incandescence, lamp, luminosity, lustre, radiance, scintillation, shimmer, sparkle, shine; comprehension, enlightenment, insight, knowledge, understanding; airy, buoyant, effervescent; ethereal, resilient, volatile; animated, blithe, capricious, cheerful, elated, hopeful, jocund, lively, sparkling, spirited, vivacious. ANT.—darkness, gloom, ignorance, obscurity, shadow; burdensome, heavy, weighty; depressed, gloomy, morose, sullen, weary.

likable, agreeable, amiable, companionable, enjoyable, friendly, good-natured, pleasant. ANT.—disagreeable, offensive, unattractive, unlikable, unpleasant.

like, akin, allied, analogous, cognate, coincident, comparable, equal, equivalent, identical, indistinguishable, parallel, related, resembling, same, similar. ANT.—contrary, disparate, dissimilar, distinct, opposed.

likeness, analogy, correspondence, counterpart, equivalence, parity, resemblance, similarity, similitude; copy, facsimile, illustration, photograph, portrait, representation. ANT.—difference, distinction, variation.

limit, border, boundary, brink, confine, edge, end, extent, extreme, frontier, limitation, line, restraint, restriction, rim, terminus. ANT.—boundlessness, endlessness, extension, infinity.

limpid, bright, clear, crystal, crystalline, glassy, lucid, pellucid, pure, translucent, transparent. ANT.—cloudy, dark, muddy, opaque, turbid.

lineage, ancestry, birth, breed, children, clan, descent, extraction, family, folk, forefathers, genealogy, nation, people, progeny, race, stock, strain, succession, tribe.

linger, abide, bide, dawdle, delay, falter, hesitate, lag, loiter, lumber, remain, rest, stay, tarry, wait. ANT.—bustle, dash, dart, hurry, speed.

link, associate, attach, bind, bond, conjoin, connect, couple, fasten, go with, join, pin, tie, unite. ANT.—cut, detach, divide, separate, sever.

liquid, dissolved, flowing, fluent, fluid, juicy, liquefied, melted, molten, sappy, serous, solvent, succulent, watery. ANT.—congealed, dense, gaseous, solid, undissolved.

listen, attend to, audit, hear, hearken, heed, list, monitor, overhear; follow, grant, obey, observe. ANT.—disregard, ignore, reject, scorn.

little, condensed, diminutive, dwarfish, elfin, infinitesimal, insignificant, meager, miniature, minute, petite, petty, puny, scanty, slight, small, tiny, trifling, trivial, wee; mean, petty, selfish. ANT.—colossal, enormous, huge, immense, mighty, titanic.

lively, active, animated, blithe, brisk bustling, ebullient, energetic, exhilarated, frolicsome, intense, rapid, spirited, sprightly, supple, vigorous, vivacious; bright, clear, fresh, glowing, sparkling, vivid. ANT.—dull, insipid, listless, stale, vapid.

load, afflict, burden, encumber, oppress, overlook, pressure, tax, trouble, weigh. ANT.—alleviate, console, ease, lighten, mitigate.

loathe, abhor, abominate, condemn, denounce, despise, detest, dislike, hate, imprecate, oppose. ANT.—admire, approve, cherish, love, respect.

location, area, locale, locality, neighborhood, place, position, post, region, site, situation, spot, station, vicinity.

lock, attachment, bar, barrier, bolt, catch, clasp, connection, fastening, grapple, hasp, hook, latch, link, padlock; curl, ringlet, tress, tuft.

lofty, dignified, elevated, exalted, grand, grandiose, high, imposing, magnificent, majestic, noble, pompous, proud, stately, sublime; arrogant, conceited, haughty, pretentious, vain. ANT.—common, humble, lowly, modest, ordinary, plebian.

logical, cogent, coherent, convincing, dialectical, discriminating, effective, efficacious, rational, reasonable, sound, strong, telling, valid, weighty. ANT.—crazy, foolish, incoherent, incongruous, weak.

lone, deserted, desolate, isolated, lonely, lonesome, secluded, unaided, unattached; alone, only, single, sole, solitary, unique. ANT.—accompanied, attended, joined, surrounded, together.

lonely, alone, cheerless, desolate, dreary, forlorn, forsaken, isolated, lonesome, secluded, sequestered, solitary. ANT.—befriended, cheerful.

long, drawn out, elongated, enduring, extended, interminable, lasting, lengthy, lingering, prolix, prolonged, protracted, tedious, wordy; distant, far-away, far-off, remote. ANT.—abridged, brief, concise, short, terse; accessible, adjacent, close, neighboring.

look, behold, contemplate, discern, distinguish, eye, gaze, glance, glimpse, perceive, scan, see, stare, survey, view, watch, witness; appear, seem; examine, inspect, investigate, observe; air, appearance, aspect, bearing, behavior, carriage, conduct, condition, department, expression, face, front, manner, mien. ANT.—avert, hide, ignore, miss, overlook.

loose, disengaged, flowing, free, indefinite, lax, limp, relaxed, separate, slack, unbound, unconfined, unfastened, untied, vague; careless, dissolute, heedless, immoral, licentious, unrestrained, wanton. ANT.—fast, taut, tied, tight; inhibited, moral, restrained.

lose, blunder, botch, drop, fail, falter, flounder, flunk, fold, forfeit, fumble, miscarry, mislay, miss, squander, stumble, waste. ANT.—accomplish, improve, master, overcome, regain.

loss, casualty, damage, death, decline, deficiency, deprivation, deterioration, detriment, disadvantage, failure, impairment, lack, retardation, want. ANT.—achievement, acquisition, advancement, gain, improvement.

lot, doom, fate, fortune, portion; award, destiny, issue, outcome, result; chance, luck; assemblage, batch, gathering, group; land parcel.

loud, blaring, blatant, clamorous, crashing, deafening, noisy, piercing, resonant, resounding, shrill, sonorous, stentorian, vociferous; coarse, ill-bred, vulgar; bright, gaudy. ANT.—dulcet, faint, inaudible, quiet, soft, subdued; tasteful.

love, adoration, affection, ardor, attachment, charity, devotion, endearment, fervor, fondness, intimacy, liking, passion, regard, respect, sentiment, warmth, worship, yearning. ANT.—aversion, dislike, enmity, hatred, indifference, scorn.

lovely, adorable, attractive, beauteous, beautiful, captivating, charming, comely, delightful, elegant, enchanting, enticing, fair, fine, graceful, handsome, inviting, lovable, pretty, satisfying, sweet, winsome. ANT.—foul, hideous, homely, repulsive, repugnant.

low, abject, contemptible, debased, degraded, despicable, disgraceful, dishonorable, groveling, ignoble, ignominious, lowly, mean, menial, servile, shameless, sordid, vile, vulgar; feeble, ill, sick, weak; cheap, inexpensive, moderate; short, small; faint, hushed, muffled, soft; blue, dejected, moody; below, beneath, deep, depressed, flat, inferior, nether, prone, prostrate, squat, sunken, supine. ANT.—esteemed, exalted, honored, lofty, noble; healthy, strong, vigorous; costly, expensive; tall, towering; blatant, clamorous, deafening, loud, thunderous; elated, exhilarated; inflated, superior.

lower, inferior, minor, poorer, secondary, subordinate; abase, adulterate, corrupt, debase, defile, degrade, deprave, depress, humiliate, impair, pervert, vitiate. ANT.—better, greater, higher, superior; enhance, improve, raise, restore, vitalize.

loyal, constant, dedicated, devoted, earnest, faithful, patriotic, steadfast, true, trustworthy, unfailing, unswerving. ANT.—disloyal, faithless, false, seditious, treacherous.

lubricate, anoint, cream, grease, lather, oil, salve, wax.

lucid, bright, clear, diaphanous, glossy, limpid, luminous, radiant, serene, transparent; sane, sound, rational; distinct, evident, explicit, intelligible, manifest, obvious, plain, understandable, unmistakable, visible. ANT.—dark, gloomy, murky, nebulous, obscure; demented, deranged; confused, cryptic, enigmatic, puzzling, unintelligible.

lucky, advantageous, auspicious, benign, conquering, favored, felicitous, flourishing, fortuitous, fortunate, happy, propitious, prosperous, successful, thriving, triumphant, victorious. ANT.—cheerless, defeated, downtrodden, ill-fated, persecuted.

lucrative, advantageous, gainful, profitable, remunerative, self-sustaining, worthwhile. ANT.—costly, failing, losing, troublesome, wasteful.

ludicrous, absurd, bizarre, comical, farcical, funny, incongruous, laughable, outlandish, ridiculous, /logical, normal, reasonable, serious, solemn.

luminous, bright, brilliant, clear, gleaming, glowing, incandescent, lucid, lustrous, radiant, shining. ANT.—dim, dull, murky, obscure, unclear.

lunacy, aberration, craziness, delirium, delusion, dementia, derangement, frenzy, hallucination, imbalance, insanity, madness, mania, psychosis. ANT.—balance, normality, rationality, sanity, stability.

lure, allure, attract, bait, bewitch, charm, coax, decoy, ensnare, entangle, entice, entrap, fascinate, induce, inveigle, lead astray, mesmerize, persuade, seduce, tempt, trick, wheedle. ANT.—alienate, antagonize, discourage, repel, revolt.

lust, appetite, avarice, carnality, concupiscence, craving, cupidity, desire, greed, hankering, hungering, longing, urge, wantonness, yearning. ANT.—chastity, purity, restraint; abomination, aversion, distaste, loathing.

luster, brightness, brilliance, brilliancy, effulgence, glossiness, luminosity, radiance, sheen, shimmer, splendor; distinction, fame, renown, repute. ANT.—cloudiness, darkness, drabness, murkiness, shade; baseness, dishonor, disrepute, reproach, shame.

luxurious, epicurean, opulent, ornate, pampered, rich, self-indulgent, sensuous, splendid, sumptuous, voluptuous, wanton. ANT.—ascetic, bare, drab, monastic, spartan.

M

machine, apparatus, appliance, automatism, contrivance, engine, implement, instrument, mechanism, motor, tool, utensil; agent, cabal, organization, system.

mad, angry, enraged, exasperated, furious, incensed, provoked, raging, upset, wrathful; crazy, daft, delirious, demented, deranged, insane, lunatic, maniacal, paranoid, psychotic, scatterbrained, unbalanced, unhinged, unsettled. ANT.—calm, cool, serene; balanced, rational, reasonable, sane, sensible.

magic, black art, charm, conjuring, demonology, divination, enchantment, hexing, hocus-pocus, illusion, jugglery, legerdemain, necromancy, occultism, omen, prediction, rune, sorcery, trickery, voodoo, witchcraft, wizardry.

magnanimous, beneficent, bountiful, charitable, chivalrous, forgiving, generous, giving, greathearted, heroic, liberal, munificent, openhanded, unselfish. ANT.—covetous, egotistical, greedy, miserly, selfish.

magnificent, elegant, excellent, glorious, gorgeous, grand, kingly, majestic, overwhelming, radiant, rich, spectacular, splendid, stately, sublime, sumptuous, superb. ANT.—common, humble, modest, ordinary, plebeian.

magnify, aggrandize, amplify, augment, embroider, enhance, enlarge, exaggerate, expand, heighten, hyperbolize, increase, overstate, romanticize, stretch. ANT.—decrease, depreciate, diminish, minimize, understate.

magnitude, amplitude, bigness, brightness, bulk, dimensions, expanse, extension, extent, girth, greatness, highness, importance, intensity, largeness, loudness, mass, power, proportions, quantity, range, size, vastness, volume. ANT.—dimness, insignificance, paucity, mediocrity, quietness.

main, cardinal, central, chief, essential, first, foremost, highest, leading, necessary, paramount, predominant, prime, principal, supreme.

ANT.—auxiliary, inessential, minor, secondary, subordinate.

maintain, continue, keep, preserve, retain, support, sustain, uphold; affirm, allege, assert, claim, confirm, contend, declare, defend, hold, justify, prove, vindicate. ANT.—abandon, discontinue, desert, forsake, quit; condemn, deny, oppose, reject, resist.

majestic, august, dignified, distinguished, eminent, exalted, grand, grandiose, high, illustrious, imperial, imposing, impressive, inspiring, lofty, magnificent, noble, pompous, prominent, splendid, stately, sublime, towering. ANT.—humble, insignificant, low, ordinary, shabby.

make, accomplish, achieve, assemble, build, carve, cause, compel, complete, compose, construct, create, do, drive, establish, execute, fabricate, fashion, force, forge, form, frame, gain, generate, invent, manufacture, mold, perfect, produce, shape. ANT.—annihilate, break, demolish, destroy, mutilate.

makeshift, alternative, expedient, momentary, provisional, short-term, stopgap, substitute, temporary. ANT.—abiding, fixed, permanent.

malady, affliction, ailment, disease, disorder, illness, indisposition, infirmity, sickness. ANT.—health, soundness, vigor, well-being.

malevolence, animosity, enmity, evil, grudge, hate, hostility, ill will, malice, malignancy, malignity, rancor, recrimination, spite, treachery. ANT.—affection, charity, love, sympathy, toleration.

malice, see **malevolence.**

malign, abuse, asperse, besmirch, calumniate, defame, detract, discredit, disparage, libel, revile, scandalize, slander, traduce, vilify; misapply, misemploy, misuse. ANT.—acclaim, celebrate, extol, praise, respect.

malignant, bitter, deadly, evil, fatal, hostile, malevolent, malign, mischievous, pernicious, spiteful, virulent. ANT.—benign, good, helpful, peaceful.

malleable, changeable, ductile, flexible, impressionable, moldable, plastic, pliant, shapeable, supple, yielding. ANT.—fixed, indomitable, resolute, rigid, unyielding.

manage, administer, command, conduct, control, direct, dominate, govern, guide, head, officiate, oversee, regulate, rule, run, steer, superintendent, supervise, watch; bridle, check, curb, repress, restrain. ANT.—abandon, bungle, mismanage, muff, spoil.

mandate, behest, charge, command, commission, decree, edict, fiat, injunction, law, order, ordinance, requirement, requisite, rule, statute, ukase.

maneuver, action, artifice, design, enterprise, execution, feint, movement, operation, performance, plan, plot, procedure, proceeding, ruse, scheme, stratagem, tactic, wile. ANT.—cessation, inaction, inactivity, rest.

mangle, cripple, crush, disfigure, dismember, fracture, hack, lacerate, maim, mutilate, rend, slash.

manifest, clear, cloudless, fair, sunny; limpid, transparent; apparent, conspicuous, defined, definite, distinct, evident, explicit, intelligible, lucid, obvious, patent, plain, unmistakable, unveiled, visible; open, unobstructed; disclose, exhibit, indicate, reveal, show. ANT.—cloudy, foul, overcast; ambiguous, complex, obscure, unclear, vague; buried, concealed, covered, hidden; conceal, distract, divert, falsify, mislead.

manipulate, bribe, compel, control, direct, feel, finger, guide, handle, lead, operate, rule, threaten.

manner, approach, custom, fashion, form, habit, method, mode, practice, style, way; air, bearing, behavior, carriage, conduct, demeanor, deportment, guise, mien.

many, countless, diverse, manifold, multifarious, multitudinous, myriad, numerous, several, sundry, various. ANT.—few, infrequent, meager, scanty, scarce, uniform.

mar, botch, bungle, damage, deface, deform, distort, harm, hurt, impair, injure, mutilate, scar, spoil, stain, twist, warp, waste. ANT.—adorn, beautify, benefit, enhance, vivify.

margin, bank, border, brim, brink, boundary, confines, fence, fringe, leeway, limit, lip, rim, shore, strand, wall. ANT.—center, extension, heart, interior, surface.

marine, aquatic, hydrographic, maritime, natatorial, nautical, naval, ocean, oceanic, oceanographic, pelagic, seafaring, seagoing. ANT.—alluvial, ashore, earthly, geodetic, terrestrial.

mark, brand, engraving, impression, imprint, scar, stamp, stigma, trace, vestige; badge, emblem, label, sign, symbol, token; characteristic, feature, indication, representation, symptom, trait; goal, target; attend to, behold, notice, observe, perceive, recognize, regard, see. ANT.—disregard, ignore, overlook, skip.

marriage, conjugality, espousal, matrimony, nuptials, oath, union, wedding, wedlock. ANT.—celibacy, divorce, separation, singleness, virginity.

marvelous, amazing, astonishing, awesome, exceptional, extraordinary, fabulous, incredible, indescribable, ineffable, miraculous, mysterious, peculiar, phenomenal, rare, remarkable, singular, superb, uncommon, unexpected, unusual, wonderful, wondrous. ANT.—commonplace, ordinary, plain, unremarkable, worthless.

masculine, aggressive, bold, brave, daring, hardy, husky, lusty, male, manly, mannish, robust, strong, vigorous, virile. ANT.—effeminate, emasculated, feminine, timorous, womanish.

mask, camouflage, cloak, conceal, cover, disguise, dissemble, falsify, hide, hoodwink, hush, muffle, mystify, screen, secrete, shield, suppress, veil, withhold. ANT.—bare, disclose, expose, reveal, unveil.

mass, body, carcass, corpse, remains; form, frame, torso; bigness, bulk, dimensions, magnitude, size; accumulation, aggregate, aggregation, assemblage, association, collection, company, heap, lump, society, sum, total, totality, whole; agglomeration, conglomeration. ANT.—mind, soul, spirit; individual, factor, part, portion.

massacre, annihilation, bloodshed, butchery, carnage, decimation, execution, extermination, genocide, killing, murder, pogrom, slaughter, slaying. ANT.—animation, preservation, protection, resuscitation.

massive, colossal, dense, heavy, huge, large, majestic, ponderous, weighty; burdensome, cumbersome, cumbrous, grievous, trying, unwieldy; gloomy, grave, serious, sluggish. ANT.—airy, delicate, light, small; flexible, pliant; animated, brisk, buoyant.

master, captain, champion, chief, commander, conqueror, director, employer, governor, head, leader, lord, manager, mentor, overseer, potentate, principal, ruler, superior, teacher, victor; holder, owner, proprietor; adept, expert. ANT.—apprentice, dependent, follower, pupil, servitor; amateur, beginner, greenhorn, neophyte, novice.

masterpiece, chef-d'oeuvre, forte, greatest accomplishment, magnum opus, masterstroke, masterwork, monument, paragon, peak.

mastery, advantage, ascendancy, command, conquest, control, domination, dominion, expertise, exultation, predominance, rule, skill, sovereignty, superiority, supremacy, sway, transcendence, triumph, victory. ANT.—defeat, failure, impotence, inferiority, subjugation.

mate, assistant, associate, attendant, chum, colleague, companion, comrade, consort, crony, friend, intimate, pal, partner, spouse; ship's officer; match, marry.

material, body, cloth, fabric, gear, matter, staple, stuff, substance; affair, cause, concern, occasion, subject, theme, thing, topic; consequence, essence, importance, moment; bodily, concrete, corporeal, palpable, physical, ponderable, sensible, solid, somatic, substantial, tangible, temporal. ANT.—nothingness; airy, bodiless, ethereal, intangible, spiritual.

matrimony, see **marriage.**

matter, see **material.**

mature, adult, aged, complete, consummate, developed, experienced, fertile, finished, full-grown, hardened, matronly, matured, mellow, prime, pubescent, ready, ripe, seasoned, virile; age, develop, perfect, ripen, season. ANT.—deficient, immature, juvenile, premature, raw, undeveloped.

mean, average, mediocre, medium, middle, model, normal; abject, base, contemptible, debased, degraded, despicable, ignoble, low, obscure, plebeian, sordid, vile, vulgar; bad-tempered, malicious, nasty, offensive; mercenary, miserly, parsimonious, penurious, selfish, stingy; contemplate, design, imply, indicate, intend, ordain, purpose, say, signify, state, suggest. ANT.—admirable, distinguished, extraordinary, high, superior; benevolent, charitable, kind; generous, indulgent, liberal, philanthropic, profuse.

meaning, acceptation, connotation, drift, explanation, gist, implication, import, intent, interpretation, purport, purpose, sense, significance, signification.

means, agent, apparatus, channel, device, expedient, factor, instrument, materials, measure, medium, method, tool, utensil, vehicle; capital, income, property, resources, riches, stock, wealth.

measure, criterion, gauge, law, principle, proof, rule, scale, standard, test, touchstone; amplitude, capacity, degree, extent, magnitude, limit, range, scope, size; amount, quantity; allotment, proportion, share; bill, design, draft, outline, plan, plot, project, proposal, proposition, scheme, sketch, suggestion.

mechanical, automated, automatic, autonomic, contrived, controlled, impulsive, instinctive, involuntary, machinelike, perfunctory, rote, routine, unreasoned.

meddle, annoy, impede, interfere, interpose, interrupt, intervene, intrude, mix, monkey, obtrude, pester, pry, tamper. ANT.—aid, avoid, encourage, shun, support.

mediocre, average, commonplace, fair, intermediate, mean, median, medium, middling, moderate, ordinary, passable. ANT.—exceptional, extraordinary, outstanding, superior, unusual.

meditate, cogitate, consider, contemplate, deliberate, muse, ponder, reason, reflect, speculate, study, think; conceive, imagine, picture, recall, recollect, remember; devise, intend, mean, plan, project, purpose, resolve. ANT.—dismiss, disregard, divert, neglect, overlook.

meek, calm, compliant, demure, docile, domestic, gentle, humble, mild, modest, obedient, pacific, patient, peaceable, subdued, submissive, tame, tolerant, unpretentious, yielding; dull, flat, insipid, tedious. ANT.—arrogant, fierce, obstinate, pompous, savage; animated, exciting, lively, spirited.

meet, collide, confront, connect, converge, cross, encounter, engage, find, greet, intersect, join, touch; answer, fulfill, gratify, satisfy; experience, suffer, undergo. ANT.—avoid, cleave, disperse, miss, separate.

melancholy, dejected, depressed, despondent, disconsolate, dismal, dispirited, doleful, forlorn, funereal, gloomy, glum, grim, joyless, moody, mournful, sad, sorrowful, sulky, wistful; grave, pensive, somber. ANT.—cheerful, happy, jubilant, spirited, vivacious.

mellow, aged, full-flavored, mature, perfected, ripe, sweet; delicate, pleasing, refined, relaxed, subdued, sweet-sounding. ANT.—dull, hard, immature, sour, stale; callous, crude, harsh, stubborn.

melody, air, aria, chant, concord, descant, euphony, harmony, lyric, mellifluence, monophony, strain, theme, tune.

member, allotment, apportionment, division, fragment, moiety, piece, portion, scrap, section, segment, share; component, constituent, element, ingredient; limb, organ, part.

memorial, commemoration, commemorative, inscription, memento, monument, remembrance, souvenir; chair, professorship, scholarship.

memory, mental trace, recollection, remembrance, reminiscence, retention, retrospection; fame, renown, reputation. ANT.—amnesia, effacement, forgetfulness, oblivion, unconsciousness.

mend, fix, patch, repair, restore, sew, touch up; ameliorate, better, correct, enhance, improve, rectify, refine, reform, refresh, remedy, renew, revive; get well, heal, recover. ANT.—damage, deform, impair, mar, wound; deteriorate, fall ill, wane, weaken.

mendicant, beggar, pauper, ragamuffin, scrub, solicitor, starveling, tatterdemalion, vagabond, wretch. ANT.—benefactor, contributor, donor, giver.

menial, abject, base, degrading, humble, ignoble, lowly, mean, servile, unimportant, unskilled. ANT.—elevated, expert, noble, professional, uplifting.

mentality, brain, capacity, comprehension, consciousness, faculties, intellect, intelligence, judgment, mind, perception, psyche, reason, reasoning, thought, understanding, wisdom; disposition, inclination, intention, purpose, will, wish. ANT.—corporeality, materiality, matter.

mentor, advisor, counselor, guide, instructor, leader, monitor, teacher. ANT.—disciple, follower, pupil, student.

mercenary, avaricious, corrupt, grasping, greedy, selfish, sordid, venal. ANT.—generous, honorable, liberal, unselfish.

merciful, beneficent, benignant, clement, compassionate, feeling, forbearing, forgiving, gracious, humane, kind, lenient, philanthropic, pitying, soft-hearted, sympathetic, tender, tolerant. ANT.—barbarous, cruel, pitiless, ruthless, tyrannical.

mercy, benevolence, benignity, charity, clemency, compassion, forbearance, forgiveness, grace, humanity, kindness, leniency, mildness, pardon, pity, tolerance. ANT.—banishment, inhumanity, oppression, punishment, vengeance.

merge, amalgamate, blend, coalesce, combine, commingle, conjoin, consolidate, fuse, integrate, join, mingle, mix, unify, unite. ANT.—decompose, divest, divide, separate.

merit, effectiveness, efficacy, force, power, strength; excellence, goodness, regard, value, virtue, worth, worthiness; reward; achieve, attain, deserve, earn, gain, obtain, win. ANT.—corruption, dishonor, evil, weakness, unworthiness; forfeit, lose, spend, waste.

merry, animated, blithe, buoyant, cheerful, ebullient, elated, exhilarated, exuberant, festive, gay, gleeful, hilarious, jocular, jolly, jovial, joyous, jubilant, light-hearted, lively, mirthful, rollicking, spirited, sprightly, vivacious. ANT.—gloomy, melancholy, morose, pessimistic, wretched.

mess, allowance, portion, ration; difficulty, dilemma, plight, predicament, problem; confusion, conglomeration, disorder, disorganization, hodgepodge, jumble, litter, medley, mélange, mixture, potpourri. ANT.—arrangement, method, order, system, tidiness.

message, indication, mark, sign, signal, symbol, token; annotation, comment, communication, dispatch, letter, memorandum, news, note, observation, remark, report, word.

method, arrangement, custom, design, fashion, form, manner, mode, order, plan, procedure, process, rule, scheme, style, system, technique, vogue, way. ANT.—chaos, confusion, disarrangement, disorder, irregularity, muddle.

meticulous, exacting, fastidious, finical, fussy, painstaking, particular, precise, punctilious, scrupulous, tidy. ANT.—careless, cursory, disheveled, sloppy, unkempt.

methodical, accurate, correct, definite, distinct, exact, formal, orderly, precise, regular, rigid, strict, systematic, unequivocal, well-regulated. ANT.—careless, informal, loose, rough, vague.

microscopic, diminutive, fine, infinitesimal, minimal, minute, tiny; detailed, exact, particular, precise. ANT.—enormous, huge, large; general.

middle, axis, center, core, focus, heart, marrow, mean, midpoint, midst, nucleus, pivot; average, axial, central, equidistant, halfway, interjacent, intermediate, mediocre, pivotal. ANT.—border, boundary, outskirts, periphery, rim; beginning, end; extreme, high, low.

might, ability, brawn, energy, force, potency, power, puissance, strength, sturdiness, sway, tenacity, vigor, vitality. ANT.—frailty, impotence, inability, vulnerability, weakness.

mighty, able, bold, concentrated, doughty, enduring, firm, forceful, great, hale, hardy, heavy, husky, immense, impregnable, indomitable, invincible, large, lusty, majestic, manful, momentous, muscular, overpowering, potent, powerful, puissant, resistless, robust, sinewy, stalwart, strapping, strong, stupendous, sturdy, tough, vigorous. ANT.—delicate, enervated, feeble, flaccid, weak.

mild, calm, genial, gentle, humane, kind, meek, mellow, moderate, pacific, patient, peaceful, placid, quiet, smooth, soft, soothing, temperate, tender, tepid, tranquil; bland, savory, sweet. ANT.—bitter, fierce, harsh, irritating, uncouth; acid, biting, bitter, sour, stringent.

militant, active, aggressive, armed, belligerent, combative, contentious, fighting, hostile, pugnacious, pushing, warring. ANT.—acquiescent, amenable, compliant, peaceful, submissive.

mimic, ape, burlesque, caricature, copy, counterfeit, duplicate, echo, feign, forge, imitate, impersonate, mock, parody, parrot, repeat, reproduce, simulate. ANT.—distort, diverge, invent.

mind, see **mentality**.

mingle, amalgamate, associate, blend, combine, commingle, compound, concoct, confound, conjoin, consort, fraternize, fuse, intermingle, intermix, join, jumble, merge, mix, participate, unite. ANT.—disjoin, distinguish, separate, sort.

miniature, abridged, bantam, diminutive, little, minuscule, minute, reduced, small, tiny. ANT.—full-size, large, normal, regular.

minimize, belittle, curtail, deduct, degrade, depreciate, derogate, detract, diminish, disparage, fault, lessen, reduce, shorten, subtract. ANT.—amplify, enlarge, exalt, expand, magnify, praise.

minister, ambassador, churchman, clergyman, cleric, consul, curate, delegate, diplomat, divine, ecclesiastic, envoy, official, padre, parson, pastor, preacher, priest, rector, representative, reverend, vicar; aid, assist, help, nourish, nurture, serve, support, sustain. ANT.—apostate, disciple, follower, layman, renegade; encumber, hinder, impede, obstruct, oppose.

minor, inconsiderable, inferior, junior, lesser, lower, petty, poorer, secondary, smaller, subordinate, unimportant, younger; adolescent, child. ANT.—first, greater, important, major; adult, of age.

minute, accurate, atomic, critical, detailed, diminutive, exact, exiguous, fine, inconsiderable, infinitesimal, insignificant, little, microscopic, miniature, minuscule, molecular, petty, precise, puny, small, tiny. ANT.—colossal, comprehensive, enormous, extensive, magnificent.

miraculous, astonishing, awesome, extraordinary, incredible, inexplicable, marvelous, metaphysical, preternatural, spectacular, spiritual, stupefying, superhuman, supernatural, unearthly. ANT.—commonplace, customary, insignificant, natural, ordinary.

mirage, apparition, delusion, dream, fantasy, figment, hallucination, illusion, phantasm, vision. ANT.—actuality, reality, substance.

miscarriage, defeat, failure, fiasco, frustration, malfunction; spontaneous abortion. ANT.—achievement, success, victory; pregnancy.

miscellaneous, assorted, dissimilar, diverse, diversified, heterogeneous, indiscriminate, mingled, mixed, motley, promiscuous, sundry, variant, varied, various. ANT.—classified, homogeneous, ordered, same, sorted.

mischief, affront, annoyance, damage, detriment, deviltry, disservice, evil, grievance, harm, hurt, ill, infliction, injury, misfortune, mishap, outrage, prank, roguery, wrong. ANT.—betterment, favor, kindness, support, vindication.

miserable, afflicted, ailing, comfortless, crushed, disconsolate, discontented, dismal, distressed, forlorn, heartbroken, pained, pitiable, sickly, sorrowful, suffering, wretched; abject, contemptible, despicable, lamentable, low, mean; insufficient, meager, paltry, poor, scanty, small, stingy. ANT.—contented, happy, lively, rejoicing; noble, respectable; fortunate, prosperous, significant.

miserly, avaricious, close, covetous, greedy, niggardly, parsimonious, penurious, rapacious, selfish, stingy, tight, tight-fisted. ANT.—altruistic, bountiful, extravagant, generous, liberal, munificent.

misery, agony, anguish, anxiety, desolation, despair, despondency, distress, grief, heartache, mortification, pain, sorrow, suffering, torment, trial, tribulation, woe, wretchedness; affliction, calamity, disaster, evil, misfortune, ordeal, trouble; illness, sickness. ANT.—bliss, delight, ecstasy, elation, joy; comfort, contentment, fortune, peace; health, salubrity, vigor.

misfortune, accident, adversity, affliction, bereavement, calamity, casualty, catastrophe, chastening, disaster, distress, hardship, harm, hurt, ill fortune, infliction, injury, loss, misadventure, mishap, privation, ruin, set-back, tribulation. ANT.—advantage, blessing, contentment, prosperity, success, well-being.

misgiving, distrust, doubt, hesitation, mistrust, suspicion, uncertainty. ANT.—certainty, security, sureness, trust.

mishap, accident, calamity, casualty, contretemps, disaster, misadventure, mischance, misfortune, reverse. ANT.—good fortune, luck.

misinterpret, distort, falsify, misconceive, misconstrue, misunderstand, pervert. ANT.—comprehend, perceive, understand.

misleading, deceitful, deceptive, delusive, delusory, fallacious, false, furtive, illusive, specious. ANT.—authentic, direct, forthright, genuine, straightforward, truthful.

misrepresent, belie, caricature, dissemble, distort, exaggerate, falsify, mislead, misstate, pervert, simulate. ANT.—delineate, depict, represent.

miss, fail, default, lack, lose, miscarry, omit, overlook, skip; crave, desire, want, yearn; drop, fumble, muff, snatch at; blunder, mishap, slip. ANT.—achieve, attain, have, succeed; detest, shun; catch, grab, hold; accomplishment, advancement, gain.

mission, activity, affair, attack, business, commission, delegation, errand, purpose; calling, duty, task, work.

mistake, aberration, blunder, downfall, error, failure, fallacy, fault, flaw, illusion, inaccuracy, lapse, misapprehension, misconception, mishap, omission, oversight, slip. ANT.—accuracy, correctness, perfection, precision, truth, veracity.

misunderstanding, confusion, difference, disagreement, discord, dissension, error, misapprehension, misconception, misinterpretation, mistake, quarrel, variance. ANT.—agreement, concord, understanding.

misuse, abuse, asperse, defame, desecrate, disparage, harm, ill-use, injure, malign, maltreat, maul, mishandle, pervert, revile, scandalize, traduce, vilify, wrong; consume, dissipate, scatter, spend, squander, waste. ANT.—cherish, honor, protect, respect, succor; accumulate, conserve, economize, preserve, retain.

mitigate, abate, allay, alleviate, ameliorate, appease, assuage, calm, decrease, dilute, diminish, extenuate, lessen, lighten, moderate, modify, mollify, relieve, soften, solace, soothe, subdue, temper, weaken. ANT.—aggravate, deepen, increase, inflate, intensify, provoke.

mix, adulterate, alloy, blend, combine, commingle, commix, compound, concoct, crossbreed, homogenize, incorporate, intermingle, intermix, fuse, join, mingle, shuffle, stir; coalesce, integrate; confound, confuse, jumble, mix up, tangle; associate, consort, fraternize, join, unite. ANT.—detach, disperse, divide, separate, sort; segregate; clarify, enlighten, unravel, untangle; abandon, desert, dissociate, divide.

mixture, assortment, change, difference, dissimilarity, diversity, heterogeneity, hodgepodge, jumble, medley, mélange, miscellany, multifariousness, olio, potpourri, variety; alloy, amalgam, blend, composite, compound, fusion; breed, strain, subspecies. ANT.—homogeneity, likeness, sameness, uniformity; isolation, purity, separation; simplicity; pedigree, purebred.

mob, assemblage, bevy, crowd, crush, drove, flock, gang, gathering, herd, horde, host, masses, multitude, populace, press, rabble, riffraff, swarm, throng.

mobilize, adapt, assemble, call up, command, gather, increase, marshal, order, organize, prepare, transport, unify, unite. ANT.—demobilize, disperse, end, scatter, separate.

mock, ape, defy, deride, fleer, flout, gibe, insult, jeer, mimic, ridicule, satirize, scoff, sneer at, taunt. ANT.—compliment, flatter, honor, praise, support.

mode, condition, course, custom, design, fashion, habit, kind, manner, method, order, plan, practice, procedure, rule, scheme, state, system, usage, vogue, way. ANT.—confusion, disorder.

model, archetype, copy, criterion, design, duplicate, example, facsimile, form, gauge, image, mold, original, paragon, pattern, prototype, replica, representation, specimen, standard, tracing, type.

moderate, abate, allay, assuage, check, curb, deaden, decrease, diminish, lessen, lower, palliate, quell, reduce, subdue, suppress, temper, weaken; abstemious, cool, dispassionate, fair, judicious, measured, mild, regulated, sparing, steady, temperate, tolerant. ANT.—agitate, anger, excite, inflame, stimulate; excessive, extravagant, liberal, outrageous, radical.

modern, contemporary, current, fashionable, fresh, latest, new, novel, present, recent, renovated. ANT.—ancient, antiquated, bygone, primitive, obsolete, outmoded.

modest, bashful, constrained, demure, diffident, humble, meek, reserved, retiring, shy, timid, unassuming, unpretentious; inconsiderable, insignificant, minute, small; chaste, pure, undefiled, virtuous. ANT.—arrogant, bold, conceited, egotistical, ostentatious; excessive, grand, huge, magnificent; immodest, indelicate, obscene, prurient, unchaste.

modification, adaptation, alteration, alternation, change, limitation, modulation, mutation, qualification, substitution, transformation, variation, variety, vicissitude. ANT.—monotony, stability, uniformity.

modify, adapt, alter, change, convert, exchange, expand, limit, lower, moderate, qualify, shape, reform, restrict, shift, soften, substitute, temper, transfigure, transform, vary, veer. ANT.—preserve, retain, stabilize.

moist, aqueous, damp, dank, dewy, dripping, fresh, humid, infiltrated, juicy, muggy, saturated, sloppy, soaked, sodden, soppy, swampy, vaporous, watery. ANT.—arid, barren, dehydrated, dry, parched, waterless.

mold, alter, carve, cast, create, fashion, forge, form, frame, influence, make, model, modify, produce, sculpt, shape. ANT.—destroy, dismantle, mutilate, wreck.

molest, aggrieve, annoy, assail, attack, bother, chafe, damage, disturb, harass, hurt, inconvenience, injure, irk, irritate, maltreat, misuse, oppress, persecute, pester, plague, tease, trouble, vex, worry. ANT.—aid, comfort, defend, encourage, protect, soothe.

moment, flash, instant, jiffy, minute, second, twinkling, wink; consequence, gravity, importance, significance, weight.

momentous, consequential, critical, crucial, decisive, far-reaching, grave, important, influential, material, memorable, pressing, prominent, relevant, salient, serious, significant, solemn, vital, weighty. ANT.—boring, commonplace, immaterial, insignificant, trivial.

monastery, abbey, cloister, convent, hermitage, lamasery, nunnery, priory.

money, assets, bills, bullion, cash, change, checks, coin, currency, finances, gold, legal tender, lucre, notes, pelf, resources, revenue, silver, specie, sterling, wherewithal; capital, funds,

opulence, property, riches, stock, wealth; payment, salary, wages.

monopolize, absorb, control, corner, direct, engross, own, possess.

monotonous, boring, burdensome, depressive, dilatory, dreary, dry, dull, flat, heavy, humdrum, irksome, prosy, repetitious, slow, sluggish, tardy, tedious, tiresome, undiversified, uninteresting, unvaried, wearisome. ANT.—appealing, entertaining, exciting, refreshing, varied, versatile.

monument, commemoration, memento, memorial, remembrance, souvenir, testimonial; gravestone, headstone, mausoleum, plaque, pyramid, shrine, statue, tomb, tombstone.

mood, behavior, conduct, disposition, frame of mind, humor, manner, nature, spirit, temper, temperament; inclination, propensity, tendency.

moral, chaste, decent, ethical, good, honest, honorable, just, noble, pure, right, righteous, scrupulous, upright, virtuous. ANT.—amoral, dishonorable, evil, immoral, unethical.

morose, acrimonious, cantankerous, churlish, crabbed, depressed, dour, fretful, gloomy, glum, grouchy, gruff, moody, morbid, petulant, splenetic, sulky, sullen, surly, unamiable. ANT.—buoyant, cheerful, exhilarated, good-natured, pleasant.

mortal, deadly, destructive, fatal, final, lethal, poisonous; extreme, serious; ephemeral, human, passing, temporal, transient. ANT.—curative, life-giving, reviving, strengthening, vivifying; trifling, trivial; external, everlasting, immortal, perpetual.

mortification, abasement, annoyance, chagrin, dissatisfaction, embarrassment, humiliation, shame, vexation; gangrene, necrosis. ANT.—elevation, happiness, praise, satisfaction, success.

motion, action, activity, change, gesture, mobility, move, movement, passage, revolution, transit, transition; proposal, proposition, recommendation, suggestion. ANT.—halt, immobility, inaction, repose, stillness.

motive, cause, determinant, encouragement, ground, impulse, incentive, incitement, inducement, influence, instigation, motivation, principle, prompting, purpose, reason, spur, stimulus, urge; mobile, motile, movable.

motley, assorted, composite, disparate, diverse, heterogeneous, incongruous, indiscriminate, miscellaneous, mixed, mottled, speckled, sundry, varied. ANT.—homogeneous, like, pure, similar, unvaried.

motto, adage, aphorism, apothegm, axiom, byword, epigram, maxim, proverb, saw, saying, sentiment, slogan.

mount, arise, ascend, aspire, climb, grow, increase, rise, scale, scramble, soar, surge, swell, tower. ANT.—collapse, decline, descend, diminish, drop, slump.

mourn, agonize, anguish, bemoan, bewail, cry, deplore, droop, fret, grieve, groan, languish, lament, miss, pray, regret, repine, rue, sigh, sing, sorrow, suffer, wail, weep (over), whimper, yearn. ANT.—celebrate, exult, laugh, rejoice, revel.

move, actuate, advance, agitate, arouse, convey, drive, excite, impel, incite, induce, influence, instigate, operate, persuade, proceed, propel, propose, push, rouse, run, shift, start, stimulate, stir, transfer, transport, travel, urge. ANT.—cease, deter, dissuade, halt, pacify, rest, suppress.

movement, see motion.

muddled, addled, befuddled, bewildered, chaotic, confounded, confused, deranged, disarrayed,

disconcerted, disordered, disorganized, indistinct, jumbled, messy, mixed, obscured, perplexed, puzzled, snarled, stupid. ANT.—distinguished, lucid, obvious, ordered, organized.

multiply, augment, enlarge, generate, grow, increase, propagate, reproduce. ANT.—divide, lessen, reduce, shrink, waste.

multitude, aggregation, army, assemblage, congregation, crowd, galaxy, gathering, horde, host, legion, mob, populace, swarm, throng. ANT.—fraction, handful, nobody, paucity, scarcity.

mundane, carnal, earthly, laic, lay, mortal, profane, secular, temporal, terrestrial, worldly; everyday, normal, ordinary. ANT.—celestial, eternal, heavenly, paradisaic, spiritual, unearthly; extraordinary, special, unique.

munificent, altruistic, beneficent, benevolent, charitable, generous, hospitable, liberal, philanthropic, princely, unselfish. ANT.—avaricious, covetous, grasping, miserly, selfish.

murder, annihilate, assassinate, butcher, choke, destroy, execute, exterminate, immolate, kill, massacre, poison, shoot, slaughter, slay, stab, victimize. ANT.—animate, propagate, nurse, refresh, restore, vitalize.

murmur, babble, complain, grouse, grumble, hum, mumble, mutter, protest, remonstrate, repine, ripple, rustle, whisper. ANT.—applaud, approve, honor, praise, recommend.

muscular, athletic, brawny, forceful, husky, powerful, sinewy, stalwart, strong, sturdy, vigorous. ANT.—feeble, flabby, infirm, puny, weak.

musical, agreeable, assonant, choral, euphonic, euphonious, harmonious, lyrical, mellow, melodic, melodious, pleasing, symphonic, tonal, tuneful, unisonant, vocal. ANT.—clashing, discordant, dissonant, grating, harsh.

muster, accumulate, amass, arrange, assemble, call, collect, congregate, convene, convoke, gather; marshal, organize, summon; cull, garner, harvest, pick, reap. ANT.—disjoin, disperse, divert, scatter, separate.

mute, calm, dumb, gagged, hushed, inarticulate, inaudible, noiseless, peaceful, quiet, silent, soundless, speechless, still, taciturn, tranquil, voiceless. ANT.—articulate, garrulous, loquacious, loud, raucous, talkative, vocal.

mutiny, anarchy, coup, insubordination, insurrection, outbreak, overthrow, rebellion, resistance, revolt, revolution, riot, upheaval, uprising.

mutter, complain, grouse, grumble, groan, grunt, maunder, moan, mumble, murmur, rumble, sputter, whisper.

mutual, analogous, common, convertible, correlative, correspondent, equivalent, identical, interchangeable, joint, like, reciprocal, self-same, shared, similar. ANT.—dissociated, divergent, separate, unlike, unshared.

mysterious, abstruse, ambiguous, baffling, cabalistic, covert, cryptic, dark, dim, enigmatical, hidden, impenetrable, incomprehensible, inconceivable, incredible, inexplicable, inscrutable, mystical, mystifying, obscure, occult, secret, surreptitious, unaccountable, unfathomable, unintelligible. ANT.—apparent, distinct, explicit, lucid, obvious.

mystery, conundrum, enigma, obscurity, perplexity, problem, puzzle, riddle, secret. ANT.—answer, key, solution.

mystical, see mysterious.

myth, allegory, chronicle, fable, fiction, folk ballad, folk tale, legend, lore, parable, saga, tale. ANT.—fact, history.

mythical, allegorical, apocryphal, fabricated, fabulous, fanciful, fantastic, fictitious, imaginary, invented, legendary, visionary. ANT.—actual, factual, historical, real, true.

N

nag, aggravate, annoy, badger, bother, browbeat, discompose, disturb, goad, harass, harry, heckle, irritate, molest, pester, plague, provoke, scold, tantalize, taunt, tease, torment, vex, worry. ANT.—comfort, delight, mollify, please, soothe.

naive, artless, guileless, inexperienced, ingenuous, innocent, natural, open, plain, provincial, simple, unaffected, unsophisticated. ANT.—crafty, cunning, experienced, sophisticated, wise.

naked, bare, exposed, nude, stripped, threadbare, unclad, unclothed, uncovered, undressed; bald, barren, unfurnished; definite, distinct, evident, exact, explicit, literal, mere, obvious, plain, simple, uncolored; defenseless, open, unprotected. ANT.—attired, clothed, dressed; furnished; artful, complex, concealed, secret; protected, shielded.

name, appellation, cognomen, denomination, designation, epithet, surname, title; character, reputation, repute; distinction, eminence, fame, renown; autograph, signature; nom de plume, pseudonym; appoint, call, characterize, christen, define, denominate, denote, designate, elect, entitle, identify, list, mark, mention, proclaim, signify, specify, term, title. ANT.—anonymity, namelessness.

narcotic, anaesthetic, anodyne, dope, drug, opiate, sedative, soporific, tranquilizer; anesthetizing, doping, drugging, nepenthic, stupefying, tranquilizing.

narrate, declaim, deliver, describe, detail, disclose, enumerate, mention, paint, picture, portray, proclaim, recite, recapitulate, recount, rehearse, relate, repeat, report, reveal, state, tell, unfold. ANT.—conceal, disguise, repress, stifle, withhold.

narrow, bigoted, dogmatic, fanatical, illiberal, intolerant, narrow-minded, prejudiced; miserly, parsimonious; close, confined, contracted, cramped, limited, restricted; scrawny, slender, spindling, thread-like. ANT.—liberal, progressive, radical, tolerant; bountiful, charitable, generous; broad, expanded, extended, wide; corpulent, fat, fleshy, stout.

nasty, dirty, foul, polluted, squalid; gross, indecent, lewd, obscene, smutty; disgusting, nauseating, offensive, repulsive, selfish; inclement, rainy, sleeting, stormy. ANT.—clean, spotless, unsullied; decent, pure; attractive, delightful, pleasant, sweet; clear, sunny.

nation, colony, commonwealth, community, country, empire, kingdom, nationality, people, principality, realm, republic, state, territory; clan, community, folk, people, populace, population, public, race, society.

native, aboriginal, congenital, domestic, endemic, inborn, indigenous, inherent, innate, local, natal, natural, original, pristine, regional, vernacular. ANT.—acquired, alien, artificial, extrinsic, foreign, imported, unnatural.

natural, characteristic, essential, fundamental, genetic, inherent, innate, intrinsic, native, original; normal, regular; artless, genuine, ingenuous, legitimate, real, simple, spontaneous, unaffected, unsophisticated. ANT.—contingent, external, extrinsic, objective; abnormal, artificial, irregular; beautified, embellished, forced, formal, unnatural.

nature, bent, character, constitution, disposition, essence, humor, individuality, kind, mood, reputation, repute, sort, temperament; creation, universe.

nauseous, abhorrent, abominable, despicable, detestable, disgusting, loathsome, nasty, offensive, repulsive, revolting, sickening, unpalatable. ANT.—ambrosial, delectable, delicious, desirable, savory.

naval, marine, maritime, nautical, navigating, ocean, oceanic, sailing, seafaring, seagoing, seaworthy.

near, abutting, adjacent, adjoining, bordering, close, contiguous, neighboring, proximate; approaching, coming, expected, imminent, impending, looming, next, prospective; dear, familiar, intimate. ANT.—far, remote; deferred, expired, postponed, stopped; distant, remote.

neat, adroit, clear, compact, correct, exact, finished, orderly, precise, proportioned, shapely, spotless, spruce, suitable, symmetrical, tidy, trim, well-done, well-ordered. ANT.—awkward, disordered, irregular, lax, slipshod, slovenly.

necessary, binding, compulsory, essential, expedient, imperative, indispensable, inevitable, inexorable, irrevocable, needed, obligatory, pressing, required, requisite, unavoidable, undeniable, urgent. ANT.—extravagant, optional, superfluous, unnecessary, worthless.

need, destitution, indigence, penury, pennilessness, poverty; distress, inadequacy, insufficiency, lack, misery, privation, shortage; emergency, necessity, obligation, requirement, urgency; lack, require, want, wish. ANT.—property, wealth; comfort, luxury, plenty; independence; competence, fullness.

neglect, apathy, carelessness, default, deferment, dereliction, disregard, disrespect, evasion, failure, heedlessness, indifference, negligence, nonchalance, omission, oversight, procrastination, recklessness, scorn, slight, thoughtlessness; defer, dismiss, disregard, fail, forget, ignore, omit, overlook, skip, slight, spurn, suspend, underestimate, undervalue. ANT.—attention, care, diligence, surveillance; accomplish, complete, perform, preserve, safeguard, work.

negotiate, accomplish, achieve, agree, arrange, bargain, compromise, confer, consult, contract, deal, debate, dicker, overcome, reflect, sell, transact.

neighborhood, community, district, environs, locality, region; adjacency, nearness, proximity, vicinity.

nerve, audacity, courage, determination, fortitude, hardihood, intrepidity, pluck, resolution, strength, vigor, vitality.

neutral, disinterested, impartial, indeterminate, indifferent, nonpartisan, unallied, unconcerned. ANT.—biased, decided, involved, positive, predisposed.

new, fresh, late, modern, novel, original, recent, strange, unaccustomed, unfamiliar, untried, up-to-date. ANT.—ancient, archaic, familiar, obsolete, outmoded.

news, advice, bulletin, communication, copy, information, intelligence, message, report, tidings.

nimble, active, agile, alert, brisk, bustling, co-ordinated, fast, flexible, lively, prompt, quick, rapid, speedy, sprightly, spry, supple, swift. ANT.—clumsy, dull, inert, lumbering, slow.

noble, aristocratic, august, dignified, distinguished, elevated, eminent, exalted, genteel, grand, honorable, illustrious, imperial, lofty, lordly, loyal, majestic, princely, regal, royal, stately, sublime, superior. ANT.—abject, base, ignoble, low, plebeian, servile.

noise, babel, blare, clamor, clangor, clatter, cry, din, hubbub, outcry, pandemonium, racket, row, sound, tumult, uproar. ANT.—calm, hush, quiet, silence, tranquility.

nonchalant, careless, inconsiderate, indifferent, negligent, unconcerned; casual, composed, cool, imperturbable, unruffled. ANT.—attentive, careful, considerate, concerned, vigilant; active, agitated, eager, enthusiastic, excitable, fervid, zealous.

nonsense, absurdity, babble, drivel, foolishness, gibberish, imbecility, inanity, inconsistency, jargon, jest, joke, rigamarole, senselessness, shallowness, silliness. ANT.—accuracy, clarify, common sense, substance, wisdom.

normal, average, common, conventional, customary, general, natural, ordinary, rational, reasonable, regular, sane, standard, steady, typical, uniform, unvaried, usual. ANT.—abnormal, exceptional, irregular, peculiar, strange.

nosy, curious, inquiring, inquisitive, interrogative, intrusive, meddling, peeping, prying, searching, snoopy. ANT.—decorous, incurious, indifferent, polite, restrained, unconcerned.

note, commentary, indication, explanation, mark, sign, symbol, token; acknowledgment, annotation, comment, dispatch, epistle, letter, memorandum, message, missive, notation, notice, observation, remark; distinction, fame, renown, reputation; contemplate, discern, notice, observe, perceive, remark, see, view.

noted, celebrated, distinguished, eminent, exalted, exceptional, extraordinary, famous, glorious, illustrious, imposing, memorable, outstanding, prominent, remarkable, renowned, significant, striking, uncommon, well-known. ANT.—common, insignificant, obscure, trivial, unknown.

notice, attend to, behold, detect, discern, discover, distinguish, examine, heed, mark, note, observe, perceive, recognize, regard, remark, see, warn; announcement, attention, bulletin, civility, cognizance, comment, consideration, heed, mention, note, observation, placard, poster, recognition, regard, respect, warning. ANT.—avoid, disregard, ignore, overlook, shun; evasion, forgetfulness, laxity, omission.

notify, acquaint, advise, alert, apprise, call, communicate, convey, disclose, divulge, enlighten, express, impart, indicate, inform, instruct, intimate, signify, specify, spread, teach, tell, warn. ANT.—conceal, deceive, delude, mystify, suppress.

notion, abstraction, belief, caprice, concept, conception, conviction, fancy, idea, image, imagination, impression, inclination, inkling, knowledge, opinion, perception, presumption, sentiment, theory, thought, understanding, view, viewpoint, whim.

novel, fiction, narrative, romance, story, tale; fresh, modern, new, original, unique, unprecedented, untried. ANT.—fact, history, reality, truth, verity; ancient, common, customary, familiar, primitive.

novice, amateur, apprentice, beginner, dabbler, dilettante, greenhorn, intern, learner, neophyte, newcomer, postulant, probationer, recruit, tenderfoot, tyro. ANT.—authority, expert, master, mentor, professional.

nude, see **naked**.

nullify, cancel, countermand, cross out, delete, destroy, discard, dispel, eliminate, erase, expunge, negate, obliterate, suppress, upset, void; abolish, abrogate, annul, invalidate, quash, repeal, rescind, revoke. ANT.—confirm, enact, enforce, execute, ratify, support.

number, aggregate, amount, quantity, sum, volume; calculate, compute, count, enumerate, figure, list, score. ANT.—nothing, nothingness, zero; estimate, guess.

numerous, see **many.**

nurture, cherish, hold dear, prize, treasure, uphold, value; feed, foster, nourish, nurse, rear, support, sustain, tend. ANT.—dislike, disregard, ignore, neglect; abandon, deprive, reject.

nutriment, aliment, diet, edibles, fare, feed, food, meal, nourishment, nutrition, provision, rations, repast, sustenance, viands, victuals. ANT.—hunger, starvation, want.

O

obdurate, adamant, callous, dogged, hard, headstrong, impenitent, indurate, inflexible, insensible, insensitive, mulish, obstinate, stubborn, tenacious, tough, unbending, unfeeling, unyielding. ANT.—amenable, compassionate, sensitive, submissive, tractable.

obedient, acquiescent, compliant, conformable, deferential, dutiful, faithful, law-abiding, loyal, submissive, surrendering, tractable, yielding. ANT.—defiant, insubordinate, intractable, lawless, obstinate, rebellious.

obese, adipose, corpulent, fat, fleshy, portly, rotund, stout, swollen, thickset, unwieldy. ANT.—emaciated, gaunt, lean, skeletal, slender, thin.

object, article, particular, thing; aim, design, end, goal, intention, mark, objective, purpose; balk, disapprove, oppose, protest, resist. ANT.—acquiesce, approve, comply, concur, sanction, welcome.

objection, argument, censure, criticism, disagreement, disapproval, dissent, opposition, protest, rejection, remonstrance, variance. ANT.—acceptance, accord, agreement, approval, compliance.

objective, aim, ambition, aspiration, design, desire, destination, end, goal, hope, intention, longing, mark, motive, object, purpose, scheme, target; dispassionate, equitable, fair, impartial, impersonal, unbiased. ANT.—biased, emotional, partial, personal, subjective.

obligation, accountability, bond, contract, duty, engagement, indebtedness, liability, pledge, promise, requirement, responsibility, stipulation. ANT.—choice, exemption, freedom.

oblige, bind, coerce, command, compel, constrain, drive, enforce, force, hinder, impel, insist, necessitate, restrain; accommodate, benefit, favor, gratify, help, please. ANT.—absolve, discharge, exempt, free, release, spare, unshackle.

obliterate, annihilate, cancel, delete, demolish, destroy, devastate, efface, eradicate, erase, exterminate, extinguish, nullify, ravage, raze, ruin, wreck.

obscene, coarse, corrupt, defiled, dirty, disgusting, filthy, foul, gross, impure, indecent, lascivious, lewd, licentious, offensive, polluted, pornographic, smutty, vulgar, wanton. ANT.—immaculate, innocent, modest, pure, virtuous.

obscure, abstruse, ambigious, blurred, cloudy, complex, complicated, concealed, cryptic, dark, dim, dusky, enigmatic, hazy, incomprehensible, indistinct, mysterious, nebulous, shadowy, unintelligible, unknown, vague, veiled. ANT.—apparent, clear, explicit, lucid, visible.

observant, alert, attentive, aware, careful, considerate, heedful, mindful, perceptive, wary, watchful; obedient, submissive. ANT.—careless, inattentive, indifferent, lax, nonobservant; disobedient, disrespectful.

observe, behold, comprehend, detect, discover, examine, eye, heed, inspect, mark, note, perceive, regard, see, view, watch; celebrate, commemorate, keep; express, mention, remark, utter. ANT.—avoid, disobey, disregard, ignore, neglect, overlook.

obsolete, ancient, antiquated, antique, archaic, disused, extinct, forgotten, obsolescent, old, old-fashioned, outdated, outmoded, out-of-date, outworn, primitive, rejected, timeworn. ANT.—current, modern, new, novel, recent, up-to-date.

obstacle, bar, barrier, block, check, difficulty, hindrance, impediment, interruption, obstruction, snag, stumbling block. ANT.—aid, blessing, boost, clearance, encouragement, help.

obstinate, contumacious, determined, dogged, firm, fixed, headstrong, immovable, indomitable, inflexible, intractable, mulish, obdurate, persistent, pertinacious, recalcitrant, resolute, stubborn, unaffected, uncompromising, unflinching, unyielding, willful. ANT.—amenable, compliant, docile, pliable, submissive.

obstruct, bar, barricade, block, choke, clog, close, cramp, cripple, curb, dam, frustrate, hamper, hinder, impede, inhibit, interfere, oppose, prevent, restrain, retard, stop, thwart. ANT.—assist, facilitate, forward, promote, support; clear, open.

obtain, acquire, assimilate, attain, collect, earn, gain, gather, get, procure, recover, secure, win. ANT.—forfeit, forsake, lose, miss, sacrifice.

obtuse, blunt, dense, dull, heavy, impassive, insensitive, phlegmatic, slow, stolid, stupid, unintelligent. ANT.—acute, brilliant, imaginative, keen, quick, sharp.

obvious, apparent, clear, comprehensible, conclusive, definite, distinct, evident, explicit, intelligible, lurid, manifest, palpable, patent, plain, precise, self-evident, unmistakable, visible. ANT.—ambiguous, confused, esoteric, obscure, puzzling.

occupation, business, calling, commerce, craft, employment, enterprise, job, mission, position, profession, pursuit, trade, vocation, work.

occupy, absorb, busy, employ, engage, engross, entertain, fill, hold, keep, monopolize; capture, invade, seize; dwell, inhabit, own, possess, tenant, use. ANT.—relinquish, surrender; abandon, empty, leave, vacate.

occurrence, affair, circumstance, episode, event, eventuality, happening, incident, issue, occasion, proceeding, transaction.

odd, abnormal, bizarre, curious, eccentric, erratic, exceptional, extraordinary, mysterious, peculiar, quaint, queer, rare, singular, strange, unique, unnatural, unusual, weird; alone, lone, remaining, single, uneven, unmatched. ANT.—common, familiar, natural, normal, ordinary; even, matched.

odious, abhorrent, base, debased, depraved, detestable, disgusting, foul, hateful, hideous, horrible, loathsome, obnoxious, repellent, repugnant, repulsive, revolting, vicious, vile, wicked; abject, ignoble, low, mean, worthless, wretched. ANT.—delightful, inviting, lovable, pleasant, refreshing; honorable, upright, wholesome.

odor, aroma, essence, fetidness, fetor, fragrance, fume, incense, perfume, redolence, reek, scent, smell, stench, stink.

offense, affront, atrocity, indignity, injury, insult, outrage; aggression, assault, attack, crime, fault, felony, injustice, misdeed, misdemeanor, scandal, sin, transgression, trespass, vice, wrong. ANT.—compliment, defense, gentleness, support; justice, morality, right.

offer, overture, proposal, proposition, suggestion; advance, bid, exhibit, extend, move, present, proffer, propose, sacrifice, submit, suggest, tender, volunteer. ANT.—denial, rejection, withdrawal; refuse, reject, withdraw, withhold.

often, commonly, frequently, generally, ofttimes, recurrently, repeatedly. ANT.—infrequently, rarely, seldom, sporadically.

old, aged, ancient, antediluvian, antiquated, antique, archaic, elderly, experienced, faded, immemorial, obsolete, old-fashioned, patriarchal, prehistoric, remote, superannuated, venerable. ANT.—contemporary, current, fresh, inexperienced, modern.

omen, augury, auspice, emblem, foreboding, foreshadow, gesture, harbinger, indication, mark, note, portent, precursor, prediction, presage, proof, sign, signal, symbol, symptom, token, warning.

omit, bar, cancel, delete, discard, disregard, drop, eliminate, evade, except, exclude, forget, ignore, miss, neglect, overlook, preclude, reject, repudiate, skip, spare. ANT.—add, enroll, enter, include, insert, introduce, notice.

onerous, arduous, burdensome, difficult, hard, heavy, laborious, oppressive, tough; exacting, intricate, perplexing, ponderous, puzzling, troublesome. ANT.—easy, effortless, facile, trivial; clear, simple.

only, barely, but, entirely, exclusively, just, merely, particularly, simply, singly, solely, totally, uniquely, utterly, wholly.

opaque, cloudy, dark, dim, dull, dusky, filmy, gloomy, misty, murky, non-transparent, obfuscated, obscure, shadowy, shady, smoky, unilluminated. ANT.—crystalline, glassy, lustrous, pellucid, transparent.

open, agape, ajar, apart, gaping, unbarred, unclosed, uncovered, unlocked, unobstructed, unsealed; clear, passable, unobstructed; available, disengaged, free, unoccupied; accessible, exposed, public, undefended, unrestricted; artless, candid, explicit, frank, honest, overt, plain, sincere, unreserved; exhibit, expand, expose, rend, reveal, show, spread, start, unbar, unfasten, unfold, unlock, unseal. ANT.—blocked, closed, locked; impassable, obstructed; busy, engaged, occupied; concealed, hidden, private; covert, crafty, cunning, designing, hypocritical; block, conceal, exclude, hinder, secrete.

operate, act, behave, comport, conduct, demean, deport, direct, execute, function, interact, manage, manipulate, perform, react, run, transact, work.

operation, act, action, agency, effort, enterprise, execution, instrumentality, maneuver, manipulation, performance, procedure, proceeding, process, transaction, working. ANT.—cessation, inaction, inactivity, inefficiency, uselessness.

operative, acting, active, busy, efficacious, efficient, effective, effectual, industrious, moving, performing, working. ANT.—dormant, inactive, inefficient, quiet, still.

opinion, belief, conclusion, consensus, conviction, determination, feeling, idea, impression, judgment, notion, persuasion, sentiment, theory, thought, verdict, view. ANT.—fact, knowledge.

opponent, adversary, antagonist, assailant, challenger, competitor, contestant, disputant, encroacher, enemy, foe, infringer, intruder, rival, violator. ANT.—ally, colleague, comrade, consort, partner.

opportunity, advantage, chance, contingency, occasion, occurrence, opening, possibility, situation, timeliness. ANT.—blockage, deterrent, disadvantage, hindrance, obstacle.

oppose, antagonize, bar, check, combat, confront, contradict, contrast, contravene, counteract, cross, defy, deny, hinder, impede, interfere, obstruct, protest, rebuff, resist, restrain, retaliate, snub, thwart, withstand. ANT.—approve, collude, endorse, fraternize, sanction, support.

opposite, antithesis, antonymous, contradictory, contrary, inverse, reverse. ANT.—compatible, counterpart, identical, like, same.

oppress, afflict, annoy, badger, burden, crush, harass, harry, hound, maltreat, overbear, overwhelm, persecute, pester, plague, torment, torture, tyrannize, vex, worry. ANT.—aid, assist, comfort, relieve, support.

optimistic, assured, confident, encouraging, enthusiastic, expectant, heartening, hopeful, inspiriting, promising, trusting. ANT.—despairing, doubtful, gloomy, hopeless, pessimistic.

option, alternative, choice, discretion, election, preference, prerogative, right, selection.

opulent, abundant, affluent, luxurious, moneyed, plentiful, profuse, rich, sumptuous, wealthy. ANT.—destitute, indigent, limited, poor, scarce, squalid.

oral, articulate, mouthed, said, spoken, uttered, verbal, vocal. ANT.—printed, recorded, written.

ordain, appoint, assign, command, commission, constitute, create, decree, delegate, destine, enact, install, institute, invest, order, prescribe, select. ANT.—abolish, abrogate, cancel, depose, dismiss, invalidate.

ordeal, affliction, agony, assay, cross, hardship, judgment, misery, misfortune, pain, strain, suffering, test, trial, tribulation. ANT.—alleviation, comfort, joy, pleasure.

order, arrangement, class, method, plan, rank, regularity, sequence, series, succession, symmetry, system; bidding, canon, command, decree, dictate, directive, injunction, instruction, law, mandate, precept, prescription, regulation, requirement, rule; appoint, arrange, bid, conduct, demand, direct, govern, exact, impose, methodize, ordain, proclaim, regulate, rule, systematize. ANT.—chaos, confusion, disorder, irregularity, muddle, perplexity; allowance, consent, liberty, permission; confuse, disorganize, misdirect, misguide.

ordinary, accustomed, average, common, consistent, conventional, customary, familiar, habitual, medium, natural, normal, regular, typical, usual; inferior, low, plain, trite, vulgar. ANT.—bizarre, eccentric, irregular, strange, unconventional; exceptional, exclusive, extraordinary, wonderful.

organic, constitutional, essential, fundamental, inherent, innate, natural, radical, structural, systematic, vital. ANT.—external, extraneous, inorganic, nonessential.

organization, arrangement, association, constitution, construction, establishment institution, method, mode, order, plan, process, regularity, rule, scheme, system. ANT.—chaos, disarray, disorganization, irregularity, labyrinth, maze.

organize, adjust, arrange, assort, classify, constitute, co-ordinate, devise, dispose, establish, form, found, frame, institute, plan, prepare, regulate, shape, systematize. ANT.—destroy, disband, disorganize, disperse, divide, scatter.

origin, beginning, birth, cause, commencement, cradle, derivation, foundation, inception, outset, rise, root, source, spring, start. ANT.—conclusion, consequence, finality, harvest, result, termination.

original, aboriginal, archetypal, causal, etiological, first, formative, inceptive, initial, primary, rudimentary; creative, fresh, inventive, model,

new, novel, unique. ANT.—consequential, derivative, emanating, evolved, terminal; banal, copied, imitated, plagiarized.

ornamental, adorning, beautifying, decorative, embellishing, garnishing, gilt, ornate.

oscillate, change, fluctuate, hesitate, swing, undulate, vacillate, vary, vibrate, waver. ANT.—halt, persist, remain, resolve, stay.

ostentation, boasting, bravado, display, exhibition, flourish, glitter, gloss, pageantry, parade, pomp, pomposity, pretension, show, tinsel, vanity, vaunting, veneer. ANT.—humility, modesty, reserve, restraint, timidity.

ostracize, banish, bar, blackball, deport, except, exclude, exile, expel, hinder, omit, prevent, prohibit, restrain. ANT.—accept, admit, embrace, include, welcome.

oust, banish, deport, depose, discharge, dislodge, dismiss, dispel, dispossess, eject, evict, exclude, exile, expatriate, expel, fire, ostracize, proscribe, reject, remove. ANT.—admit, appoint, empower, harbor, retain, shelter.

outcome, conclusion, consequence, destiny, effect, end, fate, fortune, issue, lot, outgrowth, portion, result, sequel, termination, upshot.

outline, alignment, boundary, brief, configuration, contour, delineation, draft, drawing, figure, form, framework, perimeter, plan, profile, representation, silhouette, skeleton, sketch, tracing.

outrage, abuse, affront, atrocity, grievance, indignity, injury, insult, maltreatment, mortification, offense, oppression, persecution, shock, transgression, trespass, vice, violation.

outrageous, abominable, abusive, atrocious, despicable, excessive, fierce, flagrant, furious, heinous, monstrous, nefarious, scandalous, villainous, violent, wanton, wicked. ANT.—calm, dispassionate, favorable, peaceable, soothing, tranquil.

outspoken, abrupt, bluff, blunt, brusque, candid, direct, forthright, frank, impolite, open, plain, rough, rude, unceremonious, unreserved. ANT.—cautious, circumspect, misleading, reserved, sincere, suave, taciturn.

outstanding, conspicuous, distinguished, dominant, eminent, exceptional, important, notable, noticeable, prominent, remarkable, salient, striking, superior; owing, unpaid, unsettled. ANT.—average, commonplace, inconspicuous, ordinary, usual; paid, settled.

overcome, beat, conquer, crush, defeat, humble, master, overpower, overthrow, quell, rout, subdue, subjugate, suppress, surmount, vanquish. ANT.—fail, lose, succumb, surrender, yield.

overflowing, abounding, abundant, ample, bountiful, copious, fruitful, plenteous, plentiful, profuse, sufficient, teeming, unlimited. ANT.—deficient, insufficient, poor, scanty, scarce.

overlook, disregard, drop, eliminate, exclude, forget, ignore, miss, neglect, omit, skip, slight; condone, excuse, forgive, pardon; dominate, examine, inspect, oversee, supervise. ANT.—note, observe, regard, see, watch; charge, indict, punish; acquiesce, serve, surrender.

oversee, administer, command, direct, engineer, execute, guide, maintain, manage, order, preside, superintend, supervise. ANT.—obey, follow, take orders.

oversight, aberration, blunder, error, failure, fault, inadvertence, inattention, lapse, mistake, neglect, omission, slip; charge, control, direction, guidance, inspection, management, regulation, superintendence, supervision, surveillance, watchfulness. ANT.—attention, care, diligence.

overt, apparent, candid, frank, honest, manifest, obvious, open, patent, plain, public, unconcealed, undisguised. ANT.—concealed, covert, hidden, latent, private, secret.

overthrow, abolish, conquer, crush, defeat, demolish, destroy, extirpate, obliterate, overcome, overpower, overturn, rout, ruin, subjugate, subvert, supplant, upset, vanquish. ANT.—assist, develop, maintain, preserve, restore, support.

overwhelm, see **overthrow.**

own, admit, allow, avow, concede, confess, control, disclose, hold, possess, recognize, retain, reveal. ANT.—deny, disavow, lack, lose, need, reject.

P

pacific, calm, composed, conciliatory, dispassionate, gentle, imperturbable, nonviolent, peaceful, placid, quiet, restful, serene, smooth, tranquil, undisturbed, unruffled, untroubled. ANT.—belligerent, combative, rough, stormy, tempestuous, turbulent.

pacify, allay, alleviate, ameliorate, appease, assuage, calm, compose, lull, mollify, placate, quell, quiet, reconcile, relieve, satisfy, soothe, still, subdue, quell, settle, tranquilize. ANT.—anger, antagonize, excite, incense, rile, roil.

pack, assemblage, amount, bag, band, bundle, collection, company, concourse, gathering, group, load, luggage, number, package, parcel, trunk, valise; arrange, bind, brace, collect, compress, condense, cram, gather, prepare, press, squeeze, stuff, tie. ANT.—allocate, distribute, dispose, loosen, scatter.

pact, agreement, alliance, arrangement, bargain, bond, cartel, compact, concord, contract, covenant, deal, league, stipulation, treaty, understanding, union.

pain, affliction, agony, anguish, discomfort, distress, grief, misery, suffering, torment, torture, woe; ache, pang, paroxysm, throe, twinge. ANT.—happiness, pleasure, solace, well-being; comfort, ease, relief.

painful, agonizing, bitter, distressing, excruciating, galling, grievous, poignant, racking; arduous, difficult, toilsome. ANT.—delightful, enjoyable, pleasant, sweet; easy, effortless, facile.

paint, adorn, color, daub, decorate, delineate, describe, explain, express, ornament, picture, portray, reveal; pigment; cosmetic, rouge.

palpable, apparent, appreciable, clear, discernible, evident, explicit, manifest, obvious, patent, perceptible, plain, prominent, self-evident, sensible, unmistakable, visible; bodily, corporeal, material, physical, real, sensible, tangible. ANT.—concealed, doubtful, mysterious, obscure, questionable; incorporeal, mental, spiritual.

paltry, abject, contemptible, despicable, insignificant, low, mean, measly, miserable, petty, picayune, pitiful, poor, puny, worthless. ANT.—important, large, momentous, rich, significant.

panic, alarm, apprehension, consternation, dismay, dread, fear, fright, horror, perturbation, terror, trembling, tremor, trepidation. ANT.—calm, composure, placidity, repose, serenity.

parade, cavalcade, cortege, file, procession, retinue, sequence, succession, train; display, expose, flaunt, publish, show, vaunt; march, strut.

paradox, absurdity, ambiguity, contradiction, enigma, inconsistency, mystery, perplexity, puzzle.

parallel, akin, alike, allied, analogous, comparable, concentric, concurrent, congruent, congruous, correlative, correspondent, corresponding, like, regular, similar, uniform. ANT.—different, divergent, incongruous, opposed, unique.

paralyze, astound, benumb, cripple, daunt, daze, deaden, demoralize, disable, dumfound, incapacitate, petrify, prostrate, stun, unnerve. ANT.—excite, revive, stimulate, vitalize.

pardon, absolve, acquit, condone, efface, exculpate, excuse, exonerate, forgive, liberate, overlook, quash, release, remit; absolution, acquittal, amnesty, deliverance, discharge, forgiveness, freedom, parole, release, remission, respite. ANT.—banish, castigate, chastise, condemn, punish; chastisement, penalty, punishment, retaliation, vengeance.

parley, chat, colloquy, conference, conversation, dialogue, interview, talk; argue, confer, converse, debate, dispute, negotiate, palaver, talk.

parody, burlesque, caricature, imitation, joke, lampoon, mimicry, mockery, spoof, travesty.

parsimonious, acquisitive, avaricious, covetous, frugal, greedy, grudging, mercenary, miserly, penurious, scrimping, sparing, stingy, tight, ungenerous. ANT.—altruistic, generous, lavish, liberal, prodigal.

part, allotment, apportionment, bit, chip, chunk, division, fragment, lump, moiety, morsel, piece, portion, scrap, section, segment, share, slice, subdivision; component, element, ingredient, member; concern, constituent, faction, interest, party, side; character, lines, role; detach, disunite, dissever, dissociate, divide, separate, sever, sunder; allot, apportion, distribute, share. ANT.—aggregate, entirety, sum, whole; combine, gather, join, unite; keep, withhold.

partiality, bent, bias, bigotry, favoritism, fondness, inclination, leaning, liking, preconception, predisposition, preference, prejudice, tendency, unfairness. ANT.—equality, fairness, honor, impartiality, justice.

participate, associate, commune, cooperate, enjoy, join, mingle, partake, share, unite, use.

particle, atom, bit, corpuscle, crumb, element, grain, iota, jot, mite, molecule, scintilla, scrap, shred, smidgen, speck, whit. ANT.—aggregate, entirety, mass, total, whole.

particular, characteristic, distinctive, exclusive, individual, peculiar, singular, specific, unusual; detailed, exact, minute, precise; careful, discrete, fastidious, meticulous, painstaking, scrupulous, squeamish; circumstance, detail, item, minutia, part, portion, section. ANT.—comprehensive, general, universal, usual; fallacious, ordinary; negligent, nonchalant, slovenly, untidy; generality.

partisan, adherent, aide, ally, assistant, attendant, backer, champion, devotee, disciple, follower, henchman, successor, supporter, votary. ANT.—chief, director, leader, master.

partner, accomplice, ally, assistant, associate, colleague, companion, comrade, confederate, consort, co-worker, crony, mate, participant, spouse. ANT.—adversary, enemy, foe, opponent, stranger.

pass, course, crossing, opening, passageway, route; license, passport, permit, ticket; lunge, thrust; advance, approve, depart, die, disappear, disregard, expire, go, ignore, move, overcome, overlook, overstep, ratify, recede, sanction, skip, surpass, transcend, vanish.

passable, acceptable, adequate, admissible, allowable, average, endurable, fair, mediocre, middling, ordinary, so-so, tolerable; navigable,

penetrable, traversable. ANT.—excellent, inferior, intolerable, superior; impassable.

passage, aisle, arcade, avenue, channel, corridor, course, gateway, hall, pass, path, road, way.

passion, ardor, craving, desire, ecstasy, eroticism, excitement, fascination, fervor, frenzy, hunger, infatuation, intensity, lust, yearning. ANT.—calm, dispassion, frigidity, indifference, restraint, tranquility.

passionate, ardent, burning, excitable, extreme, fervent, fervid, feverish, fiery, glowing, hot, impetuous, intense, irascible, quickened, vehement, violent. ANT.—apathetic, calm, cool, dull, impassive, phlegmatic.

passive, cold, dull, idle, inactive, indifferent, inert, quiet, receptive, relaxed, resigned, stoical, submissive, supine, unresisting. ANT.—active, assertive, dynamic, operative, resistant.

patch, fix, mend, rebuild, renew, repair, restore, revamp, sew; ameliorate, better, correct, improve, rectify, remedy. ANT.—damage, destroy, impair, injure, ravage.

patent, apparent, clear, conspicuous, evident, manifest, obvious, open, overt, plain, unconcealed, unmistakable. ANT.—concealed, covered, covert, hidden, obscure.

path, access, avenue, channel, course, lane, passage, pathway, read, route, runway, sidewalk, street, thoroughfare, track, trail, walk, way.

pathetic, affecting, distressing, heart-rending, moving, piteous, pitiable, pitiful, plaintive, poignant, sad, touching. ANT.—cheering, comical, funny, happy, joyful.

patience, composure, constancy, endurance, forbearance, fortitude, imperturbability, moderation, perseverance, persistence, resignation, submission, sufferance, tolerance. ANT.—disquietude, excitability, impatience, petulance, perturbation, rage.

patient, assiduous, calm, composed, enduring, forbearing, gentle, imperturbable, indulgent, lenient, long-suffering, passive, placid, resigned, serene, stoical, submissive, tolerant, uncomplaining. ANT.—clamorous, high-strung, hysterical, irritable, turbulent, ungovernable.

pattern, archetype, blueprint, conformation, copy, exemplar, guide, ideal, model, mold, norm, original, outline, paradigm, paragon, plan, prototype, sample, standard.

pause, delay, demur, desist, doubt, falter, halt, hesitate, intermit, stop, vacillate, waver, wait; break, cessation, discontinuance, hesitation, intermission, interruption, lull, recess, suspension. ANT.—continue, persevere, proceed, resolve; continuance, continuity, extension, persistence, progression.

pay, allowance, compensation, earnings, fee, indemnity, payment, recompense, remuneration, reparation, retribution, reward, salary, settlement, stipend, wages; compensate, defray, discharge, expend, liquidate, offer, recompense, refund, reimburse, remunerate, reward, settle. ANT.—default, expenditure, expense, forfeiture, nonpayment, outlay, penalty; bilk, cheat, defraud, swindle, victimize.

peace, accord, agreement, amity, armistice, calm, conciliation, concord, harmony, hush, order, pacifism, quiescence, quiet, repose, serenity, silence, stillness, tranquility. ANT.—conflict, discord, disruption, fracas, uproar, warfare.

peaceful, calm, complacent, composed, gentle, mellow, mild, pacific, placid, quiet, serene, still, tranquil, undisturbed, unruffled. ANT.—agitated, noisy, perturbed, turbulent, upset, violent.

peak, acme, apex, climax, consummation, crest, culmination, height, high point, pinnacle, spire,

summit, top, zenith. ANT.—abyss, base, bottom, lowest point, nadir.

peculiar, abnormal, bizarre, eccentric, exceptional, extraordinary, idiosyncratic, odd, rare, singular, strange, striking, unusual; characteristic, distinctive, especial, individual, particular, special, specific. ANT.—common, normal, ordinary, regular, visual.

peculiarity, attribute, characteristic, eccentricity, feature, idiosyncrasy, irregularity, mark, oddity, property, quality, singularity, trait. ANT.—normality, regularity, uniformity.

pedantic, academic, bookish, erudite, formal, impractical, learned, precise, professorial, scholarly, scholastic, theoretical; affected, dry, dull, stilted, stuffy, tedious. ANT.—ignorant, practical, simple; interesting, lively, stimulating.

peer, colleague, companion, compeer, equal, fellow, match, mate; aristocrat, knight, lord, nobleman. ANT.—commoner, inferior, superior.

peevish, acrimonious, cantankerous, cross, faultfinding, fractious, fretful, grouchy, grumbling, ill-natured, ill-tempered, irritable, moody, petulant, snappish, sulky, testy, touchy, ungracious, waspish. ANT.—affable, genial, gracious, pleasant, soothing.

penalty, chastisement, damages, fine, forfeiture, punishment, retribution; disadvantage, handicap. ANT.—benefit, compensation, forgiveness, prize, remuneration, reward.

penetrating, abstruse, deep, profound, recondite, solemn; acute, astute, clever, discerning, discriminating, incisive, keen, piercing, sagacious, sharp, shrewd. ANT.—shallow, slight, superficial, trivial; dull, idiotic, muddled, obtuse, stupid.

penitent, contrite, regretful, remorseful, repentant, sorrowful, sorry. ANT.—impenitent, incontrite, obdurate, remorseless.

penniless, beggared, destitute, empty-handed, fortuneless, impecunious, indigent, needy, poor, poverty-stricken. ANT.—affluent, opulent, prosperous, rich, wealthy.

pensive, contemplative, dreamy, grave, introspective, meditative, musing, reflective, serious, solemn, speculative, thoughtful. ANT.—careless, extroverted, heedless, rash, thoughtless, unconcerned.

penurious, avaricious, cheap, covetous, grasping, greedy, mercenary, miserly, parsimonious, stingy, tight, ungenerous. ANT.—altruistic, bountiful, charitable, generous, liberal, philanthropic.

people, citizens, community, inhabitants, populace, population; family, kindred, relations, siblings; humanity, human race, mankind; nationality, race, tribe; crowd, folk, masses, mob, multitude, rabble.

perceive, conceive, discern, note, notice, observe, recognize, see, sense; apprehend, comprehend, realize, understand. ANT.—confuse, ignore, miss, overlook; misapprehend, misunderstand.

perceptible, apparent, appreciable, apprehensible, discernible, noticeable, palpable, sensible, tangible, visible. ANT.—absurd, impalpable, imperceptible, invisible, obscure.

perception, acumen, acuteness, apprehension, cognizance, comprehension, discernment, insight, keenness, recognition, sharpness, understanding.

perceptive, alert, apprised, aware, cognizant, incisive, keen, observant. ANT.—dense, ignorant, mindless, obtuse, unaware.

perfect, complete, consummate, entire, finished, whole; blameless, faultless, flawless, immaculate, impeccable, ideal, infallible, inviolate, irreproachable, supreme, unblemished, unqualified. ANT.—deficient, incomplete, lacking, unfinished; blemished, defective, flawed, imperfect, worthless.

perform, accomplish, achieve, act, conduct, do, effect, execute, fulfill, impersonate, play, pretend. ANT.—fail, loaf, neglect, refrain, rest.

performance, accomplishment, achievement, action, deed, demonstration, entertainment, exploit, feat, production, show, spectacle, stunt.

perhaps, conceivably, haply, maybe, mayhap, peradventure, perchance, possibly, reasonably. ANT.—certainly, definitely, impossibly.

peril, danger, exposure, hazard, insecurity, jeopardy, liability, menace, pitfall, risk, snare. ANT.—immunity, protection, safety, security.

perimeter, ambit, border, boundary, circuit, circumference, compass, edge, periphery. ANT.—center, core, heart, hub, middle.

period, age, circuit, cycle, date, duration, epoch, era, interim, interval, limit, season, span, spell, tempo, term, time.

perish, cease, decay, decease, depart, die, expire, pass away, succumb, vanish. ANT.—exist, flourish, live, survive, thrive.

permanent, abiding, changeless, constant, durable, enduring, established, everlasting, fixed, indelible, indestructible, invariant, lasting, perpetual, persistent, stable, unalterable, unchangeable, unchanging. ANT.—ephemeral, mutable, temporary, transitory, vacillating, variable.

permeate, drench, imbue, impregnate, infiltrate, infuse, ingrain, penetrate, pervade, saturate, soak, steep.

permission, allowance, approval, authority, authorization, confirmation, consent, dispensation, enfranchisement, grace, leave, liberty, license, permit, sanction, tolerance, toleration, verification. ANT.—denial, opposition, prohibition, refusal, veto.

permit, admit, allow, approve, authorize, empower, endorse, give, grant, let, recognize, sanction, suffer, tolerate, yield; charter, law, license, pass, passport, patent, permission, warrant. ANT.—bar, forbid, inhibit, oppose, restrain; ban, embargo, inhibition, injunction, restriction.

perpendicular, erect, plumb, straight, upright, upstanding, vertical. ANT.—horizontal, level, oblique, slanting.

perpetrate, accomplish, do, commit, enact, execute, inflict, perform. ANT.—fail, miscarry, ignore, neglect.

perpetual, ceaseless, continual, constant, deathless, endless, enduring, eternal, everlasting, immortal, incessant, infinite, interminable, lasting, permanent, timeless, unceasing, undying, uninterrupted. ANT.—ephemeral, evanescent, finite, fleeting, temporal.

perplex, annoy, baffle, bewilder, complicate, confound, confuse, disconcert, disorganize, dumfound, entangle, fluster, mislead, muddle, mystify, puzzle, snarl, trouble, worry. ANT.—clarify, explain, illumine, inform, instruct.

perplexing, bewildering, complex, complicated, compound, confusing, difficult, intricate, involved, mystifying, puzzling. ANT.—clear, lucid, manifest, obvious, plain, simple.

persecute, abuse, afflict, aggrieve, annoy, badger, bother, castigate, gall, harass, harry, hound, maltreat, oppress, pester, plague, punish, rile, scourge, tease, torment, torture, vex, victimize, worry. ANT.—aid, assist, comfort, gladden, nurture, support.

persevere, abide, continue, endure, last, persist, prevail, pursue, remain, survive, sustain.

ANT.—cease, desist, surrender, vacillate, waver.

perseverance, assiduity, constancy, determination, diligence, grit, industry, persistence, persistency, pertinacity, pluck, resolution, steadfastness, tenacity. ANT.—cessation, idleness, inertia, laziness, procrastination, sloth.

persist, see persevere.

persistence, see perseverance.

persistent, constant, determined, enduring, firm, fixed, immovable, indefatigable, lasting, persevering, resolute, steadfast, steady, tenacious; contumacious, dogged, headstrong, importunate, insistent, obstinate, pertinacious, perverse, stubborn. ANT.—dawdling, doubtful, hesitant, unsure, vacillating, wavering; humble, pliable, reasonable, submissive, yielding.

personality, being, character, disposition, identify, individuality, nature, oneself, self, style, temper, temperament; celebrity, cynosure, notable, star.

perspicuity, clarity, clearness, discrimination, distinctness, explicitness, intelligibility, lucidity, preciseness. ANT.—confusion, mystification, obscurity, perplexity, vagueness.

persuade, allure, arouse, cajole, coax, convince, entice, exhort, incite, induce, influence, lead, lure, move, prevail upon, prompt, provoke, urge, win over. ANT.—deter, dissuade, divert, hinder, repress, restrain.

persuasion, allegiance, belief, conviction, creed, faith, religion; enticement, incitement, inducement, influence, suasion.

pertain, appertain, apply, belong (to), concern, refer (to), relate (to).

pertinacious, constant, contumacious, determined, dogged, firm, headstrong, immovable, inflexible, intractable, obdurate, obstinate, persistent, resolute, stubborn, tenacious, unyielding. ANT.—compliant, docile, flexible, submissive, yielding.

pertinent, applicable, appropriate, apropos, apt, fit, fitting, germane, material, proper, relating, relevant, suited. ANT.—alien, extraneous, foreign, improper, irrelevant, unrelated.

perturb, agitate, aggravate, annoy, bother, discommode, disquiet, harass, heckle, irk, irritate, perplex, pester, plague, vex, worry. ANT.—assist, calm, delight, help, please.

pervade, diffuse, extend, fill, imbue, impregnate, infiltrate, overspread, penetrate, permeate, run through, saturate, spread.

perverse, cantankerous, contrary, contumacious, disobedient, dogged, forward, fractious, intractable, irascible, obstinate, peevish, petulant, resolute, splenetic, stubborn, ungovernable, unyielding; perverted, sinful, wayward, wicked. ANT.—agreeable, docile, manageable, obliging, tractable; angelic, saintly, virtuous.

perversion, abasement, abuse, corruption, debasement, degradation, depravity, desecration, falsification, humiliation, maltreatment, misuse, outrage, profanation, reviling, vitiation, wickedness. ANT.—elevation, enhancement, improvement, respect, veneration.

pessimistic, blue, cynical, depressed, desolate, despairing, despondent, doleful, downcast, foreboding, forlorn, gloomy, glum, hopeless, melancholy, misanthropic, rueful, spiritless. ANT.—bright, enthusiastic, hopeful, optimistic, trusting.

pester, annoy, badger, bait, bother, chafe, disturb, fret, harass, harry, heckle, inconvenience, irk, irritate, molest, plague, provoke, tease, torment, trouble, vex. ANT.—accommodate, comfort, delight, gratify, soothe, support.

petition, appeal, application, entreaty, invocation, plea, prayer, proposal, request, requisition, suit, solicitation, supplication.

petrify, calcify, deaden, fossilize, harden, lapidify, mineralize, ossify, solidify; amaze, astonish, benumb, frighten, paralyze, shock, stun, stupefy.

petty, childish, frivolous, insignificant, negligible, nugatory, paltry, puny, shallow, slight, small, trifling, trivial, unimportant, weak, worthless. ANT.—important, momentous, serious, significant, vital.

petulant, acrimonious, choleric, cranky, cross, crusty, fretful, ill-humored, ill-natured, ill-tempered, irascible, irritable, peevish, querulous, snappish, sullen, surly, testy, touchy, unamiable, waspish. ANT.—affable, congenial, good-natured, pleasant, temperate.

philanthropic, altruistic, beneficent, benevolent, charitable, compassionate, generous, gracious, humanitarian, liberal, magnanimous, munificent. ANT.—antisocial, cruel, egotistical, merciless, selfish.

phlegmatic, cold, dispassionate, impassive, inexcitable, passionless, stoical, stolid, unemotional, unfeeling. ANT.—ardent, demonstrative, enthusiastic, lively, passionate.

phobia, aversion, avoidance, disgust, dislike, distaste, fear, hatred, resentment. ANT.—attraction, endurance, liking, love, tolerance.

phraseology, diction, expression, idiom, language, locution, manner, phrasing, speech, style, usage, vocabulary, wording.

physical, anatomical, bodily, carnal, corporal, corporeal, material, mortal, natural, palpable, real, sensible, somatic, tangible, visible. ANT.—abstract, immaterial, incorporeal, spiritual, unreal.

pick, acquire, choose, cull, elect, gather, opt, prefer, select, single, take. ANT.—decline, refuse, reject.

picture, advertisement, appearance, blueprint, cartoon, cinema, design, draft, drawing, effigy, engraving, etching, facsimile, figure, film, illustration, image, landscape, likeness, lithograph, outline, pageant, painting, panorama, photo, photograph, portrait, portrayal, print, representation, scene, sketch, spectacle, tableau, tracing, view; delineate, depict, draw, represent, sketch.

piece, amount, bit, chunk, fraction, fragment, hunk, morsel, part, portion, scrap, section, segment, shred; combine, patch, repair, unite. ANT.—all, entirety, sum, total, whole.

pigment, brilliance, color, coloration, coloring, complexion, dye, hue, intensity, oil paint, paint, shade, stain, taint, tincture, tinge, tint, wash.

pinnacle, acme, apex, chief, climax, crest, crown, culmination, head, peak, summit, top, zenith. ANT.—base, bottom, depths, foot, foundation, nadir.

pious, blessed, consecrated, devotional, devout, divine, godly, hallowed, holy, prayerful, pure, religious, reverent, sacred, saintly, sanctified, seraphic, spiritual, unworldly. ANT—blasphemous, evil, irreverent, profane, sacrilegious, wicked.

pitch, cast, chuck, fling, heave, hurl, launch, propel, sling, throw, thrust, toss; decline, slant, slope. ANT.—catch, grab, receive.

pitiful, clement, compassionate, lenient, merciful, tender, tender-hearted, sympathetic; abject, contemptible, despicable, vile, wretched; cheerless, doleful, lamentable, miserable, mournful, piteous, sad, sorrowful, tearful. ANT.—dignified, exalted, grand, joyful, noble, sublime.

pity, charity, clemency, commiseration, compassion, condolence, empathy, kindness, mercy, philanthropy, sympathy, tenderness. ANT.—brutality, cruelty, inhumanity, ruthlessness, vengeance.

place, allocate, allot, arrange, assign, deposit, dispose, distribute, group, install, invest, locate, plant, put, set, store, stow; abode, dwelling, home, residence; area, locality, point, position, post, region, site, situation, spot, station. ANT.—disarrange, disturb, empty, remove, unsettle.

placid, calm, composed, dispassionate, equable, gentle, imperturbable, pacific, peaceful, quiet, serene, still, tranquil, undisturbed, unmoved, unruffled. ANT.—agitated, disturbed, excited, stormy, turbulent, wild.

plague, see persecute.

plain, even, flat, level, smoothe; apparent, clear, distinct, evident, exposed, lucid, manifest, obvious, palpable, perceptible, recognizable, unmistakable, visible; candid, definite, explicit, frank, open, simple, sincere, unpretentious; absolute, unqualified. ANT.—broken, rough, uneven; abstruse, ambiguous, cloudy, enigmatical, obscure, puzzling; adorned, embellished, feigned, insincere, pretentious; qualified.

plan, chart, contrive, create, delineate, design, devise, invent, map, plot, prepare, scheme, shape; intent, mean, purpose; depict, draw, illustrate, outline, sketch; arrangement, blueprint, chart, contrivance, delineation, design, device, diagram, draft, drawing, map, method, model, outline, plot, policy, program, project, proposal, proposition, prospectus, sketch, view.

plant, complex, establishment, factory, foundry, mill, shop; bush, flower, herb, organism, shoot, shrub, sprout, vegetable; establish, locate, place, put, set, settle; bed, implant, pot, sow.

plastic, ductile, flexible, formable, formative, impressible, malleable, pliant, resilient; artificial, counterfeit, fabricated, false, simulated. ANT.—brittle, hard, rigid, stiff; authentic, genuine, real.

plausible, acceptable, believable, credible, defensible, feasible, justifiable, likely, possible, practical, probable, reasonable, specious. ANT.—implausible, impossible, incredible, unlikely, visionary.

play, amusement, diversion, enjoyment, entertainment, fun, game, pastime, pleasure, recreation, relaxation, sport; caper, frisk, frolic, gambol, revel, romp, skip, sport, stake, toy, wager; execute, perform, work; act, impersonate, personate, pretend; finger, pedal, pipe, sound, strum, thrum; dissemble, feign, imagine, pretend, simulate; drama piece, musical, theatrical; compete, engage, participate, rival.

plead, appeal, ask, beg, beseech, crave, entreat, implore, petition, press, request, solicit, supplicate, urge; advocate, argue, attest, claim, contend, declare, defend, indicate, maintain, proclaim, profess, pronounce, state, swear.

pleasant, acceptable, agreeable, amiable, attractive, charming, comforting, cordial, delightful, engaging, enjoyable, gratifying, honeyed, mellifluous, melodious, pleasing, pleasurable, suitable, welcome, winning. ANT.—disagreeable, hateful, obnoxious, offensive, painful, repellent, repulsive.

pleasing, see pleasant.

pleasure, amusement, bliss, comfort, contentment, delight, diversion, ease, ecstasy, enjoyment, entertainment, felicity, exhilaration, gladness, gratification, happiness, indulgence, light-heartedness, joy, rapture, satisfaction. ANT.—affliction, distress, grief, hopelessness, misery, suffering.

pledge, affirmation, agreement, assertion, assurance, commitment, contract, covenant, declaration, engagement, guarantee, oath, pact, promise, security, token, troth, vow, word; candidate; affirm, agree, bind, commit, declare, deposit, engage, guarantee, hypothecate, obligate, promise, swear, vouch, vow, wage. ANT.—break faith, deceive, deny, renounce.

plentiful, abundant, ample, bounteous, bountiful, copious, inexhaustible, lavish, liberal, luxurious, plenteous, profuse, replete, rich, teeming, unsparing. ANT.—deficient, drained, impoverished, scanty, scarce, stripped.

pliable, adaptable, adjustable, compliant, docile, ductile, elastic, flexible, limber, manageable, pliant, resilient, supple, tractable, wavering, yielding. ANT.—brittle, intractable, rigid, stiff, unyielding.

plot, artifice, cabal, conspiracy, design, development, intrigue, machination, plan, progress, scheme, stratagem, trick, unfolding; chart, diagram, draft, graph, outline, sketch; contrive, frame, plan, scheme; area, land, lot, parcel.

plump, buxom, chubby, corpulent, fleshy, paunchy, portly, pudgy, puffy, rotund, round, stout, swollen, thickset. ANT.—emaciated, gaunt, lean, slender, slim.

poignant, affecting, heart-rending, moving, pitiable, sad, tender, touching; acute, biting, penetrating, piercing, pungent, trenchant. ANT.—painless, pleasant; blunt, dull, insipid, numb, obtuse.

point, aim, designate, direct, indicate, level, punctuate, sharpen, show; acme, apex, characteristic, end, gist, goal, intent, juncture, location, meaning, object, peak, place, position, promontory, prong, purpose, significance, summit, trait.

pointed, acute, biting, caustic, cutting, keen, knifelike, penetrating, piercing, razor-edged, sarcastic, severe, sharp, spiked, stinging, trenchant. ANT.—bland, blunt, dull, gentle, unsharpened.

poise, balance, equilibrium, equipoise, gravity; class, composure, culture, dignity, self-possession, serenity, stateliness.

poisonous, corrupt, deadly, deleterious, destructive, evil, fatal, malignant, morbid, noisome, noxious, pestilential, toxic, venomous, virulent. ANT.—curative, harmless, healthful, invigorating, nourishing, wholesome.

policy, contract, course, handling, management, method, order, outline, plan, plank, platform, procedure, strategy, system, tactic.

polish, art, breeding, courtesy, culture, elegance, finish, glaze, gloss, glossiness, grace, luster, politeness, refinement, skill, smoothness, suavity, tact, training; brighten, burnish, civilize, discipline, refine, refinish, rub, shine, smooth, wax. ANT.—baseness, crudity, harshness, lowliness, roughness; debase, dull, mar, roughen, ruin.

polite, accomplished, attentive, civil, considerate, cordial, courteous, cultivated, decorous, diplomatic, genteel, mannerly, polished, refined, tactful, urbane, well-bred, well-mannered. ANT.—abusive, coarse, discourteous, impudent, offensive, rude.

pollute, adulterate, befoul, contaminate, corrupt, defile, demoralize, infect, pervert, poison, soil, sully, taint, vitiate. ANT.—clean, disinfect, purge, purify, sanitize.

pomp, boasting, display, flourish, glory, grandeur, magnificence, ostentation, pageantry, parade, show, splendor, vaunting. ANT.—humility, modesty, plainness, shabbiness, simplicity, tawdriness.

pompous, august, dignified, grand, high, imposing, lofty, magnificent, majestic, noble, spectacular, stately, sublime; arrogant, boastful, domineering, egotistical, flaunting, haughty, inflated, ostentatious, pretentious, swaggering. ANT.—banal, common, humble, lowly, ordinary; bashful, demure, modest, reserved, submissive.

ponder, calculate, cogitate, contemplate, deliberate, devise, examine, investigate, meditate, muse, reflect, ruminate, scrutinize, study, weigh. ANT.—forget, ignore, neglect, overlook.

ponderous, burdensome, cumbersome, heavy, massive, unwieldy, weighty; dull, gloomy, grave, spiritless; important, momentous, serious, significant. ANT.—airy, fluffy, light; animated, brisk, buoyant, volatile; insignificant, petty, trivial, unimportant.

poor, destitute, impecunious, impoverished, indigent, insolvent, needy, penniless, poverty-stricken, substandard, underprivileged; bad, defective, deficient, inferior, insignificant, mediocre, miserable, shabby, unfavorable. ANT.—affluent, opulent, rich, solvent, wealthy; ample, commendable, excellent, favorable, superior.

popular, common, current, familiar, general, lay, ordinary, plebeian, prevailing, prevalent, public, universal; admired, approved, desired, favorite, liked. ANT.—esoteric, exclusive, restricted; disliked, disreputable, shunned, unpopular.

pornographic, coarse, corrupt, debauched, depraved, dirty, disgusting, filthy, gross, immoral, indecent, lascivious, lecherous, lewd, obscene, prurient, smutty. ANT.—chaste, decent, modest, pure, refined.

port, anchorage, bay, berth, cove, dock, door, entrance, gateway, harbor, haven, inlet, portal, shelter; bearing, carriage, deportment, demeanor, manner, mien, presence.

portion, allotment, consignment, cutting, dividend, division, fraction, fragment, measure, morsel, parcel, part, piece, quota, ration, section, segment, share, slice, subdivision. ANT.—aggregation, entirety, mass, sum, total.

portray, act, characterize, copy, delineate, depict, describe, draw, figure, impersonate, paint, picture, represent, reproduce, reveal, show, sketch.

position, bearings, environment, ground, locality, location, place, post, seat, site, situation, spot, station; caste, condition, place, rank, standing, status; berth, employment, incumbency, job, occupation, office, post, profession, situation; attitude, belief, judgment, opinion, view; bearing, carriage, pose, posture.

positive, absolute, affirmative, assertive, assured, certain, concrete, decided, definite, dogmatic, emphatic, firm, fixed, incontrovertible, indubitable, inevitable, resolute, secure, sure, uncompromising, undeniable, unmistakable, unquestionable. ANT.—ambiguous, doubtful, dubious, hazy, questionable, uncertain.

possess, appropriate, control, dominate, have, hold, keep, obtain, occupy, own, reserve, retain, seize, take. ANT.—abandon, lack, lose, need, renounce, surrender.

possessions, assets, belongings, capital, commodities, effects, equity, estate, goods, holdings, investments, lands, legacy, merchandise, property, resources, stock, wares, wealth.

possibility, chance, contingency, event, feasibility, happening, hope, incident, occasion, occurrence, opening, opportunity, outside chance, plausibility, potentiality. ANT.—disadvantage, impossibility, hindrance, obstacle.

possible, achievable, attainable, conceivable, contingent, credible, feasible, liable, likely, obtainable, performable, plausible, potential, practical, probable. ANT.—foolish, impossible, inconceivable, unattainable, unreasonable.

postpone, adjourn, defer, delay, discontinue, interrupt, pigeonhole, procrastinate, protract, remand, retard, shelve, stall, stay, suspend, table, waive. ANT.—accelerate, continue, maintain, persevere, persist, proceed.

potent, capable, cogent, compelling, effective, efficacious, enduring, firm, forceful, forcible, great, hardy, influential, intense, irresistible, mighty, overpowering, powerful, puissant, robust, staunch, strong, sturdy, vigorous, virile. ANT.—delicate, enervated, fragile, impotent, weak.

pound, batter, beat, buffet, clout, club, crush, dash, drum, flail, hammer, hit, knock, pelt, pulverize, pummel, punch, smite, strike, thrash, thump, whack; palpitate, pulsate, pulse, throb.

poverty, dearth, deficiency, destitution, distress, exigency, inadequacy, indigence, necessity, need, pauperism, penury, privation, scarcity, want. ANT.—abundance, affluence, opulence, riches, wealth.

power, ability, capability, capacity, competence, efficacy, efficiency, endowment, potency, skill, talent; energy, force, might, stamina, strength, vigor; authority, command, control, dominion, government, influence, jurisdiction, mastery, predominance, preponderance, sway, sovereignty, superiority, supremacy. ANT.—impotence, inability, ineptitude; debility, infirmity, weakness; servitude, subjection, subservience.

powerful, see potent.

practical, balanced, down-to-earth, effective, feasible, functional, operative, pragmatic, rational, realistic, reasonable, sensible, sound, unromantic, useful, utilitarian, workable. ANT.—foolish, idealistic, imperceptible, impractical, outlandish, useless.

practice, application, custom, drill, exercise, fashion, habit, manner, method, mode, recitation, rehearsal, repetition, system, training, usage, use; clients, patients.

praise, acclaim, admire, applaud, approve, boost, commend, compliment, endorse, exalt, extol, flatter, glorify, laud, magnify, recommend, sanction. ANT.—admonish, berate, condemn, impugn, reproach, upbraid.

precarious, critical, dangerous, deadly, hazardous, insecure, menacing, perilous, risky, threatening, treacherous, unsafe, unstable; doubtful, dubious, unassured, uncertain. ANT.—protected, safe, secure, stable; assured, certain, unquestionable.

precept, adage, belief, canon, code, commandment, direction, creed, doctrine, dogma, injunction, instruction, law, mandate, maxim, regulation, rule, teaching, tenet.

precious, beloved, costly, darling, dear, esteemed, excellent, expensive, exquisite, high-priced, inestimable, invaluable, priceless, profitable, select, superior, superlative, unequaled, useful, valuable, worthy. ANT.—cheap, insignificant, trifling, valueless, worthless.

precipitate, accelerate, hasten, quicken, speed; abrupt, hasty, headlong, impetuous, rash, sudden. ANT.—check, delay, moderate, preclude, retard, slow; deliberate, intentional, reflective, thoughtful.

precise, accurate, correct, definite, distinct, exact, meticulous, punctilious, rigorous, scrupulous, strict, unequivocal; ceremonious, formal, prim,

prudish, rigid, stiff. ANT.—ambiguous, fallacious, inexact, negligent, slipshod; casual, informal, loose, relaxed.

predicament, bind, corner, crisis, difficulty, dilemma, fix, mess, muddle, perplexity, pinch, plight, puzzle, quandary, scrape, situation, strait. ANT.—comfort, ease, security, solace, tranquility.

prediction, augury, divination, foreboding, forecast, foretelling, fortunetelling, horoscope, omen, presage, prognosis, prognostication, prophecy.

predominant, cardinal, chief, controlling, distinguished, dominant, essential, first, foremost, highest, leading, main, notable, paramount, preponderant, prevailing, prevalent, principal, reigning, ruling, sovereign, supreme. ANT.—insignificant, minor, obscure, subordinate, subsidiary.

preface, beginning, foreword, introduction, overture, preamble, prelude, prologue. ANT.—addendum, afterword, conclusion, ending, epilogue.

preference, alternative, choice, decision, election, favorite, option, pick, selection.

prejudice, animosity, antipathy, apartheid, aversion, bias, contempt, detriment, dislike, enmity, intolerance, objection, partiality, pique, preconception, predilection, prejudgment, prepossession, repugnance, revulsion, unfairness. ANT.—approval, benevolence, kindness, regard, respect, tolerance.

premature, anticipatory, early, green, hasty, immature, incomplete, precipitate, precocious, rash, raw, sudden, unanticipated, unexpected, unfinished, unprepared, unripe, unseasonable, untimely. ANT.—anticipated, completed, expected, fully developed, matured, tardy.

premeditated, calculated, contemplated, deliberate, designed, intended, intentional, planned, plotted, prearranged, predetermined, studied, voluntary. ANT.—accidental, casual, fortuitous, spontaneous, unforeseen.

premise, assumption, basis, criterion, evidence, foundation, groundwork, justification, postulate, presumption, presupposition, principle, proof, proposition, reason. ANT.—derivative, superstructure, trimming.

premium, appreciation, award, bonus, boon, bounty, enhancement, favor, gift, gratuity, present, prize, recompense, remuneration; best, choicest, highest quality, top grade. ANT.—inferior, low grade, poor, third rate.

preoccupied, absorbed, abstracted, distracted, engrossed, inattentive, musing, oblivious, unobservant. ANT.—attentive, watchful.

prepare, adjust, adapt, anticipate, arm, arrange, concoct, cook, develop, devise, equip, fit, fix, foresee, form, furnish, outfit, plan, predispose, prime, provide, qualify, ready, settle. ANT.—forget, ignore, neglect, overlook.

prerogative, authority, birthright, claim, grant, immunity, liberty, license, perquisite, privilege, right. ANT.—duty, injustice, limitation, obligation, violation.

present, advance, assign, award, bestow, confer, deliver, endow, exhibit, extend, give, grant, introduce, offer, proffer, propose, sacrifice, show, tender; boon, donation, gift, grant, gratuity; instant, now, today. ANT.—accept, receive, reject, spurn, take.

preserve, conserve, defend, guard, hold, keep, maintain, protect, rescue, safeguard, save, secure, shield, spare, support, sustain, uphold. ANT.—abandon, abolish, abrogate, destroy, forego, waste.

pressing, absorbing, compelling, constraining, critical, crucial, crying, distressing, exigent, impelling, imperative, important, importunate, insistent, necessary, serious, urgent, vital. ANT.—insignificant, meaningless, petty, superficial, trivial.

pressure, burden, compression, encumbrance, force, stress, tension, thrust, weight; affliction, coercion, compulsion, constraint, exigency, hurry, obligation, persuasion, stress, urgency. ANT.—relief, release; assistance, ease, encouragement, leniency, relaxation.

prestige, ascendancy, authority, credit, effect, fame, glory, honor, influence, power, rank, renown, repute, supremacy, weight. ANT.—impotence, insignificance, weakness, unimportance.

presume, assume, believe, conclude, conjecture, consider, guess, hypothesize, imagine, posit, presuppose, regard, speculate, suppose, surmise, theorize, think. ANT.—ascertain, confirm, demonstrate, manifest, prove.

pretense, affectation, affection, cloak, deceit, disguise, dissimulation, evasion, excuse, fabrication, falsification, garb, mask, pomposity, pretension, pretext, prevarication, ruse, semblance, sham, show, simulation, subterfuge, trickery, wile. ANT.—candor, frankness, honesty, sincerity, truth, veracity.

pretty, see handsome.

prevalent, accepted, catholic, common, comprehensive, controlling, familiar, frequent, general, ordinary, popular, predominant, prevailing, sweeping, ubiquitous, universal, usual, widespread, world-wide. ANT.—exceptional, extraordinary, infrequent, isolated, sporadic.

prevent, avert, block, check, foil, forestall, halt, hinder, impede, inhibit, interrupt, obstruct, obviate, preclude, prohibit, repress, stop, thwart. ANT.—allow, assist, expedite, further, promote, stimulate.

previous, aforesaid, antecedent, anterior, earlier, foregoing, former, preceding, prefatory, preliminary, preparatory, prior. ANT.—ensuing, latter, pursuant, subsequent, succeeding.

pride, arrogance, conceit, egoism, egotism, haughtiness, loftiness, pomposity, pretension, self-esteem; self-glorification, self-love, self-respect, superciliousness, vanity. ANT.—humility, meekness, modesty, reserve, self-effacement.

primary, basic, beginning, chief, earliest, elementary, first, fundamental, initial, leading, main, opening, original, prime, primeval, primitive, principal, pristine; chief, foremost. ANT.—following, hindmost, last, latest; inferior, least, secondary, subordinate.

primeval, first, initial, original, primary, primordial, pristine; creative, fresh, inventive, new, novel. ANT.—derivative, subsequent, terminal; banal, trite.

primitive, aboriginal, ancient, antiquated, archaic, early, old, primary, primeval, primordial, pristine; barbaric, crude, first, fundamental, rudimentary, simple, uncivilized, untaught. ANT.—civilized, complex, modern, polished, sophisticated.

primordial, see primeval.

principal, cardinal, chief, dominant, essential, first, foremost, greatest, highest, leading, main, paramount, predominant, preeminent, prime, supreme; chief, commander, director, executive, head, leader, master. ANT.—accessory, auxiliary, inferior, minor, negligible, unimportant; attendant, follower, pupil, subordinate.

principle, axiom, base, canon, doctrine, formula, foundation, ground, guide, law, maxim, method, order, policy, precept, reason, regulation, rule, statute, system, teaching, theorem; belief, conviction, faith; integrity, rectitude, uprightness.

prior, see previous.

private, clandestine, concealed, covert, hidden, latent, secluded, secret, sequestered, surreptitious, unknown, unrevealed; individual, personal. ANT.—disclosed, exposed, known, open, public.

privation, see poverty.

privilege, advantage, benefit, exemption, favor, franchise, freedom, immunity, liberty, license, perquisite, prerogative, right, sanction; chance, event, occasion, opportunity. ANT.—deprivation, disallowance, inhibition, limitation, prohibition, restriction.

prize, accolade, advantage, award, bonus, booty, bounty, citation, compensation, honor, inducement, laurel, possession, premium, privilege, recompense, remuneration, requital, reward, spoil. ANT.—charge, earnings, forfeiture, penalty, punishment.

problem, conundrum, difficulty, dilemma, enigma, intricacy, mystery, obstacle, perplexity, plight, puzzle, quandary, query, riddle. ANT.—answer, certainty, clarification, explanation, solution.

procedure, arrangement, course, custom, fashion, form, formula, habit, manner, method, mode, order, plan, practice, proceeding, process, routine, rule, style, system, technique, way.

proceed, advance, continue, forge ahead, improve, move, progress, rise, thrive. ANT.—recede, regress, retire, retreat, withdraw.

proceeds, crop, fruit, earnings, gain, gross, harvest, income, net, produce, product, profits, reaping, receipts, result, return, store, yield. ANT.—costs, expenses, outlay.

proclaim, advertise, affirm, announce, assert, aver, broadcast, circulate, declare, divulge, express, make known, profess, promulgate, protest, publish, reveal, state, tell, voice. ANT.—camouflage, conceal, mask, repress, suppress.

procrastinate, adjourn, dally, dawdle, defer, delay, extend, loiter, postpone, prolong, protract, retard, stall, suspend, tarry. ANT.—accelerate, hasten, hurry, persevere, quicken.

produce, aftermath, consequence, crop, effect, fruit, gain, goods, harvest, outcome, outgrowth, proceeds, product, profit, realization, reaping, result, return, store, yield; bear, breed, conceive, generate, hatch, procreate, propagate, sire, yield; fabricate, make, manufacture, supply; bring forward, exhibit, present, show; accomplish, author, cause, create, institute, issue, originate.

production, authoring, bearing, creation, erection, generation, harvest, making, origination, output, performance, procreation, product, project, rendering, work, yield.

profess, see proclaim.

proficient, able, accomplished, adept, adroit, agile, clever, competent, cunning, deft, dexterous, expert, gifted, ingenious, masterful, practiced, skilled, skillful, talented, versed. ANT.—bungling, incapable, incompetent, inept, maladroit, unskilled.

profit, advantage, benefit, earnings, emolument, gain, improvement, interest, proceeds, receipts, remuneration, return, returns, service, use. ANT.—destruction, detriment, failure, loss, ruin.

profligate, see corrupt.

profound, abstruse, abysmal, consummate, deep, erudite, heartfelt, heavy, intense, mysterious,

penetrating, recondite, scholarly, serious, solemn. ANT.—frivolous, shallow, superficial, trivial, unenlightened, unlearned.

profuse, abundant, copious, excessive, extravagant, exuberant, immoderate, improvident, lavish, liberal, luxuriant, overflowing, plentiful, prodigal, redundant, superfluous, wasteful. ANT.—barren, deficient, inadequate, meager, scanty.

progress, advance, advancement, attainment, betterment, development, growth, headway, improvement, increase, locomotion, movement, proficiency, progression; advance, improve, move onward, press on, proceed, rise, thrive. ANT.—deferment, delay, moratorium, regression, suspension; backtrack, regress, resign, retard, retreat.

prohibit, ban, block, check, circumscribe, debar, deny, exclude, forbid, hinder, inhibit, interdict, preclude, prevent, proscribe, refuse, restrain, restrict, taboo, veto, withhold. ANT.—allow, empower, endorse, license, permit, sanction.

project, contrivance, design, device, idea, outline, plan, plot, procedure, projection, scheme, undertaking, working draft.

prolific, bountiful, breeding, fecund, fertile, fruitful, luxuriant, plenteous, productive, propagating, rich, swarming, teeming. ANT.—barren, sterile, unfruitful, unproductive.

prolong, amplify, augment, continue, elongate, extend, increase, lengthen, protract, stretch, sustain. ANT.—condense, curtail, shorten, shrink.

prominent, celebrated, conspicuous, distinguished, eminent, famous, illustrious, influential, leading, noteworthy, outstanding, popular, remarkable, salient, renowned, well-known; convex, extended, jutting, projecting, protruding. ANT.—common, humble, obscure, ordinary, unknown; concave, depressed, flat, level, sunken.

promise, affirmation, agreement, assurance, bestowal, betrothal, commitment, consent, contract, covenant, engagement, fulfillment, guarantee, insurance, oath, obligation, pact, pledge, swearing, troth, undertaking, vow.

promote, advance, aggrandize, aid, assist, contribute, cultivate, dignify, elevate, encourage, endow, exalt, facilitate, forward, foster, further, help, push, raise, urge. ANT.—degrade, discourage, hinder, impair, impede, obstruct.

prompt, arouse, cause, evoke, incite, induce, inspire, make, occasion, originate, provoke; active, alert, direct, early, immediate, instant, keen, precise, punctual, quick, ready, swift, timely, vigilant. ANT.—dilatory, late, overdue, slow, tardy.

promulgate, see proclaim.

proof, affidavit, attestation, confirmation, corroboration, credentials, data, demonstration, evidence, facts, reasons, substantiation, test, testimony, verification, warrant, witness. ANT.—aberrancy, failure, fallacy, invalidity, misconception, untruth.

propagate, beget, breed, create, develop, diffuse, disseminate, engender, father, generate, grow, increase, multiply, originate, procreate, produce, publish, raise, reproduce, sire, spread, teach. ANT.—annihilate, destroy, exterminate, extinguish, kill, ravage.

propel, actuate, agitate, drive, force, impel, induce, instigate, move, persuade, push, start, thrust, urge. ANT.—delay, discourage, drag, halt, hinder, stop.

propensity, aim, aptitude, bent, bias, drift, flair, gift, inclination, knack, leaning, penchant, predilection, predisposition, prejudice, proclivity,

proneness, tendency, trend. ANT.—antipathy, aversion, deviation, disinclination, dislike.

proper, appropriate, befitting, conventional, correct, decent, fair, fit, formal, just, legitimate, meet, pertinent, respectable, right, seemly, suitable; individual, peculiar, special. ANT.—improper, inaccurate, objectionable, unfit, unsuitable.

property, assets, belongings, capital, commodities, effects, equity, estate, goods, holdings, lands, merchandise, plot, possessions, premises, resources, stock, wares, wealth; attribute, characteristic, peculiarity, quality, trait.

propitious, auspicious, encouraging, favorable, fortunate, kindly, hopeful, lucky, opportune, promising.

proportion, balance, composure, dimension, equilibrium, equivalence, poise, relationship, share, stability, steadiness, symmetry. ANT.—fall, imbalance, inequality, instability, unsteadiness.

proposal, offer, overture, presentation, proposition, recommendation, suggestion, tender; design, idea, intention, outline, plan, program, prospectus, scheme. ANT.—acceptance, refusal, rejection, withdrawal.

proposition, see proposal.

proprietor, heritor, holder, keeper, landlady, landlord, master, owner, possessor, proprietary, title holder. ANT.—leaseholder, renter, resident, servant, tenant.

propriety, appropriateness, aptness, conventionality, correctness, decency, decorum, dignity, fitness, righteousness. ANT.—impropriety, misconduct, unfitness, unseemliness.

prosper, achieve, advance, be fortunate, bloom, blossom, flourish, flower, gain, increase, prevail, rise, succeed, thrive, win. ANT.—fail, lose, miscarry, miss, perish.

prosperous, affluent, flourishing, luxurious, moneyed, opulent, rich, sumptuous, wealthy, well-off, well-to-do. ANT.—destitute, indigent, needy, poor, poverty-stricken.

protect, see preserve.

protection, bulwark, camouflage, covering, fence, refuge, safeguard, screen, shelter, shield; assurance, certainty, defense, guard, invulnerability, reassurance, security, stability, strength. ANT.—exposure, insecurity, fragility, frailty, weakness.

protest, challenge, clamor, demonstration, difference, disagreement, dissent, dissentience, mass meeting, moratorium, noncompliance, nonconformity, objection, opposition, recusancy, rejection, remonstrance, tumult, turmoil, variance. ANT.—acceptance, agreement, assent, compliance, peace, recognition.

protract, continue, defer, delay, distend, distort, elongate, expand, extend, lengthen, postpone, procrastinate, prolong, spread, strain, stretch. ANT.—abridge, condense, curtail, hasten, reduce, shorten.

proud, arrogant, dignified, disdainful, exalted, haughty, imperious, lofty, lordly, majestic, overbearing, stately, supercilious, vain. ANT.—ashamed, humble, lowly, meek, modest.

prove, confirm, corroborate, demonstrate, establish, justify, manifest, show, substantiate, test, try, verify. ANT.—contradict, deny, disprove, expose, refute.

proverb, adage, aphorism, apothegm, axiom, bromide, byword, dictum, epigram, maxim, moral, motto, platitude, precept, saying, teaching, tenet, theorem, truism.

provide, afford, arm, cater, contribute, endow, equip, fit, fit out, furnish, give, produce, purvey, replenish, stock, store, supply, yield. ANT.—denude, deprive, divest, remove, strip, withhold.

provident, careful, cautious, discreet, economical, foresighted, frugal, prudent, saving, sparing, thoughtful, thrifty, wise. ANT.—extravagant, lavish, prodigal, profuse, wasteful.

provision, accumulation, arrangement, emergency equipment, fund, hoard, outline, plan, preparation, procurement, reserve, stock, store, supply; prerequisite, requirement, stipulation, terms.

provoke, see disturb.

proximate, adjacent, adjoining, beside, bordering, close, contiguous, handy, near, neighboring, nigh; approaching, imminent, impending. ANT.—distant, far, remote, removed.

prudent, careful, cautious, circumspect, discerning, discreet, judicious, reasonable, sensible, sound, vigilant, wary, watchful, wise. ANT.—absurd, foolish, impetuous, rash, reckless, stupid, unaware.

prying, curious, inquisitive, interfering, meddling, nosy, peeping, peering, searching, seeking, snoopy, spying. ANT.—aloof, incurious, indifferent, nonchalant, uncaring, unconcerned.

pseudo, bogus, counterfeit, fake, false, imitation, mock, phony, quasi, sham, simulated, spurious. ANT.—genuine, honest, real, sound, true.

public, complimentary, free, gratis, known, open, unrestricted. ANT.—charged, costly, personal, private, restricted.

publish, announce, broadcast, circulate, communicate, declare, disclose, disseminate, divulge, impart, issue, post, print, proclaim, promulgate, publicize, reveal, utter.

pull, drag, draw, haul, lift, stretch, tow, tug; extract, pluck, remove, take out, unsheathe; allure, attract, entice, induce, lure, persuade.

pulse, beat, oscillation, palpitation, throb, vibration.

punctual, dependable, early, exact, meticulous, particular, precise, prompt, punctilious, ready, scrupulous, strict, timely. ANT.—careless, desultory, dilatory, late, tardy.

punish, afflict, castigate, chasten, chastise, correct, discipline, fine, flog, imprison, inflict, pummel, scold, strike. ANT.—acquit, exonerate, forgive, free, pardon, reward.

puny, decrepit, delicate, diminutive, dwarfish, enervated, exhausted, faint, feeble, frail, impaired, inferior, infirm, languid, powerless, small, stunted, undeveloped, weak. ANT.—mighty, robust, strong, sturdy, vigorous.

purchase, see obtain.

pure, clean, clear, genuine, immaculate, perfect, spotless, stainless, unadulterated, unblemished, unmixed, untainted; chaste, guiltless, holy, incorrupt, innocent, modest, undefiled, virginal, virtuous; absolute, bare, sheer. ANT.—adulterated, foul, polluted, rotten, tainted; corrupt, defiled, licentious, immodest, obscene.

purge, see eliminate.

purify, chasten, clarify, clean, cleanse, clear, correct, deodorize, disinfect, filter, fumigate, mop, purge, refine, revise, scrub, sweep, wash. ANT.—debase, dirty, pollute, stain, tarnish, vitiate.

purpose, aim, design, determination, end, goal, inclination, intent, intention, object, objective, resolve, view. ANT.—accident, chance, fate, hazard.

pursue, chase, follow, hound, hunt, persist, seek, shadow, track, trail. ANT.—abandon, elude, flee, ignore, stop.

push, butt, compel, crowd, drive, elbow, force, impel, jostle, nudge, press, propel, shove, thrust; hasten, expedite, promote, urge. ANT.—drag, halt, pull, retreat; discourage, ignore, oppose.

put, assign, deposit, establish, imbed, insert, install, lay, locate, lodge, place, plant, settle. ANT.—displace, misplace, oust, remove, transfer.

putrid, contaminated, corrupt, decayed, disgusting, polluted, purulent, rotten. ANT.—clean, fragrant, pure, wholesome, uncontaminated.

puzzle, complexity, conundrum, enigma, intricacy, labyrinth, maze, mystery, perplexity, problem, riddle; baffle, bewilder, confound, confuse, disconcert, entangle, mystify, perplex. ANT.—answer, key, solution; clarify, elucidate, explain, reveal, solve, unravel.

Q

quack, charlatan, cheat, counterfeiter, deceiver, faker, imposter, phony, pretender, swindler.

quaint, anomalous, antique, curious, droll, eccentric, fanciful, odd, old-fashioned, peculiar, queer, strange, unique, unusual, whimsical. ANT.—common, familiar, fashionable, regular, usual.

quake, flutter, quail, quiver, shake, shiver, shudder, totter, tremble, vibrate; earthquake, temblor.

qualified, able, adequate, capable, clever, competent, efficacious, efficient, eligible, experienced, fitted, skillful, tempered. ANT.—incapable, ineffectual, inept, unfit, unqualified.

quality, attribute, character, characteristic, condition, distinction, feature, nature, peculiarity, property, qualification, trait; caliber, grade, rank, status, value.

quantity, abundance, amount, bulk, capacity, extent, mass, measure, multitude, number, pile, portion, sum, volume.

quarrel, affray, altercation, argument, bickering, brawl, clash, contention, disagreement, dispute, dissension, feud, fray, fuse, row, spat, squabble, strife, tiff, wrangle. ANT.—agreement, armistice, harmony, peace, silence.

quaver, see quake.

queer, see quaint.

query, ask, challenge, dispute, doubt, examine, inquire, interrogate, probe, quest, question, quiz, search, seek. ANT.—answer, reply, respond, retort, state.

quest, adventure, crusade, enterprise, examination, expedition, exploration, inquiry, inspection, interrogation, investigation, journey, pursuit, research, scrutiny, search, seeking, survey, trek.

question, see query.

quick, brisk, expeditious, fast, fleet, hasty, immediate, instantaneous, lively, precipitate, prompt, rapid, speedy, swift; excitable, impatient, impetuous, irascible, mercurial, rash, sharp, testy, touchy; active, acute, alert, clever, discerning, keen, ready, sensitive, sharp, shrewd, vigorous. ANT.—slow, sluggish; apathetic, drowsy, languid, lazy, listless; dull, insipid, obtuse, vapid.

quicken, see hurry.

quiescent, abeyant, calm, dormant, hidden, inactive, latent, motionless, peaceful, placid, quiet, resting, secret, serene, smooth, still, tranquil, undeveloped, undisturbed, unruffled. ANT.—active, dynamic, manifest, spirited, stirring, vivacious.

quiet, hushed, motionless, muffled, mute, pacific, peaceful, placid, quiescent, secluded, serene, soundless, still, tranquil, undisturbed; calm, contented, gentle, meek, mild, passive, patient, silent; allay, alleviate, appease, assuage, calm, compose, cool, gratify, lull, moderate, pacify, placate, please, quell, relax, relieve, restrain, smooth, soothe, still, tranquilize. ANT.—loud,

noisy, strident; agitated, excited, impatient, perturbed; arouse, excite, incense, inflame, provoke.

quiet, abandon, cease, depart, desert, desist, discontinue, forsake, leave, stop; give up, relinquish, resign, surrender, withdraw, yield. ANT.—continue, endure, keep, persevere, remain, retain, stay.

quiver, see quake.

quiz, see query.

quotation, blurb, citation, citing, excerpt, extract, passage, quote, recitation, reference, repetition, selection; estimate, price, rate.

R

race, ancestry, breed, clan, cultural group, family, folk, lineage, mankind, nation, nationality, people, stock, strain, tribe.

racket, see noise.

radiant, beaming, bright, brilliant, dazzling, effulgent, glittering, glorious, glowing, grand, luminous, lustrous, magnificent, resplendent, shimmering, shining, sparkling, splendid. ANT.—cloudy, dark, dim, dull, obscure.

radiate, brighten, broadcast, circulate, diffuse, disperse, disseminate, emanate, emit, gleam, glitter, illumine, propagate, shed, shine, spread, transmit. ANT.—absorb, concentrate, converge, gather.

radical, complete, entire, total, thorough; basic, congenital, constitutional, essential, fundamental, inborn, ingrained, inherent, inherited, innate, intrinsic, native, natural, organic, original; communistic, excessive, extreme, fanatical, insurgent, leftist, liberal, militant, progressive, revolutionary, ultra, uncompromising, violent. ANT.—incomplete, partial; extraneous, extrinsic, nonessential, superficial; casual, conservative, moderate, stable, traditional.

rage, anger, animosity, choler, exasperation, explosion, frenzy, fury, hysterics, indignation, ire, irritation, outburst, passion, petulance, storm, tantrum, temper, uproar, vehemence, wrath; boil (over), foam, fume, rail at, rant, rave, roar, scold, scream, seethe, splutter, yell. ANT.—conciliation, forbearance, patience, peace, self-control, tranquility; appease, calm, lull, placate, quiet, soothe.

raise, elevate, erect, exalt, heave, heighten, hoist, honor, lift, uplift; breed, cultivate, grow, produce, rear; collect, gather, levy, muster; advance, aggrandize, amplify, augment, boost, increase, intensify, magnify. ANT.—abase, degrade, depreciate, destroy, lower, reduce.

ramble, deviate, digress, drift, meander, range, roam, rove, saunter, straggle, stray, stroll, traipse, wander.

rancor, see malice.

rank, column, file, line, order, range, row, series, string, tier; class, division, grade, order; degree, position, seniority, standing, station; dignity, distinction, eminence, reputation.

rapid, see quick.

rapture, bliss, delight, ecstasy, enchantment, exultation, felicity, gladness, happiness, joy, passion, transport. ANT.—depression, grief, melancholy, misery, pain, suffering.

rare, infrequent, occasional; odd, peculiar, strange, unusual; choice, exceptional, extraordinary, incomparable, precious, remarkable, scarce, singular, uncommon, unique, unparalleled, unprecedented. ANT.—frequent, habitual, incessant, recurring; common, normal, ordinary, regular, typical; cheap, worthless.

rash, see impetuous.

rate, appraise, assess, calculate, determine, estimate, evaluate, measure, price, rank, value; succeed, triumph; comparison, degree, fixed amount, measure, percentage, proportion, quota, ratio, relationship, standard.

ration, see portion.

rational, deductive, discriminating, intelligent, judicious, logical, prudent, reasonable, sagacious, sensible, wise; conscious, lucid, sane, sober, sound. ANT.—absurd, foolish, inconsistent, ridiculous, stupid; insane, irrational, unconscious.

ravage, see devastate.

ravenous, see hungry.

raw, callow, coarse, crude, green, harsh, ill-prepared, immature, inexperienced, rough, rude, undisciplined, unfinished, unpolished, unprepared, unrefined, unripe. ANT.—adult, courteous, mature, polished, ripe, seasoned, well-prepared.

raze, annihilate, demolish, destroy, devastate, dismantle, efface, eradicate, exterminate, extinguish, level, obliterate, overthrow, ravage, ruin, topple, wreck. ANT.—build, construct, erect, raise, repair, restore.

reach, extend to, span, stretch, touch; accomplish, achieve, arrive at, attain, earn, gain, get to, join, overtake. ANT.—bungle, fail, fall short, leave, miss.

react, act, answer, reciprocate, rejoin, reply, respond; be affected, be involved, be moved, feel. ANT.—disregard, ignore, overlook; be insensitive to.

read, apprehend, browse, comprehend, decipher, discern, glance over, grasp, interpret, learn, perceive, peruse, scan, skim, study, translate, understand, unravel.

ready, active, available, complete, consummate, disposed, equipped, finished, fit, mature, mellow, prepared, prompt, ripe, seasonable, suitable, willing; concoct, condition, equip, fit, furnish, make ready, order, predispose, prepare. ANT.—immature, unavailable, undeveloped, unready.

real, see genuine.

reality, actuality, authenticity, entity, existence, realness, substance, tangibility, truth, verity. ANT.—fantasy, fiction, imagination, nonentity.

realization, accomplishment, achievement, attainment, completion, performance; appreciation, awareness, comprehension, perception, understanding. ANT.—defeat, failure; blindness, disregard, ignorance.

realm, area, department, district, domain, estate, farm, kingdom, land, province, region, sphere, territory, vicinity.

reap, accumulate, acquire, collect, cut, earn, gain, garner, gather, glean, harvest, hoard, obtain, pick, win. ANT.—lose, plant, seed, sow.

rear, bring up, elevate, foster, lift, nurture, raise, support, train; build, erect.

reason, account, aim, argument, basis, cause, design, end, foundation, ground, motive, object, purpose, sake, view; intelligence, intuition, judgment, mind, rationality, sense, understanding; analyze, argue, conclude, contend, debate, deduce, deliberate, discuss, establish, infer, judge, question, reflect, speculate, study, trace. ANT.—bewilder, confuse, fabricate, guess.

reasonable, see rational.

rebellion, coup, disorder, disturbance, insurrection, mutiny, outbreak, overthrow, revolt, revolution, riot, sedition, tumult, upheaval, uprising. ANT.—conciliation, law, order, peace, submission.

rebellious, contumacious, defiant, disobedient, insubordinate, intractable, mutinous, pugnacious, recalcitrant, refractory, undutiful, unmanageable, unruly. ANT.—docile, dutiful, manageable, obedient, subservient, tractable.

rebuke, accuse, admonish, berate, censure, chide, condemn, criticize, implicate, punish, reprimand, reproach, reprove, scold, upbraid. ANT.—approve, exonerate, laud, praise, reward.

recall, recollect, remember, remind, reminisce, review, revive; annul, disqualify, revoke; reassemble, reconvene, summon. ANT.—forget, ignore, overlook; reestablish, restore; disperse, separate, terminate.

recede, abate, decline, ebb, fade, lessen, regress, retire, retreat, revert, shrink from, withdraw. ANT.—advance, approach, gain, increase, near, rise.

receive, accept, acquire, catch, gain, get, obtain, take, win; admit, shelter; entertain, welcome. ANT.—bequeath, donate, give, return; evict, expel, oust; deny, refuse, reject.

recent, contemporary, foregoing, fresh, late, latter, modern, new, newfangled, novel, original, preceding, retiring, streamlined, young. ANT.—ancient, antiquated, archaic, obsolete, old-fashioned.

recite, address, convey, declaim, delineate, deliver, describe, detail, discourse, enumerate, explain, impart, mention, narrate, quote, read, recapitulate, recount, rehearse, relate, repeat, report, state, tell.

reckless, careless, daring, foolhardy, heedless, impetuous, imprudent, precipitate, rash, wild. ANT.—cautious, circumspect, prudent, wary.

recognize, accede, accept, acknowledge, admit, apprehend, concede, confess, distinguish, identify, know, perceive, realize, recollect, remember. ANT.—forget, ignore, overlook, renounce, repudiate.

recommend, advise, allude, counsel, hint, imply, insinuate, intimate, offer, prescribe, propose, refer, suggest, urge; acclaim, advocate, applaud, approve, commend, endorse, extol, praise, sanction. ANT.—demand, dictate, insist; condemn, denigrate, disapprove.

reconcile, accommodate, adapt, adjust, arrange, conciliate, conform, correct, harmonize, mediate, mitigate, pacify, placate, rectify, regulate, reunite, settle. ANT.—alienate, annoy, bother, divide, irritate, separate.

record, account, archive, chronicle, docket, document, inventory, memorandum, note, register, registry, report, schedule; inscription, mark, memorial, trace, vestige; achievement, career, experience, history; catalogue, enroll, enter, file, list, note, register, report, tape.

recover, cure, heal, mend, rally, recuperate, revive; recapture, recoup, redeem, regain, renew, renovate, repossess, restore, retrieve, salvage. ANT.—perish, regress, relapse, wane, weaken; forfeit, lose, mislay.

recreation, amusement, diversion, entertainment, frolic, fun, game, pastime, play, refreshment, relaxation, relief, sport. ANT.—drudgery, labor, task, toil, work.

rectify, adjust, amend, correct, fix, improve, mend, purify, refine, reform, remedy, repair, revise, right. ANT.—adulterate, debase, falsify, ruin, spoil.

recuperate, see recover.

redeem, atone, deliver, emancipate, expiate, extricate, free, liberate, propitiate, ransom, recoup, recover, regain, repair, repurchase, rescue, retrieve, save. ANT.—abandon, forfeit, ignore, neglect, overlook, shun.

reduce, abate, abbreviate, abridge, assuage, condense, contract, curtail, decimate, decrease, degrade, diminish, impoverish, lessen, lower, moderate, modify, shorten, subdue, suppress, thin, weaken. ANT.—amplify, enlarge, increase, magnify, strengthen.

redundant, copious, diffuse, excessive, extra, profuse, prolix, repetitious, verbose, wordy. ANT.—concise, laconic, succinct, terse.

refer, advert, allude, appeal, apply, ascribe, attribute, belong, cite, commit, concern, connect, consign, consult, deliver, include, involve, pertain, point, quote, regard, relate, submit, suggest.

refinement, breeding, civilization, clarification, cultivation, culture, delicacy, education, elegance, enlightenment, finesse, poise, polish, purification, purity. ANT.—barbarism, coarseness, crudity, rusticity, vulgarity.

reflect, cogitate, concentrate, consider, contemplate, deliberate, meditate, muse, ponder, reason, ruminate, speculate, study, think, weigh; copy, echo, imitate, mirror, reproduce; rebound, revert.

reform, amend, better, correct, freshen, improve, mend, reconstruct, rectify, redress, renew, renovate, reorganize, repair, restore, revise, right, transmute. ANT.—aggravate, corrupt, damage, impair, ruin, vitiate.

refrain, abstain, avoid, check, curb, desist, forebear, restrain, withhold; burden, chorus, undersong. ANT.—continue, indulge, persevere, persist.

refresh, air, animate, brace, cheer, enliven, freshen, invigorate, renew, renovate, rest, restore, revive, stimulate. ANT.—bore, exhaust, fatigue, tire, weary.

refuge, asylum, fortress, harbor, haven, hideaway, protection, retreat, sanctuary, seclusion, shelter, stronghold. ANT.—danger, exposure, hazard, jeopardy, pitfall, risk.

refuse, decline, deny, disavow, disown, negate, protest, rebuff, reject, renounce, repel, repudiate, spurn, veto, withhold; dross, garbage, junk, litter, rubbish, rubble, scoria, sweepings, trash, waste. ANT.—accept, consent, grant, present, sanction, welcome; assets, resources, valuables.

refute, confound, confute, controvert, disprove, expose, falsify, invalidate, overthrow, parry, rebut, repel, stultify. ANT.—assist, defend, encourage, sanction, strengthen, uphold.

regal, courtly, dignified, imperial, kingly, lordly, magnificent, majestic, monarchial, noble, princely, queenly, royal, sovereign, splendid, stately, sublime. ANT.—common, ignoble, lowly, ordinary, plebeian, servile.

regard, attention, concern, consideration, notice, observation; reference, relation, respect; affection, esteem, estimation, liking; honor, revere; contemplate, notice, observe, view, watch; believe, hold, imagine, reckon, suppose, think. ANT.—avoidance, neglect; antipathy, disgust; deride, insult, mock; forget, ignore, neglect, omit, overlook.

register, admit, chronicle, declare, enroll, enter, establish, express, fix, indicate, insert, list, note, record, save, table; annal, archive, catalogue, list, roll, roster, schedule.

region, area, belt, climate, district, domain, locale, locality, location, neighborhood, place, quarter, realm, sector, site, spot, station, territory, vicinity, zone.

regression, backsliding, deterioration, ebb, recession, recidivism, retrogression, return, reversion, withdrawal. ANT.—advancement, headway, progress, progression.

regret, bitterness, compunction, contrition, disappointment, grief, heartache, lamentation, penitence, qualm, remorse, repentance, repining, self-reproach, sorrow, vexation, worry; bewail, deplore, lament, repent, repine, rue, sorrow. ANT.—contentment, impenitence, induration, obduracy, satisfaction, tranquility; celebrate, cheer, enjoy, exult, rejoice.

regular, consistent, conventional, customary, homogeneous, homologous, invariable, methodical, natural, normal, orderly, ordinary, periodic, punctual, steady, symmetrical, systematic, uniform, unvaried, usual. ANT.—anomalous, erratic, inconsistent, infrequent, rare, strange, unusual.

regulate, adapt, adjust, allocate, arrange, classify, control, correct, direct, fix, govern, legislate, organize, readjust, reconcile, rectify, rule, systematize. ANT.—confuse, disarrange, disorganize, entangle, jumble, sunder.

rehabilitate, overhaul, reawaken, rebuild, reconstitute, reconstruct, recreate, reestablish, refinish, refresh, reinstate, reinvigorate, renew, renovate, repair, replenish, restore, revamp, revive.

reinforce, augment, buttress, energize, fortify, invigorate, pillar, strengthen, support. ANT.—detract, weaken.

reject, decline, deny, discard, dismiss, eject, eliminate, exclude, rebuff, refuse, renounce, repudiate, spurn, veto, withhold. ANT.—accept, admit, choose, select, welcome.

relate, describe, detail, narrate, recite, recount, rehearse, report, state, tell; apply, associate, compare, connect, correlate, link, parallel, pertain, refer.

relation, alliance, bearing, connection, correlation, correspondence, likeness, reference, relationship, relevancy, similarity; affinity, bond, family connection, filiation, kindred, kinship, link, sibling, tie, union.

relationship, see relation.

relative, appositive, cognate, comparative, conditional, contingent, definite, dependent, germane, particular, pertinent, referable, relevant, respecting, special; connection, kin, relation.

relaxation, abatement, amusement, comfort, diversion, ease, leisure, loosening, mitigation, peacefulness, reclining, recreation, relief, repose, respite, rest, slackening, tranquility. ANT.—drudgery, exertion, labor, striving, struggle, toil.

release, deliver, discharge, emancipate, free, liberate, set free; absolution, acquittal, deliverance, discharge, dispensation, emancipation, exoneration, freedom, liberation, relinquishment, surrender. ANT.—confine, imprison, oppress; restriction, subjugation.

relent, abdicate, accede, acquiesce, capitulate, cede, comply, defer, quit, relinquish, resign, submit, succumb, surrender; abate, bend, bow, relax, soften, subside, yield. ANT.—assert, persevere, persist, strive, struggle; harden, stiffen.

relentless, fierce, hard, implacable, inexorable, inflexible, obdurate, pitiless, rigid, rigorous, ruthless, strict, stringent, unyielding, vindictive. ANT.—compassionate, gentle, lenient, merciful.

relevant, see pertinent.

reliable, certain, conscientious, constant, definite, dependable, faithful, firm, positive, reputable, responsible, safe, secure, solid, stable, staunch, steadfast, sterling, strong, sure, tried, true, trustworthy, unimpeachable. ANT.—dangerous, dubious, insecure, questionable, undependable, unreliable.

relief, aid, alleviation, assistance, backing, comfort, ease, help, mitigation, palliation, succor, support. ANT.—aggravation, agitation, distress.

relieve, abate, aid, allay, alleviate, assist, assuage, calm, comfort, disburden, disentangle, ease, extricate, facilitate, free, lighten, mitigate, pacify, redress, remedy, solace, soothe. ANT.—disturb, irritate, trouble, vex.

religious, believing, canonical, devout, divine, ecclesiastical, ethical, god-fearing, godly, holy, ministerial, moral, pietistic, pious, reverent, sacred, sanctimonious, spiritual, theological; careful, methodical, scrupulous, thorough. ANT.—atheistic, free-thinking, immoral, impious, profane, secular; careless, indifferent, negligent, slovenly.

relinquish, abandon, abdicate, abjure, acquiesce, capitulate, cede, deny, desert, discard, dismiss, forego, forsake, quit, reject, renounce, resign, revoke, sacrifice, spare, submit, surrender, vacate, yield. ANT.—conquer, keep, perpetuate, persist, pursue, retain.

relish, appetizer, seasoning, spice; appreciation, enjoyment, gratification, gusto, inclination, partiality, preference, satisfaction, zest. ANT.—disfavor, distaste.

reluctant, averse, backward, demurring, disinclined, doubtful, hesitant, indisposed, loathe, opposed, slow, tardy, unready, unwilling. ANT.—amenable, disposed, eager, enthusiastic, ready, willing.

rely, bank, confide, count, depend, lean, trust. ANT.—distrust, doubt.

remain, abide, continue, dwell, endure, inhabit, last, reside, rest, stay, survive. ANT.—depart, dissipate, go, leave, terminate.

remainder, balance, dregs, excess, leavings, leftovers, remains, remnant, residue, residuum, rest, surplus.

remark, comment, mention, note, observation, point, saying, statement, utterance; assert, declare, express, maintain, mention, observe, relate, say, speak, talk, tell, utter.

remarkable, arresting, awesome, commanding, distinguished, exceptional, exciting, extraordinary, great, impressive, memorable, moving, notable, peculiar, prominent, rare, special, stirring, striking, wonderful, uncommon, unusual. ANT.—common, inconspicuous, normal, regular, unimpressive, usual.

remedy, antidote, bracer, cure, help, medicant, medication, nostrum, panacea, redress, relief, reparation, restorative; ameliorate, amend, better, correct, cure, fix, heal, improve, mend, rectify, redress, reform, relieve, renew, repair, restore. ANT.—burden, hindrance, impediment, ruination; aggravate, intensify, neglect, worsen.

remember, memorize, recall, recollect, remind, reminisce, retain, retrace, review. ANT.—disregard, forget, obliterate, overlook, repress, suppress.

remembrance, commemoration, keepsake, memento, memoir, memorial, memory, recollection, reminiscence, reminder, souvenir, token, trophy. ANT.—forgetfulness, nirvana, oblivion.

remit, absolve, alleviate, defer, discontinue, excuse, exempt, forgive, mitigate, moderate, overlook, pardon, postpone, relax, release, relinquish, restore, soften; compensate, make payment, pay, reimburse, remunerate. ANT.—avenge, bind, control, dominate, restrict, suppress; deceive, swindle, victimize.

remorse, see regret.

remorseless, see inhuman.

remote, alien, distant, far, faraway, foreign, inaccessible, indirect, removed, secluded, unconnected, unrelated. ANT.—adjacent, close, near, proximate, related.

remove, depart, dislodge, displace, evacuate, leave, migrate, move, separate, shift, transfer, transport, vacate; discharge, dismiss, eject, evict, oust, unseat; eliminate, extract, pull, uproot, wrench; destroy, kill. ANT.—dwell, place, remain; establish, maintain; imbed, plant, root; preserve.

renew, continue, reestablish, refresh, regenerate, reiterate, renovate, repeat, replace, replenish, restore, resume, resuscitate, revive. ANT.—deplete, diminish, enfeeble, exhaust.

renounce, abandon, abdicate, desert, drop, forego, forsake, quit, relinquish, resign, sacrifice, secede, surrender; deny, disavow, disclaim, disown, recant, reject, repudiate, retract, revoke. ANT.—maintain, persevere, persist, remain; acknowledge, assert, claim.

renovate, see rehabilitate.

renowned, see eminent.

repair, amend, correct, darn, fix, mend, patch, rectify, refit, remedy, remodel, renew, renovate, replace, restore. ANT.—damage, destroy, mar, neglect, ruin.

repeal, abolish, abrogate, annul, cancel, invalidate, nullify, quash, recall, rescind, revoke, veto. ANT.—continue, keep, maintain, renew, validate.

repeat, duplicate, echo, iterate, quote, recapitulate, recite, recur, rehearse, reiterate, relate, reproduce, tell.

repentance, compunction, contrition, penitence, regret, regretfulness, remorse, self-disgust, self-reproach, sorrow. ANT.—callousness, complacency, impenitence, recusancy, shamelessness.

replace, reconstitute, reconstruct, refund, rehabilitate, reinstate, repay, restore, return, substitute, succeed, supersede, supplant. ANT.—alter, change, diversify, modify, transform.

replicate, see duplicate.

reply, acknowledge, answer, counter, echo, react, rejoin, respond, retort; answer, rejoinder, repartee, response, retort. ANT.—ask, disregard, ignore, question; examination, inquiry, question, summoning.

report, advertise, announce, broadcast, chronicle, communicate, declare, describe, detail, disclose, herald, impart, inform, mention, notify, proclaim, promulgate, publish, recite, relate, specify, state, tell; account, announcement, chronicle, communication, description, dispatch, hearsay, intelligence, message, narration, narrative, news, publication, recital, record, statement, story, tidings. ANT.—conceal, delete, mask, screen, veil; concealment, evasion, deletion, reserve, secrecy, suppression.

repose, calm, calmness, comfort, ease, hush, leisure, peace, quiescence, quiet, quietude, relaxation, respite, rest, serenity, silence, stillness, tranquility. ANT.—activity, disturbance, noise, tumult, turmoil.

represent, delineate, depict, describe, draw, imitate, impersonate, paint, personate, picture, portray, show, sketch, symbolize, typify.

repress, bridle, check, choke, constrain, curb, dull, hinder, inhibit, overpower, quell, restrain, silence, smother, still, stop, subdue, suppress. ANT.—advance, assist, encourage, exhilarate, invigorate, stimulate.

reprimand, admonish, berate, blame, censure, chide, lecture, punish, rebuke, reprehend, reproach, reprove, revile, scold, upbraid, vilify, vituperate. ANT.—approve, commend, forgive, laud, praise, reward.

reproach, see blame.

reproduction, casting, copy, duplicate, exemplar, facsimile, imitation, print, replica, representation, tracing, transcript; generation, procreation, propagation. ANT.—archetype, original, pattern, prototype; infertility, sterility.

repugnant, abhorrent, adverse, antagonistic, contrary, disagreeable, disgusting, distasteful, hostile, invidious, obnoxious, offensive, opposed, refractory, repellent, revolting, unbearable. ANT.—agreeable, appealing, conciliatory, harmonious, pleasant.

repulsive, abhorrent, abominable, detestable, disgusting, gross, gruesome, hideous, homely, horrible, horrid, nauseating, obnoxious, odious, offensive, repellent, repugnant, revolting, ugly, uncomely. ANT.—alluring, captivating, enticing, inviting, pleasing.

reputation, acceptability, character, class, credit, dependability, description, esteem, honor, kind, name, nature, prestige, reliability, repute, respectability, sort, standing, trustworthiness; eminence, notoriety, prominence.

repute, see reputation.

request, appeal, apply, ask, beg, beseech, bid, entreat, implore, importune, invite, petition, plead, pray, seek, solicit, sue, summon, supplicate.

requirement, behest, bidding, call, charge, claim, command, decree, demand, essential, exigency, injunction, mandate, necessity, need, pinch, requisite, requisition, urgency, want.

requisite, basic, binding, compelling, compulsory, crucial, essential, expedient, fundamental, imperative, important, indispensable, intrinsic, mandatory, necessary, needed, obligatory, required, urgent, vital. ANT.—accidental, expendable, extrinsic, nonessential, optional.

rescue, deliver, disenthrall, extricate, free, liberate, preserve, ransom, recapture, reclaim, recover, redeem, release, retrieve, save. ANT.—abandon, bind, enslave, hinder, incarcerate.

research, analysis, examination, experimentation, exploration, inquiry, interrogation, investigation, observation, query, quest, question, scrutiny, study, testing.

resemblance, affinity, agreement, analogy, correspondence, facsimile, likeness, match, purity, semblance, similarity, simile, similitude. ANT.—contrast, deviation, dissimilarity, distinction, inconsistency, variance.

resentment, acerbity, anger, animosity, annoyance, bitterness, displeasure, exasperation, grudge, huff, indignation, ire, irritation, perturbation, pique, rancor, rankling, umbrage. ANT.—affection, concord, geniality, good humor, happiness, harmony.

reserved, aloof, bashful, cautious, demure, detached, diffident, distant, formal, modest, restrained, reticent, retiring, shy, taciturn, timorous, undemonstrative, wary; booked, preserved, saved. ANT.—affable, blatant, expansive, uninhibited; unreserved.

residue, see remainder.

resign, abandon, abdicate, abjure, cede, eschew, forego, quit, relinquish, renounce, retract, surrender, vacate, waive, withdraw, yield. ANT.—accept, receive, remain, retain, stay.

resilient, buoyant, elastic, flexible, spirited, springy, supple. ANT.—inflexible, stiff, tense, unbending.

resist, attack, check, confront, contest, counteract, defy, frustrate, hinder, impede, impugn, neutralize, obstruct, oppose, thwart, withstand. ANT.—acquiesce, assist, collaborate, comply, defer, submit, yield.

resolution, constancy, courage, decision, determination, devotion, firmness, fortitude, persistence, resolve, stamina, steadfastness, zeal. ANT.—caprice, hesitation, indecision, uncertainty, vacillation.

resolve, adjudicate, choose, close, conclude, decide, decree, determine, elect, end, fix, propose, purpose, settle, terminate. ANT.—hesitate, procrastinate, vacillate, waver.

respect, admiration, consideration, deference, esteem, fealty, honor, recognition, regard, reverence, veneration; admire, appreciate, consider, heed, honor, note, notice, prize, regard, revere, reverence, treasure, uphold, value, venerate. ANT.—contempt, disdain, irreverence, scorn; abuse, blame, censure, deride, despise.

respectable, adequate, becoming, comely, decent, decorous, estimable, honorable, mediocre, moderate, presentable, proper, seemly, suitable, tolerable, upright, virtuous, worthy. ANT.—dishonorable, improper, indecent, reprehensible, scandalous, unworthy.

resplendent, see radiant.

respond, see reply.

response, see reply.

responsible, accountable, amenable, answerable, liable, obligatory, subject; dependable, reliable, trustworthy. ANT.—arbitrary, exempt, free, immune, unbound; careless, irresponsible, lax, negligent, unreliable.

restful, calm, comfortable, cozy, easy, mild, peaceful, placid, quiet, relaxing, reposeful, serene, soothing, still, tranquil, untroubled. ANT.—alarming, annoying, disconcerting, disturbing, upsetting.

restless, agitated, anxious, changeable, disquieted, disturbed, fidgety, fitful, irresolute, nervous, sleepless, uneasy, unsettled, worried; active, moving, roving, transient, wandering. ANT.—calm, composed, placid, tranquil, unperturbed.

restore, see rehabilitate.

restrain, see repress.

restrict, bind, bridle, check, confine, constrain, curb, fence, hinder, impede, inhibit, limit, obstruct, repress, restrain, stop, suppress. ANT.—enlarge, expand, extend, free, release.

result, conclusion, consequence, determination, effect, end, eventuality, fruit, issue, outcome, product, resolution, resolve, termination, upshot; accrue, arise, come, eventuate, flow, follow, issue, originate, proceed, resolve, spring.

retain, detain, employ, engage, hire, hold, keep, maintain, preserve, reserve, secure, withhold. ANT.—discard, dismiss, jettison, relinquish, surrender.

retaliate, avenge, match, punish, reciprocate, repay, requite, retort, return, vindicate. ANT.—forget, forgive, ignore, pardon.

retard, arrest, check, clog, delay, detain, hamper, hinder, impede, interrupt, postpone, stay. ANT.—accelerate, advance, hasten, speed.

retire, see relinquish.

retort, see reply.

retract, abjure, abnegate, abrogate, annul, cancel, deny, disclaim, disown, nullify, recall, recant, renounce, reverse, revoke. ANT.—affirm, confirm, endorse, ratify, uphold.

retrogress, backslide, decline, degenerate, deteriorate, regress, relapse, retreat, retrograde, revert. ANT.—advance, develop, improve, proceed, progress.

return, reappear, recur, retreat, revert; reciprocate, repay, replace, reply, requite, restore. ANT.—appropriate, retain, take.

reveal, announce, betray, confess, disclose, divulge, explain, expose, express, impart, inform, open, publish, show, uncover, unfold, unmask, unveil. ANT.—conceal, deceive, disguise, mask, secrete.

revenge, avenging, implacability, malevolence, reprisal, requital, retaliation, retribution, vengeance, vindictiveness. ANT.—forgiveness, mercy, pardon, reconciliation, remission.

reverence, admiration, adoration, approbation, awe, deference, dignity, esteem, fame, glory, homage, honor, praise, regard, renown, respect, veneration, worship. ANT.—contempt, derision, execration, dishonor, irreverence, mockery.

reverse, alter, convert, invert, modify, shift, transpose, turn about; overthrow, overturn, subvert, upset; annul, cancel, countermand, invalidate, nullify, repeal, rescind, retract, revoke, undo.

revert, go back, recur, repeat, retreat, return, reverse. ANT.—advance, go forward, proceed.

review, consider, examine, inspect, reconsider, rehearse, retrace, survey; analyze, correct, criticize, edit, judge, revise; commentary, criticism, critique, examination, inspection, reconsideration, reflection, retrospection, revision, study, survey; digest, journal, periodical; abstract, outline, summary, synopsis.

revision, see review.

revive, animate, awaken, freshen, improve, invigorate, reanimate, recall, refresh, reinforce, renew, renovate, repair, reproduce, resuscitate, revivify, rouse. ANT.—decay, decline, fade, perish, waste, wither.

revoke, see repeal.

revolting, see repulsive.

revolution, anarchy, *coup d'état*, disorder, foment, insubordination, insurrection, mutiny, overthrow, rebellion, revolt, tumult, uprising; gyration, revolving, rotation, spin, swirl, twirl.

revolve, circle, circulate, eddy, gyrate, orbit, roll, rotate, spin, turn, twirl, wheel, whirl; brood over, consider, ponder, ruminate, study.

reward, acknowledgment, amends, award, bonus, bounty, compensation, gain, gratuity, indemnity, payment, premium, prize, recompense, recoupment, redress, remuneration, requital, retribution, return, satisfaction. ANT.—assessment, charge, deprivation, divestment, forfeiture, levy, seizure.

rhythm, accent, beat, cadence, lilt, measure, meter, periodicity, pulsation, regularity, swing, tempo.

rich, ample, bountiful, costly, elegant, exorbitant, expensive, generous, luscious, luxurious, opulent, resplendent, splendid, sumptuous, superb, valuable; abundant, exuberant, fecund, fertile, fruitful, lush, luxuriant, plentiful, profuse, prolific; intense, strong, vivid; affluent, moneyed, prosperous, wealthy, well-to-do. ANT.—drab, plain, unadorned; barren, sterile, unfruitful, unproductive; faint, powerless, unsubstantial, weak; destitute, impoverished, indigent, penniless, poor.

riddle, see mystery.

ridicule, banter, contempt, derision, disdain, disparagement, gibe, irony, jeering, mockery, persiflage, raillery, sarcasm, satire, scorn, sneering. ANT.—approval, commendation, honor, praise, respect.

ridiculous, absurd, bizarre, comic, droll, farcical, foolish, funny, hilarious, inconsistent, irrational, laughable, ludicrous, nonsensical, odd, preposterous, self-contradictory, silly, unreasonable. ANT.—conventional, rational, reasonable, sensible, wise.

right, ethical, fair, honest, just, lawful, legitimate, reasonable, rightful; accurate, correct, true, valid; appropriate, proper, suitable; direct, erect, straight, upright; authority, exemption, immunity, liberty, license, prerogative, privilege; equity, honesty, integrity, justice, morality, propriety, rectitude, uprightness, virtue. ANT.—dishonest, illegitimate, unethical, unreasonable; false, inaccurate, invalid; improper, inappropriate, unsuitable; crooked, devious, dishonest, twisted; encroachment, injustice, violation, wrong; dishonesty, immorality, inequity, injustice, vice.

righteous, chaste, commendable, conscientious, decent, equitable, ethical, good, honorable, just, pure, right, scrupulous, virtuous, worthy; devout, godly, pious, religious, saintly. ANT.—amoral, corrupt, immoral, licentious, unethical; impious, irreligious.

rigid, austere, exacting, harsh, precise, relentless, rigorous, scrupulous, severe, stern, stony, strict, stringent, unyielding; inelastic, inflexible, petrified, stiff, unbending. ANT.—compassionate, considerate, forbearing, indulgent, lenient, tolerant; elastic, flexible, limber, mobile, pliant.

rigorous, austere, blunt, coarse, cruel, exacting, grating, gruff, hard, harsh, inflexible, jarring, oppressive, rigid, rough, severe, stern, stiff, strict, stringent, uncompromising, unfeeling. ANT.—easy, easygoing, lax, lenient, mild, soft, tender.

rim, border, brim, brink, brow, curb, edge, fringe, hem, limit, lip, margin, outskirts, terminus, top, verge. ANT.—center, core, interior, middle.

ring, arena, band, chime, circle, clangor, clique, confederation, coterie, faction, gang, hoop, resonance, reverberation; chime, circle, clang, encircle, enclose, girdle, jingle, knell, peal, resound, surround, tinkle, toll.

riot, altercation, commotion, fray, insurgence, melee, pandemonium, protest, rebellion, row, strife, tumult, turmoil, uprising. ANT.—order, peace, quiet, regularity, tranquility.

rip, burst, cleave, cut, disunite, lacerate, rend, rive, separate, sever, shear, shred, slash, slit, split, sunder, tear. ANT.—join, mend, unite.

ripe, complete, consummate, developed, finished, full-grown, mature, matured, mellow, perfect, ready, ripened, seasonable, seasoned. ANT.—budding, green, immature, undeveloped, unfit, unseasoned.

rise, arise, ascend, begin, climb, commence, grow, increase, mount, originate, proceed, progress, prosper, scale, soar, spring, start, thrive, tower. ANT.—decline, descend, fall, recede, sink, tumble.

risk, danger, hazard, imperilment, jeopardy, peril; chance, gamble, opportunity, prospect, uncertainty, venture; endanger, expose, hazard, jeopardize, venture. ANT.—defense, immunity, protection, safety; certainty, guarantee; defend, insure, protect, secure, shield.

risky, chancy, critical, dangerous, hazardous, insecure, jeopardous, menacing, perilous, precarious, threatening, uncertain, unsafe. ANT.—certain, protected, safe, sure.

rite, ceremony, custom, duty, formality, liturgy, observance, ordinance, parade, pomp, protocol, ritual, sacrament, service, solemnity.

ritual, see rite.

rival, adversary, antagonist, combatant, competitor, contestant, disputant, emulator, enemy, foe, opponent; antagonize, attack, battle, challenge, combat, compete, conflict, confront, contend, contest, dispute, emulate, fight, oppose, struggle, wrestle. ANT.—advocate, ally, assistant,

helper, partner, patron, supporter; assist, champion, cooperate, encourage, support, uphold.

roam, deviate, digress, err, gallivant, hike, meander, prowl, ramble, range, rove, saunter, straggle, stray, stroll, traipse, traverse, wander. ANT.—halt, lodge, settle, stay.

rob, appropriate, burglarize, cheat, defraud, embezzle, fleece, forge, loot, pilfer, pillage, plunder, purloin, rifle, sack, steal, strip.

robber, bandit, burglar, despoiler, forager, forger, marauder, pillager, pirate, plunderer, poacher, raider, rustler, swindler, thief.

robust, brawny, hale, hardy, healthy, muscular, powerful, sound, strapping, strong, sturdy, tough, vigorous, well. ANT.—debilitated, feeble, flabby, frail, sickly, weak.

rock, boulder, cliff, crag, gravel, jewel, pebble, promontory, reef, slab, stone; defense, foundation, support; agitate, convulse, jiggle, jolt, oscillate, roll, shake, shove, sway, swing, tremble, vibrate.

role, acting, character, characterization, function, impersonation, part, performance, presentation, task.

roll, catalogue, document, inventory, list, register, rota, schedule, scroll; bind, enfold, flatten, fluctuate, level, press, resound, reverberate, revolve, rotate, rumble, smooth, swathe, tumble, turn, undulate, wallow, wheel, whirl.

romantic, charming, chimerical, chivalrous, courtly, dreamy, enchanting, extravagant, fanciful, fantastic, fictitious, ideal, idealistic, imaginary, imaginative, improbable, picturesque, poetic, sentimental. ANT.—definite, practical, pragmatic, realistic, solid.

roomy, ample, broad, capacious, commodious, extensive, grand, immense, large, spacious, vast, wide. ANT.—condensed, cramped, inconsiderable, little, small, tiny.

root, base, basis, bottom, foundation, groundwork, substructure, support, underpinning; cause, motive, reason; etymon, radical, radix, stem.

rot, corrode, decay, decline, decompose, decrease, degenerate, disintegrate, dwindle, ebb, fade, putrefy, spoil, wane, waste, weaken, wither. ANT.—bloom, flourish, grow, thrive.

rotate, circle, circulate, eddy, gyrate, invert, loop, revolve, roll, spin, swirl, swivel, turn, twirl, twist, wheel, whirl.

rough, bumpy, craggy, irregular, jagged, rugged, scabrous, scraggy, scratchy, serrated, uneven; approximate, coarse, cursory, imperfect, incomplete, unfinished, unpolished, unrefined; hard, harsh, severe, stormy, tempestuous, violent; austere, blunt, burly, crude, gruff, impolite, indecent, rude, uncivil. ANT.—even, level, sleek, smooth; complete, finished, polished, refined, thorough; gentle, mild, placid; courteous, cultivated, polite.

round, annular, circular, cylindrical, discoid, globular, orbed, orbicular, rotund, spherical; bulging, convex, protuberant; arched, bowed, coiled, curled, looped.

rouse, agitate, animate, arouse, awaken, excite, inflame, inspire, inspirit, motivate, provoke, raise, revive, stimulate, urge, whet. ANT.—calm, lull, pacify, tranquilize.

route, avenue, beat, channel, circuit, course, detour, digression, divergence, meandering, passage, path, rambling, road, rounds, street, thoroughfare, track, trail, walk, way.

routine, course, custom, cycle, fashion, habit, method, practice, round, system, usage, use; conventional, customary, habitual, methodical.

royal, august, courtly, dignified, elevated, grand, high, honorable, imperial, kingly, lofty, lordly,

majestic, monarchial, noble, princely, regal, reigning, resplendent, ruling, sovereign, stately, sublime, superior, supreme, worthy. ANT.—low, plebeian, proletarian, servile, unadorned.

rude, abusive, arrogant, blunt, boorish, brash, brazen, brusque, churlish, crass, crusty, discourteous, disrespectful, gross, gruff, impertinent, impolite, impudent, insolent, insulting, obstreperous, rough, saucy, surly, uncouth, ungracious, vulgar; barbarous, coarse, crude, ignorant, ill-bred, illiterate, inelegant, primitive, raw, rough, savage, uncivilized, uncouth, unpolished, unrefined, untaught; harsh, inclement, rough, stormy, turbulent, violent; approximate, guessed, unprecise. ANT.—affable, considerate, engaging, genial, tactful; chivalrous, civilized, courtly, cultured, genteel, refined; gentle, peaceful, placid, tranquil; exact, precise.

rugged, arduous, brawny, broken, corrugated, craggy, difficult, furrowed, harsh, husky, irregular, jagged, rough, scabrous, scratchy, uneven. ANT.—delicate, even, feeble, gentle, level, refined.

ruin, see destroy.

rule, axiom, canon, criterion, edict, formula, guide, law, maxim, method, norm, order, precept, prescript, principle, propriety, regulation, ruling, standard, statute, system; administration, authority, control, direction, domination, dominion, dynasty, empire, government, jurisdiction, mastery, regency, regime, reign, sovereignty, sway; command, control, dictate, direct, dominate, domineer, govern, influence, manage, prevail, regulate, restrain, superintend, sway. ANT.—accident, chance, hazard, irregularity; anarchy, chaos, disorder, disorganization, servility; abandon, follow, forsake, submit, yield.

rupture, break, burst, cleave, crack, crush, demolish, destroy, disjoin, fracture, gash, infringe, pound, puncture, rack, rend, rive, sever, shatter, slash, slice, smash, split, squeeze, sunder, tear. ANT.—join, mend, renew, repair, restore.

rural, agrarian, agrestic, agricultural, agronomic, backwoods, bucolic, country, countrified, farm, nonurban, pastoral, ranch, rustic, suburban. ANT.—commercial, industrial, urban, urbane.

rush, accelerate, bolt, bustle, dash, expedite, fly, gallop, hasten, hurry, precipitate, press, quicken, scurry, scuttle, speed, sprint, tear, zoom; activity, demand, haste, hurry. ANT.—delay, detain, hinder, procrastinate, tarry.

rustic, agrestic, agricultural, country, pastoral, rural; coarse, homely, inelegant, plain, simple; boorish, bucolic, countrified, rough, rude, uncouth, unpolished, unsophisticated; artless, unaffected. ANT.—commercial, industrial, urban; cultured, elegant, polished, refined, urbane; artificial, insincere, pretentious, unnatural.

rut, channel, crevice, furrow, groove, hollow, track, trench; course, custom, habit, practice, procedure, routine, rote, tedium.

ruthless, barbarous, bestial, brutal, brutish, coarse, cruel, ferocious, gross, harsh, implacable, inhuman, malevolent, merciless, pitiless, rancorous, relentless, remorseless, rough, rude, savage, tyrannical, unforgiving, unkind, vengeful, vindictive. ANT.—benevolent, charitable, compassionate, humane, merciful, sympathetic.

S

sack, demolish, despoil, devastate, loot, pillage, plunder, ravage, ruin, strip, waste; bag, pack, package, pocket.

sacred, blessed, consecrated, devout, divine, hallowed, holy, inviolable, pious, religious, sacrosanct, sanctified, saintly, spiritual, venerable. ANT.—blasphemous, evil, profane, sacrilegious, temporal, worldly.

sacrifice, abnegation, atonement, giving up, immolation, libation, loss, oblation, offering, self-denial, surrender, tribute; destroy, forfeit, forgo, give up, immolate, lose, offer, relinquish, renounce, surrender, yield.

sad, cheerless, dejected, depressed, despondent, disconsolate, dismal, doleful, downcast, funereal, gloomy, lugubrious, melancholy, mournful, pathetic, piteous, plaintive, somber, sorrowful, unhappy, woeful. ANT.—blithe, cheerful, elated, happy, joyful.

safe, certain, dependable, harmless, immune, impregnable, intact, invulnerable, protected, reliable, secure, snug, sure, trustworthy, unharmed, unscathed. ANT.—endangered, hazardous, insecure, perilous, unsafe.

safeguard, bulwark, fence, palladium, protection, refuge, shelter, shield; convoy, defense, escort, guard, guardian, security.

safety, asylum, custody, escape, harbor, haven, preservation, protection, refuge, sanctuary, security, shelter, surety; exemption, immunity. ANT.—danger, hazard, jeopardy, peril, risk.

sag, bend, crumple, decline, droop, incline, lean, list, settle, sink, slant, slope, stoop, strain, sway, tend, tilt, waver, weaken. ANT.—ascend, climb, mount, rise, straighten.

sage, intellectual, philosopher, professor, pundit, savant, scholar. ANT.—dolt, dunce, fool, idiot, lunatic.

salary, allowance, commission, compensation, earnings, fee, pay, payment, recompense, redress, reimbursement, remuneration, settlement, stipend, wages.

salient, clear, conspicuous, distinguished, impressive, manifest, marked, notable, noticeable, obvious, outstanding, prominent, significant, striking, visible. ANT.—hidden, inconspicuous, insignificant, minor, obscure, unimportant.

salubrious, see healthy.

same, alike, analogous, corresponding, duplicate, equal, equivalent, identical, indistinguishable, invariable, isomeric, like, matching, twin, uniform. ANT.—contrary, different, disparate, distinct, opposed.

sample, case, cutting, example, exemplification, illustration, instance, model, part, pattern, prototype, representation, slice, specimen; check, examine, experiment, inspect, judge, smell, taste, test, try.

sanction, allowance, approbation, approval, assent, authority, authorization, commendation, consent, endorsement, permission, permit, praise, privilege, ratification, support; allow, approve, authorize, confirm, endorse, favor, let, permit, promote, ratify, suffer, support, sustain, tolerate. ANT.—censure, denunciation, objection, prohibition, stricture; ban, exclude, forbid, prevent, refuse, veto.

sanctuary, see safety.

sane, healthy, lucid, normal, rational, reasonable, self-possessed, sensible, sober, sound, sound-minded, steady, wholesome. ANT.—delirious, demented, insane, irrational, maniacal.

sap, debilitate, deplete, drain, enervate, enfeeble, exhaust, impair, impoverish, mine, subvert, tunnel, undermine, unsettle, weaken.

sarcastic, acrimonious, biting, bitter, caustic, cutting, derisive, hostile, ironic, mocking, sardonic, satirical, scornful, sneering, taunting.

ANT.—affable, agreeable, amiable, courteous, gracious, respectful.

sate, cloy, content, fill, fill up, glut, gorge, gratify, pervade, please, quench, satiate, satisfy, saturate, slake, stuff. ANT.—deplete, drain, empty, exhaust, frustrate.

satire, abuse, banter, burlesque, derision, invective, irony, lampoon, mockery, parody, quip, raillery, ridicule, sarcasm, twist, wit.

satisfaction, comfort, content, contentment, delight, fulfillment, gladness, gratification, happiness, joy, pleasure, relief, serenity; amends, atonement; recompense, reimbursement, reparation. ANT.—despair, discontent, dissatisfaction, misery, sadness.

satisfactory, acceptable, adequate, ample, enough, fitting, gratifying, pleasing, satisfying, sufficient, suitable. ANT.—deficient, inadequate, insufficient, lacking, scanty.

satisfy, appease, cheer, comfort, compensate, content, gladden, gratify, please, remunerate, satiate; indemnify, repay; accomplish, complete, do, fill, fulfill, meet requirements, perform, qualify, suffice. ANT.—annoy, displease, fail to do, frustrate, neglect.

saturate, diffuse, drench, drown, fill, flood, immerse, impregnate, infiltrate, overfill, penetrate, permeate, pervade, run through, soak, steep, wet. ANT.—dehydrate, desiccate, dry, wipe.

savage, see ruthless.

save, accumulate, amass, collect, store; conserve, defend, deliver, economize, extricate, free, guard, hoard, keep, liberate, maintain, preserve, prevent, protect, redeem, rescue, reserve, safeguard, secure, shield, spare, uphold. ANT.—spend, waste; abandon, condemn, desert, impair, injure, leave.

savory, see delicious.

say, affirm, allege, articulate, assert, cite, declare, express, mention, pronounce, recite, rehearse, speak, state, talk, tell, utter.

saying, adage, affirmation, aphorism, apothegm, assertion, byword, citation, declaration, dictum, maxim, motto, pronunciation, proverb, quotation, remark, saw, statement, utterance.

scalding, blazing, blistering, burning, hot, red-hot, scorching, searing, torrid; ardent, fervent, fiery, flaming, passionate; peppery, pungent, spicy. ANT.—cold, freezing, frigid, frozen; apathetic, indifferent, phlegmatic, unconcerned; bland, dull, tasteless.

scan, audit, browse, consider, examine, inspect, investigate, regard, scrutinize, skim, survey, thumb over.

scandal, see disgrace.

scandalize, abuse, asperse, backbite, defame, detract, disgrace, disparage, libel, malign, offend, revile, shock, slander, traduce, vilify. ANT.—applaud, eulogize, honor, praise, respect.

scandalous, despicable, discreditable, disgraceful, disgusting, scarce, scrimpy, dishonorable, disreputable, flagrant, gross, hellish, ignominious, infamous, infernal, outrageous, shameful. ANT.—admirable, creditable, esteemed, honorable, respectable.

scanty, bare, few, inadequate, insufficient, lacking, limited, little, meager, narrow, pinched, ragged, scarce, scrimpy, skimpy, small, sparse, thin. ANT.—abundant, ample, plentiful, profuse, sufficient.

scarce, deficient, expensive, infrequent, isolated, limited, occasional, precious, rare, scanty, sparse, uncommon, unique, unplentiful. ANT.—cheap, customary, frequent, numerous, profuse.

scare, alarm, astound, cow, daunt, dismay, frighten, horrify, intimidate, petrify, shock, startle, terrify, terrorize, threaten. ANT.—calm, compose, encourage, inspirit, pacify, soothe.

scared, afraid, alarmed, apprehensive, faint-hearted, fearful, frightened, nervous, petrified, startled, timorous, trembling, upset, worried. ANT.—assured, bold, composed, confident, self-assured.

scatter, see disperse.

scene, display, exhibition, pageant, panorama, representation, scenery, setting, show, sight, spectacle, tableau, view.

scent, aroma, bouquet, essence, fragrance, fume, incense, odor, perfume, redolence, smell, stench, stink, sweetness.

scheme, arrangement, cabal, conspiracy, design, intrigue, machination, method, plan, plot, procedure, project, stratagem, system; chart, diagram, draft, graph, outline, sketch; conspire, contrive, delineate, design, devise, engineer, frame, intend, invent, map, outline, plan, plot, prepare, project, shape, sketch.

scholar, apprentice, disciple, learner, novice, pupil, student; intellectual, philomath, sage, savant. ANT.—dolt, dunce, fool, ignoramus, numskull, simpleton.

scholarly, see learned, pedantic.

scholarship, see knowledge.

scoff, deride, fleer, flout, gibe, jeer, mock, rail, ridicule, scorn, sneer, taunt, twit. ANT.—applaud, approve, commend, laud, praise.

scold, see reprimand.

scope, amount, area, compass, degree, expanse, extent, field, length, magnitude, measure, purview, range, reach, room, size, space, span, stretch, sweep, width.

scorch, blaze, brand, burn, char, incinerate, kindle, parch, roast, scald, sear, shrivel, singe. ANT.—douse, extinguish, quench, snuff out, stifle.

scorn, see contempt, disdain.

scrap, apportionment, bit, crumb, fragment, moiety, morsel, part, particle, piece, portion, section, segment, share; trash, waste material; brawl, fight, quarrel, squabble.

screen, camouflage, cloak, conceal, cover, defend, examine, guard, hide, inspect, protect, separate, shield, sift, sort, winnow.

scrub, clean, cleanse, purify, rub, scour, wash. ANT.—dirty, pollute, soil, stain, smirch.

scrupulous, see honest, just.

scrutinize, analyze, appraise, criticize, evaluate, examine, inspect, investigate, observe, probe, review, scan, search, stare, study, view. ANT.—disregard, ignore, neglect, overlook, slight.

search, examination, exploration, hunting, inquiry, investigation, pursuit, quest, research, seeking out; examine, explore, ferret out, hunt, investigate, look for, probe, ransack, rummage, scour, scrutinize, seek, shadow, track down, trail. ANT.—abandonment, cession, resignation, withdrawal; forgo, quit, relinquish, waive, vacate.

searching, see inquisitive.

season, age, complete, develop, mature, perfect, ripen; acclimate, accustom, harden, inure; flavor, spice.

seclusion, alienation, aloofness, apartness, concealment, insulation, isolation, loneliness, privacy, quarantine, quiet, refuge, remoteness, retirement, retreat, segregation, separation, sequestration, solitude, tranquility, withdrawal. ANT.—association, communion, connection, exposure, union.

secondary, see inferior.

secret, see clandestine.

secrete, see disguise, mask.

section, component, division, fragment, part, piece, portion, segment, share, slice, subdivision; country, district, division, domain, locality, province, realm, region, sector, territory, vicinity, zone.

secular, see lay, mundane.

secure, adjusted, assured, bound, certain, confident, definite, fastened, firm, fixed, immovable, indemnified, indubitable, inevitable, positive, safe, stable, sure, tight, undeniable, unharmed, unquestionable; accomplish, achieve, acquire, attain, earn, gain, get, grasp, obtain, possess, procure, realize, receive, win; assure, ensure, guarantee; defend, guard, protect, shield; adjust, bind, fasten, moor, settle, tighten. ANT.—doubtful, dubious, indefinite, questionable, uncertain; abandon, fail, forsake, relinquish; deny, disaffirm, disclaim, renounce; desert, leave, quit, relinquish, withdraw; detach, loosen, release, unfasten.

security, see refuge, safeguard.

sedate, calm, composed, demure, dignified, earnest, grave, imperturbable, proper, serene, serious, sober, solemn, staid. ANT.—excitable, flighty, frivolous, lively, mercurial.

see, behold, contemplate, descry, detect, discern, distinguish, espy, examine, gaze, grasp, heed, inspect, mark, mind, note, notice, observe, perceive, recognize, regard, scan, scrutinize, spy, stare, survey, understand, view, watch, witness; accompany, attend, escort; consult, discuss, interview, visit.

seek, see search.

seeming, apparent, external, ostensible, pretending, specious, superficial. ANT.—certain, definite, real, specific, true.

segment, allotment, apportionment, compartment, component, department, division, element, fraction, fragment, ingredient, moiety, parcel, part, piece, portion, scrap, section, share. ANT.—aggregate, entirety, sum, total, whole.

seize, see hinder, restrain.

select, adopt, appoint, choose, cull, decide, designate, elect, nominate, opt, pick, prefer, single out, specify. ANT.—eliminate, rebuff, refuse, reject.

selection, adoption, alternative, appropriation, choice, determination, election, favorite, option, pick, preference, reservation; assortment, collection.

self-contradictory, see irrational.

self-denial, see abstinence.

selfish, covetous, egoistic, egotistical, grasping, greedy, illiberal, mercenary, miserly, narrow, narrow-minded, parsimonious, rapacious, self-centered, self-indulgent, self-seeking, stingy, uncharitable, ungenerous. ANT.—altruistic, charitable, generous, liberal, magnanimous, philanthropic.

send, carry, cast, consign, convey, delegate, deliver, discharge, dispatch, drive, emit, fling, forward, hurl, impel, project, propel, ship, sling, throw, toss, transfer, transmit. ANT.—get, hold, keep, receive, retain.

senile, aged, ancient, decrepit, doddering, elderly, enfeebled, feeble, infirm, old, superannuated. ANT.—alert, strong, young, youthful, vigorous.

senior, advanced, chief, dean, elder, older, superior.

sensation, consciousness, excitement, feeling, passion, perception, response, sense, sensibility, sentiment. ANT.—apathy, insensibility, lethargy, narcosis, stupor.

sense, apprehension, connotation, consciousness, discernment, drift, explanation, feeling, gist,

implication, import, insight, intent, interpretation, judgment, meaning, notion, opinion, purport, purpose, reason, sagacity, sensation, sensibility, sentiment, significance, signification, understanding, view, wisdom.

senseless, absurd, brainless, dense, dull, dumb, fatuous, foolish, idiotic, insensible, nonsensical, obtuse, ridiculous, silly, stupid, unconscious, unwise, witless. ANT.—alert, brilliant, clever, discerning, perceptive.

sensibility, awareness, consciousness, delicacy, discernment, emotion, feeling, impressibility, insight, sensation, sense, sensitiveness, subtlety, susceptibility, sympathetic response, sympathy, taste. ANT.—anesthesia, coldness, detachment, indifference, insensitivity, nonchalance.

sensible, apprehensible, perceptible; alive, attentive, awake, aware, cognizant, comprehending, conscious, informed, perceiving, sentient; capable, careful, discreet, intelligent, judicious, keen, prudent, rational, reasonable, sagacious, sage, sharp, shrewd, sober, sound, thoughtful, wise. ANT.—foolish, half-witted, inattentive, insensitive, unaware.

sensitive, alert, aware, conscious, delicate, impressionable, liable, painful, perceptive, predisposed, prone, responsive, sentient, subject, susceptible, sore, tender; irritable, high-strung, nervous, tense. ANT.—heartless, indifferent, obdurate, unconscious, unfeeling; calm, placid, relaxed, serene, tranquil.

sensual, arousing, carnal, debauched, dissolute, earthy, fleshly, intemperate, lascivious, lecherous, lewd, licentious, orgiastic, pleasure-loving, salacious, self-indulgent, sensory, sensuous, sybaritic, unspiritual, voluptuous, wanton. ANT.—ascetic, chaste, moderate, self-controlled, spiritual, temperate.

sentence, see condemn.

sentiment, sensation; affection, emotion, feeling, passion, sensibility, sympathy, tenderness; impression, judgment, notion, opinion, perception, remark, thought; maxim, saying, toast.

sentimental, dreamy, effusive, emotional, fanciful, gushing, idealistic, imaginative, languishing, maudlin, mushy, mawkish, overemotional, poetic, romantic, sappy, tender, unrealistic, visionary. ANT.—factual, literal, matter-of-fact, pragmatic, realistic.

separate, detach, disconnect, disjoin, dissociate, dissolve, disunite, divide, isolate, part, rend, segregate, sequester, sever, sunder, withdraw; alone, apart, disjoined, distinct, disunited, divergent, independent, parted, private, radial, unconnected, unique. ANT.—assemble, attach, combine, fuse, intertwine; associated, connected, joined, mixed, united.

separation, alienation, disconnection, disengagement, disjunction, dissolution, disunion, division, divorce, insulation, isolation, loneliness, partition, quarantine, retirement, rupture, seclusion, segregation, sequestration, severance, solitude, withdrawal. ANT.—association, communion, connection, relationship, union.

sequence, arrangement, chain, following, graduation, order, progression, series, string, succession, train; consequence, result, sequel.

serene, see quiescent, quiet.

serenity, see peace, repose.

series, see sequence.

serious, great, important, momentous, weighty; austere, deep, earnest, grave, profound, sedate, sober, solemn, somber, staid, thoughtful; alarming, critical, dangerous, risky. ANT.—flippant, insignificant, small, trifling, trivial; informal, reassuring, relaxed, safe.

serve, advance, aid, answer, assist, attend, benefit, content, contribute, distribute, forward, give, help, promote, requite, satisfy, succor, suffice, supply, support, treat, uphold, wait on. ANT.—attack, combat, impede, oppose, rival.

service, advantage, assistance, avail, behalf, benefit, co-operation, favor, gain, good, help, interest, profit, use, utility; ceremony, ritual, rite, worship; business, duty, employment, function, labor, ministry, office.

serviceable, advantageous, applicable, beneficial, conducive, contributive, favorable, good, helpful, important, practical, profitable, salutary, usable, useful, valuable, wholesome. ANT.—deleterious, detrimental, impractical, ineffective, useless.

servile, see contemptible, ignoble.

set, adjust, anchor, appoint, arrange, deposit, dispose, establish, expose, fix, lay, locate, mount, place, plant, predetermine, put, regulate, settle, situate, stand, station; coagulate, congeal, harden, jell, solidify, thicken; established, firm, fixed, formal, immovable, located, placed, positive; arrangement, association, attitude, circle, class, club, cluster, collection, company, coterie, group, party, position, posture, series.

settle, adjudicate, close, conclude, confirm, decide, determine, dispose, end, reconcile, resolve, terminate; drop, fall, sink, subside; calm, pacify, quiet, tranquilize; colonize, domesticate, people; establish, fix, locate, place, put, set, station; adjust, arbitrate, regulate, stabilize, straighten. ANT.—doubt, hesitate, suspend, vacillate, waver; anger, antagonize, roil, stir; destroy, disestablish, raze, ruin, unsettle; confuse, disarrange, disorganize, disrupt, entangle.

settlement, close, completion, conclusion, end, finale, issue, termination; decision, deduction, inference, judgment; colonization, colony, community, establishment; adjustment, compensation, pay, recompense, reimbursement, remuneration, reward; agreement, arrangement, compact, contract, covenant, pledge, understanding.

sever, see divide, separate.

several, different, distinct, divers, diverse, manifold, many, numerous, quite a few, separate, sundry, unlike, various. ANT.—one, none.

severe, acute, arduous, austere, despotic, distressing, domineering, drastic, exacting, extreme, forbidding, grim, hard, harsh, inflexible, intense, obdurate, oppressive, relentless, rigid, rigorous, sharp, stern, stiff, strict, stringent, uncompromising, unmitigated, unrelenting, unyielding, violent; plain, simple, unadorned. ANT.—compassionate, courteous, gentle, lenient, placid; beautified, decorated, embellished.

sew, baste, bind, fasten, fix, mend, patch, piece, refit, repair, restore, seam, stitch, tack, tailor. ANT.—deface, destroy, hurt, rend, ruin.

shabby, see inferior, poor.

shade, brilliance, color, complexion, dye, hue, paint, pigment, saturation, stain, tincture, tinge, tint; shadow, umbrage; cloud, darken, dim, eclipse, obscure. ANT.—achromatism, paleness, transparency; brighten, illuminate, manifest, reveal.

shake, agitate, convulse, discourage, dishearten, dissuade, flutter, intimidate, jar, joggle, jolt, jounce, oscillate, quake, quiver, rock, shiver, shudder, sway, totter, tremble, trill, vibrate, wave, waver.

shallow, cursory, exterior, flimsy, frivolous, imperfect, inconsiderable, senseless, silly, simple, slight, stupid, superficial, trifling, trivial. ANT.—bottomless, complete, deep, intelligent, profound, thorough, unfathomable.

sham, affect, assume, dissimulate, feign, imitate, personate, pretend, simulate; counterfeit, deceit, delusion, dissimulation, fake, fakery, fraud, humbug, imitation, mockery, pretense, pretext, ruse, stratagem, trick, wile. ANT.—disclose, expose, reveal, unmask, unveil; actuality, fact, reality, substance, truth.

shame, abash, degrade, discomfit, discredit, dishonor, embarrass, humiliate, mortify; abashment, chagrin, discomfiture, embarrassment, humiliation, mortification, remorse; baseness, contempt, disfavor, disgrace, dishonor, disrepute, ignominy, infamy, odium, opprobrium, reproach, scandal. ANT.—encourage, glorify, honor, respect, uphold; contentment, impenitence, satisfaction, serenity, tranquility; dignity, glory, honor, praise, respect.

shameful, see scandalous.

shape, appearance, aspect, build, cast, configuration, conformation, construction, contour, cut, figure, form, frame, guise, image, mold, outline, pattern; arrange, cast, combine, compose, constitute, construct, create, develop, devise, direct, discipline, fashion, forge, form, frame, invent, make, make up, model, mold, organize, produce, regulate, sketch. ANT.—contortion, deformity, distortion, malformation, mutilation; destroy, disfigure, distort, injure, mar, wreck.

shapeless, amorphic, amorphous, deformed, disfigured, formless, irregular, misshapen, unshapely, unsymmetrical. ANT.—proportionate, proportioned, shapely, symmetrical, well-formed.

share, allotment, bit, contingent, dividend, division, dole, dose, fraction, fragment, helping, parcel, part, percentage, piece, portion, quota, ration, section, segment; administer, allot, apportion, appropriate, assign, deal, dispense, distribute, divide, experience, parcel, partake, participate in, partition, portion. ANT.—bulk, entirety, sum, totality, whole; aggregate, amass, combine, unite, withhold.

shared, see mutual.

sharp, acute, honed, keen, pointed, razor-edged, sharpened; acrid, barbed, biting, bitter, cutting, peppery, piquant, pungent, sour, spicy, stinging; excruciating, penetrating, piercing, severe, shrill; astute, brilliant, clever, cunning, discerning, incisive, intelligent, quick, sagacious, shrewd, wily, wise, witty; abrupt, harsh, precipitous, rough, rugged, steep. ANT.—blunt, dull, pointless, unsharpened; bland, tasteless, unsavory; delicate, faint, low, melodious, mild, soft; dull-witted, inept, insipid, stupid, vapid; even, flat, gradual, level, smooth.

shatter, see break.

shattered, broken, collapsed, crushed, demolished, destroyed, flattened, fractured, hurt, interrupted, mutilated, reduced, ruptured, separated, slivered, smashed, splintered, wrecked. ANT.—intact, integral, repaired, sound, united.

shelter, asylum, harbor, haven, refuge, retreat, sanctuary; cover, defense, lee, protection, safety, screen, security, shield; cloak, clothe, conceal, cover, curtain, defend, disguise, ensconce, envelop, guard, harbor, hide, house, mask, preserve, protect, safeguard, screen, secure, shield, shroud, veil. ANT.—danger, exposure, hazard, jeopardy, menace, threat; endanger, expose, ignore, neglect, uncover.

shield, avert, forbid, repel; also see shelter.

shift, displace, exchange, remove, substitute; adapt, adjust, alter, change, convert, moderate, modify, transfigure, transform, vary; move, stir, turn,

veer. ANT.—keep, retain; continue, establish, preserve, stabilize; cease, halt, rest, stop.

shifting, see fickle.

shine, beam, blaze, dazzle, flare, flash, glare, gleam, glimmer, glisten, glitter, glow, irradiate, radiate, scintillate, shimmer, sparkle, twinkle; excel, surpass; buff, burnish, polish, wax.

shining, see magnificent, radiant.

ship, consign, convey, dispatch, forward, remit, route, send, transmit, transport; deport, dismiss, send away.

shock, alarm, amaze, appall, astonish, astound, disconcert, dumfound, embarrass, flabbergast, frighten, horrify, offend, startle, stun, surprise, terrify, terrorize. ANT.—calm, console, mitigate, pacify, prepare, soothe.

shocking, see horrible.

shoot, cast, catapult, dart, discharge, eject, emit, expel, fire, hit, hurl, propel; kill, wound; bloom, bud, germinate, sprout; branch, channel, chute, offshoot, scion, sprout, sucker, trough, twig.

shore, bank, beach, border, brink, coast, margin, seacoast, seaside, strand; brace, buttress, prop, stabilize, support.

short, compact, diminutive, little, low, slight, small, tiny; abbreviated, abridged, abrupt, brief, compendious, compressed, concise, condensed, laconic, pithy, precise, succinct, summary, terse; deficient, inadequate, insufficient, lacking, limited, scanty; abrupt, curt, uncivil. ANT.—colossal, enormous, gigantic, titanic, towering; diffuse, jumbled, redundant, repetitive, wordy; abundant, adequate, excessive, profuse, sufficient; civil, courteous, gracious, patient, polite.

shortcoming, see defect, imperfection.

shorten, see contract, diminish.

shout, acclaim, bellow, call out, clamor, cry, cry out, ejaculate, exclaim, howl, roar, scream, screech, shriek, vociferate, yell, yelp. ANT.—intimate, murmur, mutter, suggest, whisper.

shove, butt, crowd, drive, elbow, force, impel, jostle, press, propel, push, ram, shoulder, thrust. ANT.—drag, halt, pull, stop.

show, array, demonstration, display, entertainment, exhibition, exposition, exposure, flourish, ostentation, pageantry, parade, performance, production, spectacle, splendor, splurge; appearance, semblance; pretense, puppetry, sham, simulation, speciousness; disclose, display, exhibit, expose, indicate, parade, present, reveal, unfold; demonstrate, evidence, explain, manifest, prove, verify; conduct, direct, guide, usher; inform, instruct, teach.

showy, affected, artificial, ceremonious, dramatic, flashy, gaudy, glaring, histrionic, melodramatic, ornate, pompous, theatrical, tinseled. ANT.—genuine, humble, modest, subdued, unaffected.

shred, bit, fragment, frazzle, jot, mite, particle, rag, scrap, smidgen, speck, strip, tatter; lacerate, rend, rip, slice, slit, split, strip, tear, wound. ANT.—aggregate, bulk, mass, quantity, volume; heal, join, mend, repair, restore, unite.

shrewd, artful, clandestine, covert, crafty, cunning, foxy, furtive, guileful, insidious, sly, stealthy, surreptitious, tricky, underhand, wily; acute, alert, astute, careful, circumspect, clever, discerning, ingenious, intelligent, knowing, mindful, observant, perspicacious, prudent, reflective, sagacious, sapient, sharp. ANT.—candid, frank, genuine, open, sincere; dense, frivolous, ignorant, impetuous, undiscerning.

shrill, see keen, severe.

shrink, balk, contract, cringe, decline, decrease, deflate, diminish, droop, dwindle, fail, flinch,

languish, lessen, quail, recoil, shrivel, waste, weaken, wilt, wince, withdraw, wither. ANT.—expand, grow, rejuvenate, renew, revive.

shun, see avoid, escape.

shut, close, lock, seal; debar, exclude, preclude; confine, immure, imprison, incarcerate; complete, conclude, end, finish, terminate. ANT.—open, unbar, unlock; clear, free, liberate, release; begin, commence, initiate, start.

shy, see modest, reserved.

sick, ailing, confined, diseased, ill, impaired, indisposed, infirm, invalid, morbid, sickly, unhealthy, unwell. ANT.—hale, hardy, healthy, robust, vigorous.

sift, analyze, discuss, evaluate, examine, investigate, probe, screen, scrutinize, separate, sort, winnow; bolt, colander, filter, grade, screen, size, sort, strain.

sign, augury, badge, emblem, gesture, identification, indication, manifestation, mark, note, notice, omen, portent, presage, proof, representation, signal, suggestion, symbol, symptom, token.

signal, alarm, cue, gesture, indicator, mark, message, sign, warning; conspicuous, famous, important, memorable, momentous, outstanding, prominent, remarkable, salient, striking.

significance, consequence, effect, force, implication, import, importance, meaning, point, purpose, relevance, substance, weight.

significant, critical, emphatic, expressive, grave, important, indicative, meaningful, momentous, notable, outstanding, prominent, remarkable, serious, suggestive, telling, vital, weighty, worthy. ANT.—inconsequential, insignificant, petty, shallow, trivial.

signify, denote, designate, disclose, express, imply, import, indicate, intimate, manifest, mean, purport, reveal, show, specify, suggest. ANT.—conceal, cover, hide, obscure, withhold.

silent, calm, hushed, mute, noiseless, peaceful, placid, quiescent, quiet, reserved, reticent, secretive, still, taciturn, tight-lipped, tranquil, uncommunicative. ANT.—clamorous, communicative, loquacious, noisy, raucous, voluble.

silhouette, configuration, conformation, contour, delineation, figure, form, outline, profile, shape.

silly, see irrational, preposterous, ridiculous.

similar, akin, alike, allied, analogous, comparable, correlative, correspondent, corresponding, facsimile, homogeneous, like, parallel, reciprocal, related, resembling. ANT.—alien, different, dissimilar, divergent, opposed, unlike.

similarity, affinity, analogy, association, comparison, concordance, conformity, correlation, correspondence, harmony, homogeneity, likeness, parallelism, parity, relation, resemblance, semblance, simile, similitude. ANT.—difference, disparity, distinction, divergence, variance.

simple, apparent, easy, effortless, elementary, facile, mere, obvious, pure, simplistic, single, unblended, uncompounded, unmixed; homely, humble, modest, plain, unadorned; artless, frank, naive, natural, open, unaffected, unpretentious, unsophisticated; asinine, credulous, foolish, gullible, ignorant, oafish, silly. ANT.—complicated, complex, difficult, intricate; decorated, embellished, opulent, ornate; contrived, deceptive, pretentious, sophisticated; discerning, intelligent, judicious, sagacious, wise.

simulate, see mimic.

simultaneous, accompanying, coeval, coincident, concomitant, concurrent, contemporaneous, synchronal, synchronous. ANT.—foregoing, following, preceding, prior, subsequent.

sin, see evil, offense.

sincere, candid, conscientious, direct, earnest, frank, genuine, guileless, heartfelt, honest, ingenuous, open, straightforward, true, trustworthy, truthful, unaffected, undisguised, unfeigned, unreserved, upright, veracious. ANT.—deceitful, deceptive, evasive, false, hypocritical, untrustworthy.

sincerity, see honesty.

sinewy, able-bodied, active, athletic, brawny, burly, energetic, firm, hardy, husky, manly, mighty, muscular, powerful, robust, stalwart, steely, strapping, strong, sturdy, tough, vigorous, virile, wiry. ANT.—delicate, emaciated, feeble, puny, weak.

sinful, see bad, corrupt, immoral.

sing, carol, chant, chirp, croon, hum, hymn, intone, lilt, trill, troll, vocalize, warble, yodel.

singe, see scorch.

single, celibate, distinctive, elemental, individual, isolated, marked, one, only, particular, pure, separate, simple, singular, sole, solitary, special, specific, unaccompanied, unique, unmixed, unwed. ANT.—associated, common, general, multiple, ordinary, universal.

singular, see eccentric, extraordinary, rare.

sinister, adverse, corrupt, deleterious, dire, disastrous, dishonest, evil, foreboding, harmful, hostile, malefic, mischievous, ominous, pernicious, perverse, threatening, unfavorable, unlucky. ANT.—auspicious, expedient, favorable, opportune, propitious.

sink, collapse, decline, decrease, descend, diminish, drop, fall, slump, subside; droop, extend downward, hang; be submerged, engulf, go down, immerse, touch bottom. ANT.—arise, ascend, climb, mount, surge; come up, float, rise, stay afloat, swim.

site, district, locality, locus, place, position, region, section, situation, spot, station.

situation, case, circumstance, condition, exigency, plight, predicament, state, status; employment, environment, job, location, place, position, post, setting, site, spot, station, surroundings, whereabouts.

size, amplitude, area, bigness, bulk, capacity, dimensions, enormity, expanse, extent, greatness, immensity, largeness, magnitude, measurement, mass, quantity, scope, space, vastness, volume.

skeleton, frame, shell, structure; also see outline.

skeptic, agnostic, apostate, cynic, deist, detractor, dissenter, doubter, free-thinker, idolator, infidel, nihilist, questioner, schismatic, unbeliever. ANT.—believer, devotee, disciple, evangelist, worshiper.

skepticism, agnosticism, cynicism, disbelief, distrust, doubt, doubting, hesitation, incredulity, infidelity, misgiving, mistrust, questioning, suspicion, wavering. ANT.—belief, certainty, conviction, faith, reliance, trust.

sketch, see outline.

skill, cunning, ingenuity, knack; also see dexterity, facility.

skillful, able, accomplished, adept, adroit, apt, capable, clever, competent, cunning, deft, dexterous, efficient, expert, handy, ingenious, masterful, practiced, proficient, ready, skilled, talented, trained, versed. ANT.—awkward, blundering, clumsy, inept, inexperienced.

skin, bark, coat, covering, cuticle, derma, dermis, epidermis, hide, husk, integument, lamina, lining, parchment, peel, pelt, plating, rind, surface, tegument, veneer.

skip, drop, miss, neglect; also see eliminate, exclude, ignore.

slack, disengaged, free, indefinite, lax, limp, loose, relaxed, slow, stagnant, unbound, unfastened, untied, vague; backward, careless, dilatory, dissolute, heedless, indifferent, negligent, remiss, tardy, unrestrained, wanton. ANT.—drawn, engaged, fast, taut, tied; alert, careful, disciplined, dutiful, restrained.

slander, see libel, scandalize.

slant, bent, bias, disposition, inclination, leaning, partiality, penchant, predilection, predisposition, prejudice, proclivity, proneness, propensity, tendency, turn; acclivity, angle, declivity, divergence, grade, list, obliquity, slope, tilt; lean, slope, tilt, tip, slope.

slavery, serfdom, thralldom, vassalage; also see captivity.

slaughter, see kill, massacre.

sleazy, feeble, flabby, flaccid, flimsy, fragile, limp, poor, tenuous, thin, trashy, weak, worthless. ANT.—excellent, fine, firm, forceful, strong.

sleek, glossy, lustrous, oily, polished, satiny, shiny, silky, slick, smooth, velvety. ANT.—coarse, dry, dull, harsh, rough.

sleep, catnap, coma, doze, dozing, drowse, hibernation, lethargy, nap, nod, repose, rest, siesta, slumber, snooze, somnolism, stupor, trance.

slender, feeble, flimsy, gaunt, lank, lean, meager, narrow, rare, scanty, scrawny, skinny, slight, slim, spare, tenuous, thin, trivial. ANT.—broad, bulky, fat, strong, thick, wide.

slide, glide, skate, skid, skim, skip, slip, slither; chute, incline, ramp.

slight, disregard, ignore, neglect, omit, overlook, skip; also see slender.

sling, cast, dangle, hang, heave, hoist, hurl, impel, pitch, propel, shove, suspend, throw, toss.

slip, blunder, boner, error, fallacy, fault, fluff, inaccuracy, indiscretion, lapse, misstep, mistake. ANT.—accuracy, perfection, precision, truth.

slope, see slant.

slothful, see lazy.

slow, crawling, creeping, dawdling, deliberate, dull, gradual, laggard, languid, leisurely, lingering, loitering, moderate, slack, torpid, unready; apathetic, dilatory, idle, indolent, lazy, lethargic, negligent, phlegmatic, procrastinating, sleepy, sluggish, tired; belated, delayed, overdue. ANT.—quick, rapid, speedy, swift; conscientious, enthusiastic, industrious, lively, zealous; prompt, punctilious, punctual, timely.

sluggish, see slow.

slumber, see sleep.

sly, artful, astute, calculating, clandestine, covert, crafty, cunning, deceitful, designing, foxy, furtive, guileful, insidious, knowing, mischievous, nimble, scheming, shifty, shrewd, stealthy, subtle, surreptitious, traitorous, tricky, underhand, wary, wily. ANT.—artless, candid, frank, genuine, open, sincere.

small, diminutive, feeble, inconsiderable, insignificant, little, microscopic, miniature, minute, petty, puny, pygmy, scanty, slender, slight, tiny, trivial, ungenerous, weak, wee, young. ANT.—enormous, generous, huge, immense, powerful.

smart, adroit, apt, clever, dexterous, quick, quick-witted, skillful, talented, witty; acute, alert, bright, intelligent, keen, sharp, shrewd; chic, dapper, modish, stylish. ANT.—awkward, bungling, clumsy, slow; dense, dull, stupid, unintelligent; dowdy, frowzy, shabby.

smash, see rupture.

smell, see odor.

smooth, even, flat, flush, level, plane; glossy, polished, silky, sleek, slick; diplomatic, glib, suave, unruffled, urbane; calm, mild, still, tranquil. ANT.—craggy, jagged, rocky, uneven; hairy, rough, rugged; blunt, rash, rude, tactless; agitated, inflamed, furious, stormy, violent.

snag, see obstacle.

snare, ambush, apprehend, arrest, capture, catch, clutch, grasp, grip, lure, net, seize, trap; artifice, deception, decoy, hoax, lure, pitfall, ruse, stratagem, trap, trick, wile. ANT.—free, liberate, release, unchain, unshackle; fact, fidelity, genuineness, honesty, truth.

sneer, fleer, scoff; also see mock.

snub, abash, crush, cut, discomfit, disdain, disregard, humble, humiliate, ignore, neglect, rebuke. ANT.—comfort, honor, love, regard, respect.

snug, compact, constricted, contracted, firm, narrow, neat, stretched, taut, tense, tight, trim; close, comfortable, cozy, warm. ANT.—lax, loose, open, relaxed, slack; cold, detached, distant, removed, uncomfortable.

soar, circle, dart, flit, float, flutter, fly, glide, hover, mount, remain aloft, sail, swoop, wing. ANT.—descend, fall, plummet, sink, topple.

sober, abstemious, austere, calm, dispassionate, earnest, grave, moderate, quiet, reasonable, sedate, serious, solemn, staid, steady, temperate, unintoxicated, unruffled. ANT.—boisterous, dissipated, drunk, excited, immoderate, joyful, overwrought.

social, affable, communicative, out-going; also see hospitable, pleasant.

soft, amenable, bland, compassionate, downy, elastic, flaccid, flexible, fluffy, gentle, impressible, indulgent, lenient, malleable, meek, mellow, merciful, mild, pliable, pliant, silky, smooth, spongy, subdued, supple, tender, tolerant, tractable, yielding. ANT.—brittle, cruel, domineering, insensible, self-possessed, unyielding.

soften, abate, allay, alleviate, diminish, dissolve, extenuate, lessen, melt, mitigate, moderate, relax, relieve, solace, soothe, tenderize, thaw, weaken. ANT.—aggravate, agitate, augment, increase, irritate, lengthen.

soil, continent, country, earth, field, ground, land, plain, region, tract; blemish, blight; also see defile.

solace, see console.

sole, alone, deserted, desolate, isolated, lonely, secluded, unaided; individual, lone, one, only, remaining, single, solitary. ANT.—accompanied, attended, surrounded; collective, multiple, public, social.

solemn, august, awe-inspiring, ceremonious, consequential, formal, imposing, impressive, majestic, momentous, precise, regular, reverential, ritualistic; austere, earnest, grave, grim, heavy, intense, reserved, sedate, serious, sober, somber, staid, stern, thoughtful. ANT.—informal, insignificant, ordinary, transitory, uneventful; animated, cheerful, frivolous, giddy, lively.

solid, compact, dense, firm, hard, rigid, sound, stable, substantial, unyielding. ANT.—liquid, porous, vaporous, vulnerable, weak.

solitary, see sole.

solitude, alienation, asylum, concealment, isolation, loneliness, privacy, quiet, refuge, retirement, retreat, seclusion, silence, stillness. ANT.—clamor, exposure, notoriety, publicity, tumult.

solve, decipher, discover, elucidate, explain, interpret, resolve, unfold, untangle. ANT.—complicate, involve, tangle.

somatic, bodily, carnal, corporal, corporeal, fleshly, human, material, natural, organic, physical, substantial, tangible, unspiritual. ANT.—ethereal, mental, spiritual.

somber, bleak, dull, funereal; also see dismal.

soon, beforehand, before long, early, quickly, shortly. ANT.—late, overdue, slow, tardy.

soothe, allay, alleviate, assuage, calm, cheer, comfort, compose, console, ease, encourage, gladden, lull, mollify, pacify, please, relieve, solace, sympathize, tranquilize. ANT.—afflict, annoy, antagonize, distress, vex.

soothing, docile, relaxed, soft; also see gentle, peaceful.

sophisticated, astute, blase, cultivated, cultured, experienced, knowledgeable, polished, refined, wise, worldly. ANT.—artless, crude, immature, ingenuous, naive.

sorcery, see magic.

sordid, base, debased, depraved, dirty, foul, loathsome, obscene, odious, revolting, squalid, vicious, vile, vulgar, wicked; abject, contemptible, degraded, despicable, ignoble, low, mean, worthless, wretched. ANT.—attractive, charming, decent, laudable; distinguished, eminent, honorable, noble, upright.

sorrow, affliction, anguish, contrition, distress, grief, heartache, lamentation, misery, misfortune, mourning, penitence, regret, remorse, sadness, trial, tribulation, woe. ANT.—comfort, delight, happiness, joy, solace.

sorrowful, see gloomy, melancholy.

sort, category, character, class, description, kind, nature, species, strain, type, variety.

sound, binding, cogent, durable, effective, efficacious, faithful, genuine, hale, healthy, intact, legal, logical, powerful, reliable, satisfactory, solvent, stable, strong, substantial, unimpaired, valid, vigorous, weighty; din, noise, note, tone. ANT.—counterfeit, defective, impaired, spurious, void; hush, quiet, stillness.

sour, acid, acrid, acrimonious, astringent, bitter, complaining, curdled, embittered, glum, grouchy, morose, peevish, querulous, rancid, sharp, spoiled, sullen, tart, vinegary. ANT.—amiable, cheerful, cordial, kindly, sugary, sweet.

source, agent, cause, determinant, incentive, inducement, motive, origin, principle, reason; beginning, birth, commencement, cradle, derivation, foundation, fountain, inception, incipience, origin, primogenitor, rise, root, spring, start, wellspring. ANT.—consequence, effect, result; harvest, issue, outcome, product, termination.

souvenir, see memorial.

spacious, see roomy.

spare, rescue, safeguard; also see preserve.

sparkle, see glare.

speak, announce, articulate, chatter, communicate, converse, debate, declaim, declare, discourse, discuss, express, proclaim, pronounce, report, say, talk, tell, utter, vocalize, voice.

special, choice, definite, determinate, distinctive, exceptional, exclusive, extraordinary, individual, particular, peculiar, proper, rare, restricted, singular, specific, uncommon, unique, unusual. ANT.—broad, commonplace, ecumenical, prevalent, universal.

specific, categorical, characteristic, concrete, definite, especial, exact, explicit, express, individual, limited, particular, peculiar, precise, special. ANT.—general, generic, indefinite, uncertain, vague.

specify, appoint, call, choose, denominate, designate, entitle, individualize, mention, name, particularize, select, single out, stipulate. ANT.—discard, generalize, hint, miscall, misname, reject.

specimen, instance, unit; see also example.

speck, crumb, smidgen; see also particle.

spectacle, parade, representation, scene, splurge; see also display.

speculate, apprehend, assume, believe, conjecture, consider, contemplate, deduce, guess, imagine, meditate, muse, ponder, presume, reflect, suppose, surmise, think, weigh. ANT.—ascertain, conclude, demonstrate, prove, substantiate.

speech, articulation, chatter, communication, diction, discourse, enunciation, lecture, locution, oration, pronunciation, report; see also conversation; language.

speed, facilitate, forward, further, promote, rush, urge; see also hasten.

spend, consume, deplete, disburse, dispense, dissipate, exhaust, expend, liquidate, pay, scatter, squander, use, waste. ANT.—cache, collect, conserve, hoard, pocket, retain.

sphere, ball, circle, compass, department, domain, globe, orb, province, realm, scope, spheroid.

spirit, apparition, ghost, phantom, specter, vision; animation, courage, energy, enthusiasm, fervor, fortitude, life, liveliness, verve, vigor, vitality, vivacity, zeal; intent, meaning; disposition, feeling, mood, nature, temper; essence, psyche, soul, substance.

spiritual, divine, ecclesiastical, ethereal, ghostly, holy, immaterial, incorporeal, pure, refined, religious, sacred, supernatural, unearthly, unworldly. ANT.—carnal, corporeal, material, physical, secular, worldly.

spite, see malice.

spiteful, antagonistic, disagreeable, hostile, ill-natured, malevolent, malicious, malign, mean, rancorous, surly, ugly, vengeful, venomous, vicious, vindictive. ANT.—forgiving, friendly, generous, helpful, merciful.

splendid, brilliant, bright, dazzling, effulgent, eminent, excellent, glorious, gorgeous, grand, illustrious, magnificent, radiant, refulgent, resplendent, shining, showy, sumptuous, superb. ANT.—drab, dull, humble, mediocre, unimpressive.

splendor, brilliance, radiance; see also luster.

split, rive, sever, shred, wound. see also rip; sever.

spoil, decay, decompose, disintegrate, putrefy, rot, waste; corrupt, damage, debase, destroy, disfigure, harm, impair, injure, mar, pervert, ruin, vitiate; booty, loot, plunder. ANT.—flourish, grow, increase, luxuriate, thrive; enhance, improve, mend, perfect, repair.

spoken, announced, expressed, oral, unwritten, uttered, verbal, vocal, voiced. ANT.—documentary, nonverbal, recorded, written.

sponsor, advertiser, advocate, backer, champion, helper, patron, protector, subscriber, supporter, surety; godparent.

spontaneous, automatic, casual, extemporaneous, impulsive, instinctive, involuntary, offhand, unbidden, unconscious, unforced, unintentional, unwilling. ANT.—deliberate, designed, intended, premeditated, rehearsed.

sport, contest, match, merriment; caper, frolic, gamble, play, revel, romp, stake, toy, wager; display, exhibit, wear; see also recreation.

spread, circulate, diffuse, dispense, disperse, disseminate, distribute, exhibit, expand, extend, open, promulgate, propagate, publish, radiate, scatter, sow, stretch, strew, unfold, unroll, unseal. ANT.—collect, conceal, condense, suppress, tighten.

sprightly, agile, animated, blithe, brisk, buoyant, cheerful, debonair, effervescent, elated, hopeful, jocund, lively, quick, spirited, sportive, vivacious. ANT.—dejected, depressed, despondent, gloomy, pessimistic.

spring, birth, cradle, derivation, foundation. see also beginning.

sprout, bud, burgeon, develop, germinate, grow, shoot. ANT.—decrease, shrink, wither.

spry, active, agile, alacritous, alert, blithe, brisk, flexible, frisky, lively, nimble, quick, spirited, sprightly, supple, vivacious. ANT.—feeble, inactive, lethargic, sluggish, torpid.

spur, cause, incitement, principle, purpose, reason; see also incentive.

squabble, see quarrel.

squalid, dirty, filthy, foul, grimy, muddy, soiled, sordid, unclean; base, contemptible, despicable, low, mean, miserable, pitiful, poor, shabby, unkempt, wretched. ANT.—clean, immaculate, pure, spotless; appealing, attractive, comfortable, inviting, presentable.

squander, abuse, consume, corrode, dissipate, drain, exhaust, expend, lavish, misspend, misuse, scatter, spend, splurge, waste. ANT.—economize, hoard, invest, preserve, retain.

squeamish, see particular.

stability, composure, steadiness; see also balance.

stable, balanced, constant, determined, durable, enduring, equable, established, firm, fixed, immovable, immutable, lasting, permanent, regular, resolute, secure, settled, solid, staunch, steadfast, steady, unwavering. ANT.—erratic, fluctuating, mercurial, mutable, vacillating.

staid, dignified, earnest, grave, reserved, sedate, serious, sober, solemn, steady, stuffy, unimaginative. ANT.—boisterous, flighty, frivolous, impulsive, volatile.

stain, befoul, blemish, blight, blot, defile, discolor, disgrace, dishonor, mark, soil, spot, sully, taint, tarnish; color, dye, tinge, tint. ANT.—cleanse, decorate, honor, purify; blanch, bleach, whiten.

stale, see insipid.

stand, abide, bear, continue, endure, hold, last, persist, prevail, remain, suffer, survive, sustain, tolerate; discontinue, halt, hold, pause, remain, rest, stay, stop. ANT.—falter, succumb, surrender, weaken, yield; advance, continue, develop, grow, progress, run.

standard, gauge, touchstone; see also criterion.

start, see commence; origin.

startle, alarm, amaze, astonish, astound, bewilder, confound, daze, disconcert, dumbfound, flabbergast, overwhelm, petrify, shock, stun, surprise, unsettle. ANT.—caution, forewarn, prepare, signal, warn.

starving, craving, dying, longing, weakening; see also hungry.

state, claim, explain, express, propound, recount, say, specify, utter; see also assert; recite; situation.

stately, courtly, lordly, monarchial, princely, regal, royal, ruling, sovereign, supreme; see also majestic.

statement, acknowledgment, affirmation, allegation, announcement, assertion, declaration, dictum, mention, profession, proposition, report, specification, thesis.

status, caste, circumstance, condition, distinction, footing, grade, place, position, rank, reputation, situation, standing, state, station.

statute, act, decree, edict, injunction, law, order, ordinance, regulation, ruling.

staunch, reliable, trusty. see also loyal.

stay, abide, delay, halt, linger, lodge, pause, persist, remain, sojourn, stand, tarry, visit, wait; arrest, check, hinder, impede, obstruct, restrain, retard. ANT.—dart, hasten, leave, progress, scurry; assist, encourage, facilitate, promote, sustain.

steady, inflexible, unswerving, unyielding; see also stable.

steal, pillage, plagiarize, snitch, swipe; see also embezzle; rob.

steep, abrupt, angular, craggy, hilly, perpendicular, precipitous, rugged, sharp, sheer, sudden, vertical. ANT.—flat, gradual, horizontal, level, smooth.

steer, control, escort, supervise; see also guide.

stench, fetidness, fetor, stink. see also odor.

sterile, arid, barren, childless, fallow, fruitless, impotent, infecund, infertile, unfruitful, unproductive, unprolific, worthless; antiseptic, decontaminated, pure, sanitary, sterilized. ANT.—fecund, fertile, fruitful, generative, prolific, proliferous; contaminated, infectious, noxious, unhygienic, unsanitary.

stern, see severe.

stiff, firm, hard, hardened, inflexible, petrified, rigid, solid, tense, unbending; see also severe.

stigma, brand, defect, disfigurement, imprint, mark, scar, stain, trace, vestige.

still, hushed, inaudible, inert, motionless, mum, mute, noiseless, quiet, quiescent, soundless, stagnant, stationary, undisturbed, unruffled; calm, gentle, meek, mild, passive, peaceful, patient, placid, silent, tranquil; besides, but, furthermore, however, yet. ANT.—clamorous, disturbed, loud, piercing, stirring, tumultuous; aggressive, dynamic, hostile, impassive, perturbed.

stilted, affected, bombastic, fustian, grandiose, grandiloquent, high-flown, high-sounding, magniloquent, pompous, pretentious, swelling, turgid. ANT.—candid, honest, humble, reserved, shy, simple.

stimulate, animate, arouse, awaken, disquiet, energize, excite, impel, incite, instigate, invigorate, irritate, kindle, pique, provoke, rouse, stir up, urge. ANT.—calm, deaden, pacify, quell, tranquilize.

stimulus, arousal, encouragement, goad, stimulant; see also incentive.

stingy, see greedy; miserly.

stir, beat, mix; impel, persuade; see also move.

stock, accumulation, fund, goods, hoard, inventory, merchandise, produce, provision, reserve, store, wares; calves, cattle, cows, herd, steers; fill, fill up, furnish, replenish, store, supply.

stoical, assiduous, forbearing, indulgent, uncomplaining; see also patient.

stone, boulder, crag, flint, gem, granite, gravel, jewel, marble, pebble, quartz, rock, rubble, shale.

stop, see cease; halt; hinder; interrupt.

store, see heap.

storm, agitation, commotion, cyclone, disturbance, fury, hurricane, outbreak, paroxysm, rage, tornado, tumult, turbulence, turmoil, upheaval, violence, whirlwind; assail, assault, attack, blow, boil, bombard, fume, hail, rage, rain, rant, snow, whirlwind. ANT.—calm, peace, placidity, repose, serenity, tranquility; assuage, ease, lull, pacify, soothe.

stormy, agitated, angry, blustery, excitable, frenzied, furious, gusty, inclement, passionate, raging, raving, roaring, rough, tempestuous, turbulent, violent, windy. ANT.—calm, clear, composed, gentle, peaceful, tranquil.

story, account, allegory, anecdote, apologue, burlesque, chronicle, epic, fable, fantasy, fiction, history, legend, memoir, myth, narration, narrative, novel, parable, report, romance, saga, satire, tale, yarn; canard, fabrication, falsehood.

stout, paunchy, pudgy, stocky, thickset; see also fat; obese.

straight, direct, erect, even, level, perpendicular, rectilinear, right, unbent, undeviating, unswerving, upright, vertical; candid, fair, honest, honorable, just, regular, reliable, trustworthy, upright. ANT.—bent, circuitous, crooked, distorted, swerving, twisted; deceptive, devious, dishonest, fraudulent, unreliable.

strain, breed, extraction, lineage, pedigree, race, stock; kind, sort, variety; effort, endeavor, overexertion, struggle; melody, tune; manner, style; anxiety, burden, mental tension, pressure, stress.

strange, abnormal, alien, anomalous, bewildering, bizarre, curious, dissociated, eccentric, exotic, extraordinary, fantastic, foreign, grotesque, inapplicable, incredible, irregular, irrelevant, misplaced, mysterious, nondescript, odd, peculiar, remote, singular, stupefying, surprising, unaccustomed, uncommon, unfamiliar, unrelated, unusual. ANT.—conventional, familiar, ordinary, prevailing, regular, typical.

stranger, alien, drifter, foreigner, immigrant, interloper, intruder, newcomer, outsider, squatter, visitor. ANT.—acquaintance, associate, companion, friend, neighbor, peer.

stratagem, artifice, cabal, conspiracy, design, device, finesse, intrigue, logistics, machination, maneuver, plan, plot, ruse, scheme, strategy, tactics, trick.

stray, err, go astray, traipse, wander; see also deviate; ramble.

stream, spout, spurt; abound, be copious. see also emanate; flow.

strength, durability, fortitude, intensity, lustiness, stamina, sturdiness, toughness; see also power.

strengthen, confirm, corroborate, substantiate, sustain, verify; brace, buttress, fortify, harden, invigorate, reinforce, rejuvenate, steel; augment, enlarge, extend, heighten, intensify, sharpen.

stress, burden, compulsion, exigency, force, press, pressure, strain, tension, urgency; accent, emphasis, importance, significance, weight.

stretch, distort, spread, strain. see also distend; extend.

strict, accurate, exact, precise, stern, rough, rugged; see also severe.

strike, hurt, knock, pummel, smite. see also hit.

striking, affecting, august, grandiose, majestic, over-powering, splendid; see also impressive.

stripped, defenseless, unprotected; see also naked.

strive, see endeavor.

strong, athletic, concentrated, durable, enduring, forcible, fortified, hale, impregnable, resistant, resolute, solid, strenuous, tough; see also mighty; sinewy.

struggle, brawl, feud, fray, quarrel, row, scuffle, skirmish; see also combat; conflict.

stubborn, adamant, contumacious, determined, dogged, headstrong, immovable, inflexible, intractable, mulish, obdurate, obstinate, pertinacious, recalcitrant, refractory, uncompromising, ungovernable, unyielding. ANT.—amenable, compliant, reasonable, submissive, tractable, yielding.

student, apprentice, disciple, learner, novice, observer, pupil, scholar.

study, cogitate, examine, investigate, scrutinize, weigh; see also contemplate.

stumble, fall, pitch, slide, slip, sprawl, tilt, topple, trip, tumble. ANT.—arise, ascend, mount, soar.

stun, amaze, astonish, disconcert, dumbfound, flabbergast, surprise; see also shock.

stupid, asinine, brainless, crass, dense, dull, dumb, feeble-minded, foolish, inane, inept, moronic, obtuse, senseless, vapid, witless. ANT.—clever, discerning, perspicacious, saga, wise.

stupor, apathy, coma, daze, drowsiness, inertness, insensibility, languor, lethargy, narcosis, numbness, stupefaction, torpor, unconsciousness. ANT.—activity, consciousness, liveliness, sensibility, vivacity.

sturdy, see mighty; sinewy; strong.

suave, adroit, affable, amiable, courteous, cultured, debonair, gallant, genteel, glib, gracious, pleasing, polished, polite, smooth, sophisticated, tactful, urbane, well-bred. ANT.—brusque, crude, displeasing, inept, rude.

subdue, beat, conquer, control, crush, defeat, humble, master, moderate, overcome, quell, restrain, rout, soften, subjugate, suppress, surmount, tame, temper, vanquish. ANT.—awaken, enrage, incite, rouse, stimulate.

subject, citizen, dependent, inferior, liegeman, subordinate, vassal; argument, case, material, matter, point, problem, question, substance, theme, thesis, thought, topic.

sublime, elevated, glorious, lofty, raised, supreme; see also majestic.

submerge, see immerse.

submit, abdicate, abide, accede, acquiesce, bear, bend, capitulate, cede, defer, obey, quit, relent, resign, succumb, suffer, surrender, yield; offer, present, propose, suggest. ANT.—defy, obstruct, resist, struggle, withstand; deny, refuse, reject, retain, withhold.

subordinate, ancillary, dependent, inferior, insignificant, junior, minor, paltry, secondary, subject, subservient, subsidiary, unimportant; control, subdue, subjugate. ANT.—chief, dominant, excellent, leading, superior; dignify, elevate, glorify, promote, revere.

subsequent, after, consequent, ensuing, following, later, next, posterior, succeeding, successive. ANT.—antecedent, anterior, earlier, preceding, prior.

subside, descend, drop, fall, sink; droop, extend downward, hang; see also collapse; decline.

substance, see material; moment.

substantiate, see confirm.

substitution, alternation, exchange, replacement, variety. see also change; modification.

subtract, deduct, remove, take away, withhold; see also decrease; lessen.

subvert, demolish, depress, destroy, extinguish, invert, overthrow, overturn, overwhelm, pervert, reverse, supplant, topple, upset. ANT.—conserve, establish, perpetuate, preserve, sustain.

succeed, achieve, accomplish, attain, conquer, defeat, flourish, gain, prevail, prosper, surmount, thrive, triumph, vanquish, win; ensue, follow, replace, supersede, supervene, supplant. ANT.—blunder, fail, lose, miscarry, miss; anticipate, herald, introduce, precede, preface.

succession, continuation, progression; see also sequence.

succinct, compendious, curt; see also concise.

sudden, abrupt, immediate, instantaneous, unexpected; see also hasty; rapid.

suffer, bear, endure, experience, feel, stand, sustain; admit, allow, indulge, let, permit, submit, tolerate; ache, agonize, undergo. ANT.—avoid, resist, surrender; deny, disallow, prohibit, refuse; heal, rally, overcome, recover, revive.

suffering, see distress; pain.

sufficient, abundant, adequate, ample, commensurate, enough, fitting, plenty, proper, satisfactory, satisfying, suitable. ANT.—deficient, inadequate, insufficient, lacking, scant.

suggest, advise, allude to, counsel, hint, imply, infer, insinuate, intimate, offer, propose, recommend, submit.

suggestion, admonition, advice, allusion, caution, counsel, exhortation, hint, idea, implication, indication, innuendo, insinuation, intimation, proposal, recommendation, thought, warning; design, layout, outline, plan, project, scheme, strategy.

suit, accommodate, adapt, adjust, alter, conform, fit, revise; fill, gratify, please, satisfy. ANT.—misapply, misfit; annoy, disturb, vex.

suitable, acceptable, accordant, adapted, agreeable, applicable, appropriate, becoming, conformable, congruous, consonant, eligible, expedient, fitting, gratifying, just, meet, pertinent, proper, relevant. ANT.—disagreeable, improper, incongruous, irrelevant, obnoxious, reprehensible.

sullen, churlish, crabbed, cross, dismal, dour, fretful, gloomy, glum, moody, morose, sour, stubborn, sulky, surly. ANT.—amiable, cheerful, genial, jovial, sociable.

sum, aggregate, amount, bulk, collection, entirety, entity, everything, gross, lump, total, totality, unity, value, whole, worth. ANT.—fraction, ingredient, part, portion.

summary, abstract, analysis, condensation, core, digest, epitome, outline, recapitulation, reduction, report, resumé, survey, syllabus, synopsis.

summit, apex, cap, crest, crown, culmination, head, height, peak, pinnacle, tip, top, vertex, zenith. ANT.—base, bottom, foot, foundation, nadir.

sunny, bright, brilliant, clear, cloudless, dazzling, fair, gleaming, shining, shiny, splendid, sunlit. ANT.—cloudy, dark, dull, foul, overcast.

superficial, cursory, desultory, exterior, external, flimsy, frivolous, hasty, ignorant, imperfect, outward, shallow, short-sighted, slight, surface, unenlightened. ANT.—careful, deep, deliberate, learned, profound, thorough.

superfluous, abounding, exaggerated, excessive, exorbitant, extra, extravagant, extreme, inexhaustible, inordinate, lavish, lush, luxuriant, needless, overmuch, profuse, redundant, spare, superabundant, unnecessary, useless. ANT.—inadequate, insufficient, scanty, scarce.

superior, above, better, distinguished, excellent, finer, greater, higher, major, preferred, sovereign, supreme, unsurpassed, upper. ANT.—below, deficient, inferior, minor, substandard.

supernatural, ghostly, metaphysical, mysterious, mystic, spectral, spiritual, superhuman, unearthly; see also miraculous.

supervise, command, dominate, manage, superintend; see also regulate.

supple, see elastic.

supplicate, adjure, importune, request; see also beg.

supply, fund, reserve; endow, fit out, produce; see also hoard; furnish.

support, base, basis, bolster, brace, buttress, foundation, fulcrum, groundwork, prop, shore, stanchion, stay; advocacy, aid, assistance, backing, comfort, contribution, encouragement, favor, help, patronage, succor; livelihood, living, maintenance, subsistence, sustenance; confirmation, evidence; advance, advocate, aid, assist, back, bear, bolster, brace, carry, contribute, defend, encourage, expedite, foster, further, help, hold, keep, maintain, preserve, prop, shore, sustain, uphold, verify. ANT.—apex, cupola, peak, pinnacle, summit; blockage, discouragement, hindrance, impediment, injury, opposition; abandonment, betrayal, denial, desertion; delusion, fantasy, illusion; check, cripple, destroy, encumber, frustrate, obstruct, undermine.

supporter, advocate, defender, devotee, pillar, sustainer, upholder, votary; see also follower.

suppose, conjecture, deduce, speculate, surmise; see also imagine.

suppress, lower, moderate; see also lessen.

supremacy, domination, predominance, sovereignty, transcendence; see also mastery.

supreme, best, cardinal, chief, dominant, essential, final, first, foremost, greatest, highest, leading, main, paramount, peerless, predominant, principal, transcendent, ultimate. ANT.—auxiliary, inferior, subordinate, subsidiary, supplemental.

sure, assured, indubitable, inevitable, secure, undeniable, unquestionable; see also definite.

surplus, see excess.

surprise, curiosity, marvel, miracle, phenomenon, oddity, prodigy, rarity, sensation, spectacle; admiration, amazement, astonishment, awe, bewilderment, curiosity, incredulity, perplexity, shock, stupefaction, wonder, wonderment; alarm, amaze, astonish, astound, bewilder, confound, dazzle, disconcert, dumbfound, flabbergast, overwhelm, shock, startle, stun. ANT.—familiarity, habit, routine, triviality; anticipation, apathy, expectation, indifference, tranquility; admonish, caution, forewarn, prepare, warn.

surrender, acquiesce, capitulate, resign, sacrifice, submit; see also relinquish.

surround, bound, confine, enclose, fence, limit; see also encircle, encompass.

surveillance, charge, control, management, superintendence; see also inspection.

suspect, disbelieve, dispute, distrust, doubt, mistrust, query, question, waver; assume, guess, imagine, presume, speculate, suppose, theorize. ANT.—believe, confide in, rely on, trust; ascertain, discern, know.

suspend, adjourn, cease, defer, delay, desist, discontinue, interrupt, postpone, stay; append, balance, dangle, hang, hitch, poise, sling, swing. ANT.—accelerate, continue, expedite, persist, proceed, support.

suspicion, incredulity, scruple, skepticism, suspense, unbelief; see also distrust.

sustain, advocate, back, bear, brace, further; see also encourage, help, preserve.

swallow, absorb, accept, assimilate, bear, believe, bolt, consume, devour, endure, engulf, envelop, imbibe, stomach, tolerate; recant, retract, suppress, withdraw. ANT.—discharge, doubt, emit, expel, reject; affirm, confirm, uphold.

swarthy, brown, dark, dusky, sable, tawny. ANT.—bright, fair, light.

sway, impel, incite, stir; see also influence.

swear, affirm, declare, protest, state; see also maintain.

sweep, brush, clean, clear, graze, mop, rake, remove, touch, traverse, whisk; amplitude, bend, compass, contour, curve, extent, range, reach, scope, stretch, swing.

sweet, engaging, gentle, honeyed, mellifluous, melodious, saccharine, sugary, winning; see also luscious.

swell, amplify, bulge, dilate, distend, expand, heave, increase, inflate, intensify, protrude, puff, rise, tumefy; bulge, crescendo, curve, elevation, intensity, power, protuberance, swelling. ANT.—compress, contract, diminish, shrink, shrivel; decline, depression, flatness, reduction, shrinkage.

swift, see fast.

swindle, cheat, chicanery, guile, imposture; bilk, dupe, fool, gull, hoax, hoodwink, victimize; see also deceit; deceive.

symbol, character, figure, mark, representative, sign, token, type.

symmetry, agreement, arrangement, balance, centrality, conformity, equality, equilibrium, equivalence, evenness, finish, form, harmony, order, proportion, regularity, shapeliness. ANT.—disagreement, disparity, distortion, imbalance, irregularity.

sympathetic, forbearing, kindly, tender, thoughtful; see also humane.

sympathize, gladden, soothe; see also comfort.

sympathy, accord, affinity, agreement, alliance, concord, condolence, congeniality, consolation, empathy, harmony, warmth. see also compassion. ANT.—antipathy, harshness, indifference, insensitivity, malevolence.

symptom, characteristic, diagnostic, evidence, feature, indication, mark, property, token, trace, trait, vestige.

synthetic, artificial, ersatz, fake, feigned, fictitious, phony, unreal; see also counterfeit.

system, network, operation, organization, policy, program; see also method.

T

tact, adroitness, dexterity, diplomacy, discretion, discrimination, finesse, knack, perception, perspicacity, poise, savoir-faire, skill, subtlety.

tactful, discreet, discriminating, judicious, politic; see also diplomatic.

take, catch, clasp, clutch, grasp, grip, procure, seize; appropriate, arrogate, capture, confiscate, ensnare, steal, usurp; apprehend, deprehend; necessitate, need, require; adopt, assume, choose, select; bear, endure, stand, tolerate; attract, captivate, charm, delight, interest; accept, obtain, receive.

tale, account, anecdote, chronicle, history, narration, narrative, report, yarn; see also fiction.

talent, cleverness, endowment, genius; see also ability, faculty.

talented, bright, sharp, smart, quick, quick-witted, witty; see also skillful.

talk, chatter, gossip, lecture, report; blab, chat, comment, gossip, harangue, jabber, mutter, plead, prattle, preach, rant, speak, spout, tattle; see also conversation; discourse, speak.

talkative, chatty, communicative, glib, voluble; see also garrulous.

tall, see high.

tame, domestic, domesticated, gentle, obedient, subdued, timid; boring, dull, flat, insipid, tedious, vapid; see also docile.

tamper, alter, discommode, inconvenience, interrupt, intervene, mix in, monkey, trouble; see also interfere.

tangible, palpable, sensible; see also corporeal.

tangle, complicate, confuse, ensnare, entrap, hinder, interfere, intertwine, involve, jumble, muddle, snare, spoil; dilemma, disorder, embarrassment, muddle, perplexity, puzzle, quandary, snarl.

tardy, detained, lax, overdue, retarded, slack; see also late.

tarnish, befoul, besmirch, blemish, blight, blot, defame, defile, discolor, disgrace, dishonor, smudge, soil, spot, stain, sully, taint. ANT.—brighten, cleanse, defend, honor, restore.

tart, see bitter.

task, assignment, burden, business, charge, chore, duty, function, job, labor, mission, office, pursuit, stint, toil, work, undertaking.

taste, flavor, gusto, piquancy, relish, savor, tang, zest; acumen, appreciation, discernment, discrimination, disposition, inclination, judgment, liking, predilection, refinement, sensibility, susceptibility. ANT.—antipathy, disinclination, indelicacy, rudeness, vulgarity.

taut, bound up, constricted, firm, fixed, snug, stretched, tight, unbending, unyielding. ANT.—lax, loose, relaxed, shaky, slack.

tax, assessment, charge, custom, dues, duty, exaction, excise, fine, impost, levy, obligation, rate, tariff, toll, tribute; burden, demand, strain, task. ANT.—gift, grant, present, remuneration, reward; comfort, ease, relaxation, rest.

teach, advise, coach, direct, educate, enlighten, explain, expound, guide, imbue, inculcate, indoctrinate, inform, instill, instruct, interpret, lecture, nurture, prepare, school, train, tutor. ANT.—follow, imbibe, learn, misguide, misinform.

tear, cleave, disunite, rive, sever, shed, sunder, wound; see also rip.

tease, aggravate, badger, bother, disturb, harry, nag; see also harass.

tedious, boring, burdensome, dilatory, dreary, drowsy, dull, fatiguing, humdrum, irksome, monotonous, slow, sluggish, soporific, tardy, tiresome, uninteresting, wearisome. ANT.—animating, exhilarating, fascinating, inspiring, refreshing.

teeming, abounding, abundant, ample, bountiful, copious, overflowing, plenteous, plentiful, profuse, prolific, replete, rich, rife. ANT.—deficient, inadequate, meager, scant, scarce.

tell, describe, narrate, recite, recount, rehearse, relate, report; assert, communicate, declare, discuss, express, mention, publish, say, speak, state, utter; announce, betray, confess, disclose, divulge, reveal; discern, discover, distinguish, recognize; acquaint, apprise, explain, impart, inform, instruct, notify; direct, order, request.

temper, anger, animosity, choler, fury, indignation, ire, irritation, petulance, rage, resentment, wrath; composition, disposition, humor, mood, nature, quality, structure, type; anneal, assuage, change, moderate, modify, mollify, qualify, soften, soothe. ANT.—composure, conciliation, patience, peace, repose; agitate, harden, intensify, strengthen, toughen.

temperament, constitution, disposition, humor, makeup, mood, nature, personality, propensity, spirit, temper.

temperate, abstemious, abstinent, frugal, mild, moderate, reasonable, self-restrained, sober, unruffled. ANT.—excessive, immoderate, impetuous, tempestuous, uncontrolled.

temporal, earthly, ephemeral, fleeting, laic, lay, mundane, profane, secular, temporary, transient, transitory, worldly. ANT.—ecclesiastical, eternal, everlasting, religious, spiritual.

temporary, brief, changeable, cyclical, ephemeral, evanescent, fleeting, impermanent, momentary, passing, provisional, shifting, short, summary, transient, transitory. ANT.—abiding, durable, endless, permanent, perpetual, timeless.

tempt, allure, bait, captivate, charm, coax, court, decoy, entice, fascinate, incite, induce, inveigle, lure, rouse, seduce, test, try. ANT.—discourage, disenchant, nauseate, repel, repulse.

tend, accompany, attend, escort, guard, keep, manage, nurse, protect, serve, watch; gravitate, incline, lean, point, verge on.

tendency, aim, aptness, bent, bias, direction, disposition, drift, inclination, learning, mood, predisposition, proclivity, proneness, propensity, susceptibility, tone, trend, turn. ANT.—apathy, aversion, deviation, disinclination, opposition.

tender, benevolent, delicate, loving, merciful, responsive, sympathetic, warm; feeble, fragile,

immature, weak, young; advance, extend, offer, present, proffer, propose, suggest, volunteer; see also mild.

tenet, belief, conviction, creed, doctrine, dogma, position, precept, principle, system, teaching, view.

tense, firm, rigid, stiff, strained, taut, tight; anxious, distraught, edgy, high-strung, nervous, overwrought, restless, troubled. ANT.—lax, limp, loose, slack; calm, placid, relaxed, tranquil, unruffled.

tentative, experimental, makeshift, probationary, provisional, temporary. ANT.—conclusive, decisive, definitive, final, permanent.

term, boundary, course, cycle, duration, interval, limit, period, phase, span, time; condition, stipulation; expression, name, nomenclature, phrase, terminology, word.

terminate, abolish, achieve, cease, close, complete, conclude, end, expire, finish, perfect, stop. ANT.—begin, commence, inaugurate, initiate, start.

terrible, alarming, appalling, awful, dire, dreadful, fearful, frightful, gruesome, hideous, horrible, horrid, severe, shocking, terrifying. ANT.—appealing, attractive, captivating, happy, pleasing.

terrify, see frighten.

territory, area, boundary, country, district, division, domain, dominion, land, place, province, quarter, region, section, township.

terror, see fear.

terse, brief, compact, compendious, concise, condensed, crisp, incisive, laconic, neat, pithy, sententious, short, succinct, summary, trenchant. ANT.—profuse, rambling, redundant, verbose, wordy.

test, assay, examine, experiment, inspect, prove, scrutinize, substantiate, try, verify; criterion, demonstration, essay, examination, proof, standard, trial.

testimony, affidavit, attestation, certification, confirmation, credentials, declaration, deposition, evidence, indication, proof, warrant, witness.

text, book, handbook, manual, manuscript, matter, passage, publication, quotation, sentence, stanza, subject, textbook, theme, topic, verse, volume, wording, writing.

texture, character, coarseness, composition, constitution, disposition, feel, fiber, firmness, flexibility, grain, makeup, nap, organization, rigidity, roughness, smoothness, structure, tissue.

thankful, appreciative, beholden, contented, grateful, gratified, pleased, satisfied. ANT.—critical, discontented, dissatisfied, faultfinding, thankless.

thaw, deliquesce, dissolve, flow, liquate, liquefy, melt, run. ANT.—chill, congeal, freeze, petrify, solidify.

theft, burglary, depredation, embezzlement, fraud, holdup, larceny, misappropriation, pillage, piracy, plagiarism, plunder, rapine, robbery, spoliation, swindle.

theme, composition, description, discourse, dissertation, essay, idea, motive, narrative, proposition, report, statement, subject, tenor, text, thesis, topic, trend, writing.

theoretical, analytical, formal, ideal, scholastic; see also learned.

theory, assumption, attribution, doctrine, guess, opinion, perception, plea, presupposition, speculation, surmise, thesis, viewpoint; see also hypothesis.

therefore, accordingly, consequently, for, hence, since, so, then, thence, wherefore.

thesis, affirmation, argument, composition, dictum, dissertation, doctrine, essay, position, proposition, report, study, theme.

thick, abundant, close, compact, compressed, condensed, crowded, dense, impenetrable, multitudinous, numerous, packed, populous, profuse, solid, swarming; coagulated, curdled, gelatinous, glutinous, gummy, heavy, miry, muddy, opaque, ropy, solidified, viscid, viscous; cloudy, dull, indistinct, turbid; doltish, dull, ignorant, obtuse, stolid, stupid; coarse, crass, gross; broad, chunky, dumpy, squat, thickset. ANT.—barren, inadequate, scattered, spacious, sparse; clear, diaphanous, gaseous, limpid, rarified, transparent; clear, distinct; acute, bright, intelligent, perceptive; genteel, polite, refined; fragile, frail, slender, thin.

thin, diaphanous, diluted, fine, gauzy, gossamer, rare, scanty, scrawny, skeletal, threadlike, wasted; see also gaunt, slender.

think, conceive, imagine, picture, recall, recollect, remember; cogitate, contemplate, deliberate, determine, examine, meditate, muse, ponder, reason, reflect, ruminate, speculate, study; apprehend, believe, conjecture, consider, deem, esteem, guess, hold, judge, opine, presume, reckon, regard, suppose, surmise; devise, intend, mean, plan, propose.

thorough, absolute, accurate, complete, concluded, consummate, ended, entire, exact, exhaustive, finished, full, painstaking, perfect, plenary, radical, scrupulous, sweeping, thoroughgoing, total, unbroken, undivided, unmitigated. ANT.—deficient, incomplete, perfunctory, sketchy, superficial.

thought, cerebration, cogitation, conception, consideration, contemplation, deliberation, fancy, idea, imagination, impression, judgment, lucubration, meditation, memory, notion, opinion, perception, recollection, reflection, regard, retrospection, sentiment, speculation, view. ANT.—emptiness, fatuity, inanity, vacancy, vacuity.

thoughtful, attentive, careful, cautious, charitable, concerned, considerate, empathic, heedful, kind, provident, prudent, sympathetic; cogitative, contemplative, engrossed, introspective, meditative, pensive, philosophic, rapt, reflective, speculative, studious. ANT.—careless, heedless, indifferent, negligent, thoughtless; fatuous, idiotic, inane, obtuse, vacuous.

thoughtless, desultory, heedless, imprudent, inaccurate, inattentive, neglectful, reckless, unconcerned. see also inconsiderate, lax.

threatening, see imminent.

thrift, conservation, economy, frugality, parsimony, providence, prudence, saving. ANT.—extravagance, prodigality, shiftlessness, waste.

thrill, excitement, flutter, sensation, shock, tingling, tremor; affect, agitate, electrify, inspire, move, penetrate, rouse, stimulate, stir, strike, tingle, touch, tremble, vibrate.

thrive, advance, bloom, flourish, grow, improve, increase, luxuriate, prosper, succeed. ANT.—decline, fail, fall, lose.

throb, beat, oscillate, palpitate, pulsate, pulse, vibrate; beating, palpitation, pulsation, vibration.

throng, aggregation, assemblage, assembly, bevy, concourse, crowd, crush, gang, horde, host, legion, masses, mob, multitude, populace, press, rabble, swarm.

throw, cast, chuck, drive, fling, hurl, impel, launch, pitch, project, propel, sling, thrust, toss. ANT.—catch, draw, haul, hold, retain.

thrust, cast, crowd, drive, extend, fling, force, impel, jostle, penetrate, pierce, press, propel, push, shove, stab, tilt; hasten, promote, urge; explosion, force, impact, pressure, propulsion, push. ANT.—drag, falter, halt, retreat; impede, obstruct, oppose; debility, powerlessness, weakness.

thwart, see frustrate.

tidy, clean, clear, methodical, neat, nice, orderly, precise, shipshape, snug, spruce, systematic, trim. ANT.—deranged, disheveled, littered, slovenly, unkempt.

tie, affinity, alliance, association, band, bond, brace, conjunction, connection, cord, coupling, ligament, ligature, link, relationship, rope, security, strap, string, tackle, union, yoke; attach, bind, confine, connect, constrain, engage, fasten, fetter, hitch, join, link, moor, obligate, restrain, restrict, secure, shackle, tether, unite. ANT.—detachment, disunion, isolation, separation, sunderance; detach, free, loosen, unbind, separate.

tight, close, compact, contracted, narrow, tense; penny-pinching; see also taut; greedy, miserly.

time, age, course, cycle, date, duration, eon, epoch, era, interim, interval, measure, period, season, sequence, span, spell, stage, succession, tempo, term, while; adjust, measure, regulate, set.

timely, appropriate, convenient, exact, opportune, precise, prompt, proper, propitious, providential, punctual, ready, seasonable, suitable, welltimed. ANT.—dilatory, inexpedient, inopportune, tardy, untimely.

timid, abashed, afraid, bashful, coy, daunted, diffident, embarrassed, faltering, fearful, hesitant, humble, irresolute, modest, recoiling, scared, shamefaced, sheepish, shy, skulking, spiritless, terrified, timorous, unspirited, vacillating, wavering. ANT.—adventurous, courageous, dauntless, determined, gregarious, intrepid.

tiny, insignificant, trivial, wee; see also small.

tire, bore, drain, exhaust, fatigue, harass, irk, jade, overtax, overwork, pall, prostrate, strain, tucker, wear out, weary, worry. ANT.—amuse, energize, invigorate, refresh, restore.

tired, collapsing, drained, drooping, drowsy, exhausted, faint, fatigued, haggard, jaded, spent, wasted, weary, wearied, worn. ANT.—active, energetic, fresh, invigorated, lively.

title, appellation, caption, cognomen, denomination, designation, epithet, heading, inscription, name; birthright, claim, due, honor, ownership, possession, prerogative, privilege, right.

toil, achievement, business, drudgery, effort, employment, grind, labor, occupation, opus, pains, performance, production, task, travail, work. ANT.—leisure, recreation, relaxation, repose, rest.

token, badge, emblem, evidence, index, manifestation, mark, memorial, note, symbol, trait; see also souvenir.

tolerant, enduring, fair, forbearing, lenient, liberal, open-minded, patient, receptive, understanding. ANT.—bigoted, discriminatory, intolerant, prejudiced, unyielding.

tolerate, allow, authorize, concede, let, license, sanction, permit; abide, bear, brook, endure, persevere, prevail, stand, stomach, sustain, swallow, undergo. ANT.—bar, forbid, hinder, inhibit, veto; avoid, evade, falter, succumb, surrender, yield.

toll, see tax.

tongue, cant, lingo, slang; see also language.

too, additionally, also, as well, besides, further, furthermore, in addition, likewise, moreover, similarly.

tool, agent, apparatus, appliance, device, equipment, implement, instrument, means, mechanism, medium, utensil, vehicle. ANT.—hindrance, impediment, obstacle, obstruction.

top, acme, apex, chief, crest, crown, culmination, head, peak, pinnacle, summit, surface, tip, vertex, zenith. ANT.—base, bottom, foot, foundation, nadir.

topic, affair, argument, issue, material, matter, motion, point, problem, proposition, question, resolution, subject, text, theme, theorem, thesis.

torment, abuse, ache, agony, anguish, cruelty, distress, excruciation, malady, martyrdom, misery, pain, persecution, rack, suffering, throe, torture, woe, wretchedness; afflict, aggravate, annoy, badger, bait, bother, distress, disturb, grill, gull, harass, harry, hurt, irritate, mistrust, nag, oppress, pain, pester, plague, provoke, rack, tantalize, taunt, tease, torture, trouble, vex. ANT.—comfort, ease, mitigation, relief, solace; console, help, mollify, please, relieve, soothe.

torrid, hot-blooded, scalding, scorching, sweltering, warm; see also hot, passionate.

torture, see torment.

toss, see throw.

total, see sum; thorough.

touch, affect, allude, brush, concern, feel, finger, glance, graze, handle, hint, impress, melt, mollify, pat, regard, soften, strike, stroke, tap; dash, feeling, infusion, palpability, sensation, sprinkling, tangency, taste, tinge, trace.

touching, affecting, heart-rending, impressive, pitiable, sad; adjacent, adjunct, bordering, tangent; see also impressive; poignant; tender.

touchy, choleric, fiery, hasty, snappish; see also irritable.

tough, adhesive, coherent, fibrous, firm, hardened, hardy, seasoned, stalwart, strong, sturdy, tenacious, wiry; difficult, formidable, hard, intricate, laborious, puzzling, rigorous, troublesome, trying; boisterous, bullying, callous, fierce, incorrigible, intractable, obdurate, obstinate, raging, savage, stubborn, turbulent, unmanageable, unyielding, vicious. ANT.—defenseless, delicate, fragile, puny, vulnerable, weak; easy, effortless, elementary, facile, simple; amenable, compliant, deferential, docile, passive, tractable, yielding.

tour, see journey.

tow, see draw, pull.

towering, see lofty.

toy, caper, frisk, frolic, gamble, gambol, play, revel, romp, sport, wager; bauble, game, pastime, plaything, trinket; little, miniature, small.

trace, mark, scar, stain, stigma, tinge; characteristic, clue, evidence, feature, fragment, impression, indication, memorial, property, record, sign, symptom, trait, vestige. ANT.—deletion, effacement, extinction, nonexistence, obliteration.

track, see pursue.

tractable, acquiescent, adaptable, amenable, compliant, deferential, docile, dutiful, governable, manageable, obedient, pliant, submissive, willing, yielding. ANT.—insubordinate, intractable, obstinate, rebellious, stubborn.

trade, barter, business, calling, commerce, contract, dealing, employment, enterprise, exchange, job, livelihood, metier, occupation, position, profession, pursuit, sales, speculation, traffic, transaction, undertaking, vocation, work; art, craft, handicraft; bargain, barter, buy, deal, exchange, patronize, purchase, sell, shop, swap.

traffic, see business; trade.

trail, course, footprint, mark, path, scent, trace, track; chase, climb, crawl, creep, drag, draw,

follow, grow, hunt, persist, pull, straggle, track. ANT.—abandon, elude, escape, evade, withdraw.

train, chain, line, procession, retinue, sequel, sequence, series, staff, string, succession, suite; accustom, aim, bend, coach, direct, discipline, drill, educate, enlighten, exercise, guide, habituate, imbue, implant, inculcate, indoctrinate, inform, infuse, innure, instruct, lead, practice, prepare, prime, rear, school, teach.

training, background, coaching, cultivation, development, direction, discipline, drilling, education, exercise, foundation, groundwork, guidance, instruction, learning, nurture, practice, preparation, schooling, study, tutelage.

trait, attribute, characteristic, distinction, earmark, feature, habit, mannerism, mark, nature, peculiarity, property, quality, style, tone, trademark.

traitorous, apostate, disloyal, faithless, false, insidious, mutinous, perfidious, rebellious, recreant, renegade, seditious, treacherous, treasonable. ANT.—constant, devoted, faithful, loyal, steadfast.

tramp, beggar, bum, derelict, hobo, indigent, landloper, nomad, rover, vagabond, vagrant, wanderer; harlot, prostitute.

tranquil, dispassionate, dulcet, imperturbable, sedative, softened, solacing, stifled, unstirred, whispering; see also peaceful, placid, quiet.

tranquility, calmness, hush, quiescence, quietude, rest, serenity; see also peace.

transact, accomplish, achieve, buy, carry on, conclude, conduct, dispatch, enact, execute, exercise, manage, negotiate, operate, perform, perpetrate, sell, settle, treat, work.

transaction, act, action, activity, affair, business, deal, deed, disposal, doing, event, execution, matter, negotiation, occurrence, performance, proceeding, purchase, sale, step, undertaking.

transfer, carry, dispatch, relegate, send, shift, transmit, transplant, transport; assign, confer, convey, dispense, give, grant, impart, sell.

transform, shift, vary, veer; see also convert.

transgression, breach, crime, delinquency, encroachment, error, fault, infraction, infringement, iniquity, injustice, invasion, misbehavior, misdeed, misdemeanor, offense, sin, slip, trespass, vice, violation, wrong. ANT.—benevolence, goodness, honor, innocence, virtue.

transient, flitting, flying, fugitive, short-lived, temporal, vanishing, volatile; see also temporary.

translate, explicate, transform, transmute. see also interpret.

transmit, broadcast, communicate, confer, convey, disclose, dispatch, divulge, forward, impart, inform, notify, pass on, relate, relay, reveal, send, tell, transfer. ANT.—conceal, hide, mask, secrete, shroud, withhold.

transparent, crystalline, thin; guileless, manifest, open, patent; see also lucid.

transport, bring, cart, haul, relocate, transplant; see also convey.

trap, ambush, artifice, bait, blind, intrigue, lure, maneuver, net, noose, pit, pitfall, plot, ruse, snare, stratagem, trick, wile; ambush, deceive, decoy, dupe, ensnare, entrap, fool, lure, mislead, outwit, seduce, swindle, victimize.

trash, debris, dregs, dross, garbage, junk, leavings, litter, rags, refuse, riffraff, rubbish, rubble, scourings, slag, sweepings, trumpery, waste. ANT.—advantages, benefits, goods, perquisites, valuables.

travel, drive, fly, go, journey, move, ramble, roam, rove, sail, tour, walk, wander; circuit, course, cruise, excursion, exodus, expedition, journey, march, migration, peregrination, pilgrimage, ramble, ride, sojourn, tour, trip, wandering.

treacherous, base, deceitful, disloyal, evil, faithless, false, foul, ignominious, inglorious, malevolent, malicious, malign, perfidious, rancorous, recreant, traitorous, treasonable, unfaithful, unreliable, venomous, vile. ANT.—dependable, faithful, honest, reliable, trustworthy.

treason, betrayal, cabal, collusion, conspiracy, deception, dishonesty, disloyalty, intrigue, machination, plot, revolution, sedition, subversion, treachery.

treasure, appreciate, cherish, foster, guard, hold dear, love, nurture, prize, sustain, value. ANT.—abandon, detest, disregard, loathe, reject.

treat, arrange, employ, handle, manage, manipulate, operate, use, utilize; administer, assist, attend, care for, doctor, heal, minister to, nurse, prescribe; amuse, divert, entertain, indulge, satisfy; comment, criticize, discuss, explain, interpret, negotiate, review. ANT.—disarrange, disorder, mismanage, spoil, waste; ignore, neglect, overlook; annoy, bore, irritate, offend, vex; befuddle, cloud, confuse, mystify, perplex.

treaty, agreement, alliance, arrangement, bargain, compact, concordat, covenant, negotiation, pact, protocol, settlement.

tremble, agitate, flutter, jar, jolt, oscillate, pulsate, quail, quake, quaver, quiver, rock, shake, shiver, shudder, sway, teeter, totter, vibrate, waver, wobble.

tremendous, alarming, amazing, appalling, astounding, awesome, colossal, enormous, gigantic, great, huge, immense, monstrous, monumental, prodigious, startling, stupendous, vast. ANT.—insignificant, miniature, tiny, trivial, unimportant.

trespass, encroach, infringe, interfere, interlope, intrude, invade, meddle, penetrate, poach, transgress, violate. ANT.—abandon, evacuate, guard, protect, relinquish, vacate.

trial, analysis, examination, experiment, proof, test; attempt, effort, endeavor, exertion; adversity, affliction, difficulty, hardship, misery, misfortune, ordeal, suffering, tribulation, trouble; arraignment, case, cross-examination, hearing, lawsuit, litigation, prosecution.

tribulation, adversity, affliction, agony, anguish, distress, grief, hardship, misery, oppression, sorrow, suffering, trial, trouble, woe, wretchedness. ANT.—consolation, delight, elation, joy, peace.

trick, antic, artifice, caper, cheat, deceit, deception, device, fraud, guile, hoax, humbug, illusion, imposture, maneuver, ploy, ruse, stratagem, stunt, subterfuge, swindle, wile. ANT.—candor, honesty, justness, openness, sincerity.

tricky, foxy, guileful, insidious, stealthy, subtle; see also covert, shrewd.

trim, clean-cut, compact, harmonious, precise, streamlined, symmetrical; bedeck, embellish, gild; clip, cut, lop, prune, scissor, shave, shear, snip; see also spruce, tidy; embellish.

trip, see journey, travel.

trite, banal, bromidic, common, driveling, dull, hackneyed, humdrum, monotonous, obvious, ordinary, prosaic, shopworn, stale, stereotyped, tedious, uninspiring, uninteresting, wearisome. ANT.—bracing, effectual, novel, original, rousing.

triumph, achievement, ascendancy, celebration, conquest, exultation, gain, joy, jubilation, mastery, ovation, prize, routing, success, trophy,

victory; celebrate, exult, flourish, glory, master, prevail, rejoice, succeed, surpass, thrive, win. ANT.—adversity, defeat, downfall, failure, subjugation; default, fail, flounder, lose, quit, succumb.

trivial, beggarly, diminutive, dribbling, frivolous, inappreciable, inconsiderable, insignificant, little, meager, minute, paltry, petty, scanty, small, trifling, unessential, unimportant, useless, valueless, worthless. ANT.—paramount, precious, significant, valuable, vital, weighty.

troop, army, band, company, crowd, group, herd, host, legion, multitude, party, squad, throng, unit.

trophy, award, citation, crown, cup, honor, laurel, loving cup, medal, memento, memorial, palm, prize, reward, token, wreath.

trouble, afflict, agitate, annoy, bother, concern, distract, distress, disturb, inconvenience, irk, irritate, molest, perturb, pester, plague, tease, upset, vex, worry; affliction, ailment, bind, crisis, difficulty, distress, effort, grief, hardship, illness, ordeal, pain, sorrow, woe; annoyance, bother, embarrassment, irritation, torment, worry; disorder, disturbance, hindrance, predicament, plight, problem; care, drudgery, effort, exertion, grind, labor, toil; altercation, argument, controversy, dispute, feud, fight, hostility, wrangle. ANT.—accommodate, console, gratify, please, soothe; delight, ecstasy, happiness, joy, pleasure; comfort, gratification, peace, quietude, repose, satisfaction, security, solace, tranquility.

troublesome, afflictive, annoying, bothersome, burdensome, damaging, difficult, distressing, disturbing, galling, harassing, irksome, tedious, trying, upsetting, wearisome. ANT.—comfortable, facile, gratifying, manageable, smooth.

true, absolute, accurate, actual, authentic, correct, definite, exact, factual, genuine, legal, legitimate, positive, precise, real, uncontradictable, valid, veracious, veritable; constant, dependable, faithful, honest, honorable, incorrupt, just, loyal, reliable, righteous, scrupulous, sincere, steadfast, straight, trustworthy, upright. ANT.—erroneous, false, fictional, imaginary, inaccurate, invalid, mythical; deceitful, disloyal, fickle, perfidious, treacherous.

trunk, body, bole, box, casing, chest, coffer, column, compartment, portmanteau, proboscis, shaft, snout, stalk, stem, stock, thorax, torso.

trust, assurance, belief, certainty, certitude, confidence, conviction, credence, credit, dependence, faith, reassurance, reliance, security; corporation, estate, holding, institution, monopoly; bank, believe, commit, confide, count on, credit, depend upon, entrust, esteem, expect, hope, intrust, presume, rely on. ANT.—disbelief, incredibility, misgiving, skepticism, suspicion; assail, disbelieve, discredit, impugn, suspect.

trustworthy, certain, constant, dependable, faithful, honest, honorable, loyal, reliable, safe, secure, sincere, steadfast, steady, sure, tried, true, truthful, upright, veracious. ANT.—deceitful, perfidious, sneaking, traitorous, underhand, unfaithful.

truth, accuracy, actuality, authenticity, candor, constancy, correctness, exactness, fact, fidelity, honesty, honor, ingenuousness, rectitude, rightness, sincerity, truthfulness, uprightness, veracity, verisimilitude, verity. ANT.—deception, duplicity, evasion, fabrication, falsehood, hypocrisy.

truthful, candid, frank, honest, just, open, reliable, sincere, true, trustworthy, veracious; accurate, correct, exact, factual, legitimate, verifiable. ANT.—deceitful, misleading, sly, venal; fictitious, inaccurate, incorrect, inexact.

try, aim, aspire, attempt, design, endeavor, essay, exert, intend, labor, mean, risk, seek, strive, struggle, tackle, undertake, venture; afflict, test, torment, trouble; adjudicate, adjudge, assay, decide, examine, hear, investigate, judge, probe. ANT.—abandon, decline, ignore, neglect, omit; comfort, console, ease, solace, support; cover, defer, hide, postpone, procrastinate.

trying, aggravating, annoying, bothersome, disquieting, distressing, disturbing, galling, irksome, irritating, perturbing, provoking, troublesome, upsetting, vexatious; arduous, backbreaking, burdensome, demanding, difficult, hard, laborious, painful, strenuous, tedious. ANT.—accommodating, encouraging, gratifying, pleasing, soothing; easy, facile, inconsiderable, manageable, paltry, simple.

tug, drag, draw, haul, labor, lug, pull, strive, struggle, tow, wrench, yank; effort, haul, jerk, pull, rending, strain, towboat, uprooting.

tumble, derange, disarrange, dishevel, disturb, fall, heave, pitch, plunge, roll, rumple, sprawl, stumble, topple, toss, trip, wallow.

tumult, disarray, hubbub, jumble, stir; see also chaos, commotion, disorder.

tune, accord, air, harmony, lyric, melody, song, strain, unison.

turbulent, agitated, blustery, brawling, disturbed, gusty, inclement, insurgent, obstreperous, restless, riotous, roaring, rough, stormy, tempestuous, tumultuous, violent, wild, windy. ANT.—calm, orderly, peaceful, placid, tranquil.

turmoil, disarray, hubbub, jumble, stir, tumult. see also chaos, commotion, disorder.

turn, circle, circulate, gyrate, invert, loop, oscillate, pivot, reel, revolve, rotate, spin, swing, swivel, twirl, twist, wheel, whirl; alter, change, convert, invert, transform, transmute, vary; avert, avoid, deflect, deviate, divert, dodge, sidetrack, swerve, veer; cycle, gyration, pirouette, revolution, rotation; bend, curve, hook, twist; climax, crisis, juncture, shift.

twist, bend, bow, coil, complicate, contort, convolve, crook, curve, deflect, distort, encircle, gnarl, incline, knot, lean, pervert, rotate, screw, squirm, turn, twine, wind, wreathe, wrench, wring, writhe.

type, emblem, figure, letter, mark, sign, symbol; assortment, breed, cast, category, character, class, description, genus, kind, nature, sort, species, stamp, variety; example, exemplar, form, model, mold, pattern, representation, sample.

typical, accustomed, average, common, conventional, customary, figurative, habitual, ideal, illustrative, indicative, middling, modal, model, normal, ordinary, plain, regular, representative, symbolic, usual. ANT.—aberrant, atypical, deviant, distinctive, rare.

tyrannous, authoritative, dictatorial, domineering, imperious, oppressive. see also despotic.

tyrant, autocrat, despot, dictator, inquisitor, martinet, oppressor, persecutor, slavedriver.

U

ugly, deformed, hideous, homely, horrible, offensive, repellent, repulsive, revolting, uncomely, unsightly; bullying, corrupt, disagreeable, disorderly, ill-natured, pugnacious, quarrelsome, rough, rude, spiteful, surly, threatening, tough, vicious, vile. ANT.—beautiful, captivating, dazzling, exquisite, magnificent; agreeable, charming, gentle, inviting, loving, pleasant.

ultimate, absolute, concluding, decisive, eventual, extreme, farthest, final, hindmost, last, latest, maximum, terminal, utmost. ANT.—beginning, first, initial, opening, preliminary, primary.

umpire, arbiter, arbitrator, assessor, censor, compromiser, inspector, judge, mediator, moderator, negotiator, peacemaker, propitiator, referee, settler.

unadulterated, see clean, clear, immaculate.

unanimity, accord, agreement, apposition, compatibility, concert, concord, concordance, conformity, congruence, correspondence, harmony, unity. ANT.—disagreement, discord, dissonance, division, variance.

unassuming, compliant, lowly, plain, simple, submissive; see also modest.

unbecoming, gauche, improper, inappropriate, indecent, indecorous, inept, maladroit, unbefitting, unfit, unseemly, unsuitable. ANT.—appropriate, becoming, fitting, proper, suitable.

unbeliever, see heretic.

unbiased, equitable, fair, honest, impartial, judicial, just, neutral, objective, reasonable, unimpassioned, unjaundiced, unprejudiced. ANT.—biased, partial, prejudiced, slanted, unfair.

uncertain, ambiguous, dim, doubtful, dubious, equivocal, hazy, indefinite, indistinct, insecure, irresolute, obscure, precarious, questionable, unclear, undecided, undetermined, unsettled, unstable, unsure, vacillating, vague. ANT.—certain, definite, explicit, lucid, precise, specific.

uncertainty, see distrust; doubt.

uncivilized, barbarian, crude, discourteous, heathenish, ignorant, low, remorseless, ruthless, uncultured, unenlightened, unrelenting. see also barbarous; cruel.

unclad, see naked.

unclean, abominable, beastly, dirty, fetid, filthy, foul, grimy, impure, nasty, obscene, offensive, repulsive, slimy, smutty, soiled, sooty, squalid, unwashed, vile. ANT.—chaste, clean, immaculate, impeccable, pure.

uncommon, different, exceptional, exotic, extraordinary, infrequent, noteworthy, occasional, odd, rare, remarkable, scarce, singular, strange, unconventional, unique, unusual, unwonted. ANT.—conventional, customary, expected, typical, usual.

uncompromising, confirmed, contumacious, determined, dogged, firm, fixed, headstrong, immovable, inflexible, intractable, intransigent, narrow, obdurate, obstinate, orthodox, pertinacious, rigid, stiff, strict, stubborn, tough, unyielding. ANT.—adaptable, amenable, compliant, flexible, submissive, yielding.

unconcern, see indifference.

unconditional, absolute, carte blanche, certain, complete, definite, entire, full, genuine, positive, thorough, unequivocal, unlimited, unqualified, unrestricted, whole. ANT.—conditional, contingent, limited, partial, qualified.

uncouth, awkward, clumsy, coarse, crass, crude, gawky, graceless, harsh, ill-prepared, raw, rough, rude, rustic, unfinished, ungainly, ungraceful, unpolished, unrefined, vulgar. ANT.—cultivated, elegant, graceful, refined, symmetrical.

uncover, betray, divulge, impart; see also open.

under, below, beneath, following, inferior, subject to, subordinate, underneath. ANT.—above, over, superior.

undergo, feel, encounter, experience, sustain; see also tolerate.

understand, accept, appreciate, experience, gather, hear, interpret, learn, realize, recognize; see also comprehend.

understanding, accordance, agreement, concord, concurrence, harmony, unison; bargain, compact, contract, covenant, pact, stipulation; comprehension, discernment, grasp, insight, intellect, intelligence, knowledge, perception, perspicacity, rationality, reason, reasoning, sapience, wisdom. ANT.—contention, disagreement, discord, dissension, variance, wrangling; fatuity, foolishness, imbecility, incapacity, stupidity.

undertaking, action, attempt, business, effort, endeavor, engagement, enterprise, essay, experiment, performance, project, task, trial, venture, work. ANT.—inertia, laziness, negligence, passivity, shiftlessness.

undisguised, genuine, open, real, true, unadulterated, uncovered; see also sincere.

undivided, intact, integral, unimpaired; see also complete.

undying, see eternal.

unearthly, metaphysical, spiritual, superhuman; see also miraculous.

uneasy, afraid, alarmed, anxious, apprehensive, disturbed, fearful, fidgety, fretful, frightened, harried, irritable, nervous, peevish, petulant, restless, shaky, troubled, uncomfortable, unquiet, wakeful, worried. ANT.—calm, content, peaceful, serene, undismayed.

uneducated, uninformed, unlettered, unschooled; see also ignorant.

unemployed, idle, inactive, inert, jobless, loafing, out of work, unoccupied. ANT.—active, busy, employed, industrious, occupied.

unequal, disparate, ill-matched, inequitable, irregular, lop-sided, odd, one-sided, unbalanced, uneven, unfair, unlike, unparallel. ANT.—balanced, coequal, even, matched, uniform.

uneven, intermittent, irregular, jagged, notched, rough, rugged, spasmodic, unequal, variable. ANT.—even, matched, regular, smooth.

unexpected, amazing, astonishing, immediate, instantaneous, rapid, surprising, unforeseen; see also hasty.

unfair, biased, dishonest, disingenuous, hypocritical, inequitable, one-sided, partial, prejudiced, slanted, unethical, unjust. ANT.—ethical, fair, honest, just, unbiased.

unfavorable, counteractive, disastrous, unlucky; see also hostile.

unfeeling, apathetic, callous, cold, cruel, hard, harsh, inconsiderate, insensate, insensible, merciless, numb, pitiless, rigorous, senseless, severe, stony, unkind, unsympathetic. ANT.—compassionate, empathic, merciful, responsive, sympathetic.

unfit, improper, inappropriate, incapable, incompetent, inexpert, objectionable, unconditioned, unhealthy, unqualified, unsuitable. ANT.—capable, competent, fit, skilled, suitable.

unfold, elaborate, evolve, mature; see also expand.

unfortunate, afflicted, burdened, calamitous, desolate, disastrous, doomed, ill-fated, ill-starred, inexpedient, inopportune, miserable, overwhelmed, ruined, troubled, unhappy, unlucky, unsuccessful, unpropitious, untimely, wretched. ANT.—advantageous, beneficial, fortunate, opportune, propitious.

unhappy, calamitous, dejected, despondent, disconsolate, dismal, distressed, dolorous, gloomy, grievous, heartsick, miserable, mournful, sad, sorrowful, troubled, unfortunate, woeful, wretched. ANT.—contented, delighted, exhilarated, gratified, peaceful, satisfied.

uniform, agreeable, agreeing, alike, comformable, consistent, constant, customary, equable, equal, even, harmonious, homogenous, homologous, methodical, natural, normal, orderly, ordinary, periodical, proportionate, regular, stable, steady, symmetrical, systematic, unchanging, undeviating, undiversified, unvaried, unvarying. ANT.—amorphous, disordered, distorted, diversified, erratic, irregular, unsystematic.

unify, ally, amalgamate, blend, combine, concentrate, conjoin, connect, consolidate, entwine, join, merge, mix, organize, rally, solidify, strengthen, unite. ANT.—disperse, disrupt, divide, separate, split.

unimportant, commonplace, immaterial, incidental, inconsequential, inferior, irrelevant, mediocre, nugatory, ordinary, picayune, poor, slight; see also trivial.

uninformed, see ignorant.

unintelligible, cloudy, dim, dusky, indistinct, vague; see also mysterious.

uninteresting, burdensome, dreary, sluggish; see also monotonous.

union, amalgamation, annexation, attachment, blending, combination, commixture, concurrence, conjunction, connection, consolidation, coupling, fusion, incorporation, joining, junction, meeting, merging, mingling, solidarity, symbiosis, unification, uniting; affinity, agreement, concord, cooperation, harmony, unanimity, unison, unity; alliance, association, coalition, concert, confederacy, federation, league, marriage, organization. ANT.—disconnection, dispersion, division, separation; clash, conflict, disagreement, discordance, rebellion; dissociation, divorce, segregation, schism.

unique, choice, different, distinctive, exceptional, individual, matchless, novel, one, only, original, peculiar, rare, remarkable, single, singular, sole, solitary, uncommon, unequaled, unlike, unmatched, unparalleled, unprecedented, unrivaled, unusual. ANT.—commonplace, conventional, familiar, ordinary, prevailing.

unite, affiliate, ally, amalgamate, annex, associate, attach, blend, coalesce, combine, concur, confederate, conjoin, connect, consolidate, cooperate, couple, embody, embrace, entwine, fuse, join, link, meet, merge, mingle, mix, solidify, strengthen, unify. ANT.—disconnect, divide, part, separate, sever.

unity, agreement, concert, concord, constancy, continuity, harmony, oneness, singleness, solidarity, unification, uniformity, union. ANT.—discord, dissimilarity, diversity, multiplicity, variety.

universal, all, all-embracing, boundless, catholic, complete, comprehensive, cosmic, cosmopolitan, ecumenical, entire, exhaustive, generic, pandemic, prevailing, sweeping, total, unlimited, whole, world-wide. ANT.—distinctive, individual, partial, singular, unique.

universe, cosmos, creation, earth, firmament, galaxy, heavens, macrocosm, nature, world.

unlawful, see illegal.

unlike, divergent, incongruous, miscellaneous, sundry, variant; see also contrary, different.

unlimited, limitless, unconfined, unconstrained, undefined, unrestrained, unrestricted; see also infinite.

unlocked, ajar, disengaged, exposed, open, unclosed, unlatched; accessible, clear, free, passable, unobstructed. ANT.—closed, locked, sealed, shut; barred, blocked, impassable, inaccessible, obstructed, unobtainable.

unmistakable, see obvious.

unpretentious, candid, frank, modest, open, plain, simple, sincere, unobtrusive, unostentatious, unpretending. ANT.—deceitful, false, hypocritical, ostentatious, pompous.

unqualified, absolute, certain, conclusive, downright, indisputable, outright, positive, unconditional, unquestionable, unrestricted, utter; inappropriate, incapable, incompetent, ineligible, inept, inexperienced, unfit, unprepared. ANT.—conditional, contingent, dependent, qualified, questionable, uncertain; capable, competent, eligible, experienced, qualified.

unreasonable, absurd, fatuous, foolish, illogical, implausible, inconsistent, irrational, ludicrous, mindless, nonsensical, preposterous, ridiculous, self-contradictory, senseless, silly, stupid, untenable. ANT.—consistent, judicious, rational, reasonable, sensible, wise.

unrestricted, accessible, accorded, allowable, available, clear, exposed, free, open, passable, permitted, public, sanctioned, unobstructed, welcoming. ANT.—denied, forbidden, private, prohibited, refused.

unruly, disobedient, fractious, headstrong, lawless, mutinous, obstreperous, rebellious, recalcitrant, refractory, stubborn, ungovernable, violent, wanton, willful. ANT.—docile, law-abiding, manageable, obedient, tractable.

unsafe, critical, dangerous, hazardous, imperiled, insecure, menacing, perilous, precarious, risky, threatening, treacherous, unreliable, unstable. ANT.—firm, harmless, protected, safe, secure.

unscrupulous, dishonorable, reckless, ruthless, unconscientious, unprincipled, unrestrained; see also dishonest.

unseemly, boorish, brutish, clownish, depraved, disgraceful, disorderly, dissolute, dowdy, gross, ill-advised, immoral, improper, imprudent, inappropriate, indecorous, inept, inexpedient, inopportune, objectionable, rowdy, slovenly, unbecoming, unfit, ungraceful, unkempt, unpolished, unsightly, unsuitable, vulgar, worthless. ANT.—commendable, cultivated, fitting, polished, proper, suave.

unselfish, see generous.

unsettled, adrift, apprehensive, changeable, fickle, inconstant, nervous, perturbed, restless, stirred, troubled, unhinged, unnerved, unstable, unsteady, vacillating, wavering; uninhabited, wild; outstanding, owing, unpaid; foul, muddy, roily, turbid. ANT.—calm, certain, constant, peaceful, secure; inhabited, settled; cleared, paid, solvent; clarified, immaculate, pure, sparkling, untainted.

unskilled, awkward, clumsy, ignorant, ill-qualified, incompetent, inept, inexperienced, maladroit, rusty, unfit, unpracticed. ANT.—accomplished, competent, efficient, expert, trained.

unsophisticated, artless, candid, frank, fresh, genuine, guileless, ignorant, ingenuous, innocent, naive, natural, open, pure, real, simple, true, unaffected, undesigning, unspoiled, unstudied, unvitiated. ANT.—experienced, guileful, hard, initiated, sophisticated, worldly.

unstable, see fickle.

unswerving, fast, inflexible, solid, unyielding; see also stable.

unusual, aberrant, abnormal, anomalous, atypical, awesome, capricious, curious, devious, distinguished, eccentric, exceptional, extraordinary, incredible, irregular, odd, rare, strange, uncommon, unique, unnatural, unparalleled, variable. ANT.—common, normal, ordinary, regular, usual.

unyielding, see unswerving.

upbraid, blame, lecture, reprehend, vituperate; see also rebuke.

uphold, see maintain.

upright, direct, right, undeviating, unswerving; erect, standing, straight, unbent, vertical; conscientious, ethical, fair, faithful, honest, honorable, incorruptible, just, moral, scrupulous, square, straightforward, true, trustworthy, virtuous. ANT.—deviating, indirect, swerving; bent, horizontal, prone; corruptible, crooked, dishonest, fraudulent, immoral, lax.

upset, disturb, haunt, inconvenience, perplex, worry; see also pester.

urbane, considerate, well-mannered; see also polite.

urge, appetite, aspiration, hungering, lust; induce, prevail upon, win over; see also desire; persuade.

urgency, importance, need, seriousness; see also emergency.

urgent, absorbing, breathless, chief, cogent, compelling, critical, crucial, demanded, essential, exigent, grave, impelling, imperative, important, importunate, insistent, instant, momentous, necessary, pressing, principal, required, salient, serious, vital, weighty. ANT.—common, insignificant, petty, trivial, unessential, uneventful.

use, apply, avail, employ, exploit, handle, manage, manipulate, operate, ply, utilize, wield; exercise, exert, practice, work; consume, exhaust, expend; accustom, familiarize, habituate, inure; application, employment, service, utilization; necessity, need; advantage, usefulness; method, technique, usage; see also habit.

useful, advantageous, applicable, beneficial, gainful, good, helpful, practical, pragmatic, profitable, remunerative, salutory, serviceable, suitable, utilitarian, valuable, wholesome. ANT.—deleterious, destructive, detrimental, harmful, noxious.

usefulness, adaptability, advantage, application, convenience, helpfulness, practicality, utility, versatility; see also merit.

useless, abortive, empty, fruitless, futile, idle, inadequate, ineffective, ineffectual, pointless, unavailing, unproductive, unserviceable, vain, valueless, vapid, worthless. ANT.—beneficial, effective, potent, profitable, valuable.

usual, accustomed, common, commonplace, conventional, current, customary, everyday, expected, familiar, frequent, general, habitual, normal, ordinary, prevailing, prevalent, prosaic, recognized, regular, stereotyped. ANT.—abnormal, exceptional, extraordinary, rare, unconventional.

utensil, apparatus, appliance, device, equipment, implement, instrument, medium, tool, vehicle, ware.

utility, adequacy, advantage, avail, benefit, convenience, efficacy, efficiency, expediency, favor, productiveness, profit, service, serviceableness, usefulness, utilitarianism, value, worth. ANT.—disadvantage, futility, inefficacy, uselessness, worthlessness.

utilize, adopt, apply, appropriate, avail, employ, exercise, exert, exploit, occupy, practice, use. ANT.—discard, discharge, expel, refuse, reject.

utmost, absolute, chief, extreme, farthest, greatest, highest, last, main, maximum, most, ultimate, unqualified, uttermost. ANT.—closest, least, merest, minimum, nearest.

utopian, chimerical, exemplary, fabulous, fancied, fantastic, faultless, ideal, illusory, imaginary, perfect, supreme, unreal, visionary. ANT.—actual, faulty, imperfect, substantial, tangible, visible.

utter, complete, entire, finished, full, perfect, thorough, total, whole; consummate, excellent, ideal, pure, superlative, supreme; absolute, downright, sheer, unconditional, unqualified, unrestricted, wholehearted; acclaim, air, announce, articulate, assert, claim, declare, disclose, divulge, emit, enunciate, express, inform, proclaim, pronounce, speak, talk, tell, vocalize, voice, whisper. ANT.—imperfect, incomplete, lacking, partial, unfinished; inferior, lesser, negligible, poor; conditional, limited, qualified, restricted; conceal, cover, hide, mask, withhold.

V

vacant, abandoned, bare, barren, blank, depleted, deserted, empty, hollow, idle, tenantless, unfilled, uninhabited, unoccupied, untenanted, unused, vacuous, void; dreaming, empty-headed, foolish, inane, silly, thoughtless. ANT.—filled, full, inhabited, occupied, overflowing; cogitative, contemplative, meditative, reflective, thoughtful, wise.

vacate, abandon, abdicate, abjure, depart, desert, empty, evacuate, forsake, leave, quit, relinquish, resign, surrender, waive. ANT.—assume, maintain, remain, stay, support.

vacillate, change, oscillate, undulate, vary; see also hesitate.

vacillation, changeableness, faltering, fluctuation, hesitation, inconstancy, indecision, irresolution, oscillation, reeling, rocking, swaying, uncertainty, unsteadiness, wavering. ANT.—certainty, constancy, dependability, firmness.

vagrant, beggar, bum, hobo, idler, loafer, rambler, rogue, rover, straggler, tramp, truant, vagabond, wanderer; changeable, digressive, discursive, divergent, erratic, fickle, fluctuating, homeless, idle, inconstant, irresolute, itinerant, nomadic, peripatetic, ranging, roaming, roving, straying, traveling, unsettled, unstable, unsteady, wandering. ANT.—gentleman, laborer, toiler, worker, workman; anchored, established, fixed, rooted, stable.

vague, cryptic, dark, doubtful, dubious, enigmatic, formless, imprecise, mysterious, nebulous, questionable, unsure, visionary; see also indefinite.

vain, abortive, bootless, delusive, empty, fleeting, frivolous, fruitless, futile, hollow, idle, ineffective, ineffectual, nugatory, pointless, shadowy, trifling, trivial, unavailing, unprofitable, unsatisfactory, useless, valueless, vapid, visionary, worthless; arrogant, conceited, egotistical, inflated, ostentatious, proud, showy, vainglorious. ANT.—advantageous, effective, potent, profitable, valuable; demure, genuine, humble, meek, modest, unpretentious.

valiant, adventurous, assertive, audacious, bold, brave, chivalrous, courageous, daring, dauntless, fearless, gallant, heroic, indomitable, intrepid, magnanimous, manly, plucky, puissant, spirited, strong-willed, unafraid, undismayed, unflinching, unshrinking, valorous, venturesome, vigorous. ANT.—cowardly, craven, fearful, timid, timorous, weak.

valid, accurate, actual, authentic, binding, cogent, conclusive, convincing, definite, effective, efficacious, efficient, factual, forceful, genuine, legal, legitimate, logical, operative, powerful, real, solid, sound, strong, substantial, sufficient, telling, tested, true, weighty. ANT.—counterfeit, erroneous, fallacious, invalid, spurious.

valor, chivalry, manliness, prowess, spiritedness; see also courage.

valuable, costly, expensive, high-priced, rare; dear, esteemed, precious, worthy; profitable, serviceable, useful. ANT.—cheap, common, unmarketable; abhorred, disliked, disrespectable, worthless; profitless, useless.

value, appreciate, cherish, esteem, hold dear, prize, treasure; appraise, assess, compute, estimate, figure, rate; advantage, appreciation, consideration, esteem, estimation, excellence, importance, merit, price, profit, quality, significance, usefulness, utility, valuation, virtue, worth, worthiness. ANT.—abandon, despise, ignore, neglect, overlook, reject; inexpedience, inutility, unfitness, uselessness, worthlessness.

vandalism, barbarism, burning, damage, destruction, looting, piracy, spoliation, wasting, wrecking. ANT.—care, preservation, protection, repair, replacement.

vanish, cease, depart, die, disappear, dissolve, evaporate, fade, go away, sink. ANT.—appear, emerge, reappear.

vanity, affectation, arrogance, conceit, conceitedness, display, egotism, ostentation, pretension, self-applause, self-glorification, selfishness, self-laudation, self-love, show, vainglory. ANT.—bashfulness, diffidence, humility, modesty, unobtrusiveness.

vanquish, beat, outwit, suppress; see also conquer.

vapid, banal, bland, commonplace, dry, dull, feeble, flat, hackneyed, inane, insipid, lifeless, prosaic, spiritless, tasteless, trite, uninteresting. ANT.—bright, fresh, original, pungent, stimulating, striking.

vapor, breath, cloud, condensation, effluvium, emanation, exhalation, fog, fume, gas, haze, mist, smoke, smog, spray, steam.

variable, see fickle.

variation, aberration, alteration, change, contrariety, contrast, departure, deviation, difference, disagreement, discord, discrepancy, disparity, dissent, dissidence, dissimilarity, dissimilitude, distinction, diversity, fluctuation, heterogeneity, incongruity, inconsistency, innovation, modification, mutation, noncomformity, oscillation, variety, vicissitude. ANT.—agreement, congruity, homogeneity, permanence, stability, uniformity.

variety, change, difference, dissimilarity, diversification, diversity, heterogeneity, medley, miscellany, mixture, multifariousness, variance; array, assortment, brand, breed, category, class, division, family, genus, grade, kind, race, rank, sort, species, stock, strain, subspecies, tribe, type. ANT.—homogeneity, likeness, monotony, sameness, uniformity, unity.

various, assorted, different, disparate, divergent, divers, diverse, manifold, many, miscellaneous, numerous, several, sundry. ANT.—alike, congruous, identical, same, uniform.

vary, exchange, substitute; shift, transfigure, veer; see also modify.

vast, ample, big, capacious, extensive, great, large; see also colossal.

vault, see jump.

vehement, ardent, burning, eager, enthusiastic, excitable, fervent, fervid, fiery, glowing, hot, impetuous, intense, irascible, passionate. ANT.—apathetic, calm, cool, indifferent, lukewarm.

veil, cloak, clothe, curtain, envelop, guard; see also conceal.

velocity, alacrity, celerity, impetus, pace, quickness, rapidity, speed, swiftness.

venerable, adored, aged, ancient, antiquated, antique, archaic, elderly, erudite, esteemed, honored, old, patriarchal, respected, revered, superannuated, time-worn, venerated, worshipped. ANT.—callow, immature, inexperienced, modern, new.

venerate, admire, adore, appreciate, approve, cherish, esteem, honor, regard, respect, revere, worship. ANT.—abhor, despise, dislike, loathe, scorn.

vengeance, reparation, reprisal, requital, spitefulness; see also revenge.

venom, acerbity, bitterness, contempt, enmity, gall, hate, malevolence, malice, malignity, poison, rancor, resentment, virulence. ANT.—benevolence, charity, fellowship, love, warmheartedness.

vent, belch, breathe, discharge, eject, emanate, emit, expel, explode, shoot, spurt, ventilate; airhole, crenel, emission, escape, hole, inlet, loophole, mouth, nostril, opening, orifice, outlet, overflow, passage, plug, spiracle, spout, tap, valve.

ventilate, aerate, air, circulate air, cool, explain, express, fan, freshen, open, oxygenate, purify, refresh, vent.

venture, adventure, attempt, business, chance, dare, enterprise, experiment, gamble, hazard, investment, peril, project, risk, speculation, stake, trial, undertaking, work; advance, assay, attempt, bet, brave, dare, experiment, gamble, grope, hazard, invest, risk, speculate, try, wager.

veracity, accuracy, candor, credibility, exactitude, fidelity, frankness, honesty, probity, reality, sincerity, truth, truthfulness. ANT.—chicanery, deception, duplicity, falsehood, misrepresentation.

verbal, announced, communicated, expressed, lingual, literal, nuncupative, oral, sounded, spoken, told, unwritten, uttered, vocal, voiced. ANT.—documentary, printed, unspoken, written.

verbose, chattering, chatty, fluent, garrulous, long-winded, loquacious, redundant, talkative, verbal, wordy. ANT.—concise, laconic, silent, stammering, taciturn, uncommunicative.

verdict, adjudication, arbitrament, conclusion, decision, decree, determination, finding, judgment, result.

verge, border, boundary, brim, brink, confine, edge, end, extreme, limit, lip, margin, rim, skirt. ANT.—body, bulk, center, inside.

verification, affirmation, attestation, authentication, confirmation, corroboration, demonstration, evidence, proof, recognition, support, testimony. ANT.—contradiction, denial, failure, fallacy, invalidity.

verify, acknowledge, affirm, approve, assure, attest, authenticate, certify, corroborate, confirm, determine, establish, fix, prove, ratify, sanction, settle, strengthen, substantiate, validate. ANT.—contradict, deny, disprove, invalidate, repudiate.

versed, acquainted, aware, cognizant, conversant, familiar, intimate, knowing, proficient, skilled. ANT.—unaware, unfamiliar, unknowing.

versatile, adaptable, apt, changeable, many-sided, movable, ready, variable. ANT.—awkward, limited, unadaptable, unchanging.

vertical, erect, perpendicular, plumb, standing, straight, upright. ANT.—flat, horizontal, inclined, oblique, prone, supine.

vestige, mark, remainder, remains, remnant, residue, scrap, sign, trace.

vex, aggravate, embitter, inflame; see also irritate.

vibrate, agitate, flicker, fluctuate, flutter, jar, jolt, oscillate, pulsate, quake, quaver, quiver, rock, shake, shiver, shudder, sway, swing, totter, tremble, undulate, wave, waver.

vice, blemish, blot, carnality, debauchery, defect, excess, fault, impropriety, impurity, iniquity, offense, perversity, sin, transgression, ungodliness; see also evil.

vicinity, district, domain, environment, environs, locality, neighborhood, realm, region, sector, territory; adjacency, nearness, proximity. ANT.—outskirts; distance, remoteness.

vicious, bad, base, corrupt, debased, degenerate, demoralized, depraved, destructive, evil, harmful, hurtful, malignant, obnoxious, pernicious, profligate, reprehensible, sinful, unruly, vile, virulent, wicked. ANT.—admirable, exemplary, honorable, noble, upright, virtuous.

victim, dupe, gull, martyr, prey, puppet, quarry, sacrifice, scapegoat, sufferer, wretch. ANT.—culprit, evil-doer, felon, swindler.

victor, champion, conqueror, hero, master, vanquisher, winner. ANT.—failure, loser, underdog, vanquished, victim.

victory, achievement, ascendancy, conquest, defeating, mastery, overcoming, subjugation, success, superiority, supremacy, triumph, win, winning. ANT.—collapse, defeat, failure, frustration, overthrow.

view, aim, belief, conception, examination, glance, glimpse, goal, impression, inspection, judgment, look, object, observation, opinion, outlook, panorama, perspective, picture, prospect, range, regard, scene, sight, survey, theory, vision, vista; behold, consider, discern, examine, eye, gaze, glance, inspect, look, observe, regard, scan, scrutinize, see, stare, survey, watch, witness. ANT.—avert, disregard, ignore, miss, overlook, sidetrack.

viewpoint, angle, aspect, attitude, disposition, light, outlook, perspective, pose, position, posture, slant, stand, standpoint.

vigilant, alert, attentive, careful, cautious, circumspect, guarded, heedful, observant, wakeful, wary, watchful, wide-awake. ANT.—careless, foolhardy, negligent, rash, reckless.

vigor, endurance, energy, force, fortitude, hardihood, health, liveliness, lustiness, spirit, strength, verge, virility, vitality, well-being, zeal. ANT.—exhaustion, languor, lassitude, listlessness.

vigorous, active, animated, blithe, brisk, energetic, flourishing, forceful, frolicsome, healthy, lively, lusty, powerful, robust, spirited, sprightly, strenuous, strong, virile, vital, vivacious. ANT.—debilitated, feeble, frail, inactive, lethargic.

vile, abject, base, brutish, cheap, contemptible, debased, depraved, despicable, disgusting, evil, foul, gross, ignoble, impure, iniquitous, loathsome, low, mean, obscene, odious, repulsive, revolting, sinful, sordid, ugly, vicious, vulgar, wicked, worthless, wretched. ANT.—attractive, decent, elevated, honorable, laudable, valuable.

vilify, abuse, asperse, ill-use, revile, scandalize; see also malign.

villainous, bad, base, evil, unsound, unwholesome; see also deleterious, iniquitous.

vindicate, advocate, assert, avenge, defend, excuse, maintain, support, uphold; see also exonerate.

vindictive, avenging, grudgeful, implacable, malevolent, malicious, rancorous, resentful, unforgiving, vengeful. ANT.—conciliatory, excusing, forgiving, placable.

violate, break, disobey, disregard, encroach, infringe, invade, transgress; debauch, defile, deflower, desecrate, dishonor, outrage, pollute, profane, rape, ravish.

violence, assault, fury, intensity, outrage, vehemence, violation, wildness; see also force.

violent, angry, convulsive, fierce, fiery, frantic, frenzied, fuming, furious, hysterical, obstreperous, passionate, raging, rampant, raving, riotous, savage, turbulent, ungovernable, uproarious, vehement, wild; acute, extreme, forceful, great, intense, mighty, potent, powerful, severe, strong. ANT.—composed, kind, pacific, peaceful, tranquil, unruffled; feeble, insignificant, mild, moderate, weak.

virgin, chaste, clean, immaculate, innocent, modest, pure, spotless, stainless, unadulterated, unblemished, undefiled, unsullied, untainted, virginal; first, fresh, genuine, natural, new, original, undisturbed, untamed, untouched. ANT.—corrupt, defiled, shameless; foul, poisoned, polluted, soiled.

virile, hardy, lusty, vigorous; see also masculine.

virtue, chastity, decency, goodness, honesty, honor, impeccability, innocence, integrity, morality, probity, prudence, purity, rectitude, sanctity, temperance, uprightness, virginity; effectiveness, efficacy, force, fortitude, power, strength; distinction, excellence, merit, superiority, value, worth. ANT.—corruption, depravity, dishonor, vileness, wickedness; debility, enervation, infirmity, weakness; deficiency, inferiority, inutility, uselessness, worthlessness.

virtuous, decent, honorable, just, right, scrupulous; see also chaste, ethical.

visible, see evident, fair, manifest.

vision, apparition, appearance, chimera, conception, daydream, discernment, dream, fancy, ghost, hallucination, hope, illusion, image, manifestation, mirage, perception, phantasm, phantom, prophecy, revelation, shadow, sight, specter. ANT.—actuality, blindness, corporality, fact, substantiality, verity.

visionary, chimerical, delusory, dreamy, fancied, fanciful, ideal, illusory, imaginary, imaginative, romantic, unreal, utopian. ANT.—actual, material, real, substantial.

vital, alive, animate, existing, living; basic, cardinal, essential, fundamental, important, indispensable, necessary, paramount, requisite, urgent. ANT.—dead, inanimate, lifeless; dispensable, excessive, insignificant, trivial, unimportant.

vitality, being, existence, life; animation, ardor, buoyancy, energy, intensity, liveliness, spirit, spunk, verve, vigor, vim, vivacity. ANT.—death, demise, extinction; apathy, lassitude, lethargy, passivity, torpor.

vitiate, abase, adulterate, alloy, annul, contaminate, corrupt, damage, debase, defile, degrade, deprave, depress, deteriorate, humiliate, impair, infect, injure, lower, nullify, pervert, poison, pollute, ruin, spoil, void. ANT.—clean, enhance, improve, purify, revive, vitalize.

vivid, animated, bright, brilliant, clear, expressive, fresh, graphic, intense, lifelike, lively, lucid, pictorial, picturesque, realistic, sprightly, striking, strong, telling, vibrant. ANT.—cloudy, dreary, dull, vague, weak.

vocal, announced, articulate, communicated, expressed, expressive, fluent, musical, oral, spoken, sung, uttered, verbal, vocalized, voiced, voluble. ANT.—printed, quiet, silent, unspoken, written.

vocation, art, business, calling, commerce, employment, engagement, enterprise, field, job, lifework, mission, occupation, office, position, profession, pursuit, role, situation, trade, trading, undertaking, work. ANT.—avocation, diversion, entertainment, hobby, pastime.

voice, accent, articulation, call, cry, enunciation, expression, intonation, noise, pronunciation, sound, speech, tongue, utterance, vocalization; choice, election, suffrage, vote; announce, assert, cry, declaim, declare, express, say, sound, speak, talk, tell, utter.

void, blank, lacking; see also empty.

volatile, airy, buoyant, changeable, effervescent, evaporable, fleeting, gaseous, inconstant, irresolute, light, resilient, vacillating, vaporous, vapory, wavering, weak; active, animated, blithe, cheerful, elated, jocund, lively, playful, vivacious. ANT.—durable, heavy, massive, soluble, weighty; dejected, despondent, hopeless, melancholy, sad.

volition, choice, decision, determination, election, intention, resolution, resolve, selection, will. ANT.—coercion, compulsion, force, persuasion, pressure.

volume, capability, power, talent; amount, extent, mass, size; book, edition, printed document, publication; see also capacity.

voluntary, deliberate, elective, free, intentional, self-determining, uncoerced, unforced, volitional, willful, willing. ANT.—compulsory, enforced, forced, instinctive, involuntary, mandatory, required.

volunteer, come forward, enlist, extend, sacrifice, submit oneself; see also offer.

vouch, affirm, assert, attest, avow, certify, confirm, declare, depose, guarantee, support, swear, testify, uphold, warrant. ANT.—abnegate, controvert, deny, disavow, repudiate.

vow, oath, pledge, promise; affirm, assert, certify, consecrate, dedicate, devote, pledge, promise, swear.

vulgar, abusive, base, brutish, cheap, coarse, common, crass, disgusting, general, gross, ignorant, ill-bred, indecent, inelegant, low, obscene, odious, offensive, plebeian, popular, profane, ribald, rough, rowdy, rude, tawdry, uncouth, uncultured, unpolished, unrefined. ANT.—aristocratic, charming, cultured, elegant, polished, refined.

vulnerable, assailable, defenseless, exposed, unprotected, unsafe; see also insecure.

W

wager, bet, chance, gage, gamble, hazard, play, punt, risk, sport, stake; betting, gambling, risk, speculation.

wages, compensation, earnings, fee, income, pay, payment, recompense, remuneration, salary, stipend. ANT.—donation, gift, gratuity.

wait, abide, bide, delay, linger, remain, rest, stay, tarry; await, expect, watch; attend, minister, serve. ANT.—act, depart, hasten, leave, proceed; disregard, neglect, reject; hamper, hinder, impede, oppose.

waive, see renounce.

wake, activate, animate, arouse, awake, awaken, call, enkindle, excite, kindle, prod, revive, rouse, stimulate, stir, wake.

wallow, flounder, grovel, immerse, revel, roll, toss, welter.

wander, deviate, digress, diverge, drift, err, journey, meander, peregrinate, ramble, range, roam, rove, saunter, straggle, stray, stroll, tour, traipse, travel, traverse. ANT.—halt, pause, remain, settle, stay.

want, aspire, covet, crave, desire, long for, wish; be destitute, lack, need, require, suffer privation; dearth, deficiency, depletion, destitution, exigency, inadequacy, indigence, insufficiency, lack, necessity, need, neediness, pauperism, penury, poverty, privation, scarcity,

starvation. ANT.—abhor, detest, dislike; enjoy, have, own, possess; abundance, affluence, opulence, riches, wealth.

ward, care, charge, custody, dependent, guardianship, minor, protection; district, division, precinct, quarter, section; defend, guard, keep, parry, protect, safeguard, watch.

warfare, armed struggle, battle, combat, conflict, contest, fighting, hostilities, military operations, mobilization. ANT.—accord, armistice, harmony, peace, truce.

wariness, see heed.

warlike, see hostile.

warm, affable, affectionate, ardent, compassionate, cordial, earnest, empathic, enthusiastic, fervent, friendly, genial, gracious, heartfelt, hearty, loving, responsive, sincere, sociable, sympathetic, tender, warmhearted; feverish, flushed, heated, lukewarm, melting, mild, sunny, temperate, tepid; comfortable, cozy, secure, sheltered, snug; chafe, foment, heat, incite, melt, thaw. ANT.—aloof, cold, detached, diffident, taciturn; cold, cool, freezing, frosty, icy; disturbed, exposed, insecure, uncomfortable, uneasy; calm, chill, freeze, soothe, temper.

warn, admonish, caution, counsel, forebode, forewarn, signal, summon; see also notify.

warning, admonition, advice, alarm, augury, caution, indication, information, notice, omen, portent, prediction, premonition, sign, signal, summons, threat.

wary, attentive, alert, awake, aware, careful, cautious, circumspect, discreet, guarded, heedful, mindful, observant, provident, scrupulous, thoughtful, vigilant, watchful. ANT.—foolhardy, impulsive, negligent, precipitate, rash.

wash, bathe, clean, cleanse, douse, immerse, launder, lave, rinse, scour, scrub, soak, soap, wet, wipe. ANT.—dirty, foul, soil, stain.

waste, abandoned, bare, bleak, deserted, desolate, discarded, empty, forlorn, forsaken, futile, lonely, pointless, solitary, uninhabited, useless, wild, worthless; abuse, consume, dissipate, exhaust, lavish, misapply, misspend, misuse, scatter, spend, squander, wear out; decay, diminish, dwindle, pine, wither; corrode, damage, despoil, destroy, devastate, pillage, plunder, ravage, ruin, sack, strip. ANT.—attended, cultivated, fertile, inhabited, productive; hoard, preserve, redeem, retain, save; grow, prosper, thrive, triumph; defend, guard, harbor, protect, shield.

wasteful, careless, destructive, dissipated, extravagant, improvident, lavish, prodigal, profligate, profuse, reckless, ruinous, squandering, thriftless, unthrifty, wild. ANT.—conservative, economical, hoarding, mercenary, thrifty.

watch, attend, behold, contemplate, descry, discern, distinguish, espy, follow, glimpse, guard, inspect, mark, mind, notice, observe, perceive, regard, scan, scrutinize, see, view, wait, witness.

watchful, alert, attentive, careful, cautious, circumspect, guarded, heedful, observant, prudent, vigilant, wakeful, wary, watchful, wideawake. ANT.—careless, inattentive, lax, neglectful, oblivious.

water, bathe, deluge, dilute, douse, drench, flood, immerse, irrigate, moisten, soak, sprinkle, steep, wash, wet. ANT.—dehydrate, drain, dry, parch, sear.

wave, billow, breaker, ripple, roller, surge, swell, undulation; beckon, flap, flutter, oscillate, shake, signal, stir, sway, swing.

waver, boggle, deliberate, dillydally, equivocate, falter, flicker, fluctuate, flutter, hesitate, oscillate, quiver, reel, shake, totter, tremble, twitch, vacillate, vibrate.

wavering, see fickle.

way, allay, approach, artery, avenue, channel, course, driveway, entrance, gateway, highway, lane, pass, passage, path, pathway, road, roadway, route, street, thoroughfare, track, trail, walk; design, fashion, form, habit, manner, means, method, mode, plan, practice, procedure, process, style, system.

weak, bending, delicate, faint, fragile, frail, pliant, soft, tender, yielding; debilitated, decrepit, enervated, exhausted, feeble, flaccid, impotent, infirm, nervous, shaky, wasted, worn; illogical, inadequate, ineffective, ineffectual, lame, poor, vague; assailable, defenseless, exposed, helpless, powerless, unguarded, unsubstantial, vulnerable. ANT.—rigid, strong, unyielding; animated, healthy, robust, vigorous; cogent, effective, efficacious, persuasive, potent; defended, protected, safe, secure, unthreatened.

weaken, attenuate, cramp, cripple, debilitate, devitalize, dilute, diminish, enervate, enfeeble, exhaust, impair, incapacitate, reduce, relax, sap, thin, undermine. ANT.—brace, energize, fortify, invigorate, strengthen.

weakness, see disability.

wealth, abundance, affluence, assets, capital, fortune, luxury, means, money, opulence, plenty, possessions, prosperity, riches, resources, securities, stock, substance, treasure. ANT.—indigence, need, poverty, privation, want.

wear, abrade, bear, carry, consume, diminish, display, endure, erode, impair, use, waste; service, use, utilization.

weariness, annoyance, disgust, ennui, exhaustion, faintness, fatigue, languor, lassitude, lethargy, prostration, tedium, tiredness. ANT.—alertness, amusement, energy, strength, vim.

weary, bored, exhausted, faint, fatigued, jaded, spent, tired, wearied, worn; anger, annoy, bore, bother, deject, depress, discourage, disgust, dishearten, dispirit, displease, distress, enfeeble, exhaust, fatigue, grieve, irk, irritate, jade, overburden, overtax, pain, prostrate, sadden, strain, tire, vex. ANT.—animated, fresh, invigorated, refreshed, rested; arouse, brace, energize, enliven, revive, strengthen.

weather, bear, bleach, discolor, disintegrate, dry, endure, expand, fade, overcome, resist, rot, shrink, split, stand, sustain, tan, toughen.

weave, braid, compose, construct, crochet, design, fabricate, form, imagine, intertwine, knit, lace, mat, twist.

wedding, see marriage.

weigh, consider, examine, heed, study; see also ponder.

weight, ballast, burden, contents, density, gravity, heaviness, load, mass, tonnage; pressure; authority, consequence, domination, emphasis, import, importance, influence, moment, power, seriousness, significance, stress, sway, value. ANT.—airiness, buoyancy, levity, lightness; insignificance, pettiness, smallness, triviality, worthlessness.

weird, curious, eerie, ghostly, mysterious, odd, peculiar, spooky, strange, supernatural, uncanny, unearthly, wild. ANT.—common, normal, ordinary, regular, usual.

welcome, accept, address, admit, embrace, entertain, greet, hail, hug, receive, recognize, salute, shelter, take in. ANT.—discharge, ignore, reject, snub, turn away.

well, adequately, admirably, competently, expertly, extremely, favorably, satisfactorily, strongly, suitably; see also healthy.

well-being, contentment, delight, felicity, fortune, gladness, happiness, health, pleasure, prosperity, satisfaction, serenity, welfare, wholeness.

ANT.—depression, distress, illness, suffering, trouble.

well-bred, see polite.

well-known, see distinguished.

wheel, bicycle, circle, disk, roller; eddy, gyrate, pirouette, revolve, roll, rotate, spin, swirl, transport, turn, twist, veer, whirl, wind.

whim, caprice, dream, fancy, fantasy, humor, idea, impulse, inclination, notion, quirk, tendency, vagary, vision, whimsy.

whimsical, curious, droll, peculiar, quaint; see also eccentric.

whole, absolute, all, complete, entire, full, inclusive, intact integral, inviolate, perfect, plenary, total, unabridged, unbroken, undivided, unimpaired; hale, healed, healthy, sound, well. ANT.—defective, fragmentary, imperfect, incomplete, partial; diseased, feeble, impaired, infirm, sickly.

wholesome, beneficial, nourishing, nutritive; hearty, robust, strong; see also healthy; whole.

wicked, atrocious, base, corrupt, criminal, deleterious, disorderly, disreputable, dissolute, erring, evil, fiendish, foul, gross, hellish, immoral, impure, infamous, iniquitous, irreligious, malevolent, murderous, nefarious, noxious, pernicious, scandalous, shameful, sinful, unrighteous, unsound, vicious, vile, villainous, wayward, wrong. ANT.—admirable, commendable, honorable, moral, noble, praiseworthy, virtuous.

wide, all-inclusive, blanket, broad, comprehensive, expanded, extensive, general, large, sweeping, universal, vast. ANT.—confined, hampered, limited, narrow, restricted.

wild, undomesticated, untamed; rough, uncultivated; impetuous, irregular, turbulent, wayward; extravagant, foolish, giddy; boisterous. see also barbarous; fierce; desolate; reckless; stormy.

will, choice, conviction, decision, desire, determination, inclination, intent, intention, mind, preference, purpose, resolution, volition, willingness, wish. ANT.—coercion, compulsion, doubt, indecision, wavering.

willful, see intentional.

win, see gain, succeed.

wind, air, blast, breeze, current, cyclone, draft, flurry, flutter, gale, gust, hurricane, squall, storm, tempest, typhoon, zephyr; coil, fold, twine, twist, wreathe; bend, crook, curve, deviate, meander, sinuate, snake, zigzag.

winding, bending, coiling, crooked, curving, devious, involuted, meandering, sinuous, turning, twining, twisting, writhing. ANT.—direct, plain, straight.

wisdom, acumen, astuteness, comprehension, depth, discernment, discretion, discrimination, enlightenment, erudition, farsightedness, foresight, insight, intelligence, judgment, knowledge, learning, perspicacity, prudence, reason, reasoning, sagacity, sense, understanding. ANT.—absurdity, fatuity, foolishness, ignorance, imprudence, misjudgment.

wise, advisable, alert, astute, calculating, deep, discerning, discreet, enlightened, erudite, foresighted, informed, intelligent, judicious, penetrating, profound, prudent, rational, sagacious, sage, sane, sensible, shrewd, smart, sound.

wish, appetite, aspiration, bid, craving, desire, hungering, longing, lust, need, petition, plea, request, urge, yearning; covet, crave, desire, hanker, hope, hunger, long, pine, thirst, want, yearn.

wit, comprehension, intellect, intelligence, mind, perception, perspicacity, reason, sagacity, sense, understanding; banter, burlesque, cleverness,

drollery, facetiousness, fun, humor, irony, jest, jocularity, playfulness, raillery, sarcasm, satire, witticism; comedian, humorist, joker, wag. ANT.—dullness, stupidity; gloom, gravity, melancholy, pessimism, solemnity; cynic, misanthrope, pessimist.

witchcraft, bewitchment, black art, black magic, charm, conjuration, conjuring, demonology, divination, enchantment, incantation, legerdemain, magic, necromancy, sorcery, spell, voodooism, witchery, wizardry.

withdraw, abandon, abjure, abstract, deduct, depart, desert, dissociate, disengage, draw, forsake, give up, go, leave, part, quit, recall, recant, relinquish, remove, renounce, retire, retract, retreat, revoke, secede, separate, sequester, shrink, vacate, wean. ANT.—abide, introduce, remain, return, stay, tarry.

wither, decay, decline, deteriorate, droop, dry up, fail, languish, shrink, shrivel, sink, waste, weaken, wilt, wizen, wrinkle. ANT.—bloom, invigorate, refresh, rejuvenate, revive.

withhold, abstain, check, conceal, deny, desist, detain, forbear, hide, hinder, keep, refrain, refuse, reserve, restrain, retain, suppress. ANT.—accord, concede, grant, indulge, persist, yield.

withstand, bar, combat, confront, contradict, counteract, defy, endure, face, hinder, hold out, obstruct, resist, thwart. ANT.—acquiesce, consent, submit, succumb, yield.

witness, attestation, confirmation, declaration, evidence, proof, testimony; attestor, beholder, bystander, corroborator, deponent, eyewitness, observer, onlooker, spectator, testifier, watcher; attest, bear witness, confirm, corroborate, mark, note, observe, see, testify, vouch, watch.

witty, droll, facetious, funny; see also clever.

wizardry, see witchcraft.

woe, see disaster; misery.

womanly, compassionate, gentle, ladylike, maidenly, modest, protective. see also feminine.

wonder, curiosity, marvel, miracle, oddity, phenomenon, portent, prodigy, rarity, sight, sign, spectacle; admiration, amazement, astonishment, awe, bewilderment, confusion, curiosity, fascination, perplexity, stupefaction, surprise, wonderment; admire, doubt, gape, marvel, ponder, query, stare. ANT.—commonness, familiarity, triviality; anticipation, apathy, expectation, indifference, stolidity; abhor, disregard, ignore, ridicule, scorn.

wordy, diffuse, digressive, long-winded, loquacious, prolix, rambling, redundant, talkative, verbose, voluble. ANT.—brief, concise, succinct, summary, terse.

work, accomplishment, achievement, action, business, calling, deed, drudgery, duty, effort, employment, exertion, function, job, labor, occupation, office, opus, performance, production, profession, pursuit, task, toil, travail; accomplish, achieve, act, control, do, form, function, labor, manage, operate, make, mold, react, serve, slave, strive, struggle, sweat, toil. ANT.—ease, idleness, leisure, recreation, relaxation; abandon, ignore, malfunction, mismanage, quit, rest.

working, see industrious; operative.

worldly, carnal, corporeal, earthly, irreligious, materialistic, mundane, opportunistic, practical, secular, sensual, temporal, terrestrial, ungodly. ANT.—exalted, incorporeal, intellectual, refined, spiritual.

worn, exhausted, faint, fatigued, jaded, shabby, spent, threadbare, tired, used, wasted, wearied, weary. ANT.—fresh, invigorated, new, rested, unused.

worry, agitation, anxiety, apprehension, care, concern, disquiet, doubt, fear, trouble, uneasiness; annoy, bother, disturb, gall, gnaw, harass, harry, haze, irritate, pain, persecute, pester, plague, tease, torment, torture, trouble, vex; fret, fume, fuss, grieve. ANT.—contentment, ease, peace, satisfaction, serenity; aid, comfort, please, soothe, support; enjoy, rejoice, relax, rest, unbend.

worship, honor, respect; see also idolize; reverence.

worth, advantage, benefit, estimation, price, usefulness, utility; see also merit.

worthless, barren, bootless, inane, insignificant, meritless, pointless, poor, profitless, unimportant, unproductive; see also futile.

worthy, charitable, creditable, decent, dependable, deserving, dutiful, exemplary, fit, good, honorable, incorrupt, incorruptible, meritorious, model, moral, noble, pure, reliable, reputable, righteous, suitable, trustworthy, virtuous, worthy. ANT.—corrupt, dishonorable, iniquitous, reprehensible, vicious, villainous.

wound, affront, dishonor, insult; disfigure, gash, scrape; see also abuse; hurt.

wrangle, affray, bickering, spat, squabble; see also dispute.

wrap, bundle, cloak, clothe, conceal, cover, curtain, disguise, enclose, enfold, envelop, furl, guard, hide, lap, mask, muffle, package, protect, roll, screen, shield, shroud, swathe, veil, wind; blanket, cape, cloak, coat, coverlet, overcoat, shawl. ANT.—bare, divulge, expose, open, reveal, unfold.

wrath, choler, irritation, petulance, provocation, tantrum; see also indignation.

wreck, annihilate, break, damage, demolish, destroy, devastate, eradicate, exterminate, extinguish, injure, obliterate, ravage, raze, ruin, shatter, smash; accident, crash, desolation, destruction, junk, litter, loss, perdition, shreds, smash, wreckage. ANT.—conserve, construct, establish, preserve, repair; gain, improvement, recovery, renewal, restoration.

wretched, see miserable.

write, compose, correspond, draft, draw, formulate, inscribe, pen, record, scrawl, scribble, sign, transcribe.

writer, author, biographer, calligrapher, composer, contributor, correspondent, creator, editor, essayist, father, inventor, journalist, maker, novelist, originator, playwright, poet, reporter, scribe, stenographer.

writing, calligraphy, composition, document, handwriting, inscription, manuscript, penmanship.

wrong, amiss, askew, awry, erroneous, fallacious, false, faulty, imprecise, inaccurate, incorrect, inexact, mistaken, untrue; improper, inappropriate, unsuitable; aberrant, abusive, bad, base, corrupt, criminal, cruel, evil, hurtful, immoral, indecent, iniquitous, injurious, malevolent, reprehensible, sinful, wicked. ANT.—accurate, correct, exact, precise, right; appropriate, becoming, fitting, proper, suitable; blameless, decent, ethical, honest, noble, virtuous.

X

xanthic, dusky, fulvous, saffron, swarthy, tawny, yellow, yellowish.

xerox, copy, ditto, duplicate, recreate, reproduce.

x-ray, radiant energy, radiation, radioactivity, radiograph, radium emanation, Roentgen ray.

xylography, woodcutting, woodengraving.

Y

yard, backyard, corral, court, courtyard, enclosure, garden, playground, terrace.

yardstick, criterion, gauge, measure, rule, ruler, standard, test, touchstone.

yearning, see wish.

yell, bawl, bellow, cry, howl, roar, scream, screech, shout, shriek, shrill, squall, squeal, vociferate, whoop, yelp.

yet, additionally, although, besides, but, despite, further, furthermore, hitherto, however, nevertheless, notwithstanding, now, still, though.

yield, crop, fruit, harvest, proceeds, produce, product, reaping, result, store; bear, breed, generate, impart, produce, supply; allow, bestow, concede, confer, grant, permit, sanction, tolerate; abdicate, accede, acquiesce, capitulate, cede, defer, quit, relent, relinquish, resign, submit, succumb, surrender, waive. ANT.—deny, forbid, oppose, prevent, refuse; assert, master, overcome, overpower, strive, struggle.

young, active, adolescent, blooming, budding, childish, childlike, fresh, green, growing, immature, inexperienced, juvenile, pubescent, puerile, strong, vibrant, vigorous, youthful. ANT.—aged, ancient, elderly, experienced, mature, withered.

youthful, see young.

Z

zeal, activity, ardor, courage, dedication, determination, devotion, eagerness, energy, enthusiasm, excitement, fanaticism, fervency, fervor, inclination, industry, inspiration, intensity, intentness, involvement, passion, perseverance, vehemence, vigilance, warmth, willingness. ANT.—apathy, detachment, ennui, indifference, nonchalance.

zealot, adherent, bigot, devotee, dogmatist, dreamer, enthusiast, fanatic, martyr, opinionist, partisan, patriot, visionary. ANT.—dawdler, idler, shirker, slacker.

zealous, alert, animated, assiduous, brisk, bustling, diligent, fervid, fiery, hustling, indefatigable, passionate, resolute, sedulous, steadfast, vivacious. see also eager.

zenith, acme, apex, apogee, cap, climax, consummation, crest, crown, culmination, eminence, height, maximum, peak, pinnacle, pitch, summit, top. ANT.—base, bottom, floor, foundation, nadir.

zero, blank, cipher, naught, nil, nobody, nonentity, nothing, nullity, unreality, unsubstantiality. ANT.—corporeality, existence, matter, object, substance.

zest, ardor, delight, desire, energy, enhancement, enjoyment, enthusiasm, exhilaration, gusto, passion, pleasure, relish, spirit; flavor, piquancy, pungency, savor, savoriness, sharpness, tang, taste.

zigzag, askew, awry, bent, crinkled, crooked, curved, devious, diagonal, erratic, fluctuating, forked, inclined, indirect, jagged, meandering, oblique, oscillating, rambling, serrated, sinuous, sloping, spiral, straggling, transverse, twisted, undulatory, vibratory, waggling, wry. ANT.—direct, even, rectilinear, straight, unbent.

zone, area, band, belt, circuit, climate, commune, district, dominion, enclosure, ground, latitude, locality, location, locus, meridian, precinct, quarter, region, section, sector, segment, site, terrain, territory, tract, ward.

World in Summary

Country	Capital	Monetary Unit	Major languages	IDD code	Telex code
Algeria	Algiers	Algerian dinar (AD) = 100 centimes	Arabic, French, Berber	213	408
Argentina	Buenos Aires	Argentine peso (Arg$) = 100 centavos	Spanish, Italian, German	—	33
Australia	Canberra	Australian dollar (A$) = 100 cents	English	61	71
Austria	Vienna	Schilling (Sch) = 100 groschen	German	43	47
Bangladesh	Dacca	Taka (TK) = 100 poisha	Bengali, English	—	780
Belgium	Brussels	Belgian franc (BFr) = 100 centimes	Flemish, French, English	32	46
Bolivia	LaPaz	Bolivian peso (B$) = 100 centavos	Spanish, Quochua, Aymara	—	309
Brazil	Brasilia	Cruzeiro (Cr) = 100 centavos	Portuguese, Italian, German, Spanish	55	38
Brunei	Bandar Seri Begawan	Brunei dollar (Br$) = 100 cents	Malay, English	673	809
Bulgaria	Sofia	Lev (Lv) = 100 Stotinki	Bulgarian, Turkish, Greek	—	67
Burma	Rangoon	Kyat (Kt) = 100 pyas	Burmese, Karen, Shan, English	—	83
Canada	Ottawa	Canadian dollar (C$) = 100 cents	English, French	1	21/26
Chile	Santiago	Chilean peso (Ch$) = 100 centavos	Spanish, German, Araucanian	56	34
China	Beijing	Yuan (Y) = 10 chiao 100 fen	Mandarin	—	85
Colombia	Bogota	Colombian peso (Col$) = 100 centavos	Spanish, Arawak, Carib	57	35
Czechoslovakia	Prague	Koruna or Crown (KCS) = 100 haler	Czech, Slovak, Hungarian	42	66
Denmark	Copenhagen	Danish Krone (DKr) = 100 ore	Danish, English	45	55
Egypt	Cairo	Egyptian pound (E£) = 100 piastres	Arabic	20	91
Finland	Helsinki	Markka (FMk) = 100 penni	Finnish, Swedish	358	57
France	Paris	Franc (Fr) = 100 centimes	French	33	42
Germany (GFR) West	Bonn	Deutsche mark (DM) = 100 pfenning	German	49	41
Germany (GDR) East	Berlin (East)	Mark (M) = 100 pfenning	German	37	69
Ghana	Accra	Cedi (C) = 100 pesewas	English, Twi, Fonti, Ewe	—	—
Greece	Athens	Drachma (Dr) = 100 lepta	Greek, Turkish	30	601
Guatemala	Guatemala	Quetzal (Q) = 100 centavos	Spanish, Mayan	502	372
Hong Kong	Victoria	Hongkong Dollar (HK$) = 100 cents	English, Chinese	852	802
Hungary	Budapest	Forint (Ft) = 100 filler	Hungarian	36	61
India	New Delhi	Indian rupee (IR) = 100 paise	Hindi, Urdu, Bengali, Telugu, Tamil	—	81
Indonesia	Jakarta	Rupiah (Rp) = 100 sen	Indonesian, Sudanese, Javanese	62	73
Iran	Teheran	Rial (Rl) = 100 dinars	Persian, Kurdish, Azkerbaijani	98	88
Iraq	Baghdad	Iraqi dinar (ID) = 20 dirhams	Arabic, Kurdish	964	491
Ireland	Dublin	Punt (1£) = 100 pighne	English, Irish	353	500
Israel	Jerusalem	She Kel (SK) = 100 new agorot	Hebrew, Arabic, English	972	606
Italy	Rome	Lira (L) = 100 centesimi	Italian, French	39	43
Ivory Coast	Abidjan	CFA fance (CFAFr) = 100 centimes	French, Dyula, Senulu, Agni, Baule	225	983
Japan	Tokyo	Yen (Y) = 100 sen	Japanese	81	72
Jordan	Amman	Jordan dinar (JD) = 1000 fils	Arabic	—	493
Kenya	Nairobi	Kenya Shilling (KSh) = 100 cents	Swahili, English, Bantu	254	987
Korea North	Pyongyang	N. Korean Won (SKW) = 100 chon	Korean	—	899
Korea South	Seoul	S. Korean Won (NKW) = 100 chon	Korean	82	801

Country	Capital	Monetary Unit	Major languages	IDD code	Telex code
Kuwait	Kuwait City	Kuwaiti dinar (KD) = 10 dirhams	Arabic	965	496
Lebanon	Beirut	Lebanese pound (L£) = 100 piastres	Arabic, French	—	494
Libya	Tripoli	Libyan dinar (LD) = 1000 dirhams	Arabic	—	901
Malaysia	Kuala Lumpur	Ringgit (Ma$) = 100 sen	Malay, Chinese, English, Tamil	—	84
Mexico	Mexico City	Mexican peso (Mex$) = 100 cntavos	Spanish, Nahuati, Maya	52	22
Mongolia	Ultan Bator	Tugrik (Tug) = 100 mongo	Mongolian	—	800
Morrocco	Rabat	Dirham (Dh) = 100 centimes	Arabic, French, Berber, Spanish	—	407
Netherlands	Amsterdam	Guilder (Gld) = 100 cents	Dutch	31	44
New Zealand	Wellington	New Zealand dollar (NZ$) = 100 cents	English, Maori	64	74
Niger	Niamey	CFA franc (CFA Fr) = 100 centimes	French, local African	227	—
Nigeria	Lagos	Naira (#) = 100 koko	English, Hausa, Yoruha, Ibo, Fulani	234	905
Norway	Oslo	Norwegian Krone (NKr) = 100 ore	Norwegian	47	56
Pakistan	Islamabad	Pakistan rupee (PR) = 100 paisa	Urdu, Punjabi, English	—	82
Panama	Panama City	Balboa (BA) = 100 centesimos	Spanish, English	—	377
Papua New Guinea	Port Moresby	Kina (Ka) = 100 toea	Pidgin English, Police Motu	675	703
Peru	Lima	Sol (S) = 100 centavos	Spanish, Quechua	—	36
Philippines	Metro Manila	Pilippine peso (PP) = 100 centavos	Philipino (Tagalog), English, Spanish	63	75
Poland	Warsaw	Zloty (zl) = 100 groszy	Polish	48	63
Portugal	Lisbon	Escudo (Esc) = 100 centavos	Portuguese	351	404
Rumania	Bucharest	Leu = 100 bani	Rumanian, Hungarian	40	65
Saudi Arabia	Riyadh	Saudi riyal (SAR) = 100 hallalas	Arabic	966	495
Singapore	Singapore	Singapore dollar (S$) = 100 cents	English, Chinese, Malay, Tamil	65	87
South Africa	Pretoria	Rand (R) = 100 cents	Afrikaans, English	27	95
Spain	Madrid	Peseta (Pa) = 100 centimos	Spanish	34	52
Sri Lanka	Colombo	Sri Lanka rupee (SLR) = 100 cents	Singhalese, Tamil, English	94	803
Sudan	Khartoum	Sudanese pound (S£) = 100 piastres	Arabic, French, Kurdish	—	984
Sweden	Stockholm	Swedish krona (SKr) = 100 ore	Swedish	46	54
Switzerland	Berne	Swiss franc (SFr) = 100 centimes	Swiss, German, French, Italian	41	45
Syria	Damascus	Syrian pound (Sy£) = 100 piastres	Arabic, French, Kurdish	963	492
Tanzania	Dares Salaam	Tanzanian Shilling (TSh) = 100 cents	Swahili, English	255	989
Thailand	Bangkok	Baht (Bt) = 100 satang	Thai, English, Chinese	66	86
Tunisia	Tunis	Tunisian dinar (TD) = 100 millimes	Arabic, French	216	409
Turkey	Ankara	Turkish Lira (TL) = 100 Kurus	Turkish, Kurdish	90	607
United Kingdom	London	Pound (£) = 100 new pence	English	44	51
U.S.A.	Washington	Dollar ($) = 100 cents	English	1	23/230
Uruguay	Montevideo	Uruguayan new peso (Urug N$) = 100 centesimos	Spanish	—	—
Venezuela	Caracas	Bolivar (B) = 100 centimos	Spanish, Arawak, Carib	—	31
Yugoslavia	Belgrade	Dinar (D) = 100 paras	Serbo-Croatian	38	62
Zaire	Kinshasa	Zaire (Z) = 100 makuta	French, Kongo, Kingwara, Luba	—	—
Zambia	Lusaka	Kwacha (K) = 100 ngwee	English, Bemba, Tonga, Nyanja	260	902
Zimbabwe	Harare	Zimbabwe dollar (Z$) = 100 cents	English African	—	907

COMMON ABBREVIATIONS

ABBREVIATIONS, ə-brē-vē-ā′shənz, are letter symbols or contractions used as shortened forms of words and phrases to facilitate writing and to save space. The practice of abbreviating goes back to antiquity; early examples of abbreviation have survived on coins and inscriptions, where lack of space made the shortening of words necessary. With the development of papyrus and, later, of parchment, writing increased and abbreviations were adopted by copyists to save labor.

In modern times the rapid growth of the sciences, technology, and business, and the increase of governmental agencies have produced a vastly increased vocabulary of abbreviations for use in some fields, symbols other than letters are employed, as in physics and mathematics. The following list of abbreviations often used in printing or writing includes only letter symbols or contractions, in the Roman alphabet.

A

A.—absolute (temperature)
A., Å, A—angstrom unit
a.—about; acre(s)
AA—Alcoholics Anonymous
A.A.—Associate in Arts
AAA—Agricultural Adjustment Administration; Amateur Athletic Association; American Automobile Association; antiaircraft artillery
AAAL—American Academy of Arts and Letters
AAAS—American Association for the Advancement of Science
AAU—Amateur Athletic Union
AAUP—American Association of University Professors
A.B.—Artium Baccalaureus (Lat.), Bachelor of Arts
A.B., a.b.—able-bodied (seaman); airborne
ABA—American Bar Association
abbr., abbrev.—abbreviation; abbreviated
ABC—American Broadcasting Company
abp.—archbishop
abr.—abridged; abridgment
ABS—American Bible Society
AC—Air Corps; Army Corps; Athletic Club
AC, A.C., a.c., a-c—alternating current
A/C, a/c, ac.—account
Ac—actinium
ac—acre(s)
acad.—academic; academy
accel.—accelerando (It.), more quickly (music)
acct.—account; accountant
ACDA—Arms Control and Disarmament Agency
ACLS—American Council of Learned Societies
ACLU—American Civil Liberties Union
ACP—American College of Physicians
ACS—American Chemical Society; American College of Surgeons
ACTH—adrenocorticotropic hormone
A.D.—anno Domini (Lat.), in the year of our Lord
ADA—American Dental Association; Americans for Democratic Action
adag.—adagio (It.), slowly (music)
ADC, a.d.c.—aide-de-camp
add.—addenda; addendum; addition; additional; address
adj.—adjacent; adjective; adjourned; adjustment; adjutant
ad lib., ad libit.—ad libitum (Lat.), at one's pleasure

adm.—administration; administrative; admiral
adv.—adverb; adversus; advertisement; advocate
ad val.—ad valorem (Lat.), according to the value
ae., aet., adtat.—aetatis (Lat.), of age, aged
AEC—Atomic Energy Commission
AEF—American Expeditionary Force
aero.—aeronautics
AF—Air Force; audio frequency
AFAM—Ancient Free and Accepted Masons
AFB—Air Force Base
AFC—automatic frequency control
AFL-CIO—American Federation of Labor-Congress of Industrial Organizations
AFTRA—American Federation of Television and Radio Artists
Ag—argentum (Lat.), silver
agr., agri., agric.—agricultural; agriculture
agt.—agent
A.H.—anno Hegirae (Lat.), in the year of Hegira (Mohammedan era)
AHA—American Historical Association
AIA—American Institute of Architects
A.I.Ch.E.—American Institute of Chemical Engineers
AID—Agency for International Development
AIEE—American Institute of Electrical Engineers
AKC—American Kennel Club
Al—aluminum
ALA—American Library Association
Ala.—Alabama
Alas.—Alaska
Alba.—Alberta
alg.—algebra
alt.—alternate; alternating; altitude; alto
Alta.—Alberta
AM—amplitude modulation
A.M., A.M., a.m.—ante meridiem (Lat.), before midday
A.M.—Artium Magister (Lat.), Master of Arts
Am—americium
AMA—American Medical Association
amb.—ambassador
A.M.E.—African Methodist Episcopal
amp.—amperage; ampere
AMS—Agricultural Marketing Service
amt.—amount
AMVETS—American Veterans (of World War II and Korea)
AN, AN.—Anglo-Norman

ANA—American Nurses Association
anal.—analogy, analysis; analytic
ANC—Army Nurse Corps
and.—andante (It.), slowly (music)
anon.—anonymous
ant.—antenna; antonym
anthrop., anthropol.—anthropological; anthropologist; anthropology
antiq.—antiquarian; antiquary
ANZAC—Australian and New Zealand Army Corps
AOH—Ancient Order of Hiberians
AP—Associated Press
APA—American Philological Association
APO—Army Post Office
app.—apparent; appended; appendix; appointed; apprentice
approx.—approximately
Apr., Apr—April
apt.—apartment
AQ—accomplishment quotient; achievement quotient
aq.—aqua; aqueous
Ar—argon
Ar.—Arabian; Arabic; Aramaic
ARA—Agricultural Research Administration; American Railway Association
A.R.A.—Associate of the Royal Academy
Arab.—Arabian; Arabic
ARC—American Red Cross
arch.—archaic; archbishop; archery; archipelago; architect; architecture
archaeol.—archaeological; archaeology
archd.—archduke
arith.—arithmetic
Ariz.—Arizona
Ark.—Arkansas
ARS—Agricultural Research Service
AS, AS.—Anglo-Saxon
As—arsenic
ASCAP—American Society of Composers, Authors and Publishers
ASCE—American Society of Civil Engineers
ASME—American Society of Mechanical Engineers
ASPCA—American Society for the Prevention of Cruelty to Animals
assn., assoc.—association
ASSR—Autonomous Soviet Socialist Republic
asst.—assistant
ASTM—American Society for Testing Materials
ASTP—Army Secialized Training Program
astrol.—astrologer; astrological; astrology

TWO-LETTER GEOGRAPHICAL ABBREVIATIONS RECOMMENDED BY THE UNITED STATES POSTAL SERVICE

ALABAMA	AL	GEORGIA	GA	MARYLAND	MD	NEW MEXICO	NM	SOUTH DAKOTA	SD
ALASKA	AK	GUAM	GU	MASSACHUSETTS	MA	NEW YORK	NY	TENNESSEE	TN
ARIZONA	AZ	HAWAII	HI	MICHIGAN	MI	NORTH CAROLINA	NC	TEXAS	TX
ARKANSAS	AR	IDAHO	ID	MINNESOTA	MN	NORTH DAKOTA	ND	UTAH	UT
CALIFORNIA	CA	ILLINOIS	IL	MISSISSIPPI	MS	OHIO	OH	VERMONT	VT
CANAL ZONE	CZ	INDIANA	IN	MISSOURI	MO	OKLAHOMA	OK	VIRGINIA	VA
COLORADO	CO	IOWA	IA	MONTANA	MT	OREGON	OR	VIRGIN ISLANDS	VI
CONNECTICUT	CT	KANSAS	KS	NEBRASKA	NE	PENNSYLVANIA	PA	WASHINGTON	WA
DELAWARE	DE	KENTUCKY	KY	NEVADA	NV	PUERTO RICO	PR	WEST VIRGINIA	WV
D. OF C.	DC	LOUISIANA	LA	NEW HAMPSHIRE	NH	RHODE ISLAND	RI	WISCONSIN	WI
FLORIDA	FL	MAINE	ME	NEW JERSEY	NJ	SOUTH CAROLINA	SC	WYOMING	WY

astron.—astronomer; astronomical; astronomy
ASV—American Standard Version
ATC—Air Transport Command
at. no.—atomic number
ATP—adenosine triphosphate
ATS—Army Transport Service
attn.—attention
atty.—attorney
atty. gen.—attorney general
at. wt.—atomic weight
A.U., A.U., a.u., a.u.—angstrom unit
Au—aurum (Lat.), gold
Aug., Aug—August
AUS—Army of the United States
aux.—auxiliary
A.V.—Authorized Version (Bible)
av.—avenue; average; avoirdupois
AVC—American Veterans Committee; automatic volume control
advp.—avoirdupois
ave.—avenue
avoir—avoirdupois
AWOL—absent without leave

B

B—bishop (chess); boron
b.—base; bass; bat; battery; bay; book; born; brother
B.A.—Baccalaureus Artium (Lat.), Bachelor of Arts; British Association (for the Advancement of Science); Buenos Aires
Ba—barium
bact.—bacteria; bacteriology
Bap., Bapt.—Baptist
bap.—baptized
B.Ar., B. Arch.—Bachelor of Architecture
Bart.—Baronet
B.B.A.—Bachelor of Business Administration
BBB—Better Business Bureau
BBC—British Broadcasting Corporation
bbl—barrel, barrels
B.C.—before Christ; British Columbia
B.C.E.—Bachelor of Civil Engineering
B.Ch.E.—Bahelor of Chemical Engineering
B.C.L.—Bachelor of Civil Law
B.D.—Bachelor of Divinity
BSDA—Business and Defense Services Administration
B.E.—Bachelor of Engineering; Bachelor of Education
Be—beryllium
Bé.—Baumé
B.Ed.—Bachelor of Education
BEF—British Expeditionary Force(s)
B.E.M.—British Empire Medal
BEV, bev—billion electron volts
bf.—boldface
Bi—bismuth
bib.—Bible; biblical
bibliog.—bibliography
biochem.—biochemistry
biog.—biographer; biographical; biography
biol.—biology
B.I.S.—Bank for International Settlements; British Information Service
Bk—berkelium
bk.—bank; block; book
bkg.—banking
B.L.—Baccalaureus Legum (Lat.), Bachelor of Laws
bldg.—building
B.Lit(t).—Baccalaureus Lit(t)erarum (Lat.), Bachelor of Literature (or Letters)
BLS—Bureau of Labor Statistics
B.L.S.—Bachelor of Library Science
blvd.—boulevard
BM—basal metabolism
B.M.—Baccalaureus Medicinae (Lat.), Bachelor of Medicine; British Museum
B.Mus.—Baccalaureus Musicae (Lat.), Bachelor of Music
BOAC—British Overseas Airways Corporation
bor.—borough

bot.—botanical, botany
bp.—bishop
b.p.—boiling point
BPOE—Benevolent and Protective Order of Elks
Br—bromine
brig.—brigade; brigadier
brig. gen.—brigadier general
bro.—brother
B.S.—Bachelor of Science
BSA—Boy Scouts of America
B.S.A.—Bachelor of Science in Agriculture
B.Sc.—Baccalaureus Scientiae (Lat.), Bachelor of Science
B.T., B.Th.—Baccalaureus Theologiae (Lat.), Bachelor of Theology
B.T.U., Btu, b.t.u., btu—British thermal unit
bu—bushel
bur.—bureau
B.V.M.—Blessed Virgin Mary

C

C—carbon
C., c.—candle; capacitance; cape; carat; cathode; cent; center; century; chapter; circa (Lat.), about; cirrus (meteor.); copyright; cubic; cup; current; cycle
C., C, c., c—centigrade; centimeter
CA—chronological age; Coast Artillery
Ca—calcium
c.a.—chartered accountant; chief accountant; commercial agent; consular agent; controller of accounts
CAA—Civil Aeronautics Administration (or Authority)
CAB—Civil Aeronautics Board; Consumers' Advisory Board
Cal.—California; large calorie
cal.—calendar; caliber; small calorie
Calif.—California
Cant.—Canticles
CAP—Civil Air Patrol
cap.—capital; capitalize
capt.—captain
CAR—Civil Air Regulations
CARE—Cooperative for American Remittances to Everywhere
Cath.—Catholic
cath.—cathedral
CAVU—ceiling and visibility unlimited
C.B.—Chirurgiae Baccalaureus (Lat.), Bachelor of Surgery; Companion of the Bath
Cb—columbium
CBC—Canadian Broadcasting Corporation
C.B.E.—Commander (of the Order) of the British Empire
CBS—Columbia Broadcasting System
cc, cc., c.c.—cubic centimeters
CCC—Commodity Credit Corporation
CCS—Combined Chiefs of Staff
Cd—cadmium
CE—Chemical Engineer; Chief Engineer; Civil Engineer; Church of England; Christian Endeavor
Ce—cerium
CEA—Council of Economic Advisers
CED—Committee for Economic Development
CEF—Canadian Expeditionary Force(s)
Celt.—Celtic
CEMA—Council for Mutual Economic Assistance
cent.—centigrade; centimeter; central; century
CENTO—Central Treaty Organization
Cf—californium
cf.—confer (Lat.), compare
CG—center of gravity; Coast Guard; commanding general; consul general
cg, cgm—centigram
cgs—centimeter-gram-second
CGT—Confédération Générale du Travail (Fr.), General Confederation of Labor

CH—clearing house; courthouse; customhouse
C.H.—Companion of Honor
ch.—chaplain; chapter; check (chess); chief; child; children; chirurgia (Lat.), surgery; church
chan.—channel
chap.—chaplain; chapter
Ch.E.—Chemical Engineer
chem.—chemical; chemist; chemistry
chm.—chairman; checkmate
Chr.—Christ; Christian
Chron.—Chronicles
chron.—chronology
CIA—Central Intelligence Agency
C.I.E.—Companion (of the Order) of the Indian Empire
CIF—cost, insurance, freight
C. in C.—Commander in Chief
CIO—Congress of (formerly Committee for) Industrial Organizations
cir., circ.—circular; circa (Lat.), about
cit.—citation; cited; citizen
civ.—civil; civilian
Cl—chlorine
clk.—clerk
C.M.—Chirurgiae Magister (Lat.), Master in Surgery
Cm—curium
cm, cm.—centimeter(s)
C.M.G.—Companion (of the Order) of St. Michael and St. George
CO—Commanding Officer; conscientious objector
Co—cobalt
co.—company; county
c.o., c/o—care of; carried over
COD, c.o.d.—cash on delivery; collect on delivery
C. of C.—Chamber of Commerce
C. of S.—Chief of Staff
Col.—Colorado; Colossians
col.—collected; collector; college; colonel; colonial; colony; column
colloq.—colloquial; colloquialism
Colo.—Colorado
Coloss.—Colossians
com.—comedy; command; commandant; commerce; commercial; commission(er); committee; commodore; common; communication; community
comdr.—commander
COMECON—Council for Mutual Economic Assistance
comr.—commissioner
con.—concerto; consolidated; consul
conf.—conference
confed.—confederate
Cong.—Congregational
cong.—congress
conj.—conjugation; conjunction
Conn.—Connecticut
consol.—consolidated
constr.—construction
cont.—containing; contents; continent; continental; continue(d)
Cor.—Corinthians
CORE—Congress of Racial Equality
corp.—corporal; corporation
cos—cosine
CP—candlepower; chemically pure; command post; Communist Party
cp.—candlepower; compare
CPA—Certified Public Accountant
cpl.—corporal
CPO—chief petty officer
Cr—chromium
cr.—credit; creditor; creek
cres., cresc.—crescendo (It.), increasingly loud (music)
crit.—criticism
CS—civil service
C.S.—Christian Science
Cs—cesium
CSA—Confederate States of America
C.S.B.—Bachelor of Christian Science
CSC—Civil Service Commission

C.S.I.—Companion of (the Order of) the Star of India
CST—Central Standard Time
ct.—carat; cent; court
Cu—cuprum (Lat.), copper
cu—cubic
CWA—Civil Works Administration
cwt—hundredweight
CYO—Catholic Youth Organization

D

D—deuterium
D., d.—dam (in pedigrees); date; daughter; day(s); dead; democrat; density; diameter; died
d.—pence, penny
D.A.—delayed action; district attorney
DAB—Dictionary of American Biography
Dan., Danl.—Daniel
DAR—Daughters of the American Revolution
DAV—Disabled American Veterans
D.B.E.—Dame Commander (of the Order of the) British Empire
D. Bib.—Douay Bible
DC, D.C., d.c., d-c—direct current
D.C.—da capo (Lat.), repeat (music); District of Columbia; Doctor of Chiropractic
D.C.L.—Doctor of Civil Law
D.C.M.—Distinguished Conduct Medal (Brit. Army)
D.C.T.—Doctor of Christian Theology
D.D.—Divinitatis Doctor (Lat.), Doctor of Divinity
D.D.S.—Doctor of Dental Surgery
Dec., Dec—December
dec.—deceased; declaration; declension; declination; decrease; decrescendo (It.), decreasing in loudness (music)
deg.—degree(s)
Del.—Delaware
Dem.—Democrat; Democratic
D.Eng.—Doctor of Engineering
dep.—department; departure; deposit; depot; deputy
dept.—department; deputy
der., deriv.—derivation; derivative
dermatol.—dermatology
Deut.—Deuteronomy
DEW—distant early warning
DFC—Distinguished Flying Cross
diag.—diagram
dial.—dialect
dict.—dictionary
dim.—diminuendo (It.), diminishing in loudness (music)
dipl.—diplomat; diplomatic
dir.—director
disc.—discount; discovered
dist.—distinguished; district
div.—dividend; division; divorced
D.Lit., D.Litt.—Doctor Lit(t)erarum (Lat.), Doctor of Literature (or, Letters)
D.L.S.—Doctor of Library Science
dm, dm.—decameter; decimeter
D.M.D.—Doctor of Medical Dentistry
D.Mus.—Doctor of Music
DNA—deoxyribonucleic acid
DNB—Dictionary of National Biography (Brit.)
D.O.—Doctor of Optometry; Doctor of Osteopathy
do.—ditto (It.), the same
DOA—dead on arrival
doc.—document
doz.—dozen
DP—degree of polymerization; diametrical pitch; displaced person
dpt.—department
D.R., D/R, d.r.—dead reckoning; deposit receipt
Dr.—doctor
dr.—debit; debtor; drachma; dram
D.S., D.Sc.—Doctor of Science
DSC—Distinguished Service Cross

DSM—Distinguished Service Medal
DSO—Distinguished Service Order
DST—Daylight Saving Time
d.t.—delirium tremens; double time
dup., dupl.—duplicate
D.V.—Deo volente (Lat.), God willing; Douay Version
D.V.M.—Doctor of Veterinary Medicine
dwt—pennyweight
Dy—dysprosium

E

E, E., e.—east, eastern
e., e—erg: errors (baseball)
ea.—each
ECA—Economic Cooperation Administration
eccl., eccles.—ecclesiastical
Eccles., Eccl.—Ecclesiastes
Ecclus.—Ecclesiasticus
ECG—electrocardiogram
ecol.—ecology
econ.—economic; economics; economy
ECSC—European Coal and Steel Community
ed.—edited; editor; edition
EDC—European Defense Community
Ed.D.—Doctor of Education
EDT—Eastern Daylight Time
EEC—European Economic Community
EEG—electroencephalogram
EFTA—European Free Trade Association
e.g.—exempli gratia (Lat.), for example
Egyptol.—Egyptology
EHF, e.h.f.—extremely high frequency
EIB—Export-Import Bank
EKG—electrocardiogram
elec., elect.—electric(al); electrician; electricity
elev.—elevation
Eliz.—Elizabeth; Elizabethan
E.M.—Engineer of Mines
EMF, e.m.f., emf—electromotive force
emp.—emperor; empire; empress
e.m.u.—electromagnetic unit
enc.—enclosed
ency., encyc., encycl.—encyclopedia
eng.—engineer; engineering; engraved
ens.—ensign
entom., entomol.—entomologist; entomology
Eph., Ephes.—Ephesians
Epis., Episc.—Episcopal
Er—erbium
ERA—Emergency Relief Administration
ERP—European Recovery Program
Es—einsteinium
ESB—Economic Stabilization Board
ESC—Economic and Social Council (United Nations)
Esk.—Eskimo
ESP—extrasensory perception
Esq., Esqr.—Esquire
EST—Eastern Standard Time
est.,—established; estimate
Esth.—Esther
et al.—et alibi (Lat.), and elsewhere; et alii (Lat.), and others
etc.—et cetera (Lat.), and so forth
ETO—European Theater of Operations
et seq.—et sequens (Lat.), and the following; et sequentes or seqentia (Lat.), and those that follow
Eu—europium
Ex.—Exodus
ex.—examined; example
exch.—exchange; exchequer
exec.—executive; executor
ex lib.—ex libris (Lat.), from the books of
Exod.—Exodus
Ez., Ezr.—Ezra
Ezek.—Ezekiel

F

F—Fahrenheit; farad; fathom; fluorine; function (math.)

F.—Fahrenheit; Fellow; Friday
f—forte (It.), loud (music)
f.—farad; father; farthing; fathom; feminine; fluid (ounce); folio; following; franc; frequency
FAA—Federal Aviation Agency
fac.—facsimile
Fahr.—Fahrenheit
FAO—Food and Agricultural Organization of the United Nations
FBI—Federal Bureau of Investigation
FCA—Farm Credit Administration
FCC—Federal Communications Commission
FCIC—Federal Crop Insurance Corporation
FDA—Food and Drug Administration
FDIC—Federal Deposit Insurance Corporation
Fe—ferrum (Lat.), iron
Feb., Feb—February
fec.—fecit (Lat.), he (she) did, or made, it
fed.—federal; federated; federation
fem.—female; feminine
FEPC—Fair Employment Practice Committee
ff—fortissimo (It.), very loud (music)
ff.—folios; following
FFA—Future Farmers of America
FHA—Farmers Home Administration; Federal Housing Administration; Future Homemakers of America
FICA—Federal Insurance Contributions Act
fig.—figure
fin.—finance
fl.—florin; flourished; fluid
Fla., Flor.—Florida
F.L.S.—Fellow of the Linnaean Society
FM—frequency modulation
Fm—fermium
FMB—Federal Maritime Board
FMCS—Federal Mediation and Conciliation Service
fn.—footnote
FOB, f.o.b.—free on board
FOE—Fraternal Order of Eagles
fol.—folio; following
F.P., f.p.—foot pound; freezing point
FPC—Federal Power Commission
FPHA—Federal Public Housing Authority
FPO—Fleet Post Office
fps—feet per second
Fr.—francium
Fr.—Father (eccl.); Frater (Lat.), brother; Friar; Friday
fr.—fragment; franc; from
F.R.A.S.—Fellow of the Royal Astronomical Society
F.R.C.P.—Fellow of the Royal College of Physicians
F.R.C.S.—Fellow of the Royal College of Surgeons
F.R.G.S.—Fellow of the Royal Geographical Society
F.R.Hist.S.—Fellow of the Royal Historical Society
Fri.—Friday
F.R.I.B.A.—Fellow of the Royal Institution of British Architects
front.—frontispiece
FRS—Federal Reserve System
F.R.S.—Fellow of the Royal Society
F.R.S.C.—Fellow of the Royal Society of Canada
F.R.S.E.—Fellow of the Royal Society, Edinburgh
F.R.S.L.—Fellow of the Royal Society of Literature; Fellow of the Royal Society, London
FSA—Farm Security Administration; Federal Security Agency
F.S.A.—Fellow of the Society of Antiquaries, or Arts
FSCC—Federal Surplus Commodities Corporation
FSH—follicle-stimulating hormone

F.S.A.—Fellow of the Society of Antiquaries, or Arts
FSCC—Federal Surplus Commodities Corporation
FSH—follicle-stimulating hormone
F.S.S.—Fellow of the (Royal) Statistical Society
ft—feet; foot
ft.—fort
FTC—Federal Trade Commission
F.Z.S.—Fellow of the Zoological Society

G

G., g.—conductance; gauge; grain; gravity; guinea; gulf
g., g—gram
GA—general agent; General Assembly
Ga—gallium
Ga.—Gallic; Georgia
Gael.—Gaelic
Gal.—Galatians; Galen
gal, gall.—gallon
GAO—General Accounting Office
GAR—Grand Army of the Republic
GATT—General Agreement on Tariffs and Trade
gaz.—gazette; gazetteer
G.B.E.—Grand (Cross, Order) of the British Empire
GCA—ground-controlled approach
G.C.B.—(Knight) Grand Cross of the Bath
GCI—ground-controlled interceptor
G.C.I.E.—(Knight) Grand Commander (of the Order) of the Indian Empire
G.C.L.H.—Grand Cross of the Legion of Honor
G.C.M.G.—(Knight of the) Grand Cross (of the Order) of St. Michael and St. George
G.C.S.I.—(Knight) Grand Commander (of the Order) of the Star of India
GCT—Greenwich civil time
G.C.V.O.—(Knight) Grand Cross of the (Royal) Victorian Order
Gd—gadolinium
Ge—germanium
Gen.—Genesis
gen.—gender; genera; general; genus
geod.—geodesy; geodetic
geog.—geographer; geographical; geography
geol.—geologic; geologist; geology
geom.—geometric; geometry
ger.—gerund
GHA—Greenwich hour angle
GHQ—General Headquarters
GI—general issue, or government issue (U.S. Army)
GI, g.i.—gastrointestinal
gloss.—glossary
GM—General Manager; George Medal (Brit.); Grand Master; guided missiles
gm—gram
GMT—Greenwich mean time
GNP—gross national product
GOP—Grand Old Party (Republican)
Goth.—Gothic
gov.—governor
govt.—government
GP—general practitioner
GPO—General Post Office; Government Printing Office
gr—grain(s); gram(s)
gram.—grammar; grammarian
GS—General Staff
GSA—General Services Administration; Girl Scouts of America
GSC—General Staff Corps

H

H—henry (elec.); hydrogen; intensity of magnetic field
h.—hard; hardness; high; hits (baseball); husband
Hab.—Habakkuk
hab. corp.—habeas corpus (Lat.), that you have the body

Hag.—Haggai
Hal.—halogen
Haw.—Hawaii
Hb—hemoglobin
H.B.M.—His (Her) Britannic Majesty
H.C.—House of Commons
H.C.M.—His (Her) Catholic Majesty
H.E.—His Eminence; His Excellency
He—helium
Heb., Hebr.—Hebrew(s)
her.—heraldry
HF—high frequency
Hf—hafnium
Hg—hydrargyrum (Lat.), mercury
H.H.—His (Her) Highness; His Holiness (the Pope)
HHFA—Housing and Home Finance Agency
HIFI—high fidelity
H.I.H.—His (Her) Imperial Highness
hist.—historical; historian; history
H.J.S.—hic jacet sepultus (Lat.), here lies buried
H.L.—House of Lords
H.M.—His (Her) Majesty
H.M.S.—His Majesty's Service, Ship, or Steamer
Ho—holmium
Hon.—Honorable
hort.—horticultural; horticulture
Hos.—Hosea
H.P., HP, h.p., hp—high pressure; horsepower
HQ, H.Q., hq, h.q.—headquarters
H.R.—Home Rule; House of Representatives
hr—hour(s)
H.R.H.—His (Her) Royal Highness
H.R.I.P.—hic requiescit in pace (Lat.), here rests in peace
H.S.H.—His (Her) Serene Highness
ht.—height

I

I—iodine
I.—Island; Isle
Ia.—Iowa (not official)
IADB—Inter-American Defense Board
ib., ibid.—ibidem (Lat.), in the same place
IBRD—International Bank for Reconstruction and Development
ICAO—International Civil Aviation Organization
ICBM—intercontinental ballistic missile
ICC—Interstate Commerce Commission; Indian Claims Commission
ichth.—ichthyology
ICJ—International Court of Justice
Id.—Idaho (not official)
id.—idem (Lat.), the same
i.e.—id est (Lat.), that is
IFC—International Finance Corporation
IGY—International Geophysical Year
IHS—the first three letters of the Greek word for Jesus
ILA—International Longshoremen's Association
ILGWU—International Ladies' Garment Workers' Union
Ill.—Illinois
ILO—International Labor Organization
I.L.P.—Independent Labour Party
IMF—International Monetary Fund
imp.—imperative; imperial; imports; imprimatur (Lat.), let it be printed
In—indium
in.—inch; inches
inc.—including; income; incorporated
Ind.—Indian; Indiana
Inf.—infantry
in loc. cit.—in loco citato (Lat.), in the place cited
INRI—Iesus Nazarenus, Rex Iudaeorum (Lat.), Jesus of Nazareth, King of the Jews
INS—International News Service

ins.—inches; insurance
inst.—instant, the present month; institute
introd.—introduction
IOF—Independent Order of Foresters
IOOF—Independent Order of Odd Fellows
IOU—I owe you
IQ—intelligence quotient
Ir—iridium
IRA—Irish Republican Army
IRO—International Refugee Organization
IRS—Internal Revenue Service
Is., is.—island(s); isle
Isa.—Isaiah
ITO—International Trade Organization
ITU—International Telecommunications Union
IU—international unit
IWW—Industrial Workers of the World

J

J—joule
J.—Justice; Judge
JA—Judge Advocate
Jan., Jan—January
Jas.—James
JCC—Junior Chamber of Commerce
J.C.D.—Juris Civilis Doctor (Lat.), Doctor of Civil Law
J.D.—Juris Doctor (Lat.), Doctor of Law
Jer.—Jeremiah
j.g.—junior grade
Jno.—John
Josh.—Joshua
jour.—journal
J.P.—Justice of the Peace
Jr., jr.—junior
J.U.D.—Juris Utriusque Doctor (Lat.), doctor of both laws (canon and civil)
jud.—judicial
Judg.—Judges (Bible)

K

K—kalium (Lat.), potassium; king (chess)
K, k.—kilogram; king
K.—Kelvin
k.—kilo, thousand
ka—kathode or cathode
Kan., Kans., Kas.—Kansas
KB—king's bishop (chess)
K.B.—King's Bench; Knight Bachelor; Knight of the Bath
K.B.E.—Knight (Commander of the Order) of the British Empire
KBP—king's bishop's pawn (chess)
K.C.—King's Counsel; Knights of Columbus
kc—kilocycle
K.C.B.—Knight Commander of the Bath
K.C.I.E.—Knight Commander (of the Order) of the Indian Empire
K.C.M.G.—Knight Commander of St. Michael and St. George
K.C.S.I.—Knight Commander of the Star of India
K.C.V.O.—Knight Commander of the Victorian Order
KEV, Kev—thousand electron volts
K.G.—Knight of the Garter
kg—kilogram
Ki.—Kings (Bible)
kilo.—kilogram; kilometer
KKK—Ku Klux Klan
K Kt—king's knight (chess)
K Kt P—king's knight's pawn (chess)
KLM—Royal Dutch Airlines
km—kilometer
KO—knockout
K. of P.—Knights of Pythias
KP—king's pawn (chess); kitchen police, assistants to cooks
K.P.—Knight of St. Patrick; Knights of Pythias
KR—king's rook (chess)
Kr—krypton
KRP—king's rook's pawn (chess)

K.T.—Knight of the Thistle; Knight Templar
Kt.—Knight
kt.—carat
kv.—kilovolt
kw—kilowatt
K.W.H., kw-h, kw-hr—kilowatt-hour
Ky.—Kentucky

L

£, L, l.—libra (Lat.), pound
L., l.—lake; left; length; liber (Lat.), book; lira
l., l—liter
l., ll.—line; lines
La—lanthanum
La.—Louisiana
Lab.—Labrador
lab.—laboratory
Lam.—Lamentations
lang.—language
Lat.—Latin
lat.—latitude
lb—libra (Lat.), pound
LC—landing craft (following letter specifies type, for example, LCI Landing Craft Infantry)
L.C.—Library of Congress
l.c.—loco citato (Lat.), in the place cited; lower case (print.)
LD—lethal dose; Low Dutch
leg.—legal; legend; legato (It.), in a smooth manner (music); legislative; legislature
legis.—legislation; legislative, legislature
Lev.—Leviticus
LG—Low German
LH—luteinizing hormone
L.H.D.—lit(t)erarum Humaniorum Doctor, *or* In Litteris Humanioribus Doctor (Lat.), Doctor of Humanities
L.I.—Long Island
Li—lithium
lib.—liberal; librarian; library
lieut.—lieutenant
ling.—linguistics
Linn.—Linnaeus; Linnaean
liq.—liquid; liquidation; liquor
lit.—literally; literary; literature
Lit.B., Litt.B.—Lit(t)erarum Baccalaureus (Lat), Bachelor of Letters *or* Literature
Lit.D., Litt.D.—Lit(t)erarum Doctor (Lat.); Doctor of Literature
LL—Late Latin; Low Latin
LL.B.—Legum Baccalaureus (Lat.), Bachelor of Laws
LL.D.—Legum Doctor (Lat.), Doctor of Laws
LL.M.—Legum Magister (Lat.), Master of Laws
loc. cit.—lococitato (Lat.), in the place cited
log.—logarithm
Lon., Lond.—London
lon., long.—longitude
LOOM—Loyal Order of Moose
loq.—loquitur (Lat.), he, or she, speaks
L.R.A.M.—Licentiate of the Royal Academy of Music
L.R.C.P.—Licentiate of the Royal College of Physicians
L.R.C.S.—Licentiate of the Royal College of Surgeons
LS—landing ship (following letter specifies type, for example, LST, Landing Ship Tank)
l.s.—locus sigilli (Lat.), place of the seal
L.S.A.—Licentiate of the Society of Apothecaries
LSD—lysergic acid diethylamide
L.S.D., ls.d., l.s.d.—librae, solidi, denarii (Lat.), pounds, shillings, and pence
lt.—lieutenant
Ltd., ltd.—limited
Lu—lutetium
Luth.—Lutheran
Lw—lawrencium

M

M—magnitude; thousand
M.—Majesty; Monsieur (Fr.), miter
m.—male; mark (German money); married; meridian; meridies (Lat.), noon; meter; mile; minute; month
MA—Maritime Administration; mental age
M.A.—Magister Artium (Lat.), Master of Arts
ma, ma., mA—milliampere
Mac., Macc.—Maccabees
Maced.—Macedonia(n)
mach.—machine; machinist
maj.—major
Mal.—Malachi
Man.—Manitoba
MAP—Military Assistance Program
Mar., Mar—March
mas., masc.—masculine
Mass.—Massachusetts
math.—mathematician; mathematics
MATS—Military Air Transport Service
Matt.—Matthew
M.B.—Medicinae Baccalaureus (Lat.), Bachelor of Medicine
M.B.A.—Master of Business Administration
MBS—Mutual Broadcasting System
M.C.—Medical Corps; Master of Ceremonies; Member of Congress
mc—megacycle
M.D.—Medicinae Doctor (Lat.), Doctor of Medicine; Medical Department
Md—mendelevium
Md.—Maryland
M.D.S.—Master of Dental Surgery
mdse.—merchandise
ME, ME., M.E.—Middle English
M.E.—Methodist Episcopal; mining or mechanical, engineer
Me.—Maine
mech.—mechanical; mechanics
med.—medical; medicine; medieval
Medit.—Mediterranean
M.E.E.—Master of Electrical Engineering
mem.—memento (Lat.), remember, memorandum
mep—mean effective pressure
Messrs.—Messieurs (Fr.), gentlemen
metal.—metallurgy
meteorol.—meteorology
Meth.—Methodist
MEV, Mev—million electron volts
mf—mezzo forte (It.), moderately loud (music); millifarad
mf, mfd—microfarad
M.F.A.—Master of Fine Arts
mfg.—manufacturing
mfr.—manufacture; manufacturer
MG—Military Government
Mg—magnesium
mg, mg., mgm—milligram
MGB—Ministerstvo Gosudarstvennoi Bezopasnosti (from the Russian), the Soviet Ministry of State Security
mgr.—manager; monsignor
MHG, M.H.G.—Middle High German
M.I.—Military intelligence
mi—mile; mill
Mic.—Micah
Mich.—Michigan
M.I.E.E.—Member of the Institution of Electrical Engineers
mil., milit.—militia; military
M.I.Mech.E.—Member of the Institution of Mechanical Engineers
M.I.Min.E., M.I.M.E.—Member of the Institution of Mining Engineers
min—Minute(s)
min.—mineralogy; minimum; mining
Minn.—Minnesota
M.Inst.C.E.—Member of the Institution of Civil Engineers
misc.—miscellaneous
Miss.—Mississippi

M.I.T.—Massachusetts Institute of Technology
ML, M.L.—Medieval, *or* Middle, Latin
M.L.—Magister Legum (Lat.), Master of Laws; Medieval, *or* Middle, Latin
ml, ml.—milliliter
MLA—Modern Language Association
MLG, M.L.G.—Middle Low German
M. Lit(t).—Magister Lit(t)erarum (Lat.), Master of Letters
Mlle.—Mademoiselle (Fr.), Miss
MM—Messieurs (Fr.), gentlemen; (Their) Majesties
mm—millimeter(s); millia (Lat.), thousands
M.M.E.—Master of Mining, or Mechanical, Engineering
Mme.—Madame (Fr.), Madam
Mn—manganese
MO, m.o.—medical officer; money order
Mo—molybdenum
Mo.—Missouri
mo.—month(s)
mod.—moderate
Moham.—Mohammedan
Mon.—Monday; Monsignor
Mont.—Montana
MOS—military occupational specialty (duty classification by serial number)
MP—military police
M.P.—Member of Parliament
mp—mezzo piano (It.), moderately soft (music)
MPH, mph—miles per hour
Mr., Mr—Mister
MRA—Moral Re-Armament
MRP—Mouvement Républicain Populaire (Fr.), Popular Republican Movement
Mrs.—Mistress
MS, Ms, ms, ms.—manuscript
M.S., M.Sc.—Master of Science
msgr.—monsignor
m.s.l.—mean sea level
MSS, MSS., mss, mss.—manuscripts
MST—Mountain Standard Time
M.S.W.—Master of Social Work
mt.—mount; mountain
MTO—Mediterranean Theater of Operations
Mt. Rev.—Most Reverend
mts.—mountains
mu—micron
mus.—museum; music; musician
Mus.B., Mus.Bac.—Musicae Baccalaureus (Lat.), Bachelor of Music
Mus. D.—Musicae Doctor (Lat.), Doctor of Music
MVA—Missouri Valley Authority
MVD—Ministerstvo Vnutrennikh Del (from the Russian), the Soviet Ministry of Internal Affairs
M.V.O.—Member of the (Royal) Victorian Order
myth., mythol.—mythology

N

N—nitrogen
N, N., n—north, northern
N., n.—navy; noon; normal (solution)
n.—natus (Lat.), born; neuter; note; noun
Na—natrium (Lat.), sodium
NAACP—National Association for the Advancement of Colored People
NAB—National Association of Broadcasters
NAD—National Academy of Design
Nah.—Nahum
NAM—National Association of Manufacturers
NAS—National Academy of Sciences
NASA—National Aeronautics and Space Administration
nat.—national; native; natural
natl.—National
NATO—North Atlantic Treaty Organization
NATS—Naval Air Transport Service

naut.—nautical
nav.—naval; navigation
N.B.—New Brunswick
N.B., n.b.—nota bene (Lat.), mark well, take notice
Nb—niobium
NBA—National Basketball Association; National Boxing Association
NBC—National Broadcasting Company
NBS—National Bureau of Standards
NC—Nurse Corps
N.C.—North Carolina
NCAA—National Collegiate Athletic Association
NCCJ—National Conference of Christians and Jews
NCO, n.c.o.—noncommissioned officer
N.D.—North Dakota
N.D., n.d.—no date
Nd—neodymium
N.Dak.—North Dakota
N.E.—New England
Ne—neon
NEA—National Education Association
Neb., Nebr.—Nebraska
NED—New English Dictionary (the Oxford English Dictionary)
neg.—negative
Neh.—**Nehemiah**
neur., neurol.—neurology
Nev.—Nevada
Newf.—Newfoundland
New M.—New Mexico
New Test.—New Testament
N.F.—Newfoundland; Norman French
NFL—National Football League
Nfld.—Newfoundland
NG—National Guard
N.G., n.g.—No good
N.H.—New Hampshire
NHA—National Housing Administration
NHG, NHG., H.H.G.—New High German
Ni—nickel
NIH—National Institutes of Health
NIRA—National Industrial Recovery Administration
N.J.—New Jersey
NKVD—from the Russian for People's Commissariat for Internal Affairs, the secret police succeeding OGPU
NL, N.L.—New Latin
n.l.—new line (print.); non licet (Lat.), it is not permitted or it is not lawful; non liquet (Lat.), it is not clear
NLRB—National Labor Relations Board
N.M., N.Mex.—New Mexico
NMU—National Maritime Union
No—nobelium
No.—north; northern
No., no.—numero (Lat.), number
noncom.—noncommissioned officer
non obst.—non obstante (Lat.), notwithstanding
non pros.—non prosequitur (Lat.), he does not prosecute
non seq.—non sequitur (Lat.), it does not follow
Nor.—Norman; North
NORAD—North American Air Defense Command
Nov., Nov—November
N.P.—nisi prius (Lat.), no protest (banking); Notary Public
Np—neptunium
n.p. or d.—no place or date
NRA—National Recovery Administration
NRAB—National Railroad Adjustment Board
N.S.—New Style (calendar); Nova Scotia
NSC—National Security Council
NSF—National Science Foundation
NSPCA—National Society for the Prevention of Cruelty to Animals
NSPCC—National Society for the Prevention of Cruelty to Children
NT., N.T.—New Testament
Num., Numb.—Numbers (Bible)
NWLB—National War Labor Board

N.W.T.—Northwest Territories
N.Y.—New York
NYA—National Youth Administration
N.Y.C.—New York City

O

O—oxygen
o—ohm
o.—ocean; order
OAS—Organization of American States
Obad.—Obadiah
O.B.E.—Officer (of the Order) of the British Empire
obit.—obituary
obj.—object, objective
obs.—observation; obsolete
OCD—Office of Civilian Defense
OCDM—Office of Civil and Defense Mobilization
OCS—Officer Candidate School
Oct., Oct—October
oct., 8vo.—octavo (print.)
O.D.—Officer of the Day; ordinary seaman; overdraft or overdrawn
ODT—Office of Defense Transportation
OE, O.E.—Old English
OECD—Organization for Economic Co-operation and Development
OED—Oxford English Dictionary
OEO—Office of Economic Opportunity
OES—Office of Economic Stabilization
O.E.S.—Order of the Eastern Star
OF, O.F.—Old French
O.F.M.—Order of Friars Minor
OHG, O.H.G.—Old High German
O.H.M.S.—On His (Her) Majesty's Service
O.K., OK—correct or approved
Okla.—Oklahoma
Old Test.—Old Testament
O.M.—Order of Merit
ON, O.N.—Old Norse
Ont.—Ontario
O.P.—Order of Preachers (Dominicans)
op. cit.—opere citato (Lat.), in the work cited
Ore., Oreg.—Oregon
orig.—original; originally
ornith.—ornithology
OS, O.S.—Old Saxon
O.S.—Old Style (calendar)
Os—osmium
O.S.A.—Order of St. Augustine
O.S.B.—Order of St. Benedict
O.S.F.—Order of St. Francis (Franciscan, or Capuchin, Order)
OSRD—Office of Scientific Research and Development
OSS—Office of Strategic Services
O.T.—Old Testament
OTS, O.T.S.—Officers' Training School
oz.—ounce (It. abbrev. of onza)

P

P—phosphorus
P., p.—pater (Lat.), father; pawn (chess); père (Fr.) father; post (Lat.), after; president; priest; prince
p—piano (It.), softly (music)
p.—page; part; participle; penny; per (Lat.), by
PA—public address (system); power of attorney
Pa—protactinium
Pa.—Pennsylvania
PAC—Political Action Committee
Pac., Pacif.—Pacific
PAL—Police Athletic League
paleon.—paleontology
par.—paragraph; parallel
parl.—parliamentary
pat., patd.—patent; patented
Pat. Off.—Patent Office
path., pathol.—pathology
PAU—Pan American Union
Pb—plumbum (Lat.), lead
PBS—Public Buildings Service

PBX—private branch exchange
PC—Preparatory Commission
P.C.—Police Constable; Privy Council; Privy Councilor
PCA—Progressive Citizens of America
pct.—percent
P.D.—Police Department
Pd—palladium
Pd.—paid
p.d.—per diem (Lat.), by the day
P.E.N.—Poets, Playwrights, Editors, Essayists and Novelists (International Association of)
pen.—peninsula
Penn., Penna.—Pennsylvania
per an.—per annum (Lat.), by the year
pers.—person; personal
Pet.—Peter
pfc, pfc.—private first class
PGA—Professional Golfers Association
*p*H—(not an abbrev.) a symbol indicating the negative logarithm of the hydrogen ion concentration.
Ph—phenyl
PHA—Public Housing Administration
phar., pharm.—pharmaceutical; pharmacology; pharmacopoeia; pharmacy
Ph.B.—Philosophiae Baccalaureus (Lat.), Bachelor of Philosophy
Ph.C.—Pharmaceutical Chemist
Ph.D.—Philosophiae Doctor (Lat.), Doctor of Philosophy
Phil.—Philemon
Phila.—Philadelphia
Philem.—Philemon
philol.—philologist; philology
philos.—philosopher; philosophy
phon.—phonetics
PHS—Public Health Service
phys.—physical; physician; physicist; physics
pizz.—pizzicato (It.), plucked (music)
pl.—plural
P.M.—Past Master; Police Magistrate; Postmaster
P.M., P.M., p.m.—post meridiem (Lat.), after noon
Pm—promethium
P.M.G.—Paymaster General; Postmaster General
Po—polonium
po.—putouts (baseball)
p.o.—petty officer; postal order; post office
POE—Port of Embarkation
pop.—population
POW, P.O.W., POWs, P.O.W.'s—prisoner(s) of war
P.P., p.p.—parcel post; parish priest; postpaid
pp—pianissimo (It.), very soft (music)
pp.—pages
P.P.C.—pour prendre congé (Fr.), to take leave
ppd.—postpaid; prepaid
P.Q.—Province of Quebec
p.q.—previous question
P.R.—Puerto Rico; proportional representation
Pr—praseodymium
PRA—Public Roads Administration
prep.—preparation; preparatory; preposition
pres.—president
Presb.—Presbyterian
prin.—principal; principle
PRO—public relations officer
proc.—proceedings; process
prod.—production
Prof., prof.—professor
prom.—promontory
pron.—pronoun; pronunciation
Prot.—Protestant
pro tem.—pro tempore (Lat.), for the time being
Prov.—Provençal; Proverbs
prov.—province; provisional; provost
prox.—proximo mense (Lat.), next month
Prus.—Prussia(n)

P.S.—Privy Seal; Public School
P.S., p.s.—post scriptum (Lat.), postscript
Ps.—Psalm(s)
pseud.—pseudonym
psi—pounds per square inch
PST—Pacific Standard Time
psychol., psych.—psychological; psychologist; psychology
Pt—platinum
pt—pint
pt.—part; payment; point; port
PTA—Parent-Teacher Association
PT boat—patrol torpedo boat
P.T.O.—please turn over
Pu—plutonium
pub.—public; published; publisher; publication
pvt.—private
PW—Prisoner of War
PWA—Public Works Administration
PWD—Public Works Department
pwt—pennyweight
PX—Post Exchange

Q

Q—Queen (chess)
Q—quasi (Lat.), as it were, almost; Quebec; queen; query; question
q.—quarto; question
QB—queen's bishop (chess)
Q.B.—Queen's Bench
QBP—queen's bishop's pawn (chess)
Q.C.—Quartermaster Corps; Queen's Counsel
Q.E.D.—quod erat demonstrandum (Lat.), which was to be proved
Q.E.F.—quod erat faciendum (Lat.), which was to be done
QKT—queen's knight (chess)
QM, Q.M.—quartermaster
QMG—quartermaster-general
QP—queen's pawn (chess)
Q.P., q.pl.—quantum placet (Lat.), as much as you please
qq.v.—quae vide (Lat.), which see (plural)
QR—queen's rook (chess)
qr.—quarter
QRP—queen's rook's pawn (chess)
qs—quantum sufficit (Lat.), as much as may suffice
qt—quart
q.t.—quiet (slang)
Que.—Quebec
ques.—question
quot.—quotation
q.v.—quod vide (Lat.), which, or whom, see

R

R—radical (hydrocarbon radical, chem.); radius; rates (math.); rook (chess)
R, r—resistance (elec.); royal; ruble
R.—Reaumur
R., r.—rabbi; rector; regina; river; road; royal; rupee
r.—radius; reigned; runs (baseball)
R.A.—Rear Admiral; Royal Academy, or Academician: Royal Artillery
Ra—radium
RAAF—Royal Australian Air Force
RAF—Royal Air Force
R.A.M.—Royal Academy of Music; Royal Arch Mason
Rb—rubidium
RBC—red blood cells; red blood count
r.b.i., rbi, RBI—run(s) batted in (baseball)
R.C.—Red Cross; Reserve Corps; Roman Catholic
RCAF—Royal Canadian Air Force
RCMP—Royal Canadian Mounted Police
R.D.—Rural Delivery
Rd., rd.—road
R.E.—real estate; Reformed Episcopal; Right Excellent; Royal Engineers
Re—rhenium
REA—Rural Electrification Administration
rec.—receipt; recipe; record; recorded

rect.—receipt; rector
ref.—referee; reference; reformed
Ref. Ch.—Reformed Church
reg.—regent; regiment; region; register; registrar; regular; regulation
Rep., Repub.—Republic; Republican
Rev.—Revelation (Bible); Reverend
Rev. Ver.—Revised Version (Bible)
RF—radio frequency
RFC—Reconstruction Finance Corporation
R.F.D.—Rural Free Delivery
Rh—rhodium
Rh factor—Rhesus factor (agglutinogen often present in human blood, biochem.)
R.I.—Rhode Island
RIBA—Royal Institute of British Architects
R.I.P.—requiescat in pace (Lat.), let him, or her, rest in peace
rit., ritard.—ritardando (It.), more slowly (music)
riv.—river
R.M.S.—Railway Mail Service
R.N.—Registered Nurse; Royal Navy
Rn—radon
RNA—ribonucleic acid
R.N.R.—Royal Naval Reserve
R.N.V.R.—Royal Naval Volunteer Reserve
Rom.—Roman; Romans (Bible)
ROTC—Reserve Officers Training Corps
R.P.—Regius Professor (Lat.), Royal Professor; Reformed Presbyterian
RPF—Rassemblement du Peuple Français (Fr.), Reunion of the French People
rpm—revolutions per minute
rps—revolutions per second
R.R.—Railroad; Right Reverend
RRB—Railroad Retirement Board
R.S.A.—Royal Society for Antiquarians; Royal Scottish Academy
RSFSR—Russian Socialist Federated Soviet Republic
RSV—Revised Standard Version (Bible)
R.S.V.P., r.s.v.p.—répondez s'il vous plait (Fr.), answer if you please
Rt. Hon.—Right Honorable
Rt. Rev.—Right Reverend
Ru—ruthenium
R.V.—Revised Version (Bible)
Ry.—Railway

S

S—sulfur
S, S., s.—south
S.—Sabbath; Samuel (Bible); Saturday; Saxon; Seaman; September; Signor; Sunday
S., s.—saint, soprano; southern
s.—second; semi-; shilling; silver; sire; solo; son
S.A.—Salvation Army
SAC—Strategic Air Command
Sam., Saml.—Samuel
Sans., Sansk.—Sanskrit
SAR—Sons of the American Revolution
S.A.S.—Societatis Antiquariorum Socius (Lat.), Fellow of the Society of Antiquaries
Sask.—Saskatchewan
Sat.—Saturday; Saturn
S.B.—Scientiae Baccalaureus (Lat.), Bachelor of Science
Sb—stibium (Lat.), antimony
SBA—Small Business Administration
SC—Security Council (United Nations)
S.S.—Sanitary Corps; Signal Corps; South Carolina; Supreme Court
Sc—scandium
Sc.—science; Scotch; Scots; Scottish
sc.—scale; scene; science; screw
s.c.—small capitals (print.)
Scan., Scand.—Scandinavia(n)
SCAP—Supreme Commander Allied Powers
Sc.B.—Scientiae Baccalaureus (Lat.), Bachelor of Science

Sc.D.—Scientiae Doctor (Lat.), Doctor of Science
sch.—school
sci.—science; scientific; scientist
Sc.M.—Scientiae Magister (Lat.), Master of Science
Scot.—Scotch; Scotland; Scottish
scr.—scruple (pharm.)
Script.—Scripture
sculp., sculp.—sculptor; sculptural; sculpture
S.C.V.—Sons of Confederate Veterans
s.d.—sine die (Lat.), without day or without appointing a day
S.Dak.—South Dakota
Se—selenium
SEATO—Southeast Asia Treaty Organization
SEC—Securities and Exchange Commission
sec—secant; second(s)
sec.—secretary
sect.—section
secy.—secretary
sen.—senate; senator
Sep.—Septuagint
Sept., Sept—September
seq., seqq.—sequentia (Lat.), following
serg., sergt.—sergeant
sf., sfz.—sforzando (It.), sudden strong accent (music)
SFSR—Soviet Federated Socialist Republic
sg, s.g.—senior grade
s.g.—specific gravity
sgt.—sergeant
SHAEF—Supreme Headquarters, Allied Expeditionary Forces
SHAPE—Supreme Headquarters Allied Powers (Europe)
Si—silicon
Sig., sig.—signature; signor (It.), mister
sin—sine
sing.—singular
S.J.—Society of Jesus
S.J.D.—Scientiae Juridicae Doctor (Lat.), Doctor of Juridical Science
Slav.—Slavic; Slavonian; Slavonic
S.M.—Scientiae Magister (Lat.), Master of Science; Sergeant Major; Soldier's Medal; State Militia
Sm—samarium
Sn—stannum (Lat.), tin
So.—South; Southern
soc.—society
S. of Sol.—Song of Solomon
sol.—solicitor
sop.—soprano
SOS—Service of Supply; the signal of distress is not an abbreviation but a prescribed code
SP—shore patrol or shore police (U.S. Navy)
sp.—special; species; specific; specimen; spelling; spirit
s.p.—sine prole (Lat.), without issue
SPARS—Women's Coast Guard Reserves (from the Coast Guard motto, "Semper Paratus—Always Ready")
SPCA—Society for the Prevention of Cruelty to Animals
spec.—special
sp gr—specific gravity
sp ht—specific heat
SPR—Society for Psychical Research
Sq.—Squadron
sq.—square; sequence
SR—Sons of the Revolution
Sr—strontium
Sr.—Senior; Señor; Sir
SRO—standing room only
SS, S.S.—Schutzstaffel (Ger.), protective force (a military unit of the Nazis)
SS, S.S., S/S—Steamship
SS.—Saints
S.S.—Sunday School
SSA—Social Security Administration

SSR—Soviet Socialist Republic
SSS—Selective Service System
St.—saint; strait; street
stacc.—staccato (It.), detached (music)
S.T.B.—Sacrae Theologiae Baccalaureus (Lat.), Bachelor of Sacred Theology
S.T.B.—Sacrae Theologiae Doctor (Lat.), Doctor of Sacred Theology
Ste.—Sainte (Fr., fem. of saint)
ster., stg.—sterling
St. Ex.—Stock Exchange
sub.—submarine; substitute; suburb
subj.—subject; subjective; subjunctive
Sun., Sund.—Sunday
sup.—superior; supplement; supply; supra (Lat.), above; supreme
supp., suppl.—supplement
supt.—superintendent
surg.—surgeon; surgery
sym.—symbol; symphony
syn.—synonym; synonymous

T

T—tantalum; temperature (absolute scale); (surface) tension; tritium
T.—Testament; Tuesday
t.—temperature; tempo; tempore (Lat.), in the time of; tenor; tense (gram.); territory; time; ton(s); town; transitive; troy (wt.)
Ta—tantalum
TAC—tactical air command
tan—tangent
TASS—Telegraphnoye Argentstvo Sovyetskovo Soyuza (Russ.), the Soviet News Agency
T.B., Tb., Tb, t.b.—tubercle bacillus; tuberculosis
Tb—terbium
tbs., tbsp.—tablespoon
TC—Trusteeship Council (United Nations); teachers college
Tc—technetium
Te—tellurium
tech.—technical; technology
tel.—telegram; telephone; telegraph
temp.—temperature; temporary
ten.—tenor; tenuto
Tenn.—Tennessee
terr., terr.—territory
Test.—Testament
Teut.—Teuton(ic)
Tex.—Texas
TF—Task Force
Th—thorium
Th.D.—Theologiae Doctor (Lat.), Doctor of Theology
theol.—theologian; theological; theology
Thess.—Thessalonians
Thur., Thurs.—Thursday
Ti—titanium
Tim.—Timothy
Tit.—Titus
TKO—technical knockout
Tl—thallium
Tm—thulium
TNT, T.N.T.—trinotrotoluene; trinitrotoluol
Tob.—Tobias
topog.—topography; topographical
tox.—toxicology
tr.—transitive; translated; translation; translator; transpose
trag.—tragedy; tragic
trans.—transaction; translation; translator; transportation
treas.—treasurer; treasury
trem.—tremolo, wavering, trembling (music)
trig., trigon.—trigonometric; trigonometry
tsp.—teaspoon
Tu., Tues.—Tuesday
TV—television; terminal velocity
TVA—Tennessee Valley Authority
TWA—Trans World Airlines
twp.—township

TWU—Transport Workers Union
typ.—typographer; typographical; typical

U

U—uranium
UAR—United Arab Republic
UAW—United Automobile Workers
U.B.—United Brethren
UDC—United Daughters of the Confederacy
UFO—unidentified flying objects
UHF—ultrahigh frequency
UK—United Kingdom
ult.—ultimate
UMT—Universal Military Training
UMW—United Mine Workers
UN, U.N.—United Nations
UNESCO—United Nations Educational, Scientific and Cultural Organization
UNICEF—United Nations Children's Fund
Unit.—Unitarian
Univ.—Universalists
univ.—universal; university
UNRRA—United Nations Relief and Rehabilitation Administration
UPI—United Press International
UPU—Universal Postal Union
U.S., US—United States
U.S.A., USA—United States Army; United States of America
USAF—United States Air Force
USCG—United States Coast Guard
USDA—United States Department of Agriculture
USES—United States Employment Service
USIA—United States Information Agency
USM—United States Mail; United States Mint
USMA—United States Military Academy
USMC—United States Marine Corps; United States Maritime Commission
USN—United States Navy
USNA—United States Naval Academy
USNG—United States National Guard
USNR—United States Naval Reserve
USO—United Service Organizations
USP—United States Pharmacopoeia
USPHS—United States Public Health Service
USS—United States Ship or Steamer
USSR—Union of Soviet Socialist Republics
U.S.W.A.—United Steel Workers of America
U.S.W.V.—United Spanish War Veterans
Ut.—Utah (not official)
U.T.W.A.—United Textile Workers of America
uv—ultraviolet

V

V—vanadium; vector (math.); velocity; victory
v.—verb; verse; versus; vide (Lat.), see; voltage; von (in German names)
VA—Veterans Administration
Va.—Virginia
VAR—visual-aural range
Vat.—Vatican
V.C.—Veterinary Corps; Vice-Chancellor; Victoria Cross
VD—venereal disease
ven.—venerable
vet.—veteran; veterinary
VFW—Veterans of Foreign Wars
V.G.—Vicar General
VHF—very high frequency
vid.—vide (Lat.), see
VIP—very important person
VISTA—Volunteers in Service to America
viz.—videlicet (Lat.), namely
V.M.D.—Veterinariae Medicinae Doctor (Lat.), Doctor of Veterinary Medicine
VNA—Visiting Nurse Association
vol.—volcano; volume
VOR—very high frequency omnirange

vox pop.—vox populi (Lat.), voice of the people
v.p.—vice president
V.R.—Victoria Regina (Lat.), Queen Victoria
V. Rev.—Very Reverend
V.S.—Veterinary Surgeon
vs.—versus (Lat.), against
vs., vss.—verse, verses
v.s.—vide supra (Lat.), see above
VSS—versions
Vt.—Vermont
VTOL—vertical take off and landing
Vulg., Vul.—Vulgate (Bible)

W

W—wolfram (Ger.), tungsten
W, W., w.—watt; west
W.—Wales; Wednesday; Welsh
W., w.—width; work (physics)
WAAF—Women's Auxiliary Air Force (Brit.)
WAAS—Women's Auxiliary Army Service (Brit.)
WAC—Women's Army Corps (U.S.)
WAF—Women in the Air Force (U.S.)
Wash.—Washington
WASP—Women's Air Force Service Pilots
WAVES—Women Accepted for Volunteer Emergency Service (U.S. Navy)
WBC—white blood cells; white blood count
WCTU—Women's Christian Temperance Union
WD, W.D.—War Department
Wed.—Wednesday
w.f.—wrong font (print.)
WFU—World Federation of Trade Unions
WHO—World Health Organization (United Nations)
Wis., Wisc.—Wisconsin
WMO—World Meteorological Organization (United Nations)
WO—warrant officer
WPA—Works Projects Administration
wpm—words per minute
WRENS, W.R.N.S.—Women's Royal Naval Service (Brit.)
wt—weight
W.Va.—West Virginia
WVS—Women's Voluntary Service (Brit.)
WW—world war
Wyo., Wy.—Wyoming

X

X—Christ; Christian
x—an abscissa (math.); an unknown quantity
Xe—xenon
Xmas—Christmas

Y

Y—yttrium
Y.—Young Men's (Women's) Christian Association
y—an ordinate (math.); an unknown quantity
Yb—ytterbium
yd—yards(s)
YMCA—Young Men's Christian Association
YMHA—Young Men's Hebrew Association
yrbk.—yearbook
yr—year(s)
YWCA—Young Women's Christian Association
YWHA—Young Women's Hebrew Association

Z

Z—atomic number; zenith distance
z—an unknown quantity
Zech.—Zechariah
zn—zinc
Z.O.A.—zoological; zoology
Zr—zirconium

MUSICAL TERMS

Term	Origin	Meaning	Term	Origin	Meaning
Accelerando	(It.)	Becoming quicker	Lento	(It.)	Slow
Adagietto	(It.)	Somewhat faster than *adagio*	Lo stesso tempo	(It.)	The same speed
Adagio	(It.)	Slow	Lourd	(F.)	Heavy
Ad libitum	(Lat.)	At the performer's discretion	Lusingando	(It.)	Flattering, coaxing
Affettuoso	(It.)	Tenderly	Lustig	(G.)	Merry, cheerful
Agitato	(It.)	Agitated	Maestoso	(It.)	Majestic
Al fine	(It.)	To the end. Usually with *da capo* or *dal segno*	Marcando, marcato	(It.)	Marked
			Meno	(It.)	Less
Alla brev	(It.)	Double the tempo (with half note as the beat)	Mesto	(It.)	Mournful
			Mezza voce	(It.)	Half voice; in instrumental music, half volume
Allargando	(It.)	Getting slower			
Allegretto	(It.)	Less movement than *allegro*	Mezzo	(It.)	Half
Allegro	(It.)	Fast	Moderato	(It.)	Moderate tempor
Andante	(It.)	In moderate walking speed	Molto	(It.)	Very
Andantino	(It.)	Modification of *andante*, whether faster or slower is not always clear	Obbligato	(It.)	Indispensable part; opposite of *ad libitum*
			Parlando, Parlante	(It.)	Speechlike
Arco	(It.)	With the bow. Cancels *pizzicato*	Piacevole	(It.)	Agreeable
			Piano	(It.)	Soft (*p*)
Assai	(It.)	Very; sometimes, rather	Pianissimo	(It.)	Very soft (*pp*)
A tempo	(It.)	Resume earlier tempo	Più	(It.)	More
Attacca	(It.)	Continue without pause	Pizzicato	(It.)	Plucked instead of bowed (*pizz.*)
Ausdrucksvoll	(G.)	With expression			
Bewegt	(G.)	With motion	Poco	(It.)	Little
Breit	(G.)	*Largo*. Also, broad	Quasi	(It.)	As if, or nearly
Brio, con	(It.)	With spirit or vigor	Rallentando	(It.)	Gradually slowing (*rall.*)
Calando	(It.)	Getting weaker and slower	Rasch	(G.)	Quick
Cantabile	(It.)	Singing, songlike	Ritardando	(It.)	Gradually slowing (*rit.*)
Cédez	(F.)	Slow down	Ritenuto	(It.)	Immediately slower
Col legno	(It.)	With the wood (of the bow)	Rubato	(It.)	Flexible melody against an inflexible accompaniment
Comodo	(It.)	Leisurely			
Crescendo	(It.)	Gradually getting louder (< or *cresc.*)	Ruhig	(G.)	Peaceful
			Scherzando	(It.)	Playfully
Da capó	(It.)	Repeat from the beginning (D.C.)	Schleppend, nicht	(G.)	Not dragging
			Schnell	(G.)	Fast
Dal segno	(It.)	Repeat from the sign: (D.S.)	Segue	(It.)	Continue without a break
Decrescendo	(It.)	Gradually getting softer (> or *decr.*)	Semplice	(It.)	Simple
			Senza	(It.)	Without
Détaché	(F.)	Broad, separate bow strokes	Sforzando	(It.)	Sudden accent (*sf.*)
Diminuendo	(It.)	Gradually getting softer (> or *dim.*)	Slentando	(It.)	Slowing down
			Soave	(It.)	Gentle
Dolce	(It.)	Sweetly	Solo	(It.)	Alone; one player
Dolente	(It.)	Sorrowful	Sordino, con	(It.)	With the mute
Doucement	(F.)	Gently, sweetly	Sospirando	(It.)	Sighing
Empfindung, mit	(G.)	With feeling	Sostenuto	(It.)	Sustained; smoothly
Ernst	(G.)	Serious	Sotto voce	(It.)	In an undertone
Espressivo	(It.)	Expressively (*espr.*)	Spiritoso	(It.)	Spirited
Feierlich	(G.)	Solemn, exalted	Staccato	(It.)	Disconnected; opposite of legato
Festivo	(It.)	Festive			
Fine	(It.)	End	Staff	(E.)	5 parallel lines used in musical notation
Flüssig	(G.)	Flowing			
Forte	(It.)	Loud (*f*)	Tace	(It.)	Silent
Fortissimo	(It.)	Very loud (*ff*)	Tempo		Rate of Speed
Fuoco, con	(It.)	With fire	Tempo giusto	(It.)	Strict time; fitting speed
Giocoso	(It.)	Playful	Tenuto	(It.)	Held, legato
Gioioso	(It.)	Joyous	Tremolo	(It.)	Rapid reiteration of a single pitch
Glissando	(mock It.)	sliding			
Grandezza, con	(It.)	With dignity, grandeur	Trill		Rapid alternation of notes
Grave	(It.)	Solemn, serious	Troppo, non	(It.)	Not too much
Gusto, con	(It.)	With style, taste	Tutti	(It.)	All (players)
Lacrimoso	(It.)	Tearful	Una corda	(It.)	Use of soft pedal on piano to achieve muting
Langsam	(G.)	Slow			
Largamente	(It.)	Broadly	Veloce	(It.)	Fast
Largo	(It.)	Slow, dignified tempo	Vif	(F.)	Lively
Legato	(It.)	Smooth, connected	Vivace	(It.)	Quick, vivacious
Leggiero	(It.)	Light	Volti subito	(It.)	Turn (the page) quickly (*v.s.*)

Purpose of This Book

The purpose of this *Handbook* is to provide a quick, easy-to-use guide to grammar, correct usage, and punctuation. It is intended for use in the business office, in the home, and in school. Secretaries, writers, teachers, and students, will find it especially useful.

The *Handbook* is divided into 25 sections or chapters each covering an important aspect or problem in English. The book is designed so that it may be used as a step-by-step complete self-study English review. But, in addition, it is a complete reference handbook for day-to-day use whenever a question arises concerning English usage or punctuation.

Special Features

Complete Table of Contents

Starting on page 1, is a detailed table of contents for use in finding subtopics within each chapter.

Clear Explanations and Examples

Throughout the book, each explanation is followed by one or more specific examples. The examples clarify the principles and rules of good English usage.

TABLE OF CONTENTS

Taken from *Instant English Handbook* by Madeline Semmelmeyer and Donald O. Bolander, © Copyrighted and reprinted by permission of Career Publishing, Inc.

1. THE PARTS OF SPEECH—I

When we speak and write, we use words to express our thoughts and ideas. The English language has thousands of words, but all of them fall into eight groups or classes known as the *parts of speech*. The following names have been given to the *parts of speech*:

Nouns   Pronouns   Verbs

Adjectives   Adverbs   Prepositions

Conjunctions   Interjections

Each group has its special work to do. *Nouns* are the names of persons, places, and things. *Pronouns* take the place of nouns. *Adjectives* and *adverbs* help express the ideas that give color and more definite meanings to nouns, verbs, and other words. *Conjunctions* are joining or connecting words.

Words, then, are the tools of communication. Like any other tool, a word may be used for different purposes at different times. For example, a word might be used as a noun in one sentence and as a verb in another sentence. Another word might be used as a preposition in one sentence and as an adverb in another sentence. All words do not have more than one use, but many words do.

The most important fact concerning any word is its *function* or use in a particular sentence. If you keep this fact in mind, you will have no difficulty in understanding the simple principles that govern the relationship of words in sentences.

NOUNS
WORDS USED AS NAMES

A **noun** is one of the most important words that you use when either speaking or writing. It is the word that tells what you are talking about. *A noun is a word that names something.* There are names for *persons, animals, places,* and *objects* that can be pointed out and recognized. There are also names for *substances, qualities, actions,* and *measures* of time or quantity. The following list includes examples of different kinds of nouns.

Persons: soldier—Jane—friend
Animals: elephant—mouse—zebra
Places: home—Chicago—camp
Objects: desk—picture—computer
Substances: iron—air—water—food
Qualities: kindness—heroism—beauty
Actions: climbing—cooking—reading
Measures: year—pound—inch—day

Nouns Used in Sentences

The words in *italics* in the following sentences are nouns.

The *soldier* is wearing his new *uniform*.
Chicago is a great industrial *city*.
Iron is a useful *metal*.

PRONOUNS
SUBSTITUTES FOR NOUNS

You will often find it necessary to refer to a *name* a number of times in a single sentence. This repetition usually results in a sentence that is very awkward or monotonous. You can readily see what might happen from the following illustration:

Jack went to *Jack's* closet and took out *Jack's* new suit because *Jack* was going to a dance given by *Jack's* company.

In this sentence the word *Jack* is stated five times. This awkward repetition of the word *Jack* and *Jack's* could be avoided by substituting another part of speech for these words.

Jack went to *his* closet and took out *his* new suit because *he* was going to a dance given by *his* company.

The words *his* and *he* used in the revision of the sentence are called **pronouns.** They are substitutes for the noun *Jack*. The prefix **pro** in the word pronoun means *for*. The word **pronoun** simply means *for a noun, or in place of a noun.*

In the following sentences, the pronouns and the nouns to which they refer are underlined.

Mary said she was going.
The men forgot their tickets.
The officer blew his whistle.

Commonly Used Pronouns

You should be familiar with the pronouns in common use. For that reason a list of pronouns is a handy reference guide. Whenever you are not certain whether a word is a pronoun, refer to the following list. In a short time you will be familiar with most of them.

I	she	this	several
my	her	that	other
mine	hers	these	another
me	it	those	anybody
we	its	all	everybody
our	they	any	nobody
ours	their	both	somebody
us	theirs	each	no one
you	them	either	someone
yours	which	neither	everyone
your	what	few	one
he	who	many	whoever
his	whose	none	whosoever
him	whom	some	anyone

VERBS
ACTION AND LINKING VERBS

The **verb** is the most important part of speech. *It is the only part of speech that can make a statement about the subject.* The subject is the part of a sentence that names the person, place, or thing that is talked about. If you wanted to write or say something about a *hunter,* you could not complete your statement without the use of a verb. You must have a verb in every sentence. The following illustration will make this clear.

The hunter *shot* the deer.
(The verb is the word *shot.*)

If you take the verb *shot* out of the sentence, you have left the words, *the hunter, the deer,* but you do not have a complete thought. You need a verb to state what the hunter did to the deer. When you supply a verb, you have a complete statement.

Most of the verbs in common use express **action.** The action is not always physical action like the action expressed in the sentence, *The hunter shot the deer.* In the sentence, *I solved the problem,* the meaning of the verb *solved* implies both mental and physical activity.

In the sentence, *The engineer built a bridge,* all the types of activity that went on until the bridge was completed are implied in the verb *built.* The same would be true of the verb *made* in the sentence, *The chef made a cake.* All the verbs in the following sentences express action of some kind:

The painter *decorated* the hall.
I *pricked* my finger.
The manager *wrote* a letter.
The president *called* a meeting.

A small, but very important group of verbs, *do not* express action. The verb **to be** is the most important verb in this group. The most common forms of the verb *to be* include *is, are, was* and *were.* Since the verb *to be* does not express action. It must have another function in the sentence. With the help of some other word or words, it makes a statement about the *condition* of the subject, or the person, place, or thing that is talked about.

In the sentence, *Henry is ill,* the verb *is* does not express action of any kind, but it serves two purposes in the sentence. With the help of the word *ill* it makes a statement about the subject, *Henry.* It also serves to connect the word *ill* with *Henry.* The sentence really means *ill Henry,* but you need the verb *is* to make the statement a complete sentence. Because the verb has this connecting function, it is called a **linking verb.**

From the following illustrations, you will see that the verb *to be* with the help of some other word describes or explains the condition of the subject in some way. The verb *is* is a form of the verb *to be.*

My uncle *is* a famous surgeon.
  (classifies uncle as surgeon)
Mother *is* very happy.
  (describes the condition of mother)
Her dress *is* beautiful.
  (describes dress)

VERB PHRASES
PRINCIPAL AND AUXILIARY VERBS

A *verb* is not always a single word. *When the verb is composed of two or more words, it is called a* **verb phrase.** The verb form at the end of the verb phrase is always the *principal verb.* It is the verb form that indicates the nature of the action, if the verb expresses action. The other verb forms in the verb phrase are called *auxiliary verbs* or *helping verbs.*

The men *work* in the fields.
The men *are working* in the fields.
The men *have been working.*
The men *must have been working.*

In the first sentence the verb consists of one word, the verb *work.* The verb *work* tells the kind of action that is going on. The verb in the second sentence consists of two words. The principal verb is *working.* The auxiliary, or helping verb is *are.* The verb phrase is *are working.* The verb phrase in the third sentence is *have been working.* The principal verb is *working,* and the two helping verbs are *have been.* The verb phrase in the fourth senpence is *must have been working.* The principal verb is *working* and the three helping verbs are *must have been.*

One of the first things you should learn to do in your study of grammar is to be able to identify the verb or the verb phrase in any sentence. Some persons have trouble in deciding what words belong in the verb phrase. You will never encounter this difficulty if you become familiar with the commonly used auxiliary verbs. A list of these auxiliary verbs follows. You should refer to this list constantly until you become familiar with the verbs that help make verb phrases.

Commonly Used Auxiliary Verbs

am	have been	could
is	had been	would
are	has been	should
was	shall	must
were	will	should have
will be	do	would have
shall be	did	must have
could be	does	should have been
have	may	could have been
has	can	must have been
had	might	

Verb Phrases Used in Sentences

In the following sentences, the words in *italics* are verb phrases.

You *will receive* the money.

He *was talking* with the manager.

The building *was destroyed* by fire.

2. THE PARTS OF SPEECH—II

Chapter One explained how *nouns, pronouns, verbs,* and *verb phrases* function in English. With these three parts of speech you can build the framework of any sentence. But it is only a framework. The sentence that contains only a noun or a pronoun and a verb is not a very interesting sentence. It does not give very specific information, or present a very interesting picture. Such sentences become very monotonous if repeated often, as you will readily see from the following illustrations:

Birds fly.	Dogs bark.
Men work.	She knits.
He swims.	They sing.

ADJECTIVES-Modifiers

You will generally find it necessary to add other parts of speech to a skeleton sentence to make the meaning clearer and more exact. You can add words to nouns and pronouns that tell *what kind, what color, which one,* etc. If you wanted to tell about the hat a woman was wearing, you would describe the hat in some way. You might say that it was a *large* hat, an *atrocious* hat, or a *red* hat, depending upon the meaning which you intended to convey.

When you add one or more of these *describing words* to hat, you give a clearer picture of what the hat is like. *Words which add new ideas to nouns and pronouns are called* **adjectives.**

The adjective not only describes by telling what kind or what color, but it may limit the meaning by telling *which* hat, *whose* hat, or the *number* of hats. For example, you might limit the meaning by saying *that* hat, *Fred's* hat, *two* hats, or *several* hats.

In grammar, we say that the adjective *modifies* the meaning of the noun or pronoun.

The word **modify** means *to change the, meaning slightly* by *describing* or *limiting* the meaning to a certain kind or to a certain number.

When we speak of a hat as an *attractive* hat, we are limiting the meaning because we are leaving out all the hats that are not attractive. If a word describes, limits, or restricts the meaning in any way, it is called a **modifier.** This is an important term that is frequently used in grammar.

The words *a, an,* and *the* are adjectives although in grammar they are called **articles.** The word *the* is called the *definite* article. The words *a* and *an* are called the *indefinite articles.* When we say, *the* book on *the* table, we are pointing out a particular book on a particular table. When we say, *I have a book,* no specific or particular book is indicated.

Adjectives Modifying Nouns

The following examples show how adjectives modify nouns and how their use makes the meaning clearer or more explicit.

long road	*good* friend	*rainy* day
rusty nail	*worthy* cause	*rapid* typist
old piano	*steep* hill	*essential* parts

ADVERBS—Modifiers

Another interesting group of words that serve as modifiers are **adverbs.** The prefix *ad* in the word adverb means *to, toward,* or *in addition to.* An adverb is a word that you *add to a verb to modify or expand the meaning of the verb.* Adverbs may also modify adjectives or other adverbs. In this unit we shall consider the adverb as a modifier of the verb. A later unit will give you the other uses of an adverb.

Adverbs are easy to identify because they usually answer the questions *when, where, how, in what manner,* or *to what extent* or *degree.* The following illustrations will make this clear:

You must set up the copy *now.*
  (*Now* tells when to set it up.)
We put the desk *there.*
  (*There* tells where it was put.)
Mary walks *gracefully.*
  (*Gracefully* tells how she walks.)

When we say, *The paper is issued weekly,* the adverb *weekly* introduces an additional idea of *time.* The adverb *weekly* makes the meaning explicit because we know *how often* or *when* the paper is issued. When we say, *Dandelions grow everywhere,* we have introduced the idea of *place,* or we tell *where* the dandelions grow. In the sentence, *We walked farther into the forest,* we have added the idea of *extent* or the *degree to which.* The adverbs in the preceding sentences are called adverbs of *time, place, manner,* or *degree.*

POSITION OF THE ADVERB

Although an adverb often modifies the verb in the sentence, it is not always placed directly after the verb. Sometimes the adverb introduces the sentence. In this position it gives more emphasis. At times the adverb is placed between the parts of the verb phrase. Study the following sentences carefully. Note the position of the adverb.

Sometimes I take a walk in the woods.
Jack *usually* leaves the house at seven.
We added a room to our house *recently.*
I have *always* admired him.

PREPOSITIONS
Words That Show a Relationship

Another important part of speech is the **preposition.** A preposition is not a modifier. The only parts of speech that are modifiers are adjectives and adverbs. The preposition has a different function to perform in the sentence. *A preposition shows the relationship that exists between certain words in a sentence.*

The word *preposition* comes from two Latin words which mean *placed before.* A preposition is a word that is *placed before some noun or pronoun.* It shows the relationship that exists between that noun or pronoun and some other word in the sentence. When we say "a bag *for* the mail," the word *for* is a preposition. It shows a relationship between *bag* and *mail.* The word *mail* which follows the preposition is called the **object** of the *preposition.*

In the sentence, *The accident occurred on the bridge,* the word *on* is a preposition. The preposition *on* is followed by the word *bridge* which is called its object. The entire group of words, *on the bridge,* is called a **prepositional phrase.** The preposition *on* shows the relation between the noun *bridge* and the verb *occurred.* The entire phrase *on the bridge* tells where the accident occurred.

We might use a number of prepositions to show the relationship between the noun *bridge* and the verb *occurred.* Each preposition would show a slightly different type of relationship, as you will readily see from the following illustrations:

The accident occurred *under* the bridge.
The accident occurred *near* the bridge.
The accident occurred *above* the bridge.
The accident occurred *behind* the bridge.
The accident occurred *beneath* the bridge.

You should become acquainted with the words that are commonly used as prepositions. A list of these prepositions is given here for your reference. Refer to this list repeatedly until you are able to identify the prepositions that are in common use.

A List of Commonly Used Prepositions

above	behind	for	since
about	below	from	to
across	beneath	in	toward
after	beside	inside	through
against	between	into	under
along	beyond	like	until
among	by	near	up
around	down	of	upon
at	during	off	with
before	except	on	within

CONJUNCTIONS—Connecting Words

In many sentences you need words that serve to join words or groups of words. In grammar, words that have this connecting function are called **conjunctions.**

The word *conjunction* comes from two Latin words which mean to *join with* or to *join together*. In the sentence, *Jane and Alice are secretaries,* the word *and* connects the two nouns, *Jane* and *Alice*. The word *and* in this sentence is a conjunction. In the sentence, *The manager or his secretary will see you,* the word *or* connects the words *manager* and *secretary*. The word *or* in this sentence is a conjunction. In the sentence, *Her small but attractive apartment is for rent,* the word *but* joins the words *small* and *attractive*.

The conjunctions that were used in the preceding illustrations were *and, but,* and *or*. These conjunctions always connect words or groups of words of equal rank. For the present, we shall limit our discussion to the use of these three conjunctions. In the following sentences, the underlined words are the words joined by the conjunction.

Mark drives too fast *and* too recklessly.
   (joins two adverbs)

He *or* I will audit the account.
   (joins two pronouns)

I fell *and* broke my arm.
   (joins two verbs)

He gave it to Mary *or* Jane.
   (joins two nouns)

It is a large *but* attractive home.
   (joins two adjectives)

INTERJECTIONS—Exclamatory Words

In English we have a number of words that are used to express strong feeling or sudden emotion. Words that serve this purpose are called **interjections.** The word *interjection* comes from two Latin words which mean *to throw between*. Interjections are really thrown into the sentence to express some type of emotion such as disgust, joy, excitement, enthusiasm, etc.

Interjections have no grammatical relation to any word or group of words in the sentence. In grammar we call words of this type *independent elements*. Sometimes words which are independent elements stand for an entire sentence. The following illustrations show the kinds of words that are commonly used as interjections. The interjections are in *italics*.

Alas! This is the end!

Hey! Where are you going?

Bah! I can't believe that.

Pshaw! Why did I do that?

The words classified as interjections in the preceding illustrations *are always interjections*. In addition to such words, nouns, pronouns, adjectives, and other parts of speech *are often used* as interjections.

Heavens! I cut my finger.

Good! I'm glad to hear that.

Horrors! Look at that hat!

Well! When are you going?

FUNCTION OF WORDS

One of the most important things to learn about the English language is the fact that *the same words are often used as different parts of speech*. A word may perform a certain function in one sentence and an entirely different function in another sentence.

Adjectives are commonly used as nouns, and nouns are frequently used as adjectives. The same word may function both as an adverb and as a preposition. Almost any type of word may be used as an interjection. The following sentences show how words function as different parts of speech:

The *light* in my study is poor.
   (*Light* is a noun.)

Please *light* the candles.
   (*Light* is a verb.)

Her hat is a *light* shade of blue.
   (*Light* is an adjective.)

Father is a *fast* driver.
   (*Fast* is an adjective.)

Father drives too *fast*.
   (*Fast* is an adverb.)

I *fast* one day every week.
   (*Fast* is a verb.)

3. THE SENTENCE

When a number of words (parts of speech) are put together in such a way that they express a **complete thought,** you have a *sentence*. The sentence may consist of one word, or it may consist of as many as three hundred words. The tendency in modern writing is to use short, effective sentences. Twenty words is about the average length in present-day writing.

Often those who are beginning the study of language find it difficult to understand what is meant by a *complete thought*. Some students punctuate parts of sentences as if they were sentences because they do not realize that some essential element is missing. None of the following groups of words are sentences, although they are punctuated as if they were complete.

The officers of our company.
Enjoyed the banquet.
On the top of the hill.

These groups of words are not sentences because they lack something that is necessary in order to express a complete thought. When you examine the first group of words, you will readily see that you know what the writer is talking about. However, the writer did not complete the sentence by telling you what the officers did. The second group of words tells you that somebody enjoyed a banquet. But the author neglected to tell you who it was. The third group of words tells you very little. You

have no way of knowing what the writer is talking about.

SUBJECT AND PREDICATE

In order to express a complete thought, a sentence must have both a *subject* and a *predicate*. These are two important grammatical terms used to describe the essential elements of a sentence.

The **subject** is the word or group of words that tells us *what or whom the speaker or writer is talking about*. The **predicate** is the part of the sentence *that makes a statement about the subject*. The *predicate* usually tells what the subject is doing, or what is happening to the subject.

Study the following sentences carefully. Note that the subjects have been separated from the predicates so that you will be able to see the relationship between the two parts more easily.

Subject	Predicates
My friend	lives in New York.
The letter	contains exciting news.
Both men	are experienced salesmen.

In the first sentence, I am talking about *my friend*. Therefore, *my friend* is the subject of the sentence. I complete the sentence by making a statement about my friend. I say that my friend *lives in New York*. The predicate is *lives in New York*. This group of words, *My friend lives in New York*, is a sentence because it expresses a complete thought. It has both a subject and a predicate. The other two sentences also have a subject and predicate.

COMPLETE SUBJECT AND COMPLETE PREDICATE

In many sentences the subject or the predicate is only a single word. But more often, the subject consists of two or more words. In grammar, we call the entire subject, regardless of the number of words, the **complete subject**. We call the entire predicate the **complete predicate.**

If the subject of a sentence is a single word, that word is the *complete subject*. If the predicate of the sentence is a single word, that word is the *complete predicate*. In the sentence, *Birds fly,* the word *birds* is the complete subject, and the word *fly* is the complete predicate.

SIMPLE SUBJECT AND SIMPLE PREDICATE

After you have learned how to identify the complete subject and the complete predicate, you can easily find the **simple subject** and the **simple predicate.**

Somewhere in the complete subject you will find the *particular word* about which something is said. That word is the *simple subject*. It is usually either a noun or a pronoun.

Somewhere in the predicate you will find a word that serves as the *key* to the predicate. That word is the *verb*, the most important word in any sentence. If the verb consists of more than one word, it is called a *verb phrase*. In the following examples the simple subjects and predicates are underlined:

The <u>ambassador</u> <u>attended</u> a conference.

The <u>hero</u> of the story <u>had</u> many adventures.

My <u>friend</u> in Boston <u>bought</u> a new car.

Sometimes you will find only one word in the subject or one word in the predicate. In that case, the single word in the subject is the simple subject. It is also the complete subject.

The single word in the predicate is the simple predicate and also the complete predicate.

Pronouns are often used as the simple subject and the complete subject. In the sentence, *We are buying a new home,* the pronoun *we* is the simple subject. It is also complete subject since there are no other words in the subject.

In the sentence, *The building collapsed,* the verb *collapsed* is the simple predicate. It is also the complete predicate since it is the only word in the predicate.

In the following illustrations, the simple subjects and simple predicates are underlined.

Fast driving is often dangerous.
The detectives on the case found the jewels.
Children play.

COMPOUND SUBJECT AND COMPOUND PREDICATE

A sentence may have two or more simple subjects and two or more simple predicates. In the sentence, *Harry and Fred joined a lodge,* there are two simple subjects, *Harry* and *Fred.* The connecting word is *and.* In grammar we say that the sentence has a **compound subject.**

In the sentence, *The stenographer wrote the letter and mailed it,* there are two predicate verbs, *wrote* and *mailed.* The connecting word is *and.* This sentence has a **compound predicate.**

Some sentences have a compound subject and a compound predicate. In the sentence, *Alice and Jane washed the curtains and ironed them,* there are two simple subjects and two simple predicates. The subject nouns are *Alice* and *Jane.* The two predicate verbs are *washed* and *ironed.* In both cases, the connecting word is *and.*

The following sentences contain either a compound subject, a compound predicate, or both.

Corn and beans are grown in the valley.
(*compound subject*)
I attended the lecture and took notes.
(*compound predicate*)
The boys and girls sang and danced at the club.
(*compound subject and compound predicate*)

SENTENCE FRAGMENTS

If you have studies this unit carefully, you will have a thorough understanding of the essential elements of a sentence. But even persons who have this knowledge often punctuate groups of words as sentences when one or both of the essential elements are missing.

Any incomplete group of words punctuated as if it were a sentence is called a *sentence fragment* or a *fragmentary sentence.* As you know, a fragment is only a piece or a part of the whole. A fragment always refers to something that is incomplete.

A fragmentary sentence always lacks one or both of the essential elements of a sentence. That is, either the subject or the predicate, or both the subject and predicate are missing. Whenever you are in doubt about a particular sentence, apply this test: Does the group of words contain both a subject and a predicate? Does it express a complete thought?

Very often the subject of the sentence is missing. The following group of words is *not* a sentence because it does not tell who it is that the writer is talking about:

Interviewed the candidate.
(This is not a sentence.)
The president interviewed the candidate.
(This is a complete sentence.)

The sentence was completed by supplying a subject, *The president.*

Sometimes the predicate is missing. The following group of words is *not* a sentence because the entire predicate is missing:

The sound of footsteps.
(This is not a sentence.)
The sound of footsteps *alarmed us.*
(This is a complete sentence.)

The use of fragmentary or incomplete sentences is an unsatisfactory way of communicating your ideas. Surprising as it may seem, sentence fragments similar to the following examples can be found repeatedly in letters sent out by reputable business firms. Check the letters of your company. You may be amazed at what you find. Be sure you do not use fragments in your own personal writing.

Received your letter this morning.
(*Subject* is missing.)
Will send order at onec.
(*Subject* is missing.)
Have shipped your order.
(*Subject* is missing.)
Hoping this meets with your approval.
(*No subject or predicate.*)

4. SENTENCE PATTERNS

In Chapter Three it was explained that a sentence must express a complete thought. It must also have both a subject and a predicate. This unit shows how it is possible to express a complete thought in a variety of ways. You should become familiar with the different ways of arranging words in sentences and the different sentence patterns that are the result of these arrangements.

KINDS OF SENTENCES

Sentences fall into four groups according to the purpose the sentence serves and the manner in which the thought is expressed. Some sentences simply *make statements.* Some sentences *ask questions.* Another type of sentence *gives a command* or *makes a request.* The last group is the kind of sentence that *expresses strong feeling* or *sudden emotion.*

In grammar, the sentence that makes a statement is called a **declarative sentence.** The sentence that asks a question is called an **interrogative sentence.** The sentence that gives a command or makes a request is called an **imperative sentence,** and the sentence that expresses strong feeling is called an **exclamatory sentence.** Following are examples of the four types of sentences:

My friend is a business executive.
(*declarative sentence*)

Have you entered the contest?
(*interrogative sentence*)

Clear the road at once!
(*imperative sentence—command*)

Please shut the door.
(*imperative sentence—request*)

What a tragedy this is!
(*exclamatory sentence*)

If you examine the preceding illustrations carefully, you will notice that the *declarative sentence* ends with a *period.* The *interrogative sentence* ends with a *question mark* (?). Sometimes the *imperative sentence* ends with an *exclamation mark* (!) and sometimes it ends with a *period.* If the command is given in a very emphatic or decisive manner, an exclamation mark is placed at the end. A mild request always ends with a period. An *exclamatory sentence* usually ends with an *exclamation mark.* Briefly summarized, then:

A **declarative** sentence *makes a statement.*

An **interrogative** sentence *asks a question.*
An **imperative** sentence gives a *command* or makes a *request.*

An **exclamatory** sentence expresses *strong feeling* or *sudden emotion.*

INVERTED ORDER

You have probably observed that the four types of sentences follow certain patterns of word arrangement. These patterns will now be discussed in more detail.

Every sentence has a basic structure or framework. This is true of all four types of sentences—*declarative, interrogative, imperative,* and *exclamatory.* This framework, as you already know, consists of the subject noun or pronoun and the predicate verb.

There are a number of ways of introducing the subject in a declarative sentence. The **normal order,** or the grammatical order, is *subject first,* followed by the predicate. If you always followed this pattern, your sentences would soon become monotonous and uninteresting. The following illustration will make this clear. The sentences in this paragraph sound very much like the sentences in a primer or in a first reader.

I like this book. It is a book about Mexico. My friend sent this book to me. My friend lives in New York. She speaks Spanish.

In this short paragraph, all the sentences follow the same pattern—subject first, followed by the predicate. You can give more variety to your sentence patterns by placing words in unusual positions.

You can put the subject after the verb or place it at the very end of the sentence. Varying the position of the subject gives you an opportunity to place other words at the beginning of the sentence to give them more emphasis. This also makes our sentences more interesting.

On my desk I found an interesting book about Mexico.

In this sentence, the subject is placed after the group of words, or the phrase, *on my desk.* This arrangement throws the phrase to the front of the sentence and gives it more emphasis.

When the subject of the sentence does not appear in its normal position, we say that the order of the sentence is inverted, or turned around. Always remember that *normal* or grammatical order *means subject first,* followed by the predicate. Examine the following sentences carefully. Note the position of the subject in the two sentences.

The *band* marched down the street.
Down the street marched the *band.*

The first sentence is in normal, or grammatical order. The subject noun *band* appears at the beginning of the sentence. The verb *marched* follows the subject.

The second sentence is the same sentence in **inverted order.** The subject noun *band* now appears at the end of the sentence. The verb *marched* comes before the subject. A phrase, *Down the street*, appears at the beginning of the sentence.

An adverb often introduces a sentence. The following sentence begins with an adverb, and not with the subject.

Suddenly the train stopped. (*inverted order*)
The train stopped *suddenly*. (*normal order*)

Some persons find it difficult to determine the true subject when a sentence is not in grammatical order. This difficulty can be avoided by *transposing* the sentence and putting it back in normal order. The only purpose in transposing a sentence is to see the grammatical relations more clearly.

Sometimes when you put a sentence back in grammatical order by transposing it, you will find that the transposed sentence is not so smooth as the original sentence. However, the following sentence is just as effective in either order.

Along the road we passed a number of army trucks.
We passed a number of army trucks *along the road.*

Whenever you are dealing with a sentence in inverted order, you should transpose it before you attempt to analyze the sentence from the grammatical point of view.

INTERROGATIVE SENTENCE PATTERNS

In asking a question, you seldon start with the subject first, as you do in a declarative sentence. For that reason, *the interrogative sentence is generally in inverted order.* Sometimes the interrogative sentence starts with the *verb*. Often it begins with an *adverb*, which is used to ask the question.

Did you bring your camera?
   (introduced by the *verb*)
Where did you buy your watch?
   (introduced by an *adverb*)

In order to see the grammatical constructions in an interrogative sentence that is inverted, you must transpose the sentence and put it in normal order. Sometimes the interrogative sentence becomes a statement when it is transposed.

You did bring your camera?
You did buy your watch where?

IMPERATIVE AND EXCLAMATORY SENTENCE PATTERNS

The imperative sentence presents a different problem. The *subject* of the sentence that gives a command or makes a request *is seldom expressed.* If the subject is not expressed, it is the word *you* understood.

Sound the alarm at once!
   (Subject is not expressed.)
(You) Sound the alarm at once!
   (Subject *you* is understood.)
Please read the announcement.
   (Subject is not expressed.)
(You) Please read the announcement.
   (Subject *you* is understood.)

Sometimes an imperative sentence begins with a noun that indicates the name of the person to whom the command or the request is given. An interrogative sentence may also begin in this way. The point to keep in mind is that such a noun *is not the subject* of the sentence. In fact, it has no grammatical connection with the rest of the sentence. It is an independent element. For that reason, it is separated from the rest of the sentence by a comma. Study the following illustrations carefully:

Imperative Sentence

Fred, please close the door.
   (*Fred* is the person addressed.)
Fred, (you) please close the door.
   (Subject is *you* understood.)

Interrogative Sentence

Alice, did you lock the door?
   (*Alice* is a noun in direct address.)
Alice, you did lock the door?
   (Subject is *you* expressed.)

In the first sentence, the word *Fred* is a noun in **direct address** because it names the person spoken to directly. It is not the subject of the sentence. The subject of an imperative sentence is *you* understood. The word *Fred* is set off from the rest of the sentence by a comma to show that it is used *independently.*

In the second sentence, the word *Alice* is a noun in direct address because it names the person spoken to directly. Since this is an interrogative sentence, the subject is expressed. When the sentence is placed in normal order, you can easily see that the subject is *you*, and not Alice.

A noun in *direct address* may appear at the beginning or at the end of the sentence. It may even appear within the sentence.

Fred, please close the door.
   (beginning of the sentence)
Please close the door, *Fred*.
   (end of the sentence)
Come here, *Fred*, and look at this book.
   (within the sentence)

The exclamatory sentence is often expressed in inverted order. In the sentence, *What a feast she spread!*, the subject and the verb appear at the end of the sentence. When the sentence is transposed, the subject appears at the beginning of the sentence and is followed by the verb.

What a feast she spread! (*inverted order*)
She spread what a feast! (*normal order*)

How beautiful the sunset is tonight! (*inverted order*)
The sunset is how beautiful tonight! (*normal order*)

What a tragedy that would be! (*inverted order*)
That would be what a tragedy! (*normal order*)

SENTENCES THAT BEGIN WITH "THERE"

Another sentence pattern that we use frequently is the sentence that begins with the word *there*. We have a very good reason for beginning some of our sentences in this way.

When the word *there* is used to introduce the sentence, it is possible to place the subject after the verb. In many cases this results in a much smoother sentence, as you will see from the following illustration:

A heavy frost was last night.
There was a heavy frost last night.

Although the first sentence is in grammatical order, it is a very awkward sentence. The second arrangement results in a much smoother style, but it presents a grammatical problem. In dealing with a sentence that begins with *there*, you must always remember that the word *there* is neither the subject of the sentence, nor an adverbial modifier. It is merely an introductory word which has a special function, that of introducing the sentence.

When the word *there* functions in this way, it is called an **expletive.** The word **expletive** comes from the Latin and means "*added merely to fill up.*" This is a very suitable term because it explains exactly what takes place.

The word *there* merely "fills up" the place normally occupied by the subject. It has no other function in the sentence. Like the noun in direct address, it is an independent construction. When the sentence is transposed, and placed in grammatical order, you should enclose the word *there* in parentheses to show that it is used independently.

There are twelve candidates for the position.
(There) twelve candidates are for the position.

It is important to transpose the sentence beginning with *there* in order to determine the true subject of the sentence. It is also important to determine whether the word *there* is used as an introductory word or whether it is used as an adverb.

There they are. (*There* is an adverb of place.)
They are *there*. (*There* is an adverb of place.)

There were ten men in the band. (*there*—expletive)
(*There*) ten men were in the band. (*there*—expletive)

The coach stood *there* watching the game. (*there*—adverb of place)

There is a telephone directory on the table. (*there*—expletive)

We met *there* last year. (*there*—adverb of place)

There will be some objection to the plan. (*there*—expletive)

The word *it* is also used as an expletive in certain sentence patterns. The use of *it* as an expletive will be discussed in later units.

5. NOUNS
KINDS OF NOUNS

Chapter One explained that a noun is a word used as a name. You also learned that some nouns begin with capital letters, and others begin with small letters. The subject of *capitalization* is very important because it is closely concerned sith the division of nouns into groups or classes.

In English, nouns are divided into two main classes called **common nouns** and **proper nouns.** A *common noun* names any one of a class of persons, places, or things. We have a name for all the chairs in the world when we use the common noun *chair*. We have a name for all the lakes in the world when we use the common noun *lake*.

But when we want to name a particular lake, we must give it a special name. The name of a particular lake might be *Lake Louise, Lake George*, or *Lake Michigan*. These particular names are called proper nouns. *A proper noun always begins with a capital letter.*

We have particular names for persons, such as *John Adams, General Eisenhower, Queen Elizabeth,* and *Governor Stevenson.* We also have particular names for certain objects, such as buildings, hotels, theaters, and clubs: *Conway Building, Congress Hotel, Harris Theater,* and *Union League Club.*

Sometimes a common noun names a collection of objects or a group of persons. When we use the word *band* in music, we include under one name all the musicians who play the different instruments. When we use the word *jury,* we include all the members who make up the jury. Nouns that name a group of persons or a collection of objects are called *collective nouns.*

A **common noun** is the name of *any one* of a class of *persons, places,* or *things.*

aviator	ocean	tiger	meat
city	book	lily	desk

A **proper noun** is the name of a *particular person, place,* or *thing.*

Pacific Ocean	Thomas Edison
Chicago	Amazon River
England	Wrigley Building
State Street	Bay of Fundy

A **collective noun** is a common noun whose singular form names a *group* of persons, objects, or acts.

herd	company	team	crowd
army	corps	audience	faculty

Some nouns are *common nouns* in one sentence and *proper nouns* in another sentence.

Common Nouns
Roy is studying to be a doctor.
John's uncle is an engineer.
I went to the theater with May.
We spent the summer at the lake.

Proper Nouns
The family called in Dr. Allen.
Uncle John is a colonel in the army.
The play was given at the Grand Theater.
Did you ever cross Lake Erie?

CAPITALIZATION OF PROPER NOUNS

A student of language should be familiar with the accepted rules regarding the capitalization of *proper nouns* and *proper adjectives.* **Proper adjectives** are adjectives derived from proper nouns.

Proper Nouns	Proper Adjectives
America	an *American* soldier
Spain	a *Spanish* house
China	a *Chinese* vase

The following list of rules for the capitalization of proper nouns follows accepted, present-day usage:

1. Capitalize names of *particular persons* and *places.*

Mr. Smith	Yankee Stadium
Helen Hayes	Radio City
Senator Clark	Ellis Island

2. Capitalize *geographic names:* continents, countries, states, cities, rivers, mountains, lakes, falls, harbors, valleys, bays, etc.

Africa	Gulf of Mexico
Montana	Rocky Moutains
Pikes Peak	New York Harbor
Cleveland	Long Island

3. Capitalize names of *definite regions, localities,* and *political divisions.*

the Orient	Third Precinct
the Bad Lands	Wheeling Township
the Arctic Circle	French Republic

4. Capitalize names of *bridges, buildings, monuments, parks, ships, automobiles, hotels, forts, dams, railroads, streets,* etc.

Brooklyn Bridge	Michigan Avenue
Fine Arts Building	Plaza Hotel
Statue of Liberty	Eiffel Tower
Central Park	Boulder Dam

5. Capitalize names of *historical events, historical periods,* and *historical documents.*

the Middle Ages	Battle of Gettysburg
World War II	Louisiana Purchase
the Crusades	Fourteenth Amendment
Magna Charta	the Civil War (American)

6. Capitalize names of *governmental bodies* and *departments.*

Bureau of Mines	Civil Service Commission
the Federal Government	Federal Trade Commission
United States Senate	the President's Cabinet
Federal Courts	Supreme Court of the United States

7. Capitalize names of *political parties, business* and *fraternal organizations, clubs* and *societies, companies,* and *institutions.*

Republicans	County Hospital
Democratic Party (or party)	John Crerar Library
	a Shriner
Chapman Chemical Company	the Elks
	Ford Motor Company
Volunteers of America	Rutgers University

8. Capitalize *titles of rank* when they are joined to a person's name.

President Lincoln	Professor Thomas
Senator Lodge	Doctor Hayden
Dr. Allen Reed	Dean Mary Allison
Chancellor Harris	Cardinal Wolsey
Secretary Henderson	His Honor the Mayor

9. Capitalize *days* of the *week, months* of the *year, holidays,* and *days* of *special observance,* such as feast and fast days.

Monday	Feast of the Passover
September	Mothers's Day
Labor Day	Good Friday
Easter Sunday	Memorial Day

10. You should not capitalize names of the seasons unless they are personified. When something is personified it is represented or considered as if it were a person. Personification is frequently used in poetry.

spring	winter
Spring's warm touch	Winter's icy breath

11. The words *north, east, south,* and *west* are capitalized when they refer to *sections* of the country. They are not capitalized when they refer to *directions.*

Sections of Countries
the Midwest
the Far West
the Near East

Directions
I travel north on my way home.
The sun rises in the east.
The southern part of Idaho is beautiful.

12. The *special names* given to planets and stars are capitalized. The words *sun, moon, star,* and *planet* are not capitalized.

Jupiter	The *sun* rose at six that morning.
Venus	The *moon* is a heavenly body.
Mars	A *planet* shines by reflected light.
Milky Way	A *constellation* is a group of stars.

SPECIAL USES OF CAPITAL LETTERS

1. Words derived from proper nouns are usually capitalized. If the word has acquired a special meaning, it is not capitalized.

Capitalized	Not Capitalized
Mongolian race	navy blue
Venetian blinds	china cabinet
Swiss cheese	morocco leather
English tweeds	chinaware
Turkish bath	turkish towel or Turkish towel

2. The principal words in *titles of books, magazines, pictures, songs, articles,* etc., are capitalized. Prepositions, conjunctions, and the articles *a, an,* and *the* are not capitalized unless the title begins with one of these words.

The Last of the Mohicans (book)
The Saturday Evening Post (magazine)
"Outside Our World" (article)
Battle Hymn of the Republic (song)
"Meet the Press" (television program)

3. The definite article *the* is not capitalized unless it is the first word of a title. Many titles do not begin with *the.* If the word *the* is within the title, it is written with a small letter. The only way to be sure about the correct form of a title is to check the official form, or the form adopted by the company, publication, etc.

The Christian Science Monitor
The John C. Harris Company
National Geographic Magazine
Pinnacle Oil Company

4. All words referring to the Deity, the Bible, books of the Bible, and other *sacred books* are capitalized.

God, the Father	the Koran
Savior	Genesis
the Trinity	Supreme Being
Talmud	Bible
Book of Job	New Testament

5. The pronoun *I* and the interjection *O* are capitalized. The word *oh* is not capitalized unless it is the first word of a sentence.

"O say! can you see, by the dawn's early light, . . ."
" 'Tis the Star Spangled Banner, oh, long may it wave. . ."

6. Names of school subjects are not capitalized unless they are names of the languages. Subjects listed in school catalogs as names of special courses are capitalized.

mathematics	History 101
French	Advanced Chemistry II
economics	Economics 345
English	Physics II

7. Capitalize words which show family relationships when they are used with a person's name. The words *father* and *mother* are not capitalized when they are preceded by a pronoun. When used without a pronoun, they are usually capitalized.

Aunt Martha   her cousin
Cousin John   their uncle
Uncle Jack   my father

8. Capitalize the first word in a *compound word that is used as a proper noun.* If the second word in the compound word is a proper noun, it should also be capitalized. Capitalize both parts of *compound titles of distinction.*

Forty-third Street un-American activities
Army-Navy game   ex-President Eisenhower
The Honorable   Rear Admiral Simpson
 John Willis

9. The names of special departments of business firms may be written with small or with capital letters. In business writing, it is considered good practice to capitalize titles such as *president, secretary, office manager, general superintendent,* etc. They may also be written with small letters.

claim department *or* Claim Department
The Company will reimburse you. (or company)
Our President will see you. (or president)

PLURAL FORMS OF NOUNS

When a noun refers to one person or thing, it is singular in number. When a noun refers to more than one person or thing, it is plural in number. Nouns have special forms to show these distinctions, as you will see from the following illustrations:

Singular Plural

boy   boys
box   boxes
leaf   leaves
tomato tomatoes

The plurals of nouns are formed in a number of different ways. Since there are exceptions to almost every one of these methods, you should consult a reliable dictionary whenever you are in doubt regarding a correct plural form. You should also be familiar with the following methods of forming the plurals of nouns:

1. Most nouns add the letter *s* to the singular to form the plural.

lamp   lamps   college   colleges
dance   dances   manager   managers
chief   chiefs   dynamo   dynamos

2. Nouns ending in *s, sh, ch, x,* or *z* form the plural by adding *es.* The plural adds another syllable in the pronunciation.

dress   dresses couch   couches
match   matches waltz   waltzes
tax   taxes   loss   losses

3. Nouns ending in *o* preceded by a vowel add *s.* Musical terms ending in *o* add *s.*

Vowel Preceding "o"   Musical Terms

patio   patios   piano   pianos
rodeo   rodeos   alto   altos

Some nouns ending in o preceded by a consonant add *s.* Others add *es.* Some form the plural either way.

Add "s"   Add "es"

kimono kimonos Negro   Negroes
zero   zeros   hero   heroes

Add "s" or "es"

cargo   cargos   cargoes
motto   mottos   mottoes

4. Nouns ending in *y* preceded by a consonant, change the *y* to *i* and add *es.*

party   parties country countries
city   cities   enemy   enemies
lady   ladies   berry   berries

5. Nouns ending in *y* preceded by a vowel, usually add *s.* In many cases the vowel before the final *y* is *e.*

alley   alleys   journey journeys
boy   boys   valley   valleys
key   keys   day   days

6. Some nouns ending in *f* or *fe* change the *f* or the *fe* to *v* and add *es.* Some nouns ending in *f* have two plurals, one in *s* and one in *ves.* Some simply add *s.*

Change to "ves"   Add "s" or Change to "ves"

wife   wifes   scarf scarfs scarves
thief   thieves wharf wharfs wharves
half   halves   hoof   hoofs   hooves

7. Some nouns form the plural by a change in the vowel.

man   men   mouse   mice
foot   feet   goose   geese
tooth   teeth   louse   lice

8. Some nouns have the same form for both singular and plural.

Singular and Plural

fish   fish   species species
sheep   sheep   series   series
Chinese Chinese salmon   salmon

9. The plurals of compound nouns are generally formed by adding *s* to the *principal word* in the compound.

mother-in-law   *mothers*-in-law
board of education *boards* of education
attorney general   *attorneys* general *or* attorney *generals*
court-martial   *courts*-martial

Sometimes *both parts* of the compound are made plural.

manservant   menservants
woman doctor   women doctors

Sometimes an *s* or *es* is added to the end of the compound. In that case, there is no important word in the compound.

forget-me-not   forget-me-nots
toothbrush   toothbrushes

Compounds ending in *ful* are made plural by adding *s* to the end of the compound. This rule applies when the same container is filled a number of times.

spoonful spoonfuls handful handfuls
bucketful bucketfuls cupful   cupfuls

10. The plurals of proper names are formed by adding *s* or *es.*

There are three *Ruths* in this class.
The two *Burnses* left the hall.
The *Joneses* and the *Smiths* attended.

The spelling of proper names must not be changed. If we followed the rule for words ending in *y* in the case of *Mary,* we would change the *y* to *i* and add *es.* The name would then be changed to *Marie,* for the plural would be *Maries.* The correct plural of *Mary* is *Marys.*

11. Titles are made plural in several ways. The plural of *Miss* is *Misses;* the plural of *Mr.* is *Messrs. Mrs.* has no plural. The plural of *Madam* is *Mesdames,* which is sometimes used for the plural of *Mrs. Misses* should not be followed by a period. It is not an abbreviation. In the first column of the following examples, the title is made plural. In the second column the name is made plural. Either form is correct.

the *Misses* Thomas *or* the Miss *Thomases*
the *Messrs.* Churchill *or* the Mr. *Churchills*

Foreign Plurals

Words taken from foreign languages usually retain their foreign plurals. Some of these words are used so commonly that they have acquired an English plural which is formed in the regular way; that is, by adding *s* or *es* to the singular.

The following list gives the foreign and English plurals for some commonly used foreign words. If no English plural is given, the foreign plural is used.

Foreign Word	Foreign Plural	English Plural
alumna (*feminine*)	alumnae	_____
alumnus (*masculine*)	alumni	_____
analysis	analyses	_____
appendix	appendices	appendixes
bacterium	bacteria	_____
basis	bases	_____
cactus	cacti	cactuses
crisis	crises	_____
criterion	criteria	criterions
curriculum	curricula	curriculums
datum	data	_____
formula	formulae	formulas
gymnasium	gymnasia	gymnasiums
hypothesis	hypotheses	_____
index	indices	indexes
madam	mesdames	_____
medium	media	mediums
memorandum	memoranda	memorandums
parenthesis	parentheses	_____
phenomenon	phenomena	_____
radius	radii	radiuses

12. The plural of numbers, letters, signs, and symbols is formed by adding the apostrophe and *s.*

Your *2's* look like your *3's.*
You use too many *ands* in your writing. (correct)
or
You use too many *and's* in your writing. (correct)
You must always cross your *t's.*
He received three *A's* and two *B's* last semester.

13. The following nouns are used only in the plural. You may find some of them used in the singular, but the general practice is to regard them as plural. When you are in doubt, consult the dictionary.

trousers shears   contents
pants   pliers   riches
scissors scales (weighing) alms
billiards nuptials   remains
clothes   gallows   victuals

6. PRONOUNS

In Chapter One you learned that a *pronoun* is a word used in place of a noun. Because pronouns can be used in place of nouns, they avoid the monotonous repetition of nouns. The following illustration shows what happens when we repeat the same noun too often in a sentence:

Alice went to **Alice's** room to dress because **Alice** was going to a reception given by **Alice's** club in **Alice's** honor.

This sentence is very awkward and monotonous because of the tiresome repetition of *Alice* and *Alice's*. When we rewrite the sentence and substitute pronouns for *Alice* and *Alice's,* we have a much better sentence.

Alice went to **her** room to dress because **she** was going to a reception given by **her** club in **her** honor.

You should not only learn how to use pronouns effectively, but you should also learn how to use them correctly. Many of the language errors that are commonly made are errors in the use of pronouns. These mistakes occur because some of the pronouns that we use constantly have a number of different forms.

As a student of English you should know how and when to use the different forms of pronouns. In order to do this, you must be familiar with the changes in form that certain pronouns undergo. To illustrate: The pronoun **I** is used as the subject of a sentence. When this same pronoun is used as the object of a preposition, the form changes to *me.* It is incorrect to say, "between *you* and *I.*" The correct form to use in this phrase is *me.*

Illustrations of Changes in the Forms of Pronouns

I saw the accident. (The pronoun **I** is the subject.)
Jane saw **me** at the game. (The pronoun *me* is the object of *saw.*)
He *won* the first prize. (The pronoun *he* is the subject).
We met **him** in the lobby. (The pronoun *him* is the object of *met.*)

In the first sentence, the pronoun *I* is used as the **subject** of the sentence. When this same pronoun is used as the **object of a verb,** the form changes to *me.* In the third sentence, the pronoun *he* is the subject of the sentence. When this same pronoun is used as the object of the verb *met,* the form changes to *him.*

KINDS OF PRONOUNS

There are five groups or classes of pronouns in English: **personal** pronouns, **interrogative** pronouns, **demonstrative** pronouns, **indefinite** pronouns, and **relative** pronouns. The personal pronouns include the *compound personal* pronouns, and the relative pronouns include the *compound relative* pronouns.

PERSONAL PRONOUNS

The personal pronouns are the most important group of pronouns. They are also the pronouns that will give you the most trouble unless you are familiar with the various forms that belong to each pronoun.

A **personal pronoun** is a pronoun that shows by its form whether it refers to the *person speaking,* the *person spoken to,* or the *person or thing spoken of.* All the personal pronouns, with the exception of the pronoun *it,* refer to persons. The following sentences show the use of personal pronouns in the first, second, and third person:

I shall spend the winter in Texas. (*I* is the *person speaking.*)
You are working too hard. (*You* is the *person spoken to.*)
He bought a new Ford. (*He* is the *person spoken about.*)
We built the garage. (*We* refers to the *persons speaking.*)
They operate two farms. (*They* refers to the *persons spoken about.*)
Ted has a new radio. **It** is a Zenith. (*It* refers to the *thing spoken about.*)
Jan has two fur coats. **They** are both mink. (*They* refers to the *things spoken about.*)

The pronoun of the **first person** is the pronoun **I** with its plural form **we.** The pronoun of the **second person** is *you.* The plural form is also *you.* The pronouns of the **third person** are *he, she,* and *it* with the common plural *they* for all three persons.

The personal pronouns also have different forms to indicate case. You will learn more about the case of pronouns in Chapter Nine. For the present, you should be familiar with all the forms of the personal pronouns and the pronoun *who* so that you will be able to identify them.

Forms of the Personal Pronouns

1. **First person**—personal pronouns referring to the *speaker*:

   I, my, mine, me (singular)
   we, our, ours, us (plural)

2. **Second person**—personal pronouns referring to the *person spoken to*:

   you, your, yours (same forms in both singular and plural)

3. **Third person**—personal pronouns referring to the *persons* or *things spoken about*:

   he, his, him, she, her, hers, it, its (singular)
   they, their, theirs, them (plural)

4. Forms of the pronoun **who:**

   who, whose, whom

COMPOUND PERSONAL PRONOUNS

Sometimes the word *self* or *selves* is added to certain forms of the personal pronouns. Pronouns formed in this way are called **compound personal pronouns.**

List of Compound Personal Pronouns

myself	herself
yourself	ourselves
himself	yourselves
itself	themselves

Compound personal pronouns are used in two ways: (1) as *reflexive pronouns* and (2) as *intensive pronouns.* A compound personal pronoun is used *reflexively* when the pronoun is the object of the verb. It tells *who* or *what* received *the* action expressed by the verb. In this case the pronoun *always refers back* to the same person or thing as the subject. The following illustration will help to make this clear.

The chef burned himself yesterday.

In this sentence the word *himself* is a compound personal pronoun used as the object of the verb *burned. Himself* refers to the same person as the subject, which is the word *chef.* In other words, *chef* and *himself* are the same person. This is called the **reflexive** use of the compound personal pronoun. It means that the pronoun *refers* or *reflects back* to the subject.

Sometimes the compound personal pronoun is used to give added emphasis to a noun or pronoun in the sentence. This is called the **emphatic** or **intensive** use of the compound personal pronoun.

When a compound personal pronoun is used in this way, it must give emphasis to some noun or pronoun that is already in the sentence. Observe the following sentences carefully. In each sentence you will find that there is a *noun* or a *pronoun* to which the compound personal pronoun refers.

I made the dress myself. (*Myself* intensifies the pronoun I.)
John himself built the canoe. (*Himself* intensifies the noun *John.*)

Incorrect Use of Compound Personal Pronouns

One of the mistakes commonly made in English is to use the compound personal pronoun when there is no word in the sentence to which it refers. These pronouns should never be used as a substitute for a personal pronoun. They should never be used as the subject of the sentence.

My wife and *myself* appreciate your courtesy. (incorrect)
My wife and **I** appreciate your courtesy. (correct)

The manager and *myself* checked the accounts. (incorrect)
The manager and **I** checked the accounts. (correct)

He sent the book to John and *myself.* (incorrect)
He sent the book to John and **me.** (correct)

The first sentence is incorrect because there is no noun or pronoun in the sentence which the pronoun *myself* refers to or gives emphasis to. The second sentence is correct because a *personal pronoun* is used.

Whenever you use a compound personal pronoun in a sentence, always remember that such a pronoun must have an *antecedent,* or a word in the sentence which refers to the same person or thing as the pronoun does. In other words, it must have its own antecedent in the sentence. Do not make mistakes like the following:

Alice and *yourself* were appointed on the committee. (incorrect)
Alice and **you** were appointed on the committee. (correct)

The owner gave Tom and *myself* his old lawn mower. (incorrect)
The owner gave Tom and **me** his old lawn mower. (correct)

Everyone in the club has a car as well as *myself.* (incorrect)
Everyone in the club has a car as well as **I.** (correct)

They sent an invitation to the Smiths and *ourselves.* (incorrect)
They sent an invitation to the Smiths and **us.** (correct)

INTERROGATIVE PRONOUNS

Interrogative pronouns are pronouns that are used in asking questions. The interrogative pronouns are *who (whose, whom), which,* and *what.* An interrogative pronoun also has another function to perform in the sentence, just as any other pronoun has. It may be the *subject* of the sentence, or it may be the *object* of the verb or of a preposition.

Who is the director of the band?

For **whom** are you waiting?

What did they say about his speech?

Which is your car?

Whose car did you borrow?

DEMONSTRATIVE PRONOUNS

Demonstrative pronouns are pronouns that point out definite persons, places, or things. There are only two demonstrative pronouns: *this* with its plural *these*, and *that* with its plural *those*.

This is my hat. (A definite hat is pointed out.)

That is your book. (A definite book is pointed out.)

These are the theater tickets. (Definite tickets are pointed out.)

Those are John's shoes. (Definite shoes are pointed out.)

INDEFINITE PRONOUNS

A large group of pronouns are called **indefinite pronouns** because they do not point out particular places, persons, or things.

Somebody took my coat. (*Somebody* is an indefinite pronoun.)

A **few** left the hall early. (*Few* is an indefinite pronoun.)

The following list contains the commonly used indefinite pronouns. Refer to this list, and to the other lists in this unit, whenever you are not sure of the classification of a pronoun.

Commonly Used Indefinite Pronouns

all	everybody	one
any	everyone	one another
anybody	everything	ones
anyone	few	other
anything	many	others
both	neither	several
each	nobody	some
each one	none	somebody
each other	no one	someone
either	nothing	something

RELATIVE PRONOUNS

A **relative pronoun** is a pronoun that joins the clause which it introduces to its own antecedent. The *antecedent* of a pronoun is the noun or pronoun to which it refers. (Clauses will be explained in later chapters.)

The relative pronouns are *who, which, that,* and *what.* The pronoun *who* has two other forms, *whose* and *whom.* When the relative pronoun is combined with *ever* or *soever,* it is called a **compound relative pronoun.**

List of Compound Relative Pronouns

whoever	whosoever	whichsoever
whomever	whatsoever	whomsoever
whatever	whosesoever	whichever

The *relative pronoun* is always found in a clause which it introduces. For that reason, we shall postpone further study of relative pronouns until we take up the study of subordinate clauses.

Use of Relative Pronouns

The following distinctions are generally observed in the use of relative pronouns. A careful writer or speaker always observes these distinctions:

Who is used when the antecedent is a *person.*

That is used to refer to either *persons* or *things.*

Which is used to refer to anything *except persons.*

She is the girl **who** won the award.
(*Who* refers only to persons.)

This is the dog **that** (or **which**) was lost.
(*That* or *which* refers to things.)

She is the girl **that** won the award.
(*That* may refer to persons.)

PRONOUNS USED AS ADJECTIVES

The *possessive forms* of the personal pronouns are often used with nouns in much the same way as adjectives are used to modify nouns. Although they function as adjectives when they are placed before the noun, they still retain the idea of possession. For that reason, they are sometimes called **possessive adjectives** to distinguish them from other types of adjectives.

In the sentence, *Herbert forgot his coat,* the possessive form of the pronoun *he,* which is *his,* is used as an adjective modifying the noun *coat.* It also shows that the coat belongs to Herbert. Therefore, it is called a possessive adjective. All the adjectives in the following sentences show possession. They are called possessive adjectives.

Possessive Forms of Personal Pronouns Used as Adjectives

These are **her** gloves. (modifies *gloves*)
I bought **their** home. (modifies *home*)
Did you bring **your** violin? (modifies *violin*)
The dog lost **its** collar. (modifies *collar*)
We like **our** new radio. (modifies *radio*)
Do you like **my** new coat? (modifies *coat*)
The manager has **his** report. (modifies *report*)

Demonstrative and *indefinite* pronouns are also used as adjectives. Demonstrative pronouns that function as adjectives are often called **demonstrative adjectives** because they have not lost their pointing out function. In the following sentences the demonstrative pronouns are used as adjectives:

This camera belongs to Jane. (modifies *camera*)
Those apples are delicious. (modifies *apples*)
That man is an army officer. (modifies *man*)
These cards are Easter cards. (modifies *cards*)

Indefinite pronouns used as adjectives are generally regarded as pure adjectives, although they may be called **indefinite adjectives.** They have no special function. The following examples illustrate their use as adjectives:

Each girl carried a flag. (modifies *girl*)
Both men received a promotion. (modifies *men*)
Neither answer is correct. (modifies *answer*)
Many soldiers were on that ship. (modifies *soldiers*)
Any mechanic could do that job. (modifies *mechanic*)
Several tables were ruined. (modifies *tables*)

Interrogative pronouns are also often used as adjectives. Since the adjective is the word that asks the question, these adjectives are called **interrogative adjectives.** In the sentence, *Which house did you buy?* the word *which* asks the question. It is also an adjective modifying the noun *house.* Note how the pronouns are used to ask questions in the following sentences:

What newspapers does he read? (modifies *newspapers*)
Whose name did he call? (modifies *name*)
Which play do you like best? (modifies *play*)

POSSESSIVE FORMS OF PRONOUNS

The possessive forms of the *personal pronouns* and the possessive form of the pronoun *who* are never written with an apostrophe. These pronouns have a special form to show possession and do not require an apostrophe. The correct forms to use in order to show possession are the following: *my, mine, yours, his, hers, its, ours, theirs, whose.* Do not place an apostrophe either before or after the **s** in any of these words.

The word *it's* is a contraction of *it is.* It is not a form of the pronoun, and should never be used to show possession. The word *who's* is a contraction of *who is* or *who has,* and should not be confused with the possessive form *whose.*

Contractions

It's on my desk. (*It is* on my desk.)
Who's speaking tonight? (*Who is* speaking tonight?)
Who's finished the test? (*Who has* finished the test?)

Indefinite pronouns do not have special forms to show possession. Therefore, it is necessary to use the apostrophe to show the possessive forms of these pronouns. Since most of these pronouns are used only in the singular, the possessive is formed by adding the *apostrophe* and **s** (**'s**). The plural of the indefinite pronoun *other* is *others.* In the case of this plural form, the apostrophe is placed after the **s**. Study these forms carefully:

Possessive Forms of Indefinite Pronouns

everybody's job	*anyone's* opinions
somebody's hat	*someone's* car
one's relatives	*each one's* duty
another's problems	*others'* affairs (plural)

When *else* is added to an indefinite pronoun, it is regarded as part of the pronoun. In this case, the apostrophe and **s** are added to *else* to form the possessive.

I came home with *somebody else's* coat.
Someone else's book was substituted for mine.

7.   AGREEMENT OF PRONOUN WITH ANTECEDENT

You have already learned that a pronoun usually refers to a noun or pronoun which precedes it in the sentence. The word to which the pronoun refers is called its antecedent. The word *antecedent* comes from two Latin words which mean *"going before."* The antecedent of a pronoun is the word which *"goes before"* the pronoun. It is the word to which the pronoun refers.

In the sentence, *Robert lost his fishing tackle,* the pronoun *his* refers to *Robert.* The word *Robert* precedes the pronoun *his* or *"goes before"* it. *Robert* is the antecedent of *his.* It is the word to which the pronoun *his* refers.

Antecedents of Pronouns

Margaret attended her class reunion. (*Margaret*—antecedent of *her*)

Every day brings its duties. (*day*—antecedent of *its*)

The men brought their golf clubs. (*men*—antecedent of *their*)

Only a few brought their equipment. (*few*—antecedent of *their*)

The professor himself did not know the answer. (*professor*—antecedent of *himself*)

AGREEMENT OF PRONOUN AND ANTECEDENT IN GENDER

Since a pronoun stands for, or replaces a noun, it must agree with that noun in person, number, and gender. We have already considered the problems of number and person in Chapters Five and Six. In this unit we shall take up the problem of gender, and show its connection with the agreement of pronoun and antecedent.

In grammar **gender** means the classification of nouns and pronouns according to distinctions in sex. There are four genders: *masculine gender, feminine gender, common gender,* and *neuter gender.*

Masculine gender denotes the male sex. **Feminine gender** denotes the female sex. **Common gender** denotes either sex. **Neuter gender** denotes absence of sex. The following are examples of nouns and pronouns in the four genders:

Masculine gender—he, him, father, kind
Feminine gender—sister, she, her, princess
Common gender—child, adult, cousin, neighbor
Neuter gender—table, book, dress, radio, it

Some nouns and a few pronouns have special forms to show gender. The following list shows the changes that occur in some words to indicate a change in the gender. Some of the distinctions formerly used to show gender are passing out of use. The words *authoress* and *poetess,* for example, are seldom used.

SPECIAL FORMS TO SHOW GENDER

Masculine	Feminine	Masculine	Feminine
uncle	aunt	god	goddess
bull	cow	aviator	aviatrix
waiter	waitress	hero	heroine
alumnus	alumna	count (title)	countess
emperor	empress	gander	goose
host	hostess	sir	madam
peacock	peahen	ram	ewe
male	female	lion	lioness
monk	nun	duke	duchess
actor	actress	nephew	niece
bachelor	spinster	prince	princess
executor	executrix	fiance	fiancee
baron	baroness	stallion	mare
he	she	father	mother
lad	lass	him	her
man	woman	boy	girl
rooster	hen	husband	wife
master	mistress	buck(stag)	doe
brother	sister	landlord	landlady
drake	duck	son	daughter

GENDER AND NUMBER OF INDEFINITE PRONOUNS

Indefinite pronouns present a problem in gender. These pronouns often refer to both sexes, masculine and feminine. When we say, *Everybody went to the game,* the indefinite pronoun *everybody* includes individuals of both genders, masculine and feminine.

The problem arises when the indefinite pronoun is the antecedent of another pronoun. In that case, the accepted practice is to *use the masculine gender for the pronoun that is used in place of the indefinite pronoun.*

In the sentence, *Everyone received his income tax form,* the indefinite pronoun *everyone* is the antecedent of the pronoun *his.* It is the word to which the pronoun *his* refers. Although *everyone* includes persons of both genders, the masculine pronoun *his* is used instead of saying *his or her* income tax form.

If the sentence shows clearly that the indefinite pronoun refers to members of only one sex, the pronoun that refers to that sex should be used.

Everyone attending the meeting of the Women's Athletic Club presented **her** membership card.

In this sentence the members are women, and the pronoun *her* is used correctly. In cases where it is not clear whether the antecedent is masculine or feminine, use the pronoun *his.*

Anyone may have **his** money refunded.
Somebody left **his** pen on my desk.

Indefinite pronouns also present a problem in number. Some of them are always singular. Some are always plural, and some may be either singular or plural.

Pronouns That Are Always Singular

The following pronouns are always singular. A pronoun that is used in place of one of these indefinite pronouns must also be singular.

anybody	everybody	neither
anyone	everyone	one
another	many a one	other
each	nobody	someone
either	no one	somebody

Study the following illustrations carefully. These sentences show the proper agreement between pronoun and antecedent when the antecedent is singular.

Neither of the men had **his** tools. (not *their*)
If **anyone** wants a pen, **he** can obtain one here. (not *they*)
One likes to do what **he** can do well. (not *they*)
Someone left **his** coat in **his** locker. (not *their*)

Pronouns That Are Always Plural

The following pronouns are always plural. A pronoun that is used in place of one of them must also be plural.

many	both	few	several	others

Notice that *many a one* is included in the list of pronouns that are always singular, whereas *many* is included in this plural list. When singular expressions, such as *a man, a one, a person,* etc., are added to *many,* the *pronoun* is singular, not plural.

Several found **their** cars unlocked. (*Several*—plural)
Only a **few** would sacrifice **their** savings. (*few*—plural)
Many brought **their** lunches with them. (*Many*—plural)
Others found **their** friends in the balcony. (*Others*—plural)

Pronouns That May Be Either Singular or Plural

The pronouns *all, any, some,* and *none* are singular or plural according to the meaning of the sentence. When these pronouns refer to **number,** they are generally regarded as plural.

When they refer to **quantity** or to a **mass,** they are regarded as singular.

The pronoun *none* is singular when it clearly means *no one,* or *not one.* It is often difficult to determine the number of this pronoun since there are sentences in which it carries a plural idea. If you want to express the singular idea use *no one,* or *not one.*

Some found **their** children in the park. (*Some* is plural.)
Some of the candy has lost **its** flavor. (*Some* is singular.)
All were waiting for **their** salary checks. (*All* is plural.)
There is no candy in the box. **All** of **it** has been eaten. (*All* is singular.)
Did **any** of the men have **their** membership cards? (*Any* is plural.)
None have arrived. (*None*—plural in use)
None of these is a typical example. (*None*—singular in use)

AGREEMENT OF THE PRONOUN WITH A COMPOUND ANTECEDENT

Sometimes the pronoun refers to two antecedents connected by *and.* If both of these antecedents are singular and refer to *different persons or things,* the antecedent is plural. The pronoun that refers to these antecedents must also be plural.

The president and the manager have outlined their plans.

If the antecedent refers to *one* person who fulfills *two* functions, the pronoun that takes the place of the antecedent is singular. In the following sentence *cook* and *housekeeper* are the same person.

The cook and housekeeper did not like her duties.

If the housekeeper were another individual, the word *the* would be placed before the word *housekeeper.*

The cook and the housekeeper did not like their duties.

When the connectives, *either—or* and *neither—nor* join singular nouns, the antecedent is singular. When they join plural nouns, the antecedent is plural. When they join nouns that differ in number, the pronoun should agree with the antecedent that is nearer to it.

Either *Jane* or *Alice* left **her** book on **her** desk. (Nouns are singular—pronoun is singular)

Either the *boys* or the *girls* left **their** books on the table. (Both nouns are plural—pronoun is plural)

Neither *Harvey* nor his *cousins* wore **their** dress suits. (Pronoun is plural—agrees with cousins)

Neither the *men* nor the *boy* could find **his** place in the line. (Pronoun agrees with *boy* which is nearer to it.)

In sentences like the last one, it is better to place the plural noun nearer to the pronoun. By doing so, you make the antecedent plural, and the sentence sounds better.

AGREEMENT OF PRONOUN WITH COLLECTIVE NOUNS

Collective nouns are singular when they designate a group *acting as a unit.* They are plural when the members who make up the group are *acting independently.* The pronoun that takes the place of the collective noun must agree with it in number. If the collective noun expresses a singular idea, the pronoun is singular. If the collective noun expresses a plural idea, the pronoun is plural.

The band played its fifth concert. (*acting as a unit*)

The band were tuning up their instruments. (*as individuals*)

You can readily see that the second sentence could not refer to the band as a unit. That would mean that the members of the band were all working on the same instrument.

AGREEMENT OF PRONOUN AND ANTECEDENT IN PERSON

A pronoun must agree with its antecedent in **person.** If the antecedent of the pronoun is in the *third person,* the pronoun that refers to it must also be in the *third person.* If the antecedent is in the *second person,* the pronoun should be in the *second person.*

One of the most common mistakes in English is to start the sentence in the *third person* and then put the pronoun that refers to the antecedent in the *second person.* Study the following examples carefully:

If anybody wants an education, you can get it. (*incorrect*)

If anybody wants an education, he can get it. (*correct*)

When one pays attention, you learn better. (*incorrect*)

When one pays attention, he (or *one*) learns better. (*correct*)

VAGUE ANTECEDENTS

A pronoun should not have two possible antecedents in the same sentence. If it is not clear which of two nouns a pronoun refers to, there will be two possible interpretations of the sentence. Observe the two possible interpretations in the following illustration:

James told his friend that **he** had been elected president.

In this sentence, does the pronoun *he* refer to *James* or to *friend?* If the antecedent of the pronoun *he* is *friend,* the sentence means that *James told his friend that he* (*the friend*) *had been elected president.* If the antecedent of the pronoun *he* is *James,* the sentence means that *James told his friend that he* (*James*) *had been elected president.*

The sentence might be rewritten in either of the two following ways, since we do not know which meaning the author intended:

James said to his friend, "You have been elected president."

James said to his friend, "I have been elected president."

Many of the errors that are made in the use of pronouns are caused by a lack of agreement between pronoun and antecedent. The pronoun should refer definitely to the noun which it represents. In the following sentence, to what does the pronoun *it* refer?

Your letter and your check arrived promptly, but we cannot ship **it** at present.

There is no antecedent for the pronoun *it* in the sentence. Neither the word *letter* nor the word *check* could be the antecedent. *It* probably refers to an order for goods which was included in the letter. If the word *it* refers

to an order for goods, the sentence might be written as follows:

Your letter and your check arrived promptly, but at present we cannot ship the goods ordered.

ADJECTIVE—PRONOUN AGREEMENT

Demonstrative adjectives should agree in *number* with the nouns they modify. The adjectives *this, that, these,* and *those* sometimes cause agreement trouble when they modify such nouns as *kind, sort, type,* and *variety.*

Keep in mind that the demonstrative adjectives *this* and *that* are singular and should be used only with singular nouns. *These* and *those* are plural and should be used only with the plural nouns.

these kind of apples **(incorrect)**
this kind of apples (or apple) **(correct)**
or **these kinds** of apples (plural)

those sort of roses **(incorrect)**
that sort of roses (or rose) **(correct)**
or **those sorts** of roses (plural)

these variety of fruits **(incorrect)**
this variety of fruits or fruit **(correct)**
or **these varieties** of fruits (plural)

The forms in italic are incorrect because the adjective does not agree with the noun in number. The forms in bold face are correct because the adjective agrees with the noun in number.

8. COMPLEMENTS OF VERBS
THE DIRECT OBJECT

Every sentence must have a basic structure in order to express a complete thought. This basic structure may consist of only two parts, a subject noun or pronoun and a predicate verb or verb phrase. Many sentences require a third part or an additional word in order to express a complete thought. This additional word or group of words is necessary to complete the idea expressed by the verb.

The group of words, *The men lifted,* contains a subject noun *men* and a predicate verb *lifted.* Still it does not express a complete thought. A word is needed to tell **what** the men lifted. The sentence might be completed by adding the word *beam.* The completed sentence, *The men lifted the beam,* expresses a complete thought.

The word *beam* completes the meaning expressed by the verb *lifted.* For that reason it is called a **complement** or a completing word. The three essential parts of this sentence are the **subject,** the **verb,** and the **complement.** The complement is *beam.*

A complement completes the meaning expressed by a verb. The *complement* of a verb that expresses *action* is called the **direct object** of the verb. A direct object usually answers the questions *what?* or *whom?* In the preceding sentence the verb *lifted* expresses action. The complement *beam* tells *what* the men lifted. Notice how the underlined complements in the following sentences complete the meaning of the verb.

I saw Evelyn at the convention.
(*Evelyn* tells whom I saw.)
The engineer stopped the train.
(*Train* tells what he stopped.)

The sailors saluted the captain.
(tells *whom* they saluted)
She refused the invitation.
(tells *what* she refused)

Some verbs that express action are complete without the addition of a complement. When such verbs are used in sentences, only two parts are essential—the *subject* and the *verb.*

Study the following illustrations. You will readily see that the thought is complete without the addition of a complement.

Jane is singing.
We have been studying.
The boys are playing.

Although the verbs in the preceding sentences do not require a complement or a completing word, a complement might be added to some of them to make the meaning more explicit. The underlined words are complements and are called *direct objects.*

Jane is singing a ballad.
(tells *what* Jane is singing)
We have been studying Spanish.
(tells *what* we have been studying)
The boys are playing games.
(tells *what* the boys are playing)

The **direct object** of a verb names the *receiver* of the action. It completes the meaning of the verb. A direct object is usually a noun or a pronoun. Adjectives and adverbs are never used as direct objects. Adjectives and adverbs are always used as modifiers. If you have any difficulty in deciding which word is the direct object, apply this test: Find the word that answers the question *what?* or *whom?* Apply the test in the following sentences:

The farmer planted the **seeds** in rows.

What did the farmer plant? The answer is, "He planted the *seeds."* The word *seeds* is the direct object of the verb planted. It tells **what** he planted.

I met *Uncle Henry* in the bank.

Whom did I meet? The answer is, "I met Uncle Henry." The direct object is *Uncle Henry.* It tells **whom** I met.

A verb may take two or more direct objects. In this case, the verb or verb phrase has a compound object.

He grows *orchids* and *lilies* in his garden.

I met *Jerry* and *Jane* at the stadium.

TRANSITIVE AND INTRANSITIVE VERBS

When an action verb takes a direct object, it is called a **transitive verb.** The word *transitive* comes from two Latin words which mean *"passing across."* When the verb is transitive, the action passes across from a **doer** (the subject) to a **receiver** of the action (the direct object). When we say that a verb is *transitive,* it is the same as saying that it has a *direct object.*

Any verb that does not take a direct object is **intransitive.** That is, the verb does *not* express action that passes over to a receiver.

A verb may be transitive in one sentence and intransitive in another sentence. The verb may express action, but the action may not pass over to a receiver. In that case the verb is intransitive. When the verb is transitive, it always takes a direct object—the receiver of the action.

The following sentences show the same verb used as a *transitive* verb with a direct object (underlined) in the first sentence and as an *intransitive* verb with no object in the second sentence:

The sexton rang the bell.
The bell rang loudly. (*no object*)

The ship sailed the seas.
The ship sails at noon. (*no object*)

I met my friend at the airport.
The delegates met yesterday. (*no object*)

THE INDIRECT OBJECT

Some verbs that express action take two objects, a direct object and an indirect object. The **indirect object** tells *to whom* the action is directed or *for whom* the action is performed.

The indirect object is used after certain verbs: *get, give, lend, offer, read, tell, buy, send, show, make, pay,* etc.

In the sentence, *Mother bought Ellen a coat,* there are two objects, a direct object and an indirect object. The word *coat* is the direct object. It tells *what* Mother bought. The word *Ellen* is the indirect object. It tells *for whom* Mother bought a coat. The indirect object *always* precedes or comes before the direct object. In the following sentences the indirect object and the direct object are underlined.

The librarian read the children a story.
Give him five dollars for his services.
The tailor made Edward a brown suit.

There are two tests that you can apply in order to identify an indirect object. One test is to determine the position of the object. *The indirect object always precedes the direct object.* The other test is to determine whether the indirect object seems to be the object of the preposition *to* or *for* understood. The following sentences illustrate this point:

The librarian read **(to)** the children a story.
Give **(to)** him five dollars for his services.
The tailor made **(for)** Edward a brown suit.

The words *to* and *for* are never expressed when a word functions as an indirect object. If we change the order of the sentence and supply the preposition, our sentence would read as follows: *The librarian read a story to the children.* In this sentence the word *children* is no longer the indirect object but is the object of the preposition *to.*

LINKING VERBS

Most verbs describe or express action. However, there are a small group that do not. The verb **to be** is the most important verb in this group. Since it is the most irregular verb in our language, you should be familiar with its various forms. The following verbs and verb phrases are forms of the verb *to be:*

Forms of the Verb "To Be"

am	will be	shall have been
are	shall be	will have been
is	have been	could have been
was	has been	would have been
were	had been	might have been

Although the verb *to be,* as well as the other verbs belonging in this group, does not express action, it has another function in the sentence. The chief purpose of this verb is to serve as a link which joins the subject to some word in the predicate that gives the meaning to the sentence. For that reason, it is called a **linking verb.**

Linking verbs have very little meaning of their own. With the help of another word, they express various ideas in regard to the subject. In the sentence, *Mary is ill,* the verb *is* (a form of *to be*) is used with the adjective *ill* to describe the condition of the subject, *Mary.* The sentence really means *ill Mary,* but you need a verb in order to make a complete statement.

In the sentence, *The young man was an aviator,* the verb *was* is a linking verb. With the help of the noun *aviator,* it identifies of classifies the young man. The noun *aviator* means the same as the subject. In the sentence, *The actress is very beautiful,* the verb *is,* with the help of the adjective *beautiful,* describes the appearance of the actress.

The verbs *become* and *seem,* like the verb *to be,* are almost always used as linking verbs. The following verbs are used both as linking verbs and as action verbs. The meaning of the sentence will show to which classification they belong:

Linking and Action Verbs

grow	look	smell	remain
turn	feel	taste	keep
prove	sound	appear	stay

This group of words is important because a great many mistakes in English are made when a speaker of writer does not understand their linking function.

When these words have a linking function, they have practically the same meaning as the verb *to be* would have in the same sentence. By supplying the the verb *to be* mentally after one of these verbs, you can readily tell whether the verb has a linking function or whether it is used as an action verb. Every one of the verbs in the following sentences is a linking verb. The verb *to be* has been supplied to show you how to interpret the sentence when the verbs have a linking function.

The cookies **are** wonderful.
(wonderful cookies)
The cookies **look** (to be) delicious.
(delicious cookies)
The cookies **smell** (to be) good.
(good cookies)
The cookies **taste** (to be) sweet.
(sweet cookies)
The cookies **seem** (to be) brittle.
(brittle cookies)
The cookies **became** (to be) stale.
(stale cookies)
The cookies **proved** (to be) sweet.
(sweet cookies)
The cookies **feel** (to be) hard.
(hard cookies)
The cookies **stayed** (to be) fresh.
(fresh cookies)
The cookies **appear** (to be) tempting.
(tempting cookies)
The cookies **remained** (to be) soft.
(soft cookies)
The cookies **kept** (to be) fresh.
(fresh cookies)

Some of the same verbs that were used in the preceding illustrations may also be used to express action. Note the differences in meaning when these verbs function as action verbs and not as linking verbs.

John **appeared** promptly.
(made his appearance)

The horticulturist **grows** orchids.
(produces by cultivation)
I **turned** the key in the lock.
We **proved** a theorem in geometry.
The doctor **felt** the broken bone.
The warden **sounded** the gong.
The chef **tasted** the sauce.
We **kept** a record of our journey.
The dog **smelled** the meat.
The judge **will stay** the trial. (postpone)
The committee **looked** at the pictures.

COMPLEMENTS OF LINKING VERBS

A *linking verb* cannot make a complete predicate. It always requires a *complement.* The group of words, *My friend is,* does not make a complete statement. The verb *is* requires some additional word to complete the meaning of the sentence. That word may be a noun, a pronoun, or an adjective.

My friend is an executive.
My friend is very ambitious.
That is he.

The noun that completes the meaning of a linking verb is called a *predicate noun* because it is found in the predicate. A **predicate noun** completes the verb and renames or explains the subject. In the preceding illustration, *executive* is a predicate noun. It renames the subject *friend* and classifies *friend* as an *executive.* The noun *friend* and the noun *executive* refer to the same person.

A pronoun that follows a linking verb functions in the same way as the noun. It completes the verb and means the same person or thing as the subject. It is called a **predicate pronoun.**

An adjective that follows a linking verb is called a **predicate adjective** because it is found in the predicate. A predicate adjective always modifies the subject.

The following sentences illustrate the use of the predicate noun, predicate pronoun, and predicate adjective:

Our manager was a former army colonel.
(*manager* and *colonel*—same person)
Our manager is very efficient.
(*efficient* modifies *manager*)
The candidate for the position is he.
(*he* and *candidate*—same person)

In the first sentence, *colonel* is a **predicate noun**. It completes the meaning of the verb *was* and refers to the same person as the subject. In the second sentence *efficient* is a **predicate adjective**. It modifies the subject noun *manager*. In the third sentence, *he* is a **predicate pronoun**. It means the same person as the subject *candidate.*

9. CASE OF NOUNS AND PRONOUNS

Nouns and pronouns have certain relationships to other words in a sentence. We call attention to these relationships by indicating the case of the noun or pronoun. The word **case** is used in grammar to indicate the *relationship* a noun or a pronoun has to other words in the sentence. The case of a noun or a pronoun is determined by the particular use of that noun or pronoun in the sentence.

There are only three cases in English: the *nominative case*, the *objective case*, and the *possessive case*. The **nominative case** is the case of the *subject*. The **objective case** is the case of the *object*. The **possessive case** is the case that shows *ownership*.

CASE OF NOUNS

Nouns present very few problems in case because the same form is used for the nominative case and the objective case. The only way to determine whether a noun is in the nominative case or in the objective case is to determine its relationship to other words in the sentence. If the noun is used as the *subject* of the sentence, it is in the *nominative case*. If the noun is used as the *object* of a verb or a preposition, it is in the *objective case*.

The **door** is open.
(*nominative case*—subject)
I closed the **door.**
(*objective case*—direct object)

In the first sentence, the noun *door* is used as the subject of the sentence. It is in the nominative case. In the second sentence, the same form *door* is used as the direct object of the verb *closed*. *Door* is in the objective case in this sentence.

Like nouns, *indefinite pronouns* have the same form for the nominative case and the objective case.

Everyone contributed five dollars.
(*nominative case*—subject)
I saw **everyone** at the game.
(*objective case*—direct object)

NOMINATIVE CASE

The word *nominative* comes from a Latin word which means *name*. The **nominative case** names the case of the subject of the sentence. It also names the case of a predicate noun. A predicate noun is in the nominative case. For this reason, it is often called a **predicate nominative.**

A *predicate noun* must agree in case with the *subject* because it refers to the same person or thing as the subject. It also follows a verb which cannot take an object. Nouns used after linking verbs are called predicate nouns. In the following sentences the subjects and the predicate nouns are underlined.

My friend is a naval officer.
The leading lady was Mary Harris.

In the first sentence, *officer* is a predicate noun. It is used after the linking verb *is* and refers to the same person as the subject. It is in the nominative case to agree with the case of the subject *friend*.

In the second sentence, *Mary Harris* is a predicate noun. It is in the nominative case to agree with the subject *lady*. *Mary Harris* and *lady* refer to the same person.

OBJECTIVE CASE

The **objective case** is the case of the *subject*. The *direct object* of a verb, the *indirect object*, and the *object* of a *preposition* are in the objective case.

Lester writes **articles** for the paper.
(*articles*—direct object)
Arthur sent the **manager** a detailed report.
(*manager*—indirect object)

In the first sentence, *articles* is the direct object of the verb *writes*. It tells **what** Lester writes. *Articles* is in the objective case. In the second sentence, *manager* is the indirect object. It tells **to whom** Arthur sent his report. *Manager* is in the objective case.

In Chapter Two you learned that a preposition is always followed by some noun or pronoun which is called the *object* of the *preposition*. The object of a preposition is always in the objective case.

Edward met his lawyer at the **bank.**
(object of preposition **at**)
We met Marvin in the **lobby.**
(object of preposition **in**)

In the first sentence, the preposition *at* is followed by the noun *bank*. The object of the preposition is *bank*, which is in the objective case. In the second sentence, *lobby* is the object of the preposition *in*. *Lobby* is in the objective case.

It is easy to remember that direct objects of verbs, indirect objects of verbs, and objects of prepositions are in the objective case because they are all called **objects** of some type. The fact that they are objects indicates that they are in the **objective case.**

CASE OF PRONOUNS

Nouns do not present any problems in case because the form of the noun is the same for the nominative case and the objective case. Pronouns do present problems in case. The *personal pronouns* and the pronoun *who* have different forms to indicate the different cases.

There are only *six pronouns* in English that have these special forms to show *case*, but the changes that occur to indicate case are very important. They are responsible for many of the errors that frequently occur in the use of pronouns. You should become familiar with the different forms of these pronouns, and you should learn how to use them correctly. The six pronouns are *I, you, he, she, it, who*. The following table gives the nominative case forms and the objective case forms of each of the six pronouns:

Nominative Case		Objective Case	
Singular	Plural	Singular	Plural
I	we	me	us
you	you	you	you
he	they	him	them
she	they	her	them
it	they	it	them
who	who	whom	whom

The pronouns *he*, *she*, and *it* all have the same plural form. *They* is the pronoun used in the nominative case in the plural for each of the three pronouns. *Them* is the pronoun used in the objective case in the plural for each of the three pronouns.

NOMINATIVE CASE OF PRONOUNS

Like nouns, pronouns are in the nominative case when they are used as the subjects of sentences, or as predicate pronouns after one of the linking verbs. Mistakes are seldom made in selecting the correct from of the pronoun to use as the subject of the sentence. Mistakes are frequently made, however, when a pronoun is used as a *predicate nominative*. The following sentences illustrate the correct use of the six pronouns in the nominative case:

Subject of the Sentence	Predicate Pronoun
I saw the accident.	It is **I.**
You have been elected.	It is **you.**
He attended the lecture.	It might be **he.**
She gave me her note book.	It could be **she.**
It is my overcoat.	Could this be **it?**
We are great friends. (plural)	It is **we.**
They arrived early. (Plural)	It was **they.** (plural)
Who came in?	**Who** was it? (It was **who?**)

The pronoun *you* does not present any problem in the plural, because the forms for the plural are the same as the forms for the singular. The form of the pronoun *you* is also the same for the nominative case and the objective case.

Interrogative sentences should always be transposed and put in normal order. When this is done, it is easy to determine the case of the pronoun.

OBJECTIVE CASE OF PRONOUNS

Pronouns are in the objective case when they are used as direct objects of verbs, or as objects of prepositions. The correct forms to use in the objective case are *me, you, him, her, it,* and *whom* in the singular, and *us, you them, whom* in the plural. The following sentences illustrate the correct use of these pronouns in the objective case:

Object of the Verb

Mother called **me.**
Jack saw **him** yesterday.
I met **you** in Paris.
The firm sent **her** to Texas.
My friend invited **us** to the game.
Sue drove **them** to the station.
Whom did you call?

Indirect Object of the Verb

Ethel gave **me** her pen.
I sent **him** a notice.
David sent **you** a ticket.
Jack offered **her** a seat.
The tailor made **us** new uniforms.
The teacher read **them** a story.

Object of a Preposition

The telegram was sent to **me.** (object of the preposition *to*)
The manager created the position for **him.** (object of *for*)
The author wrote an article about **us.** (object of *about*)
The waiter placed their table near **us.** (object of *near*)
We distributed the gifts among **them.** (object of *among*)

THE POSSESSIVE CASE OF NOUNS

The **possessive case** shows *ownership* or *possession*. The use of the possessive case does not present much of a problem in speaking, but it does present a problem in writing and spelling. Although the rule for forming the possessive case of nouns is very simple, many persons have considerable difficulty in spelling and writing the forms correctly.

One simple rule applies to all cases: If the singular form of the noun does not end in **s**, add the *apostrophe* and **s** (**'s**). If the singular ends in **s**, add the *apostrophe* (**'**). Study the following examples carefully and try to apply the rule:

Singular		Plural	
boy	boy's	boys	boys'
lady	lady's	ladies	ladies'
hero	hero's	heroes	heroes'
man	man's	men	men's
Charles	Charles'	Charleses	Charleses'
child	child's	children	children's

There is one fact that you must always keep in mind in order to form the possessive case correctly; that is, the sign of the possessive is something that is *added* to the word. It is not something that is inserted within the word. You must be absolutely sure of the correct form for the singular and the correct form for the plural before you add the sign of the possessive.

Take the proper name, *Dickens*, for example. This is a proper noun in the singular which ends in **s**. The sign of the possessive must be added to the complete word and not inserted within the word. The possessive form is often incorrectly written as *Dicken's*. That would be the possessive form of the name *Dicken*, and not the possessive form of the name *Dickens*. The singular possessive form of *Dickens* is *Dickens'* as shown below:

Oliver Twist is one of **Dicken's** novels. (incorrect)
Oliver Twist is one of **Dickens'** novels. (correct)

The possessive forms of proper nouns are formed according to the rule. If the singular form of the name does not end in **s**, add the *apostrophe* and **s**. If the singular ends in **s**, add the *apostrophe*. The same rule applies to the plural.

Singular		Plural	
Mary	Mary's	Marys	Marys'
Jones	Jones'	Joneses	Joneses'
Henry	Henry's	Henrys	Henrys'
Burns	Burns'	Burnses	Burnses'

There is one slight modification of the rule which may be followed in the case of the possessive singular of nouns that end in **s**. If you want the sound of the additional **s**, the *apostrophe* and **s** may be added

This is **Charles'** fishing rod. (correct)
This is **Charles's** fishing rod. (correct)
I saw **Doris'** picture at the studio. (correct)
I saw **Doris's** picture at the studio. (correct)

In modern practice, the first form (*Charles' fishing rod*) is the form that is generally used. It follows the rule given, and is the simpler form to use in writing and in pronunciation. This rule also applies to nouns ending in **x** and **z**.

I bought a jar of **Heinz'** pickles. (correct)
She has always worn **Knox'** hats. (correct)
I bought a jar of **Heinz's** pickles. (correct)
She has always worn **Knox's** hats. (correct)

USE OF THE POSSESSIVE —SPECIAL FORMS

As a rule, it is better practice not to use the possessive forms for inanimate objects. Inanimate objects cannot possess anything in the sense that animate objects can. Avoid expressions such as *the table's top, the book's ending, the lake's shore,* and *the shop's window*. It is much better to use the phrase with *of* in such cases.

the top **of the table**   the shore **of the lake**
the ending **of the book**   the window **of the shop**

There are certain exceptions to this rule. Usage has established authority for using expressions such as the following:

the earth's surface   the sun's rays
the world's progress   today's edition
the law's delay   time's flight
the season's greetings   the water's edge

Certain expressions relating to *time, distance,* and *value* are also written with the sign of the possessive case. The apostrophe is generally used in expressions like the following:

a moment's delay   a stone's throw
two weeks' salary   a week's journey
a month's vacation   ten cents' worth
a few minutes' quiet   thirty days' notice

The singular possessive and the plural possessive of compound nouns are formed by adding the sign of the possessive to the end of the compound word.

Singular	Plural
sister-in-law's	sisters-in-law's
editor-in-chief's	editors-in-chief's
maid of honor's	maids of honor's

Joint ownership is shown by making the last word in the series possessive. Individual ownership is shown by making both parts possessive.

Baker and Johnson's factory. (joint ownership)
Baker's and Johnson's factories. (individual ownership)

Asia and China's problems. (common to both)
Asia's and China's problems. (separate problems)

Some trade names and names of organizations and institutions are written with the sign of the possessive case, and some are not. In writing letters, one should follow the form established by the organization.

When the apostrophe and **s** (**'s**) are not used, the word which would ordinarily be written as a possessive is regarded as an adjective modifier. In the name of an institution, such as *Teachers College*, the apostrophe is not used. The word *Teachers* is regarded as an adjective modifying *College*. It tells the type of college. It does not mean that the teachers possess the college.

The following illustrations show the methods used in writing place names, institutional names, and titles of publications:

With the Apostrophe	Without the Apostrophe
Harper's Magazine	Womens Athletic Club
Hansen's Pharmacy	Bricklayers Union
Queen's College (Oxford)	Executives Club
Charles Scribner's Sons	Pikes Peak
Young Men's Christian Association	Downers Grove
Working Girl's Club	Harris Brothers Company
Illinois Chirldren's Home and Aid Society	Citizens League
Nowak's Optical Service	American Bankers Association
Ladies' Home Journal	Buzzards Bay
Martha's Vineyard Island	Peoples Finance Company

THE POSSESSIVE CASE OF PRONOUNS

The indefinite pronouns do not have special forms to show case. The possessive case of indefinite pronouns is formed in the same way as the possessive case of nouns. Indefinite pronouns are seldom used in the plural. Two of the indefinite pronouns, *one* and *other*, have the plural forms *ones* and *others*. The following are illustrations of the possessive case form of indefinite pronouns:

everyone's opinion   one's relatives (singular)
someone's hat   somebody's car
anybody's guess   another's choice

The *personal pronouns* and the pronoun *who* have special forms to show the possessive case: *my, mine, our, ours, your, yours, her, hers, his, its, their, theirs,* and *whose*. These forms are never written with an apostrophe. To add an apostrophe would be adding a possessive sign to a word that is already possessive.

Whose report did you check? (not *Who's*)
The automobile was **theirs**. (not *their's*)
I did not know that book was **yours**. (not *your's*)
The ship lost **its** anchor in the storm. (not *it's*)
That ranch type house is **ours**. (not *our's*)

PERSONAL PRONOUNS

Singular and Plural

First Person

Nominative	I
	we
Possessive	my, mine
	our, ours
Objective	me
	us

Second Person

Nominative	you
	you
Possessive	your, yours
	your, yours
Objective	you
	you

Third Person

Nominative	he she it
	they
Possessive	his her, hers its
	their, theirs
Objective	you
	you

RELATIVE AND INTERROGATIVE PRONOUN "WHO"

Singular and Plural

Nominative	who
Possessive	whose
Objective	whom

10. MODIFIERS: ADJECTIVES

Adjectives give life and color to language. They also help us give more exact pictures of what we are telling about, if we know how to select them carefully. As you improve your skill in using these words, your language will become more interesting and more explicit.

Let us assume that you were telling someone about a man whom you had seen. You might start out with a sentence like this: "I met a man walking down the street." This sentence does not give us an interesting description or very accurate information. It tells very little about the man, his manner of walking, or the street down which he walked.

Someone who has skill in selecting words that would give a more definite and colorful description might change the sentence into something like this:

I met a **weary** and **disheartened** old man hobbling down the **narrow, winding** street.

This sentence has been made more colorful and more accurate by the use of the adjectives *weary, disheartened,* and *old* to describe the man, and by the use of the adjectives *narrow* and *winding* to describe the street.

In order to use adjectives effectively, you must know the exact shade of meaning that you wish to convey. Then you must be able to select the adjective or adjectives that express that shade of meaning.

You might want to use an adjective to describe a certain type of individual, and you are not sure whether to use the adjective *sly* or the adjective *cunning.* Whenever you are in doubt, consult a reliable, up-to-date dictionary. In most dictionaries these differences in meaning are pointed out.

The adjective *sly* always implies that the individual is working or acting secretly, or is using underhand methods. The adjective *cunning* implies the use of intelligence, skill, or ingenuity. The two words do not mean exactly the same thing.

The following exercise will give you excellent practice in learning how to select the adjective that expresses the exact meaning you would like to convey. The adjectives listed below are divided into groups of three. Each adjective in a group of three expresses a different shade of meaning. Try to write sentences using these words. Be sure that your sentences show the differences in meaning. The dictionary will be a great help.

1. small—diminutive—little
2. funny—strange—queer
3. strong—robust—sturdy
4. beautiful—handsome—lovely
5. bright—shining—brilliant

"OVERWORKED" ADJECTIVES

There is a tendency on the part of many people to use the same adjective to apply to a number of different situations. When a person does this, the assumption is that he has a very limited vocabulary. As a result, he is not able to express his meaning precisely. For example, he may use the word *lovely* to describe many different things. In certain cases, the adjective *lovely* is appropriate. In other cases, it is not the most appropriate or the most precise word to use. Study the following illustrations.

a *lovely* time	a *lovely* view
a *lovely* dress	a *lovely* voice
a *lovely* picnic	a *lovely* program
a *lovely* picture	a *lovely* day
a *lovely* street	a *lovely* necktie

If you wanted to describe a dress, instead of using the word *lovely,* you might use any one of the following adjectives: *becoming, stylish, fashionable, smart, colorful, modish, dashing, beautiful,* etc. The careful speaker or writer would choose the one that expressed the most exact shade of meaning he wished to convey. This requires careful analysis, but it is worth the effort.

Adjectives that are applied in many different types of situations are often called "overworked" or "shopworn" adjectives. The following adjectives belong in this list:

fine	lovely	swell
grand	nice	adorable
funny	terrible	keen
awful	crazy	sweet

KINDS OF ADJECTIVES

There are two kinds of adjectives: *descriptive* adjectives and *limiting* adjectives. **Descriptive adjectives,** as the name implies, give color and vividness to the persons, places, or things we talk or write about. **Limiting adjectives** indicate number or quantity.

Descriptive adjectives tell *what kind, what color, what size, what shape,* etc. Limiting adjectives tell *how many, how much, which one, whose,* etc.

three checks (limiting)	**brilliant** speaker (descriptive)
high mountain (descriptive)	**one** airplane (limiting)
a **new** car (descriptive)	a **few** children (limiting)
two branches (limiting)	a **sympathetic** listener (descriptive)

Adjectives derived from proper nouns are called **proper adjectives.** They are usually written with a capital letter. They are usually descriptive adjectives.

Canadian bacon	**Turkish** tobacco
American industries	**Norwegian** sardines
Mexican pottery	**Danish** silver
United States flag	**Swedish** crystal
English wool	**Indian** summer

PREDICATE ADJECTIVES

Adjectives that complete the meaning of the verb and modify the subject are called **predicate adjectives.** If an adjective is found in the predicate and modifies a noun in the predicate, it is not a predicate adjective. The adjective must follow a linking verb and modify the subject in order to be classified as a predicate adjective. The predicate adjective usually *describes* the subject noun or pronoun.

The list of linking verbs which was given in Chapter Eight is repeated here for reference. You should become familiar with this important list of verbs. It will help you identify the predicate adjectives that are used after linking verbs.

Linking Verbs

is	grow	look	smell	remain
become	turn	feel	taste	keep
seem	prove	sound	appear	stay

Illustrations

The predicate adjectives are underlined in the following sentences.

The cookies are delicious. (*delicious* cookies)

Corn is plentiful in Illinois. (*plentiful* corn)

The street has become very muddy. (*muddy* street)

Position of the Adjective

An adjective is usually placed directly before the noun it modifies. Sometimes the adjective follows the word it modifies. The predicate adjective is always found in the predicate after the verb it completes.

1. Adjectives placed before the noun.
   An **old, gnarled** tree lay across the stream.
2. Adjectives placed after the noun.
   A tree, **old** and **gnarled,** lay across the stream.
3. Predicate adjectives, placed after the verb.
   The tree was **old** and **gnarled.**

NOUNS USED AS ADJECTIVES

The use of pronouns as adjectives was explained in Chapter Six. Nouns are also frequently *used as adjectives.* The nouns in the following expressions are used as adjectives:

college credits (modifies *credits*)
dress accessories (modifies *accessories*)
window sash (modifies *sash*)
Fourth of July speech (modifies *speech*)
summer clothes (modifies *clothes*)
table lamp (modifies *lamp*)

A noun in the *possessive case* is often placed before another noun which it modifies. In such cases, the noun in the possessive case is used as an adjective although it has not lost the function of showing ownership or possession. Nouns used in this way are sometimes called **possessive adjectives.** Sometimes they are described as nouns in the possessive case used as adjectives. Observe how nouns in the possessive case are used in the following sentences:

John's car was wrecked in the crash. (*John's* modifies *car.*)

I like to shop in **Macy's** store. (*Macy's* modifies *store.*)

I am wearing my **sister's** coat. (*sister's* modifies *coat.*)

COMPARISON OF ADJECTIVES

The form of an adjective is often changed to show the extent or degree to which a certain quality is present. In grammar, this change in form to show a difference in degree is called *comparison.*

There are three degrees of comparison in English: the *positive degree,* the *comparative degree,* and the *superlative degree.*

The **positive degree** is really not a degree of comparison because no comparison is indicated when the positive degree is used. The positive degree is the simple form of the adjective. It shows that the quality is present, but it does not show a comparison with anything else. The adjectives in the following sentences are all positive degree:

That is a **beautiful** rose.
It is a very **cold** day.
Peter is very **energetic.**
Jane is **studious.**
The **old** house was sold.
It was a very **warm** day.

In the preceding illustrations, the adjective simply shows that the quality is present. No comparison is made with any other person or thing.

The **comparative degree** of the adjective is used when a comparison *is* made between **two** persons or things. The comparative degree shows that the quality expressed by the adjective exists to a *greater* or to a *lesser* degree in one of the two persons or things that are being compared.

The comparative degree of almost all adjectives of *one* syllable is formed by adding **er** to the positive degree, or to the simple form of the adjective; for example, *colder, smoother, longer, greater, stronger, firmer, thicker,* etc.

John is **stronger** than Michael. (*two persons* compared)

This table is **larger** than that table. (*two objects* compared)

In the first sentence, *two persons* are compared as to strength. According to the sentence, John possesses this quality of strength to a greater degree than Michael. The comparative degree of the adjective is used because a comparison is made between *two* persons.

In the second sentence, *two tables* are being compared as to size. The comparative degree of the adjective *large* is used because a comparison is made between *two objects*.

The **superlative degree** of the adjective is used when **more than two** persons or things are compared. The superlative degree indicates that the quality (expressed by the adjective) is possessed to the *greatest* or to the *least* degree by one of the persons or things included in the comparison.

Our house is the **largest** house in the block. (More than two are compared.)
Louis is the **smallest** boy in his class. (More than two are compared.)

In the first sentence, *more than two* houses are being compared. The superlative degree of the adjective *large* is used to show this fact. The house that possesses the quality expressed by the adjective *large* to the greatest degree is *our* house. It is the *largest* house in a block which contains more than two houses.

In the second sentence, more than two boys are being compared as to size. Louis possesses this quality to the *least* degree. The superlative degree of the adjective *small* is used to show this fact.

DEGREES OF COMPARISON

Adjectives of One Syllable

Positive	Comparative	Superlative
neat	neater	neatest
sharp	sharper	sharpest
dark	darker	darkest
keen	keener	keenest
long	longer	longest

Adjectives of *two or more syllables* are usually compared by prefixing the words *more* and *most* to the simple form of the adjective. *More* is used to indicate the comparison between two persons or things. *Most* is used to indicate the comparison between more than two persons or things. *Less* and *least* are used in a similar way.

Positive	Comparative	Superlative
fragrant	*more* fragrant	*most* fragrant
famous	*less* famous	*least* famous
precious	*more* precious	*most* precious
difficult	*less* difficult	*least* difficult

Sometimes adjectives of *one syllable* are compared by prefixing *more* and *most*. Sometimes adjectives of *more than one syllable* are compared by adding **er** and **est**. There is no rule to follow for making these exceptions. It is usually a matter of sound. If one form of comparison sounds better than the other, that is the form of comparison to use. It sounds better to say *crisp, more crisp, most crisp,* than to say *crisp, crisper, crispest*. Therefore, the comparison with *more* and *most* is preferred.

Adjectives of more than one syllable that end in *y* are usually compared by adding **er** and **est**. Notice the change in spelling in the comparative and in the superlative degrees. The **y** changes to **i** before the addition of **er** or **est**.

Positive	Comparative	Superlative
silly	sillier	silliest
dainty	daintier	daintiest
clumsy	clumsier	clumsiest
handy	handier	handiest
noisy	noisier	noisiest

IRREGULAR COMPARISON OF ADJECTIVES

Some adjectives are compared *irregularly*. The forms for the comparative degree and for the superlative degree usually show a marked

change in the form of the word; for example, *many, more, most*. You should be familiar with these changes in order to use the correct forms for the comparative and superlative degrees.

Adjectives Compared Irregularly

Positive	Comparative	Superlative
bad, evil, ill	worse	worst
far	further	furthest
far	farther	farthest
good, well	better	best
little	less	least
many	more	most
much	more	most
out	outer	outmost or outermost

Farther refers to *distance* or remoteness in space. **Further** refers to remoteness in *time*, to *degree, extent,* or *quantity*. It is also used to express the idea of something *more* or *additional*.

The garage is **farther** than I thought. (distance in space)
I shall give you **further** instructions tomorrow. (*additional* instructions)

The distinctions between *farther* and *further* are passing out of use. These words are now used interchangeably. There is also a tendency to use *further* to express all the meanings discussed. (See latest dictionaries.)

ADJECTIVES NOT COMPARED

There are a number of adjectives that should not be compared because the **simple** form of the adjective expresses the quality to the highest possible degree. For example, if an answer to a problem is *correct*, another answer could not possibly be *more correct*. If a circle is absolutely *round*, another circle could not be *more round*. If a bottle is *empty*, another bottle could not be *more empty*.

The following are some of the adjectives that are not compared for the reasons given:

perfect	unique	square	universal
single	supreme	fatal	empty
vertical	full	alone	dead
final	mortal	round	deadly
straight	blind	everlasting	wrong

The expression, *more nearly round*, is often used when comparing two things, one of which is *more nearly round* than the other. In this case, however, neither of the things compared is round. A line could be *more nearly straight* than another line if neither of the lines was absolutely straight.

Sometimes an adjective such as the word *honest* is used in the comparative and superlative degrees. In such cases, we have no standard of absolute honesty. What the writer or speaker means is that one person approaches the absolute state of honesty to a greater or to a lesser degree than another person. The adjective *perfect* is often used in the same way.

11. MODIFIERS: ADVERBS

Chapter Two explained the uses of the adverb as a modifier of the verb, telling *how, when, where,* and *to what degree* the action is performed. This unit presents other uses of the adverb, and the relation of adverbs to adjectives and to other adverbs.

FORMS OF ADVERBS

Some people have the idea that all adverbs end in **ly**. There are a great many adverbs that do end in **ly**, but there are probably just as many that do not end in **ly**. Many adverbs are formed by adding **ly** to the adjective form:

Adjective	Adverb	Adjective	Adverb
strange	strangely	awkward	awkwardly
sudden	suddenly	necessary	necessarily
calm	calmly	strict	strictly
sure	surely	forcible	forcibly
usual	usually	extreme	extremely
swift	swiftly	similar	similarly
rapid	rapidly	slight	slightly

The following are some of the adverbs that do not end in **ly**:

seldom	little	why	fast
again	here	now	twice
soon	there	then	too
very	rather	since	much
almost	often	well	quite
late	when	near	yonder
hard	where	far	how

Many adjectives end in **ly**. They should not be confused with adverbs that end in **ly**. The following words ending in **ly** are commonly used as adjectives. Some of them might also be used as adverbs:

stately	lovely	saintly	manly
lonely	womanly	lively	courtly

Some adjectives have the same form as the adverb. In such cases, the only way you can tell whether the word is an *adjective* or an *adverb*, is to determine its use in a particular sentence. Study the following illustrations carefully:

That was a **hard** task. (*hard* adjective, modifies *task*)
Our janitor works **hard**. (*hard* adverb, modifies *works*)
We arrived at the airport **early**. (*early* adverb, modifies *arrived*)
We had to make an **early** start. (*early* adjective, modifies *start*)
That was a **cowardly** act. (*cowardly* adjective, modifies *act*)
He acted **cowardly** in that situation. (*cowardly* adverb, modifies *acted*)

INTERROGATIVE ADVERBS

An adverb is often used at the beginning of a sentence to ask a question. When an adverb is used in this way, it is called an **interrogative adverb**. An *interrogative adverb* also modifies some word in the sentence.

When did you arrive? (*When* interrogative adverb)
Where did you put my hat? (*Where* interrogative adverb)
How many books have you read? (*How* interrogative adverb)

In the first sentence, the adverb *When* asks the question. It also modifies the verb *did arrive*. (You *did arrive* when?) In the second sentence, the adverb *Where* asks the question and modifies the verb *did put*. (You *did put* my hat where?) In the third sentence, the adverb *How* asks the question and modifies the adjective *many*. (You have read how *many* books?)

YES, NO, AND NOT

The affirmative adverb *yes* and the negative adverb *no* are used independently. They are usually set off by commas. *Not* is an adverb. It is never used as part of the verb, although it often comes between the parts of a verb phrase. The adverb *not* makes the verb express an idea which is the exact opposite of the regular meaning of the verb.

Yes, I shall take the course.

I did *not* give him the plans. (No plans were given.)

No, we are *not* going to Florida this winter.

ADVERBS OF DEGREE

Adverbs of degree tell *how large, how small, how long, how much, to what extent*, etc. They answer the questions *"How much?" "To what extent?" "In what degree?"* Adverbs of degree usually modify adjectives or other adverbs. In the following illustrations the adverbs of degree modify *adjectives*:

This apple is very sour. (*very* modifies the adjective *sour*)

The play was rather dull. (*rather* modifies the adjective *dull*)

The price is too high. (*too* modifies the adjective *high*)

In the first sentence, the adverb of degree *very* modifies the predicate adjective *sour*. It tells to what degree the apple is sour, or how sour it is. In the second sentence, the adverb *rather* modifies the predicate adjective *dull*. It tells the extent to which the play was *dull*. In the third sentence, the adverb *too* modifies the predicate adjective *high*. It tells the extent to which the price is *high*. The adverbs *very, too,* and *rather* are commonly used as adverbs of degree.

In the following sentences, the adverbs of degree modify other *adverbs*:

The old man moved too slowly. (*too* modifies the adverb *slowly*)

John swims much faster than Ned. (*much* modifies the adverb *faster*)

Don't talk so loud. (*so* modifies the adverb *loud*)

In the first sentence, the adverb of degree *too* modifies the adverb *slowly*. It tells the extent to which the old man moved *slowly*. In the second sentence, the adverb of degree *much* modifies the adverb *faster*. The adverb of degree tells that John swims fast to a greater degree than Ned. In the third sentence, the adverb of degree *so* modifies the adverb *loud*. The sentence means that you should not talk loud to the extent expressed by the adverb *so*. In this sentence, the short form of the adverb (*loud*) is used instead of the longer form, *loudly*.

NOUNS USED AS ADVERBS

Nouns that express *time, size, place, measurement, degree,* or *number* are often used as adverbs. We identify these nouns by calling them *nouns used as adverbs*. Such nouns are not only used as adverbs, but they retain an important characteristic of nouns; namely, they may take an *adjective modifier*.

I am going *home*. (*home* noun used as an adverb)

Horace will arrive *Monday*. (*Monday* noun used as an adverb)

We worked all *day*. (*day* noun used as an adverb)

The fish weighed five *pounds*. (*pounds* noun used as an adverb)

In the first sentence, the noun *home* tells **where** I am going. It performs the same function as an **adverb of place.** In the second sentence, the noun *Monday* tells **when** Horace will arrive. It performs the same function as an **adverb of time.** In the third sentence, the noun *day* tells **how long** we worked, or the extent to which we worked. In the last sentence, the noun *pounds* tells the amount, or **how much** the fish weighed.

The noun *pounds* in the last sentence is modified by the adjective *five*. Although the noun *pounds* functions as an adverb, it may take an adjective modifier. It still retains that particular characteristic of a noun. It functions as two parts of speech at the same time both as a **noun** and as an **adverb.**

Some persons have difficulty in understanding the use of a noun as an adverb. A noun used as an adverb is really the equivalent of a phrase. The following illustrations will help make this clear:

I am going home. This sentence really means that I am going to *my home*. The noun *home* is the equivalent of the phrase, *to my home*.

Horace will arrive Monday. This sentence means that Horace will arrive *on Monday*. The noun *Monday* is the equivalent of the phrase, *on Monday*.

We worked all day. This sentence means that we worked for the period or to *the extent of a day*.

The fish weighed five pounds. This sentence means that the fish weighed to the extent or *to the amount of five pounds*.

COMPARISON OF ADVERBS

Adverbs are compared in exactly the same way as adjectives are compared. They have the same three degrees of comparison: the *positive degree*, the *comparative degree*, and the *superlative degree*.

A few adverbs form the comparative degree by adding **er** to the positive degree. They form the superlative degree by adding **est** to the positive degree.

Positive	Comparative	Superlative
late	later	latest
hard	harder	hardest
soon	sooner	soonest
fast	faster	fastest
near	nearer	nearest
quick (*short form*)	quicker	quickest
slow (*short form*)	slower	slowest

Most adverbs are compared by placing *more* (for the comparative degree) and *most* (for the superlative degree) before the positive forms. *Less* and *least* are used in the same way as *more* and *most*.

Positive	Comparative	Superlative
carefully	more carefully	most carefully
discreetly	more discreetly	most discreetly
abruptly	more abruptly	most abruptly
gratefully	more gratefully	most gratefully
efficiently	more efficiently	most efficiently
awkwardly	less awkwardly	least awkwardly
favorably	less favorably	least favorably
gracefully	less gracefully	least gracefully

IRREGULAR COMPARISON OF ADVERBS

A few adverbs are compared *irregularly*. In the following list you will find some words that were also in the list of adjectives that are compared irregularly. Such words are used both as *adjectives* and as *adverbs*.

Positive	Comparative	Superlative
far	farther	farthest
far	further	furthest
badly	worse	worst
little	less	least
much	more	most
well	better	best

Some adverbs are not compared. The following adverbs can not be used in the comparative or in the superlative degrees:

before	never	now	there	very	by
ever	no	so	thus	past	back
here	not	then	too	yes	whenever

The comparative degree of adverbs is used when comparing two things. The superlative degree is used when comparing more than two.

We drove *more slowly* than our guide. (Comparative)

Of the three speakers, the senator spoke *most convincingly*. (Superlative)

12. PRINCIPAL PARTS OF VERBS

Studies have shown that more than half of the errors made in English are errors in the use of verbs. Most of this trouble occurs because of confusion in the use of the principal parts.

Every verb has *three basic forms* which are called the *principal parts* of the verb. These three forms are the **present tense**, the **past tense**, and the **past participle.** They are called the principal parts of the verb because (with a few exceptions) the six tenses of the verb can be built from them.

Tense is a property that belongs to verbs. In grammar, *tense* means *time*. Every verb has certain forms which show the *time* of the *action* or the *time* of the *state of condition*. When we want to indicate that a certain action is going on now, or that a certain state of condition exists at the present time, we use the **present tense.**

Present Tense

I **drive.** (Action occurs at the *present time*.)

He **sings.** (Action occurs at the *present time*.)

Florence **is** ill. (state of condition exists at the *present time*.)

When we want to indicate that the action occurred yesterday, or in some past time, we use the **past tense** of the verb. With a few exceptions, the past tense of the verb is not the same form as the present tense of the verb.

Past Tense

I **drove.** (The action occurred in the *past*.)

He **sang** at the concert. (The action occurred in the *past*.)

Florence **was** ill yesterday. (State of condition existed in the *past*.)

In the preceding illustrations, the forms, *drive* and *sings*, are used to show that action is going on at the present time. The forms, *drove* and *sang*, are used to show that action occurred at some time in the past. The forms *drive* and *sings* are the present tense of the verbs *drive* and *sing*. The forms *drove* and *sang* are the past tense of the verbs *drive* and *sing*.

The **past participle** of the verb is a verb form that is used with *have, has,* or *had* to form the perfect tenses. The past participle cannot function as the predicate verb. It is always combined with an auxiliary, such as *have, has,* or *had.* It is a part of the verb phrase.

Past Participles

I <u>have</u> **called** her every day this week. (*called* past participle)

We <u>have</u> **driven** there often. (*driven* past participle)

The three forms, the *present tense, past tense,* and the *past participle,* constitute the **principal parts** of a verb. Become familiar with the principal parts of certain verbs so that you will be able to use them correctly. The verbs that cause most of our verb troubles are the verbs that form the principal part irregularly. We shall make a special study of these verbs.

REGULAR AND IRREGULAR VERBS

Verbs are divided into two classes on the basis of the way in which the past tense and the past participle are formed. Some are called *regular* or weak verbs, and others are called *irregular* or strong verbs.

A **regular verb** is a verb that forms the past tense and the past participle by adding **ed** or **d** to the form of the present tense. Sometimes the **ed** or **d** changes to **t**: *build, built, built.*

Verb	Past Tense	Past Participle
call	called	called
bake	baked	baked
build	built	built

The past tense and the past participle of the verb *call* are formed by adding **ed** to the form of the present tense: *call**ed**.* The past tense and the past participle of the verb *bake* are formed by simply adding **d** to the form of the present tense: *bake**d**.* The past tense and the past participle of the verb *build* are formed by changing the **d** to **t**. The old form of the verb build was *builded* in the past tense. That form is no longer used. The simpler form *built* has taken its place.

An **irregular verb** is a verb that does *not* form the past tense and the past participle in the regular way; that is, by adding **d** or **ed** to the form of the present tense. The past tense and the past participle of irregular verbs are formed in various ways. The most common way is by a change in the vowel; for example, *sing, sang, sung.* In the case of a few verbs, the same form is used for the present tense, the past tense and the past participle: *hurt, hurt, hurt.*

Verb	Past Tense	Past Participle
sing	sang	sung
drive	drove	driven
begin	began	begun
go	went	gone
burst	burst	burst

The past tense and the past participle of the verb *sing* are formed by a change in vowel. The **i** in *sing* changes to **a** in the past tense (*sang*) and to **u** in the past participle (*sung*). The verb *begin* follows a similar change in the vowel. The verb *go* has a different form for the past tense and for the past participle: *go, went, gone.* The verb *burst* has the same form for the present tense, the past tense, and the past participle.

VERBS ADDED TO THE LANGUAGE

New verbs are added to the English language as the need arises. Practically all of new verbs form the past tense and the past participle by adding **ed** or **d**; that is, they follow the pattern of the regular verbs. To form the past tense or the past participle of these verbs add **ed** or **d**.

Verb	Past Tense	Past Participle
activate	activated	activated
radio	radioed	radioed
camouflage	camouflaged	camouflaged
audition	auditioned	auditioned
laminate	laminated	laminated

THE TROUBLESOME VERBS

The *regular verbs* cause very little trouble in speaking and writing because the past tense and the past participle usually follow the rule of forming the past tense and the past participle by adding **d** or **ed**. It is the *irregular verbs* that are responsible for most of the verb errors.

Errors are frequently made in using the *past tense* and the *perfect tense* forms of irregular verbs. This is due to the fact that these verbs form the past tense and the perfect tenses irregularly. In order to use these verbs correctly, it is highly important for you to become familiar with the principal parts of the irregular verbs that are in common use. You will learn these forms by checking constantly until you are familiar with the correct forms for the past tense and the past participle.

Mistakes are commonly made in using the wrong form for the **past tense:** *done* for *did; seen* for *saw; come* for *came; swum* for *swan; dove* for *dived; run* for *ran; drunk* for *drank.* Mistakes are also made in using the wrong form for the **past participle:** *went* for *gone; did* for *done; swam* for *swum; tore* for *torn; began* for *begun; came* for *come.* The past participle is used in forming the perfect tenses.

Correct Forms for the Past Tense

I <u>did</u> the work assigned to me. (not *done*)

We <u>saw</u> the parade yesterday. (not *seen*)

He <u>came</u> from Ireland two years ago. (not *come*)

She <u>swam</u> across the English Channel last summer. (not *swum*)

The swimming teacher <u>dived</u> off the pier. (not *dove*)

The boy <u>ran</u> through the traffic. (not *run*)

We <u>drank</u> all the milk in the pitcher. (not *drunk*)

Correct Forms for the Past Participle

The delegates **have gone** home. (not *have went*)

He **has done** the work well. (not *has did*)

She **has swum** the channel several times. (not *has swam*)

The actress **has torn** her dress. (not *has tore*)

They **have begun** to check the accounts. (not *have began*)

Has the mail **come**? (not *has came*)

In the first sentence, the past participle is *gone.* It is combined with the auxiliary *have* to form the verb phrase *have gone.* The form *went* should never be used with *have, has* or *had.*

In the second sentence, the past participle is *done.* It is the correct form of the verb to combine with *has.* In the third sentence, the past participle is *swum.* It is correctly used

with *has. Tore* should never be used with *have, has,* or *had* The correct form is *have, has,* or *had torn.*

Began is the correct form for the past tense. It should not be used for the past participle. The correct form for the past participle is *begun.* Never use the forms *have began, had began,* or *has began.* The correct forms are *have begun, had begun,* and *has begun.*

The following table gives the principal parts of the irregular verbs that cause most of the verb errors. You should become familiar with the principal parts of these verbs. Consult this list whenever you are in doubt about the correct form to use. If the verb you want is not in this list, consult a reliable, up-to-date dictionary. The principal parts of verbs are given in most dictionaries.

PRINCIPAL PARTS OF TROUBLESOME VERBS

Present Tense (present time)	Past Tense (past time)	Past Participles (used with have, has, had)
awake	awaked awoke	awaked awoke
be (am)	was	been
beat	beat	beaten
become	became	become
begin	began	begun
bid (offer)	bid	bid
bid (command)	bade	bidden, bid
blow	blew	blown
break	broke	broken
bring	brought	brought
broadcast	broadcast broadcasted	broadcast broadcasted
burst	burst	burst
catch	caught	caught
choose	chose	chosen
climb	climbed	climbed
come	came	come
cut	cut	cut
dive	dived	dived
do	did	done
drag	dragged	dragged
draw	drew	drawn
drink	drank	drunk
drive	drove	driven
drown	drowned	drowned
eat	ate	eaten
fall	fell	fallen
flow	flowed	flowed
fly	flew	flown
forget	forgot	forgotten, forgot
freeze	froze	frozen
get	got	got, gotten
give	gave	given
go	went	gone
hang (a picture)	hung	hung
hang (a criminal)	hanged	hanged
know	knew	known
lay (to place, to put)	laid	laid
lead	led	led
leave	left	left
lend	lent	lent
let	let	let
lie (recline)	lay (not laid)	lain (not laid)
lie (false)	lied	lied
lose	lost	lost
prove	proved	proved

ride	rode	ridden
ring	rang	rung
rise	rose	risen (not rose)
run	ran	run
say	said	said
see	saw	seen
send	sent	sent
set	set	set
shake	shook	shaken
shine (light)	shone	shone
shine (polish)	shined	shined
show	showed	shown, showed
shrink	shrank	shrunk
sing	sang	sung
sink	sank	sunk
sit	sat	sat
spring	sprang, sprung	sprung
steal	stole	stolen
swear	swore	sworn
swim	swam	swum
swing	swung	swung
take	took	taken
teach	taught	taught
tear	tore	torn
tell	told	told
think	thought	thought
throw	threw	thrown
try	tried	tried
understand	understood	understood
wake	waked, woke	waked
wear	wore	worn
weave	wove	woven
weep	wept	wept
wind	wound	wound
wring	wrung	wrung
write	wrote	written

SIX CONFUSING VERBS

Six of the irregular verbs require special attention and study because they are so frequently confused. As a result, they are used incorrectly more often than any of the other irregular verbs. These forms of the verbs in each pair are somewhat similar, but the meanings are quite different. We shall make a special study of these verbs so that you will be able to use them correctly.

LIE AND LAY

There are two different verbs that are spelled alike (*lie*). One means to tell a falsehood. This is a regular verb and causes no difficulty, either in speaking or in writing. The verb that is confused with *lay* is the verb *lie*, which means *to recline, to rest,* or *to remain in a reclining position.* This verb is an irregular verb. The principal parts are *lie, lay,* and (*have, has, had*) *lain.* The present participle, the form that ends in *ing,* is *lying.*

There are two important facts regarding the verb *lie* (to recline) that you should always keep in mind: (1) There is no form ending in **d** that belongs to the verb *lie,* meaning *to recline.* The form *laid* should never be used when you mean *to recline, rest,* or *remain in a reclining position.* (2) The verb *lie* never takes an object.

Mother **lies** down every afternoon. (*rests, reclines*)
Mother **lay** on the couch all afternoon. (not *laid*)
Mother **is lying** on the couch. (not *laying*)
Mother **has lain** on that couch often. (not *has laid*)

The verb *lie* is also the verb to use when we speak about inanimate objects that are in a reclining or in a *lying down* position.

The pen **lies** on my desk. (not *lays*)
The pen **lay** on my desk all day. (not *laid*)
The pen **is lying** on my desk. (not *is laying*)
The pen **has lain** on my desk all week. (not *has laid*)

The verb **lay,** that is so often confused with *lie,* means *to put something down, to place something somewhere.* The principal parts of this verb are *lay, laid,* (*have, has,* or *had*) *laid.* The present participle is *laying.* The verb *lay* always takes an object.

John **lays** carpets for Macey's store. (*carpets* object of *lays*)
John **laid** carpets all week. (*carpets* object of *laid*)
John **has laid** carpets for many years. (*carpets* object of *has laid*)

In the first sentence, the verb *lays* is the present tense of the verb *lay,* which means to put something down. The word *carpets* is the direct object of the verb *lays.* It tells what John put down. In the second sentence, the verb *laid* is the past tense of the verb *lay.*

When we use the form *laid,* we must supply an object telling what we *laid,* or *what we put down. Carpets* is the direct object of the verb *laid.* It tells what John *laid.* In the last sentence, *laid* is the correct form of the verb *lay* to combine with *has.* It helps form the verb phrase *has laid.*

SIT AND SET

The verb *sit* means to *assume a sitting position* or *to occupy a seat.* The principal parts of the verb *sit* are *sit, sat,* (*have, has, had*) *sat.* The present participle is *sitting.* The verb *sit* never takes an object. The form *set* does not belong to this verb.

Joe **sat** very still, watching the game.
The children **were sitting** on the floor.
I always **sit** near the fireplace when I read.
My aunt likes **to sit** in a rocking chair.
She **has sat** in the same chair for many years.

The verb **set** means *to place, to put something in position, to make rigid, solid,* or *stiff.* The principal parts of the verb *set* are *set, set,* (*have, has, had*) *set.* The present participle is *setting.* The verb *set* usually takes an object. There are a few idiomatic uses of the verb in which it does *not* take an object. The verb *set* takes an object in the following sentences:

Esther **set** the basket on the table. (*basket* direct object)
We **set** the clock back yesterday. (*clock* direct object)
The operator **set** her hair beautifully. (*hair* direct object)
The buyer **has set** the price too low. (*price* direct object)

Idiomatic Uses

The verb *set* is used *without an object* in the following sentences. Study the types of situations in which the verb *set* is used without an object. These are idiomatic uses of the verb *set.*

The sun **was setting** when we left the lodge.
The cement **will set** in two hours.
We **set** out on a long journey.
The men **set** to work at once.
Jelly **sets** as it cools.

RISE AND RAISE

The verb *rise* means *to ascend, to go up, to extend upward, to swell up,* as bread dough in fermentation, *to increase in value, force* or *intensity.* The principal parts of the verb *rise* are *rise, rose,* and (*have, has, had*) *risen.* The present participle is *rising.* The verb *rise* expresses action, but it does not take an object.

The building **rises** to a height of eighty feet.
This river **rises** in the north.
The tide **was rising.**
Dan **has risen** in his profession.
The plane **rose** steadily.
The sun **will rise** at six o'clock tomorrow.
The cliffs **rise** far above the sea.

The verb *raise* means *to lift up something* or cause it *to go up, to increase the amount or price, to collect a number of things,* etc. The verb *raise* always takes an object. You can't raise without raising something. The verb *raise* is a regular verb. The principal parts are *raise, raised, raised.* The present participle is *raising.*

I **raised** my arm. (to lift up)
Don't **raise** so much dust! (to cause to rise)
The leader **raised** an army. (collected)
We **shall raise** the flag at sunrise. (to cause to go up)
The farmer **raises** wheat. (to cause to grow)
The landlord **raised** the rent. (increased)
Do not **raise** your voice. (to make louder)

13. THE TENSES OF VERBS

THE SIX TENSES

A verb is the most important word in any sentence because more constructions depend upon the verb than upon any other part of speech. Verbs have a number of properties which other parts of speech do not have. One of the properties that belongs exclusively to verbs and verb forms is tense.

Chapter 12 explained that in grammar *tense* means *time.* Verbs have **six tenses** which show differences in the time of *action* or the time of the *state of being* or *condition* (linking verbs).

I *see* a robin on the fence. (**present** time)
I *saw* a robin on the fence yesterday. (**past time**)
I *shall see* a number of birds when I go to the woods. (**future** time)

These sentences do not mean the same thing. The meaning depends to a large extent upon the verb form that is used; that is, the verb form that is used to show the *time* of the action.

The first sentence means that the action expressed by the verb *see* is going on now. The second sentence means that the action expressed by the verb *saw* happened at some time in the past (yesterday). The third sentence means that the action expressed by the verb *shall see* will occur at some future time.

The verbs used in the three sentences are forms of the verb *see.* The verb *see* in the first sentence is the form used in the present tense. It expresses or denotes *present time.* The verb *saw* in the second sentence is the form used to express *past time.* The verb *shall see* is the form used to express *future time.*

Remember, there are six tenses in English. The three tenses which you have just studied are called the **simple tenses.** The other three tenses are called the **perfect tenses.** The only difference between the simple tenses and the perfect tenses is that the perfect tenses include the idea of completion. In grammar, the word *perfect* refers to an action or state of being that is completed at the time of speaking or writing.

Simple Tenses	Perfect Tenses
present tense	*present perfect* tense
past tense	*past perfect* tense
future tense	*future perfect* tense

THE SIMPLE TENSES

The present tense denotes *present time*. It is also used to express *habitual action*, or to express an idea that is *generally accepted as true*.

I *hear* the bell. (present time)
Oscar *works* in an airplane factory. (habitual action)
"Honesty *is* the best policy.' (generally accepted truth)

The present tense is often used to express *future time*. Examine the following sentences carefully. In all of them the present tense expresses a future idea:

If it *rains*, we shall not go to the woods.
If the bill *passes*, the tax will be removed.
Our lease on the factory *expires* tomorrow.

The past tense denotes *past time*. The past tense of **regular verbs** is formed by adding *d* or *ed* to the present tense form: call, call*ed*; dive, div*ed*. Sometimes the *d* at the end of the present tense form changes to *t* in the past tense: build, buil*t*.

I *mailed* the letter yesterday. (addition of *ed*)
We *dived* into the pool. (addition of *d*)
The hunter *built* a cabin in the woods. (change of *d* to *t*)

The past tense of **irregular verbs** is formed in various ways. Sometimes there is a change in the vowel: s*i*ng, s*a*ng; sw*i*m, sw*a*m; beg*i*n, beg*a*n; dr*i*ve, dr*o*ve; break, broke. Sometimes the same form is used in the past tense and in the present tense: bid, bid; hurt, hurt; cut, cut; slit, slit.

The future tense denotes *future time*. The future tense is formed by combining the auxiliary *shall* or *will* with the present tense form of the verb. Use *shall* with the pronouns **I** and *we*. Use *will* with the pronouns *you, he, she, it, they*.

I *shall see* you tomorrow. (*shall* first person)
I am sure that you *will be* late. (*will* second person)
The speaker *will arrive* at seven. (*will* third person)

To express future time, use *shall* in the first person and *will* in the second and third persons.

THE PERFECT TENSES

You can remember the *perfect tenses* easily, if you remember that the work **perfect** is always used in identifying them. The three perfect tenses are the *present perfect tense*, the *past perfect tense*, and the *future perfect tense*.

The present perfect tense denotes *action that is completed* at the time of speaking or writing. It may also indicate action that is *continuing into the present*.

The present perfect tense is formed by combining the auxiliary *have* or *has* with the past participle of the principal verb. The auxiliary *has* is always used in the third person singular: He *has spoken* to the manager.

I *have seen* three of Shaw's plays. (*have seen* first person)
You *have earned* a promotion. (*have earned* second person)
John *has washed* the car. (*has washed* third person)

In the first sentence, the verb phrase is *have seen*. It is in the present perfect tense. The verb phrase is made up of the auxiliary *have* and the past participle of the verb *see*, which is *seen* (*have seen*). In the third sentence, the auxiliary *has* is used instead of *have* (*has washed*).

The past perfect tense denotes *action that was completed* before some definite time in the past. The past perfect tense is formed by combining the auxiliary *had* with the past participle of the principal verb: *had walked, had known, had given, had drunk, had become, had been*, etc.

In the following sentences, verbs in the past tense are underlined once. Verbs in the past perfect tense are underlined twice.

By the time the officer <u>arrived</u>, the thief <u><u>had disappeared</u></u>.
I <u>liked</u> the speaker better after I <u><u>had heard</u></u> him the second time.
The agent <u><u>had sold</u></u> all the tickets before I <u>applied</u> for mine.

The future perfect tense denotes *action that will be completed* at some definite time in the future. The future perfect tense is seldom used in informal speaking or writing.

The future perfect tense is formed by combining the auxiliaries *shall have* or *will have* with the past participle of the principal verb. *Shall have* is used in the first person, and *will have* in the second and third persons. The *italicized* words are in the future perfect tense.

My friend *will have sailed* before I reach the pier.
By January, the committee *will have completed* the investigation.
I *shall have crossed* the river three times before noon.

Many verb errors are made because the writer or speaker is not familiar with the forms for the past tense and the past participle. Whenever you are not sure of one of these forms, consult the tables in Chapter 12. If the verb you are interested in is not listed, consult a reliable, up-to-date dictionary. You will find these forms listed after the verb.

You can also avoid verb errors if you know the auxiliaries that indicate the tense:

shall and *will* for the future tense
have and *has* for the present perfect tense
had for the past perfect tense
shall have or *will have* for the future perfect tense

THE VERB "TO BE"

Every person should be thoroughly familiar with the forms of the verb **to be**. It is the most irregular, and also the most important verb in the English language. The verb *to be* is used as an independent verb, and is also used as an auxiliary verb. The entire passive voice and all the progressive forms of other verbs are formed by using the verb *to be* as an auxiliary or helping verb. You should become familiar with the forms for the six tenses of this important verb.

On the following pages you will find reference tables for the tenses of three verbs: the verb *to be*, the regular verb *call*, and the irregular verb *ring*. Study these tables carefully.

REFERENCE TABLE

SIX TENSES OF THE VERB "TO BE"
Singular and Plural

PRESENT TENSE

First person:	I am
	we are
Second person:	you are
	you are
Third person:	he, she, it is
	they are

PAST TENSE

First person:	I was
	we were
Second person:	you were
	you were
Third person:	he, she, it was
	they were

FUTURE TENSE

First person:	I *shall* be
	we *shall* be
Second person:	you *will* be
	you *will* be
Third person:	he, she, it *will* be
	they *will* be.

Singular and Plural
PRESENT PERFECT TENSE

First person:	I *have* been
	we *have* been
Second person:	you *have* been
	you *have* been
Third person:	he, she, it *has* been
	they *have* been

PAST PERFECT TENSE

First person:	I *had* been
	we *had* been
Second person:	you *had* been
	you *had* been
Third person:	he, she, it *had* been
	they *had* been

FUTURE PERFECT TENSE

First person:	I *shall have* been
	we *shall have* been
Second person:	you *will have* been
	you *will have* been
Third person:	he, she, it *will have* been
	they *will have* been

THE SIX TENSES OF A REGULAR VERB
VERB "CALL" ACTIVE VOICE

PRESENT TENSE
Singular and Plural

First person:	I call
	we call
Second person:	you call
	you call
Third person:	he, she, it *calls*
	they call

VERB "CALL" ACTIVE VOICE (Cont'd)
Singular and Plural

PAST TENSE

First person: I called
we called

Second person: you called
you called

Third person: he, she, it called
they called

FUTURE TENSE

First person: I *shall* call
we *shall* call

Second person: you *will* call
you *will* call

Third person: he, she, it *will* call
they *will* call

PRESENT PERFECT TENSE

First person: I *have* called
we *have* called

Second person: you *have* called
you *have* called

Third person: he, she, it *has* called
they *have* called

PAST PERFECT TENSE

First person: I *had* called
we *had* called

Second person: you *had* called
you *had* called

Third person: he, she, it *had* called
they *had* called

FUTURE PERFECT TENSE

First person: I *shall have* called
we *shall have* called

Second person: you *will have* called
you *will have* called

Third person: he, she, it *will have* called
they *will have* called

SIX TENSES OF AN IRREGULAR VERB
VERB "RING" ACTIVE VOICE
Singular and Plural

PRESENT TENSE

First person: I ring
we ring

Second person: you ring
you ring

Third person: he, she, it *rings*
they ring

PAST TENSE

First person: I *rang*
we *rang*

Second person: you *rang*
you *rang*

Third person: he, she, it *rang*
they *rang*

FUTURE TENSE

First person: I *shall* ring
we *shall* ring

Second person: you *will* ring
you *will* ring

Third person: he, she, it *will* ring
they *will* ring

PRESENT PERFECT TENSE

First person: I have *rung*
we have *rung*

Second person: you have *rung*
you have *rung*

Third person: he, she, it has *rung*
they have *rung*

PAST PERFECT TENSE

First person: I had *rung*
we had *rung*

Second person: you had *rung*
you had *rung*

Third person: he, she, it had *rung*
they had *rung*

FUTURE PERFECT TENSE

First person: I shall have *rung*
we shall have *rung*

Second person: you will have *rung*
you will have *rung*

Third person: he, she, it will have *rung*
they will have *rung*

PROGRESSIVE FORMS OF VERBS

In addition to the forms which have already been given to show tense, a verb has special forms to show that the *action is continuing*. These forms are called the **progressive forms** of a verb. The *progressive forms* are used to show that an action is *continuing* or *progressing* at the time indicated by a particular tense.

I *am studying* English. (The action is continuing.)

He *is planning* a trip to Mexico. (The action is continuing.)

The progressive form of a verb is made up by using some form of the verb *to be* with the *ing* form of the principal verb. The form of a verb that ends in *ing* is called the **present participle.**

In the first sentence, the progressive form of the verb is *am studying*. It is made up of a form of the verb *to be*, which is *am*, and the present participle of the principal verb, which is *studying*. In the second sentence, the progressive form of the verb, *is planning*, is made up in a similar way.

The following are the progressive forms of the verb *call* for the six tenses (first person, singular).

I *am calling* you. (present progressive)

I *was calling* you. (past progressive)

I *shall be calling* you. (future progressive)

I *have been calling* you. (present perfect progressive)

I *had been calling* you. (past perfect progressive)

I *shall have been calling* you. (future perfect progressive)

The present tense, progressive form often expresses a future idea. The verb *to go* is commonly used in this way:

I *am going* to New York next week. (in the future)

He *is going* to buy a new home in the suburbs. (in the future)

VERB "CALL"
PROGRESSIVE FORMS ACTIVE VOICE
Singular and Plural

PRESENT TENSE

First Person: I *am* calling
we *are* calling

Second person: you *are* calling
you *are* calling

Third person: he, she, it *is* calling
they *are* calling

PAST TENSE

First person: I *was* calling
we *were* calling

Second person: you *were* calling
you *were* calling

Third person: he, she, it *was* calling
they *were* calling

FUTURE TENSE

First person: I *shall be* calling
we *shall be* calling

Second person: you *will be* calling
you *will be* calling

Third person: he, she, it *will be* calling
they *will be* calling

PRESENT PERFECT TENSE

First person: I *have been* calling
we *have been* calling

Second person: you *have been* calling
you *have been* calling

Third person: he, she, it *has been* calling
they *have been* calling

PAST PERFECT TENSE

First person: I *had been* calling
we *had been* calling

Second person: you *had been* calling
you *had been* calling

Third person: he, she, it *had been* calling
they *had been* calling

FUTURE PERFECT TENSE

First person: I *shall have been* calling
we *shall have been* calling

Second person: you *will have been* calling
you *will have been* calling

Third person: he, she, it *will have been* calling
they *will have been* calling

EMPHATIC FORMS OF THE VERB

The **emphatic forms** of a verb are often used to give greater emphasis to the idea expressed by the verb. The auxiliaries *do, does,* and *did* are used to give this additional emphasis. The emphatic forms are used in only two tenses, the *present tense* and the *past tense.*

I *do agree* with you. (present tense)
Jane *did send* the letter. (past tense)
The editor *does need* to know the facts. (present tense)

EMPHATIC FORMS —*PRESENT TENSE*

Singular and Plural

First person:	I *do* call
	we *do* call
Second person:	you *do* call
	you *do* call
Third person:	he *does* call
	they *do* call

EMPHATIC FORMS—*PAST TENSE*

First person:	I *did* call
	we *did* call
Second person:	you *did* call
	you *did* call
Third person:	he *did* call
	they *did* call

When *do, does,* and *did* are used in questions, the form is not used for emphasis. The use of *do, does,* and *did* in questions is an idiomatic way of asking question in English. In the following questions *do, does,* and *did* are not the emphatic form of the verb:

Did he buy that hat last week?
Do you know her?
Does he want to pay the bill?

Also, when *do, does,* and *did* are used to mean *accomplish, carry out,* etc., the form is not used for emphasis in these cases. This sentence is an example:

We *did* our homework quickly.

THE USE OF SHALL AND WILL

Many of the precise distinctions concerning the use of *shall* and *will* are rapidly passing out of informal speaking and writing. Careful writers, however, still observe some of these distinctions. The following are some of the distinctions that are most generally observed:

Simple Futurity

Use *shall* in the first person and *will* in the second and third persons to express **simple futurity.** Simple futurity means anticipation or expectation of what is likely to happen, or what one is likely to do. It follows the regular forms of the future tense:

First person:	I *shall* go
	we *shall* go
Second person:	you *will* go
	you *will* go
Third person:	he *will* go
	they *will* go

Determination, Threat, Promise

If you want to express determination, compulsion, threat, or promise (willingness to do something), reverse the order of *shall* and

will. Use *will* in the first person, and *shall* in the second and third persons.

First person:	I *will* go
	we *will* go
Second person:	you *shall* go
	you *shall* go
Third person:	he *shall* go
	they *shall* go

Special Cases

When *shall* and *will* are followed by such expressions as *be glad, be sorry, be happy, be delighted, be pleased,* etc., use *shall* in the first person, and *will* in the second and third persons. If *will* is used in the first person, it would mean that you are determined *to be glad, sorry, delighted,* etc. If *shall* is used in the second and third persons, it would mean that you are compelling someone *to be glad, sorry,* etc. The following are the accepted ways of using such expressions:

I shall be glad to see you. (not *will*)
We shall be delighted to help you. (not *will*)
You will be sorry to learn of his misfortune. (not *shall*)
He will be pleased to see you at four. (not *shall*)

In giving courteous commands, you should use *will* in the second and third persons instead of *shall.* This is the form that is generally followed in giving military orders and instructions:

Corporal Smith will report to Captain Allen. (not *shall report*)
You will hand in your report on Wednesday. (not *shall*)
The meeting will come to order. (not *shall*)
Mr. Ames, you *will meet* with the committee today. (not *shall*)

SHOULD AND WOULD

Should is the past tense of *shall* and in general, follows the same rules that apply to the use of *shall. Would* is the past tense of *will* and follows the same rules that apply to the use of *will.*

Both *should* and *would* have special uses. *Would* is used in all three persons to express *habitual* or *customary* action. *Should* is often used in all three persons to express *obligation. Ought* and *should* both express obligation and are used interchangeable.

Every evening we *would play* cards for hours. (*habitual action*)
You *should read* something worth while every day. (*obligation*)
You *ought to read* something worth while every day. (*obligation*)

Study the following sentences carefully. Note especially the explanations given in parentheses. This will help you understand the distinctions which have been made in the preceding discussion:

I shall go to the theater this evening. (*simple futurity expectation*)
I will not see him today. (*determination* on the part of the speaker)
You will enjoy meeting him. (*simple futurity* or *expectation*)
He will enter Harvard in September. (*simple futurity*)
I will accompany you to the clinic. (*promise willingness*)
He shall report to the judge every month. (*I am determined* that he shall.)
You shall have any assistance that you may need. (*I am determined* that you shall.)

We shall be pleased to grant you an interview. (*simple futurity*)
You would drown if you ventured out in deep water. (*simple futurity*)
He would drown if he ventured out in deep water. (*simple futurity*)
We should be very happy if *you would call* for us. (*simple futurity*)
I should be the first one to volunteer. (*obligation*)
You should read good books. (*obligation*)
They should offer their services to the committee. (*obligation*)

MIXED TENSES

Unless there is a good reason for making a change, the tenses of the verbs in a sentence or in a paragraph should agree. If you start out with a verb in the *past tense,* you should not change to another verb in the *present tense.* If you start with a verb in the *present tense,* you should not change to the *past tense.*

Tense means *time,* and when you change the tense, you also change the time. Tenses must be consistent; that is, there must be a logical sequence of time. It is illogical to shift from one tense to another tense. Study the following illustrations carefully:

Dr. Smith *examined* the patient and *calls* the nurse. (*incorrect*)

In this sentence, the verb *examined* is in the past tense. It is followed by the verb *calls* which is in the present tense. There is a shift from the past tense to the present tense. Both verbs should be in the past tense or both verbs should be in the present tense.

Dr. Smith *examines* the patient and *calls* the nurse. (*correct*)
or
Dr. Smith *examined* the patient and *called* the nurse. (*correct*)

I *went* into the hall and there I *see* a strange man. (*incorrect*)
I *went* into the hall and there I *saw* a strange man. (*correct*)

The officer *stopped* the car and *speaks* to the driver. (*incorrect*)
The officer *stopped* the car and *spoke* to the driver. (*correct*)

THE "OF" ERROR

Careless speakers and writers often use the preposition *of* in place of the auxiliary verb *have.* The word *of* is a preposition and should never be used as part of a verb phrase.

The "*of*" error is generally caused by the use of contractions or by careless enunciation on the part of a speaker. The mistake is commonly made after the words *could, might, ought to, should,* and *would.* When *have* is used following any of these words, and the two words are contracted, the resulting combination sounds as if *of* were being used rather than *have: could've* sounds like *could of, should've* sounds like *should of,* etc.

Since in speech the contracted form of *have* cannot readily be distinguished from *of,* many persons have the mistaken belief that *of* is the word being said and that it is the correct word to use. As a result they carry over the mistake from their speech into their writing, and never know they are in error. To avoid making the "*of*" error when you are speaking, never contract *have* to *'ve.*

Study the following examples. The preposition *of* should never be used in place of *have* as part of a verb phrase.

We should *of* been more careful. (*incorrect*)
We shoud *have* been more careful. (*correct*)

He must *of* taken it. (*incorrect*)
He must *have* taken it. (*correct*)

They might *of* notified us. (*incorrect*)
They might *have* notified us. (*correct*)

I should *of* prepared the report. (*incorrect*)
I should *have* prepared the report. (*correct*)

14. VERBS: VOICE AND MOOD

ACTIVE AND PASSIVE VOICE

A verb not only undergoes certain changes to show *tense*, or the time of the action, but it changes in form to show *voice*. **Voice** is a grammatical term which is used to *tell whether the subject of the sentence is acting or is receiving the action expressed by the verb.*

When the subject is acting, we say that the subject is the *doer*. When the subject is receiving the action, we say that the subject is the *receiver*. If you keep these two terms, *doer* and *receiver*, in mind, you will have no difficulty in understanding what *voice* means in grammar.

Study the following sentences carefully. Note the changes that occur in the form of the verb. Note the change that occurs in the subject of the sentence:

Ned washed the car. (*Ned* is the *doer* of the action.)

The car was washed by Ned. (*Car* is the *receiver* of the action.)

In the first sentence, the subject is *Ned*. He is the *doer*, the one who is performing the action expressed by the verb *washed*. The *car* is receiving the action. In grammar we say that the verb in this sentence is in the **active voice** because the subject is the *doer*, or is doing the washing. The car is the *receiver* of the action.

The second sentence is written in the reverse order. The subject is now the receiver of the action instead of the doer. In order to express this idea, it was necessary to use another verb form, *was washed*. What happened to *Ned*, the doer? *Ned* is still in the sentence but is now in a phrase introduced by the preposition *by*.

The verb *was washed* is in the **passive voice** because it represents the subject of the sentence as the receiver of the action. In other words, the subject is not acting, but is *passive*. The doer, or the actor, appears in a phrase introduced by the preposition *by*.

A verb in the passive voice is *never* a simple verb. It is always a verb phrase. In the sentence, *Our car was stolen yesterday*, the verb *was stolen* is in the *passive voice*. The subject is the receiver of the action. Since the doer is unknown, the "*by* phrase" is omitted. But we know that it was stolen by someone. If we discover who stole the car, the doer might be added to the sentence:

Our car was stolen yesterday by two strangers.

If a verb is in the **active voice**, *the subject is the doer of the action.* If a verb is in the **passive voice,** *the subject is the receiver of the action.* When a verb is in the passive voice, the doer is often omitted. Sometimes the doer is unknown, and sometimes the doer is so evident that it is not necessary to include the "*by* phrase."

HOW THE PASSIVE VOICE IS FORMED

You cannot express an idea in the passive voice without using an auxiliary or helping verb. The verb *to be* is the auxiliary verb that is used to help form the six tenses of the passive voice. If you are familiar with the conjugation of the verb *to be*, you will have no difficulty in forming the passive voice of any verb that takes an object.

The passive voice is formed by combining the verb *to be* with the **past participle** of the principal verb. The principal verb is the verb that names the action.

The verb *was washed* in the sentence, *The car was washed by Ned*, is made up of the auxiliary verb *was*, which is a form of the verb *to be*. The *past participle* of the principal verb is added to the auxiliary *was*. The past participle of the verb *wash* is *washed*. The verb phrase is *was washed*. It is a verb phrase in the passive voice.

The verb phrases in the following sentences are in the *passive voice*. They are formed by combining some form of the verb *to be* with the past participle of the principal verb, or the verb that names the action.

The plans will be made by the general.

Trees have been planted in the park by the commissioners.

The verb in the first sentence is *will be made*. It is made up of the auxiliary *will be*, which is a form of the verb *to be* and the past participle of the verb *make*, which is *made* (*will be made*).

The verb in the second sentence is *have been planted*. It is made up of the auxiliary verb *have been*, which is a form of the verb *to be* and the past participle of the verb *plant* (*planted*).

The six tenses of the verb *call* were given in Chapter Thirteen for the *active voice*. The forms for the *passive voice* follow. If you examine these forms carefully, you will see that the tenses follow the regular conjugation of the verb *to be*. The past participle of the verb *call* (*called*) is added to the forms of the verb *to be*.

SIX TENSES OF THE VERB "CALL"

PASSIVE VOICE
Singular and Plural

PRESENT TENSE

First person:	I *am* called
	we *are* called
Second person:	you *are* called
	you *are* called
Third person:	he *is* called
	they *are* called

PAST TENSE

First person:	I *was* called
	we *were* called
Second person:	you *were* called
	you *were* called
Third person:	he *was* called
	they *were* called

FUTURE TENSE

First person:	I *shall be* called
	we *shall be* called
Second person:	you *will be* called
	you *will be* called
Third person:	he *will be* called
	they *will be* called

PRESENT PERFECT TENSE
Singular and Plural

First person:	I *have been* called
	we *have been* called
Second person:	you *have been* called
	you *have been* called
Third person:	he *has been* called
	they *have been* called

PAST PERFECT TENSE

First person:	I *had been* called
	we *had been* called
Second person:	you *had been* called
	you *had been* called
Third person:	he *had been* called
	they *had been* called

FUTURE PERFECT TENSE

First person:	I *shall have been* called
	we *shall have been* called
Second person:	you *will have been* called
	you *will have been* called
Third person:	he *will have been* called
	they *will have been* called

SIX TENSES OF THE IRREGULAR VERB "KNOW"

PASSIVE VOICE

Singular and Plural
PRESENT TENSE

First person:	I *am* known
	we *are* known
Second person:	you *are* known
	you *are* known
Third person:	he *is* known
	they *are* known

PAST TENSE

First person:	I *was* known
	we *were* known
Second person:	you *were* known
	you *were* known
Third person:	he *was* known
	they *were* known

FUTURE TENSE

First person:	I *shall be* known
	we *shall be* known
Second person:	you *will be* known
	you *will be* known
Third person:	he *will be* known
	they *will be* known

PRESENT PERFECT TENSE

First person:	I *have been* known
	we *have been* known
Second person:	you *have been* known
	you *have been* known
Third person:	he *has been* known
	they *have been* known

PAST PERFECT TENSE

First person:	I *had been* known
	we *had been* known
Second person:	you *had been* known
	you *had been* known
Third person:	he *had been* known
	they *had been* known

SIX TENSES OF THE IRREGULAR VERB "KNOW" (Cont'd)

FUTURE PERFECT TENSE

First person:
I *shall have been* known
we *shall have been* known

Second person:
you *will have been* known
you *will have been* known

Third person:
he *will have been* known
they *will have been* known

WHEN TO USE THE PASSIVE VOICE

Since you may show that the subject is either the doer or the receiver of the action, the question naturally arises, "Which form is better?" The use of the passive voice often results in a roundabout, awkward method of expression.

In the large majority of cases the *active voice is the better form to use.* Never use the passive voice, either in speaking or writing, when the active voice would be more natural or more direct. The following illustrations show clearly that the active voice would be more natural and more direct than the passive voice.

The concert was enjoyed by us. (*passive voice*)
We enjoyed the concert. (*active voice*)

Your order was sent by us by express today. (*passive voice*)
We sent your order by express today. (*active voice*)

The stranger was barked at by a dog. (*passive voice*)
A dog barked at the stranger. (*active voice*)

As a rule, the active voice is preferred for business writing, and for and other form of writing that requires the direct approach. The use of the *active voice increases vividness.* The passive voice expresses reversed action, since the receiver comes before the doer. Active verbs are often used in newspaper headlines because they are more vivid and take less space. The following headlines are all in the active voice:

"Lion Gets Out of Cage"
"White Sox Capture First Title"
"Urges France to Begin Defense Plan"
"Governor Advises Aid for Workers"

The passive voice is generally used when the subject of the sentence is *indefinite, general,* or *unimportant.* In the sentence, *They mine coal in Pennsylvania,* the subject is so indefinite that it is not clear what is meant by *they.* It might mean the miners, the people, or the companies. This sentence, and sentences like it, are improved by putting the verb in the passive voice.

They *mine* coal in Pennsylvania. (*poor*)
Coal *is mined* in Pennsylvania. (*better*)

They *grow* wheat in many of our states. (*poor*)
Wheat *is grown* in many of our states. (*better*)

They *use* tractors on most farms. (*poor*)
Tractors *are used* on most farms. (*better*)

The passive voice is also used when *what was done,* is more important than the doer of the action. Study the following sentences:

The play, "Man and Superman," *was written* by Shaw. (*passive*)
Shaw *wrote* the play "Man and Superman." (*active*)

America *was discovered* by Columbus. (*passive*)
Columbus *discovered* America. (*active*)

In the first sentence, if you wish to emphasize the play more than the author, put the verb in the passive voice. In the third sentence, if you wish to emphasize the discovery more than the discoverer, put the verb in the passive voice.

The use of the passive voice is generally used when you want to emphasize the *receiver* rather than the *doer.* However, in the great majority of cases the active voice is more effective than the passive voice.

MOOD OF VERBS

In addition to tense and voice, verbs have another property which is called **mood** (or *mode*). The word *mood* comes from a Latin word which means *manner.* When we apply the term mood to verbs, we mean *the manner in which the verb expresses the action or state of being.*

There are three moods in English, the *indicative mood,* the *imperative mood,* and the *subjunctive mood.* The *indicative mood* is used *to make statements* and *to ask questions.* Most of the verbs that you commonly use are in the indicative mood.

The stenographer *wrote* the letter. (*statement of fact*)
Did you hear the President's address? (*question*)

The imperative mood is used to *express a command* or *a request.* The imperative mood is found only in the present tense, second person. The subject is always the pronoun *you,* which is seldom expressed.

Come here at once! (*command*)
Close the door, Jane. (*request*)

The subjunctive mood is used to *express a wish* or *a condition which is contrary to fact.* By contrary to fact we mean something which is not true. A contrary to fact condition is usually introduced by the word *if* or *as if.*

If *he were* here, I would give him the keys. (*He is not here.*)
I wish *I were* in Florida. (*expresses a wish*)

The indicative and the imperative moods do not present any problems in English. The verb has the same form to express a statement or to ask a question. You can identify the imperative mood easily because the subject is *you,* which is usually understood. The imperative mood always expresses a command or a request.

Although most of the forms for the subjunctive have disappeared from our language, there are a few forms left that you should be able to recognize and to use. The verb *to be* still retains more of the subjunctive forms than any other verb. In the following, the subjunctive forms of the verb *to be* are given.

Reference Table

SUBJUNCTIVE FORMS OF VERB "TO BE"

PRESENT TENSE——SINGULAR AND PLURAL
First person:
(If) I *be*
(If) we *be*

Second person:
(If) you *be*
(If) you *be*

Third person:
(If) he *be*
(If) they *be*

PAST TENSE——SINGULAR
First person: (If) I *were*
Second person: (If) you *were*
Third person: (If) he *were*

PRESENT PERFECT TENSE——SINGULAR
First person: (If) I *have* been
Second person: (If) you *have* been
Third person: (If) he *have* been

The subjunctive with *be* (present tense) is almost never used in informal speaking and writing. The subjunctive form *have been* instead of *has been* is also passing out of use.

In the preceding table, the forms for the subjunctive that are different from the indicative are printed in *italics;* that is, *be* in the present tense; *were* in the past tense, first person, singular, and third person, singular; *have* in the present tense, third person, singular.

There is only one change that occurs in the subjunctive in the case of other verbs. In the present tense, third person, singular, the *s* is dropped in the subjunctive.

The verb *have* has only one form in the subjunctive that is different from the indicative. In the present tense, third person, singular, *have* is used in place of *has:*

If he *have* the time, he will meet with you. (*subjunctive*)
He *has* the time, he will meet with you. (*indicative*)

If he fail—— (not *fails*)
If he have—— (not *has*)
If he call—— (not *calls*)

The word *if* is not a part of the subjunctive. The forms for the subjunctive are usually given with the word *if* because the group of words in which the subjunctive is used is very frequently introduced by the word *if.*

Although the subjunctive mood is rapidly passing out of use in informal speaking and writing, there are certain uses that are still observed by discriminating writers and speakers. The subjunctive expressing a *wish* and the subjunctive in a *contrary to fact condition* are two of these uses.

USES OF THE SUBJUNCTIVE MOOD

You have just learned that careful writers and speakers use the subjunctive to express a wish, a condition that is contrary to fact (not true), and a condition of uncertainty (it may be true or not true). Sometimes careful writers and speakers also use the subjunctive *in making a suggestion, in making a demand,* or *in expressing a need.*

I wish I *were* a millionaire. (wish)
If I *were* you, I should give up the contest. (contrary to fact)
If this plan *fail,* we shall give up the project. (condition of uncertainty)
I suggest that he *work* full time in the future. (suggestion)
The supervisor insists that the bookkeeper *prove* his report. (a demand)
It is imperative that the play *begin* at once. (a necessity)

The subjunctive is used in certain parliamentary expressions, such as the following:

I move that the nominations *be closed.*
He moved that the report of the committee *be accepted.*

She moved that the minutes *be adopted* as read.
I move that the meeting *be adjourned*.

The *two most important* uses of the subjunctive are the subjunctive expressing a wish and the subjunctive in a contrary to fact, condition after *if, as if,* and *as though*.

15. AGREEMENT OF SUBJECT AND VERB

One of the common errors made both in speaking and writing is the lack of agreement between the subject noun or pronoun and the predicate verb. In order to have harmonious relations between the parts of the sentence, you must have this agreement.

AGREEMENT IN PERSON AND NUMBER

The grammatical principle upon which agreement of subject and verb depends is very simple: *The verb must agree with its subject in person and number.* If the subject of the sentence is singular, the verb must also be in the singular. If the subject is plural, the verb must also be plural. If the subject is in the first person, the verb must also be in the first person. If the subject is in the second or third persons, the verb must agree.

He *doesn't* know the answer. (correct—— subject and verb are in third person)
He *don't* know the answer. (incorrect——lack of agreement)
You were invited to the meeting. (correct—— subject and verb are in second person)
You was invited to the meeting. (incorrect—— —lack of agreement)

In the first sentence the subject and verb agree. The subject *He* is in the third person, singular. The verb *doesn't* is also in the third person, singular. In the second sentence, *He don't* is incorrect. The incorrect form for third person, singular is *doesn't* not *don't*.

Although the rule is very simple, there are a number of problems involved in agreement of subject and verb. These problems are responsible for the errors that are commonly made. Sometimes the speaker or writer does not know whether the subject should be regarded as singular or plural. Sometimes he is not sure about the form of the verb for the singular and for the plural. Sometimes he does not know which word is the real subject of the sentence.

In this unit you will consider some of the problems that are responsible for the errors that occur in making the subject and the verb agree. Your first problem will be the one that occurs when you have a sentence with a compound subject.

AGREEMENT OF VERB WITH COMPOUND SUBJECT

The parts of a compound subject are usually connected by *and, or, nor, either-or,* and *neither-nor*. Usually, when two or more subjects are connected by *and,* the subject is plural and requires a plural verb. The following examples have compound subjects:

Mary and Jane are taking Spanish.
The *president and the vice-president* speak at every meeting.

In the first sentence, the two parts of the compound subject are connected by *and*. The subject is plural and takes a plural verb, *are*. In the second sentence, the two parts of the compound subject are also connected by *and*. The subject takes the plural form of the verb which is *speak*.

There is one exception to the "and" rule. Sometimes the two subjects connected by *and* form a unit. In this case, *the subject is regarded as singular and takes a singular verb*.

Bacon and eggs is a popular combination. (*Verb is singular.*)

The Stars and Stripes flies overhead. (*Verb is singular.*)

When two subjects connected by *and* refer to the same person or thing, the subject is *singular*.

His companion and friend is very devoted to him. (*same person*)
The secretary and treasurer was present at the meeting. (*same person*)

If the subjects in the preceding sentences referred to *two individuals*, the verbs would be plural. The sentences would read as follows:

His companion and his friend are very devoted to him.
The secretary and the treasurer were present at the meeting.

By placing the word *his* before friend and the word *the* before treasurer, you clearly indicate that there are two individuals.

Subjects Connected by 'Or' or 'Nor'

When two singular subjects are connected by the word *or,* the subject is singular. The sentence means *either the one or the other*. It does not mean *both*. The same rule applies when *nor* is used to join two singular subjects. *Either or* and *neither nor* follow the same rule.

Mary or Jane is going to the fashion show. (*the one or the other*)
Neither the man nor the boy was responsible. (*neither the one nor the other*)

When one of the subjects connected by *or, nor, either or, neither nor* is singular and the other is plural, the verb agrees with the subject that is *nearer to* it. If both subjects are plural, the verb is also plural.

Neither the boy nor the men were responsible. (*Verb is plural.*)
Neither the men nor the boy was responsible. (*Verb is singular.*)
Neither the men nor the boys were responsible. (*Verb is plural.*)

In the first sentence, the plural subject is nearer to the verb. In the second sentence, the singular subject is nearer to the verb. In the third sentence, both subjects are plural. When one of the subjects is singular and the other is plural, you should put the plural subject nearer to the verb. It makes the verb plural and sounds better.

Either I or they are responsible for the small attendance.

This sentence would sound better if it were written as follows:

Either I am responsible for the small attendance, or they are.

AGREEMENT OF VERB WITH COLLECTIVE NOUNS

A **collective noun** is a noun that represents a group or a collection of objects usually considered as a unit. Words like *crowd, troop, herd, people, flock,* and *jury* are collective nouns.

A collective noun that is singular in meaning requires a singular verb. A collective noun that is plural in meaning requires a plural verb.

If the collective noun in a particular sentence represents the individuals acting as a unit, the noun is singular. If the sentence indicates clearly that the individuals are acting separately, the noun is plural. The following examples will help you see this distinction:

The *committee is opposed* to the plan. (*acting as a unit*)
The *board of directors is* in session. (*as a unit*)
The *jury returned its* verdict. (*as a unit*)
The *jury have returned* to their homes. (*as individuals*)
The *family have given* their contributions. (*as individuals*)

In most cases where the individuals composing a group are acting separately, it is better to use such expressions as *the members of the jury, the members of the family,* etc. These expressions sound better and clearly indicate that the individuals are acting separately.

The members of the jury have returned to their homes.
The people in the audience were waving their hands.

INTERVENING PHRASES

Sometimes the subject is followed by prepositional phrases or such expressions as *accompanied by, in accordance with, together with, as well as, including,* etc. The subject of the sentence is not affected in any way by the introduction of such phrases. You will never find the subject of the sentence in a prepositional phrase or in any one of the expressions listed in the following sentences:

A *package* (of books) *was delivered* today.
Materials (for the building) *have been shipped*.
Important *papers,* as well as his will, *were found* in his desk.
The *checks,* including a statement, *were mailed* today.

In the first sentence, the subject is the word *package*. Since package is singular, the verb must be singular. In the second sentence, the subject is the word *Materials*. Since the subject is plural, the verb must be plural. The prepositional phrases, of *books,* and *for the building,* do not affect the number of the subject.

The subject of the third sentence is *papers,* which is plural. The verb must also be plural to agree with the subject. The group of words, *as well as his will,* does not affect the number of the subject. In the fourth sentence, the expression. *including a statement,* does not affect the number of the subject. The subject is *checks,* which is plural. The verb must also be plural, to agree with the subject.

AGREEMENT OF SUBJECT WITH CONTRACTIONS

Contractions are verbs that have been shortened by the omission of one or more letters. The omission of the letters is indicated by the use of an apostrophe. Many persons make mistakes in agreement of subject and verb when they use contractions. The use of the contractions *don't* and *ain't* are responsible for a great many of these errors.

Although the word *ain't* is frequently heard in informal conversation, most educated persons consider its use incorrect and unacceptable.

Do not use *ain't* for *am not, are not,* or *isn't.* The contraction *aren't* should be used for *are not.* There is no contraction for the words *am not.*

I am not interested in the position. (not *ain't*)
We are not going to the theater. (not *ain't*)
We aren't going to the meeting. (not *ain't*)
Isn't this a beautiful day! (not *ain't*)

Another error commonly made is the use of **don't** for **doesn't. Don't** is a contraction for *do not.* It should not be used in the third person, singular. The expressions, *it don't, he don't* and *she don't* are incorrect. Do no misuse them for *it doesn't, he doesn't,* and *she doesn't.*

It *don't* make any difference. (incorrect)
It *doesn't* make any difference. (correct)

He *don't belong to our union.* (incorrect)
He *doesn't* belong to our union. (correct)

AGREEMENT OF VERB WITH INDEFINITE PRONOUNS

The indefinite pronouns *one, no one, anyone, everyone, someone, anybody, nobody, everybody, somebody, each, either,* and *neither* are always singular. Since these pronouns are singular, they take a singular verb.

Only *one* of the candidates is eligible. (*singular verb*)
Each of these bags has been examined. (*singular verb*)
Neither has lost his ticket. (*singular verb*)
Somebody is responsible for the accident. (*singular verb*)
Anyone has the right to offer criticism. (*singular verb*)
Nobody has access to the vault. (*singular verb*)

When *many a, each,* and *every* are used to introduce a sentence and function as adjectives, the *subject* is singular.

Many a *man* wishes that he had gone to college.
Each *window* and *door* was locked securely.
Every *man, woman,* and *child* is expected to report.

The indefinite pronouns *several, few, both* and *many* are always plural.

Several were called to the platform. (*plural verb*)
A *few* were opposed to the bill. (*plural verb*)
Both were anxious to receive the award. (*plural verb*)
Many in the audience objected to his speech. (*plural verb*)

The indefinite pronouns *some, none, any,* and *all* are singular or plural according to the meaning of the sentence. When these words refer to a *quantity* or a *mass* taken as a whole, they are generally considered as singular. When they refer to a *number,* they are regarded as plural in meaning.

Some are going by plane. (*more than one*——plural)
Some of the ice cream *is* left. (*mass or quantity*——singular)
Are any of the men going by plane? (*more than one*——plural)

Is there *any* gasoline in the tank? (*mass or quantity*——singular)
None of these apples *are* ripe. (*more than one*——plural)
We needed a ball but none was available. (*not one*——singular)
All of the gasoline *has been sold.* (*mass or quantity*——singular)
All of the women *have brought* gifts. (*more than one*——plural)

Some nouns are plural in form, but singular in meaning. Examples of nouns that take a singular verb are *mumps, measles, news, summons, physics, mathematics.*

Physics is a very interesting subject. *Verb is singular.*)
The *news* this week *is* startling. (*Verb is singular.*)
Measles is a contagious disease. (*Verb is singular.*)
Mathematics was his favorite study. (*Verb is singular.*)

SPECIAL CASES OF AGREEMENT

1. Words like *pants, trousers, pliers, scissors, shears,* and *tongs* are plural and take a plural verb. When the word *pair* is used as the subject, the subject is regarded as singular and takes a singular verb.

The *scissors* are very sharp. (*plural*)
A *pair* of scissors was left on the desk. (*singular*)

2. A plural noun which shows *weight, extent,* or *quantity* is singular, and takes a singular verb. Ten *miles* is a long distance to walk. (*singular*)
Five *dollars* is the price of the hat. (*singular*)
Twelve *inches* is the proper length. (*singular*)

3. The words *half* and *part* are singular or plural according to the meaning of the sentence. When these words refer to a *mass* or a *section,* they are singular. When they refer to a *number* of individuals or things, they are plural.

Half of the boys *are* in camp. (*number*——plural)
Half of the pie *is* left. (*mass or section*——singular)
Part of the roof *was* destroyed. (*mass or section*——singular)
Part of the guests *have* arrived. (*number*——plural)

4. When the word *number* is preceded by the article *a,* it takes a plural verb. When it is immediately preceded by the article *the,* it takes a singular verb.

A *number* of men *were working* on the project. (*plural*)
The *number* of men present *was* small. (*singular*)

5. The name of a firm is often regarded as singular even when there is a plural form in the title. If the entire name carries a plural idea, the name is regarded as plural.

Harrison Brothers are having a sale on furs. (*plural*)

The Lexicon Company publishes books. (*singular*)
Tractors *are* uGeneral Motors Company has declared a dividend. (*singular*)

6. Sometimes a sentence begins with the word *there* or *here.* Neither of these words could be the subject of the sentence. The word *there* is used either as an expletive or as an adverb. The word *here* is an adverb. When a sentence begins with *here* or *there,* you should transpose it so that the true subject will appear at the beginning of the sentence. Then it will be possible for you to determine whether the subject is singular or plural.

There are six men on the committee.
Six *men are* on the committee. (*plural subject*——*plural verb*)
Here comes the general with his staff.
The *general comes* here with his staff. (*singular subject and verb*)

Sometimes a sentence beginning with the introductory *there* or *here* has a *compound subject,* which requires a plural verb. Mistakes in the number of the verb are frequently made because the speaker or the writer does not realize that the subject is *compound.* When the sentence is transposed, it is easy to determine whether the subject is simple or compound. The following sentences have compound subjects:

There goes the boy and his mother. (incorrect)
There go the boy and his mother. (correct)
The *boy and his mother go* there. (*compound subject*——*plural verb*)

Here comes John and Mary. (incorrect)
Here come John and Mary. (correct)
John and Mary *come* here. (*compound subject*——*plural verb*)

16. PREPOSITIONAL PHRASES

Chapter Two explained that a preposition is a word that shows the relation between its object and some other word in the sentence. In this unit you will study the function of the phrase which the preposition introduces.

A *prepositional phrase consists of the preposition and its object.* Sometimes the noun which serves as the object of the preposition has modifiers, but the important words in the phrase are the two words–the *preposition* and the *object.* The prepositions and their objects are underlined.

I walked down the winding street.
The girl with red hair is an artist.

In the first sentence, the preposition is the word *down.* The object is *street.* The entire phrase is *down the winding street.* The two important words in the phrase are the preposition *down* and the object *street.*

In the second sentence, the preposition is *with* and the object is *hair.* The prepositional phrase is the group of words, *with red hair.*

In grammar, a **phrase** is a group of words, *without a subject and predicate,* that functions as *a single part of speech.* A prepositional phrase is a phrase that functions as an *adjective* or an *adverb.* Since adjectives and adverbs are modifiers, the prepositional phrase is also a modifier.

ADJECTIVE PHRASES

An *adjective phrase* is a prepositional phrase that modifies a *noun* or a *pronoun*. An adjective phrase is often the equivalent of an adjective, as you will readily see from the following illustrations:

The man *at the gate* sold us the tickets.
We followed the path *near the river.*

In the first sentence, the prepositional phrase is *at the gate.* It is an adjective phrase because it modifies the noun *man.* The phrase, *at the gate,* is the equivalent of an adjective because it means the *gate* man.

In the second sentence, the prepositional phrase is *near the river.* This is also an adjective phrase because it modifies the noun *path.* The sentence means that we followed the *river path.* The phrase *near the river* is the equivalent of an adjective.

Like the adjective, the adjective phrase *describes* or *limits* the noun or pronoun which it modifies.

She wore a hat *with blue trimming.* (describes the hat)
He lives in the house *to your right.* (limited to a particular house)

An adjective phrase may follow the noun which it modifies, or it may be used in the predicate after a linking verb.

The accident *on the bridge* was not serious. (follows the noun)
The injured man seemed *in a daze.* (follows a linking verb)

You will not acquire skill in recognizing prepositional phrases unless you become familiar with the words that are commonly used as prepositions. This list appeared in Chapter Two, and it is repeated here for reference. Refer to this list until you are able to identify the prepositions that are in common use.

Commonly Used Prepositions

above	at	by	into	toward
about	before	down	like	through
across	behind	during	near	under
after	below	except	of	until
against	beneath	for	off	up
among	between	in	since	with
around	but	inside	to	within
	(except)			

The fact that a word appears in this list does not mean that it is always used as a preposition. Many of the words that are commonly used as prepositions are also used as adverbs.

Planes were flying *above the city.* (*Above* is a preposition.)
Planes were flying *above.* (*Above* is an adverb.)

ADVERBIAL PHRASES

An *adverbial phrase* is a prepositional phrase that modifies a *verb,* an *adjective,* or an *adverb.* Like the adverb, the adverbial phrase answers the questions: *when? where? how?* and *to what extent?* Adverbial phrases express *time, place, manner,* and *degree.*

I shall return *at noon.* (Phrase expresses *time.*)
The sailor was working *on the deck.* (Phrase expresses *place.*)
Tell the story *in your own words.* (Phrase expresses *manner.*)

In the first sentence, the adverbial phrase is *at noon.* The phrase tells *when* or at what time I shall return. It modifies the verb *shall return.*

The adverbial phrase in the second sentence is *on the deck.* This phrase tells *where* or *at what place* the sailor was working. It modifies the verb *was working.* The adverbial phrase in the third sentence is *in your own words.* It tells *how* or *in what manner* you should tell the story. The phrase modifies the verb *tell.*

Adverbial phrases that modify verbs are very easy to identify. Those that modify adjectives and adverbs are not always easy to identify. The adverbial phrase that modifies an adjective usually follows that adjective. Study the following illustration carefully:

The child seemed afraid *of the noise.* (modifies *afraid*)

In this sentence, the adverbial phrase *of the noise* modifies the predicate adjective *afraid.* Adverbial phrases that modify adjectives usually follow this pattern.

COMPOUND OR PHRASAL PREPOSITIONS

A preposition is not always a single word. There are a number of prepositions in common use that are made up of a group of two or more words. Such prepositions are called **compound prepositions** or **phrasal prepositions.**

Although the *compound preposition* consists of two or more words, it is regarded as a unit, or as a single preposition. The following list includes the compound prepositions that are in common use:

according to	in consideration of
along side of	in apposition with
along with	in front of
because of	in regard to
by means of	in respect to
by reason of	in spite of
by way of	instead of
contrary to	on account of
for the sake of	out of
in addition to	with reference to
in accordance with	with regard to
in case of	with respect to

Compound Prepositions in Sentences

In compliance with his request, we closed the account.
According to our schedule, the job will be completed tomorrow.
The president resigned *on account of illness.*

PRONOUNS USED AS OBJECT OF PREPOSITIONS

You have already learned that the object of a preposition is always in the **objective case.** When nouns are used as objects of prepositions, they do not present a problem because nouns do not have different forms for the objective case.

Pronouns do present a problem in case because some of the *personal pronouns* and the pronoun *who* have one form for the nominative case and another form for the objective case. When a pronoun is used as the object of a preposition, the form for the objective case must be used.

It is incorrect to use the forms *I, he, she, we, they,* or *who* as objects of prepositions. They are **nominative case** forms. The correct forms to use are *me, him, her, us, them,* and *whom.* In the following sentences, all the pronouns that are used as objects of prepositions are in the **objective case:**

The speaker spoke to **me** after the meeting. (*me*——objective case)
I went to the Art Institute with **her.** (*her*——objective case)
We looked at **him** while he was dancing. (*him*——objective case)
The women prepared a dinner for **them.** (*them*——objective case)
The librarian found the books for **us.** (*us*——objective case)
For **whom** are you working now? (*whom*——objective case)

Watch the two words, *but* and *like,* carefully when they are followed by pronouns. The word *but* is a preposition when it means *except.* When the word *but* is used as a preposition, it must be followed by the objective case. Similarly, when the word *like* is used as a preposition, it must be followed by the objective case of the pronoun. As a preposition, *like* means *similar to,* or *in a manner similar to.* (Other uses of the word *like* will be found in Chapter 19.)

No one knew the answer **but** me. (*but*—— preposition)
His son looks **like** him. (*like*——preposition)

THE CORRECT USE OF PREPOSITIONS

Many of the common prepositions are often used incorrectly. Since a preposition expresses a relationship between the object and some other word in the sentence, the preposition that you use must be selected with care. Very often the speaker or writer is not aware of the distinctions in meaning that careful writers and speakers observe in using prepositions. The following are some of the prepositions that you should use with discrimination.

Differences in Meaning

1. **Around, about.** *Around* means encircling. *About* often means approximately. Do not use *around* when you mean approximately.

The fish weighed *around* three pounds. (incorrect)
The fish weighed *about* two pounds. (correct)
She tied a ribbon *about* her head. (incorrect)
She tied a ribbon *around* her head. (correct)

2. **Agree to, agree with.** One *agrees to* a proposal, but *agrees with* a person.

The members *agreed with* the president. (correct——person)
I *agree to* your plan for saving money. (correct——proposal)

3. **Beside, besides.** *Beside* means by the side of. *Besides* means in addition to.

Margaret sat *beside* her father. (*by the side of*)
There were three *besides* Jerry in the boat. (*in addition to*)

4. **Between, among.** *Between* is used when referring to two. *Among* is used when referring to more than two.

Frank and Harry divided the money *between* them. (*two persons*)
The money was divided *among* the five heirs. (*more than two*)

5. **Differ with, differ from.** One differs *with* a person in the matter of opinion. A person or thing *differs from* another in certain respects; that is, the person or thing is *unlike* another in certain respects.

I *differ with* you about his qualifications. (*matter of opinion*)

Maine *differs from* Florida in many ways. (*in certain respects*)

6. **Different from, different than.** *Different from* is correct. Do not use *different than*, which is incorrect.

The motion picture is *different from* the book. (correct)

The motion picture is *different than* the book. (incorrect)

7. **In, into.** The preposition *in* indicates location or motion within a place. *Into* indicates motion *toward the inside* of a place from the outside.

The tea was held *in* the garden. (*within a place*)

The swimmer jumped *into* the pool. (*from the outside*)

He swam *in* the pool. (*motion within a place*)

8. **In back of, behind.** *In back of* should never be used for *behind*.

The car is *in back* of the house. (incorrect)
The car is *behind* the house. (correct)

9. **Over, more than.** *Over* expresses the idea of *place*. *More than* expresses the idea of *quantity*.

The actress has *over* a hundred dresses. (incorrect)

The actress has *more than* a hundred dresses. (correct)

She wore a cape *over* her shoulders. (correct——*place*)

10. **Outside of, except.** Do not use *outside of* when you mean *except*.

No one went *outside of* James. (incorrect)
No one went *except* James. (correct)

11. **To, too.** The preposition *to* should not be confused with the adverb *too*.

I am going *to* the Dunes. (preposition *to*)
Will you go, *too*? (adverb, meaning *also*)

12. **Within, inside of.** Do not use *inside of* to express time. Use *within*.

He will leave *inside of* a week. (incorrect)
He will leave *within* a week. (correct)

13. **In regard to, with regard to.** Do not say *in regards to* or *with regards to*. The correct expressions are *in regard to* and *with regard to*.

In regards to your order (incorrect)
In regard to your order (correct)

14. **Unnecessary prepositions.** Do not use *off of* for *off*. The *of* should not be added. Always omit the unnecessary prepositions in sentences like the following:

He jumped *off of* the pier. (*of* is superfluous)
He jumped *off* the pier. (correct)
Where is he *at*? (incorrect)
Where is he? (correct)
Where is he going *to*? (incorrect)
Where is he going? (correct)
Is the rain over *with*? (incorrect)
Is the rain over? (correct)

POSITION OF THE PREPOSITION

Many persons believe that it is incorrect to end a sentence with a preposition. Very often it is more natural and more emphatic to place the preposition at the end of the sentence. In many questions, the preposition comes naturally at the end. But a preposition should not be used at the end of a sentence if it sounds awkward or changes the meaning of the sentence. The following sentences end with a preposition. The prepositions fall naturally and correctly at the end.

Whom are you looking *for*?
What kind of plane is he traveling *in*?
They sold the car you were looking *at*.

Ordinarily, the preposition should not be placed at the end of the sentence. However, many of our best writers and speakers occasionally end sentences in this way.

17. THE COMPOUND SENTENCE

Chapter Four explained that there are four types of sentences: *declarative, interrogative, imperative,* and *exclamatory sentences.* A particular sentence falls into one of these groups according to the purpose which it serves.

When you make a statement, you use a declarative sentence, but when you ask a question, you use an interrogative sentence. If your purpose is to issue a command or make a request, you use the imperative sentence. When you want to express strong feeling or sudden emotion, you use an exclamatory sentence.

KINDS OF CLAUSES

There is still another way of classifying sentences. This classification is based upon the internal structure of the sentence or the way in which it is built up. Thus far, we have been dealing with the sentence that has the simplest form of internal structure——the *simple sentence.* We have been dealing with the simple sentence because our chief problem has been the relationships that words have to each other.

In this unit you will begin a study of the more complicated sentence patterns. You will learn how to build up sentences in a number of different ways. This knowledge will enable you to express your ideas in a variety of ways and will give you more power over language.

The type of classification of sentences which you will study is based upon the *number* and *kinds* of **clauses** which a sentence contains. According to this classification, sentences are divided into four groups: *simple, compound, complex,* and *compound complex.* In this unit we shall limit our study to the simple sentence and the compound sentence.

Before you can understand the difference between a simple sentence and a compound sentence, you must have a very clear idea of what is meant by a clause in grammar.

A **clause** is a group of words that has a *subject* and a *predicate.* There are two kinds of clauses: *independent* or *main* clauses and *dependent* or *subordinate* clauses.

INDEPENDENT CLAUSES

An **independent clause** is a group of words that has a subject and a predicate. An independent clause does not depend upon anything else for its meaning. It expresses a complete thought. An independent clause is a simple sentence when it stands alone.

The officer blew his whistle and the cars stopped.

In this sentence, there are two independent clauses. The first independent clause is *The officer blew his whistle.* The second independent clause is *the cars stopped.* These clauses could be written as two simple sentences by omitting the conjunction *and.* The conjunction *and* does not belong to either of the independent clauses. It simple brings the two independent clauses together in one sentence.

The officer blew his whistle. The cars stopped.

SUBORDINATE CLAUSES

A **subordinate clause** is a group of words that has a subject and a predicate, *but the clause cannot stand alone.* A subordinate clause does not express a complete thought. It depends upon the main clause for its meaning. The connective, or the word that introduces the subordinate clause, plays an important part in making it a dependent clause. In the following sentence the subordinate clause is underlined.

The cars stopped when the officer blew his whistle.

In this sentence, the group of words, *when the officer blew his whistle,* is a subordinate clause. It cannot stand alone although it has both a subject and a predicate. The word *when,* which introduces the clause, makes the words which follow it dependent upon the main clause for the meaning. That is the reason why the clause, *when the officer blew his whistle,* is called a dependent or a subordinate clause.

The group of words, *the cars stopped,* is an independent clause. It could stand alone. It is the main clause in the sentence because it states the main idea in the sentence.

THE SIMPLE SENTENCE

A **simple sentence** is a sentence having *one* subject and *one* predicate, either or both of which may be *compound.* A simple sentence consists of one and only one independent clause. All of the following sentences are simple sentences, but some have compound subjects or predicates. The last sentence has both a compound subject and a compound predicate.

John joined the Navy. (simple subject and predicate)

John and Fred joined the Marines. (compound subject)

Mary sang and played at the concert. (compound predicate)

Mary and Jane sang and played at the concert. (compound subject and predicate)

Note that a compound subject does not mean two subjects. It means the *one* subject is made up of two or more nouns or pronouns. A *compound predicate* does not mean two predicates. It means that *one* predicate is made up of two or more verbs or verb phrases.

THE COMPOUND SENTENCE

A **compound sentence** is a sentence that *contains two or more independent clauses.* The independent clauses of a compound sentence must be joined in some way to indicate that the independent clauses form one sentence.

When you put two independent clauses or two simple sentences together to form one longer sentence, you have a compound sentence:

John joined the Navy. (simple sentence)
Harry joined the Marines. (simple sentence)

If you join these two simple sentences in order to make a compound sentence, you have the problem of punctuation and the problem of using a conjunction. The following sentences show the ways in which two simple sentences might be joined to form one compound sentence:

John joined the Navy, **but** Harry joined the Marines. (*comma and conjunction*)

John joined the Navy; Harry joined the Marines. (*semicolon*)

John joined the Navy **but** Harry joined the Marines. (*conjunction only*)

From these illustrations you can see that the independent clauses of a compound sentence may be connected in one of three ways:

1. By using a comma before a conjunction
2. By using a semicolon without a conjunction
3. By using a conjunction without a comma

All three methods of writing a compound sentence are correct. However, you will use the first method, a comma before a conjunction, much more frequently than the other two methods. You will learn more about each method of punctuation as you progress in this unit.

IDENTIFYING THE COMPOUND SENTENCE

Some persons have difficulty in distinguishing between a simple sentence with a compound subject or predicate, and a compound sentence. The point to keep in mind is that the compound sentence must be the equivalent of at least *two complete simple sentences*. Examine the following illustration carefully:

The Indian squaw cooks, sews, and builds the wigwam.

This is not a compound sentence. It is a simple sentence with a compound predicate. You could not possibly make two independent clauses out of the sentence as it is written. In order to turn it into a compound sentence, you would have to supply another subject and write the sentence as two independent clauses:

The Indian squaw cooks and sews, **and** she builds the wigwam.

COORDINATE CONJUNCTIONS

The independent clauses of a compound sentence are often connected by a coordinate conjunction. **Coordinate** means of the *same rank* or *of equal rank*. **Coordinate conjunctions** are used to connect words, phrases, and clauses of equal rank. The independent clauses of a compound sentence are of the same rank; therefore, we use a coordinate conjunction to connect them. The coordinate conjunctions that are commonly used for this purpose are *for, and, but, or, not,* and *while* when it means the same as *but*.

Use of the Comma and Coordinate Conjunction

When a coordinate conjunction is used in a compound sentence, it is usually preceded by a comma. The comma should not be omitted unless the independent clauses are very short and the thought is closely connected. Observe the use of the comma and the coordinate conjunction in each of the following compound sentences. The independent clauses are underlined.

Arthur washed our new car, **and** Ned polished it.

I may consider your plan, **or** I may disregard it.

I did not seek the position, **nor** do I want it.

Michael likes tennis, **but** he prefers to play golf.

Their team was untrained, **while** ours was highly trained.

Jack went to bed early, **for** he was very tired.

In modern writing, the comma is often omitted before the conjunctions *and* and *or*. Careful writers, however, usually place a comma before the conjunctions *but* and *for*. If a comma is not placed before the word *for* when it is used as a coordinate conjunction, *for* might be mistaken for a preposition.

USE OF THE SEMICOLON IN THE COMPOUND SENTENCE

You have learned that a comma and a coordinate conjunction are often used to separate the clauses of a compound sentence. Sometimes the ideas combined in a compound sentence are so closely related that it is not necessary to use a conjunction. In that case, a semicolon is used to separate the two clauses. The following are two important uses of the semicolon in the compound sentence:

1. A semicolon should be used between the independent clauses of a compound sentence *when they are not joined by a coordinate conjunction*. In the following sentence, there is no conjunction between the two independent clauses; therefore, a semicolon is used.

The doctor came in late; he did not stop to read the telegram.

2. When the independent clauses of a compound sentence are very long, or have *internal punctuation*, a semicolon is generally used before the coordinate conjunction. **Internal punctuation** means that there are commas within one or both of the independent clauses.

Shakespeare, a great dramatist, wrote a great many plays; and he also wrote a number of sonnets.

Temperamental and lazy, John managed to get along without working; but he was never contented or happy.

Both of these sentences have one or more commas in the first independent clause; that is, the first clause has *internal punctuation*. A semicolon is used between the two independent clauses even though a coordinate conjunction is used.

THE "COMMA FAULT"

You have just learned that two independent clauses may be joined by a semicolon when no conjunction is used. You have also learned that two independent clauses are often joined by a coordinate conjunction and a comma. The point to keep in mind is that two independent clauses should not be joined by a comma unless a coordinate conjunction is used. When a writer uses a comma between the independent clauses of a compound sentence, he makes an error known as the "comma fault." The following sentence illustrates the "comma fault."

The author wrote many stories for children, she also wrote a number of historical novels. (*comma fault*)

In this sentence, two independent clauses are joined by means of a comma. This is known as the "comma fault" because the comma is the sole connection between two independent clauses. This error may be eliminated by punctuating the sentence in any one of the three ways that have been given in this unit:

1. Use a coordinate conjunction after the comma:

The author wrote many stories for children, and she also wrote a number of historical novels. (*correct*)

2. Use a semicolon between the two independent clauses:

The author wrote many stories for children; she also wrote a number of historical novels. (*correct*)

3. Punctuate the two independent clauses as two simple sentences:

The author wrote many stories for children. She also wrote a number of historical novels. (*correct*)

A skillful writer sometimes puts commas between the independent clauses of a compound sentence. This is done deliberately for the purpose of producing a certain effect. The clauses are usually very short and similar in length and structure. The following sentence is a famous example:

"I came, I saw, I conquered.'

THE RUN ON SENTENCE

The **run on sentence error** is very similar to the "comma fault." The only difference is that the run on sentence consists of two or more independent statements that are run together without any mark of punctuation, or without any connecting word. The following sentence is an illustration of the run on sentence:

Money provided by stockholders has helped the company purchase equipment and supplies it has also enabled the company to expand its production.

In this sentence, two independent statements have been run together without any punctuation or without any connecting word or words. The sentence might be correctly written by following any of the suggestions given for removing the "comma fault."

Since the run on sentence error is commonly made, you should check your writing carefully. Be sure that you do not run sentences together without punctuation or proper connectives.

TRANSITIONAL WORDS

There is another type of connecting word that you may use between the independent clauses of a compound sentence. The words that belong in this group are not coordinate conjunctions. They are sometimes called **transitional words** because they are not pure conjunctions.

Some of these words have a slight connecting force. Others have some adverbial force. But they all belong to the independent clause which they introduce or in which they are found. Connectives that belong to this group *are always preceded by a semicolon*.

Since many of these words are regarded as independent elements, they are usually set off by commas. Words like *moreover, however, therefore,* and *nevertheless* are usually set off. Words like *then, still, yet,* and *so* are seldom set off by commas when they retain their adverbial force.

Sometimes the connection is made by a group of words. Expressions like the following are transitional words and are regarded as a single connecting word: *in fact, on the other hand, that is,* etc. Study the following illustrations carefully:

The road was unpaved; **nevertheless,** we drove on in the rain.

I missed the first boat; **however,** I arrived on time.

The president introduced the speaker; **then** he sat down.

Ethel was sick; **in fact,** she had one of her usual colds.

We arrived early; **as a result,** we had time to visit with our friends.

We cannot get materials; **consequently,** we cannot finish the job.

I became tired of doing his work; **moreover,** I had my own work to do.

I did not dislike the play; **on the contrary,** I enjoyed it immensely.

Commonly Used Transitional Words

Following is a list of transitional words which are used frequently. Become familiar with them.

accordingly	indeed	as a result
afterwards	likewise	at last
again	meanwhile	at the same time
anyhow	moreover	for example
besides	namely	for instance
consequently	nevertheless	for this reason
doubtless	next	in any case
eventually	otherwise	in fact
evidently	perhaps	in like manner
finally	possibly	in short
furthermore	still	on the contrary
hence	then	on the other hand
however	therefore	that is
yet	thus	in addition

18. THE COMPLEX SENTENCE

Chapter 17 explained how to form a compound sentence by combining two or more simple sentences into one longer sentence. It also explained how to punctuate the compound sentence when a coordinate conjunction is used, when transitional words are used, and when no conjunction is used.

The compound sentence is an important type of sentence because it enables us to combine two or more related ideas. However, it is just as ineffective to use a number of compound sentences strung along with *ands* and *buts* as it is to use a number of short, choppy sentences.

In this unit you will learn how to use a type of sentence that will enable you to put less important ideas in subordinate positions in the sentence. This type of sentence is called the *complex sentence.*

A **complex sentence** is a sentence that consists of one *independent clause* and *one or more subordinate clauses.* Subordinate means lower in rank, power, or importance. A subordinate clause is less important than an independent clause because it depends upon the independent clause for its meaning. The independent clause is also called the *main* or the *principal* clause. An independent clause is

a group of words that has a subject and a predicate, and does not depend upon anything else for its meaning. It expresses a complete thought, and can stand alone.

A **subordinate clause** is a group of words that has a subject and a predicate, but *cannot stand alone.* A subordinate clause does not express a complete thought. It should never be punctuated as if it were a complete sentence.

A subordinate clause is usually introduced by some type of *subordinate conjunction* or by a *relative pronoun.* These connecting words make it clear that the clause expresses an idea that is subordinate to the main clause. They also join the subordinate clause to some word in the independent clause. In the following sentences, the independent clauses and the subordinate clauses are underlined.

Complex Sentences

I shall be at the station when you arrive.

I shall not go to the park if it rains.

She wore a beautiful dress which her grandmother had worn.

In the first sentence, the subordinate clause is *when you arrive.* The clause is introduced by the **subordinate conjunction** *when.* The group of words, *when you arrive,* has a subject and a predicate, but it cannot stand alone. That is the reason why the clause is called a *subordinate clause.* It depends upon the main clause for its meaning.

The subordinate clause in the second sentence is *if it rains.* This group of words cannot stand alone. The clause is introduced by the subordinate conjunction *if.* This conjunction helps the subordinate clause express the idea that there is a condition upon which *my going* depends.

The subordinate clause in the third sentence is *which her grandmother had worn.* This clause is introduced by the relative pronoun *which.* The word *which* refers to the word *dress* in the independent clause. It also introduces the subordinate clause. A **relative pronoun** always joins a clause to the *antecedent* of the pronoun. In this sentence, the antecedent of the relative pronoun is *dress. Dress* is the word to which the pronoun refers.

The relative pronoun also has an important function in the subordinate clause. It might be the subject of the clause, the object of the verb in the clause, the object of a preposition, or a predicate pronoun after a linking verb.

KINDS OF SUBORDINATE CLAUSES

There are three kinds of subordinate clauses: *adverbial clauses, adjective clauses,* and *noun clauses.* Each of these different types is used as a part of speech. That is why subordinate clauses are called adverbial clauses, adjective clauses, and noun clauses.

The **adverbial clause** functions as an adverb. The **adjective clause** functions as an adjective, and the **noun clause** functions as a noun.

Adverbs modify verbs, adjectives, and other adverbs. Adverbial clauses also modify verbs, adjectives, and adverbs. Adjectives modify nouns and pronouns. Adjective clauses also modify nouns and pronouns. Nouns are used as subjects of sentences, as objects of verbs, and as objects of prepositions. Noun clauses are used in the same ways.

Subordinate Clauses

The man who received the medal was my uncle. (adjective clause)

We always stop working when the bell rings. (adverbial clause)

I believe that the bookkeeper is honest. (noun clause)

In the first sentence, the subordinate clause is the group of words, *who received the medal.* The subordinate clause is an **adjective clause** and modifies the word *man.* In the second sentence, the subordinate clause is *when the bell rings.* It is an **adverbial clause** and modifies the verb *stop.* This clause expresses *time* just as an adverb expresses *time.* The subordinate clause in the third sentence is the group of words, *that the bookkeeper is honest.* This subordinate clause is a **noun clause** and is used as the object of the verb *believe.*

ADJECTIVE CLAUSES

An **adjective clause** is *a subordinate clause that functions as an adjective.* Adjectives are used to describe or limit nouns or pronouns. An adjective clause is also used to describe or limit a noun or a pronoun.

An adjective clause is usually introduced by a relative pronoun. A **relative pronoun** is *a pronoun that joins an adjective clause to some word in the independent or main clause.* The word to which it joins the clause is the *antecedent* of the relative pronoun. The relative pronouns used in this way are *who* (*whom*), *which,* and *that.*

Adjective Clauses Introduced by Relative Pronouns

John brought the books that you ordered. (*that* —— relative pronoun)

I favored the plan which the senator proposed. (*which*——relative pronoun)

Men who are thinkers look for facts. (*who*—— relative pronoun)

I saw the salesman whom I met at the office. (*whom*——relative pronoun)

The subordinate clause in the first sentence is *that you ordered.* It is an adjective clause and modifies the noun *books.* This clause is introduced by the relative pronoun *that.* The antecedent of the relative pronoun *that* is the word *books.* The pronoun *that* joins its clause to the word *books* in the main clause.

The subordinate clause in the second sentence is *which the senator proposed.* It is an adjective clause and modifies the noun *plan.* The antecedent of the relative pronoun *which* is the word *plan.* The adjective clause limits the meaning to the *plan which the senator proposed.*

The subordinate clause in the third sentence is *who are thinkers.* The main clause is *Men look for facts.* In this sentence the subordinate clause comes between the subject and the predicate of the main clause. The subordinate clause is introduced by the relative pronoun *who.* The antecedent of *who* is *men.*

The adjective clause in the fourth sentence is *whom I met at the office.* This clause is introduced by the relative pronoun *whom.* The antecedent of the pronoun is the word *salesman.*

Relative Adjectives

Sometimes an adjective clause is introduced by the word *whose,* which is the possessive form of the pronoun *who.* In such cases the word *whose* modifies a noun which follows it. When the word *whose* is used in an adjective clause, it is called a **relative adjective.** The word *relative* is used to show that the word *whose* refers to its antecedent in the main clause.

That is the *man* **whose** car was stolen. (*man*——antecedent)

In this sentence the word *whose* is a relative adjective, modifying the word *car*. The antecedent of *whose* is the word *man* in the main clause. The word *whose* connects the clause *whose car was stolen* to the word *man*.

Adjective Clauses Introduced by Relative Adverbs

Adjective clauses are often introduced by the relative adverbs *where, when,* and *why*. When these adverbs introduce adjective clauses they relate to some word in the main clause in much the same way as a relative pronoun does. A relative adverb always has an antecedent and joins its clause to that antecedent. In addition, a relative adverb performs the function of an adverb in its own clause. It is called a *relative adverb* because it relates to an antecedent.

I found the house where the poet lived. (*where*——relative adverb)

The doctor selected a time when I was not working. (*when*——relative adverb)

I discovered the reason why he is leaving. (*why*——relative adverb)

In the first sentence, the relative adverb is *where*. It introduces the clause, *where the poet lived*. It also refers to its antecedent, *house*. As an adverb, it modifies the verb *lived* in the subordinate clause.

The relative adverb in the second sentence is *when*. Its antecedent is *time*. The relative adverb *when* joins the clause, *when I was not working*, to its antecedent *time*. It also functions as an adverb, modifying the verb *was working*.

The relative adverb in the third sentence is *why*. Its antecedent is *reason*. It modifies the verb *is leaving* in its own clause.

The only difference between a relative adverb and a simple adverb is the fact that the relative adverb is found in an adjective clause and refers to its antecedent in the main clause. Both relative adverbs and simple adverbs modify verbs.

"WHO" AND "WHOM" IN SUBORDINATE CLAUSES

It is often difficult to determine whether to use "who" or "whom" when one of these words is used to introduce a subordinate clause. Always keep in mind that *who* is the correct form for the nominative case, and *whom* is the correct form for the objective case.

When a relative pronoun introduces a clause, it has a double function. It joins the clause to its antecedent which is in the main clause, and in addition it performs one of the following three functions in the subordinate clause:

1. The pronoun may be the *subject* of the subordinate clause.
2. The pronoun may be used as a *predicate pronoun* after a linking verb.
3. The pronoun may be used as the *object* of the verb or a preposition.

In order to determine how the pronoun is used, it is often necessary to put the subordinate clause in grammatical order, or to transpose it.

Allen was the one *who published the report.* (*who*——subject)

In this sentence, it is clear that *who* is the subject of the subordinate clause. The form *who* is correct because the subject is in the nominative case.

The president is a man *whom everyone admires.* (*whom*——direct object)

In this sentence, the word *whom* is the direct object of the verb *admires*. By transposing the clause, you will be able to see this clearly: *everyone admires whom.* The subject of the clause is *everyone*, not *whom*.

Jack is the boy *to whom they gave the camera.* (*whom*——object of preposition)

In this sentence, the pronoun *whom* is the object of the preposition *to*. When the subordinate clause is transposed, the use of *whom* becomes clear: *they gave the camera to whom. They* is the subject of the clause, not *whom*.

RESTRICTIVE AND NONRESTRICTIVE CLAUSES

Adjective clauses present a problem in meaning and in punctuation. Sometimes the adjective clause is set off by commas. Sometimes the adjective clause is not set off by commas. The following sentences are illustrations of adjective clauses that are *not* set off by commas:

I spoke to the woman *who was giving the demonstration.*
This is the man *who discovered the leak in the pipe.*
I dislike driving in a town *where there are no stop signals.*

In the first sentence, the adjective clause is *who was giving the demonstration*. If you leave the clause out, the meaning of the sentence is changed. The sentence now gives no indication of *who* the woman was. Since the clause identifies that woman, it is essential to the meaning of the sentence.

In the second sentence, the clause is *who discovered the leak in the pipe*. This clause identifies the man and is essential to the meaning of the sentence. The clause restricts the meaning of the sentence to the man *who discovered the leak in the pipe*. Therefore, it is essential to the meaning of the sentence.

The third sentence does not mean that *I dislike driving in a town*. The meaning is restricted to driving in a certain type of town; that is, in a town *where there are no stop signals.*

Clauses that are necessary to the meaning of the sentence are called *restrictive clauses*. A restrictive clause is not set off by commas. A **restrictive clause** identifies the word it modifies.

Some adjective clauses are not essential to the meaning of the sentence. They give added information, but the essential meaning of the sentence would not be changed if such clauses were omitted. Study the following sentences carefully:

Mr. Miller, *who lived next door*, moved to Canada.
Will James, *who was once a cowboy*, wrote many stories.
Father, *who was working in the garden*, missed the broadcast.

The speaker, *who was accompanied by his wife*, left early.

In the first sentence, the clause, *who lived next door*, gives additional information about Mr. Miller, but the meaning of the sentence is not changed if you leave the clause out. The clause does not place any restrictions on the meaning. Therefore it is called a *nonrestrictive clause*. Nonrestrictive clauses are set off by commas.

A **nonrestrictive clause** is a clause that is *not* essential to the meaning of the sentence. All the clauses in the preceding illustrations are nonrestrictive clauses. They are set off by commas. They are not needed in the sentence to identify the person who is mentioned in the main clause.

A nonrestrictive clause functions more like an appositive or a parenthetical expression. You might call it a thrown in remark. That is the reason why the nonrestrictive clause is set off by commas.

19. ADVERBIAL CLAUSES

Chapter Eighteen explained that an adjective clause functions in the same way as an adjective functions. Adjectives modify nouns and pronouns. Adjective clauses also modify nouns and pronouns.

An *adverbial clause* functions in the same way as an adverb functions. Adverbs tell *how, when, where,* and *to what extent* the action is performed. Adverbial clauses answer the same questions and, in addition, express several other ideas which the simple adverb does not express.

Adverbs modify verbs, adjectives, and other adverbs. Adverbial clauses also modify verbs, adjectives, and adverbs. The adverbial clause modifies a verb more often than it modifies an adjective or an adverb.

SUBORDINATE CONJUNCTIONS

An adverbial clause is usually introduced by a *subordinate conjunction*. This connecting word is called a subordinate conjunction because it makes the idea expressed by its clause *subordinate to the main idea in the sentence*. The subordinate conjunction also shows the relation between the subordinate clause and the word in the main clause which the subordinate clause modifies.

The **subordinate conjunction** is used to show that the clause which it introduces is a subordinate clause, and not a main clause. The subordinate conjunction also indicates the exact type of relationship that the subordinate clause has to the main clause.

The following illustrations will make clear the function of the *subordinate conjunction* in a subordinate clause:

We listened to the radio because we wanted to hear the news. (adverbial clause—modifies listened)
She will find the telegram on her desk when she returns. (adverbial clause—modifies will find)

In the first sentence, the subordinate clause is *because we wanted to hear the news*. It is an adverbial clause and modifies the verb *listened* in the main clause. The subordinate conjunction is the word *because*.

If you leave out the word *because*, the words that follow no longer express a subordinate idea. They express a complete thought. It is the word *because* that makes the group of words, *we wanted to hear the news*, subordinate to the main clause. The **subordinate conjunction** is the key to the adverbial clause.

You should become familiar with the subordinate conjunctions that are commonly used to introduce *adverbial clauses*. The subordinate conjunction will help you identify the adverbial clause. It will also help you determine the **kind** of adverbial clause which it introduces.

WORDS USED AS SUBORDINATE CONJUNCTIONS

after	even though,	till
although	except	though
as	if	unless
as—as	in order that	until
as if	provided	when
as long as	provided that	whenever
as soon as	since	where
as though	so—as	wherever
because	so that	whether
before	than	while
even if	that	

KINDS OF ADVERBIAL CLAUSES

Adverbial clauses are used to express a number of different ideas. The following are the ten important ideas which are expressed by adverbial clauses: *time, place, manner, degree, comparison, purpose, result, condition, concession, cause (reason).*

Since the subordinate conjunction helps the adverbial clause express the idea intended, you should become familiar with the conjunctions that are used to express certain ideas, such as *time, place,* etc. The following is a list of the subordinate conjunctions commonly used in adverbial clauses of the various types:

Time: after, before, when, whenever, since, until, as soon as, while
Place: where, wherever
Manner: as, as if, as though
Degree: that, as—as, not so—as, than
Comparison: as, than, so—as, as—as
Purpose: that, so that, in order that
Result: that, so that
Condition: if, provided, provided that, unless
Concession: although, though, even if
Cause: as, because, since

Ideas Expressed by Adverbial Clauses

Time: I watched the crowd while I was waiting for you.

Place: Put the notice where it can be seen.

Manner: The soldier walks as if he were lame.

Degree: Marvin is not so industrious as his brother (is industrious).

Comparison: The train was later than it usually is.

Purpose: Ted practiced every day so that he might win the contest.

Result: The salesman was so persuasive that I finally bought the car.

Condition: I shall attend the meeting if I have the time.

Concession: Frances will sing at the concert although she has a cold.

Cause or Reason: Gerald read the book because I recommended it.

CLAUSES OF DEGREE

An *adverbial clause of degree* that is introduced by the subordinate conjunction *that* usually expresses a **result** idea as well as the idea of **degree**. The degree idea is expressed by words like *such, such a,* and *so* which precede the subordinate clause.

Jane practiced so long that she became very tired.

Harold made such a poor sales record that he lost his position.

In both these sentences, the adverbial clauses introduced by *that* express a *degree idea* and a *result idea.*

An adverbial clause of degree usually modifies an adjective or an adverb in the main clause.

He talked so loud that he annoyed the speaker.

In this sentence, the adverbial clause *that he annoyed the speaker* is introduced by the subordinate conjunction *that.* The adverbial clause modifies the adverb *so* in the main clause.

THE POSITION OF THE ADVERBIAL CLAUSE

In all of the preceding illustrations, the adverbial clause follows the main clause. An adverbial clause is often placed at the beginning of the sentence for emphasis, or for variety in sentence patterns. When the subordinate clause precedes the main clause, it is usually set off by a comma.

He went to the office when it was convenient.
(follows main clause)
When it was convenient, he went to the office.
(precedes main clause)

The men work overtime whenever it is necessary. (follows main clause)
Whenever it is necessary, the men work overtime. (precedes main clause)

In the first sentence, the adverbial clause *follows* the main clause. In the second sentence, the same adverbial clause *precedes* the main clause. The adverbial clause is placed at the beginning of the sentence for emphasis. Since the adverbial clause is in inverted or transposed order, it is set off by a comma.

The adverbial clause in the third sentence *follows* the main clause. In the fourth sentence, this same clause is placed at the beginning of the sentence for emphasis. The adverbial clause is set off by a comma because it is in transposed order.

Sometimes it is necessary to change the position of a noun and a pronoun when the adverbial clause is placed at the beginning of a sentence:

I shall visit **Margaret** in Texas if she sends me her address.
If Margaret sends me her address, I shall visit **her** in Texas.

CLAUSES OF COMPARISON

In both speaking and writing, words are often omitted that are necessary to the grammatical completeness of the sentence. Certain words are sometimes omitted because the meaning of the sentence is perfectly clear without them. Sometimes they are omitted in order to avoid using a sentence that is awkward or monotonous.

Certain words are usually omitted in an *adverbial clause of comparison* for the reasons just given. The verb is often omitted because it can be readily supplied. It is important to realize that the verb has been omitted in order to decide upon the correct form of the pronoun that should be used as the subject of the verb. We often hear sentences like the following, which are incorrect:

I am younger than **him**. (incorrect)
John can run as fast as **us**. (incorrect)

In both sentences the *incorrect form* of the pronoun is used in the adverbial clause of comparison. If the speaker had finished the clause, he would have used the correct form of the pronoun. When the clause is finished, it becomes evident that the pronoun is the *subject* of the clause. A pronoun used as the subject should be in the *nominative case.*

I am younger than **he** (is young). (*he*—subject)
John can run as fast as **we** (can run). (*we*—subject)

In the unfinished clause of comparison the word *than* is a conjunction, and not a preposition. The word *than* introduces a clause which must be finished grammatically. When we supply the words that are necessary to complete the clause, we realize that the form of the pronoun should be *he* and not *him. He* is the correct form to use for the subject. The subject requires the *nominative case.*

Study the following illustrations carefully. Pay special attention to the form of the pronoun used in the *adverbial clause of comparison.*

You have lived longer than *I* (have lived). (not *me*)
Martha sews as well as *she* (sews). (not *her*)
Some of the men worked harder than *we* (worked). (not *us*)
I speak as correctly as *he* (does). (not *him*)

"As—As" and "Not So—As" In Comparisons

The connectives *as—as* and *not so—as* are often used in sentences that contain adverbial clauses of comparison. Careful writers and speakers make a distinction in the use of these combinations. They use *as—as* when the comparison is **positive,** and *not so—as* when the comparison is **negative.**

The comparison is said to be positive when the two things compared are approximately the same or equal. The comparison is said to be negative when there is an inequality between the two things compared. An illustration will help make this clear.

John is **as** tall **as** his brother. (positive comparison)
John is **not so** tall **as** his father. (negative comparison)

In the first sentence, the comparison is *positive.* The two persons compared are approximately *equal* in height. The combination *as—as* is used to indicate this type of comparison. In the second sentence, the combination *not so—as* is used to show an *inequality* in height, or a *negative* comparison.

In speaking and in informal writing *as—as* is commonly used to show both types of comparison—positive and negative. However, in formal writing it is advisable to observe the distinctions that discriminating writers make.

Use of "Like" in Clauses

The word *like* is commonly used as a preposition. When the word *like* is used as a preposition, it should be followed by an object.

If the object is a pronoun, the pronoun should be in the *objective case.* This usage was explained in Chapter 16.

Many careful speakers and writers feel that *like* should not be used as a conjunction to introduce a subordinate clause of manner or comparison. The words *as, as if,* and *as though* should be used to introduce this type of clause.

I shall write the letter *like* you advised me. (colloquial)
I shall write the letter *as* you advised me. (preferred)

You look *like* you were tired. (colloquial)
You look *as if* you were tired. (preferred)

It looks *like* it might snow. (colloquial)
It looks *as if* it might snow. (preferred)

In the last few years, the colloquial use of *like* as a conjunction has increased. This use sometimes appears in print. We often hear the word *like* used as a conjunction in popular television programs. However, in general, it has not been accepted as standard English for written use.

When *like* is used as a preposition, it means *similar to,* or *in a similar manner to.*

Mary's hat is *like* the one I bought in Paris. (*like*—preposition)
John is *like* his father in temperament. (*like*—preposition)

20. NOUN CLAUSES

Chapters Eighteen and Nineteen explained the form and function of two types of subordinate clause—the *adjective clause* and the *adverbial clause.* In this unit you will study the form and function of another type of subordinate clause—the *noun clause.*

You have learned that adjective clauses and adverbial clauses are used as *modifiers* in the same way that adjectives and adverbs are used as modifiers. Noun clauses are not used as modifiers. They perform tha same functions that a *noun* performs.

FUNCTION OF THE NOUN CLAUSE

Noun Clause — Subject of a Sentence

A noun is commonly used as the *subject* of a sentence. A *noun clause* may also be used as the **subject** of a sentence. The following illustrations show how the noun clause is used as the subject of a sentence. The whole clause is the subject.

What the chairman proposed was not practical.
How you manage on your income is a puzzle to me.
That their house is for sale is a well-known fact.
Where we could find an apartment was our problem.

The subject of a sentence usually tells what we are talking about. The noun clause in the first sentence tells *what* was not practical; namely, *What the chairman proposed.* In the second sentence, the subject, or the noun clause, tells *what* it is that is a puzzle to me; namely, *How you manage on your income.* In the third sentence, the noun clause tells *what* is a well-known fact; namely, *That their house is for sale.* The noun clause in the last sentence tells *what our problem was.*

If you examine the preceding illustrations, you will see that the following words introduce the noun clauses: *what(how, that,* and *where.* These same words are often used to introduce adjective or adverbial clauses. The only way to be sure that you are dealing with a *noun clause* is to determine how the clause is used in the sentence. If it functions in the way that a noun functions, it is a noun clause.

Noun Clause — Direct Object of a Verb

A *noun clause* is frequently used as the **direct object** of a verb. A noun used as an object completes the meaning of the verb and answers the question *What?* A noun clause used as the direct object of a verb completes the verb and in almost all cases answers the question *What?* Study the following illustrations. They show how noun clauses are used as objects of verbs:

I hope (*what?*) that you will be promoted. (object of *hope*)
We knew (*what?*) where we could park the car. (object of *knew*)
Tell the manager (*what?*) why you are leaving. (object of *tell*)
I believe (*what?*) that it is going to rain. (object of *believe*)
He understood (*what?*) what we were trying to do. (object of *understood*)

The noun clause in the first sentence tells *what I hope.* It is used as the object of the verb *hope.* The noun clause in the second sentence tells *what we knew.* It is the object of the verb *knew.* The noun clause in the third sentence tells *what you should tell the manager.* It is the object of the verb *tell.* The noun clause in the fourth sentence tells *what I believe.* The noun clause in the last sentence tells *what he understood.*

Noun Clause — Predicate Noun

A *noun clause* may be used as a **predicate noun** after one of the linking verbs. Like the predicate noun, a noun clause used after a linking verb means the same as the subject. It is also used to complete the verb. The noun clauses in the following sentences are used as *predicate nouns* after linking verbs:

The rumor was that he had left the city. (means the same as *rumor*)
That is what we agreed to do. (means the same as *that*)
My first impression was that I had seen him before. (means the same as *impression*)
The report was that he was drowned. (means the same as *report*)

The noun clause in the first sentence is *that he had left the city.* It completes the verb *was* and means the same as the subject *rumor.* The noun clause in the second sentence is *what we agreed to do.* It completes the linking verb *is* and means the same as the subject *that.* The noun clause in the third sentence is *that I had seen him before.* It completes the linking verb *was* and means the same as the subject *impression.* The noun clause in the last sentence means the same as *report* and completes the linking verb *was.*

Noun Clause — Object of a Preposition

Like the noun, a *noun clause* is sometimes used as the **object of a preposition.** You may often find it difficult to determine whether the noun clause is the object of the preposition or whether some word in the clause is the object of the preposition. If you study the following illustrations carefully, you will see why an entire *clause* is the object of the preposition.

Give the message to whoever is in the office. (noun clause—object of the preposition *to*)
We did not agree about what the doctor ordered. (noun clause—object of the preposition *about*)
Do the job in whatever way you wish. (noun clause—object of *in*)

In the first sentence, the noun clause *whoever is in the office* is the object of the preposition *to.* Whoever could not be the object of the preposition because it is the subject of the clause. In addition, the sentence does not mean that you should give the message to *whoever.* It means that you should give the message to *whoever is in the office.* The entire clause is the object of the preposition *to.*

In the second sentence, the noun clause *what the doctor ordered* is the object of the preposition *about.* The sentence does not mean that we did not agree about *what.* It means that we did not agree about *what the doctor ordered.* The word *what* could not be the object of the preposition because it has another function to perform in the clause. It is the object of the verb *ordered.*

The noun clause in the third sentence must be the object of the preposition. The word *way* could not be the object of the preposition because that is not the meaning intended. The sentence does not mean that you should do the job in *whatever way,* but it means that you should do the job in *whatever way you wish.* The entire clause is the object of the preposition *in.*

OMISSION OF THE CONNECTING WORD

Sometimes the word that introduces a subordinate clause is omitted. The reason for this omission is to bring the main idea and the subordinate idea closer together. Although the best writers and speakers often omit the connecting word, you should supply it whenever there is any doubt about the construction of the clause.

I believe that you will be promoted. (*that*—subordinate conjunction)
I believe you will be promoted. (subordinate conjunction omitted)

NOUN CLAUSE USED AS AN APPOSITIVE

A noun is often used *in apposition* with another noun. The word **apposition** comes from two Latin words which mean "*placed by*" or "*put near to.*" A word in *apposition* is placed near another word to explain it or to identify it in some way. We often speak of a person and then add something to explain who the person is, or to identify him in some way.

Mike, our *janitor,* is very accommodating.
We called on Dr. Allen, a famous *scientist.*
Paris, a *city* in France, is famous as a fashion center.

In the first sentence, the noun *janitor* is in apposition with the noun *Mike.* It explains who Mike was. In the second sentence, *scientist* is in apposition with *Dr. Allen.* It identifies him as a scientist. In the third sentence, *city* is in apposition with *Paris.*

In all three sentences the nouns that are in apposition with other nouns are set off by commas. Sometimes the appositive is so closely connected with the noun that no commas are required. It is not good practice to set off the appositive by commas in sentences like the following:

My brother Andrew is in London.
The poet Whittier wrote "Snowbound."

Like the noun, a *noun clause* is often used in **apposition** with a word or a group of words. When the noun clause is used in apposition, it usually explains such words as *idea, fact, belief, report, rumor,* etc. Noun clauses used in apposition are not set of by commas.

The rumor that John would be elected spread rapidly.
The fact that the contract was signed was important.
The announcement that the strike was over was received with cheers.
We entertained the hope that the crew had survived.

NOUN CLAUSE AND THE INTRODUCTORY "IT"

Sometimes a sentence begins with the introductory word *it*. In sentences of this type the word *it* is not the real subject of the sentence. The grammatical or real subject appears later. The real subject is often a *noun clause.* Sentences are arranged in this way either for emphasis or for smoothness.

It is obvious that you do not have the money.
(It) That you do not have the money is obvious.
  (*transposed order*)

This sentence begins with the introductory word *it.* The real or grammatical subject appears later in the sentence. The subject is the noun clause, *that you do not have the money.* When the sentence was transposed, the word *it*, which has no grammatical connection with any part of the sentence, was dropped, and the real subject was put in its proper place.

The word *it* has only one purpose in sentences of this type. It fills in the place normally occupied by the subject. Its function is similar to that of the introductory word *there*, which was explained in Chapter Four. When the word *it* is used in this way, it is called an **expletive.**

Sentences that begin with *it* as an expletive, or "filling in" word, are easily recognized because they always follow the same pattern:

It is important that you see him at once.
(It) That you see him at once is important.
  (*transposed order*)

WORDS THAT INTRODUCE NOUN CLAUSES

A *noun clause* may be introduced by a **subordinate conjunction.** The subordinate conjunctions commonly used in this way are *that, whether,* and *whether or.* The sole duty of the subordinate conjunction is to connect the noun clause to the main clause.

I wonder *whether* they will recognize me.
John knows *that* he will be nominated for an office.

Whether (not *if*) should be used to introduce noun clauses used as the direct object of the verbs *say, learn, understand, know, doubt, ask, tell, discover, wonder,* etc.

Ask John *if* he has washed the car.
  (incorrect)
Ask John *whether* he has washed the car.
  (correct)
I did not know *if* he would leave or stay.
  (incorrect)
I did not know *whether* he would leave or stay.
  (correct)

A noun clause is often introduced by a **relative pronoun:** *who, what, whatever, whoever, whomever, whichever. Whoever* and *whomever* are seldom used in informal writing and speaking.

The agent does not know *what* he should do about repairs.
Give to the fund *whatever* you can afford.
A copy of the speech was given to *whoever* wanted it.

The relative pronoun that introduces a noun clause is sometimes called an **indefinite relative pronoun** because it does not have an antecedent expressed in the sentence.

Sometimes the relative pronoun is used as an *adjective* in the noun clause. A pronoun used in this way is called a **relative adjective,** or an **indefinite relative adjective** because it has no antecedent.

I shall accept *whatever salary* is offered me.
  (*whatever*—adjective modifies *salary*)
The manager always knows *what course* he should follow. (*what*—adjective modifies *course*)

Noun clauses are also introduced by the adverbs *how, when, why,* and *where.* The introductory adverb also modifies the verb in the noun clause. The noun clause is underlined in the following sentences.

How we should invest the money is the question. (*how*—adverb)
He asked where the president lived. (*where*—adverb)
I do not know when the speaker will arrive.
  (*when*—adverb)

21. PARTICIPLES

THE NATURE OF VERBALS

There are three verb forms in English that are known as **verbals:** *participles, gerunds,* and *infinitives.* Participles are discussed in this unit, gerunds in Chapter 22, and infinitives in Chapter 23. These verb forms are called *verbals* because they are derived from verbs and retain many of the characteristics of the verb.

A **verbal** may take any kind of modifier or any kind of complement that a verb might take. In addition to this verb like function, a verbal has a special function of its own. A verbal usually performs the work of two parts of speech at the same time.

There is one function that a *verbal* cannot perform. It cannot function as the predicate verb in a sentence because it is an incomplete form of the verb. A verbal cannot make a statement or ask a question.

A **participle** is a verbal (verb form) which is *used as an adjective.* Since a participle is a verb form and partakes of the nature of a verb, it may take modifiers and complements.

Participles do not always take modifiers or complements. Very often they are used as **pure**

adjectives and are placed directly before the nouns which they modify. Sometimes they are used as **predicate adjectives** after linking verbs. The following illustrations show the participle used as a simple adjective:

He conducts a *flourishing* business. (*flourishing* —— modifies *business*)
The reports were *discouraging*. (*discouraging*——modifies *reports*)
We are reading an *interesting* book. (*interesting*——modifies *book*)

The participle that is most commonly used as an adjective is the participle that ends in *ing.* This is called the **present participle.** In the following illustrations the *present participles* are placed directly before the nouns which they modify. When used in this way, they are generally regarded as pure adjectives.

running water	*singing* brook
shaking knees	*rustling* leaves
murmuring pines	*dangling* modifiers
coming events	*whistling* boy
soaring prices	*sleeping* child

The participles found in the preceding illustrations are *running, shaking, murmuring, coming, soaring, singing, rustling, dangling, whistling,* and *sleeping.* All these forms derived from verbs.

Many participles are used as pure adjectives. When the participle is used as a pure adjective, it is usually placed directly before the noun which it modifies. When the participle is used as a **predicate adjective,** it is found in the predicate and modifies the subject.

The game was *exciting*. (*exciting*——used as a predicate adjective)
The book is *interesting*. (*interesting*——predicate adjective)
The rumors were *startling*. (*startling*——used as a predicate adjective)

In the first sentence, the participle *exciting* is used as a predicate adjective, modifying the noun *game.* The participle *interesting*, in the second sentence modifies the noun *book.* In the third sentence, the participle *startling* is used as a predicate adjective, modifying the subject noun *rumors.* The participles *exciting, interesting,* and *startling* are forms of verbs.

FORMS OF THE PARTICIPLE

There are three participles that are commonly used as adjectives: the *present participle* (active voice); the *past participle* (passive voice); and the *perfect participle* (active voice). There is no active past participle in English.

These participles are easily recognized. The **present participle** always ends in *ing;* the **past participle** usually ends in *ed, d, t, n,* or *en.* The past participles of some of the irregular verbs do not have distinctive endings: *swum, drunk, gone, sung,* etc. The **perfect participle** is always formed by prefixing the word *having* to the past participle: *having sung, having called, having driven, having seen,* etc.

Regular Verbs		
Present Participle	**Past Participle**	**Perfect Participle**
(*active*)	(*passive*)	(*active*)
calling	called	having called
watching	watched	having watched
Irregular Verbs		
singing	sung	having sung
driving	driven	having driven
going	gone	having gone

PAST PARTICIPLES AND PERFECT PARTICIPLES

The past participle ending in *ed* is commonly used as an adjective. The following illustrations show how *past participles* function as *adjectives*:

A doctor, **called** to the scene, examined the injured man.
The **neglected** and **forgotten** child was picked up by an officer.
The army, **surprised** by the attack, fled into the woods.
The street was littered with paper, **thrown** from the windows.

In the first sentence, the past participle, *called* is used as an adjective to modify *doctor*. The participle is modified by the adverbial phrase, *to the scene*. There are two past participles in the second sentence, *neglected* and *forgotten*. One ends in *ed* and the other ends in *en*. These participles modify the noun *child*. In this sentence, the participles are placed directly before the noun *child*, which they modify.

The past participle *surprised* in the third sentence modifies *army*. The participle is modified by the adverbial phrase *by the attack*. The past participle *thrown* in the last sentence is modified by the adverbial phrase *from the windows*. The participle *thrown* modifies the noun *paper*.

The following sentences show the adjective use of the *perfect participle*:

Having finished the dress, Mary packed it carefully in a box.
Having completed the job, the men left early.
Having accomplished his mission, the ambassador returned home.
Having recovered completely, Ted left the hospital.

The perfect participles in the preceding illustrations are *having finished, having completed, having accomplished,* and *having recovered*. The first three take direct objects——*dress, job,* and *mission*. The last one, *having recovered,* is modified by the adverb *completely*. They are all in the active voice.

The perfect participle, *having finished,* modifies the noun *Mary. Having completed* modifies the noun *men; having accomplished* modifies *ambassador,* and *having recovered* modifies *Ted*. These participles are used as adjectives.

THE PARTICIPIAL PHRASE

Since the participle is derived from a verb, it retains many of the characteristics of a verb. Like the verb, a participle may take **modifiers** and **complements.** The participle with its *modifiers* or *complements,* or with both complements and modifiers is called a **participial phrase.**

MODIFIERS OF PARTICIPLES

A participle is often modified by an adverb or an adverbial phrase:

Looking up suddenly, Robert saw a rainbow in the sky.
Coming close to the rock, we saw a strange sight.

In the first sentence, the participle *looking* modifies the noun *Robert*. The participle *looking* is modified by the adverb *up* and the adverb *suddenly. Looking up suddenly* is a **participial phrase.**

In the second sentence, the participle *coming* modifies the pronoun *we.* The participle *coming* is modified by the adverb *close* and the adverbial phrase *to the rock. Coming close to the rock* is a **participial phrase.**

The participles in the following sentences also take *adverbial modifiers:*

Trembling with excitement, Sara waited for her friends.

(Participial phrase modifies the noun *Sara.*)
The house, remodeled recently, is very attractive.

(Participial phrase modifies the noun *house.*)
We saw an old man lying on the road.
(Participial phrase modifies the noun *man.*)

In the first sentence, the participial phrase consists of the participle *trembling* and its modifier, the adverbial phrase *with excitement.* The phrase, taken as a whole, modifies the noun *Sara.* The participial phrase *trembling with excitement* is used as an adjective, modifying *Sara.*

In the second sentence, the participial phrase consists of the participle *remodeled* and the adverbial modifier, the adverb *recently.* The entire phrase, *remodeled recently,* is used as an adjective, modifying the noun *house.*

In the third sentence, the participial phrase is *lying on the road.* It consists of the participle *lying* and the adverbial phrase *on the road.* The entire phrase, *lying on the road,* modifies the noun *man.*

COMPLEMENTS OF PARTICIPLES

1. Like the verb, a participle may take a direct object if the verb expresses action.

Carrying a suitcase, the porter entered the train.
Realizing the danger, the captain ordered a retreat.

In the first sentence, the noun *suitcase* is the direct object of the participle *Carrying.* The entire expression, *Carrying a suitcase,* is a participial phrase. The participial phrase modifies the noun *porter.*

In the second sentence, the noun *danger* is the direct object of the participle *realizing.* The entire expression, *Realizing the danger,* is a participial phrase. The participial phrase modifies the noun *captain.*

2. Like the verb, a participle may be followed by a predicate noun or a predicate adjective.

Participles that take predicate nouns or predicate adjectives as complements are forms of *linking verbs.*

Being an invalid, he could not climb the steep hill.
Becoming weary, the traveler sat down to rest.

In the first sentence, the participle *being* is followed by the predicate noun *invalid.* The noun *invalid* refers to the same person as the subject *he.* The entire expression, *being an invalid,* is a participial phrase. The participial phrase modifies the subject pronoun *he. Being* is a form of the linking verb *to be.*

In the second sentence, the participle *becoming* is followed by the predicate adjective *weary.* The entire expression, *becoming weary,* is a participial phrase, modifying the noun *traveler. Becoming* is a form of the linking verb *to become.*

PARTICIPLES USED IN INDEPENDENT CONSTRUCTIONS

Sometimes a participle is used with a noun in an independent construction; that is, the participle and the noun which it modifies are not related grammatically to any other part of the sentence. Such a construction is called the **nominative absolute construction.**

The term *absolute* is used because the entire expression is an *independent construction.* It forms part of a sentence, but is not connected with the rest of the sentence grammatically. The term *nominative* is used because the noun which the participle modifies is in the *nominative case.* The following illustrations will make this use of the participle clear. The independent constructions are underlined.

The sun having set, we decided to return home.
The train being late, the soldiers missed the boat.

In the first sentence, the expression, *The sun having set,* consists of the perfect participle *having set* and the noun *sun* with its modifier *The.* The entire expression, *The sun having set,* is used *absolutely* or independently. It has no grammatical connection with the rest of the sentence. The noun *sun* is in the nominative case.

The expression, *The train being late,* in the second sentence is also a *nominative absolute construction;* that is, it has no grammatical relation to the rest of the sentence. The noun *train* is in the nominative case. It is modified by the expression *being late,* which consists of the participle *being* and the predicate adjective *late.*

DANGLING PARTICIPLES

Participles are often used incorrectly in speaking and writing. One of the most common mistakes in English is to use what is commonly referred to as the **dangling participle.** Anything that dangles is said *to hang loosely,* without secure attachment. A participle "dangles" when there is no word in the sentence which it could properly modify, or when it seems to be related to a word which does not convey the meaning intended.

It is easy to detect these loose participial modifiers. Sometimes the use of a *dangling modifier* gives a ridiculous or a humorous slant to the meaning of the sentence. You can avoid this error if you think through your sentences carefully and relate the participle to the proper word.

When the participial phrase is placed at the beginning of a sentence, it should refer to the subject. When it could not possibly modify the subject from the standpoint of meaning, the sentence must be rewritten and a suitable subject supplied which it could logically modify.

Walking through the tunnel, a wallet was picked up.
Entering the harbor, the Statue of Liberty came into view.
Taking the test, the teacher gave me a passing grade.

In the first sentence, the participial phrase *walking through the tunnel* modifies the subject of the sentence, which is *wallet.* A participle used at the beginning of a sentence modifies the subject. It is evident that the wallet was not walking through the tunnel; however, that is the meaning conveyed by the sentence as it is written. Very often the best way to get rid of a dangling participle is to substitute a clause for it.

While we were walking through the tunnel, we picked up a wallet.

In the second sentence, the participial phrase modifies *Statue of Liberty*. But it was not the *Statue of Liberty* that was entering the harbor. The phrase seems to be related to a word which it could not modify. The word which the participial phrase really modifies is not in the sentence. The sentence might be revised as follows:

As we entered the harbour, the Statue of Liberty came into view.

In the last sentence, the participial phrase modifies the word *teacher*. If you read the sentence carefully, you will readily see that it was not the teacher who took the test. The sentence would be correctly written if a clause were substituted for the dangling phrase.

After I took the test. the teacher gave me a passing grade.

MISPLACED MODIFIERS

Sometimes there is a word in the sentence which the participial phrase properly modifies, but the participle is not placed correctly. As a result, the meaning is confused. This error is commonly referred to as a **misplaced modifier.**

Jumping into the water, the children were rescued by the life guard.
Several soldiers passed by in their uniforms recently drafted.

If you read the first sentence carefully, you will see that the word which the participle modifies is in the sentence. It is the word *lifeguard*. It was the *lifeguard* who jumped into the water. It was not the *children*. The trouble with the sentence is that the participial phrase should modify the subject. As the sentence is written, the subject is *children*. The subject should be the word *lifeguard*. The sentence might be rewritten as follows:

Jumping into the water, the lifeguard rescued the children.

In the second sentence, a participial modifier is also misplaced. As the sentence is written, the participial phrase modifies the word *uniforms*. But it was not the *uniforms* that were recently drafted; it was the *soldiers*. The sentence might be rewritten as follows:

Several recently drafted soldiers passed by in their uniforms.

PARTICIPLES USED IN VERB PHRASES

Participles are not always used as adjectives. One of their most important uses is to help form a *verb phrase*. When the participle forms part of a verb phrase, it is not considered as a separate word, but as part of the verb phrase.

A participle is never used alone as the predicate verb in a sentence because it is an incomplete form of the verb. It is used as part of a verb phrase. The following illustrations show how the participle is used as part of a verb phrase:

The janitor is washing the windows. (*washing*——part of verb phrase)
The gardener has planted the shrubs. (*planted*——part of verb phrase)

In the first sentence, the verb phrase *is washing* is made up of the auxiliary verb *is* and the present participle of the verb *wash*, or the *ing* participle, *washing*. In the second sentence, the verb phrase *has planted* is made up of the auxiliary *has* and the past participle of the verb *plant*, which is *planted*.

Sometimes it is difficult to determine whether the participle is part of the verb phrase, or whether it is used as an adjective modifying the subject. This is often true when a participle follows a linking verb. The meaning of the sentence will help you determine which use is intended by the speaker or writer. Study the following sentences carefully:

The talk was *inspiring*. (participle, used as an *adjective*)
We *were inspired* by his talk. (participle, part of *verb phrase*)

In the first sentence, the verb is *was*, not *was inspiring*. The verb *was* is a linking verb and requires a complement. In this sentence the complement is *inspiring*, which is used as a predicate adjective modifying the noun *talk*. The sentence means *inspiring talk*. *Inspiring* is a participle used as an adjective.

In the second sentence, the verb is *were inspired*. In this sentence, the past participle *inspired* is part of the verb phrase, *were inspired*. Study the following sentences carefully. Try to determine whether the participle is used as an adjective or is part of the verb phrase:

Robert was elected secretary at our last meeting. (*elected*——part of the verb phrase)
The old man looked neglected. (*neglected*—— participle used as adjective)
The milk seems frozen. (*frozen*——participle used as adjective)
The house was furnished by an interior decorator. (*furnished*——part of verb phrase)
I have been sitting here for an hour. (*sitting*——part of verb phrase)

22. GERUNDS

Nature of the Gerund

If you understand the dual nature of the participle, you will have little difficulty in understanding the dual nature of the **gerund.** You have already learned that the participle is both *verb* and *adjective*. The gerund is both *verb* and *noun*.

Gerunds are like participles in many respects. Gerunds and participles are verbals; that is, they are *forms derived from verbs*. Both participles and gerunds have the same "*ing*" forms. Both take the same kinds of complements and modifiers that verbs take.

Gerunds differ from participles in one fundamental respect. **Gerunds** *are verb forms used as nouns*. Participles are verb forms used as adjectives. Because a gerund functions as a noun, it can take certain modifiers that a participle cannot take. Like the noun, a gerund is often modified by an *adjective* or by an *adjective phrase*. Participles cannot take adjective modifiers.

Since the gerund functions as a noun, it may be used as the *subject* of a sentence, the *direct object* of a verb, the *object of a preposition*, or

as a *predicate noun* after one of the linking verbs. Gerunds are often called *verbal nouns* because they are derived from verbs.

Painting is Martha's hobby. (gerund used as *subject*).
Martha enjoys painting. (gerund used as direct object
Martha earns a living by painting. (gerund used as *object of a preposition*)
Martha's hobby is painting. (gerund used as a *predicate noun*)

In the first sentence, the word *painting* is a gerund. It is a verb form that is used as a noun. *Painting* is the subject of the sentence. In the second sentence the same verb form *painting* is used as the direct object of the verb *enjoys*. . In the third sentence *painting* is used as the object of the preposition *by*, and in the fourth sentence it is used as a predicate noun after the linking verb *is*.

The Gerund Phrase

Like the participle, the gerund retains many of the characteristics of a verb. Because the gerund is a verb form, it may take any of the complements or any of the modifiers that a verb might take. The gerund with its complements and modifiers is called a **gerund phrase.**

COMPLEMENTS OF GERUNDS

Like the verb, a *gerund* may take a **direct object.** Study the following sentence carefully. You will readily see that although the gerund is used as a noun, it retains the characteristics of a verb because it takes a *direct object*.

Sweeping the floor was one of Jack's duties.

In this sentence the *sweeping* is a gerund. It is used as the *subject* of the sentence. This is its noun function. Since the gerund is a verb form. it retains some of the characteristics of a verb. The verb *sweep* is an action verb and may take a *direct object*. The gerund *sweeping* may also take a direct object. In this sentence the direct object of the gerund *sweeping* is the noun *floor*.

Some verbs take both a direct and an indirect object. Gerunds formed from such verbs may also take a **direct** and an **indirect object.**

Giving the girls a holiday will please them.

In this sentence, *giving* is a gerund used as the subject of the sentence. This is its use as a **noun.** As a **verb form,** it takes the direct object *holiday* and the indirect object *girls*. The entire expression, *giving the girls a holiday* is a **gerund phrase.**

If the gerund is a form of a linking verb, it may take a **predicate noun** or a **predicate adjective** as a *complement*. Study the following sentences carefully. In both sentences the gerund requires a complement to complete its meaning. The gerunds are forms of linking verbs.

His becoming a captain involved certain responsibilities.
I had not heard of Jane's being ill.

In the first sentence, the gerund *becoming* takes the predicate noun *captain* as a complement. In the second sentence, the gerund *being* takes the predicate adjective *ill* as a complement.

ADVERBIAL MODIFIERS OF GERUNDS

The gerund, like the participle, may be modified by an **adverb** or an **adverbial**

phrase. You should have no trouble in identifying the adverbial modifiers of the gerunds in the following sentences:

Sitting on a park bench was his favorite
   pastime.
Driving a truck in the city is difficult.

I do not advise your seeing him now.

The gerund *sitting* in the first sentence is modified by the adverbial phrase *on a park bench.* The gerund *driving* in the second sentence is modified by the adverbial phrase *in the city.* The gerund *seeing* in the third sentence is modified by the adverb *now.*

ADJECTIVE MODIFIERS OF GERUNDS

Because the gerund functions as a noun, it may be modified by an *adjective,* or by a *noun* or a *pronoun* used as an *adjective.*

The slow driving in the mountains irritated
   Max.
(*slow*—adjective, modifying the gerund *driving*)
The dog's barking saved the child's life.
(*dog's*—noun used as an adjective, modifying
   barking)
The critics praised her wonderful dancing.
(*her*—pronoun used as an adjective, modifying
   dancing)
(*wonderful*—adjective, modifying *dancing*)

In the first sentence, the gerund *driving* is modified by the adjective *slow.* In the second sentence, the gerund *barking* is modified by the word *dog's,* which is a noun in the possessive case used as an adjective. In the third sentence, the gerund *dancing* is modified by the possessive adjective *her* (pronoun used as an adjective) and the adjective *wonderful.*

Like the noun, a gerund is often modified by an *adjective phrase.* In the following sentences, the gerunds take adjective phrases as modifiers:

We heard the rustling of the leaves.
The villagers listened to the tolling of the bell.

In the first sentence, the gerund *rustling* is modified by the adjective phrase *of the leaves.* You can readily see that the adjective phrase modifies *rustling* because the sentence means that we heard the *leaves' rustling.* The second sentence means that the villagers listened to the *bell's tolling.*

THE POSSESSIVE CASE BEFORE THE GERUND

The gerund is frequently modified by a noun or a pronoun in the *possessive case.* A mistake commonly made is to forget to put the noun or pronoun in the possessive case to show that it is a modifier. The important word in such sentences is the *gerund,* and not the modifier. The following illustration will help to make this clear:

The men objected to me playing on the team.
   (*incorrect*)

The men objected to my playing on the team.
   (*correct*)

The first sentence is incorrect because it conveys the wrong meaning. The sentence does not mean that the men objected to *me.* The word *me* is not the object of the preposition *to.* The object of the preposition *to* is the gerund *playing.* The sentence means that the men objected to the *playing.* The use of the form *me* before the gerund is incorrect. The possessive form *my* should be used.

The following sentences are incorrect because the wrong form of the noun or pronoun is used before the gerund:

I am interested in William advancing in his profession (*incorrect*)

Mother did not like me taking part in the contest. (*incorrect*)

The first sentence does not mean that I am interested in *William* primarily. but that I am interested in *Williams's advancing.* The object of the preposition *in* is the gerund *advancing,* and not the proper noun *William.* Since the noun is a modifier of the gerund, it must be put in the possessive case (*William's* advancing).

The second sentence does not mean that Mother did not like *me.* It means that she *did* not like the *taking part in the contest.* The correct form of the pronoun before the gerund is *my* (*my* taking part).

THE DANGLING GERUND

Gerunds are often found in prepositional phrases which are placed at the beginning of the sentence. The gerund or gerund phrase is the *object of the preposition.* The entire prepositional phrase should modify some work in the main part of the sentence. If there is no such word, the phrase "*dangles*" in the sentence; that is, the phrase is an unattached modifier.

The gerund almost always expresses action. There must be some word in the sentence to indicate the *doer* of this action. That word would logically be the subject of the sentence. Examine the following sentence carefully:

Upon receiving the telegram, the trip was
   cancelled.

This sentence begins with a prepositional phrase. The object of the preposition *upon* is the gerund phrase, *receiving the telegram.* The gerund *receiving* implies that someone received the telegram. The way the sentence is written, the *trip received the telegram.* The trouble with the sentence is that the subject has no logical relation to the gerund. The subject of the sentence should indicate *who* is doing the *receiving.* The following sentences are written correctly:

Upon receiving the telegram, *we* cancelled the
   trip.
   or
After we had received the telegram, we
   cancelled the trip.

This error might be corrected in one of two ways as shown in the preceding illustration:

1. By supplying the word which the prepositional phrase logically refers to.
2. By substituting a subordinate clause for the gerund phrase.

When the gerund phrase at the beginning of a sentence does not have a logical relation to the subject of the sentence, the result is often humorous. The careful study of a sentence like the following will help you understand the error and the reason for the correction:

By pressing a button, the table comes out of the
   wall. (*incorrect*) (*pressing* dangling gerund)

This sentence clearly indicates that *someone must press a button* before *the table* will come out of the wall. According to the way in which the sentence is written, *the table* performs that function. Such an interpretation would be absurd.

The trouble with the sentence is that the *subject* has no logical relation to the *gerund.* The subject of the sentence should be a word that would indicate the *doer* of the action expressed by the gerund. That word does not

appear in the sentence as it is written. The sentence would be correctly written in either one of the following ways:

By pressing a button, you will release the table
   from the wall.

If you press a button, the table will come out of
   the wall.

23. INFINITIVES

Nature of the Infinitive

Participles, gerunds, and *infinitives* are called **verbals** because they are derived from verbs and function like verbs in many respects. They are unlike verbs because they cannot function as the predicate verb in a sentence. They are incomplete forms that cannot be used to make statements, ask questions, or give commands or requests. This is an important fact regarding verbals that you should always keep in mind.

You have learned how to recognize a participle or a gerund by its form. The infinitive is very easy to identify because it carries a definite sign which indicates that it is an infinitive. An infinitive is usually preceded by the word **to,** which is commonly called the *sign of the infinitive.*

When the word *to* is used with a verb form to complete the infinitive, it is *not a preposition.* It is merely the *sign* of the infinitive. The way to be sure that the expression is an infinitive, and not a prepositional phrase, is to look at the word which follows *to.* If this word is a verb form, the expression is an infinitive, and not a prepositional phrase.

Like the gerund, the infinitive is *used as a noun.* It may also function as an *adjective* or as an *adverb.* An infinitive may take any complement or any modifier that a verb might take.

The sign of the infinitive (*to*) is usually omitted after certain verbs in order to avoid awkward or stilted expressions. The *to* is usually omitted after the following verbs: *bear, feel, watch, let, dare, help, see, make, please, bid, need,* etc.

USES OF THE INFINITIVE

You have already studied the two sided character of the participle and the gerund. The participle functions as an adjective and retains some of the characteristics of a verb. The gerund functions as a noun and also retains some of the characteristics of a verb. The **infinitive** retains its verb nature, and in addition may function as a *noun,* an *adjective,* or an *adverb.*

The noun function of an infinitive is very similar to the noun function of a gerund. An infinitive may be the *subject* of a sentence, the *direct object* of a verb, the *object of a preposition,* or a *predicate noun* after a linking verb.

To write was his ambition. (*subject*)
His ambition was to write. (*predicate noun*)
He did nothing except (to) write. (*object of
   preposition*)
He likes to write. (*direct object*)

In the first sentence, the infinitive *To write* is the subject of the sentence. In the second sentence, the infinitive *to write* is used as a predicate noun after the linking verb *was.* In the third sentence, the infinitive *to write* is used as the object of the preposition *except.* In this sentence, the sign of the infinitive is omitted. In the fourth sentence, the infinitive *to write* is used as the direct object of the verb *likes*.

INFINITIVES USED AS ADJECTIVES

The infinitive is often used as an *adjective* or an *adverb*. When the infinitive is used as an adjective, it usually modifies a noun which precedes it. It is easy to identify the adjective use of the infinitive because an adjective could be readily substituted for the infinitive. Study the following illustrations carefully:

The desire **to win** was apparent. (*the winning desire*)

They asked permission **to leave**. (*leaving permission*)

He obtained a permit **to build**. (*building permit*)

We had fresh water **to drink**. (*drinking water*)

In the first sentence, the infinitive *to win* is used as an adjective. It modifies the noun *desire*. In the second sentence, the infinitive *to leave* modifies the noun *permission*. In the third sentence, the infinitive *to build* modifies the noun *permit*. In the last sentence, the infinitive *to drink* modifies water.

INFINITIVES USED AS ADVERBS

The infinitive is often used as an *adverb* to modify a verb, an adjective, or an adverb. When the infinitive is used as an adverb, it usually expresses *purpose* or *degree*.

It is easy to identify an infinitive used as an adverb when it modifies a verb. In almost every case, the infinitive expresses *purpose*. It tells why, or for what purpose the action is performed. When an infinitive is used in this way, it is often called the *infinitive of purpose*. The infinitives in the following illustrations express purpose and modify the verb:

The traveler stopped **to rest**. (*to rest—expresses purpose*)

The composer came **to listen**. (*to listen—expresses purpose*)

The officer returned **to help**. (*to help—expresses purpose*)

In the first sentence, the infinitive *to rest* modifies the verb *stopped*. The infinitive expresses purpose; that is, it tells why the traveler stopped. The infinitive *to listen* modifies the verb *came*. The infinitive also expresses purpose. It tells why the composer came. The infinitive in the third sentence tells why the officer returned. It modifies the verb and expresses purpose.

An infinitive used as an adverb frequently modifies an *adjective*. This use of the infinitive is also easy to identify. In most cases, the infinitive modifies an adjective which follows a linking verb. Examine the following illustrations carefully:

The cake was ready **to bake**. (*to bake modifies the adjective ready*)

The men were anxious **to work**. (*to work modifies the adjective anxious*)

We are sorry **to leave**. (*to leave modifies the adjective sorry*)

I shall be glad **to help**. (*to help modifies the adjective glad*)

In the first sentence, the linking verb *was* is followed by the predicate adjective *ready*. The adjective *ready* is modified by the infinitive *to bake* which is used as an adverb. As you have learned, only adverbs can modify adjectives. The sentence means that the cake was ready *for baking*. The infinitive *to bake* could readily be turned into an adverbial phrase. This should make its adverbial function clear.

In the second sentence, the linking verb *were* is followed by the predicate adjective *anxious*. The adjective *anxious* is modified by the infinitive *to work*. In the third sentence, the predicate adjective *sorry* is modified by the infinitive *to leave*. In the last sentence, the predicate adjective *glad* is modified by the infinitive *to help*.

In all of the preceding illustrations a linking verb is followed by a predicate adjective. The predicate adjective is modified by an infinitive which is used as an adverb.

COMPLEMENTS OF INFINITIVES

Like the gerund and the participle, the infinitive may take any kind of complement a verb might take. Sometimes the infinitive takes a *direct object*. Sometimes it takes both a *direct* and an *indirect object*. If the infinitive is a form of a linking verb, it may take a *predicate noun* or a *predicate adjective* as a complement.

Arlene wanted to buy a fur coat. (*coat* object of *to buy*)

The tailor promised to make me a suit. (*me* indirect object) (*suit* direct object)

John would like to be an aviator. (*aviator* predicate noun)

His ambition is to become rich. (*rich* predicate adjective)

In the first sentence, the infinitive *to buy* takes the direct object *coat*. In the second sentence, the infinitive *to make* takes both an indirect object and a direct object. *Me* is the indirect object and *suit* is the direct object. In the third sentence, the infinitive *to be* takes the predicate noun *aviator* as a complement. In the last sentence, the infinitive *to become* takes the predicate adjective *rich* as a complement.

MODIFIERS OF INFINITIVES

1. Like the verb, an infinitive may be modified by an *adverb* or by an *adverbial phrase*.

The boys like to swim fast. (*fast* adverb, modifies *to swim*)

The boys like to swim in Lake Michigan. (adverbial phrase modifies *to swim*)

To write well is an accomplishment. (*well* adverb modifies *To write*)

To fish in that stream is a pleasure. (adverbial phrase modifies *To fish*)

2. Sometimes the infinitive has both a complement and a modifier.

To do the job properly would require a month's time.

In this sentence the infinitive *To do* takes the direct object *job*. The infinitive is also modified by the adverb *properly*.

THE INFINITIVE PHRASE

In the preceding illustration, the entire phrase, *To do the job properly*, regarded as a whole, is the **complete subject** of the sentence. This group of words is called an **infinitive phrase**. An *infinitive phrase* consists of an infinitive with its complements or its modifiers, or both if it takes both.

Ted's aim was to please others. (infinitive with a *direct object*)

We did not want to travel by plane. (infinitive with an *adverbial phrase* as a modifier)

The men would like to begin the project now. (infinitive with a *direct object* and an *adverb* as modifier)

The infinitive phrase in the first sentence is *to please others*. The phrase consists of the infinitive *to please* and its object *others*. The infinitive phrase in the second sentence is *to travel by plane*. It consists of the infinitive *to travel* and the adverbial phrase *by plane*, which modifies the infinitive. The infinitive phrase in the last sentence is *to begin the project now*. The infinitive takes the direct object *project* and the adverbial modifier *now*.

THE OMISSION OF THE SIGN 'TO'

You have learned that the sign of the infinitive (*to*) is omitted when the infinitive is used after certain verbs. The sign is not used because the sentence would sound awkward or stilted with the sign placed before the verb form. You should become familiar with the verbs that are followed by the infinitive without the sign "*to*."

The sign of the infinitive is usually omitted when the infinitive is used after the following verbs: *hear, feel let, watch, dare, help, see, make, please, bid, need, do*, etc. The following sentences illustrate the use of the infinitive without the sign. The *to* is enclosed in parentheses to show you that you should supply it mentally in order to recognize the infinitive construction.

1. I felt the floor (to) shake under me.
2. We heard him (to) sing some old ballads.
3. I saw her (to) enter the theater.
4. They bid us (to) leave immediately.
5. They dare not (to) create a disturbance.
6. Help me (to) carry the luggage.
7. Let his friend (to) help him.
8. They made him (to) wait for an hour.

24. PROBLEMS IN THE USE OF INFINITIVES

THE INFINITIVE CLAUSE

Sometimes the infinitive has its own *subject*. With this subject, the infinitive is used in a construction which is commonly called the **infinitive clause**. *The infinitive clause is not a true clause* because the infinitive cannot function as a predicate verb. An infinitive cannot function as the predicate verb in a clause because it is an incomplete verb form. The following illustrations will help make this clear:

The officers want the men to sing at the Rotary Club.

We believed him to be capable.

In the first sentence, the group of words, *the men to sing at the Rotary Club*, is called an **infinitive clause**. This expression is called a clause because the infinitive has a subject, and the entire group of words functions in the same way as a **noun clause** would function. The *infinitive clause* is used as the direct object of the verb *want*.

In the second sentence, the group of words *him to be capable* is an infinitive clause. The subject of the infinitive is the pronoun *him*. The entire expression *him to be capable* is used as the direct object of the verb *believed*, but it is not a true clause. The infinitive *to be* is not a predicate verb.

Jean asked me to go with her. (*me* subject of the infinitive *to go*)

Father advised <u>him to buy the bonds</u>. (*him* subject of the infinitive *to buy*)

He believed <u>her to be honest</u>. (*her* subject of the infinitive *to be*)

We want <u>them to build a house</u>. (*them* subject of the infinitive *to build*)

The underlined expression in each of the preceding sentences is the **object** of the preceding verb. In the first sentence, *me to go with her* is the object of the verb *asked*. The sentence does not mean that she asked *me*. It means that she asked *me to go with her*. The entire expression, *me to go with her*, is the object of the verb *asked*.

The group of words, *me to go with her*, is called an "infinitive clause." It consists of the subject *me* and the infinitive *to go* with the modifier of the infinitive, the adverbial phrase *with her*. You can readily see that this is not a true clause because the infinitive *to go* is an incomplete verb form and cannot function as the predicate verb.

The important fact to keep in mind about this construction is that the *subject* of the infinitive is always in the **objective case.** This is an *exception* to the rule that subjects of sentences and subjects of clauses are always in the nominative case.

Examine the preceding illustrations again. In the second sentence, *him* is the subject of the infinitive clause, *him to buy the bonds*. *Him* is in the objective case. In the third sentence, *her* is the subject of the infinitive clause, *her to be honest*. *Her* is in the objective case. In the last sentence, *them* is the subject of the infinitive clause *them to build a house*. *Them* is in the objective case.

You will not have any difficulty with the **case** of the subject of the infinitive. No one would think of saying, "Jean asked *I* to go with her," or "Father advised *he* to buy the bonds." It is natural to use the *objective case* as the subject of the infinitive. However, it is important to keep the following rule in mind. It will help you understand some of the other problems connected with the use of infinitives.

Sometimes the sign of the infinitive is omitted in the "infinitive clause." You must learn how to recognize such "clauses" even if the sign is omitted.

The manager made <u>Mary copy the report again.</u>
The manager made <u>Mary (to) copy the report again.</u>

I saw <u>her dance at the carnival.</u>
I saw <u>her (to) dance at the carnival.</u>

In the first sentence, the infinitive clause, *Mary (to) copy the report again*, is the direct object of the verb *made*. The sign of the infinitive *(to)* is omitted in this sentence. In the second sentence, the infinitive clause *her (to) dance at the carnival* is the object of the verb *saw*. The sign of the infinitive is omitted before *dance*.

VERB 'TO BE' IN AN INFINITIVE CLAUSE

When we use the infinitive *to be* in an "infinitive clause," we have a problem in agreement of subject and complement which is often confusing. You have just learned that the subject of an infinitive is always in the objective case. This rule applies in the case of *action verbs* and *linking verbs*.

The problem arises when the infinitive is a form of a linking verb. You learned in your previous study that the noun or pronoun used after a linking verb is in the *nominative case* to agree with the subject of the sentence. Up to this point, every word used as the subject of a sentence or of a clause has been in the nominative case. In the case of the "infinitive clause" we are dealing with a subject that is in the **objective case.**

The verb *to be*, as well as other linking verbs, always takes the same case after it as it takes before it. If the case before it is the *objective case*, the *objective case* must follow it. A noun or pronoun following a linking verb must be in the same case as the subject. Since the noun or pronoun that follows a linking verb means the same person or thing as the subject, it must agree with the subject in case. Therefore, the noun or pronoun that follows the verb *to be* in an infinitive clause is in the objective case to agree with the *subject*, which is in the objective case. This is the logical agreement of *subject* and *complement* after a linking verb functioning as an infinitive in an infinitive clause.

A few illustrations will make this clear. Notice the form of the pronoun after the linking verbs in the "infinitive clauses."

I should like <u>the chairman to be him.</u> (*chairman* objective case, *him* objective case)
Many of the guests thought <u>us to be them.</u> (*us* objective case, *them* objective case)

In the first sentence, the subject of the infinitive clause is *chairman*, which is in the objective case. The infinitive *to be* is followed by the predicate pronoun *him*. The pronoun used as the complement of a linking verb must agree in case with the subject. Since the subject is in the objective case, the pronoun must be in the objective case to agree with the subject.

In the second sentence, the pronoun *us* is the subject of the infinitive clause. *Us* is in the objective case. The pronoun that follows the infinitive *to be* must be in the same case as the subject. *Them* is in the object case to agree with the case of the subject, *us*.

THE SPLIT INFINITIVE

The parts of an infinitive (*to* with a verb form) are regarded as a unit. They should not be separated unless there is a good reason for doing so. The usual method of separating the parts of the infinitive is to place an adverb between the *to* and the *verb form*. When the parts of the infinitive are separated in this way, we refer to the infinitive as a **"split infinitive."** The adverbial modifier "splits" the infinitive.

As a rule, the infinitive should *not* be split by a modifier. Sometimes it is both desirable and effective to split the infinitive, as many authorities in grammar are pointing out. Ordinarily, it is not the best practice, as you will readily see from the following illustrations:

I asked you **to** immediately **return** my camera.
The judge was determined **to** intently and carefully **examine** the evidence.

In the first sentence, the infinitive is *to return*. The adverbial modifier, *immediately,* is placed between the sign of the infinitive and the verb form. In this particular sentence there is no justifiable reason for splitting the infinitive. The sentence would sound much better if it were written as follows:

I asked you **to return** my camera immediately.

In the second sentence, two adverbial modifiers connected by *and* are placed between the parts of the infinitive. This sentence would sound better if the infinitive were not split in this matter.

The judge was determined **to examine** the evidence intently and carefully.

Many authorities in English call our attention to the fact that some of the best writers split infinitives. When writers do this, they have a good reason for the "split." They also know how to do it so that the sentence will not sound awkward or stilted. When a writer splits an infinitive, his purpose is to throw the emphasis in a certain direction. The following are examples of split infinitives found in good writing:

1. "I feel like inviting them to <u>first</u> consider."
2. "I desire to <u>so</u> arrange my affairs"
3. "his ability to <u>effectually</u> carry on"
4. "to enable him to <u>properly</u> perform his work"
5. "to <u>better</u> acquaint myself with the problems"
6. "Our object is to <u>further</u> cement trade relations."
7. "He worked silently and swiftly, hoping to <u>speedily</u> end his patient's discomfort."

Although there is plenty of evidence that good writers sometimes split the infinitive, ordinarily it is better practice to keep the parts of the infinitive together. A writer or speaker should certainly avoid using such awkward sentences as the following:

Edwin was eager for me to <u>especially</u> see the art exhibit. *to se* infinitive)
Eugene promised to <u>never again</u> be late to work. *to be* infinitive)
The committee wanted to)<u>beautifully</u> decorate the hall. *to decorate* infinitive
I want to <u>next year</u> go to Europe. *(to go* infinitive)

In the first sentence, the infinitive *to see* is "split" by placing the adverb *especially* between the sign of the infinitive *to* and the verb form *see*. In the second sentence, two adverbial modifiers "split" the infinitive. In the third sentence, the adverb *beautifully* "splits" the infinitive. In the fourth sentence, the adverbial modifier *year* is placed between the sign *to* and the verb form, *go*. *Year* is a noun used as an adverb.

SPECIAL USES OF THE INFINITIVE

The infinitive is often used in **apposition** with a noun to explain or identify that noun. This is a very useful construction, for it enables us to explain the noun in a very few words. The infinitive used as an *appositive* is usually set off by commas. Sometimes a dash is used.

His first proposal, <u>to borrow money</u>, was rejected.
We were given our orders <u>to finish the job</u> before ten.

In the first sentence, the infinitive phrase, *to borrow money*, is in apposition with the word *proposal*. It explains the nature of the proposal or tells what the proposal was. In the second sentence, the infinitive phrase, *to finish the job before ten*, is in apposition with the word *orders*. It explains what our orders were.

The infinitive is also used as the **delayed subject** in a sentence that begins with the introductory word *it.* In this case *it* is an **expletive.**

It always pays to tell the truth.
(It) To tell the truth always pays.

It is your duty to protect your interests.
(It) To protect your interests is your duty.
Sentences that begin with the pronoun *it* used as an expletive should always be transposed in order to see the grammatical relations more clearly.

THE THREE SIDED CHARACTER OF THE INFINITIVE
NOUN USES OF THE INFINITIVE

1. **Subject** of the sentence
2. **Direct object** of a verb
3. **Object** of a *preposition*
4. **Predicate noun** after a *linking verb*
5. **Appositive**
6. **Delayed subject** after an expletive
7. May take an *adjective modifier*

The Infinitive As A Modifier

1. May function as an **adjective,** modifying a noun
2. May function as an **adrerb** expressing purpose or degree

Verb Characteristics Of The Infinitive

1. Expresses *action* or *state of being,* but *cannot* function as the predicate verb in a sentence
2. May take a complement: *direct object, indirect object, predicate noun,* or *predicate adjective*
3. May take modifier: *adverbs* and *adverbial phrases*
4. May form part of an infinitive clause.

25. PUNCTUATION REVIEW

All punctuation marks are "signals" from the writer to the reader. A period shows that a sentence has been ended or that an abbreviation has been used. A comma may show a slight break in thought, separate the two parts of a compound sentence, or be used in one of several other ways.

Keep in mind that *some sentences may be punctuated in more than one way* and that, in some instances, a punctuation mark may or may not be used at the writer's discretion.

Remember, also, that *some professions and businesses have their own style of punctuation.* A journalist, for example, may omit some punctuation marks which normally are included in a business letter. A lawyer, on the other hand, uses many more punctuation marks when preparing a legal form than are essential for most types of business writing.

OPEN AND CLOSED PUNCTUATION

The terms *open* and *closed* punctuation apply only to the business letter and only to the heading and inside address of the letter. They do not apply to the salutation and complimentary close. If your company uses *open* punctuation, as most firms do, *omit all commas and periods at the ends of lines in the heading and inside address* unless the line ends in an abbreviation. If your firm uses *closed* punctua-

tion, *include commas and periods at the ends of the lines in the heading and in the inside address.* The following examples illustrate the two styles of punctuation. Remember that most firms prefer open punctuation.

Open Punctuation	Closed Punctuation
Acme Rug Cleaners	Acme Rug Cleaners,
1823 Timber Avenue	1823 Timber Avenue.
New York, New York	Mahwah, New Jersey.
10016	07430

The salutation and complimentary close of a business letter are usually punctuated by a colon after the salutation and a comma following the complimentary close, regardless of open or closed punctuation.

USE OF THE PERIOD

1. The period (.) is used after a declarative or an imperative sentence.

She went to the office. (declarative)
Close the car door. (imperative)

Exception: If you wish to give a declarative or an imperative sentence the force of an exclamatory sentence, use an exclamation point rather than a period.

I was so shocked that I was speechless! (declarative)
Bring the Pulmotor quickly! (imperative)

2. After requests, use a period rather than a question mark.

May I send you a copy of our latest bulletin. (request)
Will you send me any further information which you have available. (request)

3. The period is used after abbreviations and initials.

Dr.	Mrs.	A.M.	Jan.
Sr.	Sat.	C. I. Jones	Inc.
B.S.	Ph.D.	U.S.A.	Gen.

Note: When a sentence ends with an abbreviation, one period is sufficient for both the abbreviation and the sentence.

Mail the package to Conley and Green, Inc.

4. The period is used to indicate the omission of words in quoted passages.

(a) Use three periods (. . .) to indicate the omission of words within a quoted passage.

"I pledge allegiance to the flag of the United States. . . one nation, indivisible, with liberty and justice for all."

(b) Use four periods (. . . .) to indicate the omission of words at the end of a quoted passage.

"Fame is the spur . . . ." John Milton

USE OF THE COMMA

1. The comma (,) is used after an adverbial dependent clause when the dependent clause precedes the main clause. When the dependent clause does not begin the sentence, the comma is usually unnecessary. (See Chapter 19 for a detailed discussion of adverbial clauses.)

After the director had read the minutes of the meeting, he called for the financial report. (comma)

The director called for the financial report after he had read the minutes of the meeting. (no comma)

2. The comma is used after a participial phrase or an absolute phrase at the beginning of a sentence. (See Chapter 21 for a detailed discussion of participial phrases and absolute constructions.)

Seeing the address across the street, he wrote a note in his little book.

The rain having stopped, we went to lunch.

3. The comma is used after an introductory infinitive phrase.

To be successful, you must read widely.

Note: When the subject of the sentence is an infinitive, do not separate the subject from the rest of the sentence.

To be successful was his goal.

4. The comma is used to set off parenthetical expressions, whether words, phrases, or clauses.

(a) Transitional words such as *however, therefore, moreover, besides, consequently* should be set off by commas.

Consequently, I did not receive an answer to his letter.

Exception: The word *also* is not set off by commas unless the writer wishes *also* to be emphasized strongly. In such a case, *also* is generally placed in an unusual position in the sentence.

We also noticed that the salaries declined after the first of the year. (no emphasis).
Also, we noticed that the salaries declined after the first of the year (emphasis intended)

(b) Phrases such as *so to speak, in short, as a result, of course* should be set off by commas.

We found, in short, many errors in his work.
Of course, there are many ways to tackle the problem.

(c) Clauses such as *I think, we suppose, he says* should be set off by commas.

Someone, I suppose, should check the report.

(d) Explanatory expressions, such as *and I agree with him, so far as he is concerned,* etc., which break the logical sequence of words should be set off by commas.

The president disliked the policy, and I agreed with him, of letting all employees name their vacation time.

5. The comma is used after introductory expressions such as *yes, indeed, surely* (when it means *yes*), *well.*

Well, the next thing we knew he had shot the deer.
Yes, I will attend to the matter.

6. The comma is used to set off a nonrestrictive clause. A nonrestrictive clause is set off because *it is not essential to complete the meaning of a sentence.* A nonrestrictive clause is similar to a parenthetical expression in that it gives added information about the word it modifies.

Restrictive clauses are never set off by commas. *A restrictive clause is a clause that is necessary to complete the meaning of the sentence* because the clause identifies the word it modifies. A restrictive clause *cannot* be left out of a sentence, whereas a nonrestrictive clause can be. (See Chapter 18 for further information on restrictive and nonrestrictive clauses.)

The girl who lives next door came to work in our office. (The clause *who lives next door* is restrictive because it is needed to identify the word *girl*. The clause is not set off by commas.)

Mary Jones, who lives next door, came to work in our office. (The clause *who lives next door* is nonrestrictive because it is not needed to identify the name *Mary Jones*. The name *Mary Jones* clearly identifies the person being talked about, and the clause merely gives added information about the person *Mary Jones*.)

7. The comma is used to set off words in apposition. An appositive is a word or phrase that defines or identifies another word. An appositive means the same as the word it defines.

Jones, our office manager, is ill.

Reverend Brown, our minister, is an intelligent man.

Note 1: An appositive at the end of a sentence should be preceded by a comma.

I sent the memorandum to Jones, our office manager.

Note 2: Very closely related appositives do not require a comma.

| my cousin Mary | Louis the Fourth |
| his friend Bill | Mary Queen of Scots |

8. The comma is used to set off words used in direct address.

We regret, Mr. Thomas, that your order was unsatisfactorily filled.

Henry, bring me the December file.

9. The comma is used to separate a series of three or more words, phrases, or clauses.

Alice planned to have steak, potatoes, beans, lettuce, and ice cream for dinner.

He stalked off the stage, turned around, came back, and glared at the audience.

At the meeting it was decided to (1) give two weeks' vacation with pay, (2) give pensions at age sixty five, (3) establish a profit sharing plan.

Note 1: A comma should always be placed before the conjunction joining the last two members of a series.

She asked for paper, pencils, and a ruler.

Note 2: A comma should separate pairs of words in a series. A comma should not be placed before a conjunction joining words of a series that are considered as one unit.

Typing and shorthand, spelling and vocabulary, grammar and punctuation are the most popular courses. (pairs of words in a series)

For breakfast she ordered orange juice, toast, coffee, and ham and eggs. (*Ham and eggs* is considered to be one unit.)

10. The comma is used to separate coordinate adjectives which modify the same noun. Adjectives are coordinate adjectives which modify the same noun. Adjectives are coordinate if the word *and* can be used between them.

The efficient, business-like secretary received an advance in pay. (Comma—the efficient *and* business-like secretary. Both adjectives modify *secretary*.)

The five silver spoons were very expensive. (No comma—you would not say *five and silver spoons*.)

11. The comma is used in a compound sentence to separate independent clauses joined by one of the coordinate conjunctions *and, but, for, or, nor,* and *while* when it means the same as *but*. See Chapter Seventeen for a detailed discussion of compound sentences.)

I dictated the letter as you ordered, but she did not transcribe it correctly.

Minneapolis is a large industrial center, and it has many cultural attractions.

(a) If the clauses of a compound sentence are very short and closely connected, the comma may be omitted.

He looked but he did not see her.

(b) Do not use a comma between two independent clauses unless a coordinate conjunction is used. The use of a comma without a coordinate conjunction between two independent clauses is called the *comma fault*. The following sentence illustrates the comma fault:

The men in the shipping department will not follow instructions, they repeatedly make serious errors. (Incorrect—comma should not be used without a coordinate conjunction.)

Note 1: The comma fault may be eliminated by punctuating the sentence in one of the three following ways:

(a) Use a coordinate conjunction after the comma:

The men in the shipping department will not follow instructions, and they repeatedly make serious errors. (correct)

(b) Use a semicolon between the two independent clauses:

The men in the shipping department will not follow instructions; they repeatedly make serious errors. (correct—see Rule 1 under semicolons.)

(c) Punctuate the two independent clauses as two simple sentences:

The men in the shipping department will not follow instructions. They repeatedly make serious errors. (correct)

Note 2: When the independent clauses of a compound sentence are very long or have *internal punctuation,* a semicolon is generally used before the coordinate conjunction. Internal punctuation means that there are commas within one or both of the independent clauses.

Copyboy, take this folder to Alan Toms, the fellow in brown over there; and be sure to come back.

Quietly efficient, Joan continued in her position; but she never got the raise.

Both of these sentences have one or more commas in the first independent clause. Since the first clause has internal punctuation, a semicolon is used between the two independent clauses even though a coordinate conjunction is used. (See Rule 3 under semicolons.)

12. The comma is used to set off words or phrases expressing contrast.

I asked you to file the contract, not destroy it.

You may be excused from the conference this time, but never again.

Children should be seen, not heard.

13. The comma is used to set off a definite place, month, or year.

Cleveland, Ohio   July 12, 1986

Cook County, Illinois in December, 1985

Or, in sentence form, the comma is used in the following manner:

The president was born April 8, 1872, at 1224 Elm Street, Cleveland, Ohio.

14. The comma is used to set off a direct quotation.

The director asked, "How many of you are in favor of this change in policy?"

15. The comma is used as a substitute for an exclamation point after a mild interjection.

Well, I'm glad that's over.

My, it's really raining.

16. The comma is used after inverted names

Thackeray, William M.

Whittier, John Greenleaf

17. The comma is used to indicate the omission of a word.

Fishing forms a quiet man; hunting, an eager man; racing, a greedy man.

18. The comma is used to set off a proper name when followed by an academic degree or honorary title. the comma is used to separate two or more degrees or titles.

Philip F. Adams, A.B., M.A., Ph.D., lecturer in English.

19. The comma is used to point off the thousands in figures of four digits or more.

1,117   20,718   1,817,000

Note: Do not use the comma in street addresses, page and policy numbers, or in years.

| the year 1985 | Policy No. 903451 |
| page 2348 | 1117 Pensacola Ave. |

20. The comma is used to separate two sets of figures or two identical words.

John told you, you should apply immediately.

Send me 10, No. 1234 and 7, No. 138.

Since 1986, 12,000 new machines have been sold.

21. The comma is used to separate a declarative clause and an interrogative clause which immediately follows.

The plane will arrive on time, will it not?

Jack is to get a promotion, isn't he?

22. The comma is used to separate a phrase from the rest of the sentence when the phrase is inverted or out of its natural order.

Like you, I think the policy is a worthwhile one.

For me, it will mean extra work and less pay.

In spite of his promise, he was late to work again.

USE OF THE SEMICOLON

The semicolon (;) is used to show a stronger separation between the parts of a sentence than does a comma. In practical writing, however, avoid using the semicolon because it is generally too stiff and formal. If you use a great many semicolons, the chances are that you are either using them incorrectly, or you are writing sentences which are too long. Semicolons produce rather involved sentence patterns. Use them sparingly.

1. The semicolon is used to separate independent coordinate clauses closely connected in meaning when no coordinate conjunction is used.

The sales staff meets every other Tuesday; the production staff meets only once a month.

He would not approve the art layout as presented; he suggested several drastic changes.

Note: An example of this rule, as used to avoid the comma fault, was given in Rule 11 under commas.

2. The semicolon is used between coordinate clauses of a compound sentence when they are joined by transitional words and phrases. The following is a list of commonly used transitional words and phrases:

accordingly	indeed	as a result
afterwards	likewise	at last
again	meanwhile	at the same time
anyhow	moreover	for example
besides	namely	for instance
consequently	nevertheless	for this reason
doubtless	next	in any case
eventually	otherwise	in fact
evidently	perhaps	in like manner
finally	possibly	in short
furthermore	still	on the contrary
hence	then	on the other hand
however	therefore	that is
yet	thus	in addition

For a further discussion of transitional words, see chapter 17.

Note: You have already learned that transitional words are usually set off by commas. When you use a semicolon in place of a comma before the transitional word, you usually put a comma after the transitional word. However, when the transitional word retains its adverbial force and is not regarded as an independent element, it is seldom set off with a comma.

The members of the board of directors approved the change in distribution; consequently, you should appeal to them.

The weather was cold and icy; therefore we didn't go.

3. The semicolon is used before a coordinate conjunction (*and, but, for, or, nor*) between two independent clauses when either one or both have internal punctuation.

The president, a well-read man, predicted a cost of living increase for the first of the year; but his prediction, which spread throughout the plant, proved to be wrong.
The staff housekeeper ordered carpets, divans, lamps, tables, and chairs; but her order was incorrectly filled.

4. The semicolon is used before such words as *for example, for instance, that is,* and *namely* that introduce an example, enumeration, or a list in a sentence. A comma is placed after such words.

These special artist's pencils are available in three colors; namely, red, green, and blue.

Many of our policies will be changed this year; for example, salesmen will be paid a commission instead of a salary.

5. The semicolon is used in lists where a comma is insufficient to separate the members clearly.

Guests at the convention were Mr. Leonard Key, the past president of the corporation; Mrs. F. K. Small, the wife of the founder; and Mr. Paul Wells, the speaker of the evening.

USE OF THE COLON

The colon (:) indicates the strongest possible break within a sentence.

1. The colon is used before a list of items or details.

Please send out the following items: No. 378, No. 315, No. 519, and No. 570.
His actions were as follows: He went to the drugstore, purchased a hypodermic needle, got into his car, and drove away.

Note 1: Capitalize the first letter of each item in a list when the list is in column form.

You should know how to use the following office machines:

1. Typewriter
2. Duplicator
3. Copy Machine
4. Calculator

Note 2: Do not capitalize the first letter of each item in a list when the items are included in a sentence.

You should know how to use the following office machines: typewriter, duplicator, copy machine, and calculator.

2. The colon is used before an appositive phrase or clause.

Our company has always had this motto: The customer is always right.
These are your duties: Sort the mail, open all that is not personal, throw away the envelopes, and bring the letters to me.

Note: Capitalize the first letter of the word which follows the colon when that word introduces a complete sentence, as in the above examples.

3. The colon is used after the salutation of a business letter.

Dear Mr. Roe: Gentlemen: My Dear Madam:
Note: Never use a semicolon after a salutation. A comma may be used after the salutation of a friendly or informal letter.

Dear Jane,   Dear Father,   Dear Jones,

4. The colon is used to divide the parts of references, titles, formulas, and numerals.

The time was 9:15 p.m.
He assigned Chapter XII: Section 19.
Grammar Unit Eight: Complements of Verbs

USE OF PARENTHESES

1. Parentheses ( ) are used to set off words, phrases, clauses, or sentences which are used by way of explanation, translation, or comment, but which are independent constructions:

Hilda (my sister's roommate at college) is coming to visit us.
The motto read as follows: *'De gustibus non disputandum est.'* (In matters of taste there is no dispute.)

2. Parentheses are used to enclose a number, letter, or symbol when used as an appositive.

She ordered twelve (12) night stands for the hotel.
The bookkeeper ornamented his letterhead with the percent symbol (%).

Note 1: When using parentheses with other punctuation marks, punctuate the main part of the sentence as if the parenthetical portion was not there. A punctuation mark comes after the second parenthesis if the punctuation mark applies to the whole sentence and not just to the parenthetical portion.

He analyzed and presented standards of evaluation (business and technical), but his conditions proved nothing.

Note 2: Place the punctuation mark inside the second parenthesis if the punctuation mark applies only to material within the parenthetical portion.

A simplified fire-fighting plan will help you. (See the back cover of this brochure.)

USE OF THE DASH

The dash (—) is used to indicate an abrupt change of ideas, but should be used sparingly. Excessive use of the dash usually indicates that the writer does not know what punctuation mark to use.

There are times you may want to use the dash for visual effect or emphasis. A glance at advertisements in a newspaper shows that copy writers make frequent use of the dash. However, in business writing, such as letters, reports, minutes, and in social correspondence, use the dash with caution.

1. The dash may be used to indicate a sudden change of thought in a sentence.

I was certain that the manager—indeed, all of the office force—wanted John to receive the promotion.

2. The dash may be used to indicate a summarizing thought or an afterthought added to the end of the sentence.

I shall make out an estimate, draw up a contract, send out a man to interpret it for you—give you every help I can.

3. The dash may be used to set off a word or phrase repeated for emphasis.

We invited them for one meeting—one meeting only—not for the entire convention!

4. The dash may be used between numbers or dates to indicate *to* and *and.*

His chapter covered from 1860—1868.
My appointment was scheduled from 12:15—1:15.

Note on the punctuation of parenthetical matter: Close study of the rules on commas, parentheses, and dashes will show you that any one of the three punctuation marks may be used to set off parenthetical words, phrases, or clauses. When should you use the commas, dash, or parentheses? No strict rule can be stated. In general, follow this practice: In punctuating parenthetical matter, use dashes mainly for visual effect; use commas if the material is short; and use parentheses if the material is long.

USE OF BRACKETS

1. Brackets [ ] are used to enclose material added by someone other than the writer; for example, editorial additions or comments.

The investigation [from June 1, 1985 to April 8, 1986] caused considerable speculation.

The poet [Robert Browning] did not approve of the excessive adulation during the meeting.

2. Brackets are used to enclose parenthetical matter within parenthetical matter.

Your order (including items No. 391, No. 394, and No. 286 [No. 288 was out of stock]) was filled last week.

Note: Brackets are rarely used in business and social writing. Generally they are found only in printed material of a scholarly or technical nature.

USE OF THE QUESTION MARK

1. The question mark (**?**) is used after all interrogative sentences that ask direct questions.

Where are the current files?
Are you going to the next meeting of the club?

Note: After requests, use a period instead of a question mark. (See Rule 2 under periods.)

2. The question mark may be used after each separate part of a sentence containing more than one question.

Can we be sure of his willingness? his capability? his honesty?

Note: If the question is not complete until the end of the sentence, place a question mark at the end only.

Will delivery be made today, tomorrow, or Friday?

3. The question mark is used in several ways when only part of the sentence is a question. In such sentences the question is generally introduced by a comma or colon; a semicolon or dash may also be used.

May I ask, what is his purpose?
This is our problem: What should be done to prevent further damage?
Our questions are, what date will you arrive? where will you stay? and, do you desire us to furnish transportation?

USE OF THE EXCLAMATION MARK

1. The exclamation mark (**!**) is used after all exclamatory sentences—sentences that express surprise, emotion, or deep feeling.

Look out for that train!
Headlines read, "Peace Treaty Signed!"
Your answer was hard to believe!

2. The exclamation mark is used after an interjection or a word used as an interjection. At times, the sentence following the interjection may be exclamatory.

Hurry! The train will pull out in three minutes!
Oh! I haven't heard that before.

3. The exclamation mark is used after statements which are commands or which imply need for immediate action.

Return the card today! Don't delay!
Hurry! Send your order now!

4. The exclamation point is used after an interrogative sentence that is exclamatory in form or intended to be exclamatory.

Oh, how could he say that!
But can he be trusted!

5. The exclamation point is sometimes used to add emphasis.

Realize what this means!
This offer absolutely expires April 6!

USE OF QUOTATION MARKS

1. Quotation marks (" ") are used to enclose a direct quotation. Each part of an interrupted quotation begins and ends with quotation marks.

The inspector said, "Well, your case is not hopeless."
"Where," he asked, "are you going to keep it?"
"What will we do?" he asked. "Where can we raise the money?"

Note: Capitalize the first word of a direct quotation. Do not capitalize the first word in the second part of an interrupted quotation unless the second part begins a new sentence. Do not use quotation marks or capital letters in an indirect quotation.

The inspector said that your case is not hopeless. (Many indirect quotations are introduced by the word *that.*)
He asked where we would keep it.

2. Quotation marks are used to enclose the titles of magazine articles, chapters of books, names of songs, titles of poems, and other titles.

The New Yorker includes a section entitled "The Talk of the Town."
She asked Ellen to sing "Because" at her wedding.
"Rabbi Ben Ezra" is one of my favorite poems.
Note: In typing or writing, underline the titles of books, magazines, operas, and any other works of art long enough to appear in book form. Underlining signifies italics for printing. The words, "The New Yorker" in the first sentence above are printed in italic type.

The anthology, Toward Liberal Education, includes A. E Housman's "Introductory Lecture" and S. I. Hayakawa's "Poetry and Advertising."
The soprano sang "If Madam Should Call You" from Mozart's Marriage of Figaro.

3. Quotation marks are used to set off words, phrases, or sentences referred to within a sentence.

The word "proceed" is frequently mispronounced.
The phrase "on the other hand" is sometimes used as a transitional phrase.
The sentence "Now is the time for all good men to come to the aid of their party" is an excellent typing exercise.

4. Quotation marks are used to set off slang words or expressions.

She said that the office party was held at a "swank" hotel.

5. If several paragraphs are quoted, use quotation marks at the beginning of each paragraph but at the end of the last paragraph only. Long quotations are usually introduced by a colon instead of a comma. Quotations of three or more lines are usually indented and set apart from the body of the text.

USE OF QUOTATION MARKS WITH OTHER PUNCTUATION

(a) The period and comma are always placed before ending quotation marks.

He said, "They are not here."
"They are not here," he said.

(b) The question mark and exclamation point are placed before quotation marks when they refer only to the quoted material.

She asked, "When are you going to be promoted?"

(c) The question mark and exclamation point follow ending quotation marks when they refer to the entire sentence.

Did she say, "You are to be promoted next month"?

(d) The semicolon and colon follow ending quotation marks unless they are part of the quoted matter.

She said, "You are to be promoted next month"; consequently, I expected to be promoted.

USE OF SINGLE QUOTATION MARKS

1. Single quotation marks are used to set off a quotation within a quotation.

"Jane," I asked, "did you tell me how to spell the word 'pathologically'?"
The irate mother said, "You must get all of this 'junk' out of the living room at once."

Note: Other punctuation marks are used with single quotation marks in the same way as with double quotation marks.

USE OF THE APOSTROPHE

1. The apostrophe (**'**) is used in nouns to show possession.

Note: Keep in mind that the sign of the possessive case is always added to a word. It is not something that is inserted within a word.

(a) If the singular form of the noun does not end in **s** or an **s** sound, add the apostrophe and **s** (**'s**).

Singular	Singular Possessive
boy	boy's
girl	girl's
lady	lady's

(b) If the singular ends in **s** or an **s** sound, add the apostrophe (**'**) or the apostrophe and **s** (**'s**) if the additional **s** sound is desired.

Singular	Singular Possessive
boss	boss' or boss's
dress	dress' or dress's
box	box' or box's

(c) If the plural form of the noun does not end in **s**, add the apostrophe and **s** (**s'**)

Plural	Plural Possessive
men	men's
children	children's
mice	mice's
teeth	teeth's
geese	geese's

(d) If the plural form of the noun ends in **s**, add the apostrophe (**'**)

Plural	Plural Possessive
boys	boys'
girls	girls'
ladies	ladies'

(e) The possessives of proper nouns are formed in the same way as the possessives of common nouns. If the singular form of the name does not end in **s**, add the apostrophe and **s**. If the singular ends in **s** or an **s** sound, add the apostrophe (**'**) or the apostrophe and **s** (**'s**). The plural possessive is always formed by adding the apostrophe to the plural form.

Proper Noun	Singular Possessive	Plural	Plural Possessive
John	John's	Johns	Johns'
Phyllis	Phyllis' or Phyllis's	Phyllises	Phyllises'
Jane	Jane's	Janes	Janes'

(f) Certain expressions relating to *time, distance,* and *value* are also written with an apostrophe.

the day's task   five cents's worth
a year's time   six miles' distance
a minute's notice   three weeks' vacation

(g) The singular possessive and the plural possessive of compound nouns are formed by adding the apostrophe to the end of the compound word.

Singular	**Plural**
brother-in-law's	brothers-in-law's
father-in-law's	fathers-in-law's

(h) Joint ownership is shown by making the last word in the series possessive. Individual ownership is shown by making both parts possessive.

Alice and Jack's apartment. (joint ownership)
Alice's and Jack's apartments. (individual ownership)

2. The apostrophe is used in indefinite pronouns to show possession. The possessive case of indefinite pronouns is formed in the same way as the possessive case of nouns.

everybody's duty   others' positions
one's coat   someone's hat

3. The apostrophe is used with **s** to form the plural of numbers, letters, signs, and symbols.

Your "r's" look like "n's."
He used twelve "r's" to decorate his paper.

4. The apostrophe is used to indicate the omission of a word, letters, or numerals.

don't	let's	o'clock
hadn't	it's	she's
isn't	'tis	wouldn't

The accident happened in '86.

SPELLING DICTIONARY

A

aard·vark
ab·a·cus
abaft
ab·a·lo·ne
aban·don
aban·doned
aban·don·ment
abase
abased
abas·ing
abase·ment
abate
abat·ed
abat·ing
abate·ment
ab·at·toir
ab·axial
ab·bey
ab·bot
ab·bess
a·bre·vi·ate
ab·bre·vi·at·ed
ab·bre·vi·at·ing
ab·bre·vi·a·tion
ab·di·cate
ab·di·cat·ed
ab·di·cat·ing
ab·di·ca·tion
ab·do·men
ab·dom·i·nal
ab·duct
ab·duc·tion
ab·duc·tor
ab·er·rant
ab·er·ra·tion
ab·er·rance
ab·er·ran·cy
abet
abet·ted
abet·ting
abet·ment
abey·ance
ab·hor
ab·horred
ab·hor·ring
ab·hor·rence
ab·hor·rent
abide
abode
abi·ded
abid·ing
abil·i·ty
abil·i·ties
ab·ject
ab·ject·ly
ab·ject·ness
ab·jure
ab·jured
ab·jur·ing
ab·ju·ra·tion
ab·late
ab·lat·ed
ab·lat·ing
ab·la·tion
ab·la·tive
able
ably
able-bod·ied
ab·lu·tion
ab·ne·gate

ab·ne·gat·ed
ab·ne·gat·ing
ab·nor·mal
ab·nor·mal·i·ty
ab·nor·mal·i·ties
abol·ish
abol·ish·a·ble
abol·ish·ment
ab·o·li·tion
ab·o·li·tion·ism
ab·o·li·tion·ist
A-bomb
abom·i·nate
abom·i·nat·ed
abom·i·nat·ing
abom·i·na·tion
abom·i·na·ble
abom·i·na·bly
ab·o·rig·i·ne
ab·o·rig·i·nal
abort
abor·tion
abor·tion·ist
abor·tive
above·board
ab·ra·ca·dab·ra
abrade
abrad·ed
abrad·ing
abra·sion
abra·sive
abreast
abridge
abridged
abridg·ing
abroad
ab·rogate
ab·ro·gat·ed
ab·ro·gat·ing
ab·ro·ga·tion
ab·rupt
ab·scess
ab·scessed
ab·scis·sa
ab·scis·sion
ab·scond
ab·sence
ab·sent
ab·sen·tee
ab·sent-mind·ed
ab·sinthe
ab·so·lute
ab·so·lute·ly
ab·so·lu·tion
ab·solve
ab·solved
ab·solv·ing
ab·sol·vent
ab·sorb
ab·sorb·ent
ab·sorp·tion
ab·sorp·tive
ab·sorb·a·ble
ab·sorb·en·cy
ab·stain
ab·sten·tion
ab·sti·nence
ab·sti·nent
ab·ste·mi·ous
ab·stract
ab·strac·tion
ab·stract·ed
ab·struce

ab·surd
ab·surd·i·ty
ab·surd·ness
abund·dant
abun·dance
abuse
abused
abus·ing
abus·er
abu·sive
abu·sive·ly
abu·sive·ness
abut
abut·ted
abut·ting
abut·ment
abys·mal
abyss
ac·a·dem·ic
ac·a·dem·i·cal
acad·e·mi·cian
acad·e·my
acad·e·mies
ac·cede
ac·ced·ed
ac·ced·ing
ac·ce·le·ran·do
ac·cel·er·ate
ac·cel·er·at·ed
ac·cel·er·at·ing
ac·cel·er·ant
ac·cel·er·a·tion
ac·cel·er·a·tor
ac·cent
ac·cen·tu·ate
ac·cen·tu·at·ed
ac·cen·tu·at·ing
ac·cen·tu·a·tion
ac·cept
ac·cept·ed
ac·cept·ance
ac·cept·a·ble
ac·cept·a·bil·i·ty
ac·cess
ac·ces·si·ble
ac·ces·si·bil·i·ty
ac·ces·sion
ac·ces·so·ry
ac·ci·dence
ac·ci·dent
ac·ci·den·tal
ac·claim
ac·cla·ma·tion
ac·cli·mate
ac·cli·mat·ed
ac·cli·mat·ing
ac·cli·ma·tion
ac·cli·ma·tize
ac·cli·ma·tized
ac·cli·ma·tiz·ing
ac·cli·ma·ti·za·tion
ac·cliv·i·ty
ac·cliv·i·ties
ac·co·lade
ac·com·mo·date
ac·com·mo·dat·ed
ac·com·mo·dat·ing
ac·com·mo·da·tive
ac·com·mo·da·tion
ac·com·pa·ny
ac·com·pa·nied
ac·com·pa·ny·ing
ac·com·pa·ni·ment

ac·com·pa·nist
ac·com·plice
ac·com·plish
ac·com·plished
ac·com·plish·ing
ac·com·plish·ment
ac·cord
ac·cord·ing
ac·cord·ance
ac·cor·di·on
ac·cost
ac·couche·ment
ac·count
ac·count·a·ble
ac·count·a·bil·i·ty
ac·count·ant
ac·count·ing
ac·cred·it
ac·cred·i·ta·tion
ac·cre·tion
ac·cre·tive
ac·cru·al
ac·crue
ac·crued
ac·cru·ing
ac·cum·u·late
ac·cum·u·lat·ed
ac·cum·u·lat·ing
ac·cum·u·la·tion
ac·cu·mu·la·tive
ac·cu·rate
ac·cu·ra·cy
ac·cu·rate·ly
ac·cu·rate·ness
ac·curs·ed
ac·curst
ac·cu·sa·tive
ac·cuse
ac·cused
ac·cus·ing
ac·cu·sa·tion
ac·cu·sa·to·ry
ac·cus·tom
ac·cus·tomed
acer·bi·ty
ac·e·tate
ace·tic
acet·i·fy
ac·e·tone
acet·y·lene
ache
ached
ach·ing
achieve
achieved
achiev·ing
achiev·a·ble
achieve·ment
ach·ro·mat·ic
ac·id
acid·ic
acid·i·fy
acid·i·ty
ac·i·do·sis
acid·u·late
acid·u·la·tion
acid·u·lous
ac·knowl·edge
ac·knowl·edged
ac·knowl·edg·ing
ac·knowl·edge·a·ble
ac·knowl·edg·ment
ac·me

ac·ne
ac·o·lyte
ac·o·nite
acous·tic
acous·tics
acous·ti·cal
ac·quaint
ac·quaint·ance
ac·qui·esce
ac·qui·esced
ac·qui·esc·ing
ac·qui·es·cence
ac·qui·es·cent
ac·quire
ac·quired
ac·quir·ing
ac·quire·ment
ac·qui·si·tion
ac·quit
ac·quit·ted
ac·quit·ting
ac·quit·tal
ac·quit·tance
acre
acre·age
ac·rid
acrid·i·ty
ac·ri·mo·ny
ac·ri·mo·ni·ous
ac·ro·bat
ac·ro·bat·ic
ac·ro·nym
ac·ro·pho·bia
across
acryl·ic
act·ing
ac·tion
ac·tion·a·ble
ac·tion·a·bly
ac·ti·vate
ac·ti·vat·ed
ac·ti·vat·ing
ac·ti·va·tion
ac·ti·va·tor
ac·tive
ac·tive·ly
ac·tive·ness
ac·tiv·ism
ac·tiv·ist
ac·tiv·i·ty
ac·tiv·i·ties
ac·tor
ac·tress
ac·tu·al
ac·tu·al·ly
ac·tu·al·i·ty
ac·tu·al·ize
ac·tu·al·i·za·tion
ac·tu·ary
ac·tu·ar·ies
ac·tu·ar·i·al
ac·tu·ate
ac·tu·at·ed
ac·tu·at·ing
ac·tu·a·tion
ac·tu·a·tor
acu·i·ty
acu·men
ac·u·punc·ture
acute
acute·ly
acute·ness
ad·age

ada·gio
ad·a·mant
ad·a·man·tine
adapt
    adapt·a·ble
    adapt·a·bil·i·ty
    ad·ap·ta·tion
    adap·tive
ad·dend
ad·den·dum
    ad·den·da
ad·dict
    ad·dict·ed
    ad·dic·tive
    ad·dic·tion
ad·di·tion
    ad·di·tion·al
    ad·di·tive
ad·dle
ad·dress
ad·dress·ee
ad·duce
ad·e·noid
    ad·e·noi·dal
adept
    adept·ly
ad·e·quate
    ad·e·qua·cy
    ad·e·quate·ly
ad·here
    ad·hered
    ad·her·ing
    ad·her·ence
ad·her·ent
ad·he·sion
ad·he·sive
    ad·he·sive·ness
ad·hib·it
adi·a·bat·ic
a·dieu
ad in·fi·ni·tum
adi·os
ad·i·pose
    ad·i·pose·ness
ad·ja·cent
    ad·ja·cent·ly
    ad·ja·cen·cy
    ad·ja·cen·cies
ad·jec·tive
ad·join
    ad·join·ing
ad·journ
    ad·journ·ment
ad·judge
    ad·judged
    ad·judg·ing
ad·ju·di·cate
    ad·ju·di·cat·ed
    ad·ju·di·cat·ing
    ad·ju·di·ca·tion
ad·junct
    ad·junc·tive
ad·jure
    ad·jured
    ad·jur·ing
    ad·ju·ra·tion
ad·just
    ad·just·a·ble
    ad·just·er
    ad·just·ment
ad·ju·tant
ad·lib
    ad·libbed
    ad·lib·bing
ad·min·is·ter
ad·min·is·trate
ad·min·is·tra·tion
    ad·min·is·tra·tive

ad·min·is·tra·tor
ad·mi·ral
ad·mi·ral·ty
ad·mire
    ad·mired
    ad·mir·ing
    ad·mi·ra·ble
    ad·mi·ra·bly
    ad·mi·ra·tion
    ad·mi·rer
    ad·mir·ing·ly
ad·mis·si·ble
    ad·mis·si·bil·i·ty
ad·mis·sion
ad·mit
    ad·mit·ted
    ad·mit·ting
    ad·mit·tance
ad·mix·ture
ad·mon·ish
    ad·mo·ni·tion
    ad·mon·i·to·ry
ado·be
ad·o·les·cence
ad·o·les·cent
adopt
    adopt·a·ble
    adopt·er
    adop·tion
    adop·tive
adore
    adored
    ador·ing
    ador·a·ble
    ad·o·ra·tion
adorn
    adorn·ment
ad·re·nal
adren·a·line
adrift
adroit
    adroit·ly
    adroit·ness
ad·sorb
    ad·sor·bent
    ad·sorp·tion
ad·u·late
    ad·u·lat·ing
    ad·u·la·tion
    ad·u·la·to·ry
adult
    adult·hood
adul·ter·ate
    adul·ter·at·ed
    adul·ter·at·ing
    adul·ter·ant
    adul·ter·a·tion
adul·tery
    adul·ter·er
    adul·ter·ess
    adul·ter·ous
ad va·lo·rem
ad·vance
    ad·vanc·ing
    ad·vance·ment
ad·van·tage
    ad·van·tag·ing
    ad·van·ta·geous
ad·vent
ad·ven·ti·tious
ad·ven·ture
    ad·ven·tur·ing
    ad·ven·tur·er
    ad·ven·ture·some
    ad·ven·tur·ous
ad·verb
    ad·ver·bi·al·ly
ad·ver·sary

ad·ver·sar·ies
ad·verse
    ad·verse·ly
    ad·verse·ness
ad·ver·si·ty
    ad·ver·si·ties
ad·vert
    ad·vert·ence
    ad·vert·ent
ad·ver·tise
    ad·ver·tised
    ad·ver·tis·ing
    ad·ver·tis·er
    ad·ver·tise·ment
ad·vice
ad·vise
    ad·vis·ing
    ad·vis·a·bil·i·ty
    ad·vis·a·ble
    ad·vis·a·bly
    ad·vis·er
    ad·vis·ed·ly
    ad·vise·ment
    ad·vi·so·ry
ad·vo·cate
    ad·vo·cat·ed
    ad·vo·cat·ing
    ad·vo·ca·cy
    ad·vo·ca·tion
ae·on
    ae·o·ni·an
aer·ate
    aer·at·ed
    aer·at·ing
    aer·a·tion
    aer·a·tor
aer·i·al
    aer·i·al·ist
aero·dy·nam·ics
aer·o·log·i·cal
    aer·ol·o·gist
aer·o·naut·ics
    aer·o·nau·ti·cal
aer·o·sol
aer·o·space
aes·thete
aes·thet·ic
    aes·thet·i·cal·ly
af·fa·ble
    af·fa·bil·i·ty
    af·fa·bly
af·fair
af·fect
    af·fect·ing
    af·fec·tive
    af·fec·ta·tion
    af·fect·ed
        af·fect·ed·ly
        af·fect·ed·ness
    af·fec·tion
        af·fec·tion·ate
af·fi·ance
af·fi·da·vit
af·fil·i·ate
    af·fil·i·at·ed
    af·fil·i·a·tion
af·fin·i·ty
af·firm
    af·fir·ma·tion
    af·firm·a·tive
af·flict
    af·flic·tion
af·flu·ence
    af·flu·ent
af·ford
af·fray
af·fright
af·front

af·ghan
afore·men·tioned
afore·said
afore·thought
afraid
Af·ri·can
Af·ri·kan·der
af·ter·birth
af·ter·burn·er
af·ter·ef·fect
af·ter·glow
af·ter·math
af·ter·most
af·ter·noon
af·ter·thought
af·ter·ward
again
against
agape
ag·ate
aga·ve
age
    aged
    ag·ing
    age·ing
age·less
agen·cy
    agen·cies
agen·da
agent
ag·glom·er·ate
    ag·glom·er·at·ing
    ag·glom·er·a·tion
ag·glu·ti·nate
    ag·glu·ti·nat·ing
    ag·glu·ti·na·tion
    ag·glu·ti·na·tive
ag·gran·dize
    ag·gran·dized
    ag·gran·diz·ing
    ag·gran·dize·ment
ag·gra·vate
    ag·gra·vat·ed
    ag·gra·vat·ing
    ag·gra·va·tion
ag·gre·gate
    ag·gre·gat·ed
    ag·gre·gat·ing
    ag·gre·ga·tion
    ag·gre·ga·tive
ag·gress
    ag·gress·ive
    ag·gress·or
    ag·gres·sion
ag·grieve
    ag·grieved
    ag·griev·ing
aghast
ag·ile
    ag·ile·ly
    agil·i·ty
ag·i·tate
    ag·i·tat·ed
    ag·i·tat·ing
    ag·i·ta·tion
    ag·i·ta·tor
agleam
ag·nos·tic
    ag·nos·ti·cism
ag·o·nize
    ag·o·niz·ing
ag·o·ny
    ag·o·nies
ag·o·ra·pho·bia
agrar·i·an
agree
    agreed
    agree·ing

agree·ment
agree·a·ble
agree·a·bil·i·ty
agree·a·bly
ag·ri·cul·ture
ag·ri·cul·tur·al
ag·ri·cul·tur·ist
agron·o·my
ag·ro·nom·ic
ag·ro·nom·i·cal
agron·o·mist
aground
ague
aide-de-camp
ai·grette
ail·ing
ail·ment
ai·ler·on
aim·less
air·less
air·borne
air·brush
air-con·di·tion
    air-con·di·tioned
    air con·di·tion·ing
    air con·di·tion·er
air·craft
air·drop
    air·dropped
    air·drop·ping
Aire·dale
air·field
air·foil
air·plane
air·port
air pres·sure
air·sick·ness
air·space
air·tight
air·wave
air·worthy
airy
    air·i·er
    air·i·est
    air·i·ness
    air·i·ly
aisle
ajar
akin
al·a·bas·ter
a la carte
alac·ri·ty
alarm
    alarm·ing
al·ba·core
al·ba·tross
al·be·it
al·bi·no
    al·bi·nos
    al·bi·nism
al·bum
al·bu·men
al·bu·min
    al·bu·mi·nous
al·che·my
    al·che·mist
al·co·hol
    al·co·hol·ic
    al·co·hol·ism
al·cove
al·der·man
alert
    alert·ness
al·fal·fa
al·fres·co
al·ga
    al·gae
    al·ge·bra

al·ge·bra·ic
al·ge·bra·ic·al
al·go·ri·thm
ali·as
ali·as·es
al·i·bi
al·ien
al·ien·a·ble
al·ien·ate
al·ien·at·ed
al·ien·at·ing
al·ien·ist
al·ien·ism
alight
alight·ed
alit
alight·ing
align
align·ment
aline·ment
alike
al·i·ment
al·i·men·tal
al·i·men·ta·ry
al·i·mo·ny
al·ka·li
al·ka·lies
al·ka·line
al·ka·lin·i·ty
al·ka·lize
al·ka·lized
al·ka·liz·ing
al·ka·li·za·tion
al·ka·loid
al·ka·loi·dal
all-Amer·i·can
all-around
al·lay
al·layed
al·lay·ing
al·lege
al·leged
al·leg·ing
al·le·ga·tion
al·lege·a·ble
al·le·giance
al·le·go·ry
al·le·go·ries
al·le·gor·ic
al·le·gor·i·cal
al·le·gret·to
al·le·gro
al·ler·gen
al·ler·gy
al·ler·gies
al·ler·gic
al·ler·gist
al·le·vi·ate
al·le·vi·at·ed
al·le·vi·at·ing
al·le·vi·a·tion
al·le·vi·a·tive
al·le·vi·a·to·ry
al·ley
al·leys
al·li·ance
al·lied
al·li·ga·tor
al·lit·er·ate
al·lit·er·at·ed
al·lit·er·at·ing
al·lit·er·a·tive
al·lit·er·a·tion
al·lo·cate
al·lo·cat·ed
al·lo·cat·ing
al·lo·ca·tion
al·lop·a·thy

al·lo·path·ic
al·lot
al·lot·ted
al·lot·ting
al·lot·ment
al·lot·ta·ble
al·low
al·low·ing
al·low·a·ble
al·low·ed·ly
al·low·ance
al·loy
all·spice
al·lude
al·lud·ed
al·lud·ing
al·lure
al·lured
al·lur·ing
al·lure·ment
al·lu·sion
al·lu·sive
al·lu·sive·ly
al·lu·vi·al
al·lu·vi·um
al·ly
al·lies
al·lied
al·ly·ing
al·li·ance
al·ma ma·ter
al·ma·nac
al·mighty
almond
almost
al·oe
aloft
alo·ha
alone
alone·ness
along
along·side
aloof
aloof·ness
al·pha
al·pha·bet
al·pha·bet·ic
al·pha·bet·i·cal
al·pha·bet·ize
al·pha·nu·mer·ic
al·ready
al·so
al·tar
al·ter
al·ter·a·bil·i·ty
al·ter·a·ble
al·ter·ant
al·ter·a·tion
al·ter·a·tive
al·ter·cate
al·ter·ca·tion
al·ter e·go
al·ter·nate
al·ter·nat·ed
al·ter·nat·ing
al·ter·nate·ly
al·ter·na·tion
al·ter·na·tor
al·ter·na·tive
al·though
al·tim·e·ter
al·ti·tude
al·to
al·to·gether
al·tru·ism
al·tru·ist
al·tru·is·tic
al·um

a·lu·min·na
alu·mi·num
alum·na
alum·nae
alum·nus
alum·ni
al·ve·o·lar
al·ways
amal·gam
amal·gam·ate
amal·gam·a·tion
am·a·ryl·lis
amass
amass·ment
am·a·teur
am·a·teur·ism
am·a·teur·ish
am·a·to·ry
amaze
amazed
amaz·ing
amaze·ment
Am·a·zon
am·bas·sa·dor
am·bas·sa·dress
am·bas·sa·do·ri·al
am·ber
am·ber·gris
am·bi·dex·trous
am·bi·dex·ter·i·ty
am·bi·ance
am·bi·ence
am·bi·ent
am·big·u·ous
am·big·u·ous·ly
am·bi·gu·i·ty
am·bi·tion
am·bi·tious
am·bi·tious·ly
am·bi·tious·ness
am·biv·a·lence
am·biv·a·lent
am·ble
am·bled
am·bling
am·bro·sia
am·bro·sial
am·bu·lance
am·bu·la·to·ry
am·bu·lant
am·bu·late
am·bu·lat·ed
am·bu·lat·ing
am·bus·cade
am·bush
am·bush·ment
ame·ba
amel·io·rate
amel·io·rat·ed
amel·io·rat·ing
amel·io·ra·ble
amel·io·ra·tion
amel·ior·a·tive
amel·io·ra·tor
ame·na·ble
ame·na·bil·i·ty
ame·na·ble·ness
ame·na·bly
amend
amend·a·ble
amend·ment
amen·i·ty
amerce
amerce·ment
Amer·i·ca
Amer·i·can
Amer·i·cana
Amer·i·can·ism

Amer·i·can·i·za·tion
am·e·thyst
ami·a·ble
ami·a·bil·i·ty
ami·a·bly
am·i·ca·ble
am·i·ca·bil·i·ty
am·i·ca·bly
amid
amidst
ami·go
am·i·ty
am·me·ter
am·mo·nia
am·mo·ni·um
am·mu·ni·tion
am·ne·sia
am·ne·sic
am·nes·ty
am·ni·on
amoe·ba
amoe·bae
amoe·bas
amoe·bic
amoe·boid
amok
among
amongst
amor·al
am·o·rous
am·o·rous·ly
am·o·rous·ness
amor·phous
am·or·tize
am·or·tized
am·or·tiz·ing
am·or·ti·za·tion
amount
amour
am·pere
am·per·age
am·per·sand
am·phet·a·mine
am·phib·i·an
am·phib·i·ous
am·phi·the·a·ter
am·ple
am·ple·ness
am·ply
am·pli·fy
am·pli·fied
am·pli·fy·ing
am·pli·fi·ca·tion
am·pli·fi·er
am·pli·tude
am·poule
am·pule
am·pu·tate
am·pu·tat·ed
am·pu·tat·ing
am·pu·ta·tion
am·pu·tee
amuck
am·u·let
amuse
amused
amus·ing
amuse·ment
anach·ro·nism
anach·ro·nis·tic
anach·ro·nous
an·a·con·da
an·aes·the·sia
an·aes·thet·ic
an·aes·the·tize
an·a·gram
an·a·gram·mat·ic
an·a·gram·mat·i·cal

anal
anus
an·al·ge·sia
an·al·ge·sic
an·a·logue
an·a·log
an·a·log·i·cal
anal·o·gize
anal·o·gy
anal·o·gies
anal·o·gous
anal·y·sis
anal·y·ses
an·a·lyst
an·a·lyt·ic
an·a·lyze
an·a·lyzed
an·a·lyz·ing
an·a·ly·za·tion
an·a·pest
an·ar·chist
an·ar·chism
an·ar·chis·tic
an·ar·chy
an·ar·chic
an·ar·chi·cal
anath·e·ma
anath·e·ma·tize
anat·o·mize
anat·o·mized
anat·o·mizing
anat·o·mi·za·tion
anat·o·my
anat·o·mies
an·a·tom·i·cal
anat·o·mist
an·ces·tor
an·ces·tral
an·ces·tress
an·ces·try
an·chor
an·chor·age
an·cho·rite
an·chor·man
an·chovy
an·cient
an·cient·ness
an·cil·lary
an·dan·te
an·dan·ti·no
and·i·ron
an·dro·gen
an·drog·y·nous
an·drog·y·ny
an·ec·dote
an·ec·do·tal
an·ec·dot·i·cal
ane·mia
ane·mic
an·e·mom·e·ter
anem·o·ne
an·er·oid
an·es·the·sia
an·es·thet·ic
an·es·the·tist
an·es·the·si·ol·ogist
an·es·the·tize
an·es·the·tiz·ing
an·eu·rysm
an·eu·rism
an·gel
an·gel·ic
an·gel·i·cal·ly
an·ger
an·gerily
an·gi·na pec·to·ris
an·gle
an·gling

angler
An·gli·can
An·gli·can·ism
An·gli·cism
An·gli·cize
An·gli·ci·za·tion
An·glo-Amer·i·can
An·glo-Sax·on
an·go·ra
an·gos·tu·ra
an·gry
an·gri·ly
an·gri·ness
ang·strom unit
an·guish
an·guished
an·gu·lar
an·gu·lar·i·ty
an·gu·la·tion
an·hy·dride
an·hy·drous
an·i·mad·vert
an·i·mad·ver·sion
an·i·mal
an·i·mal·ism
an·i·mal·i·ty
an·i·mal·ize
an·i·mate
an·i·mat·ed
an·i·mat·ing
an·i·ma·tion
an·i·mism
an·i·mis·tic
an·i·mos·i·ty
an·i·mus
an·ise
an·i·sette
an·kle
an·klet
an·ky·lose
an·ky·lo·sis
an·nals
an·nal·ist
an·nal·is·tic
An·nap·o·lis
an·neal
an·ne·lid
an·nex
an·nex·a·tion
an·ni·hi·late
an·ni·hi·lat·ed
an·ni·hi·lat·ing
an·ni·hi·la·tion
an·ni·hi·la·tor
an·ni·ver·sa·ry
an·ni·ver·sa·ries
an·no Do·mi·ni
an·no·tate
an·no·tat·ed
an·no·tat·ing
an·no·ta·tion
an·no·ta·tor
an·nounce
an·nounced
an·nounc·ing
an·nounce·ment
an·nounc·er
an·noy
an·noy·ance
an·nu·al
an·nu·i·ty
an·nu·i·tant
an·nul
an·nulled
an·nul·ling
an·nul·ment
an·nu·lar
an·nun·ci·ate

an·nun·ci·at·ing
an·nun·ci·a·tion
an·nun·ci·a·tor
an·ode
an·od·ize
an·o·dyne
anoint
anoint·ment
anom·a·ly
anom·a·lism
anom·a·lous
anon·ymous
an·o·nym·i·ty
anon·y·mous·ly
an·oth·er
an·swer
an·swer·a·ble
ant·ac·id
an·tag·o·nist
an·tag·o·nism
an·tag·o·nis·tic
an·tag·o·nize
an·tag·o·niz·ing
ant·arc·tic
Ant·arc·ti·ca
an·te
ant·eat·er
an·te-bel·lum
an·te·cede
an·te·ced·ed
an·te·ced·ing
an·te·ced·ence
an·te·ced·ent
an·te·cham·ber
an·te·date
an·te·di·lu·vi·an
an·te·lope
an·te me·ri·di·em
an·ten·na
an·ten·nae
an·ten·nas
an·te·pe·nult
an·te·ri·or
an·te·room
an·them
an·thol·o·gy
an·thol·o·gies
an·thol·o·gist
an·thra·cite
an·thrax
an·thro·po·cen·tric
an·thro·poid
an·thro·pol·o·gy
an·thro·po·log·ic
an·thro·po·log·i·cal
an·thro·pol·o·gist
an·thro·pom·e·try
an·thro·po·mor·phic
an·ti·air·craft
an·ti·bac·te·ri·al
an·ti·bal·lis·tic
an·ti·bi·ot·ic
an·ti·body
an·ti·bod·ies
an·tic
An·ti·christ
an·tic·i·pate
an·tic·i·pat·ed
an·tic·i·pat·ing
an·tic·i·pa·tion
an·tic·i·pa·tive
an·tic·i·pa·to·ry
an·ti·cler·i·cal
an·ti·cli·max
an·ti·cli·mac·tic
an·ti·dote
an·ti·dot·al
an·ti·freeze

an·ti·gen
an·ti·his·ta·mine
an·ti·log·a·rithm
an·ti·ma·cas·sar
an·ti·mis·sile
an·ti·mo·ny
an·ti·pas·to
an·tip·a·thy
an·ti·pa·thet·ic
an·ti·pode
an·ti·quar·i·an
an·ti·quary
an·ti·quar·ies
an·ti·quate
an·ti·quat·ed
an·ti·quat·ing
an·tique
an·tiqued
an·tiq·uing
an·tique·ness
an·tiq·ui·ty
an·ti-Sem·i·tism
an·ti·sep·sis
an·ti·sep·tic
an·ti·sep·tical·ly
an·ti·se·rum
an·ti·slav·ery
an·ti·so·cial
an·tith·e·sis
an·tith·e·ses
an·ti·thet·i·cal
an·ti·tox·in
an·ti·tox·ic
an·ti·trust
ant·ler
ant·lered
an·to·nym
anus
an·vil
anx·i·e·ty
anx·i·e·ties
anx·ious
anx·ious·ness
any·body
any·bod·ies
any·how
any·more
any·one
any·place
any·thing
any·way
any·where
any·wise
aor·ta
aor·tal
aor·tic
apace
apart
apart·heid
apart·ment
ap·a·thy
ap·a·thet·ic
ap·a·thet·i·cal·ly
aper·ri·tif
ap·er·ture
apex
apex·es
api·ces
ap·i·cal
apha·sia
aphid
aph·o·rism
aph·o·rist
aph·o·ris·tic
aph·ro·dis·i·ac
api·ar·i·an
api·a·rist
api·ary

api·ar·ies
api·cul·ture
api·cul·tur·al
api·cul·tur·ist
apiece
ap·ish
aplomb
apoc·a·lypse
apoc·a·lyp·tic
apoc·o·pe
apoc·ry·pha
ap·o·dic·tic
ap·o·gee
apol·o·get·ics
apol·o·gist
apol·o·gize
apol·o·gized
apol·o·giz·ing
apol·o·gy
apol·o·gies
apol·o·get·ic
apol·o·get·i·cal
ap·o·plec·tic
ap·o·plex·y
apos·ta·sy
apos·tate
apos·ta·tize
a pos·te·ri·o·ri
apos·tle
apos·to·late
ap·os·tol·ic
ap·os·tol·i·cal
apos·trophe
apoth·e·cary
apoth·e·car·ies
ap·o·thegm
apoth·e·o·sis
apoth·e·o·size
Ap·pa·la·chi·an
ap·pall
ap·palled
ap·pal·ling
ap·pa·rat·us
ap·pa·rat·us
ap·pa·rat·us·es
ap·par·el
ap·par·ent
ap·pa·ri·tion
ap·peal
ap·peal·a·ble
ap·peal·ing·ly
ap·pear
ap·pear·ance
ap·pease
ap·peased
ap·peas·ing
ap·pease·ment
ap·peas·er
ap·pel·late
ap·pel·lant
ap·pel·la·tion
ap·pel·la·tive
ap·pend
ad·pen·dage
ap·pend·ant
ap·pen·di·ci·tis
ap·pen·dec·to·my
ap·pen·dix
ap·pen·dix·es
ap·pen·di·ces
ap·per·cep·tion
ap·per·tain
ap·pe·tite
ap·pe·tiz·er
ap·pe·tiz·ing
ap·plaud
ap·plause
ap·ple

ap·pli·ance
ap·pli·ca·ble
ap·pli·ca·bil·i·ty
ap·pli·cant
ap·pli·ca·tion
ap·pli·ca·to·ry
ap·pli·ca·tor
ap·pli·que
ap·ply
ap·plied
ap·ply·ing
ap·point
ap·point·ee
ap·poin·tive
ap·point·ment
ap·por·tion
ap·por·tion·ment
ap·pose
ap·posed
ap·pos·ing
ap·po·site
ap·po·si·tion
ap·pos·i·tive
ap·praise
ap·praised
ap·prais·ing
ap·prais·er
ap·prais·al
ap·pre·ci·a·ble
ap·pre·ci·a·bly
ap·pre·ci·ate
ap·pre·ci·at·ing
ap·pre·ci·a·tion
ap·pre·ci·a·tive
ap·pre·hend
ap·pre·hen·si·ble
ap·pre·hen·sion
ap·pre·hen·sive
ap·pren·tice
ap·prise
ap·prised
ap·pris·ing
ap·proach
ap·proach·a·ble
ap·pro·ba·tion
ap·pro·ba·to·ry
ap·pro·pri·ate
ap·pro·pri·at·ed
ap·pro·pri·at·ing
ap·pro·pri·ate·ness
ap·pro·pri·a·tion
ap·prov·al
ap·prove
ap·proved
ap·prov·ing
ap·prox·i·mate
ap·prox·i·mate·ly
ap·prox·i·ma·tion
ap·pur·te·nance
ap·pur·te·nant
ap·ri·cot
a pri·o·ri
apron
ap·ro·pos
apt
apt·ly
apt·ness
ap·ti·tude
aq·ua
aqua·cul·ture
aq·ua·lung
aq·ua·ma·rine
aq·ua·naut
aq·ua·plane
aquar·i·um
aquat·ic
aq·ue·duct
aque·ous

aq·ui·line
ar·a·besque
Ara·bi·an
Ara·bic
ar·a·ble
arach·nid
ar·ba·lest
ar·bi·ter
ar·bi·trary
ar·bi·trar·i·ly
ar·bit·ra·ment
ar·bi·trate
ar·bi·trat·ed
ar·bi·trat·ing
ar·bi·tra·tor
ar·bi·tra·tion
ar·bor
ar·bo·re·al
ar·bo·re·tum
arc
arced
arc·ing
ar·cade
ar·chae·ol·o·gy
ar·che·ol·o·gy
ar·chae·o·log·i·cal
ar·che·o·log·i·cal
ar·chae·ol·o·gist
ar·che·ol·o·gist
ar·cha·ic
ar·cha·ism
arch·an·gel
arch·bish·op
arch·dea·con
arch·di·o·cese
arch·di·oc·e·san
arch·du·cal
arch·duke
arch·duch·ess
arch·er
ar·chery
ar·che·type
arch·fiend
ar·chi·e·pis·co·pal
ar·chi·pel·a·go
ar·chi·tect
ar·chi·tec·ton·ic
ar·chi·tec·ture
ar·chi·tec·tur·al
ar·chive
ar·chi·val
ar·chi·vist
arc·tic
ar·cu·ate
ar·dent
ar·dor
ar·du·ous
ar·ea
are·na
ar·go·sy
ar·got
ar·gue
ar·gued
ar·gu·ing
ar·gu·a·ble
ar·gu·ment
ar·gu·men·ta·tion
ar·gu·men·ta·tive
ar·gu·men·tive
ar·gyle
aria
ar·id
arid·i·ty
arise
arose
aris·en
aris·ing
aris·to·crat

aris·to·crat·ic
ar·is·toc·ra·cy
ar·is·toc·ra·cies
arith·me·tic
arith·met·i·cal
arith·me·ti·cian
arm
armed
arm·ing
ar·ma·da
ar·ma·dil·lo
Ar·ma·ged·don
ar·ma·ment
ar·ma·ture
ar·mi·stice
ar·moire
ar·mor
ar·mored
ar·mory
ar·mor·ies
ar·my
ar·mies
aro·ma
ar·o·mat·ic
ar·o·mat·i·cal
around
arouse
aroused
arous·ing
arous·al
ar·peg·gio
ar·raign
ar·raign·ment
ar·range
ar·ranged
ar·rang·ing
ar·range·ment
ar·rant
ar·ray
ar·ray·al
ar·rear
ar·rear·age
ar·rest
ar·rest·er
ar·rive
ar·rived
ar·riv·ing
ar·ri·val
ar·ro·gant
ar·ro·gance
ar·ro·gant·ly
ar·ro·gate
ar·ro·gat·ed
ar·ro·ga·tion
ar·row
ar·row·head
ar·royo
ar·se·nal
ar·se·nic
ar·son
ar·son·ist
ar·te·ri·al
ar·te·ri·o·scle·ro·sis
ar·tery
ar·ter·ies
ar·te·sian
art·ful
art·ful·ly
ar·thri·tis
ar·thrit·ic
ar·thro·pod
ar·ti·choke
ar·ti·cle
ar·tic·u·lar
ar·tic·u·late
ar·tic·u·lat·ed
ar·tic·u·lat·ing
ar·tic·u·late·ly

ar·tic·u·late·ness
ar·tic·u·la·tor
ar·tic·u·la·tion
ar·ti·fact
ar·te·fact
ar·ti·fice
ar·ti·fi·cial
ar·ti·fi·ci·al·i·ty
ar·ti·fi·cial·ly
ar·til·lery
ar·ti·san
art·ist
ar·tiste
ar·tis·tic
ar·tis·ti·cal·ly
art·ist·ry
art·less
arty
ar·ti·ness
as·bes·tos
as·bes·tus
as·cend
as·cend·ance
as·cend·ence
as·cend·an·cy
as·cend·en·cy
as·cend·ant
as·cend·ent
as·cent
as·cen·sion
as·cer·tain
as·cer·tain·a·ble
as·cer·tain·ment
as·cet·ic
as·cet·i·cism
as·cot
as·cribe
as·cribed
as·crib·ing
as·crib·a·ble
as·crip·tion
asep·sis
asep·tic
asex·u·al
asex·u·al·i·ty
ashamed
asham·ed·ly
ash
ash·en
ash·es
ashy
Asi·at·ic
as·i·nine
as·i·nin·i·ty
askance
askew
asleep
aso·cial
as·par·a·gus
as·pect
as·pen
as·per·i·ty
as·perse
as·persed
as·pers·ing
as·per·sion
as·phalt
as·phyx·ia
as·phyx·i·ate
as·phyx·i·at·ed
as·phyx·i·at·ing
as·phyx·i·a·tion
as·pic
as·pir·ant
as·pi·rate
as·pi·rat·ed
as·pi·rat·ing
as·pi·ra·tion

as·pi·ra·tor
as·pire
as·pir·ing
as·pi·rin
as·sail
as·sail·a·ble
as·sail·ant
as·sas·sin
as·sas·si·nate
as·sas·si·nat·ed
as·sas·si·nat·ing
as·sas·si·na·tion
as·sas·si·na·tor
as·sault
as·say
as·say·er
as·sem·blage
as·sem·ble
as·sem·bled
as·sem·bling
as·sem·bler
as·sem·bly
as·sem·blies
as·sem·bly·man
as·sent
as·sen·ta·tion
as·sert
as·ser·tion
as·ser·tive
as·ser·tive·ness
as·sess
as·sess·a·ble
as·sess·ment
as·sess·or
as·set
as·sev·er·ate
as·sev·er·at·ed
as·sev·er·at·ing
as·sev·er·a·tion
as·si·du·i·ty
as·sid·u·ous
as·sign
as·sign·a·ble
as·sign·a·bly
as·sign·ment
as·sig·na·tion
as·sim·i·late
as·sim·i·lat·ed
as·sim·i·lat·ing
as·sim·i·la·ble
as·sim·i·la·tion
as·sist
as·sist·ance
as·sist·ant
as·size
as·so·ci·ate
as·so·ci·at·ed
as·so·ci·at·ing
as·so·ci·a·tion
as·so·ci·a·tive
as·so·nance
as·so·nant
as·sort
as·sort·ed
as·sort·ment
as·suage
as·suaged
as·suag·ing
as·suage·ment
as·sua·sive
as·sume
as·sumed
as·sum·ing
as·sump·tion
as·sure
as·sured
as·sur·ing
as·sur·ance

as·sur·ed·ly
as·sur·ed·ness
as·ter·isk
as·ter·oid
asth·ma
asth·mat·ic
astig·ma·tism
as·tig·mat·ic
as·ton·ish
as·ton·ish·ing
as·ton·ish·ment
as·tound
astrad·dle
as·tra·khan
as·tral
astray
astride
as·trin·gent
as·trin·gen·cy
as·tro·dome
as·tro·labe
as·trol·o·gy
as·trol·o·ger
as·trol·log·ic
as·tro·log·i·cal
as·tro·naut
as·tro·nau·tics
as·tro·nau·ti·cal
as·tro·nom·ic
as·tro·nom·i·cal·ly
as·tron·o·my
as·tron·o·mer
as·tro·phys·ics
as·tro·phys·i·cist
as·tute
as·tute·ly
as·tu·cious
asun·der
asy·lum
asym·me·try
asym·met·ric
asym·met·ri·cal
at·a·vism
at·a·vis·tic
at·el·ier
athe·ism
athe·ist
athe·is·tic
athe·is·ti·cal
ath·er·o·scle·ro·sis
ath·lete
ath·let·ic
ath·let·ics
ath·let·i·cal·ly
athwart
at·las
at·las·es
at·mos·phere
at·mos·pher·ic
at·mos·pher·i·cal
at·oll
at·om
atom·ic
atom·i·cal
at·om·ism
at·om·ize
at·om·ized
at·om·iz·ing
at·om·iz·er
atonal
ato·nal·i·ty
atone
atoned
aton·ing
atone·ment
atri·um
atro·cious
atroc·i·ty

atroc·i·ties
at·ro·phy
  at·ro·phies
  at·ro·phied
  at·ro·phy·ing
  atroph·ic
at·tach
  at·tach·ment
at·ta·che
at·tack
at·tain
  at·tain·a·ble
  at·tain·ment
at·tain·der
at·taint
at·tar
at·tempt
at·tend
  at·tend·ance
at·tend·ant
at·ten·tion
  at·ten·tive
at·ten·u·ate
  at·ten·u·at·ed
  at·ten·u·at·ing
  at·ten·u·a·tion
at·test
  at·test·ta·tion
at·tic
at·tire
  at·tired
  at·tir·ing
  at·tire·ment
at·ti·tude
at·ti·tu·di·nize
at·tor·ney
  at·tor·neys
at·tract
at·trac·tive
at·trac·tion
at·tri·bute
  at·tri·but·ed
  at·tri·but·ing
  at·tri·but·a·ble
  at·tri·bu·tion
  at·trib·u·tive
at·tri·tion
  at·trite
at·tune
  at·tuned
  at·tun·ing
atyp·i·cal
au·burn
auc·tion
  auc·tion·eer
au·da·cious
  au·dac·i·ty
au·di·ble
  au·di·bil·i·ty
  au·di·bly
au·di·ence
au·dio
au·dio·phile
au·dio·vis·u·al
au·dit
au·di·tion
au·dit·or
au·di·to·ri·um
au·di·to·ry
aught
aug·ment
aug·men·ta·tion
au grat·in
au·gust
  au·gust·ly
auld·lang syne
au·ral
  au·ral·ly

au·re·ate
au·re·ole
au·re·o·my·cin
au re·voir
au·ri·cle
  au·ric·u·lar
au·ro·ra
au·ro·ra aus·tra·lis
au·ro·ra bor·e·al·is
aus·pice
  aus·pic·es
aus·pi·cious
aus·tere
  aus·ter·i·ty
au·then·tic
au·then·ti·cate
  au·then·ti·cat·ed
  au·then·ti·cat·ing
  au·then·ti·ca·tion
  au·then·tic·i·ty
au·thor
  au·thor·ess
  au·thor·ship
au·thor·i·tar·i·an
au·thor·i·ta·tive
au·thor·i·ty
  au·thor·i·ties
au·thor·ize
  au·thor·ized
  au·thor·iz·ing
  au·thor·i·za·tion
au·to·bi·og·ra·phy
  au·to·bi·og·ra·phies
  au·to·bi·og·ra·pher
  au·to·bi·o·graph·ic
  au·to·bi·o·graph·i·cal
au·toc·ra·cy
  au·toc·ra·cies
au·to·crat
  au·to·crat·ic
  au·to·crat·i·cal·ly
au·to·graph
au·to·mate
  au·to·mat·ed
  au·to·mat·ing
au·to·mat·ic
  au·to·mat·i·cal
au·to·ma·tion
au·tom·a·tism
  au·tom·a·ton
au·to·mo·bile
au·to·mo·tive
au·ton·o·mous
  au·to·nom·ic
au·ton·o·my
  au·ton·o·mies
au·top·sy
au·tumn
  au·tum·nal
aux·il·ia·ry
  aux·il·ia·ries
avail
  avail·a·ble
  avail·a·bil·i·ty
av·a·lanche
  av·a·lanch·ing
avant·garde
av·a·rice
  av·a·ri·cious
Ave Ma·ria
avenge
  avenged
  aveng·ing
  aveng·er
av·e·nue
aver
  averred
  aver·ring

aver·ment
av·er·age
  av·er·aged
  av·er·ag·ing
averse
  averse·ly
  aver·sion
avert
  avert·a·ble
avi·ary
  avi·ar·ies
avi·a·tion
avi·a·tor
avi·a·trix
av·id
  avid·i·ty
  av·id·ly
av·o·ca·do
av·o·ca·tion
avoid
  avoid·a·ble
  avoid·ance
av·oir·du·pois
avow
  avow·al
  avowed
avun·cu·lar
await
awake
  awoke
  awaked
  awak·ing
  awak·en
award
aware
  aware·ness
away
awe
  awed
  aw·ing
aweigh
awe·some
awe·strick·en
  awe·struck
aw·ful
  aw·ful·ly
  aw·ful·ness
awhile
awhirl
awk·ward
  awk·ward·ness
awn·ing
awry
ax
  ax·es
ax·i·om
  ax·i·o·mat·ic
  ax·i·o·mat·i·cal
ax·is
  ax·es
  ax·i·al
ax·le
aza·lea
az·i·muth
az·ure

B

bab·bitt
bab·ble
  bab·bled
  bab·bling
ba·boon
ba·bush·ka
ba·by
  ba·bies
  ba·bied

ba·by·ing
ba·by·sit
  ba·by·sit·ting
  ba·by·sit·ter
bac·ca·lau·re·ate
bac·ca·rat
bac·cha·nal
  bac·cha·na·li·an
bach·e·lor
ba·cil·lus
  ba·cil·li
back·ache
back·bite
back·board
back·bone
back·drop
back·field
back·fire
back·gam·mon
back·ground
back·hand
back·hand·ed
back·ing
back·lash
back·log
back·side
back·slide
  back·slid·den
  back·slid·er
back·spin
back·stage
back·stairs
back·stop
back·talk
back·ward
  back·ward·ness
back·wash
ba·con
bac·te·ria
  bac·te·ri·um
  bac·te·ri·al
bac·te·ri·cide
  bac·te·ri·ci·dal
bac·te·ri·ol·o·gy
  bac·te·ri·ol·o·gist
  bac·te·ri·o·log·i·cal
bad
  worse
  worst
badge
badg·er
bad·i·nage
bad·land
bad·ly
bad·min·ton
baf·fle
  baf·fled
  baf·fling
bag
  bagged
  bag·ging
bag·a·telle
ba·gel
bag·gage
bag·gy
  bag·gi·er
  bag·ging
ba·gnio
bag·pipe
ba·guette
bail·a·ble
bail·iff
bail·i·wick
bails·man
baize
bake
  baked
  bak·ing

bak·er
bak·er·y
  bak·er·ies
bak·sheesh
bal·a·lai·ka
bal·ance
  bal·anced
  bal·anc·ing
  bal·anc·er
bal·co·ny
  bal·co·nies
bald
  bald·ness
bal·der·dash
bald·head
bale
  baled
  bal·ing
bale·ful
balk
balky
  balk·i·est
bal·lad
bal·last
bal·le·ri·na
bal·let
bal·lis·tic
  bal·lis·tics
  bal·lis·ti·cian
bal·loon
bal·lot
  bal·lot·ed
  bal·lot·ing
ball·room
bal·ly·hoo
balmy
  balm·i·er
ba·lo·ney
bal·sa
bal·sam
bal·us·ter
  bal·us·trade
bam·bi·no
bam·boo
bam·boo·zle
  bam·boo·zled
  bam·boo·zling
ban
  banned
  ban·ning
ba·nal
  ba·nal·i·ty
ba·nana
band·age
  band·aged
  band·ag·ing
ban·dana
  ban·dan·na
ban·deau
ban·de·role
ban·dit
  ban·dit·ry
ban·do·leer
  ban·do·lier
band·stand
band·wag·on
ban·dy
  ban·died
  ban·dy·ing
bane·ful
ban·gle
ban·ish
  ban·ish·ment
ban·is·ter
  ban·nis·ter
ban·jo
bank·book
bank·er

bank·ing
bank·rupt
  bank·rupt·cy
  bank·rupt·cies
ban·ner
banquet
ban·quette
ban·shee
ban·tam
ban·ter
  ban·ter·ing·ly
ban·yan
ban·zai
bap·tism
  bap·tis·mal
Bap·tist
bap·tis·tery
bap·tize
  bap·tized
  bap·tiz·ing
bar
  barred
  bar·ring
bar·bar·ic
  bar·bar·i·an
  bar·ba·rism
  bar·ba·rous
bar·bar·i·ty
  bar·bar·i·ties
bar·be·cue
  bar·be·cued
  bar·be·cu·ing
bar·ber
bar·bi·can
bar·bi·tal
bar·bi·tu·rate
bar·ca·role
bare
  bare·ness
bare·back
bare·faced
bare·foot
bare·ly
bar·gain
barge
  barged
  barg·ing
bar·i·tone
bar·i·um
bar·ley
bar mitz·vah
bar·na·cle
bar·o·graph
ba·rom·et·er
  bar·o·met·ric
bar·on
  bar·on·ess
  ba·ro·ni·al
bar·on·et
ba·roque
bar·rack
bar·ra·cu·da
bar·rage
bar·rel
  bar·reled
  bar·rel·ing
bar·ren
  bar·ren·ness
bar·rette
bar·ri·cade
  bar·ri·cad·ed
  bar·ri·cad·ing
bar·ri·er
bar·row
bar·ten·der
bar·ter
  bar·ter·er
ba·sal

bas·al·ly
ba·salt
base
  based
  bas·ing
base·ball
base·less
base·ment
bash·ful
  bash·ful·ly
ba·sic
  ba·si·cal·ly
ba·sil
ba·sil·i·ca
bas·i·lisk
ba·sin
ba·sis
  ba·ses
bas·ket·ball
bas·ket·ry
bas-re·lief
bas·si·net
bas·so
  bas·sos
bas·soon
bas·tard
  bas·tard·ize
  bas·tard·ly
baste
  bast·ed
  bast·ing
bat
  bat·ted
  bat·ting
  bat·ter
bate
  bat·ed
  bat·ing
bathe
  bathed
  bath·ing
bath·y·sphere
ba·tiste
bat·on
bat·tal·ion
bat·ten
bat·ter
bat·tery
bat·tle
  bat·tled
  bat·tling
bat·tle·field
bat·tle·ment
bau·ble
baux·ite
bawdy
bay·o·net
bay·ou
ba·zaar
ba·zoo·ka
beach·comb·er
beach·head
bea·con
bead·ed
bead·like
beak·er
beamed
bear
  bore
  borne
bear·ing
bear·a·ble
  bear·a·bly
beard·ed
beard·less
bear·ish
beast
  beast·li·ness

beast·ly
beat
  beat·en
  beat·ing
be·a·tif·ic
be·at·i·fy
  be·at·i·fied
  be·at·i·fy·ing
  be·at·i·fi·ca·tion
be·at·i·tude
beat·nik
beau
  beaus
  beaux
beau geste
beau·te·ous
beau·ti·cian
beau·ti·fy
  beau·ti·fied
  beau·ti·fi·ca·tion
beauty
  beau·ti·ful
beaux-arts
bea·ver
be·calm
be·cause
beck·on
be·cloud
be·come
  be·came
  be·com·ing
bed
  bed·ded
  bed·ding
be·daz·zle
  be·daz·zled
  be·daz·zling
  be·daz·zle·ment
be·dev·il
  be·dev·iled
  be·dev·il·ing
  be·dev·il·ment
be·dim
  be·dimmed
  be·dim·ming
bed·lam
bed·drag·gle
  be·drag·gling
bed·rid·den
bed·room
beech-nut
beef
  beeves
beef·eat·er
beef·steak
beefy
  beef·i·er
bee·hive
bee·line
Bee·tho·ven
bee·tle
be·fall
  be·fell
  be·fall·en
  be·fall·ing
be·fit
  be·fit·ted
  be·fit·ting
be·fog
  be·fogged
  be·fog·ging
be·fore
be·friend
be·fud·dle
  be·fud·dled
  be·fud·dling
beg
  begged

beg·ging
be·get
  be·got
  be·got·ten
beg·gar
  beg·gar·ly
be·gin
  be·gan
  be·gun
  be·gin·ning
be·gin·ner
be·gone
be·go·nia
be·got·ten
be·grime
be·grudge
  be·grudged
  be·grudg·ing
be·guile
  be·guiled
  be·guil·ing
be·half
be·have
  be·haved
  be·hav·ing
  be·hav·ior
    be·hav·ior·ism
    be·hav·ior·ist
be·head
be·he·moth
be·hest
be·hind
be·hold
  be·held
  be·hold·ing
be·hold·en
be·hoove
beige
be·ing
be·la·bor
be·lat·ed
  be·lat·ed·ly
be·lay
  be·layed
  be·lay·ing
belch
be·lea·guer
bel·fry
  bel·fries
be·lie
  be·lied
  be·ly·ing
be·lief
be·lieve
  be·lieved
  be·liev·ing
  be·liev·a·ble
  be·liev·er
be·lit·tle
  be·lit·tled
  be·lit·tling
bel·la·don·na
belles let·tres
bel·li·cose
  bel·li·cos·i·ty
bel·lig·er·ence
  bel·lig·er·en·cy
bel·lig·er·ent
  bel·lig·er·ent·ly
bel·low
bel·ly
  bel·lies
  bel·lied
  bel·ly·ing
bel·ly·ache
  bel·ly·ach·ing
be·long
  be·long·ings

be·loved
be·low
belt·ed
be·mire
  be·mired
  be·mir·ing
be·moan
be·muse
  be·mused
  be·mus·ing
bend
  bent
  bend·ing
be·neath
ben·e·dict
ben·e·dic·tion
  ben·e·dic·to·ry
ben·e·fac·tion
ben·e·fac·tor
  ben·e·fac·tress
ben·e·fice
  ben·e·ficed
  ben·e·fic·ing
be·nef·i·cent
  be·nef·i·cence
ben·e·fi·cial
ben·e·fi·ci·ar·y
  ben·e·fi·ci·ar·ies
ben·e·fit
  ben·e·fit·ed
  ben·e·fit·ing
be·nev·o·lence
  be·nev·o·lent
be·night·ed
be·nign
  be·nign·ly
be·nig·nant
  be·nig·nan·cy
be·numb
ben·zene
ben·zine
be·queath
be·quest
be·rate
  be·rat·ed
  be·rat·ing
be·reave
  be·reaved
  be·reft
  be·reav·ing
be·ret
ber·ga·mot
ber·i·beri
ber·ke·li·um
ber·ret·ta
  bir·ret·ta
ber·ry
  ber·ries
ber·serk
berth
ber·yl
be·ryl·li·um
be·seech
  be·sought
  be·seeched
  be·seech·ing
be·set
  be·set·ting
be·side
be·siege
  be·sieged
  be·sieg·ing
  be·sieg·er
be·smear
be·smirch
be·sot·ted
be·speak
  be·spoke

be·spok·en
be·speak·ing
bes·tial
bes·tial·ly
bes·ti·al·i·ty
be·stir
be·stirred
be·stir·ring
be·stow
be·stow·al
be·stride
be·strode
be·strid·den
be·strid·ing
bet
bet·ted
bet·ting
bet·tor
be·take
be·took
be·tak·en
be·tak·ing
be·ta·tron
be·tel
beth·el
be·tide
be·tid·ed
be·tid·ing
be·to·ken
be·tray
be·tray·al
be·tray·er
be·troth
be·troth·al
be·trothed
bet·ter
bet·ter·ment
bet·tor
be·tween
be·twixt
bev·el
bev·eled
bev·el·ing
bev·er·age
bevy
bev·ies
be·wail
be·ware
be·wil·der
be·wil·der·ing·ly
be·wil·der·ment
be·witch
be·witch·ing
be·witch·ment
be·yond
bi·an·nu·al
bi·as
bi·ased
bi·as·ing
bi·ax·i·al
bi·be·lot
Bi·ble
Bib·li·cal
bib·li·og·ra·phy
bib·li·og·ra·phies
bib·li·og·ra·pher
bib·li·o·graph·ic
bib·li·o·ma·nia
bib·li·o·ma·ni·ac
bib·li·o·phile
bib·u·lous
bi·cam·er·al
bi·car·bo·nate
bi·cen·ten·ni·al
bi·cen·te·nary
bi·ceps
bi·chlo·ride
bick·er

bi·cus·pid
bi·cy·cle
bi·cy·cled
bi·cy·cling
bi·cy·cler
bi·cy·clist
bid
bade
bid·den
bid·ding
bid·da·ble
bid·der
bide
bode
bid·ed
bid·ing
bi·en·ni·al
bi·en·ni·al·ly
bi·en·ni·um
bier
bi·fo·cals
bi·fur·cate
bi·fur·ca·tion
big
big·ger
big·gest
big·a·my
big·a·mist
big·a·mous
big-heart·ed
big·ot
big·ot·ed
big·ot·ry
bi·jou
bi·ki·ni
bi·la·bi·al
bi·lat·er·al
bilge
bi·lin·gual
bil·ious
billed
bill·ing
bil·let
bil·let-doux
bil·liards
bil·lion
bil·lionth
bil·lion·aire
bil·low
bil·low·y
bi·met·al·lism
bi·month·ly
bi·na·ry
bind
bound
bind·ing
bind·er
bind·ery
binge
bin·go
bin·na·cle
bi·noc·u·lar
bi·no·mi·al
bi·o·chem·is·try
bi·o·chem·i·cal
bi·o·chem·ist
bio·de·grad·able
bi·o·e·col·o·gy
bi·o·en·gi·neer·ing
bi·o·gen·e·sis
bi·og·ra·phy
bi·og·ra·pher
bi·o·graph·ic
bi·o·graph·i·cal
bi·ol·o·gy
bi·o·log·i·cal
bi·ol·o·gist
bi·om·e·try

bi·o·met·rics
bi·on·ics
bi·o·nom·ics
bi·o·phys·ics
bi·op·sy
bi·op·sies
bi·par·ti·san
bi·par·tite
bi·ped
bi·plane
bi·po·lar
bi·ra·cial
birch
bird·brained
bird·ie
bird's-eye
bi·ret·ta
be·ret·ta
birth·day
birth·mark
birth·place
birth·stone
bis·cuit
bi·sect
bi·sec·tion
bi·sec·tor
bi·sex·u·al
bish·op
bish·op·ric
bis·muth
bi·son
bisque
bis·tro
bitch
bit·chy
bite
bit
bit·ten
bit·ing
bit·ter
bit·ter·ly
bit·ter·ness
bit·tern
bi·tu·men
bi·tu·mi·nous
bi·va·lent
bi·va·lence
bi·valve
bi·val·vu·lar
biv·ou·ac
biv·ou·acked
biv·ou·ack·ing
bi·week·ly
bi·zarre
bi·zarre·ness
blab
blabbed
blab·bing
black·ball
black·ber·ry
black·bird
black·board
black·en
black·eyed
black·guard
black·head
black·jack
black·ly
black·mail
black·out
black·top
blad·der
blade
blad·ed
blame
blamed
blam·ing
blam·a·ble

blame·less
blame·wor·thy
blanch
blanc·mange
bland
bland·ly
bland·ness
blan·dish
blan·dish·ment
blank
blank·ly
blan·ket
blare
blared
blar·ing
blar·ney
bla·se
blas·pheme
blas·phemed
blas·phem·ing
blas·phem·er
blas·phem·ous
blas·phemy
blas·phem·ies
blast·ed
bla·tant
bla·tan·cy
bla·tant·ly
blaze
blazed
blaz·ing
bleach·er
bleak
bleak·ly
bleary
blear·i·ness
bleed
bled
bleed·ing
blem·ish
blend·er
bless·ed
blest
bles·sing
blind
blind·ing
blind·ness
blind·er
blink·er
bliss·ful
blis·ter
blithe·ly
blitz·krieg
bliz·zard
block·ade
block·ad·ed
block·ad·ing
block·bus·ter
blond·ness
blood·curd·ling
blood·hound
blood·less
blood·shed
blood·shot
blood·stained
blood·suck·er
blood·thirsty
bloody
blood·i·est
blood·ied
blood·y·ing
bloom
bloom·ing
bloop·er
blos·som
blot
blot·ted
blot·ting

blotch
blotchy
blot·ter
blow
blew
blown
blow·ing
blow·er
blow·torch
blub·ber
bludg·eon
blue
blu·est
blu·ing
blue·ness
blue·bell
blue·ber·ry
blue·bird
blue·blood·ed
blue·col·lar
blue·print
blun·der
blun·der·ing
blun·der·buss
blunt·ly
blunt·ness
blur
blurred
blur·ring
blur·ry
blush
blushed
blush·ing
blus·ter
blus·ter·ing·ly
blus·ter·ous
blus·tery
boar
board·er
board·walk
boast
boast·fulness
boast·ing·ly
boat·house
boat·swain
bob
bobbed
bob·bing
bob·bin
bob·ble
bob·bled
bob·bling
bob·o·link
bob·sled
bob·white
bode
bod·ed
bod·ing
bod·ice
bod·kin
bod·y
bod·ies
bod·i·ly
bod·y·guard
bog
bog·gy
bo·gey
bog·gle
bog·gled
bog·gling
bo·gus
bogy
bo·he·mi·an
boil·er
bois·ter·ous
bois·ter·ous·ness
bold
bold·ly

bold·face
bo·le·ro
boll·worm
bo·lo
bo·lo·gna
bo·lo·ney
Bol·she·vik
  Bol·she·vism
bol·ster
  bol·ster·er
bolt
  bolt·ed
bom·bard
  bom·bard·ment
bom·bar·dier
bom·bast
  bom·bas·tic
  bom·bas·ti·cal·ly
bomb·er
bomb·proof
bomb·shell
bomb·sight
bo·na fide
bo·nan·za
bon·bon
bond·age
bond·ed
bond·man
bone
  boned
  bon·ing
bone·head
bon·fire
bon·go
bon·ho·mie
bon·net
bon·ny
bo·nus
  bo·nus·es
bon voy·age
bony
  bon·i·er
boo·by
  boo·bies
boo·by trap
boo·dle
book·bind·er
book·case
book·end
book·ie
book·ish
book·keep·ing
  book·keep·er
book·let
book·mark
book·mo·bile
book·plate
book·sell·er
book·shelf
book·worm
boom·er·ang
boon·dog·gle
boor
  boor·ish
boost
  boost·er
booth
boot·leg
  boot·legged
  boot·leg·ging
  boot·leg·ger
boot·ty
booze
  booz·er
  boozy
bo·rax
Bor·deaux
bor·der

bor·dered
bor·der·land
bor·der·line
bore
  bored
  bor·ing
  bor·er
  bore·dom
bor·ough
bor·row
  bor·row·er
borsch
borscht
bos·om
bossy
  boss·i·est
  boss·i·ness
bo·sun
bot·a·ny
  bo·tan·i·cal
  bot·a·nist
  bot·a·nize
botch
  botchy
  botch·i·est
both·er
  both·er·some
bot·tle
  bot·tled
  bot·tling
  bot·tle·ful
bot·tle·neck
bot·tom
  bot·tom·less
bot·u·lism
bou·doir
bouf·fant
bough
bought
bouil·lon
boul·der
boul·e·vard
bounce
  bounced
  bounc·ing
bound
bound·a·ry
  bound·a·ries
bound·less
boun·te·ous
boun·ti·ful
boun·ty
  boun·ties
bou·quet
bour·bon
bour·geois
bour·geoi·sie
bou·tique
bou·ton·niere
bo·vine
bow·el
bow·er
bow·ery
bow·ie
bow·ing
bow·knot
bowl
bow·leg
  bow·leg·ged
bowl·er
bow·line
bowl·ing
bow·string
box·car
box·er
box·ful
box·ing
boy

boy·hood
boy·ish
boy·cott
boy·friend
boy·sen·ber·ry
brace
  braced
  brac·ing
brace·let
brac·er
bra·ces
brack·et
brack·ish
brad
  brad·ded
  brad·ding
brag
  bragged
  brag·ging
brag·ga·do·cio
brag·gart
Brah·ma
Brah·min
  Brah·man
braid
  braid·ing
braille
brain·child
brain·less
brain·pow·er
brain·storm
brain·wash·ing
brainy
  brain·i·er
  brain·i·est
braise
  braised
  brais·ing
brake
  brak·ing
bram·ble
  bram·bly
branch
  branch·ed
brand
  brand·er
bran·dish
bran·dy
  bran·dies
  bran·died
bra·sier
bras·siere
brassy
  brass·i·er
brat
  brat·tish
  brat·ty
bra·va·do
brave
  braved
  brav·ing
  brave·ness
  brav·ery
  brav·er·ies
bra·vo
bra·vu·ra
brawl
  brawl·er
brawn
  brawny
  brawn·i·er
  brawn·i·ness
braze
bra·zen
bra·zier
breach
bread
  bread·ed

bread·win·ner
break
  broke
  bro·ken
  break·ing
  break·a·ble
break·age
break·down
break·er
break·fast
break·neck
break·out
break·through
break·wa·ter
breast·bone
breath
breathe
  breathed
  breath·ing
breath·less
breath·tak·ing
breathy
breech·es
breech·load·er
breed
  bred
  breed·ing
breeze
  breezy
  breez·i·ness
breth·ren
bre·vet
  bre·vet·ted
  bre·vet·ting
bre·vi·a·ry
  bre·vi·a·ries
brev·i·ty
brew·ery
  brew·er·ies
bri·ar
bribe
  bribed
  brib·ing
  brib·a·ble
brib·ery
  brib·er·ies
bric·a·brac
brick·lay·er
brick·yard
bride
  brid·al
bride·groom
brides·maid
bridge
bridge·work
bri·dle
  bri·dled
  bri·dling
brief
  brief·ly
brief·ing
bri·er
bri·gade
brig·a·dier
brig·and
brig·an·tine
bright
  bright·ness
  bright·en
bril·liance
  bril·lian·cy
  bril·liant
brim·ful
brim·ming
brim·stone
brine
  briny
bring

brought
bring·ing
brink
bri·quette
  briquet
brisk
  brisk·ly
  brisk·ness
bris·ket
bris·tle
  bris·tled
Brit·ain
  Bri·tan·nia
  Brit·ish
  Brit·on
Brit·ta·ny
britch·es
brit·tle
broach
  broached
  broach·ing
broad·cast
  broad·cast·ed
  broad·cast·ing
broad·cloth
broad·mind·ed
broad·side
bro·cade
  bro·cad·ed
  bro·cad·ing
broc·co·li
bro·chure
broque
broil·er
bro·ken
bro·ken-heart·ed
bro·ker
bro·ker·age
bro·mide
bron·chi
bron·chi·al
bron·chi·tis
bron·co
bron·to·sau·rus
bronze
  bronzed
  bronz·ing
brooch
brood
  brood·ing
broth·el
broth·er
  broth·er·hood
broth·er-in-law
broth·er·ly
  broth·er·li·ness
brow·beat
  brow·beat·en
brown
brown·ie
browse
  browsed
  brows·ing
bru·in
bruise
  bruised
  bruis·ing
  bruis·er
bru·net
brush-off
brusque
  brusk
bru·tal
  bru·tal·i·ty
  bru·tal·ize
  bru·tal·ized
  bru·tal·iz·ing
  bru·tal·i·za·tion

brut·ish
bub·ble
bub·bled
bub·bling
bu·bon·ic
buc·ca·neer
buck·a·roo
buck·board
buck·et·ful
buck·le
buck·ram
buck·skin
buck·tooth
buck·wheat
bu·col·ic
bud
bud·ded
bud·ding
Bud·dha
Bud·dhism
Bud·dhist
bud·dy
budge
budg·et
buf·fa·lo
buf·fa·loed
buff·er
buf·fet
buf·foon
buf·foon·ery
bug
bugged
bug·ging
bug·a·boo
bug·gy
bu·gle
bu·gling
bu·gler
build
built
build·ing
bulb
bul·bous
bulge
bulged
bulg·ing
bulgy
bulk·head
bulky
bulk·i·er
bulk·i·ness
bull·doze
bull·dozed
bull·doz·ing
bull·doz·er
bul·let
bul·le·tin
bul·let·proof
bull·fight
bull·frog
bull·head·ed
bul·lion
bull·ock
bull's-eye
bul·ly
bul·lies
bul·lied
bul·ly·ing
bul·rush
bul·wark
bum
bummed
bum·ming
bum·ble·bee
bump·er
bump·kin
bump·tious
bumpy

bump·i·est
bump·i·ness
bunch
bunchy
bun·co
bun·dle
bun·dled
bun·dling
bun·ga·low
bun·gle
bun·gled
bun·gling
bun·ion
bunk·er
bun·ny
bun·nies
Bun·sen burner
bun·ting
bu·oy
buoy·ant
buoy·an·cy
bur·den
bur·den·some
bu·reau
bu·reaus
bu·reaux
bu·reauc·ra·cy
bu·reauc·ra·cies
bu·reau·crat
bu·reau·crat·ic
bur·geon
bur·gess
bur·gher
bur·glar
bur·glar·ize
bur·glar·ized
bur·glar·iz·ing
bur·gla·ry
bur·gla·ries
bur·gle
bur·gled
bur·gling
Bur·gun·dy
bur·i·al
bur·lap
bur·lesque
bur·lesqued
bur·les·quing
bur·ly
bur·li·ness
burn
burned
burnt
burn·ing
burn·er
bur·nish
bur·noose
burr
burred
bur·ring
bur·ro
bur·row
bur·sa
bur·sar
bur·sa·ry
bur·si·tis
burst
burst·ing
bury
bur·ied
bur·y·ing
bus
bus·es
bush·el
Bu·shi·do
bush·ing
bush·man
bush·mas·ter

bush·whack
bushy
bus·i·ly
busi·ness
busi·ness·like
busi·ness·man
bus·tle
bus·tled
bus·tling
busy
bus·ied
bus·y·ing
bus·i·ly
bus·i·er
bu·tane
butch·er
butch·ery
but·ler
butt
butte
but·ter
but·ter·fin·gered
but·ter·fly
but·ter·flies
but·ter·scotch
but·tery
but·tock
but·ton·hole
but·ton·hol·ing
but·tress
bux·om
buy
bought
buy·ing
buy·er
buz·zard
buzz·er
by·law
by·line
by·pass
by·play
by·prod·uct
by·stand·er
byte
by·way
by·word
Byz·an·tine

C

ca·bal
ca·ball·ed
ca·ball·ing
ca·bal·le·ro
ca·ba·na
cab·a·ret
cab·bage
cab·in
cab·i·net
ca·ble
ca·bled
ca·bling
ca·ble·gram
ca·boose
cab·ri·o·let
ca·cao
cache
cached
cach·ing
ca·chet
cack·le
cack·led
cack·ling
ca·coph·o·ny
ca·coph·o·nous
cac·tus
cac·ti

cad
cad·dish
ca·dav·er
ca·dav·er·ous
cad·die
cad·died
cad·dy·ing
cad·dy
ca·dence
ca·den·za
ca·det
cadge
cadged
cadg·ing
cad·mi·um
ca·dre
ca·du·ce·us
Cae·sar
cae·sar·e·an
ces·ar·ean
ca·fe au lait
caf·e·te·ria
caf·feine
caf·tan
cage
caged
cag·ing
cagey
ca·gi·ly
cai·man
cais·son
ca·jole
ca·joled
ca·jol·ing
Ca·jun
cake
caked
cak·ing
cal·a·bash
cal·a·boose
cal·a·mine
ca·lam·i·ty
ca·lam·i·ties
ca·lam·i·tous
cal·ci·fy
cal·ci·fied
cal·ci·fy·ing
cal·ci·fi·ca·tion
cal·ci·mine
cal·ci·um
cal·cu·la·ble
cal·cu·la·bil·i·ty
cal·cu·late
cal·cu·lat·ed
cal·cu·lat·ing
cal·cu·la·tion
cal·cu·la·tor
cal·cu·lus
cal·dron
cal·en·dar
calf
calves
cal·i·ber
cal·i·brate
cal·i·brat·ed
cal·i·brat·ing
cal·i·bra·tion
cal·i·co
cal·i·coes
cal·i·per
ca·liph
cal·is·then·ics
cal·lig·ra·phy
cal·lig·ra·pher
call·ing
cal·li·o·pe
cal·lous
cal·loused

cal·low
cal·lus
calm·ly
ca·lor·ic
cal·o·rie
cal·o·ries
cal·um·ny
cal·um·nies
cal·lum·ni·ate
ca·lum·ni·at·ed
ca·lum·ni·at·ing
ca·lum·ni·a·tion
Cal·va·ry
calve
calved
calv·ing
ca·lyp·so
ca·ma·ra·de·rie
cam·ber
cam·bric
cam·el
ca·mel·lia
Cam·em·bert
cam·eo
cam·era
cam·i·sole
cam·ou·flage
cam·ou·flaged
cam·ou·flag·ing
cam·paign
camp·er
cam·phor
cam·pus
cam·pus·es
cam·shaft
can
canned
can·ning
Can·a·da
Ca·na·di·an
ca·nal
can·a·pe
ca·nary
ca·nas·ta
can·can
can·cel
can·celed
can·cel·ing
can·cel·la·tion
can·cer
can·de·la·brum
can·de·la·bra
can·des·cent
can·des·cence
can·did
can·di·da·cy
can·di·da·cies
can·di·date
can·died
can·dle
can·dled
can·dling
can·dor
can·dy
can·dies
can·died
cane
caned
can·ing
ca·nine
can·is·ter
can·ker
canned
can·nery
can·ner·ies
can·ni·bal
can·ni·bal·ism
can·ni·bal·ize

can·ni·bal·iz·ing
can·non
can·ny
can·ni·ly
can·ni·ness
ca·noe
ca·noed
ca·noe·ing
ca·noe·ist
can·on
can·on·ize
can·on·iz·ing
can·on·i·za·tion
can·o·py
can·o·pies
can·o·pied
can·o·py·ing
can·ta·loupe
can·ta·lope
can·tan·ker·ous
can·ta·ta
can·teen
can·ter
can·ti·lev·er
can·to
can·tor
can·vas
can·vass
can·yon
cap
capped
cap·ping
ca·pa·bil·i·ty
ca·pa·bil·i·ties
ca·pa·ble
ca·pa·bly
ca·pa·cious
ca·pac·i·tate
ca·pac·i·tat·ed
ca·pac·i·tat·ing
ca·pac·i·ty
ca·pac·i·ties
ca·per
cap·il·lar·i·ty
cap·il·lary
cap·il·lar·ies
cap·i·tal
cap·i·tal·ism
cap·i·tal·is·tic
cap·i·tal·ist
cap·i·tal·ize
cap·i·tal·i·za·tion
cap·i·tal·ly
cap·i·ta·tion
ca·pit·u·late
ca·pit·u·lat·ed
ca·pit·u·lat·ing
ca·pit·u·la·tion
ca·pon
ca·pric·cio
ca·price
ca·pri·cious
cap·ri·ole
cap·ri·oled
cap·ri·ol·ing
cap·size
cap·siz·ing
cap·stan
cap·sule
cap·su·lar
cap·tain
cap·tain·cy
cap·tion
cap·tious
cap·ti·vate
cap·ti·vat·ed
cap·ti·vat·ing
cap·ti·va·tion

cap·tive
cap·tiv·i·ty
cap·tor
cap·ture
cap·tured
cap·tur·ing
car·a·cole
car·a·cul
ca·rafe
car·a·mel
car·at
car·a·van
car·a·way
car·bide
car·bine
car·bohy·drate
car·bol·ic
car·bon
car·bo·na·ceous
car·bo·na·tion
car·bon di·ox·ide
car·bon·ize
car·bon·ized
car·bon·iz·ing
car·bon·i·za·tion
car·bon mon·ox·ide
car·bo·run·dum
car·boy
car·bun·cle
car·bu·re·tor
car·cass
car·cin·o·gen
car·cin·o·gen·ic
car·ci·no·ma
car·da·mom
card·board
car·di·ac
car·di·gan
car·di·nal
car·di·o·graph
car·di·og·ra·phy
car·dio·vas·cu·lar
card·sharp
care
cared
car·ing
ca·reen
ca·reer
care·free
care·ful
care·ful·ly
care·less
care·less·ness
ca·ress
ca·ress·ing·ly
car·et
care·tak·er
car·go
Car·ib·be·an
car·i·bou
car·i·ca·ture
car·i·ca·tured
car·i·ca·tur·ing
car·i·ca·tur·ist
car·il·lon
car·mine
car·nage
car·nal
car·nal·i·ty
car·nal·ly
car·na·tion
car·nel·ian
car·ni·val
car·ni·vore
car·niv·o·rous
car·ol
car·oled
car·ol·ing

car·om
ca·rouse
ca·roused
ca·rous·ing
ca·rous·al
car·ou·sel
car·pen·ter
car·pen·try
car·pet
car·pet·bag·ger
car·pet·ing
car·rel
car·riage
car·ri·er
car·ri·on
car·rot
car·roty
car·ry
car·ried
car·ry·ing
cart·age
carte blanche
car·tel
car·te·lize
car·ti·lage
car·ti·lag·i·nous
car·tog·ra·phy
car·tog·ra·pher
car·to·graph·ic
car·ton
car·toon
car·tridge
carve
carved
carv·ing
car·y·at·id
ca·sa·ba
cas·cade
cas·cad·ed
cas·cad·ing
case
cased
cas·ing
case·ment
ca·se·ous
cash·ew
cash·ier
cash·mere
ca·si·no
cas·ket
cas·sa·ba
cas·se·role
cas·sette
cas·sock
cast
cast·ing
cas·ta·net
cast·a·way
caste
cast·er
cast·ing
cas·ti·gate
cas·ti·gat·ed
cas·ti·gat·ing
cas·ti·ga·tion
cast i·ron
cas·tle
cas·tor
cas·trate
cas·trat·ed
cas·trat·ing
cas·tra·tion
cas·u·al
cas·u·al·ness
cas·u·al·ty
cas·u·al·ties
cas·u·ist
cas·u·is·tic

cas·u·ist·ry
cat·a·clysm
cat·a·clys·mal
cat·a·clys·mic
cat·a·comb
cat·a·falque
cat·a·lep·sy
cat·a·lep·tic
cat·a·log
cat·a·logue
cat·a·loged
cat·a·log·ing
ca·tal·y·sis
cat·a·lyt·ic
cat·a·lyst
cat·a·lyze
cat·a·lyz·ing
cat·a·ma·ran
cat·a·pult
cat·a·ract
ca·tarrh
ca·tas·tro·phe
cat·as·troph·ic
Ca·taw·ba
catch
caught
catch·ing
catch·er
catchy
catch·i·er
cat·e·chism
cat·e·chize
cat·e·chized
cat·e·chiz·ing
cat·e·chi·za·tion
cat·e·chist
cat·e·gor·i·cal
cat·e·go·ry
cat·e·go·ries
cat·e·go·rize
cat·e·go·riz·ing
ca·ter
ca·ter·er
cat·er·pil·lar
cat·er·waul
cat·fish
ca·thar·sis
ca·thar·tic
ca·the·dral
cath·e·ter
cath·ode
cath·o·lic
cath·o·lic·i·ty
ca·thol·i·cize
Cath·o·lic
Ca·thol·i·cism
cat·nap
cat·nap·ping
cat·nip
cat·tle
cat·tle·man
cat·ty
cat·ti·ness
Cau·ca·sian
cau·cus
cau·cus·es
cau·cus·ing
caul·dron
cau·li·flow·er
caulk
caus·al
cau·sal·i·ty
cause
caused
caus·ing
cau·sa·tion
cause·less
cause·way

caus·tic
cau·ter·ize
cau·ter·ized
cau·ter·iz·ing
cau·ter·i·za·tion
cau·tery
cau·tion
cau·tion·ary
cau·tious
cav·al·cade
cav·a·lier
cav·al·ry
cave
caved
cav·ing
ca·ve·at
cav·ern
cav·ern·ous
cav·i·ar
cav·il
cav·iled
cav·il·ing
cav·i·ty
cav·i·ties
ca·vort
cay·enne
cay·man
cay·use
cease
ceased
ceas·ing
cease·less
cease·fire
ce·dar
cede
ced·ed
ced·ing
ceil·ing
cel·e·brate
cel·e·brat·ing
cel·e·bra·tion
cel·e·brant
cel·e·bra·tor
ce·leb·ri·ty
ce·leb·ri·ties
ce·ler·i·ty
cel·ery
ce·les·tial
cel·i·ba·cy
cel·i·bate
cel·lar
cel·lo
cel·list
cel·lo·phane
cel·lu·lar
cel·lu·lose
ce·ment
cem·e·tery
cem·e·ter·ies
cen·o·taph
cen·ser
cen·sor
cen·so·ri·al
cen·sor·ship
cen·so·ri·ous
cen·sure
cen·sured
cen·sur·ing
cen·sur·er
cen·sur·a·ble
cen·sus
cen·sus·ing
cen·taur
cen·te·nar·i·an
cen·te·na·ry
cen·te·na·ries
cen·ten·ni·al
cen·tes·i·mal

cen·ter·board
cen·ter·piece
cen·ti·grade
cen·ti·gram
cen·ti·li·ter
cen·ti·me·ter
central
cen·tral·ize
  cen·tral·ized
  cen·tral·iz·ing
cen·tri·fuge
  cen·trif·u·gal
cen·trip·e·tal
cen·tro·bar·ic
cen·tu·ri·on
cen·tu·ry
  cen·tu·ries
ce·ram·ic
  ce·ram·ics
ce·re·al
cer·e·bral
  cer·e·bel·lum
cer·e·bric
  cer·e·brum
cer·e·mo·ny
  cer·e·mo·nies
  cer·e·mo·ni·al
  cer·e·mo·ni·ous
ce·rise
cer·tain
  cer·tain·ly
cer·tain·ty
  cer·tain·ties
cer·tif·i·cate
  cer·ti·fi·ca·tion
cer·ti·fy
  cer·ti·fied
  cer·ti·fy·ing
cer·ti·fi·a·ble
  cer·ti·fi·er
cer·ti·tude
ce·ru·le·an
cer·vix
  cer·vi·cal
ce·sar·ean
  cae·sar·ean
ces·sa·tion
ce·ta·cean
Cha·blis
chafe
  chafed
  chaf·ing
chaff
cha·grin
  cha·grined
  cha·grin·ing
chain
chair·man
  chair·per·son
  chair·wom·an
chaise longue
chal·et
chal·ice
chalk
  chalky
chal·lenge
  chal·lenged
  chal·leng·ing
cham·ber
cham·bray
cha·me·le·on
cham·ois
cham·pagne
cham·pi·on
  cham·pi·on·ship
chance
  chanced
  chanc·ing

chancy
chan·cel·lor
chan·de·lier
change
  changed
  chang·ing
  change·a·ble
  change·ful
  change·less
chan·nel
  chan·nel·ing
chan·teuse
chan·tey
chan·ti·cleer
cha·os
  cha·ot·ic
chap
  chapped
  chap·ping
chap·ar·ral
cha·peau
chap·el
chap·e·ron
chap·lain
chap·ter
char
  charred
  char·ring
char·ac·ter
  char·ac·ter·is·tic
char·ac·ter·ize
  char·ac·ter·ized
  char·ac·ter·iz·ing
  char·ac·ter·i·za·tion
cha·rade
char·coal
charge
  charged
  charg·ing
char·ge d'af·faires
charg·er
char·i·ot
  char·i·ot·eer
cha·ris·ma
char·i·ta·ble
  char·i·ta·bly
char·i·ty
  char·i·ties
char·la·tan
charm
  charm·er
  charm·ing
char·ter
char·treuse
chary
  char·i·er
  char·i·est
chase
  chased
  chas·ing
chasm
chas·sis
chaste
  chaste·ness
  chas·ti·ty
chas·ten
  chas·tise
  chas·tis·ing
  chas·tise·ment
chat
  chat·ted
  chat·ting
cha·teau
chat·tel
chat·ter
chat·ty
  chat·ti·ly
  chat·ti·ness

chauf·feur
chau·vin·ist
  chau·vin·ism
  chau·vin·is·tic
cheap
  cheap·ness
  cheap·en
cheap·skate
cheat
  cheat·er
check·book
check·er·board
check·list
check·mate
check·point
check·room
ched·dar
cheek·bone
cheeky
  cheek·i·ness
cheer·ful
  cheer·ful·ness
  cheer·less
cheery
  cheer·i·er
  cheer·i·ness
cheese
  cheesy
chee·tah
chef
chem·i·cal
  chem·i·cal·ly
che·mise
chem·ist
  chem·is·try
chem·o·ther·a·py
che·nille
cher·ish
cher·ry
  cher·ries
cher·ub
  cher·ubs
  che·ru·bic
chess·man
chest·nut
chesty
  chest·i·er
chev·ron
chew
  chew·er
  chewy
Chi·an·ti
chi·a·ro·scu·ro
chi·can·ery
chi·chi
chick·a·dee
chic·ken
chic·le
chic·o·ry
chide
  chid·ed
  chid·ing
chief
  chief·ly
chief·tain
chif·fon
chif·fo·nier
chig·ger
chi·gnon
Chi·hua·hua
chil·blain
chil·dren
child·bear·ing
child·birth
child·hood
child·ish
child·like
chili

chill
  chill·ing
chilly
  chill·i·er
  chill·i·ness
chime
  chim·ing
chim·ney
chim·pan·zee
chin
  chinned
  chin·ning
chi·na
Chi·na
  Chi·nese
chin·chil·la
chintz
chintzy
chip
  chipped
  chip·ping
chip·munk
Chip·pen·dale
chip·per
chi·rog·ra·phy
  chi·rog·ra·pher
chi·rop·o·dist
chi·ro·prac·tic
  chi·ro·prac·tor
chis·el
  chis·eled
  chis·el·ing
  chis·el·er
chit·chat
chit·ter·ling
chiv·al·ry
  chiv·al·ric
  chiv·al·rous
chlo·rine
chlo·ro·form
chlo·ro·phyll
chock·full
choc·o·late
choice
  choice·ness
choir·boy
choke
  choked
  chok·ing
chok·er
chol·er
chol·era
cho·les·te·rol
choose
  chose
  cho·sen
  choos·ing
choosy
  choos·i·est
chop
  chopped
  chop·ping
chop·per
chop·py
  chop·pi·ness
chop su·ey
cho·ral
  cho·ral·ly
cho·rale
chord
chore
cho·reo·graph
  cho·re·og·ra·phy
  cho·re·og·ra·pher
  cho·re·o·graph·ic
chor·tle
  chor·tled
  chor·tling

cho·rus
  cho·rus·es
chor·is·ter
  cho·rus·ing
chos·en
chow·der
chow mein
Christ
chris·ten
  chris·ten·ing
Chris·ten·dom
Chris·tian
  Chris·ti·an·i·ty
  Chris·tian·ize
  Chris·tian·ized
Christ·like
Christ·mas
chro·mat·ic
  chro·mat·i·cal·ly
  chro·mat·ics
chrome
chro·mi·um
chro·mo·lith·o·graph
chron·ic
  chron·i·cal·ly
chron·i·cle
  chron·i·cled
  chron·i·cling
chron·o·log·i·cal
chro·nol·o·gy
  chro·nol·o·gies
chro·nom·e·ter
chrys·a·lis
chry·san·the·mum
chub·by
  chub·bi·ness
chuck·full
chuck·le
  chuck·ling
chuck·ker
chum·my
chunk
  chunky
  chunk·i·est
church
  church·li·ness
church·go·er
church·man
church·war·den
church·yard
churl·ish
  churl·ish·ness
churn·ing
chut·ney
chutz·pah
ci·ca·da
cic·e·ro·ne
ci·der
ci·gar
cig·a·rette
cil·ia
  cil·i·ar·y
cinc·ture
cin·der
cin·e·ma
cin·e·mat·o·graph
  cin·e·ma·tog·ra·pher
cin·e·rar·i·um
cin·na·bar
cin·na·mon
ci·pher
cir·ca
cir·cle
  cir·cled
  cir·cling
cir·clet
cir·cuit
cir·cu·i·tous

cir·cu·lar
cir·cu·lar·ize
  cir·cu·lar·iz·ing
  cir·cu·lar·i·za·tion
cir·cu·la·tion
  cir·cu·late
  cir·cu·lat·ed
  cir·cu·lat·ing
  cir·cu·la·tive
  cir·cu·la·to·ry
cir·cum·am·bi·ent
cir·cum·cise
  cir·cum·cised
  cir·cum·cis·ing
  cir·cum·ci·sion
cir·cum·fer·ence
cir·cum·flex
cir·cum·flu·ent
cir·cum·fuse
cir·cum·lo·cu·tion
  cir·cum·lo·cu·to·ry
cir·cum·nav·i·gate
  cir·cum·nav·i·ga·tion
cir·cum·scribe
  cir·cum·scrip·tion
cir·cum·spect
cir·cum·stance
cir·cum·stan·tial
  cir·cum·stan·ti·ate
  cir·cum·stan·ti·a·tion
cir·cum·vent
  cir·cum·ven·tion
cir·cus
  cir·cus·es
cir·rho·sis
cir·rus
cis·soid
cis·tern
cit·a·del
cite
  cit·ed
  cit·ing
  cit·ta·tion
cit·i·zen
  cit·i·zen·ship
cit·i·zen·ry
  cit·i·zen·ries
cit·re·ous
cit·ron
cit·ron·el·la
cit·rus
city
  cit·ies
civ·ic
civ·ics
civ·il
civ·il·ly
ci·vil·ian
ci·vil·i·ty
  ci·vil·i·ties
civ·i·li·za·tion
civ·i·lize
  civ·i·lized
  civ·i·liz·ing
civ·et
claim
  claim·a·ble
  claim·ant
clair·voy·ance
  clair·voy·ant
clam
  clammed
  clam·ming
clam·my
  clam·mi·ness
clam·or
  clam·or·ous
clamp·er

clan
  clan·nish
clan·des·tine
clang·or
  clang·or·ous
clans·man
clap
  clapped
  clap·ping
clap·board
clap·per
claque
clar·et
clar·i·fy
  clar·i·fied
  clar·i·fy·ing
  clar·i·fi·ca·tion
clar·i·net
  clar·i·net·ist
clar·i·on
clar·i·ty
clas·sic
clas·si·cal
clas·si·cism
clas·si·cist
clas·si·fy
  clas·si·fied
  clas·si·fy·ing
  clas·si·fi·ca·tion
classy
  class·i·er
clat·ter
clause
  claus·al
claus·tro·pho·bia
clav·i·chord
clav·i·cle
clay·ey
clean·cut
clean·er
clean·ly
  clean·li·ness
cleanse
  cleansed
  cleans·ing
  cleans·er
clear
  clear·ly
  clear·ness
clear·ance
clear·cut
clear·ing
clear·sight·ed
cleav·age
cleave
  cleaved
  cleav·ing
cleav·er
clef
cleft
clem·en·cy
clem·ent
cler·gy
  cler·gies
cler·gy·man
cler·ic
  cler·i·cal
cler·i·cal·ism
clev·er
  clev·er·ness
clev·is
clew
cli·ché
cli·ent
cli·en·tele
cli·mac·ter·ic
cli·mate
  cli·mat·ic

cli·mat·i·cal
cli·max
  cli·mac·tic
climb
  climb·er
clinch·er
cling
  clung
  cling·ing
clin·ic
  clin·i·cal
clink·er
clin·quant
clip
  clipped
  clip·ping
clip·per
clique
  cliqu·ish
clit·o·ris
clo·a·ca
clob·ber
clock·wise
clod
  clod·dish
clog
  clogged
  clog·ging
cloi·son·ne
clois·ter
  clois·tral
close
  closed
  clos·ing
  clos·est
  close·ly
  close·ness
clos·et
  clos·et·ed
  clos·et·ing
close·up
clo·sure
clot
  clot·ted
  clot·ting
clothe
  clothed
  cloth·ing
cloth·ier
cloth·ing
clo·ture
cloud·burst
cloudy
  cloud·i·ness
clo·ven
clo·ver
clown
  clown·ish
cloy
  cloy·ing·ly
club
  clubbed
  club·bing
club·foot
club·house
clue
clump
clum·sy
  clum·si·ly
  clum·si·ness
clus·ter
clut·ter
coach·man
co·ag·u·late
  co·ag·u·lat·ed
  co·ag·u·lat·ing
  co·ag·u·la·tion
co·a·lesce

co·a·lesced
co·a·les·cing
co·a·les·cence
co·a·les·cent
co·a·li·tion
coarse
  coars·en
  coarse·ness
coast·er
coast·guard
coast·line
coat·ing
co·au·thor
coax
  coax·ing·ly
co·balt
cob·ble
  cob·bler
cob·ble·stone
co·bra
cob·web
co·ca
co·caine
coc·cyx
cock·ade
cock·a·too
cock·er·al
cock·le
cock·le·bur
cock·le·shell
cock·ney
cock·roach
cock·tail
cocky
  cock·i·ly
  cock·i·ness
co·coa
co·co·nut
co·coon
cod·dle
  cod·dled
  cod·dling
code
  cod·ed
  cod·ing
co·deine
codg·er
cod·i·cil
cod·i·fy
  cod·i·fied
  cod·i·fy·ing
  cod·i·fi·ca·tion
co·ed
co·ed·u·ca·tion
co·ef·fi·cient
co·e·qual
co·erce
  co·erced
  co·erc·ing
  co·er·cion
  co·er·cive
co·ex·ist
  co·ex·ist·ence
co·ex·tend
cof·fee
cof·fer
cof·fin
co·gent
  co·gen·cy
  co·gent·ly
cog·i·tate
  cog·i·tat·ed
  cog·i·tat·ing
  cog·i·ta·tive
co·gnac
cog·nate
  cog·nat·tion
cog·ni·tion

cog·ni·tive
cog·ni·zance
cog·ni·zant
co·hab·it
  co·hab·i·ta·tion
co·here
  co·hered
  co·her·ing
co·her·ent
  co·her·ence
  co·her·ency
  co·her·ent·ly
co·he·sion
  co·he·sive
  co·he·sive·ness
co·hort
coif
coif·feur
coif·fure
coin·age
co·in·cide
  co·in·cid·ed
  co·in·cid·ing
  co·in·ci·dence
  co·in·ci·dent
  co·in·ci·den·tal
co·i·tion
  co·i·tus
col·an·der
cold
  cold·ly
  cold·ness
cold·blood·ed
cole·slaw
col·ic
  col·icky
col·i·se·um
co·li·tis
col·lab·o·rate
  col·lab·o·rat·ed
  col·lab·o·rat·ing
  col·lab·o·ra·tion
  col·lab·o·ra·tor
col·lage
col·lapse
  col·lapsed
  col·laps·ing
  col·lap·si·ble
col·lar
col·late
  col·lat·ed
  col·lat·ing
  col·la·tion
col·lat·er·al
col·league
col·lect
  col·lect·ed
  col·lect·i·ble
  col·lect·or
  col·lec·tion
col·lec·tive
col·lec·tiv·i·ty
col·lec·tiv·ism
  col·lec·tiv·ize
  col·lec·tiv·i·za·tion
col·lege
col·le·gian
col·le·giate
col·lide
  col·lid·ed
  col·lid·ing
  col·li·sion
col·lie
col·li·mate
col·lin·e·ar
col·lo·cate
col·loid
col·lo·qui·al

col·lo·qui·al·ly
col·lo·qui·al·ism
col·lo·quy
col·lu·sion
col·lu·sive
col·logne
co·lon
colo·nel
co·lo·ni·al
co·lo·ni·al·ism
co·lo·ni·al·ist
col·on·nade
col·o·ny
col·o·nist
col·o·nies
col·o·nize
col·o·niz·ing
col·o·ni·za·tion
col·or
col·or·ful
col·or·ing
col·or·a·tion
col·or·blind
col·or·less
co·los·sal
Col·os·se·um
co·los·sus
Co·lum·bia
col·um·bine
col·umn
co·lum·nar
col·um·nist
co·ma
co·ma·tose
com·bat
com·bat·ed
com·bat·ing
com·bat·ant
com·bat·ive
comb·er
com·bi·na·tion
com·bi·na·tive
com·bine
com·bined
com·bin·ing
com·bus·ti·ble
com·bus·tion
com·bus·tive
come
came
come
coming
co·me·di·an
co·me·di·enne
com·e·dy
com·e·dies
come·ly
come·li·ness
com·et
come·up·pance
com·fort
com·fort·a·ble
com·fort·er
com·ic
com·i·cal
com·ma
com·mand
com·man·dant
com·man·deer
com·mand·er
com·mand·ment
com·man·do
com·mem·o·rate
com·mem·o·rat·ed
com·mem·o·rat·ing
com·mem·o·ra·tion
com·mem·o·ra·tive
com·mence

com·menc·ing
com·mence·ment
com·mend
com·mend·a·ble
com·men·da·tion
com·men·su·rate
com·men·su·ra·tion
com·ment
com·men·tary
com·men·tar·ies
com·men·ta·tor
com·merce
com·mer·cial
com·mer·cial·ism
com·mer·cial·ize
com·mer·cial·i·za·tion
com·mis·er·ate
com·mis·er·at·ed
com·mis·er·at·ing
com·mis·er·a·tion
com·mis·sar
com·mis·sary
com·mis·sar·ies
com·mis·sion
com·mis·sioned
com·mis·sion·er
com·mit
com·mit·ted
com·mit·ting
com·mit·ment
com·mit·tee
com·mode
com·mo·di·ous
com·mod·i·ty
com·mod·i·ties
com·mo·dore
com·mon
com·mon·al·ty
com·mon·place
com·mons
com·mon·weal
com·mon·wealth
com·mo·tion
com·mu·nal
com·mune
com·muned
com·mun·ing
com·mu·ni·cant
com·mu·ni·cate
com·mu·ni·cat·ed
com·mu·ni·cat·ing
com·mu·ni·ca·ble
com·mu·ni·ca·tive
com·mu·ni·ca·tion
com·mun·ion
com·mu·ni·qué
com·mun·ism
com·mun·ist
com·mu·nis·tic
com·mu·ni·ty
com·mu·ni·ties
com·mu·nize
com·mu·niz·ing
com·mu·ta·tion
com·mute
com·mut·ed
com·mut·ing
com·mut·a·ble
com·mut·er
com·pact
com·pac·tor
com·pan·ion
com·pan·ion·a·ble
com·pan·ion·ship
com·pa·ny
com·pa·nies
com·pa·ra·ble
com·pa·ra·bil·i·ty

com·par·a·tive
com·pare
com·pared
com·par·ing
com·par·i·son
com·part·ment
com·part·ment·ed
com·part·men·tal·ize
com·pass
com·pas·sion
com·pas·sion·ate
com·pat·i·ble
com·pat·i·bly
com·pat·i·bil·i·ty
com·pa·tri·ot
com·peer
com·pel
com·pelled
com·pel·ling
com·pen·di·um
com·pen·sate
com·pen·sat·ing
com·pen·sa·tive
com·pen·sa·to·ry
com·pen·sa·tion
com·pete
com·pet·ed
com·pet·ing
com·pet·i·tor
com·pe·ti·tion
com·pet·i·tive
com·pe·tent
com·pe·tence
com·pe·ten·cy
com·pile
com·piled
com·pil·ing
com·pi·la·tion
com·pla·cent
com·pla·cence
com·pla·cen·cy
com·plain
com·plain·ant
com·plaint
com·plai·sance
com·plai·sant
com·plect·ed
com·ple·ment
com·ple·men·ta·ry
com·plete
com·plet·ed
com·plet·ing
com·ple·tion
com·plex
com·plex·i·ty
com·plex·ion
com·pli·ance
com·pli·an·cy
com·pli·ant
com·pli·cate
com·pli·cat·ed
com·pli·cat·ing
com·pli·ca·tion
com·plic·i·ty
com·plic·i·ties
com·pli·ment
com·pli·men·ta·ry
com·pli·men·ta·ri·ly
com·ply
com·plied
com·ply·ing
com·po·nent
com·port
com·port·ment
com·pose
com·posed
com·pos·ing
com·pos·er

com·pos·ite
com·po·si·tion
com·post
com·po·sure
com·pote
com·pound
com·pre·hend
com·pre·hen·si·ble
com·pre·hen·si·bil·i·ty
com·pre·hen·sion
com·pre·hen·sive
com·press
com·press·ing
com·press·i·ble
com·pres·sion
com·pres·sor
com·prise
com·prised
com·pris·ing
com·pro·mise
com·pro·mised
com·pro·mis·ing
comp·trol·ler
com·pul·sion
com·pul·sive
com·pul·so·ry
com·punc·tion
com·pute
com·put·ed
com·put·ing
com·pu·ta·tion
com·put·er
com·put·er·ize
com·put·er·iz·ing
com·put·er·i·za·tion
com·rade
con
conned
con·ning
con·cave
con·cav·i·ty
con·ceal
con·ceal·ment
con·cede
con·ced·ed
con·ced·ing
con·ceit
con·ceit·ed
con·ceive
con·ceived
con·ceiv·ing
con·ceiv·a·ble
con·ceiv·a·bly
con·cen·trate
con·cen·tra·ted
con·cen·trat·ing
con·cen·tra·tion
con·cen·tric
con·cen·tri·cal
con·cept
con·cep·tu·al
con·cep·tion
con·cep·tu·al·ize
con·cep·tu·al·i·za·tion
con·cern
con·cerned
con·cern·ment
con·cert
con·cert·ed
con·cer·ti·na
con·cer·to
con·ces·sion
con·ces·sion·aire
conch
con·cierge
con·cil·i·ate
con·cil·i·at·ed
con·cil·i·at·ing

con·cil·i·a·tion
con·cil·i·a·to·ry
con·cise
con·cise·ness
con·cise·ly
con·clave
con·clude
con·clud·ed
con·clud·ing
con·clu·sion
con·clu·sive
con·coct
con·coc·tion
con·com·i·tant
con·cord
con·cord·ance
con·cord·ant
con·course
con·crete
con·cret·ed
con·cret·ing
con·cre·tion
con·cu·bine
con·cu·pis·cent
con·cur
con·curred
con·cur·ring
con·cur·rence
con·cur·rent
con·cus·sion
con·cus·sive
con·demn
con·dem·na·ble
con·dem·na·tion
con·dense
con·densed
con·dens·ing
con·den·sa·tion
con·dens·er
con·de·scend
con·de·scend·ing
con·de·scen·sion
con·di·ment
con·di·tion
con·di·tion·al
con·di·tion·er
con·di·tioned
con·dole
con·doled
con·dol·ing
con·do·lence
con·do·min·i·um
con·done
con·doned
con·don·ing
con·do·na·tion
con·dor
con·duce
con·duced
con·duc·ing
con·du·cive
con·duct
con·duct·ance
con·duc·tion
con·duc·tor
con·duit
con·fer·ence
con·fess
con·fess·ed
con·fes·sion
con·fes·sion·al
con·fes·sor
con·fet·ti
con·fi·dant
con·fi·dante
con·fide
con·fid·ed
con·fid·ing

con·fi·dence
con·fi·dent
con·fi·den·tial
con·fig·u·ra·tion
con·fine
con·fined
con·fin·ing
con·fine·ment
con·firm
con·firmed
con·fir·ma·tion
con·fir·ma·tive
con·fir·ma·to·ry
con·fis·cate
con·fis·cat·ed
con·fis·cat·ing
con·fis·ca·tion
con·fis·ca·tor
con·fis·ca·to·ry
con·fla·gra·tion
con·flict
con·flict·ing
con·flic·tion
con·flu·ence
con·flu·ent
con·flux
con·form
con·form·ist
con·form·a·ble
con·form·ance
con·for·ma·tion
con·form·i·ty
con·found
con·found·ed
con·front
con·fron·ta·tion
Con·fu·cius
con·fuse
con·fused
con·fus·ing
con·fu·sion
con·fute
con·fut·ed
con·fut·ing
con·fu·ta·tion
con·ga
con·geal
con·geal·ment
con·gen·ial
con·ge·ni·al·i·ty
con·gen·ial·ly
con·gen·i·tal
con·gest
con·ges·tion
con·ges·tive
con·glom·er·ate
con·glom·er·at·ed
con·glom·er·at·ing
con·glom·er·a·tion
con·grat·u·late
con·grat·u·lat·ed
con·grat·u·lat·ing
con·grat·u·la·to·ry
con·grat·u·la·tion
con·gre·gate
con·gre·gat·ed
con·gre·gat·ing
con·gre·ga·tion
con·gre·ga·tion·al
con·gress
con·gres·sion·al
con·gress·man
con·gress·wom·an
con·gru·ent
con·gru·ent·ly
con·gru·ence
con·gru·en·cy
con·gru·ous

con·gru·ous·ly
con·gru·ous·ness
con·gru·i·ty
cone
con·ic
con·i·cal
co·ni·fer
con·jec·ture
con·jec·tured
con·jec·tur·ing
con·jec·tur·al
con·join
con·joint
con·ju·gal
con·ju·gal·ly
con·ju·gate
con·ju·gat·ed
con·ju·gat·ing
con·ju·ga·tion
con·ju·ga·tive
con·junc·tion
con·junc·tive
con·jure
con·jured
con·jur·ing
con·jur·a·tion
con·nect
con·nec·tor
con·nec·tion
con·nec·tive
con·nip·tion
con·nive
con·nived
con·niv·ing
con·niv·ance
con·nois·seur
con·note
con·not·ed
con·not·ing
con·no·ta·tion
con·no·ta·tive
con·nu·bi·al
con·quer
con·quer·a·ble
con·quer·or
con·quest
con·quis·ta·dor
con·san·guin·e·ous
con·san·guin·i·ty
con·science
con·sci·en·tious
con·scion·able
con·scious
con·scious·ly
con·scious·ness
con·script
con·scrip·tion
con·se·crate
con·se·crat·ed
con·se·crat·ing
con·se·cra·tor
con·se·cra·tion
con·sec·u·tive
con·sen·sus
con·sent
con·se·quence
con·se·quent
con·se·quent·ly
con·se·quen·tial
con·ser·va·tion
con·ser·va·tion·ist
con·serv·a·tive
con·serv·a·tism
con·serv·a·tive·ly
con·serv·a·to·ry
con·serv·a·to·ries
con·serve
con·served

con·serv·ing
con·sid·er
con·sid·er·ing
con·sid·er·able
con·sid·er·a·bly
con·sid·er·ate
con·sid·er·a·tion
con·sign
con·sign·er
con·sign·or
con·sign·ment
con·sist
con·sist·en·cy
con·sist·en·cies
con·sist·ence
con·sist·ent
con·sis·to·ry
con·so·la·tion
con·sol·a·to·ry
con·sole
con·soled
con·sol·ing
con·sol·a·ble
con·sol·i·date
con·sol·i·dat·ed
con·sol·i·dat·ing
con·sol·i·da·tion
con·som·mé
con·so·nant
con·sort
con·sor·ti·um
con·spic·u·ous
con·spic·u·ous·ness
con·spire
con·spired
con·spir·ing
con·spir·a·cy
con·spir·a·cies
con·spir·a·tor
con·spir·a·to·ri·al
con·spir·er
con·sta·ble
con·stab·u·lary
con·stant
con·stan·cy
con·stel·la·tion
con·ster·na·tion
con·sti·pa·tion
con·sti·pate
con·stit·u·en·cy
con·stit·u·en·cies
con·stit·u·ent
con·sti·tute
con·sti·tu·tion
con·sti·tu·tion·al
con·sti·tu·tion·al·i·ty
con·sti·tu·tion·al·ly
con·strain
con·strained
con·straint
con·strict
con·stric·tive
con·stric·tion
con·stric·tor
con·struct
con·struc·tor
con·struc·tion
con·struc·tive
con·strue
con·strued
con·stru·ing
con·stru·a·ble
con·sul
con·su·lar
con·sul·ship
con·su·late
con·sult
con·sul·ta·tion

con·sult·ant
con·sume
con·sumed
con·sum·ing
con·sum·a·ble
con·sum·er
con·sum·er·ism
con·sum·mate
con·sum·mat·ed
con·sum·mat·ing
con·sum·ma·tion
con·sump·tion
con·sump·tive
con·tact
con·ta·gion
con·ta·gious
con·ta·gious·ness
con·tain
con·tain·er
con·tain·ment
con·tam·i·nate
con·tam·i·nat·ed
con·tam·i·nat·ing
con·tam·i·nant
con·tam·i·na·tion
con·tem·plate
con·tem·plat·ed
con·tem·plat·ing
con·tem·pla·tion
con·tem·pla·tive
con·tem·po·ra·ne·ous
con·tem·po·rary
con·tem·po·rar·ies
con·tempt
con·tempt·i·ble
con·tempt·i·bly
con·temp·tu·ous
con·tend
con·tend·er
con·tent
con·tent·ment
con·tent·ed
con·tent·ed·ness
con·ten·tion
con·ten·tious
con·ter·mi·nous
con·test
con·test·a·ble
con·test·ant
con·text
con·tex·tu·al
con·tex·ture
con·tig·u·ous
con·ti·gu·i·ty
con·ti·gu·i·ties
con·tig·u·ous·ly
con·ti·nent
con·ti·nence
con·ti·nen·cy
con·ti·nent
con·ti·nen·tal
con·tin·gent
con·tin·gen·cy
con·tin·gen·cies
con·tin·u·al
con·tin·u·al·ly
con·tin·ue
con·tin·ued
con·tin·u·ing
con·tin·u·a·tion
con·tin·u·ance
con·ti·nu·i·ty
con·tin·u·ous
con·tin·u·um
con·tort
con·tor·tion
con·tor·tion·ist
con·tour

con·tra·band
con·tra·cep·tive
con·tra·cep·tion
con·tract
con·tract·ed
con·trac·tu·al
con·trac·tion
con·trac·tive
con·trac·tile
con·trac·tor
con·tra·dict
con·tra·dic·tion
con·tra·dic·to·ry
con·tra·dis·tinc·tion
con·tral·to
con·trap·tion
con·tra·pun·tal
con·tra·ri·wise
con·tra·ry
con·tra·ri·ly
con·tra·ri·ness
con·trast
con·trast·ing·ly
con·tra·vene
con·tra·ven·ing
con·trib·ute
con·trib·ut·ed
con·trib·ut·ing
con·trib·ut·a·ble
con·trib·u·tor
con·trib·u·tory
con·tri·bu·tion
con·trite
con·trite·ness
con·tri·tion
con·trive
con·trived
con·triv·ing
con·triv·ance
con·trol
con·trolled
con·trol·ling
con·trol·la·ble
con·trol·ler
con·tro·ver·sy
con·tro·ver·sies
con·tro·ver·sial
con·tro·vert
con·tu·ma·cy
con·tu·me·ly
con·tuse
con·tused
con·tus·ing
con·tu·sion
co·nun·drum
con·va·lesce
con·va·lesced
con·va·les·cence
con·va·les·cent
con·vec·tion
con·vene
con·vened
con·ven·ing
con·ven·ience
con·ven·ient
con·vent
con·ven·tion
con·ven·tion·al
con·ven·tion·al·ism
con·ven·tion·al·ize
con·verge
con·verg·ing
con·ver·gence
con·ver·gent
con·ver·sant
con·verse
con·versed
con·vers·ing

con·verse·ly
con·ver·sion
con·vert
con·vert·er
con·vert·i·ble
con·vex
con·vex·i·ty
con·vey
con·vey·a·ble
con·vey·ance
con·vey·er
con·vey·or
con·vict
con·vic·tion
con·vince
con·vinced
con·vinc·ing
con·vinc·i·ble
con·viv·i·al
con·viv·i·al·ity
con·voke
con·voked
con·vok·ing
con·vo·cation
con·vo·lute
con·vo·lut·ed
con·vo·lut·ing
con·vo·lute·ly
con·vo·lu·tion
con·voy
con·vulse
con·vulsed
con·vuls·ing
con·vul·sion
con·vul·sive
cook·e·ry
cook·ie
cool
cool·ish
cool·ly
cool·ness
cool·ant
coo·lie
coop·er·age
co·op·er·ate
co·op·er·at·ed
co·op·er·at·ing
co·op·er·a·tion
co·op·er·a·tive
co·or·di·nate
co·or·di·nat·ed
co·or·di·nat·ing
co·or·di·na·tor
co·or·di·na·tion
co·part·ner
cope
coped
cop·ing
cop·i·er
co·pi·lot
co·pi·ous
co·pi·ous·ly
cop·per
cop·pery
cop·pice
copse
cop·ra
cop·u·la
cop·u·late
cop·u·lat·ed
cop·u·lat·ing
cop·u·la·tion
cop·u·la·tive
copy
cop·ies
cop·ied
copy·ing
copy·right

co·quet
co·quet·ry
co·quette
cor·al
cord·age
cor·dial
cor·dial·i·ty
cor·dial·ly
cord·ite
cor·don
cor·do·van
cor·du·roy
core
cored
cor·ing
cor·nea
cor·ner
cor·net
cor·nice
cor·nu·co·pia
corny
corn·i·er
corn·i·est
co·rol·la
cor·ol·lary
co·ro·na
cor·o·nary
cor·o·na·tion
cor·o·ner
cor·o·net
cor·po·ral
cor·po·rate
cor·po·rate·ly
cor·po·ra·tive
cor·po·ra·tion
cor·po·re·al
corps
corps·man
corpse
cor·pu·lent
cor·pu·lence
cor·pus
cor·pus·cle
cor·pus·cu·lar
cor·ral
cor·ralled
cor·ral·ling
cor·rect
cor·rect·a·ble
cor·rect·ness
cor·rec·tion
cor·rec·tion·al
cor·rec·tive
cor·re·late
cor·re·lat·ed
cor·re·lat·ing
cor·re·la·tion
cor·rel·a·tive
cor·re·spond
cor·re·spond·ing
cor·re·spond·ence
cor·re·spond·ent
cor·ri·dor
cor·ri·gi·ble
cor·ri·gi·bil·i·ty
cor·rob·o·rate
cor·rob·o·rat·ed
cor·rob·o·rat·ing
cor·rob·o·rat·tion
cor·rob·o·ra·to·ry
cor·rode
cor·rod·ed
cor·rod·ing
cor·ro·sion
cor·ro·sive
cor·ru·gate
cor·ru·gat·ed
cor·ru·gat·ing

cor·ru·ga·tion
cor·rupt
cor·rup·ti·ble
cor·rup·ti·bil·i·ty
cor·rupt·ly
cor·rupt·ness
cor·rup·tion
cor·sage
cor·sair
cor·set
cor·tege
cor·tex
cor·ti·cal
cor·ti·sone
co·run·dum
cor·us·cate
cor·vette
co·sig·na·to·ry
cos·met·ic
cos·me·tol·o·gist
cos·mic
cos·mi·cal·ly
cos·mog·o·ny
cos·mog·o·nist
cos·mog·ra·phy
cos·mog·ra·pher
cos·mol·o·gy
cos·mol·o·gist
cos·mo·naut
cos·mo·pol·i·tan
cos·mop·o·lite
cos·mos
cos·mo·tron
cost·ly
cost·li·er
cos·tume
cos·tumed
cos·tum·ing
cos·tum·er
co·sy
co·si·er
co·tan·gent
co·te·rie
co·til·lion
cot·tage
cot·ter
cot·ton
cot·tony
couch
couch·ant
cough
coun·cil
coun·cil·or
coun·cil·man
coun·sel
coun·seled
coun·sel·ing
coun·se·lor
count
count·a·ble
count·down
coun·te·nance
coun·te·nanced
coun·te·nanc·ing
count·er
coun·ter·act
coun·ter·ac·tive
coun·ter·at·tack
coun·ter·charge
coun·ter·claim
coun·ter·claim·ant
coun·ter·clock·wise
coun·ter·cul·ture
coun·ter·es·pi·o·nage
coun·ter·feit
coun·ter·feit·er
coun·ter·in·tel·li·gence
coun·ter·mand

coun·ter·meas·ure
coun·ter·of·fen·sive
coun·ter·pane
coun·ter·part
coun·ter·point
coun·ter·poise
coun·ter·rev·o·lu·tion
coun·ter·sign
coun·ter·sig·na·ture
coun·ter·sink
coun·ter·spy
coun·ter·weight
coun·tess
count·less
coun·tri·fied
coun·try
coun·tries
coun·ty
coun·ties
coup de grace
coup d'e·tat
cou·pé
coup·le
coup·ling
coup·ler
coup·let
cou·pon
cour·age
cou·ra·geous
cour·i·er
course
coursed
cours·ing
cours·er
cour·te·ous
cour·te·son
cour·te·sy
cour·te·sies
court·house
cour·ti·er
court·ly
court·li·ness
court·mar·tial
courts·mar·tial
court·room
court·ship
cous·in
cou·tu·rier
cov·e·nant
cov·er
cov·ered
cov·er·ing
cov·er·ess
cov·er·age
cov·er·all
cov·er·let
cov·ert
cov·ert·ly
cov·er·up
cov·et
cov·et·ous
cov·ey
cow·ard
cow·ard·li·ness
cow·ard·ice
cow·er
cow·er·ing
cowl
co·worker
cow·ry
cow·rie
cox·swain
coy
coy·ness
coy·o·te
coz·en
coz·en·er
co·zy

co·zi·ly
co·zi·ness
crab
crabbed
crab·bing
crab·by
crack·down
crack·er
crack·ing
crack·le
crack·led
crack·ling
crack·up
cra·dle
cra·dled
cra·dling
crafts·man
crafty
craft·i·ly
crag
crag·ged
crag·gy
crag·gi·ness
cram
crammed
cram·ming
cran·ber·ry
crane
craned
cran·ing
cra·ni·um
cranky
crank·i·ly
crank·i·ness
cran·ny
cran·nies
cran·nied
crap·shooter
crass
crass·ly
crate
crat·ed
crat·ing
cra·ter
cra·tered
cra·vat
crave
craved
crav·ing
cra·ven
craw·fish
crawl
cray·fish
cray·on
craze
crazed
craz·ing
cra·zy
cra·zi·er
cra·zi·ness
creak
creak·i·ly
creaky
cream
cream·i·ness
creamy
crease
creased
creas·ing
creasy
cre·ate
cre·at·ed
cre·at·ing
cre·a·tion
cre·a·tive
cre·a·tiv·i·ty
cre·a·tor
cre·a·ture

crèche
cre·dence
cre·den·tial
cre·den·za
cred·i·ble
 cred·i·bil·i·ty
 cred·i·bly
cred·it
 cred·it·a·ble
 cred·it·a·bil·i·ty
 cred·it·a·bly
cred·i·tor
cre·do
cred·u·lous
cre·du·li·ty
creek
creel
creep
 crept
 creep·ing
creepy
 creep·i·ness
creep·er
cre·mate
 cre·mat·ed
 cre·mat·ing
 cre·ma·tion
cre·ma·to·ry
 cre·ma·to·ri·um
cren·el·ate
 cren·el·la·tion
Cre·ole
cre·o·sote
crepe de Chine
crepe su·zette
cre·pus·cu·lar
cres·cen·do
cres·cent
crest
 crest·ed
 crest·less
crest·fall·en
cre·ta·ceous
cre·tonne
cre·vasse
crev·ice
crew·ed
crib
 cribbed
 crib·bing
crib·bage
crick·et
crim·i·nal
 crim·i·nal·i·ty
 crim·i·nal·ly
crim·i·nol·o·gy
 crim·i·nol·o·gist
crim·son
cringe
 cringed
 cring·ing
crin·kle
 crin·kled
 crin·kling
 crin·o·line
crip·ple
 crip·pled
 crip·pling
cri·sis
 cri·ses
crisp
 crisp·ness
crispy
 crisp·i·er
criss·cross
cri·te·ri·on
 cri·te·ria
crit·ic

crit·i·cal
crit·i·cal·ly
crit·i·cism
crit·i·cize
 crit·i·cized
 crit·i·cizing
 crit·i·ciz·a·ble
cri·tique
croaky
cro·chet
 cro·cheted
 cro·chet·ing
crock·ery
croc·o·dile
cro·cus
crois·sant
cro·ny
 cro·nies
crook·ed
croon·er
crop
 cropped
 crop·ping
cro·quet
cro·quette
cross·bar
cross·breed
cross·coun·try
cross·ex·am·ine
 cross·ex·am·i·na·tion
cross·fer·ti·li·za·tion
cross·ing
cross·pol·li·na·tion
 cross·pol·li·nate
cross·ref·er·ence
crotch·ety
 crotch·et·i·ness
crouch
croup
crou·pi·er
crou·ton
cru·cial
 cru·ci·al·i·ty
cru·ci·ble
cru·ci·fix
cru·ci·fix·ion
cru·ci·form
cru·ci·fy
 cru·ci·fied
 cru·ci·fy·ing
crude
 crud·est
 crude·ness
cru·di·ty
cru·el
 cru·el·ly
 cru·el·ness
 cru·el·ty
cru·et
cruise
 cruised
 cruis·ing
cruis·er
crul·ler
crum·ble
 crum·bling
crum·my
 crum·mi·est
crum·pet
crum·ple
 crum·pled
 crum·pling
crunchy
 crunch·i·er
cru·sade
 cru·sad·er
crush·er
 crush·ing

crus·ta·cean
crusty
 crust·i·ly
crutch
crux
cry
 cried
 cry·ing
cry·o·gen·ics
crypt
cryp·to·gram
 cryp·to·graph
crys·tal
 crys·tal·line
 crys·tal·lize
 crys·tal·li·za·tion
cube
 cubed
 cub·ing
cu·bic
 cu·bi·cal
cu·bi·cle
cub·ism
cuck·old
cuck·oo
cu·cum·ber
cud·dle
 cud·dled
 cud·dling
 cud·dle·some
cudg·el
 cudg·eled
 cudg·el·ing
cue
 cued
 cu·ing
cui·sine
cul-de-sac
cu·li·nary
cul·mi·nate
 cul·mi·nat·ed
 cul·mi·nat·ing
 cul·mi·na·tion
cu·lottes
cul·pa·ble
 cul·pa·bil·i·ty
 cul·pa·bly
cul·prit
cult
 cul·tist
cul·ti·vate
 cul·ti·vat·ed
 cul·ti·vat·ing
 cul·ti·va·tion
 cul·ti·va·tor
cul·tur·al
cul·ture
 cul·tured
 cul·tur·ing
cul·vert
cum·ber
 cum·ber·some
 cum·brance
cum lau·de
cum·mer·bund
cu·mu·late
 cu·mu·la·tion
 cu·mu·la·tive
cu·mu·lo·nim·bus
cu·mu·lus
 cu·mu·lous
cu·ne·i·form
cun·ning
 cun·ning·ly
 cun·ning·ness
cup
 cupped
 cup·ping

cup·board
cup·ful
cu·pid·i·ty
cu·po·la
cur·a·ble
 cur·a·bil·i·ty
cu·rate
cur·a·tive
cu·ra·tor
curb·ing
curb·stone
cur·dle
 cur·dled
 cur·dling
cure
 cured
 cur·ing
cur·few
cu·rio
cu·ri·o·sa
cu·ri·os·i·ty
 cu·ri·os·i·ties
cu·ri·ous
 cu·ri·ous·ness
curl·i·cue
curl·ing
curly
 curl·i·ness
cur·rant
cur·ren·cy
 cur·ren·cies
current
cur·ric·u·lum
 cur·ric·u·la
 cur·ric·u·lar
cur·rish
curry
 cur·ried
curse
 curs·ing
 curs·ed·ness
cur·sive
cur·so·ry
 cur·so·ri·ly
curt
curt·ly
 curt·ness
cur·tail
 cur·tail·ment
cur·tain
curt·sy
 curt·sied
 curt·sy·ing
cur·va·ceous
cur·va·ture
curve
 curved
 curv·ing
cur·vi·lin·e·ar
cush·ion
cushy
 cush·i·est
cus·pid
cus·pi·dor
cuss·ed
 cuss·ed·ness
cus·tard
cus·to·di·an
cus·to·dy
 cus·to·di·al
cus·tom
cus·tom·ary
 cus·tom·ar·i·ly
cus·tom·er
cus·tom·ize
 cus·tom·ized
 cus·tom·iz·ing
cut

cut·ting
cur·ta·ne·ous
cute
 cut·est
 cute·ness
cu·ti·cle
cut·lass
cut·lery
cut·let
cut·throat
cut·tle·fish
cy·a·nide
cy·ber·net·ics
cyc·la·men
cy·cle
 cy·cled
 cy·cling
 cy·clist
cy·clic
 cy·cli·cal
cy·clone
cy·clo·pe·di·a
cy·clo·rama
 cy·clo·ram·ic
cy·clo·tron
cyg·net
cyl·in·der
 cy·lin·dric
 cy·lin·dri·cal
cym·bal
cyn·ic
 cyn·i·cism
 cyn·i·cal
cy·no·sure
cy·pher
cy·press
cyst
czar

D

dab
 dabbed
 dab·bing
dab·ble
 dab·bled
 dab·bling
 dab·bler
dachs·hund
dac·tyl
 dac·tyl·ic
daf·fo·dil
daf·fy
dag·ger
da·guerre·o·type
dahl·ia
dai·ly
 dai·lies
dain·ty
 dain·ti·est
 dain·ti·ly
 dain·ti·ness
dai·qui·ri
dairy
 dair·ies
da·is
dai·sy
 dai·sies
dal·ly
 dal·lied
 dal·ly·ing
 da·li·ance
Dal·ma·tian
dam
 dammed
 dam·ming
dam·age

dam·aged
dam·ag·ing
dam·ask
damn
  dam·na·ble
  dam·na·bly
  dam·na·tion
  damned
damp·en
damp·er
damp·ness
dam·sel
dam·son
dance
  danced
  danc·ing
dan·de·li·on
dan·der
dan·dle
  dan·dled
  dan·dling
dan·druff
dan·dy
  dan·dies
  dan·dy·ism
dan·ger
dan·ger·ous
dan·gle
  dan·gled
  dan·gling
dank
  dank·ness
dan·seuse
dap·per
dap·ple
  dap·pled
  dap·pling
dare
  dared
  dar·ing
dare·dev·il
dark
  dark·ish
  dark·ly
  dark·ness
dark·en
dark·room
dar·ling
  dar·ling·ness
Dar·win·ism
dash·board
dash·ing
das·tard
  das·tard·li·ness
  das·tard·ly
da·ta
date
  dat·ed
  dat·ing
  dat·a·ble
date·less
date·line
da·tive
da·tum
  da·ta
daub
daugh·ter
daugh·ter-in-law
daunt·less
dau·phin
dav·en·port
dav·it
daw·dle
  daw·dled
  daw·dling
  daw·dler
dawn
  dawn·ing

day·break
day·dream
day·light
day·time
daze
  dazed
  daz·ing
  daz·ed·ly
daz·zle
  daz·zled
  daz·zling
dea·con
dea·con·ess
de·ac·ti·vate
  de·ac·ti·va·tion
dead·beat
dead·en
dead·end
dead·line
dead·lock
dead·ly
  dead·li·ness
deaf
  deaf·ness
deaf·en
  deaf·en·ing·ly
deaf·mute
deal
  dealt
  deal·ing
dean·ship
dear
  dear·ness
dearth
death
  death·less
  death·ly
death·blow
death's·head
death·watch
de·ba·cle
de·bar
  de·barred
  de·bar·ring
  de·bar·ment
de·bark
  de·bar·ka·tion
de·base
  de·based
  de·bas·ing
  de·base·ment
de·bate
  de·bat·ing
  de·bat·a·ble
  de·bat·er
de·bauch
  de·bauch·er
  de·bauch·ment
  de·bauch·ery
deb·au·chee
de·ben·ture
de·bil·i·tate
  de·bil·i·tat·ed
  de·bil·i·tat·ing
  de·bil·i·ta·tion
de·bil·i·ty
  de·bil·i·ties
deb·it
deb·o·nair
de·brief
de·bris
debt·or
de·bunk
de·but
deb·u·tante
de·cade
dec·a·dent
  dec·a·dence

dec·a·dent·ly
dec·a·gon
dec·a·gram
dec·a·he·dron
de·cal
Dec·a·logue
de·camp
  de·camp·ment
de·cant
de·cant·er
de·cap·i·tate
  de·cap·i·tat·ed
  de·cap·i·tat·ing
  de·cap·i·ta·tion
dec·a·pod
de·cath·lon
de·cay
de·cease
  de·ceased
  de·ce·dent
de·ceit
  de·ceit·ful
  de·ceit·ful·ness
de·ceive
  de·ceived
  de·ceiv·ing
  de·ceiv·er
de·cel·er·ate
  de·cel·er·at·ed
  de·cel·er·at·ing
  de·cel·er·a·tion
de·cen·cy
  de·cen·cies
de·cen·ni·al
de·cent
  de·cent·ly
de·cen·tral·ize
  de·cen·tral·ized
  de·cen·tral·iz·ing
  de·cen·tral·i·za·tion
de·cep·tion
  de·cep·tive
dec·i·bel
de·cide
  de·cid·ed
  de·cid·ing
  de·cid·ed·ly
de·cid·u·ous
dec·i·mal
dec·i·mate
  dec·i·mat·ed
  dec·i·mat·ing
  dec·i·ma·tion
de·ci·pher
  de·ci·pher·a·ble
de·ci·sion
de·ci·sive
de·claim
  dec·la·ma·tion
  de·clam·a·tory
de·clare
  de·clared
  de·clar·ing
  de·clar·a·tive
  de·clar·a·to·ry
  dec·la·ra·tion
de·clas·si·fy
  de·clas·si·fied
  de·clas·si·fy·ing
de·clen·sion
dec·li·na·tion
de·cline
  de·clined
  de·clin·ing
  de·clin·a·ble
de·cliv·i·ty
  de·cliv·i·ties
de·code

de·cod·ed
de·cod·ing
de·cod·er
de·colle·tage
de·com·mis·sion
de·com·pose
  de·com·posed
  de·com·pos·ing
  de·com·po·si·tion
de·com·press
  de·com·pres·sion
de·con·tam·i·nate
  de·con·tam·i·nat·ed
  de·con·tam·i·nat·ing
  de·con·tam·i·na·tion
de·con·trol
  de·con·trolled
  de·con·trol·ling
de·cor
dec·o·rate
  dec·o·rat·ed
  dec·o·rat·ing
  dec·o·ra·tion
  dec·o·ra·tive
  dec·o·ra·tor
dec·o·rous
de·co·rum
de·coy
de·crease
  de·creased
  de·creas·ing
de·cree
  de·creed
  de·cree·ing
de·cre·ment
de·crep·it
  de·crep·i·tude
  de·crep·it·ly
de·cre·scen·do
de·cry
  de·cried
  de·cry·ing
  de·cri·al
ded·i·cate
  ded·i·cat·ed
  ded·i·cat·ing
  ded·i·ca·to·ry
  ded·i·ca·tion
de·duce
  de·duc·i·ble
de·duct
  de·duct·i·ble
de·duc·tion
  de·duc·tive
deep
  deep·ness
  deep·en
deep·root·ed
deep·seat·ed
de·es·ca·late
  de·es·ca·lat·ed
  de·es·ca·lat·ing
  de·es·ca·la·tion
de·face
  de·faced
  de·fac·ing
  de·face·ment
de fac·to
de·fal·cate
  de·fal·ca·tion
de·fame
  de·famed
  de·fam·ing
  def·a·ma·tion
  de·fam·a·to·ry
de·fault
de·feat
  de·feat·ism

de·feat·ist
def·e·cate
  def·e·cat·ed
  def·e·cat·ing
  def·e·ca·tion
de·fect
de·fec·tion
  de·fec·tor
  de·fec·tive
de·fend
  de·fend·er
  de·fend·ant
de·fense
  de·fense·less
  de·fen·si·ble
  de·fen·si·bil·i·ty
  de·fen·sive
de·fer
  de·ferred
  de·fer·ring
  de·fer·ment
def·er·ence
  def·er·en·tial
de·fi·ance
  de·fi·ant
de·fi·cient
  de·fi·cien·cy
  de·fi·cien·cies
def·i·cit
de·file
  de·filed
  de·fil·ing
  de·file·ment
de·fine
  de·fined
  de·fin·ing
  de·fin·a·ble
def·i·nite
  def·i·nite·ly
def·i·ni·tion
  de·fin·i·tive
de·flate
  de·flat·ed
  de·flat·ing
  de·fla·tion
  de·fla·tion·ary
de·flect
  de·flec·tion
  de·flec·tive
  de·flec·tor
de·flow·er
de·fo·li·ate
  de·fo·li·at·ed
  de·fo·li·at·ing
  de·fo·li·a·tion
de·for·est
  de·for·est·a·tion
de·form
  de·for·ma·tion
  de·formed
de·form·i·ty
  de·form·i·ties
de·fraud
de·fray
  de·fray·al
  de·fray·ment
de·frost
deft
  deft·ness
de·funct
de·fy
  de·fied
  de·fy·ing
de·gen·er·ate
  de·gen·er·at·ed
  de·gen·er·at·ing
  de·gen·er·ate·ly
  de·gen·er·a·cy

de·gen·er·a·tion
de·grade
de·grad·ed
de·grad·ing
de·grad·able
deg·ra·da·tion
de·gree
de·his·cence
de·his·cent
de·hu·mid·i·fy
de·hy·drate
de·hy·drat·ed
de·hy·drat·ing
de·hy·dra·tion
de·i·fy
de·i·fied
de·i·fy·ing
de·i·fi·ca·tion
deign
de·ist
de·ism
de·is·tic
de·is·ti·cal
de·i·ty
de·i·ties
de·ject·ed
de·ject·ed·ly
de·jec·tion
de ju·re
de·lay
de·lec·ta·ble
de·lec·ta·bly
de·lec·ta·tion
del·e·gate
del·e·gat·ed
del·e·gat·ing
del·e·ga·tion
de·lete
de·let·ed
de·let·ing
de·le·tion
del·e·te·ri·ous
delft·ware
de·lib·er·ate
de·lib·er·at·ed
de·lib·er·at·ing
de·lib·er·ate·ly
de·lib·er·a·tion
del·i·ca·cy
del·i·ca·cies
del·i·cate
del·i·cate·ly
del·i·ca·tes·sen
de·li·cious
de·li·cious·ness
de·light
de·light·ed
de·light·ed·ly
de·light·ful
de·light·ful·ly
de·lim·it
de·lim·i·ta·tion
de·lin·e·ate
de·lin·e·at·ed
de·lin·e·at·ing
de·lin·e·a·tion
de·lin·e·a·tor
de·lin·quent
de·lin·quen·cy
de·lin·quen·cies
del·i·quesce
de·lir·i·um
de·lir·i·ous
de·liv·er
de·liv·er·er
de·liv·er·ance
de·liv·ery
de·liv·er·ies

de·louse
de·loused
de·lous·ing
del·phin·i·um
del·ta
del·toid
de·lude
de·lud·ed
de·lud·ing
del·uge
del·uged
del·ug·ing
de·lu·sion
de·lu·sive
de·lu·so·ry
de·lu·sive·ly
de·luxe
delve
delv·ing
de·mag·ne·tize
dem·a·gogue
dem·a·gogu·ery
dem·a·gog·ic
dem·a·gog·i·cal
de·mand
de·mar·cate
de·mar·ca·tion
de·mean
de·mean·or
de·ment·ed
de·men·tia
de·mer·it
de·mesne
dem·i·god
dem·i·john
de·mil·i·ta·rize
de·mil·l·tar·i·za·tion
de·mise
de·mised
de·mis·ing
dem·i·tasse
de·mo·bi·lize
de·mo·bi·lized
de·mo·bi·liz·ing
de·mo·bi·li·za·tion
de·moc·ra·cy
de·moc·ra·cies
dem·o·crat
dem·o·crat·ic
dem·o·crat·i·cal·ly
de·moc·ra·tize
de·moc·ra·tized
de·moc·ra·tiz·ing
de·moc·ra·ti·za·tion
de·mog·ra·phy
de·mog·ra·pher
dem·o·graph·ic
de·mol·ish
de·plor·a·bly
de·plore
de·plored
de·plor·ing
de·ploy
de·ploy·ment
de·pol·ar·ize
de·pop·u·late
de·pop·u·lat·ed
de·pop·u·lat·ing
de·pop·u·la·tion
de·port
de·por·ta·tion
de·port·ment
de·pose
de·posed
de·pos·ing
de·pos·a·ble
de·pos·it
de·pos·i·tor

dep·o·si·tion
de·pos·i·to·ry
de·pot
de·prave
de·praved
de·prav·ing
de·prav·i·ty
de·pra·va·tion
dep·re·cate
dep·re·cat·ed
dep·re·cat·ing
dep·re·ca·tion
dep·re·ca·to·ry
de·pre·ci·ate
de·pre·ci·at·ed
de·pre·ci·at·ing
de·pre·ci·a·tion
de·pre·ci·a·to·ry
dep·re·diate
dep·re·dat·ed
dep·re·dat·ing
dep·re·da·tion
de·press
de·pres·sant
de·pressed
de·pres·sion
de·prive
de·prived
de·priv·ing
dep·ri·va·tion
depth
dep·u·rate
dep·u·ta·tion
de·pute
de·put·ed
de·put·ing
dep·u·tize
dep·u·tized
dep·u·tiz·ing
dep·u·ty
dep·u·ties
de·raign
de·raign·ment
de·rail
de·rail·ment
de·range
de·ranged
de·rang·ing
de·range·ment
der·by
der·e·lict
der·e·lic·tion
de·ride
de·rid·ing
de·ri·gueur
de·ri·sion
de·ri·sive
de·ri·so·ry
der·i·va·tion
de·riv·a·tive
de·rive
de·riv·ing
de·riv·a·ble
der·ma·ti·tis
der·ma·tol·o·gy
der·ma·to·log·i·cal
der·ma·tol·o·gist
der·mis
der·o·gate
der·o·gat·ed
der·o·gat·ing
der·o·ga·tion
de·rog·a·to·ry
de·rog·a·to·ri·ly
der·rick
der·rin·ger
der·vish
de·sal·i·nate

des·cant
de·scend
de·scend·ed
de·scend·ing
de·scend·ant
de·scend·ent
de·scent
de·scribe
de·scribed
de·scrib·ing
de·scrib·a·ble
de·scrip·tion
de·scrip·tive
de·scry
de·scried
de·scry·ing
des·e·crate
des·e·crat·ed
des·e·crat·ing
des·e·cra·tion
de·seg·re·gate
de·seg·re·gat·ed
de·seg·re·gat·ing
de·seg·re·ga·tion
de·sen·si·tize
des·ert
de·sert
de·sert·ed
de·sert·er
de·ser·tion
de·serve
de·served
de·serv·ing
de·served·ly
des·ha·bille
des·ic·cate
des·ic·cated
des·ic·cat·ing
des·ic·ca·tion
de·sid·er·a·tum
de·sign
de·signed
de·sign·ing
de·signed·ly
de·signer
des·ig·nate
des·ig·nat·ed
des·ig·nat·ing
des·ig·na·tion
de·sire
de·sired
de·sir·ing
de·sir·a·ble
de·sir·a·bil·i·ty
de·sir·ous
de·sist
des·o·late
des·o·lat·ed
des·o·lat·ing
des·o·la·tion
de·spair
de·spair·ing
des·per·a·do
des·per·ate
des·per·ate·ly
des·per·a·tion
des·pic·a·ble
des·pic·a·bly
de·spise
de·spised
de·spis·ing
de·spite
de·spoil
de·spoil·ment
de·spo·li·a·tion
de·spond
de·spond·en·cy
de·spond·ence

de·spond·ent
des·pot
des·pot·ic
des·pot·i·cal·ly
des·pot·ism
des·sert
des·ti·na·tion
des·tine
des·tined
des·tin·ing
des·ti·ny
des·ti·nies
des·ti·tute
des·ti·tu·tion
de·stroy
de·stroy·er
de·struc·tion
de·struct·i·ble
de·struct·i·bil·i·ty
de·struc·tive
de·struc·tive·ness
des·ue·tude
des·ul·to·ry
des·ul·to·ri·ly
de·tach
de·tached
de·tach·a·ble
de·tach·ment
de·tail
de·tain
de·tain·ment
de·tain·er
de·ten·tion
de·tect
de·tect·a·ble
de·tec·tion
de·tec·tor
dc·tec·tive
dé·tente
de·ten·tion
de·ter
de·terred
de·ter·ring
de·ter·gent
de·te·ri·o·rate
de·te·ri·o·rat·ed
de·te·ri·o·rat·ing
de·te·ri·o·ra·tion
de·ter·mine
de·ter·mined
de·ter·min·ing
de·ter·mi·na·ble
de·ter·mi·nant
de·ter·mi·nate
de·ter·mi·na·tion
de·ter·mined·ly
de·ter·min·ism
de·ter·rent
de·ter·rence
de·test
de·test·a·ble
de·tes·ta·tion
de·throne
de·throne·ment
det·o·nate
det·o·nat·ed
det·o·nat·ing
det·o·na·tion
det·o·na·tor
de·tour
de·tract
de·trac·tion
de·trac·tor
det·ri·ment
det·ri·men·tal
de·tri·tus
deuce
de·value

de·val·u·ate
de·val·u·at·ed
de·val·u·at·ing
de·val·u·a·tion
dev·as·tate
dev·as·tat·ed
dev·as·tat·ing
dev·as·ta·tion
de·vel·op
de·vel·op·ment
de·vel·op·er
de·vi·ate
de·vi·at·ed
de·vi·at·ing
de·vi·ant
de·vi·a·tion
de·vice
dev·il
dev·il·ment
dev·il·try
dev·il·tries
dev·il·ry
dev·il·ish
de·vi·ous
de·vi·ous·ness
de·vise
de·vised
de·vis·ing
de·vis·a·ble
de·vis·al
de·vi·see
de·vi·sor
de·void
de·volve
de·volved
de·volv·ing
dev·o·lu·tion
de·vote
de·vot·ed
de·vot·ing
de·vote·ment
dev·o·tee
de·vo·tion
de·vo·tion·al
de·vour
de·vour·ing
de·vout
de·vout·ly
de·vout·ness
dewy
dew·i·ness
dew·y·eyed
dex·ter·ous
dex·ter·i·ty
dex·ter·ous·ly
dex·trose
di·a·be·tes
di·a·bet·ic
di·a·bol·ic
di·a·bol·i·cal
di·a·crit·ic
di·a·crit·i·cal
di·a·dem
di·ag·nose
di·ag·nosed
di·ag·nos·ing
di·ag·no·sis
di·ag·nos·tic
di·ag·nos·ti·cian
di·ag·o·nal
di·a·gram
di·a·gramed
di·a·gram·ing
di·a·gram·matic
di·a·gram·mat·i·cal
di·al
di·aled
di·al·ing

di·a·lect
di·a·lec·tal
di·a·lec·tic
di·a·lec·ti·cal
di·a·lec·ti·cian
di·a·logue
di·am·e·ter
di·a·met·ric
dia·mond
di·a·pa·son
dia·per
di·aph·a·nous
di·a·phragm
di·ar·rhea
di·a·ry
di·a·ries
di·as·to·le
di·as·tol·ic
di·as·tro·phism
di·a·ther·my
di·a·ton·ic
di·a·tribe
dice
diced
dic·ing
di·chot·o·my
di·chot·o·mies
di·chot·o·mous
di·cho·tom·ic
dick·ey
dic·tate
dic·tat·ed
dic·tat·ing
dic·ta·tion
dic·ta·tor
dic·ta·tor·ship
dic·ta·to·ri·al
dic·ta·to·ri·al·ly
dic·tion
dic·tion·ary
dic·tion·ar·ies
dic·tum
di·dac·tic
di·dac·ti·cal
di·dac·ti·cism
die
died
dy·ing
die·sel
di·et
di·e·tary
di·e·tet·ic
di·e·tet·ics
di·e·ti·cian
dif·fer
dif·fer·ence
dif·fer·ent
dif·fer·en·tial
dif·fer·en·ti·ate
dif·fer·en·ti·a·tion
dif·fi·cult
dif·fi·cul·ty
dif·fi·cul·ties
dif·fi·dent
dif·fi·dence
dif·fuse
dif·fused
dif·fus·ing
dif·fuse·ly
dif·fuse·ness
dif·fu·sion
dig
dug
dig·ging
di·gest
di·gest·i·ble
di·gest·i·bil·i·ty
di·ges·tion

di·ges·tive
dig·ger
dig·gings
dig·it
dig·it·al
dig·i·tal·is
dig·ni·fy
dig·ni·fied
dig·ni·fy·ing
dig·ni·tary
dig·ni·tar·ies
dig·ni·ty
dig·ni·ties
di·gress
di·gres·sion
di·gres·sive
di·he·dral
di·lap·i·date
di·lap·i·dat·ed
di·lap·i·dat·ing
di·lap·i·da·tion
dil·a·ta·tion
di·late
di·lat·ed
di·lat·ing
di·la·tion
dil·a·to·ry
dil·a·to·ri·ly
di·lem·ma
dil·et·tan·te
dil·i·gence
dil·i·gent
dil·ly·dal·ly
dil·ly·dal·lied
di·lute
di·lut·ed
dil·lut·ing
di·lu·tion
di·lu·vi·al
dim
dim·mer
dimmed
dim·ming
dim·ly
dim·ness
di·men·sion
di·men·sion·al
di·min·ish
di·min·ish·ing
di·min·u·en·do
dim·i·nu·tion
di·min·u·tive
dim·ple
dim·wit·ted
din
dinned
din·ning
dine
dined
din·ing
din·er
di·nette
din·ghy
din·ghies
din·gy
din·gi·ness
din·ner
di·no·saur
di·o·cese
di·oc·e·san
di·o·rama
di·ox·ide
dip
dipped
dip·ping
diph·the·ria
diph·thong
di·plo·ma

di·plo·ma·cy
di·plo·ma·cies
dip·lo·mat
dip·lo·mat·ic
dip·lo·mat·i·cal·ly
dip·so·ma·nia
dip·so·ma·ni·ac
dire
dire·ness
di·rect
di·rect·ness
di·rec·tion
di·rec·tive
di·rect·ly
di·rec·tor
di·rec·to·ri·al
di·rec·to·rate
di·rec·to·ry
di·rec·to·ries
dirge
di·ri·gi·ble
dirndl
dirty
dirt·i·ness
dis·a·ble
dis·a·bled
dis·a·bling
dis·a·bil·i·ty
dis·a·ble·ment
dis·a·buse
dis·a·bused
dis·a·bus·ing
dis·ad·van·tage
dis·ad·van·taged
dis·ad·van·tag·ing
dis·ad·van·ta·geous
dis·af·fect
dis·af·fec·tion
dis·af·fect·ed
dis·a·gree
dis·a·greed
dis·a·gree·ing
dis·a·gree·a·ble
dis·a·gree·ment
dis·al·low
dis·al·low·ance
dis·ap·pear
dis·ap·pear·ance
dis·ap·point
dis·ap·point·ment
dis·ap·prove
dis·ap·proved
dis·ap·prov·ing
dis·ap·prov·al
dis·ap·pro·ba·tion
dis·arm
dis·ar·ma·ment
dis·ar·range
dis·ar·ranged
dis·ar·rang·ing
dis·ar·range·ment
dis·ar·ray
dis·as·sem·ble
dis·as·so·ci·ate
dis·as·ter
dis·as·trous
dis·a·vow
dis·a·vow·al
dis·band
dis·band·ment
dis·bar
dis·barred
dis·bar·ring
dis·bar·ment
dis·be·lieve
dis·be·lieved
dis·be·liev·ing
dis·be·lief

dis·be·liev·er
dis·burse
dis·bursed
dis·burs·ing
dis·burse·ment
dis·burs·er
disc
disk
dis·card
dis·cern
dis·cern·ing
dis·cern·i·ble
dis·cern·i·bly
dis·cern·ment
dis·charge
dis·charged
dis·charg·ing
dis·char·ger
dis·ci·ple
dis·ci·pline
dis·ci·plined
dis·ci·plin·ing
dis·ci·pli·nary
dis·cl·pli·nar·i·an
dis·claim
dis·claim·er
dis·close
dis·closed
dis·clos·ing
dis·clo·sure
dis·coid
dis·col·or
dis·col·or·a·tion
dis·com·fit
dis·com·fi·ture
dis·com·fort
dis·com·mode
dis·com·mod·ed
dis·com·mod·ing
dis·com·pose
dis·com·posed
dis·com·pos·ing
dis·com·po·sure
dis·con·cert
dis·con·cert·ing
dis·con·cert·ed
dis·con·nect
dis·con·nec·tion
dis·con·nect·ed
dis·con·so·late
dis·con·so·late·ly
dis·con·tent
dis·con·tent·ment
dis·con·tent·ed
dis·con·tin·ue
dis·con·tin·ued
dis·con·tin·u·ing
dis·con·tin·u·ance
dis·con·tin·u·a·tion
dis·con·tin·u·ous
dis·cord
dis·cord·ance
dis·cord·an·cy
dis·cord·ant·ly
dis·co·théque
dis·count
dis·cour·age
dis·cour·ag·ing
dis·cour·age·ment
dis·course
dis·coursed
dis·cours·ing
dis·cour·te·ous
dis·cour·te·ous·ly
dis·cour·te·sy
dis·cour·te·sies
dis·cov·er
dis·cov·er·a·ble

dis·cov·er·er
dis·cov·er·y
dis·cov·er·ies
dis·cred·it
dis·cred·it·a·ble
dis·creet
dis·creet·ly
dis·crep·ant
dis·crep·an·cy
dis·crep·an·cies
dis·crete
dis·cre·tion
dis·cre·tion·ary
dis·crim·i·nate
dis·crim·i·nat·ed
dis·crim·i·nat·ing
dis·crim·i·nate·ly
dis·crim·i·na·tion
dis·crim·i·na·to·ry
dis·cur·sive
dis·cur·sive·ness
dis·cus
dis·cuss
dis·cus·sion
dis·dain
dis·dain·ful
dis·ease
dis·eased
dis·eas·ing
dis·em·bark
dis·em·bar·ka·tion
dis·em·bark·ment
dis·em·body
dis·em·bod·ied
dis·em·bod·y·ing
dis·em·bod·i·ment
dis·em·bow·el
dis·em·bow·eled
dis·em·bow·el·ing
dis·em·bow·el·ment
dis·en·chant
dis·en·chant·ment
dis·en·cum·ber
dis·en·fran·chise
dis·en·fran·chised
dis·en·fran·chis·ing
dis·en·gage
dis·en·gaged
dis·en·gag·ing
dis·en·gage·ment
dis·en·tan·gle
dis·en·tan·gled
dis·en·tan·gling
dis·en·tan·gle·ment
dis·es·tab·lish
dis·es·tab·lish·ment
dis·fa·vor
dis·fig·ure
dis·fig·ured
dis·fig·ur·ing
dis·fig·ure·ment
dis·fran·chise
dis·fran·chised
dis·fran·chis·ing
dis·fran·chise·ment
dis·gorge
dis·gorged
dis·gorg·ing
dis·grace
dis·graced
dis·grac·ing
dis·grace·ful
dis·grun·tle
dis·grun·tled
dis·grun·tling
dis·guise
dis·guised
dis·guis·ing

dis·gust
dis·gust·ed
dis·gust·ing
dis·ha·bille
dis·har·mo·ny
dis·har·mo·nies
dis·heart·en
dis·heart·en·ing
di·shev·eled
dis·hon·est
dis·hon·est·ly
dis·hon·es·ty
dis·hon·es·ties
dis·hon·or
dis·hon·or·a·ble
dis·hon·or·a·bly
dis·il·lu·sion
dis·il·lu·sion·ment
dis·in·cline
dis·in·clined
dis·in·clin·ing
dis·in·cli·na·tion
dis·in·fect
dis·in·fect·ant
dis·in·fec·tion
dis·in·gen·u·ous
dis·in·her·it
dis·in·her·i·tance
dis·in·te·grate
dis·in·te·grat·ed
dis·in·te·grat·ing
dis·in·te·gra·tion
dis·in·ter
dis·in·terred
dis·in·ter·ring
dis·in·ter·ment
dis·in·ter·est
dis·in·ter·es·ted
dis·join
dis·joint
dis·joint·ed
dis·junc·tion
disk
disc
dis·like
dis·liked
dis·lik·ing
dis·lik·a·ble
dis·lo·cate
dis·lo·cat·ing
dis·lo·ca·tion
dis·lodge
dis·lodged
dis·lodg·ing
dis·lodg·ment
dis·loy·al
dis·loy·al·ly
dis·loy·al·ty
dis·mal
dis·mal·ly
dis·man·tle
dis·man·tled
dis·man·tling
dis·may
dis·mem·ber
dis·mem·ber·ment
dis·miss
dis·mis·sal
dis·mount
dis·o·bey
dis·o·be·di·ence
dis·o·be·di·ent
dis·or·der
dis·or·dered
dis·or·der·ly
dis·or·der·li·ness
dis·or·gan·ize
dis·or·gan·ized

dis·or·gan·i·za·tion
dis·o·ri·ent
dis·o·ri·en·ta·tion
dis·own
dis·par·age
dis·par·aged
dis·par·ag·ing
dis·par·age·ment
dis·pa·rate
dis·pa·rate·ly
dis·par·i·ty
dis·par·i·ties
dis·pas·sion
dis·pas·sion·ate
dis·patch
dis·patch·er
dis·pel
dis·pelled
dis·pel·ling
dis·pen·sa·ble
dis·pen·sa·bil·i·ty
dis·pen·sa·ry
dis·pen·sa·ries
dis·pense
dis·pensed
dis·pens·ing
dis·pen·sa·tion
dis·perse
dis·persed
dis·pers·ing
dis·per·sion
dis·place
dis·placed
dis·plac·ing
dis·place·ment
dis·play
dis·please
dis·pleas·ing
dis·pleas·ure
dis·port
dis·pose
dis·pos·ing
dis·pos·a·ble
dis·po·si·tion
dis·pos·sess
dis·pos·ses·sion
dis·pro·por·tion
dis·pro·por·tion·ate
dis·prove
dis·prov·ing
dis·pute
dis·put·ed
dis·put·ing
dis·put·a·ble
dis·pu·tant
dis·pu·ta·tious
dis·qual·i·fy
dis·qual·i·fied
dis·qual·i·fy·ing
dis·qual·i·fi·ca·tion
dis·qui·et
dis·qui·etude
dis·qui·si·tion
dis·re·gard
dis·re·pair
dis·re·pute
dis·rep·u·ta·ble
dis·re·spect
dis·re·spect·ful
dis·robe
dis·robed
dis·rob·ing
dis·rupt
dis·rup·tion
dis·rup·tive
dis·rupt·er
dis·sat·is·fy
dis·sat·is·fac·tion

dis·sat·is·fac·to·ry
dis·sat·is·fied
dis·sat·is·fy·ing
dis·sect
dis·sect·ed
dis·sec·tion
dis·sem·ble
dis·sem·blance
dis·sem·bled
dis·sem·bling
dis·sem·i·nate
dis·sem·i·nat·ed
dis·sem·i·nat·ing
dis·sem·i·na·tion
dis·sent
dis·sent·ing
dis·sen·sion
dis·sen·tious
dis·sent·er
dis·sen·tient
dis·ser·tate
dis·ser·ta·ted
dis·ser·ta·ting
dis·ser·ta·tion
dis·serve
dis·served
dis·serv·ing
dis·serv·ice
dis·si·dence
dis·si·dent
dis·sim·i·lar
dis·sim·i·lar·i·ty
dis·sim·i·late
dis·sim·i·lat·ed
dis·sim·i·lat·ing
dis·sim·i·la·tion
dis·si·mil·i·tude
dis·sim·u·late
dis·sim·u·lat·ed
dis·sim·u·lat·ing
dis·sim·u·la·tion
dis·si·pate
dis·si·pat·ed
dis·si·pat·ing
dis·si·pa·tion
dis·so·ci·ate
dis·so·ci·at·ed
dis·so·ci·at·ing
dis·so·ci·a·tion
dis·sol·u·ble
dis·so·lute
dis·so·lu·tion
dis·solve
dis·solv·ing
dis·solv·a·ble
dis·so·nance
dis·so·nant
dis·suade
dis·suad·ed
dis·suad·ing
dis·sua·sion
dis·taff
dis·tance
dis·tant
dis·taste
dis·taste·ful
dis·tem·per
dis·tend
dis·ten·sion
dis·ten·tion
dis·till
dis·tilled
dis·till·ing
dis·til·la·tion
dis·til·late
dis·till·er
dis·till·ery
dis·till·er·ies

dis·tinct
dis·tinc·tion
dis·tinc·tive
dis·tin·guish
dis·tin·guished
dis·tort
dis·tort·ed
dis·tor·tion
dis·tract
dis·tract·ing
dis·trac·tion
dis·trait
dis·traught
dis·tress
dis·tress·ing
dis·tress·ful
dis·tress·ing
dis·trib·ute
dis·trib·ut·ed
dis·trib·ut·ing
dis·tri·bu·tion
dis·trib·u·tor
dis·trict
dis·trict at·tor·ney
dis·trust
dis·trust·ful
dis·turb
dis·turb·ance
dis·turbed
dis·u·nite
dis·u·nit·ed
dis·u·nit·ing
dis·u·ni·ty
dis·un·ion
dis·use
dis·used
dis·us·ing
ditch
dith·er
dit·to
dit·to·ing
dit·ty
di·u·ret·ic
di·ur·nal
di·va
di·va·gate
di·va·ga·tion
di·van
dive
dived
dove
div·ing
di·verge
di·verged
di·verg·ing
di·ver·gence
di·ver·gent
di·verse
di·ver·si·fi·ca·tion
di·ver·si·fy
di·ver·si·fied
di·ver·si·ty
di·ver·si·ties
di·ver·sion
di·ver·sion·ary
di·vert
di·vide
di·vid·ed
di·vid·ing
di·vis·i·ble
di·vi·sion
di·vi·sive
di·vi·sor
div·i·dend
di·vine
di·vin·i·ty
di·vin·i·ties
di·vorce

di·vorc·ing
di·vor·cee
di·vulge
di·vulged
di·vulg·ing
di·vul·gence
diz·zy
diz·zi·est
diz·zied
diz·zy·ing
diz·zi·ly
diz·zi·ness
do
did
done
do·ing
does
Do·ber·man pin·scher
doc·ile
doc·tor
doc·tor·al
doc·tor·ate
doc·trine
doc·tri·nal
doc·tri·naire
doc·u·ment
doc·u·men·ta·tion
doc·u·men·tary
dod·der
dodge
dodg·ing
doesn't
dog
dogged
dog·ging
dog·eared
dog·ged
dog·ged·ly
dog·ger·el
dog·ma
dog·mas
dog·mat·ic
dog·mat·i·cal
dog·ma·tism
dog·ma·tist
doi·ly
doi·lies
dol·drums
dole
doled
dol·ing
dole·ful
dol·lar
dol·or·ous
dol·phin
dolt
dolt·ish
do·main
dome
domed
dom·ing
do·mes·tic
do·mes·ti·cal·ly
do·mes·ti·cate
do·mes·ti·cat·ed
do·mes·ti·cat·ing
do·mes·ti·ca·tion
do·mes·tic·i·ty
do·mes·tic·i·ties
dom·i·cile
dom·i·ciled
dom·i·cil·ing
dom·i·nant
dom·i·nance
dom·i·nancy
dom·i·nate
dom·i·nat·ing
dom·i·na·tion

dom·i·neer
dom·i·neer·ing
do·min·ion
dom·i·no
dom·i·noes
don
donned
don·ning
do·nate
do·nat·ed
do·nat·ing
do·na·tor
do·na·tion
do·nor
don·key
doo·dle
dooms·day
dope
doped
dop·ing
dop·ey
dop·i·ness
dor·mant
dor·man·cy
dor·mer
dor·mered
dor·mi·to·ry
dor·mi·to·ries
dor·sal
dose
dosed
dos·ing
dos·age
dos·si·er
dot
dot·ted
dot·ting
dot·age
dote
dot·ed
dot·ing
dou·ble
dou·bled
dou·bling
doub·ly
dou·ble·breast·ed
dou·ble·cross
dou·ble·deck·er
dou·ble·faced
dou·ble·head·er
dou·ble·joint·ed
dou·ble·time
doubt
doubt·ful
doubt·ful·ly
doubt·less
douche
douched
douch·ing
dough
dough·ty
dough·ti·ness
dour
dour·ness
douse
doused
dous·ing
dove·cote
dove·tail
dow·a·ger
dow·dy
dowd·i·ly
dow·di·ness
dow·el
dow·eled
dow·el·ing
dow·er
down

down·i·ness
downy
down·grade
down·grad·ed
down·grad·ing
down·heart·ed
down·stream
down·town
down·trod·den
dow·ry
dow·ries
dox·ol·o·gy
doze
dozed
dozing
doz·en
doz·enth
drab
drab·ness
dra·co·ni·an
draft
draft·ee
drafts·man
drafty
draft·i·er
drag
dragged
drag·ging
drag·net
drain
drain·age
drake
dra·ma
dra·mat·ic
dra·mat·ics
dram·a·tist
dram·a·tize
dram·a·ti·za·tion
drape
draped
draping
dra·pery
dra·per·ies
dras·tic
drast·i·cal·ly
draught
draw
drew
drawn
draw·ing
draw·bridge
draw·er
drawl
dread
dread·ful
dream
dreamed
dreamt
dream·ing
dream·er
dream·i·ly
dreamy
dream·i·est
dreary
drear·i·er
drear·i·ly
drear·i·ness
dredge
dredged
dredg·ing
dredg·er
dreg
dreg·gy
drench
dress
dressed
dres·sing
dress·er

dressy
dress·i·est
drib·ble
drib·bled
drib·bling
dri·er
drift
drift·age
drift·er
drill·ing
dri·ly
drink
drank
drunk
drink·ing
drink·a·ble
drink·er
drip
dripped
drip·ping
drip·py
drive
drove
driv·en
driv·ing
driv·el
driv·eled
driv·el·ing
driz·zle
driz·zled
driz·zling
driz·zly
droll
drol·ly
droll·ery
drom·e·dary
drom·e·dar·ies
drone
droned
dron·ing
drool
droop
droop·ing·ly
droop·y
drop
dropped
drop·ping
drop·let
drop·per
drop·sy
dross
drought
drought·y
drought·i·est
drove
drowned
drowse
drows·ing
drow·sy
drow·si·ness
drub
drubbed
drub·bing
drudge
drudg·ing
drudg·ery
drug
drugged
drug·ging
drug·gist
dru·id
drum
drummed
drum·ming
drum·mer
drunk·ard
drunk·en
drunk·en·ly

drunk·en·ness
dry
dry·ing
dri·er
dried
dry·ad
du·al
du·al·i·ty
du·al·ism
du·al·is·tic
dub
dubbed
dub·bing
du·bi·ous
du·bi·e·ty
du·bi·ous·ly
du·cal
du·cat
duch·ess
duchy
duck·ling
ducky
duck·i·est
duct·less
duc·tile
dudg·eon
du·el
du·eled
du·el·ing
du·el·ist
du·en·na
du·et
duf·fel
duff·er
dug·out
duke·dom
dul·cet
dul·ci·mer
dull
dull·ard
dull·ness
du·ly
dumb
dumb·ness
dum·dum
dum·found
dum·my
dum·mies
dump·ling
dumpy
dump·i·er
dump·i·ness
dun
dunned
dun·ning
dunce
dun·der·head
dune
dung·hill
dun·ga·ree
dun·geon
dun·nage
du·o·dec·i·mal
du·o·de·nal
du·o·de·num
dupe
duped
dup·ing
du·plex
du·pli·cate
du·pli·cat·ed
du·pli·cat·ing
du·pli·ca·tion
du·pli·ca·tor
du·plic·i·ty
du·plic·i·ties
du·ra·ble
du·ra·bil·i·ty

dur·ance
du·ra·tion
du·ress
dur·ing
dusk
  dusk·i·ness
  dusky
dust·er
dust·less
dusty
  dust·i·er
  dust·i·ness
du·ti·a·ble
du·ti·ful
  du·ti·ful·ly
du·ty
  du·ties
dwarf
  dwarf·ish
dwell
  dwelt
  dwelled
  dwell·ing
dwindle
  dwin·dled
  dwin·dling
dye
  dyed
  dye·ing
dy·ing
dy·nam·ic
  dy·nam·i·cal·ly
  dy·na·mism
dy·nam·ics
dy·na·mite
  dy·na·mit·er
dy·na·mo
dy·na·mo·tor
dy·nas·ty
  dy·nas·ties
dy·na·tron
dys·en·tery
dys·func·tion
dys·pep·sia
  dys·pep·tic
dys·tro·phy
  dys·tro·phic·

E

ea·ger
  ea·ger·ness
ea·gle
ea·gle·eyed
ea·glet
ear·ache
ear·drum
earl·dom
ear·ly
  ear·li·est
  ear·li·ness
ear·lobe
ear·mark
earn
earn·ings
ear·nest
  ear·nest·ness
ear·ring
ear·shot
ear·split·ting
earth·bound
earth·en
earth·en·ware
earth·ly
earth·quake
earth·shaking
earth·work

earth·worm
earthy
  earth·i·ness
ease
  eased
  eas·ing
ea·sel
ease·ment
eas·i·ly
  eas·i·ness
east·er·ly
east·ern
East·ern·er
east·ward
easy
  eas·i·er
  eas·i·est
eas·y·go·ing
eat
  ate
  eat·en
  eat·ing
eau de co·logne
eaves·drop
  eaves·dropped
  eaves·drop·ping
  eaves·drop·per
ebb
  ebb·ing
eb·ony
ebul·lience
  ebul·lient
  eb·ul·li·tion
ec·cen·tric
  ec·cen·tric·i·ty
ec·cle·si·as·tic
  ec·cle·si·as·ti·cal
ech·e·lon
echo
  ech·oes
  ech·oed
  ech·o·ing
eclair
ec·lec·tic
  ec·lec·ti·cal·ly
  ec·lec·ti·cism
eclipse
  eclipsed
  eclips·ing
eclip·tic
ecol·o·gy
  ec·o·log·ic
  ec·o·log·i·cal
  ecol·o·gist
eco·nom·ic
  eco·nom·i·cal
  eco·nom·ics
  econ·o·mist
econ·o·mize
  econ·o·miz·ing
econ·o·my
  econ·o·mies
ec·ru
ec·sta·sy
  ec·sta·sies
ec·stat·ic
  ec·stat·i·cal
ec·u·men·ic
  ec·u·men·i·cal
  ec·u·men·ism
ec·ze·ma
  ec·zem·a·tous
e·da·cious
ed·dy
  ed·dies
  ed·died
  ed·dy·ing
edel·weiss

ede·ma
edge
  edged
  edg·ing
edgy
  edg·i·ness
ed·i·ble
  ed·i·bil·i·ty
edict
ed·i·fice
ed·i·fy
  ed·i·fied
  ed·i·fy·ing
  ed·i·fi·ca·tion
ed·it
edi·tion
ed·i·tor
ed·i·to·ri·al
  ed·i·to·ri·al·ly
  ed·i·to·ri·al·ize
  ed·i·to·ri·al·iz·ing
ed·u·cate
  ed·u·cat·ed
  ed·u·cat·ing
  ed·u·ca·ble
  ed·u·ca·tive
ed·u·ca·tion
  ed·u·ca·tion·al
  ed·u·ca·tor
educe
  educed
  educ·ing
  educ·i·ble
  educ·tion
eel
  eely
ee·rie
  ee·ri·ly
  ee·ri·ness
ef·face
  ef·faced
  ef·fac·ing
  ef·face·ment
ef·fect
  ef·fec·tive
  ef·fec·tive·ness
  ef·fec·tive·ly
ef·fec·tu·al
ef·fec·tu·ate
  ef·fec·tu·at·ed
  ef·fec·tu·at·ing
ef·fem·i·nate
  ef·fem·i·na·cy
  ef·fem·i·nate·ly
ef·fer·vesce
  ef·fer·vesc·ing
  ef·fer·ves·cence
  ef·fer·ves·cent
ef·fete
ef·fi·ca·cy
  ef·fi·ca·cies
  ef·fi·ca·cious
ef·fi·cient
  ef·fi·cient·ly
ef·fi·gy
  ef·fi·gies
ef·flo·resce
  ef·flo·resced
  ef·flo·resc·ing
  ef·flo·res·cence
  ef·flo·res·cent
ef·flu·ent
  ef·flu·ence
ef·flu·vi·um
  ef·flu·vi·al
ef·fort
  ef·fort·less
ef·fron·tery

ef·fron·ter·ies
ef·ful·gent
  ef·ful·gence
ef·fuse
  ef·fused
  ef·fus·ing
ef·fu·sion
ef·fu·sive
egal·i·tar·i·an
  egal·i·tar·i·an·ism
ego·cen·tric
ego·ism
  ego·ist
  ego·is·tic
ego·tism
  ego·tist
  ego·tis·tic
  ego·tis·ti·cal
egre·gious
egress
e·gre·sion
egret
eight
  eighth
eight·een
  eight·eenth
eight·fold
eighty
  eight·ies
  eight·i·eth
ei·ther
ejac·u·late
  ejac·u·lat·ed
  ejac·u·lat·ing
  ejac·u·la·tion
  ejac·u·la·to·ry
eject
  ejec·tion
  eject·ment
  ejec·tor
eke
  eked
  ek·ing
elab·o·rate
  elab·o·rat·ed
  elab·o·rat·ing
  elab·o·rate·ness
  elab·o·ra·tion
elapse
  elapsed
  elaps·ing
elas·tic
  elas·ti·cal
  elas·tic·i·ty
elate
  elat·ed
  elat·ing
  ela·tion
el·bow
eld·er
  eld·er·ly
  eld·er·li·ness
  eld·est
elect
  elec·tion
elec·tion·eer
elec·tive
elec·tor
  elec·tor·al
elec·tor·ate
elec·tric
  elec·tri·cal
  elec·tri·cian
  elec·tric·i·ty
elec·tri·fy
  elec·tri·fied
  elec·tri·fy·ing
  elec·tri·fi·ca·tion

elec·tro·car·di·o·gram
elec·tro·cute
  elec·tro·cut·ed
  elec·tro·cut·ing
  elec·tro·cu·tion
elec·trode
elec·tro·dy·nam·ics
elec·tro·en·ceph·a·lo·gram
elec·trol·y·sis
  elec·tro·lyze
  elec·tro·lyzed
  elec·tro·lyz·ing
  elec·tro·lyte
  elec·tro·lyt·ic
elec·tro·mag·net
  elec·tro·mag·net·ism
  elec·tro·mag·net·ic
elec·tron
elec·tron·ic
  elec·tron·ics
  elec·tron·i·cal·ly
elec·tro·plate
  elec·tro·plat·ed
  elec·tro·plat·ing
elec·tro·ther·a·py
el·ee·mos·y·nary
el·e·gant
  el·e·gance
  el·e·gan·cy
  el·e·gant·ly
el·e·gy
  el·e·gies
  el·e·gize
  el·e·giz·ing
el·e·ment
el·e·men·tal
el·e·men·ta·ry
  el·e·men·ta·ri·ly
ele·phant
el·e·phan·ti·a·sis
el·e·phan·tine
el·e·vate
  el·e·vat·ed
  el·e·vat·ing
  el·e·va·tion
  el·e·va·tor
elev·en
  elev·enth
elf
  elves
  elf·in
elic·it
el·i·gi·ble
  el·i·gi·bil·i·ty
elim·i·nate
  elim·i·nat·ed
  elim·i·nat·ing
  elim·i·na·tion
elite
  elit·ism
  elit·ist
elix·ir
Eliz·a·beth·an
el·lipse
el·lip·sis
el·lip·ti·cal
  el·lip·tic
el·o·cu·tion
  el·o·cu·tion·ary
  el·o·cu·tion·ist
elon·gate
  elon·gat·ed
  elon·gat·ing
  elon·ga·tion
elope
  eloped
  elop·ing
  elope·ment

el·o·quence
el·o·quent
elu·ci·date
  elu·ci·dat·ed
  elu·ci·dat·ing
  elu·ci·da·tion
elude
  elud·ed
  elud·ing
  elu·sion
elu·sive
  elu·so·ry
  elu·sive·ness
ema·ci·ate
  ema·ci·at·ed
  ema·ci·at·ed
  ema·ci·a·tion
em·a·nate
  em·a·nat·ed
  em·a·nat·ing
  em·a·na·tion
eman·ci·pate
  eman·ci·pat·ed
  eman·ci·pat·ing
  eman·ci·pa·tor
emas·cu·late
  emas·cu·lat·ed
  emas·cu·lating
  emas·cu·la·tion
em·balm
  em·balm·ment
em·bank·ment
em·bar·go
  em·bar·goes
  em·bar·go·ing
em·bark
  em·bar·ka·tion
  em·bark·ment
em·bar·rass
  em·bar·rass·ed
  em·bar·rass·ing
  em·bar·rass·ment
em·bas·sy
  em·bas·sies
em·bat·tle
  em·bat·tled
  em·bat·tling
  em·bat·tle·ment
em·bed
  em·bed·ded
  em·bed·ding
em·bel·lish
  em·bel·lish·ment
em·ber
em·bez·zle
  em·bez·zled
  em·bez·zling
  em·bez·zle·ment
  em·bez·zler
em·bit·ter
  em·bit·ter·ment
em·bla·zon
  em·blaz·on·ment
em·blem
  em·blem·at·ic
  em·blem·at·i·cal
em·bod·y
  em·bod·ied
  em·bod·y·ing
  em·bod·i·ment
em·bold·en
em·bo·lism
em·bo·lus
em·boss
  em·boss·ment
em·bou·chure
em·brace
  em·brac·ing

em·bra·sure
em·bro·cate
em·broi·der
  em·broi·dery
em·broil
  em·broil·ment
em·bryo
  em·bry·os
  em·bry·on·ic
  em·bry·ol·o·gy
em·cee
  em·ceed
  em·cee·ing
emend
  emen·da·ble
  emen·da·tion
em·er·ald
emerge
  emerged
  emerg·ing
  emer·gence
  emer·gent
  emer·gen·cy
  emer·gen·cies
emer·i·tus
em·ery
emet·ic
em·i·grant
em·i·grate
  em·i·grat·ing
  em·i·gra·tion
émi·gré
em·i·nence
  em·i·nent
  em·i·nent do·main
em·is·sary
  em·is·sar·ies
emis·sion
  emis·sive
emit
  emit·ted
  emit·ting
emol·lient
emol·u·ment
emote
  emot·ed
  emot·ing
  emo·tive
emo·tion
  emo·tion·al·ly
  emo·tion·al·ism
em·pan·el
em·pa·thize
  em·pa·thized
  em·pa·thiz·ing
em·pa·thy
  em·pa·thet·ic
  em·path·ic
em·per·or
em·pha·sis
  em·pha·ses
em·pha·size
  em·pha·sized
  em·pha·siz·ing
em·phat·ic
  em·phat·i·cal·ly
em·phy·se·ma
em·pire
em·pir·i·cal
em·pir·i·cism
em·place·ment
em·ploy
  em·ploy·a·ble
  em·ploy·ee
  em·ploy·er
  em·ploy·ment
em·po·ri·um
em·pow·er

em·press
emp·ty
  emp·tied
  emp·ty·ing
  emp·ti·ness
em·u·late
  em·u·lat·ing
  em·u·la·tion
emul·si·fy
  emul·si·fied
  emul·si·fy·ing
  emul·si·fi·ca·tion
  emul·si·fi·er
emul·sion
  emul·sive
en·a·ble
  en·a·bled
  en·a·bling
en·act
  en·act·ment
enam·el
  enam·eled
  enam·el·ing
  enam·el·ware
en·am·or
  en·am·ored
en·camp
  en·camp·ment
en·cap·su·late
  en·cap·sul·lat·ed
  en·cap·su·lat·ing
  en·cap·sule
en·case
  en·cased
  en·cas·ing
en·ceinte
en·ceph·a·li·tis
en·chant
  en·chant·ing
  en·chant·ment
  en·chant·ress
en·chi·la·da
en·cir·cle
  en·cir·cled
  en·cir·cling
  en·cir·cle·ment
en·clave
en·close
  en·closed
  en·clos·ing
  en·clo·sure
en·code
  en·cod·ed
  en·cod·ing
en·com·pass
en·core
en·coun·ter
en·cour·age
  en·cour·aged
  en·cour·ag·ing
  en·cour·age·ment
en·croach
  en·croach·ment
en·crust
  en·crus·ta·tion
en·cum·ber
  en·cum·brance
en·cy·clo·pe·dia
en·cy·clo·pe·dic
en·dan·ger
  en·dan·ger·ment
en·dear
  en·dear·ment
en·deav·or
en·dem·ic
  en·dem·i·cal
en·dive
end·ing

end·less
en·do·crine
en·do·cri·nol·o·gy
en·dog·a·mous
en·dorse
  en·dors·ing
  en·dor·see
  en·dor·ser
  en·dorse·ment
  en·do·scope
endow
  en·dow·ment
en·due
  en·dued
  en·du·ing
en·dure
  en·dur·ing
  en·dur·a·ble
  en·dur·ance
  en·dur·ing·ness
en·e·ma
en·e·my
  en·e·mies
en·er·get·ic
  en·er·get·i·cal·ly
en·er·gize
  en·er·gized
  en·er·giz·ing
  en·er·giz·er
en·er·gy
  en·er·gies
en·er·vate
  en·er·vat·ed
  en·er·vat·ing
  en·er·va·tion
en·fee·ble
  en·fee·bled
  en·fee·bling
  en·fee·ble·ment
en·fold
en·force
  en·forced
  en·forc·ing
  en·force·ment
en·fran·chise
  en·fran·chised
  en·fran·chis·ing
  en·fran·chise·ment
en·gage
  en·gaged
  en·gag·ing
  en·gage·ment
en·gen·der
en·gine
  en·gi·neer
En·gland
En·glish
en·gorge
  en·gorged
  en·gorg·ing
  en·gorge·ment
en·grave
  en·graved
  en·grav·ing
  en·grav·er
en·gross
  en·grossed
  en·gross·ing
  en·gross·ment
en·gulf
  en·gulf·ment
en·hance
  en·hanced
  en·hanc·ing
  en·hance·ment
enig·ma
  en·ig·mat·ic
  en·ig·mat·i·cal

en·join
  en·join·ment
en·joy
  en·joy·a·ble
  en·joy·ment
en·large
  en·larged
  en·larg·ing
  en·larg·er
  en·large·ment
en·light·en
  en·light·en·ment
en·list
  en·list·ed
  en·list·ment
en·liv·en
en·masse
en·mesh
en·mi·ty
  en·mi·ties
en·no·ble
  en·no·bled
  en·no·bling
  en·no·ble·ment
en·nui
enor·mi·ty
  enor·mi·ties
enor·mous
enough
en·plane
  en·planed
  en·plan·ing
en·quire
  en·quiry
en·rage
  en·raged
  en·rag·ing
en·rap·ture
  en·rap·tured
  en·rap·tur·ing
  en·rapt
en·rich
  en·rich·ment
en·roll
  en·roll·ment
en route
en·sconce
  en·sconced
  en·sconc·ing
en·semble
en·shrine
  en·shrined
  en·shrin·ing
en·shroud
en·sign
en·si·lage
  en·si·laged
  en·si·lag·ing
en·slave
  en·slaved
  en·slav·ing
  en·slave·ment
en·snare
  en·snared
  en·snar·ing
  en·snare·ment
en·sue
  en·sued
  en·su·ing
en·sure
  en·sured
  en·sur·ing
en·tail
  en·tail·ment
en·tan·gle
  en·tan·gled
  en·tan·gling
  en·tan·gle·ment

en·tente
en·ter
  en·ter·ing
en·ter·prise
  en·ter·pris·ing
en·ter·tain
  en·ter·tain·ing
  en·ter·tain·er
  en·ter·tain·ment
en·thrall
  en·thralled
  en·thrall·ing
  en·thrall·ment
en·throne
  en·throned
  en·thron·ing
  en·throne·ment
en·thuse
  en·thused
  en·thus·ing
en·thu·si·asm
en·thu·si·ast
en·thu·si·as·tic
en·thu·si·as·ti·cal·ly
en·tice
  en·ticed
  en·tic·ing
  en·tice·ment
en·tire
  en·tire·ly
  en·tire·ness
  en·tire·ty
en·ti·tle
  en·ti·tled
  en·ti·tling
  en·ti·tle·ment
en·ti·ty
  en·ti·ties
en·tomb
  en·tomb·ment
en·to·mol·o·gy
en·tou·rage
en·trails
en·train
en·trance
en·trant
en·trap
  en·trapped
  en·trap·ping
  en·trap·ment
en·treat
  en·treat·ment
  en·treaty
en·tree
en·trench
  en·trench·ment
en·tre·pre·neur
en·trust
  en·trust·ment
en·try
  en·tries
en·twine
  en·twined
  en·twin·ing
enu·mer·ate
  enu·mer·at·ed
  enu·mer·at·ing
  enu·mer·a·tion
  enu·mer·a·tor
enun·ci·ate
  enun·ci·at·ed
  enun·ci·at·ing
  enun·ci·a·tion
en·vel·op
  en·vel·op·ing
en·ve·lope
en·vi·a·ble
en·vi·ous

en·vi·ous·ness
en·vi·ron
  en·vi·ron·ment
en·vis·age
  en·vis·ag·ing
en·vi·sion
en·voy
en·vy
  en·vies
  en·vied
  en·vy·ing
  en·vi·able
en·vi·ous
en·zyme
  en·zy·mat·ic
en·vi·ron·ment
  en·vi·ron·men·tal
ep·au·let
epergne
ephed·rine
ephem·er·al
ep·ic
  ep·i·cal
epi·cen·ter
epi·cure
  epi·cu·re·an
ep·i·dem·ic
ep·i·der·mis
  ep·i·der·mal
  ep·i·der·mic
ep·i·glot·tis
ep·i·gram
  ep·i·gram·mat·ic
ep·i·graph
ep·i·lep·sy
  ep·i·lep·tic
ep·i·logue
epis·co·pal
  epis·co·pa·cy
  epis·co·pate
  Epis·co·pa·lian
ep·i·sode
  ep·i·sod·ic
  ep·i·sod·i·cal
epis·te·mol·o·gy
epis·tle
ep·i·taph
ep·i·thet
epit·o·me
  epit·o·mize
ep·och
  ep·och·al
ep·oxy
equa·ble
  eq·ua·bil·i·ty
  eq·ua·ble·ness
  eq·ua·bly
equal
  equaled
  equal·ling
  equal·ly
  equal·ness
equal·i·tar·i·an
equal·i·ty
  equal·i·ties
equal·ize
  equal·ized
  equal·iz·ing
  equal·i·za·tion
equa·nim·i·ty
equate
  equat·ed
  equat·ing
equa·tion
  equa·tion·al
equa·tor
  equa·to·ri·al
eques·tri·an

eques·tri·enne
equi·dis·tant
  equi·dis·tance
equi·lat·er·al
equi·li·brate
  equi·li·brat·ed
  equi·li·brat·ing
  equi·li·bra·tion
  equi·lib·ri·um
equine
equi·nox
  equi·noc·tial
equip
  equipped
  equip·ping
equip·ment
equi·poise
eq·ui·ty
  eq·ui·ties
eq·ui·ta·ble
  eq·ui·ta·bly
equiv·a·lent
  equiv·a·lence
equiv·o·cal
equiv·o·cate
  equiv·o·cat·ed
  equiv·o·cat·ing
  equiv·o·ca·tion
erad·i·cate
  erad·i·cat·ed
  erad·i·cat·ing
  erad·i·ca·ble
  erad·i·ca·tion
  erad·i·ca·tor
erase
  erased
  eras·ing
  eras·a·ble
  eras·ure
erect
  erect·a·ble
  erec·tive
  erect·ly
  erect·ness
  erec·tor
erec·tile
erec·tion
er·mine
erode
  erod·ed
  erod·ing
  ero·sion
  ero·sive
erot·ic
  erot·i·cal·ly
  erot·i·cism
err
  err·ing·ly
er·rand
er·rant
er·rat·ic
  er·rat·i·cal·ly
er·ra·tum
  er·ra·ta
er·ro·ne·ous
er·ror
  er·ror·less
er·satz
erst·while
er·u·dite
  er·u·dite·ness
  er·u·di·tion
erupt
  erup·tion
  erup·tive
es·ca·lade
es·ca·late

es·ca·lat·ed
es·ca·lat·ing
es·ca·la·tion
es·ca·la·tor
es·cal·lop
es·ca·pade
es·cape
  es·caped
  es·cap·ing
  es·ca·pee
  es·cap·ist
  es·cap·ism
es·ca·role
es·carp·ment
es·chew
  es·chew·al
es·cort
es·crow
es·cutch·eon
Es·ki·mo
esoph·a·gus
es·o·ter·ic
  es·o·ter·i·cal
es·pal·ier
es·pe·cial
  es·pe·cial·ly
Es·pe·ran·to
es·pi·o·nage
es·pla·nade
es·pouse
  es·poused
  es·pous·ing
  es·pous·al
es·prit de corps
es·py
  es·pied
  es·py·ing
es·quire
es·say
  es·say·ist
es·sence
es·sen·tial
  es·sen·tial·ly
es·tab·lish
  es·tab·lish·ment
es·tate
es·teem
es·thet·ic
es·ti·ma·ble
  es·ti·ma·bly
es·ti·mate
  es·ti·mat·ed
  es·ti·mat·ing
  es·ti·ma·tor
  es·ti·ma·tion
es·trange
  es·tranged
  es·trang·ing
  es·trange·ment
es·tro·gen
es·tu·ary
  es·tu·ar·ies
et cet·era
etch
  etch·ing
eter·nal
  eter·nal·ly
  eter·ni·ty
  eter·nize
  eter·ni·za·tion
eth·a·nol
ether
ethe·re·al
  ethe·re·al·ly
  ethe·re·al·ize
  ethe·re·al·i·za·tion
eth·ic
  eth·i·cal

eth·ics
eth·nic
  eth·ni·cal
eth·nog·ra·phy
eth·nol·o·gy
eth·yl
eti·ol·o·gy
  eti·o·log·i·cal
et·i·quette
etude
et·y·mol·o·gy
  et·y·mo·log·i·cal
eu·ca·lyp·tus
Eu·cha·rist
  Eu·cha·ris·tic
  Eu·cha·ris·ti·cal
eu·chre
eu·gen·ic
  eu·gen·i·cal·ly
eu·lo·gize
  eu·lo·gized
  eu·lo·giz·ing
eu·lo·gy
  eu·lo·gies
  eu·lo·gis·tic
eu·nuch
eu·phe·mism
  eu·phe·mist
  eu·phe·mis·tic
  eu·phe·mis·ti·cal
eu·phe·mize
  eu·phe·mized
  eu·phe·miz·ing
eu·pho·ny
  eu·phon·ic
  eu·phon·i·cal
  eu·pho·ni·ous
eu·pho·ria
  eu·phor·ic
Eu·rope
  Eu·ro·pe·an
eu·tha·na·sia
evac·u·ate
  evac·u·at·ed
  evac·u·at·ing
  evac·u·a·tion
  evac·u·ee
evade
  evad·ed
  evad·ing
eval·u·ate
  eval·u·at·ed
  eval·u·at·ing
  eval·u·a·tion
  eval·u·a·tor
ev·a·nesce
  ev·a·nesced
  ev·a·nesc·ing
  ev·a·nes·cent
evan·gel·i·cal
  evan·gel·ic
  evan·gel·i·cal·ism
  evan·gel·i·cal·ly
evan·ge·lism
  evan·ge·lis·tic
  evan·ge·lis·ti·cal·ly
  evan·ge·list
evan·ge·lize
  evan·ge·lized
  evan·ge·liz·ing
  evan·ge·li·za·tion
evap·o·rate
  evap·o·rat·ed
  evap·o·rat·ing
  evap·o·ra·tion
  evap·o·ra·tor
eva·sion
  eva·sive

eva·sive·ness
even
  even·ly
eve·ning
event·ful
  event·ful·ly
even·tu·al
  even·tu·al·ly
  even·tu·al·i·ty
even·tu·ate
  even·tu·at·ed
  even·tu·at·ing
ev·er·green
ev·er·last·ing
evert
  ever·sion
ev·ery·body
ev·ery·day
ev·ery·one
ev·ery·thing
ev·ery·where
evict
  evic·tion
  evic·tor
ev·i·dence
  ev·i·denced
  ev·i·denc·ing
ev·i·dent
  ev·i·dent·ly
  ev·i·den·tial
evil
  evil·do·er
  evil·ly
  evil·ness
  evil·mind·ed
evince
  evinced
  evinc·ing
  evin·ci·ble
evis·cer·ate
  evis·cer·at·ed
  evis·cer·at·ing
  evis·cer·a·tion
evoke
  evoked
  evok·ing
  ev·o·ca·tion
ev·o·lu·tion
  ev·o·lu·tion·al
  ev·o·lu·tion·ary
  ev·o·lu·tion·ism
  ev·o·lu·tion·ist
evolve
  evolved
  evolv·ing
  evolve·ment
ew·er
ex·ac·er·bate
  ex·ac·er·bat·ed
  ex·ac·er·bat·ing
  ex·ac·er·ba·tion
ex·act
  ex·act·a·ble
  ex·act·ing
  ex·act·ing·ly
  ex·act·i·tude
  ex·act·ly
ex·ag·ger·ate
  ex·ag·ger·at·ed
  ex·ag·ger·at·ing
  ex·ag·ger·a·tion
ex·alt
  ex·al·ta·tion
  ex·alt·ed
ex·am·ine
  ex·am·ined
  ex·am·in·ing
  ex·am·in·er

ex·am·i·na·tion
ex·am·ple
  ex·am·pled
  ex·am·pling
ex·as·per·ate
  ex·as·per·at·ed
  ex·as·per·at·ing
  ex·as·per·a·tion
ex·ca·vate
  ex·ca·vat·ed
  ex·ca·vat·ing
  ex·ca·va·tion
  ex·ca·va·tor
ex·ceed
  ex·ceed·ed
  ex·ceed·ing
ex·cel
  ex·celled
  ex·cel·ling
ex·cel·lent
  ex·cel·lence
  ex·cel·len·cy
ex·cel·si·or
ex·cept
  ex·cept·ing
  ex·cep·tion
  ex·cep·tion·al
  ex·cerpt
  ex·cerp·tion
ex·cess
  ex·ces·sive
ex·change
  ex·changed
  ex·chang·ing
  ex·change·a·bil·i·ty
  ex·change·a·ble
ex·cheq·uer
ex·cise
  ex·cised
  ex·cis·ing
  ex·cis·a·ble
  ex·ci·sion
ex·cit·a·ble
  ex·cit·a·bil·i·ty
ex·cite
  ex·cit·ed
  ex·cit·ing
  ex·ci·ta·tion
  ex·cit·ed·ly
  ex·cite·ment
ex·claim
  ex·cla·ma·tion
  ex·clam·a·to·ry
ex·clude
  ex·clud·ed
  ex·clud·ing
  ex·clud·a·ble
  ex·clu·sion
ex·clu·sive
  ex·clu·sive·ness
  ex·clu·siv·i·ty
ex·com·mu·ni·cate
  ex·com·mu·ni·cat·ed
  ex·com·mu·ni·cat·ing
  ex·com·mu·ni·cant
  ex·com·mu·ni·ca·ble
  ex·com·mu·ni·ca·tion
ex·co·ri·ate
  ex·co·ri·at·ed
  ex·co·ri·at·ing
  ex·co·ri·a·tion
ex·cre·ment
  ex·cre·men·tal
ex·cres·cent
  ex·cres·cence
ex·cre·ta
  ex·cre·tal
ex·crete

ex·cret·ed
ex·cret·ing
ex·cre·tion
ex·cru·ci·ate
  ex·cru·ci·at·ing
  ex·cru·ci·a·tion
ex·cul·pate
  ex·cul·pat·ed
  ex·cul·pat·ing
  ex·cul·pa·tion
  ex·cul·pa·to·ry
ex·cur·sion
  ex·cur·sion·al
  ex·cur·sion·ary
ex·cur·sive
ex·cuse
  ex·cused
  ex·cus·ing
  ex·cus·a·ble
  ex·cus·a·bly
  ex·cus·a·to·ry
ex·e·cra·ble
  ex·e·cra·bly
ex·e·crate
  ex·e·crat·ed
  ex·e·crat·ing
  ex·e·cra·tive
  ex·e·cra·tor
  ex·e·cra·tion
ex·e·cute
  ex·e·cut·ed
  ex·e·cut·ing
  ex·e·cut·er
  ex·e·cu·tion
  ex·e·cu·tion·er
ex·ec·u·tive
ex·ec·u·tor
  ex·ec·u·trix
ex·e·ge·sis
  ex·e·ge·ses
ex·em·plar
  ex·em·pla·ry
  ex·em·pla·ri·ly
ex·em·pli·fy
  ex·em·pli·fied
  ex·em·pli·fy·ing
  ex·em·pli·fi·ca·tion
ex·empt
  ex·emp·tion
ex·er·cise
  ex·er·cised
  ex·er·cis·ing
  ex·er·cis·er
ex·ert
  ex·er·tion
ex·fo·li·ate
  ex·fo·li·at·ed
  ex·fo·li·at·ing
  ex·fo·li·a·tion
ex·hale
  ex·haled
  ex·hal·ing
  ex·ha·la·tion
ex·haust
  ex·haust·ed
  ex·haust·ing
  ex·haus·tion
  ex·haus·tive
ex·hib·it
  ex·hib·i·tor
  ex·hi·bi·tion
  ex·hi·bi·tion·ism
  ex·hi·bi·tion·ist
ex·hil·a·rate
  ex·hil·a·rat·ed
  ex·hil·a·rat·ing
  ex·hil·a·ra·tion
  ex·hil·a·ra·tive

ex·hort
  ex·hor·ta·tive
  ex·hor·ta·tion
  ex·hor·ta·to·ry
  ex·hort·ing·ly
ex·hume
  ex·humed
  ex·hum·ing
  ex·hu·ma·tion
ex·i·gen·cy
  ex·i·gen·cies
ex·i·gent
  ex·i·gent·ly
ex·ig·u·ous
ex·ile
  ex·iled
  ex·il·ing
ex·ist
  ex·ist·ence
  ex·ist·ent
  ex·is·ten·tial
  ex·is·ten·tial·ism
ex   li·bris
ex·o·dus
ex of·fi·cio
ex·og·a·my
  ex·og·a·mous
ex·og·e·nous
ex·on·er·ate
  ex·on·er·at·ed
  ex·on·er·at·ing
  ex·on·er·a·tion
  ex·on·er·a·tive
ex·or·bi·tant
  ex·or·bi·tance
  ex·or·bi·tant·ly
ex·or·cise
  ex·or·cised
  ex·or·cis·ing
  ex·or·cism
  ex·or·cist
ex·ot·ic
  ex·ot·i·cal·ly
  ex·ot·i·cism
ex·pand
  ex·pand·er
  ex·pand·able
ex·panse
ex·pan·si·ble
  ex·pan·si·bil·i·ty
ex·pan·sion
  ex·pan·sion·ism
  ex·pan·sion·ist
ex·pan·sive
  ex·pan·sive·ly
  ex·pan·sive·ness
ex·pa·ti·ate
  ex·pa·ti·at·ed
  ex·pa·ti·at·ing
  ex·pa·ti·a·tion
ex·pa·tri·ate
  ex·pa·tri·at·ed
  ex·pa·tri·at·ing
  ex·pa·tri·a·tion
ex·pect
  ex·pect·a·ble
  ex·pect·a·bly
  ex·pect·ing·ly
  ex·pect·an·cy
  ex·pect·ant
  ex·pec·ta·tion
ex·pec·to·rate
  ex·pec·to·rat·ed
  ex·pec·to·rat·ing
  ex·pec·to·ra·tion
ex·pe·di·ent
  ex·pe·di·en·cy
ex·pe·dite

ex·pe·dit·ed
ex·pe·dit·ing
ex·pe·dit·er
ex·pe·di·tious
ex·pe·di·tion
ex·pel
  ex·pelled
  ex·pel·ling
ex·pend
  ex·pend·a·ble
  ex·pend·a·bil·i·ty
  ex·pend·i·ture
ex·pense
  ex·pen·sive
ex·pe·ri·ence
  ex·pe·ri·enced
  ex·pe·ri·enc·ing
  ex·pe·ri·en·tial
ex·per·i·ment
  ex·per·i·men·tal
  ex·per·i·men·ta·tion
ex·pert
  ex·pert·ly
  ex·pert·ness
ex·per·tise
ex·pi·ate
  ex·pi·at·ed
  ex·pi·at·ing
  ex·pi·a·tion
  ex·pi·a·to·ry
ex·pire
  ex·pired
  ex·pir·ing
  ex·pi·ra·tion
  ex·pir·a·to·ry
ex·plain
  ex·plain·a·ble
  ex·pla·na·tion
  ex·plan·a·to·ry
ex·ple·tive
ex·pli·cate
  ex·pli·cat·ed
  ex·pli·cat·ing
  ex·pli·ca·ble
  ex·pli·ca·tion
  ex·pli·ca·tive
ex·plic·it
  ex·plic·it·ly
  ex·plic·it·ness
ex·plode
  ex·plod·ed
  ex·plod·ing
ex·plo·sion
  ex·plo·sive
ex·ploit
  ex·ploit·a·ble
  ex·ploi·ta·tion
  ex·ploit·er
  ex·ploit·ive
ex·plore
  ex·plo·ra·tion
  ex·plor·a·to·ry
ex·po·nent
  ex·po·nen·tial
ex·port
  ex·port·a·ble
  ex·por·ta·tion
  ex·port·er
ex·pose
  ex·posed
  ex·pos·ing
  ex·pos·er
ex·po·sure
ex·po·se
ex·po·si·tion
  ex·pos·i·tor
  ex·pos·i·to·ry
ex·pos·tu·late

ex·pos·tu·lat·ed
ex·pos·tu·lat·ing
ex·pos·tu·la·tion
ex·pos·tu·la·to·ry
ex·po·sure
ex·pound
ex·press
ex·press·i·ble
ex·pres·sion
ex·pres·sive
ex·press·ly
ex·pres·sion·ism
ex·pres·sion·ist
ex·pro·pri·ate
ex·pro·pri·at·ed
ex·pro·pri·at·ing
ex·pro·pri·a·tion
ex·pul·sion
ex·pul·sive
ex·punge
ex·punged
ex·pung·ing
ex·pur·gate
ex·pur·gat·ed
ex·pur·gat·ing
ex·pur·ga·tion
ex·pur·ga·to·ry
ex·qui·site
ex·qui·site·ly
ex·qui·site·ness
ex·tant
ex·tem·po·re
ex·tem·po·rize
ex·tem·po·rized
ex·tem·po·riz·ing
ex·tem·po·ri·za·tion
ex·tem·po·ra·ne·ous
ex·tend
ex·tend·ed
ex·tend·i·ble
ex·ten·si·ble
ex·ten·sion
ex·ten·sive
ex·tent
ex·ten·u·ate
ex·ten·u·at·ed
ex·ten·u·at·ing
ex·ten·u·a·tion
ex·te·ri·or
ex·ter·mi·nate
ex·ter·mi·nat·ed
ex·ter·mi·nat·ing
ex·ter·mi·na·tion
ex·ter·nal
ex·ter·nal·ly
ex·ter·ri·to·ri·al
ex·tinct
ex·tinc·tion
ex·tin·guish
ex·tin·guish·a·ble
ex·tin·guish·er
ex·tin·guish·ment
ex·tir·pate
ex·tir·pat·ed
ex·tir·pat·ing
ex·tir·pa·tion
ex·tol
ex·tolled
ex·tol·ling
ex·tol·ment
ex·tort
ex·tort·er
ex·tor·tive
ex·tor·tion
ex·tor·tion·ary
ex·tor·tion·ate
ex·tor·tion·er
ex·tor·tion·ist

ex·tra
ex·tract
ex·trac·tive
ex·trac·tor
ex·trac·tion
ex·tra·cur·ric·u·lar
ex·tra·dite
ex·tra·dit·ed
ex·tra·dit·ing
ex·tra·dit·a·ble
ex·tra·di·tion
ex·tra·ne·ous
ex·traor·di·nary
ex·trap·o·late
ex·trap·o·la·tion
ex·tra·sen·so·ry
ex·tra·ter·res·tri·al
ex·tra·ter·ri·to·ri·al
ex·trav·a·gant
ex·trav·a·gance
ex·trav·a·gan·cy
ex·trav·a·gan·za
ex·treme
ex·treme·ly
ex·trem·ist
ex·trem·ism
ex·trem·i·ty
ex·trem·i·ties
ex·tri·cate
ex·tri·cat·ed
ex·tri·cat·ing
ex·tri·ca·tion
ex·trin·sic
ex·tro·vert
ex·tro·ver·sion
ex·trude
ex·trud·ed
ex·trud·ing
ex·tru·sion
ex·u·ber·ant
ex·u·ber·ance
ex·ude
ex·ud·ed
ex·ud·ing
ex·u·da·tion
ex·ult
ex·ult·ant
ex·ul·ta·tion
ex·ult·ing·ly
ex·ur·bia
ex·ur·ban·ite
eye
eyed
eyeing
eye·ball
eye·glass·es
eye·o·pen·er
eye·wit·ness

F

fa·ble
fa·bled
fab·ric
fab·ri·cate
fab·ri·cat·ed
fab·ri·cat·ing
fab·ri·ca·tion
fab·ri·ca·tor
fab·u·lous
fa·cade
face
faced
fac·ing
fac·et
fa·ce·tious
fa·cial

fa·cial·ly
fac·ile
fac·ile·ly
fa·cil·i·tate
fa·cil·i·tat·ed
fa·cil·i·tat·ing
fa·cil·i·ty
fa·cil·i·ties
fac·sim·i·le
fac·tion
fac·tion·al
fac·tion·al·ism
fac·ti·tious
fac·tor
fac·to·ry
fac·to·ries
fac·to·tum
fac·tu·al
fac·tu·al·ly
fac·ul·ty
fad·dist
fade
fad·ed
fad·ing
fade·less
fag·
fagged
fag·ging
fag·got
Fahr·en·heit
fa·ience
fail·ing
fail·ure
faint·ly
faint·ness
faint·heart·ed
fair·ly
fair·mind·ed
fair·ness
fairy
fair·ies
faith·ful
faith·less
fake
faked
fak·ing
fak·er
fa·kir
fal·con
fall
fell
fall·en
fall·ing
fal·la·cious
fal·la·cy
fal·li·ble
fal·li·bil·i·ty
Fal·lo·pi·an
fal·low
false
false·ly
false·ness
false·hood
fal·si·fy
fal·si·fied
fal·si·fy·ing
fal·si·fi·ca·tion
fal·si·ty
fal·ter
fal·ter·ing
famed
fa·mil·ial
fa·mil·iar
fa·mil·i·ar·i·ty
fa·mil·iar·ize
fa·mil·iar·ized
fa·mil·iar·iz·ing
fa·mil·iar·i·za·tion

fam·i·ly
fam·i·lies
fa·mil·ial
fam·ine
fam·ish
fam·ished
fa·mous
fan
fanned
fan·ning
fa·nat·ic
fa·nat·i·cal
fa·nat·i·cism
fa·nat·i·cize
fan·ci·ful
fan·ci·ful·ly
fan·cy
fan·cies
fan·ci·er
fan·ci·est
fan·cied
fan·cy·ing
fan·ci·ly
fan·ci·ness
fan·dan·go
fang
fanged
fan·ta·sia
fan·tas·tic
fan·tas·ti·cal
fan·tas·ti·cal·ly
fan·tas·ti·cal·ness
fan·ta·sy
fan·ta·sies
far
far·ther
far·thest
far·ther·most
far·a·way
farce
farced
farc·ing
far·ci·cal
fare
fared
far·ing
fa·ri·na
farm·er
farm·ing
far·reach·ing
far·see·ing
far·sight·ed
far·sight·ed·ness
far·ther·most
fas·cia
fas·ci·cle
fas·ci·cled
fas·ci·nate
fas·ci·nat·ed
fas·ci·nat·ing
fas·ci·na·tion
fas·cism
fas·cist
fa·scis·tic
fash·ion
fash·ion·a·ble
fash·ion·a·ble·ness
fash·ion·a·bly
fas·ten
fas·ten·er
fas·ten·ing
fas·tid·i·ous
fat
fat·ter
fat·test
fat·ted
fat·ten
fat·ting

fat·ty
fat·ti·ness
fat·ness
fa·tal
fa·tal·ly
fa·tal·i·ty
fa·tal·i·ties
fa·tal·ism
fa·tal·ist
fa·tal·is·tic
fate
fat·ed
fat·ing
fate·ful
fa·ther
fa·ther·hood
fa·ther·li·ness
fa·ther·ly
fa·ther·land
fa·ther-in-law
fa·thers-in-law
fath·om
fath·om·a·ble
fath·om·less
fa·tigue
fa·tigued
fa·tig·uing
fat·i·ga·ble
fat·i·ga·bil·i·ty
fa·tu·i·ty
fa·tu·i·ties
fat·u·ous
fat·u·ous·ly
fau·cet
fault
fault·find·ing
fault·less·ly
faulty
fault·i·er
fault·i·ly
fault·i·ness
fau·na
fau·nas
fau·nae
faux pas
fa·vor
fa·vored
fa·vor·ing
fa·vor·a·ble
fa·vor·a·ble·ness
fa·vor·a·bly
fa·vored·ness
fa·vor·ite
fa·vor·it·ism
fawn
faze
fazed
faz·ing
fe·al·ty
fear·ful
fear·ful·ness
fear·less
fear·less·ness
fear·some
fear·some·ness
fea·si·ble
fea·si·bil·i·ty
fea·si·ble·ness
fea·si·bly
feath·er
feath·ered
feath·er·bed·ding
fea·ture
fea·tured
fea·tur·ing
fea·ture·less
fe·brile
Feb·ru·ary

Feb·ru·ar·ies
fe·ces
  fe·cal
fe·cund
  fe·cun·di·ty
fe·cun·date
  fe·cun·dat·ed
  fe·cun·dat·ing
  fe·cun·da·tion
fed·er·al
  fed·er·al·ism
  fed·er·al·ist
  fed·er·al·ly
fed·er·al·ize
  fed·er·al·ized
  fed·er·al·iz·ing
  fed·er·al·i·za·tion
fed·er·ate
  fed·er·at·ed
  fed·er·at·ing
fe·do·ra
fee·ble
  fee·bler
  fee·bly
fee·ble-mind·ed
feed
  fed
  feed·ing
  feed·er
feel
  felt
  feel·ing
  feel·er
feign
  feigned
  feign·ing
  feign·er
feint
feisty
  feist·i·est
fe·lic·i·tate
  fe·lic·i·tat·ed
  fe·lic·i·tat·ing
  fe·lic·i·ta·tion
  fe·lic·i·tous
fe·lic·i·ty
  fe·lic·i·ties
fe·line
  fe·lin·i·ty
fel·la·tio
fel·low·ship
fel·on
fel·o·ny
  fel·o·nies
  fe·lo·ni·ous
fe·male
fem·i·nine
  fem·i·nine·ness
  fem·i·nin·i·ty
fem·i·nism
  fem·i·nist
  fem·i·nis·tic
fem·i·nize
  fem·i·nized
  fem·i·niz·ing
  fem·i·ni·za·tion
fe·mur
fence
  fenced
  fenc·ing
fenc·er
fen·der
fe·ra·cious
fe·ral
fer·ment
  fer·men·ta·tion
fe·ro·cious
  fe·ro·cious·ness

fe·ro·cious·ly
fe·ro·ci·ty
fer·ret
Fer·ris wheel
fer·ro·con·crete
fer·ro·mag·net·ic
fer·ru·gi·nous
fer·rule
fer·ry
  fer·ries
fer·tile
  fer·tile·ness
  fer·til·i·ty
fer·ti·lize
  fer·ti·lized
  fer·ti·liz·ing
  fer·ti·liz·er
  fer·ti·li·za·tion
fer·ule
fer·vent
  fer·ven·cy
  fer·vent·ly
fer·vid
  fer·vid·ness
fer·vor
fes·ter
fes·ti·val
fes·tive
  fes·tive·ness
  fes·tiv·i·ty
fes·toon
fe·tal
fetch
  fetch·ing
fete
fet·id
  fet·id·ness
fet·ish
  fet·ish·ism
  fet·ish·ist
fet·lock
fet·ter
fet·tle
fe·tus
feud
  feud·ist
feu·dal
  feu·dal·ism
  feu·dal·is·tic
  feu·dal·i·za·tion
  feu·dal·ize
fe·ver
  fe·ver·ish
  fe·ver·ish·ness
  fe·ver·ous
fez·zes
fi·an·ce
fi·an·cee
fi·as·co
fi·at
fib
  fibbed
  fib·ber
fi·ber
  fi·bered
fi·bril
fi·broid
fi·brous
fib·u·la
fick·le
  fick·le·ness
fic·tion
  fic·tion·al
fic·ti·tious
  fic·ti·tious·ness
fid·dle
  fid·dler
  fid·dled

fid·dling
fi·del·i·ty
fidg·et
  fidg·ety
fi·du·ci·ary
fief
field·er
fiend
  fiend·ish
fierce
  fierce·ness
fiery
  fier·i·est
  fier·i·ly
  fier·i·ness
fif·teen
  fif·teenth
fif·ty
  fif·ti·eth
fight
  fought
  fight·ing
  fight·er
fig·ment
fig·ur·ate
  fig·u·ra·tion
fig·u·ra·tive
fig·ure
  fig·ured
  fig·ur·ing
  fig·ure·less
fig·ur·ine
fil·a·ment
  fil·a·men·ta·ry
  fil·a·ment·ed
  fil·a·men·tous
file
  filed
  fil·ing
fi·let
fi·let mi·gnon
fil·i·al
  fil·i·al·ly
fil·i·bus·ter
fil·i·gree
  fil·i·greed
  fil·i·gree·ing
Fil·i·pi·no
fill·er
fil·let
fill·ing
fil·lip
fil·ly
  fil·lies
filmy
  film·i·est
  film·i·ness
fil·ter
  fil·ter·able
fil·tra·tion
filth
  filth·i·ness
  filthy
  filth·i·est
fin
  finned
  fin·ning
  fin·less
fi·na·gle
  fi·na·gled
  fi·na·gling
  fi·na·gler
fi·nal
fi·na·le
fi·nal·ist
fi·nal·i·ty
  fi·nal·i·ties
fi·nal·ize

fi·nal·ized
fi·nal·iz·ing
fi·nal·ly
fi·nance
  fi·nanced
  fi·nanc·ing
  fi·nan·cial
  fi·nan·cial·ly
fin·an·cier
finch
find
  found
  find·ing
fine
  fin·er
  fin·est
  fine·ness
fin·ery
  fin·er·ies
fi·nesse
  fi·nessed
  fi·nes·sing
fin·ger
fin·ger·ing
fin·ger·print
fin·i·cal
  fin·icky
fin·is
fin·ish
  fin·ished
  fin·ish·er
fi·nite
  fi·nite·ly
  fi·nite·ness
Fin·land
  Finn·ish
fire
  fired
  fir·ing
fire·arm
fire·crack·er
fire·fight·er
fire·fly
  fire·flies
fire·man
fire·place
fire·pow·er
fire·proof
fire·trap
firm
  firm·ly
fir·ma·ment
first·born
first·hand
first·rate
first·string
fis·cal
  fis·cal·ly
fish·er·man
  fish·er·men
fish·ery
  fish·er·ies
fish·ing
fishy
fis·sion
  fis·sion·able
fis·sure
  fis·sured
  fis·sur·ing
fist·i·cuffs
fit
  fit·ter
  fit·test
  fit·ted
  fit·ting
  fit·ly
  fit·ness
fit·ful

fit·ful·ness
fit·ting
  fit·ting·ly
five·fold
five-and-ten
fix
  fix·a·ble
  fixed
  fix·ed·ly
  fix·er
fix·a·tion
fix·a·tive
fix·ings
fix·i·ty
fix·ture
fiz·zle
  fiz·zled
  fiz·zling
  fiz·zy
fjord
flab·ber·gast
flab·by
  flab·bi·er
  flab·bi·est
  flab·bi·ly
  flab·bi·ness
flac·cid
fla·con
flag
  flagged
  flag·ging
flag·el·lant
flag·el·late
  flag·el·lat·ed
  flag·el·lat·ing
  flag·el·la·tion
fla·gi·tious
flag·on
fla·grant
  fla·grant·ly
flail
flair
flake
  flaked
  flak·ing
flaky
  flak·i·est
  flak·i·ness
flam·boy·ant
  flam·boy·ance
  flam·boy·an·cy
  flam·boy·ant·ly
flame
  flamed
  flam·ing
  flam·ing·ly
flam·ma·ble
fla·men·co
fla·min·go
flange
flank
  flank·er
flan·nel·ette
flap
  flapped
  flap·ping
  flap·per
flare
  flared
  flar·ing
flare-up
flash·back
flash·light
flashy
  flash·i·est
  flash·i·ness
flask
flat

flat·ly
flat·ted
flat·ting
flat·ness
flat·ten
flat·foot·ed
flat·ter
flat·ter·er
flat·ter·ing·ly
flat·tery
flat·ter·ies
flat·u·lent
flat·u·lence
flat·u·len·cy
fla·tus
flat·ware
flaunt
flaunt·ed
flaunt·ing·ly
flaunty
fla·vor
fla·vored
fla·vor·less
fla·vor·ing
flawed
flaw·less
flax·en
flea·bit·ten
flec·tion
fledge
fledged
fledg·ing
fledg·ling
flee
fled
flee·ing
fleece
fleeced
fleec·ing
fleecy
fleec·i·ness
fleet
fleet·ly
fleet·ness
fleet·ing
flesh·ly
flesh·li·est
fleshy
flesh·i·ness
fleur·de·lis
flex·i·ble
flex·i·bil·i·ty
flex·i·bly
flex·ure
flib·ber·ti·gib·bet
flick·er
flick·er·ing
fli·er
flight
flight·less
flighty
flight·i·est
flight·i·ly
flight·i·ness
flim·flam
flim·flammed
flim·flam·ming
flim·sy
flim·si·est
flim·si·ly
flim·si·ness
flinch
flinch·ing
fling
flung
fling·ing
flinty
flint·i·ness

flip
flipped
flip·ping
flip·flop
flip·pant
flip·pan·cy
flip·pant·ly
flip·per
flir·ta·tion
flir·ta·tious
flit
flit·ted
flit·ting
flit·ter
float·a·ble
float·a·tion
float·er
float·ing
floc·cu·lent
floc·cu·lence
flocked
floe
flog
flogged
flog·ging
flog·ger
flood·light
flood·light·ed
flood·lit
flood·light·ing
floor·ing
floo·zy
floo·zies
flop
flopped
flop·ping
flop·per
flop·house
flop·py
flop·pi·est
flop·pi·ness
flo·ra
flo·rae
flo·ral
flo·res·cence
flo·res·cent
flo·ret
flo·ri·cul·ture
flo·ri·cul·tur·ist
flor·id
flo·rid·i·ty
flor·id·ness
flo·rist
floss
flossy
flo·ta·tion
flo·til·la
flot·sam
flounce
flounced
flounc·ing
floun·der
floury
flour·ish
flour·ish·ing
flout·er
flow
flow·er
flow·ered
flow·er·ing
flow·ery
flub
flubbed
flub·bing
fluc·tu·ate
fluc·tu·at·ed
fluc·tu·at·ing
fluc·tu·a·tion

flue
flu·ent
flu·en·cy
flu·ent·ly
fluff
fluff·i·ness
fluffy
flu·id
flu·id·i·ty
flu·id·ness
fluke
fluky
flun·ky
flun·kies
flu·o·resce
flu·o·resced
flu·o·resc·ing
flu·o·res·cence
flu·o·res·cent
fluor·i·date
fluor·i·da·tion
fluor·i·dat·ed
fluor·i·dat·ing
fluoro·scope
flur·ry
flur·ries
flur·ried
flur·ry·ing
flus·ter
flute
flut·ed
flut·ing
flut·ist
flut·ter
flut·ter·ing
flut·tery
flux·ion
fly
flew
flown
flying
fly-by-night
fly·er
fly·leaf
fly·pa·per
fly·wheel
foal
foam
foam·i·ness
foamy
fo·cal
fo·cal·ly
fo·cal·ize
fo·cal·ized
fo·cal·iz·ing
fo·cus
fo·cus·es
fo·cused
fo·cus·ing
fod·der
foe·tus
foe·tal
fog
fogged
fog·ging
fog·gy
fog·gi·ly
fog·gi·ness
fo·gy
fo·gies
fo·gy·ish
foi·ble
fold·er
fol·de·rol
fo·li·a·ceous
fo·li·age
fo·li·ate
fo·li·at·ed

fo·li·at·ing
fo·li·a·tion
fo·lio
folk·lore
folk·sy
folk·si·ness
fol·li·cle
fol·lic·u·lar
fol·low
fol·low·er
fol·low·ing
fol·ly
fol·lies
fo·ment
fo·men·ta·tion
fo·ment·er
fon·dant
fon·dle
fon·dled
fon·dling
fond·ly
fond·ness
fon·due
food·stuff
fool·ery
fool·er·ies
fool·har·dy
fool·har·di·ness
fool·ish
fool·ish·ly
fool·proof
foot·age
foot·ball
foot·can·dle
foot·hold
foot·lights
foot·note
foot·path
foot·print
foot·step
fop
fop·pery
fop·pish
for·age
for·aged
for·ag·ing
for·ay
for·bear
for·bore
for·borne
for·bear·ing
for·bear·ance
for·bid
for·bade
for·bid·den
for·bid·ding
for·bid·dance
force
forced
forc·ing
force·a·ble
force·less
force·ful
force·ful·ly
for·ceps
for·ci·ble
for·ci·bly
ford·a·ble
fore·bode
fore·bod·ed
fore·bod·ing
fore·castle
fore·cast
fore·cast·ed
fore·cast·ing
fore·cast·er
fore·close
fore·closed

fore·clos·ing
fore·clo·sure
fore·fa·ther
fore·fin·ger
fore·gath·er
fore·go
fore·went
fore·gone
fore·go·ing
fore·ground
fore·hand·ed
for·eign
for·eign·er
fore·know
fore·knew
fore·known
fore·know·ing
fore·knowl·edge
fore·man
fore·most
fore·name
fore·noon
fo·ren·sic
fore·or·dain
fore·or·di·na·tion
fore·quar·ter
fore·run·ner
fore·see
fore·saw
fore·seen
fore·see·ing
fore·see·a·ble
fore·shad·ow
fore·short·en
fore·sight
fore·skin
for·est
for·est·a·tion
for·es·ter
for·est·ry
fore·stall
fore·taste
fore·tell
fore·told
fore·tell·ing
fore·tell·er
fore·thought
for·ev·er
for·ev·er·more
fore·warn
fore·woman
fore·word
for·feit
for·fei·ture
for·gath·er
forge
forged
forg·ing
forg·er
for·gery
for·ger·ies
for·get
for·got
for·got·ten
for·get·ting
for·get·ta·ble
for·get·ful
for·give
for·gave
for·giv·en
for·giv·ing
for·giv·a·ble
for·give·ness
for·go
for·went
for·gone
for·go·ing
forked

fork·lift
for·lorn
   for·lorn·ly
for·mal
   for·mal·ly
for·mal·ism
for·mal·i·ty
   for·mal·i·ties
for·mal·ize
   for·mal·ized
   for·mal·iz·ing
   for·mal·i·za·tion
for·mat
for·ma·tion
form·a·tive
for·mer
   for·mer·ly
form·fit·ting
for·mi·da·ble
   for·mi·da·bly
form·less
   form·less·ness
for·mu·la
   for·mu·las
for·mu·lary
   for·mu·lar·ies
for·mu·late
   for·mu·lat·ed
   for·mu·lat·ing
   for·mu·la·tion
   for·mu·la·tor
for·ni·cate
   for·ni·cat·ed
   for·ni·cat·ing
   for·ni·cat·or
   for·ni·ca·tion
for·sake
   for·sook
   for·sak·en
   for·sak·ing
   for·sak·en
for·swear
   for·swore
   for·sworn
   for·swear·ing
fort
   for·ti·fi·ca·tion
   for·ti·fy
   for·ti·fied
   for·ti·fy·ing
forte
for·te
forth·com·ing
forth·right
forth·with
for·tis·si·mo
for·ti·tude
fort·night
for·tress
for·tu·i·tous
   for·tu·i·tous·ness
for·tu·nate
   for·tu·nate·ly
for·tune
for·tune·tell·er
for·ty
   for·ties
fo·rum
   fo·rums
for·ward
   for·ward·ness
fos·sil
   fos·sil·ized
   fos·sil·iz·ing
   fos·sil·i·za·tion
fos·ter
   fos·tered
   fos·ter·ing

fought
fou·lard
found
foun·da·tion
   foun·da·tion·al
found·er
found·ling
found·ry
   found·ries
foun·tain
four·flush·er
four·fold
four·post·er
four·score
four·some
four·teen
   four·teenth
fourth
   fourth·ly
foxy
   fox·i·ly
   fox·i·ness
foy·er
fra·cas
frac·tion
   frac·tion·al
frac·tious
frac·ture
   frac·tured
   frac·tur·ing
frag·ile
   fra·gil·i·ty
frag·ment
   frag·men·tal
   frag·men·tary
   frag·men·ta·tion
   frag·ment·ize
fra·grance
   fra·grant
   fra·grant·ly
frail
   frail·ty
   frail·ness
frame
   framed
   fram·ing
frame·work
franc
France
fran·chise
   fran·chised
   fran·chis·ing
   fran·chise·ment
Fran·cis·can
fran·gi·ble
fran·gi·pan·i
frank
   frank·ly
   frank·ness
frank·furt·er
frank·in·cense
fran·tic
   fran·ti·cal·ly
frap·pe
fra·ter·nal
   fra·ter·nal·ly
fra·ter·ni·ty
   fra·ter·ni·ties
frat·er·nize
   frat·er·nized
   frat·er·niz·ing
   frat·er·ni·za·tion
frat·ri·cide
   frat·ri·cid·al
fraud·u·lent
   fraud·u·lence
   fraud·u·lent·ly
fraught

fräz·zle
   fraz·zled
freak
   freak·ish
freaky
   freak·i·est
freck·le
   freck·led
   freck·ling
   freck·led
free
   fre·er
   fre·est
   free·ly
   free·bie
free·boot·er
free·dom
free·lance
   free·lanced
   free·lanc·ing
Free·ma·son
free·stand·ing
free·spo·ken
free·think·er
freeze
   froze
   fro·zen
   freez·ing
freeze·dry
freez·er
freight·age
freight·er
fre·net·ic
   fre·net·i·cal·ly
fren·zy
   fren·zies
   fren·zied
   fren·zy·ing
fre·quen·cy
   fre·quen·cies
fre·quent
   fre·quent·ly
fres·co
   fres·coes
   fres·coed
   fres·co·ing
fresh
   fresh·en
   fresh·ness
fresh·man
fret
   fret·ted
   fret·ting
   fret·ful
   fret·ful·ly
Freud·i·an
fri·a·ble
fri·ar
fric·as·see
   fric·as·seed
   fric·as·see·ing
fric·tion
   fric·tion·al
   fric·tion·less
friend
   friend·less
   friend·ship
friend·ly
   friend·li·est
   friend·li·ness
frieze
fright·en
   fright·en·ing
   fright·ful
frig·id
   fri·gid·i·ty
   frig·id·ness
frilly

frill·i·est
fringe
   fringed
   fring·ing
frip·pery
frisky
   frisk·i·ness
frit·ter
friv·o·lous
   fri·vol·i·ty
   fri·vol·i·ties
   friv·o·lous·ly
frizz
   friz·zi·ness
   friz·zy
friz·zle
frog
   frogged
   frog·ging
frol·ic
   frol·icked
   frol·ick·ing
   frol·ic·some
front·age
fron·tal
fron·tier
   fron·tiers·man
fron·tis·piece
frost
   frost·ed
   frost·bite
   frost·bit
   frost·bit·ten
   frost·bit·ing
   frost·ing
frosty
   frost·i·ly
   frost·i·ness
froth
   froth·i·ness
   frothy
frou·frou
fro·ward
frown
frow·zy
fro·zen
   fro·zen·ness
fruc·ti·fy
   fruc·ti·fi·ca·tion
fruc·tose
fru·gal
   fru·gal·i·ty
   fru·gal·i·ties
   fru·gal·ly
fruit·ful
   fruit·ful·ly
   fruit·ful·ness
fru·i·tion
fruit·less
frump
   frump·ish
   frumpy
frus·trate
   frus·trat·ed
   frus·trat·ing
   frus·tra·tion
fry
   fried
   fry·ing
fuch·sia
fud·dle
fud·dy-dud·dy
fudge
   fudged
   fudg·ing
fu·el
   fu·eled
   fu·el·ing

fu·gi·tive
fugue
ful·crum
ful·fill
   ful·filled
   ful·fil·ling
   ful·fill·ment
full
   full·ness
   ful·ly
full-fledged
ful·mi·nate
   ful·mi·nat·ed
   ful·mi·nat·ing
   ful·mi·na·tion
ful·some
fum·ble
   fum·bled
   fum·bling
   fum·bler
fume
   fumed
   fum·ing
   fum·ing·ly
fu·mi·gate
   fu·mi·gat·ed
   fu·mi·gat·ing
   fu·mi·ga·tion
   fu·mi·ga·tor
func·tion
   func·tion·al
   func·tion·less
func·tion·ary
   func·tion·ar·ies
fun·da·men·tal
   fun·da·men·tal·ly
   fun·da·men·tal·ism
   fun·da·men·tal·ist
fu·ner·al
   fu·ne·re·al
fun·gi·cide
   fun·gi·cid·al
fun·gus
   fun·gi
fu·nic·u·lar
fun·nel
   fun·neled
   fun·nel·ing
fun·ny
   fun·ni·er
   fun·ni·est
   fun·nies
   fun·ni·ness
fur
   furred
   fur·ring
fur·be·low
fur·bish
fu·ri·ous
   fu·ri·ous·ly
fur·long
fur·lough
fur·nace
fur·nish
   fur·nish·ings
fur·ni·ture
fu·ror
fu·rore
fur·ri·er
fur·row
fur·ry
fur·ther
   fur·ther·ance
   fur·ther·more
   fur·ther·most
   fur·thest
fur·tive
   fur·tive·ly

fu·ry
  fu·ries
fuse
  fused
  fus·ing
fu·se·lage
fu·si·ble
  fu·si·bil·i·ty
fu·sil·lade
  fu·sil·lad·ed
  fu·sil·lad·ing
fu·sion
fussy
  fuss·i·ness
fus·tian
fu·tile
fu·til·i·ty
  fu·til·i·ties
fu·ture
  fu·tu·ri·ty
  fu·tu·ri·ties
fu·tur·ism
  fu·tur·is·tic
fuzzy
  fuzz·i·ness

G

gab
  gabbed
  gab·bing
gab·ar·dine
gab·ble
gab·by
ga·ble
  ga·bled
  ga·bling
gad
  gad·ded
  gad·ding
gad·a·bout
gad·fly
gad·get
  gad·get·ry
gag
  gagged
  gag·ging
gai·e·ty
  gai·e·ties
gai·ly
gain·er
gain·ful
gain·say
  gain·said
gait
ga·la
gal·axy
  gal·ax·ies
  ga·lac·tic
gal·lant
  gal·lant·ry
  gal·lant·ries
gal·lery
  gal·ler·ies
gal·ley
gal·li·mau·fry
gall·ing
gal·li·vant
gal·lon
gal·lop
gal·lows
gall·stone
ga·lore
ga·losh·es
gal·van·ic
gal·va·nize
  gal·va·nized

gal·va·niz·ing
gal·va·nom·e·ter
gam·bit
gam·ble
  gam·bled
  gam·bling
  gam·bler
gam·bol
game
  gam·ing
games·man·ship
gam·in
gam·ma
gam·ma   glob·u·lin
gam·ut
gamy
  gam·i·ly
  gam·i·ness
gan·der
gang·land
gan·gling
gan·gly
gan·grene
  gan·gre·nous
gang·ster
gant·let
gan·try
gaol
gap
  gapped
  gap·ping
ga·rage
  ga·raged
  ga·rag·ing
gar·bage
gar·ble
  gar·bled
  gar·bling
gar·den
gar·gan·tu·an
gar·gle
  gar·gled
  gar·gling
gar·goyle
gar·ish
gar·land
gar·ment
gar·ner
gar·net
gar·nish
gar·nish·ee
  gar·nish·eed
  gar·nish·ee·ing
gar·nish·ment
gar·ni·ture
gar·ret
gar·ri·son
gar·rote
  gar·rot·ed
  gar·rot·ing
gar·ru·lous
gar·ter
gas
  gassed
  gas·sing
  gas·e·ous
gas·i·fy
  gas·i·fied
  gas·i·fy·ing
  gas·i·fi·ca·tion
gas·ket
gas·light
gas·o·line
gas·sy
  gas·si·ness
gas·tric
gas·tri·tis
gas·tro·en·ter·ol·o·gy

gas·tro·in·tes·ti·nal
gas·tron·o·my
  gas·tro·nom·ic
gath·er
  gath·er·ing
gauche
gau·che·rie
gau·cho
gaudy
  gaud·i·ly
  gaud·i·ness
gauge
  gauged
  gaug·ing
gaunt
gaunt·let
gauze
  gauz·i·ness
gauzy
gav·el
ga·votte
gawky
  gawk·i·ly
  gawk·i·ness
gay·e·ty
gay·ly
gaze
  gazed
  gaz·ing
ga·ze·bo
ga·zelle
ga·zette
gaz·et·teer
gear·shift
gear·wheel
Gei·ger count·er
gei·sha
gel
  gelled
  gel·ling
gel·a·tin
  ge·la·ti·nize
  ge·lat·i·nous
  ge·la·tion
geld
  geld·ed
  gelt
  geld·ing
gel·id
  ge·lid·i·ty
gem
  gemmed
  gem·ming
gem·i·nate
  gem·i·nat·ed
  gem·i·nat·ing
  gem·i·nate·ly
  gem·i·na·tion
Gem·i·ni
gem·ol·o·gy
  gem·o·log·i·cal
  gem·ol·o·gist
gen·darme
gen·der
gene
ge·ne·al·o·gy
  ge·ne·a·log·i·cal
  ge·ne·al·o·gist
gen·er·al
gen·er·al·is·si·mo
gen·er·al·ist
gen·er·al·i·ty
  gen·er·al·i·ties
gen·er·al·ize
  gen·er·al·ized
  gen·er·al·iz·ing
  gen·er·al·i·za·tion
gen·er·ate

gen·er·at·ed
gen·er·at·ing
gen·er·a·tive
gen·er·a·tion
gen·er·a·tor
ge·ner·ic
  ge·ner·i·cal
gen·er·ous
  gen·er·os·i·ty
  gen·er·os·i·ties
gen·e·sis
  gen·e·ses
ge·net·ic
  ge·net·i·cal·ly
  ge·net·ics
  ge·net·i·cist
gen·ial
  ge·ni·al·i·ty
ge·nie
gen·i·tal
  gen·i·ta·lia
  gen·i·tals
gen·i·tive
ge·nius
  gen·ius·es
gen·o·cide
  gen·o·ci·dal
gen·re
gen·teel
gen·tian
gen·tile
gen·til·i·ty
gen·tle
  gen·tlest
  gen·tly
gen·tle·man
gen·tle·wom·an
gen·try
gen·u·flect
  gen·u·flec·tion
gen·u·ine
  gen·u·ine·ness
ge·nus
ge·o·cen·tric
  ge·o·cen·tri·cal·ly
ge·o·chem·is·try
  ge·o·chem·i·cal
  ge·o·chem·ist
ge·ode
ge·o·des·ic
geo·d·e·sy
geo·o·gra·phy
  ge·o·gra·phies
  ge·o·gra·pher
  ge·o·graph·ic
  ge·o·graph·i·cal
ge·ol·o·gy
  ge·ol·o·gies
  ge·o·log·ic
  ge·o·log·i·cal
  ge·o·log·i·cal·ly
  ge·ol·o·gist
ge·o·mag·net·ic
  geo·o·mag·ne·tism
ge·o·met·ric
ge·om·e·try
  ge·om·e·tries
ge·o·phys·ics
  ge·o·phys·i·cal
  ge·o·phys·i·cist
ge·o·pol·i·tics
  ge·o·pol·i·tic
  ge·o·po·lit·i·cal
  ge·o·po·lit·i·cal·ly
ge·o·ther·mal
ge·ra·ni·um
ger·bil
ger·i·at·rics

geri·at·ric
ger·i·a·tri·cian
ger·i·at·rist
ger·mane
Ger·ma·ny
ger·mi·cide
  ger·mi·cid·al
ger·mi·nate
  ger·mi·nat·ed
  ger·mi·nat·ing
  ger·mi·na·tion
ger·on·tol·o·gy
  ger·on·tol·o·gist
ger·ry·man·der
ger·und
Ge·stalt
ge·sta·po
ges·tate
  ges·tat·ed
  ges·tat·ing
  ges·ta·tion
ges·tic·u·late
  ges·tic·u·lat·ed
  ges·tic·u·lat·ing
  ges·tic·u·la·tion
  ges·tic·u·la·to·ry
ges·ture
  ges·tured
  ges·tur·ing
ge·sund·heit
Geth·sem·a·ne
gew·gaw
gey·ser
ghast·ly
  ghast·li·er
  ghast·li·est
  ghast·li·ness
gher·kin
ghet·to
ghost·ly
  ghost·li·est
  ghost·li·ness
ghost·write
  ghost·writ·ten
ghoul
gi·ant
gib·ber·ish
gib·bon
gib·bous
gibe
  gib·ing·ly
gib·let
gid·dy
  gid·di·ly
  gid·di·ness
gift·ed
gi·gan·tic
  gi·gan·tism
gig·gle
  gig·gled
  gig·gling
  gig·gly
gig·o·lo
gild·ed
gilt-edged
gim·let
gim·mick
  gim·mick·y
gin·ger·bread
gin·ger·ly
  gin·ger·li·ness
ging·ham
gip·sy
gip·sies
gi·raffe
gird·er
gir·dle
  gir·dled

gir·dling
girl·hood
girl·ish
girth
gist
give
  gave
  giv·en
  giv·ing
giz·zard
gla·cial
gla·cier
glad
  glad·der
  glad·dest
  glad·ly
  glad·ness
  glad·den
glad·i·a·tor
  glad·i·a·to·ri·al
glad·i·o·lus
  glad·i·o·lus·es
  glad·i·o·la
glam·or·ize
  glam·or·ized
  glam·or·iz·ing
  glam·or·i·za·tion
glam·or·ous
  glam·or·ous·ness
glam·our
glance
  glanced
  glanc·ing
glan·du·lar
glare
  glared
  glar·ing
  glar·i·ness
  glary
glass·blow·ing
glass·ful
glass·ware
glassy
  glass·i·er
  glass·i·est
  glass·i·ly
  glass·i·ness
glau·co·ma
glaze
  glazed
  glaz·ing
gla·zier
gleam
  gleam·ing
  gleamy
glean
  glean·er
  glean·ing
glee
  glee·ful
  gleee·ful·ly
  glee·ful·ness
glib
  glib·best
  glib·ly
  glib·ness
glide
  glid·ed
  glid·ing
glim·mer
glimpse
  glimpsed
  glimps·ing
glis·san·do
glis·ten
glit·ter
glit·tery
gloam·ing

gloat
  gloat·er
  gloat·ing
glob·al
  glob·al·ly
globe·trot·ter
  globe·trot·ting
glob·u·lar
glob·ule
glock·en·spiel
gloomy
  gloom·i·er
  gloom·i·ly
  gloom·i·ness
glo·ri·fy
  glo·ri·fied
  glo·ri·fy·ing
  glo·ri·fi·ca·tion
glo·ri·ous
  glo·ri·ous·ly
glo·ry
  glo·ries
  glo·ried
  glo·ry·ing
glos·sa·ry
glossy
  gloss·i·er
  gloss·i·ly
  gloss·i·ness
glot·tis
glove
glow
  glow·er
  glow·ing
glu·cose
glue
  glued
  glu·ing
glum
  glum·mer
  glum·mest
glut
  glut·ted
  glut·ting
glu·ten
  glu·ten·ous
glu·ti·nous
glut·ton
  glut·ton·ous
  glut·tony
glyc·er·in
  glyc·er·ine
gnarl
  gnarled
gnash
gnat
gnaw
  gnawed
  gnaw·ing
gnome
gnu
go
  went
  gone
  go·ing
goad·ed
goal·ie
goat·ee
goat·skin
gob·ble
  gob·bled
  gob·bling
  gob·ble·dy·gook
  gob·bler
gob·let
gob·lin
god·child
  god·daugh·ter

god·son
god·dess
god·fa·ther
god·head
god·less
  god·less·ness
god·ly
  god·li·ness
god·moth·er
god·send
go·get·ter
gog·gle
  gog·gled
  gog·gling
go·ing
goi·ter
gold·en·rod
go·nad
gon·do·la
gon·do·lier
gon·or·rhea
good
  better
  best
good-by
  good-bye
good-heart·ed
good·ish
good-look·ing
good·ly
good-na·tured
good·ness
good-tem·pered
goofy
  goof·i·er
  goof·i·est
  goof·i·ness
goose·ber·ry
go·pher
gore
  gored
  gor·ing
gorge
  gorged
  gorg·ing
gor·geous
  gor·geous·ness
gory
  gor·i·er
  gor·i·est
gos·ling
gos·pel
gos·sa·mer
gos·sip
  gos·sip·ing
  gos·sipy
Goth·ic
gouge
  gouged
  goug·ing
gou·lash
gourd
gour·mand
gour·met
gout
  gouty
gov·ern
  gov·ern·a·ble
gov·ern·ess
gov·ern·ment
  gov·ern·men·tal
gov·er·nor
gowned
grab
  grabbed
  grab·bing
  grab·ber
grace

graced
grac·ing
grace·ful
  grace·ful·ly
grace·less
gra·cious
grack·le
gra·da·tion
grade
  grad·ed
  grad·ing
gra·di·ent
grad·u·al
  grad·u·al·ly
  grad·u·al·ness
grad·u·ate
  grad·u·at·ed
  grad·u·at·ing
  grad·u·a·tion
graf·fi·ti
graft
  graft·age
  graft·er
  graft·ing
gra·ham
grain
grainy
  grain·ness
gram
gram·mar
  gram·mar·i·an
  gram·mat·i·cal
gra·na·ry
grand
  grand·ly
grand·child
gran·dee
gran·deur
gran·dil·o·quence
  gran·dil·o·quent
gran·di·ose
  gran·di·ose·ly
grange
gran·ite
gran·ny
gran·u·lar
  gran·u·lar·i·ty
gran·u·late
  gran·u·lat·ed
  gran·u·lat·ing
  gran·u·la·tion
gran·ule
grape·fruit
graph·ic
  graph·i·cal
graph·ite
graph·ol·o·gy
  graph·ol·o·gist
grap·nel
grap·ple
  grap·pled
  grap·pling
  grap·pler
grasp·ing
grass
  grassy
  grass·i·est
grass·hop·per
grass·land
grate
  grat·ed
  grat·ing
grate·ful
grat·i·fy
  grat·i·fied
  grat·i·fy·ing
  grat·i·fi·ca·tion
grat·ing

gra·tis
grat·i·tude
gra·tu·i·tous
gra·tu·i·ty
  gra·tu·i·ties
grave
  graved
  grav·en
  grav·ing
  grav·er
  grave·ly
  grave·ness
grav·el
  grav·eled
  grav·el·ing
  grav·el·ly
grav·i·tate
  grav·i·tat·ed
  grav·i·tat·ing
  grav·i·ta·tion
grav·i·ty
gra·vy
gray·ness
gray·ling
graze
  grazed
  graz·ing
grease
  greased
  greas·ing
greasy
  greas·i·ness
great
  great·ness
Great Brit·ain
Gre·cian
Greece
greedy
  greed·i·er
  greed·i·est
  greed·i·ly
  greed·i·ness
green·house
green·ing
green·ish
greet
  greet·ing
gre·gar·i·ous
  gre·gar·i·ous·ly
  gre·gar·i·ous·ness
grem·lin
gre·nade
gren·a·dier
gren·a·dine
grey·ness
grid·dle
grid·i·ron
grief
griev·ance
grieve
  grieved
  griev·ing
  griev·ous
grill
gril·lage
grille
grim
  grim·ly
  grim·ness
grim·ace
  grim·aced
  grim·ac·ing
grime
  grimy
  grim·i·ness
grin
  grinned
  grin·ning

grind
  ground
  grind·ing
grin·go
grip
  gripped
  grip·ping
gripe
  griped
  grip·ing
  grip·er
grippe
gris·ly
  gris·li·ness
gris·tle
  gris·tly
grit
  grit·ted
  grit·ting
  grit·ty
  grit·ti·ness
griz·zled
griz·zly
groan
gro·cer
gro·cery
  gro·cer·ies
grog·gy
  grog·gi·ly
  grog·gi·ness
groin
grom·met
groom
groove
  grooved
  groov·ing
  groov·er
grope
  groped
  grop·ing
gros·grain
gross
  gross·ly
  gross·ness
gro·tesque
  gro·tesque·ly
  gro·tesque·ness
grot·to
grouch
  grouchy
  grouch·i·ness
  grouch·i·ly
ground·less
ground·work
group
  group·ing
grouse
  groused
  grous·ing
grov·el
  grov·eled
  grov·el·ing
grow
  grew
  grown
  grow·ing
growl
  growl·er
  growl·ing
grown·up
growth
grub
  grubbed
  grub·bing
grub·by
  grub·bi·ness
grub·stake
grudge

grudged
grudg·ing
gru·el
  gru·el·ing
grue·some
gruff
  gruff·ly
  gruff·ness
grum·ble
  grum·bled
  grum·bling
grumpy
  grump·i·ly
  grump·i·ness
grunt
  grunt·ed
  grunt·ing
gua·no
guar·an·tee
  guar·an·teed
  guar·an·tee·ing
guar·an·tor
guar·an·ty
  guar·an·ties
  guar·an·tied
  guar·an·ty·ing
guard·ed
  guard·ed·ly
guard·house
guard·i·an
guards·man
gua·va
gu·ber·na·to·ri·al
gudg·eon
guern·sey
guer·ril·la
guess
  guess·ing
guess·work
guest
guf·faw
guid·ance
guide
  guid·ed
  guid·ing
gui·don
guild
guile
  guile·ful
  guile·less
guil·lo·tine
guilt
  guilt·less
guilty
  guilt·i·er
  guilt·i·ly
  guilt·i·ness
guin·ea
guise
gui·tar
  gui·tar·ist
gul·let
gul·li·ble
  gul·li·bil·i·ty
  gul·li·bly
gul·ly
  gul·lies
gum
  gummed
  gum·ming
  gum·my
  gum·mi·ness
gum·bo
gump·tion
gun
  gunned
  gun·ning
gun·ner

gun·nery
gun·ny
gun·wale
gup·py
  gup·pies
gur·gle
  gur·gled
  gur·gling
gu·ru
gush·er
gush·ing
gushy
  gush·i·er
  gush·i·est
  gush·i·ness
gus·set
gus·ta·to·ry
gus·to
gusty
  gust·i·er
  gust·i·est
  gust·i·ly
  gust·i·ness
gut
  gut·ted
  gut·ting
gut·less
gut·ter
gut·tur·al
  gut·tur·al·ly
guz·zle
  guz·zled
  guz·zling
gym·na·si·um
  gym·na·si·ums
gym·nast
gym·nas·tic
gy·ne·col·o·gy
  gy·ne·co·log·i·cal
  gy·ne·col·o·gist
gyp
  gypped
  gyp·ping
gyp·sum
gyp·sy
  gyp·sies
gy·rate
  gy·rat·ed
  gy·rat·ing
  gy·ra·tion
  gy·ra·tor
gy·ro·com·pass
gy·rom·e·ter
gy·ro·plane
gy·ro·scope
gy·rose
gy·ro·sta·bi·liz·er
gy·ro·stat·ics

H

ha·be·as· cor·pus
hab·er·dash·ery
ha·bil·i·ment
hab·it
hab·it·a·ble
hab·i·tat
hab·i·ta·tion
ha·bit·u·al
  ha·bit·u·al·ly
  ha·bit·u·al·ness
ha·bit·u·ate
  ha·bit·u·at·ed
  ha·bit·u·at·ing
  ha·bit·u·a·tion
ha·bit·ue
ha·ci·en·da

hack·le
  hack·led
  hack·ling
hack·ney
hack·neyed
hack·saw
had·dock
Ha·des
had·n't
hag·gard
  hag·gard·ness
hag·gis
hag·gle
  hag·gled
  hag·gling
  hag·gler
ha·gi·og·ra·phy
hag·i·ol·o·gy
hail·storm
hair·breadth
hair·dress·er
hair·rais·ing
hairy
  hair·i·er
  hair·i·est
hale
  haled
  hal·ing
half
  halves
half·heart·ed
half·wit·ted
hal·i·but
hal·i·to·sis
hal·le·lu·jah
hall·mark
hal·lo
hal·low
  hal·lowed
Hal·low·een
hal·lu·ci·nate
  hal·lu·ci·nat·ed
  hal·lu·ci·nat·ing
  hal·lu·ci·na·tion
ha·lo
halt
  halt·ing
hal·ter
halve
  halved
  halv·ing
halves
hal·yard
ham·burg·er
ham·let
ham·mer
ham·mock
ham·per
ham·ster
ham·string
  ham·strung
hand·ed
hand·ful
hand·i·cap
  hand·i·capped
  hand·i·cap·ping
  hand·i·cap·per
hand·i·craft
hand·i·ly
  hand·i·ness
hand·i·work
hand·ker·chief
han·dle
  han·dled
  han·dling
hand·made
hand·picked
hand·some

hand·som·est
hand·some·ness
hand·writ·ing
handy
  hand·i·er
  hand·y·man
hang
  hung
  hanged
  hang·ing
hang·ar
hang·er
hang·o·ver
hank·er
han·som
Ha·nuk·kah
hap·haz·ard
  hap·haz·ard·ly
hap·less
hap·pen
  hap·pen·ing
  hap·pen·stance
hap·py
  hap·pi·ly
  hap·pi·ness
ha·ra·ki·ri
ha·rangue
  ha·rangued
  ha·rang·uing
har·ass
  har·ass·ment
har·bin·ger
har·bor
hard·bit·ten
hard·boiled
hard·en
  hard·en·er
har·di·hood
hard·i·ness
hard·ly
hard·ware
hard·wood
har·dy
  har·di·er
  har·di·est
  har·di·ly
hare·brained
hare·lip
har·em
har·ken
har·le·quin
har·lot
  har·lot·ry
harm·ful
  harm·ful·ly
  harm·ful·ness
harm·less
  harm·less·ly
  harm·less·ness
har·mon·ic
  har·mon·i·cal·ly
har·mon·i·ca
har·mon·ics
har·mo·ni·ous
har·mo·nize
  har·mo·nized
  har·mo·niz·ing
har·mo·ny
  har·mo·nies
har·ness
harp·ist
har·poon
harp·si·chord
har·ri·dan
har·row
har·ry
  har·ried
  har·ry·ing

harsh
  harsh·ly
  harsh·ness
har·um-scar·um
har·vest
har·ves·ter
hash·ish
  hash·eesh
has·n't
has·sle
  has·sled
  has·sling
has·sock
haste
has·ten
hast·y
  hast·i·ly
  hast·i·ness
hatch·ery
hatch·et
hate
  hat·ed
  hat·ing
hate·ful
  hate·ful·ly
  hate·ful·ness
ha·tred
haugh·ty
  haugh·ti·ly
  haugh·ti·ness
haul
  haul·age
haunch
  haunch·es
haunt·ed
haunt·ing
hau·teur
have
  had
  hav·ing
  has
ha·ven
have·n't
hav·er·sack
hav·oc
Ha·waii
hawk
  hawk·ish
haw·ser
haz·ard
  haz·ard·ous
  haz·ard·ous·ness
haze
  hazed
  haz·ing
ha·zel·nut
ha·zy
  ha·zi·ly
  ha·zi·ness
head·ache
head·dress
head·first
  head·fore·most
head·hunt·er
head·ing
head·line
  head·lined
  head·lin·ing
head·long
head·quar·ters
heady
  head·i·ly
  head·i·ness
heal·er
health·ful
  health·ful·ly
healthy
  health·i·er

health·i·est
  health·i·ly
  health·i·ness
heaped
hear
  heard
  hear·ing
heark·en
hear·say
hearse
heart·ache
heart·break
  heart·brok·en
heart·burn
heart·en
hearth·stone
heart·less
  heart·less·ly
  heart·less·ness
heart·rend·ing
heart·sick
hearty
  heart·i·ly
  heart·i·ness
heat·ed
heat·er
heath
hea·then
heath·er
heave
  heaved
  heav·ing
heav·en
  heav·en·ly
  heav·en·ward
heavy
  heav·i·ness
heav·y-hand·ed
heav·y-heart·ed
heav·y·weight
He·brew
  He·bra·ic
heck·le
  heck·led
  heck·ling
  heck·ler
hec·tare
hec·tic
  hec·ti·cal·ly
hec·to·gram
hec·to·li·ter
hec·to·me·ter
hedge
  hedged
  hedg·ing
  hedg·er
he·don·ism
  he·don·ist
  he·do·nis·tic
heed·ful
heed·less
hefty
  heft·i·er
he·gem·o·ny
heif·er
height·en
hei·nous
  hei·nous·ness
heir·ess
heir·loom
heist
hel·i·cop·ter
he·li·um
he·lix
  he·lix·es
he·li·cal
hel·lion
hell·ish

hell·ish·ness
hel·lo
helm
  helm·less
hel·met
  hel·met·ed
helms·man
help·er
help·ful
  help·ful·ly
  help·ful·ness
help·ing
help·less
  help·less·ness
hel·ter-skel·ter
hem
  hemmed
  hem·ming
he·ma·tol·o·gy
hem·i·sphere
  hem·i·spher·i·cal
hem·lock
he·mo·glo·bin
he·mo·phil·ia
hem·or·rhage
  hem·or·rhag·ing
hem·or·rhoid
hem·stitch
hence·forth
hench·man
hen·na
hep·a·ti·tis
her·ald
  he·ral·dic
her·ald·ry
herb
  her·ba·ceous
her·bi·cide
her·biv·o·rous
her·cu·le·an
he·red·i·ty
  he·red·i·tary
  he·red·i·tar·i·ly
her·e·sy
  her·e·sies
her·e·tic
  he·ret·i·cal
her·it·a·ble
  her·it·a·bil·i·ty
her·it·age
her·maph·ro·dite
  her·maph·ro·dit·ism
her·met·ic
  her·met·i·cal·ly
her·mit
her·nia
  her·ni·al
he·ro
  he·roes
  her·o·ine
  her·o·ism
he·ro·ic
  he·ro·i·cal·ly
her·o·in
her·on
her·pes
her·pe·tol·o·gy
her·ring·bone
her·self
hes·i·tant
  hes·i·tan·cy
  hes·i·tance
  hes·i·tant·ly
hes·i·tate
  hes·i·tat·ed
  hes·i·tat·ing
  hes·i·ta·tion
het·er·o·dox

het·er·o·doxy
het·er·o·ge·ne·ous
het·er·o·ge·ne·i·ty
het·er·o·ge·ne·ous·ness
het·er·o·sex·u·al
het·er·o·sex·u·al·i·ty
hew
  hewed
  hewn
  hew·ing
hex·a·gon
  hex·ag·o·nal
hexa·gram
hi·a·tus
hi·ba·chi
hi·ber·nate
  hi·ber·nat·ed
  hi·ber·nat·ing
  hi·ber·na·tion
hi·bis·cus
hic·cup
  hic·cuped
  hic·cup·ing
hick·o·ry
hid·den
hide
  hid
  hid·den
  hid·ing
hide·bound
hid·e·ous
  hid·e·ous·ness
hi·er·ar·chy
  hi·er·ar·chal
  hi·er·ar·chic
  hi·er·ar·chi·cal·ly
hi·er·o·glyph
  hi·er·o·glyph·ic
high-grade
high·hand·ed
high·mind·ed
high·ness
high-pres·sure
  high-pres·sured
  high-pres·sur·ing
high-spir·it·ed
high-ten·sion
high-toned
high·way
hi·jack
  hi·jack·er
  hi·jack·ing
hike
  hiked
  hik·ing
hi·lar·i·ous
  hi·lar·i·ous·ly
  hi·lar·i·ous·ness
  hi·lar·i·ty
hill·bil·ly
  hill·bil·lies
hill·ock
hilly
  hill·i·er
  hill·i·est
him·self
hin·der
  hind·er·er
hind·most
hind·quar·ter
hin·drance
hind·sight
Hin·du·ism
hinge
  hinged
  hing·ing
hin·ter·land
hipped

Hip·poc·ra·tes
Hip·po·crat·ic
hip·po·drome
hip·po·pot·a·mus
hire·ling
hir·sute
His·pan·ic
his·ta·mine
his·to·ri·an
his·tor·ic
his·tor·i·cal
  his·tor·i·cal·ly
  his·tor·i·cal·ness
his·to·ry
  his·to·ries
his·tri·on·ic
  his·tri·on·i·cal·ly
  his·tri·on·ics
hit
  hit·ting
hitch·hike
  hitch·hiked
  hitch·hik·ing
  hitch·hik·er
hith·er
hith·er·to
hit·ter
hoard
  hoard·er
  hoard·ing
hoar·frost
hoarse
  hoarse·ly
  hoarse·ness
hoary
  hoar·i·ness
hoax
  hoax·er
hob·ble
  hob·bled
  hob·bling
hob·by
  hob·bies
  hob·by·ist
hob·gob·lin
hob·nail
hob·nob
  hob·nobbed
  hob·nob·bing
ho·bo
  ho·boes
hock·ey
ho·cus-po·cus
hodge·podge
hoe
  hoed
  hoe·ing
hoe·down
hog
  hogged
  hog·ging
  hog·gish
hogs·head
hog·tie
hoi·poi·loi
hoist·ing
ho·kum
hold
  held
  hold·ing
hole
  holed
  hol·ing
  holey
hol·i·day
ho·li·ness
Hol·land
hol·low

hol·low·ness
hol·ly
hol·ly·hock
hol·o·caust
hol·o·graph
Hol·stein
hol·ster
ho·ly
  ho·li·er
  ho·li·est
  ho·li·ness
hom·age
hom·bre
home·com·ing
home·less
home·ly
  home·li·ness
ho·me·op·a·thy
home·spun
home·stead
home·ward
homey
  hom·i·ness
hom·i·cide
  ho·mi·cid·al
hom·i·let·ics
hom·i·ly
hom·i·ny
ho·mo·ge·ne·ous
  ho·mo·ge·ne·i·ty
ho·mog·e·nize
  ho·mog·e·nized
  ho·mog·e·niz·ing
hom·o·graph
hom·o·nym
hom·o·phone
Ho·mo sa·pi·ens
ho·mo·sex·u·al
  ho·mo·sex·u·al·i·ty
hone
  honed
  hon·ing
hon·est
  hon·est·ly
hon·es·ty
  hon·es·ties
hon·ey
hon·ey·moon·er
hon·ey·suck·le
honk·y·tonk
hon·or
hon·or·a·ble
  hon·or·a·bly
hon·o·rar·i·um
hon·or·ary
hon·or·if·ic
hood·ed
hood·lum
hoo·doo
hood·wink
hoof
  hoofs
  hooves
  hoofed
hooked
hook·er
hoo·li·gan
hoop
  hooped
hop
  hopped
  hop·ping
hope
  hoped
  hop·ing
hope·ful
  hope·ful·ness
hope·less

hope·less·ness
hop·head
hop·per
hop·scotch
horde
  hord·ed
  hord·ing
ho·ri·zon
hor·i·zon·tal
  hor·i·zon·tal·ly
hor·mone
horn
  horned
  horny
hor·net
horn·swog·gle
ho·rol·o·gy
  ho·rol·o·gist
hor·o·scope
hor·ren·dous
hor·ri·ble
  hor·ri·bly
hor·rid
  hor·rid·ly
  hor·rid·ness
hor·ri·fy
  hor·ri·fied
  hor·ri·fy·ing
  hor·ri·fi·ca·tion
nor·ror
hors d'oeu·vre
horse
  hors·es
  horsed
  hors·ing
horse·back
horse·man
horse op·era
horse·play
horse·pow·er
horse·rad·ish
horse·whipped
hors·ey
hor·ta·to·ry
hor·ti·cul·ture
  hor·ti·cul·tur·al
  hor·ti·cul·tur·ist
ho·san·na
hose
ho·siery
hos·pice
hos·pi·ta·ble
  hos·pi·ta·bly
hos·pi·tal
hos·pi·tal·i·ty
  hos·pi·tal·i·ties
hos·pi·tal·i·za·tion
hos·pi·tal·ize
  hos·pi·tal·ized
  hos·pi·tal·iz·ing
hos·tage
hos·tel
  hos·tel·ry
host·ess
hos·tile
  hos·tile·ly
hos·til·i·ty
  hos·til·i·ties
hot
  hot·ter
  hot·test
  hot·ly
hot·blood·ed
ho·tel
hot·head·ed
hound
hour·glass
hour·ly

house
  hous·es
  housed
  hous·ing
house·bro·ken
house·hold
house·keep·er
house·warm·ing
house·wife
  house·wives
hov·el
hov·er
  hov·er·ing
how·ev·er
how·itz·er
howl·er
hoy·den
  hoy·den·ish
hub·bub
huck·le·ber·ry
huck·ster
hud·dle
  hud·dled
  hud·dling
huffy
  huff·i·ness
hug
  hugged
  hug·ging
  hug·ger
huge
  huge·ness
hulk·ing
hum
  hummed
  hum·ming
  hum·mer
hu·man
hu·mane
hu·man·ism
hu·man·i·tar·i·an
hu·man·i·ty
hu·man·ize
hum·ble
  hum·bled
  hum·bling
  hum·ble·ness
  hum·bly
hum·bug
hum·drum
hu·mer·us
hu·mid
hu·midi·fy
  hu·mid·i·fied
  hu·mid·i·fy·ing
  hu·mid·i·fi·er
hu·mid·i·ty
hu·mi·dor
hu·mil·i·ate
  hu·mil·i·at·ed
  hu·mil·i·at·ing
  hu·mil·i·a·tion
hu·mil·i·ty
hum·ming·bird
hum·mock
hu·mor
hu·mor·ist
hu·mor·ous
  hu·mor·ous·ness
hump
  humped
  humpy
hump·back
hu·mus
hunch·back
hun·dred
  hun·dredth
hun·dred·weight

hun·ger
hun·gry
  hun·gri·ly
  hun·gri·ness
hunt
  hunt·er
  hunt·ing
  hunts·man
hur·dle
  hur·dled
  hur·dling
  hur·dler
hur·dy-gur·dy
hurl·er
hur·rah
hur·ri·cane
hur·ry
  hur·ried
  hur·ry·ing
hurt·ful
hurt·ing
hur·tle
  hur·tled
  hur·tling
hus·band
hus·band·ry
husk·er
husky
  husk·i·ly
  husk·i·ness
hus·sy
hus·tings
hus·tle
  hus·tled
  hus·tling
  hus·tler
hutch
huz·zah
hy·a·cinth
hy·brid
  hy·brid·ize
  hy·brid·ized
  hy·brid·iz·ing
  hy·brid·i·za·tion
hy·dran·gea
hy·drant
hy·drate
  hy·dra·ted
  hy·dra·ting
  hy·dra·tion
hy·drau·lic
  hy·drau·li·cal·ly
hy·drau·lics
hy·dro·car·bon
hy·dro·chlo·ric ac·id
hy·dro·dy·nam·ics
  hy·dro·dy·nam·ic
hy·dro·e·lec·tric
hy·dro·gen
  hy·drog·e·nous
hy·drol·y·sis
hy·drom·e·ter
hy·dro·pho·bia
hy·dro·plane
hy·dro·pon·ics
hy·dro·ther·a·py
  hy·dro·ther·a·pist
hy·drous
hy·drox·ide
hy·e·na
hy·giene
  hy·gi·en·ic
  hy·gi·en·i·cal·ly
  hy·gien·ist
hy·grom·e·ter
hy·men
hy·me·ne·al
  hy·me·ne·al·ly

hymn
  hym·nal
hy·per·bo·la
hy·per·bo·le
  hy·per·bo·lize
  hy·per·bo·lized
  hy·per·bo·liz·ing
hy·per·bol·ic
hy·per·crit·i·cal
hy·per·sen·si·tive
  hy·per·sen·si·tiv·i·ty
hy·per·ten·sion
hy·per·thy·roid·ism
hy·phen
hy·phen·ate
  hy·phen·at·ed
  hy·phen·at·ing
hyp·no·sis
hyp·not·ic
hyp·no·tism
  hyp·no·tist
  hyp·no·tize
  hyp·no·tized
  hyp·no·tiz·ing
hy·po·chon·dria
  hy·po·chon·dri·ac
hy·poc·ri·sy
  hy·poc·ri·sies
hyp·o·crite
hy·po·der·mic
hy·po·gly·ce·mia
hy·po·sen·si·tize
hy·po·ten·sion
hy·pot·e·nuse
hy·poth·e·cate
  hy·poth·e·cat·ed
  hy·poth·e·cat·ing
  hy·poth·e·ca·tion
hy·poth·e·sis
  hy·poth·e·ses
  hy·poth·e·size
  hy·poth·e·sized
  hy·poth·e·siz·ing
hy·po·thet·i·cal
hys·ter·ec·to·my
hys·ter·e·sis
hys·te·ria
  hys·ter·ic
  hys·ter·i·cal
  hys·ter·i·cal·ly
hys·ter·ics

I

iamb
  iam·bic
ibid
ibi·dem
ice
  iced
  ic·ing
  icy
  ici·ness
ice cream
ice-skate
  ice-skat·ed
  ice-skat·ing
ich·thy·ol·o·gy
  ich·thy·o·log·i·cal
  ich·thy·ol·o·gist
ici·cle
ici·ly
icon
icon·o·clast
  icon·o·clasm
  icon·o·clas·tic
idea

ide·al
  ide·al·ly
  ide·al·ism
  ide·al·ist
  ide·al·is·tic
ide·al·ize
  ide·al·ized
  ide·al·iz·ing
  ide·al·i·za·tion
ide·ate
  ide·a·tion
iden·ti·cal
  iden·ti·cal·ly
  iden·ti·cal·ness
iden·ti·fi·a·ble
  iden·ti·fi·a·bly
iden·ti·fy
  iden·ti·fied
  iden·ti·fy·ing
  iden·ti·fi·ca·tion
iden·ti·ty
  iden·ti·ties
ide·ol·o·gist
ide·ol·o·gy
  ide·ol·o·gies
ides
id·i·o·cy
  id·i·o·cies
id·i·om
  id·i·o·mat·ic
  id·i·o·mat·i·cal·ly
id·i·o·syn·cra·sy
  id·i·o·syn·cra·sies
  id·i·o·syn·crat·ic
id·i·ot
  id·i·ot·ic
  id·i·ot·i·cal·ly
idle
  idler
  idlest
  idled
  idling
  idle·ness
  idly
idol
idol·a·try
  idol·a·tries
  idol·a·ter
  idol·a·trous
idol·ize
  idol·ized
  idol·iz·ing
  idol·i·za·tion
idyll
  idyl·lic
  idyl·lic·al·ly
ig·loo
ig·ne·ous
ig·nite
  ig·nit·ed
  ig·nit·ing
  ig·nit·er
  ig·nit·a·ble
  ig·nit·a·bil·i·ty
  ig·ni·tion
ig·no·ble
  ig·no·bil·i·ty
  ig·no·ble·ness
  ig·no·bly
ig·no·miny
  ig·no·min·ies
  ig·no·min·i·ous
ig·no·ra·mus
ig·no·rant
  ig·no·rance
  ig·no·rant·ly
ig·nore
  ig·nored

ig·nor·ing
i·gua·na
ikon
ill
  worse
  worst
ill-ad·vised
ill-bred
il·le·gal
  il·le·gal·i·ty
  il·le·gal·ly
il·leg·i·ble
  il·leg·i·bil·i·ty
  il·leg·i·ble·ness
  il·leg·i·bly
il·le·git·i·mate
  il·le·git·i·ma·cy
  il·le·git·i·ma·cies
  il·le·git·i·mate·ly
ill-fat·ed
ill-fa·vored
ill-got·ten
il·lib·er·al
il·lic·it
il·lim·it·a·ble
il·lit·er·ate
  il·lit·er·a·cy
ill·ness
il·log·i·cal
ill-tempered
ill-timed
il·lu·mi·nate
  il·lu·mi·nat·ed
  il·lu·mi·nat·ing
  il·lu·mi·na·tor
  il·lu·mi·na·tion
il·lu·mine
  il·lu·mined
  il·lu·min·ing
ill-us·age
il·lu·sion
il·lu·sive
  il·lu·sive·ness
il·lu·so·ry
  il·lu·so·ri·ness
il·lus·trate
  il·lus·trat·ed
  il·lus·trat·ing
  il·lus·tra·tion
  il·lus·tra·tive
  il·lus·tra·tor
il·lus·tri·ous
  il·lus·tri·ous·ness
im·age
  im·aged
  im·ag·ing
im·age·ry
  im·age·ries
  im·a·ge·ri·al
im·ag·ine
  im·ag·ined
  im·ag·in·ing
  im·ag·i·na·ble
  imag·i·na·bly
  im·ag·i·nary
  imag·i·nar·i·ly
  im·ag·i·na·tion
  im·ag·i·na·tive
im·bal·ance
im·be·cile
  im·be·cil·ic
  im·be·cil·i·ty
im·bed
  im·bed·ded
  im·bed·ding
im·bibe
  im·bibed
  im·bib·ing

im·bro·glio
im·bue
  im·bued
  im·bu·ing
im·i·tate
  im·i·tat·ed
  im·i·tat·ing
  im·i·ta·tor
  im·i·ta·tion
  im·i·ta·tive
im·mac·u·late
  im·mac·u·la·cy
  im·mac·u·late·ness
  im·mac·u·late·ly
im·ma·nent
  im·ma·nence
  im·ma·nen·cy
  im·ma·nent·ly
im·ma·te·ri·al
  im·ma·te·ri·al·ness
  im·ma·te·ri·al·i·ty
im·ma·ture
  im·ma·ture·ly
  im·ma·ture·ness
  im·ma·tu·ri·ty
im·meas·ur·a·ble
  im·meas·ura·bly
im·me·di·a·cy
  im·me·di·a·cies
im·me·di·ate
  im·me·di·ate·ly
im·me·mo·ri·al
im·mense
  im·mense·ness
  im·men·si·ty
im·merge
  im·merged
  im·merg·ing
  im·mer·gence
im·merse
  im·mersed
  im·mers·ing
  im·mer·sion
im·mi·grate
  im·mi·grat·ed
  im·mi·grat·ing
  im·mi·gra·tion
im·mi·grant
  im·mi·gra·tor
im·mi·nent
  im·mi·nence
im·mo·bile
  im·mo·bil·i·ty
  im·mo·bi·lize
  im·mo·bi·lized
  im·mo·bi·liz·ing
im·mod·er·ate
  im·mod·er·ate·ly
im·mod·est
  im·mod·est·ly
  im·mod·es·ty
im·mo·late
  im·mo·lat·ed
  im·mo·lat·ing
  im·mo·la·tion
  im·mo·la·tor
im·mor·al
  im·mo·ral·i·ty
  im·mo·ral·i·ties
  im·mor·al·ly
im·mor·tal
  im·mor·tal·i·ty
  im·mor·tal·ize
  im·mor·tal·ized
  im·mor·tal·iz·ing
  im·mor·tal·ly
im·mov·a·ble
  im·mov·a·bil·i·ty

im·mov·a·bly
im·mune
  im·mu·ni·ty
  im·mu·nize
  im·mu·nized
  im·mu·niz·ing
  im·mu·ni·za·tion
im·mu·nol·o·gy
im·mure
  im·mured
  im·mur·ing
im·mu·ta·ble
  im·mu·ta·bil·i·ty
  im·mu·ta·ble·ness
  im·mu·ta·bly
im·pact
  im·pac·tion
  im·pact·ed
im·pair
  im·pair·ment
impala
im·pale
  im·paled
  im·pal·ing
  im·pale·ment
im·pal·pa·ble
  im·pal·pa·bil·i·ty
im·pan·el
  im·pan·eled
  im·pan·el·ing
im·part
im·par·tial
  im·par·ti·al·i·ty
  im·par·tial·ness
  im·par·tial·ly
im·pass·a·ble
  im·pass·a·bil·i·ty
  im·pass·a·ble·ness
  im·pass·a·bly
im·passe
im·pas·si·ble
  im·pas·si·bil·i·ty
  im·pas·si·ble·ness
im·pas·sion
  im·pas·sioned
  im·pas·sioned·ness
im·pas·sive
  im·pas·sive·ly
  im·pas·sive·ness
  im·pas·siv·i·ty
im·pa·tient
  im·pa·tience
  im·pa·tient·ly
im·peach
  im·peach·a·ble
  im·peach·ment
im·pec·ca·ble
  im·pec·ca·bil·i·ty
  im·pec·ca·bly
im·pe·cu·ni·ous
  im·pe·cu·ni·ous·ness
im·pede
  im·ped·ed
  im·ped·ing
  im·ped·i·ment
im·pel
  im·pelled
  im·pel·ling
im·pend
  im·pend·ing
im·pen·e·tra·ble
  im·pen·e·tra·bil·i·ty
im·pen·i·tent
  im·pen·i·tence
im·per·a·tive
  im·per·a·tive·ness
im·per·cep·ti·ble
  im·per·cep·ti·bil·i·ty

im·per·cep·ti·bly
im·per·cep·tive
im·per·fect
  im·per·fect·ly
  im·per·fect·ness
  im·per·fec·tion
im·pe·ri·al
  im·pe·ri·al·ly
  im·pe·ri·al·ism
  im·pe·ri·al·ist
  im·pe·ri·al·is·tic
  im·pe·ri·al·is·ti·cal·ly
im·per·il
  im·per·iled
  im·per·il·ing
  im·per·il·ment
im·pe·ri·ous
  im·pe·ri·ous·ly
  im·pe·ri·ous·ness
im·per·ish·a·ble
  im·per·ish·a·bil·i·ty
im·per·ma·nent
  im·per·ma·nence
  im·per·ma·nen·cy
  im·per·ma·nent·ly
im·per·me·a·ble
  im·per·me·a·bil·i·ty
  im·per·me·a·ble·ness
im·per·son·al
  im·per·son·al·ly
im·per·son·ate
  im·per·son·at·ed
  im·per·son·at·ing
  im·per·son·a·tion
  im·per·son·a·tor
im·per·ti·nent
  im·per·ti·nence
  im·per·ti·nent·ly
im·per·turb·a·ble
  im·per·turb·a·bly
im·per·vi·ous
  im·per·vi·ous·ly
  im·per·vi·ous·ness
im·pe·ti·go
im·pet·u·ous
  im·pet·u·os·i·ty
  im·pet·u·ous·ly
  im·pet·u·ous·ness
im·pe·tus
im·pi·e·ty
  im·pi·e·ties
im·pinge
  im·pinged
  im·ping·ing
  im·pinge·ment
im·pi·ous
  im·pi·ous·ly
  im·pi·ous·ness
im·plac·a·ble
  im·plac·a·bil·i·ty
  im·plac·a·ble·ness
  im·plac·a·bly
im·plant
  im·plan·ta·tion
im·plau·si·ble
  im·plau·si·bly
  im·plau·si·bil·i·ty
im·ple·ment
  im·ple·men·tal
  im·ple·men·ta·tion
im·pli·cate
  im·pli·cat·ed
  im·pli·cat·ing
  im·pli·ca·tion
im·plic·it
  im·plic·it·ly
  im·plic·it·ness
im·plode

im·plod·ed
im·plod·ing
im·plo·sion
im·plo·sive
im·plore
im·plored
im·plor·ing
im·plo·ra·tion
im·ply
im·plied
im·ply·ing
im·po·lite
im·po·lite·ly
im·po·lite·ness
im·pol·i·tic
im·pol·i·tic·ly
im·pon·der·a·ble
im·pon·der·a·bil·i·ty
im·pon·der·a·ble·ness
im·port
im·port·a·ble
im·port·er
im·por·ta·tion
im·por·tance
im·por·tant
im·por·tant·ly
im·por·tu·nate
im·por·tune
im·por·tuned
im·por·tun·ing
im·pose
im·posed
im·pos·ing
im·po·si·tion
im·pos·si·ble
im·pos·si·bil·i·ty
im·pos·si·bil·i·ties
im·pos·si·bly
im·pos·tor
im·pos·ture
im·po·tent
im·po·tence
im·po·ten·cy
im·po·tent·ly
im·pound
im·pound·age
im·pov·er·ish
im·pov·er·ish·ment
im·prac·ti·cal
im·prac·ti·ca·ble
im·prac·ti·ca·bil·i·ty
im·prac·ti·ca·ble·ness
im·pre·cate
im·pre·cat·ed
im·pre·cat·ing
im·pre·ca·tion
im·preg·na·ble
im·preg·na·bil·i·ty
im·preg·na·ble·ness
im·preg·nate
im·preg·nat·ed
im·preg·nat·ing
im·preg·na·tion
im·preg·na·tor
im·pre·sa·rio
im·pre·sa·ri·os
im·press
im·press·i·ble
im·press·ment
im·pres·sion
im·pres·sion·ist
im·pres·sion·a·ble
im·pres·sion·a·bly
im·pres·sion·ism
im·pres·sion·ist
im·pres·sion·is·tic
im·pres·sive
im·pres·sive·ly

im·pres·sive·ness
im·pri·ma·tur
im·print
im·prin·ter
im·pris·on
im·pris·on·ment
im·prob·a·ble
im·prob·a·bil·i·ty
im·prob·a·ble·ness
im·prob·a·bly
im·promp·tu
im·prop·er
im·prop·er·ly
im·prop·er·ness
im·pro·pri·e·ty
im·pro·pri·e·ties
im·prove
im·proved
im·prov·ing
im·prov·a·bil·i·ty
im·prov·a·ble
im·prove·ment
im·prov·i·dent
im·prov·i·dence
im·prov·i·dent·ly
im·prov·i·sa·tion
im·prov·i·sa·tion·al
im·pro·vise
im·pro·vised
im·pro·vis·ing
im·pru·dent
im·pru·dence
im·pru·dent·ly
im·pu·dent
im·pu·dence
im·pugn
im·pugn·er
im·pug·na·tion
im·pulse
im·pul·sion
im·pul·sive
im·pu·ni·ty
im·pure
im·pure·ness
im·pu·ri·ty
im·pu·ri·ties
im·pute
im·put·ed
im·put·ing
im·pu·ta·tion
in·a·bil·i·ty
in ab·sen·tia
in·ac·ces·si·ble
in·ac·ces·si·bil·i·ty
in·ac·ces·si·bly
in·ac·cu·rate
in·ac·cu·ra·cy
in·ac·cu·ra·cies
in·ac·tion
in·ac·ti·vate
in·ac·ti·va·tion
in·ac·tive
in·ac·tive·ly
in·ac·tiv·i·ty
in·ad·e·quate
in·ad·e·qua·cy
in·ad·e·qua·cies
in·ad·mis·si·ble
in·ad·mis·si·bly
in·ad·vert·ent
in·ad·vert·ence
in·ad·vert·en·cy
in·al·ien·a·ble
in·al·ien·a·bil·i·ty
in·al·ien·a·bly
in·al·ter·a·ble
in·ane
in·ane·ness

in·an·i·ty
in·an·i·mate
in·ap·pli·ca·ble
in·ap·pre·cia·bly
in·ap·pro·pri·ate
in·ap·pro·pri·ate·ly
in·apt
in·ap·ti·tude
in·apt·ly
in·ar·tic·u·late
in·as·much as
in·at·ten·tion
in·at·ten·tive
in·au·di·ble
in·au·di·bly
in·au·gu·ral
in·au·gu·rate
in·au·gu·rat·ed
in·au·gu·rat·ing
in·au·gu·ra·tion
in·aus·pi·cious
in·bred
in·breed
in·breed·ing
in·cal·cu·la·ble
in·cal·cu·la·bil·i·ty
in·can·des·cent
in·can·des·cence
in·can·ta·tion
in·ca·pa·ble
in·ca·pa·bly
in·ca·pac·i·tate
in·ca·pac·i·tat·ed
in·ca·pac·i·tat·ing
in·ca·pac·i·ty
in·ca·pac·i·ties
in·ca·pac·i·ta·tion
in·car·cer·ate
in·car·cer·at·ed
in·car·cer·at·ing
in·car·cer·a·tion
in·car·nate
in·car·nat·ed
in·car·nat·ing
in·car·na·tion
in·cen·di·a·ry
in·cense
in·censed
in·cens·ing
in·cen·tive
in·cep·tion
in·cer·ti·tude
in·ces·sant
in·cest
in·ces·tu·ous
in·cho·ate
in·ci·dence
in·ci·dent
in·ci·den·tal
in·cin·er·ate
in·cin·er·at·ed
in·cin·er·at·ing
in·cin·er·a·tion
in·cin·er·a·tor
in·cip·i·ent
in·cise
in·cised
in·cis·ing
in·ci·sion
in·ci·sive
in·ci·sor
in·cite
in·cit·ed
in·cit·ing
in·cite·ment
in·ci·ta·tion
in·ci·vil·i·ty
in·clem·ent

in·clem·en·cy
in·cline
in·clined
in·clin·ing
in·cli·na·tion
in·clude
in·clud·ed
in·clud·ing
in·clu·sion
in·clu·sive
in·cog·ni·to
in·cog·ni·zant
in·co·her·ent
in·co·her·ence
in·com·bus·ti·ble
in·come
in·com·ing
in·com·men·su·rate
in·com·men·su·ra·ble
in·com·mode
in·com·mo·di·ous
in·com·mu·ni·ca·ble
in·com·mu·ni·ca·do
in·com·pa·ra·ble
in·com·pa·ra·bly
in·com·pat·i·ble
in·com·pat·i·bil·i·ty
in·com·pe·tent
in·com·pe·tence
in·com·pe·ten·cy
in·com·plete
in·com·ple·tion
in·com·pre·hen·si·ble
in·com·pre·hen·sion
in·con·ceiv·a·ble
in·con·ceiv·a·bly
in·con·clu·sive
in·con·gru·ous
in·con·gru·i·ty
in·con·se·quen·tial
in·con·sid·er·a·ble
in·con·sid·er·ate
in·con·sis·tent
in·con·sis·ten·cy
in·con·sol·a·ble
in·con·spic·u·ous
in·con·stant
in·con·stan·cy
in·con·test·a·ble
in·con·test·abil·i·ty
in·con·ti·nent
in·con·ti·nence
in·con·ti·nen·cy
in·con·trol·la·ble
in·con·ven·ient
in·con·ven·ience
in·con·ven·ienced
in·con·ven·ienc·ing
in·cor·po·rate
in·cor·po·rat·ed
in·cor·po·rat·ing
in·cor·po·ra·tion
in·cor·po·re·al
in·cor·rect
in·cor·ri·gi·ble
in·cor·ri·gi·bil·i·ty
in·cor·ri·gi·ble·ness
in·cor·rupt·i·ble
in·cor·rupt·i·bil·i·ty
in·cor·rupt·i·bly
in·crease
in·creased
in·creas·ing
in·creas·a·ble
in·cred·i·ble
in·cred·i·bil·i·ty
in·cred·i·bly
in·cred·u·lous

in·cre·du·li·ty
in·cre·ment
in·cre·men·tal
in·crim·i·nate
in·crim·i·nat·ed
in·crim·i·nat·ing
in·crim·i·na·tion
in·crust
in·crus·ta·tion
in·cu·bate
in·cu·bat·ed
in·cu·bat·ing
in·cu·ba·tion
in·cu·ba·tor
in·cul·cate
in·cul·cat·ed
in·cul·cat·ing
in·cul·ca·tion
in·cul·pate
in·cul·pat·ed
in·cul·pat·ing
in·cul·pa·tion
in·cum·bent
in·cum·ben·cy
in·cur
in·curred
in·cur·ring
in·cur·a·ble
in·cur·a·bly
in·cu·ri·ous
in·cur·sion
in·cur·sive
in·debt·ed
in·de·cent
in·de·cen·cy
in·de·ci·sion
in·de·ci·sive
in·de·co·rous
in·de·co·rum
in·deed
in·de·fat·i·ga·ble
in·de·fat·i·ga·bil·i·ty
in·de·fat·i·ga·bly
in·de·fea·si·ble
in·de·fen·si·ble
in·de·fen·si·bil·i·ty
in·de·fen·si·bly
in·de·fin·a·ble
in·def·i·nite
in·def·i·nite·ly
in·del·i·ble
in·del·i·bly
in·del·i·cate
in·del·i·ca·cy
in·dem·ni·fy
in·dem·ni·fied
in·dem·ni·fy·ing
in·dem·ni·fi·ca·tion
in·dem·ni·ty
in·dent
in·den·ta·tion
in·dent·ed
in·den·ture
in·den·tur·ing
in·de·pend·ent
in·de·pend·ence
in·de·pend·en·cy
in·de·scrib·a·ble
in·de·scrib·a·bil·i·ty
in·de·struct·i·ble
in·de·struct·i·bil·i·ty
in·de·ter·mi·nate
in·de·ter·mi·na·cy
in·de·ter·mi·na·tion
in·dex
in·di·cate
in·di·cat·ed
in·di·cat·ing

in·di·ca·tion
in·dic·a·tive
in·dic·a·tor
in·dict
  in·dict·a·ble
  in·dict·ment
in·dif·fer·ent
  in·dif·fer·ence
  in·dif·fer·ent·ly
in·dig·e·nous
in·di·gent
  in·di·gence
in·di·ges·tion
  in·di·gest·i·ble
  in·di·gest·i·bil·i·ty
  in·di·gest·i·ble·ness
in·dig·nant
  in·dig·nant·ly
  in·dig·na·tion
in·dig·ni·ty
in·di·go
in·di·rect
  in·di·rec·tion
in·dis·creet
  in·dis·cre·tion
in·dis·crete
in·dis·crim·i·nate
  in·dis·crim·i·nat·ing
  in·dis·crim·i·na·tion
in·dis·pen·sa·ble
  in·dis·pen·sa·bil·i·ty
  in·dis·pen·sa·ble·ness
in·dis·posed
  in·dis·po·si·tion
in·dis·put·a·ble
in·dis·sol·u·ble
  in·dis·sol·u·bil·i·ty
in·dis·tinct
in·dis·tin·guish·a·ble
in·di·vid·u·al
  in·di·vid·u·al·ly
  in·di·vid·u·al·is·tic
  in·di·vid·u·al·i·ty
  in·di·vid·u·al·ize
in·di·vis·i·ble
in·doc·tri·nate
  in·doc·tri·nat·ed
  in·doc·tri·nat·ing
  in·doc·tri·na·tion
in·do·lent
  in·do·lence
in·dom·i·ta·ble
  in·dom·i·ta·bil·i·ty
  in·dom·i·ta·bly
in·du·bi·ta·ble
  in·du·bi·ta·bil·i·ty
  in·du·bi·ta·bly
in·duce
  in·duced
  in·duc·ing
  in·duce·ment
in·duct
  in·duct·ee
in·duc·tion
  in·duct·ance
  in·duc·tive
in·dulge
  in·dulged
  in·dulg·ing
  in·dul·gence
  in·dul·gent
in·dus·try
  in·dus·tries
  in·dus·tri·al
  in·dus·tri·al·ize
  in·dus·tri·al·i·za·tion
  in·dus·tri·al·ist
  in·dus·tri·ous

in·e·bri·ate
in·e·bri·at·ed
in·e·bri·at·ing
in·e·bri·a·tion
in·ed·i·ble
in·ef·fa·ble
  in·ef·fa·bil·i·ty
  in·ef·fa·bly
in·ef·fec·tive
in·ef·fec·tu·al
in·ef·fi·ca·cy
in·ef·fi·cient
  in·ef·fi·cien·cy
in·el·e·gant
in·el·i·gi·ble
  in·el·i·gi·bil·i·ty
in·ept
  in·ept·i·tude
in·e·qual·i·ty
in·erad·i·ca·ble
in·er·rant
in·ert
in·er·tia
  in·er·tial
in·es·cap·a·ble
in·es·sen·tial
in·es·ti·ma·ble
  in·es·ti·ma·bly
in·ev·i·ta·ble
  in·ev·i·ta·bil·i·ty
  in·ev·i·ta·bly
in·ex·act
in·ex·cus·a·ble
in·ex·haust·i·ble
  in·ex·haust·i·bil·i·ty
in·ex·o·ra·ble
  in·ex·o·ra·bil·i·ty
  in·ex·o·ra·bly
in·ex·pe·ri·ence
  in·ex·pe·ri·enced
in·ex·pert
in·ex·pi·a·ble
  in·ex·pi·a·bly
in·ex·pli·ca·ble
  in·ex·pli·ca·bil·i·ty
  in·ex·pli·ca·bly
in·ex·press·i·ble
  in·ex·press·i·bil·i·ty
  in·ex·press·i·bly
in·ex·pres·sive
in·ex·tin·guish·a·ble
in·ex·tri·ca·ble
  in·ex·tri·ca·bil·i·ty
  in·ex·tri·ca·bly
in·fal·li·ble
  in·fal·li·bil·i·ty
  in·fal·li·bly
in·fa·mous
in·fa·my
  in·fa·mies
in·fan·cy
  in·fan·cies
in·fant
  in·fant·hood
in·fan·ti·cide
in·fan·tile
  in·fan·tine
in·fan·try
  in·fan·tries
in·fat·u·ate
  in·fat·u·at·ed
  in·fat·u·at·ing
  in·fat·u·a·tion
in·fect
  in·fec·tion
  in·fec·tious
  in·fec·tive
in·fe·lic·i·ty

in·fer
  in·ferred
  in·fer·ring
  in·fer·a·ble
in·fer·ence
  in·fer·en·tial
in·fe·ri·or
  in·fe·ri·or·i·ty
in·fer·nal
in·fer·no
  in·fer·nos
in·fest
  in·fes·ta·tion
in·fi·del
  in·fi·del·i·ty
  in·fi·del·i·ties
in·field
  in·field·er
in·fight·ing
  in·fight·er
in·fil·trate
  in·fil·trat·ed
  in·fil·trat·ing
  in·fil·tra·tion
  in·fil·tra·tor
in·fi·nite
  in·fi·nite·ness
in·fin·i·tes·i·mal
in·fin·i·tive
  in·fin·i·tive·ly
in·fin·i·ty
  in·fin·i·ties
in·firm
in·fir·ma·ry
  in·fir·ma·ries
in·fir·mi·ty
  in·fir·mi·ties
in·flame
  in·flamed
  in·flam·ing
in·flam·ma·ble
  in·flam·ma·bil·i·ty
  in·flam·ma·ble·ness
in·flam·ma·tion
in·flam·ma·to·ry
in·flate
  in·flat·ed
  in·flat·ing
  in·flat·a·ble
in·fla·tion
  in·fla·tion·ary
in·flect
  in·flec·tion
  in·flec·tion·less
  in·flec·tive
in·flex·i·ble
  in·flex·i·bil·i·ty
  in·flex·i·bly
in·flict
  in·flict·a·ble
  in·flic·tion
in·flo·res·cence
in·flu·ence
  in·flu·enced
  in·flu·enc·ing
  in·flu·en·tial
in·flu·en·za
in·flux
in·form
  in·formed
  in·for·mer
in·for·mal
  in·for·mal·i·ty
  in·for·mal·ly
in·form·ant
in·for·ma·tion
  in·for·ma·tion·al
  in·for·ma·tive

in·for·ma·to·ry
in·frac·tion
in·fran·gi·ble
  in·fran·gi·bil·i·ty
  in·fran·gi·bly
in·fra·red
in·fra·son·ic
in·fra·struc·ture
in·fre·quent
  in·fre·quen·cy
in·fringe
  in·fringed
  in·fring·ing
  in·fringe·ment
in·fu·ri·ate
  in·fu·ri·at·ed
  in·fu·ri·at·ing
  in·fu·ri·a·tion
in·fuse
  in·fused
  in·fus·ing
  in·fus·i·ble
  in·fu·sion
in·gen·ious
in·gé·nue
in·ge·nu·i·ty
  in·gen·u·ous
in·gest
  in·ges·tion
in·glo·ri·ous
in·got
in·grain
in·grate
in·gra·ti·ate
  in·gra·ti·at·ed
  in·gra·ti·at·ing
  in·gra·ti·a·tion
in·grat·i·tude
in·gre·di·ent
in·gress
in·grow·ing
  in·grown
in·hab·it
  in·hab·it·a·ble
  in·hab·i·ta·tion
  in·hab·it·ed
  in·hab·it·ant
in·hal·ant
  in·ha·la·tion
  in·ha·la·tor
in·hale
  in·haled
  in·hal·ing
in·har·mo·ny
  in·har·mon·ic
in·here
  in·hered
  in·her·ing
  in·her·ence
  in·her·ent
in·her·it
  in·her·i·tor
  in·her·i·tance
in·hib·it
  in·hib·i·tive
  in·hib·i·to·ry
  in·hib·i·ter
  in·hi·bi·tion
in·hos·pi·ta·ble
  in·hos·pi·tal·i·ty
in·hu·man
  in·hu·man·i·ty
  in·hu·mane
  in·hu·ma·tion
in·im·i·cal
in·im·i·ta·ble
  in·im·i·ta·bly
in·iq·ui·ty

in·iq·ui·ties
in·iq·ui·tous
in·i·tial
  in·i·tialed
  in·i·tial·ing
  in·i·tial·ly
in·i·ti·ate
  in·i·ti·at·ed
  in·i·ti·at·ing
  in·i·ti·a·tion
  in·i·ti·a·tor
in·i·ti·a·tive
in·ject
  in·jec·tion
  in·jec·tor
in·ju·di·cious
in·junc·tion
in·jure
  in·jured
  in·jur·ing
  in·ju·ri·ous
in·ju·ry
  in·ju·ries
in·jus·tice
ink·blot
ink·ling
inky
  ink·i·er
in·law
in·lay
  in·laid
  in·lay·ing
in·let
in·mate
in me·mo·ri·am
in·most
in·nards
in·nate
in·ner
  in·ner·most
  in·ner·sole
  in·ner·vate
  in·ner·vat·ed
  in·ner·vat·ing
  in·ner·va·tion
in·ning
inn·keep·er
in·no·cent
  in·no·cence
in·noc·u·ous
in·no·vate
  in·no·vat·ed
  in·no·vat·ing
  in·no·va·tion
  in·no·va·tive
  in·no·va·tor
in·nu·en·do
  in·nu·en·dos
  in·nu·en·does
in·nu·mer·a·ble
  in·nu·mer·ous
  in·nu·mer·a·bly
in·nu·tri·tion
in·ob·serv·ance
  in·ob·serv·ant
in·oc·u·late
  in·oc·u·lat·ed
  in·oc·u·lat·ing
  in·oc·u·lant
  in·oc·u·la·tion
in·of·fen·sive
in·op·er·a·ble
  in·op·er·a·tive
in·op·por·tune
  in·op·por·tu·ni·ty
in·or·di·nate
in·or·gan·ic
in·pa·tient

in·pour
in·put
in·quest
in·qui·e·tude
in·quire
in·quired
in·quir·ing
in·quir·er
in·quiry
in·quir·ies
in·qui·si·tion
in·quis·i·tive
in·quis·i·tor
in·road
in·sa·lu·bri·ous
in·sane
in·san·i·ty
in·san·i·ties
in·san·i·tary
in·sa·ti·ate
in·sa·tia·ble
in·sa·tia·bil·i·ty
in·sa·tia·bly
in·scribe
in·scribed
in·scrib·ing
in·scrip·tion
in·scrip·tive
in·scru·ta·ble
in·scru·ta·bil·i·ty
in·scru·ta·bly
in·seam
in·sect
in·sec·ti·cide
in·sec·ti·cid·al
in·se·cure
in·se·cu·ri·ty
in·sem·i·nate
in·sem·i·nat·ed
in·sem·i·nat·ing
in·sem·i·na·tion
in·sen·sate
in·sen·si·ble
in·sen·si·bil·i·ty
in·sen·si·tive
in·sen·si·tiv·i·ty
in·sen·ti·ent
in·sep·a·ra·ble
in·sep·a·ra·bil·i·ty
in·sep·a·ra·bly
in·sert
in·sert·er
in·ser·tion
in·set
in·set·ting
in·shore
in·side
in·sid·er
in·sid·i·ous
in·sight
in·sig·nia
in·sig·nif·i·cant
in·sig·nif·i·cance
in·sin·cere
in·sin·cer·i·ty
in·sin·cer·i·ties
in·sin·u·ate
in·sin·u·at·ed
in·sin·u·at·ing
in·sin·u·a·tor
in·sin·u·a·tion
in·sip·id
in·si·pid·i·ty
in·sip·id·ness
in·sist
in·sist·ence
in·sist·ent
in·so·bri·e·ty

in·so·cia·ble
in·so·cia·bil·i·ty
in·so·cia·bly
in·so·far
in·so·lent
in·so·lence
in·sol·u·ble
in·sol·u·bil·i·ty
in·sol·u·bly
in·solv·a·ble
in·sol·vent
in·sol·ven·cy
in·som·nia
in·som·ni·ac
in·so·much
in·sou·ci·ant
in·sou·ci·ance
in·spect
in·spec·tion
in·spec·tor
in·spire
in·spired
in·spir·ing
in·spi·ra·tion
in·spir·it
in·sta·ble
in·sta·bil·i·ty
in·stall
in·stalled
in·stall·ing
in·stal·la·tion
in·stall·ment
in·stance
in·stant
in·stan·ta·ne·ous
in·state
in·stat·ed
in·stat·ing
in·state·ment
in·stead
in·step
in·sti·gate
in·sti·gat·ed
in·sti·gat·ing
in·sti·ga·tion
in·sti·ga·tor
in·still
in·stilled
in·still·ing
in·stil·la·tion
in·stinct
in·stinc·tive
in·stinc·tu·al
in·sti·tute
in·sti·tut·ed
in·sti·tut·ing
in·sti·tu·tion
in·sti·tu·tion·al
in·sti·tu·tion·al·ism
in·sti·tu·tion·al·ize
in·sti·tu·tion·al·ized
in·sti·tu·tion·al·iz·ing
in·struct
in·struc·tion
in·struc·tive
in·struc·tor
in·stru·ment
in·stru·men·tal
in·stru·men·ta·list
in·stru·men·ta·tion
in·sub·or·di·nate
in·sub·or·di·na·tion
in·sub·stan·tial
in·sub·stan·ti·al·i·ty
in·suf·fer·a·ble
in·suf·fer·a·bly
in·suf·fi·cient
in·suf·fi·cience

in·suf·fi·cien·cy
in·su·lar
in·su·lar·i·ty
in·su·late
in·su·lat·ed
in·su·lat·ing
in·su·la·tion
in·su·la·tor
in·su·lin
in·sult
in·sup·port·a·ble
in·sup·press·i·ble
in·sure
in·sured
in·sur·ing
in·sur·a·ble
in·sur·a·bil·i·ty
in·sur·ance
in·sur·gent
in·sur·gence
in·sur·gen·cy
in·sur·mount·a·ble
in·sur·rec·tion
in·sus·cep·ti·ble
in·tact
in·ta·glio
in·take
in·tan·gi·ble
in·tan·gi·bil·i·ty
in·tan·gi·ble·ness
in·tan·gi·bly
in·te·ger
in·te·gral
in·te·grate
in·te·grat·ed
in·te·grat·ing
in·te·grant
in·te·gra·tion
in·teg·ri·ty
in·tel·lect
in·tel·lec·tu·al
in·tel·lec·tu·al·ism
in·tel·lec·tu·al·ize
in·tel·lec·tu·al·ly
in·tel·li·gent
in·tel·li·gence
in·tel·li·gent·sia
in·tel·li·gi·ble
in·tel·li·gi·bil·i·ty
in·tel·li·gi·bly
in·tem·per·ate
in·tem·per·ance
in·tend
in·tend·ant
in·tense
in·tense·ness
in·ten·si·fy
in·ten·si·fied
in·ten·si·fy·ing
in·ten·si·fi·ca·tion
in·ten·sion
in·ten·si·ty
in·ten·si·ties
in·ten·sive
in·tent
in·ten·tion
in·ten·tion·al·ly
in·ter
in·terred
in·ter·ring
in·ter·ment
in·ter·act
in·ter·ac·tion
in·ter·ac·tive
in·ter·breed
in·ter·bred
in·ter·breed·ing
in·ter·ca·late

in·ter·cede
in·ter·ced·ed
in·ter·ced·ing
in·ter·cept
in·ter·cept·or
in·ter·cep·tion
in·ter·ces·sion
in·ter·ces·sor
in·ter·change
in·ter·changed
in·ter·chang·ing
in·ter·change·a·ble
in·ter·change·a·bil·i·ty
in·ter·col·le·gi·ate
in·ter·com
in·ter·com·mu·ni·cate
in·ter·com·mu·ni·cat·ed
in·ter·com·mu·ni·cat·ing
in·ter·com·mu·ni·ca·tion
in·ter·con·nect
in·ter·con·nec·tion
in·ter·con·ti·nen·tal
in·ter·course
in·ter·cul·tur·al
in·ter·de·nom·i·na·tion·al
in·ter·de·part·men·tal
in·ter·de·pend·ent
in·ter·de·pend·ence
in·ter·dict
in·ter·dic·tion
in·ter·dis·ci·pli·nary
in·ter·est
in·ter·est·ed
in·ter·est·ing
in·ter·face
in·ter·faith
in·ter·fere
in·ter·fered
in·ter·fer·ing
in·ter·fer·ence
in·ter·fer·on
in·ter·ga·lac·tic
in·ter·im
in·te·ri·or
in·ter·ject
in·ter·jec·tion
in·ter·jec·to·ry
in·ter·lay·er
in·ter·leaf
in·ter·leave
in·ter·line
in·ter·link
in·ter·lock
in·ter·lo·cu·tion
in·ter·loc·u·tor
in·ter·loc·u·to·ry
in·ter·lope
in·ter·loped
in·ter·lop·ing
in·ter·lop·er
in·ter·lude
in·ter·lu·nar
in·ter·lu·na·ry
in·ter·mar·ry
in·ter·mar·riage
in·ter·me·di·ate
in·ter·me·di·at·ing
in·ter·me·di·a·tion
in·ter·me·di·ary
in·ter·me·di·a·tor
in·ter·mi·na·ble
in·ter·min·gle
in·ter·min·gled
in·ter·min·gling
in·ter·mis·sion
in·ter·mit
in·ter·mit·ted
in·ter·mit·ting

in·ter·mit·tence
in·ter·mit·ten·cy
in·ter·mit·tent
in·ter·mix
in·ter·mix·ture
in·tern
in·terne
in·ter·nal
in·ter·nal·ize
in·ter·nal·i·za·tion
in·ter·na·tion·al
in·ter·na·tion·al·i·ty
in·ter·na·tion·al·ly
in·ter·na·tion·al·ize
in·ter·na·tion·al·ized
in·ter·na·tion·al·iz·ing
in·ter·na·tion·al·i·za·tion
in·ter·na·tion·al·ism
in·tern·ee
in·tern·ist
in·tern·ment
in·ter·nun·cio
in·ter·of·fice
in·ter·pen·e·trate
in·ter·pen·e·tra·tion
in·ter·plan·e·tary
in·ter·play
in·ter·po·late
in·ter·po·la·tion
in·ter·po·la·tor
in·ter·pose
in·ter·posed
in·ter·pos·ing
in·ter·po·si·tion
in·ter·pret
in·ter·pret·er
in·ter·pre·tive
in·ter·pre·ta·tion
in·ter·ra·cial
in·ter·re·late
in·ter·re·lat·ed
in·ter·re·lat·ing
in·ter·ro·gate
in·ter·ro·gat·ed
in·ter·ro·gat·ing
in·ter·ro·ga·tion
in·ter·rog·a·tive
in·ter·rupt
in·ter·rup·tion
in·ter·scho·las·tic
in·ter·sect
in·ter·sec·tion
in·ter·space
in·ter·sperse
in·ter·spersed
in·ter·spers·ing
in·ter·sper·sion
in·ter·state
in·ter·stel·lar
in·ter·tid·al
in·ter·twine
in·ter·ur·ban
in·ter·val
in·ter·vene
in·ter·vened
in·ter·ven·ing
in·ter·ven·tion
in·ter·view
in·ter·weave
in·ter·wove
in·ter·weav·ing
in·ter·wo·ven
in·tes·tate
in·tes·tine
in·tes·ti·nal
in·ti·mate
in·ti·mat·ed
in·ti·mat·ing

in·ti·ma·tion
in·ti·mate
in·ti·mate·ness
in·ti·mate·ly
in·tim·i·date
in·tim·i·dat·ed
in·tim·i·dat·ing
in·tim·i·da·tion
in·to
in·tol·er·ant
in·tol·er·a·ble
in·tol·er·ance
in·tomb
in·to·nate
in·to·nat·ed
in·to·nat·ing
in·to·na·tion
in·tone
in·toned
in·ton·ing
in·tox·i·cate
in·tox·i·cat·ed
in·tox·i·cat·ing
in·tox·i·ca·tion
in·trac·ta·ble
in·trac·ta·bil·i·ty
in·tra·mu·ral
in·tra·mu·ral·ly
in·tran·si·gent
in·tran·si·gence
in·tran·si·gen·cy
in·tran·si·tive
in·tra·state
in·tra·u·ter·ine
in·tra·ve·nous
in·trench
in·trep·id
in·tre·pid·i·ty
in·tri·cate
in·tri·ca·cy
in·tri·ca·cies
in·trigue
in·trigued
in·tri·guing
in·trin·sic
in·trin·si·cal·ly
in·tro·duce
in·tro·duced
in·tro·duc·ing
in·tro·duc·tion
in·tro·duc·to·ry
in·tro·spect
in·tro·spec·tion
in·tro·spec·tive
in·tro·ver·sion
in·tro·vert
in·trude
in·trud·ed
in·trud·ing
in·trud·er
in·tru·sion
in·tu·i·tion
in·tu·i·tive
in·tu·mes·cent
in·tu·mes·cence
in·un·date
in·un·dat·ed
in·un·dat·ing
in·un·da·tion
in·ure
in·ured
in·ur·ing
in·vade
in·vad·ed
in·vad·ing
in·vad·er
in·va·lid
in·va·lid·ism

in·val·id
in·val·u·a·ble
in·var·i·a·ble
in·var·i·a·bil·i·ty
in·var·i·ant
in·va·sion
in·vec·tive
in·veigh
in·vei·gle
in·vent
in·ven·tion
in·ven·tive
in·ven·tor
in·ven·to·ry
in·ven·to·ries
in·ven·to·ried
in·ven·to·ry·ing
in·verse
in·ver·sion
in·vert·ed
in·vert
in·ver·te·brate
in·vest
in·ves·tor
in·ves·ti·gate
in·ves·ti·gat·ed
in·ves·ti·gat·ing
in·ves·ti·ga·tion
in·ves·ti·ture
in·vest·ment
in·vet·er·ate
in·vid·i·ous
in·vig·or·ate
in·vig·or·at·ed
in·vig·or·at·ing
in·vig·or·a·tion
in·vin·ci·ble
in·vin·ci·bil·i·ty
in·vin·ci·bly
in·vi·o·la·ble
in·vi·o·la·bil·i·ty
in·vi·o·la·bly
in·vi·o·late
in·vis·i·ble
in·vis·i·bil·i·ty
in·vite
in·vit·ed
in·vit·ing
in·vi·ta·tion
in·vo·ca·tion
in·voice
in·voke
in·voked
in·vok·ing
in·vol·un·tary
in·vol·un·tar·i·ly
in·vo·lute
in·vo·lu·tion
in·volve
in·volved
in·volv·ing
in·volve·ment
in·vul·ner·a·ble
in·vul·ner·a·bil·i·ty
in·ward
in·ward·ly
in·weave
in·wove
in·weaved
in·wov·en
in·weav·ing
in·wrought
io·dine
ion
ion·ic
ion·ize
ion·i·za·tion
ion·o·sphere

io·ta
ip·so fac·to
iras·ci·ble
iras·ci·bil·i·ty
irate
Ire·land
ir·i·des·cent
ir·i·des·cence
iris
iris·es
Irish·man
irk·some
iron
iron·er
iron·clad
iron·hand·ed
iron·heart·ed
iron·ic
iron·i·cal
iron·stone
iron·ware
iron·work
ir·ra·di·ate
ir·ra·di·at·ed
ir·ra·di·at·ing
ir·ra·di·a·tion
ir·rad·i·ca·ble
ir·ra·tion·al
ir·ra·tion·al·i·ty
ir·re·claim·a·ble
ir·rec·on·cil·a·ble
ir·rec·on·cil·a·bil·i·ty
ir·re·cov·er·a·ble
ir·re·deem·a·ble
ir·re·duc·i·ble
ir·ref·u·ta·ble
ir·reg·u·lar
ir·reg·u·lar·i·ty
ir·rel·e·vant
ir·rel·e·vance
ir·rel·e·van·cy
ir·re·li·gious
ir·re·me·di·a·ble
ir·re·mis·si·ble
ir·re·mov·a·ble
ir·rep·a·ra·ble
ir·re·place·a·ble
ir·re·press·i·ble
ir·re·proach·a·ble
ir·re·sist·i·ble
ir·re·sist·i·bil·i·ty
ir·res·o·lute
ir·res·o·lu·tion
ir·re·spec·tive
ir·re·spon·si·ble
ir·re·spon·si·bil·i·ty
ir·re·spon·sive
ir·re·triev·a·ble
ir·re·triev·a·bil·i·ty
ir·rev·er·ence
ir·rev·er·ent
ir·re·vers·i·ble
ir·re·vers·i·bil·i·ty
ir·rev·o·ca·ble
ir·rev·o·ca·bil·i·ty
ir·ri·gate
ir·ri·gat·ed
ir·ri·gat·ing
ir·ri·ga·tion
ir·ri·ta·ble
ir·ri·ta·bil·i·ty
ir·ri·tant
ir·ri·tate
ir·ri·tat·ed
ir·ri·tat·ing
ir·ri·ta·tion
ir·rupt
Is·lam

Is·lam·ic
Is·lam·ism
is·land
isle
is·let
iso·bar
iso·late
iso·lat·ed
iso·lat·ing
iso·la·tion
iso·la·tion·ist
iso·met·ric
iso·met·ri·cal
isos·ce·les
iso·therm
iso·ther·mal
iso·ton·ic
iso·tope
iso·top·ic
Is·ra·el
Is·rae·li
is·sue
is·sued
is·su·ing
is·su·ance
isth·mus
Ital·ian
ital·ic
ital·i·cize
ital·i·cized
ital·i·ciz·ing
ital·i·ci·za·tion
It·a·ly
itch
itch·i·ness
itchy
item
item·ize
item·ized
item·iz·ing
it·er·ate
it·er·a·tion
itin·er·ant
itin·er·ate
itin·er·a·tion
itin·er·ary
itin·er·ar·ies
ivo·ry
ivy
ivied
ivies

J

jab
jabbed
jab·bing
jab·ber
jack·al
jack·ass
jack·et
jack·et·ed
jack·ham·mer
jack·knife
jack-of-all-trades
jack-o'-lan·tern
jack rab·bit
jade
jad·ed
jad·ing
jag
jagged
jag·ging
jag·uar
jail·bird
jail·break

ja·lopy
ja·lop·ies
jal·ou·sie
jam
jammed
jam·ming
jam·mer
jamb
jam·bo·ree
jan·gle
jan·gled
jan·gling
jan·i·tor
jan·i·to·ri·al
Jan·u·ary
Ja·pan
Jap·a·nese
jar
jarred
jar·ring
jar·ful
jar·di·niere
jar·gon
jas·mine
jaun·dice
jaun·diced
jaunt
jaun·ty
jaun·ti·ly
jaun·ti·ness
jave·lin
jaw·bone
jaw·break·er
jay·walk
jazz
jazzy
jazz·i·ly
jazz·i·ness
jeal·ous
jeal·ousy
jeal·ous·ies
jeer·er
Jef·fer·son
Je·ho·vah
Jek·yll
jel·li·fy
jel·ly
jel·ly·fish
jen·ny
jeop·ar·dy
jeop·ar·dize
jeop·ar·dized
jeop·ar·diz·ing
jerk
jerk·i·ly
jerk·i·ness
jerky
jer·kin
jer·ry·build
jer·ry·built
jer·sey
Je·ru·sa·lem
jes·sa·mine
jest·er
Jes·u·it
Je·sus
jet
jet·ted
jet·ting
jet·lin·er
jet-pro·pelled
jet·sam
jet·ti·son
jet·ty
jew·el
jew·el·er
jew·el·ry
Jew·ish

Jew·ry
jew's-harp
Jez·e·bel
jibe
jif·fy
jig
  jigged
  jig·ging
jig·gle
  jig·gled
  jig·gling
  jig·gly
jilt·er
Jim Crow·ism
jim-dan·dy
jim·my
  jim·mied
  jim·my·ing
jin·gle
  jin·gled
  jin·gling
jin·go·ism
jin·rik·i·sha
jinx
jit·ney
jit·ter
  jit·ters
  jit·tery
jit·ter·bug
  jit·ter·bug·ging
job
  jobbed
  job·bing
job·ber
job·hold·er
jock·ey
  jock·ey·ing
jock·strap
jo·cose
  jo·cos·i·ty
joc·u·lar
  joc·u·lar·i·ty
joc·und
  jo·cun·di·ty
jodh·pur
jog
  jogged
  jog·ging
  jog·ger
jog·gle
  jog·gled
  jog·gling
join·er
joint
  joint·ed
  joint·ly
joist
joke
  joked
  jok·ing
  joke·ster
jol·ly
jolt
  jolt·ing·ly
  jolty
jon·quil
jos·tle
  jos·tled
  jos·tling
jot
  jot·ted
  jot·ting
joule
jour·nal·ism
jour·nal·ist
  jour·nal·is·tic
jour·ney
joust

jo·vi·al
  jo·vi·al·i·ty
jowl
joy·ful
joy·less
joy·ous
joy·ride
ju·bi·lant
  ju·bi·lance
  ju·bi·la·tion
ju·bi·lee
Ju·da·ism
Ju·da·ic
  Ju·da·i·cal
judge
  judged
  judg·ing
  judg·ment
ju·di·cial
ju·di·ci·ary
ju·di·cious
ju·do
jug·ger·naut
jug·gle
  jug·gled
  jug·gling
  jug·gler
jug·u·lar
juice
juic·er
juicy
  juic·i·er
  juic·i·ness
ju·jit·su
ju·jube
juke·box
ju·lep
ju·li·enne
jum·ble
  jum·bled
  jum·bling
jum·bo
jump
  jump·ing
  jump·i·ness
  jumpy
junc·tion
  junc·ture
jun·gle
jun·ior
ju·ni·per
junk
  junky
junk·et
junk·ie
jun·ta
Ju·pi·ter
ju·ris·dic·tion
  ju·ris·dic·tion·al
ju·ris·pru·dence
  ju·ris·pru·dent
  ju·ris·pru·den·tial
ju·rist
ju·ror
ju·ry
  ju·ries
just
  just·ness
jus·tice
  jus·tice·less
jus·ti·fy
  jus·ti·fied
  jus·ti·fy·ing
  jus·ti·fi·a·ble
  jus·ti·fi·ca·to·ry
  jus·ti·fi·ca·tion
jut
  jut·ted

jut·ting
jute
ju·ve·nes·cent
ju·ve·nile
  ju·ve·nil·i·ty
jux·ta·pose
  jux·ta·posed
  jux·ta·pos·ing
  jux·ta·po·si·tion

K

ka·bob
kai·ser
ka·lei·do·scope
  ka·lei·do·scop·ic
ka·mi·ka·ze
kan·ga·roo
ka·o·lin
  ka·o·line
ka·pok
ka·put
kar·a·kul
kar·at
ka·ra·te
kar·ma
ka·ty·did
kay·ak
kayo
kedge
  kedged
  kedg·ing
keel·haul
keel·son
keen·ly
  keen·ness
keep
  kept
  keep·ing
keep·sake
keg·ler
kelp
ken·nel
  ken·neled
ke·no
ker·a·tin
ker·chief
ker·nel
ker·o·sene
kes·trel
ketch·up
ke·tone
ket·tle·drum
key
  keyed
key·board
key·hole
key·note
  key·not·ing
key·stone
khaki
kha·lif
khan
kib·butz
  kib·but·zim
kib·itz·er
kick·back
kick·off
kid
  kid·dish
  kid·dish·ness
  kid·ded
  kid·ding
kid·nap
  kid·naped
  kid·napped
  kid·nap·ing

kid·nap·ping
  kid·nap·er
  kid·nap·per
kid·ney
kill·deer
kill·ing
kill·joy
kiln
kilo
kil·o·cy·cle
kil·o·gram
kil·o·li·ter
kil·o·me·ter
kil·o·volt
kil·o·watt
kilt
kilt·er
ki·mo·no
kin·der·gar·ten
kind·heart·ed
kin·dle
  kin·dled
  kin·dling
kind·ly
  kind·li·est
  kind·li·ness
kin·dred
kin·e·mat·ics
  kin·e·mat·ic
  kin·e·mat·i·cal
kin·e·scope
ki·net·ic
  ki·net·ics
kin·folk
king·bolt
king·dom
king·fish·er
king·ly
  king·li·ness
king·pin
king·size
  king·sized
kinky
  kink·i·est
kins·folk
kin·ship
kins·man
  kins·wom·an
ki·osk
kip·per
kis·met
kiss·a·ble
kitch·en
kitch·en·ette
kitch·en·ware
kite
  kit·ed
  kit·ing
kit·ten
kit·ten·ish
kit·ty
  kit·ties
kit·ty-cor·ner
ki·wi
klatch
klep·to·ma·nia
  klep·to·ma·ni·ac
knack
knap·sack
knave
  knav·ish
knead
knee
  kneed
  knee·ing
knee·cap
knee·deep
kneel

knelt
  kneeled
  kneel·ing
knell
knick·ers
  knick·er·bock·ers
knick·knack
knife
  knives
  knifed
  knif·ing
knight
  knight·hood
  knight·ly
knight-er·rant
knit
  knit·ted
  knit·ting
knob
  knobbed
  knob·by
  knob·bi·er
knock
  knock·down
  knock·er
knock-kneed
  knock·out
knoll
knot
  knot·ted
  knot·ting
  knot·less
  knot·ty
knot·hole
knout
know
  knew
  known
  know·ing
  know·a·ble
  know·ing·ly
know-how
knowl·edge
  knowl·edge·a·ble
know-noth·ing
knuck·le
  knuck·led
  knuck·ling
knurl
  knurled
  knurly
ko·a·la
kohl·ra·bi
ko·la
ko·lin·sky
kook
  kooky
  kook·i·er
kook·a·bur·ra
Ko·ran
Ko·rea
ko·sher
Krem·lin
krim·mer
Krish·na
kryp·ton
Ku·blai Khan
ku·dos
ku·miss
küm·mel
kum·mer·bund
kum·quat

L

la·bel
  la·beled

la·bel·ing
la·bel·er
la·bi·al
la·bi·ate
la·bile
la·bi·o·den·tal
la·bi·um
la·bor
la·bor·er
lab·o·ra·to·ry
la·bored
la·bo·ri·ous
la·bo·ri·ous·ly
la·bor-sav·ing
la·bur·num
lab·y·rinth
lab·y·rin·thine
lab·y·rin·thi·an
lace
laced
lac·ing
lacy
lac·i·est
lac·er·ate
lac·er·at·ed
lac·er·at·ing
lac·er·a·tion
lach·ry·mal
lach·ry·mose
lach·ry·mose·ly
lack·a·dai·si·cal
lack·ey
lack·lus·ter
la·con·ic
la·con·i·cal·ly
lac·quer
la·crosse
lac·tate
lac·tat·ed
lac·tat·ing
lac·ta·tion
lac·te·al
lac·tic
lac·tose
la·cu·na
la·cus·trine
lad·der
lad·die
lade
lad·ed
lad·en
lad·ing
la·dle
la·dled
la·dling
la·dy·bug
la·dy·fin·ger
la·dy-in-wait·ing
la·dy-kil·ler
la·dy's-slip·per
lag
lagged
lag·ging
lag·gard
la·ger
la·gniappe
la·goon
La Guar·dia
lair
lais·sez faire
la·i·ty
lake·side
lal·la·tion
lam
lammed
lam·ming
la·ma
la·ma·sery

La·ma·ism
La·ma·ist
lam·baste
lam·bast·ed
lam·bast·ing
lam·bent
lam·bent·ly
lam·bre·quin
lamb·skin
lame
lamed
lam·ing
lame·ness
la·mé
la·ment
lam·en·ta·ble
lam·en·ta·bly
lam·en·ta·tion
lam·i·nate
lam·i·nat·ed
lam·i·nat·ing
lam·i·na·tion
lamp·black
lam·poon
lam·prey
lance
lanced
lanc·ing
lan·ce·o·late
lan·cet
lan·dau
land·ed
land·fall
land·hold·er
land·ing
land·la·dy
land·locked
land·lord
land·lub·ber
land·mark
land·own·er
land·scape
land·scap·ing
land·scap·er
land·slide
land·ward
lang·syne
lan·guage
lan·guid
lan·guish
lan·guish·ing
lan·guor
lan·guor·ous
lank·ness
lanky
lank·i·ness
lan·o·lin
lan·tern
lan·yard
lap
lapped
lap·ping
la·pel
lap·ful
lap·i·dary
lap·in
lap·is   laz·u·li
lap·pet
lapse
lapsed
laps·ing
lar·board
lar·ce·ny
lar·ce·nous
larch
lar·der
large
larg·er

larg·est
large·ness
large·ly
large-scale
lar·gess
lar·ghet·to
lar·go
lar·i·at
lark·spur
lar·va
lar·ynx
la·ryn·ge·al
la·ryn·gi·tis
las·civ·i·ous
las·civ·i·ous·ly
la·ser
lash
lash·ing
las·si·tude
las·so
last·ing
last·ly
latch·key
late
lat·er
lat·est
late·ness
late·ly
la·teen
la·tent
la·ten·cy
la·tent·ly
lat·er·al
lat·er·al·ly
la·tex
lath
lath·ing
lathe
lath·er
lath·ery
Lat·in-A·mer·i·can
lat·i·tude
lat·i·tu·di·nal
lat·i·tu·di·nar·i·an
la·trine
lat·ter
Lat·ter-day Saint
lat·tice
lat·ticed
lat·tic·ing
lat·tice·work
laud·a·ble
laud·a·bly
lau·da·num
laud·a·to·ry
laud·a·tive
laugh
laugh·ing
laugh·a·ble
laugh·a·bly
laugh·ter
launch
launch·er
laun·der
laun·dress
Laun·dro·mat
laun·dry
lau·re·ate
lau·rel
la·va
lav·a·liere
lav·a·to·ry
lav·a·to·ries
lav·en·der
lav·ish
lav·ish·ness
law-a·bid·ing
law·break·er

law·ful
law·ful·ly
law·ful·ness
law·less
law·less·ness
law·mak·er
law·mak·ing
lawn
law·suit
law·yer
lax
lax·i·ty
lax·ness
lax·a·tive
lay
laid
laying
lay·er
lay·ette
lay·man
lay·off
lay·out
lay·o·ver
la·zy
la·zi·est
la·zi·ly
la·zi·ness
leach
lead
led
lead·ing
lead·en
lead·er
lead·er·ship
leaf·age
leaf·less
leaf·let
leaf·stalk
leafy
leaf·i·ness
league
leak
leak·age
leak·i·ness
leaky
lean
lean·ness
lean·ing
lean-to
leap
leaped
leapt
leap·ing
learn
learned
learnt
learn·ing
learn·er
lease
leased
leas·ing
leash
least·wise
least·ways
leath·er
leath·er·neck
leath·ery
leave
left
leav·ing
leav·en
leaves
leave-tak·ing
Leb·a·nese
Leb·a·non
lech·er
lech·er·ous
lech·ery

lec·tern
lec·ture
lec·tured
lec·tur·ing
lec·tur·er
ledge
ledg·er
leech
leek
leer·ing·ly
leery
lee·ward
lee·way
left-hand·ed
left·ist
left·o·ver
left-wing
leg
legged
leg·ging
leg·a·cy
leg·a·cies
le·gal
le·gal·ly
le·gal·ism
le·gal·ist
le·gal·is·tic
le·gal·i·ty
le·gal·i·ties
le·gal·ize
le·gal·ized
le·gal·iz·ing
le·gal·i·za·tion
leg·ate
leg·a·tee
le·ga·tion
le·ga·to
leg·end
leg·end·ary
leg·er·de·main
leg·gy
leg·horn
leg·i·ble
leg·i·bil·i·ty
leg·i·bly
le·gion
le·gion·ary
le·gion·naire
leg·is·late
leg·is·lat·ed
leg·is·lat·ing
leg·is·la·tive
leg·is·la·tor
leg·is·la·tion
leg·is·la·ture
le·git·i·mate
le·git·i·mat·ed
le·git·i·mat·ing
le·git·i·ma·cy
le·git·i·mate·ly
le·git·i·mize
le·git·i·mized
le·git·i·miz·ing
leg·ume
le·gu·mi·nous
lei
leis
lei·sure
lei·sure·ly
lei·sure·li·ness
leit·mo·tif
lem·ming
lem·on
lem·on·ade
le·mur
lend
lent
lend·ing

length
length·en
length·wise
lengthy
length·i·ly
length·i·ness
le·ni·ent
le·ni·ence
le·ni·en·cy
len·i·tive
len·i·ty
lens
Lent·en
len·til
le·o·nine
leop·ard
le·o·tard
lep·er
lep·ro·sy
lep·rous
lep·re·chaun
les·bi·an
les·bi·an·ism
le·sion
les·see
less·en
less·er
les·son
les·sor
least
let
let·ting
le·thal
le·thal·ly
leth·ar·gy
le·thar·gic
le·thar·gi·cal
let·ter
let·ter·er
let·tered
let·ter·head
let·ter·ing
let·ter-per·fect
let·ter·press
let·tuce
leu·ke·mia
leu·ko·cyte
lev·ee
lev·el
lev·eled
lev·el·ing
lev·el·ness
lev·el-head·ed
lev·er
lev·er·age
le·vi·a·than
lev·i·tate
lev·i·tat·ed
lev·i·tat·ing
lev·i·ta·tion
lev·i·ty
levy
lev·ies
lewd
lewd·ly
lewd·ness
lex·i·cog·ra·phy
lex·i·cog·ra·pher
lex·i·co·graph·ic
lex·i·con
li·a·bil·i·ty
li·a·bil·i·ties
li·a·ble
li·ai·son
li·ar
li·ba·tion
li·bel
li·beled

li·bel·ing
li·bel·er
li·bel·ous
lib·er·al
lib·er·al·ly
lib·er·al·i·ty
lib·er·al·ism
lib·er·al·ize
lib·er·al·ized
lib·er·al·iz·ing
lib·er·al·i·za·tion
lib·er·ate
lb·er·at·ed
lib·er·at·ing
lib·er·a·tion
lib·er·a·tor
lib·er·tine
lib·er·tin·ism
lib·er·ty
lib·er·ties
li·bid·i·nous
li·bid·i·nous·ness
li·bi·do
li·bid·in·al
li·brary
li·brar·ies
li·brar·i·an
li·bret·to
lice
louse
li·cense
li·censed
li·cens·ing
li·cen·see
li·cens·er
li·cen·ti·ate
li·cen·tious·ness
li·chen
lic·it
lick·e·ty-split
lic·o·rice
lid·ded
lie
lay
lain
lay·ing
lie
lied
ly·ing
Lieb·frau·milch
Lie·der·kranz
lien
lieu
lieu·ten·ant
lieu·ten·an·cy
life·blood
life·boat
life·guard
life·less
life·like
life·line
life·sav·er
life-size
life-style
life·time
life·work
lift-off
lig·a·ment
lig·a·ture
light·en
light·er
light-fin·gered
light·foot·ed
light-head·ed
light·heart·ed
light·house
light·ing
light·ly

light-mind·ed
light·ning
light·weight
light-year
lig·nite
like
liked
lik·ing
like·a·ble
like·li·hood
like·ly
like·li·est
lik·en
like·ness
like·wise
li·lac
lilt·ing
lily
limb
lim·ber
lim·bo
Lim·burg·er
lime
limed
lim·ing
limy
lime·light
lim·er·ick
lime·stone
lim·it
lim·it·a·ble
lim·i·ta·tive
lim·i·ta·tion
lim·it·ed
lim·it·less
lim·ou·sine
limp
limp·ing·ly
limp·ly
lim·pet
lim·pid
lim·pid·ness
Lin·coln
lin·den
line
lined
lin·ing
lin·age
lin·er
lin·e·age
lin·e·al
lin·e·a·ment
lin·e·ar
line·back·er
line·man
lin·en
lin·ger
lin·ger·ing·ly
lin·ge·rie
lin·go
lin·gua fran·ca
lin·gual
lin·guist
lin·guis·tics
lin·guis·tic
lin·i·ment
link
linked
link·er
link·age
lin·net
li·no·le·um
lin·seed
lint
linty
lint·i·er
lin·tel
li·on

li·on·ess
li·on·heart·ed
li·on·ize
li·on·ized
li·on·iz·ing
li·on·i·za·tion
lip·py
lip·stick
liq·ue·fy
liq·ue·fied
liq·ue·fy·ing
liq·ue·fac·tion
liq·ue·fi·a·ble
li·queur
liq·uid
li·quid·i·ty
liq·uid·ness
liq·ui·date
liq·ui·dat·ed
liq·ui·dat·ing
liq·ui·da·tion
liq·ui·da·tor
liq·uor
lisle
lisp
lis·some
lis·some·ness
list
list·ing
lis·ten
lis·ten·er
list·less
lit·a·ny
lit·a·nies
li·tchi
li·ter
lit·er·al
lit·er·al·i·ty
lit·er·al·ly
lit·er·al·ism
lit·er·ary
lit·er·ar·i·ness
lit·er·ate
lit·er·a·cy
lit·er·a·ti
lit·er·a·ture
lithe
lithe·some
li·thog·ra·phy
li·thog·ra·pher
lith·o·graph·ic
lit·i·gate
lit·i·gat·ed
lit·i·gat·ing
lit·i·ga·tion
lit·mus
lit·ter
lit·ter·bug
lit·tle
lit·to·ral
lit·ur·gy
lit·ur·gist
li·tur·gic
li·tur·gi·cal
liv·a·ble
live·a·ble
live·li·hood
live·ly
live·li·est
live·li·ness
liv·en
liv·er
liv·er·wurst
liv·ery
liv·er·ied
live·stock
liv·id
liv·id·i·ty

liv·id·ly
liv·ing
liz·ard
lla·ma
lla·no
load
load·ed
loaf
loaves
loamy
loath
loathe
loathed
loath·ing
loath·some
lob
lobbed
lob·bing
lob·by
lob·bies
lob·by·ist
lobe
lo·bar
lobed
lob·ster
lo·cal
lo·cal·ly
lo·cale
lo·cal·i·ty
lo·cal·i·ties
lo·cal·ize
lo·cal·ized
lo·cal·iz·ing
lo·cal·i·za·tion
lo·cate
lo·cat·ed
lo·cat·ing
lo·ca·tion
lo·ca·tor
lock·a·ble
lock·er
lock·et
lock·jaw
lock·out
lock·smith
lock·up
lo·co·mo·tion
lo·co·mo·tive
lo·cus
lo·ci
lo·cust
lo·cu·tion
lode·star
lode·stone
lodge
lodged
lodg·ing
lodg·er
lodg·ment
lofty
loft·i·est
loft·i·ly
loft·i·ness
lo·gan·ber·ry
log·a·rithm
log·a·rith·mic
loge
log·ger
log·ger·head
log·ic
lo·gi·cian
log·i·cal
log·i·cal·ly
log·i·cal·ness
lo·gis·tics
lo·gis·tic
lo·gis·ti·cal
log·roll·ing

lo·gy
loin·cloth
loi·ter
  loi·ter·er
lone·ly
lone·li·ness
  lone·some
lon·er
lon·gev·i·ty
long·hair
long·hand
long·ing
lon·gi·tude
  lon·gi·tu·di·nal
long-lived
long-play·ing
long-range
long·shore·man
long-suf·fer·ing
long-term
long-wind·ed
look·out
loony
  loon·ies
  loon·i·est
  loon·i·ness
loop·hole
loose
  loosed
  loos·ing
  loos·er
  loos·est
  loose·ness
  loos·en
loot·er
lop
  lopped
  lop·ping
lope
  loped
  lop·ing
  lop·er
lop·sid·ed
lo·qua·cious
  lo·qua·cious·ness
  lo·quac·i·ty
lord·ly
  lord·li·est
  lord·li·ness
lor·gnette
lor·ry
lose
  lost
  los·ing
  los·a·ble
  los·er
lot
  lot·ted
  lot·ting
lo·tion
lot·tery
lo·tus
loud
  loud·ness
loud-mouthed
loud·speak·er
lounge
  lounged
  loung·ing
lousy
  lous·i·ness
lout
  lout·ish·ness
lou·ver
love
  loved
  lov·ing
  lov·a·ble

lov·a·bil·i·ty
lov·a·ble·ness
lov·a·bly
love·less
love·ly
  love·li·er
  love·li·est
lov·er
lov·ing
  lov·ing·ness
low·born
low·boy
low·brow
low-down
low·er
low·er-case
low·er·ing
low·keyed
low·land
low-lev·el
low·ly
  low·li·est
  low·li·ness
low-mind·ed
low-pres·sure
low-ten·sion
loy·al
  loy·al·ist
  loy·al·ly
  loy·al·ty
  loy·al·ties
loz·enge
lu·au
lub·ber
lu·bri·cate
  lu·bri·cat·ed
  lu·bri·cat·ing
  lu·bri·cant
  lu·bri·ca·tion
  lu·bri·ca·tor
lu·bri·cious
lu·cid
  lu·cid·i·ty
  lu·cid·ness
luck
  luck·i·est
  luck·i·ly
  luck·i·ness
  lucky
lu·cra·tive
  lu·cra·tive·ness
lu·cre
lu·cu·brate
  lu·cu·bra·tion
lu·di·crous
  lu·di·crous·ness
lug
  lugged
  lug·ging
lug·gage
lug·ger
lu·gu·bri·ous
luke·warm
lull·a·by
  lull·a·bies
lum·ba·go
lum·bar
lum·ber
lum·ber·ing
lum·ber·jack
lu·men
lu·mi·nary
  lu·mi·nar·ies
lu·mi·nous
  lu·mi·nous·ness
lu·mi·nes·cence
lu·mi·nes·cent
lum·mox

lumpy
  lump·i·est
  lump·i·ness
lu·nar
lu·nate
lu·na·tic
  lu·na·cy
  lu·na·cies
lunch
  lunch·eon
lunge
  lunged
  lung·ing
lunk·head
lu·pine
lurch
lure
  lured
  lur·ing
lu·rid
  lu·rid·ly
  lu·rid·ness
lurk
  lurk·er
lus·cious
  lus·cious·ly
  lus·cious·ness
lush
  lush·ness
·lust
  lust·ful·ness
lus·ter
  lus·ter·less
  lus·trous
lusty
  lust·i·ly
  lust·i·ness
Lu·ther·an
lux·u·ri·ate
  lux·u·ri·at·ed
  lux·u·ri·at·ing
  lux·u·ri·a·tion
lux·u·ry
  lux·u·ries
  lux·u·ri·ous
  lux·u·ri·ant
  lux·u·ri·ance
ly·ce·um
ly·ing
lymph
  lym·phat·ic
lynch
  lynch·ing
lynx
lyre
ly·ric
  lyr·i·cal
  lyr·i·cism
  lyr·i·cist

M

ma·ca·bre
mac·ad·am
  mac·ad·am·ize
ma·caque
mac·a·ro·ni
mac·a·roon
ma·caw
mace
  maced
  mac·ing
mac·er·ate
  mac·er·at·ed
  mac·er·at·ing
  mac·er·a·tion
Mach

ma·chete
Mach·i·a·vel·li·an
mach·i·nate
  mach·i·nat·ed
  mach·i·nat·ing
  mach·i·na·tion
ma·chine
  ma·chined
  ma·chin·ing
  ma·chin·ery
  ma·chin·ist
mack·er·el
mack·i·naw
mack·in·tosh
mac·ra·mé
mac·ro·cosm
ma·cron
mac·ro·scop·ic
mad
  mad·den
  mad·dest
  mad·ly
  mad·ness
mad·am
  mad·ame
  mes·dames
Ma·dei·ra
mad·e·moi·selle
Ma·don·na
mad·ras
mad·ri·gal
mael·strom
maes·tro
Ma·fia
mag·a·zine
ma·gen·ta
mag·got
  mag·goty
mag·ic
  mag·i·cal
  ma·gi·cian
mag·is·trate
mag·is·te·ri·al
  mag·is·tra·cy
  mag·is·tra·cies
mag·ma
Mag·na Car·ta
mag·nan·i·mous
  mag·na·nim·i·ty
mag·nate
mag·ne·sia
mag·ne·si·um
mag·net
  mag·net·ic
  mag·net·i·cal·ly
  mag·net·ism
mag·net·ize
  mag·net·ized
  mag·net·iz·ing
mag·ne·to
mag·ne·tom·e·ter
mag·nif·i·cent
  mag·nif·i·cence
  mag·nif·i·cent·ly
mag·ni·fy
  mag·ni·fied
  mag·ni·fy·ing
  mag·ni·fi·ca·tion
  mag·ni·fi·er
mag·nil·o·quent
mag·ni·tude
mag·no·lia
mag·num
mag·pie
ma·ha·ra·jah
  ma·ha·ra·ni
ma·hat·ma
mah-jongg

ma·hog·a·ny
ma·hout
maid·en
maid·en·hair
maid·en·head
mail·a·ble
mail·box
mail·man
maim
main·land
main·ly
main·mast
main·sail
main·spring
main·stream
main·tain
  main·tain·a·ble
  main·te·nance
maî·tre d'hô·tel
maize
ma·jes·tic
  ma·jes·ti·cal
maj·es·ty
ma·jol·i·ca
ma·jor
ma·jor-do·mo
  ma·jor-do·mos
ma·jor·i·ty
  ma·jor·i·ties
make
  mak·a·ble
  ma·ker
  mak·ing
make-be·lieve
make·shift
make-up
mal·a·dapt·ed
  mal·ad·ap·ta·tion
mal·ad·just·ment
mal·ad·just·ed
mal·ad·min·is·ter
  mal·ad·min·is·tra·tion
mal·a·droit
  mal·a·droit·ness
mal·a·dy
  mal·a·dies
ma·laise
mal·a·prop
  mal·a·prop·ism
ma·lar·ia
  ma·lar·i·al
ma·lar·key
mal·con·tent
mal de mer
mal·e·dic·tion
  mal·e·dic·to·ry
mal·e·fac·tion
  mal·e·fac·tor
ma·lef·ic
ma·lef·i·cent
ma·lev·o·lent
  ma·lev·o·lence
  ma·lev·o·lent·ly
mal·fea·sance
  mal·fea·sant
mal·for·ma·tion
  mal·formed
mal·func·tion
mal·ice
ma·li·cious
  ma·li·cious·ly
ma·lign
  ma·lign·ly
ma·lig·nant
  ma·lig·nan·cy
  ma·lig·nan·cies
  ma·lig·nant·ly
ma·lin·ger

ma·lin·ger·er
mal·lard
mal·le·a·ble
  mal·le·a·bil·i·ty
  mal·le·a·ble·ness
mal·let
mal·low
mal·nour·ished
mal·nu·tri·tion
mal·oc·clu·sion
mal·o·dor
  mal·o·dor·ous
mal·prac·tice
  mal·prac·ti·tion·er
malt
  malty
mal·tose
mal·treat
  mal·treat·ment
mam·bo
mam·ma
  ma·ma
mam·mal
  mam·ma·li·an
mam·ma·ry
  mam·ma·ries
mam·mon
mam·moth
mam·my
man
  manned
  man·ning
man·a·cle
  man·a·cled
  man·a·cling
man·age
  man·aged
  man·ag·ing
  man·age·a·ble
  man·age·a·bil·i·ty
  man·age·a·ble·ness
  man·age·a·bly
  man·age·ment
man·ag·er
  man·ag·er·ship
  man·a·ge·ri·al
ma·ña·na
man·a·tee
man·da·mus
man·da·rin
man·date
  man·dat·ed
  man·dat·ing
  man·da·to·ry
  man·da·to·ri·ly
man·di·ble
man·do·lin
man·drake
man·drel
man·drill
man·eat·er
  man·eat·ing
ma·nege
ma·neu·ver
  ma·neu·ver·a·bil·i·ty
  ma·neu·ver·a·ble
man·ful
  man·ful·ly
man·ga·nese
mange
  man·gy
  man·gi·ness
man·ger
man·gle
  man·gled
  man·gling
man·go
man·grove

man·han·dle
Man·hat·tan
man·hole
man·hood
man·hour
man·hunt
ma·nia
  man·ic
ma·ni·ac
  ma·ni·a·cal
man·ic-de·pres·sive
man·i·cure
  man·i·cured
  man·i·cur·ing
  man·i·cur·ist
man·i·fest
  man·i·fest·ly
man·i·fes·ta·tion
man·i·fes·to
man·i·fold
man·i·kin
  man·a·kin
  man·ni·kin
ma·nil·la
ma·nip·u·late
  ma·nip·u·lat·ed
  ma·nip·u·lat·ing
  ma·nip·u·la·ble
  ma·nip·u·la·tion
  ma·nip·u·la·tive
  ma·nip·u·la·tor
  ma·nip·u·la·to·ry
man·kind
man·like
man·ly
  man·li·er
  man·li·ness
man-made
man·na
manned
man·ne·quin
man·ner
man·nered
man·ner·ism
man·ner·ly
man·nish
man-of-war
  men-of-war
ma·nom·e·ter
man·or
  ma·no·ri·al
man·pow·er
man·sard
man·sion
man-sized
man·slaugh·ter
man·slay·er
man·tel
  man·tle
man·til·la
man·tis
man·tle
man·u·al
  man·u·al·ly
man·u·fac·ture
  man·u·fac·tured
  man·u·fac·tur·ing
  man·u·fac·tur·er
man·u·mis·sion
ma·nure
man·u·script
many
  more
  most
man·y-sid·ed
map
  mapped
  map·ping

ma·ple
mar
  marred
  mar·ring
ma·ra·ca
mar·a·schi·no
mar·a·thon
ma·raud
  ma·raud·er
mar·ble
  mar·bled
  mar·bling
  mar·ble·ize
mar·cel
  mar·celled
  mar·cel·ling
march·er
mar·chion·ess
mar·ga·rine
mar·ga·ri·ta
mar·gin
  mar·gi·nal
  mar·gin·al·ly
mar·gue·rite
mar·i·gold
ma·ri·jua·na
ma·rim·ba
ma·ri·na
mar·i·nade
mar·i·nate
  mar·i·nat·ing
ma·rine
mar·i·ner
mar·i·on·ette
mar·i·tal
mar·i·time
mar·jo·ram
marked
  mark·ed·ly
mark·er
mar·ket
  mar·ket·a·ble
  mar·ket·a·bil·i·ty
  mar·ket·ing
  mar·ket·place
mark·ing
marks·man
  marks·man·ship
mar·lin
  mar·line
mar·ma·lade
mar·mo·set
mar·mot
ma·roon
mar·que·try
mar·quis
  mar·quess
  mar·quise
  mar·qui·sette
mar·riage
  mar·riage·a·ble
mar·row
  mar·rowy
  mar·row·bone
mar·ry
  mar·ried
  mar·ry·ing
mar·shal
  mar·shaled
  mar·shal·ing
marsh·mal·low
marshy
  marsh·i·ness
mar·su·pi·al
mar·tial
Mar·tian
mar·ten
mar·tin

mar·ti·ni
mar·tyr
  mar·tyr·dom
mar·vel
  mar·veled
  mar·vel·ing
  mar·vel·ous
Marx·ism
  Marx·ist
mar·zi·pan
mas·cara
mas·cot
mas·cu·line
  mas·cu·lin·i·ty
  mas·cu·lin·ize
mask
  masked
mas·och·ism
  mas·och·ist
  mas·och·is·tic
ma·son
  ma·son·ic
ma·son·ry
masque
mas·quer·ade
  mas·quer·ad·ing
Mas·sa·chu·setts
mas·sa·cre
  mas·sa·cred
  mas·sa·cring
mas·sage
  mas·saged
  mas·sag·ing
mas·seur
  mas·seuse
mas·sive
mass-pro·duce
  mass-pro·duc·tion
mas·tec·to·my
mas·ter
  mas·ter·ful
  mas·ter·mind
  mas·ter·piece
  mas·tery
mast·head
mas·ti·cate
  mas·ti·ca·ting
  mas·ti·ca·tion
mas·tiff
mas·to·don
mas·toid
mas·tur·bate
  mas·tur·ba·tion
mat
  mat·ted
  mat·ting
mat·a·dor
match·mak·ing
mate
  mat·ed
  mat·ing
ma·te·ri·al
  ma·te·ri·al·ly
ma·te·ri·al·ism
  ma·te·ri·al·ist
  ma·te·ri·al·is·tic
  ma·te·ri·al·is·ti·cal·ly
ma·te·ri·al·ize
  ma·te·ri·al·ized
  ma·te·ri·al·iz·ing
  ma·te·ri·al·iza·tion
ma·te·ri·el
ma·ter·nal
  ma·ter·nal·is·tic
  ma·ter·nal·ly
ma·ter·ni·ty
math·e·mat·ics
math·e·mat·i·cal

math·e·ma·ti·cian
mat·i·nee
ma·tri·arch
  ma·tri·ar·chal·ism
  ma·tri·ar·chy
mat·ri·cide
ma·tric·u·late
  ma·tric·u·lat·ed
  ma·tric·u·lat·ing
  ma·tric·u·lant
  ma·tric·u·la·tion
ma·tri·lin·e·al
mat·ri·mo·ny
  mat·ri·mo·ni·al
ma·trix
  ma·tri·ces
ma·tron
  ma·tron·ly
mat·ter
mat·ter-of-course
mat·ter-of-fact
mat·ting
mat·tress
ma·ture
  mat·u·rate
  mat·u·rat·ing
  mat·u·ra·tion
  ma·tu·ri·ty
mat·zo
maud·lin
maul
mau·so·le·um
mauve
mav·er·ick
mawk·ish
max·im
max·i·mal
max·i·mize
  max·i·mized
  max·i·miz·ing
max·i·mum
may·be
may·flow·er
may·hem
may·on·naise
may·or
  may·or·al
  may·or·al·ty
maze
  mazed
  maz·ing
  ma·zy
mead·ow
mead·ow·lark
mea·ger
  mea·ger·ness
mealy
  meal·i·ness
meal·y-mouthed
mean
  meant
  mean·ing
  mean·ing·ful
  mean·ing·ful·ly
  mean·ing·less
mean·ly
  mean·ness
me·an·der
mean·time
mean·while
mea·sles
mea·sly
  mea·sli·est
meas·ur·a·ble
  meas·ur·a·bil·i·ty
  meas·ur·a·bly
meas·ure
  meas·ur·er

meas·ured
meas·ure·ment
meat
  meaty
  meat·i·ness
mec·ca
me·chan·ic
me·chan·i·cal
me·chan·ics
mech·an·ism
mech·a·nis·tic
mech·a·nize
  mech·a·nized
  mech·a·niz·ing
  mech·a·ni·za·tion
med·al
  med·aled
  med·al·ist
me·dal·lion
med·dle
  med·dled
  med·dling
  med·dler
med·dle·some
me·dia
me·di·al
me·di·an
me·di·ate
  me·di·at·ed
  me·di·at·ing
  me·di·a·tion
  me·di·a·to·ry
  me·di·a·tor
med·ic
med·i·ca·ble
Med·i·caid
med·i·cal
  med·i·cal·ly
Med·i·care
med·i·cate
  med·i·cat·ed
  med·i·cat·ing
med·i·ca·tion
me·dic·i·nal
med·i·cine
me·di·e·val
  me·di·e·val·ism
me·di·o·cre
  me·di·oc·ri·ty
med·i·tate
  med·i·tat·ed
  med·i·tat·ing
  med·i·ta·tor
  med·i·ta·tion
  med·i·ta·tive
Med·i·ter·ra·ne·an
me·di·um
  me·dia
  me·di·ums
med·ley
meet
  met
  meet·ing
meet·ing·house
meg·a·cy·cle
meg·a·lo·ma·nia
  meg·a·lo·ma·ni·ac
meg·a·lop·o·lis
meg·a·phone
meg·a·ton
meg·a·watt
mel·an·choly
  mel·an·cho·lia
  mel·an·chol·ic
  mel·an·chol·i·ness
mé·lange
mel·a·no·ma
me·lee

mel·io·rate
mel·io·rat·ed
mel·io·rat·ing
mel·io·ra·ble
mel·io·ra·tion
mel·io·ra·tor
mel·lif·lu·ous
  mel·lif·lu·ent
mel·low
me·lo·de·on
mel·o·dra·ma
  mel·o·dra·mat·ic
  mel·o·dra·mat·i·cal·ly
mel·o·dy
  mel·o·dies
  me·lod·ic
  me·lod·i·cal·ly
  me·lo·di·ous
  me·lo·di·ous·ness
mel·on
melt
  melt·ed or mol·ten
  melt·ing
  melt·a·ble
mem·ber
  mem·ber·less
  mem·ber·ship
mem·brane
  mem·bra·nous
me·men·to
memo
mem·oir
mem·o·ra·bil·ia
mem·o·ra·ble
  mem·o·ra·bly
mem·o·ran·dum
me·mo·ri·al
  me·mo·ri·al·ly
  me·mo·ri·al·ize
  me·mo·ri·al·ized
  me·mo·ri·al·iz·ing
  me·mo·ri·al·i·za·tion
  me·mo·ri·al·ly
mem·o·rize
  mem·o·rized
  mem·o·riz·ing
  mem·o·ri·za·tion
mem·o·ry
  mem·o·ries
men·ace
  men·aced
  men·ac·ing
mé·nage
me·nag·er·ie
mend
  mend·a·ble
men·da·cious
  men·dac·i·ty
men·di·cant
me·ni·al
  me·ni·al·ly
men·in·gi·tis
me·nis·cus
Men·no·nite
men·o·pause
  men·o·pau·sal
men·sal
men·ses
men·stru·al
men·stru·a·tion
  men·stru·ate
  men·stru·at·ed
  men·stru·at·ing
men·su·ra·ble
men·su·ra·tion
men·tal
  men·tal·ly
  men·tal·i·ty

men·tal·i·ties
men·thol
  men·tho·lat·ed
men·tion
  men·tion·a·ble
men·tor
menu
me·phit·ic
mer·can·tile
mer·can·til·ism
mer·ce·nary
  mer·ce·nar·ies
mer·cer·ize
  mer·cer·ized
mer·chan·dise
  mer·chan·dised
  mer·chan·dis·ing
  mer·chan·dis·er
mer·chant
mer·cu·ri·al
mer·cu·ro·chrome
mer·cu·ry
mer·cy
  mer·cies
  mer·ci·ful
  mer·ci·ful·ly
  mer·ci·less
mere·ly
mer·e·tri·cious
  mer·e·tri·cious·ness
merge
  merged
  merg·ing
  mer·gence
merg·er
me·rid·i·an
me·ringue
mer·it
  mer·it·ed
  mer·it·ed·ly
  mer·it·less
  mer·i·to·ri·ous
mer·maid
mer·ry
  mer·ri·est
  mer·ri·ness
  mer·ri·ment
merry-go-round
  mer·ry·mak·er
  mer·ry·mak·ing
me·sa
mes·cal
mes·dames
mes·de·moi·selles
mesh·work
mes·mer·ism
  mes·mer·ic
  mes·mer·i·cal·ly
mes·mer·ize
  mes·mer·ized
  mes·mer·iz·ing
  mes·mer·i·za·tion
Meso·zo·ic
mes·quite
mess
  mess·i·ly
  mess·i·ness
  messy
mes·sage
mes·sen·ger
Mes·si·ah
Mes·si·an·ic
mes·sieurs
mes·ti·zo
me·tab·o·lism
  met·a·bol·ic
  met·a·bol·i·cal
me·tab·o·lize

me·tab·o·lized
me·tab·o·liz·ing
met·al
  met·aled
  met·al·ing
met·al·ize
  met·al·ized
  met·al·iz·ing
me·tal·lic
met·al·loid
met·al·lur·gy
  met·al·lur·gic
  met·al·lur·gi·cal
  met·al·lur·gist
met·al·work
met·a·mor·phism
  met·a·mor·phic
met·a·mor·phose
  met·a·mor·phosed
  met·a·mor·phos·ing
  met·a·mor·pho·sis
met·a·phor
  met·a·phor·ic
  met·a·phor·i·cal
met·a·phys·ic
  met·a·phys·ics
  met·a·phys·i·cal
met·a·tar·sus
Met·a·zo·a
mete
  met·ed
  met·ing
me·te·or
  me·te·or·ic
  me·te·or·ite
  me·te·or·oid
me·te·or·ol·o·gy
  me·te·or·o·log·i·cal
  me·te·or·ol·o·gist
me·ter
  me·tre
me·ter-kil·o·gram-sec·ond
meth·a·done
meth·ane
meth·a·nol
meth·od
  me·thod·i·cal
Meth·od·ist
meth·od·ize
meth·od·ol·o·gy
  meth·od·o·log·i·cal
  meth·od·ol·o·gist
me·tic·u·lous
  me·tic·u·los·i·ty
  me·tic·u·lous·ly
mé·tier
met·ric
met·ri·cal
  met·ri·cal·ly
met·ro
met·ro·nome
  met·ro·nom·ic
me·trop·o·lis
met·ro·pol·i·tan
met·tle
met·tle·some
Mex·i·can
Mex·i·co
mez·za·nine
mez·zo
mi·as·ma
mi·ca
Mi·chel·an·ge·lo
mi·cro·a·nal·y·sis
mi·crobe
  mi·cro·bi·al
  mi·cro·bi·ol·o·gy
  mi·cro·copy

mi·cro·cosm
mi·cro·fiche
mi·cro·film
mi·cro·gram
mi·cro·groove
mi·crom·e·ter
mi·cro·mi·cron
mi·cro·mil·li·me·ter
mi·cron
mi·cro·or·gan·ism
mi·cro·phone
mi·cro·pho·to·graph
mi·cro·read·er
mi·cro·scope
mi·cro·scop·ic
  mi·cro·scop·i·cal·ly
mi·cros·co·py
mi·cro·sec·ond
mi·cro·wave
mid·day
mid·dle
mid·dle-aged
mid·dle·man
mid·dle·weight
mid·dling
mid·dy
  mid·dies
midg·et
mid·land
mid·most
mid·night
mid·point
mid·riff
mid·sec·tion
mid·ship·man
midst
mid·sum·mer
mid·term
mid·way
mid·wife
mid·year
mien
mighty
  might·i·er
  might·i·est
  might·i·ly
  might·i·ness
mi·graine
mi·grant
mi·grate
  mi·grat·ed
  mi·grat·ing
  mi·gra·tion
  mi·gra·tor
  mi·gra·to·ry
mi·ka·do
mi·la·dy
  mi·la·dies
mild
  mild·ly
  mild·ness
mil·dew
  mil·dewy
mile·age
mil·er
mile·stone
mi·lieu
mil·i·tant
  mil·i·tan·cy
  mil·i·tant·ness
mil·i·ta·rism
  mil·i·ta·ris·tic
  mil·i·ta·ris·ti·cal·ly
  mil·i·ta·rize
  mil·i·ta·ri·za·tion
mil·i·tary
  mil·i·tar·i·ly
mi·li·tia

milk
milk·er
milky
milk·i·ness
milk·maid
milk·man
milk·weed
mil·len·ni·um
mil·len·nia
mil·len·ni·al
mill·er
mil·let
mil·li·gram
mil·li·li·ter
mil·li·me·ter
mil·li·ner
mil·li·nery
mill·ing
mil·lion
mil·lionth
mil·lion·aire
mil·li·sec·ond
mill·pond
mime
mimed
mim·ing
mim·er
mim·ic
mim·icked
mim·ick·ing
mim·i·cal
mim·ick·er
mim·ic·ry
mim·ic·ries
mi·mo·sa
min·a·ret
mi·na·to·ry
mince
minced
minc·ing
minc·er
minc·ing·ly
mince·meat
mind·ed
mind·less
min·er
mine·field
min·er·al
min·er·al·ize
min·er·al·ized
min·er·al·iz·ing
min·er·al·i·za·tion
min·er·al·o·gy
min·er·al·og·i·cal
min·er·al·o·gist
min·e·stro·ne
mine·sweep·er
min·gle
min·gled
min·gling
min·i·a·ture
min·i·a·tur·ize
min·i·a·tur·ized
min·i·a·tur·iz·ing
min·i·a·tur·i·za·tion
min·im
min·i·mal
min·i·mal·ly
min·i·mize
min·i·mized
min·i·miz·ing
min·i·mi·za·tion
min·i·mum
min·ing
min·ion
min·is·cule
min·is·ter
min·is·te·ri·al

min·is·trant
min·is·tra·tion
min·is·try
min·is·tries
min·now
mi·nor
mi·nor·i·ty
mi·nor·i·ties
min·strel
mint·age
min·u·end
mi·nus
mi·nus·cule
min·ute
mi·nute
mi·nut·est
min·ute·man
mi·nu·tia
minx
mir·a·cle
mi·rac·u·lous
mi·rage
mire
mired
mir·ing
miry
mir·ror
mirth
mirth·ful·ly
mirth·ful·ness
mirth·less
mis·ad·ven·ture
mis·ad·vise
mis·al·li·ance
mis·an·thrope
mis·an·throp·ic
mis·an·thro·py
mis·ap·ply
mis·ap·plied
mis·ap·ply·ing
mis·ap·pli·ca·tion
mis·ap·pre·hend
mis·ap·pre·hen·sion
mis·ap·pro·pri·ate
mis·ap·pro·pri·at·ed
mis·ap·pro·pri·at·ing
mis·ap·pro·pri·a·tion
mis·be·have
mis·be·haved
mis·be·hav·ing
mis·be·ha·vior
mis·belief
mis·believ·er
mis·cal·cu·late
mis·cal·cu·lat·ed
mis·cal·cu·lat·ing
mis·cal·cu·la·tion
mis·cal·cu·la·tor
mis·call
mis·carry
mis·car·ried
mis·carry·ing
mis·carrige
mis·ce·ge·na·tion
mis·cel·la·ne·ous
mis·cel·la·ny
mis·chance
mis·chief
mis·chie·vous
mis·ci·ble
mis·ci·bil·i·ty
mis·con·ceive
mis·con·ceived
mis·con·ceiv·ing
mis·con·cep·tion
mis·con·duct
mis·con·strue
mis·con·strued

mis·con·stru·ing
mis·con·struc·tion
mis·count
mis·cre·ant
mis·cue
mis·cued
mis·cu·ing
mis·deal
mis·dealt
mis·deal·ing
mis·deed
mis·de·mean·or
mis·di·rect
mis·di·rec·tion
mis·do
mis·did
mis·done
mis·do·ing
mis·em·ploy
mis·em·ploy·ment
mi·ser
mi·ser·li·ness
mi·ser·ly
mis·er·a·ble
mis·er·a·ble·ness
mis·er·a·bly
mis·ery
mis·er·ies
mis·es·ti·mate
mis·fea·sance
mis·fire
mis·fired
mis·fit
mis·fit·ted
mis·fit·ting
mis·for·tune
mis·giv·ing
mis·gov·ern
mis·gov·ern·ment
mis·guide
mis·guid·ed
mis·guid·ing
mis·guid·ance
mis·han·dle
mis·han·dled
mis·han·dling
mis·hap
mish·mash
mis·in·form
mis·in·orm·ant
mis·in·form·er
mis·in·for·ma·tion
mis·in·ter·pret
mis·in·ter·pre·ta·tion
mis·in·ter·pret·er
mis·judge
mis·judged
mis·judg·ing
mis·judg·ment
mis·lay
mis·laid
mis·lay·ing
mis·lead
mis·lead·ing
mis·lead·er
mis·man·age
mis·man·aged
mis·man·ag·ing
mis·man·age·ment
mis·match
mis·mate
mis·mat·ed
mis·mat·ing
mis·name
mis·named
mis·nam·ing
mis·no·mer
mi·sog·a·my

mi·sog·y·ny
mi·sog·y·nist
mi·sog·y·nous
mis·place
mis·placed
mis·plac·ing
mis·place·ment
mis·play
mis·print
mis·pri·sion
mis·prize
mis·pro·nounce
mis·pro·nounced
mis·pro·nounc·ing
mis·pro·nun·ci·a·tion
mis·quote
mis·quot·ed
mis·quot·ing
mis·quo·ta·tion
mis·read
mis·read·ing
mis·rep·re·sent
mis·rep·re·sen·ta·tion
mis·rep·re·sen·ta·tive
mis·rule
mis·ruled
mis·rul·ing
mis·sal
mis·shape
mis·shaped
mis·shap·ing
mis·shap·en
mis·sile
miss·ing
mis·sion
mis·sion·ary
mis·sion·ar·ies
mis·sive
mis·spell
mis·spelled
mis·spelt
mis·spel·ling
mis·spend
mis·spent
mis·spend·ing
mis·state
mis·stat·ed
mis·stat·ing
mis·state·ment
mis·step
mist
mist·i·ly
mist·i·ness
mis·tak·a·ble
mis·take
mis·took
mis·tak·en
mis·tak·ing
mis·tak·en·ly
mis·tak·en·ness
Mis·ter
mis·tle·toe
mis·treat
mis·treat·ment
mis·tress
mis·tri·al
mis·trust
mis·trust·ful
mis·trust·ful·ly
mis·trust·ing·ly
misty
mist·i·er
mist·i·ness
mis·un·der·stand
mis·un·der·stood
mis·un·der·stand·ing
mis·use
mis·used

mis·us·ing
mis·us·age
mis·val·ue
mi·ter
mi·tre
mit·i·gate
mit·i·gat·ed
mit·i·gat·ing
mit·i·ga·tion
mit·i·ga·tive
mit·i·ga·tor
mit·i·ga·to·ry
mi·to·sis
mitt
mit·ten
mix
mixed
mix·ing
mix·er
mix·ture
miz·zen
mne·mon·ic
mne·mon·ics
mob
mobbed
mob·bing
mob·bish
mo·bile
mo·bil·i·ty
mo·bi·lize
mo·bi·lized
mo·bi·liz·ing
mo·bi·li·za·tion
mob·ster
moc·ca·sin
mo·cha
mock
mock·er
mock·ing·ly
mock·ery
mock·ing·bird
mock-up
mod·al
mo·dal·i·ty
mod·al·ly
mod·el
mod·eled
mod·el·ing
mod·er·ate
mod·er·at·ed
mod·er·at·ing
mod·er·ate·ness
mod·er·a·tion
mod·er·a·tor
mod·ern
mod·ern·ism
mod·ern·ist
mod·ern·ist·ic
mod·ern·ize
mod·ern·ized
mod·ern·iz·ing
mod·ern·i·za·tion
mod·est
mod·est·ly
mod·es·ty
mod·i·cum
mod·i·fi·ca·tion
mod·i·fy
mod·i·fied
mod·i·fy·ing
mod·i·fi·a·ble
mod·i·fi·er
mod·ish
mod·ish·ly
mod·ish·ness
mo·diste
mod·u·late
mod·u·lat·ed

mod·u·lat·ing
mod·u·la·tion
mod·u·la·to·ry
mod·ule
mod·u·lar
mo·dus o·pe·ran·di
mo·dus vi·ven·di
mo·gul
mo·hair
Mo·ham·med
moi·e·ty
moi·ré
mois·ten
  moist·en·er
mois·ture
  mois·tur·ize
  mois·tur·ized
  mois·tur·iz·ing
  mois·tur·iz·er
mo·lar
mo·las·ses
mold
  mold·a·ble
  mold·er
mold·ing
moldy
  mold·i·er
  mold·i·ness
mol·e·cule
  mo·lec·u·lar
mole·skin
mo·lest
  mo·les·ta·tion
  mo·lest·er
mol·li·fy
  mol·li·fied
  mol·li·fy·ing
  mol·li·fi·ca·tion
  mol·li·fi·er
mol·lusk
mol·ly·cod·dle
molt
  molt·er
mol·ten
mo·lyb·de·num
mo·ment
mo·men·tary
  mo·men·tar·i·ly
mo·men·tous
  mo·men·tous·ness
mo·men·tum
mon·ad
  mo·nad·ic
  mo·nad·i·cal
mon·arch
  mo·nar·chal
mo·nar·chic
  mo·nar·chi·cal·ly
mon·ar·chism
  mon·ar·chist
mon·ar·chy
  mon·ar·chies
mon·as·tery
  mon·as·te·ri·al
mo·nas·tic
  mo·nas·ti·cal
  mo·nas·ti·cism
mon·au·ral
  mon·au·ral·ly
mon·e·tary
  mon·e·tar·i·ly
mon·e·tize
  mon·e·tized
  mon·e·tiz·ing
  mon·e·ti·za·tion
mon·ey
mon·eyed
  mon·ied

mon·ger
Mon·gol·ism
  mon·gol·oid
mon·goose
mon·grel
mon·i·ker
mon·ism
  mo·nis·tic
  mo·nis·ti·cal·ly
mo·ni·tion
mon·i·tor
  mon·i·to·ri·al
monk
  monk·ish
mon·key
  mon·keys
  mon·keyed
  mon·key·ing
  mon·key·shines
mon·o·chro·mat·ic
  mon·o·chro·mat·i·cal·ly
mon·o·chrome
  mon·o·chro·mic
  mon·o·chro·mi·cal
  mon·o·chro·mi·cal·ly
mon·o·cle
mon·o·dist
mon·o·dy
  mo·nod·ic
mo·nog·a·my
  mo·nog·a·mist
  mo·nog·a·mous
mon·o·gram
  mon·o·grammed
  mon·o·gram·ming
  mon·o·gram·mat·ic
mon·o·graph
  mo·nog·ra·pher
  mon·o·graph·ic
mon·o·lith
mon·o·logue
  mon·o·log
  mon·o·logu·ist
  mon·o·log·ist
mon·o·ma·nia
  mon·o·ma·ni·ac
mon·o·met·al·lism
  mon·o·me·tal·lic
mo·no·mi·al
mon·o·nu·cle·o·sis
mon·o·plane
mo·nop·o·lize
  mo·nop·o·lized
  mo·nop·o·liz·ing
  mo·nop·o·li·za·tion
  mo·nop·o·liz·er
mo·nop·o·ly
  mo·nop·o·lies
mon·o·rail
mon·o·so·di·um glu·ta·mate
mon·o·syl·lab·ic
mon·o·the·ism
  mon·o·the·ist
  mon·o·the·is·tic
mon·o·tone
mo·not·o·ny
  mo·not·o·nous
mon·o·type
mon·ox·ide
mon·sei·gneur
mon·sieur
  mes·sieurs
Mon·si·gnor
mon·soon
mon·ster
  mon·stros·i·ty
  mon·strous
mon·tage

Mon·tes·so·ri
month·ly
  month·lies
mon·u·ment
  mon·u·men·tal
  mon·u·men·tal·ly
mooch
  mooch·er
moody
  mood·i·er
  mood·i·ly
  mood·i·ness
moon·beam
moon·light·ing
moon·scape
moon·shine
moor·ing
moot·ness
mop
  mopped
  mop·ping
mope
  moped
  mop·ing
mop·pet
mo·raine
mor·al
  mor·al·ly
mo·rale
mor·al·ist
  mor·al·is·tic
mo·ral·i·ty
mor·al·ize
  mor·al·ized
  mor·al·iz·ing
  mor·al·i·za·tion
  mor·al·iz·er
mo·rass
mor·a·to·ri·um
mo·ray
mor·bid
  mor·bid·ly
  mor·bid·i·ty
  mor·bid·ness
mor·dant
  mor·dan·cy
more·o·ver
mo·res
mor·ga·nat·ic
morgue
mor·i·bund
Mor·mon·ism
morn·ing
morn·ing-glo·ry
mo·roc·co
mo·ron
  mo·ron·ic
  mo·ron·i·cal·ly
mo·rose
  mo·rose·ly
  mo·rose·ness
mor·pheme
mor·phine
mor·phol·o·gy
  mor·pho·log·ic
  mor·pho·log·i·cal
  mor·phol·o·gist
mor·row
mor·sel
mor·tal
  mor·tal·ly
mor·tal·i·ty
  mor·tal·i·ties
mor·tar
mor·tar·board
mort·gage
  mort·gaged
  mort·gag·ing

mort·ga·gee
mort·ga·ger
mor·ti·cian
mor·ti·fy
  mor·ti·fied
  mor·ti·fy·ing
  mor·ti·fi·ca·tion
mor·tise
  mor·tised
  mor·tis·ing
mor·tu·ary
  mor·tu·ar·ies
mo·sa·ic
mo·sey
  mo·seyed
  mo·sey·ing
Mos·lem
mosque
mos·qui·to
  mos·qui·toes
  mos·qui·tos
moss
  moss·like
  mossy
  moss·i·er
moss·back
most·ly
mo·tel
mo·tet
moth·ball
moth-eat·en
moth·er
  moth·er·less
  moth·er·hood
  moth·er·ly
  moth·er·li·ness
moth·er-in-law
  moth·ers-in-law
moth·er·land
moth·er-of-pearl
mo·tif
mo·tile
  mo·til·i·ty
mo·tion
  mo·tion·less·ness
mo·ti·vate
  mo·ti·vat·ed
  mo·ti·vat·ing
  mo·ti·va·tion
  mo·ti·va·tion·al
mo·tive
mot·ley
mo·tor
mo·tor·bike
mo·tor·boat
mo·tor·bus
mo·tor·cade
mo·tor·car
mo·tor court
mo·tor·cy·cle
  mo·tor·cy·cled
  mo·tor·cy·cling
  mo·tor·cy·clist
mo·tor·ist
mo·tor·ize
  mo·tor·ized
  mo·tor·iz·ing
  mo·tor·i·za·tion
mo·tor·man
mot·tle
  mot·tled
  mot·tling
mound
mount
  mount·a·ble
moun·tain
moun·tain·eer
moun·tain·ous

moun·te·bank
mount·ing
mourn
  mourn·er
mourn·ful
  mourn·ful·ly
mourn·ing
mouse
mous·er
mousse
mous·tache
mousy
  mous·i·er
mouth
  mouthed
mouth·ful
mouth·piece
mouthy
  mouth·i·ness
mou·ton
mov·a·ble
  mov·a·bil·i·ty
  mov·a·bly
move
  moved
  mov·ing
move·ment
  mov·ie
mow
  mowed or mown
  mow·ing
  mow·er
mox·ie
mu·ci·lage
  mu·ci·lag·i·nous
muck
  mucky
muck·rake
  muck·raked
  muck·rak·ing
  muck·rak·er
mu·cous
  mu·cos·i·ty
mu·cus
mud
  mud·ded
  mud·ding
mud·dle
  mud·dled
  mud·dling
  mud·dler
mud·dy
  mud·di·er
  mud·di·ness
mu·ez·zin
muf·fin
muf·fle
  muf·fled
  muf·fling
  muf·fler
muf·ti
mug
  mugged
  mug·ging
  mug·ger
mug·gy
  mug·gi·ness
mu·lat·to
  mu·lat·toes
mul·ber·ry
mulch
mulct
mu·le·teer
mul·ish
  mul·ish·ness
mul·let
mul·li·gan
mul·li·ga·taw·ny

mul·lion
mul·lioned
mul·ti·col·ored
mul·ti·far·i·ous
mul·ti·far·i·ous·ness
mul·ti·lat·er·al
mul·ti·lev·el
mul·ti·mil·lion·aire
mul·ti·par·tite
mul·ti·ple
mul·ti·ple-choice
mul·ti·ple scle·ro·sis
mul·ti·pli·cand
mul·ti·pli·ca·tion
mul·ti·plic·i·ty
mul·ti·pli·er
mul·ti·ply
mul·ti·plied
mul·ti·ply·ing
mul·ti·pli·a·ble
mul·ti·tude
mul·ti·tu·di·nous
mum·ble
mum·bled
mum·bling
mum·bler
mum·bo jum·bo
mum·mer
mum·mi·fy
mum·mi·fied
mum·mi·fy·ing
mum·mi·fi·ca·tion
mum·my
mum·mies
munch
mun·dane
mu·nic·i·pal
mu·nic·i·pal·ly
mu·nic·i·pal·i·ty
mu·nif·i·cent
mu·nif·i·cence
mu·nif·i·cent·ly
mu·ni·tion
mu·ral
mu·ral·ist
mur·der
mur·der·er
mur·der·ess
mur·der·ous
mur·der·ous·ly
mu·ri·at·ic ac·id
murky
murk·i·er
murk·i·ness
mur·mur
mur·mur·er
mur·mur·ing
mur·rain
mus·cat
mus·ca·tel
mus·cle
mus·cled
mus·cling
mus·cle-bound
mus·cu·lar
mus·cu·lar·i·ty
mus·cu·lar dys·tro·phy
mus·cu·la·ture
muse
mused
mus·ing
mu·se·um
mush
mushy
mush·i·ness
mush·room
mu·sic
mu·si·cal

mu·si·cal·ly
mu·si·cal·ness
mu·si·cale
mu·si·cian
musk
musky
musk·i·ness
mus·kel·lunge
mus·ket
mus·ket·eer
mus·ket·ry
musk·mel·on
musk·rat
Mus·lim
mus·lin
muss
mussy
mus·sel
mus·tache
mus·tang
mus·tard
mus·ter
mus·ty
mus·ti·ly
mus·ti·ness
mu·ta·ble
mu·ta·bil·i·ty
mu·ta·ble·ness
mu·ta·bly
mu·tant
mu·ta·tion
mu·tate
mu·tat·ed
mu·tat·ing
mu·ta·tion·al
mute
mut·ed
mut·ing
mute·ly
mute·ness
mu·ti·late
mu·ti·lat·ed
mu·ti·lat·ing
mu·ti·la·tion
mu·ti·la·tor
mu·ti·neer
mu·ti·ny
mu·ti·nied
mu·ti·ny·ing
mu·ti·nous
mut·ter
mut·tered
mut·ter·ing
mut·ton
mu·tu·al
mu·tu·al·i·ty
mu·tu·al·ly
muu·muu
muz·zle
muz·zled
muz·zling
my·col·o·gy
my·col·o·gist
my·na
my·o·pia
my·op·ic
myr·i·ad
myrrh
myr·tle
my·self
mys·te·ri·ous
mys·te·ri·ous·ly
mys·tery
mys·ter·ies
mys·tic
mys·ti·cal
mys·ti·cal·ly
mys·ti·cism

mys·ti·fy
mys·ti·fied
mys·ti·fy·ing
mys·ti·fi·ca·tion
mys·tique
myth
myth·i·cal
myth·i·cal·ly
my·thol·o·gy
myth·o·log·ic
myth·o·log·i·cal
my·thol·o·gist

N

nab
nabbed
nab·bing
na·bob
na·celle
na·cre
na·cre·ous
na·dir
nag
nagged
nag·ging
nag·ger
nain·sook
na·ive
na·ive·ly
na·ive·ness
na·ive·te
na·ked
na·ked·ness
nam·by-pam·by
name
named
nam·ing
name·less
name·ly
name·sake
nan·keen
nan·ny
nap
napped
nap·ping
na·palm
nape
naph·tha
naph·tha·lene
nap·kin
Na·po·leon
nar·cis·sism
nar·cism
nar·cis·sist
nar·cis·sis·tic
nar·cis·sus
nar·co·sis
nar·cot·ic
nar·co·tize
nar·co·tized
nar·co·tiz·ing
nar·cot·ism
nar·rate
nar·rat·ed
nar·rat·ing
nar·ra·tor
nar·ra·tion
nar·ra·tive
nar·row
nar·row·ly
nar·row-mind·ed
na·sal
na·sal·i·ty
na·sal·ize
na·sal·ized
na·sal·iz·ing

na·sal·ly
nas·cent
nas·cence
nas·cen·cy
na·stur·tium
nas·ty
nas·ti·er
nas·ti·ly
nas·ti·ness
na·tal
na·tal·i·ty
na·tant
na·ta·to·ri·al
na·ta·to·ri·um
na·tion
na·tion·hood
na·tion·al
na·tion·al·ly
na·tion·al·ism
na·tion·al·ist
na·tion·al·is·tic
na·tion·al·i·ty
na·tion·al·i·ties
na·tion·al·ize
na·tion·al·ized
na·tion·al·iz·ing
na·tion·al·i·za·tion
na·tion-wide
na·tive
na·tive·ly
na·tive·ness
na·tiv·ism
na·tiv·ist
na·tiv·i·ty
na·tiv·i·ties
nat·ty
nat·ti·ly
nat·ti·ness
nat·u·ral
nat·u·ral·ly
nat·u·ral·ness
nat·u·ral·ism
nat·u·ral·ist
nat·u·ral·is·tic
nat·u·ral·ize
nat·u·ral·ized
nat·u·ral·iz·ing
nat·u·ral·i·za·tion
na·ture
naught
naugh·ty
naugh·ti·est
naugh·ti·ly
naugh·ti·ness
nau·sea
nau·se·ate
nau·se·at·ed
nau·se·at·ing
nau·seous
nau·seous·ness
nau·ti·cal
nau·ti·cal·ly
nau·ti·lus
nau·ti·lus·es
Nav·a·ho
na·vel
nav·i·ga·ble
nav·i·ga·bil·i·ty
nav·i·ga·ble·ness
nav·i·gate
nav·i·gat·ed
nav·i·gat·ing
nav·i·ga·tion
nav·i·ga·tor
na·vy
na·vies
na·val
Naz·a·reth

Na·zi
Na·zism
Na·si·ism
Ne·an·der·thal
near
near·ly
near·ness
near·by
near-sight·ed
neat
neat·ly
neat·ness
Neb·u·chad·nez·zar
neb·u·la
neb·u·lae
neb·u·lous
neb·u·lar
neb·u·lous·ness
neb·u·los·i·ty
nec·es·sary
nec·es·sar·ies
nec·es·sar·i·ly
ne·ces·si·tate
ne·ces·si·tat·ed
ne·ces·si·tat·ing
ne·ces·si·ty
ne·ces·si·ties
neck·er·chief
neck·lace
neck·tie
ne·crol·o·gy
ne·crol·o·gies
nec·ro·man·cy
nec·ro·man·cer
ne·crop·o·lis
nec·tar
nec·tar·ine
need·ful
need·ful·ly
nee·dle
nee·dled
nee·dling
nee·dle·point
need·less
need·less·ly
nee·dle·work
needy
need·i·est
need·i·ness
ne'er-do-well
ne·far·i·ous
ne·far·i·ous·ness
ne·gate
ne·gat·ed
ne·gat·ing
ne·ga·tion
neg·a·tive
neg·a·tive·ness
neg·a·tiv·i·ty
neg·a·tiv·ism
ne·glect
ne·glect·ful
ne·glect·ful·ly
neg·li·gee
neg·li·gent
neg·li·gence
neg·li·gent·ly
neg·li·gi·ble
neg·li·gi·bly
neg·li·gi·bil·i·ty
ne·go·ti·a·ble
ne·go·ti·a·bil·i·ty
ne·go·ti·ate
ne·go·ti·at·ed
ne·go·ti·at·ing
ne·go·ti·a·tion
ne·go·ti·a·tor
Ne·gro

Ne·groes
Ne·groid
neigh
neigh·bor
neigh·bor·ing
neigh·bor·ly
neigh·bor·li·ness
neigh·bor·hood
nei·ther
nem·a·tode
nem·e·sis
ne·o·clas·sic
ne·o·clas·si·cal
ne·o·clas·si·cism
ne·o·lith·ic
ne·ol·o·gism
ne·ol·o·gy
ne·on
ne·o·phyte
neo·prene
neph·ew
ne·phri·tis
nep·o·tism
nep·o·tist
nerve
nerve·less
nerve·rack·ing
nerve·wrack·ing
nerv·ous
nerv·ous·ness
nervy
nerv·i·ness
nes·tle
nes·tled
nes·tling
net
net·ted
net·ting
neth·er
Neth·er·lands
neth·er·most
net·tle
net·tled
net·tling
net·tle·some
net·work
neu·ral
neu·ral·gia
neu·ras·the·nia
neu·ri·tis
neu·riti·c
neu·rol·o·gy
neu·ro·log·i·cal
neu·rol·o·gist
neu·ron
neu·ro·sis
neu·ro·ses
neu·rot·ic
neu·rot·i·cal·ly
neu·ter
neu·tral
neu·tral·i·ty
neu·tral·ly
neu·tral·ism
neu·tral·ist
neu·tral·ize
neu·tral·ized
neu·tral·iz·ing
neu·tral·i·za·tion
neu·tral·iz·er
neu·tron
nev·er
nev·er·more
nev·er·the·less
new
new·ish
new·ness
new·born

new·com·er
new·el
new·fan·gled
new·ly·wed
news·cast·er
news·pa·per
news·print
news·reel
news·stand
New Test·a·ment
New Zea·land
nex·us
ni·a·cin
Ni·ag·a·ra
nib·ble
nib·bled
nib·bling
Nic·a·ra·gua
nice
nice·ly
nice·ness
ni·ce·ty
ni·ce·ties
niche
nick·el·o·de·on
nick·name
nic·o·tine
nic·o·tin·ic
niece
nif·ty
nif·ti·est
Ni·ge·ria
nig·gard
nig·gard·li·ness
nig·gard·ly
nig·gling
night·fall
night·gown
night·in·gale
night·ly
night·mare
night·mar·ish
night·time
ni·hil·ism
ni·hil·ist
ni·hil·is·tic
nim·ble
nim·ble·ness
nim·bly
nim·bus
nim·rod
nin·comp·poop
nine·teen
nine·teenth
nine·ty
nine·ties
nine·ti·eth
nin·ny
ninth
nip
nipped
nip·ping
nip·per
nip·ple
Nip·pon
nip·py
nir·va·na
Ni·sei
nit·pick
ni·trate
ni·tra·tion
ni·tric
ni·tro·gen
ni·trog·e·nous
ni·tro·glyc·er·in
nit·ty-grit·ty
nit·wit
no·bil·i·ty

no·ble
no·bler
no·blest
no·ble·man
no·ble·ness
no·bly
no·blesse oblige
no·body
noc·tur·nal
noc·turne
nod
nod·ded
nod·ding
node
nod·al
nod·ule
nod·u·lar
no·el
nog·gin
noise
noised
nois·ing
noise·less
noi·some
noisy
nois·i·ly
nois·i·ness
no·lo con·ten·de·re
no·mad
no·mad·ic
no·mad·i·cal·ly
no·mad·ism
nom de plume
no·men·cla·ture
nom·i·nal
nom·i·nal·ly
nom·i·nate
nom·i·nat·ed
nom·i·nat·ing
nom·i·na·tion
nom·i·na·tive
nom·i·nee
non·age
non·align·ment
non·cha·lant
non·cha·lance
non·cha·lant·ly
non·com
non·com·bat·ant
non·com·mis·sioned
non·com·mit·tal
non·con·duc·tor
non·con·form·ist
non·con·form·i·ty
non·de·script
non·en·ti·ty
none·the·less
non·in·ter·ven·tion
non·met·al
non·me·tal·lic
non·pa·reil
non·par·ti·san
non·plus
non·plused
non·plus·ing
non·prof·it
non·res·i·dent
non·res·i·dence
non·res·i·den·cy
non·re·sis·tance
non·re·stric·tive
non·sched·uled
non·sec·tar·i·an
non·sense
non·sen·si·cal
non·sen·si·cal·ly
non se·qui·tur
non·stop

non·sup·port
non·un·ion
non·vi·o·lence
non·vi·o·lent·ly
noo·dle
noon
noon·day
noon·time
noose
nor·mal
nor·mal·cy
nor·mal·i·ty
nor·mal·ly
nor·mal·ize
nor·mal·ized
nor·mal·iz·ing
nor·mal·i·za·tion
Norse·man
North Amer·i·ca
north·east
north·east·ern
north·east·ern
north·east·er
north·east·er·ly
north·east·ward
north·er
nor·ther·ly
north·er·li·ness
north·ern
north·ern·most
north·ern·er
north·ward
north·wards
north·ward·ly
north·west
north·west·ern
north·west·ward
Nor·we·gian
nose
nosed
nos·ing
nose·gay
nos·tal·gia
nos·tal·gic
nos·tril
nos·trum
nosy
nos·i·ly
nos·i·ness
no·ta·ble
no·ta·ble·ness
no·ta·bil·i·ty
no·ta·bly
no·ta·rize
no·ta·rized
no·ta·riz·ing
no·ta·ri·za·tion
no·ta·ry
no·ta·tion
no·ta·tion·al
notch
notched
note
not·ed
not·ing
not·ed
not·ed·ness
note·wor·thy
note·wor·thi·ness
noth·ing
noth·ing·ness
no·tice
no·ticed
no·tic·ing
no·tice·a·ble
no·tice·a·bly
no·ti·fy
no·ti·fied

no·ti·fy·ing
no·ti·fi·ca·tion
no·tion
no·to·ri·ous
no·to·ri·ous·ness
no·to·ri·e·ty
no-trump
nought
nour·ish
nour·ish·ing
nour·ish·ment
no·va
No·va Sco·tia
nov·el
nov·el·ist
nov·el·is·tic
nov·el·ette
nov·el·ty
nov·el·ties
no·ve·na
nov·ice
no·vi·ti·ate
no·vo·cain
now·a·days
no·where
no·wise
nox·ious
noz·zle
nu·ance
nub·bin
nu·bile
nu·cle·ar
nu·cle·ate
nu·cle·on
nu·cle·onics
nu·cle·us
nu·clei
nude
nude·ness
nu·di·ty
nud·ism
nud·ist
nudge
nudged
nudg·ing
nu·ga·to·ry
nug·get
nui·sance
null
nul·li·ty
nul·li·fy
nul·li·fied
nul·li·fy·ing
nul·li·fi·ca·tion
nul·li·fi·er
numb
numb·ly
numb·ness
num·ber
num·ber·less
nu·mer·al
num·er·al·ly
nu·mer·a·ble
nu·mer·ate
nu·mer·at·ed
nu·mer·at·ing
nu·mer·a·tion
nu·mer·a·tor
nu·mer·i·cal
nu·mer·ous
nu·mis·mat·ics
nu·mis·mat·ic
nu·mis·ma·tist
num·skull
numb·skull
nun·cio
nun·nery
nun·ner·ies

nup·tial
nup·tial·ly
nurse
nursed
nurs·ing
nurse·maid
nurs·ery
nurs·er·ies
nur·ture
nur·tured
nur·tur·ing
nut
nut·ty
nut·crack·er
nut·hatch
nut·meg
nu·tri·ent
nu·tri·ment
nu·tri·tion
nu·tri·tion·al
nu·tri·tion·al·ly
nu·tri·tion·ist
nu·tri·tious
nu·tri·tive
nut·shell
nut·ty
nuz·zle
nuz·zled
nuz·zling
ny·lon
nymph
nym·pho·ma·nia
nym·pho·ma·ni·ac

O

oaf
oaf·ish
oak·en
oa·kum
oar·lock
oars·man
oa·sis
oath
oat·meal
ob·bli·ga·to
ob·du·rate
ob·du·ra·cy
ob·du·rate·ness
obe·di·ence
obe·di·ent
obei·sance
obei·sant
ob·e·lisk
obese
obese·ness
obes·i·ty
obey
ob·fus·cate
ob·fus·ca·ted
ob·fus·ca·ting
ob·fus·ca·tion
obit·u·ary
obit·u·ar·ies
ob·ject
ob·ject·less
ob·ject·or
ob·jec·tion
ob·jec·tion·a·ble
ob·jec·tion·a·bly
ob·jec·tive
ob·jec·tive·ly
ob·jec·tive·ness
ob·jec·tiv·i·ty
ob·jet d'art
ob·jur·gate
ob·jur·gat·ed

ob·jur·gat·ing
ob·jur·ga·tion
ob·jur·ga·to·ry
ob·late
ob·la·tion
ob·li·gate
ob·li·gat·ed
ob·li·gat·ing
ob·li·ga·tion
ob·lig·a·to·ry
oblige
obliged
oblig·ing
ob·lique
ob·lique·ly
ob·liq·ui·ty
ob·lit·er·ate
ob·lit·er·at·ed
ob·lit·er·at·ing
ob·lit·er·a·tion
ob·lit·er·a·tive
ob·liv·i·on
ob·liv·i·ous
ob·long
ob·lo·quy
ob·nox·ious
oboe
obo·ist
ob·scene
ob·scene·ly
ob·scene·ness
ob·scen·i·ty
ob·scure
ob·scured
ob·scur·ing
ob·scure·ness
ob·scu·ri·ty
ob·se·qui·ous
ob·se·quy
ob·ser·va·to·ry
ob·serve
ob·served
ob·serv·ing
ob·serv·er
ob·serv·a·ble
ob·serv·a·bly
ob·ser·vance
ob·ser·vant
ob·ser·va·tion
ob·sess
ob·ses·sive
ob·ses·sion
ob·sid·i·an
ob·so·les·cent
ob·so·les·cence
ob·so·lete
ob·so·lete·ness
ob·sta·cle
ob·stet·rics
ob·stet·ric
ob·stet·ri·cal
ob·ste·tri·cian
ob·sti·nate
ob·sti·na·cy
ob·sti·nate·ly
ob·sti·nate·ness
ob·strep·er·ous
ob·strep·er·ous·ness
ob·struct
ob·struc·tive
ob·struc·tor
ob·struc·tion
ob·struc·tion·ism
ob·struc·tion·ist
ob·tain
ob·tain·a·ble
ob·tain·ment
ob·trude

ob·trud·ed
ob·trud·ing
ob·tru·sion
ob·tru·sive
ob·tuse
ob·tuse·ness
ob·verse
ob·verse·ly
ob·vert
ob·vi·ate
ob·vi·at·ed
ob·vi·at·ing
ob·vi·a·tion
ob·vi·ous
ob·vi·ous·ness
ob·vo·lute
oc·a·ri·na
oc·ca·sion
oc·ca·sion·al
oc·ca·sion·al·ly
oc·ci·dent
oc·ci·den·tal
oc·clude
oc·clud·ed
oc·clud·ing
oc·clu·sive
oc·clu·sion
oc·cult
oc·cult·ism
oc·cult·ist
oc·cu·pa·tion
oc·cu·pa·tion·al
oc·cu·pa·tion·al·ly
oc·cu·py
oc·cu·pied
oc·cu·py·ing
oc·cu·pi·er
oc·cu·pan·cy
oc·cu·pant
oc·cur
oc·curred
oc·cur·ring
oc·cur·rence
oc·cur·rent
ocean
oce·an·ic
oce·a·nog·ra·phy
oce·a·nog·ra·pher
oce·a·no·graph·ic
oce·a·no·graph·i·cal
oce·lot
ocher
ochery
o'clock
oc·ta·gon
oc·tag·o·nal·ly
oc·ta·he·dron
oc·ta·he·dra
oc·ta·he·dral
oc·tane
oc·tave
oc·ta·vo
oc·tet
oc·to·ge·nar·i·an
oc·to·pus
oc·to·roon
oc·u·lar
oc·u·list
odd
odd·ness
odd·ball
odd·i·ty
odd·i·ties
odi·ous
odi·ous·ness
odi·um
odom·e·ter
odor

odored
odor·less
odor·ous
odor·if·er·ous
od·ys·sey
Oed·i·pus
of·fal
off·beat
off·col·or
of·fend
of·fend·er
of·fense
of·fense·less
of·fen·sive
of·fen·sive·ly
of·fer
of·fer·er
of·fer·ing
of·fer·to·ry
of·fer·to·ries
of·fer·to·ri·al
off·hand
off·hand·ed·ness
of·fice
of·fice·hold·er
of·fic·er
of·fi·cial
of·fi·cial·ly
of·fi·cial·dom
of·fi·ci·ate
of·fi·ci·at·ed
of·fi·ci·at·ing
of·fi·ci·a·tion
of·fi·ci·a·tor
of·fi·cious
of·fi·cious·ly
off·ing
off·set
off·set·ting
off·shoot
off·shore
off·side
off·spring
off·stage
off-the-record
of·ten
of·ten·times
ogle
ogled
ogling
ogler
ogre
ogre·ish
ohm
ohm·age
ohm·ic
ohm·me·ter
oil·cloth
oil·skin
oily
oil·i·ness
oint·ment
okra
old
old·er
old·est
old·en
old·ish
old·ness
old-fash·ioned
old·ster
Old Test·a·ment
old-tim·er
old-world
ole·ag·i·nous
ole·o·mar·ga·rine
ol·fac·tion
ol·fac·to·ry

ol·i·gar·chy
ol·i·gar·chic
oli·gar·chi·cal
ol·i·garch
ol·i·gop·o·ly
ol·ive
Olym·pi·an
O·lym·pic
om·buds·man
ome·ga
om·e·let
omen
om·i·nous
om·i·nous·ly
omis·sion
omit
omit·ted
omit·ting
om·ni·bus
om·nip·o·tence
om·nip·o·tent·ly
om·ni·pres·ent
om·ni·pres·ence
om·nis·cience
om·nis·cient
om·niv·or·ous
on·com·ing
on·er·ous
one·self
one-sid·ed
one-up·man·ship
one-way
on·go·ing
on·ion
on·iony
on·look·er
on·ly
on·o·mat·o·poe·ia
on·o·mat·o·poe·ic
on·o·mat·o·poe·i·cal·ly
on·rush·ing
on·set
on·shore
on·slaught
on·to
onus
on·ward
on·yx
oo·dles
ooze
oozed
ooz·ing
oo·zi·ness
oo·zy
opac·i·ty
opal
opal·es·cence
opal·es·cent
opaque
opaque·ly
open
open·ly
open·ness
open·hand·ed
open house
open·ing
open-mind·ed
open-mouthed
open ses·a·me
open·work
opera
op·er·at·ic
op·er·a·ble
op·er·a·bil·i·ty
op·er·a·bly
op·er·ate
op·er·at·ed
op·er·at·ing

op·er·a·tion
op·er·a·tive
op·er·a·tor
op·er·et·ta
oph·thal·mic
oph·thal·mol·o·gist
oph·thal·mol·o·gy
opi·ate
opin·ion
opin·ion·at·ed
opi·um
opos·sum
op·po·nent
op·por·tune
op·por·tune·ly
op·por·tun·ism
op·por·tun·ist
op·por·tun·is·tic
op·por·tu·ni·ty
op·por·tu·ni·ties
op·pose
op·posed
op·pos·ing
op·pos·er
op·po·site
op·po·site·ness
op·po·si·tion
op·press
op·pres·sor
op·pres·sion
op·pres·sive
op·pro·bri·um
op·pro·bri·ous
op·tic
op·ti·cal
op·ti·cal
op·ti·cian
op·tics
op·ti·mal
op·ti·mism
op·ti·mist
op·ti·mis·tic
op·ti·mis·ti·cal·ly
op·ti·mize
op·ti·mized
op·ti·miz·ing
op·ti·mi·za·tion
op·ti·mum
op·tion
op·tion·al
op·tom·e·try
op·to·met·ric
op·tom·e·trist
op·u·lent
op·u·lence
op·u·lent·ly
opus
opus·es
or·a·cle
orac·u·lar
oral
oral·ly
or·ange
orang·u·tan
orate
orat·ed
orat·ing
ora·tion
ora·tor
or·a·tor·i·cal
or·a·to·ry
or·a·to·rio
or·bic·u·lar
orbit
or·bit·al
or·chard
or·ches·tra
or·ches·tral

or·ches·trate
or·ches·trat·ed
or·ches·trat·ing
or·ches·tra·tion
or·chid
or·dain
or·dain·er
or·dain·ment
or·deal
or·der
or·dered
or·der·ly
or·der·li·ness
or·di·nal
or·di·nance
or·di·nar·i·ly
or·di·nary
or·di·nar·i·ness
or·di·na·tion
ord·nance
oreg·a·no
or·gan
or·gan·dy
or·gan·ic
or·gan·i·cal·ly
or·gan·ism
or·gan·ist
or·gan·i·za·tion
or·gan·i·za·tion·al
or·gan·ize
or·gan·ized
or·gan·iz·ing
or·gan·iz·a·ble
or·gan·iz·er
or·gasm
or·gas·mic
or·gi·as·tic
or·gi·as·ti·cal·ly
or·gy
or·gies
ori·ent
Ori·en·tal
ori·en·tate
ori·en·tat·ed
ori·en·tat·ing
ori·en·ta·tion
or·i·fice
orig·i·nal
orig·i·nal·i·ty
orig·i·nal·ly
orig·i·nate
orig·i·nat·ed
orig·i·nat·ing
orig·i·na·tion
orig·i·na·tor
orig·i·na·tive
or·i·son
or·mo·lu
or·na·ment
or·na·men·tal
or·na·men·ta·tion
or·nate
or·nate·ness
or·nery
or·ner·i·ness
or·ni·thol·o·gy
or·ni·tho·log·ic
or·ni·thol·o·gist
oro·tund
oro·tun·di·ty
or·phan
or·phan·age
or·tho·don·tics
or·tho·don·tic
or·tho·don·tist
or·tho·dox
or·tho·dox·ly
or·tho·dox·ness

or·tho·doxy
or·thog·o·nal
or·thog·ra·phy
or·tho·graph·ic
or·tho·pe·dics
or·tho·pe·dic
or·tho·pe·dist
os·cil·late
os·cil·lat·ed
os·cil·lat·ing
os·cil·la·tion
os·cil·la·tor
os·cil·la·to·ry
os·cil·lo·scope
os·cu·late
os·cu·la·tion
os·mo·sis
os·mot·ic
os·prey
os·si·fy
os·si·fied
os·si·fy·ing
os·si·fi·ca·tion
os·ten·sive
os·ten·si·ble
os·ten·si·bly
os·ten·sive·ly
os·ten·ta·tion
os·ten·ta·tious
os·te·op·a·thy
os·te·o·path
os·te·o·path·ic
os·tra·cize
os·tra·cized
os·tra·ciz·ing
os·tra·cism
os·trich
oth·er
oth·er·ness
oth·er·wise
oti·ose
ot·ter
ot·to·man
ought
ounce
our·self
our·selves
oust·er
out·bid
out·bid·ding
out·board
out·bound
out·brave
out·break
out·build·ing
out·burst
out·cast
out·come
out·cry
out·cries
out·dat·ed
out·dis·tance
out·do
out·door
out·er
out·er·most
out·er space
out·face
out·field
out·flank
out·grow
out·growth
out·land·ish
out·last
out·law
out·let
out·ly·ing
out·mod·ed

out·num·ber
out-of-date
out·post
out·rage
out·ra·geous
out·range
out·rank
out·right
out·sid·er
out·skirts
out·spo·ken
out·stand·ing
out·strip
out·ward
out·wear
out·weigh
ova
oval
oval·ness
ova·ry
ova·ries
ovar·i·an
ovate
ova·tion
ov·en
over
over·act
over·age
over·bear·ing
over·board
over·charge
over·charged
over·charg·ing
over·come
over·com·pen·sa·tion
over·con·fi·dence
over·dose
over·drawn
over·em·pha·sis
over·es·ti·mate
over·flow·ing
over·gen·er·ous
over·growth
over·hand
over·hang·ing
over·haul·ing
over·in·dul·gence
over·joyed
over·much
over·night
over·pass
over·pow·er
over·rat·ed
over·reach
over·ride
over·rule
over·sexed
over·shad·ow
over·shoot
over·sight
over·sim·pli·fy
over·state·ment
over·stepped
overt
overt·ly
over·take
over-the-coun·ter
over·throw
over·time
over·ture
over·weight
over·whelm
over·worked
ovip·a·rous
ovoid
ovu·late
ovu·la·tion
ovum

ova
owe
owed
ow·ing
owl·ish
own·er
ox·en
ox·ford
ox·i·da·tion
ox·ide
ox·i·dize
ox·i·dized
ox·i·diz·ing
ox·y·a·cet·y·lene
ox·y·gen
ox·y·gen·ate
ox·y·gen·at·ed
ox·y·gen·at·ing
ox·y·gen·a·tion
oys·ter
ozone

P

pab·u·lum
pace
paced
pac·ing
pac·er
pace·mak·er
pachy·derm
pa·cif·ic
pa·cif·i·ca·tion
pa·cif·i·ca·tor
pa·cif·i·ca·to·ry
pac·i·fi·er
pac·i·fism
pac·i·fist
pac·i·fy
pac·i·fied
pac·i·fy·ing
pack·age
pack·ag·er
pack·er
pack·et
pack·ing
pack·sad·dle
pad
pad·ded
pad·ding
pad·dle
pad·dled
pad·dling
pad·dock
pad·dy
pad·lock
pa·dre
pae·an
pa·gan
pa·gan·ism
page
paged
pag·ing
pag·eant
pag·eant·ry
pag·i·nate
pag·i·na·tion
pa·go·da
pail·ful
pain
pain·ful·ly
pain·less
pains·tak·ing
paint·er
paint·ing
pais·ley
pa·jam·as

pal·ace
pa·lan·quin
pal·at·a·ble
  pal·at·a·bil·i·ty
  pal·at·a·bly
pal·ate
pa·la·tial
  pa·la·tial·ly
pal·a·tine
pa·lav·er
pale
  paled
  pal·ing
  pale·ly
  pale·ness
pa·le·og·ra·phy
Pa·le·o·lith·ic
pa·le·on·tol·o·gy
  pa·le·on·tol·o·gist
Pa·le·o·zo·ic
pal·ette
pal·ing
pal·i·sade
  pal·i·sad·ed
  pal·i·sad·ing
pal·la·di·um
pall·bear·er
pal·let
pal·li·ate
  pal·li·at·ed
  pal·li·at·ing
  pal·li·a·tion
  pal·lia·tive
pal·lid
pal·lor
palm
pal·mate
pal·met·to
palm·is·try
  palm·ist
pal·o·mi·no
pal·pa·ble
  pal·pa·bil·i·ty
  pal·pa·bly
pal·pate
  pal·pat·ed
  pal·pat·ing
  pal·pa·tion
pal·pi·tate
  pal·pi·tat·ed
  pal·pi·tat·ing
  pal·pi·ta·tion
pal·sy
  pal·sied
pal·try
  pal·tri·ness
pam·pas
pam·per
pam·phlet
  pam·phle·teer
pan
  panned
  pan·ning
pan·a·ce·a
pa·nache
Pan-Amer·i·can
pan·cake
  pan·caked
  pan·cak·ing
pan·chro·mat·ic
pan·cre·as
  pan·cre·at·ic
pan·da
pan·dem·ic
pan·de·mo·ni·um
pan·der
  pan·der·er
pan·el

pan·eled
pan·el·ing
pan·el·ist
pang
pan·han·dler
pan·ic
  pan·icked
  pan·ick·ing
pan·nier
pan·o·ply
pan·o·rama
  pan·o·ram·ic
  pan·o·ram·i·cal·ly
pan·sy
  pan·sies
pan·ta·loon
pan·the·ism
  pan·the·ist
  pan·the·is·tic
pan·the·on
pan·ther
pan·tie
pan·ty
pan·to·mime
  pan·to·mimed
  pan·to·mim·ing
  pan·to·mim·ic
  pan·to·mim·ist
pan·try
  pan·tries
pant·y·hose
pa·pa
pa·pa·cy
pa·pal
pa·pau
pa·pa·ya
pa·per
  pa·per·er
  pa·pery
pa·per·back
pa·per·weight
pa·per·work
pa·pier·ma·che
pa·pil·la
pa·poose
pap·ri·ka
pa·py·rus
par·a·ble
pa·rab·o·la
par·a·chute
  par·a·chut·ed
  par·a·chut·ing
  par·a·chut·ist
pa·rade
  pa·rad·ed
  pa·rad·ing
par·a·digm
par·a·dise
  par·a·di·si·a·cal
par·a·dox
  par·a·dox·i·cal
par·a·dox
  par·a·dox·i·cal
par·af·fin
par·a·gon
par·a·graph
Par·a·guay
par·a·keet
par·al·lax
  par·al·lac·tic
par·al·lel
  par·al·leled
  par·a·lel·ing
  par·al·lel·o·gram
pa·ral·y·sis
  par·a·lyt·ic
par·a·lyze
  par·a·lyzed

  par·a·lyz·ing
  par·a·ly·za·tion
par·a·med·ic
pa·ram·e·ter
par·a·mount
  par·a·mount·cy
par·a·mour
par·a·noia
  para·noi·ac
  par·a·noid
par·a·pet
par·a·pher·nal·ia
par·a·phrase
  par·a·phrased
  par·a·phras·ing
par·a·ple·gia
  par·a·ple·gic
par·a·psy·chol·o·gy
par·a·site
  par·a·sit·ic
  par·a·sit·i·cal·ly
  par·a·sit·ism
par·a·sol
par·a·troop·er
par·boil
par·cel
  par·celed
  par·cel·ling
parch·ment
par·don
  par·don·a·ble
  par·don·a·bly
pare
  pared
  par·ing
par·e·gor·ic
par·ent
  par·en·tal
par·ent·age
pa·ren·the·sis
  pa·ren·the·ses
  par·en·thet·ic
  par·en·thet·i·cal
pa·re·sis
par·fait
pa·ri·ah
par·i·mu·tu·el
par·ish
  pa·rish·ion·er
par·i·ty
par·ka
par·lance
par·lay
  par·layed
  par·lay·ing
par·ley
  par·leyed
  par·ley·ing
par·lia·ment
  par·lia·men·tar·i·an
  par·lia·men·ta·ry
par·lor
pa·ro·chi·al
par·o·dy
  par·o·died
  par·o·dy·ing
  par·o·dist
pa·role
  pa·roled
  pa·rol·ing
  pa·rol·ee
par·ox·ysm
  par·ox·ys·mal
par·quet
  par·queted
  par·quet·ing
  par·quet·ry
par·ra·keet

par·ri·cide
par·ry
  par·ried
  par·ry·ing
parse
par·si·mo·ny
  par·si·mo·ni·ous
  par·si·mo·ni·ous·ness
par·sley
pars·nip
par·son
  par·son·age
par·take
  par·took
  par·tak·en
  par·tak·ing
  par·ta·ker
part·ed
par·the·no·gen·e·sis
par·tial
  par·tial·ly
  par·ti·al·i·ty
par·tic·i·pate
  par·tic·i·pat·ed
  par·tic·i·pat·ing
  par·tic·i·pant
  par·tic·i·pa·tion
  par·tic·i·pa·tive
  par·tic·i·pa·tor
par·ti·ci·ple
  par·ti·cip·i·al
par·ti·cle
par·ti·col·ored
par·tic·u·lar
  par·tic·u·lar·i·ty
  par·tic·u·lar·ize
par·tic·u·late
part·ing
par·ti·san
  par·ti·san·ship
par·tite
  par·ti·tion
  par·ti·tive
part·ly
part·ner
  part·ner·ship
par·tridge
par·tu·ri·ent
par·tu·ri·tion
par·ty
  par·ties
par·ve·nu
pas·chal
pa·sha
pass·a·ble
  pass·a·bly
pas·sage
  pas·sage·way
pas·se
pas·sen·ger
pass·er·by
pass·ing
pas·sion
  pas·sion·less
pas·sion·ate
  pas·sion·ate·ly
  pas·sion·ate·ness
pas·sive
  pas·siv·i·ty
Pass·over
pass·word
pas·ta
paste
  pas·ted
  pas·ting
paste·board
pas·tel
pas·teur·ize

pas·teur·ized
pas·teur·iz·ing
pas·teur·i·za·tion
pas·tille
pas·time
pas·tor
pas·tor·ate
pas·to·ral
pas·tra·mi
pas·try
  pas·tries
pas·ture
  pas·tured
  pas·tur·ing
  pas·tur·age
pasty
  past·i·ness
pat
  pat·ted
  pat·ting
patchy
  patch·i·est
pâ·té
pat·ent
  pa·ten·cy
  pat·ent·ly
pat·ent·ee
pat·er·nal
  pat·ter·nal·ly
  pat·ter·nal·ism
pa·ter·nal·is·tic
  pa·ter·ni·ty
pa·ter·nos·ter
pa·thet·ic
  pa·thet·i·cal·ly
patho·gen·ic
pa·thol·o·gy
  path·o·log·ic
  path·o·log·i·cal
  pa·thol·o·gist
pa·thos
pa·tient
  pa·tience
  pa·tient·ly
pat·i·na
pa·tio
pat·ois
pa·tri·arch
  pa·tri·ar·chy
  pa·tri·ar·chal
pa·tri·cian
pat·ri·cide
pat·ri·mo·ny
pa·tri·ot
  pa·tri·ot·ic
  pa·tri·ot·i·cal·ly
  pa·tri·ot·ism
pa·trol
  pa·trolled
  pa·trol·ling
  pa·trol·ler
pa·trol·man
pa·tron
  pa·tron·ess
pa·tron·age
pa·tron·ize
  pa·tron·ized
  pa·tron·iz·ing
pat·ro·nym·ic
pat·sy
  pat·sies
pat·ter
pat·tern
  pat·terned
pat·ty
  pat·ties
pau·ci·ty
paunch

paunch·i·ness
paunchy
pau·per
  pau·per·ism
  pau·per·ize
pause
  paused
  paus·ing
pave
  paved
  pav·ing
pave·ment
pa·vil·ion
Pav·lov
pawn
  pawn·bro·ker
pay
  paid
  pay·ing
  pay·ee
  pay·ment
  pay·a·ble
peace
  peace·a·ble
  peace·a·bly
  peace·ful
  peace·ful·ly
peach
pea·cock
peak·ed
peal
pea·nut
pearl
  pearly
peas·ant
  peas·ant·ry
peaty
peb·ble
  peb·bled
  peb·bling
  peb·bly
pe·can
pec·ca·dil·lo
pec·tin
pec·to·ral
pec·u·late
  pec·u·la·tion
pe·cu·liar
  pe·cu·liar·ly
  pe·cu·li·ar·i·ty
  pe·cu·li·ar·i·ties
pe·cu·ni·ary
ped·a·gogue
  ped·a·gog·ic
  ped·a·gog·i·cal
  ped·a·go·gy
ped·al
  ped·aled
  ped·al·ing
ped·ant
  pe·dan·tic
  pe·dan·ti·cal·ly
  ped·ant·ry
ped·dle
  ped·dler
ped·es·tal
pe·des·tri·an
pe·di·at·rics
  pe·di·at·ric
  pe·di·a·tri·cian
  pe·di·at·rist
ped·i·cure
  ped·i·cur·ist
ped·i·gree
  ped·i·greed
ped·i·ment
pe·dol·o·gy
pe·dom·e·ter

peel·ing
peer
peer·age
  peer·ess
  peer·less
peeve
  peeved
  peev·ing
  peev·ish
peg
  pegged
  peg·ging
pei·gnoir
pe·jo·ra·tive
Pe·king·ese
pe·koe
pel·age
pe·lag·ic
pel·i·can
pel·la·gra
pel·let
pell-mell
pel·vis
  pel·vic
pem·mi·can
pen
  penned
  pen·ning
pe·nal
pe·nal·ize
  pe·nal·ized
  pe·nal·iz·ing
  pe·nal·i·za·tion
pen·al·ty
  pen·al·ties
pen·ance
pen·chant
pen·cil
  pen·ciled
  pen·cil·ing
pend·ant
pend·ent
  pend·en·cy
  pend·ent·ly
pend·ing
pen·du·lous
pen·e·trate
  pen·e·trat·ed
  pen·e·trat·ing
  pen·e·tra·tive
  pen·e·tra·ble
  pen·e·tra·bil·i·ty
  pen·e·tra·ble·ness
  pen·e·tra·bly
  pen·e·tra·tion
pen·guin
pen·i·cil·lin
pen·in·su·la
  pen·in·su·lar
pe·nis
pen·i·tent
  pen·i·tence
  pen·i·ten·tial
  pen·i·tent·ly
  pen·i·ten·tia·ry
  pen·i·ten·tia·ries
pen·knife
pen·man·ship
pen·nant
Penn·syl·va·nia
pen·ny
  pen·nies
  pen·ni·less
  pen·ny an·te
  pen·ny pinch·er
pe·nol·o·gy
  pe·no·log·i·cal
  pen·nol·o·gist

pen·sion
  pen·sion·a·ble
  pen·sion·er
pen·sive
  pen·sive·ness
pen·ta·cle
pen·ta·gon
  pen·tag·o·nal
pen·tam·e·ter
pen·tath·lon
Pen·te·cost
  Pen·te·cos·tal
pent·house
pen·tom·ic
pe·nult
pe·num·bra
pe·nu·ri·ous
pen·u·ry
pe·on
  pe·on·age
pe·o·ny
peo·ple
  peo·pled
  peo·pling
pep
  pepped
  pep·ping
pep·lum
pep·per
pep·per·corn
pep·per·mint
pep·pery
  pep·per·i·ness
pep·py
  pep·pi·er
  pep·pi·ness
pep·sin
pep·tic
per·am·bu·late
  per·am·bu·lat·ed
  per·am·bu·lat·ing
  per·am·bu·la·tion
  per·am·bu·la·to·ry
per an·num
per·cale
per cap·i·ta
per·ceive
  per·ceived
  per·ceiv·ing
  per·ceiv·a·ble
  per·ceiv·a·bly
per·cent
  per·cent·age
  per·cen·tile
per·cept
  per·cep·ti·ble
  per·cep·ti·bil·i·ty
  per·cep·ti·bly
  per·cep·tion
  per·cep·tive
  per·cep·tu·al
per·chance
Per·che·ron
per·cip·i·ent
  per·cip·i·ence
per·co·late
  per·co·lat·ed
  per·co·lat·ing
  per·co·la·tion
  per·co·la·tor
per·cus·sion
  per·cus·sive
per di·em
per·di·tion
per·du·ra·ble
per·e·grine
  per·e·gri·na·tion
per·emp·to·ry

per·emp·to·ri·ly
per·emp·to·ri·ness
per·en·ni·al
  per·en·ni·al·ly
per·fect
  per·fect·er
  per·fect·ness
  per·fect·i·ble
  per·fect·i·bil·i·ty
  per·fec·tive
  per·fec·tion
  per·fect·ly
per·fi·dy
  per·fid·i·ous
per·fo·rate
  per·fo·rat·ed
  per·fo·rat·ing
  per·fo·ra·tor
  per·fo·ra·tion
per·force
per·form
  per·form·a·ble
  per·form·er
  per·for·mance
per·fume
  per·fumed
  per·fum·ing
  per·fum·ery
per·func·to·ry
  per·func·to·ri·ly
  per·func·to·ri·ness
per·haps
per·go·la
per·i·gee
per·il
  per·iled
  per·il·ing
  per·il·ous
  per·il·ous·ly
pe·rim·e·ter
  per·i·met·ric
  per·i·met·ri·cal
pe·ri·od
pe·ri·od·ic
  pe·ri·o·dic·i·ty
  pe·ri·od·i·cal
  pe·ri·od·i·cal·ly
per·i·pa·tet·ic
pe·riph·ery
  pe·riph·er·al
  pe·riph·er·al·ly
per·i·phrase
per·i·scope
  per·i·scopic
per·ish
  per·ish·a·ble
  per·ish·a·bil·i·ty
  per·ish·a·ble·ness
  per·ish·a·bly
per·i·stal·sis
  per·i·stal·tic
per·i·style
per·i·to·ni·tis
per·i·win·kle
per·jure
  per·jured
  per·jur·ing
  per·jur·er
  per·ju·ri·ous
  per·ju·ry
perky
  perk·i·est
perma·frost
per·ma·nent
  per·ma·nen·cy
per·me·ate
  per·me·at·ed
  per·me·at·ing

per·me·a·ble
  per·me·a·bil·i·ty
  per·me·a·bly
  per·me·a·tion
  per·me·a·tive
per·mis·si·ble
  per·mis·si·bil·i·ty
  per·mis·si·bly
per·mis·sion
per·mis·sive
per·mit
  per·mit·ted
  per·mit·ting
per·mute
  per·mu·ta·tion
per·ni·cious
per·o·rate
  per·o·ra·tion
per·ox·ide
per·pen·dic·u·lar
per·pe·trate
  per·pe·trat·ed
  per·pe·trat·ing
  per·pe·tra·tion
  per·pe·tra·tor
per·pet·u·al
  per·pet·u·al·ly
per·pet·u·ate
  per·pet·u·at·ed
  per·pet·u·at·ing
  per·pet·u·a·tor
per·pe·tu·i·ty
per·plex
  per·plexed
  per·plex·ing
  per·plex·i·ty
per·qui·site
per se
per·se·cute
  per·se·cut·ed
  per·se·cut·ing
  per·se·cu·tive
  per·se·cu·tor
  per·se·cu·tion
per·se·vere
  per·se·vered
  per·se·ver·ing
  per·se·ver·ance
per·si·flage
per·sim·mon
per·sist
  per·sist·ence
  per·sis·ten·cy
  per·sist·ent
per·snick·ety
per·son
  per·son·a·ble
  per·son·age
  per·son·al
  per·son·al·i·ty
  per·son·al·ize
  per·son·al·ized
  per·son·al·iz·ing
  per·son·al·ly
per·so·na non gra·ta
per·son·ate
  per·son·at·ed
  per·son·at·ing
  per·son·a·tion
  per·son·a·tor
per·son·i·fy
  per·son·i·fied
  per·son·i·fy·ing
  per·son·i·fi·ca·tion
per·son·nel
per·spec·tive
per·spi·ca·cious
  per·spi·cac·i·ty

per·spi·cu·i·ty
per·spic·u·ous
per·spire
per·spired
per·spir·ing
per·spi·ra·tion
per·suade
per·suad·ed
per·suad·ing
per·suad·a·ble
per·sua·sion
per·sua·sive
pert
pert·ly
pert·ness
per·tain
per·ti·na·cious
per·ti·nac·i·ty
per·ti·nent
per·ti·nence
per·ti·nent·ly
per·turb
per·turb·a·ble
per·tur·ba·tion
pe·ruse
pe·rused
pe·rus·ing
pe·rus·al
per·vade
per·vad·ed
per·vad·ing
per·vad·er
per·va·sion
per·va·sive
per·verse
per·verse·ness
per·ver·si·ty
per·ver·sion
per·vert
per·vert·ed
per·vi·ous
pes·ky
pesk·i·ness
pes·si·mism
pes·si·mist
pes·si·mis·tic
pes·si·mis·ti·cal·ly
pes·ter
pes·ti·cide
pes·tif·er·ous
pes·ti·lent
pes·ti·lence
pes·ti·len·tial
pes·tle
pet
pet·ted
pet·ting
pet·al
pet·aled
pet·i·ole
pe·tite
pe·tite·ness
pet·it four
pe·ti·tion
pe·ti·tion·ary
pe·ti·tion·er
pet·rel
pet·ri·fy
pet·ri·fied
pet·ri·fy·ing
pet·ri·fac·tion
pe·tro·chem·is·try
pe·trog·ra·phy
pet·rol
pe·tro·le·um
pe·trol·o·gy
pet·ti·coat
pet·ti·fog

pet·ti·fogged
pet·ti·fog·ging
pet·tish
pet·tish·ness
pet·ty
pet·ti·ly
pet·ti·ness
pet·u·lant
pet·u·lance
pet·u·lan·cy
pe·tu·nia
pew·ter
pe·yo·te
pha·e·ton
pha·lanx
phal·lus
phal·lic
phan·tasm
phan·tas·mal
phan·tas·ma·go·ria
phan·tas·ma·gor·ic
phan·ta·sy
phan·ta·sies
phan·tom
phar·aoh
phar·ma·ceu·ti·cal
phar·ma·ceu·tic
phar·ma·ceu·tics
phar·ma·cist
phar·ma·col·o·gy
phar·ma·col·o·gist
phar·ma·co·poe·ia
phar·ma·co·poe·ial
phar·ma·cy
phar·ynx
phase
phased
phas·ing
pheas·ant
phe·no·bar·bi·tal
phe·nom·e·non
phe·nom·e·na
phe·nom·e·nal
phi·al
phi·lan·der
phi·lan·der·er
phi·lan·thro·py
phi·lan·thro·pies
phil·an·throp·ic
phil·an·throp·i·cal
phi·lan·thro·pist
phi·lat·e·ly
phil·a·tel·ic
phi·lat·e·list
phil·har·mon·ic
Phil·ip·pine
phil·o·den·dron
phi·lol·o·gy
phi·lol·o·gist
phil·o·lo·gi·an
phil·o·log·i·cal
phi·los·o·phy
phi·los·o·pher
phil·o·soph·i·cal
phil·o·soph·ic
phi·los·o·phize
phil·ter
phle·bi·tis
phle·bot·o·my
phlegm
phleg·mat·ic
phleg·mat·i·cal
phlox
pho·bia
pho·bic
phoe·be
phoe·nix
phone

phoned
phon·ing
pho·neme
pho·ne·mic
pho·net·ics
pho·net·ic
pho·net·i·cal·ly
phon·ic
phon·ics
pho·no·graph
pho·nol·o·gy
pho·no·log·ic
pho·ny
pho·ni·ness
phos·phate
phos·pho·resce
phos·pho·res·cence
phos·pho·resced
phos·pho·resc·ing
phos·pho·res·cent
phos·pho·rus
pho·to·copy
pho·to·cop·ies
pho·to·cop·ied
pho·to·cop·y·ing
pho·to·en·grave
pho·to·en·grav·ing
pho·to·gen·ic
pho·to·graph
pho·tog·ra·pher
pho·tog·ra·phy
pho·to·graph·ic
pho·to·gra·vure
pho·to·stat
pho·to·syn·the·sis
phrase
phrased
phras·ing
phra·se·ol·o·gy
phre·net·ic
phre·nol·o·gy
phre·nol·o·gist
phy·lac·tery
phy·log·e·ny
phy·lum
phys·ic
phys·ick·ing
phys·i·cal
phys·i·cal·ly
phy·si·cian
phys·ics
phys·i·cist
phys·i·og·no·my
phys·i·og·nom·i·cal
phys·i·og·no·mist
phys·i·og·ra·phy
phys·i·o·graph·ic
phys·i·ol·o·gy
phys·i·o·log·i·cal
phys·i·ol·o·gist
phys·i·o·ther·a·py
phy·sique
pi·a·nis·si·mo
pi·ano
pi·an·o·for·te
pi·az·za
pi·ca
pic·a·dor
pic·a·resque
pic·a·yune
pic·a·yun·ish
pic·ca·lil·li
pic·co·lo
picked
pick·er·el
pick·et
pick·et·er
pick·ing

pick·le
pick·led
pick·ling
pick·pock·et
picky
pick·i·est
pic·nic
pic·nick·ing
pic·nick·er
pic·to·ri·al
pic·ture
pic·tured
pic·tur·ing
pic·tur·esque
pid·dle
pid·dled
pid·dling
pidg·in
piece·meal
piece·work
pierce
pierced
pierc·ing
pi·e·ty
pi·geon·hole
pi·geon·toed
pig·gish
pig·gy·back
pig·head·ed
pig·ment
pig·men·ta·tion
pik·er
pi·las·ter
pile
piled
pil·ing
pil·fer
pil·fer·age
pil·fer·er
pil·grim
pil·grim·age
pil·lage
pil·laged
pil·lag·ing
pil·lag·er
pil·lar
pil·lion
pil·lo·ry
pil·lo·ried
pil·low
pi·lot
pi·lot·age
pi·lot·less
pi·men·to
pim·ple
pim·pled
pim·ply
pin
pinned
pin·ning
pin·a·fore
pince-nez
pin·cers
pinch
pinch·er
pin·cush·ion
pine
piney
pined
pin·ing
pine·ap·ple
pin·feath·er
ping·pong
pin·ion
pin·na·cle
pin·nate
pi·noch·le
pin·to

pin·wheel
pi·o·neer
pi·ous
pi·ous·ness
pipe·line
pip·er
pi·pette
pip·ing
pip-squeak
pi·quant
pi·quan·cy
pi·quant·ness
pique
piqued
pi·quing
pi·ra·nha
pi·rate
pi·rat·ed
pi·rat·ing
pi·rat·i·cal
pi·ra·cy
pi·rogue
pir·ou·ette
pir·ou·et·ted
pir·ou·et·ting
pis·ca·to·ri·al
pis·ta·chio
pis·til
pis·til·late
pis·tol
pis·toled
pis·tol·ing
pis·ton
pit
pit·ted
pit·ting
pitch·black
pitch·blende
pitch·er
pitch·fork
pitchy
pith
pithy
pith·i·ness
pit·man
pi·ton
pit·tance
pi·tu·i·tar·y
pity
pit·ied
pit·y·ing
pit·e·ous
pit·i·a·ble
pit·i·ful
pit·i·less
piv·ot
piv·ot·al·ly
pixy
pix·ie
pix·ie·ish
piz·za
piz·ze·ri·a
piz·zi·ca·to
plac·a·ble
plac·a·bil·i·ty
plac·a·bly
plac·ard
pla·cate
pla·cat·ed
pla·cat·ing
pla·ca·tion
pla·ca·tive
place
plac·ed
plac·ing
pla·ce·bo
place·ment
pla·cen·ta

pla·cen·tal
plac·er
plac·id
  pla·cid·i·ty
  plac·id·ness
  plac·id·ly
plack·et
pla·gia·rize
  pla·gia·rized
  pla·gia·riz·ing
  pla·gia·riz·er
  pla·gia·rism
  pla·gia·rist
  pla·gia·ris·tic
  pla·gia·ry
plague
  plagued
  pla·guing
plaid
plain
  plain·ness
plain·clothes man
plain·spo·ken
plain·tiff
plain·tive
  plain·tive·ly
plait
  plait·ing
plan
  planned
  plan·ning
  plan·less
plane
  planed
  plan·ing
plan·et
plan·e·tar·i·um
plan·e·tary
plan·e·toid
plan·ish
plank·ing
plank·ton
plant
plant·a·ble
  plant·er
plan·tain
plan·ta·tion
plaque
plas·ma
plas·ter
  plas·tered
  plas·ter·ing
  plas·ter·er
  plas·ter·work
plas·ter·board
plas·tic
  plas·ti·cal·ly
  plas·tic·i·ty
plat
  plat·ted
  plat·ting
plate
  plat·ed
  plat·ing
pla·teau
plate·ful
plate·let
plat·en
plat·form
plat·i·num
plat·i·tude
  plat·i·tu·di·nal
  plat·i·tu·di·nous
  plat·i·tu·di·nize
pla·ton·ic
  pla·ton·i·cal·ly
pla·toon
plat·ter

plat·y·pus
plau·dit
plau·si·ble
  plau·si·bil·i·ty
  plau·si·ble·ness
  plau·si·bly
play·act·ing
play·back
play·boy
play·ful
  play·ful·ly
play·ground
play·house
play·mate
play·wright
pla·za
plea
plead
  plead·ed
  plead·ing
  plead·a·ble
pleas·ant
  pleas·ant·ly
  pleas·ant·ry
please
  pleased
  pleas·ing
  pleas·ing·ly
pleas·ure
  pleas·ur·a·ble
  pleas·ur·a·bly
pleat
  pleat·ed
plebe
ple·be·ian
pleb·i·scite
plec·trum
pledge
  pledged
  pledg·ing
  pledg·ee
Pleis·to·cene
ple·na·ry
ple·nip·o·tent
  plen·i·po·ten·ti·ar·y
plen·ty
  plen·i·tude
  plen·te·ous
  plen·ti·ful
  plen·ti·ful·ly
pleth·o·ra
pleu·ri·sy
plex·us
pli·a·ble
  pli·a·bil·i·ty
  pli·a·ble·ness
  pli·a·bly
pli·ant
  pli·an·cy
  pli·ant·ness
  pli·ant·ly
pli·ers
plight
plod
  plod·ded
  plod·ding
  plod·der
plop
  plopped
  plop·ping
plot
  plot·ted
  plot·ting
  plot·ter
plov·er
plow
  plow·a·ble
  plow·er

plow·share
pluck
plucky
  pluck·i·ly
  pluck·i·ness
plug
  plugged
  plug·ging
plum·age
plumb·er
plumb·ing
plume
  plumed
  plum·ing
plum·met
plump
  plump·ish
  plump·ly
  plump·ness
plun·der
  plun·der·er
plunge
  plunged
  plung·ing
plung·er
plu·ral
  plu·ral·ly
  plu·ral·ize
  plu·ral·iza·tion
plu·ral·ism
  plu·ral·ist
  plu·ral·is·tic
plu·ral·i·ty
  plu·ral·i·ties
plush
  plush·i·ness
  plushy
  plush·i·est
plu·toc·ra·cy
  plu·to·crat
  plu·to·crat·ic
plu·to·ni·um
plu·vi·al
ply
  plied
  ply·ing
ply·wood
pneu·mat·ic
  pneu·mat·i·cal·ly
pneu·mo·nia
poach
  poach·er
pock·et·book
pock·et·ful
pock·et·knife
pock·mark
pod
  pod·ded
  pod·ding
  pod·like
po·di·a·try
  po·di·a·trist
po·di·um
po·em
  po·et·ic
  po·et·i·cal
  po·et·i·cal·ly
po·e·sy
  po·e·sies
po·et
  po·et·ess
  po·et·ize
  po·et·lau·re·ate
  po·et·ry
po·grom
poign·ant
  poign·an·cy
  poig·nant·ly

poin·ci·ana
poin·set·tia
point
  point·ed
  point·ed·ly
  point·er
  point·less
poin·til·lism
poise
  poised
  pois·ing
poi·son
  poi·son·er
  poi·son·ing
  poi·son·ous
poke
  poked
  pok·ing
pok·er
poky
po·lar
Po·lar·is
po·lar·i·ty
  po·lar·i·za·tion
  po·lar·ize
  po·lar·ized
  po·lar·iz·ing
pole
  poled
  pol·ing
  pole·less
po·lem·ic
  po·lem·i·cal
  po·lem·i·cist
po·lice
  po·liced
  po·lic·ing
pol·i·cy
  pol·i·cies
pol·i·cy·hold·er
po·lio
pol·i·o·my·e·li·tis
pol·ish
po·lite
  po·lite·ly
  po·lite·ness
pol·i·tic
pol·i·tics
  po·lit·i·cal
  po·lit·i·cal·ly
  pol·i·ti·cian
  po·lit·i·cize
  po·lit·i·cized
  po·lit·i·ciz·ing
pol·i·ty
pol·ka
  pol·kaed
  pol·ka·ing
poll
  poll·ee
  poll·er
  poll·ster
pol·len
pol·li·nate
  pol·li·nat·ed
  pol·li·nat·ing
  pol·li·na·tion
  pol·li·na·tor
pol·li·wog
pol·lute
  pol·lut·ed
  pol·lut·ing
  pol·lu·tant
  pol·lu·ter
  pol·lu·tion
po·lo
  po·lo·ist
pol·o·naise

pol·ter·geist
pol·y·an·dry
  pol·y·an·drous
pol·y·chro·mat·ic
pol·y·chrome
  pol·y·chro·mat·ic
pol·y·es·ter
pol·y·eth·yl·ene
po·lyg·a·my
  po·lyg·a·mous
  po·lyg·a·mist
pol·y·glot
pol·y·gon
  po·lyg·o·nal
pol·y·graph
po·lyg·y·ny
  po·lyg·y·nous
pol·y·he·dron
pol·y·mer
  pol·y·mer·ize
  po·lym·er·i·za·tion
pol·y·mor·phism
Poly·ne·sia
pol·y·no·mi·al
pol·yp
pol·y·phon·ic
  po·lyph·o·ny
pol·y·sty·rene
pol·y·syl·lab·ic
  pol·y·syl·la·ble
pol·y·tech·nic
pol·y·the·ism
  pol·y·the·ist
  pol·y·the·is·tic
pol·y·un·sat·u·rat·ed
po·made
pome·gran·ate
pom·mel
  pom·meled
  pom·mel·ing
pom·pa·dour
pom·pa·no
pom·pon
pomp·ous
  pom·pos·i·ty
pon·cho
pon·der
  pon·der·a·ble
  pon·der·ous
pon·gee
pon·iard
pon·tiff
pon·tif·i·cal
  pon·tif·i·cal·ly
pon·tif·i·cate
  pon·tif·i·cat·ed
  pon·tif·i·cat·ing
pon·toon
po·ny
  po·nies
poo·dle
poor
  poor·ish
  poor·ly
pop·ery
  pop·ish
pop·eyed
pop·in·jay
pop·lar
pop·lin
pop·per
pop·py
  pop·pies
pop·py·cock
pop·u·lace
pop·u·lar
  pop·u·lar·ly
  pop·u·lar·i·ty

pop·u·lar·ize
pop·u·lar·ized
pop·u·lar·iz·ing
pop·u·lar·i·za·tion
pop·u·late
pop·u·lat·ed
pop·u·lat·ing
pop·u·la·tion
pop·u·lous
por·ce·lain
por·cine
por·cu·pine
pore
pored
por·ing
pork·er
por·nog·ra·phy
por·nog·ra·pher
por·no·graph·ic
por·no·graph·i·cal·ly
po·rous
po·ros·i·ty
po·rous·ness
por·poise
por·ridge
port·a·ble
port·a·bil·i·ty
port·a·bly
por·tage
por·taged
por·tag·ing
por·tal
por·tend
por·tent
por·ten·tous
por·ter
port·fo·lio
port·hole
por·ti·co
por·tion
port·ly
port·li·er
port·li·ness
por·trait
por·trait·ist
por·trai·ture
por·tray
por·tray·er
por·tray·al
Por·tu·gal
Por·tu·guese
pose
posed
pos·ing
pos·er
pos·seur
pos·it
po·si·tion
pos·i·tive
pos·i·tive·ly
pos·i·tive·ness
pos·i·tiv·ism
pos·i·tron
pos·se
pos·sess
pos·ses·sor
pos·sessed
pos·ses·sion
pos·ses·sive
pos·si·bil·i·ty
pos·si·ble
pos·si·bly
pos·sum
post·age
post·date
post·dat·ed
post·dat·ing
post·er

pos·te·ri·or
pos·te·ri·or·i·ty
pos·ter·i·ty
post·grad·u·ate
post·haste
post·hu·mous
pos·til·ion
post·lude
post·man
post·mark
post·mas·ter
post·mis·tress
post me·rid·i·em
post mor·tem
post·na·sal
post·na·tal
post·paid
post·par·tum
post·pone
post·poned
post·pon·ing
post·pon·a·ble
post·pone·ment
post·script
pos·tu·lant
pos·tu·late
pos·tu·lat·ed
pos·tu·lat·ing
pos·tu·la·tion
pos·tu·la·tor
pos·ture
pos·tured
pos·tur·ing
post·war
po·sy
po·sies
pot
pot·ted
pot·ting
po·ta·ble
pot·ash
po·tas·si·um
po·ta·to
po·ta·toes
pot·bel·ly
pot·bel·lied
po·tent
po·ten·cy
po·tent·ly
po·ten·tate
po·ten·tial
po·ten·ti·al·i·ty
po·ten·tial·ly
pot·hole
po·tion
pot·luck
pot·pour·ri
pot·tage
pot·ter
pot·tery
pouch
pouched
pouchy
poul·tice
poul·try
pounce
pounced
pounc·ing
pound·age
pound-fool·ish
pour
pour·a·ble
pout
pov·er·ty
pov·er·ty-strick·en
pow·der
pow·dery
pow·er

pow·er·ful
pow·er·ful·ly
pow·er·ful·ness
pow·er·less
pow·wow
prac·ti·ca·ble
prac·ti·ca·bil·i·ty
prac·ti·ca·ble·ness
prac·ti·ca·bly
prac·ti·cal
prac·ti·cal·i·ty
prac·ti·cal·ly
prac·tice
prac·ticed
prac·ti·tion·er
prae·di·al
prae·to·ri·an
prag·mat·ic
prag·mat·i·cal
prag·mat·i·cal·ly
prag·ma·tism
prag·ma·tist
prag·ma·tis·tic
prai·rie
praise
praised
prais·ing
praise·wor·thy
pra·line
prance
pranced
pranc·ing
prank
prank·ish
prank·ster
prate
prat·ed
prat·ing
prat·fall
prat·tle
prat·tled
prat·tling
prawn
prawn·er
prayer
prayer·ful
preach
preach·er
preach·ment
preachy
pre·ad·o·les·cence
pre·ad·o·les·cent
pre·am·ble
pre·ar·range
pre·ar·ranged
pre·ar·rang·ing
pre·ar·range·ment
pre·as·signed
pre·can·cel
pre·car·i·ous
pre·car·i·ous·ness
pre·cau·tion
pre·cau·tion·ary
pre·cede
pre·ced·ed
pre·ced·ing
prec·e·dence
prec·e·dent
pre·cept
pre·cep·tive
pre·cep·tor
pre·cep·to·ri·al
pre·ces·sion
pre·cinct
pre·cious
pre·ci·os·i·ty
pre·cious·ness
prec·i·pice

pre·cip·i·tous
pre·cip·i·tant
pre·cip·i·tate
pre·cip·i·tat·ed
pre·cip·i·tat·ing
pre·cip·i·ta·tive
pre·cip·i·ta·tor
pre·cip·i·ta·tion
pre·cip·i·tous
pre·cis
pre·cise
pre·cise·ness
pre·ci·sion
pre·ci·sion·ist
pre·clude
pre·clud·ed
pre·clud·ing
pre·clu·sion
pre·clu·sive
pre·co·cious
pre·co·cious·ness
pre·coc·i·ty
pre·cog·ni·tion
pre·cog·ni·tive
pre·con·ceive
pre·con·ceiv·ing
pre·con·cep·tion
pre·con·di·tion
pre·cook
pre·cur·sor
pre·cur·so·ry
pre·date
pred·a·tor
pred·a·to·ry
pre·de·cease
pred·e·ces·sor
pre·des·ti·nate
pre·des·ti·nat·ed
pre·des·ti·nat·ing
pre·des·ti·na·tion
pre·des·tine
pre·des·tined
pre·de·ter·mine
pre·de·ter·mined
pre·de·ter·min·ing
pre·de·ter·mi·na·tion
pred·i·ca·ble
pred·i·ca·bil·i·ty
pred·ic·a·ment
pred·i·cate
pred·i·ca·tion
pred·i·ca·tive
pre·dict
pre·dict·a·ble
pre·dict·a·bly
pre·dict·a·bil·i·ty
pre·dic·tion
pre·dic·tive
pre·di·lec·tion
pre·dis·pose
pre·dis·posed
pre·dis·pos·ing
pre·dis·po·si·tion
pre·dom·i·nant
pre·dom·i·nance
pre·dom·i·nan·cy
pre·dom·i·nate
pre·dom·i·nat·ed
pre·dom·i·nat·ing
pre·dom·i·na·tion
pre·em·i·nent
pre·em·i·nence
pre·empt
pre·emp·tor
pre·emp·tion
pre·emp·tive
pre·ex·ist
pre·ex·ist·ence

pre·ex·ist·ent
pre·fab·ri·cate
pre·fab·ri·cat·ed
pre·fab·ri·cat·ing
pre·fab·ri·ca·tion
pref·ace
pref·aced
pref·ac·ing
pref·a·to·ry
pre·fer
per·ferred
pre·fer·ring
pref·er·a·ble
pref·er·a·ble·ness
pref·er·a·bil·i·ty
pref·er·a·bly
pref·er·ence
pref·er·en·tial
pre·fer·ment
pre·fix
pre·flight
pre·form
preg·nant
preg·nan·cy
preg·na·bil·i·ty
pre·heat
pre·hen·sile
pre·his·tor·ic
pre·judge
pre·judged
pre·judg·ing
pre·judg·ment
prej·u·dice
prej·u·diced
prej·u·dic·ing
prej·u·di·cial
prel·ate
pre·lim·i·nary
pre·lim·i·nar·ies
pre·lim·i·nar·i·ly
prel·ude
prel·ud·ing
pre·ma·ture
pre·ma·ture·ness
pre·ma·tu·ri·ty
pre·med·i·cal
pre·med·i·tate
pre·med·i·tat·ed
pre·med·i·tat·ing
pre·med·i·ta·tive
pre·med·i·ta·tion
pre·men·stru·al
pre·mier
pre·miere
prem·ise
prem·ised
prem·is·ing
pre·mi·um
pre·mo·ni·tion
pre·mon·i·to·ry
pre·mon·i·to·ri·ly
pre·na·tal
pre·na·tal·ly
pre·oc·cu·py
pre·oc·cu·pied
pre·oc·cu·py·ing
pre·oc·cu·pa·tion
pre·op·er·a·tive
pre·or·dain
pre·pare
pre·pared
pre·par·ing
prep·a·ra·tion
pre·par·a·to·ry
pre·par·a·to·ri·ly
pre·pared·ness
pre·pay
pre·paid

pre·pay·ing
pre·pay·ment
pre·plan
pre·planned
pre·plan·ning
pre·pon·der·ant
pre·pon·der·ance
pre·pon·der·an·cy
pre·pon·der·ant·ly
pre·pon·der·ate
pre·pon·der·at·ed
pre·pon·der·at·ing
pre·pon·der·at·ing·ly
pre·pon·der·a·tion
prep·o·si·tion
pre·pos·sess
pre·pos·sess·ing
pre·pos·ses·sion
pre·pos·ter·ous
pre·puce
pre·re·cord
pre·req·ui·site
pre·rog·a·tive
pres·age
pres·aged
pres·ag·ing
Pres·by·te·ri·an
pres·by·tery
pre·school
pre·scind
pre·sci·ence
pre·sci·ent
pre·scribe
pre·scribed
pre·scrib·ing
pre·script
pre·scrip·tion
pre·scrip·tive
pre·sea·son
pres·ence
pre·sent
pre·sent·er
pres·ent
pre·sent·a·ble
pre·sent·a·bil·i·ty
pre·sent·a·ble·ness
pre·sent·a·bly
pres·en·ta·tion
pres·ent·ly
pre·serve
pre·served
pre·serv·ing
pre·serv·a·ble
pres·er·va·tion
pre·serv·a·tive
pre·side
pre·sid·ed
pre·sid·ing
pres·i·dent
pres·i·den·tial
pres·i·den·cy
pre·sid·i·um
pre·sig·ni·fy
press·ing
pres·sure
pres·sured
pres·sur·ing
pres·su·rize
pres·su·rized
pres·su·riz·er
pres·su·ri·za·tion
press·work
pres·ti·dig·i·ta·tion
pres·it·dig·i·ta·tor
pres·tige
pres·tig·ious
pres·tis·si·mo
pres·to

pre·sum·a·ble
pre·sum·a·bly
pre·sume
pre·sumed
pre·sum·ing
pre·sump·tion
pre·sump·tive
pre·sump·tu·ous
pre·sup·pose
pre·sup·posed
pre·sup·pos·ing
pre·sup·po·si·tion
pre·tend
pre·tend·ed
pre·tend·er
pre·tense
pre·ten·sion
pre·ten·tious
pret·er·it
pret·er·i·tion
pre·ter·nat·u·ral
pre·test
pre·text
pret·ti·fy
preti·ti·fi·ca·tion
pret·ty
pret·ti·ly
pret·ti·ness
pret·zel
pre·vail
pre·vail·ing
prev·a·lent
prev·a·lence
pre·vent
pre·vent·a·ble
pre·vent·a·bil·i·ty
pre·ven·ta·tive
pre·ven·tion
pre·ven·tive
pre·view
pre·vi·ous
pre·vi·sion
pre·war
prey
prey·er
price·less
prick·le
prick·ly
prick·li·ness
pride
prid·ed
prid·ing
pride·ful·ly
prie-dieu
priest
priest·ess
priest·hood
priest·ly
priest·li·ness
prig
prig·gish
prim
primmed
prim·ming
prim·ness
pri·ma·cy
pri·ma don·na
pri·ma fa·cie
pri·mal
pri·ma·ri·ly
pri·ma·ry
pri·mar·ies
pri·mate
prime
primed
prim·ing
prime me·rid·i·an
prim·er

pri·me·val
prim·i·tive
pri·mo·gen·i·tor
pri·mo·gen·i·ture
pri·mor·di·al
prim·rose
prince·ly
prince·li·ness
prin·cess
prin·ci·pal
prin·ci·pal·ly
prin·ci·pal·i·ty
prin·ci·pal·i·ties
prin·ci·ple
prin·ci·pled
print·a·ble
print·ing
print·out
pri·or
pri·or·ess
pri·or·i·ty
pri·or·i·ties
pri·o·ry
prism
pris·mat·ic
pris·on
pris·on·er
pris·sy
pris·si·ness
pris·tine
pri·va·cy
pri·vate
pri·vate·ly
pri·va·tion
priv·et
priv·i·lege
priv·i·leged
priv·i·leg·ing
priv·y
priv·ies
prize
prized
priz·ing
prize·fight·er
prob·a·ble
prob·a·bly
prob·a·bil·i·ty
prob·a·bil·i·ties
pro·bate
pro·bat·ed
pro·bat·ing
pro·ba·tion
pro·ba·tion·al
pro·ba·tion·ary
pro·ba·tion·al·ly
pro·ba·tion·er
pro·ba·tive
pro·ba·to·ry
probe
probed
prob·ing
prob·lem
prob·lem·at·ic
pro·lem·at·i·cal
pro·bos·cis
pro·ce·dure
pro·ce·dur·al
pro·ce·dur·al·ly
pro·ceed
pro·ceed·ing
pro·ceeds
proc·ess
pro·ces·sion
pro·ces·sion·al
pro·claim
proc·la·ma·tion
pro·cliv·i·ty
pro·cliv·i·ties

pro·con·sul
pro·cras·ti·nate
pro·cras·ti·nat·ed
pro·cras·ti·nat·ing
pro·cras·ti·na·tion
pro·cras·ti·na·tor
pro·cre·ate
pro·cre·at·ed
pro·cre·at·ing
pro·cre·a·tion
pro·cre·a·tive
pro·cre·a·tor
pro·cre·ant
proc·tor
proc·to·ri·al
pro·cure
pro·cured
pro·cur·ing
pro·cur·a·ble
pro·cur·ance
pro·cure·ment
pro·cur·er
prod
prod·ded
prod·ding
prod·der
prod·i·gal
prod·i·gal·i·ty
prod·i·gal·ly
pro·di·gious
pro·di·gious·ness
prod·i·gy
pro·duce
pro·duced
pro·duc·ing
pro·duc·er
prod·uct
pro·duc·tion
pro·duc·tive
pro·duc·tiv·i·ty
pro·fane
pro·faned
pro·fan·ing
pro·fan·a·to·ry
pro·fane·ness
pro·fan·er
pro·fan·i·ty
pro·fess
pro·fessed
pro·fess·ed·ly
pro·fes·sion
pro·fes·sion·al
pro·fes·sion·al·ism
pro·fes·sion·al·ize
pro·fes·sion·al·ized
pro·fes·sion·al·iz·ing
pro·fes·sor
pro·fes·so·ri·al
pro·fes·so·ri·al·ly
pro·fes·sor·ship
prof·fer
pro·fi·cient
pro·fi·cien·cy
pro·file
pro·filed
pro·fil·ing
prof·it
prof·it·less
prof·it·a·ble
prof·it·a·bil·i·ty
prof·it·a·ble·ness
prof·it·a·bly
prof·it·eer
prof·li·gate
prof·li·ga·cy
pro·found
pro·fun·di·ty
pro·fuse

pro·fuse·ly
pro·fu·sion
pro·gen·i·tor
prog·e·ny
prog·no·sis
prog·nos·tic
prog·nos·ti·cate
prog·nos·ti·cat·ed
prog·nos·ti·cat·ing
prog·nos·ti·ca·tion
prog·nos·ti·ca·tive
prog·nos·ti·ca·tor
pro·gram
pro·grammed
pro·gram·ming
pro·gramed
pro·gram·ing
pro·gram·mer
pro·gram·er
prog·ress
pro·gres·sion
pro·gres·sive
pro·hib·it
pro·hi·bi·tion
pro·hi·bi·tion·ist
pro·hib·i·tive
pro·hib·i·to·ry
pro·ject
pro·jec·tile
pro·jec·tion
pro·jec·tion·ist
pro·jec·tive
pro·jec·tive·ly
pro·jec·tiv·i·ty
pro·jec·tor
pro·le·tar·i·at
pro·le·tar·i·an
pro·lif·er·ate
pro·lif·er·at·ed
pro·lif·er·at·ing
pro·lif·er·a·tion
pro·lif·er·a·tive
pro·lif·ic
pro·lif·i·ca·cy
pro·lif·ic·ness
pro·lif·i·cal·ly
pro·lix
pro·lix·i·ty
pro·loc·u·tor
pro·lo·gue
pro·long
pro·lon·ga·tion
prom·e·nade
prom·e·nad·ed
prom·e·nad·ing
prom·e·nad·er
prom·i·nence
prom·i·nent
prom·i·nent·ly
pro·mis·cu·ous
pro·mis·cu·ous·ly
pro·mis·cu·ous·ness
pro·mis·cu·i·ty
prom·ise
prom·ised
prom·is·ing
prom·ise·ful
prom·is·so·ry
prom·on·to·ry
pro·mote
pro·mot·ed
pro·mot·ing
pro·mot·a·ble
pro·mot·er
pro·mo·tion
pro·mo·tive
prompt
prompt·er

prompt·ly
prompt·ness
promp·ti·tude
prom·ul·gate
prom·ul·gat·ed
prom·ul·gat·ing
prom·ul·ga·tion
prone
prone·ness
prong
pro·noun
pro·nounce
pro·nounced
pro·nounc·ing
pro·nounce·a·ble
pro·nun·ci·a·tion
pro·nounce·ment
pron·to
proof
proof·read·er
prop
propped
prop·ping
prop·a·gan·da
prop·a·gan·dist
prop·a·gan·dis·tic
prop·a·gan·dis·ti·cal·ly
prop·a·gan·dism
prop·a·gan·dize
prop·a·gan·dized
prop·a·gan·diz·ing
prop·a·gate
prop·a·gat·ed
prop·a·gat·ing
prop·a·ga·tive
prop·a·ga·tor
prop·a·ga·tion
prop·a·ga·tion·al
pro·pane
pro·pel
pro·pelled
pro·pel·ling
pro·pel·lant
pro·pel·ler
pro·pen·si·ty
pro·pen·si·ties
prop·er
prop·er·ly
prop·er·ty
prop·er·ties
prop·er·tied
proph·e·cy
proph·e·cies
proph·e·sy
proph·e·sied
proph·e·sy·ing
proph·et
pro·phet·ic
pro·phet·i·cal·ly
pro·phy·lac·tic
pro·phy·lax·is
pro·pin·qui·ty
pro·pi·ti·ate
pro·pi·ti·at·ed
pro·pi·ti·at·ing
pro·pi·ti·a·tion
pro·pi·ti·a·to·ry
pro·pi·tious
pro·pi·tious·ly
pro·po·nent
pro·por·tion
pro·por·tion·a·ble
pro·por·tion·a·bly
pro·por·tion·al
pro·por·tion·al·i·ty
pro·por·tion·ate
pro·pose
pro·posed

pro·pos·ing
pro·pos·al
pro·pos·er
prop·o·si·tion
pro·pound
pro·pri·e·tary
pro·pri·e·tor
pro·pri·etress
pro·pri·e·ty
pro·pri·e·ties
pro·pul·sion
pro·pul·sive
pro·rata
pro·rate
pro·rat·ed
pro·rat·ing
pro·ra·tion
pro·sa·ic
pro·sa·i·cal·ly
pro·sa·ic·ness
pro·scribe
pro·scribed
pro·scrib·ing
pro·scrib·er
pro·scrip·tion
pro·scrip·tive
pros·e·cute
pros·e·cut·a·ble
pros·e·cu·tion
pros·e·cu·tor
pros·e·lyte
pros·e·ly·tism
pros·e·ly·tize
pros·pect
pros·pec·tor
pro·spec·tive
pro·spec·tus
pros·per
pros·per·i·ty
pros·per·ous
pros·tate
pros·the·sis
pros·thet·ic
pros·tho·don·tics
pros·tho·don·tist
pros·ti·tute
pros·ti·tut·ed
pros·ti·tut·ing
pros·ti·tu·tion
pros·ti·tu·tor
pros·trate
pros·trat·ed
pros·trat·ing
pros·tra·tion
pro·tag·o·nist
pro·te·an
pro·tect
pro·tect·ing
pro·tec·tive
pro·tec·tive·ness
pro·tec·tor
pro·tec·tion
pro·tec·tion·ism
pro·tec·tion·ist
pro·tec·tor·ate
pro·te·ge
pro·tein
Prot·er·o·zo·ic
pro·test
prot·es·ta·tion
Prot·es·tant
Prot·es·tant·ism
pro·to·col
pro·ton
pro·to·plasm
pro·to·type
pro·to·zo·an
pro·tract

pro·trac·tion
pro·trac·tive
pro·trac·tile
pro·trac·tor
pro·trude
pro·trud·ed
pro·trud·ing
pro·trud·ent
pro·tru·sion
pro·tru·sive
pro·tu·ber·ance
pro·tu·ber·ant
proud
proud·ly
prove
proved
prov·en
prov·ing
prov·a·ble
prov·a·bly
prov·erb
pro·ver·bi·al
pro·vide
pro·vid·ed
pro·vid·ing
pro·vid·a·ble
pro·vid·er
prov·i·dence
prov·i·den·tial
prov·i·dent
prov·ince
pro·vin·cial
pro·vin·ci·al·i·ty
pro·vin·cial·ly
pro·vin·cial·ist
pro·vin·cial·ize
pro·vin·cial·ized
pro·vin·cial·iz·ing
pro·vin·cial·ism
pro·vi·sion
pro·vi·sion·al
pro·vi·sion·al·ly
pro·vi·sion·ary
pro·vi·so·ry
pro·vi·so
pro·voke
pro·voked
pro·vok·ing
pro·vok·ing·ly
prov·o·ca·tion
pro·voc·a·tive
prov·ost
prow·ess
prowl
prowl·er
prox·i·mal
prox·i·mate
prox·im·i·ty
proxy
prox·ies
prude
prud·ery
prud·ish
pru·dence
pru·dent
pru·den·tial
prune
pruned
prun·ing
pru·ri·ent
pru·ri·ence
pru·ri·en·cy
pry
pried
pry·ing
psalm·book
psalm·ist
Psal·ter

pseu·do
pseu·do·nym
pseu·don·y·mous
pseu·do·sci·ence
pseu·do·sci·en·tif·ic
pshaw
pso·ri·a·sis
psy·che
psych·e·del·ic
psy·chi·a·try
psy·chi·at·ric
psy·chi·at·ri·cal·ly
psy·chi·a·trist
psy·chic
psy·chi·cal
psy·chi·cal·ly
psy·cho·a·nal·y·sis
psy·cho·an·a·lyt·ic
psy·cho·an·a·lyt·i·cal
psy·cho·an·a·lyze
psy·cho·an·a·lyzed
psy·cho·an·a·lyz·ing
psy·cho·an·a·lyst
psy·cho·bi·ol·o·gy
psy·cho·dra·ma
psy·cho·dy·nam·ic
psy·cho·dy·nam·i·cal·ly
psy·cho·gen·e·sis
psy·cho·ge·net·ic
psy·cho·gen·ic
psy·cho·gen·i·cal·ly
psy·cho·log·i·cal
psy·cho·log·ic
psy·cho·log·i·cal·ly
psy·chol·o·gy
psy·chol·o·gist
psy·cho·met·ric
psy·cho·met·ri·cal·ly
psy·cho·mo·tor
psy·cho·neu·ro·sis
psy·cho·neu·ro·ses
psy·cho·neu·rot·ic
psy·cho·path
psy·cho·pa·thol·o·gy
psy·cho·pa·thol·o·gist
psy·cho·path·o·log·ic
psy·cho·path·o·log·i·cal
psy·chop·a·thy
psy·cho·path·ic
psy·cho·path·i·cal·ly
psy·cho·sis
psy·cho·ses
psy·chot·ic
psy·chot·i·cal·ly
psy·cho·so·mat·ic
psy·cho·so·mat·i·cal·ly
psy·cho·ther·a·py
psy·cho·ther·a·peu·tics
psy·cho·ther·a·peu·tic
psy·cho·ther·a·peu·ti·cal·ly
psy·cho·ther·a·pist
pto·maine
pu·ber·ty
pu·bes·cence
pu·bes·cen·cy
pu·bes·cent
pu·bic
pub·lic
pub·lic·ly
pub·lic·ness
pub·li·cist
pub·lic·i·ty
pub·li·cize
pub·li·cized
pub·li·ciz·ing
pub·lish
pub·lish·er
pub·li·ca·tion

puck·er
pud·ding
pud·dle
pud·dled
pud·dling
pudgy
pudg·i·ness
pueb·lo
pu·er·ile
pu·er·il·i·ty
pu·er·per·al
Puer·to· Ri·co
puff
puff·i·ness
puffy
pu·gil·ism
pu·gil·ist
pu·gil·is·tic
pug·na·cious
pug·na·cious·ness
pug·nac·i·ty
puke
puked
puk·ing
pul·let
pul·ley
pul·mo·nary
pul·mo·tor
pulp
pulp·i·ness
pulpy
pul·pit
pul·sar
pul·sate
pul·sat·ed
pul·sat·ing
pul·sa·tion
pul·sa·tor
pulse
pulsed
puls·ing
pul·ver·ize
pul·ver·ized
pul·ver·iz·ing
pul·ver·iz·a·ble
pul·ver·i·za·tion
pul·ver·iz·er
pu·ma
pum·ice
pum·mel
pum·meled
pum·melled
pum·mel·ing
pum·mel·ling
pump
pump·a·ble
pump·er
pum·per·nick·el
pump·kin
pun
punned
pun·ning
punch
punch-drunk
punc·til·io
punc·til·i·ous
punc·tu·al
punc·tu·al·i·ty
punc·tu·al·ly
punc·tu·al·ness
punc·tu·ate
punc·tu·at·ed
punc·tu·at·ing
punc·tu·a·tion
punc·ture
punc·tured
punc·tur·ing
punc·tur·a·ble

pun·dit
pun·gent
  pun·gen·cy
  pun·gent·ly
pun·ish
  pun·ish·a·ble
  pun·ish·ment
pu·ni·tive
pun·ster
pu·ny
  pu·ni·er
  pu·ni·est
  pu·ni·ness
pu·pa
pu·pil
pup·pet
  pup·pet·eer
  pup·pet·ry
pup·py
  pup·pies
  pup·py·ish
pur·chase
  pur·chased
  pur·chas·ing
  pur·chas·a·ble
  pur·chas·er
pure
  pure·ly
  pure·ness
  pu·ri·fy
  pu·ri·ty
pu·ree
pur·ga·tive
  pur·ga·tion
pur·ga·to·ry
  pur·ga·to·ri·al
purge
  purged
  purg·ing
pu·ri·fy
  pu·ri·fied
  pu·ri·fy·ing
  pu·ri·fi·ca·tion
  pu·ri·fi·er
pur·ism
  pur·ist
  pu·ris·tic
pu·ri·tan
  pu·ri·tan·i·cal
  pu·ri·tan·i·cal·ly
pu·ri·ty
purl
pur·loin
  pur·loin·er
pur·ple
  pur·plish
pur·port
  pur·port·ed·ly
pur·pose
  pur·pose·ful·ly
  pur·pose·ly
  pur·pos·ive
purse
  pursed
  purs·ing
purs·er
pur·su·ant
  pur·su·ance
pur·sue
  pur·sued
  pur·su·ing
  pur·su·er
  pur·suit
pu·ru·lent
  pu·ru·lence
  pu·ru·len·cy
  pu·ru·lent·ly
pur·vey

pur·vey·or
pur·vey·ance
pur·view
pushy
  push·i·ly
  push·i·ness
push·cart
push·o·ver
pu·sil·lan·i·mous
  pu·sil·la·nim·i·ty
  pu·sil·lan·i·mous·ly
puss·y·foot
puss·y·wil·low
pus·tule
put
  put
  put·ting
pu·ta·tive
pu·tre·fy
  pu·tre·fied
  pu·tre·fy·ing
  pu·tre·fac·tion
pu·trid
  pu·trid·ness
putt
  putt·ed
  putt·ing
put·ter
put·ty
puz·zle
  puz·zled
  puz·zling
  puz·zler
  puz·zle·ment
pyg·my
py·lon
py·or·rhea
pyr·a·mid
  py·ram·i·dal
pyre
py·ro·ma·nia
  py·ro·ma·ni·ac
  py·ro·ma·ni·a·cal
py·rom·e·ter
py·ro·tech·nics
py·thon

Q

quack·ery
quad·ran·gle
  quad·ran·gu·lar
quad·rant
  quad·ran·tal
quad·rate
  quad·rat·ed
  quad·rat·ing
quad·rat·ic
  quad·rat·ics
quad·ra·ture
qua·dren·ni·al
quad·ri·lat·er·al
qua·drille
quad·ril·lion
  quad·ril·lionth
quad·roon
quad·ru·ped
quad·ru·ple
  quad·ru·pled
  quad·ru·pling
  quad·ru·plet
  quad·ru·pli·cate
quaff
quag·mire
quail
quaint·ly
quake

quaked
quak·ing
Quak·er
qual·i·fy
  qual·i·fied
  qual·i·fy·ing
  qual·i·fi·a·ble
  qual·i·fi·ca·tion
qual·i·ta·tive
qual·i·ty
  qual·i·ties
qualm
  qualm·ish
quan·da·ry
quan·ti·fy
  quan·ti·fied
  quan·ti·fy·ing
  quan·ti·fi·a·ble
  quan·ti·fi·ca·tion
quan·ti·ta·tive
quan·ti·ty
  quan·ti·ties
quan·tum
quar·an·tine
  quar·an·tin·a·ble
quar·rel
  quar·reled
  quar·rel·ing
quar·rel·some
quar·ry
  quar·ries
  quar·ried
  quar·ry·ing
quart
quar·ter
quar·ter·back
quar·ter·ing
quar·ter·ly
quar·ter·mas·ter
quar·tet
qua·sar
quash
qua·si
qua·si·ju·di·cial
qua·ter·nary
quat·rain
qua·ver
  quav·er·ing·ly
quay
quea·sy
  quea·si·ly
  quea·si·ness
queen
  queen·li·ness
  queen·ly
queer
  queer·ness
quell
quench
  quench·a·ble
quer·u·lous
que·ry
  que·ried
  que·ry·ing
quest
  quest·ing·ly
ques·tion
  ques·tion·er
ques·tion·a·ble
  ques·tion·a·ble·ness
  ques·tion·a·bil·i·ty
  ques·tion·a·bly
  ques·tion·naire
queue
  queued
  queu·ing
quib·ble
  quib·bled

quib·bling
quick
  quick·en
quick·ness
quick·freeze
quick·sand
quick·sil·ver
quick-tem·pered
quick-wit·ted
qui·es·cent
  qui·es·cence
qui·et
  qui·et·ly
  qui·et·ness
qui·e·tude
quill
quilt
  quilt·ing
quince
qui·nine
quin·quen·ni·al
quin·tes·sence
  quin·tes·sen·tial
quin·tet
quin·til·lion
  quin·til·lion·th
quin·tu·ple
  quin·tu·pled
  quin·tu·pling
  quin·tu·plet
quip
  quipped
  quip·ping
  quip·ster
quirk
  quirk·i·ness
  quirky
quis·ling
quit
  quit·ted
  quit·ting
quit·claim
quit·tance
quite
quit·ter
quiv·er
quix·ot·ic
  quix·ot·i·cal·ly
quiz
  quiz·zes
  quizzed
  quiz·zing
  quiz·zi·cal
quoit
quon·dam
Quon·set
quo·rum
quo·ta
  quo·ta·tion
quote
  quot·ed
  quot·ing
  quot·able
quo·tid·i·an
quo·tient

R

rab·bet
  rab·bet·ed
  rab·bet·ing
rab·bi
  rab·bis
rab·bin·i·cal
  rab·bin·i·cal·ly
rab·bit
rab·ble

rab·id
  rab·id·ly
ra·bies
race
  raced
  rac·ing
race·horse
rac·er
race·track
ra·cial
  ra·cial·ly
rac·ism
  ra·cial·ism
  rac·ist
rack·et
  rack·et·eer
rac·on·teur
racy
  rac·i·ly
  rac·i·ness
ra·dar
ra·di·al
  ra·di·al·ly
ra·di·ate
  ra·di·at·ed
  ra·di·at·ing
  ra·di·ance
  ra·di·an·cy
  ra·di·ant
  ra·di·a·tion
  ra·di·a·tor
rad·i·cal
  rad·i·cal·ly
  rad·i·cal·ism
ra·dio
  ra·di·oed
  ra·di·o·ing
ra·di·o·ac·tive
  ra·di·o·ac·tiv·i·ty
ra·di·o·fre·quen·cy
ra·di·o·gram
ra·di·o·graph
ra·dio·iso·tope
ra·di·ol·o·gy
  ra·di·ol·o·gist
ra·di·os·copy
rad·ish
ra·di·um
ra·di·us
ra·don
raf·fia
raf·fish
raft·er
rag
ragged
rag·a·muf·fin
rage
  raged
  rag·ing
rag·ged
  rag·ged·ness
rag·time
rag·weed
raid·er
rail·ing
rail·lery
rail·road
rail·way
rai·ment
rain·bow
rain·coat
rain·fall
rainy
  rain·i·er
  rain·i·ly
  rain·i·ness
  rainy
raise

raised
rais·ing
rai·sin
rake
raked
rak·ing
rak·ish
rak·ish·ness
ral·ly
ral·lied
ral·ly·ing
ram
rammed
ram·ming
ram·ble
ram·bled
ram·bling
ram·bler
ram·bunc·tious
ram·i·fy
ram·i·fied
ram·i·fy·ing
ram·i·fi·ca·tion
ram·page
ram·paged
ram·pag·ing
ramp·ant
ram·pan·cy
ram·pant·ly
ram·part
ram·rod
ram·shack·le
ran·cid
ran·cid·i·ty
ran·cid·ness
ran·cor
ran·cor·ous
ran·dom
ran·dom·ly
ran·dom·ness
ran·dom·ize
range
ranged
rang·ing
rangy
rang·i·ness
ran·kle
ran·kled
ran·kling
ran·sack
ran·som
rant·er
rap
rapped
rap·ping
ra·pa·cious
ra·pa·cious·ly
ra·pac·i·ty
rape
rap·ist
rap·id
ra·pid·i·ty
rap·id·ly
rap·id·ness
rap·id·fire
ra·pi·er
rap·ine
rap·port
rap·proche·ment
rap·scal·lion
rapt
rapt·ly
rap·ture
rap·tur·ous
rap·tur·ous·ly
rare
rar·er
rar·est

rare·bit
rar·e·fy
rar·e·fied
rar·e·fy·ing
rar·e·fac·tion
rar·e·fied
rare·ly
rar·i·ty
rar·i·ties
ras·cal
ras·cal·i·ty
ras·cal·ly
rash
rash·ly
rash·ness
rasp
rasp·ing·ly
raspy
rasp·ber·ry
rat
rat·ted
rat·ting
rat·a·ble
rate·a·ble
ratch·et
rate
rat·ed
rat·ing
rath·er
rat·i·fy
rat·i·fied
rat·i·fy·ing
rat·i·fi·ca·tion
rat·i·fi·er
ra·tio
ra·tios
ra·ti·oc·i·na·tion
ra·tion
ra·tion·al
ra·tion·al·i·ty
ra·tion·al·ly
ra·tion·ale
ra·tion·al·ism
ra·tion·al·ist
ra·tion·al·is·tic
ra·tion·al·is·ti·cal·ly
ra·tion·al·ize
ra·tion·al·ized
ra·tion·al·iz·ing
ra·tion·al·i·za·tion
ra·tion·al·iz·er
rat·tan
rat·tle
rat·tled
rat·tling
rat·tle·brain
rat·tler
rat·tle·snake
rat·ty
rat·ti·est
rau·cous
rau·cous·ly
raun·chy
raun·chi·er
rav·age
rav·aged
rav·ag·ing
rav·ag·er
rave
raved
rav·ing
rav·el
rav·eled
rav·el·ing
ra·ven
rav·en·ous
ra·vine
ra·vi·o·li

rav·ish
rav·ish·ment
rav·ish·ing
raw
raw·ness
ray·on
raze
razed
raz·ing
ra·zor
raz·zle-daz·zle
reach·able
re·act
re·ac·tive
re·ac·tion
re·ac·tion·ary
re·ac·ti·vate
re·ac·ti·vat·ed
re·ac·ti·vat·ing
re·ac·tor
read·a·ble
read·a·bil·i·ty
read·a·ble·ness
re·ad·just
re·ad·just·ment
ready
read·ied
read·y·ing
read·i·ly
read·i·ness
read·y·made
re·a·gent
re·al
re·al·ism
re·al·ist
re·al·is·tic
re·al·is·ti·cal·ly
re·al·i·ty
re·al·i·ties
re·al·ize
re·al·ized
re·al·iz·ing
re·al·iz·a·ble
re·al·i·za·tion
re·al·ly
realm
re·al·tor
re·al·ty
ream·er
re·an·i·mate
re·an·i·mat·ed
re·an·i·mat·ing
re·an·i·ma·tion
reap·er
re·ap·pear
re·ap·pear·ance
re·ap·por·tion
re·ap·por·tion·ment
rear ad·mi·ral
re·arm
re·ar·ma·ment
re·ar·range
re·ar·ranged
re·ar·rang·ing
re·ar·range·ment
rea·son
rea·son·er
rea·son·a·ble
rea·son·a·bil·i·ty
rea·son·a·ble·ness
rea·son·a·bly
rea·son·ing
re·as·sem·ble
re·as·sem·bled
re·as·sem·bling
re·as·sem·bly
re·as·sume
re·as·sump·tion

re·as·sure
re·as·sured
re·as·sur·ing
re·as·sur·ance
re·bate
re·bat·ed
re·bat·ing
reb·el
re·bel
re·belled
re·bel·ling
re·bel·lion
re·bel·lious
re·bel·lious·ness
re·birth
re·born
re·bound
re·buff
re·build
re·built
re·build·ing
re·buke
re·buked
re·buk·ing
re·but
re·but·ted
re·but·ting
re·but·ter
re·but·tal
re·cal·ci·trant
re·cal·ci·trance
re·cal·ci·tran·cy
re·call
re·cant
re·can·ta·tion
re·cap
re·capped
re·cap·ping
re·cap·pable
re·ca·pit·u·late
re·ca·pit·u·lat·ed
re·ca·pit·u·lat·ing
re·ca·pit·u·la·tion
re·cap·ture
re·cap·tured
re·cap·tur·ing
re·cast
re·cede
re·ced·ed
re·ced·ing
re·ceipt
re·ceiv·a·ble
re·ceive
re·ceived
re·ceiv·ing
re·ceiv·er
re·ceiv·er·ship
re·cent
re·cent·ly
re·cen·cy
re·cent·ness
re·cep·ta·cle
re·cep·tion
re·cep·tion·ist
re·cep·tive
re·cep·tive·ly
re·cep·tive·ness
re·cep·tiv·i·ty
re·cess
re·ces·sion
re·ces·sion·ary
re·ces·sion·al
re·ces·sive
re·charge
re·charged
re·charg·ing
re·cid·i·vism
re·cid·i·vist

rec·i·pe
re·cip·i·ent
re·cip·i·ence
re·cip·i·en·cy
re·cip·ro·cal
re·cip·ro·cal·ly
re·cip·ro·cate
re·cip·ro·cat·ed
re·cip·ro·cat·ing
re·cip·ro·ca·tion
re·cip·ro·ca·tive
rec·i·proc·i·ty
re·ci·sion
re·cit·al
re·cite
re·cit·ed
re·cit·ing
rec·i·ta·tion
rec·i·ta·tive
reck·less
reck·less·ness
reck·on
reck·on·ing
re·claim
re·claim·able
rec·la·ma·tion
re·cline
re·clined
re·clin·ing
re·clin·er
rec·luse
re·clu·sion
re·clu·sive
rec·og·nize
rec·og·nized
rec·og·niz·ing
rec·og·niz·a·ble
rec·og·niz·a·bly
rec·og·ni·tion
re·cog·ni·zance
re·coil
re·coil·less
rec·ol·lect
rec·ol·lect
rec·ol·lec·tion
rec·om·mend
rec·om·mend·a·ble
rec·om·mend·er
rec·om·men·da·tion
re·com·mit
re·com·mit·tal
rec·om·pense
rec·om·pensed
rec·om·pens·ing
rec·on·cile
rec·on·ciled
rec·on·cil·ing
rec·on·cil·a·ble
rec·on·cil·a·bly
rec·on·cil·er
rec·on·cil·i·a·tion
rec·on·cile·ment
rec·on·dite
re·con·di·tion
re·con·firm
re·con·fir·ma·tion
re·con·noi·ter
re·con·noi·tered
re·con·noi·ter·ing
re·con·nais·sance
re·con·sid·er
re·con·sid·er·a·tion
re·con·sti·tute
re·con·struct
re·con·struc·tion
re·cord
re·cord
re·cord·er

re·cord·ing
re·count
re·coup
re·course
re·cov·er
re·cov·ery
re·cov·er·able
rec·re·ant
re·cre·ate
re·cre·at·ed
re·cre·at·ing
re·cre·a·tion
rec·re·a·tion·al
rec·re·a·tive
re·crim·i·nate
re·crim·i·nat·ed
re·crim·i·nat·ing
re·crim·i·na·tion
re·crim·i·na·tive
re·crim·i·na·to·ry
re·cruit
re·cruit·er
re·cruit·ment
rec·tal
rec·tan·gle
rec·tan·gu·lar
rec·ti·fy
rec·ti·fied
rec·ti·fy·ing
rec·ti·fi·a·ble
rec·ti·fi·ca·tion
rec·ti·fi·er
rec·ti·lin·e·ar
rec·ti·tude
rec·tor
rec·to·ry
rec·tum
re·cum·bent
re·cum·ben·cy
re·cum·bent·ly
re·cu·per·ate
re·cu·per·at·ed
re·cu·per·at·ing
re·cu·per·a·tion
re·cu·per·a·tive
re·cur
re·curred
re·cur·ring
re·cur·rence
re·cur·rent
re·cy·cle
red
red·der
red·ness
red·den
red·dish
red-blood·ed
re·dec·o·rate
re·dec·o·rat·ed
re·dec·o·rat·ing
re·dec·o·ra·tion
re·ded·i·cate
re·ded·i·cat·ed
re·ded·i·cat·ing
re·ded·i·ca·tion
re·deem
re·deem·a·ble
re·deem·er
re·demp·tion
re·demp·tive
re·demp·to·ry
red-hand·ed
re·di·rect
re·di·rec·tion
re·dis·trib·ute
re·dis·tri·bu·tion
re·dis·trict

red-let·ter
re·do
re·did
re·done
re·do·ing
red·o·lent
red·o·lence
red·o·len·cy
re·dou·ble
re·dou·bled
re·dou·bling
re·doubt·a·ble
re·doubt·a·bly
re·dress
re·duce
re·duced
re·duc·ing
re·duc·er
re·duc·i·ble
re·duc·tion
re·dun·dant
re·dun·dance
re·dun·dan·cy
re·dun·dan·cies
re·dun·dant·ly
re·du·pli·cate
re·du·pli·cat·ed
re·du·pli·cat·ing
re·dup·li·ca·tion
re·echo
re·ech·o·ing
re·ech·oes
re·ed·u·cate
re·ed·u·ca·tion
reedy
reed·i·ness
re·e·lect
re·e·lec·tion
re·em·pha·size
re·em·pha·sized
re·em·pha·siz·ing
re·em·ploy
re·en·act
re·en·force
re·en·forced
re·en·forc·ing
re·en·force·ment
re·en·list
re·en·list·ment
re·en·ter
re·en·trance
re·en·try
re·es·tab·lish
re·es·tab·lish·ment
re·ex·am·ine
re·ex·am·ined
re·ex·am·in·ing
re·ex·am·i·na·tion
re·fer
re·ferred
re·fer·ring
re·fer·a·ble
re·fer·ral
ref·er·ee
ref·er·eed
ref·er·ee·ing
ref·er·ence
ref·er·enced
ref·er·enc·ing
ref·er·en·dum
ref·er·ent
ref·er·en·tial
ref·er·en·cy
re·fer·ral
re·fill
re·fill·a·ble
re·fi·nance
re·fine
re·fined

re·fin·ing
re·fine·ment
re·fin·ery
re·fin·ish
re·fit
re·fit·ted
re·fit·ting
re·flect
re·flec·tion
re·flec·tive
re·flec·tive·ly
re·flec·tor
re·flex
re·flex·ive
re·for·est
re·for·est·a·tion
re·form
re·formed
re·form·er
re·form·ist
ref·or·ma·tion
re·form·a·to·ry
re·form·a·tive
re·fract
re·frac·tive
re·frac·tion
re·frac·to·ry
re·frac·to·ri·ness
re·frain
re·fran·gi·ble
re·fresh
re·fresh·ing
re·fresh·ment
re·frig·er·ate
re·frig·er·at·ed
re·frig·er·at·ing
re·frig·er·ant
re·frig·er·a·tion
re·frig·er·a·tor
ref·uge
ref·u·gee
re·ful·gent
re·ful·gence
re·fund
re·fur·bish
re·fuse
re·fused
re·fus·ing
re·fus·al
ref·use
re·fute
re·fut·ed
re·fut·ing
re·fut·a·ble
ref·u·ta·tion
re·gain
re·gal
re·gal·ly
re·gale
re·galed
re·gal·ing
re·ga·lia
re·gard
re·gard·ful
re·gard·ing
re·gard·less
re·gat·ta
re·gen·cy
re·gen·er·ate
re·gen·er·at·ed
re·gen·er·at·ing
re·gen·er·a·cy
re·gen·er·a·tion
re·gen·er·a·tive
re·gent
re·gime
reg·i·men
reg·i·ment

reg·i·men·tal
reg·i·men·ta·tion
re·gion
re·gion·al
re·gion·al·ly
reg·is·ter
reg·is·tered
reg·is·trant
reg·is·trar
reg·is·tra·tion
reg·is·try
re·gress
re·gres·sion
re·gres·sive
re·gret
re·gret·ted
re·gret·ting
re·gret·ta·ble
re·gret·ta·bly
re·gret·ful·ly
re·gret·ful·ness
reg·u·lar
reg·u·lar·i·ty
reg·u·late
reg·u·lat·ed
reg·u·lat·ing
reg·u·la·tive
reg·u·la·tor
reg·u·la·to·ry
reg·u·la·tion
re·gur·gi·tate
re·gur·gi·tat·ed
re·gur·gi·tat·ing
re·gur·gi·ta·tion
re·ha·bil·i·tate
re·ha·bil·i·tat·ed
re·ha·bil·i·tat·ing
re·ha·bil·i·ta·tion
re·ha·bil·i·ta·tive
re·hash
re·hears·al
re·hearse
re·hearsed
re·hears·ing
reign
re·im·burse
re·im·bursed
re·im·burs·ing
re·im·burse·ment
rein
re·in·car·nate
re·in·car·na·tion
rein·deer
re·in·fec·tion
re·in·force
re·in·forced
re·in·forc·ing
re·in·force·ment
re·in·state
re·in·stat·ed
re·in·stat·ing
re·in·state·ment
re·in·sur·ance
re·in·ter·pre·ta·tion
re·is·sue
re·it·er·ate
re·it·er·at·ed
re·it·er·at·ing
re·it·er·a·tion
re·ject
re·jec·tion
re·joice
re·joiced
re·joic·ing
re·join
re·join·der
re·ju·ve·nate
re·ju·ve·nat·ed

re·ju·ve·nat·ing
re·ju·ve·na·tion
re·kin·dle
re·kin·dled
re·kin·dling
re·lapse
re·lapsed
re·laps·ing
re·late
re·lat·ed
re·lat·ing
re·la·tion
re·la·tion·al
re·la·tion·ship
rel·a·tive
rel·a·tive·ly
rel·a·tiv·i·ty
re·lax
re·lax·a·tion
re·lay
re·laid
re·lay·ing
re·lay
re·layed
re·lay·ing
re·lease
re·leased
re·leas·ing
rel·e·gate
rel·e·gat·ed
rel·e·gat·ing
rel·e·ga·tion
re·lent
re·lent·less
rel·e·vant
rel·e·vance
rel·e·van·cy
re·li·a·ble
re·li·a·bil·i·ty
re·li·a·ble·ness
re·li·a·bly
re·li·ant
re·li·ance
rel·ic
re·lief
re·lieve
re·lieved
re·liev·ing
re·liev·a·ble
re·li·gion
re·li·gi·os·i·ty
re·li·gious
re·lin·quish
rel·ish
re·live
re·lived
re·liv·ing
re·lo·cate
re·lo·cat·ed
re·lo·cat·ing
re·lo·ca·tion
re·luc·tant
re·luc·tance
re·ly
re·lied
re·ly·ing
re·main
re·main·der
re·mand
re·mark
re·mark·a·ble
re·mark·a·ble·ness
re·mark·a·bly
re·me·di·al
re·me·di·a·ble
rem·e·dy
rem·e·dies
rem·e·died

rem·e·dy·ing
re·mem·ber
re·mem·brance
re·mind
re·mind·er
rem·i·nisce
rem·i·nisced
rem·i·nisc·ing
rem·i·nis·cence
rem·i·nis·cent
re·miss
re·mis·sion
re·mit
re·mit·ted
re·mit·ting
re·mit·tance
rem·nant
re·mod·el
re·mon·strate
re·mon·strat·ed
re·mon·strat·ing
re·mon·strance
re·morse
re·morse·ful·ly
re·morse·less
re·mote
re·mote·ly
re·mote·ness
re·mount
re·move
re·moved
re·mov·ing
re·mov·a·ble
re·mov·al
re·mu·ner·ate
re·mu·ner·at·ed
re·mu·ner·at·ing
re·mu·ner·a·tion
re·mu·ner·a·tive
ren·ais·sance
re·nas·cence
re·nas·cent
rend
rend·ed
rend·ing
ren·der
ren·di·tion
ren·dez·vous
ren·dez·voused
ren·dez·vous·ing
ren·e·gade
re·nege
re·neged
re·neg·ing
re·new
re·new·al
re·nom·i·nate
re·nounce
re·nounced
re·nounc·ing
ren·o·vate
ren·o·vat·ed
ren·o·vat·ing
ren·o·va·tion
re·nown
re·nowned
rent·al
re·nun·ci·a·tion
re·or·gan·ize
re·or·gan·ized
re·or·gan·iz·ing
re·or·gan·i·za·tion
re·pair
rep·a·ra·ble
rep·a·ra·tion
rep·ar·tee
re·past
re·pa·tri·ate

re·pa·tri·at·ed
re·pa·tri·at·ing
re·pa·tri·a·tion
re·pay
re·paid
re·pay·ing
re·pay·ment
re·peal
re·peat
re·peat·a·ble
re·peat·ed
re·peat·er
re·pel
re·pelled
re·pel·ling
re·pel·lent
re·pent
re·pent·ance
re·pent·ant
re·per·cus·sion
rep·er·toire
rep·er·to·ry
rep·e·ti·tion
rep·e·ti·tious
re·pet·i·tive
re·place
re·placed
re·plac·ing
re·place·a·ble
re·place·ment
re·plen·ish
re·plete
re·ple·tion
rep·li·ca
re·ply
re·plied
re·ply·ing
re·plies
re·port
re·port·able
re·port·ed·ly
re·port·er
rep·or·to·ri·al
re·pose
re·posed
re·pos·ing
re·pos·i·tory
re·pos·sess
re·pos·ses·sion
rep·re·hend
rep·re·hen·si·ble
rep·re·hen·sion
rep·re·sent
rep·re·sen·ta·tion
rep·re·sent·a·tive
re·press
re·pres·sion
re·prieve
re·prieved
re·priev·ing
re·pri·mand
re·pris·al
re·proach
re·proach·ful·ly
rep·ro·bate
rep·ro·ba·tion
re·pro·duce
re·pro·duced
re·pro·duc·ing
re·pro·duc·tion
re·pro·duc·tive
re·proof
re·prove
re·proved
re·prov·ing
rep·tile
rep·til·i·an
re·pub·lic

re·pub·li·can
re·pu·di·ate
re·pu·di·at·ed
re·pu·di·at·ing
re·pu·di·a·tion
re·pug·nant
re·pug·nance
re·pug·nan·cy
re·pulse
re·plused
re·puls·ing
re·pul·sion
re·pul·sive
rep·u·ta·ble
rep·u·ta·bly
rep·u·ta·bil·i·ty
rep·u·ta·tion
re·pute
re·put·ed
re·put·ing
re·quest
req·ui·em
re·quire
re·quired
re·quir·ing
re·quire·ment
req·ui·site
req·ui·si·tion
re·quit·al
re·quite
re·run
re·run·ning
re·scind
re·scis·sion
res·cue
res·cued
res·cu·ing
re·search
re·search·er
re·sem·ble
re·sem·bled
re·sem·bling
re·sem·blance
re·sent
re·sent·ful
re·sent·ment
re·serve
re·served
re·serv·ing
res·er·va·tion
re·serv·ist
res·er·voir
re·set
re·set·ting
re·side
re·sid·ed
re·sid·ing
res·i·dence
res·i·den·cy
res·i·dent
res·i·den·tial
res·i·due
re·sid·u·al
re·sign
res·ig·na·tion
re·signed
re·sil·ient
re·sil·ience
re·sil·ien·cy
res·in
res·in·ous
re·sist
re·sist·er
re·sist·i·ble
re·sist·ance
re·sist·ant
re·sis·tor
res·o·lute

res·o·lu·tion
re·solve
re·solved
re·solv·ing
res·o·nant
res·o·nance
res·o·nate
res·o·nat·ed
res·o·nat·ing
res·o·na·tor
re·sort
re·sound
re·source
re·spect
re·spect·ful·ly
re·spect·ful·ness
re·spect·a·ble
re·spect·a·bil·i·ty
re·spect·ing
re·spec·tive
res·pi·ra·tion
res·pi·ra·to·ry
res·pi·ra·tor
re·spire
re·spired
re·spir·ing
res·pite
re·splend·ent
re·splend·ence
re·spond
re·spond·ent
re·sponse
re·spon·sive
re·spon·si·ble
re·spon·si·bil·i·ty
re·spon·si·bil·i·ties
res·tau·rant
res·tau·ra·teur
rest·ful·ly
res·ti·tu·tion
res·tive
re·store
re·stored
re·stor·ing
res·to·ra·tion
re·stor·a·tive
re·strained
re·straint
re·strict
re·strict·ed
re·stric·tion
re·stric·tive
re·sult
re·sult·ant
re·sume
re·sumed
re·sum·ing
re·sump·tion
re·su·me
re·sur·gent
re·sur·gence
res·ur·rect
res·ur·rec·tion
re·sus·ci·tate
re·sus·ci·tat·ed
re·sus·ci·tat·ing
re·sus·ci·ta·tion
re·sus·ci·ta·tor
re·tail·er
re·tain·er
re·take
re·took
re·tak·en
re·tak·ing
re·tal·i·ate
re·tal·i·at·ed
re·tal·i·at·ing
re·tal·i·a·tion

re·tal·i·a·to·ry
re·tard
re·tard·ant
re·tar·da·tion
re·tard·ed
retch
re·tell
re·told
re·telling
re·ten·tion
re·ten·tive
re·ten·tiv·i·ty
ret·i·cent
ret·i·cence
re·tic·u·lar
ret·i·na
ret·i·nue
re·tire
re·tired
re·tir·ing
re·tire·ment
re·tort
re·touch
re·trace
re·traced
re·trac·ing
re·tract
re·trac·tion
re·trac·tor
re·trac·tile
re·tread
re·treat
re·trench
re·trench·ment
re·tri·al
ret·ri·bu·tion
re·trieve
re·trieved
re·triev·ing
re·triev·er
ret·ro·ac·tive
ret·ro·fire
ret·ro·grade
ret·ro·gress
ret·ro·gres·sion
ret·ro·gres·sive
ret·ro·rock·et
ret·ro·spect
ret·ro·spec·tion
ret·ro·spec·tive
re·turn
re·turn·a·ble
re·turn·ee
re·un·ion
re·u·nite
re·u·nit·ed
re·u·nit·ing
rev
revved
rev·ving
re·value
re·val·u·ate
re·val·u·a·tion
re·vamp
re·veal
rev·e·la·tion
rev·eil·le
rev·el
rev·el·ry
re·venge
re·venged
re·veng·ing
re·venge·ful
rev·e·nue
rev·e·nu·er
re·ver·ber·ate
re·ver·ber·at·ed
re·ver·ber·at·ing

re·ver·ber·a·tion
re·vere
re·vered
re·ver·ing
rev·er·ence
rev·er·enced
rev·er·enc·ing
rev·er·end
rev·er·ent
rev·er·en·tial
rev·er·ie
re·ver·sal
re·verse
re·versed
re·vers·ing
re·vers·i·ble
re·ver·sion
re·vert
re·view
re·vile
re·viled
re·vil·ing
re·vise
re·vised
re·vis·ing
re·vi·sion
re·vi·sion·ist
re·vi·tal·ize
re·vi·tal·iza·tion
re·viv·al
re·viv·al·ist
re·vive
re·vived
re·viv·ing
re·viv·i·fy
rev·o·ca·tion
re·voke
re·voked
re·vok·ing
rev·o·ca·ble
rev·o·ca·tion
re·volt
rev·o·lu·tion
rev·o·lu·tion·ary
rev·o·lu·tion·aries
rev·o·lu·tion·ist
rev·o·lu·tion·ize
re·volve
re·volved
re·volv·ing
re·volv·er
re·vue
re·vul·sion
re·wak·en
re·ward
re·wind
re·wound
re·wind·ing
re·write
re·wrote
re·writ·ten
re·writ·ing
rhap·sod·ic
rhap·sod·i·cal·ly
rhap·so·dize
rhap·so·dized
rhap·so·diz·ing
rhap·so·dy
rhap·so·dies
rhap·so·dist
rhe·o·stat
rhe·sus
rhet·o·ric
rhe·tor·i·cal·ly
rhet·o·ri·cian
rheu·mat·ic
rheu·ma·tism
rheu·ma·toid

rhine·stone
rhi·noc·er·os
rhi·zome
rho·do·den·dron
rhom·boid
rhom·bus
rhu·barb
rhyme
rhymed
rhym·ing
rhythm
rhyth·mic
rhyth·mi·cal
rhyth·mi·cal·ly
rib
ribbed
rib·bing
rib·ald
rib·ald·ry
rib·bon
ri·bo·fla·vin
rib·bo·nu·cle·ic
rich·es
rich·ness
rick·ets
rick·ety
rick·et·i·ness
rick·shaw
ric·o·chet
ric·o·cheted
ric·o·chet·ing
rid
rid·ded
rid·ding
rid·dance
rid·dle
rid·dled
rid·dling
ride
rode
rid·den
rid·ing
rid·er
ridge
ridged
ridg·ing
rid·i·cule
rid·i·culed
rid·i·cul·ing
ri·dic·u·lous
rif·fle
rif·fled
rif·fling
ri·fle
ri·fled
ri·fling
rig
rigged
rig·ging
rig·ger
right·eous
right·ful·ly
right·hand·ed
right-of-way
right·wing·er
rig·id
ri·gid·i·ty
rig·ma·role
rig·or
rig·or·ous
ri·gor mor·tis
rile
riled
ril·ing
rim
rimmed
rim·ming
ring

ringed
ring·ing
ring
rang
rung
ring·ing
ring·lead·er
ring·mas·ter
rinse
rinsed
rins·ing
Rio de Ja·nei·ro
ri·ot·er
ri·ot·ous
rip
ripped
rip·ping
ri·par·i·an
rip·en
ripe·ness
rip·ple
rip·pled
rip·pling
rise
rose
ris·en
ris·ing
ris·i·ble
ris·i·bil·i·ty
risky
risk·i·er
risk·i·ness
ris·que
rite
rit·u·al
rit·u·al·ism
rit·u·al·ist
rit·u·al·is·tic
ritzy
ritz·i·er
ri·val
ri·val·ry
ri·val·ries
riv·er·side
riv·et·er
riv·i·era
riv·u·let
roach·es
road·bed
road·block
road·run·ner
roast·er
rob
robbed
rob·bing
rob·ber
rob·bery
rob·ber·ies
robe
robed
rob·ing
rob·in
ro·bot
ro·bot·ics
ro·bust
rock-bound
rock·er
rock·et
rock·et·ry
rock-ribbed
rocky
rock·i·ness
ro·co·co
ro·dent
ro·deo
roent·gen
rogue
ro·guish

ro·guery
roist·er
roll·er bear·ing
roll·er coast·er
roll·er-skate
rol·lick
rol·lick·ing
roll·ing mill
ro·ly-po·ly
ro·maine
ro·mance
ro·manced
ro·manc·ing
ro·man·tic
ro·man·ti·cism
ro·man·ti·cist
ro·man·ti·cize
ro·man·ti·cized
ro·man·ti·ciz·ing
romp·er
roof·ing
rook·ery
rook·ie
room·mate
roomy
room·i·er
room·i·ness
roost·er
rope
roped
rop·ing
ropy
ro·sa·ry
ro·sa·ries
ro·se·ate
ro·sette
Rosh Ha·sha·nah
ros·in
ros·ter
ros·trum
rosy
ros·i·ness
rot
rot·ted
rot·ting
rot·ten
ro·tate
ro·tat·ed
ro·tat·ing
ro·ta·ry
ro·ta·tion
ro·tis·ser·ie
ro·tund
ro·tun·di·ty
ro·tun·da
rou·e
rouge
rouged
roug·ing
rough·age
rough-and-tum·ble
rough·en
rough-hewed
rough·house
rough·neck
rough·rid·er
rough·shod
rou·lette
round·a·bout
round·ed
round·er
round-shoul·dered
rouse
roused
rous·ing
roust·a·bout
rout
route

rout·ed
rout·ing
rou·tine
rou·tin·ize
rou·tin·ized
rou·tin·iz·ing
rove
roved
rov·ing
row·dy
row·dies
row·di·ly
row·di·ness
roy·al
roy·al·ly
roy·al·ist
roy·al·ty
roy·al·ties
rub
rubbed
rub·bing
rub·ber
rub·bery
rub·ber·ize
rub·ber·ized
rub·ber·iz·ing
rub·bish
rub·ble
ru·bel·la
ru·bi·cund
ru·bric
ru·by
ru·bies
ruck·sack
ruck·us
rud·der
rud·dy
rud·di·ness
rude
rude·ly
rude·ness
ru·di·ment
ru·di·men·tal
ru·di·men·ta·ry
rue
rued
ru·ing
rue·ful·ly
rue·ful·ness
ruf·fi·an
ruf·fle
ruf·fled
ruf·fling
rug·ged
rug·ged·ness
ru·in
ru·in·a·tion
ru·in·ous
rule
ruled
rul·ing
rum·ba
rum·ble
rum·bled
rum·bling
ru·mi·nant
ru·mi·nate
ru·mi·nat·ing
ru·mi·na·tion
rum·mage
rum·mag·ing
rum·my
ru·mor
ru·mor·mon·ger
rum·ple
rum·pled
rum·pling
rum·pus

run
　ran
　run
　run·ning
run·a·way
run·ner-up
run·ny
runt
　runty
　runt·i·est
run·way
rup·ture
　rup·tured
　rup·tur·ing
ru·ral
　ru·ral·ly
　ru·ral·ized
　ru·ral·i·za·tion
rus·set
Rus·sia
Rus·sian
rus·tic
rus·ti·cate
　rus·ti·cat·ed
　rus·ti·cat·ing
　rus·ti·ca·tion
　rus·tic·i·ty
rus·tle
　rus·tled
　rus·tling
rus·tler
rusty
　rust·i·ness
rut
　rut·ted
　rut·ting
ru·ta·ba·ga
ruth·less
　ruth·less·ness
rut·ty
　rut·ti·est

S

Sab·a·oth
Sab·bath
sab·bat·i·cal
sa·ber
sa·ble
sab·o·tage
　sab·o·taged
　sab·o·tag·ing
　sab·o·teur
sac·cha·rin
sac·cha·rine
sac·er·do·tal
sa·chet
sack·ful
sack·ing
sac·ra·ment
sa·cred
　sa·cred·ly
　sa·cred·ness
sac·ri·fice
　sac·ri·ficed
　sac·ri·fic·ing
　sac·ri·fi·cial
sac·ri·lege
　sac·ri·le·gious
sac·ris·ty
sac·ro·il·i·ac
sac·ro·sanct
　sac·ro·sanc·ti·ty
sad
　sad·der
　sad·ly
　sad·ness

sad·den
sad·dle
　sad·dled
　sad·dling
sad·ism
sad·ist
sa·dis·tic
　sa·dis·ti·cal·ly
sa·fa·ri
safe
　saf·er
　saf·est
safe-con·duct
safe-de·pos·it
safe-keep·ing
safe·ty
saf·flow·er
saf·fron
sag
　sagged
　sag·ging
sa·ga
sa·ga·cious
　sa·gac·i·ty
sage
　sage·ness
Sag·it·ta·ri·us
sail·ing
sail·or
saint·hood
saint·ed
saint·ly
　saint·li·ness
sa·ke
sa·laam
sale·a·ble
　sal·a·bil·i·ty
sa·la·cious
sal·ad
sal·a·man·der
sa·la·mi
sal·a·ry
　sal·a·ries
sales·man
sales·per·son
sales·wom·an
sa·li·ent
　sa·li·ence
　sa·li·en·cy
　sa·li·ent·ly
　sa·li·ent·ness
sa·line
　sa·lin·i·ty
sa·li·va
　sal·i·vary
sal·i·vate
　sal·i·vat·ed
　sal·i·vat·ing
　sal·i·va·tion
sal·low
sal·ly
　sal·lied
salm·on
sal·mo·nel·la
sa·lon
sa·loon
salt·cel·lar
salt·ed
salt·ine
salt·shak·er
salt-wa·ter
salty
　salt·i·ness
sa·lu·bri·ous
sal·u·tary
sal·u·ta·tion
sa·lu·ta·to·ry
sa·lute

sa·lut·ed
sa·lut·ing
sal·vage
　sal·vaged
　sal·vag·ing
　sal·vage·a·ble
sal·va·tion
salve
　salved
　salv·ing
sal·vo
sam·ba
same·ness
sam·o·var
sam·ple
　sam·pled
　sam·pling
sam·pler
san·a·to·ri·um
sanc·ti·fy
　sanc·ti·fied
　sanc·ti·fy·ing
　sanc·ti·fi·ca·tion
sanc·ti·mo·ny
　sanc·ti·mo·ni·ous
sanc·tion
　sanc·tion·a·ble
sanc·ti·ty
sanc·tu·ary
sanc·tum
san·dal
sand·bag
　sand·bagged
　sand·bag·ging
sand-cast
　sand-cast·ed
　sand-cast·ing
sand·pa·per
sand·pi·per
sand·wich
sandy
　sand·i·ness
sane
　sane·ly
　sane·ness
sang-froid
san·gria
san·gui·nary
san·guine
san·i·tar·i·um
san·i·tary
　san·i·tar·i·ly
　san·i·ta·tion
san·i·tize
　san·tized
　san·i·tiz·ing
san·i·ty
San·ta Claus
sap
　sapped
　sap·ping
sa·pi·ent
　sa·pi·ence
　sa·pi·en·cy
　sa·pi·en·tial
sap·ling
sap·phire
sap·py
sap·suck·er
sa·ran
sar·casm
　sar·cas·tic
　sar·cas·ti·cal·ly
sar·co·ma
sar·coph·a·gus
sar·dine
sar·don·ic
　sar·don·i·cal·ly

sa·ri
sa·rong
sar·sa·pa·ril·la
sar·to·ri·al
sa·shay
Sas·katch·e·wan
sas·sa·fras
sas·sy
　sas·si·ness
sa·tan·ic
　sa·tan·i·cal
satch·el
sate
　sat·ed
　sat·ing
sa·teen
sat·el·lite
sa·ti·a·ble
　sa·ti·a·bly
　sa·ti·a·bil·i·ty
　sa·ti·a·ble·ness
sa·ti·ate
　sa·ti·at·ed
　sa·ti·at·ing
　sa·ti·a·tion
sa·ti·e·ty
sat·in
　sat·iny
sat·ire
　sa·tir·i·cal·ly
　sat·i·rist
sat·i·rize
　sat·i·rized
　sat·i·riz·ing
sat·is·fac·tion
sat·is·fac·to·ry
　sat·is·fac·to·ri·ly
sat·is·fy
　sat·is·fied
　sat·is·fy·ing
　sat·is·fi·a·ble
sat·u·rate
　sat·u·rat·ed
　sat·u·rat·ing
　sat·u·ra·ble
　sat·u·ra·tion
sat·ur·nine
sa·tyr
　sa·tyr·ic
sauce
sau·cer
sau·cy
　sau·ci·ness
Sau·di Ara·bia
sau·er·bra·tne
sau·er·kraut
sau·na
saun·ter
sau·sage
sau·te
　sau·teed
　sau·tee·ing
sau·terne
sav·age
　sav·age·ness
　sav·age·ry
sa·van·na
sa·vant
save
　saved
　sav·ing
sav·ior
sa·vior-faire
sa·vor
sa·vory
　sa·vor·i·ly
　sa·vor·i·ness
sav·vy

sax·o·phone
sax·o·phon·ist
say
　said
　say·ing
scab
　scabbed
　scab·bing
scab·bard
scab·by
　scab·bi·ness
sca·bies
scaf·fold
　scaf·fold·ing
scal·a·wag
scald
　scald·ing
scale
　scaled
　scal·ing
　scal·i·ness
scal·lion
scal·lop
scalp
　scalp·er
scal·pel
scaly
　scal·i·ness
scamp·er
scan
　scanned
　scan·ning
　scan·ner
scan·dal
scan·dal·ize
　scan·dal·ized
　scan·dal·iz·ing
　scan·dal·i·za·tion
scan·dal·mon·ger
scan·dal·ous
Scan·di·na·via
scant
　scant·ness
scanty
　scant·i·ness
scape·goat
scap·u·la
scar
　scarred
　scar·ring
scar·ab
scarce
　scarce·ness
　scar·ci·ty
scare
　scared
　scar·ing
scarf
　scarfs
　scarves
scar·i·fy
　scar·i·fied
　scar·i·fy·ing
　scar·i·fi·ca·tion
scar·let
scarp
scary
　scar·i·er
　scar·i·est
scat
　scat·ted
　scat·ting
scathe
　scathed
　scath·ing
scat·ter
scat·ter-brained
scav·enge

scav·enged
scav·eng·ing
scav·en·ger
sce·nar·io
sce·nar·ist
scen·ery
sce·nic
sce·ni·cal
scent
scep·ter
sched·ule
sched·uled
sched·ul·ing
sche·ma
sche·mat·i·cal·ly
sche·ma·tize
sche·ma·tized
sche·ma·tiz·ing
scheme
schem·er
schem·ing
scher·zo
schism
schis·mat·ic
schis·mat·i·cal
schiz·oid
schiz·o·phre·nia
schiz·o·phren·ic
schol·ar
schol·ar·ly
schol·ar·li·ness
schol·ar·ship
scho·las·tic
scho·las·ti·cal
scho·las·ti·cism
school board
school·ing
school·teach·er
schoon·er
sci·at·ic
sci·at·i·ca
sci·ence
sci·en·tif·ic
sci·en·tif·i·cal·ly
sci·en·tist
scim·i·tar
scin·til·la
scin·til·lant
scin·til·late
scin·til·lat·ed
scin·til·lat·ing
scin·til·la·tion
sci·on
scis·sors
scle·ro·sis
scoff·er
scoff·ing·ly
scoff·law
scold·ing
scol·lop
sconce
scone
scoop·er
scoop·ful
scoot·er
scope
scorch
scorched
scorch·ing
score
scored
scor·ing
score·less
scor·er
score·keep·er
scorn
scorn·er
scorn·ful·ness

scor·pi·on
scot-free
scot·tie
scoundrel
scoun·drel·ly
scour
scour·er
scourge
scourged
scourg·ing
scout·ing
scout·mas·ter
scowl
scrab·ble
scrab·bled
scrab·bling
scrag
scragged
scrag·ging
scrag·gly
scrag·gy
scram
scrammed
scram·ming
scram·ble
scram·bled
scram·bling
scrap
scrapped
scrap·ping
scrape
scraped
scrap·ing
scrap·per
scrap·py
scrap·pi·ness
scratch
scratchy
scratch·i·ness
scrawl
scrawny
scrawn·i·ness
scream·er
scream·ing
screech
screen
screen·er
screen·ing
screw·driv·er
screwy
scrib·ble
scrib·bled
scrib·bling
scrib·bler
scribe
scribed
scrib·ing
scrim·mage
scrim·maged
scrim·mag·ing
scrim·mag·er
scrimpy
scrimp·i·ness
scrim·shaw
script
scrip·ture
scrip·tur·al
script·writ·er
scriv·en·er
scroll-work
scrooge
scro·tum
scrounge
scroung·er
scroung·ing
scrub
scrubbed
scrub·bing

scrub·by
scruffy
scruff·i·ness
scrump·tious
scru·ple
scru·pu·lous
scru·pu·los·i·ty
scru·pu·lous·ness
scru·pu·lous·ly
scru·ta·ble
scru·ti·nize
scru·ti·nized
scru·ti·niz·er
scru·ti·niz·ing·ly
scru·ti·ny
scu·ba
scuf·fle
scuf·fled
scuf·fling
scul·lery
sculp·tor
sculp·tress
sculp·ture
sculp·tured
sculp·tur·ing
sculp·tur·al
scum
scum·my
scup·per
scur·ri·lous
scur·ril·i·ty
scur·ry
scur·ried
scur·ry·ing
scur·vy
scur·vi·ness
scut·tle
scut·tled
scut·tling
scut·tle·butt
scythe
scythed
scyth·ing
sea·far·ing
sea·far·er
sea·go·ing
seal·ant
sea lam·prey
seal·skin
sea·man·ship
seam·stress
seamy
seam·i·ness
se·ance
search
search·er
search·ing
search·light
sea·scape
sea·shell
sea·shore
sea·sick·ness
sea·side
sea·son
sea·son·er
sea·son·ing
sea·son·a·ble
sea·son·al
sea·son·al·ly
seat·ing
sea·wor·thy
sea·wor·thi·ness
se·ba·ceous
se·cant
se·cede
se·ced·ed
se·ced·ing
se·ces·sion

se·ces·sion·ist
se·clude
se·clud·ed
se·clud·ing
se·clud·ed·ness
se·clu·sion
se·clu·sive
sec·ond
sec·ond·ary
sec·ond·ar·i·ly
sec·ond-best
sec·ond-class
sec·ond-guess
sec·ond·hand
sec·ond-rate
se·cret
se·cre·cy
sec·re·tar·i·at
sec·re·tary
sec·re·tar·ies
sec·re·tar·i·al
se·crete
se·cret·ed
se·cret·ing
se·cre·tion
se·cre·tive
se·cre·to·ry
sec·tar·i·an
sec·tar·i·an·ism
sec·tion
sec·tion·al
sec·tor
sec·to·ri·al
sec·u·lar
sec·u·lar·ism
sec·u·lar·ize
sec·u·lar·ized
sec·u·lar·iz·ing
sec·u·lar·i·za·tion
se·cure
se·cured
se·cur·ing
se·cur·a·ble
se·cure·ness
se·cu·ri·ty
se·cu·ri·ties
se·dan
se·date
se·date·ness
se·da·tion
se·dat·ed
se·dat·ing
sed·a·tive
sed·en·tary
sed·en·tar·i·ness
sed·i·ment
sed·i·men·ta·ry
sed·i·men·ta·tion
se·di·tion
se·di·tion·ary
se·di·tious
se·duce
se·duced
se·duc·ing
se·duc·er
se·duc·i·ble
se·duce·a·ble
se·duc·tion
se·duce·ment
se·duc·tive
sed·u·lous
se·du·li·ty
sed·u·lous·ness
see
saw
seen
see·ing
seed·ling

seedy
seed·i·er
seed·i·est
seed·i·ly
seed·i·ness
seek
sought
seek·ing
seem·ing
seem·ly
seem·li·est
seem·li·ness
seep
seepy
seep·age
se·er
seer·ess
seer·suck·er
see·saw
seethe
seethed
seeth·ing
seg·ment
seg·men·tal
seg·men·tary
seg·men·ta·tion
seg·re·gate
seg·re·gat·ed
seg·re·gat·ing
seg·re·ga·tion
seg·re·ga·tion·ist
seine
seined
sein·ing
seis·mic
seis·mo·graph
seis·mog·ra·phy
seis·mol·o·gy
seis·mol·o·gist
seize
seized
seiz·ing
sei·zure
sel·dom
se·lect
se·lect·ed
se·lec·tor
se·lec·tion
se·lec·tive
se·lec·tiv·i·ty
self
selves
self-a·base·ment
self-ab·ne·ga·tion
self-a·buse
self-ad·dressed
self-ad·just·ing
self-ag·gran·dize·ment
self-ag·gran·diz·ing
self-as·sur·ance
self-as·sured
self-cen·tered
self-col·lect·ed
self-com·posed
self-con·fessed
self-con·fi·dence
self-con·fi·dent
self-con·scious
self-con·scious·ness
self-con·tained
self-con·trol
self-con·trolled
self-cor·rect·ing
self-crit·i·cism
self-de·cep·tion
self-de·cep·tive
self-de·feat·ing
self-de·fense

self-de·ni·al
self-de·ter·mi·na·tion
self-dis·ci·pline
self-ed·u·cat·ed
self-ef·fac·ing
self-em·ployed
self-es·teem
self-ev·i·dent
self-ex·plan·a·to·ry
self-ex·pres·sion
self-ful·fill·ment
self-gov·ern·ment
  self-gov·ern·ing
self-im·age
self-im·por·tance
self-im·posed
self-im·prove·ment
self-in·crim·i·na·tion
self-in·duced
self-in·dul·gence
self-in·flict·ed
self-in·ter·est
self·ish
  self·ish·ness
self·less
  self·less·ness
self-liq·ui·dat·ing
self-made
self-op·er·at·ing
self-per·pet·u·at·ing
self-pity
self-pol·li·na·tion
self-pos·sessed
self-pres·er·va·tion
self-pro·pelled
self-pro·tec·tion
self-re·al·i·za·tion
self-re·li·ance
self-re·spect
self-re·straint
self-right·eous
self-sac·ri·fice
self-sat·is·fied
  self-sat·is·fac·tion
  self-sat·is·fy·ing
self-serv·ice
self-serv·ing
self-suf·fi·cient
  self-suf·fi·cien·cy
self-sup·port
self-taught
sell
  sold
  sell·ing
sell·er
sell·out
sel·vage
selves
se·man·tics
  se·man·tic
  se·man·ti·cal
sem·a·phore
sem·blance
se·men
se·mes·ter
sem·i·an·nu·al
  sem·i·an·nu·al·ly
sem·i·ar·id
sem·i·au·to·mat·ic
sem·i·cir·cle
  sem·i·cir·cu·lar
sem·i·clas·si·cal
  sem·i·clas·sic
sem·i·co·lon
sem·i·con·duc·tor
  sem·i·con·duct·ing
sem·i·con·scious
sem·i·de·tached

sem·i·fi·nal
  sem·i·fi·nal·ist
sem·i·flu·id
sem·i·for·mal
sem·i·liq·uid
sem·i·month·ly
sem·i·nal
sem·i·nar
sem·i·nary
  sem·i·nar·i·an
sem·i·of·fi·cial
se·mi·ot·ic
sem·i·per·ma·nent
sem·i·per·me·a·ble
sem·i·pre·cious
sem·i·pri·vate
sem·i·pro·fes·sion·al
sem·i·pub·lic
sem·i·skilled
sem·i·sol·id
Sem·ite
Sem·it·ic
Sem·i·tism
sem·i·trail·er
sem·i·trop·ics
  sem·i·trop·i·cal
sem·i·week·ly
sem·i·year·ly
sen·a·ry
sen·ate
sen·a·tor
  sen·a·to·ri·al
send
  sent
  send·ing
se·nes·cent
  se·nes·cence
se·nile
  se·nil·i·ty
sen·ior
  sen·ior·i·ty
se·nor
  se·nors
se·no·ra
se·no·ri·ta
sen·sate
sen·sa·tion
sen·sa·tion·al
  sen·sa·tion·al·ly
  sen·sa·tion·al·ism
sense
  sensed
  sens·ing
sense·less
  sense·less·ness
sen·si·bil·i·ty
  sen·si·bil·i·ties
sen·si·ble
  sen·si·ble·ness
  sen·si·bly
sen·si·tive
  sen·si·tiv·i·ty
sen·si·tize
  sen·si·tized
  sen·si·tiz·ing
  sen·si·ti·za·tion
  sen·si·tiz·er
sen·sor
sen·so·ry
sen·so·ri·al
sen·su·al
  sen·su·al·i·ty
  sen·su·al·ly
  sen·su·al·ism
  sen·su·al·ize
  sen·su·al·ized
  sen·su·al·iz·ing
  sen·su·al·i·za·tion

sen·su·ous
sen·tence
  sen·tenced
  sen·tenc·ing
sen·tient
sen·ti·ment
sen·ti·men·tal
  sen·ti·men·tal·ly
  sen·ti·men·tal·i·ty
  sen·ti·men·tal·i·ties
  sen·ti·men·tal·ize
  sen·ti·men·tal·ized
  sen·ti·men·tal·iz·ing
  sen·ti·men·ta·li·za·tion
sen·ti·nel
sen·try
  sen·tries
sep·a·ra·ble
  sep·a·ra·bil·i·ty
  sep·a·ra·bly
sep·a·rate
  sep·a·rat·ed
  sep·a·rat·ing
  sep·a·rate·ness
  sep·a·ra·tion
sep·a·ra·tist
  sep·a·ra·tism
sep·a·ra·tive
sep·a·ra·tor
se·pia
sep·sis
sep·ten·ni·al
sep·tet
sep·tic
  sep·ti·cal·ly
  sep·tic·i·ty
sep·tu·a·ge·nar·i·an
sep·tu·ple
sep·ul·cher
  se·pul·chral
se·quel
se·quence
se·quen·tial
  se·quen·tial·ly
se·ques·ter
  se·ques·tered
  se·ques·tra·ble
  se·ques·tra·tion
se·quin
se·quoia
se·ra·pe
ser·aph
  ser·aphs
  ser·a·phim
  se·raph·ic
ser·e·nade
  ser·e·nad·ed
  ser·e·nad·ing
ser·en·dip·i·ty
se·rene
  se·ren·i·ty
serf·dom
serge
ser·geant
se·ri·al
  se·ri·al·ly
  se·ri·al·i·za·tion
  se·ri·al·ize
  se·ri·al·ized
  se·ri·al·iz·ing
se·ries
se·ri·ous
  se·ri·ous·ly
  se·ri·ous·ness
se·ri·ous-mind·ed
ser·mon
  ser·mon·ize
  ser·mon·ized

  ser·mon·iz·ing
  ser·mon·iz·er
se·rous
ser·pent
ser·pen·tine
ser·rate
  ser·rat·ed
  ser·rat·ing
  ser·ra·tion
se·rum
serv·ant
serve
  served
  serv·ing
serv·ice
  serv·iced
  serv·ic·ing
serv·ice·a·ble
  serv·ice·a·bil·i·ty
  serv·ice·a·ble·ness
  serv·ice·a·bly
ser·vile
  ser·vil·i·ty
  ser·vile·ness
ser·vi·tude
ser·vo·mech·an·ism
ses·a·me
ses·qui·cen·ten·ni·al
ses·sion
set
  set
  set·ting
set·tee
set·ter
set·tle
  set·tled
  set·tling
set·tle·ment
set·tler
sev·en
  sev·enth
  sev·en·teen
  sev·en·teenth
  sev·en·ty
  sev·en·ti·eth
sev·er
  sev·er·a·bil·i·ty
  sev·er·a·ble
  sev·er·ance
sev·er·al
  sev·er·al·ly
se·vere
  se·ver·est
  se·vere·ness
  se·ver·i·ty
sew·age
sew·er
sew·er·age
sew·ing ma·chine
sex·less
sex·tant
sex·tet
sex·ton
sex·tu·ple
sex·tu·plet
sex·u·al
  sex·u·al·ly
  sex·u·al·i·ty
sexy
  sex·i·er
  sex·i·est
  sex·i·ness
shab·by
  shab·bi·er
  shab·bi·ly
  shab·bi·ness
shack·le
  shack·led

shack·ling
shade
  shad·ed
  shad·ing
shad·ow
  shad·owy
shady
  shad·i·er
  shad·i·ly
  shad·i·ness
shaft·ing
shag
  shagged
  shag·ging
  shag·ged
shag·gy
  shag·gi·er
  shag·gi·ly
  shag·gi·ness
shake
  shook
  shak·en
  shak·ing
  shak·er
Shake·spear·e·an
shaky
  shak·i·ly
  shak·i·ness
shal·lot
shal·low
  shal·low·ness
sham
  shammed
  sham·ming
sha·man
sham·bles
shame
  shamed
  sham·ing
shame·faced
shame·ful
  shame·ful·ly
shame·less
  shame·less·ly
  shame·less·ness
sham·mer
sham·poo
  sham·pooed
  sham·poo·ing
sham·rock
shang·hai
  shang·haied
  shang·hai·ing
shan·tung
shan·ty
  shan·ties
shape
  shaped
  shap·ing
  shap·a·ble
  shap·er
shape·less
shape·ly
  shape·li·est
  shape·li·ness
share
  shared
  shar·ing
  shar·er
share·crop
  share·crop·per
  share·cropped
  share·crop·ping
share·hold·er
shark·skin
sharp·en
  sharp·en·er
sharp·eyed

sharp·ie
sharp·shoot·er
sharp-tongued
sharp-wit·ted
shat·ter
shat·ter·proof
shave
shaved
shav·en
shav·ing
shawl
sheaf
sheaves
shear
sheared
shear·ing
sheath
sheathe
sheathed
sheath·ing
sheath·er
she·bang
shed
shed·ding
sheen
sheeny
sheep·herd·er
sheep·ish
sheep·skin
sheer
sheer·ness
sheet·ing
sheik
shelf
shelves
shell
shelled
shel·ly
shel·lac
shel·lacked
shel·lack·ing
shel·ter
shelve
shelved
shelv·ing
she·nan·i·gan
shep·herd
shep·herd·ess
sher·bet
sher·iff
sher·ry
shib·bo·leth
shield
shift
shift·ing·ness
shift·less
shifty
shift·i·er
shift·i·ly
shift·i·ness
shil·le·lagh
shil·ling
shil·ly-shal·ly
shim·mer
shim·mery
shim·my
shim·mied
shin
shinned
shin·ning
shin·dig
shine
shined
shone
shin·ing
shin·er
shin·gle
shin·gled

shin·gling
shin·gles
shin·ing
shiny
shin·i·ness
ship
shipped
ship·ping
ship·pa·ble
ship·build·ing
ship·mate
ship·ment
shirk
shirk·er
shish   ke·bab
shiv·er
shiv·ery
shoal
shock·er
shock·ing
shod·dy
shod·di·ly
shod·di·ness
shoe·mak·er
shoe·string
shoot
shot
shoot·ing
shop
shopped
shop·ping
shop·lift·er
shop·lift·ing
shop·per
shore·line
short
short·ly
short·ness
short·age
short-change
short-changed
short-chang·ing
short·cir·cuit
short·com·ing
short·cut
short-cut·ting
short·en
short·en·ing
short·hand
short-hand·ed
short-lived
short-sight·ed
short-tem·pered
short-wind·ed
shot·gun
shot·gunned
shot·gun·ning
should
shoul·der
shout·ing
shove
shoved
shov·ing
shov·el
shov·eled
shov·el·ing
show
showed
shown
show·ing
show·case
show·cased
show·cas·ing
show·er
show·ery
show·man·ship
showy
show·i·ly

show·i·ness
shrap·nel
shred
shred·ded
shred·ding
shred·der
shrew
shrew·ish
shrewd
shrewd·ly
shrewd·ness
shriek
shrill
shril·ly
shrill·ness
shrimp
shrine
shrink
shrunk·en
shrink·a·ble
shrink·age
shrive
shriv·el
shriv·eled
shriv·el·ing
shroud
shrub·bery
shrug
shrugged
shrug·ging
shud·der
shuf·fle
shuf·fled
shuf·fling
shuf·fle·board
shun
shunned
shun·ning
shun·ner
shunt
shut·ter
shut·tle
shut·tled
shut·tling
shy
shied
shy·ing
shy·ly
shy·ness
shy·ster
Si·a·mese
sib·i·lant
sib·i·lance
sib·ling
sick·en
sick·en·ing
sick·le
sick·ly
sick·li·ness
sick·ness
sid·ed
side·line
side·lined
side·lin·ing
si·de·re·al
side·split·ting
side·step
side·stepped
side·step·ping
side·swipe
side·swiped
side·swip·ing
sid·ing
si·dle
si·dled
si·dling
siege
si·er·ra

si·es·ta
sieve
sift·er
sift·ings
sigh·ing
sight·ed
sight·less
sight·ly
sight-read·ing
sight·see·ing
sight·see·er
sig·nal
sig·naled
sig·nal·ing
sig·na·to·ry
sig·na·ture
sig·net
sig·nif·i·cance
sig·nif·i·cant
sig·ni·fi·ca·tion
sig·ni·fy
sig·ni·fied
sig·ni·fy·ing
si·lage
si·lence
si·lenced
si·lenc·ing
si·lenc·er
si·lent
sil·hou·ette
sil·hou·et·ted
sil·hou·et·ting
sil·ica
sil·i·co·sis
sil·i·cone
silk·en
silky
silk·i·est
silk·i·ly
silk·i·ness
sil·ly
sil·li·er
sil·li·est
sil·li·ly
sil·li·ness
si·lo
si·los
si·loed
si·lo·ing
silt
silt·a·tion
silty
sil·ver
sil·ver·fish
sil·ver-tongued
sil·ver·ware
sil·very
sil·ver·i·ness
sim·i·an
sim·i·lar
sim·i·lar·i·ty
sim·i·lar·i·ties
sim·i·le
si·mil·i·tude
sim·mer
si·mon·ize
si·mon·ized
si·mon·iz·ing
sim·per
sim·per·ing·ly
sim·ple
sim·pler
sim·plest
sim·ple·ness
sim·ple-mind·ed
sim·ple·ton
sim·plex
sim·plic·i·ty

sim·pli·fy
sim·pli·fied
sim·pli·fy·ing
sim·pli·fi·ca·tion
sim·plis·tic
sim·plis·ti·cal·ly
sim·ply
sim·u·late
sim·u·lat·ed
sim·u·lat·ing
sim·u·la·tion
sim·u·la·tive
sim·u·la·tor
si·mul·cast
si·mul·ta·ne·ous
si·mul·ta·ne·ous·ness
si·mul·ta·ne·i·ty
sin
sinned
sin·ning
sin·ner
Si·nai
sin·cere
sin·cer·i·ty
si·ne·cure
sin·ew
sin·ewy
sin·ful
sin·ful·ly
sin·ful·ness
sing
sang
sung
sing·ing
singe
singed
singe·ing
sing·er
sin·gle
sin·gled
sin·gling
sin·gle·ness
sin·gle-breast·ed
sin·gle-hand·ed
sin·gle-mind·ed
sin·gle-space
sin·gle-spaced
sin·gle-spac·ing
sin·gle·ton
sin·gle-track
sin·gly
sing·song
sin·gu·lar
sin·gu·lar·i·ty
sin·gu·lar·i·ties
sin·is·ter
sink
sank
sunk
sink·ing
sink·a·ble
sink·er
sink·hole
sin·less
sin·ner
sin·u·ate
sin·u·at·ed
sin·u·at·ing
sin·u·ous
sin·u·os·i·ty
sin·u·ous·ness
si·nus
si·nus·i·tis
sip
sipped
sip·ping
si·phon
sire

sired
sir·ing
si·ren
sir·loin
si·roc·co
sis·sy
sis·ter
sis·ter·li·ness
sis·ter·ly
sis·ter-in-law
sit
sat
sit·ting
sit·ter
sit·ting
sit·u·ate
sit·u·at·ed
sit·u·at·ing
sit·u·a·tion
six-shoot·er
six·teen
six·teenth
sixth
six·ty
six·ti·eth
siz·a·ble
siz·a·ble·ness
siz·a·bly
size
sized
siz·ing
siz·zle
siz·zled
siz·zling
skate
skat·ed
skat·ing
skein
skel·e·ton
skel·e·tal
skep·tic
skep·ti·cal
skep·ti·cism
sketch
sketchy
sketch·i·ly
sketch·i·ness
skew·er
ski
skied
ski·ing
ski·er
skid
skid·ded
skid·ding
skiff
skilled
skil·let
skill·ful·ly
skim
skimmed
skim·ming
skimp
skimp·i·ly
skimp·i·ness
skimp·y
skin
skinned
skin·ning
skin-dive
skin-dived
skin-diving
skin·ny
skin·ni·er
skin·ni·est
skip
skipped
skip·ping

skip·per
skir·mish
skit·ter
skit·tish
skoal
skul·dug·ger·y
skulk·er
skunk
sky·div·ing
sky·jack·er
sky·rock·et
sky·scrap·er
sky·writ·ing
slab
slabbed
slab·bing
slack
slack·ness
slack·en
slack·er
slake
slaked
slak·ing
sla·lom
slam
slammed
slam·ming
slan·der
slan·der·er
slan·der·ous
slang
slang·i·ness
slangy
slant
slant·ways
slant·wise
slap
slapped
slap·ping
slap·hap·py
slap·stick
slasher
slash·ing
slat
slat·ted
slat·ting
slate
slat·ed
slat·ing
slat·tern
slat·tern·li·ness
slat·tern·ly
slaugh·ter
slave
slaved
slav·ing
slav·ery
slav·ish
sla·vish·ly
slay
slew
slain
slay·ing
slea·zy
slea·zi·ly
slea·zi·ness
sled
sled·ded
sled·ding
sledge
sleek
sleek·ness
sleep·less·ness
sleep·walk·ing
sleepy
sleep·i·ly
sleep·i·ness
sleet

sleety
sleet·i·ness
sleeve
sleeved
sleev·ing
sleeve·less
sleigh
sleight
slen·der
slen·der·ize
sleuth
slice
sliced
slic·ing
slick·er
slick·ness
slide
slid
slid·ing
slight
slim
slimmed
slim·ming
slim·mest
slim·ness
slime
slimy
slim·i·ness
sling
slung
sling·ing
slink
slunk
slink·ing
slinky
slip
slipped
slip·ping
slip·page
slip·per
slip·pery
slip·per·i·er
slip·per·i·est
slip·per·i·ness
slip·shod
slip·stream
slit
slit·ting
slith·er
slith·ery
sliv·er
slob·ber
sloe-eyed
slog
slogged
slog·ging
slo·gan
slo·gan·eer
sloop
slop
slopped
slop·ping
slope
sloped
slop·ing
slop·py
slop·pi·ly
slop·pi·ness
sloshy
slot
slot·ted
slot·ting
sloth
sloth·ful·ly
slouch
slouch·i·ly
slouchy
slough

sloughy
slov·en
slov·en·ly
slov·en·li·ness
slow-down
slow-mo·tion
sludge
sludgy
slug
slugged
slug·ging
slug·gard
slug·gard·li·ness
slug·gish
sluice
sluiced
sluic·ing
slum
slummed
slum·ming
slum·ber
slum·ber·er
slum·ber·ous
slump
slumped
slur
slurred
slur·ring
slush
slush·i·ness
slushy
slut
slut·tish
sly
sly·ly
sly·ness
smack·ing
small·pox
smart
smart·ness
smart al·eck
smash·ing
smat·ter·ing
smear
smeary
smear·i·ness
smell
smelled
smel·ling
smelly
smelt
smelt·er
smid·gen
smile
smil·ling·ly
smirch
smirk
smirk·ing·ly
smite
smote
smit·ten
smit·ting
smith·er·eens
Smith·so·ni·an
smock·ing
smog·gy
smoke
smoked
smok·ing
smok·er
smoke·house
smoke·stack
smoky
smok·i·ness
smol·der
smooth
smooth·ness
smooth·en

smor·gas·bord
smoth·er
smudge
smudged
smudg·ing
smudg·i·ness
smudgy
smug
smug·gest
smug·ly
smug·ness
smug·gle
smug·gled
smug·gling
smug·gler
smut
smut·ty
smut·ti·ness
snaf·fle
sna·fu
sna·fued
snag
snagged
snag·ging
snag·gy
snail
snake
snaked
snak·ing
snak·i·ly
snaky
snak·i·ness
snap
snapped
snap·ping
snap·drag·on
snap·py
snap·pish
snare
snared
snar·ing
snarl
snarly
snatch
snatchy
snaz·zy
snaz·zi·est
sneak·er
sneak·ing
sneaky
sneak·i·ly
sneak·i·ness
sneer
sneer·ing·ly
sneeze
sneezed
sneez·ing
sneezy
snick·er
snif·fle
snif·fled
snif·fling
snif·fy
snif·fi·ly
snif·ter
snig·ger
snip
snipped
snip·ping
snipe
sniped
snip·ing
snip·py
snip·pi·ness
snitch·er
sniv·el
sniv·eled
sniv·el·ing

snob
snob·bery
snob·bish·ness
snoop
snoopy
snoop·er
snooty
snoot·i·ness
snooze
snoozed
snooz·ing
snore
snored
snor·ing
snor·kel
snort
snort·ed
snot·ty
snot·ti·ness
snout
snow·blow·er
snow·man
snow·mo·bile
snowy
snow·i·er
snow·i·ness
snub
snubbed
snub·bing
snuf·fle
snuf·fled
snuf·fling
snuffy
snuff·i·ness
snug
snugged
snug·ging
snug·ness
snug·gle
snug·gled
snug·gling
soak·ing
soap
soapy
soap·i·ness
soar
soaring
sob
sobbed
sob·bing
so·ber
so·ber·ness
so·bri·e·ty
so·bri·quet
soc·cer
so·cia·ble
so·cia·bil·i·ty
so·cia·ble·ness
so·cia·bly
so·cial
so·ci·al·i·ty
so·cial·ly
so·cial·ism
so·cial·ist
so·cial·is·tic
so·cial·ite
so·cial·ize
so·cial·ized
so·cial·iz·ing
so·cial·i·za·tion
so·ci·e·ty
so·ci·e·ties
so·ci·e·tal
so·ci·o·ec·o·nom·ic
so·ci·ol·o·gy
so·ci·o·log·i·cal
so·ci·ol·o·gist
so·ci·o·po·lit·i·cal

sock·et
sod
sod·ded
sod·ding
so·da
so·dal·i·ty
sod·den
sod·den·ness
so·di·um
sod·omy
so·fa
soft
soft·ness
sof·ten
soft-heart·ed
soft-ped·al
soft-ped·aled
soft-ped·al·ing
soft-spo·ken
sog·gy
sog·gi·ness
soi·ree
so·journ
sol·ace
sol·aced
sol·ac·ing
so·lar
so·lar·i·um
so·lar·ize
so·lar·ized
so·lar·iz·ing
so·lar·i·za·tion
so·lar   plex·us
sol·der
sol·dier
sol·e·cism
sole·ly
sol·emn
sol·emn·ly
sol·emn·ness
so·lem·ni·ty
sol·em·nize
sol·em·nized
sol·em·niz·ing
sol·em·ni·za·tion
sole·ness
so·le·noid
so·lic·it
so·lic·i·ta·tion
so·lic·i·tor
so·lic·i·tous
so·lic·i·tude
sol·id
so·lid·i·ty
sol·id·ness
sol·i·dar·i·ty
so·lid·i·fy
so·lid·i·fied
so·lid·i·fy·ing
so·lid·i·fi·ca·tion
sol·id·state
so·lil·o·quize
so·lil·o·quized
so·lil·o·quiz·ing
so·lil·o·quy
so·lil·o·quies
sol·i·taire
sol·i·tary
sol·i·tar·i·ness
sol·i·tude
so·lo
so·loed
so·lo·ing
so·lo·ist
sol·stice
sol·u·ble
sol·u·bil·i·ty
sol·u·ble·ness

sol·u·bly
sol·ute
so·lu·tion
solve
solved
solv·ing
solv·a·ble
solv·a·bil·i·ty
solv·a·ble·ness
sol·vent
sol·ven·cy
so·mat·ic
som·ber
som·ber·ness
som·bre·ro
some·body
som·er·sault
some·thing
some·where
som·nam·bu·late
som·nam·bu·lat·ed
som·nam·bu·lat·ing
som·nam·bu·lant
som·nam·bu·la·tion
som·nam·bu·lism
som·nam·bu·list
som·no·lent
som·no·lence
som·no·len·cy
so·nant
so·nar
so·na·ta
song·ster
song·stress
son·ic
son-in-law
son·net
son·ny
son·nies
so·no·rous
so·nor·i·ty
so·no·rous·ness
soothe
soothed
sooth·ing
sooth·say·er
sooty
soot·i·ness
sop
sopped
sop·ping
soph·ist
soph·ism
so·phis·tic
so·phis·ti·cal
so·phis·ti·cate
so·phis·ti·cat·ed
so·phis·ti·cat·ing
so·phis·ti·ca·tion
soph·ist·ry
soph·o·more
soph·o·mor·ic
sop·o·rif·ic
sop·py
so·pra·no
Sor·bonne
sor·cer·er
sor·cer·ess
sor·cery
sor·cer·ous
sor·did
sor·did·ness
sore
sor·est
sore·ly
sore·ness
sor·ghum
so·ror·i·ty

so·ror·i·ties
sor·rel
sor·row
sor·row·ful·ly
sor·ry
sor·ri·ly
sor·ri·ness
sort·a·ble
sor·tie
sot
sot·ted
sot·tish·ness
sot·to vo·ce
sou·bri·quet
souf·fle
souf·fleed
sought
soul·ful
soul·ful·ly
soul-search·ing
sound
sound·a·ble
sound·ly
sound·ness
sound·ing
sound·less·ly
soupy
soup·i·er
sour
sour·ish
sour·ness
source
souse
soused
sous·ing
south·east·er·ly
south·east·ern
south·er·ly
south·ern
south·ern·er
south·west·er·ly
south·west·ern
sou·ve·nir
sov·er·eign·
sov·er·eign·ty
so·vi·et
so·vi·et·ism
sow
sowed
sown
sow·ing
soy·bean
space
spaced
spac·ing
space·craft
space·ship
spa·cious
spa·cious·ness
spack·le
spack·led
spack·ling
spade
spad·ed
spad·ing
spade·ful
spa·ghet·ti
span
spanned
span·ning
span·gle
span·gled
span·gling
Spain
Span·iard
Span·ish
span·iel
spank·ing

spar
sparred
spar·ring
spare
spared
spar·ing
spare·ness
spar·ing·ness
spar·kle
spar·kled
spar·kling
spar·kler
spar·row
sparse
sparse·ness
spasm
spas·mod·ic
spas·mod·i·cal·ly
spas·tic
spas·ti·cal·ly
spat
spat·ted
spat·ting
spa·tial
spa·cial
spa·ti·al·i·ty
spa·tial·ly
spat·ter
spat·u·la
spav·in
spawn
speak
spok·en
speak·ing
speak-easy
speak·er
spear·head
spear·mint
spe·cial
spe·cial·ly
spe·cial·ist
spe·cial·ize
spe·cial·ized
spe·cial·iz·ing
spe·cial·i·za·tion
spe·cial·ty
spe·cial·ties
spe·cie
spe·cif·ic
spec·i·fi·a·ble
spe·cif·i·cal·ly
spec·i·fic·i·ty
spec·i·fy
spec·i·fied
spec·i·fy·ing
spec·i·fi·ca·tion
spec·i·men
spe·cious
spe·ci·os·i·ty
spe·cious·ness
speck·le
speck·led
speck·ling
spec·ta·cle
spec·tac·u·lar
spec·ta·tor
spec·ter
spec·tral
spec·tro·scope
spec·tros·co·py
spec·trum
spec·u·late
spec·u·lat·ed
spec·u·lat·ing
spec·u·la·tion
spec·u·la·tor
spec·u·la·tive
speech·i·fy

speech·less
speed
　speed·ed
　sped
　speed·ing
speed·om·e·ter
speedy
　speed·i·ly
　speed·i·ness
spe·le·ol·o·gy
　spe·le·ol·o·gist
spell
　spelled
　spell·ing
spell·bound
　spell·bind·ing
spe·lun·ker
spend
　spent
　spend·ing
　spend·a·ble
spend·thrift
sper·ma·ceti
sper·mat·ic
sper·ma·to·zo·on
　sper·ma·to·zo·a
　sper·ma·to·zo·ic
spew·er
sphag·num
sphere
　sphered
　spher·ing
　spher·ic
　sphe·ric·i·ty
spher·i·cal
sphe·roid
　sphe·roi·dal
sphinc·ter
sphinx
spice
　spiced
　spic·ing
spi·cule
spicy
　spic·i·er
　spic·i·est
　spic·i·ly
　spic·i·ness
spi·der
spi·dery
spiel
spiffy
　spiff·i·ness
spig·ot
spike
　spiked
　spiky
spill
　spilled
　spill·ing
spil·lage
spin
　spun
　spin·ning
spin·ach
spi·nal
spin·dle
　spin·dled
　spin·dling
spin·dly
spine·less
spin·et
spin·na·ker
spin·ner
spin·ning
spin·ster
spiny
　spin·i·ness

spi·ra·cle
spi·ral
　spi·raled
　spi·ral·ing
　spi·ral·ly
spire
　spired
　spir·ing
spir·it
　spir·it·ed
　spir·it·less·ness
　spir·i·tous
spir·it·u·al
　spir·it·u·al·ism
　spir·it·u·al·ist
　spir·it·u·al·i·ty
　spir·it·u·al·ize
　spir·it·u·al·ized
　spir·it·u·al·iz·ing
　spir·it·u·al·i·za·tion
spir·it·u·ous
　spir·it·u·os·i·ty
spi·ro·chete
spit
　spat
　spit·ting
spite
　spit·ing
　spite·ful
spit·tle
spit·toon
splash
　splashy
　splash·i·ness
splat·ter
splay·foot
spleen
　spleen·ful
　sple·net·ic
splen·did
splen·dif·er·ous
splen·dor
splice
　spliced
　splic·ing
splin·ter
split
　split·ting
split-lev·el
split-sec·ond
splotch
　splotchy
splurge
　splurged
　splurg·ing
splut·ter
spoil
　spoiled
　spoil·ing
spoil·age
spoil·er
spoke
spo·ken
spokes·man
　spokes·wom·an
spo·li·a·tion
sponge
　sponged
　spong·ing
spong·er
spon·gy
　spon·gi·ness
spon·sor
spon·ta·ne·i·ty
spon·ta·ne·ous
　spon·ta·ne·ous·ness
spook
　spooky

spook·i·ness
spoon·er·ism
spoon-feed
　spoon-fed
spoon·fuls
spo·rad·ic
　spo·rad·i·cal·ly
spo·ran·gi·um
spore
sport
　sport·ful·ly
　sport·ing
　spor·tive
sports·cast·er
sports·man
sports·man·ship
sporty
　sport·i·ness
spot
　spot·ted
　spot·ting
spot·less·ness
spot·ty
　spot·ti·ly
　spot·ti·ness
spouse
sprained
sprawl
spray·er
spread
　spread·ing
spread-ea·gle
spread·er
sprig
spright·ly
　spright·li·ness
spring
　sprang
　sprung
　spring·ing
spring-clean·ing
spring·time
springy
　spring·i·ness
sprin·kle
　sprin·kled
　sprin·kling
　sprink·ler
sprint
　sprint·er
sprock·et
spruce
　spruced
　spruc·ing
　spruce·ly
spry
　spry·ness
spume
　spumed
　spum·ing
　spum·ous
spunky
　spunk·i·ness
spur
　spurred
　spur·ring
spu·ri·ous
　spu·ri·ous·ness
spurner
spurt
　spur·tive
sput·nik
sput·ter
spu·tum
spy
　spies
　spied
　spy·ing

squab·ble
　squab·bled
　squab·bling
squad·ron
squal·id
　squal·id·ness
squall
　squally
squal·or
squan·der
square
　squared
　squar·ing
　square·ness
　squar·ish
square-danc·ing
squash
squashy
　squash·i·ness
squat
　squat·ted
　squat·ting
　squat·ness
squat·ter
squat·ty
squawk
　squawky
squeak
　squeak·er
　squeak·ing·ly
　squeaky
squeal
　squeal·er
squeam·ish
　squeam·ish·ness
squee·gee
squeeze
　squeezed
　squeez·ing
　squeez·er
squelch
squib
squid
squig·gle
　squig·gled
　squig·gling
squint
　squint·er
　squint·ing·ly
　squinty
squire
squirm
　squirmy
squir·rel
squirt
squish
　squishy
stab
　stabbed
　stab·bing
　stab·ber
sta·bile
sta·bil·i·ty
　sta·bil·i·ties
sta·bi·lize
　sta·bi·lized
　sta·bi·liz·ing
　sta·bi·li·za·tion
　sta·bi·liz·er
sta·ble
　sta·bled
　sta·bling
stac·ca·to
sta·di·um
staff
stag
　stagged
　stag·ging

stage
　staged
　stag·ing
　stagy
stag·ger
　stag·ger·ing
stag·nant
　stag·nan·cy
stag·nate
　stag·nat·ed
　stag·nat·ing
　stag·na·tion
staid·ness
stain
　stained
stain·less
stake
　staked
　stak·ing
stake·hold·er
sta·lac·tite
sta·lag·mite
stale
　stale·ness
stale·mate
　stale·mat·ed
　stale·mat·ing
stalk
　stalked
　stalky
stalled
stal·lion
stal·wart
sta·men
stam·i·na
stam·mer
　stam·mer·ing·ly
stam·pede
　stam·ped·ed
　stam·ped·ing
stance
stand
　stand·ing
stand·ard
stand·ard·ize
　stand·ard·ized
　stand·ard·iz·ing
　stand·ard·i·za·tion
stand·point
stan·za
staph·y·lo·coc·cus
sta·ple
　sta·pled
　sta·pling
　sta·pler
star
　starred
　star·ring
starchy
　starch·i·ness
star·dom
stare
　stared
　star·ing
star·gaze
　star·gazed
　star·gaz·ing
stark·ly
star·let
star·ling
star·ry
　star·ri·ness
star·ry-eyed
star-span·gled
start·er
star·tle
　star·tled
　star·tling

star·va·tion
starve
  starved
  starv·ing
starve·ling
sta·sis
state
  stat·ed
  stat·ing
  state·ment
state·craft
state·hood
state·less
state·ly
  state·li·er
  state·li·ness
states·man
  states·man·ship
stat·ic
  stat·i·cal·ly
sta·tion
sta·tion·ary
sta·tion·er
sta·tion·ery
stat·ism
  stat·ist
sta·tis·tic
  sta·tis·ti·cal
  sta·tis·ti·cal·ly
stat·is·ti·cian
sta·tis·tics
sta·tor
stat·u·ary
stat·ue
stat·u·esque
stat·u·ette
stat·ure
sta·tus
sta·tus quo
stat·ute
  stat·u·to·ry
staunch
stave
  staved
  stav·ing
stay
  stayed
  stay·ing
stead·fast
  stead·fast·ness
steady
  stead·ied
  stead·y·ing
  stead·i·ly
  stead·i·ness
steal
  stol·en
  steal·ing
stealth
  stealthy
  stealth·i·ly
  stealth·i·ness
steam·er
steam·fit·ter
steam·roll·er
steam·ship
steamy
  steam·i·ness
sted·fast
steel·work·er
steely
  steel·i·ness
steep
  steep·ly
  steep·ness
steep·en
stee·ple
stee·ple·chase

steer
  steer·a·ble
steer·age
stein
stel·lar
stem
  stemmed
  stem·ming
  stem·less
stem·wind·ing
stench
sten·cil
  sten·ciled
  sten·cil·ing
ste·nog·ra·pher
ste·nog·ra·phy
sten·o·graph·ic
sten·o·graph·i·cal·ly
sten·to·ri·an
step
  stepped
  step·ping
step·broth·er
step·child·ren
step·daugh·ter
step·fa·ther
step·lad·der
step·moth·er
steppe
step·ping·stone
ster·eo
ster·e·o·phon·ic
  ster·e·o·phon·i·cal·ly
ster·e·o·scope
  ster·e·o·scop·ic
ster·e·o·type
  ster·e·o·typed
  ster·e·o·typ·ing
ster·ile
  ste·ril·i·ty
ster·i·lize
  ster·i·lized
  ster·i·liz·ing
  ster·i·li·za·tion
  ster·i·liz·er
ster·ling
stern
  stern·ly
  stern·ness
ster·num
ster·oid
steth·o·scope
ste·ve·dore
stew·ard
  stew·ard·ess
stick
  stuck
  stick·ing
stick·er
stick·ler
stick-to-it·ive·ness
sticky
  stick·i·ness
stiff
  stiff·ness
  stiff·en
sti·fle
  sti·fled
  sti·fling
stig·ma
  stig·ma·tic
  stig·mat·i·cal·ly
stig·ma·tize
  stig·ma·tized
  stig·ma·tiz·ing
  stig·ma·ti·za·tion
stile
sti·let·to

still·born
still·ness
stilt·ed
stim·u·late
  stim·u·lat·ed
  stim·u·lat·ing
  stim·u·lant
  stim·u·la·tion
  stim·u·la·tive
  stim·u·lus
  stim·u·li
sting
  stung
  sting·ing
stin·gy
  stin·gi·ness
stink
  stank
  stunk
  stink·ing
  stinky
stint·ing
sti·pend
stip·ple
  stip·pled
  stip·pling
stip·u·late
  stip·u·lat·ed
  stip·u·lat·ing
  stip·u·la·tion
  stip·u·la·to·ry
stir
  stirred
  stir·ring
stir-rup
stitch
stock·ade
stock·brok·er
stock·hold·er
stock·ing
stock·pile
  stock·piled
  stock·pil·ing
stocky
  stock·i·ness
stodgy
  stodg·i·ness
sto·ic
  sto·i·cal
stoke
  stoked
  stok·ing
stol·id
  sto·lid·i·ty
  stol·id·ly
stom·ach
stom·ach·ache
stone
  stoned
  ston·ing
stone·ma·son
stony
  ston·i·er
  ston·i·ness
stop
  stopped
  stop·ping
stop·page
stop·per
stor·age
store
  stored
  stor·ing
sto·ried
stormy
  storm·i·ness
story
  sto·ries

sto·ry·tell·er
stout
  stout·ly
  stout·ness
stout-heart·ed
stove
  stoved
  stov·ing
stow·age
stow·a·way
strad·dle
  strad·dled
  strad·dling
strafe
  strafed
  straf·ing
strag·gle
  strag·gled
  strag·gling
  strag·gler
strag·gly
straight·a·way
straight-edge
straight·en
straight·for·ward
straight·way
strain·er
strait·en
strait·jack·et
strait-laced
strange
  strang·er
  strang·est
  strange·ly
  strange·ness
stran·ger
stran·gle
  stran·gled
  stran·gling
  stran·gler
stran·gu·la·tion
  stran·gu·late
  stran·gu·lat·ed
  stran·gu·lat·ing
strap
  strapped
  strap·ping
  strap·less
strat·a·gem
stra·te·gic
  stra·te·gi·cal·ly
strat·e·gy
  strat·e·gies
  strat·e·gist
strat·i·fy
  strat·i·fied
  strat·i·fy·ing
  strat·i·fi·ca·tion
stra·to·cu·mu·lus
strat·o·sphere
  strat·o·spher·ic
stra·tum
stra·tus
straw·ber·ry
  straw·ber·ries
stray·ing
streak
  streaky
stream·er
stream·line
  stream·lined
  stream·lin·ing
street·walk·er
strength·en
stren·u·ous
  stren·u·os·i·ty
  stren·u·ous·ly
strep·to·coc·cus

strep·to·my·cin
stress
  stress·ful·ly
stretch
  stretch·a·bil·i·ty
  stretch·a·ble
stretch·er
strew
  strewed
  strew·ing
stri·ate
  stri·at·ed
  stri·at·ing
  stri·a·tion
strick·en
strict
  strict·ly
  strict·ness
stric·ture
stride
  strode
  strid·den
  strid·ing
stri·dent
  stri·den·cy
strid·u·late
  strid·u·la·tion
  strid·u·lous
strife
  strife·less
strike
  struck
  strick·en
  strik·ing
strike·break·er
string
  strung
  string·ing
strin·gent
  strin·gen·cy
  strin·gent·ly
stringy
  string·i·ness
strip
  stripped
  strip·ping
strip·crop·ping
stripe
  striped
  strip·ing
strip·ling
strip·per
strip·tease
strive
  strove
  striv·en
  striv·ing
stro·bo·scope
  stro·bo·scop·ic
stroke
  stroked
  strok·ing
stroll·er
strong
  strong·ly
  strong·ness
strong-mind·ed
strop
  stropped
  strop·ping
struc·tural
  struc·tur·al·ly
struc·ture
  struc·tured
  struc·tur·ing
strug·gle
  strug·gled
  strug·gling

strug·gler
strum
  strummed
  strum·ming
strum·pet
strut
  strut·ted
  strut·ting
strych·nine
stub
  stubbed
  stub·bing
  stub·by
stub·ble
  stub·bled
  stub·bly
stub·born
  stub·born·ly
  stub·born·ness
stuc·co
  stuc·coed
  stuc·co·ing
stud
  stud·ded
  stud·ding
stu·dent
stud·ied
  stud·ied·ness
stu·dio
stu·di·ous
  stu·di·ous·ly
  stu·di·ous·ness
study
  stud·ies
  stud·ied
  stud·y·ing
stuff·er
stuff·ing
stuffy
  stuff·i·ness
stul·ti·fy
  stul·ti·fied
    stul·ti·fy·ing
    stul·ti·fi·ca·tion
stum·ble
  stum·bled
  stum·bling
stump
  stumpy
stun
  stunned
  stun·ning
stunt
  stunt·ed
  stunt·ed·ness
stu·pe·fy
  stu·pe·fied
  stu·pe·fy·ing
  stu·pe·fac·tion
stu·pen·dous
  stu·pen·dous·ly
  stu·pen·dous·ness
stu·pid
  stu·pid·i·ty
  stu·pid·ly
  stu·pid·ness
stu·por
  stu·por·ous
stur·dy
  stur·di·est
stur·geon
stut·ter
  stut·ter·ing·ly
style
  styled
  styl·ing
styl·ish
  styl·ish·ness

styl·ist
sty·lis·tic
sty·lis·ti·cal
sty·lis·ti·cal·ly
styl·ize
  styl·ized
  styl·iz·ing
  styl·i·za·tion
sty·lus
sty·mie
  sty·mied
  sty·mie·ing
styp·tic
sty·rene
suave
  suave·ly
  suave·ness
  suav·i·ty
sub
  subbed
  sub·bing
sub·al·tern
sub·arc·tic
sub·as·sem·bly
  sub·as·sem·bler
sub·atom·ic
sub·base·ment
sub·chas·er
sub·com·mit·tee
sub·con·scious
  sub·con·scious·ness
sub·con·ti·nent
sub·con·trac·tor
sub·cul·ture
sub·cu·ta·ne·ous
sub·di·vide
  sub·di·vid·ed
  sub·di·vid·ing
  sub·di·vi·sion
sub·due
  sub·dued
  sub·du·ing
sub·en·try
  sub·en·tries
sub·freez·ing
sub·group
sub·hu·man
sub·ject
  sub·jec·tion
  sub·jec·tive
  sub·jec·tive·ly
  sub·jec·tive·ness
  sub·jec·tiv·i·ty
sub·join
sub·ju·gate
  sub·ju·gat·ed
  sub·ju·gat·ing
  sub·ju·ga·tion
sub·junc·tive
sub·lease
  sub·leased
  sub·leas·ing
sub·let
  sub·let·ting
sub·li·mate
  sub·li·mat·ed
  sub·li·mat·ing
  sub·li·ma·tion
sub·lime
  sub·lim·est
  sub·lime·ly
  sub·lime·ness
  sub·lim·i·ty
sub·lim·i·nal
  sub·lim·i·nal·ly
sub·ma·chine
sub·mar·gin·al
sub·ma·rine

sub·merge
  sub·merged
  sub·merg·ing
  sub·mer·gence
  sub·mer·gi·ble
sub·merse
  sub·mersed
  sub·mers·ing
  sub·mers·i·ble
  sub·mer·sion
sub·mi·cro·scop·ic
sub·mis·sion
sub·mis·sive
  sub·mis·sive·ly
  sub·mis·sive·ness
sub·mit
  sub·mit·ted
  sub·mit·ting
sub·nor·mal
  sub·nor·mal·i·ty
sub·or·bit·al
sub·or·di·nate
  sub·or·di·nat·ed
  sub·or·di·nat·ing
  sub·or·di·nate·ly
  sub·or·di·nate·ness
  sub·or·di·na·tion
  sub·or·di·na·tive
sub·orn
  sub·or·na·tion
sub·poe·na
  sub·poe·naed
  sub·poe·na·ing
sub·re·gion
sub·rosa
sub·scribe
  sub·scribed
  sub·scrib·ing
  sub·scrib·er
  sub·scrip·tion
sub·se·quent
  sub·se·quence
  sub·se·quent·ly
  sub·se·quent·ness
sub·ser·vi·ent
  sub·ser·vi·ence
  sub·ser·vi·en·cy
  sub·ser·vi·ent·ly
sub·side
  sub·sid·ed
  sub·sid·ing
  sub·sid·ence
sub·sid·i·ary
  sub·sid·i·ar·ies
sub·si·dize
  sub·si·dized
  sub·si·diz·ing
  sub·si·di·za·tion
sub·si·dy
  sub·si·dies
sub·sist
sub·sist·ence
sub·soil
sub·son·ic
sub·spe·cies
sub·stance
sub·stand·ard
sub·stan·tial
  sub·stan·ti·al·i·ty
  sub·stan·tial·ly
  sub·stan·tial·ness
sub·stan·ti·ate
  sub·stan·ti·at·ed
  sub·stan·ti·at·ing
  sub·stan·ti·a·tion
  sub·stan·ti·a·tive
sub·stan·tive
  sub·stan·ti·val

sub·stan·ti·val·ly
sub·stan·tive·ly
sub·stan·tive·ness
sub·sta·tion
sub·sti·tute
  sub·sti·tut·ed
  sub·sti·tut·ing
  sub·sti·tut·able
  sub·sti·tu·tion
  sub·sti·tu·tion·al
sub·stra·tum
  sub·stra·ta
sub·struc·ture
sub·sume
  sub·sumed
  sub·sum·ing
  sub·sum·a·ble
  sub·sump·tive
  sub·sump·tion
sub·teen
sub·tend
sub·ter·fuge
sub·ter·ra·ne·an
  sub·ter·ra·ne·ous
sub·ti·tle
sub·tle
  sub·tle·ness
  sub·tle·ty
  sub·tle·ties
  sub·tly
  sub·tly
sub·tract
  sub·tract·er
  sub·trac·ion
  sub·trac·tive
sub·tra·hend
sub·trop·i·cal
  sub·trop·ic
sub·urb
  sub·ur·ban
  sub·ur·ban·ite
sub·ur·bia
sub·vene
  sub·ven·tion
sub·ver·sion
  sub·ver·sion·ary
  sub·ver·sive
  sub·ver·sive·ly
  sub·ver·sive·ness
sub·vert
  sub·vert·er
sub·way
suc·ceed
  suc·ceed·ing
suc·cess
  suc·cess·ful·ly
  suc·cess·ful·ness
suc·ces·sion
  suc·ces·sion·al
suc·ces·sive
  suc·ces·sive·ly
  suc·ces·sive·ness
suc·ces·sor
suc·cinct
  suc·cinct·ly
  suc·cinct·ness
suc·cor
  suc·cor·er
suc·co·tash
suc·cu·lent
  suc·cu·lence
  suc·cu·len·cy
  suc·cu·lent·ly
suc·cumb
suck·er
suck·le
  suck·led
  suck·ling

su·crose
suc·tion
sud·den
  sud·den·ly
  sud·den·ness
sudsy
  suds·i·er
sue
  sued
  su·ing
  su·er
suede
su·et
suf·fer
  suf·fer·a·ble
  suf·fer·a·bly
  suf·fer·er
  suf·fer·ing
  suf·fer·ance
suf·fice
  suf·ficed
  suf·fic·ing
  suf·fi·cien·cy
  suf·fi·cien·cies
  suf·fi·cient
  suf·fi·cient·ly
suf·fix
suf·fo·cate
  suf·fo·cat·ed
  suf·fo·cat·ing
  suf·fo·ca·tion
  suf·fo·ca·tive
suf·ra·gan
suf·frage
suf·fra·gette
suf·frag·ist
suf·fuse
  suf·fused
  suf·fus·ing
  suf·fu·sion
  suf·fu·sive
sug·ar
  sug·ary
  sug·ar·coat
sug·gest
  sug·gest·i·ble
  sug·gest·i·bil·i·ty
  sug·ges·tion
  sug·ges·tive
  sug·ges·tive·ly
  sug·ges·tive·ness
su·i·cide
  su·i·cid·al
suit·a·ble
  suit·a·bil·i·ty
  suit·a·ble·ness
  suit·a·bly
suite
suit·ing
suit·or
sul·fa·nil·a·mide
sul·fate
sul·fide
sul·fur
  sul·fu·ric
  sul·fur·ous
sulky
  sulk·i·ly
  sulk·i·ness
sul·len
  sul·len·ly
  sul·len·ness
sul·ly
  sul·lied
  sul·ly·ing
sul·tan
  sul·tana
  sul·tan·ate

sul·try
sul·tri·ly
sul·tri·ness
sum
summed
sum·ming
su·mac
sum·ma·rize
sum·ma·rized
sum·ma·riz·ing
sum·ma·ri·za·tion
sum·ma·ry
sum·ma·ries
sum·mar·i·ly
sum·mar·i·ness
sum·ma·tion
sum·ma·tion·al
sum·mer
sum·mit
sum·mon
sum·mons
sump·tu·ary
sump·tu·ous
sump·tu·ous·ly
sump·tu·ous·ness
sun
sunned
sun·ning
sun·bathe
sun·bathed
sun·bath·ing
sun·bath·er
sun·burn
sun·burned
sun·burnt
sun·burn·ing
sun·dae
sun·der
sun·der·ance
sun·di·al
sun·dry
sun·dries
sun·flow·er
sun·glass·es
sunk·en
sun·ny
sun·ni·er
sun·ni·ness
sun·shine
sun·spot
sun·stroke
sup
supped
sup·ping
su·per·a·bun·dant
su·per·a·bun·dance
su·per·a·bun·dant·ly
su·per·an·nu·ate
su·per·an·nu·at·ed
su·per·an·nu·at·ing
su·per·an·nu·a·tion
su·perb
su·perb·ly
su·perb·ness
su·per·car·go
su·per·charge
su·per·charged
su·per·charg·ing
su·per·charg·er
su·per·cil·i·ous
su·per·cil·i·ous·ly
su·per·cil·i·ous·ness
su·per·e·go
su·per·e·rog·a·to·ry
su·per·fi·cial
su·per·fi·ci·al·i·ty
su·per·fi·ci·al·i·ties
su·per·fi·cial·ly

su·per·fi·cial·ness
su·per·fine
su·per·flu·ous
su·per·flu·i·ty
su·per·flu·ous·ly
su·per·flu·ous·ness
su·per·high·way
su·per·hu·man
su·per·im·pose
su·per·im·posed
su·per·im·pos·ing
su·per·im·po·si·tion
super·in·duce
su·per·in·tend
su·per·in·tend·ence
su·per·in·tend·en·cy
su·per·in·tend·ent
su·pe·ri·or
su·pe·ri·or·i·ty
su·pe·ri·or·ly
su·per·la·tive
su·per·la·tive·ly
su·per·la·tive·ness
su·per·man
su·per·mar·ket
su·per·nal
su·per·nat·u·ral
su·per·nat·u·ral·ism
su·per·nat·u·ral·ly
su·per·nat·u·ral·ness
su·per·nu·mer·ary
su·per·pow·er
su·per·scribe
su·per·scrip·tion
su·per·script
su·per·sede
su·per·sed·ed
su·per·sed·ing
su·per·son·ic
su·per·son·i·cal·ly
su·per·sti·tion
su·per·sti·tious
su·per·sti·tious·ly
su·per·sti·tious·ness
su·per·struc·ture
su·per·tank·er
su·per·vene
su·per·vened
su·per·ven·ing
super·ven·tion
su·per·vise
su·per·vised
su·per·vis·ing
su·per·vi·sion
su·per·vi·sor
su·per·vi·so·ry
su·pine
su·pine·ness
sup·per
sup·plant
sup·plan·ta·tion
sup·ple
sup·plest
sup·ple·ness
sup·ple·ment
sup·ple·men·tal
sup·ple·men·ta·ry
sup·ple·men·ta·tion
sup·pli·ant
sup·pli·cate
sup·pli·cat·ed
sup·pli·cat·ing
sup·pli·cant
sup·pli·ca·tion
sup·pli·ca·to·ry
sup·ply
sup·plied
sup·ply·ing

sup·plies
sup·pli·er
sup·port
sup·port·a·ble
sup·port·a·bly
sup·port·er
sup·port·ive
sup·pose
sup·posed
sup·pos·ing
sup·pos·a·ble
sup·pos·a·bly
sup·pos·ed·ly
sup·po·si·tion
sup·po·si·tion·al·ly
sup·pos·i·to·ry
sup·press
sup·press·i·ble
sup·pres·sion
sup·pres·sor
sup·pu·rate
sup·pu·rat·ed
sup·pu·rat·ing
sup·pu·ra·tion
su·prem·a·cy
su·prem·a·cist
su·preme
su·preme·ly
su·preme·ness
sur·cease
sur·charge
sur·charged
sur·charg·ing
sur·cin·gle
sure
sur·er
sur·est
sure·ly
sure·ness
sure-foot·ed
sure·ty
surf
surf·board
surf·ing
sur·face
sur·faced
sur·fac·ing
sur·feit
surge
surged
surg·ing
sur·geon
sur·gery
sur·gi·cal
sur·gi·cal·ly
sur·ly
sur·li·ly
sur·li·ness
sur·mise
sur·mised
sur·mis·ing
sur·mount
sur·mount·a·ble
sur·name
sur·pass
sur·pass·a·ble
sur·pass·ing
sur·plice
sur·plus
sur·plus·age
sur·prise
sur·prised
sur·pris·ing
sur·pris·al
sur·re·al·ism
sur·re·al·ist
sur·re·al·is·tic
sur·re·al·is·ti·cal·ly

sur·ren·der
sur·rep·ti·tious
sur·rep·ti·tious·ly
sur·rep·ti·tious·ness
sur·rey
sur·ro·gate
sur·ro·gat·ed
sur·ro·gat·ing
sur·round
sur·round·ings
sur·tax
sur·veil·lance
sur·veil·lant
sur·vey
sur·vey·ing
sur·vey·or
sur·vive
sur·vived
sur·viv·ing
sur·viv·al
sur·vi·vor
sus·cep·ti·ble
sus·cep·ti·bil·i·ty
sus·cep·ti·ble·ness
sus·cep·ti·bly
sus·pect
sus·pend
sus·pend·er
sus·pense
sus·pen·sion
sus·pi·cion
sus·pi·cious
sus·pi·cious·ly
sus·pi·cious·ness
sus·tain
sus·tain·a·ble
sus·tain·er
sus·tain·ment
sus·te·nance
su·ture
su·tured
su·tur·ing
su·ze·rain
svelte
svelte·ly
svelte·ness
swab
swabbed
swab·bing
swad·dle
swad·dled
swad·dling
swag·ger
swag·ger·ing
swal·low
swa·mi
swamp
swampy
swamp·i·ness
swank
swank·i·ly
swank·i·ness
swanky
swan dive
swap
swapped
swap·ping
sward
swarthy
swarth·i·er
swarth·i·ness
swash·buck·ling
swas·ti·ka
swat
swat·ted
swat·ting
swat·ter
swathe

swathed
swath·ing
sway
sway·a·ble
sway·backed
swear
swore
sworn
swear·ing
swear-er
sweat
sweat·ing
sweat·i·ly
sweat·i·ness
sweaty
sweat·er
Swe·den
Swed·ish
sweep
swept
sweep·ing
sweep·ing·ness
sweep·stakes
sweet
sweet·ish
sweet·ly
sweet·ness
sweet·en
swell
swelled
swoll·en
swell·ing
swel·ter
swel·ter·ing
swerve
swerved
swerv·ing
swift
swift·ly
swift·ness
swig
swigged
swig·ging
swill
swim
swam
swum
swim·ming
swim·mer
swin·dle
swin·dled
swin·dling
swin·dler
swine
swin·ish
swing
swung
swing·ing
swing·a·ble
swing·er
swipe
swip·ed
swip·ing
swirl
swirl·ing·ly
swirly
swish
swishy
switch
switch·blade
switch·board
switch-hit·ter
Switz·er·land
swiv·el
swiv·eled
swiv·el·ing
swiz·zle
swoon

swoon·ed
swoon·ing·ly
swoop
swop
swopped
swop·ping
sword
swords·man
syc·a·more
syc·o·phant
syc·o·phan·cy
syc·o·phan·tic
syc·o·phan·ti·cal
syl·lab·ic
syl·lab·i·cate
syl·lab·i·ca·tion
syl·lab·i·fy
syl·lab·i·fi·ca·tion
syl·la·ble
syl·la·bus
syl·lo·gism
syl·lo·gis·tic
sylph·like
syl·van
sym·bi·o·sis
sym·bol
sym·bol·ic
sym·bol·i·cal
sym·bol·ism
sym·bol·ize
sym·bol·ized
sym·bol·iz·ing
sym·bol·i·za·tion
sym·me·try
sym·met·ric
sym·met·ri·cal
sym·pa·thet·ic
sym·pa·thet·i·cal·ly
sym·pa·thize
sym·pa·thized
sym·pa·thiz·ing
sym·pa·thiz·er
sym·pa·thiz·ing·ly
sym·pa·thy
sym·pa·thies
sym·pho·ny
sym·pho·nies
sym·phon·ic
sym·po·si·um
sym·po·sia
symp·tom
symp·to·mat·ic
symp·to·mat·i·cal
symp·to·mat·i·cal·ly
syn·a·gogue
syn·a·gog·al
syn·a·gog·i·cal
syn·chro·nism
syn·chro·nis·tic
syn·chro·nis·ti·cal
syn·chro·nis·ti·cal·ly
syn·chro·nize
syn·chro·nized
syn·chro·niz·ing
syn·chro·ni·za·tion
syn·chro·niz·er
syn·chro·nous
syn·chro·nous·ly
syn·chro·nous·ness
syn·chro·tron
syn·co·pate
syn·co·pat·ed
syn·co·pat·ing
syn·co·pa·tion
syn·co·pa·tor
syn·cre·tism
syn·cre·tic
syn·di·cate

syn·di·cat·ed
syn·di·cat·ing
syn·di·ca·tion
syn·di·ca·tor
syn·drome
syn·ec·do·che
syn·ecol·o·gy
syn·er·gism
syn·od
syn·od·al
syn·o·nym
syn·on·y·mous
syn·on·y·my
syn·op·sis
syn·op·tic
syn·tax
syn·tac·tic
syn·tac·ti·cal
syn·the·sis
syn·the·sist
syn·the·size
syn·the·sized
syn·the·siz·ing
syn·thet·ic
syn·thet·i·cal
syn·thet·i·cal·ly
syph·i·lis
syph·i·lit·ic
sy·ringe
syr·up
syr·upy
system
sys·tem·at·ic
sys·tem·at·i·cal
sys·tem·at·i·cal·ly
sys·tem·at·ic·ness
sys·tem·a·tize
sys·tem·a·tized
sys·tem·a·tiz·ing
sys·tem·a·ti·za·tion
sys·tem·a·tiz·er
sys·tem·ic
sys·tem·i·cal·ly
sys·to·le
sys·tol·ic

T

tab
tabbed
tab·bing
Ta·bas·co
tab·by
tab·er·na·cle
tab·er·nac·u·lar
ta·ble
ta·bled
ta·bling
tab·leau
tab·le d'hote
ta·ble·spoon·fuls
tab·let
tab·loid
ta·boo
ta·booed
ta·boo·ing
ta·bor
tab·o·ret
tab·u·lar
tab·u·lar·ly
tab·u·late
tab·u·lat·ed
tab·u·lat·ing
tab·u·la·tion
tab·u·la·tor
ta·chom·e·ter
tac·it

tac·it·ly
tac·it·ness
tac·i·turn
tac·i·tur·ni·ty
tack
tacked
tack·ing
tack·le
tack·led
tack·ling
tack·ler
tacky
tack·i·ness
ta·cos
tact
tact·ful·ly
tact·ful·ness
tact·less
tac·tics
tac·ti·cal
tac·ti·cian
tac·tile
tac·til·i·ty
tad·pole
taf·fe·ta
taf·fy
tag
tagged
tag·ging
tail
tailed
tail·less
tail·gate
tail·gat·ed
tail·gat·ing
tai·lor
tai·lored
tai·lor·ing
taint
taint·ed
take
took
tak·en
tak·ing
take·off
tal·cum
tale·bear·ing
tal·ent
tal·ent·ed
tal·is·man
talk·a·tive
talk·a·tive·ly
talk·a·tive·ness
talky
talk·i·er
talk·i·est
tal·low
tal·lowy
tal·ly
tal·lies
tal·lied
tal·ly·ing
tal·ly·ho
Tal·mud
Tal·mud·ic
Tal·mud·i·cal
tal·on
tal·oned
ta·ma·le
tam·a·rack
tam·a·rind
tam·bour
tam·bou·rine
tame
tamed
tam·ing
tam·a·ble
tame·ly

tame·ness
tam-o'·shan·ter
tam·per
tam·pon
tan
tanned
tan·ning
tan·nish
tan·a·ger
tan·bark
tan·dem
tang
tangy
tang·i·er
tan·ge·lo
tan·gent
tan·gen·cy
tan·gen·tial
tan·ge·rine
tan·gi·ble
tan·gi·bil·i·ty
tan·gi·ble·ness
tan·gi·bly
tan·gle
tan·gled
tan·gling
tan·gle·ment
tan·go
tan·goed
tan·go·ing
tank·age
tank·ard
tank·er
tan·nery
tan·nin
tan·ta·lize
tan·ta·lized
tan·ta·liz·ing
tan·ta·mount
tan·trum
tap
tapped
tap·ping
tape
taped
tap·ing
ta·per
ta·per·ing·ly
tap·es·try
tap·es·tries
tap·es·tried
tap·es·try·ing
tap·i·o·ca
ta·pir
tar
tarred
tar·ring
tar·ry
tar·an·tel·la
ta·ran·tu·la
ta·ran·tu·las
ta·ran·tu·lae
tar·dy
tar·di·ly
tar·di·ness
tar·get
tar·iff
tar·nish
tar·nish·a·ble
ta·ro
tar·pau·lin
tar·pon
tar·ra·gon
tar·ry
tar·ried
tar·ry·ing
tart
tart·ness

tar·tan
tar·tar
tar·tar·ic
tar·tar·ous
tas·sel
tas·seled
tas·sel·ing
taste
tast·ed
tast·ing
taste·ful
taste·ful·ly
taste·ful·ness
taste·less
taste·less·ness
tasty
tast·i·ness
tat
tat·ted
tat·ting
tat·ter·de·ma·lion
tat·tered
tat·tle
tat·tled
tat·tling
tat·tle·tale
tat·too
tat·tooed
tat·too·ing
taught
taunt
taunt·ing·ly
taut
taut·ly
taut·ness
tau·tol·o·gy
tau·to·log·i·cal
tau·to·log·i·cal·ly
tav·ern
taw·dry
taw·dri·ly
taw·dri·ness
taw·ny
taw·ni·ness
tax
tax·a·bil·i·ty
tax·a·ble
tax·a·tion
tax·ex·empt
taxi
tax·i·cab
tax·i·der·my
tax·i·der·mic
tax·i·der·mist
tax·on·o·my
tax·o·nom·i·cal
tax·o·nom·i·cal·ly
tax·on·o·mist
tax·pay·er
teach
taught
teach·ing
teach·a·ble
teach·a·ble·ness
teach·a·bil·i·ty
teach·er
teak·wood
tea·ket·tle
team·mate
team·ster
tear
tore
torn
tear·ing
tear·ful
tear·ful·ly
tear·ful·ness
teary

tease
  teased
  teas·ing
tea·sel
  tea·seled
  tea·sel·ing
tea·spoon·fuls
teat
tech·ni·cal
  tech·ni·cal·ly
  tech·ni·cal·ness
  tech·ni·cal·i·ty
  tech·ni·cian
tech·nique
tech·noc·ra·cy
  tech·no·crat
  tech·no·crat·ic
tech·nol·o·gy
  tech·no·log·i·cal
  tech·no·log·ic
  tech·nol·o·gist
tec·ton·ic
te·di·ous
  te·di·ous·ly
  te·di·ous·ness
te·di·um
tee
  teed
  tee·ing
teem
  teem·ing
teen·ag·er
tee·pee
tee·ter
teethe
  teethed
  teeth·ing
tee·to·tal
  tee·to·tal·er
  tee·to·tal·ist
  tee·to·tal·ism
  tee·to·tal·ly
teg·u·ment
tel·e·cast
  tel·e·cast·ing
  tel·e·cast·er
tel·e·com·mu·ni·ca·tion
tel·e·gram
tel·e·graph
  tel·e·graph·ic
  te·leg·ra·phy
tele·ki·ne·sis
tele·me·ter
te·le·ol·o·gy
te·lep·a·thy
  tel·e·path·ic
  tel·e·path·i·cal·ly
  tel·lep·a·thist
tel·e·phone
  tel·e·phoned
  tel·e·phon·ing
  tle·phon·ic
tel·e·pho·to
tel·e·pho·tog·ra·phy
  tel·e·pho·to·graph·ic
Tel·e·promp·ter
tel·e·ran
tel·e·scope
  tel·e·scoped
  tel·e·scop·ing
tel·e·scop·ic
  tel·e·scop·i·cal
tel·e·thon
Tel·e·type
tel·e·vise
  tel·e·vised
  tel·e·vis·ing
  tel·e·vi·sion

tell
  told
  tell·ing
  tell·er
tem·blor
te·mer·i·ty
tem·per
  tem·per·a·bil·i·ty
  tem·per·a·ble
  tem·pered
  tem·per·er
tem·pera
  tem·per·a·ment
  tem·per·a·ment·al
  tem·per·ance
tem·per·ate
  tem·per·ate·ly
  tem·per·ate·ness
  tem·per·a·ture
tem·pest
  tem·pes·tu·ous
  tem·pes·tu·ous·ly
  tem·pes·tu·ous·ness
tem·plate
tem·ple
tem·po
tem·po·ral
  tem·po·ral·i·ty
  tem·por·ral·ly
  tem·por·ral·ness
tem·po·rary
  tem·po·rar·i·ty
  tem·po·rar·i·ness
tem·po·rize
  tem·po·ri·za·tion
  tem·po·riz·er
  tem·po·riz·ing·ly
tempt
  tempt·a·ble
  temp·ta·tion
  tempt·ing
ten·a·ble
  ten·a·bil·i·ty
  ten·a·ble·ness
  ten·a·bly
te·na·cious
  te·na·cious·ly
  te·na·cious·ness
  te·nac·i·ty
ten·ant
  ten·an·cy
  ten·an·cies
  ten·ant·a·ble
ten·den·cy
  ten·den·cies
ten·den·tious
  ten·den·tious·ly
  ten·den·tious·ness
ten·der
  ten·der·ly
  ten·der·ness
ten·der·foot
ten·der·ize
  ten·der·ized
  ten·der·iz·ing
  ten·der·iz·er
ten·der·loin
ten·don
ten·dril
te·neb·ri·ous
ten·e·ment
ten·et
ten·nis
ten·on
ten·or
tense
  tensed
  tens·ing

tense·ly
tense·ness
ten·si·ty
ten·sile
  ten·sil·i·ty
ten·sion
  ten·sion·al
  ten·sion·less
  ten·sive
ten·ta·cle
  ten·ta·cled
  ten·tac·u·lar
ten·ta·tive
  ten·ta·tive·ly
  ten·ta·tive·ness
tenth
te·nu·i·ty
ten·u·ous
  ten·u·ous·ly
  ten·u·ous·ness
ten·ure
  ten·ured
  ten·u·ri·al
  ten·u·ri·al·ly
te·pee
tep·id
  te·pid·i·ty
  tep·id·ness
te·qui·la
ter·cen·te·nary
  ter·cen·ten·ni·al
ter·gi·ver·sate
ter·i·ya·ki
ter·ma·gant
ter·mi·nal
  ter·mi·nal·ly
ter·mi·nate
  ter·mi·nat·ed
  ter·mi·nat·ing
  ter·mi·na·ble
  ter·mi·na·tion
  ter·mi·na·tive
  ter·mi·na·tor
ter·mi·nol·o·gy
  ter·mi·nol·o·gies
  ter·mi·no·log·i·cal
  ter·mi·no·log·i·cal·ly
ter·mi·nus
ter·mite
ter·na·ry
terp·sich·o·re·an
ter·race
  ter·raced
  ter·rac·ing
ter·ra-cot·ta
ter·ra fir·ma
Ter·ra·my·cin
ter·ra·pin
ter·rar·i·um
ter·raz·zo
ter·res·tri·al
  ter·res·tri·al·ly
ter·ri·ble
  ter·ri·ble·ness
  ter·ri·bly
ter·ri·er
ter·rif·ic
  ter·rif·i·cal·ly
ter·ri·fy
  ter·ri·fied
  ter·ri·fy·ing
ter·ri·to·ry
  ter·ri·to·ri·al
  ter·ri·to·ri·al·i·ty
ter·ror
  ter·ror·less
ter·ror·ism

ter·ror·ist
  ter·ror·is·tic
  ter·ror·less
ter·ror·ize
  ter·ror·ized
  ter·ror·iz·ing
  ter·ror·i·za·tion
  ter·ror·iz·er
ter·ry
terse
  ters·er
  terse·ly
  terse·ness
ter·ti·ary
tes·sel·late
  tes·sel·lat·ed
  tes·sel·lat·ing
  tes·sel·la·tion
tes·ta·ment
  tes·ta·men·ta·ry
tes·tate
tes·ta·tor
  tes·ta·trix
tes·ti·cle
  tes·tic·u·lar
tes·ti·fy
  tes·ti·fied
  tes·ti·fy·ing
tes·ti·mo·ni·al
tes·ti·mo·ny
  tes·ti·mo·nies
tes·tis
  tes·tes
tes·tos·ter·one
tes·ty
  tes·ti·ly
  tes·ti·ness
tet·a·nus
tete-a-tete
teth·er
tet·ra·eth·yl
tet·ra·he·dron
tex·tile
tex·tu·al
tex·ture
  tex·tur·al
  tex·tur·al·ly
  tex·tured
thank
  thank·ful·ly
  thank·ful·ness
thank·less
  thank·less·ly
  thank·less·ness
thanks·giv·ing
thatch
  thatch·ing
thaw
the·a·ter
  the·a·tre
the·at·ri·cal
  the·at·ri·cal·ism
  the·at·ri·cal·i·ty
  the·at·ri·cal·ly
the·ism
  the·ist
  the·is·tic
theme
  the·mat·ic
  the·mat·i·cal·ly
them·selves
thence·forth
the·oc·ra·cy
  the·oc·ra·cies
  the·o·crat
  the·o·crat·ic
  the·o·crat·i·cal
  the·o·cart·i·cal·ly

the·ol·o·gy
  the·ol·o·gies
  the·o·lo·gian
  the·o·log·ic
  the·o·log·i·cal
  the·o·log·i·cal·ly
the·o·rem
  the·o·re·mat·ic
the·o·ret·i·cal
  the·o·ret·ic
  the·o·ret·i·cal·ly
the·o·rize
  the·o·rized
  the·o·riz·ing
the·o·re·ti·cian
the·o·rist
  the·o·ri·za·tion
  the·o·riz·er
the·o·ry
  the·o·ries
the·os·o·phy
  the·o·soph·ic
  the·o·soph·i·cal
  the·o·soph·i·cal·ly
  the·os·o·phist
ther·a·peu·tic
  ther·a·peu·ti·cal
  ther·a·peu·ti·cal·ly
ther·a·peu·tics
  ther·a·peu·tist
ther·a·py
  ther·a·pist
there·fore
ther·mal
  ther·mal·ly
ther·mo·dy·nam·ics
  ther·mo·dy·nam·ic
  ther·mo·dy·nam·i·cal
ther·mo·e·lec·tric
ther·mom·e·ter
  ther·mo·met·ric
ther·mo·nu·cle·ar
ther·mo·plas·tic
ther·mos
ther·mo·stat
  ther·mo·stat·ic
the·sau·rus
the·sis
  the·ses
thes·pi·an
thi·a·mine
thick
  thick·ish
  thick·ly
  thick·ness
  thick·en
thick·et
  thick·et·ed
thick-head·ed
thief
  thieves
thieve
  thieved
  thiev·ing
  thiev·ish
  thiev·ish·ness
thiev·ery
  thiev·er·ies
thim·ble
thin
  thin·ner
  thin·nest
  thinned
  thin·ning
  thin·ly
  thin·ness
thine
thing

think
  thought
  think·ing
third·ly
thirsty
  thirst·i·er
  thirst·i·est
  thirst·i·ly
  thirst·i·ness
thir·teen
  thir·teenth
thir·ti·eth
thirty
  thir·ties
this·tle
thith·er
thong
tho·rax
tho·ri·um
thorn
  thorny
  thorn·i·ness
thor·ough
  thor·ough·ly
  thor·ough·ness
thor·ough·bred
thor·ough·fare
thor·ough·go·ing
though
thought·ful
  thought·ful·ly
  thought·ful·ness
thought·less
thou·sand
  thou·santh
thrall
  thrall·dom
thrash·er
thrash·ing
thread
thread·bare
thready
  thread·i·ness
threat·en
  threat·en·ing·ly
three-deck·er
three-di·men·sion·al
three·fold
three·quar·ter
three·score
three·some
thren·o·dy
thresh·er
thresh·old
thrice
thrift·less
thrifty
  thrift·i·ly
  thrift·i·ness
thrill
  thrill·ing
thrive
  throve
  thrived
  thriven
  thriv·ing
throat
throaty
  throat·i·ly
  throat·i·ness
throb
  throbbed
  throb·bing
throe
throm·bo·sis
throne
throng
throt·tle

throt·tled
throt·tling
through
through·out
through·way
  thru·way
throw
  threw
  thrown
  throw·ing
  throw·a·way
  throw·back
thrum
  thrummed
  thrum·ming
thrust
  thrust·ing
thud
  thud·ded
  thud·ding
thug
  thug·gery
  thug·gish
thumb
  thumb·nail
  thumb·screw
  thumb·tack
thump·ing
thun·der
  thun·der·ous
  thun·der·bolt
  thun·der·cloud
  thun·der·head
  thun·der·show·er
  thun·der·storm
  thun·der·struck
thwack
thwart
thyme
thy·mus
thy·roid
ti·ara
tib·ia
tic
tick
  tick·er
  tick·et
  tick·ing
  tick·le
    tick·led
    tick·ling
  tick·lish
    tick·lish·ness
  tick-tack-toe
ti·dal
tid·bit
tid·dly·winks
tide
tide·land
tide·water
ti·dings
ti·dy
  ti·di·ly
  ti·di·ness
tie
  tied
  ty·ing
tier
ti·ger
  ti·gress
  ti·ger·ish
tight
  tight·ly
  tight·ness
tight·en
tight-fist·ed
tight-lipped
tight·rope

tight·wad
til·de
tile
  tiled
  til·ing
till
  till·a·ble
  till·age
tilt
  tilt·ed
tim·bal
tim·ber
  tim·bered
  tim·ber·line
tim·bre
tim·brel
time
  timed
  tim·ing
time-con·sum·ing
time-hon·ored
time·keep·er
time·less·ness
time·out
time-shar·ing
time·ta·ble
tim·id
  tim·id·ly
  tim·id·i·ty
  tim·id·ness
tim·or·ous
  tim·or·ous·ly
  tim·or·ous·ness
tim·o·thy
tim·pa·ni
  tim·pa·nist
tin
  tinned
  tin·ning
tinc·ture
  tinc·tur·ing
tin·der
tinge
  tinged
  tinge·ing
tin·gle
  tin·gled
  tin·gling
  tin·gly
tink·er
tin·kle
  tin·kled
  tin·kling
tin·ny
  tin·ni·ly
  tin·ni·ness
tin·sel
  tin·seled
  tin·sel·ing
tint
  tint·er
  tint·ing
tin·tin·nab·u·la·tion
ti·ny
  ti·ni·er
  ti·ni·ness
tip
  tipped
  tip·ping
tip·ple
  tip·pled
  tip·pling
  tip·pler
tip·sy
  tip·si·ly
  tip·si·ness
tip·toe
  tip·toed

tip·to·ing
tip·top
ti·rade
tire
  tired
  tir·ing
  tire·less
tire·some
  tire·some·ness
tis·sue
ti·tan
  ti·tan·ic
tithe
  tithed
  tith·ing
ti·tian
tit·il·late
  tit·il·lat·ed
  tit·il·lat·ing
  tit·il·la·tion
ti·tle
  ti·tled
tit·mouse
tit·ter
  tit·ter·ing
tit·u·lar
tiz·zy
toady
  toad·y·ing
  toad·y·ism
toast·er
toast·mas·ter
  toast·mis·tress
to·bac·co
to·bog·gan
toc·sin
to·day
tod·dle
  tod·dled
  tod·dling
  tod·dler
tod·dy
toe
  toed
  toe·ing
toe·nail
tof·fee
tog
  togged
  tog·ging
to·ga
to·geth·er
  to·geth·er·ness
tog·gle
  tog·gled
  tog·gling
toil·er
toi·let
toi·let·ry
toil·some
to·ken·ism
To·kyo
tol·er·a·ble
  tol·er·a·ble·ness
  tol·er·a·bil·i·ty
  tol·er·a·bly
tol·er·ant
  tol·er·ance
tol·er·ate
  tol·er·at·ed
  tol·er·at·ing
  tol·er·a·tion
  tol·er·a·tive
toll·booth
tom·a·hawk
to·ma·to
tom·boy
  tom·boy·ish

tomb·stone
tom·cat
tom·fool·ery
to·mor·row
tom·tit
tom-tom
tone
  ton·al
  to·nal·i·ty
  ton·al·ly
  tone·less
tongue
  tongue-lash
  tongue-tied
ton·ic
to·night
ton·nage
ton·neau
ton·sil
ton·sil·lec·to·my
ton·sil·li·tis
ton·so·ri·al
ton·sure
  ton·sured
  ton·sur·ing
ton·tine
tool·mak·er
tooth
  teeth
  tooth·ache
  tooth·brush
  tooth·less
  tooth·paste
  tooth·pick
  tooth·some
toothy
  tooth·i·ness
top
  topped
  top·ping
to·paz
tope
  toped
  top·ing
  top·er
to·pi·ary
top·ic
top·i·cal
  top·i·cal·i·ty
to·pog·ra·phy
  to·pog·ra·pher
  top·o·graph·i·cal
  top·o·graph·i·cal·ly
to·pol·o·gy
  top·o·log·i·cal
top·ping
top·ple
  top·pled
  top·pling
top-se·cret
top·sy-tur·vy
toque
To·rah
torch·bear·er
torch·light
tor·e·a·dor
to·re·ro
tor·ment
  tor·ment·ing
  tor·men·tor
tor·na·do
  tor·na·dos
  tor·nad·ic
tor·pe·do
  tor·pe·doed
  tor·pe·do·ing
tor·pid
  tor·pid·i·ty

tor·pid·ly
tor·por
torque
tor·rent
    tor·ren·tial
tor·rid
    tor·rid·i·ty
    tor·rid·ness
    tor·rid·ly
tor·sion
    tor·sion·al
tor·so
tort
torte
tor·til·la
tor·toise
tor·to·ni
tor·tu·ous
    tor·tu·ous·ly
    tor·tu·ous·ness
tor·ture
    tor·tured
    tor·tur·ing
    tor·tur·er
    tor·ture·some
tossing
to·tal
    to·taled
    to·tal·ing
    to·tal·i·tar·i·an
    to·tal·i·tar·i·an·ism
    to·tal·i·ty
    to·tal·i·za·tor
    to·tal·ly
tote
    tot·ed
    tot·ing
to·tem
    to·tem·ic
    to·tem·ism
    to·tem·ist
    to·tem·is·tic
tot·ter
    tot·ter·ing
tou·can
touch
    touched
    touch·ing
    touch·a·ble
    touchy
    touch·i·ness
touch·down
tou·ché
tough
    tough·ness
tough·en
tou·pee
tour de force
tour·ism
tour·ist
tour·ma·line
tour·na·ment
tour·ney
tour·ni·quet
tou·sle
    tou·sled
tout·er
tow·age
to·ward
tow·boat
tow·el
    tow·eled
    tow·el·ing
tow·er
    tow·ered
    tow·er·ing
    tow-head·ed
town·ship

tox·e·mia
tox·ic
tox·ic·i·ty
tox·i·col·o·gy
    tox·i·co·log·i·cal
    tox·i·co·log·i·cal·ly
    tox·i·col·o·gist
tox·in
tox·oid
trace
    traced
    trac·ing
    trace·a·ble
    trace·a·bly
trac·ery
tra·chea
tra·che·ot·o·my
tra·cho·ma
track·age
track·er
tract
trac·ta·ble
    trac·ta·bil·i·ty
    trac·ta·ble·ness
    trac·ta·bly
trac·tion
    trac·tion·al
    trac·tive
trac·tor
trade
    trad·ed
    trad·ing
trade·mark
trades·man
tra·di·tion
tra·di·tion·al
    tra·di·tion·al·ism
    tra·di·tion·al·ist
    tra·di·tion·al·ly
tra·duce
    tra·duced
    tra·duc·ing
    tra·duce·ment
traf·fic
    traf·ficked
    traf·fick·ing
    traf·fick·er
tra·ge·di·an
    tra·ge·di·enne
trag·e·dy
    trag·e·dies
trag·ic
    trag·i·cal
    trag·i·cal·ly
    trag·i·cal·ness
tragi·com·e·dy
trail·blaz·er
    trail·blaz·ing
trail·er
train
    train·a·ble
    train·er
    train·ing
traipse
    traipsed
    traips·ing
trait
trai·tor
    trai·tor·ous
    trai·tor·ous·ly
tra·jec·to·ry
    tra·jec·to·ries
tram·mel
    tram·meled
    tram·mel·ing
tramp·ing
tram·ple
    tram·pled

tram·pling
tram·po·line
tram·po·lin·ist
trance
tran·quil
    tran·quil·li·ty
    tran·quil·ly
    tran·quil·ness
tran·quil·ize
    tran·quil·ized
    tran·quil·iz·ing
    tran·quil·iz·er
trans·act
    trans·ac·tor
    trans·ac·tion
    trans·ac·tion·al
trans·at·lan·tic
trans·ceiv·er
tran·scend
    tran·scend·ent
tran·scen·den·tal
    tran·scen·den·tal·ly
    tran·scen·den·tal·ism
trans·con·ti·nen·tal
tran·scribe
    tran·scribed
    tran·scrib·ing
    tran·scrib·er
tran·script
    tran·scrip·tion
    tran·scrip·tion·al
    tran·scrip·tive
tran·sect
    trans·sec·tion
tran·sept
    tran·sep·tal
    tran·sep·tal·ly
trans·fer
    trans·ferred
    trans·fer·ring
    trans·fer·al
    trans·fer·a·ble
    trans·fer·ence
trans·fig·ure
    trans·fig·ured
    trans·fig·ur·ing
    trans·fig·ure·ment
    trans·fig·u·ra·tion
trans·fix
    trans·fixed
    trans·fix·ing
    trans·fix·ion
trans·form
    trans·form·a·ble
    trans·for·ma·tion
    trans·form·a·tive
trans·form·er
trans·fuse
    trans·fused
    trans·fus·ing
    trans·fus·a·ble
    trans·fu·sion
trans·gress
    trans·gres·sive
    trans·gres·sor
    trans·gres·sion
tran·sient
    tran·sience
tran·sis·tor
tran·sis·tor·ize
    tran·sis·tor·ized
    tran·sis·tor·iz·ing
trans·it
tran·si·tion
    tran·si·tion·al
    tran·si·tion·al·ly
tran·si·tive
    tran·si·tive·ly

tran·si·tive·ness
tran·si·tiv·i·ty
tran·si·to·ry
    tran·si·to·ri·ly
    tran·si·to·ri·ness
trans·late
    trans·lat·ed
    trans·lat·ing
    trans·lat·a·bil·i·ty
    trans·lat·a·ble
    trans·la·tor
trans·la·tion
    trans·la·tion·al
    trans·la·tive
trans·lit·er·ate
    trans·lit·er·at·ed
    trans·lit·er·at·ing
    trans·lit·er·a·tion
trans·lu·cent
    trans·lu·cence
    trans·lu·cen·cy
    trans·lu·cent·ly
trans·me·rid·i·o·nal
trans·mi·grate
    trans·mi·grat·ed
    trans·mi·grat·ing
    trans·mi·gra·tion
    trans·mi·gra·tor
    trans·mi·gra·to·ry
trans·mis·sion
    trans·mis·si·bil·i·ty
    trans·mis·siv·i·ty
    trans·mis·si·ble
    trans·mis·sive
trans·mit
    trans·mit·ted
    trans·mit·ting
    trans·mit·ta·ble
    trans·mit·tal
trans·mit·ter
trans·mute
    trans·mut·ed
    trans·mut·ing
    trans·mut·er
    trans·mut·a·ble·ness
    trans·mut·a·bil·i·ty
    trans·mut·a·bly
    trans·mu·ta·tion
    trans·mut·a·ble
trans·o·ce·an·ic
tran·som
tran·son·ic
trans·pa·cif·ic
trans·par·ent
    trans·par·en·cy
    trans·par·en·cies
    trans·par·ent·ly
    trans·par·ent·ness
tran·spire
    tran·spired
    tran·spir·ing
    tran·spi·ra·tion
trans·plant
    trans·plant·a·ble
    trans·plan·ta·tion
trans·port
    trans·port·a·bil·i·ty
    trans·port·a·ble
    trans·port·er
    trans·por·ta·tion
trans·pose
    trans·posed
    trans·pos·ing
    trans·pos·a·ble
    trans·po·si·tion
trans·ship
    trans·shipped
    trans·ship·ping

trans·ship·ment
trans·verse
    trans·verse·ly
trans·ves·tism
    trans·ves·tite
trap
    trapped
    trap·ping
tra·peze
tra·pe·zi·um
trap·e·zoid
trap·per
trap·pings
trap·shoot·ing
trash
    trash·i·est
    trash·i·ness
    trashy
trau·ma
    trau·mat·ic
    trau·mat·i·cal·ly
    trau·ma·tize
tra·vail
tra·vel
    tra·vel·ed
    tra·vel·ing
trav·e·logue
    trav·e·log
trav·erse
    trav·ersed
    trav·ers·ing
    tra·vers·a·ble
    tra·vers·al
trav·es·ty
trawl·er
treach·er·ous
    treach·er·ous·ly
    treach·er·ous·ness
treach·ery
    treach·er·ies
tread
    trod
    trod·den
    tread·ing
trea·dle
trea·son
    trea·son·a·ble
    trea·son·ous
    trea·son·a·bly
treas·ure
    treas·ured
    treas·ur·ing
    treas·ur·a·ble
treas·ur·er
treas·ury
    treas·ur·ies
treat
    treat·a·ble
    treat·ment
trea·tise
trea·ty
    trea·ties
tre·ble
    tre·bled
    tre·bling
    tre·bly
tre·foil
trek
    trekked
    trek·king
trel·lis
trem·ble
    trem·bled
    trem·bling
    trem·bly
tre·men·dous
    tre·men·dous·ly
    tre·men·dous·ness

trem·o·lo
trem·or
   trem·or·ous
trem·u·lous
   trem·u·lous·ly
   trem·u·lous·ness
trench·ant
   trench·an·cy
   trench·ant·ly
trench·er
trend
   trendy
tre·pan
   tre·panned
   tre·pan·ning
   trep·an·a·tion
tre·phine
trep·i·da·tion
tres·pass
   tres·pass·er
tres·tle
tri·ad
   tri·ad·ic
tri·al
tri·an·gle
   tri·an·gu·lar
   tri·an·gu·lar·i·ty
   tri·an·gu·lar·ly
tri·an·gu·late
   tri·an·gu·lat·ed
   tri·an·gu·lat·ing
   tri·an·gu·la·tion
tribe
   trib·al
   tribes·men
trib·u·la·tion
tri·bu·nal
trib·une
trib·u·tary
   trib·u·tar·ies
   trib·u·tar·i·ly
trib·ute
trice
tri·ceps
trich·i·no·sis
tri·chot·o·my
trick·ery
trick·le
   trick·led
   trick·ling
trick·ster
tricky
   trick·i·er
   trick·i·ly
   trick·i·ness
tri·col·or
tri·cus·pid
tri·cy·cle
tri·dent
   tri·den·tate
tri·di·men·sion·al
tri·en·ni·al
tri·en·ni·um
tri·fle
   tri·fled
   tri·fling
   trif·ler
   tri·fling·ness
tri·fo·cals
trig·ger
trig·o·nom·e·try
   trig·o·no·met·ric
   trig·o·no·met·ri·cal
   trig·o·no·met·ri·cal·ly
tri·lin·gual
tril·lion
   tril·lionth
tril·o·gy

trim
   trimmed
   trim·ming
   trim·mer
   trim·mest
   trim·ly
   trim·ness
tri·mes·ter
tri·mes·tral
tri·mes·tri·al
tri·month·ly
Trin·i·tar·i·an
Trin·i·ty
trin·ket
trio
trip
   tripped
   trip·ping
tri·par·tite
trip·ham·mer
tri·ple
   tri·pled
   tri·pling
   tri·ply
tri·plet
trip·li·cate
   trip·li·cat·ed
   trip·li·cat·ing
   trip·li·ca·tion
tri·pod
trip·tych
tri·sect
   tri·sec·tion
   tri·sec·tor
trite
   trite·ly
   trite·ness
trit·u·rate
tri·umph
   tri·um·phal
   tri·um·phal·ly
   tri·um·phant
   tri·um·phant·ly
tri·um·vi·rate
triv·et
triv·ia
triv·i·al
   triv·i·al·i·ty
   triv·i·al·i·ties
   triv·i·al·i·za·tion
   triv·i·al·ly
tri·week·ly
tro·che
trog·lo·dyte
troi·ka
troll
trol·ley
trol·lop
trom·bone
   trom·bon·ist
troop·er
tro·phy
   tro·phies
trop·ic
   trop·i·cal
trop·o·sphere
trot
   trot·ted
   trot·ting
   trot·ter
trou·ba·dour
trou·ble
   trou·bled
   trou·bling
   trou·ble·mak·er
   trou·ble·shoot·er
   trou·ble·some
trough

trounce
   trounced
   trounc·ing
troupe
   trouped
   troup·ing
troup·er
trou·sers
trous·seau
trow·el
tru·ant
   tru·an·cy
   tru·an·cies
   tru·ant·ry
truck·age
truck·er
truck·ing
truc·u·lent
   truc·u·lence
   truc·u·lent·ly
trudge
   trudged
   trudg·ing
true
   tru·er
   tru·est
   true·ness
truf·fle
tru·ism
   tru·is·tic
tru·ly
trump
   trump·er·y
trum·pet
   trum·pet·er
trun·cate
   trun·cat·ed
   trun·cat·ing
   trun·ca·tion
trun·cheon
trun·dle
   trun·dled
   trun·dling
truss
   truss·ing
trust
trus·tee
   trus·teed
   trus·tee·ing
   trus·tee·ship
trust·ful
   trust·ful·ly
trust·wor·thy
   trust·wor·thi·ly
   trust·wor·thi·ness
trusty
   trust·i·est
   trust·i·ness
truth·ful
   truth·ful·ly
   truth·ful·ness
try
   tried
   try·ing
tryst
tsu·na·mi
tu·ba
tu·bal
tub·by
   tub·bi·ness
tube
   tubed
   tub·ing
tu·ber
tu·ber·cle
tu·ber·cu·lo·sis
tu·ber·cu·lar
tu·ber·ous

tu·bu·lar
tu·bule
tuck-point
tuft·ed
tu·i·tion
tu·la·re·mia
tu·lip
tulle
tum·ble
   tum·bled
   tum·bling
tum·ble-down
tum·bler
tum·ble·weed
tu·mes·cent
tu·mid
   tu·mid·i·ty
tu·mor
   tu·mor·ous
tu·mult
   tu·mul·tu·ous
   tu·mul·tu·ous·ly
   tu·mul·tu·ous·ness
tu·na
tun·dra
tune
   tuned
   tun·ing
   tun·a·ble
   tune·ful
tung·sten
tu·nic
tun·nel
   tun·neled
   tun·nel·ing
tuque
tur·ban
tur·bid
   tur·bid·i·ty
   tur·bid·ness
tur·bine
tur·bo
tur·bo·fan
tur·bo·jet
tur·bo·prop
tur·bot
tur·bu·lent
   tur·bu·lence
   tru·bu·len·cy
tu·reen
turf
tur·gid
   tur·gid·i·ty
   tur·gid·ness
tur·key
tur·mer·ic
tur·moil
turn·coat
turn·ing
tur·nip
turn·key
turn·pike
turn·ta·ble
tur·pen·tine
tur·pi·tude
tur·quoise
tur·ret
tur·tle
tur·tle·dove
tur·tle·neck
tusk
   tusked
tus·sle
   tus·sled
   tus·sling
tu·te·lage
tu·tor
   tu·tor·age

tu·to·ri·al
tu·ti-fru·ti
tu·tu
tux·e·do
twad·dle
twain
twang
   twangy
tweak
tweed
   tweedy
   tweed·i·ness
tweet·er
tweez·ers
   tweeze
   tweezed
   tweez·ing
twelve
   twelfth
twen·ty
   twen·ties
   twen·ti·eth
twid·dle
   twid·dled
   twid·dling
twig
   twig·gy
twi·light
twilled
twin
   twinned
   twin·ning
twine
   twined
   twin·ing
twinge
   twinged
   twing·ing
twin·kle
   twin·kled
   twin·kling
twirl
   twirl·er
   twirly
twist·er
twit
   twit·ted
   twit·ting
twitch
twit·ter
   twit·tery
two-di·men·sion·al
two-faced
two-fist·ed
two-sid·ed
two·some
two-time
ty·coon
tym·pan·ic
type
   typed
   typ·ing
   typ·ist
type·face
type·set·ter
type·set
type·write
   type·writ·ten
   type·writ·ing
type·writ·er
ty·phoid
ty·phoon
ty·phus
typ·i·cal
   typ·i·cal·ly
   typ·i·cal·ness
   typ·i·cal·i·ty
typ·i·fy

typ·i·fied
typ·i·fy·ing
typ·i·fi·ca·tion
ty·pog·ra·phy
ty·pog·ra·pher
ty·po·graph·ic
ty·po·graph·i·cal
ty·po·graph·i·cal·ly
ty·pol·o·gy
ty·ran·ni·cal
ty·ran·nic
ty·ran·ni·cal·ly
ty·ran·nous
tyr·an·nize
tyr·an·nized
tyr·an·niz·ing
tyr·an·niz·er
tyr·an·ny
ty·rant
ty·ro

U

ubiq·ui·ty
ubiq·ui·tous
ubiq·ui·tary
ubiq·ui·tous·ly
ubiq·ui·tous·ness
ud·der
ug·ly
ug·li·er
ug·li·est
ug·li·ly
ug·li·ness
uku·le·le
ul·cer
ul·cer·ous
ul·cer·ate
ul·cer·at·ed
ul·cer·at·ing
ul·cer·a·tion
ul·ster
ul·te·ri·or
ul·te·ri·or·ly
ul·ti·mate
ul·ti·mate·ly
ul·ti·mate·ness
ul·ti·ma·tum
ul·tra
ul·tra·con·serv·a·tive
ul·tra·fash·ion·a·ble
ul·tra·lib·er·al
ul·tra·ma·rine
ul·tra·mod·ern
ul·tra·re·li·gious
ul·tra·son·ic
ul·tra·vi·o·let
ul·u·late
ul·u·la·tion
um·bel
um·ber
um·bil·i·cal
um·bra
um·brage
um·bra·geous
um·bra·geous·ly
um·bra·geous·ness
um·brel·la
u·mi·ak
um·laut
um·pire
um·pired
um·pir·ing
un·a·bashed
un·a·ble
un·a·bridged
un·ac·cep·ta·ble

un·ac·com·pa·nied
un·ac·count·ed
un·ac·count·a·ble
un·ac·count·a·bly
un·ac·cus·tomed
un·ac·quaint·ed
un·a·dorned
un·a·dul·ter·at·ed
un·ad·vised
un·ad·vis·ed·ly
un·ad·vis·ed·ness
un·af·fect·ed
un·af·fect·ed·ly
un·af·fect·ed·ness
un·a·fraid
un·aligned
un-A·mer·i·can
unan·i·mous
una·nim·i·ty
unan·i·mous·ly
unan·i·mous·ness
un·an·swer·a·ble
un·an·swered
un·ap·peal·a·ble
un·ap·peal·ing
un·ap·pe·tiz·ing
un·ap·pre·ci·at·ed
un·ap·pre·ci·a·tive
un·ap·pro·pri·at·ed
un·ap·proach·a·ble
un·ap·proach·a·ble·ness
un·armed
un·a·shamed
un·asked
un·a·spir·ing
un·as·sail·a·ble
un·as·sailed
un·as·sum·ing
un·at·tached
un·at·tain·a·ble
un·at·tained
un·at·tended
un·au·thor·ized
un·a·vail·a·ble
un·a·vail·a·bil·i·ty
un·a·vail·a·bly
un·a·void·a·ble
un·a·void·a·bil·i·ty
un·a·void·a·bly
un·a·ware
un·a·ware·ness
un·a·wares
un·backed
un·bal·anced
un·bar
un·barred
un·bar·ring
un·bear·a·ble
un·bear·a·ble·ness
un·bear·a·bly
un·beat·en
un·beat·a·ble
un·be·com·ing
un·be·com·ing·ness
un·be·known
un·be·lief
un·be·liev·a·ble
un·be·liev·a·bly
un·be·liev·er
un·be·liev·ing
un·bend
un·bend·ed
un·bend·ing
un·bend·ing·ness
un·be·seem·ing
un·bi·ased
un·bid·den
un·bind

un·blem·ished
un·blush·ing
un·blot
un·born
un·bos·om
un·bound
un·bound·ed
un·bound·ed·ness
un·bowed
un·bred
un·break·a·ble
un·bri·dled
un·bro·ken
un·buck·le
un·bur·den
un·but·ton
un·called-for
un·can·ny
un·can·ni·ly
un·can·ni·ness
un·cap
un·capped
un·cap·ping
un·ceas·ing
un·ceas·ing·ly
un·ceas·ing·ness
un·cere·mo·ni·ous
un·cere·mo·ni·ous·ly
un·cere·mo·ni·ous·ness
un·certain
un·certain·ly
un·certain·ness
un·certain·ty
un·chal·lenged
un·change·a·ble
un·changed
un·chang·ing
un·char·i·ta·ble
un·char·i·ta·ble·ness
un·char·i·ta·bly
un·chart·ed
un·chris·tian
un·cir·cum·cised
un·civ·il
un·civ·il·ly
un·civ·i·lized
un·clad
un·class·i·fi·a·ble
un·clas·si·fied
un·cle
un·clear
un·clean·ly
un·clean·li·ness
un·clothe
un·clothed
un·clut·tered
un·com·fort·a·ble
un·com·fort·a·ble·ness
un·com·fort·a·bly
un·com·mit·ted
un·com·mon
un·com·mon·ly
un·com·mon·ness
un·com·mu·ni·ca·tive
un·com·mu·ni·ca·tive·ness
un·com·pre·hend·ing
un·com·pro·mis·ing
un·com·pro·mised
un·com·pro·mis·ing·ly
un·com·pro·mis·ing·ness
un·con·cerned
un·con·cern·ed·ly
un·con·cern·ed·ness
un·con·di·tion·al
un·con·di·tion·al·ly
un·con·firmed
un·con·for·mi·ty
un·con·nect·ed

un·con·nect·ed·ness
un·con·quer·a·ble
un·con·quered
un·con·scion·a·ble
un·con·scion·a·ble·ness
un·con·scion·a·bly
un·con·scious
un·con·scious·ly
un·con·scious·ness
un·con·sti·tu·tion·al
un·con·sti·tu·tion·al·i·ty
un·con·sti·tu·tion·al·ly
un·con·strained
un·con·test·ed
un·con·trol·la·ble
un·con·trolled
un·con·ven·tion·al
un·con·ven·tion·al·i·ty
un·con·ven·tion·al·ly
un·count·ed
un·cou·ple
un·cour·te·ous
un·couth
un·couth·ly
un·couth·ness
un·cov·er
un·cov·ered
un·crit·i·cal
unc·tion
unc·tu·ous
un·daunt·ed
un·daunt·ed·ly
un·daunt·ed·ness
un·de·ceived
un·de·ceiv·ing
un·de·cid·ed
un·de·cid·ed·ness
un·de·fined
un·de·fin·a·ble
un·de·mon·stra·tive
un·de·mon·stra·tive·ly
un·de·mon·stra·tive·ness
un·de·nied
un·de·ni·a·ble
un·de·ni·a·ble·ness
un·de·ni·a·bly
un·de·pend·a·ble
un·de·pend·a·bil·i·ty
un·de·pend·a·ble·ness
un·der·a·chiev·er
un·der·a·chiev·ment
un·der·act
un·der·age
un·der·armed
un·der·bid
un·der·brush
un·der·car·riage
un·der·charge
un·der·class·man
un·der·clothes
un·der·coat·ing
un·der·cov·er
un·der·cur·rent
un·der·cut
un·der·cut·ting
un·der·de·vel·oped
un·der·de·vel·op·ing
un·der·dog
un·der·es·ti·mate
un·der·es·ti·mat·ed
un·der·es·ti·ma·tion
un·der·ex·pose
un·der·go
un·der·went
un·der·gone
un·der·go·ing
un·der·grad·u·ate
un·der·ground

un·der·growth
un·der·hand·
un·der·hand·ed
un·der·hand·ed·ness
un·der·lie
un·der·lay
un·der·lain
un·der·ly·ing
un·der·line
un·der·lined
un·der·lin·ing
un·der·ling
un·der·mine
un·der·mined
un·der·min·ing
un·der·most
un·der·neath
un·der·nour·ished
un·der·paid
un·der·pass
un·der·pin·ning
un·der·play
un·der·priv·i·leged
un·der·rate
un·der·rat·ed
un·der·score
un·der·scored
un·der·scor·ing
un·der·sea
un·der·sec·re·tary
un·der·sec·re·tar·ies
un·der·sell
un·der·sold
un·der·shirt
un·der·shoot
un·der·side
un·der·signed
un·der·sized
un·der·slung
un·der·stand
un·der·stood
un·der·stand·ing
un·der·stand·a·bil·i·ty
un·der·stand·a·ble
un·der·stand·a·bly
un·der·state
un·der·stat·ed
un·der·stat·ing
un·der·state·ment
un·der·study
un·der·stud·ied
un·der·stud·y·ing
un·der·take
un·der·took
un·der·tak·en
un·der·tak·ing
un·der·tak·er
un·der-the-coun·ter
un·der·tone
un·der·tow
un·der·val·ue
un·der·wa·ter
un·der·wear
un·der·weight
un·der·world
un·der·write
un·der·wrote
un·der·writ·ten
un·der·writ·ing
un·der·writ·er
un·de·sign·ing
un·de·sir·a·ble
un·de·sir·a·bil·i·ty
un·de·sir·a·ble·ness
un·de·sir·a·bly
un·de·ter·minded
un·de·vel·oped
un·di·gest·i·ble

un·dip·lo·mat·ic
un·dip·lo·mat·i·cal·ly
un·di·rect·ed
un·dis·ci·plined
un·dis·closed
un·dis·posed
un·dis·tin·guished
un·di·vid·ed
un·do
  un·did
  un·done
  un·do·ing
un·doubt·ed
  un·doubt·ed·ly
  un·doubt·ing
un·dress
  un·dressed
  un·dress·ing
un·due
un·du·lant
un·du·late
  un·du·lat·ed
  un·du·lat·ing
  un·du·la·tion
  un·du·la·tory
un·du·ly
un·dy·ing
un·earned
un·earth
un·earth·ly
  un·earth·li·ness
un·easy
  un·ease
  un·eas·i·ly
  un·eas·i·ness
un·ed·u·cat·ed
un·em·ployed
  un·em·ploy·ment
  un·em·ploy·a·ble
un·end·ing
un·e·qual
  un·e·qual·ly
  un·e·qualed
un·e·quiv·o·cal
  un·e·quiv·o·cal·ly
un·err·ing
  un·err·ing·ly
un·es·sen·tial
un·eth·i·cal
  un·eth·i·cal·ly
un·e·ven
  un·e·ven·ly
  un·e·ven·ness
un·event·ful
un·ex·am·pled
un·ex·cep·tion·al
  un·ex·cep·tion·a·ble
un·ex·pect·ed
  un·ex·pect·ed·ly
  un·ex·pect·ed·ness
un·ex·pres·sive
un·fail·ing
  un·fail·ing·ly
un·fair·ness
un·faith·ful
  un·faith·ful·ly
  un·faith·ful·ness
un·fa·mil·iar
  un·fa·mil·i·ar·i·ty
un·fast·en
un·fath·om·a·ble
un·fa·vor·a·ble
  un·fa·vor·a·ble·ness
  un·fa·vor·a·bly
un·feel·ing
  un·feel·ing·ly
  un·feel·ing·ness
un·feigned

un·fet·ter
  un·fet·tered
un·fin·ished
un·fit
  un·fit·ness
  un·fit·ting
un·flat·ter·ing
un·flinch·ing
un·fold
un·for·get·ta·ble
  un·for·get·ta·bly
un·for·giv·a·ble
un·formed
un·for·tu·nate
  un·for·tu·nate·ly
  un·for·tu·nate·ness
un·found·ed
un·fre·quent·ed
un·friend·ly
  un·friend·li·ness
un·fruit·ful
un·gain·ly
  un·gain·li·ness
un·gen·er·ous
un·god·ly
  un·god·li·ness
un·gov·ern·a·ble
un·grace·ful
un·gra·cious
  un·gra·cious·ly
  un·gra·cious·ness
un·gram·mat·i·cal
un·grate·ful
  un·grate·ful·ly
  un·grate·ful·ness
un·grudg·ing
un·guard·ed
un·guent
un·ham·pered
un·handy
un·hap·py
  un·hap·pi·ly
  un·hap·pi·ness
un·harmed
un·healthy
  un·health·i·ness
un·heard
un·heed·ed
un·heed·ful
un·heed·ing
un·hinge
un·ho·ly
  un·ho·li·ly
  un·ho·li·ness
un·hook
un·hur·ried
uni·cel·lu·lar
uni·corn
uni·cy·cle
uni·form
  uni·formed
  uni·form·i·ty
  uni·form·ly
  uni·form·ness
uni·fy
  uni·fied
  uni·fy·ing
  uni·fi·ca·tion
uni·lat·er·al
  uni·lat·er·al·ly
un·im·ag·i·na·ble
un·im·paired
un·im·peach·a·ble
  un·im·peach·a·bly
un·im·por·tance
  un·im·por·tant
un·im·proved
un·in·hib·it·ed

un·in·tel·li·gent
  un·in·tel·li·gi·ble
un·in·ten·tion·al
un·in·ter·est·ed
  un·in·ter·est·ing
un·in·ter·rupt·ed
un·ion
un·ion·ism
  un·ion·ist
un·ion·ize
  un·ion·ized
  un·ion·iz·ing
  un·ion·i·za·tion
unique
  unique·ly
  unique·ness
uni·sex
uni·son
unit
Uni·tar·i·an
unite
  unit·ed
  unit·ing
Unit·ed Ar·ab Emir·ates
Unit·ed King·dom
Unit·ed Na·tions
Unit·ed States
uni·ty
uni·valve
uni·ver·sal
  uni·ver·sal·i·ty
  uni·ver·sal·ly
  uni·ver·sal·ness
uni·verse
uni·ver·si·ty
  uni·ver·si·ties
un·just
  un·just·ly
  un·just·ness
un·kempt
un·kind
  un·kind·ly
  un·kind·ness
  un·kind·li·ness
un·know·ing
un·known
un·law·ful
  un·law·ful·ly
  un·law·ful·ness
un·learn
  un·learned
  un·learn·ed
un·leash
un·less
un·let·tered
un·like
  un·like·ness
un·like·ly
  un·like·li·hood
  un·like·li·ness
un·lim·ber
un·lim·it·ed
un·list·ed
un·load
un·lock
un·looked-for
un·loose
  un·loos·en
un·lucky
  un·luck·i·est
  un·luck·i·ly
  un·luck·i·ness
un·make
  un·made
  un·mak·ing
  un·mak·er
un·man·ly
un·manned

un·man·ner·ly
un·mask
un·mean·ing
  un·mean·ing·ly
un·men·tion·a·ble
un·mer·ci·ful
  un·mer·ci·ful·ly
un·mind·ful
un·mis·tak·a·ble
  un·mis·tak·a·bly
un·mit·i·gat·ed
un·nat·u·ral
  un·nat·u·ral·ly
  un·nat·u·ral·ness
un·nec·es·sary
  un·nec·es·sar·i·ly
un·nerve
  un·nerved
  un·nerv·ing
un·num·bered
un·ob·jec·tion·a·ble
un·ob·tru·sive
un·oc·cu·pied
un·or·gan·ized
un·or·tho·dox
un·pack
un·par·al·leled
un·par·don·a·ble
un·pleas·ant
  un·pleas·ant·ly
  un·pleas·ant·ness
un·plumbed
un·pop·u·lar
  un·pop·u·lar·i·ty
un·prec·e·dent·ed
un·pre·dict·a·ble
un·prej·u·diced
un·pre·ten·tious
un·prin·ci·pled
un·print·a·ble
un·pro·fes·sion·al
un·prof·it·a·ble
un·prom·is·ing
un·qual·i·fied
  un·qual·i·fied·ly
un·ques·tion·a·ble
  un·ques·tion·a·bly
un·ques·tioned
un·rav·el
  un·rav·eled
  un·rav·el·ing
un·ready
  un·read·i·ness
un·re·al
un·re·al·is·tic
un·re·al·i·ty
un·rea·son·a·ble
  un·rea·son·a·ble·ness
  un·rea·son·a·bly
un·rea·son·ing
un·re·con·struct·ed
un·re·fined
un·re·gen·er·ate
un·re·lat·ed
un·re·lent·ing
un·re·mit·ting
un·re·serve
  un·re·serv·ed·ly
un·rest
un·re·strained
un·ri·valed
un·ruf·fled
un·ru·ly
  un·ru·li·ness
un·sad·dle
un·said
un·sat·u·rat·ed
un·sa·vory

un·scathed
un·schooled
un·sci·en·tif·ic
un·scram·ble
un·screw
un·scru·pu·lous
  un·scru·pu·lous·ness
un·seal
un·sea·son·a·ble
  un·sea·son·a·bly
un·seat
un·seem·ly
  un·seem·li·ness
un·seg·re·gat·ed
un·self·ish
un·set·tle
  un·set·tled
  un·set·tling
un·sheathe
un·shod
un·sight·ly
  un·sight·li·ness
un·skilled
un·skill·ful
un·snap
  un·snapped
  un·snap·ping
un·snarl
un·so·phis·ti·cat·ed
  un·so·phis·ti·ca·tion
un·sought
un·sound
  un·sound·ness
un·spar·ing
un·speak·a·ble
un·spot·ted
un·sta·ble
  un·sta·ble·ness
un·steady
  un·stead·i·ly
un·stop
  un·stopped
  un·stop·ping
un·stressed
un·strung
un·stud·ied
un·suc·cess·ful
un·suit·a·ble
un·sung
un·tan·gle
un·taught
un·think·a·ble
un·think·ing
un·ti·dy
  un·ti·di·ness
un·tie
  un·tied
  un·ty·ing
un·til
un·time·ly
  un·time·li·ness
un·to
un·told
un·touch·a·ble
un·to·ward
un·truth·ful
un·tu·tored
un·used
un·u·su·al
  un·u·su·al·ness
un·ut·ter·a·ble
un·var·nished
un·veil
un·war·rant·ed
un·wary
  un·war·i·ness
un·well
un·whole·some

un·wieldy
un·wield·i·ness
un·will·ing
un·will·ing·ness
un·wind
un·wound
un·wind·ing
un·wise
un·wit·ting
un·wit·ting·ly
un·wont·ed
un·world·li·ness
un·wor·thy
un·wor·thi·ly
un·wor·thi·ness
un·wrap
un·wrapped
un·wrap·ping
un·writ·ten
un·yield·ing
up-and-com·ing
up-and-down
up·beat
up·braid
up·bring·ing
up·com·ing
up·coun·try
up·date
up·dat·ed
up·dat·ing
up·grade
up·grad·ed
up·grad·ing
up·heav·al
up·heave
up·hold
up·held
up·hold·ing
up·hol·ster
up·hol·stery
up·keep
up·land
up·most
up·on
up·per·class
up·per·cut
up·per·most
up·pish·ness
up·pi·ty
up·raise
up·raised
up·rais·ing
up·rear
up·right
up·right·ness
up·ris·ing
up·roar
up·roar·i·ous
up·root
up·set·ting
up·shot
up·stage
up·staged
up·stag·ing
up·stairs
up·stand·ing
up·start
up·state
up·stream
up·swing
up·take
up-to-date
up·town
up·trend
up·turn
up·ward
ura·ni·um
Ura·nus

ur·ban
ur·bane
ur·bane·ness
ur·ban·i·ty
ur·ban·ize
ur·ban·ized
ur·ban·iz·ing
ur·ban·i·za·tion
ur·chin
ure·mia
ure·ter
ure·thra
urge
urged
urg·ing
ur·gent
ur·gen·cy
ur·gent·ly
uri·nal
uri·nal·y·sis
uri·nary
uri·nate
uri·na·tion
urine
urol·o·gy
uro·log·ic
Uru·guay
us·a·ble
us·a·ble·ness
us·a·bil·i·ty
us·age
use
used
us·ing
use·ful
use·ful·ly
use·ful·ness
use·less·ness
ush·er
usu·al
usu·al·ly
usurp
usur·pa·tion
usurp·er
usu·ry
usu·ri·ous
uten·sil
uter·us
util·i·tar·ian
util·i·ty
util·i·ties
uti·lize
uti·lized
uti·liz·ing
uti·li·za·tion
ut·most
Uto·pia
Uto·pi·an
ut·ter
ut·ter·a·ble
ut·ter·ance
ut·ter·most
uvu·la
ux·o·ri·ous

V

va·can·cy
va·can·cies
va·cant
va·cate
va·cat·ed
va·cat·ing
va·ca·tion
vac·ci·nate
vac·ci·nat·ed
vac·ci·nat·ing

vac·ci·na·tion
vac·cine
vac·il·late
vac·il·lat·ed
vac·il·lat·ing
vac·il·la·tion
vac·il·la·tor
va·cu·i·ty
vac·u·ous
vac·u·ous·ness
vac·u·um
vag·a·bond
vag·a·bond·age
va·gary
va·gar·i·ous
va·gi·na
vag·i·nal
va·grant
va·gran·cy
vague
vague·ness
vain
vain·ly
vain·ness
vain·glo·ry
vain·glo·ri·ous
vain·glo·ri·ous·ness
val·ance
val·anced
val·e·dic·tion
val·e·dic·to·ri·an
val·e·dic·to·ry
va·lence
va·len·cy
val·en·tine
val·et
val·iant
val·iant·ly
val·iant·ness
val·id
val·id·ly
val·id·ness
val·i·date
val·i·dat·ed
val·i·dat·ing
val·i·da·tion
va·lid·i·ty
va·lise
val·ley
val·leys
val·or
val·or·ous
val·or·ous·ly
val·or·ous·ness
val·or·ize
val·or·i·za·tion
val·u·a·ble
val·u·a·ble·ness
val·u·a·bly
val·u·a·tion
val·u·a·tion·al
val·ue
val·ued
val·u·ing
val·ue·less
valve
valve·less
val·vu·lar
va·moose
vam·pire
vam·pir·ic
van·dal
van·dal·ism
van·dal·ize
van·dal·ized
van·dal·iz·ing
vane
vaned

vane·less
van·guard
va·nil·la
van·ish
van·i·ty
van·i·ties
van·quish
van·quish·a·ble
van·quish·er
van·tage
vap·id
va·pid·i·ty
vap·id·ness
vap·id·ly
va·por
va·por·er
va·por·ish
va·por·ish·ness
va·por·es·cence
va·por·ize
va·por·ized
va·por·iz·ing
va·por·i·za·tion
va·por·iz·er
va·por·ous
va·por·ous·ly
va·que·ro
var·i·a·ble
var·i·a·bil·i·ty
var·i·a·ble·ness
var·i·a·bly
var·i·ance
var·i·ant
var·i·a·tion
var·i·a·tion·al
var·i·a·tion·al·ly
var·i·col·ored
var·i·cose
var·i·cos·i·ty
var·ied
var·ied·ness
var·i·e·gate
var·i·e·gat·ed
var·i·e·gat·ing
var·i·e·ga·tion
va·ri·e·tal
va·ri·e·tal·ly
va·ri·e·ty
va·ri·e·ties
var·i·o·rum
var·i·ous
var·i·ous·ly
var·i·ous·ness
var·mint
var·nish
var·si·ty
var·si·ties
vary
var·ied
var·y·ing
var·y·ing·ly
vas·cu·lar
vas·cu·lar·i·ty
vas·ec·to·my
Vas·e·line
vas·o·mo·tor
vas·sal
vas·sal·age
vast·ness
vas·ti·tude
vat
vat·ted
vat·ting
Vat·i·can
vaude·ville
vaude·vil·lian
vault
vault·ed

vault·er
vault·ing
vaunt
vaunt·er
vaunt·ing·ly
vec·tor
vec·to·ri·al
veer·ing
veg·e·ta·ble
veg·e·tal
veg·e·tar·i·an
veg·e·tar·i·an·ism
veg·e·tate
veg·e·tat·ed
veg·e·tat·ing
veg·e·ta·tion
veg·e·ta·tion·al
veg·e·ta·tion·less
veg·e·ta·tive
ve·he·ment
ve·he·mence
ve·he·men·cy
ve·hi·cle
ve·hic·u·lar
veil
veiled
veil·ing
vein
veiny
vein·ing
vel·lum
ve·loc·i·ty
ve·loc·i·ties
vel·our
ve·lum
vel·vet
vel·vet·ed
vel·vety
vel·vet·een
ve·nal
ve·nal·i·ty
ve·nal·ly
ve·na·tion
ve·na·tion·al
vend·er
vend·or
ven·det·ta
vend·i·ble
vend·i·bil·i·ty
ve·neer
ve·neer·ing
ven·er·a·ble
ven·er·a·bil·i·ty
ven·er·a·ble·ness
ven·er·a·bly
ven·er·ate
ven·er·a·tion
ven·er·a·tor
ve·ne·re·al
venge·ance
venge·ful
venge·ful·ness
ve·ni·al
ve·ni·al·i·ty
ve·ni·al·ness
ve·ni·al·ly
ven·i·son
ven·om
ven·om·ous
ven·om·ous·ness
ve·nous
ve·nous·ly
ve·nous·ness
vent
vent·ed
vent·ing
ven·ti·late
ven·ti·lat·ed

ven·ti·lat·ing
ven·ti·la·tion
ven·ti·la·tor
ven·tral
ven·tri·cle
ven·tril·o·quism
ven·tri·lo·qui·al
ven·tril·o·quist
ven·tril·o·quize
ven·tril·o·quized
ven·tril·o·quiz·ing
ven·ture
ven·ture·some
ven·tur·ous
ven·tur·ous·ness
ven·ue
ve·ra·cious
ve·ra·cious·ness
ve·rac·i·ty
ve·rac·i·ties
ve·ran·da
ver·bal
ver·bal·ly
ver·bal·ize
ver·bal·ized
ver·bal·iz·ing
ver·bal·i·za·tion
ver·ba·tim
ver·be·na
ver·bi·age
ver·bose
ver·bose·ness
ver·bos·i·ty
ver·bo·ten
ver·dant
ver·dan·cy
ver·dict
ver·di·gris
ver·dure
ver·dured
ver·dur·ous
verge
verged
verg·ing
verify
ver·i·fied
ver·i·fy·ing
ver·i·fi·a·bil·i·ty
ver·i·fi·a·ble·ness
ver·i·fi·a·ble
ver·i·fi·ca·tion
ver·i·fi·er
ver·i·si·mil·i·tude
ver·i·ta·ble
ver·i·ta·ble·ness
ver·i·ta·bly
ver·i·ty
ver·i·ties
ver·meil
ver·mi·cel·li
ver·mic·u·lar
ver·mic·u·late
ver·mi·fuge
ver·mil·ion
ver·min
ver·min·ous
ver·mouth
ver·nac·u·lar
ver·nac·u·lar·ism
ver·nal
ver·nal·ly
ver·ni·er
Ver·sailles
ver·sa·tile
ver·sa·tile·ness
ver·sa·til·i·ty
versed
ver·si·fy

ver·si·fi·ca·tion
version
ver·sion·al
ver·sus
ver·te·bra
ver·te·brae
ver·te·bral
ver·te·brate
ver·tex
ver·tex·es
ver·ti·cal
ver·ti·cal·i·ty
ver·ti·cal·ness
ver·ti·cal·ly
ver·ti·go
ver·tig·i·nous
verve
ves·i·cant
vas·pers
ves·sel
ves·tal
vest·ed
ves·ti·bule
ves·tige
ves·tig·i·al
ves·tig·i·al·ly
vest·ment
vest-pock·et
ves·try
ves·tries
vet·er·an
vet·er·i·nar·i·an
vet·er·i·nary
ve·to
ve·toed
ve·to·ing
ve·to·er
vex
vexed
vex·ing
vex·a·tion
vex·a·tious
vi·a·ble
vi·a·bil·i·ty
vi·a·bly
vi·a·duct
vi·al
vi·and
vi·brant
vi·bran·cy
vi·brate
vi·brat·ed
vi·brat·ing
vi·bra·tion
vi·bra·to
vi·bra·tor
vi·bra·to·ry
vi·bur·num
vic·ar
vic·ar·age
vi·car·i·ous
vi·car·i·ous·ly
vi·car·i·ous·ness
vice-ad·mi·ral
vice-chan·cel·lor
vice-con·sul
vice-con·su·lar
vice-con·su·late
vice-con·sul·ship
vice-pres·i·dent
vice-pres·i·den·cy
vice-pres·i·den·cies
vice-pres·i·den·tial
vice·roy
vice ver·sa
vi·chys·soise
vi·cin·i·ty
vi·cin·i·ties

vi·cious
vi·cious·ly
vi·cious·ness
vi·cis·si·tude
vic·tim
vic·tim·ize
vic·tim·ized
vic·tim·iz·ing
vic·tim·i·za·tion
vic·tor
Vic·to·ri·an
vic·to·ri·ous
vic·to·ri·ous·ly
vic·to·ri·ous·ness
vic·to·ry
vic·to·ries
vict·ual
vi·cu·na
vid·eo
vid·e·o·tape
vid·e·o·taped
vid·e·o·tap·ing
vie
vied
vy·ing
vi·er
Vi·et·nam·ese
view·er
view·point
vig·il
vig·i·lance
vig·i·lant
vig·i·lan·te
vig·i·lan·tism
vi·gnette
vig·or
vig·or·ous
vig·or·ous·ly
Vi·king
vile
vil·er
vil·est
vile·ly
vil·i·fy
vil·i·fied
vil·i·fy·ing
vil·i·fi·ca·tion
vil·la
vil·lage
vil·lain
vil·lain·ous
vil·lain·ous·ly
vil·lain·ous·ness
vil·lainy
vil·lain·ies
vil·lein
vil·lous
vin·ai·grette
vin·ci·ble
vin·ci·bil·i·ty
vin·di·cate
vin·di·cat·ed
vin·di·cat·ing
vin·di·ca·tion
vin·di·ca·tor
vin·dic·tive
vin·dic·tive·ly
vin·dic·tive·ness
vin·e·gar
vin·e·gary
vine·yard
vi·ni·cul·ture
vi·nous
vin·tage
vint·ner
vi·nyl
vi·ol
vi·o·la

vi·o·list
vi·o·la·ble
vi·o·la·bil·i·ty
vi·o·late
vi·o·lat·ed
vi·o·lat·ing
vi·o·la·tor
vi·o·la·tion
vi·o·lence
vi·o·lent
vi·o·let
vi·o·lin
vi·o·lin·ist
vi·o·list
vi·o·lon·cel·lo
vi·o·lon·cel·list
vi·per
vi·ra·go
vi·ral
vi·reo
vir·gin
vir·gin·al
vir·gin·al·ly
vir·gin·i·ty
vir·gule
vir·ile
vi·ril·i·ty
vi·rol·o·gy
vi·rol·o·gist
vir·tu·al
vir·tu·al·ly
vir·tue
vir·tu·os·i·ty
vir·tu·o·so
vir·tu·ous
vir·tu·ous·ly
vir·tu·ous·ness
vir·u·lent
vir·u·lence
vir·u·len·cy
vi·rus
vi·rus·es
vi·sa
vis·age
vis-a-vis
vis·cera
vis·cer·al
vis·cid
vis·cid·i·ty
vis·cid·ly
vis·cid·ness
vis·cos·i·ty
vis·cos·i·ties
vis·count
vis·count·ess
vis·cous
vis·i·bil·i·ty
vis·i·ble
vi·sion
vi·sion·ary
vis·it
vis·i·tant
vis·i·ta·tion
vis·it·ing
vis·i·tor
vi·sor
vis·ta
vis·u·al
vis·u·al·ly
vis·u·al·ize
vis·u·al·ized
vis·u·al·iz·ing
vis·u·al·i·za·tion
vi·tal
vi·tal·ly
vi·tal·i·ty
vi·tal·ize
vi·tal·ized

vi·tal·iz·ing
vi·tal·i·za·tion
vi·tals
vi·ta·min
vi·ti·ate
vi·ti·at·ed
vi·ti·at·ing
vi·ti·a·tion
vit·re·ous
vit·re·os·i·ty
vit·ri·fy
vit·ri·fied
vit·ri·fy·ing
vit·ri·fi·a·ble
vit·ri·fi·ca·tion
vit·ri·ol
vit·ri·ol·ic
vit·tles
vi·tu·per·ate
vi·tu·per·at·ed
vi·tu·per·at·ing
vi·tu·per·a·tion
vi·va
vi·va·cious
vi·vac·i·ty
vi·var·i·um
vi·va vo·ce
viv·id
viv·i·fy
viv·i·fied
viv·i·fy·ing
viv·i·fi·ca·tion
vi·vip·a·rous
vivi·sect
vivi·sec·tion
vix·en
vi·zier
vi·zor
vo·cab·u·lary
vo·cab·u·lar·ies
vo·cal
vo·cal·ic
vo·cal·ist
vo·cal·ize
vo·cal·ized
vo·cal·iz·ing
vo·cal·i·za·tion
vo·ca·tion
vo·ca·tion·al
vo·cif·er·ate
vo·cif·er·ous
vod·ka
vogue
vogu·ish
voice
voiced
voic·ing
voice·print
void·a·ble
voile
vol·a·tile
vol·a·til·i·ty
vol·can·ic
vol·can·i·cal·ly
vol·ca·no
vol·ca·noes
vol·ca·nos
vo·li·tion
vol·ley
vol·leys
vol·leyed
vol·ley·ing
vol·ley·ball
volt·age
vol·ta·ic
vol·u·ble
vol·u·bly
vol·u·bil·i·ty

vol·ume
vo·lu·mi·nous
  vo·lu·mi·nous·ly
  vo·lu·mi·nous·ness
vol·un·tary
  vol·un·tar·i·ly
vol·un·teer
vo·lup·tu·ary
vo·lup·tu·ous
vo·lute
vom·it
voo·doo
  voo·doo·ism
  voo·doo·ist
  voo·doo·is·tic
vo·ra·cious
  vo·rac·i·ty
vor·tex
  vor·tex·es
  vor·ti·ces
vo·ta·ry
  vo·ta·ries
vote
  vot·ed
  vot·ing
  vot·er
vo·tive
vouch·er
vouch·safe
  vouch·safed
  vouch·saf·ing
vow·el
vox po·pu·li
voy·age
  voy·aged
  voy·ag·ing
  voy·ag·er
vo·yeur
  vo·yeur·ism
  voy·eur·is·tic
vul·can·ize
  vul·can·ized
  vul·can·iz·ing
  vul·can·i·za·tion
vul·gar
  vul·gar·ism
  vul·gar·i·ty
vul·gar·ize
  vul·gar·ized
  vul·gar·iz·ing
  vul·gar·i·za·tion
Vul·gate
vul·ner·a·ble
  vul·ner·a·bil·i·ty
  vul·ner·a·bly
vul·ture
vul·tur·ous
vul·va

W

wab·ble
  wab·bled
  wab·bling
wacky
  wack·i·er
  wack·i·est
  wack·i·ly
  wack·i·ness
wad
  wad·ded
  wad·ding
wad·dle
  wad·dled
  wad·dling
  wad·dler
  wad·dly

wade
  wad·ed
  wad·ing
wa·fer
waf·fle
waft
wag
  wagged
  wag·ging
wage
  waged
  wag·ing
wa·ger
wag·gery
wag·gish
wag·gle
  wag·gled
  wag·gling
wag·on
wa·hi·ne
Wai·ki·ki
wain·scot
  wain·scot·ing
wain·wright
waist·band
waist·coat
waist·line
wait·er
  wait·ress
  wait·ing
waive
  waived
  waiv·ing
  waiv·er
wake
  waked
  wok·en
  wak·ing
wake·ful
  wake·ful·ly
  wake·ful·ness
wak·en
wale
  waled
  wal·ing
walk·a·way
walk·er
walk·ie-talk·ie
walk·out
walk·o·ver
walk-up
walk·way
wal·la·by
  wal·la·bies
wall·board
wal·let
wall·flow·er
wal·lop
wall·pa·per
wall-to-wall
wal·nut
wal·rus
waltz
wam·pum
wan
  wan·ner
  wan·ness
wan·der
wan·der·lust
wane
  waned
  wan·ing
wan·gle
  wan·gled
  wan·gling
want·ing
wan·ton
war

warred
war·ring
war·ble
  war·bled
  war·bling
war·bler
war·den
ward·er
ward·robe
ware·house
war·fare
war·head
warm
  warm·er
  warm·est
warm-blood·ed
warm-heart·ed
war·mong·er
warmth
warn·ing
war·path
war·rant
war·ran·ty
war·ren
war·ri·or
war·ship
war·time
wary
  war·i·er
  war·i·est
  war·i·ly
  war·i·ness
wash·a·ble
wash·ba·sin
wash·bowl
wash·cloth
wash·er
wash·ing
Wash·ing·ton
wash·out
wash·room
wash·tub
wasp·ish
  wasp·ish·ness
was·sail
wast·age
waste
  wast·ed
  wast·ing
  waste·ful
waste·bas·ket
waste·land
waste·pa·per
wast·rel
watch·dog
watch·ful
watch·man
watch·tow·er
watch·word
wa·ter·borne
wa·ter·col·or
wa·ter·course
wa·ter·cress
wa·ter·fall
wa·ter·fowl
wa·ter·front
wa·ter·less
wa·ter lev·el
wa·ter lily
wa·ter line
wa·ter·logged
wa·ter main
wa·ter·mark
wa·ter·mel·on
wa·ter moc·ca·sin
wa·ter·pow·er
wa·ter·proof
wa·ter-re·pel·lent

wa·ter·side
wa·ter-ski
  wa·ter-skied
  wa·ter-ski·ing
wa·ter·spout
wa·ter·tight
wa·ter·works
wa·tery
  wa·ter·i·ness
watt·age
watt-hour
wat·tle
  wat·tled
  wat·tling
wave
  waved
  wav·ing
wave·length
wave·let
wa·ver
wav·y
  wav·i·ly
  wav·i·ness
wax
  waxed
  wax·ing
wax·en
wax·wing
wax·work
waxy
  wax·i·er
  wax·i·ness
way·far·er
  way·far·ing
way·lay
  way·laid
  way·lay·ing
way·side
way·ward
weak·en
weak-kneed
weak·ling
weak·ly
  weak·li·er
  weak·li·ness
weak-mind·ed
weak·ness
wealthy
  wealth·i·er
  wealth·i·est
  wealth·i·ness
wean
weap·on
weap·on·ry
wear
  wore
  worn
  wear·ing
wea·ri·some
wea·ry
  wea·ried
  wea·ry·ing
  wea·ri·ly
  wea·ri·ness
wea·sel
weath·er
weath·er·a·bil·i·ty
weath·er-beat·en
weath·er·cock
weath·er·glass
weath·er·ing
weath·er·man
weath·er·proof
weath·er·vane
weave
  wove
  weaved
  wov·en

weav·ing
web
webbed
web·bing
web-foot·ed
wed·ding
wedge
wedged
wedg·ing
wed·lock
weedy
weed·i·er
weed·i·ness
week·day
week·end
week·ly
weep
wept
weep·ing
wee·vil
weigh
weight
weighty
  weight·i·er
  weight·i·est
  weight·i·ness
weird
weird·er
weird·est
wel·come
  wel·comed
  wel·com·ing
wel·fare
well-ad·vised
well-be·ing
well·born
well-bred
well-dis·posed
well-done
well-found·ed
well-groomed
well-ground·ed
well-known
well-mean·ing
well-off
well-read
well-spo·ken
well·spring
well-timed
well-to-do
well-wish·er
well-worn
wel·ter
wel·ter·weight
were·wolf
west·er·ly
west·ern
West·ern·er
west·ern·ize
  west·ern·ized
  west·ern·iz·ing
  west·ern·i·za·tion
west·ern·most
west·ward
wet
wet·ter
wet·test
wet·ting
wet·back
whale
whaled
whal·ing
whale·boat
whale·bone
whal·er
wharf
wharves
wharf·age

what·ev·er
what·not
what·so·ev·er
wheal
wheat
whee·dle
　whee·dled
　whee·dling
wheel·bar·row
wheel·chair
wheeled
wheel·house
wheeze
　wheezed
　wheez·ing
wheezy
　wheez·i·ness
whelm
whelp
whence·so·ev·er
when·ev·er
where·a·bouts
where·as
where·by
where·fore
where·in
where·on
where·so·ev·er
where·to
where·up·on
wher·ev·er
where·with
where·with·al
wher·ry
whet
　whet·ted
　whet·ting
wheth·er
whet·stone
which·ev·er
while
whim·per
whim·sy
　whim·si·cal
whine
　whin·ed
　whin·ing
whin·ny
　whin·nied
　whin·ny·ing
whip
　whipped
　whip·ping
whip·lash
whip·per·snap·per
whip·pet
whip·poor·will
whir
　whirred
　whir·ring
whirl·i·gig
whirl·pool
whirl·wind
whisk·er
whis·key
　whis·ky
whis·per
whist
whis·tle
　whis·tled
　whis·tling
whis·tler
white
　whit·er
　whit·ish
white·col·lar
white·faced
whit·en

white·wash
whith·er
whit·tle
　whit·tled
　whit·tling
whiz
　whizzed
　whiz·zing
　whiz·zes
whoa
who·ev·er
whole·heart·ed
whole·sale
　whole·sal·ing
　whole·sal·er
whole·some
whol·ly
whom·ev·er
whom·so·ev·er
whoop·ing
whop·per
whop·ping
whore
whorled
whose·so·ev·er
who·so·ev·er
wick·ed
wick·er·work
wick·et
wide
　wid·er
　wid·est
wide-a·wake
wide-eyed
wid·en
wide·spread
widg·eon
wid·ow
wid·ow·er
width
wield·er
wieldy
wie·ner
wife·ly
　wife·li·ness
wig·gle
　wig·gled
　wig·gling
　wig·gly
　wig·gli·est
wig·wag
　wig·wagged
　wig·wag·ging
wig·wam
wild·cat
　wild·cat·ted
　wild·cat·ting
wil·der·ness
wild-eyed
wild·fire
wild·fowl
wild·life
wild·wood
wile
　wil·i·ly
　wil·i·ness
wily
willed
will·ful·ly
will·ing
will-o'-the-wisp
wil·low
wil·lowy
wil·ly-nil·ly
win
　won
　win·ning
wince

winc·ing
wind
　wound
　wind·ing
wind·break
wind·ed
wind·fall
wind·jam·mer
wind·lass
wind·mill
win·dow
win·dow·pane
win·dow-shop
　win·dow·shop·ping
wind·pipe
wind·shield
wind·storm
wind·up
wind·ward
windy
　wind·i·er
　wind·i·ness
wine
　wined
　win·ing
win·ery
winged
wing·span
wing·spread
win·na·ble
win·ner
win·ning
win·now
win·some
win·ter
win·ter·green
win·ter·ize
　win·ter·ized
　win·ter·iz·ing
　win·ter·i·za·tion
win·try
　win·ter·y
　win·tri·ness
wipe
　wiped
　wip·ing
wire-haired
wire·less
wire·tap
　wire·tapped
　wire·tap·ping
　wire·tap·per
wir·ing
wiry
　wir·i·er
　wir·i·ness
wis·dom
wise
　wis·er
　wis·est
　wise·ly
wise·crack
wish·bone
wish·ful·ly
wish·y-washy
wisp
　wispy
　wisp·i·er
wis·te·ria
wist·ful·ly
witch·craft
witch·ery
witch·ing
with·al
with·draw
　with·drew
　with·drawn
　with·draw·ing

with·draw·al
with·er
with·hold
　with·held
　with·hold·ing
with·in
with·out
with·stand
　with·stood
　with·stand·ing
wit·less
wit·ness
wit·ti·cism
wit·ting
　wit·ting·ly
wit·ty
　wit·ti·est
　wit·ti·ly
　wit·ti·ness
wiz·ard
　wiz·ard·ry
wiz·en
　wiz·ened
wob·ble
　wob·bled
　wob·bling
　wob·bly
woe·be·gone
woe·ful·ly
wolf·hound
wolf·ram
wol·ver·ine
wom·an
　wom·en
wom·an·ly
　wom·an·li·ness
wom·an·hood
wom·an·ish
wom·an·kind
womb
won·der·ful
won·der·land
won·der·ment
won·drous
wont·ed
wood·bine
wood·chuck
wood·cock
wood·craft
wood·ed
wood·en
wood·land
wood·peck·er
wood·pile
woods·man
woodsy
wood·wind
wood·work
woody
woo·er
woof·er
wool·en
wool·gath·er·ing
wool·ly
　wool·li·ness
　wool·ly-head·ed
woozy
　wooz·i·ly
　wooz·i·ness
word·ing
word·less
wordy
　word·i·est
　word·i·ly
　word·i·ness
work·a·ble
work·a·bil·i·ty
work·a·day

work·bench
worked-up
work·er
work·horse
work·ing
work·ing·man
work·man
work·man·like
work·man·ship
work·out
work·room
work·shop
work·ta·ble
world·ly
　world·li·er
　world·li·est
　world·li·ness
world·ly-wise
world-wea·ry
world-wide
worm-eat·en
wormy
worn-out
wor·ri·some
wor·ry
　wor·ried
　wor·ry·ing
　wor·ries
　wor·ri·er
wor·ry·wart
wors·en
worship
　wor·ship·ful
wor·sted
worth·less
worth·while
wor·thy
　wor·thi·er
　wor·thi·est
　wor·thi·ly
　wor·thi·ness
would-be
wound·ed
wrack
wraith
wran·gle
　wran·gled
　wran·gling
　wran·gler
wrap
　wrapped
　wrap·ping
　wrap·per
wrath·ful
wreak
wreath
wreathe
　wreathed
　wreath·ing
wreck·age
wrench
wres·tle
　wres·tled
　wres·tling
wretch
wretch·ed
wrig·gle
　wrig·gled
　wrig·gling
　wrig·gly
　wrig·gler
wring
　wrung
　wring·ing
wring·er
wrin·kle
　wrin·kled
　wrin·kling

wrin·kly
write
  wrote
  writ·ten
  writ·ing
  writ·er
writhe
  writhed
  writh·ing
wrong·do·er
  wrong·do·ing
wronged
wrong·ful·ly
wrong-head·ed
wrought
wry
  wri·er
  wri·est
  wry·ly

X

xan·thous
xe·bec
xe·non
xen·o·phobe
  xen·o·pho·bia
X-ray
  x·ray
xy·lem
xy·lo·graph
  xy·log·ra·phy
xy·loid
xy·lo·phone
  xy·lo·phon·ist

Y

yacht
yacht·ing
yachts·man
ya·hoo
yak
yam
yam·mer
yank
Yan·kee
yap
  yapped
  yap·ping
yard·age
yard·arm
yard·mas·ter
yard·stick
yarn
yar·row
yawl
yawn
year·book
year·ling
year·long
year·ly
yearn
  yearn·ing
year-round
yeast
  yeasty
yel·low
  yel·low·ish
yel·low·bird
yel·low fe·ver
yel·low·ham·mer

yel·low jack·et
yelp
yen
  yenned
  yen·ning
yeo·man
  yeo·men
ye·shi·va
yes·ter·day
yes·ter·year
yew
Yid·dish
yield
  yield·ing
yip
  yipped
  yip·ping
yo·del
  yo·deled
  yo·del·ing
  yo·del·er
yo·ga
yo·gi
yo·gurt
yoke
  yoked
  yok·ing
yo·kel
yolk
Yom Kip·pur
yon·der
yore
young
  young·er
  young·ish
young·ling

young·ster
your·self
  your·selves
youth·ful
  youth·ful·ly
yowl
yuc·ca
yule·tide

Z

za·ny
  za·nies
  za·ni·er
  za·ni·est
  za·ni·ly
  za·ni·ness
zeal
  zeal·ot
  zeal·ous
ze·bra
ze·bu
ze·nith
zeph·yr
zep·pe·lin
ze·ro
  ze·ros
  ze·roes
zest
  zesty
  zest·i·er
  zest·ful
  zest·ful·ly
zig·zag
  zig·zagged
  zig·zag·ging

zinc
  zinced
  zinc·ing
zing
zin·nia
Zi·on
Zi·on·ism
  Zi·on·ist
zip
  zipped
  zip·ping
zip·per
zip·py
  zip·pi·er
  zip·pi·est
zir·con
zir·co·ni·um
zith·er
zo·di·ac
  zo·di·a·cal
zom·bie
zon·al
  zon·al·ly
zone
  zoned
  zon·ing
zoo
  zoos
zoo·ge·og·ra·phy
zo·ol·o·gy
  zo·o·log·ical
  zo·o·log·i·cal·ly
  zo·ol·o·gist
zuc·chet·to
zuc·chi·ni
zwie·back
zy·gote

Metric Measurement

JOULE (J) = the work done when the point of application of a force of 1 newton is displaced through a distance of 1 metre in the direction of the force.

erg = 1 dyn acting through a distance of 1 centimetre = 100^7J

watt (W) = the power which in 1 second gives rise to energy of 1 joule.

metric horsepower (ch or CV or cv or PS or pk) = the power which raises 75 kilograms against the force of gravity through a distance of 1 metre per second = $75 \times 9.806\,65$ joules per second = 735.498 75 watts.

coulomb (C) = the quantity of electricity carried in 1 second by a current of 1 ampere.

volt (V) = the difference of electric potential between two points of a conducting wire carrying a constant current of 1 ampere, when the power dissipated between these points is equal to 1 watt.

ohm (Ω) = the electric resistance between two points of a conductor when a constant potential difference of 1 volt, applied to these points, produces in the conductor a current of 1 ampere, the conductor not being the seat of any electromotive force.

siemens (S) = 1 ampere per volt, being the unit of electric conductance; this unit has also been known as the reciprocal ohm (ohm^{-1}) or 'mho'.

farad (F) the capacitance of a capacitor between the plates of which there appears a difference of electric potential of 1 volt when it is charged by a quantity of electricity of 1 coulomb.

weber (Wb) = the magnetic flux which, linking a circuit of 1 turn, would produce in it an electromotive force of 1 volt if it were reduced to zero at a uniform rate in 1 second.

henry (H) = the inductance of a closed circuit in which an electromotive force of 1 volt is produced when the electric current in the circuit varies uniformly at the rate of 1 ampere per second.

tesla (T) = the flux density in vacuum produced by a magnetic field of strength 1 ampere per metre; this is the unit of magnetic flux density and equals 1 weber per square metre.

lumen (lm) = the luminous flux emitted within unit solid angle of 1 steradian by a point source having a uniform luminous intensity of 1 candela. lux (lx) = an illuminance of 1 lumen per square metre.

LENGTH

1000 picometres	= 1 nanometre
1000 nanometres	= 1 micrometre
1000 micrometres	= 1 millimetre
10 millimetres	= 1 centimetre
100 millimetres	= 1 decimetre
10 centimetres	= 1 decimetre
1000 millimetres	= 1 metre
100 centimetres	= 1 metre
10 decimetres	= 1 metre
100 metres	= 1 hectometre
1000 metres	= 1 kilometre
10 hectometres	= 1 kilometre
1000 kilometres	= 1 megametre
1852 nautical metres	= 1 international nautical mile

AREA

100 sq millimetres	= 1 sq centimetre
100 sq centimetres	= 1 sq decimetre
10 000 sq centimetres	= 1 sq metre
100 sq decimetres	= 1 sq metre
100 sq metres	= 1 are
10 ares	= 1 dekare
10 000 sq metres	= 1 sq hectometre
	= 1 hectare
100 ares	= 1 hectare
10 dekares	= 1 hectare
100 sq hectometres	= 1 sq kilometre
100 hectares	= 1 sq kilometre

MASS

1000 nanograms	= 1 microgram
1000 micrograms	= 1 milligram
200 milligrams	= 1 metric carat
1000 milligrams	= 1 gram
5 metric carats	= 1 gram
25 grams	= 1 metric ounce
100 grams	= 1 hectogram
1000 grams	= 1 kilogram
100 kilograms	= 1 quintal
1000 kilograms	= 1 megagram
10 quintals	= 1 megagram
	= 1 tonne

ENERGY (WORK & HEAT)

10 000 ergs	= 1 millijoule
1000 millijoules	= 1 joule
1000 joules	= 1 kilojoule
1000 kilojoules	= 1 megajoule
3.6 megajoules	= 1 kilowatt hour
1000 megajoules	= 1 gigajoule
1000 gigajoules	= 1 terajoule

POWER

1000 microwatts	= 1 milliwatt
1000 milliwatts	= 1 watt
1000 watts	= 1 kilowatt
1000 kilowatts	= 1 megawatt
1000 megawatts	= 1 gigawatt
1000 gigawatts	= 1 terawatt

VOLUME & CAPACITY

1000 cu millimetres	= 1 cu centimetre
1000 cu centimetres	= 1 cu decimetre
1000 cu decimetres	= 1 cu metre
1000 cu metres	= 1 dekametre
1000 cu dekametres	= 1 cu hectometre
1000 cu hectometres	= 1 cu kilometre
1000 microlitres	= 1 millitre
	= 1 cu centimetre
10 millilitre	= 1 centilitre
10 centilitres	= 1 decilitre
1000 millilitres	= 1 litre
100 centilitres	= 1 litre

100 litres	= 1 hectolitre
1000 litres	= 1 kilolitre
	= 1 cu metre
10 hectolitres	= 1 kilolitre

PRESSURE AND STRESS

1000 micropascals	= 1 millipascal
100 millipascals	= 1 microbar
1000 millipascals	= 1 pascal
10 microbars	= 1 pascal
1000 microbars	= 1 millibar
100 pascals	= 1 millibar
1000 pascals	= 1 kilopascal
10 millibars	= 1 kilopascal
	= 1 pieze
1000 millibars	= 1 bar
	= 1 hectopieze
1000 kilopascals	= 1 megapascal
100 bars	= 1 hectobar
1000 bars	= 1 kilobar
1000 megapascals	= 1 gigapascal

ELECTRICITY & MAGNETISM

1000 picoamperes	= 1 nanoampere
1000 nanoamperes	= 1 microampere
1000 microamperes	= 1 milliampere
1000 milliamperes	= 1 ampere
1000 amperes	= 1 kiloampere
1000 millicoulombs	= 1 coulomb
1000 coulombs	= 1 kilocoulomb
1000 microvolts	= 1 millivolt
1000 millivolts	= 1 volts
1000 volts	= 1 kilovolt
1000 kilovolts	= 1 megavolt
1000 microhm	= 1 milliohm
1000 milliohm	= 1 ohm

1000 ohms	= 1 kilohm		1000 kilograms per	= 1 tonne per
1000 kilohms	= 1 megohm		cu metre	cu metre
1000 megohms	= 1 gigohm			= 1 kilogram per
1000 millisiemens	= 1 siemens			cu decimetre
1000 millihenrys	= 1 henry			
1000 milliteslas	= 1 tesla			

FORCE

10 micronewtons	= 1 dyne
1000 micronewtons	= 1 millinewton
10 millinewtons	= 1 centinewton
1000 millinewtons	= 1 newton
1000 newtons	= 1 kilonewton
1000 kilonewtons	= 1 meganewton

TIME

1000 nanoseconds	= 1 microsecond
1000 microseconds	= 1 millisecond
1000 milliseconds	= 1 second
1000 seconds	= 1 kilosecond

FREQUENCY

1000 hertz	= 1 kilohertz
1000 kilohertz	= 1 megahertz
1000 megahertz	= 1 gigahertz
1000 gigahertz	= 1 terahertz
1000 terahertz	= 1 petahertz
1000 petahertz	= 1 exahertz

DENSITY & CONCENTRATION

1 gram per cubic metre	= 1 milligram per cu decimetre
1000 milligrams per cu decimetre	= 1 gram per cu decimetre
	= 1 kilogram per cu metre

3.6 kilometres per hour	= 1 metre per second
3 600 kilometres per hour	= 1 kilometre per second

Metric Conversions

CONVERSION FORMULAE
Non-metric to metric

LENGTH

To convert	Multiply by
milli-inches into micrometres	25.4
inches into millimetres	25.4
inches into centimetres	2.54
inches into metres	0.0254
feet into millimetres	304.8
feet into centimetres	30.48
feet into metres	0.3048
yards into metres	0.9144
fathoms into metres	1.8288
chains into metres	20.1168
furlongs into metres	201.168
miles, statute into kilometres	1.609344
miles, nautical into kilometres	1.852

VOLUME & CAPACITY

To convert	Multiply by
cubic inches into cubic centimetres	16.387064
cubic inches into litres	0.016387
cubic feet into cubic metres	0.0283168
cubic feet into litres	28.316847
pints into litres	0.5682613
quarts into litres	1.1365225
cubic yards into cubic metres	0.7645549
gallons into litres	4.54609
fluid ounces into cubic centimetres	28.413063

AREA

To convert	Multiply by
square inches into square millimetres	645.16
square inches into square centimetres	6.4516
square feet into square centimetres	929.0304
square feet into square metres	0.092903

square yards into square metres	0.836123
square yards into ares	0.0083613
acres into square metres	4046.8564
acres into ares	40.468564
acres into hectares	0.4046856
square miles into hectares	258.9988
square miles into square kilometres	2.589988

MASS

To convert	Multiply by
grains into milligrams	64.79891
grains into metric carats	0.323995
grains into grams	0.064799
pennyweights into grams	1.555174
drams into grams	1.77185
ounces into grams	28.349523
ounces troy into metric carats	155.5174
ounces into kilograms	0.0283495
pounds into kilograms	0.4535924
stones into kilograms	6.3502932
hundred weights into kilograms	50.802345
tons into kilograms	1016.0469
tons into metric tonnes	1.01604
tahils into grams	37.799
kati into kilograms	0.60479

POWER

To convert	Multiply by
foot pounds-force per second into watts	1.35582
horsepower into watts	745.7
foot pounds-force per second into kilowatts	0.001356
horsepower into kilowatts	0.7457
horsepower into metric horsepower	1.01387

Metric to non-metric

VOLUME & CAPACITY

To convert	Multiply by
cu.centimetres into cu.inches	0.06102
cu.metres into cu.feet	35.3147
cu.metres into cu.yards	1.30795
litres into cu.inches	61.03
litres into pints	1.7598
litres into quarts	0.8799
litres into U.K. gallons	0.219976
litres into U.S. gallons	0.264178

MASS

To convert	Multiply by
grams into ounces	0.03527
grams into grains	15.4324
grams into tahil	0.02646
kilograms into pounds	2.2046
kilograms into tons	0.0009842
kilograms into katis	1.653
kilograms into stones	0.1575
kilograms into hundredweights	0.01968

VELOCITY

To convert	Multiply by
centimetres per second into feet per second	0.03281
metres per second into feet per minute	196.9
metres per second into feet per second	3.281
kilometres per hour into miles per hour	0.6214

POWER

To convert	Multiply by
kilowatts into horsepower	1.341
metric horsepower into	
horsepower	0.98632
metric horsepower into	
foot pounds—force per second	542.48

FORCE

To convert	Multiply by
newtons into pounds force	0.2248
newtons into pounds	7.2330

LINEAR

To convert	Multiply by
millimetres into feet	3.281×10
millimetres into inches	0.03937
centimetres into inches	0.3937
metres into yards	1.09361
metres into feet	3.281
kilometres into yards	1093.61
kilometres into miles	0.62137

AREA

To convert	Multiply by
sq.millimetres into sq.inches	1.550×10^{-3}
sq.centimetres into sq.inches	0.1550
sq.metres into sq.feet	10.7639
sq.metres into sq.yards	1.19599
sq.metres into acres	2.47105×10^{-4}
sq.kilometres into sq.miles	0.3861
sq.kilometres into acres	247.105
hectares into acres	2.47105

LENGTH

Inches		Millimetres
0.03937	. 1 .	25.40
0.07874	. 2 .	50.80
0.11811	. 3 .	76.20
0.15748	. 4 .	101.60
0.19685	. 5 .	127.00
0.23622	. 6 .	152.40
0.27559	. 7 .	177.80
0.31396	. 8 .	203.20
0.35433	. 9 .	228.60

inches		Centimetres
.393700	. 1 .	2.540
.787402	. 2 .	5.080
1.181102	. 3 .	7.620
1.574803	. 4 .	10.160
1.968504	. 5 .	12.700
2.362205	. 6 .	15.240
2.755906	. 7 .	17.780
3.149606	. 8 .	20.320
3.543307	. 9 .	22.860

Feet		Metres
3.280840	. 1 .	.3048
6.561680	. 2 .	.6096
9.842520	. 3 .	.9144
13.123359	. 4 .	1.2192
16.404199	. 5 .	1.5240
19.685038	. 6 .	1.8288
22.965878	. 7 .	2.1336
26.246718	. 8 .	2.4384
29.527558	. 9 .	2.7432

Yards		Metres
1.093613	. 1 .	0.91440
2.187226	. 2 .	1.82880
3.280839	. 3 .	2.74320
4.374452	. 4 .	3.65760
5.468065	. 5 .	4.57200
6.561678	. 6 .	5.48640
7.655291	. 7 .	6.40080
8.748904	. 8 .	7.31520
0.842517	. 9 .	8.22960

Miles		Kilometres
.621371	. 1 .	1.60934
1.242742	. 2 .	3.21869
1.864113	. 3 .	4.82803
2.485484	. 4 .	6.43738
3.106855	. 5 .	**8.04672**
3.728226	. 6 .	9.65606
4.349597	. 7 .	11.26541
4.970968	. 8 .	12.87475
5.592339	. 9 .	14.48410

VOLUME & CAPACITY

Cu. Inches		Cu. Centimetres
.061024	. 1 .	16.38706
.122048	. 2 .	32.77413
.183072	. 3 .	49.16119
.244096	. 4 .	65.54826
.305120	. 5 .	81.93532
.366144	. 6 .	98.32238
.427168	. 7 .	114.70945
.488192	. 8 .	131.09651
.549216	. 9 .	147.48358

Metric Conversions

009VOLUME & CAPACITY

Fluid ounces		Cu. Centimetres
0.03520	. 1 .	28,4131
0.07039	. 2 .	56.8261
0.10009	. 3 .	85.2392
0.14078	. 4 .	113.6522
0.17598	. 5 .	142.0653
0.21117	. 6 .	170.4784
0.24637	. 7 .	198.8914
0.28156	. 8 .	227.3045
0.31676	. 9 .	255.7176

Quarts		Litres
.87988	. 1 .	1.13652
1.75976	. 2 .	2.27304
2.63964	. 3 .	3.40956
3.51952	. 4 .	4.54608
4.39940	. 5 .	5.68260
5.27928	. 6 .	6.81912
6.15916	. 7 .	7.95564
7.03904	. 8 .	9.09216
7.91892	. 9 .	10.22868

Cwt.		Kiloframs
0.19684	. 1 .	50.80234
.039368	. 2 .	101.60469
.059052	. 3 .	152.40704
.078736	. 4 .	203.20938
.098420	. 5 .	254.01173
.118104	. 6 .	304.81408
.137788	. 7 .	355.61642
.157472	. 8 .	406.41977
.177156	. 9 .	457.22112

VOLUME & CAPACITY

Tons		Kilograms
.000984	. 1 .	1016.0469
.001968	. 2 .	2032.0938
.002952	. 3 .	3048.1407
.003936	. 4 .	4064.1876
.004920	. 5 .	5080.2345
.005904	. 6 .	6096.2814
.006888	. 7 .	7112.3283
.007872	. 8 .	8128.3752
.008856	. 9 .	9144.4221

Cu. Feet		Litres
0.035315	. 1 .	28.3168
0.070630	. 2 .	56.6337
0.105940	. 3 .	84.9505
0.140588	. 4 .	113.2674
0.176574	. 5 .	141.5842
0.211888	. 6 .	169.9011
0.247203	. 7 .	198.2179
0.282518	. 8 .	226.5348
0.317832	. 9 .	254.8516

Gallons		Litres
.21997	. 1 .	4.54609
.43994	. 2 .	9.09218
.65991	. 3 .	13.63827
.87988	. 4 .	18.18436
1.09985	. 5 .	22.73045
1.31982	. 6 .	27.27654
1.53979	. 7 .	31.82263
1.75976	. 8 .	36.36872
1.97973	. 9 .	40.91481

POWER

Horsepower		Kilowatts
1.341022	. 1 .	.7457
2.682044	. 2 .	1.4914
4.023066	. 3 .	2.2371
5.364088	. 4 .	2.9828
6.705110	. 5 .	3.7285
8.046132	. 6 .	4.4742
9.387154	. 7 .	5.2199
10.728176	. 8 .	5.9656
12.069198	. 9 .	6.7113

Cu. Feet		Cu. Metres
35.31467	. 1 .	0.02832
70.62934	. 2 .	0.05664
105.94401	. 3 .	0.08496
141.25868	. 4 .	0.11328
176.57335	. 5 .	0.14160
211.88802	. 6 .	0.16992
247.20269	. 7 .	0.19824
282.51736	. 8 .	0.22656
317.83203	. 9 .	0.25488

MASS

Ounces		Grams
.035274	. 1 .	28.34952
.070548	. 2 .	56.69905
.105812	. 3 .	85.04857
.141096	. 4 .	113.39809
.176370	. 5 .	141.74762
.211644	. 6 .	170.09714
.246918	. 7 .	198.44666
.282192	. 8 .	226.79618
.317466	. 9 .	255.14571

AREA

Sq. Inches		Sq. Centimet
.15500	. 1 .	6.45160
.31000	. 2 .	12.90320
.46500	. 3 .	19.35480
.62000	. 4 .	25.80640
.77500	. 5 .	32.25800
.93000	. 6 .	38.70960
1.08500	. 7 .	45.16120
1.24000	. 8 .	51.61280
1.39500	. 9 .	58.06440

Cu. Yards		Cu. Metres
1.30795	. 1 .	.76455
2.61590	. 2 .	1.52910
3.92385	. 3 .	2.29365
5.23180	. 4 .	3.05820
6.53975	. 5 .	3.82275
7.84770	. 6 .	4.58730
9.15565	. 7 .	5.35185
10.46360	. 8 .	6.11640
11.77155	. 9 .	6.88095

Grains		Grams
15.4324	. 1 .	0.06480
30.8648	. 2 .	0.12960
46.2972	. 3 .	0.19440
61.7296	. 4 .	0.25920
77.1620	. 5 .	0.32400
92.5944	. 6 .	0.38880
108.0268	. 7 .	0.45360
123.4592	. 8 .	0.51840
138.8916	. 9 .	0.58320

Pints		Litres
1.75976	. 1 .	.56826
3.51952	. 2 .	1.13652
5.27928	. 3 .	1.70478
7.03904	. 4 .	2.27305
8.79880	. 5 .	2.84131
10.55856	. 6 .	3.40957
12.31832	. 7 .	3.97783
14.07808	. 8 .	4.54609
15.83784	. 9 .	5.11435

Pounds		Kilograms
2.204622	. 1 .	.453592
4.409244	. 2 .	.907184
6.613866	. 3 .	1.360776
8.818488	. 4 .	1.814368
11.023110	. 5 .	2.267960
13.227732	. 6 .	2.721552
15.432354	. 7 .	3.175144
17.636976	. 8 .	3.628736
19.841598	. 9 .	4.082328

Sq. Feet		Sq. Metres
10.76391	. 1 .	0.09290
21.52782	. 2 .	0.18580
32.29173	. 3 .	0.27870
43.05564	. 4 .	0.37160
53.81955	. 5 .	0.46450
64.58346	. 6 .	0.55740
75.34737	. 7 .	0.65030
86.11128	. 8 .	0.74320
96.87519	. 9 .	0.83610

Sq. Yards			Sq. Metres	Acres				Hectaares	Sq. Miles				Sq. Kilometres
1.19599	.	1	.	0.83613	2.47105	.	1	.	.40469	.38610	.	1	.	2.58999
2.39198	.	2	.	1.67226	4.94210	.	2	.	.80938	.77220	.	2	.	5.17998
3.58797	.	3	.	2.50839	7.41315	.	3	.	1.21407	1.15830	.	3	.	7.76997
4.78396	.	4	.	3.34453	9.88420	.	4	.	1.61876	1.54440	.	4	.	10.35996
5.97995	.	5	.	4.18065	12.35525	.	5	.	2.02345	1.93050	.	5	.	12.94995
7.17594	.	6	.	5.01678	14.82630	.	6	.	2.42814	2.31660	.	6	.	15.53994
8.37193	.	7	.	5.85291	17.29735	.	7	.	2.83283	2.70270	.	7	.	18.12993
9.56792	.	8	.	6.68904	19.76840	.	8	.	3.23752	3.08880	.	8	.	20.71992
10.76391	.	9	.	7.52517	22.23945	.	9	.	3.64221	3.47490	.	9	.	23.30991

Metric System

Multiples and Submultiples

The multiples and submultiples of the base and other units are formed by applying established prefixes, which are the same whichever unit is used. Examples are: milligram (mg), millimetre (mm), kilowatt (kW).

Only one multiplying prefix is applied at one time to a given unit. Thus one thousandth of a milligram is not referred to as a milli-milligram but as a microgram (g). There are a few cases where, in attaching a prefix to the name of a unit, a contraction of the prefix name is made for convenience in pronunciation; for example me-gohm, microhm and hectare. Unit names take a plural 's' when associated with numbers greater than 1, eg 1.5 metres; the names hertz, lux and siemens are, however, the same in the plural. Symbols are not altered in the plural form; eg 1.5 m.

The names and values of prefixes in use are given below; also indicated are the equivalent powers to base 10 of the multiplying factors which can be used to relate any multiple or submultiple to the main unit: for example $1 \text{ mm} = 10^{-3}\text{m}$ and $1 \text{ MN} = 10^6 \text{ N}$. The general use of prefixes representing 10 raised to a power which is multiple of ± 3 is recommended in SI; for example, millimetre (10^{-3} m), metre (m) and kilometre (10^3 m). Other prefixes, notably centi, deci, deka and hecto can be used where others are inconvenient. Myria, as a prefix symbol, is not an SI multiple, but is included for reference.

Prefix name	Prefix symbol	Factor by which the unit is multiplied			Description
atto	a	10^{-18}	=	0 000 000 000 000 000 001	one million million millionth
femto	f	10^{-15}	=	0 000 000 000 000 001	one thousand million million millionth
pico	p	10^{-12}	=	0 000 000 000 001	one million millionth
nano	n	10^{-9}	=	0 000 000 001	one thousand millionth
micro	m	10^{-6}	=	0 000 001	one millionth
milli	m	10^{-3}	=	0 001	one thousandth
centi	c	10^{-2}	=	0 01	one hundredth
deci	d	10^{-1}	=	0 1	one tenth
deca (or deka)	da	10^1	=	1 0	ten
hecto	h	10^2	=	10 0	one hundred
kilo	k	10^3	=	1 00 0	one thousand
myria	my	10^4	=	10 00 0	ten thousand
mega	M	10^6	=	1 000 00 0	one million
giga	G	10^9	=	1 000 000 00 0	one thousand million
tera	T	10^{12}	=	1 000 000 000 00 0	one million million
peta	P	10^{15}	=	1 000 000 000 000 00 0	one thousand million million
exa	E	10^{18}	=	1 000 000 000 000 000 00 0	one million million million

METRIC STANDARD ABBREVIATIONS

A	= ampere	cP	= centipoise	EHz	= exahertz	hm^2	= square hectometre
a	= are	cSt	= centistokes	F	= farad	hm^3	= cubic hectometre
bar	= bar	daa	= dekare	g	= gram	hpz	= hectopièze
C	= coulomb	dag	= dekagram	GHz	= gigahertz	Hz	= hertz
°C	= Celsius	dal	= dekalitre	GJ	= gigajoule	J	= joule
cc	= cubic centimetre	dam	= dekametre	GΩ	= gigohm	kA	= kiloampere
cg	= centigram	dam^2	= square dekametre	GPa	= gigapascal	kbar	= kilobar
cl	= centilitre	dam^3	= cubic dekametre	GW	= gigawatt	kC	= kilocoulomb
cm	= centimetre	dB	= decibel	h	= hour	kg	= kilogram
cm^2	= square centimetre	dg	= decigram	H	= henry	kgf	= kilogram-force
cm⅔	= square centimetre per second	dl	= decilitre	ha	= hectare	kgf m	= kilogram-force metre
		dm	= decimetre	hbar	= hectobar		
cm^3	= cubic centimetre	dm^2	= square decimetre	hg	= hectogram	kHz	= kilohetz
CM	= metric carat	dm^3	= cubic decimetre	hl	= hectolitre	kJ	= kilojoule
cN	= centinewton	dyn	= dyne	hm	= hectometre	kl	= kilolitre

km	= kilimetre	mg	= milligram	mW	= milliwatt	Ω	= ohm
km²	= square kilometre	Mg	= megagram	MW	= megawatt	p	= pond
km³	= cubic kilometre	mH	= millihenry	μA	= microampere	P	= poise
km/h	kilometre per hour	MHz	= megahertz	μbar	= microbar	pA	= picoampere
km/s	= kilometre per second	mJ	= millijoule	μC	= microcoulomb	Pa	= pascal
		MJ	= megajoule	μF	= microfarad	Pa s	= pascal second
kN	= kilonewton	ml	= millilitre	μg	= microgram	pC	= picocoulomb
kΩ	= kilohm	Mm	= megametre	μH	= microhenry	pF	= picofarad
kp	= kilopond	mm	= millimetre	μl	= microlitre	pH	= picohenry
kPa	= kilopascal	mm²	= square millimetre	μm	= micrometre	PHz	= petahertz
ks	= kilosecond	mm²/s	= square millimetre per second	μN	= micronewton	pm	= picometre
kS	= kilosiemens			μΩ	= microhm	pz	= pièze
kV	= kilovolt	mm³	= cubic millimetre	μPa	= micropascal	q	= quintal
kW	= kilowatt	mN	= millinewton	μS	= microsecond	s	= second
kWh	= kilowatt hour	MN	= meganewton	μS	= microsiemens	S	= siemens
l or L	= litre	mΩ	= milliohm	μT	= microtesia	sn	= sthène
m	= metre	MΩ	= megohm	μV	= microvolt	St	= stokes
m/s	= metre per second	mPa	= millipascal	μW	= microwatt	t	= tonne
m²	= square metre	MPa	= megapascal	N	= Newton	T	= tesla
m²/s	= square metre per second	mPa s	= millipascal second	nA	= nanoampere	THz	= terahertz
		ms	= millisecond	nC	= nanocoulomb	TJ	= terajoule
m³	= cubic metre	m/s	= metre per second	ng	= nanogram	TW	= terawatt
mA	= milliampere	mS	= millisiemens	nH	= nanohenry	V	= volt
mbar	= millibar	mT	= millitesia	nm	= nanometre	W	= watt
mC	= millicoulomb	mV	= millivolt	ns	= nanosecond		
MC	= megacoulomb	MV	= megavolt	nT	= nanotesia		

ANNUAL PERCENTAGE RATE TABLE FOR MONTHLY PAYMENT PLANS

ANNUAL PERCENTAGE RATE

(FINANCE CHARGE PER $100 OF AMOUNT FINANCED)

NUMBER OF PAYMENTS	10.00%	10.50%	11.00%	11.50%	12.00%	12.50%	13.00%	13.50%	14.00%	14.50%	15.00%	15.50%	16.00%	16.50%	17.00%	17.50%	18.00%
1	0.83	0.87	0.92	0.96	1.00	1.04	1.08	1.12	1.17	1.21	1.25	1.29	1.33	1.37	1.42	1.46	1.50
2	1.25	1.31	1.38	1.44	1.50	1.57	1.63	1.69	1.75	1.82	1.88	1.94	2.00	2.07	2.13	2.19	2.26
3	1.67	1.76	1.84	1.92	2.01	2.09	2.17	2.26	2.34	2.43	2.51	2.59	2.68	2.76	2.85	2.93	3.01
4	2.09	2.20	2.30	2.41	2.51	2.62	2.72	2.83	2.93	3.04	3.14	3.25	3.36	3.46	3.57	3.67	3.78
5	2.51	2.64	2.77	2.89	3.02	3.15	3.27	3.40	3.53	3.65	3.78	3.91	4.04	4.16	4.29	4.42	4.54
6	2.94	3.08	3.23	3.38	3.53	3.68	3.83	3.97	4.12	4.27	4.42	4.57	4.72	4.87	5.02	5.17	5.32
7	3.36	3.53	3.70	3.87	4.04	4.21	4.38	4.55	4.72	4.89	5.06	5.23	5.40	5.58	5.75	5.92	6.09
8	3.79	3.98	4.17	4.36	4.55	4.74	4.94	5.13	5.32	5.51	5.71	5.90	6.09	6.29	6.48	6.67	6.87
9	4.21	4.43	4.64	4.85	5.07	5.28	5.49	5.71	5.92	6.14	6.35	6.57	6.78	7.00	7.22	7.43	7.65
10	4.64	4.88	5.11	5.35	5.58	5.82	6.05	6.29	6.53	6.77	7.00	7.24	7.48	7.72	7.96	8.19	8.43
11	5.07	5.33	5.58	5.84	6.10	6.36	6.62	6.88	7.14	7.40	7.66	7.92	8.18	8.44	8.70	8.96	9.22
12	5.50	5.78	6.06	6.34	6.62	6.90	7.18	7.46	7.74	8.03	8.31	8.59	8.88	9.16	9.45	9.73	10.02
18	8.10	8.52	8.93	9.35	9.77	10.19	10.61	11.03	11.45	11.87	12.29	12.72	13.14	13.57	13.99	14.42	14.85
24	10.75	11.30	11.86	12.42	12.98	13.54	14.10	14.66	15.23	15.80	16.37	16.94	17.51	18.09	18.66	19.24	19.82
30	13.43	14.13	14.83	15.54	16.24	16.95	17.66	18.38	19.10	19.81	20.54	21.26	21.99	22.72	23.45	24.18	24.92
36	16.16	17.01	17.86	18.71	19.57	20.43	21.30	22.17	23.04	23.92	24.80	25.68	26.57	27.46	28.35	29.25	30.15
42	18.93	19.93	20.93	21.94	22.96	23.98	25.00	26.03	27.06	28.10	29.15	30.19	31.25	32.31	33.37	34.44	35.51
48	21.74	22.90	24.06	25.23	26.40	27.58	28.77	29.97	31.17	32.37	33.59	34.81	36.03	37.27	38.50	39.75	41.00
54	24.59	25.91	27.23	28.56	29.91	31.25	32.61	33.98	35.35	36.73	38.12	39.52	40.92	42.33	43.75	45.18	46.62
60	27.48	28.96	30.45	31.96	33.47	34.99	36.52	38.06	39.61	41.17	42.74	44.32	45.91	47.51	49.12	50.73	52.36
66	30.41	32.06	33.73	35.40	37.09	38.78	40.49	42.21	43.95	45.69	47.45	49.22	51.00	52.79	54.59	56.40	58.23
72	33.39	35.21	37.05	38.90	40.76	42.64	44.53	46.44	48.36	50.30	52.24	54.21	56.18	58.17	60.17	62.19	64.22
78	36.40	38.40	40.41	42.45	44.49	46.56	48.64	50.74	52.85	54.98	57.13	59.29	61.46	63.66	65.86	68.09	70.32
84	39.45	41.63	43.83	46.05	48.28	50.54	52.81	55.11	57.42	59.75	62.09	64.46	66.84	69.24	71.66	74.10	76.55
90	42.54	44.91	47.29	49.70	52.13	54.58	57.05	59.54	62.05	64.59	67.14	69.72	72.31	74.93	77.56	80.22	82.89
96	45.67	48.22	50.80	53.40	56.03	58.68	61.35	64.05	66.77	69.51	72.28	75.06	77.88	80.71	83.57	86.44	89.34
102	48.84	51.59	54.36	57.16	59.98	62.83	65.71	68.62	71.55	74.51	77.49	80.50	83.53	86.59	89.67	92.78	95.91
108	52.05	54.99	57.96	60.96	63.99	67.05	70.14	73.26	76.40	79.58	82.78	86.01	89.27	92.56	95.87	99.21	102.57
114	55.30	58.43	61.61	64.81	68.05	71.32	74.63	77.96	81.33	84.73	88.15	91.61	95.10	98.62	102.17	105.74	109.35
120	58.58	61.92	65.30	68.71	72.17	75.65	79.17	82.73	86.32	89.94	93.60	97.29	101.02	104.77	108.56	112.37	116.22
180	93.43	98.97	104.59	110.27	116.03	121.85	127.74	133.70	139.71	145.79	151.93	158.12	164.37	170.67	177.02	183.42	189.88
240	131.61	139.61	147.73	155.94	164.26	172.67	181.18	189.77	198.44	207.20	216.03	224.93	233.90	242.94	252.03	261.19	270.39
300	172.61	183.25	194.03	204.94	215.97	227.11	238.35	249.69	261.13	272.65	284.25	295.92	307.67	319.47	331.34	343.26	355.23
360	215.93	229.31	242.84	256.50	270.30	284.21	298.23	312.35	326.55	340.84	355.20	369.63	384.11	398.65	413.24	427.88	442.55

DAILY COMPOUNDING INTEREST TABLE

ANNUAL PERCENTAGE RATE

(WHAT A $1 DEPOSIT WILL GROW TO IN THE FUTURE)

NUMBER OF YEARS	5.00%	5.25%	5.50%	5.75%	6.00%	6.50%	7.00%	7.50%	8.00%	8.50%	9.00%	9.50%	10.00%
1	1.0520	1.0547	1.0573	1.0600	1.0627	1.0681	1.0735	1.0790	1.0845	1.0900	1.0955	1.1011	1.1067
2	1.1067	1.1123	1.1180	1.1237	1.1294	1.1409	1.1525	1.1642	1.1761	1.1881	1.2002	1.2124	1.2248
3	1.1642	1.1731	1.1821	1.1911	1.2002	1.2186	1.2373	1.2562	1.2755	1.2950	1.3148	1.3350	1.3554
4	1.2248	1.2373	1.2499	1.2626	1.2755	1.3016	1.3282	1.3555	1.3832	1.4115	1.4404	1.4699	1.5001
5	1.2885	1.3049	1.3215	1.3384	1.3555	1.3903	1.4259	1.4625	1.5001	1.5386	1.5781	1.6186	1.6601
6	1.3555	1.3762	1.3973	1.4187	1.4405	1.4850	1.5308	1.5781	1.6268	1.6770	1.7288	1.7822	1.8372
7	1.4259	1.4515	1.4774	1.5039	1.5308	1.5861	1.6434	1.7027	1.7642	1.8279	1.8940	1.9624	2.0332
8	1.5001	1.5308	1.5622	1.5942	1.6268	1.6941	1.7642	1.8373	1.9133	1.9924	2.0749	2.1607	2.2502
9	1.5781	1.6145	1.6518	1.6899	1.7288	1.8095	1.8940	1.9824	2.0749	2.1718	2.2731	2.3792	2.4902
10	1.6602	1.7028	1.7465	1.7913	1.8373	1.9328	2.0333	2.1390	2.2502	2.3672	2.4903	2.6197	2.7559
15	2.1391	2.2219	2.3080	2.3975	2.4904	2.6871	2.8993	3.1284	3.3755	3.6421	3.9298	4.2402	4.5751
20	2.7561	2.8994	3.0502	3.2087	3.3756	3.7357	4.1343	4.5753	5.0634	5.6036	6.2014	6.8629	7.5950
25	3.5512	3.7834	4.0309	4.2946	4.5755	5.1936	5.8952	6.6915	7.5955	8.6215	9.7861	11.1080	12.6085
30	4.5756	4.9370	5.3270	5.7478	6.2019	7.2204	8.4061	9.7866	11.3937	13.2648	15.4430	17.9790	20.9313

ANNUAL PERCENTAGE RATE

(WHAT A $1 DEPOSIT WILL GROW TO IN THE FUTURE)

NUMBER OF YEARS	10.50%	11.00%	11.50%	12.00%	12.50%	13.00%	13.50%	14.00%	14.50%	15.00%	15.50%	16.00%	16.50%
1	1.1123	1.1180	1.1236	1.1294	1.1351	1.1409	1.1467	1.1525	1.1583	1.1642	1.1701	1.1761	1.1821
2	1.2372	1.2498	1.2626	1.2754	1.2884	1.3016	1.3148	1.3282	1.3417	1.3554	1.3692	1.3832	1.3973
3	1.3762	1.3973	1.4187	1.4404	1.4625	1.4849	1.5076	1.5307	1.5542	1.5780	1.6022	1.6267	1.6516
4	1.5308	1.5621	1.5941	1.6268	1.6601	1.6941	1.7287	1.7641	1.8003	1.8371	1.8748	1.9131	1.9523
5	1.7027	1.7464	1.7912	1.8372	1.8843	1.9327	1.9823	2.0331	2.0853	2.1388	2.1937	2.2500	2.3077
6	1.8939	1.9524	2.0127	2.0748	2.1389	2.2049	2.2730	2.3432	2.4155	2.4901	2.5669	2.6462	2.7279
7	2.1067	2.1827	2.2615	2.3432	2.4278	2.5155	2.6063	2.7004	2.7980	2.8990	3.0037	3.1121	3.2245
8	2.3433	2.4402	2.5412	2.6463	2.7558	2.8698	2.9886	3.1122	3.2410	3.3751	3.5147	3.6601	3.8115
9	2.6064	2.7281	2.8554	2.9886	3.1281	3.2741	3.4269	3.5868	3.7541	3.9293	4.1127	4.3046	4.5054
10	2.8992	3.0499	3.2084	3.3752	3.5507	3.7353	3.9294	4.1337	4.3486	4.5746	4.8124	5.0625	5.3256
15	4.9364	5.3263	5.7470	6.2009	6.6907	7.2191	7.7892	8.4044	9.0681	9.7843	10.5570	11.3907	12.2902
20	8.4053	9.3019	10.2941	11.3922	12.6074	13.9522	15.4404	17.0873	18.9099	20.9269	23.1589	25.6290	28.3625
25	14.3116	16.2447	18.4390	20.9295	23.7564	26.9651	30.6072	34.7410	39.4332	44.7590	50.8040	57.6653	65.4531
30	24.3683	28.3697	33.0281	38.4513	44.7649	52.1150	60.6719	70.6336	82.2307	95.7318	111.4493	129.7470	151.0484

COMPOUND INTEREST TABLE

ANNUAL PERCENTAGE RATE

(FUTURE VALUE OF $1—PRINCIPAL PLUS ACCUMULATED INTEREST)

NUMBER OF PERIODS	1.00%	1.50%	2.00%	2.50%	3.00%	3.50%	4.00%	4.50%	5.00%	6.00%	7.00%	8.00%	9.00%	10.00%	12.00%	14.00%	16.00%	18.00%
1	1.010	1.015	1.020	1.025	1.030	1.035	1.040	1.045	1.050	1.060	1.070	1.080	1.090	1.100	1.120	1.140	1.160	1.180
2	1.020	1.030	1.040	1.051	1.061	1.071	1.082	1.092	1.103	1.124	1.145	1.166	1.188	1.210	1.254	1.300	1.346	1.392
3	1.030	1.046	1.061	1.077	1.093	1.109	1.125	1.141	1.158	1.191	1.225	1.260	1.295	1.331	1.405	1.482	1.561	1.643
4	1.041	1.061	1.082	1.104	1.126	1.148	1.170	1.193	1.216	1.262	1.311	1.360	1.412	1.464	1.574	1.689	1.811	1.939
5	1.051	1.077	1.104	1.131	1.159	1.188	1.217	1.246	1.276	1.338	1.403	1.469	1.539	1.611	1.762	1.925	2.100	2.288
6	1.062	1.093	1.126	1.160	1.194	1.229	1.265	1.302	1.340	1.419	1.501	1.587	1.677	1.772	1.974	2.195	2.436	2.700
7	1.072	1.110	1.149	1.189	1.230	1.272	1.316	1.361	1.407	1.504	1.606	1.714	1.828	1.949	2.211	2.502	2.826	3.185
8	1.083	1.126	1.172	1.218	1.267	1.317	1.369	1.422	1.477	1.594	1.718	1.851	1.993	2.144	2.476	2.853	3.278	3.759
9	1.094	1.143	1.195	1.249	1.305	1.363	1.423	1.486	1.551	1.689	1.838	1.999	2.172	2.358	2.773	3.252	3.803	4.435
10	1.105	1.161	1.219	1.280	1.344	1.411	1.480	1.553	1.629	1.791	1.967	2.159	2.367	2.594	3.106	3.707	4.411	5.234
11	1.116	1.178	1.243	1.312	1.384	1.460	1.539	1.623	1.710	1.898	2.105	2.332	2.580	2.853	3.479	4.226	5.117	6.176
12	1.127	1.196	1.268	1.345	1.426	1.511	1.601	1.696	1.796	2.012	2.252	2.518	2.813	3.138	3.896	4.818	5.936	7.288
14	1.149	1.232	1.319	1.413	1.513	1.619	1.732	1.852	1.980	2.261	2.579	2.937	3.342	3.797	4.887	6.261	7.988	10.147
16	1.173	1.269	1.373	1.485	1.605	1.734	1.873	2.022	2.183	2.540	2.952	3.426	3.970	4.595	6.130	8.137	10.748	14.129
18	1.196	1.307	1.428	1.560	1.702	1.857	2.026	2.208	2.407	2.854	3.380	3.996	4.717	5.560	7.690	10.575	14.463	19.673
20	1.220	1.347	1.486	1.639	1.806	1.990	2.191	2.412	2.653	3.207	3.870	4.661	5.604	6.727	9.646	13.743	19.461	27.393
22	1.245	1.388	1.546	1.722	1.916	2.132	2.370	2.634	2.925	3.604	4.430	5.437	6.659	8.140	12.100	17.861	26.186	38.142
24	1.270	1.430	1.608	1.809	2.033	2.283	2.563	2.876	3.225	4.049	5.072	6.341	7.911	9.850	15.179	23.212	35.236	53.109
26	1.295	1.473	1.673	1.900	2.157	2.446	2.772	3.141	3.556	4.549	5.807	7.396	9.399	11.918	19.040	30.167	47.414	73.949
28	1.321	1.517	1.741	1.996	2.288	2.620	2.999	3.430	3.920	5.112	6.649	8.627	11.167	14.421	23.884	39.204	63.800	102.967
30	1.348	1.563	1.811	2.098	2.427	2.807	3.243	3.745	4.322	5.743	7.612	10.063	13.268	17.449	29.960	50.950	85.850	143.371
32	1.375	1.610	1.884	2.204	2.575	3.007	3.508	4.090	4.765	6.453	8.715	11.737	15.763	21.114	37.582	66.215	115.520	199.629
34	1.403	1.659	1.961	2.315	2.732	3.221	3.794	4.466	5.253	7.251	9.978	13.690	18.728	25.548	47.143	86.053	155.443	277.964
36	1.431	1.709	2.040	2.433	2.898	3.450	4.104	4.877	5.792	8.147	11.424	15.968	22.251	30.913	59.136	111.834	209.164	387.037
38	1.460	1.761	2.122	2.556	3.075	3.696	4.439	5.326	6.385	9.154	13.079	18.625	26.437	37.404	74.180	145.340	281.452	538.910
40	1.489	1.814	2.208	2.685	3.262	3.959	4.801	5.816	7.040	10.286	14.974	21.725	31.409	45.259	93.051	188.884	378.721	750.378
42	1.519	1.869	2.297	2.821	3.461	4.241	5.193	6.352	7.762	11.557	17.144	25.339	37.318	54.764	116.723	245.473	509.607	1044.827
44	1.549	1.925	2.390	2.964	3.671	4.543	5.617	6.936	8.557	12.985	19.628	29.556	44.337	66.264	146.418	319.017	685.727	1454.817
46	1.580	1.984	2.487	3.114	3.895	4.867	6.075	7.574	9.434	14.590	22.473	34.474	52.677	80.180	183.666	414.594	922.715	2025.687
48	1.612	2.043	2.587	3.271	4.132	5.214	6.571	8.271	10.401	16.394	25.729	40.211	62.585	97.017	230.391	538.807	1241.605	2820.567
50	1.645	2.105	2.692	3.437	4.384	5.585	7.107	9.033	11.467	18.420	29.457	46.902	74.357	117.391	289.002	700.233	1670.704	3927.357
52	1.678	2.169	2.800	3.611	4.651	5.983	7.687	9.864	12.643	20.697	33.725	54.706	88.344	142.043	362.524	910.023	2248.099	5468.452
54	1.711	2.234	2.913	3.794	4.934	6.409	8.314	10.771	13.939	23.255	38.612	63.809	104.962	171.872	454.751	1182.666	3025.042	7614.272
56	1.746	2.302	3.031	3.986	5.235	6.865	8.992	11.763	15.367	26.129	44.207	74.427	124.705	207.965	570.439	1536.992	4070.497	10602.113
58	1.781	2.372	3.154	4.188	5.553	7.354	9.726	12.845	16.943	29.359	50.613	86.812	148.162	251.638	715.559	1997.475	5477.260	14762.381
60	1.817	2.443	3.281	4.400	5.892	7.878	10.520	14.027	18.679	32.988	57.946	101.257	176.031	304.482	897.597	2595.919	7370.201	20555.140

MONTHLY SALARY TABLE

MONTHLY RATE	ANNUAL	QUARTERLY	WEEKLY	DAILY	HOURLY	¼ HOURLY
$ 300	$ 3,600	$ 900	$ 69.23	$13.85	$1.73	$0.43
325	3,900	975	75.00	15.00	1.87	0.47
350	4,200	1,050	80.77	16.15	2.02	0.51
375	4,500	1,125	86.54	17.31	2.16	0.54
400	4,800	1,200	92.31	18.46	2.31	0.58
425	5,100	1,275	98.08	19.62	2.45	0.61
450	5,400	1,350	103.84	20.77	2.60	0.65
475	5,700	1,425	109.61	21.92	2.74	0.69
500	6,000	1,500	115.38	23.08	2.88	0.72
550	6,600	1,650	126.92	25.38	3.17	0.79
600	7,200	1,800	138.46	27.69	3.46	0.87
650	7,800	1,950	150.00	30.00	3.75	0.94
700	8,400	2,100	161.54	32.31	4.04	1.01
750	9,000	2,250	173.08	34.62	4.33	1.08
800	9,600	2,400	184.61	36.92	4.62	1.16
850	10,200	2,550	196.15	39.23	4.91	1.23
900	10,800	2,700	207.69	41.54	5.19	1.30
950	11,400	2,850	219.23	43.85	5.48	1.37
1,000	12,000	3,000	230.77	46.15	5.77	1.44
1,100	13,200	3,300	253.85	50.77	6.35	1.58
1,200	14,400	3,600	276.93	55.38	6.93	1.73
1,300	15,600	3,900	300.00	60.00	7.50	1.88
1,400	16,800	4,200	323.08	64.61	8.08	2.02
1,500	18,000	4,500	346.15	69.23	8.65	2.16

40 Hours a Week—5 Days of 8 Hours

ANNUAL SALARY TABLE

ANNUAL RATE	QUARTERLY	MONTHLY	WEEKLY	DAILY	HOURLY	¼ HOURLY
$ 5,000	$1,250	$ 416.67	$ 96.15	$19.23	$2.40	$0.60
5,500	1,375	458.33	105.77	21.15	2.64	0.66
6,000	1,500	500.00	115.38	23.08	2.88	0.72
6,500	1,625	541.67	125.00	25.00	3.13	0.78
7,000	1,750	583.33	134.62	26.92	3.37	0.84
7,500	1,875	625.00	144.23	28.85	3.60	0.90
8,000	2,000	666.67	153.85	30.76	3.84	0.96
8,500	2,125	708.33	163.47	32.72	4.09	1.02
9,000	2,250	750.00	173.08	34.62	4.33	1.08
9,500	2,375	791.67	182.70	36.54	4.57	1.14
10,000	2,500	833.33	192.31	38.46	4.81	1.20
11,000	2,750	916.67	211.54	42.31	5.29	1.32
12,000	3,000	1,000.00	230.77	46.15	5.77	1.44
13,000	3,250	1,083.33	250.00	50.00	6.25	1.56
14,000	3,500	1,166.67	269.23	53.84	6.73	1.68
15,000	3,750	1,250.00	288.46	57.69	7.21	1.80
16,000	4,000	1,333.33	307.69	61.53	7.69	1.92
17,000	4,250	1,416.67	326.92	65.38	8.17	2.04
18,000	4,500	1,500.00	346.15	69.23	8.65	2.16
19,000	4,750	1,583.33	365.38	73.07	9.13	2.28
20,000	5,000	1,666.67	384.61	76.92	9.61	2.40

40 Hours a Week—5 Days of 8 Hours

MULTIPLICATION TABLE

To multiply two numbers find one of the numbers along the side of the table and follow this row to the column headed at the top by the other number. Thus $12 \times 17 = 204$

×	2	3	4	5	6	7	8	9	10	11	12	13	14	15	16	17	18	19	20	21	22	23	24	25	26	27	28	29	30
1	2	3	4	5	6	7	8	9	10	11	12	13	14	15	16	17	18	19	20	21	22	23	24	25	26	27	28	29	30
2	4	6	8	10	12	14	16	18	20	22	24	26	28	30	32	34	36	38	40	42	44	46	48	50	52	54	56	58	60
3	6	9	12	15	18	21	24	27	30	33	36	39	42	45	48	51	54	57	60	63	66	69	72	75	78	81	84	87	90
4	8	12	16	20	24	28	32	36	40	44	48	52	56	60	64	68	72	76	80	84	88	92	96	100	104	108	112	116	120
5	10	15	20	25	30	35	40	45	50	55	60	65	70	75	80	85	90	95	100	105	110	115	120	125	130	135	140	145	150
6	12	18	24	30	36	42	48	54	60	66	72	78	84	90	96	102	108	114	120	126	132	138	144	150	156	162	168	174	180
7	14	21	28	35	42	49	56	63	70	77	84	91	98	105	112	119	126	133	140	147	154	161	168	175	182	189	196	203	210
8	16	24	32	40	48	56	64	72	80	88	96	104	112	120	128	136	144	152	160	168	176	184	192	200	208	216	224	232	240
9	18	27	36	45	54	63	72	81	90	99	108	117	126	135	144	153	162	171	180	189	198	207	216	225	234	243	252	261	270
10	20	30	40	50	60	70	80	90	100	110	120	130	140	150	160	170	180	190	200	210	220	230	240	250	260	270	280	290	300
11	22	33	44	55	66	77	88	99	110	121	132	143	154	165	176	187	198	209	220	231	242	253	264	275	286	297	308	319	330
12	24	36	48	60	72	84	96	108	120	132	144	156	168	180	192	204	216	228	240	252	264	276	288	300	312	324	336	348	360
13	26	39	52	65	78	91	104	117	130	143	156	169	182	195	208	221	234	247	260	273	286	299	312	325	338	351	364	377	390
14	28	42	56	70	84	98	112	126	140	154	168	182	196	210	224	238	252	266	280	294	308	322	336	350	364	378	392	406	420
15	30	45	60	75	90	105	120	135	150	165	180	195	210	225	240	255	270	285	300	315	330	345	360	375	390	405	420	435	450
16	32	48	64	80	96	112	128	144	160	176	192	208	224	240	256	272	288	304	320	336	352	368	384	400	416	432	448	464	480
17	34	51	68	85	102	119	136	153	170	187	204	221	238	255	272	289	306	323	340	357	374	391	408	425	442	459	476	493	510
18	36	54	72	90	108	126	144	162	180	198	216	234	252	270	288	306	324	342	360	378	396	414	432	450	468	486	504	522	540
19	38	57	76	95	114	133	152	171	190	209	228	247	266	285	304	323	342	361	380	399	418	437	456	475	494	513	532	551	570
20	40	60	80	100	120	140	160	180	200	220	240	260	280	300	320	340	360	380	400	420	440	460	480	500	520	540	560	580	600
21	42	63	84	105	126	147	168	189	210	231	252	273	294	315	336	357	378	399	420	441	462	483	504	525	546	567	588	609	630
22	44	66	88	110	132	154	176	198	220	242	264	286	308	330	352	374	396	418	440	462	484	506	528	550	572	594	616	638	660
23	46	69	92	115	138	161	184	207	230	253	276	299	322	345	368	391	414	437	460	483	506	529	552	575	598	621	644	667	690
24	48	72	96	120	144	168	192	216	240	264	288	312	336	360	384	408	432	456	480	504	528	552	576	600	624	648	672	696	720
25	50	75	100	125	150	175	200	225	250	275	300	325	350	375	400	425	450	475	500	525	550	575	600	625	650	675	700	725	750
26	52	78	104	130	156	182	208	234	260	286	312	338	364	390	416	442	468	494	520	546	572	598	624	650	676	702	728	754	780
27	54	81	108	135	162	189	216	243	270	297	324	351	378	405	432	459	486	513	540	567	594	621	648	675	702	729	756	783	810
28	56	84	112	140	168	196	224	252	280	308	336	364	392	420	448	476	504	532	560	588	616	644	672	700	728	756	784	812	840
29	58	87	116	145	174	203	232	261	290	319	348	377	406	435	464	493	522	551	580	609	638	667	696	725	754	783	812	841	870
30	60	90	120	150	180	210	240	270	300	330	360	390	420	450	480	510	540	570	600	630	660	690	720	750	780	810	840	870	900

TABLE OF SQUARES, CUBES, SQUARE ROOTS, AND CUBE ROOTS

No.	Square	Cube	Square Root	Cube Root	No.	Square	Cube	Square Root	Cube Root
1	1	1	1.000	1.000	51	2,601	132,651	7.141	3.708
2	4	8	1.414	1.260	52	2,704	140,608	7.211	3.732
3	9	27	1.732	1.442	53	2,809	148,877	7.280	3.756
4	16	64	2.000	1.587	54	2,916	157,464	7.348	3.780
5	25	125	2.236	1.710	55	3,025	166,375	7.416	3.803
6	36	216	2.449	1.817	56	3,136	175,616	7.483	3.826
7	49	343	2.646	1.913	57	3,249	185,193	7.550	3.848
8	64	512	2.828	2.000	58	3,364	195,112	7.616	3.871
9	81	729	3.000	2.080	59	3,481	205,379	7.681	3.893
10	100	1,000	3.162	2.154	60	3,600	216,000	7.746	3.915
11	121	1,331	3.317	2.224	61	3,721	226,981	7.810	3.936
12	144	1,728	3.464	2.289	62	3,844	238,328	7.874	3.958
13	169	2,197	3.606	2.351	63	3,969	250,047	7.937	3.979
14	196	2,744	3.742	2.410	64	4,096	262,144	8.000	4.000
15	225	3,375	3.873	2.466	65	4,225	274,625	8.062	4.021
16	256	4,096	4.000	2.520	66	4,356	287,496	8.124	4.041
17	289	4,913	4.123	2.571	67	4,489	300,763	8.185	4.061
18	324	5,832	4.243	2.621	68	4,624	314,432	8.246	4.082
19	361	6,859	4,359	2.668	69	4,761	328,509	8.307	4.101
20	400	8,000	4.472	2.714	70	4,900	343,000	8.367	4.121
21	441	9,261	4.583	2.759	71	5,041	357,911	8.426	4.141
22	484	10,648	4.690	2.802	72	5,184	373,248	8.485	4.160
23	529	12,167	4.796	2.844	73	5,329	389,017	8.544	4.179
24	576	13,824	4.899	2.884	74	5,476	405,224	8.602	4.198
25	625	15,625	5.000	2.924	75	5,625	421,875	8.660	4.217
26	676	17,576	5.099	2.962	76	5,776	438,976	8.718	4.236
27	729	19,683	5.196	3.000	77	5,929	456,533	8.775	4.254
28	784	21,952	5.292	3.037	78	6,084	474,552	8.832	4.273
29	841	24,389	5.385	3.072	79	6,241	493,039	8.888	4.291
30	900	27,000	5.477	3.107	80	6,400	512,000	8.944	4.309
31	961	29,791	5.568	3.141	81	6,561	531,441	9.000	4.327
32	1,024	32,768	5.657	3.175	82	6,724	551,368	9.055	4.344
33	1,089	35,937	5.745	3.208	83	6,889	571,787	9.110	4.362
34	1,156	39,304	5.831	3.240	84	7,056	592,704	9.165	4.379
35	1,225	42,875	5.916	3.271	85	7,225	614,125	9.219	4.397
36	1,296	46,656	6.000	3.302	86	7,396	636,056	9.274	4.414
37	1,369	50,653	6.083	3.332	87	7,569	658,503	9.327	4.431
38	1,444	54,872	6.164	3.362	88	7,744	681,472	9.381	4.448
39	1,521	59,319	6.245	3.391	89	7,921	704,969	9.434	4.465
40	1,600	64,000	6.325	3.420	90	8,100	729,000	9.487	4.481
41	1,681	68,921	6.403	3.448	91	8,281	753,571	9.539	4.498
42	1,764	74,088	6.481	3.476	92	8,464	778,688	9.592	4.514
43	1,849	79,507	6.557	3.503	93	8,649	804,357	9.644	4.531
44	1,936	85,184	6.633	3.530	94	8,836	830,584	9.695	4.547
45	2,025	91,125	6.708	3.557	95	9,025	857,375	9.747	4.563
46	2,116	97,336	6.782	3.583	96	9,216	884,736	9.798	4.579
47	2,209	103,823	6.856	3.609	97	9,409	912,673	9.849	4.595
48	2,304	110,592	6.928	3.634	98	9,604	941,192	9.899	4.610
49	2.401	117,649	7.000	3.659	99	9,801	970,299	9.950	4.626
50	2,500	125,000	7.071	3.684	100	10,000	1,000,000	10,000	4.642

INVESTMENT AND MONETARY GLOSSARY

ADR American Depository Receipt. This receipt is issued by various American banks for shares of a stock in a foreign company. The stock certificates are deposited by the bank and the **ADR's** are traded in their place.

ANNUITY A contract with an insurance company to pay you a fixed amount periodically (monthly, yearly, etc.) over a given period of time or for life.

ARBITRAGE The purchase of an asset in one market accompanied by a simultaneous sale of the same (or a similar asset in a different market, to take advantage of differences in price. The arbitrage principle can be applied to simultaneous buying and selling of related currencies, commodities, or securities, the same commodity with different delivery dates, etc.

BALANCE OF PAYMENTS A nation's exports less its imports.

BANKNOTE A unit of currency in paper form, as opposed to a bank deposit.

BANKNOTE A unit of currency in paper form, as opposed to a bank deposit.

BARTER The trading of one commodity for another; in modern usage, any exchange that doesn't involve the use of money or money substitutes.

BID PRICE The price at which a dealer or trader offers to buy.

BLACK MARKET A free market operating without the government's legal sanction.

BULLION Refined bars of gold or silver.

BULL MARKET OR BULLISH When prices are going up in value, or are expected to.

CALL OPTION The right to buy a given asset at a fixed price any time to a specified date.

CARRYING CHARGES In futures trading, the difference between the spot price and a future price—usually equal to the cost of interest and storage for the period of time involved.

CASH:(1)Money substitutes in paper form. (2) The absence of credit.

CENTRAL BANK An agency created by a government to issue its currency and to supervise the nation's banking system.

CERTIFICATE OF DEPOSIT A deposit with a fixed time period and a fixed rate of interest.

COIN Real money (gold or silver) transformed into a recognizable shape and weight in order to facilitate exchange.

CONSERVATIVE Involving a minimum of risk.

CONTENT The metal in a coin or token.

CONVERTIBILITY The metal in a coin or token.

CONVERTIBILITY The ability to receive gold in exchange for currency, at a stated rate of exchange, from the agency that issued the currency.

CURRENCY Correctly, receipts for real money in storage; in modern practice, any money substitues in use—even if not backed by real money (synonymous with *paper money*).

CURRENT ACCOUNT A bank deposit that can be withdrawn by the depositor at any time.

DEFLATION A decrease in the amount of money substitutes that have been issued in excess of the real money in storage. (The opposite of *inflation*).

DEMAND DEPOSIT A bank deposit that can be withdrawn by the depositor at any time.

DEPOSIT ACCOUNT A bank deposit in which interest is earned and withrawals are limited.

DEPRESSION A period during which most people are no longer able to maintain their previous standards of living. It is caused by the General Market's attempts to cleanse itself of the misguided uses of resources that have been encouraged by government intervention to productive activity more desired by consumers.

DEVALUATION Repudiation of the government's promise to redeem its money substitutes at the stated rate of exchange, causing a new rate for convertibility.

DIRTY FLOAT A period during which the government intervenes in the foreign exchange market while claiming that it isn't. (See also *floating exchanges rates* and *fixed exchange rates.*)

DOWNSIDE RISK The possible depth to which the price of an investment can drop.

ECONOMICS The study that seeks to allocate limited resources in ways that will provide maximum happiness (whether on a personal, commercial, national, or international scale); the art of making decisions.

ENTREPRENEUR An individual who forecasts future demand for a product or service and arranges a business enterprise to respond to that demand.

EQUITY The value of an investment after deduction of all claims against it— loan amount, interest, commissions, and any other fees.

EUROCURRENCY Currency that is circulating outside the nation where it was issued.

EXCHANGE CONTROLS Governmental regulations limiting or prohibiting the exporting or importing of currencies.

EXCHANGE RATE The price of a currency as expressed in units of another currency. (Synonymous with *foreign exchange rate.*)

FACE VALUE The legal tender value of a coin, toke, or banknote. On bonds, the amount that will be paid to the holder at maturity.

FIAT MONEY The extent to which bullion is pure gold or silver to back it with.

FINESS The extent to which bullion is pure gold or silver, expressed as a decimal of the total gross weight involved. For example, gold bullion of .995 fineness means that 99.5% of the total weight is pure gold.

FIXED DEPOSIT ACCOUNT A bank deposit for a fixed period of time.

FIXED EXCHANGE RATES Currency exchange rates that are prevented from fluctuating by governmental purchases and sales of the currencies involved.

FLOATING EXCHANGE RATES Currency exchange rates that fluctuate freely because governments are *not* stabilizing the rates through purchases and sales. (See *dirty float* and *fixed exchange rates*.)

FLUCTUATION A change in price—upward or downward.

FOREIGN EXCHANGE RATE The price of a currency as expressed in units of another currency. (Synonymous with *exchange rate*.)

FRACTIONAL RESERVE BANKING A banking system in which money that is payable upon demand to depositors is lent to others by the bank; in other words, a system in which the bank doesn't maintain 100% reserves against demand deposits.

FREE MARKET A market free of governmental intervention.

FUTURES CONTRACT a contract for delivery of a commodity or currency in the future at a price determined in the present.

GAP A condition created on a price graph when the prices for one day's trading do not overlap the previous day's range.

GOVERNMENT The institution of greatest economic, political, and police power in a given area.

GRAM Used in gold weights; there are 31.1042 grams to a troy ounce; one gram = 03215 troy ounces. A kilogram in 1,000 grams; there are 1,000 milligrams to a gram.

HARD MONEY Silver and gold.

INCOME (INVESTMENT) Dividends or interest received from an investment.

INCONVERTIBILITY The inability to receive gold in exchange for currency from the agency that issued the currency.

INFLATION An increase in money substitutes above the stored stock of real money; the conterfeiting of money receipts.

INFLATIONARY DEPRESSION A depression within a period of inflation.

LEGAL TENDER A form of money that an individual is legally required to accept in payment of debts.

LEVERAGE In investments, the ability to purchase more than a monetary investment could purchase on a cash basis.

LIQUIDATION: Normally, the sale of an investment. With regard to depressions, *liquidation* refers to the acceptance of losses and the closing of businesses that existed only because of the miscalculations caused by inflation.

LIQUIDITY The availability of spending money.

LONG The expectation that a price will go up; buying before selling. (See also *short*).

LOT In gold coins, the basic unit of trading. A lot contains 100 British sovereigns, 30 Mexican 50-peso pieces, or 20 U.S. double eagles.

MARGIN In a margin account, the amount of one's equity expressed as a percentage of the total current market value of the investment; also, it can refer to the amount of cash equity.

MARGIN ACCOUNT An investment account in which the investment purchase is increased by borrowing money and using the investment as collateral.

MARGIN CALL In a margin account, a request by the lender for the borrower to make a payment on his loan.

MARGIN SALE A sale forced by margin call conditions.

MARKET (1) A group of transactions integrated by geography or items traded. (2) An opportunity to exchange.

MARKET-MAKER A *dealer* who continually offers to buy and sell a given investment.

MARKETABLE Salable in liquid market. (See also *Liquidity*.)

MATURITY The date on which a contractual obligation such as repayment of a bond) falls due.

MONETARY INFLATION An increase in the *money supply*.

MONEY An asset that is generally accepted in exchange with the intention of trading it for something else; normally, usage is confined to gold, bank notes, bank deposits, coins, or tokens.

MONEY MARKET FUND A *mutual fund* that invests only in short-term interest-earning securities.

MONEY MARKET PAPER Easily marketable short-term notes and bills carrying little risk of default.

MONEY SUPPLY Currency held outside of the commercial marketplace.

OPTION The privilege to buy or sell something at a specific price within a specified time.

OUT OF THE MONEY For an *option* (or a *warrant*), the condition that exists when the price of the *underlying investment* is lower than the striking price of the option.

PAR (1) See *Par value.* (2) Equal in value.

PAR VALUE The nominal or face value of a security or currency. (A currency is often referred to as being at par value when it is trading at the price announced as official by the government.)

PERMANENT PORTFOLIO An assortment of ivestments that remains unchanged from year to year.

PORTFOLIO An assortment of investments held by an individual or company.

POWER OF ATTORNEY *Signature authority.*

PREMIUM (1) The amount by which a security is priced above its *face value, book value,* or inherent value. (2) The amount by which the *forward price* exceeds the *spot price.*

PRIME RATE The interest rate charged by commercial banks to their best customers.

PUBLIC MARKET An investment market in which most relevant information is publicly available.

PUBLICLY TRADED INVESTMENT FUND A *closed-end investment company.*

PURCHASING POWER The value of a unit of money or other asset, measured by the quantity of goods and services it will purchase.

PURCHASING POWER PARITY The exchange rate at which a country's price level is equivalent to price levels in other countries.

PURCHASING POWER PARITY THEORY The system of currency forecasting that maintains that exchange rates will gravitate toward their *purchasing power parities.*

PUT OPTION The right to sell a given asset at a fixed price any time prior to a specified date.

RATIO SCALE On a graph drawn to a ratio scale, a given percentage change in value will cover the same vertical distance, no matter at what level it occurs—so that the significance of the change is graphically illustrated. On a *linear scale,* a given absolute change will cover the same vertical distance, no matter at what level it occurs.

REDEMPTION The repurchase of a security by by its issuer.

RESERVE An allocation of capital for possbile losses or to meet a statutory requirement.

RESISTANCE LEVEL An investment price level at which an unusually large volume of selling is expected.

RESTRIKE A coin that was minted after the date marked, but is otherwise genuine.

RUNAWAY INFLATION A period of intense inflation in which vast "paper money" increases cause all retail prices to zoom upward. During this inflationary period prices can increase daily. As bad as inflation is today (1981), we are not yet in a true state of runaway inflation.

SHORT The expectation that a price will drop; the sale of a commodity the seller doesn't own, with the exception of buying the commodity at a lower price later. (See also *long.*)

SPECIAL DRAWING RIGHTS (SDRs) A currency issued by the International Monetary Fund, used only by governments in place of gold as a monetary reserve.

SPECIE Gold or silver.

SPECULATIVE Involving more than a minimum of risk.

SPOT PRICE The price charged in a sale made for delivery today—as opposed to a price quoted for future delivery.

SUBSIDY Payment to an individual or a company by other than a customer or investor; or a purchase at a price higher than the market price; or a loan that doesn't carry a rate of interest commensurate with normal marketplace interest for the risk involved.

SWAPS An arrangement by which one government borrows another government's currency in order to buy its own currency in the marketplace—in order to keep its own currency from sinking in price.

TAX Property coercively taken from its owner by a government.

TAX HAVEN A country where government offers tax advantages to foreigners. Usually in the hopes that wealthy foreigners will come and help boost the economy.

TECHNICAL ANALYSIS A system, usually related to the stock market, in which supply and demand factors are considered.

TECHNOLOGY The increase of productive output from a given unit of human effort—through the use of machines or improved skills.

TERM INSURSANCE Insurance in which the benefits are payable only upon the death of the insured.

TIME DEPOSIT A bank deposit that isn't payable on demand.

TOKEN A money substitute in metallic form (includes gold and silver if the legal tender face value of the token is considerably above the market value of the gold or silver content).

TON, METRIC See *Gram.*

TRADE BALANCE A nation's product exports less its product imports. (See also *Balance of payments* and *Current account.*)

TRADING Buying and/or selling.

TREND A persistent movement in one direction.

TROY OUNCE The unit of weight used to measure gold and silver. One troy ounce equals 1.097 avoirdupois ounces.

TRUST ACCOUNT A **Discretionary** account.

UNDERLYING INVESTMENT For an *option* (or a *warrant* or other *convertible security*), the investment for which the option provides the right of purchase or sale.

UNEARNED INCOME Interest, dividends, rents, and royalties, when measuring taxable income.

UPSIDE POTENTIAL The probability of an increase in price, and its potential extent.

UPVALUATION (Colloquial) The opposite of a *devaluation;* a *revaluation.*

VALUE DATE The date on which payment is considered to have been made, and from which interest charges will be computed.

VARIABLE PORTFOLIO An assortment of investments that is altered as investment prospects change.

WARRANT An option to purchase a share of stock at a fixed price until a specified date. (A warrant differs from a *call option* in that a warrant is issued by the company whose stock is involved.)

WEAK HANDS Investors holding a given investment who are prone to be easily influenced in their trading by short-term trends or events.

WEALTH Resources that can be used or sold.

THE
NEW WEBSTER'S
Handbook
of
Practical
Information

Donald O. Bolander, M.A., Litt. D.

LEXICON PUBLICATIONS, INC.

Chapter 1

EFFECTIVE LETTER WRITING

In commerce and industry, there are three kinds of contacts between business firms and their customers, suppliers, and others — *personal contacts, telephone calls,* and *letters.* By far the majority of business contacts are made by letter!

But good letter writing is equally important for those in education, government, fund-raising and other private organizations, clubs, church groups, and many others.

In the pages that follow you will be given a solid working knowledge of good letter writing. You will easily and quickly be able to understand the principles and techniques presented. However, you must then put them into practice in your own work or activities.

EVERY LETTER A SELLING LETTER

First of all, remember that your letters represent you, your company, or your organization to the recipient or reader. If the person has not met or talked with you, his or her opinion of you or your organization depends on the way they react to your letter.

If the reaction is favorable, you have sold yourself to the person. If the reaction is negative, you have not sold the reader your idea.

The fundamental principle of good letter writing, then, is this: **Every letter is a selling letter.** The aim of every letter is to sell one or more ideas. The one idea that should be included and sold in every letter is *good will.* Additional ideas included in the letter will depend upon the writer's purpose.

Of course, certain business letters are specifically called sales letters. They are designed to get an order or to aid in getting an order for some product or service. In the average business organization, sales letters are considered the most important of all. But consider the selling problem of the writer who must refuse an adjustment, refuse credit, or demand payment, but who still wants to retain the good will of the customer. He, indeed, has a difficult problem.

But letters other than business letters must sell, too. Fund-raising letters must convince the reader to send in a contribution. Letters from a club or other organization may be to sell the member on attending the next meeting or perhaps just to convey information. But even so, the letters are selling the value of the organization, its benefits, the pride the member can feel in the group.

Keep in mind, then, that all letters should have the aim of being silent salesmen of good will, but in addition a letter will usually include other ideas. How does a successful letter sell its ideas? It does so in two ways: first by its *appearance,* and second by its *contents.*

APPEARANCE OF THE LETTER

Letters, like salesmen and window displays, depend upon their appearance for a favorable first impression. If a letter is slovenly, carelessly written, or unattractive, it gives the same impression as a salesman with unshined shoes and unpressed clothes. If the appearance is not attractive, the potential customer may reject the messenger — whether by salesman or letter — before he hears or reads the message.

Based on the principle that every letter is a selling letter, the first rule of effective letter writing is that *the letter must be pleasing in appearance and correct in form.*

The appearance of your letter depends upon many things. The color and quality of stationery, the way the letter is set on the page, its form, the perfection of the typing — all these create the fleeting, but important, first impression.

So that you may recognize the main features of good mechanical layout of a letter, they are discussed briefly here. This discussion applies to all correspondence as well as business letters.

Page Arrangement:

1. A letter should be framed within its margins, with narrow margins for a long letter and wide margins for a short letter.

2. There should be a little more space at the bottom than at the top of a typed letter to balance it properly, since the optical center of a page is slightly higher than the actual center.

3. The date should be placed close to the body of the letter rather than near the letterhead, either four or six spaces above the inside address, depending upon the length of the letter.

4. If a letter is more than one page, the heading of each subsequent page should show the name of the recipient, the page number, and the date as follows:

Mr. H. J. James   Page 2   June 30, 19___

5. Single spacing between lines is normally used rather than double spacing because single spacing is more economical and more attractive. When single spacing is used, two spaces are left between paragraphs.

Letter Styles:

As mentioned, a part of the success of any letter is its appearance. On the pages which follow, types of letter layout or format are shown. The *full-block* and *modified-block* are the most widely used. However, the *simplified* form is often used particularly when the letter is not addressed to a specific person.

Note: In business, a company may have a standard format which they want all typists to use. If so, follow company instructions.

Full Block Format

```
_____(Date)

_____
_____(Inside Address)
_____
_____: (Salutation)

_____
_____
_____(Body)_____
_____
_____
_____(Body con't)_____
_____, (Complimentary Close)

_____(Signature)

____(Typist's initials)
____(Enclosure or cc: line)
```

The *full-block format* starts all writing at the left-hand margin. This makes it unnecessary to set tab stops for indenting the date line and the complimentary close. A colon is placed after the salutation and a comma is placed after the complimentary close.

Note: The above sample layout illustrates the typed portion only. This typed portion, of course, would be on a letterhead with white margins left, right, and bottom.

Modified Block Format

```
                    (Date) _____

_____
_____(Inside Address)
_____
_____: (Salutation)

_____
_____
_____(Body)_____
_____
_____
_____(Body con't)_____
(Complimentary Close) _____

            (Signature) _____

____(Typist's Initials)
____(Enclosure or cc: line)
```

In the *modified-block format,* the date line and complimentary close and signature line are indented to the right. All other lines start flush left.

Note: Some writers also indent the first line of each paragraph five spaces. This is called *mixed style.*

Simplified Format

```
_____(Date)

_____
_____(Inside Address)
_____

_____(Subject    or    Attention
          Line)
_____
_____(Body)_____
_____
_____(Body con't)_____
_____

_____(Signature Line-underline)
_____(Typed Name and Title)

____(Typist's Initials)
____(Enclosure or cc: line)
```

The *simplified format* is similar to the full-block format in that all items begin at the left margin. The salutation is replaced by a subject line or an attention line; e.g., Attention: Accounts Receivable Department.

OTHER LETTER ELEMENTS

Punctuation — The most widely-accepted style of punctuation uses no end punctuation for the date and address but retains the colon after the salutation and the comma after the complimentary close. Use this punctuation unless your company specifies otherwise. For complete punctuation rules, see the *Punctuation Rules* section of this handbook.

Postscripts — If you want to add a friendly personal comment or reminder as a handwritten postscript to a typed letter, by all means do so. Typewritten postscripts, although they should not be overused, are permissible and actually are very effective when used judiciously. Start the postscript at the bottom of the letter, three or four spaces below the signature line. Place it even with the left-hand margin or indent to conform with the other paragraphs.

Abbreviations — Good form forbids the use of abbreviations in the date line (Sept. 26, 19—) or in the address (St., W., Co.). Even though it takes a little more time to write out Street, West, and Company, the appearance of your letter is important enough to merit the extra effort. There is one exception to this no-abbreviation rule. If the corporate name of the company you are addressing contains the abbreviation *Co.* or *Inc.*, use it. Always use such widely accepted abbreviations as *Mr., Mrs., Jr., Sr., Dr., D.C.,* and *St.* as in *St. Louis.* For more information, see the *Rules for Abbreviations* sections of this handbook.

Spelling — Be extremely careful to spell correctly the name of either a company or an individual to whom a letter is addressed. Verify spellings, if you have the slightest doubt.

Note: Elsewhere in this book you will find a complete presentation of *Spelling Rules,* a listing of commonly *Misspelled Words,* plus a special listing of *Words Confused and Misused.*

Spelling includes the correct division of words at the end of lines. The pronounciation of words governs their division or syllabication. Your reader might well be bewildered by such incorrect division as *daug-hter, cynical, progr-ess.*

Note: See the section on *Word Division* in this book.

Readability — Does your letter look inviting and easy to read? It won't, if it is composed of long, solid, difficult-looking paragraphs. Vary the length of your paragraphs. Usually they should not exceed ten lines. Don't be afraid of a one-sentence or two-line paragraph, especially if you want an important idea to stand out. Your sentences, too, should be short enough to read easily.

CONTENTS OF THE LETTER

The appearance of your letter is important because from it your reader gets his first impression of you and your message. But the contents are even more important in making sure that every letter is a selling letter.

Fundamentally, your letters will sell *only if they are written from the other person's point of view* rather than from your own. Much has been said and written — and properly so — about the "you" attitude in business letters, and it is equally important in social correspondence. There are still far too many letters which begin almost every paragraph with *I* or *we* because the writer is thinking of himself rather than the reader.

BE COURTEOUS AND CONSIDERATE

The "you" attitude is not merely an appeal to vanity or pride. If it were, it would be insincere and ineffective. The real "you" attitude is the ability to put yourself in the other person's place and to govern your actions — or write your letters — accordingly. This assures the sincerity that is essential to the effectiveness of any letter.

To accomplish your aim of making every letter a selling letter, therefore, your second rule is: *Be courteous and considerate.*

Certain words or phrases should never appear in a courteous, considerate letter. They invariably cause resentment and hostility by connotation, if not by denotation. Consider the words *you claim* or *your claim, you state* or *your assertion.* If you use these words, you might as well add, *but we don't believe you,* for that is the impression you will give.

Obviously is another word to shun as you would poison ivy, for it almost always has a

bad effect on the reader. Here is an example from an adjustment letter which lost a valuable customer for a retail store: "Obviously you did not read our last letter carefully or you would have understood that the credit would be shown on next month's bill."

It didn't matter to the customer that her complaint was unjustified and that the adjustment had been made. She had been insulted by a discourteous correspondent who, in effect, had said, "If you're so stupid that you can't understand what we write, we'll just have to point out that *obviously* the credit will appear next month." The customer retaliated by sending back her credit card. Since her account had averaged more than $100 a month, this was truly an expensive letter.

How much better it would have been to say, "Our last letter evidently was not clearly expressed. We are glad to assure you that the credit will be shown on next month's bill. Thank you for writing us."

Evidently, apparently, and *manifestly* are other adverbs which should be used with care. Although you can safely say, *we evidently* or *we apparently,* don't say, *you evidently* or *you apparently.* Keep the other person's viewpoint in mind, and your letters will be courteous and considerate.

"Thank you" is one phrase that never becomes trite. You may say thank you in nine letters out of ten, and yet never sound stale to your reader. It is one positive way of putting the you before the I in your letters. How many letters do you receive or write which begin, "We have your letter . . . ." or "In response to your letter of . . . ." or even "On receipt of your letter . . . ."? If it is necessary to acknowledge the receipt of a letter — and in business it is sometimes helpful in keeping files in proper order — why not simply say, "Thank you for your letter of . . . ." or "Thank you for writing us about . . . ."?

This simple, natural way of expressing friendly appreciation illustrates the third rule in making every letter a selling letter: *Be informal and natural.*

BE INFORMAL AND NATURAL

There are varying degrees of formality in both written and spoken communication. Conversation is the most informal kind of spoken communication, and letters should be the most informal written communication. Personal letters are even more informal than business letters.

Conversation does not require the same degree of organization as the letter, and it has the added advantage of immediate give-and-take. The letter is documentary in nature (although it should never read like a legal document) and must await a reply. Although you cannot say everything in a letter that you would in conversation (the "Hi ya, Joe, whadda yu know'' type conversation), you might safely follow this rule: If you wouldn't say it, don't write it — but don't write everything you'd say. Don't let the idea of writing become too high a hurdle. What you are really doing is *talking* to the other person — on paper.

TRITE WORDS AND PHRASES

To be natural and informal, watch your letters carefully until you have eliminated all the cliches — hackneyed, trite, old-fashioned words and phrases — which make a letter sound stilted and formal. You would never dream of using such a vocabulary if you were talking to the other person.

Would you in talking, for instance, use such obsequious language as *your kind favor, your esteemed favor, your obedient servant,* or *I beg to state*? These are hangovers from the nineteenth century. Many a modern, progressive business fails to sell its ideas by letter because of antiquated phraseology. In social correspondence as well, the artificially exaggerated expressions of courtesy have given way to friendly informality.

Approach all your correspondence with an analytical mind. If a word or phrase jars you, question its importance and meaningfulness. Ask yourself if you would use it in talking with the other person. If you would not, the word probably would not be effective in a letter, Apply the "Would I say it?" test with judgment, of course, remembering that you do not want your letters — except the most personal — to be chatty or intimate. You merely want them to be friendly and informal.

BE CLEAR AND CONCISE

Have your facts clearly in mind before starting to write. Otherwise, your reader may misunderstand, necessitating additional, expensive correspondence. The second letter is always more difficult to write, for it is harder to explain a misunderstanding which has arisen because of confused information than it is to say it right the first time.

The fourth general rule, then, to make every letter a selling letter is: *Be clear and concise.*

Take time to analyze the situation before you begin. Ask yourself, "What do I have to say?" Then marshal your facts, mentally or by penciled notation, and put your ideas in logical order. Finally, express what you have to say clearly and simply. When you read your mail, you may find it helpful to put small dots or question marks or even brief penciled notes in the margin opposite the sentences you want to answer. Then, when you are ready to reply, you will not need to reread the letter word for word.

If you are explaining or questioning several different items on a bill, or a number of insurance policies, or various steps in assembling a piece of machinery, use one paragraph for each item or each stem.

Test the clarity of your letter by reading it from the other person's viewpoint before you mail it. Does it answer every question? Does it anticipate those which might result from this correspondence? Is the information given in simple, clear, concise language?

Concise does not mean abrupt or curt. By definition, it means to express much in a few words. It means, therefore, that you should express your thoughts completely but briefly. Do not be disturbed if you find that a letter must be long to cover the information completely. A letter is not ineffective merely because it is long. It is ineffective if it is incomplete. Short letters are manifestly more economical than long ones, but don't make a letter short at the expense of courtesy or completeness.

For conciseness, try to eliminate from your letter the "cluttering" words — words which do not advance an idea. If you are doubtful of a word or phrase, ask yourself, "Does it advance the idea or hinder its advancement?" If it does not advance the idea, drop it! You will find that your ideas are more clearly expressed and your letters more interesting and effective.

INTRODUCTIONS AND CONCLUSIONS

An important aspect of letter writing is how to open and close your letter. Frequently you hear letter writers exclaim, "If I could just get started, I'd be all right" or "I wish I knew how to end this thing." It is true that a lame beginning or ending will detract from the effectiveness of a letter. A poor beginning fails to capture attention — the first essential of a good letter as well as a good speech. A weak ending will leave the other person feeling let down instead of stimulated to action as he should be.

TYPES OF OPENING SENTENCES

Here are some suggestions that will aid you in writing effective openings:

"Thank You" Opening — Like the salesman, you want to make your first words count. The beginning of a letter is the most important place to express the "you" attitude, and there is no better "you" than a "thank you." For example, *Thank you for your letter asking for information about our computer software programs.*

Positive Opening — Shun negative ideas in your openings, and minimize them as much as possible throughout your letter. Don't open a letter with *We are sorry to learn* or *It was most unfortunate.* For every negative there is a positive, and if you have made a mistake, the other person will be glad to know it has been corrected. Instead of apologizing, make positive statements such as *You will be glad to know* or *Fortunately, we were able to.*

Summary Opening — Try the journalistic approach. Summarize the facts or give the main idea in your opening sentence as is done in this example: *The adjustment you requested in your letter of October 10 has been made, and the credit will appear on your November bill.*

Question Opening — Don't be afraid to open with a question if it is natural and sensible to do so. For example, *Have you had an opportunity to consider the proposition we outlined in our letter of April 10?*

"Please" Opening — Use a "please" opening occasionally when it is important that you have immediate action. *Please give us the dates of the bills which are past due.* Or, *Please tell us when you returned the merchandise referred to in your letter of March 5 so that we can check our records.*

"If" Opening — Does an "if" opening seem unusual? Because it is different, it is frequently effective in arousing attention and stimulating action. Watch for opportunities to use the "if" opening, as shown in these examples: *If you will give us the name of the salesman you wrote us about last week, we will check the order with him.* Or, *If you can come in to our office next week, we shall be glad to talk with you about the proposition you suggested in your letter.*

Remember that every sentence in your letter is important, but none is more important than the first sentence. It is there that you gain or lose the reader's interest.

TYPES OF CLOSING SENTENCES

Of only secondary importance to the opening is the closing sentence. Here is where salesmen apply what is known as the "hook," a slang term meaning *stimulus to action.* Like a firecracker which fails to explode, a letter which fizzles out is a "dud." Don't spoil the effectiveness of a letter with an ending that fizzles.

Use definite, to-the-point statements that are not high pressure but emphatic enough to induce action. Here is the place where the word *we* can be used to advantage. *As soon as we hear from you, we will,* or *If we can answer any questions, we shall be glad to do so.*

Avoid long, vague generalizations and negatives. Be sure to leave a clear idea of what you expect. You can do this by calling attention to some idea previously expressed, or by summarizing the main purpose of the letter, or by saving your most important idea for the last, as a climax to your letter.

Use questions. A question may formulate a courteous request such as, *Will you please give us this information before the end of the week?* Or, *Will you please handle this promptly?* Other questions might be, *Can you arrange to handle this shipment?* or *What is your opinion?* You can change the courteous request to a courteous demand by changing from the interrogative to the imperative mood. *Please give us this information* or *Please handle this.*

Avoid connections. The last sentence of your letter should never be connected with the complimentary close. Do not say, *Awaiting your reply, we are — Yours very truly.* It is also incorrect to say, *With best wishes, we are,* or *With kindest regards, we are.*

Because *Please accept my best wishes* sounds stilted, try to find some other friendly closing idea. Occasionally, when letter writers are close friends, just the words *best wishes* or *best regards* may be used as a breezy, personal closing. Such phrases should never take the place of the complimentary close in a business letter. They should be placed as a separate, final paragraph.

ANALYZING LETTERS

Now that you have considered the general principles of letter writing, you are ready to analyze and evaluate specific types of correspondence, both business and social. The most effective method of analysis is to ask questions that will train you to detect the good and bad points of any letter.

The following check list gives a series of questions that you should ask yourself about the specific letter which you are analyzing. This list is called the Four-A Check List since, when you are writing, you are concerned with the *aim, appearance, accuracy,* and *attitude* of a letter.

FOUR-A CHECK LIST
For Business and Social Letters

Aim
  a. What are the specific purposes of the letter?
  b. Does it accomplish these purposes?
Appearance
  c. Is the letter pleasing in appearance?
  d. Is it correct and consistent in mechanics according to the style used?
Accuracy
  e. Is the letter grammatical?
  f. Are spelling, syllabication, capitalization, punctuation, and abbreviations correct?
  g. Are the sentences and paragraphs varied in length?
  h. Are the ideas presented in logical order?
  i. Is the letter clear and concise? Does it include any irrelevant ideas or use any unnecessary words?
  j. Is the choice of words fully effective?
Attitude
  k. Does the letter have the "you" attitude — not merely through the use of the pronoun "you" but through ideas expressed from the other person's viewpoint?
  l. Does the letter have words that are negative or words that will have a bad effect on the reader?
  m. Does it include, whenever necessary, courteous expressions of thanks, appreciation, etc?
  n. Are trite or old-fashioned words and phrases avoided?
  o. Is the letter informal and natural in tone?
  p. Is abrupt or curt wording avoided?

  q. Does the closing thought leave the reader with the desired idea?

Using the Check List

You will find that the questions in the Four-A Check List are easy to apply to any letter. When you begin to analyze your letters, have the check list open in front of you and check your letter carefully against each question in the list. You will soon be able to detect faults almost automatically and will need to refer to the list only occasionally.

LETTER PARTS

As discussed earlier in this section, the appearance of your letter creates either a favorable or unfavorable impression. Here is a brief explanation of the specific parts of a letter so that your letters conform to generally accepted usages.

Sender's Address: If you are writing on printed stationary, your name and address or the name of your company or organization is given on the letterhead. However, if you are writing a personal letter on plain paper, place your address immediately above the date line.

670 Walnut Street
Little Falls, NJ 07424
June 27, 19—

Date Line: Do not abbreviate dates. Spell out the month and do not use ordinals (*nd, rd, st, th*). Do not use the military version except in military correspondence.

No: 9/21/87
No: Sept. 21st, 1987
No: 21 September 87 (military)
Yes: September 21, 1987

Receiver's Address: Use the proper complimentary title (*Mr., Mrs., Ms., Dr.*) with the person's name, his or her position if known, and the name of the company or organization followed by the complete address.

Mr. Robert Costantini
Director of Publications
Hexagon Publishers, Inc.
1000 Lexington Avenue
New York, NY 10018

Apartment or suite numbers may be placed either on the same line with the address or if the address is too long, on a separate line immediately above it.

Note 1: For titles of educational, governmental, military, and religious dignitaries, see the *Forms of Address* section of this book.

Note 2: If writing to an individual at a home address, only the name and address would be given.

Salutations: The salutation should follow two

spaces after the inside address. It is generally followed by a colon, but some writers omit the colon. The choice of the salutation depends on the relationship with the reader. Unless you know the reader quite well, use a moderately dignified salutation.

Recommended Salutations
Dear Mr. Henderson:
Dear Mrs. Chambers:
Dear Ms. Risner:

Salutations To Be Avoided
Dear Sir: Dear Madam:
Gentlemen: Mesdames:

If you are not writing to a specific person, use a *subject* line or *attention* line as explained for the simplified letter format.

Instead of a salutation some modern writers recommend an opening *attention getting phrase* which is generally part of the first sentence as follows:

It was great seeing you again, Tom . . .
. . . at the annual convention.

Thank you for the time . . .
. . . you gave me yesterday, Mr. Henderson, to review my qualifications.

It's true, Mrs. Jordan,
— It was our error. Your account has not been credited.

Body of the Letter: Begin the body of the letter two spaces below the salutation or subject line. Unless the letter is very brief, it should be single-spaced with a double space between paragraphs. If double spacing is used, the first line of each paragraph should be indented.

Complimentary Close: Complimentary closes should be followed by commas, capitalizing only the first word. Here are some accepted closes.

Sincerely,   Cordially,
Sincerely yours,   Best regards,
Very truly yours, Regards,

The close *Respectfully yours* may be used for a top business executive, government official, or church dignitary. Other complimentary closes are given in the *Forms of Address* section of this book.

Signature and Writers Identification: Type the writer's name and title immediately below the complimentary close. Leave three to five spaces for the signature.

Sincerely yours,

Henry K. Peters
Director of Public Relations

Typist's Initials: The initials should be placed two spaces below the writer's title or name and flush left with the margin. The writer's initials need not be shown.

No: HKP: dob   *Yes*: dob

Enclosure Line: Use an enclosure line when other items are included in the letter. If there is more than one enclosure indicate the number. Place the enclosure line two spaces below the typist's initials.

Enclosure   Enclosures (3)

Carbon Copy Notation: If copies of the letter are being sent to other people note their names one or two spaces (depending on letter length) below the typist's initials or enclosure line. If necessary, give the person's title so the addressee knows his identity.

cc: Mr. Harry Rigio   cc: Walter Brown
    Ms. Jane Friedlan   Sales Coordinator

Chapter 2

FORMS OF ADDRESS

The following are preferred forms and correct use of titles:

Business Names and Titles

1. All titles in a business address should be capitalized. The "Zip" code should be placed two spaces after the state name without separating punctuation. Do not abbreviate *Company* or *Incorporated* unless the firm uses the abbreviations on its official letterhead.

Mr. John Rae, President
Graphic Products, Inc.
Monroe, Michigan 48048

Mr. Richard Greene
Chairman of the Board
General Dynamics Company
Quincy, Maine 02169

2. An educational or business title may be used with a personal title or degree for the same person.

Dr. Jay Howard
Director of Research
Dexter Electronics, Inc.

Thruman Hardwick, Ph.D.
Professor of History
Cornell University

3. A position title may be placed either on the same line, or on a separate line, based on length and convenience.

Mr. James Gordon, Superintendent
Riverdale Public Schools
Riverdale, Illinois

Mr. James Gordon
Superintendent of Schools
Riverdale, Illinois

4. The salutation *Gentlemen* may be used

if the letter is not addressed to a specific person within the company, even though the letter is marked for the attention of that person.

Gould Incorporated
Chicago, Illinois
   Attention: Mr. Andrew Williams
Gentlemen:

Titles for Addressing Men

1. The title *Mr.* always precedes the name when addressing letters to a man, if he has no professional title.

Mr. Gary Jones
   or
Mr. Gary Jones, Manager

Salutation: Dear Sir:
   or
Dear Mr. Jones:

2. For two or more men who have no professional title, *Mr.* should precede each name.

Mr. James North
Mr. Leo James

Salutation: Dear Sirs:
   or
Gentlemen:

3. The proper title for a boy under 12 is *Master*. From ages 12 to 18 usually no title is used. *Mr.* becomes the correct title at age 18.

Master Tommy Burns
Masters Tommy and Jim Burns

Salutation: Dear Tommy and Jim:

4. Designations such as Sr., Jr., III, etc., should be capitalized and usually are separated from the name by commas.

Mr. R.J. Hooker, Sr.
Peter Brady, Jr., Ph.D.
Dr. Arnold Smith, III
Mr. Raymond Gallo, Sr., President

Titles for Professional Men and Women

1. The title *Doctor* is designated for persons who have attained that degree.

Martin Gould, Ph.D.
   or
Dr. Martin Gould

Martha Merk, M.D.
   or
Dr. Martha Merk

Salutation: Dear Dr. Merk:

2. *Dr.* and *Mr.* should not be used with the same name.

Martin Gould, Ph.D.
   not
Dr. Martin Gould, Ph.D.

3. College or university teachers who hold professional rank are called *Professor* or *Prof.*

Professor Lenore Klein
   not
Professor Mrs. Klein

Professor Donald Boone
   not
Prof. Boone

4. A professional man and his wife are addressed as:

Dr. and Mrs. Richard Warner
Professor and Mrs. James Donalson

5. The title *Messrs.* (*Messieurs*) precedes

the name of two or more professional men jointly engaged in practice.

Messrs. Carl Bunker and Robert Black
Attorneys at Law

Titles for Addressing Women

1. The title *Miss* is used when addressing an unmarried woman. Authorities prefer the use of the title *Ms* for a woman whose marital status is unknown.

Miss Jean Peterson
Secretary to the President

Ms Shelly Streeter, Office Manager
Turner Supply Company

Misses is recommended when addressing two or more unmarried women.

The Misses Baker and Frederickson
The Misses Lena and Sarah Bronson

2. To address a married woman you should use *Mrs.* In business correspondence, the woman's personal first name is preferred. In social correspondence, her husband's name should be used.

Mrs. Linda Reisman
(business)
Mrs. John Reisman
(social)

For two or more married women *Mesdames* is used (or if one is married and one is single, *Mesdames* is also suggested).

Mesdames Elyse Brown
and Cynthia Birch

Dear Ladies:
Mesdames:
Ladies:

3. The wife of a doctor or professor should not be addressed as Mrs. Dr. John Toomey or Mrs. Prof. B.T. Brown. The correct form is Mrs. B. T. Brown.

4. A divorced woman may use either her married name or her maiden name, and *Ms, Miss* or *Mrs.* are all correct. The preferred usage by the divorced woman should be followed.

Military Titles

1. Military personnel should be addressed with the rank or grade held. If the military title contains a prefix as in Brigadier, the prefix may be omitted in the salutation. Military personnel may be greeted with Dear Sir: for example.

Brigadier General Mark Reis, U.S.A.
Address
Dear General Reis:
or
Dear Sir:

2. Naval commissioned officers below the rank of *Commander* may be addressed either with their rank or addressed as *Mr.* in the salutation.

Lieutenant Fred Buckner, U.S.N.
Address
Dear Lieutenant Buckner:
or
Dear Mr. Buckner:

The Complimentary Close

1. There are various complimentary closes which are acceptable for business correspondence. The preferred close is largely determined by the writer and the degree of friendliness he has with the person being written to. The first word of the close is always capitalized.

Sincerely,	Yours very truly,
Sincerely yours,	Respectfully,
Yours truly,	Respectfully yours,
Very truly yours,	Cordially,

2. Any of the following may be used for government officials:

Respectfully yours,	Very truly yours,
Respectfully,	Yours very truly,
Yours respectfully,	Sincerely yours,

3. For dignitaries of the church, any of the following may be used:

Faithfully yours	Yours in Christ
Respectfully yours,	Sincerely yours in Christ,
Respectfully,	Sincerely yours,

Chapter 3

TABLES OF ADDRESSES AND SALUTATIONS FOR GOVERNMENT, SCHOOL, AND CHURCH DIGNITARIES

Admiral (Four Star)
Adm. Robert Stone, USN
Address

Dear Admiral Stone:

Ambassador, American
The Honorable John Adams
The American Ambassador
Address

Sir:
Dear Mr. Ambassador:

Ambassador, Foreign

His Excellency Ronald Scala
The Ambassador of Italy
Address

Sir:
Excellency:
Dear Mr. Ambassador:

Archbishop (Catholic)
Most Rev. Robert Carson
Archbishop of (Ecclesiastical Province)
Address

Dear Archbishop Carson:

The Most Reverend Archbishop
of (Ecclesiastical Province)
Address

Most Reverend Sir:
Your Excellency:
Your Grace:

Archdeacon (Episcopal)
The Venerable Alexander Roth
Archdeacon of (Diocese)
Address

Venerable Sir:

The Venerable Archdeacon
of (Diocese)
Address

Venerable Sir:

Attorney General
Hon. Charles Scott
Attorney General of the State
of (State Name)
Address

Dear Mr. Scott

The Attorney General of the State
of (State Name)
Address
Subject Line

Attorney
Ms. Nancy T. Bell
Attorney-at-Law
Address

Dear Ms. Bell:

Bishop (Catholic)
Most Rev. Stephen Lewis
Bishop of (Diocese)
Address

Dear Bishop Lewis
Your Excellency:
Most Reverend Sir:

Bishop (Episcopal)
Right Rev. Gerald Berg
Bishop of (Diocese)
Address

Dear Bishop Berg:
Your Excellency:
Right Reverend Sir:

Bishop, Other Denominations
Rev. Thomas Birch
Bishop of (Diocese)
Address

Dear Bishop Birch:

The Reverend Bishop Birch
Bishop of Memphis
Address

Reverend Sir:
Dear Bishop:
Dear Sir:

Brother
Brother James Dunne,*
LaSalle University
Address
*Add abbreviation of order

Dear Brother:

Dear Brother Dunne:

Cabinet Officer (Federal or State)
The Honorable Samuel Stern
Secretary of ＿＿(State, etc.)
Address

Sir:
Dear Sir:
Dear Mr. Secretary:

Cardinal
His Eminence Martin,
Cardinal ＿＿＿
Address

Your Eminence:

Chancellor
Dr. Patrick Bacon
Chancellor of Pace University
Address

Dear Dr. Bacon:

The Chancellor
Pace University
Address

Subject Line:

Chaplin
Chaplain Donald Folley
Captain, U.S. Army
Address

Dear Chaplain:
Dear Chaplain Folley:

City Council
The City Council
City of Toledo
Address

Honorable Sirs:
Honorable Gentlemen:

Clerk of the Court
Sally T. Brown, Esq.
Clerk of the Court of Illinois
Address

Dear Ms. Brown:

The Clerk of the Court of Illinois
State Capital, State Zip

Subject Line:

Colonel
Col. Terrence Black, USA (or USAF
or USMC)
Address

Dear Colonel Black:

Commodore
Com. Robert James, USCG (or USN)
Address

Dear Commodore James:

Congressman or State Representative
The Honorable Dean Shelly
The House of Representatives
Address

Sir:
Dear Mr. Shelly:
Dear Congressman Shelly:
(United States only)

Consul, American
The American Consul

(or: Gerald Dole, Esquire)
American Consul
Address

Sir:
Dear Sir:
Dear Mr. Consul:

Consul, Foreign
The Spanish Consul
Address

Sir:
Dear Sir:
Dear Mr. Consul:

Dean (Church)
The Very Reverend Timothy Bello
St. Patrick's Church
Address

Very Reverend Sir:
Dear Dean:

Dean (College)
Dean Gina Hawes,*
LaFayette University
Address
*Add abbreviation of degree.

Dear Dean (Dr.) Hawes:
Dear Madam: (or Sir)
Dear Dean:

General (Four Star)
Gen. Richard Cornwall, USA
(or USAF or USMC)
Address

Dear General Cornwall:

Governor
The Honorable William Mason
Governor, State of New Jersey
Address

Dear Sir:
Dear Governor:

Judge
The Honorable Daniel Galton
Judge of the Circuit Court
Address

Dear Sir:
Dear Judge:

Judge, Federal
Hon. Nancy Bell
Judge of the U.S. District
Court of (District)
Address

Dear Judge Bell:

Mayor
The Honorable Robert Benson
Mayor, City of Richmond
Address

Sir:
Dear Mr. Mayor:
Dear Mayor:

Minister, American
Hon. Donald Brown
American Minister
Foreign City, Country

Dear Mr. Brown:

Minister, Foreign
Hon. Mary Marquette
Minister of (Country)
Washington, DC Zip

Dear Ms. Marquette:

Minister (Protestant)
The Reverend Jessie Burke
First Methodist Church
Address

Dear Sir:
Dear Doctor: (if D.D.)
Dear Mr. Burke:

Monsignor
The Right Reverend
  Monsignor Ben Stacey
  Name of Church
Address

Right Reverend Sir:
Dear Monsignor:
Right Reverend and
  Dear Monsignor:

The Pope
His Holiness, Pope _____
The Vatican
Vatican City, Italy

Your Holiness:
Most Heavenly Father:

Postmaster General
Hon. Victor Johns
The Postmaster General
Washington, DC 20540

Dear Mr. Johns:

The Postmaster General
Washington, DC 20540

Subject Line:

President (College or University)
William Buchner,*
President, Indiana University
Address
*Add abbreviation of highest degree.

Dear Sir:
Dear Mr. President:

President of the United States
The President
The White House
Washington, D.C.

Sir:
Dear Mr. President:

Priest
The Reverend Stephen Wilson,*
University of Minnesota
Address
*Add abbreviation of order.

Reverend Father:
Dear Reverend Father:
Dear Father:

Principal
Dr. (Ms.) Martha Truman
Principal of Paterson High School
Address

Dear Dr. (Ms.) Truman

Rabbi
Rabbi Nathan Greene
(or: The Reverend Nathan Greene)
Sinai Congregation
Address

Dear Rabbi Greene:

(With Doctor's Degree)
Rabbi Nathan Greene, D.D.
(Name of Synagogue)
Address

Dear Rabbi (or Dr.) Greene:

Rear Admiral
Rear Admiral Dean Thelander, USCG
(or USN)
Address

Dear Admiral Thelander:

Rector
The Very Reverend Timothy Hart
Name of Church
Address

Dear Father Hart:
Very Reverend Sir:
Dear Reverend Hart:

Secretary of State (Treasurer
or Commissioner)
Hon. Mark Andrews
Secretary of State of (State)
Address

Dear Mr. Andrews:

Senator (U.S. or State)
The Honorable Charles Nutley
United States Senate
(or: The State Senate)
Address

Sir:
Dear Senator:
Dear Senator Nutley:

Sister
Sister Catherine Mary,*
St. Elizabeth's Convent
Address
*Add abbreviation of order.

Dear Sister:
Dear Sister Mary:

Superintendent of Schools
Dr. (Mr.) Raymond McArdle
Superintendent of Glencoe City
  School System
Address

Dear Dr. (Mr.) McArdle:

Superior of Sister Order
Mother Teresa Mullens,*
Mother General
Address
*Add abbreviation of order.

Reverend Mother:
Dear Mother General:
Dear Sister Superior:

Supreme Court: Chief Justice
Hon. Joseph Tiernan
Chief Justice of the Supreme Court
  of (State)
Address

Dear Mr. Chief Justice:

Vice-President
The Honorable Justine Smith
The Vice-President of the
  United States
Washington, D.C. 20025

Sir:
Mr. Vice-President:
Dear Mr. Vice-President:

Chapter 4

IMPROVING YOUR SPELLING

To write a letter, report, or article that contains misspelled words is an almost unforgivable error. Frequent misspellings in business writing may prevent a person from being promoted to a position for which he or she is otherwise qualified. In high school or college a lower grade may be given to papers or reports that contain several misspelled words. Misspellings in social correspondence or in minutes, reports, etc. for club or church groups often affect a person's social or personal standing because errors create an impression of a lack of education or cultural background.

Suggestions for Improvement

Learning to spell well is not difficult, particularly if you set up a spelling improvement program for yourself. The program is simple and consists of the following steps:

1. **Learn the six basic spelling rules.** The rules are given on the following pages. The rules for forming plurals are also given.

2. **Keep a notebook of words you misspell.** Go over the words frequently until you are sure you know their correct spelling. You will be surprised how effective this notebook system will be and how little of your time it will take. Continue keeping the notebook until you have learned to spell correctly the majority of words you regularly use in your writing.

3. **Don't guess about the spelling of a word.** Look up any word you are not sure of in a spelling dictionary or regular dictionary. If you find you have misspelled a word, add it to your spelling notebook. Looking up words in a dictionary takes a little time, but it prevents embarrassing mistakes.

In addition, immediately following this section you will find a list of 400 words which are frequently misspelled. Go over this list just as you do your notebook to help eliminate any errors you may now make. You will be pleased with how rapidly your spelling will improve.

SIX BASIC SPELLING RULES

Following are six basic spelling rules which will guide you in your program of spelling improvement. Each rule is illustrated by examples, and exceptions (if any) are noted.

Note: In another section of this handbook, a list of word roots, prefixes, and suffixes is given.

Rule 1. Words ending with a silent **e** usually drop the **e** when a suffix beginning with a vowel is added.

Root Word	Suffix		Complete Word
survive	+ al	=	survival
divide	+ ing	=	dividing
fortune	+ ate	=	fortunate
abuse	+ ive	=	abusive

Exceptions to the rule:

a. Words containing the soft sounds of **g** or **c** retain the **e** before the suffixes **able** or **ous**. *Examples*: Courageous, advantageous, peaceable, noticeable, changeable, manageable, serviceable.

b. Retain the **e** in words that might be mistaken for another word if the rule were applied. *Examples*: singe, singeing; dye, dyeing; shoe, shoeing; canoe, canoeing.

c. Words ending in **ie** drop the **e** and change the **i** to **y** when the suffix **ing** is added. This is done to prevent two **i's** from coming together. Examples: die, dying; tie, tying; lie, lying.

d. In the words *mileage, acreage, lineage*, the **e** is not dropped before the suffix **age**.

Rule 2. Words ending with a silent **e** usually retain the **e** before a suffix beginning with a consonant.

Word	Suffix		Complete Word
arrange	+ ment	=	arrangement
awe	+ some	=	awesome
forgive	+ ness	=	forgiveness
safe	+ ty	=	safety
shame	+ less	=	shameless

Exceptions to the rule: judge, judgment; acknowledge, acknowledgment; argue, argument; true, truly; nine, ninth; pursue, pursuant; value, valuation; wise, wisdom; whole, wholly; awe, awful.

Rule 3. Words ending in a single consonant preceded by a single vowel, usually double the final consonant before a suffix beginning with a vowel.

run	+ ing	=	running
big	+ est	=	biggest
hot	+ er	=	hotter
plan	+ ing	=	planning
bag	+ age	=	baggage

If the word ends with two or more consonants, or if the final consonant is preceded by two vowels instead of one, the rule does not apply.

Two Consonants

debt	+ or	=	debtor
calm	+ est	=	calmest

Two Vowels

frail	+ est	=	frailest
swear	+ ing	=	swearing
sweet	+ er	=	sweeter

Rule 4. Words of two or more syllables, that are accented on the final syllable and end in a single consonant preceded by a single vowel, double the final consonant before a suffix beginning with a vowel. If the accent is not on the last syllable, the final consonant is not doubled.

Accent on Last Syllable

refer	+ ing	=	referring
regret	+ able	=	regrettable
occur	+ ence	=	occurrence

Accent Not on Last Syllable

benefit	+ ed	=	benefited
differ	+ ence	=	difference
travel	+ er	=	traveler

If the word ends in two consonants, if the final consonant is preceded by two vowels, or if the accent shifts to the first syllable when the suffix is added, the rule does not apply.

perform + ance = performance (two consonants)
repeal + ing = repealing (two vowels)
refer + ence = reference (accent shifts)

Rule 5. Use of "ei" and "ie." Use **i** before **e** except when the two letters follow **c** and have a long **e** sound, or when the two vowels are pronounced long **a**.

Long e after c	Long a sound	After letters other than c
conceit	vein	shield
deceive	weight	believe
ceiling	veil	grieve
receipt	freight	niece
perceive	neighbor	mischievous

Exceptions to the rule:

weird	foreign	seize	leisure
either	forfeit	height	ancient
neither	sleight	surfeit	sovereign

Words that end in **ie** change the **ie** to **y** when the suffix **ing** is added.

lie - lying   die - dying   vie - vying

Rule 6. Words ending in **y** preceded by a consonant usually change the **y** to **i** before any suffix except one beginning with an **i**.

beauty + ful = beautiful
lady + es = ladies
lovely + ness = loveliness
ratify + es = ratifies
accompany + ment = accompaniment
accompany + ing = accompanying

Exceptions to the rule:

shy + ness = shyness
baby + hood = babyhood
plenty + ous = plenteous
lady + like = ladylike
beauty + ous = beauteous
wry + ly = wryly

If the final **y** is preceded by a vowel, the rule does not apply.

journey + s = journeys
buy + s = buys
essay + s = essays
obey + ing = obeying
repay + ing = repaying
attorney + s = attorneys

Note: This rule will be referred to later in the section on forming plurals.

FORMING PLURALS OF NOUNS

If a word is incorrectly pluralized, it is, of course, misspelled. There are thirteen rules on forming plurals listed here, together with examples and exceptions to the rules.

1. Plurals of most nouns are formed by adding **s** to the singular word.

Singular	Plural	Singular	Plural
bell	bells	pencil	pencils
college	colleges	tablet	tablets

2. When nouns end in **y** preceded by a consonant, the plural is formed by changing the **y** to **i** and adding **es**.

Final y preceded by a consonant:		Final y preceded by a vowel:	
Singular	**Plural**	**Singular**	**Plural**
baby	babies	valley	valleys
century	centuries	donkey	donkeys
lady	ladies	turkey	turkeys

Note: See Rule 6 under Basic Spelling Rules in this unit.

3. When nouns end in **ch, sh, ss, s, x,** or **z**, add **es** to form the plural.

Singular	Plural	Singular	Plural
dress	dresses	church	churches
fox	foxes	dish	dishes

4. The plurals of nouns ending in **f, ff,** or **fe** are formed by adding **s** to the singular. However, some nouns with these endings change the **f** or **fe** to **v** and add **es**.

Add s for plural		Change f to v and add es	
Singular	**Plural**	**Singular**	**Plural**
cliff	cliffs	wife	wives
handkerchief	hankerchiefs	leaf	leaves
safe	safes	self	selves

5. (a) The plurals of nouns ending in **o** preceded by a vowel usually are formed by adding **s** to the singular. Musical terms ending in **o** add **s** although the final **o** is not always preceded by a vowel.

Singular	Plural	Singular	Plural
studio	studios	piano	pianos
ratio	ratios	trio	trios
portfolio	portfolios	soprano	sopranos

(b) Nouns ending in **o** preceded by a consonant usually add **es** to form the plural.

Singular	Plural	Singular	Plural
motto	mottoes	hero	heroes
tomato	tomatoes	echo	echoes
potato	potatoes	Negro	Negroes

(c) Some nouns ending in **o** have two plural forms. In the following examples, the preferred plural form is given first:

Singular	Plural
memento	mementos or mementoes
cargo	cargos or cargoes
zero	zeros or zeroes

6. (a) Plurals of compound nouns are formed by adding **s** to the important word or most essential part of the compound.

Singular	Plural
sister-in-law	sisters-in-law
passer-by	passers-by
editor-in-chief	editors-in-chief
co-editor	co-editors

(b) Sometimes both parts of a compound are made plural.

manservant	menservants

(c) Compounds ending in **ful** form the plural by adding **s** to the ending of the compound.

Singular	Plural	Singular	Plural
cupful	cupfuls	handful	handfuls
spoonful	spoonfuls	tubful	tubfuls

(d) If there is no important word in the compound, or if both words are equal in importance, make the last part of the compound plural.

Singular	Plural
clothesbrush	clothesbrushes
scrubwoman	scrubwomen
washcloth	washcloths

7. Plurals of some nouns are formed either by a change in the vowel or by a complete change of spelling.

Singular	Plural	Singular	Plural
man	men	foot	feet
child	children	woman	women
mouse	mice	goose	geese
ox	oxen	tooth	teeth

8. Some nouns have the same form in both the singular and plural.

Examples: athletics, corps, deer, fish, moose, sheep, species

9. Some nouns are plural in form but are almost always considered to be singular in usage.

Examples: economics, ethics, news, mathematics, politics

10. Some nouns are rarely or never used in the singular.

Examples: cattle, cosmetics, scissors, statistics, trousers

11. Some words derived from a foreign language retain their foreign plurals.

Singular	Plural	Singular	Plural
datum	data	analysis	analyses
alumnus	alumni (masc.)	alumna	alumnae (fem.)
stratum	strata	synopsis	synopses

Sometimes, however, the English plurals are used instead of the foreign plurals.

Singular	Plural
referendum	referendums or referenda
curriculum	curriculums or curricula
trousseau	trousseaux or trousseaus

12. The plurals of proper nouns are formed by adding **s** if the name does not end in **s**, or by adding **es** if the name ends in **s**.

There are two **Marys** in our family.
Three **Besses** answered the roll call.
The **Adamses** have a new automobile.
The **Joneses** and the **Halls** are old college friends.

13. Plurals of letters, symbols, and numbers are formed by adding an apostrophe and **s** (**'s**).

Examples: A's x's 2's ?'s
+'s if's $'s 100's

FORMING POSSESSIVES

The apostrophe (') is a mark to show that a noun (or indefinite pronoun) is possessive, or to indicate a contraction. Just as a word is misspelled if it is pluralized incorrectly, so is it misspelled if the apostrophe is omitted or inserted in the wrong place in a word that shows possession.

1. If the singular form of the noun does not end in **s**, add the apostrophe and **s** (**'s**). If the singular ends in **s**, add the apostrophe (**'**).

Note: In the possessive singular of nouns that end in **s**, if you want the sound of an additional **s**, the apostrophe and **s** (**'s**) may be added.

Singular	Possessive	Singular	Possessive
boy	boy's	Harold	Harold's
child	child's	woman	woman's
Ross	Ross'	Davis	Davis'
	(or Ross's)		(or Davis's)

2. If the plural does not end in **s**, add the apostrophe and **s** (**'s**). If the plural ends in **s**, add the apostrophe (**'**).

Helpful hint: Make the word plural first; then make it possessive.

Plural	Possessive	Plural	Possessive
calves	calves'	bosses	bosses'
boys	boys'	children	children's
men	men's	sheep	sheep's
weeks	weeks'	Joneses	Joneses'

Caution: Be sure that you always add the apostrophe to the end of a word and that you do not insert it within the word. For example, take the proper name Jones. If you insert the apostrophe before the **s** (Jone's), it would mean that the proper name was Jone.

3. Possessive personal pronouns do not require an apostrophe.

my, mine	you, your
he, his	we, ours
she, hers	they, theirs
it, its	who, whose

Note: *It's* is a contraction of *it is* not the possessive of *it*.

4. Possessives of indefinite pronouns are formed by adding an apostrophe and **s** (**'s**).

else's	someone's	everybody's
somebody's	everyone's	one's

5. Possession of a compound word is shown at the end of the word, regardless of which part of the compound may be pluralized.

Singular	Singular Possessive
tradesman	tradesman's
editor-in-chief	editor-in-chief's
secretary-treasurer	secretary-treasurer's

Plural	Plural Possessive
brothers-in-law	brothers-in-law's
menservants	menservants'
freshmen	freshmen's

FORMING CONTRACTIONS

The second use of the apostrophe is to show the omission of one or more letters in words that are contracted.

it's (it is)	wouldn't (would not)
can't (cannot)	haven't (have not)
don't (do not)	hadn't (had not)
I've (I have)	isn't (is not)
I'm (I am)	you're (you are)
doesn't (does not)	won't (will not)
couldn't (could not)	who's (who is)

Chapter 5

440 WORDS
FREQUENTLY MISSPELLED

In business letters and reports and in reports or papers prepared by students in high school and college, there are certain words which are misspelled more often than others. Following is a list of words which are frequently misspelled. Refer to the list if you are unsure of the spelling of a word. If the word you are seeking is not in the list and you still are not sure, refer to a spelling dictionary or a regular dictionary.

abeyance	advantageous	ascertain	bureau	commodities	convincing
absence	advisable	assessment	business	comparatively	correlation
abundance	aggravate	assistant	calendar	competent	correspondence
accelerate	aggressive	association	cancel	competition	courteous
acceptable	allege	attendance	canceled	concede	criticism
acceptance	allowance	attorney	cancellation	conceivable	criticize
accessible	amendment	automatically	candidate	conferred	crucial
accidentally	among	auxiliary	capital	confidence	debtor
accommodate	analysis	available	capitol	confidentially	deceive
accompanying	analyze	bankruptcy	career	consummation	deductible
accomplish	announce	bargain	catalog	controlled	defendant
accumulate	annoyance	beginning	category	conscience	deferred
accurate	apologize	belief	certain	conscientious	deficiency
accustom	apparatus	believe	changeable	conscious	deficit
achievement	apparent	believing	chargeable	consistent	definite
acknowledgment	appealing	belligerent	collateral	conspicuous	dependent
acknowledging	appearance	beneficial	collectible	continuously	description
acquaintance	appreciate	beneficiary	column	controlling	desirable
acquisition	approach	benefited	commission	controversial	despair
acquitted	appropriate	bookkeeping	commitment	counterfeit	detrimental
across	argument	budget	committed	convenient	develop
actually	arrangement	bulletin	committee	conversant	difference

disappearance
disappoint
disastrous
disbursement
discipline
discussion
dissatisfaction
distribute
divide
efficiency
efficient
eighth
either
elaborate
eligible
eliminate
embarrass
eminently
emphatically
encouraging
endeavor
enforceable
enthusiastic
entirely
environment
equipment
equipped
equivalent
erroneous
especially
exaggerate
exceed
excellent
exhaustible
exhibition
existence
existent
exorbitant
expense
experience
explanation
extension
extraordinary
facilities
familiar
feasible
February
finally
financially
financier
forbade
foreign

forfeit
forty
forward
foresee
fourth
freight
fulfill
generally
government
grammar
grateful
guidance
handling
happiness
harass
height
hierarchy
hindrance
hurriedly
hygiene
image
immediately
immensely
imminent
impossible
incidentally
incredible
independent
indispensable
inevitable
influence
install
insistence
integrity
intelligence
intelligent
intentionally
interfere
interrupt
irrelevant
itinerary
judgment
judiciary
knowledge
knowledgeable
labeled
laboratory
laissez-faire
legible
legitimate
leisure
liable

liability
license
likable
likely
liquidate
lucrative
lying
maintenance
manageable
management
maneuver
manual
manufacturer
meant
mileage
millionaire
miniature
minute
miscellaneous
misspelled
monotonous
moral
morale
mortgage
movable
necessary
negligible
negotiate
neither
ninety
ninth
noticeable
oblige
obstacle
occasionally
occupant
occur
occurred
occurrence
offered
omission
omitted
oneself
operate
opinion
opportunity
ordinance
originally
paid
pamphlet
parallel
partially

particularly
pastime
patient
patronize
perceive
permanent
permissible
perseverance
personnel
persuade
pertain
pertinent
physically
plausible
pleasant
policies
possession
possible
possibly
practical
practically
precede
predictable
predominant
prejudice
prefer
preferable
preference
preferred
preparation
prerogative
presumptuous
prevalent
principal
principle
privilege
probably
procedure
proceed
programmed
programmer
propaganda
proportion
psychology
pursue
quality
quantity
questionnaire
realize
recede
receipt
receivables

receive
recipient
recognize
recommend
recruit
refer
reference
referred
regrettable
relevant
relieve
repetition
representative
requirement
rescind
research
resistance
responsibility
restaurant
rhythm
ridiculous
sacrifice
safety
salable
salient
schedule
secretary
seize
separate
severely
signature
significant
similar
simultaneous
sincerely
sizeable
skillful
source
specialized
specifically
strenuous
subtle
subtlety
succeed
success
suffered
sufficient
summarize
superintendent
supersede
supplies
suppress

surely
surprise
susceptible
symmetrical
sympathize
technique
temperament
temperature
temporarily
tendency
therefore
thorough
through
totaled
toward
transferred
transferring
transient
tremendous
typical
unanimous
undoubtedly
unnecessary
unusual
unwieldy
usage
useful
usually
vacillate
vacuum
valuable
variable
various
vegetable
vengeance
vice versa
victim
voluntary
warehouse
warrant
Wednesday
weather
weight
whether
wholly
write
writing
written
yield

Chapter 6

WORDS OFTEN CONFUSED AND MISUSED

Many words, for whatever reason, are often confused with another word and therefore misused. Sometimes the words look or sound somewhat alike, or they may have a somewhat similar meaning but have different accepted usages. Following are words often confused and misused. Examples of the correct use of the words is given following the definitions.

accept -- except:

Accept means to receive or to agree to something.

He did not *accept* the position.

Except means to exclude or leave out.

Everyone *except* John is here.

adapt -- adept -- adopt:

Adapt means to adjust to or to modify.

She did not *adapt* to her new job.

Adept means skillful.

She is an *adept* typist.

Adopt means to embrace or accept.

We will *adopt* a child.

They *adopted* the plan.

advice -- advise:

Advice is a noun meaning a recommendation that is given.

He gave me his *advice*.

Advise is a verb meaning an act of guidance.

Advise her what she should do.

affect -- effect:

Affect is a verb meaning to influence.

His attitude will *affect* his chances.

Effect is a noun indicating result or outcome.

What *effect* will the new plan have?

Effect is occasionally used as an action verb meaning to bring about.

We did *effect* your instructions.

aggravate -- irritate:

Aggravate means to make worse (a situation or condition).

His actions *aggravated* the situation.

The rubbing *aggravated* the wound.

Irritate means to annoy or to make sore.

The loud noise *irritated* me.

My skin is quite *irritated*.

allusion -- delusion -- illusion:

Allusion is an indirect reference to something.

She made an *allusion* to the mistake.

Delusion is a false or irrational belief.

He had a *delusion* that he would be made president.

He had *delusions* that he was being persecuted.

Illusion is a wrong idea or concept, or an optical misconception (In some usages, illusion and delusion mean about the same).

He had the *illusion* that he was to become president.

The mirage was strictly an *illusion*.

all ready -- already:

All ready means all prepared, i.e., a state of readiness.

The students were *all ready* to go.

Already is an adverb meaning previously.

The students had *already* gone.

all together -- altogether:

All together means a group as a whole.

The tools were *all together* on the bench.

Altogether means completely.

The two plans were *altogether* different.

among -- between:

Among is used when more than two persons or things are involved.

The supplies were divided *among* the group.

Between is used when only two persons or things are involved.

Jim and Ed divided the supplies *between* them.

amount -- number:

Amount, except for money, is used when mentioning something that cannot be counted.

The bill *amounted* to $64.50.

She had a large *amount* of cash.

He has a great *amount* of courage.

Number is used for things that can be counted.

A *number* of dogs were in the kennel.

A great *number* voted "no".

anxious -- eager:

Anxious means to have a degree of anxiety or fear.

I am *anxious* to hear the results of the operation.

Eager means pleasant anticipation.

I am *eager* to meet her.

any one -- anyone:

Any one is used to refer to one of several things or persons.

I do not like *any one* of the plans.

Any one who wishes may go.

Anyone is a pronoun meaning any person.

Has *anyone* arrived yet?

avenge -- revenge:

Avenge is used when there is a moral intention to right a wrong.

I will try to *avenge* the injustice done to him.

Revenge is a desire to inflict a punishment for an insult or injury.

He is so angry that he is going to seek *revenge*.

bad -- badly:

Bad is an adjective meaning disagreeable, offensive, defective.

Mother feels *bad* this morning.

The sales results were very *bad*.

There is a *bad* odor in the room.

Badly is an adverb meaning in a bad manner.

He behaved *badly* at the meeting.

best -- better:

Best is used when comparing more than two persons or things.

His plan was the *best* of those submitted.

Better is used when comparing two people or things.

His plan is the *better* of the two.

borrow -- lend:

Borrow means that the person is taking or wishes to take.

May I *borrow* your car?

Lend means to give or to let use.

I am going to *lend* him my car.

can -- may:

Can means to be able or capable of doing something.

He *can* operate the machine. (is able to)

Can he operate the machine? (does he know how?)

May means to seek or give permission.

He *may* operate the machine. (giving permission)

May he operate the machine? (seeking permission)

capital -- capitol:

Capital refers to a city where a national, state, or province government is located; also to monetary possessions, including money.

Washington, D.C. is the *capital* of the United States.

He invested most of his *capital* (money) in the new company.

Capitol refers to the main government building.

His office is in the *capitol*. (building)

complement -- compliment:

Complement refers to people or things that go well or work well together.

The advertising program *complemented*

the increased sales effort.

Compliment means to praise.

They *complimented* us on the increased sales.

counsel -- council -- counsul:

Counsel as a verb means to give advice; as a noun it means a lawyer or other person who gives advice.

He *counseled* us on the strategy we should use.

He is our company legal *counsel*.

Council is a group of people who discuss and/or take action on various matters.

The city *council* is meeting today.

Counsul is a government official appointed to represent citizens of his country in a foreign country.

The new *counsul* is leaving for Mexico tomorrow.

continual -- continuous:

Continual refers to something that occurs regularly, but with interruption.

His *continual* complaints are irritating.

Continuous means something that occurs without pause.

The *continous* noise in the shop is irritating.

emigrate -- immigrate:

Emigrate means to leave one's country to settle in another.

To avoid political persecution, he *emigrated* from Russia.

Immigrate means to enter a new country to settle there.

Because of political persecution, he *immigrated* to the United States.

eminent -- imminent:

Eminent means prominent or distinguished.

He is an *eminent* author.

Imminent means about to occur or threatening to occur.

A strike appeared to be *imminent*.

fewer -- less:

Fewer is used for things that can be counted.

We have had *fewer* plant accidents this year.

Less is used for things or ideas that cannot be counted.

He is *less* qualified than she is.

farther -- further:

Farther pertains to distance.

How much *farther* do we have to go?

Further refers to degree or extent but not to distance.

She can go no *further* in that type of work.

good -- well:

Good is an adjective that describes something positive.

She has a *good* educational background.

Well is an adjective meaning skillful, satisfactory, or thorough. It is also used to describe a state of health.

He is doing *well* in his new job.

The office manager does not look *well* today.

imply -- infer:

Imply means a hint or indirect suggestion.

He *implied* that he was going to quit.

Infer means to draw a conclusion from or interpret the meaning.

From what he said, I *infer* he may quit.

in -- into:

In indicates that something is already at a place or location.

The computers are *in* the next room.

Into indicates that someone or something is moving from the outside to the inside of a place.

He went *into* the computer room.

lay -- lie:

Lay means to put something down, to place something somewhere.

The principal parts are *lay*, *laid*, (*have*, *has*, or *had*) *laid*.

The present participle form is *laying*. The verb *lay* always takes an object.

He *lays* tile for the Regal store.

He *laid* tile for the Petersons.

He *has laid* tile for our neighbors.

He is *laying* tile today.

(Tile is the object of all the above sentences.)

Lie means to recline, to rest, or to remain in a reclining position.

The principal parts are *lie*, *lay*, (*have*, *has* *had*) *lain*.

The present participle form is *lying*.

He *lies* down every afternoon.

He *lay* on the couch all afternoon.

He *has lain* on the couch at times.

He *is lying* on the couch.

The verb *lie* is also the verb to use when speaking of inanimate objects that are in a reclining or in a *lying-down* position.

The report *lies* on my desk.

The report *lay* on my desk for a week.

The report *has lain* on my desk for weeks.

The report *is lying* on my desk.

There is another verb *lie* which means falsehood. It causes no special problems. Its principal parts are *lie*, *lied*, *lying*.

learn -- teach:

Learn indicates that knowledge or behavior is being acquired.

He should *learn* from that experience.

He *learned* Spanish in college.

Teach indicates that knowledge is being provided.

That experience should *teach* him a lesson.

He was *taught* conversational Spanish in college.

liable -- likely:

Liable is used either to indicate legal responsibility or the likelihood of an undesirable possibility.

If you injure someone, you are *liable* for damages.

If you don't change your ways, you are *liable* to be fired.

Likely indicates the probability of something.

She is *likely* to be the next one promoted.

It is *likely* you will be fired if you don't change your ways.

precede -- proceed:

Precede means to come or go before someone or something.

The band will *precede* the float.

Careful investigation should *precede* any action.

Proceed means to go on, usually after an interruption.

We can now *proceed* with the plan.

principal -- principle:

Principal means 1) something that is most important, 2) the amount of money owed or invested, 3) the head officer of a school, 4) the employer of a person to act in his behalf.

The *principal* purpose of the plan is to reduce expenses.

The *principal* amounts to $100,000.

She is *principal* of the Bergen Grade School.

The lawyer did his best to protect the interests of his *principal*.

Principle is used to indicate a law, basic truth, rule of conduct, or guidance.

Democracies are based on the *principle* of self-government.

The *principles* of his religion govern his action.

quite -- quiet:

Quite is an adverb meaning completely or very.

The new plan is not *quite* ready.

I am *quite* sure he will agree.

Quiet means still, calm, motionless, silent.

After hearing the announcement, the audience remained *quiet*.

raise -- rise:

Raise means to lift or raise. It requires an object.

Those who agree, *raise* your hand.

We will have to *raise* our prices.

Rise means to get up or go up. It requires no direct object.

Please *rise* when the President enters.

The audience *rose* (stood up) when the President arrived.

Our taxes seem to *rise* every year.

set -- sit:

Set means to put something down or in a certain place, or to bring to a specified state or condition.

He *set* the books on the president's desk.
The trees were *set* on fire.
She has *set* her heart on going.
Sit means to be seated.
Please do not *sit* on the desk.

stationary, stationery:
Stationary means inmovable, not moving, or unchanging.

Once the machine is installed, it will be *stationary*.
The troops stood *stationary* until the flag was past.
Stationery refers to writing paper, envelopes, and other office supplies.
Our new *stationery* order has just arrived.

whose -- who's:
Whose is an adjective showing possession.
He is the one *whose* car was stolen.
Who's is a contraction of *who* and *is*. In writing, its use should be avoided.
Who's going to be at the meeting?

Chapter 7

WORD PREFIXES, SUFFIXES, AND ROOTS

Following are some of the important word prefixes used in English. The prefix is indicated in boldface type followed by the basic meaning of the prefix. Examples of the prefixes used in words are given in italic type.

ab-, a-, abs-, away from, *abduct, avert, abstain*

a-, an-, not, less, without, *agnostic, atheist, anarchy*

ad-, a-, ac-, af-, to, toward, *adhere, ascribe, accord, affirm*

ag-, al-, an-, *aggressor, allude, annex*

ap-, ar-, as-, at-, to, toward, *associate, attend*

ante-, before, *antedate, antecedent*

anti-, ant-, against, *antiseptic, antipathy, antacid*

ana-, up, through, throughout, *analysis, anatomy*

be-, by or near, *below, beside*

bene-, good, well, *benevolent, beneficial*

bi-, two, twice, *bicycle, biennial*

circum-, around, all round, *circumstance, circumvent*

com-, con-, col-, together, *combine, confound, collate*

contra-, against, *contradict, contravene*

de-, from, down away, *depart, descend, denude*

dis-, di-, apart, apart from, *distract, divert*

ex-, ef-, e-, out, out of, *export, effect, emit*

hypo-, under, beneath, *hypodermic, hypothesis*

in-, in, into, *intrude, inside, include, insight*

in-, im-, il-, ir-, un-, not, *inactive, impress, illicit, irresistible, unreal*

inter-, between, *intermingle, interstate*

intra-, intro-, within, *intramural, introduction*

mal-, bad, *malcontent, malnourished*

mis-, wrong, *misdeed, mislead*

non-, not, *nonentity, nonconformist*

ob-, against, *object, objective*

par-, para-, beside, beyond, *paradox, parallel*

per-, through, throughout, *persist, pervade*

peri-, around, *periscope, perimeter*

post-, after, *postpone, postscript*

pre-, before, *prefer, predict*

pro-, before, forward, *prologue, promote, pronoun*

re-, back, again, *refer, report, review*

retro-, backward, *retroactive, retrogress*

se-, apart, *seduce, sedate*

semi-, half, *semicircle, semiconscious*

sub-, under, *submit, subordinate*

super-, supra-, above, over, *supernatural, suprarational*

syn-, sym-, with, *synopsis, symphony, synonym*

trans-, tra-, across, *transfer, traverse*

un-, not, reversal of action, *uncovered, untie*

uni-, single, *unity, universal*

vice-, instead of, *vice-president, vice-consul*

with-, against, back, *withdraw, withhold*

Word Suffixes

Following are some of the important word suffixes used in English. The suffix is indicated in boldface type followed by the basic meaning of the suffix. Examples of the suffixes used in words are given in italic type.

-able, -ible, -ble, capable of being, as *bearable, reversible, voluble*

-ac, -ic, pertaining to, as *cardiac, angelic*

-ac, -ic, condition or quality of, as *maniac, mechanic*

-acious, characterized by, as *pugnacious, tenacious*

-acity, quality of, as *tenacity, veracity*

-acy, having the quality of, as *accuracy, fallacy*

-age, collection of, state of being, as *garbage, marriage, storage*

-al, -el, -le, pertaining to, as *fanatical, novel, single*

-an, -ian, belonging to, one who, as *American, physician, historian*

-ance, relating to, as *reliance, distance*

-ancy, -ency, denoting state or quality, as *occupancy, dependency*

-ant, -ent, one who, as *tenant, correspondent*

-ar, -ary, ory, relating to, as *popular, dictionary, mandatory*

-ate, act, as *mandate, confiscate*

-ation, action, as *elation, separation*

-cle, -ule, -ling, diminutive, as *article, globule, suckling*

-cracy, rule, as *democracy, autocracy*

-cy, quality, as *idiocy, ascendency*

-dom, state of being, as *freedom, kingdom*

-ee, one who is acted upon, as *employee, trustee*

-ence, relating to, as *confidence, abstinence*

-er, -or, -ar, one who, as *butler, actor, scholar*

-ful, abounding in, as *grateful, sinful*

-fy, -efy, -ify, to make, as *deify, liquefy, solidify*

-hood, condition, as *fatherhood, falsehood*

-ic, pertaining to, as *historic, democratic*

-ice, act of, as *justice, police, practice*

-il, -ile, pertaining to, capable of being, as *civil, juvenile, mobile*

-ity, -ty, state or condition, as *sanity, acidity, safety*

-ious, full of, as *laborious, rebellious*

-ist, one who, as *pianist, machinist*

-ity, ty, state or condition, as *sanity, acidity, safety*

-ize, -yze, to make like, as *sympathize, analyze*

-less, without, as *careless, needless, hopeless*

-ly, manner, like, as *bodily, truthfully*

-ment, result, as *management, fragment*

-meter, measurement, as *thermometer, hydrometer*

-ness, state of being, as *sickness, happiness*

-nomy, pertaining to laws or government, distribution, arrangement, as *economy, harmony, astronomy*

-ory, place where, as *directory, rectory*

-ous, -ious, -eous, -uous, full of, as *dangerous, melodious, beauteous, strenuous*

-ose, full of, as *morose, verbose*

-ship, state or quality, as *friendship, worship*

-some, like, full of, as *gruesome, tiresome*

-ster, one who, person doing something, as *gangster, songster*

-sion, -tion, act or state of being, as *conception, perception*

-tude, condition, as *fortitude, magnitude*

-ty, ity, condition, as *clarity, peculiarity, sanity*

-ule, little, as *globule, granule*

-ure, act of, as *departure, manufacture*

-ward, direction of course, as *backward, forward, downward*

-y, full of, characterized by, as *filthy, icy, soapy*

Latin and Greek Word Roots

Following are Latin and Greek word roots which are used in English words. Word roots give the word its basic meaning, whereas prefixes or suffixes modify or change the root word. The root word is given in bold face type followed by the meaning of the root. Examples of the roots are printed in italic type. Many word roots are generally used only as prefixes or suffixes. However, as you examine the examples, you will note that many appear at the beginning, in the middle, or at the end of the English word.

aero, air, as *aerodynamics, aerospace*

ag, ac, to do, as *agenda, action*

agr, agri, agro, farm, as *agriculture, agronomy*

anthropo, man, as *anthropology, anthropoid, misanthrope*

aqua, water, as *aqueous, aquatic*

arch, rule, principle, chief, as *archbishop, archenemy, anarchy*

astra, astro, star, as *astronomy, astral, astronomical*

aud, audi, audio, hearing, as *audience, auditor, audiovisual*

auto, self, oneself, as *automatic, autograph*

biblio, bib, book, as *bibliophile, Bible*

bio, life, as *biology, biosphere*

cad, cas, fall, as *cadence, cascade, casual*

cant, sing, as *cantata, chant*

cap, cep, take, as *captive, accept*

capit, head, as *capital, capitate*

cat, cath, down, through, as *cataract, catheter*

ced, cess, go, yield, as *procedure, cession, antecedent*

cide, cis, kill, cut, as *suicide, excise, incision*

clud, clus, close, as *include, inclusion, preclude*

cred, believe, as *creditor, creditable, creed*

dec, ten, as *decimal*

dem, people, as *democracy, demagogue*

dent, tooth, as *indent, dental*

derm, skin, as *dermatology, taxidermist*

dic, dict, say, speak, as *diction, dictate, predicate*

duc, lead, as *induce, ductile*

equ, equal, as *equivalent, equitable, equality*

fac, fec, make, do, as *manufacture, infection*

fring, break as *infringement*

fract break as *fracture, fractious*

frater, brother, as *fraternal, fraternize*

fund, fus, pour as *refund, confuse*

gam, gamos marriage as *monogamous, bigamist, polygamous*

gen, produce as *generate, generation*

geo, earth as *geology, geometry, geography*

gastro, gast, stomach as *gastronomy, gastritis*

greg, group as *gregarious*

gress, grad walking, moving as *progress, degrade, retrograde*

gyn, woman as *gynecologist*

hemo, blood, as *hemorrhage, hemorroid*

homo, man, same as *homocide, homogeneous*

hydr, water as *dehydrate, hydralic*

idio, own, private, as *idiocy, idiosyncrasy*

iso, equal as *isothermal, isomorph*

ject, throw as *reject, project*

jud, jur, right as *judge, jury*

logy, study of as *psychology, biology*

loqu, speak as *loquacious, eloquent*

mand, order as *remand, command, demand*

manu, hand as *manuscript, manual*

mater, mother as *maternal, matricide*

meter, measure, as *thermometer, barometric*

micro, small as *microscopic, microbe*

mit, mis send as *permit, commission*

mono, mon, single, one as *monotony, monogram, monarch*

mort, death as *mortician, mortal*

nom, law as *economy, astronomy*

onym, name as *synonym, pseudonym*

pathos, feeling as *pathology, pathos*

philo, love as *philosophy, philosophical*

phobia, fear as *claustrophobia, hydrophobia*

porto, carry as *portable, export, report, transport*

pseudo, false as *pseudonym, pseudo*

psych, mind as *psychiatry, psychic, psychology*

scope, see as *telescope, microscope*

scrib, write as *inscription, description*

sec, cut as *dissect, bisect, resection*

sens, feel as *sensuous, sensitive*

sequ, follow as *sequence, inconsequent*

spec, spect, look as *specimen, inspect, spectacular*

spir, breath as *inspire, respiratory*

state, stand as *status, statutory*

ten, hold as *retention, detention*

term, end as *terminal, interminable*

typ, print as *typography, typewriter*

ven, vent, come as *prevent, convene, adventure*

vert, vers, turn as *divert, subversion, controversy*

vict, conquer as *evict, victim*

vid, vis, see as *video, visual, revise*

voc, call as *vocal, vocation*

Chapter 8

GUIDE FOR COMPOUNDING WORDS AND USE OF HYPHENS

A compound is two or more words joined together either with a hyphen or without a hyphen. Many words have become compound words through custom or usage because they are regularly used in succession or because the meaning is somewhat more clear or precise when the words are combined. The hyphen, when used in a compound word, is a mark of punctuation. Its purpose is to join the parts of a compound but also to separate the parts for better readability and clearer understanding. When in doubt about the compounding or hyphenation of a word, always consult your dictionary.

1. General Rule. Two or more words are not compounded unless the compounding aids understanding or readability. If the first word is principally an adjective describing the second word the words usually are not joined.

real estate	martial law	machine shop
book value	marble cake	fish hawk
tail wind	sun parlor	roller bearing

2. Nouns. Many nouns are formed by two other nouns (including gerunds) and are written as one word either by repeated usage or because as one word they better express a single thought or idea.

redhead	northeast	eggplant
locksmith	raindrop	doorman
eyewitness	laughingstock	bathroom

3. Verb and Adverb Compounds. Verbs and adverbs are often joined together or with nouns to express a literal or nonliteral figurative thought.

viewpoint	striptease	outwork
upgrade	rearmost	pushover
troublesome	pennywise	breakdown

4. Compound Personal Pronouns. Write compound personal pronouns as one word.

myself	himself	ourself
yourself	herself	themselves

5. Any, Every, Some, No. When these words are combined with *body, thing* or *where*, they should be written as one word. When *one* is the second element, and the meaning is a single or particular person, group, or thing, write as two words. *No one* is always two words.

anybody	everywhere	nowhere
anything	somebody	nothing
everyone	something	no one

Everyone came. *but*: Every one of the boys came.

6. Compound Modifiers (Adjectives). When words or numerals are combined to modify a noun, they should be hyphenated when they precede the word modified. However, see the rules which follow.

long-term lease	two-time candidate
short-wave radio	reddish-brown color
2-volume set	single-engine plane

(a) Certain types of unit modifiers should not be hyphenated. A precise rule can not be given. However, in general the two modifying words are words that are regularly used together in other contexts, the first word is a modifier of the second word, and then the two words together serve to identify or describe the third word.

life insurance policy	high school student
special delivery mail	civil rights law
income tax return	real estate tax
atomic energy plant	social security law

(b) Omit the hyphen in a unit modifier when it follows the word modified.

The area is middle class.
but: It is a middle-class area.
The company is well financed.
but: It is a well-financed company.

(c) Omit the hyphen in a unit modifier if the first word is a comparative or superlative.

lower priced stock	low-priced stock
best developed plan	well-developed plan
highest salaried group	high-salary group

(d) Descriptive words are not hyphenated when one of the words is an adverb.

happily awaited event	suprisingly long time
socially accepted custom	lovely young girl

(e) If a series of two or more compounds has the same basic word and this word is omitted except as the last term, retain all the hyphens.

first-, second-, and third-class mail
part- or full-time work
4-, 5-, and 6-foot lumber

(f) Omit the hyphen in foreign phrases used as modifiers.

prima facie evidence	bona fide signature
per diem payment	ex officio chairman

7. Miscellaneous Rules.

(a) Compound words containing proper nouns and beginning with the prefixes *anti-, ex, pro,* and *un,* as well as those ending with the suffix *elect,* are hyphenated.

ex-President Carter	Senator-elect Harris
pro-British	un-American

(b) Use hyphens to connect capital letters to words forming adjectives or nouns.

an A-line skirt	a V-line blouse
an S-curve	a T-square

(c) Compound numbers over twenty and less than one hundred are hyphenated.

twenty-one	one hundred eighty-six
sixty-three	six hundred forty-two

(d) Two-word fractions are hyphenated only when they are used as adjectives. They are not hyphenated when functioning as nouns.

A two-thirds majority voted in favor, (an adjective)
Two thirds of the members voted in favor. (a noun)

(e) A range in numbers or in the alphabet is indicated by a hyphen.

10-31 (meaning 10 through 31)
M-S (meaning M through S)

(f) Compound nouns and adjectives with the prefix *self* are hyphenated.

self-restraint (n)	self-induced (a)
self-interest (n)	self-service (a)

Chapter 9

RULES FOR WORD DIVISION

1. Avoid dividing a word at the end of a line unless necessary to maintain good margins. Do not divide the last word in a paragraph or the last word on a page.

2. If it is necessary to divide, divide a word only between syllables; but even then, apply the following rules:

3. Do not separate a single letter syllable from the rest of the word.

Right: emo-tion   Wrong: e-motion
Right: abu-sive   Wrong: a-busive

4. Avoid dividing a word before or after a two letter syllable.

Avoid: el-evate   Better: ele-vate
Avoid: cavi-ty   Better: cav-ity

5. Do not divide words of five or fewer letters even if the word has more than one syllable.

Wrong: In-dia, Indi-a   Correct: India
Wrong: i-deal, ide-al   Correct: ideal

6. Where the final consonant is doubled before a suffix, the added consonant goes with the suffix. However, if the root word ends with a double letter, divide after the double letter.

Right: assess-ing   Wrong: asses-sing
Right: allot-ted   Wrong: allotted

7. Words of one syllable should never be divided. Examples: whom, mend, passed, scrubbed.

Chapter 10

PUNCTUATION RULES

When you are writing, punctuation marks are signals from you to your reader. A period indicates that you have ended a sentence or that an abbreviation has been used. A comma may mean that there is a slight break in thought, indicate two separate parts of a compound sentence; or it may be used in one of several other ways.

Some sentences may be punctuated in more than one way; and, in some instances, a punctuation mark is a matter of choice by the writer. To help you punctuate expertly, the following rules and examples are given.

THE PERIOD (.)

1. Use a period at the end of a declarative or imperative sentence. (Also see Rule 5 under quotations.)

> The letter arrived this morning. (declarative)
> Ship our order immediately. (imperative)

2. Use a period rather than a question mark after an indirect question or courteous request.

> He asked if you had received it yet. (indirect question)
> Will you please ship it today. (courteous request)

3. Use a period after abbreviations, initials, and contractions. Abbreviations do not have internal spacing.

> Mr.   qt.   P.M.   etc.   U.S.A.

4. At the end of a sentence, a period is sufficient for both an abbreviation and the sentence.

> Send it to McDonald and Son, Inc.

5. Use three periods (ellipis marks) to indicate the omission of words from a quotation.

> "Democracy is the government of the people . . . for the people." --Abraham Lincoln

6. Use four periods when the omission comes at the end of a quoted passage.

> "Get your facts first, and then you can distort them . . . ." --Mark Twain

Note: Do not use a period at the end of a title of a book, magazine article, poem, etc. unless the title ends a sentence. In typed material, there should be two spaces between a period ending a sentence and the beginning of the next sentence.

THE QUESTION MARK (?)

1. Use the question mark after all direct questions.

Did you receive the report?
Have you shipped our order yet?

2. In a sentence containing more than one question each separate query may use a question mark.

> Are you certain of the place? the time? the date?

But if a question is not complete until the final word of the sentence, the question mark should be at the end only.

> Do you want to meet me at two p.m., three p.m., or four p.m.?

3. The question mark may also be used when only part of the sentence is a question, and in such sentences, the question is often introduced by a comma or colon; a semicolon or dash is sometimes used.

> Please tell me, why are you going?
> We must analyze the problem: Have you any suggestions?
> I have explained the problem: Have you any suggestions?

Note: In typed material, leave two spaces after the question mark and the beginning of the next sentence.

THE EXCLAMATION MARK (!)

1. Use the exclamation mark after all exclamatory sentences which convey surprise, strong emotion, or deep feeling.

> I can't believe you failed to complete the job!
> What a lovely thing to do!

2. Use the exclamation mark after interjections or after statements which emphasize commands or which suggest immediate action.

> Please! Ship our order immediately.
> Act now! Don't wait!

3. Use the exclamation mark after an interrogative sentence that is intended to be exclamatory.

> Oh no, how can you tell him that!
> Isn't she too young to understand!

4. The exclamation mark is also used to add emphasis.

> Your deadline is midnight!
> This is your last chance!

Note: In typed material, use two spaces after an exclamation mark and before the beginning of the next sentence.

THE COMMA (,)

1. When a dependent clause precedes the main clause, use the comma to separate the introductory clause. However, the comma is usually unnecessary when the dependent clause does not begin the sentence.

> When he completed his assignment, he went to see the dean. (comma)
> The chairman asked for the voting to begin after everyone was in the room. (no comma)

2. Use the comma after an absolute phrase or a participial phrase at the beginning of a sentence.

> The snow storm having begun, we decided to stay at home.
> Having completed the test in less than an hour, she left the room.

3. Use the comma after an introductory infinitive phrase. But do not separate the subject from the rest of the sentence when it is an infinitive.

> To be helpful, you must know when to offer help.
> To be helpful was her wish.

4. Use the comma to set off parenthetical elements in a sentence, such as words, phrases, clauses, or expressions. (Also see Rule 1 under parenthesis and Rule 1 under the dash.)

(a) Transitional words should be followed by commas (*besides, consequently, however, moreover, therefore*).

> However, I did not feel it was necessary.

Phrases, such as *in short, as a result, of course,* or *so to speak,* should be set off by commas.

> As I wrote before, there is, of course, a way out.
> As a result, our losses will be less than expected.

Use the comma to set off clauses (*I think, he says, we suppose*).

> The president, I think, will be concerned.

Expressions should be set off by commas when the logical progression of words is interrupted (*so far as she is concerned,* and *I respect his view*).

> The chairman did not object, and I respect his view, to staggering vacation time over a two-month period.

5. Introductory expressions are set off by commas (*indeed, yes, surely,* meaning *yes, well*).

Yes, I am going to attend.
Well, I would not have accepted the report.

6. A nonrestrictive clause is set off by a comma because it gives added information about the word it modifys, but it is not needed to complete sentence meaning.

A restrictive clause is needed to complete the meaning of a sentence, and, therefore, is never set off by commas.

The new manager, who is thirty-three, certainly is doing a good job. (The non-restrictive clause *who is thirty-three* gives added information but is not needed to complete the meaning of the sentence.)

The new manager who came from sales is now in charge. (The restrictive clause *who came from sales* is necessary to identify the word *manager*. Therefore, no commas are used.)

7. Use a comma to separate a word in opposition that defines or identifies another word with a noun.

Mary, my secretary, is very efficient.
My secretary, Mary, is very efficient.

8. Use a comma to separate words that indicate direct address.

Scott, please read the enclosed report.

9. Use a comma to separate a series of words, phrases, or clauses.

The recipe calls for, eggs, cream, and sugar.
She ran down the street, into a driveway, back to the curb, and sat down crying.
If we accept the proposal, it means that: (1) we will have three weeks vacation, (2) we will be paid for overtime, (3) we will have maternity leave.

10. Use the comma to separate coordinate adjectives which modify the same noun if the word *and* can be substituted for the comma.

The new, efficient machine will increase our production. (The new *and* efficient machine.)
The present operating plan will be changed. (No comma. You would not say present *and* operating.)

11. Use a comma before the conjunctions *and, but, for, or, nor,* and *yet* when they join the independent clauses of a compound sentence.

I sent the letter as you requested, and we should have a reply soon.
She asked for him on the telephone, but no one was there by that name.

(a) The comma may be omitted between most short clauses and between some long clauses when the meaing is clear.

He searched but did not find the report.

(b) When the comma is used without a coordinate conjunction between two independent clauses it is called the *comma fault.*

The children going to school do not cross at the intersection, they repeatedly jay-walk. (Incorrect -- a coordinate conjunction should be used after the comma.)

To eliminate the comma fault, the sentence may be punctuated in any one of the three following ways:

The children going to school do not cross at the intersection, and they repeatedly jay-walk. (using a coordinate conjunction)
The children going to school do not cross at the intersection; they repeatedly jay-walk. (using a semicolon)
The children going to school do not cross at the intersection. They repeatedly jay-walk. (using two simple sentences)

Use a semicolon before the coordinate conjunction when the independent clauses of a compound sentence are very long or contain internal punctuation.

The children going to school do not cross at the intersection; and, as a result, they repeatedly jay-walk.

12. Use the comma to separate words or phrases that express contrast.

The supervisor, not the foreman, offered to help.

13. Use the comma to set off a month, year or definite place.

He was born December 3, 1954, at 1612 Fardale Road, Jenkintown, Pennsylvania.

14. Use the comma to set off a direct short quotation. (See rule 4 under Quotations.)

The employer asked, ''Where do you expect to be in the next five years?''

15. Use the comma to separate a declarative clause and an interrogative clause which follows it.

Terry will receive the award, will she not?

16. Use the comma to set off a sentence element when it is out of its natural order or when it separates inverted names, or phrases.

That she could accept the suggestion, none of us seriously doubted.
Buckley, William S.
Like you, I feel the time is not right.

17. Use a comma to indicate the omission of a word.

Mark is extremely sensitive to the feelings of others; Scott, totally indifferent. (The word *is* has been omitted.)

18. Use the comma to separate a proper name from an academic degree or honorary title. Also use a comma between two or more degrees or titles.

Mary Jones, B.S.N., M.S., F.A.A.N., Director of Nursing.

19. Use a comma to separate the thousands in figures of four digits or more.

1,200   22,200   3,000,000

20. Use a comma to separate two sets of figures or two identical words.

Bring me 5, No. 1040, and 10, No. 1140.
Where he is, is not known.

Note: In typed material, use one space after a comma.

THE SEMICOLON (;)

The semicolon (;) indicates a more complete separation between sentence elements than does the comma. Overuse of the semicolon should be avoided.

1. Use the semicolon to separate independent coordinate clauses that are related in meaning when no coordinate conjunction is used. (Rule 11 under Comma.)

The staff members desired a change in direction; they were eager to offer suggestions.

2. Use the semicolon between coordinate clauses of a compound sentence when they are united by transitional words.

The freeholders approved the building plans; as a result, construction will resume next spring.

Commonly used transitional words:

accordingly	furthermore	nevertheless
as a result	however	otherwise
besides	in addition	that is
consequently	indeed	therefore
finally	in fact	thus
for example	moreover	yet
for this reason	namely	

3. Use the semicolon before a coordinate conjunction (*and, but, for, or, nor*) to separate two independent clauses with internal punctuation. (Rule 11 under Commas.)

The meeting, which ran overtime, was boring; but some decisions were made in spite of weak presentations.

4. Use the semicolon before words such as *for example, for instance, namely,* or *that is* which introduce an example, enumeration, or items in a series.

The committee was represented by four officers; namely, the president, vice-president, secretary, and treasurer.

5. Use the semicolon in clarifying listings where a comma is insufficient to separate the items clearly.

Committee members who attended were James Farley, president; Timothy Sullivan, vice-president; and Jean Shelley, secretary.

Note: In typed material use one space after a semi-colon.

THE COLON (:)

1. Use the colon before a list of items or enumerations.

See if we have the following merchandise in stock: No. 42, No. 63, and No. 67.

My itinerary included: going on a bus trip, visiting several museums, and shopping for jewelery.

(a) When the list of items is in a column, capitalize the first letter.

You must hire someone who has technical skills in the following areas:
1. Computer programming
2. Audio/Video camera
3. Software production

(b) When the items are presented in a sentence it is not necessary to capitalize the first letter.

You must hire someone who has technical skills in the following areas: computer programming, audio/visual camera, and software production.

2. Use the colon before an appositive phrase.

The jury rules were simply stated: no radio, no television, no visitors.

3. Use the colon following the salutation of a business letter.

Dear Mr. Greene: Gentlemen:

Do not use a semicolon after a salutation. However, a comma may be used after the salutation of an informal letter.

Dear Kathy,   Dear Mother,

4. Use the colon to divide the parts of formulas, numbers, references, or titles.

The conferences will begin at 10:30 A.M.

The pastor quoted from Chapter VI: Page 10.

PARENTHESES ( )

1. Use parentheses to separate words, phrases, clauses, or sentences which enclose

material that explains, translates or comments. (Rule 4 under commas. Rule 1 under the dash.)

She swam 1500 meters (somewhat less than a mile).

He stated, "E pluribus unum." (One out of many.)

2. Use parentheses to enclose letters, numbers, or symbols when referring to an appositive.

We made reservations for fifteen (15) days.

(a) Use parentheses with other punctuation marks. If the punctuation mark is connected to the entire sentence and not just to the parenthetical part, the punctuation mark follows the second parenthesis.

They carefully analyzed and evaluated the standards (legal and moral), but could not reach a decision.

(b) The punctuation mark should be placed within the second parenthesis if it applies only to material concerning the parenthetical section.

You may save a life by giving first-aid to someone who is choking. (See the back cover of this pamphlet.)

- THE DASH (—)

The dash should be used to indicate a sudden change of ideas, but should be used sparingly. The dash may be used for emphasis or for visual effect.

1. Use the dash to indicate an abrupt change of thought in a sentence or strong parenthetical expressions.

She feels — how can I say that? — like an outcast.

I was annoyed — no, shocked to be more specific — by his behavior.

2. Use the dash to set off a summary or an afterthought that is added to a sentence.

The educational team will make an evaluation and draw up a plan — in fact, they will provide a complete special program for the child.

3. Use the dash to emphasize a word or phrase that is repeated.

The president stated that we had one week — one week only — to make a decision.

4. Use a dash to mark limits between dates, numbers, places, and times.

The admissions office is open 9:00 — 4:30 daily.
Read pages 22-40.

THE QUOTATION MARK (" ")

1. Use quotation marks to enclose all direct quotations.

"Yes," she said, "I did help to raise funds."

The teacher asked, "Did I give you the date for the test?"

Rules governing the use of quotation marks: Capitalize the first word of a direct quotation. The first word in the second section of an interrupted quotation is not capitalized unless it begins a new sentence. Quotation marks or capital letters are not used in an indirect quotation.

The teacher asked if she gave you the date for the test.

2. Use quotation marks to enclose the chapters of a book, names of songs, titles of magazine articles or poems, and other similar titles. In typing or writing, underline titles of books, magazines, operas, and any other work long enough to appear in book form. Underlining of titles signifies italics for printing.

The National Geographic includes a section called "Members Forum."

"The Owl and the Pussy Cat" is a child's favorite poem.

3. Use quotation marks to set off words, phrases, or sentences referred to within a sentence or to emphasize a word. (Italics may also be used in such cases.)

The sentence "you can't take it with you" has deep meaning for some people.

The word "judgement" is often misspelled.

What was the real "meaning" of his asking?

4. Use quotation marks at the beginning of each paragraph if several paragraphs are quoted, and at the end of the last paragraph. Very long quotations are frequently introduced by a colon instead of a comma. (Rule 14 under commas.) Usually indent quotations of three or more lines from the body.

5. Using quotation marks with other punctuation:

(a) Place a period or comma before ending quotation marks.

She said, "No one is home."
"No one is home," she said.

(b) Place the question mark before quotation marks when they refer to the quoted content, or after when they refer to the complete sentence.

He said, "Why do you want to see her"?
Did he say, "Why do you want to see her?"

(c) Place the semicolon and colon after ending quotation marks unless they are part of the quoted material.

He said, "You are to be our next president"; therefore, I hope you you will consider me for your present job.

Chapter 11

RULES OF CAPITALIZATION

1. Capitalize the first word of a sentence.

Your order has been shipped.

2. Capitalize the first word of a line of poetry.

"Poems are made by fools like me...."

3. Capitalize the first word of a direct quotation.

He asked, "Where are the parts?"

4. Capitalize *proper nouns* (names of specific persons, places, or things).

New York City	Henry Jones	Wall Street
Lake Michigan	Brazil	Holiday Inn

5. Capitalize *proper adjectives* (adjectives formed from proper nouns).

American	Spanish	Southern
Communistic	Chinese	Russian

6. Capitalize names of *specific organizations* or *institutions*.

Northwestern University	Republican Party
American Red Cross	Ford Motor Company

7. Capitalize *days of the week, months of the year, holidays,* and *days of special observance.*

Sunday	August	Yom Kippur
Mother's Day	Easter	Christmas
Feast of the Passover	St. Valentines Day	

8. Capitalize *names of the seasons* only if they are personified.

Personified	*Season*
Springs warm touch	spring breezes
Winter's icy breath	winter's snow

9. Always capitalize *languages* but not other school subjects unless they are names of specific courses.

English	Chemistry 101	but: chemistry
French	Economics 102	economics
Spanish	Composition 200	composition

10. Capitalize *races, religions,* and *ethnic groups.*

Negro	Catholic	Moslem
Eurasian	Presbyterian	Japanese

11. Capitalize references to the *Diety* and to the *titles of holy books.*

God, the Father	the Trinity	the Koran
Supreme Being	Genesis	Talmud

12. Capitalize *titles of people* when they are followed by a name.

President Henderson	Senator Hutchins
Cardinal Wilson	Professor Stark
Doctor Allison	Reverend Harmon

13. Capitalize sections of a *country,* but do not capitalize directions.

Sections	*Directions*
the Midwest	I traveled west.
the Near East	The sun rose in the east.
the South	They went south.

14. Capitalize titles of *works of literature, art,* and *music.* However, in such titles do not capitalize short prepositions, articles, and conjunctions unless they are the first word.

War and Peace	Battle Hymn of the Republic
The Angelus	Beethoven's Fifth Symphony
Book of Job	The Last of the Mohicans

15. Capitalize *names of governmental bodies* and *departments.*

President's Cabinet	Civil Service Commission
Supreme Court	Bureau of the Census
United States Senate	the Federal Government

16. Capitalize *words which show family relationships* when they are used with a person's name or when they stand unmodified as a substitute for a person's name.

Aunt Alyce	my aunt
Grandfather Scott	his grandfather

I sent a package to Mother. (but: My mother will be there.)

17. Capitalize names of *definite regions, localities,* and *political divisions.*

the Orient	Fourth Precinct
the Artic Circle	First Ward (of a city)
French Republic	Bergen County

18. Capitalize names of *historical events, historical periods* and *historical documents.*

the Middle Ages	Magna Carta
World War II	the Crusades
Bill of Rights	Third Amendment

19. The names of separate departments of a business may be written with either capital or small letters. Business titles such as president, office manager, superintendent, etc. may be written either way.

The Company will pay your expenses. (or company)

Our President will see you June 6. (or president)

Research Department *or* research department.

20. The pronoun *I* should always be capitalized.

It is I who will go.

Chapter 12

POST OFFICE INFORMATION

Air Mail: The post office now moves all first-class mail within distant cities in the United States by air. Do not waste money by sending letters within the United States via airmail. However, much time can be saved by sending letters and packages to foreign countries (including Canada and Mexico) by air. To overseas countries, regular mail by sea may take one to three months for delivery. By airmail, delivery will usually take place in one to three weeks. If time is important, it may pay to send even some bulky materials by airmail. Air-freight companies or export brokers can give you information about shipping materials and supplies by air using their services.

Bulk Rate: See Third-class Mail.

Bulk Mail: If your company, club, etc. makes simultaneous mailings of fifty or more items with any frequency, you can secure a bulk mail permit. Items that carry a permit or are meter stamped and presorted by postal zones may be mailed at a special reduced rate. Larger mailings receive still lower rates. Since rates change from time to time, check with your postoffice for specific rates and requirements.

Business Reply Permits: If your company is making large mailings to secure orders or to seek a reply, you generally can increase response by paying the return postage. Rather than apply postage to each return envelope or card (which is costly since many envelopes will not be returned), businesses or individuals can secure business reply permits by paying an annual fee. The envelopes must carry certain insignia and facing identification marks (series of horizontal and vertical bars) printed from negatives that are available free at the post office. Upon return of envelopes or cards the regular postage is paid plus an extra fee which almost doubles the total postage. However, postage is paid only for items actually returned.

C.O.D. Mail: First-, third-, and fourth-class mail may be sent *collect on delivery*. The post office carrier collects the amount due from the receiver at the time of delivery. The sender must prepay the postage and a collection fee. However, the mailer may include the charges in the amount to be collected from the addressee.

Insurance is included in the fee, and a return receipt may be requested. The addressee (receiver) is not allowed to inspect the contents before paying for the item.

Certified Mail: First-class mailings in the U.S. of items having no insurance value but for which assured delivery is desired may be sent *certified mail*. Delivery may be restricted to the addressee (only the addressee may sign for it) by writing the words *Restricted Delivery* above the address. A return receipt showing the addressee's signature and date of delivery may also be requested. There is an extra fee for these services.

Electronic-mail System: The U.S. Post Office provides a system whereby businesses may send communications through government computers. E-COM (Electronic-Computer Originated Mail) accepts material up to two pages in length for mailing to multiple addresses. Messages are routed to an E-Com center where they are placed in local mail for the next scheduled delivery. There is an annual subscriber fee plus a per page charge. A somewhat similar service is available through Western Union where the same letter can be sent to multiple addresses with next day delivery by mail.

Express Mail: Any item from a letter to a 70-pound package may be mailed from a designated post office (ask the post office for a list) before 5:00 p.m. with delivery guaranteed by 3:00 p.m. the next day (except Sunday). Or, if addressed to someone in care of a post office, the addressee may pick up the item at any time after 10:00 a.m. Postage is determined by weight and distance and the cost is relatively high. However, the post office refunds the full amount if delivery is made later than promised. Special labels and envelopes for this service are available at your post office. Private air-express companies also offer the same service.

First-class mail: Letters, bills, checks, receipts, orders, etc. as well as post cards must be mailed first-class mail. Postage on the first ounce is the price of a regular first-class stamp with slightly lower rates for additional ounces. Inter-city mail of any distance is sent by air without extra charge. The weight limit is 70 pounds with a size limitation from 2 by 4$\frac{1}{4}$ inches to a maximum of 100 inches in combined length and girth (the measurement around the package).

Stamp all large envelopes and packages *first-class* so that post office employees will not mistake them as being third-class. First-class mail, such as letters, may be included in second-, third-, or fourth-class mail provided you note on the outside of the package *letter enclosed*, etc. and affix the additional first-class postage to the package. Or you may attach a stamped envelope containing a letter, etc. to the outside of the package. Any item weighing more than 12 ounces is classified as *priority mail*, described later in this section.

Fourth-class Mail (Parcel Post): Items weighing 16 ounces or more and not shipped first-, second-, or third-class mail are designated *Parcel Post*. Postage is based on weight and distance. Weight cannot exceed 70 pounds and size cannot exceed 108 inces of combined length and girth (distance around the package).

Special delivery is available for fourth-class mail. However, sending a package by priority mail (first-class mail) is oftentimes better and less costly then fourth-class, special delivery.

Special fourth-class rates are available for books, educational materials, manuscripts, catalogs, films, records, etc. Check with your post office for details.

General Delivery: For persons not permanently located in a city, mail may be sent to the destination post office in that person's name. Write *General Delivery* above the person's name and then the post office (or a specific branch) address (city, state, and zip code). The person addressed will have to call at the post office and provide identification to secure his mail.

Insured Mail: Insured mail is available for only third- and fourth class mail. In the event of loss, the post office will pay only the cost value of the item sent.

International Mail: First-class mail, air mail, and parcel post service are available to other countries. However, the rates and mailing rules vary from country to country. Check with your post office for the specific rates, etc. for the country to which you are mailing.

A copy of *International Postage Rates and Fees* may also be secured from the U.S. Postal Service without charge.

Metered Mail: Small businesses may buy or rent manual meters. However, larger businesses usually have electically powered meter machines that automatically feed, seal, meter-stamp, and count the mail. The sealed meter box is taken to the post office to replenish the postage.

Money Order: A *postal money order* for up to $500 may be purchased or cashed at any U.S. post office.

National Zip Code Directory: A large directory listing zip codes by state, city, and street may be secured at any post office for a nominal fee.

Parcel Post: See fourth-class mail.

Post Cards: Cards ranging in size from 3$\frac{1}{2}$ by 5 inches to 4$\frac{1}{4}$ by 6 inches may be mailed at rates lower than first-class envelope mail. A post card carrying first-class prepaid postage may be purchased at your local post office.

Post Office Box: Boxes or bins may be rented at any post office. A box enables a business or individual to pick up mail at anytime that post office lobbies are open. Many larger businesses may rent several boxes so that their mail is automatically presorted by box number (such as for payments, new orders, sales reports, etc.).

Priority Mail (Air Parcel Post): All first-class mail weighing from 13 ounces to 70 pounds is classified as *Priority Mail*. Priority mail receives air service the same as other first-class mail.

Registered Mail: First-class mail that is registered is kept locked and separate from other mail. It is the safest way for mailing valuable documents or other papers that are uninsurable. All items that are irreplaceable or difficult to replace should be registered (such as money, stock certificates, manuscripts, signed documents, jewelry of unusual value, etc.).

At the time of mailing, the sender receives a numbered receipt and the post office maintains a record of the number. As proof of delivery a return receipt may be requested.

In addition, to first-class postage and return receipt fee, the sender must pay a registration fee based on the declared value (up to $10,000) of the item.

Second-class Mail: This mail class provides special rates for publishers who have permits to mail magazines or newspapers, for publications of certain non-profit organizations, or for individuals mailing complete publications. The wrapper must be marked *second-class* and no other communication may be included without making all the items subject to first-class postage.

Special Delivery: A special delivery fee may be paid for all classes of mail. For this fee, in addition to regular postage, delivery is assured immediately after arrival at the destination post office.

Third-class Mail: This class mail may be used for individual or bulk mailings of advertising material such as booklets, circulars, and catalogs, and for merchandise, seeds, bulbs, and plants that weigh less than 16 ounces apiece. Items weighing more than 16 ounces are classified as fourth-class (parcel post). Third-class mail must be left unsealed for postal inspection, or if sealed, marked *bulk mail* or *third-class mail*. it must not include written messages or directions on the outside. Check with your post office for the specific requirements for the type of item you are mailing.

Chapter 13

TIME CHANGE

Business today in many industries is done on a worldwide basis. Government and military personnel, too, often must communicate with others in many foreign countries. There is often a need, then, for knowing the time in other locations or other travel itineraries. The listings on the pages which follow will enable you to quickly determine the time in other locations.

In the listing, if all of a country is in one time zone, only the name of the country is given. Where there is more than one zone, the principal cities of the country are given with their time zone.

The *Eastern Standard Time* Zone in the United States is used as a base. If you are in that zone, you only need to add or subtract the number of hours indicated after the name of the country or city whose time you are determining.

For example, if you are in New York or New Jersey or any other Eastern Time Zone area, and wish to know the time in Rome, Italy, look up *Italy*. You will find it has only one time zone indicated as +6. Simply add 6 hours to your time. In other words, if it is 12 o'clock where you are, it is 6 p.m. in Rome.

If you are not in the Eastern Standard Time Zone, follow these steps:

1. In the list, find the name of the country or city *where you are* or near.
2. Reverse the sign given for your location; e.g. change a +3 to a −3. Then add or subtract that number from the actual time where you are.
3. Find the name of the country whose time you wish to know and add or subtract the figure you arrived at in step 2 above.

For example, if you are in San Francisco and wish to know the time in Hong Kong when your time is 2 p.m.:

1. Locate San Francisco in the list.
2. Change the −3 to +3 and then add that amount to your actual time. Your time 2 p.m. plus 3 = 5 p.m.
3. Look up Hong Kong which shows + 13. Add that amount to the time from step 2 above: 5 p.m. + 13 = 18 or, in other words, it would be 11 a.m. in Hong Kong when the time is 2 p.m. in San Francisco.

Note: If Daylight Savings Time is in effect in your time zone, *subtract* one hour from the result you found by following the steps above. In the example above, you would subtract one hour from 6 a.m. making it 5 a.m. You would then not want to call until after 5 p.m. San Francisco time to reach someone in Hong Kong after 8 a.m.

Afghanistan $+9\frac{1}{2}$	Bolivia +1	Canada	Czechoslovakia +6	Ghana +5	Semarang +13
Algeria +6	Botswana +7	Montreal 0	Dahomey +6	Greece +7	Surabaya +12
Angola + 6	Brazil	Ottawa 0	Denmark +6	Greenland +2	Iran $+8\frac{1}{2}$
Argentina +1	Belo Horizonte +2	Toronto 0	Dominican Rep. 0	Guatemala −1	Iraq +8
Australia	Brasilia +2	Vancouver −3	Ecuador 0	Guinea +5	Ireland +6
Adelaide $+14\frac{1}{2}$	Campo Grande +1	Winnipeg −1	Egypt +7	Guyana +2	Italy +6
Brisbane +15	Recife +2	Central Africa	El Salvador −1	Haiti 0	Ivory Coast +5
Canberra +15	Pôrto Velho +1	Republic +6	Equatorial	Honduras −1	Jamaica 0
Darwin $+14\frac{1}{2}$	Rio de Janeiro +2	Chad +6	Guinea +6	Hong Kong +13	Japan +14
Melbourne +15	Sao Luis +2	Chile +1	Ethiopia +8	Hungary +6	Jordan +7
Perth +13	Sao Paulo +2	China +13	Finland +7	Iceland +4	Kenya +8
Sydney +15	Bulgaria +7	Columbia 0	France +6	India $+10\frac{1}{2}$	Korea +14
Austria +6	Burma $+11\frac{1}{2}$	Congo, Rep. of +6	Gabon +6	Indonesia	Kuwait +8
Bangladesh +11	Burundi +7	Costa Rica −1	Gambia +5	Bandung +12	Laos +12
Barbados +1	Cambodia +12	Cuba 0	Germany, East +6	Djakarta +12	Lebanon +7
Belgium +6	Cameroon +6	Cyprus +6	Germany, West +6	Irian Jaya +14	Lesotho +7

Liberia + 5¾	Newfoundland +1½	South Africa +7	Kharkov +8	Boston 0	Oklahoma City −1
Libya +7	New Zealand +17	Spain +6	Kiev +8	Buffalo 0	Phoenix −2
Luxembourg +6	Nicaragua −1	Sri Lanka +10½	Kuybyshev +9	Chicago −1	Pittsburgh 0
Malagasy Rep. +8	Niger + 6	Sudan +7	Leningrad +8	Cincinnati 0	Philadelphia 0
Malawi +7	Nigeria +6	Sweden +6	Minsk +8	Cleveland 0	St. Louis −1
Malasia +12½	Nova Scotia +1	Switzerland +6	Moscow +8	Columbus 0	San Antonio −1
Maldive Is. +10	Pakistan +10	Syria +7	Novosibirsk + 12	Dallas −1	San Francisco −3
Mali +5	Panama 0	Taiwan +13	Odessa +8	Denver −2	Seattle −3
Malta +6	Paraguay +1	Tanzania +8	Omsk + 12	Detroit 0	Washington 0
Mauritania +5	Peru 0	Thailand + 12	Perm + 12	Ft. Worth −1	Upper Volta +5
Mauritius +9	Philippines + 13	Togo Rep. +5	Rija +8	Honolulu −5	Uruguay +2
Mexico	Poland +6	Trinidad and	Rostov +9	Houston −1	Venezuela +1
Guadalajara −1	Portugal +6	Tobago +1	Tashkent + 11	Indianapolis −1	Vietnam + 13
Mexico City −1	Rhodesia +7	Tunisia +6	Vladivostok +15	Kansas City −1	Yemen +8
Monterey −1	Rumania +7	Turkey +7	Volgograd +9	Memphis −1	Yugoslavia +6
Mazatlán −2	Samoa, W. −6	Uganda +8	United Kingdom +6	Minneapolis −1	Zaire
Mongolian Rep. + 13	Saudia Arabia +9	USSR	United States	New York 0	Kinshasa +6
Morocco +5	Senegal +5	Alma-Ata + 11	Anchorage −5	Los Angeles −3	Lumbumbashi +7
Nepal +10½	Singapore + 12½	Baku +9	Atlanta 0	Milwaukee −1	Zambia +7
Netherlands +6	Somalia +8	Gorki +9	Baltimore 0	New Orleans −1	

Chapter 14

ROMAN NUMERALS

Roman numerals are not widely used, but used often enough so you should be able to read or interpret them. Following is a table of Arabic numerals and their equivalent Roman Numerals.

Table of Roman Numerals

Arabic Numeral	Roman Numeral	Arabic Numeral	Roman Numeral
1	I	50	L
2	II	60	LX
3	III	70	LXX
4	IV	80	LXXX
5	V	90	XC
6	VI	100	C
7	VII	200	CC
8	VIII	300	CCC
9	IX	400	CD
10	X	500	D
11	XI	600	DC
12	XII	700	DCC
13	XIII	800	DCCC
14	XIV	900	CM
15	XV	1,000	$\overline{\text{M}}$
16	XVI	4,000	$\overline{\text{MV}}$
17	XVII	5,000	$\overline{\text{V}}$
18	XVIII	10,000	$\overline{\text{X}}$
19	XIX	15,000	$\overline{\text{XV}}$
20	XX	20,000	$\overline{\text{XX}}$
30	XXX	100,000	$\overline{\text{C}}$
40	XL	1,000,000	$\overline{\text{M}}$

The following examples illustrate the use and meaning of Roman Numerals.

1. A Roman Numeral or letter preceding *a letter of greater value* subtracts from it:

V = 5	IV = 4
L = 50	XL = 40
C = 100	XC = 90

2. A letter preceding *a letter of equal or lesser value* adds to it.

V = 5	VI = 6
L = 50	LX = 60
C = 100	CXI = 111

3. You will quickly, of course, be able to remember and recognize smaller numbers.

XVI = 16
  X (10) + VI (6) = 16

XLIV = 44
  XL (40) + IV (4) = 44

XCI = 91
  XC (90) + I (1) = 91

For larger numbers simply examine the numbers and break it down into its elements and you will readily interpret the number. You will be able to recognize the elements or parts by applying rules 1 and 2 given above or by looking at the table of Roman Numerals.

CDXCIII = 493
  CD (400) + XC (90) + III (3) = 493
DCXCIX = 699
  DC (600) + XC (90) + IX (9) = 699
MDCLXXV = 1,675
  M (1,000) + DC (600) + LXX (70)
    + V (5) = 1,675

4. A bar over a Roman Numeral multiplies it by 1,000.

$\overline{\text{MV}}$ = 4,000	$\overline{\text{V}}$ = 5,000
$\overline{\text{XV}}$ = 15,000	$\overline{\text{XX}}$ = 20,000

Chapter 15

PERPETUAL CALENDAR

The use of this perpetual calendar will enable you to determine the day of the week on which any date fell or will fall during the two centuries from 1901 to 2100. To locate a date and day of the week, first locate the year in which you are interested in the list below. Following the year is a letter to tell you which calendar to use on the pages which follow. In addition, if you are planning schedules, etc. for the next year or two and do not yet have copies of those calendars, simply look up the year and the calendar letter, and you will then have a calendar for the entire year in question.

1901 C	1918 C	1935 C	1952 J	1969 D	1986 D	2003 D	2020 K	2037 E	2054 E	2071 E	2088 L
1902 D	1919 D	1936 K	1953 E	1970 E	1987 E	2004 L	2021 F	2038 F	2055 F	2072 M	2089 G
1903 E	1920 L	1937 F	1954 F	1971 F	1988 M	2005 G	2022 G	2039 G	2056 N	2073 A	2090 A
1904 M	1921 G	1938 G	1955 G	1972 N	1989 A	2006 A	2023 A	2040 H	2057 B	2074 B	2091 B
1905 A	1922 A	1939 A	1956 H	1973 B	1990 B	2007 B	2024 I	2041 C	2058 C	2075 C	2092 J
1906 B	1923 B	1940 I	1957 C	1974 C	1991 C	2008 J	2025 D	2042 D	2059 D	2076 K	2093 E
1907 C	1924 J	1941 D	1958 D	1975 D	1992 K	2009 E	2026 E	2043 E	2060 L	2077 F	2094 G
1908 K	1925 E	1942 E	1959 E	1976 L	1993 F	2010 F	2027 F	2044 M	2061 G	2078 G	2095 H
1909 F	1926 F	1943 F	1960 M	1977 G	1994 G	2011 G	2028 N	2045 A	2062 A	2079 A	2096 C
1910 G	1927 G	1944 N	1961 A	1978 A	1995 A	2012 H	2029 B	2046 B	2063 B	2080 I	2097 C
1911 A	1928 H	1945 B	1962 B	1979 B	1996 I	2013 C	2030 C	2047 C	2064 J	2081 D	2098 D
1912 I	1929 C	1946 C	1963 C	1980 J	1997 D	2014 D	2031 D	2048 K	2065 E	2082 E	2099 E
1913 D	1930 D	1947 D	1964 K	1981 E	1998 E	2015 E	2032 L	2049 F	2066 F	2083 F	2100 F
1914 E	1931 E	1948 L	1965 F	1982 F	1999 F	2016 M	2033 G	2050 G	2067 G	2084 N	
1915 F	1932 M	1949 G	1966 G	1983 G	2000 N	2017 A	2034 A	2051 A	2068 H	2085 B	
1916 N	1933 A	1950 A	1967 A	1984 H	2001 B	2018 B	2035 B	2052 I	2069 C	2086 C	
1917 B	1934 B	1951 B	1968 I	1985 C	2002 C	2019 C	2036 J	2053 D	2070 D	2087 D	

A
(JANUARY, FEBRUARY, MARCH, APRIL, MAY, JUNE, JULY, AUGUST, SEPTEMBER, OCTOBER, NOVEMBER, DECEMBER — monthly calendar grids, columns S M T W T F S)

B
(monthly calendar grids)

C
(monthly calendar grids)

D
(monthly calendar grids)

E
(monthly calendar grids)

F
(monthly calendar grids)

G
(monthly calendar grids)

H
(monthly calendar grids)

I

JANUARY	MAY	SEPTEMBER
S M T W T F S	S M T W T F S	S M T W T F S
1 2 3 4 5 6	5 6 7 8 9 10 11	8 9 10 11 12 13 14
7 8 9 10 11 12 13	12 13 14 15 16 17 18	15 16 17 18 19 20 21
14 15 16 17 18 19 20	19 20 21 22 23 24 25	22 23 24 25 26 27 28
21 22 23 24 25 26 27	26 27 28 29 30 31	29 30
28 29 30 31		

FEBRUARY	JUNE	OCTOBER
S M T W T F S	S M T W T F S	S M T W T F S
1 2 3		1 2 3 4 5
4 5 6 7 8 9 10	2 3 4 5 6 7 8	6 7 8 9 10 11 12
11 12 13 14 15 16 17	9 10 11 12 13 14 15	13 14 15 16 17 18 19
18 19 20 21 22 23 24	16 17 18 19 20 21 22	20 21 22 23 24 25 26
25 26 27 28 29	23 24 25 26 27 28 29	27 28 29 30 31
	30	

MARCH	JULY	NOVEMBER
S M T W T F S	S M T W T F S	S M T W T F S
1 2		1 2
3 4 5 6 7 8 9	7 8 9 10 11 12 13	3 4 5 6 7 8 9
10 11 12 13 14 15 16	14 15 16 17 18 19 20	10 11 12 13 14 15 16
17 18 19 20 21 22 23	21 22 23 24 25 26 27	17 18 19 20 21 22 23
24 25 26 27 28 29 30	28 29 30 31	24 25 26 27 28 29 30
31		

APRIL	AUGUST	DECEMBER
S M T W T F S	S M T W T F S	S M T W T F S
1 2		1 2 3 4 5 6 7
7 8 9 10 11 12 13	4 5 6 7 8 9 10	8 9 10 11 12 13 14
14 15 16 17 18 19 20	11 12 13 14 15 16 17	15 16 17 18 19 20 21
21 22 23 24 25 26 27	18 19 20 21 22 23 24	22 23 24 25 26 27 28
28 29 30	25 26 27 28 29 30 31	29 30 31

K

JANUARY	MAY	SEPTEMBER
S M T W T F S	S M T W T F S	S M T W T F S
	1 2	1 2 3 4 5
12 13 14 15 16 17 18	10 11 12 13 14 15 16	13 14 15 16 17 18 19
19 20 21 22 23 24 25	17 18 19 20 21 22 23	20 21 22 23 24 25 26
26 27 28 29 30 31	24 25 26 27 28 29 30	27 28 29 30
	31	

FEBRUARY	JUNE	OCTOBER
S M T W T F S	S M T W T F S	S M T W T F S
	1	1 2 3
2 3 4 5 6 7 8	7 8 9 10 11 12 13	4 5 6 7 8 9 10
9 10 11 12 13 14 15	14 15 16 17 18 19 20	11 12 13 14 15 16 17
16 17 18 19 20 21 22	21 22 23 24 25 26 27	18 19 20 21 22 23 24
23 24 25 26 27 28 29	28 29 30	25 26 27 28 29 30 31

MARCH	JULY	NOVEMBER
S M T W T F S	S M T W T F S	S M T W T F S
1 2 3 4 5 6 7		1 2 3 4 5 6 7
8 9 10 11 12 13 14	12 13 14 15 16 17 18	8 9 10 11 12 13 14
15 16 17 18 19 20 21	19 20 21 22 23 24 25	15 16 17 18 19 20 21
22 23 24 25 26 27 28	26 27 28 29 30 31	22 23 24 25 26 27 28
29 30 31		29 30

APRIL	AUGUST	DECEMBER
S M T W T F S	S M T W T F S	S M T W T F S
1 2 3 4		1 2 3 4 5
5 6 7 8 9 10 11	2 3 4 5 6 7 8	6 7 8 9 10 11 12
12 13 14 15 16 17 18	9 10 11 12 13 14 15	13 14 15 16 17 18 19
19 20 21 22 23 24 25	16 17 18 19 20 21 22	20 21 22 23 24 25 26
26 27 28 29 30	23 24 25 26 27 28 29	27 28 29 30 31
	30 31	

M

JANUARY	MAY	SEPTEMBER
S M T W T F S	S M T W T F S	S M T W T F S
1 2	1 2 3 4 5 6 7	1 2 3
10 11 12 13 14 15 16	15 16 17 18 19 20 21	4 5 6 7 8 9 10
17 18 19 20 21 22 23	22 23 24 25 26 27 28	11 12 13 14 15 16 17
24 25 26 27 28 29 30	29 30 31	18 19 20 21 22 23 24
31		25 26 27 28 29 30

FEBRUARY	JUNE	OCTOBER
S M T W T F S	S M T W T F S	S M T W T F S
1 2 3 4 5 6	1 2 3 4	1
7 8 9 10 11 12 13	5 6 7 8 9 10 11	2 3 4 5 6 7 8
14 15 16 17 18 19 20	12 13 14 15 16 17 18	9 10 11 12 13 14 15
21 22 23 24 25 26 27	19 20 21 22 23 24 25	16 17 18 19 20 21 22
28 29	26 27 28 29 30	23 24 25 26 27 28 29
		30 31

MARCH	JULY	NOVEMBER
S M T W T F S	S M T W T F S	S M T W T F S
1 2 3 4 5		1 2 3 4 5
6 7 8 9 10 11 12	3 4 5 6 7 8 9	6 7 8 9 10 11 12
13 14 15 16 17 18 19	10 11 12 13 14 15 16	13 14 15 16 17 18 19
20 21 22 23 24 25 26	17 18 19 20 21 22 23	20 21 22 23 24 25 26
27 28 29 30 31	24 25 26 27 28 29 30	27 28 29 30
	31	

APRIL	AUGUST	DECEMBER
S M T W T F S	S M T W T F S	S M T W T F S
1 2	1 2 3 4 5 6	1 2 3
3 4 5 6 7 8 9	7 8 9 10 11 12 13	4 5 6 7 8 9 10
10 11 12 13 14 15 16	14 15 16 17 18 19 20	11 12 13 14 15 16 17
17 18 19 20 21 22 23	21 22 23 24 25 26 27	18 19 20 21 22 23 24
24 25 26 27 28 29 30	28 29 30 31	25 26 27 28 29 30 31

J

JANUARY	MAY	SEPTEMBER
S M T W T F S	S M T W T F S	S M T W T F S
1 2 3 4 5	1 2 3	1 2 3 4 5 6
6 7 8 9 10 11 12	4 5 6 7 8 9 10	7 8 9 10 11 12 13
13 14 15 16 17 18 19	11 12 13 14 15 16 17	14 15 16 17 18 19 20
20 21 22 23 24 25 26	18 19 20 21 22 23 24	21 22 23 24 25 26 27
27 28 29 30 31	25 26 27 28 29 30 31	28 29 30

FEBRUARY	JUNE	OCTOBER
S M T W T F S	S M T W T F S	S M T W T F S
1 2	1 2 3 4 5 6 7	1 2 3 4
3 4 5 6 7 8 9	8 9 10 11 12 13 14	5 6 7 8 9 10 11
10 11 12 13 14 15 16	15 16 17 18 19 20 21	12 13 14 15 16 17 18
17 18 19 20 21 22 23	22 23 24 25 26 27 28	19 20 21 22 23 24 25
24 25 26 27 28 29	29 30	26 27 28 29 30 31

MARCH	JULY	NOVEMBER
S M T W T F S	S M T W T F S	S M T W T F S
1		1
2 3 4 5 6 7 8	6 7 8 9 10 11 12	2 3 4 5 6 7 8
9 10 11 12 13 14 15	13 14 15 16 17 18 19	9 10 11 12 13 14 15
16 17 18 19 20 21 22	20 21 22 23 24 25 26	16 17 18 19 20 21 22
23 24 25 26 27 28 29	27 28 29 30 31	23 24 25 26 27 28 29
30 31		30

APRIL	AUGUST	DECEMBER
S M T W T F S	S M T W T F S	S M T W T F S
1 2 3 4 5 6	1 2 3	1 2 3 4 5 6
6 7 8 9 10 11 12	3 4 5 6 7 8 9	7 8 9 10 11 12 13
13 14 15 16 17 18 19	10 11 12 13 14 15 16	14 15 16 17 18 19 20
20 21 22 23 24 25 26	17 18 19 20 21 22 23	21 22 23 24 25 26 27
27 28 29 30	24 25 26 27 28 29 30	28 29 30 31
	31	

L

JANUARY	MAY	SEPTEMBER
S M T W T F S	S M T W T F S	S M T W T F S
1 2 3	1 2 3	1 2 3 4
4 5 6 7 8 9 10	2 3 4 5 6 7 8	5 6 7 8 9 10 11
11 12 13 14 15 16 17	9 10 11 12 13 14 15	12 13 14 15 16 17 18
18 19 20 21 22 23 24	16 17 18 19 20 21 22	19 20 21 22 23 24 25
25 26 27 28 29 30 31	23 24 25 26 27 28 29	26 27 28 29 30
	30 31	

FEBRUARY	JUNE	OCTOBER
S M T W T F S	S M T W T F S	S M T W T F S
1 2 3 4 5 6 7	1 2 3 4 5	1 2
8 9 10 11 12 13 14	6 7 8 9 10 11 12	3 4 5 6 7 8 9
15 16 17 18 19 20 21	13 14 15 16 17 18 19	10 11 12 13 14 15 16
22 23 24 25 26 27 28	20 21 22 23 24 25 26	17 18 19 20 21 22 23
29	27 28 29 30	24 25 26 27 28 29 30
		31

MARCH	JULY	NOVEMBER
S M T W T F S	S M T W T F S	S M T W T F S
1 2 3 4 5 6	1 2 3	1 2 3 4 5 6
7 8 9 10 11 12 13	4 5 6 7 8 9 10	7 8 9 10 11 12 13
14 15 16 17 18 19 20	11 12 13 14 15 16 17	14 15 16 17 18 19 20
21 22 23 24 25 26 27	18 19 20 21 22 23 24	21 22 23 24 25 26 27
28 29 30 31	25 26 27 28 29 30 31	28 29 30

APRIL	AUGUST	DECEMBER
S M T W T F S	S M T W T F S	S M T W T F S
1 2 3	1 2 3 4 5 6 7	1 2 3 4
4 5 6 7 8 9 10	8 9 10 11 12 13 14	5 6 7 8 9 10 11
11 12 13 14 15 16 17	15 16 17 18 19 20 21	12 13 14 15 16 17 18
18 19 20 21 22 23 24	22 23 24 25 26 27 28	19 20 21 22 23 24 25
25 26 27 28 29 30	29 30 31	26 27 28 29 30 31

N

JANUARY	MAY	SEPTEMBER
S M T W T F S	S M T W T F S	S M T W T F S
1	1	1 2 3 4
2 3 4 5 6 7 8	7 8 9 10 11 12 13	5 6 7 8 9 10 11
9 10 11 12 13 14 15	14 15 16 17 18 19 20	12 13 14 15 16 17 18
16 17 18 19 20 21 22	21 22 23 24 25 26 27	19 20 21 22 23 24 25
23 24 25 26 27 28 29	28 29 30 31	26 27 28 29 30
30 31		

FEBRUARY	JUNE	OCTOBER
S M T W T F S	S M T W T F S	S M T W T F S
1 2 3 4 5	1 2 3	1 2
6 7 8 9 10 11 12	4 5 6 7 8 9 10	3 4 5 6 7 8 9
13 14 15 16 17 18 19	11 12 13 14 15 16 17	10 11 12 13 14 15 16
20 21 22 23 24 25 26	18 19 20 21 22 23 24	17 18 19 20 21 22 23
27 28 29	25 26 27 28 29 30	24 25 26 27 28 29 30
		31

MARCH	JULY	NOVEMBER
S M T W T F S	S M T W T F S	S M T W T F S
1 2 3 4	1 2 3 4 5 6 7	1 2 3 4 5 6
5 6 7 8 9 10 11	2 3 4 5 6 7 8	7 8 9 10 11 12 13
12 13 14 15 16 17 18	16 17 18 19 20 21 22	14 15 16 17 18 19 20
19 20 21 22 23 24 25	23 24 25 26 27 28 29	21 22 23 24 25 26 27
26 27 28 29 30 31	30 31	28 29 30

APRIL	AUGUST	DECEMBER
S M T W T F S	S M T W T F S	S M T W T F S
1	1 2 3 4 5	1 2
2 3 4 5 6 7 8	6 7 8 9 10 11 12	3 4 5 6 7 8 9
9 10 11 12 13 14 15	13 14 15 16 17 18 19	10 11 12 13 14 15 16
16 17 18 19 20 21 22	20 21 22 23 24 25 26	17 18 19 20 21 22 23
23 24 25 26 27 28 29	27 28 29 30 31	24 25 26 27 28 29 30
30		31

SPACE EXPLORATION

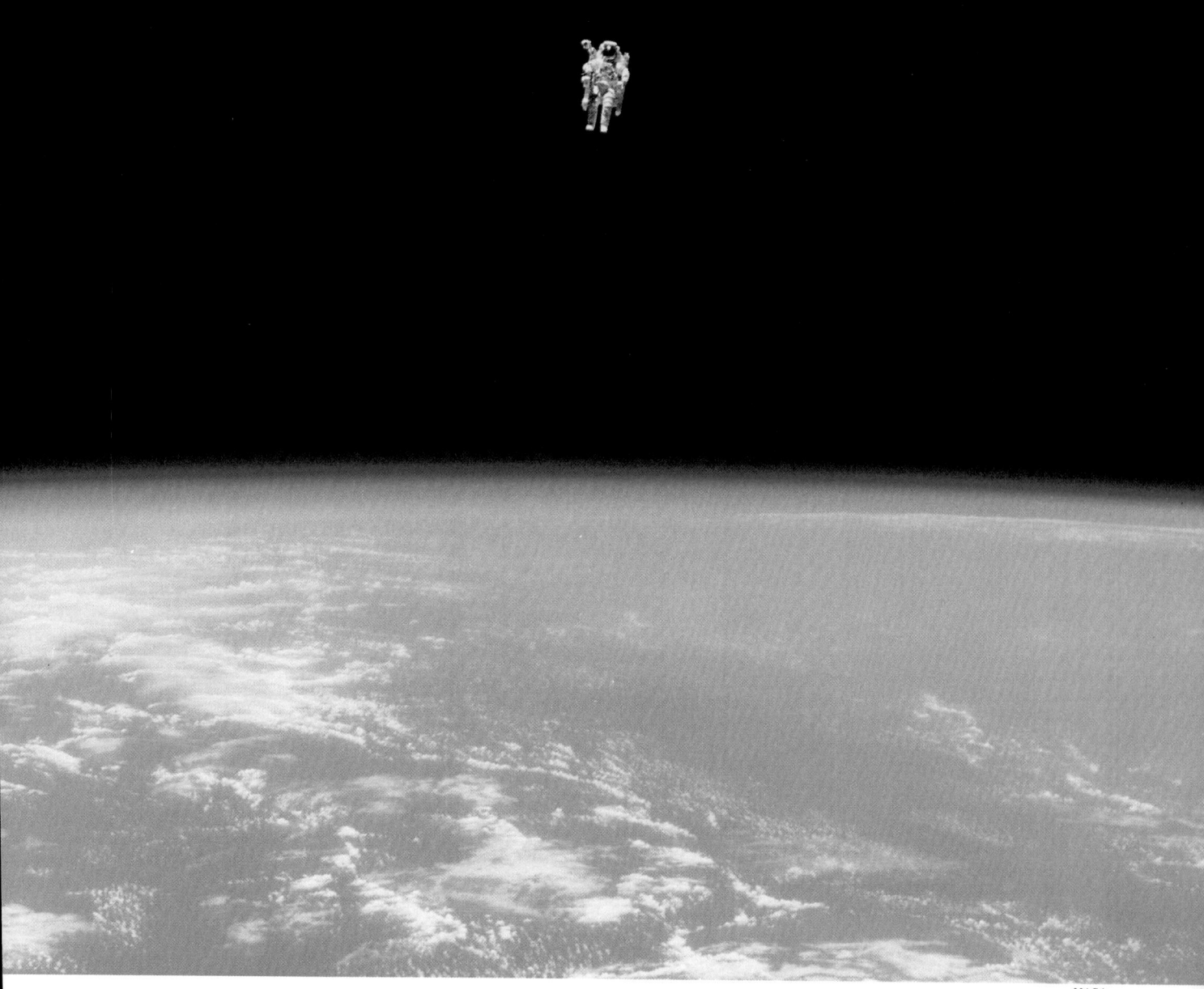

NASA

Expanding Our Horizons

"That's one small step for a man, one giant leap for mankind." These memorable words were spoken by Neil A. Armstrong on July 20, 1969, as he became the first person to step onto the moon. Armstrong's words aptly describe not only the mission that landed people on the moon but space exploration in general. For as President Lyndon B. Johnson had pointed out, "the moon trip is just one of the many goals" of space exploration.

Some of the goals, such as landing people on the moon and sending unmanned craft to other planets, have been achieved. But with each accomplishment new goals are set, new plans made for the future. By the late 1980s, scientists were looking toward the time when people would visit Mars, when permanent manufacturing facilities would operate in space, when contact would be made with life on other worlds.

The knowledge gained from space exploration has been immense. Instruments aboard spacecraft discovered the Van Allen belt (a zone of radiation encircling Earth) and previously unknown moons circling around Jupiter, Saturn, and Uranus. They have provided much data on such phenomena as solar flares, planetary rings, exploding galaxies, and binary stars. They have yielded valuable information about natural processes occurring on Earth, and about people and how they function in strange environments.

There also have been many practical rewards from the space program. Space-based sensors identify areas that are likely to have petroleum or other mineral deposits. They help forecast harvests and find new fishing grounds in remote waters. They monitor the movement of storms, air pollutants, and volcanic debris. They aid in search-and-rescue missions for lost ships, monitor temperatures to warn farmers of an approaching freeze, enable the evacuation of people from the paths of hurricanes. Thanks to communication satellites, previously isolated communities receive radio and television service.

The transfer of space technology to everyday life has been enormous: new systems for purifying and treating water and wastes . . . the rapid development and miniaturization of computers . . . new food preservation methods . . . .

Epoxy graphite materials that are light yet strong and rigid were developed for use in spacecraft, and now are also used to make ski poles and fishing rods. High-intensity flashlights developed to mimic the effects of sunlight on spacecraft are now used by campers and search-and-rescue teams. And in 1985 the first commercial products actually made in space became available: tiny latex spheres all exactly the same size. These spheres are used for instrument calibration in medical and industrial work, and they cannot be produced on Earth because of the adverse effects of gravity.

Finally, space exploration has changed forever the way we view our planet. Color photographs taken from outer space show how very beautiful Earth is—and how very different from the barren surfaces of other planets. No other planet in the solar system has the lush greenery, the sparkling oceans, the oxygen-filled atmosphere that form our most precious heritage.

A CHRONOLOGY

The following chronological review of the highlights of space exploration is divided into three broad groups: earth satellites, planetary and lunar missions, and manned space missions.

Earth Satellites

Earth-orbiting satellites are the oldest type of spacecraft—the first one, Sputnik 1, was launched on Oct. 4, 1957. Since then thousands more have been launched; these vehicles have become the workhorses of communications, navigation, weather forecasting, and intelligence gathering. (The date at the beginning of each entry is the craft's launch date.)

1957

Oct. 4: Sputnik 1 (USSR). The first successful artificial satellite.
Nov. 3: Sputnik 2 (USSR). The second satellite and the first to carry a living organism—a dog named Laika—into space.

1958

Jan. 31: Explorer 1 (U.S.). The first American satellite. Discovered the inner (Van Allen) radiation belt.
March 17: Vanguard 1 (U.S.). Contained two transmitters, one operating on solar power supply.
May 15: Sputnik 3 (USSR). A geophysical laboratory.
Dec. 18: Score (U.S.). A military communications relay satellite. On Dec. 19, transmitted a prerecorded tape of President Eisenhower's Christmas message to the nation.

Sputnik 1, the first artificial satellite, was a metal ball 23 inches (58 centimeters) in diameter. It circled Earth for 1 hour 36.2 minutes.

Tass/Sovfoto

1959

Aug. 7: Explorer 6 (U.S.). Gathered radiation, magnetic field, and micrometeorite data. Took the first TV photographs of Earth as seen from space.

1960

April 1: Tiros—Television and Infrared Observation Satellite (U.S.). The first weather satellite. During a period of 2½ months it sent back 22,952 photographs of global cloud conditions.
May 24: Midas 2 (U.S.). The first missile launch detection satellite. It was equipped with infrared sensors capable of picking up the exhaust heat from a ballistic missile as it left the ground.
Aug. 10: Discoverer 13 (U.S.). Ejected a 300-lb (136-kg) reentry capsule recovered from the Pacific Ocean—the first object recovered from space.
Aug. 12: Echo 1 (U.S.). The first passive communication satellite. Reflected communications between the U.S. and the United Kingdom (U.K.).

1961

Feb. 16: Explorer 9 (U.S.). The first satellite launching by an all-solid-propellant rocket vehicle.
June 29: Transit 4A, Injun 1, and **Solrad 3** (U.S.). The first triple launch. The first nuclear power supply in space.
Dec. 12: Oscar—Orbiting Satellite Carrying Amateur Radio (U.S.). The first privately built satellite, constructed by radio hams. It transmitted for 18 days.

1962

March 7: OSO 1—Orbiting Solar Observatory (U.S.). Carried out the first comprehensive study of the sun from a satellite.
April 26: Ariel 1 (U.S.-U.K.; launched by U.S.). The first international satellite. Conducted atmospheric studies.
July 10: Telstar 1 (U.S.). The first commercially financed communications satellite and the first satellite to transmit live TV and telephone conversations across the Atlantic, between the U.S., U.K., and France.
Sept. 28: Alouette 1 (Canada; launched by U.S.). The first satellite to be wholly designed and built by a nation other than the U.S. or USSR. Conducted ionospheric measurements.
Oct. 31: Anna 1-B (U.S.). The first in a series of geodetic satellites.

1963

July 26: Syncom 2 (U.S.). The first synchronous communications satellite.
Sept. 28: Transit 5-B (U.S.). The first satellite to be completely powered by a nuclear isotope generator.
Oct. 16: Vela 1 and **Vela 2** (U.S.). Designed to detect nuclear explosions.

Nov. 1: Polyot 1 (USSR). The first satellite capable of maneuvering in all directions and able to change its orbit.

1964

Jan. 30: Electron 1 and **Electron 2** (USSR). The first Soviet dual launch. The craft measured Earth's radiation belt.
March 27: Ariel 2 (U.K.; launched by U.S.). Britain's second satellite.
Aug. 28: Nimbus 1 (U.S.). The first of a new type of weather satellite. Unlike Tiros, its cameras moved to keep Earth's surface in view at all times.
Sept. 4: OGO 1—Orbiting Geophysical Observatory (U.S.). Carried 20 coordinated geophysical experiments.
Dec. 15: San Marco 1 (Italy; launched in U.S.). Launched by an Italian crew.

1965

Feb. 16: Pegasus 1 (U.S.). The first in a series of satellites designed to evaluate the danger of a puncture of a spacecraft by micrometeorites and dust in the vicinity of Earth.
April 6: Intelsat 1 (U.S.). Also known as Early Bird. The first commercial communications satellite in synchronous orbit.
April 23: Molniya 1A (USSR). The first Soviet communications satellite.
April 3: Snapshot (U.S.). Tested the performance of the SNAP 10-A (Systems Nuclear Auxiliary Power) system under space conditions. The first known launch of a nuclear-fission reactor into Earth orbit.
Nov. 26: A-1 (France). France thereby became the third nation to launch satellites by its own means.
Dec. 6: FR-1 (France; launched jointly by France and U.S.).

1966

Feb. 3: ESSA 1 (U.S.). An Environmental Sciences Services Administration satellite. Together with ESSA 2, launched Feb. 28, marked the beginning of regular operational use by the U.S. Weather Bureau of information gained from cloud-covered observations. The two satellites were placed into nearly polar orbits, enabling them to survey Earth's entire surface every day.
Feb. 22: Cosmos 110 (USSR). Carrying two dogs, orbited Earth for 22 days. Helped determine the effects of radiation and long periods of weightlessness.
Dec. 6: ATS 1—Applications Technology Satellite (U.S.). Proved the possibility of two-way communications between ground stations and aircraft in flight.

1967

Apr. 26: San Marco 2 (Italy). Italy thereby became the fourth nation to launch satellites by its own means.
Sept. 7: Biosatellite 2 (U.S.). Aboard were plants, insects, amoebas, frog eggs, and other specimens. Tested the effects of weightlessness and radiation.
Nov. 28: WRESAT 1 (Australia). Australia became the fifth nation to launch satellites by its own means.

1968

April 14-15: Cosmos 212 and **Cosmos 213** (USSR). Docked and undocked automatically in space.
May 17: ESRO 2B—European Space Research Organization. (A ten-nation international group; launched by U.S.). The satellite studied space physics and Earth's environment.
July 4: Explorer 38 (U.S.). The first of a series of radio astronomy satellites.

1969

April 14: Nimbus 3 (U.S.). The first weather satellite to provide radiometric data for determining vertical temperature and water-vapor profiles (needed for numerical weather prediction).

COMSTAT

Intelsat V, launched in late 1980, is part of a global communications system established by the International Telecommunications Satellite Consortium.

Nov. 8: Azur (West Germany; launched by U.S.). The first West German satellite. Studied Earth's atmosphere and radiation belt.

1970

Feb. 11: Ohsumi (Japan). The first satellite launched by Japan.
April 24: China 1 (China). The first satellite launched by China. It transmitted music and telemetric signals.
Nov. 9: OFO—Orbiting Frog Otolith (U.S.). Two frogs with microelectrodes implanted in their inner ears were monitored to study the effects of weightlessness and simulated gravity conditions.

1971

Oct. 28: Prospero (U.K.; launched in Australia). Britain's first technology satellite.
Dec. 27: Aureole (USSR). The first satellite launched by the USSR with French assistance. It studied the upper atmosphere in high latitudes and the polar lights.

1972

July 23: ERTS 1—Earth Resources Technology Satellite (U.S.). Carried remote sensing devices to gather data on Earth's resources. Later renamed Landsat 1.
Aug. 21: OAD 3—Orbiting Astronomical Observatory; also named Copernicus (U.S.). Studied stellar ultraviolet radiation. Operated until Dec. 30, 1980.
Nov. 10: Anik 1 (Canada). Canada's first domestic communications satellite.

1973

Oct. 31: Cosmos 605 (USSR). An animal flight test of manned spaceflight systems.

1974

May 17: SMS-1 (U.S.). The first meteorological satellite placed in a synchronous orbit.

1975

April 19: Aryabhata (India; launched by USSR). India's first satellite.

1976

Feb. 19: Marisat 1 (U.S.). The first of a new class of maritime satellites designed to enable merchant ships to transmit voice, data, facsimile, and telex messages to U.S. shore stations interconnected with domestic terrestrial networks.
May 4: Lageos—Laser Geodynamics Satellite (U.S.). Conducted long-term geodetic studies.
July 8: Palapa 1 (Indonesia; launched by U.S.). Provided transmission of television, voice, and data throughout Indonesia.

1977

Aug. 12: HEAO 1—High Energy Astronomy Observatory (U.S.). Surveyed and mapped X-ray sources.
Sept. 18: Cosmos 954 (USSR). Ocean surveillance craft with a nuclear reactor. In Jan. 1978, disintegrated and fell over northern Canada; no known injuries.
Nov. 22: Meteosat 1 (ESA; launched by U.S.). The first of a series of five global weather satellites sponsored by a total of 145 nations.
Dec. 15: Sakura (Japan; launched by U.S.). An experimental communications satellite that tested the relay of various communication signals among the Japanese islands.

1978

April 26: HCMM—Heat-Capacity-Mapping Mission (U.S.). Measured day and night temperature differences on Earth's surface.
Aug. 12: ISEE—International Sun Earth Explorer-C (U.S.). Monitored sun spots, solar flares, and the solar wind. In Dec. 1983, was renamed International Cometary Explorer (ICE) and redirected to intercept comet Giacobini-Zinner. On Sept. 11, 1985, passed through the tail of Giacobini-Zinner—the first spacecraft to probe a comet.
Oct. 24: Nimbus 7 (U.S.). The first pollution monitoring satellite.
Nov. 13: HEAO 2 (U.S.). Also known as the Einstein Observatory. Studied pulsars, quasars, black holes, and exploding galaxies.

1979

June 27: NOAA-6 (U.S.). Weather and earth-resources satellite orbited for the National Oceanic and Atmospheric Administration. It and Tiros-N (launched Oct. 13, 1978) provided round-the-clock scanning of Earth's surface and atmosphere and monitored solar radiation levels above the atmosphere.
Sept. 20: HEAO 3 (U.S.). Measured cosmic and gamma radiation.
Oct. 30: MAGSAT—Magnetic Field Satellite (U.S.). Provided a complete survey of Earth's magnetic field for use in updating maps. Assisted in the search for mineral resources on Earth.

1980

Feb. 14: Solar Maximum Mission or Solar Max (U.S.). Examined the physics of solar flares and their effects on Earth.
Sept. 9: GOES-4—Geostationary Operational Environmental Satellite (U.S.). The first in a series of weather satellites placed into synchronous orbits to provide high-resolution images over large areas of North and South America and surrounding oceans at least every 30 minutes. Part of the Global Weather Watch project.

Satellites have proven invaluable. Communications craft (*top*: AUSSAT) provide radio, TV, and telephone services. Weather craft (*above*: Tiros) monitor storms. Surveying craft (*facing page, left*: ERTS) map natural resources. Astronomical craft (*facing page, right*: IRAS) study heavenly bodies.

1981

June 19: Meteostat 2, a European Space Agency (ESA) weather satellite, and Apple, a communications satellite for India. The first satellite launched by ESA.
Aug. 3: Dynamics Explorers 1 and 2 (U.S.). Studied space around Earth from the limits of the upper atmosphere to distances far out in Earth's magnetic field.
Oct. 6: Solar Mesosphere Explorer (U.S.). Studied reactions between sunlight and molecules in the atmosphere.
Dec. 20: MARECS-1—Maritime Communications Satellite (ESA). Part of a global communications system designed to provide voice, data, and teleprinter services between ship and land stations.

1982

May 17: Iskra 2 (USSR). An amateur radio satellite placed into orbit by cosmonauts aboard Salyut 7—believed to be the first launch of a satellite from an orbiting space station.
Nov. 11: SBS 3—Satellite Business System (U.S.). and Anik C (Canada). The first satellite deployed from a space shuttle.

1983

Jan. 25: IRAS—Infrared Astronomical Satellite (U.S.). Provided first direct evidence of the possible existence of other planetary systems.

April 5: TDRS—Tracking and Data Relay Satellite (U.S.). Designed to provide a communication link between space shuttles and ground stations. Launched by Mission STS 6.

1984

Jan. 23: Yuri 2A (Japan). The first high-power direct TV broadcast satellite, designed for transmission to remote areas and urban areas inhibited by high buildings.

Aug. 16: AMPTE—Active Magnetospheric Particle Tracer Explorers (U.S.). Three satellites from West Germany, the U.K., and the U.S. launched simultaneously to study the interaction of the solar wind with Earth's magnetosphere. On Dec. 27, the German satellite released two containers of barium, which discharged their contents to form a dense cloud—the first artificial comet.

1985

Feb. 8: Arabsat-1 (Arab League; launched by Arianespace). The first of a series of satellites designed to provide the 22-member states of the Arab League with various TV and communications services.

July 10: Cosmos 1667 Biosatellite (USSR). Carried two rhesus monkeys, one of which was equipped with sensors provided by the U.S. On July 17, returned to Earth; flight data provided to American investigators for analysis.

1986

Feb. 21: SPOT (France). A commercial remote-sensing satellite that provides extremely detailed photographs of Earth's surface.

An artist's rendition of an unmanned Surveyor craft on the moon's surface, with Earth on the horizon, some 240,000 miles (386,000 kilometers) distant.

Planetary and Lunar Missions

Unmanned space probes are the pioneers of the solar system and, indeed, of the universe itself. Such planetary and lunar missions were the first to visit the moon, to orbit the sun, to visit other planets. One such probe has left the solar system. (The date at the beginning of each entry is the craft's launch date.)

1959

Jan. 2: Luna 1 (USSR). The first successful lunar probe. Passed within 3,728 mi (6,000 km) of the moon.
March 3: Pioneer 4 (U.S.). The first successful U.S. lunar probe. Passed within 37,300 mi (60,000 km) of the moon.
Sept. 12: Luna 2 (USSR) moon probe. The first spacecraft to hit the moon's surface. Obtained magnetic field, cosmic and solar radiation, micrometeoroid, and gas composition data.
Oct. 4: Luna 3 (USSR) moon probe. Took the first photographs of the moon's far side.

1960

March 11: Pioneer 5 (U.S.) solar satellite. Radioed back data on the interplanetary magnetic field and the interaction of Earth's magnetic field with the solar wind.

1962

March 7: OSO 1 (U.S.) solar satellite. Obtained data on solar flares.

April 23: Ranger 4 (U.S.) lunar probe. An apparent electronics failure caused it to impact on the moon—the first U.S. spacecraft to make contact with the moon's surface. No scientific data obtained.
Aug. 27: Mariner 2 (U.S.) launched toward Venus. On Dec. 14, passed within 22,000 mi (35,400 km) of Venus—the first spacecraft to visit another planet. Radioed back information on Venus' atmosphere, surface temperatures, and cloud cover.

1964

July 28: Ranger 7 (U.S.) moon probe. Transmitted more than 4,300 photographs of the lunar surface before impact.
Nov. 28: Mariner 4 (U.S.) Mars probe. On July 14, 1965, passed within 6,200 mi (9,980 km) of Mars—the first spacecraft to visit the planet. During the 25-minute encounter it took 21 photographs of the Martian surface.

1965

Feb. 17: Ranger 8 (U.S.) lunar probe. Impacted on the moon Feb. 20. Transmitted more than 7,100 photographs of the lunar surface.
March 21: Ranger 9 (U.S.) lunar probe. Impacted on the moon March 24. Transmitted more than 5,800 photographs.
July 18: Zond 3 (USSR) lunar probe. On July 20, flew past the far side of the moon, photographing the surface.
Nov. 16: Venera 3 (USSR) launched toward Venus. On March 1, 1966, hit Venus—the first spacecraft to impact another planet. Failed to return planetary data.
Dec. 16: Pioneer 6 (U.S.) solar satellite. Obtained a wealth of data on the sun.

1966

Jan. 31: Luna 9 (USSR) lunar probe. On Feb. 3, became first spacecraft to soft-land on the moon. For three days it transmitted photographs of the lunar surface.
March 31: Luna 10 (USSR) lunar probe. On April 3, became the first probe to enter a lunar orbit.
May 30: Surveyor 1 (U.S.) moon probe. On June 2, became the first U.S. probe to soft-land on the moon. Transmitted 11,150 photographs of itself and the lunar surface before ceasing transmission on July 14.
Aug. 10: Lunar Orbiter 1 (U.S.) moon satellite. First U.S. lunar orbiting probe. Photographed the lunar surface for studies of possible Apollo landing sites.
Aug. 17: Pioneer 7 (U.S.) solar satellite. Investigated phenomena of interplanetary space.
Aug. 24: Luna 11 (USSR). Launched into an orbit around the moon.
Oct. 22: Luna 12 (USSR). Launched into an orbit around the moon. Transmitted photographs and scientific data.
Nov. 6: Lunar Orbiter 2 (U.S.) moon probe. Provided photographs and data that helped in selecting locations for a manned lunar landing.
Dec. 21: Luna 13 (USSR) lunar probe. Landed on the moon Dec. 24. Returned photographs and soil density data.

1967

April 17: Surveyor 3 (U.S.). Landed on the moon April 20. Took photographs and soil samples.
June 12: Venera 4 (USSR) Venus probe. On Oct. 18, the main body of the probe crashed into the planet's surface. As it approached, it ejected a capsule that parachuted to the surface. Instruments in the capsule returned data on the Venusian atmosphere during the descent.
June 14: Mariner 5 (U.S.) Venus probe. On Oct. 19, passed within 25,000 mi (40,230 km) of Venus.
July 19: Explorer 35 (U.S.). Placed into a lunar orbit. Measured Earth's magnetic tail every 29.5 days.
August 1: Lunar Orbiter 5 (U.S.). Last in a series of moon probes. On Aug. 5, entered a lunar polar orbit. Photographed areas not previously covered.
Sept. 8: Surveyor 5 (U.S.). Landed on the moon Sept. 11. Transmitted soil analysis data and 19,000 photographs.

Nov. 7: Surveyor 6 (U.S.) moon probe. On Nov. 10, landed on the moon. On Nov. 24, its three engines were fired to lift it slightly off the lunar surface and move sideways about 8 ft (2.4 m)—the first lateral movement on the moon's surface. It then photographed the spot where it originally stood.

Dec. 13: Pioneer 8 (U.S.) solar satellite. Studied solar phenomena.

1968

Jan. 7: Surveyor 7 (U.S.) moon probe. Landed on the moon Jan. 10—the only Surveyor to land in lunar highlands and in the debris of a relatively young crater. Relayed 21,000 photographs and soil-analysis data. The last of the Surveyor series.

April 7: Luna 14 (USSR) moon probe. On April 10, entered a lunar orbit. Provided data on Earth-Moon mass relationship and the moon's gravitational field.

Sept. 15: Zond 5 (USSR) moon probe. First unmanned round-trip flight to moon. On Sept. 21, returned to Earth.

Nov. 8: Pioneer 9 (U.S.) launched into a solar orbit. Provided data on solar radiation and the space environment between Mars and Venus.

Nov. 10: Zond 6 (U.S.) moon probe. Unmanned circumlunar flight. On Nov. 17, returned to Earth.

1969

Jan. 5: Venera 5 (USSR) Venus probe. On May 16, descent capsule entered Venusian atmosphere and returned 53 minutes of data as it parachuted toward the planet's surface.

Jan. 10: Venera 6 (USSR) Venus probe. On May 17, descent capsule entered Venusian atmosphere but did not transmit data.

Feb. 24: Mariner 6 (U.S.) Mars probe. On July 31, passed Mars at a distance of 2,200 mi (3,540 km). Transmitted photographs of the Martian surface.

March 27: Mariner 7 (U.S.) Mars probe. On Aug. 5, flew over the south pole of Mars. Transmitted 126 photographs.

July 13: Luna 15 (USSR) moon probe. Orbited the moon 52 times before crashing onto the surface on July 21.

Aug. 8: Zond 7 (USSR). Unmanned circumlunar flight. Returned to Earth Aug. 14.

1970

Aug. 17: Venera 7 (USSR) Venus probe. On Dec. 15, reached Venus and released an instrumented capsule that parachuted down to the surface. The capsule transmitted data for 23 minutes—the first time that data was received on Earth from the surface of another planet.

Sept. 12: Luna 16 (USSR) moon probe. On Sept. 20, landed on the Sea of Fertility. Drilled 14 in (35 cm) into the surface and extracted a 3.5-oz (109-g) core, which was placed into Luna's upper stage. On Sept. 24, the upper stage returned to Earth.

Oct. 20: Zond 8 (USSR) moon probe. Unmanned circumlunar flight. On Oct. 27, returned to Earth.

Nov. 10: Luna 17 (USSR) moon probe. On Nov. 17, landed on the Sea of Rains. Released Lunokhod 1, the first automated moon-roving vehicle, which moved over the lunar surface making observations and telemetering data back to Earth.

1971

May 19: Mars 2 (USSR) Mars probe. First Soviet craft to land on Mars.

May 22: Kosmos 422 (USSR) launched into an orbit around Mars.

May 28: Mars 3 (USSR) Mars probe.

May 30: Mariner 9 (USSR) Mars probe. On Nov. 13, entered into an orbit around Mars. Transmitted photographs and data.

Sept. 2: Luna 18 (USSR) moon probe. Completed 54 orbits of the moon. On Sept. 11, impacted on the lunar surface.

Sept. 28: Luna 19 (USSR) moon probe. Entered an orbit around the moon. Photographed the lunar surface.

1972

Feb. 14: Luna 20 (USSR) moon probe. On Feb. 21, landed on the Sea of Fertility. Collected lunar rock and soil samples. On Feb. 25, returned to Earth.

March 2: Pioneer 10 (U.S.) launched toward Jupiter and outer space. On Dec. 3, 1973, passed within 81,000 mi (130,000 km) of Jupiter—the first spacecraft to visit the planet. Transmitted photographs of Jupiter and several of its moons, and sent back data on the planet's atmosphere and magnetic field. On June 13, 1983, crossed the orbit of Neptune, the most distant planet, becoming the first man-made object to go beyond the solar system.

March 27: Venera B (USSR) launched toward Venus. On July 22, reached Venus and released a descent capsule that landed on the planet's sunlit side—the first daylight landing on Venus. Capsule instruments transmitted data on the atmosphere and the landing site.

1973

Jan. 8: Luna 21 (USSR) moon probe. On Jan. 16, landed on the moon; unloaded Lunokhod 2 vehicle, which traveled 23 mi (37 km) on the lunar surface during next four months, transmitting pictures and data.

April 5: Pioneer 11 (U.S.). The second probe to the outer planets. On Dec. 2, 1974, flew within 26,600 mi (42,800 km) of Jupiter; transmitted many photographs, including the first pictures of planet's polar regions. On Sept. 1, 1979, made closest approach to Saturn—the first spacecraft to visit the planet; returned photographs and data. Continued on path to escape solar system.

June 10: Explorer 49 (U.S.). Placed in a lunar orbit. Measured galactic and solar radio noise.

July 25: Mars 5 (USSR) Mars probe. Orbited the planet and returned high-resolution photographs.

Nov. 3: Mariner 10 (U.S.) Venus and Mercury probe—the first spacecraft to explore two planets in the course of a mission and the first to reconnoiter with Mercury. On Feb. 5, 1974, flew past Venus at distance of about 3,600 mi (5,800 km); photographed the planet's thick cloud cover. On March 29, 1974, came with 460 mi (740 km) of Mercury; sent back about 2,000 photographs of the innermost planet. On Sept. 21, 1974, and March 16, 1975, made two additional flybys of Mercury.

Photographs of Jupiter taken by Pioneer 10 in 1973 revealed that the Great Red Spot, the planet's most prominent feature, has a "pinwheel" structure.

NASA

Detailed studies of Mars began with the Viking 1 and 2 probes. Here, two television cameras aboard the Viking 1 orbiter scan the planet's surface.

1974

May 29: Luna 22 (USSR) moon probe. In orbit around moon.
Oct. 28: Luna 23 (USSR). Placed in a lunar orbit. Relayed limited data.
Dec. 10: Helios 1 (West Germany; launched by U.S.) solar probe. Obtained data on interplanetary space in the region near the sun.

1975

June 8: Venera 9 (USSR) Venus probe. On Oct. 22, entered an orbit around Venus and landed an instrument-laden capsule on the planet, which during its 53-minute operational life returned data and the first photographs of the planet's surface.
June 14: Venera 10 (USSR) Venus probe. On Oct. 25, entered an orbit around Venus and landed a capsule, which during its 65-minute operational life returned data and photographs.
Aug. 20: Viking 1 (U.S.) Mars orbiter-lander. On July 20, 1976, the lander made a soft landing on Mars. It sent back the first photographs from the planet's surface and much data. On Aug. 7, 1980, the orbiter, which had mapped the Martian surface, was shut off by radio command.
Sept. 9: Viking 2 (U.S.) Mars orbiter-lander. On Sept 3, 1976, the lander made a soft landing on the Martian surface. Mission objectives similar to those for Viking 1.

1976

Jan 15: Helios 2 (West Germany; launched by U.S.). Solar probe. Three of the ten experiments on board were built by the United States and seven by West Germany. These instruments measured solar wind, magnetic fields, solar and galactic cosmic rays, as well as electromagnetic waves.
Aug. 9: Luna 24 (USSR) lunar probe. Landed on the Sea of Crises and collected a core of lunar soil about 6 ft (1.8 m) long. Returned to Earth Aug. 22.

1977

Aug. 20: Voyager 2 (U.S.) probe to the outer planets. On July 9, 1979, reached Jupiter; transmitted photographs and data. On Aug. 25, 1981, flew past Saturn; transmitted more than 18,000 images of Saturn's rings and satellites. On Jan. 24, 1986, flew within 51,000 mi (82,000 km) of Uranus—the first spacecraft to visit the planet; returned photographs and a wealth of new data. The probe was scheduled to visit Neptune in 1989.
Sept. 5: Voyager 1 (U.S.) probe of outer planets. On March 5, 1979, made closest approach to Jupiter; transmitted photographs of the planet and its moons. On Nov. 12, 1980, made closest approach to Saturn; returned photographs and data; discovered unknown rings and moons.

1978

May 20: Pioneer Venus 1 (U.S.) Venus probe. On Dec. 4, placed in orbit around Venus. Returned data on the atmosphere and weather of Venus.

Aug. 8: Pioneer Venus 2 (U.S.) Venus probe. On Dec. 9, entered an orbit around Venus; five payloads entered the planet's atmosphere to measure temperature, chemical composition, and weather conditions.

Sept. 9: Venera 11 (USSR) Venus orbiter. On Dec. 25, deployed a probe that landed on Venus and transmitted data for 95 minutes.

Sept. 14: Venera 12 (USSR) Venus orbiter. On Dec. 21, deployed a probe that descended to the planet's surface transmitting data for 110 minutes.

1981

Oct. 30: Venera 13 (USSR) Venus probe. On March 1, 1982, parachute-landed on the planet's surface. Survived 127 minutes before the planet's intense heat put it out of commission. Radioed back eight photographs and information on water vapor content of the atmosphere. Inert gases of neon, krypton, and possibly xenon also were discovered in an atmosphere that is composed principally of carbon dioxide.

Nov. 4: Venera 14 (USSR) Venus probe. On March 5, 1982, parachute-landed on the planet. Operated for about an hour. Provided spectra obtained from Venusian soil samples.

1983

June 2: Venera 15 (USSR) Venus probe. On Oct. 10, 1983, arrived at Venus. Conducted high-resolution radar-mapping of the planet's surface.

June 7: Venera 16 (USSR) Venus probe. On Oct. 14, 1983, arrived at Venus. Conducted high-resolution radar mapping of the planet's surface.

1984

Dec. 15: Vega 1 (USSR). On June 11, 1985: flew past Venus, deploying a descent module containing a balloon probe and a lander, which gathered data on the planet's atmosphere and soil composition. On March 6, 1986, flew within 5,500 mi (8,850 km) of Comet Halley's core, transmitting the first views of the comet's nucleus.

Dec. 21: Vega 2 (USSR). On June 15, 1985: flew past Venus, deploying a descent module containing a balloon probe and a lander, which gathered data on the planet's atmosphere and soil composition. On March 9, 1986, flew within 5,200 mi (8,360 km) of Comet Halley's nucleus, sending data to Earth on the comet's structure.

1985

Jan 8: Sakigake (Japan) launched toward an encounter with Comet Halley. It flew within 4.3 million mi (6.9 million km) of the comet on March 11, 1986, for an examination of solar winds and magnetic fields.

July 2: Giotto (ESA) probe launched toward an encounter with Comet Halley. On March 14, 1986, came within 335 mi (539 km) of the comet's nucleus, sending back the closest pictures ever taken of the object.

Aug. 19: Suisei (Japan) probe launched toward an encounter with Comet Halley. On March 8, 1986, passed within 94,000 mi (151,000 km) of the comet, transmitting data on the interaction between the solar wind and the comet's enveloping gases.

Space probes have sent back to Earth a great deal of information about other planets. Venera probes revealed that Venus (*top*), hidden beneath thick clouds that telescopes on Earth cannot penetrate, has a crated surface. Voyagers 1 and 2 discovered previously unknown moons circling Saturn (*middle*) and revealed that this planet has more than 100 rings. Voyager 2 detected unknown moons and a tenth ring around Uranus (*bottom*), and determined that Uranus has a magnetic field that is only about a third the strength of Earth's.

NASA, Hansen Planetarium

NASA

JPL

Manned Space Missions

Of all the space missions, the manned one have most captured people's imaginations. Such missions began after unmanned vehicles had helped perfect the necessary technologies and studies had been conducted to determine how to overcome the hazards of weightlessness, radiation, and other perils faced by people in a space environment. (A single date at the beginning of an entry denotes a one-day mission or the date of launch. A combined date, e.g. Dec. 10-March 16, 1968, is the date of the flight. It was launched on Dec. 10, 1967, and concluded on March 16, 1968.)

1961

April 12: Vostok 1 (USSR). Crew: Yuri A. Gagarin—the first person in space. Completed one orbit of Earth. The flight lasted 1 hour 48 minutes.

May 5: Freedom 7 (U.S.). Crew: Alan B. Shepard, Jr.—the first American in space. A suborbital flight, lasting 15 minutes.

July 21: Liberty Bell 7 (U.S.). Crew: Virgil I. Grissom. A suborbital flight, lasting 16 minutes.

Aug. 6-7: Vostok 2 (USSR). Crew: Gherman S. Titov. The flight lasted 25 hours 18 minutes and completed 17 orbits of Earth.

1962

Feb. 20: Friendship 7 (U.S.). Crew: John H. Glenn, Jr. The first U.S. manned orbital mission. The flight lasted 4 hours 56 minutes and completed three orbits of Earth.

May 24: Aurora 7 (U.S.). Crew: M. Scott Carpenter. Completed three orbits of Earth.

Aug. 11-15: Vostok 3 (USSR). Crew: Andrian G. Nikolayev.

Aug. 12-15: Vostok 4 (USSR). Crew: Pavel R. Popovich. Together with Vostok 3, the first Soviet "group flight." At their closest approach the two craft were about 3 mi (4.8 km) apart.

Oct. 3: Sigma 7 (U.S.). Crew: Walter M. Schirra, Jr. Completed six orbits of Earth.

1963

May 15-16: Faith 7 (U.S.). Crew: L. Gordon Cooper, Jr. The last flight of the Mercury program.

June 14-19: Vostok 5 (USSR). Crew: Valery F. Bykovsky.

June 16-19: Vostok 6 (USSR). Crew: Valentina Tereshkova—the first woman in space. Together with Vostok 5, the second Soviet "group flight." The two craft came within 3 mi (4.8 km) of each other.

1964

Oct. 12-13: Voskhod 1 (USSR). Crew: Vladimir M. Komarov, Konstantin P. Feoktistov, and Boris B. Yegorov. The first craft to carry more than one person into space.

1965

March 18-19: Voskhod 2 (USSR). Crew: Pavel I. Belyayev and Aleksei A. Leonov. Leonov spent ten minutes outside the spacecraft—the first walk in space.

March 23: Gemini 3 (U.S.). Crew: Virgil I. Grissom and John W. Young. The first U.S. two-member crew in space.

June 3-7: Gemini 4 (U.S.). Crew: James A. McDivitt and Edward H. White 2d. Secured by umbilical and tether lines, White spent 21 minutes outside the spacecraft—the first American to walk in space.

Aug. 21-29: Gemini 5 (U.S.). Crew: L. Gordon Cooper, Jr., and Charles Conrad, Jr. The first use of fuel cells instead of conventional batteries for electric power. Carried out rendezvous maneuvers with a hypothetical target.

Dec. 4-18: Gemini 7 (U.S.). Crew: Frank Borman and James A. Lovell, Jr.

Dec. 15-16: Gemini 6 (U.S.). Crew: Walter M. Schirra, Jr., and Thomas P. Stafford. Rendezvoused within 1 ft. (0.3 m) of Gemini 7.

1966

March 16: Gemini 8 (U.S.). Crew: David R. Scott and Neil A. Armstrong. Docked with an unmanned Agena—the first docking in space with a previously launched target vehicle.

June 3-6: Gemini 9 (U.S.). Crew: Thomas P. Stafford and Eugene A. Cernan. Rendezvoused with an orbiting Agena. Cernan spent 2 hours 5 minutes outside the spacecraft.

July 18-21: Gemini 10 (U.S.). Crew: Michael Collins and John W. Young. Docked with an orbiting Agena. During extravehicular activity (EVA), Collins retrieved a test package from Agena—the first retrieval of a space object.

Sept. 12-15: Gemini 11 (U.S.). Crew. Charles Conrad, Jr., and Richard F. Gordon, Jr. Docked with an Agena target vehicle. Gordon made a brief space walk.

Nov. 11-15: Gemini 12 (U.S.). Crew: James A. Lovell, Jr., and Edwin E. Aldrin, Jr. Docked with an Agena target vehicle. Aldrin spent more than five hours outside the spacecraft.

1967

Jan. 27: Apollo (U.S.). During a check of the ship on the launch pad, a fire destroyed the module and killed the three astronauts on board: Virgil I. Grissom, Edward H. White 2d, and Roger B. Chaffee.

April 23-24: Soyuz 1 (USSR). Crew: Vladimir M. Komarov. Cosmonaut killed in reentry accident—the first actual space fatality.

1968

Oct. 11-22: Apollo 7 (U.S.). Crew: Walter M. Schirra, Jr., Donn F. Eisele, and R. Walter Cunningham. The first flight of the three-person Apollo command module.

Oct. 25-28: Soyuz 2 (USSR). Unmanned.

Oct. 26-30: Soyuz 3 (USSR). Crew: Georgi T. Beregovoi. The cosmonaut maneuvered Soyuz 3 to within 650 ft (198 m) of Soyuz 2. Returned to Earth after 64 orbits.

Dec. 21-27: Apollo (U.S.). Crew: Frank Borman, James A. Lovell, Jr., and William A. Anders. The first manned flight around the moon. Completed ten orbits of the moon.

1969

Jan. 14-17: Soyuz 4 (USSR). Crew: Vladimir A. Shatalov.

Jan. 15-18: Soyuz 5 (USSR). Crew: Boris V. Volynov, Aleksei S. Yeliseyev, and Yevgeny V. Khrunov. Docked with Soyuz 4. Yeliseyev and Khrunov transferred to Soyuz 4 and landed with it.

March 3-13: Apollo 9 (U.S.). Crew: James A. McDivitt, David R. Scott, and Russell L. Schweikart. Tested the lunar module.

May 18-26: Apollo 10 (U.S.). Crew: Thomas P. Stafford, Eugene A. Cernan, and John W. Young. Completed 31 orbits of the moon. Descended in the lunar module to within 9 mi (14.5 km) of the moon's surface.

July 16-24: Apollo 11 (U.S.). Crew: Neil A. Armstrong, Edwin E. Aldrin, Jr., and Michael Collins. First manned landing on the moon. Armstrong and Aldrin landed on *Mare Tranquillitatis* and on July 20 became the first people to walk on the lunar surface.

Oct. 11-16: Soyuz 6 (USSR). Crew: Georgy Shonin and Valery Kubasov. Conducted the first welding experiments in space.

Oct. 12-17: Soyuz 7 (USSR). Crew: Anatoly Filipchenko, Vladislav Volkov, and Viktor Gorbatko.

Using a Manned Maneuvering Unit and a life-support system on his back, an astronaut has left the space shuttle to make an untethered spacewalk.

Photo: NASA

NASA from FPG International

Pioneers in the exploration of space. *Above:* Yuri Gagarin, who on April 12, 1961, became the first human being to travel in space when he completed one orbit of Earth aboard Vostok 1. *Top right:* John Glenn, who on Feb. 20, 1962, became the first American to orbit the Earth, piloting Friendship 7. *Bottom right:* Valentina Tereshkova, who on June 16, 1963, became the first woman to fly in space, piloting Vostok 6 for 48 orbits of Earth.

Oct. 13-18: Soyuz 8 (USSR). Crew: V. Shatalov and A. Yeliseyev. Part of a group flight with Soyuz 6 and 7, although the three craft did not dock with one another. Each conducted experiments plus observations of Earth and stars.

Nov. 14-24: Apollo 12 (U.S.). Crew: Charles Conrad, Jr., Richard F. Gordon, Jr., and Alan L. Bean. The second manned lunar landing. Conrad and Bean landed on *Oceanus Procellarum*. They spent a total of 7 hours 39 minutes outside the lunar module, exploring the moon's surface and visiting the Surveyor 3 probe, which landed on the moon April 20, 1967.

1970

April 11-17: Apollo 13 (U.S.). Crew: James A. Lovell, Jr., Fred W. Haise, Jr., and John L. Swigert, Jr. The planned lunar landing was aborted after the oxygen tank in the service module ruptured.

June 2-19: Soyuz 9 (USSR). Crew: Andrian G. Nikolayev and Vitaly I. Sevastyanov. The cosmonauts performed space navigation experiments and made Earth and celestial observations. The flight tested people's reactions to long periods of weightlessness.

1971

Jan. 31–Feb. 9: Apollo 14 (U.S.). Crew: Alan B. Shepard, Jr., Stuart A. Roosa, and Edgar D. Mitchell. The third manned lunar landing, Shepard and Mitchell landed on the *Fra Mauro* highlands. They spent two periods outside their craft, for a total of 9 hours 19 minutes.

April 19: Salyut 1 (USSR). The first space station, launched unmanned into an orbit around Earth.

April 23-25: Soyuz 10 (USSR). Crew: Vladimir A. Shatalov, Aleksei S. Yeliseyev, and Nikolai N. Rukavishnikov. Docked with Salyut 1 but did not board the space station.

June 6-30: Soyuz 11 (USSR). Crew: Georgi T. Dobrovolsky, Vladislav N. Volkov, and Viktor I. Patsayev. Docked with Salyut 1 and occupied the space station for 22 days. The crew died as they returned to Earth, when a faulty valve caused cabin decompression.

July 26–Aug. 7: Apollo 15 (U.S.). Crew: David R. Scott, James B. Irwin, and Alfred M. Worden. The fourth manned lunar landing. Scott and Irwin landed on Hadley Rill. They made three exploratory trips, spending a total of 18 hours 37 minutes outside their craft. They made the first use of the lunar roving vehicle.

Tass/Sovfoto

1972

April 16-27: Apollo 16 (U.S.). Crew: John W. Young, Charles M. Duke, Jr., and Thomas K. Mattingly, II. The fifth manned lunar landing. Young and Duke landed in Descartes crater. They made three lunar excursions, spending a total of 20 hours 14 minutes outside their craft. They used the lunar roving vehicle and launched a lunar orbiter.

Dec. 7-19: Apollo 17 (U.S.). Crew: Eugene A. Cernan, Harrison Schmitt, and Ronald E. Evans. The sixth and last U.S. manned lunar landing. Cernan and Schmitt landed in Taurus-Littrow Valley. They made three lunar excursions, spending a total of 22 hours 5 minutes outside their craft.

1973

April 3: Salyut 2 (USSR) space station launched, unmanned. Not visited by any crews.

May 14: Skylab (U.S.). The first U.S. space station, launched unmanned and placed into Earth orbit at an altitude of 271 mi (436 km). On July 11, 1979, entered Earth's atmosphere and broke up over Australia, without causing any injury or damage.

May 25–June 22: Skylab 1 (U.S.). Crew: Charles Conrad, Jr., Joseph P. Kerwin, and Paul J. Weitz. Launched aboard an

Apollo spacecraft and docked with Skylab. Conducted studies of space, sun, and Earth. Tested people's ability to endure long periods in space.

July 28–Sept. 26: Skylab 2 (U.S.). Crew: Alan L. Bean, Jack R. Lousma, and Owen K. Garriott. Launched aboard an Apollo spacecraft and docked with Skylab. Conducted photographic surveys of Earth's surface. During a 6 hour 31 minute space walk, Lousma and Garriott erected a sunshade on Skylab and loaded new film in the solar telescope cameras.

Sept. 27-29: Soyuz 12 (USSR). Crew: Vasily Lazarev and Oleg Makarov. Test of an improved Soyuz craft, in which chemical batteries replaced solar cell arrays found on earlier models.

Nov. 16–Feb. 8, 1974: Skylab 3 (U.S.). Crew: Gerald P. Carr, Edward G. Gibson, and William R. Pogue. Launched in an Apollo spacecraft and docked with Skylab. Conducted extensive studies of Earth and sun. Photographed comet Kohoutek.

Dec. 18-26: Soyuz 13 (USSR). Crew: Pyotr Klimuk and Valentin Lebedev. Tested experiments related to the Salyut program.

1974

June 24: Salyut 3 (USSR) space station launched, unmanned.

July 3-19: Soyuz 14 (USSR). Crew: Pavel Popovich and Yuri Artyukhin. Docked with Salyut 3. Performed wide range of experiments.

Aug. 26-28: Soyuz 15 (USSR). Crew: Gennady Sarafanov and Lev Demin. Attempt to dock with Salyut 3 failed because of fault in automatic control system.

Dec. 2-8: Soyuz 16 (USSR). Crew: Anatoly V. Filipchenko and Nikolai N. Rukavishnikov. Tested docking system of Soyuz and reduction of cabin pressure as required for future joint docking experiment with Apollo.

Dec. 26: Salyut 4 (USSR) space station launched, unmanned.

1975

Jan. 11–Feb. 9: Soyuz 17 (USSR). Crew: Aleksei Gubarev and Georgi Grechko. Docked with Salyut 4. Conducted medical tests and observations of Earth's atmosphere and surface, as well as research into space.

May 24–July 26: Soyuz 18 (USSR). Crew: Pyotr Klimuk and Vitaly Sevastyanov. Docked with Salyut 4. Conducted various astronomical studies, surveyed the USSR, and tended a small space greenhouse.

July 15-24: Apollo (U.S.). Crew: Thomas P. Stafford, Donald K. Slayton, and Vance D. Brand. Together with Soyuz 19, launched on the same date, the first cooperative international space flight. The craft linked up for two days, during which the crews visited one another and conducted a series of experiments. (The last Apollo mission and last U.S. manned mission until April 1981.)

July 15-21: Soyuz 19 (USSR). Crew: Aleksei A. Leonov and Valery N. Kubasov. Two-day linkup with Apollo launched on same date.

Nov. 17–Feb. 19, 1976: Soyuz 20 (USSR). Unmanned mission. Docked with Salyut 4. Test of a resupply and rescue system needed for the development of permanent space stations.

1976

June 22: Salyut 5 (USSR) space station launched, unmanned, into orbit.

July 6–Aug. 24: Soyuz 21 (USSR). Crew: Boris Volynov and Vitaly Zholobov. Conducted geographical and meteorological studies and various scientific experiments.

Sept. 15-23: Soyuz 22 (USSR). Crew: Valery F. Bykovsky and Vladimir Aksenov. Carried out a photographic survey of Earth.

In 1969 humans first walked on the moon. During their 2½-hour walk on the surface, Edwin Aldrin (*below*) and Neil Armstrong (photographer) collected rocks and soil samples and set up a series of instruments to relay scientific data to Earth.

NASA

Oct. 14-16: Soyuz 23 (USSR). Crew: Vyacheslav Zudov and Valery Rozhdestvensky. A malfunction prevented the craft from docking with Salyut 5. An emergency landing was made.

1977

Feb. 7-25: Soyuz 24 (USSR). Crew: Viktor Gorbatko and Yuri Glazkov. Docked with Salyut 5. Conducted research on the effects of weightlessness. Carried out extensive photographic studies of Earth.
Sept. 29: Salyut 6 (USSR). space station launched, unmanned, into orbit. During its nearly five years in orbit, 17 manned craft docked with Salyut 6.
Oct. 9-11: Soyuz 25 (USSR). Crew: Vladimir Kovalenok and Valery Ryumin. Attempt to dock with Salyut 6 failed.
Dec. 10–March 16, 1978: Soyuz 26 (USSR). Crew: Yuri Romanenko and Georgi M. Grechko. First ship to dock with Salyut 6. Conducted numerous experiments. Hosted two groups of visiting cosmonauts; employed the first resupply of a space station by an unmanned tanker/transport spacecraft, Progress 1. Crew returned to Earth in Soyuz 27.

1978

Jan. 10-16: Soyuz 27 (USSR). Crew: Vladimir Dzhanibekov and Oleg Makarov. Docked with Salyut 6/Soyuz 26 complex—the first time that two spacecraft were simultaneously docked with a space station. Crew returned to Earth in Soyuz 26.

Each Apollo mission ended with an ocean landing of the command module. Large parachutes slowed the module's speed for a gentle "splashdown."

Photos, NASA

March 2-10: Soyuz 28 (USSR). Crew: Aleksei A. Gubarev and Vladimir Remek (Czechoslovakia). Docked with Salyut 6/Soyuz 27 complex.
June 15–Nov. 2: Soyuz 29 (USSR). Vladimir Kovalenok and Alexandr Ivanchenkov. Docked with Salyut 6. Performed experiments in biology, physics, and technology. Hosted two visiting pairs of cosmonauts. Resupplied by three Progress tanker/transport vehicles.
June 27–July 5: Soyuz 30 (USSR). Crew: Pyotr Klimuk and Miroslaw Hermaszewski (Poland). Docked with Salyut 6/Soyuz 29 complex.
Aug. 26–Sept. 3: Soyuz 31 (USSR). Crew: Valery Bykovsky and Sigmund Jaehn (East Germany). Docked with Salyut 6/Soyuz 29 complex.

1979

Feb. 26–Aug. 19: Soyuz 32 (USSR). Crew: Vladimir Lyakhov and Valery Ryumin. Docked with Salyut 6. Performed scientific research. Resupplied by Progress 5, 6, and 7. Progress 5 also boosted the Salyut 6/Soyuz 32 complex into a higher orbit. Crew returned aboard Soyuz 34, launched unmanned on June 6.
April 10-12: Soyuz 33 (USSR). Crew: Nikolai Rukavishnikov and Georgi Ivanov (Bulgaria). The craft's docking mechanism failed and it returned to Earth rather than link up with Salyut 6.
Dec. 16: Soyuz T-1 (USSR). Unmanned. Test flight of new generation of manned spacecraft. Docked with Salyut 6.

1980

April 9–Oct. 11:Soyuz 35 (USSR). Crew: Valery Ryumin and Leonid Popov. Docked with Salyut 6. Hosted four visiting pairs of cosmonauts. Crew returned aboard Soyuz 37.
May 26–June 3: Soyuz 36 (USSR). Crew: Valery Kubasov and Bertalan Farkas (Hungary). Docked with Salyut 6/Soyuz 35 complex. Crew returned aboard Soyuz 35.
June 5-9: Soyuz T-2 (USSR). The first manned flight of a new generation of manned space ship. Crew: Yuri Malyshev and Vladimir Aksenov. Docked with Salyut 6/Soyuz 36 complex.
July 23-31: Soyuz 37 (USSR). Crew: Viktor Gorbatko and Pham Tuan (Vietnam). Docked with Salyut 6/Soyuz 36 complex. Crew returned in Soyuz 36.
Sept. 18-26: Soyuz 38 (USSR). Crew: Yuri Romanenko and Arnaldo Tamayo Mendez (Cuba). Docked with Salyut 6.
Nov. 27–Dec. 10: Soyuz T-3 (USSR). Crew: Leonid Kizim, Oleg Makarov, and Gennady Strekalov. Docked with Salyut 6. Made repairs to Salyut 6 to extend its life.

1981

March 12–May 26: Soyuz T-4 (USSR). Crew: Vladimir Kovalenok and Viktor Savinykh. Docked with Salyut 6. Conducted a wide range of experiments and did repair work. Hosted two visiting groups of cosmonauts.
March 22-30: Soyuz 39 (USSR). Crew: Vladimir Dzhanibekov and Jugderdemidiyn Gurragcha (Mongolia). Docked with Salyut 6/Soyuz T-4 complex.
April 12-14, Space Transportation System 1 (STS-1): *Columbia* (U.S.). The first test flight of the first reusable space shuttle. Crew: John W. Young and Robert L. Crippen. Like all succeeding shuttle missions, *Columbia* lifted off from a launchpad but landed on a runway like a conventional airplane.
May 14-22: Soyuz 40 (USSR). Crew: Leonid Popov and Dumitru Prunariu (Rumania). Docked with Salyut 6/Soyuz T-4 complex.
Nov. 12-14, STS-2: *Columbia* (U.S.). Crew: Joe H. Engle and Richard H. Truly. Conducted tests of the shuttle's mechanical arm, which would be used to launch and retrieve satellites.

1982

March 22-30, STS-3: *Columbia* (U.S.). Crew: Jack R. Lousma and C. Gordon Fullerton. Tested the vehicle's ability to withstand the extreme temperatures of space.

April 19: Salyut 7 (USSR) space station launched, unmanned, to an altitude of 186 mi (300 km).

May 13–Dec. 10: Soyuz T-5 (USSR). Crew: Anatoly Berezovoy and Valentin Lebedev. Docked with Salyut 7. Conducted a variety of experiments. Hosted two groups of visiting cosmonauts. Crew returned aboard Soyuz T-7.

June 27–July 4, STS-4: *Columbia* (U.S.). Crew: Thomas K. Mattingly II and Henry Hartsfield, Jr. The final test flight of the shuttle. Carried a secret military payload. Landed at Edwards Air Force Base, California, the first shuttle landing on a hard-surface runway.

June 24–July 2: Soyuz T-6 (USSR). Crew: Vladimir Dzhanibekov, Aleksandr Ivanchenkov, and Jean-Loup Chrétien (France). Docked with Salyut 7/Soyuz T-5 complex.

Aug. 19-27: Soyuz T-7 (USSR). Crew: Leonid Popov, Aleksandr Serebrov, and Svetlana Savitskaya (the second woman in space). Docked with Salyut 7/Soyuz T-5 complex. Crew returned aboard Soyuz T-5.

Nov. 11-16, STS-5: *Columbia* (U.S.). Crew: Vance Brand, Robert Overmyer, William Lenoir, and Joseph Allen. Launched two communications satellites—the first deployment of satellites by the shuttle.

1983

April 4-9, STS-6: *Challenger* (U.S.). Maiden flight of the second American space shuttle. Crew: Paul Weitz, Karol Bobko, Story Musgrave, and Donald Peterson. Two crew members took a space walk, the first U.S. extravehicular activity since 1972.

April 21: Soyuz T-8 (USSR). Crew: Vladimir Titov, Aleksandr Serebrov, and Gennady Strekalov. The mission was aborted when the ship's rendezvous radar failed to deploy, preventing docking with Salyut 7.

June 18-24, STS-7: *Challenger* (U.S.). Crew: Robert L. Crippen, John M. Fabian, Frederick H. Hauck, Norman E. Thagard, and Sally K. Ride (the first American woman in space). Launched two communications satellites and tested the shuttle's 50-ft. (15-m) robotic arm.

June 27–Nov. 23: Soyuz T-9 (USSR). Crew: Vladimir Lyakhov and Aleksandr Aleksandrov. Docked with Salyut 7. Conducted a series of scientific and technical experiments, including materials processing, Earth observations, and medical and biological studies.

Aug. 30–Sept. 5, STS-8: *Challenger* (U.S.). Crew: Daniel C. Brandenstein, Dale A. Gardner, William E. Thornton, Richard H. Truly, and Guion S. Bluford, Jr. Launched a weather and communications satellite. Conducted further tests of the shuttle's robotic arm.

Sept. 27: Soyuz (USSR). Crew: Vladimir Titov and Gennady Strekalov. The crew was saved by an emergency escape system seconds before the SL-4 booster rocket exploded on the launchpad.

Nov. 28–Dec. 8, STS-9: *Columbia* (U.S.). Crew: Owen K. Garriott, Byron K. Lichtenberg, Robert A. Parker, Brewster H. Shaw, John W. Young, and Ulf Merbold (West Germany). The first use of Spacelab, a research facility developed by ESA.

1984

Feb. 3-11, STS-10: *Challenger* (U.S.). Crew: Vance D. Brand, Robert L. Gibson, Bruce McCandless II, Ronald E. McNair, and Robert L. Stewart. The first use of jet-propelled backpacks known as Manned Maneuvering Units, which allow astronauts to make untethered spacewalks.

Feb. 9–Oct. 2: Soyuz T-10 (USSR). Crew: Leonid Kizim, Oleg Atkov, Vladimir Solovyov. Docked with Salyut 7. Performed five extravehicular activities to repair the Salyut propulsion system. Hosted two groups of visiting cosmonauts. Crew returned to Earth aboard Soyuz T-11.

The space shuttle can be launched into Earth orbit, then fly back to a conventional landing on a runway. It has three main parts: two solid-fuel rocket boosters, a large external fuel tank, and a piloted delta-wing orbiter.

Tass/Sovfoto

Space stations, such as Mir (seen prior to launch in the assembly and testing shop), enable people to work in space for weeks or months at a time.

April 3-11: Soyuz T-11 (USSR). Crew: Gennady Strekalov, Yuri Malyshev, Rakesh Sharma (India). Docked with Salyut 7/Soyuz T-10 complex. Crew returned to Earth aboard Soyuz T-10.

April 6-13, STS-11: *Challenger* (U.S.). Crew: Robert L. Crippen, Terry J. Hart, George D. Nelson, Francis R. Scobee, James D. van Hoften. Retrieved and repaired Solar Max, a satellite launched in Feb. 1980 to study the sun's outer surface. Deployed the Long Duration Exposure Facility, a satellite carrying 57 materials-processing experiments.

July 17-29: Soyuz T-12 (USSR). Crew: Vladimir Dzhanibekov, Igor Volk, and Svetlana Savitskaya. Docked with Salyut 7/Soyuz T-11 comples. Savitskaya performed the first spacewalk by a woman.

Aug. 30–Sept. 5, STS-12: *Discovery* (U.S.). Maiden flight of the third American space shuttle. Crew: Henry W. Hartsfield, Jr., Michael L. Coats, Steven A. Hawley, Richard M. Mullane, Judith A. Resnik, and Charles D. Walker. Launched three communications satellites.

Oct. 5-13, STS-13: *Challenger* (U.S.). Crew: Robert L. Crippen, David C. Leestma, Jon A. McBride, Sally K. Ride, Paul Scully-Power, Kathryn D. Sullivan, and Mark Garncau (Canada). Sullivan became the first American woman to walk in space.

Nov. 8-16, STS-14: *Discovery* (U.S.). Crew: Frederick H. Hauck, Joseph P. Allen, Dale A. Gardner, David M. Walker, and Anna L. Fisher. Retrieved and brought back to Earth two communications satellites that had misfired into useless orbits after their launch by STS-10.

1985

Jan. 24-27, STS-15: *Discovery* (U.S.). Crew: James F. Buchli, Thomas K. Mattingly II, Ellison S. Onizuka, Gary E. Payton, and Loren J. Shriver. The first shuttle mission devoted exclusively to secret military objectives. It was believed to have included the deployment of an intelligence-gathering satellite.

April 12-19, STS-16: *Discovery* (U.S.). Crew: Karol J. Bobko, S. David Griggs, Jeffrey A. Hoffman, M. Rhea Seddon, Charles D. Walker, Donald E. Williams, and Sen. Jake Garn of Utah, the first member of Congress to participate in a space mission. Two communications satellites were deployed. One, Leasat-3, failed to activate and efforts to repair it were unsuccessful.

April 29-May 6, STS-17: *Challenger* (U.S.). Crew: Frederick D. Gregory, Donald L. Lind, Robert F. Overmyer, Norman Thagard, William Thornton, Lodewijk van den Berg, and

Taylor G. Wang. Conducted investigations in crystal growth, materials and fluid processing, and weightlessness.

June 7-Sept. 26: Soyuz T-13 (USSR). Crew: Vladimir Dzhanibekov and Viktor Savinykh. Manually docked with Salyut 7, which had lost all its electrical power by the beginning of 1985. The men spent ten days repairing and reactivating the space station. On August 2, using equipment carried up by an unmanned Progress 24 on June 21, the men installed additional solar panels on Salyut 7.

June 17-24, STS-18: *Discovery* (U.S.). Crew: Daniel C. Brandenstein, John O. Creighton, John M. Fabian, Shannon W. Lucid, Steven R. Nagel, Patrick Baudry (France), and Sultan Salman al-Saud (Saudi Arabia). Three communications satellites and the Spartan payload carrier for studies of galactic X-ray emissions were deployed; the latter was subsequently retrieved and carried back to Earth.

July 29–Aug. 6, STS-19: *Challenger* (U.S.). Crew: Loren W. Acton, John-David F. Bartoe, Roy D. Bridges, Jr., Anthony W. England, C. Gordon Fullerton, Karl G. Henize, and F. Story Musgrave. Conducted a series of astronomical observations using Spacelab's experiment mounting structure to carry several large telescopes.

Aug. 27–Sept. 3, STS-20: *Discovery* (U.S.). Crew: Richard O. Covey, Joe H. Engle, William F. Fisher, John M. Lounge, and James D. van Hoften. Three communications satellites were deployed. The mission's primary accomplishment was the capture, repair, and redeployment of Leasat-3, a communications satellite that failed to activate when launched by STS-16.

Sept. 17–Nov. 21: Soyuz T-14 (USSR). Crew: Georgi Grechko, Vladimir Vasyutin, and Alexander Volkov. Docked with Salyut 7/Soyuz T-13 complex. On Sept. 26, Grechko and Dzhanibekov returned to Earth aboard Soyuz T-13—the first in-flight rotation of space crews. On Sept. 27, a new unmanned module docked to Salyut 7, nearly doubling the station's size. On Nov. 21, Vasyutin became ill and the three cosmonauts returned to Earth in Soyuz T-14.

Oct. 3-7, STS-21: *Atlantis* (U.S.). Maiden flight of the fourth American space shuttle. Crew: Karol J. Bobko, Ronald J. Grabe, David C. Hilmers, William A. Pailes, and Robert C. Stewart. A secret mission, it was believed to have deployed two Department of Defense communications satellites.

Oct. 30–Nov. 6, STS-22: *Challenger* (U.S.). Crew: Guion S. Bluford, Jr., James F. Buchli, Bonnie J. Dunbar, Henry W. Hartsfield, Jr., Steven R. Nagel, Reinhard Furrer (W. Germany), Ernst Messerschmid (W. Germany), and Wubbo Ockels (Netherlands). A scientific mission directed by West Germany—the first shuttle mission paid for and dedicated to a payload provided by another nation. Investigations focused on microgravity research, communications, and navigation.

Nov. 26–Dec. 3, STS-23: *Atlantis* (U.S.). Crew: Mary L. Cleave, Bryan D. O'Connor, Jerry L. Ross, Brewster H. Shaw, Jr., Sherwood C. Spring, Charles D. Walker, and Rodolfo Neri (Mexico). Three communications satellites were launched and construction methods designed to be used in building a space station were tested.

1986

Jan. 12-18, STS-24: *Columbia* (U.S.). Crew: Robert L. Gibson, Steven A. Hawley, Robert J. Cenker, Charles F. Bolden Jr., George D. Nelson, Franklin R. Chang-Diaz, and Rep. Bill Nelson of Florida. A communications satellite was launched and various scientific experiments were performed.

Jan. 28: *Challenger* (U.S.). Exploded seconds after liftoff, killing the crew: Francis R. Scobee, Michael J. Smith, Judith Resnik, Ellison S. Onizuka, Ronald E. McNair, Gregory B. Jarvis, and Christa McAuliffe, a Concord, NH, high-school teacher. Subsequent investigation indicated the accident was caused by the rupture of seals on the booster rockets.

Feb. 20: Mir (USSR). space station launched, unmanned, into a slightly elliptical orbit at an altitude of 210 mi (338 km).

March 13–July 16: Soyuz T-15 (USSR). Crew: Leonid Kizim and Vladimir Solovyov. Docked with Mir. On May 5, the cosmonauts flew to Salyut 7 in Soyuz T-15, the first transfer of crew from one space station to another. Various activities of the crew were televised live during the mission.

Science Encyclopedia

absorption of light

When light passes through a vacuum there is nothing to stop it: nothing for it to bump into. However, when light passes through anything else it will collide with the molecules, or tiny particles, that make up the substance. And any light ray which does strike a molecule will give up some of its energy to that molecule. The energy will be absorbed by the molecule. If all of the light energy is absorbed the light will no longer be visible. But if some light is reflected off a molecule, only some of the energy is absorbed.

Even substances which appear to be transparent, such as air or clear glass, absorb energy from any light passing through. Even a highly polished mirror absorbs energy from light reflected off it. Every time light strikes anything, some of its energy is absorbed.

The amount of energy absorbed from light depends on three things: the wavelength of the light, the sort of molecules it strikes, and how the molecules are arranged.

White light is a mixture of all the colours. Each colour has its own wavelength. If the colours are arranged according to wavelength, we have what is called a spectrum. Towards one end of the spectrum is violet light, which has short waves. Towards the other is red light, which has long waves. Waves longer than red light are called infra-red waves. They are not seen as light but felt as heat.

At the other end of the spectrum, and even shorter than violet light waves, are the ultra-violet rays. In very small doses they are good for us. When absorbed by the skin they build up vitamin D in the body. They also give us a sun-tan. In larger doses, however, they can cause blistering and skin damage.

Sunlight contains a lot of ultra-violet rays. However, because they are very short waves, which are most easily absorbed by the ozone in the atmosphere, we do not suffer. This is why some scientists are worried by airliners like Concorde, which would fly in the upper atmosphere and might burn up all the ozone.

The sun appears redder than usual when seen through a haze. This is because there are more particles in the air. These absorb more of the shorter, bluer, wavelengths. The longer, redder, wavelengths are less affected. So if we see sunlight through haze it is redder than on a clear day.

Sunglasses filter the sunlight by absorbing light energy. Even the very best sunglasses will alter slightly the colours we see. But they do give valuable protection from the sun's harmful ultra-violet rays.

Astronauts who walk in space or on the Moon do not have the protection of the atmosphere to absorb the intense heat and ultra-violet rays in sunlight. This is why they wear reflective suits in space.

Infra-red waves are used by doctors to treat rheumatism. They can also be used to cook food. Both the rheumatic tissue and the food absorb heat energy from the infra-red waves. Although infra-red waves are not visible, they can be used in photography. Aerial photography can use infra-red techniques to detect patterns on the land's surface which are not apparent in ordinary light. This can help archeologists to choose sites for excavation.

We see things as coloured because they do *not* absorb particular wavelengths. For instance, a piece of green paper appears green because its molecules have absorbed all the colours in white light *except* green. Light passing through red glass is red because the energy of all the other wavelengths is absorbed by the molecules in the glass. Anything which absorbs light of all wavelengths appears black. Anything which reflects visible light of all wavelengths appears white. If its molecules are arranged to form a very flat surface, it will act as a mirror.

Energy which has been absorbed from light does not just vanish. It may have been lost to the light but it survives in some other form. Usually it is turned into heat in the substance absorbing the energy. Sometimes it is given out again as light of a different colour. This is called 'fluorescence'.

Absorbed light energy can also start chemical reactions. An example is in photosynthesis. This is the process by which green plants use sunlight to make their food. We are able to see because of another chemical reaction started by light energy. When light passes into the eye it lands on the retina, the screen at the back of the eye. There its absorbed energy starts chemical reactions. These send nerve impulses, or electrical messages, to the brain. The brain can then form a picture of what is being seen.

Dark objects absorb more light and heat energy than lighter-coloured objects do. They also give out the energy more rapidly. So a house with a dark roof will be hotter in summer than one with a white roof. This also explains why houses in hot sunny climates tend to be painted light colours.

The ability of molecules to absorb light is used in the laboratory to identify substances and to determine their concentration. This technique is called colorimetry. A sample in liquid form or in solution is placed in a clear-sided container and held against an illuminated screen. The amount of light absorbed in passing through the liquid depends on the concentration of molecules. And the type of molecule will determine what kind of light is absorbed and what allowed to pass through.

See also *light, photosynthesis, radiation.*

Find out by doing

To demonstrate that dark materials absorb and radiate more light and heat energy than lighter coloured materials: wrap a piece of white cloth around the bulb of a thermometer and place it in sunlight. Note the temperature after five minutes. Then do the same with black cloth. Look at the sky through red cellophane, such as a candy wrapper, on a day when there are clouds as well as clear sky. Can you explain why the contrast between cloud and blue sky is greater? (Clue: *clouds reflect white light.*)

To think about

Why do people wear light-coloured clothes in the tropics?

acceleration

When the speed of an object increases, it is said to accelerate. For example, suppose a car is traveling at 40 fps (feet per second). If it speeds up to 50 fps, it has accelerated by 10 fps. If it does this in two seconds, its rate of acceleration is 5 feet per second per second.

An object accelerates only when a force is applied to it. Otherwise it remains at rest or continues at its original speed. When a bullet is fired, it accelerates from rest until it reaches the end of the gun barrel. It then has maximum speed. After it leaves the muzzle, no further force is applied behind it. Air resistance slows it down, and gravity drags it to the ground. If there were no air resistance or gravity, the bullet would move at constant speed in a straight line for ever.

A rocket's engine continues to fire for a long time after take-off. The rocket keeps on accelerating as long as the engine is firing. If the thrust could continue long enough, the rocket would eventually accelerate until it reached the speed of light.

If there were no air present to resist the motion, a feather and a cannon ball would fall at the same rate. The force that causes them to fall is gravity. The acceleration due to gravity is 32 fps per second. A falling object reaches a velocity of 32 fps after one second, 64 fps after two seconds, and so on. This rate of acceleration is called one gravity, or simply 1g.

It is possible for the speed of an object to *increase* in one direction while it *decreases* in another direction. For example, suppose a car is traveling at 50 mph (miles per hour) due north. It then goes round a bend at constant speed so that it is now traveling eastward at 50 mph. Its eastward speed has increased from zero to 50 mph, so that it has accelerated in an eastward direction. Its northward speed is now zero, so it has decelerated by 50 mph.

This means that whenever a moving object changes direction, an accelerating force is needed to make this change.

An object which travels at constant speed in a circle is always changing its direction of motion toward the center. In other words, it is constantly accelerating toward the center.

A force is required to maintain this acceleration. If a stone is whirled in a circle on a piece of string, the pull on the string provides the force. The Moon is held in its orbit by the force of the Earth's gravity, which is always directed toward the center of the Earth.

We have all felt the sensations that acceleration causes in our bodies. An elevator that is beginning to rise makes its occupants feel heavier than normal. When it starts to descend they feel lighter, and perhaps have a moment of sickness.

Fighter pilots and astronauts have serious problems with the effects of acceleration. When a plane is in a tight turn, its pilot may feel an acceleration of 4g or 5g for several seconds. It is difficult for his heart to pump blood to the upper parts of his body. He may lose his vision for a few seconds because the blood supply to his eyes is reduced. At higher accelerations he may lose consciousness.

The G-suit is designed to help his heart. It applies pressure to parts of his body at the right moments and forces the blood upwards.

Astronauts lie flat during the launch, thus giving their hearts less work to do. They may experience accelerations up to about 10g.

See: *ballistics, gravity.*

Find out by doing

Gravity acts upon falling objects so that they tend to accelerate at the rate of 1g, or 32 fps per second, regardless of weight or size. However, air resistance does affect some falling bodies more than others. You can demonstrate this with a sheet of aluminum foil and a pebble, or similar spherical object. Hold up one in each hand and let them go at the same moment. The pebble will land on the floor before the foil. Now screw the foil up into a small hard ball and repeat the experiment. This time the objects will land at the same moment. This is because the foil meets less air resistance the second time.

To think about

Look at the water from a faucet that is dripping fairly rapidly. Why do the drops get farther apart as they fall?

acoustics

The study of sound and how it travels from place to place. A knowledge of acoustics is of value in designing buildings and streets so that they have desirable sound effects.

Sound is made by vibrating air. The faster the air vibrates, the higher the pitch of the sound. Noise is any sound that is unwanted.

Sound vibrations radiate in all directions. The farther the listener is from a source of sound, the weaker the sound he will hear. This is because the sound energy is spread thinly over a large area. Sound energy is absorbed by any matter in its path. Even the air absorbs some sound energy as it transmits sound. Walls and furniture can absorb sound strongly.

In a room sound waves are reflected back and forth from the walls. They may last for several seconds before dying away. The sound waves going direct to the listener are heard first, followed by waves reflected from the walls. This is called reverberation. Reverberation adds richness to sound. A certain amount of reverberation is desirable for orchestral music and even more for organ and choral music in church. Less reverberation is desirable for speech because echoes can make it hard to understand. The preacher in a church has to speak slowly so that the echoes can die between each word. Otherwise there would be a jumble of new sounds mixed with old ones still reverberating.

Fortunately we can control the reverberation in a room. If a room is designed so that its surfaces are sound absorbent, echoes will die quickly. We call such a room 'dead' as opposed to a 'live' reverberant, room. The 'reverberation time' of a room is the time it takes for a sound to die away to one millionth of its original loudness. For speech, the reverberation time should not be more than one second. For orchestral music two seconds is better. In some churches it can be five to ten seconds.

Rooms and concert halls should be shaped to distribute sound correctly. There should be a direct line between sound source and listener. The first reflection to reach the listener should arrive only a short time after the direct sound. They cannot be distinguished from the direct sound and serve to reinforce it. Reflections arriving later only confuse more recent direct sounds. In large concert halls reflectors hung from the ceiling can help to shorten the path of the first reflections. The reflectors should be convex to spread the sound over the auditorium. Concave reflectors would tend to focus reflections on just a few seats.

Side reflections

In a concert hall, reflections from the side walls are also important in determining the quality of sound. They add to the feeling of space. Without good side reflections, listening to an orchestra can be like listening to music through a single loudspeaker. With good side reflections, however, it is like listening on a good-quality stereo system. In fact, of course, the sound heard in a well-designed hall with fine acoustics is far superior to the sound that can be produced by any stereo system.

Fan-shaped halls are not ideal for orchestral music because the side walls do not bounce much sound back into the audience. Rectangular rooms are generally better. The side reflections are strongest if the room is fairly narrow, perhaps no more than 20 metres (21 yards) or so in width. Some of the world's best concert halls are indeed narrow, rectangular rooms that were built in the nineteenth century, without any scientific knowledge of acoustics.

In the twentieth century, however, architects have wanted to break away from these well-tried designs. They have also wanted to seat larger audiences, and to build halls which can be used for anything from a poetry recital to a rock concert. This produces a challenge for the acoustical engineer.

The larger a hall is the more difficult it is to make the acoustic effects evenly good. There is also a greater likelihood of echoes. Halls which are used for speech-making and music recitals have to compromise between the requirements of each. Even different kinds of music require different acoustic effects. Think of a string quartet or a full sized choir and orchestra in turn using the same hall. The hall's acoustics would not suit both types of performance.

Systems are being developed to meet this situation. We can reduce true reverberation to the minimum and use artificial reverberation.

The direct sound can be played back through loudspeakers a fraction of a second late and this has the effect of reverberation. The advantage is that the delay can be controlled to suit different needs.

In some halls, the reflecting canopy over the stage can be raised and lowered by motors. There are even halls where the whole ceiling moves up and down. Lowering the ceiling has the effect of reducing reverberation, so speech can be clearly heard. With the ceiling raised, there is more space for the sound to bounce around in. This added reverberation, however, would be wanted for an orchestral concert.

Another way to adjust the acoustics of a multi-purpose hall is by adding or removing areas of sound-absorbing material. This can be in the form of heavy retractable banners hung from the ceiling.

When an auditorium has been successfully designed for its internal acoustics there is still noise from outside or from adjoining rooms to be considered. To counteract this we use sound insulation. Heavy walls are very effective in stopping sound. They do not vibrate very readily when sound waves strike them and therefore do not carry the vibration through to the air on the other side. Low-pitched sounds are transmitted more readily than high-pitched sounds, because the wall can take up the slower vibrations more easily. Two thin walls separated by a gap are more efficient at shutting out sound than one wall of the same weight of material. However, this insulation is spoiled if there are any holes such as windows or ventilators in the wall. Even minute cracks will spoil the insulation.

Ordinary windows transmit more sound than a brick wall even if they are kept shut. This is because glass is much lighter than brickwork and so vibrates more easily. Windows can be improved by making them double, with a space of about six inches between the layers.

Mechanical ventilation will be required if windows are kept shut. This creates more problems because noise can enter through the ducts. Also, the motors which move the air make noise which can travel along the ducts.

To reduce this noise, mufflers have to be inserted in the ducts. They will also catch external noise coming in through the ducts. The mufflers absorb the noise energy by passing the incoming air through vanes, called 'splitters', made of sound absorbent material.

Sound does not travel between rooms by direct routes only. All the walls, the floor and the ceiling vibrate and so sound energy can reach the next room by side routes. This is called 'flanking sound'. Quite often as much sound is conveyed by flanking paths as by direct transmission.

A special form of flanking transmission occurs when machinery is fixed to a floor and vibrates the structure of the building directly. The remedy is to 'isolate' the machine on resilient mountings. Footsteps on a floor have the same effect. They can be softened by carpeting, or the floor itself can be isolated – that is it can be constructed on a resilient layer. The characteristics of a floor can be measured using a standard impact generator known as a 'footsteps machine'.

Architects and town planners have to consider the levels of noise in cities. Concert halls and theatres can be protected by heavy walls and roofs and they can be ventilated with air conditioning. Buildings such as hospitals and office blocks need large windows for daylight, thus tending to let in noise. The windows can be made double and kept shut, provided mechanical ventilation is acceptable.

Acoustical oddities

Some of the world's famous buildings have acoustical oddities. High above the floor of St Paul's Cathedral in London, just below the great dome, there is a 'whispering gallery'. The smooth, curving wall of this circular gallery has a focussing effect on sound, so that two people standing anywhere in the gallery can hold a conversation in low voices as if they were standing side by side. The sound actually travels along the wall, and it works best if both speaker and listener hold their heads close to the wall.

There is an open-air example of a whispering gallery at the Temple of Heaven in Peking, China. It is a popular spot for overseas tourists as well as Chinese families. Standing round the edge of the walled, circular courtyard you can see many people apparently talking to themselves. In fact, they are calling out to their friends or families far away at another part of the wall.

The same courtyard has a famous echo. If you stand on a particular paving stone near the centre and clap, you will hear a single echo. Step forward a pace and clap again and you will hear two distinct echoes. Another step forward and this time you are able to hear three echoes of your clap.

In most buildings, of course, effects like these would be quite undesirable. Acoustic designers are well aware of the echoes and focussing effects in circular and elliptical buildings and generally try to avoid designing such shapes.

Town-planners try to site houses, apartments and schools as far away as possible from main roads and other noise sources. It is also sensible to build houses facing away from roads rather than onto them. Planning should take account of prevailing winds, because noise travels more readily downwind than upwind. Belts of trees do not provide much noise protection unless they are very wide and dense. Barriers (including other buildings in which quietness is not important) can help to prevent noise from spreading to housing sites.

As machinery becomes more widespread and powerful in every sphere of life, noise increases everywhere. It should be regarded as a form of pollution. Excessive noise can cause discomfort, pain and even deafness in people who are exposed to it for long periods. In consequence, much more attention is now being given to research into noise control – how to make machines quieter, how to stop noise from travelling far, how to insulate buildings more effectively and more cheaply. In most countries certain minimum standards of sound insulation or noise control are already legally enforced.

Sound against sound

One new method of noise control is to fight sound with sound. A sound wave has peaks of high pressure and troughs of low pressure. A second wave, with peaks where the first has troughs (and vice-versa) is able to cancel out the first. So-called 'anti-sound' that is fed to an airplane pilot's headphones can protect him from the deafening noise in his cockpit.

The levels of noise and the behaviour of sound at various sites can be studied with instruments carried in specially-equipped vehicles. The acoustic properties of materials, and of buildings planned for the future, are best studied in the laboratory. The 'anechoic' chamber is a room lined with blocks of acoustically absorbent material. The blocks are shaped so that the small amount of sound reflected is not directed into the body of the room. It is reflected to fall on the walls again so that further absorption quickly takes place. The noise output of sound sources can be measured in such a chamber. The 'reverberant' chamber, on the other hand, has walls of highly sound-reflecting material, and sounds linger for a long time. The sound absorption properties of various specimens of materials can be measured in such a chamber.

Reverberant and anechoic chambers are also used to test the quality of sound recordings and reproduction equipment. For instance, a recording played in an anechoic chamber will display only the reverberation qualities recorded during the original performance. Because there are none in the chamber, the quality of the recording can be assessed.
See: *sound*.

Find out by doing

Demonstrate that a concave reflector can focus sound waves. Set up two umbrellas as shown in the picture. You will be able to hear the ticking from a distance of three or four yards.

To show that materials of different weights absorb sound differently: place a balloon in front of your radio loudspeaker so that it touches. Put your ear against it and you will find that you can hear the radio as clearly as if nothing were in the way. Now do the same with a cushion of the same thickness as the balloon. The sound will be heavily muffled. A heavy book in front of the speaker will dampen the sound much more, even though it is not as thick as either the balloon or the cushion.

aerodynamics

The science that explains what happens when gases move past objects and when objects move through gases. Aerodynamics explains what keeps an airplane flying but it is concerned with many other subjects. Automobile designers must study aerodynamics for it affects fast-moving cars. Architects must keep in mind the effects of winds on the buildings they design.

Sailboat designers must use aerodynamics to make sure that sails get the maximum power from the wind.

Some of the forces that air can exert have long been known. Breezes can disturb leaves and hurricanes can destroy buildings. Windmills and sailing-ships put the winds to good work. But only in the eighteenth century did the scientific study of mechanics reveal new ways of harnessing the power of the air.

The most important law to be discovered was called Bernoulli's Principle, after the Swiss scientist Daniel Bernoulli. He studied moving liquids in tubes. The laws that govern these are similar to those that control moving gases.

If a tube contains an obstruction, or if it becomes narrower at one point, liquid flowing through it has to speed up at that place. Bernoulli found that when the liquid was forced to speed up in this way, the pressure that it exerted in all directions became less.

This general fact about liquids and gases is used in the design of an airplane wing. The shape that would be obtained if a wing were sliced through from front to back is called an airfoil. It is fairly flat underneath, but strongly curved above.

Air that flows over the wing must travel a greater distance than air traveling beneath the wing. This means that it has to travel faster. And by Bernoulli's Principle, its pressure drops.

So the pressure the air exerts on the lower side of the wing is greater than the pressure that it exerts on the top surface. The wing feels an upward force called lift.

The lift that a wing generates overcomes the plane's weight. The lift is greater the faster the plane moves through the air. But the plane also experiences a backward resisting force from the air called drag. This also increases with the plane's speed and puts a top limit to it. The problem of the airplane designer is to get as much lift for as little drag as possible.

Streamlining

Planes, cars and trains are designed with smooth curved bodies. This helps the air flow over them quickly and so reduces drag. This is called streamlining. When the machines are being designed, models are tested in wind tunnels.

If smoke is introduced in a wind tunnel it will show how the air flows around a body in the tunnel. This helps designers to decide whether the body has desirable aerodynamic qualities.

An airplane creates a disturbance that spreads through the air with the speed of sound. This disturbance travels on ahead of a plane that is traveling slower than sound, and makes the plane's flight easier. When a plane travels faster than sound the air has no time to get out of its way.

When a plane reaches the speed of sound it experiences a sudden increase in drag. This resistance is called the sound barrier. Drag continues to increase as speed increases.

A car is shaped in such a way that air passing over it has to travel faster than air passing underneath it. This produces a lifting force. The whole car acts as an airfoil. This can be dangerous in a racing car travelling fast because the wheels grip the road less firmly.

Many modern racing cars now have upside-down airfoils mounted on them. These create a downward push on the car at high speed and press the wheels more firmly onto the road.

Low speed aerodynamics applies to sail-boats. It is not so well understood as high-speed aerodynamics, but its broad principles are known. A sailboat can let itself simply be pushed by the wind. But when it is sailing into the wind – 'tacking' – Bernoulli's Principle applies.

When the front edge of the sail meets the wind, the sail forms a curve like an airfoil. Air has to go farther round one side than the other, and a force is developed at right angles to the sail. The shape of the hull only permits the boat to move in the desired direction.

Architects have problems with the forces that the wind produces. They have to know how much force winds can exert on tall buildings. When a number of tall buildings are grouped close together, the air is funnelled by the buildings. Strong gusts can be produced at ground level, as well as high stresses on the buildings themselves for brief periods.

air

We hardly ever notice the mixture of gases that surround us. We only realize it if there is a strong wind, or when fog or smog cuts off our view into the distance. Yet we depend on the air in many ways. It provides the oxygen that we breathe. Plants, on which all animals depend for food, could not live without the carbon dioxide in the air. And it is a barrier, hundreds of miles deep, protecting us from the burning ultra-violet rays of the sun. Fast-moving pieces of stone called meteoroids are burnt up when they enter the atmosphere from space, before they can reach the ground. And cosmic rays, which are made up of fragments of atoms travelling from distant parts of space, are slowed down before they can do damage.

To the Ancient Greeks, air was one of the four basic elements (see: *elements*). Everything was supposed to be made from mixtures of fire, water, earth and air. The picture has become a little more complicated since then. We know now that air itself is mainly composed of two basic chemical elements, oxygen (about one-quarter by weight) and nitrogen (about three-quarters). There are also small amounts of water vapour and carbon dioxide, along with the 'rare gases' (argon, krypton, xenon, neon and helium).

The air has not always had its present composition throughout the history of the earth. Early in the earth's development (more than three thousand million years ago) there was no atmosphere at all. The surface of the earth was extremely hot, and gases and steam were produced by volcanic action. They were so hot that when they came to the surface they escaped into space. As the earth cooled down it became possible for these gases to be captured by the force of gravity (see: *gravity*). An atmosphere of nitrogen and carbon dioxide was formed, and the steam condensed to make the first oceans. The development of life, and the process called 'photosynthesis', led to the presence of oxygen in the air (see: *photosynthesis*).

Animals and plants depend on one another to keep the quantities of oxygen and carbon dioxide in the air constant. Plants take carbon dioxide and water from the earth and energy from sunlight. They build up sugars from carbon and water, and they give out oxygen. This is photosynthesis. But animals, including humans, 'burn' sugar in their muscles, and turn the oxygen that they breathe back into carbon dioxide and water.

About seven hundred million years ago the first plants began to manufacture oxygen from carbon dioxide in the atmosphere. Most of the carbon dioxide was used up in about one hundred million years. The new conditions enabled animals as we know them to develop.

All animals breathe in oxygen and breathe out carbon dioxide. But at the same time fires, automobiles, industrial processes, jet aircraft and so on generate large quantities of the gas. At present the green plants on the earth are able to cope with all this carbon dioxide and keep the proportion of oxygen in the air steady.

The nitrogen in the air is also essential to life. Many of the complicated molecules in living tissues contain nitrogen. Almost all the nitrogen in living things has been part of the air at some time. Most plants and animals can use it only after combining it with other substances to make new chemicals like ammonia or nitric acid. This is called 'fixing' the nitrogen.

Two main 'fixing' processes occur naturally. In a flash of lightning some nitrogen from the air may interact with oxygen and water vapour to form nitric acid. There are also bacteria that 'fix' atmospheric nitrogen into nitrates. Some of these bacteria live in the nodules that you can find on the roots of pea and bean plants. They help peas and beans to form green leaves.

The weight of the air

Air can be very strong when it is compressed. When workmen dig up the roadway they use a drill driven by compressed air to break up hard concrete.

We live under about a hundred miles of air. Why are we not squashed by it? We are not squashed, strangely enough, because our bodies are soft and so everything in our bodies is at the same pressure as the air around us. This causes trouble only if the pressure around us is increased or reduced too quickly. For instance, if we fly in an airplane when we have a head cold, we may get severe pains in our ears. The pressure of the surrounding air is reduced when the airplane goes up. But there is air at ground-level pressure trapped inside our ears, because a head cold blocks the tubes from the nose that let this air flow in and out.

To measure air pressure we use a barometer. A simple barometer consists of a glass tube that has only one end open. If this tube is filled with water or mercury and then held upright with the open end still in the liquid bath, some of the liquid will remain in the tube. It is held there, above the level of liquid in the bath, by air pressure acting on the surface of the liquid.

We can measure air pressure by the length of the column of liquid that it will hold up. In the case of water the length is about 34 ft (1,033 cm) at sea level. Mercury is usually used to measure air pressure. It is much denser than water, and a column only about 30 in (75 cm) high will balance the pressure of air at ground level. This is why we refer to atmospheric pressure in inches of mercury.

Air pressure also varies with the weather. Water vapour is lighter than oxygen, nitrogen or carbon dioxide. So, if the air is damp it weighs less and the air pressure is lower. When a barometer falls, showing that the air pressure is decreasing, it means that the air is growing moister and therefore that rain is likely.

Sound is transmitted through the air because of the way air can be compressed. A radio loudspeaker is a sort of high speed piston. It pushes and pulls very rapidly, hundreds or thousands of times every second, depending on the pitch of the sound. This first compresses the air nearby, then decompresses it. This air pushes against the air further away, and makes waves from one layer of air to the next, until they reach our eardrums. The waves then push and pull against the eardrum and cause a vibration, which we recognize as sound.

The speed of sound through the air depends on the way one layer of air pushes against the next layer. This is affected by the temperature of the air. Sound travels more slowly in colder air. At normal temperatures the speed of sound is over 700 miles per hour.

In watching moon flights on television you may be surprised to notice how easily the astronauts talk to each other on the surface of the moon. The moon has no air, because its gravity is not strong enough to stop an atmosphere from escaping into space. Sound cannot be carried without air, so that the astronauts must use built-in walkie-talkie radios in their space suits – even when they are standing face to face two feet apart.

But light does behave in the same way both on earth and on the moon. Light is a wave motion too. It is not composed of disturbances in the air itself. Visible light, like radio waves, radar, X-rays and gamma-rays, is a form of 'electromagnetic radiation'. It usually travels through air as easily as it travels through the vacuum at the surface of the moon. But in mist or cloud there are tiny water drops in the air, which scatter light. These sometimes cause a rainbow, or a 'ring' round the moon or sun.

Dirty air may scatter light too. Fine dust, carried up to the top of the atmosphere, scatters blue light more than red light, so that the sun appears redder (see: *absorption of light*).

Even clean air is slightly different from a vacuum in the way it transmits light: light travels a tiny fraction slower in the air. The speed is also affected by the temperature of the air. This bends the light, as you can see in the shimmering of the air above a hot stove.

Even when the air feels dry it still has water vapour in it. On a dry summer day a bottle that has just been taken out of a refrigerator is soon covered with tiny drops of water. These have been condensed out of the air. When the air contains as much water vapour as it can hold without mist appearing, we say the humidity has reached 100 per cent. Cool air can hold less water vapour than hot air. A block of dry ice (solid carbon dioxide) generates a mist because it cools the air close to it, and causes the humidity of that air to rise above 100 per cent. Clouds are formed when warm moist air rises and is cooled due to its expansion.

As far as life is concerned, it is only the few miles of atmosphere nearest the earth that are important. Three-quarters of the atmosphere (by weight) lies within seven miles of the Earth's surface and nine-tenths of it is within ten miles of the surface.

The weather is 'made' even nearer the earth. Most of the water vapour, which forms rain-clouds, is contained in the lowest 10,000 feet and half of it is in the lowest 7,500 feet.

The higher you go into the atmosphere the colder it is, but this gradual chilliness stops after a certain height. The point where the temperature stops dropping is called the 'tropopause'. The atmosphere below this height is called the 'troposphere'. Above it is the beginning of the 'stratosphere'.

At about 50 miles up the layer is called the 'mesosphere'. Above it comes the 'ionosphere'.

The ionosphere is so called because the air molecules are bombarded by the sun's ultraviolet rays to become electrically charged (ionized). The ionized particles form layers which reflect radio waves back to earth. This is why we can send radio signals round the world instead of the signals going into space.

The very top level of the atmosphere where the air is very rarefied and gases escape into space is sometimes called the exosphere.
See: *aerodynamics, light, sound.*

Find out by doing

Place a tumbler in a bowl of water right way up. You need to push to make the tumbler go right to the bottom, to overcome the upthrust of the water against the bottom of the tumbler. Next push the tumbler into the water upside down. The force of your push is probably about the same. This time the water is pushing on the air trapped in the tumbler, which is partly compressed.

Lay a tumbler down in a bowl of water so that it completely fills up. Then try and pick it up, bottom first. If you do it carefully you can lift almost the whole tumbler out of the bowl without a bubble getting in. The water is held up inside the tumbler by the pressure of the air on the water in the bowl outside the tumbler.

Invert a glass jar over some wet nails, iron filings, or wire, standing over water, as illustrated. As the iron rusts over a period of days and weeks, it uses up oxygen in the jar. The water will rise to fill the space formerly occupied by the oxygen in the jar.

Pour an inch or two of boiling water into a large square can and screw the lid on tight. Pour cold water over it. The water vapour in the can will condense rapidly, reducing the pressure inside. If the metal of the can is not too thick it will be crushed by the pressure of the atmosphere.

Rising currents of air can be revealed with the paper spiral shown, balanced on a pinpoint. Held over a radiator or a hot kitchen cooker it will begin to rotate as it is driven round by the rising air.

alchemy

An early kind of chemistry that was largely concerned with trying to turn ordinary metals into gold. When this possibility was eventually disproved, alchemists turned their attention to other things, and the science of modern chemistry was born.

One of the most distinguished of the early alchemists was an Arabian called Jabir, who lived in the eighth century. He is often referred to by the Latin form of his name, Geber. One of the processes he described for making gold involved distilling water 700 times. This, he said, would make it white, brilliant, cold and no longer moist. He was wrong, and the whole elaborate process was a complete waste of time. But it was described absolutely seriously and was accepted, although probably nobody attempted to carry it out.

We do not know when alchemy started, but the earliest reliable records date from the time of Christ. It was seriously studied from then until the eighteenth century when it was discredited in the eyes of most sensible people. In this period it was mainly concerned with turning 'base' metals, such as lead and copper, into 'noble' ones, such as gold. This is called 'transmuting'.

Alchemists also tried to find or prepare the 'philosopher's stone'. It was supposed that this would transmute any metal it touched. Another of their dreams was to prepare the 'Elixir of Life', which would give eternal life to anyone who drank it.

'Alkahest' was a mythical liquid that would dissolve anything. Alchemists tried desperately to make it but do not seem to have considered what they would have kept the alkahest in, since it would have dissolved its container.

We now know that attempts to make gold by their methods are hopeless. Although we can transmute individual atoms using nuclear physics, it is not feasible to make gold in worthwhile quantities.

The early experimenters had strange ideas about the nature of metals. They thought all metals were made of the same matter, but that each had different properties.

Lead was matter with the added properties of greyness and easy melting. Heating lead 'destroyed' it by turning it into a red powder, which did not have these properties. Gold was the same matter, but with the added properties of yellowness and indestructibility.

The alchemists tried to remove the properties of lead and replace them with properties of yellowness and indestructibility. They believed they would then have gold.

Alchemists were also inclined to think that metals act like people do. It was thought that man is resurrected to a purer life after death. Gold was metal that had died and been resurrected in its pure form. If copper is dissolved in nitric acid and heated to dryness it forms a black powder. Alchemists said it had died and needed only to be resurrected as gold.

This religious approach to alchemy continued for a long time. The language of alchemy was used by people who were not alchemists to describe their religious beliefs. Religion has always used myths and fairy tales to describe mystical ideas, which are difficult to express in plain words. The language and ideas of alchemy were put to the same use.

Because of this, many texts that appear to be alchemical are really religious parables and have little to do with science.

The earliest texts about alchemy say that it started in Egypt. However, this may not be true. At that time, if someone wanted to put forward a theory he would look for some great authority in the past who had said the same, or nearly the same, thing. This would gain respect for his theory. If he could not find such an authority to back him up, he would just invent one. The early European alchemists may have invented their Egyptian links to lend dignity to their work. The Ancient Egyptians were certainly very clever, particularly at gold-plating and making alloys, or mixtures of metals.

The Egyptians could make an alloy of copper and gold. To the alchemists, the result looked like gold. Therefore the Egyptian had created gold. He had transmuted the copper.

The Arabs were keen students of alchemy. In fact the word comes from Arabic. Geber, the Arab alchemist we mentioned earlier, is credited with a great many discoveries that may not have been his. He may have got the credit from some later alchemists who used Geber's name to give their ideas authority.

Geber's great contribution to alchemy was to define the nature of metals. He said that they were all combinations of mercury with different amounts of sulphur. He said that metals were formed underground by the blending of vapours of mercury and sulphur. If the alchemist could copy the natural process he would be able to make gold.

Although Geber's recipes for gold-making were incorrect, he did give the first clear and accurate account of how to make nitric acid. He also made 'aqua regia', a mixture that dissolves gold. Some of his drawings show very useful furnaces and stills.

Ramon Llull, a Majorcan who died in 1315, gave a perfectly clear description of how to make gold. It certainly would not work and yet he presents it as if he had done it. It may be that the experiment took so long that nobody ever managed to finish it. Another possibility is that his followers believed he was not talking about making gold metal but about some sort of mystical idea.

Alchemy attracted many swindlers. Chaucer's *The Canterbury Tales* describes one—as does Ben Johnson's play, *The Alchemist*.

However it also attracted the interest of eminent scientists. Isaac Newton (1642-1727) spent a great deal of time doing alchemical experiments.

Alchemy eventually died out when scientists began to understand the nature of matter and its construction.
See: *chemistry*.

algebra

A branch of the science of mathematics. It is like arithmetic, but as well as using numbers it uses letters of the alphabet to symbolize numbers.

One reason for using symbols in place of numbers is that we often do not know what the number we are interested in is. We are trying to find out what it is.

Suppose a boy tells us that he wants to buy something costing £5 and he needs another £2. We could say this algebraically by writing $x + 2 = 5$. Here x stands for the number of pounds he already has. We can then go on to work out what number x actually is. Later we shall look at some ways of doing this.

Algebra can be thought of as a form of shorthand. For addition and subtraction we use the familiar signs + and −. In arithmetic we use × as the multiplication sign. We avoid using it in this way in algebra, because x is often used to stand for an unknown number. To show that two numbers are to be multiplied together, we usually place them side by side with no symbol between them. For example, $2x$ means 2 multiplied by the number that x stands for. And ab means the number that a stands for multiplied by the number that b stands for.

For division we use the idea of fractions. $\frac{x}{3}$ means x divided by 3. If we need to show a number multiplied by itself several times we use small index numbers called 'exponents'. For example, x^2 means x multiplied by x. x^4 means $x\,x\,x\,x$; that is, four x's multiplied together. 2 and 4 are the exponents.

Here is an algebraic expression using some of the above 'shorthand': $x^2 + 2xy - 3y$. The symbols x and y stand for two unknown numbers. If, for example x stands for the number 3 and y stands for the number 5 the expression becomes: $(3 \times 3) + (2 \times 3 \times 5) - (3 \times 5)$ or $9 + 30 - 15$, which is 24. The brackets show which parts to work out first.

Algebraic statements
To make a complete statement using numbers we must have a 'verb'. We use 'equals' or 'is greater than' or 'is less than'. The signs for these verbs are =, > and <. Using ordinary numbers, we can then write: $2 + 3 = 5$; $2 + 3 > 4$; $2 + 3 < 6$.

We can also use symbols instead of numbers. For example: $2x + 3 = 7$. This is an 'equation'. It says that twice the number that x stands for, with 3 added to it, is equal to 7. The statement is true if x stands for the number 2, but not true if it stands for any other number.

An equation is a statement that is only true for certain values of the unknown number. These values are called *solutions* of the equation.

An *inequality* is a statement like $2x + 3 > 7$. This statement is true for a range of values of x. It is true in fact for all values greater than 2. To solve an equation or inequality means to find the number or set of numbers that make it a true statement.

An equation can be thought of as a see-saw or balance. The illustration shows $2x + 3$ in the left-hand tray 'balanced' by 11 in the right.

If one side is changed the other side must be changed in the same way to preserve the balance. In the example: take 3 from each side; the equation becomes $2x = 8$. So $x = 4$.

In solving an equation the aim is to finish up with another equation that tells us at once what the unknown number is. This final equation has the unknown number on one side only. Nothing unknown must appear on the other side.

Arithmetic only makes statements about particular numbers. For example, $3 + 2 = 5$ is an arithmetical statement. But sometimes we wish to make a statement that is true for all numbers, or a wide range of them. For example, suppose we wish to say that $3 + 2 = 2 + 3$, and $4 + 6 = 6 + 4$, and so on for *all* possible pairs of numbers. We can do this with the single algebraic statement $a + b = b + a$, in which a stands for any number and b stands for any other number. We are saying that when adding two numbers together, it does not matter in which order we add them.

A very important example of a general statement in geometry is known as Pythagoras' Theorem. Let the length of the longest side of a right-angled triangle be called a. Let the length of the other sides be called b and c. The Theorem says: $a^2 = b^2 + c^2$. In words, this is: 'the square on the longest side is equal to the sum of the squares of the other two sides'. This is a general statement because it is true for every right-angled triangle. But it is not true for *any* three numbers. Two possible sets of solutions are: $a = 5$, $b = 4$, $c = 3$ and: $a = 13$, $b = 12$, $c = 5$.

Algebra has given us the power to discover – or invent – new kinds of numbers. The 'negative' numbers are examples of this.

Suppose that a boy walks 2 miles north from his home. We can write this distance as 2. If he walks another 3 miles north we can write $2 + 3 = 5$.

If he now walks 2 miles south we know that he will be only 3 miles north of his home. We

write $5 - 2 = 3$. So 2 miles has to be subtracted when it is in a southward direction.

If the boy now walks 4 miles south, he will be 1 mile south of his home. We write $3 - 4 = -1$. The minus sign shows that the 1 mile is to the south. -1 is called a 'negative' number. Ordinary numbers are called 'positive' numbers.

Negative numbers could also represent, say, the number of gallons by which the water in a cistern is *below* its normal level. Positive numbers would represent the number of gallons by which it is *above* that level.

When the water in the reservoir is 3 gallons above its normal level there is more water than when it is only 2 gallons above normal. So we can write $3 > 2$.

When the water in the reservoir is 3 gallons below its normal level, there is less water than when it is 2 gallons below normal. So we can write $-3 < -2$.

Algebra can be applied not just to arithmetic, but to many other parts of mathematics. One example is set theory.

A set is a collection of objects of any kind: apples, numbers, geometrical figures, and so on. They can be labeled with letters.

All the girls who are students at a particular school, considered together, are a set. Call this set G. All the students who happen to be in one classroom make up a different set, C. These two sets will probably overlap; if there are any girl students in the classroom they will belong to both sets.

We can join two sets together to make a larger set. The set of boy students, B, and the set of girl students, G, at a school together make the set of all the students at that school, S. S is called the *union* of B and G, and in set notation is written: $S = B \cup G$.

When two sets overlap they are said to intersect. In the example above, the set of girl students, G, and the set of students in one classroom, C, overlap. The set of people who are members of both sets is called the *intersection* of the two sets. If we call this set Q we write: $Q = G \cap C$. It is just the set of girl students in the classroom.

With the aid of symbols it is possible to perform calculations with sets just as we can with numbers.

Solving problems

Many problems can be solved using algebra. The first step is to construct an equation or an inequality that describes the problem in algebraic 'code'.

Suppose we want to find two numbers that add up to 12, and one of the numbers must be twice as big as the other.

First, let one number be represented by x. Then the other number equals $2x$. The equation says that they add up to 12; that is, $x + 2x = 12$.

This is the same as saying $3x = 12$. Dividing both sides by 3 gives $x = 4$. So one number is 4. The other one is $2x$, which is 8.

Some problems lead to equations with two unknown quantities. For example: three pieces of wood must add up to 10 feet in length when laid end to end. Two pieces are the same length. Suppose they are each y feet long. Suppose the other piece of wood is x feet long. Then we can say: $x + 2y = 10$. Some possible solutions are: $x = 2$ and $y = 4$, or $x = 4$ and $y = 3$, or $x = 5\frac{1}{2}$ and $y = 2\frac{1}{4}$. The set of solutions has no end and the equation is said to be 'indeterminate'.

But suppose we know that one piece of wood must be 1 foot longer than each of the others, we can form another equation: $x - y = 1$. There are many solutions for this equation too; they include $x = 2$ and $y = 1$, $x = 4$ and $y = 3$, $x = 8$ and $y = 7$ and so on. However, there is only one solution that is the same for both equations: $x = 4$ and $y = 3$. A pair of equations solved together in this way are called 'simultaneous' equations.

The solutions to the two simultaneous equations can be shown on a graph as follows: for the solution $x = 2$, $y = 4$ of the first equation, mark a point in red whose distance is 2 units from the left-hand side of the graph, and 4 units from the bottom. Do the same for other solutions of the first equation, $x = 3$, $y = 3\frac{1}{2}$ and so on.

Then mark the solutions of the second equation with blue points. By joining up the points in each set, we get two straight lines, called the 'graphs' of the equations. Every point on the red line represents a solution of the first equation, every point on the blue line represents a solution of the second.

There is one point which lies on both lines – the point where they cross. This represents the solution of the simultaneous equations, $x = 4$, $y = 3$.

Algebra is a very old subject. Babylonian tablets dating from nearly four thousand years ago discuss algebraic problems. Later the Greeks made great advances. They were interested mainly in geometry, and it influenced their algebra just as it influenced the rest of their mathematics.

There were great students of algebra among the Arabs and the Indians. The name 'algebra' comes from the title of a book by the Arabian mathematician al-Khwarizmi. It means literally 'joining together'. The subject of algebra flourished in Europe from the fourteenth century, thanks to Arabian knowledge.

Most of our modern algebraic symbols were in use in Europe by 1650. The letters x, y, z were used to represent unknowns by the great philosopher and mathematician Descartes. He was also responsible for the great advance of applying algebra to geometry in a way that the Greeks never dreamed of.

arithmetic

Arithmetic is the art and science of using numbers. It forms part of mathematics along with algebra, geometry and trigonometry.

Before man could count, he had a rough idea of number. He could tell that one herd of animals contained more animals than another herd. But he could not tell how many more. Man made a big jump in his thinking when he had the idea of matching each animal with a mark on a stick or a scratch in the ground.

His next big advance was to invent more convenient systems to keep track of what he counted. We still use the earliest way of writing down numbers, tally marks. When you keep score for a game, you often simply make a mark for each point and later add them all up. Your score card might look like this: //// //// //// ///

Grouping the tally marks makes it easier to add up the total. The groups could be any size. They might be groups of 3 or 4 or 6. But they must all contain the same number of marks.

The next step is to invent symbols that stand for the numbers. Many different systems have been invented by different civilizations. One that you sometimes see today is the Roman system. Roman numerals were invented more than 3,000 years ago. They seem to be based on tally marks.

The Romans counted: I, II, III, IV, V, VI, VII, VIII, IX, X. This number system introduces a new idea, the idea of 'place'. A number sometimes had to be added and sometimes subtracted. Which it was depended on its position. Two numbers are added together when the one on the right is smaller or has the same value. For example, VI is 6 and XX is twenty.

When the left-hand number is smaller, it is subtracted from the one on the right. So IV is 4.

The symbol for 10 is X. So IX is 9 and XI is 11.

The only other numbers the Romans used were: L = 50, C = 100, D = 500 and M = 1,000.

This is certainly a quicker way to write a number than using tally marks. It is very clumsy for calculating, though. Try to multiply XXXIII by LXII (33 × 62).

Our number system

Our system uses the position of a number in a different way. Each of the first nine numbers is written with its own symbol: 1, 2, 3, 4, 5, 6, 7, 8 and 9. Each of these symbols is called a 'digit'. The place that this symbol occupies is called the 'units' column. To write higher numbers we use the place on the left of the units column to show how many tens there are in the number. 43, for example, tells us that there are 4 tens and 3 units. These are 'Arabic' numerals.

This second column is called the 'tens'

column. With its aid we can now write numbers up to 99. The place on its left can be used to show how many hundreds there are in the number. 336 is made up of 3 hundreds, 3 tens and 6 units.

Our system could not work without a symbol to show when one column is empty. This symbol is zero. Without zero, we could not tell the difference between 23, 203, and 230.

Our system needs to use two numbers for ten. It is called a 'decimal' system from the Latin word meaning ten. Several ancient number systems, however happened to be based on other numbers.

Suppose we wanted to base our numbers on five instead of ten. We should only use the symbols 1, 2, 3, 4 and 0. When we wanted to count past 4 we could use the column on the left of the units column to show how many *fives* there were in the number. So now the figures 10 would represent *five*. 11 would represent six, 12 would represent seven, and so on.

The highest number we could write using two columns would be 44, meaning 4 fives and 4 units, or twenty-four. Then we would have to use the third column. 100 would represent twenty-five, 101 would represent twenty-six, and so on.

You can see that numbers take up more space in a system based on five than in a system based on ten. The binary system is based on two, and only needs two symbols: 0 and 1. Numbers are very long to write out, but the binary system is the one actually used in computers (see: *binary number*).

Addition is the basis of all arithmetic. Even subtraction can be thought of as using the idea of addition. When one number is to be subtracted from another – for example, 2 from 7 – we can ask the question, 'What must be added to the smaller number to give the larger number?' Since 2 must be added to 5 to give 7, 2 is the result of subtracting 5 from 7.

Division is related to subtraction. Just as multiplication is repeated addition, division is repeated subtraction. To divide 24 by 6, we could subtract 6, subtract 6 again, and so on until we reached zero. The number of subtractions needed would be the answer. In this case, 6 would have to be subtracted 4 times.

This method is very slow when done by people. Desk calculators can subtract quickly, and this is the method by which they usually divide. It is quicker for a person to ask: 'What must I multiply 6 by to get 24?' Since 6×4 equals 24, 24 divided by 6 equals 4.

Fractions
The numbers used to count animals in a herd or children in a group are called 'whole' numbers, because they are used to count *whole* things. But there are some things that can be cut into pieces. When you talk about how much cake you have, it may only be a piece of cake. Or the money you have may only be half a penny. To express ideas like these, men invented fractional numbers. 'Fractional' means, literally, 'broken'.

A pie can be cut into several pieces. If it is cut into 4 equal pieces, the size of each can be represented by $\frac{1}{4}$. If it is cut into 3 equal pieces, each is represented by $\frac{1}{3}$, and so on.

We say that a piece of pie of size $\frac{1}{3}$ 'goes into' a whole pie 3 times. But there are some pieces that will not go into one pie a whole number of times. For example, consider a piece which is slightly larger than $\frac{1}{3}$ of a pie. It must go into a whole pie less than 3 times. But if that same piece is also smaller than $\frac{1}{2}$ of a pie, it must go into the whole pie more than 2 times. So it cannot go into the whole pie a whole number of times at all.

But the size of the piece can be written down. It can be regarded as made up of smaller pieces. For example, it might be 5 times as large as a piece $\frac{1}{12}$ the size of the whole pie. This is written as $\frac{5}{12}$ which means five twelfths.

If we write $\frac{17}{239}$ we can regard this as an 'instruction' telling us how to obtain the fraction. It tells us to imagine one unit divided into 239 parts and to take 17 of these parts together.

In the decimal system, we write whole numbers according to how many hundreds, tens and units they contain. In a similar way, we write fractional numbers according to how many tenths, hundredths, and so on, they contain. The digits describing the fractional part of the number are written after the stop. called the decimal point. $\frac{3}{4}$ is written in the decimal system as 0.75, meaning that it contains 75 hundredths, or 7 tenths and 5 hundredths.

Not all fractions can be written exactly in the decimal system. Sometimes the series of digits needed never ends. For example, $\frac{1}{9}$ is the series 0.1111..., with the 1 repeated forever. Another example is $\frac{1}{7}$, which has the pattern 0.142857 142857..., and so on.

Most money systems break up their basic unit into a hundred parts. The pound contains 100 pence, and £$4\frac{3}{4}$ contains £4 and 75 pence.

Negative numbers
You are standing on a hill 50 metres (164 feet) above sea level. You then walk down into a hollow 100 metres (328 feet) lower. What is your altitude? The answer is: 50 metres (164 feet) *below sea level*.

Today's temperature is 5 degrees. Tonight it will fall by 10 degrees. It will then be 5 degrees *below zero*. Another way of saying this is 'minus five'. Minus five is what we call a *negative number*.

Negative numbers are not used to count

things, but they are useful in measuring. We cannot imagine 'minus five bricks', but we know what 'minus five degrees' feels like. It's cold!

Minus five is written −5. Ordinary, above zero numbers are known as 'positive' numbers. We can do arithmetic with negative and positive numbers together. For example:

$$5 - 10 = -5$$
$$2 \times (-5) = -10$$

The brackets are used to show that we mean a negative number, not a subtraction sum.

Precision

We often have to work with quantities that are not known exactly. Suppose we want to know the area of a rectangle which has sides of 1.57 and 3.28. (You find the area by multiplying together the lengths of the sides.) So 1.57×3.28 equals 5.1496. That would be the answer if we were sure those were the *exact* lengths of the sides. But real measurements are never exact. The shorter side of the rectangle might have been 1.571 or 1.568, but perhaps 1.57 was the nearest mark on the ruler.

It would be wrong to state the answer – the area – in a way which suggests greater precision. In this particular case we can safely say that the area is '5.15, correct to three significant figures'. Note that we say 5.15 rather than 5.14. The reason is because 5.1496 is closer to 5.15 than it is to 5.14.

Zeroes at the beginning of a decimal, or at the end of a large number, are not regarded as significant because they do not add to the precision. Does this seem strange? We can say that a man is 1.7 metres (5 foot 7 inches) tall, or 1700 millimetres, or (for the sake of argument) 0.0017 kilometres. Is any of these measurements more or less precise than the others? No – they all tell us the same thing.

In long calculations it is better to work with one or two more significant numbers than you will eventually need.

Fast figuring

There are many ways to make calculating easier. Here are a few.

In all kinds of calculations it is often useful to get an approximate answer by changing the numbers into nearly equal numbers which are more convenient. For example, 18×27 is approximately equal to 20×25, which is quickly worked out to be 500. The right answer is actually 486.

The main use of approximations like this is as a quick check that your proper calculation has produced a reasonable answer. If an exact answer is not necessary for your purposes, it is allowable to use an approximation.

When making an approximate calculation, round each number off to the nearest 10. That is, if the number is 51 to 54, round it off to 50.

If it is 56 to 59, round it off to 60. If it is 55, you can round it up or down. Numbers can be rounded off to the nearest hundred, too. 623×291 could be simplified to 600×300, telling you that the answer is somewhere near 180,000.

It is sometimes useful to know quickly whether a number can be divided by another number. Some 'rules of divisibility' exist to help us find out.

A number is divisible by 2 if it is even.
A number can be divided by 3 if the sum of its digits is divisible by 3. *Example: 972 is divisible by 3, since $9+7+2=18$, which is divisible by 3.*
A number can be divided by 4 if the number formed by the last 2 digits can be divided by 4. *Example: 13,628 is divisible by 4 since 28 is divisible by 4.*
If a number ends in 5 or 0 it can be divided by 5.
A number is divisible by 6 if it is both even and divisible by 3.
To test whether a number can be divided by 11, add up the first, third, fifth, and so on, digits. Then add up the ones you skipped. If the difference between the two totals is divisible by 11, or if it is zero, the original number can be divided by 11. *Example: 64,207 is divisible by 11, because: $6 + 2 + 7 = 15$, and $4 + 0 = 4$, and the difference between 4 and 15 is 11, which is divisible by 11.*

Many 'calculating machines' have been invented over the centuries. They have usually been simple devices that permit the operator to carry out a complicated calculation, such as a multiplication, by performing simpler operations, such as addition. The abacus is one of the earliest of these devices. The operator could perform lengthy additions very rapidly by counting off beads strung on wires or rods.

Multiplications can be reduced to additions very easily by means of a set of marked rods. The rods are lengths of wood, one for each number from zero to nine. The number is written at the top and multiples of that number are written down the rod. For instance, the 3 rod carries the numbers 3, 6, 9, 12 and so on.

To use the rods to multiply 4×137, start by placing the 1, 3 and 7 rods together, as the diagram on page 58 shows. Then look at the numbers in the fourth row. These are: 4 on the first rod, 12 on the next rod, and 28 on the last.

Starting from the left, add the numbers that are side by side, but on different rods. That is, add $4 + 1 = 5$, and $2 + 2 = 4$. The 8 on the last rod stays as it is. So 4×137 equals 548.

To multiply 137 by 43, multiply 137 by 40 and then by 3, and add the two results. To work out

40 x 137, multiply by 4 and add a zero at the end of the result.

Many ancient peoples, including the Greeks, thought numbers had magic powers. They studied each number and found that some had special properties.

The Greeks were especially interested in prime numbers. Prime numbers – also called simply 'primes' – are numbers that cannot be divided by any other – except, of course, 1. 19, 23, 29 and 37 are examples.

The first few primes are: 2, 3, 5, 7, 11, 13 and 17. (Mathematicians have decided not to count 1 itself as a prime). A simple method of finding the prime numbers up to a particular number is called the Sieve of Eratosthenes.

First write down all the numbers in order, starting at 2, up to the number you have chosen, say 100. Cross out every multiple of 2, that is, all the even numbers except 2 itself. The next number after 2 not crossed out is 3. Cross out all multiples of 3, except 3 itself. Moving on from 3, we find that 4 has been crossed out. The next number still remaining is 5. Cross out all multiples of 5 and so on. Continue in this way. The numbers not crossed out at the end are the prime numbers up to 100.

When Greek civilization was just beginning, the Chinese invented the first magic square. The numbers in each row, each column and the two long diagonals of a magic square must add up to the same number. No number may appear more than once in the square. If the square has three numbers to a side, it is called a 3×3 square. It contains the numbers from 1 to 9. A 4×4 square contains the numbers up to 16.

Albrecht Durer made one 4×4 square famous by including it in one of his pictures. Each column, row and diagonal adds up to 34. Besides this, there are four 2×2 magic squares in the corners and one in the middle. The rows, columns and diagonals in these smaller squares add up to 34. So do the four smaller single squares that form the corners.

Arithmetic is usually regarded as the simplest part of school maths. But mathematicians find 'number theory' – the study of the properties of numbers – endlessly fascinating.
See: *algebra, computer, mathematics.*

Find out by doing

Make a set of multiplying rods like those described in the text. You will need nine strips of stiff card about an inch wide. Mark off each strip into half-inch divisions and divide each of these into a left-hand and a right-hand section. On the '7' strip write in the multiples of 7 as shown in the diagram. Do this for all the other numbers, and then try some multiplications.

Make a 3×3 magic square. See how many 4×4 magic squares you can find.

Find the first 25 prime numbers using the Sieve of Eratosthenes.
(Answer: 2, 3, 5, 7, 11, 13, 17, 19, 23, 29, 31, 37, 41, 43, 47, 53, 59, 61, 67, 71, 73, 79, 83, 89, 97.)

astronomy

A few thousand years ago, Man did not even know whether the Earth was round or flat. A few hundred years ago, he knew it was round, but did not know whether it was the centre of the Universe, or just one of many planets orbiting the Sun. Today he is beginning to wonder whether there is life elsewhere in the Universe. And, if there are intelligent beings, how we can get in touch with them.

For several thousand years Man has wondered and wondered about the nature and the behaviour of all the things to be seen in the sky. He has learned a great deal from watching the Sun, the Moon, the stars, planets, meteors, comets and other heavenly bodies. Our Sun is a star. The bodies orbiting a star are known as planets. Those orbiting planets are known as moons. Astronomy is the study of all these heavenly bodies.

Some people may think it strange that a science that began several thousand years ago cannot yet answer the question: 'Is there life elsewhere?' But when we consider the huge distances and the time involved, it is amazing that we know as much as we do.

We know that our solar system was born at least 5,000 million years ago. This is calculated by estimating the age of the oldest rocks on Earth and by studying the Sun. Also, we can guess when the end of the solar system will come. The atomic reactions now raging in the centre of the Sun will go on for another 5,000 million years at least. Then the Sun will expand into a huge red ball of gas. It will swallow up the closest planets – Mercury, Venus and Earth – as this happens. Of course, this means that any life existing on these planets at that time will be destroyed.

Five thousand million years is a long time, but many parts of the Universe are thought to be much, much older. The world's largest telescopes have detected the faint light of distant systems of stars, called galaxies, estimated to lie nearly 10,000 million light years away. This means that their light has taken nearly 10,000 million years to reach us. Radio telescopes, in particular the world's largest one in Puerto Rico, have probed even further.

The distances in which astronomy deals are vast – so vast that it is difficult for us to imagine them. Pluto, for instance, the outermost known planet in our solar system, has a path around the Sun which is some 7,350 million miles in diameter. But our solar system is only one tiny part of the Milky Way galaxy. This galaxy is a huge family of stars, planets, satellites, asteroids and gas and dust. We are the merest speck in space. The Milky Way has an estimated diameter of 80,000 light years. If the Milky Way were Europe, our solar system would be a postcard lying somewhere on its surface. Even 80,000 light years might sound like a manageable distance, if said quickly. But a light year is the distance travelled by light in one year. That is about 6 million million miles.

In turn, the diameter of the known Universe is about 10,000 million light years. This means that the Milky Way would fit across it 125,000 times. With distances such as these, it is no wonder that many astronomers have given up trying to understand it all. They are content to concentrate on their favourite aspect of astronomy.

Even if we just think of our own solar system it strains the imagination. It covers an area almost too large to conceive of.

To help us, many kinds of word 'pictures' are used. One such picture supposes that the Sun is reduced to the size of a beach ball which is 12 inches in diameter. If the Sun were this size, then the planet sizes and distances could be represented as follows:

Mercury	:	a grape seed 164 feet away
Venus	:	a pea 284 feet away
Earth	:	a bigger pea 430 feet away
Mars	:	a raisin 654 feet away
Jupiter	:	an orange half-a-mile away
Saturn	:	a tangerine four-fifths of a mile away
Uranus	:	a plum just over a mile away
Neptune	:	a plum two and a half miles away
Pluto	:	a grain of rice three miles away

On the same reduced scale, the nearest star to our own Sun – Alpha Centauri – would lie at a distance of 8,000 miles! This shows how alone in space we are.

Just as amazing is the way in which man has reached his present knowledge of the Universe. He has observed, measured and calculated and sometimes made inspired guesses. He never set foot on another body outside Earth until July 1969 when Neil Armstrong took his first historic steps on the Moon.

Even so, there is good reason to assume that most of our major ideas about other heavenly bodies are correct. Certainly, allowing for one or two geological facts, this has proved to be the case with the Moon. The pictures taken by the astronauts and the rocks they brought back supported our theories. All the same, one of the most fascinating things about astronomy is how much we do not know. It was only as a result

of the space probes of the 1970s that we learnt much about the planet Venus, with its thick cloud cover. And Venus is our nearest neighbour planet.

Astronomers are also often wrong. It used to be thought that Mars contained little or no water vapour. But data transmitted by the spacecraft Mariner 9 now suggests that this may not be true.

There is also the interesting case of Vulcan. Vulcan was a planet which one or two astronomers last century claimed went round the Sun within the orbit of Mercury. This was dismissed by other astronomers, who said it was merely a figment of the imagination. Recently, however, certain disturbances in the orbits of Mercury and Venus suggest that Vulcan may well exist. And there may even be another planet still unseen, circling outside the orbit of Pluto.

The birth of astronomy
When did man first start to think about the stars? The answer lies in pre-history.

Most of the early people who noticed the movements of heavenly bodies in the night skies were probably hunters or shepherds. They could not write, so we have no idea of what they saw and thought.

Everybody would have noticed the daily rising and setting of the Sun, and how it was lower in the sky in winter than in summer. They would see the regular changes in shape, the phases, of the Moon, and wonder what was happening. People invented stories to explain what they saw. And they worshipped the heavenly bodies as gods.

The cleverest people in those days were the priests. We know that Ancient Egyptian priests used to study the movements of heavenly bodies in a systematic way some 2000 years BC. And the Chinese invented the 365-day calendar year, which we now use, as early as 1600 BC. But the first of the great astronomers was Greek. He was called Thales of Miletus and lived from 624 to 546 BC. He is thought to be the first person to have stated that the Earth is a globe.

But the real credit for this discovery must go to two other Greeks. The first was Aristotle (385-325 BC), the great philosopher. He pointed out that sometimes the Earth came between the Sun and the Moon, and that the Earth's shadow on the Moon is curved. This is what we call an eclipse.

The second was Eratosthenes (276-194 BC) who was the keeper of the great library of Alexandria in Egypt. He calculated the distance around the Earth, and said it was 24,662 miles. We now know that the true distance is 24,861 miles, so his was a remarkable achievement. This feat was based on measuring shadows at noon in two different places, and thus the curvature of the Earth's crust.

The next notable astronomer was Ptolemy. He was the royal astronomer of Egypt and lived in the second century AD. Ptolemy's theories were wrong. But unfortunately they were believed for more than 1300 years. This held back progress in astronomy for all that time.

Ptolemy believed that the Earth was the centre of the Universe, with the Moon, Mercury, Venus, the Sun, Mars, Jupiter and Saturn, in that order, orbiting round it. His theory was thought to be right until 1543. In that year a Polish priest, Copernicus, declared that the Earth and Mars were in orbit around the Sun.

The next famous name in astronomy is Johannes Kepler (1571–1630). He is known for his three laws of planetary motion. The first law stated that the planets move round the Sun in elliptical (oval) and not circular paths.

The second law stated that the speed of a planet changes with its distance from the Sun. As it gets nearer the Sun the speed increases, and, as it goes away from the Sun, the speed decreases. For example, the Earth's orbital speed is highest at the position called 'perihelion'. This happens in January, when the speed reaches 67,800 mph. At this point in time the Earth is closest to the Sun. When the Earth is farthest from the Sun, in June, it is at the position known as the 'aphelion'. At this position the speed falls to 65,600 mph.

Kepler's third law stated that for any planet, the time taken to complete one orbit round the Sun is related to the cube of the planet's distance from the Sun. The time taken for planet to complete one orbit is known as the 'sidereal period'.

Putting Earth in its place

Galileo, who was born in 1564, was the first man to examine the heavens with a telescope. This instrument had just been invented in Holland by Hans Lippershey.

Galileo first used it during the winter of 1609–1610. He pointed it upwards into the night skies and made many exciting discoveries. He helped people to realize that the Sun, Moon and planets were not 'magic' in any way – they are just masses of matter in space like our own planet. Through this telescope he saw mountains and valleys on the surface of the moon. He was able to detect four of Jupiter's twelve moons, the 'rings' around Saturn, and the dark areas on the Sun known as 'sunspots'. Unfortunately, Galileo's work was such a strain on his eyes that he became blind in later life.

Galileo also backed up the idea of another Italian astronomer, Giordano Bruno. He had been burned to death by the Church for declaring, amongst other things, that the Earth was not the centre of the Universe, but that it moved

round the Sun. Galileo was tried by the Church court and threatened with the same fate. He pretended he had changed his mind. But, after the trial he is reported to have whispered: 'Nevertheless, it does move!'

Galileo died in 1642, and in the same year Isaac Newton was born. His genius revealed many astronomical truths. His celebrated findings on gravity in 1687 explained why bodies, such as our Earth, kept orbiting round the Sun instead of shooting off into space.

From Newton's work, too, we came to realize that our solar system is in balance. Each planet's pull, or gravity, acts on every other one. If, for example, our moon were to disappear suddenly, this would upset the Earth's orbit. And if the Earth's orbit changed, then the orbit of Mars would change slightly too, and so on.

Since Newton's day there have been generations of distinguished astronomers. William Herschel discovered binary or twin stars, which spin round one another. Friedrich Bessel in 1838 first measured the distance of nearby stars. He did this by measuring the apparent changes of stars' positions. Great American astronomers such as Edwin P. Hubble and V. M. Slipher are remembered for working out the size and structure of galaxies. They also found out what stars are made of, from the study of starlight. This was in the early part of this century.

Among other things, he is studying bodies known as 'quasars' or quasi-stellar objects. They are only about one hundredth of the size of stars of the Milky Way, but they radiate 50 to 150 times as much energy.

'Pulsars', which are stars that emit radio signals at fixed intervals, are also being studied. Again, man is constantly watching and listening for signs of life elsewhere.

Astronomers have begun to probe the sky for other types of radiation such as X-rays and infrared radiation. Space probes and satellites as well as increasingly sophisticated telescopes are helping too.

Chemists have joined the astronomers in analysing the signals received by these various pieces of equipment. Already they have confirmed the existence of large carbon-based molecules in the clouds of hydrogen gas that lie between the stars.

The possibility of finding intelligent life on other planets remains the most exciting challenge to scientific research. At one time, it was believed that the planets of the solar system had been formed from material 'dragged' out of a passing star by the gravity of our own Sun. This could have meant our being the only inhabited world in the whole Milky Way and possibly in the Universe.

However, this theory has been rejected. There is now evidence that most, if not all, of the stars we can see from Earth have their own planets. Some of them we have certain knowledge of because we can observe disturbances in their paths.

But this is considering only one tiny corner of the Milky Way. Throughout the galaxy as a whole, there could be as many as 600 to 1,000 million planets on which the human race could thrive. And our own galaxy is but one of millions upon millions in the known Universe.

At one time, man thought that the Earth was the centre of the Universe. We now know how wrong he was. We now have some idea of the size and age of the Universe. It contains an inconceivable number of suns and planets. Today we could be just as wrong if we thought of ourselves as the only intelligent life in the Universe.

See: *relativity, solar system, star.*

Find out by doing

Make a pinhole in some card. Hold it up in sunlight so that it casts a shadow on a wall. The hole will form a circular spot of light in the middle of the shadow. This spot is an image of the Sun. In eclipses it becomes a crescent. This 'pinhole camera' also shows large sunspots occasionally.

WARNING: *never look directly at the sun.*

To think about

Light travels six million million miles in a year. What was happening in history when the light by which we see the following stars set out on its journey? *Alpha Centauri (25 million million miles); Altair (100 million million miles); Canopus (1,400 million million miles); Antares (2,200 million million miles). In Britain a million million is called a billion. In the U.S.A. a thousand million is called a billion, and a million million is a trillion.*

atom

If you dissolve some cooking salt in water it disappears. It is still there, so how do we account for its disappearance? It has disappeared because the tiny particles of which salt is made have slipped in among the tiny particles of water. The particles are so small that they cannot be seen with the naked eye, nor even with a microscope.

The same is true of the smallest particles of all other substances although they do not necessarily mix like salt and water.

The smallest particles of chemical substances are called atoms. An atom of iron, say, is exactly the same as every other atom of iron. It is also different from atoms of anything else

– aluminium for instance – which are also identical to each other. A piece of pure iron would contain millions upon millions of iron atoms and nothing else.

Invisible 'suns' and 'planets'

We now know that atoms are like miniature solar systems, with the equivalent of a sun in the centre and planets in orbit around. To give an idea of the size of an atom, 200,000,000 hydrogen atoms side by side makes only one inch. At the centre of the atom is the 'nucleus' (plural: 'nuclei'), which has a positive electrical charge. In orbit around the nucleus are 'electrons', which have a negative electrical charge. The number of negative charges equals the number of positive charges. They balance out and the atom is neutral.

A substance which is made up of only one kind of atom is called an element. But atoms of different kinds can combine to form substances other than elements. When two or more atoms join up they become what we call a 'molecule'.

Each molecule of water, for instance, contains two atoms of hydrogen linked to one atom of oxygen. The atoms of the molecule can be separated again to make hydrogen and oxygen gases. But the bond of the molecule is quite strong. Even if you boil water, the molecules will stay whole. The water turns into water vapour, which is a gas. But this vapour still consists of water molecules.

Water and all the other substances that have more than one kind of atom in them are called chemical compounds. This distinguishes them from the elements, which have only one kind of atom each.

'Uncuttable' particles

The idea of atoms was first considered by the Ancient Greeks. In 400 BC the philosopher Democritus decided on the name for these tiny particles. It comes from the Greek *atomos* which means 'uncuttable'. He chose that name because he thought that if you cut a piece of anything in half, and then in half again, and again, and again, you must come to a point when minute particles are produced which simply could not be cut any smaller. Democritus said that everything was made up of such particles. He even put forward the idea that substances were different because they were made up of different sorts of atoms, or mixtures of them. Other philosophers laughed at Democritus and his ideas were rejected. Now, over 2,000 years later, we can see that Democritus was pretty close to the truth.

The first man to demonstrate that matter is composed of atoms was the English chemist John Dalton at the beginning of the nineteenth century. He also showed that the atoms of various elements differed in their weight. Iron atoms are heavier than hydrogen atoms, for example, and oxygen atoms are heavier than hydrogen atoms, but lighter than iron atoms. Dalton's work inspired other chemists. They were interested in measuring how the weights of different atoms compared, so that they could arrange them in order. It might be possible to group the elements into classes. The Russian Mendeléev first classified them.

He showed that it was possible to range all the known elements according to weight in a table. This was the beginning of the 'periodic table'.

Until about 1890, scientists still thought of atoms as being small 'uncuttable' particles, probably rather like very tiny solid balls. Then the electron was discovered.

Electricity had been studied for a very long time. Scientists could make electric currents flow, but they had no idea what they were made of. In fact, they consist of electrons in movement. Whenever an electric current flows, electrons leave their atoms and begin to move.

A strange glow

Electrons were discovered when electric currents were passed through tubes from which nearly all the air had been pumped out. The electrons flowed from a metal terminal called the cathode, to another one called the anode. If the anode was set off to one side, as in the diagram, some of the electrons would 'overshoot' and strike the glass wall of the tube. The glass glowed at the place where they struck it.

Scientists quickly realized that the glow was caused by rays of some kind travelling from the cathode, and called them 'cathode rays'. They did not know at first whether they were waves of some kind, like light, or whether they were particles. Sir William Crookes found evidence that cathode rays consisted of particles. He showed that when a magnet was placed near them, the rays were bent. Waves would not have behaved like this.

Crookes also showed that the rays could push round a light metal vane when it was placed in their path. This also helped to show that the rays were made of particles with weight.

In 1897 the question was settled by the famous scientist J. J. Thomson. He showed that the 'rays' could be bent by nearby electric charges – and very strongly. This indicated that they were tiny negatively-charged particles. Experiments showed that each particle was less than one thousandth of the weight of a hydrogen atom – the lightest atom known.

So it seemed that atoms were not the smallest existing particles of matter after all. The newly-discovered electron was to revolutionize science. All the previous ideas about atoms suddenly seemed to be wrong.

The 'raisin cake' picture

Scientists changed their picture of the atom from being like a solid ball to being like a raisin cake. The 'cake' had a positive charge, and in it were the 'raisins', the negatively charged electrons. The opposite charges cancelled out. The atoms as a whole therefore had no charge.

Positive and negative electronic charges attract each other. This attraction held the parts of the atoms together. Under certain conditions, however, 'raisins' could be knocked off the 'cake'. In other words, electrons could be knocked off the atom – that is what had happened in the cathode ray tube. The atom would then have more positive charge than negative. It would be positively charged. An atom with an electron missing, or with an extra electron, is called an ion.

Then came the discovery of radioactive elements (see: *radioactivity*). These substances gave out three kinds of radiation. The three sorts were named alpha, beta and gamma rays, after the first three letters of the Greek alphabet. Beta rays could penetrate thin sheets of metal. They were found to be ordinary electrons. Gamma rays were quickly found to be similar to the highly penetrating X-rays that had been discovered earlier (see: *X-rays*). But alpha rays were quite new.

Atoms without electrons

Alpha radiation was found to be made up of larger particles than electrons. In England, Ernest Rutherford showed that streams of alpha particles were bent, like electrons, by a magnetic field. But they were bent in the opposite direction, and much less strongly.

Rutherford decided that this kind of particle had a positive charge. We now know that alpha particles are helium atoms that have lost their electrons. They are about four times as heavy as hydrogen atoms.

Rutherford was able to explore the atom using alpha particles. He sent alpha particles given off by radioactive elements towards thin metal sheets. Most of the particles went straight through. But some were scattered and even bounced back. Rutherford decided that some of the particles, the ones that did not go straight through, were hitting a dense target, a core inside the atom. Since only a few bounced back, the core must be extremely small.

Rutherford put all the evidence together and decided there would have to be a new picture of what the atom was like. Atoms were certainly not like small hard balls. But again they must be different from the raisin-cake idea, with electrons simply sticking on the sides. In fact the only picture that would fit the facts was of an atom that was mainly empty space.

Rutherford suggested the idea of a nucleus

consisting of positively-charged particles called protons. Surrounding this was a cloud of orbiting electrons. The charges balanced, and this explained why the atom was neutral.

Now it became possible to visualize the differences between the atoms of different elements. Hydrogen, the lightest element, had a nucleus consisting of only one proton. Helium had a nucleus of two protons and two orbiting electrons. Lithium had three protons and three electrons – and so on for all the elements. It was the number of protons that the nucleus contained that decided what the element was.

However, there was now another mystery to explain. Except in the case of hydrogen, the weights of different atoms were not what would be expected. Helium, as we have stated above, was known to have two protons in its nucleus. It weighed as much as if it had four. Again, oxygen was known to have eight protons, but it weighed as much as if it had sixteen.

It was not until 1932 that the mystery was solved. A new kind of particle was found. The new particles were as heavy as protons, but had no electrical charge. They were given the name 'neutrons'.

The existence of non-charged particles was a key to several problems. Immediately it became possible to explain the mystery of the apparent extra weight of various atoms. Except in the case of hydrogen, which had only a proton, there are protons *and* neutrons in the nucleus of each atom. Thus helium has two protons and two neutrons, explaining why it is four times the weight of hydrogen, not just twice the weight. Oxygen has eight neutrons in the nucleus as well as eight protons, and so weighs sixteen times as much as hydrogen, not just eight times as much.

The neutrons do not change the electrical charge of the nucleus. They hold the nucleus together and add to the weight. The electrons in orbit around the nucleus are only a very small part of the weight of the atom. Although each has as much electrical charge as a proton, it has only about one 1,800th of the weight. Knowing that the difference in weight between an electron and a neutron was so great, and that neutrons had no charge, was very helpful.

It also became possible now to explain another puzzling thing. It had been found that different samples of the same element did not always show the same atomic weight. The reason for this was now clear. There could be extra neutrons in the nuclei of an element. This would not alter what element it was, because that was decided by the number of protons.

The number of protons in the nucleus of an atom is called the *atomic number* of that element. All the atoms of an element have the same atomic number. Atoms with the same atomic number, but with different numbers of neutrons in the nucleus, have a different atomic weight. These different forms of one element are called *isotopes* of that element.

'Heavy' water
Nearly all elements have isotopes, and some of them are radioactive. Hydrogen has three isotopes. Ordinary hydrogen, H^1, has just a proton as its nucleus. An isotope with an additional neutron in the nucleus, H^2, is called deuterium. The form with two neutrons in the nucleus, H^3, is called tritium. 'Heavy water' is water composed of oxygen combined with hydrogen, like ordinary water. However, the hydrogen in each molecule is one of the 'heavy' isotopes of hydrogen, H^2.

The electrons in orbit around an atom are arranged in 'shells', rather like the layers of an onion. Only two electrons can be in the innermost shell, but the next shell can contain eight. The arrangement gets more complicated as the number of electrons increases.

A filled outer shell is a stable arrangement. That is, it will tend to remain as it is, neither losing nor gaining electrons. Atoms always tend to become stable. They will share electrons if necessary. Atoms that are sharing electrons are joined closely together forming a new chemical substance. Atoms can also give electrons to other atoms. This joins them closely, too.

Making molecules
The chemical behaviour of an atom depends on the electrons in its outermost shell. These are called 'valence electrons'.

For example, an atom of hydrogen has only one electron. It can combine with another atom of hydrogen so that they share the two electrons between them. The innermost shells are thus both filled. This is why nearly all hydrogen gas is in molecules formed from two hydrogen atoms linked together.

Helium has two electrons. Its innermost shell is filled, so it is a very stable atom and does not combine with others. Lithium, with three electrons, has a filled innermost shell and only one electron in the next shell, which can take up to eight. So it will give up the solitary electron to an atom of another element. It then has one filled shell, which is a stable state.

Common salt is made of sodium and chlorine. Sodium has two full shells but also one electron in the third shell, further out. Chlorine needs only one electron to fill its third shell. When sodium and chlorine combine, the sodium atom loses its outer electron to the chlorine atom. The sodium atom is left with two full shells and the chlorine atom with three full shells.

Because the sodium atom has given up a negatively-charged electron, it now has an overall positive charge. The chlorine is negatively charged because it has gained a negative electron. They have become ions, and their opposite charges hold them together as a stable chemical compound.

Elements which have the same number of electrons in their outer shells all tend to be similar in chemical properties. Those with completely filled outer shells, such as helium, neon and argon, are all very unreactive. In fact they are usually known as the 'inert', or inactive, gases, and were once called the 'noble' gases.

The arrangement of electrons also explains why some elements, like metals, are good conductors of electricity, but others are not. In general, metals have one or more electrons in the outer shell of their atoms. They are not too tightly bound to the nucleus, and can move from one nucleus to another quite easily. Such electrons can be looked on as 'free' electrons. When they do jump from one atom to another they pass electrical charge along. Insulators, such as rubber and wood, have no free electrons and will not pass electricity along.

It is possible to knock electrons right out of atoms. Because electrons have a negative charge, this leaves the atoms of the element with a positive charge. With some materials, simply rubbing the surface will knock electrons out of the atoms. If amber is rubbed with a piece of silk or fur, electrons are taken from the amber, and the amber becomes electrically charged. This kind of electricity is called 'static electricity.' Objects that are charged with static electricity attract things that have the opposite charge.

The Ancient Greeks noticed that if a piece of amber was rubbed briskly it could be used to pick up pieces of fluff. But of course they had no idea why this happened. It was from the Greek word for amber (elektron) that we got our words 'electricity', 'electron' and so on. (See: *electricity*.)

Electrons have another characteristic which is important. They can move, or jump, from one orbit into another. To jump to an outer orbit takes energy. On the other hand, when an electron jumps to an inner orbit it must lose energy. The energy appears as radiation, such as visible light.

From experiments using small particles as missiles it has now become clear that a proton-neutron idea of the nucleus was rather too simple. The study of cosmic rays and their effects has also shown that the picture is more complex. Cosmic rays are very energetic particles coming from space and entering the Earth's atmosphere. The particles smash into atoms and molecules in the atmosphere and produce showers of so-called 'secondary' particles.

Thanks to experiments using particle accelerators, (see *accelerator*) which artifically produce showers of particles similar to those found in cosmic rays, physicists are now fairly sure that protons and neutrons are themselves constructed out of even smaller building blocks called 'quarks'. Quarks have an electric charge of either $2/3$ or $-1/3$ the charge on the proton. The proton contains three quarks (charges $2/3 + 2/3 - 1/3 = 1$) and the neutron has a different combination of three (charges $2/3 - 1/3 - 1/3 = 0$). No lone quarks have ever been observed in nature – hence the name 'gluon' for the particle that holds the quarks together.

Radioactive atoms have nuclei that are unstable. They can be thought of as trying to reorganize themselves to become stable. They do this by giving out energy in the form of alpha, beta or gamma radiation. They give out radiation at a definite rate which nothing can change. It is measured as a 'half life', which is the time needed for half the atoms in a sample to complete their radiation. It can vary from less than a millionth of a second to a hundred million years.

'Looking-glass' atoms
We know that atoms are composed of protons, electrons and neutrons. However, we also know that positrons exist. Positrons could be called 'anti-electrons' because they are like electrons, except that they have opposite electric charges. They also have other properties which are the opposite of electrons. If there are also anti-protons and antineutrons, they could make up atoms whose properties would be in every way opposite to ordinary atoms.

We call these theoretical atoms 'antimatter' as opposed to 'matter'. Antimatter does not exist naturally on earth. If it did it would immediately collide with ordinary matter and be destroyed. But antimatter appears for very brief periods in atomic experiments and it is possible that other galaxies are composed entirely of antimatter.

See: *chemistry, electricity, physics, radiation.*

automation

The first step in automating any process is to replace human or animal muscles by machines. This is called mechanization. Since very early times the power of water and wind have been used to turn the millstones that grind corn. When sails were first put up on ships the labour of oarsmen was replaced by wind power.

Industrial revolution
For most of his history man has used no other

forms of power than animals, wind and water. The first great advance in man's use of natural forces occurred when the powers of steam were harnessed.

This marked the beginning of the Industrial Revolution. Huge factories were built in which steam engines drove looms on which cotton fabrics were woven. People and freight could now be transported rapidly and in large numbers on steam-driven railroad trains and ships. In the industrial nations the traditional farming way of life began to give way to manufacturing.

The petrol engine was developed towards the end of the nineteenth century. Mechanized transport could now be used by private individuals, and automobiles began to compete with railroads.

Electricity, too, brought wide mechanization. The new form of power could be used in many new types of machines and could be transmitted by cable to the places where it was needed. Electricity has mechanized every aspect of our lives. Homes, offices and vehicles all use electricity to power heaters, windows, cleaners or cookers.

In factories, drills, cranes, trucks and handling equipment are powered by electric motors, petrol engines, or steam. Man's muscle power has been helped out enormously by these new machines.

The next step after mechanizing an activity is to make it *automatic*, so that the process can work for a long time without attention.

One of the earliest automatic processes was devised by the American inventor Oliver Evans in 1785. He used water power to run a flour mill. The wheat was carried to an upper level by a moving belt for grinding. No operators were required for the grinding or for pounding the flour produced to make it fine.

Since then many other processes have been made automatic. One of the most advanced is car manufacture and assembly.

The first step in making a car engine, for example, is drilling a block of steel in a very complicated way. A series of drilling machines is required, each of which is completely automatic. When one machine has finished its work the block is passed to the next automatically.

The body, wheels, engine and other parts of an automobile are put together on an assembly line. The partly built car moves along on a conveyor belt, and further parts are added. Some of these are attached by human workers, but many are attached completely automatically. put into it – the 'input' – must be of unchanging quality. If a slight change in the product – the 'output' – is required, a human being must step in and change the process. A process is fully automated when machines are able to change the working of the process according to circumstances. They must be able to make measure-

ments on the product, compare it with what it should be, and make the necessary changes.

One of the most common automated processes

Machines never sleep
Machines sometimes break down. But they do not need rest and sleep every day, and they can be many times faster than human workers. This has led to huge increases in production of many goods. But such a process can only repeat the same activity over and over again. The materials is the heating of ordinary homes, offices and factories. When the temperature reaches a preset level such as 21°C or 70°F, a switch called a thermostat which is sensitive to temperature turns the heating off. The area served by the heater begins to grow cooler. When the temperature falls below 21°C or 70°F, the heater is switched on again.

The temperature of the area being heated is the 'output' of this particular process. It corresponds to the articles manufactured in an assembly line, or the gasoline produced in an automated oil refinery.

The switch 'senses' this output. It compares this measured value with the desired value of 21°C or 70°F. According to the difference, the input – the rate of heating – is changed.

The information about the output has to be sent back to a device that controls the input. This process is called 'feed-back'. It is an essential part of any fully automated process.

Some processes have more than one input and output. In the chemical industry many ingredients may be fed into a chemical reaction, and several substances of value may be produced. The changes that have to be made in the inputs in order to keep all the outputs up to the required standard will be very complicated. A computer that can perform calculations automatically may be needed.

Airplanes can be kept on their course automatically. The system that does this is called the autopilot and may include a small computer. It can be set to keep the plane flying straight and level in one direction. The height, direction and angle of tilt of the plane have to be kept constant. Instruments detect slight changes and correct the motion.

Railways are automating their work more and more. Many underground railways in the world are automatically controlled. The position of every train is automatically indicated at a central control point.

Today automation is making many traditional jobs unnecessary. Fewer workers are needed to make the same number of goods. But modern societies continually demand new kinds of products and greater quantities of the old ones. And many workers will be faced with the need to change their jobs and learn new skills several times during their working lives.

Automation is also changing the traditional office. Many records are now kept on computers: bank statements, driving licences, airline tickets and retail stocks are examples encountered in everyday life. Offices use computers to compose and print invoices, letters and documents.
See: *computer, robot.*

Find out by doing
Time the traffic signals in your neighbourhood. Do they show 'stop' and 'go' for fixed times, or do they change the times according to the flow of traffic?
See the effect of opening the door of your refrigerator. How long is it before the thermostat switches the motor on?
Find out how many machines in your household use feedback. Your radio, water- and room-heating systems, food mixer and iron are worth thinking about.

ballistics

This is the study of how objects behave when they are thrown into the air. It deals with the flight of bullets, shells, rockets and arrows which are fired, bombs which are dropped, and spears and stones which are thrown.

All of these can be called missiles. A ballistic missile is one which is under control only at the beginning of its journey. If, like some rocket weapons, and spaceships, it can be steered during flight, it is called a guided missile.

One part of the science deals with the behaviour of bullets and shells before they leave a gun. It also studies what happens to the gases inside a rocket motor while it is firing. The design of the gun barrel and the shape of the bullet influence the accuracy of the bullet's path. When the charge in the cartridge explodes, very great heat and pressure are produced by the gases which are formed. The barrel must be strong enough to withstand these forces without bursting or becoming distorted. At the same time, the missile must be designed to fit the barrel properly, travel through it smoothly and leave it at great speed.

When a bullet or shell leaves a gun, an arrow leaves a bow, a rocket stops firing, or a stone leaves a slingshot, it can no longer be controlled. The path that it now follows is called its trajectory. This is in the form of a curve, of the sort called a parabola. It is not a straight line because several forces now act on the missile. Air resistance slows it down. The force of gravity tends to pull it towards the earth. Wind pressure may push it sideways. Ballistics experts are able to work out how all these forces are going to change the shape of the curve. Knowing the speed at which a shell leaves a gun barrel (the muzzle velocity) is important in ballistics. The greater the shell's speed, the further it will travel before gravity pulls it to earth. Streamlining of the missile also increases the distance it will travel, by reducing friction with the air. To prevent shells and bullets turning end over end in flight, which would slow them down, they are given a spin. This is done by spiral grooves (rifling) in the gun barrel.

The angle at which a missile is fired also determines the trajectory. A bullet fired upwards at an angle of 45 degrees will travel further than one fired at either a greater or lesser angle. Gunnery experts can work out trajectories precisely for different weapons, so that targets can be hit accurately. A separate branch of ballistics deals with bomb trajectories, and designing bomb sights for aircraft.

Ballistics is also helpful in police work. It is possible to determine whether a bullet has been fired from a particular gun by examining the scratches on it. Experts can often tell from what direction and distance a bullet has been fired.

Find out by doing
If you have a bow, a slingshot or a toy spring-gun, try firing it at various angles to the horizontal. Find out what angle gives you the greatest range. Try throwing a ball straight up while running. Where do you think the ball will fall?

binary number

Computers can perform lengthy arithmetic calculations in a few minutes that would take you days or weeks. But to do this they need a special number system called the binary system, which is simpler than the number system that we use.

Our number system is called the denary, or decimal, system. This is because it is based on tens. Numbers are arranged in columns. Going from right to left, each column has ten times the value of the one before it. The far right column holds units, the next left tens, the next hundreds and so on.

The binary number system is so called because it is based on twos. The far right column has a value of one and each column going left has twice the value of the previous one. The second column from the right is the twos column, the third is the fours column, the fourth is the eights column, and so on.

Any number can be made up from these values. You may wish not to count a particular column, in which case you put a 0 in that column. Those columns that you do wish to count are marked with 1s. Thus the decimal number 5 appears in the binary system as 101. We can show this as:

$$5 = 101$$

decimal   binary   (one 4, plus no 2s, plus one 1).

We can see right away that binary numbers are clumsier than decimal numbers. But they have the advantage that only two symbols are needed. In each column there can only be either 1 or 0. In the decimal system each column may show any of ten different symbols ranging from 0 – 9.

Addition in the binary system is very simple. The two numbers to be added are set out one above the other. Where a 0 occurs above a 0 the result is given as 0. If two digits in a column are a 0 and a 1 the result is 1. Where there are two 1s the result is 10. The 0 stays in the same column and the 1 moves one column to the left. This process is reversed in subtraction.

The multiplication process in the binary system is as follows: $0 \times 0 = 0$; $0 \times 1 = 0$; and $1 \times 1 = 1$. Division is performed in the same way as in the decimal system.

The way in which the binary system is used in computers is simple. Each digit in a number is represented on one electrical circuit. If the digit is 1 then the switch in that circuit is on. If the digit is 0, then the switch is off. For large numbers there have to be many circuits, but each one is simply either off or on.

As human beings, we have ten fingers, and so find it convenient to count things in tens, on the decimal system. It would be possible to make a computer that worked on the decimal system, but the circuits would have to be much more complicated, and take up more space. For computers, the binary system is ideal, and makes calculation very rapid.

See: *arithmetic, computer*.

Find out by doing

Write out the decimal number 365 in binary terms. There will be nine digits in the number, the one at the far left having the value 256 (decimal).

biology

Biology is the science that studies living things. It investigates how the bodies of plants and animals are made, what they look like, how they get food, breathe and reproduce, and how they behave.

We can all see that a dog is alive and a stone is not. But there is a borderline where the difference between living and non-living is no longer clear. It is really rather difficult to define 'life'.

If something can move by itself, you might say that it is alive. But many animals, and almost all plants, cannot move. Life may mean the ability to grow and reproduce. But a flame does both these things. As long as you give it enough fuel, a flame will grow. If you put some paper near enough to it, the flame will produce a new little flame. But we do not think that the flame is alive in the sense that a tree or a dog is alive.

Perhaps, then, life includes a structure, a body with a definite shape and surrounded by some sort of skin. It seems that the idea of life includes all these ideas and at least one more. This is the ability to react to changes in the surroundings. A plant, as it grows, turns towards the sun. A snail goes into its shell when it senses danger. A fish swims towards food. All these are responses and are essential to life.

Another question is, what is the difference between plants and animals? Again, it is easy to see differences between large plants like flowers and large animals like horses. Plants usually stay in one place. Most plants are green because they contain chlorophyll. Using this chemical and the energy from sunlight, they make their food out of air and water. This is called photosynthesis. Most animals move around. They must do this to find food, for they cannot make it. Yet some plants are not green, some, like some fungi and parasitic plants, eat other organisms, and some move. Also, many sea animals stay fixed in one place and let their food come to them.

Because plants and animals share so many of the basic processes and structures of life, we often simply use the word 'organism' to refer to a living thing. An organism is made up of cells. It must take in food, water and oxygen and convert these into energy and new cells. It must excrete waste products. Its cells wear out or are injured and need to be replaced, while new cells must be made for growth and to produce young. The organism, if it is bigger than a single cell, needs a circulatory system to carry food and other chemicals all through its body. This body has a definite size and shape. Its young inherit this size, shape and structure.

These characteristics apply to all living things. Once the basic processes of life are understood, how they are applied in individual cases has more meaning. Although they all share the basic processes of life, a seaweed, a flowering plant, a worm, a snail, a fish, and man have found unique ways of working them.

The earliest written records of biology we have were made in Greece around 500 BC. They describe some parts of the human body. By 400 BC, the arteries, which carry blood from the heart to all parts of the body, had been described. Because only dead bodies were studied and the blood leaves the arteries after death, they were thought to be passageways for carrying air.

Aristotle, who lived from 384 BC to 322 BC, thought that the heart contained the intelligence. Except for a few guesses like this, he observed carefully. He described the habits and the bodily structure (anatomy) of many animals, birds and fish. Another Greek, Galen, who lived in the second century AD, performed biological experiments. Both careful observation of living things and experiments are used today in the study of biology. Galen observed and described the internal anatomy of the human body. He described many parts that he saw in the body. But he was not always careful. He sometimes described what he expected to see and did not look carefully to see what was really there. For centuries after Galen, people studied anatomy from his books instead of trusting their own observations.

Then, around 1400, came the rebirth of knowledge that we call the Renaissance. People began again to think and question and look at the world around them. Artists and sculptors, such as Leonardo da Vinci, (1452-1519), measured, dissected (cut up) and made drawings of bodies in order to be able to show them more accurately in their art. They also studied and drew plants and animals. In medical schools too, students of anatomy dared to believe that some of Galen's descriptions might be wrong. For the first time since Ancient Greek civilization, scientists learned by using their own eyes and brains.

The Renaissance artists were among the first anatomists. Anatomy is the study of where each part of the body and each organ lies, its shape, size, and appearance, and how it is related to the structures around it.

The mental awakening that began during the Renaissance produced discoveries in many fields. Explorers travelled to new countries and brought back tales of strange plants and animals. Printing was invented and books of drawings and descriptions of animals, plants and the human body were published in many copies for the first time. During the seventeenth century, microscopes were first used. Anton van Leeuwenhoek discovered one-celled organisms, which could not be seen before he made his lenses.

Discovering how blood moves

People used to think that the blood ebbs and flows like the tides. Then William Harvey (1578-1657) discovered that the blood circulates through the body. He showed that the valves in the blood vessels leaving the heart allow the blood to flow only one way, away from the heart.

Harvey was the first physiologist. Physiology is the branch of biology that studies how living things work. In animals, physiology covers subjects like circulation, digestion, breathing (respiration), and metabolism, which is how the body converts food into energy and new tissue. In plants, physiologists also study respiration and metabolism. But in addition they study the special processes of plants. One of these is photo-synthesis, by which green plants make their food. Another is transpiration, the loss of water from leaves.

Classification is another branch of biology that has developed steadily over the centuries. In order to understand living things, it is necessary to learn how they are related to each other. Also, for scientists to know what plant or animal is being discussed, it must have its own name. And the name should be understood by scientists who speak different languages.

From Aristotle's time, naturalists had arranged plants and animals on a scale with simple things at the bottom and man at the top. But each person used a different system. Our present system describes each living thing by a double Latin name. Latin is used because it was internationally understood by all learned people. A flower has a different name in every language, and may have several names in some languages, but it can always be identified correctly by its Latin name.

The double Latin name system was created by Linnaeus, who lived from 1707-1778. He grouped plants into classes and divided the classes into orders according to the details of their flowers. Animals were divided into mammals, birds, reptiles, fish, insects and worms, in his system. The double name includes the two smallest groups the organism belongs to. These are the 'genus' and 'species'. Linnaeus' system was well thought out, but he considered only the external appearance of his specimens.

Georges Cuvier is one of the most famous of the scientists who made classification more accurate. He dissected animals and compared their internal structure. He also studied fossil animals. These are the remains of animals that lived long ago. Sometimes their bones have been found. Other times the animals became covered by mud after death, and this mud hardened into rock. Many outlines of primitive plants or animals are found in limestone. Cuvier compared these fossils with the bodies of animals alive today and showed how they must be related. This was the beginning of paleontology.

Today, classification has developed into the field of taxonomy. Taxonomists consider an organism's microscopic structure, its chemistry and sometimes even behaviour, in classifying it. They also use complicated mathematical methods to evaluate all the information about the organism. Classification changes as more living things are discovered and more is learned about them.

Living things are now divided into two kingdoms, the plants and the animals. Sometimes one-celled organisms are put into a separate kingdom, the protists. But usually they are classified as either plants or animals. Each kingdom is subdivided into smaller and smaller groups, including: phyla (singular, phylum), classes, orders, families, genera (singular, genus) and species (same singular and plural). The animal kingdom is grouped into the invertebrates, animals without backbones, and vertebrates, animals with backbones. A few of the invertebrate phyla are: Protozoa (one-celled animals), sponges, Coelenterata (including sea anemones), flat worms, round worms, segmented worms (including the earthworm), Arthropoda (including insects, crabs, lobsters), Mollusca (snails, clams and their relatives), and Echinodermata (including starfish and sea urchins). The vertebrates are only one phylum Chordata. They include fish, eels, amphibians, reptiles, birds and mammals. In the plant kingdom, there are many phyla of one-celled and other simple plants. These include bacteria, fungi and algae, among which are the seaweeds. 'Higher' plants are grouped into three phyla. The bryophytes include mosses and liverworts; the second phylum, the pteridophytes, include horsetails and ferns; the seed-bearing and flowering plants are called spermatophytes.

For an example of how this works, consider the domestic dog. It is a vertebrate – it has a backbone – and so it belongs to the phylum Chordata. Within this phylum, it is in the class Mammalia, animals that feed their young with milk. Its order is Carnivora, meat-eating vertebrate mammals, and its family, Canidae, includes dog-like animals like dogs, wolves and foxes. Dogs and wolves belong to the same genus *Canis*. Since tame dogs live with human families, their species is called *familiaris*. So the domestic dog is correctly called *Canis familiaris*.

The nineteenth century was another period of exciting discoveries in biology. So many details of plant and animal life were known that theories could be made to explain them. It was no longer enough to observe life. Now biologists were ready to try to understand how and why living things and processes have developed into their present states.

Selection and evolution

One of the most important advances was the theory that evolution occurs due to natural selection, proposed by Charles Darwin and Alfred Russel Wallace in 1858. People had always assumed that plants and animals were created in the same shape as they are today. The discovery of fossils had shown that this was not true, but it was not known how fossil organisms had changed into their present shapes.

Darwin's travels introduced him to many new animals and to many variations on the animals he knew in Europe. He decided that each animal or plant fits into certain surroundings. This includes weather, the availability of water, the type and amount of food available, competition for food and water, the animals that prey on the organism and other advantages and dangers.

Each organism differs slightly from all others. Those that are most suited to a certain environment will be healthiest and live longest. They will have more offspring, and these will inherit the favourable characteristics. If the environment changes, another type of organism may fit it better. So Darwin's theory of natural selection and the survival of the fittest says that species are constantly changing. If two groups of a species become separated and live in different environments, for instance, on separate islands, their descendants eventually develop into separate species.

People used to think that living things could appear out of dead rotting meat. This sudden creation of life was called 'spontaneous generation'. That this was certainly not true was first shown by Francesco Redi in 1668. He put some rotting meat in a container covered by a piece of gauze. Maggots appeared on the gauze where flies were crawling, but not on the meat. He showed that the maggots came from the flies' eggs and did not arise out of the meat.

But people still thought that there was some magical life force in the air that could cause new living things to appear. Louis Pasteur proved that this was wrong. He prepared a bottle with a long tube for a neck. This tube stuck out to one side and curved like an S lying on its side. Air could get into the bottle through the tube, but particles of dust in the air would fall into the bends before reaching the bottle. Pasteur put broth, a rich soup, into the bottle and boiled it until the steam sterilized the bottle and its neck. When it cooled, no bacteria grew. Then he broke the neck so that dust could fall on the broth. Bacteria grew. Pasteur showed that among the dust particles in air are tiny bacterial spores. These are bacteria in protective capsules. When they land on food, they grow. So bacteria do not arise from magic.

Genetics

An Austrian monk, Gregor Mendel, working in his vegetable garden, discovered in 1866 how characteristics are passed on from parent plants to their offspring. He crossed pea plants that had different coloured flowers and different types of peas. From the results, he worked out several basic laws of inheritance. Although he published his work, no one paid any attention to it until 1900 when it was rediscovered

Mendel's laws began the science of genetics. They also explained how the gradual changes in species, which Darwin had noticed, were passed on to succeeding generations.

Biochemistry

Yet another nineteenth century discovery was essential to the development of modern biology. This was the realization that the chemicals that make up living tissue can be studied in the laboratory.

Chemists were used to studying inorganic chemicals. These include metals and minerals. If you heat a metal, it melts. When you cool it, it becomes hard, as it was before. If you melt a metal figure, you can pour the molten metal into a mould and make it back into the figure. Chemists recognized another group of chemicals, organic ones. These include living tissue and its products. If you burn wood, you get only ashes. There is no way to turn the ashes back into a log. If you boil an egg, you cannot change it back into a raw egg. Nor, if you bake a cake, can you change it back into flour.

Until the nineteenth century, chemists thought that the chemicals in living creatures were so special that they could not be studied. Then they discovered that certain chemicals can be combined in the laboratory into substances found in the body. Now they knew that these chemicals could be experimented with. A system of symbols and writing to describe organic compounds was developed. After more study, scientists learned how organic chemicals attach themselves to each other to form organic compounds.

The chemicals that make up living tissue are made mostly out of atoms of carbon and hydrogen. To these other atoms are often joined. The atoms are attached to each other in a definite order to form a structure of a definite shape called a molecule. The cell and the structures within it are built of molecules. Many cells of the same type together form a tissue, such as wood, bark, muscle, fat or bone, which has a definite structure and function. Tissues are often arranged into organs to perform a specialized job. Organs include leaves, flowers, kidneys and the heart. All these cells, tissues and organs together make up the organism's body.

Plant cells and animal cells have the same basic components. The 'average' cell can be discussed and drawn although all cells differ according to the work they must perform. For instance, plant cells have a rigid wall of cellulose which helps to give plant tissue its strength.

Three main types of organic compounds make up most of living tissue. These are carbo-hydrates, fats and proteins. Carbohydrates are sugars and starches. Fats or lipids include butter and oils like cooking oil. Both of these types of compound are made up of carbon and hydrogen atoms. They are used or stored by the plant or animal as a supply of energy. Proteins are very complicated molecules made up of carbon, hydrogen and nitrogen. They are the building blocks from which all tissue is made. They also have another function. Some proteins are enzymes. These are chemicals that control the rate of organic reactions. The reaction would happen without the enzyme, but too slowly or too quickly to support life.

Living jelly

The cell is a mass of jelly-like substance called protoplasm, with a nucleus inside an envelope called a membrane. The protoplasm is made up of very large molecules which form a definite but flexible structure. An average cell contains 15 per cent fat, 15 per cent protein, 0.5 per cent sugars, 4.5 per cent salts. The rest, 65 per cent, is water. The salts and sugars are mostly dissolved in the water, while the proteins and fats link together to form the membranes. Membrane-lined channels extend all through the cell. There are several small organs within the cell, called organelles. Except in the simplest one-celled organisms, these are covered by membranes. The nucleus too is enclosed in membrane. Membranes have the important function of controlling what chemicals enter the cell. Some molecules pass through easily, some cannot pass, and some are carried across the membrane when the cell has need of them. How the membrane does this is not yet completely understood.

The nucleus, which lies near the centre of the cell, controls its activities. It contains the genetic information with which the cell makes new chemical compounds to repair itself, grow, and divide into new cells. All the actions of our organs, such as breathing, exercise, digestion, and reproduction, are the result of the work of millions of tiny cells.

The equations of life

Animals need chemical energy to run on. The main source of chemical energy on Earth is the activity of plants. Green plants contain a special chemical, chlorophyll, in tiny organelles within their leaves and stems. It absorbs the energy of sunlight and converts it into chemical energy by the process of photosynthesis. During photosynthesis, the plant takes carbon dioxide from the air and water from the soil and from their atoms makes a sugar called glucose, and oxygen. This is the source of the oxygen in the air we breathe. Carbon dioxide + water + energy = glucose + oxygen.

The energy stored in glucose is used by both plants and animals to perform work and build their tissues. To release this energy they combine the glucose with oxygen and 'burn' it. This is the opposite of photosynthesis, and is called respiration: glucose + oxygen = energy + carbon dioxide + water.

You can see a similar process when you burn a piece of wood. The carbohydrates in the wood are combined with oxygen from the air and give off energy in the form of heat. This energy can be harnessed and used to run machines like steam engines.

Glucose in the living body is not burned all at once. It is changed in several complicated series of tiny steps into one chemical after another. Unlike fire, where the energy is given off intensely, this produces a slow controlled release of energy. Every few steps a small packet of energy is released and stored in a special molecule called ATP. The end products of respiration, carbon dioxide and water, are breathed out through the lungs and excreted through the skin and kidneys. In plants the end products pass out through the leaves.

Each step in the series of reactions has one or more specific enzymes to control its rate. The total process of converting food into energy and new tissues is called metabolism.

The study of nutrition in plants and animals is an important part of biology. It is the science of the chemicals they need to take in to support their metabolism. An animal requires food containing carbohydrates, fats, proteins and tiny amounts of minerals and vitamins. If a person or an animal eats too much, his body changes the extra carbohydrates and proteins into fat and stores it. If he eats too little, the stored fat is changed back into glucose and used for energy. If the animal starves, even the protein in its muscles will be used up to provide energy so that it can stay alive as long as possible.

It is not enough to eat a lot of food. The diet must contain all the molecules that the organism needs for its metabolism. Since the human body cannot make vitamins and minerals, our diet must contain all of the ones we need. Plants can make their own sugars, proteins, fats and vitamins. But they need to be given minerals, which they get from the soil. When a farmer fertilizes his fields, he is putting minerals into the soil.

Vitamins are important to our health because they work together with enzymes. Many enzymes need to combine with a vitamin before they can act. If an enzyme cannot act, the body cannot use food properly for its metabolism and becomes sick. One such illness is scurvy— due to lack of vitamin C. This vitamin is found in citrus fruits, like oranges and lemons, and in fresh vegetables. Sailors, who used to live on salted meat and biscuits, often got this disease, which starts with bleeding gums and leads to weakness and sometimes death.

Biophysics

A new field of biology has developed during the twentieth century that studies the physical and chemical processes that occur within the cell, its organelles and its membranes. This is biophysics. It developed when several important new tools gave biologists new insight into the workings of the cell. One is the electron microscope. With this microscope, small structures within the cell, its membranes, and even large molecules can be seen and photographed. Another new method is the use of radioactive isotopes. A molecule can be labelled with a radioactive isotope of carbon (see: *radioactivity*). Then what happens to the molecule as it enters the cell and is metabolized can be traced. Each of the carbon atoms in glucose has been labelled and the pathway of each of these atoms during metabolism has been followed.

For centuries man has exploited biological processes – winemaking, brewing, cooking and baking are a few examples. In the next few decades we may expect to see a number of new industries based on a better understanding of biology. We already manufacture edible protein and produce drugs on a large scale using existing organisms. We can expect to see biological materials replace products from precious petroleum, and further advances in producing drugs and vaccines in large quantities are just on the horizon.

These developments depend on progress in understanding and controlling how organisms pass information on to their offspring – and sometimes even changing this information in specified ways. Such research will also help scientists to combat the unexplained diseases we call cancer.

chemistry

Everything in the universe – ourselves, our food, the atmosphere, the furthest corners of space – is made of chemicals. The water that we drink is a chemical, and quite a pure one too. Sugar and salt, chalk and charcoal – all these are simple chemical substances. There are also much more complex chemicals, such as the proteins that make up much of plant and animal bodies.

Chemistry is concerned with chemicals: with two kinds known as elements and compounds. There are just over 100 elements known at present and they are the building bricks of chemistry. Some elements occur in nature: metals like gold and mercury and silver, and non-metals like sulphur, carbon and oxygen.

More often, the elements occur combined together into compounds. Carbon will combine with oxygen to give the very poisonous gas carbon monoxide. This is found in the exhaust fumes of a car. More oxygen will combine to give carbon dioxide. The air always contains about 0.03 per cent carbon dioxide, and green plants use it to make sugars (see: *photosynthesis*).

Physicists are interested in atoms and parts of atoms such as electrons and neutrons (see: *atom*). But the chemist's practical interest is in atoms, which are the smallest indentifiable parts of an element. Each atom of iron, for instance, is chemically exactly like every other atom of iron. But it is different from an atom of copper, or an atom of sulphur.

The chemist is interested in the properties of elements and compounds. The pure element iron will always melt at exactly the same temperature. The liquid metal mercury has an exact temperature at which it will boil. If it is cooled down enough it will freeze solid; the temperature at which this happens is its freezing point. When it is warmed again it will melt. The melting point will be the same as the freezing point.

There are many other properties that can be measured. There is hardness, heaviness, colour, ability to dissolve other things, and so on. These are called the 'physical properties'. The ways in which an element or compound combines or reacts with other things are its 'chemical properties'.

Not all chemicals occur naturally pure. In iron ore, the iron is combined with oxygen as iron oxide. But this is also mixed with various other minerals that do not contain iron, and that are not wanted in the process of obtaining the iron from the ore. They are impurities. If there are many of them, it may not be worthwhile trying to make iron from the ore.

First of all, then, a chemist is interested in substances whose properties are always the same ('constant'). To obtain these substances with constant properties, he has to make sure that they are pure. And the fact that they have these properties shows them to be pure.

The beginnings of chemistry
This emphasis on purity and constant properties comes from the early days of chemistry. Man's first chemical studies were concerned with drugs and making metals. The drugs were natural ones extracted from plants. Many of them could be dangerous, and so it was important to remove any impurities. And to sell valuable metals, they had to be pure.

So both the doctors and the metalworkers looked for ways to refine their products. They found two tools of the greatest importance: fire and water. Fire itself is the product of chemical change. It is the result of, for example, charcoal burning in air: that is, carbon combining with oxygen. And with fire men found that they could melt metals out of ore, and also burn away the impurities.

With water they could obtain the drugs they wanted, and with fire they could boil off the water to recover the drugs. Plunging a metal weapon into water after working it at the forge helped to make it harder. And the water itself was pure. It could be frozen solid or heated with fire until it vanished as steam.

The Ancient Egyptians were skilled metal workers. Many of them knew how to mix gold with other metals to produce something that still looked like gold. To the Arabs who saw this it seemed that the Egyptians were creating gold from less valuable metals. The Arabs called the Egyptians' skills *al quemia*, from which we get the words 'alchemy' and 'chemistry' (see: *alchemy*).

For a thousand years alchemy survived as a mystical study. The alchemists worked hard and experimented to find ways to purify themselves as well as the substances they studied. The theories they held were strange and impractical, but if it had not been for alchemists almost no advance would have been made in science.

Some chemical words that we still use today, like alcohol and alkali, come straight from Arabic. The Arabs discovered distillation. Most of the simpler apparatus that is still used in chemical laboratories has hardly changed from the earlier days.

But alchemy was not a science. The alchemists made observations and wrote down what they saw. But often they saw, not the truth, but what they wanted to see. And they seldom tried to draw conclusions from what they saw, or to plan further experiments from the conclusions.

Chemistry as a science
It was in the fifteenth century that the beginnings of scientific method emerged. Any theory had to be proved by practical experiments and the experiments had to be repeatable by anyone who followed the right instructions.

Chemistry could quite easily follow this principle. Chemists worked with simple substances, in small quantities which they kept in bottles and jars. The purer these substances were the better they could be stored. And the easier it was to get the same experiment to work again and again. Chemists came to recognize more and more compounds, such as sulphuric acid, ammonia, metal oxides and many different crystalline substances.

Alchemical theories still persisted, however. They held that all things were made of different mixtures of four basic 'elements' – fire, air, water and earth – which combined two of the four 'qualities' – dry, hot, wet and cold.

Fire, for instance, is hot and dry; earth is dry

and cold. Water, wet and cold, is heated with fire; it turns into steam, which is wet and hot. So the alchemists' experiments were concerned with heating and cooling, liquefying and drying. They hoped to change one substance into another by changing the mixture of 'elements' and 'qualities' that made it.

Robert Boyle is often called the 'father of chemistry'. In the 17th century, he defined 'element'. He said that any substance that could not be broken down into simpler substances was an element. If it could be broken down it was a mixture or a compound. Only experiments could show which substances were elements, and there might be many more than the four 'elements' of the ancients.

The final break away of chemistry from alchemy came when the theory of phlogiston was proved wrong. This theory was put forward by the German Georg Stahl in the 18th century. He said that phlogiston was a substance given out when things burn. Things that contained phlogiston would burn; those that did not would not burn. The more phlogiston present, the more imflammable the substance.

Many people studied this theory, like the well-known British chemist Joseph Priestley. It became generally accepted that phlogiston explained the burning of substances. It was the French scientist Lavoisier who finally proved this wrong.

In 1774, he repeated one of Priestley's experiments and weighed everything carefully. He heated mercury in a closed vessel. A dark crust was formed on the surface of the mercury. He found that the mercury had increased in weight while it was burning, and that the amount of air in the vessel had decreased. Thus he concluded that the mercury had not given off phlogiston. Instead it had taken in something from the air. This something he called oxygen. He found it was possible to get back this oxygen by heating the crust of mercury vigorously. In this way, the oxygen was released again.

Many new chemical substances were discovered after this time. They were given names in a logical way by Lavoisier and his followers. Chemists now began to try to make chemicals in their laboratories, starting with simple substances and trying to make them react and combine. Later on, with the help of electricity, they were able to break down natural mineral products and build them up again. But it did not seem possible to do this with products from animals and plants. These chemicals were called 'organic' because they came from living things (see: *carbon*). Organic and inorganic chemistry eventually became two distinct branches of science.

For many years, it was believed that there was something missing, a 'vital principle' that was lost – rather like phlogiston – when an organic substance was broken down into its component parts. The chemist Wohler, in 1828, accidentally changed the inorganic chemical ammonium cyanate (which he got from strictly mineral sources) into the organic chemcial urea (which occurs in urine). This was the start of a new approach to chemistry.

Atoms, molecules and equations
The chemist deals in very exact quantities: only precise numbers of atoms or molecules react with each other. And he needs to know exactly what quantities of chemicals to mix together. For this reason he states his chemical facts in a mathematical form.

First of all he needs a set of symbols to represent all the different elements. Lavoisier was the first to give the elements logical names like oxygen ('acid-maker') and hydrogen ('water-maker'). The symbols for these elements are now O and H. Other symbols are equally obvious: S for sulphur, P for phosphorus, C for carbon, Ca for calcium ('chalk metal'), and so on. Other elements were given symbols derived from their Latin names: Na for sodium, from natrium; K for potassium, from kalium.

In 1808 John Dalton published his theory of the atomic nature of matter. His suggestions have had to be slightly modified as we have found out more about atoms, but they are basically unchanged. In brief: every element is made up of atoms, which do not break up during chemical reactions. All atoms of any one element are the same in weight and other properties. But atoms of different elements differ from one another. Chemical compounds are formed by atoms of different kinds joining together.

The symbol of an element, therefore, is used to represent one atom of an element. Compounds are represented by combinations of the atomic symbols, showing how many of each kind of atom there are in one molecule. Oxygen, for instance, exists normally as a gas with molecules that contain two atoms. We write this O_2. Hydrogen similarly exists as the gas H_2. If we mix hydrogen and oxygen together and explode them with an electric spark, water is formed.

But to make water, we need two molecules of hydrogen to every one of oxygen:
$$2H_2 + O_2$$
This will give us two molecules of water:
$$2H_2 + O_2 = 2H_2O$$
This is a chemical equation, and it tells us very simply about the chemicals that have reacted together, the quantities of each, their molecular structure and what the reaction has produced.

In the same way, one molecule of oxygen,

containing two atoms, and one atom of carbon will produce one molecule of carbon dioxide:

$$C + O_2 = CO_2$$

The chemical equation is just like an equation in algebra; the numbers of molecules that are involved are reduced to the smallest whole number. But in reality, of course, many millions of molecules are present.

Different elements combine together in different proportions. It is as if the atoms had little hooks with which they could attach themselves to other atoms. (In fact, this is due to the number of electrons present in the outer orbits of the atom.) Hydrogen has only one hook, H-. Oxygen however has two hooks, -O-. This is why two atoms of hydrogen and one of oxygen make water, H-O-H.

The number of hooks of this kind that an atom possesses is called its valence. Hydrogen has a valence of only 1; oxygen has a valence of 2. Calcium also has a valence of 2, aluminium has a valence of 3, and carbon has a valence of 4.

Some elements have more than one valence. Iron, for instance, can have a valence of 2 or 3: nitrogen has a valence of 3 or 5; sulphur has a valence of 2, 4, or 6 (see: *element, valence*).

In the summary of Dalton's atomic theory above, we mentioned the weight of atoms. It is not possible, of course, to weigh a single atom. But it is quite easy to weight a certain volume of oxygen and show that it weighs 16 times as much as the same volume of hydrogen (at the same temperature and pressure). Various experiments prove that equal volumes of gas contain equal numbers of molecules. The molecules of oxygen and hydrogen both contain 2 atoms, so the oxygen atom must weigh 16 times as much as the hydrogen atom. Hydrogen is the lightest element, and so we give it the atomic weight 1; oxygen has the atomic weight 16. Scientists can also work out the atomic weights of elements that do not occur as gases.

At first the chemical elements were thought to be separate and unrelated to one another. But in 1869, the Russian chemist Dmitri Mendeléev discovered that a list of elements in order of their atomic weights showed similar properties occurring at regular intervals. He was able to arrange the elements that he knew into a table. There were eight main columns, and each contained elements that had related chemical properties. In particular, the valence changed for each column across the table.

Valences in the eighth column were variable. Much later a ninth column was added to contain the 'inert gases', which exist in the air but which are very unreactive.

The important point about Mendeléev's table was that it included a number of gaps. He suggested that elements could be found to fill these gaps, and he predicted what their properties would be. This idea was scoffed at as mysticism rather than science. But seven of the ten elements he predicted have since been discovered. And the gaps that would have held the others no longer exist in the modern form of the table.

Modern knowledge about the structure of the atom has shown that Mendeléev's table reflects the electronic structure of the elements. Scientists have now made artificial elements of high atomic weights. In honour of Mendeleev, one of these was named mendelevium in 1955 (see: *physics*).

What chemists do

As we have seen, all chemistry is divided into inorganic and organic chemistry. This is a rather artificial division, but it recognises the difficulty that the early chemists had in dealing with the products of living things.

Roughly speaking, inorganic chemistry is concerned with mineral substances. The possible number of inorganic chemicals is limited. Most naturally occurring minerals are either simple compounds of a metal with chlorine, oxygen or sulphur, or with sulphuric, phosphoric or carbonic acid. Or they are rather more complex structures held together by the element silicon. Most of the inorganic chemist's work concerns finding better ways of preparing pure elements, methods of separating pure compounds, and ways to make different mixtures of metals (alloys) that have special properties.

Organic chemistry is concerned with substances that are compounds of carbon with one or more other elements. Carbon has very special properties. It can make many thousands of compounds and these include the most complex substances known.

Silicon can also form many complex compounds. It is similar in its properties to carbon. Some important organic substances – silicones – have been made, in which silicon partly replaces carbon. It has been suggested that life on some other planets could be based on compounds of silicon rather than carbon compounds.

Organic chemists concern themselves with analysis. When they discover a new compound they try to find out what elements it is made of and how they are put together in the molecule. Then they try to make the compound in the laboratory. This is called synthesis. If they succeed in making the compound, they often try to make other compounds like it, but which may be even more useful.

Chemistry in industry

Some of the world's earliest industries were chemical ones: drugs, brewing, mining and metallurgy. The chemists of the 18th century laid the foundations of today's 'heavy chemical' industry. They found that by heating coal in closed vessels coal gas was formed. This could be used for lighting and heating. A number of liquids and a residue of tar were also formed. The liquids could be separated from each other by distillation. Most of them were oily, imflammable compounds of carbon and hydrogen. The organic chemists analysed these substances and gave them names: the hydrocarbons benzene, toluene, napthalene and anthracene; the phenols carbolic acid, cresol and so on.

Organic chemists everywhere now turned their attentions to improving on natural products. They took the separate compounds obtained from coal tar and experimented with them. They tried to find ways to change them into other compounds by adding or taking away groups of atoms. They made drugs like aspirin, lots of different dyes, explosives, fruit flavours and perfumes. They also started to make substitutes like margarine, and celluloid (see: *cellulose*), rayon and saccharine. Later they made detergents and artificial rubber from the by-products of the oil industry.

Chemists have also devised fertilizers that are now indispensable to modern farming, and additives, colorants and preservatives to alter the properties of food and cosmetics. Useful as they are in providing us with convenient products, some of these chemicals can be a threat to health. Many people now prefer to buy food that is free from artificial substances or that has not been grown with synthetic fertilizers.

The foundations of the plastics industry were laid when Otto Baekeland heated two simple chemicals – phenol and formaldehyde – together and made bakelite. This artificial resin is formed by many molecules joining together and giving off water. The very large molecule that is formed in this way is called a polymer.

Many substances occurring in nature are polymers of this kind. Silk and rubber are examples. In 1930 the American chemist Carothers began to study polymerization, and in 1935 he produced a polymer that was very similar to the protein in silk. Nylon was developed from this discovery. Carothers's research also led to the synthesis of rubber. Nylon was the first synthetic textile fibre developed.

cold

Every day we use the words 'hot' and 'cold' to describe things around us. We say that the Sun is hot and that ice cream is cold. We tend to think of hot and cold as being two separate and different qualities. But of course they are really not separate at all. They are just opposite ends of the same scale.

We say the Sun is hot because it contains a great deal of heat – and we can feel the heat being given out. It is tempting to think of cold in the same way. You might think that an ice cream contained a great deal of something called 'cold' – and that the 'cold' given out by it affected your lips and tongue as you ate the ice cream. But that is not true at all. Cold is simply the absence of heat. Ice cream contains less heat than your mouth. So as you eat it, the ice cream takes heat from your mouth and produces the sensation of coldness.

Hot and cold are not exact words. They are useful for comparing one thing with another, but it depends what things you are comparing. If you jump into a swimming pool, you might say that the water is cold. But compared with a glass of water taken from a refrigerator, the water in the swimming pool would be warm. To express how hot something is exactly, we have to use a temperature scale. Temperature is a measurement of hotness. The higher its temperature, the hotter a thing is, and the lower the temperature, the colder it is. Temperature is measured in degrees, by means of a thermometer.

Temperature

Temperature is not the same thing as heat, and it is important to understand the difference. Heat is one form of energy. The atoms that make up all substances are moving around all the time, although of course we cannot see them (see: *atom*). In gases the atoms are free to move around a great deal. In liquids they can also move a considerable amount, but in solids they cannot move so much. They can move only from side to side, or vibrate. The more heat energy a substance contains, the faster the atoms move around. If you put a pan of cold water on a hot stove, the energy from the electricity or gas passes into the water. The atoms in the water begin to move faster and faster the more heat energy they receive. The water becomes hotter and hotter, and its temperature rises.

The opposite happens if you put a pan of water in the freezing compartment of a refrigerator. Energy is taken from the atoms of water, and they move around less and less. Eventually they move around so little that the liquid turns into a solid – ice. While the atoms are slowing down like this, the temperature of the water is gradually falling.

Even in ice the atoms are moving to some extent. This means that although we think of ice as being cold, it still contains some heat energy. It is possible to imagine a state when all the atoms in a substance were perfectly still. In this case they would have no heat energy at all, and they would have the lowest temperature possible. This temperature is called absolute zero. In fact it has been found that there is still some movement even at absolute zero.

Just as there are different scales by which we can measure distances, using inches and feet, or centimetres and metres, so there are different temperature scales. This can cause confusion, and it is very important to state what scale you are using when you write a temperature.

A scale commonly used is called the Celsius scale. On this system the temperature at which water freezes into ice is called zero, or 0°C (the sign ° means a degree, or unit of temperature). The temperature at which water boils into steam is 100°C. Anything colder than the freezing point of water is measured in minus degrees, for example -10°C or -50°C. This scale is now standard in Britain.

Another scale is called the Fahrenheit scale. On this scale water freezes at 32°F, and boils at 212°F.

We have already mentioned that absolute zero is the coldest temperature possible. This is zero on another special scale, called the Kelvin scale. Absolute zero can be written 0°K. On the Celsius scale this is about -273°C, and on the Fahrenheit scale -460°F.

Scientists have not yet managed to lower anything to a temperature of absolute zero, although they have come pretty close. It is hard to imagine what would happen if absolute zero were reached, because strange things happen to substances that are cooled, even a long way above that point.

Cooling a substance makes the atoms move less and less, and come closer together. So a gas turns into a liquid, and then into a solid. The gas carbon dioxide, for example, which we breathe out, becomes solid at a temperature of -78°C (-108°F) This is what we call dry ice.

Although temperatures in the Arctic and Antarctic do not drop so low that the gases in the air become solid, or even liquid, they do affect other things. Mercury, which is liquid at normal temperatures, becomes solid metal at -39°C (-38°F). So it is useless to use a thermometer containing mercury in these regions, where the temperature may fall to -40°C (-40°F) or even -45°C (-49°F) Alcohol must be used instead. This has a lower freezing point and still stays liquid inside the glass of the thermometer.

At very low temperatures, the resistance of metals to electric currents is reduced. The metals are said to become 'superconductive'. When mercury is cooled to near absolute zero an electric current will flow in it for weeks with no outside source of energy. Another strange thing happens to helium near absolute zero. It appears to defy gravity. At this temperature it is a liquid, not a gas. If the liquid is put in a glass, it flows up the sides and out over the rim by itself.

The study of the strange things that happen near absolute zero has become a branch of science in itself. It is called 'cryogenics', from the Greek words for 'ice-making.' Scientists working in cryogenics are hoping to develop a theory to explain the odd behaviour of substances at these low temperatures.

They have already found some useful effects. For example, some materials at very low temperatures can be made to sustain very strong magnetic fields. Another effect may prove so useful in making high density computer memories that it would justify the cost of cooling the equipment down to temperatures close to absolute zero.

Cryogenics is of interest to physicists. But what of the more ordinary sort of cold – the low temperature that anyone might encounter? How does it affect our bodies?

Cold slows down the processes of life. It makes all the chemical reactions in our bodies go slower, so that, at a low enough temperature, they stop completely. Human beings are warm-blooded animals. This means that we are able to regulate the temperature of our bodies to keep ourselves not just comfortable, but working efficiently. The temperature at which the human body works most efficiently is about 37°C. Above this temperature the important chemicals in our body cells called enzymes (see: *enzyme*), that control the reactions going on inside, are destroyed. And below this temperature the enzymes are unable to work. So the body has means of reducing the loss of heat when the outside temperature drops, as well as means of increasing the loss of heat when the outside temperature rises.

One reaction to the cold is that the blood vessels in our skin tighten up. This means there is less blood flowing in an area where its heat could be lost into the air. One effect of the lessened blood supply is that the hairs on our skin stand on end, causing 'gooseflesh'.

Also, the way that we shiver in the cold is simply a defence mechanism. The very rapid quivering of the muscles makes them warm, and so the whole body is kept warm. Babies are unable to shiver until about the age of two, and this is one reason why they are very susceptible to the cold.

All these means of defence against cold, including the natural ones, such as shivering, and the artificial ones, such as clothing, are to prevent possible illness or death. The body cannot survive cold because all the chemical reactions inside it have to happen at a certain temperature. The blood is always a constant temperature, except in illness. So is the flesh of our bodies. In the cold, so much heat can be lost from the surface of the body that the temperature is no longer constant. Then, when our bodies cool down, all the chemical reactions are slowed down or changed. This is so un-natural that the body cannot survive it.

Mountaineers are accustomed to the problem of cold and they wear the right protective clothing. Most people in our cities and towns do so too, and they have their homes to go back to. The people in greatest danger from the cold are often the young and the old. Babies, as we have said, cannot easily survive even a slightly cold environment. They have very delicate and fragile bodies. Old people are also very delicate, and when they have no proper heating or clothing, their temperature can fall very low. Many old people die every year because of this, in Great Britain and in many other countries.

Adaptation

People who live in very cold countries can adapt to the cold. Their bodies become accustomed to the low temperature, and are not so likely to be damaged by it. This is called adaptation to cold. It may be that people from warm countries can also adapt to the cold if they go to the Arctic for a long enough time. But the changes in their bodies are of far lesser importance than the artificial means of protection: fire, clothing and shelter. Indeed, the same is true even of people like the Eskimoes. Their bodies are more used to the cold, but it is really their skill with fur clothing and safe shelters that ensures their health and survival.

Animals, too, must live in the cold. The ones that survive best in cold climates do so because of their protective 'clothing'. The fur of a polar bear, and the feathers of birds, give good insulation against loss of heat from the body. Animals that live in warmer countries need fur too, although not so much.

Other animals cope with the problem in different ways. Those that hibernate, for example, are protected by their fur, but they keep their bodies only just 'ticking over', so that the food they have in the autumn lasts them until the spring.

Some more primitive species do not keep their temperature constant. It varies according to the weather. These, the cold-blooded animals, are able to survive the cold because their body's chemical reactions are not disastrously affected, as ours are. It may sound like a very useful thing to be cold-blooded, but in fact the complicated organization of the human body could never exist that way. A constant body temperature is one of the factors that makes advanced life possible.

Some of the very lowest and most primitive forms of animal life, including germs and the tiny one-celled protozoa that live in ponds, can survive cold spells by changing almost completely. Bacteria, plants, and fungi – all these have ways of altering themselves to a very hardy form which will stay just barely alive

through the crisis. Some form spores, tiny specks that are wafted on the wind until they land somewhere warmer. Plants 'die', or appear to die, leaving all the life in their underground bulbs or seeds, ready to grow again later.

Refrigeration

Man has been very ingenious with cold. Besides protecting himself from it, he has harnessed it for his own purposes. An obvious example is the refrigerator. At low temperatures, as we have mentioned, the processes of life slow down. This means that the tiny organisms responsible for making food decay are slowed down. So food keeps better, and stays fresh, when frozen. The bacteria cannot get to work to spoil the food. Refrigeration has made possible the storage of food for long periods and its transportation to prospective purchasers many miles away.

Cold has uses in surgery, too. When the body is cooled, its chemical reactions are slowed down. Less oxygen is needed by the cells, so that it is possible to interrupt the circulation of the blood without dangerously affecting the body. Deliberately cooling a patient's body – 'hypothermia' – has made possible many surgical operations, particularly on the heart, that would otherwise have been too dangerous to undertake.

The surgical instrument called a 'cryoprobe' uses extreme cold to destroy diseased tissue. It is a fine tube of metal, with a bulb at the end that can be cooled with a refrigerating gas expanding from an even finer tube within. The cryoprobe is sometimes used in eye surgery, to remove a diseased lens of the eye. The lens comes away cleanly, frozen to the tip of the cryoprobe, without breaking, as might otherwise happen. The instrument can also be used to freeze and destroy tiny areas of diseased tissue deep in the brain, without harming the surrounding healthy tissue.

It is perhaps rather strange that although cold is not a 'thing', but an absence of something – heat – we can talk about it. We can talk about protecting ourselves from it, and we can talk about using it in various ways to our advantage.

See: *energy, heat.*

computer

Imagine life without such things as the electric light bulb, television, the jet engine or penicillin. These, and thousands of other discoveries, have had great effects on our way of life. But the invention of the computer will probably have a greater effect than any of these.

A computer can do some of the things the human brain can do—and it can do them better. For example, a computer can work out mathematical problems faster than the human brain can; it doesn't make as many mistakes as the human brain makes; and it can remember more facts than the human brain can remember.

A computer can make decisions. It can choose to follow one course of action or another. Even if it is only doing a simple calculation on a series of numbers, it must be able to decide when to stop.

But when a computer is making thousands of decisions a second, its behaviour becomes very complex. It seems to have a mind of its own. You may have felt this when playing a video game—which is a kind of computer.

Some people believe a computer can think. They point out that a computer can, for example, play an excellent game of chess. Other people say that the computer is only carrying out the instructions of the person who programmed it, and this cannot be called 'thinking'.

It is true that a computer only acts on instructions. That is all a computer 'program' is: a list of instructions.

It is also true that a computer program can find a good move in a chess position, for example, which has never been seen on this earth before.

How is it that a machine which merely carries out instructions, can react to a new situation with what appears to be an original, intelligent response? It comes down to the computer's decision-making ability. The individual decisions a computer makes are not very subtle. Usually it is just a matter of examining the result of a previous calculation: if the result is, say, zero, the machine does one thing; if not, it does another.

Even quite complex decisions, involving many factors and many possible courses of action, can be broken down into simple yes/no decisions like this. That is part of the job of the programmer.

We tend to think that a machine obeying orders must act in a repetitive, stereotyped way. This is because most machines can only be told 'do this, do that'. But a computer can be ordered: 'here are the rules for making decisions—decide for yourself!' What is more, a computer program can learn from experience. It can improve its own performance.

Is this 'thinking'? Decide for yourself! There is still one important difference between computers and people making decisions. The choices for a computer program are always limited. Even the best chess program can only decide between good and bad chess moves. But *you* can wake up in the morning and ask 'what shall I do today?'

The decision-making ability of computers is important, because almost every program uses it. Most of the work done by computers would not require very deep thought if done by human beings. Most computers perform routine clerical work for businesses, or lengthy (but routine) arithmetic for scientists; or else they act as filing clerks, building up and searching through vast libraries of information. Certainly those computers which control industrial machinery are not expected to think of new and original solutions.

How computers work

As we have seen, a computer is a machine which carries out instructions, step by step. The instructions tell it to carry out operations on information, or 'data' as it is called. Data in computers is expressed in 'binary' form (so, for that matter, are instructions). Binary code uses just two symbols, 0 and 1. Numbers can be expressed in this form (see: *arithmetic, binary number*). So can letters and other symbols.

There is a standard code used for communicating with computers, in which D, for example, is 1000100 and 5 is 0110101. Different codes may be used inside the computer.

Since computers only operate on data, you cannot instruct a computer to 'lift up that weight'. But the computer may be connected to another machine which *can* lift weights. There might be an agreed signal from the computer which means 'lift!' Computers really can make things happen in the outside world.

Charles Babbage designed (but never completed) a computer in the last century, using wheels and shafts. Future computers may use guided laser beams. But all today's computers are electronic (see: *electronics*). Tiny electric charges and currents represent 0s and 1s inside the machine. Binary code is convenient since an electrical circuit can clearly either be 'on' or 'off'.

The central processing unit

The two most important parts of a computer are the central processing unit and the memory. The central processing unit (CPU) is in overall control of the computer. It carries out all the operations on the data which are ordered by the program.

Data is handled by computers in standard-length segments called 'words'. The length may be anything from eight binary digits (0s and 1s) to as many as sixty-four. Data 'words' have nothing to do with words in the English language.

Instructions may tell the CPU to move a data word from one place to another, or to alter it in some way, to compare it with another word, or to treat two words as numbers and add or subtract them.

A simple CPU might only understand 60 or 70 different instructions. But this is enough. Bigger computers have more instructions but these merely provide short cuts. The essence of a computer is that it does complicated things in simple steps.

When the CPU has finished one instruction, it 'fetches' the next instruction from the memory. The memory is where programs are stored. Data, too, is stored in the memory. The CPU uses the memory rather as you use pencil and paper when doing arithmetic: you write down things which you can't hold in your head.

Since the program in its memory tells the computer everything it has to do, it can work automatically, without human supervision. The other important parts of a computer are input devices (such as a keyboard) and output devices (such as a video screen or printer). Input devices are needed for two purposes: first, to put programs into the computer; and second, to supply a program with data to work on.

When they are built as small units separate from the computer itself, input and output devices are known as 'terminals'. A computer terminal with a screen and a keyboard is called a visual display unit or VDU. Sometimes the screen can show only letters and numbers; sometimes it can show 'graphics' (i.e. diagrams and pictures). The display on a screen can change very fast in response to the user's actions. Computer games take advantage of this.

A terminal may be right next to the computer, or it may be in another continent. Satellites, cables and radio links may be used to link a terminal to a computer, or one computer to another. The simplest way, though not very reliable, is to use an ordinary dialled telephone call. Devices called 'modems' allow computers to 'talk' to each other—in a high-pitched warbling sound—on the telephone.

Printers

Printers are an important part of computer systems. Large computers often use high-speed 'line printers'. These have a printing mechanism which extends the whole width of the paper and prints a whole line at once. Line printers can print hundreds of lines per minute.

'Daisywheel' printers have a flower-shaped printing wheel with the raised shapes of letters on the petal-like spokes of the wheel. A hammer hits one of the spokes and presses it against a ribbon (which is inked or carbon-coated). This leaves an impression of a letter on the paper. Different letters are selected rapidly by spinning the wheel. Daisywheel printers are not very fast, but their printing is very clear and readable. They are often used to print business letters.

Some printers build up the shapes of letters from tiny dots. You can often make out the dots if you look closely at something printed by a computer. In one type of printer, thin wires or needles shoot out and hit a ribbon to make dots. Another, the 'ink jet' printer, squirts tiny drops of ink at the paper. Other types use heat, light or electric sparks to make marks on specially coated paper.

Storing information

Since a powerful computer carries out millions of instructions every second, its memory must be able to find an item almost immediately—in a good deal less than a millionth of a second. But memory circuits which can do this are expensive. Most computers have back-up storage of a cheaper type, where large amounts of less urgently-needed data can be kept.

Small computers often use flexible or 'floppy' discs. These are discs of a soft plastic material, usually $5\frac{1}{4}$ or 8 inches across, with a magnetic coating. The disc is sealed into a square envelope. It can turn inside the envelope.

Equipment which uses rigid or 'hard' discs is more expensive. Hard discs hold more data than floppy discs, and operate faster. Magnetic tape can store even more data, but it takes longer to find an item of data on a tape than on a disc. All these magnetic recording devices used with computers work on the same principle as the ordinary tape recorder used to record sound.

Very large amounts of information are stored in some computer systems. The computers have special programs for entering, altering and finding items of information. The data must be arranged systematically, like books in a library. An organized collection of data of this kind is called a 'database'. A scientist might use a database to find out what is known about a particular chemical; databases for lawyers contain details of laws and court decisions. A person who has a computer terminal can consult such databases from almost anywhere in the world.

Not all databases are for public use. Banks, government departments, police authorities, and large financial and commercial organizations have information about millions of citizens in their computers. Such information is confidential. The computer system must be carefully designed to stop unauthorized persons looking at the data or altering it. Criminals have obtained large sums of money by secretly altering information in computers owned by banks and insurance companies.

Secret passwords, cyphers, and other methods are used to protect computer data. Many companies guard their computers as carefully as they guard their cash.

Now computers can be made so powerful that programmers have developed 'expert systems'. These will store all the experience of a number of experts in such a way that the information can be used to make deductions and plan an appropriate course of action. The computer could make a medical diagnosis, identify a chemical substance or plan a survey to search for oil.

Software

People often think that if you use a computer, you yourself must 'program' it. This is not true. Of course you are always free to write your own programs. But most people who use computers buy programs already written, or have them written by professionals. Programs for small computers often come recorded on a 'floppy' disc. Programs for large systems may be contained on reels of magnetic tape. All that the person using the computer has to do is fit the disc or tape to the machine, and carry out a simple procedure to 'load' the program into the computer's memory.

Programs are known as 'software' to distinguish them from the machinery or 'hardware'. Software is an important part of any computer system. Software is a product like any other. It takes the work of many people for many months to produce some of the more complex programs.

Languages

A computer can only act directly on instructions given in a binary number code called 'machine code'. Machine code is not easy for people to understand. It is easier if each instruction is given a name instead of a number. This set of names for the things the computer can do is called an 'assembly language'. Programs written in assembly language are translated into machine code by a special program called an 'assembler'.

Even in assembly language, programming is slow and difficult. You have to know exactly how your computer works. High-level languages such as Fortran, Cobol, Basic and Pascal look rather more like English. They allow the person programming to concentrate on the problem in hand, without bothering exactly how a particular computer will solve it. 'Compilers' and 'interpreters' are programs which turn high-level language into machine code. To use Basic programs, for example, you must have a Basic interpreter for your computer.

Automation

Computers help to control many industrial machines and processes. Usually a factory which uses computers can make more goods with fewer workers. But this is not entirely a good thing, since some workers may lose their jobs. Often computers create new jobs, but these may not be as skilled or interesting as the old jobs.

Computers are useful in the 'process' industries which make such things as oil, steel, chemicals and food. In an oil refinery, a computer can monitor and control pressures, temperatures and flow rates in all parts of the plant. It can adjust them for efficient operation, and give warning if dangerous conditions develop. It can also help with day-to-day decisions which affect the refinery's profits: for example, how much gasoline the plant should produce, and exactly how it should be blended.

The engineering industry works in a different way. The parts of a product are made separately by many different machines. Then they are put together or assembled. Computers can assist engineers with all the decisions which go into the design of a gearbox, a food mixer or an airplane: not only what it will look like, but how it will be made, how it will work, and what it will cost. The computer can print drawings, lists of parts needed, and other paperwork.

When the design is complete, the computer can prepare punched paper tapes which tell automatic machine tools how to cut out, shape and drill the various parts. Then the parts must be assembled. This is often still a job for human hands. But there are machines with mechanical 'arms' and 'hands' which can pick up parts and fit them together. They are called industrial robots. They are controlled by computers or microprocessors. Some can 'see' with TV cameras. Already there are factories where robots make robots.

A completely automatic factory has been designed in Japan. Parts and materials are carried by conveyor belts from one automatic machine to another. Robots lift parts on and off the moving belts.

Computers now play a vital part in scientific research. They control experiments and record data and can even be used to analyse photographs and graphs for particular combinations of events or objects. Some scientists use computers to make detailed models of complex systems and calculate what experiments would show if their theories were correct.

Office automation

Word processors are now used in many offices. A word processor is like a typewriter with an electronic memory. Words typed in do not appear on paper immediately. They can be corrected or rearranged first. Often you can see what you have just typed, on a video screen. Standard letters, long reports, or even whole books can be prepared on a word processor.

A word processor looks like a computer, and inside, it works like one. Instead of having computers or word processors, in the future people in offices may simply have a 'work station' with a keyboard, a screen and a telephone, all connected to a communications network. Through the 'work station' it will be possible to send and receive messages to store and retrieve information, and to use the power of big computers in the same building or many miles away. Paperwork will be reduced, but probably never eliminated.

Microcomputers

Integrated circuits (see: *electronics, silicon*) came into use in computers during the 1960s. By 1971 it was possible to make an integrated circuit or 'chip' containing some thousands of transistors. It became feasible to put an entire central processing unit on a chip. Such a device came to be called a 'microprocessor'.

Like any central processing unit, a microprocessor works according to a program. Some microprocessors are given a simple fixed program and installed inside a machine—perhaps a cash register or a washing machine—where they do a routine job which could probably be done in other ways. But a microprocessor can also become the heart of a small but general-purpose computer system. Computers based on microprocessors are generally known as microcomputers. In principle a microcomputer can solve any problem a big computer can solve. But in practice there are limitations on its speed, the size of its memory, the number of other devices that can be connected to it, and so on.

Some microcomputers are used as 'personal computers' by scientists or business people. Some are used as home computers. Some are in factories. Some of the more powerful ones can be used by more than one person at once, and are found in medium-sized businesses.

Cheap and flexible computers are also helping the handicapped to tackle tasks they could never have dreamed of before. And in schools and at home they can help children to learn languages, music and math. More and more schools are now teaching the skills they will need for the revolution in information technology.
See: *automation, binary number, electronics.*

cosmic ray

A cosmic ray is not a ray in the same sense as a ray of light. Cosmic rays are streams of tiny electrically-charged particles, smaller than an atom, which bombard the Earth from space. Cosmic rays are striking us all the time, but they are so infinitely small that we do not feel them.

Cosmic rays were first discovered early in this century. At that time, scientists in Europe and the United States were carrying out many experiments connected with electric charges (see: *electricity*). There was one thing in particular that puzzled these scientists. They measured electric charge with a device in an airtight jar, called an electroscope. But the charge was always lost eventually. This happened even though the box was protected by insulating material, which would not allow electricity to flow through it. The scientists believed that this charge could be lost in only one way. It must have been balanced or 'neutralized' by particles of opposite charge arriving from outside.

The questions that now puzzled the scientists were these: What were these mysterious electrically-charged particles that found their way into the box – despite all efforts to cut it off from any electrical influence? And where did the particles come from?

The answers to these questions first began to take shape in 1912. In that year, an Austrian physicist, Victor Hess, took three electroscopes in a balloon 5 kilometres (three miles) above the Earth. Hess found that the higher he ascended the more rapidly the charge given to the electroscope was lost. He decided this could have only one meaning. The neutralising influence must come from somewhere above the Earth, and not from the Earth itself.

Hess concluded that the Earth was under constant bombardment from some outside source by electrically-charged particles. Some would have a negative charge and some a positive charge.

At first, other scientists doubted Hess's theory. But gradually their experiments began to confirm what he had stated. In particular, an American professor, Robert Millikan, was completely convinced by his own experiments that the theory was true. Because they came from the cosmos – the depths of space – Millikan named the mysterious radiation 'cosmic rays'.

Since then, cosmic rays have been intensively investigated, using all types of equipment. Instruments have often been flown in balloons. In recent years, many satellites and space vehicles have been used.

Cosmic rays are divided into two classes – 'primary' and 'secondary'. Primary rays are the tiny particles that first enter the Earth's atmosphere. They are travelling at immense speeds, close to that of light – which covers 299,792 kilometres (186,282 miles) per second.

In Earth's upper atmosphere, these primary rays strike atoms of nitrogen, oxygen and the other gases that make up our air (see: *air*). So great is the energy of the cosmic rays that they completely break up these atoms into smaller particles. The particles produced in this way are the secondary cosmic rays. The rays that eventually reach Earth are almost all secondary.

It is now known that primary cosmic rays are positively-charged particles of very high energy. They consist of atoms of every kind that have lost their electrons leaving only the 'core' or 'nucleus' (plural, 'nuclei') of the atom (see: *atom*). Over 80 per cent of cosmic rays are nuclei of hydrogen. About 12 per cent are nuclei of helium. After these the commonest elements present are carbon, nitrogen and oxygen.

Hydrogen and helium are the lightest nuclei that exist. They are common elements in the universe as a whole, not just in cosmic rays.

Cosmic ray particles that come near the Earth are 'guided' by the Earth's magnetic field. The result is that more cosmic rays strike the Earth near the magnetic poles.

But not all the particles travel straight to the Earth. Many are stored in the Van Allen belts, zones of very strong radiation high above the Earth. One is strongest about 16,000 km (10,000 miles) up, the other one about 4,000 km (2,500 miles) up. After being trapped here for a time the particles are likely to find their way into the atmosphere.

Secondary rays have been detected by sensitive instruments over 900 metres (3,000 feet) below an ocean surface. The rays had passed through an amount of material equivalent to 90 metres (300 feet) of solid lead.

The main question scientists ask themselves about cosmic rays is: where do they come from?

The theory now most widely accepted is that they have two main sources. One is our own Sun. At times when 'flares' or explosions are seen to be occurring on the Sun, increased amounts of cosmic rays hit the Earth. But the increase is only in the rays of lower energy. So it is believed that the higher-energy, more powerful rays come from some unknown point in our own galaxy, or even in other galaxies. We cannot find out where this point is by seeing which direction the particles came from. The particles have changed direction so many times on their long journey that they hit the Earth from all sides and from every angle.

One source of cosmic radiation may be the 'supernovae'. This is the name given to stars as they suddenly explode towards the end of their existence. Such explosions release enormous quantities of energy.

It is possible to 'see' cosmic rays. Astronauts reported seeing flashes when they were travelling in space. They were found to be caused by cosmic rays of high energy passing through the retinas of the astronauts and stimulating nerves of vision. The effect has been repeated on Earth using particles produced by the huge accelerating machines used in atomic research.

Cosmic rays have the same effect on living tissues as radioactivity (see: *radioactivity*). As each particle passes through it leaves a tiny trail of damaged cells, which the body has to repair. If a living creature is exposed to strong radiation, or weaker radiation for a long time, sickness and possibly death may follow. Future astronauts may be exposed to the full force of primary cosmic radiation during journeys lasting months or even years. High-flying passenger jets of the future may need shielding from cosmic rays, too.

density

A piece of cork will float on water because cork is less dense than water. By the same principle, a lump of steel will sink because steel is more dense than water. But steel will float on mercury. Steel is less dense than mercury.

The density of a substance is measured as its weight per unit volume. In scientific work, the weight is measured in grams. The volume of a substance is the amount of space it takes up. It is measured in cubic centimetres (cc). The density of a substance is therefore given in grams per cc. For example, one cubic centimetre of steel has a weight of approximately 8.5 grams, and so the density of steel is 8.5 grams per cc.

The density of a substance is related to the distances between the atoms or molecules from which it is built. The closer together these are packed, the denser the substance will be. For example, diamonds and soot are built from identical carbon atoms; but the atoms are arranged differently, and so the two densities are different.

The densest matter that we certainly know of occurs in 'white dwarfs'. These tiny, faint stars are the remains left when large stars explode. One handful of a white dwarf's substance would weigh as much as several elephants.

But astronomers believe they have discovered even denser objects. 'Pulsars' are almost certainly made up entirely of neutrons (see: *atom*). If so, then a handful of a pulsar would weigh perhaps a billion tonnes (See: *pulsar*.) And astronomers think that matter may become even more dense in certain circumstances.

The density of a substance can vary. For example, it is affected by changes in temperature and pressure. As a general rule, an increase in temperature at a constant pressure, or a decrease in pressure at a constant temperature, will decrease the density of a substance by making it expand. This effect is small in liquids and solids, but it is important in gases.

Any substance has three states: solid, liquid or gas. Generally, a substance is most dense when it is in its solid state, and least dense when it is in its gaseous state.

There are exceptions to this rule, however. For example, water has its maximum density at 4° Celsius, (39°F) (at atmospheric pressure). At higher or lower temperatures, water is less dense. This gives scientists a useful standard to compare other densities with. At 4° Celsius, at atmospheric pressure, the density of water is exactly one gram per cc. (The gram was first defined as the mass of one cubic centimetre of water in these conditions.)

Find out by doing

Make your own hydrometer (density-measurer) from a drinking straw. Weight it with a small

piece of modeling clay at one end. It will float at different levels in different liquids. In less dense liquids it floats lower than in denser ones.
Compare the densities of water, milk, cooking oil, motor oil and petrol.

eclipse

One of the most beautiful – and perhaps terrifying – sights in nature is the darkening of the Sun in daytime. Sometimes, at the time of New Moon, a small, round notch will appear at the edge of the Sun's disc. It grows, turning the Sun into a crescent. If it covers the whole disc of the Sun, the sky turns completely dark and the stars shine. Then, after only a few minutes, a thin crescent of the Sun reappears, and grows to a full disc. This is an eclipse of the Sun.

What happened was that the Moon moved between the Earth and the Sun, and its shadow fell on the Earth. It is also possible for the Earth to come between the Moon and the Sun. The Moon passes into the Earth's shadow and becomes almost completely dark. This is an eclipse of the Moon.

Eclipses of the Sun
The Moon is about 3,200 kilometres (2,000 miles) across. The Sun is very much larger – about one-and-a-half million kilometres (nearly a million miles) across. But because the Sun is about 400 times as far away, they look about the same size to us. During a solar eclipse the Moon's disc almost exactly covers the Sun as seen from the centre of the Moon's shadow.

The part of the Earth from which the Sun's disc is completely blotted out may be only a few kilometres across. People inside this area see a 'total' eclipse. Over a much wider area, the Moon is 'off-centre' and covers only part of the Sun's disc. This kind of eclipse is 'partial'.

During a partial eclipse the sky darkens but does not become completely black. Only one or two of the brightest stars appear.

A total eclipse is much more spectacular, for when the light of the Sun's disc is cut off the Sun's atmosphere becomes visible. Surrounding the Moon, and going out to a great distance, a halo of pearly white light called the corona ('crown') can be seen. From the rim of the Moon, red thread-like 'prominences' stick out. Though they look tiny to us, they are colossal fountains of glowing hydrogen gas tens of thousands of kilometres long, rising from the Sun's surface.

You should not look at an eclipse directly, even through dark glass, because the light of the corona can burn the eyes (see: *astronomy*).

Eclipses of the Moon
An eclipse of the Moon is visible from anywhere on the night-time part of the Earth. It does not happen every month because the Moon's orbit is tilted so the Moon, Earth and Sun do not often make a straight line. In eclipse, the Moon slowly disappears until it is just a thin crescent. At total eclipse it does not become completely invisible. It has a dull, coppery-red colour because it is lit by red sunlight bent into the Earth's shadow by our atmosphere. The total eclipse can last nearly two hours.
See: *Moon, Sun.*

elasticity

If you pull a piece of elastic it stretches and springs back when you let go. Elasticity is the ability of something to go back to its original shape after being stretched, squeezed or bent.

If you squeeze a tennis ball, your fingertips make little dents in it. You have to press very hard because the dents try to spring out again. This is what happens when a ball bounces. The ball flattens where it hits the ground. As it springs back into shape, the ball bounces up.

When you drop a book on the floor it does not bounce. The book and floor do not collide elastically. Try dropping your tennis ball on the floor. Don't bounce it – just let it fall. How high does it bounce? It does not reach the height you dropped it from. The ball lost some energy when it hit the floor. Each bounce is smaller than the last. The collision would be 'perfectly elastic' if it could bounce up to the same height each time.

Tennis balls are not perfectly elastic. But balls made of special synthetic rubber are very nearly so. You can get an idea how well a ball will bounce by squeezing it with your fingers. It won't bounce high if it is soft. A bouncy ball feels hard because it springs back against your fingers when you try to squeeze it.

The great 17th century scientist, Robert Boyle, realised that sound travels through air because air is elastic. When a pop-gun fires, tiny particles of air – called molecules – are pushed away by the sudden movement of the cork. But they hit other molecules and bounce back. Boyle said that each molecule behaved as if it had springs fixed all over it so that it bounced. When molecules hit each other, they bounce away and hit others. But molecules are not perfectly elastic, so they bounce less each time. This movement of the air molecules spreading outwards and growing fainter is a sound wave.

All elastic things have an elastic limit. If you overload an elastic object beyond this limit, it will not go back to its original shape when the load is removed. For example if you put too great a weight on a spring it will stretch. Not only will the spring be longer but it will also have lost its elasticity.

Wood is elastic. When you jump on a springboard the planks bend and spring back into shape. As the plank bends downwards it stretches on top and is squeezed underneath. It will break if it is bent too much.

Steel beams bend elastically. High buildings are made of steel and reinforced concrete. These materials flex in a strong wind. If they did not bend, steel bridges and skyscrapers would be brittle and they would break easily.

Engineers have to know the elasticity of the building materials they use. They must be sure that they will be able to bend without breaking.

One way to test a beam is to load it until it breaks. Then you know that other beams of the same size, shape and material are safe for smaller loads.

Nowadays engineers prefer to use tests that don't destroy the thing they are testing. They can use sound to find out the elasticity of the beam. They use 'ultrasound', which is too high-pitched to hear. But electronic apparatus can detect it. Engineers calculate the elasticity of the beam by comparing the strength of the sound that went in with the strength of the sound that comes out.
See: *sound*.

electricity

Ancient civilisations thought that thunder and lightning were signs that their gods were angry. Now we know that lightning is a powerful discharge of electrical energy, and that its passage through the air causes thunder.

Modern man has learned how to produce electricity, and how to make it work for him. Electricity has become one of the most important forms of energy in our everyday lives. Without it we would have no lights in our houses and streets, no radio, television or telephone, very little transport, and almost no industry.

The earliest discovery about electricity was made more than 2500 years ago by a Greek named Thales. He found that a yellow substance called amber, when rubbed with a woollen cloth, attracted dust, leaves and other light dry objects. Thales could not explain this strange behaviour, because he knew nothing of electricity. More than 2000 years later, in 1570, an English scientist named William Gilbert showed

that other materials also had this strange property. To describe it he used the word 'electrics', which he got from the Greek word *elektron*, which means amber.

Electric charges
Both the Greek Thales and the English scientist Gilbert, had discovered 'static electricity'. You can copy these experiments yourself. If you rub a glass rod with a piece of silk, you will find that it will attract small pieces of dry paper. If you run a plastic comb through your hair, the comb will also cause small pieces of dry paper to jump and cling to it. Both the glass rod and the comb have acquired an electric charge. To understand static electricity, we must first understand the structure of the atom.

All matter is made up of atoms. These are tiny particles, and the atoms themselves are made up of even tinier particles. An atom consists of a nucleus (the central part) and a number of electrons. The electrons revolve round the nucleus in orbits – rather like the planets revolve in orbits round the Sun. Scientists have found that electrons carry a tiny electric charge. The nucleus of an atom is built up from two other kinds of particle. These two particles are the neutron and the proton. The proton also carries an electric charge. Scientists also found that the two charges carried by the electron and the proton were different. We say that the electron's charge is negative, and that the proton's charge is positive. Although the charges are very tiny, powerful charges are made by large numbers of them building up and 'joining forces'.

This explains how material such as glass can be charged with electricity by rubbing it with a piece of silk. Ordinarily a piece of glass has the same number of electrons as it has protons. Therefore the positive charges and negative charges cancel each other out. But when the glass is rubbed with silk, the silk attracts some of the electrons away. Then the glass has more protons than electrons, and therefore has more tiny positive charges than negative charges. The glass has a positive charge, which is equal to the combined charges of the extra protons.

The discovery that there were two kinds of electric charges – positive and negative – was made by a French scientist named Charles Dufay, in 1733. Again you can copy his experiments yourself. Rub two inflated balloons with a woollen cloth, and hold the balloons close together. They will try to spring apart. Rub two pieces of nylon on a sheet of paper, and then hold them close together. Again, they will try to spring apart. Now hold one balloon and one piece of nylon close together. This time the nylon clings to the balloon.

This is what has happened. The two balloons have taken electrons from the woollen cloth and so have acquired a negative charge. The two pieces of nylon have lost electrons to the sheet of paper, and so have acquired a positive charge. The experiment shows one of the most important laws of electricity: like charges repel and unlike charges attract. The two negative charges (on the balloons) tried to push each other away. The two positive charges (on the pieces of nylon) also tried to push each other away. But the unlike charges, the balloon and the nylon, tried to move closer together. You will see the importance of this law when we examine electric current and how electric current is produced.

The word 'static' means 'at rest', and static electricity is electric charges which are at rest in an object. If we can make these charges move in some way, we produce electric current.

What is electric current?
The structure of the atom plays a vital part in the flow of an electric current. In some materials, the electrons in the outermost orbit of the atoms are loosely held. These electrons can easily be set free from their orbits, and for this reason they are called free electrons. Materials which have lots of free electrons are called conductors. If a body with a negative charge is connected through a conductor to a body with a positive charge, electrons will flow from the negative charge through to the positive charge. This flow of electrons is called an electric current.

Volts, ohms and amps
There has to be some 'driving force' that makes electrons flow in a conductor. But what is this force and where does it come from? As a simple example, think of the piece of glass that was rubbed with silk. The glass lost some of its electrons and so became positively charged. The silk gained extra electrons and became negatively charged. The difference between the two charges is called the potential difference. This is the driving force. If a conductor such as a piece of wire were now made to join up the glass and the silk, electrons would flow back through the wire. The difference in charge would disappear. There would be no potential difference or driving force any more.

The potential difference between two ends of a conductor can be measured. Another name for it is the voltage, and the units that it is measured in are volts. These names come from the Italian scientist Alessandro Volta, who, as we shall see later, found a simpler way of producing a potential difference than by rubbing glass with silk.

The larger the voltage, the larger will be the current in a conductor. This relationship between voltage and current was first described by a German scientist named Georg Ohm in 1827. He found that doubling the voltage doubled the current in a given wire conductor, and that halving the voltage halved the current and so on.

Current is measured in units called amperes, usually shortened to amps. This describes how much electricity passes a given point in one second.

Some materials allow electric currents to flow more easily than other materials. Most metals, for example, are good conductors. But other materials, such as rubber and dry wood, have few free electrons and conduct little or no electric current. Materials like this are called insulators.

An English scientist, Henry Cavendish, said that all materials resisted the flow of electrons. Good conductors resisted the flow of electrons much less than did bad conductors (insulators). We say that good conductors have low resistance, and that bad conductors have high resistance.

Georg Ohm also discovered a relationship between resistance and electric current. He found that the current would be halved if a wire of twice the resistance was used, or that the current would be doubled if a wire of half the resistance was used. Ohm's two discoveries resulted in the most famous electric law: Ohm's Law. Ohm's Law states that the current in a conductor is proportional to the voltage, and inversely proportional to its resistance. This law is written as an equation:-

$$\frac{voltage}{resistance} = current$$

Resistance is measured in a unit called an ohm, after Georg Ohm. Ohm's Law written in units is:

$$\frac{volts}{ohms} = amperes$$

The electric circuit
Before an electric current can flow, there must be a difference in potential between one end of a conductor and the other. The current must have somewhere to flow to.

In most cases electricity flows from a source of current (say a battery), through a conductor and back again to the source. We say that the electric current follows a closed circuit. For example, when an ordinary flashlight is switched off, nothing happens. We say that the circuit is open. When you switch the flashlight on, you complete the circuit. Electricity flows from the battery, through the bulb and back to the battery.

Light switches in your house work in a similar way. When they are switched on, they complete a circuit and allow electricity to flow through the light bulbs. When switched off, they break the circuit and no electricity flows through the bulbs.

The electrical energy which flows through a circuit can be used by changing it into heat and light. For example, when you switch on your flashlight, the bulb 'lights up', and when you switch on an electric heater, the element glows red and gives out heat.

To understand why this happens, we have to go back again to the structure of the atom. When an electric current flows along a conductor, the free electrons constantly bump into the atoms in the conductor. When things bump together heat is produced. If the current is strong enough, so much heat is produced that the conductor glows.

In a flashlight bulb there is a very thin coil of wire, which heats up very quickly. When an electric current flows through this thin coil of wire, so much heat is produced that the wire becomes first of all red-hot and then white-hot, and gives out bright light. In passing through the metal, electrical energy is turned into two other forms of energy – heat and light.

Sources of electricity
From the time of the Ancient Greeks, people have known about electricity. But it was probably not until about two hundred years ago that anyone could produce a steady flow of current. Scientists were able to build up quite large static electric charges in objects at this time by friction – by rubbing objects and collecting the charges. They could even store this electricity. A device called a Leyden jar became very popular. This was a glass jar, coated with metal, with a metal rod sticking through a cork in the opening. The rod could be given a powerful electric charge, and would keep it until a conductor was brought near. Then a current of electricity would discharge, by jumping in a crackling spark, just like a tiny flash of lightning. But the jar was not a steady source of electricity. It only stored a static charge.

An Italian scientist called Luigi Galvani was interested in the effects of electricity on muscles. He knew that it would make the muscles in a frog's leg twitch, even if the frog had just been killed. He also knew that there was electricity in the air during a thunderstorm. So he wondered whether a frog's muscles would twitch when there was lightning, as they twitched when held near a charged Leyden jar. He took some frogs' legs, hung them on brass hooks, and put them on the iron bars near his window to wait for a thunderstorm.

To Galvani's surprise the legs twitched even though the thunderstorm he was expecting had not yet arrived. He knew that there must be electricity around – but what was making it?

Galvani decided and for years insisted, that the electricity was coming from the frog's muscles themselves, in contact with the brass and iron. But he was wrong, because the electricity was coming from the two metals, not the frog's legs. Another Italian scientist, called Alessandro Volta, realized the truth and showed that Galvani was wrong. He found that when any two metals of different kinds were put together they would make electricity. They produced a potential difference. And if they were joined by a wire, this would produce a current. At last a steady source of current had been found.

Volta took discs of silver, zinc and cardboard soaked in salt water. He stacked them in a pile, in order from the bottom, silver, zinc, cardboard, silver, zinc, cardboard and so on. If now he joined a wire from the silver disc at the bottom to a zinc disc at the top, a steady current would flow in it. This device, called a 'voltaic pile', was the first ancestor of our modern batteries.

Electrolysis
An important branch of the study of electricity is concerned with what happens when an electric current is passed through a liquid. If a positive and negative electrode are put into a conducting liquid, then very often chemical changes take place in the liquid. The electrodes might be simply wires connected to the two poles of a battery, dipping into water which has been made slightly acid. When a circuit is completed in this way, the current produces a chemical change in the water, around each electrode. The water actually breaks down into the elements of which it is made – the gases hydrogen and oxygen. From around the positive electrode, the anode, bubbles of oxygen rise to the surface, and from around the negative electrode bubbles of hydrogen arise. This breaking up of a conducting liquid by electricity is called electrolysis. The liquid is called the electrolyte.

Chemical changes like this can be produced in nearly every conducting liquid. Mercury, of course, is an obvious exception, because it is itself both a metal and an element. Nothing happens if electrodes are dipped into a container of oil, because it does not conduct electricity.

Electrolysis does not always produce bubbles of gas at the electrodes, because the elements of which electrolytes are made are not all gases. If, for example, the electrolyte is molten sodium hydroxide (soda lye), then metallic sodium will gradually build up around the cathode. This way of producing metals from their compounds is very important in industry. The metal can be produced in a state of great purity from compounds that occur naturally in minerals.

Electrolysis has other important uses than

obtaining metals. It is the basis of electroplating, whereby a layer of metal can be deposited upon an object used as a cathode, dipped into an electrolyte. The anode is made of the metal to be used for plating, and as the electric current passes it dissolves in the electrolyte, and the metal forms a layer on the cathode.

Movement and electricity
A battery is a steady source of electricity but it produces only a small voltage. Today, to light and heat our cities, and to keep factories running, we need vast quantities of electricity. Batteries are not powerful enough for this. A source of electricity many millions of times more powerful is needed. We use machines called generators. These change, not just the energy of different chemicals in contact, but many other forms of energy into electricity. In particular, we rely on the conversion of the energy of movement into electricity.

To understand how something moving can be made to make electricity, we must go back to the scientists just after Galvani and Volta, who discovered that electricity and magnetism were in fact quite closely related. At that time, very little was known about magnetism. Scientists knew that a magnetized length of metal, suspended, turns to point north-south. It forms a compass. And that another piece of magnetic metal, such as iron, held nearby, affects this compass and makes it swing. It produces movement. A piece of zinc or copper wire does not make the compass swing.

In 1819, the Danish scientist Hans Oersted found that, if an electric current was passed through a copper wire, then a compass needle held nearby would move, just as though the wire was magnetic. A year later, two French scientists called Ampère and Arago found that a coil of wire carrying a current acted as an even stronger magnet. By now it was clear that magnetism and electricity had something in common. They produced invisible forces that acted at a distance, and could make other things move, without touching them.

The English scientist Michael Faraday was fascinated by these forces. He imagined that there must be magnetic 'lines of force' spreading out invisibly from magnets and from wires carrying electric currents. And he thought that these could repel or attract other objects producing lines of force, and could move them. If electricity could make things move, perhaps it could be made to do useful work. And perhaps, even, the other way round – moving things might be made to produce magnetic lines of force, and so electricity.

The simplest form of electric motor consists of a coil of wire between the two poles of a magnet. (A magnet has two poles, a north pole and a south pole – see: *magnet*.)

When electric current flows through the coil the coil is magnetized. Like poles repel and unlike poles attract, so the magnetized coil swings round until its south pole lines up with the north pole of the magnet. At this point the electric current is reversed. This reverses the magnetic poles of the coil. The north pole becomes the south, and vice versa. The coil swings round again to line up opposite poles. If the current in the coil is reversed several times a second, the coil will spin round rapidly.

Faraday was not content with this idea. He thought that the process could be reversed. He found that if a magnet was moved backwards and forwards inside a coil of wire it would produce a current in the wire. This is called 'inducing' a current. This new discovery meant that mechanical energy could be changed into electrical energy.

This discovery was very important. Today almost all our electrical energy is supplied by inducing currents in the coils of wire in electrical generators.

The coils can be turned by falling water, steam engines using coal or oil, or by atomic power. Without generators, we would rely on batteries for our electricity supplies.

When a conducting wire is attached to the terminals of a battery, electrons flow from the negative terminal to the positive terminal. This one-way electron flow is called direct current or DC for short.

Our electricity supply
The electric current supplied to your home from the power station is alternating current or AC for short. AC reverses its direction of flow 120 times every second. It flows 60 times in the one direction, say to the power station; and 60 times in the other direction, say from the power station. AC is easier to generate than DC (remember – the poles of the generator coil reverse several times a second). Another reason that AC is used for house power supplies is that its voltage can be changed by a device called a transformer.

Huge quantities of electrical energy are produced by a power station. These quantities of electricity must be sent out across the country to houses, stores and factories. To 'push' the electricity over these distances, very high voltages are needed. But when the electricity reaches its destination, lower voltages are needed because high voltages are very dangerous.

The high voltages are 'stepped-down' by means of a transformer. The transformer is another invention of Michael Faraday. It consists of two coils of wire, one coil having many more turns of wire than the other. If AC is passed through one coil, it induces moving lines of magnetic force. These in turn induce an electric current in the other coil. Suppose coil A has half as many turns as coil B. Then the voltage induced in it will be half the voltage in coil B. In this way the voltage can be reduced. At the same time the current can be increased.

The power supply from the power station is stepped-down by transformers from hundreds of thousands of volts to 240 volts for household use. Houses are wired with electric circuits. Electricity coming into the house passes through a meter. This measures the amount of current used so that the supplier can charge for it. The current also passes through a fuse box. This protects electrical appliances from over-loading. If too much power is taken, a wire in the fuse gets hot and so it melts, so breaking the circuit and acting as a 'switch'.

When we want to use an electric appliance, all we need to do is plug it into the circuit and switch on to complete the circuit. The energy of electricity is essential to our modern lives. An interesting exercise is to make a list of all the electrical appliances in your home. You might be surprised how many there are.

It is very dangerous to play with an electric appliance when it is plugged in. Accidentally touching a live wire can make an electric current flow through your body. This is an electric shock and it can kill.

See: *electronics*.

electronics

Do you enjoy watching television? A television set is an electronic machine. So is a tape recorder, a computer and a radar set.

All these machines depend upon the very accurate control of tiny electric currents. Without this control none of them could work.

An electric current is a flow of electrons (see: *electricity*). Electronics is the science that deals with the control of electron flow, and therefore with the control of electric currents.

Electrons are minute particles found in atoms. They orbit round the central nucleus of the atom. The nucleus itself consists of two other kinds of particle – protons and neutrons (see: *atom*). Electrons carry a tiny negative charge of electricity, and protons carry a tiny positive charge of electricity.

In some substances, the electrons can move easily from their orbits round the nucleus of each atom. Such electrons are called free electrons. Electric current is the movement of free electrons in a particular direction.

A direct current flows steadily in one direction. An alternating current reverses its direction, usually many times each second. Both kinds of current are important in electronics.

There are some currents in electronic equipment which should change as little as possible. These are the currents used to supply power and create the correct operating conditions for electronic circuits. But the current which drives the loudspeaker of your radio is not like this. It changes all the time. And those changes mean something. Currents of this kind are called signals. A radio picks up a weak signal from the transmitter and turns it into something powerful enough to fill a room with music. Electronic circuits can strengthen or amplify a signal.

Amplification is needed in almost every electronic device. In a radio it is needed because the signal is very weak to start with. In computers the signals are stronger but amplification is still needed to prevent them fading away as they travel on complex branching paths.

Electronic components which can amplify a signal or add to its power are called 'active' components. A transistor is an active component (see: *transistor*) made from a solid material of the type known as a semiconductor.

Electronics also uses 'passive' components such as resistors, capacitors, inductors and diodes. A resistor resists or limits the flow of current. A capacitor does not allow electrons to pass but transmits electric forces: energy can pass through it in the form of an alternating current. An inductor is a coil of wire which resists rapid changes in current. A semiconductor diode lets current flow in one direction only.

Before the introduction of semiconductors, electronics relied on electron tubes. The simplest is the diode, which (like its semi-conductor counterpart) acts as a one-way valve. In electron tubes, electrons travel through empty space (a vacuum) or very thin gas. The diode has a heated wire or piece of metal called the cathode which gives off electrons. There is a metal plate nearby called the anode. If the plate is given a positive charge it attracts the negatively charged electrons. A current flows. But no current can flow in the reverse direction. The anode is cool and no electrons can leave it. Diodes can turn alternating current into direct current. They can also turn a radio signal into an audio or sound signal.

One of the most useful electronic tubes is called the triode. Tri means three – there are three electronic parts in the tube. In addition to the emitter and the plate, there is a grid, which is placed between the two. If a negative electric charge is applied to the grid, the electrons from the emitter will be repelled, for although unlike charges attract one another, like charges repel one another. This means that few electrons will pass through the grid, and so very little current will flow in the plate. On the other hand, if a positive charge is applied to the grid, many more electrons will be attracted from the emitter, and a strong current will pass through the tube.

Another kind of electron tube is the cathode ray tube. It has a fluorescent screen which gives off light when electrons hit it. It is best known as the TV picture tube. Other uses are in radar, computers, instruments and office machines.

There are also semiconductor devices which emit light. Red, green and yellow light emitting diodes or LEDs are used as indicator lamps. More complicated arrangements of LEDs can display numbers on a calculator.

Many calculators and electronic watches have 'liquid crystal displays', which are special chemicals with electrically charged molecules. Electrical signals can make the molecules turn to point in different directions. This alters the way the molecules act on light rays.

Electronic or electrical devices exist which can detect and measure light, temperature, pressure, magnetic fields, mechanical force and motion, and other physical and chemical quantities. They are used in electronic measuring instruments and control equipment.

Engineers are constantly trying to make electronic devices which are smaller and use less power. Electron tubes the size of medicine bottles were replaced by matchhead-sized transistors. Now, thousands of transistors and other components can be formed in a 'chip' of silicon a few millimetres square (see: *silicon*). One of the first uses of 'chips' or integrated circuits was in guided missiles. In the late 1960s and 1970s they came to be used in electronic equipment of all kinds, such as pocket calculators, electronic watches, miniature television sets, compact Citizens Band radios, and microcomputers.

In the 1980's complete computers have been built on a handful of chips – opening up the era of the cheap personal computer.

energy

We cannot pick up a handful of energy and weigh it on a balance. But we can sometimes see energy, and we can sometimes feel it. We can see light and feel heat – and both light and heat are forms of energy. And there are ways of measuring energy. Energy is the ability to do work, and by 'work' we mean 'moving something against resistance'.

For example, if you pick up a book against the pull of gravity, or drive a stake into the ground against the resistance of the earth, you are doing work. When you pedal your bicycle you are doing work.   And to do it you are using up energy. Work and energy are both measured according to the distance an object is moved and the force that must be overcome to move it.

You might have seen a pile-driving machine on a construction site. These machines are used to drive steel girders into the ground against the resistance of the hard-packed soil. They work by dropping a weight on one end of the girder, and it is the motion of the falling weight which does the work. The moving weight is said to have kinetic energy – the energy of motion. (The word 'kinetic' comes from a Greek word meaning 'motion'). Any moving body has kinetic energy, because any moving body can do work.

But the weight in the pile-driving machine has kinetic energy only when it is falling. Only then can it do work. While the weight is being held above the girder, its ability to do work is only 'potential'. 'Potential' means that the ability to do work will exist as soon as the weight is moving, but doesn't exist at the moment. The weight can't do any work while it is being held still. For this reason, we say that the weight held in the air has potential energy. In this case, the potential energy is due to the weight's position. If the weight is pulled up to a greater height, it has more potential energy. It can do more work – for example by driving a girder a greater distance into the soil. There are other forms of potential energy, which will be discussed later in this article.

Several kinds of energy are connected with electricity. When an electric current flows through electrical machines, work has to be done to keep the current moving. The energy to do this work may come from a battery (see: *battery*) or from the machines called generators in the power stations which make the current flow.

Not only is energy used in keeping a current flowing. Every electric current has a magnetic field around it (see: *magnetism*). If an electric current passes through wire coiled round a bar of iron, a strong magnetic field is produced, turning the iron bar into a magnet. This is an electromagnet, and they are widely used in industry for lifting and transporting heavy pieces of metal. When an electromagnet is switched on above a metal object, the object flies up and is held to the magnet. Work is done by the magnet in lifting this weight against the force of gravity. And the energy that is used in doing this work comes from the power station that generates the current.

Another form of energy is chemical energy. Chemical compounds are built up of atoms (see: *atom*). The atoms are held in place by attractions between them. The atoms are made of parts that are held together by electrical forces. In the outer parts of the atom are tiny particles called electrons. (Moving electrons make up ordinary electric currents.) When the atoms join to form new compounds, some electrons are rearranged. Energy may be given out as this happens, or it may have to be taken in from outside. When large amounts of energy are given out very quickly, there is an explosion. Energy given out in chemical reactions comes from chemical energy.

Chemical energy is very important in everyday life. For example, the burning of petrol in a car engine is a chemical change. As oxygen from the air combines with the petrol, energy is released and used to drive the wheels. Chemical compounds in an electric battery react with each other to produce an electric current. Human beings must eat food to live. The food is broken down in the body in complicated chemical reactions. The chemical energy released is used by the body.

Heat is a form of energy, too. In any hot object, atoms and molecules are vibrating fast. The hotter the object is, the faster they vibrate. So heat is a form of kinetic energy of atoms and molecules.

Whenever two things strike each other – water hitting the rocks at the bottom of a water fall, a high speed jet hitting molecules of air as it travels faster than sound, or the atoms on the surface of a drill-tip boring through rock – the molecules of the two objects are set vibrating. Kinetic energy of the moving objects is turned into kinetic energy of the molecules. Motion is turned into heat.

In a car's brakes, rough pads press against a metal disc or cylinder attached to the wheels. The brakes grow very hot as the car slows down. Kinetic energy of the car's forward motion is being turned into the heat energy of the atoms in the brakes.

At the centre of every atom is a tiny particle called the nucleus of the atom. The nucleus is itself made up of even tinier particles. The forces that hold the nucleus together are even stronger than the electrical forces which hold the electrons in place. Tremendous amounts of energy are stored in the nucleus. They are released when a nuclear bomb is exploded. This energy is called nuclear energy.

Yet another form of energy appears in light waves, radio waves and X-rays. All these forms of energy are basically the same, except for their wavelength (see: *wave*). Huge amounts of energy are constantly falling on the Earth in the form of sunlight. When an electric light glows, it is sending out energy in the form of light.

Sound waves carry energy too. They are vibrations of the molecules in the air, and so these molecules have kinetic energy. When any thing is making sound, energy is being carried away from it in the sound waves.

One of the most important things to know about energy is that any form of energy can be changed into any other form. For example, chemical energy is changed into heat energy when combustion (burning) of gasoline takes place in an automobile engine. Some of this heat energy is then turned into the energy of the car's movement. Electrical energy is changed into energy in the form of heat and light when an electric current passes through a wire. The kinetic energy of a spinning turbine is changed into electrical energy in a generator (see: *electricity*).

Imagine an explosives expert in a quarry. The explosives he uses are really stored chemical energy. His job is to release that energy safely and make it work for him by loosening the rock in the quarry.

He detonates (sets off) the explosive and the chemical energy is released. Some of it is changed into heat energy and light energy. We can see the light energy as the flash of the explosion. Some energy is released as sound energy, and we can hear the sound of the explosion. If the explosives expert has placed his explosive in the right place, most of the energy will be absorbed (taken in) by the rock. This will cause the rock to vibrate, split, and loosen. This energy finally spreads out among the molecules of the rock as heat, flowing away from the point of explosion.

In this example, one form of energy – chemical – has changed into a number of other forms of energy. But if we could measure all the energy released in these different forms, we would find that the total amount was equal to the amount of chemical energy we started with.

This is another very important idea concerning energy. Energy can be changed from one form to another, but it is never created and never destroyed. This idea is known as the law of conservation of energy.

Sometimes it might seem that energy has been destroyed. For example, if you boil a kettle of water, then turn out the flames under it, the water will slowly cool down to room temperature. The heat energy seems to have been destroyed or to have disappeared. But it hasn't. It has just spread out through the air. A bouncing ball also seems to lose energy as it rolls to a standstill. Its kinetic energy has been changed to heat energy. This happens as the ball pushes the air aside as it moves, and as it strikes the ground. The energy is still there – spreading out in the form of heat energy.

So we can say that energy never disappears. It changes from one form to another and always ends up as heat energy.

Sources of energy

Most of the energy that is used by men, and by plants and animals, comes from the Sun. Light from the Sun warms the atmosphere and heats the Earth's surface. Without this source of energy, the Earth would be a frozen, lifeless mass of ice and rock. Most of the light is absorbed by the sea and land. It sets molecules vibrating, and the land and sea become warm.

A tiny – but very important – part of sunlight is used by green plants. This is the energy upon which every animal and human being depends for life.

Plants contain a substance called chlorophyll, which can absorb sunlight. When this happens, the energy of the sunlight is used to join carbon dioxide from the air, with water from the soil. This chemical reaction produces starch and other complicated substances. The sunlight's energy is now stored as chemical energy in these substances. A few oxygen atoms are left over in each reaction, and these are given off into the air by the plants.

In this way, plants use the radiant energy from the Sun to make food and oxygen from carbon dioxide and water. The process is called photosynthesis. The food product contains the chemical energy we need to live (see: *photosynthesis*).

What happens when we get chemical energy from food we have eaten? The food contains atoms of the element carbon (which came from the carbon dioxide), and atoms of hydrogen (which came from the water). The carbon atoms and hydrogen atoms are attached by chemical bonds. In our bodies, the attachment is broken. The carbon atoms combine with oxygen atoms to form carbon dioxide. The hydrogen atoms combine with oxygen atoms to form water. And we end where we started – with carbon dioxide and water. But the chemical energy contained in the food has been released. The energy may appear as heat, or it may be stored as chemical energy in special molecules. These molecules are carried in the blood to the parts of the body where the energy is needed. Some of it is used in building up our tissues, some is changed into kinetic energy when we move our muscles. Even if we lie completely still, we use energy. We use it to breathe and to keep our blood circulating around our bodies. Some of the chemical energy is changed into electrical energy and used in our nerves. (The 'messages' that are sent along our nerves are electrical signals.) We need energy to keep warm.

Remember, the law of conservation of energy says that energy is never destroyed. Our bodies don't destroy energy, they just change it into different forms. Eventually, most of the energy we get from our food is changed into heat energy and radiates away from our bodies. If you hold your hand close to your forehead you may be able to feel the heat radiating from it.

We do not get our energy only from eating plants. We can, for example, get energy from eating meat. But the chemical energy we get from meat can be traced back to photosynthesis. Whatever animal we are eating got its energy from plants, or from eating other animals which ate plants. Some of that energy was stored away in the body of the animal, and it is this energy we are getting when we eat meat.

Man harnesses energy
Energy is the ability to do work, and therefore it follows that no work can be done without energy. Early man could use only the energy in his body – the energy he obtained from his food. He did not know how to harness the sources of energy around him, or how to put this energy to work.

The natural movements of the air and flowing water are both sources of energy. Both can easily be put to work. Perhaps these were the first natural sources of energy to be used by our ancestors. Imagine, for example, one of these primitive men using a current to help him float downstream on a log; or running with the wind to help him run faster.

Eventually man learned how to make fire. This meant that he could change the chemical energy stored in wood into heat energy and light energy. This was a very important step in man's development, for it meant that he could cook food, keep warm in winter and drive away wild animals from his home. It also led to man making metal tools and weapons.

The water wheel is one of the earliest machines used by man. The water pushes against the wheel, making it turn. The turning wheel can be put to work – for example, it can be made to turn a heavy stone which grinds grain into flour. The work comes from the kinetic energy of the flowing water.

The amount of kinetic energy in the water depends on the amount of water flowing, and the speed at which it flows. The faster the current, the faster the water wheel turns, and the greater the work done in each minute.

The energy of moving water is becoming more important as the years go by. Some parts of the world, such as areas of Scandinavia, Canada and the United States, rely on hydroelectric power to light and heat towns and drive the machinery in factories. 'Hydroelectricity' means 'electricity from water'. In a hydro-electric power station, flowing water turns huge water wheels called turbines. The turbines turn generators, so producing electricity.

Turbines must turn at a constant speed so that a constant regular electricity supply is produced. This means that the flow of water must be controlled in some way. This is done by building dams, like the Hoover Dam on the Colorado River, or the Aswan Dam in Egypt. These dams create lakes or 'store-houses' of water. Special gates allow water to flow from the lake to the turbines at a constant rate.

The kinetic energy of water – like the chemical energy of food – is derived from the energy of sunlight. The warmth of sunlight turns the waters of the seas and lakes into water vapour, which is water in gas form. The air over areas of water is damp. The damp air rises and is carried over high land by the winds. This is potential energy. As it rises, it condenses (changes back into drops of water or ice crystals). These drops or ice crystals have potential energy, because they are at a great height. But they do not fall as rain until they have grown to a certain size.

The rain collects in streams and rivers. Some of these rivers flow into lake 'store-houses' behind dams. And this water may be used to provide hydroelectric power. So there is a long chain of processes connecting the Sun's energy absorbed by seas and lakes and the electrical energy provided by the hydroelectric station.

The energy of moving air can also be traced back to the energy of sunlight. The Sun warms the air. Warm air rises, and colder air rushes in to take its place. These moving currents of air are the winds.

Wind energy can be made to work in much the same way as water energy. The moving air turns a wheel, which turns heavy grinding stones or operates some form of machinery. Windmills are still used today in some parts of the world – Holland for example. Usually, modern windmills have huge propellers and special gears which ensure the energy is used at a constant rate (see: *machine*). They are used mostly to pump water and produce electricity, but some are still used to grind grain.

Coal and energy

The chemical energy of wood also comes from the Sun. When wood is burnt this chemical energy is released in the form of heat energy and light energy. Millions of years ago huge forests covered the surface of the Earth. These forests changed the energy of the sunlight into chemical energy by photosynthesis, just as modern plants did. As the centuries passed, the forests died and were buried under layers of new vegetation. Eventually they came under tremendous heat and pressure and formed coal. But the chemical energy of the forests remained. When man discovered that this energy could be released by burning he found a vast new source of energy. Coal does not contain any more chemical energy than the wood from which it is formed. But it is a more convenient fuel, because it is dry and light compared with wood.

Scientists think that oil is the remains of tiny sea creatures. So oil too contains chemical energy from the Sun.

Though wood, coal and oil could be used for heat and light, it was a long time before they could be used to drive machinery. The problem was to change the chemical energy into kinetic energy in some way. The problem was solved with the invention of the steam engine.

About 250 years ago, engineers learned how to use steam to drive engines. This discovery meant that huge supplies of cheap energy were available for the first time. Factories were built, new industries sprang up and new methods of travel were invented. So much change took place in such a short time, that this period is called the Industrial Revolution.

In the last hundred years, man has used up supplies of energy at ever-increasing rates. Our oil and coal supplies will soon be used up, so scientists are searching for new sources of energy to replace them. There are many possibilities.

For example, scientists have learned how to make use of what is called nuclear energy. In some countries this nuclear energy is changed into electrical energy. It may also be possible to use a kind of hydrogen atom as a source of nuclear energy. There is so much hydrogen, particularly in the seas that, if a method is found, we would have energy supplies for thousands of years.

See: *nuclear energy, power*.

engineering

Modern living is completely dependent on engineering. Almost everything in our homes, from the kitchen stove to a packet of frozen food or a box of chocolates, owes its existence to engineers. Even the house itself was designed by engineers.

Civil engineering

Civil engineering has changed the face of our cities. Twentieth century engineering is replacing traditional building methods. Skyscrapers and highway overpasses are designed by civil engineers.

Concrete and steel have revolutionized building methods. Modern buildings are supported by a steel framework covered by glass or concrete. Others are built of concrete, reinforced with steel.

As men learned to use the new building materials they were able to build higher and higher buildings. But the new techniques are more complicated than the traditional building crafts that use bricks and mortar, wood or stone. Modern building is the work of engineers.

When a new block of flats is built, civil engineers survey the building site and decide exactly what kind of construction is suitable. They decide what materials to use and draw up plans for the building. They not only design the building itself; they plan the drainage, heating, water and air-conditioning systems.

Traditionally, buildings were designed by architects who did not need to know much about engineering. Nowadays, architects and engineers co-operate. Unfortunately, many ugly apartment blocks, offices and factories are engineered with little care for their appearance. Engineers and architects work together when they can, to make buildings with striking new designs. The Frank Lloyd Wright House in Pennsylvania shows just what can be achieved when the best architects and engineers get together.

Big construction jobs, like building a new town, need precise planning. This can involve building housing, shops and entertainment centres, all at once. A lot of time and money can be wasted by tackling the problem in a muddled way. Civil engineers use computers to help them. They use critical path programs to find out what order to do tasks in, and how to use manpower best. 'Critical path' programs enable the engineers to plan, in advance, just when to tackle each project and how much labour is available to work on each.

The Highway Department employs civil engineers to plan highways and transportation systems. Civil engineers also build dams, bridges, subways, oil-wells and pipe-lines.

Electrical and electronic engineering

When we switch on the light, electric heaters, the hairdryer or television, we are switching on electric power. Most of us take electricity very much for granted. We only have to flick a switch to produce electricity, as if by magic. But a power failure is looked on as a national disaster. We shiver in darkened homes, we can't watch T.V., father can't use his electric razor and mother can't cook. Old people may be in serious danger when their room heating fails. We suddenly realize how much we depend on electricity.

Electrical engineers design and operate the generators that produce electric power from coal, waterfalls or atomic energy. They design the systems that supply this power to our cities. Electrical machines in factories and the electrical circuits in cars are other examples of electrical engineering (see: *electricity*).

Radio, telephones, telegraphs and television are examples of electrical engineering applied to communications. This field overlaps with electronics. Electronics engineers design television and radar systems and controls for missiles and satellites. Computers are an important product of electronic engineering (see: *electronics*).

Mechanical engineering

In 1903, the Wright brothers invented the first aircraft, and called it Flyer. Flyer flew at 50 km/h (30 mph), about four metres (12 feet) above the ground. Only sixty-two years later, in 1965, a Lockheed YF-12A jet-plane made a world record speed of 3,330 km/h (2,070 mph).

In 1968, a Lockheed submarine set a record for the deepest dive by a submarine. It dived to 2,530 metres – over 2½ kilometres (1½ miles) below the surface of the sea. The US Navy bought its first submarine in 1900. It could submerge for only a few hours at a time. The submarines used in the Second World War had to surface every night to charge their batteries and renew their air supply. Today's nuclear submarines stay under water for 2 or 3 months at a time. In 1958, the US nuclear submarine, *Nautilus*, made history by crossing under the ice at the North Pole.

Mechanical engineering has made immense strides in this century. From Wright's Flyer, man has progressed to the Apollo Moon shots. Space travel was just a fairy-tale when your parents first went to school.

Mechanical engineers do not only make engines. They also design the car, ship or aircraft that the engine will move. Moving at high speed through the air creates problems in design.

Aeronautical engineers specialise in designing aircraft. They study the way air flows round the plane when it is flying. They do this in a wind tunnel. Blowing a stream of air fast past a stationary plane has the same effect on the plane as flying it fast through the air. The engineers make a scaled-down model of the body of the aircraft, an exact copy which is smaller. They put the model plane in the wind tunnel and watch what happens when a blast of air is blown down the tunnel. (See: *aerodynamics*.)

Not only planes must be 'streamlined'. Cars are made with sleek bodies. Ships and boats are streamlined to help them move through wind and water.

Production engineering

It takes mechanical engineers, electrical engineers and production engineers to design the machines that produce the box of chocolates you buy in a sweet shop. You may think that is a lot of people to make such a simple thing. You can probably make sweets yourself, but the chocolates we buy are made and packaged by the million – they are mass-produced. The machines used for mass production are designed and maintained by engineers.

In industrialised countries, like the British Isles, nearly everything that comes out of a factory is manufactured by machines. Manufactured used to mean made by hand, now it means made on a machine. Things made without machines are now so rare that they are usually labelled 'Hand-made' and sold at a higher price.

It is much quicker to make things on machines than by hand. The cost of labour is high in the British Isles. That means that it costs too much to pay a man to make something slowly by hand. It is much cheaper to build an expensive machine that can make the same thing a hundred times in the time a man could make it once. But in 'developing' countries, like India or China, far more things are hand-made. One of the reasons for this is that workers are paid very much less than in the UK. So most of the things you can buy in a British store are mass-produced. Production engineers plan the mass-production.

Suppose a factory is going to mass-produce a new sports car. First, the factory's production engineers need an exact description of every part of the car. They have to design machines to make each part. Some machines will just make a tiny name-plate, others will make large body panels, like the doors. So production engineers must know a lot about metals. They must design tools for cutting metals and for pressing them into shape.

As well as designing machines to make each part, the production engineers must arrange the machines in the motor-works so that they work together to produce a whole car. The right machines should be next to each other so that no time is wasted going back and forth. Suppose we are working out how to make a door. First the inside and outside panels must go from the metal-presses where they were made to the welding machine which fastens them together. Then they go on to the paint-spraying machine. Afterwards they go to the assembly line. At the same time, windows and window frames are being made. The doors, window frames and windows must all arrive at the assembly line at the right place and time to be fitted together.

So before building a motor-works, production engineers must work out exactly where each machine is going to go, and how the parts will go from one machine to the other. An efficient system will produce the cheapest cars.

The production engineers also may test their designs by making a miniature model of the factory. But the engineers often work first with computer programmers to find out how to arrange the machines and work-schedules in the motor-works.

Chemical engineering is a specialized branch of production engineering. Chemical engineers work out processes for mass-producing chemicals like fertilizers, detergents, medicines, synthetic fibres like nylon or plastic, and many other useful things. They also help design oil refineries and manufacturing processes for petroleum products.

When a scientist discovers a new product in the laboratory, he makes it in small amounts. He works with test tubes, jars and other rather small equipment. If the product is useful – if it is a new drug, for instance – large amounts must be made. The chemical engineer designs the system that can produce it in thousands of litres or tonnes.

Millions of litres of drinking water must be produced every day. City water supplies usually come from lakes or rivers. This dirty water must be purified before we can use it for washing or drinking. Chemical engineers design water purification systems.

Becoming an engineer
If you enjoy the sciences and mathematics, you might like to be an engineer. Most engineering courses in university take four years. Students spend the first two years studying mostly physics, mathematics and chemistry. This gives them time to decide which specialized engineering courses to study in the last two years at university. Most universities offer a wide choice, such as Aerospace Engineering, Naval Architecture and Marine Engineering, Mechanical Engineering, Electrical Engineering and Civil Engineering.
See: *electricity, electronics*.

ergonomics

No-one needs a left-handed coffee cup, because the standard model is as well suited to one handedness as the other. But if you were a left-handed golfer you really would appreciate a set of clubs that had been designed to suit you. And the same set would not be of much use to a right-handed golfer. The study of the relationship between man and his tools and machines that he uses is called ergonomics.

Of course, ergonomics is applied not just to rare problems of matching man to his machines. A housewife may find her electric sewing machine a great help. But if she has to stretch to reach the on/off switch she might develop backache. The science of ergonomics can be applied to every situation in which people operate mechanical systems.

The word ergonomics comes from Greek and means the law of work. It is applied in a broader sense to the study of man in relation to the machines and tools that he uses and the places in which he uses them.

Ergonomics therefore involves many of the traditionally separate fields of science. On the human side it involves physiology, psychology, statistics and anthropometry – the measurement of people's physical dimensions. On the machine side it involves engineering, physics and technology.

Ergonomics became a science during and after World War II. Previously designers had simply applied common sense to the job of making their products comfortable or easy to handle. In the war situation, pilots and the like found themselves in charge of highly sophisticated technological equipment for long periods and under the severe stress of their lives being in danger. This showed that common sense was not enough. In fact it never had been adequate but it took the war situation to reveal this.

Ergonomics should really have been recognized as an important science during the Industrial Revolution when machines suddenly took on a new significance in human society. But industrialists enjoyed such a boom in production as a result of using machinery that they were not greatly concerned about small losses in production and efficiency caused by bad ergonomics.

An example of 'pre-ergonomic' design is the type of engineering equipment that was widely used in industry for decades. Ergonomists who assessed the design of the machine reported that it was well suited for operation by a very broad-shouldered dwarf. However, the machines were not being operated by dwarfs but by ordinary people, who suffered from its bad design. Re-designing the lathes ergonomically to suit the operator resulted in better production, happier workers and a drop in absenteeism caused by minor ailments. Very often this is the aim of applying ergomonics to industry.

Ergonomics is also applied to safety and protecting man from his own machines. The motor car, for instance, can be a very useful machine. But if it is so designed that the driver cannot keep his eyes on the road and at the same time operate the vehicle's controls accurately and quickly, it becomes a menace. Ergonomics is an important part of automobile design.

Exactly the same ergonomic problems arise in the design of an aircraft and space rockets but the life and property at risk is on a greater scale. The pilot of the jumbo jet is responsible for the safety of as many as 400 passengers at a time. Ergonomists are responsible for designing the flight deck so that the pilot can see his dials clearly; so that he can reach the controls quickly and identify them correctly; and so that he is positioned and supported comfortably and does not suffer any unnecessary distracting physical strain.

The Apollo space missions were manned by only three astronauts. They were handling the most sophisticated technology that man has yet produced and were involved in the most advanced of scientific programmes.

Obviously they could not be expert in every aspect of this project; they had to be 'all-round' scientists. Only the best of ergonomic design could make it possible for only three all-rounders to operate at the frontiers of all the sciences.

Closer to home you can see the work of ergonomists in the design of domestic appliances. For instance, your mother probably uses a vacuum cleaner. When vacuum cleaners were first put on the market they were designed so that the machinery – the heaviest part – was pushed along the floor on the end of a long handle. The whole machine was pushed or pulled over the area that had to be cleaned. Ergonomics has changed this. Most modern machines have a light weight flexible tube extending from the suction end of the machine. The brush or nozzle at the end of the tube may be passed over the floor while the vacuum machine remains stationary. Not only is the cleaning of the floor made easier, the extension tube can easily be lifted to clean shelves, stairs, curtains, etc.

The chairs in your classrooms are also designed ergonomically. In each form they are made for children of the height that is average for that age group. The desks are designed to the same formula. So the desks of one form would not suit the chairs of another – and together they would suit none of the pupils.

Find out by doing

Is your kitchen sink well-designed ergonomically? Or is it too high, or too low, so that the people who use it regularly are likely to suffer backache? Are the storage shelves within easy reach? What improvements should be made? Your mother or father may have some helpful suggestions to make to you about the re-design.

feedback

A guitar player in a pop group. A refrigerator. A central heating system. Automatic machinery in a factory. An automatic pilot in an airplane. A cricketer hitting a run. All these different things have one thing in common – they use a process called feedback.

Let's see how feedback is used in an ordinary refrigerator. The purpose of a refrigerator is to keep food cool. Most have special switches which allow you to select the temperature you require.

Say you select a temperature of 4° Celsius (40°F). An electric motor pumps a cold liquid or gas around the walls of the refrigerator, thus lowering the temperature. When the temperature falls to 4°C, a switch called a thermostat, which is sensitive to temperature, turns the motor off. After a while, the temperature rises above 4°C and the thermostat switches the motor on again. By switching the motor on and off, a constant temperature of 4°C is obtained.

The thermostat measures the temperature inside the refrigerator and compares it with the set value of 4°C. According to the difference in the two values, the rate of cooling is changed. The information sensed by the thermostat is 'feedback' and used to operate a switching device on the 'input' – the motor.

A household central heating system works in much the same way. A pre-set thermostat measures the temperature in a room, and an electric pump is switched on or off according to the difference from the set temperature. The pump drives hot water or air through the pipes and radiators, thus warming the room.

The principle of feedback is very important in automatic machinery. For example, imagine that you own a factory which produces 50 kilogram bags of fertilizer mixture. Because labour is expensive, you have installed automatic machinery to measure out the ingredients, mix them together and pack the bags.

Every so often, you must take a bag from the 'production line' and check that the machine is doing its job properly. If anything goes wrong, you must stop the machine and change the control process in some way. This is not a very satisfactory checking method, and it takes up valuable production time. It is much better to use a feedback device and allow the machinery to check its own work.

Special instruments could measure the amount of each ingredient in the mixture. If the amounts vary, the information would be fed back to the machinery which controls the input. In this way the amounts of each ingredient can be automatically changed and adjusted.

Another feedback process could be installed to check that exactly 50 kilos of fertilizer are packed in each bag. Each bag would be weighed. Any variation in weight would be fed back to the packing machinery and adjustment would be made. The faulty bag would be rejected.

This basic idea holds for any process involving feedback. Information about an output is fed back to some device that controls the input. The input changes accordingly. Sometimes the input and output are quantities of materials – as they were in the fertilizer factory. Sometimes they are measurements of weight, temperature, electric current and so on.

Electric guitarists can use feedback to create exciting effects. The input of an electric guitar is the vibration of its string. The output is the sound produced by the 'speakers'. If the player holds his guitar close enough to a speaker, the sound vibrations that the speaker sends out will set the strings vibrating more strongly. This feedback will increase the speaker's sound output even more. The result is a drawn-out, whining note that the player can control by moving the guitar back and forth near the speaker.

Scientists and engineers are finding dozens of new ways of using the feedback process. For example, ships and aircraft can be kept on course using feedback. Information regarding any change in course, height or speed is picked up by special instruments. The information is fed back to more instruments which cause the control surfaces on the wings or rudder to move, so correcting the change.

Feedback is not only used in automatic machinery. It is also used in many processes in living things. For example, when a batsman hits a ball, he is using the principle of feedback. He sees the ball coming towards him and measures its position and speed by eye. Messages are passed along the optic nerve to the brain. The brain receives these messages, decodes them, and sends further messages, which instruct the muscles to move in certain ways. The batter begins to swing his bat.

As the ball moves through the air, a stream of messages pass to the brain and out again to the muscles. The whole process happens very quickly indeed, and is referred to as co-ordination.

Feedback is also used to give our bodies a built-in temperature control. Body temperature must keep as close to 37°C (98.4°F) as possible. Sensitive nerve endings in the skin send messages to the brain, telling it whether the body is too hot or too cold. If the body is too hot, small blood vessels near the surface of the skin expand. This allows more blood to flow and so more heat is given off. If the body is too cold, the opposite process takes place. The blood vessels shrink and less heat is lost through the body surface. In this case, the 'output' is the body temperature and the 'input' is the quantity of blood flowing through the blood vessels close to the surface of the skin. When the temperature of the body has been corrected the blood flow returns to normal.

gas

Have you ever wondered why water is 'wet' or why it 'flows'? Or why brick is 'hard' and has a definite shape? Or why you cannot 'see' the air around you, although it is certainly there?

The answer to these questions is that water, brick and air are three different states of matter. All matter is made up of tiny particles called atoms (see: *atom*). What a substance looks and behaves like depends upon the kinds of atom, and how they are arranged. The bubbles you see when you open a bottle of Coca Cola are matter in the gaseous state. They are bubbles of carbon dioxide. Air is a mixture of gases: oxygen, nitrogen, carbon dioxide and so on.

Scientists arrange· substances into three groups: solids, liquids and gases. These are sometimes called the states of matter. Brick and iron are examples of matter in the solid state. Water and petrol are examples of matter in the liquid state.

The atoms in a solid are packed close together, and stay in place. This means that a solid, such as a brick or an iron bar, has a definite shape. A solid also has a definite volume (it fills up a definite space).

The particles in a liquid are packed less closely together than those in a solid. They can move about, and we say that a liquid 'flows'. A liquid has no definite shape. It usually takes the shape of the container holding it. For example, a liquid in a tall thin glass takes up that shape. If we poured this liquid into a short fat glass, it would take up a short fat shape. But the volume of liquid wouldn't change. A liquid has a definite volume, although it doesn't have a definite shape.

The particles in a gas can move about and flow even more freely than the particles in a liquid. They spread out as widely as possible. If a quantity of gas is placed in a container, it spreads out and fills the whole container. If the same quantity of gas is placed in a container twice as large, it spreads out and fills that, too. The gas takes up twice as much space as it did before, so its volume has doubled. Therefore, a gas has no definite shape, nor has it a definite volume.

Liquids and gases are both states of matter that can flow, so they are grouped together as 'fluids'. Many people think of fluids as meaning only liquids, but air is a fluid, and so are all gases. When a gas is held in a container, the moving particles constantly strike the walls and bounce ·off – rather like balls striking the cushions of a pool table. Each time a particle strikes the wall of the container, it gives a little 'push'. The total effect of all these tiny pushes is called the pressure of the gas. You can feel the pressure if you try to squeeze a car tyre or a blown-up balloon.

When the volume of a gas increases, the particles have more space to move around in. Fewer particles strike the walls of the container at any time. This means that there are fewer 'pushes', and therefore the pressure of the gas is lower.

The reverse is also true. If a quantity of gas is moved from a large container to a small one, its volume decreases. The particles have less space to move around in. More of them strike the walls each second, and so the pressure is greater.

This relationship between pressure and volume was first discovered by an English scientist named Robert Boyle in 1660. He found that by halving the volume of a sample of air, he doubled the pressure. And by doubling the volume of the air, he halved the pressure. This idea became known as Boyle's Law. Although he used air in his experiments, the 'Law' can be applied to any gas. Boyle's Law states that: 'For a given amount of gas, the pressure multiplied by the volume equals a constant'. (A 'constant' is a number which always remains the same.)

Boyle's Law only works when the temperature of the gas stays the same. If a gas is heated, its particles move more quickly. They strike the walls of the container with greater force. This means that the pressure increases. The extra force of the particles tries to push the walls of the container back to make more space. If the walls can move (in the case of a rubber balloon, for example) then the volume of the gas can become greater.

Therefore, we can say that if the temperature of a gas rises, the volume increases if the pressure is kept the same. This is another of the laws that govern the behaviour of gases. It was first discovered by a French scientist named Jacques Charles in 1787, and is known as Charles's Law. Another scientist, working separately from Charles, made the same discovery a few years later. His name was Gay-Lussac, and so Charles's Law is sometimes called Gay-Lussac's Law.

If the temperature of a gas is lowered, the particles slow down and move less quickly. If the temperature is lowered enough, the particles tend to stay close to each other. They no longer fill the whole space of a container. When this happens, the gas has become a liquid. If the temperature is lowered still further, the particles become even more organized. The liquid becomes a solid.

The process can also go the other way. If the temperature of a solid substance is raised sufficiently, the solid melts. It becomes a liquid. If the temperature is raised even higher, the liquid becomes a gas. The most familiar example is ice, which melts to water, and then turns to steam, when heated. But even a metal like iron can be turned into a gas if the temperature is raised high enough. At very high temperatures all matter is in the form of gases. For example, the Sun contains no solid or liquid matter. It is a huge ball of very hot gases.

Scientists found that oxygen can combine

chemically with many different substances to form new compounds. They called this process oxidation, and the compounds were called oxides. They discovered that burning is really oxidation. When a material such as wood burns, the atoms of carbon and hydrogen in the wood combine with the atoms of oxygen in the air to form new compounds.

When oxidation occurs, energy is released, as heat. This is what happens when a fuel is burnt. We get a hot flame. But if oxidation occurs slowly we don't notice it happens. For example, rusting is slow oxidation. The atoms of iron combine with the atoms of oxygen to form 'rust'. The chemical name for rust is iron oxide.

Lavoisier's discovery that oxygen was present in air paved the way for many more chemical discoveries. Scientists have since discovered many other gases, and studied their properties.

Nitrogen is the most abundant gas on Earth. Air contains about four parts of nitrogen for every part of oxygen. Nitrogen has no colour, no taste and no smell. Nitrogen compounds are necessary for the growth of plants and animals, and so nitrogen is an important gas.

Carbon dioxide is another very important gas. It is a compound of carbon and the gas oxygen. Small amounts are present in the air, and it is also produced in our bodies. The air we breathe out contains carbon dioxide. Carbon dioxide is used by green plants in the food-making process (see: *photosynthesis*).

Hydrogen is rare as gas. But it combines well with other substances. It is found combined with oxygen in water. Hydrogen atoms are also present in all living things and in fuels such as wood and coal. Hydrogen gas is the lightest of the gases. It is also very dangerous and explodes easily when mixed with air.

geology

How were the Earth's mountains raised? What forces shape the surface of the land? The science of geology tries to answer these and similar questions.

The Ancient Greeks made many brilliant discoveries about the changing surface of the Earth. The historian Herodotus (5th century BC) realized that Egypt's soil had been laid down largely by the Nile River. He and other thinkers also knew that sea shells are frequently found far inland. They realized that the places where they are found must once have been covered by ancient seas. The shells belonged to creatures that had lived in those seas. Two thousand years later an Italian, Leonardo da Vinci, studied the rock that such shells were found in. He pointed out that it was a type of rock formed from the deposits laid down by seas, lakes and rivers. Similar remains, both of plant and animal life, are still being found in deep mines today.

Such remains are also found in mountainous areas. This suggests that not only has the sea advanced and retreated during the Earth's history, but that the land has been lifted to great heights. The English scientist Robert Hooke stated in the 17th century that the British Isles had once been beneath the sea and later lifted.

It is not only the bodies of animals and plants long since dead that can be preserved. Sometimes a hollow is left in stone in the shape of the creature. Sometimes certain parts of the creature's body are gradually replaced by rock and a kind of permanent copy of it is formed. These remains are called fossils.

Only in the early 19th century were fossil remains first put to full use as evidence of the age of rocks. Several investigators had studied and classified fossils and compared them with living plants and animals. But they had not noticed that each layer of rock has its own kind of fossils, different from the fossils in other layers. If rocks in two different places contain similar fossils, we can be sure that the rocks are about the same age. This means that fossils are a reliable way of dating the rocks they occur in.

This method was first used by William Smith in England, whose job was to study the ground in places where canals were to be built. He made a map of Britain showing that older rocks occur at the surface in the north-west of the country, and younger rocks in the south-east. Many of the names he made up are still in wide use in geology. For example, a certain part of the Earth's history is now called the Devonian Period (405-340 million years ago) because the rocks found in Devon were mostly laid down at that period in our planet's life. At the same time that Smith was working in England, Cuvier was making the same kind of study in France.

A rich procession of life was revealed over the years as rocks of different ages were studied. It was realized that the fossils represented the appearance, slow change and, often, disappearance of countless different species, over a period of millions of years. Man was only a recent arrival in this long story of life.

The oldest rocks containing many fossils are called Cambrian (from Cambria, a Latin name for Wales, where Smith first found rocks of this kind). We now know that the Cambrian period began over 570 million years ago. Yet this is less than a sixth of the age of the Earth's oldest rocks. Rocks older than the Cambrian are called Precambrian, and they contain a few remains of very simple creatures. Because they had no hard parts to their bodies these creatures rarely formed fossils. But there were probably many of these ancient living creatures by the beginning of the Cambrian.

The interval from about 570 million years ago to 225 million years ago is called the Paleozoic (meaning 'ancient life') Era. Fishes and the first land creatures appeared during this era.

The interval from the end of the Paleozoic to about 70 million years ago was named the Mesozoic (middle life) Era. It was the age of the dinosaurs, and mammals made their first appearance. The era in which we now live is the Cenozoic (recent life) Era. It extends from the end of the Mesozoic to the present. It has seen the appearance of the apes and of man.

Many kinds of rock appear in definite layers. The sides of the Grand Canyon clearly show where the Colorado River has cut through layer after layer. Rocks of this kind are called sedimentary because they were formed from sediments, which are the deposits laid down by water. Geologists have a special name for these rock layers. They call them strata (singular: stratum). The study of such rocks is called stratigraphy.

Sediments are laid down by lakes, rivers and seas. Streams carry fragments of stone along with them. Near the source of the river the pieces are large and rough-edged. As they are carried downstream the stones become worn by rolling over the river bed. They become smaller, smoother and rounder. At the mouth of the river the solid matter that the river carries along is mainly sand, mud and grains of clay.

In the oceans sediment is constantly settling to the sea floor. It may be sand or mud, washed into the sea by the rivers. It may be dissolved matter that cannot stay dissolved because the water has become cool. The remains of dead animals and plants, from the large to the microscopic, also settle.

Over many centuries, thick layers of the sediments build up. The deeper layers are pressed down by the huge weight of the layers above. The grains are 'cemented' together by clay or some other binding material. The sediments are changed into hard, firm rocks.

Sandy sediments form sandstone, and mud forms the kind of stone called shale. Plant and animal remains are fossilized. The remains of tiny shells become limestone, dolomite or chalk. During the geological period called the Cretaceous, thick layers of limestone and chalk were laid down in the world's oceans. Other remains of animals and plants hardened to form coal deposits. Great layers of coal were formed in the Carboniferous period.

Layers of sedimentary rock are level when they are first formed. And sometimes they remain undisturbed for millions of years, like the upper layers of the Grand Canyon today. But they may be distorted by huge pressures caused by Earth movements. Sometimes the layers are pushed up into huge folds. The Alps on the northern border of Italy, the Andes in South America, and the Appalachians and Rockies in North America, are all examples of this kind of mountain-building.

When a mountain is raised above the level of surrounding land, wind, rain and frost immediately begin to wear it down. The softer parts of the rock are worn away faster than the harder parts. The smooth outline of the original folds becomes jagged. But beneath the surface the smooth curves of the folding can still be seen in the rock layers.

Sometimes a whole block of surface rock may slip downwards. Or it may be pushed upwards by pressures from below the surface. Where this happens a great crack, known as a fault, appears in the strata. On each side of the fault the strata no longer line up.

Some mountain ranges are formed by huge blocks raised by faulting. The Sierra Nevada in the western United States is an example of such a range. Fault-block mountains usually have one side very much steeper than the other. In the case of the Sierra Nevada, the eastern face is the steeper.

Not all rocks are formed from sediments. Igneous rocks are another very important class. They are formed from hot molten rock from the depths of the Earth. This rock may reach the surface in the lava thrown up by volcanic eruptions. When this happens it often forms thick, 'ropey' masses of rock. Seen under the microscope the rock can be seen to be made up of tiny crystals. Solidified lava is often glassy. The crystals of this kind of rock are very small.

Molten rock may travel slowly upwards from hot, high-pressure zones to levels nearer the surface, where the temperature and pressure are lower. The rock cools and becomes solid underground. Centuries later the rock above may be worn away, and the igneous rock becomes visible at the surface.

Rock that cools underground does so very slowly. The crystals that form have time to grow large. Granite has grain-like crystals that are visible to the naked eye.

The lava that flows from volcanoes, together with cinders and ashes, builds up over long periods of time to form conical volcanic mountains (see: volcano).

When sedimentary rocks are heated by nearby molten rock, their chemical nature changes. Substances dissolved in the molten rock will pass into the changing sedimentary rock. Great pressures also change the nature of the sedimentary rocks. Asbestos is an example of rock formed by such processes. Rocks that have been changed in this way are called metamorphic.

One of the most important causes of the wearing away (erosion) of mountains in regions away from the tropics has been glaciers. These great 'rivers of ice' carve out U-shaped valleys, polishing the floor and sides smooth as they crawl along at speeds from a few centimetres to many metres per day.

The landscapes of the whole of northern Europe and much of North America show signs of erosion by glaciers. The deep valleys that lead into the sea on the coasts of Norway were hollowed out by ancient glaciers. We now know that during the last two million years the ice-caps have several times grown to many times their present size. They stretched down as far south as Germany and the northern United States during these 'ice ages'.

All the evidence about the past history of the Earth that has been discussed above is obtained by studies of the surface rocks. But geologists can 'X-ray' the Earth. They use, not real X-rays, but the shock waves sent out by earthquakes. Some of these waves travel through the Earth, before appearing at the surface, possibly thousands of kilometres away. These waves are studied at centres all over the world. From the speed of travel and paths followed by the waves it is possible to tell what kind of material the waves have travelled through.

Over short distances geologists can use the shock waves sent out by artificial 'earthquakes', made by explosive charges planted underground.

The study of earthquake waves is called seismology. Automatic 'moonquake' recorders set up by the Apollo astronauts, are now operating on the Moon. The information they are providing is helping scientists to understand the Moon's interior better.

Seismological studies have given us a fairly reliable picture of the structure of the Earth. They tell us that the rock of the continents forms a light, thin crust floating on heavier rock up to 65 kilometres (40 miles) thick. Below this layer, and stretching down about half-way to the centre of the Earth, is the mantle, probably made of a kind of rock called olivine. Very pure olivine sometimes occurs on the surface, and is valued as a gemstone. At the centre of the Earth is the molten core, 6,500 kilometres (4,000 miles) in diameter (half the diameter of the Earth). Probably the huge pressures existing this deep make the core solid at its very centre.

One of the earliest theories to explain the building of mountains suggested that the Earth began its existence as a ball of molten rock. As millions of years passed, the theory said, the Earth cooled and shrank. The outer skin 'wrinkled', and the wrinkles were mountains.

This theory is no longer held. We now know that radioactive materials are distributed throughout the Earth's interior. These are constantly giving out heat. Because of this radioactive heating, the temperature of our planet has probably not decreased for the last few thousand million years.

These radioactive materials provide the geologist with his most powerful method of dating rocks. Uranium, for example, is present in many rocks. In one second in any sample of uranium some atoms turn into atoms of lead, sending out radiation as they do so. The age of the rocks containing the uranium can be worked out by measuring the amount of lead present in a small sample of uranium. Another radioactive substance useful for age measurements is strontium, which turns into the element rubidium. The oldest rocks that have been dated by measuring their radioactivity are about four billion years old.

It is now believed that the most important force in the lifting of mountains is the collision of continents. The idea that continents move over the surface of the Earth was first seriously argued in 1915. But it was only in the 1950s that the theory began to be generally accepted. The evidence that was collected then depended on measurements of the magnetism of rocks. This rock magnetism is an important clue to the position of the rock when it was first formed. It can tell the geologist whether the rocks were formed near the poles or near the equator, and whether they have turned to lie in a new direction since then. Measurements made on seabed rock have shown that the floor of the great oceans are spreading. New sea floor material is constantly appearing in the centres of the ocean floor. So, for example, Europe and Africa have been drifting away from North and South America. Rock magnetism measurements and other lines of study show that over millions of years the continents have drifted around, collided and sometimes split up.

Geologists have discovered not only that the Earth's surface is constantly active in ways they had not dreamed of previously. They have extended their knowledge of the surface to new fields. They have mapped unexplored regions from the air. They have measured the depths of the oceans and found that the greatest mountain ranges in the world lie hidden beneath them. They have used space satellites to measure more accurately the Earth's shape. Now they are applying their knowledge to the study of the Moon and the planets. These studies may reveal more information about the origin of the Earth.

Find out by doing

Look out for signs in soil and rock that tell you about their history. You may see layers of rock in the walls of river valleys. If so, is there any evidence that the rock layer has shifted since it was laid down? Does the cross section of the valley leave the V-shape made by water, or the U-shape made by a glacier?

Can you recognize any igneous rock?

Compare what you find on river beds in the mountains with what you find near river mouths. How do you explain the difference?

Swirl fine sand, coarse sand and pebbles in a jar of water. Leave the jar for a few minutes. materials will settle in layers with the pebbles at the bottom and the finest particles at the top. Added clay will provide still smaller particles, but will take some hours to settle.

geometry

How do you tell a car from a truck? Or a table from a chair? Or a holly leaf from a maple leaf? You tell them apart because they have different shapes and sizes. Different kinds of shapes and sizes are all we see in a black and white photo. Yet it is usually all we need to recognize or identify things in the photo.

Geometry is the mathematics of shape and size. It is part of our everyday lives. Geometry helps us fit different shapes together. No one could design a car, airplane or sky-scraper without knowing a lot about geometry.

What do you know about shapes and sizes? A baseball and a basketball do not look the same. They are the same shape but a basketball is bigger. In mathematics, things that are the same shape are called 'similar'. Which of these are similar: an egg and an orange; a violin and a double bass; a model jumbo jet and a real jumbo jet?

A model airplane is a 'scale model' of a real airplane. A scale model is exactly similar, but it is a different size. If the real airplane is 600 times longer than the model, it must be 600 times wider as well. Every part of the plane is 600 times bigger than the same part of the model.

What shapes can you make with toothpicks? A ring of three toothpicks, placed so that each end of each toothpick is touching an end of another, makes a triangle. Four toothpicks make a square. Five make a pentagon and six make a hexagon. All these shapes are called 'polygons'. Polygon means 'with many corners'. The polygons you make with toothpicks are 'regular' – that is each side is the same length as the other. The US Department of Defence is in a building called the Pentagon because it is pentagon-shaped (five-sided).

Trace out the polygons (triangles, squares, rectangles, pentagons and hexagons) in the diagram and cut them out in stiff paper. Make at least six of each. If possible, use a different colour of paper for each kind of polygon. Can you fit the squares together without leaving any spaces in between? What polygons can you make by fitting squares or triangles together? See what patterns you can make by fitting polygons together, without leaving any gaps between them.

Who is the tallest person in your family? You can easily find out, using a ruler or tape-measure. But which is the biggest room in your home? Can you say which is the next biggest and so on, until you reach the smallest? That's not so easy because rooms are all sorts of shapes. How do you tell whether a rectangular room is bigger than a square one?

When we measure length we divide it up into many units–such as centimetres and metres. We measure a surface – such as a floor – in the same way. The size of a surface is called an 'area'. We measure an area by dividing it up into lots of little areas. We could choose a square floor tile as one unit of area. Suppose 100 floor tiles cover the square floor. And only 64 floor tiles cover the rectangular floor. The square floor is bigger. We measured the area by dividing it into lots of little squares and counting them up.

Squares are a good shape for comparing floor sizes. But how do you compare the areas of two triangles? Draw two large triangles and use your paper squares to see which is bigger. How much larger is it? Are you sure that your answer is right? You cannot be sure because you cannot completely fill a triangle with squares. There is always some space left over. But you can completely fill a triangle with little triangles.

How can you compare the areas of a square and a triangle? You can cover the square with little squares and cover the triangle with little triangles. But the little squares must be the same size as the little triangles. They must have the same area. A square with one-centimetre sides has an area of one 'square centimetre'. A triangle with each side about one-and-a-half centimetres long has an area of one square centimetre. They are both made of one square centimetre of paper. This is useful for measuring the area of triangles and some other polygons.

You need not cut out lots of little squares and triangles to measure areas. You can draw them on the area to be measured with a pencil. This is called a 'grid'.

How many things did you turn today? You probably turned the doorknob, the knob on the radio or TV and the cap on your toothpaste tube. And you must have turned yourself round several times. How do we measure turns?

You make a whole turn when you turn all the way round so that you face the same way again. The hour hand of a clock makes a whole turn when it goes from midday to midnight. It makes a half-turn between twelve and six o'clock. And it makes a quarter turn between twelve and three o'clock.

We use the word 'angle' for the amount of turning. A 'right angle' is another name for a quarter turn. An 'acute angle' is smaller than a quarter turn. A turn bigger than a quarter turn is called an 'obtuse angle'.

In geometry we measure small turns in 'degrees'. There are 360 degrees in a circle or whole turn. We can also measure corners in degrees. A quarter turn makes the corner of a square. How many degrees is that?

Look at yourself in the mirror. How is your reflection different from the way other people see you? Is your hair parted on the same side? Move your right hand. Which hand did your reflection move?

Your reflection is a 'mirror image' of you. It is just like you, but the wrong way round. Similarly, your left side is a mirror image of your right side. Both sides have one eye, ear, leg and arm. But your right eye is on the right side of your nose and your left eye is on the left side of your nose. Another word for having one half of something the mirror image of the other half is 'symmetry'. Left and right symmetry is called 'bilateral symmetry'.

How many places can you put a fold down the middle of a sweater, so that it folds exactly in half? There is only one possibility – along the midline from top to bottom. A sweater has 'one-fold' symmetry. How many ways can you fold a square handkerchief exactly in half? The answer is four. Find out how many ways you can fold your paper polygons in half.

Polygons are shapes that you can draw on paper. They are flat. The mathematical name for a flat shape is a 'plane figure'. But the things that we handle – like cups, toys or animals – are solid shapes. Plane figures have width and length but no thickness. Solid shapes have thickness.

A polygon with thickness is called a 'polyhedron'. Polyhedron means 'with many faces'. Each face (side) of a polyhedron is a polygon. There are special names for different kinds of polyhedron. A square box is a 'cube'. A cube is a polyhedron with six square faces. Some milk cartons are tetrahedrons. A tetrahedron is a polyhedron with four sides – all triangles.

Why do we use some solid shapes more than others? Some shapes fit together better. Bricks are a good shape for building because they fit together exactly. And they stack together without falling down. Square and rectangular boxes are good for packaging because they pack into a container without leaving any gaps. No space is wasted. And tetrahedrons pack together without wasting any space.

Most cans are 'cylinders'. They have circular ends. Cylinders pack well but they waste space. You cannot fit circles together without leaving space between them. But we do use cylindrical cans. This is partly because they are easy to open. It is hard to turn a can opener round corners. But it is also because they are easy to make and handle. You can make a paper cylinder by just joining opposite edges of a sheet of paper together.

Solids can be solid all through – like a brick. You can make this kind of solid out of plasticine. Or solids can be hollow – like a can or a box. How can you make a hollow cube out of stiff paper? You could cut out six identical squares and join them together. But you could more easily make a cube by cutting the correct shape out of paper and folding it. Open out a carton and see how it is made. There are several possible ways. Each shape that can be folded to make a cube is called a 'net' of a cube.

Nets are useful for finding the shortest distance between points on different sides of a solid. The net is flat, so you can join the two spots with a straight line.

You can make a polyhedron 'skeleton' with drinking straws. Use a straw for each edge. A cube has twelve edges so you need twelve straws. Three straws meet at each corner. You can put pipecleaners in the straws to make the corner joints.

The area of a solid is the surface size – the amount of paper you need to make a net. Volume is the amount of solid size – the amount of plasticine you would need to make a solid. Volume can also tell us how much we can put inside a hollow solid.

When you go to a supermarket, you can see bottles and packages of all shapes and sizes. Can you guess which bottle contains more shampoo? Does the tall, flat bottle really hold more than the short round bottle? Which has the greater volume? We can easily make mistakes when comparing the volumes of differently shaped bottles. It is safest to read the labels.

You can compare the volume of two bottles by filling one with water and emptying it into the other. How many tumblers fill a pitcher? Do your tumblers hold more than your teacups. It is surprising how some shapes look bigger than they really are.

How do we measure volume? We divide the volume into lots of little volumes and count them up. We could divide a cube into lots of little cubes. We could choose a sugar cube as our unit of volume. Then if 144 sugar cubes fill a small box, its volume is 144 sugar cubes. But measuring a volume in sugar cubes does not help us much. So we measure volumes in cubic centimetres or cubic metres. A cubic metre is the volume of a cube that has each side one metre long. One hundred layers of one-centimetre cubes could be stacked in the big cube. Each layer would contain 100 rows of 100 cubes. Therefore you can put $100 \times 100 \times 100 = 1,000,000$ one centimetre cubes in a one-metre cube.

Geometry has been used by man for many thousands of years. In Ancient Babylonia and Egypt, geometrical knowledge was applied to practical problems of land measurement and building. But in Ancient Greece geometry was studied as an independent subject, though much of the knowledge gained was useful to builders and land surveyors.

In the third century BC the Greek mathematician Euclid organized the knowledge that he and previous geometers had gained into a deductive science. A deductive science is one in which all statements are proved, step by step, from a small number of basic statements.

Some of Euclid's basic statements were definitions, like: 'a point is that which has no size'. Others were statements that Euclid thought were obvious and could not be proved from any simpler statement. He called these statements postulates. An example of a postulate is: 'only one line can be drawn through any point parallel to a given straight line'.

From a small number of definitions and postulates Euclid was able to prove a huge number of geometrical facts.

The facts that Euclid proved from his basic definitions and postulates he called theorems.

Some of Euclid's 'obvious' postulates were later challenged. Alternative systems of geometry were devised using different assumptions. Different systems correspond to different physical environments. As in all mathematics what can be proved depends on the definitions and postulates you start from.

Geometry is concerned with distances and angles, and hence with the shapes of things. There is a modern branch of mathematics called topology, that is similar to geometry in some ways, but is not concerned with these things.

Imagine drawing a figure 8 on a flat sheet of rubber, not paper. Then you start stretching and squeezing the rubber. The shape of the figure changes completely, and so does its size. Only one thing about it stays the same. Whatever shape the 8 has become, there is always a place where two lines cross. The centre point of the 8 is still recognizable. It is important not to cut or tear the sheet. Otherwise the cross point could be removed by cutting the 8 through the middle.

Other properties stay the same during all these changes. Suppose six points are marked round the 8 and numbered in order. Their order will stay the same through all the changes. The line will never run through the points in the order 1, 3, 2, 4, 6, 5, for example.

Topology is interested in the properties that do not change – things like the ordering of points and the crossing points of lines.

Solid objects can be imagined to change in shape by being squeezed or stretched. Such a change would turn a basketball into a football shape. Topologically these two shapes are 'equivalent'. But a sphere could never be changed into a flat plane. A hole would need to be made at some point. The surface remaining would then need to be stretched over the plane. See: *algebra*, *topology*.

gravity

The Earth's gravity is the force that pulls everything near the Earth towards its centre. The oceans, the air and all objects on the surface are held there by gravity. The Moon and orbiting spacecraft are held in their paths by the Earth's gravity.

But not only the Earth has gravitational influence. Any quantity of matter – a mountain, a boulder, a pin, even an atom – exerts gravitational force on other matter. The Sun holds the Earth and the other planets in their orbits by its gravitational attraction. The Sun belongs to a great system of stars, gas and dust called the Galaxy, which is held together by the gravitational forces of its members.

The gravitation force of an object depends on the mass of the object – that is, on the amount of matter of which it is composed. For example, the Sun's mass is greater than that of the Earth, so the Sun's gravitational attraction is greater than that of the Earth.

We describe the mass of objects as being so many pounds or so many kilograms. One kilogram is just over two pounds. The more mass an object has, the more resistance it has to being moved. A stalled ten-tonne truck needs a harder push to get it moving on a level road than does a family car. This is true even if the wheels are turning smoothly. We say that the truck has a greater mass than the car. A locomotive has a greater mass still. It is harder to move than either the truck or the car.

The mass of an object does not depend on its location. It would be the same on the surface of the Moon or any of the planets. You would need just as great an effort to start the truck rolling on a level road on the Moon as on Earth.

Yet the weight of a quantity of matter does depend on where it is. The car, truck and locomotive would all weigh much less on the Moon than they do on Earth. In fact they would have only one-sixth their Earth weight.

The Earth has a greater gravitational pull on objects with a large mass than objects that have a small mass. It pulls the locomotive towards itself with a greater force than the truck, and it pulls the truck with a greater force than the car. This greater force shows itself in many ways. A more powerful crane is needed to lift the locomotive than the truck. The truck uses more energy in climbing a hill than the car does.

The strength of the Earth's pull on an object is measured by weighing machines such as spring balances. Scientists describe this force in terms of a unit called the newton. Half a kilo of vegetables, or half a kilo of sweets, is pulled towards the Earth with a force of about five newtons. This force is called the object's weight.

The Moon has a smaller gravitational attraction than the Earth for objects on its surface. The locomotive, car and truck would all weigh less on the Moon. But the locomotive would still weigh more than the truck, and the truck more than the car.

The mass of an object determines not only how strongly it is attracted by other objects, but also how strongly it attracts them. More massive objects have stronger gravitational pulls. The Earth has a stronger pull than the Moon because the Earth is more massive. The Sun has a still stronger pull, because it has a third of a million times as much mass as the Earth.

So the weight of an object on the surface of a planet depends on its own mass and on the planet's mass.

While an apple weighing 100 grams is being pulled downward by the Earth, the apple is pulling the Earth upward. In fact, the two forces are exactly equal. The Earth's strong gravity is acting on the small mass of the apple. The apple's small gravity is acting on the huge mass of the Earth. The result is that the Earth pulls the apple with just the same force as the apple pulls the Earth. If the apple starts to fall from the tree to the ground, the Earth starts to 'fall' upwards to meet the apple. But the massive Earth is shifted by an amount so tiny that the movement could never be detected.

The Moon also pulls the Earth, with a force equal to the pull of the Earth's gravity on the Moon. This is huge, and has a much greater effect on the Earth than does the pull of the apple. The Earth 'wobbles' slightly as the Moon goes round it each month. The Moon's attraction also makes the oceans rise slightly, roughly along the Earth-Moon line. This results in daily changes in sea level of several metres, which we call the tides.

We have seen earlier that a truck weighs more than a car because it has more mass.

Because it has more mass, the truck has a stronger gravitational attraction for all other objects than does the car. So it is possible to 'weigh' the truck and the car by measuring how strongly they attract other things.

It would be easier to drive the truck onto a large weighing machine. But it is not possible to do this with a mountain. So a mountain is 'weighed' by finding out how strongly it attracts nearby things. One way of doing this is to measure how much it pulls a nearby hanging weight away from the true vertical.

People often think that heavy objects fall faster than light ones. And at first sight this seems true of the things we come across every day. Very light things, such as feathers, paper, balsa wood, take longer to reach the ground than heavy objects such as bricks. But the air interferes to some extent with the fall of an object. The amount of air resistance depends on the shape of the falling object. This resistance has a greater slowing effect on light things than on heavy things of the same shape. But when a light object and a heavy object are allowed to fall together in a container out of which the air has been pumped, they reach the bottom at the same time. On the Moon, which is airless, heavy and light objects take the same time to fall a given distance.

A falling object accelerates – picks up speed (see: *acceleration*). Near the Earth's surface falling objects gain an extra 975 centimetres (32 feet) per second of speed in every second (ignoring air resistance). They are said to accelerate at 975 centimetres per second per second.

If an object – any object – were fired from the Earth's surface with a speed of 40,000 kph (25,000 mph) – 11 kilometres per second – it would never stop travelling as long as it did not hit anything. It would never need another boost. This is called the Earth's escape speed. The escape speed from Mars is only 5 kps (3 mps), and from the Moon, only two and a half kilometres per second.

When an Apollo spacecraft is on the right course for the Moon, its engines are turned off. It coasts towards the Moon, but the craft is gradually slowed down by the Earth's gravity.

If the craft came to a stop it would begin to fall back toward the Earth. But before this happens, it reaches a point where the Moon's gravity is stronger than the Earth's. It now begins to fall toward the Moon. During the whole of this time, the engines are not needed, except perhaps for small corrections to the craft's course. Gravity is the only influence on the spaceship's movements. This condition is called 'free-fall'.

In free fall, the craft and its crew move together, just as falling objects do on Earth (if there is no air resistance). So the crew have no weight. On the Earth the ground held them up.

In space when the rocket was firing, the motors were pushing the craft and the crew along. But in free fall nothing is 'holding up' the crew. There is a condition of weightlessness.

It was in 1687 that Sir Isaac Newton published his theory of gravitation. He was able to explain the tides and the movements of the planets and the Moon. Nothing fundamental was added to his theory for over 200 years.

Then, in this century, Albert Einstein revolutionized our knowledge and concept of gravity. He showed that gravity would affect measurements of space and time themselves. And he showed that light rays would be bent by gravity. His prediction was confirmed by astronomers. They observed stars lying almost in the same direction as the Sun. As the Sun passed in front of them, their light was bent into new paths. This made the stars look as if they were lying in new positions. Since then other predictions of Einstein have been confirmed.

Scientists have now observed the effect of the Earth's gravity on subatomic particles. In 1979 astronomers observed a double image of a star-like body called a quasar. Many believe that the double image was formed by the action of a 'gravitational lens' – a heavy object such as a galaxy that bends and focuses the light from the quasar.

See: *acceleration, astronomy, ballistics.*

Find out by doing

Arrange two poles as shown in the diagram, so that they point together and the closer ends are lower. Put a beach ball on the poles. You may be surprised to see which way it rolls. Look closer. Is the ball really rolling uphill?

heat

Until about 1800 scientists thought heat was a fluid, like water or air. They called the fluid 'caloric'. Because nobody had seen it they decided that caloric must be invisible. And because things weighed the same hot and cold, caloric must be weightless as well as invisible. According to this theory, caloric was present in all substances, and how hot they were depended on the amount of caloric that they possessed.

The caloric theory was disputed as long ago as 1620 by Francis Bacon. But it was not until the end of the 18th century that Benjamin Thompson, an American scientist, carried out experiments to prove that heat could be manufactured in unlimited quantity.

This remarkable man was created Count Rumford by the Bavarian government in return for reorganizing their army. For a while he was in charge of an arsenal. In the arsenal he investigated the heat that developed when the barrel of a cannon was being bored out. He could produce enough heat to boil water in a kettle on the cannon. Furthermore, the water went on boiling as long as the borer worked.

Rumford concluded that the turning movement of the borer was being turned into heat, and that there was no limit to the amount of heat that could be so produced. This suggested that heat is actually a form of motion.

At about the same time Humphry Davy, the famous English chemist, performed a similar experiment. He discovered that blocks of ice melted if they were rubbed against each other. He decided that the rubbing motion was being turned into heat, which was melting the ice.

The caloric theory was not abandoned until precise experiments had been made over many years. Many of the experiments were done during the 1840s by James Prescott Joule, an English physicist. His work was so important that we have named a unit of energy after him – the joule.

The idea that heat is a form of motion is an old one. The experiments of Rumford, Davy and those who came after them were the first experimental evidence for the theory.

We now call energy of motion 'kinetic' energy (see: *energy*). If you throw a ball at a window, the kinetic energy in the moving ball is what breaks the glass. All matter is made up of countless tiny particles called atoms. In some substances the atoms occur singly. In others they form groups, called molecules. Atoms are moving all the time and so they, too, have kinetic energy. The heat energy of any object is simply the kinetic energy of its moving atoms. The faster they move, the hotter the body is.

In the end, every method of creating heat turns out to be a way of making the atoms move faster. When you put a red hot poker in water the water gets hotter. This is because the fast-moving atoms in the poker give the atoms of the water next to them a hard push, and that starts them moving fast too.

Heat energy can be changed into other forms of energy. The heat in the boiler of an old-fashioned steam locomotive is converted to mechanical energy to drive the train. The heat generated by the burning fuel in a jet or rocket engine is turned into the kinetic energy of the hot gases, which as they blast out backwards, push the craft forward. The change can happen the opposite way round, for other kinds of energy can be changed into heat. For example, when an electric heater is switched on electrical energy is turned into heat and light.

It is important to understand the difference between heat and temperature.

Try boiling two identical saucepans, one containing a little water, and the other containing a lot of water. When boiling, the water in each will be at the same temperature of 100° Celsius. But the larger quantity of water will have taken longer to reach boiling point. This is another way of saying it needed more heat to make it boil. Temperature changes with the speed at which the individual molecules are moving, in other words, with their individual kinetic energy. The heat contained in the water is the sum of the kinetic energies of all the moving molecules in the water. The larger quantity of water contains more heat. We shall see that heat and temperature are measured in different ways.

The amount of heat needed to raise the temperature of a substance by one degree Celsius is its 'heat capacity'. The larger amount of water has the larger heat capacity.

A gram of copper needs more heat to raise its temperature by one degree Celsius than does the same weight of platinum. The amount of heat needed to raise the temperature of one gram of any substance by one degree Celsius is called the 'specific heat capacity' of that substance.

Heating a substance can do more than change its temperature. It can change the pattern in which the atoms of the substance are arranged. In solids the individual molecules are not free to wander around, though they can vibrate around a fixed position. The molecules may form a geometrical pattern, as in a crystal. Or there may be no order or arrangement, as in solids like glass. If, however, the solid is heated the molecules will vibrate faster, meaning that the temperature is rising. Usually the atoms move farther apart, too, so that the solid grows larger. But at a certain temperature the vibrations become so strong that the atoms are no longer bound to fixed places in the substance. They can move around and over each other. In an undisturbed glass of water, two molecules that are closer at one time may be far apart a short time later. But the spacing between molecules of a liquid is always small. The atoms of a liquid are constantly vibrating, as in a solid.

As the solid turns into a liquid, it takes in heat, but its temperature does not change. As ice melts, for example, it remains at 0° Celsius. If the heating continues when the ice has turned entirely into water, the temperature of the water will rise.

Molecules are constantly escaping from the surface of a liquid. Water left in a dish for a time will disappear as it turns into water vapour in the air. As the liquid is warmed, molecules escape at a greater rate. A temperature is reached at which the molecules in the liquid cannot stay together. Boiling begins, and the liquid turns into gas.

In the gas state, the molecules of the substance move around independently of each other, moving through the whole available space.

While a liquid is turning into a gas, it is taking in heat. But the temperature stays the same. The temperature of boiling water is 100° Celsius (at normal atmospheric pressure).

Solids expand when they are heated. This is why engineers leave spaces between the concrete blocks of a freeway. Otherwise the blocks would expand in the heat of the Sun and press against each other, causing buckling.

You can see an increase of size with temperature most obviously if you put a mercury thermometer in hot water. As the mercury grows hotter, its atoms move faster. The mercury expands and rises up the stem of the thermometer.

The rule that substances expand when heated, and contract when cooled, has some exceptions. When water is cooled from 100°C, it contracts until it reaches a temperature of about 4°C. Then it expands as it is cooled to 0°C. There is a further expansion as it freezes. So a given weight of ice occupies more space than the same weight of water. For this reason ice floats in water.

As we have seen, heat can be changed into other forms of energy, and it can be obtained from other forms of energy. The branch of science called 'thermodynamics' deals with changes from one sort of energy to another. The rules that govern such changes are known as the laws of thermodynamics.

The first law of thermodynamics states that energy may change its form but that in doing so no energy is created or lost. This is called conservation of energy. In Rumford's experiments one form of energy – mechanical energy provided by the cannon-borer's power source – was turned into heat. A steam engine or petrol engine does the reverse. It takes a certain amount of heat and makes it do mechanical work, by driving a vehicle or lifting loads. But in all cases, the total amount of energy in its different forms is the same after any process as it was before. Energy cannot be created or destroyed and the total amount in the universe does not change. So the first law of thermodynamics is also known as the law of conservation of energy.

Heat will not flow of its own accord from a cooler place to a hotter one. This is the second law of thermodynamics, and its workings can be seen in everyday life. If a hot plate is placed on a cold table, heat cannot flow from the table to make the plate even hotter. The table will receive heat from the plate until both are at the same temperature. If the plate is very hot the rate of cooling will be much faster than if there is only a slight difference of temperature between the two bodies.

When the hot plate and the cool table are in contact, their temperatures even out. The degree of 'evenness' of temperature in bodies is called entropy. The entropy of the plate and the table is low when they are at different temperatures. It increases as they gradually come to the same temperature. This is true of all processes, both natural and artificial. The entropy of the universe never decreases during a process (though it may stay the same). In fact, the second law can be stated in the form: 'the total entropy of the universe is constantly increasing'. (See: *universe*.)

Although heat will not flow the 'wrong' way – from a cold object to a hot one – of its own accord, it can be forced to do so. This is what a refrigerator does. Your household refrigerator constantly draws heat from the air in the cold compartment. This heat passes into the air of the room. So there is a transfer of heat from the lower temperature of the refrigerator to the higher temperature of the room.

Energy of movement – kinetic energy – is converted to heat according to the law of conservation of energy. Friction always generates heat. In Rumford's experiments with the cannon, it was friction that was creating the heat. You can see it happen when the tyres of racing cars smoke as they spin wildly against the tarmac at the start of a race. You can even feel the heat caused by friction when you rub your hands together. This heat is frequently a nuisance, and we go to great lengths to reduce it by lubricating engine surfaces that rub against one another.

Another way of converting kinetic energy to heat is by hammering or percussion. This is how people used to make fire. They struck a flint so that the fragment, made white hot by the blow, fell onto dry tinder, which caught fire.

We cannot hammer a gas, but we can compress it and that, too, leads to a rise in temperature. The energy used to compress the gas is changed to heat. In a diesel engine the heat produced is so great that the mixture of air and petrol vapour in the cylinder explodes and drives the piston.

These are all ways in which we convert other forms of energy to heat. But they are not sources of heat. Some heat comes to us from the molten core of the Earth itself. It appears in hot geysers, in really deep mines, and, most vividly, in volcanos sending out red-hot masses of lava.

The stars give out huge quantities of heat. They are masses of intensely hot gas, just as our Sun is. But they are so far away from the Earth that very little of their heat reaches us (see: *star*). The Sun is not a specially hot star, but it is comparatively close – only 93 million miles away. Nearly all our warmth comes to us from the Sun, directly or indirectly. It comes directly in the warmth of sunlight. But it also comes to us indirectly, whenever we burn coal or oil.

Coal and oil were formed from the remains of plants that grew long ago. When the plants were alive they stored the energy of sunlight in their tissues (see: *photosynthesis*). When we burn them we get back that energy.

When we knock steel against flint to make a spark we are using our own muscular energy. But we have to eat to get that energy. Everything we eat grew by obtaining energy from the Sun, or by eating something else that did so.

Even hydroelectric power depends on energy from the Sun. Hydroelectric power stations are driven by flowing water in rivers and waterfalls. The rivers are fed by rain, and rainwater is formed from water vapour in the air. This vapour is created as lakes and seas are warmed by the sunlight. So it is energy from sunlight that is raising this huge weight of water. We get back a tiny fraction of the energy in hydroelectric power stations as the water finds its way back to the seas.

The only energy we use that does not come from the Sun, either now or in the past, is nuclear energy. This comes from the very centres of atoms such as uranium or hydrogen. It was 'locked into' these atoms when they were created, billions of years ago.

Heat is only useful when it moves. You can boil water only because the heat from the stove moves to the kettle. On a larger scale, we have seen that the Sun is the source of nearly all our heat, but this is only because the Sun's heat can travel to the Earth. There are three ways in which heat can travel.

The first way heat travels is by 'radiation', that is, in invisible waves through space or through air. Heat waves are transmitted from the Sun just as light waves are. Light waves and heat waves travel at the same speed of 299,000 kilometres (186,000 miles) per second. Heat and light waves are, in fact, identical except for their wavelengths. The length of a wave is the distance from one wave peak to the next. Heat waves are longer than the longest visible light waves. Because they lie beyond red light in the wavelength scale they are called 'infrared' waves. Some of the heat from an open fire travels in the same way as the light, so we do not have to touch the fire to feel its warmth. It is described as 'radiant heat'.

Another way in which heat travels is by 'conduction'. This happens when two bodies are touching one another. We have seen how a red-hot poker warms water when the agitated atoms of the poker push the water molecules into motion. If the poker is put in the fire the heat from the fire will eventually travel right up to the handle in the same way. Some materials, such as the metals, are good conductors of heat. Others are not. Substances that come from living things, like wood, are generally not good conductors. The end of a stick placed in the same fire as the poker would probably burst into flames before the end you were holding even became warm.

The third way in which heat travels is by 'convection'. Warm air rises and this is convection. We know that heat causes molecules to move apart, and because there is more space between them the warm air is less dense than cold air, and floats upward. Sparks from a bonfire often fly upward, borne on the currents of hot air. Heat movement by convection is possible only with liquids and gases.

Heat energy cannot be picked up and weighed, or measured with a ruler. But we need a unit of measurement. The unit of measurement of heat energy was once the 'calorie'. It is the amount of heat required to raise the temperature of one gram of water by one degree Celsius.

Scientists and engineers now prefer to measure heat in joules, the same units used for all other forms of energy. One calorie is just over four joules. (The calories we count in diets are actually kilocalories. A kilocalorie is equal to one thousand calories.)

Many scales of temperature have been devised. Some are based on the difference between the freezing and boiling points of water at a definite atmospheric pressure. (Both the freezing point and boiling point of water depend on the pressure of the air.) Sir Isaac Newton devised a scale from 0° to 12°, but this was too rough to measure small variations in temperature. The first really practical scale was announced to the world in 1724 by Gabriel Fahrenheit, a German physicist. It was named after him. The Fahrenheit scale has 32° as the freezing point of water and 212° as its boiling point.

Another scale, used throughout the world, runs from 0° to 100° and was proposed by Anders Celsius, a Swedish professor, in 1742. He called it the Centigrade (meaning '100 degrees') scale. It is still often known by that name, although it is officially renamed the Celsius scale.

When dealing with very low temperatures we avoid negative numbers by using the Kelvin scale, named after Lord Kelvin, the great 19th century British scientist. One unit of the scale is called a degree Kelvin (°K), or simply a kelvin. It is equal to a Celsius degree. On this scale water freezes at 273 kelvins and boils at 373 kelvins. So any temperature can be converted from the Celsius scale to the Kelvin scale simply by adding 273. The coldest temperature that can exist in theory is 0 kelvins. At

this point the movement of molecules would come almost to a stop. This temperature is called 'absolute zero' and is equivalent to -273.2°C, or -459.7°F. Another law of thermodynamics states that absolute zero can never be reached, though experiments have come within a fraction of a degree of achieving it. The coldest temperature in nature is about 3 kelvins for interstellar dust.

For most everyday purposes we measure temperature with a thermometer. Thermometers use a material that has some property that changes when the temperature changes, and that can be measured. The ordinary clinical thermometer uses mercury. As it gets hotter the mercury expands up the stem of the thermometer and we can measure the point at which it stops.

Very high temperatures, of course, would melt glass thermometers. And mercury thermometers cannot be used to measure temperatures at a distance, such as the surface of the Sun. Very much more complex instruments are required to deal with problems like this. Some of them use quite different principles from mercury thermometers. A 'pyrometer', for example, has a metal filament. This is heated until it glows. Its colour is the same as the colour of light from a hot object, such as a star (see: *star*). Then the star's temperature will equal the filament's known temperature.

See: *absorption of light, cold, energy, light, nuclear energy, power, radiation.*

Find out by doing

Make your own air thermometer. You will need a long narrow glass tube, two empty ink bottles, a one-holed rubber stopper and some wax. Place the rubber stopper in one of the ink bottles and push the glass tube through the hole. Seal the hole with some wax to make the connection completely airtight. Heat the empty bottle, either by clasping it tightly with your hands or covering it with a hot cloth. As the temperature of the air inside the bottle increases the air expands.

Turn the bottle upside down and place the other end of the glass tube in the second ink bottle, which you have half-filled with coloured ink. The diagram shows you how to set up the apparatus.

When you remove your hands from the top bottle, the air in it gets cooler and contracts. The pressure is now lower in the top bottle and there is a partial vacuum in it. The coloured ink will rise up the tube to fill this space. The level of the ink now represents room temperature. If you heat or cool the top bottle now, the ink will go up or down the glass tube.

You can do a similar experiment using an empty bottle with a balloon attached to it. When the bottle is heated strongly by standing on a radiator the balloon will inflate as the air expands.

holography

Holography is a photographic technique for making three-dimensional ('3-D') pictures. A 3-D object has depth as well as length and breadth. Ordinary photographic film is used but the picture, or hologram, has to be 'taken' and viewed in special light.

A hologram is remarkably different from an ordinary photo to look at. You can see past objects in the foreground of the picture to objects in the background, just by moving your head. To understand how this is possible it is necessary to know about light and photography.

You can read this book because it is reflecting light waves into your eyes. Light waves are being reflected from it in different directions. The waves that arrive at your eye pass through the lens at the front of your eyeball (see: eye). The lens bends these waves so that when they reach the back of the eyeball they are arranged in a pattern similar to the object that reflected them. This pattern is called an image.

An ordinary photographic camera works on the same principles. The image is formed on light-sensitive film and this is chemically processed to make a photograph. If there were no lens the light waves would not be focussed and would form a blur on the film instead of an image.

The image formed in a camera is a pattern of brightness and darkness that corresponds to the scene photographed. But it does not tell us which parts of the scene are nearest the camera and which farther away. We can often work this out for ourselves. For instance, suppose the picture shows a man and a skyscraper, and the image of the man is larger than the image of the skyscraper. We know that skyscrapers are much larger than men. The reason why the man's image is larger is that he was nearer the camera at the time the photo was taken. But we might still be wrong. The skyscraper might have been a small scale model and might have been nearer the camera than the man was. We might not be able to tell from the photograph.

This confusion would not arise with a hologram of two objects because it records information about the distances of the objects from the film as well as their shape. This is what gives holography its 3-D effect.

Laser light

A hologram is made using special light produced by a laser (see: laser). And it shows up best in the same kind of light. The difference between ordinary light and laser light is in the organization of the light waves. Ordinary light is of various wavelengths, and the waves are out of step with each other. The light waves are jumbled. Laser light waves are all of one length and they are all in step with each other.

To make a hologram a laser beam is directed at the object to be holographed. A mirror is placed half-way along the beam to reflect half of it onto the light-sensitive film. This half of the beam is called the reference beam. The other half of the beam illuminates the object. This light is reflected by the object and some of it bounces back to the light-sensitive film. This part of the beam is called the signal beam.

Some of the laser waves have farther to travel than others. Waves travelling from the laser to the foreground travel a shorter distance than those reflected by the background. Those that travel farther take longer. But the waves in the reference beam travel the same distance all the time. So they all have the same journey time.

When the waves of light leave the laser they are all in step. But when they meet again at the film, some are out of step with others. The 'peaks' of some waves arrive at the same time as the 'troughs' of other waves, cancelling them.

At the point on the film where the waves of the signal and reference beams are in step they reinforce each other, producing bright light. This is recorded on the film as a clear patch. At places where the waves are completely out of step, they cancel each other out and there is a dark patch on the film. So the pattern of dark and clear patches recorded tells us not only what shape the object is but which parts are nearer than others. But when viewed in ordinary white light the pattern does not look like the object. The film is covered with what seems to be a meaningless jumble of lines and spots.

A picture of the original scene can be obtained by shining laser light through the developed film. The light passes through the clear parts of the film, and is stopped by the parts that are dark. On the far side of the film the light emerges in a pattern of brightness and darkness. This pattern is identical with the pattern made by the overlapping reference beam and reflected signal beam.

One of the amazing properties of the hologram is that it can be cut into small pieces and each piece will give, not a part of the picture, but the whole picture. It is just like looking through a small window instead of a large one. But there is a loss of picture quality and the image is blurred if only a small part of the film is used.

Holography could lead to an entirely new system of 3-D movies, and one day holographic TV will probably be developed. So far however, the main uses of holography have been either artists striving after new effects or the storage of various types of digital information – here the property that all the information is distributed throughout the image is particularly important, for it means that a lost or deleted item can be retrieved.

hydroponics

Hydroponics is the science of growing plants and seeds without using soil. The name comes from the Greek words meaning 'water' and 'labour'.

We know that all plants grow according to the conditions around them. Plants need heat, moisture, light and air in order to grow. Plants take in carbon dioxide through their leaves and give out oxygen (see: *photosynthesis*). They need oxygen in the water around their roots. Also, plants require large amounts of seven important chemicals that are found in the soil. These chemicals are potassium, magnesium, calcium, nitrogen, phosphorus, sulphur and iron. They also need five other chemicals, but in such tiny quantities that these are known as 'trace elements'. Sometimes, one or more of these chemicals is missing from the soil. Gardeners then use fertilizers that provide the missing chemical.

If the roots of a plant can take in enough dissolved oxygen from the water, they can grow well in water that contains the required chemicals. For instance, suppose we were to put some seeds in a small bowl with water containing all the important chemicals that a plant requires for growth. We would be doing practically the same thing as growing the plants in good fertile soil. Instead of using a bowl, we could use a tray containing material such as coarse sand, or crushed rock, or vermiculite. This material must not dissolve in water, or react with the chemicals in the water. It will provide the support needed for the plants in our tray. As the roots of the plant spread out, they anchor the plant.

There is one other important thing that is required in hydroponics. This is air. The roots of the plants must have air as well as liquid food from the water.

Once we have planted our seeds in the tray, we should water them with the dissolved chemicals. This should be done regularly each day. Excess water drains out into a tank beneath the tray. As it drains and passes through the tray it sucks air in after it. This can be used by the roots.

Over a period of time the chemicals in the water solution are used up by the plants. They must be continually replaced. In commercial projects for growing plants hydroponically, the solution is pumped in from a tank. The pump is controlled automatically. The solution is tested every two to three weeks to see that it still contains the right proportions of different chemicals.

What are the advantages of growing plants by hydroponic methods? Although it is a rather expensive method of growing plants, it is much easier to add fertilizer than when they are grown in soil. Also, they do not need watering. The main advantage is that crops can be grown in areas that are desert or have very poor soil. In hot, dry places such as the Negev Desert in Israel, and the Cape Verde Islands in the Atlantic, plants suffer severely from the weather. In these places, hydroponics has proved of great value in growing crops.

Hydroponics succeeds best in warm areas, such as California, and especially in greenhouses where crops and flowers are grown under glass in large numbers. It was used during World War II to provide fresh fruit and vegetables for American forces stationed on some of the Pacific Islands.

See: *photosynthesis*.

laser

Imagine a beam of light many billions of times more concentrated than the sunlight focussed by a magnifying glass. A beam so intense that it will burn a hole in a steel plate, or even through a diamond, the hardest natural material known to man. Such a beam can be produced by a modern source of light called a laser. Laser light is used for communication, for extremely accurate measurements, for surgery and dentistry, and for many different purposes in engineering and science.

To understand the properties that make a laser beam so unusual and useful, it is necessary first to understand the nature of ordinary light. Light is one form of energy. Like sound it travels in waves, but unlike sound it can travel through 'empty' space. Some other forms of energy that do this are radio waves, infra-red and ultraviolet waves, X-rays, and gamma rays. They are called electromagnetic waves because they consist of rapidly-changing electric and magnetic fields travelling through space.

A major difference between the various kinds of electromagnetic wave is in their wavelength. The wavelength is the distance between two successive crests of the travelling wave. Radio waves have wavelengths in the range from a few metres to about two thousand metres (six thousand feet). But some X-rays have wavelengths of one fifty-millionth of a centimetre, and gamma rays are even shorter. The waves that we call visible light occupy only a very small part of the wavelength range, or electromagnetic spectrum. We cannot see any of the waves outside this part of the spectrum. The shortest wavelength that we can see is that of violet light – about 35 millionths of a centimetre. The longest wavelength we can see is that of red light – about 70 millionths of a centimetre.

This 'wave theory' helps us to understand the nature of light. But, in addition to thinking of light as travelling in waves, physicists have proved that the energy in a light beam is in the form of small 'packets' of energy, called photons. A photon is the smallest amount of light energy of a particular wavelength that can exist. You cannot have half a photon.

Light is usually given out, or emitted, by atoms (or ions – electrically charged particles). To make atoms give out light, it is necessary first to give them additional energy. An atom that has more energy than usual is said to be in an 'excited' state. It is unable to remain in this excited, or higher state and falls back almost instantly to its normal, or ground, state. As it does so, it emits energy, in the form of light waves.

The light from a burning candle comes from atoms that have been heated by the chemical changes releasing energy in the flame. The glow on a television screen comes from a beam of fast-moving electrons.

Atoms can also be excited by absorbing light, and this is what happens in a laser. Ordinary light is used to excite atoms which then give out laser light. Unlike ordinary light, laser light is all of the same wavelength and the waves travel in step with each other – all their crests and troughs are together. Laser light spreads out very little from its source. It is a nearly parallel beam.

The first laser, built in 1960, consisted of a rod of synthetic ruby with a flash tube coiled around it. Synthetic ruby is man-made, as opposed to natural (see: *gemstone*). It is made mainly of aluminum oxide, which is a clear and colourless substance. The redness of the ruby results from the presence of a small amount of chromium. The chromium atoms are arranged in an orderly way throughout the ruby crystal. The ruby laser crystal was in the form of a long cylinder. In this type of laser, the chromium atoms in the ruby are first excited by a very intense flash of ordinary light from a flash tube. Then the atoms drop back part of the way to the ground state. They are then in a 'metastable', or partly stable, state. Next, some of the atoms lose more energy and drop into the ground state. Their energy is emitted as red light. This consists of 'packets' of energy, or photons, as we mentioned earlier. This stage of the process is called 'spontaneous emission'.

Some of the photons pass out through the sides of the ruby cylinder, and are lost. But others travel along its length. One of these photons hits another chromium atom that is still metastable. It makes this atom fall back into its ground state. As it does so, the atom gives out a photon that is identical to the photon causing the emission. This process is called 'stimulated emission'. The second photon is 'in step' with the first one.

There are now two photons, where there was only one before. These two photons go on to hit other metastable chromium atoms. Each atom hit releases another, identical photon of light, of exactly the same wavelength and energy. The new photons are always in step with the stimulating photons. The process continues in this way. All the time the beam of red light grows stronger as more photons are emitted.

The ends of the ruby cylinder are coated with silver so that they act as mirrors. One of the mirrors is only partly silvered, and hence is slightly transparent. Though most of the light falling on it is reflected, a small part travels through. Reflected photons travel back and forth. They cause more atoms in the metastable state to drop back to the ground state. The number of photons travelling back and forth along the crystal increases until no more atoms are left in the metastable state. Those that are not travelling almost exactly parallel to the length of the crystal are lost through the sides.

The light then 'leaks away' through the partly silvered end of the crystal. This escaping light is the laser's flash, lasting perhaps only a hundred-millionth of a second.

So in the ruby laser, energy from the ordinary white light of a flash tube is stored in excited atoms. Then it is released as a pulse of red laser light.

A ruby laser produces light of precise wavelength. 'Ordinary' red light consists of a mixture of light waves of different wavelengths. Although we think of it as one colour, it is a mixture of colours. Each wave of laser light is in phase with all the others. Such light is called 'coherent' light ('coherent' means 'sticking together'; the waves stay together). Ruby lasers were the first source of intense coherent light.

The coherent laser beam is almost exactly parallel when it emerges from the laser. This is very different from the non-coherent light from 'ordinary' sources, which quickly spreads out in all directions. In 1962, a laser beam only a few centimetres across was directed at the Moon. After having crossed about 400,000 kilometres of space, it had spread out into an area only about three kilometres across.

Today there are lasers that produce continuous beams. They use gases in a tube with mirrored ends. The gas carbon dioxide can be used to produce a beam, not of visible light, but of infra-red waves. Other lasers can be made that produce ultraviolet waves. Devices similar to lasers, called masers, amplify radio microwaves, that is make them stronger. A weak beam of microwaves emerges from a maser as a much stronger beam of waves.

Lasers have great possibilities in communications. It is easy to transmit many messages at one time using coherent light waves. They can be used for transmitting television signals, although this development is still at the experimental stage. It is possible for a laser beam of visible light to carry 80 million television channels or 800 million telephone channels without interference between them.

Communication by laser beams, instead of radio waves, may soon be used for contact between satellites and spacecraft. Unfortunately, light is easily scattered by clouds or fog so that laser communication through the Earth's atmosphere is not possible at all times. An exciting development of the laser is the production of three-dimensional ('solid'-looking) photographs (see: *holography*).

The amount of energy in a laser pulse may not be very great. But when the laser beam is flashed onto an object, the energy arrives in a short space of time. The surface of the object cannot lose the heat very quickly. So that small area of the surface is raised to a high temperature. Laser beams can be used for drilling, cutting, etching and welding metals. A powerful laser beam can burn a hole through a thick steel plate in less than a second.

Surgeons have used very fine beams to perform delicate operations on the tissues at the back of the eye. Dental surgeons also can use laser beams to burn away small portions of teeth that have become decayed.

The concentrated power of the laser can help to persuade atoms to fuse together to become a new element in a novel form of reactor that may one day supply some of our energy needs.

Lasers can help scientists to make accurate determinations of standard units, or induce and observe chemical reactions that last for only tiny fractions of a second. They can help to determine very long distances and so help to guide space craft and aircraft.

See: *holography, light.*

lenses and mirrors

Every day we look at ourselves in mirrors. We see through lenses that are part of our eyes. To see clearly, we may also need to wear eyeglasses, which have lenses. Lenses and mirrors help us in many other ways too. The camera and magnifying glass are familiar devices employing lenses. There are lenses and mirrors in microscopes, telescopes, and many measuring instruments that scientists use.

When you stand right in front of a mirror you see your own face in it. By changing the position of the mirror suitably you can see other objects. The mirror forms a 'picture' of the objects in front of it. The 'picture' of each object is called an image.

It is the purpose of lenses and mirrors to make images. An ordinary mirror's images look just the same as their objects except that they are 'inverted' – your left hand becomes the image's right hand. But lenses and mirrors can be used to make images that are small or large and changed in shape.

A lens is a piece of material such as glass or plastic, with one or two curved surfaces. It is transparent, meaning that light can pass through it. But a lens bends the light going through it. It changes the direction that light moves in. The bending is called 'refraction'.

A mirror is an object with a very smooth surface that light cannot go through. The surface may be either flat or curved. It is usually made by coating glass with a metal like silver. The mirror bounces back the light that hits it. This is known as 'reflection'.

The study of lenses and mirrors is known as geometrical optics. Optics is the science of light. It is named after the Greek word for eye. Geometry is the mathematical language that we use to describe shapes and directions (see: *geometry*). Lenses and mirrors of different shapes change the direction of light in different ways. Such changes are described by the laws of geometrical optics.

Light is a form of energy (see: *energy*). The light travelling from this printed page to your eyes is carrying energy to your eyes. (See: *light.*) But we do not need to think about the nature of light to find out how lenses and mirrors affect it. The way in which light moves was studied and understood long before it was discovered what light is.

Light can travel through materials like glass, water, or air. Such materials are called media (singular: medium). Empty space is also a medium, for light can travel freely through it. This movement can be studied by thinking of 'light rays'. A light ray is a very thin beam of light.

As long as light moves in a single medium, and does not come near other media, it goes straight. But when it reaches another medium, its direction can be changed. This happens if a light ray hits the surface of a lens or mirror. It approaches and leaves the surface in straight lines. But it changes direction as it hits the surface. In the case of a lens, the light is bent slightly, and continues through the surface.

Draw a straight line. Imagine that it is the surface of a flat mirror seen from the side. Then draw a straight ray of light approaching the surface. This 'incident' ray hits the surface at a certain point. Draw another straight line through that point, at right angles to the surface, or 90°. This line is a 'perpendicular' line, or 'normal'.

The incident ray makes an angle with the normal line, called the angle of incidence. Where the incident ray hits, a reflected ray must bounce off, on the other side of the normal. The reflected ray makes an angle with the normal line, called the angle of reflection.

The law of reflection says that the angles of incidence and reflection are equal. So we draw the reflected ray making the same angle with the normal line as the incident ray does.

If a light ray meets the mirror head on it travels along the normal. The reflected ray travels away from the surface along the normal also. Then both the angles are 0°.

If the incident ray skims the surface before meeting the mirror it travels at nearly 90° to the normal. The reflected ray travels away from that point at the same angle, also skimming the surface.

The light ray behaves something like a billiard ball bouncing off the side of a billiard table. The ball moves away from the side of the table at roughly the same angle as it struck it.

Now suppose that an object is put in front of the mirror. Light rays spread from each point of the object. Many of them hit the mirror. Each ray obeys the law of reflection. The rays change direction and travel away from the mirror. But they continue to spread. Now they seem to spread from a point somewhere behind the mirror. It is as if the object were there.

This seeming object 'behind' the mirror is the image of the object.

With the flat mirror, an image is the same size as the object. And it is the same distance behind the mirror as the object is in front of the mirror.

All objects reflect some of the light that falls on them. If this were not so we should not be able to see them. Why don't we see images in the surfaces of every object? What is special about the surface of a mirror?

Mirrors form images because they have very smooth surfaces. Most objects – even a piece of glossy paper – have rough surfaces by comparison. Light striking a rough surface obeys the same law of reflection as light striking a smooth surface. But the rough surface sends the reflected rays in many different directions so that images are completely confused.

A 'convex' mirror produces images similar to those of a flat mirror. Its surface is not flat, but curved outward. The surface of a ball, or the outside of a cup is convex. The surface of a convex mirror is usually spherical – part of a sphere. Mirrors in department stores and cars are often convex. In a convex mirror, the image of an object is smaller than the object. The image also appears to be the wrong shape, or 'distorted'.

Not only are the sizes of images reduced by convex mirrors. The images are closer to the mirror surface than the objects. In the convex rear-view mirror of a car, following cars seem to be closer than they really are. Drivers have to learn to judge their true distances.

We can imagine each small area of a convex mirror to be flat. In the same way we see our small region of the Earth's curved surface as flat. So each ray is reflected exactly as it would be reflected from a flat surface.

The normal that goes through a convex mirror's centre is called the mirror's axis. Objects on the axis form images that lie on the axis behind the mirror's surface.

The back of a soup spoon is a convex mirror. The inside of the bowl of the spoon makes a concave surface. Whereas convex mirrors make small images, concave mirrors make images of things close to them that are larger than the objects. Shaving mirrors are concave.

The trick mirrors you find in amusement parks have wavy surfaces. So they are concave in some parts and convex in others. The mirror makes some parts of you look small, and other parts large.

Concave mirrors make a different kind of image when the object is far away. If you stand well back from a shaving mirror you will see a small image of yourself that is upside down. And it is not behind the mirror, but in front of it.

This kind of image is called a 'real' image. This simply means that light rays pass through the place where the image is located. The image made by an ordinary mirror seems to lie behind the mirror. No light rays are actually passing through that spot. The same is true of the magnified images of nearby objects that concave mirrors form. This kind of image is called 'virtual'.

The largest astronomical telescopes use concave mirrors and are called reflectors. The Hale reflector on Mount Palomar, California, has a mirror 508 centimetres (200 inches) across. It forms images of the stars. Usually these are allowed to form on a photographic plate, so that a photograph of them is obtained.

Apart from mirrors, the other main method of forming images is the lens. Lenses are frequently made by grinding discs of glass into the correct shape and then polishing them.

When light passes through a lens its direction is changed. To understand what happens it is necessary to know what happens when a light ray meets a single flat surface of a medium like glass or water.

Whenever light travels from one medium to

another it is bent. This bending is called refraction.

Draw a straight line, showing the surface between two media, such as air and glass. Then draw an incident ray of light coming through air. Where it hits the glass, draw a normal line. At this point, the light will go through the surface into the glass, and become a 'refracted ray'. The refracted ray will make a certain angle with the normal line, called the angle of refraction. And the refracted ray will be on the other side of the normal line to the incident ray.

In this case, the law of refraction says that the angle of refraction is smaller than the angle of incidence. So the light is bent toward the normal line as it goes through the surface. Only if it hits the surface 'head on' – at right angles – will it not be bent. Then the two angles will both be zero, and the ray will go straight through the surface.

Now draw an incident ray coming through the glass. It hits the surface, and becomes a refracted ray in the air. Now the angle of refraction lies in the air, not the glass. The same law says, in this case, that the angle of refraction is bigger than the angle of incidence. The light bends away from the normal line when going through the surface.

These two cases are similar. The angle in the air is always bigger than the angle in the glass. Glass is denser than air (see: *density*). The angle is smaller in the denser medium. The same is true for other media than air and glass. When light is refracted between air and water, the angle is smaller in the water since water is denser than air.

When light goes from air into another medium, it bends by an amount that depends on the density of the other medium. The greater this density is, the more the light will be bent. The amount of bending is shown by a number called the 'refractive index'. Denser media have higher refractive indexes.

Like mirrors, lenses work by changing the direction of light rays. After passing through a lens rays from an object spread from a different point. There seems to be an image at that new point.

A magnifying glass is a 'biconvex' lens – it has two convex surfaces. You can use a magnifying glass to focus the rays of the Sun to form a bright spot of light on paper. You have then formed a real image of the Sun. You can form an image of a window in the same way.

Hold an ordinary magnifying glass at arm's length and look at distant objects through it – but not the Sun. The light from the objects is brought together at points between the lens and your eye. Light spreads out from there to your eye. So you can see real images. They are upside down.

Small telescopes, binoculars, and many astronomical telescopes use a convex lens to make a real image of the object. This image is viewed by the observer through the eyepiece, a special combination of smaller lenses.

As objects come nearer to a convex lens, the real image is formed farther from the lens. When the object is very close, no real image is formed at all. Instead, a magnified virtual image is formed on the same side of the lens as the object. When you examine a plant or a small insect under a magnifying glass, you are looking at a virtual magnified image of it.

A magnifying glass does not have to be biconvex. It can have one convex surface and a flat surface. This type is called 'planoconvex'. Or it can have one convex and one concave surface. It is necessary only that it should be thicker in the middle than at the edge. Then it has the effect of bringing light rays together, or at least of making them spread less.

A lens that is thinner at the middle than at the edges cannot be used as a magnifying glass. It forms virtual images that are smaller than the objects. As the diagrams show, it cannot form real images of objects. The lenses in spectacles are often of this kind.

You can photograph any object or its image with a camera. The camera has a biconvex lens. It forms real images on the film.

The human eye contains a biconvex lens. It forms real images on the back of the eye, which is called the retina. The retina turns the coloured pattern of light and shade in the image into electrical signals that are passed to the brain.

Unlike man-made lenses, the shape of the human eye lens can be changed. When it is most strongly curved, it forms sharp images of nearby objects. When it is completely relaxed, it is least strongly curved. It is then thinnest and flattest and sharp images of distant objects are formed on the retina.

The lens of a camera has a fixed shape. To bring objects at different distances into focus, the lens has to be moved. This brings the real image of the object to the surface of the film.

Lenses and mirrors are never perfect. When their surfaces are spherical a blurred image can result. The rays from a point on the object do not focus at a single point on the image. They meet at many slightly different points. This is called 'spherical aberration'. It can be partly corrected in lenses by using surfaces with a shape that is not exactly spherical. But in practice spherical lenses are nearly always used.

A lens can also produce a blurred image because of 'chromatic aberration'. Each colour of light from an object is focussed slightly differently. This is because glass and any other transparent medium refract different colours of light by different amounts. The object's image is really a blur of many coloured images. The result is that images seem to have coloured fringes. Chromatic aberration is corrected by combining two or more lenses. The lenses are made of glasses of different indexes of refraction.

Not all the light falling on a lens passes through it. Some light is reflected from each surface. You see your reflection in a window for the same reason. Unwanted reflections can spoil the images formed in optical instruments. To reduce reflection, lenses are coated with a transparent non-reflective chemical.

If light goes from a more dense medium into a less dense one, it bends away from the normal line. It may bend so much that the refracted ray skims the surface. This occurs at an angle of incidence called the 'critical angle'. When the angle of incidence is greater than the critical angle, there is no more refraction. All the light is reflected back into the more dense medium. This effect is known as 'total internal reflection'.

Total internal reflection is used in the science of 'fibre optics'. Light is guided down a plastic or glass fibre like water along a pipe. The light shines in one end of the fibre. Any that strikes the surface of the fibre is reflected back inside again. No light escapes through the surface into the air.

See: *light, microscope.*

Find out by doing

You can make a periscope by fixing two small mirrors on the ends of a ruler with plasticine. Place them parallel to each other, and both at an angle with the ruler, as the drawing shows. Hold the ruler upright. Light from an object hits the upper mirror, is reflected down to hit the lower mirror, and is then reflected into your eye.

Make a ray diagram like the following one. Put a coin in front of a mirror, on a sheet of paper. By 'aiming' with a ruler at the coin's image in the mirror, draw lines from your eye to the mirror. You are tracing rays of light backwards to where the mirror reflects the rays coming from the coin. Then draw a line along the edge of the mirror. Remove the mirror, and extend the light rays. They meet behind the mirror, showing where the coin's image was located. The lines prove that the image is as far behind the mirror as the coin is in front of the mirror.

light

Men have always worshipped and wondered at light. The Ancient Greek philosophers recognized over 2,000 years ago that men depended on light from the Sun or from fire to see things.

But light was also believed to resemble streams of particles, or perhaps a kind of liquid, flowing extremely fast. And it was believed that the eye grasped things it was looking at with invisible 'feelers'. The Ancients thought of vision as a kind of touching.

We now know that when we look at an object nothing travels outwards from our eyes. Light travels from the object to the eyes, passing into them through the opening called the pupil, and falling on the back of the eye.

We cannot see any light that does not enter our eyes. The shafts of sunlight that break through clouds are visible to us only because of dust or water drops in the air. They scatter a small part of the sunlight and some of this enters our eyes.

Light can be created in various ways. Hot materials glow. The light of a wood fire is due to the hot gases in the flame, and the wood made hot by its own burning. An iron heated in the fire will glow when it is taken out. It will give out less and less light as it cools down. The Sun and the stars are masses of intensely hot gas. The light of an electric light bulb comes from a hot glowing wire. But not all sources of light are hot. Fluorescent light tubes are much cooler than light bulbs of the same brightness.

A source of light is any object that actually creates light. But the light by which we see an object may not have been created by it. You are reading this book by sunlight or electric light that has fallen on the book and been sent back – reflected – to your eyes. When this happens, only part of the light is sent back. The rest is taken in by the reflecting object. Bright-looking objects reflect a lot of the light that falls on them. Dark-looking objects reflect only a small part of the light that falls on them.

Light is a form of energy (see: *energy*). Energy cannot be destroyed, only turned into other forms of energy. When light is absorbed by this book, it is converted into heat. In the light meter on a camera, the energy of light is turned into the energy of an electric current.

Light travels outward from its source until it falls on something. Then the reflected light travels outward from this new object. It travels in straight lines, as shown by the sunbeams shining through breaks in a cloud, or by sunlight shining through a hole in a window shade. Because it 'radiates' outward from its source, light is described as a form of 'radiation'.

The Sun and stars are natural sources of light. Because they generate light they are called 'luminous'.

Most of the objects around us are not luminous. We see them by the light that they reflect.

Light can travel through completely empty space. It is quite unlike sound, which is a vibration of air, water or a solid. Sound cannot reach us from beyond the Earth's atmosphere, but light travels many millions of kilometres to the Earth from the Sun and stars.

The first great advance in understanding the nature of light was made by Sir Isaac Newton, the great English physicist, in the seventeenth century. Newton made a pinhole in a shade covering the window of his study.

A thin ray of sunlight shone through the pinhole, making a white spot on a screen. Then Newton put a triangular glass prism – a wedge-shaped glass block – into the ray. The spot of light on the screen shifted, because the prism changed the direction of the light passing through it. And the spot was 'stretched' into a bright-coloured band. Newton called the coloured band a spectrum (plural: spectra)

All the colours that we see in the rainbow were present in this band. And they were in the same order that they appear in the rainbow – red, orange, yellow, green, blue, indigo and violet shading smoothly from one into the next.

Newton realised that sunlight was a mixture of light of different colours. When this mixture enters our eyes we see white light. We cannot see the colours in white light until they have been separated.

When white light passes through a prism, its direction is changed. But every colour of light is changed in direction by a different amount. Red rays are bent least. Violet rays are bent most. So the white light is spread out into the colours that make it up.

Newton allowed the spectrum to form on a screen with a hole in it, so that the red light passed through. This red ray was bent by a second prism. But it stayed the same colour. This showed that the prisms were not adding colours to the light.

After splitting white light into its different colours, Newton was able to mix them again to obtain white light. He did this by passing the light through a second prism, arranged so as to bend the rays the opposite way.

Prisms are not the only things that can produce a spectrum like the one seen by Newton. Spectra of sunlight are often produced by chance. Patches of light reflected from mirrors or glass tumblers and dishes are often broken up into rainbow colours. Rainbows themselves are spectra of sunlight. They are made by falling raindrops splitting up sunlight and sending the colours back to our eyes.

It is possible to split up any kind of light to make a spectrum, and to learn a great deal about the source from which the light is coming. Astronomers have learned a lot about the Sun by studying its spectrum. They have found that its outer surface, the part we can see, is at a temperature of 5,000° Celsius. They have been able to tell what substances the Sun is made of (see: *Sun*). The stars, which are similar to the Sun, but much farther away, have spectra similar to the Sun's.

It is important to be able to study the amount of light of each colour in a spectrum of, say, a star. It is done by measuring how much energy is given out in each second by the star as light of that colour.

The light from an ordinary electric light bulb is yellowish compared with sunlight. It contains more red, orange and yellow light, and our eyes see this mixture as a yellowish colour. Light from a fluorescent lamp contains more colours near the blue end of the spectrum.

The colours contained in the light are often a guide to the temperature of the light source. When a piece of iron is heated strongly, it first glows red. As its temperature rises it begins to give out light that is farther towards the blue end of the spectrum. First it turns orange, then yellowish. When it is very hot it gives out light of all the colours from red through blue, and glows white. This happens at a temperature of 1,350 °C, before it melts. The surface of the Sun glows white because it is at about 5,000 °C.

The star called Betelgeuse has more red light and less blue light in its spectrum than does the Sun. This tells astronomers that the surface of Betelgeuse is cooler than the surface of the Sun. The spectrum of the hot star Sirius has more blue light, proportionally, than the Sun.

Another great step forward in our understanding of light was made by the astronomer William Herschel in 1800. He was studying the heating effect of light. Sunlight warms the things it falls on. Herschel wanted to know whether different colours of light have different heating effects. He put a thermometer at different positions in the spectrum of sunlight. To his surprise he found the highest thermometer reading when the thermometer was placed just beyond the red end of the spectrum.

Invisible light

Herschel decided that sunlight contained radiation that is invisible to the human eye. He gave it the name infrared ('below red') radiation. The infrared radiation was bent by the prism even less than red light was.

We now know that other creatures, such as snakes, can detect infrared radiation. And we have photographic films that can register infrared radiation. When these infrared photos are developed, the infrared radiation in the picture may show as white or coloured areas according to the kind of film used.

Green plants reflect most of the green light, and also some of the infrared radiation, that falls on them. So in an infrared photo green plants show up as white or coloured areas.

Infrared photos taken from orbiting space satellites can tell experts whether a particular piece of land is covered with forest, crops, buildings, or other features, so that land-use maps can be prepared. They can also reveal crop diseases, such as potato blight.

Herschel realised that infrared light must be the same kind of thing as visible light. We now know what the relation between them is.

Light is made up of waves. They can be thought of as rather like the waves that spread outward in all directions when you disturb water with your hand. Light waves spread from a disturbance that is the light source. Sound consists of waves too. But sound waves are vibrations of the air, of water, or of a solid (see: sound). The vibrations of light are not vibrations of air or any other substance. They can take place in empty space.

All waves have a 'wavelength'. This is the distance from the crest of one wave to the crest of the next. Ocean waves can have a wavelength of several metres. Sound waves can have a wavelength of around 30 centimetres (one foot). Light waves have a wavelength far shorter – about fifty millionths of a centimetre. Blue light has the shortest – about forty millionths of a centimetre.

When white light passes through a prism it is bent according to its wavelength. The shorter waves are bent the most.

Infrared radiation

Radiations exist with wavelengths shorter than blue light and longer than red light. These are the invisible radiations. The infrared radiation that Herschel discovered covers a range of wavelengths from 75 millionths of a centimetre to half a centimetre.

Though we cannot see infrared radiation, we can feel it as warmth on the skin. Any warm object, such as the top of an electric stove or a hot car engine, gives out infrared radiation. Photos made with infrared-sensitive film will show these hot objects looking bright. Coal fires and electric heaters give out more infrared than visible light. But very hot objects, like the Sun and most stars, give out more visible light than infrared radiation.

Infrared radiation is used by doctors in a new technique to help in the treatment of patients with severe burns. Previously, it was difficult to discover which burned areas were damaged enough to need skin grafts. The doctor uses a special camera that turns the infrared radiation from the skin into electrical charges that can be converted into a picture on a television screen. Badly damaged or dead skin is colder than less damaged or healthy skin and shows up darker on the TV picture.

Another kind of invisible radiation, just beyond the other end of the visible spectrum, was discovered by the German physicist Johann Ritter. He was studying the effect of light in turning a solution of a silver compound dark. The light breaks down the silver compound and causes grains of silver to form. These grains are dark. A similar process takes place when a photographic film is exposed and developed. Ritter found that the silver darkened most quickly when it was placed just beyond the violet end of the spectrum. He realized there was another kind of invisible radiation in the Sun's spectrum. He named it ultraviolet ('beyond violet') radiation.

The wavelength of ultraviolet light extends from that of violet light, forty millionths of a centimetre, to about one two-millionth of a centimetre.

Modern photographic films are very sensitive to ultraviolet radiation. There is usually some ultraviolet present in light from the sky, and this makes the sky look bright in photographs. To make the sky look darker an ultraviolet 'filter' is attached to the camera lens. This absorbs the ultraviolet radiation before it can pass through the lens and affect the light-sensitive coating of the film. The white light from clouds is not affected, and so the clouds show up bright against a dark sky in the photograph.

Ultraviolet radiation is responsible for the tanning of the skin in sunlight. The darkening of the skin is a protection against the ultraviolet, which can be harmful. Most of the ultraviolet radiation in sunlight is absorbed high in the Earth's atmosphere by a layer of ozone gas. Without this, life would not be possible.

Adding and subtracting colours

We saw earlier that an object's colour depends on the colour of light that it sends to our eyes. But this, in turn, depends on many things. Painters, lighting technicians in theatres and TV studios, printers and many other people need to understand the process involved in seeing colour.

Yellow paint is yellow because it reflects yellow light. When white light (which is a mixture of light of all the rainbow colours) falls on a yellow painted surface the light of the other colours (as well as a small part of the yellow light), is absorbed by the paint. But the yellow light is reflected to the eyes.

If yellow light is shone onto the paint, the light is reflected and the paint still looks yellow. But if a pure blue light is shone onto the paint, the light is absorbed. The paint will look black (or nearly black). A blue handkerchief placed in blue light will reflect the blue light. Its colour will show clearly.

So the colours of things can change with the colour of the light that you shine on them. Clothes often look a different colour in daylight from the colour they look in the artificial lighting of the store where they were bought. Two cloths that looked the same colour in the store may look different from each other in sunlight.

A green object is likely to reflect a little blue and yellow light as well as green light. A red object will probably reflect some orange light. This fact makes it possible to mix paints to give new colours.

Blue paint can be mixed with yellow paint to make green paint. The blue paint by itself reflects some green light. The yellow paint reflects some green light as well as some orange. The only kind of light that both paints reflect is green so the mixture appears that colour.

Similarly, red and yellow paint can be mixed to give orange. Orange light is the only colour of light that both paints reflect.

The kind of colour mixing given by paints is called 'subtractive' colour mixing. Some of the colour that each paint reflects is 'subtracted', or absorbed, by other paints in the mixture.

There is another way of mixing colours, called additive colour mixing. When red light is shone onto a white screen it is reflected, because white objects reflect all the colours that fall on them. If green light is shone onto the same place at the same time, it too is reflected. So both red and green light comes from this place. What do we see?

The answer is that we see a mixture of red and green light as yellow. Red and blue light give the shade called magenta. And blue and green light give the shade called cyan. Magenta and cyan do not occur in the spectrum, because they are not pure colours.

Colour television

Additive colour mixing is used in TV. In a part of the screen that is yellow at a particular moment, there are actually red and green dots glowing. Our eyes combine these colours to give an effect of yellow. All colours can be shown by red, green and blue dots glowing with the correct brightness.

Every object – even a shiny highly-reflecting metal object – absorbs some of the light that falls on it. It also gives out radiation. Every object around you at this moment is sending out radiation. But this radiation is mostly infrared and so invisible.

The radiation energy absorbed by an object is turned into heat. When an object absorbs more radiation in every second than it sends out, it warms up. As it warms up it sends out more and more energy. When its temperature is steady it is sending out exactly as much energy as it is taking in.

A dark object takes in more radiation energy every second than a light object of the same size and shape. It must send out more energy too, when they are both at the same steady temperature. So we have the rule that dark objects absorb more radiation and send out more radiation than light objects of the same size and shape at the same temperature. So buildings and clothing for use in the polar regions should be light-coloured, to keep down the rate at which they lose heat. Polar bears, Arctic foxes and snowy owls, which are found in Arctic regions, all have white bodies, and send out less heat than they would if they were darker. The white colouring is also good camouflage in the snowy surroundings that exist there. The same is seen in hot countries where many travellers wear light-coloured clothes which absorb little heat.

The Sun is a giant powerhouse pouring heat and light into space. Life on the Earth depends on this light and heat. But only a tiny fraction falls on the Earth. The rest travels off into space. As it travels it is spread out more and more thinly.

Imagine a space satellite in orbit about the Earth. The satellite has two large 'paddles' covered with 'solar cells' that it keeps turned toward the Sun. The solar cells are powerful photoelectric cells. The sunlight falling on the solar cells generates electrical power for the satellite's instruments.

The Earth is 40 times closer to the Sun than is the planet Pluto. In Earth orbit, the satellite's solar cells receive 1,600 times as much energy in sunlight as they would if the satellite were in orbit round Pluto. Even if it were possible to send a satellite to orbit Pluto, it could not function on such a small amount of power. And life could not exist on Pluto for the same reason.

The speed of light

Light travels at an enormous speed. It covers about 299,500 kilometres (just over 186,000 miles) in every second. Light takes one and one-third seconds to reach the Earth from the Moon. It takes only just over eight minutes to cover the 150 million kilometres (93 million miles) to the Earth from the Sun. Yet light from Pluto takes five and a half hours to reach us. It takes four years to travel from the nearest star system.

Light travelling in empty space is the fastest thing we know of. In fact, the great physicist Einstein showed that nothing can travel faster than light (see: *relativity*). But when light enters transparent substances – diamond, glass, even air – it is slowed down. In glass, light travels at only about 195,000 kilometres (120,000 miles) per second, two-thirds of its speed in empty space. In air it is slowed down by only 95 kilometres (60 miles) per second. But when light that has passed through, for example, glass, comes out into air it travels at its full air speed. It is not permanently slowed down.

When light changes its speed, its path may be

changed. If a glass of water is placed near a newspaper lying on a table, the words and pictures seen through the glass will seem to be distorted. The light rays from the paper are bent as they travel through the glass and water. The bending of light rays by transparent substances is called 'refraction'.

Blue light is slowed down more than red light in transparent substances. For this reason the path of blue light is bent more than the path of red light, as when white light is broken up by a prism.

Diamond slows light more than glass. It bends light and breaks it up more than glass. This is what makes diamonds sparkle and flash so much more than glass imitation jewels.

Man puts refraction to use in the lenses of cameras, telescopes and microscopes, as well as many other optical instruments (see: *lenses and mirrors*).

Refraction can also deceive us. Mirages are illusions often seen in hot, level country, such as deserts, or over sea, especially in polar regions. They are created by layers of warm air, either lying close to the ground, or high above it, bending the light from objects in unusual ways.

The behaviour of waves
Because light is made up of waves, it never casts perfectly sharp shadows. This is because the direction of a wave is bent as it passes an obstacle. This bending of waves is something quite different from refraction. Sea waves passing through a hole in a breakwater spread out slightly on the far side. Sound waves, too, bend round things.

So if the wave theory is true it should never be possible to get a sharp-edged shadow. And this is correct. When the shadow cast by a straight edge is examined with a microscope, it is found that there is no sharp boundary between light and dark. Instead the shadow of the edge seems to be fringed with light and dark bands. The behaviour of light in this case is complicated, but the wave theory can explain it fully.

Light passing through a small opening or slit behaves in a similar way. This spreading of light is called 'diffraction'.

Light shows other strange kinds of behaviour that suggest that it is made up of waves. When light beams overlap they do not always produce greater brightness.

You can show a similar effect for yourself with water. Splash the water at one end of a bathtub with both hands in a steady rhythm. You will set up two series of waves spreading outwards from the two hands.

At the sides of the bath you can see the result of their overlap. In some places the waves arrive in step. The result is a stronger wave,

with the water rising and falling farther than it would in either of the waves singly. At other places the two waves arrive out of step. The water is still.

Light can be made to do this. Beams can be made to overlap so that at some places they add to give bright light. And at other places they cancel each other out so that they produce darkness.

What kinds of things are the waves? Ocean waves are movements of water. The sound waves of your voice are movements of air. What is moving in a light wave?

The answer was given by the Scottish physicist and mathematician James Clerk Maxwell, around 1870. He said that light waves consist of fast-changing electric and magnetic fields (see: *electricity, magnet*). Now, take as an example a light ray travelling horizontally. Along the path of the ray there are electric and magnetic fields, constantly changing in strength. The directions of the fields are at right angles to the path of the ray.

When the field is strongest the light wave has a 'crest'. The strength of the field changes a few hundred million million times each second in visible light.

All other kinds of electromagnetic radiation consist of electric and magnetic fields varying at different rates.

Light is a kind of wave motion called 'transverse'. Transverse motion is motion from side to side. The waves that you send along a rope by flicking one end are transverse waves. Each point on the rope moves from side to side (or up and down) while the wave shape travels along the rope.

In the case of the light waves there is no sideways movement. But the electric and magnetic fields point sideways.

In a light beam travelling horizontally the vibrations are up and down, side to side, and at all the angles in between. If the light beam passes through a sheet of a special kind of plastic material, only light vibrations in one direction are allowed through. For example, the transmitted light may have its vibrations in the up and down direction only, while the side to side vibrations are absorbed by the plastic. If the plastic sheet is rotated through a right angle, the side to side vibrations will be allowed through, and the others will be absorbed.

Polarized light
Light that has its vibrations in one direction only is called 'polarized light'. Polarized light looks just like unpolarized light. Engineers use polarized light a great deal.

Light that is unpolarized is usually polarized partly after being reflected or refracted. Polarizing sunglasses make use of this effect. The glare from water and road surfaces on a sunny day consists partly of polarized light. The glasses allow only a small part of the polarized light to pass through. The brightness of un-polarized light is less strongly reduced.

In 1900 Max Planck, a great German physicist, showed that the energy of electromagnetic radiation is not given out continuously from a hot or luminous body. It is given out in short bursts. Each burst is one 'quantum' (plural: quanta) of radiation.

The energy of a quantum is very small. It depends on the wavelength of the radiation. A quantum of red light has an energy of about one third of a million-million-millionth of a joule. Quanta of light of shorter wavelengths have more energy. Quanta of visible light are often given the special name 'photons'.

Matter has been known for centuries to consist of tiny particles – atoms. But it has been shown in modern times that it has some properties that need a wave theory – the quantum theory of matter (see: *matter*). So the basic physics of matter and of light are not so different after all. Both have wave-like and particle-like properties.

See: *absorption of light, electricity, magnet, matter, radiation, wave.*

Find out by doing

Make a pinhole camera like the one shown in the diagram. You can use a can or cardboard box, after removing top and bottom. Cover one end with thick paper and make a pinhole in it. Cover the other end with thin tissue paper to act as a screen. Light from a scene passes through the pinhole in straight lines and forms an image on the tissue paper. You can view the image if you cover your head and the camera with a cloth to keep out stray light from the surroundings. What happens to the image of, say, a window if you change your distance from the window? What happens to the image if you enlarge the pinhole?

magnet

Thousands of years ago man noticed that lumps of a special black rock attracted pieces of iron to them. The strange force of attraction came to be called magnetism, and the pieces of rock were named magnets. These words probably came from the name of the place in Asia Minor where much of the black rock was found. This place was called Magnesia by the Ancient Greeks. The Ancient Greeks and Romans had many theories to explain the force of magnetism. One idea was that there were tiny hooks on the surface of the iron. This idea seemed to show why the iron stuck to the rock.

The earliest known use of magnetism was by sailors travelling in the Far East in about 1100AD. But it is almost certain that the Vikings used magnets on their long ocean voyages in northern seas in about 1000AD. These sailors used small pieces of the magnetic rock to make compasses. The compasses helped them to navigate when the sky was too cloudy to see the Sun or stars. Men had invented the compass by noticing an important fact. If they hung a bar of the magnetic rock by a thread so that it could swing freely, one end always pointed north. For this reason the magnetic rock was called lodestone, or leading stone.

In 1269, a French crusader, Petrus Maricourt, wrote about a pivoted compass much like the simple compasses we use today. He took a chunk of lodestone that had been cut into the shape of a ball. He put a compass at different points on its surface. For each point he marked a line on the ball showing the direction in which the compass needle set. When he had finished, the lines covering the ball looked like the lines of longitude that are drawn from south to north on a map of the Earth. Maricourt noticed that all the lines passed through two points, one at each end of the ball. He called the points 'poles', because they reminded him of the geographical Poles of the Earth. He did more tests with magnets. He found that the poles were the places where the magnetic power was strongest. He thought that magnets got their power from the sky.

It was now known that every magnet had a pole at each end. At one end was a south-seeking (or south) pole. At the other end was a north-seeking (or north) pole. When brought near each other, similar poles pushed each other away. Dissimilar poles pulled towards each other. It was not possible to make a magnet with only one pole. No matter how many times a magnet was broken in two, it always had two poles. Pieces of iron could be made into magnets by stroking one end of the iron in one direction with one pole of a magnet, then the other end with the other pole.

Over 300 years passed before much more was discovered about magnetism. In 1600, William Gilbert, the physician of Queen Elizabeth I, made a large sphere of magnetic iron. By experiments with the sphere he proved that the Earth itself acts as a huge magnet. He also found that iron when heated lost its magnetism, but regained it when cooled.

The next advances came at the beginning of the 19th century. For some time scientists had thought that there might be a connection between magnetism and electricity. After many experiments, the French physicist André Ampère and the Danish chemist Hans Oersted discovered in 1820 that a coil of wire with an electric current flowing through it acted like a magnet.

In 1825 William Sturgeon in England found that a stronger magnetic effect could be produced by winding the coil of wire on an iron rod, or core. The American scientist Joseph Henry made a much more efficient version in 1828. Such magnets, which use an electric current to produce a magnetic effect, are called electromagnets. (See: *electricity*.)

The next discovery was to prove very important in the development of the modern machine age. It was made independently by Joseph Henry and the English scientist Michael Faraday. They reasoned that if an electric current could produce a magnetic effect, then a magnet should be able to produce a current. In 1822, Faraday wrote in his notebook: 'Convert magnetism into electricity.'

Earlier, Faraday had done a simple experiment that had been described by Maricourt more than 500 years earlier. He sprinkled iron filings on a piece of paper under which he had put a magnet. When he tapped the paper gently, the filings formed a pattern on the paper round the magnet. They formed lines that curved from the south pole to the north pole of the magnet. These lines Faraday called magnetic lines of force. They formed a magnetic field. Such lines show the direction of the magnetic force. They indicate the direction in which a compass needle would point when put at different places near the magnet.

In 1831, Faraday did a new experiment to produce an electric current from a magnetic field. He took an iron ring and wound a coil of wire round one part of it. Around another part he wound a second coil of wire. Then he connected the first coil to a battery. He thought that the current passing through the first coil would, as Ampère had shown, act like a magnet and produce a magnetic field. This magnetic field would be concentrated in the iron core and would pass through the second coil. Now, Faraday reasoned, the magnetic field should cause a current to flow in the second coil.

He connected the second coil to an instrument for measuring current. When he switched on the current in the first coil, however, no steady current flowed in the second coil. But he noticed that there was a brief flow of current in the second coil, just when he switched on the current in the first coil. There was another brief flow when he turned the current off. He realized that it was not the magnetism itself but the change in the magnetic field that caused a current to flow in the second coil. As the current in the first coil was switched on or off a magnetic field built up or collapsed. The changing magnetic lines of force passed through the second coil and produced the brief flow of current. This second current was 'induced' by the current in the first coil. (The word 'induce' means simply 'to bring about'.)

This discovery was very important. It led to the development of the dynamo, to produce electricity, and the electric motor to drive machines. Faraday himself built several electric motors and dynamos.

Such inventions enabled men to make and use electricity on a large scale for the first time. Until then, only small amounts of electricity had been produced using batteries and clumsy friction machines.

How is it that some materials make good magnets while others do not? The answer lies in the fact they are often made up of tiny units. Each unit acts like a magnet with a north pole at one end and a south at the other. In the case of a magnetic material in the unmagnetized state, these little units point in all directions. So their magnetic fields cancel out, and the material does not act like a magnet. But, if the material is placed in a strong magnetic field, the little units all line up. Their north poles face one way and their south poles face the opposite way. Then the material acts like a magnet. It has a north pole at one end and a south pole at the other. In a piece of iron, the unit can stay lined up in this way after the strong magnetic field is removed. The iron can become a permanent magnet.

What causes these unit magnets? During the 1820s, André Ampère suggested that they might be caused by tiny electric currents flowing inside the particles that make up the material. His idea proved correct, but physicists now have a better theory. Matter is made of very small particles called atoms. Every atom contains still smaller particles. The smallest are known as electrons. They are very light particles with a negative electric charge. Their motion inside the atom creates a tiny electric current, and, according to Ampère, a current causes a magnetic force. Thus it is the movement of the electrons inside the atoms that causes magnetism. Part of the magnetism is due to the circling of electrons round the centre of the atom. Another part is a result of each electron spinning round on its own axis, like a top. Most substances are made of atoms in which the magnetic forces are weak. These kinds of substance are very weakly magnetic and commonly called 'nonmagnetic'. But, a few materials are made of atoms in which the magnetic forces are strong. These are the materials, such as iron, cobalt, and nickel, that are commonly called 'magnetic'. (See: *atom, matter*.)

How big are the unit magnets? Physicists have recently discovered that they are large clusters of atoms. They are called domains. All the atom magnets in a domain are lined up in the same direction. Although each domain may contain billions of atoms, domains are still very small. Often they are only about one thousandth of a centimetre across.

Domains are formed only in the strongly magnetic materials. Once formed they are stable, and so provide 'permanent' magnets. But such a magnet can lose its magnetism if it is hit hard. The shock moves the atoms in the domains out of their lined-up arrangement. It is possible to make a bar of iron magnetic by hitting it while it is in line with the Earth's magnetic field. The atoms in the domains vibrate and the Earth's field pulls them into line with it, in parallel north-south positions. Heating a magnetic material above a certain temperature, called its Curie point, destroys its 'permanent' magnetism.

The strength of a magnetic field is measured in units called gauss. The strength of the Earth's field is only about half a gauss. A strong horseshoe magnet may produce a field of a few hundred gauss. The strongest field that can be produced by a permanent magnet is about 9,000 gauss. Electromagnets can produce magnetic fields even stronger than this. One huge electromagnet at the National Magnet Laboratory in Cambridge, Massachusetts, can produce a field of 255,000 gauss. An immense amount of heat is generated by the huge currents needed, so the magnet must be cooled to prevent it melting.

Strong fields can be made using superconductors. These are materials in which huge currents flow easily. Metals, such as zirconium or niobium, when cooled to nearly $-273\,^\circ$C (0 K), almost the lowest possible temperature, become superconductors. A wire coil made of such metals carrying a large current can be a powerful electromagnet at very low temperatures.

Each year several million tons of iron are used to make magnets all over the world. Modern permanent magnets are often made of alloys, or mixtures of metals, such as steel. Alnico is another magnetic alloy. It contains aluminium, cobalt, nickel, and iron. Permanent magnets are used in many devices, including loudspeakers, telephones, small motors, and measuring instruments. Temporary magnets and electromagnets are needed when a magnetic field must be switched on and off frequently. They are used in electric bells, motors, and generators.

The linear induction motor

Magnetism has a lot of other uses, too. For example, it is used in an exciting new device called the linear induction motor. The motor generates a moving magnetic field. The field may move a metal object along, such as a steel plate.

Or, a train can carry the motor, which generates a backward-moving field in the rail. The magnetic field tends to pull the rail backward. Since the rail cannot move, the train is pulled forward.

The linear induction motor can produce rapid acceleration and high speeds, perhaps up to 400 kph (250 mph). It also has the advantage of having no moving parts. Research into its uses is being done in the USA, Britain, France, and Japan. Some designs use a magnetic field to keep the train stable. The track is made of bricks of a magnetic material. They are arranged so that all their south poles are uppermost. On the underside of the train is a flat metal plate, magnetized so that its south pole faces downward. Similar poles push each other away, so the train is supported on the tracks.

Magnetic North

The simplest use of magnetism is in the compass. This invention has helped travellers for many centuries. But there are few places on the Earth where a compass needle will point to True North. True North is the direction toward the North Pole, which is the north end of the Earth's axis. The direction in which a compass points is called Magnetic North. The angle between Magnetic and True North is known as the magnetic declination. This angle varies widely from place to place and also from year to year. In the USA it can be up to about 20 degrees east or west of True North. Sailors must use special charts showing angles of declination, in order to navigate with a compass.

Declination at a particular place varies with time. There are small daily changes. Bigger changes occur over many years. Sudden changes, often very large, occur too. They are called magnetic storms. These storms are caused by the eruption of charged particles from the Sun. Some of the particles travel toward the Earth. They move about the Earth, like an electric current that produces its own magnetic field. This field is added to the Earth's magnetic field, causing a magnetic storm. It can make compass needles swing wildly. (See: *Sun*.)

mathematics

The mathematics classes of a good modern school are very different in the early forms from the classes of thirty or forty years ago. In the old classes, children sat in rows, while the teacher stood at the front. They worked singly. Their only tools, apart from books, were pencils, rulers and compasses. The books consisted of text with a few black and white diagrams.

The classroom of today is likely to be noisy. It is filled with children who are active. They are making models, or measuring the room, or weighing, or counting. They are working together in pairs or in groups. In the course of these activities the children are learning about all the different things that mathematics actually is.

Very young children learning about numbers will use all sorts of different materials. They may use counters. They may use rods of various lengths, each length representing a number. They may draw charts in which numbers are laid out in patterns. Some children learn best when using shapes, others when counting, others when colours help them. But in the end they learn that facts about numbers do not depend on what kind of material you use.

In learning about mathematics, very young children have problems that older people find hard to understand. A child may not be able to work out whether 34 is an even number, because he or she is confused by the fact that 3 is odd. Explaining in words may not be much help. But the child can certainly find out the answer, given the chance to experiment with rods or counters. The teacher must not be too quick to help. The adult's way of seeing things will probably not be the child's. And a discovery, such as '34 is even', made after many mistakes, will not easily be forgotten by the child.

In learning about numbers, it is important to study their factors. The factors of a number are all the smaller numbers that divide into it without leaving a remainder. For example, the factors of 12 are 1,2,3,4 and 6. Young children can discover factors with the help of heaps of counters or with rods of various lengths.

With the help of number charts they can reach the same understanding from a different direction. For example, they can number a hundred squares in order. Then they can shade in all the numbers that are multiples of 3 – 3,6,9 and so on. The pattern they obtain is a valuable lesson about numbers in itself. When they go on to shade in the multiples of 4, they obtain another pattern. Where a square is shaded twice, that number is a multiple of both 3 and 4. It has both 3 and 4 for factors. One such number is 12.

The child shading in every third square is following a rule. And following the rule makes a pattern. Part of the job of mathematics is to study patterns.

Natural processes follow rules. And so patterns often become visible in nature. Children in present-day maths classes study the patterns that occur in nature. They find that there is a mathematical rule that describes the spiral shape of a coiled shell. At each turn of the spiral the shell gets bigger. And the increase in size follows a rule.

Snow crystals grow as new water molecules – the smallest possible particles of water – attach themselves. The building-up process follows rules. The result is the beautiful shapes that snow crystals show under the microscope.

Snow crystals illustrate an important idea

that is taught in modern mathematics lessons. They show several kinds of symmetry. If you imagine a perfectly formed crystal to be divided down the middle, the left-hand side will look like the reflection in a mirror of the right side. We say that the crystal has reflection symmetry. The human face has reflection symmetry too. The left half looks like a reflection of the right half. But the snow crystal has more symmetry than the human face. For example, you can imagine dividing it horizontally. The lower half looks like a reflection of the upper half.

Symmetry is important not only to mathematicians – artists and designers constantly create symmetrical patterns.

Maths teaching once included much practice in computing (adding, subtracting, multiplying and dividing). Now we increasingly use electronic machines to work out lengthy sums. In well-equipped schools children may have the use of small calculating machines. And they are likely to make their own simple 'computers'. The diagram shows how a number chart and strips of paper of various lengths can be used for addition. Children can make their own slide rules for multiplication problems.

The point of these 'labour-saving' devices is that making them and using them teaches the child a lot about arithmetic. Long calculations are not an important part of mathematics.

Teaching standard formulas and making students practice them can prevent real understanding. Countless children in the past have learned that the area of a rectangle is equal to its 'length times breadth'. This formula will not help them when they meet shapes with more sides, especially if they are curved.

The emphasis in present-day maths teaching is on reaching an understanding of the basic mathematical processes. Some of the most basic ideas of mathematics have only in the last few years been brought into the classroom.

The idea of a set, for example, is fundamental to all modern mathematics. A set is any group of objects. The members of the set do not have to be connected, or similar to each other, or even near to each other. We can think of the set of all red-haired people, for example, or the set of all English words beginning with D, or the set of all the objects on a certain table.

The idea of sets is basic to counting. For when we say that two collections contain the same number of objects, we are saying that the members of one of those sets can be matched with the members of the other set one-to-one. There are no unmatched members left over in either set.

The members of some sets cannot be counted. A straight line is a set of points that is 'infinite' in number – the points cannot be counted. In modern maths it is treated as such. And a triangle is treated as a set of three straight lines.

Many adults can do complicated multiplication and division without really understanding what they are doing. Children today are taught the 'basic laws of arithmetic' on which all computation rests. There are the commutative laws of addition and multiplication. They say simply that the order of numbers does not matter in addition and multiplication:

$$4 + 5 = 5 + 4$$
$$3 \times 6 = 6 \times 3$$

and so on.

These laws are used constantly in calculation without being noticed. There are no commutative laws for subtraction and division. It is false to say:

$$4 - 5 = 5 - 4$$
or: $$3 \div 6 = 6 \div 3$$

There is another basic law called the distributive law. It gives the rule for the use of brackets:

$$5 \times (8 + 7) = (5 \times 8) + (5 \times 7)$$

We have given these laws using particular sets of numbers. The maths student of today learns very early how to use algebra to make statements about any set of numbers. Thus he or she will write the commutative law of addition as:

$$x + y = y + x$$

Here the letters x and y can be replaced by any pair of numbers. In the language of modern maths teaching they are called place-holders. (See: *algebra*.)

The young maths student of today will also learn a little about topology, a branch of maths that does not involve numbers or shapes. An example of a topological problem is very old and famous: Walk across the seven bridges of Koenigsberg and return to your starting point without crossing any of them twice. This is a mathematical problem. It was a mathematician who first gave an answer by proof, rather than trial and error.

See: *algebra, arithmetic, topology*.

matter

Think of the knife, fork and spoon with which you ate dinner yesterday. They were made completely or partly of a metal, steel. Though they were three different objects they were probably made of the same kind of steel. We say that the steel is one kind of matter.

The leather of a pair of shoes is another kind of matter. The same kind of matter was used in making thousands of other pairs of shoes. Each shoe may also contain rubber, and metal (around the holes for the laces).

Matter is what things are made of. One kind of matter can make up countless different objects. And a single object can be made of many different kinds of matter.

Though there are many different kinds of matter we can group them into three main forms. You can see all three in a glass containing a fizzy drink.

Solids are the first form of matter. They have a definite size and shape which can be hard to change. The glass itself is a solid. If it isn't hit or squeezed too hard, it keeps its shape.

The drink is an example of the second form of matter, the liquids. Liquids don't have a definite shape. They take the shape of the container they are poured into. But they take up a definite amount of space. A litre of milk is still a litre, whatever shape of container it is poured into.

The bubbles in the drink are an example of the third form of matter, the gases. A quantity of gas can take any shape. And it can take almost any size. If you look closely, you may be able to see the bubbles getting bigger as they rise.

The air around us is a gas. When you pump up a bicycle tyre, you are putting air into the tyre. You are pushing it into a smaller space.

Most matter can exist in any of these three forms. The ice that you skate on in winter, for example, is solid. In spring it melts, and becomes the water of the pond. In dry weather the level of the water in the pond may fall. The water hasn't simply vanished. It has turned into water vapour, the gas form of water. Water vapour is invisible. It spreads out through the atmosphere.

You can see the same thing on a small scale. Leave a glass containing ice cubes standing in a room for a few days. First the ice changes from the solid form to liquid water. Then the water slowly disappears as it turns into gas, spreading out through the air of the room.

The solid, liquid and gas forms are called the three 'states' of matter. Nearly all matter can exist in all three forms. Air, even when dry, can be turned into a liquid by making it cold enough. A gas can also be turned into the solid form by further cooling.

So, too, even solids like iron can be turned into liquids by heating. And in the Sun and stars, iron and many other kinds of matter exist as intensely hot gases.

Ancient ideas of matter

Earlier than 500BC, philosophers in Ancient Greece tried to explain how matter can exist in so many different forms.

One idea was that any piece of matter is a mixture of several different substances, called elements. There were supposed to be four elements making up the matter around us, Earth, Air, Fire and Water. The heavenly bodies were made of a fifth element, Ether.

Democritus, a Greek of the fifth century BC, tried to explain the kinds of matter in a different way. He suggested that all matter is made up of tiny particles. The particles could not be cut into smaller pieces, so he called them atoms, meaning 'uncuttable'. The difference between, say, a rough solid and a smooth one was due to the different shapes of their atoms and the way they were joined together. In a solid the atoms were joined together strongly. In a liquid like water, the atoms were smooth and round, and so could slide over each other easily. Flames were supposed to be painful because their atoms were pointed, like thorns.

It was not until 2,000 years after these early Greeks that scientists began to make experiments to find out how matter is made up. It was soon discovered that elements exist. That is, there are certain basic substances from which all others are made up. But there are far more elements than the five that the Greeks believed in. Nearly a hundred occur in nature. And they do not include Earth, Air, Fire or Water. Air for example, is a mixture consisting mainly of the elements oxygen and nitrogen in the gas state. Water consists of the elements hydrogen and oxygen. 'Earth' can be the name of many different kinds of substance, none of which is an element. Fire can consist of many different kinds of gas, produced by burning. These gases glow merely because they are hot.

Scientists learned more and more about atoms. They found Democritus was right in many ways. The atoms of a particular element are all the same (except that they may have several slightly different weights). The atoms of each element are different from the atoms of all other elements. Atoms join together in small groups called molecules. In each molecule of water, for example, two atoms of hydrogen are joined to one atom of oxygen. Today we call a substance an element only if its molecules consist of one kind of atom. Oxygen is an element because the two atoms of each molecule are both oxygen atoms. If the molecules of a substance contain more than one kind of atom, we call that substance a compound.

Scientists could even measure the weight of atoms. They found that each atom of oxygen in the air, for example, weighs only about one fifty-million-millionth of a milligram. They found that atoms are about one forty-millionth of a centimetre across. (See: atom.)

Inside the atom

Around 1900, scientists began to learn how atoms themselves are built up. Tiny though the atom is, most of its mass is concentrated into an even smaller space at its centre. This central part of the atom is called the nucleus (plural: nuclei). The nucleus is itself a collection of smaller particles called protons and neutrons.

Round the nucleus, particles called electrons circle. Sometimes electrons can be separated from their atoms. When you switch on a light, the electric current flowing through the light bulb and the wires is made up of countless slowly moving electrons. (See: electricity.) In the Sun and stars, the huge temperatures and pressures break atoms up. The hot gases of the Sun and stars are made of electrons and nuclei, not whole atoms. Gases like these, made of electrically charged particles, are known to scientists as plasmas.

Knowing what matter is made of is only part of the job of understanding matter. We also need to know what holds each atom together.

Gravitational attraction is one of the pulls holding matter together. Every single piece of matter in the universe attracts every other piece of matter. There is an attraction now between you and this book and every other object in the room. But the pull is very weak. Gravity is important only with big objects like the Earth, other planets and the stars. You are kept on the ground by the pull of the Earth's gravity. The planets are held in their paths round the Sun by gravity, and the Sun and stars are kept together by gravity.

But electrons are held in their paths round the nucleus of each atom by a much stronger pull than gravity. There are two kinds of electricity. Electrons carry one kind called negative electricity. We say that they have negative electric charge. Protons carry the other kind, called positive electricity. They have positive electric charge. There is a strong pull between the two kinds of electric charge. So electrons and nuclei pull on each other very strongly.

But positive electric charge pushes away any other positive charge. Similarly, negative charge pushes away other negative charge. So the positive charges of the nucleus tend to push away from each other. The nucleus would break up, except that there are even stronger forces holding its particles together.

Some nuclei actually do break up. The forces holding them together are not strong enough. Uranium atoms, for example, break up to form other, smaller kinds of atom. Much more uranium existed in the Earth when it was formed than does now. Fortunately, most atoms are 'stable' – they will last for ever.

Matter and antimatter

To scientists, it is surprising that an atom's positive charge is in the nucleus, and the negative charge all in the outer parts. Why do we not find atoms with negative nuclei and positive electrons?

Positive electrons, or positrons, exist, and they can be produced in the laboratory. They do not last very long because they soon collide with an electron. When that happens, the electron and positron both disappear completely, sending out a flash of radiation.

So positrons and other kinds of 'antiparticle' cannot exist for long on Earth. There is probably very little 'antimatter' in our Galaxy – the collection of stars, gas and dust to which our Sun belongs. But it is possible that some of the other star systems that astronomers can see through telescopes are made completely of antimatter. Negatively charged electrons would be as short-lived there as positrons are on Earth.

It was once thought that matter could never be created or destroyed. The amount of matter in the universe was supposed to be always the same. But as we have just seen, when a particle such as an electron collides with its corresponding antiparticle, they both vanish.

Although the particle and antiparticle disappear, they send out radiation. Later new matter could be formed, for radiation can be turned into matter. An X-ray passing close to the nucleus of an atom may disappear and be replaced by a particle and an antiparticle. The photo on this page shows tracks left by an electron and a positron separating from the point where they were created together. (The path of the X-ray does not show in the photo.)

Radiation – which includes light, radio waves and X-rays – behaves like matter in many ways. It travels in 'packets' called **quanta** (singular: **quantum**), which sometimes act like particles. When light shines onto an object, that object gets a tiny push from the stream of quanta. Rays of light and other kinds of radiation are bent by the gravitational pull of planets and stars, just as streams of particles would be.

The beginning of matter
How was the matter in the universe created originally? And when did it appear?

Astronomers can see billions of star systems or galaxies. They are travelling away from each other at high speeds. They are moving as if they were thrown out by a gigantic explosion over ten billion years ago. Most astronomers believe that this really happened. What happened before the 'big bang', they cannot say.

In the early days of the universe, according to this theory, all matter consisted of the gas hydrogen. Hydrogen has the smallest, simplest atoms. Stars appeared from this hydrogen. Inside them, heavier atoms were built up. They were atoms of the elements other than hydrogen. Some of the stars exploded, scattering these elements into space. The planets of our solar system, including our Earth, were formed from this matter. (See: *solar system, star.*)

A different theory of the origin of matter has been suggested. According to this theory, there was no 'big bang'. Atoms of hydrogen are being created all the time, everywhere, from nothing. New galaxies form from these. This would mean that new matter is appearing in, for example, your room – but at the rate of one atom of hydrogen in millions of years. So far, no such creation of matter has been discovered. See: *energy, gravity, physics, universe.*

measurement

How big? How far? How heavy? How hot? How fast? When? These are commonplace questions. And we need measurements to answer each one of them. We need to measure distance to answer 'how big' or 'how far'. We must measure temperature to answer 'how hot', weight to answer 'how heavy', speed to answer 'how fast' and time to answer 'when'.

We can use a ruler to measure distance and size. We can use a thermometer to measure temperature, a speedometer to measure speed and a clock to measure time. Most homes have at least one clock, thermometer and ruler. Every car has a speedometer.

We measure length by splitting it up into many smaller lengths and counting them up. The small lengths are called 'length units'. A ruler is marked in millimetres and centmetres, or feet and inches. These are length units. You can easily measure the cover of this book with a ruler. What you are really doing is counting the number of centimetres each length.

In ancient times, people used body measurements instead of rulers or tape measures. Many of the measuring units we still use come from body measurements. A foot was originally the length of a man's foot. At first, it was any man's foot, but later it became the length of a specific foot, such as the chief's or headman's foot. A mile was a thousand strides, as defined by the Romans. A stride was about five Roman feet. Mile comes from *mille*, the Latin word for thousand.

The 'cubit' was an Ancient Egyptian measure, meaning the distance from a man's elbow to the tip of his middle finger. Cubit comes from the Latin word for elbow. We no longer use cubits but we do still use yards. A yard began as 'two cubits'. A fathom is a man's armspan – the distance between his fingertips with arms stretched out on either side. Traditionally, sailors measure depth of water by 'casting the lead'. A weight is attached to the end of a rope. The sailor sees how many fathoms of rope are needed to drop the rope to the bottom of the water. Depth of water is still measured in fathoms. One fathom is defined as six feet.

A system of personal units is very useful. By putting one foot in front of the other, heel to toe, you can measure out your room or your driveway. You might find cubits or fathoms more useful for measuring out cloth. But although your personal measurements are useful to you, they do not tell much to someone who is not your size. We should all use the same measuring units.

Throughout history men have needed to measure three things in particular, length, time and mass. (Mass is what you are interested in when, for example, buying food. It tells you how much food there is. In everyday life we measure mass by weighing and express the result in kilos or pounds. (See: *gravity*.)

So agreed units are needed for measuring length, time and mass. Tradesmen are required by law to use correct weights and measures. In Britian, the Imperial System has been used until recent years. The units are the same in the US Customary System, established in 1832, although some quantities differ slightly. The US gallon, for example is smaller than the British gallon. The Imperial System is now being replaced by the metric system used in Europe.

The Imperial System is only one of the many systems of weights and measures used in the world today. Measurement is very important to trade and science. Using so many different ways of measuring makes international trade and science difficult. Science is international, so measurements should be meaningful to scientists in all countries. Scientists and engineers throughout the world use the International System of Units, or SI. You will find a table of SI units in Volume 8.

In the SI, length is measured in metres, time is measured in seconds, and mass is measured in kilograms. A metre equals about 39.57 inches. A kilogram is about 2.2 pounds.

It is convenient to have units of different sizes for different purposes. We do not want to discuss the distance from the Earth to the Moon in inches, or the weight of an atom in pounds. In Imperial units inches, feet, yards and miles are used as units of length. Ounces, pounds and tons are used as units of mass. Seconds, minutes, hours, days and years are used as units of time.

A decimal system

The SI is a decimal system, meaning that it is based on ten. Larger units are 10, 100, 1,000, and so on, times the size of the basic units. A thousand metres are one kilometre. 'Kilo' means one thousand. Smaller units are named in a similar way. A centimetre is one hundredth of a metre. 'Centi' means one hundred.

Rulers must agree with some standard of length. The standard yard used to be marked on a brass bar called the Trouton Scale. The distance between two fixed marks on the Trouton Scale at a fixed temperature was defined as one yard. A metal bar gets longer when it is warmed, so temperature is important.

Nowadays, the yard is defined to be exactly equal to 0.9144 metres. The metre was first introduced at the end of the eighteenth century in France. One metre was defined as one ten-millionth of the distance from the North Pole to the Equator along a path passing through Paris. A platinum bar, later replaced by a platinum-iridium bar, was used as the standard metre until 1960.

We now use the 'light wave standard' for the metre. The metre is defined as 1,650,763.73 wavelengths of orange light from the element krypton-86. (A wavelength is the distance from one crest of a wave to the next. See: *wave*.)

Light waves are used as a standard of length because they always have exactly the same wavelength. But light is also useful for actually making exact measurements. Distances can be measured to within a fraction of a wavelength of light. The wavelength of light is around sixty millionths of a centimetre. The wave length of orange light is 59.62 millionths of a centimetre. The thickness of a film of oil only one molecule thick can be measured. (See: *light*.)

Even smaller distances can be measured with X-rays. The wavelength of X-rays is ten thousand times smaller than the wavelength of visible light. X-rays can travel through substances which are not transparent to light. Layers of atoms in a metal reflect X-rays, just as a mirror reflects light. The reflected X-rays give us information about the spacing of atoms in the metal.

Weighing balances

An old fashioned weighing balance has a rod with a scale-pan hanging at each end. The rod is pivoted at the middle and can move up and down like a seesaw. One pan holds the material to be weighed. Weights are put in the other pan. The scales balance when there is an equal weight in each pan. If one pan is heavier than the other, the heavy pan sinks.

Exactly the same principle is used in the most accurate of modern balances. The slightest change in temperature during a weighing will cause the arms of the balance to change in length by a tiny amount. So, in very accurate measurements, the operator remains outside the weighing room. He makes the measurement by remote control. Thus it will not be influenced by his body heat.

In ancient times, goods were weighed by putting stones in the weight pan. Wheat grains were used for measuring light things, like small quantities of herbs and medicines. Weights called stones and grains are still used in some countries.

The SI unit of mass is the kilogram. The standard kilogram is a cylinder made of platinum-iridium, like the old standard metre. The pound is now defined in terms of the kilogram. It is roughly 0.45 kilograms.

Many countries possess their own copies of the international standard kilogram. From time to time they are compared with the standard. Their weights are generally found to be in agreement to within one part in 50 million.

We use clocks or watches to measure time. Long before clocks were invented, people used the Sun, the Moon and the stars to mark the passage of time.

A sundial used the Sun to measure time. The most primitive kind of sundial is just an upright stick in the ground. As the day goes on, the stick's shadow moves round in an arc of a circle. The sundial helped man to divide the day into smaller time intervals. The Ancient Egyptian and Babylonian sundials were the first to divide the daylight hours into twelve equal parts. Summer days are longer than winter days so the length of these ancient units varied with the time of year.

The invention of mechanical clocks meant that man could measure time more exactly. Fairly accurate mechanical clocks were made in the 14th century. Clocks enabled man to divide the day into 24 equal parts, called hours. As clocks were made more accurate, the hour was divided into smaller parts. Sixty minutes make an hour and 60 seconds make a minute.

The sundial is adequate for one kind of time measurement. It can tell – though only roughly – the time at which an event happens. You can arrange to meet someone at, say, 'the sixth hour'. All correctly-made sundials will agree upon when this is. This kind of time measurement is called a measurement of 'epoch'. The epoch of an event is simply the time when it happened. Calendars, sundials and ordinary clocks state epochs.

Another kind of time measurement tells how much time passes between two events. This is the time 'interval' between them. For measuring time intervals, units of equal size are needed. Sundials could be marked to indicate hours of roughly equal length. But this was not frequently done until mechanical clocks began to replace sundials.

Accurate clocks

Mechanical clocks measure time intervals. Modern clocks can do so with great accuracy. Clocks that can keep time to one part in a million million can be built. This is a variation of about one minute in two million years.

The standard SI time unit is the second. The SI second is the time taken by 9,192,631,770 wavelengths of a certain kind of light to pass a fixed point. The light is given out by the radioactive element cesium-133.

The second was once defined so that the average day was 86,400 seconds long. But the length of the day varies. So a more constant standard was chosen.

The SI system has only seven basic units. They include units of mass, length, time, electric current and temperature. From these a large number of other units are defined. The unit of energy, for example, is called the joule (see: *energy*). It is equal to the energy of movement of a mass of one kilogram travelling at a speed of one metre per second.

Measurement is essential to science. Most scientific experiments depend on it. Scientific measurements are only as exact as our measuring instruments. Scientists and technologists are always trying to improve measuring techniques.

Find out by doing

See how you can use your body measurements as a rough measure. How big is your personal foot, inch or fathom? Are they the same as the inch, foot and fathom we use today? Which of your own body measurements compare best with modern measuring units? Maybe your 'cubit' is exactly a foot, or your hand is six inches long.

Make an instrument to measure small distances. Stand a bottle with a screw cap on a table. Next to it, hold a ruler which is marked in millimetres. Tape a needle across the top of the cap, pointing at the ruler. Give the cap one complete turn. Measure how far the needle moves up or down. Then mark ten lines at equal intervals around the edge of the cap. Turn the cap by an amount equal to one of these intervals. The needle will move up or down by a smaller distance. This smaller distance is one-tenth of the distance it moves in a complete turn of the cap.

microscope

One of nature's most wonderful creations is the human eye. Yet our eyes cannot see objects smaller than a few thousandths of a centimetre. This is less than the width of a hair, but is still larger than many living organisms. A whole world of very tiny things, ranging from particles of dust to bacteria, is closed to us if we use only our eyes. The microscope opens that world for us to study and enjoy. Its name is taken from the Greek words meaning 'small' and 'look'.

The first microscopes were invented in the

17th century. Anton van Leeuwenhoek, a Dutch merchant, made a simple homemade microscope. He ground tiny but perfect glass lenses. With each one he could magnify the object at which he was looking about 200 times. In 1665, Robert Hooke, an English scientist, discovered and identified the cell, the basic unit of all living matter. He used a compound microscope, that is, one with several lenses in it. Hooke did not invent his microscope. It is thought that two Dutch eyeglass makers, Hans and Zacharias Janssen, invented it in 1590. With time, compound microscopes reached the high degree of precision they have today.

Most modern microscopes use the same principles as the older ones. They are called light, or optical, microscopes, since they use light to see objects, just as our eyes do. But more powerful microscopes have been developed recently, for example the electron microscope which uses a beam of electrons instead of ordinary light.

Today, the microscope plays an important role in all fields of medicine and biology. It also helps the geologist to analyse minerals, and the chemist or physicist to discover the structure of matter. It has even revealed the history of ancient civilisations to the archeologist, by showing him what has been dug out of the earth.

The purpose of any microscope is to 'magnify' objects – make them look bigger. It will multiply the object's apparent height and width by an amount called the magnifying power. This power can be up to about 18 thousand for some optical microscopes. An ordinary magnifying lens has a power of, at most, eight or ten. Electron microscopes can magnify objects several hundred thousands of times.

A microscope's quality depends on its magnifying power. It also depends on its ability to separate the details of an object. Two points very close together on the object may be blurred by the microscope. They look like one larger point. If this happens, they remain blurred even when they are greatly magnified. We cannot see the two separate points. The microscope's ability to separate them is called its power of resolution, or resolving power. Resolving power is the smallest distance between two points that the microscope can show clearly.

An optical microscope blurs objects in this way because of the nature of light. We know that light consists of tiny waves. To see an object with the microscope, we shine light on it. The light waves spread out slightly as they travel from each point on the object.

Light from points on the object that are very close together may overlap, blurring into one point. The points cannot be separated, or resolved. This occurs when the points are closer than about half the length of a light wave. Therefore, the microscope's resolving power is

about half the wavelength of the light we are using. Visible light has wavelengths of around 50 millionths of a centimetre. So, the resolving power is half that. Blue light has a shorter wavelength than red light. The resolving power is better if we use blue light.

An electron microscope can also blur objects. The electrons which it uses behave like little bundles of waves. However, the wavelength of the electron waves is several hundred times shorter than that of light. So, the electron microscope's resolving power is hundreds of times better than that of an optical microscope. For this reason, it can separate details that are only a few atoms apart. The optical microscope can show only details that are thousands of atoms apart.

How does a microscope work? A light microscope contains lenses. Lenses are pieces of curved glass that bend the light going through them. This is called refraction. (See: *lenses and mirrors*.) The lenses produce a magnified image, or picture, of the object. What we see is the image. The simplest light microscope has only one lens. It is a magnifying glass. Its magnifying power is small. It can have many imperfections which blur or distort the image, so that the image does not look like the object. Therefore a better kind of microscope, called the compound microscope, is used by scientists. It has a number of lenses.

One group of lenses makes up the condenser. This focuses light on the object from below. The light usually comes from an electric light bulb and is reflected onto the condenser by a mirror. Another group of lenses makes up the objective, which creates a magnified image. Last of all is the eyepiece, which magnifies the image again and presents it to our eyes.

Sometimes there are several objective lenses with different magnifying powers. They can be changed to let us see different sizes of image. Because of such refinements, a good microscope can be very expensive.

To use the microscope well, you must practice with it until you can focus and see easily. The light which shines on the object should be adjusted carefully. The 'stage' supporting the object may also be adjustable. And the object itself must be prepared in the right way. A specimen of material often has to be stained, or dyed, for details to be seen. The specimen may be a thin slice of material, or a liquid, so that light can shine through it. Or it may be a solid object. In this case, light from a lamp at the side of the microscope may be directed down on the object by a mirror above the object. The object reflects the light to the eyepiece.

The scientist has many kinds of microscope available to him. One kind uses invisible ultraviolet light. It has a wavelength even shorter than blue light, and the power of resolution is thus better. But the image must be photographed, because it cannot be seen by the human eye. Also, ultraviolet light cannot go through ordinary glass, so special lenses are needed. And it kills living cells, so it cannot be used for live specimens.

The electron microscope does not use lenses to bend light, like an optical microscope does. Instead, it uses electric and magnetic fields to bend beams of electrons. Electrons are tiny particles with a negative electric charge. They travel in straight lines through an empty space, or vacuum. But their path is changed when they move through an electric or magnetic field. An electric field is produced by a battery. A magnetic field can be produced by an ordinary magnet. (See: *electricity*, *magnet*.)

In an electron microscope, the electrons are shot out into a vacuum by an 'electron gun'. They 'boil off' a heated metal filament and are accelerated by a very high voltage. This voltage can be up to a million volts. The higher it is, the smaller will be the wavelength of the electrons, and the better resolving power the microscope has. Then the electrons shoot through a hole into the microscope tube, which also contains no air. This vacuum is needed because air would disturb the electron beam. Next the electrons go through a magnetic lens that focusses them onto the specimen. Living material cannot be used, since it would be killed by the electrons. The specimen must be sliced very thin, to let the electrons go through it. Higher voltage electrons go through thicker specimens. The electrons are scattered by the material, and travel onward, passing through other lenses. Finally they hit a fluorescent screen, which glows at the points where they hit. This works like a TV screen. The screen can be viewed or photographed from the other side.

The most powerful kind of microscope used today is called the field ion microscope. It was invented by a German physicist, Erwin Müller, in 1958. It can reveal details even finer than those shown by an electron microscope. At present it can be used only for studying certain metals. Its resolving power is so good that the arrangement of atoms in metal crystals can be seen clearly. The atoms form a pattern (see: *atom*). Magnifications of three million are possible when the metal is cooled to low temperatures.

The X-ray microscope could be the next big advance. X-rays have wavelengths a thousand times smaller than light, and they do less damage to a sensitive sample, such as a living cell, than an electron microscope. However, it is difficult to produce a sufficiently intense beam of X-rays, and even if you have one (as is now possible with certain types of particle accelerators) it is difficult to make the beam bend and focus. Now both of these problems seem soluble, and scientists have already made fascinating images of several different types of cell.

Moon

Nearly half a million kilometres from us the Moon, our nearest neighbour in space, travels round the Earth. The Moon is a ball of rock 3,475 kilometres (2,160 miles) across its centre. It always has the same scarred face towards the Earth. Until the first space probes travelled round it, less was known about its far side than about stars millions of times farther away.

The Moon is an airless, waterless, lifeless body. It is roasted by the Sun during the lunar day, which lasts for two of our weeks. It is then frozen during the lunar night, which also is two weeks long. Near the lunar poles the temperature is never above freezing point. Seen from the Earth, the Moon appears much larger than the planets and the stars, and as large as the Sun. In fact, it is smaller than any of these, but it is much nearer to Earth.

Scientists have always been fascinated by the nature of the Moon. Galileo, the Italian astronomer, was one of the first to draw a map of the Moon, in the year 1610. Newton was the first to explain the motion of the Moon, in terms of his theory of gravity.

But the greatest advances in our knowledge of the Moon have been made in the 20th century. In the 1960s unmanned spacecraft from the Soviet Union and the United States brought back excellent pictures of the Moon's surface. Then, on July 20th 1969, Neil Armstrong, an American, first stepped on the Moon. Much information has been gathered since then.

The Earth and the Moon are parts of the solar system. At the centre of the solar system is the Sun. The planets are the large bodies that revolve in paths, called orbits, round the Sun. Around some of the planets smaller bodies, called satellites, revolve in orbits. The Moon is the satellite of the planet Earth.

The Earth has only one satellite but some of the other planets have several. For instance, Jupiter has 13 satellites, or moons. Saturn has 10. Some planets' satellites, are larger than our Moon. But, although our Moon is not the largest satellite in the solar system, it is the largest compared with the size of the planet that it circles. So, the Earth and the Moon are sometimes described as a 'double planet'.

Every object in the universe exerts a force of attraction, called a gravitational force, on every other object. The Sun exerts a powerful gravitational pull on the planets. This pull is responsible for keeping the planets in their orbits. Without the gravitational pull of the Sun, the planets would travel on in straight lines into space. Instead, they follow clearly defined orbits which are elliptical – shaped like an ellipse. An ellipse is a flattened, or stretched-out, circle. The Moon's orbit around the Earth is elliptical too.

The Moon's own gravitational pull has an effect on the Earth. The tides are due mainly to the Moon's gravitational pull on the Earth's oceans. The tides are the twice-daily rise and fall of the water level in the oceans on the Earth.

The Moon seems to shine brightly in our sky at night. It can sometimes be seen in the day too. But the Moon, like the planets, does not have light of its own. It merely reflects some of the light from the Sun. From the Earth, the Moon at night seems very bright and pale. But, in fact, most Moon rock is dark. Samples brought back by the *Apollo* astronauts confirm this. Moon rock reflects on average only about seven per cent of the light that strikes it from the Sun.

At any moment, half the Moon is lit up by the Sun. But at different stages of the Moon's orbit, different amounts of the lighted area can be seen from the Earth. Sometimes the entire half of the Moon shining with the reflected light of the Sun faces the Earth. This is called a full Moon. At other times only a thin strip of the lighted half of the Moon can be seen. This is called a crescent Moon. The different appearances of the Moon as seen from the Earth are called the phases of the Moon.

The Moon passes through all its phases in $29\frac{1}{2}$ days. The Moon's phases are so regular that they have been used for the measurement of time. One 'lunar month' is the time taken for the Moon to pass through one complete cycle of its phases – $29\frac{1}{2}$ days. It is not the same as our calendar month.

When the Moon lies roughly between the Earth and the Sun, the far side of the Moon, which cannot be seen from the Earth, is lit. This phase, when the Moon is invisible to us, is called the new Moon. After a day or two the Moon has moved far enough for the edge of the lighted portion to be seen from the Earth. This is the crescent Moon.

The crescent grows, or waxes, until, about a week after new Moon, you can see one half of the lighted portion. This phase is called the first quarter. Then the Moon has travelled through about one quarter of its orbit.

At the 'waxing gibbous' phase, three quarters of the lighted portion of the Moon can be seen. And at full Moon, about two weeks after new Moon, the whole of the lighted side faces the Earth. At this stage the Earth lies roughly between the Sun and the Moon.

After full Moon, the part of the lighted half that is visible from the Earth shrinks, or wanes. The Moon passes through the phases 'waning gibbous' and 'last quarter'. Finally it returns to 'new Moon'.

Strange as it may seem at first, the Moon takes less than one lunar month to complete one orbit of the Earth. The time taken for one complete orbit, called the sidereal month, is $27\frac{1}{3}$ days. But, as we have seen, it takes two days longer than this for the Moon to pass through a complete cycle of its phases.

The reason for this difference is that while the Moon completes one orbit round the Earth, the Earth moves some distance in its own orbit around the Sun. This means that the Earth-Sun line moves. Although the Moon has completed an orbit, it does not yet lie between the Earth and the Sun. It has not reached the Earth-Sun line. The Moon reaches this position after travelling for a further two days.

The Moon's orbit is slightly tilted and so the Moon does not usually pass directly between the Earth and the Sun. But occasionally it does, and the Moon then casts a shadow on the daylight side of the Earth. People on the Earth, within the Moon's shadow, see the Sun partly or wholly hidden by the Moon. This hiding of the Sun is called an eclipse of the Sun, or 'solar' eclipse. The Moon's shadow travels across the Earth at over 1,500 kilometres per hour. In any one district the eclipse of the Sun never lasts more than $7\frac{1}{2}$ minutes. (See: *eclipse*.)

An eclipse of the Sun occurs only at new Moon. The dark side of the Moon faces Earth – the Sun lighting up the far side. On the other hand, an eclipse of the Moon, or 'lunar' eclipse, will occur at full Moon. But it will occur only on those occasions when the Earth lies exactly between the Sun and the Moon. In a lunar eclipse the shadow of the Earth passes across the sunlit half of the Moon. The Moon takes some time to pass through the Earth's shadow. So, a lunar eclipse can last for up to $3\frac{1}{2}$ hours.

The Moon is constantly turning, or rotating on its axis. In fact the Moon goes through one complete rotation in exactly the same time that it takes to complete one orbit – $27\frac{1}{3}$ days. As a result, the Moon keeps the same face turned toward the Earth at all times. We can never see the far side of the Moon from the Earth.

The Moon rotates at a constant speed, but its movement round the Earth regularly speeds up and slows down slightly. At intervals the position of the Moon in its orbit becomes temporarily out of step with its rotation. So, the Moon appears to rock to and fro. First, we can see slightly round one edge of the far side. Later, we can see slightly round the other edge. This effect is called libration. At any given moment we can see only 50 per cent of the Moon's surface. But, because of the Moon's librations, we can observe 59 per cent of the Moon's total surface, over a period of time. This leaves 41 per cent of the Moon's surface, on the far side, which is never visible from the Earth.

The best times to study the surface features of the Moon are around the first and last quarters. At these phases sunlight is striking the side of the Moon, as seen from Earth. Irregularities on its surface cast long shadows and can be detected. You might think that the best time to study the Moon is when it is full.

But at this phase, sunlight shines straight on the Moon. There are few shadows and the height and depth of features are hard to judge.

You can see many of the main features of the near side of the Moon. Look at it on a clear night through an ordinary pair of binoculars or through a small telescope. Use the Moon map with its grid as a guide to help you to identify what you can see. Through an ordinary astronomical telescope you will see the Moon upside down. Through a telescope designed for looking at things on Earth, and through binoculars, the Moon will appear the right way up, with north at the top.

You will see that the Moon's surface is broken up into light and dark areas. Probably the first thing you will notice will be the numerous 'craters'. Craters are circular depressions like saucers, surrounded by raised ridges. Some of the craters are as much as 250 kilometres (about 150 miles) across, and the ridges that surround them rise 6,000 metres (20,000 feet) above the surrounding plain. Only since the recent Moon probes have we known that the Moon's surface is also spotted with millions of small craters, some being only 60 centimetres (about two feet) in diameter.

The large dark patches on the Moon that are visible to the naked eye are called maria (singular: mare) – the Latin word for seas. But there is no water on the Moon. These areas are relatively flat, broad plains.

When you look at the Moon during its waxing phase, at around the first quarter, you will see the right side of the Moon illuminated. The Mare Serenitatis (Sea of Serenity) is a large dark area toward the north. The Mare Tranquillitatis (Sea of Tranquillity) was the landing site for *Apollo 11*. From this spacecraft stepped Neil Armstrong, the first man to set foot on the Moon. Look out for the Mare Crisium (Sea of Crises) and the Mare Foecunditatis (Sea of Fertility).

If you look at the Moon during its waning phase, at about the time of the last quarter, you will be able to see the left side of the Moon. The principal maria to look out for are the Mare Imbrium (Sea of Showers), Oceanus Procellarum (Ocean of Storms), Mare Humorum (Sea of Humours), and the Mare Nubium (Sea of Clouds). Several craters are prominent. Look out for Plato on the upper edge of the Mare Imbrium, and Aristarchus on the Ocean of Storms, the brightest crater on the whole Moon. Copernicus is a crater with a diameter of 90 kilometres (56 miles). The mountains that surround it rise to 3,000 metres (10,000 feet) above its floor. Clavius, not far from the south pole of the Moon, has a diameter of 235 kilometres (146 miles).

Moon features that show up best at full Moon are the bright streaks, called rays. The rays radiate like the spokes of a wheel from certain craters. The crater Tycho, which is slightly north of Clavius, has the most spectacular ray system. Scientists are still not certain of the nature and the origin of the rays. They must certainly consist of material thrown out at the time the central crater was formed.

Until the Russian probe of 1959, the nature of the far side of the Moon remained a mystery. An unmanned Russian vessel, *Lunik 3*, went on an orbital flight of the Moon and transmitted back to Earth the first photographs of the far side. Between 1966 and 1968 the United States *Lunar Orbiter* programme carried out an extensive survey of the Moon's far side. The far side of the Moon is best photographed at new Moon, when the whole of the far side is lit by the Sun.

From the photographs of the Moon's hidden side we know that there are few maria on that side. The Mare Orientale is the most extensive. However, the whole of the Moon's hidden side is pitted with numerous craters. Probably the most prominent is the one named after the Russian scientist Tsiolkovsky. He pioneered the idea of using rockets for space flight. This crater has a very dark floor and a bright central mountain.

In spite of the great success of the recent Moon probes there are still several questions that remain to be solved. How, for instance, were the craters on the Moon formed? How did the Moon itself originate?

There are three main theories about the origin of the craters on the Moon. Scientists who support the first theory believe that the craters were formed by volcanic activity on the Moon's surface. According to the second theory, the craters were formed by the impact of meteorites hitting the Moon's surface at high speeds. Meteorites are pieces of rock or iron moving through space. It is now certain that both meteoric and volcanic activity occurred. But rock samples from Apollo missions have so far failed to show which was more important.

Scientists who support the third theory suppose that early in the Moon's history gases were released from the interior of the Moon. These gases caused loose material on the Moon's surface to 'bubble' like a liquid. After the gases had disappeared the craters remained where the bubbles had formed.

Was the Moon once joined to the Earth? An early theory of the Moon's origin suggested that the Moon was formed from a lump of rock that broke away from the Earth. A more likely theory is that the Earth and the Moon used to follow independent orbits as planets around the Sun. Eventually, the Earth with its strong gravitational pull drew the Moon into orbit around it. Another theory supposes that the Earth and the Moon, and perhaps even Mars, were formed at the same time, close to each other, from a single cloud of material.

Samples of Moon rock show it to be similar to igneous (volcanic) Earth rock. The Earth and Moon are probably the same age. The Moon, though, has changed little over millions of years. Some Moon soil samples astronauts brought back have been found to be about 4,600 million years old. The Earth itself is believed to be 4,700 million years old.

We can be certain that there is no life on the Moon and never has been. The Moon's lack of atmosphere means that there is no oxygen, or protection from harmful radiations from the Sun and space. There is most probably no water either. On Earth, the temperature varies only slightly between night and day. On the Moon, though, the temperature reaches 120°C (250°F) on the side heated by the Sun. In areas of darkness, the temperature drops to –162°C (–260°F). See: *solar system, Sun.*

motion

Rain falls downward. Rockets climb upward. Motor cars and locomotives move along the ground. These are all forms of motion.

The Earth itself is in motion. It is moving round the Sun all the time. The Earth completes one path, or orbit, round the Sun in one year. The Earth spins as well. It spins round once in every twenty four hours.

We say that an object is moving relative to another one whenever it is changing its position compared with that second object. When we do this we are taking the second object as being 'at rest.'

Thus we say that a car is moving relative to the Earth. But the Earth itself is moving relative to the Sun.

The rate at which an object moves is its speed. So the speed depends on the object that we are comparing it with. Whenever we state a speed we must make it clear what the 'reference body' is – what we are assuming to be at rest.

When talking about moving objects, scientists use imaginary 'frames of reference'. One such frame of reference could be this. Imagine three lines drawn through your present position. One is the north-south line, the second is the east-west line, the third is the vertical line. Imagine that this frame stays at the same position on the surface of the Earth. As long as you are sitting still, you are at rest in this frame of reference. If you now start moving

round the house, your movement can be described relative to this frame of reference. You may move so many metres north or south, so many metres east or west, so many metres up or down.

But suppose you set up a second frame of reference on the planet Mars. Relative to this frame of reference, our first frame, on the Earth, is moving rapidly. It shares in the daily rotation of the Earth, and in its yearly movement round the Sun.

Yet the second frame of reference is itself moving at high speed. Mars turns once in just over 24 hours. And it also travels round the Sun. In addition to all those movements, the Sun itself is travelling among the stars.

It can be a complicated problem to work out what an object's motion relative to a new frame of reference will be. Consider a swimmer crossing a river that flows from north to south. A natural frame of reference for him would be the water. Relative to this frame of reference he is moving at, say, five kilometres per hour from east to west. But relative to a frame of reference that is fixed on the land, he has a southward motion as well. Suppose the river is flowing at six kilometres per hour southward. Then the swimmer's motion relative to the frame of reference on the land is in roughly a south-west direction. His speed relative to the land is, in fact, seven kilometres per hour.

Everything around us is made up of atoms collected together in groups called molecules (see: *atom*). The molecules are constantly moving. A substance may exist as a solid, a liquid, or a gas. These different states of a substance depend upon the motion of its molecules.

The molecules of a gas move freely all the time (see: *gas*). The molecules of a liquid are in constant motion too, but they cannot move as far as the gas molecules (see: *liquid*). The molecules of most solids are packed together to form regular structures called crystals. The molecules in crystals move, but their motion is very limited. Individual molecules may move away from their position in the crystal, but they move back again.

Atoms themselves contain moving particles. An atom consists of a central core called the nucleus surrounded by electrons. The electrons are in constant motion around the nucleus.

The study of motion is as old as science itself. The Greek philosopher Aristotle, who was born in 384BC, proposed theories of motion. They were accepted right up to the 16th century.

Aristotle classified motion as of two types: 'natural' motions, and 'violent' motions. Natural motions were those that took place without the interference of man. Violent motions were those for which man was responsible.

Aristotle believed (wrongly) that the Sun

revolved round the Earth, as the Moon does. This was one type of natural motion. He thought that both the Sun and the Moon moved in circular paths.

Another type of natural motion, according to Aristotle, was the motion of heavy bodies toward the ground. He thought that heavy bodies fall because they wish to reach their proper positions on the Earth. And they fall in a straight line as this is the quickest way that they can reach this natural position. Light substances, such as gases, move straight upward, he thought, so that they can quickly reach their natural positions above the Earth.

Pitching a baseball would have been called a violent motion by Aristotle. He called a motion violent if it was neither circular, nor in a straight line, but was along some other kind of curve.

Aristotle's laws may seem convincing at first sight but they do not agree with the facts. Aristotle could not easily explain why a stone continues to move after being thrown. When the hand is no longer touching the stone, it can no longer exert a force.

Another view held by Aristotle, and unquestioned by scientists up to the 16th century, was that heavy bodies fall faster than light ones. This theory was finally disproved by the great Italian scientist Galileo, who was born in the year 1564. According to an old story, Galileo tested Aristotle's theory by dropping objects from the top of the leaning tower of Pisa. When stones of different weights were dropped at the same time, they reached the ground almost together.

Galileo was right about the stones, though he probably did not perform this particular experiment. So you may wonder why feathers and snowflakes take so long to reach the ground. They take so long to fall because they have a large surface area relative to their weight. The air resists the fall of any object to some extent. The larger the surface area, the greater is the resistance to its fall. On the Moon there is no air. A stone and a feather reach the ground at the same time if they are released together.

Galileo found that falling objects travel faster and faster as they fall – they accelerate. The acceleration of any falling body is constant in a vacuum. This means that as it falls, a body's speed is increased by the same amount in every second. On Earth, a falling body's speed increases in every second by 9.8 metres (32.2 feet) per second.

Galileo died in the same year that the great English scientist, Isaac Newton, was born. Newton used Galileo's work as the basis of his own study of motion. As well as his famous theory of gravitation (see: *gravity*), Newton said that all forms of motion were governed by three general laws. Newton's laws of motion form part of the foundations of modern physics.

Newton's first law of motion states that a body in motion will move in a straight line and with a constant speed, unless it is acted upon by a force. This is the principle of inertia. Inertia is the tendency of a body to maintain its state of motion or rest.

When you think of Newton's first law, it is difficult to see how it can be true. When you throw a stone into the air, or roll a ball along the ground, they both soon come to rest. According to Newton's law they should continue in motion unless acted upon by a force. Now the force that brings a thrown stone to the ground is the force of gravity. The Earth's gravity acts upon the stone. It pulls it toward the centre of the Earth.

A ball rolling along the floor is also acted upon by the forces of gravity. And although the rolling ball cannot fall, its weight presses it against the floor. As the ball presses against the floor another force, called friction, is produced. Friction is a force that resists the movement of surfaces in contact. There is always friction between any surfaces that roll or slide over one another. The rougher the surfaces, the greater is the frictional resistance to motion. Friction brings the ball to rest.

In space there is no air and so there is no frictional resistance to motion. Far from any star or planet, the force of gravity is weak. A moving body in space will keep moving practically in a straight line. A rocket ship in space will travel in a straight line until the engines are fired to provide a force that makes it change its state of motion.

So Newton's first law, the principle of inertia, says that objects do not accelerate if there are no forces acting on them. His second law states that the acceleration of a body is larger if the force is larger. And the change of speed is in the same direction as the force.

This is very different from Aristotle's idea of force. Aristotle had said that a particular force produces a particular speed in an object. According to Newton's law, the force can give any speed to the object, if it acts for long enough.

When a stone is thrown straight upward into the air, it would keep travelling at a constant speed if gravity and air resistance did not act on it. Gravity makes the stone lose upward speed – which is equivalent to gaining downward speed. It slows down until it comes to rest. Then it accelerates downward.

A force does not produce the same acceleration in every object. A car engine at full power will make the car accelerate more rapidly when unloaded than when loaded.

The loaded car is said to have more mass than

the unloaded car. A body with a large mass is harder to accelerate than a body with a small mass. It is also harder to stop. A big lorry moving at 80 kilometres per hour (50 mph) needs stronger brakes than a small car moving at the same speed.

Newton's third law of motion states that for every 'action' there is an equal and opposite 'reaction'. It just means that, when a body is pushed one way by a force, another force is produced that pushes the opposite way with equal strength.

A good example of this is the recoil of a rifle. When a rifle is fired, the bullet is pushed out by the explosion of the gunpowder. At the same time the rifle recoils – it is pushed back, sometimes even bruising the shoulder of the person who fired the shot. The explosion exerts an equal and opposite force on the rifle.

We use the third law all the time in moving around. When we walk, our feet push backwards against the ground. There is a reaction that pushes us forward. A power boat's propeller constantly throws water backwards. The reaction drives the boat forward. Jets and rockets blast out a stream of exhaust gases. A reaction force pushes them forwards.

In this century, Newton's laws of motion have been slightly modified. Albert Einstein put forward his Special Theory of Relativity in 1905. He claimed that, as any object travels faster and faster, it becomes harder to give it more speed. In other words, its mass increases.

Einstein was right. Atom-smashing machines accelerate tiny particles to very high speeds (see: *accelerator*). Yet they cannot make any particle travel faster than light.

See: *acceleration*, *matter*, *physics*, *relativity*.

To think about

Imagine you are standing in the aisle of an airliner travelling at a steady speed of 800 kph (500 mph). You hold a ball directly above a mark on the floor of the plane. If you drop the ball, will it fall onto the mark? Or will it hit the floor towards the rear of the plane?

navigation

Every day people make many thousands of journeys. Life in the modern world depends greatly on transportation over long distances. But travel would be difficult, or impossible, if we used only our eyes and our sense of direction to avoid getting lost. Navigation helps us travel to places by sea, by air and in space.

It is easy to drive through a town or a city without losing your way. The signs by the roadside and the arrangement of the streets help you. Going from one city to another is not much harder, if you have a map and can read it. But when we travel on water instead of land, there are usually no aids such as signs and roads to guide us. An aircraft navigator has an even more complicated task. An aircraft moves up and down, as well as forward and sideways like cars or ships do. The astronaut's job is the most difficult of all. He has to man-oeuvre his spacecraft very accurately, yet he frequently can see nothing outside his cabin.

The science of navigation dates back as far as the first sailors, but it is still growing to meet the needs of today's travellers. A modern navigator uses many methods and instruments.

The word navigation comes from the Latin verb to sail. But this science is much older than the Romans. Men began to travel on water at least 10,000 years ago. They did so only occasionally and knew little about their surroundings. Therefore, they had to sail near the coasts to see where they were and in which direction they were moving. They navigated by observing landmarks, or familiar points on land, and by paying attention to natural aids like the Sun and stars.

Primitive man thus discovered the two main activities of every navigator. One is to find his location. The other is to figure out how to get to a certain place, and is called 'plotting a course'. The course is the path the traveller must take in order to reach his chosen destination. The first activity is really part of the second. A navigator must first find his position to plot a course toward his destination, or to be sure that he is on the right course.

Plotting a course requires other information too. The direction in which the destination lies is most important. The distance to a destination and the speed of the traveller's vehicle are needed to tell how long it will take him to get there. This time shows how much fuel or food should be carried. Conditions during the trip, such as currents and winds, must also be known. They influence the vehicle's speed and direction and can even be dangerous. So can other vehicles, which the navigator has to avoid hitting by keeping track of their positions. If he is on a ship, he must know the depth of water along its course so that the ship does not run aground. If he is in a plane, he has to know the heights of any mountains beneath its path, to avoid them.

Celestial navigation

By 2000BC, men had learned to sail by the stars. This is called celestial navigation. It was made possible by the study of astronomy.

The directions of sunrise and sunset, which depend on the time of year, led to an exact definition of east and west. North could be found by looking at the Pole Star, which is directly above the North Pole. The time of day or night was measured by using a sandglass, which is like an old-fashioned egg timer. Speed was estimated by throwing a piece of wood overboard, and seeing how long the ship took to go past it.

By such methods, sailors in the Near East began to make long voyages, well out of sight of land. Merchants and whole navies crossed the seas, stimulating the growth of early civilizations. Information helpful to the navigator was spread by word of mouth, and eventually written in books. (See: *astronomy, star.*)

But the great disadvantage of celestial navigation is that stars cannot be seen by day or in bad weather. This problem made navigation very difficult for centuries. Then in about 1100AD, the compass was invented. No one is sure whether the Chinese or Arabs were first (see: *compass*). The compass soon became, and has remained, a standard tool of navigators all over the world. A compass shows directions with its needle, which points toward Magnetic North. It is not a perfect instrument, since it may give inaccurate readings if placed near magnetic materials such as iron, and it must be kept very steady. Nevertheless, many kinds of improved compasses have been developed, and can be used under most conditions.

The compass enables sailors to draw and use reliable sea charts. Maps had already been invented, but they were not very accurate, even on land. Now the navigator could record more exact distances and directions between ports. This information produced great advances in geography.

It meant that even longer voyages could be made, from Europe to Africa and the Far East, and at last to America. Ships brought back knowledge of currents and winds. By the 16th century, atlases, globes, and maps drawn using the famous Mercator projection were in use. The most amazing feat of navigation in history, until our recent trips to the Moon, occurred then. A Portuguese crew, led by the navigator Ferdinand Magellan, sailed around the world. It took them three years, from 1519 to 1522.

Two important methods of navigation were developed at this time. One is called dead reckoning. It tells a navigator his position. He begins by marking his last known position on a chart. Next he draws a line from there in his direction of travel as shown by a compass. He knows how long he has been moving at a certain speed, so that he can calculate the distance he has travelled. Finally he marks off this distance on the line, and finds his present position. But corrections must be made because currents and winds are influencing the direction and speed at which the vehicle is travelling.

The sextant

In the second method, the navigator determines his position by finding his latitude and his longitude. Latitude is the angle between two imaginary lines. One is drawn from the Earth's centre to the Equator, and the other from the Earth's centre to the navigator's position. Latitude is measured in degrees. There are 90° of latitude north of the Equator and 90° south of it. For example, the latitude is zero degrees if the navigator is on the Equator, and ninety degrees north if he is at the North Pole. Latitude is easily found. At the Equator, the Pole Star seems to lie on the horizon. At the North Pole, it is directly overhead. For all other places, the height of the Pole Star above the horizon is equal to the latitude of that place. So a navigator can find his latitude by measuring the Pole Star's height above the horizon. A number of devices have been invented to do this. The best is called the sextant.

A sextant can also be used to find latitude from the Sun instead of from the Pole Star. A navigator measures the Sun's height above the horizon at noon. This angle must be corrected according to the time of year, using astronomical tables.

During the eighteenth century, a very precise clock, usually called a chronometer, was invented in England for use at sea.

By the twentieth century, many improvements in navigation had been made. Dangers to shipping were marked by buoys and lighthouses In addition, charts and pilot books enabled the sailor to travel near any coast and enter crowded harbours. Laws of navigation were passed to prevent accidents, and to protect the rights of each country's sailors. The old magnetic compass was replaced by the gyrocompass (see: *gyroscope*). And scientists learned about the behaviour of sound in water. They developed the depth sounder, which shows the depth of water. It sends sound from the surface to the bottom, and receives the echo that bounces back. The time between sending and receiving tells the depth. Another invention was sonar.

Modern navigation

But the most important developments were in telecommunications. By the beginning of the First World War, radio signals could be sent over long distances. This led to the use of radio direction-finding equipment. A navigator could find his position quickly, and in any weather, by receiving signals from transmitters on land.

Later, a more accurate and complicated

method was introduced. Several transmitters can produce a pattern of signals, spread out over a great area.

The Loran system was invented during the Second World War in the United States. It is used all over the world by ships and aircraft. Its signals are radio pulses. They are very short bursts of radio waves, at a low frequency. The pulses are transmitted at regular intervals by three stations on land. The navigator listens first to only two, the master station and a slave station. Their pulses reach him at the same time if he is at an equal distance from the two stations. If he is not the same distance from each station the pulses arrive at different times.

Next, he listens to the other slave station and the master station. By measuring the delay between their pulses, he finds a second line on which his position must lie. He draws the two lines on a map. The point where the lines intersect is his position, as it lies on both lines.

Such methods were the beginning of electronic navigation. It became even more important as aircraft travel increased. A second electronic aid to navigation is radar (short for 'radio detection and ranging'). This invention is like sonar, but it uses radio pulses instead of sound. Navigators need radar in bad weather or at night to help them plot courses and keep clear of dangerous obstacles. (See: radar.)

Modern aircraft use many additional methods of navigation. The pilot plots his course on a flight plan before he takes off. After take-off, an altimeter tells his height or 'altitude' above the ground or water. Instruments controlled by gyroscopes show whether he is climbing or turning. Another instrument informs him of 'drift' from his chosen course. An automatic pilot can navigate the plane while he rests. Satellites in orbit around the Earth give him information about the weather and his position. When he lands, radio beacons guide him down to the runway.

The Space Age has created new problems in navigation. A spacecraft must find its way over longer distances, at higher speeds, and with less chance of rescue in an emergency than does any ship or aircraft.

But little of the navigation in space is done by the astronauts. Most of it is done by the highly-trained ground crews back on Earth, and by automatic equipment. Computers are programmed with astronomical information (see: computer). When the spacecraft is launched on its course, it is guided by radio signals from the Earth. The signals operate both the main engines of the spacecraft and smaller steering rockets. Radar is used to measure the spacecraft's speed and distance from the Earth. Its position is given by latitude and longitude, not on the Earth's surface, but on a celestial sphere. This can be thought of as an imaginary sphere with the same centre as the Earth, but much bigger.

Such methods are very successful. Dozens of astronauts have travelled into space and come back safely. Yet as man's space trips grow longer, he will need to learn even more about navigation.

Man is not the only navigator. Animals have always travelled great distances to find food and shelter and to breed. For example, a turtle, seal or seabird may navigate over thousands of kilometres of open ocean with amazing accuracy to reach a particular stretch of beach in migration. How they do so is still being studied by scientists. Some creatures, such as many birds, and eels, seem to be born with knowledge of how to reach their destinations without ever having learned the route. But other animals can learn to find their way along new routes. Dogs and homing pigeons can find their way home from places they have never visited before (see: homing). Man may discover new methods of navigation by observing those used by animals.

nuclear energy

Without energy no natural process or human activity could occur. There are many kinds of energy. Each kind can be turned into any other kind. Man uses more energy than other forms of life or nature do. He takes energy in food for his body needs. In addition he uses energy to heat and light his homes, to drive machines, and for many other purposes. As his demands for energy increase and existing energy sources are used up, so he has to discover new sources. The largest source he has ever found is that of nuclear energy, sometimes also called atomic energy.

The secret of nuclear energy lies in the atom (see: atom). Atoms are among the smallest particles of matter. They were not well understood until our own century, and nuclear energy was thus discovered only recently. Atoms consist of tiny particles. Every atom has a nucleus, or central core, surrounded by electrons, each of which has a negative charge. The nucleus itself is a group of particles called protons and neutrons which are tightly packed together. The protons have a positive electric charge, while the neutrons have no charge.

The particles in the atom are held together by very strong nuclear forces. The positive charge of the protons and the negative charge of the electrons balance each other. So, overall, the atoms have no charge.

Fission and fusion

There are two ways of getting energy from nuclei. Some nuclei can break apart to release energy. This is called fission. Other nuclei can be put together to make a new nucleus, while giving out energy. We call this process fusion. Fission and fusion are different processes, but both produce enormous amounts of energy. Fission is a simpler process than fusion, and was discovered earlier. The difficulties of controlling fusion to generate useable power have not yet been overcome. Today fission is still the main method of producing nuclear energy.

In fission, a nucleus is broken apart by being hit with a neutron. The neutron can hit the nucleus because it has no electric charge. When the nucleus breaks up, new particles appear. Some of them are new nuclei which contain less energy than the original nucleus did. The rest of them are neutrons that have been released by the nucleus.

The first nucleus gives part of its energy to the new nuclei and part to the new neutrons. The energy of the new neutrons is called kinetic energy, or energy of motion. The kinetic energy of the neutrons is soon transferred to the atoms of the surroundings as heat. Heat energy is simply the kinetic energy of atoms. We make use of this heat.

In fusion, a nucleus is built up by making two smaller nuclei hit each other and join. This cannot happen unless the electrons are removed from the atoms to expose the nuclei. The atoms of a gas are heated to a high temperature. They then move so fast that they collide and knock off each other's electrons. All the resulting nuclei are now left with a positive charge, because of the protons in them. Since positively charged bodies repel, or push against, each other, the nuclei cannot easily be made to touch.

Scientists reckon that fusion will take place if two conditions are met. The temperature must be around 100 million degrees C, and there must be a way of keeping the mutually repelling nuclei together so that they come close enough to interact. There need to be 500 million nuclei in every cubic centimetre (this may sound a lot, but it is about a thousand times thinner than hydrogen gas at room temperature and pressure), and they must be confined at this density for at least 200 microseconds for fusion to take place and be maintained.

So far fusion has been achieved in big expensive experimental reactors, but it is likely to be some time before scientists and engineers can make the fusion reaction yield more energy than it takes to start it up.

Other particles, often neutrons, are released too. They move away rapidly. So they have the kinetic energy that we want to obtain. Fusion is frequently called a 'thermonuclear reaction', because heat is needed to start it ('thermo' means heat).

Each process uses a different material, or nuclear fuel, to produce energy. Fission needs nuclei that are not hard to break apart. It usually takes less effort to break up a big nucleus than a small one. This is because the forces of repulsion among protons inside the nucleus are strong. Each proton's positive electric charge pushes against the charge of every other proton. Such repulsion becomes stronger the more protons there are, and thus the larger the nucleus is. So fission requires relatively large nuclei.

Fusion needs nuclei that are small. Therefore we require opposite types of material for the processes of fission and fusion. Fission is often produced by using the nuclei of uranium atoms, which are very large. Fusion energy is created from hydrogen atoms which are the smallest of all atoms. Hydrogen and uranium are two of the many elements in nature.

Fission also needs moving neutrons to break up the nuclei. Fusion needs fast-moving nuclei to hit each other. In both cases, we must supply kinetic energy. At first we must supply energy from a different source. Once the process has begun, it continues by itself, and produces enough energy to keep itself going and to provide us with energy.

A fission process that continues by itself is called a chain reaction. It depends on the fact that a nucleus, when broken up with a neutron, releases its own neutrons. We can then use the new neutrons to break up other nuclei. This creates additional neutrons to break up more nuclei, and so on.

The problem with a chain reaction is that if a neutron is moving too fast, it will not break up a nucleus. Instead, it will pass by the nucleus and escape. So, either neutrons must be slowed down after they are created, or else we must have enough nuclei to keep neutrons from escaping.

Pieces of the nuclear fuel are placed in a material called a moderator. The neutrons, after being created by the fuel, hit the atoms of the moderator. They lose speed until they go slowly enough to break up more nuclei of the fuel. Graphite and water are good moderators.

A chain reaction can only continue if each neutron has a good chance of hitting a fuel nucleus. This can only happen if a certain minimum amount of fuel, known as the 'critical mass', is brought together in one place.

In fission, not all the neutrons are produced immediately. 'Delayed' neutrons appear some seconds after a nucleus has split. They are essential in maintaining a controlled, steady chain reaction in a reactor.

If a fairly small amount of very concentrated nuclear fuel is brought together in a small space, a chain reaction can develop which is so vigorous that it does not need the help of delayed neutrons. The result is a nuclear explosion.

In a star, fusion occurs easily. Stars contain a large amount of material. The centre of a star consists of matter that is packed together at tremendous pressure. Particles cannot escape, and the fusion continues. The light we see from stars is the energy produced by the fusion of their nuclei. (See: *light, star*.)

Reactors and fuels

The generators that produce nuclear energy are called reactors. A fission reactor is made of several parts. It has a core that contains the nuclear fuel and the moderator material. There may also be control rods, which are made of some material that absorbs neutrons. The reaction can be stopped by inserting the control rods into the core. The reaction can be started by partly withdrawing them.

Next, a mechanism is used to collect the nuclear energy that is produced in the core. This energy appears as kinetic energy of the new neutrons that are produced. The neutrons collide with their surroundings, such as the fuel and moderator, so that their kinetic energy heats up these materials. The heat can boil water and make steam to drive an electrical generator.

Finally, a shield is needed to protect people from the reactor. The fast-moving particles and other kinds of radiation resulting from fission are very dangerous (see: *radiation*). A thick wall of concrete is a good shield.

The new nuclei into which each fuel nucleus divides during fission are often radioactive. They too create dangerous radiation. They gradually accumulate inside the reactor.

Other radioactive elements are formed when uranium nuclei absorb neutrons without splitting. One of them, plutonium, can itself be used as nuclear fuel. A type of reactor called a 'breeder' is specially designed to produce large amounts of plutonium. But all types of reactor produce radioactive waste.

The task of removing this waste presents a great problem. As more reactors are built throughout the world, it becomes ever harder to find a place where radioactive waste can be put without harming people. Today, the usual method is to enclose waste materials in a shield and bury them underground. The process of fusion may be our answer to pollution. Fewer harmful wastes are created by fusion.

Reactors also produce a lot of waste heat. The waste heat is removed by water, which then flows into a nearby lake or river. It can thus change the temperature of our environment, enough to harm fish and plant life.

The manufacture of nuclear fuel is a growing industry. Every fuel must contain not only a particular chemical element, but also a certain 'isotope' of that element. An isotope of an element is one of the several kinds of atoms of that element. The isotopes of an element are different from each other, because their nuclei have differing numbers of neutrons.

Hydrogen has three different isotopes. One is ordinary hydrogen, which is part of water. The other two isotopes are deuterium and tritium. These two can be used in fusion.

Deuterium occurs in nature. Unlimited amounts could be extracted from seawater. Tritium is made by a nuclear process from the metal lithium. But eventually lithium may no longer be needed if scientists succeed in producing a fusion reaction using deuterium alone.

Fission uses an isotope of uranium. This isotope is called uranium 235, because its nucleus contains 235 protons and neutrons. It exists in nature as a tiny part of the uranium found in the earth. Some reactors use natural uranium. Others use 'enriched' uranium with an increased proportion of uranium 235. Since uranium is so important for nuclear energy, it has now become a valuable resource of some countries. The United States and Canada possess about half of all the world's uranium mines.

The first nuclear reactor was built during the Second World War. American scientists, led by the Italian physicist Enrico Fermi, succeeded in producing a chain reaction with uranium, using a graphite moderator. Since then, hundreds of fission reactors have gone into operation for many purposes. They provide electricity, radioactive materials that are used in medicine, heat for applications in industry, and power to propel ships. Spacecraft on long journeys may one day be powered by nuclear reactors.

perpetual motion

By the side of a lake, a complicated machine is working. A spiral device, or 'waterscrew', is turning continually. It raises water from the lake to a tank. Water is also flowing down from the tank. The falling water turns a paddlewheel. This wheel is turning large millstones that grind corn. And the wheel is turning the waterscrew too. So the falling water enables the wheel to do useful work, and to lift more water to keep the tank full.

Does this machine sound strange? If you doubt that it can work, you are right. It was suggested centuries ago, but nobody has ever built it. It is an example of a 'perpetual motion machine'. Perpetual means 'lasting forever'. This machine could go on moving forever, once it was started. It would keep itself moving, as well as doing work. Yet scientists now believe that such machines are impossible to build.

There are two main reasons why a machine cannot run forever by itself. First, the moving parts of a machine invariably cause friction. They rub against each other and their surroundings. So work is being done in the machine while it moves. If it were left by itself, it would use up all its ability to do work in this way, and would eventually stop running.

But the second reason is more important. Every machine does work, not only to overcome friction, but to be useful – for example, by turning millstones. The ability to do work is called energy. (See: energy, machine.) By doing work, a machine transfers its energy to something else, so that the energy is used. In this way, the machine must lose energy, even if it has little or no friction. To avoid losing all its energy and stopping, the machine must obtain more energy to replace the lost energy. How can a machine obtain energy if it is left by itself?

We give machines energy to replace the energy that they lose by doing work. We give them fuel which contains energy, or we connect them to an outside source of power which uses fuel (see: fuel, power). But a perpetual motion machine would not be given energy. So it would have to create its own energy. No energy would go into it, and yet energy would continually come out of it while it did work. It would be an inexhaustible source of energy. This is why people have wanted to build it, and why it cannot be built.

Physicists have found that energy can be neither created nor destroyed. This fact is called the Law of Conservation of Energy. Energy is 'conserved', that is, it never changes in quantity. It can only be changed from one form into another form. Machines work by changing the form of energy. A windmill that pumps water, for example, takes energy from the movement of wind. And the wind's energy comes from the heat of the Sun. The Sun gets energy from the tiny particles inside it. Energy has probably been stored in them since the beginning of the universe. (See: Sun, universe, wind.)

The perpetual motion machine described above, for grinding corn with a water wheel, would break the Law of Conservation of Energy. Suppose that we start the machine, by putting a tonne of water in the tank. To raise this water from the lake to a certain height, we must give it a definite amount of 'potential' energy. Then the machine is left alone. As the water falls back to the lake, its potential energy changes into the 'kinetic' energy of movement. Its kinetic energy is transferred to the water

wheel, which turns. Some of the wheel's energy is used to overcome friction. Some is used in doing work to grind the corn.

The rest of the wheel's energy must be used to lift another tonne of water from the lake, to keep the tank full. But this remaining amount of energy would be too small to do so. For it would be less than the original amount of energy we supplied, by lifting the first tonne of water to the tank. To make up the difference in energy, the machine would have to create some energy, which is impossible.

Machines that run for a long time all by themselves have been built. There are clocks that will go for a year on one winding. But they stop eventually, and must be wound again. The winding stores energy in the mainspring of a clock. Self-winding watches are also common. Yet they take energy from movements of the wearer's hand. As such a watch is shaken during the day, energy is supplied to it. The watch stores the energy and gradually uses it up in turning the hands of the watch. Just as animals need a supply of food to live, machines need a supply of energy to do work. No machine has ever been built that creates energy by itself alone.

The device we have described is called a perpetual motion machine of the first kind. There is a second kind of perpetual motion machine too. This kind would not create energy, and would not break the Law of Conservation of Energy. It would need an outside source of energy. If the source were taken away, this kind of machine would stop moving. So its motion is not truly perpetual. But it is just as impossible to build as the first kind of machine. It is supposed to use only heat as its energy source.

Everything contains heat, even substances that seem very cold. Heat is a form of energy (see: heat). In an electrical power station, heat is changed into electrical energy. Water is heated to make steam, which turns large wheel-like turbines that generate electricity (see: electricity, turbine). This process suggests the following design for a perpetual motion machine of the second kind.

Pump water continually from a lake, and freeze it to make ice. As the water freezes, it gives up heat to its surroundings. This heat is then used to produce steam that can generate electricity. The ice is returned to the lake, where the Sun melts it back into water. So the same water can be used again.

The flaw in this plan is that energy must be used in freezing the lake water. Just as your home refrigerator needs electrical power, any machine needs energy to freeze water. In fact, all the energy we could get from the steam would be needed to make the ice in such a machine.

The illustrations on these pages show a few of

the many perpetual motion machines that have been proposed through the ages. With an increased understanding of machines, and of heat, scientists have decided that all such machines are impossible to build. But inventors still try to design perpetual motion machines, and to get patents for them. The United States Patent Office requires a working model to be built, before it will even consider the application for a patent. The British Patent Office simply refuses to accept such applications.

Could the Law of Conservation of Energy be wrong? This is always possible. Like every other scientific conclusion, the law may need to be altered and corrected some day. We can only say that the law has been proved true in our past experience. As long as it remains true, and the laws of heat are still true too, we cannot obtain energy from perpetual motion machines.

Sources of energy are very important in modern society. Soon we may be able to get almost unlimited amounts of energy from the nucleus of the atom, and in a safe way as well. See: *atom, nuclear energy, physics.*

photosynthesis

Heat which warms us and light by which we see are both forms of energy. Another form of energy is hidden inside substances. It is called chemical energy. Substances are made of tiny particles called molecules. The molecules are made of even tinier parts, called atoms, linked together. Chemical energy is held in the links between the atoms. From the chemical energy in food substances animals and plants get their energy. They need energy to move, grow, and carry out all the activities of living things.

Animals must take food into their bodies by eating. But green plants can make their own food. They make their food from the atoms of simpler chemicals. The chemicals are linked together to make molecules of food substances. Plants can trap energy in the form of light. Then they change it into chemical energy held in the food substances. The way they do this is called photosynthesis. The name comes from Greek words meaning 'light' and 'to put together'. Atoms are put together to make food substances, using the energy of light.

Atoms of carbon, hydrogen, and oxygen are put together to make molecules of sugar – a carbohydrate food substance. The carbon comes from carbon dioxide gas in the air. Air enters through holes, called stomata, in the plant's leaves. The hydrogen and oxygen come from water. The water is taken up from the soil by the plant's roots. The light energy is trapped by a special chemical called chlorophyll. Chlorophyll is green and gives green plants their colour. The gas oxygen is left over at the end of photosynthesis and goes into the air. Simply:

carbon dioxide + water + energy = sugar + oxygen

Only plants that contain chlorophyll can make food by photosynthesis. Non-green plants, such as mushrooms and other fungi, live on dead plant and animal matter. Chlorophyll is made and stored within structures called chloroplasts. Chloroplasts are found in most cells of the leaves and other green parts. Inside the chloroplasts are stacks of plates called grana (singular: granum). Each granum holds millions of molecules of chlorophyll.

In the chloroplasts, the plant makes a substance that is turned into chlorophyll by daylight, or by artificial light. If the plant is kept in the dark, this substance builds up. A plant grown in the dark is whitish. When moved into the light, the plant soon becomes green. Some plants have red leaves. The red pigment masks the chlorophyll so that you do not see it. But it is there underneath, working exactly like any other chlorophyll.

Chlorophyll takes in, or absorbs, light. It absorbs green light least. Most of the green light is reflected and so chlorophyll looks green (see: *light*). Chlorophyll passes on this light energy, now minus the green light, to be stored as chemical energy until it is needed.

Photosynthesis can be thought of as two sets of reactions. One set is the light reactions. The other set is the dark reactions. They both occur in the chloroplasts. The light reactions can happen only in light. When light shines on a molecule of chlorophyll, some of the light energy is taken by the molecule. The atoms of each chlorophyll molecule are made of tiny particles, called electrons. These move in orbits round a central nucleus. The light energy is taken up by one of these electrons. It now has extra energy. Scientists say it is 'excited'. It becomes so excited that it leaves the chlorophyll molecule completely.

The excited electron is taken by another molecule called an acceptor. It is then passed along a chain of acceptors. Each acceptor takes some of the electron's energy as the electron hops from one to the other. Finally the electron returns to the chlorophyll molecule, having lost its extra energy. The energy taken by the acceptors is passed to a special chemical called ATP (adenosine triphosphate). The energy is trapped in high-energy links between atoms in ATP. The energy of light has been changed into chemical energy.

While this is happening, another reaction takes place. Excited electrons cause water to split up into hydrogen and oxygen. The oxygen goes out of the plant through the stomata.

The hydrogen from the water and the ATP are used in the dark reactions. Carbon dioxide from the air is combined with the hydrogen. A sugar called glucose is made, and water. The energy from ATP is used for these reactions. This process is happening in a plant most of the time. But they are called dark reactions because they can happen without light, as long as hydrogen, ATP and carbon dioxide are present.

Animals cannot make sugar in this way. They must eat plants or other animals that in turn live on plants. Thus all life depends on the Sun's energy. Most of our fuel energy too was created by photosynthesis. Coal and oil were made from plants that lived long ago. Wood is from plants that lived more recently.

The oxygen passes out of the plant into the air. Long ago, there was no oxygen in the atmosphere. Almost all the oxygen present has been supplied by green plants. This is still happening. Animals take in oxygen and give off carbon dioxide in the process of getting energy from their food substances. This is called respiration (see: *respiration*). Without green plants to replace the oxygen, animal life would soon die out.

As air is only 0.03 per cent carbon dioxide, it takes a lot of air to keep a plant healthy. One thousand cubic metres of air hold enough carbon dioxide to make a half kilogram of glucose. (One thousand cubic metres are about the size of ten largish rooms in a house.) Plants grow best in an atmosphere of 1-5 per cent carbon dioxide, as supplied in many greenhouses.

Plants use the glucose for energy and to build up their cells by another series of reactions called respiration. This process also occurs in animals. During this process, plants use oxygen and give off carbon dioxide. The same happens in animal respiration. In the light, plants give off more oxygen than respiration uses up.

If we are to grow enough food to feed the Earth's increasing population, it is important to learn how to increase photosynthesis. We can grow plants that make more food by photosynthesis than the chemicals and energy they use. Algae, simple water plants, contain chlorophyll all over so that photosynthesis can occur in every part of them. Land plants have parts such as roots, wood, flowers, and fruits, which have no chlorophyll. These parts use food substances but do not make any. Such plants are more wasteful than algae. The Japanese eat some seaweeds, which are types of algae. Algae could be especially useful on spaceships. They would be a source of food. They would replace the oxygen used up by the crew. Also, they would take up little room.

Find out by doing

You can show that light is necessary for photosynthesis. The sugar made in the leaves soon becomes starch. Brown iodine solution, called tincture of iodine, reacts with starch, making it dark blue. (You can show this by adding a drop of iodine solution to household starch.) Cut a hole in a strip of foil. Wrap the foil round part of a leaf on a plant to cover both surfaces. Kangaroo vine is a suitable plant. Hold the foil in place with paper-clips. Leave the plant in sunlight for a week or so. Then mix one spoonful of iodine in nine spoonfuls of water. Pick the experimental leaf, and remove the foil. Place the leaf in boiling water for one to two minutes to kill it. Spread the now pale leaf out in a saucer. Pour the iodine over it and watch. In about 15 minutes the parts that were covered with foil will still be pale. The parts exposed to the light will be dark indicating starch is there. (You will see dark blue-green rather than blue because of the green chlorophyll.)
If you carefully cut the letters out of the foil, you can 'print' your initial.

physics

Physics is the most fundamental science. Its name comes from the Greek word for nature. All the things that exist and happen in nature are studied by the physicist. He describes them in great detail, and organizes our knowledge of them in an orderly way. He tries to explain them by finding physical laws that give us a basic understanding of nature. And he can often predict things which no one has seen yet, so that our awareness of the physical world may be increased.

The study of matter is an important part of physics. Matter is what makes up every object in nature. Tiny atoms containing even smaller particles are matter. So are the enormous star systems which are the largest groupings of matter that we know of. The physicist is also concerned with energy, which is closely related to matter. Radiations such as heat, light, radio waves, and X-rays are kinds of energy. They are caused by matter, have effects on matter, and sometimes even become matter. (See: *matter*.)

Physics also deals with the movement of matter and energy. It tells us about the motion of atoms in a hot object, and the way that light travels through a substance like water. We learn, too, about the different forms in which matter and energy appear to us. The physicist shows why a solid metal can become a liquid when it is heated, and become a gas if it is heated still more. He finds out how some tiny particles are created, destroyed, or changed into other kinds.

The discoveries of physics are used in every

field of science. Knowledge of the atom helps an astronomer to understand the past history and future of the stars. The activities of living organisms (plants and animals and people) are explained largely with basic physical laws. A physicist may investigate forces that control the flight of birds and aircraft. He studies the flow of electricity in thunderclouds, and in the little transistors that are used in a radio or computer. The Earth's magnetism, and the slow shifting of continents on its surface, are problems that must be solved by physics. So are the calculation of the orbit of a spacecraft, and the design of instruments that it carries into space.

Many articles in this encyclopedia describe what physicists are doing now. But physics has had a long history of its own. It grew from countless theories and observations, made throughout several centuries, and in different countries. At first, all these observations did not belong to a single science. They were brought together only gradually, to form the organized study of nature which forms the modern science of physics.

The Greek physicists
The Early Greeks had many ideas about nature. But they did not observe it as closely as we do. Their ideas were seldom found, or tested, by performing experiments as a scientist does today. Still, they contributed much to the development of later theories in physics.

Around 600BC, Thales, who lived in the Greek city of Miletus, taught that everything in the world was made of different forms of water. This seems silly to us. Yet it was an attempt to explain all the kinds of matter around us by a smaller number of simple and basic substances. Physicists have been making the same attempt ever since then.

Democritus proposed a similar theory in the fifth century BC. He invented the idea of atoms. According to him, if a piece of matter was continually divided, you would eventually obtain pieces that could not be divided any further. He called such a piece *atomos*, meaning uncuttable or indivisible. The atoms could have many different shapes, and could join to make the kinds of substance found in nature. It was 2,000 years before this valuable theory was studied experimentally. (See: *atom*.)

The great philosopher Aristotle lived in the fourth century BC. He too wanted to find a few simple substances that made up matter. He believed there were five 'elements': Earth, Air, Fire, Water, and the Ether of which the stars were made. Some elements were drier, hotter or heavier than others. These properties were given to the substances that resulted when the elements combined.

Aristotle thought that each element had its 'natural' place. It would move there if it was not prevented from doing so. Smoke rises because it is largely made of the element Fire, and the natural place of Fire is above the element of Air. Aristotle had many other ideas about motion, but he did not try to test them by performing experiments (see: *motion*).

Other Greek thinkers, such as Pythagoras in the sixth century BC, and Archimedes in the third century BC, were closer to our own idea of the natural scientist. Both these men made experiments. They used mathematics to express the results of experiments, and to state their theories exactly. Pythagoras studied the production of musical sounds by vibrating strings. (See: *sound*.)

Archimedes was the greatest experimental physicist in the ancient world. He studied the behaviour of levers in machines. And he investigated how solid objects float or sink when they are placed in liquids. The laws that he discovered are still being used by engineers.

Scientific development stopped when the Greek civilization died out. The Romans were great builders and engineers, but they did not learn more about nature. However, they preserved many of the theories of the Greeks, especially the ideas of Democritus on atoms.

The Arabs
Arabian civilization suddenly arose in the seventh century AD. It was very active in the sciences. The Arabs were excellent at mathematics and astronomy, and did experimental work too. They discovered much about the movement of light as it passes through lenses and is reflected from mirrors.

The Arabs studied many Greek writings that had been lost in Europe. From the eleventh century AD, Arabic translations of Greek works came to Europe and were translated there. Europe rediscovered Aristotle, but adopted his scientific mistakes along with the valuable parts of his teaching. Since he was greatly respected, it took a long time to shake off his influence. This was done largely by Roger Bacon in England, in the 13th century. He insisted that the truth about nature could be found only by making experiments. He did not simply accept the ideas of past thinkers. It was not until the beginning of the 17th century that scientists accepted this principle.

A universal physics
Many theories in physics were proposed long before they could be proved by experiments. For example, to show that atoms exist, we can use experimental equipment that Democritus did not have when he said that they exist. Another such theory was the idea that the Earth goes around the Sun. This was believed by some Greeks, and was revived by Copernicus in the 16th century. Despite this, most people

thought the idea was wrong, and considered the Earth to be the centre of the whole universe.

The Earth-centred view of the universe was weakened by Johannes Kepler, an astronomer of the early 17th century. He found laws of planetary motion which indicated that the Earth, like other planets, goes around the Sun. This was not experimental proof, but it made the idea of Copernicus more likely to be true.

Aristotle had emphasized the differences between the heavens and the Earth. He saw the heavens as perfect and unchanging. Now Kepler's work encouraged scientists to think that the heavenly bodies obey the same laws as objects on or near the Earth. This very important idea was accepted by one of the greatest of physicists in the world, Galileo Galilei, in Italy in the 17th century.

From 1609 onwards, Galileo observed the skies with his telescope. He found evidence that the heavens were quite different from what Aristotle had said they were. For one thing, they were not at all unchanging. Galileo saw four satellites, or moons, revolving around the planet Jupiter. He knew that comets moved in the distant parts of the solar system, and not in the air as had been thought (see: *comet*). And he knew that new stars sometimes appeared or faded away.

Galileo also experimented with falling bodies on Earth. He discovered the law that showed that a falling body's speed does not depend on its weight. Aristotle had claimed that heavy bodies fall faster than light bodies do, and now he was proved wrong.

Galileo recognized, too, though not very clearly, that an object does not need a force to keep it moving as Aristotle had thought. It needs a force to change its speed or its direction of movement. We now call such a change an acceleration (see: *acceleration*). When a spacecraft moves between the Earth and Moon, for example, almost no force is acting on it, and yet it keeps moving.

Sometimes Galileo was very stubborn. He refused to believe that the Moon influenced the Earth's tides. And he made mistakes. For example, he put forward some false arguments for the Earth's daily rotation. Perhaps he did not even do all the experiments he claimed to have done. But his approach, at best, was that of the modern scientist, combining bold theories with careful experiments.

The achievement of Newton

Galileo's findings, about both astronomy and falling bodies, had to be explained by a new and more general theory. This was provided in 1687 by Newton when he published his great book called *Mathematical Principles of Natural Philosophy*. The theory Newton propounded had every feature that we now think a good theory in physics should have.

First, it used only a few simple assumptions to explain complicated things. Newton found three basic laws of motion. They included the first clear definition of force. Newton's theory also included something quite new: his law of gravitation.

The law of gravitation stated that every particle of matter in the universe attracts every other particle with a force called 'gravitational' force. This force acts not only between heavenly bodies, but between the Earth and objects on it.

The second feature of the theory was that it was mathematical. Newton used mathematics to express his laws, just as Pythagoras and Archimedes had done in a more basic way. He described the movements of planets and of falling objects by means of mathematics.

Third, the theory claimed to be universal. It was meant to be true for all matter, in any location and under any circumstances.

Fourth, the theory agreed with all of the known facts about the motion of falling bodies, planets, and satellites of planets. It was also able to explain earlier laws. Kepler's laws of planetary motion, as well as Galileo's law of falling bodies, follow from Newton's basic principles or laws.

A fifth feature of the theory was that it successfully predicted new facts. Thus, it indicated that Kepler's laws would be obeyed by any planets and satellites that were ever discovered in the future. And the theory correctly suggested that the Earth bulges at the Equator, because of its spinning.

Sixthly, the theory was a unifying theory. It brought together many facts and laws in different fields of science. This kind of unity became an important goal of physicists in their continuing search for basic knowledge of nature.

After Newton

Many scientists hoped that Newton's theories would be able to explain all known physical processes – electricity, magnetism, chemical reactions, light, and so on. Everything might be studied in terms of tiny particles, which obeyed the laws of motion and gravity. Perhaps some other forces would have to be added to that of gravitation, but nothing more.

Electricity was investigated intensively in the 18th century. Machines were made that could store large 'static' electric charges. Simple batteries were developed to supply electrical currents. Electrical force was found to be very similar to gravitational force. Magnetism was being explored too. Soon these two fields were joined in the single study of electromagnetism. (See: *electricity*, *magnet*.)

James Clerk Maxwell, a British physicist,

found a mathematical theory of electricity and magnetism. He showed how certain kinds of waves, called 'electromagnetic' waves, could be produced by moving electric charges. The waves move at the speed of light. (See: *light, wave*.)

This theory helped Maxwell to explain the known laws of light. He also predicted the existence of new types of electromagnetic wave radiation (see: *radiation*). Radio waves are one type, and were created in 1888 by Heinrich Hertz (see: *radio*). Physicists used the theory to understand how such waves act on matter. So Maxwell succeeded in partly unifying the laws of matter and radiation. This was a great breakthrough in the science of physics.

Atomism revived

The ancient idea of atoms was revived in the 19th century. Progress was slow in finding whether atoms existed, and what properties they had. Dalton proved first that the atomic theory could explain some chemical facts. He was able to compare the weights of different atoms, by making chemical measurements. (See: *chemistry*.)

An early achievement of the atomic theory was to explain the behaviour of gases. A gas was assumed to be made of many atoms moving rapidly. The atoms bounced off the walls of the container of the gas, and created a push against the walls in this way. If they were crowded together more, by making the container smaller, they would bounce off its walls more often. Their push would then increase. Thus the theory showed why the pressure of a gas increases if it is in a smaller volume.

The atomic theory was developed until it also explained the properties of liquids and solids. Next, in the twentieth century, men began to study how the atoms themselves are built up. Atoms were no longer 'uncuttable' as Democritus had thought in Ancient Greece. Through these investigations, chemistry was united with the wider field of physics.

One of the greatest unifying ideas in physics was the idea of energy (see: *energy*). The basic principle was that the total amount of energy remained constant during any process. This was true for all kinds of energy: energy of motion, gravitational energy, electrical energy, heat energy and so on. This was the principle of 'conservation of energy'. It related all the different kinds of energy to each other, and showed how one kind changes into another. We can use it to solve many problems of science.

As physics has progressed, much new knowledge has continued to appear. But the goal of a single, united physics is still far away. Probably we will always discover things faster than we are able to find laws relating them to each other.

Revolutions in physics

In our century, physicists have learned a surprising fact. Even the most well-tested theories may have to be replaced by others. Newton's ideas, for example, prove false in some cases. They do not apply to objects moving at very high speeds, or to strong gravitational forces, or to tiny particles inside the atom. For such cases, new and quite different theories were needed. These were supplied largely by Albert Einstein, possibly the greatest physicist in history.

Einstein developed his famous theory of 'relativity' shortly after 1900. It was an enormous improvement over Newton's views, since it explained many things that Newton could not. It also achieved an important unification. It showed the close connection between space, time, and gravity. And it led to surprising predictions. One of them was that matter and energy could be changed into each other. The two are simply different forms of the same thing. This idea enabled man to split the atom and later to obtain large amounts of useful energy. (See: *nuclear energy, relativity*.)

Another revolutionary idea was that of the quantum. This is a small, basic amount of a certain thing (see: *quantum*). Larger amounts of the same thing are just multiples of the quantum. But they cannot be measured in any amounts less than a quantum. Energy, for example, often exists only as a number of these basic amounts or 'quanta'. Yet Newton had thought that energy could exist in any amount at all. Again, the new quantum theory was able to improve his explanations of nature. It allowed physicists at last to understand light, and the structure of the atom.

Physics is no longer as 'deterministic' as in Newton's day. We do not try, for example, to determine exactly where a tiny particle is, or just how fast it is going. Instead we must speak of where it is likely to be, or how fast it is probably moving. This 'probabilistic', or statistical, point of view seems strange. But it has proved to be necessary in many theories of physics. (See: *statistics*.)

Today, there are very many basic questions, both new and old, to be answered by physicists. The smallest 'elementary' particles in matter are still unexplained. So is the amazing energy of the faraway 'quasars'. And between these two extremes, even some of Einstein's ideas are being improved. Thus physics is certain to continue growing because there will always be more things to discover about the world we live in.

Physics as a career

Every industrial country now employs thousands of physicists. They work directly for governments, in universities and research institutes, and in industry. To receive the training required, large numbers of students enter colleges and universities.

To begin a college physics course, a student must have studied physics and mathematics at school. It takes three years of study before a student can take the examinations for the Bachelor of Science, or BSc, degree. Mathematics will be important throughout the course. At the same time the student will be learning how to use advanced equipment in laboratories, and perhaps carry out a small piece of research.

A person with a BSc degree can work in industry or teach in secondary schools and in certain colleges. But to do more advanced work in physics, or to teach physics in most colleges, it is necessary to take a 'higher' degree. The PhD (Doctor of Philosophy) degree needs a further four or more years of hard study. An important part of the student's work for a PhD is research. Here he is making his own contribution to scientific knowledge, and not just learning about the results of others.

The work of a physicist may be theoretical – developing his own or other people's theories so that they can be used to make definite predictions that can be tested by experiment. Theoretical work is highly mathematical, and often needs the use of computers.

Or the physicist may be an experimentalist, actually making measurements and perhaps inventing new kinds of equipment to do so. Increasingly, experimentalists are working in teams. They use equipment that is worth millions of pounds, like the huge 'atom-smashers'.

The physicist's work may be useful quickly. He may study such things as the strength of packaging materials or how to reduce the noise of machines. But even if he studies, for example, processes inside other planets, there is the chance that one day his results will be not only interesting but also useful.

See: *chemistry, matter.*

power

If you look up the word 'power' in a dictionary, you will find that it means 'the ability to do something'. This could include being able to send a rocket to the Moon, being able to tell somebody to do something, or being able to lift a heavy weight. But a scientist usually uses the word in a more exact sense. Power is the rate at which something uses up or produces energy. A powerful car can start off and accelerate more quickly than a less powerful one. More power means spending a certain amount of energy in less time. Or, put another way, less power means spending less energy in a certain time.

Power should not be confused with energy. Energy is the ability to do work. If you are to lift a weight from the ground to waist height, you need a certain amount of energy. But the amount of power you produce depends on how quickly you lift the weight. Energy is your ability to do the work of lifting the weight to your waist. Power is how rapidly you lift it.

There are many kinds of energy. Examples are the energy of electricity and light, chemical energy, mechanical energy and the energy of sound. Each kind can be changed into others. But energy cannot be created or destroyed. It can only change from one form into another. If energy is changed at a certain rate, a certain amount of power is generated.

Our own bodies change chemical energy into mechanical energy. The chemical energy is stored, first in the food that we eat, and then in our muscles. It changes into mechanical energy when we do physical work, as when we lift a weight. The faster this change can take place, the more powerful our bodies are.

The energy for doing work comes from a fuel. Fuels, then, are sources of energy and power. The source of nearly all the power on Earth for millions of years has been the Sun, our nearest star. The other stars are so far away that the energy we receive from them is only a very, very tiny amount. The Sun's energy that we receive is mostly in the form of radiation. This energy creates the changes in the atmosphere that make up the world's weather. For example, winds are produced because the Sun heats up the Earth's surface, causing warm air to rise. Cooler air moves in to take the place of the warm air. A movement of air is the result. This we call 'wind'.

Part of the Sun's energy is 'trapped' by green plants. They turn it into chemical energy which is stored in their cells. We can get some of this energy by eating plant food, or by eating animals that have eaten plants. We also obtain some of the energy in plants when we burn them, for example when we burn logs to heat a room.

Plants and animals have lived on Earth for millions of years. Sunlight energy kept them alive just as it does present-day organisms. Many of these ancient plants and animals – including whole forests of trees – were buried under mud and water over the course of time. Eventually, their remains became 'fossilized', or partly preserved (see: *fossil*). Over millions of years, some of these decomposed so much that they became changed into what we often call the 'fossil fuels' – coal, oil and natural gas.

Fossil fuels are an example of 'primary' fuels. These are the ones that occur naturally. Most radioactive substances used to produce nuclear power, such as uranium and plutonium, are also examples of primary fuels (see: *nuclear energy, radioactivity*).

Secondary fuels are those made by man. Examples are coal gas and man-made electricity. Man now uses about twenty times more fuel than he did a hundred years ago. Most of this increase is due to his increasing ability to make secondary fuels.

Man's first power source for doing work was his own body. Buildings as vast as the pyramids of the ancient Egyptians and the temples of the South American Incas were built mainly by human muscle power. Man also learnt early in his history to use animals as a source of power – horses and oxen for ploughing, for example. And he also learnt to use the natural power of wind and water. Water wheels were built. They used the energy produced by falling water. We still use water power in the modern devices called water turbines (see: *turbine*). These develop power by changing the direction and the speed of a stream of water that is passed through them. They can be used to turn electric generators that generate large amounts of electricity.

Wind power is also an ancient method of obtaining energy. But it is used less today, except in non-industrialized parts of the world. Wind-driven sailing ships were replaced by ships using steam power and later by ships powered by diesel engines. Windmills, too, were replaced by steam-driven engines, and later by electric or diesel engines.

The Sun supplies us directly with some power for each square metre of the Earth's surface it shines on. This energy can be concentrated by means of mirrors to produce intense heat. But this is not a very convenient process and has been little used. The Sun's energy can also be converted directly into electricity by means of 'solar cells'. By combining many of these cells, electrical power can be generated. This process is expensive and used only in special cases. Space satellites use such solar power for producing electricity to operate cameras and communication equipment.

Man has invented many devices that change energy from one form into another. Engines are devices in which power is applied to do work. Many engines change the energy of a fuel into heat energy. This heat energy may then be changed into mechanical energy.

The steam engine is one of the most important devices of this kind, although more efficient engines, such as the internal combustion engine, are now used. Steam engines burn fuel such as coal to heat water. The resulting steam is used to move a piston up and down. The movement of the piston produces mechanical power, which can be used to drive machinery. Another device using steam is the steam tur-bine. It has a big wheel that turns when steam is blown against the outside of the wheel.

Mechanical energy can also be used to produce electrical energy. This is done with a machine called a dynamo or generator. An electrical power station uses such devices to produce electrical energy at a high rate. The mechanical energy may come from steam engines. The energy needed to heat the water to make the steam comes from the burning of fuel or from a nuclear reactor. A very small amount of nuclear fuel can be changed gradually into huge amounts of heat energy.

Electrical energy can be produced in other ways too. A battery generates it from chemical energy. And it can also be generated from heat energy by a new technique known as 'magnetohydrodynamics'. A gas is heated to an extremely high temperature, when it becomes what is called a 'plasma'. A plasma consists of 'ions'. Ions are electrically-charged particles. The plasma is made to flow between the poles of a magnet. This produces an electric current near the poles.

The most important way of getting cheap power is to use cheap fuel. But today man is gradually using up the primary fuels, such as coal and oil.

Scientists are therefore looking for other cheap sources of power. A new interest in windmills has grown. Metal windmills have been made as wind generators to change wind power into electrical power. Also, the centre of the Earth is a natural source of heat energy. Its temperature measures thousands of degrees. In hot springs and geysers, for example, a useful amount of this heat comes to the surface. The steam from steam wells in Italy is already used for steam generators. Similar sources in other parts of the world, the hot lakes in New Zealand for instance, could be brought into use. But these sources are unlikely to add a great deal to our supplies of power.

Scientists are developing methods for using nuclear power more efficiently. One day we may be able to produce electricity by a process called nuclear fusion. This process uses water as a raw material and could possibly provide all the power man would need for thousands of years to come.

pressure

As you read a book, physical pressure is being exerted. Your hands may be pressing on the cover and pages. The book may be pressing on a table that supports it. All around you, the air presses on your body and the book.

Whenever two things touch, pressure is exerted between them. Anything that has weight, and is supported by something else, exerts pressure. And a substance presses on the sides of the container holding it.

We often speak of forces that push against objects. But pressure is different from force. If you stand on your toes, a force equal to your weight is pushing on the floor. And the floor is given a certain pressure. Yet if you stand flat on your feet, the force is the same, and the pressure is less. Your feet have a larger area than your toes do. They spread the force over a larger area of the floor. This spreading out of the force is what we mean by a smaller pressure.

Pressure has a clear definition in the sciences, such as physics. It is equal to the amount of force divided by the area on which the force is exerted. Thus, the same force on a larger area, or a smaller force on the same area, gives a smaller pressure. In this way, scientists can describe more easily how forces act.

All forms of matter – gases, liquids, and solids – exert pressure. They do so because of the tiny particles that they are made of. Each particle pushes against its surroundings with a very small force. But a quantity of matter may contain a huge number of particles. Thus the pressure can be huge. (See: *atom, matter.*)

In a gas, the particles can move around freely. They go quite fast, and continually hit each other. If placed in a container, they also bounce off its walls, and create pressure. The pressure is the same on every part of the walls. And the walls push back on the gas, to keep it contained in a certain space, or 'volume'. This pushing force of the gas can be measured to find the pressure. (See: *gas.*)

To increase the pressure of a gas, three things may be done. If more gas is put in a container, more particles will hit each area of the walls, so there is more pressure. And if the gas is heated, its particles will move faster (see: *heat*). Then they hit the walls with greater force, raising the pressure.

Finally, if the volume of the gas is made smaller, the particles are crowded together more closely. They will hit the walls more often. And the walls of a smaller container must have a smaller area too. The pressure will thus be increased. Boyle's Law tells us the amount of the increase. For example, if the volume is halved, the pressure is doubled. This law was discovered by Robert Boyle in the seventeenth century. His experiments with gases were among the first scientific studies undertaken of pressure.

The Earth's atmosphere is a mixture of gases. It is 'contained' by the downward pull of gravity. And its weight is supported by the Earth's surface upon which it exerts atmospheric pressure. At sea level, there is an average pressure of about 1 kilo per square centimetre (15 pounds per square inch). This pressure acts on all parts of your body. The pressure inside your body balances the air pressure outside. (See: *gravity.*)

Atmospheric pressure changes with time and place on the Earth. Such differences in air pressure influence the weather. They force air to move from places of high pressure to those of low pressure. In this way, winds and storms are created. Air pressure can be measured with a special instrument called a barometer.

Air exerts pressure on every surface it touches. But if it moves past the surface, the pressure decreases. This decrease is the 'Bernoulli effect', which enables an aircraft to fly. It creates a difference in pressure between the bottom and top of an aircraft's wing. The pressure difference supports the aircraft.

The pressure in a liquid is also produced by tiny particles, moving in all directions rapidly. These particles are closer together than those of a gas. Thus they create a much greater pressure. The pressure increases with depth, so as to support the weight of the liquid. And it is exerted on every surface inside the liquid. There can be a Bernoulli effect too, for example when the liquid flows through a pipe. A liquid moves from a place of high pressure to one of low pressure. This is how currents of water flow in the ocean.

The particles inside a solid body are not free to move as they are in a gas or a liquid. Normally, the pressures on them are evenly balanced and the particles do not push against each other. But, they can press against each other if something squeezes them together. The pressure inside a solid body, like a rubber ball you can squeeze, may then be great.

Huge pressures are often found in nature. They exist, for example, in the liquid matter deep inside the Earth. There they may make the Earth's solid outer crust bend and buckle, causing an earthquake (see: *earthquake*). The crust may even crack, so that matter bursts out of the Earth as a volcano (see: *volcano*).

Pressure is often useful to us. We need 'compressed' air to inflate tyres. Such air enables people to breathe in the 'pressurized' cabin of a high-flying aircraft. It allows a diver to breathe under water. Machines, such as the hydraulic press, and steam engines, depend on pressure for the work they do.

Find out by doing

You can make a fountain in a glass jar. Half fill a small bottle with water. Seal it with a cork through which a thin glass tube passes. Stand it on a plate holding a few sheets of wet paper. Heat a large jar gently over a candle flame. Put the jar over the bottle, and press it down onto the wet paper. Soon the air in the jar will cool, decreasing the pressure there. But the air in the bottle will have a higher pressure. So water will be forced out of the bottle through the tube, because of the difference in air pressure.

pulsar

Most of the stars you see in the sky at night shine steadily. They may seem to be twinkling, but this is caused by the Earth's atmosphere, which dims their light. There are, however, stars that really do change in brightness. These are known to astronomers as 'variable stars'. The light of a variable star often changes from bright to dim, then to bright again, in just a few days or even hours.

There is another kind of star whose brightness changes. It is a pulsar. But it is different from a variable star. Nearly all pulsars are invisible from Earth. They give out little light, or are too far from the Earth to be seen. But they give out radio waves. So they can be detected with radio equipment. This is done by huge radio telescopes (see: *radioastronomy*).

The radio waves from a pulsar come in very short bursts, or pulses. The time between two pulses is always constant. It may be a little more than a second, or only a fraction of a second. Such fast, regular signals are as regular as the tick of a clock. Scientists do not know why some pulsars tick faster than others, or how this pulsing behaviour can happen at all.

The first pulsar was discovered in 1968 by radio astronomers at Cambridge in England. Soon many more pulsars were found by other radio telescopes throughout the world. One pulsar is located in the Crab Nebula, which is a massive cloud of gas. This pulsar 'ticks' about 30 times each second. And it gives out visible light that flashes at the same rate. It was the first pulsar actually to be seen. Astronomers at the Steward Observatory in Arizona observed it early in 1969 with their ordinary optical telescope.

Some pulsars, such as the one in the Crab Nebula, give out a double pulse. About halfway between the main pulses is a weaker pulse called the 'interpulse'. The radio waves from pulsars have other strange properties that must be explained too.

Radio signals from a pulsar are very weak. But, if they are magnified through an amplifier, they can be heard. A pulsar in the Leo constellation sends four pulses a second which sound like a musical beat.

Several theories have been proposed to explain pulsars. Most scientists now think that a pulsar is a 'neutron star'. It is an old star that has almost burned itself out, and has collapsed under the force of its own gravity. It is made of the tiny particles called neutrons. (See: *atom*.) They are packed so tightly together that the pulsar is no bigger than the Earth, which is more than a million times smaller than the nearest star, the Sun. (See: *Sun*.) But the pulsar contains much more matter than the Earth.

According to this theory, the pulsar is spinning. It rotates on an axis as the Earth does, but much faster. And radio waves are given off from two places on the pulsar. We 'see' these two spots on the pulsar each time the pulsar spins round once. But, as the diagram shows, we may get a better view of one of the spots than of the other one. We receive a stronger burst of radio waves from that spot. This theory would explain why some pulsars have double pulses.
See: *astronomy, star*.

qualitative and quantitative analysis

Everybody wants to know what things are made of. Your mother may wonder how her neighbour makes such delicious lemonade. You may ask if the stars are made of rock, just like the Earth. Doctors may want to know whether a special food is good for babies. A police detective may ask if a bloodstain has been left by a particular person. We can help to answer all these questions – and more – by chemical analysis.

Two kinds of analysis are done. We can discover *what* substances are in a sample. This is qualitative analysis. Or we can discover *how much* of each substance is in the sample. This is quantitative analysis.

How can we go about this? The methods we use really depend on what we want to know. For instance: how much mud is there in the water of your local river? You can get a sample of the water, and let it stand in a tall narrow glass. Soon all the solids in the water will begin to settle to the bottom. Eventually, there will be clear water at the top of the glass and solid matter, which we call sediment, at the bottom. This is an example of a kind of analysis called sedimentation analysis.

So far we do not know much about the mud. Perhaps it is made up of many different substances. Maybe there is some heavy iron ore, or much of it may be sand. There may be chalk or other powdery minerals that sink very slowly. And there will certainly be lots of dead vegetable matter. You may see different layers, but because you let your sample settle slowly, the different substances are probably mixed up. All you can say for certain is how much mud you have.

But suppose we put your river sample into a strong glass tube and spin it around very fast in a machine called a centrifuge. This speeds up sedimentation.
Then, the heaviest of the particles will sink very quickly, and even the lightest will sink quickly. The result will be that the mud will separate into layers. When you look through the side of the tube, you will be able to see the layers. They may even be different colours. Now we can say not only how much mud is in the water; we can also make a guess at what the mud is made of.

But this is still a guess. Each of those layers must be analyzed separately. Are they single substances, or are they mixtures? Looking at them under a microscope may help; it will certainly show us the dead vegetation. But most probably we shall find that each layer is still a mixture.

We have to find a way to separate the mixture. Substances in the mixture can be identified by their different properties. This is done by testing the mixture in a number of ways. For example, when acid is added to a sample, some of the mixture may dissolve, leaving the rest behind. The mixture is this separated into two different parts. Then, testing with a magnet may show that some of one part is attracted to the magnet while the rest is not. Another part is thus separated.

We can continue our analysis by more tests, until we have separated each substance. When we cannot find any way of separating the mixture further, the substances we are left with are what we call chemical compounds, such as iron oxide.

But there is still the clear water to deal with, which was separated from the mud. Probably there are chemical compounds dissolved in it. There may be small plants and animals, such as bacteria. It is the job of someone called an analyst to keep a check on what is in the water of a river supplying, say, a town.

We can find out what is dissolved in the water by boiling it until all the water is changed into steam. Some solid will be left. We can heat this solid part, which we call a residue, further, until anything that can be burnt away has gone. What we are left with is the 'ash content'. Or we can separate the residue in the same way we separate the sediment – into compounds.

Now we have a great many compounds, and we have to find out what they are. Already we may have a good idea what some of them are. That shiny metallic dust that will only dissolve in a strong acid, is it gold? No, it is probably iron pyrites. The small cubic crystals left when we heated the water are most likely to be common salt (sodium chloride).

By analysis we can find out what elements are in the compound. An element contains only one type of atom (see: *element*). We can test for it with chemicals called reagents. For instance, a solution of ammonia is the reagent that gives a bright blue colour with the elements copper and nickel. A solution of barium chloride is the reagent that gives a thick white solid or precipitate with any solution containing a sulphate. We can heat the compound in a flame and see if the flame is coloured. Calcium will make a bright red flame; sodium a yellow one.

Organic compounds – that is, most of the compounds of carbon – are harder to identify than inorganic chemicals, like minerals. This is because organic compounds break down easily into their elements. Organic compounds make identifiable smells and colours. Sometimes they can be separated and identified by chromatography. This makes use of a column of material, such as chalk, through which we pass a solution of our sample. The different compounds come out from the solution at different levels.

Finally we need to know how much there is of everything. We can take measured quantities of substances, burn them in a flame and measure how bright the flame is. We do this in an instrument called a spectro-photometer. We can also make precipitates, dry them, and weigh them.

Enzymes are chemicals that are made by living cells. They alter the speed of chemical reactions. Enzymes can be extracted from bacteria, or from other living things, and used to measure the quantity of a particular chemical by the rate at which they break it down. This is called biochemical analysis (see: *biology*). It has opened up a whole new way of analysis, and is particularly valuable in the analysis of organic substances.

New and more complicated methods of analysis, both qualitative and quantitative, are being devised. They are used in medicine, in industry, in astronomy, in crime detection – anywhere that anybody asks the questions: what is it made of, and how much of it is there?

quantum

When you look at an electric light bulb in your home it seems to shine steadily. But in fact, the light that pours from it is made up of vast numbers of tiny 'packages' of light. The light is more like a spray, made up of many droplets, than a smoothly flowing stream. Each of the packages of light is called a quantum (plural: quanta). 'Quantum' means 'quantity', and is a Latin word.

Until 1900, scientists did not realize that quanta existed. The idea of quanta was suggested by the German physicist Max Planck to solve several puzzling problems. One of these was the 'photoelectric effect'.

When light is shone onto many metals and metal-like substances, it knocks electrons out of them. Electrons are tiny particles that make up part of every atom. They have electrical charge. Electric currents are made up of moving electrons. (See: *atom, electricity*.)

The photoelectric effect

When electrons are knocked out of a substance by light, they make a weak electric current, which can be measured. This action of light is called the photo-electric effect (*photo* means light).

Photographers' lightmeters use the photo-electric effect. The meter is pointed at a scene, and produces electric current according to how bright the scene is.

Scientists say that the light gives up energy to the electrons. To say that the light has energy means that it can do such things as set electrons moving, heat up the things it shines on, and so on. (See: *energy*.)

The wave theory

At the time the photoelectric effect was discovered, in the 19th century, scientists pictured light as a kind of wave motion.

Ocean waves are movements in water. Sound waves are movements of the air. Scientists thought there was a substance, called the ether, that filled all space. Light waves were vibrations of this substance. (This ether had nothing to do with the chemical called ether, which doctors once used to send people to sleep.) The light waves, like other kinds of wave, carried energy.

So the photoelectric effect could be thought of as being like the pounding of ocean waves on a beach. In a storm, big breakers can fling pebbles high into the air. The ocean waves transfer a little of their energy to the pebbles, setting them moving. Similarly, it was thought, light waves transfer energy to electrons and throw them out of the metal.

But when studying the photo-electric effect, scientists realized that the wave theory of light is not the whole truth. Suppose you were walking along the seashore on a calm day, when the waves were gentle. You would be very surprised if, from time to time, you saw a pebble thrown high into the air by the waves. Each wave has only a little energy. How could each pebble get enough energy all at once.

This could never happen with sea waves. Yet something like it happens with light and electrons. In faint light, the waves are weak. Scientists did not expect that faint light would be able to knock electrons out of metals. They were amazed when they found that weak light would produce a slight photo-electric current. Though only a few electrons were knocked out of the metal, each one had received a comparatively large amount of energy from the light.

The photon

In 1905, the great physicist Albert Einstein suggested how each electron could receive so much energy even from faint light. He suggested that the energy of light exists in separate 'packages', which he called photons. The word photon is still used today, meaning a quantum of light. But photons are only one kind of quantum.

According to Einstein's idea, photons are sent out in great numbers by any source of light, like drops of water sprayed from a lawn-sprinkler. From a less powerful lamp, fewer photons are sent out each second.

In the photo-electric effect, each electron is knocked out of (for example) the substance selenium by a single photon. The photon disappears completely, giving up all its energy. The photon never gives up part of its energy.

When weak light is shone onto selenium, comparatively few photons arrive each second. So comparatively few electrons are knocked out of the selenium. But each one that is knocked out gets all the energy of a photon.

The idea of photons explained the photo-electric effect and some other problems of physics. But then physicists were puzzled by what light is really like. In some cases, such as the photo-electric effect, light behaves like a stream of particles. In other cases, such as the diffraction, or breaking up, of light into dark and light bands, light behaves like waves. (See: *light*.)

Wavelength and energy

In experiments in which light acts like waves, physicists could measure its 'wavelength'. Sixteen thousand waves of yellow light take up only one centimetre. Physicists say that yellow light has a wavelength of one sixteen-thousandth of a centimetre (one forty-thousandth of an inch). Red light has longer waves – about one fourteen-thousandth of a centimetre. Blue and violet light have shorter waves than yellow light – about one twenty-four-thousandth of a centimetre.

Invisible infrared light waves are longer than visible light waves. TV and radio waves are longer still; they can be kilometres long.

Waves of invisible ultraviolet light are shorter than visible light waves. X-rays and gamma rays have wavelengths down to a thousand-millionth of a centimetre and less.

All these waves are called 'electromagnetic' waves (see: *light*). And they all carry energy. Their energy comes in quanta.

Physicists found that the longer the wavelength of light, the less energy its quanta had. For example, each quantum sent out by TV transmitters has about one ten-millionth of the energy of a visible-light quantum (that is, a photon).

Electrons knocked out of a substance by violet (short-wavelength) light have more energy than if they are knocked out by yellow (longer-wavelength) light. Each photon of violet light has more energy to give up to the electron than each photon of yellow light.

Scientists say that the energy of light and other forms of electromagnetic radiation is 'quantized', simply meaning that it comes in quanta. Other kinds of energy are quantized.

For example, electrons inside atoms have quantized energy. Every atom is made up partly of electrons. We can think of them as travelling round the centre of the atom in orbits, like planets round the Sun, or artificial satellites round the Earth. In each orbit, the electrons have a definite amount of energy.

In the same way, a space satellite moving round the Earth has a definite amount of energy. If the satellite is given more energy (by firing its rocket engine) it moves out to a larger orbit. If it loses energy it will move in to a smaller orbit.

But the energy of a space satellite is not quantized. It can be given any amount of energy, and it will follow an orbit of corresponding size. The orbits of electrons in an atom can have only certain definite sizes. So the electrons' energy is quantized.

The fact that electron orbits can have only certain sizes explains why electrons do not fall into the centre of the atom. Only certain orbits are 'allowed' to the electrons. And each orbit can hold only a certain number of electrons. For example, the innermost orbit can hold only two electrons, the second orbit only eight. When the inner orbits are filled with electrons, an electron in an outer orbit cannot move inward. All the places on the inner orbits are filled, and there is no place for the outer electron to move into.

Particles or waves?

We saw above that, when the quantum theory was first suggested, scientists were puzzled as to whether light and other kinds of radiation consisted of particles or waves. Now they think that it is neither of these things. In certain situations, such as experiments with photoelectricity, we can think of radiation as consisting of particle-like quanta. In other situations we must think of radiation as consisting of waves, if we are to be able to explain the way in which it behaves.

Not only must we do this for radiation – we must also do it for what we usually call 'particles'. Streams of electrons and other tiny particles that make up atoms sometimes behave as if they were actually made up of waves. Their wavelength can even be measured. It is found that fast-moving (high-energy) electrons have shorter wavelengths than slow-moving electrons. So shorter wavelengths go with higher energies of particle motion, just as they go with higher quantum energies of radiation.

quasar

Until recently, quasars were thought to be ordinary stars. 'Quasar' is short for 'quasi-stellar' (starlike) 'radio source'. Quasars send out radio waves that can be picked up by the huge antennas used by radio astronomers (see: *radioastronomy*). Radio waves from a quasar come from a point in the sky. Astronomers can often photograph blue starlike objects lying at the position of a quasar.

Astronomers study the light of stars, like that from other objects in the sky, by splitting it up into its colours (see: *light*). At first the light from the quasars seemed to make no sense. It was quite different from the light of any star. Then, in 1963, Maarten Schmidt, a Dutch astronomer working in California, realised what was happening.

As the light from a quasar travelled through space, its wavelength seemed to increase. The light given out by a quasar might be violet (short wavelength and invisible). This would appear as visible blue light (greater wavelength) to an observer on Earth. The wavelengths of light from some quasars had increased so much that they would appear to be double to an observer on Earth.

A similar 'wavelength shift' exists with the light from galaxies. Galaxies are huge systems of gas, dust and stars. Our Sun is just one star in the Milky Way galaxy. And astronomers know that there are billions more galaxies in the Universe. It is nowadays believed that the galaxies are travelling rapidly away from us. This motion causes a Doppler effect – a 'stretching' of the light waves.

The quasars' wavelength shift is probably also due to a rapid motion away from us. Astronomers think that some quasars are travelling away from us at almost the speed of light. Light travels at about 300,000 kilometres (186,000 miles) per second.

The farther a galaxy is from us, the faster it is found to be travelling. Most astronomers assume that the same rule is true for quasars. If this is true, then, the quasars are as far away as the galaxies, or farther.

This reveals the quasars as amazing objects. To appear like even the faintest star to us they must be hundreds of times brighter than whole galaxies. Yet they are small compared with galaxies. Their radiation comes from a region less than one light year across. Our own Galaxy is 100,000 light years across.

Scientists do not know how so much energy can be released so fast in such a small volume. One suggestion has been that in the quasars matter is colliding with antimatter (see: *matter*). If this were to happen the matter and antimatter would disappear and be turned completely into energy. Another suggestion is that large quantities of matter are collapsing, releasing gravitational energy.

Some astronomers have suggested that quasars are not really distant, bright objects at all. They might, for example, be objects thrown out from our own Galaxy at high speed. But most evidence points the other way. Some laws of physics may need to be changed in order to explain quasars.

See: *astronomy, star, Sun, universe.*

radar

A pilot flying an aircraft through a thick fog needs to rely on more than just his eyes. He cannot see very far in a fog. Radar is a system that helps a pilot 'see' if, for example, there are other aircraft nearby. Our eyes cannot measure speeds very accurately either. Radar also shows a pilot how fast other aircraft are moving.

The basic idea of radar is a simple one. When you shout inside a cave or a large hall, you sometimes hear an echo. The echo is the sound 'reflected' from the walls. Sound waves from your mouth travel to the walls of the hall. They

bounce off the walls back to your ears. The sound waves take time to travel to the walls and back. This causes the delay between your shout and the echo. The farther the walls are from you, the longer the delay is.

Radar works on the same principle. But, instead of using sound waves, radar uses short radio waves. Radio waves travel farther than sound waves in air. They also travel very much faster. Radio waves travel at the speed of light. This is about 300,000 kilometres per second.

'Catching' echoes

A radar set sends out short bursts, or 'pulses', of radio waves. If there is an object in the path of the waves, an aircraft for example, some of the waves bounce off it. These waves return to the radar set, just like an echo of the transmitted pulse.

There is a delay between the waves being sent out and returning to the radar set. This is just like the delay between your shout and the echo. The radio waves take time to travel to the aircraft and back.

The time taken is measured automatically in the radar set. The speed of the waves is known. From this it is possible to work out how far away the aircraft is. This is what the radar set does. In fact, the name 'radar' is taken from the words '*radio detection and ranging*'. 'Ranging' means measuring how far away an object is.

The radar set has a 'transmitter' device. This produces radio waves and sends them out. The set also has a receiver. This detects the echoes.

Only some of the waves that are sent out are reflected back to the radar set. The pulses that are sent out must be kept very powerful so that they produce a strong echo. To keep their power, they must not spread out as they travel. That is why they are aimed in a narrow beam.

An 'antenna' is used to focus the waves. Sometimes, this device is shaped like a big metal dish. It moves round and round or swings back and forth. Thus, it beams over a wide area. The antenna may be completely enclosed by a 'radome'. This is a spherical plastic structure. Though you cannot see through the radome, radar waves can pass easily through it. It protects the antenna from wind and rain.

The antenna receives the echoes as well as sending out the waves. Usually, radar waves are not sent out in a continuous stream. They are sent out in short bursts, or pulses. In most radar sets, each pulse lasts about one millionth of a second. The time between pulses is much longer. It is about one hundredth of a second. During this time, no waves are sent. This is when the echoes are received.

A radar set can also show the direction of an object. The antenna beams the waves like a searchlight. When the antenna 'picks up' reflections from an object, that object is in the direction that the antenna is pointing.

The strength of the radar echo depends on the size and shape of the reflecting object and what it is made of. Metals reflect radar waves more strongly than non-metals. Larger objects give stronger echoes. This may be useful to a ship's captain, for example. He may need to know whether a ship 50 kilometres away is a destroyer, say, or an aircraft carrier.

Distance finder

Radar echoes are usually shown on a screen like a television screen. One type of radar screen is a 'plan position indicator', or PPI, for short. This is a round screen showing a map of the area around the radar station. The station is at the centre of the screen. Circles may be marked on the screen. These show distances from the station. Around the edge of the screen is a scale indicating compass directions. This shows directions from the radar station.

On the screen there is a bright line called the 'trace'. The trace sweeps round and round the screen. It represents the wave sent out from the radar station. It moves at the same rate as the antenna turns. As it does so, bright spots appear on it from time to time. They remain glowing on the screen as the trace moves on. These are called 'blips'. They are produced by the echoes returning to the station. They show the position of fixed objects, such as buildings or mountains. They also show moving objects, such as ships or aircraft, whose echoes have been picked up by the radar station.

Each blip slowly fades away. When the trace sweeps over that part of the screen again, a new spot is formed, showing the new position of the aircraft or ship. The past positions are maked by a trail of several fading blips.

One kind of radar set can show how fast an object is moving. This is done by a measurement of 'wavelengths'. The wavelength is measured from the 'crest', or top, of one radio wave to the crest of the next wave. Radar uses short radio waves called microwaves. These have a wavelength of between one and ten centimetres. This is less than one thousandth of the wavelength of ordinary radiowaves. Waves of a fixed wavelength are sent out.

The waves that are reflected from an object, such as an aircraft, may be longer or shorter than the waves sent out. The wavelength is shorter if the aircraft is approaching. And the wavelength is longer if the aircraft is moving away. The speed of the aircraft is worked out from the difference in the wavelengths.

Radar can show the positions of aircraft and ships many hundreds of kilometres away. A radar set can be carried on a ship or aircraft or fixed to the ground. Radar was developed during the Second World War. It has many military uses. It can be used to aim a gun or missile at a target. Radar stations can detect missiles moving into the area they cover.

But radar also has peaceful uses. Ships and aircraft use it for navigation. The Doppler type of radar set is also an essential part of the air traffic control system of every major airport. In bad weather, when the pilot may not be able to see the ground, an operator in the control tower can use radar to follow the exact position of the aircraft. He then talks the pilot down, giving him precise instructions for a safe landing. This technique is called 'ground controlled approach', or GCA.

Radar is also used by weathermen to detect storms and hurricanes. Astronomers use it to detect meteors and study planets such as Mercury and Venus. And it is also often used by traffic police to measure the speed of vehicles in order to enforce speed limits on roads.

radiation

When you throw a stone into a pond, drops of water splash up from the place where the stone goes in. Ripples spread out from this place over the surface of the pond. And, although you cannot see under the surface as easily, the water is disturbed there too. Waves spread out underwater from the point where the stone entered the pond. And they spread out from the stone as it sinks to the bottom of the pond. Fish in the pond can feel the disturbance the stone makes. You can see the ripples or be splashed by the water.

The ripples and disturbances in the water are examples of radiation. Radiation is the spreading out of energy from a point. The name 'radiation' comes from the Latin word for the spokes of a wheel. We still use this Latin word when we speak of the 'radius' of a circle. Spokes go out from a wheel's centre in several directions. Similarly, waves 'radiate' from a point in all directions.

As radiation spreads, energy is carried outward. Energy is the ability to do work – for example, to set things moving (see: *energy*). Energy is transferred when you throw the stone into the pond. It is carried away from the place where the stone hits. For example, ripples set pieces of floating driftwood bobbing up and down. The wood is given energy of movement. It comes from the stone, carried by the ripples.

Wave radiation

The sound that you hear when the stone hits the water has reached you by radiation. It travels like the disturbance that the fish feels, except that the sound waves travel through the air. The sound waves spread out from the place where the stone hits the water. These waves carry sound energy that makes your ear-drums vibrate. (See: *sound*.)

Light is another form of radiation. Most of the light we see comes from the Sun. The light travels across millions of kilometres of space. When we look at an object, this page for example, in the daylight, what we see is light from the Sun that has bounced off, or been 'reflected' from, the page. Light, too, consists of waves carrying energy. (See: *light*.)

Many forms of radiation are useful. For example, the radio waves that bring us radio and television programmes are a form of radiation. And so, also, is part of the warmth that we get from a 'radiator' in our houses. The X-rays that enable a doctor to see bones inside the body also are a form of radiation.

These types of radiation, and light itself, are called electromagnetic radiation. They are different from sound radiation. Electromagnetic radiation can travel through empty space. For example, radioastronomers pick up radio waves from space with special receivers. These waves are given out naturally by some objects in space, such as distant stars. But sound cannot travel through space. It needs matter – a 'medium' – to move through. The medium may be a gas, such as air, a liquid, such as water, or a solid, such as wood.

Every wave is a disturbance. In a wave, something changes. In a sound wave the positions of tiny particles in the air change. The particles of air move back and forth, or 'oscillate'.

Electromagnetic waves do not consist of moving particles. They can travel in space where there are no particles to move up and down. They are called 'electromagnetic' waves because they have various electrical and magnetic effects. For example, electromagnetic waves can set tiny electric currents flowing in matter. (See: *electricity*.)

Wavelength and frequency

Waves are measured by their 'wavelength' and their 'frequency'.

Wavelength, in water for instance, is the distance between ripples, measured from the top of one wave to the top of the next wave. Wavelength is usually measured in metres. (One metre is just over three feet.) If it takes 10 waves, say, to cover a distance of one metre, then the length of one wave is a tenth of a metre, or 10 centimetres. This is a short wave length.

Frequency is the number of waves per second that pass a point. It is measured in units called hertz (Hz for short). These were named after Heinrich Hertz, the German physicist who discovered radio waves. A frequency of one wave, or 'cycle', per second is one hertz. This is a very low frequency. A frequency of 1,000 cycles per second is a kilohertz (kHz).

Different kinds of radiation have different frequencies. We can only hear sound waves within a certain range of frequency. This range is about 16 hertz to 20 kilohertz (16 cycles per second to 20,000 cycles per second). High-pitched sounds, such as the sound of a whistle, have high frequencies. Low-pitched sounds, such as the bass notes of a church organ, have low frequencies.

When sound waves have a frequency that is less than about 16 hertz, the waves are called infrasonic. We cannot hear these waves. But we can sometimes feel them as vibrations. You may have felt infrasonic waves from the bass notes of an organ or from heavy machinery, for example.

When the frequency of sound waves is more than 20 kilohertz, we again cannot hear them. We call these waves ultrasonic. Some animals, for example dogs, can hear sounds that have frequencies that are ultrasonic for human beings.

Most electromagnetic waves have even higher frequencies than ultrasonic waves. Radio waves range from a few hertz to several hundred thousand million hertz. Above this range are heat waves, known as 'infrared' radiation. Light waves have still higher frequencies.

All electromagnetic radiations travel at the same speed – about 300,000 kilometres (186,000 miles) per second. In short-wavelength radiation, there are more waves per second than in long-wavelength radiation. Imagine a small child walking with his father. They both move at the same speed, walking the same distance in the same time. But the child's steps are shorter than his father's. The child must therefore take more steps than his father. The length of the steps is comparable with wavelength, and the number of steps is the frequency. Similarly, then, the number of waves each second is more for shorter wavelengths than for longer. The shorter the wavelength, the higher the frequency. The longer the wavelength, the lower the frequency.

Light waves have very high frequencies. So they also have short wavelengths. Their wavelengths are so short that we measure them in nanometres. There are a thousand million nanometres in a metre. The wavelength of visible light – light that we can see – ranges from 770 nanometres for deep red colours to about 380 nanometres for violet. There is another kind of light, invisible to us, with wavelengths shorter than violet light. It is called ultraviolet radiation, meaning 'beyond the violet'. And X-rays have even shorter wavelengths. They can be as short as a picometre –

a thousandth of a nanometre. The shortest wavelengths of any electromagnetic radiation are found in cosmic rays from outer space.

Your eyes see only visible light. But your skin can feel infrared radiation as heat. Infrared radiation is a form of invisible light with wavelengths longer than red light. 'Infrared' means 'beneath the red'. The kind of film that is used by an ordinary camera is sensitive only to visible light and to ultraviolet radiation. But special film can be made that is sensitive to infrared radiation.

Infrared photographs taken automatically from spacecraft, for example on the Apollo missions, are useful in mapping areas. They give information which would otherwise take a lot more time and money to obtain. For example, photographs may indicate the bottom of a river, and the kinds of crops in an area of vegetation. Infrared radiation has several other applications. For instance, it can be used in a special oven to heat up small amounts of food and liquid very quickly.

Energy of radiation

All waves carry energy. The ripples on a pond carry energy. When they reach the edge of the pond they can do work. They may shake loose some dirt, or move grains of sand. A sound wave also carries energy. It carries energy to your ear by moving the air that is next to it.

The energy of radiation can be dangerous. Your eyes will be harmed if you look directly at the Sun, which sends out high-energy radiation. So never do this.

The intensity of radiation can be decreased in various ways before it reaches you. Radiation may be absorbed by other matter that it hits. Then, less reaches you. Sound waves are absorbed by the medium they travel through. Part of their energy is turned into heat.

The Sun sends out a lot of ultraviolet light. Ultraviolet light is good for us. It builds up vitamin D in the body. This vitamin helps make strong bones and teeth. In small doses, ultraviolet light gives a suntan. In larger doses it burns the skin and is dangerous. On its way through the atmosphere, ultraviolet light is partly absorbed by particles of the gas called ozone. By the time it reaches us, the intensity of the Sun's ultraviolet light is reduced. (See: *absorption of light*.)

The intensity of radiation reaching you is less the farther away you are from the source. For example, sources of light always appear dimmer the farther away we are from them.

Electromagnetic waves are given out, or 'emitted', by matter whenever electrically charged particles move. Radio waves are emitted from a metal rod or wire called an 'antenna'. Inside the antenna, electrons (tiny particles of electricity) are moving backward and forward. This produces a wave of electromagnetic radiation which travels away from the antenna. The receiving antenna is a rod or wire similar to the emitter. When a wave hits it, electrons in it are set moving, just as floating wood is set moving by ripples on a pond. These moving electrons are an electric current. The current is 'amplified', or strengthened, by the radio receiver. Then, it is used to produce sound from loudspeakers in the radio set.

Heat waves are emitted in a similar way by the vibration of the atoms of an object. The higher the temperature of the object, the faster the atoms vibrate.

Wave radiation often acts like a stream of tiny particles, called quanta (singular: quantum). Quanta cannot be held and weighed, as real particles can. But their energy makes them act like real particles in some ways. For example, they exert a 'radiation pressure', a push, on whatever they hit.

A quantum 'starts' inside an atom. Each atom has a centre called the nucleus. Other particles, the electrons, spin round the nucleus in orbits, like planets spinning round the Sun. When a moving particle hits an atom, an electron may be knocked into a 'higher' orbit – one farther from the centre. When it is knocked into a higher orbit, the electron 'absorbs', or picks up, a quantum of energy. But the electron soon falls back into its original orbit. As it does so, it emits energy. It may fall back in one jump, giving out one quantum of energy. Or it may fall back in several jumps, each time giving out a quantum of energy.

Electrons, as we have said, are particles of electricity. Scientists say they have a negative electric 'charge'. The nucleus of an atom also has an electric charge but of a different kind, called positive.

X-rays are emitted when a fast-moving charged particle, such as an electron, slows down suddenly. This may happen if the electron passes near another charged particle, such as the nucleus of an atom in matter that it hits. The electron is slowed down by the electric force between the two particles. The electron must lose some energy. This is given off as X-radiation. This is always happening naturally in stars, such as the Sun, which emit X-rays. And it can be made to happen artificially in an X-ray machine.

High-speed particles

The 'particles' of electromagnetic radiation disappear when they are absorbed. They only exist while they are moving. Other kinds of radiation consist of high-speed particles, which do not disappear when they are slowed down or stopped. One source of these particles is the atoms of 'radioactive' substances.

A radioactive substance sends out several sorts of high-speed particle. Alpha radiation is composed of particles from the nucleus of a radioactive atom (see: *radioactivity*). Beta particles are just electrons. Particles called neutrons may also be emitted.

These high-speed particles are absorbed by hitting other matter. When they hit an atom, they may knock the electrons out of it. An atom that has lost electrons is called an 'ion'. It is said to be 'ionized'. The high-speed particles produced by radioactive atoms are therefore often called 'ionizing radiation' by scientists.

Cosmic rays consist partly of high-speed 'protons'. These are small particles with a positive electric charge. Protons are the nuclei of hydrogen atoms. But cosmic rays also contain the nuclei of heavier atoms, and electrons. When very energetic cosmic ray particles hit atoms of the Earth's atmosphere, they can break them apart. This can produce still more high-speed particles.

Like X-rays, high-speed particles can cause ionization, and they are more dangerous. The ionization of atoms in living organisms may cause chemical changes. These changes are called 'radiation sickness', and can result in death.

People near sources of X-radiation or high-speed particles – for example, people who work in nuclear power stations – have to be protected by special clothing. They are also 'shielded' from the radiation source by thick layers of lead.

To make sure they are not getting too high a dose of radiation, people who work in nuclear power stations often wear a badge containing a piece of special film on their coat lapels. This is called a 'dosimeter'. If ionizing radiation hits the film, it becomes 'fogged'. The film has to be developed to show the fogging. The fogging indicates how much radiation the wearer has received.

radioactivity

Imagine that you are holding a watermelon. Suddenly, for no apparent reason, one of its seeds comes flying out through the thick skin. At the same time, the watermelon turns into a grapefruit. Before you can say a word, the grapefruit spits out a seed and turns into an apple. As you are about to bite into the apple, a seed shoots out of it, and you are left with an orange. Then, the orange throws out a seed and becomes a lemon. Since you do not like to eat lemons, you wait for it to turn into a grape. But it remains a lemon.

If you ever had such an experience, you might think that some magician was trying to keep you from eating. Luckily, we never find one kind of fruit changing into another in this way. Yet, a very similar process can occur inside many atoms. This process is called radioactivity.

Atoms are tiny particles that make up all matter. At the centre of each atom is a much smaller 'nucleus'. The nucleus is a group of even tinier particles, known as protons and neutrons.

The nucleus of a radioactive atom can throw out one or more of these tinier particles. Such a nucleus is said to decay, or break apart. By this decay, one type of atom is changed into a different type. To understand how this happens, we must look more closely at the atom. There are over 100 basic types of atom. Each atom is part of a particular chemical element.

The nucleus in each type of atom has a definite number of protons and neutrons. An atom of oxygen, for example, has eight protons and eight neutrons. An atom of one kind of carbon has six protons and six neutrons, and an atom of another kind of carbon has six protons and seven neutrons. If the number of protons inside a nucleus changes, the nucleus of a different element is formed. The nucleus of an atom of iron, for example, has 26 protons, and the nucleus of an atom of cobalt has 27 protons.

When a nucleus has more than about 83 protons, we find that it cannot stay together. It will decay and is said to be radioactive. For example, radium has 88 protons in its atoms and is a radioactive element.

Nuclei can decay in various ways. The simplest way is called 'alpha decay'. A group of two protons and two neutrons shoots out of the nucleus. They are joined together, making a single particle called an alpha particle. The original nucleus becomes a new nucleus. It has lost two protons and two neutrons. Because it has a different number of protons, the nucleus belongs to a different element. An atom of radium, with 88 protons and 138 neutrons, by giving off alpha particles, decays into the radioactive gas called radon. An atom of radon has 86 protons and 136 neutrons.

Another way in which nuclei change is by 'beta decay'. In the usual kind of beta decay, a neutron inside the nucleus changes into a proton. In the process, a very small 'beta particle' is given off. This is just a high-speed electron – the same particle that moves in an electric current. The nucleus then has one neutron less and one proton more than the original nucleus. A new element has been formed. For example, one form of the radioactive element thorium has 90 protons and 144 neutrons in its atoms. It decays by beta decay into the radioactive element protactinium. An atom of protactinium has 91 protons and 143 neutrons.

Most atoms are not radioactive. Their nuclei are 'stable', meaning that they do not decay. An ordinary object, such as an apple, has millions and millions of atoms with stable nuclei, so it stays the same. We call a radioactive nucleus 'unstable', because it can decay.

When a radioactive nucleus decays, both the number of protons and the number of neutrons can change. The resulting nucleus may be stable or it, too, may be radioactive. If it is radioactive, it decays to form a new nucleus, which may be radioactive as well. Thus, a 'decay series' can occur. Each kind of chemical element in the series changes into the next kind. Finally, the series ends with an element, such as lead, that is not radioactive. The atoms in this element are stable. They do not decay.

A very long series begins when an atom of uranium decays. The uranium atom is the heaviest atom that occurs in nature. (Scientists can produce heavier ones.) Each uranium atom contains 92 protons. It may have 142, 143, or 146 neutrons.

A uranium atom that begins with 142 neutrons will decay by throwing out two protons and two neutrons. An atom of thorium will be left, containing 90 protons and 140 neutrons. This new atom will decay in the same way, becoming an atom of radium with 88 protons and 138 neutrons. This changes into an atom of radon gas, with 86 protons and 136 neutrons. The atom of radon in turn changes into an atom of polonium, with 84 protons and 134 neutrons.

Further decay follows. The series ends only when stable atoms are formed. Lead, which has 82 protons in its atoms, is the stable end-product of the uranium decay series. In many of the Earth's rocks, uranium is slowly changing into lead in just this way.

Not all the atoms of a particular chemical element are radioactive. Every element is a mixture of several kinds of atom, which are called 'isotopes'. As we have said, nuclei with the same number of protons can have different numbers of neutrons. These different kinds of atom are isotopes. The element carbon, for example, has six known isotopes. Four of these carbon isotopes are radioactive, but two are stable.

Radioactive isotopes occur in nature in small amounts. They are continually breaking apart into stable isotopes. But they can be produced artificially in the laboratory.

We cannot tell when a radioactive nucleus will decay, or influence it in any way. But we can predict how many of a large number of such nuclei will decay. Half of them will decay in a certain time. Then, half of the remaining number will decay in an equal time. Next, half of the nuclei that are still left will decay in the same time.

The time for half the nuclei to decay is called the 'half life' of the isotope. Every radioactive isotope has a different half life. It might be thousands of millions of years or just a fraction of a second. For example, one isotope of uranium has a half life of 4½ thousand million years. But the half life of one isotope of polonium is less than a millionth of a second.

Radioactive energy

When a radioactive atom decays, it gives off energy. Alpha and beta particles move very fast and thus have enormous energy (see: *energy*). An alpha particle may travel at about one tenth of the speed of light. A beta particle travels at about nine tenths of the speed of light (see: *light*).

A radioactive nucleus can also give off 'gamma rays' when it decays. These are similar to visible light rays and also to X-rays (see: *quantum, X-rays*), except that they have much shorter wavelengths. Gamma rays occur more often in alpha decay than in beta decay.

These particles and rays differ in the way they behave when they hit another object, such as an atom. They may set the atom moving, for example, or knock some of the electrons out of the atom they hit. An alpha particle will be stopped and lose all its energy of motion in this way, after travelling through only a few centimetres of air. A beta particle can go much farther. And gamma rays can go through several centimetres of solid iron.

This is why radioactive materials must be handled carefully in special containers. Otherwise, the particles and rays they send out might hit people and cause great harm. Radioactive 'fallout' material, created by nuclear weapons, is even more dangerous. (See: *radiation*.)

The energy produced by radioactivity can be useful. An example is another kind of decay process, called 'fission'. It occurs when a nucleus splits into two big parts and a few small particles, which usually are neutrons. The energy released in fission appears as heat. This can be used to turn water into steam and so generate electricity.

Radioactivity serves many other purposes in science and industry. Gamma rays from an isotope of cobalt are used in the treatment of certain diseases, such as cancer. Isotopes of some elements are used as 'tracers' in scientific research and medicine. Their radioactivity enables scientists to locate them, even inside a living body. One isotope of carbon, known as carbon-14, has a long half life. It is contained in the bones and wood that an archaeologist digs up. Its radioactivity allows him to find their age. Instruments have been invented to measure radioactivity. They are used to search for valuable radioactive materials, such as uranium.

Radioactivity was discovered only in 1896 by

the French scientist A. H. Becquerel. Becquerel was interested in substances that can take in the energy of sunlight and give out their own light, or 'fluoresce' (see: *fluorescence*). He wanted to find out if they give out X-rays when they fluoresce. X-rays will go through paper and mark photographic film. Becquerel put some fluorescent substance on film that he had covered in black paper. He put this in a drawer while he waited for sunny weather. After a few dull days, he decided to develop the film anyway. To his surprise it was marked. The substance could not have fluoresced in the dark drawer. It must have given out something else. This was called radioactivity by Marie Curie, a scientist who did a lot of work on radioactivity. In 1901, Becquerel found the radioactive part of his fluorescent substance. It was uranium.
See: *atom, nuclear energy*.

radioastronomy

If your eyes suddenly became able to see radio signals, the world would look very different. A radio station's tall antenna would seem as bright as a bonfire. But the Sun would be much fainter than it normally looks to us. Nearly all the stars would be invisible. On the other hand, there would be many other strange new objects in the sky. They would be visible night and day, and in cloudy weather.

Of course our eyes cannot detect radio waves. We can see only ordinary light. Astronomers study the heavens by looking at the light from stars, planets, and other matter. They use optical telescopes, which, because they are large, collect more light than our eyes can. But objects in space also send out radio waves. These waves are received by radio telescopes, and studied in the science of radioastronomy.

This science was developed after 1930. Yet already it has greatly increased man's knowledge of the universe. It tells us much about objects in space whose light cannot be seen. Many objects that give out no light at all can be detected by the radio waves they send out.

Radio waves from space were discovered in 1931 by Karl Jansky in America. They came from the centre of our star system, known as the Galaxy. This region is hidden from optical astronomers by dark clouds of gas and dust in space. Such clouds stop light, but radio waves can pass through them.

Later, radio waves from the Sun and Jupiter were detected.

Recently, radio telescopes have been used to listen for signals from other intelligent life in the universe. So far this search has been unsuccessful. But new mysteries are continually being revealed. In 1968, very regular radio signals were detected by astronomers at Cambridge in England. They occurred regularly every one and one-third seconds. At first they were thought to be artificial. But, although strange, these signals certainly come from natural objects. These objects are now called pulsars. (See: *pulsar*.)

The radioastronomer records the wavelengths of radio waves that he receives. These wavelengths range from less than a centimetre up to many metres. They are much longer than the wavelengths of visible light. (See: *light, waves*.)

Radio telescopes are basically huge radio antennas. One kind is a wide metal dish. It is curved like the mirror of an optical reflecting telescope, but it is much bigger (see: *telescope*). Radio waves bounce off the dish, just as light reflects from a mirror. Waves that come from the direction the antenna is pointing in, focus, or come together, in a small region in front of the dish. Here there is a 'receiver'.

The receiver turns radio signals into electric currents. The currents must be 'amplified' – strengthened – before they can be studied, for the radio signals from space are extremely weak. When you pick up this encyclopedia, you use far more energy than all the radio telescopes ever built have received.

A radio telescope picks up some interference. The amplified signals are therefore fed into computers which sort out the space signals. So as not to interfere, radio programmes are transmitted on wavelengths different from the wavelengths that come from space.

Finally, the amplified signals can be fed into a loudspeaker and heard. Or they can be recorded automatically.

The great dish antenna at Jodrell Bank in England is 76 metres (250 feet) wide. Its surface is made of solid metal plates. The 64-metre (210-foot) dish at Parkes in Australia is an open mesh of steel wires. Some antennas are protected from the wind by plastic domes, such as the 36-metre (120-foot) dish at Haystack Hill in Massachusetts. Radio waves pass through the plastic just like light passes through glass.

Such a telescope is usually steerable. It can be pointed at any part of the sky. And it can follow an object that moves across the sky as the Earth rotates. Thus the object may be observed for some time. But some telescopes are fixed, not steerable. The 300-metre (1,000-foot) dish antenna at Arecibo in Puerto Rico is of this kind. It is made of wire mesh, hung over the floor of a natural crater in a mountain top.

Many radio telescopes are not dish-shaped. They have various arrangements of wires and rods, often like giant home TV antennas. Some are shaped like a cross with arms over a kilometre long.

To allow more accurate observation, two telescopes can be used together. They are separated by a few kilometres or thousands of kilometres. When telescopes are kilometres apart, they can map the sky in greater detail. The two are linked so that their signals can be compared. They both observe the same area of sky at the same time. Their signals may be sent by cable, or even by a radio link, to a laboratory where they are combined. Or they may be recorded separately, to be combined later. Radio telescopes in Australia and the United States have been used together in this way. Radio-astronomers have been able to map details 300 kilometres (less than 200 miles) apart. This is better than any photograph shows.

With such equipment, radioastronomers can map the sky in great detail. They have detected the signals from invisible 'radio galaxies', and have discovered the amazing objects called quasars (see: *quasar*).

Radio telescopes have other uses. They enable scientists to receive signals from spacecraft launched from the Earth. Radio waves have been sent from space probes as they passed 'behind' Mars. The radio waves passed through the atmosphere of Mars on their way to Earth. They were affected slightly, giving scientists valuable information about the Martian atmosphere.

As well as telescopes, radioastronomers use radar sets to study the Moon and nearby planets. Radar has been used to track meteors, or 'shooting stars', in a similar way to tracking aircraft (see: *meteor*, *radar*). The signals travel outward, then back to the receiver, at the speed of light. So the time between sending them and receiving them shows how far they have travelled. In this way, the distance from Earth to the planet Venus has been measured very accurately. Radio waves also penetrate the thick clouds surrounding Venus. They were used to measure the planet's slow rotation.

relativity

In this book you will often find phrases like 'the speed of a spacecraft relative to the Earth', or 'the speed of a car relative to another car'. What does this word 'relative' mean in these cases?

Speed is rate of change of distance. By the speed of a train we mean the distance it travels along the track in every second or minute or hour – say, 150 kilometres per hour. Now, what is the speed of a man in the train walking toward the front? The value we give for this speed depends on what distance we measure.

If we think of the walking passenger's distance from a seated passenger, his speed is quite small – say, about five kilometres per hour. This is his speed relative to the seated passenger. But if we think of his movement relative to a man standing by the track, his speed is much greater – about 155 kph.

So when we talk about speeds we ought always to say what the speeds are relative to. Wouldn't it be best to talk only about speeds relative to the ground? For many everyday purposes – when talking about trains, cars, runners and so on – we do this. But drivers often have to think about their speed relative to other cars, for example when a driver wants to pass the car in front. Pilots of planes often have to think about their speed relative to other planes.

We know that the Earth itself is moving. At different times astronauts have to think about their speed relative to the Earth, the Moon, other spacecraft or the Sun. And astronomers have to think about the movement of the Sun among the other stars of the Galaxy.

When we talk about speeds relative to the Earth we are taking the Earth as our 'standard of rest'. We are thinking of the Earth as if it was fixed, not moving. When we talk about speeds, relative to, say, the Sun, we are taking the Sun as our standard of rest.

The ether sea

A hundred years ago physicists thought they could use a standard of rest called 'the ether'. The ether, they thought, was a kind of fluid – a little like a liquid or gas – filling all space. (It had nothing to do with the ether that doctors once used to make patients unconscious before they operated on them.) Because it was everywhere, it was not noticed, just as we do not notice the air that surrounds us. But the ether carried light just as the air carries sound. Light waves were thought to be vibrations in the ether. (See: *light*.) If the ether existed, it should have been possible to measure all speeds as being relative to it.

In 1887, Albert Michelson and Edward Morley, American physicists, set out to measure the speed of the Earth through the ether. A passenger on the deck of a moving ship feels a breeze blowing because he is moving through the air. Michelson and Morley reasoned that, in a similar way, there must be an ether 'wind' blowing past the moving Earth. This ether 'wind' would affect the motion of light. A light ray that travelled against the 'wind' would be slowed down relative to the Earth. A ray that travelled in the same direction as the 'wind' would be speeded up.

Michelson and Morley performed a very accurate experiment to compare the speeds of light rays in different directions. But they could find no difference. They repeated the experiment at different times of year, when the Earth was moving in different directions as it went round the Sun. But they could never find any difference in the speed of the light rays. It seemed that the speed of light was always the same in space. (Light is slowed down when travelling in transparent substances like glass and water. Here, we are thinking only about light in space.)

Other experiments confirmed this result. The speed of light from stars is not affected by their motion, for example.

In 1905 Albert Einstein published what we now call the Special Theory of Relativity. Einstein knew that the ether theory was being questioned. And possibly he knew about the Michelson-Morley experiment.

Einstein took as his starting point this assumption: the laws of physics are the same for all observers, provided the observers move at constant speed, and in a constant direction, relative to each other.

Imagine a train that is travelling perfectly smoothly at 150 kph. According to the theory of relativity a physicist would get exactly the same results for any experiment he did on the train as he would if he did it on the ground. A ball dropped onto the floor would fall in just the same time, for example. In fact, if the curtains were drawn on the train the physicist would have no way of knowing that he was moving. And suppose he did look out of the window and saw people and houses moving past. He would be perfectly entitled to assume that he was at rest and they were moving.

The situation is different if the train is changing its speed or direction, or if it is not riding smoothly. If it brakes suddenly, things on the floor will slide forward, coffee will spill and so on. If the train goes round a curve fast, everything in it will tend to slide over to one side of the train. Yet there will be nothing visibly pushing or pulling these moving objects. So even if he cannot see out of the windows, the physicist will know that it is the train that is changing its motion. But Einstein's theory of 1905 covered only the case of constant speed and direction.

The examples given deal with moving objects. Physicists already knew that an experiment done in a train would give the same result as the same experiment done on the ground. They knew that moving objects acted the same way for any observer, whether the observer was standing still or moving smoothly at a constant speed. But Einstein added a further assumption. He said that the speed of light would be the same for all such observers.

This new assumption had some results that seemed impossible. Suppose a physicist on board the train shines a ray of light forward along the aisle of the car and measures its speed. According to Einstein he will get the usual result 300,000 kilometres (186,000 miles) per second.

But a physicist standing still on the ground can make measurements on exactly the same ray of light. We should expect him to find a speed that was 150 kph greater. If the light ray travelled backward along the train we should expect him to find a speed 150 kph less than usual.

But Einstein's theory says that both physicists will find exactly the same speed for the light ray. The speed of light does not depend on the motion of the observers. The result of the Michelson-Morley experiment is one example of this fact. The Earth is moving, but Michelson and Morley found the same result as they would have if the Earth was at rest.

How is it possible for the speed of light not to depend on the motion of the observer? The answer is that measurements of speed involve measurements of distances and times. And these measurements depend on the motion of the observer making them.

To see the effect of motion on time measurement, think of this simplified case. A scientist on the ground has a clock that makes use of light flashes. A flash of light is sent from a lamp to a mirror fixed above the lamp. The flash is reflected back and triggers another flash. The distance between the light and the mirror is set so that the light flashes take one nanosecond (one thousand millionth of a second) to travel to the mirror and back. So this is a clock that marks off nanoseconds.

Suppose a scientist on a spaceship has an identical clock. As far as he is concerned it marks off nanoseconds. But relative to people on the Earth the flashes of the space clock follow the path shown in the diagram. In going to the mirror and returning they travel a greater distance than the flashes of the Earth clock, because of their sideways movement.

So in the time that it takes the space clock to 'tick' once, the ground clock 'ticks' more than once. In other words the moving space clock is running slower than the ground clock.

Einstein's theory says that every observer sees clocks that are moving relative to him as running slow.

The crew of the spaceship won't think the ship's clock is running slow. The human body itself is a kind of 'clock'. We feel hungry and tired at certain times because of chemical reactions taking place in our bodies. On the spaceship the crew's 'body clocks' will slow down too. They will feel hungry and tired at the usual times, according to the ship's clock. They will even age more slowly, compared to clocks on Earth. But because their bodies have slowed down at the same rate as the ship's clock, they will not see the ship's clock as running slow.

Einstein's theory says that there is no meaning in the idea that the Earth is truly at rest while the spaceship is really moving. The observers on the ship judge that Earth clocks run slow compared with their own clocks. And their judgment is just as correct as the judgment of the Earth scientists.

So this apparent change in the rate of moving clocks is not due to some defect in the clocks. The slowing predicted by relativity doesn't depend on how the clock is built. It affects all kinds of process equally. So we can say that time slows down on a moving object.

The meson clock
Is it true? Do moving clocks run slow?

Yes, it is true. The tiny particles called mesons, smaller than atoms, are a kind of clock. When they are at rest they 'live' for only two millionths of a second. Then they change into other kinds of particle. But fast-moving mesons in nature and in the laboratory live longer. The faster they move the longer they last. So two millionths of a second for a moving meson is longer than for a stationary meson. The moving meson's 'clock' is running slow.

Fast-moving mesons are created high up in our atmosphere. They travel downwards at high speed. Their lifetimes are increased by their fast motion. Many of them reach the ground before they decay.

Clocks have been carried round the world in opposite directions by planes. They had the same speed relative to the ground. But the Earth, with its atmosphere is turning from west to east, so the eastward-flying plane actually travelled farther. When the clocks were brought together and compared, the east-flying clock – which had been travelling faster – was a tiny amount slower than the other clock.

Not only are measurements of time affected by motion. Measurements of distance are affected as well.

According to relativity, every observer measures moving objects as being slightly shortened in the direction of motion.

So, for example, a fast-moving rocket is reduced in length – but not in width – very slightly. In present-day rockets, travelling at 40,000 kph (25,000 mph), this shortening is one part in a thousand million – about one millionth of a centimetre.

At normal, everyday speeds, the strange effects of relativity are impossible to observe. Even at the speeds of our fastest rockets they are tiny, as the example above shows. Only near the speed of light do objects shorten and time slow down greatly. At half the speed of light

(nearly 150,000 kilometres per second) a spaceship would have about 85 per cent of its length when at rest. And its clocks would run at 85 per cent of their normal rate. At nine-tenths the speed of light the spaceship would have less than about 45 per cent of its rest length. And clocks would run at 45 per cent of their rest rate. The only thing that we can raise to these speeds as yet are tiny sub-atomic particles.

No matter how great the shrinking of the rocket was, no one on board would notice it. Everything would be equally affected. And when they observed the Earth, the crew would find that it was contracted in turn. Once again, their point of view would be just as correct as the viewpoint of an Earth observer.

This is why the theory of relativity is so called. For it says that not only speeds but also time intervals and lengths are relative to the observer who is measuring them.

Earlier in this article we considered a man on a train that was travelling at 150 kph. If he walks forward at 5 kph relative to the train, we would expect his speed relative to the ground to be 155 kph. But according to relativity speeds do not add in this way. His speed relative to the ground will actually be slightly less than 155 kph. The difference is actually so small at these speeds that it could never be detected.

A universal speed limit
Another consequence of the Special Theory is that, as a body moves faster, it becomes harder to give it more speed. In the machine called a synchrotron, sub-atomic particles are pushed round and round. They travel very fast. But as they approach the speed of light the increase of speed at each revolution becomes smaller. In fact, according to the theory of relativity they cannot reach the speed of light.

The resistance that a body offers to being pushed is called its mass (see: *gravity*). So we say that a body's mass increases as its speed increases.

Can anything travel faster than light? Not if it starts off with less than the speed of light. But recently physicists have suggested that there may be particles that *always* travel faster than light. They could not be slowed below that speed. These supposed particles are called tachyons. Nobody yet knows if they exist.

It takes light four years to reach us from the nearest star, Alpha Centauri. No spaceship could take less than four years to travel to Alpha Centauri, as measured by Earth clocks. But if the ship travelled close to the speed of light, time would pass slowly on board. The crew might be only a few weeks older after a return trip that took eight years of Earth time.

In 1915 Einstein extended his theory to cover all kinds of motion. This General Theory of

Relativity was a theory of gravity as well. It replaced the theory of Isaac Newton, which had lasted over 200 years.

The new theory explained a puzzling fact that had been known for a long time. The planet Mercury's orbit is an ellipse, a flattened circle, as are all the other planets' orbits. What was surprising was that the length of the ellipse slowly turns in space. According to Newton a planet's orbit should be an ellipse fixed in space. Einstein's theory showed that the orbit of any planet would turn slowly.

The general theory also predicted some new and surprising facts. According to the theory light rays should be bent as they pass near the Sun. This effect was found by a famous expedition sent to an island off West Africa to observe the total eclipse of 1919.

According to the general theory, measurements of space and time are affected by gravitational fields. A clock on the Earth would run slow compared to a clock far out in space. A clock on the ground runs slow compared with a clock at the top of a tower, because gravity is slightly stronger at the bottom of the tower. This effect has been confirmed.

We might be able to decide between these rival theories by observing regions of high gravity in space. Astronomers are now looking for so-called 'black holes'. Some stars collapse in on themselves. When this happens they get smaller and denser. Their gravitational fields get stronger. It is possible that a star could collapse in on itself so much that it would form a 'black hole' in space. The gravitational field would be so strong that anything that fell into it could never escape. Even light would not be able to get out again, so we would not be able to see into a black hole. We do not yet know whether black holes exist.

The two great innovations in modern physics, quantum theory and relativity, were both developed by Albert Einstein. Paul Dirac brought the two together into a single theory, that, among other predictions, suggested the existence of antimatter, subsequently verified by experiment.

Special relativity showed Newton's theory of motion to be only approximately true. In a similar way general relativity shows special relativity to be only approximate. When gravity is very strong, the basic assumptions of special relativity are not true. The speed of light, for example, need not be the same in all circumstances. The most important insight of relativity is that measurements of time and space depend on the observer who makes them.
See: *gravity, matter, physics, universe*.

robot

A robot is an automatically-operated machine that can perform some of the actions or mimic the behaviour of a human being. Unlike other machines, some robots can direct their own actions. Some robots are able to walk and climb over obstacles. Others are able to clear a dinner table. Some can even learn to find their way through a maze by themselves.

The word 'robot' was originally used in a more limited sense as a name for mechanical devices that not only acted like men, but looked like them as well. It was first used by the Czech writer Karel Capek in his play *RUR* (Rossum's Universal Robots), written in 1920. The word 'robot' comes from the Czech word for 'work'. Capek's play describes an imaginary factory in which the robot workers finally arise and overthrow their human masters.

The American engineer and architect Buckminster Fuller once described the human body as if it were a machine. He wrote about it in terms of joints, pumps, batteries and so on. The human body is a wonderful piece of machinery. It is extremely complicated and can do many things. And it does some things remarkably well. For example, a person with normal colour vision can tell the difference between over a million different shades of colour.

But the human body also has its limitations. It may suffer from damage and disease. It tires easily, and it grows old. The bodies of some people do not work as well as others. A human body is out of action for periods of sleep and needs rest periods and vacations. There are many tasks that a machine can do more reliably than a man. And some of these can be done best of all by completely automatic robots.

For example, robot devices are sometimes used on the production lines of factories. They may perform tasks that are unpleasant or dangerous for humans. They may handle white-hot metals, or radioactive substances, for instance. Or the robots may be used to assemble the tiny parts that make up a transistor radio or television set. In this work they are more precise than any human worker could ever be.

Some robots are used in testing motor cars in simulated crashes, for testing ejector seats in aircraft, and to test conditions inside nuclear fallout shelters during a nuclear explosion. These robots are often called 'simocs , short for 'simulated occupants'. They do not carry out a task so much as gather information. They are also sometimes called 'phantoms'.

The idea of building a robot is not new. Man has long been interested in making man-like and animal-like machines. These were called automata (singular: automaton). In 1738, the French inventor Jacques de Vaucanson constructed an artificial duck that ate, drank and quacked. He also made an automatic flute-player. For a long time, automatic clockwork toys like these have been built, especially in Switzerland. These include birds that can sing and fly.

In the nineteenth century a German inventor demonstrated a robot that could play chess. But there was a man hidden inside to decide on the moves. (Today, there are electronic computers that can play chess.) In 1939 a robot called the 'Voder' was shown to the public in Philadelphia, Pennsylvania. It could speak whole sentences in English when an operator worked the keyboard and foot pedal attached to it. Its 'vocal cords' were electronic circuits.

Many early robots were built so that they looked like mechanical men. They had heads, bodies, arms and legs. Today, robots may have more or less any shape. Many look simply like large metal boxes. They may walk about on mechanical legs or roll on wheels.

Modern robots have a variety of devices that imitate human senses. Senses are the things that let us know what is happening in our surroundings. The human senses are sight, taste, hearing, smell and touch (see: *senses*). Some robots have electrical 'copies' of our senses. For example, they may have cells that are sensitive to light, just like the photo-electric cells in the light-meter of a camera. These cells are a kind of electrical copy of human eyes. Human eyes also contain cells that are sensitive to light.

The robot's 'sense organs' create electrical signals which are passed to a control centre, the robot's 'brain'. This is an imitation of the way our sense-organs send tiny electrical impulses to the brain via the nervous system (see: *brain, nervous system*). The robot's 'brain' sends its commands to motors that work the robot's limbs. These motors act as the robot's muscles.

Robots often have built into them a system of 'feedback control'. To see how this works, imagine a robot that is designed to move toward a light until the light appears too bright, when it moves away again. The light-sensitive cells measure the amount of light falling on the robot. This information is constantly being passed to the robot's 'brain'. The robot's brain has also been programmed with information about how strong the light should be for it to move away. The robot compares this with the information it receives from the light-sensitive cells about how much light is actually hitting it. The difference between the two is called the 'error'. When this error is zero, the robot moves away from the light, but not before.

There are various methods of programming the actions or behaviour of a robot. The programme may be fed into its 'brain' on recording tape or punched cards. Or the robot's actions may be controlled by pressing buttons.

It is difficult to design and build a robot. And it is even more difficult to make one that can learn. But robots capable of learning simple facts have been built. An example is Theseus, an electronic 'mouse'. Theseus can learn to find its way out of a maze. It has a 'brain' that stores memories like a computer.

Robots can be important tools in helping scientists to study the workings of the human brain and nervous system. Devices have been made that work like the human eye and ear. Experiments can then be done to find out more about human vision and hearing.

Because of feedback, a robot can sometimes act in a way that seems intelligent. Theseus can act in different ways in different situations. But the number of choices it can make are limited. Human beings have a much greater choice of action. People have imagination which allows them to work out beforehand how they will act in a new situation. But there are robot-like machines that may be used in close association with a human operator. His decisions can be converted into action by the robot, which may be a long way away. The robot now has the power to adapt to different situations as it encounters them.

Such a system is called a 'telechiric' system. The word comes from the Greek words *tele*, meaning 'distant' and *cheir*, meaning 'hand'. 'Slave arms' are used to handle radioactive substances. The operator controlling them sits safely behind a protective shield. Telechiric machines can go where it is difficult or dangerous for men to go. They can be sent into a damaged nuclear reactor to repair it. They were used to recover an unexploded hydrogen bomb accidentally dropped by the US Air Force off the Mediterranean coast of Spain in 1966.

Telechiric devices are important generally in undersea research, rescue and exploration. The Mobot is an undersea robot developed in the United States about 1962. It was designed for work on underwater oil wells. It can turn screws automatically, adjust valves and brush a surface to remove anything that is fouling it. And it can do all this at a depth of 300 metres (1,000 feet). The Mobot 'sees' by TV and can detect objects by a sonar device that bounces sound waves off objects to measure the objects' distance and size. (See: *sound*.)

Telechiric devices mimic the movements of their operators. For example, the right arm and hand of the robot may be controlled by the operator's right arm and hand, the left arm by the operator's left arm. The robot faithfully imitates the actions of its human operator who may be many miles away. And the operator's actions may be greatly magnified by the robot. For instance, the robot may be able to lift great weights or take giant strides.

Today there are many different kinds of robot doing many different jobs. Some control driver-less tractors, lorries and trains; others are automatic draughtsmen, drawing up accurate plans from information given to them in the form of figures; yet others operate telephone exchanges. There are robot lawnmowers and robot navigation systems for aircraft, space rockets and ships. Robots will be of great use in helping disabled people to cope with everyday problems such as setting tables and sweeping floors. One day, robots may man space stations or bases on planets where conditions are hostile to man.

See: *automation, computer.*

solar system

Our planet Earth moves through space as it orbits the Sun. Other planets and heavenly bodies are also travelling around the Sun. This 'family' of the Sun, together with the Sun itself, is called the solar system ('solar' means 'of the Sun'). It includes nine planets and 33 moons that we know of. It also includes many thous-ands of minor planets, or asteroids. It includes moving objects, called comets, which are masses of gas, dust, and ice. And it includes gas and dust spread out over the whole system.

The Sun is at the centre of the system. It is an enormous ball of glowing gas. A line from one side of a ball to the other through its centre is called its diameter. The diameter of the Sun is 1,392,000 kilometres (865,000 miles). Earth's diameter is only 13,000 kilometres (8,000 miles). More than a million Earths could be placed inside the Sun.

The Sun's surface is yellow-hot. The intense light and heat that it sends into space make life impossible on Mercury, the planet nearest to the Sun. Life is equally impossible on the farthest planets because they are so far away that they are always frozen. Life exists only on Earth, as far as we know.

As well as heat and light, the Sun sends out a stream of tiny electrically charged particles. These are actually fragments of atoms, called ions. Sometimes gigantic explosions on the Sun, called flares, send very strong bursts of ions into space. They would be deadly if they reached the Earth's surface. But ions are trapped by the Earth's magnetic field before they can do any harm.

The planets move round the Sun in paths called orbits. The orbits are elliptical – shaped like flattened circles. Most of them are very nearly circular. Except for the orbit of Pluto, they lie nearly in one plane – that is, they are not greatly tilted. Most of the planets have moons in orbit around them.

The nearest planet to the Sun, Mercury, is about 60 million kilometres (36 million miles) from the Sun. This might seem like a huge distance. But Pluto, the farthest known planet, has an average distance from the Sun over a hundred times as great. Light from the Sun, travelling at over 300,000 kilometres (186,000 miles) per second, takes about five and a half hours to reach Pluto.

Even if there are no other planets beyond Pluto, we know that there are more distant members of the solar system. Many of the comets that make spectacular journeys through our skies come from beyond Pluto. It is possible that there are huge numbers of comets out there. Only when its orbit is disturbed for some reason does a comet plunge in toward the Sun.

The Sun itself is a star. It is one star among thousands of millions of stars. The system of stars that includes our Sun is called the Galaxy. The Galaxy is vast. It is the second largest known galaxy in space. The largest galaxy we know of is called Andromeda. The Sun, with its family of planets, moves slowly around the centre of the Galaxy. The Sun takes 225 million years to complete one journey.

Our solar system is only a small part of the Galaxy. Although the stars appear close to-gether in the night sky, they are huge distances apart. The nearest star to the Sun is so far away that light takes just over four years to reach us from it. This star is called Proxima Centauri.

Discovering the solar system
It took man many centuries to realize what the solar system is really like. Ancient astronomers saw that the movements of the planets were very different from the movements of the stars. They thought that the planets were at roughly the same distance as the stars, but had no idea how far that might be. They thought that both stars and planets moved round the Earth. Not having telescopes, they did not suspect that the planets are in any way like Earth, or that some of them have moons.

Some ancient astronomers suggested that the Earth goes round the Sun. This idea was not taken seriously, however, for 2,000 years. Then, in the 16th century, the Polish astronomer Copernicus showed that the Earth and other planets move around the Sun in the same direction.

This idea gave a simple explanation for some seemingly complicated movements of the planets. For example, against the background of the stars, Mars often appears to slow down in its movement. It moves 'backward' for a while, and then goes forward again.

The reason is that the Earth is closer to the Sun than Mars, and so it travels in a smaller orbit. It takes less time than Mars to go once round the Sun. The Earth 'overtakes' Mars roughly every two years. At these times Mars seems to move backward in the sky. At other times, we can see the forward motion of Mars.

Copernicus was able to calculate the distances of the planets from the Sun, compared with the Earth's distance. He got good values. But, since he did not know exactly how far the Earth was from the Sun, he did not know any of the other distances exactly, either.

Copernicus clearly separated the planets from the stars. And he realized that the stars must be at huge distances compared with the planets.

In about 1609 Galileo began to study the skies with a simple telescope. His discoveries supported Copernicus's ideas. He found that Mercury and Venus certainly go around the Sun. This made it easier to believe that the other planets do the same. He found that there were mountains and plains on the Moon. He could even estimate the height of the mountains. This showed that the Moon is a world something like the Earth.

Later in the 17th century, in 1687, Isaac Newton published his theory of gravitation. The force that pulls a falling apple to the ground is called gravity. Newton showed that the same force pulls on the Moon, causing it to stay in orbit round Earth. It would otherwise follow a straight path out into space. The farther away from Earth, the weaker its gravity. Newton proved that because of this, the Moon's orbit is not a circle, as was believed, but an ellipse.

The Moon also has a gravitational force, which pulls on Earth. It causes the oceans to move, resulting in the daily tides. Newton said that gravity acts between all bodies in the Universe. He proved that the gravity of an object depends on how massive it is. Earth's gravity is stronger than the Moon's since Earth is more massive. The Sun's gravity is even greater. It holds all the planets in their elliptical paths round the Sun.

From this time on, men had a basically correct picture of the solar system. But the picture was far from complete. Only five planets, other than Earth, were known. These were Mercury, Venus, Mars, Jupiter, and Saturn. With the use of increasingly powerful telescopes, other members of the solar system were discovered.

In 1781 Sir William Herschel found that a faint 'star', which had often been seen before, looked like a disc in the telescope. At first he thought it was a comet. But it was soon shown that it followed a nearly circular orbit far beyond Saturn (the farthest planet previously known). The new planet was called Uranus.

Uranus was observed over a long time, and its orbit was found to be strange. It was as if it were being disturbed by the gravitational pull of another, unseen, planet. Unknown to each other, Adams (English) and Le Verrier (French) calculated the orbit of the unseen planet. In 1846 the planet was found, close to the predicted position. This, the eighth known planet (including the Earth), was given the name Neptune.

However, the influence of Neptune was not enough to explain the disturbance of Uranus completely. Neptune's orbit too, was found to be irregular. In the 20th century a search was carried out for a planet beyond Neptune. One was found in 1930 near the expected position. This, the farthest known planet from the Sun, was called Pluto.

The strange thing is that Pluto seems much too small to account for the peculiar movement of Uranus and Neptune. So, the search for other planets is continuing.

In the 18th century, astronomers suspected that there might be an undiscovered planet between Mars and Jupiter. The distance between these two planets seemed to be too big. A committee of astronomers was formed to search for a new planet. One was found in 1801, and named Ceres. It was tiny, less than 800 kilometres (500 miles) across. Within ten years three more of these tiny planets were found, all moving between Mars and Jupiter. In the 19th century hundreds more were found. Many are now discovered every year.

The orbits of about 2,000 of these minor planets, called asteroids, are now accurately known. Though they mostly lie between Mars and Jupiter, some of them come much closer to, or go much farther from, the Sun. Some share the orbit of Jupiter. Some, such as Eros and Geographos, come close to the Earth – though still not as close as the Moon, which is 400,000 kilometres (a quarter of a million miles) away.

Today's picture of the solar system

The Sun, at the centre of the system, is an intensely hot ball of glowing gas. At its centre it has a temperature of millions of degrees Celsius. At its surface, which is the hot disc that we see, the temperature is about 6,000 °C.

The Sun is the largest object in the solar system. Most of the matter of the Sun is the gas hydrogen. It is being slowly turned into the gas helium, releasing energy. The Sun has been sending out light and heat for five thousand million years.

The four innermost planets are made up mostly of rocks and metals. They contain very little hydrogen and helium, which are the most common substances in the universe as a whole.

The closest planet to the Sun, 60 million kilometres away on average, is tiny Mercury. It is only about 5,000 kilometres (3,000 miles) in diameter, which is roughly the distance between London and New York. Mercury takes 88 of our days to travel once round the Sun. This is one year on Mercury. If there is any air on Mercury it must be in thin traces only. The great heat on the sunlit side of Mercury would drive gases off into space.

Venus is 108 million kilometres (67 million miles) from the Sun. It is nearly the same size as the Earth. Dense clouds completely hide its surface. Once it was thought that beneath the clouds was a world not too different from ours. But space probes have discovered that towards its surface Venus is very hot, 400-500°C. The air pressure is about 100 times the pressure of the air on Earth at ground level. And the air of Venus is nearly all carbon dioxide. There is little hope of finding life on Venus.

The third planet, 150 million kilometres (93 million miles) from the Sun, is the Earth. Compared with the other planets it has huge amounts of oxygen and water. Its surface temperatures are suitable for the development of life, even at its frozen poles or in its hottest deserts.

The Earth's companion, the Moon, is just over a quarter the diameter of the Earth. There are bigger moons in the solar system, but these are tiny compared with the planets they travel round. Perhaps Earth and Moon should be regarded as a double planet. Or perhaps the Moon was once a separate planet that was 'captured' by the pull of Earth's gravity.

Mars can be regarded as the most Earth-like planet. It has seasons, just as Earth does. Though generally colder than Earth, it can be as warm as 21°C (70°F) on a summer's day at the equator. But Mars is in fact very different from our planet. Its air is thin and consists mainly of carbon dioxide. It has little oxygen or water. Mars has glistening polar caps, but these are mainly frozen carbon dioxide, not ice. The rest of its surface consists of rocky and sandy deserts. Yet this is the most promising place in the solar system to search for life. But it could be only very simple life.

The giant planets and the asteroids
Beyond the four inner planets is the region of the asteroids. Once they were thought to be the pieces of a planet that had exploded. But if all the asteroids were put together, they would probably make a planet far smaller than our Moon. It is more likely that the asteroids consist of material left over after the planets had formed. Perhaps it was prevented from forming

into a planet by the gravitational pull from the giant planet Jupiter.

The next four planets from the Sun are very different from the four inner planets. They are huge. The largest of all, Jupiter, is over 129,000 kilometres (80,000 miles) across, more than ten times the diameter of the Earth. Saturn is somewhat less than ten times, Uranus and Neptune between three and half and four times, the diameter of the Earth.

These numbers refer to the discs that we can see. These are actually the tops of the planets' deep, thick atmospheres. We can never see the solid surfaces. The atmospheres are rich in hydrogen and probably also in helium, like the Sun. The poisonous gas methane is present and there is probably frozen ammonia, too.

The tops of the atmospheres are always freezing cold. On Jupiter, the nearest giant planet to the Sun, the temperature is about 140°C below the freezing point of water. Neptune, the farthest giant planet, is 220°C below freezing.

Beyond the giant planets lies the small planet Pluto. At its farthest, it is 50 times as far from the Sun as is the Earth. At its closest, it is 30 times the distance of the Earth from the Sun and within Neptune's orbit. Pluto takes nearly 250 years to complete its vast orbit.

The beginning of the solar system
We believe that the planets and the Sun began to form at the same time. Our present ideas of the beginnings of the solar system are roughly as follows.

The Sun was born at the same time as many of the other stars in the Galaxy, about five thousand million years ago. It formed from a swirling cloud of gas and dust, mostly hydrogen, part of the much larger cloud from which the rest of the stars in the Galaxy formed. The gas in the cloud came together under the pull of its own gravitational force.

Particles of hot matter move faster than particles of cold matter (see: *heat*). As the particles of swirling gas were pulled closer and closer together, they were more likely to bump into and bounce off each other. The more squashed the gas became, the more often the particles collided, and the faster they moved. Thus, the mass of gas became hotter and hotter as it was pulled together by its own gravity. Gradually, the primitive Sun appeared – a glowing ball of hot hydrogen at the centre of a swirling disc of gas.

In the disc, gas began to collect at certain places, again under gravitational force. But these 'lumps' in the gas disc were smaller than the Sun. They did not become hot enough for nuclear reactions to begin. They did not turn into stars, but planets. Round them, smaller lumps appeared. They became the moons.

The early planets and moons grew as their gravitational pull swept up gas and dust from around them. The disc gradually vanished.

What each planet was made of depended on how far it was from the Sun. Near the Sun the gas was hot, and so its molecules moved fast. The molecules could escape from the Sun's pull more easily. The planets near the Sun, including the Earth, are made of the heavier gases and rocky minerals. Only a small part of the disc consisted of these.

Farther out, where the temperature was lower, the growing planets could capture and hold the lighter hydrogen and helium gas. This is why the outer planets are gas giants.

Pluto is hard to explain. It does not seem to be a normal planet. But it has been suggested that it was once a moon of Neptune that has somehow strayed into a new orbit.
See: *astronomy, star, Sun.*

sound

It is hard to imagine a world without sound. Even the quietest night is not completely silent. Traffic noise, or the sound of the wind or of night creatures can enter a room. And there are faint sounds within the room. To achieve complete silence special 'soundproof' rooms have to be made. They let in no sound from outside.

Yet hundred of kilometres above Earth, in space, there is no sound. And there is no sound on the Moon. For in space and on the Moon there is no air. The sounds we hear on Earth travel through air and cannot exist without it. Astronauts on the Moon have to talk to each other using radio, because there is no air.

The fact that sound cannot exist without air is sometimes demonstrated by a simple experiment. An electric buzzer is placed under a glass dome or 'bell jar'. When it is switched on, the buzzer can be clearly heard through the glass of the jar. Then the air in the jar is pumped out. As more and more air is removed the sound of the buzzer becomes fainter. Finally it cannot be heard at all.

The air is a mixture of gases. Sound can travel through other gases too. So there can be sound on other planets that have atmospheres quite different from our own, such as Mars and Venus.

Sound can also travel through solids and liquids. If we hear someone speaking in the next room when the doors are closed, we are hearing sound that has travelled through air, then through the wall and floor, and then through the air of the room we are in. The crew of a submarine can hear the engines of ships on the surface near them. The sound they hear has travelled through the water, then through the steel hull of the submarine and finally through the air inside to reach them.

When the string of a musical instrument is plucked, the string vibrates. The vibration of cymbals and of gongs is easily seen. All sounds are caused by vibration, though the vibrations are often too small to be seen. When you tap a table, you set it vibrating for a moment. When a bell is struck, its vibrations take a much longer time to die away. So the sound of a tap is brief, while the note of a bell is long drawn out.

To see how vibrating objects cause sound, imagine throwing a stone into a pond. Waves spread from the place where the stone breaks the surface. The waves get weaker as they travel. If you watch the movement of floating leaves and twigs, you will see that the waves make them bob up and down. But they are not carried along in the direction of the waves. For water is not being carried outward. At each place the water has been set in motion, up and down and back and forth. This disturbance passes through the water, but the water does not move outwards. The waves are like a rumour passing through a theatre audience. The rumour may travel fast, but the people who pass it on do not move from their seats. (See: *wave.*)

Sound, too, consists of waves. Let us think first of all about sound in air only. Air consists of countless tiny gas particles called molecules. (Each molecule is a group of atoms. See: *atom.*) These molecules are constantly moving at high speeds and bumping into each other.

Suppose a bell has been struck once and set vibrating. Imagine that you can 'freeze' the sound waves and bring them to a stop. And now imagine that you can examine the air molecules with a microscope more powerful than any real one. What would you find?

You would find that in some places air molecules are crowded together more closely than usual. We say that the air is 'compressed' there. And in other places the molecules would be spread out more. We say the air is 'rarefied' there. The regions where the air is compressed form spheres, or globes, centered on the bell. Between these spherical zones are the zones where the air molecules are more spaced out. The distance from a sphere of compression to the one outside it may be from a centimetre to 15 metres, depending on the sound.

These spheres of compression and rarefaction are the sound waves. They are formed near the bell as its vibration disturbs the nearby air. The disturbances are like the jostling of people in a crowd.

Now imagine that the waves are no longer 'frozen', but are moving outwards as they really do. How fast do they travel? The answer is about 340 metres per second, (about 1,100 feet per second). If you see a lightning stroke three kilometres (two miles) away, the sound will take about ten seconds to reach you. (The light from the lightening flash takes about a hundred-thousanth of a second to reach you).

If you watch a pile-driver on a construction site from a few hundred metres away, you will be able to notice the delay of a fraction of a second between each blow and your hearing the sound.

All sounds travel at almost exactly the same speed. But deep sounds travel farther than high-pitched sounds. Thunder from a nearby lightning stroke sounds like the crack of a giant whip. It is a mixture of sounds from high to low pitch. But at a distance the thunder is a rumbling sound, because the higher-pitched parts of the sound are weakened much more by their journey than the deep-pitched sounds.

When a sound wave strikes a solid object or the surface of a liquid, like a lake or the sea, a weakened wave travels on through that body. Thus sound travels through walls and floors, and so on. But a weak sound wave will also be sent back from the surface of the object. It will be reflected, just as light is reflected from shiny objects (see: *light*), or as a ball bounces off the ground or a wall. Such reflections cause echoes. Echoes can often be heard very clearly when you shout across a valley. If the sound of your call bounces off a rocky surface a kilometre away, you will hear the echo after about five seconds. It takes that long because the sound travels a kilometre before being reflected, and a kilometre back to you. There may be other echoes as the sound is reflected several times.

Echoes that are delayed by only fractions of a second can be heard in tunnels, large halls, in the open near large buildings, and in many other places. Every sound you make in even a small room sets up echoes. But you usually do not notice them. Firstly there are many different echoes from various points, with different delays, which become mixed and confused. Secondly, echoes from soft chairs, curtains, carpets and people's bodies are very weak. We say that these objects 'absorb' sound. You may have noticed that, in a new house before furniture and carpets are moved in, echoes are strong.

Architects who design concert halls have to think about the echoes that music and speech produce in them. They even have to take account of the fact that echoes are stronger when there is a small audience than when there is a large one. Such problems are studied by acoustic engineers. Acoustics is the scientific study of sound. (See: *acoustics*.)

Ships use echoes to measure the depth of the water they are in. A device in the bottom of the ship called an echo-sounder sends out short bursts of sound waves. The sound waves are reflected from the sea bottom and an echo is detected. The sounder automatically calculates the distance the sound has travelled, using the speed of sound in water and the time taken. Echo sounders can also be used by fishing ships to detect shoals of fish, which reflect strong echoes.

Sound can 'bend' around obstacles. If you stand close to a concrete pillar you will not be able to hear the sound of, say, a clock ticking on the other side. But if you stand some distance from the pillar, you may be able to hear the clock. The sound waves bend around the pillar to reach you. This bending of sound is called diffraction. We can often hear voices through an open door when the speaker is just out of sight. Light cannot reach our eyes from the speaker, because it travels in straight lines. So we cannot see him or her. But sound can spread out after passing through the doorway, to reach us.

Sometimes sound travelling upwards is bent back towards the ground. This happens when the sound enters a layer of air that is warmer than the air beneath. (This is unusual; normally the air gets colder with increasing height.) The sound may then be heard far from its source, while it cannot be heard at nearby places. This is rather like a mirage.

When a sound wave enters a human ear it sets up vibrations in a tissue called the ear drum. These vibrations pass along bones and fluid in the ear. Finally the vibrations set up tiny electrical currents in nerves running from the ear to the brain. The brain interprets these currents as sound.

One sound is louder than another one if the air molecules in the waves of the first sound are packed together tighter in the compression and more loosely in the rarefaction. The louder sound makes stronger vibrations in the eardrum and bones of the ear. These in turn cause more frequent electric impulses which are sent to the brain.

One way of measuring loudness uses the unit called the decibel (symbol dB). Usually the sound is compared with the faintest sound that the average person can hear. This faintest sound is said to have a loudness of zero decibels. Then the voice of someone you are talking to has a loudness of about 60 decibels. In a busy street the noise of traffic has a loudness of about 75 dB. A very noisy factory reaches noise levels of 130 dB. Sounds louder than this cause actual pain. People who work in noisy factories or near aircraft wear ear plugs. Without them, their hearing would be damaged.

One of the most noticeable things about a sound apart from its loudness is its pitch. The jingling bells of a child's toy are higher in pitch than the bells of a church tower. Children's voices have a higher pitch than the voice of an adult man. Nearly all musical instruments can make sounds over a range of pitch.

When you listen to a high-pitched note more sound waves reach your ear each second than when you hear a low note. When the note that musicians call 'A above middle C' is played, 440 waves reach your ear each second. If middle C is played, 262 waves per second reach your eardrum.

The number of waves per second in a sound is called the frequency of that sound. Scientists describe the frequency of middle C as 262 hertz, (or 262 cycles per second) after Heinrich Hertz, a German physicist of the nineteenth century.

When a jet plane warms up its engines before take off, the pitch of the sound rises as the engines speed up. The same thing happens as a car engine is revved up. As the engines work faster, they send out more waves per second, making higher-pitched noises.

The note given out by the siren of a police car or ambulance appears to be higher in pitch as the vehicle approaches you, and lower in pitch after it has passed you. This is caused by a change in the number of sound waves per second reaching you as the source of the sound approaches or recedes from you. It is called the Doppler effect, after the Austrian scientist who explained it in 1842.

The average adult person can hear sound frequencies up to about 20,000 cycles per second. Children can hear higher frequencies. As we grow older, it becomes harder to hear high-pitched sounds. Many animals can hear sounds of much higher pitch than can humans. Some whistles used for calling dogs give out sounds that human beings cannot hear. Bats send out squeaks of as high as 100,000 hertz, which we are unable to hear. The echoes of these squeaks tell the bat the positions of obstacles in its path and of insects in flight that it hunts.

Sounds that are too high in pitch for human beings to hear are called ultrasonic. There is no definite lowest limit of the pitch we can hear. Very low notes, such as the bottom notes of a church organ, which might have a frequency of around 10 hertz, can be felt, rather than heard, as a throbbing in the building. Such sounds are called infrasonic.

Human voices can range from about 75 hertz (in the case of men) up to about 1,400 hertz (in women). The majority of musical instruments can produce sounds above and below this frequency range. The top note of a full-sized piano has a frequency of 4,100 hertz, whilst the frequency of its bottom note is only 30 hertz.

The frequency of a sound corresponds to the rate at which the object making the sound vibrates. The high notes of a piano or harp are made by strings that vibrate fast, compared with the lower strings. The rate at which a string vibrates depends on many things. If a string is stretched with a stronger force, its pitch rises. You may have noticed how the twang of a piece of elastic rises in pitch if you stretch it. The strings of harps, pianos and other stringed instruments are set to the right pitch by stretching them with just the right force.

The pitch of a vibrating string also depends on its length. Suppose you have a short string and a long string made of the same material, with the same thickness, and held taut by the same force. The short string will vibrate faster than the long string, and give out a higher note. Acoustic guitarists and violinists use the fingers of their left hands to change the length of string that is free to vibrate. The vibrating string then sets the body of the instrument vibrating. A relatively small part of the sound from a stringed instrument comes from the actual strings.

The rate of vibration of a string depends on the material of the string, and on its thickness. The bottom strings of an instrument are thicker than the top strings and perhaps made of a different material.

Drums, cymbals, bells and xylophones all vibrate to produce their sounds. In wind instruments, such as trumpets and flutes, the vibrations are set up in the air inside the instrument. If you blow across the top of an empty bottle, you will be able to produce a note. Your blowing has made the air in the bottle vibrate at a certain frequency. If you put a little water into the bottle and blow across the top again, you will get a higher note.

Organs have a large number of pipes of different lengths and widths. Air is blown through them. The air in the longer pipes vibrates with lower frequency and makes a deeper note.

A trumpet consists of a single pipe. Old-fashioned trumpets were long and straight. The pitch of the note they made depended on their length, though the player could control the pitch to some extent with his lips. The bugle of today is a trumpet bent into a loop to make it shorter.

The modern valve trumpet is bent like the bugle. It is equipped with piston valves on the top of the instrument. By pressing these, the trumpeter can make the air follow a longer path through the instrument. It is as if he could change the length of the trumpet from moment to moment. When there is a longer air path in the trumpet, a deeper note is made.

So far we have talked as if sounds always have a single definite pitch. But nearly all the sound we hear is a mixture of high- and low-pitched sounds. The noise of conversation or of traffic in the street consists of sounds of a wide range of pitch, mixed together. When an orchestra is playing it is producing many different notes at each moment. A combination of several notes is called a chord. Musicians choose the notes in a chord so that they sound 'harmonious', or pleasing.

But even the single note sounded by a musical instrument does not have completely pure pitch. Sound of other, higher, frequencies is always mixed with the main sound. For example, when middle C is played on a piano, the main sound is a note with a frequency of 262 hertz. But weaker notes with frequencies twice as great, three times as great, and so on, are mixed with this main sound.

This is true of the notes produced by every musical instrument. The purest musical notes are made by tuning forks. (A tuning fork looks like the fork you eat with except that it has only two prongs. It gives out a musical sound when the 'handle' is struck.) But even the note of tuning fork contains 'overtones', as the higher-frequency sounds are called. Completely pure notes can be produced only by electronic machines. TV stations sometimes transmit pure notes when they are not broadcasting. They sound 'flat' and unmusical.

When middle C is played on a piano, it sounds quite different from middle C on a violin. The two instruments can be easily recognized. The difference is due to the overtones that they produce. The strength of the higher-frequency notes is different in the two cases. Different human voices singing the same song at the same pitch sound different because of the different overtones that each voice produces.

Loudspeakers in radios, TVs and record-playing equipment have to produce sounds that are good copies of the original sounds. To do this loudspeakers must cover a wide range of frequencies. A 'high-fidelity' loudspeaker system will have several different loudspeakers. Some will deal with low frequencies, others produce high-frequency sounds, including some beyond the range of even the best human hearing. The loudspeaker which is used in the earpiece of a telephone is of much lower quality. It can only produce a true 'copy' of a narrow range of frequencies. Voices sound distorted on the telephone, and are often hard to tell apart.

Ultrasonic sound

Ultrasonic sound waves, those that are too high-pitched for human beings to hear, are being used in more and more ways. The echo sounders described above use ultrasonic waves. Ultrasonic waves can be focused into a narrow beam, rather as light can. A beam of lower-frequency waves would soon spread out, but ultrasonic beams do not. 'Searchlight beams' of ultrasonic waves can be used by surface ships to find the positions of submarines. The echoes of the ultrasonic waves from the submarine give information about its direction and distance.

Ultrasonic sound is used by doctors. When an ultrasonic beam falls on a human body it passes through, like ordinary lower-frequency sound. But bones, muscles and other tissues, and hollow spaces like the stomach, send back echoes. Certain diseases and injuries can be studied in this way. For example, metal splinters that have entered the body can be detected. Here sound is being used like X-rays. (See: X-ray.)

Ultrasonic waves are used in industry for cleaning. For example, dirt can be removed faster from metal objects in a bath of detergent, if ultrasonic waves are sent into the liquid. The waves literally shake the dirt off.

spectrum

Have you ever noticed the rainbow effect of oil in a puddle? Or perhaps you have seen a spot of different colours of light on the wall on a sunny day. These spots of colour are called spectra (singular: *spectrum*).

You can see a spectrum more clearly if you hold a prism, which is a triangular-shaped block of glass, in the path of a ray of white light such as sunlight. The ray of light becomes a short rainbow-like band of colours.

There is another way to see the effect of this breaking up of light. Look through the prism at the objects around you (but not at the Sun – its brightness could damage your eyes). The objects will seem to be surrounded by coloured fringes. These fringes show where the colours in the light from objects have been separated by the prism.

White light is actually a mixture of many different colours of light. When light passes through a substance, such as glass, its direction of travel may be changed. This 'bending' of light is called refraction (see: *lenses and mirrors*). Some colours of light are refracted more than others. So, when white light goes through a prism, its colours travel away in different directions and are separated. Then, these 'spectral colours' may form a rainbow-like band on a surface that the light hits.

Other hard materials, such as diamonds, can also act as prisms by refracting light. Diamonds give particularly dazzling colour because they can bend light more than any other transparent (see-through) substance.

Jewels are shaped by jewel-cutters so that they will sparkle and flash as brilliantly as possible. You can often catch glimpses of spectra formed by chance in glass bowls and dishes, in the edges of mirrors and in broken glass.

When you look at a rainbow you are seeing a spectrum that is formed by water droplets. The droplets may be falling rain in the distance. They reflect sunlight toward you while breaking it up into its colours. You can often see similar coloured bands in the spray of a water sprinkler or a fountain on a sunny day. Rainbows may appear in the spray of waterfalls when the Sun shines.

Scientists study spectra with instruments called spectroscopes. The spectroscope has a telescope which is pointed at a light source. This might be a hot flame or electric sparks made in the laboratory. Or it might be the Sun or a star.

The light passes from the telescope to a prism, or to another device called a diffraction grating. A grating is a flat plate of glass with many parallel lines scratched on it. The grating splits up light like a prism does. The spectrum made by the prism or grating is viewed through a second telescope. Cameras can be attached to the spectroscope to photograph the spectrum.

If you hold a long playing record at a certain angle to the light, you will notice a rainbow sheen on the surface. The ridges on the record are like the thin parallel lines on the grating. As the light hits the ridges it is broken up into its colours. The colours are determined by the spacing of the ridges and the angle from which they are viewed. Similar colours can be seen in fur coats or in animals' fur.

Astronomers can use the spectroscope to photograph the spectra of stars. An ordinary photograph would show the stars in some part of the sky as small white spots. A colour photograph taken with a spectroscope shows each spot 'stretched' out into a rainbow-coloured band. Since the stars look small, the astronomer picks out particular stars to take more detailed photographs of their spectra later.

The colours in a spectrum are always in the same order – red, orange, yellow, green, blue, indigo and violet. These colours can be remembered in the right order by their initials which make up the name Roy G. Biv. These seven colours are picked out just for convenience. There are many more colours in the spectrum, each shading into the next. Beyond the colours that we can see there are also infrared and ultraviolet light. The human eye cannot see these, but photographic film can record them.

The spectroscope can be used by scientists to find out the elements in minerals, fossils and even in the samples brought back from the Moon. The sample is made to give out light by heating it to give the atoms energy. The light is passed through a narrow slit and then through a glass prism or grating. This breaks up the light into a spectrum which consists of a series of lines, side by side. These lines are called 'spectral lines'. They show the colours of light that the flame is sending out. But the fact that they are line-shaped is simply due to the shape of the slit.

The pattern made by spectral lines can tell the scientist what substance is sending out light. Sodium, for example, makes two yellow lines that are very close together. These lines appear in the spectrum when ordinary salt is burned in a flame. They show that salt is partly made of sodium.

Chemists often identify chemicals by studying the light that they send out. Just as sodium-containing substances give out yellow light, so substances containing the metal calcium, for example, send out reddish light when they burn. Barium-containing substances burn with a yellowish-green light. Such colours can be studied more accurately with a spectroscope than with our eyes alone.

Absorption spectrum

Every substance sends out light in its own particular pattern of lines, when it is hot. But a substance can also take in, or absorb, exactly the same colours. Suppose a yellow sodium flame is placed between a spectroscope and a source of white light. The white light forms a continuous spectrum – a band of colours without breaks. But crossing this band of colour there are fine dark lines. These show where certain colours of light are being absorbed.

Among these lines are two very close together. They are at the same places where two bright lines appear in the spectrum from the sodium flame by itself.

The spectrum of the Sun is like this. There is a background of colour, which is a continuous spectrum. Crossing this are thousands upon thousands of fine dark lines. These are formed by a thin layer of cooler gas surrounding the Sun. The lines show us what this cooler gas is made of – mostly hydrogen and helium, with many other substances found on Earth. In fact the gas helium was first discovered by its lines in the Sun's spectrum.

The spectroscope is an instrument of great value in many branches of science. It can tell the astronomer how hot distant stars are, and what they are made of. And it can help the scientist to identify tiny samples of a substance in the laboratory.

The sample is heated in a flame or by electric sparks. It may be destroyed in an instant. But the brief flash of light it gives out is photographed with a spectroscope. The spectrum may be complicated. But after study the scientist can identify the substance that produced it.

Find out by doing

You can make a spectrum for yourself by observing the effect of sunlight reflected from a mirror which is placed in a dish of water as shown in the photograph. Partly fill the dish with water and place a mirror in it, leaning against the side of the dish. Place the dish near a window, where light can shine on the water. Hold a piece of white paper about a metre in front of the dish at an angle of 90° to the light coming in from the window. You will be able to see a spectrum formed on the paper. What is acting as the prism to break up the light into its colours?

star

Look up at the sky on a clear night. Nearly all of the bright dots that you see are distant stars. If you tried to count all the stars that you can see in the night sky, you would probably give up after a while.

Yet there are many more stars. More stars can be seen through a telescope. Still more can be detected with other scientific instruments. And there are even more stars that cannot be detected with scientific instruments, and perhaps never will be. The total number of stars in the universe is unknown.

Stars are objects in outer space, beyond the atmosphere of our Earth. The nearest star to us is the Sun. The Earth orbits the Sun. The Sun is about 150 million kilometres (93 million miles) from us. The other stars are millions of millions of kilometres away from us and from each other.

Starlight

We see stars because they produce light. Their light travels to us at a high speed – 300,000 kilometres (186,000 miles) per second. In one year, light travels a distance called a 'light year'. This is about 9.5 million million kilometres (6 million million miles). The nearest star is Proxima Centauri. It is about 4.3 light years away. The farthest stars that we can see with telescopes are thousands of millions of light years away. The light that we see from these stars today was produced by them thousands of millions of years ago.

Light is a kind of 'radiation', or energy, given off from a source. Stars produce other kinds of radiation too. They send out heat, radio waves, and X-rays. (See: *radiation*.)

You must have heard the rhyme that begins

'Twinkle, twinkle, little star'. Stars often appear to 'twinkle'. Their brightness seems to change very quickly. This is because starlight must pass through the air to reach us on the Earth. Movements in the Earth's atmosphere cause the 'twinkling' effect.

Some stars really do change greatly in brightness. The amount of radiation that they produce is changing. But most stars shine more or less steadily. They continue to shine during the daytime. The blue light of the sky stops us from seeing the stars during the daytime. This blue skylight is actually sunlight scattered by particles of air.

The Sun is a typical star. It is almost round in shape like the Earth. But it is much bigger than the Earth. The Sun is not made up of solid material like the Earth. It consists of hot gases. Their tiny particles are continually whirling about. Much of it is pure hydrogen gas, which is rare on Earth. In the central core of the Sun, a reaction, called fusion, occurs between particles. This releases nuclear energy (see: *nuclear energy*). The nuclear energy is turned into radiation. The Sun produces vast amounts of radiation. It has been shining for thousands of millions of years. And it will go on shining for even longer.

The Sun moves through space. And we move with it. Distant stars move through space too. Yet they are so far away from us that these movements are difficult to see.

But all stars seem to move across the sky at night. They move from east to west. On a long winter night, you can watch stars come up in the east and go down in the west. This happens because you are on Earth, which is turning from west to east on its axis. As you turn with it, the stars seem to move in the opposite direction.

The movement of stars

The arrangement of stars in the night sky can be understood better if you imagine that the sky is a large sphere. At the centre of the sphere is the Earth, which is turning. As we look from the Earth, we see the inner surface of the sphere. All over that surface, the stars are located. Astronomers call this imaginary sphere of the sky the 'celestial sphere'.

At any particular time, we can see only a part of the celestial sphere. This is the half of the sphere that lies above us. From where we stand it is above the horizon. The other half of the sphere is hidden from us by the Earth. But if we go to a different part of the Earth, we see a different part of the celestial sphere.

As the Earth turns, different parts of the celestial sphere come into view. They rise above the eastern horizon, while other parts disappear below the western horizon. So it seems to us that the celestial sphere is turning around the

Earth. There seems to be an axis, with two poles, about which the celestial sphere turns. One of these, the northern celestial pole, lies directly above the North Pole of the Earth. This pole is roughly marked today by the position of Polaris, the Pole Star.

A star's position on the celestial sphere changes very slowly. This movement may not be noticeable for several centuries. So the distant stars are often called 'fixed' stars.

Stars form patterns on the celestial sphere. Ancient peoples named these patterns, or 'constellations', after the things they thought they resembled.

One familiar constellation is Ursa Major, or the Great Bear. The seven brightest stars of this constellation make the pattern known as the Plough, or Big Dipper. Their position on the celestial sphere is near the Pole Star.

Not all the bright dots that you see in the night sky are stars. Venus, for example, is sometimes mistaken for a very bright star. Venus is a planet. Like Earth, it moves in an orbit round the Sun. Planets do not give off light as stars do. We can see planets because they reflect the light of the Sun. Planets change their position from night to night.

The positions of stars have been observed accurately for thousands of years. But today the science of astronomy can explain a great deal more about stars. In fact, the name 'astronomy' comes from Greek words meaning 'the laws of the stars'.

We now know more about how stars move through space. Stars are grouped into large collections called galaxies. A galaxy consists of thousands of millions of stars. The stars are kept together by the force of gravity between them (see: *gravity*). A galaxy spins slowly like a huge top. The Sun is part of a galaxy sometimes called the Milky Way. The Sun moves round the centre of this galaxy once every 225 million years.

Star groups
Not all stars move independently in galaxies. Some stars are 'binaries', or double stars. To the naked eye, a binary may look like one star. But it really consists of two stars. Some binaries can be seen to consist of two stars through a telescope. The two stars move around each other because of the force of gravity between them. At the same time, they are both moving through space.

Sirius, called the Dog Star, is a binary. It is the brightest star we can see. But its smaller companion, known as the Pup, is too faint to be seen except with a telescope. The Pup was first discovered by observing the motion of Sirius. Sirius slowly changes its position compared with the other stars. In 150 years it moves a distance equal to the width of the full Moon.

Sirius would move in a straight line if it were a single star moving alone. Instead, Sirius is seen to move along a wobbly path. It moves from side to side as it goes around its companion. After this 'wobble' had been discovered, the companion star was observed. The two stars are now called Sirius A and B.

An 'eclipsing' binary is one kind of binary system. It looks like a single star whose brightness changes in a regular way. As its two stars move around each other, one star comes between us and the other star. Then the first star 'eclipses' the second star – blocks some of the light from it. So the star looks fainter to us for a while. This happens again when the second star comes in front of the first star. A larger decrease in brightness occurs as the brighter of the two stars is eclipsed. One such binary system is called Algol.

Stars can belong to groups of three, four or more. In fact few stars are single, as our Sun is. The nearest star to the Sun, Proxima Centauri, is a member of a triple system. The other two members form the bright star Alpha Centauri.

Some stars look to us as if they are close together, although they are not. This is because they are seen in the same direction in the sky. To find out whether they really are in the same system, we have to find out how far away they are.

One way of finding the distance of stars is by measuring their apparent movement. A nearby star seems to move during the year. As our Earth travels round the Sun, we see the star from different parts of the Earth's path. Thus we see it from slightly different directions. The star seems to move in a tiny circle or oval against the background of more distant stars.

This apparent movement of a star is called its 'parallax'. The distance the Earth moves is known. Using that distance, and the parallax of a star, we can figure out the distance of the star.

A star's parallax is only a fraction of a degree of angle. It is too small even to be measured accurately if the star is more than about 150 light years away. So for stars at greater distances than this, other methods must be used.

The brightness of a star is a clue to its distance. The less bright it looks to us, the more distant it may be from us. But we must also know how bright the star really is. For if it is really not producing much light, it will not look bright to us even though it is near. And if it is really producing a lot of light, it may look bright although it is very far away from us.

For example, imagine that you see a motorcycle light and a bicycle light at night. If the two lights look equally bright to you, the motorcycle must be farther away.

Astronomers can often figure out how bright

a star really is. That is, they know how much light it is producing. The amount of light a star produces is called its 'luminosity'. Some stars are much more luminous than the Sun. They look fainter only because they are much farther away from us than the Sun is.

Suppose that all the stars, including the Sun, were placed at the same distance from us. Then, if a star were more luminous than the Sun, it would look brighter than the Sun. And if less luminous, it would look less bright. In this manner, stars can be compared in their luminosity. They are marked on a scale showing their 'brightness relative to the Sun', if viewed from the same distance. The brightness of the star Rigel is over ten thousand times that of the Sun on this scale. And the nearest star, Proxima Centauri, is less than one ten-thousandth as bright as the Sun on this scale.

Many stars change in brightness. These are called variable stars. One important kind is known as a Cepheid. It grows bright, then faint, then bright again, in a period of several days. This period is longer for a Cepheid that is more luminous. So we can find the luminosity by measuring the period. Then the luminosity is compared with the star's apparent brightness, as we see it. Thus its distance from us is figured out. This method is used to find the distances of far away galaxies that contain Cepheid stars.

A 'nova' is another kind of variable star. A nova simply grows to great brightness, then fades away. It is a star whose outer regions are exploding. A 'supernova' is a whole star that explodes. Its luminosity becomes millions of times that of the Sun. One famous supernova was seen in 1054. The explosion left behind a cloud of gas called the Crab Nebula.

The Sun is a star that has planets, such as Earth, in orbit around it. Any planets orbiting other stars would be too small to be seen even through a powerful telescope. But, if a star does have planets, they alter the path it follows. The path of the red dwarf star, called Barnard's Star, shows that it may have at least one planet. It is possible that a star exists that has a planet similar to Earth.

The nature of stars

Astronomers can tell what a star is made of. They study the spectrum of its radiation. The spectrum is the range of all the kinds of waves – light, heat, radio, and X-rays - that are radiated. Different kinds of radiation are produced by different substances in the star. Thus the chemical elements in the star can be identified.

A star's spectrum also shows whether it is moving towards or away from us, and how fast. Its motion towards us or away from us changes its spectrum, according to the Doppler effect (see: *Doppler effect*). A star's temperature, too,

can be found by studying its spectrum. A star's temperature is thousands of degrees at the star's outer surface, and millions of degrees at its centre. If its surface is very hot, it looks white or blue to us. If cooler, it appears reddish, or yellow like the Sun.

The temperature and luminosity of a star can be used to figure out how big it is. The Sun is a star of average size. But there are 'dwarf' stars only about 128,000 kilometres (80,000 miles) across. The diameter of a 'giant' star may be a thousand times as great, or 100 times bigger than the Sun's diameter. And a 'supergiant' is even bigger than that.

Astronomers describe stars with the help of the Hertzsprung-Russell, or H-R, diagram. Each star is represented by a point in the diagram. The distance of a point from the left of the diagram indicates the star's temperature. The hotter a star is, the farther to the left it is placed. The distance of a point from the bottom of a diagram shows how bright the star is. The brighter stars are placed higher up in the diagram.

Stars fall into groups when they are plotted on the H-R diagram. Most of them lie on the 'main sequence', which runs from hot bright stars near the top left to cool faint stars near the bottom right. Our Sun also lies on the 'main sequence'. Lying above the main sequence and to the right are the giant and supergiant stars. Some are very cool and glow a dull red, like Antares and Betelgeuse. But they are so big that they send out huge quantities of light and heat. This is why they are so bright. Below the main sequence are stars that, while they may be hot, are so small that they do not send out much light and heat. These are the white 'dwarf' stars. Sirius B is one of these.

Stars have a life cycle. They are 'born' from gas clouds, nebulas. This process is almost certainly happening now in, for example, the Orion Nebula. Despite this, most stars in our galaxy were born about the same time, five thousand million years ago. Nebulas consist almost wholly of hydrogen. Stars are formed when the hydrogen gathers together in various places, owing to gravitational attraction.

As the gas gathers together it heats up. When it becomes hot enough, a process called nuclear fusion begins. Atoms of hydrogen fuse, or join together, to form atoms of the gas helium. (See: *nuclear energy*.) This releases heat. The inside of the star heats up to millions of degrees and the star begins to shine. The more gas there is in the star, the hotter and brighter it is, and the faster it turns hydrogen into helium. Thus, the brightness of a star at this early stage of its life depends on how much hydrogen went to make up the star as it was formed.

When they begin to turn hydrogen into

helium, all stars lie on the main sequence. Stars about the size of the Sun stay there for thousands of millions of years. Bigger stars may stay there for only a few million years.

When the star's supplies of hydrogen begin to run low, the star swells and becomes cooler.

Stars that have less than about 1½ times the mass of the Sun expand, during their lifetimes, to become red giants. The Sun will probably grow to about 250 times its present size, taking in Mercury, Venus, and the Earth in the process. Then it will get smaller again. While it gets smaller, the Sun will turn atoms of helium into heavier atoms, releasing further energy. Still heavier atoms will be built up from these.

The Sun will grow so small that finally all its matter will be packed into a space not much larger than the Earth. This tiny star will be a white dwarf. Finally, the process of building heavier atoms will come to an end. The white dwarf will stop shining and become a 'dead' black dwarf.

Supernovas

Stars that have masses greater than 1½ times the mass of the Sun may explode as supernovas. Perhaps as much as 90 per cent of an exploding star's material is scattered into space. The rest of the star's matter remains as a collapsed core. This core is called a neutron star. By comparison with the smallest white dwarf, a neutron star is tiny, say, 4 kilometres (2½ miles) in diameter. A ping-pong ball filled with material from a neutron star would have the mass of a small planet.

If the core left by a supernova is big enough, it may not even end as a neutron star. It may go on collapsing until it becomes a 'black hole'. The gravity of a black hole would be so strong that anything that fell into it would not be able to escape again. Not even light would be able to escape from a black hole, so we would never be able to see into one.

We do not know if black holes actually exist. A black hole could not be seen through a telescope. But it could be detected by its gravitational influence on nearby stars. So up to now we still do not know for certain if a black hole is one of the ways in which a star's 'life' may end.

statistics

For many hundreds of years, governments have been interested in collecting information of a rather special kind. This information is about numbers of things or people that make up certain groups. For example, they may want to know the number of people in a country, or the number of people who have farms. Rulers used to send out people to collect these facts or 'data'. Because the facts were useful to the state, they came to be known as statistics.

Statistics, then, is concerned with 'quantitive information'. Quantitive information is information about quantities or numbers of people or things. We use the word 'statistics' to mean two things. It can mean the actual data or facts that have been collected. Or it can mean the science of collecting and analyzing data and making use of it.

Nowadays, almost everyone is interested in statistics. When you compare the grades you get in school with the grades of your classmates, you are making use of data. The data in this case is the information about the grades. Big businesses make use of statistics to help them develop new products. For example, they may want to know if enough people would be interested in buying a new product.

The people who collect and analyze statistical data are called statisticians. They are experts at statistical predictions or inference. They may have a lot of information about a small section of a large group. From this information, they 'infer' what will happen in the large group. In other words, they can use the information they have to make predictions. Making accurate predictions like this is a very important part of a statistician's work. One technique which helps statisticians to do this is known as sampling.

Imagine that your mother has just baked an apple pie. She asks you to taste it to see if it is good. You don't find out by eating the whole pie. Instead you sample it by taking a slice. You sample a part of it, and this part gives you an idea of what the whole is like. But you must choose your sample with care. You must sample both the pastry and the apple filling to get a fair idea of the pie. You could not get a good idea of the pie if you tasted only the pastry, or only the apple.

Suppose you have a box containing 1,000 ball point pens. And you want to find out if they all write well. It would take a long time to test each one. So what you must do is to take a sample. Suppose you select 20 pens. You try them out, and they all work. You might take this as a clue that all the pens work.

But supposing you had taken 20 pens from the top of the box. There might be a lot of faulty pens 'hidden' at the bottom. In order to make sure it is a fair sample, you must select pens from all parts of the box – not just the part nearest your hand. You must take what is known as a random sample. If you take some pens from the top, some pens from the middle and some from the bottom, you can be more sure that faulty pens are not hidden anywhere.

Random sampling is very important. It is a way of making sure that you get an accurate picture of what is going on. If your sample is not random, the results of your tests may be misleading. Supposing that there had been faulty pens in the box. Supposing all these had been packed at the bottom. If your sample had only been made up of pens from the top, you might have assumed that all the pens were good. But if you had taken a random sample, you would probably have discovered that there were some faulty pens. You might not have found all of them. But your knowledge of the pens would be more accurate. You would know that they were not all perfect.

Let us look at another example which shows the importance of random sampling. Supposing someone wanted to find out how many people in Britain live in flats and how many in houses. And supposing he took his sample from people who lived in a large city. He would get a very misleading figure. Most people who live in large cities live in flats. So if the sample consisted only of city-dwellers, the figure for the number of people living in flats would be much higher than it really is. The statistician should have made sure his sample was a random one. He should have included city dwellers and country dwellers in his sample.

These examples show how important random samples are. Unless the statistician has a random sample, he cannot make accurate conclusions.

The statistician cannot be absolutely sure he is right when he makes a prediction. But he can use mathematics to find out what chance his prediction has of being right or wrong. The branch of mathematics that enables him to do this is called probability. Probability is the science of chance. It is one of the most useful branches of mathematics, and it is still being developed. The theory of probability involves complicated mathematics. But we can get some idea of it by looking at the basic principles.

Suppose you have 3 cups of coffee in front of you. Only one of them has sugar in it. You have to choose the one with the sugar. What are your chances of picking the correct one? You have 3 chances to find the sweetened coffee. You can test each one by tasting it. With one of the tests out of the three, you are bound to find the sweetened coffee. Mathematicians say that your chances of finding the coffee are 1:3 or $\frac{1}{3}$. You have one chance in three of picking the sweetened coffee on your first try.

How do you get this figure for the probability of an event happening?

First, you have to find out the number of times that the event can happen. You can only choose the sweetened coffee once. That gives you the figure one. Then you must find out the total number of times that the event can happen

plus the number of times it might not happen. You can choose the sweetened coffee once. But you might make two wrong choices. So not finding the sweetened coffee could happen twice. Add these, and you get the total number of possibilities which is 3. In the same way you can calculate that your chances of not picking the sweetened coffee are $\frac{2}{3}$ or 2:3.

If an event has a probability of one, it is certain to happen. And if it has a probability of 0, it is certain not to happen.

Imagine you have three cups of coffee. This time they all contain sugar. And you have to pick one with sugar. The number of times you can succeed is 3. No matter which of the three cups you choose, you will pick a coffee with sugar. And the total number of times you can succeed or fail is also three. This gives us the probability of picking a sweetened coffee as 3/3 or one. In this case you cannot fail to pick a cup of sweet coffee.

Supposing, though, you had three cups of non-sweet coffee. Then someone asks you to pick a sweet one. The number of times you could succeed is zero. You have no chance of picking a sweet coffee from three cups all containing non-sweet coffee. The total number of times you can succeed or fail – the number of times the event can happen and not happen – is three. This gives us a probability of 0/3 or 0. The event, in this case picking a sweet coffee, is certain not to happen.

The probabilities that we have been considering are called theoretical probabilities. These are worked out by using mathematics. But there is another kind of probability called empirical probability. Empirical probability is based on experiment or observation, rather than theory. Statisticians use the mathematics of empirical probability to find out what chance their predictions have of being right.

Another important use of statistics is in summarizing data that has been collected. One way of doing this is by using averages. Finding the average of something means that one figure can be used to represent a whole list of figures.

There are three kinds of average. These are called the mean, the median and the mode.

You may have heard the phrase 'mean annual rainfall'. This means the average amount of rain that falls in a year. One figure is used to give some idea of the amount of rainfall. It is easier to do this than to give you a long list of figures that tell you exactly how much rain fell in each year, over say, a 20-year period. The mean is the kind of 'average' you will probably know best.

In order to find the mean, you add up all the figures you have, and then divide by the number of figures. Supposing we want to find the mean annual rainfall and we have collected data which tells us how much rain fell each year from 1953-1972. We have 20 figures – one for each year. We add them up and suppose the total comes to 1440 centimetres. In 20 years, 1440 centimetres of rain have fallen. So, on average, in each year 1440/20 centimetres of rain falls. This gives us a value of 72 centimetres for the mean annual rainfall.

It doesn't mean that exactly 72 centimetres of rain fell each year. Maybe some years were dry and only 50 centimetres of rain fell. And some years may have been very wet when 100 centimetres fell. But the mean gives us a general picture. Probably in most years, the rainfall was about 72 centimetres. Having worked out an average like this also means that it can be used as a standard that can be compared with other figures.

It is possible that the mean of a set of numbers may give you a misleading idea about the numbers. Suppose four people each take ten minutes to walk to school. A fifth person takes 30 minutes. If we work out the mean time it takes to walk to school, it works out at 14 minutes. But it is not really a very true and informative value. In this case it would be better to use the kind of average known as the mode. The mode of a set of numbers is the one that occurs most often. In this example, 10 occurs most often. So we assume that it takes most of the group ten minutes to walk to school – which give us a more accurate picture of the situation.

Sometimes you may get a list of figures that are all roughly the same except for one. This one may have a much higher or lower value than the others. It is not possible to use the mode, as no number occurs more than once. So, in this case, you would use the median to find the average.

For example, imagine that there are five people, let us call them A, B, C, D and E. A reads 3 books a week, B2, C4, D11, and E5. To find the median of a set of numbers, you arrange them so that each number is either larger than or the same as the one before it. So you would arrange the numbers like this – 2, 3, 4, 5, 11. The number in the middle is the median – in this case, it is 4.
See: *mathematics*.

Sun

All living things depend on the Sun. If the Sun were to disappear now, the Earth would be plunged into an endless night. No life would be possible. The seas and even the gases of the air would freeze.

Even if the brightness of the Sun were to change by only a small amount, the temperature of the Earth would rise or fall sufficiently to make life impossible. Many millions of years from now the Sun will grow larger and scorch life from the Earth. But until then it will shine steadily on as it has done for millions of years.

Though there is no real change in the Sun's brightness from day to day, it can look very different at different times. At dawn and sunset it may look yellowish compared with its appearance at midday.

This is an effect caused by the air through which we see the Sun. Sunlight is white light, which is actually a mixture of all colours of light (see: *light*). The blue part of this light is scattered as it passes through the air.

When the Sun is high in the sky we see it through a fairly thin layer of air. Most of the air belongs to a layer 320 kilometres (200 miles) thick. Some blue light is scattered by the air. The Sun then looks more yellowish than it does to an astronaut outside the atmosphere. The blue light is scattered in all directions, making the sky look blue to us on the ground.

When the Sun is near the horizon we see it through a much greater thickness of air. So much blue light is scattered out of the sunlight that the Sun's disc appears reddish.

The Sun also looks flattened when it is near the horizon. This is due to bending of the light rays by the air. This bending makes the Sun seem to be slightly higher than it really is. When the Sun is just below the horizon its light rays are bent over the horizon so that the Sun can still be seen. So the Sun sets a few minutes before we see it set, and rises a few minutes after we see it rise.

The apparent raising of the Sun by the air is greater near the horizon. So the lower part of the Sun is raised more than the higher part. The result is that the Sun's disc seems to be squeezed, making it look oval. This effect is noticeable only near the horizon.

The Sun can look bigger near the horizon than when it is higher. This, too, is an illusion. The Sun does not change in size and shape.

Ancient man was fascinated by the Sun. He often believed that it was a god who could help or harm him. And he depended on it for many purposes. It enabled him to tell the time with inventions like the sundial. He could use it to find directions when travelling.

The nature of the Sun
The Sun is the main body in the solar system. This is the group of planets, their moons, comets, meteors, and other bodies that go around the Sun. The Earth is one of the nine known planets. It is the third planet from the Sun. It moves completely around the Sun every 365¼ days. This is the length of one year.

The Sun is about 150,000,000 kilometres (93,000,000 miles) from the Earth. This distance changes only slightly during the year. The Sun's diameter is about 1,400,000 kilometres (865,000 miles), over a hundred times the Earth's diameter. A million Earths could be put into the Sun and there would still be plenty of room to spare.

But the Sun contains only 333,000 times more matter than the Earth does. So each cubic metre of matter in the Sun contains, on average, only one quarter as much matter as does the Earth. Scientists say that its average density is one quarter the Earth's average density. But the Sun's density varies from place to place. Its centre is 60 times as dense as solid rock. Its outer regions are less dense than the air we breathe. (See: *density*.)

The Sun is a star. It is one of the millions of stars in a group called the Milky Way galaxy. It is about 290 thousand billion kilometres, or 30,000 'light-years', from the centre of the galaxy. And it moves around the centre, once every 200 million years. Thus it is moving through space, and our Earth moves with it. However, many other stars are larger than the Sun. But they do not look as big, because they are much more distant from the Earth.

The Sun only seems to move around the Earth each day. In reality, the Earth turns around on its own axis. The axis is a line through the Earth, from its North to South Pole. One complete turn, or 'rotation', is made in about 24 hours. And the direction of rotation is from west to east. Therefore the Sun appears to move across the sky from east to west.

The Earth's axis is not 'upright' relative to its path round the Sun, but tilted. The tilt of the axis scarcely changes during a year, always pointing roughly toward the distant Pole Star. For part of the year, the North Pole is tilted toward the Sun. Then the Northern Hemisphere has its summer. At the same time, the Southern Hemisphere has its winter.

Six months later, the Earth is on the other side of the Sun. Then the North Pole is tilted away from the Sun. The Northern Hemisphere has its winter, while the Southern Hemisphere has its summer.

The Sun, too, rotates on its axis. Every complete rotation of the Sun takes about one month. But not all parts of it turn at the same rate. Those near the Sun's two poles turn more slowly than those near its equator. The equator is an imaginary line around its middle, just halfway between the poles, as on the Earth.

Thus only 25$\frac{1}{3}$ days are needed for each rotation at the Sun's equator. Several days more are required at places near the poles. This difference does not occur on the Earth. All parts of the Earth take the same time, one day, to rotate once around its axis.

It is possible for different parts of the Sun to rotate in different times because the Sun is not a solid body like the Earth. Even though the Sun is so incredibly dense at its centre, it is made wholly of gas. Gases consist of tiny particles of matter, as solid material does. But the particles are not held together in fixed positions. They are free to move independently of each other. So they can easily rotate at different rates about the Sun's axis.

The matter of the Sun is held together by gravity. Gravity is the force of attraction that each piece of matter has for all other matter. Gravity holds the planets in orbit round the Sun, and the Sun in orbit round the centre of the Galaxy. It also holds the matter in each planet or star together. The objects around us have weight because they are pulled downward by the Earth's gravitation. (See: *gravity*.)

Because there is so much matter in the Sun, the strength of gravitation is huge there. An object on the Sun's surface would weigh 28 times as much as it would on Earth. An average man would weigh over two tonnes on the Sun.

The Sun's activity
The Sun produces enormous amounts of heat and light. In every second it sends out into space as much energy as three thousand million power stations could produce in a year.

This vast energy output could not be provided by ordinary burning, like the burning of a coal fire. It comes from a process called nuclear fusion. Fusion here means 'joining'. In the Sun, atoms of hydrogen are fused, or joined together, to make heavier atoms of helium. Heat and light are given out in this process.

The enormous heat and pressure in the Sun break down atoms into parts. Normal whole atoms contain a central core called the nucleus. Round the nucleus circle the tiny particles called electrons. In the Sun atoms are torn apart and electrons and nuclei move separately. Sometimes hydrogen nuclei collide and build up helium nuclei in several steps. This is the fusion process.

When the Sun was first formed it may have been entirely made of hydrogen. Today there are about eight helium nuclei for every hundred hydrogen nuclei.

The temperature at the centre of the Sun is over 15 million degrees C. Scientists are trying to achieve similar temperatures on Earth to create controlled fusion. If they can imitate the processes going on in the Sun, nearly unlimited supplies of energy will be available to man. (See: *nuclear energy*.)

Light is only one kind of radiation that the Sun sends out. It also radiates heat, radio waves, and even X-rays. This radiation travels away from the Sun at the speed of light. It reaches the Earth just over eight minutes later.

The Sun sends out tiny particles as well. This stream of particles is called the solar wind. It consists mostly of hydrogen nuclei and electrons. They travel more slowly to the Earth. When the solar wind is very strong it can disturb the atmosphere greatly and interfere with radio communication. (See: *cosmic rays, radiation.*)

Many processes in our atmosphere depend on the Sun's radiation. But the atmosphere also shields us from dangerous radiation, especially ultraviolet light. Ultraviolet light is invisible, and causes suntanning and sunburn. If the Earth had no atmosphere, ultraviolet light reaching the surface would be so strong that life would be impossible.

The Sun has an atmosphere too. In fact, there are several outer layers of gas. The bright, visible surface of the Sun is called the photosphere. Its temperature is a few thousand degrees – much cooler than the middle of the Sun. We cannot see more than a few hundred kilometres into it. The Sun's inner regions must be studied indirectly by examining the radiation from the photosphere.

The photosphere is too dazzlingly bright to be looked at with unprotected eyes. You should *never* look directly at the Sun, with the naked eye, binoculars, or a telescope.

Above the photosphere is the chromosphere. This is a much less dense layer of gases. Its name comes from a Greek word which means colour. It produces light of a reddish colour. It can be seen only with special instruments.

The outermost region of the Sun is called the corona. This is the least dense of all. It stretches millions of kilometres out from the Sun into space. Its atoms are moving very rapidly. They produce a white glow of light around the Sun. Some of them are the atoms of heavy elements like iron and nickel.

Eclipse of the Sun

The Sun's outer layers are difficult to observe. But they can be studied easily during a total eclipse. This happens when the Moon comes between the Earth and the Sun. The Moon completely covers the bright photosphere of the Sun, and the sky darkens. Then the chromosphere is visible as a red rim round the black disc of the Moon. Red 'bristles' can be seen sticking out from the chromosphere. These are called prominences, great eruptions of gas thrown up from the surface of the Sun and falling back again.

The corona is also visible during a total eclipse – a pearly white glow several times the diameter of the Sun.

One device used to study the Sun's light is the spectroscope. It separates sunlight into different colours. Thus it shows which kinds of atom produce the light. In this way, many chemical elements have been found to exist in the Sun. They include most of the elements known on Earth. (See: *spectrum.*)

Sunspots are comparatively dark areas of the Sun's surface. They would seem intensely bright if they were not surrounded by the even brighter photosphere. They are often vast, far larger than the Earth.

Energy from the Sun enables organisms to live on Earth. It is stored by green plants through the process called photosynthesis (see: *photosynthesis*). Animals absorb the stored energy by eating plants. And we acquire it by eating both plants and animals as food. We also use the stored energy of sunlight when we burn coal and oil, which were formed from dead plants. Devices for producing 'solar power' are also being built. They can change sunlight directly into electricity (see: *power*). Winds are caused by the heating of the atmosphere by sunlight, too.

How old is the Sun? It was formed about 5 thousand million years ago from a gigantic cloud of gas, part of the larger gas cloud from which all the other stars in the Milky Way galaxy formed. The atoms of the gas cloud that one day would become the Sun were pulled together by gravity. As the atoms fell in toward the centre of the cloud they moved faster. This meant that the cloud heated up. (In hot objects atoms move faster than in cold bodies. See: *heat.*)

Eventually the atoms were broken up into their electrons and nuclei by the high temperature in the cloud. As the cloud shrank and became even hotter, the nuclei began to collide and fuse.

The Sun has become slightly brighter since then. It will continue to grow brighter in future. Its nuclear fuel will burn at an even faster rate. Even now it is using up 593 million tonnes of hydrogen each second.

This is why the Sun will not last forever. It contains only a limited amount of hydrogen. As this fuel is used up, the Sun will become redder and larger. Its radiation will make the nearby planets, including the Earth, so hot that they will burn up. Life on Earth will become impossible. Long after that, the Sun will stop shining altogether.

Find out by doing

Sunspots are dark patches that appear on the Sun's surface. We know very little about what causes them but you can use them as 'landmarks' in observing the Sun. But you must protect your eyes. *Never* look at the Sun directly.
You can use a telescope or a pair of binoculars to throw an image of the Sun onto a screen made of white paper or card. A small adjustment of the eyepiece will bring the Sun into focus as a white disc. If there are any large sunspots on the nearside of the Sun at that time, they

will be visible as black dots. If you follow a sunspot over a period of time you will see that it moves across the Sun's disc. This is because the Sun is turning on its axis and carrying the spots along with it. You will find that it takes a group of spots 13½ days to go all the way from one side of the Sun's disc to the other. It will then be on the far side of the Sun for 13½ days and therefore invisible from the Earth. If the spot group has not faded away it will reappear round the side of the disc.

To think about

From the above observation it seems to take a spot 27 days to return to its original position. But the Sun in fact takes 25 days to revolve once. Can you explain the difference?
(*Clue: the Earth is moving around the Sun.*)

surface tension

There are some small insects that can walk on water. They seem to 'skate' over the surface of ponds on long legs. If you could look closely at one of these insects you would see the water surface at the end of each leg pressed down by the insect's weight. But the leg wouldn't go through.

You can make a needle 'float' on the surface of water. It must be placed very gently on the surface. Lay it on a small piece of blotting paper and float the paper on the water. The paper will soak up water and sink, leaving the needle floating. Push the needle beneath the surface and it will immediately sink.

The water acts as if it were covered with a thin elastic skin, just strong enough to hold up light objects. This effect is due to a property that all liquids have, called surface tension.

Molecular attraction

All matter is made up of tiny particles called molecules. Molecules that are very close together attract each other. This happens only when the distance between them is less than a few times the diameters of the molecules themselves.

In solids these forces between molecules hold the solid together, so that it keeps its shape. In liquids molecules are farther apart. The forces of attraction hold the liquid together, but molecules can slide over each other, so that the liquid can flow. In gases the molecules are comparatively far apart. They only rarely come close enough to attract each other.

A molecule in a liquid is surrounded by other molecules. Unless it is very near the surface it is pulled in all directions, and the pulls cancel out. But in the top few layers of molecules, the situation is different. Each molecule has more neighbours below than above, and tends to be pulled downwards.

The effect of this pull is to make the surface of the liquid like an elastic skin stretched over the surface. The surface layer is a few molecules thick.

Surface tension (tension just means a stretching force) is responsible for the spherical shape of small drops of water. The attraction on the surface molecules pulls the drop into a ball shape. Larger drops of water are not spherical. They are flattened out by their own weight.

The tension in the skin of a rubber balloon leads to an inward pull. The air pressure inside the balloon is greater than the pressure outside, balancing this inward pull. In a similar way surface tension pulls soap bubbles into a spherical shape. There is excess air pressure inside the bubble to balance the inward pull.

If you look closely at water in a glass you will see that its surface curves upwards at the edge. This curve is called a meniscus. It is surface tension that causes the meniscus. The meniscus can curve upwards or downwards.

Just as molecules of water attract each other, so water molecules and glass molecules attract each other. Water molecules at the edge of the surface 'climb over each other' to get closer to the glass. The water piles up next to the glass.

The attraction of the glass on the sloping water is in an upward direction. In narrow tubes water can be pulled up several centimetres by the glass.

Mercury atoms

Atoms of the liquid metal mercury attract each other more strongly than they attract glass. A mercury surface curves downward next to a glass container.

Soap and detergents work by decreasing the surface tension of water. This helps oil clinging to cloth fibres to form itself into droplets under the action of the oil's own surface tension. These droplets can then easily be shaken off the cloth by the movement of water during washing and rinsing.
See: *matter*.

Find out by doing

Place a needle on a small piece of blotting paper and float it on a bowl of water. The needle will stay on the surface as the paper sinks. Then add a drop of detergent to the water. The needle will sink as the surface tension is weakened.

Cut a piece of stiff paper or card to make a boat. It need only be roughly boat-shaped with a pointed bow and a wider stern. Cut two small slits in the stern. Put a small piece of soap in each slit. The boat will move forward across the surface of the water in a bowl or sink. The dissolving soap lowers the surface tension behind the boat. So the pull of the water surface is greater at the front of the boat than behind, and the boat is pulled forwards.

The boat will not move for long. As the whole surface becomes soapy, surface tension becomes equal everywhere.

time

Your everyday routine is probably like this. At eight o'clock in the morning you wake up. By nine or so, you begin school. Each class lasts a certain time. At about one o'clock in the afternoon, you may have lunch. And at other times you eat dinner and go to bed.

Thus you do a particular thing at the same time every day. Most other people do so too. They may have a different time from you. In some parts of the world, people are waking up just at the moment when you are going to bed. This is because, as the Earth turns on its axis, the Sun's light reaches different parts. While some are in daylight, others are in darkness.

Time is not a real object or a process. We cannot see, hear, touch, taste, or smell it. Time is a kind of measurement. It indicates when things happen and how long they last. Man has invented many useful ways of measuring time.

We have countless names for time. 'Now' is the present time. Past time comes before this. Future time comes after it. Life is the time during which we exist. If two things happen at different times, the time between them is called an interval. If they happen at the same time, they are said to be 'simultaneous'.

Man observes nature so as to measure time. He names the regular intervals that he sees. Thus, the Earth takes one 'year' to go around the Sun. This time is divided into seasons, months, weeks, and days. The Earth takes a 'day' for each turn on its axis. This 'day' is divided into daytime, night-time, hours, minutes, and seconds.

A calendar tells us what day and month of the year it is. A watch or clock shows the hour, minute, and second of the day. Many other devices have been developed for measuring time. They all work in a very regular way so they can 'keep step' with time. The sundial and hourglass are old instruments of this kind. The pendulum is one that you can easily build yourself.

Each method for measuring time uses some process that repeats itself regularly and reliably. Many clocks use the swinging of pendulums. Wristwatches use the movements of thin springs, called hairsprings. The atomic clocks, for very accurate time-keeping, use the vibrations of atoms in crystals.

Geologists – scientists who study the structure of the Earth – have to measure periods of millions of years. They need to know how old rocks are and when mountains formed. At first, they could calculate these only roughly. They used such things as the rate at which glaciers and rivers carve out their beds, or wind and rain wear away mountains. Now, it is possible to date many kinds of natural and artificial object by using radioactivity.

Every living thing contains radioactive carbon, whose atoms break down at a steady rate to form nitrogen atoms. A piece of wood from an ancient tomb, say, can be dated by measuring how much radioactive carbon is left in it. Rocks contain other radioactive atoms. They enable the age of rocks to be measured back to the beginnings of the Earth, thousands of millions of years ago.

It was once assumed that the rate at which time passes would be the same for all observers. In 1905, Albert Einstein published his revolutionary theory of relativity. This showed that the rate at which time passes is different for observers moving at different speeds. On a fast-moving plane, clocks and all processes, such as radioactive decay, take place very slightly slower than they do on the ground. This difference can be measured, but it would be important only on craft moving close to the speed of light – 300,000 kilometres per second. The theory raises the possibility that high-speed space travellers of the future may age less than the people they leave behind on Earth. See: *astronomy, measurement, relativity.*

time zones

What is the best way of measuring time? One accurate method is to observe the heavenly bodies. We can watch the movements of the stars or the Sun. But the Sun is easiest to use. We see the Sun rise and set regularly each day. It seems to do so because the Earth is turning around, and we turn with the Earth. The time for one complete turn of the Earth is the length of one day – about 24 hours.

The Earth has a North and a South Pole. These are the ends of the imaginary axis through the Earth. The Earth turns around its axis. Other lines can be imagined on the Earth's surface. They stretch between the two poles. They are called meridians of longitude. Your meridian is the imaginary line running from North Pole to South Pole through the place where you live.

As the Earth turns, you can see the Sun crossing the sky. It seems to go from east to west. At noon, the Sun is exactly halfway along its path. It is at its highest point for that day. Then, the Sun is crossing your meridian. Its position at noon is said to be in the 'zenith'.

We often say that noon is 12 o'clock. But at this time, the Sun is almost never exactly in the zenith. This is because the hours of the day do not quite agree with the Earth's turning. The day is rarely 24 hours long exactly. It has this length on only four days of the year. These are April 15, June 14, September 1, and December 24.

The time of noon does not occur at just the same moment everywhere on Earth. Not all people on Earth can see the Sun in the zenith at the same moment. When you see the Sun at its zenith, people to the west of you will not have seen it in its zenith yet. Noon will not yet have occurred. The Sun will not yet have crossed to their meridians, because it moves across the sky from east to west. But, people to the east of you will have seen the Sun at its zenith already. Noon will have already occurred. Thus, at places to the west of you the time will be before noon, and to the east of you it will be some time after noon.

The difference in time between one place and another exists at all moments, not just at noon. In the past, it was not very important. People thought only of their own 'local' time. But, during the past century, the time difference became very troublesome. People travelled over longer distances. They began to communicate with each other all over the world. They had to know the time in places far away.

Time zones are the solution to this problem. They were established in the 1880s, by an agreement among many countries. Each time zone is an area on the Earth. It runs from north to south, but is not very wide from east to west. Its width is decided as follows.

In 24 hours, the Earth turns through one complete circle of 360°. Thus, it turns by 15° of longitude each hour. And you see the Sun move by 15° across the sky in each hour. During one hour after noon, the Sun moves from your zenith to the zenith of another place. This place lies 15° west of you on the Earth. So, noon there, occurs one hour later than it does at your location.

The time zones were designed to be 15° wide. Each zone has a time one hour earlier than the zone just to its east. Two people 15° of longitude apart are in different time zones. And their times are just one hour apart. But in the same zone, all places keep the same time. The time in a zone does not depend on the latitude of a place. Latitude shows how far you are north or south of the Earth's Equator.

For example, New York and Chicago have about the same latitude. But their longitudes differ greatly. They are in two different time zones, one hour apart. However, New York has about the same longitude as Port au Prince in Haiti. These two cities are thus in the same time zone, although they are in different latitudes.

The time zones are numbered from Greenwich, in England. There are 12 zones to its east and 12 to its west. Its meridian is called the 'prime' meridian of 0° longitude. The time there is usually known as Greenwich Mean Time. It fixes the time for places all over the world. It is measured with very accurate clocks which use, for instance, the vibrations of quartz crystals.

The borders of time zones do not always run straight north and south. In many areas they follow the borders of countries. This is more useful for the people living there. Some countries, though, are especially wide in longitude. These have several time zones. In the United States, different zones have particular names for time. There are, for example, Eastern Time, Central Time, Mountain Time, and Pacific Time.

When you travel from east to west over a long distance, you 'gain' time. You must set your watch back one hour for each time zone that you cross. When going from west to east, you 'lose' time. Your watch must be set forward instead. If you fly from New York to London, you 'lose' five hours. This does not mean that you are five hours older. Your body is really the same age as before. You can 'gain' the same five hours by simply flying back to New York, from east to west.

What happens if you travel the whole way around the Earth? Suppose that where you live it is one minute past 12 noon on May 8th. At places farther to the west, the time is earlier. So, at a place that is 12 zones to the west of you, the time is 12 hours earlier. This means it is one minute past midnight at the beginning of the same day – May 8th. At a place 12 zones to your east, the time is 12 hours later. There, it is one minute after midnight at the beginning of the next day – May 9th.

These two places are really the same place, because they are both halfway round the world from you. But, how can it be one minute past midnight on May 8th and one minute past midnight on May 9th at the same place?

To solve this problem, the International Date Line was created. This imaginary line runs along the 180° meridian for most of its length. It is halfway around the world from the Greenwich prime meridian. If you cross the Date Line from east to west, you lose a day. The date will be one day later. If it were May 8th just east of the line, you would go straight into May 9th by crossing to west of the line. If you cross the line from west to east, you gain a day instead. From May 9th, say, you go back to May 8th again, on crossing the line.

The Date Line does not go through areas where many people live. Most of it lies over the Pacific Ocean. It goes around small island areas. The people there are all in a common time zone with the same date. Thus, the Date Line is usually crossed only by people who travel very far. They may be going from America to Japan, for example.

President Truman of the United States once celebrated the same birthday twice in this way. He crossed the Date Line from west to east on the night of his birthday. So, he gained a day. The date changed to the night of the day before his birthday. The next day, east of the Date Line, was his birthday again.

Some countries use 'daylight saving time'. This means that each time-zone uses the time of the zone just to its east. Its clocks are set forward one hour. So, if the Sun sets at 7:00 pm standard time, it would set at 8:00 pm in daylight saving time. Such a system is used in the summer season. Then, the Sun rises earlier, when many people are still in bed. The total number of daylight hours is still the same, but by advancing their clocks, people will get up earlier and have more daylight time to use.

topology

Suppose that you invite a friend to your house and he has never been there before. You might draw a rough street map, to help him find your house. Your map would look different from an accurate map of the same streets. Distances and directions would be wrong. But your map could be exactly right in important details. It would show that you had to take, say, the third turning on the left, then the second on the right. It would show where there was a street connecting two places, but no street connecting two other places. Thus your map would be a squeezed and stretched version of a truly accurate map.

There is a branch of mathematics that deals with squeezing and stretching. It can study their effects on diagrams and solid objects. It is called topology. To the topologist, your rough map is 'equivalent' to a truly accurate map, because your map does show the correct connections between places. A 'tube' map shows a traveller which routes connect which places. But, it shows all routes as straight lines and does not give correct distances.

Solid figures can be squeezed and stretched too. There are spheres, such as tennis balls or footballs. By squeezing and stretching a sphere, it can be changed into an egg-shape, say, or a cube like a sugar lump. To a topologist, these are all the same kind of shape as a sphere. They are 'equivalent' to a sphere.

An example of a shape that is certainly not equivalent to a sphere is a doughnut. You cannot turn a sphere into a doughnut unless you punch a hole in the sphere. This is because the doughnut is shaped like a ring. It has a hole through the middle.

A jar, or a cup without a handle, is equivalent to a sphere. But, if you imagine a handle added, the shape is equivalent to a doughnut shape.

If you draw a joined-up line, such as a circle, on a sphere, you divide the surface of the sphere into two areas. These are the inside and outside of the closed curve that you draw. If you wanted to join a point inside the closed curve to a point outside it, you would have to cross the curve itself. You may think that any closed curve divides a surface into an outside and an inside area. But this is not true for a doughnut shape. Some closed loops do divide the surface of a doughnut into two regions. But you can draw some loops that do not. Imagine a line drawn right around the outside surface of the doughnut. Now take two points, one on each side of the line. You can join those points by a second line without crossing the first line. This is done if you just go through the hole in the middle of the doughnut. The loop does not really divide the doughnut's surface into an outside and an inside area.

A closed curve also divides a flat surface, such as a piece of paper, into two regions – an outside and an inside. For very complicated curves, it may be difficult to tell at first whether a certain point is inside the curve or outside. But, as the diagram shows, there is an easy way to find out. Join the point by a line to another point that is definitely seen to be outside the curve. If the line crosses the curve an even number of times, like 2 or 4 or 6, the first point is outside the curve. If the line crosses the curve an odd number of times, the point is inside the curve.

Map-makers try to show the surface of the Earth on flat paper. But the surface of a sphere and a flat surface are not topologically equivalent. No amount of stretching and of squeezing will turn a sphere into a flat surface. Maps therefore always distort the areas they show. For instance, many maps do not show the North and South Poles. And others show the world as a disc whose outside edge may represent the South Pole.

Many problems can be solved only by topology. Draw three squares on a piece of paper, in any position you like. These represent houses. Now draw circles, representing the offices of the water, electricity, and telephone companies. Each office must be connected to each house by a line. (But the offices are not connected to each other.) Can you draw the lines so that none of them cross?

However hard you try not to, you will have

to make two of the lines cross. This is a topo-logical problem because, on different kinds of surface, the results are different. For example, if the houses and the company offices are drawn on the surface of a doughnut shape, the problem can be solved.

One problem in topology is called the four-colour problem. Imagine that you want to colour a map so that every country has a different colour from its neighbours. Two countries can have the same colour provided they are not next door to each other. You will never need more than four colours in order to shade a map in this way. This was proved in 1976 by a computer program that looked at a large number of possible maps, taking 120 hours of computer time. See: *geometry, mathematics*.

trigonometry

Trigonometry is the study of triangles. It is a branch of the science of mathematics. Its name comes from the Greek words meaning 'measurement of triangles'. It makes use of the angles and sides of triangles, and the relationships between them.

How can you measure the width of a river without crossing it? Or how can you find the height of a tall building without climbing to its top? Trigonometry helps in solving such problems. Navigators on ships and aircraft also use trigonometry to calculate their routes.

Thus, trigonometry allows us to find out distances when we are unable to measure them directly with rulers or tapes. This is done by using known distances and angles to find unknown distances. The unknown distances can be calculated by drawing triangles.

For example, suppose you want to know the height of a tall building. You could climb up to the top and hang a tape from the roof. But this might be difficult and dangerous. Instead, you notice that the building casts a shadow on the ground. The length of its shadow can be measured easily. The angle at which the Sun's rays hit the ground at the edge of the shadow can also be measured, by using a special instrument such as a sextant, which is used in navigation.

The side of the building, and the length of the shadow, make two sides of a triangle. They are the sides BC and AB in the diagram of the triangle ABC which is illustrated. The third side AC is the imaginary line of a ray of sunlight. This comes over the top of the building and hits the ground at the end of the shadow. The triangle also has three angles. One angle, at point A, is the angle at which the Sun's rays hit the ground.

Suppose that you have measured the length of the shadow and found that it is 7·5 metres (25 feet). You have also found out that the angle of the Sun's rays is 60°. With this information, you can draw the triangle ABC that is formed. It is not necessary to draw a triangle with a side that is 7·5 metres long. You can make a scale drawing. You could let one centimetre represent a metre for example. Then you would get a triangle that is exactly the same shape as the real triangle, but smaller. Next, you measure the length BC, which represents the height of the building. Using your scale, you change this measurement of centimetres to metres. Thus you find the height of the building in metres. Your result should be about 13 metres (43 1/3 feet).

This method of finding out lengths is not very practical. Scale drawings take a long time to do accurately. Instead, you can use trigonometry to find the height of the building from the same information.

There is a special relationship between the height of the building, the length of the shadow, and the angle of the Sun's rays. This relationship is called the 'tangent' of the angle. The tangent of the angle equals the height of the building divided by the length of the shadow. In the triangle ABC, it is the side BC divided by the side AB.

This relationship can also be stated in the following way. The building's height equals the length of the shadow multiplied by the tangent of the angle. You know that the length of the shadow is 7·5 metres. What is the tangent of the angle of 60°? It is 1.732. This value can be found in a list of tangents of various angles. Such a list is called a mathematical table, and it is in many books of mathematics and science. A short table of this kind is illustrated with the triangle labelled PQR.

Now, you need only to multiply 7·5 metres by 1·732 to find the height of the building. The result is 13 metres. This answer is very accurate, and requires no scale drawing.

Besides the tangent, there are other useful relationships between the sides and angles of triangles. Among these are the 'sine' and 'cosine'. To see what they mean, suppose that we want to find the length of side AC in the triangle ABC. This side is part of the line of the ray of sunlight.

The length of the shadow (side AB) divided by the length of the ray (side AC) equals the 'cosine' of the angle of 60° in triangle ABC. The ray's length equals the length of the shadow divided by the angle's cosine. We can find the cosine of 60° listed in a mathematical table. It is $\frac{1}{2}$, or 0.500. By dividing this into the measured shadow length of 7·5 metres we find that the length of the ray AC is exactly 15 metres (50 feet).

Suppose we want to find the height of the

building by using the length of the ray. The 'sine' of the angle of 60° is equal to the building's height (side BC) divided by the ray's length (side AC). The height equals the length of the ray multiplied by the sine of the angle. We can look up the sine of 60° in a mathematical table; it is 0.866. Multiplying this by the length of the ray, which was just found to be 15 metres we get 13 metres. The same answer for the building's height was found using the tangent of the angle of 60°.

A similar problem would be to calculate the height of a wall and the length of a ladder leaning against the wall, by measuring the angle of leaning and the distance from the wall to the bottom of the ladder.

These relationships are the most important ones used in trigonometry. The sine, cosine, and tangent are usually called sin, cos, and tan for short. They relate the three sides of a triangle to each other, using one angle of the triangle. Such a triangle must be a 'right' triangle. This means that one of its angles is a right angle of 90°. In the right triangle ABC, the angle of 90° is between the building and the ground. With other kinds of triangle, more complicated relationships are used.

The three basic relationships are shown in the illustration of triangle DEF. This has a particular angle which is marked X. The size of X may be anything between 0° and 90°. The side opposite the angle X is called the opposite side. The side opposite the right angle is called the hypotenuse. The third side, which is one side of the angle X, is called the adjacent side. These names are used to state the definitions of the sine, cosine, and tangent of the angle X.

The sine of angle X is found by dividing the length of the opposite side by the length of the hypotenuse. The cosine of X is found by dividing the length of the adjacent side by the length of the hypotenuse. The tangent of X is found by dividing the length of the opposite side by the length of the adjacent side.

The sine, cosine, and tangent depend only on the size of the angle X. They do not depend on the size of the whole triangle. They are the same for any two triangles, if both of the triangles have the same size angle X. You can see this in the illustration of the two triangles each having an angle of 35°. One triangle has sides measured in kilometres on a map. The other triangle has sides that may be measured in centimetres on a sheet of paper. Yet the sine, cosine, and tangent of 35° are found to be the same in both triangles.

Any sine, cosine, or tangent is a 'ratio' of two lengths. It is one length divided by the other length. Thus, it is not counted in units, such as feet. It is simply a number. The number changes as the angle changes in size. As X changes length. Thus, it is not counted in units, such as

centimetres. It is simply a number. This changes gradually from 1 to 0. But the tangent of X changes gradually from 0 to 'infinity' — a number so large that it cannot even be calculated. In the illustration of triangle PQR, you can see how the sine, cosine, and tangent change as the size of the angle X increases.

Values of the sine, cosine, and tangent for many different angles can be found in mathematical tables. Such tables list the values for angles only between 0° and 90°. But the sine, cosine, and tangent also have values for angles greater than 90°. Angles up to almost 180° exist in some triangles. Other kinds of figure may have angles up to 360°, which is a full circle.

The sine, cosine, and tangent values for angles greater than 90° are defined in a more complicated way than for angles less than 90°. These values can be calculated by knowing the values for angles less than 90°.

See: *astronomy*, *geometry*, *mathematics*, *navigation*.

universe

How far can you see without the help of a device such as a telescope? You can see the Moon, for instance, which is about 400,000 kilometres away. When you are looking at a star, you are seeing something that is millions of kilometres from Earth.

Beyond the constellation (group of stars) called Triangulum, there is a faint patch of light. This light comes from the most distant thing that can be seen with only our eyes. This is a spiral galaxy — a system of gas, dust, and millions of stars. It looks like a fiery wheel, when seen through a large telescope. It is over 20 million, million, million kilometres away.

Fainter and more distant galaxies become visible through a telescope. Objects even farther away can be photographed by fitting a camera. Their light is directed by a large telescope onto the camera film for many hours. Thus we get pictures of galaxies that are thousands of times more distant than the galaxy in Triangulum.

To describe such great distances in space, we use the time that light takes to travel. Light travels very fast – at over 300,000 kilometres per second. In a year it travels about 9·5 million million kilometres. This distance is a 'light-year'. The galaxy in Triangulum is over two million light-years away. The Pole Star is nearly eight hundred light-years away. The closest star is over four light-years away.

When we look at these faraway objects, we are not only looking across space. We are also looking back into time. Light takes almost eight hundred years to reach us from the Pole Star. We are seeing the Pole Star as it was eight centuries ago. Many millions of years are needed for light to reach us from very distant galaxies. Their light began its journey before our planet Earth was formed. (See: *light*.)

How far back in time can we look? Did the 'universe' (meaning 'everything there is') have a beginning, which we cannot see beyond? Or, has it existed forever? How long will it exist in the future? These questions about time are related to questions about space. How big is the universe? Does it have an edge that we may see through a powerful telescope someday? Or, does it go on and on with no limit?

The universe includes the largest things that we know of – the galaxies. It includes the smallest things – the tiny particles that make up atoms of matter.

The ancient Greek word for the universe was 'cosmos'. Scientists who study problems such as the size and age of the universe are now called cosmologists. The study of the universe is part of the science of physics, which deals with both matter and energy (see: *energy*). Astronomers and other scientists contribute much to this study as well.

An expanding universe

Our Earth belongs to a galaxy known as the Milky Way, named after its milky appearance in the sky. There are countless other galaxies in the universe. Galaxies are not standing still in space. Their distances from each other are continually changing. They are said to be moving through space. In general, the change is an increase in distance. Thus, other galaxies seem to be rushing away from us. They are getting ever farther away. We say that the universe is expanding.

We can tell this from the light that the galaxies send out. Light consists of tiny waves. The light waves from a galaxy are 'stretched' by its movement away from us. The waves are longer than they would be if the galaxy were not moving away. The colour of the light is different too. This is because the colour and wavelength of light are related.

Such a change in wavelength is called a 'Doppler shift'. It can be measured exactly by studying the light from galaxies. The larger the shift is, the faster the galaxies are moving away from us. Their speeds can therefore be found.

We find that the farther away a galaxy is, the faster it is moving. A galaxy 10 million light-years away is moving away from us at over 160 kilometres (100 miles) per second. A galaxy 500 million light-years away is moving at 8,880 kilometres (5,500 miles) per second.

This does not mean that our own galaxy is not moving. It is not in a special position such as the centre of the universe. If you were in another galaxy, you would see our galaxy rushing away from you. All the other galaxies would seem to be moving away from you as well. At any position in the universe, you seem to be at the centre of the expansion.

The big bang

The galaxies are rushing ever further apart. Thus they must once have been much closer together than they are now. There may have been a time when they were all together in one place. According to this theory, their matter was thrown outward in a huge explosion. The galaxies were formed from this expanding matter. Since then, the galaxies that have been moving fastest have moved farthest. The slowest-moving galaxies have moved the least distance.

Most astronomers now accept this idea of the beginning of the universe. It is called the Big Bang theory. When did the explosion happen? The time is easily found from the present distances and speeds of the galaxies. Apparently the Big Bang occurred about 16 thousand million years ago.

Galaxies are grouped into 'clusters'. The clusters are held together by the attraction of gravity between galaxies. Our galaxy is in a small cluster with 20 members. Some clusters have thousands of galaxies.

It is the clusters that are moving apart, not individual galaxies. The clusters are now so far apart that their gravitational pull on each other is very small. There is not enough backward pull to slow them down as they move apart. Thus, the universe may go on expanding forever.

There is also much matter in space between the clusters. Most of it consists of dead galaxies, or of gas that has never collected into galaxies. If there is enough of it, this matter might have enough pull of gravity to slow down the existing galaxies. In that case, the universe could eventually stop expanding, thousands of millions of years from now.

Then, the universe would begin to contract. The galaxies would move toward each other. They would fall inward and finally collide. All their matter would be crushed together in a gas hot enough to smash atoms. This would be the reverse of the Big Bang.

A cyclic universe?

Such a contraction would have to stop at some point. Another huge explosion would occur. The universe would start expanding again. So, we may be in a 'cyclic' universe, whose matter has been expanding and contracting in turn throughout time.

The idea of a Big Bang is not the only theory of the universe. Another has been suggested, called the Steady State theory. According to

vacuum

this idea, there was never any beginning of the universe, such as a huge explosion. The universe has always been as it is now, and always will be.

This theory tells us that new galaxies are continually being formed. They appear in the space between older galaxies. Old galaxies are constantly moving apart. So the number of galaxies in each part of the universe should always be about the same.

The new galaxies are thought to be formed from hydrogen gas. This gas is created in the space between the galaxies. Its atoms simply appear from nowhere. Such continuous creation of matter is not easily explained by the Steady State theory. Neither is the fact that the galaxies begin to move apart after they have formed.

If this theory were true, we would expect all parts of the universe to look the same. A part that is ten thousand million light-years away was created over ten thousand million years ago. And it should be similar to another nearer part that was created a shorter time ago.

The different parts of the universe do not seem to be so similar. There seem to be more galaxies in distant parts than in nearer parts. And the faraway galaxies are closer together than nearby ones. This is what the Big Bang theory would lead us to expect. For, in that theory, galaxies were closer together in the distant past.

There is another difference between near and distant galaxies. The distant ones seem to be slowing down in their expansion away from us. This fact cannot be explained by the Steady State theory, in which the universe should always expand at the same rate. For these reasons, most astronomers now believe that the Steady State theory is wrong.

The future of the universe
What will the universe be like, millions of years from now? According to the Steady State theory, it would look just as it does today. New galaxies would simply have replaced the old ones whose stars had stopped shining.

If this theory is wrong, then we may be living in a cyclic universe. The universe would still have an endless life ahead of it. After each Big Bang, stars and galaxies, and probably life, would reappear.

Instead, we may be living in an ever-expanding universe. There may not be anything to replace the galaxies whose stars stop burning. Eventually, the whole universe would be dark, with no light at all.

Such possibilities are not important for our lives. But they are of great interest to cosmologists, astronomers, and physicists.

Scientists also study the shape of the universe. But we do not have enough information about the whole universe to decide this yet.

All the things around us are made of matter. They may be solid, like a book. Or they can be liquid, like water. Or, they may be gaseous, like air. Every piece of matter occupies some space, or volume, that can be measured. But, is every space occupied by matter? Suppose that the matter in a space could be completely removed from it. Then, the space would be a perfect 'vacuum'. A vacuum is a space containing little or no matter.

A perfect vacuum with no matter has never been made by man. A partial vacuum with very little matter can be created. Partial vacuums are used in science and technology. They also exist in nature.

The effects of vacuums make them useful. For example, what happens when you drink lemonade through a straw? You suck air out of the straw with your mouth. This forms a partial vacuum at the top of the straw. Then, the vacuum seems to suck the lemonade up the straw and into your mouth.

Actually the lemonade is being pushed up the straw. The push is given by air outside the straw. This air presses down on the surface of the lemonade. This is because the air is made of tiny moving particles, which are continually hitting the surface. So the lemonade is pushed into the straw and upward. The vacuum at the top of the straw contains fewer particles of air. Their downward push is not great enough to keep the lemonade from rising in the straw.

A vacuum cleaner works similarly. It has a fan that produces a partial vacuum. This is done by blowing air out of a space inside the cleaner. Then air from outside pushes into the partial vacuum in the cleaner. Dust and dirt are pulled in with the air.

A perfect vacuum would be too difficult to create. It is easy enough to remove all the solid objects, like books, from a space. It is almost as easy to take away the liquids, like water. But the difficulty is caused by gases, like air. Gases, and all other forms of matter are made of tiny particles called molecules. Yet gas particles are the hardest to control. (See: *atom*.)

The molecules of a gas are too small to be seen or held. They move fast. They do not stick together in big pieces. Thus, they are hard to remove from a space. Any space made by man must be enclosed in a container, such as a box or a bottle. The container may leak, so that particles can get in from outside. This prevents a vacuum from being perfect.

Some vacuums in nature are better than any made by man. An example is outer space. It is almost a perfect vacuum. The best man-made vacuums have millions of times more matter than exists in outer space.

To create a good partial vacuum, care is

needed. The box, bottle, or other container must be sealed tightly. Then it will leak as little as possible. Equipment is used to get as much matter as possible out of the container. This is called 'evacuating' it.

To produce good vacuums, a vacuum pump is used (see: *pump*). A simple vacuum pump takes air or other gases out of a container. It may be a machine attached to the container. The gas particles enter the machine. Then they are pushed out into the atmosphere. Other kinds of vacuum pump are used too.

How is a vacuum measured? The 'pressure' of the moving gas particles in it is found. This is the force on each square centimetre of the container's walls. The particles cause the force by hitting the walls as they move about. The fewer the particles, the smaller their pressure is. (See: *pressure*.)

Pressure is very low in a good partial vacuum. It is less than one thousand millionth of the atmosphere's pressure at sea level. But it is still millions of times greater than the pressure in outer space. A perfect vacuum would have no pressure at all.

Good vacuums are needed in valves. These are still used in radio and television equipment. In a valve, a stream of particles, called electrons, moves through a space. This stream helps, for example, to make a radio or TV signal stronger after it is received by your radio or TV set. But the stream would be disturbed if the electrons hit other matter such as air in the tube. The space in the valve must be evacuated.

The first man-made vacuum was created by Evangelista Torricelli of Italy, over 300 years ago. He used the method shown in the illustration. A long glass tube is filled with mercury, a heavy liquid metal. Then it is placed upside down in a bowl containing mercury. Some mercury falls out of the tube into the bowl, but most of it remains in the tube. Thus, an empty space is created above the mercury at the top of the tube.

This space is a vacuum. It cannot contain air, since the tube was filled with mercury. The vacuum has only some mercury particles, with almost no pressure to push down on the mercury in the tube. But the outside air is pressing on the mercury in the bowl. The pressure of the atmosphere supports a column of mercury in the tube. The height of this column is normally about 76 centimetres (30 inches). It changes with the atmosphere's 'barometric' pressure, which it can thus measure.

Today, the physicist often uses vacuums in his experiments. Vacuums are also needed to make many products in industry. Salt can be removed from sea water by a vacuum freeze process to provide fresh water for countries, like Israel, where it is in short supply. You can create vacuums yourself with the simple equipment illustrated on this page.

valence

The matter around us is made of tiny atoms. These particles join together to form bigger ones called molecules. They do this in definite ways. For example, one atom of the element chlorine can combine with one atom of the element hydrogen to form hydrochloric acid, but never with two or three.

The way in which a particular atom joins with a definite number of other atoms is described by a number called its valence. If an element combines with hydrogen, its valence is given by the number of hydrogen atoms with which each atom of the element combines. For example, the valence of chlorine is one, because it combines with one atom of hydrogen.

The valence of any atom can be found easily if it combines with something whose valence is already known. Sodium combines with chlorine. We know chlorine combines with one atom of hydrogen and has a valence of one. Sodium, then, must also have a valence of one.

Valences depend on the structures of atoms. An atom contains tiny 'electron' particles. It can usually lose or gain electrons too. Then it becomes an 'ion' (see: *ion*). This can combine with other ions to form molecules.

The number of electrons lost by an atom is called a positive valence. If a number is gained, instead, this is a negative valence. In the formation of hydrochloric acid, the atom of hydrogen loses one electron, and the atom of chlorine gains that electron. Thus, the valence is $+1$ for hydrogen and -1 for chlorine.

The valence of sodium is $+1$ too. An atom of this element combines with one hydrogen atom. Thus, a molecule of sodium hydride is formed. The sodium atom loses an electron, and the hydrogen atom gains one. Then the valence of hydrogen is -1.

Since the valence is $+1$ for sodium and -1 for chlorine, these elements may be able to combine with each other. The chlorine atom should gain an electron from the sodium atom. This actually happens. A molecule of sodium chloride, or common table salt, is formed.

The valence is larger than one for many kinds of atom. For an oxygen atom, it is -2. This kind combines with two hydrogen atoms. Then, a molecule of water is formed.

Some atoms have more than one valence, such as $+1$ or -1 for hydrogen. A copper atom may have a valence of $+1$ or $+2$. It combines with one or two chlorine atoms, to form cuprous chloride or cupric chloride.

Some kinds of atom have a valence of zero. These atoms cannot lose or gain any electrons. They do not combine with any other atoms. They belong to substances called inert gases. An example is helium (see: *gas*).

A different type of combination of atoms is known as 'covalent'. Here the atoms do not lose or gain electrons. They share each other's electrons. A hydrogen molecule contains two hydrogen atoms. Each atom shares one of its electrons with the other atom. Larger molecules may contain many different kinds of atom in such a combination.

See: *atom, chemistry, electricity.*

volcano

In February 1943, the people of the Mexican village of Paricutin saw a volcano erupting right out of their cornfields. It began as a crack in the ground. Gases and hot ash soon billowed out from the crack. Then rocks were thrown out high into the air. Some of the rocks were red-hot and set fire to nearby trees and crops. By the next morning a cone 9 metres (30 feet) high had been built around the crack, and the explosions were heard 320 kilometres (200 miles) away. At the end of 1943, the volcano of Paricutin stood over 300 metres (1,000 feet) above the cornfields, and its rock outflow had buried two towns.

Volcanoes have always been a source of wonder to man. Their name comes from Vulcano, one of the Lipari Islands near Sicily. This was thought to be the home of Vulcan, the ancient Roman god of fire, because it spewed out smoke-like vapour. Much earlier, in about 6000BC, a painting was made of a volcano, on the wall of a house at Catal Huyuk in Turkey. And many archeologists believe that the volcano of Thera or 'Santorin' in Greece destroyed the great Minoan civilization there in 1500BC.

Today, volcanoes are still fascinating. Scientists called vulcanologists study them to learn about the inside of the Earth. This is possible because the products of a volcano come from deep inside the Earth.

A volcano is an opening where gas and rock are thrown out of the Earth onto its surface. Usually the rock is 'molten' or melted. Such rock is called 'magma' by scientists. Magma contains gases that are mixed or 'dissolved' in it (see: *solutions and solvents*).

To explain the origin of volcanoes, it was once supposed that the whole inside of the Earth was a seething mass of molten rock and hot gases. These could escape through weak parts in the Earth's outer crust, which acted as safety valves. This became known as the 'central fire theory'.

But later it was proved that the material thrown out by a volcano comes from within only 32 kilometres (20 miles) or so of the Earth's surface. And it is now known that most of the Earth is solid rock. Only part of the central core of the Earth is liquid. Magma seems to come from the thick, normally solid layer between the crust and the central core.

Then how does the rock become molten, and what force brings it to the Earth's surface? This can be answered more clearly by finding out what volcanoes are made of, and where in the world they occur. They occur in 'belts', as shown in the map.

Volcanic rock

A volcano usually looks like a mountain with the shape of a cone. But we can tell the difference between ordinary mountains and volcanoes by their different kinds of rock. The most important volcanic rock is 'lava'. Lava is magma that has reached the surface but has lost most of its dissolved gases. The gases bubble out of the lava and escape as it cools into solid rock on the surface.

Magma and lava usually contain crystals of minerals in some form. While the lava is very hot, the crystals remain completely dissolved. But they separate from the lava as it cools. If it cools slowly, the crystals may grow up to 2·5 centimetres (1 inch) long. Yet if it cools quickly, the crystals have no time to grow, and the lava cools into a glass-like solid.

This volcanic glass is of two important kinds. One, called pumice, is formed when the lava becomes solid while the bubbles of gas are escaping. Then the bubbles leave holes in the solid lava. Pumice often looks like a grey rock, but is not heavy and can float on water because of air trapped in the holes. Pumice is widely used as an 'abrasive' for grinding things. The other kind, called obsidian, is formed when the lava becomes solid more rapidly, and some gas is left inside it. Obsidian may look like black glass, and is very sharp and shiny. It has been used for thousands of years to make knives and jewellery.

The smallest particles in lava are called volcanic ash. Ash is thrown high into the air by an eruption, and may be carried far away by the winds. Sometimes the particles spread all around the world, and can cause beautiful sunsets by reflecting sunlight, before they finally fall back to Earth.

Usually a volcano has the shape of a cone. The cone is built around a central hole, or vent, from which the lava flows out. Some kinds of lava cool very slowly and continue to flow over large areas before turning into solid rock. When this happens, the cone is not formed. Instead a plateau, or a lake of lava, is formed. This may be thousands of metres deep and many kilometres wide.

There are several thousand volcanoes on the Earth's surface. Only one quarter of these are active today. A volcano that has not erupted since ancient times is called extinct, and it is not expected to erupt again. But new volcanoes are being built up, often on the ocean floor. Over 50 volcanoes have recently been discovered under the sea.

The most famous eruption in history was probably that of Mount Vesuvius in Italy. This was thought to be an extinct volcano. But it erupted violently in 79AD. Nearby Roman towns such as Pompeii were buried so deep with ash and rocks that they were not rediscovered for over 1,500 years.

Another huge eruption was that of Krakatoa, a volcanic island in Indonesia, in Southeast Asia. This occurred in August of 1883. The explosion of Krakatoa was heard thousands of kilometres away. It disturbed the ocean around the island, and created a great 'tidal wave' which drowned 36,000 people on nearby coasts. Later, scientists came to study the effects of the eruption. (See: *wave*.)

On the map of volcanic activity, you can see where the Earth's active volcanoes are located. They are concentrated into three 'belts'. One belt circles the Pacific Ocean, and is called the ring of fire. Another belt runs from east to west through Indonesia and the Mediterranean Sea. And the third runs from north to south through the Atlantic Ocean.

Mountains of the future

In these belts, the rocks of the Earth's crust have been lifted up and crushed to form mountains, in regions such as Italy, Indonesia, and Central America. Such belts of earth movement will become the mountain ranges of the future – as the Himalayas and the Alps are at present.

When these earth movements occur, they make breaks in the Earth's crust. This is one reason why volcanoes occur along the same belts. But another reason must be some extra heating in the upper 40 or so kilometres of the crust. For the rocks must become molten to reach the surface through these breaks.

This extra heat could be supplied by a lot of 'radioactive' minerals under the ground. The particles of such minerals break apart and produce much heat (see: *radioactivity*). Gases that are trapped in the rock can also mix together and create heat.

But most of the heat is probably caused by friction. The Earth's crust is made up of many 'plates'. These move very slowly, yet rub against each other with great force. This friction is believed by vulcanologists to produce enough heat to form volcanoes.

The friction within the Earth raises the temperature sufficiently to melt the rock. The molten rock expands and rises from below. It does this by moving along a crack, or by melting the rocks through which it passes.

The main gas in lava is steam. This may be formed by the boiling of water that has seeped down from the surface through cracks in the crust. Steam is also formed when hydrogen gas combines chemically with oxygen gas inside the Earth.

The steam is dissolved in the magma just as carbon dioxide gas is dissolved in a bottle of lemonade. As the magma rises to the surface, pressure is decreased, and the steam is released. Similarly, when you open a bottle of lemonade, the pressure inside the bottle is reduced, and the gas bubbles out of the liquid. And if the pressure is reduced suddenly, the gas will rush out rapidly, causing a volcanic explosion.

When a volcano erupts, more energy is produced than from any nuclear bomb. The energy is mostly heat. Since man is using up energy from other sources in the world, scientists are trying to harness the energy given out by volcanoes. But they have not yet had much success. (See: *energy*.)

Volcanic steam was first used to generate electric power at Larderello in northern Italy. This has been done more recently in Iceland, in New Zealand, and at the geysers located in California. A geyser is a spring where boiling water and steam shoot high into the air at regular intervals.

Most scientists think that volcanoes will be important to man in the future. But the main contribution that volcanoes make now to human life is in agriculture. Nearly all volcanic regions are very fertile. Volcanic ash contains minerals that plants need.

To have a complete understanding of the life of a volcano, from its first eruption to its extinction, vulcanologists must study volcanoes continuously. They investigate the changing chemical and mineral composition of the rocks and gases. Such research may allow scientists to predict volcanic eruptions
See: *gas, geology*.

wave

You may have seen ocean waves at the seashore. They reach the shore one by one, all day and night long. There they may 'break' on the sand or rocks, throwing water high into the air. They have travelled to the shore from far away over the sea. And often they carry seaweed or driftwood onto the shore.

Such waves travel on the surface of the water. They are caused by a disturbance of the water. This is usually produced by the winds that blow across the sea's surface. The waves also disturb the water as they travel. They make each part of the surface move up and down as they pass it.

The highest part of a wave is called the crest. The lowest part of a wave is known as the trough. The crest and trough of the wave travel together, one after the other. And they are followed by the crest and trough of another wave. Waves do not carry water along with them. They move across the surface.

Water is the material, or medium, through which such waves travel. It consists of tiny particles called molecules (see: *atom*). Each particle of the water's surface is disturbed by a passing wave. As the crest goes by, the particle rises. It also moves forward a little way in the direction of the wave's travel. As the trough goes by, the particle falls. Then it moves backward in the direction that is opposite to the wave's direction of travel. Thus it stays in about the same place, while the wave travels onward to other particles.

Waves of the most simple kind are equally spaced. The same space, or distance, exists between each wave and the next. This can be measured from the crest of one wave to the crest of the next. Or it can be measured between the troughs of the two waves. It is called the wavelength of the waves.

Waves have a certain 'frequency' too. In each second of time, a definite number of waves travel past a place on the surface of the water. The number might be two waves per second. Or five, or more, waves per second might pass that place. This number is the frequency.

Frequency is measured in cycles per second, or 'hertz'. A cycle is one complete wave, with one crest and one trough.

Waves travel at a particular speed. This speed may be measured in metres per second, or kilometres per hour. The speed always equals the frequency multiplied by the wavelength.

Waves can be made on the surface of liquids other than water. They travel more slowly on a liquid such as oil. The speed of waves always depends on the medium that they are travelling through. For surface waves, the speed also depends on how deep the liquid is.

Waves can bounce off an object. This is called reflection. You can see it by making waves on water in a swimming pool. The waves approach one side of the pool. They hit the side and are reflected. The reflected waves are seen going away from the side. And these waves make a definite angle with the side of the pool.

Waves can also be 'refracted'. That is, they change their direction of travel without hitting any object. This happens to ocean waves when the depth of the water changes. Suppose that the waves approach a shore at an angle. They go from deeper into shallower water. Their direction of travel changes so that they travel more directly toward the shore. The path of the waves bends. The amount of bending can be described by a law of refraction.

Waves on the surface of a liquid travel horizontally. But they make the tiny particles of the liquid move up and down, or vertically. So they are an example of 'transverse' waves. This means that the particles do not travel in the same direction as the waves. They travel at right angles to that direction.

There is another kind of wave called a 'longitudinal' wave. Longitudinal waves can exist deep inside a liquid. Such a wave makes the particles move back and forth in the same direction that the wave travels.

Both transverse and longitudinal waves can exist inside a solid material as well. This may be a metal object. If the object is suddenly hit or twisted, it vibrates. The vibrations are waves that go through it and along its surface.

Sound waves are the most important example of longitudinal waves. They can travel in a gas like air. They are caused by a vibrating object that disturbs the air. Then the waves travel away from the object to reach our ears. They make our eardrums vibrate, and we hear.

Electromagnetic waves are an important example of transverse waves. Light, radio signals, and X-rays such as those that a doctor uses, are all electromagnetic waves. They can travel even through empty space.

xerography

Run a plastic comb through your hair several times, and then hold the comb near some small pieces of paper. The pieces will jump onto the comb and stick there. The force making the pieces of paper stick to the comb is called an electrostatic force.

Effects like this have been observed by man for thousands of years. But today the force is put to use in a process of copying, known as xerography.

Most methods of copying bills, letters, and other documents, use wet chemicals. But the xerography process is a dry one. Its name comes from the Greek word *xeros*, which means 'dry'. Xerography is faster than most other methods. So xerographic machines are used mainly in offices, where copying must be done quickly and accurately.

Anyone can use a xerographic machine, for the process is now automatic. All you do is slide the document you want to copy into the machine and press a button. In about one second you have a fresh copy. Any number of copies can be made from the same document.

Inside a xerographic machine is a surface coated with a semi-conductive material. This material conducts electricity in the light, but acts as an insulator in the dark.

The surface is covered with electrostatic charges in the dark. Then a strong light is made to shine on the document that you want to copy. The light bounces off the document and onto the semi-conductive surface. This makes a reflection of the document on the surface.

Where the light touches the surface, the electrostatic charge disappears. But charge remains on the dark parts of the surface. The dark parts are like shadows, made by the solid lines or the printing on the document.

Next, a black powder is sprinkled onto the surface. The powder sticks only to the dark parts, where the electrostatic charge remains, just as the bits of paper stick to your comb. So the powder makes a 'reverse image' of the document on the semi-conductive surface.

A clean sheet of ordinary paper is now laid on the surface. Another electric charge is applied to the back of the paper. Thus the powder is attracted from the surface and sticks to the paper. Since the image on the surface was reversed, the copy on the paper comes out the right way around.

Finally the paper is heated, and the powder melts and sticks permanently to the paper.

In early xerographic machines, the surface with semi-conductive material was a flat plate. But modern machines use a revolving drum. It turns past fixed electrodes, which supply the electric charge. This is faster than moving the electrodes across a flat surface.

Xerography was invented by Chester Carlson of the United States in the 1930s. Today it is used widely in business of all kinds.
See: *electricity*.

X-ray

X-rays are like beams of light. They are able to pass through many substances, just as light can go through a glass window. But X-rays can pass through materials that normally stop light. They are used in science, industry and medicine.

A doctor often uses X-rays. He takes an X-ray photograph of the inside of a person's body. The person may have a broken bone in an arm or leg. This limb is placed in front of a machine that produces X-rays. Behind the limb is a piece of photographic film. Then the machine is turned on for just a few seconds. X-rays go straight through the soft parts of the limb, such as skin and flesh. They hit the film and show up as a dark area. But X-rays cannot pass so easily through hard parts such as the bones. These slow down X-rays and make much lighter areas on the film. So by looking at the film, the doctor can see where the bone is broken.

A dentist may take X-ray pictures of your teeth. They show if the teeth have any decayed parts that need to be filled. All but the inside of healthy teeth is solid and can stop X-rays. But when these parts become decayed, the decayed parts are softer and allow the X-rays to pass through and expose the film.

Such a photograph cannot be taken with an ordinary camera. This is because it depends on light, which cannot go through the body. Why do X-rays have so much penetrating power?

Producing X-rays

You have probably thrown a stone into a pond. Water splashes up where the stone hits the pond's surface. And the harder you throw the stone, the higher it makes the water splash. This is because the moving stone has 'kinetic' energy of movement. The faster it moves, the more energy it has. When it hits the water and slows down, it gives some of its energy to the water. Then some water splashes up with kinetic energy of movement. Thus the stone 'does work' by moving the water. The more energy the stone has the more work it can do. (See: *energy*.)

X-rays are produced in a very similar way. But instead of stones, tiny particles called electrons are used. Instead of a surface of water, there is a hard surface of a material such as metal. The metal does not splash, but X-rays are created and shoot away at a great speed. They are created from the energy of the moving electrons that hit the metal surface.

An X-ray machine contains a special tube. This is made of glass and metal. Inside, it is a vacuum – an empty space with almost no air (see: *vacuum*). Air would slow down the beam of electrons that move through the tube. The electrons move between two parts of the tube, called the cathode and anode.

The cathode is a metal filament, a piece of wire. It is heated by passing an electric current through it. Then it gives off many electrons into the space. Electrons are particles with a negative electric charge. They are attracted toward anything which has a positive electric charge. This is provided by the anode, within the X-ray tube. (See: *electricity*.)

The anode is a flat piece of metal. It pulls electrons through the space from the cathode. They speed up as they move toward the anode, and finally hit it. This speed depends on the size of the anode's positive electric charge which is pulling the electrons.

The anode is charged by being connected to a source of electric voltage outside the X-ray tube. This voltage is much higher than the voltage with which you are familiar at home of about 220-240 volts. It ranges from several thousand volts up to a few million volts. It is usually higher than the voltages used in television picture tubes, or in electron microscopes. These devices contain 'electron guns' which also move electrons from a cathode to an anode. (See: *microscope.*

When the electrons hit the surface of the anode, they suddenly slow down. Almost all their kinetic energy of movement is lost. Some of the energy – normally less than one per cent – is changed into X-rays. But the rest of the energy turns into heat. The anode might be heated so much by the electrons hitting it that it would melt. To prevent this, the anode must be cooled by other equipment in the X-ray machine. (See: *heat.*)

The X-rays have greater energy as the voltage in the X-ray tube is increased. With up to about 20,000 volts, they are known as 'soft' X-rays. With higher voltages, they are called 'hard' X-rays, which are the most useful kind. X-rays leave the tube through a thin glass window. The rest of the tube is shielded by a thick covering of lead. This stops other X-rays which are produced in the tube from emerging, and protects the surroundings from them.

The nature of X-rays

Why are X-rays created when the electrons slow down at the anode? The main reason is that the electrons have an electric charge. When any charged particle is speeded up or slows down, it gives out energy as 'radiation'. This radiation is a stream of tiny waves. They are not waves in a material, like the waves of water on a pond. They are called 'electromagnetic' waves. For they consist of electric and magnetic fields. They can travel through materials or empty space. (See the entry for *wave.*)

X-rays are electro magnetic radiation. So are many other kinds of wave. These include radio waves, light waves, and 'gamma' rays. They all travel at the speed of light, which is 300,000 kilometres (186,000 miles) per second. (See: *light, radio.*) But, they have different wavelengths. The wavelength is the distance between the crests, or high points, of two successive waves. Radio wavelengths range from hundreds of metres down to hundredths of a centimetre. Light that we can see has wavelengths of millionths of a centimetre. And X-ray wavelengths are less than a hundredth of visible light wavelengths.

The shorter the wavelength of such waves, the greater their energy is. So X-rays have much more energy than light waves. This is why X-rays can go through materials that stop light waves. But X-rays can be stopped by a piece of a solid material like lead that is thick enough. Then their energy is lost to the material's particles. They are 'absorbed' in the same way that light can be absorbed (see: *absorption of light*).

X-rays can be created by another process too, not only by radiation from electrons slowing down. When the electrons hit the anode, they may 'ionize' some of its atoms. Atoms are the tiny particles that make up the material of the anode. An atom contains even smaller particles, including electrons. If an electron is knocked out of the atom, the atom becomes an ion (see: *atom, ion*). This happens when the electrons moving in the X-ray tube hit the atoms of the anode.

After an electron is lost from an atom, another electron in the atom may move into its place. As this occurs, electromagnetic radiation is given out in the X-ray region of the spectrum.

The amount of X-ray energy created in an X-ray tube depends partly on the anode's material. This is often called the 'target' material. If it is made of light atoms, they will not be able to slow down the moving electrons very much. But heavy atoms can slow down the electrons easily. So the anode is made of heavy metals such as tungsten.

X-rays are useful but they are dangerous too—they can damage and kill the cells of the body. Those who work with them have to take great care to minimise the dose that reaches their bodies.

Doctors also use the harmful properties of X-rays to treat certain forms of cancer.

An X-ray picture is often blurred, since it shows overlapping images of tissues in different layers of the body. This problem is overcome by X-ray scanning. The scanner rotates round the patient's body, firing X-rays. The strength of the X-rays that pass through the body is measured at each step. Many thousands of these measurements are made, and a computer uses them to build up a picture of a slice through the body. The computer adds colour to show the different organs clearly.

ABDOMEN, DISTENDED Enlargement of structures within the abdomen will lead to distention, a bulging contour. By far the most common cause of this is pregnancy. By the end of the third month, the pregnant uterus has grown out of the pelvic cavity and may be felt just above the pelvic bones in the bladder region. By the sixth month, the pregnant uterus has reached the level of the umbilicus; by the ninth month, it is close to the lowermost portion of the breastbone. The only comparable enlargement is that found with certain very large cysts of the ovary. In the course of such abdominal enlargement there may be a stretching and cracking of the connective tissue of the skin resulting in linear markings over the lower abdomen known as striae; these generally appear pink during pregnancy, but afterwards turn white. During a succeeding pregnancy new pink markings dispersed among the older ones may be seen. Neither abdominal supports nor other measures will prevent such markings. The number vary from individual to individual. There are some who never show striae, or in whom they are inconspicuous.

ABDOMINAL PAINS Most of the important abdominal organs have muscles in their walls. Food and wastes are moved along by contractions of these muscles, but ordinarily one is not aware of such muscular activity. However, when inflammation or obstruction is present, severe and painful contractions may occur. These pains generally come and go rhythmically, may mount in intensity and then decrease somewhat, and are often referred to as painful spasms, colic, or griping pains.

Severe colicky pains may be experienced with the movement of gallstones or urinary stones, or when intestinal obstruction is present. The pain of appendicitis often starts as a colicky pain perhaps due to obstruction in the canal within the appendix. Colicky pains felt in the lower abdomen preceding a bowel movement, as in dysentery and diarrhea, generally point to involvement of the large intestine. In certain disorders the pain may also be felt in the back and occasionally may radiate to other parts of the body. Thus the pain of gallbladder disease may be felt not only in the back but also in the right shoulder, and occasionally a kidney stone may produce pain which shoots down to the groin and upper thigh.

Sometimes the pain of inflammation within the abdomen is a steady one. This is true in appendicitis once the initial crampy pains have subsided. The pain then experienced will be a localized pain in the region of the appendix itself. A somewhat similar course of events may occur in inflammation of the gallbladder, the pancreas, the colon, and other organs. Often such pain is accompanied by nausea and sometimes by vomiting. In addition, a few points to remember about abdominal pain are:

1. Never assume that abdominal pain is due to constipation nor take a laxative when you are experiencing pain, unless so directed by a doctor.

2. Most forms of abdominal pain can be helped to some degree by heat, as by a heating pad.

3. Abdominal pain is only a symptom: an explanation for it should be forthcoming. Check it out with the doctor. Thus in pregnancy acute appendicitis may produce atypical abdominal pains felt in a location higher or different from the usual one. Sometimes a blood count or other special tests may be necessary to determine the cause of any particular pain. (See also APPENDICITIS.)

ABORTION An abortion is properly defined as any interruption in a pregnancy prior to the time that the fetus (unborn child) can live independently—that is, about the sixth month.

Spontaneous abortion (often referred to as a miscarriage) may result from any number of conditions, some of which are identifiable, others not. Falls or blows to the abdomen, a severe febrile illness such as influenza or typhoid fever, or operative procedures are sometimes the cause. Very often no cause is found, although careful study sometimes indicates that the embryo was abnormal. Spontaneous abortion is by no means rare; perhaps one in every four or five pregnancies will result in such an abortion. One uncertainty in estimating their number is the fact that abortion early in pregnancy may be difficult to recognize. It is quite likely that some of the delayed periods reported by women represent an early and unrecognized abortion. A small but distressing percentage of women may abort with virtually every pregnancy. They are sometimes referred to as "chronic aborters." In most instances the reasons for this are not understood. Occasionally the pregnancy may be carried to term by bedrest, hormone administration, removal of fibroids, and other measures.

Therapeutic abortion is one performed for a sound medical reason, as for instance psychiatric disease. German measles (in the first three months of pregnancy), active tuberculosis, certain cardiac conditions, and other disturbances. A therapeutic abortion is generally performed in a hospital setting, requires the signature of at least two doctors, and is a safe procedure ordinarily.

Criminal abortion is an illegal operation for terminating pregnancy. It is often performed surreptitiously, and not always in the most sanitary or most skillful fashion. Some risk may therefore be attached to it, despite which it has been estimated that as many as a million such operations are performed per year.

Induced abortion is a general term for an abortion produced by some procedure or drug. In fact, however, most drugs used to stimulate the uterus to evacuate its contents are singularly unsuccessful.

ABSCESS An abscess is any localized collection of pus in the body. An abscess forms as a result of invasion by bacteria or other organisms, with consequent breakdown of tissue. Abscesses are often described in terms of their locations. Thus an *appendiceal abscess* is one occurring within the abdominal cavity in close relation to the appendix, and generally subsequent to a ruptured appendix, i.e., appendicitis.

A *lung abscess* frequently follows an inflammation in the lung caused by certain organisms such as the staphylococcus, or as a result of violent mixed infections that may occur if vomited material is aspirated into the lungs.

Boils and carbuncles are essentially abscesses within the skin. Since they normally come to a "head," thereby instituting drainage (which is desirable in healing), they pose less of a threat than similar kinds of inflammations in the organs.

Breast abscess, a fairly common form of abscess, occurs in the tissue of the breast; this is seen most often in post-

Taken from *Instant Medical Adviser* by Jeanne Smith, M.D. and Isadore Rossman, M.D., © Copyrighted and reprinted by permission of Career Publishing, Inc.

partum women and in nursing mothers. Most of these abscesses are due to an invasion of the breast tissue by skin organisms which either enter via some minute crack in the nipple or work their way down through the breast duct system. A breast abscess manifests itself as a warm tender swelling, sometimes accompanied by chills or fever. It may respond to local compresses and antibiotics by mouth. If it does not, the swelling will continue and may become fluctuant (soft), at which point an incision to produce drainage may be necessary. Once drainage is established, the abscess empties itself and healing generally occurs without incident.

A *pelvic abscess* is one which forms in the pelvic cavity and is often secondary to inflammations of a pelvic organ. Inflammations of the tube and ovary may lead to this, but so also may inflammations of the large intestine. Suppuration of the appendix may also drain off into the pelvic cavity and produce an abscess there.

Abscesses are now a great deal less common than in bygone years. Before the introduction of antibiotics, one of the frequent results of inflammation was abscess formation, and a great deal of surgery was performed to permit drainage of such abscesses. The control of the original inflammation by antibiotics has made resort to surgery far less common. However, a surgical approach is still highly desirable for certain abscesses, since antibiotics penetrate established abscesses very slowly and sometimes not at all. Thus an amoebic abscess, caused by an amoebi invasion and breakdown of tissue, often requires surgical incision. An alveolar abscess, also known as a dental abscess, occurs in the jaw in relation to a tooth. Removal of the tooth will permit drainage; occasionally an attempt is made to spare the tooth if this is at all feasible. (See also BOILS.)

ACCIDENT PREVENTION IN THE HOME
Infancy and childhood are periods of development in which physical abilities outstrip understanding and caution. Inevitably they are periods of accidents—some trivial, some quite serious. Every mother must "set up shop" as a safety engineer, and the best safety engineer is the one who faces all of the possibilities, however unpleasant they may be. Some of the questions that could well be asked are: Can my child get at the aspirin in the medicine chest? (Aspirin is the most common cause of childhood poisoning.) Has my child access to bleaches, furniture polishes, and the like in my kitchen? Are there window guards for every window?

One might well make a cold-eyed tour through the house, looking not at the furniture and decorating but at the potential hazards to the toddler whose mother has lost track of him for a few minutes while busy in the kitchen. Though the chances may be thousands-to-one against certain accidents occurring, one wants to protect the child against even the remote ones.

The following are some of the guidelines which will enable parents to profit by the experiences of others:

1. Never leave a small child unattended in the home.
2. Close all doors leading to basement stairs. Insert gates at the heads of stairs. Put window guards on the windows. All these measures will certainly cut down on serious falls in the younger age groups.
3. Keep medicines in a *locked* medicine chest; if the medicine chest cannot be locked, find some other place for drugs. (A sliding bolt on the bathroom door that can be reached only by the adults may be a useful solution to the bathroom medicine chest threat.)
4. Never take or dispense a medicine in the dark, or without checking the label and the appearance of the medication itself.
5. Make sure that bleaches, polishes, detergents, bowl cleaners, perfumes, and pesticides are inaccessible to young children.
6. Never store cleaning agents, turpentines, paint removers, or other chemicals in soda bottles or milk bottles, nor keep them on food shelves. Since they also represent a fire hazard, buy a small quantity when necessary and throw the unused portions away.
7. Use night lights in some bedrooms and hallways, nonskid backing for scatter rugs, and rubber mats in bathtubs or shower stalls; these will prevent falls in all age groups.
8. Obtain a small fire extinguisher, and a supply of universal antidote for possible poisonings; these items are more useful pieces of equipment than many kitchen gadgets. (See also POISONS.)

ACQUIRED IMMUNE DEFICIENCY SYNDROME (AIDS)
AIDS results from infection by HTLV-III virus that is associated with debilitating, and often fatal diseases. A great deal of fear and anxiety results from misinformation or lack of information. Many thousands of cases of AIDS have been reported and the number increases each year. Those at high risk are homosexual/bisexual men, parenteral (intravenous) drug users, and hemophiliacs.

Surveillance of known cases suggest a pattern of transmission resembling that of hepatitis B virus by blood and body fluids. Researchers agree on the routes of transmission: sexual, intravenous transfusion of blood and blood products, and mother to fetus. What is unknown is which cofactors make an infected host more likely to develop the complications of AIDS. It is believed that AIDS occurs only in persons whose immune systems are already vulnerable.

Sexual transmission is the most common cause of acquiring AIDS, and the greatest risk of transmission is among homosexual men. Heterosexual transmission has been apparant since the beginning of the epidemic, though the incidence is relatively low. Male-to-female transmission may be the most common (rather than female-to-male) since semen can carry infected lymphocytes. Most of the evidence is based on patients who have had sustained or recurrent relationships with a person with AIDS or a person in a high incidence group, or who has had multiple sexual contacts. Multiple sexual contacts place both heterosexual men and women at risk.

HTLV-III virus has been isolated in lymphocytes from saliva, but the probability of transmission by oral-genital contact or salivary exchange remains unknown.

IV (intravenous) drug users are described as the bridge to other potential risk groups: heterosexuals with AIDS who have had sexual contact with an IV drug user; homosexual/bisexual men with AIDS who have used IV drugs; children with AIDS who have at least one parent who used IV drugs. Both men and women who use IV drugs are at equal risk.

About 1% of AIDS cases occur in children under 13 with both males and females affected equally. In this population, the mortality rate is 40% but is much greater for infants who have symptoms of AIDS. A high percentage of children with AIDS have at least one parent who has been diagnosed with AIDS or, as mentioned, a parent with a history of IV drug use. Another cause of AIDS in children results from transfusion to hemophiliacs.

Household spread of AIDS infection has not been documented. In a 3-year study that followed up siblings with AIDS, all other siblings remained both immunologically normal and seronegative.

Transfusion-associated cases of AIDS represent about 2 percent of adult cases and 12 percent of pediatric cases involving whole blood, cellular components, plasma, and clotting factor concentrates.

To avoid acquiring AIDS, emphasis is placed on the importance of knowing one's partner and practicing healthy sex which means no exchange of body fluids (including semen, urine, saliva, feces, or blood), or contact of body fluids with mucous membranes. Attention to risk reducing behavior is most important even among persons who already are infected with HTLV-III.

The advice to drug users emphasizes the importance of using clean, disposable needles, syringes, and other paraphernalia and not sharing such items, which is difficult to do because of the illegal activity and transient population of drug users.

The U.S. Health Service recommends delaying pregnancy in women who are seropositive because of the risk of infecting the fetus and the danger of complications for the mother.

Educating the public about AIDS has already been effective because incidence of sexually transmitted diseases, other than AIDS among homosexual men, has been reduced, and many drug users are buying disposable needles and syringes.

Health care workers exposed to AIDS have been under surveillance with documented parenteral or mucous membrane exposure to blood or body fluid of patients with AIDS. In a 12-month follow up of 261 health care workers tested for HTLV-III antibody, none was positive. Based on this study, it is believed that the risk to health care workers is very small.

To diagnose AIDS, physical examination and lab tests are given. Serum is collected and tested for HTLV-III antibody which identifys the presence of the virus (seropositive). Further research is necessary to provide effective treatment and possible cure.

ALCOHOL SPONGE RUB (BATH) An alcohol sponge rub is a rapid way of lowering the body temperature during high fevers. It will also remove accumulated skin oils and perspiration. By killing surface bacteria it also has a disinfectant action.

A properly conducted alcohol sponge rub will lower body temperature by several degrees within half an hour, but care to avoid chilling should be exercised. If the patient complains of chilliness, it is probably best to stop the sponging. Other precautions are to avoid getting alcohol fumes into the eyes and to bypass the face, and the anal and genital areas.

Sponging can be done with straight rubbing alcohol, or with a mixture of half alcohol and half tepid water. (The latter is less drying and less chilling.)

In addition to a basin with alcohol, one will need two washcloths and one or two large towels. A light blanket (or bath towel) can be used for covering the patient during the procedure. One should be sure to protect any furniture against splashing with alcohol since it may spoil the finish. Newspapers or plastic covers will be helpful.

An alcohol sponge rub is performed as follows:
1. Bring the patient toward the side of the bed.
2. Remove gown or pajamas.
3. Wring out one washcloth in the alcohol or alcohol-water mixture and place on the abdomen; renew frequently throughout the procedure.
4. Dip the other washcloth in alcohol and in rotation sponge the arms, the trunk, and the legs. Place a bath towel under each part being sponged to protect the bedding.
5. Turn the patient over and sponge the back; this may be followed up with rubbing in a body lotion.
6. Spend about five minutes each on the arms, chest, and the legs.
7. Check temperature in a half hour.

ALLERGY Allergy is a condition of hypersensitivity or altered tissue reactivity. Antigens (sensitizing agents) are found in various foods, bacteria, drugs, medications, pollens (inhalants). These sensitizing agents produce antibodies in the blood of allergic people. As a consequence of antigen-antibody reaction, certain symptoms occur. These can resemble common colds with running nose, sneezing, watering of the eyes; colic with abdominal pains, distention, gas; croup with wheezing, cough, rashes, bronchitis, stomach aches, vomiting, itchy sensations, etc.

More than half of all allergic symptoms are found in the first few years of childhood. They can appear in any organ of the body, but are most common in those systems where there is exposure to foreign substances, such as the respiratory tract, the skin, and the gastrointestinal tract. With young infants who are on a limited diet, it may be relatively easy to determine what foods cause allergy in the first few months of life. If an infant breaks out with a skin rash soon after being introduced to orange juice, egg, or a cereal, it is possible to assume that one of them is the allergic substance. One may then withdraw the food from the diet, use ointments to clear the rash, and observe the patient. If the rash does not recur after the offending food has been eliminated, it is good evidence that the food was causing the allergic response.

In some children there is a history of "keeping a cold all winter long," of wheezing the minute they get outside into the cold air, and inability to take a bath without catching cold the following morning (presumably due to exposure with a change in temperature). These children are sometimes also unable to go swimming in the summer because the chilling water and change of temperature predisposes them to catching cold. These may be signs of upper-respiratory infection allergy and may be associated with wheezing and a clinical picture resembling asthma. While this may not be true asthma, it is considered asthmatic bronchitis because it occurs whenever the child has some slight chilling or upper-respiratory infection. These children are frequently allergic to bacteria. The onset of a cold triggers a wheezing episode. They can usually be treated and desensitized with a respiratory vaccine. This causes a reduction in the frequency, severity, and duration of these symptoms. (See also ASTHMA.)

Drug Allergy Many persons are sensitive to the chemicals in drugs. This reaction is not caused by an overdose but by a particular sensitivity. Children, in particular, may have an unexpected reaction to a medication—an effect quite opposite to what was intended. For instance, if the drug is a sedative, the child may become excited and agitated. Children often do not respond to many preparations which are designed to cure their illness.

Symptoms. The symptoms produced by drug allergy reaction are usually the same as those produced by pollen, house dust, food, inhalants, or other substances. There may be swelling of the mucous membranes of the nose and throat, hives, rashes, headache, mental dullness, wheezing, etc.

Treatment. Treatment involves eliminating these particular medications. Adrenalin and cortisone may also be used.

Gastrointestinal Allergy The symptoms of this form of allergic reaction are: headaches, vomiting, diarrhea, and recurring abdominal pain. Small infants may have repeated bouts of vomiting if they are allergic to cow's milk protein. Their stools may become loose and watery. They may tense up and cry with pain, indicating colic. They may also break out with various skin rashes, such as hives, or have eczema or generalized itching without any evidence of rash.

For infants and children the most frequent allergenic foods are: cow's milk, orange juice, tomatoes and tomato juice, chocolate, eggs, fish, nuts, and the various citrus fruits. Children who are allergic to one of these may frequently be sensitive to all of them.

Treatment. Treatment depends upon finding the food

or drink which causes the reaction. Attacks may be relieved by eliminating these foods and by giving injections of adrenalin. Antihistamines may also be of help.

Serum Sickness Serum sickness is a response to certain injections which contain horse serum. The patient may be allergic to certain immunization procedures and should be tested before receiving them. Injection material made from horse serum, or incubated on egg yolk, may cause sensitivity. The symptoms are headache, nausea, vomiting, and fever, and hives, with swelling of the glands. Joints may become swollen and painful. The treatment is adrenalin, antihistamines, and cortisone.

Hay Fever This disorder is due to a state of allergy or hypersensitivity primarily involving the nose and eyes, producing cold-like symptoms. The usual complaints are of nasal congestion, watery secretion, sneezing, itching of the eyes, and tearing. Predisposition is inherited: a hay fever sufferer will generally be found to have one or more close relatives (his parents, brothers and sisters, or aunts and uncles) who share the same discomfort. Hypersensitivity is most often to the pollens of certain grasses, trees, and weeds—although not infrequently multiple sensitivities exist, such as allergic reactions to dusts, bacterial infections, and/or various food items.

A normal individual can inhale air containing large amounts of ragweed pollen with no reaction whatsoever. In contrast, the hay fever victim will show immediate reactions of the sort mentioned earlier. Because of the sensitivity, there is local production in the tissues of a chemical called histamine. Histamine results in prompt swelling and inflammation. Its production in the tissues will go on quite continuously throughout the time of exposure, which in the case of the ragweed season generally runs from about mid-August until the first frost. The existence of the excessive sensitivity can also be shown by appropriate skin tests. Injection of a tiny amount of even very diluted extracts of the offending agents will produce a marked skin reaction in the sensitized individual.

Various methods are available for the treatment of hay fever:

1. In desensitization, progressively increasing amounts of the extract of the offending substances are injected under the skin.

2. A group of drugs known as the antihistamines seem to neutralize or antagonize the local effects of histamine.

3. Steroid (cortisone-type) drugs have as one of their general properties the ability to abolish reactions of hypersensitivity.

4. Drugs related to atropine and ephedrine may also have a marked drying effect on the swollen, congested nasal linings.

5. A change of location to a low pollen count area may give the hay fever victim relief.

Testing for Allergy An allergic child or adult should have a complete physical examination, history, and laboratory tests, such as blood count, urinalysis, and nasal smear. Following this there are three types of skin tests which can be performed to determine the allergies.

The most frequently used is the *scratch test* in which a small amount of specific substance is introduced onto the skin and a small scratch made, usually on the forearm. If a small wheal (which looks like a small mosquito bite) develops, this is a suspicious, positive reaction to the allergen in question. Some patients may show a positive skin-test reaction to substances which they have never eaten or been exposed to. Such a reaction does not necessarily indicate that they are allergic to these substances.

An *intradermal test* is one in which the antigen is injected into the dermal (deeper) layer of the skin with a tiny needle. This test is more sensitive and may give a strongly positive reaction if the person is allergic to the material. A *patch test,* in which the allergic material is placed on the skin as a sort of patch and left for twenty-four to forty-eight hours, is another method of testing for sensitivity.

Passive transfer is a special method which is used when the skin cannot be involved in testing, as in severe eczema, or with children who are too difficult to test. It is also used to spare the individual the test procedures. The serum obtained from the allergic person is injected into the skin of a number of areas of a normal person. A few days later the allergic extracts are introduced into the same areas on the skin and the tests are read.

Allergy can also be tested by placing a drop of antigen into the eye of a sensitive person. The reaction is noted by comparing it with the response to a normal control.

Many cases of allergy are called "psychosomatic," indicating that they are "emotional in origin." This is frequently the case and may be demonstrated at times in older children. It takes the form of a strong dislike for, or bad association with certain specific foods, to such a degree that when a child is forced to eat them he becomes sick. Frequently the conscious representation of the dislike is forgotten, so that all that remains is the unconscious dislike of the food. It is expressed in the body language which rejects the food and causes a strong reaction of nausea, vomiting, hives, etc. The most common types of allergy are those due to offending foods, house dust, animal dander, pollens, and contact materials.

ALZHEIMER'S DISEASE (AD) *What is Alzheimer's Disease?* Alzheimer's Disease is a progressive disorder of the brain causing loss of memory or serious mental deterioration. Little is known about the cause of this disorder, but research shows that nerve endings in the cortex of the brain degenerate and disrupt the passage of electrochemical signals between the cells. The areas of degeneration have a characteristic appearance under the microscope and are called "plaques." In addition, the nerve cells, themselves, develop abnormal fibers called neurofibrillary tangles. The larger the number of these two abnormalities—plaques and tangles—the greater the disturbance in intellectual function and memory.

The condition is not caused by hardening of the arteries, nor is it contagious. It is estimated that the disease affects from 500,000 to 1.5 million middle-aged and older Americans, or about 2–3 percent of the general population over 60 years of age. AD does not usually affect more than one member of the family.

What are the symptoms? There are many patterns in the type, severity, and sequence of mental changes in AD. Usually, the symptoms are progressive but vary greatly in the rate of change from person to person. In a few cases, there may be rapid mental deterioration, but often, there are long periods in which little change is noted. However, the progressive deterioration which occurs is a source of deep concern and frustration for both the victim and the family.

As the disease progresses, the changes in the nerve cells produce simple forgetfulness and increasingly more noticeable memory loss. Changes in thought, language, personality, and behavior can eventually render the person incapable of taking care of himself or communicating his needs to others.

How is the Diagnosis Made? The diagnosis of Alzheimer's Disease is made after other illnesses (affecting memory loss) are ruled out; such as, brain tumors, strokes, infections, and spinal-cord abnormalities. Diagnostic techniques are needed to differentiate the various causes of dementia. These techniques include computer tomography (CT scan), studies of the spinal fluid system and electroencephalography (EEG). Comprehensive blood studies and metabolic tests are also conducted.

A thorough physical, neurological, and psychiatric examination is necessary to rule out several other conditions which mimic the symptoms of AD. Some of these related disorders are Creutzfeld-Jakob disease, Pick's disease, or cerebral vascular disease. A diagnosis of AD can be made on the basis of history, mental status and course of the disease.

What is the Treatment? Medical care can *relieve many of the symptoms* of AD but prevention or cure of the disease is not known. Counseling can help the victim and his family in coping with the illness. A neurologist, psychiatrist, or family physician should closely monitor treatment and have the time and interest to answer the variety of questions that arise. Medication can be prescribed to improve sleeping patterns. Proper nutrition, exercise and physical therapy can aid difficulties that arise in physical functioning. Social contacts should be encouraged. A list of daily tasks, written reminders, and safety measures can assist the individual in day-to-day living. It is best to maintain an ordered environment so that the afflicted person does not have to continuously learn new things.

ANEMIA The function of the red blood cells is to carry oxygen and nutrition to the tissues and carbon dioxide from the tissues. The main element of red blood cells is hemoglobin, which is made from stores of iron and protein in the body. These are derived from food and from the destruction of hemoglobin in the body for the iron is reused.

Anemia is a lowering of the red blood cells, or hemoglobin, below the normal value for the age of the person. It may or may not produce symptoms such as fatigue, weakness, or headaches. The diagnosis of anemia is made by drawing a drop of blood from the finger, diluting it in a standard solution, and examining and counting the cells directly under a microscope. The cells are also stained with dye and the colors and shapes examined on a slide. A defect of the red blood cells, or hemoglobin, reflects a disturbance of the production of iron, or a loss of destruction of these elements.

Anemias of Pregnancy Anemia is a good deal more common in women than in men, due to the loss of iron women experience with each menstrual period. Anemia is therefore more likely to develop with heavy and frequent periods.

Pregnancy may be another contributory factor, for the developing baby will draw on maternal iron stores. It is quite common, therefore, to prescribe iron supplements during pregnancy. Prenatal vitamin supplements often have calcium and iron added to them in recognition of the extra need for these two elements. Although, as a rule, blood loss at the time of delivery creates no problem, it may be sufficient to result in mild anemia. In such an event the doctor will probably prescribe iron supplements to be taken for some time after the delivery. As can be seen, the crucial factor in most of the anemias that affect women is the availability of iron.

There are some rare anemias in pregnancy known as megaloblastic anemias. These are not due to iron deficiency but rather to an inadequate supply of folic acid, a member of the B group of vitamins; the condition is remedied by giving folic acid by injection. Occasionally also, considerable amounts of bleeding from hemorrhoids or from disorders not necessarily associated with pregnancy (such as a bleeding peptic ulcer) may contribute to anemia. Occurrences of this sort should be reported to the doctor who will in any case routinely check for anemia in pregnancy.

Hemolytic Anemias These anemias refer to destruction *within the bloodstream* of the red blood cells. They may be due to congenital or hereditary disorders which result in defects in the production of red blood cells and/or hemoglobin. As the red blood cells are destroyed, part of the hemoglobin is released from these cells and the bile pigment (bilirubin) formed leads to an increase in the bilirubin level in the blood. This eventually gives a yellowish color to the skin called jaundice. In severe, chronic, hemolytic anemias, there may also be an accumulation of iron-containing pigment in the body tissues, leading to an enlargement of the liver and a characteristic gray-green discoloration of the skin.

In some of these anemias the spleen, which is the main organ for the destruction of the blood, is often enlarged, and one may be able to feel its outlines in the abdomen.

Iron Deficiency Anemia This is due to deficient or poor nutrition, chronic illness, or excess loss of iron. The red cells are usually small (microcytic) and are filled with very small amounts of hemoglobin, indicating that they are hypochromic (without much color).

The symptoms of this anemia are varied, and may include poor appetite, decrease in normal activity, irritability, behavior disorders, pale skin. The poor appetite leads to a further poor intake of iron and exaggerates the degree of anemia. The condition is slowly progressive and may lead to serious disorders of the heart and respiration. It should, therefore, be corrected as soon as possible. The patient must be supplied with food rich in iron, or with medications, sometimes called "tonics," containing iron salts. Periodic blood counts should be taken to indicate the progress of the anemia or its correction. (See also BLOOD.)

APPENDICITIS The appendix is a small, dead-end pouch, situated just below the point where the small intestine empties into the large; it is, therefore, located in the right lower fourth of the abdomen. The appendix performs no useful digestive function, its chief importance arising from the fact that it occasionally becomes inflamed—appendicitis—and can pose a threat of serious and spreading infection within the abdomen.

Although appendicitis is generally regarded as a disease of children and young adults, it can occur in all age groups, including the elderly. Its symptoms may be deceptively mild, particularly at the beginning, and can easily be dismissed as "an upset stomach." Typically, it starts with cramping abdominal pains experienced in the upper abdomen, generally above the level of the "belly button" (navel). There is usually an associated loss of appetite which may progress to nausea and occasionally to vomiting. Over the course of the next six to twelve hours there is increasing localization of pain in the abdominal region of the appendix.

The appendix is inches below and to the right of the navel. The pain here will be steady, and will increase if the patient coughs or is asked to "blow out" the abdomen. When the doctor makes his examination, he will look for such signs as:

1. *Tenderness* to pressure in the area.
2. *Guarding*—involuntary tightening up of the abdominal muscle overlying the inflamed appendix.
3. *Rebound*—the sudden sharp increase in pain produced when manual pressure in this region is suddenly released.

There may not always be certainty in diagnosing acute appendicitis; among some of the conditions that imitate it are ovulation with the release of an egg and certain inflammations, generally viral, of the abdominal lymph glands. It may therefore be considered wise to hospitalize a suspected case of appendicitis for repeated blood cell counts and observations before the diagnosis can be established.

Treatment. There are no first-aid measures of any value in appendicitis. An icebag placed over the region may produce some relief of pain. Nothing should be given by mouth. Above all *be sure to avoid the use of laxatives.* It is a grievous error to mistake acute appendicitis as "gas pains" or "spastic constipation" and take a laxative, for this may produce rupture of the inflamed appendix and a spreading peritonitis. Clearly, both diagnosis and treatment require the skill of a doctor, who must check the patient. Remember that there are unusual cases of appendicitis in which the person feels "a little sick," has a little soreness over the region of the appendix, and yet proves to have a severely inflamed appendix when surgery is performed. The degree of inflammation cannot be judged by fever; this seldom exceeds 100°F. by mouth throughout the early stages.

Mesenteric Adenitis A non-surgical condition which resembles appendicitis is called mesenteric adenitis. The mesentery is a lining covering the intestines. It contains blood vessels and lymph glands. When acute infection exists, such as in cases of tonsillitis, bronchitis, pneumonias, etc., these abdominal glands may become swollen, tender, and painful, causing nausea, vomiting and abdominal pain. It resembles acute appendicitis very closely. However, antibiotic treatment of the general infection will usually make these glands subside and the symptoms will disappear. In true acute appendicitis the symptoms usually do not disappear. However, in many cases, surgical intervention may be necessary because of the danger of missing an acute appendix. (See also ABDOMINAL PAINS.)

ARTERIES, HARDENING OF (ATHEROSCLEROSIS) This is by far the most common and most important abnormal condition found in the human body. The basic process consists of deposits of fatty materials which are readily visible as yellow streaks and mounds in the inner lining of the arteries. The deposits tend to be irregular in extent and location; they can be present to an excessive degree in one location, as for example, in the coronary arteries of the heart, with only slight-to-moderate involvement elsewhere.

When it is widespread and advanced, the condition is sometimes spoken of as "generalized arteriosclerosis;" disorders produced by this condition are traceable to impairment of the circulation. Decreased circulation results from the fatty deposits, which encroach on the caliber of the blood vessel. In addition, there is a local slowing of the bloodstream, which can result in the formation of thromboses or clots. When this occurs in an artery of the heart, a coronary thrombosis (heart attack) is the result: if the vessel involved happens to be one in the brain, a stroke (with paralysis) may result. If the clot is in an important vessel going to the lower extremities, death (gangrene) of the tissue there will follow.

It was formerly thought that atherosclerosis was a normal aging phenomenon in arteries. It is now regarded as a disease process which tends to increase with aging but which is variable and partially, if not largely, preventable. Many factors can contribute to the degree of atherosclerosis, although there is uncertainty about their relative importance. Some of these are:

1. The level of such *blood fats* as the neutral fats called triglycerides and the waxlike fat called cholesterol; when these are elevated, the degree of atherosclerosis is increased. (See CHOLESTEROL.)

2. *High blood pressure,* which tends to increase atherosclerosis.

3. *Sex hormones.* All else being equal, female sex hormone protects against, and male sex hormone tends to favor, atherosclerosis. Hence, till the menopause, the female has a distinct advantage over the male in this respect.

4. *High saturated-fat diets.* It appears that diets in which the saturated fats are reduced and the polyunsaturated fats increased may favorably affect atherosclerosis.

5. *Cigarette smoking.* This appears to increase the likelihood of coronary thrombosis—presumably by some effect on atherosclerosis there.

6. *Metabolic disorders* such as diabetes and hypothyroidism. These significantly increase the rate of atherosclerosis.

The possibility that atherosclerosis may be controllable by diet has excited widespread attention and has resulted in a changing pattern in the fat consumption of Americans. Probably overweight also tends to increase atherosclerosis. (See also CORONARY THROMBOSIS.)

ARTHRITIS Most bones of the body interact with others at a site called the joint. Most joints are so constructed as to permit some freedom of motion; this freedom may be very extensive (as in the shoulder or the elbow) or quite restricted (as in the joints found in the spinal column). In many, though not all, joints the bony surface concerned is covered by a layer of cartilage (gristle) and the joint may have a special delicate lining (the synovium).

Diseases of the joints are termed "arthritis." Despite their relatively simple structure, the joints are involved in a great many local and general disorders. Some are related to the allergic disorders, as is seen in the acute arthritis of rheumatic fever or of a penicillin reaction. Damage to a joint, as through a fall or blow, may produce fractures in the bones, as well as a filling-up of the joint with an increased amount of secretion; this is spoken of as traumatic arthritis. In gout, deposits of a chemical (uric acid) may occur in and about the joints, leading to the condition known as gouty arthritis.

It is also important to know that not all of the pains and discomforts around joints are due to arthritis; many are due to disorders of the muscular tendons and are known as *tendonitis.* (Tendonitis in the shoulder joint is frequently referred to as "Charley-horse.") The two major forms of arthritis which must be reckoned with are osteoarthritis and rheumatoid arthritis.

Osteoarthritis Osteoarthritis, a disorder that almost everyone will experience as he gets older, is marked by a proliferation of the bone at the joint site. This is of very variable degree. Minor forms of osteoarthritis produce no symptoms or discomfort. The thickening of the finger joints seen in many individuals past age fifty is an example of this form of arthritis. In a small percentage, thickening leads to deformity and moderate amounts of pain, the latter most likely to be experienced on arising in the morning. Other joints that may be involved in osteoarthritis in the elderly are the hip and the knee—the more so if overweight is present. Symptoms include mild achiness and stiffness which are made worse by resting or by exposure to cold. Other common sites at which osteoarthritis occurs are the joints of the spine, the shoulders, and the elbows. When necessary, the condition is treated by such simple drugs as aspirin and its derivatives, and by local heat.

Rheumatoid arthritis is a far more serious and crippling condition. This probably represents a chronic allergic type of disorder involving the joints with production of increased fluid, heat, and pain. Sometimes all the major joints are attacked to produce generalized or disseminated rheumatoid arthritis. In other instances (especially in the early stages) the spine alone, or only the hands and the feet, are attacked. Neither the basic nature of nor basic therapy for rheumatoid arthritis is yet known. Immediate control of even severe rheumatoid arthritis can be secured by the use of steroid drugs (cortisone-type drugs). Other treatments that have been used include injections of gold and such drugs as aspirin and butazolidine, perhaps supplemented by such pain-killing agents as the codeine group of drugs.

Many doctors rely heavily on physical therapy. Rheumatoid arthritis must be regarded as a troublesome affliction which can be helped—but not cured. The patient must learn to live with the disease and do what he can despite it.

ARTIFICIAL RESPIRATION Artificial respiration should be used on anyone whose breathing is greatly slowed or stopped; this includes victims of poisoning, drowning, and accidents. All previous methods of artificial respiration have now been replaced by the mouth-to-mouth method, which is performed as follows:

1. Clear the victim's mouth of any dirt, sand, clothing, or other foreign matter.

2. Place the victim flat on his back with head extended. Kneel alongside, at the victim's shoulder level. With the fingers of one hand hook the under-surface of the victim's jaw and pull on it so that it juts forward.

3. Press your mouth against the victim's mouth so as to form a relatively airtight connection. With a small child, the rescuer's mouth should cover both the victim's mouth and nose. With an adult, the rescuer should pinch the victim's nostrils together with his free hand.

4. Blow air into the victim's mouth with quick, deep puffs, as in blowing out a candle. (The puffs are bigger for an adult than for a child and should produce movement of the victim's chest like that in deep breathing.) Repeat twelve to fifteen times per minute for an adult, up to twenty times per minute for a child.

5. Allow the lungs of the victim to deflate between breaths. (Gentle pressure with one hand on the victim's abdomen will help deflation.)

6. Artificial respiration should be maintained *without halt* until a physician arrives at the scene or while transporting the patient to a hospital.

ASTHMA The bronchial tubes have muscles in their walls which can contract, thus narrowing the size of the tube. Excessive degrees of contraction of the bronchial muscle is referred to as bronchospasm; much of the difficulty that occurs in asthma is traceable to bronchospasm. If, in addition, there is accumulated secretion within the bronchial tube, the difficulty in getting air in and out may become marked. An obvious wheezing is often noted and the emptying of air out of the lungs (normally an easy process not requiring any effort) may be difficult and prolonged. All of this to a lesser or greater degree is observed in asthma. Even in moderate degrees of asthma the effort of breathing may be painful to behold. The victim has to labor to get air in and out, and like anyone else who is working hard may be drenched in perspiration.

Most cases of asthma are due to allergy, that is, a hypersensitivity to some offending substance. In the most common type, that due to pollens, the disease is often combined with hay fever. (This form of asthma is also known as seasonal asthma.) A good guess as to the cause may be based on observation of the time that the disease is active, and a knowledge of the local pollens. Thus, asthma that occurs in the spring is generally due to the pollens of the grasses and trees, while the common asthma that starts in the late summer or early fall is generally traceable to ragweed. Sometimes molds and dust may be at fault; less often, an allergic response to something that the person has eaten may produce asthma.

In another form of the disease the asthmatic response seems to be brought about by bronchitis, the sensitivity apparently being due to bacteria or their products associated with the bronchitis. This is known as *asthmatoid bronchitis*. It is more likely to come on in the middle years (as compared to ordinary asthma which appears earlier in life),

is made worse by respiratory infections, and may be present all year 'round.

Treatment. There are various approaches a doctor may use in the treatment of asthma: (1) desensitization to the offending agent, (2) bronchodilator drugs, or (3) steroid drugs. (See also ALLERGY; BRONCHITIS.)

BABY-SITTERS There are about a million persons who do baby-sitting in the United States. Most baby-sitters are teenagers and fortunately they usually like youngsters, but the parent must remember that a baby-sitter is not the parent and therefore there are definite limits that must be set for the baby-sitter. Baby-sitters should not be asked to perform the functions of a nurse or doctor.

A new baby-sitter should be given an orientation talk which will include information about what the child likes, how the home is run, situations the baby-sitter is to be particularly alerted to, especially those that are likely to result in accidents. But, of course, the most important lesson you must get across to the baby-sitter is that his or her main job is to watch the child, so that you will find your child safe when you return home.

When you have special instructions, *put them in writing*. Such writing should include your policy of not permitting the baby-sitter to have visitors or to monopolize the telephone. Write out very clearly specific or extra chores that you may want the baby-sitter to perform. Of course other information should be written down, and this includes the following:

Important Telephone Numbers:

Where parents can be reached _____
Where doctor can be reached _____
Close friend or neighbor _____
Police Department: Dial "Operator" or _____
Fire Department: Dial "Operator" or _____

Special Information

Bedtime _____
Meal (or snack) time _____
TV rules for children _____
Other Things Your Baby-sitter Should Know:
Names (and nicknames) of children
Sleeping arrangements
Where clothing and special equipment are kept
Favorite stories, games, and activities
Where the children play
Special habits or problems of children
Sitter's privileges (TV, radio, refrigerator)

BACKACHE Backache can occur in a variety of conditions. It is a fairly common complaint during "flu," menstruation, acute kidney inflammations, arthritis; in some elderly individuals it is caused by shrinkage and collapse of the vertebrae due to loss of calcium. By far and away, however, the most common cause is acute and chronic stress-and-strain on the muscles and ligaments supporting the spine. Pain is most commonly experienced low in the back, either in the small of the back or in the bony region just below it (the sacroiliac region). In acute low backache severe pain may come on in seconds. The sufferer often states that he reached over to pick up something, experienced a stabbing pain in the back region, and found himself so doubled up by pain as to be unable to straighten up. A backache of this sort may be utterly incapacitating and require narcotics for relief of pain. The patient may have to be helped into bed and kept there for several days. Attempts to turn in bed may be most painful. The victim usually finds a comfortable position by trial and error. This is frequently flat on the back with a pillow underneath the knees.

Treatment. Heat from a heating pad, aspirin, and similar pain-killers—and occasionally cortisone-type drugs—may help to relieve the pain. (There are some patients who experience a few such attacks of acute sacroiliac pain at widely spread intervals throughout their lifetime.)

Chronic Low Backaches These may come on after a bout of acute sacroiliac strain, or may develop in a slow and progressive fashion until finally the person realizes he is having backaches a good deal of the time. Such backache is usually described as dull, persistent, and made worse under such circumstances as prolonged standing, driving, slumping in a chair, or (at times) on arising in the morning. Occasionally a single factor, such as a sagging mattress or a strain or position at work, can be identified as the cause; with correction of such a factor the backache disappears. More often, however, the patient finds that the backaches are frequent and recurrent, and that special efforts seem to be needed to help them. Among the measures that are useful are:

1. A firm mattress is generally desirable. Particularly if the pain comes on in the morning on arising, an inadequate bed should be suspected as a major contributing factor. It may be necessary to put a bed board between mattress and box spring.

2. Attention should be directed to avoiding positions which strain the back. Chairs should have a good back support; most chairs are too deep and the victim of backache will need a pillow for adequate support. A sitting position in which the knees are at a somewhat higher level than the lower back or hips may be the most relaxing. This may be achieved by having low footstools available both at home and at work. The basic principle is to avoid positions which accentuate arching of the back.

3. Systematic daily exercises.

Exercises for Backache Victims of chronic low backache find that exercise is the most effective therapy for their condition. Exercises should be done once or twice a day, either on a firm bed or on the floor. Among useful exercises are:

1. Lying flat on the back, raise both legs off the floor to a vertical position and slowly return to starting point.

2. In the same position, bring the legs up and over as far as possible (which will require lifting the lower back off the supporting surface).

3. Starting flat on the back, raise up the trunk, bringing arms forward until the fingertips reach the ankles.

4. "Kissing the knees:" Starting flat on the back, come up to a sitting position, at the same time drawing up the knees, thus bringing the face up to the knees.

5. From a standing position—with knees slightly bent, not with straight knees—bend the trunk, bringing arms down to ankles or toes, then return to starting position.

6. With the hands supported by top of a table or bureau and knees slightly bent—slowly do a few knee bends, then return to original position.

All these exercises can be done in sequence, with brief rest periods between them. The average sedentary person may be able to do only a few to begin with, but should be able to work up to ten to fifteen each within a period of a few weeks. In addition to their tonic and trimming effect, exercises may cause mild backaches to disappear. Although some backaches may be relieved by special belts and girdles, such devices in some cases may weaken rather than strengthen the important supporting muscles of the back and abdomen. Properly exercised and developed muscles are a better support.

BALDNESS Baldness refers to any form of hair loss, temporary or longer lasting, in which, because of the thinning of hair, the underlying scalp becomes more readily visible. The most common form of baldness is hereditary, sex-linked, and is found in men; this form is inherited through the mother and passed on to the son. (It does not occur in women even when they carry and transmit the characteristic.) Being a female (with the accompanying female hormones) protects against this form of baldness, while being a male with male hormones predisposes. Thus a woman whose brothers are bald may pass the characteristic on to her own son even though her husband, the father of the boy, has a good head of hair. The extent of hair loss in sex-linked baldness is variable, as is also the age at which it becomes obvious. There is no treatment of significant value for this form of baldness in men, although many ingenious approaches (including the rubbing-in of female sex hormones) have been tried.

There are temporary states of hair loss in women which may unnecessarily trouble them because of the fear of significant baldness; such women may be reassured that this will not occur. Such hair loss may be seen following pregnancy, some women complaining that hair is "coming out by the handful." This form of hair loss is completely compensated for in the ensuing months.

Similar states of temporary hair loss may be seen following feverish illnesses, of which typhoid fever was once a prime example. It may be seen after some of the more common infectious diseases. Some glandular disorders may lead to noticeable hair loss; these include certain disorders of the adrenal glands and, perhaps somewhat more commonly, over- and under-function of the thyroid gland. With proper diagnosis and treatment for these conditions, however, regrowth of hair can be anticipated. Cracking and splitting of the hairs and increased shedding may occur because of some procedures applied to the hair. "Ponytails" and other styling procedures which pull unnecessarily on the hair may do this and are best avoided.

Alopecia Areata A rather peculiar form of baldness seen in both sexes has been termed alopecia areata. In this disorder a circular patch of scalp loses hair. The area involved seldom exceeds the size of a quarter. After a period of some weeks or months, a regrowth of hair will occur in the bald patch. The cause of this disorder and the reason for its peculiar localization is unknown; it sometimes seems related to nervous stresses and is seen more frequently in tense, hypersensitive persons.

In elderly women, as well as in elderly men, some degree of thinning-out of the hair is generally observed. It occurs also with body hair, such as pubic and armpit hair. A somewhat similar process is being observed more frequently in a relatively small percentage of middle-aged women, no particular agent or hormonal disturbance seemingly being involved. This pattern of hair thinning in middle age seems to have arisen only in the past two decades and is still under investigation. In no way does it resemble the kinds of baldness seen in men. Women exhibiting this condition can at least be told that it is not unrestrainedly progressive; currently, hormones and other agents are being evaluated in its treatment. For practical purposes, the average woman with an average head of hair can be reasonably certain that she will keep it indefinitely, and whatever episodes of hair loss she may encounter will always be temporary ones.

BEHAVIOR AND EMOTIONS

Emotions in Childhood The development of emotions or feelings begins in infancy. This refers to positive emotions (pleasure, happiness, contentment, love, etc.) as well as negative emotions (fear, anger, anxiety, depression, unhappiness, etc.). The infant is born helpless and depends for the satisfaction of his needs entirely on his mother and father. He is born into the world with certain hereditary and temperamental qualities. The development of his emotions will depend upon the nature of the interaction between him and the person who supplies his needs, usually the mother.

Inconsistent attention, stimulating or threatening behavior, punishment and hostility will give the child a sense of fear and mistrust of his environment. Sensitive mothering, with reasonable satisfaction of the emotional needs of infancy, will establish a sense of basic trust in the environment. The mother, as the recipient of signals of need from the child, has a responsibility in taking care of those needs. Her failure to do so produces in the infant feelings of anger, helplessness, insecurity, futility, and even despair. The groundwork of stable emotional development occurs during the first six to eight months of life. Overwhelming anxiety or trauma during this period can severely maim the emotional development of the child.

If a child is treated with tolerance, he learns to be patient.

If he lives with encouragement, he learns to be confident.

If he lives with praise, he learns to be appreciative.

If he lives with recognition, he learns that it is good to have a goal.

If he lives with honesty, he learns what truth is.

If he lives with security, he learns to have faith in himself and those about him.

If he lives with acceptance, he learns to love.

If he lives with friendliness, he learns the world is a nice place in which to live.

However, if he lives with criticism, he learns to condemn.

If he lives with hostility, he learns to fight.

If he lives with jealousy, he learns to feel guilty.

And if he lives with fear, he learns to be apprehensive.

The emotional climate which a child experiences in his home, school, and outer world molds his development.

Behavior Disturbances in Children   Child behavior reflects temperament, organic problems, and social situations. Experimental evidence based on studies of children's individual primary reaction patterns, has shown what we all have more or less known for many years, namely, that different children respond to parental care practices in different ways. For instance, children may respond differently to the *same* approach on the part of the *same* parent regarding feeding, sleeping, toilet training, or general discipline. Each child seems to have a characteristic way of responding to new situations, and this response appears consistently time and again, even in more complex situations as he gets older.

Individual temperament, which consists of a number of primary reaction patterns, is one of the very important factors in the development of behavior disturbances between child and parent. A short description of some of the most important primary reaction patterns will help to clarify this concept.

1. *Adaptive and non-adaptive behavior* refers to the ability of the child to adapt to new situations and the ease with which he responds if the situation is repeated.

2. *Approach-withdrawal* refers to responses to anything new, such as foods, toys, people. Some children will approach immediately and make contact, whereas some will always be hesitant or withdrawn and have great difficulty in making contact with people and objects.

3. *Intensity* refers to the quality of a child's response to tension, hunger, new foods, attempts to discipline or restrain, dress, diapers, etc. This may be mild or extremely intense in its nature and is important in the overall picture of a child's response to various new training problems. If a child is a high intensity reactor and so is his mother, it is almost inevitable that temper tantrums and behavior disorders will occur. If the child is a mild reactor and the mother

an intense person, this may still result in interpersonal difficulties. However, if both are mild reactors, presumably there is going to be less friction.

4. *Distractibility and persistence* refer to the ease with which a child can be diverted from what he is doing to doing something else. A child who is very easily distracted is going to be difficult to train. He will not be able to pay attention long enough to absorb commands. He will also probably have learning difficulties.

5. *Positive and negative moods* represent expressions of pleasure, pain, friendliness, unfriendliness, joy, and crying. A child with a high degree of negative mood responses is going to be less agreeable than a child whose responses are generally positive.

Behavior Problems, Causes of It   It is important to differentiate behavior problems in children who have real organic brain damage (See BRAIN DISORDERS) and those whose temperament and ability to respond to training procedures reflect struggles with the way their parents are handling them. Disturbed functioning may represent a distortion of the characteristics of primary temperament, so that the parents respond with growing annoyance and pressure to the demonstration of the child's initial way of responding. In turn, the child's continuing negative responses arouse parental hostility, and this leads to constant fights and recriminations within the family.

The importance and the understanding of individuality in psychological functioning cannot be overestimated. It takes sensitivity, tact, and observation for parents to see in what way their child will best respond. Usually, gentle persuasion, soft tones, and firm discipline within the framework of love and kindness will get the best results. Many behavior problems are secondary to primary disturbances, such as nightmares which result after prolonged hospitalization, or feeding problems which are secondary to prolonged illness, etc. It is necessary to have expert pediatric or psychiatric advice in cases of emotional disturbances in children.

Social situations may also create behavior disturbances in children. As children observe adults and their own friends and have a wider sampling of people to imitate, they often start imitating the disturbed behavior of classmates or of characters they see on television, in the movies, etc. They may read certain things and become influenced by them. As they grow older, various fads, customs, and social mores become standards on which they base their behavior. Children coming from one culture to another may show varieties of behavior patterns which they did not show in their original country. Gang warfare on city streets is certainly not attributable to parents but is a social phenomenon which children, unfortunately, imitate. Children who have been inadequately supervised and improperly disciplined are likely to develop serious behavior problems. Correction of severe behavior disorders of either children or adults usually requires the services of a qualified psychiatrist.

Discipline   Discipline is a matter of teaching limits to one's child. It is the process of giving the child with no life experience the benefit of the adult's experience. Discipline teaches children to set limits on their impulsive behavior, to value the rights of others, and to learn the general rules of behavior, in order to be socially accepted.

Children *require* limits. They lack a knowledge of what is good and bad for them, nor can they see far enough ahead to develop the qualities of character and internal discipline which will be necessary for their later performance as adults. Self-restraint, limitation of activities, postponement of gratification for further or future rewards are important tasks for a child to learn. He has to be able to realize that breaking the rules of discipline will bring some kind of punishment, even if it is only a rebuke or an angry scolding.

Parents who continually say "no" to a child in a tone of voice which indicates contempt, anger, or scorn will soon destroy the effectiveness of this as a method of discipline. Treating a child with consideration and kindness, asking "Please do this for me," or *requesting* certain behavior is much more agreeable to anyone (including a child) than a harsh and angry command.

One of the most important aspects of obedience is the maintaining of *consistent standards of behavior* and the *maintaining of a uniform standard between both parents.* If a mother forbids something and the child says, "I'll ask father," and the father permits it, this child will soon be playing one parent off against the other in an attempt to dominate and get his own way. If the parents stick together, are firm in agreeing on methods of discipline and decisions regarding behavior, the child will have no alternative but to obey, even if unwillingly.

When repeated training and discipline take effect, the child learns inner control, so that he can begin to discipline himself in life situations and get along without the constant help of his parents. Discipline involves guidance, assistance, acceptance, and permitting growth while imposing limits on unacceptable behavior. His self-discipline will enhance his self-esteem and give him confidence in life. But remember, the language of love and authority can be the same.

Temper Tantrums Temper tantrums are a form of manipulative behavior on the part of a child, characterized by screaming, kicking, breath-holding, and extreme agitation. This response is often seen in infants or very young children when they are frustrated or refused something they badly want. They may become angry or jealous and may use this method to blackmail parents into giving in to them. It is a fairly common behavior reaction in children from one to four. Temper tantrums which occur in older age groups (children of eight, nine, or adolescents) are a more serious behavior disorder and will require different treatment.

If a temper tantrum is met with indifference and nonchalance, the child will soon observe that kicking and screaming serve no good purpose and are self-defeating procedures. If a child is given what he wishes because the parents become intimidated, he will learn that he can do this whenever he wishes to get his way. It is a very bad emotional habit to encourage. It is not usually necessary to punish the child who has temper tantrums. Just refusing to acknowledge him and handling the situation with calm and firm tolerance is probably the best procedure.

Impulse control and its mastery are a requirement of normal emotional development. Temper tantrums may sometimes occur in neurologically damaged or defective children because of inability to control their impulses. In these cases it may be necessary to treat them with medication and sedation.

Neurosis in Childhood Neuroses and mental disturbances begin to exist in childhood. The manner in which a child deals with his environment and with his relations to parents and other significant persons determines many of the characteristics of his behavior in later life.

Neurotic character disorders are characterized by very fixed and prevading attitudes in which the child has a distorted impression of other people's attitudes, behavior and motives. A child may think that every person he meets is going to behave in a threatening or destructive manner toward him and adopt a character pattern of defensive hostility, aggression, or withdrawal. If this expectation of threatening behavior becomes inflexible, the child will react to every person in his environment in exactly the same abnormal manner.

In order to prevent serious adult character neuroses, children with these behavior disorders should be treated by a child psychiatrist or a psychologist early in the disturbance. Otherwise the disorder becomes magnified, ingrained into the personality, and is extremely difficult, if not impossible, to erase later in life.

Phobias and anxiety reactions in children may be real or may be irrational. A child may become frightened of the water after having a near-drowning experience, but usually the reaction to this, if he develops normally, should be gradual restoration of confidence in his ability to go into the water and learn how to swim. A child may be frightened by a horse or a dog, but later on becomes adjusted to the idea that not all dogs or horses are dangerous. If this ability to change fails to develop, various phobias and fears may appear, with many of the more irrational ones, which are incomprehensible and baffling to parents, representing substitutions for deeper-hidden fears. These require unraveling by a qualified child psychiatrist.

Bed-wetting (Enuresis) Bed-wetting is involuntary urination during sleep or in daytime. It may be caused by infections or abnormalities of the urinary system. It may be caused by inability of the bladder to hold enough fluid. It is usually only a problem if it persists beyond the age of three or four and if its occurrence is frequent.

Most children who can develop speech have the ability to hold urine long enough to notify their parents when they have to urinate. Bed-wetting may sometimes represent a regression to a previous immature state during periods of emotional stress or upset. Some cases of bed-wetting are purely psychological, and it will take a trained physician to determine whether this is so. Even if it is psychological, however, it is usually not conscious or voluntary, so that the child is actually unable to control it. He may have to be retrained and reconditioned. There are some devices available for conditioning children. They generally involve a bell which rings as the child starts to urinate. Feeding of small amounts of salty foods at bedtime, and limiting fluids after 6 P.M., may help to control night bed-wetting. It is not advisable to humiliate or punish children for this difficulty. Such an approach may simply aggravate the condition.

Nail-biting (Onychophagy) This is a common sign of nervousness, tension, excitement, or worry in a child. It may indicate fear and anxiety or may be an expression of repressed anger.

Treatment is directed to allaying the fear, anxiety, or nervousness and to trying to provide more stable emotional support for the child. Punishment for this habit is usually useless and often only aggravates the condition. Putting ill-tasting medicine on the nails and shaming or punishing the child usually intensifies nail-biting. A child who bites his nails out of boredom or lack of interests should be directed toward some meaningful activity to keep his hands occupied.

Nightmares (Night Terrors) Nightmares, night terrors, and bad dreams occur in children who may be restless, emotionally upset, neurotic, or suffering from some mild illness. Many of these episodes represent dreams of anxiety, psychic conflict, and fears. They may reflect a frightening or traumatic situation which the child has experienced during the day. He may relive these fearful experiences at night and wake with fears and anxiety. Sometimes frightening things seen on television or in movies may distress the child and he will dream about them. They may represent fear resulting from a disturbed relationship with or between the parents. They may also represent displacement of anxiety in the form of phobic fears.

During an attack of night terrors, the child suddenly wakes up, cries out or screams, trembling and perspiring. He may be incoherent and not understand what has frightened him. He may or may not remember the occurrence in the morning.

The immediate treatment of a frightening dream is to try

to reassure the child, comfort him, and try to get him back to sleep. If the child is old enough to comprehend, he can be told it was "only a bad dream." Since many children dream about frightening experiences (such as watching horror shows), stimulating television or movie programs should be avoided by these sensitive children. Any child who persistently has nightmares or night terrors should be evaluated by a psychiatrist to determine whether there is an emotional disorder present. A complete psychological and psychiatric examination is often required.

Oedipus Complex and Electra Complex A complex is a group of associated ideas (which may be partly unconscious) that have strong emotional overtones. They may significantly influence attitudes and associations.

The Oedipus complex, first described by Sigmund Freud, refers to the attachment of the male child for his parent of the opposite sex accompanied by feelings of envy and aggression toward the parent of his own sex. Attitudes arising during critical phases of infantile emotional development and largely repressed (made unconscious) because of fear of punishment by the parent of the same sex are responsible for the complex. Originally the term was used only in relation to male children. A parallel type of complex has long been recognized as existing in girls and is called the Electra complex. Both of these terms are derived from Greek mythology.

Inadequate mastery of the emotions during the "oedipal" period results in prolonged (unconscious) emotional attachments and persistence of emotional disorders resulting in neurosis.

Extroversion and Introversion *Extroversion* is the name given to a personality type whose attention and energies are directed outward from the self, as opposed to *introversion,* in which interest is directed primarily toward one's own self. In the latter condition there is a reduction of interest in the outside world. Naturally, there are gradations and degrees of both personality types, and there are times in the life of any person when he may become more introverted than he normally is (states of grief, sadness, depression). The degree to which these states become exaggerated and, therefore, pathological is a criterion for normal or abnormal mental states.

Depression Depression is one of the most universal of all human emotions. No one can expect to go through life without experiencing depressions. A depression brought about by sad events, failures, or financial reverses (and thus one which is entirely understandable) is sometimes referred to as a reactive depression. It is not always possible to identify the causes of depressions, however. Some seem to arise almost spontaneously from within; to put it another way, the events that trigger them seem to be insufficient causes. Some of the depressions that are seen in middle-aged individuals fall into this category and are sometimes referred to as endogenous depressions.

Some of the cyclic depressions to which women may be subject are essentially transitory. Their widespread occurrence suggests that they may depend on hormonal or other processes going on within the system. Thus the premenstrual tension and depression which affect a considerable number of women have been related to hormones with fluid-retaining properties. These psychic complaints appear with, and seem to be more marked in women who complain of considerable bloating and swelling. The depression often ends quite promptly with the onset of menstruation, at which time there is an abrupt drop-off in the hormones responsible.

Depressive Reactions Depressive reactions can occur under other circumstances than the reproductive ones, such as menstruation and delivery. Some individuals (for reasons that often become clear only when their whole life history is reviewed) may be subject to recurrent bouts of depression. There are some families in which several members may from time to time be afflicted with fairly severe depressions. Some of these troublesome depressions are associated with feelings of inferiority, self-blame, and self-attack, deep feelings of pessimism about life and the desirability of living, etc. Depressive reactions of this sort can be brought about by any of a great number of major events and having a baby is only one of them.

Drugs may be helpful in at least alleviating such depressive states, but when there is a pattern of recurrent depressions some form of psychotherapy may well be the answer and provide a more permanent and superior solution. The aim in psychotherapy is for the patient to find out why he or she has feelings of inadequacy, poor self-esteem, convictions of unworthiness, and other similar ideas which often form the basis for depression. Psychotherapy may take time and is frequently quite expensive, nevertheless there are circumstances in which it is wise to consider it, or at least discuss the possibility of such treatment with a physician.

Psychopathic Personality This refers to a child or adult who is unable to be disciplined, who performs impulsive antisocial acts without any understanding of the feelings of others, and without any qualms regarding his disturbed behavior. It also refers to a person *who has never been taught limits:* that he sometimes should delay or postpone gratification, that a sense of guilt should follow wrongdoing. It implies the inability to develop a "conscience" or a sense of self-limitation. It implies the inability to see reality properly or to learn from experience or disaster. A child who is habitually cruel, destructive, intolerant of the feelings of others, shows characteristics of this disorder. These children urgently require treatment; otherwise they will grow up to become serious delinquent and criminal problems.

Most behavior problems which begin in childhood and continue untreated into adolescence will show up as adolescent character disorders. Personality traits may carry over, show feelings of self-contempt and unworthiness, attitudes of arrogance and contempt, hostility and exploitation. Or on the other hand, they may show continued dependency and inability to rely on the self. Children may also show attitudes of excessive ingratiation or an attempt to please others, which is equally abnormal since it does not show an adequate concern for one's self as an individual.

The aim of raising children is to raise mature, independent, functioning adults. The mentally healthy person can deal with reality even at its worst, find satisfaction in struggle (including adversity which can be turned into achievement). The mentally healthy person is relatively free from tensions and anxieties, relates consistently to others with mutual satisfaction and helpfulness. He accepts present frustration in the hopes of future gains, profits from experience, and can direct and divert hostile feelings into creative or constructive outlets. Finally, he has the capacity to love, the most essential quality of human behavior.

Psychosis in Children This indicates a state of clinical "insanity" which may occur in a child who has normal capacity but has been so traumatized, so badly treated and handled in childhood, that he becomes quite abnormal. Some of these children are called schizophrenic. Psychoses in children also refer to the behavior of children who have brain disturbances and are damaged. Their behavior is fragmented, irrational hyperactive, and very disordered— but on the basis of an organic condition. Some children who are mentally defective or retarded may also show behavior disturbances which are classified as psychotic. (See also BRAIN DISORDERS.)

Psychotherapy Psychotherapy is a form of medical

treatment for emotional and mental illness which attempts to uncover the meanings and the origins of the disorder. Unlike other procedures (which may also be useful)—such as the taking of drugs, changes in the environment, or electroconvulsive treatment—most psychotherapy involves a series of discussions between patient and doctor. Generally the patient discusses his symptoms, his feelings, and many aspects of his personal development. From time to time the psychotherapist may organize and interpret this material in a new and meaningful way. By this process the patient develops insight and, as a result of the deepened understanding he gains of himself, many behavioral changes can follow. One of the key concepts that may emerge is the patient's understanding of anxiety. It is anxiety experienced early in life which can lead to later difficulties in a person's behavior—whether in the family, at work, or in the sexual or social areas.

For adults, the most sophisticated form of psychotherapy is known as analysis. In the course of this, the patient speaks out freely, letting his thoughts come out as they may and using dreams or daily events as points of departure. This technique is know as free association and can lead to surprising insights.

Although with adults it is possible to interchange ideas through talk, this may not be the case with a young child, for whom a type of treatment is used known as "play therapy." In one form of play therapy, a large number of dolls which can be perceived as parents, children and pets are made available to the child, and his behavior with them is studied. A skilled child therapist will make available to the child appropriate toys and games to reveal his disturbance. Psychotherapy has been criticized from time to time as being an imperfect instrument; but imperfect or not, it is at present the only instrument available for the treatment of some emotional difficulties in children as well as adults.

BIRTH CONTROL Birth control refers to any of those procedures which will diminish or do away with the probability of pregnancy; it is also known as family planning and contraception. Besides the inadequate methods, such as *coitus interruptus,* and tap-water douche, that have been employed, the more effective or better known ones are the following:

1. *Birth-control pills.* Their effectiveness is approximately 100 percent. Many kinds are dispensed in a special package containing 20 pills. Counting the first day of menstruation as day 1 of the cycle, the pill is taken on the morning of day 5 and every morning thereafter through day 25. Within a few days of stopping—roughly therefore around day 28—menstruation occurs. Again one waits till day 5 and repeats the daily taking of the pill. The pills work by preventing the growth and release of the egg from the ovary so that a woman remains infertile throughout her cycle. Once the pills are stopped, the possibility of pregnancy promptly recurs; thus it is necessary for the pill to be taken daily. Occasionally pink staining may occur while taking the pills; this may necessitate a temporary increase in the amount taken. Other difficulties are occasional symptoms of nausea or bloating. An increased amount of clotting in the veins was reported for the first pill in use. Since then, a reduction in dose and newer combinations have been made available, and original difficulties may now be reduced.

2. *Diaphragm.* This is a rubber dome mounted on a flexible rubber-covered metal circle. When properly inserted, it fits into the upper portion of the vagina, covering the opening to the uterus (the cervix). Usually a special sperm-killing jelly or cream is used to seal the edges of the diaphragm.

3. *Condom.* Sometimes referred to as "a rubber," this is a device worn by the male. It is convenient, and widely used.

4. *Foams and jellies.* These are sperm-killing materials injected or placed within the vagina just before intercourse. They rapidly immobilize and kill the sperm. They are fairly effective, generally non-irritating, and lessen the need for the fitting or insertion of a diaphragm.

5. *Rhythm method.* Sometimes also referred to as the "safe period."

"Safe Period" (Rhythm System) The "safe period" is the time in a woman's menstrual cycle when she cannot become pregnant. In the average woman it generally refers to a few days after the end of menstruation and to a period of about a week-and-a-half before the expected onset of her next menstruation. A knowledge of the safe cycle is basic to the rhythm method of birth control. It is based upon the following considerations.

1. An egg is released (ovulation) from a woman's ovary only once during a menstrual cycle.

2. The egg can be fertilized by the sperm of the male only during about twenty-four hours after its release. After that time the egg undergoes degenerative changes and can no longer initiate a pregnancy.

3. Although the sperm supplied by the male can live for a somewhat longer period within the female reproductive tract, they probably cannot fertilize the egg more than two or three days after their release.

4. If one could time the ovulation exactly, and if no sperm were supplied for approximately three days before, and for a day or two afterwards, pregnancy could not occur. The time in the cycle just before and just after the release of the egg is the time of highest fertility in a woman; other parts of the menstrual cycle would therefore be "safe."

The difficulty arising with this approach is that the menstrual cycle is subject to some fluctuation. Even very regular women find, when they start charting their cycle on the calender, that it fluctuates either way by several days. It is also known that ovulation may occur somewhat earlier in some cycles and be somewhat later in other cycles, although most ovulations in a woman with a twenty-eight-day cycle tend to occur around days 12, 13, and 14 of the cycle (day 1 of the cycle is the first day of menstruation).

To take into account the different menstrual cycles the following has been proposed. A woman should keep track of the length of her menstrual cycles for approximately a year. By subtracting 18 from her shortest cycle and 11 from her longest cycle she can calculate the time of her highest fertility. Intercourse without contraception during this time would be the most likely to result in pregnancy. Furthermore, it cannot be applied to a woman whose cycles fluctuate a good deal—if one menstrual cycle is twenty-three days and another thirty-three days the method will not be reliable.

BIRTHMARKS, FRECKLES, AND MOLES
Angioma Angiomas are small skin lesions characterized by an elevated red area having small dilated capillaries radiating from it like a spider's legs. These are called *spider nevi*. They are usually birthmarks and frequently disappear. If they persist, they may be treated with electrolysis or electrocautery.
Cavernous Angioma This is the most common birthmark. It is more deep-seated than the others and is sometimes called a strawberry angioma because of its resemblance to a strawberry. It varies in size. The treatment is usually with sclerosing agents which are injected at intervals into the lesion until it disappears. Carbon dioxide snow is also used to shrink the involved vessels. Some types which are very extensive may require surgical removal.

Port-wine Mark This is a more extensive birthmark, involving larger areas of the skin. The port-wine discoloration of the skin is caused by a network of fine capillaries. It becomes redder if the child cries or strains. Most of these marks are somewhat disfiguring when they appear on the face. There are waterproof cosmetics available at a drug store which cover marks temporarily.

Freckles Freckles are flat, vari-colored, pigmented areas of the skin. Freckling is usually hereditary and appears in darkly pigmented as well as light-skinned peoples. Sunlight causes freckles to increase. They are harmless. However, one form, which is blue-black in color and is slightly raised, may be pre-malignant. This form is called a melanoma. It is dangerous to remove these lesions, as they may spread to other areas of the body. Surgical removal requires wide excision. Doctors with skill and experience should be consulted regarding removal of any freckle.

Moles Few, if any of us, are lacking in at least a small number of moles, and in some individuals there are literally hundreds of them. Most are small, perhaps ¼-½ inch in length, and are to be found almost anywhere on the skin. They are mostly tan, brown, or blue-black in color, often slightly elevated, and may bear a few hairs. It is not practical to remove most moles, nor is it necessary. If a mole is considered to be a cosmetic problem the doctor can easily remove it, often by as simple a procedure as cauterizing. This will, of course, result in a small scar. In general moles are to be regarded as harmless.

An exceedingly rare tumor related to moles is known as a melanoma. Melanomas may arise in a pre-existent type of mole (known as the junctional nevus) which appears as a generally flat, blue to black, hairless pigment spot in the skin. Some also appear to arise in apparently normal skin without a preceding nevus. Melanomas occur most often on the hands, feet or genitals. Any mole that enlarges, becomes darker or develops nearby new pigment spots, ulcerates or bleeds should be called to the doctor's attention.

None of these moles is in any way related to the patchy pigmentation of the skin that occurs in some pregnancies. This is most marked on the face and resembles patches of tan. It is sometimes so extensive as to be called "the mask of pregnancy." It is probably due to a pigment-controlling secretion from the pituitary gland. The pigmentation recedes after the delivery.

BITES, ANIMAL, INSECT AND SNAKE

Animal Bites Most animal bites present no special problems of infection, with a few exceptions. The risk of infection is cut further if one permits some bleeding from the wound or even encourages bleeding with slight pressure, as in the case of puncture wounds produced by a cat. One may then wash the wound with soap and water which may be all the first-aid procedures that are needed. If there is free bleeding, such as may occur from a dog-inflicted laceration, a clean compress can be applied and firm pressure maintained. If the skin is not penetrated by a bite, there need be no further concern. This can be the case when a dog bites through heavy clothing, or in the relatively uncommon bites from a horse; both may produce a bruising injury only, for which application of an ice bag may be useful in cutting down swelling and bleeding within the skin. Very rarely, and only after the passage of some weeks, scratches or bites from cats may produce fever and swelling of the nearby lymph glands. This is known as cat-scratch fever. Rabies following a dog bite is even rarer. However, if the dog is a stray, is known not to have been immunized, behaves peculiarly, or runs about snapping and biting aimlessly, it should be captured and turned over to the authorities for further examination. If this is not done and a question arises as to whether or not the dog might have been rabid, it may be-

come necessary to give the bite victim a course of special injections known as the Pasteur treatment.

Insect Bites *Bites of mosquitoes and gnats* will produce immediate itching, and itching may recur thereafter for one or more days. They are generally disregarded. However, a paste of soda bicarbonate or a pledget of cotton dipped in household ammonia diluted with three parts of water may be dabbed on the bite. Calamine lotion may be applied for recurrent itching.

Bee bites can be treated by removal of the stinger with a forceps or tweezer, followed by local application of ice, then by calamine lotion or a paste of bicarbonate of soda. Bee bites can be dangerous and even fatal to sensitive individuals. Indications of such sensitivity are unusual local swelling, and marked general reactions such as weakness, faintness or collapse. If any such unusual reactions do occur with a child or adult, hypersensitivity exists and any further exposure to bee bites can be most hazardous. Extracts for producing desensitization are available and should be used in such cases. Otherwise strict avoidance of the countryside and areas where bee bites can occur is necessary. If exposure is unavoidable and undue sensitivity may still be present, tablets to be placed under the tongue (Isuprel®) or an adrenalin inhaler such as is used by asthmatics should be carried on the person. The fact is that there are more fatalities from the bee bite than from snakebite or any other kind of animal bite.

A few *spider bites* present special threats: the black widow spider, which is recognizable by the orange hourglass figure on its abdomen, injects a toxin which can produce serious general reactions including painful contractions of all muscles and collapse. It is found mostly in the southern United States. The brown recluse spider is found most commonly in the southwestern United States, most often in the cellars and basements of buildings. It does not attack unless disturbed. Its bite can produce a marked local breakdown of the skin as well as general reactions.

Scorpion bites also lead to an introduction of a toxin under the skin. They are not likely to be serious except in very small children. First aid for all of these bites may consist of tying a tourniquet above the site of the bite, much as for snakebite, and the application of ice to the area of bite. The patient should be taken to any nearby doctor's office or medical facility.

Snakebites Most United States snakes are harmless. Poisonous snakes have fangs—specialized teeth through which a poison can be injected under the skin as with a hypodermic needle. The bite is characteristically two needle-like puncture wounds side by side. The only four poisonous snakes in the United States are the rattlesnake, the cottonmouth moccasin, the copperhead, and the coral snake. First aid for their bites includes the following:

1. *Immediately apply a tourniquet* some inches above the wound at a level where the soft tissues can be compressed; tighten the tourniquet to a point where the veins swell up and the skin becomes flushed.

2. With a sharp razor blade or knife *make an X-shaped incision* over each of the fang marks. The cut can be up to one quarter of an inch deep. Avoid prominent skin vessels such as veins, or any tendons.

3. *Suck out the venom,* which will be mixed with blood. Spit it out from time to time but keep sucking as strongly as possible for at least an hour. If there are no open cuts in the mouth the venom is harmless, and it is equally harmless if swallowed.

4. *Have the victim lie down* and keep the suction going while he is being taken to a hospital or the doctor's office.

5. A snakebite kit may well be kept in the car or with camping equipment if one is going into areas where poisonous snakes are known to exist.

BLADDER DISORDERS

Cystitis The most common disorder affecting the bladder is an inflammation termed cystitis. It is a good deal more common in women than in men. Cystitis produces an entire set of uncomfortable symptoms, among which are:

1. *Frequent desire to urinate.* Although the bladder feels as though it is full, so that the desire to urinate may be quite urgent, only small amounts of urine are passed; nonetheless the patient may find it necessary to go to the bathroom every few minutes throughout the day.

2. Frequent complaint of *painful urination.* This is often described as a burning pain.

3. Sometimes, because of painful spasm around the bladder opening, it is *difficult to start urination,* and the urine may come in weak, dribbling fashion.

4. Not uncommonly, there is *some bleeding* associated with cystitis. It is seldom more than enough to color the urine in an obvious fashion and is sometimes mistaken for vaginal bleeding.

Treatment. Fortunately, these distressing symptoms will generally respond within a day or so to the administration of antibiotic or sulfa drugs. In fact, the symptoms often improve markedly, even though some pus and bacteria can still be found in the urine. Cystitis is generally treated for a matter of some days, or even longer; the urine should be checked, not only when the treatment is discontinued but also at some intervals thereafter. The aim is to avoid any lurking, low-grade, or chronic infection which can go unnoticed but may serve as a source of reinfection and flare-up of cystitis later. Most cases of cystitis, if untreated, tend to get progressively worse. There is very often an ascending spread of the infection to the kidneys, at which point symptoms such as chills and fever often occur.

Cystocele This is the medical term for a sagging of the bladder produced by a relaxation of the tissues supporting it. It is limited to women who have been pregnant and is seen as an occasional sequel to pregnancy and delivery. Only a small minority of mothers, however, develop cystocele of any consequence, and mild degrees of cystocele can be disregarded.

A large cystocele is detected easily enough by inspection. The patient is told to bear down as though she were having a bowel movement. The increased pressure within the abdomen will push the sagging bladder down into the upper wall of the vagina, thus producing a bulge at the vaginal opening. It is this anatomical fact that leads to the difficulties of cystocele, for it may be difficult or impossible to evacuate the bladder completely. This alone may lead to frequency of urination. It is also a general fact that infection is likely to occur whenever the bladder cannot be completely emptied. Thus there may be frequent episodes of cystitis with all the discomfort that these can bring. It is sometimes possible, at least partially, to correct the difficulty produced by a cystocele by inserting a pessary into the vagina to support the bladder.

For cystocele of a degree that produces frequent symptoms or infections, surgery is recommended. The aim is to fashion a sling of supporting tissue that will hold the bladder in a normal location. When this is done, the symptoms due to cystocele disappear.

Rectocele Very often, in addition to cystocele, rectocele may be present. This is an anatomically similar condition, but in this case it is the rectum that bulges into the lower wall of the vagina. A rectocele may produce relatively few symptoms except when quite large, and is generally disregarded. However, it is possible surgically to repair a rectocele at the same time that the cystocele is repaired.

BLEEDING

Cuts and Lacerations Bleeding from a large cut or laceration can be brisk if one of the larger veins or arteries is cut. The best generally applicable method for control of such bleeding is to *exert firm pressure, using a cloth compress, against the area.* In an emergency one can employ a wad of facial tissue, a handkerchief, towel, shirt, or a pillowcase suitably folded on itself so as to make the compress. Press it against the bleeding site, and if the cut is on a limb, elevate the limb, for this too diminishes bleeding. Maintain pressure for five to ten minutes. One may then lift part of the compress to judge whether the bleeding has come under control. If it has not, pressure can be maintained for a longer period or even indefinitely if necessary.

Nosebleed In principle a nosebleed is treated in the same manner. Almost all nosebleeds occur from the septum, the central partition that separates the nostrils. This is made of cartilage (gristle). It has a rich blood supply, chiefly of smaller blood vessels. To control bleeding from this, grasp the fleshy portion of the nose firmly between the thumb and forefinger, and keep it compressed for five to ten minutes.

Pressure Points Pressure points are places where major arteries can be directly compressed—often against a bone—thus cutting down the circulation to a limb or other part of the body. A knowledge of pressure points and their use forms part of advanced first-aid courses and requires considerable practice and training. Two such points that everyone might readily become familiar with are the brachial and femoral. The brachial artery can be felt high up on the inner surface of the arm just below the armpit. It can be recognized by its pulsation, and the vessel can be readily compressed against the unyielding arm bone alongside of it. It is the major artery supplying the entire upper extremity. The corresponding artery for the entire lower extremity, the femoral artery, can be located in the crease between thigh and abdomen. The arterial pulse can be felt at about the middle of the crease, and the vessel is readily compressed against the firm tissues beneath it.

Tourniquets—Severe Bleeding Another first-aid method occasionally needed *to control severe bleeding* is the tourniquet. A tourniquet can be improvised by tying a handkerchief, a strip of cloth, or rope of clothesline diameter (a tourniquet that is too narrow may cut into the tissues.) Next a stick, heavy pencil, or even a butter knife is placed between the skin and the encircling handkerchief. Turn this one or more times, thus tightening the encircling cloth. If the pressure is inadequate, the part of the limb below the tourniquet will turn reddish, the veins will increase in size and bleeding may actually increase. If the constricting pressure is raised above the level of the pressure in the arteries, the portion of the limb below the tourniquet turns white and bleeding should stop or markedly subside. The pressure of a tourniquet can be released (preferably by a doctor) at ten-to-fifteen-minute intervals to check on whether bleeding has stopped. Overlong use (longer than one hour or so) of a tourniquet may put the limb in jeopardy.

Internal Bleeding There are no first-aid measures for hemorrhage of internal organs; indeed, it is not often easy to recognize it. Thus a person with a bleeding peptic ulcer may vomit blood, or pass a very black stool; sometimes he merely becomes very dizzy or faints. Large-scale internal bleeding can be recognized by weakness, pallor, rapid pulse. The patient should lie down, and no whiskey or other stimulants should be given. If there is any possibility of delay in securing a doctor, precious time is best saved by rushing the patient directly to a hospital.

Hemophilia This is a hereditary disease occurring in males and transmitted by females. A disease of excessive and easy bleeding, it is believed to be caused by a deficiency of plasma thromboplastinogen. Formation of thrombin, needed for clot formation, is lacking, and consequently, no blood clot forms.

Bleeding may be controlled by application of cold packs locally; otherwise, plasma transfusions and transfusions of antihemophiliac globulin and 50 percent fibrinogen transfusions have been helpful. There is no cure.

Thrombocytopenic Purpura This disease is characterized by small, spontaneous hemorrhages into the skin, the mucous membrane, and other tissues of the body. It occurs most often in females under the age of twelve.

Symptoms. Bleeding may be from the nose or mouth, and there may be black-and-blue marks over the surface of the body. It may be due to infection, drugs, diseases, vitamin deficiency, or no particular cause may be found for it. There is usually a lack of platelets in the peripheral blood, which produces a defect in the clotting mechanism. Since clots do not form at the torn capillaries, bleeding time is prolonged.

Treatment. Newer drugs, such as ACTH and cortisone, have been used with limited success. Occasionally, removal of the spleen is required in long-standing cases.

BLOOD, THE Two groups of cells are moved along the circulating blood. One, the red blood cells, is involved in the transfer of oxygen to the tissues and is responsible for the red color of blood; the other, the white blood cells, takes part in the body's defense, as in inflammation. There are several groups of white blood cells—lymphocytes, plasma cells, polymorphonuclear leukocytes—each with different properties and making different contributions to defense. The polymorphonuclear leukocytes, for example, are involved in acute inflammation against bacteria; thus they are the major cells found in pus.

Enumeration of blood cells, known as a *blood count,* is a routine and basic examination in medicine. A complete blood count may call for several more bits of information:

1. An estimate of hemoglobin (the essential component of the red blood cell).

2. A differential white blood cell count, in which the white blood cells are stained and the different kinds counted.

3. Occasionally, a platelet count—a count of the tiny cellular fragments, or platelets, which play an important role in blood-clotting.

The blood count is an important diagnostic clue. In anemia both the red blood cell count and the hemoglobin count fall. In leukemia, the white blood cells are abnormal and often very high in number. The white blood cell count is generally high when there is infection due to bacteria, but barely elevated and sometimes even low in many infections due to viruses. The white cells increase as an infection worsens and decrease as it subsides. In allergic disorders a special kind of white cell known as the eosinophil may be considerably increased. Changes in white cells occur in infectious mononucleosis. Low counts for all types of cells may be found in certain disorders of the spleen and bone marrow. (See also ANEMIA.)

Albumin Albumin is an important protein manufactured in the liver, which circulates in the blood stream. Human albumin is a pale, somewhat sticky material, quite like the white of an egg. In certain disorders albumin may pass through the small blood vessels of the kidney and appear in the urine. One of the basic tests in medicine is, therefore, the test for albuminuria—the presence of albumin in urine. Here albumin may be found as a result of acute or chronic inflammation of the kidneys; as a result of the effect of high blood pressure in the kidneys, or in circulatory disorders affecting the kidneys, such as heart failure.

Some drugs and poisons may damage the kidneys sufficiently to produce albuminuria. This condition may also be due to quite innocuous causes, such as fever. In a few individuals, albumin appears in the urine when they assume the upright position, although not present when they are lying down. This is known as orthostatic albuminuria; it is of no great concern but may lead to diagnostic difficulties. One of the few threatening disorders associated with pregnancy, known as eclampsia, has various warning symptoms and findings, such as rise in blood pressure, headache, and puffiness around the eyes and elsewhere. Generally associated with these is the finding of albumin in the urine. Eclampsia illustrates one of the reasons for doing routine urinalysis during pregnancy.

One rather serious affliction of the kidneys—the nephrotic syndrome—results from various kinds of inflammations and also from advanced diabetes; large amounts of albumin are poured out into the urine and because of the loss of this important protein, marked swelling of the various tissues (edema) occurs. The major change that underlies all forms of this disorder is loss of albumin into the urine.

Gamma Globulin Second in amount to the albumin in the circulating blood are the globulins. These are a group of diverse proteins which can be separated from one another by appropriate chemical procedures. The most important one which is now commercially available is gamma globulin. It is formed by the lymphocyte-plasma cell group of the white blood cells, and is part of the body's chemical defenses against infection.

The disease-fighting globulins are sometimes referred to as *antibodies;* without antibodies it would be impossible to develop immunity, and we would be fighting the same disease battles over and over again. As it is, one successful battle may result in the production of enough antibodies to protect the individual against that organism for the rest of his life. For this reason, an adult who has had measles or hepatitis can be exposed to a child with the disease and not reacquire it. In fact, such antibodies are produced even when the disease is nipped in the bud; thus a person may be exposed to the viruses of polio, hepatitis, or mumps and overcome them without the characteristic signs of the disease, be it the paralysis of polio or the jaundice of hepatitis. These brief battles may produce relatively few symptoms beyond fever and grippal sensations, often cannot be diagnosed, but nonetheless produce immunity. Hence commercially obtained gamma globulin made from a pool derived from many individuals is a storehouse filled with all sorts of specialized weapons capable of fighting a variety of infective processes.

The value of gamma globulin is pointed up by recorded cases of a relatively rare condition known as agammaglobulinemia. Some babies are born with this condition, while some children and adults acquire it later in life. These individuals are unable to form adequate amounts of antibodies and are subject to repetition of the same illnesses, most often respiratory illnesses with bouts of pneumonia. They may also have the same contagious disease more than once and it may not be possible to immunize them successfully. Indeed, one way of diagnosing the condition is to demonstrate the inability of a child to form antitoxins to scarlet fever or diptheria toxins. Such children, however, may be given some degree of enhanced protection against infections by repeated doses of gamma globulin.

The most common use of gamma globulin is in preventing certain infections in exposed individuals or in diminishing the severity of an illness. It is common medical procedure to give small doses of gamma globulin to all household contacts when a case of infectious hepatitis appears. In children who have been exposed to measles, a small dose of gamma globulin given at the appropriate time may diminish the severity of the measles attack, producing "modified measles." A more recent application is the administration of gamma globulin in a small dose at the time of a measles vaccination. A very mild form of measles results and the child develops immunity despite the mildness of the modified disease. It is occasionally recommended that a large dose of gamma globulin be given to individuals who are traveling into areas with a high incidence of hepatitis, such as India. The dose gives protection for a period of about six weeks and has been shown statistically to diminish the possibility of hepatitis developing. Various other claims have been made for the protective value of gamma globulin, such as an ability to cut down the number of respiratory infections in children, but they have not been verified.

BLOOD PRESSURE Determination of blood pressure yields two measurements: the *systolic*, which measures the height of the pressure produced by the thrust of the heart; and the *diastolic*, which measures the constant "head of pressure" that exists between the beats. A blood pressure of 120/80, for example, would record a normal systolic and a normal diastolic pressure.

Blood pressure may vary considerably in the same individual at different times in his life. In may show a rise under the influence of emotions, in cold weather, as an effect of drugs, and (sometimes) during the course of pregnancy. It may be lower in hot weather, when the person is resting or has taken sedatives, during a fainting spell, or as a result of shock. In contrast, it may also be remarkably stable from year to year.

The cutoff point at which high or low blood pressure is diagnosed is somewhat arbitrary and many people have borderline readings or may be somewhat high on one occasion and normal on another. Systolic blood pressure readings of less than 100 would be regarded as rather low for an adult; however, they are encountered in many perfectly healthy persons. In the diagnosis of high blood pressure or hypertension the diastolic blood pressure is of the greater importance. A diastolic blood pressure of 90–95 may be regarded as borderline elevation, and most doctors would agree that once it exceeds 100, high blood pressure exists. The diastolic blood pressure is more important because it represents a constant pressure to which the arteries are subjected. Thus a blood pressure reading of 130/100 might be regarded as a case of hypertension which should be treated, whereas one of 170/80 could well be regarded as normal, particularly for an elderly person, and in any case not presenting a need for treatment.

Hypertension (High Blood Pressure) When levels of blood pressure significantly exceed normal, hypertension or high blood pressure is said to exist. A rise in blood pressure may occur acutely, as when a person is frightened, angry, or even as a result of the anxiety that some people are apt to experience when they go to the doctor's office. On relaxation, such a person's blood pressure may return to normal. A fairly sustained rise in blood pressure may occur throughout a pregnancy, with a return to normal soon after the delivery; this is often associated with an unusual degree of fluid retention and is thought to be due to secretions emanating from the pregnant uterus. Certain tumors of the adrenal glands known as pheochromocytomas may similarly produce secretions that raise the blood pressure, and there are many disorders of the kidney in which rises in blood pressure occur.

A great majority of cases of hypertension have no ascertainable causes of this sort and are spoken of as *essential hypertension*. Essential hypertension is found in about 20 percent of the population and runs through some families, so that a constitutional factor seems to be involved. It is sometimes possible to identify individuals who will develop sustained hypertension later in life by abnormal rises in response to tension or to cold exposure. There are sound reasons for identifying and treating hypertension early in its course. Hypertension increases the work of the heart, the muscular wall of the left ventricle (whose contraction

pumps out the blood) undergoing enlargement because of it. After many years of carrying the extra burden, the overworked heart muscle may fail, with resultant symptoms of shortness of breath due to lung congestion and such evidences of fluid retention (edema) as swollen ankles. The arteries everywhere show involvement: atherosclerosis and degenerative changes appear much earlier than usual, a sort of premature aging of the vascular system. Circulatory problems are all increased in individuals with hypertension: they show an increased incidence of strokes, heart attacks, and kidney difficulties.

Treatment. A variety of drugs and treatments have now changed the whole course of hypertension. Depending on the severity of the hypertension and the patient's response, various combinations of these drugs are employed. Among them are:

1. Rauwolfia derivatives—rauwolfia being the Indian root whose extract contains both tranquilizing and blood-pressure-lowering properties. The purified derivatives include reserpine (Serpasil®) and an agent called Singoserp®. These drugs may be sufficient for mild cases of hypertension; if not, other drugs can be added to the treatment program.

2. Diuretic drugs—a number of drugs known collectively as the chlorothiazide drugs—promote the excretion of salt and water by the kidneys. For reasons still unknown this also serves to lower blood pressure, sometimes quite effectively. These drugs may be given daily, produce an obvious increase in the amount of urine, and are basic drugs in the treatment of hypertension.

3. Apresoline—a drug which has no other equivalent—apparently acts on the brain centers that control blood pressure levels. It is often combined with the preceding drugs.

4. Ganglionic-blocking agents—drugs that block the transmission of nerve impulses to the small arteries which are narrowed in hypertension. As these small arteries dilate, the blood pressure levels drop.

BODY ODORS Nature did not give the human body the pleasant odors she gave to the flowers—a situation partially rectified by perfume manufacturers. Although human sweat has practically no odor, it rather quickly develops one due to chemical changes produced by the ever-present bacteria on the skin. Such odorous changes are particularly likely to occur on the feet and between the toes, where a variety of organisms flourish. By removing the accumulation of materials on the skin surface (as well as many of the organisms), ordinary soap-and-water cleanliness makes a substantial contribution to decreasing odor.

Even more improvement can be achieved by using cleansing agents containing a medication known as hexachlorophene; this is a germ-killing agent which has a residual effect. Thus, when such substances are used day after day, the bacterial count of the skin diminishes markedly. (Hexachlorophene is the active ingredient often used by surgeons in scrubbing up prior to operations.) It is not generally necessary to use such agents over the entire surface, but they may be useful in special areas such as the feet, the groin, and the armpits. In the latter site the problem is further complicated by the presence of special glands whose secretion has a rather pungent odor. All individuals possess these glands, and in women, they have been shown to undergo changes throughout the menstrual cycle.

Most sprays, ointments, and liquids applied to the armpits contain aluminum salts. These decrease perspiration considerably and are sometimes combined with other agents which will decrease odor. Most of them work quite satisfactorily, although in individuals who perspire freely from the armpits, and especially in hot weather, more frequent applications may be necessary. A few individuals present special difficulties because of a condition of excessive perspiration, known as hyperhidrosis; the doctor may be able to suggest some special agents for controlling this.

Menstrual odors are by no means as common nor as marked as some hypersensitive women think. Appropriate powdering and frequent changes of napkins are of value. In some instances a tampon may be of further help. Masking scents (perfumes and powders with a pleasant odor of their own) can be helpful in concealing an objectionable odor.

Halitosis Unpleasant odors on the breath are referred to as halitosis; these may be produced by diet, and are often only temporary after consumption of such items as liquor, onions and garlic, various spices, wines, etc. The degree to which halitosis is found objectionable varies with different groups; furthermore, if everyone partakes of the offending item, no one complains. Thus smokers generally have no objection to "tobacco breath," though non-smokers may complain. Poor mouth hygiene is sometimes a cause of halitosis and may require more frequent brushing of the teeth, perhaps combined with the use of dental floss or other cleansing techniques. Dentures should not be worn continuously and require cleaning from time to time.

Disordered digestion and certain conditions of the nose or respiratory passages may also make the breath odorous. The doctor will direct treatment to the underlying cause in these instances. Where the cause of an offensive odor cannot be tracked down or treated, a masking scent may be the only practical suggestion. Mints and similar items are, of course, widely used for such purposes.

BOILS AND CARBUNCLES A boil is a local area of inflammation or abscess formation in the skin. A boil generally manifests itself initially as a hard, tender, reddish area. Later this softens; and if it comes to a "head," a variable amount of pus will be discharged. As compared to a pimple, a boil is somewhat larger and more deeply situated. A carbuncle is in turn larger still and involves more tissue destruction than a boil and, unlike the boil, a carbuncle has many heads through which pus may be discharged.

All three of these conditions may be regarded as basically interrelated, the common offending organism responsible for these suppurative infections of the skin being the staphylococcus organism. Since the staphylococcus is constantly found on the skin, it is not always possible to determine what has tipped the balance in favor of the invading germ. In some instances chafing or rubbing may be a factor, as when a boil develops under a tight collar or where the inner surfaces of the thighs rub against each other.

Boils sometimes develop in areas of the body where the circulation is less active, where sweating is excessive, as a complication of acne, or as a result of infection following the scratching of insect bites or other itching lesions of the skin. It is only infrequently that some systemic factor such as diabetes is found to be playing a role. Indeed, sometimes boils can be seen to come and go in crops in individuals who seem to be in excellent health.

A simple boil may not require much more attention than the application of hot wet compresses. These help to bring it to a head, and as a rule, once the pus has been discharged, progressive healing occurs without difficulty. If boils come and go frequently, more extensive treatment may be deemed desirable. This may include washing the skin with a soap containing an agent such as hexachlorophene, which destroys bacteria and has a residual effect also. In addition, antibiotics known to be effective against the staph group of organisms may be taken by mouth or in the form of ointments applied locally. Simple soap-and-water cleanliness seems to be all that is necessary in the handling of boils, and it is quite rare to see evidence of transmission of the bacteria in the usual boil from one member of a household to another. (See also ABSCESS.)

BRAIN DISORDERS IN CHILDREN

Brain Tumors For purposes of description, the brain is divided roughly into two cerebral hemispheres and the posterior fossa (cerebellum, or brainstem). The dividing line between the hemispheres and brainstem is called the tentorium. In children, 60 to 70 percent of brain tumors occur below the tentorium. Because of this difficult location, they cannot be completely removed. Sometimes they cannot even be reached.

The tumors are classified according to the area of the brain in which they occur and the particular cell type of tumor. The most frequently occurring brain tumors in childhood (75 percent) are gliomas. About two-thirds of these are astrocytomas and medulloblastomas. The remainder are different forms of cell types. The location and cell pattern of the tumor determines whether the symptoms are major or minor. In infants under one or two years of age, a brain tumor will cause the head to get larger and produce signs of increasing intracranial pressure. This may become quite noticeable since the skull bones in the infant are soft and the suture lines allow growth and distention. As the head becomes large, there is compression of the brain due to the obstruction of the flow of cerebrospinal fluid. This fluid bathes the brain, its linings, and structures. When the pressure inside the brain has been markedly increased, the symptoms of headache, vomiting, weakness, lethargy, irritability, and poor appetite occur.

In children above three years of age, where the tumor is located in the cerebellum, signs of a disorder of balance occur. There may be a staggering gait (ataxia), tremors, swallowing and urinary difficulties, slurred speech, facial paralysis, cross-eyes, and other eye disorders. If the sixth nerve in the brain is involved, there may be loss of vision and nystagmus (horizontal or vertical oscillating eye movements), double vision, or complete blindness. Marked personality changes may occur. The signs may be temporary or progressive. Other disorders of equilibrium show in clumsiness and difficulty in handling toys. Playful and active children may become listless and lethargic. Other neurological signs depend upon the specific nerves involved. They are called *focal signs*. It is essential to hospitalize all children in whom such a diagnosis is suspected.

Organic Brain Damage Behavior problems in children often reflect certain real and serious organic brain damage. Not all behavior disturbances are "psychological." A damaged or defective child has difficulty in the entire area of perceiving, learning, repeating, and reproducing desired behavior. These children are characteristically restless, hyperactive, easily excited, and easily distracted. They show unpredictable variations in their behavior, alternating from fairly normal to unpredictable, with outbursts of anger, destructiveness, and irritability. They often provoke fights, or tease and annoy others without cause. They are impulsive and act without thinking. They have difficulty in learning the concepts of reward, punishment, and competition. They have severe learning problems characterized by inability to pay attention for a prolonged period of time, difficulty with abstract thinking (particularly reading and arithmetic) and inability to form "concepts."

Only properly given psychological tests can determine whether these children are defective or damaged. There are special treatment methods for children who have difficulties in any of these learning areas. Retraining is the treatment of choice.

Hydrocephalus Hydrocephalus is a condition characterized by an increase in the accumulation of cerebrospinal fluid in the brain. The cerebrospinal fluid represents a lake between the arteries and the brain and is the fluid which bathes the membranes of the brain. If there is some obstruction, or block, to the passage of this fluid, a dam is set up in which the fluid pressure builds up, causing a rapid increase in size of the head, with a separation of the bony sutures. The scalp veins become distended and the spaces between the bones (fontanels) become markedly enlarged. Growth and development are retarded. Increased pressure on the brain may also cause neurological symptoms.

Another form of hydrocephalus is called "communicating." This is the most common form; the block is in the intracranial subarachnoid space.

The imbalance occurs because absorption of cerebrospinal fluid does not equal its production; the head becomes quite spherical due to the increased cerebrospinal pressure. Treatment is therefore directed to getting rid of the excess cerebrospinal fluid. It is best to treat this condition as early as possible. Diagnosis is by X-ray and spinal tap.

Treatment is usually by means of some form of shunt or insertion of a polyethylene valve or tube which will permit the cerebrospinal fluid to drain into another area. Many cases of hydrocephalus remain minimal and require no surgical interference.

Mongolism (Down's Syndrome) This is the name given to a type of mental retardation in which the child is born with certain typical characteristics. The eyes slant upward and outward, and the eye sockets are smaller than normal. The nose is small with an underdeveloped bridge, and the tongue usually protrudes. The fifth finger is short and incurved, and the first and second toes are spaced widely apart. The skin may be dry with poor muscle tone and marked looseness of the joints. Mongoloid children are usually affectionate and pleasant but do not develop beyond the level of idiot or moron. They are very susceptible to infections and have a higher than average rate of leukemia.

The cause of mongolism is a specific chromosome abnormality. Sometimes the chromosones number forty-seven instead of the normal forty-six, and an abnormally shaped chromosome may be found (Philadelphia chromosome). The condition is hereditary. Mongoloid children account for about 7 to 10 percent of institutionalized mental defectives.

There is no treatment except home or institutionalized care, with recognition that these children are permanently retarded. The families are usually warned that they may possibly give birth to other children with this abnormality. (See also INTELLIGENCE—Mental Retardation.)

BRAIN, INFLAMMATION AND INFECTION
Encephalitis Encephalitis means an inflammation of the brain. The symptoms consist of either gradual or sudden headache, fever, drowsiness, lethargy, and coma. In infants, convulsions may occur. Sometimes bizarre symptoms such as hyperactivity, nervousness, mental disorders, palsies, speech disorders, weakness, instability, and reflex changes are seen.

Encephalitis, like meningitis, may be caused by many different organisms. Some of them are: the virus of measles, infectious mononucleosis, insect-borne viruses, entero viruses, herpes, mumps, and smallpox virus. Other forms are: influenzal virus, lymphocytic choriomeningitis, St. Louis encephalitis, equine encephalitis, epidemic encephalitis, Von Economo's disease (encephalitis lethargica). There is no specific treatment for these diseases. However, patients should be in the hospital for supportive and symptomatic treatment.

Encephalitis may resemble poisonings with various metals such as lead, insecticides, etc., and drug intoxications, such as bromides, etc. In these cases, however, there is usually no fever.

Meningitis Meningitis is an acute infectious disease of the meninges, or linings covering the brain.

Cause. Any number of different organisms, such as meningococcus, streptococcus, staphylococcus, pneumococcus, tubercle bacilli, and influenzal and a variety of other viruses.

Incubation period. Varies depending on infecting organism.

Symptoms. These vary slightly, depending upon the causative organisms. In general, however, in young children the most striking symptoms are: severe headache, fever, and great irritability and crankiness, particularly on being touched or bothered. There may be nausea, vomiting, and usually a stiff neck is a prominent sign. Convulsions and coma are often seen. Any child who has these complaints should be hospitalized immediately, and a spinal tap performed to confirm or rule out the diagnosis. A spinal tap is a procedure in which some of the spinal fluid is withdrawn by a syringe for study of the cell count, bacterial culture, and pressure.

The symptoms of meningitis frequently resemble those of polio, therefore a physician should always be called when any of these conditions is suspected. Various antibiotics are available to treat and usually cure meningitis. There is no specific immunization for meningitis. During epidemics, however, antibiotics may be used prophylactically to prevent cases.

BREASTS The breasts are made up of a large number of glands which, when stimulated, produce milk. They are supported in a framework of connective tissue and fat. The size and shape of the breasts are determined particularly by the supporting elements, and in the non-pregnant state the glandular elements may be relatively inconspicuous. A variety of factors will affect breast size. Hereditary factors which determine body build are sometimes obvious determinants of breast size also. Thus in some families many of the women run to large busts, in others to small busts, and this regardless of such features as height and even, to a lesser extent, of weight. In general, however, breast size will vary up and down parallel to body weight.

The glands of the breasts have a series of ducts or canals which converge toward the areola, the pigmented circular area surrounding the nipple. Here the ducts merge with one another and curve in so as to converge on the nipple. The actual openings of the milk ducts are scattered over the end of the nipple. Sometimes a nipple instead of protruding from the end of the breast may be virtually flush with the skin surface or even beneath it, a condition known as inverted nipple.

The glandular tissue of the breasts goes through cycles of growth and stimulation with every menstrual cycle. Just as the lining of the uterus is stimulated by the ovarian hormones, so too stimulation of the glandular elements of the breasts occurs. The degree to which this happens is more marked with some women and in some cycles than in others. However, it may be sufficient to result in obvious swelling of the breasts, and tenderness, which is most noticeable for a few days before menstruation. In pregnancy the breasts enlarge considerably because of specific and often intense stimulation of the glandular elements in preparation for nursing. Small amounts of secretion may collect on the nipple and dry there. This is known as colostrum, and need only be washed away with soap and warm water. (See also CHILDBIRTH—Delivery, Breasts After Delivery.)

BREAST EXAMINATION FOR CANCER A simple 3-step procedure could save or prolong your life by finding breast cancer early. Most breast lumps are benign (non-malignant) and are first discovered by women themselves.

It is recommended that you examine your breasts once a month about a week after your period. After menopause, it is suggested that you check your breasts on the first day of each month.

1. Examine your breasts with fingers flat during a bath or shower by gently moving over every part of each breast. Use the right hand to examine the left breast, and the left hand for the right breast. Check for any lump or thickening.

2. Sit or stand in front of a mirror with your arms relaxed at your sides. Next, raise your arms over your head. Look for any puckering, swelling, or dimpling of skin, and for changes in the nipples.

Then, rest palms on your hips and press down firmly on your hips in order to flex the muscles in your chest. The left and right breast will not exactly match—very few women's breasts do. Regular inspection will show you the normal appearance of your breasts and will increase your confidence in examining your own breasts.

3. Lie down on your bed. To examine the right breast, put a pillow or a folded towel under your right shoulder and place your right hand under your head. (This procedure will distribute breast tissue more evenly.) With your left hand, fingers flat, press gently in small circular motions around an imaginary clock face. Begin, at the outermost top of your right breast for 12 o'clock, then move to 1 o'clock, and so on in a circle back to 12 o'clock. The ridge of tissue in the lower curve of each breast is normal.

Then, move an inch inwards in the direction of the nipple, and keep circling in order to inspect every part of your breast including the nipple. Slowly repeat the same procedure on your left breast with a folded towel under your left shoulder and your left hand behind your head.

Lastly, gently squeeze the nipple of each breast between your thumb and index finger. Any discharge, lump, or dimple should be reported to your doctor at once. Most breast lumps or changes are not cancer, but only your doctor can make the diagnosis.

Breasts, Tumors of Various disorders of the glands and ducts may lead to tumors in the breasts. One such condition, considered to be due to unusual hormonal stimulation, is known as chronic cystic mastitis or fibrocystic disease. It is perhaps the most common cause of painful breasts in women, with the pain being most marked in the days prior to the menstrual period. The pain is usually felt in both breasts, the breasts are tender to palpation, and generally feel as though they are filled with shot. Usually all of these findings improve with the onset of menstruation; moreover, the condition can vary from one menstrual cycle to the next.

Sometimes one or several large tumors may be found in the breasts. They may be marble-sized, generally are not tender, and are known as fibroadenomata. The more serious tumors of the breasts generally do not produce pain at all, and are often felt accidentally or incidentally, as for example while soaping in a shower. More serious tumors of the breasts are hard and sometimes produce a dimpling of the overlying skin.

It is often not possible to make a correct diagnosis of a lump in the breast without removing a portion of it for examination under the microscope. This procedure is called a biopsy. A woman who finds a lump in her breast should know first of all that even an expert may not be sure of its exact nature without such a biopsy, hence she is in no position to pass judgment on it herself. Secondly, she should be cautioned against unnecessary delay in establishing a diagnosis, and not allow precious time to pass in waiting for it to go away.

BRONCHITIS The windpipe or trachea divides into a right and a left main stem bronchus in the upper part of the chest. These two major bronchi further subdivide into a system of pipelike channels which go to the five lobes into which the two lungs are divided (three on the right, two on the left). Within each lobe of the lung the bronchi undergo further division, and with each subdivision the size of the channel diminishes. This whole complex of branching tubes is referred to as the bronchial tubes and infection within them is termed bronchitis.

The many forms of bronchitis differ a great deal. Perhaps the chief thing they have in common is the symptom of cough, a prime indicator that something is going on in the trachea or bronchi. Thus certain viral inflammations of the respiratory tract, often termed tracheobronchitis, may produce relatively little phlegm but a good deal of irritative cough, so that people sometimes refer to "dry bronchitis" and the doctor to a nonproductive cough. Various bacterial inflammations, however, will cause a great deal of phlegm production. The phlegm may be thick, yellowish or greenish white, and abundant amounts may be brought up with each cough. Rattling sounds may be produced by the flapping about of mucus with breathing and coughing, and the abundant phlegm or coughing is spoken of as a productive cough.

Since many viral inflammations may be succeeded by mixed infections with various bacteria, it is not uncommon to see a change from the dry hacking cough to a more productive one as a respiratory illness progresses. Indeed, occasionally a further stage is reached which is the extension of the bronchial infection down into the finer subdivisions of the lung—at which point we can speak of pneumonia or bronchopneumonia. Still another form of bronchitis can be produced by inhalation of irritant gases and fumes. The most common example of this is produced by cigarette smoking, which is by far the most frequent cause of chronic bronchitis.

Bronchitis, Chronic It is often easier to clear up a pneumonia than to clear up a bronchitis. One reason for this is that pneumonia occurs in the lung substance proper and the antibiotic drugs which are administered can be brought to this region in large amounts. It is not possible to attain the same concentration of the antibiotic inside the larger bronchial tubes, so that inflammation here is resolved with greater difficulty.

In a few individuals wheezing due to narrowing and spasm of the bronchial tubes may occur in association with infection. This is spoken of as asthmatoid bronchitis, since it bears some resemblance to bronchial asthma. Indeed, somewhat similar drugs are used in the treatment of both conditions.

Treatment. Treatment will consist of cessation of smoking and the administration of antibiotics and other appropriate drugs. Sometimes special medicinal agents designed to liquefy the muscus may be administered. Maintaining a high humidity in room air, as for example by vaporizers, may be useful in all forms of bronchitis. It is clear that any form of bronchitis that hangs on, is associated with wheezing, or keeps recurring should be brought to the doctor's attention. (See also ASTHMA.)

BURNS Burns are generally described in terms of their extent and the depth of the injury produced by heat. A burn of the back, for example, would be classified as an 18 percent burn, one of the upper extremity as a 9 percent burn. The depth of injury is classified in degrees: a *first degree burn* produces reddening of the skin; a *second degree burn* produces blistering; a *third degree burn* extends below the surface of the skin and produces injury to underlying tissues.

First and second degree burns, unless very extensive, can be treated in the doctor's office or in the home; third degree burns must be treated in a hospital setting. Immediate first aid may be helpful in cutting down the degree of injury due to a burn. Thus, if someone spills hot coffee over his hand, immediate immersion in cold running water might diminish the injury and would certainly help relieve the pain. Burns of the hands are usually quite painful, but pain can be relieved by immersing the hand in ice cold water. Such immersion for relief of pain can be maintained off-and-on for as long as seems necessary.

Blisters on the hands and the fingers are a fairly common second degree injury. When large, they are nuisances since they interfere with the use of the fingers. There is no reason why they should not be evacuated, and collapse of the blister actually promotes the rate of healing. In the doctor's office they will be aspirated by the use of a syringe and a small needle. If they are treated at home, it is best to start by painting the blister with a germ-killing solution. One end of the blister can then be pierced with a needle that has been flamed or dipped into alcohol for several minutes and then allowed to dry, and the fluid allowed to run out. It is best to prick the end of the blister which will be in the lowermost position when the hand is kept in the usual down position. First and second degree burn areas should be covered with vaseline and a dressing. Some of the common ointments available for first-aid use in the kitchen contain tannic acid, which should be applied only to very small areas and never to the face or genital regions.

CANCER New cells are constantly being formed in the body. Where replacement needs are high, as in the skin, the intestine, or the bone marrow (blood formation), the cells may be found multiplying at a correspondingly high rate. The new cells take their proper place and function. This kind of growth is orderly and necessary.

In cancer, the growth process goes astray. Here the new cells may not be organized properly, perform no useful function and, on the contrary, may destroy neighboring normal cells by the pressure they exert. A group of cancer cells may lie dormant for years or may for unknown reasons enlarge rapidly. At first the growth is local only. It may remain that way, and sometimes very large growths are encountered still in their site of origin. Some cancers, however, do not conform to normal boundary lines. Groups of cells may slip away and show up in a distant location, an event known as metastasis. Some cancers have been successfully treated even after metastasis has occurred. But generally once the growth has metastasized, the golden opportunity for cure is gone. Hence the emphasis on early detection, when the growth is still localized and cure can be achieved.

It should be remembered that the term "cancer" covers a whole spectrum of growths. Some are progressive, others very slow-growing. Some may pose relatively little threat—as, for example, the fairly common cancers of the skin and some of the cancers arising in the thyroid gland and the prostate gland. Acute leukemia in a child is a most serious illness, but chronic lymphatic leukemia in an elderly person is compatible with years of uneventful existence.

Although this variability may produce uncertainty in dealing with cancer, it also leads to hope. In general, the layman is more pessimistic about cancer than the doctor, who knows that many cancers can be cured and others can be lived with. Significant advances continue to be made; among them are the relatively recent discoveries that cancer of the lung can be largely avoided by abstaining from cigarette smoking, that early curable cancer of the uterus can be readily detected, and that even advanced cancer of the breast and of the prostate can show considerable response to hormonal drugs.

Hodgkin's Disease (Lymphogranulomatosis) This is a malignant tumor whose cause is unknown. It affects the lymph nodes and lymphatic system. The spleen and lymph nodes enlarge and weakness, loss of weight and appetite usually occur. The nodes may enlarge in the neck or groin. Microscopic examination of the tissue of these enlarged nodes will give the diagnosis.

Treatment is usually radical surgery followed by X-ray. There are many new drugs which have proven useful in delaying what is ultimately a poor prognosis. However, there have been some long survivals.

Leukemia This is a fatal disease suspected of being caused by a virus. It is characterized by uncontrolled production of white blood cells and of their immature forms. Leukemias are classified according to the predominant cell type which is involved, and also according to whether they are acute or chronic. Lymphocytes, monocytes, and myelocytes are most commonly involved. The disease is seen most frequently in the first five years of childhood, also in the eighth to ninth years.

The general symptoms are fever, weakness, weight loss, fatigue, pallor, bleeding, frequent and repeated infections, and easy bruising. The lymph nodes and the spleen may be enlarged. Bleeding from the mucous membranes (mouth) should make one suspicious of this condition. Normally, the white blood count is 8,000 to 10,000 cells/cu. mm. In leukemias there are blood counts of 200,000 cells per cubic mm. and more. Immature forms of white blood cells are often seen in the peripheral blood smears.

Modern treatment of leukemias with various chemicals has arrested some of the more acute cases. There were also some cases which remain chronic for many years. However, this disease does not have a very good long-term prognosis.

Neuroblastoma Neuroblastoma is one of the most common malignant tumors in children. It is a tumor of the peripheral nerve cells derived from primitive sympathetic nerve tissue. Many arise from adrenal tissue or the chain of glands along the posterior portion of the chest. Their cell type varies, as does their degree of malignancy. The most frequent symptom is that of an abdominal tumor mass. If the tumor is very small, other symptoms such as fever, high white blood count, or a spread of this tumor to bone, liver, or eye, may occur. It is often found on both sides of the body, in contrast to another malignant tumor of childhood called Wilms' tumor. A sample of diseased tissue is examined under the microscope to determine the diagnosis.

Present treatment includes X-ray therapy and surgical excision followed by administration of various chemicals (chemotherapy) such as nitrogen mustard or antimetabolites.

Wilm's Tumor This is a tumor of the kidney which arises from the embryonal cells. It is the most common kidney tumor in children, occurs during the first four years of life, and is usually limited to one side. It is one of the most common abdominal tumors of early years.

The first sign is that of an enlarging abdomen. Other signs, such as blood in the urine, painful urination, anemia, fever, malnutrition, high blood pressure, constipation, etc., may arouse suspicion of this area. Wilms' tumor most frequently spreads to the lungs.

Surgical removal is followed by X-ray treatment and chemotherapy. There are many new drugs which have been used with some success in arresting this tumor. In general, however, the prognosis is poor.

CANCER, DETECTION OF About half of all the cancer found in women is in relatively accessible locations where early detection is possible—in the breast where it can be detected by palpation or by special X-ray methods, and in the cervix where it can be detected by the "Pap" smear method.

In other organs cancer sometimes makes it presence

known by departures from normal functioning. Thus cancer of the digestive tract may produce alterations in appetite, in capacity for food, or change in bowel habits such as constipation and diarrhea. Symptoms such as these, particularly in middle-aged and older individuals, may call for appropriate X-ray studies.

An annual physical examination—whether or not there are symptoms of any kind—is highly desirable. Many doctors feel that every woman should have a check of her breasts and of her reproductive organs twice a year, particularly past the age of thirty or thirty-five. Early localized cancer is in most instances readily cured, either with surgery or by X-ray. The American Cancer Society has issued a useful list in its program of education. Its early warning signals are the following:

1. Unusual bleeding or discharge.
2. A lump or thickening in the breast or elsewhere.
3. A sore that does not heal.
4. Change in bowel or bladder habits.
5. Persistent hoarseness or cough.
6. Persistent indigestion or difficulty in swallowing.
7. Change in a wart or mole.

"Pap" Smear This is a cancer detection procedure developed by the Greek-American anatomist George Papanicolaou. The basic principle derives from the observation that in many locations in the body a growing tumor, just like adjacent normal tissue, will undergo some shedding of the surface cells. When placed on a slide, stained, and examined under a microscope, it is possible to distinguish between normal and suspicious or obviously malignant cells. As a routine procedure, the "Pap" smear has been most successful when applied to the study of the uterus, particularly the cervix.

It seems both theoretically and practically possible to wipe out cancer of the cervix by routinely doing "Pap" smears on all women. It has been clearly shown that the "Pap" smear will pick up very early stages of cancer of the cervix, at a time when cure is relatively easy. In fact the "Pap" smear technique has demonstrated that this early non-invasive stage goes on for some years, throughout which time the "Pap" smear is consistently positive although nothing may be seen on naked-eye inspection.

The "Pap" smear procedure is very simple: a speculum is inserted into the vagina as is customarily done in routine pelvic examinations. The cervix, which protrudes into the upper part of the vagina is thereby readily visualized. An ordinary cotton-tipped swab is inserted into the opening of the cervix, briefly rotated and removed. The swab is then streaked across an ordinary microscope slide. This can be stained at any convenient time thereafter.

By one system of classification the findings under the microscope are grouped into a series of grades ranging from 1 to 5. Class 1 is clearly normal, class 5 is clearly a malignant tumor; intermediate stages are suspicious and may require repeated follow-up or perhaps a biopsy of the cervix for further clarification. A negative "Pap" smear does not necessarily rule out disease, but when correctly done the "Pap" smear is a valuable cancer detection technique which should be far more widely employed.

CANKER SORE (APTHOUS STOMATITIS) This mouth condition occurs both in children and adults. It is caused by the virus of *herpes simplex*. The lesions are characterized by groups of blisters which become ulcerated. They appear on the mucous membranes of the lips, cheeks, and tongue. Sometimes they extend into the throat area and involve the tonsils. The gums frequently start to swell and bleed. They may cause fever and swollen glands. Eating becomes painful and difficult. Prophylaxis and proper mouth hygiene are important in preventing this condition.

Since it is contagious, the eating utensils should be kept separate and boiled.

Treatment. Treatment is with bland diet, mild antiseptic mouth washes and antibiotics by injection and by mouth. Penicillin and aureomycin have been used with success. The ulcers may also be treated locally with applications of silver nitrate, a caustic agent which helps to heal them. The condition usually clears within five to seven days.

CATHETERIZATION Catheterization is the passing of a plastic or rubber tube into a channel or hollow organ of the body. The most common kind of catheterization is performed on the urinary bladder. It is done most often because of inability to urinate, which may be encountered after a general anesthetic or after childbirth. In men difficulty in urinating is most often due to enlargement of the prostate.

Catheterization used to be done almost routinely during deliveries, and not infrequently afterwards, if the need arose. However, it is best to try other alternatives such as the following: hot compresses or ice-cold compresses to the pubic region; running a water tap; bypassing the bedpan in favor of the commode or toilet. In some cases it is necessary to keep a catheter in the bladder for some time. It may be referred to as an "inlying catheter." One form of this is the Foley catheter, which has a small balloon. After this is inflated it will keep the catheter securely situated within the bladder.

Cardiac Catheterization Cardiac catheterization is a procedure which has been developed over recent years for evaluating disorders of the heart. It is used particularly to evaluate the departures from normal in congenital heart disease, or in estimating the degree of damage in a rheumatic heart. In cardiac catheterization a very long catheter is passed up the vein into a heart chamber, where pressure measurements can be taken and samples withdrawn for analysis of oxygen content. Cardiac catheterization is an invaluable diagnostic aid that is performed almost routinely before cardiac surgery.

CELIAC SYNDROME Celiac syndrome combines a number of specific symptoms which occur in children who are unable to digest starches or fats, or both. In cases of fat intolerance, there will be a defect in the absorption of fatty acids from the intestines. There may be a single defect, the absorption of starch, or, there may be a combination of both. A more severe form of the latter is called cystic fibrosis of the pancreas.

Celiac disease is a chronic nutritional disturbance occurring generally from the age of ten months to five years. Children affected with this condition fail to grow and thrive. They develop enlarged protuberant abdomens with weak, wasted muscles, particularly in the buttocks and extremities. They show evidence of vitamin deficiencies and pass large, bulky, foul-smelling stools. The stools will float if they are placed in water because of their large fat and starch content. These children are extremely cranky and irritable. Even though they may be receiving adequate food and nutrition, they are really malnourished, suffering from a serious defect in the absorption of foods. Normal stood contains a fat content of approximately 20 percent or even less. Celiac stools contain anywhere from 30 to 60 percent fat. The body is unable to absorb and utilize this fat; therefore, it has to be excreted.

As a result of the absorption deficiency, rickets, thinning of the bones (osteoporosis), hemorrhagic disease due to vitamin K deficiency, and secondary anemias develop.

Celiac disease has been shown to be a deficiency in absorption of gliadin, which is the active ingredient found in the protein fraction of wheat (gluten). Feeding even small amounts of gluten to children with celiac disease will induce severe diarrhea crises. A slice of bread or a cracker will cause abdominal pain, vomiting, and shock within hours. Most investigators feel that starch plays a more significant role than fat in the development of celiac syndrome.

Treatment. Celiac disease is treated with the Dorothy Anderson diet which starts with protein milk and banana powder, then graduates to scraped beef and tomato juice, ripe bananas, pot cheese, gelatin, squash, peas, celery, spinach. As improvement occurs, other meats, eggs, baked apples, and vegetables are added to the diet. Toast, bread, cereals, potatoes, whole milk, and butter are the very last to be added.

True cures of this condition are rare, and one generally speaks of remission rather than cure.

CERVIX The cervix is the lowest, narrowed portion of the uterus, and projects into the upper part of the birth canal (vagina). The normal cervix has a pink-white, solid appearance which is quite uniform. At its center is a small opening—the "os" or mouth—which leads into a narrow canal running the length of the cervix and entering the uterine cavity. A sampling of the tissue within the os, generally taken by a swab and placed on a microscope slide, is the basis of the "Pap" smear, an important diagnostic procedure for cancer. (See CANCER—Pap Smear.)

Many contraceptive devices and techniques act as barriers, preventing sperm from entering the os. In a non-pregnant woman it is a small circular opening; after one or more deliveries, however, it is larger and may appear as a slightly irregular slit running traversely. Women who use a diaphragm become familiar with the firm consistency of the cervix. (See BIRTH CONTROL.)

One of the remarkable changes that occurs in delivery is the virtual disappearance of the cervix as an indentifiable structure. When fully dilated at the time of delivery, the opening of the cervix permits the baby's head to descend into the vagina. That this thin-walled and distended segment can return within a matter of weeks to a size and shape somewhat resembling that before pregnancy is truly remarkable. (See CHILDBIRTH AND PREGNANCY—Labor.)

Infection within the cervix known as endocervicitis may lead to a mucous discharge. There may (sometimes in association with endocervicitis, but also independently) be a change in the appearance of the cervical tissue adjacent to the os. Instead of a dull opaque white, the os may appear thinner and redder; this is known as erosion. The doctor will often treat endocervicitis and erosion by a procedure known as cauterization, which promotes the return of the tissue to normal.

CHICKEN POX (VARICELLA) Contagious.

Cause. Virus.

Incubation period. 2 to 3 weeks.

Symptoms. Slight illness, including loss of appetite, feelings of malaise, and mild fever, may be present before the rash breaks out. The rash starts with small, red, flat patches which become raised and then blistered. The blisters fill with cloudy fluid. There are all stages of eruption present at the same time. It appears first on the body, then spreads to the face and head (including mucous membranes of the mouth, vulva, etc.). Very few pox appear on the legs and arms. After the fluid-filled blisters dry, they crust and become scabs. If the child scratches them, they may become infected. The rash, which causes severe itching, continues to break out for three to five days, and is often seen inside the mouth and in the hair.

The lymph glands in the body also become enlarged. Ear infections, pneumonia, and other complications have been known to follow this disease. There is no known prevention. However, one attack usually gives permanent immunity.

Treatment. Local starch baths, or starch applications, and soothing lotions and creams to suppress itching are helpful. Children should be prevented from picking the scabs off before they are completely dry, as ugly, pitted scars may result if they are prematurely loosened. It is advisable not to give the child a complete tub bath until all the scabs have fallen off. Premature soaking will only loosen them and cause scars. A physician should always be called to determine whether the case is chicken pox or smallpox, which it resembles. However, smallpox is rarely seen in this country due to mass vaccination programs.

CHILDBIRTH AND PREGNANCY

Pregnancy Tests Most of the pregnancy tests used are based upon the observation that large amounts of hormones are produced when pregnancy occurs. These hormones are secreted by the developing embryo; they are passed on into the blood of the mother and some are excreted through the kidney and urine. Hence pregnancy tests can be done on either blood or urine specimens.

The particular hormones tested for are known as the gonadotropins, hormones which stimulate the sex glands—the ovaries or the testes. In the case of the commonly performed Friedman's test (Friedman-Lapham test, or rabbit test) the course of events is as follows: It is known that the isolated female rabbit has in her ovaries ripe follicles ready to shed their eggs. Injection of a small amount of an ovar-stimulating hormones, such as may be found in the urine or blood of a pregnant woman, will produce rupture of these follicles with release of their eggs—ovulation. The test is simple to perform. An extract of an overnight urine specimen or the serum of a blood specimen from the pregnant woman is injected into the rabbit's ear vein. Twenty-four hours later an abdominal incision is made and the rabbit's ovaries inspected. If ovulation has occurred, the alteration in the appearance of the ovary is easily seen by naked-eye inspection. This would be a positive pregnancy test.

There are other forms of pregnancy testing which include: (1) the original A-Z (Aschheim-Zondek) test, based upon observation of stimulation by the pregnant woman's hormones of the immature testes or ovaries of a rat; (2) the frog or toad test, based upon the fact that these same hormones of pregnancy will produce extrusion of sperm in a frog or a toad. The frog test may be read within a few hours. Recently newer pregnancy tests have been devised which do away with experimental animals altogether. They are based upon delicate testing of the immunization type.

None of these tests is 100 percent accurate very early in pregnancy. But this level of accuracy is almost reached two weeks or more after the menstrual period is missed. Hence a positive test means more than a negative test, and a negative test does not always rule out the possibility of early pregnancy. If other signs indicate a possible pregnancy and a first test is reported negative, another test should be run.

Fetal Development This term refers to the growth of the unborn baby. Its development in the uterus during the 280 days following the missed menstrual period is the greatest and most complex growth process in nature. It transforms the tiny fertilized ovum, invisible to the naked eye, into the six-to-eight pound human infant whose lusty birth cry marks the appearance of a new human being. Development proceeds somewhat as follows, with times representing averages from the first day of the last menstrual period:

14 days—sperm penetrates the egg, fertilization
14–17 days—fertilized egg proceeds down the tube
24 days—fertilized egg, now a little ball of cells, burrows into the lining of the uterus

30 days—embryo well embedded in uterine lining. Multiple little processes have sprouted like roots for taking up nourishment.

6 weeks—head, spinal canal, and vertebrae forming. Rudiments of eyes, ears, and nose have appeared.

8 weeks—one inch long. Head is proportionately large, rudimentary extremities. Eyes, face, and features forming.

12 weeks—3 inches long. Arms, legs, hands, and feet formed. Distinct fingers and toes with soft nails. External sex organs begin to show differences between male and female.

16 weeks—4.6 inches long; 2-4 ounces in weight. Fine downy hair (lanugo) covers skin. Obvious external sex organs.

20 weeks—12 inches long; ¾ of a pound in weight. Fetal movements begin, heart sounds may be heard by doctor.

24 weeks—1½ pounds in weight. Skin is wrinkled, eyebrows and lashes are formed. If child is born it cannot survive.

28 weeks—2½ pounds in weight. Eyes open. Well-developed head hair.

32 weeks (end of seventh month)—16 inches long; 3½ pounds in weight. The child looks like a "little old man," with not much fat in the skin.

36 weeks—18 inches long; 5 pounds in weight. Face is less wrinkled, because of fat deposits.

40 weeks (full term infant)—19–20 inches long; 6 ½–8 pounds in weight. Scalp hair is dark, the skin smooth and covered with white secretion. There are well-developed nails and head hair. Eyes are slate-colored, but the final color cannot be predicted.

Prenatal Care A routine form of professional care for a pregnant woman, generally given by a doctor or nurse, is called prenatal care. The objectives of prenatal care are to keep the mother as healthy as possible throughout the pregnancy, avoiding or minimizing the various disorders that may be associated with the pregnant state and insuring that the unborn baby is well nourished and developed. The routines involved may vary somewhat, as will the time and frequency of the visits.

Basic elements of prenatal care will include keeping track of weight, blood pressure and urine to avoid toxemia of pregnancy. Attention will be paid to diet since pregnancy calls for special measures such as increased calcium and iron as well as maintenance of a well-balanced high vitamin diet. Influenza and polio are somewhat more hazardous to women who are pregnant, and appropriate immunizations may be called for. The dangers of German measles, especially to the fetus, are well known. Swelling of the legs, development of varicose veins, obesity and vaginal infections may occur. (See VAGINITIS.) Heartburn, excess salivation, constipation, nausea and vomiting are some of the diegestive problems frequently encountered. The doctor is able to treat or alleviate most of these.

"Morning Sickness" A significant number of pregnant women experience nausea of varying degrees during the first third of their pregnancies. There is no doubt that some physical change in the digestive tract underlies this complaint. Thus women have been known to complain of nausea before they missed their menstrual period—i.e., before they had reason to believe they might be pregnant. Worries and anxieties about the pregnancy may increase complaints regarding nausea, much as tension may increase a headache or stomach cramps. In addition, anything that can produce or contribute to nausea in the non-pregnant state will do the same to a pregnant woman—whether it be an unpleasant sight or thought, greasy food, or unpleasant odors. The complaint is most marked on arising and shortly thereafter. Both physical and psychological factors may be involved in "morning sickness."

Treatment. Various procedures may be helpful:

1. Before retiring for the night, place two or three dry crackers at the bedside; these should be eaten on awakening in the morning without getting up. After a wait of twenty minutes or so, one can arise.

2. Overloading the stomach, particularly in the morning, should be avoided. Breakfast should be small and should be followed a few hours later by a mid-morning snack.

3. Avoid fats and fried or greasy foods.

4. All else being equal, a meal consisting largely of solids will sit more easily than one containing much fluid—it may be preferable to save the fluid intake for later in the day.

5. Various mild sedatives and tranquilizers will help allay nausea, but none should be taken without first checking with the doctor.

Toxemia of Pregnancy This term refers to an abnormality found in the last two to three months of pregnancy and occasionally in the period immediately following the delivery. Its causes are unknown, but the condition is specific to pregnancy and is more common during first pregnancies, or if twins are present. It is sometimes impossible to distinguish mild degrees of this disorder from many of the normal events in pregnancy. As the doctor sees it, there is a rise in blood pressure, an unusual amount of edema (puffiness), and albumin in the urine.

The pregnant woman may feel entirely well but should be aware of the possibilities of toxemia if she undergoes rapid weight gain (on the order of two to three pounds per week), if the fingers swell up so that rings become tight, or if the face becomes puffy. Headaches or blurring of vision usually indicate that toxemia is well established. Any pregnant woman experiencing any of these symptoms should communicate with her doctor at once and not let matters slide until the next regular appointment. Toxemia is rare where there has been good prenatal care; when caught early, it is generally easily reversed.

Treatment. The measures that the doctor prescribes will include rest, restriction of salt in the diet, and perhaps also the taking of such drugs as the diuretics, which promote the excretion of fluid, or drugs designed to lower the blood pressure. If the blood pressure is unusually high, or if the other findings warrant it, the doctor may well advise a few days' stay in the hospital for observation. Mild degrees of toxemia are by no means rare—especially toward the very end of pregnancy. That the condition is somehow related to secretions coming from the uterus, perhaps the placenta, is indicated by the usually prompt disappearance of the puffiness and the drop in blood pressure that occurs upon delivery.

Weight Gain in Pregnancy It is the doctor's hope in most instances that the weight gain in pregnancy should not exceed twenty pounds. The exception would be a painfully thin woman for whom some filling-out would be desirable. For her, pregnancy may be a good opportunity to put on some desired weight. The twenty-pound figure for normal pregnancy gain is based on adding together the following: the baby, seven pounds; enlargement of the uterus, three pounds, placenta and uterine fluid, two pounds; increase in breast weight, up to two pounds. Adding approximately six pounds of retained fat and fluid to this total of fourteen pounds can be regarded as reasonable. During the first three months of pregnancy some women exhibit no weight gain because of nausea; others gain as much as four to five pounds. During the last six months of pregnancy the weight gain should not be at a rate faster than two-thirds to three-fourths of a pound per week. The rate at which this weight is gained fluctuates from week to week and cannot be exact. However, rapid weight gains such as one to two pounds per week—especially when accompanied by obvious puffiness of the face and around the eyes and by headaches—should be reported to the doctor.

Many women experience an inordinate stimulation of appetite during pregnancy. If intake is not restrained, very large weight gains are possible. A woman who throws caution to the winds can gain thirty to forty pounds and, of course, will find that putting it on is much easier than taking it off. It is wise to avoid weight gains in pregnancy beyond an upper limit of approximately twenty-four pounds.

The Pelvis and Childbirth   The bones that make up the pelvis are put together in such a manner as to form an oval basin-like enclosure. The largest of the bones, the innominate, extends from the sacrum in the midline of the back and forms a curve which runs up to the front and, again in the midline, meets the pubic bones. The junction of the two pubic bones in the midline in front is called the pubic symphysis. It is only some two inches in height and can be easily felt just above the genital region.

Late in pregnancy the pubic symphysis actually becomes looser and more mobile in preparation for the baby's birth. When looked at from below, the opening through the pelvis is much narrower; it is called the pelvic outlet. The size of the pelvic outlet is of major importance in obstetrics. If it is small, and if the baby's head is proportionately large, Caesarean section may be necessary.

Although it is impossible to measure the pelvic outlet precisely, the doctor can take a series of measurements of the pelvis at different points and draw quite accurate conclusions as to the size of the outlet. In a few cases (as when the pelvis has been deformed because of poliomyelitis with paralysis early in life) it may be obvious that normal delivery cannot be expected.

Sometimes the measurements taken by the doctor may be borderline, so that he cannot be sure whether a normal-sized baby can be delivered from below. The doctor may therefore decide to observe the course of labor before coming to a decision as to whether or not Caesarean section is necessary. This is known as "trial of labor." In the overwhelming percentage of cases, of course, such mechanisms as the loosening-up of the pubic symphysis, the relaxation of other ligaments binding the pelvis, and the molding of the baby's head will all be factors that will abet a normal delivery. Nature is often further aided when the doctor performs the procedure known as episiotomy.

Labor   The baby is brought into the world by painful contractions of the uterus. These pains are labor pains. Exactly what initiates them, after nine months of relative quiet, is unknown. In some women painful uterine contractions may occur for a period of some hours about a week or two before true labor begins. Such pains may even result in a woman's being brought to the hospital before the pains, instead of increasing, decrease and then disappear. This is sometimes referred to as "false labor."

In contrast, true labor pains are characterized by regular rhythmicity, increasing intensity, and a progressive shortening of the interval between contractions. It is sometimes wise to time the intervals between the pains to determine precisely whether the intervals are diminishing. As soon as it is clear that true labor pains have commenced, the doctor should be contacted. He is the one to determine the time at which hospitalization seems desirable. His decision in this respect will be influenced by the knowledge of whether or not this is a first baby, whether there is a history of rapid deliveries in the past, and whether a woman may not feel more secure in a hospital setting. The total duration of labor is generally somewhere between twelve and eighteen hours, but it can be either longer or shorter by another six hours. It is generally shorter in women who have had one or more previous children (multiparas, from *multi,* many; *para,* birth).

It is customary to divide labor into stages. In the *first stage* there is a gradual dilatation and softening-up of the cervix, the lowermost portion of the uterus which protrudes into the vagina. (See CERVIX.) The extent of this dilatation can be judged by rectal examination. When the opening of the cervix has reached approximately 2½ inches, the woman is said to be "fully dilated." Approximately 90 percent of the total duration of the labor is involved in reaching this point. During the second stage of labor, the baby passes through the uterus and the vagina on his way into the outside world. The second stage may take one to two hours in a woman having her first baby, generally considerably less in others.

The *second stage* may tax the skill of the doctor and require good patient cooperation. Depending on how things are going, the doctor may ask the mother to bear down, which aids in the delivery process, or to avoid bearing down, perhaps to avoid a precipitate delivery with possible tissue damage. In the case of a breech delivery, the doctor may have to work rapidly. During the second stage the powerful uterine contractions may push the baby's head periodically up to the vaginal entrance, an event known as "crowning." At about this point the doctor may elect to do an episiotomy to widen the opening.

An episiotomy makes the delivery of the baby easier for both mother and infant. In hospital practice it is almost routine to do an episiotomy, especially for women having their first delivery. Another indication for doing an episiotomy would be evidence of undue stretching as the baby's head comes down, suggesting the possibility that a tear may occur. Instead of running the risk of such a tear, which may be irregular, deep, or lead to complications, an episiotomy will be done to control the threatening situation. Other advantages of episiotomy are: (1) It substitutes a surgical incision which is easily repaired for lacerations which may be difficult to repair. (2) It is easier on the baby's head and avoids some of the risk of damage to it. (3) It shortens labor.

The *third stage* of labor consists of delivery of the afterbirth or placenta. This generally takes about fifteen minutes and completes the act of labor.

CHILDBIRTH—DELIVERY

Natural Childbirth   Natural childbirth is a term generally used to describe a program of care and instruction during pregnancy which emphasizes physical and psychological preparation for the delivery. Its exponents have emphasized that feelings of fear and isolation, coupled with the complete ignorance about labor which used to be true of most women, lead to anxiety and muscular tension; these in turn increase the pain, may perhaps prolong the labor, and therefore increase the woman's difficulties. Natural childbirth has also emphasized the importance of a positive and supportive relationship between the woman in labor and those about her. Since isolation may increase the pain and anxiety, natural childbirth requires support for the woman in the labor room, which may include visiting by the husband.

Some hospitals sponsor classes of instruction based upon natural childbirth. There are lectures and demonstrations which discuss the anatomy of pregnancy and the mechanism of delivery. Instruction is also given in the various methods of breathing which will be of importance during labor. Systematic exercises and methods for producing relaxation, both of value during delivery, are part of the instruction. In some hospital settings the area of the unknown is further reduced by a tour through the obstetric wards, inspection of the labor rooms, and introduction to the nursing personnel who may be present at the time of delivery. There is generally one lecture for the expectant fathers.

Various books dealing with the subject of natural childbirth and descriptions of the exercises used are readily available. There can be no doubt that natural childbirth and programs derived from it have diminished previous fears based on ignorance and, therefore, diminish the impact of labor pains. Proponents of natural childbirth never claim that it can make labor a painless process, but rather that a woman who is not tense and who knows what is happening will experience considerably less discomfort. Thus natural childbirth does not mean that pain-killing drugs or anesthetics are unnecessary.

Caesarean Birth A Caesarean birth is a delivery made through an incision into the abdomen and uterus. The most frequent reason for this kind of delivery is a contracted pelvis—a pelvis whose dimensions are too small to permit a normal (natural) delivery. Sometimes the operation is decided upon after a trial of labor indicates that vaginal delivery will be very difficult or impossible. However, if it has become clear that a Caesarean section will be necessary, the mother may be admitted to a hospital late in the ninth month of pregnancy and delivered by Caesarean procedure before labor pains have commenced. Such a planned Caesarean birth is known as an elective Caesarean section. It is often done on women who have had a previous Caesarean, the thought being that the scar into the uterus from the previous operation represents a weak spot and, therefore, a potentially troublesome one if labor is permitted.

"Once a Caesarean always a Caesarean" is still a pretty general rule. Accordingly, some women have had three, four or even more babies by the Caesarean route. A Caesarean section is sometimes done after a too-early separation of the placenta (the afterbirth), since otherwise the baby's life is endangered. Still another reason might be a first pregnancy late in a woman's life: doing a Caesarean delivery may mean less of a risk to the baby, and in a sense will insure that the mother will have at least one successful pregnancy.

Breech Delivery In about 3 percent of all births, the legs or buttocks rather than the head present first. Such presentations are referred to as breeches. The reason for the breech presentation is unknown. Occasionally attempts may be made before delivery to shift the baby's position within the womb into the head-down position. Once labor has begun, such a maneuver may not be possible. Unfortunately, even if it is successful at first, it may be found that the baby may again return to the breech position some time before the delivery.

A breech presentation makes the delivery somewhat more difficult from the doctor's point of view. So far as the mother is concerned no difference in the labor will be noted. Various technical maneuvers are available to the obstetrician in expediting the second stage of labor when a breech presentation occurs. In the delivery of twins or other multiple births, one or more of the babies may come out in the breech position. The problem here is eased somewhat, however, by the fact that the infants are generally smaller and hence more easily maneuvered.

The Umbilical Cord (Navel) The umbilical cord is the cord through which nourishment is supplied to the fetus. The cord, containing a vein and two umbilical arteries, is attached to the mother's placenta and to the infant at the middle of the abdomen.

At birth, the cord is cut a few inches from the abdomen and clamped so that it does not bleed. It is permitted to dry, whereupon it falls off, leaving the depression known as the navel or "belly button." Sometimes the cord oozes pus or may separate and bleed a little. Pressure for five or ten minutes will stop the bleeding. The drainage from a healing cord can be cleansed with alcohol. Antibiotic ointments may also be required.

It is advisable not to bathe the infant in a tub until the cord has dried and fallen off, since it may become infected with dirty bath water. Sometimes there is incomplete closure of the inner portion of the cord, and a protrusion results. This is called an *umbilical hernia*. It usually enlarges when the infant strains at stool or cries. If it becomes very large, it runs the danger of becoming an *incarcerated umbilical hernia*. If this occurs, an emergency operation is required. Sometimes the doctor will advise taping the umbilical hernia with adhesive tape to prevent it from enlarging.

Premature Infants An infant who weighs five and a half pounds or less is termed premature. This definition applies whether the child is born at the full nine months or earlier. Children who are born before term usually weigh less than normal and therefore, automatically, are called premature ("preemies"). These babies are generally a bit weaker than normal. They may cry in a more feeble manner; the skin is loose and wrinkled and their temperature is unstable and generally lower than normal. They may lose more weight in the beginning than heavier babies, and their general gain is not as rapid. They require extra warmth in an incubator and special precautions to prevent infection. Many premature infants require feeding from tubes (gavage feeding) or feeding from a dropper. Their sucking and swallowing reflexes and muscles are not well developed.

Premature babies have many other immature features. However, they generally catch up with full-term babies and their subsequent development is not necessarily damaged by the fact of their prematurity. Because of their anatomic and physiological immaturity, premature babies are particularly susceptible to many illnesses, including circulatory, respiratory, gastrointestinal, urinary, and other difficulties. Prematurity is the leading cause of infant deaths. The prevention of prematurity depends on excellent professional obstetrical care and on early diagnosis and treatment of conditions in the mother which may dispose to prematurity.

Premature infants are fed nothing by mouth during the first twenty-four to forty-eight hours. Then boiled sugar water (5 percent solution) is given. Formulas for prematures should be high in protein, low in fat, and high in calcium. One-half powdered skim milk and one-half fresh skimmed or evaporated milk is generally used. In the second week, vitamins are added to the formula (vitamins A, B, and C). Most of these babies eat more often than every four hours in the beginning months. They may have more frequent bowel movements. This has sometimes been mistaken for "diarrhea" and caused alarm. It is not diarrhea, but is merely due to the infant's limited capacity. The frequency of movements lessens in time as the infant's capacity to hold more ounces of food grows.

Twins and Multiple Births Twins occur approximately once in ninety births, triplets once in 9,300 pregnancies, quadruplets once in 490,000 pregnancies, and quintuplets approximately once in 8 million deliveries. The peak incidence for twins occurs in women between 35 and 40, is more common in women with previous pregnancies, more common in Negroes than in Caucasians, and is least common among the Japanese.

Most often twins come about because two eggs are released simultaneously rather than the usual one. The resulting offspring have no more resemblance to one another than is usual between brothers and sisters. They are referred to as fraternal (non-identical) twins. Occasionally a single fertilized egg can divide into two identical halves, each of which is capable of complete development. There then results a pair of what are called identical twins. Identical twins are always of the same genetic constitution and therefore have the same sex, look alike to the point of being difficult to tell apart, and possess the same temperament, intellect, etc.

In the case of triplets, quadruplets, and multiple births generally, any combination of fraternal or identical babies may be found in the offspring. Thus triplets may be identical, consist of two identical and one fraternal twin, or be derived from three separate eggs and be entirely fraternal. Since the babies are generally smaller in multiple births, the actual delivery may be physically easier. However, breech presentations and prematurity are often complicating factors.

Breasts After Delivery The production of milk is the result of stimulation of the breasts by a pituitary hormone. This milk-producing principle is inhibited throughout pregnancy by the sex-hormone production of the placenta, the afterbirth, an interesting example of nature's wisdom. Thus during the latter part of pregnancy and for the first couple of days after the delivery, only a clear fluid known as colostrum may exude from the nipples. Milk production begins often in a dramatic way, about three days after the delivery. The breasts may suddenly become full, hard, and tender, an event known as engorgement. The network of veins may visibly develop in the skin of the breasts, becoming much more prominent.

If the decision is made to nurse the infant, the pain and fullness of the breast will promptly be helped by the breast feeding. This emptying of the breast is also a strong stimulus to further milk production. If the mother decides not to nurse, she may have some discomfort for several days while the breasts learn to adjust to this situation. Several steps may be of value during this time: (1) The pain of engorgement will be relieved by aspirin, codeine, or similar drugs. (2) Ice bags may be applied to the breasts, an hour on and an hour off. (3) A well-fitting snug bra giving uplift and support will be useful. (See also INFANT FEEDING.)

Care of Nipples The nipples need no special care during pregnancy. However, if a nipple is flat or inverted, and especially if nursing is planned, the doctor or nurse may show procedures for bringing the nipple out and making it more prominent. One technique consists of cuppling the hand around the aerola—the pigmented circular area around the nipple—and gently pressing down the tissue around the nipple so as to make it more prominent. With the fingers of the other hand, the nipple can be gently pulled on and stripped. The procedure can be repeated for a minute or two; in conjunction with the enlargement that occurs during pregnancy anyway, a flat nipple can thus be "brought out" reasonably well.

Cracking of the nipples is not uncommon in nursing mothers; perhaps half of them will develop some cracks or fissures at one time or another. There are some events which predispose the nipples to such cracking. Falling asleep while nursing may lead to maceration and cracking of the nipples; a mother should stay awake while nursing and see that the baby "attends to business." Forceably pulling the baby away from the nipple is also an occasional cause. A fissure makes nursing quite painful; this is true even when it is a hairline in width. There may occasionally be some bleeding from a crack, some of the blood being taken by the baby while nursing. If, after nursing, the baby regurgitates milk with some blood in it, the most likely source is the nipple. The cracked nipple will not heal so long as nursing is continued; hence, the baby should be promptly removed. This alone will generally lead to rapid cure.

The nipples should be protected and kept dry. Sometimes a nipple shield is recommended so as to permit continued nursing; however, the nipple may be drawn against one side of the shield and further injured. A cracked nipple may thus mean abandoning nursing; if cracking persists, a change to formula may become necessary. A heat lamp may promote healing; all that is necessary in addition is to protect the nipple with sterile gauze. (See also BREASTS.)

Involution of Uterus After the birth of a baby the uterus begins to undergo shrinkage, a process known as involution. This process is remarkable both for the amount of shrinkage that occurs and the rapidity with which it occurs. Indeed no comparable process occurs anywhere else in the body. Within a six-week period the two-pound uterus will shrink down to two ounces. A large organ well up in the abdomen becomes a small one well down in the pelvis.

Thus, immediately after the delivery the uterus is above the level of the umbilicus (belly button). Within twenty-four hours it sinks below this level. By the fourth day after delivery it is halfway between the umbilicus and the pubic symphysis, the bony landmark felt just above the vaginal area. By the eighth day it is one-third of the way between umbilicus and symphysis, and by the tenth it has sunk below the symphysis and can no longer be felt by abdominal palpation.

During the first few days in the hospital the doctor will check on the process of involution. If it seems to be going too slowly he may prescribe medications for contracting the uterus. Nursing the infant, through an interesting tie-in between the breasts and the uterus, tends to hasten involution. It does this by increasing the contractions of the uterus, sometimes to such a point that nursing may increase afterpains. Sometimes nursing may produce a spurt in the lochia, the reddish discharge which occurs after delivery, the spurt representing increased uterine contraction. This increased vigor of the uterine contractions is desirable.

Another remarkable aspect of the involution of the uterus is that it tends to return to its old tipped-forward position in the pelvis, immediately behind the bladder. At one time it was considered that the return to this normal tipped-forward position might be aided by special exercises such as "monkey-trots," an exercise in which a woman went around on all fours for several minutes several times a day. Another procedure designed with the same end in mind was adopting the knee-chest position one or more times daily for several minutes. In this position, with the knees spread approximately eighteen inches apart, air can get into the vagina. It was felt that this might be of aid in returning the uterus to a good position. It is now generally felt, however, that the normal process of involution can be relied upon to return the structures to the usual nonpregnant state and position.

Activity After Childbirth The amount of activity that will be permitted or encouraged during the first two weeks after delivery of the child will be dependent in part on how the pregnancy and labor went. If the labor was an easy one and not exhausting, obviously the mother will feel stronger and will be able to do more. If it was a first labor, or a difficult one perhaps associated with some blood loss and an episiotomy, the new mother can hardly be blamed for not feeling too energetic for the first day or two. She may well be advised to remain in bed during this time and use a bedpan rather than the bathroom.

However, the experience of the past twenty years has indicated that it is better for the mother to be up and about so far as possible and not to remain in bed for as long as a week or more as was formerly the practice. Muscle strength is restored earlier and activity also diminishes the possibility of clotting in the veins of the legs. In fact, if the mother has to remain in bed longer than the usual time, the doctor may well advise her to wiggle her feet at the ankles and bend them at the knees repeatedly throughout the day to stimulate the circulation. The advantages of being up and around should in no way contradict the need for rest; frequent rest periods and naps during the day are desirable.

The mother's work during delivery has correctly been called "labor," and rest is needed to accelerate the repair process. This requires mental relaxation also. A constant flow of visitors is not conducive to such relaxation, and in many maternity hospitals the number of visitors is wisely limited, sometimes to no more than two per day.

In the ordinary course of events, the average mother will be discharged around the sixth day following delivery. The return home may pose problems, since she will be faced with a great many more activities and responsibilities than existed in the hospital. In addition to running the home, there may be the needs of other family members, including perhaps other children. If this is added to the round-the-clock demands of the newborn baby, the load may be heavy indeed. A willing husband may be pressed into service, but even better is a practical nurse or a "baby nurse"—often an older woman with some experience in the field—or perhaps a mother or other close woman relative. Help of this sort will enable the mother to have adequate rest periods during the morning and the afternoon and an uninterrupted night's sleep may become possible.

For the first few days at home it may be best for her to remain on one floor if at all possible. If the home is such that it is necessary to negotiate stairs, this should be kept at a minimum. Showers and even tub baths may be permitted once a woman has returned home, but this should be checked with the doctor. If an episiotomy incision still remains open, local hot compresses or sitz baths may also be advised by the doctor. A woman can usually figure on taking short walks within a few days after she has returned home. She can be driven around in a car in about two weeks after the delivery and do the driving herself in about three to four weeks.

Soon after her return home, and perhaps even earlier if so advised, various exercises for firming up the abdomen may be advisable. Sexual relations are generally advised against until the first post-partum checkup at the doctor's office, generally at six weeks. (See SEXUAL RELATIONS AFTER CHILDBIRTH.)

Post-Patrum Conditions   *Afterpains.*   A fair number of women who have had more than one baby, and occasionally a woman who has had only one, may experience pains due to contractions of the uterus for several days after delivery. The pains may recur at fairly regular intervals and are more likely to be noticed if the baby is nursed. With some of these contractions, there may be an expulsion of secretion or a blood clot. The pains are sometimes sufficiently sharp to warrant taking some medication, and various pain-killing drugs will be ordered by the doctor as indicated.

Lochia.   For several weeks after the delivery there is a vaginal discharge called the lochia. For the first three or four days the lochia is blood-colored, somewhat resembling a menstrual period. About the third to tenth day the discharge becomes more watery and less red in color. It then decreases in amount and may become almost colorless but will generally continue for about three weeks, when it disappears. Occasionally a slight brown discharge may persist somewhat longer. The changing appearance and amount of the lochia reflect healing changes going on within the uterus. The separation of the placenta (afterbirth) leaves a large wound surface within the uterus which contributes to the red lochia of the first days. As this area heals, the white lochia makes its appearance. The lochia has a somewhat pungent but not offensive odor; it does not ordinarily contain blood clots. It is quite normal for the amount of lochia to increase somewhat when a woman gets up and about. Sudden or unusual changes in the lochia, such as the apperance of blood clots, should be called to the doctor's attention.

Depression.   "Baby blues" (post-partum depression) is a common term to describe the depressions that many women experience soon after their labor and delivery. It has been estimated that at least 60 percent, and probably more, of new mothers experience significant depression during the first week after the delivery. Some women are ashamed to admit this and are indeed puzzled by it: the nine-month period of pregnancy has terminated successfully; the delivery has gone well; and the baby is beautiful and well-formed. What possible reason can there be for unhappiness?

Nevertheless, by about the third day following labor, a woman may find herself feeling low, lacking in energy and interest, and sometimes may burst into tears which she is unable to control. It may well be that various emotionally tinged thoughts occur to the new mother. She may feel that her having at long last fulfilled her biological role and become a mother is an important step toward aging—she is now a changed and older person. She may well also have doubts and fears about the responsibilities of motherhood and the day-in, day-out commitments this represents.

Not infrequently, however, the new mother can find no explanation to account for her tears; this in itself may add to her feelings of annoyance and depression; she merely realizes she is in the grip of an emotion she cannot readily account for and which, in fact, seems uncalled for. She should, however, be reassured that "baby blues" are very widespread in every maternity hospital; that they are generally quite temporary and almost predictably tend to disappear when the mother goes home with her new baby. There certainly is no need, nor is it advisable, to conceal her feelings. She should by all means discuss them with her doctor.

Post-partum Exercises   These are exercises that may be embarked on at some time shortly after the delivery, designed to hasten the return to normal strength and to the figure of the non-pregnant state. Many post-partum changes will tend to occur naturally; thus the uterus shrinks spontaneously and many varicose veins tend to diminish or disappear. The abdominal muscles, despite the considerable stretching they undergo during pregnancy—which can be the despair of a woman who prides herself on a good figure—will undergo considerable contraction once the uterus has pushed the baby into the outer world. However, what Nature will do can be helped along and somewhat improved with appropriate exercises. Not only will these exercises tighten up the abdomen, but they also tend to improve posture and are useful in the treatment of backache. The woman who is naturally the athletic sort will find them easy. If one is sedentary, do not overdo; it is better to do a small number of exercises frequently than do too large a number once or twice. Exercises can be started while in the hospital or after one returns home, as directed by the doctor. Some of them are:

1.   Position: lying flat on the back. Bring right leg up eight or ten inches, let it come down slowly; repeat with the left leg, and perform this eight to ten times for each. As the days go by, one should be able to elevate each leg to approximately a right angle.

1a.   After a few days this same exercise can be done with both legs. At first elevate both legs only a few inches off the bed or floor. Repeat eight to ten times. On successive days the legs can be elevated higher and higher, and lowered more and more slowly—which increases the effectiveness of the exercise. After several weeks, one should be able to bring both legs well over toward one's head. Come up and go down slowly and repeat six to ten times.

2.   Position: flat on the back, arms crossed over chest. Lift the head up a few inches, then return to original position. Repeat six to ten times. As the days pass by, try raising the head higher. In four to six weeks one should be able to attain the sitting position.

3.   Position: flat on the back, legs drawn up. Contract the muscles around the vaginal and rectal openings as though trying to hold back a bowel movement. Repeat ten to twelve times.

4. Position: on hands and knees, weight equally distributed on all four extremities. By contracting the buttocks and stomach muscles, tilt the pelvis forward. Relax and repeat up to twelve times. This "pelvic rocking" helps relieve lumbosacral (lower back) strain.

CHOLESTEROL Cholesterol is a wax-like member of the varied chemical family of fats. It is found in all body cells, where it is an essential structural component. In common with many other fatty substances it is constantly found circulating in the bloodstream. Here its level is remarkably constant in most individuals. The level at which it is established, however, does vary a good deal. In some families many members tend to have high blood cholesterols, a condition known as hypercholesterolemia. Similar elevations of the blood cholesterol are frequently found in diabetes and in underfunctioning of the thyroid gland, and slight rises are reported to occur under the stress of deadlines and similar pressures.

The present interest in cholesterol is based upon the fact that it has been incriminated in the process of atherosclerosis, popularly referred to as "hardening of the arteries." Cholesterol is indeed found in the fatty deposits in the arteries, although it is by no means the only fat present there. However, in a special long-term study being conducted in the population of Framingham, Mass., it has been found that elevated blood cholesterol cannot be disregarded as a factor in the background of coronary heart disease.

On the basis of such lines of evidence, certain nutritionists have advocated a reduction in the fat and cholesterol content of the American diet. Food particularly rich in cholesterol include whole milk and its derivatives (butter, cream, most cheeses, ice cream), eggs, and the fatter cuts of meat. It is now recognized that the problem is somewhat more complicated; for in addition to the restriction of fats and cholesterol, a balance between saturated and unsaturated fats is also important (see DIET). Since cholesterol is laid down in new cells, there seems to be no reason for concern over the cholesterol intake of the growing young. Indeed, in milk and in eggs nature seems to have furnished cholesterol with this in mind.

Cholesterol must not be thought of as being all villain. In addition to being an essential part of every living cell, it is the base molecule from which the sex hormones and the hormones of the adrenal gland are formed. (See also ARTERIES, HARDENING OF.)

CIRCUMCISION Circumcision consists of surgical removal of some of the foreskin, the excess skin which conceals the head of the penis. Sometimes the foreskin is quite tight so that it may be difficult or even impossible to pull it back. Irritation of the penis then occurs because of retained secretions (known as smegma) or even from the accumulation of small amounts of urine in this location. Circumcision performed as a religious ceremony has been practiced by the Jews and Moslems for centuries. The operation has become increasingly popular in ethnic groups, for it has health aspects of concern to both sexes: (1) Circumcision enables the penis to be kept clean with minimal effort. (2) Irritation of the head of the penis by smegma is avoided and its sensitivity is decreased, which may be an advantage in sexual performance. (3) Cancer of the penis, although a rare disease, is even less likely to be found in a circumcised individual. (4) More importantly, cancer of the cervix (the opening of the womb) appears to have some relationship to circumcision in the male partner in marriage. Thus cancer of the cervix is extremely rare in Jewish women; when it does occur it may well be found that the husband is not circumcised.

All the above-mentioned considerations have led to a considerable increase in the number of circumcisions. The procedure is often performed on babies within the first week or two of life, when no anesthesia is needed. In boys and men, circumcision may sometimes be necessary because the foreskin cannot be retracted, a condition called phimosis. Phimosis in babies who have not been circumcised can be prevented by pulling the foreskin back routinely whenever the baby is bathed and, if the doctor so instructs, at other times also.

COLDS, COMMON The treatment of a common cold is generally simple. However, in a small infant, even a mild cold can make both mother and infant very uncomfortable. The child's nose is "all stopped up," which means that it is blocked with mucus. Frequently he will refuse the bottle because, as he eats with nose and mouth blocked, he has no way to get air. He therefore becomes fearful of eating.

One of the most important things in this case is to keep the nasal passages clear so he may breathe. In order to do this, the nostrils should be cleansed with cotton swabs first. You may enter the nose at least half an inch in depth, or until resistance does not permit you to go any further. Children usually cry when this is done, not because it is painful but because it is annoying. If this mechanical cleansing of the nostrils is not effective, you should consult a doctor. He may recommend the use of a specific type of nose drop. Do not use nose drops on infants, however, unless this treatment is recommended by a doctor.

Frequently there are lumps of solid mucus in the nasal passages which block the entry of nose drops. When you place three or four drops into the nostrils and they shoot out immediately, or if they well up instead of going down into the nose, you may be sure that there is some blockage. It may be necessary to use eight or ten drops and close the infant's mouth while he is breathing *in* so that he may suck the nose drops through the nasal passage into the throat and unblock the passageway. Sometimes the drops cause him to sneeze out solid mucus. The suction apparatuses which take mucus from the nose are generally ineffective in clearing it completely. They can only reach what is in the front part of the nose. If there is blockage farther down in the passageway leading to the back of the throat, it will not be cleared. Nose drops can usually be used every three to four hours.

There are many new antihistamines with nasal decongestants which have been effective in diminishing the amount of nasal secretions. These are helpful additions in the treatment of colds and upper respiratory infections. It is usually not advisable to bathe the child when he has a cold. You may wash him off or give him a sponge bath with alcohol, or with soap and water.

Aspirin, in dosages prescribed by the doctor, can be used to reduce low-grade and higher fevers. Other medications (antibiotics) may be prescribed, not so much to cure the cold but to prevent the complications of colds, such as bronchitis and pneumonia. Cough medicines relieve cough. These should not be given unless a physician so advises.

COLITIS, FUNCTIONAL Colitis is a general term used to refer to a large number of disorders of the colon or large intestine. Although strictly speaking *colitis,* like any medical word ending in *itis,* refers to inflammation, the term is often used to refer to disorders of motility in the large bowel without true inflammation occurring.

Disorders of functioning in the colon without inflammation are far more common than ulcerative or amebic colitis. Known as "functional colitis," the chief symptoms are either frequency of bowel movements or irregular patterns of bowel behavior in which sometimes constipation alternates with diarrhea. One pattern may consist of having two or three loose stools which may be limited only to the morning. Functional colitis is often related to stressful situations and nervous tension. Sometimes cramps and other evidences of hyperactivity of the colon are noted for which the terms "spastic colitis" or "spastic colon" are sometimes employed. Colitis is generally found in tense hypersensitive individuals, frequently of a high level of intelligence. It is felt that in these persons the large intestine is the organ that reacts to stress in a manner comparable to the organs which produce the headache or rise in blood pressure which others may experience under tension. The particular organ that thus reacts to stress is sometimes referred to as a "target organ."

Treatment. Functional colitis is treated in a variety of ways. Some of the common approaches are the following:

1. Bland diets. Most varieties of bland diets call for easily digested non-irritating types of food. Spices, condiments, alcohol, fried and greasy foods are avoided. Stimulating or laxative foods, including raw fruits and vegetables, may be restricted or omitted.

2. A variety of drugs are used to diminish hyperirritability of the colon. They may sometimes be administered in combination with tranquilizers.

3. Episodes of diarrhea may be controlled by taking paregoric or allied drugs.

4. Avoidance of tension-producing situations, a change in jobs, the talking-over of difficulties with the doctor or psychiatrist may all be useful approaches to controlling the stress that gives rise to functional colitis.

COMPRESS A compress is a folded cloth, pad, or equivalent which can be applied to some part of the body, usually with moderate pressure. A compress may be wet or dry, hot or cold. A hot wet compress may be used to bring pimples and boils to a head, to relieve the pain of an arthritic joint, to increase the local blood supply and therefore aid bodily defenses. In many instances it will also relieve pain. A basin of hot water with two washcloths used in rotation will serve the purpose quite well.

A somewhat more convenient method is to apply the wet cloth to the area and cover it with plastic film or saran wrap. A hot-water bottle or heating pad can then be applied to maintain the heat of the compress. Care should be taken not to wet the heating pad unless is it a waterproof one. A heating pad alone is the equivalent of a hot dry compress, but for certain purposes this may not be as good as a hot wet compress. If the skin is delicate or if hot wet compresses are to be applied continuously for long periods, a prior application of cold cream or vaseline is desirable.

Cold compresses may consist of cloths wrung out of cold running water or ice water. An ice bag containing ice cubes may often conveniently serve the same purpose. Cold compresses are used for sprains and bruises, for headaches, and for relieving the discomfort of some sore throats. Paradoxically, a cold compress may sometimes serve better than a recommended hot one—for example, in bursitis, where the cold produces a numbing effect while heat, by increasing congestion, occasionally increases pain. The cold compress can be applied for five to fifteen minutes or even longer; if, however, it produces uncomfortable sensations of cold, it should be used in an on-and-off manner: for example, five minutes on and five minutes off.

The immediate effect of cold applications on sprains or bruises is to cut down pain and swelling, and to diminish any bleeding that may result from the injury. Often within the first twelve to twenty-four hours cold compresses are advocated, which are then to be followed by heat. Thus, after removal of a tooth or other dental manipulation, the immediate application of cold will diminish swelling and pain; application of heat the following day will promote the rate of healing.

CONCUSSION A fall or the impact of a blow to the head may produce an injury which results in a brief loss of consciousness. This is referred to as a concussion. Sometimes the victim appears dazed after he recovers, may be confused as to the events that led to the injury or have a loss of memory in relation to events for some longer period of time prior to the injury. There are all degrees of concussion—from relatively brief losses of consciousness with virtually no aftereffect, on to more prolonged episodes with greater memory damage. Some of the latter are followed by what is known as the post-concussive syndrome, in which the individual complains of recurrent headaches, feelings of faintness, or other symptoms.

Fortunately the brain receives excellent protection from the fluid immediately surrounding it and the sturdy box we call the skull. Most bumps on the head will not affect it at all. Occasionally, however, bleeding may occur from one of the blood vessels within the skull. There may be a brief period of unconsciousness, often regarded as a concussion, from which the person recovers. After a variable period during which he appears conscious or perhaps somewhat dazed, the victim may lapse into unconsciousness again. This sequence is generally due to bleeding within the skull, a common form of which is known as subdural hematoma. It will need prompt medical attention.

CONGENITAL DISORDERS
Congenital Megacolon This is a disorder due to a defect in the nerve cells of the rectosigmoid portion of the intestines which results in an absence of normal bowel movements. Stool accumulates and cannot be pushed out. This causes progressive constipation with enlargement of the colon and abdomen. It usually begins in early infancy and is characterized by passage of stool every four to five days.

The treatment of this condition is surgical. The disordered section of bowel is eliminated, and the condition cured.

Phenylketonuria (PKU) Phenylketonuria is an inherited protein disorder of the metabolism transmitted by an autosomal recessive gene. If a family has one child with this disease, the chance of a second occurring is one in four, or 25 percent. Although PKU occurs frequently (one in every 40,000 babies in the United States), it is treatable. Untreated cases account for 1 per cent of the institutionalized mental defectives. PKU is caused by lack of the liver enzyme *phenylalanine hydroxylase* which converts phenylalanine to tyrosine. Excessive accumulation of L-phenylalanine in the blood, eventually excreted in the urine as phenylacetyl glutamine, accounts for the typical mousy, musty odor of the baby's urine.

Children with PKU may appear normal at birth. They frequently are blond with blue eyes, and suffer from eczema. They fail to develop mentally and often show epileptic seizures and an abnormal electroencephalogram. Diagnosis is made by testing the suspected urine for phenylpyruvic acid with a specially prepared piece of filter paper. Chemical tests for measuring phenylalanine blood levels confirm the diagnosis.

Treatment is with a diet low in phenylalanine. In general, children treated early enough (before six months of age) have a better chance of avoiding severe retardation. Treatment before two years of age results in children who are educable but mentally handicapped. A child over two years of age may be too retarded to train, although there are isolated cases of untreated phenylketonurics who are of average intelligence. Many hospitals now have a screening process for PKU in newborn infants.

Pyloric Stenosis Infants with this disease are born with it (congenital). Pyloric stenosis is a thickening of the muscle around the duodenum where the stomach enters the intestines. Occurring mostly in boys, the main symptom is projectile vomiting of all foods before seven or eight weeks of age. The child is normally hungry and has a good appetite, but after swallowing a few ounces of milk, shoots it out immediately. Most normal babies do spit up a small amount when they are burped, when the stomach is compressed, or if they are placed on their stomachs after a feeding.

Mechanical pressure will cause some spitting up. However, the type of vomiting seen in pyloric stenosis is persistent and unremitting. There is never any bile in the vomit, indicating that the vomiting comes from an obstructed area above the bile-duct entrance into the intestines. The infant becomes constipated and loses weight. Frequently a small, olive-size tumor mass may be felt in the child's abdomen. He may become dehydrated due to fluid loss from vomiting. Corrective treatment is usually surgical if medical management fails.

CONSTIPATION Constipation should be regarded as the passage of hard, dried, or pellety stools rather than the failure to have regular or daily bowel movements. Thus, constipation can exist even in the presence of daily movements. Since a good deal of the bulk of the stool is its water content, people who are constipated generally complain that the stools are smaller. They sometimes regard this as evidence that they are retaining wastes, which is an erroneous supposition. Many of the ills ascribed to constipation are exaggerated; some individuals, however, do experience mild headache, a sub-par feeling, abdominal distention, and "gas." Symptoms end with a satisfactory evacuation.

Constipation is quite common during pregnancy, in part because the intestinal musculature seems to be relaxed and because the enlarged uterus may exert pressure against the lower part of the large intestine.

Treatment. There are several measures that may be helpful:

1. Sipping a cup of hot water the first thing in the morning.

2. Increasing the amount of fruits and fruit juices in the diet—particularly prunes, prune juice, figs, apples. Salads and green leafy vegetables are bulk stimulants.

3. Consumption of six to eight glasses of water daily.

4. Possible use of mineral oil, stool softeners, and other laxatives (See DRUGS AND REMEDIES.)

5. Glycerine or Ducolax® suppositories, or prepackaged enemas containing sodium phosphate (Fleet enema, Travad enema) act within a few minutes to relieve constipation.

Your doctor may have other suggestions and diets that may be of use. In general, constipation that comes on with pregnancy promptly disappears after the delivery. Admittedly also, constipation becomes more of a problem in the later years and is a common complaint in the older age groups. Any of the measures mentioned above may be applicable. (See CONGENITAL DISORDERS—Congenital Megacolon.)

CONVULSIONS Convulsions, commonly called "fits" or seizures, are caused by many different conditions. The eyes roll up into the head, the jaws are clamped shut, and one loses consciousness as the body stiffens. Parts of the body then shake with twitching or convulsive movements. There may be difficulty in breathing, and the color of the skin may change to reddish purple or bluish. There may be some frothing at the mouth. Sometimes high fever or the onset of some illness may cause a convulsion. More serious causes of convulsions are brain disorders (epilepsy, brain tumors) and poisoning. Most convulsions are self-limited: one may be unconscious for one or two minutes, then come around.

When there is a convulsive seizure there is also spasm of the throat muscles. Grinding motions may injure the tongue; later, the tongue may fall back into the throat; nasal and respiratory passages fill with mucus. It is important to pry open the teeth with a wooden or metal tool (the handle of a knife or a spoon) and draw the tongue forward. It can be held with a towel—this will guard against choking. The mucus may be wiped from the back of the mouth and, if possible, mouth-to-mouth resuscitation performed. If there is any rubber tubing handy, it can be inserted into the nose or mouth, and with suction much of the mucus may be removed. This is an emergency measure which permits air to enter.

In many cities an emergency oxygen service exists as part of the police department. A call to the police will often bring the emergency squad to administer oxygen to a convulsing person. The victim should be placed in a lukewarm bath until help arrives, making sure, of course, that his nose and mouth are kept out of the water. This will often relax him and stop the convulsion.

Hospitalization is important after a convulsive seizure to determine its cause. It will also ensure proper treatment in case one convulsion is followed by a second.

CORONARY THROMBOSIS The coronary arteries are the main channels which conduct blood to the heart. Formation of a clot within the vessel, known as a thrombosis, will cut off the circulation to a portion of heart muscle. As a consequence the muscle tissue dies off and is replaced by scar tissue. Such a clot never forms in a normal artery and is most commonly seen in arteries in which the fat depositions of atherosclerosis have previously occurred.

Coronary thrombosis is associated with severe pain, usually felt under the breast bone, which commonly radiates to the arms or to the neck. The pain may last for hours and require narcotics for relief. Various disorders of the heart rate and of the circulation may accompany this, one of the more critical ones being a severe drop in blood pressure with a shock-like state. This may require the emergency use of special drugs designed to raise blood pressure. Occasionally the symptoms are less marked, or they may be referred to the digestive tract, with symptoms such as nausea and vomiting perhaps secondary to congestion there. Or acute congestion may occur in the lungs, producing marked shortness of breath.

Once the acute symptoms have been treated, an enforced rest will be the next step. It is known that it takes at least three to four weeks for a firm scar to form within the damaged heart muscle. During this time the patient may be kept in bed, although some physicians may permit him to sit in a bedside chair for parts of the day. Anticoagulant drugs, which diminish the rate of clot formation of the blood, may be given to the patient with a coronary thrombosis, and may even be kept up for months afterwards. There are some risks inherent in this method of treatment, and not all physicians subscribe to the benefits to be derived therefrom.

With current methods of treatment, the great majority of victims of a coronary thrombosis recover and can be expected to resume usual activities. In some instances the impaired efficiency of the heart as a pump may necessarily lead to restriction of physical activities. In recent years the use of diets emphasizing polyunsaturated fats for victims of coronary thrombosis has been advocated by the American Heart Association.

Up until about the age of fifty, heart attacks are a good deal more common in men than in women. Thereafter the coronary thrombosis rate begins to rise in women, and at sixty and beyond the rate in women approximates that in men. It has therefore been concluded that the female sex hormone produced by a woman's ovaries protects her against coronary thrombosis and other vascular disorders but that the protection disappears after the menopause. (See also ARTERIES, HARDENING OF.)

CRAMPS AND COLIC

Cramps Cramps are painful contractions of muscles. They may occur either in the voluntary muscles, those we use in movement, or the involuntary muscles, sometimes called smooth muscles. (The latter are found in such internal organs as the uterus, urinary bladder, and gallbladder and in the stomach and intestines.)

Muscular cramps occur most frequently in the legs, often at night when they produce awakening from sleep. They are complained of by young individuals with good circulatory systems and hence are not necessarily a sign of a poor circulation. They are also a fairly frequent complaint during pregnancy where possibly they are related to the pressure of the enlarging uterus on the great veins running up from the extremities. Various drugs are used for leg cramps, including large doses of calcium and tranquilizers with muscle-relaxing properties. At times nothing works too well and the only relief may be secured by getting out of bed and walking about briefly.

"Abdominal cramps" is a general term applied to recurrent pains arising in the digestive tract or in an associated organ. They are sometimes referred to as "colicky pains" and typically come in waves, rise to a certain level, then decrease until the next wave of contractions begins. Various kinds of inflammations, the passage of stones, toxins, or irritants may all be causative. Many of the factors that lead to vomiting will produce crampy pains in the upper abdomen, and similarly the many causes of diarrhea will set up colicky pains in the large intestine. Consultation with the doctor, and sometimes X-rays or other procedures, may be indicated.

Colic of Early Infancy Colic is a condition of painful abdominal cramps. It is produced by many different conditions occurring in the first three to six months of life. It may be caused by hunger or distention of the abdomen from swallowing too much air ("gas pains"). Infants get red in the face, draw their legs up and cry with extreme pain. If the infant is able to burp the gas, or pass it through the rectum, he is generally relieved and the crying stops.

Overfeeding (too many ounces of milk, or too rich a formula) may cause colic. Allergies to certain milks may cause colicky pains. There may also be mechanical causes: for example, a nipple which does not have holes adequate to permit enough milk to come through will cause the infant to suck mostly air (and gas). He will not really be properly nourished, and the air or gas cause distention and pain.

Treatment. The treatment of colic depends on the cause. If the child is allergic, is on a heavy formula which disagrees with him, or is taking solid foods too early, obviously the elimination of the causes will relieve the cramps. There are also some symptomatic measures which will relieve the pain, such as a hot-water bottle applied to the abdomen, sedatives, and antispasmodics. Frequently burping in order to get the gas up will be helpful, as will be warm baths. Introduction of an enema bone to help the child pass gas through the rectum may relieve the pain. Usually colic subsides after the first three or four months.

CYSTIC FIBROSIS

CYSTIC FIBROSIS Cystic fibrosis of the pancreas combines a fat and starch deficiency with a defect in the mucus-secreting glands of the entire body. It is an inborn error of metabolism affecting the exocrine glands, such as the mucus, sweat, and salivary glands. The affected glands produce an abnormally thick and tenacious mucus which in turn produces lung, pancreas, and liver changes by obstructing the flow of air and fluid in these organs. The sweat glands secrete abnormally increased amounts of sodium and chloride (salt).

Chronic respiratory disease is the most prominent part of cystic fibrosis. Bronchial mucus obstruction predisposes to recurring infections with progressive damage to lung tissue. The insufficiency of pancreatic trypsin, lipase, and amylase (pancreatic enzymes) causes intestinal malabsorption. The stools are malodorous, greasy, and bulky in spite of a normal food intake. A very reliable diagnostic test in these infants, if they are over six weeks of age, is the sweat electrolyte test. Infants with this disease show increased excretion of sodium, chloride, and potassium in their perspiration. The test is made by placing a hand print on an agar plate. The sweat chlorides react with the silver nitrate and potassium chromate in the agar, producing a positive test. Other tests to confirm the diagnosis examine duodenal enzymes and muscus secretions.

Treatment. Treatment of cystic fibrosis is a high calorie, high protein, and low fat diet. Pancreatic extracts have to be given in addition. The frequent respiratory infections must be prevented and treated immediately when they do occur. Children with cystic fibrosis are particularly liable to heat prostration in summer due to abnormal loss of salts in their sweat. They may develop severe crisis of shock and dehydration.

DEMENTIA, SENILE The terms pre-senile and senile dementia are used to describe any kind of severe mental impairment in older individuals. Approximately one-half of such persons are victims of Alzheimer's Disease; about another quarter have diseased blood vessels and the remainder suffer from a variety of other disorders such as brain tumors, thyroid dysfunction and pernicious anemia. Diagnosis of the specific type of senile or pre-senile dementia is very important since some types, other than Alzheimer's Disease, can be effectively treated.

DIABETES INSIPIDUS Diabetes Insipidus is a disorder of water metabolism caused by deficiency of the antidiuretic hormone, vasopressin. The predominant symptom is polyuria, an enormous dilute urine output of 6 to 40 quarts daily. The urine contains no abnormal substances such as sugar or albumin. Some cases are secondary to lesions of the brain in the region of the pituitary gland where treatment is focused. Other cases are primary since no lesion can be found and may be caused by circulatory changes in the kidneys. These changes are due to a dysfunction of the posterior lobe of the pituitary gland or by a midbrain lesion.

Primary symptoms may first appear at birth. In adults, polyuria may have a gradual onset or it may occur suddenly and often is related to fright or an injury. Generally, overall health and duration of life are little affected by this disease. Diabetes Insipidous cannot be controlled by limiting fluid intake. Because of the volume output of urine, inconvenience and great embarrassment interfer with daily activities.

To treat Diabetes Insipidus the medication vasopressin, the only known remedy to control the disease, is administered by subcutaneous injection, by spray, or by cotton pledgets inserted into the nasopharynx.

DIABETES MELLITUS Diabetes mellitus is a disorder of carbohydrate metabolism. It is rare in early childhood. Approximately 10 percent of the cases begin before fifteen years of age, and are usually inherited. There are associated abnormalities in fat and protein metabolism producing high amounts of sugar in the blood and urine.

The exact cause is not known. However, the following facts are important in the development of the disease. Insulin, the important secretion of the pancreas, is necessary for the storage of glycogen (sugar) in the liver. If insulin is not produced, no glycogen can be stored, consequently the body burns fat and protein instead, at a very high rate. Metabolism of fat and protein produces ketone bodies which cannot be excreted in the urine and cannot be further metabolized by muscles. They accumulate in the blood and cause acidosis. In order to remove these organic acids through the bloodstream, base (substance reacting with acid to produce salt and water) is lost by the kidney, thus increasing the degree of acidosis. Large amounts of water are necessary for the kidneys to excrete the sugar and acid products. This leads to dehydration. Symptoms of thirst and excess excretion of water occur.

Symptoms. The classical symptoms of diabetes, therefore, are: polyuria (excessive urination), polyphagia (excessive eating), and polydipsia (excessive drinking). Weight is lost in spite of adequate eating. Diabetics show unusually high levels of sugar in both bloodstream and urine. The glucose tolerance test which is specific for diabetes shows a blood sugar curve rising above normal levels and a slower return to fasting levels. The blood cholesterol and fat levels in many cases are high, and there may be chemical findings of acidosis.

Treatment. The treatment of diabetes is replacement with insulin. The insulin metabolizes the glucose from the blood stream and prevents the formation of ketone bodies. There are many different forms of insulin. Protamine zinc insulin acts over a period of twenty-four to forty-eight hours. Diet and calorie control are important in the treatment of diabetes, particularly in children. In infants of "uncontrolled" diabetic mothers, a condition of temporary hyperinsulism resulting in low blood sugar may occur.

Several new pills have been developed which can be taken by mouth and effectively lower the blood sugar. However, these have not been effective in the treatment of children, and therefore *they* must still take their insulin by injection. With treatment and proper medication, diabetes can be maintained under reasonable control.

Diabetic children are particularly susceptible to infections. Any child who is diabetic and has fever with infection should be carefully supervised by a physician. Diabetic coma and insulin shock are major problems in the management of diabetic children. The symptoms of insulin shock (too much insulin) are: tingling sensations, sweating, irritability, pallor, followed by delirium, unconsciousness, and convulsions. It is treated by giving sugar immediately either by mouth or injection.

Diabetic coma is characterized by apathy, drowsiness, restlessness, and deep rapid breathing. The skin is dry, the lips cherry red, and the breath may have a fruity (acetone) odor. Vomiting and headache may occur. Treatment is insulin.

DIAGNOSTIC PROCEDURES

Cystoscopy This procedure through which the bladder is visualized by passing an instrument (cystoscope) up the urethra (urinary channel) and thus into the bladder. The instrument has a lens system and a special bulb at the tip which furnishes light. Infection, tumors, stones may be directly observed.

Proctoscopy Here a similar but larger instrument is passed into the rectal region, thus permitting direct inspection to a level as high as six or seven inches.

Electrocardiograph (ECG) This is an instrument which picks up the electrical currents generated by the beating heart, amplifies them, and transmits them to a moving stylus. A tracing is inscribed which may reveal abnormalities such as irregularities (arrhythmias), or areas of damage such as result from a coronary attack.

Electroencephalogram (EEG) This is a similar instrument which records brain waves. It is of help in diagnosing various forms of epilepsy, brain tumors, damage produced by circulatory changes, etc.

DIAPER CARE Advanced technology has greatly aided mothers by providing disposable diapers of various sizes, increased comfort, and greater absorbable qualities. However, there are times when a disposable diaper should not be worn by an infant, especially when a stubborn rash persists or when the baby is sensitive to the disposable materials.

A baby may use up to a dozen or more diapers a day, depending on how much he is awake. Diapers need to be soft, light in weight, and not clumsy. If they are cloth, the material they are made of should soak up moisture well, wash easily, and dry fast. Those made of birdseye or of knit goods are much used. Gauze diapers absorb moisture well and dry very fast. They are made of two thin layers woven together at the edges instead of hemmed. They wear as well as those of heavier material.

As your baby gets older and takes larger amounts of liquid, you may find he gets so wet at night that you feel he will be more comfortable with a waterproof diaper cover that keeps his bed from getting wet and chilly. Try out moisture-proof pants for overnight use. You can soon tell whether your baby is one of those whose skin is too sensitive to make their use safe for hours at a time.

When you wash the diapers at home put them to soak in a covered pail of cold water as soon as you take them off the baby. If the diaper is soiled, shake or scrape off as much as you can of the stool, and rub a little soap into the stained parts before putting it to soak. To wash diapers use any mild soap, soap powder, or detergent in plenty of hot water. The rinsing is just as important as the washing, for unless you get all the soap out, the baby's tender skin is liable to become irritated. If the water in your locality is soft, two or three rinsings may be enough. With hard water, three or four rinses are usually necessary to completely rid the diapers of soap. It is all right to use a little bleach in the wash water if you put the diapers through several rinse waters. If you can dry diapers outdoors, the sunlight will take out most stains. It is usually unnecessary to boil diapers if they are thoroughly washed and rinsed. They are softer if dried outdoors, and bacteria have little chance of remaining in diapers dried in the sun.

If your baby has a tender skin that makes him get diaper rash easily, you will need to use special care to keep him free of the irritation caused by wet diapers. You can prevent the ammonia odor in wet diapers and protect your baby's skin either by boiling the diapers, ironing them with a hot iron, or by putting in the last rinse water some product your doctor suggests.

A baby whose diapers are free of soap and are changed promptly is quite unlikely to have much, if any, trouble with diaper rash. But if your baby's buttocks tend to break out with a rash very easily, you may feel that boiling or ironing his diapers is a small price to pay for his comfort. Leaving off a baby's diaper and exposing his skin to the sun and air or to the warmth of an electric light helps to do away with diaper rash. If an electric light is used, be sure that it has a wire mesh protective covering and it is placed at a safe distance from the baby, so that he cannot be burned.

DIARRHEA AND DYSENTERY There are many causes for diarrhea, ranging from spoiled or laxative foods, emotional upsets and tensions, to a group of inflammations of the colon produced by various organisms. The latter are frequently referred to as dysentery. It is not always easy to distinguish among these causes: thus the symptoms of a viral diarrhea and a mild food poisoning might be quite indistinguishable, with cramps, frequency of bowel movements, perhaps with little or no fever. Both types of disorders might respond equally to a bland diet, antispasmodic drugs, paregoric, perhaps also to a heating pad applied to the abdomen.

Viral dysentery is the mildest form of dysentery. It is often seen in epidemics, particularly during the winter and spring. Although it may produce severe abdominal pains, more often the cramps are relatively mild. This diarrhea seldom lasts more than a few days and there is no bloody mucus in the bowel movements.

Bacillary dysenteries generally produce frequent odorous stools and often contain pus and blood. Within a day or so the colon usually has emptied itself and the stools that are passed consist largely of mucus. For bacillary dysenteries the physician will prescribe antibiotics or certain drugs of the sulfonamide group.

Amebic dysentery is uncommon in the United States. The diagnosis can be made by examining a portion of freshly passed stool under the microscope. Several of the antibiotics, or Atabrine® (a drug used in malaria) and Carbarsone® (an arsenical drug), are useful in the treatment of amebic dysenteries.

Most of the simple diarrheas are more of a nuisance than a threat, although in infants the loss of large amounts of fluid may produce a grave situation and call for emergency measures. Consult your doctor immediately.

In older age groups it is traditional to limit the diet to such foods as tea and toast, and binding foods such as farina, oatmeal, tapioca, and mashed potatoes. Later, relatively bland and digestible foods are added, such as chicken, eggs, fish, and broiled meats. Kaopectate®, a suspension of kaolin in pectin, and paregoric are frequently employed. Certain drugs that relax the large bowel and diminish its activity, known as antispasmodics, may also be prescribed. Some of the weakness produced by diarrhea is due to the loss of salts, particularly sodium and potassium, from the body. Non-laxative fruit juices such as apple juice or tomato juice, to which a sprinkle of salt has been added, will be useful in compensating for these lost salts.

DIET, CALCIUM REQUIREMENTS Calcium is a widely distributed and basic mineral found in the blood and in all the tissues. It is the chief mineral that goes into the structure of bones. Calcium is involved in the formation of blood clots, and it regulates the performance of muscle tissue. Dietary calcium is of particular concern to women because of the increased need for it during pregnancy and during lactation (nursing). Every mother should also know that the calcium needs of her children are considerably higher than those of the adult because of bone growth. Even after the period of reproduction and child-rearing has ended, calcium still continues to be of concern.

At least 20 per cent of the women of the United States will develop osteoporosis, a condition in which the bones become brittle. (This accounts for the frequency of fractures in aging women.) Nutritional studies indicate that many adults as well as adolescents fail to get recommended daily allotments of calcium. In three out of ten households the average diet contains less than the recommended amounts of calcium; in fact, of all the nutrients we eat calcium is most likely to be lacking. Recommended daily allowances for calcium are as follows:

Adults, all ages and sexes—0.8 gm.
Women, pregnant (second half)—1.5 gm.
Women, nursing—2.0 gm.
Children, 1 to 10—1.0 gm.
Teenagers, 13 to 19—1.3-1.4 gm.
From a practical point of view it is difficult to get enough calcium without drinking milk, one quart of which will supply 1 gm. Two cups of milk will thus supply about ¾ of the adult's daily requirement. For those who worry about calories, skimmed milk has the same calcium value as whole milk. A pregnant woman should probably drink at least one quart of milk per day, a nursing mother a quart and a half.

Other good sources of calcium are some of the cheeses, but this is variable. Swiss and cheddar cheese contain about 250 mg., (¼ gm.), in a one-ounce portion, but one ounce of cottage cheese contais only 25 mg. and cream cheese only 18. A medium serving of ice cream has about 115 mg. Vegetables and fruits are the next best source of calcium. One cupful of most vegetables furnishes 35 to 70 mg. Vegetables particularly rich in calcium are broccoli, kale, collards, and turnip and mustard greens. Whole wheat flour contains two or three times the calcium of white flour.

DIET, CRASH AND FORMULA These are nutritionally restricted diets which can be embarked upon for only a few days, and with which a daily multiple vitamin supplement is necessary. Crash diets may produce an encouraging weight loss and enable one to go on to a more orthodox reducing diet. Examples of crash diets applicable to both lunch and dinner are: (1) One or two bananas plus a glass of skimmed milk. (2) Three-fourths cup of cottage cheese plus a glass of skimmed milk. (3) One or two hard-boiled eggs plus one quarter head of lettuce sprinkled with lemon juice and a glass of skimmed milk. In addition, chewing raw celery or carrots for between-meal hunger is permitted.

Formula diets, such as Metrecal® or equivalents, generally consist of skimmed-milk products to which vitamins and sometimes oils are added. A typical portion contains 225 calories, and if unsweetened tea or coffee are taken in addition, three or four meals would amount to 675 to 900 calories per day. The formula diet works, at least initially, because of their restriction in calories and the fact that no choice is permitted. Also, the oil that some of the products contain leads to a feeling of satiety. Some digestive disturbances may be encountered because of the oil, however.

Appetite-curbing drugs, many of which are derived from the amphetamine family, enable some people markedly to reduce their calorie intake without feeling hungry or having such symptoms as weakness or faintness.

For individuals with low basal metabolism, thyroid is sometimes prescribed as part of a weight-loss program. Also, if there are evidences of fluid retention on a reduction program, a pill to produce loss of water (a diuretic) may be prescribed. Obviously drugs in any of these classes can be taken only under a doctor's supervision. (See also DIET, REDUCING.)

DIET, FOOD GUIDE The U.S. Department of Agriculture has developed a simplified and basic approach to healthful eating. It is based on sound findings developed by nutritional scientists and is sometimes known as the basic food guide. Nutritionists everywhere use it as a base for the developments of all kinds of special diets. Whether a diet is low in calories, high or low in salt, or has other special features, one is likely to find the basic food guide forming its foundation. It consists of the following four groups:

1. MILK GROUP. The following amounts of milk should be used daily: Children, 3 to 4 glasses; teenagers, 4 or more glasses; adults, 2 or more glasses; mothers-to-be, 4 or more; nursing mothers, at least 6 glasses. Cheese, ice cream, and other milk-derived foods can supply part of the daily milk requirement. In terms of the calcium content in milk, count one slice of cheese (1 ounce) as 2/3 glass of milk, ½ cup of cottage cheese as 1/3 glass, ¼ pint of ice cream as ¼ glass of milk.

2. MEAT GROUP. Two or more servings daily of beef, veal, pork, lamb, poultry, fish, or eggs. Dried beans,

peas, and nuts may be used as occasional alternatives. A serving is 2 to 3 ounces (without bone) of lean cooked meat, poultry, or fish (1 slice to 2 thin slices); 2 eggs; 1 cup of cooked dried beans, dried peas, or lentils; 4 tablespoons of peanut butter.

3. VEGETABLE-FRUIT GROUP Four or more servings daily. Include a citrus fruit or other source of vitamin C and also a dark green or deep yellow vegetable for vitamin A at least every other day. Other vegetables and fruits can make up the suggested servings. A serving consists of ½ cup of vegetable or fruit, or a portion ordinarily served, such as a medium-sized apple, banana, orange, or half a medium-sized grapefruit or cantaloupe.

Vitamin C Group. Fruit and vegetables important for vitamin C include oranges and grapefruit and their juices, cantaloupe, fresh strawberries, broccoli, and peppers. Less rich sources of vitamin C, two servings of which equal one serving of the above, include: asparagus tips, Brussels sprouts, cabbage, collards, garden cress, kale, kohlrabi, mustard greens, potatoes or sweet potatoes cooked in their jackets, spinach, tomatoes and tomato juice, and turnip greens. Other fruits include honeydew melon, tangerine, tangerine juice, lemons and lemon juice, and watermelon.

Vegetables for Vitamin A Broccoli, carrots, chard, collards, cress, kale, spinach, turnip greens, and other dark green leaves, sweet potatoes, pumpkin, or winter squash. (Apricots and cantaloupe can also serve as a source of vitamin A.)

4. BREAD-CEREAL GROUP. Four or more servings daily of the whole grain, enriched or restored kinds. (Check the label to be sure that they are "enriched.") A serving consists of one slice of bread, 1 ounce of ready-to-eat cereal, ½ to ¾ cup of cooked cereal, corn meal, grits, macaroni, noodles, rice, or spaghetti.

DIET, PRUDENT The Bureau of Nutrition of New York City's Department of Health has developed a dietary program referred to as the Prudent Diet, which emphasizes the unsaturated fats. There is evidence that individuals who have had a heart attack are less likely to have a second one if they follow this diet; at present it would also seem reasonable to eat in this way to avoid having heart attacks or other forms of hardening of the arteries. The Prudent Diet emphasizes substantial cuts in most meats, eggs, whole milk, whole-milk cheeses, sweet and sour cream, ice cream, butter, etc. The following are the highlights of the program:

1. FISH, MEAT, EGGS. Fish and shell fish at least four to five times a week, for any meal. The fat in fish is an excellent source of polyunsaturated fatty acids. Poultry may be taken often; it is low in fat. Veal may be taken frequently—it is a lean meat; beef, pork, and lamb not more than three to four times a week, with the serving not to exceed four ounces of cooked meat. Eggs, not more than four a week for adults; four to seven a week for children. Avoid very fat meats, bacon, sausage, corned beef, pastrami. Select lean cuts of all meats. Trim off all visible fat. Keep portions moderate—four to six ounces before cooking (four ounces after cooking).

2. MILK AND MILK PRODUCTS. The fat in whole milk is predominantly saturated and is not recommended. Two cups of skimmed milk daily for adults—two to four cups of milk daily for children; two cups of this milk allowance may be whole milk. More than four cups of milk are not recommended for children, even for adolescents. Cottage, pot, or farmer cheese often. Avoid butter, cream, ice cream, cream cheese, hard cheese, and other whole-milk cheeses.

3. FATS. Vegetable oils should be used for their polyunsaturated fatty acids. To have more of these than saturated fatty acids, use vegetable oils daily. Use 1½ ounces (3 tablespoons) daily in cooking and at table. Make salad dressings with oil. Substitute oil for other fats in cooking and baking. Butter, ordinary margarine, and other hydrogenated fats must be kept at a minimum.

DIET, REDUCING There is no satisfactory long-term answer to overweight that does not call for some self-discipline. Losing weight, however rapidly, only to regain it however slowly or rapidly, only leads to cycles of self-torture and aggravation which in the long run may be hardly worthwhile. It is better to find a more stable solution, whether this means giving up rich desserts, bread, carbonated sweet beverages and candy, or increasing one's exercise. Among the dietary programs that may be applicable are:

1. A HIGH-PROTEIN REDUCING DIET. The program focuses on a small-to-moderate-sized portion of meat, poultry, or fish for both lunch and dinner. To this is added a salad with a low-calorie dressing and 5 percent vegetables, such as string beans, asparagus, broccoli, zucchini, etc. No bread, rolls, or sweet desserts are permitted, though half a grapefruit or cantaloupe, or their equivalent, can be included. Two cups of skimmed milk per day may be taken, and can be used for the mid-afternoon snack, or before retiring. The success of this diet is dependent on the high-satiety value of meats.

2. BALANCED LOW-CALORIE DIETS. These are diets in which the various food items normally consumed are represented, but are selected as to quantity (smaller portions), or as to quality (low as against high-calorie desserts, 5 per cent vegetables as against 15 per cent vegetables, etc.). It is seldom practicable to reduce the total calorie intake of the day below 1000 calories. Numerous diets are available in which the calories are totaled up, but rather than following them rigidly it is probably better to grasp their essence and follow the principles. Instead of bacon, eggs, butter, and cream in the course of the morning breakfast, one would have juice, a small portion of a dry cereal with skimmed milk, and coffee with a little whole milk. For lunch and supper one could choose from a protein, such as listed above, or a scoop of cottage cheese, or one to two eggs, to which will be added a salad or 5 per cent vegetable, 1 slice of bread, and a fruit or other low-calorie dessert. Contrast for example pie (350 calories) or ice cream (250 calories) with half a grapefruit (50 calories) or half a cantaloupe (40 calories), a tangerine (40 calories), or an apple (70 calories).

DIET, REDUCING
First Day
LOW CALORIE—1,200 Calories
BREAKFAST
Grapefruit..½ medium
Wheat flakes...1 ounce
Skim milk..1½ cups
Coffee (black), if desired.
LUNCH
Chef's salad:
Julienne chicken...1 ounce
Cheddar cheese..½ ounce
Hard-cooked egg..½ egg
Tomato...1 large
Cucumber..6 slices
Endive..½ ounce
Lettuce..⅛ head
French dressing...2 tablespoons
Rye wafers..4 wafers
Skim milk...1 cup
DINNER
Beef pot roast...3 ounces
Mashed potatoes...⅓ cup

Green peas ....½ cup
Whole-wheat bread ....1 slice
Butter or margarine ....½ teaspoon
Fruit cup:
  Orange...½ small
  Apple...½ small
  Banana...½ medium

Second Day
BREAKFAST
Orange juice ....½ cup
Soft-cooked egg...1 egg
Whole-wheat toast...1 slice
Butter or margarine ....1 teaspoon
Skim milk ....1 cup
Coffee (black), if desired.
LUNCH
Sandwich:
  Enriched bread..2 slices
  Boiled ham...1½ ounces
  Mayonnaise..2 teaspoons
  Mustard
  Lettuce...1 large leaf
Celery...1 small stalk
Radishes..4 radishes
Dill pickle ....½ large
Skim milk ....1 cup
DINNER
Roast lamb...3 ounces
Rice, converted..½ cup
Spinach...¾ cup
Lemon ....¼ medium
Salad:
  Peaches, canned...1 peach half
  Cottage cheese..⅓ cup
  Lettuce...1 large leaf
BETWEEN-MEAL SNACK
Apple..1 medium

Third Day
BREAKFAST
Tomato juice...½ cup
French toast:
  Enrich bread...1 slice
  Egg..½ egg
  Milk
Butter or margarine ....1 teaspoon
Jelly..1½ teaspoons
Skim milk ....1 cup
Coffee (black), if desired.
LUNCH
Tunafish salad:
  Tunafish...2 ounches
  Hard-cooked egg ....½ egg
  Celery..1 small stalk
  Lemon juice ....1 teaspoon
  Salad dressing..1½ tablespoons
  Lettuce...1 large leaf
Whole-wheat bread ....2 slices
Butter or margarine ....1 teaspoon
Carrot sticks...½ carrot
Skim milk ....1 cup
DINNER
Beef liver ....3 ounces
Green snap beans..⅔ cup
Shredded cabbage..⅔ cup
  with vinegar dressing.
Roll, enriched ....1 small
Butter or margarine ....½ teaspoon
Grapes...1 small bunch
BETWEEN-MEAL SNACK
Orange..1 medium

DIET REQUIREMENTS IN CHILDHOOD— MALNUTRITION

Caloric Requirements *Infants:* 45 to 55 calories per pound of expected body weight and for age of the child.

Children: 1,000 calories basic plus 100 calories for each year. Example: an eight-year-old child should have 1,000 plus 800, or 1,800 calories per day.

Protein Requirements *Infants:* 2 grams per pound of body weight. Thus if a child takes one and three-quarter ounces of whole milk per pound per day, or a little less than one ounce of evaporated milk per pound per day, this will assure adequate protein intake.

Children: 1 gram per pound of body weight until the age of eleven or twelve. Later, slightly more is required. If approximately 20 percent of the required calorie intake is protein, this will be adequate.

Minerals (Daily Requirements)
Calcium: 1 to 1.5 grams
Phosphorous: 1.5 grams
Iron: 16 milligrams
Iodine: 100 to 200 micrograms
The following daily diet composition will satisfy basic growth needs:
Milk: ¾ to 1 quart
Meat, poultry or fish: 1 serving (5 or 6 weekly)
Liver: 1 serving weekly
Eggs: 2 (5 or 6 weekly)
Vegetables: 1 raw, 1 pigmented—2 servings daily
Fruit, fresh: 1 citrus—2 or more servings daily
Butter: 2 teaspoons daily
Bread, enriched or whole grain, and cereals: enough to meet caloric needs.
Cod liver oil: 1 teaspoon or equivalent in multiple vitamins daily.

Malnutrition This refers to a state of poor nutrition which may be caused by inadequate vitamin intake (leading to rickets or scurvy) or inadequate intake of specific nutritional elements. Inadequate calorie or protein intake will result in different forms of diseases.

Symptoms. Failure to gain weight and progressive emaciation occur. The abdomen may be distended, and the infant may take on the appearance of a withered old man. Specific vitamin deficiencies will produce evidence of rickets, scurvy, beriberi, pellagra, and other conditions. Protein deficiency produces kwashiorkor. In this condition, there may be pot belly, skin rash, and hair color changes; the hair frequently falls out.

Chronically malnourished children may not necessarily be underweight. They may show increased susceptibility to infection, pale skin, muddy complexion, poor teeth, delayed bone development, and may find it difficult to pay attention in school. Fatigue, restlessness, and nervousness are common.

Treatment. Preventive treatment is accomplished by providing a diet adequate in calorie, protein, fat, carbohydrate, and vitamin content. Treatment of malnutrition, once it has been established, is directed towards providing an adequate diet containing all the above-mentioned elements in addition to extra vitamins if these are indicated.

DIETS FOR CHILDREN
A Sample Day's Meals for a 4-Year-Old
BREAKFAST
Orange
Oatmeal (½ cup) with milk (⅓ cup).
Whole-wheat toast (2 thin slices) with butter or fortified margarine (2 teaspoonfuls).
Milk (½ pint).
DINNER
Ground beef ball (1 small) or boneless fish.
Baked potato (1 small) with butter or fortified margarine (1 teaspoonful).
Green beans (¼ cup) with butter or fortified margarine (½ teaspoonful).
Custard (⅓ cup).
Milk (½ pint).

SUPPER
  Poached egg.
  Carrot strip (3 pieces).
  Enriched bread (1 slice) with butter or fortified margarine (1 teaspoonful).
  Applesauce (½ cup) with milk (2 tablespoonfuls).
  Milk (½ pint).

A Sample Day's Meals for a 10-Year-Old
BREAKFAST
  Tomato juice (¾ cup).
  Hot whole-wheat cereal (⅔ cup) with milk (½ cup).
  Toast (2 slices) with butter or fortified margarine (2 teaspoonfuls).
  Milk (½ pint).
LUNCH
(If served at school or at home)
  Creamed eggs (¾ cup).
  Green beans (½ cup) with butter or fortified margarine (1 teaspoonful).
  Oatmeal muffins (2) with butter or fortified margarine (2 teaspoonfuls).
  Milk (½ pint).
(If brought from home)
  Sandwich—peanut butter and raw carrot on buttered whole-grain or enriched bread.
  Sandwich—chopped dried fruit on buttered whole-grain or enriched bread.
Supplemented at school by—
  Orange
  Milk soup (1 cup) or cocoa (1 cup).
DINNER
  Meat loaf (1 serving).
  Scalloped potatoes (⅔ cup).
  Cole slaw with red and green peppers (½ cup).
  Whole-wheat bread or enriched bread (2 slices) with butter or fortified margarine (2 teaspoonfuls).
  Applesauce (½ cup).
  Molasses cookies (2 thin).
  Milk (½ pint).
  Reprinted from *Nutrition and Healthy Growth*, Children's Bureau publication, U.S. Department of Health, Education, and Welfare.

DIETS, VITAMINS AND ESSENTIAL MINERALS
Vitamins and minerals are essential chemicals in the diet, and are found in foods. They are crucial in the formation of the structure of muscles, bones, tissues, and various organs of the body. Vitamin and mineral deficiencies cause specific diseases. A well-balanced diet containing all the various vitamins and minerals is the best protection against these diseases. In childhood, supplementary vitamins and minerals are taken as added protection against deficiencies. Unless there is a poor dietary intake, poor absorption due to gastroenteritis, vomiting, celiac syndrome, or increased excretion of vitamins, a normal well-balanced diet will provide adequate nutrients for good nutrition and growth.

VITAMIN A. Deficiencies of vitamin A may cause, among other symptoms, dryness and scaliness of the skin, and small, dry spots on the conjunctiva. Vitamin A poisoning or hypervitaminosis is a condition caused by a history of prolonged and excessive dosage of vitamin A. The treatment of vitamin A poisoning is to stop the administration of vitamin A. Sources of vitamin are milk, beef, liver, egg yolk and various fish oils.

VITAMIN B_1 (THIAMINE CHLORIDE). Severe deficiency of this vitamin causes beriberi, which may affect the heart and peripheral nerves. Sources of vitamin B_1 are milk, liver, pork, eggs, vegetables, wheat bran, soybeans, and fruits.

VITAMIN B_2 (RIBOFLAVIN). Riboflavin deficiency may produce various eye symptoms alone or in combination, such as burning, itching, difficulty in looking at light (photophobia), cracks at the corner of the mouth, ulcers and fissures at the corners and inside the mucous membranes of the mouth, greasy scales on reddish skin, particularly around the nose, or a magenta-colored, smooth, painful tongue. Sources of riboflavin are milk, liver, pork, eggs, vegetables, cereals and fruit.

VITAMIN C (ASCORBIC ACID). Deficiency in vitamin C causes scurvy. This is a disease of increased capillary fragility in which there are hemorrhages under the lining of the bone(subperiosteal). Good sources of vitamin C are citrus fruit and tomatoes.

VITAMIN D (ANTIRACHITIC VITAMIN). Early signs of vitamin D deficiency occur in the skull, with softening and thinning of the bone, so that when it is pressed in, it cracks like a ping pong ball. Later signs of rickets show bulging of the frontal (forehead) bones, pigeon breast, and grooves in the rib insertions of the diaphragm. The legs are usually bowed, and walking is usually difficult. Vitamin D is found in fish, fish-liver oils, sunlight, and activated steroids.

VITAMIN K. A lack of this important vitamin may cause a bleeding disorder in the newborn child. Administration of synthetic vitamin K to the mother before delivery, and later to the newborn infant, will prevent this condition. Vitamin K is found in many foods and especially in cabbage, cauliflower, liver, pork, soybeans, spinach, and alfalfa.

NIACIN (NICOTINIC ACID). This is the anti-pellagra factor. Symptoms of niacin deficiency may be found singly or in combinations, pellagra itself being characterized by dermatitis, diarrhea, and dementia. Poor power of concentration, mental confusion, irritability and depression may occur. Sources of niacin in diet are liver, meat, whole milk, and wheat.

BIOTIN. Deficiency of biotin in humans is rare but if present will cause skin lesions, lassitude, and muscle pain. Good sources of boitin are beef liver, roasted peanuts, chocolate, and eggs.

FOLIC ACID. Deficiency may result in megaloblastic erythropoesis. Good sources of folic acid are meat and chicken livers, wheat bran, asparagus, and dry lima beans.

PANTOTHENIC ACID. Because almost any daily diet contains foods with a pantothenic acid content, deficiency signs in humans are not fully identified, but evidence exists that dizziness, constipation, and numbness of hands and feet are among some of the symptoms produced by pantothenic acid deficiency. Almost all foods are sources of pantothenic acid, but especially beef and pork liver, wheat germ, lamb kidney, and broccoli.

VITAMIN B_6 (PYRIDOXINE). Deficiency, although rare, could produce seborrheic dermatitis in the area of the eyes and mouth. Sources of vitamin B_6 are blackstrap molasses, soybeans, wheat bran, and whole rice.

VITAMIN B_{12}. Deficiency of vitamin B_{12} may result in some form of anemia. Good sources of vitamin B_{12} are meat livers, meat kidneys, and fish.

MINERALS. Deficiency or absence in the diet of the essential minerals may cause metabolic disruptions with associated diseases. The essential minerals (some sources of each mineral are given in the parentheses) are calcium (milk), phosphorus (almonds, whole wheat grain), magnesium (cocoa, peanuts, whole wheat flour), sodium (salt), potassium (eggs, meats, skim milk, soybean flours), manganese (oatmeal, whole wheat flour), iron (beef, lamb, and hog liver, soybean flours, yeast), copper (liver, oysters), cobalt (cabbage, spinach, lettuce), iodine (iodized salt), sulfur (eggs, chicken, salmon), zinc (herrings, wheat bran, yeast), and flourine (mackerel, salmon, sardines).

DILATATION AND CURETTAGE (D&C)
This is a surgical procedure in which part or most of the lining of the uterus is removed. It is sometimes referred to by the lay

man as a "scraping." The procedure is done by the vaginal route. In essence it consists of dilating the os, *i.e.,* the opening of the uterus. Next the curette—a long rod with a shallow cuplike head—is introduced into the uterine cavity and portions of the lining removed.

A D&C is an important and useful diagnostic procedure, since the tissue removed can be examined for abnormalities. Thus, in the presence of abnormal or frequent uterine bleeding, a D&C may be necessary to determine which of many possible conditions may be present. By examining tissue samples it may be possible to determine the existence of chronic hormonal stimulation, polyp formation, cancer, chronic inflammation, or the presence of benign tumors known as fibroids. Some cases of continued bleeding after childbirth are due to retention within the uterus of parts of the placenta. It may be necessary to remove these by a curettage.

In addition to its value in diagnosis, a D&C may also cure certain abnormal conditions of the lining. A thorough scraping will remove all the abnormal tissue and leave the uterus in a state somewhat similar to that at the end of menstruation. A more normal cycle of growth and development in the lining may then follow. A D&C performed on a pregnant woman is known as an abortion. Where menstrual cycles have been irregular and the possibility of pregnancy exists, many hospitals may require a pregnancy test before permitting a D&C. This is done to rule out the possibility of unwittingly tampering with an early pregnancy.

The course of events after the D&C somewhat resembles those of a menstrual period. Several days of bleeding, necessitating the wearing of a napkin, generally follow. Bleeding that is unusually heavy or profuse, or fever and discharge, should be reported to the doctor. The procedure itself is generally done in a hospital setting. An injection to prevent pain or some brief form of general anesthesia is generally required. In the usual course of events the patient will be discharged within a day or so.

DIPHTHERIA *Cause.* Bacterial, *Corynebacterium diphtheriae.*

Incubation period. 2 to 7 days.

Symptoms. This disease is spread by contact with cases or carriers. The symptoms are caused by a membrane which forms on the tonsils, pharynx, and lining of the throat. This narrows breathing capacity and also produces a toxin (poison) which is absorbed by the blood and causes the most severe symptoms of this disease. In order to neutralize this poison, diphtheria antitoxin has to be used early in the disease. Otherwise the antitoxin will have no effect. The diphtheria toxin has a special attraction for cardiac (heart), renal (kidney), and nervous tissues.

Diphtheria in the throat area is characterized first by swelling of the tonsils and glands of the neck, with pus spots and a yellowish white membrane covering the tonsils. Fever, rapid heart rate, malaise, and weakness occur. Classical symptoms of croup with noisy, obstructed breathing, brassy cough, hoarseness, and "pulling" (retractions) of the chest follow. This is caused by obstruction to the air passages. If this obstruction is not relieved, death may result from heart failure, exhaustion, or choking.

Diphtheria is rare during the first six months of life, as passive immunity is obtained by the newborn child from antibodies of the mother (if the mother is immune). If the mother is susceptible to diphtheria, so is the child. Diphtheria occurs in epidemics throughout the world and is more frequent in the winter. The sickness and death rate from diphtheria has declined rapidly in the United States since 1920, when active immunization became widely established. Not everyone who recovers from diphtheria develops immunity, and secondary attacks have been known to occur.

The Schick test was developed to test whether a person is susceptible to diphtheria. It is not in general use today because immunization is so widespread.

Complications. These may include paralysis as a result of peripheral neuritis. Selective paralysis of eye muscles, palate, and other areas of the body may occur.

Treatment. Cases of diphtheria should be hospitalized. Antitoxin, antibiotics, and oxygen may be required. In severe cases, tracheotomy (an operation to open the windpipe) may be necessary. This operation makes an artificial airway into the trachea below the area blocked by the membrane in the throat.

Prevention. Immunization with diphtheria toxoid should be started within the first year of life, followed by booster doses every two to three years. This may be administered in the form of triple toxoid or individual diphtheria toxoid. Children who have been exposed to diphtheria should be Schick-tested, and those with positive Schick tests should receive passive immunization.

DIVERTICULITIS A diverticulum (plural, diverticula) is an outpouching of an organ, generally with an internal lining similar to that of the organ itself. Common locations for diverticula are in the urinary bladder and in any portion of the digestive tract including the esophagus, stomach, and small and large intestine.

By far the most common location is the large intestine. Indeed, diverticula of the colon are found in such a large number of middle-aged individuals that they are not considered particularly unusual. They are generally multiple and more common in the descending colon, which is on the left side of the abdomen, but do occur at other points. On an X-ray of the large intestine they generally appear as tiny outgrowths on slim stalks. Even the wider ones are generally considerably smaller than a small grape. Ordinarily their presence arouses no concern. In a few individuals, and for reasons that are not always clear, diverticula may become inflamed, producing the condition known as diverticulitis. This occurs perhaps more commonly in the lower left fourth of the abdomen, so that diverticulitis is sometimes referred to as "left-sided appendicitis." There may be crampy abdominal pain, tenderness in the affected region, and some degree of fever.

Treatment. Diverticulitis is most often treated conservatively by putting the digestive tract to rest, giving feedings intravenously, by use of antibiotics, and similar measures. It is seldom necessary to operate. Rarely, local abscess-formation or some degree of intestinal obstruction may necessiate surgery. However, the chances are thousands to one against surgery becoming necessary. Another (equally rare) complication of diverticulitis is bleeding; a history of passing blood with the bowel movement may lead the doctor to consider diverticulitis as a possible cause. Generally no special diet or alteration in the way of life is made necessary by the presence of diverticula. It is generally advised that constipation be avoided, perhaps by taking a stool softener or doses of mineral oil.

Meckel's Diverticulum Meckel's diverticulum is a rather small protrusion from the small intestine near the ileocecal valve. It may remain quiet as an unnecessary remnant, or it may produce symptoms. It may produce the same symptoms as an acutely inflamed appendix, or give the signs and symptoms of acute intestinal obstruction. It may bleed, producing the picture of a bleeding ulcer. It is usually only diagnosed during surgery, when it can be observed and confirmed.

DIZZINESS, MOTION SICKNESS Dizziness is also known as motion sickness and technically vertigo. True vertigo arises from a disturbance of the semicircular canals located in the inner ear or of the nerve pathways running from it to the brain centers. The canals are filled with a fluid which, if set into sudden or violent motion, may produce sensations of giddiness and nausea. When vertigo is marked, the patient will complain that everything seems to be reeling, his gait may stagger, and his nausea may increase and lead to vomiting. He may be unable to remain upright and even when lying down may complain of dizziness which is increased by every motion of the head.

Motion sickness refers to this disturbance when it is produced as a result of the movement of the body through space, and is commonly encountered on shipboard—seasickness—and occasionally in autos—car sickness. Generally children are more susceptible to car sickness than adults.

In certain viral respiratory illnesses, the semicircular canals may be involved and extreme dizziness may result. This condition, sometimes referred to as labyrinthitis, may also be encountered after the use of certain drugs, such as the barbiturates, or large doses of alcohol. A severe form of labyrinthitis which comes in episodes, particularly in middle age and later, is known as Meniere's syndrome. The person may be suddenly seized with severe dizziness, nausea and vomiting and may be completely incapacitated.

Various other sensations in the head are sometimes incorrectly described as dizziness. These include certain forms of lightheadedness to which individuals with low or very high blood pressures may be subject, and the somewhat similar sensations complained of when sleep has been inadequate or as a result of a "hangover" from either alcohol or sleeping pills. Elderly persons with some evidence of hardening of the arteries may have bouts of unsteadiness described as "dizziness."

Treatment. For motion sickness, Meniere's syndrome, and allied disorders there are several drugs useful in prevention or treatment. They should not be taken, however, without the advice of a physician.

DOUCHE A douche is the introduction into the vagina of a watery solution of a medication or drug. It is no longer considered necessary or even desirable for a woman to douche unless some special indication for it is present. It would be well to discuss the advisability of douching with the doctor; some physicians advise against it any time during pregnancy, except in very special circumstances.

Douches are most often advised in the following situations: (1) Vaginitis, or vaginal infections by certain organism. Here the douche is generally medicated. Sometimes a simple vinegar douche, made by adding three tablespoons of white vinegar to two quarts of warm water, may be prescribed. Or various medicines or specially prepared powders may be advised. (2) Excessive secretions, such as may necessitate the wearing of a sanitary napkin. Here, a cleansing douche is sometimes prescribed. (3) Douches, are sometimes used as a birth-control measure. Such douching, however, is not reliable: whatever advantage is gained by it calls for its immediate use after intercourse.

Douching requires a bag with rubber tubing connected to a hard rubber or plastic nozzle. A cutoff clamp on the rubber tubing will also prove useful. Douching is most conveniently carried out in a bathtub. The douche bag should be no higher than two feet above the level of the hips. After making up the solution in the bag, preferably at about body temperature, the nozzle is inserted approximately two or three inches into the vagina. No attempt should be made to bring the lips of the vagina around the tubing, as free escape of the fluid is necessary.

A convenient position for douching is to recline in the tub with the knees partially drawn up. The douche fluid is allowed to circulate freely into and out of the vagina. It is seldom necessary to douche more than several times a week and often less. For certain kinds of stubborn vaginal infection, daily douching may be prescribed by the doctor.

DRUGS AND REMEDIES

Antibiotics An antibiotic is a substance secreted by one organism which will kill other organisms—specifically bacteria and fungi. The first and best-known of the antibiotics is penicillin. Its successors include streptomycin, tetracycline, and terramycin. Less well known are mycostatin, griseofulvin, kanamycin, and others which have limited but useful special application. Recently, chemically modified forms of the naturally occurring penicillin have appeared; these have useful new properties, including the ability to attack certain penicillin-resistant organisms.

The sulfonamide drugs preceded the antibiotics, then for a long time were displaced by them. They are synthetic chemicals which come out of the chemists' test tube and not out of a fermentation vat. Between the antibiotics and the sulfa drugs, today's doctor has a wide choice of infection-fighting agents. These drugs can be used against an almost endless list of infections, ranging from pimples and boils to pneumonia and meningitis. Constant advances are made in the antibiotic field. Thus at one time streptomycin was extensively used in the treatment of tuberculosis but has now been largely supplanted by a very simple chemical related to one of the vitamin B group—isonicotinic hydrazide (INH). Some antibiotics should be used only when all other measures fail; thus, although griseofulvin is effective when taken by mouth for the treatment of athlete's foot and similar fungus infections, one would certainly try local measures first.

The most important limiting factor in the treatment of infections is the absence of agents that will kill off viruses. For instance, there is no presently available drug that can be used in the treatment of acute poliomyelitis, measles, influenza, the common cold, and other virus-produced illnesses. The first step the doctor must take is to decide the nature of an infection; only then can an antibiotic drug be correctly prescribed.

Sometimes a resistant organism is encountered which does not respond to the usual antibiotic. The usual countermeasure is either to increase the dose or switch to another antibiotic. There are also certain drawbacks to be kept in mind: at least 5 percent of the population will develop an allergy to penicillin. This may be manifested by hives, joint pains, fever, and occasionally by a collapse following a penicillin injection. Tetracycline may occasionally produce somewhat similar reactions, and in addition may encourage an overgrowth of certain organisms usually kept in check. This may result in diarrhea or in vaginal itching. With pregnant women it is now generally considered a good rule to take drugs only for good reason and under a doctor's direction.

Anticoagulants These form an important group of drugs which diminish the clotting power of the blood. They can prevent the extension of a clot that has already formed, or can be used prophylactically to prevent clots. Heparin was the first drug with anticoagulant properties to be used. It has to be given by injection and produces a prompt drop in the coagulability of the blood. Because of its expense and the necessity for injection, another group of drugs without these disadvantages has been developed (dicumarol, coumadin, and others). With these it is possible to maintain long-term treatment, and some patients have been on anticoagulant drugs for years.

The correct dose of the drug to be taken is arrived at by

frequent testing of blood samples. It is impossible to predict in advance how much will be needed. Sometimes the dose has to be changed because of fluctuations in blood clotting capacity. In overdose there may be noted easy bruising, so that black-and-blue marks appear in the skin with slight bumps or even without apparent injuries. Bleeding in the urinary tract with reddish urine, and occasionally into the digestive tract with a reddish-to-blackish stool, may also occur from overdosage. This is easily corrected by giving the appropriate antidote, vitamin K. The great majority of patients do very well on anticoagulants. Some can be allowed to go for relatively long periods of time between routine checks. Hence the need for testing may diminish from almost daily down to weekly and even monthly.

Clotting (thrombosis) in a large vein is one common condition for which anticoagulants may be prescribed. Thrombosis is more likely to occur in patients who are compelled to stay in bed for days or weeks, as in the treatment of a heart attack. Some, though not all, doctors may consider it worthwhile to give such a patient an anticoagulant drug. The drugs have also been used, though again there are differences of opinion here, for the long-term treatment of patients who have had a heart attack. It is felt that there may be less risk of a second attack if the clotting power of the blood is diminished. Recent studies suggest that this particular effect diminishes considerably after the first year.

In certain elderly individuals, impaired circulation to the brain results in transient bouts of visual difficulties, weakness, and dizziness; anticoagulants seem to be useful in cutting down and even eliminating such episodes. However, if high blood pressure is present, it is generally considered less safe to use the anticoagulants. Since the anticoagulants are relatively recent drugs on the medical scene, precise opinions as to their range of usage are still being formed.

Barbiturates The important chemical compound, barbituric acid, was synthesized at the turn of the century; it and its derivatives are widely used in medical practice. They have sedative and sleep-producing properties and, although much maligned and abused, are important and useful drugs. Collectively, these compounds are known as the barbiturates. Perhaps the best known is phenobarbital, widely employed as a sedative. In moderate doses, it allays anxiety and is hence used to assuage feelings of tension, restlessness, and for sleep difficulties. It may produce some dulling, with feelings of drowsiness. It is also useful in psychosomatic disturbances—that is, in such disorders as "nervous headaches," "nervous stomach," spastic colitis—and has some value in the treatment of nausea. Hence many of the compounds used for the treatment of disorders of the digestive tract incorporate phenobarbital as one of the ingredients. It is also used to diminish overstimulation produced by such drugs as ephedrine, a medication used in the treatment of asthma and other conditions. In some patients use of phenobarbital may produce a rash.

The other widespread application of the barbiturates is in the treatment of insomnia and other sleep disorders. A dose of one of these compounds taken at bedtime will generally induce sleep, often for five or more hours. Depending on dosage and individual response, one may awake feeling refreshed or somewhat sleepy and heavy-headed. Some tolerance generally develops to sleeping pills after they have been taken for a time. In ordinary dosages, however, there is no danger of addiction or habit formation. Those who have to take sleeping pills night after night do not do so because of addiction, but rather because the reasons for insomnia (whatever they may be) are often constant and well-established ones. Hence, whatever produces the need for sleeping pills in the beginning will again become apparent if the sleeping pills are omitted.

Diuretics Diuretics are substances which increase the production of urine. The caffeine found in coffee and tea and the theobromine found in cocoa are examples of natural diuretic substances. Certain acidifying salts, of which ammonium chloride is an example, will also increase urine production. Much more potent diuretics than these are now available. A single dose may lead to a 3 to 5-pint increase in urine production within the following twenty-four hours. This in turn would mean a 3 to 5-pound loss of body weight, since a pint of fluid weighs a pound.

The first potent group of diuretics were known as the mercurial diuretics, since their active ingredient was an organic compound of mercury. Mercurial diuretics are generally given by injection and induce a very prompt and often extensive urinary increase. In recent years some potent drugs which are effective by mouth have been synthesized. They are sometimes collectively referred to as the chlorothiazide group of drugs. One or two of these pills may produce a diuresis equivalent to that following a mercurial drug. In addition to promoting the excretion of sodium chloride, which is common salt, these pills also increase the excretion of potassium from the body. To compensate for this the pills may be combined with potassium salts. Otherwise their frequent or long-continued use may lead to states of serious potassium depletion, manifested by muscular weakness.

Diuretics are invaluable drugs in all fields of medicine. With them it is possible to get rid of fluid accumulations which otherwise may be annoying, troublesome, or even massive. Diuretics may be used by women with troublesome fluid accumulations during the last part of their menstrual cycles. Also during pregnancy, when fluid accumulation is marked or the blood pressure is rising too high, the doctor may prescribe diuretics. A clot in a large vein of the lower extremity may result in troublesome chronic leg swelling. This too may be controlled, at least partially, by the diuretics.

A second most important application of these drugs is in the treatment of high blood pressure. For reasons that are not entirely clear, promoting the excretion of salt and water from the body tends to lower blood pressure. Hence these drugs are one of the basic approaches in the drug treatment of hypertension. On the whole they produce relatively few unpleasant effects. Sometimes, when the rate of urine production is quite brisk, muscular cramps due to rapid loss of salts may be noted. This may be an indication for decreasing the dose somewhat. Diuretic drugs, however, should not be taken for trivial reasons, nor without some form of medical supervison.

Laxatives Laxatives are agents which promote the evacuation of the large intestine. The old distinction drawn between laxatives, cathartics, and purgatives is not a practical one. Originally the laxatives were regarded as the least active and the purgatives as the most active evacuants. The distinction is in part due to dosage; a small dose of a specific medicine will have a mild laxative effect, but increasing it may produce a great number of watery stools—a purgative action. There are many stimulants that move the bowel, and their mechanisms of action are different. Thus castor oil stimulates the muscle of the small intestine as well as the large one, and produces copious watery movements. In addition, it stimulates the muscle of the uterus and hence should not be used during pregnancy. Other laxatives have a bulk or mechanical effect.

One classification based upon action is the following:

1. *Saline cathartics.* These draw fluid out into the intestinal canal because of their salt concentration, and so will produce one or more bowel movements that are more watery than usual. Saline cathartics include Epsom salts (magnesium sulphate), phospho-soda (sodium phosphate),

citrate of magnesia (magnesium citrate solution), and Seidlitz powders (potassium and sodium tartrate).

2. *Bulk-lubricant group.* These increase the bulk of the intestinal contents, hence stimulate the bowel to evacuation and may have a lubricating effect. Mineral oil is a common example of this. Other bulk agents include bran, psyllium or its extracts, and agar.

3. *Stool-softeners.* These are wetting agents which keep the stool moist and therefore bulkier. They are usually taken daily, are well tolerated, and are used in all age groups including babies. With them the small, hard, or pellety stool of chronic constipation becomes larger, bulkier, and moister.

4. *Irritant cathartics.* These include many plant extracts and fruits such as prunes used for centuries in the treatment of constipation.

5. *Suppositories.* These are sometimes a convenient way of emptying the rectum promptly.

Steroid Drugs The two hormones of the ovary, a group of adrenal hormones, and the male hormone all bear considerable resemblance to each other.

These hormones are collectively spoken of as the "steroid hormone."

Sulfonamide (Sulfa) Drugs This is a group of germ-killing drugs created synthetically and first introduced in the early 1930s. The first one, sulfanilamide, is now of historical importance only and has been succeeded by a number of derivatives with varying properties. For a time the sulfonamide drugs were pushed aside by the new antibiotics, but they are now returning to their rightful place and have widespread usage. In some cases they are good alternatives to the antibiotics. Thus, in children who have rheumatic fever, a daily dose of penicillin or a sulfonamide drug should be taken to prevent recurrences. If the child is sensitive to penicillin, he will have no choice except to take the sulfa drug. For many urinary tract infections, infections of the sinuses, sore throats, etc., the choice of whether it is to be a sulfa drug or an antibiotic may be in part a matter of personal preference on the part of the physician. He will be guided especially by any knowledge of past difficulties with the drugs that the patient may have experienced; reactions such as nausea, vaginal itching, or drug eruptions. In meningitis and certain other infections the sulfa drugs may be the preferred ones.

Most of the sulfa drugs have to be taken at frequent intervals, perhaps every four to six hours, since they tend to be rapidly excreted through the urine; it is sometimes advised that extra water be drunk to prevent any crystallization of the drug in the urine. Recently, longer-acting and more slowly excreted derivatives have been created which need to be taken only once every twelve hours.

There is also a group of poorly absorbed sulfonamide drugs which can be taken by mouth in large quantities. These are particularly effective in infections of the intestinal tract. Because of poor absorption from the intestine, large amounts can be given and high concentrations achieved. This propery is useful in certain dysenteries and in preparing the intestine for certain operative procedures; these drugs are sometimes referred to as the intestinal sulfonamides. In certain severe infections, a sulfonamide drug can be injected directly into the vein for high concentrations in the bloodstream.

Tranquilizers A tranquilizer is a drug which will diminish nervous tension and its manifestations. A perfect tranquilizer would diminish anxiety without impairing the ability to think. In practice, depending in part on the drugs and the person taking it, some slowing up or sedative effect is likely to be noted. There is, therefore, only a difference of degree between some of the new tranquilizers and some of the older sedative drugs, such as phenobarbital. This differ-ence may be of some value, since there may be less sleepiness with a tranquilizer. Hence, for the woman who has difficulty falling asleep, a tranquilizer might be preferred if she wants to get up during the night to give the baby a formula; after the usual dose of a barbiturate a woman might find herself too sleepy or dizzy to function well. A distinction is sometimes drawn between minor tranquilizers—such as meprobamate (Miltown®, Equanil®), which is used for minor symptoms of anxiety like nervous headache, jitteriness, difficulty in falling asleep, etc.—and major tranquilizers which can be used in severe mental disturbances, such as states of great agitation and overactivity or various psychotic disorders.

The first major tranquilizer—and still one of the most widely employed—is thorazine. Various drugs, some more or less closely related to thorazine, have appeared in the last ten years and have greatly improved treatment of mental disorders. In full dosage, such as may be given only in a hospital setting, a major tranquilizer may greatly suppress delusions, hallucinations, and hyperactivity in an agitated psychotic. Through their use, long periods of institutionalization have been so drastically cut that the major tranquilizers are said to have introduced a new era in the treatment of mental disorders. Small doses of tranquilizers may be effective against nausea.

EAR CONDITIONS

Hearing Disability There may be organic causes for hearing defects, such as ear malformations, trauma, infections and diseases of the nose, throat, and ear. Other defects due to hereditary or birth injuries may cause a delay in hearing. This, of course, will cause delay in speech development.

It is difficult to discover a hearing defect in a very young infant. However, most parents will be able to tell whether the child wakes on hearing a loud noise, or responds to music or the sound of a voice. As a child approaches school age, accurate audiometric evaluation (hearing tests) is possible. It is extremely necessary to treat all ear infections in children until they are cleared, otherwise many such infections may result in impaired hearing.

Treatment of hearing defects includes speech therapy, lip reading, acoustic training, hearing aids, and sometimes schooling in a special school for the hard-of-hearing.

Otitis (Ear Infection) The ear is divided into the external, middle, and internal (inner) ear. These units conduct sound and maintain equilibrium. Acute otitis media is a term describing inflammation of the lining membrane of the middle ear. It is usually a result of an infection carried from the throat or tonsil area through the eustachian tube. In children, the most outstanding symptom is ear pain which results from pressure of fluid behind the drum, or from inflammation of the drum. Hearing may be impaired, and sometimes noises and ringing may be heard.

In small infants who have no demonstrable sign of illness, fretting, crying, screaming with pain, head-banging, or handling of the ear may indicate an ear infection. It can only be diagnosed by looking into the ear with an otoscope.

Ear infections should be treated with antibiotics. If they are not treated early, pus accumulates behind the eardrum, the drum may rupture, and chronic draining ear may develop. This will predispose to the development of mastoiditis and possibly meningitis. Hearing loss and deafness may also develop.

Acute Mastoiditis Acute mastoiditis usually occurs as a complication of middle ear infections. Since the advent of antibiotics, which usually cure most middle ear infections, it has become a rare condition.

The signs of this condition are: persistent fever, pain in the ear and behind the ear, hearing loss, and general toxicity. There is tenderness over the mastoid area (the bone just behind the ear) and X-ray will show destruction of the mastoid cells. If pus discharges from the ear and remains untreated, mastoiditis is very likely to develop. The treatment is usually surgery plus antibiotics.

EYES—CROSS-EYES OR SQUINT (STRABISMUS)
Squint is caused by abnormalities in the nerves or the ocular muscles. The person fixes one eye on an object while the other eye turns so that the image does not fall on the center portion of the eye. This condition may involve one or both eyes.

Paralytic squint is due to either partial or complete paralysis of one or more of the eye muscles. This may cause a turning of the eye to one side, double vision, or restriction of motion.

Concomitant squint is a muscle imbalance which involves both eyes equally. It does not involve paralysis or loss of function of one single muscle. These squints may be intermittent or alternating, converging or diverging and/or vertical. In children this condition is usually caused by an imbalance between the ciliary muscle and the internal recti muscles.

Treatment. Surgical treatment is usually necessary if the squint has been present since birth. Early surgery, between the ages of two and three years, produces a better result and prevents more complications. Since the brain and cerebral structures are involved in correct eye functioning, a delay in surgery may lead to loss of vision in one of the eyes.

Medical treatment alone is usually only successful in infants who have developed cross-eyes after the age of eighteen or twenty-four months. It is possible to test eyes of infants and young children to determine whether they require glasses. Sometimes glasses will convert squinting eyes to normal. However, training and special eye exercises may often be necessary in addition to glasses.

EYES, INFLAMMATION OF
Conjunctivitis Conjunctivitis is an inflammation of the conjunctiva, the lining of the eye. In health the conjunctiva appears pale and glistening; it has relatively few visible blood vessels traversing it. As a result of the inflammation it turns quite red (hence the term "pink eye"), and whitish or yellowish secretion may accumulate. Sometimes, particularly after a night's sleep, the accumulated secretion may fuse the eyelashes together to such an extent that opening the eye is difficult or temporarily impossible. Washing this dried exudate away will generally relieve this condition. Conjunctivitis can result from the irritation of chemicals, smoke, or dusts, and is occasionally allergic in origin. Most cases, however, are due to inflammations set up by various bacteria. Thus, epidemics of conjunctivitis have been reported due to a germ known as the Koch-Weeks bacillus. More common organisms such as the staphylococcus and the streptococcus are also to be found in isolated cases of conjunctivitis. In many instances conjunctivitis occurs in both eyes, or if it appears in one eye first it will infrequently spread to the other.

Treatment. Mild cases due to smoke, dusts, and mechanical irritants will subside by themselves. Even mild cases due to bacterial inflammation may not require special treatment, since the bodily defenses can generally handle them. It is possible to get a very high local concentration of a sulfa drug or an antibiotic into the area of conjunctivitis, however. A drop or two from an eyedropper will do this, and as a rule conjunctivitis will respond quite promptly to instillations of such drugs.

As a precaution against the possibility of the newborn baby developing conjunctivitis from an unsuspected gonor-rheal infection in the mother, many states require that silver nitrate drops be placed in the eyes immediately after birth. This routine has virtually eliminated gonorrheal conjunctivitis in the newborn. Infants may acquire other forms of conjunctivitis, however, including some due to viruses. Generally speaking, none of these is serious, and response to treatment is generally prompt and satisfactory.

Sty This is an inflammation and infection of the eyelid. A hair follicle may become red, enlarged, and cause an accumulation of pus. The eyelid becomes red and painful; tears and a pus discharge may occur.

Treatment. Warm boric acid eyewashes, or compresses, in addition to antibiotics by mouth and by injections will usually suffice.

EYES—VISUAL DIFFICULTIES
Most visual difficulties can be understood only if one has some basic knowledge of the structures within the eye. The eye can be compared to the camera; it has a clear portion admitting light (the cornea), a variable lens opening (the pupil, controlled by the iris), and beyond this a lens whose thickness can be modified and which throws the image onto the back part of the eye (the retina). Difficulties in focusing the image correctly are called refractive errors. Compensating lenses can partially or wholly correct such errors, and these are the lenses we wear as eyeglasses.

Common refractive errors include:

1. *Myopia.* In this condition the eyeball is relatively long so that the image transmitted through the lens focuses in front of the retina. It is corrected by a concave lens (thinner in the middle than at the sides). Myopia runs in some families and has a hereditary aspect.

2. *Hypermetropia.* This condition is known as farsightedness. Here the reverse of myopia exists, the eyeball being somewhat shorter than it should be. The visual difficulty is most marked with images that are close up, not with objects that are at a distance. A lens which is convex, the opposite of the one used for nearsightedness, will be prescribed for this condition.

3. *Presbyopia.* There is a loss of elasticity in the lens of the eye as we grow older. Because of this some of its power to focus on nearby objects is lost past the age of forty to fifty. Fine print cannot be read at the usual distance, though for a time it may be readable when held out at arm's length. A lens similar to that used for farsightedness will help—"reading glasses."

4. *Astigmatism.* Slight distortions in the cornea, the transparent window-like opening at the front of the eye, will produce blurring in some parts of the transmitted image. It may be associated with other difficulties but may also exist alone.

Various conditions, such as fatigue or some illnesses, may affect the refractive behavior of the eye. Some people do not focus as well when they are very tired or when they first get up in the morning. Diabetes, by temporarily altering the various fluids within the eyeball, may lead to a refractive error which is correctable when the diabetes is brought under control. In addition, diabetes tends to increase the rate at which cataracts (opacifications) form within the lens. Some of the antispasmodic drugs may cut down on the ability to focus; this is also temporary and reversible.

Blindness The most extreme visual difficulty is, of course, blindness. Recognition of blindness in a young infant may be difficult within the first few months. After that, it can be recognized by a failure to respond to normal stimulation by the parent. The child does not smile appropriately or follow objects with his eyes and appears to stare vacantly.

Blind children present special problems in learning and development. Blindness also creates emotional problems for the parents, family, and friends. Blind children require specialized schools which teach them to develop a sense of independence and self-sufficiency. At such schools they are taught touch systems (the Braille alphabet) or reading and special methods of getting around in the street. The parents as well as the children must learn how to handle the problem of the visually handicapped. Given proper training, blind children can grow up into useful, productive adults.

FAINTING A fainting episode is associated with a marked drop in blood pressure which results in a temporary decline in the circulation to the brain. Hot and crowded surroundings, a painful injection, a sudden unpleasant sight or upsetting news are among the common causes. There may be some warning signals, such as pallor, perspiraton, complaints of dizziness, or "spots before the eyes." If the victim is quickly stretched out or if the head is lowered at once, fainting may be avoided. Otherwise unconsciousness may ensue, sometimes in associaton with brief muscular twitching.

Cold applications, chafing of the hands and forearms, and allowing the person to inhale aromatic spirits of ammonia are old, well-established measures. The losses of consciousness just described are sometimes called simple faints. They are to be differentiated from fainting due to such causes as bleeding, internal hemorrhage, overdoses of insulin, and other episodes which will require medical attention.

FALLS AND FRACTURES It is not always possible to tell whether a fall has resulted in a bruise, a sprain, or a serious fracture—a break in the bone. A fracture may be looked for when a person has fallen from a considerable height or has suffered severe or multiple impacts, as in falling down stairs or in auto accidents. However, in the elderly fractures may occur with relatively little impact because of brittleness of the bones in old age. A fracture may also be suspected if there is an obvious deformity, a shortening of an extremity, or if crepitus (a grating sound) is produced on gentle touching of the injured part. *If there is any possibility of a fracture involving the backbone, no attempts should be made to move the person or to help him to his feet,* as occasionally serious damage to the spinal cord may occur.

For other fractures, immobilization by splints is necessary before any movement is attempted. The splints can be sticks of wood, boughs, broom handles, umbrellas, or anything else which can be satisfactorily applied to the limb. The splint is placed so as to run to the joint above and the joint below the site of the fracture and so that it can be secured in place with handkerchiefs, twine, or any other binding available.

Where only bruises and sprains have resulted from the injury, the best first-aid measure is application of cold. Thus, compresses wrung out of icewater or an icebag may be applied to the area. Cold can be maintained continuously (or intermittently, if uncomfortable) for hours; it results in diminishing pain, swelling, and bleeding. Generally, starting in about twenty-four hours, local heat can be used. This may be in the form of a heating pad, hot wet compresses, or a heat lamp. Heat treatments may be given for as long as a half hour and can be repeated several times a day. An X-ray of the region may be necessary to rule out fracture. Aspirin and other pain-killing medications are frequently necessary.

FEVER Even an everyday event like fever still defies complete explanation. Most often, in the presence of infection, the temperature-regulating center in the mid-brain, which functions like a thermostat, allows the "setting" to go somewhat higher. It is thought that higher body temperatures may accelerate the rate of bodily defenses.

The degree of fever provides some rough estimate of the severity of infection. But it is only a crude estimate: for example, there is no significant difference between a fever of 101° or 102°F. One may also be quite sick without having appreciable fever, as is often true of patients with hepatitis, who may have liver inflammation, be quite jaundiced, and yet have normal body temperature. In describing a fever one should specify whether oral or rectal temperatures were taken. Normal rectal temperature is about 99.6°F., or one degree higher than normal mouth temperature, despite the fact that both kinds of thermometers indicate the normal at 98.6°F.

Whatever the value of fever, people with markedly elevated temperatures generally feel better if it is lowered somewhat. Aspirin in the usual doses possesses the property of lowering fevers. For a bacterial infection one would, of course, want to use an antibiotic to cure the infection. For fever associated with viral infection (one against which an antibiotic will not work) aspirin still remains the most useful drug.

Another measure for reducing high fevers is an alcohol sponging. For the rare but severe fever produced by sunstroke or certain viral infections in which the temperature can go to 104°-105°F., rapid decreases in body temperature are in order. This reduction can be achieved by direct applications of ice, wrapping in a cool wet sheet. Fevers of lesser magnitude generally present no emergency and do not call for heroic measures designed to beat the temperature down a degree or two. Moderate fever may be regarded as a help, not a hindrance, to bodily defenses. (See also TEMPERATURE, TAKING.)

FIBROID A fibroid is a benign tumor occurring in the heavy muscular wall of the uterus. As is also true of tumors elsewhere, we do not know why fibroid tumors develop as often as they do. More than half of all women develop fiboids of some size. The tumors are frequently multiple and vary from marble-sized to orange-sized and even larger. Stimulation by the hormones produced by the ovary may increase their size. When there is a drop-off in ovarian hormones fibroid tumors may shrink, an event frequently seen after the menopause.

Because of the stimulating effect of hormones, fibroids may increase in size in women taking hormone injections or birth-control pills and also, for the same reason, during a normal pregnancy. Fibroids often reach larger size without producing any symptoms of any kind. In the absence of symptoms even a large uterine fibroid does not need to be removed. The difficulties produced by fibroids are the following: (1) Pressure symptoms—large fibroids can exert pressure on nearby organs such as the bladder and the rectum. The symptoms produced will be those of frequent urination, small bladder capacity, or difficulties in bowel function. (2) Abnormal bleeding may be produced by fibroids, with patterns of increased flow or more frequent menstruation; anemia may then result. (3) In some instances fibroids may contribute to sterility, either by interfering with conception or with the progress of pregnancy. (4) Sometimes because of impaired blood supply or for other reasons a fibroid may undergo degenerative changes and produce pain and fever.

Treatment. The treatment of fibroids must necessarily be very individualized. The doctor will want to be sure that there is no other associated condition producing abnormal symptoms. Up to a point it is possible to live with fibroids that are producing symptoms. Beyond this point surgery is often recommended. Complete removal of the uterus is the operation called hysterectomy. In younger women who still want to have children and where there is a reasonable chance that they may become pregnant, a surgical procedure known as a myomectomy may be performed instead. In such a case the surgeon will try to remove the fibroids alone, to the extent that this is possible, hoping to spare the uterus for further functioning. However, it is not always possible to do a myomectomy. Since fibroids tend to shrink after the menopause, a woman approaching it may sometimes put up with symptoms due to fibroids in the hope that spontaneous improvement will occur.

FIRST AID

The following 18-page *Emergency First Aid Guide* (adapted from a United States Government publication) presents instructions for use in a wide variety of emergency situations. Other emergency and medical problems are discussed throughout the text in more detail.

Use this handy First Aid Guide for instant answers to emergency questions.

Call a physician immediately for serious injuries, poisoning, and drug overdoses.

FORMULA

Kinds and Amounts Most babies thrive on very simple formulas. Formulas are usually mixtures of cow's milk, water, and sugar. As a baby grows older, water and sugar are gradually cut down until he is taking milk alone.

Your doctor will tell you how to make your baby's formula and how to change it from time to time. However, if you are unable to get in touch with your doctor, a formula that suits most young babies is:

Evaporated milk	4 ounces
Water	8 ounces
Sugar	1 tablespoon (level

or

Whole milk	8 ounces
Water	4 ounces
Sugar	1 tablespoon (level)

This mixture may be divided into 6 bottles of about 2 ounces each or eight bottles of about 1½ ounces each. This amount of feeding usually satisfies a newborn baby from about the second or third day to the end of the first week.

As soon as your baby is no longer satisfied with this amount of feeding, double the amounts in the original formula. Later, when the baby wants it, use 3 times the amount of each item in the formula.

Most babies do well if they are given as much of this milk mixture as they wish when they are hungry, which will usually be about every 3 to 4 hours. After your baby is 2 weeks old he will need in each 24 hours from 2 to 3 ounces of this milk mixture for each pound that he weighs. If in 24 hours your baby usually takes less than 2 ounces of this formula for each pound that he weighs, tell your doctor about that.

A formula which has less water in it may be quite satisfactory for your baby, particularly when he is 2 or 3 months old. Gradually cut down the amount of water until he is taking whole milk or until he is taking equal parts of evaporated milk and water.

When your baby is taking other foods, it is time to stop adding sugar to the milk. If sugar is cut down slowly, your baby will probably not miss it. (See also INFANT FEEDING.)

In general, there are two simple ways of making a formula safe for a baby. The first way is to mix the formula, pour it, unboiled, into bottles that have been washed but not sterilized, put on the nipples, and last, sterilize the filled bottles. The second method is to sterilize the equipment, boil the formula, and then pour the boiled milk into the sterilized bottles. Either way is all right. You can, if you like, try both ways and see which seems simpler to you.

Feeding Equipment The standard-sized nursing bottle holds 8 ounces. Lines are marked where the ounces come, so there need be no guesswork when you pour in the formula. Bottles of heat-resistant glass or of boilable plastic cost more, but you will probably save in the long run by getting them. Buy bottles that are easy to clean with a bottle brush. The neck of the bottle as well as the bottom should slope into the sides, so there are no sharp, hard-to-clean corners.

Buy as many bottles as you will need in a 24-hour period. A dozen will be none too many, and a few more will come in handy in case you break any. In addition to the number of bottles you use for feedings, you will need two or three for water and orange juice. These can be 4-ounce bottles. Bottles are easier to clean if you rinse them after each feeding and fill them with cold water.

If you can, buy enough nipples so that you will not have to boil them but once a day. This will mean having one for each feeding and one for each drink of water or orange juice. You may have to make the holes in the nipples larger. Try out the nipples by putting one on a bottle with water in it and turning it upside down. Watch to see if there is a steady drip. Remembering that water will come through faster than milk because it is thinner.

If the holes seem too small, heat the point of a fine needle in the flame of a match. While the point is red hot, poke it quickly through one or more holes in the nipple. Be sure to use a small needle as it is easy to ruin a nipple by burning too large holes in it. After each feeding, wash the nipple and squeeze water through the holes. Dry it and keep it in a covered jar until you are ready to sterilize the day's supply.

Nipple caps or covers are made of glass, plastic aluminum, or paper. Paper caps are the cheapest, but since they can be used only once, they may not be the most economical in the long run.

Equipment for Making It is convenient to have a set of utensils that you use only in preparing your baby's food. In any case, keeping utensils together will make the sterilizing and formula preparation go more speedily.

Kettle for sterilizing. If you are going to bottle-feed a baby for a long time, it may pay you to buy a kettle specially made for this purpose. Such a kettle has a tight-fitting cover and a rack inside to hold the bottles.

If you do not want to go to this expense, any kettle large enough to hold the bottles and other equipment will do. If you have a large enough pressure cooker, you can use it as a kettle.

In addition to the kettle you will need:

A wire rack or a pie tin (upside down) that fits the bottom of the kettle, for holding the bottles.

A bottle brush with a long handle and with stout bristles to scrub the inside of the bottles. It should be one that is bent at the tip so that the bristles clean the bottom of the bottle and not just the sides.

A set of measuring spoons is handy.

A measuring cup marked in ounces, with a pouring lip.

A 2-quart saucepan with a pouring lip to mix the formula in.

A small saucepan with a lid, in which to boil and keep the nipples.

A funnel makes it easier to pour the formula into the bottles, but if your saucepan has a lip that pours well you may be able to get along without one. If you get a plastic one, make sure it is the kind which can be boiled.

A long-handled spoon.

A can opener that punches holes (if you use canned milk).

A small wide-mouthed jar with a cover, for used nipples.

Bottles to hold a 24-hour supply of formula.

Nipples and nipple caps.

A pair of tongs is convenient.

Making the Formula—Method I (Terminal Sterilization)

1. Wash thoroughly with hot water and detergent all the articles you will use. With the bottle brush scrub the inside of the bottles and nipple covers and the inside and outside of the nipples.

2. Rinse all articles well. Drain. Squeeze clean water through nipple holes.

3. Measure the milk, water, and sugar or syrup into a large saucepan. If you use granulated sugar, level off measuring spoon with back of table knife. If you use syrup, pour from the bottle into the measuring spoon. If the milk you use is not homogenized, shake the bottle well to mix the cream before measuring. If you use evaporated milk, wash the top of the can with soap and water and rinse it off well before opening.

4. Divide the milk mixture among the number of bottles the baby is likely to need in 24 hours.

5. Put nipples and nipple covers on the bottles. Do not push or screw nipple covers down tight, because during sterilization the hot air may blow the caps off.

6. Put the bottles of formula on the rack in the kettle. Put one or two bottles of drinking water, covered with nipple and cap, in at the same time. Pour water into the kettle until it comes about halfway up on the bottle. Cover the kettle.

7. Bring the water in the kettle to a boil. *Boil actively for 25 minutes* by the clock. As soon as the bottles cool enough to handle, take them out of the kettle. Tighten nipple caps.

8. After the bottles cool, put them in your refrigerator at once. In an ice refrigerator, place the bottles near the ice. A rack to hold the bottles upright is very convenient.

Method II (Standard Clean Technique) *Sterilizing the equipment.* You may like to sterilize ahead of the time when you make the formula. Then the things in the sterilizing kettle will have a chance to cool down before you need to handle them in making the formula.

1. Wash the bottles, nipple covers, funnel and nipples thoroughly in hot water with a detergent. With the bottle brush scrub the inside of the nursing bottles and nipple covers, and inside and outside of the nipples.

2. Rinse all these articles well. Squeeze clean water through the nipple holes.

3. If your sterilizing kettle has a rack to hold the bottles, set each bottle in it, upside down. Fit the other articles between the bottles. If your kettle has no rack, lay the bottles on their sides in the kettle, with the other equipment on top.

4. If your kettle has a rack and a tight-fitting cover, pour in 1 or 2 inches of water and put on the cover. When the water boils actively, steam will form and will sterilize the equipment. Keep the water boiling for at least 5 minutes by the clock. If your kettle doesn't have a tight-fitting lid, put in enough water to completely cover the bottles and all the other things to be sterilized. Boil for at least 5 minutes after the water has come to a boil.

5. If you put enough water in the kettle to cover the bottles and other articles, they will cool more quickly if you drain off some of the water. Leave the things in the covered kettle until ready to use.

6. Drop the nipples into boiling water in a small pan, cover, and let boil for 5 minutes. Then pour the water off, let the steam escape and leave the nipples in the covered pan until you use them.

Sterilizing the formula.

1. Measure the milk, water, and sugar or syrup into a large saucepan. To make up for water lost during boiling you can put an ounce or so more water than your formula calls for. If you use granulated sugar, level off measuring spoon with back of table knife. If you use syrup, pour from the bottle into the measuring spoon. If the milk you use is not homogenized, shake the bottle well to mix the cream before measuring. If you use evaporated milk, wash the top of the can with soap and water and rinse it off well before opening it.

2. Bring the mixture to a boil and keep boiling (bubbling) gently for 5 minutes by the clock. Stir constantly with a large stirring spoon.

3. Take the milk mixture off the stove and let it cool for a few minutes. Stirring it will make it cool faster. If you use fresh milk, stirring will keep scum from forming.

4. Take the nursing bottles out of the sterilizer without touching the tops, using tongs if you have them. If you use a funnel take it out of the sterilizer without touching its rim or stem, and set it in one of the bottles.

5. Divide the milk mixture among the number of bottles the baby is likely to need in 24 hours.

6. Put sterile rubber nipples on the bottles without touching the rim of the bottle or the nipple except by the tab or outer edge. Cover the nipples at once with sterile nipple caps, being careful not to touch nipples or lip of nipple caps. (Follow the directions that come with whatever kind of nipple and bottle you use.)

7. Put the bottles in the refrigerator at once. In an ice refrigerator, place the bottles near the ice.

GALLBLADDER, DISEASES OF The gallbladder is roughly comparable in size and shape to a small pear. It is located in the upper right quarter of the abdomen. Its location can be approximated as being in the area where a line dropped from the right nipple meets the lowermost rib. The pain of gallbladder disease is most often felt in this location. In addition, it may also be felt at approximately the same point in the back and occasionally in the tip of the right shoulder.

The movement of stones out of the gallbladder—termed biliary colic—may produce paroxysms of intense pain which radiate to the upper central abdomen. Gallstones may vary from the size of a pinhead to that of a marble, and will develop at one time or another in 10 or 20 per cent of the inflammation of the gallbladder itself, and may or may not produce symptoms.

Acute inflammation of the gallbladder, known as *cholecystitis,* usually comes on suddenly. It produces pain in the region of the gallbladder, often accompanied by nausea and vomiting and a variable degree of fever. It may be mild and subside, or severe, in which case, like acute appendicitis, rupture and peritonitis may result. Hence, depending on the course of events, it may be allowed to subside or urgent operation may be necessary. It may occur in bouts weeks to years apart, and is often associated with gallstones. The acute disorder may give way to a chronic one in which there are many repeated bouts of pain in the right upper abdomen with bloating and nausea, often brought on by dietary indiscretions such as eating certain fats.

Gallbladder disease is often regarded as a surgical and not a medical disorder, for the following reasons: (1) Once any sort of gallbladder disorder, be it acute inflammation or colic, has occurred, repeated attacks can be expected. (2) There is no known medical treatment which will do away with gallstones once they have formed. (3) It is easier on both patient and surgeon to remove a diseased gallbladder at a time other than that of an acute attack, even though the patient has to be persuaded to be operated on when he is well, not sick. Exceptions to the rule of surgery may occur if the patient is old and in poor physical condition, if one or two large stones are found on an X-ray but no symptoms are referable to them, or if a long period has passed since an attack without any evidence of progression.

During an acute attack of gallbladder disease the usual

treatment will consist of strict food abstinence (though fluids are occasionally permitted) and pain-killing drugs. Where bacterial infection is suspected, antibiotics (tetracyclines) may be given.

Gallstones, common in adults, do occur in children, but only rarely as part of a disease called cholelithiasis. Cholelithiasis is sometimes seen in congenital hemolytic anemia and sickle-cell anemia. In these conditions there is excess destruction of red blood cells, and the pigment released forms stones in the gallbladder. These may obstruct the gallbladder duct or cause inflammation. Jaundice may result and the gallbladder may have to be surgically removed.

GENES The genes are the units of heredity. They can be looked upon as an exceedingly long list of directions which determine the structure and much of the functioning of the offspring. The enormous number of genes present in each of us is indicated when one reflects on the innumerable characteristics that are unique to one individual as compared to another: height; weight; eye, skin, and hair color; nose size; jaw formation; body build; sex; hair distribution; intelligence (I.Q.); and musical and mathematical abilities—not to mention all of the disorders or illnesses that have a family background, such as high blood pressure, diabetes, high blood cholesterol, gout, etc. Many thousands of messengers are obviously needed to transmit the appropriate instructions.

Recent investigations have indicated that the chemical messengers involved are highly specialized components of desoxyribonucleic acid (DNA) contained within the nucleus of the cell; various arrangements of molecules of nucleoprotein lead to various kinds of messages. All the genes are laid out in linear fashion on strands called chromosomes which become apparent under the microscope, particularly during the process of cell division. There are forty-six chromosomes in all of the cells in human beings, with one exception: only half this number is present in the sex cells, the ovum of the female and the sperm of the male. When the sperm fertilizes the egg, the twenty-three chromosomes of each sex cell are combined, thus restoring the count of forty-six in the fertilized egg. In usual cell division, which occurs countless times within the body in all of its growing tissues—such as the skin, the blood cells, or the lining of the intestines—the cell with forty-six chromosomes undergoes a reduplication of its chromosomes during division. This produces two daughter cells, each with the appropriate number of forty-six chromosomes.

There is one dissimilar pair of chromosomes found in males known as the XY pair. In females a corresponding pair of chromosomes known as XX is found. It is possible to take a few cells, as for example, blood cells or cells from the inner surface of the cheek, stain them, and (with the microscope) tell whether they came from a male or a female, because the XX pair of chromosomes produces a dot within the nucleus of the cell which is not found in males. It is of interest that the sex of the offspring is contributed by the male, not by the female. This occurs because half the male's sperm contain an X chromosome, half a Y chromosome, whereas all egg cells contain only an X chromosome. If an X-bearing sperm fertilizes the egg, the offspring will have an XX pair and be a female. If a Y-bearing sperm fertilizes it, the offspring is XY or male. Certain disorders associated with the X or Y chromosome are referred to as sex-linked. The most common are the varying degrees of baldness in the male which are transmitted on the X chromosome of the mother. Thus, baldness in a son can be anticipated from looking at the mother's brothers, not by looking at his father. (See also BALDNESS.)

Rare abnormalities referable to the XY pair of chromosomes may occur because of a failure to separate in the formation of the egg cell or the sperm cell. This can lead to odd and unusual combinations in which the offspring may have forty-seven or even more chromosomes, with combinations such as XXY, XXXY, and others. Some of these combinations are associated with defects in sex organ formation, infertility, short stature, and other deviations.

GENITAL HYGIENE, INFANT The practice of cleaning the genital area is about the same as for other areas of the body. A daily bath with soap and water is desirable. In girl infants and little girls, the labia (lips) should be separated and the parts cleansed so that mucous secretions do not accumulate in the creases and folds. Uncircumcised boys should have the foreskin gently drawn back so that accumulations of mucus (smegma) may be removed. Thorough drying is advisable to prevent moisture accumulation with chafing and irritation of the skin. A lotion or talcum powder may be used to prevent irritating rashes in these areas.

GENITOURINARY DISEASES Genitourinary infections are those which involves any areas of the urinary tract, the kidneys, bladder, and ureters (tubes leading from the kidney to the bladder carrying urine).
Pyelitis Symptoms of urinary tract infection may include abdominal pain, vomiting, diarrhea, back pain, fever, burning on urination, frequency of urination, urgency to urinate, and tenderness in the kidney area. Examination of the urine in this condition shows pus and bacteria in some specimens, with occasional casts and red blood cells. Treatment is with antibiotics. These infections may sometimes recur secondarily as a result of other, upper respiratory or generalized, systemic infections.
Postinfectious Hemorrhagic Nephritis This type of kidney infection frequently follows tonsillitis or other respiratory infections. It may be caused by a streptococcus. Ankle swelling, puffiness around the eyes, fever, pallor, malaise, with smoky or frankly bloody urine, may appear. Headaches and other signs of high blood pressure may occur. Microscopic examination of the urine shows blood or albumin and casts. Treatment involves antibiotics, fluids, and other measures if complications occur. Most cases recover. If the condition progresses, it may develop into a chronic one.
Nephrosis Nephrosis is a kidney disease characterized by excess loss of albumin and proteins in the urine. Nephrosis causes swelling around the eyes, ankles, and in the abdomen. It is usually preceded by some infection. The urine shows large amounts of albumin, casts, and fatty substances. There may be high cholesterol in the blood. This is a chronic disease and extends over many years. Recent treatment with ACTH and steroids has improved the prognosis of this disease.

GROWTH AND DEVELOPMENT—CRITICAL NORMS It is obvious that your child's stage of development will determine his ability to respond to your requirements and your demands upon him. The critical norms of development for parents to be aware of are listed below:

1. *Head control.* If your baby is unable to hold his head erect and steady without support by four months, there should be some investigation as to why he is unable to do this.

2. *Vision.* If the child does not follow objects moving across his line of vision by four months.

3. *Hearing.* If your child does not turn in the direction of a loud noise, say a telephone bell or a voice, by seven months.

4. *Grasping.* If your child does not reach out to grasp objects, hold them for several minutes, and/or transfer them from one hand to the other by seven months of age.

5. *Sitting*. If the infant does not sit up on a flat surface without support for a few minutes at a time by ten months of age.

6. *Babbling*. If your child does not make recognizable babbling sounds of two syllables, such as, "Dada," "Baba," "Mama," by ten months.

7. *Prehension*. If your child cannot grasp small objects with the thumb and index finger by ten months.

8. *Feeding*. If your child does not hold a glass and drink from it or use a spoon to feed himself by eighteen months.

9. *Walking*. If your child does not take steps across the room without support and without falling down by eighteen months.

10. *Speaking*. If your child does not use several words spontaneously and appropriately, that is, saying "milk" or "ball" upon seeing the object, by eighteen months.

11. *Climbing*. If your child does not try climbing on and off a chair, bed, or stair by twenty-four months.

12. *Sentences*. If your child does not speak in sentences by three years. A sentence is defined as two or more words which do not usually go together in a familiar phrase. "Baby wants ball" is a sentence.

If your infant or child fails to develop according to these general levels, a complete evaluation should be made by your physician or a neurologist.

GROWTH AND DEVELOPMENT—THE FIRST SIX MONTHS Growth is increase in size. Development is increase in maturity and function. There are many factors which influence the normal development of a child, such as nationality, heredity, individuality, nutrition, endocrine factors, disease, environment, and social and economic conditions. There is, therefore, considerable variation in height, weight, and achievements at every age. The following are some of the average descriptions of babies.

1 Month. The baby moves his arms and legs at random and kicks aimlessly. He sucks, swallows, sneezes, and can generally put his fist, or sometimes a finger, into his mouth. He generally can look only straight ahead and not too much around him. If something is put into his hand he drops it fairly soon. His head generally sags a bit. He makes small noises, gurgles, and stares continuously at things around him. His eyes follow light but he cannot really focus or see too much.

2 Months. Real smiles of recognition may be seen and he will become more responsive. He may be able to gurgle and coo and listen to the sound of his own voice.

3 Months. He may develop head control while lying on his back.

4 Months. Usually the head will be steady while the baby is sitting and he can lift it up when he is on his stomach. His eyes will follow moving objects well, and his arms will start to move when he sees a toy. He will take the toy in his hand and/or put it to his mouth, and he looks at objects much more carefully. He may laugh out loud, become excited and show a spontaneous smile when greeted. He plays with things in his hand and he fingers objects. He follows moving objects with his eyes. There is some hand control at this time and his head can be kept still.

5 Months. He sometimes can roll back and forth on his abdomen and back and may turn over.

6 Months. He tries to sit up by himself.

GROWTH AND DEVELOPMENT—7 MONTHS TO 18 MONTHS *7 Months*. He may sit up erect by himself, may call, and may transfer objects from one hand to the other. At 7 months he has a one-hand approach and a grasp of toys. He may shake and bang a rattle and transfer a toy from one hand to the other. He may be able to put his toes into his mouth, make certain vowel sounds, and make noises called "vocalizing" when he is crying or babbling.

8 Months. He may be able to put his thumb and forefinger together, which is called prehension. This enables him to manipulate objects and toys that interest him.

9 Months. He may stand by himself or if held. He may bounce on standing.

10 Months. He may creep or crawl and sit up perfectly steadily by himself. He may pull himself to his feet at a rail. He may say "Mama" or "Dada," or one other word. He can probably feed himself a cracker or a piece of something and hold his own bottle.

11 Months. He may walk with or without support, or simply pull himself up to a standing position and remain standing for some time.

12 Months. He may walk with or without support. He may stand alone. He plays with objects and may say "Mama" and "Dada," and he sometimes will give a toy on request and cooperate in dressing.

16 to 18 Months. He climbs, runs, and develops some small skills with toys. He may turn the pages of a book or put blocks in a hole. He may use a spoon. He may say a few words. He may discard the bottle and indicate when he is wet.

18 Months. He usually walks without falling, turns the pages of a book, may build a tower of three to four cubes and imitate pencil strokes with a crayon. He may have six to ten words and may be able to carry out two directions. He may also have his toilet habits regulated in the daytime by this time.

GROWTH AND DEVELOPMENT—TWO YEARS TO NINE YEARS *2 Years of Age*. By this time he can point to his eyes, nose, ears and *may* be toilet-trained during waking hours. He runs well without falling, can go up and down stairs alone, may kick a ball. He may use three-word sentences and may tell you when he needs to go to the bathroom. He may put on simple clothing himself and mimic certain play.

3 Years of Age. He may talk in short sentences, feed himself, and is generally toilet-trained. He alternates his feet going upstairs instead of putting one foot on a step and then bringing the other one to the same step. He may ride a tricycle. He can build a nine- or ten-cube tower. He can copy a circle and a cross. He can give his name and state whether he is a boy or a girl and usually obeys a few simple commands. He may feed himself well and be able to put on shoes and unbutton buttons. He may know some songs or rhymes and understand what it means to take turns.

4 Years of Age. He can walk downstairs alternating his feet. He can throw a ball and hop on one foot. He can draw the figure of a man with at least two parts to it, and copy a cross. He can count three objects and correctly point to them. He may name one or more colors accurately and obeys about five commands. He may be able to wash and dry his face; brush his teeth; tell the back from the front of clothes; lace his shoes and go on errands outside the home. He can play games and repeat four numbers.

5 Years of Age. He can speak in sentences of ten syllables; knows three or four colors; can name a nickel, a penny and a dime; can dress and undress without help; may ask the meaning of words; can draw a man with a body, head, and arms; can copy a triangle and circle; can count to ten; and can skip, alternating his feet.

6 Years of Age. He can tell his right from his left hand; can count to thirteen or thirty, can draw a man with neck, hands, and clothes; can add and subtract within 5; can repeat four numbers; can tie shoelaces; knows the difference between morning and night.

7 Years of Age. He knows the names of the days of the week and can repeat five numbers.

8 Years of Age. He can count backwards from 20.

9 Years of Age. By this age he can repeat the months, knows how to tell time, and can give change from a quarter.

GROWTH AND DEVELOPMENT—PHYSICAL

Height The average birth length of a child is about 20 inches (50 cm.). In the first 6 months the child grows 1 inch a month; the second 6 months he grows one-half inch a month. At the end of the first year your child has increased his birth length by 50 per cent. By the fourth year he has doubled it. After that, the height increase is averaged at about 2 or 3 inches per year. By the thirteenth year, the birth length has tripled. From 1 to 7 years height increases 3 inches a year. From 8 to 15 years it increases 2 inches a year. From 16 to 20, it increases only 1 inch a year.

Weight Birth—6 to 7½ to 9 pounds is the usual birth weight. The infant loses approximately 10 per cent of the birth weight during the first three or four days. This actually represents water loss, not weight. It is usually regained by the eighth or tenth day. First 6 months, gain is 6 to 8 ounces per week. Second 6 months, gain is 3 to 4 ounces per week. 5 months—birth weight doubles (14 pounds). 1 year—birth weight triples (21 pounds). 2½ years—birth weight quadruples (28 pounds). 5 years—weight at 1 year has doubled (42 pounds). 10 years—weight at 1 year has tripled (63 pounds). 13 to 14 years—weight at 1 year has quadrupled (84 pounds). Generally speaking, the average weight increase after the age of 2 is about 5 pounds per year until the ninth or tenth year. After this the weight curve decreases slowly. There is a rapid gain in weight during adolescence. A rough idea of weight during preschool and early school years can be gotten by using the following formula:

Age (in years) x 5, plus 18, equals weight in pounds.

Chest Measurements The chest measurement at birth is about one half inch smaller than the head. At 1 year of age the chest is equal to, or slightly greater, than the head measurement, and after that it grows more rapidly. The circumference of the abdomen is generally about the same as that of the chest during the first year.

Heartrate At birth, the heartrate is 140 beats per minute. At 6 months, 110 beats per minute; at 1 year, 100 beats per minute; at 3 to 4 years, 95 beats per minute; at 5 to 10 years, 90 beats per minute; at 10 to 15 years, 85 beats per minute; over 15 years, 75 to 80 beats per minute.

Breathing Rate At birth, breathing rate is 40 per minute; at 6 months, 30 per minute; at 1 year, 28 per minute; at 3 to 4 years, 25 per minute; at 5 to 10 years, 24 per minute; at 10 to 15 years, 20 per minute; over 15, 12 to 18 per minute.

Speech In the infant, all early sounds are impulsive and aimless. By two months of age they have generally become cooing and gurgling sounds; at four months there are consonants followed by vowels; at eight months, certain syllables and then "Mama" and "Dada." At eighteen months, words may be accompanied by movements and gestures. At twenty-four months, short sentences of three to four words, not necessarily grammatical, are heard.

Sight When an infant is born, the pupils react to light but light is generally avoided. At one month of age, the child can follow a moving light. At seven weeks, he will close his lids when a light is brought close. At two months, familiar objects and faces are recognized. At four months, the infant reaches for objects. At six to eight months, he transfers them from one hand to the other. At twelve months, he may distinguish colors in the following order: yellow, red, and then blue.

Taste, Touch, Smell The sense of taste is present at birth, but it is not known whether the child can differentiate sour, salt, and bitter tastes. By two or three months, taste is acute and the child can notice a change in the amounts of sugar or other substances in his food. He begins to salivate at about the third month. The lips and tongue of the infant are developed at birth. Localization of touch is developed by the fifth month.

Sense of smell is present in the premature and normal-term infant, but this develops slowly. It becomes more acute later on. Most infants can smell milk.

Hearing Hearing develops after the first few days of life, but a deaf infant may show no signs of deafness for many months. One of the first things noted in a deaf child would be less-than-normal vocalization and not much laughter and smiling. After about one month of age, the child can localize and recognize where noises are coming from. By three months of age he can recognize familiar voices, and after six months may respond pleasurably to music. If the child is extremely attentive visually, it may be a sign that hearing is not normal. This should be quickly investigated, since a hearing defect threatens a child's contact with his environment and may distort his entire behavior.

Sleep Infants require a great deal of sleep during the first few months of life—about eighteen to twenty hours per day up until about six months of age, and by one year, fourteen to sixteen hours. At two years the requirements are twelve to fourteen hours, and at five years, ten to twelve hours. The need for sleep varies in children as it does in adults, and many children may give up naps earlier than others.

GROWTH AND DEVELOPMENT—BONES

The story of growth is basically the story of the bones. These are to the body as structural steel is to a building; both determine height and shape. Growth in the body is a most complex process and is more than a simple multiplication of cells. If one compares the face of the infant with that of the adult, it is easy to see the many changes in proportion that only *differential growth* can produce: the nose and the jaws must necessarily become larger, whereas the bones encasing the brain grow proportionately less prominent. Similar differential in growth occurs in the rest of the body, most notably, perhaps, in the lower extremities, in which relative shortness is found in infancy and early childhood.

Most growth that occurs around puberty seems to center in the region of the knees. Many complex factors operate in all this; one factor is the genes which will decree what the ultimate height and appearance of the individual will be. The various secretions of the endocrine glands are also necessary to set the stage properly for correct bone development. Thus, in hypothyroidism (underactive thyroid) there is a marked lag in skeletal growth. The administration of thyroid hormone produces a marked acceleration of growth; in fact, mildly hyperthyroid children tend to be taller. The vitamin D the child receives and the amount of calcium-made available in the diet are also controlling factors in bone growth. It must be remembered also that there is a range of variability to growth. Some children lag behind others for no very definite reasons that can be ascertained. The gap is sometimes made up suddenly. A sex factor is also involved; girls may grow more rapidly than boys, and even exceed them in height, but with the onset of puberty and menstruation the female rate of growth decreases sharply; at the equivalent point, the boy may undergo a considerable and sustained spurt of growth.

Estimating Age by Bone Growth Many bones are formed from a cartilaginous model. Within the cartilage, centers for bone formation appear at stated times; these are known as centers of ossification. A good deal is known about the location and sequence of appearance of such centers. Thus, a few appropriately taken X-rays may enable the doctor to give an estimate of age. This figure is known as the bone age. If adverse influences have been operative (such as prolonged illness or poor nutrition) the bone age may lag behind the child's calendar age. Determination of bone age may be of value in such a situation as is presented by an adolescent of short stature; if bone age is less than calendar age, further growth and acceleration in height may be anticipated.

During early years, hands and wrists give excellent X-ray pictures for estimating bone age because of the numerous little bones present there and the sequence in which centers of ossification appear: at one year, there are two centers among the little bones of the wrist; at three, a third center appears (the triangularis); at four, a fourth center appears (the lunate); at five, two more appear (major multangulum and navicular); at six years a seventh center appears; and at ten years an eighth one. If, therefore, the wrist of a six-year-old fails to show either major and minor multangulum centers, or the navicular, although the lunate is present, bone age would be about four and a half—obviously well behind chronologic age. Similar useful data can be obtained later in childhood by X-raying such areas as the pelvis.

GROWTH AND DEVELOPMENT—HEAD The progress of growth is from the head down. Therefore, at birth, the head is relatively large, the trunk long, and the lower extremities relatively short. The arms are usually longer than the legs and the middle part of the body is about three-quarters of an inch above the umbilical cord. The extremities grow much more rapidly than the trunk, and the head grows the least. By approximately two years of age, the middle point of the body is slightly below the umbilicus. There are two "soft" spots on the head. The front one (fontanelle) is quadrangular in shape; it closes gradually as the cranial bones grow together. The soft spot represents the space between the cranial bones to permit expansion of the brain. It is generally closed by sixteen to eighteen months of age. The posterior fontanelle is closed at six to eight weeks. This is a triangular area at the back of the head.

Measurements of the Head Circumference at birth is thirteen to fourteen inches. There is an increase of about one-half an inch a month, making a total of two inches (5 cm.) in the first four months of life. Another two-inch increase in the next eight months makes a total growth of over four inches (10 cm.) for the first year (to measure 17 to 18 inches). Second year growth is one inch (total 18 to 19 inches). From the end of the first year to the age of twenty, the head increases by only four inches in all, with growth between ages three to five years at the rate of one-half inch per year (19½ to 20½ inches), and one-half inch every five years thereafter until adult (20½ to 21½ inches).

GROWTH AND DEVELOPMENT—SPEECH DISORDERS Development of speech in a child begins at birth and continues in regular and progressive developmental manner with increasing complexity for the rest of his life. This development of speech implies that the child's brain and central nervous system are normal. However, there are many reasons, both organic and psychological, which may impede, prevent, or disturb the development of proper communication, such as serious childhood illnesses, metabolic disorders, or malnutrition. Cleft palate and harelip, which result from embryonic defects, are organic causes of speech delay.

Many palsied children have difficulty in communication, ranging from complete inability to speak to disturbances in pronunciation and intelligibility.

Another organic cause of speech defect and inability to develop speech is called "congenital aphasia." This may result from an accident or illness before the speech process began. It is usually connected with brain damage.

Deafness will interfere with a child's learning to talk normally. This may cause him to appear mentally retarded.

The steps or phases of speech development are listed below:

1. *At birth,* and up until six to ten months, the child will gurgle, coo, babble, and make general vowel and consonant sounds.

2. *At ten months* most children will say "Mama" or "Dada."

3. *At eigtheen months* the vocabulary contains about ten to twenty words and there may be small phrases.

4. *At thirty months* sentences involving a few words are usually developed. There may be some difficulty in articulating certain consonants such as *"s," "r" "l."* This slight difficulty in pronunciation frequently disappears. If it does not, speech therapy may be required.

5. *At thirty-six months* the child has all the mechanics of language at his command, and after this his speech development consists of vocabulary and grammar.

Speech Defects, Psychological Causes of Speech, as communication of needs and desires, is a primary need. Its frustration always has consequences. These may be reactions of aggression, hostility, and resentment. Since such emotions are not rewarding ones, they produce secondary developments of feelings of discouragement, inferiority, shame, and insecurity. A speech defect may result from a poor relationship of the child with his parents or may impair the relationship. Speech defects often have long-range and serious lifetime consequences. They may reduce his earning power by limiting his ability to work; alter his personality by undermining his self-esteem and personal adjustment; interfere with personal relationships and his general ability to communicate.

Children who have been given psychological tests to determine what factors were important in their poor speech development showed that *lack of a feeling of achievement, a feeling of anxiety and insecurity coupled with hostility and no hope of escape* were factors involved in their difficulties. Sometimes these findings may be secondary, as a *result* of an organic speech defect which causes interpersonal difficulties between the child and his parents. Some children are punished for not speaking properly. They are scolded, slapped, given whippings, and otherwise rigidly disciplined. Many of these children withdraw and respond with silence. Some of them develop stammering and stuttering. Any child who does not have understandable speech by the age of three years should certainly have a complete physical and psychological evaluation.

GROWTH AND DEVELOPMENT—PUBERTY Puberty begins earlier in girls than in boys. It may start at eleven or twelve in girls, at thirteen to fifteen in boys. It is marked by extra growth in height and weight, and the development of secondary sexual characteristics—menstruation, breast and pubic hair development in girls, and voice change and development of genital hair in boys. Emotionally, puberty is a stage between the giving up of childhood and its dependence on the parents, and the development of adolescence and independence. It is usually marked by a stormy course of emotional swings between rebellion and compliance. It marks the insurgence of sexual feelings and the desire to experiment. It is a period where the balance between freedom and license may be difficult to impose. If a youngster has had a good and stable relationship with his parents all of his life, he can usually emerge from adolescence with very little difficulty. Children who have had a disturbed emotional development become more disturbed with the pressures of puberty. Puberty is a period when there is still a need for parental guidance, but also a recognition that it is necessary to separate from the parents and become an independent, mature, functioning adult able to carry on one's own life. Parents often do not recognize this need and may prolong the period of dependence because of their own unsatisfied emotional needs.

Serious behavior disorders and delinquencies which occur at this time of the child's life usually require professional psychiatric help. The parents may also require treatment.

A condition that often disturbs parents of boys reaching puberty is nocturnal emission (wet dreams). Nocturnal emissions are experienced by adolescent boys as an emission of seminal fluid during the night when they are asleep. They awaken to find that the bedclothes are wet. These emissions are unconsciously produced, frequently due to the emerging sexual dreams and fantasies of this age. They are very common and harmless and should not be taken seriously. They are considered normal phenomena.

HEADACHE The number of causes of headache are legion. Some of the more common ones include psychologic tension, inadequate sleep, respiratory and other viral illnesses, hangovers, menstruation, high blood pressure, eye strain, and various digestive disorders (including in some cases constipation). More serious but fortunately rare causes of headache will include certain inflammations of the brain, such as meningitis, brain tumors, and suppurative infections of the skull.

Some headaches are descriptively classified as simple headache (not due to any significant underlying causes), vascular headache (one with a throbbing quality), and tension headache which arises from tightening-up of the muscles at the back of the head and in the scalp. Migraine, also known as "sick headache," is a vascular headache which often starts with visual difficulties, is generally one-sided, and terminates with nausea and vomiting. It runs in families and occurs most often in tense, perfectionistic people with high standards and higher-than-average intelligence. Migraine is one of the few headaches with a specifically reversible cause: a vasoconstrictive drug known as ergotamine when taken early in the attack may successfully reverse it. In many instances it is not possible to identify a special cause for headache.

Treatment. Treatment is therefore directed against the symptom—that is, the pain—and consists of various painkilling medications starting with such drugs as aspirin and working upwards to drugs such as Darvon®, codeine and its derivatives, and even some of the narcotics. Most patients who have repeated headaches find it worthwhile to experiment with several medications to see which is most effective. Sometimes combinations of aspirin with small doses of benzedrine (Edrisal®, Daprisal®) may help some vascular headaches—particularly if one's blood pressure tends to be on the low-normal or low side. Another product found to help many chronic headache sufferers at the Montefiore Hospital Headache Clinic is Fiorinal®. Relief can sometimes be gotten by as simple a device as an icebag, or by taking aspirin and a short nap. Chronic or repeated headache can be the subject of elaborate investigation including skull X-rays, brain-wave patterns, and detailed neurological examination. Even these elaborate or refined techniques may fail to uncover an underlying disease process. The headache victim may well furnish meaningful clues by close observations of the past pattern of his headaches, and report the data he secures to the doctor.

HEARTBURN Heartburn is a term used for a burning sensation generally felt high in the upper central abdomen. It is experienced by many people after eating spicy, rich, greasy, or fried foods or after they have taken too much coffee or alcohol. It is a common complaint during pregnancy, when it is due to various functional changes in the behavior of the digestive tract. Heartburn is probably not due to "excess acidity," but neutralizing stomach acids will help heartburn as well as other digestive complaints.

Treatment. Many over-the-counter remedies are sold for heartburn but they often contain bicarbonate of soda, too much of which is particularly undesirable during pregnancy. A milk-of-magnesia tablet is probably preferable for the pregnant woman and there are other alkalinizers—Amphogel®, Gelusil®, Maalox®, Riopan®, Titralac®, etc.—free of bicarbonate of soda. Many come in either liquid or tablet form, and whichever is easier to take can be used. Generally, one or two tablets or a teaspoonful or two of these medications will give some relief. It may be necessary to repeat the dose within an hour or two. Repeated or frequent heartburn may require consultation with a doctor. Occasionally further investigations, including stomach X-rays, may be in order if a ready explanation is not at hand. (See also HERNIA, HIATUS.)

HEART DISEASE, CONGENITAL The symptoms of congenital heart disease may be noted from time of birth. A murmur may be heard immediately or within a few months after birth. Certain symptoms such as a bluish tinge to the skin, difficulty in breathing, and poor growth and development may be seen early. There is usually no history of rheumatic heart disease.

Congenital heart disease is divided into two main classifications: those which cause bluish discoloration of the skin (cyanotic) and those which do not (acyanotic). There are also "late cyanotic" ones. In the latter cases the blue color does not develop until the child is older.

In cyanotic congenital heart disease there is an abnormal communication between the pulmonic and systemic circulations. Fresh blood from the lungs mixes with bluish blood from the returned systemic circulation, and the result is a mixture which causes the bluish discoloration of the skin.

In the acyanotic group there is no abnormal communication between the left and right side, therefore no mixture of blood and no bluish discoloration. However, other conditions which cause abnormalities may give a very poor prognosis for life and health.

In the late cyanotic groups, there is an arterial venous shunt (communication between the right and left sides of the heart, or between the systemic and pulmonic circulation). Normally, the pressure on the left side of the heart is higher than that of the right. However, if there is a complication in which the pressure on the right side is raised above that on the left, there will be a reversal of blood flow, the shunt will become venous to arterial, and cyanosis will develop. This may be a late finding in certain forms of heart abnormalities.

The prognosis for children with certain forms of congenital heart disease has been improved tremendously by the modern advances of open heart surgery. Even for children who have destructive valvular lesions due to rheumatic heart disease, such as mitral stenosis and other valvular insufficiencies, the prognosis is also much better due to new surgical techniques. There is now a pulmonary-circulation machine which continuously oxygenates the blood during heart surgery.

HEAT REACTIONS Reactions to excessive heat may take several forms. *Heat exhaustion* occurs most often during spells of hot, humid weather. The person will complain of faintness, dizziness, weakness. The skin will be moist but not hot. Occasionally there will be nausea and muscular or abdominal cramps. The following steps should be followed for heat exhaustion: (1) Have the person stretch out in as cool and open a spot as is available. (2) Give small frequent sips of cold drinks, such as fruit juices, to which extra salt has been added. If there has been a good deal of perspiration, salt tablets can be given. Stimulants such as coffee or tea, iced or otherwise, may also be given. The face and extremities may be rubbed down with cold cloths.

Heat stroke is most often seen after considerable exposure to the sun, at the beach or in the country. In heat stroke the body's temperature-regulating mechanism goes astray, and the victim is obviously very hot to the touch. In fact, temperatures ranging up to 106 degrees have occurred in heat stroke. The skin is hot and dry, the pulse rapid and strong. Weakness and headache are the usual complaints.

Treatment. The victim should be helped out of the sun into as cool a spot as possible. Measures designed to reduce the body temperature should be instituted properly. These may range from dousing the person with cold water to applications of ice to various parts of the body. Alcohol may be freely applied, as it too may efficiently lower body temperature. Cold applications should be continued if the patient is transported to a hospital.

HEMORRHOIDS Hemorrhoids are small distended veins in the region of the anus or rectal opening. The ones just inside the opening are covered by the lining of the anus and are called internal hemorrhoids; those exterior to this are covered by skin and are called external hemorrhoids. Anything that raises the pressure within the veins of the rectal region may bring on or aggravate hemorrhoids. Pregnancy is one of the most common aggravating factors, as are also chronic constipation and straining at stool.

Many individuals have one or two hemorrhoids without being aware of them, and certainly such asymptomatic hemorrhoids need cause no concern. Sometimes, however, hemorrhoids appear in clusters like small grapes and are readily felt externally when wiping after a movement. They become quite painful, until sitting is uncomfortable or impossible. Such pain is often brought on by a clotting within the hemorrhoid—a thrombosed hemorrhoid. Occasionally, because of impaired blood supply to the skin over the hemorrhoid, an ulcer may form with severe pain resulting.

Hemorrhoids often present a problem of acute or emergency nature and certain first aid measures may be useful: (1) Cold compresses of plain water or of half water, half witch hazel may provide relief. (2) Hot sitz baths may also relieve the pain of hemorrhoids and help stop bleeding. A sitz bath is prepared by drawing four to six inches of hot water in the tub and sitting in it. (3) Sometimes hemorrhoids will produce annoying oozing or staining for which a sanitary napkin applied to the rectum may be useful. (4) During the painful stage of hemorrhoids a rubber ring, or the adjustment of two small pillows so that the buttocks are supported without pressure against the anal region, may make life more tolerable.

The doctor may, after a preliminary anesthetic to the area, cut into a thrombosed hemorrhoid and evacuate the clot; this will often relieve the pain or at least diminish it considerably. Generally, a hot sitz bath is prescribed after this procedure. For multiple hemorrhoids which are chronic and annoying, or which bleed frequently, surgical removal is generally curative. Considerable relief may be secured by the local application of hemorrhoid ointment, or the insertion into the anus of special suppositories containing anesthetics and certain healing agents. (See also SUPPOSITORIES.)

HEPATITIS Hepatitis refers to a variety of inflammations of the liver, including those produced by viruses, amoebas, and even various drugs. Unless otherwise qualified, however, it generally refers to a virus-produced condition, *viral hepatitis* (for which the synonyms are "infectious hepatitis" and also "serum hepatitis"). Viral hepatitis seems to be on the increase in recent years. The early symptoms may be grippe-like, with chilly feelings, headache, fever, and a loss of appetite. At about the same time it may be noted that the urine is darker than usual. This is brought about by an excess of bile pigments in the blood, which spill over into the urine. In jaundiced cases, there is a yellow tint to the skin and whites of the eyes. This usually deepens so that over the course of the next week or two deep yellow staining may become obvious. The stools are generally lighter than normal. The jaundice is produced because the damaged liver cells can no longer perform their proper functions, one of which is to transfer bile pigments out of the bloodstream and into the intestines. Even mild cases seldom clear in less than three to four weeks, and a six- to eight-week period of illness is by no means uncommon. Complete recovery is the rule, although in a small minority the condition may become chronic.

Viral hepatitis is a contagious disease, although it is not common to see more than one case in a household. Probably most cases are the result of contamination of food by an infected person who may not have symptoms. In fact, most cases of this disease do not produce obvious jaundice and are referred to as anicteric (non-jaundice) cases. Hence many adults without a history of jaundice have, in fact, had the disease and are immune.

A disease quite indistinguishable from naturally occurring hepatitis can be transmitted by blood transfusion and blood products; it is therefore known as *serum hepatitis*. It may come on a month or more after receiving a blood transfusion which contained the virus.

Treatment. The disease is customarily treated by rest, which is not necessarily strict bed rest, a high-carbohydrate diet (high also in proteins, if the patient can tolerate them), and in a few instances steroid drugs may be employed. It is customary to give an injection of gamma globulin to household contacts, and it has been demonstrated in institutional outbreaks that gamma globulin injections can stop an epidemic. Some recent work indicates that serum hepatitis may also be reduced in intensity, if not prevented, by giving one large dose of gamma globulin at the time of the transfusion and another approximately one month later.

HERNIA A hernia is an abnormal protrusion of a bodily organ into a canal or opening. The opening may be one normally present in the body but abnormally enlarged, or it may be an opening artificially created—as, for example, after surgery. Most common hernias are in close relation to the abdominal cavity and frequently contain a portion of the digestive tract. One common form of hernia seen in infants, and occasionally in adults, occurs at the "belly button" (umbilicus) and is called an *umbilical hernia*. In infants it is often temporary and requires only adhesive-taping.

The inguinal canal in males is a frequently site for *inguinal hernia*. This is the oblique canal which penetrates the abdominal musculature, and through which runs the spermatic cord that sends sperm up from the testicles. Normally, the fibrous connective tissue and muscle defining the inguinal canal snugly enclose the spermatic cord and resist any encroachment from adjacent structures. Occasionally, perhaps because of a slight defect in construction of the canal or from excessive intra-abdominal pressure, a "knuckle" of intestine may work its way into the aperture. As time goes by the aperture tends to widen, hence hernias tend to grow larger. In a full-fledged inguinal hernia, a fair-sized loop of bowel may have worked its way down into the scrotum. Generally it can be tucked back into the abdomen and is referred to as a *reducible* hernia.

Apart from being a nuisance, the hernia may present no threat; many individuals get along without paying much attention to them. The chief threat may not arise for years, if at all—this threat being a twisting or swelling within the herniated bowel loop following which it can no longer be replaced. This is known as an *incarcerated* hernia. Incarceration may present all the features of an intestinal obstruction; in addition, the bowel may become acutely inflamed because its own blood supply can be cut off. This produces a surgical emergency requiring active intervention.

For uncomplicated hernia, belts with padding (trusses) may be arranged so as to keep the hernia tucked within the abdominal cavity. But individuals who wear these trusses often complain of some discomfort from the pressure they exert. Another drawback is that the truss has to be worn constantly. To avoid both the risks and discomfort of hernia, surgical repair is often advised. The procedure is known as a herniorrhaphy. Inguinal hernias also occur in women, though to a lesser extent than in men. Relatively more common in women are hernias which present in the upper portion of the thigh just beneath the abdominal crease. They are called *femoral hernias* and have much the same significance as does an inguinal hernia.

HERNIA, HIATUS The food-pipe (esophagus) is a long, slender, muscular tube which runs from the back of the throat down to the stomach. Just before it opens into the stomach it penetrates the diaphragm through a special opening known as the hiatus. Several factors may produce widening of the hiatus, which in turn leads to the appearance of a portion of stomach above the level of the diaphragm. It may take a special maneuver to reveal the widening, since the stomach is not always herniated through the opening.

Most cases of hiatus hernia cause no distress or discomfort. They may be discovered as an incidental finding in an X-ray study. However, a hiatus hernia may lead to symptoms of pressure—often interpreted as a heart pain—and palpitations or cardiac irregularities. Upper-abdominal discomfort is sometimes also felt in the back, with associated symptoms such as burping and belching. Attacks may be intermittent and are sometimes relieved by shifting from the lying to the standing position. There is a tendency to ascribe too many symptoms to a really innocent hiatus hernia.

Many common forms of indigestion and such everyday symptoms as heartburn or burping occur in individuals without hiatus hernia. In the few cases where it is clear that a hiatus hernia is producing frequent symptoms or contributing to chronic anemia, an operation may be advised. This consists basically of "taking tucks" into the widened hiatus and thereby narrowing the opening. Since no organ needs to be cut into in this repair, the operative procedure generally poses no particular difficulty.

Treatment. Medical treatment of hiatus hernia resembles that used for the treatment of peptic ulcer. Alkalinizers, to be taken at frequent intervals throughout the day, may be prescribed. Since overdistention of the stomach should be avoided, the patient with hiatus hernia will do better to eat small frequent meals rather than a few large ones. In a few instances, raising the head of the bed may prevent night attacks; weight reduction may also be quite helpful.

HOME CARE DURING ILLNESS
Caring For a Sick Child The following are a few important considerations to keep in mind when taking care of a sick child:

1. Do not give any medicine, patent or otherwise, except perhaps aspirin, unless you have consulted your doctor.

2. Do not follow the recommendations of your neighbor who gave her child a particular medicine. Chances are her child had a totally different illness although the symptoms may have seemed similar.

3. Do not give enemas without the consent or advice of your doctor. *You* may think the child's bellyache is merely constipation or "something he ate." It may really be acute appendicitis. It is extremely dangerous to introduce water under pressure when the appendix is inflamed, since this may cause the appendix to rupture.

4. Do not give laxatives routinely to "clean a child out." This is an unnecessary habit and is potentially harmful. The child who has difficulty passing stools should have medical advice and investigation to determine the reason for this.

5. Severe and prolonged illnesses in children create special problems. Diseases such as tuberculosis, rheumatic fever, or paralytic polio create secondary psychological dependency problems in the child and often produce great anxiety in the parents. As a result, the child may become a chronic invalid, mentally as well as physically. It is important to give these children as much psychological freedom as possible so that their physical illness does not permanently warp their personalities. It is much safer not to discuss the child's illness, length of illness, future, etc., in his presence either with the doctor or with relatives. Nor should it be discussed with his playmates. It may cause misunderstandings and result in severe permanent psychological damage. A child can be kept busy, active, and interested in various forms of occupational therapy while he is ill, so that he can make progress in other areas and not have time to brood about his condition.

Feeding a Sick Child Most sick children have no appetite for solid foods. The best thing to do is to nourish them with some form of fruit or fruit juices, liquids, such as bouillon, weak tea, clear soup, sodas, milk, and even ice cream. A mashed banana may be given in orange juice, or other fresh fruit mashed in fruit juice. This provides glucose (sugar) and fluid. Other foods which are both good and easy to take are soft things such as Jello, custard, rice pudding, mashed potatoes, or any easy-to-swallow food. If a child continues to vomit there is medicine which can be given to stop the vomiting. For children who have to maintain a high nutrition and calorie intake, there are prepared food supplements which can be bought. They are effective in providing all the nourishment (calories, protein, fat, and carbohydrates) which a growing child requires, in a liquid form.

Giving Medicine Some children will take any medicine which is offered to them. Others will take it providing it does not taste very bad. But there are some who are extremely particular and will refuse anything that tastes strange. In such cases it is possible to get medication into these children, sometimes a drop at a time, if it can be mixed with something pleasant-tasting which the child already likes. It may be mixed, drop-by-drop, with one or two ounces of cherry soda, ice cream, applesauce, or jam. Sometimes it can be placed in rice pudding, tapioca, or malted milks. Most modern medications are so pleasant (or tasteless) that they can be mixed into almost any pleasant food. For children who absolutely refuse anything by mouth, many medications can be administered by injection; others can be administered rectally. Aspirin is available in the form of rectal suppositories, and so are other painkilling drugs. Your physician will advise you whether this is necessary.

How to Give an Enema You will need an enema bag with tubing and an enema tip; a bedpan, newspaper, some toilet paper, vaseline or cold cream, and a small rubber sheet or oilcloth. There are some prepared enemas which can be bought in the drugstore in a prepared plastic bottle with a nozzle. After being lubricated, the appropriately sized nozzle is simply inserted into the child's rectum and the material in the bottle is squeezed into the rectal area. In a homemade enema, the water should be lukewarm and, generally, mild soapsuds used. The water is placed under the child. The bag is hung low enough so that the water goes into the rectum very slowly. The enema solution should be retained by the patient for two to five minutes if possible. Then the child may be placed on the bedpan or the toilet and the contents expelled. You always wash your own hands and the patient's hands after enemas. The enema bag should be cleansed thoroughly after use; the enema bone may be sterilized by boiling for five minutes.

Another type of enema for a very constipated stool is the oil-retention enema. Two to four ounces of mineral oil are inserted into the rectum and held there for five to ten minutes so that the stool may be softened. Then it is expelled.

Setting up the Sick Room The behavior of a child who is sick will depend directly upon how severe his illness is. With an extremely high fever—103° or 104°F.—he will not be anxious to play. He is *really* sick: he may be cranky, irritable, fussy or want to sleep most of the time, in which case it is best to let him do so. Many children who are sick cannot concentrate on games, television, or other activities which normally interest them. However, a child who is bed-ridden but not very toxic requires distraction and things to play with because he becomes annoyed and bored at being confined to bed. There are things which may make a child more comfortable and will divert him (and permit you to do less running around). If he has the following items near his bedside it will be much easier to keep him happy and occupied: Drinking water or soda with ice cubes, a glass, a spoon, and tissues are essentials; also a bag for waste material pinned to the mattress or a small wastebasket placed by the bed. A large shopping bag can contain most of his toys, crayons, paint books, magazines, or other handicraft material. A small radio, or possibly a television set which is not too far from the foot of the bed so that he can manipulate the dials, is a welcome diversion.

Materials which encourage creative interest and skills are excellent diversions for a sick child. Coloring paper, pencils, art handicraft supplies, knitting, embroidery and sewing things are interesting. Tropical fish, a bird or other pets may create diversion. Hobbies such as stamp-collecting, shell-collecting, making a scrapbook, or keeping a diary can be encouraged at this time. Modeling with clay is also very useful. If a child has to be kept in bed, he may be permitted to lie in the living room on the couch rather than in bed. This allows him to partake in the general family life rather than feeling isolated.

The most important thing in caring for a sick child is not to permit him to become so accustomed to overwhelming attention that when he gets well his personality will again become directed to absorbing all this attention toward himself. It is important not to hover over him to the point where he becomes helpless and dependent. When he is again well, he should be treated without the concern and anxiety you naturally felt when he was ill.

Recognizing Illness in Children up to Two Years of Age How do you know when a child who cannot speak is ill? By the time your child is one or two years old, you know him pretty well. You know his moods, his general behavior, and whether he is cheerful, contented, happy, playful. You know when he is wet, when he wishes to be picked up, when he's hungry, tired, or needs a nap. If your child is behaving in a manner which is not up to his usual standard, he may be coming down with some illness. It is wise to check his temperature at this time. If he is extremely irritable, cranky, fussy, refuses to eat, doesn't play with his toys,

seems listless, apathetic, sleeps a lot, etc., these may be signs of illness. Some mothers think they can tell a child's temperature by feeling his forehead. This is usually not accurate since a low-grade temperature of 100°F. or so is not always felt on touching the skin. If the temperature is over 100°, one can assume that an illness is developing. It is wise to check the temperature again within an hour or so. Many children with temperatures of 103° or 104°F. appear perfectly normal, cheerful, active, and show no signs of illness, whereas others with only slight temperatures may show listlessness and a lack of playful activity. (See also FEVER.)

Preparing Children for Hospital Children who are ill and must undergo hospitalization or surgery should be prepared for it beforehand if their age permits. Most children of four, five, and up can understand what you tell them. These children should be informed (depending on their age level and degree of understanding) in a calm, matter-of-fact manner as to what they are to expect. Fear and anxiety should be minimized. If they are left alone in a hospital where painful things are done to them in a strange atmosphere without any explanation, they may become very frightened and traumatized. Sudden experiences with anesthesia are often interpreted by the child as being "smothered." This, too, can have traumatic psychological effects. A good general rule is to realize that it is not wise to lie to children about their future experiences in any area. It may be necessary to give explanations which are not completely accurate and descriptive, but adequate at least to the level of their own understanding. If children find that you lie to them, trick them and disappoint them often, they will lose confidence in you and never believe anything you say. This will shake their belief and trust in people in general and make them uncertain of themselves and their experiences.

Failure to prepare children for painful experiences often results in behavior disturbances. They start having nightmares, phobias, nervousness, wakefulness, and sometimes permanent impairment of the personality may result from shock. Modern practice today is to permit the parents to be in the same room with the child following an operation or, whenever possible, at least to be present when the child emerges from anesthesia and is out of danger.

With the use of modern antibiotics, only acute emergencies, accidents, severe croup, convulsions, meningitis, appendicitis, poisonings, and elective surgery require hospitalization. Most pneumonia can be treated at home providing there are no complications. Even tuberculosis is often treated at home. Diseases for which hospitalization is required have been enormously reduced in number in the past twenty years. Most doctors will attempt to take care of a child at home if at all possible.

HORMONES AND GLANDS The hormones are "chemical messengers" produced by glands located in various parts of the body. One feature they share in common is that the secretion is poured directly into the bloodstream and affects the function of an organ or organs in a distant location. (The organ affected is sometimes referred to as the "target organ.") The glands are sometimes collectively termed the endocrines. Some of the more important glands and hormones are described below:

1. *Pituitary*. This tiny gland at the base of the brain has a dominant role because many of its target organs are other endocrine glands. The pituitary secretes gonadotropic hormones which stimulate the overy and testicle to secrete the sex hormones. Other pituitary hormones are *ACTH*, which stimulates the adrenal gland to secrete hydrocortisone and related chemicals; the mammotropic hormone, which stimulates the breast to produce milk and becomes particularly

operative toward the end of pregnancy, and the somatropic hormone, which stimulates growth. Somatotropic hormone is in short supply but has been shown experimentally to increase the growth of human dwarfs.

2. *Sex hormones.* These include testosterone in the male, which is secreted by the testicles, and in the female, estrogen and progesterone secreted by the ovaries. Small amounts of sex hormones are also secreted by the adrenals in both sexes.

3. *Adrenal.* This pair of glands produces a complex group of hormones which regulate such basic processes as the formation of fats and sugars, the secretion of urine, and bodily responses to inflammation.

4. *Thyroid.* Controlled by a pituitary factor known as TSH (thyroid stimulating hormone), the thyroid gland in turn produces a hormone, thyroxin, which stimulates all processes in all cells of the body.

5. *Insulin.* This is a hormone (produced by the pancreas) which regulates the level of the blood sugar and controls the rate at which the blood sugar enters cells.

6. *Miscellaneous other hormones include:* Secretin, a digestive tract hormone which stimulates the pancreas; cholecystokinin, a similar hormone, which stimulates the gallbladder to contract; ADH, a hormone produced by the posterior part of the pituitary gland, which regulates urine formation, and oxytocin, another posterior pituitary substance, which produces contractions of the uterus.

Endocrine Diseases The thyroid, pituitary, pineal, adrenal, parathyroid, ovary, testes, and pancreas are endocrine glands, or glands of internal secretion. They secrete chemicals (called hormones) which have a complex funtional interrelationship in both health and disease.

During the first few weeks of life there may be carry-over effects of the mother's hormones, producing various conditions in the infant, such as swollen breasts, vaginal discharge, and uterine bleeding. They may cause secretion of milk in the breasts of both male and female infants. The thyroid and pituitary glands are usually well-developed at birth.

Hypoparathyroidism (under-development of parathyroid gland) may cause symptoms of tetany in the newborn, i.e., crowing breathing, generalized convulsions, and carpopedal spasm (in which the wrist is flexed, the hand bent back, and the thumb is in the cupped palm). There is a decrease in the amounts of ionized calcium in the blood, causing hyperirritability of the neuromuscular system. There may be other causes of tetany, but an under-developed parathyroid gland is most common.

Hypothyroidism may be present at birth or acquired later. It is also called cretinism. The absence or lack of thyroid gland in non-goitrous geographic areas causes the "occasional" form of cretinism. In goitrous areas the condition is due to deficiency of thyroid hormone secretion (endemic form).

Cretinism is a condition of mental retardation due to lack of thyroid hormone, associated with the following signs: coarse brittle hair, cool thick skin, stunted height, delayed teething, large tongue, infantile face and body proportions, pot-belly with poor muscle tone, and intolerance to cold. Cretinous children show physical, mental, and emotional retardation. There are characteristic laboratory blood findings and X-ray findings. Usually the protein-bound serum-iodine level is low, testing with radioactive iodine showing low or absent levels.

The treatment of cretinism is substitution therapy with thyroid hormone. Naturally, the earlier these children are diagnosed and treated, the better the prognosis.

Hyperthyroidism is a condition of excess secretion of thyroid hormone due to a nodule (toxic adenoma) or Graves' disease (toxic goiter). The latter, more common in younger persons, is due to overstimulation of the thyroid gland by the pituitary. These patients show hyperactivity, nervousness, tremors, rapid heart rate, high blood pressure, bulging eyes (exophthalmos), loss of weight with accelerated growth in children, and emotional instability. Blood tests of protein-bound iodine in the serum and uptake of radioactive iodine show increased levels. The basic metabolic rate is increased.

Treatment of hyperthyroidism is directed towards suppressing the effect of the overactive thyroid gland with medicine. If the symptoms of hyperthyroidism do not subside on medical management, surgical removal of the thyroid gland may be necessary.

HYSTERECTOMY Surgical removal of the uterus (womb) is the operation referred to as a hysterectomy. In some instances the cervix may be left in, the operation then being termed a supracervical hysterectomy. When the cervix too is removed, the procedure is referred to as a complete hysterectomy. Still another variant is a panhysterectomy, in which the tubes and ovaries are also removed (pan = all).

The most common cause of hysterectomy is the growth of the benign tumors known as fibroids. A uterus enlarged because of fibroids may produce uncomfortable pressure symptoms and interference with the function of nearby organs, most often the bladder. Very heavy and prolonged menstrual periods or other forms of frequent and recurrent uterine bleeding, when not controllable by other measures, may necessitate a hysterectomy. Cancer of the uterus is often treated in this way, sometimes after a preliminary period of irradiation. Rather rarely, some severe and life-threatening infections of the uterus may also lead to hysterectomy.

When the ovaries are removed in a premenopausal woman, a surgical menopause follows. Like the naturally occurring menopause, it too may be marked by flushes and sweats, and these may sometimes be severe. It too may require the use of hormones for a variable period of time. The tides of medical opinion have changed over the years as to whether or not it is wise to remove the ovaries at the time of hysterectomy.

One of the arguments for a panhysterectomy is that since tumor formation is by no means rare in the ovaries, their removal at the time of the hysterectomy can be regarded as justifiable prophylaxis. A decisive factor may be age; a surgeon would certainly feel less hesitant about removing the ovaries of a woman in her mid-forties, presumably approaching the menopause anyway. Fortunately, most of the mandatory reasons for doing hysterectomies are found in women in the older age group. In most instances these women have had their families so that the loss of the uterus has far less impact on them. A hysterectomy need in no way impair a woman's sexual life thereafter.

IMMUNIZATION OF YOUR CHILD There are many diseases today which your child will never get if he is immunized against them. In previous years thousands of children used to die, during epidemics, of diseases which can now be prevented. It is therefore important and necessary for you to give your child all the injections which have been developed to protect him. Epidemics still can and do break out, but if this occurs your child will be protected. You can get in touch with your physician to arrange for this vital protection.

Long-term immunity can be given against smallpox, tuberculosis, polio, tetanus, whooping cough, diphtheria, and measles. If you are traveling outside the United States, especially to a tropical area, there are other diseases against which your child can be protected, such as typhoid-paratyphoid fever, yellow fever, cholera, typhus, and a few other very specialized diseases. Lifelong immunity cannot really be given against any disease by a single inoculation; therefore it is necessary at various ages to reinforce first injections with booster shots of the immunizing substance.

Temporary immunity can often be given a child against a disease to which he has been exposed before being inoculated against it. For example, if your child has been exposed to measles before he has received the measles vaccine, let your doctor know at once. The doctor will treat him with gamma globulin, which produces temporary immunity and will make the attack milder.

The ideal time for a child to start having his injections is about two to three months after birth. Always contact your physician during an epidemic, even if your child has received immunization; additional protection may be received in the form of booster doses. It is important to keep a record of the dates of your child's immunizations, so that you will know what he has been given and when it is time for booster injections. This record will be required almost every year that he registers in school, so keep it some place where you will have it readily available.

INFANT AND CHILDHOOD DISORDERS

Intussusception Intussusception is an acquired form of intestinal obstruction and occurs mostly in young male children. A portion of the lower intestine turns inside of itself and blocks the linings and passage of food. It causes severe colicky pain, fever, and typical currant-jelly bowel movements. This represents some passage of blood in the stools. A sausage-shaped mass may sometimes be felt in the abdomen.

This condition requires immediate attention. The longer one delays diagnosis, the more difficult it is to treat. If it exists for more than twelve hours, strangulation of the bowel and gangrene may occur. The intussusception may sometimes reduce itself without treatment and not require surgery.

Infantile Tetany (Spasmophilia) This is a neuromuscular hyperexcitability produced by inadequate amounts of ionized calcium in the blood. It is commonly associated with rickets, and is most frequently seen in male children during the first two years of life. A typical sign is "carpopedal spasm," in which the wrist is flexed, with the fingers extended and the hand abducted (turned), with the thumb in the cupped palm. Convulsions and crowing sounds when breathing in may occur. A blood test will show low calcium. The treatment is replacement therapy with intravenous or oral calcium.

Cleft Palate (Harelip) During the fifth and eighth weeks in the developing embryo, the maxillary and premaxillary palatal processes fuse. A failure in fusion may result in either cleft lip or cleft palate, or both. The exact cause is unknown, but any abnormal influence occurring at a critical developmental level will cause defects in the developing embryo. This disorder is more frequent in males, and occurs in one in 800 births. Due to the space created, it may cause immediate feeding problems. Special methods of nursing may be required for these children. Most of these lesions are correctable with plastic surgery. This is performed at optimum growth periods, when all the available tissue may be used.

Thrush This is an acute, sub-acute, or chronic infection caused by a yeastlike fungus called *monilia*. It may cause infections in any area of the body, but the most common type observed in newborn infants involves the mucous membranes of the mouth. Mouth thrush is characterized by white plaques on the tongue, cheek lining, and throat. It may be very painful and cause feeding difficulties.

Diagnosis can usually be made by simple observation or by culturing the fungus. *Candida albicans* usually causes these infections. The antibiotic Mycostatin is effective in clearing the lesions. Painting the mouth with aqueous gentian violet solution is also effective.

INFANT FEEDING

Breast-feeding Breast-feeding of infants is generally to be encouraged because mother's milk is a truly natural source of food. It is more digestible than prepared milks and causes few feeding difficulties. The breasts should be emptied by the nursing child. The mother's diet should be adequate in nutritious food, vitamins, calories, and minerals. A relaxed attitude and freedom from tension and irritation are important factors in insuring an adequate breast-milk supply. Emptying the breasts is the best stimulus to refilling them. If breast-feeding is not possible, or if it is not desired, formula feeding is widely and generally accepted as an excellent substitute. If breast-feeding is only partially satisfactory, supplementary feedings with formula may be added. At four to six months, the infant can be weaned by the gradual substitution of formula feedings for breast-feeding.

The total daily fluid requirements for infants are approximately 2½ ounces per pound of body weight per day. Evaporated milk provides 40 calories to the ounce. Cow's or breast milk provides 20 calories per ounce. Sugar (2 tablespoons) equals 120 calories per ounce, corn syrup, 120 calories per 2 tablespoons. Dextri-maltose equals 120 calories per 4 tablespoons.

Formulas Most infants are given formulas made of either evaporated or whole milk. There are many other excellent prepared formulas on the market to which only water need be added. (See FORMULAS.)

Supplementary Foods Vitamins are generally added to the infant's diet at about three weeks of age. There are many standardized excellent multiple vitamin preparations available. They contain 50 mgm. of vitamin C, so that it is not absolutely necessary to introduce fruit juice (orange juice) at this time.

Solid Foods Many infants are very hungry at birth, and frequently it may be necessary to introduce cereal, vegetables, fruits as early as 6 weeks to 2 months. However, *not all infants will tolerate the addition of these new foods.*

Frequency, Quantity, Burping The frequency and amounts of feeding at each meal vary in all infants. There is now general agreement that a modified self-demand schedule satisfies more children better than a rigid time-clock schedule. This is also easier on the mother. Small infants of six pounds tend to eat every two or three hours because their capacity is small. As they gain weight, they will tend to get hungry at longer intervals. Up to two months of age, six or seven feedings may be necessary.

After the second or third month, the 2 A.M. feeding is usually discontinued with most babies. The total fluid intake does not have to exceed more than thirty-two ounces per day, and the maximum fluid per meal does not have to be greater than eight ounces. If the entire amount is not taken in the form of milk, it can be provided with water (sweetened or unsweetened), juices, and fluids diluted into the cereals and solid foods.

Burping or bubbling the infant is necessary to get rid of gas or air which accumulates in the stomach. If this is not done, the air may cause discomfort, cramps, and mechanical vomiting. The latter is readily seen when the child brings up a great deal of food along with a large amount of gas. In these cases, it may be necessary to burp the baby before and, frequently, during a feeding, as well as afterwards.

When the infant weighs approximately twelve to fifteen

pounds, regular whole milk may be substituted for formula feeding. In areas where water is purified and sanitation modern, sterilization of bottles and boiling of water may be discontinued when the baby is six weeks to two months old. In periods when the child has diarrhea or is ill with some gastrointestinal disturbance it may be necessary to go back to sterilizing bottles.

New Foods New foods should be introduced gradually, preferably one at a time for a few days, to see whether there is any adverse reaction. It may be necessary to mix the vegetables and meats with a little water to make them more fluid so that the child can swallow them more easily. A toothless infant cannot manipulate sticky or pasty foods. He is accustomed to swallowing liquids and may reject undiluted solids. Following is a schedule of approximate ages for the introduction of new solid foods:

6 weeks to 3 months. Introduce precooked cereals, mashed banana (fresh or canned), some vegetables or other fruits.

4 months. Introduce cooked cereals, fruits, vegetables, hard-boiled egg yolk.

5 months. Introduce meat soups (chicken, bouillon, beef broth), pureed vegetables, meats.

6 to 8 months. Introduce whole milk, zweiback, puddings, custards, cheese.

8 to 12 months. The child may go on 3 meals a day—hard-boiled egg white may be introduced first, then boiled egg with the white incompletely cooked may be tried.

12 to 18 months. The child may eat most adult foods except fish with bones.

"Junior" foods, or chopped foods, are often refused until the child has sufficient teeth to chew lumpy masses. Since such food is just as nutritious in strained form, there is no particular advantage in forcing junior foods before the child is willing to accept them. Fillet or canned salmon and tuna fish may be used as protein substances.

Some children are allergic to cow's milk protein. This may show up as a series of digestive disturbances characterized by diarrhea, vomiting, intestinal cramps and colic, rash, a general irritability and disagreeableness. There are many non-allergenic milks made from soybeans. Your doctor will advise you whether it is necessary for your child to switch to this type of milk. Another form of milk, good for digestive disturbances, is lactic acid milk. Powdered protein milks are often used for the treatment of intestinal disturbances and for the feeding of premature infants.

INFLUENZA Influenza, or "flu," is a virus disease which occurs in epidemics, generally in the winter and spring. The usual symptoms are sudden onset of muscular aches, headache, fever, and symptoms referable to the respiratory tract, such as nasal stuffiness, sore throat, and dry cough. The illness generally lasts for some days. The flu is noted for producing a prolonged period of debility, many victims feeling weak and sub-par for some weeks. The fever during the first few days may be on the order of 101°-102°F., and occasionally even higher. It generally abates within three days but occasionally may last longer.

Treatment. None of the known antibiotics are of value in treatment. Probably the most useful drug is aspirin, one to two tablets four times a day, which lowers the temperature and relieves much of the aching. For severe headache small doses of codeine or a similar pain killer may also be used. An alcohol sponge bath may be of value for high fever. Epidemics in recent years have indicated that elderly individuals, patients with chronic heart or lung disease, and pregnant women are more susceptible to flu, and a higher death rate has been reported in these three groups. Immunization against flu, using a vaccine made of several strains, should be given to susceptible individuals and pregnant women. The immunization lasts for only a year and must be repeated at the start of each respiratory season.

There are a large number of viruses which can produce other respiratory illnesses which are also sometimes called flu or grippe. These produce less muscular aching, less fever (as a rule), and more head-cold symptoms. True influenza has no particular effect on the digestive tract. It only rarely causes nausea or vomiting, and does not produce diarrhea.

INSOMNIA Inability to fall asleep, light slumber with repeated episodes of wakefulness, or early morning awakening with inability to go back to sleep comprise some of the forms of insomnia. Sleep difficulties are not uncommon, especially toward the end of pregnancy; abdominal enlargement may interfere with restful positioning and turning, and there seem to be times in the quiet of the night when the thrashing about of the unborn baby seems to be almost deliberately intended to keep the mother awake. Hot weather may further add to the difficulties encountered.

Sometimes psychological factors such as worry, anxiety, or fear may lead to insomnia. Having a baby often changes a woman's sleep patterns temporarily if not permanently. New babies are notoriously unaware of day-and-night differences. The need for 2 A.M.(feedings may not be bypassed for some months, while older babies may regularly wake at 5 A.M., fresh and playful. These interruptions of sleep do not constitute insomnia, although some mothers complain of difficulty in going back to sleep once they have been up.

There is often no wholly satisfactory answer to the insomnia problem. Among the suggested solutions are: (1) A warm (not necessarily hot) tub bath. (2) A light meal or a glass of warm milk shortly before retiring; occasionally beer or wine may produce sleepiness. (3) A whole host of drugs, which are not barbituates (the classical sleeping pills) may prove of use. Even mild ones may be adequate. They include antihistamines—the drugs used for allergic reactions—which are mildly sleep-inducing, the oldtimer phenobarbital, meprobamate (Miltown®, Equanil®), Doriden® and many others. (4) The standard sleeping pills include Seconal® (red), Nembutal® (yellow), sodium amytal (blue), Tuinal® (blue and red), Carbrital® (white with a blue band), and various others; they can be secured only on a doctor's prescription. For temporary use there is certainly no major objection to any one of these. Their use should, however, be discouraged in favor of other possibilities. Nevertheless, as many weary victims of insomnia, and their doctors too, will point out, one thing worse then taking a sleeping pill is insomnia. Tranquilizers or psychotherapy may be better solutions than barbituates.

INTELLIGENCE AND MENTAL RETARDATION
Intelligence Tests *The Wechsler Intelligence Scale* is made up of ten tests, each testing a different process of intellectual functioning. Five of these sub-tests are *verbal,* which means that the child answers questions on the tasks presented to him. The other five are *performance* tests, which means the child manipulates materials in order to solve the tasks presented to him.

The berbal sub-tests test information, comprehension, arithmetic, similarities, vocabulary, and digit span. Similarities test the formation of concepts. This relates to the ways in which similar things belong together, such as a pear and an apple, which are both fruit. This tests the ability to think in abstractions and is often interfered with by organic brain damage. In another test, the child repeats series of digits which become progressively longer. This gives a measure of his ability to maintain continuous concentration and retain units of information and their relationships.

On the performance sub-tests, the picture arrangements

sub-test is a series of pictures which the child is asked to rearrange so that they make a meaningful story. This test measures planning, anticipation, and the ability to see relationships between events.

The picture completion sub-test consists of twenty drawings which are presented one at a time, and the child is asked to tell what important element is missing in each drawing. This tests the child's ability to discover inconsistencies and incompleteness.

The block design sub-test consists of seven geometric designs; the child is asked to assemble colored blocks of wood so that they reproduce a specific design. This test measures visual-motor coordination. It utilizes two intellectual processes; the child must first differentiate the pattern into its parts, then must take these parts and reassemble the design. This particular sub-test is designed especially to test brain-damaged children. Those who have organic brain damage show great difficulty with this test.

The object assembly sub-test consists of four puzzles which the child is asked to assemble. This is also a measure of visual-motor coordination. Children who fail in this test are unable to determine the correct interrelationship of the parts.

The coding sub-tests the ability to maintain correct spatial relationships while transporting a mental symbol. Brain-damaged children frequently reverse or invert symbols when copying them. It is another test of visual-motor coordination.

The Bender Motor Gestalt Test is a series of eight geometric designs presented to a child who is asked to copy them on a sheet of paper. This tests the ability to perceive order and organize the parts of a design and their interrelationship, and to reproduce this design. It is basically a visual-motor coordination test, but also tests other psychological functions. Brain damage is frequently diagnosed by failures in this test.

The Rorschach Test is a series of ten ink blots printed on ten cards—five in black-and-white and five in color. The child is asked to look at each of these designs and tell what it looks like, or what it reminds him of. This tests shows up conflict areas, impulses, personality devices, and the ability of the child to integrate and make use of information. It is helpful in diagnosing neurologically damaged children.

The Thematic Apperception Test. Here the child is shown pictures of either humans or animals in various situations and is asked to tell a story about what is going on in the picture. These tests provide information on how the child sees himself, his environment, and his relationship with others.

Mental Retardation (Feeblemindedness) The intelligence quotient (I.Q.) is a convenient and descriptive numerical device for defining intelligence. The intelligence quotient is arrived at by dividing the child's mental age (derived after tests) by his chronological age and multiplying the result by 100.

An average of normal I.Q. is between 90 and 110. A score above 130 indicates superior intelligence, and one above 140, very superior intelligence. Idiots have an I.Q. range from 0 to 20, and they do not develop beyond a mental age of 3. Imbeciles' I.Q. is 20 to 50. These never develop beyond a mental age of 3 to 7. Morons' I.Q. is 50 to 70. These do not reach a level higher than age 10 or 11.

Causes of mental retardation. Mental retardation is only a symptom of poor development of various mental faculties, and may be caused by many different conditions. Heredity, neurological diseases, virus or other infections in the mother (German measles, toxoplasmosis, syphilis). Rh incompatibility, endocrine disorders (cretinism), and chromosome abnormality (mongolism) are some causes of mental retardation.

Birth trauma, hemorrhage in the brain, lack of oxygen immediately following birth, etc., may also cause developmental abnormalities resulting in defective intelligence.

After birth, infections of the nervous system, such as encephalitis, convulsions, meningitis, brain trauma (fractured skulls), etc., may also cause retardation. Severe emotional disturbances, and lack of proper training and of mental stimulation may retard mental growth temporarily.

JAUNDICE Jaundice is a yellow discoloration of the skin and eyes produced when red blood cells disintegrate; they release hemoglobin which is changed to bilirubin (a bile pigment). This causes the yellow color.

Physiologic jaundice (icterus neonatorum) occurs during the first few days of life. There is increased destruction of red blood cells and decreased excretion of the bile pigment by the infant's immature liver. The jaundice usually appears from the second to the fourth day and disappears by the seventh or fourteenth day. This jaundice is perfectly normal and is seen in about 40 per cent of all newborn infants. There is no associated enlargement of the liver or spleen. The blood tests are normal in this condition.

However, there are a few other conditions at birth which cause jaundice due to abnormalities.

1. *Malformations of the bile tract,* such as stenosis of the common bile duct, or absence of the hepatic or common ducts, may cause obstruction and jaundice. A plug of bile or mucus in the common bile duct may also cause obstruction. In this condition, the jaundice may occur at birth or a few weeks later. The liver is usually enlarged and stools may be clay colored. Special blood tests and X-rays are necessary to confirm it.

2. *Syphilitic jaundice.*

3. *Sepsis with jaundice.* This is a condition of severe infections with organisms causing marked toxicity and jaundice.

4. *Erythroblastosis fetalis* (Rh disease). This is a hemolytic disease of the newborn. It is due to the fetus (baby in uterus) producing antibodies to the RH negative blood cells of the mother.

5. *Icterus praecox.* This is a mild form of hemolytic disease of the newborn due to ABO blood-group incompatibility between the mother and infant. It resembles erythroblastosis. Transfusion with Group O blood is usually necessary. It occurs in first-born infants, whereas erythroblastosis fetalis occurs mainly in subsequent births.

Other causes of jaundice are infectious mononucleosis Cooley's anemia, infectious hepatitis, sickle cell anemia, and acute hemolytic anemias, either congenital or acquired.

LARYNGITIS Inflammation of the larynx (voice box) is commonly seen in various respiratory infections. The most common symptoms are huskiness of voice, weakness of the voice—it can be reduced almost to a whisper—cough, and, frequently, sore throat. Other parts of the respiratory system may be affected so that there may also be stuffy nose, sinusitis, or perhaps bronchitis with cough and phlegm production. There is no prompt cure for laryngitis; most of the trouble is due to inflammatory swelling, which even under the best of circumstances may take several days to disappear.

Treatment. Various measures that are helpful are: (1) Voice rest. In severe cases there may be an absolute ban on speaking and the victim may have to communicate by using pencil and paper. (2) Antibiotics may or may not be used, depending on whether the symptoms are considered to be primarily viral or not. Purely viral inflammations do not as a rule respond to antibiotics. (3) Maintaining high humidity in the room by having a vaporizer going or placing pans of water on radiators is soothing. By contrast, inhalation of very dry hot air may be irritating. (4) Hot drinks, often tea or tea-and-honey mixtures, may allay soreness and coughing. (5) Cough may be an annoying symptom and in itself may tend to keep the larynx irritated. Cough suppressants such as codeine or related medicines may then be of value.

Chronic laryngitis is very often due to excessive cigarette smoking. The symptoms may be much like those described above, except they are not associated with respiratory infections and tend to persist the year 'round. Finally, polyps and other growths on the vocal cords, most commonly seen in the middle-aged, may produce hoarseness and voice weakness and thus simulate laryngitis.

LEGS, SWELLING OF Swelling of the legs is generally due to accumulation of fluids in the skin which results in a puffiness, easily demonstrated by pressing firmly with a finger. This will leave a dent which will fill in only slowly. When marked, it is called dropsy, but is generally referred to by physicians as edema.

A variety of causes, mostly not at all serious, may produce swelling of the legs. In pregnancy it is due to pressure on the great veins bringing the blood back to the heart. In addition, in pregnancy the great amounts of hormones that are secreted tend to increase the edema. Considerable amounts of salt will always aggravate any tendency to such swelling.

Apart from the various circulatory disorders of the veins mentioned above, the circulatory changes produced by weakness of the heart muscle may produce edema. Marked swelling may result. The condition generally requires treatment with digitalis, which strengthens the heart, and with diuretic drugs which promote the excretion of fluid from the system.

Various disorders of the kidneys may underlie some cases of leg swelling. Any disorder which leads to a significant loss of albumin into the urine will lower the amount of this substance present in the blood. One of the sequels to this is that some of the fluid normally kept within the bloodstream will tend to diffuse out into the tissue so that puffiness results. Such edema due to kidney disease may produce obvious puffiness of the hands and of the face, in contast to that found in heart disease which tends to be limited to the lower extremities. In the childhood disease known as nephrosis there is general swelling in all the tissues, associated with a marked drop in the albumin of the blood.

Treatment. For swelling due to kidney disease, restriction of salt, diuretic drugs, and other measures are useful. When the swelling is due to local circulatory causes such as those in the veins of the extremities, elastic hose are often useful. Some of these are sold commercially, but they can also be made up to order. By exerting compression on the veins, fluid accumulation is diminished. Keeping the legs elevated as far as possible is a further useful measure.

LONGEVITY There are important hereditary aspects to longevity. We all know families in which everyone lives to a ripe old age, and the contrary is also known to be true; in trying to evaluate this factor in one's own family, death from such events as accidents, influenza or other infections, operations, or similar incidents or accidents are to be excluded.

Progress in medical science has shed some light on the factors involved in long life, and whether or not longevity runs in one's family, certain important factors have been evaluated. Some of the leading ones follow:

1. *One's sex.* Everything else being equal, women have, on the average, a seven-year-longer life span than men. Mainly this can be ascribed to the fact that a woman's cardiovascular system stands up better because of the protec-

tion afforded throughout the first fifty years or so by her own female hormones.

2. *Cigarette smoking.* As with other forms of exposure to toxic substances, cigarette smoking ages the organism. As long ago as 1938 it was shown that heavy smokers lived on the average four years less than non-smokers.

3. *Overweight.* The majority of individuals who reach a ripe old age are slender, sometimes even underweight. A body weight 10 per cent above the desirable range has a significant effect in shortening life, and this effect increases with the degree of overweight. There is an increased incidence of heart attacks, high blood pressure, and diabetes in overweights as compared to normals.

4. *Elevated blood pressure.* More than half of all deaths in the United States are due to disease of the heart and blood vessels; any factor that increases or decreases this will affect many millions of individuals. High blood pressure tends to age the blood vessels and can seriously increase the work of the heart. Hence heart attacks and strokes occur more frequently in hypertensives as compared to normotensives. Combinations of overweight and elevated blood pressure are considerably more serious than either of these conditions alone.

MASTURBATION Masturbation is a practice of handling one's own genitals for the purpose of sexual excitation and pleasure. It occurs to some degree in all children as part of the general desire to see, touch, and be curious. Since sexual feelings are a normal part of growing up, it is to be expected that sexual exploration and experimentation will occur. Children are not aware that the adult world considers this a shameful or disgusting practice.

Parents should be informed that masturbation is not harmful, will not (as was once believed) cause insanity, and does not in itself have any bad effects. However, if a child is made to feel that such pleasurable activity is completely wrong, sinful, harmful, and that he may be threatened with removal of his organ because of it, it may create a permanent and terrible inhibition regarding sex which will cause a neurosis, or sexual disturbance, in later life.

MEASLES (RUBEOLA) Contagious.

Cause. Virus.

Incubation period. 10 to 12 days.

Symptoms. Before the typical spots of measles break out there is a severe cold, frequently with high fever, harsh brassy cough, red eyes and an expression of general misery. The cold does not get better with the usual antibiotics and cough medicines—rather, it seems to get worse until the rash appears. The skin rash is preceded by a rash inside the mouth, called "Koplik's spots." These are tiny white specks, like salt sprinkled on the mucous lining of the mouth, very small and difficult to see without magnification. The rash of measles appears first around the ears and neck, then spreads to the face, arms, and body. They are typical flat, round, red spots, approximately the size of a small split pea. The rash disappears between the fourth and fifth day, fading first where it first appeared. The cough and fever diminish slowly after the rash has reached its full bloom, then the patient improves. Cough may persist, however, and the skin may show some dark pigmented areas and peel.

Complications. Swollen glands, measles pneumonia, ear infections, and sometimes encephalitis (brain fever) may follow measles. Encephalitis is a rare but dangerous complication of measles characterized by high fever, lethargy, delirium, convulsions, and/or coma. The result of severe measles encephalitis may be permanent brain damage.

Treatment. Most simple cases of measles respond to aspirin, cough medicines, soothing skin applications (to relieve itching), and a fluid or light diet. The lights should be kept dim because children with measles find it difficult to look at bright light. Persistence of fever, or cough, after seven to ten days requires the attention of a physician.

Prevention. There are now two measles vaccines available for producing permanent immunity. One is a killed-virus vaccine, the other a live attenuated-virus vaccine. The latter is administered with gamma globulin in order to modify any side effects. In cases where there is not sufficient time after exposure to immunize the child with permanent vaccine, an injection of gamma globulin provides some temporary immunity lasting about a month. It also will modify a severe case if given early enough.

German Measles (Rubella) Contagious.

Cause. Virus.

Incubation period. 14 to 21 days.

Symptoms. A general feeling of illness, mild fever, swelling of the glands in the back of the neck and head, followed by a pink rash which appears first on the face, then spreads over the head, arms, and body. It rarely covers the legs. The rash resembles measles the first day, scarlet fever the second; it fades on the third.

The particular danger of this disease occurs when pregnant women get it within the first three months of pregnancy. During this period there is crucial development of certain parts of the developing fetus. It has been observed that when German measles affects the developing fetus, the children are born with various abnormalities, including blindness and deafness.

Treatment. Injections of gamma globulin may be helpful. In cases where the disease is contracted by a woman during the first three months of pregnancy, it is frequently an indication for legal therapeutic termination (abortion) of the pregnancy.

MENOPAUSE Menopause is sometimes referred to as the "change of life," or the "climacteric." The menopause marks the halt of usual cyclic activity of the ovaries. Production of egg cells (ovulation) and all the accompanying changes in the uterus which mark the menstrual cycle end with the menopause.

The menopause sometimes comes on quite abruptly, but more often is marked by a gradual onset with scantier periods, and skipping of periods. A frequent accompanying symptom is hot flashes (flashes)—a circulatory disturbance in which a wave of heat is felt, most often over the face but sometimes over a larger part of the body. This is frequently accompanied by a transient sweat and obvious flushing. Hot flushes occur erratically (sometimes many times a day) and may be increased by emotional upset, weather fluctuations, fatigue, etc. Onset of the menopause is variable; it may occur as early as the late thirties, as late as the mid-fifties. A diagnosis of the menopause canot be made so long as a woman is menstruating regularly. Thus, a woman in her forties who is still menstruating is wrong to ascribe irritability, depression, joint pains, changes in blood pressure, etc., to the menopause.

Treatment. When menopausal symptoms are severe and the menopause occurs very early, the doctor may well advise the taking of female hormones. There is no reason to fear the possibility, once raised, that taking such hormones might increase the number of tumors in the female reproductive tract; indeed, quite to the contrary, some doctors hold that women should continue female hormones at some dosage level since this protects them against aging changes in the blood vessels and bones.

There has been an increasing tendency in recent years to give women female hormones if they go into an early menopause, or if a heart attack has been experienced. The routine very often is to prescribe the hormones for about three weeks at a time, to be alternated with a period off the drug.

This may result in the appearance of a menstrual flow similar to, though perhaps scantier than, that which the woman previously experienced.

One of the reasons for permitting menstruation to occur in this way is that by the shedding of the uterine lining an unduly prolonged hormonal stimulation is avoided. The artificial cycle thus imitates natural ones, just as, in women who take the birth-control pills, stopping the pills will generally result in a menstrual flow several days later. Occasionally, in women taking these hormones, a pink staining may appear which resembles a light flow. This is known as "break-through bleeding" and may be an indication for increasing the dose of the drug for at least a short period. There is much current discussion on this matter; it is conceivable that a medical opinion will eventually favor extended use of hormones, which will thus abolish the menopause.

MENSTRUATION AND OVULATION

Menstruation The formation of an egg in the ovary is associated with hormone secretions which produce a cycle of growth and development in the lining of the uterus (womb). If the egg is fertilized and pregnancy initiated, the fertilized egg will implant itself in the uterine lining which has been especially prepared to receive it. In the absence of pregnancy much of the prepared lining is cast off to the accompaniment of bleeding, a process termed menstruation.

Many aspects of menstruation are subject to variability. Although the interval is generally supposed to be twenty-eight days, many perfectly normal women have cycles which are definitely shorter or longer—for example, twenty-four day or thirty-five day cycles. Even greater irregularity may be associated with normal fertility. A nervous upset, a trip, worry over a possible pregnancy, a variety of illnesses, all may lead to a postponement of the menstrual period or even a complete skipping of the cycle. Some women regularly menstruate for only two days, others for seven or more, and the amount of the flow may similarly be quite variable. Adolescent girls frequently have menstrual irregularities, but with the passage of years more regular patterns tend to be established. Definitely scanty periods are referred to as oligomenorrhea, frequent periods as polymenorrhea, painful periods as dysmenorrhea.

Dysmenorrhea generally takes the form of painful cramps, particularly on the first day or two of menstruation. In addition, many women complain of such other symptoms as heaviness and congestion in the pelvic area, backache, and a subpar feeling—"being unwell." Menstrual cramps may be helped by a hot-water bottle, antispasmodic drugs such as are used for disorders of the digestive tract, aspirin and other pain killers, including one useful combination which incorporates small doses of benzedrine with aspirin.

Ovulation Ovulation is the release of an egg cell from the ovary; it is the basic event of reproduction. Failure to ovulate (which is rare) will, of course, produce sterility. Ovulation most often occurs about mid-menstrual cycle. Where the length of the menstrual cycles is variable, there is evidence that the variability is due to fluctuation in the time before ovulation occurs. Thus ovulation may occur as early as the eighth or ninth day in a short cycle, and as late as the eighteenth or nineteenth day in a longer one. The interval between ovulation and menstruation is considered to be less variable, most often about two weeks. Ovulation generally occurs without a woman having any awareness of it. A few women do experience a lower abdominal pian, which has been termed *Mittelschmerz.*

Ovulatory pain can sometimes imitate appendicitis. It is often associated with bloating and an increased amount of vaginal secretion, which may be pink-tinged. When ovulation produces a definite discomfort, it may be useful to take note of this on a menstrual calendar. An exceptional woman may be able to base her family planning on the regular occurrence of mid-cycle pain or other discomfort. Women who take their temperature every morning for sterility studies will note a slight drop in mouth temperature at about the time of ovulation; this is succeeded by a rise which is maintained in a steady fashion until the time of menstruation. The mid-cycle temperature drop, followed by a rise, may also be a useful indicator of the probability of ovulation.

MONONUCLEOSIS, INFECTIOUS This disease, which is probably caused by a virus, is of low-grade contagiousness. The incubation period is about four to fourteen days and it is rare in infancy.

Symptoms. The symptoms are fever, swollen glands, signs of upper respiratory infection, sometimes a rash. There may be more severe symptoms with headache, blurred vision, mental confusion, etc. The most important laboratory finding is a large number of abnormal lymphocytes in the blood smear. Another test which confirms the diagnosis is that of a high heterophil antibody titer.

Treatment. The condition lasts two to four weeks and there is no specific treatment except for general supportive measures.

MULTIPLE SCLEROSIS (MS) MS is a chronic, progressive disease of the central nervous system causing neurological symptoms; such as, difficulty in walking (major cause of disability), speech disorders, mental changes, sensory loss, and visual disturbances. In some individuals, symptoms progress to tremors and complete paralysis. It is estimated that one-quarter of a million Americans have MS with approximately 200 new cases diagnosed every week. Onset manifests itself in early adult life and is frequently associated with sexual dysfunction and urinary problems.

MS is the third most common cause of severe disability between ages 15 and 50 years. The cause is unknown, and there is no cure of specific treatment that will arrest the disease. Medications such as ACTH and corticosteroids may shorten the length of an acute exacerbation, but these drugs do not appear to alter the long-term course. There are no agents that will restore damaged nerve tissues or fibers and their functioning. Multiple Sclerosis appears to be an autoimmune disease in which the immune system is misdirected and turns against healthy body tissue, namely, the myelin sheath that surrounds nerve axons. To date, the best available treatment for MS patients is in symptomatic intervention (treatment to alleviate symptoms as they occur).

The long course of MS may span 30 years or more from onset to death. The disease may be separated into four stages of varying length.

1. The first stage is from the appearance of a neurological symptom to the first medical examination, and may vary from one day to several years.

2. The second stage begins with the first examination and the diagnosis, varying in length from a day to several years.

3. The third stage is from disclosure of MS to a spontaneous remission. If no remission occurs and the course of the disease is progressive, it merges into a fourth stage.

4. The fourth and final stage begins from the first remission (if it occurs) to the termination of the disease, or death.

Disabling symptoms can be categorized as primary, secondary, or tertiary, and involve specific treatments for each cluster of symptoms, with good results for each group of symptoms except for coordination, tremors, and diplopia (double vision).

MS patients should avoid strenuous exercise, and provide for adequate rest periods. Well-balanced meals and correction of obesity are suggested. Counseling may be recom-

mended to relieve stressful situations, and to encourage participation in activities of daily living.

The prognosis of MS is variable. Some patients never manifest symptoms while others appear to have a severe, progressive illness resulting in death. The average patient lives 35 years after onset of the disease. MS patients have a fairly good outlook for an active life when compared to patients with other neurological disorders that lead to disability.

MUMPS (EPIDEMIC PAROTITIS)
Cause. Virus.
Incubation period. 2 to 3 weeks.
Symptoms. There is painful swelling of the salivary glands, mainly the parotids which are located in the cheeks. Frequently the glands under the tongue and under the jawbone may be involved. The swelling may be on one or both sides and begins just in front of the lobe of the ear. Eating becomes painful because saliva, which is produced during chewing, irritates the gland. This may be noted particularly when sour or tart foods (juices and pickles) are eaten. There is usually fever, headache, vomiting, and lack of appetite, although some cases may be very mild and show none of these symptoms.

Complications. There may be swelling of the sex glands during the first week of mumps, but this rarely occurs in children under twelve to fifteen. If it occurs in males, it may produce sterility. In females, both adult and adolescent, the ovaries may become inflamed and this will produce lower-abdominal pain and tenderness without, however, causing sterility.

Occasionally a neurological complication such as encephalitis may occur. This is characterized by headaches, vomiting, irritability, or lethargy. A physician should always be called for this complication.

Treatment. For mild cases there is no specific treatment except bedrest, aspirin, and soothing or warm applications to the swelling. A bland diet will prevent pain on swallowing or chewing. Swelling is usually over within five to seven days.

Prevention. Injection of a mumps hyperimmune serum is available. It will prevent mumps temporarily (for about a month). In children, mumps is usually such a mild disease that routine use of this serum is not common.

Because there are many other conditions which resemble it (glands swollen from tonsilitis, tumors of the parotid gland, etc.), children with mumps should be seen by a physician.

MUSCULAR CONTROL, DISEASES AFFECTING
Cerebral Palsy Cerebral palsy is a disorder of the nervous system which produces many complex symptoms. It may be caused by: (1) congenital malformation of the brain (defects occurring in the development of the brain); (2) brain damage from difficult birth (lack of oxygen or brain hemorrhage); or (3) infection of the brain, with damage, after birth (encephalitis or poisoning).

Symptoms. The symptoms vary, depending upon the area of the brain affected and the severity of the damage. The child who doesn't walk, talk, sit, or develop moving abilities may have this condition. It frequently produces spastic limbs. If one limb is involved, this is called monoplegia. In hemiplegia, the arm and the leg on one side are affected. In paraplegia both legs are affected and in quadriplegia all four limbs. Most of the cerebral palsy lesions produce a spasticity (tenseness) of the muscles, so that moving and walking are difficult. About 60 per cent of palsied persons are spastic. In other forms, when the base of the brain is involved, movements may be bizarre, slow and wormlike (athetoid movements). Because of the excess of involuntary movements, these persons may have extreme difficulty in manipulating things with their hands, and in walking.

Treatment. The treatment for this condition is usually rehabilitation and corrective surgery. Sometimes medications are successful in reducing extra movements.

Epilepsy Epilepsy is a disease characterized by recurring attacks of convulsions. Sometimes the disorder is a hereditary one, while other cases may be of acquired origin. Tumors or brain disease (damage) may cause secondary convulsions. "Grand mal" is a major seizure, followed by tonic and clonic spasms of the arms or legs associated with loss of consciousness. There may be a warning (aura) that the attack is about to occur. This may come in the form of sensations of light, sound or smell.

"Petit mal" is a milder form of the same disease, and is characterized by minimal temporary loss of consciousness. The head may drop, and the patient may appear to be staring blankly.

Neurological investigation should be done in all cases of convulsions. The electroencephalogram, which records brain waves, may determine the specific type of epilepsy present. There are many drugs which will prevent epileptic seizures, without actually curing the disease.

Muscular Dystrophy, Progressive This is a hereditary and familial disease characterized by progressive weakness and wasting of the muscles. There is difficulty in learning to stand or walk, then a waddling gait due to weakness of the muscles of the buttocks. Persons with this disease fall frequently and have difficulty coordinating their movements. A typical feature of muscular dystrophy is the inability to rise steadily to a standing position from a sitting one on the floor. Physiotherapy for general supportive measures are important, but there is no specific treatment for this condition.

NAUSEA AND VOMITING A great many disorders may produce symptoms of nausea and vomiting. During pregnancy symptoms of this kind characteristically occur in the morning but are very variable, and some women seem to escape them altogether. (See CHILDBIRTH AND PREGNANCY, Morning Sickness.) Other common causes are food poisoning, certain viral or infectious disease, overindulgence in alcohol, some disorders of the inner ear, and a whole range of disorders involving the upper digestive tract. Among the latter are ulcer, tumors, functional spasms, and reaction to some drugs such as aspirin in overdosage as well as to the heart medicine digitalis. Migraine often produces nausea and vomiting, hence the term "sick headache." Obviously many of these conditions will require a doctor's diagnosis and advice. When the cause is an obviously temporary one, the chief practical problem will revolve about the procedures that will make the transition back to normal easiest.

Treatment. There are some drugs which will diminish or do away with nausea, and some of these (as in the case of seasickness remedies) are available over-the-counter. Small doses of sedatives or tranquilizers will usually help diminish nausea. Other points to be kept in mind are the following: (1) Only small amounts of liquid should be taken at a time. Sudden distention of the stomach, even drinking only a cupful of tea, may provoke another bout of vomiting. Small frequent sips will be better. (2) Sucking on chips of ice may help, and sips of a cold carbonated beverage, such as ginger ale or a cola drink, may be retained when other items are not. (3) Small doses of cola syrup at ten-to-fifteen-minute intervals may often stay down and seem to have a sedative effect on the stomach. Check this treatment and the dosage with your doctor.

Once it is clear that small quantities of such fluids are being retained, one can cautiously expand to somewhat larger quantities and start adding solids. Small amounts of bland cereals such as farina or oatmeal are very commonly employed after gastrointestinal upsets. These can be followed by toast with jams or jellies, small amounts of eggs or milk (only if the patient likes them, however); as performance improves, chicken, potatoes, various soups, chopped meats and the like can be added.

Vomiting in Infancy Vomiting occurs in many illnesses. It may be one of the first symptoms of any febrile disease (a disease accompanied by fever). A child may appear perfectly well and then suddenly vomit a meal. This is an indication that the temperature should be checked, as he may be developing some illness. Excess air-swallowing, too rich a formula, indigestion from foods introduced too early, may all cause vomiting. Conditions of the intestine such as abdominal obstruction (blocking of the passage of food) may cause vomiting.

Emotional and psychological factors in vomiting are common causes. If a child is very angry or disturbed, is punished or scolded during a meal or shortly afterwards, this may cause him to become so upset he will vomit his food.

A child may have no fever at the onset of vomiting. However, if the temperature is checked within an hour or two and is rising, this may give some indication of oncoming illness.

Congenital defects in the abdomen, such as pyloric stenosis, cause a persistent projectile vomiting within the first seven weeks of life. This condition can usually only be relieved by surgical operation.

NECK, STIFFNESS OF What is generally referred to as "stiff neck" is a musculoskeletal condition, generally temporary, which produces pain and tightening-up of a neck muscle. Sometimes the painful spasm of the neck muscle makes it stand out quite prominently and even throws the neck to one side, a condition known as "wry neck," called torticollis by medical men. Any of a considerable number of stresses, torn fibers, or inflammations involving the bones, ligaments, or muscles of the neck may underlie this complaint.

A stiff neck is sometimes noted in the morning on awakening, and a person may be aware that he has slept with his neck at an uncomfortable angle, perhaps off the pillow. Drafts or exposure to cold and dampness may also produce a stiff aching muscle in the neck region. A stiff painful neck may come on almost instantly after certain kinds of twisting motions, as in athletic contests; this is comparable to the acute lumbosacral strains (low backaches) which can arise from as simple a motion as leaning over to pick up a shoe. Probably the twisting motion of the spinal vertebrae produces a slippage between their facets or a slight tear in some of the ligamentous fibers running between them. A painful spasm of the nearby muscles, designed by nature to prevent further motion, will then be the result. Many of these acute painful conditions of the neck last for several days.

Stiffness of the neck is also seen in meningitis and poliomyelitis as well as several other disabling diseases, including infection or irritation in the central nervous system. In these diseases, fever and other evidences of a general infection differentiate the condition from muscular or arthritic involvement of the neck region.

Treatment. The usual treatment for a musculoskeletal condition may include manipulation or stretching, ointments or liniments that produce local heat (known as counterirritants), hot compresses or a heating pad, aspirin, or other pain-killing drugs. (See also POLIOMYELITIS.)

NEUROLOGICAL CONDITIONS
Neuritis Various kinds of inflammation or degenerative change in a nerve may be spoken of as "a neuritis." Viral

inflammations, decreases in circulation, mechanical pressure, cuts and blows, lack of vitamin B₁((thiamine) are among some of the numerous causes. Since many nerves transmit sensations, disorders of sensation are frequent in cases of neuritis. Most commonly there is a pain which may have a burning, tingling, or knifelike quality. Curiously, the area to which the nerve goes is often numb to the touch. If the nerve also goes to muscles, these too are weak.

Some of the commoner forms of neuritis follow:

1. *Shingles* is produced by the herpes zoster virus, which is related to the viruses of chicken pox and cold sores. It generally affects a single nerve on one side, most often on the trunk. It produces a patchy or bandlike eruption usually with severe burning pain and exquisite tenderness.

2. *Bell's palsy* affects the facial nerve and produces a characteristic weakness and drooping of the lower side of the face around the lips. Since no sensation is transmitted by this nerve, only the muscle weakness will be complained of.

3. *Sciatica* affects the largest nerve of the body, the sciatic. There is usually pain along the course of the nerve, and a mixture of disordered sensations and muscle weakness. The common causes include the pressure of disks or of the bony spurs produced by arthritis, and inflammations.

4. In *polyneuritis,* many nerves are involved due to a generally acting rather than a local cause. The long nerves going to the limbs are usually the more seriously affected. Pain and weakness are the common complaints. The muscular weakness can lead to inability to raise the wrists or the feet—wrist-drop and foot-drop.

Treatment. To treat neuritis properly one must ascertain the cause. Shingles and Bell's palsy may be helped by steroids. Sciatica may be helped by bedrest, and sometimes traction on the lower spine is employed. Neuritis of nutritional origin is treated by large doses of the vitamins. A traumatic neuritis such as may occur with a fall or a fracture may simply require the passage of time for recovery, but in general neuritis tends to heal slowly.

Multiple Sclerosis (M.S.) This is a disease of the nervous system that usually attacks young adults under the age of forty, causing neurological symptoms such as difficulty in walking, speech, and vision. Later on, tremors and complete paralysis may occur. (See separate article on Multiple Sclerosis.)

NOSE, CONGESTION OF THE The nose performs various useful functions in relation to breathing. It secretes mucus which traps foreign bodies and many bacteria and it warms and humidifies the air we breathe in. Some of this work is done by an exceedingly rich network of small blood vessels which, when completely filled up, can produce much swelling. When swelling is marked, the air space is cut down, and breathing through the nose may be difficult or impossible. In an infant this may produce great difficulties when at the breast or on the bottle. Sucking has to be interrupted frequently so that air can be breathed in through the mouth.

Nasal congestion is common with the common cold; hence many individuals often misdiagnose their nasal congestion as being evidence of a "head cold." There are many other causes including:

1. *Hay fever.* In this condition a hypersensitivity reaction to pollens may produce intense nasal congestion, clear watery discharge, tearing and itching of the eyes. Depending upon the pollens to which the person is allergic it may be experienced in the spring (trees and grasses), in the late summer (ragweed), etc.

2. *Allergies* to dusts, molds, danders (especially of cats and dogs) may produce similar symptoms.

3. *Hormone reaction.* A small group of women experience nasal congestion, sometimes quite intense, during pregnancy. It is considered to be a reaction to hormones whose amounts are increased in pregnancy.

4. *Vasomotor rhinitis.* This is regarded as a functional disturbance which is often made worse by psychologic stress. In some tense individuals the condition is often chronic. The symptoms in many ways resemble those of nasal allergy but can occur at any time of year. It may be seen in children as well as in adults, but often does not come on until middle age.

5. *Physical allergy,* or reactions to changes in temperature or humidity, may set off nasal congestion. Thus some individuals show marked nasal reactions to humidity and to chilling.

Treatment. Despite the varied origins of these kinds of nasal swelling, many persons will show at least some useful response to antihistamines. Thus the running nose and stuffiness produced either by a common cold or by hay fever can be improved with the same medication. Some antihistamines may work better than others with a particular patient, and it may well be worth trying several to determine which is most beneficial. Some are put up in long-acting form so that the duration of effect from a single dose may be twelve hours or longer. Many antihistamines produce sleepiness, and individuals who have to drive a car, take an examination, or otherwise remain alert should be cautioned against this. Nose drops can be used sparingly to decrease nasal congestion, whatever the cause; but their overuse may tend to prolong or intensify nasal congestion. Steroid drugs are sometimes given to break up episodes of intense congestion, and sometimes may work in relatively small dosage. Another group of drugs useful in nasal congestion are called the sympathomimetic amines, drugs of the ephedrine-neosynephrine group. They may be combined with antihistamines and taken by mouth. Patients with elevated blood pressure are generally advised not to take such drugs, however. (See also ALLERGY.)

ORTHOPEDIC CONDITIONS

Club Foot or Talipes Equinovarus This is a congenital deformity and requires skilled orthopedic treatment. About 90 per cent of uncomplicated club feet can be treated successfully by manipulation and casting. Severe cases may require surgery.

Flat Feet This describes a varying degree of flattening of the longitudinal arch of the foot. The arch itself does not develop in children under the age of two and a half. However, since the bones in the child under two are cartilaginous, the foot must be supported in the correct position until he is four or five years old so that the stress on the bones can be changed and any incipient deformity will not progress. The usual treatment for this deformity is a medial heel wedge, either one eighth or one quarter of an inch high. If the child is very heavy, further measures may be required, such as a heel extension along the medial border of the heel.

Hip, Congenital Dislocation of This is a disorder occurring more commonly in females than in males, and one which is not usually noticed until the child begins to walk. There is inability to stand and walk properly, and a waddle is prominent. When examining an infant with this condition, abduction, or pulling of the thigh to the side, is painful and difficult. X-rays of the hips are required in order to make an accurate diagnosis. The treatment is placing the hip in a particular position for a certain period until the hip joint becomes normal. If this condition is not noticed until after two years of age, surgery for this deformity may be required.

Internal or External Rotation of One or Both Feet
This usually involves rotation of the entire lower leg. Children with the condition show toeing in or toeing out. If there is no deformity around the hips, shoes with a proper heel or sole wedge may be used as correctives. If this is not effective, a Denis Browne bar or similar device is utilized. Here the shoes are fastened to a board, with the heels against the lower edge and the feet toed outward or inward, depending upon whether the child is pigeon-toed or slew-footed. These shoes fastened to the splint are to be worn every night for approximately four months. It takes about five or six weeks for changes to appear.

Knock-knee Knock-knee is a condition in which the knees touch and the legs flare, giving the appearance of bow-legs. This may be due to heredity or to rickets. In the latter case the bones are soft and flexible. Heavy infants often appear to have this condition. Certain congenital abnormalities (achondroplasia) may be one cause. Mild degrees of knocking-knee and bow-legs usually correct themselves within the limits of their heredity. Extreme deformities may require braces or surgical correction.

Metatarsus Varus This is the condition which consists of a turning-in of the outer border of the foot. It is sometimes called a third of a club foot. The condition may tend to correct itself. However, in moderately severe cases, the application of firm "holding" casts for several three-week periods is the treatment of choice. If the foot straightens out and becomes corrected, the child can wear straight-last, normal shoes.

PALPITATIONS This term is generally applied to sensations of forceful beating of the heart or to such irregularities as skipped beats. Very often both of these sensations are experienced together. Skipped beats are generally described as consisting of a beat which occurs somewhat ahead of time in the normal sequence and is then followed by a pause of longer duration than usual. Doctors describe this phenomenon as a premature beat with a compensatory pause. To determine the exact nature of this will generally require an electrocardiogram. In the overwhelming majority of instances, the symptoms described as palpitations are not signs of organic heart disease.

Palpitations occur in some individuals when they have drunk too much coffee or tea, have smoked too much, are excited, under stress or fatigued, or have had insufficient sleep. There sometimes seems to be no identifiable cause: the palpitations may come on abruptly on a particular day, leave as abruptly, and not recur for very long periods.

Far less common than these causes for palpitations, but sometimes described as palpitations, are runs of very fast heart action. The technical name for this is *paroxysmal tachycardia* or *paroxysmal fibrillation*. Such a symptom will certainly need a doctor's attention, and may call for special medication such as digitalis or reserpine. Individuals who can take their own pulse should take careful note of the pulse during these episodes, as such information may be of value to the doctor, especially when the complaint is not present at the time of the office visit.

PARKINSON'S DISEASE Parkinson's disease is a slowly progressive disorder of the central nervous system characterized by tremor in muscles that are at rest, or muscular slowness, weakness, and rigidity. In most cases the cause is unknown. However, known causative factors are: arteriosclerosis, cerebral vascular disease, head injuries, syphilis, toxic agents such as carbon monoxide and manganese, and drugs. Family history is also a factor. Researchers believe that part of the basal ganglia in the brain is the center that produces much of the tremor and stiffness of Parkinson's disease due to atrophy and destruction of nerve cells.

More men than women are affected by Parkinson's disease and it generally occurs between ages fifty to sixty. For some persons, the onset of symptoms is mild marked by slight tremor and stiffness on one side that does not impair functioning. For others, the symptoms develop quickly and within months of the onset the person may require total care. There is a characteristic appearance of a person affected with Parkinson's disease. His skin may appear unusually greasy, especially the face. He has an unblinking, wide-eyed, masklike staring facial expression. He may hold his mouth slightly open and drool saliva from the corners. He walks with a slow, shuffling gait with head bent a little forward and arms flexed and held stiffly at his sides. If pushed slightly, he may break into a run spontaneously faster and faster (propulsion), or if pushed back, he tends to run backward with retropulsion. Mental faculties are unimpaired. A characteristic tremor involving the forearm, the hand, and the thumb in a pill-rolling motion ceases when he makes a voluntary motion. Emotional excitement or fatigue intensifies the tremor. Speech may also be impaired.

Diagnosis is readily determined by the clinical picture presented by the patient. Early diagnosis of Parkinson's disease may easily be mistaken for involutional depression, or more rarely, intracranial tumors.

There is no cure for Parkinson's disease, however, treatment with medication, physical therapy, warm baths, stretching exercises, and surgery as a last resort, may relieve symptoms. Maintaining a cheerful mental attitude should be encouraged, and an effort should be made to keep the patient active as long as possible.

PLEURISY The lungs and the inner side of the rib cage forming the chest cavity are lined with a thin glistening membrane called the pleura. Inflammation of the pleura is known as pleuritis or pleurisy. Sometimes a fluid is formed which collects around the lung; it is known as a pleural effusion and is sometimes referred to by laymen as "wet pleurisy." With the aid of a little local anesthetic and a needle, the doctor can tap this fluid and examine it, a procedure which may be important for diagnosis. Not all such fluid collections are due to inflammation. A common cause is a weakness of the heart muscle; the resulting congestion may produce a leakage of fluid into the pleural space.

Pleurisy used to be a common accompaniment to old-fashioned lobar pneumonia, where there was often a severe infection of the pleural space known as an empyema. Since the advent of antibiotics empyema has become a rare complication. Somewhat more common are collections of pleural fluid due to virus infections. Some mild inflammations of the pleural lining may result in pain on breathing, though without a significant accumulation of fluid. This is sometimes referred to as pleuritis or "dry pleurisy." Most chest pains that people complain of, including those aggravated by deep breathing, have nothing to do with the pleura or with fluid collections, however. Rather, they arise in ribs or in the muscular spaces between the ribs—the intercostal spaces—and pain results when these structures are set in motion on breathing.

Treatment. Pain may be considerably relieved by strapping that part of the chest area with adhesive tape; this produces some immobilization, with resulting relief of pain. Lying on the affected side and taking aspirin or similar pain killers may also be useful. The presence of a collection of fluid in the pleura may indicate different disorders in different age groups, and may well call for a series of diagnostic steps.

PNEUMONIA The bronchial tubes divide and subdivide, finally ending in clusters of air sacs in the lungs. These air sacs are called alveoli, and it is in them that the actual exchange of oxygen between the inspired air and the bloodstream takes place. Inflammation involving the alveoli is called pneumonia or pneumonitis and will produce much more systemic reaction than will bronchitis. The symptoms will generally consist of chills, fever, weakness, shortness of breath, or rapid respiration. Pneumonia may follow bronchitis as the inflammation extends down into the alveoli; this produces a patchy form of inflammation called bronchopneumonia. The classical pneumonia of bygone years, produced by the organism known as the pneumococcus, produced inflammation in an entire lobe of a lung (there are five lobes altogether) and hence was termed lobar pneumonia. Before the introduction of antibiotics, this was a dreaded disease with a high mortality rate.

Rather more common in recent years has been a form of pneumonitis produced by several viruses and referred to as virus pneumonia. Virus pneumonia may involve part or all of the lobe of a lung, usually with some cough, but with relatively little secretion of phlegm. There is usually some fever, but not always, so that sometimes victims of virus pneumonia may be up and about, seemingly not too sick—hence the term "walking pneumonia." In recent years it has been definitely established that the usual organism producing virus pneumonia, the Eaton agent, shows some response to the antibiotic tetracycline. Virus pneumonia can last for some weeks and, like other viral infections, be associated with prolonged debility. In contrast, bronchopneumonias and other pneumonias produced by bacteria usually respond quite promptly to antibiotics, with X-rays showing clearing in a matter of a day or a few days.

POISON IVY The poison ivy plant produces an acute spreading and weeping eruption of the skin, either by direct or indirect contact with a secretion of the plant. Similar contact irritants are found in poison oak and poison sumac; the skin reactions to all of these are quite similar. Poison ivy tends to spread for a period of some days and produces annoying burning and itching. The involved skin appears red, and little blisters appear which may enlarge and then burst, producing oozing and crusting.

Treatment. Good preventive first-aid treatment following contact with poison ivy is to wash the exposed areas with an alkaline soap, such as yellow laundry soap. If eruption does occur, calamine lotion or lotions containing a chemical called zirconium may be drying and soothing; antihistamines taken by mouth will also help the itching; certain sedative and tranquilizing drugs also have anti-itching properties. For extensive cases of poison ivy, adrenal steroid drugs (cortisone-type drugs) may be taken by mouth or applied locally. They will cut down inflammation and associated symptoms, as well as the tendency of the condition to spread. They are not, however, generally used except for very extensive eruptions in highly sensitive individuals. None of the various attempts to immunize people against poison ivy has proved particularly successful. Individuals known to be sensitive to poison ivy, when exposure to it is unavoidable, should keep all skin areas covered as much as possible.

POLIOMYELITIS (POLIO) Contagious.

Cause. 3 separate types of viruses.

Incubation period. 5 days to 3 weeks.

Symptoms. Its special symptoms are caused by varying degrees of nerve involvement, with special injury to the anterior horn cells and the motor nuclei of the brain stem. Infections may be caused by one, two, or mixed types, and the symptoms depend almost entirely on the location and severity of the damaged nerve cells. If there is simple injury,

the damage may be reversible, and function may return after an initial paralysis.

Polio is classified in the following way:

1. *Abortive.* In abortive cases one sees headache, nausea, sore throat, malaise, and vomiting. These cases are recognized during polio epidemics but do not have muscular or paralytic involvement.

2. *Spinal paralytic.* In this form there is weakness of the neck, trunk, diaphragm, thorax, abdomen, or extremities, due to involvement of the nerves. Preliminary symptoms may occur resembling minor upper respiratory infections, such as headache, sore throat, vomiting, diarrhea, stiff neck, etc. Meningeal irritation and signs of meningitis may occur. There may be muscle pain on extension of the legs and bending of the neck and back.

3. *Bulbar.* In this form, the cranial nerves and centers of breathing and circulation are affected. Symptoms involve the breathing and swallowing mechanisms. Because of moderate paralysis of the swallowing muscles there is difficulty in swallowing fluids, and they may be brought up through the nose. If the breathing center in the brain is involved, paralysis of the muscles of breathing may occur.

4. *Encephalitic.* In this variety there is drowsiness, irritability, disorientation, and tremors. The picture is the same as encephalitis from other causes.

Hospitalization with physical therapy and muscle reeducation are the modern methods of treating polio. In recent years, mass immunization programs with Salk (killed) or Sabin (live attenuated) vaccine have virtually eliminated polio in many countries.

PULSE AND RESPIRATION RATE, HOW TO MEASURE Pulse rate registers the frequency of the heartbeat per minute. The pulse rate varies in children as well as in adults, and is higher when fever is present. The average normal rate for adults is between 70 and 90 and in children between 80 and 100. In very small infants it can be as high as 110 to 140. The best place for feeling the pulse is directly below the thumb on the wrist. A rapid pulsation will be felt there. If one uses the second hand on a watch, the frequency of the counted beats determines the pulse rate. The rate is recorded as beats per one minute. A pulse rate that is so fast it can hardly be counted is abnormal, and the doctor should be notified. Heartbeat is the same as pulse rate.

Breathing is an automatic function, and we do not regulate or think about it. It just continues. In sick children as in adults, however, the respiratory rate is affected by many factors. Fever, disease, the state of acid base metabolism in the body, all affect the normal rate of respiration which, in adults, is usually sixteen to twenty every minute. In children, it is slightly more frequent. Respiration is counted by observing the number of excursions of the chest per minute. The quality of breathing may also be noted; whether it is regular, irregular, shallow, or deep. It is recorded as breaths taken per minute. The respiratory rate is increased in diseases with fever, such as bronchitis, pneumonia, diabetes, etc. When it returns to normal it is an indication of general improvement. Extremely depressed, infrequent respiration is a serious condition and should be reported to the physician. Respiration rates below ten or twelve per minute are not normal. They may be an indication of impending coma or central nervous system depression. (See also TEMPERATURE.)

RABIES (HYDROPHOBIA)

Cause. Virus.

Incubation period. Varies from 4 to 8 days up to 3 months.

Symptoms. The primary symptom of the nervous system in rabies is that of severe and painful spasm of the muscles

POISONS AND TREATMENT

POISON	PROCEDURE
ACIDS often fume and are corrosive to tissues	*Avoid vomiting.* Give large amounts of milk, repeated tablespoon doses of milk of magnesia, or household remedies for heartburn.
ALKALIES produce corrosive burns around lips and mouth. Examples: lye (used in many products for stopped-up drains), ammonia, quicklime.	*Avoid vomiting.* Give large amounts of citrus fruit juices, or diluted vinegar or large amounts of milk.
ARSENIC is found in some ant, mouse and rat poisons, and in some plant sprays. It produces burning stomach pain, thirst, constriction in throat.	*Induce vomiting.* Give large amounts of milk, milk of magnesia, egg whites, or universal antidote.
ASPIRIN is a common ingredient in headache and pain remedies. Poisoning produces flushing, ringing in the ears, gastric irritation, heavy breathing.	*Induce vomiting.* Give bicarbonate of soda (baking soda) in water, one or two teaspoons.
ATROPINE and related drugs (belladonna, hyoscine) are used for spastic disturbances of the digestive tract. Overdosage produces excitement, confusion, dilated pupils, pounding of the heart.	*Induce vomiting,* and alternate with strong tea or universal antidote.
BARBITURATES are found in many sleeping pills and sedatives. Overdosage produces increasing sleepiness, depressed respiration, and coma.	*Induce vomiting,* unless victim is comatose. Follow with strong coffee. If victim is comatose, give artificial respiration.
CHLORINE is the active agent in various bleaches, produces burning and nausea.	Give milk or emetic and *induce vomiting.*
CONCENTRATED HOUSEHOLD BLEACHES requiring dilution for use.	Treat as for *alkalies.*
CLEANING FLUIDS should be checked to see if benzine, kerosene, gasoline, or "petroleum distillate" are present.	*Avoid vomiting.* Give strong coffee or tea. Artificial respiration may be necessary.
CARBON TETRACHLORIDE or most "spot removers."	*Induce vomiting.* Give tea or coffee.
CARBON MONOXIDE (motor exhaust fumes) produces headache, weakness, coma.	Give artificial respiration and strong coffee.
DEMEROL (also *morphine, codeine, paregoric*) is a narcotic, used chiefly as a pain killer. Overdosage produces drowsiness, coma, constricted pupils, and depressed breathing.	Give universal antidote or strong tea. *Induce vomiting.* If breathing slows markedly, give artificial respiration.
DETERGENTS.	Give milk. *Induce vomiting.* Repeat with milk and *again induce vomiting.*
DIGITALIS is a widely-used heart medication. Its derivatives (digoxin, digitoxin, gitaligen) are similar. They produce weakness, headache, slow pulse, collapse, and delirium.	If no more than one half hour or so has passed since taking, *induce vomiting.* Give strong tea repeatedly. Have victim lie down.
FLUORIDES are the active ingredient of many ant and mouse poisons.	*Induce vomiting.* Give large amounts of milk.
IODINE produces stomach and throat pains.	Give any starchy substance—cornstarch, flour, or bread. Then *induce vomiting.*
LEAD, found in some paints and in white and red lead, produces pain in throat and stomach, vomiting, convulsions, collapse.	*Induce vomiting.* Give large amounts of milk or Epsom salts, and *induce vomiting again.*
OIL OF WINTERGREEN is chemically related to aspirin and produces similar symptoms. It is very toxic if swallowed.	Give 1 or 2 teaspoons of baking soda in water. *Induce vomiting.* Repeat the baking soda, and allow it to be absorbed.
PHOSPHORUS, found in roach and rodent poisons, often has a disagreeable garlicky odor.	*Avoid vomiting.* Give half a glass of hydrogen peroxide.
STRYCHNINE is found in rodent poisons.	*Induce vomiting.* Give strong tea and the universal antidote.
TURPENTINE produces burning pain, excitement, weakness, nausea, shock.	*Avoid vomiting.* Give 1 to 2 ounces of Epsom salts in a pint of water.

of the throat (pharynx and larynx) at the sight of food or liquid. The disease is therefore given the name "hydrophobia," meaning literally, fear of water. Rabies is an acute infectious disease which attacks the nervous system. The virus is transmitted to man by the bite of an infected dog, cat, fox, squirrel, or other wild animal. The virus enters the nervous system and travels by the peripheral nerves to the central nervous system. Degeneration of certain nerves is responsible for the extensive symptoms of spasm, muscle weakness, and finally paralysis. This severe and progressive disease is almost always followed by death. The incubation period of rabies may be much shorter if the bite is around the head and neck. The virus has a shorter distance to travel to the brain.

The symptoms of rabies appear in three phases. The first is characterized by certain peripheral nerve sensations, such as numbness, itching, tingling, and burning, followed by sensations of irritation, restlessness, salivation, perspiration, insomnia, drowsiness, or depression. In the second phase there is excitation. Apprehension and terror appear at this time. The neck may become stiff, and delirium with twitching or convulsive movements may appear. During this second stage, the intensely painful spasm of the throat while attempting to swallow appears. The third phase is represented by increasing paralysis, coma, and death. It is a terminal phase.

Treatment. Rabies in some ways resembles tetanus, but there are many differences. The prognosis for rabies is very poor. Consequently, the best form of treatment is prevention.

Prevention. Most important in preventing rabies is immunizing dogs and other animals who may become contaminated with the virus. If a dog has been bitten by an animal suspected of being infected with rabies, he is either destroyed or isolated for observation to see whether he comes down with the disease. Any animal who has bitten a person should be isolated and observed. Since rabies is such a severe disease, passive immunization with hyperimmune antirabies serum is now an established procedure. Louis Pasteur was the first man to demonstrate the virus in the central nervous system of rabbits, and he developed a vaccine for it.

The immunization treatment against rabies is painful and long. It is therefore important to have all animals and pets immunized against the disease. Bites from animals should be properly cauterized and thoroughly cleansed, and a doctor should be alerted to observe the progress of the case. The antirabies serum should be followed by intramuscular immunization with the vaccine. However, once the disease has developed, all these sera and vaccines are of no value.

RECTUM   The last six inches or so of the large intestine is relatively straight and is called the rectum. In a well-functioning digestive tract the rectum may be quite empty except at the time of having a bowel movement. Indeed, the distention of the rectum produced by the movement of stool into it is the usual signal for the need to evacuate, and it is this that the infant has to learn in the course of his bowel training. Inflammation in this area, called proctitis, may also stimulate the desire to move the bowels even though in fact the rectum may be empty.

If the signal to have a bowel movement is neglected, as it may be when people are in a hurry to leave the house in the morning or when it is otherwise inconvenient to have a movement, stool may accumulate in the rectum. Some of its water content may be reabsorbed, thus leading to a hard, dried-out stool such as is seen in constipation. Occasionally (also in weak or bedridden individuals who are unable to recognize or act on the signal for defecation), large amounts of dried-out stool may accumulate in the rectum, which is somewhat distensible. This is spoken of as an impaction. An impaction may necessitate vigorous measures, such as repeated enemas or even removal by hand.

The opening of the rectum is guarded by a circular muscle called the sphincter ani. Paralysis of this muscle occurs in certain conditions and may lead to inability to hold back the stool. One of the rare but distressing tears that may occur in childbirth can also damage the sphincter and lead to difficulty in rectal control. A more common problem, also related to delivery, is a weakening of the muscles of the pelvic outlet which encircle and support the lower rectal region. This may result in the dilatation of the rectum known as rectocele. Minor degrees of rectocele are of no consequence, but more advanced stages may require plastic surgical repair. Various fluids and medicines may be introduced into the rectum for different purposes—to move the bowels, to soothe local inflammation, or to produce some systemic effect, as when an aminophylline suppository or enema is used in the treatment of asthma.

RHEUMATIC FEVER   Rheumatic fever is caused by the toxic effect of streptococcus infections in children. These tonsillitis and strep throat infections occur more commonly in the spring in the eastern United States and on the West Coast during the winter. The disease may run in families and is also common where there is poverty, malnutrition, and poor hygiene.

Symptoms. The symptoms of rheumatic fever vary, depending on the severity of the infection. The heart and its valves may be involved early, producing characteristic murmurs. In severe cases there is fever, heart murmur, arthritis (inflammation of the joints—generally the ankles, knees, and wrists—with redness and painful swelling). There may be a rash, nosebleeds, abdominal pain, pallor, malaise, and difficulty in breathing. Severe cases may result in heart failure. Laboratory findings in these conditions show a high white blood count and sedimentation rate, typical electrocardiogram, X-ray, and fluoroscopy changes.

Treatment. Rheumatic fever treatment consists of bedrest, antibiotics, sometimes steroids (cortisone). All children who have had rheumatic fever should be placed on preventative treatment with antibiotics to prevent future infections.

Milk attacks of rheumatic fever may go unnoticed and show minimal signs of join pains and other symptoms. Even with mild attacks, there may be heart involvement. However, the disease may be so mild that it is simply considered inactive rheumatic heart disease. Most patients with acute rheumatic fever should be kept in bed for three to six months. After this they may be permitted out of bed if their blood tests remain normal for two weeks and they look fairly well.

SCARLET FEVER (SCARLATINA)   Contagious.
Cause. Streptococcus.
Incubation period. 2 to 7 days. This is an acute contagious infection, caused by (most frequently) the Group A betahemolytic streptococcus. It may be contracted directly from an active case by droplet infection, or from books, clothing, toys, and other contaminated objects. The incubation period is two to seven days. In the period before the rash breaks out, fever, sore throat, and vomiting usually occur. The temperature may be as high as 104°F. Most cases of scarlet fever occur between the ages of two and eight.

A second attack of scarlet fever usually does not follow the immunity which one attack provides. However, repeated streptococcal infections such as tonsillitis, sinusitis, and ear infections are possible with other strains of streptococcus germs; but a rash does not usually occur with all these diseases.

Symptoms. Children with scarlet fever usually appear very sick. The rash, which resembles red "goose flesh," starts around the neck and chest, spreading over the rest of the body. It is rarely seen on the face. The throat is usually very red, and the tonsils may be inflamed and covered with pus. Glands in the neck are often swollen. At first there is a whitish coating on the tongue; when this disappears, the papillae of the tongue enlarge, leaving what is called a "strawberry tongue." This is a beefy red tongue with tiny swellings (tongue glands). After the height of the eruption (three to seven days) the rash fades and is followed by a slight peeling of the skin.

Complications. Ear, gland, kidney infections, rheumatic fever, and arthritis frequently follow scarlet fever. In recent years the use of penicillin by mouth and by injection has prevented many of these complications. In very severe cases, a convalescent serum can be used.

Immunity. Infants may be immune to this condition up to nine months of age if their mothers are immune. Both convalescent serum and scarlet fever antitoxin may be used to confer immunity. These are not often used; however, permanent immunity may be acquired after having the disease or by five weekly subcutaneous injections of scarlet fever toxin.

Treatment. Children exposed to scarlet fever may be given penicillin or sulfonamides, which may either prevent or at least modify the course of the disease.

SEX EDUCATION This is a complex subject to cover briefly, and it becomes all the more difficult because of the variability of values and standards of sexual behavior and education in this country. Certain religious groups are very strict about what they consider proper sex education for children. Other psychoanalytically-oriented groups have much more lenient and flexible standards.

The first two or three years of the infant's life are crucial in the development of his feelings. He learns warmth and responsiveness from the way his mother handles him, plays with him, talks to him, feeds and tends him. And he develops an "outgoing" feeling of love and affection, tenderness, and a desire to please and oblige.

Early loving is directed toward the parents, and the children become very attached to them during the first few years of life. Once the child is able to walk and play and have contact with other individuals, he detaches himself a little from his close dependence on the parents and seeks out friendships and affection outside the family circle. Usually sexual feelings go into a "latency" or dormant period until approximately puberty (twelve to fifteen years of age). In the intervening years the child sublimates, or deflects, sexual striving toward other aims, and becomes interested in school, sports, play, and other activities.

The development of sexual feelings is a natural process of growth. Young children make discoveries about their bodies and will frequently experiment with themselves and with each other.

Proper sex information can be given at various stages of the child's life if the parents' attitudes have been "normal." Very often the parents themselves have confused, fearful, guilty attitudes of sin toward sex. These attitudes will often be communicated to the children in the form of shame or punishment. Many parents are too embarrassed to discuss sex matters with their children. A matter-of-fact attitude and a tone of voice which does not unduly indicate disaster in relation to this area of life are the best approaches to take. Children should be informed that sexual and tender, loving feelings should go together. A great deal of sexual difficulty arises when a split exists between sexual feelings and tender, loving feelings. If the parents' ideas and feelings about sex are unclear or uncertain, this will usually be communicated to the children. If discussion regarding this area is too embarrassing or distasteful to the parents, there are books which can be bought for the children, and possibly discussions with the family physicians or psychiatrist would be helpful.

SEX ORGANS, FEMALE The external female sex glands are, together, known as the *vulva*. This includes the larger and smaller vaginal lips, the clitoris, the urinary and vaginal openings, and the hymen. The larger lips (labia majora) mark out the entire vulva. They are essentially folds of skin containing a small amount of fatty tissue, and are covered with hair. Below, they meet and blend into the skin overlying the central area between the vaginal and rectal openings. This central area is sometimes referred to as the perineum. The small lips (labia minora) are two thinner folds of reddish tissue, a good deal smaller than the larger external lips, and are hairless. They meet above in the region of the clitoris, pass downward around the vagina, then blend imperceptibly together below the vaginal openings.

The *clitoris* is a small (perhaps 1/2 inch), highly sensitive structure with erectile tissue and is analogous to the penis of the male. Stimulation of the clitoris contributes importantly to the pleasure of intercourse. Between the clitoris and the vaginal opening is the urethral opening, the channel for the passage of the urine.

The *hymen* is a rather variable membranous fold at the vaginal opening. In rare cases, a hymen may completely block the vaginal opening, a condition known as imperforate hymen. Usually the hymen will admit at least one finger, occasionally two. It is generally partially ruptured at the time of first intercourse, and only vestiges are left after childbirth.

The *vagina* is an extensible pouchlike structure approximately three to five inches in length, the upper end of which is a blind vault into which the lower portion of the cervix projects. The internal lining of the vagina has a corrugated appearance because of its folds. The walls of the vagina normally lie in contact with one another but are capable of considerable distention, as during intercourse and childbirth. The vagina is kept moist by secretions from the uterus. At its opening are also special glands which secrete a lubricant substance, particularly during sexual stimulation.

In its nonpregnant state the *uterus* (womb) is a small pear-shaped muscular organ. It measures two to three inches in length and consists of an upper larger triangular portion, the corpus, and a lower narrowed cylindrical portion, the neck or cervix. The *cervix* projects into the vagina and there presents a small opening, the *os,* which is the beginning of the canal which runs into the uterus. (In the familiar cancer-detection procedure known as the "Pap" smear, the physician rotates a swab placed just within the os to get a sample of cells.)

Extending outward to the sides of the pelvic cavity and acting as a support for the uterus are membranous folds known as the broad ligaments. Along the upper portion of these ligaments run the *fallopian tubes,* the channels which run from the uterus up to the ovary. Each tube has a trumpet-shaped widening at its ovarian end which receives the egg.

The *ovaries* are almond-shaped structures in which the eggs (ova) are formed. All the eggs of the ovary are present in the newborn female infant, and no more are formed in her lifetime. These tiny structures, known as the primordial follicles, are present by the thousands just below the surface of the ovary; about five hundred of them will come to maturity during a woman's total reproductive lifetime and will discharge a ripe egg capable of being fertilized. At the time of ovulation, one egg bursts out of the ovarian surface and is momentarily free in the abdominal cavity. Apparently, however, it is soon "scooped up" by the fallopian tube.

SEX ORGANS, MALE The important sex organs of the male are all externally located, in contrast to those of the female. Those internally situated—the *prostate,* the *seminal vesicles*—are of secondary importance. The male external organs are the *penis* (the organ of copulation, whose dimensions vary depending upon sexual stimulation) and the *scrotum* (a container for the *testes*—or testicles—in which the sperm are manufactured). The scrotum is a pouch of skin whose size and appearance is, curiously enough, dependent upon temperature: in hot weather, or after a hot bath, the scrotum hangs quite low and appears smooth and thin-walled; after exposure to cold, it shrinks considerably and has a thicker-walled, corrugated, or wrinkled appearance.

An inadequate erection, or absence of erection in appropriately-stimulating circumstances, will make intercourse impossible and is referred to as impotence. Hostility toward the woman, fatigue, the debility associated with certain illnesses, or neurotic patterns often going back to childhood may contribute to impotence, which may be either a temporary or a long-standing complaint in some men. Aging also plays a part in this diminished capacity to perform sexually, as there is an increasing percentage of impotence occurring in men past forty. Because of the complex psychological features that have a bearing on it, a man may be impotent on one occasion—including even his wedding night—and fully potent on others, when he is less nervous or anxious. A squabble or other marital difficulty may produce the same symptom, although paradoxically it sometimes heightens sexual desire.

The testes are firm, ovoid structures, approximately one and a half inches long. They contain two important groups of cells. One group is in almost constant division, undergoing changes which result in the formation of sperm (spermatogenesis). Not only does this type of change alter a large rounded cell into an elongated whiplike one, but there is at the same time a halving of the total number of chromosomes—from 46 to 23. The second group of cells within the testes secretes a substance called testosterone, referred to as the male hormone. It is this which is related to the increased muscle mass, body hair, and beard of the male, as well as such other features as the heavier bones, the lower-pitched voice, and perhaps some behavioral and psychologic characteristics. Sperm formed in the testicles undergo maturation in the *epididymis* and in the spermatic cord—a pair of channels which runs from the testes through the *inguinal canal* and into the pelvic cavity. Close to the internal portions of the spermatic cords are the *seminal vesicles* and the *prostate,* both of which secrete fluids added to the semen at the time of ejaculation.

Undescended Testicles (Cryptorchidism) Sometimes a boy is born with either one or both testicles undescended. The missing testicle or testicles may have remained higher up in the abdomen, or halfway down in the testicular canal. Frequently, undescended testicles do descend spontaneously into the scrotal sac. If this does not occur by the time the child is six to nine years old, injections of anterior pituitary hormone or testosterone (male sex hormone) are given. Testicles which remain in the abdomen or the canal may become atrophic and result in sterility. If hormone treatment is unsuccessful, surgery is usually necessary.

SEXUAL HARMONY There is much more to marriage than sex, but a good sexual relationship is a powerful foundation. The sex act can contribute a deep and ever-renewable pleasure; it can allay conflicts, even when nothing is said. Since this is a vital part of marriage, it is unfortunate that even today sex still remains a somewhat taboo topic.

To the extent that sex is not guided by instinct—and in humans instinct is a small part—it is subject to learning and to improvement. Sex education should therefore be looked upon as normal, desirable, and (like a college education) worthy of time and effort. In general, most of the difficulties, and perhaps most of the learning of new lessons, confront the woman. This is not to deny that many men are too hasty and must learn to "slow down," as well as to be more thoughtful or considerate in their approach.

Women often face biological and psychological obstacles to sexual enjoyment. Their sexual drives are more delicately poised and therefore more readily thrown off by fatigue, worry, fear of pregnancy, or other emotions. A fair number of women seem to be unable to achieve an orgasm (climax) even in relatively favorable circumstances. Then, too, there is the lifelong accumulated burden produced by the upbringing which says that sex is not "nice," that a girl should be wary of a man's advances, that a woman cannot be too careful, and so forth. Although there is often a sound basis for these feelings in the young girl emerging into adolescence and in the young unmarried woman, negative feelings about men and sex should not be carried into marriage. The marital state will be happier if more positive feelings toward sexual relationships are developed.

Some common complaints made by husbands are that wives are uninterested, unresponsive, and unwilling. Possibly some men cannot be satisfied with less than a veritable "tiger," while others are simply searching for something that does not exist. Nonetheless, some of the difficulties they complain of *do* exist.

Based on the many things that marriage counselors hear, the following suggestions can be made to the wife: (1) to give freer expression to one's positive feelings—a woman can both speak of and show love in many ways: with a warm (not a routine) kiss, an affectionate caress, the sex act itself; (2) avoidance of a necessarily passive, silent, and acquiescent role in the sexual act—a woman can contribute actively to preliminary love-making as well as to the act itself; (3) demonstration of that "infinite variety" for which Cleopatra was praised—sexual variety can be the spice of life and one should therefore experiment with new approaches and new techniques; (4) recognition that it is not always possible to match up sexual desire—even if a woman's desire is slight on a particular occasion it is still possible to be a loving and responsive partner in the sexual act; and finally (5) when problems *do* come up, one must not hesitate to discuss them with either the husband or the doctor.

Frigidity Lack of responsiveness in sexual intercourse, sometimes to the point of absolute distaste, is referred to as frigidity in women. Frigidity is a complex state: it may exist at some times and not at others, and with one man but not another. In many women frigidity may be traced to severe or restrictive upbringing resulting in conscious or unconscious inhibiting feelings of guilt, and poor information or misinformation on the subject of sex. A woman who is brought up to believe that sex is an act of aggression on the part of the man rather than an act of mutual love may find that she is fearful and unresponsive in sexual situations. Also, in our society, there are contradictory attitudes toward sex at all levels. On the one hand, sex is always being emphasized in our entertainment, advertising, movies, and literature. On the other hand, it is simultaneously regarded as "not nice," as an activity that one has to be very secretive about, or as the one major aspect of living that has shameful associations. Were this not so, the fable that it is the stork who brings the baby would not have been invented.

In the more severe degrees of frigidity, fear and hostility always play a part. Fear of the man, fear of being hurt, fear of becoming pregnant may dominate a woman's thoughts and make her sexually unresponsive. If, for one or another reason traceable to her experiences with this or some other man, she has negative feelings toward him, then too she is likely to be frigid. There is little doubt that moderate degrees of frigidity, or at least inhibition about sex, are by no means uncommon among women. However, these inhibitions may be resolved by the progress of a successful marriage and by repetition of successful acts of sexual intercourse. Thus many women who early in marriage fail to experience a climax may do so as they grow more relaxed in the sexual relationship. Often coupled with increased responsiveness on their part is increased expertness on the part of the husband.

At worst, frigidity can break up a marriage; at best, it is bound to be a drag on it. It should, therefore, be dealt with as a serious problem and not be disregarded. The fact that a frigid woman can still have intercourse does not alter the desirability of improving this area of the marital relationship. The problem should be discussed with the family doctor or the gynecologist and, if considered advisable, with a psychotherapist. The great majority of cases of frigidity are susceptible of considerably improvement.

SEXUAL RELATIONS AFTER CHILDBIRTH As a general rule it can be predicted that there will be no significant changes in the sexual life after childbirth. True, there is first stretching, followed by shrinkage of the various parts. Then there is the healing of the incision which may have been made by the doctor to facilitate childbirth (episiotomy). However, the vagina and adjacent parts will resume their usual dimensions and sensitivity with respect to sexual functioning. A few woman may find that the vaginal opening seems tight after an episiotomy. A warm tub and the use of a lubricant will facilitate intercourse for them. As sexual relations are continued the feeling of tightness disappears.

The post-partum discharge, at first red, then white, called the lochia continues for some three weeks. In many women, by the time the lochia clears the usual sexual desires may be experienced. It is generally advised that sexual relations be postponed till the six-week visit to the doctor. In this, as in other matters, one should be guided by one's own doctor's advice regarding resumption of sex. A few doctors believe that sexual relations a bit earlier than this need not fall under an absolute ban, and certainly the husband is not likely to object.

Marked changes in attitude toward sexual relations are generally founded on emotional, not a physical, basis. A woman who has had a difficult pregnancy, a hard labor, and perhaps various kinds of discomfort afterward, may sometimes shrink from intercourse. She may harbor the thought that pregnancy and a new cycle of discomfort may result, even when contraceptive measures are practiced. In a few instances fear of pregnancy and therefore of intercourse may lead to frigidity. It may help such a person if she can be made to understand that with the new birth control pill 100% freedom from pregnancy can be guaranteed. Persistent fear in this kind of situation may require some form of psychotherapy. The reverse may also occur—a woman who has successfully and happily become a mother, is anxious to have more children, and has a good basic relationship with her husband may be more desirous and responsive sexually.

SEXUAL RELATIONS DURING PREGNANCY If all goes well, there is no need for change in a couple's usual pattern of sexual relations during most of a pregnancy. Intercourse may be continued as frequently as formerly, and if the wife is accustomed to having a climax, she may expect to continue to have one. In women with a history of frequent abortions (spontaneous miscarriages), or where there has been bleeding in the presence of pregnancy, sexual relations may be temporarily forbidden by the doctor; in some instances intercourse at about the time when a menstrual period would have appeared may thus be advised against for the first three months. Most doctors also advise that abstinence should be practiced during the last one to two months of the pregnancy. Intercourse is difficult at this time, especially during the last month, and there is a possibility—however remote—of injury or precipitation of labor.

After delivery, it is customary to advise against sexual relations until the six-week checkup visit. Among the contributing reasons for this are the presence of the vaginal discharge (*lochia*) and possibly also a healing *episiotomy*.

Some women experience tightness or pain after the healing of an episiotomy. The liberal use of lubricants may be of help, as is also a preliminary hot tub-bath. If the problem continues, the doctor should be consulted, since gentle dilation may sometimes be of value. Ordinarily an episiotomy will, if anything, contribute to enhanced sexual gratification.

As a rule, a woman, if nursing her child, will not be likely to ovulate and will therefore remain infertile. The probability is therefore high that she may have intercourse without contraception for at least the first few months of nursing. In the absence of nursing, her fertility will return much sooner; it is quite possible for such a woman to conceive even before she has had her first menstrual period after the delivery. Certainly with resumption of menstruation—i.e., with the first menstrual period—the possibility of a new pregnancy does return.

SHOCK (ELECTRIC) Most of the electric shocks sustained in the household are not likely to be dangerous unless one is wet and grounded as, for example, when someone standing in the bathtub touches a live electrical outlet. Serious shocks most often result from contact with a main power line which carries high voltages. Contact with such a line may lead to weakness or complete paralysis; unconsciousness may result, together with burns at the contact point.

It is of utmost important that rescuers should avoid touching not only the line but also the victim so long as the latter is in contact with it. If the line can be switched off promptly, do so! Otherwise push the line away from the victim, using a nonconductive material, such as wood, paper, or rubber. If the victim appears to have stopped breathing, artificial respiration should be started at once; this should be maintained until the doctor arrives, or until the victim is brought to the hospital.

SICKLE CELL ANEMIA Sickle cell anemia is the result of deformity of red blood cells which are crescent-shaped causing a crystallization of the hemoglobin within the cells, and resulting in the clogging of blood vessels. The cause of this chronic inherited defect is a fault in the DNA of a gene controlling the production of the abnormal S hemoglobin in the bone marrow. This disease affects 1 in 500 American Negroes and is marked by severe anemia, jaundice, abdominal, muscular, and joint pain, skin ulcerations, especially of the lower extremities, formation of bilirubin gallstones, bony absorption, recurrent infarctions of the spleen, kidneys, liver, and bowels, and many other complications.

The severity of the disease depends on the number of abnormal red blood cells and the quality of the blood flow at the arteriole-capillary-venule level. Sickle cell anemia is not life-threatening, however, it does restrict the freedom of the patient to participate in many of life's activities. Treatment of sickle cell may include analgesic medication, a hyperbaric oxygen chamber to reverse the sickling process and to re-establish the blood flow throughout the body. Blood transfusion is rarely necessary.

SKIN CARE   The care of the skin is not nearly so complicated as many cosmetic ads intimate. Also contrary to the ads, oiling, creaming, or moisturizing the skin will not prevent such aging changes as wrinkles. Wrinkling is due to changes in the subcantaneous tissue—the connective tissue underlying the epidermis—and agents applied to the surface of the skin will generally have no effect on the underlying connective tissue nor on the unknown and still uncontrolled connective tissue changes that occur with age.

Some women avoid the use of soap and water because they fear a drying effect. The most likely thing that would result from any oversoaping would be a slight flaking of the skin, which in actual fact seldom happens. The skin of the face generally has enough oil glands so that any drying produced by soap is very temporary, and surface film from oil secretion is rather quickly re-formed.

There is no objection to women creaming their faces as a cleansing procedure to substitute for use of soap if it produces no difficulty—it may occasionally lead to a case of acne or seborrhea. The skin of the body, being less oily than the face, *can* be overly dried by soaping. This is seen particularly during the winter, when the amount of secretion is diminished, and the skin tends to be overly dried because of overheated homes. Under these circumstances, in scrupulously clean individuals who like to take an overall soaping daily, some dryness and roughness of the skin with itching may occur. The itching is generally mild and is often referred to as "winter itch." The treatment is to decrease the amount of soaping, to use a soap containing cold cream or a similar agent, or to add oils to the tub or the washcloth. In the older age group particularly, because of decreased oil production, such special measures for replenishing and adding oils to the skin with the bath may be desirable.

Premature Aging   Probably the most important common factor in premature aging skin is excessive exposure to the sun. It has been convincingly shown that all of the characteristic changes that occur in the skin with the aging process are greatly accelerated by overexposure to sunlight. The deep tan developed by the sun worshipper gives a healthy outdoor look at the time, but in the long run will produce an unhealthy, leathery, aged skin. In addition, chronic exposure to the sun greatly increases the possibility of developing cancer of the skin. It would thus certainly be preferable to avoid a way of life of constant sunbathing which increases this likelihood. (The importance of this factor is illustrated by data which show that cancer of the skin of the face is a thousand times more common in Texas than in New York.)

One substance which seems to slow down the aging process in the skin is the female sex hormone. This hormone seems to increase the water content of the skin and decrease aging changes. Various methods of taking advantage of this effect of the female hormone have been tried. One has been to rub female hormone-containing creams into the skin. It has been shown that the hormone will get to the underlying connective tissues and exert an effect there. This approach has been frowned upon because the hormone thus absorbed could have indirect effects on the ovaries of women prior to the menopause, and conceivably on the breasts as well. In recent years, however, there has been a reconsideration of the effects of female hormone, with an increasing tendency to give the hormone to women past the menopause for a variety of sound reasons.

SKIN CARE DURING INFANCY   The newborn child has a skin which is soft, smooth, tender, and velvety. When he is born, he is covered with some blood and a cheesy material called "vernix caseosa." The skin becomes red later; then when it turns lighter again, peeling occurs. It has long been considered axiomatic that every newborn infant required a soap-and-water bath. However, many physicians now realize that the vernix caseosa has a protective character and prevents infections and irritations of the skin if left on for a few days following birth.

When bathing infants, ordinary castile soap may be used. The skin should never be rubbed, but only patted gently. Perfumed soaps are not necessary, and may even be harmful because they may act as irritants and sensitize the skin. It is not usually necessary to use oils on a baby's skin unless it is extremely dry or peeling. Oils produce a blocking of the sweat ducts and glands. They block the bacteria normally found on the skin and produce postules and clogged glands. Many of the baby oils available contain certain chemicals which either irritate the skin or act as sensitizers.

On the other hand, a mildly astringent liquid, such as pure witch hazel, is cleansing and cooling and does not irritate the skin. Unscented talcum powder may be used instead of fancy perfumed dusting powders. It is now thought best to avoid the use of boric acid as a powder, ointment, or wet dressing. Boric acid is a poison, and instances of death have been reported from its absorption through the skin.

SKIN CONDITIONS AND INFECTIONS

Acne   Acne may be regarded as one of the tolls exacted for becoming an adult; unknown in children prior to puberty, acne's onset is associated with sexual development. For reasons not well understood, puberty seems to exert a stimulating effect on the oil glands, chiefly those of the face and upper trunk. The most active hormone in this respect is the male sex hormone; acne is thus worse in males. Some of the secretions of the ovary and the adrenals in women, however, also contribute to acne.

The first stage of acne, that of the "blackhead," is caused by accumulation of secretion in the little duct of an oil gland which may have become plugged up. Chemical changes in the secretion turn it dark, resulting in the blackhead itself. Enlargement and inflammation of the oil gland may then occur, resulting in pimple formation. A variety of other factors may increase or decrease the severity of this process. Lack of sunshine, poor general health, the imminence of menstruation—perhaps also emotional stress—may aggravate acne; so, too, will an excess of certain food items, such as chocolate, nuts, candy, and fatty foods (and perhaps also food items rich in iodide, such as shellfish). Secondary infection by some of the bacteria that are generally present on the skin, notably the staphylococcal organisms, will aggravate the process.

Most cases of acne leave no scarring; with more severe forms, healing results in the formation of "pits." Even in the absence of scarring, many teenagers find acne a distressing disorder which increases their doubts about their appearance and makes them feel unhappily conspicuous; this condition should therefore not be dismissed as a passing growth-event. A normal teenager interested in appearance will appreciate parental and medical attention directed to acne.

Treatment. Although acne is treated in different ways by various doctors, the following are generally useful hints:

1. Soap-and-water cleanliness is important. The face should be washed several times daily. One of the newer germ-killing soaps may be helpful in keeping down the element of infection.

2. A cotton pledget soaked in rubbing alcohol may be wiped across the forehead, nose, or other oily and broken-

out area several times daily. Prepackaged pledgets moistened with alcohol are available in tinfoil and are easily carried about.

3. Lotions and creams which cut down the activity of the oil glands can be applied one or more times daily as directed; most contain sulphur, salicylic acid, and similar ingredients, and have a drying and peeling effect.

4. Sunlight—to the point of slight tanning and burning— is good for acne. The acne patient should get plenty of sun in the summertime and might well take ultraviolet lamp treatments throughout the winter.

5. Where pus formation and the element of infection seem important, antibiotics may be prescribed.

Acne Rosacea This is a skin disorder, predominantly of the face, which bears some resemblance to ordinary acne. It is, however, more common in women, particularly past the age of thirty, and especially in those with a lifelong tendency to easy blushing. Redness of the skin is an almost constant finding, usually associated with oiliness, enlargement of the oil glands, and pustule formations; it is made worse by sunlight, hot beverages, alcoholic drinks, and emotional tension. It has been found that many patients with acne rosacea lead psychologically stressful lives and have difficulty in relaxing. The nose, which is most often the first area involved, usually shows some degree of redness much of the time; later the forehead, cheeks, and chin tend to show involvement. The tiny blood vessels of the skin become more prominent, and this may persist even after treatment.

Treatment. Treatment somewhat resembles that for acne, except that sun should be avoided, along with extremes of weather and hot or alcoholic beverages. Sulphur ointment is useful when applied to the skin, and frequent washing with soap and water is desirable. Learning a "take-it-easy" attitude may well be made part of the treatment.

Athlete's Foot This is a common fungus infection of the feet, often chronic, and difficult to eradicate because of the hardiness of the organism responsible for it. In most instances it is more of a minor nuisance than a major skin disorder. However, a relatively mild form may spread in hot weather with great rapidity. Minor forms are found in the skin between the toes, most commonly between the third, fourth, and fifth toes and seldom involving the big toe. The skin has a soggy or opaque appearance, or may appear thinner than usual and be reddened. Oozing and cracking can occur and produce itching and pain. Occasionally the eruption spreads over the sole of the foot and produces patches of redness, swelling, and moisture. Sometimes infection with other organisms occurs; increased swelling, and pain and pus formation, may follow. However, in another form of the disease the eruption is dry and scaly. In certain sensitive individuals an eruption—known as the "id" reaction— which resembles tiny blisters may appear on the palms and fingers. This is not an actual infection of the skin of the hands but is rather an allergic reaction to some substance produced by the fungi in the feet; the id eruption clears up when the fungi infection of the feet is brought under control.

Treatment. Treatment of athlete's foot will depend upon the extent and kind of infection present. For an acute, spreading, weeping, or secondarily-infected eruption the patient may have to get off his feet for a time. Soaking in potassium permanganate solution or Burow's solution may be useful at this stage. Once this acute stage is controlled, the usual measures can be employed. These include the following:

1. Applying Whitfield's ointment.

2. Applying solutions and ointments containing fatty acids.

3. Washing feet daily with a bacteria-killing soap.

4. Wearing open-toed shoes or sandals, with as much exposure of the feet as possible. The organism cannot grow on a dry foot.

5. Wearing cotton hose since they are more absorptive than synthetic or wool.

6. Continuing the powders and ointments even after the condition seems to have cleared, since athlete's food is notorious for recurring.

Dandruff Dandruff, referred to by doctors as seborrheic dermatitis, can vary from a little flakiness deposited on the hair and clothing to larger, reddened or crusty patches on the scalp. It is considered a disturbance of the oil glands of the scalp; it is not uncommonly found together with acne or with seborrheic dermatitis of the chest and face—all of which involve some disordered function of the oil-making (sebaceous) glands. Most cases of dandruff are mild and need not cause concern, for they do not worsen with the passage of time. Sometimes if a shampooing is skipped, particularly if the hair grows thickly, some itching may occur. This may also be aggravated by oily or greasy hairdressings and by hair-styling which plasters the hair down and prevents airing of the scalp.

Milder cases of dandruff can be kept under control simply by shampooing once or twice a week. Tincture of green soap, available at the drugstore counter, may be more efficacious than ordinary soap. In addition there are various prepared shampoos specifically designed to be of aid in dandruff control. Many of these can be bought over the counter, but other effective ones are available on the doctor's prescription.

Eczema Eczema is an allergic skin disorder characterized by itching, scaling, and oozing lesions. (In urticaria, a less severe form, hives appear which are raised red wheals of either small or giant size; these are extremely itchy.) The itching causes scratching which in turn produces bleeding; frequently secondary infection appears. In infants, eczema usually appears first on the face, the cheeks, and the creases and folds of the arms and legs. Eczema may be caused by sensitivity to milk, eggs, wool, soaps, oils, etc.

Treatment. Treatment of eczema is directed toward removing the offending allergen and applying soothing lotions and ointments to the skin in order to heal it. Wet, oozing types of eczema can be treated with Burow's solution compresses, or with soaking in potassium permanganate. More severe cases require medication such as cortisone and cortisone-containing ointments. Treatment can also be accomplished by desensitization with specific antigens.

Impetigo Contagiosa This is a contagious disease of the skin characterized by postules and crusts. The crusted type is caused by *streptococcus pyogenes;* the bulbous type is caused by *staphylococcus pyogenes.* It is a common secondary invader of any irritation or rash. It appears most commonly on the face, hands, neck, ears, and upper and lower extremities. It starts as a pimple which becomes a blister, filling with pus. Then the yellowish material drains out and produces a raw, wet, pustular surface. Impetigo is treated with antibiotics, both in ointment form and by injection.

Neurodermatitis This is an often stubborn skin reaction which generally occurs in older children. It is characterized by itchy, dry, red, raised, scaly lesions which become thickened so that they appear lichenified. The most common areas for this rash are in the creases of the elbows, the back of the neck, and the creases behind the knees. Treatment is the same as for many allergic conditions of the skin.

Psoriasis This is a common chronic skin disorder which tends to run in some family groupings. A major feature of the disorder is scale formation; the scales are white, are often shed in large numbers, and are most commonly found over the knees, elbows, and the scalp. There is seldom any itching. Although psoriasis can occur at any age, it is not common before the age of four. Various general infections and menstruation make psoriasis worse; pregnancy often improves it. Small localized forms of the disease can be left alone. More extensive forms may be discouragingly conspicuous. It is important to recognize that, although psoriasis is chronic, it can be helped and the lesions may stay cleared for many months after successful treatment.

Treatment. Sunlight often helps psoriasis, this being the basis for the approach known as the Goekerman treatment. In this, a coal tar ointment is applied to the area of psoriasis, and increasing doses of ultraviolet from an ultraviolet lamp are given daily. The ultraviolet exposure is built up in ordinary tanning treatments, by increasing the exposure slightly each day. After the treatment, the scales can be scrubbed away and more ointment rubbed into the area. Another form of treatment suitable when the disease is not too extensive involves application of a steroid (cortisone-type) ointment. The area is then covered with Saran® wrap. The Saran wrap may be left undisturbed for several days, and the treatment may be repeated as directed by the physician. Sometimes dietary approaches, such as low-protein intake, may be tried.

Ringworm (Tinea Circinata)   Ringworm of the skin is a contagious fungus disease, showing a circular lesion with a raised border. It may be contracted from animals, household pets or from direct contact with infected persons. It appears first as a small pink-to-reddish round patch (the size of a small pea to that of a quarter), with some scaliness in the center. It is very itchy. Treatment is by the proper use of fungicidal remedies. Tincture of iodine, sulfur, ammoniated mercury, and other drugs have been used with success.

Scabies   This is a highly contagious itching rash which consists of little papules, vesicles (blisters), and crusts resulting from secondary infection and scratching. It is caused by an organism, *Sarcoptes scabiei* (mite), also called the "itch mite." Usually, if one member of a family has this condition, others become infected. It is frequently seen as a wavy line on the palms of the hands, the soles of the feet, or on other areas of the body. The itching usually occurs at night. It is generally necessary for a physician to make the diagnosis; he can then prescribe the proper medication to clear up the condition.

Urticaria (Hives) and Angioneurotic Edema   Hives are small, red, raised lesions of the skin which break out and cause severe itching. They may appear in single pimples or in clusters and may be large in diameter or very tiny.

Giant hives are characterized by very large areas of swelling (edema) which may appear in any part of the skin or mucous membranes. There may be swelling and puffiness of the eyes and lids, and puffiness of the throat in which there may be a sensation of choking. The skin may become red and itchy. The causes are generally the same as those of hives, that is, some specific allergen or possibly a psychological cause. The treatment is the same as for other allergies.

SKIN CONDITIONS IN INFANTS

Cradle Cap (Seborrheic Dermatitis)   This is a condition in infants characterized by thick yellow-brown crusts on the scalp. It occasionally appears on the brows and behind the ears. It is often due to inadequate cleansing of the scalp.

Bland oils (olive oil, sweet almond oil, petrolatum, etc.) are used to soften the crusts. Then the hair can be washed and the crusts fine-combed out. If this home treatment does not effectively clear the scalp, consult your doctor.

Diaper Rash (Ammonia Dermatitis)   This is a rash characterized by red, raised pimples and flat areas around the surfaces of the thighs, buttocks, and frequently on the lower half of the abdomen. There is usually a strong odor of ammonia present in the diapers.

The treatment of this condition, first of all, is to remove the wet diaper as soon as possible, so that it does not remain in contact with the tender skin. Use of ointments or powders to prevent bacterial decomposition in this area will help. There are also pills, to be given by mouth, which metabolize the ammonia in the urine to its less toxic product and prevent its further formation. Severe diaper rash may go on to secondary infection and require use of antibiotics. Special superabsorbent diaper liners are also helpful in reducing rash.

Intertrigo   This is a chafing from the effects of heat and moisture, and is seen in the creases of the skin, particularly in fat babies. It usually occurs in the groin, neck and underneath the armpits. Proper cleansing and proper washing of the skin, as well as changing soiled diapers frequently, is important in the prevention of this condition.

Perianal Dermatitis   This is an area of redness, inflammation, and rash localized around the anus and rectal area. Its cause is not known, but sometimes the stool and its chemicals produce it by irritating the skin around the rectum. It may be confused with typical "diaper rash," which usually has a strong ammonia odor associated with it. In perianal dermatitis there is usually no odor of ammonia.

Proper cleansing of the perianal region by using cotton moistened by warm water or vaseline, with care to remove all the stool from the area, is important. It may be necessary to leave the diaper off and expose the child to a 100-watt bulb, placed about 18 inches above the buttocks. This will dry the rash and help to clear it.

Prickly Heat (Miliaria)   This is caused by overheating and excessive clothing. Approximately 75 to 80 per cent of body heat loss occurs through the skin by evaporation or perspiration. Prickly heat occurs during the hot summer days and is characterized by tiny, red, raised pimples all over the skin. Witch hazel water is an excellent evaporating lotion for the prevention and treatment of this condition. It may be patted on the skin daily, and followed by dusting with ordinary cornstarch or an unscented talc. Bathing in starch or bicarbonate of soda is helpful in overcoming skin irritation.

Roseola Infantum   Contagious.

Cause. Virus.

Incubation period. 1 to 2 weeks.

Symptoms. Convulsions frequently usher in roseola with high fever up to 105° and 106°F. There is little to account for the sudden onset and marked irritability in these infants except, sometimes, a slight sore throat. The fever remains high and fluctuating for three or four days. Then it suddenly drops and a rash breaks out, usually on the trunk, subsequently spreading to the arms and neck, occasionally on the face. The rash is light pink, flat, approximately the size of small split peas. It fades within twenty-four to forty-eight hours.

There is no treatment necessary because by the time the rash breaks out and the disease is recognized, it is over. Roseola resembles regular measles, allergic drug rashes, and German measles. It is usually necessary for a doctor to distinguish which condition is present.

SMALLPOX (VARIOLA)   Contagious.

Cause. Virus.

Incubation period. Usually 12 to 14 days, but may be as long as 16 to 21 days.

Symptoms. The disease is transmitted by droplet infection via the respiratory tract. There is usually a long period of mild symptoms, such as fever, headache, malaise, and back pain, before the rash breaks out. A slight rash, which resembles measles or scarlet fever, may appear during the first two days. Then it becomes raised and pustular and begins to look exactly like smallpox vaccinations. These are first distributed mainly on arms and legs, then travel toward the trunk and body. Then tend to be deeper and the centers are depressed. Whereas in chicken pox there are different stages of the rash present at the time, in smallpox they are all more or less at the same stage at each phase of the disease.

Prevention. Vaccination with the virus of cow pox is performed on the skin during the first year of life. In three or four days a pimple forms which becomes a blister, then fills with pus. There may be a red ring around the vaccination about the size of a dime or quarter. After five to seven days a fever may develop, and the child may become irritable and fretful. The scab which forms on the vaccination should be protected with a bandage until it falls off spontaneously; otherwise it may leave a deep, pitted scar. If the vaccination does not "take" the first time, it should be repeated after a few months. It is extremely dangerous to vaccinate a child who has any open sores, allergic rashes, or eczema until the rash is cleared completely. Nor should vaccine be administered to a child in whose family any of the above skin rashes exist (unless the others have already been vaccinated). Open skin lesions will attract the virus and start a case flaring with scattered smallpox lesions. This condition, in a child who has eczema, is called "eczema vaccinatum" and will leave serious skin scars.

SMOKING The only form of smoking that has been particularly singled out as a health hazard is the smoking of cigarettes. The risks associated with smoking pipes and cigars are markedly less. The case against cigarettes has been building up for many years and was given impressive endorsement by the Surgeon General's Report in 1964; however, as early as 1938 it had been demonstrated that heavy smokers, on average, lived four years less than non-smokers. Cigarette smoking unquestionably contributes to a great many major lung diseases, ranging from lung cancer to chronic bronchitis and a condition known as emphysema which produces breathlessness on effort. There is some evidence that it also increases the work of the heart and that the incidence of heart attacks is higher in smokers. The major problem is not with establishing the truth of the accusations, but rather with the difficulty cigarette smokers encounter in giving up the habit. A lucky few find it can be given up with ease; the majority find it difficult and trying. Nevertheless, medical men who best know the facts deplore the willingness of smokers to run the risks involved.

Surveys indicate that the highest percentage of ex-smokers is to be found among doctors. If men who know tobacco best have quit—why shouldn't you? Insofar as pregnancy is concerned, there is no evidence that cigarette smoking has any significant effect on the development of the child. Some evidence does indicate that the child may be slightly smaller in cigarette-smoking mothers, but the difference is not very significant. However, our knowledge about tobacco is only a recently acquired one and is still undergoing change.

Since no one pretends to know it all, it might not be considered unreasonable to include tobacco in a general ban against all drugs—except the necessary ones—during pregnancy. Since the nausea often experienced in early pregnancy tend to do away with the desire to smoke anyway, giving up cigarettes for the duration, if not longer, may be a relatively easier step at that time. Certainly heavy smoking, one or two packs a day or more, is best drastically cut down. Statistics indicate that all of the difficulties produced by tobacco increase considerably above the ten-cigarette per day limit.

SPINAL COLUMN The spinal column consists of a series of vertebrae which extend from the skull down to a terminal portion. The latter can be felt adjacent to the rectal region and is known as the coccyx or tailbone. The vertebrae are sometimes referred to in terms of their location; the cervical vertebrae, of which there are seven, form the neck region; the twelve thoracic vertebrae have ribs extending from them and from the main bony support to the trunk; the five lumbar vertebrae form the small of the back. These twenty-four vertebrae are capable of movement. Below them are the five sacral segments which contribute to the posterior aspect of the pelvis, and below those, the four little segments which make up the coccyx. The sacral and coccygeal segments are sometimes referred to as false or fixed vertebrae, and lack motion.

Between the true vertebrae there are fibrous disks with a central more gelatinous portion called the *nucleus pulposus*. Occasionally the nucleus pulposus works loose from its central location and impinges on one of the spinal nerves. This produces a radiating type of neuritis which may be quite severe and is sometimes referred to as a radiculitis; it is a common cause of sciatica. Between the vertebrae are openings for the spinal nerves, called the intervertebral foramina. Occasionally bony spurs that form because of osteoarthritis can produce pressure on the emerging nerves—another form of neuritis.

Disorders of the Spinal Column The infant has a backbone which is a single long curve from the head down to the buttocks. As the child grows and assumes the upright position, a series of curves normally appears in the vertebral column. This produces two hollows, one in the neck, the other in the small of the back, plus two outward bowings, one in the trunk and the other in the sacral region. It is thought that the curve in the lumbosacral region is one of the anatomical "facts of life" which leads to the frequency of backache in human beings; it can be regarded as one of the penalties for assuming our erect position.

Curvature of the spine to one side or the other is most often seen in the thoracic region and produces a condition known as scoliosis. Unequal rates of growth in the centers which lay down the bone of the vertebrae can lead to scoliosis. There is also a hereditary background, for it may be seen in more than one member of a family. Mild degrees of this disorder can be disregarded, but in other instances the curvature may be progressive. This can lead to various types of chest deformities. There are usually associated pains in the chest and there may be interference with lung function. Various orthopedic procedures for correcting scoliosis are available.

Since the vertebrae encase the spinal cord, injuries to them pose a special threat. Cord damage can produce symptoms varying from pain to weakness and on to paralysis. Hence the reason for caution in treating accident victims who may have a back injury. Some of the loss of height seen in elderly individuals, particularly women, is due to narrowing of the vertebrae. This is a condition known as osteoporosis—a loss of substance and calcium from bone. The vertebrae, being subject to the stress of weight bearing, may be among the first bones to give indication of this disorder. Various factors contribute to this condition, including inadequate calcium intakes over the years and the diminishing hormones after the change of life.

STEAM INHALATIONS, HOW TO PREPARE Steam inhalations may be prescribed when children have croup, hoarseness, sore throat, or difficulty in breathing. Breathing a warm, moist mixture of air usually relieves the swelling in the tissues of the nose and throat and eases breathing. There are many good commercial vaporizers for sale. If you buy one, it is important to get the kind which will run automatically all night so that you do not have to get up every few hours to replace the water in it.

If you wish to make a homemade vaporizer, these are the things you will require: a hotplate with a teakettle, a long funnel which you can make out of newspapers or aluminum foil, an umbrella, and some sheets. The umbrella is used to make a canopy over the child's bed. The sheet is draped over the umbrella so that it makes a tent. This permits the steam to enter only the area in the child's bed and not dissipate itself in the rest of the room. A blanket may be used over the sheet. Since there will be a great deal of moisture, it may be well to wrap the child's head in a towel or scarf, so that the wet hair does not become uncomfortable.

The teakettle, with water in it, is placed on the hotplate on a stool or chair near the side of the bed. The funnel is directed so that the steam does not hit the child directly in the face, nor should it be close enough to cause a steam burn. It is very important to avoid scalding. The water can be kept boiling as long as treatment is required. Fresh water may be added as needed. It is important to make sure that the kettle is not within reach of the child's hand. It is best to stay with him while the treatment is continuing.

STERILITY AND INFERTILITY Sterility is said to exist in a woman when, despite normal sexual relations, she fails to become pregnant. A somewhat related condition consists of difficulty in becoming pregnant as often as is desired, as may occur when a couple has one or two children although they attempt to have more. If no contraceptive methods are used, a young, sexually vigorous couple can anticipate that pregnancy will occur within a year, and it may, of course, occur quite a bit sooner. If it becomes clear with the passage of time that the marriage is a sterile one, a "sterility work-up" may be called for.

Since a sterile marriage can be due to the male rather than the female, and since the male partner's role is easy to evaluate, the husband may be checked first. After establishing that he is in good health and suffers no endocrine or other disease which might affect sexual performance, a semen examination will generally be the next step. By examining such a specimen the doctor can determine whether a normal number of sperm cells are being furnished, and whether these cells appear normal under the microscope.

The equivalent question to be answered in the case of the woman is whether or not she is ovulating, that is, whether an egg is being formed and released from the ovaries each month. There are various ways of establishing this, some simple, others complicated. One of the simplest is the daily temperature record. This involves taking the temperature with a specially designed thermometer the first thing in the morning before arising, and recording the temperature. In a normal cycle there is generally a slight temperature rise at about the middle of the cycle, corresponding to the time of ovulation. The temperature rise remains for the next two weeks, then rapidly declines with the onset of menstruation. Such a temperature change around mid-cycle is fairly good, though not conclusive, evidence of ovulation.

Sometimes a blockage of the tubes which run from the ovary to the uterus may be responsible for sterility. This can be determined by a tubal insufflation test. In this procedure air is blown up into the tubes and the pressure recorded by a measuring device. An X-ray can be taken simultaneously. The test will reveal whether or not a blockage of the tubes is present. Other tests that may be performed include analysis of the urine for its hormone content, which may also give evidence for ovulation, and biopsies.

Both general and specific measures are often indicated in cases of infertility. Moderate to marked degrees of overweight in women may be associated with menstrual irregu-

larity and lack of fertility, so that a reducing program may be advised. Some doctors almost routinely give some of their patients thyroid by mouth, on the theory that its generally stimulating value may be of use. It is often advised that sexual relations be restricted to the time of ovulation, or at least more frequently indulged in then. It is also sometimes advised that women lie on their backs with their legs drawn up for perhaps a half hour after intercourse. Occasionally plastic operations on the tubes if there is evidence of blockage, or for repositioning a uterus that is very markedly tipped backwards, are advised. In the rare instances where failure to form eggs in the ovary is the cause for sterility, with the tubes and everything else seemingly normal hormone preparations designed to produce ovulation have been experimented with successfully.

SUNBURN The sun's rays are capable of producing injury to the skin quite comparable to that produced by a flame. One of the chief differences is that in sunburn the extend of the injury may be seen only after some hours, and its development is gradual. In addition to marked reddening and burning sensations, blistering may occur. When a considerable skin area is involved, the individual may feel sick and have chilly sensations, weakness, and perhaps also headache and some fever.

In most instances sunburn is due to an overenthusiastic attempt to become tanned too rapidly. It sometimes results from falling asleep while out in the sun, something that is often avoidable. Blondes and redheads are generally more susceptible than brunettes, and infants and children are more susceptible than adults. Certain drugs, as some of the sulfonamides, may also sensitize the skin to the sun. Remember, too, that pregnancy also increases susceptibility to sunburning.

A brunette should probably have no more than one or two fifteen-minute exposures at the first sunning. As pigmentation develops, skin tolerance increases and the periods of exposure can be lengthened. Blondes and other with sensitive skins should probably get no more than five minutes of sun under the same circumstances. Reflections from sand, water, and ice increase the intensity of the exposure time. Numerous commercial preparations are available for screening out the skin-damaging components of sunshine while permitting tanning to occur.

Mild cases of sunburn are often disregarded; the discomfort can be somewhat relieved by powders containing zinc oxide and zinc stearate, or by local dabbing with calamine lotion or with cold cream. Where there has been some blistering, oatmeal or starch baths will be soothing. A starch bath is prepared by mixing two cups of cornstarch with water to form a paste and adding it to a tub bath. After soaking in this, the individual may allow the starch to dry on the skin. Aspirin and other pain-diminishing drugs may be used for the burning pain. Steroids are sometimes prescribed to diminish the reaction in the skin. Peeling of the skin and tanning are the usual consequences of a sunburn, and these may be more marked in a pregnant woman. For a severe sunburn, especially if there is any sign of infection in the blisters, a doctor should be consulted.

SUPPOSITORIES Suppositories are specially designed and molded solids which are inserted into a bodily orifice. Their composition is such that they melt at body temperature and release their medicinal agents. Rectal and vaginal suppositories are by far the most common. Occasionally, a suppository destined to be introduced into the urethra, the urinary channel, may be prescribed. Many suppositories have a cocoa-butter base or other ingredients which soften at room temperature, particularly on hot days. This may make them more difficult to insert, in which case they are probably best kept in the refrigerator.

Hemorrhoidal suppositories generally contain a mixture of medicines designed to promote healing in combination with a local anesthetic which will relieve some of the pain or discomfort. When both external and internal hemorrhoids are present, the external ones may be lightly coated by rubbing them with the suppository before insertion. The familiar glycerine suppository, generally dispensed in adult and child sizes, releases glycerine as it melts. This produces a local irritant effect and initiates a desire to move the bowels. More recent suppositories for the same purpose contain agents which stimulate the bowel musculature and may produce a movement within five to ten minutes. A variety of drugs are available in suppository form. They are particularly useful when nausea or vomiting occur.

Vaginal suppositories are widely used, particularly for the treatment of infections such as trichomoniasis and moniliasis. Vaginal suppositories contain such varied agents as antibiotics, and even so simple an agent as lactose, a sugar which in the course of its breakdown will raise the vaginal acidity.

TEETH The milk teeth, or temporary teeth (deciduous) are all erupted by two and half years of age. There are twenty of them. They appear in approximately the following order:

6 to 8 months—2 lower central incisors
8 to 12 months—4 upper incisors; 2 lower lateral incisors
12 to 16 months—4 anterior molars
16 to 20 months—4 canines
12 to 30 months—4 posterior molars

In order to determine approximately how many temporary teeth should be present in your child, subtract six from the age of the child in months. That is, at ten months your child should have approximately four teeth.

There are thirty-two permanent teeth. These appear in approximately the following order:

6 years of age—4 first molars
7 to 9 years of age—8 incisors
10 to 12 years—8 bicuspids
11 to 12 years—4 canines
13 years—4 second molars
17 to 22 years—4 third molars

Salivation begins at about three or four months of age. In most instances, infants drool and do not swallow the saliva. This usually indicates that teething will begin shortly. Many infants become slightly irritable and fussy, with occasional low fevers and insomnia, during the period preceding the eruption of teeth. The temperature usually does not go above 100° or 100.5°F. The gums may be painful and sore, and there are many medications which can be rubbed on them to relieve the pain. In addition, aspirin and teething rings may be used. If fever persists, call your doctor.

Fluorides Fluorides retard the development of cavities in the teeth of children, hence some communities have fluoridated their water supplies. If your water supply is fluoridated, it will not be necessary to give your child supplementary fluorides in his vitamins. However, there is considerable controversy regarding the safety of administering fluorides, which have been the subject of many large-scale studies and series for years. If your child should develop mottling, or speckling of the teeth, it may be an indication that fluorides should be stopped.

TEETH, CARE OF Children can be taught to brush their own teeth from about the age of two. It has recently been shown that children who from infancy drink water containing minute quantities of fluoride do not develop as many cavities as those who do not. If your community does not have fluoridated water, it may be desirable to add fluoride to your child's diet in the form of fluoridated vitamins.

Regular visits to the dentist will help in maintaining healthy teeth. Healthy teeth are important for general good health. They make us more attractive, help us speak well, and help us digest food by chewing it properly. Good nutrition with all the essential food elements is necessary to develop and maintain healthy teeth and gums. When food particles are left between the teeth, bacteria in the mouth produce acids that dissolve the enamel and form cavities. It is, therefore, advisable, to brush teeth after eating in order to remove trapped food.

Brushing should be performed away from the gums instead of toward them so that food will not be pushed under the gum margin. Separate toothbrushes should belong to each member of the family and not be used interchangeably.

Pyorrhea (Periodontitis) This is a condition that attacks the tissues around the teeth. It causes the tooth sockets to become loose, and finally the teeth either fall out or must be removed. The infection begins with an inflammation of the gums called gingivitis. The gums bleed easily and food wedges in the spaces between the teeth. If there is also malocclusion (upper and lower teeth which do not fit together), it may contribute to infections of the gum. In cases where the upper and lower teeth do not fit together properly, a dentist may decide that braces or other treatment may be necessary to get them into proper alignment.

TEETH—MALOCCLUSION Malocclusion refers to departures from the normal in the way in which the teeth meet. As with many other facial features, hereditary factors may play a part. Thus, one may see "buckteeth" and other disorders in several members of one family. Because of the genes determining the size of the upper and lower jaw may be inherited separately from the two parents, a structural disharmony with malocclusion may result.

Too early loss of baby teeth may allow a shifting from the normal position of some of the permanent teeth. In fact, even in the adult, loss of teeth frequently leads to shifts in the position of adjacent teeth, and production of an acquired malocclusion. In the young child, such a shift is sometimes prevented by placing a device between the remaining teeth so that they will not move together and crowd a tooth that is still to come; such a device is referred to as a "space saver." Other causes for malocclusion are: failure of certain teeth to erupt; eruption of teeth in such a manner that significant spaces exist; or out-of-line eruption of teeth.

Much of the loss of teeth experienced by middle-aged individuals is not due to dental decay but to bad bite. As a result of bad bite, there is a resorption of bone around the sockets, with loosening of the teeth. This can lead to their ultimate loss.

Malocclusion also increases the incidence of dental decay; hence most dentists believe that correction of most malocclusions is well worth the time, effort, and expense. Usually wires or molds are used to slowly push some of the teeth into a more desirable location. In order to do this and achieve a good bite, several teeth may sometimes have to be pulled—as in those instances where the jaw is small and the teeth are crowded. Children wearing the various braces and bands that are necessary may be somewhat more subject to dental decay. They should accordingly be cautioned against eating candy or sweet and sticky foods, drinking carbonated beverages, and chewing gum.

TEMPERATURE, TAKING Temperature indicates the heat of the body. It may be taken in many ares of the body.

In infants and children the rectal area is the one generally accepted since it determines the internal temperature of the body most readily. Small children should not be permitted to hold a glass thermometer in the mouth. They will often bite it off or permit it to drop and break.

There are two types of thermometers—rectal and oral. The rectal thermometer has a blunt, short bulb containing the mercury. The oral thermometer has a long thin bulb. A thermometer should be held at the end opposite to the mercury. It should never be placed or cleansed in hot water, since this would shoot the mercury up past the level at which the temperature is calibrated and break the thermometer. Normal temperature is about 98.6° to 99.4°F. with fluctuations of 0.2 to 0.6 degrees. It may sometimes be as low as 97°F.

To take a child's temperature, the child should be placed on one's lap, lying prone or on his back, and the thermometer lubricated with vaseline (or some other lubricant) and inserted about one-third to halfway into the rectum. It is held there for about two to three minutes, removed, and cleansed with a piece of alcohol-soaked cotton. The temperature is read and recorded, than the thermometer is shaken down with a snapping motion of the wrist. This reduces the mercury to below the normal level. If this is not done, then when one takes the temperature again it will show a recording at a higher-than-normal level.

Temperature taken by mouth may be slightly lower than the taken by rectum. Sometimes there is as much as one degree of difference.

Temperature can be taken under the armpits or in the groin by placing the thermometer in one of these areas, with instructions to keep the arm or leg close to the body. It may be necessary to keep the thermometer in this position for five to seven minutes in order to get an accurate reading. Temperature should be taken every three or four hours, and if the fever is high, every hour. (See also FEVER.)

TETANUS (LOCKJAW) Contagious.
Cause. Bacterial. *Clostridium tetani.*
Incubation period. 1 to 3 weeks.

The infection is via a contaminated wound. The organism which causes this disease is widely distributed in the soil in many parts of the world. Under certain conditions, it gets into the skin and bloodstream and produces several poisons. One of these destroys red blood cells, another injures white blood cells and produces a poison which causes the muscle rigidity and spasm for which this disease is noted. There is no suitable skin test to determine immunity. Any type of wound may give rise to tetanus if the germs enter that area. Any injury or skin cut which has been contaminated by dirt should therefore be carefully cleansed and treated, and immunization given to prevent tetanus. Tetanus is also popularly known as "lockjaw." The reason for this name is that during the onset, which is gradual, there is increasing spasm of the neck and jaw muscles (trismus) with difficulty in swallowing and opening the mouth.

Symptoms. They include irritability, fever, chills, pains, headaches, convulsions, and coma. The spasm is quite characteristic in which the body is rigid as a board. The head is drawn back with the legs and feet extended. The arms are stiff and the hands clenched. The spasm of the facial muscles results in a fixed expression which looks like a sardonic grin.

Treatment. Tetanus is a very serious disease. The mortality rate, even with treatment, is about 50 per cent. Immediate hospitalization is necessary and tetanus antitoxin plus sedatives are required. It is extremely important to prevent choking. Antibiotics and antitoxin are usually used.

Prevention. Tetanus toxoid injections, either singly or in triple toxoid form, followed by booster injections, should be started during the first year of life.

THUMB-SUCKING
Sucking is reflex activity in newborn infants. Stroking the lips produces sucking as soon as the infant is given a nipple. It is one of the child's first pleasures and satisfactions. Unless adequate sucking is given to children, many develop unsatisfied "oral" needs in later life. This may be seen in overeating, smoking, chewing, and other oral excesses. Some babies finish the bottle rapidly, not really getting enough sucking. They may continue to suck on their thumbs or fingers because it is pleasurable. Pacifiers are sucked instead of fingers by some infants.

Sucking needs usually diminish after the children are able to drink from a cup or glass, but many of them continue to suck their thumbs for years afterwards. This persistence of immature gratification may be an indication of unsatisfied emotional needs, inadequate attention to the child so that he has to look to himself for gratification; or it may be a habit which the parents have never really taken the trouble to discourage. If thumb-sucking persists into later years, and there is pushing of the dental arch, disorders of the teeth and gums may occur. Parents can often divert young children from sucking their fingers by playing with them and keeping them occupied in other ways.

Most cases of finger- or thumb-sucking are outgrown after the age of two or so, when the child is able to move about on his own and is not entirely dependent upon parents for the satisfaction of needs. Most children who feel a firm family affection and receive sufficient attention do not need to resort to thumb-sucking for their own emotional satisfaction. If sucking persists into older years, psychological treatment may be necessary.

THYROID GLAND DISORDERS
Goiter Enlargement of the thyroid gland is termed goiter. The gland is located in the lower portion of the neck, with its two main lobes on either side of the trachea or windpipe. Hence any significant goiter may be readily visible on inspection of the neck, particularly if the head is thrown backwards. Various terms are used by doctors to classify thyroid enlargements.

A toxic goiter is one producing excessive amounts of thyroid hormone; the associated symptoms are nervousness, tremor, rapid pulse, weight loss, crying spells. A non-toxic goiter is one that does not produce excess thyroid hormone. A diffuse goiter is one in which the enlargement occurs quite equally throughout the entire gland. A nodular goiter is one in which generally small nodules or lumps are felt scattered throughout the thyroid substance.

Sometimes the cause or a significant symptom is referred to, as in iodine-deficiency goiter, in which lack of iodine in the diet produces the enlargement; or exophthalmic goiter, a common form of goiter associated with prominent, "staring" appearance of the eyes. Virtually all enlargements of the thyroid are benign, but occasionally one is not, and may be referred to as a malignant goiter. Even so, many cancers of the thyroid are classified as low-grade tumors with little propensity to spread, and curiously enough, some may be controlled by thyroid administration.

Treatment. Treatment of a goiter is dependent upon its type. A toxic goiter may be treated by surgery, radioactive iodine, or certain antithyroid drugs. Some forms of goiter respond well to the administration of thyroid by mouth, and in iodine-deficiency goiter some form of iodine or iodized salt may be prescribed. Minor degrees of enlargement may remain untreated. The thyroid gland is normally slightly larger in women than in men, and may undergo some further enlargement in pregnancy. This represents an enlargement compatible with the need for increased output. No special measures are indicated for this sort of size increase.

Hyperthyroidism Overactivity of the thyroid gland leads to the condition known as *hyperthyroidism*. Common complaints here are loss of weight, a ravenous appetite, sensations of great warmth, tremors, nervousness, palpitations and other disorders of the heart, and sometimes diarrhea. This condition is usually associated with an obvious enlargement of the thyroid gland, and—particularly in younger individuals—prominence of the eyes. Some of the diagnostic aids used to determine the degree of hyperthyroidism include: (1) The basal metabolism test, a test of the amount of oxygen consumed; this rises in hyperthyroidism. (2) The protein-bound iodine (PBI) test. In this, determination is made of the amounts of thyroid hormone circulating in the blood. (3) The radioactive iodine uptake test. In this, a minute amount of radioactive iodine is taken as a drink—the "atomic cocktail." Next, measurements are made over the thyroid gland to determine the amount of iodine that has been picked up there. In over-activity of the thyroid, more than twice the normal amount may be taken up.

Hypothyroidism Underfunctioning of the thyroid gland, called *hypothyroidism* and sometimes referred to as "sluggish thyroid," is seen most often in women in their middle years. The condition develops slowly and stealthily, so that it is difficult for the patient herself to fix the time of onset. The complaints are usually of a progressive degree of weakness, fatigability, sensitivity to cold, dryness of the skin and hair, menstrual changes, constipation. The hair may become thin, the skin dry and yellowish, the voice low and cracked, thinking and the emotions slowed down and blunted. Widespread disorders of so many organs point up the fact that thyroid hormone acts on all body cells. Hypothyroidism is easily corrected by taking thyroid hormone by mouth.

Thyroiditis Thyroiditis refers to various forms of inflammation in the thyroid gland. Some have been observed in relation to respiratory illnesses and are thought to be of viral origin. In most forms of thyroiditis, however, no organisms can be found. Acute thyroiditis may begin with an obvious swelling in the thyroid gland, with pain and tenderness, and even with mild symptoms of hyperthyroidism due to excessive release of the hormone. The condition is generally treated with steroid drugs. Chronic forms of thyroiditis—in which the process goes on at a slow rate for months and for years—also occur, though they are rare. An obvious goiter may be formed. Treatment varies but may consist of thyroid hormone, steroid drugs, and occasionally surgery.

TOILET TRAINING Successful toilet training is a complex procedure for the young child. All normal children accomplish this eventually, and it is therefore simply a matter of time before the process is completely mastered. Hence it is wise to be patient and wait until the child is sufficiently mature to master this procedure.

Voluntary and involuntary nerve impulses maintain control of the urine and bowels. In the early weeks and months of life, the muscles which guard the opening for the passage of waste materials remain contracted until a certain "fullness" is obtained which stimulates the relaxation of the sphincter muscle control. The amount of stimuli and the time vary in different infants. Some voluntary activity as the infant strains and squeezes may operate very early in life. Sometimes it is a difficult process for a small infant in a lying-down position to expel the stool by himself. It may be helpful to sit him in a propped-up position as he strains so that the force or effect of gravity will help.

Children usually wish to gain approval; until your child is able to cooperate when you let him know you want him to use the toilet, he may not be able to meet your demands. Keeping a child on the toilet for long periods, expressing anger, disapproval, and shame, will only confuse him and make him resentful. It may lead to a bitter struggle. It is not possible to force a child to learn to control his bowels without serious trauma to the personality.

Occasional accidents and lapses may occur after a child is completely trained, and certain situations of stress may be responsible for lapses in ability to hold urine and stool. Attitudes which shame or humiliate the child will only delay and impair training. This may leave character traits of a more undesirable nature. Punishments, scoldings, spankings, threats are usually useless, and may be harmful. An attitude of encouragement, reassurance, tolerance, and praise are the best approaches to encourage toilet training.

TONSILS AND ADENOIDS

Tonsils The tonsils are two groups of lymphoid tissue located on each side of the back of the throat. Tonsils (and the adenoids which are located near them) are frequently the source of chronic and recurrent upper respiratory infections in children. Some children are particularly susceptible to tonsil infection. Frequently the infection extends into the ear. There is usually fever which can go as high as 104o, a sensation of sore throat, inability to swallow, lack of appetite, nasal obstruction, and possibly impaired hearing.

Many mild cases of tonsillitis will clear by themselves without the use of antibiotics. Aspirin may be helpful in reducing the pain and fever. However, many cases require the use of penicillin and other antibiotics. Most cases clear within seven to ten days. In other cases tonsillectomy may be required.

The indications for tonsillectomy in children are: chronic tonsillitis attacks with adenoidal and ear complications; extreme cases of mouth breathing due to enlarged and obstructive adenoids; and peritonsillar abscess with chronic draining glands. Children who have repeated attacks of tonsillitis accompanied by rheumatic fever or other complications should be considered for tonsillectomy. Massive tonsils which cause obstruction in eating and difficulties in speech and phonation should be removed. Except in unusual cases, it is advisable for the child to be at least four or five years old before tonsils are removed.

Adenoids These are masses of lymphoid tissue located on the posterior throat wall and roof of the mouth, in the area above the tonsils. They commonly enlarge and block the nasopharynx, causing mouth-breathing, running nose, and snoring.

Chronic adenoiditis may cause a nasal or "adenoidal" quality in the voice, offensive breath, and impairment of taste and smell. It has been known to alter the facial expression so much that the child appears dull or stupid. Cough, particularly at night, may occur. Deafness may sometimes be a complication if the eustachian tube (the tube leading from the ear to the throat) is blocked. Enlarged adenoids may be seen with the use of a pharyngeal mirror. The most effective treatment is surgical removal. This is usually done along with tonsillectomy.

TUBERCULOSIS Contagious.

Cause. Bacterial. *Mycobacterium tuberculosis.*

Incubation period. Highly variable, up to years.

Symptoms. Tuberculosis may occur in any organ of the body and may frequently resemble other diseases. The diagnosis is made by recovering and growing the organism in a culture or examining a typical X-ray picture, particularly of the lungs. There are certain changes in tissues which are characteristic of this germ.

In children, *primary tuberculosis* refers to the first infection of an individual with the tubercle bacillus. The primary focus (Ghon tubercle) is usually in the lungs and is the original site of entry of the germ. This first lesion heals over and becomes calcified. It is seen on X-ray as an old but inactive lesion. Many people have initial, original infections of this sort which never spread.

Lung lesions in older people are generally larger, and the bacilli may travel to and colonize in the regional lymph glands. Infections may spread to bones, kidney, brain, etc., and it is possible to have tuberculosis without many symptoms. Such lesions remain in a quiescent state, but may also break down in the future and spread.

Tuberculosis is classified according to the organ and form in which it occurs.

Since symptoms of this disease may continue obscure until the disease is well under way, diagnostic *tuberculin testing* is of great importance. There are patch tests and intradermal skin tests in different strengths. Further tests, such as X-rays, sputum cultures and spinal fluid examination, may be required to recover the tubercle bacilli and confirm the diagnosis.

Treatment. Tuberculosis is now considered curable as a result of the development of new drugs, which have been extremely successful in arresting early and even relatively advanced infections. More severe conditions may not be curable by drug treatment and may require prolonged hospitalization or surgical procedures. The drugs used are: INH (isonicotinic acid hydrazide), streptomycin, and PAS (para-aminosalicylic acid).

Prevention. Periodic chest X-rays and skin testing locate existing lesions and prevent spread by contacts. All contacts who show signs of disease should be treated. Exposure to known positive cases should be carefully avoided. Passive immunization to tuberculosis is available with BCG (bacillus Calmette-Guerin). This is a vaccine composed of bovine (cow) tubercle bacilli whose virulence has been modified by special procedures. Vaccination with this material produces a limited immunity to infection with tuberculosis. It is especially indicated for persons who live in areas with high tuberculosis rates and those who have intimate contact with arrested cases.

ULCER, PEPTIC A peptic ulcer is a defect in the lining of the digestive tract, produced by a process of self-digestion and generally due to stomach secretions. The most common location for a peptic ulcer is in the top part of the small intestine, called the duodenum. Less common, but by no means infrequent, are peptic ulcers of the stomach lining, and least frequent are those found in the lower part of the esophagus, the tubelike structure running from the mouth to the stomach. Based on their location, therefore, peptic ulcers are sometimes referred to as *duodenal, gastric,* or *esophageal.* Peptic ulcers form at one time or another in about 10 per cent of the population, but only a very small group are diagnosed.

A peptic ulcer will produce pain of a burning or gnawing character felt in the upper abdomen and sometimes also in the back. The pain is generally helped by eating, drinking milk, or taking an alkalinizing medication. Because food helps ulcer pain, the symptoms tend to go away after eating, only to recur several hours later; between-meal pain and discomfort and therefore a common complaint. They can also occur during the night, so that peptic ulcer victims often wake during the night with reactivation of pain. In about 95 per cent of the cases the diagnosis can be proved by taking an X-ray.

Treatment. The treatment of peptic ulcer consists of a bland diet with omission of spices; fried, smoked, or greasy foods; liquor; and preferably also smoking. Neutralization of acids is promoted by small frequent feedings, frequent consumption of milk or milk-cream mixtures, and the taking of alkalinizers which are available in the form of a great many commercial products (Maalox®, Gelusil®, Amphojel®, Titralac®, etc.). One satisfactory program calls for eating some one item in any of these three categories—bland food, milk, alkalizer—ever hour throughout the day. If pain recurs regularly at night, an alarm clock may be set so as to wake the sleeper before the expected discomfort, which can then be forestalled by eating, or by drinking milk.

UPPER RESPIRATORY INFECTIONS
Croup (Acute Laryngotracheobronchitis) This is an upper respiratory infection due either to virus or bacteria (streptococcus, pneumococcus, staphylococcus). It involves one or more of the structures of the voice box (larynx) and throat. Infants and children have an airway only about the diameter of a pencil. Upper respiratory infections which cause swelling of this area are therefore of a more serious nature than is the case with adults. The infections may involve the tonsils, the lower portion of the trachea, the larynx, and the lungs.

Symptoms. The symptoms of this infection cause difficulty in breathing *in.* This results in a harsh, barking cough and a noisy, groaning inspiration. There may be such difficulty breathing in that the face becomes red and the expression anxious. The skin may turn bluish due to lack of oxygen. The child is "pulling," and the breathing is labored. A great deal of mucus accumulates in the tracheobronchial tree, and the air passages may become obstructed. It is very hard for these infants to cough up mucus. They struggle with both the inability to get air in and the inability to cough up the obstructive phlegm. The stridor (difficult breathing) also manifests itself by retractions at the neck and the sternal notch. Intercostal retractions between the ribs also occur.

Treatment. The two measures which are most useful in relieving the breathing distress are: (1) To place the child in a room or atmosphere filled with warm, moist steam. One method is to turn on the hot shower and hot-water tap in the bathroom, close the door, and sit with the child in this steamy atmosphere for fifteen to twenty minutes. This will usually relieve some of the congestion, and the child will breathe easier. (2) The child can be helped to vomit. This will bring up a great deal of the trapped, thickened mucus. If the child is unable to vomit, he may be given one teaspoon of syrup of ipecac followed by some warm water; your doctor may prescribe a larger dosage for a child over two years old. This is a nauseating agent. If it is given, the child should remain in a seated position so that when he vomits he will not choke on the vomitus.

Children who have been "pulling" or breathing with stridor and difficulty for more than six to eight hours are in danger of exhaustion.

Children with croup should always be seen by a physician. If croup becomes very severe, it may be necessary to operate and perform a tracheotomy. This procedure opens an airway through the trachea (windpipe) below the area of swelling and obstruction. A metal tube is inserted and kept in place, and suctioning of mucus is performed so that the child may breathe with ease. Such cases must usually be hospitalized. When the infection has cleared and the child is able to breathe well by himself, the opening can be closed.

Strep Throat This is a throat infection caused by streptococcus. The bacillus can usually be cultured from the throat. Beta-hymolytic streptococcus is the most virulent. It produces toxic substances, high fever, and severe disease. The group A beta-hemolytic streptococcus is responsible for scarlet fever, streptococci have been implicated in rheumatic fever.

Treatment. Most streptococcus infections can be cured with penicillin and other antibiotics.

VAGINITIS Vaginitis is any inflammation of the vagina. It generally consists of an annoying discharge, and in severe cases there is pain, burning, itching, and a scalding sensation with the passage of urine. One of the common organisms that may produce this condition is called *Trichomonas,* so that the disorder is sometimes referred to as trichomoniasis.

The organism can sometimes be passed from a woman to her husband and vice versa, so that in stubborn cases both may have to be treated. Various suppositories, insufflation with powders, douches, and a recently developed medication to be taken by mouth may all be used. The infection often flares up after the time of menstruation, and it is generally advisable to continue the treatment through at least two menstrual cycles and even throughout menstruation.

Another form of vaginitis is caused by a fungus known as *Candida,* hence the term candidiasis. This is, perhaps, the most common form of vaginitis to appear during pregnancy. Here too, inflammation may vary from mild to almost intolerable, usually with a thin, somewhat odorous discharge. Another condition which may produce this form of vaginitis is diabetes, since the sugar in the urine favors the growth of the organism. Various suppositories, jellies, and douches may be used in treatment. Both of these organisms may sometimes be found together, producing a mixed form of vaginitis.

Senile vaginitis is sometimes seen in post-menopausal women. At this time, in the absence of hormone treatment, the lining of the vagina is thin and has a low resistance to infection. There may be slight bleeding as well as a discharge which is thin and irritating. One of the most widely employed forms of treatment for this is the use of female hormone, either by suppository or by mouth. This thickens the vaginal lining, increases its resistance, and is generally sufficient to abolish the infection. Occasionally *Trichomonas* and other organisms may be found, and treatment will have to be directed against these organisms. Vaginitis may be most troublesome and annoying, and may call for great patience.

VENEREAL DISEASES Venereal diseases are generally transmitted by sexual intercourse. The two most common are *gonorrhea* and *syphilis.*
Gonorrhea The symptoms of gonorrhea appear, on the average, five days after exposure. In the male they consist of a milky-white to yellowish discharge from the penis, with redness and irritation around its opening. In a woman, similar discharge with irritation of the vaginal and urinary channels occurs.

Since various kinds of vaginal discharges and urinary symptoms due to other causes are common in women, a gonorrheal infection may not seem quite so alarming or striking in the female. Also, undoubtedly some of these infections are milder than others. In the more serious forms of the disease an untreated gonorrheal infection may ascend through the uterus and produce considerable inflammation in the tubes and the ovaries. One of the unfortunate consequences of such tubal infection when it heals is that it may produce sterility. In mild cases the doctor may have to do smears or special cultures to determine the existence of gonorrhea.

Gonorrhea responds quite promptly to various sulfa drugs and antibiotics. A vast decrease in the amount of gonorrhea is indicated by the fact that with most men a discharge from the penis will turn out to be "non-specific"—not due to a gonorrheal infection. Very occasionally gonorrhea may be transmitted by a non-venereal route. This is occasionally seen in young children to whom an infection may be transmitted by careless handling by an adult having the disease. The eyes, particularly, are subject to infection with the organism of gonorrhea. In the presence of such an infection scrupulous cleanliness is necessary to avoid a spread.
Syphilis Syphilis does not produce a discharge but appears first as a local sore. In the male the sore is seen most frequently near the head of the penis, is generally less than dime-sized, and has a moist ulcerated appearance. It is known as a chancre. It will clear up within a few weeks, even without treatment. Since in women the chancre will be internally situated in the vagina or the cervix, it will not be obvious externally. Hence primary syphilis in the female may go completely unnoted. Though the chancre will disappear without treatment, the syphilitic infection will not. Syphilis is notorious for remaining in the system for years without producing evident harm. During this time, however, important organs including the aorta, the large blood vessel leading from the heart, and also the nervous system may become involved. The former may result in syphilitic heart disease, the latter in various forms of paralysis and insanity.

The long silent stage in syphilis that follows the chancre would be most difficult to detect were it not for the important test known as the *Wassermann test* and some of the more recent modifications of this test. Sometimes referred to simply as "a blood test," it is required by law in many states before a marriage certificate can be issued. It is generally routinely done on pregnant women, and indeed is often done as a routine test in hospital admissions. Rather rarely the test may be positive in a person who, one is reasonably sure, never had a syphilitic infection. This is referred to as a biological false-positive. As a rule, however, a positive test generally calls for a course of treatment. Fortunately, since the advent of penicillin and related drugs, the treatment of syphilis has been enormously simplified. Despite successful treatment and eradication of the syphilitic infection, the Wassermann test may remain positive for years thereafter. When this happens, the individual is said to be "Wassermann-fast."

WARTS A wart is a benign (harmless) skin growth and is known to be produced by a virus; why some individuals are susceptible to this virus at certain stages in their lives is not known. Warts are most commonly seen in children and young adults. The most frequent site is on the fingers or the back of the hands, but warts may also occur on the face and, not uncommonly, on the sole of the foot. In the latter location, they tend to be pushed into the skin by one's weight and therefore do not protrude above the surface; these are known as plantar warts. One evidence of the infectious nature of warts is sometimes seen in their distribution in a line which can occur from scratching the original wart and distributing the virus in the line of the scratch.

Treatment. Warts will often disappear spontaneously, the individual waking up one day to find them gone. Another peculiarity of warts is that they are the only form of skin growth known which can disappear by suggestion; painting them with a completely harmless and inert coloring agent may make them disappear if a strong suggestion to this effect is given simultaneously. Occasionally, for large numbers of warts, hypnosis will even be effective. Such suggestion will take one to two weeks, during which time it becomes obvious that the wart is shrinking and being cast off.

Other treatments that have been used include touching the wart with acids, castic alkalies, or extract of podophyllin; freezing with carbon dioxide ice; and (occasionally) X-ray treatments. A recent suggestion has been the immersion of the wart in hot water (about 116°F.) for half an hour; this hot-water treatment may clear up warts if repeated on a daily basis.

Plantar warts are particularly stubborn because the wart is buried in the skin, often quite deeply. Repeated applications of caustic agents or X-ray treatments may be necessary. Some of the results that are achieved are doubtless due to the self-limited nature of the wart.

WHOOPING COUGH (PERTUSSIS) Contagious.

Cause. Bacterial, *Hemophilus pertussis.*

Incubation period. 5 days to 3 weeks.

Symptoms. This disease occurs most commonly in January and February in northern climates and in May in southern climates. It may occur at any age but is particularly serious if it occurs in infants below one year of age. In typical cases there is a mild period in the beginning, characterized by a cough which becomes more frequent at night and in the next ten days to two weeks becomes more severe. It develops into a series of repeated spasms of cough, ending in a forced inspiration which is called "the whoop." This is called the spasmodic or paroxysmal stage. Frequently this stage is followed by vomiting or coughing up large amounts of thick mucus. Small infants may turn blue or black from lack of oxygen. In severe cases, they develop nosebleeds or hemorrhages in the eyes due to the great effort of coughing. The disease may last from four to six weeks.

Complications. Bronchitis, bronchopneumonia, etc., are common. Dehydration as a result of prolonged vomiting may occur.

Treatment. Small infants should be hospitalized as they may require oxygen. Antibiotics and hyperimmune serum may be necessary. Sedating cough mixtures help lessen cough spasms.

Prevention. Active immunization of all infants should be started by the third month of age. This consists of an injection of DPT (combined diphtheria, pertussis, tetanus) vaccine. It is usually given in monthly injections for three months, followed by booster doses at one year of age and every three years thereafter. If triple vaccine immunization is not provided, individual immunization with whooping cough vaccine may be given.

The treatment of mild cases is aspirin for the fever and cough medicine to modify the coughing spells. In infants, special care must be taken to prevent their breathing in the vomit and mucus.

WORMS OR PARASITES Many different types of worms may infest the intestinal tracts. The most common ones are the pinworm, the whipworm, and the roundworm.

Pinworms are white, threadlike worms one-half to three-quarters of an inch long. Their eggs are deposited on the mucous lining and skin around the rectum. The worms may frequently be seen coming out of the rectum and mixed with stool.

Whipworms resemble pinworms but may be larger.

Roundworms are considerably larger, anywhere from six to eight inches long and one-eighth to one-quarter inch in diameter. They are unmistakable.

The symptoms of "worms" vary and may be minimal or severe. There may be no signs or symptoms except vague complaints of poor appetite, poor growth and development, vague abdominal pains, occasional diarrhea, or bloody, tarry stools. Itching or scratching around the rectal area may also be a complaint. If the worms are actually seen, they may be saved and examined. Different worms may require different chemicals for treatment.

A worm which is eaten in uncooked or undercooked pork causes a disease called *trichinosis.* In this condition the eyes become puffy and swollen. There may be a rash, itching, intestinal symptoms, etc. Pork should always be well cooked before serving in order to avoid this condition.

A tropical parasite which does not commonly occur in the United States is the *amoeba* which produces *amoebic dysentery.* This causes severe symptoms of diarrhea, bloody stools, loss of weight, etc. Another worm which occurs in tropical and semi-tropical countries is *hookworm.* It also appears in the southern part of the United States.

The diagnosis of most worm diseases is made by isolating and identifying the worm or its egg in the stool of the patient. It may be necessary to test repeated samples of stool to find eggs or worms. Practically all worm infestations are treatable. However, some are more difficult to cure than others.

FIRST AID

BASIC PROCEDURES FOR FIRST AID

When a person is injured or ill, someone must take charge, send for a doctor, and apply first aid. The person taking charge must make a rapid but effective examination to determine the nature of the injuries.

Do not move the injured person until you have a clear idea of the injury and have applied first aid, unless the victim is exposed to further danger at the accident site. If the injury is serious, if it occurred in an area where the victim can remain safely, and if medical aid is readily obtainable, it is sometimes best not to attempt to move the person, but to employ such emergency care as is possible at the place until more highly qualified emergency personnel arrive.

When making an initial survey, a first aider will consider what witnesses to the accident tell him about the accident, what he observes about the victim, and what the victim tells him.

The first aider must not assume that the obvious injuries are the only ones present because less noticeable injuries may also have occurred. Look for the causes of the injury, this may provide a clue as to the extent of physical damage.

While there are several conditions that can be considered life-threatening, respiratory arrest and severe bleeding require attention first.

In all actions taken during the initial survey the first aider should be especially careful not to move the victim any more than necessary to support life. Any unnecessary movement or rough handling should be avoided because it might aggravate undetected fractures or spinal injuries.

Once respiratory arrest and severe bleeding have been alleviated, attention should be focused on other obvious injuries—open chest or abdominal wounds should be sealed, open fractures immobilized, burns covered and less serious bleeding wounds dressed. Again remember to handle the victim carefully.

Once the obvious injuries have been treated, the secondary survey can be made to detect less easily noticed injuries that can be aggravated by mishandling. If a victim with a spinal injury is mishandled, he could suffer spinal damage, leading to paralysis. Also a closed fracture can become an open fracture if not immobilized. The secondary survey is a head to toe examination. Start by examining the victim's head, then neck, trunk, and extremities looking for any type of abnormalities such as swelling, discoloration, lumps, and tenderness that might indicate an unseen injury.

FIRST AID PROCEDURES FOR LIFE THREATENING CONDITIONS

This section outlines the first aid measures that should be used when life-threatening conditions exist. These conditions include: **impaired breathing, heart failure, severe bleeding,** and **shock.** Obviously, of first and paramount concern is immediate recognition and correction of these conditions. Emergency treatment should be given in this order, as necessary:

1. **CLEAR THE AIR PASSAGE.**
2. **RESTORE BREATHING AND HEARTBEAT.**
3. **STOP BLEEDING.**
4. **ADMINISTER TREATMENT FOR SHOCK.**

IMPAIRED BREATHING

CAUSES
1. Suffocation
2. Gas poisoning
3. Electrical shock
4. Drowning
5. Heart failure

SIGNS/SYMPTOMS
1. The chest or abdomen does not rise and fall.
2. Air cannot be felt exiting from the nose or mouth.

FIRST AID TREATMENT
There are several methods of artificial ventilation. Mouth-to-mouth is the most effective. Use the mouth-to-nose method if the victim has a severe jaw fracture or mouth wound, or has his jaws tightly closed. Simply breathe into his nose instead of his mouth.

Use back pressure method only when mouth-to-mouth cannot be used: for example, if the victim has severe facial injuries, is trapped or pinned face down, or when you are in a toxic environment and both you and the victim are wearing masks which do not contain a resuscitation device.

MOVE FAST
Seconds count when a person is not breathing. Start artificial ventilation at once. Don't take time to move the victim unless the accident site remains unsafe.

MOUTH-TO-MOUTH (NOSE) TECHNIQUE

1. Position victim on his back. If it is necessary to roll the victim over, try to roll him over as a single unit, keeping the back and neck straight. This is to avoid aggravation of any possible spinal injury.

2. Kneeling at the victim's side, tilt victim's head back so chin is pointing up by placing one hand under the neck and the other hand on the forehead.

3. Quickly glance in victim's mouth for any obstruction (e.g., food, tobacco, blood, dentures). If an obvious obstruction is present, carefully turn the victim on his side, tilt his head down, and sweep his mouth out with your fingers. When the mouth is clear move the victim onto his back again and tilt his head back.

For at least 5 seconds listen and feel the air exchange and look for chest movements.

4. Check for breathing by bending over the victim, placing your ear close to victim's mouth and nose. For at least 5 seconds listen and feel for air exchange and look for chest movements.

If the person is not breathing, pinch the nose closed, form an airtight seal by placing your mouth over the victim's mouth and breathe into the victim's mouth until the chest rises.

5. If no breathing is present, pinch the nose closed with the hand that is resting on the forehead, form an airtight seal by placing your mouth over the victim's mouth, and breathe into the victim's mouth until his chest rises. (If using the mouth-to-nose method, seal the victim's mouth with your hand and breathe in through his nose.

6. Breathe into the patient a total of four times as quickly as possible. If you feel or hear no air exchange, re-tilt his head and try again. If you still feel no air exchange, again sweep the mouth of foreign objects (Step 3), and breathe into the victim again. If you still have no air exchange, turn victim on side and slap the victim on the back between his shoulder blades. Again sweep his mouth to remove foreign matter. (Note: If none of the above steps clears the air passage, repeat the blows to the back and tilt the head.)

7. Repeat breathing. Remove mouth each time to allow air to escape. Repeat 12 times per minute for an adult—20 times for a small child or infant. Use deep breaths for an adult, less for a child, gentle puffs of the cheeks for infants. As the victim begins to breathe, maintain head tilt. If it is impossible to do mouth-to-mouth or mouth-to-nose, use the following:

BACK PRESSURE ARM LIFT METHOD

1. Place victim face down. Clean mouth. Bend his elbows and place his hands one upon the other at eye level under victim's head. Turn his head to one side, making sure the chin juts out. This method will be done on a five beat count.

Kneel at the victim's head, place your hands on the victim's back.

2. Kneel at victim's head. Place your hands on victim's back so palms lie just below an imaginary line between armpits. **(Count 1)**

Rock forward until your arms are vertical.

3. Rock forward until arms are vertical and the weight of your body exerts steady pressure on your hands. **(Count 2)**

Rock back grasping the victim's elbows.

4. Rock back grasping victim's elbows **(Count 3)** and draw victim's arms up toward you until you feel resistance at his shoulders. **(Count 4)**

5. **Lower victim's arms to the ground. (Count 5)** Repeat about 12 times per minute (every 5 seconds). Keep checking to see if mouth is clean, airway open, and the heart is beating. If heart is not beating, begin external cardiac compression (circulatory failure).

DON'T STOP

Continue artificial ventilation until victim breathes normally, a doctor pronounces him dead, a more qualified person takes charge, or you are physically unable to continue. If he must be moved, continue artificial ventilation.

SIGNS/SYMPTOMS
1. The victim gasps for breath
2. Has violent fits of coughing
3. Quickly turns pale then blue
4. Cannot talk or breathe

FIRST AID TREATMENT
1. Open victim's mouth and grasp foreign object with fingers (index and middle), trying to remove obstruction.
2. Place head lower than body or roll victim on his side and slap him on the back.
3. If these methods do not work, try this third method:
   a. Rescuer stands behind the choking victim with arms around the victim just above the navel and below the rib cage.
   b. Lean the victim forward at the waist with his head and arms hanging down.
   c. The rescuer grasps his wrist then exerts sudden strong pressure against the victim's abdomen. This will force air out of the lungs and may expel the obstruction.

CIRCULATORY FAILURE

CAUSES
1. Heart attack
2. Impaired breathing
3. Shock
4. Electrical shock

SIGNS/SYMPTOMS
1. No breathing
2. No pulse

FIRST AID TREATMENT

Don't Waste Time! Cardiac arrest (heart stops beating) means certain death if CPR (cardiopulmonary resuscitation) is not attempted.

If you have been trained in CPR:

1. **CHECK FOR RESPONSE**—Gently shake the victim and shout "Are you OK."
2. **CHECK AIRWAY**—Open the victim's airway by tilting his head back (Victim should be on his back.)

Check for breathing.

3. **CHECK BREATHING**—For at least **5** seconds listen and feel for air exchange and look for chest movement.

If not breathing, give four quick full breaths.

4. **IF NOT BREATHING**—Give four quick full breaths using the mouth-to-mouth technique.

Check pulse.

5. **CHECK PULSE**—After giving four quick breaths, check the pulse using the carotid artery in the neck. To find the carotid artery, locate the voice box and slide two fingers into the groove between the voice box and the large neck muscle. Press firmly but gently to feel for the pulse and hold for at least **5** seconds. If a pulse is not present, begin cardiac compressions immediately.

To determine the pressure point for cardiac compressions, locate the bony tip of the breastbone with your ring finger and place two fingers just above that point.

6. **CARDIAC COMPRESSIONS**— Kneel at the victim's side near his chest. (Victim should be on a hard, flat surface.) To determine the pressure point for cardiac compressions, locate the bony tip of the breastbone (sternum) with your ring finger and place two fingers just above that point. Place the heel of one hand adjacent to your fingers and the second hand on top of the first.

Place the heel of your hand adjacent to your fingers and the second hand on top of the first.

Position your shoulders directly over victim's breastbone and press downward, keeping arms straight. Depress the sternum 1½ to **2** inches for an adult. The time spent depressing and releasing the sternum should be equal.

If there is only one rescuer, compressions should be at a rate of **80** per minute with **2** breaths (artificial ventilation) after each **15** compressions. Remember, after the two breaths, check your hand position on the sternum before resuming compressions.

If there are two rescuers, they should be on opposite sides of the victim. One rescuer should perform compressions at a rate of **60** per minute, while the second rescuer is interposing a breath (artificial ventilation) after every fifth compression. Compressions should not be interrupted to breathe for the victim.

CARDIOPULMONARY RESUSCITATION FOR INFANTS AND SMALL CHILDREN

1. **Airway**—be careful not to overextend the infant's head when tilting it back; it is so pliable that you may block breathing passage instead of opening it.

2. **Breathing**—you can cover both mouth and nose with your mouth and use less volume of air; give a breath every three seconds.

3. **Circulation**—In both infants and small children only one hand is used for compressions. For infants, use only the **tips** of the index and middle fingers to depress the mid-sternum ½ to ¾ of an inch at a rate of 80 to 100 compressions per minute. For small children, use only the heel of the hand to depress the chest at mid-sternum and depress the mid-sternum ¾ to 1½ inches, depending on the size of the child. The rates should be 80 to 100 compressions per minute.

In both small children and infants, breaths should be interposed after every fifth chest compression.

BLEEDING

SIGNS/SYMPTOMS
Blood coming from an artery, vein, or capillary:

a. **Artery**—spurting blood, bright red in color

b. **Vein**—continuous flow of blood, dark red in color

c. **Capillary**— blood oozing from a wound

Cover the wound with the cleanest cloth immediately available.

FIRST AID TREATMENT
1. Cover wound with the cleanest cloth immediately available or your bare hand and apply **direct pressure** on the wound. Most bleeding can be stopped this way.

2. **Elevate** the arm or leg as you apply pressure, if there is no broken bone.

3. **Digital pressure** at a pressure point is used if it is necessary to control bleeding from an arterial wound (bright red blood spurting from it.) Apply your fingers to the appropriate pressure point—a point where the main artery supplying blood to the wound is located (see diagram). Hold pressure point tightly for about 5 minutes or until bleeding stops. The three pressure points in the head and neck should only be used as a last resort if there is a skull fracture and direct pressure can't be used. If direct pressure can be used, it will stop bleeding on the head in about 95% of the injuries.

4. A tourniquet should be applied to an arm or leg **only** as a **last resort** when all other methods fail. A tourniquet is applied between the wound and the point at which the limb is attached to the body, as close to the wound as possible but never over a wound or fracture. Make sure it is applied tightly enough to stop bleeding completely.

In the case of an improvised tourniquet, the material should be wrapped twice around the extremity and half knotted. Place a stock or similar object on the half knot and tie a full knot. Twist the stick to tighten the tourniquet only until the bleeding stops—**no more.** Secure the stick or

Apply pressure to the pressure point closest to the wound and between the wound and the heart.

level in place with the loose ends of the tourniquet, another strip of cloth, or other improvised material.

Once the tourniquet is put in place, **do not** loosen it. Mark a "**T**" on the victim's forehead and get him to a medical facility as soon as possible. Only a doctor loosens or removes a tourniquet.

Note: A tourniquet can be improvised from a strap, belt, handkerchiefs, necktie, cravat bandage, etc. (Never use wire, cord or anything that will cut into the flesh.)

A tourniquet should be applied to an arm or leg only as a *last resort.*

INTERNAL BLEEDING

SIGNS/SYMPTOMS
1. Cold and clammy skin
2. A weak and rapid pulse
3. Eyes dull and pupils enlarged
4. Possible thirst
5. Nauseous and vomiting
6. Pain in affected area

FIRST AID TREATMENT
1. Treat victim for shock
2. Anticipate that victim may vomit, give nothing by mouth
3. Get the victim to professional medical help as quickly and safely as possible.

SHOCK

Shock may accompany any serious injury: blood loss, breathing impairment, heart failure, burns.

Shock can kill—treat as soon as possible and continue until medical aid is available.

SIGNS/SYMPTOMS
1. Shallow breathing
2. Rapid and weak pulse
3. Nausea, collapse, vomiting
4. Shivering
5. Pale, moist skin
6. Mental confusion
7. Drooping eyelids, dilated pupils

FIRST AID TREATMENT
1. Establish and maintain an open airway.
2. Control bleeding.
3. Keep victim lying down.
   Exception: Head and chest injuries, heart attack, stroke, sun stroke. If no spine injury, victim may be more comfortable and breathe better in a semireclining position. If in doubt, keep the victim flat.
4. Elevate the feet unless injury would be aggravated by this position.

Elevate the feet unless injury would be aggravated.

Maintain normal body temperature. Place blankets under and over victim.

5. Maintain normal body temperature. Place blankets under and over victim.
6. Give nothing by mouth, especially stimulants or alcoholic beverages.
7. Always treat for shock in all serious injuries and watch for it in minor injuries.

INTRODUCTION TO SPECIFIC INJURIES

This section describes special methods which you should follow for specific injuries or illnesses other than the four life threatening conditions discussed in Section 1. For quick reference this section has been arranged alphabetically by the injury.

Reddened skin.

Reddened skin, blisters.

Skin destroyed, tissues damaged, charring.

BURNS—HEAT

FIRST DEGREE

SIGNS/SYMPTOMS
Reddened Skin

FIRST AID TREATMENT
Immerse quickly in cold water or apply ice until pain stops.

SECOND DEGREE

SIGNS/SYMPTOMS
Reddened Skin, Blisters

FIRST AID TREATMENT
1. Cut away loose clothing.
2. Cover with several layers of cold moist dressings of if limb is involved immerse in cold water for relief of pain.
3. Treat for shock

THIRD DEGREE

SIGNS/SYMPTOMS
Skin destroyed, tissues damaged, charring

FIRST AID TREATMENT
1. Cut away loose clothing (do not remove clothing adhered to skin.)
2. Cover with several layers of sterile, cold, moist dressings for relief of pain and to stop burning action.
3. Treat for shock.

BURNS—CHEMICAL

FIRST AID TREATMENT
1. Flood affected area with water for at least 20 minutes until all chemical is removed.
2. Remove victim's clothing because chemical may be retained in clothing.

Flood affected area with water until all chemical is removed.

GENERAL CARE FOR ALL BURNS

1. Administering Liquids—If medical help is not available within an hour and the victim is conscious and not vomiting and requests something, give him ½ glass solution of ½ teaspoon salt, ½ teaspoon baking soda to a quart of water, every 15 minutes.
2. Separate any burned areas that might come in contact with each other when bandaging. (fingers, toes, ear and head)
3. Get medical attention as soon as possible.
4. Do not break blisters.
5. Do not use ointments.

Cover with an airtight material.

CHEST, WOUNDS

FIRST AID TREATMENT
1. Cover wound with an airtight material (aluminum foil or plastic wrap) after the victim has exhaled. If no airtight material is available, use your hand.
2. Place the victim on the injured side to allow expansion room for the uninjured lung.
3. Get the victim to the hospital as soon as possible.

DIABETIC EMERGENCIES

DIABETIC COMA

SIGNS/SYMPTOMS
1. Skin: red and dry
2. Temperature: lowered
3. Sickly sweet odor of acetone on breath
4. Breathing: rapid and deep

FIRST AID TREATMENT
1. Treat as you would for shock
2. Place in a semi-reclining position.
3. In case of vomiting turn head to one side.
4. Do not give sugar, carbohydrates, fats or alcoholic beverages.

INSULIN SHOCK

SIGNS/SYMPTOMS
1. Skin: pale, moist, clammy and covered with cold sweat.
2. Breathing: normal or shallow.
3. No odor of acetone

FIRST AID TREATMENT
This is a hurry situation and should be done quickly.

1. If the victim is conscious, give him sugar (sugar, candy bar or orange juice)
2. If unconscious, put sugar under the tongue.

Because it is often difficult to determine the difference between the diabetic emergencies, sugar should be given to any unconscious or semiconscious diabetic even though he may be suffering from diabetic coma (too much sugar). The reason for giving sugar is that an insulin reaction (too little sugar) resulting in unconsciousness can quickly cause brain damage or death.

EPILEPTIC SEIZURE

SIGNS/SYMPTOMS
1. Loses consciousness
2. Convulsions

3. Severe spasms of the muscles of the jaw (may bite tongue)
4. Victim may vomit
5. Face may be livid, with veins of the neck swollen.
6. Breathing may be loud and labored with a peculiar hissing sound.
7. Seizure usually lasts only a few minutes but it may be followed by another.

FIRST AID TREATMENT

1. Keep calm.
2. Do not restrain victim; prevent injury by moving away any object that could be dangerous.
3. Place light padding under victim's head to protect from rough ground (jacket, shirts, rug).
4. There is a danger of the victim biting his tongue so place a padded object between his jaws on one side of his mouth. A shirt tail and a stick can be used for the padded object. However do not try to force jaws open if they are already clamped shut.
5. When the seizure is over loosen clothing around the neck.
6. Keep the victim lying down.
7. Keep victim's airway open.
8. Prevent his breathing vomit into lungs by turning his head to one side or by having him lie on his stomach.
9. Give artificial respiration if breathing stops.
10. After the seizure, when consciousness is regained allow the victim to sleep or rest.

EYE INJURIES

FOREIGN BODIES IN THE EYE

FIRST AID TREATMENT

1. Never rub eyes.
2. Try to flush out with clean water.
3. If object is on upper lid, lift eyelid, and remove object with sterile gauze.
4. If foreign object is on the eye and can't be washed out, cover eye and take victim to a doctor.

If object is on upper lid, lift eyelid, and remove object with sterile gauze.

FIRST AID TREATMENT

1. Leave object in victim; it should only be removed by a doctor.
2. Place sterile gauze around eye, apply no pressure.
3. Cover with paper cup or cardboard cone to protect it and prevent object from being further driven into eye.
4. Cover both eyes, and explain to victim why both eyes are covered, one eye cannot move without the other eye moving. Calm and reassure the victim—he may panic with both eyes covered.

For chemical burns to the eyes see Burns—Chemical

IMPALED OBJECTS

Cover with paper cup to protect the eye and prevent object from being further driven into it.

FRACTURES—DISLOCATIONS

CLOSED FRACTURE (simple): broken bone but no open wound.

FRACTURES

SIGNS/SYMPTOMS
a. Deformity
b. Irregularity
c. Swelling
d. Discoloration
e. Grating sound
f. Exposed bone (open fracture)
g. Pain

OPEN FRACTURE (compound): broken bone with open wound

DISLOCATIONS

SIGNS/SYMPTOMS
a. Deformity
b. Pain
c. Loss of function

DISLOCATION: separation of two bones that come together to form a joint.

FIRST AID TREATMENT FOR FRACTURES AND DISLOCATIONS

1. If fracture is suspected immobilize.
2. "Splint them where they lie."
3. Handle as gently as possible. This work should be done in pairs, one person to immobilize the limb and one to apply the splint.
4. Place a **fracture** in as near normal position as possible by applying slight traction. Traction is applied by grasping the affected limb gently but firmly, with one hand above and below the location of the fracture, and pulling the limb between your hands. This is maintained until the splint is secured in place. **Caution:** never try to straighten if a joint of spine is involved.
5. Immobilize **dislocated joints** in the position they are found, do not attempt to reduce or straighten any dislocation.
6. Splints
   a. Should be long enough to support joints above and below fracture or dislocation.
   b. Rigid enough to support the fracture or dislocation.
   c. Improvised splints should be padded enough to insure even contact and pressure between the limb and the splint and to protect all bony prominences.
   d. Types of splints; air splint, padded boards, rolled blanket, tools, newspapers, magazines.
7. Applying improvised splints
   a. Apply slight traction to the affected limb.

   b. A second person (if available) should place the padded splint under, above or alongside the limb.

c. Tie the limb and splint together with bandaging materials so the two are held firmly together. Make sure the bandaging material is not so tight that it impairs circulation. Leave fingers and toes exposed, if they are not involved, so that the circulation can be checked constantly.

8. Applying inflatable splints
   a. Inflatable splints can be used to immobilize fractures of the lower leg or forearm.
   b. To apply an air splint gather splint on your own arm so that the bottom edge is above your wrist.
   c. Help support the victim's limb—or have someone else hold it.

   d. **Inflate by mouth only** to desired pressure. It is inflated to the point where your thumb would make a slight indentation.
   e. If it is a zipper type air splint lay the victim's limb in the unzipped air splint, zip it and inflate. Traction cannot be maintained when applying this type of splint.
   f. Change in temperature can effect this type of splint—going from cold area to warm area will cause the splint to expand. It may be necessary to deflate the splint until proper pressure is reached.

FROSTBITE

Most frequently frostbitten: toes, fingers, nose, and ears.

CAUSE
Exposure to cold

SIGNS/SYMPTOMS
1. Skin becomes pale or a grayish-yellow color
2. Parts feel cold and numb
3. Frozen parts feel doughy

FIRST AID TREATMENT
1. Until victim can be brought inside, he should be wrapped in woolen cloth and kept dry.
2. Do not rub, chafe or manipulate frostbitten parts.
3. Bring victim indoors.
4. Place in warm water (102° to 105°) and make sure it remains warm. Test water by pouring on inner surface of your forearm. Never thaw if the victim has to go back out into the cold which may cause the affected area to be refrozen.

5. Do not use hot water bottles or a heat lamp, and do not place victim near a hot stove.
6. Do not allow victim to walk if feet are affected.
7. Once thawed, have victim gently exercise parts.
8. For serious frostbite, seek medical aid for thawing because pain will be intense and tissue damage extensive.

HEART ATTACK

SIGNS/SYMPTOMS
1. Shortness of Breath
2. Anxiety
3. Crushing pain in chest, under breastbone, or radiating down left arm.
4. Ashen color
5. Possible perspiration and vomiting.

FIRST AID TREATMENT
1. Place victim in a semi-reclining or sitting position.
2. Give oxygen if available.
3. Loosen tight clothing at the neck and waist.
4. Administer nitroglycerine pill if victim is carrying them and asks you to get them (they are administered by putting one under the tongue).
5. Keep onlookers away.
6. Comfort and reassure him.
7. Do not allow him to move around.
8. Give no stimulants.

HEAT CRAMPS

Affects people who work or do strenuous exercises in a hot environment.

SIGNS/SYMPTOMS
1. Painful muscle cramps in legs and abdomen.
2. Faintness
3. Profuse perspiration

FIRST AID TREATMENT
1. Move victim to a cool place
2. Give him sips of salted drinking water (one teaspoon of salt to one quart of water)
3. Apply manual pressure to the cramped muscle

PREVENTION
1. Men at hard work in high temperatures should drink large amounts of cool water.
2. Add a pinch of salt to each glass of water.

HEAT EXHAUSTION

Pale and clammy skin, perspiration.

SIGNS/SYMPTOMS
1. Pale and clammy skin
2. Profuse perspiration
3. Rapid and shallow breathing
4. Weakness, dizziness, and headache

FIRST AID TREATMENT
1. Care for victim as if he were in shock.
2. Remove victim to a cool area, do not allow chilling.
3. If body gets too cold, cover victim.

HEAT STROKE

Red and flushed, skin hot and dry.

SIGNS/SYMPTOMS
1. Face is red and flushed
2. Victim becomes rapidly unconscious
3. Skin is hot and dry with no perspiration

FIRST AID TREATMENT
1. Lay victim down with head and shoulders raised.

2. Reduce the high body temperature as quickly as possible.
3. Apply cold applications to the body and head.
4. Use ice and fan if available.
5. Watch for signs of shock and treat accordingly.
6. Get medical aid as soon as possible.

HYPOTHERMIA
(Exposure)
Chills the inner core of the body so the body can't generate heat to stay warm.

SIGNS/SYMPTOMS
1. Entire body affected
2. Shivering
3. Numbness
4. Low body temperature
5. Drowsiness, mumbling, incoherence
6. Muscular weakness

FIRST AID TREATMENT
1. Bring victim into a warm room as quickly as possible.
2. Remove wet clothing.
3. Wrap victim in prewarmed blankets, put in a warm tub of water, or next to one or between two people for body warmth.
4. Give artificial respiration, if necessary.
5. If victim is conscious, give warm drink (no alcohol).
6. Get medical help as soon as possible.

INSECT BITES AND STINGS

(from bees, wasps, yellow jackets, hornets, mosquitoes, ticks, fleas, and bedbugs)

SIGNS/SYMPTOMS
1. Local irritation and pain
2. Moderate swelling and redness
3. Itching and/or burning, may be present

FIRST AID TREATMENT
1. If stinger is left in the wound, withdraw it.
2. Apply paste of baking soda and water.
3. Immediate application of ice or ice water to the bite or sting relieves pain.
4. For people who are allergic to certain insects, use a constricting bandage (if on an extremity) and ice. Get medical help immediately.

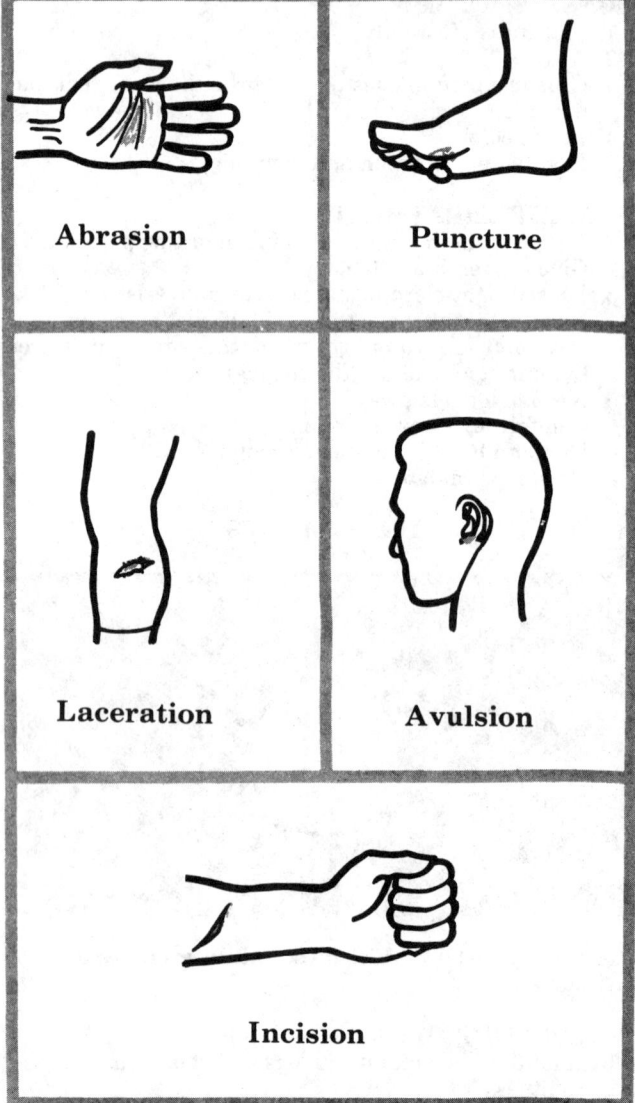

Abrasion

Puncture

Laceration

Avulsion

Incision

OPEN WOUNDS

FIRST AID TREATMENT
1. Stop bleeding.
2. Cover with cleanest cloth immediately available. (Preferably a sterile dressing.)
3. Wash with soap and water—those wounds which involve surface area with little bleeding.

Do not remove imbedded objects.

Cut clothing from injury site.

Bandages and dressings

PRINCIPLES OF BANDAGING
1. Never tie a tight bandage around the neck. It may cause strangulation.
2. A bandage should be tight enough to prevent slipping, but not so tight as to cut off circulation.

Stabilize object with bulky dressings.

Apply paper cup, if available, to prevent movement.

4. Impaled Objects
   a. Do not remove embedded objects.
   b. Cut clothing away from injury site.
   c. Stabilize objects with bulky dressing.
   d. Apply bandage and paper cup (if available) to prevent movement.
   e. If large object, cut off only enough to allow for transportation of victim.

3. Leave fingers and toes exposed, if uninjured, to watch for swelling or changes of color and feel for coldness, which signal interference with circulation.
4. Loosen bandages immediately if victim complains of numbness or a tingling sensation.
5. Once a dressing is in place do not remove. If blood saturates the dressing, put another on top of it.

POISONS

FIRST AID TREATMENT

1. Dilute by drinking large quantities of water.
2. Induce vomiting except when poison is corrosive or a petroleum product.
3. Call the poison control center or a doctor.

PROTRUDING INTESTINES

FIRST AID TREATMENT
1. Do not try to replace intestine.
2. Leave organ on the surface.
3. Cover with non-adherent material (aluminum foil or plastic wrap).
4. Cover with outer dressing to hold it in place.

Bind arm to chest with two medium cravats.

FIRST AID TREATMENT
1. Bandage should be tightened during exhalation.
2. Place arm of injured side across chest.
3. Bind arm to chest with two medium cravats.
4. Repeat with two additional cravats, overlapping bandages slightly.
5. Tie fourth cravat along angle or arm for support.
6. It is important to make certain that the binding is not too tight, as a fractured rib might puncture a lung.

SKULL FRACTURE

(suspected)

SIGNS/SYMPTOMS
1. Unconsciousness
2. Deformity of the skull
3. Open wound
4. Blood or clear water-like fluid coming from ears or nose
5. Pupils may be unequal in size.

FIRST AID TREATMENT
1. Maintain an open airway.
2. Check for spinal injury.
3. Keep victim quiet.

Raise head and shoulders. If there is no suspected neck injury turn head so it does not rest on fracture . . .

. . . Or place in a three-quarter prone position.

4. If there is no suspected neck injury, turn head so it does not rest on fracture.
5. Raise head and shoulders or place in a three-quarter prone position.
6. Use ice pack to stop severe bleeding.
7. Do not stop bleeding from ears or nose.

Cover with nonadherent material.

RIB FRACTURES

SIGNS/SYMPTOMS
1. Pain is usually localized to site of fracture. By asking the victim to place his hand on the exact area of pain (if he is conscious), the first aider can determine the location of the injury.
2. Possible rib deformity or lacerations.
3. Deep breathing, coughing or movement is painful.
4. The victim often leans toward the injured side with his hand held over the injury site in an attempt to ease the pain and immobilize the chest.

Check upper extremities for paralysis of neck.

SNAKEBITES

SIGNS/SYMPTOMS
1. Puncture marks
2. Severe burning, pain and spreading swelling
3. Nausea and vomiting
4. Respiratory distress
5. Shock

Puncture marks at the site of the bite.

FIRST AID TREATMENT
1. Immobilize the victim immediately, with injured part lower than the rest of the body. Any activity will stimulate spread of poison.
2. Remove rings, watches, and bracelets.
3. Apply a constricting band above swelling caused by the bite. It should be tight, but not tight enough to stop arterial circulation.
4. Make an incision, no more than ⅛ inch deep nor more than ½ inch long, length wise through fang marks. Press around cut to make it bleed.
5. Suction wound with device found in snakebite kit. If no kit is available, use your mouth (if you have no open sores in your mouth or on your lips) and spit out the blood. Cutting and suction is of no value unless done immediately. Do not cut if bite is near a major vessel.
6. If swelling continues past the constricting band, put another past the swelling and loosen the first band.
7. Treat the victim for shock. **Do not** give the victim any stimulants or alcohol.
8. Identify snake if possible. If snake can be killed, take it to the hospital with the victim.
9. For persons who frequent regions infested with poisonous snakes, it is recommended that any of the pocket-size snakebite kits be retained.

SPINE FRACTURE OR DISLOCATION

(back and neck)

SIGNS/SYMPTOMS
1. Pain in back or neck
2. Paralysis
3. Deformation
4. Cuts and bruises
5. Swelling

SURVEY—for a conscious victim
1. Ask if the victim feels pain in the back.
2. Look for cuts, bruises, and deformation.
3. Feel along back for tenderness to your touch.
4. Check for paralysis by having victim move fingers and toes.

Can victim feel your touch?

Can victim grasp your hand?

Can victim raise arms and wiggle fingers?

Check lower extremities for paralysis of back.

Can victim feel your touch?

Can victim press against your hand?

Can he wiggle his toes?

SURVEY—for an unconscious victim
1. Look for cuts, bruises, and deformation.
2. Feel along back for deformation.
3. Ask others what happened.
4. Gently jab victim (with something sharp) lightly on the soles of feet or ankles (for back) or hand (for neck)—if cord is intact foot or hands may react.

Lightly jab hands or feet with something sharp.

A spine fracture or dislocation is difficult to tell in the unconscious victim with any accuracy. If the accident looks as if it could have produced a spinal injury, treat for one even through there are no other signs.

FIRST AID TREATMENT

1. Do not try to straighten the deformity to make splinting easier—straighten only to help open an airway.
2. Apply traction to the head, supporting head in line with the body. The head should be held until the victim is secured to the plint.

3. Restore airway and make sure breathing is adequate.
4. If there is a suspected neck fracture and the victim is found on his face, apply traction to the head and roll the victim over keeping the head in line with the body. A minimum of three people is needed for this.
5. Do not bend or twist back or neck. Support head in line with body.
6. Control serious bleeding.
7. Immobilize before moving victim.
8. Lift victim only high enough to slide stretcher under victim.
9. In case of a suspected neck fracture, the head should be kept from moving after the victim has been put on the stretcher—by rolling a blanket around the head and securing it to the stretcher with two cravat bandages.
10. Do not move the victim until there are enough rescuers and an adequate splint available.
11. The stretcher must be rigid, an ordinary canvas stretcher is not suitable. An improvised stretcher can be made from two long boards, 84 by 6 by 1 inch; and 3 short boards, each 22 by 4 by 1½ inches. The three short boards will be cross pieces under the two long boards, nailed or tied at points corresponding to where the person's shoulders, hips, and heels will be. Pad the long boards with blankets and secure in place. The victim is then placed on the stretcher and tied on with fifteen cravat bandages.

Apply traction to victim's head.

Victim is secured to an improvised stretcher board with 15 cravat bandages.

SPRAINS

Ligaments or other tissues around joints are torn or stretched.

SIGNS/SYMPTOMS
1. Pain on movement.
2. Swelling.
3. Discoloration.

FIRST AID TREATMENT
1. Elevate injured part.
2. Apply cold compresses.
3. Treat as a fracture.

Note: Sprains present basically the same signs and symptoms as fractures. Because of this factor, treat all injuries to the bones and joints as fractures.

STRAINS

Strains are caused by overstretching of a muscle or tendon.

Overstretching of a muscle or tendon

SIGNS/SYMPTOMS
1. Intense pain
2. Moderate swelling
3. Pain and difficulty in moving

FIRST AID TREATMENT
1. Rest

STROKE

Pupils are unequal in size. There may be paralysis on one side of the body.

(a blood clot or rupture of a blood vessel in the brain)

SIGNS/SYMPTOMS
1. Usually unconscious.
2. Face flushed and warm but may sometimes appear ashen gray.
3. Pulse first slow and strong; later rapid and weak.
4. Respiration slow with snoring.
5. Pupils unequal size.
6. Paralysis on one side of face and/or body.

FIRST AID TREATMENT
1. Keep an open airway; do not allow tonuge or saliva to block air passage.
2. Keep the victim warm.
3. Place victim in a semi-reclining position if breathing is satisfactory.
4. Keep the victim quiet.
5. Reassure victim if he is conscious.

TRANSPORTATION

After receiving first aid care, a seriously injured person often requires transportation to a hospital, to a physician's office or to his home. It is the responsibility of the first aid person to insure that the victim is transported in such a manner as to prevent further injury and is subjected to no unnecessary pain or discomfort. No matter how expert the first aid care has been, improper handling and careless transportation often add to the severity of the original injuries, increases shock, and frequently endangers life.

Never move a victim until a thorough examination has been made and all injuries have been protected by proper dressings. (Unless the victim and the first aider are in immediate danger at the accident site.)

Seriously injured persons should be moved only in a lying down position. If proper transportation is not immediately available, continue care of the victim to conserve his strength until adequate means of transportation can be found.

If the person must be pulled or dragged to safety, pull in the direction of the long axis of the body.

If a person is in a life threatening situation and must be pulled or dragged to safety, he should be pulled in the direction of the long axis of his body, preferably from the shoulders, not sideways. Avoid bending or twisting the neck or trunk.

If available use a blanket, board or cardboard to move the victim.

Various carries can be used in emergencies, but the stretcher is the preferred transportation method. Carrying in the arms, carrying over the back, and the two-man carry should be used only when it is positively known that no injury will be aggravated by such handling of the victim.

Various carries can be used in emergencies.

The Two-Man Carry.

THREE OR FOUR MAN LIFT AND CARRY

An injured person can be moved or carried with a minimum of further injury or discomfort with the three or four man lift and carry. It is used where an injured person is to be carried a short distance, transported through narrow passageways, or where a stretcher is not available.

The lift is used also when an injured person is being placed or removed from a stretcher.

Three persons are required for this lift and a fourth is desirable (a fourth is necessary for a spinal injury to hold the head). Proper lifting must be done by commands of a leader or one of the bearers, usually the one at the victim's head.

Each of the three men kneels (on his knee nearest the victim's feet) one opposite the victim's shoulders, another opposite his hips, and the third opposite his knees. Unless the nature of the victim's injuries makes it undesirable, the bearers kneel by the victim's uninjured or least injured side.

Position of the hands: First man—hands under shoulders and neck; second man—hands under thighs and small of the back; third man—hands under victim's ankles and knees; fourth man—helps support trunk from opposite side, to prevent rolling.

Step 1: The leader will tell the bearers "Prepare to lift victim."

Step 2: The leader will then say "Lift victim." The bearers slowly lift the victim and support him on their knees. If a stretcher is available, stop in this position and slide stretcher under the victim. Then lower the victim on command of the leader. If stretcher is not available and cannot be brought to the victim go to Step 3.

Step 3: The leader will tell the bearers "Prepare to rise with victim." Bearers turn victim slowly to his side until he rests against their chests.

Step 4: When the leader says "Rise with victim," the bearers rise slowly with the victim.

Position of hands: neck and shoulders, thighs and small of back, ankles and knees.

If stretcher is not available, the bearers will have to rise with the victim and carry him away from the scene of the accident.

STRETCHERS
Stretcher should be tested before placing victim on it. Use a person of about equal weight as the victim. The person should be face down so that if the stretcher should break or tear when it is picked up, the person will be able to catch himself.

Bearers slowly lift the victim and support him on their knees.

Improvised Blanket Stretcher, partly folded

Stretcher Board (with foot rest)

STRETCHER BOARDS
Stretcher boards can be made from a wide board, approximately one and one-half inches thick, or from laminated plywood, about three-quarters of an inch thick. They are usually about 78 inches in length and about 18 inches in width. They have slots about 1 inch wide placed along the edges, through which cravat bandages are passed to secure the victim to the board. The slots may also serve as hand holds. Some variations have additional slots in the center of the boards so that each leg may be secured separately to the board.

IMPROVISED STRETCHERS
A stretcher may be improvised with a blanket, brattice cloth of similar size, a rope, or a strong sheet and two poles or pieces of pipe each 7 to 8 feet long. Place one pole or pipe about 1 foot from the center of the unfolded blanket. Fold the short side of the blanket over the pole toward the other side. Place the second pole or pipe on the two thicknesses of blanket about 2 feet from the first pole and parallel to it. Fold the remaining side of the blanket over the second pole toward the first pole. When the injured person is placed on the blanket, the weight of the body secures the folds.

Place the stretcher under the victim.

Medical Dictionary

A

abarticulation, joint dislocation.

abasia, inability to walk due to incoordination.

abatement, decrease in severity of pain or other symptom.

abdomen, area of body between thorax and pelvis.

abdominoscopy, examination of the abdominal cavity by an instrument.

abduct, to draw an extremity away from the body.

aberration, deviation from normal state or action.

ablation, removal or separation by surgery.

abnormal, variation from normal.

abortion, the termination of pregnancy, spontaneous or induced.

abrade, chafing of skin by friction.

abrasion, a scraping injury to the outer layer of skin.

abscess, a localized collection of purulent matter in any part of the body that may cause pain or swelling.

abscission, the removal of a growth by surgical means.

absolute, pure or perfect.

absorb, to take in by soaking up.

abuse, improper use, frequently cited in connection with drugs or alcohol misuse or mistreatment of children.

acariasis, a skin disease caused by a mite or acarid. See scabies.

acclimation, becoming accustomed to a different climate or situation.

accomodation, adjustment of the eye for seeing varied distances.

accouchement, act of delivery in childbirth or confinement.

acetabulum, the cavity in the hip bone which receives the head of the femur or thigh bone.

acetic, having properties of vinegar.

acetic acid, used as a reagent. An aqueous solution containing alcohol.

acetone, a volatile, colorless and inflammable liquid useful as a solvent; found in the blood and urine of diabetics.

acetylcholine, an acid found in various organs and tissues necessary for the transmission of nerve impulses.

acetylicysalic acid, used to relieve symptoms of pain and fever. Syn: aspirin.

achalasia, inability of muscles or sphincters to relax.

ache, a continued dull or severe pain.

Achilles tendon, connects the muscles of the calf of the leg to the heel bone.

achlorhydria, abscence of hydrochloric acid in stomach.

acholic, absence of bile.

achondroplasia, dwarfism caused by a defect in the formation of cartilage in which the trunk of the body is of normal size but the limbs are abnormally short.

acroma, an absence of normal pigmentation; albinism.

achromatin, found in a cell nucleus which lacks staining properties.

acid, a sour tasting compound containing hydrogen that easily combines with metals; also, informal term for the hallucinogenic drug LSD.

acid-fast, pertaining to bacteria which are not easily decolorized after staining but retain the red dyes.

acidity, a sour stomach due to an excess of hydrochloric acid.

acidosis, an accumulation of acids causing a disturbance in the acid-base balance of the body often seen in diabetic acidoses or renal disease.

acne, a disease of the sebaceous glands and hair follicles of the skin characterized by blackheads and pimples which usually occurs during adolescence.

acoria, ingestion of large amounts of food; gluttony.

acoustic, relating to hearing or sound.

acoustics, the science of sound.

acquired, originating outside the organism.

acrid, biting or irritating.

acriflavine, an orange granulated powder used as an antiseptic.

acromegaly, excessive growth of the extremities -- fingers, toes, jaw and nose; caused by an overactive pituitary gland.

acromion, the highest extension of the shoulder.

acrophobia, an abnormal fear of high places.

ACTH, a pituitary hormone; adrenocorticotropic hormone that stimulates a specific area of the adrenal glands.

actin, a muscle protein.

actinodermatitis, an inflammation to the skin caused by excessive exposure to the sun or X-rays.

actinomcete, a parasite that causes a fungus disease in animals; sometimes communicated to man.

actinomycin, an anti-bacterial substance effective against gram-positive organisms.

acuity, clarity of vision; sharpness.

acupuncture, method of treatment used for a variety of disorders by puncturing specific points on the body with long needles; a technique first used by the ancient Chinese.

acute, a sudden onset of an illness that is attended by a brief course and severe symptoms.

adactyly, congenital absence of digits of hands or feet.

Adam's apple, prominence on the front of throat produced by the thyroid cartilage.

adaptation, ability of an organism to adjust to its environment for survival.

addict, one who exhibits addiction.

addiction, the state of being physically or psychologically dependent on some agent such as drugs or alcohol.

Addison's Disease, a condition caused by underactive adrenal glands characterized by pigmentation of skin, weakness, fatigue, and digestive disturbances.

additive, a substance added to another to enhance its appearance, or nutritional value.

adduct, the movement of an extremity toward the body's main axis.

adduction, the movement of a limb, the trunk, or head toward the median axis of the body.

adductor, the muscle that adducts.

adenalgia, pain in a gland.

adenectomy, surgical removal of a gland.

adenine, white, crystaline substance found in plant and animal tissues; a decomposition product of nuclein.

adenitis, inflammation of lymph nodes or a gland.

adenocarcinoma, malignant tumor cells occurring in glandular tissue.

adenofibroma, benign tumor cells arising from connective tissue frequently found in the uterus.

adenoids, lymph glands in the upper pharynx which function to trap germs which can enlarge to the point of hindering nasal breathing.

adenoidectomy, the removal of the adenoids by excision.

adenoiditis, inflammation of the adenoids.

adenoma, a benign epithelial tumor in a gland.

adenomatosis, the development of multiple grandular growths.

adenomyofibroma, a fibroma containing muscular and glandular elements.

adenopathy, enlargement and morbid change of glands and lymph nodes.

adenosarcoma, a malignant tumor composed of both glandular and sarcomatous elements.

adenosine, derived from nucleic acid consisting of adenine and the pentose sugar D--ribose.

adenosis, abnormal development of a gland; gland disease.

adenovirus, virus causing disease of the upper respiratory tract.

adermia, absence of skin, congenital or acquired.

adhesion, the abnormal joining of structures or organs which have been separated by incision.

adhesive, adhering; sticky.

adipose, pertaining to fat accumulations in cells.

adiposis, an increase of fat in the body; obesity.

adjuvant, an additive to a drug which enhances the action of a principal prescription.

adnerval, near or toward a nerve.

adnexa, accessory parts of a structure or organ.

adnexopexy, attaching the fallopian tube and ovary to the abdominal wall.

adolescence, beginning of puberty until maturity.

adrenal, pertaining to the kidney or its function.

adrenal gland, an endocrine gland attached to the kidney.

adrenalectomy, excision of the adrenal glands.

adrenalin, epinephrine, a drug used as a heart and circulatory stimulant.

adrenaline, the hormone epinephrine.

adrenergic, activated by epinephrine.

adrenocortical, pertaining to the cortex of the adrenal gland./

adrenocorticotropic hormone, ACTH, an anterior pituitary hormone that stimulates the adrenal cortex of the adrenal glands.

adsorb, to attract and retain other substances.

adsorption, the action of a substance in attracting and retaining other materials to its surface.

adult, having reached full maturity.

adventitia, the outer coat of a structure or organ.

aeration, an exchange of carbon dioxide for oxygen by the blood in the lungs.

aerobe, a microorganism that lives and thrives only in the presence of free oxygen.

aeroembolism, an obstruction within the blood vessel by air or gas.

aeroneurosis, a nervous disorder occurring to aviators.

aerophagia, habitual air-swallowing.

aerosol, a drug or suspension that is dispensed in a fine spray.

afebrile, without fever.

affect, cognitive display of emotion reflecting a mental state.

affective, pertaining to the emotions.

afferent, transporting impulses toward a center.

affinity, a tendency to unite with another object or substance.

afflux, a sudden rush of blood to a part of the body.

afterbirth, after childbirth, the placenta and membranes that are expelled from the uterus.

afterhearing, sensations of sound heard after the stimulus has ceased.

afterimage, the persistence of images after the cessation of stimulus.

afterpains, cramplike pains after expulsion of placenta in the uterus.

aftertaste, a persistent taste after cessation of stimulus.

agar, a colloidal substance from red algae used in solid culture media for microorganisms; also used as a treatment for constipation.

agensia, an imperfect development; sterility.

agglutination, the clumping together of bacteria when exposed to immune serum; a process in wound healing.

agglutinogen, a substance that stimulates the production of agglutinin.

aggregation, a clumped mass of material such as platelets induced by agents.

aglaucopsia, inability to distinguish bluish-green and green tints.

aglossia, the absence of a tongue at birth.

aglossostomia, the absence of the tongue and mouth opening at birth.

agnosia, inability to comprehend sensory impressions.

agonad, an individual without sex glands.

agoraphobia, an extreme fear of open spaces.

agranulocytosis, a marked decrease in the number of granulocytes in the white blood cell count characterized by high fever and prostration.

agraphia, a loss of ability to express thoughts in writing.

agromania, morbid desire to live in solitude.

ague, intermittent malerial fever, characterized by fever, sweating, and chills.

ahypnia, insomnia; sleeplessness.

ailurophobia, unusual fear of cats.

air embolism, an obstruction of a blood vessel brought about by a bubble of air.

akatamathesia, inability to comprehend.

akathisia, motor restlessness due to anxiety.

akinesia, lacking muscular movement.

ala, resembling a wing; winglike appendage.

alalia, unable to speak because of vocal organs paralysis or defect.

alanine, a natural amino acid.

albinism, congenital absence of normal pigmentation; albino.

albumin, a water-soluble protein found in blood, milk, and the white of an egg.

albuminuria, albumin found in urine indicating a kidney disorder.

alcohol, organic compound which can be used as an astringent or antiseptic. Also a common name for ethyl alcohol found in alcoholic beverages.

alcoholism, an addictive disease characterized by a craving for alcohol which interferes with an individual's health, relationships, and economic functioning.

aldehyde, a colorless, flammable liquid resulting from the oxidation of a primary alcohol.

aldosterone, a hormone secreted by the adrenal cortex which regulates the electrolyte and water balance of the organism.

aleukemia, absence of white blood cells.

aleukocytosis, deficiency of white blood cell production.

alexia, inability to read; form of aphisia.

algae, various water plants, including the seaweeds.

algesia, increased sensitivity to pain.

algogenic, producing pain; lowering body temperature.

algophobia, unusual fear of pain.

alienation, a mental disorder; insanity.

alimentary, pertaining to nutrition and digestion.

alkalemia, abnormal alkalinity of the blood.

alkali, a caustic base such as sodium or potassium hydroxide that can neutralize acids to form salts.

alkalinuria, alkali found in urine.

alkaosis, an accumulation of high concentrations of alkali in blood and tissues.

allele, one of two alternative forms of a gene, dominant or recessive, which occupy the same locus on a designated pair of chromosomes that determine heredity.

allergen, any substance inducing hypersensitivity or allergy.

allergist, a specialist in allergies.

allergy, sensitivity to an allergen.

allopathy, a treatment based on producing a condition antagonistic to the condition being treated.

allorhythmia, an irregular heart beat or pulse that recurs regularly.

allotropism, possessing different forms of the same element with unlike properties.

aloe, a plant whose juices are used in pharmaceutical preparations.

alopecia, baldness; an absence of normal body hair.

alum, a crystaline substance used as an astringent and stypic.

aluminosis, chronic inflammation of the lungs due to aluminum-bearing dust.

alveolar, the cavities or sockets found in the jaw for the teeth.

alveolus, a small hollow; socket of a tooth; an air cell of the lungs.

Alzheimer's Disease, a mental disease causing deterioration similar to senility.

A.M.A., American Medical Association.

amalgam, an alloy containing mercury; mixture; blend.

amara, bitters.

amarthritis, inflammation of more than one joint.

amaurosis, loss of vision in which there is no evidence of pathology within the eye itself.

ambidextrous, one who is able to use either hand with equal proficiency.

ambivalence, simultaneous conflicting feelings or emotions toward a goal, person, or object.

Amblyomma, hard-bodied ticks.

amblyopia, dullness of vision without a detectable cause sometimes called "lazy eye".

ambulatory, able to move about and not confined to bed.

ameba, a single celled protozoan which moves about and absorbs food by completely surrounding it. Some amebae cause amebic dysentery in man. Also known as amoeba.

amebiasis, ulceration and infection of mucous membranes of the intestinal walls with Entameoba histolytica, the causative agent of amebic dysentery.

amelioration, the improvement of a condition.

amelodentinal, pertaining to dentin or dental enamel.

amenorrhea, the absence or suppression of menstruation which is normal before puberty, after menopause, and during pregnancy or lactation.

amentia, feeble-mindedness or mental deficiency marked by mental confusion and subnormal intelligence.

ametropia, an abnormal condition of the eye in which vision is affected due to imperfect focus of images on the retina as in astigmatism, hyperopia, and myopia.

amino acid, one of a group of organic compounds containing both an amino and a carboxyl radical which are the building blocks of protein.

aminopyrine, an antipyretic and analgesic which has longer lasting effects in smaller doses than an antipyrine.

aminuria, accumulations of nitrogen-containing compounds found in the urine.

amitosis, cell division without changes in the nucleus or formation of chromosomes.

amitriptyline, an antidepressant drug.

amniocentesis, a surgical procedure which penetrates the uterus for aspiration of amniotic fluid to determine genetic defects.

amnion, the inner membrane which surrounds the fetus and holds the amniotic fluid.

amniotic fluid, the albuminous fluid within the amniotic sac which is colorless and functions to protect the floating fetus.

amnionitis, inflammation of the amnion.

amoeba, see: ameba.

amorphous, shapeless and having no specific form.

amphetamine, a drug used to stimulate the central nervous system. Misuse may lead to drug dependence.

amphoteric, showing or having opposite characteristics and capable of neutralizing both acids and bases.

ampule, a small container for hypodermic solutions.

ampulla, a dilatated end of a tubular structure such as a canal or duct.

amputation, the act of cutting off a limb or appendage by a surgical procedure.

amusia, loss of ability to produce or recognize musical sounds.

A.M.W.A., American Medical Women's Association.

amyelia, absence of the spinal cord at birth.

amygdaline, shaped like an almond; pertaining to a tonsil.

amylaceous, resembling starch.

amylase, pancreatic and salivary juices with enzymes that convert starch into sugar.

amyloid, starchlike, translucent material formed in a variety of diseases and deposited intercellularly.

amylolysis, the conversion of starch into sugar by enzymes in the process of digestion.

amylopsin, an enzyme in pancreatic juice which converts starch into sugar maltose.

amylum, corn starch used as dusting powder.

amyocardia, weakness of the heart muscle.

amyosthenia, muscular weakness and lacking muscle tone.

amyotrophy, muscular wasting that is painful.

amyxorrhea, an absence of mucous secretion.

ana, used in medical ingredients meaning in equal proportions or of each.

anabiosis, restoration of life after an apparent cessation of vital processes.

anabolism, opposed to catabolism in the metabolic process by which the body substance is built up.

anabolite, a complex substance of anabolism.

anadipsia, intense thirst.

anaerobe, a microorganism that thrives without oxygen.

anakusis, total deafness.

anal, a ring, pertaining to the rectal opening; near the anus.

analeptic, drug that gives strength and is restorative.

analgesic, drug that relieves pain without loss of consciousness.

anallergic, not allergic or hypersensitive.

analysis, separation and or act of determining the compound parts of a substance; separation into compound parts; psychoanalysis involving diagnosis and treatment.

analyst, one who analyzes.

anamnesis, recollection; past history of a patient and his family.

anaphase, third stage in mitosis between metaphase in which longitudinal halves of chromosomes separate and move toward opposite poles.

anaphia, diminished sense of touch.

anaphoresis, insufficient activity of the sweat glands.

anaphrodisia, loss of sexual desire.

anaphrodisiac, a substance that represses sexual desire.

anaphylaxis, an increased sensitivity to a drug, so that a second dose brings about a severe reaction, severe enough to cause serious shock.

anaplasia, an alteration in cells which is believed to produce characteristics of tumor tissue.

anaplastic, restoring of an absent part.

anarthria, speechlessness resulting from the loss of the ability to articulate words.

anasarca, severe generalized edema.

anastaltic, very astringent.

anastomosis, the surgical formation of a passage between two normally distinct organs or spaces; the joining together of parts such as nerves or connective tissue fibers; the union of arteries or veins.

anatomist, one skilled in anatomy.

anatomy, the scientific study of structures of organisms.

anconal, pertaining to the elbow.

ancylostomiasis, infestation with hookworms which gain entrance into the body through the skin of the bare foot of a person causing inflammation, itching, allergic reactions, pneumonia-like symptoms, nausea, and diarrhea. Excessive blood loss leads to anemia.

androgen, a substance producing male characteristics, as testosterone.

androgynous, resembling an androgynoid and without definite sexual characteristics.

androsterone, a male hormone found in urine.

anemia, a reduction in hemoglobin, or in the volume of packed red blood cells. It occurs when hemoglobin is less than 13--14 gm. per 100 ml. for males or 11--12 gm. per 100 ml. for women.

anemic, having anemia.

anencephaly, an absence of brain and spinal cord, a congenital defect.

anesthesia, a lost sense of feeling due to disease or induced to permit the performance of surgery and other painful procedures.

anesthesiology, a branch of medicine which studies the administration of anesthetics.

anesthetist, a person trained to administer anesthetics.

anesthetize, to place under an anesthetic agent.

aneurin, thiamine, or Vitamin B1.

aneurysm, a widening of a blood vessel due to pressure on weakened tissues causing the formation of a sac of blood that may become clotted.

angiasthenia, a loss of tone in the vascular system.

angiitis, inflammation of the coats of either blood or lymph vessels.

angina, a choking, spasmodic, or suffocating pain that characterizes any disease.

angina pectoria, severe pain about the heart that radiates to the shoulder and down the left arm, usually caused by interference with the oxygen supply to the heart muscle.

angiocardiogram, a film produced by an X-ray of the heart and the great vessels after intravenous injection of a radiopaque solution.

angiocarditis, inflammation of the heart and the great blood vessels.

angiography, an examination of blood vessels and lymphatics by roentgen rays which are made visible by injection of a diagnostic solution.

angiology, the scientific study of blood vessels and lymphatics.

angioma, a tumor which is usually benign believed to be misplaced fetal tissue consisting of blood vessels and lymphatics.

angiomyosarcoma, a tumor consisting of a mass of blood vessels or lymphatics resembling elements of angioma, myoma, and sarcoma.

angioneurectomy, excision of blood vessels and nerves.

angioplasty, reconstruction of blood vessels by surgery.

angiospasm, excessive contractions of blood vessels.

angiostaxis, trickling of blood; oozing of blood as in Hemophilia.

angiostenosis, narrowing of a blood vessel.

angulation, angular loops which form in the intestine.

anhidrosis, deficiency of secretion of sweat.

anhydremia, deficiency of the normal fluid content in the blood.

anhydrous, without water.

anhypnia, insomnia.

animation, the quality of being alive, or active. **(suspended,** a. temporary suspension of vital activities).

aniridia, absence of the iris at birth.

anisocoria, inequality in size of the pupils, a normal condition or congenital.

anisocytosis, excessive variations in size of red blood cells indicating an abnormal condition.

ankle, the joint between leg and foot.

ankylo-, combining word form meaning bent or crooked.

ankylocolpos, pathological closure of the vagina.

ankylosis, partial or complete rigidity of a joint as a result of disease, injury, or surgical procedure.

ankyroid, hook-shaped.

anlage, the beginning of cell formation in an embryo which will develop specific tissue, organ, or part.

annular, ring-shaped.

annulus, a ring-shaped structure.

anococcygeal, refering to the anus and coccyx.

anodyne, a medication that relieves pain.

anomalous, irregular or abnormal.

anomaly, deviation from normal resulting from congenital or hereditary defects; a malformation.

anoia, idiocy.

anomia, inability to name objects or to recognize names of persons.

anonychia, without nails.

anopheles, widely distributed mosquitoes, many of which are vectors of malaria.

anopsia, defective vision resulting from strabismus, cataract, or refractive errors.

anorexia, loss of appetite for food.

anorexia nervosa, a lack or complete loss of appetite usually seen in girls and young women; sometimes the disease is accompanied by induced vomiting, emaciation, and amenorrhea. The psychophysiologic condition may also occur in males.

anosmia, absence of the sense of smell.

anostosis, defective development of bone.

anovarism, absence of the ovaries.

anoxemia, reduced oxygen level in the blood.

anoxia, absence of oxygen to body tissues despite adequate blood supply.

ant-, anti-, prefix meaning opposed to or counteracting.

Antabuse, trademark for disulfiram used in treatment of alcoholism.

antacid, an alkali that neutralizes acids in the stomach.

antagonism, opposition between similar muscles, medicines, or organisms.

antagonist, counteracting the action of anything.

antalkaline, neutralizing alkalinity.

ante-, prefix meaning before.

antefebrile, before a fever.

anteflexion, the foreward bending of an organ; the normal foreward bending of the uterus.

antemortem, occurring before death.

antenatal, before birth.

antepartum, before labor commences.

anterior, directed toward the front.

anterolateral, in front and situated to one side.

anteversion, tipping forward of an organ.

anthelmintic, an agent which is destructive to parasitic intestinal worms.

anthemorrhagic, medication for preventing hemorrhage.

anthracosis, a pneumoconiosis due to the inhalation of coal dust.

anthrax, a disease man contracts from animal hair or waste; a carbuncle; the disease may be of two forms, one on the skin and the other in the lungs. If untreated, anthrax may often be fatal.

anthropo-, prefix denoting relation to man.

anthropogeny, origin of man.

anthropoid, resembling man; tailless apes such as the gorilla, orangutan, and chimpanzee.

anthropology, the science of man in relation to origin, classification, race, physical and mental constitution, environmental and social relations, and culture.

anthropometry, the science of measuring the size, weight, and proportions of the human body.

anthropophobia, a morbid fear of a particular person, or of society. May be the onset of mental illness.

anthypnotic, hindering sleep.

anti-, prefix meaning against.

antianaphylaxis, desensitization to antigens.

antiarrhythmic, an agent alleviating cardiac arrhythmias.

antibacterial, destroying or hindering the growth of bacteria.

antibiotic, a substance produced by a microorganism which has the capacity to inhibit or destroy other microorganisms. Antibiotics are produced by bacteria and fungi and can be made synthetically.

antiblennorrhagic, a substance used to prevent or cure gonorrhea or catarrh.

antibody, a protein produced by the body in response to the presence of an antigen.

anticholingeric, an agent that blocks the passage of impulses through the parasympathetic nerves; parasympatholytic.

anticoagulant, acting to prevent clotting of blood; any substance which prevents or delays the coagulation of blood.

anticonvulsive, inhibiting or relieving convulsions.

antidepressant, acting to relieve or prevent depression.

antidiuretic, a substance that acts to suppress excretion of urine by the kidneys.

antidotal, acting as an antidote.

antidote, an agent which neutralizes poison or its effects.

antiemetic, an agent that prevents or alleviates nausea and vomiting.

antienzyme, an agent which inhibits enzymatic action; an enzyme produced by the body retarding the activity of another enzyme.

antiepileptic, an agent that combats epilepsy.

antifebrile, relieving fever.

antigalactic, an agent that suppresses the secretion of milk.

antigen, any substance which induces the formation of antibodies when bacteria or foreign blood cells are introduced into the body.

antihistamine, a substance which counteracts the effects of histamine such as used in treatment of allergies.

antihypertensive, reducing high blood pressure.

antimalarial, acting to relieve or prevent malaria, such as quinine.

antimicrobial, preventing or destroying the development of microbes.

antimony, a metallic element with a crystalline structure used in medicine.

antimycotic, preventing the growth of fungi.

antiparkinsonian, an agent used in treatment of parkinsonism.

antipathy, aversion or disgust; a chemical incompatibility.

antiperistalsis, the peristalic contractions moving toward the oral end of the gastrointestinal tract.

antiphlogistic, relieving inflammation.

antiprothrombin, anticoagulant.

antipyretic, an agent effective against fever.

antipyrine, an odorless, white crystalline powder used to reduce pain and fever.

antiscabious, relieving or preventing scabies.

antiscorbutic, effective against scurvy such as Vitamin C.

antisepsis, pertaining to sepsis, preventing the growth of germs.

antiserum, a serum containing antibodies specific for the antigen.

antispasmodic, relieving or preventing spasms.

antitoxin, a substance produced by the body capable of neutralizing a specific poison or toxin.

antitussive, an agent which relieves or prevents coughing.

antivenin, a substance used in treatment of animal venom poisoning.

antiviral, an effective agent inhibiting a virus.

antivitamin, an antagonistic substance which inhibits certain vitamins.

antrum, any nearly closed chamber or cavity in bones.

anuresis, a condition in which the kidneys fail to secrete urine.

anuria, failure to produce urine.

anus, outlet of the rectum leading from the bowel.

anvil, one of the three small bones of the middle ear between the stirrup and the hammer.

anxiety, an emotional feeling indicating uneasiness and apprehension; a psychological term.

aorta, the main artery arising from the left ventricle of the heart.

aortic stenosis, a narrowing of the aorta due to lesions of the wall with scar tissue from infection often seen resulting from rheumatic fever or embryonic anomalities.

aortitis, inflammation of the aorta.

apandria, an aversion to men.

apaneuria, impossibility of cloitus.

apathetic, indifferent; lacking interest.

apathy, sluggish; without feeling or emotion.

aperient, a mild laxative usually given at night on an empty stomach.

aperitive, an appetizer; a gentle purgative.

aperture, an opening.

apex, the extremity of anything; used to indicate the uppermost part of a body organ.

aphagia, inability to swallow.

aphakia, absence of crystalline lens behind the pupil of the eye.

aphasia, inability to express oneself through speech; a loss of verbal comprehension.

aphemia, loss of speech due to a central lesion.

aphonia, lack of voice with intact inner speech due to chronic laryngitis, hysteria, psychological problems, or diseases of the vocal cords.

aphrasia, inability in using connected phrases in speaking.

aphrodisia, extreme or morbid sexual passion.

aphrodisiac, a substance that excites sexual desire.

aphtha, a white spot or small ulcer occurring in the mouth.

aphthous stomatitis, recurring blister-like ulcers inside the mouth and on the lips; canker sores.

aphylaxis, absence of immunity.

aplasia, defective development of an organ or tissue.

apnea, temporary cessation of breathing due to reduction of stimuli to respiratory center; may occur during Cheyne-Stokes respiration.

apocrine, cells which lose part of their cytoplasm while functioning, especially mammary gland and certain sweat gland cells.

apodal, having no feet.

apomorphine, a morphine derivative used as an emetic and expectorant.

aponeurosis, a fibrous sheet of connective tissue which attaches muscle to bone or other tissues at insertion.

apophysis, a projection from a bone; an outward growth without a center of ossification.

apoplectic, pertaining to apoplexy.

apoplexy, sudden loss of consciousness followed by paralysis resulting from rupture of a blood vessel of the brain; a stroke.

appendage, anything attached to a larger part.

appendectomy, surgical removal of the vermiform appendix.

appendicitis, inflammation of the vermiform appendix.

appendix, an appendage; the vermiform appendix attached to the cecum.

appestat, a section of the brain, centrally located, controlling the appetite.

appetite, chiefly a desire for food, not necessarily hunger.

apraxia, loss of ability to carry out familiar purposeful movements without motor or sensory impairment.

apyrexia, absence of fever; nonfebrile period of an intermittent fever.

aqua, water; solution.

aquaphobia, unusual fear of water.

aqueous, containing water.

aqueous humor, watery transparent liquid produced by the iris, ciliary bodies, and cornea which circulates through the anterior and posterior chambers of the eye.

arachnoid, resembling a web.

arachnoid membrane, the thin, transparent center membrane that covers the brain and spinal cord.

Aran-Duchenne disease, muscular atrophy beginning in the extremities and progressing to other parts of the body; a progressive muscular atrophy.

archiform, bow-shaped.

arcus, an arc or arch.

arcus senillis, the opaque white ring which appears around the periphery of the cornea, seen in aged persons due to lipoid degeneration.

areola, a small area in a tissue; a small space between tissues that surrounds a skin lesion such as a boil; the colored circle surrounding the nipple; the part of the iris that surrounds the pupil.

areolar, containing small cavities in a tissue such as the glands lying beneath the breasts with ducts opening on its surface; connective tissue within the innerspaces of the body.

ariboflavinosis, a condition caused by a deficiency of riboflavin (Vitamin B2 or G).

arnica, a substance derived from plants used as an application to wounds.

aromatic, a drug or medicine having a fragrant odor.

arrectores pilorum, involuntary muscle fibers contracting under the influence of cold or fright and raising the hair follicles resulting in ''gooseflesh''.

arrhythmia, a disturbance of rhythm in the heartbeat.

arrhythmic, without regularity; abnormal rhythm of the heartbeat.

arsenic, a poisonous chemical element used in medicine and industry.

ateria, an artery.

arterial, pertaining to an artery or arteries.

arterial bleeding, bright-red blood pumped out of an artery, may be arrested by pressure on the proimal side of the blood vessel nearest the heart.

arterialization, changing venous blood to arterial by aeration.

arteriogram, a radiograph of arterial pulse.

arteriography, radiography of an artery or arterial system after injection of a contrast medium into the blood stream.

arteriola, arteriole, a minute artery, especially one which leads into a capillary at its distal end.

arterioplasty, surgical reconstruction of an artery.

arteriosclerosis, a thickening or hardening and loss of elasticity of the blood vessels and arteries.

arteriospasm, pain in an artery caused by spasms.

arteriostenosis, constriction of an artery.

arteriovenous, pertaining to both arteries and veins.

arteritis, inflammation of an artery.

artery, one of the many vessels carrying blood from the heart to the tissues of the body.

arthralgia, pain in a joint.

arthritic, pertaining to a joint; pertaining to arthritis; a person afflicted with arthritis.

arthritis, inflammation of the joints.

arthrography, an x-ray of a joint after injection with an opaque solution.

arthropathy, any joint disease.

arthroplasty, a surgical procedure upon a joint to make it function.

arthrosclerosis, stiffening of the joints, occurring especially in the aged.

arthrosis, a joint; degeneration of a joint.

arthrosynovitis, inflammation of the synovial membrane of a joint.

articular, pertaining to the joint.

articulation, connection of bones or joints; clearly enunciated speech; in dentistry, the contact relationship of the surfaces of the teeth.

artifact, artificially produced; a structure produced in a tissue or cell by staining.

artificial, not natural; formed in imitation.

artificial insemination, mechanical injection of seminal fluid within the vagina or cervix.

artificial respiration, maintaining respiratory movements by mouth-to-mouth breathing or by mechanical means.

artus, a joint or limb.

arytenoid, resembling a ladle, usually referring to the larynx and relating to cartilage or ligaments.

arytenoiditis, inflammation of arytenoid cartilage.

asaphia, inability to articulate normally due to a cleft palate.

asbestosis, lung disease caused by the inhalation of asbestos particles.

ascaris, infestation of an intestinal parasite.

ascites, excessive fluid accumulation in the peritoneal cavity or abdominal cavity.

ascorbic acid, Vitamin C which occurs naturally or may be produced synthetically.

asepsis, absence of germs; sterile, free from microorganisms.

aseptic, free from germs.

asexual, not sexual.

Asiatic cholera, an acute infectious disease of epidemic proportion.

aspergillosis, a condition produced by Aspergillus fungi producing mycotic nodules in the lungs, liver, kidneys, or on any mucous surface.

aspermia, lack of semen, or failure to ejaculate sperm.

asperous, minute, uneven elevations; roughness.

asphyxia, an interruption of effective gaseous exchange, oxygen and carbon dioxide, resulting in respiratory interference or suffocation.

asphyxiate, to cause asphyxia.

aspirate, to remove by suction; to inhale.

aspiration, to draw foreign bodies in or out by suction through the nose, throat, or lungs; withdrawal of fluid from a body cavity with an instrument called an aspirator.

aspirin, a derivative of acetylsalicylic acid used as an analgesic, antipyretic, and antirheumatic.

astasia, motor incoordination resulting in the inability to sit, stand, or walk normally.

asteatosis, an absence of sebaceous secretion.

asternal, not connected to the sternum.

asthenia, loss of strength; weakness originating in muscular or cerebellar disease.

asthenic, pertaining to asthenia.

asthenopia, tiring or weakness of eye muscles due to fatigue; painful vision.

asthma, a chronic condition characterized by difficulty in breathing and wheezing due to spasmodic bronchial contractions.

asthmatic, pertaining to asthma; one who suffers from asthma.

astigmatic, pertaining to astigmatism.

astigmatism, an imperfection of the eye caused by differences in curvature of the lens and refractive surfaces of the eye so that light rays are not focused properly on the retina.

astragalus, the talus, or anklebone of the foot.

astraphobia, unusual fear of lightening and thunderstorms.

astringent, styptic or contracting; an agent that has an astringent effect; a constricting or binding effect which checks hemorrhages and secretions.

astrocyte, a neuroglial cell resembling a star-shape, collectively named astroglia.

astrocytoma, a malignant tumor composed of astrocytes.

asynergia, incoordination between muscle groups.

asynovia, insufficient secretion of synovial fluid of a joint.

asystole, abnormal contractions of ventricles of the heart.

atactilia, inability to distinguish tactile impressions.

ataractic, a drug that produces ataraxia.

atavism, reappearance of a disease or abnormality experienced by an ancestor.

ataxia, muscular incoordination affecting voluntary muscular movements.

atelectasis, partial or total collapse of the lung; a condition in which lungs of a fetus remain unexpanded at birth.

atelencephalia, congenital anomaly, an imperfect development of the brain.

atelocardia, congenital anomaly, an incomplete development of the heart.

atelocephalus, having an incomplete head.

atelocheilia, incomplete development of the lip; harelip.

atheroma, a sebaceous cyst; a thickening of the wall of larger arteries.

atherosclerosis, localized accumulations of deposits of lipids within the inner surfaces of blood vessels, one of the causes of arterial occlusion.

athetosis, repeated involuntry, purposeless, muscular distortion involving the entire body, especially hands, fingers, feet, and toes.

athlete's foot, a fungus infection of the foot which is contagious; ringworm of the foot.

athrombia, defective blood clotting.

athymia, without emotion or feeling.

atlas, the first cervical vertebra which supports the head.

atom, the smallest particle of an element.

atomizer, a device for dispensing liquid into a fine spray.

atonic, lack of normal tone.

atony, flaccidy and lack of strength; lack of muscular tone.

atopy, a group of diseases of an allergic nature; an acquired or inherited hypersensitivity of the skin to an agent.

atresia, closure of a normal body opening or congenital absence of a body orifice such as anus or vagina.

atrioventricular, pertaining to an atrium and ventricle of the heart.

atrium, the auricles; receiving chambers of the heart.

atrophic, pertaining to or characterized by atrophy.

atrophy, degeneration of the body or of an organ or part.

atropine, an anticholinergic alkaloid which acts to block stimulation of muscles and glands and used as a smooth muscle relaxant; used to dilate the pupil of the eye.

attenuation, the act of thinning or weakening.

attic, the upper part of the tympanic cavity of the ear.

audiogram, a drawing of the audiometer.

audiometer, an instrument for testing the acuity of hearing.

auditory nerve, a sensory nerve of hearing leading to the brain; the eighth cranial nerve.

aura, a subjective feeling that precedes the onset of an attack, such as experienced in epilepsy or hysteria.

aural, pertaining to the ear; pertaining to an aura.

aureomycin, a trademark for chlortetracycline, an antibiotic.

auricle, auricula, the external ear; pina or flap; the atrium of the heart.

auricular, pertaining to an auricle or to the ear.

auriscope, an instrument for making an aural examination.

aurotherapy, treatment of rheumatoid arthritis using gold salts.

auscultate, to examine by listening to the sounds of the viscera.

ascultation, process of listening for sounds produced in the body cavities such as the chest and abdomen to detect abnormalities with a stethoscope.

autism, a self-centered mental state in which thoughts and behavior are not subject to correction by external information.

autistic, self-centered; living in a phantasy of wish fulfillment.

autoclave, an airtight apparatus used to sterilize materials by steam pressure for a specified length of time.

autodigestion, digestion of tissue by their own secretion.

autogenous, self-produced; originating within the body.

autograft, a tissue graft taken from one part of a person's body and transferred to another part of the same body.

autohypnosis, self-induced hypnosis.

autoinfection, infection by microorganisms present within one's own body.

autoinoculation, inoculation of organisms obtained from another part of the body.

autointoxication, poisoning within the body by toxic substances produced within the body.

autolysis, digestion of tissue or cells by ferment in the cells themselves, even after death.

automatism, automatic actions and behavior without conscious volition; the activity of tissues or cells spontaneously such as the movement of cilia or the contractions of smooth muscles or organs removed from the body.

autonomic nervous system, spontaneous control of involuntary bodily functions as part of the nervous system which innervates glands, smooth muscle tissue, blood vessels, and the heart.

autophobia, abnormal fear of being alone.

autoplasty, a replacement of diseased or injured parts with a graft taken from the patient's own body.

autopsy, dissection of a body after death to determine the cause of death; a postmortem examination of a body.

autosome, any non-sex-determining chromosome of which there are 22 pairs in man.

autosuggestion, suggestion or thought originating within one's self.

autotoxemia, self-poisoning due to absorption of a poisonous substance generated within the body.

autotoxin, a toxin generated within the body upon which it acts.

avitaminosis, a condition caused by a lack of vitamins in the diet; a deficiency disease.

avivement, a procedure to hasten wound healing by refreshing the edges of the wound.

avulsion, a forcible pulling away of a part or structure.

axalein, a red dye.

axanthopia, yellow blindness.

axilla, armpit.

axion, pertaining to the brain and spinal cord.

axis, a line, real or imaginary, that runs through the center of the body; the second cervical vertebra of the neck on which the head turns.

axon, axone, a process of a nerve cell which conducts impulses away from the cell body.

azoospermia, absence of spermatozoa from the semen.

azotenesis, a condition caused by an excess of nitrogen in the body.

azoturia, an increased accumulation of nitrogenous compounds in urine.

azygous, singled, not in pairs.

azymia, lack of an enzyme.

B

Babes-Ernst bodies, metachromatic bodies seen in bacterial protoplasm.

Babinski reflex, backward flexion of the great toe when the sole of the foot is stroked, a normal reaction found in children up to one year of age. When the reflex is found in adults it indicates pyramidal tract involvement.

bacillary, relating to or being caused by bacilli, rod-like structures.

bacillemia, presence of bacilli in the blood.

bacilluria, bacilli in the urine.

bacitracin, an antibiotic effective against a wide range of infections.

back, posterior surface of the body; the region of the body from neck to pelvis.

backbone, vertebral or spinal column.

bacteria, bacterium, plant-like microorganisms without chlorophyll.

bacterial, pertaining to, or caused by bacteria.

bactericidal, being able to destroy bacteria.

bactericide, an agent capable of destroying bacteria.

bacteriology, the scientific study of bacteria.

bacteriolysis, destroying bacteria or dissolving them by a specific antibody.

bacteriophagia, destruction of bacteria by a virus capable of inducing lysis.

bacterioscopy, a microscopic examination of bacteria.

bacteriostasis, arresting bacterial growth.

bacterium, (singular of bacteria) single-celled microorganisms called Schizomycetes, having rod-shaped, round, or spiral bodies found in animal tissue, soil, and water.

bacteriuria, bacteria found in urine.

bag-of-waters, the amnion that surrounds the fetus.

baker's itch, eczema caused by yeast irritation.

baker's leg, knock-knee.

balanitis, inflammation of the glans penis.

balanus, the glans penis or glans clitoridis.

barbiturate, a salt used for its sedative effects; hypnotic.

basal metabolism, the process and measurement of cellular activity necessary to maintain life in the fasting and resting state based on oxygen requirements of the individual.

Basedow's disease, Graves's disease; exopthalmic goiter.

basiphobia, morbid fear of walking.

basocytopenia, a decrease of basophil leukocytes in the blood.

basocytosis, excess of basophil leukocytes in the blood.

basophil, applied to cells which are readily stained with basic dyes; a type of white blood cell.

bathophobia, extreme fear of looking downwards from high places.

bathycardia, a condition in which the heart is fixed in an abnormally low position.

battarism, stuttering.

B complex, see Vitamin B complex.

bedsore, see decubitus.

bedwetting, see enuresis.

behavior, conduct; the observable actions and activity of an individual.

behaviorism, a psychological theory based upon objective observation and measurable data, rather than subjective ideas and emotions.

belch, an involuntary escape of gas from the stomach through the mouth.

belladona, a poisonous plant from which a drug is manufactured to relieve spasmodic disorders; active principle of atropine.

Bell's palsy, paralysis of facial nerves and muscles; an acute inflammatory reaction causing distortion to facial muscles.

belly, stomach.

bends, a decompression illness caused by bubbles of nitrogen in the blood and tissues.

benign, not malignant.

Benzedrine, proprietary name for amphetamine; a central nervous system stimulant.

benzocaine, a nontoxic local anesthetic; found in an ointment.

beriberi, a deficiency caused by faulty nutrition and the lack of Vitamin B, uncommon in the United States.

bicarbonate, a salt containing two parts of carbonic acid and one part of a base.

biceps, a muscle with two heads; a major muscle in the upper arm and in the thigh.

bicuspid, premolar tooth; having two cusps; mitral valve between left atrium and left ventricle of the heart.

bifid, split into two parts; cleft or forked.

bifocal, having two foci as seen in eyeglasses that correct both near and far vision.

bifurcate, having two distinct branches; forked.

bifurication, a division into two branches.

bilateral, relating to two sides of the body.

bile, a bitter secretion of the liver which aids digestion.

bile acids, complex acids which occur as salts and which are important to the digestion of fats in the intestines.

bile duct, a tube which conveys the liver secretion as it leaves the gall bladder.

biharzia, a term used for Schistosoma, the human blood fluke.

biliary, pertaining to the bile or gallbladder or to the passages conveying bile.

bilifulvin, bilirubin mixed with other substances, resulting in a tawny pigment.

bilious, an excess of bile due to a disorder of the liver.

bilirubin, a reddish-yellow pigment in bile, also found in blood and urine.

biliverdin, a greenish pigment found in bile formed in oxidation of bilirubin.

bilobate, having two lobes.

bilocular, divided into two cells or compartments.

bimaxillary, afflicting both jaws.

binocular, pertaining to two eyes.

binovular, derived from two ova.

bioassay, determining the strength of a drug by observing its effects on test animals and comparing these effects with a standard substance.

biocatalyst, a biochemical that dissolves; an enzyme.

biochemistry, the scientific study of living things and the chemical changes that occur during vital processes.

bioclimatology, pertaining to the relations or effect of climate on living things.

biodynamics, the science of energy; biophysiology.

biogenesis, the origin of living organisms.

biokinetics, the science of movement occurring in the developing of organisms.

biological, pertaining to biology; medical preparations used in the treatment or prevention of disease such as serums and vaccines.

biological block, pertaining to the internal mechanism in living organisms that direct the rhythmic cycles of varied involuntary processes.

biologist, a specialist who studies biology.

biology, the scientific study of life and living things; the study of plants and animals.

biometry, the study and computation of life expectancy.

bion, any living organism.

bionomy, the science pertaining to vital functions within the organism.

biophysics, the scientific study of living organisms using the principles of physics.

biopsy, tissue excised from a living organism for examination under the microscope.

biostatics, vital statistics.

biotics, pertaining to the law of living things.

biotin, a component of the vitamin B complex of which the therapeutic value has not been proven.

biotomy, vivisection on living animals for physiological and pathological study.

biotype, a genotype; the basic constitution of an organism.

biovular twins, twins from two separate ova.

biparous, giving birth to twins.

biramous, having two branches.

birth, the act of being born.

birth control, the prevention of pregnancy; any method used to prevent conception such as artificial devices or drugs.

birthmark, a permanent mark from birth injury found on the skin of an infant; nevus.

birth trauma, the emotional stress experienced by an infant at birth which may be a source of neurosis as an adult according to psychoanalytic theory.

bisexual, having both sexes in one individual; hermaphroditic; possessing genital and sexual characteristics of both man and woman.

bisferious, having a double pulse; dicrotic.

bismuth, a silvery white metallic element; it is used in its salt form as an antiseptic, astringent, sedative, and in treatment of diarrhea.

bistoury, a small surgical knife, used for minor surgery.

bitemporal, referring to both temporal bones in the skull.

bituminosis, pneumoconiosis originating from inhalation of dust or soft coal.

black death, a contagious and malignant disease known as bubonic plague.

blackhead, a fatty deposit of dried sebum in a sebaceous gland.

blackout, a sudden temporary loss of consciousness and vision.

blackwater fever, a form of malaria characterized by a sudden rise in body temperature, enlarged liver and spleen, epigastric pain, vomiting, jaundice, dark bloody urine, and shock.

bladder, collecting sac for urine; a reservoir.

bland, mild or soothing; pertaining to diet in which irritating food is avoided.

Blandin's glands, glands near tip of tongue.

blastocyst, a group of undifferentiated cells, the bastula, which develop into an embryo; a stage in the development of an embryo which follows the morula.

blastogenesis, the transmission of characteristics from parents to offspring by genes.

blastoma, a granular tumor.

blastomere, one of the cells into which fertilized ovum separate into segments.

blastomyces, pathogenic yeastlike organisms producing disease.

blastula, an early stage in the development of an ovum that develops into an embryo.

bleb, a blister or pustule.

bleeder, one who bleeds an abnormal amount; see hemophilia.

bleeding time, a natural stoppage of bleeding from a wound or cut, usually about three minutes or less.

blennorrhagia, an accumulative amount of discharge from mucous membranes, esp. gonorrheal discharge from the genital or urinary tract; gonorrhea.

blepharitis, inflammation of the eyelids involving hair follicles and glands causing swelling, redness and crusting.

blepharon, the eyelid.

blindness, inability to see partially or totally; visual impairment as a result of disease, irritation, or accident.

blind spot, a region on the retina where the optic nerve enters the eye and that is insensitive to light.

blister, a collection of fluid under the skin due to pressure or injury.

bloated, an abnormal swelling beyond normal size.

blood, the fluid which circulates throughout the body carrying nourishment and oxygen to the cells and tissue, and, at the same time, takes away waste matter and carbon dioxide.

blood bank, a storing place and processing center for reserve blood kept for emergency transfusions.

blood cell, a minute chamber; a corpuscle in the blood; red or white corpuscle.

blood clot, a coagulated mass of blood cells which forms when blood vessels are injured.

blood corpuscle, a circulating cell in the blood; a red cell, erythrocyte, or a white cell, leukocyte.

blood count, determination of the number and type of red and white blood cells per cubic millimeter of blood.

blood group, a classification into which human blood can be based or grouped; blood groups are designated as O, A, B, and AB.

bloodletting, an old method for treating disease by opening a vein and allowing a person to bleed for the specific purpose to reduce blood volume and hence the amount of work required by the heart; phlebotomy.

blood plasma, the colorless fluid of the blood separated by centrifuging.

blood poisoning, a diseased condition caused by the entrance of toxins or microorganisms into the blood stream; toxemia; pyremia, septicemia.

blood pressure, the pressure existing against the inner walls of the large arteries at the height of the pulse when the heart contracts, systolic pressure, and when the heart relaxes, diastolic pressure.

blood serum, the clear liquid that separates from the blood when it is allowed to clot; blood plasma from which fibrogen has been removed.

bloodshot, excessive congestion of capillaries causing inflammation and redness of the eyes.

blood smear, a drop of blood spread on a slide for microscopic examination.

blood sugar, glucose circulating in the blood, normally 60--90 mg. per 100 ml. of blood.

blood test, test of blood sample to determine blood type or the contents (such as sugar) of the blood.

blood transfusion, a technique for transferring the blood from one individual to another directly without being exposed to air.

blood type, determining classification of blood according to blood groups such as O, A, B, or AB.

blood vessel, vessels of the body that transport blood; three major types of blood-vessel: artery, capillary, and vein.

blotch, usually a red or pink spot on the skin.

blue baby, an infant born with a bluish color due to a mixture of venous and arterial blood caused by a defect in the heart.

boil, a microbic infection of the skin; a furuncle.

bolus, a pill-shaped mass.

bone, the hard, dense connective tissue consisting of bone cells that form the skeleton.

bone reflex, a reflex action resulting from a tapping; actually a tendon or muscle response or reflex.

borborygmus, a rumbling sound in the bowels; intestinal flatus.

boric acid, an odorless, white, crystalline powder used as a mild antiseptic, especially for the eyes, mouth, and bladder. In large amounts taken by children it may be poisonous.

botulinic acid, a toxic substance found in putrid meat.

botulism, severe food poisoning containing the toxin produced by Clostridium botulinum.

bougie, an instrument for dilating canals and passages of the body.

boulimia, abnormal hunger sensation after a meal.

bowels, see intestines.

bowleg, an outward bending of the leg.

brachialgia, extreme pain in the arm.

brachium, pertaining to the upper arm from shoulder to elbow.

brachycardia, slowness of heartbeat.

brachycephalic, short headed.

brachydactylia, shortness of fingers.

brachymetropia, nearsightedness; myopia.

bradycardia, unusually slow heart action.

bradykinesia, extremely slow movements.

bradyphagia, slowness in eating.

bradypnea, abnormally slow breathing.

bradyrhythmia, slow pulse rate.

bradyuria, slowness in passing urine.

brain, a large mass of nerve tissue which fills the cranium of man and other vertebrates.

brain fever, meningitis.

brain storm, a temporary outburst of mental excitement often seen in paranoia.

breakbone fever, a sudden febrile disease of epidemic proportion.

breast, the upper anterior aspect of the chest; mammary gland.

breath, inhaled and exhaled air in act of respiration.

breathing, respiration; taking in air and exhaling carbon dioxide.

breech, the buttocks.

breech presentation, the appearance of the buttocks or feet first instead of the head in childbirth occurring in about 3% of all labors.

bregma, the junction of the coronal and sagittal sutures on the surface of the skull.

Bright's disease, a disease of the kidneys usually associated with faulty uric acid elimination and high blood pressure.

broad-spectrum, any antibiotic that is effective against a wide variety of bacteria.

Brocca's area, the speech center in the left hemisphere of the brain which controls the movements of the tongue, lips, vocal cords, or motor speech.

bromides, the salts of bromine used in medication as a sedative and a hypnotic.

bromism, brominism, state of poisoning due to prolonged use of bromides.

bromomania, psychosis induced by use of bromides.

bromopnea, an offensive breath.

bronchadenitis, inflammation of the bronchial glands.

bronchi, plural of bronchus; primary divisions of the thrachea.

bronchial, pertaining to the bronchi or bronchioles.

bronchial tubes, the bronchi that lead from the trachea or windpipe.

bronchiectasis, a condition arising from inflammed bronchial tubes, usually secreting large amounts of offensive, infectious pus.

bronchiole, the smallest branch of the bronchi within the lungs.

bronchitis, an inflammation of the membranes lining the bronchi.

bronchopneumonia, inflammation of the bronchi and lungs caused by various types of pneumococci, pathogenic bacteria as well as viruses, rickettsias, and fungi.

bronchoscope, an instrument for examination of the interior of the bronchi.

bronchospasm, contractions of the smooth muscles of the bronchi which occurs in asthma.

bronzed skin, characteristic of Addison's disease due to adrenal cortical insufficiency.

brow, the forehead; the prominence over the eyes.

brucellosis, an infectious disease which primarily affects cattle, swine, and goats but sometimes affects man; caused by bacteria Brucella.

bruise, a contusion; an injury produced by impact without skin breakage but causing blood vessels to rupture and discolor surrounding tissues.

bruit, a murmur or sound heard in auscultation by means of a stethoscope.

bruxism, the grinding of teeth while sleeping.

bubo, an inflammed or enlarged lymph node, especially in the groin or axilla.

bubonic plague, an acute, infectious disease, frequently fatal, caused by infected rats and ground squirrels who carry the rat-flea which ultimately infects man through its bite; the black death of the Middle Ages.

buccal, pertaining to the cheek or mouth.

Buerger's disease, a recurring inflammatory disease affecting the veins and arteries of the limbs, seen mostly in males between the ages of 15 and 50 years.

bulbous, bulb-shaped; swollen or enlarged.

bulimia, unusual hunger experienced a short time after eating a meal.

bulla, a large blister; a skin vesicle or bubble filled with a watery fluid; the dilated portion of the bony external meatus of the ear.

bundle, group of fibers; a bundle of fibers of the impulse-conducting system of the heart.

bundle branch block, formation of a heart block in which the two ventricles contract independently of each other.

bunion, inflammation and thickening of the bursa of the joint of the great toe resulting from chronic inflammation.

burn, injury to the tissues of the skin as a result of excessive high heat, chemical, or radio-active exposure; burns are classified according to the extent of damage to the layers of skin.

bursa, a sac lined with synovial membrane containing synovial fluid which acts as a lubricant and reduces friction between joints and surrounding structures.

bursectomy, surgical removal of the bursa.

bursitis, inflammation of a bursa.

butacaine, used as a local anesthetic.

butalbital, a sedative.

buttocks, the fleshy prominence formed by the gluteal muscles of the lower back which joins the thighs.

bypass, a shunt performed by surgery creating an alternate pathway for the blood to bypass an obstructed main artery.

bysma, a plug.

byssinosis, a pulmonary disease from inhalation of cotton dust.

byssus, growth of pubic hair.

C

cachet, a wafer in which medicine is placed; capsule.

cachexia, a condition of malnutrition and wasting occurring in chronic illness in the later stages.

cachinnation, hysterical laughter.

cadaver, corpse; dead body.

cadaverous, resembling the appearance or color of a corpse.

caduceus, a symbol of the medical profession.

caesarean, see cesarean.

caffeine, an alkaloid found in coffee and tea which is used as a stimulant, diuretic, and as a treatment for headache.

caffeinism, chronic effects from excessive use of coffee causing heart palpitations, trembling, general depression, anxiety, insomnia, and agitated states.

caisson disease, a painful condition occurring in divers when air pressure is reduced too rapidly after coming to the surface causing nitrogen in the blood and tissues to be released as bubbles; the bends.

calamine, a pink, watery substance composed of zinc and iron oxides used externally as a protective astringent, skin lotion or ointment.

calcaneus, heel bone.

calcar, a spurlike process or projection.

calcareous, containing calcium carbonate; chalky.

calcemia, an excess of calcium in the blood.

calcic, pertaining to calcium or lime.

calcicosis, a pulmonary condition caused by inhaling dust from limestone, especially by marblecutters.

calciferol, vitamin D2 derived from ergosterol; used in treatment of rickets and hypocalcemic tetany.

calcification, the deposit of calcium in the tissues and bone.

calcinosis, an abnormal condition caused by deposits of calcium in tissues.

calcipenia, a calcium deficiency in the body.

calcium, a silvery white metallic element; the basic element of lime, necessary to skeletal structure and body function.

calcium carbonate, a white tasteless powder used as an antacid.

calculus, resembling a stone composed of mineral salts, found in kidneys, bladder, urethra, or other organs and ducts in the body under abnormal conditions.

calf, the fleshy part on the back of the leg below the knee.

calibrator, an instrument for measuring openings.

calisthenics, a systematic exercise routine for improving health, strength, and flexibility in movement.

callus, a thickening or horny layer of skin; the osseous material at the ends of a fractured bone and eventually replaced by new bone growth.

caloric, relating to heat or calories.

calorie, calory, a unit of heat; a measure of energy intake and output of the body; the amount of heat necessary to raise the temperature of one gram of water one degree centigrade.

calorimeter, an apparatus for determining the heat of the body.

calosity, callositas, the formation of thick skin due to pressure, friction, or irritation.

calvaria, human skull cap; cranium skull.

calvities, alopecia, baldness.

calyx, a cup-shaped organ or cavity such as the cup-like structure of the kidney pelvis.

camphor, a gum derived from an Asian evergreen tree used as a topical antipruitic.

camphorated, containing camphor.

canal, a passage or duct.

canaliculus, a tubular small channel or passage.

cancellate, latticelike or porous.

cancer, a malignant tumor; neoplasm; sarcoma or carcinoma characterized by abnormal growth of cells which spread to other tissues.

cancerous, pertaining to malignant growth.

cancroid, appearance of a cancer; skin cancer.

cancrum, a rapidly spreading cancer or ulcer.

canine, pertaining to upper and lower teeth between the incisors and molars of which there are four in number.

canker, a mouth ulcer; thrush; gangrenous inflammation of the mouth.

canker sore, an ulceration of the lips or mouth.

cannabis, the dried tops of hemp plants which produces euphoric states when used as a narcotic; hashish and marijuana.

cannula, a tube used for insertion into a duct or cavity for the purpose of withdrawing fluid or injecting medication into the body.

cannular, a hollow needle.

cantharis, a strong substance derived from crushed blister beetles used in medicine as a diuretic stimulant to reproductive or urinary organs; Spanish fly.

canthectomy, excision of a canthus.

canthitis, inflammation of the canthus.

canthus, the junction or angle of the upper and lower corner of both sides of the eyelids.

capiat, an instrument for removing foreign materials from body cavities, especially the uterus.

capillaritis, inflammation of the capillaries.

capillarity, action by which the liquid's surface is elevated or depressed at the point of contact with a solid.

capillary, minute blood vessel which connects the smallest arteries with the smallest veins.

capital, pertaining to the head.

capitate, head-shaped; having a rounded end.

capitatum, small capitate bone in the hand.

capitellum, the rounded projection or knob of the humerus articulating with the radial head.

capsitis, crystalline lens.

capsula, resembling a capsule; internal capsule of the brain.

capsular, referring to a capsule.

capsulation, enclosed within a capsule.

capsule, a covering usually of gelatin which envelops medication; a small membranous sac.

caput, head; upper part of an organ.

carbohydrase, an enzyme such as amylase and lactase that aids in the digestion of carbohydrates.

carbohydrates, a group of compounds including starches, sugars, celluloses, and gums; organic compounds composed of carbon, oxygen, and water, and classified as monosaccharides, disaccharides, and polysaccharides; carbohydrates provide 47% of calories in the diet and are one of the major sources of nourishment.

carbolic acid, used as an antiseptic and disinfectant derived from coal tar.

carbon, a nonmetallic element found in all living matter in various forms; coal is a common form, a diamond is a crystallized form, and in food it is a fuel which creates heat in animal life.

carbon 14, used in cancer research and archaeological studies.

carbon dioxide, an acid-tasting gas which is heavier than air and exhaled by all living animals; found in the atmosphere as a colorless, odorless non-combustible gas necessary to all plant life.

carbon monoxide, a colorless, odorless, tasteless, poisonous gas which is formed as a result of incomplete combustion and oxidation.

carbon monoxide poisoning, poisoning produced as a result of breathing in carbon monoxide gas and mixing with the hemoglobin of the blood which prevents oxygen from being carried to the tissues of the body causing difficult breathing, dizziness, pounding of the heart, headache, reddish color to face and chest, faintness, and nausea. If the victim can inhale fresh air, he will recover, but if not found in time convulsions, paralysis, and death may occur.

carbuncle, large boil.

carcinogenic, causing cancer.

carcinoid, a benign epithelial growth resembling a cancer.

carcinoma, a cancer; a malignant tumor which infiltrates connective tissues and spreads.

carcinomatophobia, extreme fear of carcinoma.

carcinomatosis, having a widespread dissemination of carcinoma throughout the body.

carcinosarcoma, pertaining to a mixed tumor of both carcinoma and sarcoma.

cardia, the region of the heart; the part of the stomach surrounding the esophagus.

cardiac, heart failure; having heart disease; referring to cardiac orifices surrounding the stomach; a heart medication.

cardiac failure, inability of the heart to pump blood in sufficient volume to meet body needs.

cardiac hypertrophy, enlargement of the heart.

cardiasthenia, weakness of the heart muscles with cardiac symptoms.

cardiataxia, very irregular heart contractions.

cardiectomy, a surgical procedure which involves the excision of the cardiac portion of the stomach.

cardiogram, record of electrical energy changes of the heart cycle.

cardiograph, apparatus for recording the heart cycle on a graph.

cardiologist, a specialist in the treatment and diagnosis of the heart.

cardiology, scientific study of the heart and its functions.

cardioneurosis, functional neurosis with cardiac symptoms such as rapid heart beat.

cardiopathy, any disorder or disease of the heart.

cardiophobia, extreme fear of heart disease.

cardiopulmonary, pertaining to the lungs and heart.

cardiopyloric, referring to both the cardiac and pyloric ends of the stomach.

cardiosclerosis, thickening and hardening of the cardiac tissues and arteries.

cardiospasm, spasm or contraction of the cardiac sphincter of the stomach when the esophagus fails to function properly.

cardiosphygmograph, an apparatus for recording movements of the heart and pulse.

cardiotomy, incision of the heart.

cardiovalvulitis, inflammation of the valves of the heart.

cardiovascular, pertaining to the heart and blood vessels.

carditis, inflammation of the heart muscles.

caries, decay and disintegration of bone or teeth.

carminative, a drug that will remove flatus from the gastrointestinal tract.

carnal, relating to the flesh.

carnophobia, abnormal fear to eat meat.

carotene, a yellow, orange, or red pigment found in some plants and animal tissues; stored in the liver and kidney and converted into Vitamin A in the body.

carotid, the main artery of the neck which divides into the left and right branch that transports the blood from the aorta to the head.

carpal, relating to the joint of the wrist.

carpophalangeal, pertaining to the carpus and the finger bones.

carpus, eight bones of the wrist.

carrier, an individual carrying disease germs without being infected himself; one who transmits a disease without suffering from it himself.

car sickness, motion sickness.

cartilage, dense connective tissue consisting of cells embedded in compact matrix but without blood vessels; gristle; the cartilage or elastic connective tissue composing the skeletal structures of the embryo is converted into bone after birth.

cartilaginous, pertaining to cartilage.

caruncle, an abnormal fleshy growth.

cascara, a laxative.

caseation, conversion of necrotic tissue into a cheese-like granular mass in some diseases; formation of casein during coagulation of milk.

case history, information about a patient's personal or family's history recorded during interview, used especially in social work, medicine, or psychiatry.

casein, the principle protein in milk occurring in milk curds.

caseous, resembling cheese.

cassia, used as a laxative derived from a plant in the form of senna.

cast, a mold made of plaster of Paris to hold a bone rigid and straight as in fractures, dislocations, and other serious injuries.

castor oil, a sticky oil used as a purgative derived from the castor bean.

castrate, to remove the testicles or ovaries.

castration, destruction or excision of the testicles or ovaries.

castration complex, morbid fear of castration.

catabasis, decline of a disease or illness.

catabolic, pertaining to catabolism.

catabolism, the breaking-down phase of metabolism in which complex substances are converted to simpler substances; the opposite of anabolism.

catalepsy, a neurosis characterized by a temporary loss of the senses and the power to move the muscles; trance-like.

catalyst, an agent that causes a chemical reaction or change.

catamenia, menses; periodic menstrual discharge from the uterus.

catamnesis, the medical history of a patient documented by the physician after the first examination including subsequent visits.

cataphasia, a speech disorder causing involuntary or constant repetition of the same phrase or word.

cataphora, lethargy with intermittent periods of waking.

cataphoria, a condition in which a downward turning of the visual axis of each eye continues after the visual stimuli have been removed.

cataplasia, degeneration change in which cells and tissues revert to earlier, more primitive conditions.

cataplasm, a poultice, usually with a medication.

cataplexy, cataplexia, resembling a stroke; sudden shock with a temporary loss of muscular weakness and muscle tone; often a result of emotional shock, sudden onset of an illness, or associated with narcolepsy.

cataract, a condition of the eye caused by a clouding of the crystalline lens or its capsule or both which prevents normal vision.

catarrh, inflammation of the mucous membranes with a discharge of mucus secretions, particularly from the upper respiratory tract.

catatonia, type of schizophrenia characterized by immobility and unresponsiveness; stupor; exhibiting fixed posturing and refusal to communicate.

catatonic, pertaining to catatonia.

catatropia, the downward turning of both eyes.

catgut, a cord or surgical thread that is sterile and absorbable used for tying or binding blood vessels, usually made of twisted sheep's intestine or silk.

catharsis, a purging of the bowels; in psychoanalysis, experiencing emotional release by recalling an event that precipitated a psychoneurosis; abreaction.

cathartic, pertaining to catharsis.

catheter, a tube of elastic, elastic web, rubber, glass, or metal used for evacuating or injecting fluids.

catheterization, inserting a catheter into a body channel or cavity.

cathexis, the attachment of emotional or mental energy to an idea or object.

cauda, taillike structure.

caudad, toward the tail or posterior direction of the body.

caudal, pertaining to any taillike structure; inferior in position.

caudate, having a taillike projection.

caul, the great omentum; membranous amnion covering the head of the fetus at birth.

causalgia, burning pain.

caustic, corroding and burning; an agent capable of destroying tissue.

cauterization, burning or cauterizing a part.

cauterize, to burn or sear with a cautery.

cautery, destroying tissue by application of electricity, heat, or corrosive chemicals.

caval, pertaining to the vena cava.

cavernous, containing hollow spaces.

cavity, hollow space; a hollow place within the body or one of the organs; hole in a tooth or a dental cavity.

cecectomy, surgical removal of part of the cecum or incision of the cecum.

cecitis, inflammation of the cecum.

cecoileostomy, an opening or stoma into the ileum.

cecoptosis, displacement of the cecum.

cecostomy, surgical creation of an artificial opening into the cecum.

cecum, a pouchlike formation at the beginning of the large intestine and bears at its lower end the vermiform appendix; any blind sac.

celiac, pertaining to the abdominal cavity.

celiac disease, a chronic intestinal disorder occurring in infants and children due to a dietary deficiency.

cell, a small enclosed chamber containing a nucleus within a mass of protoplasm which is the basic structure of all living things.

cellular, pertaining to, or composed of cells.

cellulase, an enzyme produced by snails or molluscs used in medicine to convert cellulose to celloboise; used as a digestive aid.

cellulitis, inflammation of connective tissues.

celluloneuritis, inflammation of nerve cells.

cellulose, a carbohydrate forming the framework of plants; plant fiber.

cell wall, boundary lying outside the cell membrane.

cementum, thin layer of bony tissue deposited by cementoblasts which form the dentine or outer surface of the root of a tooth.

cenogenesis, appearance of characteristics in a person which are absent in ancestors and which do not have a phylogenetic importance.

cenotype, common or original type.

centigrade, pertaining to a thermometer in which the boiling point is 100° and the freezing point is 0°.

central nervous system, abrr. CNS, brain and spinal cord, including nerves and end organs which control voluntary action; voluntary nervous system.

centrifuge, an apparatus used in testing corpuscles in the blood, and solids in urine by employing centrifuging force which hastens sedimentation.

cephalad, toward the head.

cephalagia, pain in the head; headache.

cephalhematoma, a swelling of the subcutaneous tissues containing blood, frequently found on the head of a newborn infant a few days after delivery.

cephalic, pertaining to the head.

cephalitis, encephalitis; inflammation of the brain.

cephalometer, an instrument for measuring the head.

cephalonia, enlarged head marked by idiocy.

cera, wax.

cerebellar, pertaining to the cerebellum.

cerebellitis, inflammation of the cerebellum.

cerebellospinal, relating to the cerebellum and spinal cord.

cerebellum, posterior portion of the brain which controls voluntary muscular movements, equilibrium, and posture.

cerebral, pertaining to the cerebrum or brain.

cerebral hemorrhage, resulting from a ruptured blood vessel in the brain associated with disease, accident, or high blood pressure.

cerebral palsy, brain damage, usually occurring at birth, characterized by incoordination of muscular activity, spasms, and abnormal speech.

cerebritis, inflammation of the brain.

cerebromalacia, softening of the brain.

cerebromeningitis, inflammation of the brain and its membranes.

cerebrosclerosis, hardening of the brain, esp. of the cerebrum.

cerebrospinal, pertaining to the brain and spinal cord.

cerebrospinal fluid, a watery substance produced by the choroid plexuses in the lateral ventricles situated at the base of the brain which acts as a cushion protecting the brain.

cerebrum, the largest part of the brain consisting of the left and right hemisphere being united by the corpus callosum and the anterior and posterior commissures.

cerumen, earwax.

cervical, pertaining to the neck of the womb.

cervicitis, inflammation of the cervix.

cervitamic acid, crystalline ascorbic acid; Vitamin C.

cervix, narrow part of the uterus; part of an organ resembling a neck.

cervix vesicae, the neck of the bladder.

cesarean, abdominal operation to remove an infant from the womb; cesarean section.

cestode, belonging to the subclass Cestoda; a parasitic tapeworm found in the alimentary tract.

cestoid, resembling a tapeworm.

cetrimonium bromide, a quaternary ammonium compound used as an antiseptic and detergent; applied topically to the skin as a disinfectant.

chafe, injury by friction or rubbing.

chalazion, a sty; small, hard sebaceous cyst developing on the eyelids.

chancre, a syphilitic ulcer usually occurring two or three weeks after infection.

chancroid, a nonsyphilitic soft veneral ulcer, highly contagious.

change of life, menopause; climacteric.

chapped skin, skin which becomes dry, split, and cracked due to overexposure to a harsh environment and decreased activity of glands in the surrounding area.

charting, recording the progress of an illness or disease which also gives information about the patient and his treatment; a clinical chart or record.

chauffage, treatment with a cautery at low heat that is applied close to the tissue.

cheek, fleshy portion of either side of the face below the eyes; pertaining to the mucous membranes within the inner surface of the mouth.

cheekbone, zygomatic bone.

cheilitis, inflammation of the lip.

cheilosis, a condition of the lips characterized by dry scaling, fissures, and reddened appearance at the angles of the mouth, resulting from Vitamin B deficiency.

cheirospasm, writer's cramp; spasms of the muscles of the hand.

chemical, pertaining to chemistry.

chemocautery, application of a caustic substance in cauterization.

chemoprophylaxis, prevention of a disease by drugs or chemical agents.

chemosis, edema of the conjunctiva of the eye.

chemosurgery, destruction of diseased tissue by chemical agents for therapeutic purposes.

chemotaxis, movement of living cells in response to a chemical stimulus.

chemotherapy, treatment of disease by chemical agents.

cherophobia, extreme fear of and aversion to gaiety.

chest, the thorax which encloses the ribs.

Cheyne-Stokes respiration, irregular type of arrhythmic breathing occurring in acute illness or in certain acute diseases of the central nervous system, heart, lungs, and occasionally involving intoxication.

chiasm, a crossing of tendons or nerves; a structure in the forebrain formed by fibers of the optic nerves.

chickenpox, varicella; a highly contagious disease characterized by vesicular eruptions on the skin and mucous membranes.

chiggers, a six-legged reddish mite larva which burrows beneath the skin producing wheals, intense itching and sever dermatitis.

chilblain, inflammation, swelling, and itching of the ears, fingers, and toes produced by frostbite.

childbed, puerperal period in childbearing.

childbirth, process of giving birth; parturition.

chill, shaking of the body when affected by cold temperatures or occurring with certain diseases such as malaria; shivering.

chiropodist, podiatrist; one who treats foot irregularities.

chiropractic, manipulative treatment based on the theory that all diseases are caused by interference with spinal nerves and can be treated by adjusting the spinal column.

chiropractor, one who practices chiropractic manipulation.

chirospasm, see cheirospasm.

chloasma, discoloration of pigment in skin occurring in yellowish brown patches or spots.

chloral, an oily, bitter tasting substance derived from chlorine and alcohol.

chloral hydrate, colorless crystalline substance used as a sedative and hypnotic.

chloramphenicol, a broadspectrum antibiotic made synthetically used especially to treat typhoid fever.

chloride, a salt of hydrochloric acid.

chlorinated, treat with chlorine.

chlorinated lime, used in solution as a bleach and as an antiseptic derived from calcium hypochlorite.

chlorine, a yellowish-green irritating gas used in compounds as a bleaching agent and germicide; a poisonous gas which can cause severe damage to the mucous membranes of the respiratory passages and cause death if inhaled in excessive amounts.

chloroform, colorless, heavy liquid with a sweet taste and ethereal odor used as a solvent, general anesthetic, locally in liniments, and internally as a carminative or a sedative.

chloroma, green cancer of the cranial bones; a greenish colored malignant tumor found in myeloid tissue.

Chloromycetin, trademark for chloramphenicol, an antibiotic.

chloromyeloma, multiple growths in bone marrow.

chlorophyll, green coloring matter found in plants and which acts in the manufacture of simple carbohydrates.

chloropsia, vision in which all things appear green.

chlorosis, iron deficiency anemia.

chlorpromazine, a major tranquilizer used in treatment of psychotic states; trademark name is Thorazine; used as an antiemetic.

chlorpropamide, an oral hypoglycemic used to treat mild diabetes.

chlortetracycline, a broad-spectrum antibiotic which destroys strains of streptococci, staphylococci, pneumococci, rickettsiae, and some viruses; trademark name is Aureomycin.

choke, to interrupt respiration by obstruction or by constriction about the neck; strangle; spasm of the larynx; suffocate.

cholangitis, inflammation of the bile ducts.

cholecystectomy, surgical removal of the gallbladder.

cholecystitis, acute or chronic inflammation of the gallbladder.

cholesystography, examination of the gallbladder by x-ray.

cholecystolithiasis, cholelithiasis, the formation of gallstones in the gallbladder.

cholecystopathy, any gallbladder disease.

cholecystotomy, incision of gallbladder to remove gallstones.

choledochitis, inflammation of the common bile duct.

choleic, pertaining to the bile.

cholelithotomy, surgical removal of gallstones.

cholemia, presence of bile pigments in the blood causing jaundice.

cholera, an acute, infectious disease caused by Vibrio cholerae, characterized by diarrhea, severe cramps of muscles, vomiting, and exhaustion.

choleretic, an agent that increases bile production.

choleric, quick-tempered; easily irritated.

cholesteatoma, a small, pearl-like tumor occurring in the brain.

cholesterol, fatty, steroid alcohol found in animal tissues, occurring in egg yolk, oils, fats, and organ tissues; constitutes the largest portion of gallstones; most of the cholesterol is synthesized in the liver, and it is important to bodily metabolism.

choline, an amine found in plant and animal tissues which is important to normal fat and carbohydrate metabolism.

cholinergic, pertaining to nerve endings which produce acetylcholine which is important in the transmission of nerve impulses.

chondral, pertaining to cartilage.

chondroma, a slow growing cartilaginous tumor.

chondromalacia, abnormal softening of cartilage.

chondropathy, any disease of the cartilage.

chorda, referring to a chord, string, or tendon.

chorditis, inflammation of the vocal cord.

chorea, muscular twitching of the limbs; known as St. Vitus' dance or Sydenham's chorea, a disease of the central nervous system; Huntington's chorea is a hereditary form marked by mental deterioration.

chorion, the outermost embryonic membrane from which chornionic villi develop and connect with the endometrium from which the fetal part of the placenta forms.

chorionic, pertaining to the chorion.

chorioretinitis, inflammation of the choroid and retina.

choroid, the vascular coat of the eye between the sclera and retina.

choroiditis, inflammation of the choroid membrane.

chromatelopsia, color blindness.

chromatid, either of the two chromosomal bodies resulting from cell division, each drawn to a different pole.

chromatin, the specific portion in the nucleus of a cell that stains readily with basic dyes, and is considered to carry hereditary characteristics in the genes.

chromatosis, pathological skin pigmentation.

chromaturia, abnormal color of the urine.

chromocystoscopy, examination of kidney functions by use of dyes.

chromoscopy, examination of renal function by color of urine after dyes have been administered; testing for color vision.

chromosomal, pertaining to chromosomes.

chromosome, found in all plant and animal cells; a structure in the nucleus containing threads of DNA responsible for transmitting genetic information; there are 23 pairs of chromosomes in man.

chronic, recurring or occurring over a long period of time; in reference to a disease that is not acute.

chyle, a milklike substance found in the intestinal lymphatic vessels, produced during digestion, especially fats.

chylopoiesis, the formation of chyle.

chylothorax, chyle in the pleural cavity or chest.

chylous, pertaining to chyle.

chyme, the liquid mixture of partially digested food and gastric juices during digestion found in the stomach and small intestine after a meal.

chymotrypsin, an enzyme found in the intestine combined with trypsin which hydrolyzes protein to peptones.

cicatrix, healed wound; scar.

cilia, hairlike projections that arise from epithelial cells as found in bronchi, which transport mucus and dust particles upward; eyelashes.

ciliary, pertaining to eyelashes and to eye structures such as ciliary body.

ciliary body, consists of ciliary processes and ciliary muscle that extends from the iris base to the choroid.

cillosis, spasmodic twitching of the eyelid.

cinchona, a tree or shrub whose bark is the source of quinine.

cinchonism, poisoning resulting from overdoses of cinchona or quinine, characterized by headache, deafness, dizziness, and ringing of the ears.

circulation, movement of blood through the blood vessels of the body maintained by the pumping action of the heart.

circulatory, pertaining to circulation.

circumcision, the cutting around or removal of the foreskin of the penis.

cirrhosis, inflammation of an organ characterized by degenerative changes, particularly the liver.

cirrhotic, affected with or pertaining to cirrhosis.

cirsectomy, surgical removal of a part of a varicose vein.

cirsotomy, treatment for varicose veins with multiple incisions.

citric acid, an acid derived from citrus fruits used to flavor pharmaceuticals; important to metabolism.

citric acid cycle, Kreb's cycle, involved and complicated reactions pertaining to the oxidation of pyruvic acid in metabolism and converting it into energy for the body.

clamp, used for surgical procedures to compress a part or structure such as a blood vessel.

clap, see gonorrhea.

claudication, lameness; limping due to severe pain in the muscles of the calf resulting from decreased blood flow.

claustrophobia, an obsessive, intense fear of closed spaces.

clavicle, collarbone; a curved bone which joins the sternum and the scapula.

clavicular, pertaining to the clavicle.

clavus, a corn.

cleft palate, a congenital malformation in the roof of the mouth which forms a communicating opening between the mouth and the nasal cavities.

cleidorrhexis, bending or fracturing the clavicles of the fetus to ease delivery.

cleptomania, the impulsive act of stealing.

climacteric, menopause; cessation of a woman's reproductive period; corresponding period in a male characterized by decreased sexual activity.

clinic, a medical center for examination, diagnosis, and treatment for non-hospitalized patients.

clinical, pertaining to a clinic; pertaining to actual observation and treatment of patients.

clinician, a specialist in clinical procedures such as a clinical physician, teacher, or nurse; practicing physician.

Clinistix, trademark for glucose oxidase reagent strips to test urine for glucose.

clitoris, an organ of the female genitalia; an erectile structure located beneath the anterior part of the vulva.

clonic, alternate contraction and relaxation of muscle groups in rapid succession.

clonicity, condition of being clonic.

clonus, opposite of tonus.

Clostridium, a genus of spore-bearing anaerobic, rod-shaped bacteria commonly found in soil and in the intestinal tract of animals and man; frequently found in wound infections and the primary cause of gangrene and tetanus.

clot, coagulated blood or lymph; a thrombus.

clotting time, see coagulation time.

clouding of consciousness, state of mental confusion characterized by disorientation of time and place, amnesia, and decreased reaction time due to illness.

cloudy swelling, degeneration of tissues which become swollen and turbid.

clubbed fingers, broadening and rounding of the fingertips due to swelling, often seen in children with congenital heart disease and adults with pulmonary disease of long duration.

club-foot, congenital foot deformity.

clumping, see agglutination.

clunes, buttocks.

clysis, injection of a cleansing fluid for washing out blood in a cavity.

C.N.S., see central nervous system.

coagulability, being capable of forming clots.

coagulant, an agent responsible for coagulation.

coagulate, cause a clot or to become clotted.

coagulation, process of clotting.

coagulation time, period of time required for blood to clot or coagulate which is indicated when fibrin appears in tiny threads; normal clotting time is between 3 to 7 minutes.

coagulum, clump of clotting blood.

coarctate, pressed together; to tighten.

coarctation, compression of vessel walls; narrowing or tightening.

coarctotomy, division of a stricture by incision.

coat, a layer in the wall of an artery.

cobalt, a chemical element; cobalt 60 is a radioisotope of cobalt used in radiation therapy.

cocaine, a bitter alkaloid obtained from coca plants used in medicine as a local anesthetic and as a narcotic.

cocarcinogenesis, the development of cancer in preconditioned cells.

coccidia, sporozoa which are commonly found in epithelial tissue of the intestinal tract, the liver, and other organs in the body.

coccygeal, pertaining to the coccyx.

coccygectomy, removal of the coccyx by surgery.

coccygodynia, pain in the coccyx and the surrounding area.

coccyx, usually referring to the last four bones of the spine which attach to the sacrum.

cochlea, a cone-shaped, winding structure in the inner ear containing the organ of corti which is the receptor for hearing.

cochleitis, inflammation of the cochlea.

cocoid, resembling a cocus.

coconscious, coconsciousness, a conscious objective state in which subconscious impressions may rise to the surface and influence the stream of consciousness.

cocoa butter, a fat obtained from cocoa seed used as a lubricant in pharmaceuticals.

cocus, a spherical bacterium; organisms of the genus staphylococcus, and micrococcus.

codeine, an alkaloid from opium or synthetically produced, used as an analgesic and hypnotic sedative.

cod liver oil, a fixed oil obtained from cod fish livers used for its Vitamin A and D.

cohabitation, sexual intercourse; living together.

coherent, sticking together; being logically consistent.

cohesion, the process of sticking together; adhering; causing particles to unite.

coitus, sexual intercourse; copulation.

colchicum, a drug derived from the Colchicum seed used to relieve symptoms of gout.

cold, common viral infection of the respiratory mucous membranes causing symptoms of nasal congestion, headache, coughing, body aches, fatigue, fever, and chills.

cold sore, a fever blister particularly around the mouth caused by herpes simplex virus.

colectomy, excision of part of the large intestine or colon.

colic, spasms accompanied by abdominal pain; pertaining to the colon; occurring in infants, especially in the first few months of life.

colicstitis, cystitis caused by Eschericia coli.

colitis, inflammation of the colon.

collagen, a substance composed of white fibers of connective tissue found in the skin, tendons, cartilage, and bone; a body protein composed of connective tissue fibers.

collapse, a sudden caving in of the walls of an organ; an extreme loss of vital functioning of organ systems producing shock or breakdown.

collarbone, the clavicle.

collecting tubules, small ducts which receive urine from the renal tubules.

Colles' fracture, fracture of the distal end of the radius (just above the wrist bone).

colliculus, small anatomical mound.

collodion, a substance applied to the skin which forms a very thin protective layer.

colloid, a gelatinous protein found normally in thyroid secretion.

colloma, colloid degeneration found in cancerous tissue.

collutory, used as a gargle or mouth wash.

collyrium, a neutral solution used as an eyewash.

coloboma, an eye defect, usually due to an abnormal closure of the fetal fissure which may affect any part of the eye.

colon, the section of the large intestine between the cecum to the rectum.

color blindness, a hereditary condition in which a person is totally or partially unable to distinguish between certain primary colors; chromatelopsia.

colostomy, a surgical procedure that provides an opening between the colon and the abdominal wall creating a stoma.

colostrum, the first secretion of the breasts after childbirth before lactation commences, within a two to three day period, containing high protein and immunity factors for the newborn.

colotomy, incision of the colon.

colpalgia, vaginal pain.

colpitis, vaginitis.

colpocystitis, inflammation of both the bladder and vagina.

copocystocele, prolapse of the bladder into the vagina.

colpohysterectomy, excision of the uterus through the vagina.

coloplasty, plastic repair involving the vagina.

colpoptosis, prolapse of the vagina.

colporrhapy, suturing the vaginal wall for the purpose of narrowing it.

colposcope, an instrument for examining the cervix and vagina.

coma, a state of abnormal unconsciousness from which a person cannot respond to external stimuli due to illness or an injury; stupor.

comatose, pertaining to coma.

comedo, a blackhead caused by dried sebum blocking a duct in the skin.

comminute, breaking into pieces such as a shattered bone.

comminution, comminuting or reducing to fine particles.

commissure, joining together of corresponding structures such as lips or eyelids; a band of nerve fibers coming together.

communicable disease, transmission of a disease from one person to another either directly or indirectly.

compensation, making up for some abnormality.

complemental, adding something that is deficient.

complex, a group of associated ideas which are usually unconscious, believed to be influencing factors of abnormal attitudes and mental states.

complication, a complex state in which disease or accident is added to an existing illness without being related specifically.

compos mentis, sane; of sound mind.

compound, a substance composed of two or more parts.

compound fracture, bone which is broken and pierces the skin.

compress, a soft pad, moist or dry, applied to a part of the body with pressure to prevent hemorrhage, or to apply medication, heat or cold.

compression, being pressed together.

compulsion, an insistent, repetitive, and unwanted urge to perform an irrational act; state of being compelled.

compulsive, exhibiting repetitive patterns of behavior.

concave, a rounded, hollowed out surface, or cavity.

concavity, a concave surface.

concavoconvex, being concave on one side and convex on the other side; pertaining to the lens of the eyes.

conceive, to become pregnant; to form a mental image or an idea.

concentration, increasing in strength of a substance by evaporation.

concept, a mental image of an idea.

conception, the beginning of pregnancy when the ovum is fertilized by a sperm forming a zygote.

concha, a structure resembling a shell; the pinna or outer ear; one of the three bones on the nasal cavity.

conchitis, inflammation of a concha.

concretion, a calculus; an inorganic mass found in a body cavity or tissues.

concubitus, sexual intercourse, copulation, coition.

concussion, an injury resulting from a collision or impaction with an object; partial or complete loss of bodily functions resulting from a violent shock or a blow to the head.

conditioned reflex, acquired response through repetition and training.

condom, a thin rubber sheath to be worm over the penis during sexual intercourse to prevent impregnation or veneral disease.

condyle, a rounded projection at the end of a bone which articulates with another bone.

condylectomy, excision or removal of a condyle.

condyloma, a wartlike lesion on the skin occurring on the mucous membranes or external genitals or near the anus.

confabulation, an unconscious replacing of imaginary experiences due to memory loss, seen principally in organic mental disorders.

confinement, period of childbirth or puerperal state.

confusion, disturbance in orientation to time, place, or person; a psychological evaluation pertaining to a disordered consciousness.

congenital, present at birth, including conditions arising from fetal development or the birth process that are not hereditary.

congest, to cause an abnormal amount of blood to accumulate in an organ.

congestion, the presence of an excess amount of fluid in an organ or in tissue.

congestive, pertaining to congestion.

conization, excision of a cone of tissue pertaining to the cervix.

conjugate, paired; working together; an important measurement in the diameter of the pelvis.

conjugation, a coupling.

conjunctiva, mucous membranes lining the eyelids and covering the anterior surface of the eyeball.

conjunctivitis, inflammation of the conjunctiva.

connective tissue, primarily functions to support or bind together bodily tissues, organs, and parts; other functions include food storage, blood formation, and defensive mechanisms.

consanguinity, kinship; blood relationship.

conscience, associated with superego; a person's set of moral values which controls his behavior and performance.

conscious, being aware of one's existence and having the ability to respond subjectively to stimuli; awake.

consciousness, awareness; being conscious.

consolidation, the process of becoming solid, referring to a condition in the lungs due to an accumulation of fluid in acute pneumonia.

constipation, irregular, difficult, or sluggish defecation.

constitution, the functional habits and physical properties of the body; a disposition, temperament, or condition of the mind.

constitutional, pertaining to the whole body.

constriction, a narrowing of a part or opening.

consultant, acting in an advisory capacity.

consultation, two or more specialists who deliberate about diagnosis and treatment of a client.

consumption, pertaining to tuberculosis; wasting away of the body.

consumptive, one afflicted with tuberculosis.

contact, one who has been exposed to a contagious disease; touching of two bodies.

contact lens, a thin concave disk which fits on the convex surface of the eyeball and floats on the fluid of the eye, helpful in correcting impaired vision.

contagion, the process of spreading a disease from one person to another by direct or indirect contact.

contagious, a readily transmitted disease either directly or indirectly from one person to another; communicable.

contaminate, the act of soiling or exposing to infectious germs into normally sterile objects; render impure by contact or mixture.

continence, the practice of self-restraint in sexual indulgence.

contortion, a spasmodic twisting or writhing of the body; distortion.

contraception, the prevention of conception.

contraceptive, an agent or device to prevent conception or impregnation.

contraction, a shortening or drawing up of a muscle; a shrinking.

contracture, a permanent contraction or shortening of a muscle due to spasm, fibrosis of tissues, or paralysis.

contraindication, a condition or circumstance that indicates that a form of treatment of medication is inappropriate in a specific case.

contralateral, affecting the opposite side of the body.

contuse, to injure or wound by bruising.

contusion, an injuring to the skin without breaking the flesh; a severe bruise.

convalescence, a recovery period after an illness, operation, or injury.

convalescent, pertaining to convalescence; a patient who is recovering from an illness, operation, or injury.

convergence, coordinating the movements of both eyes toward a common point.

convex, having an elevated or rounded surface.

convexoconcave, having one convex and one concave surface, especially the lens.

convolute, rolled or coiled up, as a scroll.

convolution, a folding or coiling of anything which is convoluted; the many folds on the surface of the brain or the intestines.

convulsant, medication or a drug which causes convulsions.

convulsion, severe involuntary muscle contractions with a temporary loss of consciousness due to many causes.

convulsive, pertaining to, characterized by convulsions.

Coombs' test, used in the diagnosis of several forms of hemolytic anemias.

coprolalia, abnormal desire to use obscene words in ordinary conversion.

coprophagy, ingesting of feces.

coprophilia, abnormal attraction to feces and defecation.

coprophobia, an abnormal disgust of filth and feces.

coprostasis, fecal impaction.

copulation, sexual coitus, or the act of copulating.

coracoid process, pertaining to the upper anterior surface of the scapula.

Coramine, trademark for nikethamide used as a respiratory stimulant.

cord, the umbilical cord; stringlike structures such as vocal cords, the spinal cord, or the spermatic cord.

cordate, heart-shaped.

corectomy, surgical removal of the iris.

corium, the dermis; the layer of skin immediately beneath the epidermis which contains vascular connective tissue, nerve endings, hair follicles, sebaceous glands, sweat glands, and smooth muscle fibers.

corn, a horny and thickened area of the skin which may be either soft or hard depending on its location on the foot due to pressure or friction.

cornea, the transparent membrane covering the iris and pupil of the eye.

corneal, pertaining to the cornea.

corneitis, inflammation of the cornea.

corneous, horn-shaped.

cornification, conversion of stratified squamous epithelium cells into keratin, or horn.

corona, resembling a crown.

coronal, pertaining to corona; referring to the suture which joins the parietal and frontal bones in the skull.

coronary, pertaining to a circle or crown.

coronary arteries, two arteries which supply blood to the heart muscles.

coronary occlusion, closure or blockage of one of the coronary arteries.

coronary thrombosis, clotting of blood in the blood vessels which supply the heart; a common cause of myocardial infarction.

coroner, a county officer who investigates any death from unknown causes or violent crimes.

corpulence, obesity.

corpulent, being stout, fat, obese.

corpus, principle part of an organ; any mass or body.

corpuscle, any minute rounded body; a blood cell.

corpusculum, corpuscle.

corpus luteum, a yellowish endocrine substance secreted by the ovary after the rupture of a Graafian follicle and the release of ovum; during pregnancy the corpus luteum persists in secreting the hormone progesterone.

corrode, to wear away by chemical action.

corrosion, disintegrating; the process of corroding.

corrosive, an agent that is destructive to the tissues.

cortex, outer portion of an organ, the brain, and the adrenal glands.

cortical, pertaining to the cortex.

corticosteroids, hormones produced by the adrenal glands.

cortin, a hormone secreted by the adrenal cortex.

cortisone, a hormone extracted from the adrenal cortex of the adrenal gland and also prepared synthetically, important to fat metabolism.

coryza, nasal catarrh resulting from inflammation of the mucous membranes; common head cold.

costa, rib.

costae, the rib cage composed of twelve ribs on each side.

costal, pertaining to the ribs.

costalgia, pain in a rib, or intercostal spaces.

costive, constipated.

costoclavicular, pertaining to the ribs and clavicle.

costovertebral, the joining of a rib to a vertebrae.

cough, a more or less violent expulsion of air from the lungs in an attempt to expel an irritant from the respiratory tract.

counterirritant, the application of an agent to reduce or relieve another irritation.

courses, menses.

cowperitis, inflammation of the Cowper's glands.

Cowper's glands, two composed tubular glands the size of a pea beneath the bulb of the urethra in males.

cowpox, pustular eruptions of milk cows on areas of udder and teats resembling smallpox in man; when virus is contained in vaccine and given to humans against smallpox, it offers some degree of immunity against the disease.

coxa, the joint in the hip or hip bone.

coxalgia, pain in the hip.

cramp, a spasmodic, involuntary contraction of a muscle or group of muscles with pain.

cranial, pertaining to the cranium or skull.

cranial nerves, originating in the brain; there are twelve pairs of cranial nerves.

craniectomy, excision of part of the skull.

craniometry, the science of skull measurement.

cranioplasty, plastic repair on the skull.

craniopuncture, an exploratory procedure in which the skull is punctured.

cranium, including all of the bones of the head that enclose the brain.

crapulent, crapulous, excessive drinking of alcohol; intoxication.

creatine, a nitrogenous compound synthesized in the body which serves as a source of high energy phosphate.

Crede's method, a procedure used in obstetrics whereby the placenta is expelled by employing a downward pressure on the uterus through the abdominal wall; treatment of the eyes of the newborn with 1% silver nitrate solution immediately after birth for prevention of infection.

cremaster, one of the fascialike muscles suspending the testicles and spermatic cord.

cremation, burning of dead bodies by heat.

crepitant, a crackling sound; making a grating sound.

cresol, a substance used as a disinfectant derived from coal tar.

crest, a ridgelike formation on a bone.

cretin, one afflicted with cretinism.

cretinism, a congenital affliction caused by abnormal thyroid secretion, characterized by stunted physical and mental development.

crevice, a small fissure or crack.

cribbing, swallowing air.

cribriform, sievelike; having many small openings.

cribriform plate, a thin, perforated bone in the skull through which many nerve filaments pass.

cricoid cartilage, the lowermost, ringlike cartilage of the larynx.

crinogenic, stimulating secretions in a gland.

crisis, the turning point of a disease marked by a sudden decrease in high temperature to normal; a turning point in illness for better or worse.

cross-eye, esotropia.

cross-matching, testing before transfusion to determine blood compatibility.

croup, a disease occurring in children characterized by inflammation of the respiratory passages causing difficult breathing, laryngeal spasm, coughing, and sometimes exudation due to the formation of a membrane.

crowning, stage in delivery when the fetal head appears at the opening of the birth canal.

crural, pertaining to the leg or thigh.

crus, the leg.

crush syndrome, renal failure following the severe crushing of the lower extremities.

crust, crusta, a scab; an outer covering.

crutch, used to support the body weight in walking. A staff which extends from the armpit to the ground.

cryanesthesia, the inability to perceive cold.

cryesthesia, having an abnormal sensitivity to cold.

cryocautery, cold cautery; a device used for application of solid carbon dioxide.

cryogenic, pertaining to low temperatures.

cryosurgery, the application of extreme low temperatures to destroy or remove diseased tissue.

cryotherapy, crymotherapy, the therapeutic use of cold.

crypt, a small sac or cavity which extends into epithelial or glandular surfaces.

cryptogenetic, of unknown origin.

cryptorchidism, a condition in which the testicles fail to descend into the scrotum.

crystalline, resembling a crystal; clear.

crystalline lens, the lens of the eye behind the pupil.

crystaluria, the appearance of crystal formations in the urine.

crystalluridrosis, urinary elements appearing on the skin as crystallized sweat.

cubital, pertaining to the forearm.

cubitus, elbow; forearm; ulna.

cuboid, referring to the outermost bone of the tatsal or instep bones which connect with the 4th and 5th metatarsus.

cul-de-sac, a blind cavity or pouch.

culdoscopy, a visual examination of the female viscera in the pelvic cavity through an endoscope introduced into the vagina.

Culex, a genus of mosquitoes found throughout the world which are vectors of malaria producing organisms.

culture, a mass of microorganisms growing in a culture medium in the laboratory.

cumulative, increasing in effect or amount; an accumulation of drugs by successive additions or dosages.

cupula, an inverted cup-shaped cap or dome over a structure.

curare, curari, an extract obtained from tropical plants used as an arrow poison by South American Indians; used in anesthesia to control convulsions, spasms, and for skeletal muscle relaxation.

curet, curette, a spoon-shaped instrument used in scraping a cavity to remove foreign matter or a diseased surface.

curettage, scraping of a cavity with a curette.

curie, a standard unit of radioactivity.

curietherapy, radium therapy.

cusp, a point of a crown of a tooth.

cuspid, a canine tooth, of which there are four; a cuspidate tooth.

cuspidate, having cusps.

cutaneous, pertaining to the skin.

cuticle, a layer of solid or semisolid nonliving skin that surrounds fingernails and toenails.

cutis, the skin.

cyanemia, dark blue-colored blood.

cyanide, a fast-acting poison.

cyanocobalamin, Vitamin B12.

cyanopsia, objects appear tinged with blue due to a defect in vision.

cyanosis, a bluish, slatelike, or dark purple skin color due to excessive concentration of reduced hemoglobin in the blood.

cyanotic, pertaining to cyanosis.

cycle, a series of events or a sequence of movements.

cyclic, pertaining to cycles.

cyclitis, inflammation of the ciliary body or ciliary region of the upper eyelid.

cyclomate, an artificial sweetener with no nutritional value.

cycloplegia, paralysis of the ciliary muscles.

cyclothyme, one afflicted with cyclothymia.

cyclothymia, a cyclic disorder of the mind characterized by recurring and alternating periods of sadness and elation.

cyesis, pregnancy.

cyst, a pouch or closed sac under the skin or in the body which contains fluid, semifluid, or solid matter.

cystadenoma, a tumor containing cysts.

cystalgia, a painful urinary bladder.

cystectomy, removal of a cyst; removal of the gallbladder; excision of the urinary bladder or part of it.

cystic, pertaining to a cyst; pertaining to the urinary bladder, or to the gallbladder.

cystic fibrosis, a disease occurring in childhood involving the exocrine glands resulting in pancreatic insufficiency and chronic respiratory disease; believed to be hereditary.

cystitis, inflammation of the bladder.

cystocele, a protrusion of the urinary bladder into the vagina.

cystocolostomy, a surgical procedure that creates a permanent communication between the gallbladder and the colon.

cystoid, resembling a cyst; bladderlike.

cystolith, having a calculus or stone in the urinary bladder.

cystolithectomy, excision of calculus from the bladder.

cystoma, a cystic tumor.

cystoplasty, plastic repair upon the bladder.

cystoscope, an instrument for examining the bladder.

cystoscopy, examination of the bladder with a cystoscope.

cystospasm, a spasmodic contraction of the urinary bladder.

cystostomy, surgical procedure of the urinary bladder to make an opening.

cytobiology, biology of the cells.

cytoblast, a cell nucleus.

cytochemistry, the scientific study of the structure and chemistry of living cells.

cytochromes, iron-containing compounds found in animal and human tissue which play an important role in cellular respiration.

cytogenesis, the origin and development of cells.

cytokalipenia, a deficiency of potassium in the body.

cytokinesis, the movement of cytoplasm into two parts during cell division.

cytology, the study of the structures and functions of cells.

cytolysis, the destruction or degeneration of cells.

cytoplasm, the protoplasm of a cell not including the nucleus.

cytosine, a component of nucleic acid common to both DNA and RNA.

cytoscopy, a diagnostic microscopic examination of cells.

cytotropism, the movement of cells in response to external stimuli.

cytula, the impregnated ovum.

cyturia, the presence of various cells in the urine.

D

dacrocystitis, dacryocystitis, inflammation of the lacrimal or tear sac.

dacryadenitis, dacroadenitis, inflammation of a lacrimal (tear) gland.

dacryocele, protrusion of a lacrimal (tear) sac.

dacryocystotomy, surgical operation of the lacrimal sac.

dacryolith, a calculus or stone in the tear duct.

dacryorrhea, excessive flow of tears.

dactyl, a finger or toe.

dactylitis, inflammation of a finger or toe.

dactylography, the study of fingerprints.

dactylology, communicating by sign language made with the hands and fingers.

dactylolysis, loss or amputation of a finger or toe.

dactylomegaly, abnormally large fingers or toes.

dactylus, referring to a finger or toe; a digit.

daltonism, color blindness, especially in differentiating between red and green.

D and C, pertaining to dilatation of the cervix and curettage of the uterus.

dandruff, dry scales of epidermis forming on the scalp which shed, sometimes due to seborrheic dermatitis.

dandy fever, an acute febrile disease which occurs in the tropics; dengue.

dartos, a fibrous layer beneath the skin of the scrotum.

darwinian ear, a congenital deformity of the helix of the ear.

deaf, lacking the sense of hearing.

deaf-mute, unable to hear or speak.

deafness, complete or partial loss of hearing.

deamination, the removal of the amino group from a compound.

dearterialization, changing arterial to venous blood by deoxygenation.

death rattle, a rattling sound heard in the throat of the dying.

debilitant, drug to reduce excitement.

debilitate, producing weakness or debility.

debility, weakened condition of the body and loss of bodily function; feebleness.

debridement, the removal of foreign matter or dead tissue from a wound.

decalcification, the removal of lime salts from bones; loss of bone calcium.

decalcify, softening of bone by removal or loss of calcium or its salts.

decannulation, to remove a cannula or tube.

decant, to pour off liquid with sediment remaining in the bottom of the flask or container.

decapitation, beheading; to remove the head from the body.

dechloridation, dechlorination, decrease sodium chloride in the body by the removal of salt from the diet.

decibel, a unit of sound measuring intensity and volume.

decidua, the endometrium when conception occurs which divides itself into three layers enveloping the impregnated ovum.

decidual, pertaining to the decidua.

deciduoma, a uterine tumor containing decidual tissue.

deciduous, shedding at a particular stage of growth, especially of temporary teeth.

decimeter, one-tenth of a meter.

declinator, an instrument used in surgery to retract or hold apart the dura matter.

decline, a declining period of a disease or illness.

decoloration, bleaching or the removal of color.

decompensation, the ability of the heart or other organs in the body to maintain adequate functioning; a term used in psychiatry which implies the failure of defense mechanisms resulting in disintegration of personality.

decomposition, decaying process.

decompression, removal of pressure, or removing of air pressure from a chamber; a normal bodily adjustment to atmospheric pressure.

decongestant, a substance or drug that reduces congestion and swelling, especially in nasal passages.

decontamination, rendering free of contamination as in an object or person contaminated by poisonous gas or radioactive substances.

decortication, removal of the surface layer from structures or organs.

decrepit, wasted or worn down by the infirmities caused by the aging process.

decrepitude, senile breaking down.

decubation, recovery stage of an infectious disease.

decubitus, a bedsore; a pressure wound.

decussate, crossing of parts.

decussation, crossing of structures or nerves which form an X; chiasma.

defecation, evacuation of the bowels, or the expulsion of fecal matter.

defective, imperfect; physically or mentally deficient.

defeminization, loss or absence of female sexual characteristics.

deferens, to carry away, as in ductus deferens, excretory duct of the testicles.

deferent, to carry downward.

deferentitis, inflammation of the ductus deferens.

defervescence, subsidence of fever to normal body temperature.

defibrillation, terminating atrial or ventricular fibrillation or irregular heart muscle contractions.

deficiency disease, any disease caused by a dietary insufficiency.

defluvium, sudden loss of air.

defluxion, a flowing down of a copious discharge of any kind.

deformation, disfiguration or malformation.

deformity, a malformation or misshapen part of the body or organ; a distortion of the body or part of the body which may be acquired or congenital.

degenerate, a sexual pervert; to deteriorate.

degeneration, impairment or deterioration of an organ or its parts.

deglutition, act of swallowing.

degradation, act of degrading; conversion of a chemical compound to one less complex.

degustation, act of tasting.

dehiscence, bursting open; separation of the layers of a surgical wound.

dehydrate, to lose moisture or water.

dehydration, excessive loss of body fluids or water; the process of dehydrating.

déjà vu, a sensation that what one is seeing is a repetition of a previous experience.

dejecta, feces.

dejection, dejecture, feeling of being downcast; a state of mental depression; excretment.

delacrimination, a constant overflow of tears.

delactation, cessation of lactation; weaning.

deleterious, injurious or harmful to health or well-being.

delinquent, antisocial, criminal, or illegal behavior, especially significant in a minor exhibiting such behavior.

deliquescence, liquefaction of salts by absorption of water from the air.

delirious, pertaining to delirium.

delirium, a temporary disorientation, usually accompanied by illusions and hallucinations due to various causes such as fever, intoxication, or trauma.

delirium tremens, an acute mental disorder characterized by delirium, trembling, great anxiety, mental distress, sweating, and gastrointestinal symptoms, caused by excessive alcohol consumption.

delivery, giving birth; parturition.

delomorphous, having a definite form or shape.

deltoid, referring to a large triangular muscle which covers the shoulder prominence.

delusion, a false belief which is firmly maintained despite obvious evidence to the contrary.

delusional, pertaining to delusions.

demented, out of one's mind; insane.

dementia, mental deterioration; organic loss of intellectual functioning.

dementia praecox, schizophrenia; an obsolete descriptive term for schizophrenia.

demineralization, abnormal loss of mineral salts from the body by excessive secretion and excretion.

demonomania, obsolete term for an irrational belief that one is possessed by demons or evil spirits.

demulcent, a substance that will soothe and soften the skin.

demyelinate, to remove the myelin sheath from a nerve or nerves.

denatured, to change the nature of a substance; to render unfit for human consumption without impairing usefulness for other purposes, as alcohol.

dengue, an infectious tropical disease carried by mosquitoes characterized by fever and severe pain in the joints and muscles.

dental, pertaining to the teeth.

dental caries, decay of the teeth.

dentalgia, toothache.

dental hygienist, one trained to clean teeth, provide instruction on general tooth care, and assist a dentist.

dentate, notched, or toothed.

denticle, a small tooth; projecting toothlike point.

dentifrice, a substance for cleaning teeth.

dentin, dentine, the main hard tissues of a tooth enclosing the pulp which is covered by enamel on the crown and cementum on the roots.

dentist, a practitioner who cares for and treats the gums and teeth.

dentistry, the branch of medicine which is concerned with the care of teeth, and with the prevention, diagnosis, and treatment of diseases of the teeth and gums.

dentition, the teeth in situ or in the dental arch.

dentures, false teeth; artificial teeth.

denudation, act of denuding; removal of a protective covering.

denutrition, malnutrition.

deodorant, an agent that masks offensive odors.

deodorize, to remove offensive and foul odors.

deossification, loss of mineral elements from bone.

deoxidation, process of depriving or reducing oxygen.

deoxycholic acid, a crystalline acid found in bile.

deoxyribonuclease, an enzyme produced by some streptococci.

deoxyribonucleic acid, see DNA.

depersonalization, a neurosis characterized by feelings of unreality and lost sense of personal identity; a lessened sense of one's perception of self, may occur in a mild form in a normal person.

depilate, to remove or pluck out hair.

depilation, the process of removing hair.

depilatory, a substance used for hair removal.

deplete, to empty or relieve, as in blood letting or purging.

deplumation, loss of eyelashes due to illness or disease.

deposit, collecting of matter in an organ part, or in an organism; sediment.

depraved, one perverted or abnormal; deteriorated.

depressant, a substance that depresses any functional body activity; an agent that depresses; sedative.

depressed, pertaining to depression.

depression, a depressed region or hallow; lowering of a body part or vital function; a morbid sadness, melancholy, or lack of hope.

depressomotor, an agent which retards muscular movements.

depressor, a device for depressing the tongue or a body part.

depurate, an agent that purifies.

deradentis, inflammation of a lymph gland in the neck.

derangement, a mental disorder.

dereistic, day dreaming.

derm, derma, true skin, beneath the epidermis.

dermal, pertaining to the true skin.

dermatitis, inflammation of the derma.

dermatoautoplasty, grafting of skin taken from the patient's own body.

dermatogen, an antigen produced from a skin disease.

dermatoid, resembling skin.

dermatologist, a skin specialist.

dermatology, the branch of medicine concerned with the skin and its diseases.

dermatomycosis, a skin infection caused by fungi; athlete's foot.

dermatomyositis, inflammation of the skin and muscles.

dermatone, an instrument used for cutting thin sections of skin for transplants.

dermatoneurosis, skin disease caused by a nervous disorder.

dermatophobia, morbid fear of contracting a skin disease.

dermatophyte, a plant parasite which infects the skin of animals and man causing diseases such as eczema and ringworm; a parasitic plant fungus.

dermatoplastic, pertaining to the grafting of skin.

dermatorrhea, excessive secretion from sebaceous glands.

dermatosis, any skin disease.

dermis, see derm, derma.

desensitization, to lessen hypersensitivity reactions by giving subsequent injections of an antogen; in treatment of phobias, a patient is intentionally exposed to emotionally distressing stimuli.

desiccant, a medication which causes drying.

desiccate, to dry up.

desmalgia, pain in a ligament.

desmectasis, stretching of a tendon.

desmitis, inflammation of a ligament.

desmoid, resembling a ligament; a very tough and fibrous tumor.

desmology, science of ligaments and tendons.

desmotomy, incision of a ligament.

desquamate, shedding of the epithelium.

desquamation, shedding of skin or cuticle.

detelectasis, collapse of an organ.

deteriorate, to become worse, to degenerate.

determinism, the theory that nothing in a person's emotional or mental life results by chance alone but rather from specific causes known or unknown.

detoxify, to decrease the toxic properties of a substance; to remove the effects of a toxic drug.

detritus, any degenerative or broken down tissue.

detrusor urinae, the longitudinal muscular layer of the bladder that helps to excrete urine.

detumescence, the subsidence of a swelling or of erectile tissue.

deutencephalon, the interbrain.

deuteranopia, defective color vision, especially an inability to distinguish between green and red.

deviant, varying from a normal standard or condition.

deviated septum, a congenital or acquired cartilaginous partition between the nostrils or septum.

devitalize, to weaken; to deprive of life or vitality.

devolution, degeneration as in catabolism.

dexter, pertaining to the right side.

dextral, pertaining to the right side.

dextrocardia, the heart positioned on the right side of the chest.

dextrose, a simple form of sugar, also known as glucose or grape sugar; a constituent of corn syrup and honey.

dextrosuria, the presence of dextrose in the urine.

diabetes, any one of various diseases which indicate the body's inability to handle glucose.

diabetes insipidus, a disease characterized by the excretion of excessive amounts of pale urine with no sugar or albumin, and extreme thirst, weakness, and dry skin.

diabetes millitus, a disorder of carbohydrate metabolism characterized by an elevated blood sugar and the presence of sugar in the urine, resulting from decreased insulin production or utilization.

diabetic, pertaining to one afflicted with diabetes.

Diabinese, trademark for chlorpropamide which is used in selected patients for management of diabetes mellitus.

diagnosis, recognition of diseases based on examination, and microscopic and chemical results of laboratory findings.

diagnostic, pertaining to diagnosis.

diagnostics, the science concerned with diagnosis of diseases.

dialysis, the passage of small molecules or solute through a membrane; a procedure used to purify colloidal substances enclosed in a thin membraneous sac, and exposing to water or solvent which continually circulates outside the sac.

dialyze, to loosen or separate by a dialyzer.

dialyzer, a membrane used in performing dialysis such as a coiled cellophane tube.

diameter, measured by a straight line passing through the center of a circle or body surface and connecting opposite points on its circumference.

diapason, a tuning fork used in diagnosing diseases of the ear.

diapedesis, the passage of blood cells outward through unruptured capillary walls.

diaphane, translucent membrane of a cell.

diaphoresis, excessive or profuse perspiration or sweating.

diaphoretic, pertaining to profuse perspiration; an agent which increases perspiration.

diaphragm, a membraneous partition separating the abdominal and thoracic cavity which serves in inspiration and expiration; any separating membrane; female contraceptive placed over the cervix.

diarrhea, an abnormal evacuation of the intestines characterized by watery and frequent stools.

diarthric, pertaining to two or more joints.

diarthrosis, an articulation in which the bones move freely; a synovial or hinged joint.

diarticular, pertaining to two joints.

diastalsis, a foreward movement due to a wave of inhibition before a downward contraction of the intestines.

diastase, an enzyme or ferment found in plant cells of grains and malt, and in the digestive juice which converts starch into sugar.

diastasis, an injury to a bone occurring during surgery in which an epiphysis is separated; pertaining to the rest period of the cardiac cycle between the diastole and the systole.

diastole, the normal period of dilatation of the heart, especially the ventricles.

diastolic, pertaining to the diastole of the heart; referring to diastolic pressure; it is the point of the greatest cardiac relaxation.

diathermia, diathermy.

diathermic, being permeable by heat waves.

diathermic surgery, the application of high frequency heat to remove tissue as in cauterization.

diathermy, therapeutic use of heat within the body in treatment of disease or injury.

diathesis, a constitutional perdisposition to certain diseases.

dichotomy, dichotomization, dividing into two parts, or dividing into pairs.

dichromasy, partial colorblindness.

diachromatic, perceiving only two colors.

dicliditis, inflammation of a cardiac valve.

dicoria, double pupil in each eye.

dicrotic, having one heartbeat for two arterial pulsations; a double pulse.

dicrotism, the state of having a double pulse.

Dicumarol, trademark for bishydroxycoumarin, an anticoagulant used in treatment of intravascular clotting.

didactylism, having only two digits on a hand or foot.

didelphic, having a double uterus.

didymitis, inflammation of the testicle.

diencephalon, second portion of the brain which includes the epithalamus, thalamus, metathalamus, and hypothalamus.

diet, one's nutritional intake; a prescribed food exchange adapted for a particular health problem; to eat sparingly according to prescribed rules to reduce body weight.

dietetic, pertaining to diet.

dietetics, science of nutrition and diet.

dietitian, one trained in dietetics and nutritional needs and who is part of the treatment team in hospitals and institutions in charge of diets.

dietotherapy, the regulation of diet in the treatment of disease.

differential blood count, microscopic determination of the number and variety of white and red blood cells in a cubic millimeter of a blood specimen.

differential diagnosis, a diagnosis of symptoms of two or more diseases by comparison.

differentiation, pertaining to distinct differences between individuals, groups or objects.

diffuse, irregular spreading or scattering of a substance; to pass through a tissue or substance.

diffusion, the process of becoming diffused; widely spread.

digest, to undergo digestion.

digestion, the process of converting food by enzymatic action into chemical substances and assimilation into the body.

digestive tract, the system responsible for the conversion of food in the body which includes the mouth, pharynx, esophagus, stomach, small intestine, large intestine, and accessory glands.

digit, a finger or toe.

digital, pertaining to digits.

digitalis, a drug obtained from common foxglove, or Eurasian herbs used in powdered form as tablets or capsules which acts as a heart stimulant and indirectly as a diuretic.

digitalism, a condition caused by the poisonous effects produced by digitalis.

digitalization, the administration of the drug digitalis in scheduled dosages designed to produce and maintain optimal therapeutic results.

digitate, having digitlike appendages.

digitoxin, a cardiotoxic, bitter-tasting glycoside obtained from Digitalis purpurea used as a heart stimulant and in treatment of congestive heart failure.

Dilantin, trademark for phenytoin used as an anticonvulsant in the treatment of epilepsy.

dilatation, enlargement or expansion of an organ or vessel; expansion of an opening with a dilator.

dilation, see dilatation.

dilator, an instrument used to dilate or stretch muscles, cavities, or openings.

dilute, rendering less potent by mixing with water.

dilution, process of diluting a substance; weakening the strength of a substance.

dimercaprol, a metal antagonist used as an antidote in heavy metal poisoning which is effective against arsenic, gold, and mercury poisoning.

diminution, act of reducing.

dimpling, a retracting of the subcutaneous tissue in the formation of a dimple which occurs in certain carcinomas.

dinical, vertigo.

Diodoquin, trademark for diodohydroxyquin used as an antiamebic drug.

diopsimeter, an apparatus for exploring the visual field.

diopter, something that can be seen through such as a lens with refractive power with focal distance of 1 meter; one diopter is used as a unit of measurement in refraction.

dioptometer, an instrument for measuring ocular refraction and accommodation.

dioptric, pertaining to refraction of light.

dioxide, a compound consisting of two atoms of oxygen and another element such as carbon dioxide.

dipeptidase, an enzyme that converts dipeptids into amino acids by hydrolysis.

dipeptide, a derived protein by hydrolysis.

diphasic, having two phases.

diphtheria, an acute infectious disease affecting the mucous membranes of the nose, throat, or larynx with symptoms of fever, pain, and respiratory obstruction; toxins produced by the causative organism Corynebacterium diphtheriae may also cause myocarditis and neuritis.

diphtheritic, pertaining to diphtheria.

diphyodont, having two sets of teeth, as in man.

diplegia, a paralysis of similar parts occuring on both sides of the body.

diplococcus, gram positive bacteria occurring in pairs.

diploe, cancelled tissue between the inner and outer walls of the skull bones.

diploetic, diploic, pertaining to the diploe.

diploid, having two sets of chromosomes, as in somatic cells.

diplophonia, diphonia, producing two different voice tones at the same time in speaking.

diplopia, having double vision.

dipsomania, having an uncontrollable craving for alcoholic beverages.

dipsophobia, abnormal fear of drinking alcohol.

dipsosis, abnormal thirst.

disaccharide, any of the group of sugars in carbohydrates yielding two monosaccharides in hydrolysis.

disarticulation, separation or amputation through a joint.

disc, disk, a round, platelike structure or organ such as the fibro-cartilaginous disc between two vertebrae in the spinal column.

disease, any interruption of the normal function of any body organ, part, or system that presents an abnormal or pathological body state.

disinfect, to free from infection or destroy bacteria by physical or chemical means.

disinfectant, a chemical agent which kills bacteria; germicide.

disjoint, to separate bones from their natural positions in a joint.

dislocate, to move out of position or joint.

dislocation, the act of dislocating.

dismemberment, amputation.

disorganization, state of being disorganized or confused.

disorientation, being disoriented; inability to perceive one's self in relation to time, place, or person; a state of confusion.

dispensary, clinic for free dispensation of medicines or medical treatment; a place in which medicines are dispensed.

displacement, a defense mechanism in which an emotion is transferred unconsciously from its original object to one more acceptable; removal from the normal or usual position such as a body part.

disposition, a natural tendency or aptitude within a person; having susceptibility to disease.

dissect, to divide or cut apart tissues for the purpose of anatomical study; to separate tissues of a cadaver.

dissection, referring to the cutting of parts or tissues and studying of same.

dissector, one who dissects such as an anatomist.

disseminated, to scatter or spread over a wide area.

dissociation, a state of being separated; a defense mechanism through which emotional attachment is separated from an object, idea, or situation, usually an unconscious process.

dissolution, the process of dissolving of one substance into another; liquefaction; death.

dissolve, to cause a solid substance to pass into solution.

distal, farthest point from the medial line or center of the body.

distemper, an infectious disease of animals.

distend, to swell up, stretch out, or to become inflated.

distill, to purify by vaporization of heat, condensing a volatile substance.

distillation, the process of purifying a liquid by vaporizing it and then condensing the substance.

districhasis, the growing of two hairs from the same follicle.

distrix, the splitting of ends of the hairs.

disulfiram, a drug used in treatment of alcoholism to deter ingestion of alcohol by producing an unpleasant reaction, nausea, and vomiting.

diuresis, abnormal secretion of urine.

diuretic, an agent which increases urinary output.

divagation, incoherent speech.

divergent, radiating or separating in different directions.

diver's paralysis, an occupational disease occurring after working under high air pressures and returning too suddenly to normal atmospheric pressure; the bends.

diverticula, pertaining to diverticulum; a pouch or sac in the walls of a canal or cavity.

diverticulitis, inflammation of the diverticulum.

diverticulosis, the presence of diverticula without inflammation.

divulsion, the act of pulling apart.

divulsor, an apparatus for dilation of a part.

diztgotic twins, fraternal twins, who are the product of two ova.

dizziness, state of being dizzy; foolish; vertigo.

DNA, deoxyribonucleic acid, a complex protein found in all cells, considered the chemical basis of heredity; a nucleic acid found in chromosomes consisting of a long chain molecule of repeated combinations of four basis (two purines, adenine and guanine, and two pyrimadines, thymine and cystosine).

doctor, one licensed to practice medicine and graduated from a college of medicine, dentistry, or veterinary medicine.

dolichocephalic, a long head; having a skull with a long front to back diameter.

dolichoderus, having a long neck.

dolichomorphic, having a thin, long body type.

dolor, pain, sorrow.

dolorific, producing pain.

dolorus, expressing pain, or grief.

domatophobia, morbid fear of being in the mouse; pertaining to a form of claustrophobia.

dominant, exerting control or influence; in genetics, the expression of a trait or characteristic which is inherited from one parent and excluding a contrasting trait from the opposite parent; a dominant allele or trait.

donor, a person who furnishes blood for transfusion or an organ for transplant.

dorophobia, morbid aversion to touching animal fur.

dorsad, toward the back.

dorsal, pertaining to the back; thoracic.

dorsalgia, pain in the back.

dorsiflect, bending backward.

dorsiflexion, backward flexion, as in bending backward either a hand or foot.

dorsolateral, pertaining to the back and the side.

dorsosacral, pertaining to the lower back.

dorsum, pertaining to the back or posterior surface of a body part.

dosage, the determination and regulation of the amount of medicine to be given at one time.

dose, a prescribed amount of medication to be taken at one time.

dosimeter, a device for measuring doses of radiation or X-rays.

dosimetry, a scientific determination of radiation; measurement of doses.

dotage, feeblemindedness or senility of old age.

double vision, seeing two images of an object at the same time.

double-blind, in reference to a study in which neither the administrator nor the subject knows which treatment the subject is getting.

douche, a stream of hot or cold water directed against a body part or cavity used for hygenic or medicinal purposes, especially the vagina.

DPT, diptheria-pertussis-tetanus vaccine.

Down's Syndrome, a common form of mental retardation caused by a chromosomal abnormality; mongolism.

drainage, the withdrawal of fluids and discharges from a cavity or wound.

dram, drachm, dr., a unit of liquid measure of the apothecaries system, containing 60 minims; a unit of weight equal to 60 grains, 1/8 ounce of the apothecaries' system.

Dramamine, trademark for dimenhydrinate, effective in the prevention and treatment of nausea, vomiting, and vertigo associated with surgery, motion sickness, and radiation sickness.

dreams, images that occur during sleep.

dressing, a protective covering for treatment of a wound caused by disease or injury to aid the healing process.

drip, to fall in drops; a slow injection of glucose or saline a drop at a time; intravenously.

drive, the urge or force that activates and motivates animals and man.

drop foot, inability to raise the foot upwards due to paralysis, of dorsal flexor muscles.

dropsy, a condition characterized by generalized accumulation of fluids in the tissues and cavities; see edema.

drug, a medicinal substance used internally or externally in treatment of disease or for diagnostic purposes.

drug addiction, a physical dependence on a drug caused by excessive or continued use of habit-forming drugs.

druggist, pharmacist.

drum, the middle ear; the tympanic membrane which serves to separate the tympanic cavity from the exterior acoustic meatus.

duct, a narrow tube or channel which serves to convey secretions from a gland.

ductless, having no duct, or secreting internally; see endocrine glands.

ductule, a small duct.

ductus arteriosus, the fetal blood vessel which communicates between the pulmonary artery and the aorta.

dumb, unable to speak; mute.

duodenal, pertaining to the duodenum.

duodenectomy, an operation excising all or part of the duodenum.

duodenitis, inflammation of the duodenum.

duodenostomy, a surgical procedure of making a permanent opening into the duodenum through the abdominal wall.

duodenum, the first segment of the small intestines connecting with the pylorus of the stomach and extending to the jejunum.

dural, pertaining to the dura mater, the outermost covering of the brain and spinal cord.

durematoma, an accumulation of blood between the arachnoid and dura membranes.

dwarf, an undersized human being.

dwarfism, being abnormally small in size.

dynamia, having vital energy or an ability to combat disease.

dynamometer, an apparatus for measuring muscular strength.

dynamoscopy, to examine the muscles by auscultation.

dysacousia, dysacousma, discomfort caused by loud noises, or having a hypersensitivity to sounds.

dysarthrosis, disease or deformity of a joint.

dyscrasia, a disordered condition of the body; an abnormal condition of the blood.

dysenteric, pertaining to dysentery.

dysentery, any of a group of intestinal disorders characterized by inflammation and irritation of the colon, with diarrhea, abdominal pain, and the passage of mucous or blood.

dysergia, incoordination in voluntary muscular movements.

dysfunction, impairment or absence of total function of the body or an organ.

dysgenesis, defective development, or malformation.

dysgenics, research study into causative factors in degeneration or deterioration in offspring.

dysgerminoma, a slow-growing, malignant tumor of the ovary; the seminoma is the counterpart in testicular neoplasm.

dysgraphia, inability to write due to a brain lesion; writer's cramp.

dyskinesia, any of a number of diseases which produce defective voluntary movements; impairment of normal movement.

dyslexia, difficulty in reading and visual confusion resulting from a brain lesion; inability to comprehend written language due to a central lesion.

dysmenorrhea, painful menstruation.

dyspepsia, indigestion due to any one of many causes.

dysphagia, difficulty in swallowing.

dysphemia, stuttering; a speech disorder.

dysphonia, any voice impairment causing difficulty in speaking; hoarseness.

dysphoria, restlessness; having a feeling of unrest and depression without cause.

dysplasia, abnormal growth of tissue, as in pathology; irregular growth in size, shape, and structure of cells.

dyspnea, difficult and labored breathing; shortness of breath, which may be accompanied by pain.

dystonia, impairment of muscle tone or tonicity.

dystrophy, defective nutrition; any disorder due to poor nutrition marked by degeneration of the muscles.

dysuria, painful urination.

E

ear, the organ of hearing and equilibrium composed of three different sections: the external, middle, and internal ear.

earache, pain in the ear usually caused by inflammation.

eardrum, the tympanic membrane.

earwax, cerumen.

eburnation, changes in bone structure causing a hardening of bone into an ivory-like mass.

ecbolic, an agent which hastens labor or abortion by causing the uterine muscles to contract.

eccentric, deviating from a center; peripheral; peculiar or abnormal behavior.

ecchondroma, a cartilaginous tumor of slow growth.

ecchymosis, a hemorrhagic, non-elevated, irregularly-formed discolored area of the skin caused by the seepage of blood beneath the epidermis.

eccrinology, the study of glandular secretions.

eccyesis, extrauterine pregnancy.

ecderon, pertaining to the epidermis or outer portion of the skin.

ecdysis, the sloughing off or shedding of skin; desquamation.

echidin, the venom of poisonous snakes.

Echinococcus, a genus of tapeworms whose larvae may develop in mammals and form cysts, especially in the liver.

echinosis, a change in the appearance of blood corpuscles such as losing their smooth outlines; crenation of red blood cells.

echolalia, uncontrollable senseless repetition of words spoken by others.

eclampsia, a major toxemia occurring in pregnancy or childbirth characterized by high blood pressure, albuminuria, decreased urine formation, edema, convulsions, and coma.

eclectic, choosing from a wide variety of sources what appears to be the best.

ecmnesia, forgetfulness of recent events, as seen in senility.

ecologist, a specialist in ecology.

ecology, the study of the physiology of organisms as affected by environmental factors.

ecomania, extreme humbleness in the presence of those in authority but having a dominating and irritable attitude toward family members; manifested in chronic alcoholism.

ecphoria, reestablishment of a memory trace.

ecthyma, an infection of the skin as a result of neglected treatment of impetigo.

ectiris, the external part of the iris.

ectoblast, ectoderm, the outer layer of cells in a developing embryo; from this outer layer, the epidermis, nails, hair, skin glands, nervous system, external sense organs, and the mucous membrane of the mouth and anus are derived.

ectodermosis, ectodermatosis, a disorder or illness resulting from congenital maldevelopment of organs.

ectogenous, developing from outside a body structure, as infection from pathogenic bacteria.

ectomere, any of the cells forming the ectoderm.

ectomorphic, having body structures that are slightly developed characterized by linearity and leanness; referring to body tissues derived predominantly from the ectoderm.

ectoparasite, pertaining to a parasite living outside the host's body.

ectopia, displacement of an organ or structure.

ectopic pregnancy, a pregnancy occurring in the abdominal cavity of a fallopian tube.

ectoplasm, the outer portion of the cell protoplasm.

ectopotomy, surgical removal of the fetus in ectopic pregnancy.

ectopy, displacement or malposition.

ectoretina, outer portion of the retina.

ectotoxemia, introduction of a toxin into the blood.

ectromelia, congenital absence of a limb or limbs.

ectropic, pertaining to complete or partial turning outward of a part such as eversion of the eyelid.

ectropion, eversion of a part or edge, especially of an eyelid.

eczema, an inflammatory condition of the skin which may be acute or chronic, characterized by itching or burning, tiny papules and vesicles, oozing, crusting, and scaling; dermatitis.

eczematous, resembling eczema.

edema, swelling of body tissues due to an excessive accumulation of fluid in connective tissue or a serous cavity.

edematous, pertaining to edema.

edentia, without teeth.

edulcorant, sweetening.

edulcorate, to sweeten; to wash out acids, or salts.

EEG, electroencephalogram.

effect, a result or consequence of an action.

effector, a motor nerve ending having the efferent process terminate in a muscle or gland cell.

effemination, having feminine qualities in a man.

efferent, conducting impulses from the brain or spinal cord to muscles, glands, and organs.

effervescence, the formation of bubbles of gas rising to the surface of a liquid; to show exhilaration or excitement.

efflorescence, a rash, eruption, or redness of the skin.

effluvium, a noxious or foul exhalation.

effusion, the escape of fluid into a cavity, as the pleural space.

egersis, extremely alert; abnormal wakefulness.

egest, excrete or discharge from the body.

egesta, excrement or waste matter eliminated from the body.

egestion, eliminating undigested matter.

egg, a female gamete or egg; a female reproductive cell before fertilization.

ego, the conscious part of the psyche that maintains its identity and tests reality; in psychoanalysis, the ego mediates between the id and the superego.

egocentric, self-centered and withdrawing from the external world; having most of one's thoughts and ideas centering on self.

ego ideal, an unconscious perfection or desired standard of character usually identified with significant others or esteemed and admired persons.

egoism, an overevaluation of self; self-seeking personal advantage at the expense of other people.

egomania, egotism developed to a pathological degree.

egotism, an overevaluation of self.

egotist, a boastful and self-centered person.

eidoptometry, measuring visual acuteness.

eighth cranial nerve, the acoustic nerve.

eikonometry, determining distance of an object by measuring the image produced by a lens with an instrument.

ejaculation, the sudden ejection of seminal fluids from the male reproductive organs.

ejaculatio precox, premature ejaculation.

EKG, electrocardiogram.

elastin, an albuminoid material forming the main constituent of yellow elastic tissue found in tendons and cartilage.

elation, emotional excitement, or joyous emotion; euphoria.

elbow, the joint of the arm and forearm.

Electra complex, the suppressed, unresolved libidinal feelings a daughter has for her father, accompanied by strong feelings of jealousy toward her mother.

electroanesthesia, a local anesthesia injected into tissues by electricity.

electrocardiogram, a record of heart action by an electrocardiograph.

electrocardiograph, an apparatus used for recording variations in heart muscle activity.

electrocardiography, the study and recording of electrocardiograms produced by an electrocardiograph of the heartbeat.

electrocatalysis, chemical decomposition using electricity.

electrocautery, cauterization by means of an instrument containing a platinum wire heated by a current of electricity.

electrocoagulation, coagulation of tissue using a high frequency electric current.

electroconvulsive, using electric current to induce convulsions in treatment of mental illness.

electroencephalogram, a record of electrical activity in various areas of the brain.

electroencephalograph, an instrument for recording electrical activity of the brain.

electroencephalography, the study of changes in electrical fluctuations of the brain made by an electroencephalograph.

electrohemostasis, stopping of hemorrhage by electrocautery.

electrolysis, the destruction of a chemical compound by an electric current passing through it; the removal of body hair by electric current.

electrolyte, a solution which is capable of conducting electricity.

electrolytic, pertaining to electrolysis, or to an electrolyte.

electromassage, application of electrization in massage.

electromyogram, a graphic record of muscle contraction resulting from electrical stimulation.

electromyography, the preparation, study, and interpretation of an electromyogram.

electronarcosis, inducing narcosis or anesthesia by the application of electricity which is used in treatment of mental illness.

electropathology, the study of electrical reaction of muscles and nerves as a means of determining a diagnosis.

electroretinograph, an apparatus for measuring the electrical responses of the retina using light stimulation.

electroshock, shock induced by an electric current used in treatment of mental illness.

electrosurgery, surgery performed by electricity.

electrotherapy, treatment of disease by use of low-intensity electricity.

electuary, a medicinal substance mixed with a powdered drug and honey or syrup to form a paste.

elephantiasis, a chronic disease due to a tropical infection characterized by inflammation and obstruction of the lymphatics, and hypertrophy of the skin and subcutaneous tissues, affecting the lower extremities and the scrotum most frequently.

elinguation, surgical removal of the tongue.

elixir, a sweetened, aromatic alcoholic liquid used in oral preparations.

elytrocleisis, surgical closure of the vagina.

elytrotomy, surgical incision into the vaginal wall.

emaciate, to become extremely thin or lean; wasting.

emaciation, wasting of flesh; the state of growing extremely thin.

emaculation, removal of spots from the skin.

emasculation, removal of the testicles; castration.

embalming, a procedure to retard decomposition in treatment of the dead.

embedding, a process by which a piece of tissue is fixated in a medium such as paraffin to keep it intact during cutting into thin sections for microscopic examination.

embolic, pertaining to or caused by embolism.

embolism, an obstruction of a blood vessel by a clot of blood or foreign substance.

embololalia, including meaningless words or phrases in a spoken sentence.

embolus, a plug or clot of blood present in a blood or lymphatic vessel having been brought from another vessel and obstructing the circulation within the smaller vessel.

emboly, invagination of one part into another such as the formation of the gastrula by the bastula.

embradure, to widen an opening.

embrocation, fomentation, such as the application of heat and moisture to a diseased or bruised part of the body; a drug rubbed into the skin.

embryectomy, the removal of an extrauterine embryo by excision.

embryo, the offspring of any organism in the process of development from the fertilized ovum; prenatal development of a mammal between the ovum and the fetus; in humans, the stage of development between the second week to the eighth week after conception.

embryogeny, study of the origin or development of the embryo.

embryology, the science of the development of the individual organism during the embryonic stage.

embryoma, a dermoid cyst; a tumor consisting of embryonic germ tissue but devoid of organization.

embryonic membrane, derived from the zygote but outside the embryo, an additional embryonic structure in vertebrates providing additional nutritive and protective value.

emesis, vomiting.

emetic, an agent or substance to induce vomiting.

emetine, a white powdered alkaloid derived from ipecac with emetic properties used as an antiamebic.

eminence, a projection or bony prominence.

emissary, providing an outlet.

emissary veins, small veins which penetrate the skull carrying blood from the sinuses.

emission, an involuntary discharge of semen by the male, particularly during sleep.

emmenagogue, a medicine that stimulates menstrual functioning.

emmenia, the menstrual flow.

emmenic, pertaining to the menses.

emmeniopathy, any menstrual dysfunction.

emmetropic, normal vision.

emollient, an agent that softens and soothes the skin.

emotion, a mental state or strong feeling accompanied by physical bodily changes; any intense state of mind such as hate, love, anger, joy, or grief which precipitates physiological changes.

empathy, an attempt to identify one's feelings with those of another; having understanding and recognition of another's feelings.

emphysema, a distention caused by accumulated air in tissues or organs; pulmonary emphysema, a disease of the lungs due to overdistention of lung tissues and atrophic changes such as loss of elasticity and thinning of lung tissues.

emphysematous, pertaining to emphysema.

empiric, based on experience and observation.

empirical, pertaining to empiric, or based on experience.

Empirin, trademark for acetylsalicylic acid, phenacetin, and caffeine combined in a tablet used as an analgesic and antipyretic compound.

empyema, accumulation of pus in certain cavities of the body such as the chest cavity.

emulsify, to make into an emulsion.

emulsion, a mixture of two liquids not mutually soluble, one being divided into droplets and dispersed throughout the other.

enamel, the hardest substance in the body forming a white, dense covering for the crown of the teeth.

enanthesis, a skin eruption or rash originating from internal disorders or diseases.

enarthritis, inflammation of a ball-and-socket joint.

enarthrosis, any ball-and-socket joint.

encanthis, a new growth at the inner angle of the eye.

encelialgia, abdominal pain; belly-ache.

endoderm, inner layer of cells of an embryo.

endosteitis, inflammation of the medullary cavity of a bone.

endosteum, the membrane lining the medullary cavity of the bone which contains the marrow.

endothelial, pertaining to the endothelium.

endothelioma, a malignant growth of the endothelial lining of blood vessels.

endothelium, a lining formed of epithelial cells which line the blood and lymphatic vessels, heart, and the serous body cavities.

endothermy, surgical diathermy.

endotoscope, an instrument to examine the ear; and ear speculum.

endotoxin, bacterial toxin present within the body of a bacterium, liberated only when the bacterium disintegrates.

end plate, the terminal mass of a motor nerve ending which joins a skeletal muscle fiber.

enema, introduction of water or solution into the rectum and colon to evacuate the contents of the lower intestines, or as a means of introducing nutrients or medicine for therapeutic purposes.

energy, having the ability to work or take part in any activity.

enervation, weakness; lack of energy or strength.

engorged, distended with blood.

engorgement, the state of being engorged or distended; vascular congestion.

engram, the lasting impression of a physical experience upon nerve cells.

enomania, a craving for alcohol; delirium tremens.

enophthalmus, -mos, recession of the eyeball into its orbit.

ensiform, sword-like structure of the lower part of the sternum.

enstrophe, turning inward, especially of the eyelids.

enteral, pertaining to the small intestine.

enteralgia, pain in the intestines; colic or intestinal cramps.

enterectomy, surgical excision of part of the intestines.

enteric, pertaining to the intestines.

enteric fever, typhoid fever.

enteritis, inflammation of the intestines, usually of the small intestines.

enterocele, intestinal hernia; posterior vaginal hernia.

enterocinesia, movement of the intestines; peristalsis.

enterococcus, any streptococcus found in the intestines of man.

enterocolitis, inflammation of the intestines and colon.

enterocolostomy, surgical joining of the small intestine to the colon.

enteroenterostomy, surgical joining between two segments of the intestine after a diseased portion has been excised.

enterogastritis, inflammation of the intestines and of the stomach.

enterogenous, originating in the intestines.

enterohepatitis, inflammation of both large and small intestines and the liver.

enterlith, an intestinal calculus.

enterology, the study of the large and small intestines.

enteromegalia, enteromegaly, abnormal enlargement of the intestines.

enteron, the alimentary canal with specific reference to the small intestine.

enteropathy, referring to intestinal diseases.

enteroplasty, surgical plastic repair of the intestine.

enteroplegia, paralysis occurring in the intestines.

enterospasm, painful peristaltic movement in the intestines; resembling colic.

enterostenosis, narrowing of the intestine; a stricture.

enterostomy, creating a permanent opening into the intestine through the abdominal wall by a surgical procedure.

entoderm, see endoderm.

entopic, pertaining to the eyeball.

entoptoscopy, examining the interior of the eye.

entropion, turning inward of the edges of the lower eyelid.

enucleate, to remove the entire tumor or structure without rupturing; to remove the nucleus of a cell.

enuresis, being incontinent, involuntary complete or partial discharge of urine.

environment, external surroundings which influence an organism.

enzygotic, developing from the same ovum.

enzyme, a complex colloidal substance produced by living cells which induces chemical changes in another substance without being changed; a catalyst in the metabolism of organisms.

enzymology, the science that studies enzymes and enzymatic activity.

eonism, sexual perversion, as in transvestism of the male.

eosin, an acid dye used for diagnostic purposes and microscopic examination.

eosinophil, a cellular structure that stains readily with eosin dye.

epencephalon, the anterior portion of the embryonic hindbrain which develops into the pons and cerebellum.

ependyma, membrous lining of cerebral ventricles and the spinal cord's central canal.

ephedrine, an alkaloid, usually produced synthetically, known for its therapeutic properties as a bronchodilator in treatment of asthma, and for its constricting effects on the nasal passages in colds.

epicardia, the abdominal part of the esophagus which extends from the diaphragm to the stomach.

epicardiac, pertaining to the epicardium.

epicardium, the visceral layer of the pericardium which forms a serous membrane surrounding the outer layer of the heart wall.

epicranium, soft section covering the cranium.

epicritic, extreme sensitivity of the skin in discriminating between varying degrees of sensation produced by touch or temperature.

epidemic, infectious disease affecting many people at the same time and in the same region; a contagious disease widely diffused and quickly spreading and of high morbidity.

epidemiology, the study of epidemic diseases.

epidermal, pertaining to the epidermis.

epidermatoplasty, grafting with pieces of skin.

epidermis, outer layer of skin.

epidermitis, inflammation of the epidermis.

epididymis, a small, oblong structure resting upon and beside the posterior section of the testes.

epididymitis, inflammation of the epididymis.

epidural space, outside of the dura matter of the brain or spinal cord.

epigastric, the upper region of the abdomen, pertaining to the epigastrium.

epigastrium, region over the pit of the stomach or belly.

epiglottis, the thin, lid-like structure behind the posterior section of the tongue which covers the entrance of the larynx when swallowing.

epilation, removal of hair by the roots.

epilepsy, an episodic disturbance of the brain function characterized by a loss of consciousness, sensory disturbance, and generalized convulsions; three major types of epilepsy are: grand mal, petit mal, and focal seizures.

epileptic, one who is afflicted with epilepsy.

epileptoid, resembling or similar to epilepsy.

epimysium, a fibrous sheath of connective tissue surrounding the skeletal muscle.

epinephrine, a hormone produced by the adrenal medulla which is a powerful stimulant of the sympathetic nervous system, and a potent vasopressor which acts on the cardiovascular system and stimulates the myocardium to increase cardiac output; other medicinal uses include increasing metabolic activity, relaxing bronchioles in treatment of asthma, and inducing uterine contractions.

epinephritis, inflammation of the adrenal gland.

epineurium, the connective tissue sheath around the trunk of a nerve.

epiphora, abnormal excessive flow of tears.

epiphylaxis, to increase defensive powers within the body.

epiphyseal, pertaining to an epiphysis.

epiphysis, the end part of a juvenile long bone separated by cartilage from the main shaft but which later becomes a part of the larger bone through ossification.

epiphysitis, inflammation of an epiphysis, mostly of the hip, knee, and shoulder in infants.

epiploic, pertaining to the omentum.

episiotomy, surgical cutting of the vaginal opening to avoid the tearing of tissues in childbirth.

epistasis, a substance which rises to the surface like scum instead of sinking; the checking of a discharge; in heredity, a presence of a determining gene which prevents another gene not allelomorphic to it from expressing itself.

epistaxis, hemorrhage from the nose.

episternum, upper part of the sternum.

epithelial, pertaining to the epithelium.

epithelioma, malignant tumor consisting of epithelial cells; a carcinoma.

epithelium, the cellular layer forming the epidermis of the skin and internal and external covering of mucous and serous membranes.

equilibrium, a balance between opposing forces.

equivalent, equal in force or value.

erection, a distended state of an organ or part, especially in erectile tissue when filled with blood; becoming rigid.

erector, muscle that raises another part.

eremophobia, morbid fear of being alone.

erepsin, an enzyme found in intestinal juice which causes a peptide-splitting action.

erethism, excessive irritability or excitement.

ereuthrophobia, morbid fear of blushing.

ergograph, a device for recording muscle contractions and measuring the amount of work done.

ergonovine, an alkaloid derived from ergot, also produced synthetically; used to prevent hemorrhage after childbirth and to relieve migraine.

ergophobia, abnormal dread of working.

ergosterol, found in animal and plant tissues, and also derived from yeast, ergot, and other fungi; resembles cholesterol, and may be converted into Vitamin D by ultraviolet radiation.

ergot, a drug derived from fungi used to cause contractions of the uterus and control hemorrhage after childbirth.

ergotamine, a crystalline substance derived from ergot, used to treat migraine and to stimulate uterine contractions.

ergotism, poisoning resulting from excessive use of ergot, or from infected rye or wheat by fungus Claviceps purpurea, producing symptoms marked by spasms, cramps, or dry gangrene.

erogenous, sexual excitability; producing sexual desire.

eroticism, excessive libido; a condition of intense but normal sexual desire.

erotomania, abnormal, unrestrained libido.

erotopathia, any perverted sexual impulse.

erotophobia, an aversion to sexual love.

erubescence, a reddening of the skin, as in blushing.

eructation, bringing up of gas from the stomach; belching.

eruption, the appearance of a skin rash which accompanies a disease such as measles; the breaking through of a tooth through the gum.

erysipelas, an infectious disease of the skin due to infection with Streptococcus pyogenes characterized by fever and vesicular and bulbous lesions.

erysipeloid, a contagious dermatitis resembling erysipelas.

erythema, unusual redness of the skin caused by capillary congestion, resulting from inflammation, as in heat or sunburn.

erythrism, unusual redness of hair with a ruddy-colored skin.

erythroblast, a nucleated cell which possesses hemoglobin; the precursor of the erythrocyte.

erythrocyte, a mature red blood corpuscle, or cell.

erythrocythemia, an increase in the number of erythrocytes in the blood.

erythrocytosis, an abnormal increase in the number of red blood corpuscles.

erythrodermia, erythroderma, abnormal redness of the skin over a large area.

erythromycin, an antibiotic effective against many gram-positive organisms, used in treating amoebic and other diseases.

erythropoiesis, producing red blood corpuscles.

eschar, a sloughing or crusting which forms on the skin after cauterization or a burn.

esophagismus, spasms of the esophagus.

esophagitis, inflammation of the esophagus.

esophagoscope, a device used to examine the esophagus.

esophagus, the muscular canal extending from the pharynx to the stomach, approximately 9 inches in length.

esophoria, a tendency for the visual lines to converge.

esophoric, pertaining to esophoria.

esotropia, a marked turning inward of one eye toward that of the other causing crossed eyes.

ester, the combination of an organic acid with an alcohol; esters usually have fruity or flowery odors in liquid form.

esterase, an enzyme that catalyzes the hydrolysis of esters.

esthesioneurosis, loss of feeling in a body part without any apparent organic lesion.

estradiol, a hormone found in the ovary with estrogenic properties used in treatment of estrogen deficiency.

estriol, a hormone found in the urine of pregnant women.

estrogen, an estrogenic hormone produced by the ovarian follicle and other structures, responsible for the development of secondary female characteristics and changes in the epithelium of the vagina and the endothelium of the uterus; the natural estrogens include estradiol, estrone, and estriol.

estrone, a female sex hormone found in urine of pregnant women, used in the treatment of estrogen deficiencies.

estrum, estrus, the recurrent period of sexual receptivity in mammals called "heat."

ether anesthetic, a thin, colorless, highly volatile, and highly inflammable liquid widely used for general anesthesia and having a great margin of safety.

ethmoid, sievelike, cribriform plate which forms the nasal fossae and part of the floor of the skull.

ethmoidal, pertaining to the ethmoid bone.

ethmoidectomy, surgical removal of ethmoid cells.

ethmoiditis, inflammation of the ethmoidal cells causing headache, pain between the eyes, and nasal discharge.

ethmoid sinus, air spaces inside the ethmoid bone.

etiology, the study of any of the causes of diseases or abnormal body states.

eucalyptus, an oily substance derived from fresh plant leaves used as an expectorant and antiseptic.

eugenics, the scientific study of inheritance and the improvement of the human offspring.

eunuch, one with testicles removed; castrated male.

euphoria, feeling of mild elation and a sense of well-being.

euplastic, healing quickly and organizing well, as in tissue repair.

eupnea, normal respiration.

eupraxic, normal functioning.

eustachian tube, the auditory tube that connects the middle ear with the pharynx.

eustachitis, inflammation of the eustachian tube.

euthanasia, known as mercy killing; the ending of life for those who have an incurable disease or condition.

evacuant, an agent which promotes evacuation; cathartic.

evacuate, to discharge or expel, especially from the bowels.

evacuation, the process of evacuating.

evagination, the protrusion of an organ or part of an organ from its natural place.

eversion, a turning inside out, or turning outward.

evert, to turn outward; to turn inside out.

evisceration, the removal of viscera, contents of a cavity, or internal organs.

evolution, a developmental process from a rudimentary to a more complex state.

evulsion, a forcible extraction, or the act of tearing away of a part.

exacerbation, an increase in the severity of symptoms in a disease.

exaltation, a state of mind characterized by excessive or abnormal feelings of joy, optimism, elation, self-importance, or personal well-being.

examination, the process of inspecting the body and its products as a means of diagnosing a disease or as to physical fitness.

exanthema, any eruptive disease accompanied by inflammation of the skin, fever, or rash, as in measles or smallpox.

exanthrope, any cause of a disease originating externally.

exarteritis, inflammation of the outer coat of an artery.

exarticulation, amputation of a limb, or partial removal of a joint.

excipient, a substance such as jelly or sugar which is added to a drug to give it more consistency.

excise, to cut off or remove.

excision, the act of cutting out or removing, as in removing an organ or part of an organ.

excitability, susceptible to being stimulated.

excitant, an agent producing excitation of vital functions of the brain.

excitation, the condition of being excited, stimulated, or irritated.

excitor, a nerve which stimulates to greater activity.

excoriate, to abrade or wear off the surface of the skin or cuticle.

excoriation, the abrasion of the skin or the coating of an organ caused by disease or injury.

excrement, excreta, feces, or dejecta.

excreta, waste material expelled from the body.

excretion, the elimination of waste materials from the body.

excretory, pertaining to excretion.

exenteration, the surgical removal of the internal organs; evisceration.

exercise, physical exertion for health improvement; voluntary muscle activity.

exfoliation, the falling off of dead tissue in scales.

exhalation, breathing outward; the opposite of inhalation.

exhaustion, state of being extremely fatigued; weariness; the using up of a supply of something.

exhibit, to administer, as a drug or medicine; to show.

exhibitionism, an abnormal compulsion to expose the genitals to the opposite sex; a psychoneurosis.

exhibitionist, one with an abnormal impulse to exhibit the genitals to attract attention.

exhumation, disinterment of a body, or corpse.

exocrine, external secretion of a gland; excretion which reaches epithelial tissue or a duct.

exodontia, dentistry concerned with tooth extraction.

exodontist, one who practices exodontics.

exoenzyme, an enzyme that functions outside the cell which secretes it.

exogastritis, inflammation of the peritoneal coat of the stomach.

exogenous, originating outside an organ.

exometritis, inflammation of the peritoneal coat of the uterus.

exophoria, visual axes diverging outward.

exophthalmia, an abnormal protrusion of the eyeballs.

exormia, any skin rash.

exoserosis, an oozing or discharge of exudate.

exostosis, a bony growth projecting from the surface of a bone capped by cartilage.

exoteric, developing outside the body.

exotoxin, a toxin excreted by a microorganism into its surrounding medium.

expectorant, an agent having the quality of liquefying sputum or phlegm.

expectoration, ejecting or expelling mucus or phlegm from the lungs and throat; spitting.

expiration, the process of breathing out air from the lungs.

expire, to exhale; to die.

exploration, examining of an organ, part of an organ, or a wound by various means.

exploratory, pertaining to exploration.

expulsion, the act of expelling.

exsanguinate, to deplete of blood; bloodless;

exsanguination, the process of draining blood from a part.

exsanguine, anemic.

exsection, to cut out; excision.

exsiccation, the process of drying by heat.

extima, the outermost layer of blood vessels.

extirpation, to cut out totally; removal by the roots.

extraction, pulling out a tooth; the process of removing the active part of a drug.

extrasystole, an abnormal or premature contraction of part of the heart.

extrauterine, occurring outside the uterus.

extravasate, to escape into the tissues from a blood vessel.

extravasation, an escape of blood into the surrounding tissues; process of being extravasated.

extravascular, occurring outside a vessel.

extremity, a limb of the body; a terminal part of a structure.

extrinsic, originating externally.

extroversion, the direction of one's energy or attention turned outward from the self and toward objects.

extrude, to push out of a normal position.

extrusion, the process of being extruded, as in a tooth being pushed out of alignment.

extubation, removal of a tube.

exudate, the accumulation of fluid or pus in a cavity.

exudation, abnormal oozing of fluids, as in inflammatory conditions.

eye, the organ of vision; a globular structure consisting of three coats: the retina, uvea, and sclera with the cornea; the three layers enclose two cavities. The anterior cavity is divided by the iris into an anterior chamber and a posterior chamber which are filled with a watery aqueous humor. The cavity behind the lens is much larger in proportion and is filled with a jelly-like substance vitreous humor.

eyebrow, the ridge containing hair above the eye.

eyedrops, ophthalmic solutions for the treatment of eye disorders.

eyeglass, a lens for aiding impaired sight.

eyelash, a cilium or stiff hair on the edge of the eyelid.

eyelid, a movable protective fold of skin which covers the eyeball.

eyesight, having the ability to see.

eyestrain, fatigue of the eye due to excessive use or to an uncorrected visual defect.

eyetooth, a cuspid or upper canine tooth.

F

fabella, small fibrocartilages which develop in the head of the large muscle of the leg, or gastrocnemius.

face, the anterior or front part of the head from the forehead to the chin.

facet, facette, a small smooth surface on a bone.

facial, pertaining to the face.

facies, a specific surface of an organ or body structure; face.

faciocephalalgia, a neuralgia affecting the face and head.

facioplasty, plastic surgery of the face.

facioplegia, facial paralysis resulting from a stroke, or injury.

factitious, artificial or not natural; contrived.

faculty, having the ability to function.

faint, syncope; to feel weak and about to lose consciousness; temporary loss of consciousness.

fainting, the loss of consciousness.

falcate, sickleshaped; hooked.

fallectomy, excision of part of the fallopian tube.

fallopian tube, one of two tubes or ducts which extend laterally from the uterus to the ovary, and that function to convey the ova from the ovary to the uterus.

fallostomy, a surgical procedure to create an opening of the fallopian tube.

Fallot, tetralogy of, stenosis of the pulmonary artery which is a congenital defect occurring in newborns.

fallotomy, surgical division of the fallopian tubes.

false ribs, the lower five ribs which are not directly attached to the sternum.

falx, a sickle-shaped structure.

familial, common to the same family.

family, members of a group descended from a common progenitor.

fantasy, mental images which satisfy unconscious wishes or desires.

faradism, an interrupted current of electricity used to stimulate muscles and nerves.

farcy, a form of glanders which is a contagious infection in animals that may be communicated to man.

farsighted, clarity of vision at a distance.

fascia, a fibrous membrane of connective tissue supporting, and separating muscles and body organs.

fascicle, fasciculus, a small bundle of muscle fibers or nerves; a synonym for tract.

fasciectomy, surgical removal of strips of fascia.

fasciola, a small group of nerve or muscle fibers.

fascioplasty, plastic repair on a fascia.

fasciotomy, surgical incision and separation of a fascia.

fascitis, inflammation of a fascia.

fastidium, aversion to eating.

fastigium, the highest point of the 4th ventricle of the brain; the period of maximum temperature during the development of acute, infectious diseases.

fasting, going without nourishment.

fat, obese; corpulent; oily consistency; a group of organic compounds composed of carbon, oxygen, and hydrogen.

fatigue, a feeling of weariness resulting from excessive mental or physical exertion; temporary loss of capacity to respond to stimulation.

fauces, a passage leading from the mouth to the pharynx or throat cavity.

faucial, pertaining to the fauces.

faucitis, inflammation of the fauces.

faveolus, a depression on the skin.

favus, a contagious skin disease which may spread all over the body and scalp which is characterized by yellowish crusts resembling honeycomb.

febricula, a mild fever of short duration.

febrifacient, fever producing.

febrifuge, an agent which lessens fever such as an antipyretic.

febrile, pertaining to a fever.

fecal, pertaining to feces.

feces, excreta, dejecta, stools; waste products of the body discharged through the anus.

feculent, containing feces; having sediment.

fecundation, fertilization; impregnation.

fecundity, having the ability to produce offspring.

feeblemindedness, mental deficiency.

fellatio, oral stimulation of the penis.

felon, a purulent infection of the deeper tissues of the distal phalanx of a finger.

feminism, having female characteristics by the male.

feminization, adopting female characteristics.

femoral, pertaining to the femur or the thigh bone.

femur, the thigh bone which extends from the hip to the knee.

fenestra, a window-like open area in the inner wall of the middle ear covered by a membrane.

fenestration, surgical operation creating an artificial opening into the labyrinth of the ear.

fermentation, decomposition of complex substances by the action of anaerobic microorganisms' enzymatic conversion.

ferric, pertaining to iron; containing iron.

ferrotherapy, therapeutic use of iron compounds.

ferrous, pertaining to iron.

ferruginous, containing the color of iron rust; pertaining to iron.

fertile, capable of reproduction.

fertility, the ability to produce offspring.

fertilization, fecundation; impregnation of a sperm cell and an ovum.

fester, to become suppurate.

fetal, pertaining to a fetus.

fetalism, the retention of fetal structures after delivery.

fetation, pregnancy.

feticide, intentional destruction of a fetus.

fetid, having an offensive or foul odor.

fetish, an object or body part which excites the libido or sexual interest.

fetishism, belief that an object has certain power, or it is symbolically endowed with special meaning, especially that of a beloved person; the attraction of an object is associated with libido gratification and sexual desire.

fetor, an offensive odor such as halitosis; stench.

fetus, the developing young in utero of humans from the eighth week after fertilization.

fever, an elevation of body temperature above 98.6°F; pyrexia; characteristic of a disease such as typhoid fever or yellow fever in which the body temperature is abnormally elevated.

fiber, a threadlike structure as in a nerve fiber; the axonal part of a neuron; in nutrition, pertaining to constituents found in a diet.

fibra, pertaining to a fiber.

fibralbumin, globulin.

fibremia, fibrin formation which causes embolism or thrombosis in the blood.

fibril, an extremely fine filament or fiber.

fibrillar, pertaining to fibrils.

fibrillation, elements composed of fibrils; a quivering of muscle fibers which are uncoordinated; rapid and tremulous action of the heart.

fibrillolytic, dissolution of fibrils.

fibrin, a whitish, elastic protein formed by the action of thrombin on fibrinogen which forms a network of red and white blood cells and platelets, causing a clot.

fibrinogen, a soluble protein in the blood which through the action of thrombin and calcium ions is converted into fibrin, responsible for the clotting of the blood.

fibrinogenic, fibrogenous, producing fibrin.

fibrinolytic, pertaining to the dissolution of fibrin.

fibrinopenia, a deficiency of fibrin and fibrinogen in the blood.

fibroadenoma, fibrous tissue adenoma, a benign tumor occurring in the breasts of young women.

fibroangioma, a fibrous tissue angioma, usually benign.

fibroblast, a cell from which connective tissue is developed.

fibrocyst, a fibrous tumor with cystic degeneration.

fibrocystic, consisting of fibrocysts.

fibroid, a fibroid tumor.

fibroma, a fibrous benign tumor, slow in growth.

fibromatosis, having multiple fibromas developing simultaneously.

fibrosarcoma, a malignant tumor consisting of connective tissue, primarily.

fibrosis, an abnormal fibrous tissue formation.

fibrositis, inflammation of white fibrous connective tissue anywhere in the body.

fibrous, resembling fibers.

fibula, the outer and smaller bone of the leg, or calf bone, connecting the ankle to the knee.

fibulocaneal, pertaining to the fibula and calcaneus.

filaria, a threadlike worm.

filariasis, a disease caused by a long filiform worm which may be found in the lymphatic ducts, circulatory system, and connective tissues of man, causing inflammation, fibrosis, or blockage of the lymph flow that results in edema.

filtration, passage of a liquid through a semipermeable membrane such as a filter.

filum, a threadlike structure.

fimbria, resembling fringe.

finger, a digit of the hand.

first aid, emergency treatment given to persons who have been injured in an accident or have an acute illness prior to regular medical care.

first cranial nerve, olfactory nerve.

fissure, a natural division, cleft, or furrow in body organs such as the brain; an ulcer; a crack or break in tooth enamel.

fistula, an abnormal passage or duct between two internal organs, or between an internal organ to the body surface.

fistulous, pertaining to a fistula.

fit, a sudden attack or convulsion.

fixation, holding in a fixed position; arresting psychosexual development at an early stage, often resulting from childhood trauma.

flaccid, absence of muscular tone; relaxed; flabby.

flagellum, hairlike processes on the extremities of protozoa and bacteria.

flatfoot, an abnormal flatness of the arch of the foot causing the sole to rest upon the ground.

flatulence, excessive gas in the stomach and the alimentary canal.

flautus, gas formed in the digestive tract and expelled through the anus.

flavedo, yellowish pigment of the skin; jaundice.

fleam, an instrument used in venesection.

flection, flexion, to bend, as in bending a limb.

fletcherism, excessive chewing of small amounts of food.

flexibility, being capable of being bent without breaking; adaptability.

flexor, a muscle that bends a joint.

flexure, a bend, or curvature to a structure.

flight of ideas, skipping from one idea to another in a continuous stream of talk.

floaters, visual spots caused by deposits in the vitreous of the eye, occurring as benign degenerative changes.

floating kidney, a kidney displaced from its normal position in the body.

floating ribs, the 11th and 12th ribs which do not directly connect with the sternum.

flora, normal bacteria living in the intestines or the skin of humans; plant life.

fluid, liquid; gaseous substance.

fluid ounce, eight fluidrams.

fluidram, measure of liquid capacity equal to one-eight part of a fluid ounce.

fluke, any of several parasitic worms in man.

fluor albus, a whitish discharge from the uterus or vagina; leukorrhea.

fluorescein, a red crystalline substance used in diagnostic examination of the eye to detect corneal lesions or foreign bodies.

fluoridation, addition of fluorides to drinking water as a means of preventing tooth decay.

fluoride, any binary compound of fluorine, especially with a radical.

fluorine, a gaseous, nonmetallic element found in the soil in combination with calcium which is important to plant and animal life.

fluoroscope, an apparatus that permits visual observation of the deep structures of the body on a fluorescent screen.

fluoroscopy, the use of a fluoroscope for medical examination and diagnosis.

fluorosis, chronic fluorine poisoning often caused by an excess of fluoride in drinking water.

flush, sudden reddening to the skin; blushing; flushing a body cavity or part with water.

flutter, a rapid pulsation or regular movement, especially of the heart.

flux, an excessive evacuation or discharge of fluid matter from the body or a cavity; diarrhea.

focal, pertaining to a focus.

focus, foci, point at which convergent light rays or sound waves intersect; that part of the body or organ in which a disease is localized.

folic acid, a B- vitamin important in the diet of humans used in treatment of pernicious and macrocytic anemia, and gastrointestinal disorders.

follicle, a small secretory cavity, sac, or gland.

follicle-stimulating hormone, a pituitary hormone that stimulates estrogen secretions and the production of Graafian follicles in the female; the follicle-stimulating hormone (FSH) in males stimulates the seminiferous tubules to produce sperm more rapidly.

follicular, pertaining to a follicle.

folliculin, the oophorin hormone produced by the ovarian follicles.

folliculitis, inflammation of a follicle.

fomentation, the application of heat and moisture to relieve pain or inflammation.

fomes, any material or substance on which infectious disease-producing agents may be transmitted.

fontanel, fontenelle, the soft spot of an infant's head lying between the cranial bones of the skull.

food, any nutritive taken into the body which provides a source of energy for physical activity, growth support, and maintenance of body tissue repair.

food allergies, allergic reactions to certain foods in one's diet caused by a sensitivity to one or more foods ingested; the most common foods that cause sensitivity are: eggs, lettuce, milk, spinach, strawberries, and tomatoes.

food poisoning, an acute digestive disorder due to ingesting foods which contain poisonous substances.

foot, the terminal part of a leg.

foot-and-mouth disease, Aphthous fever, a disease of cattle characterized by ulcers in the mouth, the hooves, teats, and udder, which can be transmitted to man.

footdrop, a condition in which the foot falls in a planter-flexed position caused by paralysis of flexor leg muscles.

foramen, an opening or communication between two cavities of an organ, or a perforation in a bone through which vessels or nerves pass.

foramen magnum, a perforation in the occipital bone through which the spinal cord unites with the medulla oblongata.

foramen ovale, an opening between the left and right cardiac atria that normally closes after birth.

forceps, a two-pronged instrument resembling a pair of tongs used for holding or extracting.

forearm, the section of the arm between elbow and wrist.

forebrain, the part of the brain which develops from the anterior portion of the embryonic brain, comprising the diencephalon and telencephalon.

forehead, the brow above the eyes.

forensic medicine, legal aspects of medicine.

foreskin, the fold of skin or prepuce which covers the glans of the penis.

formaldehyde, a pungent, colorless gas used in solution as a disinfectant, preservative, astringent, and fumigant.

formalin, an aqueous solution of formaldehyde with the addition of methanol.

formication, a creeping sensation as if ants were crawling upon the body; form of paresthesia.

formula, a prescription of ingredients with proportions in the preparation of medicine.

formulary, book of formulas.

fornication, voluntary sexual intercourse on the part of an unmarried person.

fornix, fornices, a vault-like band of a fibrous formation connecting the cerebral lobes; an arch-like space formed by such a structure.

fossa, a hollow or depressed area in the body.

fossette, a small, deep corneal ulcer; a small fossa.

fourchet, fourchette, a transverse fold of mucous membrane connecting the posterior ends of the labia minora which forms the margin of the vulva.

fovea, a small pit or depression, often indicating the central fovea of the retina.

Fowler's position, a semi-sitting position with the back rest elevated or the head of the patient placed on several pillows to relieve dyspnea.

fracture, a break or rupture, especially in a bone.

fragilitas, a brittleness or fragility.

fragility, state of being brittle or frail.

fragmentation, breaking into small pieces.

fraternal twin, derived from two separate fertilized ova.

freckle, a small, localized brownish spot on the skin, often due to exposure to the sun.

fremitus, palpation of vibratory tremors felt through the chest wall.

frenum, a membranous fold which connects two parts, one more or less restrained in movement, as in the underside of the tongue.

frenzy, state of violent mental agitation; wild excitement; delirium.

Freudian, pertaining to Sigmund Freud, founder of psychoanalysis, and to his theories regarding the causes and treatment of neurosis and psychosis.

friable, easily pulverized or broken down into crumbs.

friction, act of rubbing.

frigidity, usually applied to the inability to respond to sexual desire or sexual stimuli; coldness.

frontal, pertaining to the forehead or the bones forming the forehead.

frontal lobe, the anterior portion of the cerebral hemisphere, the cerebrum.

frostbite, damage occurring by the freezing of part of the body such as nose, fingers, or toes causing numbness.

frottage, rubbing; massage; sexual gratification by rubbing against a person of the opposite sex.

frotteur, one who practices frottage.

fructose, fruit sugar; levulose.

FSH, see follicle stimulating hormone.

fugue, physical flight from home on a hysterical impulse; a state of personality dissociation accompanied by amnesia.

fulguration, destruction of tissue by electricity.

fulminating, pain occurring with rapidity and severity.

fumigation, exposing to poisonous fumes or gases for the purpose of destroying living organisms such as vermin; disinfecting of rooms by gases.

functional, pertaining to function and not to structure.

functional disease, one not organic but in which there is a pathological alteration in the functioning of an organ.

fundus, referring to the base part or body of a hollow organ; the part most remote from its opening.

fungicide, a bactericide which destroys fungi.

fungoid, resembling fungus.

fungus, fungi, any of a group of eukaryotic protists such as yeasts, molds, or mushrooms that subsist on organic matter.

funiculus, small structure resembling a cord; small bundle of nerve fibers; umbilical or spermatic cord.

funny bone, outer part of the elbow where part of the ulnar nerve passes by the internal codyle of the humerus.

furfur, dandruff.

furfuraceous, resembling dandruff; flaky or scaling.

furuncle, a boil.

furunculosis, a condition marked by the presence of boils on the skin.

fusiform, spindle-like structures.

Fusobacterium, a genus of gram-negative anaerobic bacteria normally found in the mouth and large intestines, and in necrotic lesions.

fusospirillosis, Vincent's angina caused by fusiform bacilli and spirochetes.

G

gag, a device to hold the mouth open; to retch or to cause to retch or vomit.

gait, a manner of moving on foot or walking.

galactacrasia, an abnormal condition occurring in the composition of milk from the breast.

galactan, a carbohydrate which forms galactose upon hydrolysis.

galactemia, an abnormal milky condition of the blood.

galactic, pertaining to flow of milk.

galactidrosis, sweat that appears milklike.

galactischia, suppression of the secreting ducts and the flow of milk.

galactophore, a milk duct.

galactophoritis, inflammation of a milk duct.

galactorrhea, excessive flow of milk after cessation of nursing.

galactstasis, cessation of breast milk secretion.

galeophobia, morbid aversion to cats.

gall, pertaining to the gallbladder bile.

gallbladder, a pear-shaped organ containing bile produced in the liver, located beneath the right lobe of the liver.

gallstone, a stonelike mass formed in the gallbladder or bile ducts.

galvanism, the use of direct electric current to the body for therapeutic purposes.

galvanometer, an apparatus that measures current strength using electromagnetic action.

galvanopalpation, the testing of nerve sensibility of the skin by galvanic current.

galvanopuncture, the use of needles to complete an electric current.

galvanoscope, a device which detects the direction of a galvanic current.

gamete, a male or female reproductive germ cell that unites to form an offspring; the spermatozoon or ovum.

gametocyte, an oocyte or spermatocyte.

gametogenesis, the formation of gametes.

gamic, sexual, especially as applied to eggs after fertilization.

gamma globulin, a blood protein containing antibodies, given by injection as a prophylactic measure against measles, poliomyelitis, and infectious hepatitis.

gamma rays, extremely short-wave length rays which penetrate radioactive material and reduce the cell nucleus; used in radiotherapy.

gamogenesis, sexual reproduction.

gamophobia, a psychoneurotic fear of being married.

ganglial, pertaining to a ganglion.

gangliectomy, ganglionectomy, surgical removal of a ganglion.

ganglioma, a tumor of a lymphatic gland; swelling which occurs in lymphoid tissue.

ganglion, a knot-like mass of nervous tissue consisting of nerve-cell bodies, located outside the brain or spinal cord; a cystic tumor which develops on a tendon, sometimes occurring on the back of the wrist due to strain.

ganglionitis, inflammation of a ganglion.

gangrene, necrosis or a gradual deterioration of an area of tissue resulting from interference of the blood supply to that part of the body.

gargle, a solution for washing the throat or mouth; to wash the mouth or throat by holding a liquid preparation in the mouth and agitating it with expired air from the lungs.

gargoylism, Hurler's syndrome, characterized by a form of dwarfism accompanied by mental deficiency, damaged vision, and grotesque facial features.

garrot, a form of tourniquet.

gaseous, having the nature of gas.

gastralgia, periodic pain in the stomach without gastric lesion.

gastrectomy, surgical removal of part or the whole of the stomach.

gastric, pertaining to the stomach.

gastric ulcer, a peptic ulcer of the stomach.

gastrin, a hormone secreted by the glands in the pyloric end of the stomach which stimulates the secretion of gastric acid and pepsin in the cardiac end of the stomach; it is a weak stimulant of pancreatic enzymes and gallbladder contraction.

gastritis, inflammation of the stomach mucous membranes.

gastrocele, hernia of the stomach.

gastrocnemius, the large muscle in the calf of the leg.

gastrocolic, pertaining to the colon and the stomach.

gastrocolic reflex, the peristaltic waves produced in the colon by the ingestion of food into an empty stomach.

gastrocolitis, inflammation of the stomach and colon.

gastrocolostomy, surgical joining of the stomach to the colon.

gastroduodenal, pertaining to the stomach and the duodenum.

gastroduodenitis, inflammation of the stomach and the duodenum.

gastroenteric, pertaining to the stomach and the intestine.

gastroenteritis, inflammation of the stomach and the intestine.

gastroenteroptosis, displacement downward of the stomach and the intestines.

gastroenterostomy, a surgical joining of the stomach wall to the small intestine.

gastroesophageal, pertaining to the stomach and the esophagus.

gastrogavage, feeding through a tube passed into the stomach.

gastrointestinal, pertaining to the stomach and the intestines.

gastrojejunostomy, surgical joining between the stomach and jejunum.

gastrology, the study of structures, functions, and diseases of the stomach.

gastromalacia, a softening of the walls of the stomach.

gastronephritis, inflammation of both the stomach and the kidneys at the same time.

gastroparalysis, paralysis of the stomach.

gastropathy, any disorder of the stomach.

gastrophrenic, referring to the stomach and the diaphragm.

gastroplegia, see gastroparalysis.

gastroptosia, abnormal falling of the stomach, usually involving the displacement of other organs.

gastrorrhagia, excessive bleeding from the stomach.

gastroscope, an instrument for examining the interior of the stomach.

gastroscopy, examination of the stomach and abdominal cavity with a gastroscope.

gastrosia, excessive secretion of hydrochloric acid in the stomach.

gastrostaxis, an oozing of blood from the mucosa of the stomach.

gastrotomy, incision of the abdominal or stomach wall.

gatophobia, fear of cats.

gauze, a thin fabric used as a bandage applied to wounds.

gavage, a tube passed through the nares, pharynx, and esophagus into the stomach for feeding purposes, or forced pumping of the stomach contents.

gene, a unit of heredity located at a specific position on a chromosome which determines characteristics in the offspring from a parent.

generic, pertaining to a genus of a drug name, not a trademark.

genetic, pertaining to the science of genetics; referring to genes.

genetics, the science concerned with individual differences of related organisms and the study of heredity.

genial, pertaining to the chin.

genicular, pertaining to the knee.

geniculate, bent as a knee; pertaining to the ganglion of the facial nerve.

genitals, genitalia, organs of the reproductive system, especially the external organs.

genitourinary, pertaining to the genital and urinary organs.

genotype, the basic hereditary constitution of the individual in a combination of genes.

gentian violet, a dye derived from coal tar used as a stain in bacteriology, cystology, and histology; therapeutic uses include an anti-infective and an anthelmintic agent.

genupectoral position, knee-chest position.

genu varum, bowleg.

genyplasty, plastic surgery on the chin.

geotragia, practice of eating earth, clay, or chalk.

gereology, the science concerned with old age.

geriatrics, the branch of medicine concerned with the problems and diseases of aging.

germ, a microorganism that causes disease; an early embryonic stage.

German measles, rubella, a viral infection with a rash and fever of short duration.

germicide, an agent destructive to germs.

germinal, pertaining to a germ or reproductive cells, egg or sperm; germination.

germinal disk, blastoderm, or disk of cells from which the embryo develops.

germination, the stage of development of an impregnated ovum into an embryo.

germ layer, one of three embryonic layers of cells: ectoderm, endoderm, mesoderm.

gerontology, the scientific study of the aging process.

gestation, period of fetal development in the womb.

gestosis, any disorder of pregnancy such as toxemia.

giantism, gigantism, abnormal growth or development of the body or its parts.

giddiness, dizziness, vertigo, or a sensation of reeling.

gingivitis, inflammation of the gums.

girdle, an area around the waist; cingulum; a structure which resembles a belt or band.

glabella, the flat surface of the frontal bone or the area of the face between the eyebrows.

glabrous, smooth and bald.

gland, specialized secretory cells in a structure or organ; a gland may be ductless or endocrine whose secretions directly enter the blood or lymph system, or a gland maybe exocrine, having ducts which transport the secretions to an epithelial surface.

glanders, a contagious disease found in horses which is communicable to man.

glandular, consisting of, or pertaining to glands.

glans, bulbous end of the penis; head of the clitoris; goiter; a gland.

Glauber's salt, a crystalline salt used as a purgative.

glaucoma, an eye disease characterized by increased intraocular pressure resulting in degeneration of the optic nerve and gradual loss of vision.

gleet, a purulent discharge from the urethra resulting from chronic gonorrhea.

glenoid, resembling a socket.

gliadin, a protein found in the gluten of wheat or rye.

glial, pertaining to glia or neuroglia.

glioma, a tumor consisting predominantly of neuroglia.

globin, a protein formed from hemoglobin.

globulin, a simple protein insoluble in water.

globus hystericus, a sensation of a lump in the throat occurring in hysteria or other neuroses.

glomerulitis, inflammation of the glomeruli.

glomerulonephritis, nephritis with inflammation of the capillary loops in the renal glomeruli which may frequently follow other infections.

glomerulus, a small rounded mass of capillary loops eclosed within the Bowman's capsule of a renal tubule and which serves as a filter in the formation of urine.

glossa, tongue.

glossal, pertaining to the tongue.

glossitis, inflammation of the tongue.

glottis, an opening at the upper part of the trachea and between the vocal cords responsible for the modulation of the voice; the vocal apparatus of the larynx.

glucagon, a hormone secreted by the alpha cells of the islets of Langerhans in the pancreas which functions in response to hypoglycemia and to stimulate the growth hormone.

glucogenic, producing glucose.

glucohemia, sugar in the blood.

glucose, a monosaccharide or dextrose found in certain foods such as nuts; an end product in the metabolism of carbohydrates and the chief source of energy for the body.

glucosuria, excessive amount of sugar in the urine.

glutamic acid, an amino acid formed in the hydrolysis of proteins; in the form of monosodium glutamate it is used as a salt substitute.

gluteal, pertaining to the buttocks, or gluteal muscles.

gluten, protein found in cereals and bread.

glycemia, sugar or glucose present in the urine.

glycerin, a clear, syrupy liquid, soluble in alcohol and water, used in medication preparation.

glycerol, transparent, syrupy liquid formed by hydrolysis of fats.

glycine, a crystalline amino acid derived from gelatin and from other proteins.

glycogen, a storage form of carbohydrate found in the liver and muscles.

glycogenesis, the formation of glycogen from glucose in the body.

glycolysis, the breakdown of carbohydrates in living organisms by enzymatic action.

glycolytic, pertaining to the hydrolysis of sugar.

glyconeogenesis, formation of carbohydrates from fat or protein.

glycosemia, excessive sugar in the blood.

glycoside, a substance derived from plants which hydrolyze into sugars.

glycosuria, sugar in the urine.

gnathalgia, pain in the jaw.

gnathitis, inflammation of the jaw.

goiter, an enlargement of the thyroid gland causing a swelling to the front part of the neck.

gomphosis, a conical process which is inserted into a socket in an immovable joint.

gonad, female or male reproductive gland that produces gametes; the sex glands in the embryo before differentiation.

gonadal, pertaining to a gonad.

gonadotrophin, gonad-stimulating hormone.

gonarthritis, inflammation of knee joint.

gonococcus, organism causing gonorrhea, Neisseria gonorrhoeae.

gonorrhea, a contagious, catarrhal disease of the genital mucous membranes of both males and females.

gonorrheal, pertaining to gonorrhea.

goose flesh, erection of skin papilae resulting from exposure to cold, shock, or fear.

gout, a metabolic disease characterized by acute arthritis and inflammation of the great toe, diagnosed by excessive accumulation of uric acid in the bloodstream.

graft, a section of skin, muscle, bone, or nerve tissue inserted into a similar substance by surgical means.

gram, basic unit of mass, equivalent to 15.432 grains.

gramicidin, an antibiotic obtained from soil bacillus, effective against gram-positive bacteria.

gram-positive, pertaining to organisms that will retain the gentian violet color when stained; gram-negative organisms will not retain the violet color when stained.

Gram's method, a method for staining organisms for identification under a microscope.

grand mal, severe epileptic attack characterized by convulsions, stupor, and temporary loss of consciousness.

granulation, new tissue formed in the process of healing; granular projections formed on the surface of an open wound.

granule, a very small grainlike body or structure.

granulocyte, a white blood cell or granular leukocyte.

granuloma, a granular growth consisting of epithelial and lymph cells which occur in diseases such as leprosy, yaws, and syphilis.

granulomatosis, multiple granulomas.

granulose, soluble part of starch.

graphobia, unusual fear of writing.

graphorrhea, the writing of meaningless words or phrases.

gravel, small calculi of crystalline dust which form in the kidneys or bladder.

gravid, being pregnant.

gravida, a pregnant woman.

gray matter, a grayish color nervous tissue; the term is applied to the gray portions of the central nervous system which include the cerebral cortex, basal ganglia, brain nuclei, and the gray spinal cord columns.

green sickness, anemia found in adolescent girls resulting from a poor diet.

gripe, grippe, sudden onset of an infectious disease characterized by fever, fatigue, headache, back pain, and phlegm from the respiratory tract.

gripes, severe intermittent pain in the bowels.

gristle, cartilage.

groin, the hollow on either side of the body between thigh and trunk; inguinal region.

growth, to develop or increase in size; abnormal cell or tissue growth, as in a tumor.

gullet, the esophagus; passage to the stomach.

gum, fleshy tissue covering the jaws' alveolar parts and the necks of the teeth.

gumboil, a gum abscess.

gumma, a soft tumor characteristic of the tertiary stage of syphilis.

gustation, taste sensation stimulated by gustatory nerve endings in the tongue.

gustatory, pertaining to sense of taste.

gut, bowel; intestine.

gutta, a drop.

guttate, a drop-like spot, as in certain skin lesions.

guttur, throat.

guttural, pertaining to the throat.

gymnophobia, unusual aversion to looking at a naked body.

gynecologist, a specialist in gynecology, or who specializes in diseases of women.

gynecology, the science of the diseases of women, especially of the genital, urinary, or rectal organs.

gynecomania, abnormal sexual desire in the male.

gynecomastia, unusually large breasts in the male.

gynephobia, aversion to female companionship.

gyrus, one of the ridges or convolutions of the cerebral hemisphere of the brain.

H

habit, a pattern or action which becomes automatic following constant repetition; a predisposition or characteristic of a person's mental makeup; clothing characteristic of a function, as a priest; bodily temperature; an addiction to drug, alcohol, or tobacco usage.

habit chorea or spasm, voluntary spasmodic movement of muscles that has become involuntary, as blinking of the eyes, coughing, or scratching.

habitual, acting in a repeated manner from force of habit.

habitus, attitude or physical appearance that indicates a tendency to certain diseases or abnormal conditions.

hachement, massaging with chopping strokes with the edge of the hands.

hacking, strokes with the edge of the hand.

hair, threadlike outgrowth from the skin.

hairball, a mass of hair in the stomach.

halation, blurring of vision due to a strong light shining in one's eyes from the direction of the object being viewed.

halazone, a disinfectant for drinking water.

Haldol, trademark for haloperidol, a psychotropic drug used in treatment of psychosis.

half-life, the time in which the radioactive atoms associated with an isotope are reduced by half through decay.

halisteresis, the lack of calcium in bones.

halitosis, foul or offensive breath.

halitus, exhalation of vapor; the breath.

hallucination, false sensory perception in the absence of an actual external cause.

hallucinogen, a chemical substance or narcotic used to produce fantastic visions and hallucinations.

hallucinogenic, pertaining to a hallucinogen.

hallucinosis, an abnormal condition marked by persistent hallucinations.

hallux, the great toe.

hallux flexus, see hammer toe.

hallux valgus, great toe displacement toward other toes.

hallux varus, great toe displacement away from other toes.

halogen, any of the group of elements astatine, bromine, chlorine, flourine, and iodine which form salt when combined with metal.

haloid, resembling salt in composition.

halothane, used as a general anesthetic.

ham, the region behind the knee; commonly used for buttock, hip, or thigh in which the hamstring muscles are located.

hamartoma, a benign tumor composed of a new growth of mature cells on existing blood vessels; a tumor resulting from faulty development of the embryo.

hammer, common name for malleus, a bone in the middle ear.

hammer toe, deformity of the toe due to abnormal dorsal flexion.

hamstring, one of three muscles on the posterior part of the thigh which flex the leg and adduct and extend the thigh.

hamulus, a hooked-shaped structure.

hand, terminal part of the arm attached to the wrist.

hangnail, a partly detached piece of skin at the base or side of the fingernail.

haphalgesia, sensation of pain when touching objects.

haphephobia, an aversion to being touched by others.

haploid, having half the normal number of chromosomes following the division of germ cells in gametogenesis.

hairlip, a congenital defect resulting from faulty fusion of the vertical fissure of the upper lip, often involving the palate; cleft lip.

haunch, hips and buttocks.

haut-mal, grand mal seizure at its height.

hay fever, an allergy to air-borne pollens marked by inflammation of mucous membranes of the nose and upper air passages, catarrh, watery eyes, headache, asthmatic symptoms, and other symptoms similar to a head cold.

head, caput; the part of the body above the neck containing the brain.

headache, diffused pain in the head.

heal, to cure or restore to health; to make whole.

healing, the process of restoring to a normal or improved condition.

health, a state of having a sound or active body and mind; a sense of well-being and the absence of disease.

healthy, enjoying or being in a state of good health.

hearing, the ability to perceive sound.

hearing aid, a small device to amplify sound waves for those with impaired hearing.

heart, a hollow muscular organ that maintains the circulation of blood throughout the body, consisting of four chambers: the lower chambers are the left and right ventricles and the upper chambers are the left and right auricles.

heart attack, a sudden decrease in the flow of blood to the heart muscle resulting in impaired heart functioning often caused by an embolism or by chronic high blood pressure.

heart block, an impairment of the conductile tissue of the heart, specifically the S-A node, A-V node, bundle of His, and Purkinje fibers which fail to conduct normal impulses resulting in altered heart rhythm.

heartburn, a sensation of burning in the esophagus behind the lower part of the sternum, sometimes accompanied by an acid-tasting liquid in the mouth.

heart disease, any pathological or abnormal condition of the heart.

heart failure, an inability of the heart to maintain sufficient circulation resulting in cessation of the heart beat.

heart-lung machine, an apparatus through which the circulation of the blood is maintained and oxygenated while the heart is opened during surgery.

heart murmur, an abnormal heart sound which is detected by a stethoscope, usually indicating either a functional or structural defect.

heat, a warm sensation; high temperature; a form of energy; sexual excitement in lower animals; to make hot.

heat exhaustion, a condition caused by prolonged exposure to high temperatures combined with fatigue; characterized by dizziness, faintness, nausea, sweating, and general weakness.

heatstroke, a condition due to excessive exposure to high temperatures or the sun, occurs especially with those who are debilitated or who have been drinking alcoholic beverages, resulting in symptoms of dizziness, nausea, weakness, spots before the eyes, ringing in the ears, reddened and dry skin, rapid pulse, and collapse.

hebephrenia, a schizophrenic disorder characterized by disorganized thinking, regressive behavior, giggling, hypochondrial complaints, and bizarre delusions and hallucinations.

hebephrenic, pertaining to hebephrenia.

hebetic, pertaining to puberty.

hebetude, mental slowness; dullness.

hebosteotomy, an enlargement of the pelvic diameter by surgery to facilitate delivery.

hectic fever, a fever that occurs with an organic disease such as pulmonary tuberculosis or kidney or liver abcess.

hedonism, preoccupation with pleasure.

helcoid, resembling an ulcer.

helicoid, resembling a helix or spiral.

heliencephalitis, inflammation of the brain due to sunstroke.

heliotherapy, therapeutic application of sunlight in treatment of disease.

helix, the whole circuit of the external ear structure.

helminth, worm-like animal including flatworms, spiney-headed worms, threadworms or roundworms, and segmented or tapeworms.

helminthiasis, the presence of parasitic worms.

helminthic, pertaining to worms; that which expels worms.

helminthicide, a worm-expelling agent.

helminthology, the study of intestinal parasitic worms.

helminthophobia, a pathological dread of worms, or delusion of being infested by worms.

heloma, callosity, or corn.

helosis, having corns.

helotomy, removal of corns by surgery.

hemacytometer, hemocytometer, an apparatus for counting blood corpuscles.

hemadostenosis, contraction of blood vessels.

hemal, pertaining to the blood or blood vessels.

hemangioma, a tumor consisting of blood vessels.

hemarthrosis, the effusion of blood into a joint.

hematemesis, the vomiting of blood.

hematherapy, the infusion of fresh blood in the treatment of disease.

hematic, referring to blood; a treatment for anemia.

hematidrosis, excreting bloody sweat.

hematimeter, an apparatus used in counting blood corpuscles in a cu. mm. of blood.

hematin, the reddish iron-containing pigment of hemoglobin.

hematinic, pertaining to blood; a medicine which increases the hemoglobin level in the blood.

hematinuria, hematin in the urine.

hematocolpos, blood accumulation in the vagina.

hematocrit, a centrifugal apparatus used to determine the percentage of red blood cells in whole blood; the volume percentage of erythrocytes or red blood cells in blood.

hematodyscrasis, pathological blood condition.

hematogenesis, the formation of blood corpuscles.

hematogenous, produced by the blood; disseminated by means of the blood stream.

hematology, the branch of medicine concerned with blood diseases.

hematoma, a swelling of blood which occurs in an organ or tissue resulting from ruptured blood vessels.

hematometra, hemorrhage in the uterus.

hematomyelia, hemorrhage of blood into the spinal cord.

hematoperitoneum, effusion of blood into the peritoneal cavity.

hematophobia, abnormal fear of the sight of blood.

hematopoiesis, formation of red blood cells.

hematorrhea, profuse bleeding.

hematosalpinx, retained menstrual flow in the fallopian tube.

hematoscopy, blood examination.

hematosis, the development of red blood cells in the formation of blood; blood oxygenation in the lungs.

hematospermia, bloody semen.

hematostatic, arresting the flow of blood in a hemorrhage; retaining blood in a part.

hematothorax, presence of blood in the chest cavity.

hematozoon, a parasitic organism in the blood.

hematuria, blood in the urine.

heme, hematin.

hemeralopia, day blindness; difficulty in seeing during the day.

hemialgia, pain in one-half of the body.

hemic, pertaining to blood.

hemicrania, affecting one side of the head, usually a migraine headache.

hemiplegia, paralysis affecting one side of the body.

hemisphere, either of two sides of the cerebellum or cerebrum.

hemispheric, pertaining to a hemisphere.

hemocytoblastoma, a tumor consisting of embryonic blood cells.

hemocytology, the scientific study of blood cells.

hemocytometer, an instrument used to determine the number of blood cells in the blood.

hemoglobin, the red oxygen-carrying pigment of red blood cells.

hemolysin, an agent or substance in a serum which dissolves red blood corpuscles.

hemolysis, destruction of red blood corpuscles with the liberation of hemoglobin.

hemophilia, an inherited blood disease of males characterized by defective coagulation and an abnormal tendency to bleed.

hemophiliac, a person afflicted with hemophilia.

hemophobia, morbid fear of the sight of blood.

hemophthalmia, hemophthalmus, escape of blood inside the eye.

hemoptysis, the spitting of blood; blood-stained sputum.

hemorrhage, excessive or profuse bleeding; an abnormally heavy flow of blood from a ruptured blood vessel.

hemorrhagenic, producing hemorrhage.

hemorrhagic, pertaining to hemorrhage.

hemorrhoid, a swelling or dilated blood vessel in the anal area.

hemorrhoidectomy, surgical excision of hemorrhoids.

hemostasis, interruption of blood flow; a stopping of bleeding; stagnation of blood.

hemostat, a device or drug which stops the flow of blood.

hemostatic, checking bleeding or hemorrhage.

hemostypic, an astringent to stop bleeding.

hemothorax, a blood fluid present in the pleural cavity due to inflammation of the lungs, as in pneumonia.

hepar, the liver.

heparin, a complex blood anticoagulant present in many body tissues, especially in the liver and lungs; an agent used in prevention and treatment of embolism and trombosis, obtained from domestic animals.

heparinize, therapeutic treatment with heparin to prolong blood clotting time.

hepatic, pertaining to the liver.

hepatitis, inflammation of the liver.

hepatogenic, being produced in the liver.

hepatography, liver roentgenography.

hepatologist, one who specializes in diseases of the liver.

hepatology, the study of the liver and its diseases.

hepatoma, a tumor of the liver.

hepatomegaly, an enlargement of liver.

hepatopathy, liver disease.

herbivorous, a vegetarian living on plants; an animal that eats plants.

hereditary, genetically transmitted from one's ancestry.

heredity, the genetic transmission of individual traits and characteristics from parent to offspring.

hermaphrodite, having genital and sexual characteristics of both male and female.

hermaphroditism, a condition characterized by the presence of both male and female sexual characteristics and genitalia.

hernia, a protrusion of an organ or part of an organ through the cavity wall that encloses it; rupture.

hernial, pertaining to a hernia.

herniated disk, the protrusion or rupture of a disk between the vertebrae, especially involving the lumbar vertebrae of the spinal column.

herniation, development of a hernia.

heroin, a morphine derivative altered to increase its potency and used to relieve pain and induce sleep; an addictive narcotic.

herpes, an inflammation of the skin and mucous membranes marked by vesicles or blisters appearing in clusters, which often spreads.

herpes simplex, a viral disease which produces clusters of blisters around the mouth or genital regions that cause itching and localized congestion. The lesions dry up within a 10-14 day period and form yellowish crusts that shed.

herpes zoster, an infectious, inflammatory skin disease; shingles.

herpetic, pertaining to herpes.

herpetiform, resembling herpes.

herterogenous, differing species or sources; dissimilar elements in contrast to homogeneous.

heterologous, consisting of abnormal cell tissue.

heterology, an abnormality; differing from the normal structure of growth.

heteropathy, an abnormal reaction to an irritation.

heterophasia, the expression of nonsensical words instead of those intended.

heterophthalmia, a difference in the color of the iris of each eye.

heteroplasty, the procedure of grafting with skin tissue from another person or animal to repair skin lesions.

heterosexual, having sexual desire for the opposite sex.

heterosexuality, sexual attraction for the opposite sex.

heterotopy, displacement of an organ or a portion of the body.

heterotropia, a defect of the eyes; not having normal bifocal vision.

heterozygosity, the state of having one or more pairs of unlike genes.

heterozygote, a person who has one or more different alleles in regard to a given character.

hexachlorophene, a bactericidal and bacteriostatic compound used as a local antiseptic and detergent in emulsions, soaps, and other skin applications.

hexadactylism, having six fingers or six toes.

hexamine, a substance used as a disinfectant of the urinary tract.

hiatus, any natural cleft or opening, as the opening in the diaphragm for the passage of the esophagus.

hiatus hernia, a protrusion of part of the stomach upward through the esophageal hiatus of the diaphragm.

hiccough, hiccup, a spasmodic closure of the glottis following a sudden involuntary intake of breath causing an abrupt, sharp sound, or inspiratory cough.

hidrosis, excessive perspiration; profuse sweating.

high blood pressure, hypertension; abnormally high pressure in the arteries at the height of the pulse wave.

hilus, a depression or an organ at the point where ducts, nerves, or vessels enter or emerge.

hindbrain, the posterior part of the brain composing the pons, cerebellum, and the medulla oblongata.

hindgut, the embryonic entodermal tube which develops into the alimentary canal including the ileum, colon, and rectum.

hip, upper portion of the thigh; hip joint on either side of the pelvis.

hipbone, innominate bone.

hip joint, ball-and-socket joint between the femur and hipbone.

Hippocrates, ancient Greek physician referred to as "the father of medicine," born in 460 B.C.

Hippocratic oath, an oath taken by graduating physicians which embodies a practicing code of ethics.

hirsute, hairy or shaggy; roughly hairy.

hirsutism, abnormal condition marked by the excessive growth of hair, sometimes in unusual places as on the face of a woman.

histaminase, an enzyme distributed throughout the body which inactivates histamine.

histamine, a bodily substance that naturally occurs whenever there is tissue damage or allergic reactions; an amine produced by the putrefactive action of bacteria; may also be synthetically produced.

histidase, an enzyme produced in the liver that converts histidine to urocanic acid.

histogenesis, the origin and development of tissue.

histologist, one who studies the microscopic structure of tissue.

histology, the scientific study of tissue, esp. their microscopic structure.

histolysis, the disintegration and breaking down of tissues.

histone, simple proteins derived from cell nuclei which yield certain amino acids resulting from hydrolysis.

histoplasmosis, a respiratory disease caused by Histoplasma capsulatum, a fungus, which produce pulmonary calcifications, sometimes mistaken for tubercular calcifications. The usually fatal infection is marked by emaciation, irregular fever, decrease in white blood cells, and enlarged spleen.

hives, an eruption of uncertain origin marked by itchy wheals; urticaria.

hoarseness, difficulty in speaking due to a harsh, rough voice, as with cold symptoms or flu.

Hodgkin's disease, a progressive disease causing an enlargement of the lymph glands, spleen, liver, and kidneys.

holarthritis, inflammation of many of the joints; polyarthritis.

homeopathy, a method of treating a disease by administering minute doses of a drug that normally causes symptoms similar to those of the disease.

homeostasis, a state of equilibrium of the internal environment of the organism; self-regulating maintenance of the metabolic or psychologic processes which are necessary for survival.

homeostatic, pertaining to homeostasis.

homergic, having the same effect.

homicide, murder; the killing of one human being by another, involving acts of manslaughter, murder, accidental killing, and justifiable homicide.

homogeneity, state of being uniform in composition or nature.

homogeneous, having the same quality or uniformity throughout; belonging to the same kind or type.

homogenesis, the reproduction and development of offspring similar to the parents in each subsequent generation.

homogenetic, pertaining to homogenesis; having a common origin.

homograft, an organ or tissue grafted from an individual or animal to another of the same species, but of a different genotype.

homologous, any organ or part which corresponds in structure and in origin.

homology, state of being homologous, or similar in structure and origin.

homosexual, one sexually attracted to another of the same sex; a homosexual person.

homosexuality, exhibiting sexual desire toward persons of the same sex.

homozygosity, having identical alleles in referring to a given character.

homozygote, an individual possessing like pairs of genes for any hereditary characteristics.

hookworm disease, a condition produced by a nematode parasite present in the intestinal tract of man and other vertebrates causing severe anemia, listlessness, and general weakness. The most common port of entry is by walking on infected soil in bare feet, and once the microscopic worms are in the body they quickly invade the heart and lungs.

hormone, a chemical substance secreted by the endocrine glands which is conveyed throughout the body and serves to regulate the activity of certain cells or organs.

host, any organism that nourishes another organism such as a parasite.

hot flashes, a condition which occurs commonly during menopause characterized by vasodilation in the skin of head, neck, and chest with a sensation of suffocation and profuse sweating.

hot line, a 24-hour telephone service which provides assistance for people who are in a crisis situation and have a need to reach a mental health professional.

humerus, the upper bone of the arm between the shoulder and the elbow.

humor, any fluid or semifluid produced in the body.

humoral, pertaining to body substances or fluids.

humpback, a curvature of the spine; kyphosis.

hunchback, a person with kyphosis.

Huntington's chorea, an inherited disease involving the central nervous system.

hyaline, a glassy, translucent nitrogenous substance.

hyaline cartilage, the typical smooth, translucent cartilage which covers bone surfaces that articulate with other bones.

hyaline membrane disease, a thin membrane inside the lung of the newborn fetus which interferes with normal respiration.

hyaluronic acid, mucopolysaccharide (polymer) found in connective tissue which holds cells together and acts as a protective agent; also found in synovial fluid, skin, and vitreous humor.

hyaluronidase, an enzyme which increases connective tissue permeability by breaking down the molecular structure of hyaluronic acid; an enzyme present in the testes, other tissues, and semen.

hybrid, a heterozygous individual; the offspring of parents who differ in one or more distinct traits.

hybridization, production of hybrids.

hydatid, hydatid cyst, a cyst-like structure formed in the tissues by tapeworm larva, especially in the liver of man and certain animals.

hydatid mole, hydatidiform mole, a degenerative process occurring in the chorionic villi, characterized by many cysts resembling a bunch of grapes, and rapid growth of the uterus with hemorrhage.

hydradenitis, inflammation of a sweat gland.

hydradenoma, a tumor of a sweat gland.

hydragogue, producing a watery discharge from the bowels; a drug which acts as a cathartic causing a watery evacuation of the bowels.

hydrarthrosis, serous accumulation in a joint cavity, with swelling.

hydrated, chemical combination of a substance with water.

hydration, act of hydrating.

hydremia, excess of watery fluid in the circulating blood.

hydriatics, the application of water in treatment of disease.

hydroa, a chronic skin disease with bullous eruptions.

hydrocarbon, a compound made up of hydrogen and carbon.

hydrocele, an accumulation of serous fluid in a saccular cavity, especially the scrotum.

hydrocephalus, an abnormal enlargement of the head due to an increased accumulation of cerebrospinal fluid resulting from developmental anomalies, infection, injury, or brain tumors.

hydrochloric acid, an aqueous solution of hydrogen chloride, a strong highly corrosive acid which is used in industry and medicine; found in gastric juices in the stomach in a diluted and neutralized form which converts pepsinogen into pepsin.

hydrocortisone, an adrenal cortical steroid which has life-maintaining properties; used in synthetic preparations for inflammations, allergies, pruritus, shock, bursitis, rheumatoid arthritis, and many other diseases.

hydrogen peroxide, a colorless liquid with an irritating odor used as a mild antiseptic, germicide, and cleansing solution.

hydrolysis, any reaction produced by combining water with a salt to produce an acid and a base, or a chemical decomposition in which a substance is broken down into simpler compounds by taking up elements of water, as the conversion of starch into maltose.

hydrometer, an apparatus which measures the specific gravity of fluids.

hydromyelocele, a protrusion of a membranous sac containing cerebrospinal fluid through a spina bifida.

hydronephrosis, an accumulation of urine in the kidney causing swelling due to an obstruction of the ureter, with atrophy of the kidney.

hydropericarditis, serous effusion around the heart with inflammation.

hydroperitoneum, an accumulation of fluid in the abdominal cavity.

hydrophobia, rabies, a disease resulting from a rabid animal bite; abnormal fear of water.

hydrops, edema or dropsy.

hydrotherapy, the application of water in treatment of disease.

hydrothorax, increased swelling of the chest due to the effusion of serous fluid into the pleural cavity.

hydroureter, an accumulation of urine or fluid causing distention of the ureter due to obstruction.

hydruria, increased water content of urine with decreased solids; polyuria.

hygiene, the study and practice of certain rules or principles for the purpose of maintaining health and cleanliness.

hygenic, pertaining to hygiene.

hygienist, a specialist in hygiene, as in the dental profession.

hygroscopy, determination of the quantity of moisture in the atmosphere by a hygroscope.

Hygroton, trademark for chlorthalidone, a diuretic.

hymen, a membranous fold of tissue covering the vaginal orifice.

hyoid, the U-shaped bone between the root of the tongue and larynx.

hyosine, scopolamine in some sedative medication.

hyoscyamine, an anticholinergic alkaloid obtained from solanaceous plants used as a sedative, mydriatic, antispasmodic, and analgesic.

hyperacidity, excessive gastric acidity.

hyperactive, pertaining to hyperactivity or hyperkinetic.

hyperactivity, abnormal and excessive activity; hyperkinesia.

hyperacusis, having an exceptionally acute sense of hearing.

hyperalgesia, extreme sensitivity to pain.

hyperkinesia, excessive motor activity.

hyperaphia, extreme sensitivity to touch.

hyperbilirubinemia, an excessive amount of bilirubin in the blood.

hypercalcemia, an excessive amount of calcium in the blood.

hyperchromic, excessive pigmentation.

hyperchromia, an abnormal increase in the hemoglobin in each red blood cell, with a decrease in the number of red blood cells.

hyperemesis, an abnormal amount of vomiting.

hyperemesis gravidarum, toxemia of early pregnancy marked by excessive vomiting.

hyperemia, an unusual amount of blood or congestion in a part which gives rise to reddened areas on the skin.

hyperesthesia, an increased sensibility to external stimuli, an oversensitivity to pain, touch, cold, or heat.

hyperglocosuria, excessive sugar in the urine.

hyperglycemia, excessive increase of blood sugar, as in diabetes.

hyperinsulinism, an excessive amount of insulin in the blood, producing hypoglycemic symptoms.

hyperinvolution, a reduction in size below normal of the uterus after parturition; a reduction in size below normal of an organ following hypertrophy.

hyperkeratosis, an overgrowth of the cornea; excessive development of the horny layer of the skin; keratosis.

hypermenorrhea, abnormal flow or frequency of menstrual periods.

hypermetropia, farsightedness; hyperopia.

hypermyatrophy, abnormal muscle wasting.

hypermyotonia, excessive muscle tonus.

hypernephroma, malignant tumor of the kidney.

hypernoia, excessive imagination or mental activity.

hyperopia, defect in eyesight in which the focal point falls behind the retina resulting in farsightedness.

hyperosmia, hypersensitivity to odors.

hyperparathyroidism, overactivity of the parathyroid glands.

hyperpiesia, having extremely high blood pressure.

hyperpituitarism, excessive pituitary gland activity resulting in increased growth hormone which produces gigantism and acromegaly.

hyperplasia, increased size of a tissue or organ due to excessive proliferation of cells.

hyperpnea, increased respiratory rate with deeper breathing or panting, such as a normal state after exercise.

hyperpyretic, pertaining to elevated body temperature; hyperpyrexia.

hyperpyrexia, a high fever.

hypersecretion, an excessive increase in secretion.

hypersensitivity, an abnormal sensitivity to a stimulus, as in drug reactions; allergic.

hypertension, persistently high arterial blood pressure.

hyperthermia, an unusually high body temperature.

hyperthymia, having excessive emotion, or morbid sensitivity.

hyperthyroidism, excessive thyroid gland activity characterized by goiter, increased metabolic rate, rapid pulse, psychic disturbances, excitement, and other symptoms.

hypertonia, an abnormal tension of the muscles or arteries.

hypertonicity, excess tonus of the muscle; intraocular pressure.

hypertrichiasis, an abnormal growth of hair.

hypertrophy, an enlargement of an organ or structure as a result of functional activity and not due to an increase in the number of cells.

hypervitaminosis, a condition caused by an excesive ingestion of vitamins, especially Vitamin A and D.

hyperventilation, an increased or forced respiration which results in carbon dioxide depletion with accompanied symptoms of lowered blood pressure, vasoconstriction, and faintness.

hypesthesia, a lessened sensation to touch.

hyphidrosis, a decrease in the amount of perspiration.

hypnagogic, inducing sleep; pertaining to dreams just before loss of consciousness.

hypnogenesis, producing sleep.

hypnogenic zones, certain areas on the body which produce sleep when stimulated, as in the elbow.

hypnoidal, pertaining to a mental state between sleep and waking, similar to sleep.

hypnolepsy, irresistible sleep; narcolepsy.

hypnophobia, pathological aversion to falling asleep.

hypnosis, a subconscious state of mind accompanied by an abnormal sensitivity to respond to impressions or verbal suggestions which allows the subject to be induced into a trance or dream state.

hypnotic, any agent that induces sleep, or dulls the senses.

hypnotism, the science concerned with hypnosis.

hypnotist, one trained in hypnosis.

hypoblast, inner cell layer or entoderm.

hypochondria, an abnormal concern about health issues and false belief of being afflicted with some disease.

hypochondriasis, preoccupation with the body and abnormal fear of diseases.

hypochondrium, the abdominal portion beneath the lower ribs on each side of the epigastrium.

hypocythemia, a deficiency in the number of red blood cells.

hypodermic, administered beneath the skin such as an injection into the subcutaneous tissue.

hypodermic syringe, a hollow tube, usually with a hollow needle used to inject a solution or medication under the skin; it may be administered subcutaneously, intramuscularly, intraspinally, or intravenously.

hypodermis, subcutaneous tissue.

hypogastric, pertaining to the hypogastrium.

hypogastrium, the area below the naval and between the right and left inguinal areas.

hypogenitalism, underdeveloped genital organs.

hypoglossal, underneath the tongue.

hypoglossal nerve, a mixed nerve which carries afferent and efferent impulses that give rise to tongue movements.

hypoglycemia, a deficiency of blood sugar marked by fatigue, restlessness, malaise, irritability, and weakness.

hypohidrosis, diminished perspiration or sweating.

hypokalemia, abnormal depletion of potassium in the circulating blood producing muscle weakness, tetany, and postural hypotension.

hypokinesia, diminished motor activity.

hypomania, a mild degree of mania without behavioral change.

hypomenorrhea, a deficient menstrual flow.

hypometropia, myopia; shortsightedness.

hypophyseal, referring to the pituitary gland.

hypophysectomy, excision of the hypophysis or pituitary gland.

hypophysis, the pituitary body.

hypophysitis, inflammation of the pituitary gland.

hypopituitarism, a condition resulting from diminished pituitary secretion of hormones.

hypoplasia, incomplete development of an organ or tissue.

hypopnea, abnormally slow depth and rate of respiration.

hypopyon, a condition seen in corneal ulcer in which purulence occurs in the anterior chamber of the eye in front of the iris.

hyposecretion, diminished amount of secretion.

hyposensitive, exhibiting reduced ability to respond to external stimuli.

hypostasis, a sedimentation; poor circulation in a body part or organ.

hypostatic, pertaining to hypostasis.

hypotension, abnormally low blood pressure.

hypothalamus, part of the diencephalon; the gray matter in the floor and walls of the third ventricle of the brain.

hypothermia, subnormal body temperature, below 37°C, or between 78 and 90°F.

hypothymia, a decreased emotional response.

hypothyroidism, a condition caused by a thyroid secretion deficiency marked by lowered basal metabolism, and cretinism.

hypotonia, reduced muscle tone or activity.

hypotonic, pertaining to decreased muscle tone or tension.

hypovolemia, a diminished blood supply.

hysterectomy, surgical excision of the uterus, either through the abdominal wall or through the vagina.

hysteria, a psychological state characterized by lack of control over emotion, abnormal self-consciousness, anxiety, simulated bodily symptoms, and impairment of both motor and sensory functions.

hysterogenic, producing hysteria.

hystero-oophorectomy, surgical excision of the uterus and one or both ovaries.

hysterotomy, incision of the uterus; a caesarean operation.

I

iatric, pertaining to medicine or the physician.

iatrogenic, caused by the treatment of a physician, resulting in an adverse condition in a patient.

iatrology, medical science.

ichor, a watery, fetid discharge from an ulcer or a wound.

ichorrhemia, septic blood poisoning caused by ichorous matter.

Ichthyol, trademark, used as an astringent, antiseptic, and to relieve pruritis.

ichthyosis, any of many skin disorders characterized by dryness, and scaliness, giving rise to eczema; a congenital skin disorder characterized by a thick, scaly skin resembling fish-skin.

ICTH, interstitial cell stimulating hormone, a male hormone which stimulates testosterone production in the interstitial cells of the testes.

icteric, pertaining to jaundice.

icteroid, resembling jaundice.

icterus, bile pigments causing jaundice in the tissues, membranes, and secretions of the body.

id, in Freudian theory, the unconscious part of the personality that deals with instinctive desires or libinal energy of the individual; a biological germ structure carrying hereditary qualities.

idea, a concept, or mental imge.

ideation, the thinking process, or the formation of mental images.

identical twins, twins exactly alike which originate from a single fertilized ovum.

identification, a defense mechanism, usually unconscious, by which a person identifies himself with another, such as a hero.

idiocy, mental deficiency; severe mental retardation.

idiopathic, pertaining to idiopathy.

idiopathy, usually in reference to disease without a known cause; a spontaneous disease.

idiosyncrasy, individual peculiarities; a quality which makes a person react differently and distinguishes him from others; an unusual susceptibility to a drug.

idiosyncratic, pertaining to idiosyncrasy.

idiot, severe mental retardation; an uncouth or foolish person.

idiot savant, one who is severely mentally retarded, yet has an outstanding mental ability developed to an unusually high degree, as in mathematics or music.

ileac, pertaining to the ileum.

ilectomy, excision of the ileum.

ileitis, inflammation of the ileum.

ileocecal, pertaining to the ileum and cecum.

ileocecum, referring to both the ileum and cecum.

ileocolic, relating to the ileum and colon.

ileocolostomy, surgical forming of a passage between the ileum and the colon.

ileostomy, the creation of a passage through the abdominal wall into the ileum by a surgical procedure.

ileum, the lower third portion of the small intestine between the jejunum and the cecum.

ileus, an obstruction of the small intestine.

iliac, pertaining to the ileum.

ilium, the haunch bone, or the wide upper part of the innominate bone; hip bone.

illness, having an ailment, or a deviation from a normal healthy state.

illusion, an inaccurate perception, or the misinterpretation of a real experience or sensation.

illusory, based on deceptive perception.

image, a mental picture with a likeness to a real object.

imagery, imagination; mental images that are products of the imagination.

imago, the unconscious, idealized mental image of an important person from one's early childhood.

imbalance, lack of balance, as in glands or muscles.

imbecile, mental deficiency, having an intelligence quotient between 25 and 50 or of about age seven.

immature, not fully developed; having not reached full growth potential.

immiscibility, state of being immiscible.

immiscible, that which cannot be mixed together such as liquids, especially oil and water.

immobilization, a part or limb that is immovable; fixed; to immobilize.

immobilize, to restrain movement, as by a cast on the arm or leg.

immune, able to resist disease; protected from certain diseases by vaccination.

immunity, having resistance, or being immune to injury, poisons, foreign proteins, or certain invading organisms.

immunization, the process of obtaining immunity to a specific disease; active immunity with a specific agent to stimulate an immune response, or passive immunity by administering serum from immune persons.

immunize, to render immune.

immunochemistry, the study of immunology as it relates to physical chemical aspects.

immunogenetics, the study of genetic factors which control individual immune responses, and how it affects succeeding generations.

immunogenic, inducing immunity to a particular disease.

immunology, the scientific study of immunity to specific diseases.

immunosuppressive, being capable of inhibiting immune responses, as the rejection of a transplant by the body.

immunotherapy, passive immunization of an organism by the administration of antibodies in serum or gamma globulin.

immunotoxin, an antitoxin.

immunotropic, enhancing immune response mechanisms.

impacted, a firmly wedged tooth in the jawbone which prevents it from emerging from the gum; in obstetrics, referring to twins being wedged firmly together preventing complete enlargement of either before delivery; accumulation of feces in the rectum.

impaction, condition of being impacted.

impalpable, not detectable by the touch.

imparidigitate, having an uneven number of fingers or toes.

impedance, self-induced resistance.

imperception, inability to perceive; faulty perception.

imperforate, having no opening.

impermeable, not allowing the passage of fluids; impenetrable.

impetigo, an inflammatory skin disease which may be highly contagious, marked by pustules that become crusted and rupture.

implant, a tissue graft, a pellet of medicine, or a radioactive substance.

implantation, the attachment of a blastcyst to the lining of the uterus which occurs within six to seven days after fertilization of the ovum; the grafting of an organ or tissue into the body.

impotence, the inability of male copulation.

impotent, unable to copulate; sterile.

impregnate, to fertilize or make pregnant; to saturate.

impregnation, the fertilization of an ovum.

impression, a depression in the surface; the effect produced upon the mind; a dental imprint of the jaw and teeth.

impulse, an instinctual urge; neural transmission through nerve fibers by electrochemical process.

impulsive, impelling emotional or involuntary behavior.

inactivate, to render inactive.

inactivation, destruction of biological activity.

inactive, being out of use or sluggish; not active; inert.

inanition, a condition of exhaustion due to lack of nourishing food which is essential to the body.

inappetence, lack of appetite or craving for food.

inarticulate, unable to express oneself verbally; not jointed.

in articulo mortis, at the time of death.

inassimilable, unable to be used as nourishment by the body.

inborn, innate characteristics which are inherited or acquired before birth; congenital or being acquired during fetal development.

inbred, producing offspring closely related.

incest, sexual intercourse between close blood relations.

incidence, the number of new cases of a disease or other condition in a given population and within a specific time period.

incipient, beginning, or about to appear.

incise, to cut into with a surgical instrument.

incision, surgical process of cutting with a knife.

incisor, one of the eight cutting teeth located in the upper and lower jaw.

inclusion, being enclosed.

inclusion bodies, stainable bodies present in the nucleus or cytoplasm of a viral-infected cell; negri bodies.

incoherent, not understandable or disorganized and rambling, as in thoughts or language.

incompatible, not capable of being mixed in solution; antagonistic or mutually unsuited.

incompetence, inability to function realistically or properly; a legal status determined by the court.

incontinence, unable to control the elimination of feces or urine.

incoordination, inability to produce rhythmic and coordinated muscular movements due to disturbances in tone or harmony between muscle groups.

incrustation, the formation of crusts or scabs.

incubation, the period between infection of a disease and the appearance of symptoms.

incubator, an apparatus for regulating and maintaining a suitable temperature, oxygen, etc. for the survival of premature infants; apparatus for cultivating bacteria or for artificially hatching eggs.

incubus, a nightmare; a heavy burden.

incurable, not able to be cured; an individual with terminal cancer.

incus, the middle of three ossicles in the ear that is shaped like an anvil.

index, the forefinger; a ratio between a given measurement compared with a fixed standard.

indication, a sign that points to the cause or treatment of a disease.

indigestion, failure of complete digestion usually marked by abdominal discomfort after meals.

indisposition, a disorder or temporary illness.

indole, a crystalline compound found in feces that is largely responsible for odor.

indolent, sluggish; inactive.

induced, to cause or produce, as in induced labor.

induction, the process of inducing, as an abortion; electric current generated by electricity when near a charged body; the interaction between an embryonic cell and inductive cells adjacent to it.

indurate, to become hardened; callous.

induration, the act of hardening; a specific area of hardened tissue.

inebriant, something that intoxicates.

inebriate, intoxicate; to make drunk.

inebriation, state of being intoxicated; drunkenness.

inert, inactive; sluggish.

inertia, inactivity; tendency to remain in repose.

in extremis, near death; reaching the point of death.

infant, a child under two years of age.

infanticide, the killing of an infant.

infantile, pertaining to infancy.

infantile paralysis, poliomyelitis.

infantilism, failure of development pertaining to the mind and body; failure to attain maturation.

infarct, a necrotic area of tissue following cessation of the blood supply.

infarction, the development of an infarct, as in myocardial infarction.

infect, to contaminate with pathogenic organisms.

infection, the condition in which the body is penetrated by a pathogenic agent such as a virus.

infectious, pertaining to a disease which is capable of being transmitted due to a microorganism, either by direct or indirect contact.

infectious hepatitis, inflammation of the liver caused by a virus which produces jaundice, nausea, and abdominal pain.

infectious mononucleosis, a contagious viral disease characterized by constant fatigue, and other symptoms which include fever, headache, sore throat, swollen glands, jaundice, and stomach irritability.

infecundity, sterility in women.

inferior, beneath; lower placement.

inferiority complex, manifested feelings of inferiority either real or imagined evolved from physical or social inadequacies that produce anxiety.

infertile, not productive; unable to produce offspring.

infertility, being sterile or barren.

infestation, harboring parasites which do not multiply within the body in contrast to infection which does multiply and spread.

infirm, feeble, or weak.

infirmary, a hospital or a place for the care of the sick or infirmed.

infirmity, having an illness or debility; state of being infirmed; feebleness or weakness.

inflammation, a tissue or organ reaction to injury or irritation characterized by pain, heat, swelling, redness, and possible loss of function.

inflammatory, a sudden onset marked by inflammation and heat.

influenza, a contagious viral infection marked by head and back pain, catarrh of the respiratory or gastrointestinal tract; grippe.

infra-auxillary, below the axilla, or armpit.

infraclavicular, below the collarbone.

infracostal, below a rib.

infraction, incomplete fracture of a bone in which the two parts do not become displaced.

inframammary, below the mammary gland.

infraorbital, beneath the orbit of the eye.

infrapubic, below the pubis.

infrared rays, invisible heat rays beyond the red end of the visible spectrum.

infrascapular, below the shoulder blade.

infrasternal, below the sternum.

infundibulum, a funnel-shaped passage; a tube which connects the frontal sinus cavity with the middle nasal cavity.

infusion, introduction of a solution into a vein.

ingesta, substances taken into the body through the mouth such as food.

ingestion, the process of taking food into the gastrointestinal tract.

ingrowing, growing inward.

inguinal, pertaining to the groin region.

inhalant, a medicinal preparation which may be inhaled.

inhalation, the process of breathing medicated vapors or oxygen into the nose and lungs; act of drawing in of breath.

inhalator, an apparatus used for administering vaporized medication by inhalation, or for breathing in oxygen.

inherent, belonging to something naturally; intrinsic.

inheritance, hereditary factors transmitted and blended in the offspring.

inherited, characteristics received from one's ancestors.

inhibition, the act of repressing or the state of being restrained; commonly applied to the unconscious defense against the sex instinct; suppression.

inhibitor, something which inhibits.

inject, to introduce a solution into the body tissue or cavity with a syringe.

injection, forcing a fluid or liquid into a body tissue or cavity using a sterile needle and syringe; injections into the skin may be subcutaneous, intramuscular, or intravenous.

inlet, a passage which leads to a cavity.

innate, inborn, or hereditary.

innervate, the supply of nerves to an organ or part of the body; to stimulate through the nerves.

innervation, stimulating a body part through the action of nerve fibers, or nervous energy; the functioning of the nervous system.

innocent, benign, not malignant.

innocuous, harmless; inoffensive.

innominate artery, the right artery arising from the aortic arch.

innominate bone, the hip bone consisting of the ilium, ischium, and pubis which form the pelvis.

innominate veins, the right and left vein from the jugular and subclavian veins which form the superior vena cava.

inoculability, being susceptible of infection transmitted by inoculation.

inoculate, to inject a virus or bacteria into the body to cause a mild disease as a prevention against certain diseases and to build immunity.

inoculation, the act of injecting serum to induce antibody formation.

inoculum, a substance introduced into the body by inoculation.

inoliomyoma, a tumor consisting of smooth muscle tissue.

inoma, a fibrous tumor.

inoperable, unsuitable for excision without danger of death.

inquest, postmortem examination to determine legally the medical cause of death; act of inquiry.

insane, unsound mind; mentally deranged.

insanitary, unhealthy; pertaining to filth.

insanity, a legal term for mental derangement or mental illness; mental incompetence; unable to distinguish "right from wrong".

insatiable, incapable of being satisfied.

insemination, discharge of seminal fluid into the vagina; fertilization of an ovum.

insensibility, the state of being insensible.

insensible, unconscious; incapable of sensory perception.

insensitive, lacking feeling or physical sensation.

insertion, the place of muscle attachment to a bone allowing movement; the act of implanting.

insidious, a gradual and deliberate development; a slow developing disease that does not exhibit early symptoms.

insight, self-understanding.

insipid, without taste; lacking animation or spirit.

in situ, in its normal position.

insolation, exposure to the rays of the sun for brief periods, as a treatment of certain skin disorders; heat therapy; heat- or sunstroke.

insoluble, incapable of being dissolved.

insomnia, disturbances in sleep patterns; chronic inability to sleep.

inspection, to visually examine the external surface of the body.

inspersion, sprinkling with powder or a solution.

inspiration, inhalation; pertaining to breathing air into the lungs; a state of being inspired.

inspiratory, pertaining to breathing in, or inspiration.

inspissate, to thicken by absorption of liquid content or by evaporation.

inspissated, being thickened by absorption, evaporation, or dehydration.

inspissation, the process of diminishing fluidity and increasing thickness.

instep, the upper surface of the foot or the arch, in front of the ankle.

instillation, dispensing a liquid drop by drop.

instinct, an inborn drive or innate urge characteristic of a species necessary for self-preservation, and which satisfies basic biological needs.

instinctive, unlearned responses determined by instinct.

instrumentation, the use of instruments, or work resulting from their use.

insudation, an accumulated substance derived from the blood, as in a kidney.

insufficiency, being inadequate for its function or purpose.

insufflate, to blow a medicated substance into a cavity such as lungs; to blow air into the lungs.

insufflation, the process of insufflating.

insufflator, a device used for insufflation.

insula, any round cutaneous body.

insulin, a pancreatic hormone secreted by the beta cells of the islets of Langerhans essential for oxidation and utilization of blood sugar. A sterile preparation of insulin is used in the treatment of diabetes mellitis.

insulinemia, the presence of too much insulin in the blood.

insulin shock, a condition resulting from an overdose of insulin which causes the blood sugar level to drop below normal, producing symptoms of hypoglycemia such as increased hunger, thirst, excitability, rapid pulse, flushing, pallor, sweating, fainting, convulsions, and coma.

insuloma, a tumor of the islets of Langerhans.

insusceptibility, having immunity.

integration, constituting a whole; assimilation.

integument, a covering such as skin; the skin.

integumentary, pertaining to a covering consisting of dermis or epidermis.

intellect, having the mental capacity to comprehend ideas and to exercise judgment; the capacity for knowledge.

intellectual, pertaining to the mind, or possessing intellect.

intellectualization, a defense mechanism that uses reasoning as a defense against conscious confrontation with unconscious conflict and its distressing mental tension.

intelligence, having the capacity to learn, to comprehend relationships, and to reason with facts and propositions.

intelligence quotient, (I.Q.), a numerical rating of intelligence, determined by dividing one's mental age, derived through intelligence test scores, by one's chronological age, then by multiplying by 100.

intemperance, excessive usages of anything.

intensive, relative to the degree or extent of activity.

interaction, the process of two or more things acting on each other.

interarticular, situated between two joints.

interatrial, situated between the atria of the heart.

interbrain, diencephalon.

intercellular, between the cells.

interchondral, between the cartilage.

interclavicular, between the clavicles.

intercostal, between the ribs.

intercourse, coitus; the sexual act; social contacts.

intercurrent, intervening; a disease that occurs during another illness.

interdental, between the teeth.

interdigital, between the fingers or toes.

interdigitation, fingerlike processes that interlock.

interfemoral, between the thighs.

interlobar, between lobes.

intermenstrual, between menstrual periods.

intermission, a temporary cessation of symptoms of a disease.

intermittent fever, an absence of symptoms between attacks of fever, as in malaria.

intermittent pulse, a pulse in which a beat is dropped at intervals, as in cardiac exhaustion.

intermuscular, between muscles.

intern, interne, a medical graduate assisting in a hospital as a resident physician or surgeon.

internal medicine, the branch of medicine concerned with diseases not usually treated by surgery.

internist, one concerned with internal diseases, and not a surgeon.

internuncial, serving as a connecting medium.

interosseous, between bones.

interosseus, a muscle lying between bones.

interpalpebral, between the eyelids.

interparietal, between walls; between the parietal bones; between the parietal lobes on the cerebrum.

intersex, a person having both male and female characteristics.

interspace, an area between two similar parts, as between ribs.

interstice, a gap or space in a tissue or an organ.

interstitial, placed between; pertaining to interstices or gaps between the cellular structures.

interventricular, between two ventricles.

intervertebral, between two adjacent vertebrae.

intestinal, pertaining to the intestine.

intestinal juice, a chemical liquid produced by the intestinal mucosa.

intestine, the alimentary canal which is divided into the small intestine and the large intestine extending from the pylorus to the anus.

intima, the innermost lining of a structure, as a blood vessel.

intolerance, the inability to endure pain; the side effects of drugs or foods.

intoxicant, an agent which intoxicates.

intoxication, the state of being intoxicated or drunk; being poisoned by a toxic substance.

intra-abdominal, within the abdomen.

intra-arterial, within the arteries.

intra-articular, within a joint.

intra-atrial, within the atrium of the heart.

intracellular, within cells.

intracranial, within the skull.

intracutaneous, within the substance of the skin or layers.

intracutaneous test, a test to determine allergic sensitivity.

intradermal, between the layers of the skin.

intradural, within the dura matter.

intraglandular, within a gland.

intra-intestinal, within the intestine.

intramammary, within the breast.

intramastoiditis, inflammation of the antrum and mastoid process.

intramural, within the substance of a wall or hollow cavity.

intramuscular, within a muscular substance.

intranasal, within the nasal cavity.

intraocular, within the eyeball.

intraoral, within the mouth.

intraorbital, within the orbit of the eye, or eye socket.

intraosseous, within the substance of a bone.

intraperitoneal, within the peritoneal cavity.

intrapleural, within the pleural cavity.

intrapsychic, originating within the mind such as conflicts; mental origin or basis.

intrapulmonary, within the lung.

intrathoracic, within the thorax.

intratracheal, introduction into the trachea.

intrauterine, within the uterus.

intravascular, within a blood vessel.

intravenous, within a vein.

intraventricular, within a ventricle.

intravital, occurring during life.

intrinsic, belonging within or pertaining essentially to a part.

intrinsic factor, a substance produced from gastrointestinal mucosa of animals which increases the absorption of Vitamin B complex in humans.

introitus, an opening into a cavity such as the vagina.

introjection, a defense mechanism in which external objects are taken within oneself symbolically.

introspection, looking into one's own mind.

introversion, a preoccupation with oneself with little interest in the outside world; turning inside out of a part or organ.

introvert, one whose interests are turned inward and away from reality.

intubation, the introduction of a tube into a body cavity, as into the larynx.

intumesce, to swell or enlarge.

intumescence, the process of enlarging.

intussusception, the prolapse of one part of the intestine into another part adjacent to it; a growth of new cells by receiving nutrients and its transformation into protoplasm.

intussuscipiens, that part of the intestine which contains the intussusceptum.

inulin, a starch of certain plants which yield fructose upon hydrolysis, used in renal function testing.

in utero, within the uterus.

invagination, folding of one part within another structural part, as in intestines; intussusception.

invalid, a weak and sickly person.

inversion, the turning inside out of an organ, especially the uterus; homosexuality; a chromosomal aberration resulting in a change in the sequence of genes.

invertase, an enzyme found in intestinal juice.

invertebrate, having no backbone.

in vitro, observable in a test tube or within an artificial environment.

in vivo, within a living organism.

involuntary, working independently of conscious control.

involution, a turning inward; the process of decreasing the size of the uterus after delivery; a degeneration of the internal organs with the aging process.

iodide, a compound of iodine.

iodine, a chemical element composed of a black, crystalline substance, essential to the body for synthesis of thyroxine, a thyroid hormone.

iodism, a poisonous condition occurring with prolonged use of iodine or its compounds.

iodoform, a yellowish crystalline substance with an offensive odor used as an antiseptic.

iodopsin, photosensitive violet pigment present in the retinal cones which are important for color vision.

ipecac, dried roots of the plant impecacuanha used in treatment against amebic dysentery; other uses are as an expectorant, emetic, and diaphoretic.

iridemia, hemorrhaging from the iris.

iridocyclectomy, surgical removal of part of the iris and of the ciliary body.

iridocystectomy, surgical procedure to form an artificial iris.

iridotomy, surgical incision of the iris without removal of a piece.

iris, the pigmented contractile membrane forming the portion of the eye containing the pupil.

iritis, inflammation of the iris.

iron, a chemical element essential for the formation of hemoglobin in the body, and the prevention of certain forms of anemia.

irradiate, to treat with radiation.

irradiation, the therapeutic use of roentgen rays, radium rays, ultraviolet and other radiation for healing purposes.

irrational, lacking reason or understanding.

irrigate, to wash out with water or solution.

irrigation, to cleanse a canal or cavity with the injection of fluids.

irritability, the state of being excitable; a condition in which an organism, organ, or body part responds excessively to stimuli.

irritant, that which causes irritation; an agent which produces local inflammation and gives rise to irritation.

irritation, a condition which produces unusual sensitivity in part of the body.

ischemia, temporary and localized anemia due to restricting circulation to a part.

ischial, pertaining to the ischium.

ischium, the lower portion of the hip bone.

ischuria, suppression or retention of urine.

islets of Langerhans, clusters of beta cells which produce insulin in the pancreas.

isoagglutinin, an antibody serum which agglutinates blood cells.

isogamete, a gamete or sex cell which conjugates with a similar cell and reproduces; a gamete of the same size as another with which it unites to form a zygote.

isoleucine, an amino acid containing fibrin and other proteins essential in the diets of man.

isomer, a compound which has the same molecular formula in each chemical substance but differing in chemical and physical properties resulting from different arrangements of the atoms in the molecule.

isomeric, pertaining to isomer arrangements.

isometric, pertaining to, or having equal dimensions.

isometric exercises, physical exertion of muscles that does not involve motion, achieved by setting one muscle against another.

isometropia, having the same refraction in the two eyes.

isosthenuria, a decreased variation of specific gravity of urine in renal dysfunction.

isothermal, having an equal degree of heat.

isotonic, of equal tone or tension, as in muscles; pertaining to a solution in the body having the same osmotic pressure.

isotope, a chemical element having the same atomic number as another, but differing in atomic mass.

isotropic, possessing the same properties in every direction such as conduction.

isthmitis, inflammation of the throat or fauces.

isthmus, a narrow connection between two cavities.

itch, an irritation of the skin that induces a desire to scratch; pruritus; scabies.

iter, a tubular passageway.

ivy poisoning, a dermatitis caused by poison ivy contact with the skin.

ixodic, caused by ticks.

J

jacket, a covering for the trunk or thorax made of plaster of Paris or leather bandage, used to immobilize the spine or to correct certain deformities.

jactition, extreme restlessness marked by tossing to and fro during an acute illness; convulsive movements.

jargon, chattering, unintelligible language or speech pattern; paraphasia.

jaundice, a yellow tinge to the skin and sclera of the eyes caused by an increase in bile pigment resulting from excess bilirubin in the blood due to obstruction of the bile ducts, excessive red blood cell destruction, or disturbances in liver cell function.

jaw, one of two bones that form the framework of the mouth.

jecur, the liver.

jejunectomy, surgical removal of part or all of the jejunum.

jejunitis, inflammation of the jejunum.

jejunocolostomy, surgical creation of a communication between the jejunum and the ileum.

jejunoileitis, inflammation of the jejunum and ileum.

jejunojejunostomy, surgical joining between two portions of the jejunum after the removal of the diseased part.

jejunotomy, surgical incision of the jejunum.

jejunum, the middle section of the small intestine extending from the duodenum to the ileum.

jerk, an abrupt muscular movement; reflex action to a stimulus.

joint, a junction or union between two bones such as at the elbow; an articulation between two bones or cartilage.

Jolles test, a test to determine the presence of biliary pigments in urine.

jugal, pertaining to the malar or zygomatic or bony arch of the cheek.

jugular, pertaining to the throat.

jugular veins, the large veins at the front of the throat which receive the blood from the head, brain, and face and returns it to the heart.

jugulate, to quickly stop or arrest a process or disease by therapeutic intervention such as a tracheotomy.

juice, body secretions.

junction, coming together of two parts as a nerve with a muscle.

junctura, an articulation or suture of bones.

juvenile, pertaining to youth; immature; young.

juxtaposition, a side by side position.

K

Kahn's test, a blood test for detecting syphilis.

kakotrophy, malnutrition.

kalium, potassium.

kaliuresis, presence of potassium in the urine.

kaolin, a mineral clay used as an adsorbent in the coating of pills and in kaolin mixture with pectin.

karyogenesis, the formation and development of a cell nucleus.

karyokinesis, division of the nucleus of a cell at an early stage of mitosis.

karyoplasm, the substance of the nucleus in a cell.

karyosome, chromatin mass within the nuclear network.

karyotype, complete characteristics of a cell's nucleus including its size, form, and chromosome number.

katabolism, catabolism, the opposite of anabolism.

katotropia, the tendency for the eyeball to drop downward; a turning downward.

keloid, scar formation consisting of dense tissue.

keloidosis, a formation of keloids.

kelotomy, operation for a strangulated hernia through the tissues of the constricting part or neck.

kenophobia, extreme fear of empty spaces.

keratalgia, a neuralgia of the cornea.

keratectasia, the conical protrusion of the cornea of the eye.

keratectomy, surgical excision of part of the cornea.

keratiasis, the formation of multiple horny warts on the skin.

keratin, a scleroprotein present in skin, hair, nails, and horny formations.

keratitis, inflammation of the cornea.

keratoconjunctivitis, inflammation of the cornea and the conjunctiva of the eye.

keratoderma, the horny layer of the skin; the cornea.

keratodermatitis, inflammation of the horny layer of the skin.

keratodermia, hypertrophy or thickening of the horny layer of the skin, especially on the palms of the hands and soles of the feet.

keratogenous, producing horny tissue development.

keratoid, resembling horn or corneal tissue layer of the skin.

keratoma, a callosity, or horny growth of tissue.

keratome, a surgical knife for incising the cornea.

keratometer, a device for measuring the curves of the cornea.

keratonosis, any disease of the horny layer of skin which is nonflammatory.

keratoplasty, plastic surgery on the cornea.

keratosis, any growth of horny tissue development on the skin.

keratotomy, surgical incision of the cornea.

kernicterus, a form of jaundice, icterus neonatorum, occurring in infants due to high levels of bilirubin in the blood resulting in severe neural symptoms and degeneration of parts of the brain.

ketamine, a general anesthetic which is rapid-acting.

ketoacidosis, acidosis caused by an accumulation of ketone bodies in the blood.

ketogenesis, the production of ketones or acetone within the body, especially in diabetes.

ketol, an organic compound formed in the intestine and pancreas during digestion and decomposition of protein.

ketone, a substance or an organic compound containing the carbonyl group (CO), as acetone.

ketone bodies, any acetone, B-hydroxybutyric acid, or acetoacetic acid produced during the oxidation of fatty acids and found in the blood and urine, especially in diabetics.

ketosis, an accumulation of ketone bodies in the body.

kidney, one of two glandular, bean-shaped organs situated at the back of the abdominal cavity which excrete urine (consisting of 95% water and 5% of solids).

kinanesthesia, the loss of perceptive power in sensations of movements.

kinesalgia, painful muscular movement.

kinesia, motion sickness.

kinesis, motion.

kinesthesia, sense of muscle movement.

kinetotherapy, treatment that employs active and passive movements, as in physiotherapy.

kinesiology, the science concerned with anatomy and muscular movement.

kinesioneurosis, a functional disorder manifested by tics and spasms which affect external muscles.

kleptomania, impulsive stealing

kleptomaniac, one afflicted with kleptomania.

klieg eye, inflamed conjunctiva, increased lacrimation and photophobia due to long periods of exposure to intense lights.

Kline test, a microscopic test for the presence of syphilis.

knee, pertaining to the knee joint between the thigh and the lower leg.

kneecap, the patella.

knee jerk reflex, a contraction of the quadriceps muscle which causes an involuntary kick when a sharp striking blow to the ligament patellae is applied by an instrument.

knock-knee, inward curvature of the legs which cause the knees to knock together when walking.

knuckle, the rounded end of the phalangeal joint of a finger.

Korsakoff's syndrome, a disease characterized by psychosis, polyneuritis, delirium, insomnia, illusions and hallucinations, as a sequel to chronic alcoholism.

kraurosis, a dryness and hardening of the skin and mucous membranes.

kymograph, a device for recording variations in motion and blood pressure changes.

kyphosis, a humpback; an abnormal backward curving of the spine.

kyphotic, humpback or hunchbacked.

kysthitis, inflammation of the vagina.

kysthoptosis, a prolapse of the vagina.

L

labia, lips; the lips of the vulva.

labial, pertaining to lips.

labia majora, two folds of adipose tissue covered with pigmented skin and hair on the outer surface and free from hair on the inner surface which lie on either side of the vaginal opening.

labia minora, two thin folds of mucous membrane located within the labia majora on either side of the vaginal opening.

labile, unsteady; fluctuating.

labium, a lip-like structure; lip.

labor, delivery; parturition; childbirth.

labyrinth, the inner ear consisting of the vestibule, the cochlea, the semicircular canals or bony labyrinth, and the membranous labyrinth.

labyrinthectomy, surgical removal of the labyrinth.

labyrinthine, pertaining to the labyrinth; intricate.

labryrinthitis, inflammation of the labyrinth.

lac, any milklike medical substance.

lacerate, to tear, or to make a ragged gash of the flesh.

laceration, the process of tearing, as a tearing injury to the vaginal opening by childbirth.

lacrima, pertaining to tears or tearing.

lacrimal, characterized by tears, or pertaining to organs that produce tears.

lacrimal gland, a gland which secretes tears, located in the orbit of the eye.

lacrimation, a discharge of tears.

lacrimonasal, pertaining to the lacrimal sac and nose.

lacrimotomy, surgical incision of the lacrimal duct or gland.

lactagogue, galactagogue, a substance that stimulates alveoli of the mammary glands to secrete milk.

lactalbumin, a protein in human milk.

lactation, secretion of milk; breast feeding.

lacteal, pertaining to milk; relating to intestinal lymphatics which transport chyle.

lactescense, becoming milky, or resembling milk.

lactic, pertaining to milk.

lactic acid, a syrup-like, colorless substance formed by fermentation of sugars by microorganisms which occur naturally in sour milk; it is also formed during muscular activity by breaking down glycogen; medical uses of lactic acid are found in antiseptics and dietary products.

lactiferous, the process of secreting and conveying milk.

lactiferous ducts, referring to the ducts of the mammary gland.

lactifuge, an agent used to cause cessation of milk secretion in the mammary glands.

lactin, pertaining to lactose, a sugar of milk.

lactobacillus, a rod-shaped, gram-positive bacteria that produce lactic acid from carbohydrates and which cause milk to sour.

lactogenic, inducing lactation, the secretion of milk.

lactose, a sugar derived from milk which yields glucose and galactose upon hydrolysis, used as a sweetening substance in foods.

lactosuria, milk sugar in the urine.

lacuna, a minute hollow found in bones where osteoblasts lie; a gap found in cartilage or bone consisting of bone cells.

lacus lacrimalis, the inner portion of the eye where tears accumulate.

lagophthalmos, lagophthalamus, incomplete closure of the eyelids.

la grippe, an acute infectious respiratory or gastrointestinal disease; influenza.

laliatry, speech disorder therapy.

lallation, infantile speech or babbling; stammering; the constant use of ''i'' instead of ''r.''

lalopathy, any speech disorder.

lalophobia, extreme reluctance to communicate verbally due to stammering.

laloplegia, a paralysis caused by a stroke which affects speech muscles but not tongue action or movements.

lalorrhea, an abnormal flow of speech.

lamella, a gelatinous disk inserted under the lower eyelid used as a medicinal application to the eye.

lamina, a thin layer of membrane; pertaining to either flattened side of the vertebral arch.

laminectomy, surgical removal of the posterior vertebral arch.

laminitis, inflammation of the lamina.

lance, a surgical instrument; to incise with a lancet.

lancet, a pointed surgical instrument with two sharp edges.

lanolin, a greasy, purified substance obtained from sheep's wool used as a base in ointments or lotions that are beneficial to the skin.

lanuginous, a lanugo or wooly covering, as in the human fetus immediately after birth.

lanugo, a downy hair covering the body of a fetus.

lapactic, cathartic; laxative.

laparocystotomy, surgical incision through the abdomen for removal of a cyst or an extrauterine fetus.

laparoenterostomy, a surgical creation of an opening through the abdominal wall into the intestine.

laparotomy, an abdominal operation; surgical opening of the abdomen.

laryngalia, neuralgia of the larynx.

laryngeal, pertaining to the larynx.

laryngectomy, surgical removal of the larynx.

laryngismus, laryngeal spasm.

laryngitic, pertaining to or resulting from laryngitis.

laryngitis, inflammation of the larynx.

laryngography, a description of larynx movements as recorded by a laryngographic device.

laryngologist, a specialist in laryngology.

laryngology, the branch of medicine concerned with the treatment of diseases of the larynx.

laryngoparalysis, paralysis of the muscles of the larynx.

laryngopharyngeal, pertaining to both the larynx and the pharynx.

laryngopharyngitis, inflammation of both the larynx and the pharynx.

laryngopharynx, the lower part of the pharynx which extends into the larynx and esophagus.

laryngoplasty, surgical repair of a defect of the larynx.

laryngoscope, an instrument with a tiny light used to examine the larynx.

laryngoscopy, an examination of the interior of the larynx by an instrument.

laryngospasm, spasm of the muscles of the larynx.

laryngostomy, operation to make a permanent opening through the throat into the larynx.

laryngotomy, surgical operation of the larynx.

laryngotracheotomy, a surgical procedure in which upper tracheal rings and the larynx are incised to form an artificial airway.

larynx, the enlarged upper portion of the trachea or organ of voice, composed of nine cartilages and the vocal cords.

laser, a device that transfers light frequencies into an extremely intense beam of radiation which is capable of emitting immense heat when focused, used in surgery, in diagnosis, and in research.

Lasix, trademark for furosemide used as a diuretic and to prevent the accumulation of fluid in the body.

lassitude, weakness; listlessness; exhaustion.

latent, hidden; present in a concealed form but capable of becoming manifest; potential.

latent content, the unconscious meaning associated with thoughts or actions, especially applied to dreams or fantasies.

latent period, the period in disease from the time of infection to the appearance of symptoms∞ psychoanalytic theory, a period of psychosexual development.

lateral, situated to the side, or directed to the side.

lateroflexion, flexion or bending to one side.

lateropulsion, the tendency to fall to one side involuntarily due to cerebellar and labyrinthine disease.

lateroversion, a tendency to turn to one side.

laudanum, tincture of opium.

laughing gas, nitrous oxide gas.

lavage, the washing out of a cavity or organ, as in the stomach in poisoning.

lax, without tension.

laxative, a gentle purgative or cathartic.

lead colic, severe abdominal pain due to lead poisoning.

lead poisoning, an acute condition of poisoning from large doses of absorbed lead, as in children who eat paint chips, the absorbed lead affects the brain, nervous and digestive systems, and the blood; a condition among workers exposed to lead products in industry.

lecithin, derived from glycerin, a fatty substance found in the blood, bile, brain, egg yolk, nerves, and animal tissue and which yield stearic acid, glycerol, phosphoric acid, and choline upon hydrolysis.

leech, a blood-sucking water worm once used as a means of blood-letting, now abandoned; a device used for drawing blood.

leg, the lower extremity; that part of the body extending from the knee to the ankle.

leiomyoma, a smooth muscle tissue tumor.

leiomyosarcoma, a malignant smooth muscle tumor.

lema, the dried secretion of the meibomian glands which collects in the inner corners of the eye.

lens, the crystalline lens behind the pupil of the eye that focuses light rays on the retina; a piece of glass or other transparent material so shaped as to converge or scatter light rays.

lenticular, lens shaped; pertaining to a lens.

lentiginous, a freckle; covered with tiny dots.

lentitis, inflammation of the crystalline lens of the eye.

leper, one afflicted with leprosy.

leprosy, an infectious disease caused by a microorganism, once believed to be incurable, marked by a gradual onset of symptoms such as general malaise, headache, chilliness, mental depression, numbness in various body parts, ulcerations, tubercular nodules, and loss of fingers and toes.

leprous, afflicted with leprosy.

leptocephalus, one possessing an abnormally small head.

leptomeninges, the two delicate structures that cover the brain and spinal cord.

leptopellic, having an abnormally narrow pelvis causing labor to be difficult or impossible indicating need for cesarean section.

Leptospira, disease infecting spirochetes which are thin, hooked-end, aerobic bacteria that sometimes infect man.

leptospirosis, a condition resulting from Leptospira infection, marked by lymphocytic meningitis, hepatitis, and nephritis occurring in combination or separately.

lesbian, a female homosexual.

lesion, an abnormal localized tissue formation; a wound resulting from disease or injury.

lethal, causing death; fatal; deadly.

lethargic, relating to lethargy; sluggish; stupor; inclined to sleep.

lethargy, a condition characterized by drowsiness, indifference or inattention.

leucine, an amino acid derived from protein digestion which is present in all body tissue and is essential for normal growth and metabolism.

leucinuria, the presence of leucine in the urine.

leucitis, inflammation of the sclera.

leucovorin, folinic acid used in treatment of megaloblastic anemias caused by a deficiency in folic acid.

leukanemia, leukemia existing with anemia.

leukemia, a progressive and fatal disease characterized by rapid and abnormal growth of leukocytes in the blood-forming organs of the body such as bone marrow, spleen, and lymph nodes, and the presence of immature white blood corpuscles in the circulating blood; cancer of the blood.

leukemic, pertaining to leukemia.

leukemoid, resembling leukemia symptoms but caused by another condition.

leukoblast, a cell that gives rise to a leukocyte.

leukoblastosis, an excessive growth of immature white blood corpuscles.

leukocyte, white blood cells or corpuscles of which there are two types: granulocytes, containing granules in cytoplasm, and agranulocytes, lacking granules in cytoplasm. The leukocytes are scavengers and are essential to fight invading bacteria within the body.

leukocythemia, a condition marked by excessive white blood corpuscles in the body, and an enlarged spleen, lymphatic glands, and bone marrow; leukemia.

leukocytic, pertaining to leukocytes.

leukocytogenesis, the formation of white blood corpuscles or leukocytes.

leukocytolysis, the dissolution or destruction of white blood cells.

leukocytopenia, an abnormally low white blood cell number in the circulating blood.

leukocytosis, an increased number of white blood cells in the blood usually indicating an infection, or it may occur due to hemorrhage, surgery, coronary occlusion, malignant tumors, some intoxications, pregnancy, and toxemias.

leukoderma, usually an acquired condition marked by a localized deficiency of pigmentation in the skin rendering a patchy effect.

leukoma, a white, corneal opacity.

leukopenia, an abnormal decrease in white blood cells, below 5,000 per cu. mm.

leukoplakia, white patches which form on the mucous membranes of the cheek or tongue that may become malignant.

leukorrhea, an abnormal condition marked by a white or creamy-yellowish discharge from the vagina resulting from acute inflammation and infection by Trichomonas vaginalis.

leukosis, excessive growth of leukocyte-producing tissue.

levator, a muscle that raises a body part; an instrument used to lift depressed portions such as part of the skull.

levitation, a sensation that one is being lifted gently or moving through the air without physical support, as in a dream state.

levulose, fruit sugar; fructose which is present in honey and many fruits, used in medicinal preparations.

libidinous, marked by intense sexual desire or lust; salacious.

libido, sexual drive; innate drives and instincts that motivate human behavior; the energy force associated with pleasure seeking and sexual instinct.

lichen, any of various forms of eruptive skin diseases which have small, firm, and closely set papules.

lid, eyelid.

Lieberkuhn crypts, tubular glands present in the intestinal wall.

lien, the spleen.

lienitis, inflammation of the spleen.

lientery, diarrhea with undigested food in the fecal matter.

ligament, a strong fibrous band of connecting tissue which binds the articular ends of bones to limit motion or to hold body organs in place.

ligamentous, pertaining to a ligament.

ligate, to apply or bind, as with a ligature.

ligation, the application of a ligature.

ligature, any material that binds, such as a band, thread, or wire, used for tying blood vessels; the process of tying.

limb, an extremity, an arm or leg; a limblike appendage of a structure.

limbus, the rim or edge of a part.

limen, the edge, or threshold.

liminal, barely noticeable; pertaining to the threshold, as in consciousness.

lingua, the tongue, or resembling a tongue.

lingual, pertaining to the tongue.

liniment, a liquid medicine containing oil, alcohol, or water for external use, applied by friction to the skin as treatment for sprains.

linin, a threadlike substance that connects the chromatin granules in the cell nucleus.

linitis, an inflammation of the gastric cellular tissue.

linkage, in genetics, two or more genes which tend to remain together in the same chromosome in the formation of gametes.

lip, the soft structure around the mouth, or a formation bordering an opening or groove.

liparous, obese; fat.

lipase, a fat-splitting digestive enzyme occurring in the pancreas, liver, and found in the blood and which breaks down fat into fatty acids and glycerol.

lipemia, an accumulation of fat in the blood.

lipid, any group of fats which are water-insoluble.

lipidosis, a disease of faulty lipid metabolism in which an abnormal accumulation of lipids form in the body, as in Tay-Sachs disease, Gaucher's disease, and Niemann-Pick disease.

lipogenic, producing fat.

lipoid, resembling fat.

lipolysis, the dissolution or breaking down of fat into fatty acids and glycerol.

lipoma, a benign fatty tumor.

lipomatosis, excessive fat deposits in the tissues; obesity.

lipomatous, pertaining to lipoma.

lipometabolism, metabolism of fat.

lipoprotein, a simple protein combined with a lipid.

lipothymia, fainting; syncope.

lipotropic, having an affinity for fat utilization, therefore decreasing fat deposits in the liver.

lipuria, fat in the urine.

liquefacient, a liquefying drug that causes solid deposits to be converted into liquid.

liquescent, becoming liquid.

liquor amnii, referring to the amniotic fluid which is a clear, watery substance that surrounds the fetus in the amniotic sac.

lithiasis, the formation of calculi and concretions, as gallstones.

lithium, a metallic element in its salt form used in the treatment of manic and hypomanic states of excitement, as in manic-depressive illness.

lithogenesis, the formation of calculi.

litholysis, disintegration or dissolution of calculi.

lithotomy, surgical incision into the bladder for removal of a stone.

lithotripsy, the crushing of a stony formation in the bladder or urethra.

lithotrite, a device used for crushing stone in the bladder.

lithuresis, the passage of calculi or crushed stone by urination.

litmus paper, a chemically treated blue paper which turns red by acids, but remains blue in alkali solutions, used to indicate the presence of acid in urine testing.

liver, the largest organ of the body, a reddish-brown glandular structure situated on the right side beneath the diaphragm and which secretes bile and aids metabolic functioning.

livid, cyanotic or bluish color to skin; discoloration.

lividity, the condition of being discolored or livid.

lobar, pertaining to a lobe of the lungs.

lobe, the globular part of an organ with well-defined boundaries; lower portion of the ear without cartilage.

lobectomy, the removal of a lobe of any organ or gland by surgical excision.

lobotomy, incision of a lobe; the severing of nerve fibers, disconnecting the diencephalon and sectioning the white matter of the brain, used in treatment of mental disturbances.

lobular, consisting of small lobes.

lobule, a small lobe.

lochia, a discharge of blood, mucus, and tissue from the uterus during the first few weeks after childbirth.

locomotion, moving from one place to another; moving the body.

locomotor, pertaining to locomotion.

locomotor ataxia, a form of sclerosis which affects the posterior columns of the spinal cord; tabes dorsalis. Charcot's arthropathy.

loculus, a small cavity.

logagnosia, a form of aphasia; word blindness.

logagraphia, unable to express ideas in writing.

logamnesia, forgetfulness, or unable to recognize spoken or written words.

logomania, excessive and continuous flow of speech with a repetitive quality.

logorrhea, a condition marked by incoherent and excessive talking seen in the insane.

loin, portion of the back between thorax and pelvis.

lordosis, an abnormal inward curvature of the spine.

lordotic, pertaining to lordosis.

LSD, lysergic acid diethylamide.

lubricant, an agent which makes the skin soft and smooth.

lucid, clarity of mind; rational.

lues, a pestilent disease, especially syphilis.

lumbago, dull back pain across loin region caused by sudden chilling of overheated lumbar muscles.

lumbar, pertaining to the loins.

lumbar vertebrae, referring to five bones of the spinal column extending from the sacrum to the thoracic vertebrae.

lumbosacral, pertaining to both the lumbar vertebrae and the sacrum.

lumbricalis, one of the muscles of either the hand or foot resembling a wormlike structure.

lumen, the space or cavity within a tube or tubular structure or organ; a unit of light; a hollow of a tube.

lunatic, one who is insane or mad.

lungs, one of two cone-shaped structures which function as respiratory organs responsible for providing oxygen for the body and discharging waste products.

lunula, the pale crescent at the root of fingernails.

lupiform, resembling lupus.

lupus, any of the skin diseases caused by tubercle bacilli characterized by lesions with raised edges and depressed centers that become scarlike when the scales shed.

lupus erythematosus, a chronic inflammation of the skin characterized by reddish macules that scale and drop off; the lesions form a butterfly pattern over the bridge of the nose and cheeks, occurring predominantly in females between puberty and menopause.

luteal, pertaining to the corpus luteus, the cells, or the hormone.

lutein, a yellowish pigment from the corpus luteum, lipochromes, fat cells, and egg yolk.

luteinization, the process involving the development of the corpus luteum within the ruptured graafian follicle.

luteinizing hormone, a substance secreted by the pituitary gland that stimulates the reproductive organs and the development of the corpus luteum.

luteoma, a tumor of the ovary containing lutein cells.

luxation, a dislocation.

lying-in, puerperal period; puerperium; confinement.

lymph, a transparent, opalalescent liquid composed of plasma and white cells found within the lymphatic vessels. The fluid is collected from the body tissues and returned to the blood through the lymphatic system.

lymphadentitis, inflammation of the lymph nodes or glands.

lymphatic, pertaining to lymph, or the lymphatic vessels.

lymph cell, a lymphocyte.

lymph node, lymph gland, a rounded body of glandular tissue found at intervals throughout the lymphatic system, varying in size from a pinhead to an olive, which produce lymphocytes and monocytes.

lymphoblast, immature cells that become lymphocytes.

lymphocyte, a white blood corpuscle or leukocyte which participates in the body's immunity.

lymphocytic, referring to lymphocytes.

lymphocytoma, a malignant lymphoma or tumor.

lymphocytosis, a condition in the blood that involves an excess of lymphocytes above normal range.

lymphogranuloma, Hodgkin's disease; inflammed lymph nodes, as in venereal disease.

lymphogranulomatosis, infection of the lymphatic system; Hodgkin's disease.

lymphoid, resembling lymph or tissue of the lymphatic system.

lymphoma, any malignant disorder of the lymphoid tissue.

lymphopoiesis, the formation of lymphocytes or lymphatic tissue.

lymphosarcoma, a malignant tumor of lymphoid tissue, but not including Hodgkin's disease.

lyse, to cause disintegration of cells; the process involving lysis.

lysergic acid, a crystalline ergot derivative composing the base of LSD.

lysine, an amino acid derived from protein digestion, essential for growth and repair.

lysis, gradual decline of a fever or disease, opposite of crisis; destruction to a cell or substance by an influencing agent.

Lysol, trademark, used as a disinfectant and antiseptic.

lysozyme, an antibacterial enzyme present in tears, saliva, and various body fluids.

M

macerate, to soften by soaking or steeping.

maceration, the softening of a solid or tissue by soaking.

macrocardius, abnormal heart enlargement.

macrocephaly, an excessively large head.

macrochelia, excessively large lips.

macrocolon, megacolon, enlargement of the colon.

macrocyte, an abnormally large red blood corpuscle.

macrocytic, pertaining to a macrocyte.

macrocytosis, an excess of macrocytes, being greater in number than normal.

Macrodantin, trademark for nitrofurantoin used in treatment of urinary tract infection caused by Escherichia coli.

macrodontia, abnormally large size of one or more teeth.

macrogamete, the larger female gamete which is fertilized by the smaller male gamete; pertaining to the female reproductive cell.

macroglossia, excessively large tongue.

macromastia, excessively large breasts.

macrophage, a large phagocytic cell derived from monocytes present in loose connective tissues and various body organs which become active when stimulated by inflammation.

macroscopy, examination of an object with the naked eye.

macula, macule, a small colored spot on the skin.

maculation, the development of macules on the skin.

maculopapular, having both macules and papules.

mad, mentally deranged; irrational; suffering from rabies.

madarosis, the loss of eyelashes or eyebrows.

magnesium, a mineral element found in soft body tissue, muscle, bone and teeth essential to the proper functioning of the body. An excellent source of magnesium is found in nuts, wholegrain products, dry beans and peas, and dark green vegetables.

maidenhead, hymen.

mal, sickness or a disorder.

mala, cheek; cheekbone.

malacia, abnormal softening of body tissue or organs.

maladjusted, an inability to adjust one's desires or needs to the environment often causing anxiety.

malady, illness.

malaise, generalized uneasiness or discomfort, as a preliminary condition of disease; morbid discontent.

malar, pertaining to the cheekbone, or cheek.

malaria, a febrile, infectious disease caused by a protozoan parasite found in red blood cells, injected by a mosquito bite and characterized by periodic attacks of chills, fever, sweating, which may cause progressive anemia and enlargement of the spleen.

malformation, deformity or abnormal structure, especially congenital.

malign, malignant.

malignancy, condition of being malignant.

malignant, virulent and becoming worse, or resisting treatment, as in cancerous growths which threaten to produce death.

malinger, to pretend to be ill, usually to gain sympathy or to escape work.

malleal, pertaining to the malleus.

malleolus, the projections on either side of the ankle joint.

malleus, one of the three bones in the middle ear shaped like a hammer.

malnutrition, insufficient or faulty nutrition due to lack of necessary food ingestion, improper absorption, or any other disorder of nutrition.

malocclusion, imperfect closure or meeting of opposing teeth caused by abnormal growth of the upper or lower jaw.

malodor, an offensive stench or odor.

malodorous, ill-smelling, fetid, or putrid.

malpighian layer, the innermost layer of the epidermis which replaces the outer cells of the skin.

malposition, an abnormal placement of a body part.

malpractice, wrong and injurious treatment implying neglectful or illegal performance of duty by one in a practicing position, as a physician, surgeon, lawyer, or public servant.

malpresentation, an abnormal position of the fetus over the pelvic inlet, as in breech, or scapula.

Malta fever, brucellosis, an infectious disease transmitted from animals to man, marked by swelling of joints and spleen, excessive perspiration, weakness, and anemia.

maltase, a salivary and pancreatic enzyme which converts maltose to glucose by hydrolysis.

maltose, a disaccharide found in malt, malt products, and seed sprouts, formed by the hydrolysis of starch; primarily used as a sweetener.

mamma, mammary glands, or breasts.

mammary, pertaining to the breasts or glands which secrete milk formed in the lactiferous ducts during lactation.

mammilla, the nipple of the breast; a nipple-like process or proturberance.

mammillary, resembling a nipple, or concerning a nipple.

mammogram, radiography of the mammary gland.

mammography, a study of the mammary structures by X-ray photography to detect cancer.

mammotomy, surgery of a breast.

mandible, the lower portion of the jaw.

mandibular, pertaining to the lower jaw bone.

manducation, chewing of food, mastication.

maneuver, a skillful procedure, as in manipulation of the fetus and placenta to aid in delivery.

mania, intense excitement; madness; violent passion or desire.

manic-depressive, one afflicted with alternating attacks of mania and depression; cyclic affective psychosis.

manifestation, the appearance of symptoms of a disease that determine diagnosis.

manifest content, the remembered content of a dream including events and images.

manubrium, the upper portion of the sternum which articulates with the clavicle and the first pair of costal cartilages.

manus, hand.

manustupration, masturbation.

marasmus, emaciation or wasting of flesh, especially in infants.

marijuana, marihuana, an intoxicating drug usually in cigarette form, illegally used in the U.S.

marrow, soft tissue consisting of red or yellow marrow occupying the inner cavities of long bones responsible for blood cell and hemoglobin production.

masculine, having male characteristics.

masochism, sexual perversion in which pleasure is derived from physical or psychological pain inflicted upon another, or being abused; any pleasure obtained from the abuse of another which gives sexual gratification to the recipient.

masochist, one addicted to masochism.

massage, methodical manipulation of the body applied by kneading or rubbing the bare skin to stimulate circulation or increase flexibility.

masseter, the principle muscle of the mouth which is used in mastication and closing of the mouth.

masseur, a man trained in massage techniques.

masseuse, a woman trained to practice massage.

mastadenitis, inflammation of the mammary gland.

mastadenoma, a benign breast tumor.

mastalgia, breast pain.

mastectomy, surgical excision of the breast.

mastication, chewing of food.

masticatory, pertaining to mastication; a substance chewed to promote salivary secretion.

mastitis, inflammation of the breast occurring mostly in women during lactation.

mastodynia, pain in the breast.

mastoid, pertaining to the mastoid process located in the temporal bone behind the ear.

mastoidal, pertaining to the mastoid.

mastoidalgia, pain in the mastoid.

mastoidectomy, surgical removal of mastoid cells.

mastoiditis, inflammation of any of the mastoid process.

mastopexy, surgical correction of large, drooping breasts.

mastoptosis, pendulous or sagging breasts.

masturbation, manustupration, self production of an orgasm by manipulation of the genitals.

materia medica, scientific study concerned with all drugs used in the treatment of diseases, their origin, ingredients, preparation, dosage, and uses.

maternal, pertaining to a mother.

maternity, the state or condition of motherhood.

matter, pus; any substance that occupies space such as gas, liquid, or solid.

maturation, maturing or ripening, as a graafian follicle.

mature, fully developed.

maturity, the state of being mature.

maxilla, the upper jawbone.

maxillary, referring to the jawbone.

M.D., Doctor of Medicine.

measles, a highly infectious viral disease, usually occurring in childhood, characterized by reddish skin eruptions appearing on the face which rapidly increase in size and spread to the trunk and extremities, elevation of temperature, loss of appetite, and bronchitis; rubeola.

meatus, a passage or opening; a duct in the body; opening of the nose or ear.

meconium, the first fecal discharge of a newborn infant, usually tarry colored, consisting of salts, mucilaginous amnii, mucous, bile, and epithelial cells; also: opium.

media, medium, pertaining to the middle, as in the wall of an artery.

mediad, in the median line of the body, or central plane.

medial, median, pertaining to the middle.

mediastrinum, a median partition of the chest cavity from the sternum backward; a septum between two main portions of an organ; the pleural folds and space between the right and left lung.

mediate, between two parts or sides.

medicable, expectation of cure; treatable.

Medicaid, medical aid for the disabled or needy of any age not eligible for social security benefits, sponsored by federal, local, and state governments.

medical, pertaining to medicine.

medicament, a remedy or substance for healing wounds; medication.

Medicare, a Federal insurance program financed by social security which provides medical care for the aged.

medication, the administration of remedies, medicine, or drugs for the treatment of diseases or the healing of wounds.

medicine, any drug or remedy; the science of diagnosis and treatment of diseases and care of the injured; nonsurgical means of treatment of diseases; the science of preserving health.

medulla, the marrow; medulla oblongata; the inner surface of an organ or part of an organ.

medulla oblongata, the lower portion of the brain stem, or enlarged part of the spinal cord in the cranium.

medullary, pertaining to the marrow or inner portion.

megacardia, an enlargement of the heart.

megacephalic, enlargement of the head.

megacephaly, the condition of having an enlarged head or megacephalic.

megacolon, extreme enlargement of the colon.

megalomania, a mental disorder characterized by extreme preoccupation with delusions of power, greatness, or goodness.

meiosis, the process of nuclear cell division of mature reproductive cells in which the number of chromosomes are reduced to half their original number before the cell divides in two, or from diploid to the haploid.

melancholia, a major affective disorder characterized by worry, anxiety, agitation, great depression, severe insomnia, and inhibition of activity; many of the observable symptoms are similar to the depressed phase of manic-depressive psychoses.

melancholy, an abnormal state of despondency or dejection; an overelaboration of sadness and grief.

melanemia, an unnatural dark pigment in the blood.

melanidrosis, black colored sweat.

melanin, the black or brown compounds which are the chief pigments produced by melanoblasts located in the deepest layers of the skin. Many factors influence skin melanin pigments such as exposure to the sun, radiation therapy, hormone deficiency, and some types of Vitamin B deficiency.

melanism, excessive amounts of black or dark pigment in the skin, hair, and eyes.

melanoleukoderma, having mottled skin.

melanoma, any tumor which is composed of melanin-pigmented cells; a malignant melanoma.

melanomatosis, the formation of widespread melanomas on or beneath the skin.

melanopathy, a diseased condition of the skin marked by dark pigmented areas.

melanosis, an abnormal deposit of black pigments in the skin found on different parts of the body.

melanosis lenticularis, a very rare skin disorder which appears in early youth marked by various pigmented areas, ulcers, and atrophy.

melanotic, blackish discoloration; pertaining to melanosis.

malenuria, dark pigments present in urine.

melissophobia, abnormal aversion or fear of bee or wasp stings.

melitemia, the presence of sugar in the blood; glycemia.

melitis, inflammation of the cheek.

membrane, a thin layer of tissue which lines a cavity or canal, covers organs, or separates one structure from another.

membranoid, resembling a membrane.

membranous, pertaining to a membrane, or relating to the nature of a membrane.

membranous labyrinth, the inner ear which is also called labyrinth because of its complicated shape. The membranous labyrinth within the bony labyrinth consists of the utricle and saccule inside the vestibule, the cochlear duct inside the cochlea, and the membranous semicircular canals inside the bony structures.

menarche, the onset of menses, normally between ages 10--17.

Mendel's laws, the fundamental rules which govern the transmission of genetic traits based on experiments with the common garden pea (Pisum sativum).

Meniere's disease, a usually progressive disease of the labyrinth characterized by a hearing loss, ringing in the ears, dizziness, and a sensation of fullness or pressure.

meningeal, pertaining to the meninges.

meninges, relating to the three membranes enveloping the spinal cord and brain including the dura mater, pia mater, and the arachnoid.

meningioma, a tumor in the meninges.

meningitis, inflammation of the membranes of the brain or spinal cord, especially of the arachnoid or pia mater.

meningocele, congenital hernia in which the meninges protrude through an opening of the skull or spinal column.

meningococcus, the microorganism, Neisseria meningitidis, that causes cerebral meningitis.

meningoencephalitis, inflammation of both the brain and its membranes.

meningoencephalomyelitis, inflammation of the brain, the spinal cord, and their membranes.

meningomyelitis, inflammation of the spinal cord and its membranes.

meniscectomy, surgical removal of meniscus cartilage of the knee.

meniscus, a crescent-shaped interarticular fibrocartilage found in joints, as in the knee joint; concavo-convex lens.

menopausal, pertaining to menopause.

menopause, the cessation of the menses; climacteric, or change of life for women between ages 45--50.

menorrhagia, excessive or profuse bleeding during the menstrual period.

menorrhea, normal menstruation; free flowing menstruation.

menses, monthly menstruation; monthly flow of blood from the female genital tract.

menstruate, the process of discharging blood from the uterus.

menstruation, the periodic discharge of blood and mucus from the uterus occurring at regular intervals of approximately 28 days during a woman's life from puberty to menopause.

menstruum, a solvent or a medium.

mensuration, the act of measuring.

mental, relating to the mind.

mental age, the age of a person's mental ability which may be determined by mental tests.

mental deficiency, mental retardation; subnormal intellectual functioning, present at birth or which may develop during early childhood, affecting areas of learning, social adjustment, and maturation.

mentality, one's mental capacity or mental power; intellectuality.

mentum, the chin.

meperidine, a synthetic narcotic used as an analgesic and sedative.

meprobamate, a tranquilizing drug used to relieve anxiety and mental tension.

merbromin, trademark Mercurochrome, used as an antiseptic and a germicide.

mercuric chloride, a compound of mercury, highly poisonous, useful as a disinfectant, fungicide, antiseptic, and preservative.

mercuric oxide, a yellowish powder used in ointments.

mercury, a metallic element soluble in hydrochloric acid, useful in two salt forms, mercurous and mercuric, in germicides.

mercury poisoning, acute poisoning due to ingestion marked by severe abdominal pain, vomiting, watery and bloody diarrhea, diminished urinary output, and digestive tract ulceration; chronic form of mercury poisoning due to absorption through the skin and mucous membranes by inhalation, and ingestion which causes inflamed tongue, bleeding gums, loosening of teeth, tremors, incoordination and other various symptoms.

Merthiolate, trademark for thimersol used as an antiseptic and germicide.

mesarteritis, inflammation of the middle coat of an artery.

mescaline, a crystalline alkaloid drug obtained from mescal cactus which causes hallucinations.

mesencephalon, the middle portion of the brain, or midbrain.

mesenchyme, a network of embryonic mesodermic cells that develop into connective tissues, blood and lymphatic systems, heart, and cartilage and bone.

mesenteric, pertaining to the msentery.

mesenteritis, inflammation of a mesentery.

mesentery, a fold of membranous tissue which attach and support various organs to the body wall such as the peritoneal fold connecting the small intestine to the posterior abdominal wall.

mesial, pertaining to the middle.

mesial plain, a median plane or division of the body longitudinally into symmetrical parts.

mesmerism, an early term for hypnosis, named after Anton Mesmer (1733--1815) which now means therapeutic hypnotism.

mesmerize, to hypnotize; to facinate.

mesoblast, the mesoderm, or an early stage in the development of the middle layer of the mesoderm.

mesocardia, a location of the heart in the middle plane of the thorax.

mesocolic, pertaining to the mesocolon.

mesocolon, the mesentery or peritoneal fold that connects the colon to the posterior wall of the abdomen.

mesoderm, the middle layer of the primary embryonic layers lying between the ectoderm and the entoderm.

mesometritis, inflammation of the uterine muscular structures.

mesomorph, a body type which is well-proportioned, muscular, and of medium height.

mesomorphic, having characteristics of mesomorphs.

mesonephroma, a malignant tumor found in the female genital tract, or in the ovary.

mesonephros, an excretory organ of the embryo.

mesosternum, the middle portion of the sternum.

mesothelium, a layer of cells derived from the mesoderm which forms the lining of the embryonic cavity.

metabolic, pertaining to metabolism.

metabolism, all physical and chemical changes within the organism involving energy and material transformations, and including two fundamental processes, anabolism (building-up process), and catabolism (breaking down process).

metabolite, any product of metabolic functions.

metabolize, to be transformed by metabolism.

metacarpal, pertaining to the metacarpus; a bone of the hand between the fingers and wrist.

metacarpus, the bony structure of the hand between the fingers and the wrist.

metaphase, the second stage of mitosis or cell division in which chromosomes align across the equatorial plane of spindle fibers prior to separation.

metaplasia, a change of one kind of tissue into a form that is abnormal for that tissue.

metamorphosis, a change in form or structure; in pathology, a change that is degenerative.

metapsychology, speculative psychology concerned with mental processes that reach beyond empirical verification.

metastasis, the movement of bacteria or diseased body cells from an organ or body part to another part of the body, usually applied to malignant cells spread by the lymphatics or blood stream.

metastatic, pertaining to metastasis.

metatarsal, a bone of the metatarsus or foot.

metatarsus, the portion of the foot between the tarsus or ankle and the phalanges or toes; including the five bones of the foot.

metencephalon, anterior portion of the hindbrain which consists of the cerebellum and pons; that part of the brain vesicles formed by a specialization of the hindbrain in the development of the embryo.

meteorism, formation of gas or flautus resulting in distention of the abdomen or intestines.

methadone, a synthetic compound with actions similar to morphine which is habit-forming; the hydrochloride is used as a potent analgesic and weak sedative, also used as an antitussive in tuberculosis, bronchiectasis, whooping cough, bronchogenic carcinoma, and congestive heart failure; used in treatment of addiction as a withdrawal substitute for morphine.

methemoglobin, present normally in the blood in small amounts, but becomes toxic when a larger portion of hemoglobin is converted into methemoglobin by the oxidation of iron, giving the blood a dark-brown color and decreasing its function to carry oxygen.

methenamine, a urinary antiseptic.

methionine, an essential amino acid important to nutrition.

metopic, pertaining to the forehead.

metopian, that part of the forehead between the frontal eminences.

metra, the uterus.

metralgia, pain in the uterus.

Metrazol, trademark for pentamethylenetetrazol used in treating certain heart conditions and as a respiratory stimulant.

metrectomy, surgical excision of the uterus; hysterectomy.

metritis, inflammation of the uterus.

metrocarcinoma, cancerous uterine tumor.

metrocystosis, the formation of many uterine cysts.

metropathy, any uterine disease.

metroptosis, a dropped uterus.

metrorrhagia, excessive or profuse bleeding from the uterus not associated with menses.

microbe, a microorganism, bacteria, or germ which produces disease.

microbic, referring to microbes.

microbiologist, a specialist in microbiology.

microbiology, the scientific study of microorganisms.

microcephalic, pertaining to a small head below 1350 cc.

microcephaly, microcephalism, an abnormal small head, a congenital anomaly, as seen in idiocy.

micrococcus, belonging to gram-positive bacteria of the Micrococcaceae family which are globular or oval and produce certain diseases in man.

microcyte, a small red blood cell less than 5 microns in diameter occurring in certain anemias.

micron, measurement of a unit of length equal to one millionth of a meter.

microorganism, a bacteria, or minute living structure which cannot be seen with the naked eye.

microscope, an optical apparatus which magnifies minute structures and microorganisms.

microscopic, pertaining to a microscope; visible only by means of a microscope.

microscopy, a microscopic examination, as in viewing specimens under a glass slide.

microsome, a minute particle or granule present in cell protoplasm.

microtome, a device for cutting thin sections of tissue for microscopic examination.

micturate, to discharge urine; urinate.

micturition, urination, or voiding of urine.

midbrain, mesencephalon, which lies below the inferior surface of the cerebrum and above the pons, consisting mainly of white matter.

middle ear, consisting of the tympanic membrane and a cavity containing the incus, malleus, and stapes.

midriff, the diaphragm.

midwife, a woman who practices midwifery; one who assists at childbirth.

midwifery, the art of assisting at childbirth or delivery.

migraine, sudden attacks of headache which usually affect the vision and may cause nausea, vomiting, constipation or diarrhea, resulting from constriction of the cranial arteries affecting one side of the head.

miliaria, an acute inflammation of the sweat glands causing vesicles to appear on the skin due to obstruction and the retention of sweat.

miliaria rubra, prickly heat, or heat rash.

miliary, resembling millet seeds; small nodules on the skin due to excessive exposure to heat.

milieu, pertaining to environment.

milium, a tiny pink and white vesicle or nodule appearing beneath the skin due to the retention of a fatty secretion of the sebaceous gland.

milk, an opaque white secretion of the mammary glands for feeding the young.

milk fever, a fever appearing with the beginning of lactation following childbirth, resulting from an infection.

milk leg, an inflammation of the iliac or femoral vein which causes pain and swelling, often a complication of childbirth.

milk tooth, a temporary or deciduous tooth occurring in childhood.

milligram, one-thousandth of a gram; abbreviated mg.

millimeter, one-thousandth meter; abbreviated mm.

millicron, one-thousandth of a micron; one-millionth of a millimeter.

mind, the psyche; having integrated brain functioning resulting in one's ability to perceive, comprehend, reason, and process information in an intelligent manner.

miosis, an abnormal contraction of the pupils.

miotic, an agent that produces contraction of the pupil.

misanthropy, hatred of mankind.

miscarriage, spontaneous abortion; referring to the interruption of pregnancy usually between the fourth month and viability.

miscegenation, marriage or sexual union between mixed races; inbreeding between different races.

miscible, having mixing capability; able to be mixed with separation.

misogamy, a hatred or fear of marriage.

misogyny, an aversion to women.

misologia, hatred for mental work.

misoneism, an aversion to new ideas; conservatism.

misopedia, an abnormal dislike for children.

mithridate, an antidote against poisoning.

mithridatism, acquiring immunity to a poison by taking small amounts and gradually increase dosages.

mitochondria, threadlike structures in cell cytoplasm.

mitosis, indirect cell division involving complex changes in the nucleus in a continuous process divided into four phases: prophase, metaphase, anaphase, and telephase.

mitotic, pertaining to mitosis.

mitral, pertaining to the bicuspid valve in the heart that prevents the blood in the left ventricle flowing back to the left auricle.

mittelschmerz, pain between menstrual periods at the time of ovulation.

modality, a method of application of any therapeutic agent.

molar, broad surfaced tooth for grinding, one of three on both sides of the upper and lower jaw.

mole, nevus; a congenital discolored spot on the skin which is slightly elevated.

molluscum, any slightly infectious skin disease marked by the formation of cutaneous tumors.

mongolism, Down's syndrome, a congenital mental deficiency.

mongoloid, a person with characteristics of mongolism.

moniliasis, candidiasis; an infection of the mucous membranes or skin caused by yeastlike fungi.

moniliform, resembling a string of beads.

monoamine, a molecule from one amino group, as serotonin, dopamine, and norepinephrine.

monocular, affecting one eye; pertaining to a single lens.

monocyte, a phagocytic leukocyte with a nucleus shaped like a kidney which is formed in bone marrow and which constitutes part of the important defense mechanism of the body.

monocytosis, having an excess of monocytes in the blood.

monodactyly, having only one digit on a foot or hand.

monomania, a mental illness marked by a morbid preoccupation with one idea or activity.

monomaniac, a person afflicted with monomania.

monomelic, affecting only one limb.

mononuclear, having a single nucleus.

mononucleosis, having an excess of monocytes in the blood stream; an infectious mononucleosis is an acute disease caused by the Epstein-Barr virus marked by fever, sore throat, general lymph node enlargement, and an abnormal increase of mononuclear leukocytes.

monoparesis, paralysis of one part of the body.

monophobia, pathological fear of being alone.

monoplegia, paralysis of one limb or one group of muscles.

mons pubis, the pubic eminence.

morbid, pertaining to, or being affected by disease; referring to an unhealthy mental state.

morbidity, the state of being diseased.

morbiliform, resembling measles with skin eruptions.

morgue, a public mortuary where dead bodies are held until identified or buried.

moribund, dying, or a state of dying.

morning sickness, nausea and vomiting that affects some women during the early stages of pregnancy.

moron, an adult who is feebleminded or mentally deficient, whose mental intellect corresponds to that of a normal child between ages 7--12 years.

morose, a gloomy or sullen disposition.

morphia, morphine.

morphine, an alkaloid found in opium used as an analgesic and sedative.

morphinism, habitual or excessive use of morphine which results in a morbid disposition.

morphinomania, madness resulting from the habitual use of morphine; a morbid and uncontrolled desire for morphine.

morphogenesis, various changes occurring during the development of an organism or part of the body.

morphology, the study of structure and form of organisms without regard to function.

mortal, causing death; destined to die; human.

mortality, state of being mortal; statistical death rate.

morula, a solid mass of cells formed by cleavage of a fertilized ovum.

mosaic, in genetics, a person exhibiting mosaicism.

mosaicism, two or more cell lines which are distinct karyotypically or genotypically and are derived from a single zygote.

motility, having spontaneity of movement; capable to perform voluntary movements.

motion sickness, a condition marked by nausea, vomiting, and dizziness caused by rhythmic, irregular, or jerky movements, as in sea sickness.

motor, a muscle, nerve, or center that conveys an impulse which produces movement.

Motrin, trademark for ibuprofen used as an anti-inflammatory agent, and possesses analgesic and antipyretic properties.

mouth, the cavity or first portion of the digestive system, consisting of the hard palate, teeth, tongue, and cheeks; essential part for speaking, and is an alternate breathing passage.

mouth-to-mouth resuscitation, a life-saving procedure to induce artificial respiration of an apneic victim by pressing the nostrils together to close the airway and at the same time blowing directly into the mouth and lungs using short, repeated, and regular breaths.

movement, motion or the act of moving; evacuation of the bowels.

mucilage, a gummy, aqueous preparation or glue used as an adhesive.

mucin, a glycoprotein which is the chief component of mucous secretions.

mucocutaneous, pertaining to an area where the skin and mucous membranes come together.

mucoid, a glycoprotein which is similar to mucin but differing in solubility.

mucoprotein, protein, containing polysaccharides, which is present in all connective and supporting tissues in the body.

mucopurulent, containing mucous and pus.

mucosa, referring to mucous membrane.

mucoserous, composed of both mucous and serum.

mucosin, mucin present in viscous, and sticky mucus.

mucous, resembling or pertaining to mucus; secreting mucus.

mucous membranes, membranes that secrete mucus.

mucoviscidosis, the disease cystic fibrosis of the pancreas.

mucus, a viscid secretion of the glands and mucous membranes, consisting of mucin, leukocytes, various salts, and desquamated cells.

multigravida, a woman pregnant for the third time or more.

multipara, a woman who has had two or more viable fetuses.

multiparous, having borne more than one child.

multiple sclerosis, MS, a progressive and degenerative disease of the central nervous system which is not contagious, marked by tremors, muscular weakness, speech disturbances, and visual complaints.

mumps, an acute contagious disease occurring mainly in childhood marked by swelling of the large salivary glands in front of the ears, but may involve the meninges and testes in postpubertal males.

mural, pertaining to the wall in any cavity of the body.

murmur, an abnormal heart sound which has a blowing or rasping quality.

muscle, an organ which produces body movement within an animal by contraction, composed of bundles of fibers of different lengths, breaths, and thicknesses.

muscular, pertaining to muscles; composed of muscle; having well-developed muscles.

muscular dystrophy, a progressive disease in which deterioration and atrophy of the muscles cause wasting and symmetrical weakening, believed to be inherited.

musculature, involving the muscular arrangement of the body or of a part.

musculoskeletal, comprising the skeleton and the muscles.

mutant, a living organism that is a product of genetic mutation.

mutate, to alter or change.

mutation, a permanent change in genetic material; an individual exhibiting such a change.

mute, one who is unable to speak.

myalgia, having muscle pain; muscular pain.

myasthenia, muscular debility or weakness.

myasthenia gravis, a neuromuscular disorder without atrophy, characterized by progressive fatigue and exhaustion of the muscular system.

myatrophy, muscle wasting.

mycete, a fungus.

Mycobacterium, a gram-positive bacteria found in swimming pools which causes granuloma.

mycology, the scientific study of fungi.

mycosis, a disease caused by fungi.

mycotic, pertaining to mycosis.

Mycostatin, trademark for nystatin used for fungus infections.

mydriasis, dilatation of the pupils.

mydriatic, an agent that dilates the pupil of the eye.

myelencephalitis, inflammation of the brain and the spinal cord.

myelencephalon, the posterior part of the embryonic hindbrain from which the medulla oblongata and the lower portion of the fourth ventricle develop.

myelin, the whitish fatlike substance that surrounds the axon of myelinated nerve fibers.

myelinic, pertaining to myelin.

myelinization, the formation of the myelin sheath around the axon.

myelin sheath, a segmented wrapping of a double layer of Schwann cells surrounding some nerve fibers.

myelitis, inflammation of the spinal cord or bone marrow.

myelocyte, a cell intermediate between a promyelocyte and a metamyelocyte in development of leukocytes found in red bone marrow.

myeloencephalitis, inflammation of the spinal cord and brain.

myelography, radiography of the spinal cord after an injection of a radiopaque substance into the subarachnoid space.

myeloid, pertaining to or resembling bone marrow; referring to the spinal cord; resembling myelocytes but not developing from bone marrow.

myeloma, a tumor originating in hematopoietic cells of bone marrow.

myocardiograph, an instrument for tracing heart movements.

myocarditis, inflammation of the myocardium.

myocardium, the thickest and middle layer of the wall of the heart, or muscle of the heart.

myogenic, originating in muscle.

myoglobin, a protein of hemoglobin in muslces, composed of one polypeptide chain and one hemp group, and carrying more oxygen and less carbon monoxide.

myograph, an apparatus used to measure muscular contraction.

myology, the study of muscles and their accessory structures such as bursae and synovial membrane.

myoma, a tumor consisting of muscular tissue.

myomatous, pertaining to a myoma.

myoneural, concerned with both muscles and nerves.

myopia, nearsightedness; defective vision in which objects can only be seen clearly when very close to the eyes.

myopic, pertaining to myopia.

myositis, inflammation of voluntary muscle tissue.

myospasm, spasm of a muscle or group of muscles.

myotomy, dissection of muscular tissue.

myringa, tympanic membrane.

myringitis, eardrum inflammation.

myringoscope, a device used to examine the eardrum.

myxedema, a condition causing nonpitting edema with abnormal deposits of mucin in the tissues, accompanied by a blunting of the senses and intellect due to hypothyroidism.

myxoma, a tumor consisting of connective tissue cells and mucous.

myxorrhea, an excessive flow of mucus.

myxovirus, a group of related viruses which produce influenza, mumps, and measles.

N

nacreous, a pear-like, iridescent luster in certain bacterial clusters.

nail, the horny cutaneous cell structure on the dorsal end of fingers and toes forming flat plates.

nalorphine, used as an antagonist of morphine and in treatment of narcotic overdose.

nanism, dwarfism; an abnormal small stature.

nape, the back of the neck.

naprapathy, a treatment of disease based on the assumption that an illness is due to faulty ligament functioning which may be corrected or adjusted by massage and manipulation of joints and muscles.

narcissism, self-love, or being interested in one's self, as opposed to the love of another person. An excess of narcissism interferes with relationships, but some degree of self-love if considered normal.

narcolepsy, an uncontrollable desire to sleep for brief periods.

narcosis, a state of unconsciousness, stupor, or insensibility produced by a chemical or narcotic drug.

narcotic, a drug which produces sleep; used in moderate doses, a central nervous system depressant which relieves pain and induces sleep; used in excessive doses, produces unconsciousness, stupor, coma, and even death.

narcotized, to become unconscious under the influence of a narcotic.

naris, nares; nostril or nostrils.

nasal, pertaining to the nose.

nascent, having just come into existence; being born.

nasofrontal, pertaining to the nasal and frontal bones.

nasolabial, pertaining to the nose and lip.

nasolacrimal, pertaining to the nose and tear ducts and glands.

nasology, the study of the nose and its diseases.

nasopalatine, pertaining to both the nose and palate.

nasopharyngeal, pertaining to the nose and pharynx.

nasopharyngitis, inflammation of the nasopharynx.

nasopharynx, that portion of the pharynx situated above the soft palate.

natal, pertaining to birth.

natality, birth rate.

nates, the buttocks.

natural selection, Darwin's theory of evolution which accounts for the origin of species. Because of limited food supply and a struggle for existence those genetic species which have particular characteristics tend to survive.

naturopathy, the therapeutic use of natural forces such as air, heat, light, massage, and water.

nausea, having an upset stomach and the inclination to vomit.

nauseant, causing one to feel nauseated; affecting nausea.

nauseate, to cause nausea.

nauseous, affecting or producing nausea, disgust, or loathing.

navel, the depression in the center of the abdomen; the umbilicus.

navicular, boat-shaped; a wrist or ankle bone.

nearsightedness, myopia; seeing clearly only objects that are near.

nearthrosis, an artificial joint due to a broken bone.

nebula, a corneal opacity; an oily liquid prepared for atomizer usage.

nebulizer, an apparatus which produces a fine spray such as an atomizer.

neck, that part of the body which connects the head to the trunk; a constricted part of an organ.

necrobiosis, a gradual degeneration and death of certain tissues or cells.

necrophilia, a pathological attraction to dead bodies or death.

necrophobia, morbid fear of death or dead bodies.

necropsy, autopsy; examination of a corpse.

necrose, to become necrotic.

necrosis, death of cells or bone caused by enzymatic degradation surrounding tissues which are healthy.

necrotic, pertaining to death of a portion of tissue.

negative, lacking confirmation of a disease by testing results, as a negative diagnosis; showing resistance.

negativism, opposition to advice; an opposite behavior to one appropriate in a specific situation.

Neisseria, a gram-positive bacteria, causing gonorrhea.

nematode, a roundworm belonging to Nematoda, a parasitic phylum whose hosts may be man, animals, or domestic plants.

nematology, the study of nematodes.

Nembutal, trademark for pentobarbital sodium used as a hypnotic and sedative prior to anesthesia and to control convulsions.

neoantigen, an intranuclear antigen present in cells which are infected by oncogenic viruses.

neogenesis, regeneration of tissues.

neomycin, a broad-spectrum antibiotic effective against various gram-negative organisms, used in skin infections, wounds, burns, and ulcers which form in the urinary tract, ear, eye, skin, and for preoperative preparation of the skin.

neonatal, pertaining to the newborn infant.

neonate, a newborn infant.

neophobia, an aversion to all unknown things or new scenes or circumstances.

neoplasia, the formation of new tissues or a neoplasm.

neoplasm, any new abnormal growth of tissue in the body; a tumor.

neoplastic, pertaining to neoplasm.

neoplasty, surgical restoration of tissue or parts.

Neo-synephrine hydrochloride, trademark for phenylephrine useful in raising blood pressure, as a decongestant, and as a mydriatic.

nephralgia, pain in a kidney.

nephralgic, pertaining to renal pain.

nephrectomy, excision of a kidney.

nephric, pertaining to the kidney or kidneys.

nephrism, various symptoms caused by chronic kidney disease.

nephritic, pertaining to nephritis; referring to a kidney.

nephritis, inflammation of the kidney.

nephrolith, a stone or calculus in the kidney.

nephrolithiasis, the presence of renal calculi.

nephrolithotomy, surgical removal of a kidney stone.

nephroma, a tumor of the kidney or its tissue.

nephron, the structural and functional unit of the kidney, approximately a million and a quarter nephrons in each kidney.

nephropathy, kidney disease.

nephrosis, a kidney disease marked by degenerative lesions of the renal tubules without inflammation.

nerve, a white cord-like structure comprising nerve fibers which conduct and convey impulses from the brain and spinal cord throughout the body.

nerve cell, a neuron.

nerve fiber, an enlongated thread-like process, or axon, which conducts impulses.

nerve impulse, an excitatory process occurring in nerve fibers by the introduction of a stimuli.

nervous, easily excited or agitated; pertaining to a nerve.

nervous breakdown, signifying any mental disorder that affects an individual's normal activities such as depression, psychosis, or neurosis.

nervousness, excitability or mental unrest.

nervous system, consisting of a network of nerve cells responsible for controlling body functions including ganglia, spinal cord, nerves, and brain; CNS, or central nervous system which acts to regulate and coordinate bodily activities and initiate responses that help the body to adjust to environmental changes.

neural, pertaining to a nerve or nerves; the nervous system.

neuralgia, sharp pain along the course of a nerve or several nerves.

neural tube, a tubular formation of nerve tissue in the embryo from which the brain and spinal cord develop.

neurasthenia, a condition following depressed states from prolonged emotional tension marked by weakness, exhaustion, headache, sweating, polyuria, ringing ears, vertigo, double vision, fear, irritability, poor concentration, insomnia, and many other symptoms.

neuraxitis, encephalitis.

neurectomy, excision of a nerve or part of a nerve.

neurectopia, an abnormal position of a nerve.

neurilemma, a thin membranous sheath surrounding a nerve fiber.

neurinoma, a peripheral nerve tumor.

neuritis, inflammation of a nerve or nerves accompanied by impaired reflexes.

neuroblastoma, a hemorrhagic malignant tumor involving nerve ganglia.

neurocirculatory, pertaining to circulation and the nervous system in the body.

neurocrine, relating to hormonal influence on nervous activity.

neurodermatitis, severe irritation and itching of the skin due to a nervous disorder.

neurodynia, pain in a nerve.

neurofibril, any of the delicate fibrils found in nerve cells which extend into the axon and dendrites.

neurofibroma, a tumor of peripheral nerves found in connecting nerve tissue.

neurofibromatosis, a conditioned marked by various sizes of tumors on peripheral nerves, muscles, bones, and skin.

neurogenic, beginning in a nerve or nerve tissue.

neurogenous, developing in the nervous system.

neuroglia, delicate connective tissue which supports the structure of nervous tissue in the central nervous system.

neuroglial, pertaining to neuroglia.

neuroglioma, a tumor consisting of neuroglial tissue.

neuroleptic, an antipsychotic drug.

neurologist, a specialist in neurology.

neurology, the branch of medicine concerned with the nervous system.

neurolysin, an agent which destroys neurons.

neurolysis, the cutting of a nerve sheath to relieve tension; stretching a nerve to reduce tension; dissolution of nerve tissue.

neuroma, a new growth composed of nerve cells and nerve fibers.

neuromalacia, an abnormal softening of the nerves.

neuromuscular, pertaining to both nerves and muscles.

neuromyopathic, affecting the nervous system and muscles including the heart.

neuron, a nerve cell, or any of the conductive cells of the nervous system.

neuronal, relating to neurons.

neuropathology, the study of the diseases of the nervous system.

neuropathy, any disease of the peripheral nervous system.

neuropharmacology, the science concerned with the effects of drugs on the nervous system.

neurophysiology, the physiology of the nervous system.

neuroplasty, surgical repair of nerves.

neuropsychiatry, the branch of medicine concerned with both neurology and psychiatry.

neurosis, an emotional disorder characterized by anxiety arising from unresolved and unconscious conflicts, considered to be less severe than psychoses because personality disorganization and distortion of reality are not manifested.

neurosurgery, surgery performed on the nervous system.

neurosyphilis, syphilis involving the central nervous system.

neurotherapy, treatment of nervous disorders.

neurotic, pertaining to one affected with neurosis; relating to nerves; an unusually nervous person.

neurotomy, surgical cutting of nerves.

neurotoxin, a poisonous substance which is destructive to nerve cells and tissue.

neurotripsy, crushing of a nerve by surgery.

neurovascular, pertaining to the nervous and vascular systems.

neutral, neither acid or alkaline.

neutrophil, a leukocyte that stains readily with neutral dyes.

nevocarcinoma, a malignant melanoma developing from a mole.

nevoid, resembling a nevus.

nevose, marked with nevi or moles.

nevus, a congenital circumscribed malformation of the skin which is not caused externally; a birthmark.

newborn, recently born infant.

Niacin, trademark for nicotinic acid essential to the body.

nicotine, a poisonous alkaloid found in tobacco used as an insecticide, and in veterinary preparations as an external parasitide.

nicotinic acid, from the complex Vitamin B group consisting of a crystalline compound occurring in various animal and plant tissues, used for its curative property in pellagra, poor peripheral circulation, and high cholesterol levels in the blood.

nictitation, the act of winking; blinking of the eyelids.

night blindness, defective vision in the dark due to lack of visual purple in the rods of the retina, or to regenerative slowness after being exposed to light.

nightmare, a terrifying and anxiety provoking dream.

nightwalking, somnambulism; a state of walking habitually in one's sleep.

nipple, mammilla papilla, a protuberance from the mammary gland from which the lactiferous ducts discharge milk in the female; any similarly shaped structure.

nit, the egg of a louse.

niter, potassium nitrate or sodium nitrate.

nitrate, a salt of nitric acid.

nitric acid, a corrosive, poisonous liquid in concentrated form widely used in industry and in the manufacture of medicinal preparations.

nitrogen mustard, used in therapeutic mustard compounds important in treating some diseases.

nitroglycerin, a vasodilator used in treatment of angina pectoris; also used in making dynamite or rocket propellants by treating glycerol with nitric and sulfuric acids.

nitrous oxide, a gas used as a general anesthetic and analgesic, especially during dental procedures and surgery; laughing gas.

noctalbuminuria, an excessive amount of albumin voided in urine at night.

nocturia, excessive urination at night; enuresis or bed-wetting.

node, a knot or swelling; a constricted area; a tiny rounded structure; a lymph gland.

nodose, knotlike projections at intervals; having nodes.

nodular, resembling nodules.

nodule, a tiny node; an aggregation of small cells.

nodulose, having nodules or small knots.

nodus, a node.

noma, a progressive gangrenous condition of the mouth and cheek spreading from the mucous membranes to cutaneous surfaces, occurring in malnourished children.

nomenclature, classified system of anatomical structures, organisms, and names signifying the genus and species of animals and plants.

nonipara, a woman who has delivered nine viable fetuses.

nonunion, the failure of a fracture to heal, especially the ends of a bone that do not unit.

nonviable, not capable of living; inadequate development.

norepinephrine, a hormone secreted by the adrenal glands, a powerful vasopressor, and used to restore blood pressure in hypotensive conditions.

normal, a standard; natural and proper functioning.

nose, the projection on the face that contains the nares, the nasal cavity, olfactory nerve endings, and functions in speech, respiration, and sense of smell.

nosebleed, epistaxia.

nosology, scientific classification of diseases.

nosomania, an assumption that one has some special illness or disease; hypochondriasis.

nosomycosis, a fungal disease; mycosis.

nosophobia, morbid fear of sickness.

nostril, one of either of the nares.

notalgia, back pain.

notochord, a rod-shaped primitive groove of the embryo which develops into the vertebral column.

Novocain, trademark for procaine hydrochloride used as a local anesthetic.

noxious, injurious to health; hurtful.

nubility, being able to marry or marriageable, said of a girl at puberty; the final stage of sex development.

nucleate, having a nucleus.

nucleic acid, an organic compound found in cells, especially the nucleus, which is important to heredity and the control of cell metabolism. It is composed of phosphoric acids, bases from purines or pyrimidines, carbohydrates, and sugars.

nucleolus, a small rounded body within the cell nucleus in which the synthesis of RNA takes place.

nullipara, a female who has never given birth to an infant.

nulliparous, having never borne an infant.

numb, having no feeling or sensation in a body part.

numbness, a state of lacking sensation in a part of the body; lacking the power to move; state of being numb.

nurse-midwife, a person trained in the two disciplines of nursing and midwifery, and having received certification from the American College of Nurse-Midwives.

nutation, involuntary nodding of the head.

nutrient, a substance that provides nourishment, as in a component of food.

nutriment, nourishment that serves to sustain the body by promoting growth and replacement of worn-out cells.

nutrition, the process of ingesting food and utilizing it in the growth, repair, and maintenance of body activities.

nutritionist, one who specializes in scientific study of nutrition.

nutritious, providing nourishment.

nutritive, pertaining to nutrition and the process of assimilating food substances.

nyctalgia, pain occurring during the night.

nyctalopia, poor vision in a faint light or at night; night blindness.

nyctophilia, an unusual preference for night.

nyctophobia, morbid fear of darkness.

nympha, small fold of mucous membrane which form the inner lips of the vulva.

nymphomania, an abnormal and excessive need for sexual intercourse in females.

nystagmus, involuntary rapid eye movements.

nyxis, paracentesis, or puncturing the abdominal cavity for the removal of fluid to relieve the pressure of ascites; piercing.

O

oarialgia, pain in an ovary.

obduction, scientific examination of a dead body to learn cause of death; autopsy.

obese, extremely corpulent; fat; overweight.

obesity, a condition of the body in which an abnormal amount of fat accumulates beyond body requirements.

oblique, a slanting or diagonal direction; involvement of two muscles of the eye, the abdomen, the head, and the ears which run at an angle, not laterally.

obsession, an uncontrollable need to dwell on a thought or an emotion, or to behave in a specific way.

obsessive, pertaining to obsession.

obstetric, pertaining to obstetrics or midwifery.

obstetrician, a physician who attends women during pregnancy, labor, and puerperium.

obstetrics, the branch of medicine concerned with prenatal care and puerperium.

obstipation, extreme constipation which is resistive to treatment and cure, usually caused by an obstruction.

obturate, to obstruct or to close.

obturator, any obstruction that closes an opening, as a plate or disk that closes an abdominal opening.

obtusion, a deadening of normal sensations.

occipital, pertaining to the occiput or the back part of the head.

occipital bone, concerning the bone in the lower posterior portion of the skull between the parietal and temporal bones in the head.

occipitocervical, pertaining to the occiput and the neck.

occipitofacial, relating to both the occiput and face.

occipitomental, pertaining to the occiput and chin.

occipitoparietal, pertaining to the occiput and parietal bones.

occipitotemporal, pertaining to the occiput and temporal bones.

occiput, the back part of the skull.

occlusion, the state of being occluded or closed; referring to closely fitting opposing teeth in the upper and lower jaw.

occlusive, pertaining to occlusion or closing up.

occult, hidden or concealed from view, as a hemorrhage.

occult blood, a minute amount of blood that can only be detected by a microscope or chemical means.

occupational disease, a functional disease caused by one's occupation, such as writer's cramp.

occupational therapy, a method of rehabilitative treatment using activities to encourage a physically or mentally disabled person to aid his own recovery by performing light work, physical exercise, creative arts, cooking, crafts, or vocational training.

ochlophobia, abnormal fear of crowds.

ocular, pertaining to the eye; concerned with the eye or vision; the eyepiece of a microscope.

oculist, one who specializes in diseases of the eye; ophthalmologist.

oculomotor, referring to movements of the eye.

oculomotor nerve, the third cranial nerve which originates in the ventral part of the midbrain and extends to the external eye muscles.

oculomycosis, any of the fungal eye diseases.

oculus, the eye.

adontalgia, a toothache.

odontectomy, excision or the removal of a tooth.

odontitis, inflammation of a tooth.

odontoblast, connective tissue cells that line the tooth pulp outer surface and form deposits of dentin on teeth.

odontoid, resembling a tooth.

odontologist, a dentist or dental surgeon.

odontology, dentistry; the study of teeth, as they relate to health, growth, diseases and structure.

odontoma, a tumor arising from dental tissues.

odontonecrosis, extensive tooth decay.

odontopathy, diseases of teeth.

odontophobia, unusual aversion to the sight of teeth; morbid fear of dental surgery.

odontorrhagia, hemorrhaging from a socket after tooth extraction.

odontosis, development or eruption of teeth.

odontotherapy, special treatment of diseased teeth.

oedipal, pertaining to the Oedipus complex.

Oedipus complex, Freudian concept; abnormal intense love of a child for a parent of the opposite sex manifested by envy and aggressive feelings toward the parent of the same sex, most commonly love of a son for his mother.

oikomania, a nervous disorder caused by unhappy home surroundings.

oikophobia, an abnormal dislike of the home.

ointment, a soft fatlike substance used in external preparations and having an antiseptic quality.

olecranal, pertaining to the olecranon.

olecranoid, resembling the olecranon or elbow joint.

olecranon, the large bony projection of the ulna forming the elbow joint.

olfaction, the process of smelling; the sense of smell.

olfactology, the study of the sense of smell.

olfactory, referring to the sense of smell.

olfactory nerves, the first pair of cranial nerves consisting of sensory fibers which conduct impulses from the mucosa of the upper part of the nasal cavity to the brain.

olfactory organ, the nose consisting of hair cells with receptors in the mucosa of the upper part of the nasal cavity which are extremely sensitive to delicate odors.

oligemia, deficiency of blood volume in the body.

oligocholia, a lack of bile.

oligocythemia, decreased number of red blood cells than normal.

oligogalactia, a deficient milk secretion.

oligohemia, an insufficiency of circulating blood in the body.

oligohydramnios, an abnormal small amount of amniotic fluid.

oligohydruria, urine that is highly concentrated.

oligopnea, having infrequent respirations.

oligospermia, a deficient number of spermatozoa in seminal fluid.

oliguria, insufficiency in the amount of urine produced.

omental, pertaining to the omentum.

omentectomy, surgical removal of a portion of the omentum.

omentitis, inflammation of the omentum.

omentum, a double fold of peritoneum which extends from the stomach to the abdominal viscera.

omphalic, pertaining to the umbilicus.

omphalitis, inflammation of the umbilicus.

omphalocele, a protrusion of a portion of the intestine through an abdominal defect in the wall at the umbilicus occurring at birth.

omphalos, umbilicus or navel.

omphalotomy, cutting the umbilical cord at birth.

onanism, coitus interruptus, or withdrawal during intercourse before ejaculation; masturbation.

oncogenesis, producing tumors.

oncology, the branch of medicine concerned with the study of tumors.

onychauxis, nail hypertrophy.

onychectomy, surgical removal of a finger or toe nail.

onychia, inflammation of a nail bed frequently causing nail loss.

onyx, a fingernail or toenail.

onyxis, ingrown nails.

oocyte, an early stage of the ovum before maturation.

oogenesis, the formation and development of the ovum after a series of cell divisions beginning with the primordial germ cells in the ovary.

oogenetic, pertaining to oogenesis.

oophorectomy, excision or surgical removal of an ovary; ovariectomy.

oophoritis, inflammation of an ovary.

operable, subject to surgical treatment with a reasonalbe chance of safety.

ophidism, poisoning caused by snakebite.

ophthalmalgia, pain the eye.

ophthalmia, inflammation of the eye or its membranes.

ophthalmic, belonging to the eye.

ophthalmologic, pertaining to ophthalmology.

ophthalmologist, a medical physician who practices ophthalmology.

ophthalmology, science of the eye; study of eye anatomy, physiology, and diseases.

ophthalmopathy, any of the eye diseases.

ophthalmoplasty, plastic surgery of the eye or the surrounding appendages.

ophthalmoplegia, paralysis of the eye musculature.

ophthalmoscope, an instrument used to examine the interior of the eye or the retina.

opiate, any medicine derived from opium; sleep inducing.

opiomania, an abnormally intense craving for opium.

opisthotonos, a tetanic spasm in which the feet and head are bent backwards and the body arched forward, sometimes seen in meningitis and tetanus.

opium, dried juice obtained from unripe poppy capsules, used in medicine for its narcotic and analgesic effect.

opsonin, an antibody that causes bacteria to become more susceptible to phagocytic destruction.

optic, pertaining to the eyes.

optical, pertaining to vision.

optic disk, optic disc, the area in the retina known as the blind spot where the optic nerve enters.

optician, a specialist who makes optical lenses or eyeglasses for correcting visual defects.

optic nerve, the second cranial nerve which functions as the sense of sight, one of a pair.

optics, the scientific study of light and vision.

optometer, an instrument which measures the eye's refractive power.

optometrist, one trained to measure the eye's refractive powers and to fit eyeglasses to correct defects in vision.

optometry, an examination and measurement of refractive powers of the eye and the correction of visual defects with eyeglasses.

oral, pertaining to the mouth.

oralogy, the study of oral hygiene and diseases of the mouth.

orbit, the bony cavity which holds the eyeball.

orbital, concerning the orbit of the eye.

orchialgia, pain in the testis.

orchidectomy, surgical removal of a testicle.

orchioplasty, plastic surgery of a testis or testes.

orchitis, inflammation of a testis.

orderly, a male hospital employee who attends especially to male needs.

organ, a body part that performs a specific function.

organelle, a specialized part of cell strucutre, such as a mitochondrion or "power plant" within a cell.

organic, pertaining to an organ; having an organized structure; pertaining to substances produced by living organisms; denoting chemical materials containing carbon.

organism, any living plant, animal, or unicellular bacteria, yeasts, or protozoa.

organoplexy, the reattachment of an organ by surgical fixation.

organotherapy, treatment of diseases by endocrine gland preparations and extractions from animals.

orgasm, a state of culminated sexual excitement; the apex of sexual intercourse.

orientation, the ability to comprehend one's self with regard to time, place, and person.

orifice, the entrance or outlet of a body cavity; foramen, meatus, or opening.

Orinase, trademark for tolbutamide used to treat uncomplicated, mild, or stable diabetes mellitus that has some functioning islet cells.

ornithosis, a disease found in birds and domestic fowl which may be transmitted to man.

oropharynx, the space between the soft palate and the upper epiglottis.

orthocephalic, having a head with a height and length index between 70--75.

orthodontia, the science of dentistry concerned with correcting teeth irregularities, malocclusion, and facial abnormalities.

orthodontist, a dentist who specializes in orthodontia.

orthogenics, eugenics, or the science that is concerned with the improvement of hereditary qualities in the human race.

orthognathics, the study of the causes and treatment of malposition of jaw bones.

orthopedics, the branch of surgery dealing with the skeletal system in preservation and restoration of its articulations, and structures.

orthopedist, an orthopedic surgeon.

orthopnea, difficulty in breathing except in an erect sitting position or standing, associated with cardiac diseases, pulmonary edema, severe emphysema, pneumonia, angina pectoris and several other conditions that affect respiration.

orthopsychiatrist, one specialized in orthopsychiatry.

orthopsychiatry, the branch of psychiatry concerned with the study and treatment of human behavior in the clinical setting and which emphasizes preventive techniques that provide healthy emotional growth of children.

orthoptic, promoting normal binocular vision.

orthoptics, treatment with ocular exercises to correct strabismus.

orthoscope, an apparatus for examining the eyes which uses a layer of water that neutralizes corneal refraction.

orthoscopic, pertaining to the correction of vision.

orthoscopy, an examination using an orthoscope.

orthotonos, orthotonus, muscular spasm which fixes the head, body, and limbs in a straight and rigid line.

os, a body opening; the mouth; a bone.

oscheitus, inflammation of the scrotum.

oscillograph, an instrument which records electric vibrations of the heart activity or blood pressure.

oscillography, a process which records alternating current waves.

oscilloscope, an electronic instrument that presents visual changes of electrical variations on the fluorescent screen of a cathode-ray tube.

osmics, the science concerned with the sense of smell.

osmidrosis, a condition in which body perspiration has a strong offensive odor.

osmose, subject to osmosis.

osmosis, the movement or diffusion of a solution through a selectively permeable, or a semipermeable membrane from an area of higher density to an area of lesser density. In the human body the cell membranes are selectively permeable which permits oxygen, blood, and nutrients to pass through cells by the process of osmosis. Waste products are removed from the blood in the kidneys through the same process of osmosis.

ossa, bones.

osseous, bonelike, or bony.

ossicle, a small bone, as in the middle ear.

ossicula auditus, the three small bones in the middle ear: incus, malleus, and stapes.

ossiculectomy, surgical excision of one of the ossicles of the middle ear.

ossiferous, forming or producing bone; bonelike tissue.

ossify, to form bone, or to turn into bone.

osteal, pertaining to bone.

ostectomy, surgical removal of a bone or part of a bone.

osteectopia, displacement of a bone.

osteitis, inflammation of bone.

osteoarthritis, a degenerative disease of the joints, especially those which bear the bodies weight.

osteoarthropathy, any disease of the joints or bones.

osteoarthrosis, a chronic bone disease which is noninflammatory.

osteoblast, arising from a fibroblast cell which matures and produces bone.

osteoblastic, pertaining to the bone-forming osteoblast.

osteclasis, the fracture or refracture of a bone by surgical means to correct deformity in the bone.

osteoclast, a large multinuclear cell present in growing bone and which functions to absorb and remove osseous tissue in the formation of canals; an instrument used for refracturing bone.

osteodermia, formation of bony tissue in the skin.

osteodystrophia, bone development that is defective.

osteodystrophy, defective bone formation.

osteogen, a substance from which bone is formed within the inner periosteal layer.

osteoid, resembling bone.

osteology, the branch of anatomy concerned with bones and the structure of bones.

osteoma, a bony tumor, or a bone-like structure which develops on a bone.

osteomalacia, softening of the bones.

osteometry, study of bone measurements.

osteomyelitis, inflammation of the bone marrow, or of both the bone and marrow.

osteopath, one trained in osteopathy.

osteopathic, pertaining to osteopathy.

osteopathy, any bone disease; the branch of medicine based on the theory that the body is able to make its own remedies against disease with favorable environmental conditions and good nutrition; its therapeutic procedure involves manipulation of the bony framework and muscles for correction or cure.

osteophyte, a bony outgrowth from the surface of a part.

osteophytic, pertaining to an osteophyte.

osteoplastic, pertaining to bone repair.

osteoplasty, plastic surgery of the bones to correct a defect.

osteoporosis, loss of bone calcareous matter and increased bone porosity.

osteosclerosis, abnormal density or hardening of the bone.

osteoseptum, the bony portion of the septum of the nose.

osteotome, a bevelled chisel for surgical cutting through bones.

osteotomy, surgical procedure for cutting through a bone, or excising part of it.

ostium, ostial, a mouth, orifice, or a small opening.

otalgia, pain in the ear.

otantritis, inflammation of the mastoid antrum.

otectomy, surgical removal of the middle ear contents.

otic, pertaining to or concerning the ear.

otitis, inflammation of the ear.

otocleisis, an occlusion of the auditory tube.

otolaryngologist, a specialist in otology, rhinology, and laryngology.

otolaryngology, the division of medicine concerned with the ear, nose, and throat.

otolith, a minute calcareous body in the inner ear composed of calcium carbonate.

otologist, one trained in diseases of the ear.

otology, the science of the ear, its diseases, and functions.

otopharyngeal, pertaining to both the ear and the pharynx.

otopharyngeal tube, eustachian tube, the passage between the tympanic cavity and the pharynx.

otosalpinx, referring to the eustachian tube or otopharyngeal tube.

otoscope, an instrument used for an ear examination.

otoscopy, the auscultation of the ear with an otoscope.

ovarian, pertaining to the ovary.

ovariectomy, excision of an ovary or part of it; oophorectomy.

ovariohysterectomy, surgical removal of the ovaries and uterus.

ovariotomy, incision into an ovary, as in an ovarian tumor procedure to excise it.

ovaritis, inflammation of an ovary.

ovary, one of two reproductive glands in females which produce ova and sex hormones.

overexertion, excessive physical activity to the point of exhaustion.

overextension, hyperextension; extension beyond a reasonable point.

overriding, having one end of a fracture slipping past the other part.

overweight, exceeding one's normal weight by 10--15%; obese.

oviduct, fallopian tube, one of two tubes which extend laterally from the ovary to the uterus and which transport the ovum from the ovary to the uterus.

ovular, pertaining to an ovum.

ovulate, to release an ovum from one of the ovaries.

ovulation, the periodic process of ovulating.

ovule, an immature ovum within a graafian follicle.

ovum, an egg, or female reproductive cell, capable of developing into a new organism of the same species after fertilization.

oxygen, an odorless, colorless gas essential to respiration of most plants and animals, which constitutes approximately 20% of the atmosphere's total volume, and is necessary to support combustion.

oxygenate, to saturate or combine with oxygen.

oxygen tent, an air-tight enclosure that allows the oxygen content of air to be raised above normal to aid the respiration of a patient.

oxygen therapy, the administration of oxygen for treating conditions resulting from a lack of oxygen such as arterial anoxia from pneumonia, pulmonary edema, breathing obstruction, or congestive heart failure.

oxyhemoglobin, the combined arterial blood of hemoglobin and oxygen.

oxytocic, an agent used to accelerate childbirth; a drug which stimulates uterine contractions.

oxytocin, a pituitary hormone that stimulates uterine contractions.

ozena, a disease of the nose marked by a thick mucopurulent discharge with an offensive odor.

ozone, a form of oxygen with three atoms to a molecule which is irritating and toxic to the respiratory system.

ozostomia, a foul breath; halitosis.

P

pabulum, food or nourishment.

pacemaker, the sinuauricular node which sets the pace of cardiac rhythm situated in the right atrium which controls the heartbeat; an artificial cardiac pacemaker, as a small electronic device.

pachycephaly, abnormal thickness of the skull bones.

pachydermatous, having an unusual thickness of the skin.

pachydermia, excessive thickening of the skin; elephantiasis.

pachymeningitis, inflammation of the dura mater in the brain.

pachyvaginitis, a chronic condition of the vaginal walls in which they become abnormally thickened.

packing, the filling of a wound or cavity with gauze or similar material.

pagetoid, resembling Paget's disease.

Paget's Disease, Osteitis Deformans; a progressive, chronic disorder of bone metabolism which causes a thickening of bones, predominantly in the skull and shin.

pain, a sensation of agony, or suffering due to the stimulation of certain nerve endings; emotional suffering such as grief.

painful, a feeling of pain; distressing.

painter's colic, a condition marked by colic accompanying lead poisoning resulting in vomiting, abdominal pain, prostration, paralysis, and collapse.

palatable, savory, or agreeable to taste.

palatal, pertaining to the palate.

palate, the partition which separates the nasal and oral cavities in the roof of the mouth.

palatitis, inflammation of the palate.

palatoglossal, pertaining to the palate and tongue.

palatognathous, a congenital cleft palate.

palatoplasty, plastic repair of the palate to correct a cleft.

palatoplegia, paralysis the musculature structure of the palate.

palatum, palate.

palilalia, an abnormal condition in which words and phrases are repeated with increasing rapidity.

palindromia, a relapse, or recurrence of an illness or disease.

palingraphia, an abnormal condition in which written letters or words are repeated.

palinphrasia, an abnormal repetition of words and phrases in speaking.

pallial, pertaining to the cerebral cortex or brain.

palliate, to sooth; to relieve symptoms.

palliative, a drug that affords relief; something that soothes pain.

pallid, having no color; pale; wan.

pallidum, the globus pallidus of the cerebral hemisphere.

pallium, the cerebral cortex.

pallor, a paleness to the skin.

palm, the hollow surface of the hand.

palmar, referring to the palm of the hand.

palmar reflex, a grasping reflex found in newborn infants which is more developed in some than in others. It persists for 4 or 5 months then gradually disappears.

palpable, able to be touched, or easily perceived.

palpation, the act of examining with the hand; the application of fingers to the surface of the body to assist in diagnosing its condition.

palpebra, the eyelid.

palpebral, pertaining to the eyelid, or situated near it.

palpitate, to cause to throb or pulsate intensely, especially associated with the heart; abnormally rapid throbbing or fluttering involving the heart.

palpitation, an abnormal rapid or irregular heart beat, usually subjective.

palsy, a temporary or permanent paralysis or loss of ability to control movement; a person so disabled.

paludism, malaria; swamp fever.

panaris, infection and inflammation around a fingernail, or toenail.

panacea, a solution or remedy to cure all diseases; a cure-all.

panarthritis, inflammation in all joints.

pancreas, an elongated gland situated behind the stomach which secretes digestive enzymes and produces insulin.

pancreatalgia, pain in the pancreas.

pancreatectomy, surgical excision of the pancreas or a portion of it.

pancreatic, pertaining to the pancreas.

pancreatic juice, contains digestive enzymes produced in the tubuloacinar units of the pancreas, important in carbohydrate metabolism.

pancreatin, a substance derived from the pancreas of hogs and cattle containing the enzymes amylase, protease, and lipase which is used as an aid to digestion.

pancreatitis, inflammation of the pancreas.

pandemic, pertaining to an epidemic of a disease which affects a major portion of a country or the world.

panagenesis, a theory by Darwin, now abandoned, which states that each cell of a parent is represented in the reproductive cell, and is capable of reproducing itself in the offspring.

panhidrosis, panidrosis, perspiration over the entire body surface.

panhysterectomy, surgical removal of the entire uterus including the cervix uteri.

panic, an overwhelming fear that produces extreme anxiety; a sudden unreasonable, contagious fear that produces mass flight.

pannus, superficial vascular tissue growth arising from the conjunctiva into the cornea of the eye.

panophobia, panphobia, a fear of everything; a vague apprehension.

pansinusitis, inflammation involving all the nasal sinuses.

pant, to gasp or breathe quickly, especially after physical exertion; pant or panting during the second stage of labor under direct supervision of a trained person which allows the woman to have some control over expulsion of the fetus.

pantalgia, pain felt over the whole body.

papilla, a tiny nipple-shaped protuberance found on the elevations of the tongue and on the fingertips; the mesodermal papilla surrounding the hair bulb; the optic disc.

papillary, resembling or referring to a papilla; pertaining to the nipple of the breast.

papillectomy, surgical excision of a papilla.

papillitis, inflammation and swelling of the optic disc.

papilloma, a benign skin tumor consisting of hypertrophied papilla.

papillomatosis, the condition of having multiple papillomas.

Pap Smear, a microscopic examination of cells collected from the vagina for early detection of cervical or uterine cancer.

papule, a small elevated lesion of the skin.

papulopustular, having both papules and pustules.

papulosis, marked by multiple papules.

para, a woman who has given birth to one or more viable offspring.

para-anesthesia, the loss of feeling in the lower part of the body, or two corresponding sides of the body.

parabiosis, the union or fusion of two individuals, as conjoined twins.

paracentesis, a puncture of a cavity for the aspiration of fluid, as in dropsy.

paracephalus, a congenital defective head and imperfect sense organs in a fetus.

parachlorophenol, used in dentistry as a local anti-infective.

parachromatopsia, color blindness.

paracusis, defective sense of hearing.

paracystitis, inflammation of the tissues surrounding the urinary bladder.

paradenitis, inflammation in tissues surrounding a gland.

parageusia, dysfunction in the sense of taste.

parahepatitis, inflammation of parts adjacent to the liver.

paralalia, an abnormal speech defect marked by producing a vocal sound different from one desired, or speaking with sound distortion.

paralambdacism, unable to sound the letter "l" and substituting another letter for it.

paraldehyde, a colorless liquid polymer characterized by an unpleasant odor used as a sedative and hypnotic in medicinal preparations.

paralexia, a condition in which one is unable to comprehend printed or written words and transposes words or syllables into meaningless combinations; dyslexia.

paralogia, a disorder of reasoning ability; psychosis.

paralysis, an impairment of motor function in one or more parts of the body due to a lesion; an impairment of sensory function which causes a loss of voluntary motion.

paralysis agitans, a progressively slow form of Parkinson's disease marked by masklike facies, fine hand tremors, slowing of voluntary muscle movement, shuffling gait, peculiar posturing, weakness, and other symptoms.

paralytic, pertaining to paralysis; a person with paralysis.

paralyze, to affect with paralysis, or to cause a temporary or permanent loss of muscular movement or sensation.

paramastitis, inflammation surrounding the breast.

paramedic, one who performs adjunctive professional medical duties.

paramenia, an abnormal or difficult menstrual period.

paramnesia, the sensation of remembering something which has never actually existed or occurred.

paranephritis, inflammation of the adrenal gland; inflammation of connective tissues which surround the kidney.

paranephros, one of two adrenal glands.

paranesthesia, see para-anesthesia.

paranoia, a rare mental disorder marked by elaborate and systematized delusions of grandeur and persecution, a condition which does not appear to interfere with the rest of a person's thinking and personality.

paranoiac, one affected with paranoia.

paranoid, a term applied to persons who are overly suspicious and who harbor grandiose or persecutory delusions, or ideas of reference; resembling paranoia.

paranoid schizophrenia, a mental disorder characterized primarily by persecutory or grandiose delusions, but frequently associated with hallucinations.

paraphasia, a type of aphasia in which wrong words are employed in senseless combinations.

paraphobia, mild form of phobia.

paraphonia, an unusual weakness in the sound of one's voice; a partial loss of the voice.

paraphrasia, a disordered arrangement of spoken words.

paraplegia, paralysis of the lower trunk and the lower limbs.

paraplegic, pertaining to paraplegia; one affected with paraplegia.

parapsoriasis, slow developing, persistent skin disorder marked by scaly red lesions.

parapsychology, the study of metapsychic phenomena which deal with psychical actions and experiences that fall outside the scope of physics or physical law, as telepathy, clairvoyance, etc.

parasalpingitis, inflammation of the tissues around a fallopian tube.

parasite, any animal or plant that lives inside or upon the body of another living organism, often at a disadvantage to the host; symbiosis.

parasitic, concerning a parasite.

parasitism, the condition of being infected with parasites.

parasitize, to infect or be infected with a parasite.

parasitology, the scientific study of parasites.

parasitosis, a disease resulting from parasitism.

parastruma, an enlargement of the parathyroid gland resulting from a goiterlike tumor.

parasympathetic nervous system, a subdivision of the autonomic nervous system. Fibers which originate from nuclei in the midbrain, medulla, and sacral region of the spinal cord, pass through the cranial and sacral nerves. Some of the effects of the parasympathetic system are: constriction of pupils, slowing of heart rate, contraction of smooth muscles, increased glandular secretions, and the constriction of bronchioles.

parasynovitis, inflammation of tissues surrounding the synovial sac.

parathyroid, one of four tiny endocrine glands, pea-size, located on the lower back portion of the thyroid gland that secretes the hormone parathormone responsible for calcium-phosphorous metabolism.

paprathyroidal, pertaining to the parathyroid glands.

parathyroidectomy, surgical removal of one or more of the parathyroid glands.

paratyphoid, an infection resembling typhoid fever caused by bacteria Salmonella.

paregoric, a mixture containing a derivative of opium, anise oil, camphor, alcohol, benzoic acid, and glycerin, used in treatment of diarrhea.

parencephalitis, inflammation of the cerebellum.

parencephalon, the cerebellum.

parenchyma, the functioning cells of an organ.

parenteral, situated or occurring outside of the digestive tract, as by injection through an alternate route or means.

paresis, an imcomplete paralysis; a weakness of an organic origin.

paresthesia, an abnormal tactile sensation, often described as creeping, burning, tingling, or numbness.

paretic, pertaining to paresis.

paridrosis, any disordered condition involving the secretion of perspiration.

paries, parietes, the enveloping wall of any hollow organ.

parietal, pertaining to the wall of a cavity.

parietal bone, one of two bones forming the top portion and sides of the skull.

Parkinson's disease, a chronic, slowly progressive nervous disorder characterized by muscular rigidity, tremors, drooling, restlessness, peculiar involuntary movements, shuffling gait, chewing movements and protrusion of the tongue, blurred vision, and other neurological symptoms.

parkinsonism, Parkinson's disease.

parodontitis, inflammation of the tissues around a tooth.

parodynia, a difficult or abnormal delivery; labor pains.

paroniria, terrifying abnormal dreaming.

paroniria ambulans, sleepwalking.

paronychia, infection of the tissues around the base of a nail.

parorexia, a perversion of the appetite marked by a craving for strange foods.

parosmia, an abnormal sense of smell.

parotid, pertaining to the parotid gland; near the ear.

parotidectomy, surgical removal of a parotid gland.

parotid gland, one of two salivary glands on other side of the face in front of each ear.

parotiditis, inflammation of a parotid gland; mumps.

parous, having given birth to at least one offspring.

paroxysm, a sudden, intense attack, or recurrence of symptoms; a seizure or spasm.

paroxymal, pertaining to paroxysms.

parrot fever, psittacosis; a disease occurring in parrots and other domestic birds that is transmitted to man, which resembles pneumonia accompanied by fever, cough, and enlargement of the spleen; ornithosis.

parturient, pertaining to birth or giving birth, as a woman in labor.

parturition, the birth process; labor; childbirth.

parulis, an abcess of the gum, especially beneath a tooth socket.

parvule, a tiny pill, granule, or pellet.

passive, not active; submissive.

pasturization, a process of heating a liquid such as milk for a definite period of time and at a moderate temperature in order to destroy specific bacteria which is undesirable.

Pasteur treatment, a method of treatment for preventing rabies by a series of injections with a virus of gradually increasing strength.

pastille, a medicated lozenge for irritated mucosa of the throat and mouth; a small cone of aromatic paste used to fumigate or disinfect the air by burning it within a room.

patch test, a skin test to determine sensitivity.

patella, kneecap.

patellar, pertaining to the kneecap.

patellar reflex, an involuntary jerk of the leg following a tapping of the patellar ligament with an instrument; knee jerk reflex.

pathetic, the causing or arousing of emotions such as pity or sorrow.

pathogen, a microorganism that causes disease.

pathogenesis, the development of disease; the pathogenic reactions occurring in the development of disease.

pathogenic, causing disease.

pathogenicity, having the ability to produce morbid changes or disease.

pathognomonic, specifically characteristic of a disease; denoting one or more symptoms indicative of a disease.

pathological, pertaining to the causes of a specific disease.

pathologist, a specialist trained in pathology.

pathology, the scientific study of the nature and causes of disease, and changes in function and structure; manifestations of a disease.

pathophobia, morbid fear of disease.

patient, a person who is receiving medical treatment; one who is enduring pain without complaining.

pavor nocturnus, night terror such as nightmares during sleep occurring in children and the aged.

peccant, producing disease; morbid; pathogenic.

pectoral, pertaining to the chest or breast; an expectorant which relieves respiratory tract disorders.

pectoralgia, pain in the chest.

pectoral girdle, the arch formed by the collarbone and the shoulder.

pectoralis, pertaining to the breast or chest; one of the four muscles of the breast.

pectus, the chest; breast; thorax.

pedal, referring to the foot.

pedatropy, marasmus; a wasting disease occurring in children; Tabes mesenterica, tuberculosis of mesenteric glands in children.

pederasty, coitus between males through anal intercourse, especially with young boys; sodomy.

pediatrician, a physician who specializes in pediatrics.

pediatrics, the branch of medicine concerned with children and their development, and the care and treatment of children's diseases.

pedicle, a footlike, narrow structure; a bony process which forms the root of the vertebral arch.

pedicular, pertaining to pediculosis.

pediculosis, being infected with lice.

pedodontia, pedodontics, the branch of dentistry concerned with the teeth and mouth care of children.

pedodontist, a dentist trained in pedodontics.

peduncle, a stemlike collection of nerve fibers that attaches a new growth such as a nonsessile tumor which hangs free on a stalk; a band connecting structures of the brain.

peduncular, relating to a peduncle.

pedunculation, developing a stalk or peduncle.

pelioma, a livid cutaneous spot; ecchymosis.

peliosis, a condition marked by purple patches on the skin and mucous membranes; purpura.

pellagra, a disease caused by niacin deficiency which affects the skin, digestive system, and nervous system.

pellagrin, one afflicted with pellagra.

pellagroid, resembling pellagra.

pellicle, a thin membrane; a film which forms on the surface of liquids.

pellucid, translucent; limpid or clear.

pelvic, pertaining to the pelvis.

pelvimeter, an apparatus for measuring the pelvis.

pelvis, the lower portion of the body trunk formed by the innominate bones, the sacrum, and the coccyx.

pemphigus, a condition marked by successive crops of watery blisters eruting on the skin and mucous membranes which disappear leaving pigmented areas.

pendulous, to hang or swing freely.

penetrometer, an instrument which measures the penetrating power of x-rays and radiation.

penicillin, one of a group of antibiotics semisynthesized from various molds, especially from the genus Penicillum, effective against most grampositive bacteria and certain gram-negative forms, also effective against some forms of mold, spirochetes, and rickettsias by inhibiting bacterial growth.

penicillium, a genus of fungi, often found in mold forms of bluish color on cheese, bread, and fruit.

penile, pertaining to the penis.

penis, the male organ for urination and copulation, a pendulous structure that is suspended from the front and the sides of the pubic arch.

penitis, inflammation of the penis.

pentobarbital, a barbiturate acid derivative, the sodium salt is effective as a hypnotic and sedative, or as an analgesic; Nembutal sodium, a trademark, reduces responsiveness to external stimuli and is often used as a sedative prior to anesthesia.

pentylenetetrazol, a bitter, white powder used in preparation of a compound that is effective as a respiratory stimulant in certain circulatory conditions, and as a convulsant analeptic.

peotomy, excision of the penis.

pepsin, the primary enzyme of gastric juice that reduces protein to proteoses and peptides; an extract obtained from the glandular layer of the stomachs of hogs, sheep, or cows, used as a digestive aid.

pepsinogen, the inactive form of pepsin, the proteolytic enzyme in gastric juice which is converted to the active form by hydrochloric acid.

peptic, concerning digestion; relating to pepsin; a medicine that aids digestion.

peptic ulcer, an ulcer found in the lower part of the esophagus, in the stomach, in the duodenum, or in the gastrojejunostomy.

peptidase, any of a group of proteolytic enzymes that hydrolyze peptides or peptones into amino acids.

peptide, the linkage of two or more amino acid units by hydrolysis.

peptone, a derived protein produced by partial hydrolysis of native protein by the action of pepsin and trypsin.

peptonize, the process of converting a native protein into peptone.

peracute, very acute.

per anum, through the opening of the anus; by way of the anus.

Percodan, trademark for a fixed preparation of oxycodone hydrochloride and oxycodone terphthalate with aspirin, caffeine, and phenacetin.

percuss, to perform percussion by tapping a body part for diagnostic purposes.

percussion, the process of striking or tapping a part of the body with quick, sharp blows in diagnosing a condition of the underlying parts by sound.

percussor, an instrument used for percussion.

percutaneous, performed through the skin, as in the application of ointment by rubbing into the skin.

perflation, the process of blowing air into a cavity in order to expand its walls or to expel its contents.

perforans, perforating or penetrating, as of nerves or muscles.

perforation, the act of puncturing a hole, as caused by ulceration; any hole made through a substance or part.

perfusion, the passage of fluids through the blood vessels of an organ; the pouring of a fluid through an organ or tissue.

periadenitis, inflammation of tissues surrounding a gland.

periarterial, surrounding an artery.

periarteritis, inflammation of the outer coats of an artery.

peribronchitis, inflammation of all tissues around the bronchi or bronchial tubes.

pericardiac, pericardial, pertaining to the pericardium.

pericardiectomy, surgical removal of part or all of the pericardium.

pericardiotomy, incision of the pericardium.

pericarditis, inflammation of the pericardium.

pericardium, the fibroserous sac that envelops the heart and the roots of the great blood vessels.

pericecal, surrounding the cecum.

pericecitis, inflammation of the tissues situated around the cecum.

perichondral, relating to the perichondrium.

perichondrium, a membrane of fibrous connective tissue covering all cartilage except at synovial joints.

pericolic, around the colon.

pericolitis, inflammation of the area surrounding the colon.

perichonchal, around the concha of the ear.

pericorneal, around the cornea of the eye.

pericranium, the periosteum or membranous covering of the skull.

pericystitis, inflammation of the tissues around the urinary bladder.

peridental, surrounding a tooth or part of it.

perihepatitis, inflammation of the peritoneal capsule of the liver and the tissues of the surrounding area.

perimeter, the outer margin of a body; a device for measuring the visual field.

perimetrium, the peritoneum covering the uterus.

perimetry, the circumference of the body; the measurement of the scope of the field of vision using a perimeter.

perineal, pertaining to the perineum.

perineorrhaphy, the repair of a laceration in the perineum following childbirth.

perineotomy, surgical incision of the perineum to facilitate childbirth.

perineum, the area between the anus and the vulva in the female, or between the scrotum and the anus in a male.

perineurium, the connective tissue sheath surrounding the bundle of fibers in peripheral nerves.

period, the menses; the time it takes for a disease to run its course.

periodic, occurring at intermittent intervals.

periodontal, pertaining to the periodontium around a tooth.

periodontics, the branch of dentistry concerned with diseases of the periodontium and their treatment.

periodontist, a dentist trained in periodontics.

periodontitis, inflammation of the periodontium.

periodontium, the surrounding supportive tissues around a tooth, including the bone and gum.

perionychia, inflammation around a finger or toe nail.

perionychium, the epidermis bordering a finger or toe nail.

periosteal, pertaining to the periosteum.

periosteotomy, surgical incision into the periosteum.

periosteum, the fibrous membrane which forms a covering of bones containing numerous blood vessels for nourishment, and a supporting structure for the attachment of muscles, and ligaments.

periostitis, inflammation of the periosteum.

periotic, around the ear; pertaining to certain bones that protect the internal ear, and constituting a portion of the temporal bone.

peripheral, pertaining to an outer surface.

periprostatitis, inflamed tissues surrounding the prostate gland.

perisalpingitis, inflammation of the peritoneal coat surrounding the oviduct.

peristalsis, normal contraction and relaxation of the hollow tubes of the alimentary canal which slowly moves the contents along for variable distances.

peristaltic, pertaining to peristalsis.

perisystole, the interval preceding the systole in the cardiac rhythm.

perithelioma, a tumor of the perithelial layer of the blood vessels.

perithelium, the fibrous outer layer, composed of connective tissue, of the smaller blood vessels and capillaries.

peritoneal, relating to the peritoneum.

peritoneum, the thin, serous membrane which lines the entire internal surface of the abdominal cavity and envelops the viscera.

peritonitis, inflammation of the peritoneum.

peritonsillar, around a tonsil.

permanent teeth, the teeth which develop at the second dentition that supplant the milk teeth.

permanganate, a purple salt which contains potassium, manganese, and oxygen, used in solution as a disinfectant and an oxidizer.

pernicious, fatal; destructive; very harmful.

pernicious anemia, a severe and often fatal blood disease caused by a progressive decrease in red blood cells resulting in muscular weakness, gastrointestinal disorders, and neural disturbances.

peroneal, pertaining to the fibula.

peroral, by mouth; given by mouth.

per os, by mouth.

peroxide, a compound containing more oxygen than other oxides of the element, for example, the peroxides of hydrogen, sodium, and nitrogen.

perspiration, the secretion of sweat; sweating.

perspire, to sweat; to excrete fluid of perspiration through the skin.

pertussis, an infectious disease marked by catarrh and cough; whooping cough.

perversion, deviation from normal, as in sexual perversion or desire.

pervert, one who is perverted, esp. sexually.

pervious, capable of being penetrated; permeable; passing through.

pes, resembling a foot; serving as a foot; foot.

pessary, a device placed into the vagina to support and correct the uterus or rectum; a medicated vaginal suppository; a contraceptive device.

pestiferous, infectious; producing a pestilence; noxious.

pestilence, a widespread contagious disease that is usually of epidemic proportion and deadly, specifically bubonic plague.

pestilential, producing an infectious and deadly disease; destructive.

petechia, a tiny red spot occurring on the skin caused by a small amount of escaping blood.

petrolatum, a semisolid, purified mixture obtained from petroleum used in ointment preparations which protect and soothe the skin.

petrosal, pertaining to the petrous portion of the temporal bone.

phagedena, a sloughing and eroding ulcer that spreads.

phagocyte, a leukocyte which has the ability to destroy bacteria by ingesting or absorbing the harmful cells.

phagocytic, concerning phagocytosis.

phagocytosis, the destruction and absorption of bacteria and particles by phagocytes.

phagomania, an abnormal craving for food.

phakitis, inflammation of the crystalline lens of the eye.

phalacrous, baldness.

phalangeal, pertaining to a phalanx.

phalangitis, an inflammation of one or more digits.

phalanx, any of the bones of the fingers or toes.

phallic, pertaining to the phallus, or penis.

phallitis, an inflammation of the phallus or penis.

phallus, the penis.

phantasy, daydream; imaginary possibilities.

phantom limb, an illusion that a limb still exists after amputation.

pharmaceutical, pertaining to drugs or to a pharmacy.

pharmaceutics, the science of preparing pharmaceutical preparations.

pharmacist, one licensed to prepare, sell, or dispense drugs, and to fill prescriptions of physicians.

pharmacodynamics, the scientific study of drug actions and effects upon the body.

pharmacognosy, the branch of pharmacology concerned with natural drugs and possible medicinal substitutes.

pharmacologist, one who specializes in pharmacology.

pharmacology, the science concerned with drugs, including origin, chemistry, nature, effects, and uses of drugs.

pharmacopoeia, an authoritative book on official listings of drugs and drug standards, such as the United States Pharmacopeia.

pharmacy, the branch of health science that deals with preparation, dispensing, and proper usage of drugs; a drug store.

pharyngeal, relating to the pharnyx.

pharyngitis, inflammation of the pharyngitis.

pharyngology, the branch of medicine that studies the larynx and its diseases.

pharyngoparalysis, paralysis of the musculature of the pharynx.

pharynx, the membraneous tube that connects the mouth and the esophagus.

phase, a stage of development; a distinct stage in mitosis.

phenacaine, a crystalline compound used in its hydrochloridic form to anesthetize the eye for removal of foreign particles and to relieve discomfort of laceration in the cornea.

phenacetin, an analgesic.

phenobarbital, a white crystalline substance used as a hypnotic, sedative, and antispasmodic.

phenolphthalein, a crystalline compound used as a laxative.

phenoluria, excretion of phenols in the urine.

phenotype, the physical appearance of a person, or the traits exhibited.

phenylketonuria, see PKU.

phial, a vial; a small container for medicine.

phimosis, a narrowness of the preputial orifice that prevents the foreskin from being pushed back over the glans penis.

phlebitis, inflammation of a vein.

phlebotomist, one trained to open a vein for blood letting.

phlebotomy, the practice of opening a vein for the letting of blood in treatment of disease.

phlegm, a thick mucus which is secreted in respiratory passages.

phlegmatic, one sluggist in temperament; apathetic.

phlyctena, a tiny watery blister or pustule.

phlyctenular, resembling a pustule; pertaining to vesicles.

phlyctenule, a tiny blister or vesicle, as on the cornea or conjuctiva.

phobia, an abnormal or exaggerated fear, usually illogical.

phonation, the utterance of vocal sounds.

phonatory, pertaining to utterance of vocal sounds.

phonetics, the science of speech and the pronunciation of words.

phonic, concerning the voice, speech, or sound.

phosphatase, an enzyme which catalyzes the hydrolysis of phosphoric esters secreted by the liver and important to the metabolism of carbohydrates.

phosphocreatine, an important form of high-energy phosphate found in muscle tissue; the source of energy in muscle contraction.

phospholipid, any group of lipids that contain phosphorus, including lecithin and cephalin, found in living cells, especially nerve tissue.

photalgia, pain in the eye caused by intense light.

photic, pertaining to light.

photochemotherapy, treating with drugs that react to sunlight or ultraviolet radiation.

photodermatitis, an abnormal skin condition caused by overexposure to light, especially from the sun.

photophobia, an abnormal intolerance to light.

photopia, vision in day-light.

photopsia, an appearance of flashes of light, occurring in certain retinal, optic, or brain conditions.

photopsin, a protein found in the cones of the retina that combines with retinal to produce photochemical pigments responsible for color vision.

photoreceptor, a receptor, or a nerve end-organ that is sensitive to light.

photosensitive, an abnormal sensitivity to sunlight, occasionally seen in certain drug reactions.

phototherapy, exposure to the sun or artificial light rays in treatment of disease. Ultraviolet phototherapy is effective in preventing dangerous levels of bilirubin in low birth weight infants with increased jaundice conditions.

phrenalgia, pain in the diaphragm; melancholia.

phrenasthenia, mental deficiency, or feeblemindedness.

phrenic, pertaining to the mind or to the diaphragm.

phrenology, the study of the shape of the skull as supposedly indicative of mental powers and character.

phylaxis, the active bodily defense against infection.

physiatrics, the branch of medicine concerned with physical therapy, and use of light, heat, water, electricity, and massage in the diagnosis and treatment of disease; physiotherapy.

physic, the art of medicine and healing; a cathartic; general drugs; to purge.

physical, pertaining to the body; relating to material things; pertaining to physics.

physician, one trained and legally qualified to practice medicine after being licensed by an appropriate board; a doctor who practices medicine as distinguished from one specializing in surgery.

physics, the study of natural forces and phenomena, and properties of energy and matter.

physiognomy, the face or quality of countenance as indicative of moral or mental character; the facial expression and bodily appearance used in diagnosis.

physiological, pertaining to physiology; normal; concerning functions of the body.

physiologist, one who specializes in physiology.

physiology, the science concerned with the functions of the living organism, its organs, and its parts; the science of the functioning of all structures in the human body.

physiotherapy, the treatment of disease by physical therapy.

physique, the organization, development, and structures of a body; body build.

physostigmine, an alkaloid obtained from the Calabar bean, used as a topical myotic in glaucoma.

pial, pertaining to pia mater.

pia mater, the highly vascular membrane forming the innermost of the three coverings which envelop the brain and spinal cord. The inner coverings consist of membranes, called meninges, which are composed of three distinct layers of tissue: the dura matter, the arachnoid membrane, and the pia mater.

pica, an unnatural craving for substances that are not food such as clay, chalk, or ashes; a depraved appetite.

pigeon breast, an abnormal projection of the sternum and the area surrounding the sternum resulting in a malformation of the chest, often seen in rickets.

pigment, coloring substance in the tissues or cells.

pigmentary, concerning a pigment.

pigmentation, a deposit of coloring matter or pigments.

pigmented, colored by a deposit of pigment.

pilar, pilary, pertaining to the hair; covered with hair.

piles, hemorrhoids.

pill, medicine in a small globular or oval shaped mass to be swallowed; a tablet.

pilose, covered with hair; hairy.

pilosis, an excessive growth of hair.

pilosity, hairiness.

pimple, a tiny elevation of the skin with an inflamed base which may form pus; pustule.

pineal, pertaining to the pineal body.

pineal body, a small, cone-shaped body in the brain believed to be an endocrine organ which secretes a hormone that stimulates the adrenal cortex; pineal gland.

pink eye, acute conjunctivitis; contagious inflammation of the eyelids affecting man and some animals; a non-infectious, sporadic condition of the conjunctiva caused by irritation from various agents.

pinna, the auricle, or the external part of the ear.

pinnal, pertaining to the pinna.

pinworm, a nematoid worm which infects the intestines; formerly called oxyuris.

pisiform, resembling a pea, or pea-shaped bone of the wrist; the smallest carpal bone.

pitting, the formation of pits or depressions in the skin, as in smallpox.

pituitary, pertaining to the pituitary gland; a substance prepared from the posterior portion of animal pituitary glands used as an antidiuretic and as a vasoconstrictor; the hypophysis cerebri.

pituitary gland, a small, grayish colored, oval-shaped endocrine gland attached to the base of the brain which secretes a number of hormones that regulate many bodily processes including growth, reproduction, and metabolic activities; referred to as the ''master gland'' of the body.

pituitrin, an extract derived from posterior lobes of the pituitary glands of cattle used to stimulate contraction of blood vessels, peristalsis in intestines, and uterine contractions to facilitate labor.

pityriasis, a skin disease marked by irregular scaly patches and shedding of branlike scales, occurring in humans and some domestic animals.

PKU, phenylketonuria, a metabolic hereditary disorder resulting in faulty metabolism of phenylalanine which causes mental retardation.

placebo, an inactive preparation given merely to satisfy the patient's demand; used in experimentation and research of the effectiveness of genuine drugs in controlled studies.

placenta, the flatlike organ attached to the wall of the uterus through which the fetus receives nourishment and oxygen, and passes off metabolic waste products.

placental, pertaining to the placenta.

placentation, the formation and attachment of the placenta to the wall of the uterus; the process or events following implantation of the embryo and the development of the placenta.

placentitis, inflammation of the placenta.

plague, a widespread contagious disease with a high mortality rate; a virulent, infectious, and acutely febrile disease caused by the Pasteurella pestis bacteria, transmitted to man by fleas from rodents; bubonic plague.

planomania, pathological desire to wander and to be free of social restraints.

planta, the sole of the foot.

plantar, pertaining to the sole of the foot.

plantar wart, a painful wart occurring on the bottom of the foot.

plaque, a rounded patch on the skin or on a mucous surface; a blood platelet.

plasma, the liquid part of the blood or lymph; cell protoplasm outside the nucleus.

plasmin, a proteolytic enzyme in the blood which causes fibrin breakdown and has the ability to dissolve blood clots.

plasmolysis, the dissolution and shrinkage of cytoplasm within a living cell caused by excessive water loss by osmosis.

plaster cast, a firm dressing made of gauze and plaster of Paris which is used to immobilize an injured part of the body, as in bone fractures.

plastic, capable of building tissue; material that can be molded.

plastic surgery, surgery utilized to restore and repair external defects, malformation, injured bones, body organs, and tissue by grafts of bone or tissues.

platelet, a minute disk-shaped structure found in the blood important in clotting of the blood, and in stimulating phagocytic action of leukocytes.

platycephalic, having a wide skull with a flattened top.

platyhelminthes, a group of worms or phylum having a flattened body, including tapeworms, planarians, and flukes.

platypodia, flatfeet.

platyrrhine, having a wide nose in proportion to length.

plethora, an excess blood volume; congestion.

plethoric, pertaining to plethora.

pleura, a serous membrane lining the walls of the thorax and enclosing the lungs.

pleural, pertaining to the pleura.

pleuralgia, pain in the pleura, or in the side.

pleurectomy, surgical removal of part of the pleura.

pleurisy, inflammation of the pleura, frequently accompanied by respiratory difficulties and fever.

pleuritic, pertaining to pleurisy.

pleuropneumonia, inflammation of the pleura and of the lungs.

plexor, a small hammer with a soft rubber head used in percussion for diagnostic purposes.

plexus, a network of vessels or nerves; a complicated network of interlacing parts.

plica, a fold.

plicate, folded or braided.

plication, a process by which folds are stitched in an organ's wall to decrease its size.

plumbism, a chronic condition caused by lead poisoning.

pneumatogram, a record made by a pneumatograph.

pneumatograph, an apparatus for registering respiratory movements.

pneumatometer, an apparatus which measures the quantity of air involved in inspiration and expiration.

pneumobacillus, the bacillus Klebsiella pneumoniae which causes pneumonia.

pneumococcal, pertaining to pneumococci.

pneumococcus, bacterium Diplococcus pneumoniae which produces lobar pneumonia and various infectious diseases.

pneumoconiosis, any lung disease due to an occupation, such as by inhaling dust particles, mineral dust, or coal dust.

pneumogastric, pertaining to the lungs and the stomach; pneumogastric nerve, or vagus nerve.

pneumoencephalography, a radiographic examination of the fluid- containing structures of the brain after cerebrospinal fluid is withdrawn by a lumbar puncture and replaced by injecting air or a gas.

pneumoenteritis, inflammation of the lungs and intestine.

pneumomyelography, a radiography of the spinal canal after the withdrawal of spinal fluid and the injection of air or gas.

pneumonectomy, pneumectomy, surgical excision of part or all of a lung.

pneumonia, inflammation of the lungs caused by microbes, chemical irritants, dusts, or allergy, characterized by chills, fever, chest pain, cough, purulent sputum often spotted with blood.

pneumonic, pertaining to the lungs; having pneumonia.

pneumothorax, the presence of air or gas in the pleural space which may occur spontaneously due to trauma, or deliberately introduced in collapsing a lung.

pock, a pustule on the skin in an eruptive disease, as in smallpox.

poockmark, a depressed scar on the skin made by smallpox or other disease.

podagra, pain in the great toe caused by gout.

podalgia, pain in the feet.

podiatrist, chiropodist; one who specializes in podiatry.

podiatry, a specialized field concerned with the care or the foot, including its anatomy, medical and surgical treatment, and its diseases.

pogoniasis, an excessive growth of the beard, especially on women.

poison, an agent or substance which may cause structural damage or functional disorders when introduced into the body by ingestion, inhalation, absorption, or injection.

polio, poliomyelitis.

polioencephalitis, inflammatory lesions of the brain involving the gray matter.

poliomyelitis, a viral disease of the gray matter of the spinal cord marked by fever, sore throat, headache, vomiting, and frequently stiffness of the neck and back.

pollex, the thumb.

pollex pedis, the great toe; hallux.

pollution, the act of making foul or impure, as air, soil, or water.

polyarteritis, a condition in which the body is affected by multiple sites of inflammatory and destructive lesions in the arteries.

polyarthritis, inflammation of several joints at the same time.

polychromatic, having many colors.

polyclinic, a hospital or clinic which treats all kinds of injuries and diseases.

polycythemia, a condition in which the total cell mass of the blood is abnormally increased; excessive red blood cells; erythrocytosis.

polypolydactylism, the presence of more than normal numbers of fingers or toes.

polydipsia, abnormal thirst, or having an excessive desire to drink.

polydysplasia, abnormal development of several organs, systems, or tissues.

polyesthesia, the feeling that several points on the body were touched on application of one stimulus to a single point.

polygalactia, excessive secretion of milk.

polygenic, pertaining to the belief that humans have their origin from more than one ancestral line.

polygraph, an apparatus for recording blood pressure, pulse, respiration, and electrical resistance of the skin all at the same time; lie-detector.

polynuclear, polymorphonuclear, having many-shaped nuclei.

polyp, polypus, protruding mass of tissue growth from a mucous membrane, commonly found in the nose, uterus, and rectum; a tumor with a footlike structure.

polyphagia, excessive eating.

polyphagous, eating many different kinds of food.

polyphobia, morbid fear of many things.

polyplegia, paralysis of several muscles.

polypnea, abnormally heavy panting or breathing.

polyposis, formation of multiple polyps.

polyptome, a surgical instrument for excision of a polyp.

polyspermia, excessive secretion of seminal fluid; polyspermy.

polyspermy, the fertilization of an ovum by more than one mature male germ cell, or spermatozoon.

polythelia, the presence of more than one nipple on a mammary gland or breast.

polyunsaturated, denoting a fatty acid, or pertaining to animal or vegetable fats having more than one double bond in its hydrocarbon chain; linoleic acid.

polyvalent, multivalent, as in vaccine which has several strains of antibodies.

pons, a broad band of nerve fibers in the brain which connects the lobes of the cerebrum, medulla, and cerebellum; pons Varolio.

popliteal, pertaining to the area behind the knee; the ham.

pore, a tiny opening in skin or tissue.

porosis, the formation of cavities or pores in repair of bone fractures; callus formation in bone repair.

porosity, state of being porous.

porous, having many open spaces or pores.

porphyrin, any of a group of metal-free pyrrole derivatives, occurring in protoplasm, forming the basis of animal and plant respiratory pigments.

porphyrinemia, presence of porphyrin in the blood.

porphyrinuria, excretion of porphyrin in the urine.

portal, concerning an entrance to an organ; pertaining to the porta hepatis, or the fissure of the liver.

portal vein, the large vein which carries blood from the stomach, intestine, pancreas, and spleen to the liver.

position, a placement of the body, or a bodily posture, as in supine, prone, or standing position.

posology, the system of dosage of medicines.

postauricular, located behind the auricle of the ear.

postcibal, after eating; postprandial.

posterior, situated at the back; behind; coming after.

postmortem, subsequent to death, as an autopsy.

postnasal, occurring behind the nose, as postnasal drip.

postnatal, occurring after birth of a newborn.

postpartum, after childbirth, referring to the mother.

postprandial, after a meal; postcibal.

postulate, something taken for granted without proof; a fundamental principle.

posthumous, occurring after death, which is said of a child delivered by cesarean section after death of the mother.

postural, pertaining to or affected by posture.

posture, an attitude or carriage of the body.

potable, fit to drink.

potassium, a mineral element which is the main cation of intracellular fluid in the body. It functions with sodium and chloride to regulate osmotic pressure and acid-base balance; in combination with calcium and magnesium ions, it is essential for normal muscle excitability, especially the heart muscle; and it is necessary in the conduction of nerve impulses.

potassium permanganate, a dark crystalline compound used as a topical anti-infective, an astrigent, and oxidizing agent.

potency, the quality of being strong or potent; ability to perform coitus; strength.

potion, a dose of liquid medicine.

Pott's disease, caries of the vertebrae caused by tubercular infection resulting in the destruction and compression of vertebrae marked by curvature of the spine.

pouch, a pocket-like space or sac.

poultice, a soft, moist dressing made of hot linseed, bread, mustard, or soap and oil which is applied to the skin to relieve inflammation, and to hasten the excretion of pus.

pox, an eruptive or pustular disease, usually caused by a virus, such as chicken pox.

practical nurse, a nurse who is not a graduate registered nurse but who has sufficient professional training and skills to provide care for the ill.

practitioner, one who practices medicine; physician.

preanesthetic, a drug given to ease the induction of a general anesthetic.

precancerous, preceding the development of a carcinoma.

precipitant, an agent that causes precipitation.

precipitation, the process by which a substance is made to separate from another in a solution and settle in solid particles to the bottom.

precipitin, an antibody formed in the blood that causes certain proteins to precipitate when it unites with its antigen.

precocious, exhibiting mature mental development at an unusually early age.

preconscious, in reference to thoughts that are not in immediate awareness but that may readily be recalled.

precursor, something that precedes.

predigestion, a partial digestion of food by artificial means to make it more readily digestible.

predisposition, having a tendency to develop certain diseases, acquired or hereditary.

pregnable, vulnerable.

pregnancy, state of being pregnant.

prpegnant, being with child; the condition of having a developing fetus in the womb.

prehensile, adapted for grasping or seizing.

prehension, the act of graspping.

premature, happening before the proper time, as a premature infant.

premaxilla, the incisive bone.

premaxillary, situated in front of the maxilla, or upper jaw.

premedical, pertaining to preparatory professional studies in medicine.

premedication, preliminary medication which produces narcosis prior to administering general anesthesia.

premolar, in front of a molar tooth, or teeth.

premorbid, occurring before the development of a disease.

prenatal, previous to birth.

preoperative, preceding an operation or surgery.

prepuce, foreskin.

preputium, pertaining to the prepuce.

presbyatrics, geriatrics.

presbyopia, defect of vision involving loss of accommodation in which near objects are seen less distinctly than those at a distance, occurring in advancing age.

presbyopic, pertaining to presbyopia.

prescription, a written order for dispensing medication which is signed by a physician.

presenile, resembling senility but occurring in early or middle life.

presentation, in obstetrics, the manner in which the fetus is presenting itself at the mouth of the uterus and which can be determined by the examining finger, such as breech, cephalic, or scapula.

pressor, stimulating or increasing the activity of a function, as a nerve or an elevation of blood pressure.

pressure sore, bed sore; decubitus ulcer.

presystole, the period of time before the systole of the heart beat.

preventive, pertaining to a vaccine or medicine that wards off disease; prophylactic.

prickly heat, a noncontagious eruption of the skin causing red pimples that itch and tingle, usually in hot weather.

primary lesion, an original lesion from which a second one develops.

primary sore, the initial sore or hard chancre of syphilis.

primipara, a woman who has given birth to her first child, or who is parturient for the first time.

primiparity, the condition of having given birth to only one child.

probang, a flexible slender rod with a ball, sponge, or tuft at one end used to remove matter from the esophagus or larynx or to apply medicine.

probe, a slender instrument for exploring wounds, body cavities, or passages.

procaine, a compound which uses hydrochloride salt in solution for a local anesthetic as a nerve block, and for spinal anesthesia.

process, a bony prominence or protuberance; a series of steps or events leading to a specific result.

procreant, pertaining to procreation.

procreate, to beget; to reproduce.

procreation, the act of producing offspring; reproduction.

proctalgia, pain in the anus or rectum.

proctectomy, surgical removal of the anus or rectum.

proctology, the branch of medicine dealing with rectal and anal disorders.

proctoplasty, plastic repair of the anus or rectum.

proctoscope, an instrument with illumination for inspecting the interior of the rectum.

proctoscopy, an examination of the lower intestine with a proctoscope.

proctostomy, surgical creation of an artificial opening into the rectum.

prodrome, a symptom which indicates an approaching disease.

professional nurse, one who is licensed by the state board of examiners, and who works with doctors in a hospital or various other settings. The professional nurse plays an important role as a member of a treatment or surgical team.

progeria, premature senility usually occurring in childhood, marked by wrinkled skin, baldness, and hardened arteries.

progestational, referring to changes in the uterus when the corpus luteum is preparing the endometrium for the fertilization and growth of the ovum.

progesterone, progestin, the hormone excreted by the corpus luteum which prepares the uterus for reception and development of the fertilized ovum. Some synthetic and natural agents are called progestins and are used in treatment of menstrual disorders.

prognathous, marked by jaws which project forward beyond the face.

prognosis, a prediction of the probable course and outcome of a disease.

prognostic, pertaining to prognosis.

progressive, advancing forward; gradually increasing in severity of symptoms.

prolactin, a hormone that stimulates lactation.

prolamin, any of a group of simple proteins found in the seeds of grain such as wheat or oats.

prolan, a hormone present in the urine of pregnant women which allows early diagnosis of pregnancy.

prolapse, falling down, or downward displacement of a part or an organ.

proliferation, the rapid growth and reproduction of similar forms, as cells.

proline, an amino acid made in the body necessary to protein synthesis which is a basic constituent of collagen.

promazine, a phenothiazine used in the form of hydrochloride salt as a major tranquilizer in psychomotor states of anxiety and agitation.

promontory, a projecting bodily protuberance.

pronation, the act of lying with the face downward, or in a prone position; the position of turning the hand so that the palm faces downward.

pronotor, a muscle of the forearm that pronates the palm.

prone, lying with the face downward and lying horizontally.

propagation, reproduction.

prophage, an intracellular lysogenic bacterial virus that provides protection to its host from active viruses.

prophase, the first stage in cell reduplication in mitosis.

prophylactic, an agent that wards off disease; pertaining to prophylaxis.

prophylaxis, a preventive measure or treatment; the prevention of disease.

proprietary, a medicine protected against free competition by a trademark or patent.

proprioceptor, a sensory nerve ending originating chiefly in muscles, tendons, and the labyrinth that are concerned with movements and position of the body.

protosis, a bulging of the eyes; a forward displacement of an organ.

propulsion, a tendency for the body to bend forward while walking, characteristic in paralysis agitans; festination.

prosection, a programmed dissection for the purpose of demonstration of the anatomic structures of cadavers.

prosencephalon, forebrain.

prosopoplegia, facial paralysis.

prostatalgia, pain in the prostate gland.

prostate gland, a gland that surrounds the male urethra at the neck of the bladder and which contributes to the secretion of semen.

prostatic, pertaining to the prostate gland.

prostatitis, inflammation of the prostate gland.

prostatocystotomy, incision of the bladder and prostate.

prostatomegaly, an enlargement of the prostate gland.

prostatovesiculectomy, surgical excision of the prostate gland and seminal vesicles.

prosthesis, an artificial part substituted for a missing part of the body, such as an arm or leg.

prosthodontics, the branch of medicine which constructs artificial teeth or oral structures to replace missing or injured parts; prosthodontia.

prosthodontist, one trained in prosthodontics.

prostrate, lying with the body extended; to exhaust.

prostration, extreme exhaustion, or lack of energy.

protamine, basic proteins found in the sperm of some fish used as an antidote to heparin overdosage.

protanopia, inability to distinguish reds and greens; red blindness.

protease, any proteolytic enzyme that assists in hydrolysis of peptide linkages in the digestive action on proteins; peptidase.

protein, found in all cells, and constitutes about 15% of human body weight; any of a group of complex organic compounds that contain carbon, hydrogen, oxygen, nitrogen, and sulfur.

proteinase, any enzyme that hydrolyzes proteins, as pepsin and rennin.

proteinic, pertaining to protein.

proteinuria, an excess accumulation of serum proteins in the urine.

proteolysis, the hydrolysis of protein into simpler compounds such as polypeptides.

proteolytic, pertaining to proteolysis.

proteose, a class of compounds produced by partial degradation of proteins by hydrolysis.

prothrombin, a complex globulin protein in the blood important to coagulation.

protodiastole, pertaining to the first of four phases of ventricular diastole.

protopathic, responding solely to gross stimuli such as pain.

protoplasm, the primary living matter which composes all vegetable and animal cells and tissues.

protoplasmic, pertaining to protoplasm.

protozoan, a microscopic, one-celled organism.

protozoology, the science of protozoans, a division of zoology.

proud, flesh, pertaining to flesh which is characterized by an excessive granulation in wounds and ulcers.

provitamin, a substance such as ergosterol that can form a vitamin when acted upon by the body.

proximal, nearest to the point of reference.

pruritogenic, causing itching or pruritus.

pruritus, an intense, chronic itching, as in the anal region.

pseudesthesia, a subjective sensation which occurs without an appropriate stimulus, such as a pain felt in an amputated limb.

pseudocyesis, false pregnancy.

pseudoplegia, paralysis due to hysteria.

pseudopregnancy, a condition in which all symptoms of pregnancy appear to be present but without being substantiated; false pregnancy; pseudocyesis.

psilocybin, a hallucinogen derived from the mushroom Psilocybe mexicana.

psittacosis, an infectious viral disease occurring in birds that may be transmitted to humans that causes pulmonary disorders, chills followed by fever, headache, nausea, constipation, and epistaxis; parrot fever.

psoriasis, a chronic skin disease of various characteristics such as the formation of red scaly patches or flat-topped papules that cause itching.

psychasthenia, an emotional disoroder marked by obsessions, compulsions, anxiety, doubts, feelings of inadequacy, and phobias.

psyche, the mind and all its mental processes both conscious and subconscious.

psychedelic, pertaining to any of several drugs that induce hallucinations, intensification of perception of the senses, psychotic states, and heightened awareness. The most commonly used psychedelics are LSD, marijuana, mescaline, psilocybin, and morning-glory seeds.

psychiatric, pertaining to psychiatry.

psychiatrist, a physician who specializes in the treatment of mental disorders, or psychiatry.

psychiatry, the medical science concerned with the origin, diagnosis, treatment and prevention of mental illness.

psychic, pertaining to the mind.

psychoanalysis, a psychologic method or theory of human development and behavior originated by Sigmund Freud that provides a system of psychotherapy which analyzes the subconscious thoughts in order to determine and eliminate physical and mental disorders.

psychoanalyst, a psychiatrist who has training in psychoanalysis.

psychoanalytic, pertaining to psychoanalysis.

psychobiology, the science concerned with the interaction between the mind and body as being an integrated unit in the formation and functioning of the personality.

psychodrama, a technique of group psychotherapy in which individuals dramatize roles enabling them to increase awareness of their emotional problems.

psychodramatic, pertaining to psychodrama.

psychodynamics, a systemized theory of human behavior and the role of unconscious motivation.

psychogenesis, the origin and development of the mind; the causation of a symptom or illness by mental or psychic factors as opposed to organic ones.

psychogenetic, pertaining to a disease which has its origin in the mind.

psychogenic, of mental origin; having a psychological origin.

psychokinesis, the alteration of motion directed by thought processes.

psycholepsy, sudden alteration of moods.

psychological, pertaining to the study of the mind.

psychologist, one who specializes in psychology.

psychology, the science concerned with mental processes and the behavior in man and animals.

psychometry, the science dealing in testing and measuring psychologic ability, efficiency, potential, and functioning.

psychomotor, pertaining to motor effects of the cerebral or psychologic functioning; causing voluntary movement.

psychoneurosis, a neurosis of a functional nature characterized by anxiety, phobias, compulsions, obsessions, and physical complaints without physical cause; neurosis.

psychoneurotic, one suffering from psychoneurosis.

psychoparesis, weakness of the mind.

psychopath, one lacking moral sensibility, but possessing normal intelligence; a mentally unstable person.

psychopathic, pertaining to a mental disorder; relating to treatment of mental disorders; abnormal.

psychopathology, the study of the causes and processes of mental disease or abnormal behavior.

psychopathy, any mental disease, especially one characterized by a defective personality.

psychopharmacology, the science of drugs as they relate to mental and behavioral effects on emotional states; the use of drugs to modify psychological symptoms.

psychophysics, the study of mental processes in relation to physical processes; the study of the relation between stimuli and the effects they produce.

psychophysiology, the physiology of the mind; the correlation between the body and mind.

phychosis, a major mental disorder of organic or emotional origin, often characterized by regressive behavior, inappropriate mood, lack of impulse control, delusions, hallucinations, loss of contact with reality, and a disintegration of personality.

psychosomatic, referring to illnesses in which bodily symptoms are of mental or emotional manifestation.

psychosomatic medicine, the branch of medical science emphasizing mental factors as the cause of functional and structural changes in disease processes.

psychosurgery, surgery of the brain to relieve certain symptoms in mental illness, as a lobotomy.

psychotherapeutic, pertaining to psychotherapy.

psychotherapist, one trained in psychotherapy.

psychotherapy, a treatment or method based primarily upon the verbal and nonverbal aspects of communication with a patient, as distinguished from the use of drugs or other measures of treatment.

psychotic, pertaining to psychosis; one exhibiting psychosis.

psychotropic, a term applied to drugs that have a special action upon the mind or psyche.

psychrophobia, an abnormal fear or sensitivity to cold.

psychrotherapy, treatment of disease by application of cold.

ptamic, that which causes sneezing.

ptarmus, spasmodic sneezing.

pterygoid, shaped like a wing; pertaining to the two large processes of the sphenoid at the base of the skull.

ptilosis, the loss of eyelashes.

ptomaine, any of a class of nitrogenous organic bases which become toxic resulting from the action of putrefactive bacteria produced in animal and vegetable matter.

ptosis, a drooping of the upper eyelid caused by paralysis of the levator muscle; the prolapse of any organ of the body.

ptotic, pertaining to ptosis.

ptyalism, excessive secretion of saliva; salivation.

ptyaloith, a salivary concretion or stone.

puberal, concerning puberty.

puberty, the period in life during which the secondary sex characteristics begin to develop and either sex becomes capable of sexual reproduction.

pubes, the pubic region; the anterior region of the innominate bone covered with pubic hair; os pubis.

pubescence, one arriving at puberty; the covering of fine hair on the body.

pubescent, reaching puberty.

pubic, pertaining to the pubes.

pubis, pubic bone, or the innominate bone.

pudendal, relating to the external female genitalia, or genitals. pudendum, external female genitals; vulva.

puerile, childlike.

puerilism, childish behavior exhibited by an adult; immature behavior.

puerperal, pertaining to puerperium.

puerperal fever, septicema following childbirth.

puerperium, the state of a woman immediately following childbirth, usually a period of 3 to 6 weeks.

pulmometry, determination of the capacity of the lungs with a pulmometer.

pulmonary, pertaining to the lungs.

pulmonary artery, an artery which conveys venous blood directly from the heart to the lungs.

pulmonary vein, any of four veins conveying oxygenated blood directly from the lungs to the heart.

pulmonectomy, surgical removal of part or all of a lung's tissue; pneumonectomy.

pulmonic, pertaining to the lungs.

pulmonitis, inflammation of the lung; pneumonia.

pulmotor, a mechanical apparatus for inducing artificial respiration by forcing oxygen into the lungs or to expel the lung contents, as in asphyxiation or drowning.

pulp, the soft part of an organ; referring to dental pulp in the interior of a tooth.

pulpy, resembling pulp.

pulsation, the process of rhythmic beat, as in the heart and blood vessels; pulse.

pulse, the rate or rhythm of the heart contractions causing the arteries to contract and expand at regularly throbbing intervals; the pulsation of the radial artery at the wrist.

pulsimeter, an instrument for measuring the frequency and force of a pulse; sphygmometer.

pulverization, the crushing of any substance into tiny particles. pulverulent, resembling powder; fine powder; dusty.

pulvis, a powder.

pump, an apparatus used to transfer or to remove fluids or gases by suction or pressure.

puncture, a hole or wound made by a sharp pointed device; to make a hole with a pointed instrument.

pupil, the round contractile orifice or opening at the center of the iris.

pupillary, concerning the pupil of the eye.

purgative, a substance that evacuates the bowels; a cathartic.

purge, a drug that causes evacuation of the bowels; to evacuate the bowels by means of a purgative.

purpura, a condition of the skin marked by purple or livid spots caused by tiny hemorrhages that invade the tissues.

purpuric, pertaining to purpura.

purulent, consisting of matter or pus; resembling pus.

pus, a yellowish-white product of inflammation composed of a thin albuminous fluid and leukocytes or particles of their remains.

pustulant, causing pustules or blisters; a pustulant medication or agent.

pustular, pertaining to or having the nature of a pustule; covered with pustules.

pustulation, the formation of pustules.

pustule, a small, elevated pus-containing lesion of the skin; any circumscribed, flat, or rounded protruberance found on the skin resembling a pimple or blister with an inflamed base and containing pus.

putrefaction, the process of putrefying; the enzymatic decomposition of animal or vegetable matter, producing a foul- smelling compound.

putrefy, to undergo putrefaction.

putrescence, the process of undergoing putrefaction; becoming putrid.

putrescine, a polyamine found in decaying meat products.

putrid, decayed or rotten; putrefied.

pyelitis, inflammation of the renal pelvis.

pyelocystitis, inflammation of the renal pelvis and the bladder.

pyelogram, the x-ray film produced by pyelography.

pyelography, a radiography of the kidneys and ureter after an injection of a contrast solution or dye.

pyelonephritis, inflammation of the whole kidney due to a bacterial infection.

pyelonephrosis, any disease of the kidney and its pelvis.

pyelotomy, surgical incision of the kidney.

pyemia, septicemia or blood poisoning caused by pyogenic bacteria.

pyknic, having a shorot, thick, and stocky body build.

pyknometer, an apparatus for determining the specific gravity of fluids.

pylephlebitis, inflammation of the portal vein.

pylic, pertaining to the portal vein.

pyloric, pertaining to the pylorus.

pylorus, the opening between the stomach and the duodenum; used to refer to the pyloric part of the stomach.

pyoderma, any purulent disease of the skin.

pyogenic, producing pus; pertaining to the formation of pus.

pyorrhea, a bacterial gum infection with a copious discharge of pus.

pyostatic, a drug that arrests suppuration.

pyothorax, an accumulation of pus in the pleural cavity; empyema.

pyramidal, pertaining to drugs which have an accumulative effect; resembling a pyramid; see extrapyramidal.

pyretic, pertaining to fever.

pyrexia, a fever; a febrile condition.

Pyridium, a brick-red powder used to treat infections of the genitourinary tract; trademark for phenazopyridine hydrochloride.

pyridoxine, one of the forms of Vitamine B6 used in its salt form to treat a deficiency of B6 in the body; sometimes used in treatment of myasthenia gravis.

pyromania, an obsessive preoccupation with fires or the compulsion to set them.

pyrosis, heartburn.

pyrotic, caustic; burning.

pyuria, the presence of pus in the urine.

Q

Q-fever, an acute infectious disease marked by fever, headache, muscular pains, chills, and loss of appetite, caused by rickettsia and transmitted by inhaling infected dust or drinking contaminated milk. Common among those who handle hides and animal products; Queensland fever.

q-sort, an assessment of personality in which the subject (or one who observes) indicates the degree to which a standardized set of descriptive statements are representative of the subject.

quack, one who pretends to have experience in medicine, as in diagnosis and treatment of disease; charlatan.

quackery, the methods used by a quack.

quadrant, a fourth of a circle; the four regions of the abdomen which are divided for diagnostic purposes.

quadriceps, having four heads, as in the large quadriceps muscle in front of the thigh.

quadripara, a woman who has produced four viable offspring.

quadripartite, having four parts.

quadriplegia, paralysis affecting all four limbs.

quadroon, the offspring of a white person and a mulatto; an individual having one-quarter Negro heritage.

quadruplet, being one of four children born to the same mother and of one birth.

quarantine, a period of detention or isolation to prevent the spread of a communicable disease.

quartan, recurring every fourth day, as in quartan fever.

Queensland fever, see Q-fever.

quenching, to suppress or extinguish by immersing in water.

querulent, fretful or complaining.

quickening, the first noticeable movement of the fetus in utero.

quinidine, a crystalline alkaloid isomer of quinine used to treat abnormal cardiac arrythmias.

quinine, a bitter-tasting alkaloid; obtained from the bark of cinchona trees, used in its salt form to treat malaria; quinine is used as an analgesic, antipyretic, oxytocic, cardiac depressant, and for other various treatments.

quinsy, an inflammation of the tonsils and the formation of abscess of the peritonsillar tissue.

quintipara, a woman who has had five viable offspring.

quintuplet, one of five offspring produced at one labor.

quotidian, occurring daily; recurring daily fever.

quotient, a number derived at by division.

Q-wave, a downward wave of an electrocardiogram that is associated with the contractions of the heart ventricles.

R

rabbetting, interlocking of the splintered edges of a bone fracture.

rabbit fever, Tularemia.

rabic, pertaining to rabies.

rabid, being affected with rabies; relating to rabies.

rabies, an acute viral disease that produces infection of the central nervous system marked by paralysis of the muscle of deglutition, glottal spasm, manic behavior, convulsions, tetany, and respiratory paralysis. May be communicated by a bite of a rabid animal, often fatal to man without proper treatment.

racemose, resembling a cluster or bunch of follicles which are divided and subdivided, as in a gland.

rachialgia, pain in the spine.

rachianesthesia, spinal anesthesia.

rachicentesis, lumbar puncture to determine the pressure of fluid and to obtain fluid for examination.

rachidial, rachidian, pertaining to the spinal column.

rachigraph, a device that outlines the curves of the spine.

rachiometer, a device that measures spinal curvatures.

rachiopathy, any disease of the spine.

rachioplegia, spinal paralysis.

rachiotome, an instrument used to divide the vertebrae.

rachiotomy, surgical incision of the vertebral column.

rachis, vertebral or spinal column.

rachitis, rickets.

radectomy, surgical excision of the root of a tooth.

radial, pertaining to the radius bone of the arm.

radiate, to spread from a common center.

radiation, emission of rays from a central point; a treatment for certain disease using a radioactive substance.

radiation syndrome, an illness due to exposure of a body part to ionizing radiations from radioactive substances marked by anorexia, headache, nausea, vomiting, and diarrhea.

radical, directed to the origin to eliminate the cause of a disease; treatment by surgical excision, usually by the total eradication of diseased tissues.

radicle, the smallest branches of a nerve or blood and lymph vessels.

radicular, pertaining to a root or radicle.

radiculitis, inflammation of the spinal nerve roots.

radioactive, pertaining to radioactivity.

radioactivity, the ability of a substance to emit alpha rays, beta rays, and gamma rays that undergo spontaneous disintegration.

radiobiologist, a specialist in radiobiology.

radiobiology, the scientific study concerned with the effects of radiant energy or radioactive material on living tissue or organisms.

radiocystitis, inflammation of the bladder following roentgen rays or radium treatment.

radiodermatitis, inflammation of the skin caused by roentgen rays or radium treatment.

radiodiagnosis, the use of x-ray in diagnosis.

radioelement, an element possessing radioactive power.

radiograph, a film produced by radiography.

radiography, the production of film records of internal structures of the body for diagnostic purposes; roentgenography.

radioisotopes, radioactive forms of chemicals used in research and in the diagnosis and treatment of certain diseases; radioactive isotopes.

radiologist, one specializing in radiology.

radiology, the branch of science concerned with roentgen rays, radium rays, and other forms of radiation and their medical uses; the process of photographing organs or bones for diagnostic purposes.

radiolucency, the quality of being partly or wholly permeable to radiant energy.

radionecrosis, disintegration of tissue exposed to radium or x-rays.

radioneuritis, neuritis caused by exposure to radiant energy.

radioresistance, resistance to radiation by certain tumors or tissues.

radiosensitive, the ability to be destroyed by radiation, as a tumor by x-rays.

radiosurgery, the use of high-energy radioactive particles in treating cancer or other diseased tissues.

radiotherapist, one who specializes in radiotherapy.

radiotherapy, treatment of disease by radioactive elements such as radium or thorium.

radiothermy, short-wave diathermy.

radioulnar, pertaining to the radius and ulna.

radium, a radioactive element found in minerals used in radiography for treating cancer.

radius, a bone in the forearm on the thumb side; a line from the center of a circle to a point on its circumference.

radix, root, as of a spinal or cranial nerve.

rage, being violently angry.

ragocyte, a cell often found in the joints of one suffering from rheumatoid arthritis.

rale, an abnormal respiratory sound heard on auscultation indicating a pathologic condition; death rattle.

ramification, a branching.

ramiform, branchlike; having the form of a branch; ramal.

ramose, having many branches.

ramulose, having many tiny branches.

ramus, a branch of an artery, nerve, or vein.

ranula, a tumor or cyst beneath the tongue, caused by obstruction and subsequent swelling of a glandular duct.

ranular, pertaining to a ranula.

rape, sexual intercourse with a female without her consent; stupration.

raphe, the line of union or seam of the two symmetrical parts or halves of an organ.

rarefaction, a condition of becoming less dense.

rash, a temporary eruption on the skin which may be in the form of red spots or patches.

raspatory, a file or rasp used in surgery.

ratbite fever, an infectious disease transmitted to humans by the bite of an infected rat, marked by recurring fever, skin eruptions, and muscular pain; sodoky.

ratio, proportion.

ration, a fixed allowance of food and drink for a certain period of time.

rational, having a sound mind; logical or reasonable; sane.

rauwolfia, any group of trees or shrubs from the genus Rauwolfia from which numerous alkaloids are derived for medicine, such as reserpine which is used as an antihypertensive and sedative.

rave, irrational verbalization; to talk irrationally, as in delirium; to be furious or raging.

reaction, a response of an organism to a stimulus; counterreaction; the specific effect caused by the action of chemical agents; a chemical transformation of one substance into another substance; the emotional state that is manifested in a particular situation.

reaction formation, a defense mechanism by which a person assumes an attitude or behavior that is the opposite of the impulse harbored, usually operating unconsciously.

reactivation, the act of causing something to become active again, especially the reactivating of an immune serum which has lost its potency.

reactive, the ability to respond to a stimulus.

reagent, a substance used to produce a chemical reaction in order to detect, measure, or produce other substances.

reagin, an antibody.

recall, to remember; the act of bringing a memory into consciousness.

rebound, the act of rebounding; resilience.

receptor, the ending of an afferent neuron that is sensitive to stimuli.

recess, a small cavity or indentation.

recessive, a tendency to recede; a hidden trait or recessive character, as opposed to a dominant character.

recidivation, recurrence of a disease; relapse; the repetition of a crime or offense.

recidivist, one who tends to relapse or return to crime; a mentally ill patient who has repeated relapses.

recipe, a prescription of a physician.

recrement, secretions, such as saliva, which are reabsorbed into the blood stream.

recrudescence, the recurrence of disease after abatement or remission.

rectal, pertaining to the rectum.

rectalgia, proctalgia; pain in the rectum.

rectectomy, surgical excision of the rectum or anus; proctectomy.

rectitis, an inflammation of the rectum; proctitis.

rectocele, the protrusion of the posterior wall of the vagina with the anterior wall of the rectum into the vagina.

rectocolitis, inflammation of the rectum and colon.

rectoscope, proctoscope.

rectostenosis, a narrowing or stricture of the rectum.

rectum, the lower portion of the large intestine between the sigmoid flexure and the anal canal.

rectus, any straight muscle.

recumbent, lying down or reclining position.

recuperate, to be restored to normal health; to recover.

recuperation, the restoration to normal health.

recurrence, the return of symptoms of an illness or disease.

recurrent, returning at intervals, as a fever; relapse.

red blood cell, a blood corpuscle containing hemoglobin; erythrocyte.

reduce, to restore to a normal place, as the ends of a fractured bone; to lose weight.

reduction, the process of restoring a dislocated bone to its normal place.

reflector, an apparatus which reflects light or sound waves.

reflex, a reflected action, or an involuntary response to a stimulus, such as a movement.

reflex arc, impulses which travel from receptors to effectors between the point of stimulation and the responding organ in a reflex action; neural pathway.

reflexogenic, producing or causing a reflex action.

reflexograph, an instrument for charting a reflex.

reflexophil, characterized by exaggerated reflex activity.

reflux, a backward flow; regurgitation.

refraction, the bending of a light ray as it passes from a medium of one density to another of different density.

refractory, stubborn or obstinate; resistant to ordinary treatment, as in some diseases; resisting stimulation.

regeneration, regrowth, repair, or restoration of part of the body or of damaged tissues.

regimen, a method of therapy to improve or restore health.

region, a particular division or area of the body.

regional, pertaining to particular regions or areas of the body.

registered nurse, a professional nurse who receives a license to practice nursing after completing a training period of 3-5 years depending on the school of nursing and passing an examination by a state or provincial board of examiners. Specialization usually requires a master's degree which prepares a nurse for teaching, supervision, or administration.

regression, reverting to an earlier or more infantile pattern of behavior; returning to a prior status in physical or mental illness.

regurgitate, to pour forth; to vomit.

regurgitation, the act of regurgitating; a backflow of blood through a defective valve of the heart.

rehabilitation, the process of restoring to health or activity, as one physically handicapped.

rehalation, a rebreathing process sometimes employed in anesthesia.

rehydration, replacement of the water or fluid content to a body or a substance that has undergone dehydration.

reimplantation, replacement of a structure or tissue in the original site from which it was previously lost.

reinfection, a recurrence of an infection by the same agent or bacteria.

reinforcement, strengthening; in behavioral science, the presentation of a stimulus (either a reward or punishment) which elicits a response.

reinforcer, that which produces reinforcement, such as a stimulus.

reinoculation, a repeated inoculation with the same organism.

relapse, recurrence of an illness or disease; to slip or slide back.

relapsing fever, a tropical disease resulting from spirochetal infections transmitted by head lice, body lice, and ticks marked by intermittent attacks of high fever.

relaxant, an agent that relaxes tension, especially in muscles.

relaxation, a reduction of tension; the act of relaxing.

relief, the removal of distressing or painful symptoms.

REM, rapid eye movements, the dream phase during the sleep cycle.

remediable, capable of being remedied.

remedial, curative; intended to improve certain skills.

remedy, anything that cures a disease or illness; a curative medication, application, or treatment; to restore to the natural state or condition.

remission, an abatement of symptoms of a disease or pain.

remit, to abate or relax.

remittent, a temporary easing; having periods of abatement and returning.

renal, pertaining to the kidneys.

reniform, having a kidney-shaped form or structure.

renin, a proteolytic enzyme secreted by the juxtaglomerular cells of the kidney, which is a powerful vasoconstrictor.

renopathy, any disease of the kidney.

reposit, to replace surgically.

repositor, an instrument used in surgery to return a displaced organ to its original position.

repress, to reject or force out of consciousness, as impulses or fears.

repressed, affected by repression; marked by repression.

repression, the act of repressing, restraining, or inhibiting; a defense mechanism in which one banishes unacceptable ideas or impulses from conscious awareness.

resect, to surgically excise a portion of an organ or a structure.

resection, surgical excision of a segment of a structure or a portion of an organ.

reserpine, an alkaloid of rauwolfia which acts centrally on the vasomotor center to decrease peripheral vasoconstriction, used as an antihypertensive and as a tranquilizer for extremely agitated patients.

residual, pertaining to that which is left as a residue; that which remains behind; an aftereffect of experience which influences later behavior.

residue, remainder; that which remains after removal of another substance.

resilience, having the quality to bounce back; elasticity; flexibility.

resilient, elastic; rebounding; coming back to original shape.

resolution, disappearance of a disease, inflammation, or tumor.

resolve, to return to normal.

resolvent, an agent that causes dispersion of inflammation.

resonance, the act of resounding; the sound produced by tapping the chest or by percussion of a body cavity.

resonant, pertaining to resonance.

respiration, the act of respiring; breathing; inspiration and expiration in exchange of oxygen and carbon dioxide.

respirator, a mechanical apparatus used to aid breathing; a device for giving artificial respiration or promoting pulmonary ventilation.

respiratory, pertaining to respiration.

respiratory system, includes the lungs, pleura, bronchi, pharynx, larynx, tonsils, and the nose.

respirometer, a device that determines the nature of respiration.

response, a reaction resulting from a stimulus.

rest, refreshing repose of the body due to sleep; the freedom from activity or bodily exertion; a remnant of embryonic tissue that persists in the adult organism.

restiform, twisted or shaped like a rope.

restitution, returning to an original position or to a former state; the spontaneous turning of the fetal head either to the left or right after it has extended through the vagina.

restorative, causing a return to health or to consciousness; a remedy or substance that is effective in the regaining of health or strength.

restore, to bring back to health, or consciousness.

restraint, to forcibly control; state of being hindered.

resuscitate, to restore life to one apparently dead.

resuscitation, the process of restoring life to one who has stopped breathing; the act of bringing one back to full consciousness. CPR or cardiopulmonary resuscitation, in which the heart and lung action is reestablished after cardiac arrest or apparent death or loss of consciousness resulting from electric shock, drowning, respiratory obstruction, and various other causes. The two important components of CPR are artificial ventilation and cardiac massage.

resuscitator, one who initiates resuscitation; a device used for producing respiration in persons who have stopped breathing.

retardation, delayed development; subnormal general intellectual and physical activity due to impairment of social adjustment or of maturation, or both; mental retardation.

retarded, one who exhibits retardation.

retch, to strain, as in vomiting.

retching, an involuntary effort to vomit.

rete, a network of blood vessels.

retention, the process of holding back or retaining in the body materials which are normally excreted, such as urine.

retial, pertaining to a rete.

reticular, having a netlike structure; resembling a net.

reticulation, formation of a network.

reticulocyte, an immature red blood corpuscle containing a network of granules; a young erythrocyte or red blood cell.

reticulocytosis, an excessive amount of reticulocytes in the peripheral blood.

reticulum, a small network of protoplasmic cells or structures.

retiform, reticular.

retina, the innermost coat of the eyeball which receives images formed by the lens, and transmits these images to the brain by the optic nerve.

retinal, pertaining to the retina.

retinene, an orange-yellow pigment formed in the retina resulting from the action of light on rhodopsin (visual purple pigment) used in dark adaptation.

retinitis, inflammation of the retina.

retinoscope, an apparatus used for measuring refractory errors.

retinoscopy, an examination of the retina to determine refractory errors.

retinosis, any nonflammatory, degenerative condition of the retina.

retractile, able to be drawn back.

retractility, the capability of retraction.

retraction, drawing back; the condition of being drawn back.

retractor, an instrument for holding open the edges of a wound; a muscle that retracts.

retral, posterior; at the back.

retrobuccal, pertaining to the back part of the mouth.

retrocedent, returning or going backward.

retroflex, to bend backward.

retroflexion, a bending backward of an organ.

retrograde, going backward; decline or deterioration; catabolic.

retrogress, to revert.

retrogression, return to an earlier and less complex state; degeneration; decline or deterioration.

retrogressive, degenerative changes; changes to a lower complexity, such as atrophy, degeneration, or necrosis.

retroinfection, the infection of a mother communicated by the fetus in the uterus.

retrolental, behind the lens of the eye.

retrolingual, behind the tongue.

retromammary gland, behind the mammary gland.

retromandibular, behind the lower jaw.

retromastoid, behind the mastoid process.

retronasal, concerning the back of the nose.

retroocular, behind the eye.

retroparotid, behind the parotid gland.

retroperitoneal, behind the peritoneum.

retroperitoneum, the space behind the peritoneum.

retroperitonitis, inflammation of the retroperitoneal space.

retropharyngeal, behind the pharynx.

retropharyngitis, inflammation of the posterior region of the pharynx.

retroplasia, degeneration of tissues into a more primitive structure.

restrospect, to reflect, or look back in thought.

retrospection, by thought, to look back into the past; a survey of past experiences.

retrospective falsification, an unconscious distortion of past experiences to conform to the emotional needs of the present.

retrosternal, behind the sternum.

retrovaccination, vaccination with a virus obtained from a calf inoculated with a smallpox virus which was first obtained from a human.

retroversion, a state of being turned back; bending backward, as part of an organ, especially the uterus.

reversion, return to a previously existing form or condition; the expression of traits possessed by a remote ancestor; atavism.

revulsion, the act of drawing blood from one part of the body to another in diverting disease; counterirritant.

revulsive, an agent causing revulsion; a counterirritant.

rhagades, painful fissures appearing at the corner of the mouth or anus, caused by movement or infection.

rhegma, a rupture, or fracture.

rheum, a catarrhal or watery discharge.

rheumatic, pertaining to rheumatism.

rheumatic fever, a systemic inflammatory disease which varies in severity, duration, and frequently followed by heart disease, usually occurring in young adults or children.

rheumatism, pain, swelling, and deformity of joints causing stiffness, or limitation of motion.

rheumatoid, resembling rheumatism.

rheumatoid arthritis, an inflammation of the joints causing stiffness, swelling, pain, and cartilaginous hypertrophy.

rheumic, pertaining to rheum.

rhexis, the rupture of a blood vessel, or an organ.

Rh factor, Rhesus factor, first detected in the blood of Rhesus monkeys; inherited antigens in red blood cells of most humans who have a Rh positive blood type and, due to a blood transfusion or pregnancy, are capable of destroying red blood cells in one who is typed Rh negative, such as a newborn infant.

rhinal, pertaining to the nose; nasal.

rhinalgia, pain in the nose; nasal neuralgia.

rhinencephalon, the portion of the brain concerned with olfactory impulses.

rhinitis, inflammation of the nasal mucous membranes.

rhinolaryngology, the branch of science concerned with the structures and diseases of the nose and larynx.

rhinologist, one who specializes in the diseases of the nose.

rhinology, the study of the nose and its diseases.

rhinopathy, any disease of the nose.

rhinophonia, having a nasal tone in speaking.

rhinoplasty, plastic surgery of the nose.

rhinopolyp, a polyp of the nose.

rhinopolypus, a nasal polyp.

rhinorrhagia, a nosebleed; epistaxis.

rhinorrhea, a thin, watery discharge from the nose.

rhinoscope, a speculum used in nasal examination.

rhinoscopy, an examination of the nasal passages with a rhinoscope.

rhizomelic, concerning the roots of the extremities, such as the hips and shoulders in man.

rhizotomy, the surgical section of a root, as a nerve or tooth.

rhodogenesis, the formation or regeneration of visual purple that has been bleached by light.

rhodophylaxis, the ability of the retina to form or regenerate rhodopsin (visual purple).

rhodopsin, visual purple, a photosensitive red pigment in the outer segment of retinal rods important to night vision.

rhombencephalon, a primary division of the embryonic brain from which the metencephalon and myelencephalon are formed.

rhoncal, rhonchial, pertaining to rhoncus or rattle in the throat.

rhonchus, a rale or rattling in the throat; a snoring sound; a dry, coarse rale that occurs in the bronchial tubes because of a partial obstruction.

rhubarb, an extract made from roots and rhizome of Rheum officinale (rhubarb), used as a cathartic and astringent.

rhypophagy, eating of filth.

rhypophobia, a morbid disgust to the act of defecation or filth.

rhythm, a measured time or movement which occurs at regular intervals, as the action of the heartbeat.

rhythmic, pertaining to a rhythm; rhythmical.

rhytidectomy, plastic surgery for the excision of wrinkles.

rhytidosis, wrinkling of the skin; wrinkling of the cornea.

rib, a bone or cartilage that forms the chest cavity and protects certain vital organs.

riboflavin, a water-soluble vitamin of the B complex family found in milk, muscle, liver, kidney, eggs, malt, and algae, essential to man; Vitamin B_2.

ribonucleic acid, RNA which is a nucleic acid containing ribose found in cytoplasm in all cells.

ribose, a monosaccharide sugar present in ribonucleic acid (RNA).

ribosome, a large particle containing RNA and protein present in the cytoplasm of cells.

ricin, a poisonous white powdery substance made from the castor bean used in medicine as an agglutinin.

ricinoleic acid, an organic acid found in castor oil in the form of glyceride which is used as a laxative.

ricinus, the castor oil plant from which ricin and castor oil are derived used as a cathartic or lubricant.

rickets, a disease occurring in infancy and childhood due to a deficiency of Vitamin D, marked by bone distortion and softening, muscle pain, and sweating of the head.

rickettsia, a genus of the Rickettsiaceae which is transmitted by lice, ticks, fleas, and mites to humans from animals causing diseases, as typhus.

ridge, a narrow, elevated edge or border.

rigidity, stiffness; immovability; inability to bend.

rigor, chill preceding a fever; a state of stiffness as in a muscle.

rigor mortis, stiffening of muscles of a dead body.

rima, a slit, fissure, or crack.

rimose, filled with fissures or cracks.

rimula, a minute fissure or slit, especially of the brain or spinal column.

ring, a round organ or band which encircles an opening.

Ringer's solution, an aqueous solution used intravenously in conditions of dehydration and for improving circulation.

ringworm, a disease caused by fungi which appears in ring formations or patches on various parts of the body, especially on the scalp.

risus, laughter.

risus sardonicus, a peculiar grin caused by muscle spasms, as seen in tetanus.

R.N., registered nurse.

RNA, ribonucleic acid.

roborant, a tonic; strengthening.

Rocky Mountain spotted fever, an infectious disease caused by a parasite, Rickettsia rickettsii, which is transmitted to man by a wood tick, resulting in fever; pain in the bones and muscles, prostration, skin eruptions, and chills.

roentgen, the unit of measurement of radiation that is used internationally, pertaining most commonly to x-rays.

roentgenogram, the film made by x-rays.

roentgenography, the x-ray pictures of internal body structures.

roentgenologic, pertaining to roentgenology.

roentgenologist, one who specializes in roentgenology.

roentgenology, the study of x-rays and technical application to medical diagnosis and therapy.

roentgenoscope, an apparatus which has a fluorescent viewing screen; fluoroscope.

roentgenoscopy, examination by means of roentgen rays.

roentgenotherapy, treatment of a disease by roentgen rays.

rongeur, a surgical instrument for cutting or removing small fragments of bone or tissue.

root, proximal end of a nerve; that portion of an organ that is implanted in tissues, such as a tooth, hair, or nail.

Rorschach test, a projective technique which seeks to determine personality traits and emotional conflicts by an analysis of subjective responses to a standard series of ten ink blots.

rosacea, a chronic disease of the skin, usually involving the nose, cheeks, and forehead, marked by flushing, papules, and acne-like pustules.

rose fever, rose cold, an allergy attributed to inhalation of rose pollen in the early part of summer.

roseola, a rose-colored rash from various causes.

rotation, the process of turning on an axis; in obstetrics, the twisting or turning of the fetal head as it follows the curves of the birth canal as it descends.

roughage, indigestible, rough material such as fibers, and cellulose which are found in certain fruits and cereals that stimulate peristalsis.

rouleau, a grouping of red blood cells arranged like a roll of coins.

roundworm, a nematode which is a parasite that thrives in the intestines.

rubedo, blushing; a temporary redness of the skin, especially the face.

rubefacient, an agent that reddens the skin; causing reddening of the skin.

rubella, German measles; an acute viral infection that resembles measles, but runs a shorter course, marked by a pink macular rash, fever, lymph node enlargement, and sometimes, a sore throat and drowsiness may occur.

rubeola, measles, rubella.

rubescent, growing red, or reddish; ruddy.

rubor, redness due to inflammation.

rudimentary, undeveloped; imperfectly developed.

ruga, a ridge, crest, or fold, especially of mucous membrane.

rugose, marked by wrinkles; ridged.

rumination, the casting up of food, or regurgitation, to be chewed the second time, as in cattle; preoccupation of the mind.

rump, the buttock; gluteal region.

rupia, a skin eruption marked by large cutaneous elevations, usually occurs in the third stage of syphilis.

rupophobia, morbid aversion to dirt or filth.

rupture, hernia; a tearing apart, as of an organ.

rutilizm, red-headedness.

Rx, symbol; a simple method for writing ''take'', ''recipe'', or prescription; treatment.

rytidosis, the contraction of the cornea preceding death which causes wrinkling of its surface.

S

sabulous, sandy or gritty.

sac, a baglike structure or organ; a pouch.

saccate, having the form of a pouch or sac; contained within a sac.

saccharide, one of the carbohydrates containing sugar; a sugar substitute.

sacchariferous, yielding sugar.

saccharification, the conversion into sugar.

saccharin, a white, crystalline compound which is several hundred times sweeter than sucrose, used as a non-nutritive sweetener.

saccharine, resembling sugar; sugary consistency.

saccharolysis, chemical splitting up of sugar.

saccharolytic, pertaining to saccharometer.

saccharometer, saccharimeter, an optical instrument used to determine the strength of sugar solutions by measuring a plane of polarized light rotations after it passes through a sugar solution.

saccharomycetes, a genus of yeasts, including brewers' yeast, used in the fermentation of sugar.

saccharomycetic, pertaining to yeast fungi.

saccharomycosis, any of several diseases caused by yeast fungi.

saccharum, sugar.

sacciform, shaped like a pouch or sac.

saccular, resembling a sac.

sacculate, having saclike expansions; containing saccules.

saccule, a little sac; applied to the smaller of two sacs in the membranous labyrinth of the ear.

sacculocochlear, relating to both the saccule and cochlea.

sacculus, a saccule.

sacrad, toward the sacrum.

sacral, pertaining to the sacrum.

sacralgia, pain in the sacrum.

sacrectomy, surgical removal of part of the sacrum.

sacrocoxitis, inflammation of sacroiliac joint.

sacrodnia, pain in the sacrum region.

sacroiliac, pertaining to the sacrum and the ilium; relating to the juncture of the hipbone and the lower spine.

sacrolumbar, pertaining to the sacrum and the loins.

sacrosciatic, pertaining to the sacrum and the ischium.

sacrospinal, pertaining to the sacrum and the spinal column.

sacrospinalis, pertaining to the large muscle on either side of the spinal column which extends from the sacrum to the head.

sacrotomy, surgical removal of part of the sacrum.

sacrouterine, pertaining to the sacrum and uterus.

sacrum, part of the vertebral column between the lumbar and coccygeal regions.

sadism, a pathological condition in which pleasure is derived from inflicting physical or psychological pain on others; a perversion or sexual deviation when it is necessary to inflict pain upon another in order to obtain sexual gratification.

sadist, one who finds pleasure in inflicting pain on others.

sadistic, pertaining to sadism.

sadomasochism, the derivation of pleasure from inflicting physical or mental pain upon others or on oneself.

sagittal, resembling an arrow; pertaining to the suture that unites the parietal bones of the skull; referring to a plane that divides a body into two halves.

Saint Vitus's dance, involuntary muscular movements; chorea.

salacious, lustful.

salicylate, a salt of salicylic acid.

salicylic acid, a powder which is soluble in water, used as a food preservative, and in medicine as an analgesic and an antipyretic. Salicylic acid is too irritating internally to be used by itself, but is widely used in the preparation of acetylsalicylic acid (aspirin).

salify, combining an acid with a base to form a salt; to infuse with a salt.

saline, consisting of salt; containing chemical salt, as an alkali metal; salty.

saline solution, sodium chloride and distilled water in a solution; an isotonic solution.

salinometer, an instrument that measures the amount of salt present in a solution.

saliva, the slightly acid fluid secreted by the glands of the mouth that serves as the first digestive enzyme, ptyalin. The saliva begins the digestive process of converting starches into various dextrins and to some maltose. Final hydrolysis of these products breakdown to glucose is completed in the small intestine.

salivary, pertaining to saliva.

salivary calculus, a minute stone in a salivary duct.

salivary glands, the three pairs of glands in the oral cavity that contribute to the formation of saliva: parotid glands, submaxillary glands, and sublingual glands.

salivation, the process of secreting saliva; ptyalism.

salivatory, producing the secretion of saliva.

Salk vaccine, a vaccine against poliomyelitis produced from inactivated poliomyelitis virus, given by injection or orally on a sugar cube.

Salmonella, any rod-shaped bacteria belonging to the family Enterobacteriaceae that cause food poisoning, intestinal inflammation, or genital-tract diseases.

salmonellosis, infestation with Salmonella bacteria which cause food poisoning.

salpingectomy, surgical removal of a fallopian tube.

salpingemphraxis, an obstruction of an eustachian tube; an obstruction of a fallopian tube.

salpingian, concerning the eustachian tube, or an oviduct.

salpingitis, an inflammation of a fallopian tube, or eustachian tube.

salpingocele, a herniated protrusion of an oviduct.

salpingocyesis, a pregnancy in an oviduct; tubal pregnancy.

salpinx, pertaining to the fallopian or eustachian tube.

salsoda, a crystalline sodium carbonate which is used as a cleaning agent, or water softener.

salsalate, an analgesic and anti-inflammatory agent.

salt, sodium chloride; common table salt.

saltation, leaping, jumping, or dancing, as in chorea; conduction along myelinated nerves; in genetics, a mutation.

saltatory, characterized by leaping, jumping, or dancing.

salt-free diet, a diet with no more than two grams of salt.

salubrious, healthful; promoting good health; wholesome.

salutary, healthful; curative; promoting health.

Salvarsan, a yellowish arsenical powder used in treatment of syphilis; trademark; rarely used since the development of penicillin.

salve, a thick, soothing ointment or cerate.

sanative, having a healing quality; curative.

sanatorium, sanitarium, an institution for the treatment of diseases, for convalescents, or patients with mental disorders.

sanatory, healing; hygienic; conducive to health.

sand-blind, having imperfect eyesight.

sandfly, flies of the family Psychodidae, a biting fly inhabiting the seashore; a fly of the genus Phlebotomus which is a blood-sucking species that transmits sandfly fever and various other diseases affecting the skin, nasal cavity, or visceral organs such as the liver or spleen.

sandfly fever, usually a three-day fever produced by a mild virus transmitted by the sandfly from the genus Phlebotomus papatasii, similar to dengue fever.

sane, of sound mind; able to anticipate and judge one's action; having reason; rational.

sanguicolous, a parasite inhabiting the blood.

sanguifacient, making blood, or forming blood.

sanguiferous, conducting blood, as the circulatory system.

sanguine, abounding in blood; pertaining to blood; hopeful.

sanguineous, bloody; abounding in blood; relating to blood.

sanguinolent, tinged with blood; containing blood.

sanies, a fetid serous discharge from a wound or ulcer, containing pus tinged with blood.

sanious, pertaining to sanies.

sanitarian, a person skilled in public health science and sanitation.

sanitary, promoting health; clean; healthful.

sanitation, the use of measures to promote conditions favorable to health.

sanitization, the process of being made sanitary.

sanitize, to disinfect, or to sterilize.

sanity, rationality; soundness of mind; reasonableness.

sap, any fluid of a living structure essential to life.

saphena, small saphenous or the great saphenous veins of the leg.

saphenous, pertaining to certain arteries, nerves, or veins.

saphenous nerve, a branch of the femoral nerve that follows the long saphenous vein in the lower leg.

sapid, savory or very tasty.

sapiens, referring to modern man, Homo sapiens.

sapor, that which affects the sense of taste.

saporific, imparting a taste; pertaining to sapor.

sapphism, lesbianism.

sapremia, a toxic condition of the blood produced by putrefactive bacteria.

saprodontia, tooth decay.

saprogen, any bacteria produced by putrefaction, or causing it.

saprogenic, resulting from putrefaction or causing it.

saprophilous, living on decaying substances, such as bacteria.

saprophyte, any organism living upon decaying matter.

saprophytic, relating to a saprophyte.

sarcitis, inflammation of muscle tissue.

sarcoid, tuberculoid; resembling a sarcoma tumor; sarcoidosis.

sarcoidosis, a chronic, progressive granulomatous reticulosis of any organ or tissue marked by the presence of tubercle-like lesions, generally affecting the skin, lymph nodes, lungs, and bone marrow.

sarcology, the branch of medicine concerned with the study of soft body tissues.

sarcoma, a malignant tumor originating in connective tissue, bone, or muscle.

sarcomatoid, resembling a sarcoma.

sarcomatosis, a condition in which many sarcomas develop at various sites in the body; sarcomatous degeneration.

sarcous, belonging to flesh or muscle.

sardonic laugh, sardonic grin, a spasmodic affectation of the muscles of the face, giving the impression of laughter; risus sardonicus.

sartorius, a narrow, ribbon-shaped muscle of the thigh, the longest muscle in the body which aids in flexing the knee, and in rotating the leg to a cross-legged position.

satiable, capable of being satisfied.

satiety, a fullness or gratification; completely satisfied.

saturated, unable to hold any more in solution of a given substance; referring to an organic compound in which only single bonds exist between carbon atoms.

saturation, the state of being saturated.

saturnine, morose or gloomy; pertaining to the absorption of lead, as in lead poisoning.

saturnism, lead poisoning.

satyriasis, an exaggerated sexual desire in males.

saxitoxin, a neurotoxin produced by poisonous mussels, clams, and plankton; gonyaulax poison.

scab, a crust formation of a superficial sore or wound.

scabicide, a substance lethal to Sarcoptes scabiei.

scabies, a contagious skin disease caused by the itch mite, Sarcoptes scabiei, resulting in intense itching and eczema.

scabious, pertaining to scabies.

scabrities, a condition of the skin marked by a roughened and scaly appearance; a sand-like roughness of the inner surface of the eyelids.

scala, a ladder-like structure, as the spiral passages of the cochlea.

scald, a burn to the flesh or skin caused by hot liquid or steam.

scalene, pertaining to the scalenus.

scalenus, one of the three muscles located in the vertebrae of the neck and attached to the first two ribs; known as scalenus anterior, medius, and posterior.

scall, a scalp disease marked by scaly eruptions.

scalp, the skin covering the cranium; hairy integument of the upper part of the head.

scalpel, a straight, small, sharp-bladed surgical knife used in dissection and surgical procedures.

scaly, resembling scales.

scan, an image produced by a sweeping beam of radiation.

scanner, an apparatus that inspects and detects certain conditions of the body, as in ultrasonography.

scanning speech, pronunciation of words in syllables in a slow and hesitating manner, usually a symptom of disease involving the nervous system.

scaphocephalic, having a deformed head, resembling a boat's keel.

scaphoid, the boat- shaped bone of the carpus on the radial side; navicular bone.

scaphoiditis, inflammation of the scaphoid bone.

scapula, the large, flat bone of the shoulder; shoulder blade.

scapulalgia, pain in the shoulder blade region.

scapular, pertaining to the shoulder blade.

scapulectomy, surgical removal of part or all of the shoulder blade.

scar, the mark left on the skin by a healing wound or sore.

scarification, having many small superficial punctures or scratches in the skin over a part, as for introduction of vaccine.

scarificator, scarifier, an instrument with many sharp points.

scarlatina, mild form of scarlet fever.

scarlatiniform, resembling scarlet fever.

scarlet fever, a contagious disease characterized by sore throat, fever, rash, and rapid pulse, usually occurring in children.

scatacratia, fecal incontinence.

scatemia, intestinal toxemia in which chemical poisons are absorbed from retained fecal matter.

scatology, the study and analysis of waste products for diagnostic purposes.

scatophagy, the eating of feces.

Schick test, test for susceptibility to diphtheria.

Schiller's test, a test for superficial cancer of the cervix.

schistoprosopia, congenital fissure of the face.

Schistosoma, a genus of blood flukes which cause infection in man by penetration of the skin while coming in contact with infected waters; schistosomiasis.

schistosomiasis, infection with Schistosoma.

schistothorax, congenital fissure of the chest or thorax.

schizogenesis, reproduction by fission.

schizoid, resembling schizophrenia; referring to a person with a schizoid personality.

schizomycete, an organism of the class of Schizomycetes, a group of plant organisms belonging to fungi.

schizomycetous, pertaining to schizomycetes.

schizont, a stage in the development of the malarial parasite following the trophozoite in which its nucleus divides into smaller nuclei.

schizonychia, splitting of fingernails and toenails.

schizophasia, muttered or disordered speech of the schizophrenic.

schizophrenia, any of a large group of severe emotional disorders, usually of psychotic proportion, characterized by disturbances of thought, mood, and behavior, such as misinterpretation of reality, delusions and hallucinations, ambivalence, inappropriate affect, and withdrawn, bizarre, or regressive behavior.

schizophrenic, one afflicted with schizophrenia.

schizotrichia, splitting of the hair at the ends.

sciatic, pertaining to the ischium or hip.

sciatic nerve, the largest nerve in the body extending from the sacral plexus on either side of the body down the back of the thigh and leg.

sciatica, inflammation of or injury to the sciatic nerve and its branches; severe pain in the leg along the course of the sciatic nerve.

scirrhoid, pertaining to a hard scirrhus or carcinoma.

scirrhoma, a hard tumor or carcinoma; scirrhus.

scirrhous, hard like a scirrhus; knotty.

scirrhus, a hard, cancerous tumor caused by an overgrowth of fibrous tissue.

scissor leg, an abnormal crossing of both legs in walking due to adduction of both hips.

sclera, the white outer coat of the eye which extends from the optic nerve to the cornea; sclerotica.

scleradenitis, inflammation and hardening of a gland.

scleral, pertaining to the sclera.

sclerectasia, a protrusion of the sclera.

sclerectoiridectomy, surgical removal of part of the sclera and iris as a treatment for glaucoma.

sclerencephalia, sclerosis of the brain.

scleriasis, progressive hardening of the skin.

scleritis, inflammation of the sclera.

scleroderma, a disease that causes the skin to become hard and rigid.

sclerodermatitis, a skin inflammation accompanied by thickening and hardening.

scleroid, having a hard texture.

scleroma, sclerosis; a hardened patch or induration of nasal or laryngeal mucous membranes.

sclerose, to become hardened.

sclerosis, a hardening of tissue or a part, due to excessive growth of fibrous connective tissue.

sclerotic, pertaining to the sclera of the eye; affected with or pertaining to sclerosis.

sclerous, hard; indurated; bony.

scolex, the round, attachment organ of a tapeworm; the larva of a tapeworm.

scoliosiometry, measurement of spinal curvature.

scoliorachitic, relating to scoliosis or rickets.

scoliosis, a lateral curvature of the spine.

scoliotic, pertaining to scoliosis.

scoop, a surgical spoon-shaped instrument used in extracting the contents of cysts or cavities.

scopolamine, an anticholinergic alkaloid obtained from the Scopolia carniolica plant, used as a sedative, mydriatic, cycloplegic.

scopophobia, a morbid fear of being seen.

scorbutic, pertaining to or affected with scurvy.

scorbutus, a disease caused by a deficiency of vitamin C; scurvy.

scotodinia, vertigo accompanied by faintness and black spots before the eyes.

scotoma, a blind gap in the visual field.

scotomatous, pertaining to scotoma.

scotometer, an instrument for diagnosing and measuring areas of depressed vision in the visual field.

scotophobia, an aversion or fear of the dark.

scotopia, night vision; the adaptation of the eye to the dark.

scotopsin, a protein that combines with retinene to form rhodopsin, important to the adjustment of vision for darkness.

scratch, a superficial injury or mark on the skin produced by scraping with a fingernail or a rough or sharp surface.

screen, a structure used in fluoroscopy on which light rays are projected for diagnostic purposes.

screening, an examination of a large segment of a population to detect a particular disease.

screwworm, the larva of a two-winged fly that deposits its eggs in wounds or in the nose; the larva, then, thrives upon the tissue of the host.

scrobiculate, marked with furrows or pits.

scrobiculus, a small groove, furrow, or pit.

scrofula, a condition of primary tuberculosis of the lymph glands of the neck characterized by swelling and degeneration.

scrofuloderma, a skin disease characterized by suppurating abscesses on the chest, neck, and in the axilla and groin area. The condition responds to ultraviolet light and chemotherapy.

scrofulous, pertaining to scrofula.

scrotal, pertaining to the scrotum.

scrotectomy, surgical excision of part of the scrotum.

scrotitis, inflammation of the scrotum.

scrotocele, hernia of the scrotum.

scrotum, the external double pouch that contains the testicles.

scruple, 20 grains of the apothecaries' unit of weight; one-third of a dram.

scurf, a desquamation of the skin, or a flaking of dry scales resembling dandruff.

scurvy, a deficiency disease due to the lack of vitamin C, marked by anemia, swollen and bleeding gums, livid skin patches and exhaustion.

scutiform, shaped like a shield.

scutulum, shoulder blade; scapula.

scutum, any shield-shaped bone; thyroid cartilage.

scyphoid, shaped like a cup.

seasickness, motion sickness; nausea, and vomiting due to unusual motion.

sebaceous, pertaining to or secreting sebum.

sebaceous cyst, a swelling formed beneath the skin due to a blockage of a duct or gland filled with sebaceous material.

sebaceous gland, an oil- secreting gland of the skin.

sebiferous, producing fatty or sebaceous matter.

sebiparous, secreting or producing sebum.

seborrhea, a functional disease of the sebaceous glands marked by an excessive increase of sebaceous secretion.

seborrheic, pertaining to seborrhea.

sebum, the fatty secretion of the sebaceous glands of the skin.

secobarbital, a short-acting barbiturate used as an hypnotic and sedative prior to anesthesia; also used to control convulsions; trademark name, Seconal.

secondary sex characteristic, any manifest characteristic due to the effect of gonadal secretions of hormones, such as the development of beards in males, and the development of mammary glands in females at puberty.

second-degree burn, a burn marked by blistering and redness without destruction of the epidermis.

secretagogue, an agent that causes secretion of glands; stimulating secretion.

secrete, to separate from the blood; to produce secretion.

secretin, a hormone secreted by the duodenal and jejunal mucosa which aids digestion; it also stimulates secretion of pancreatic juice and bile.

secretion, the cellular process of releasing a specific product; any substance produced by secretion of glands.

secretory, pertaining to secretion; a secretory organ or gland.

section, the act of separating by cutting, as in surgery; a segment of material for microscopic examination.

sector, a separate part; an area of the body.

secudines, afterbirth.

sedation, the act of alleviating distress, pain, or tension by administering a sedative.

sedative, a tranquilizer; an agent allaying irritability or excitement; quieting.

sedentary, habitually sitting; inactive; staying in one locale.

sediment, the material settling at bottom of a liquid.

sedimentation, a formation of sediment; settling out of sediment.

sedimentator, a centrifuge apparatus for separating sediment from urine.

segment, a part of a whole, especially of an organ; a division or section.

segmental, pertaining to a portion; resembling segments.

segmentation, a division into parts that are similar.

segregation, separating; in genetics, the separation of paired genes into different gametes during meiosis.

seismotherapy, sismotherapy, treatment of disease by vibratory or mechanical massage.

seizure, a sudden attack of a disease or of a symptom; a convulsion, or epileptic attack, heart attack, or a stroke.

selectivity, the degree to which a single dose of medicine produces the desired effect.

self-antigen, the ability of the body's tissues to stimulate autoimmunity.

self- destruction, the destruction of oneself, as in suicide.

self- hypnosis, self-induced hypnosis, often used to overcome bad habits or to accomplish a specific feat.

self-limited, influenced by one's own peculiarities; a disease that runs a precisely limited course.

self-tolerance, individual tolerance of immunity to self-antigens.

semeilogy, the study of symptoms; symptomatology.

semeiotic, pertaining to symptoms or signs; symptomatic.

semen, the viscous secretion at ejaculation in the male containing spermatozoa.

semicanal, a passage or channel open at one end.

semicircular canals, three small tubular canals in the labyrinth of the ear responsible for maintaining equilibrium.

semilunar, resembling a half-moon, or a crescent shape.

semilunar bone, crescent shaped bone of the carpus or wrist.

semilunar valves, the valves of the aorta and pulmonary artery.

seminal, pertaining to semen.

seminal vesicle, one of two sac-like glands lying in back of the bladder of the male, which join the ductus deferens on each side.

semination, insemination; introduction of semen into the vagina.

seminiferous, producing or carrying semen.

semipermeable, permeable only to certain molecules, as a membrane that permits passage of a solvent but not the solute.

semisynthetic, produced by chemical manipulation of substances that occur naturally.

senescence, the process of aging, or growing old.

senile, pertaining to old age; decline of mental faculties.

senilism, premature aging, or old age.

senility, the physical and mental deterioration that accompanies old age.

senna, any of various leguminous herbs, shrubs, or trees of the genus Cassia, the dried leaves of which are used as a cathartic.

senopia, an improvement of vision in the aged usually a sign of incipient cataract.

sensation, an impression produced by impulses through the sense organs; the power of feeling or sensing; an awareness of stimulus to the nervous system.

sense, perceived through the nervous system or a sense organ; the normal power of understanding.

sense organ, any organ of the body that transmits impulses to the brain, such as the nose, ear, eye, and skin; receptor.

sensibility, an ability to feel or perceive; sensitivity.

sensitive, able to respond to stimuli; unusually responsive to stimulation; reacting quickly.

sensitivity, the quality of being sensitive; the state of being acutely affected by the action of a chemical or other agents.

sensitization, a condition of being made sensitive to certain stimulus; the exposure of a person to a specific antigen by repeated injections of it, as a serum; anaphylaxis.

sensorimotor, being both sensory and motor.

sensorineural, pertaining to a sensory nerve.

sensorium, the sensory nerve center in the cerebral cortex that receives and coordinates impulses sent to individual nerve centers; the special sensory perceptive powers and their integration in the brain; having a clear, accurate memory together with a correct orientation for time, place, and person; consciousness.

sensory, pertaining to sensation.

sensuous, pertaining to the senses; appealing to the senses; readily affected through the senses or susceptible to influence.

sentient, capable of sensation.

sepsis, the presence of pathological microorganisms or their toxins in the blood; a state of poisoning of the system caused by the spread of infection through the blood.

septal, pertaining to a septum.

septate, divided by a septum.

septectomy, surgical removal of a septum or part of it.

septic, pertaining to sepsis.

septicemia, blood poisoning, or a systemic disease caused by the presence of pathological microorganisms or their toxins in the bloodstream.

septicemic, pertaining to septicemia.

septic sore throat, an inflammation of the throat caused by streptococcus bacteria, accompanied by fever and prostration.

septicophlebitis, septic inflammation of a vein.

septimetritis, septic inflammation of the uterus.

septometer, an instrument that measures the width of the nasal septum.

septonasal, pertaining to the nasal septum.

septotome, an instrument used for surgical cutting of a section of the nasal septum.

septotomy, surgical incision of the nasal septum.

septum, a dividing membrane or partition; a partition of tissue.

septuplet, one of seven children born of one pregnancy.

sequel, sequela, the consequence of an illness or disease; a morbid condition occurring as a consequence of another condition.

sequestration, the formation of sequestrum; isolation of a patient.

sequestrectomy, surgical excision of a sequestrum.

sequestrum, a portion of dead bone which has separated from sound bone due to necrosis.

sera, plural of serum.

seroalbuminuria, the presence of serum albumin in the urine.

serocolitis, inflammation of the serous coat of the colon.

seroculture, bacterial culture on blood serum.

seroenteritis, inflammation of the serous coat of the intestine.

serohepatitis, inflammation of the peritoneal covering of the liver.

serologist, one who specializes in serology.

serology, the science concerned with the nature and reactions of blood serum.

serolysin, a bacterial substance occurring in blood serum.

serosa, serous membrane, as peritoneum, pleura, and pericardium.

serositis, inflammation of a serous membrane.

serotherapy, therapeutic measure in treatment of disease by injecting blood serum, either human or animal, containing antibodies.

serotonin, a hormone and neurotransmitter found in certain cells that causes muscle contraction and vasoconstriction.

serous, resembling serum; producing or containing serum.

serous membrane, any thin membrane lining a serous cavity such as the peritoneum.

serpiginous, creeping; having a wavy border.

serpigo, a creeping eruption, especially ringworm.

serum, any serous fluid that moistens the surfaces of serous membranes; the fluid portion of the blood after coagulation; serum from the blood of an animal that has been rendered immune to some disease, given by inoculation as an antitoxin; consisting of plasma minus fibrogen.

serum albumin, a simple protein found in blood serum.

serum globulin, a plasma protein that may be separated into three blood fractions, alpha, beta, and gamma globulin responsible for the body's resistance to certain infections.

serum sickness, an eruption of purpuric spots accompanied by pain in the limbs and joints following a serum injection.

sesamoid, a small nodular bone that is embedded in a tendon or joint capsule; sesamoid bone, resembling a sesame seed.

setaceous, bristle-like; resembling a bristle; bristly, or hairy.

seventh cranial nerve, the facial nerve.

sex, the distinctive characteristics which differentiate between males and females; activities related to sexual attraction; sexual reproduction; sexual intercourse.

sex chromosome, a chromosome that carries sex-linked traits, as determined by the presence of the XX (female) or XY (male) genotype in somatic cells.

sex hormone, a hormone that affects the growth or function of the sexual organs and the development of secondary sex characteristics in males and females.

sex-linked, transmitted by a gene which is located on the X chromosome.

sexological, pertaining to sexology.

sexologist, one specializing in sexology.

sexology, the study of sexual behavior in humans.

sextuplet, one of six children born at the same birth.

sexual, pertaining to sex.

sexual intercourse, copulation; coitus; sexual relations.

sexuality, state of having sex; the collective characteristics differentiating between the male and female; the constitution of a person relating to sexual behavior and attitudes.

sexual organs, genitalia; genitals.

shaft, the long slender portion of a long bone.

shakes, shivering due to a chill; fine vibrations of the hands, often seen in chronic alcoholics.

shaking palsy, a basal ganglion disease marked by progressive rigid tremulousness, affected gait, muscular contraction and weakness, often seen in Parkinson's disease.

shank, leg, or shin; tibia.

sheath, a tubular encasement or enveloping structure.

shedding, loss of deciduous teeth; casting off the top layer of the epidermis or skin.

shell shock, a form of psychoneurosis, often seen during military service and in training camps; war neurosis.

shield, a protective covering.

Shigella, a genus of nonmotile, gram- negative rods belonging to the family Enterobacteriaceae, which produce digestive disturbances ranging from mild diarrhea to dysentery.

shin, the anterior edge of the tibia or leg, between the ankle and the knee; shinbone.

shingles, a viral infection involving the central nervous system causing eruption of acute, inflammatory vesicles or blisters on the skin along peripheral nerves which are painful; herpes zoster.

shiver, slight tremor; involuntary shaking, as with cold, fear, or excitement.

shivering, an involuntary shaking or tremor of the body, as with cold.

shock, a sudden debilitating disturbance of bodily functions resulting from acute peripheral circulatory failure due to hemorrhage, severe trauma, burns, dehydration, infection, surgery, or drug toxicity. Outstanding symptoms of shock are: prostration, pallor, perspiration, rapid pulse, pulmonary deficiency, coldness of skin, and often anxiety.

shock therapy, a treatment in mental illness involving three different types: electric shock therapy, insulin shock therapy, or metrazol shock therapy.

shortsightedness, unable to see distant objects clearly; myopia, or nearsightedness.

shoulder, joining of the clavicle and scapula, where the arm joins the trunk.

shoulder-blade, scapula.

shoulder dislocation, displacement of the shoulder joint caused by falling on an outstretched arm.

shoulder girdle, the bony semicircular band which forms an arch, serving as supporting structure for the upper extremities.

show, appearance of a discharge of blood prior to labor; menstruation.

shudder, temporary convulsive shaking of the body resulting from fright, fear, or anxiety; tremor.

shunt, to turn to one side or to bypass; a passage between two blood vessels or between two sides of the heart that has an abnormal opening in its wall partition; a surgical creation of an anastomosis.

sialaden, a salivary gland.

sialadenitis, inflammation of a salivary gland.

sialadenocus, tumor of a salivary gland.

sialagogic, pertaining to sialagogue.

sialagogue, an agent that increases the flow of saliva.

sialaporia, a deficiency in saliva secretion.

sialemesis, vomiting caused by excessive secretion of saliva.

sialine, concerning saliva.

sialism, sialismus, excessive secretion of saliva; ptyalism.

sialoadenectomy, surgical removal of a salivary gland.

sialoadenitis, an inflammation of a salivary gland; sialadenitis.

sialoaerophagia, swallowing of saliva and air.

sialoangitis, inflammation of a salivary duct.

sialocele, a salivary cyst.

sialolith, a salivary calculus, or stone.

sialolithiasis, formation of several salivary calculi, or stones.

sialoncus, a tumor under the tongue caused by obstruction of a salivary duct.

sialorrhea, ptyalism.

sialosis, the flow of saliva; ptyalism.

Siamese twins, any twins born joined together, usually at the hips or buttocks; twins congenitally united.

sib, a blood relative; kinsman descended from a common ancestor; sibling.

sibilant, hissing or whistling.

sibling, offspring of the same parents; a brother or sister.

sibship, brothers and sisters of the same family group.

siccus, dry.

sick, not well; affected by disease; nauseous.

sickle cell, an abnormal crescent-shaped red blood cell.

sickle cell anemia, a hereditary form of anemia in which the presence of crescent-shaped red blood cells causes a crystallization of the hemoglobin within the cells, resulting in the clogging of blood vessels. This disease affects about 1 in 500 American Negroes and is marked by severe anemia, jaundice, abdominal, muscular, and joint pains, skin ulcerations, formation of bilirubin gallstones, and many other complications.

sicklemia, sickle cell anemia.

sickly, not robust; habitually indisposed; in poor health.

sickness, state of being affected with disease; illness.

side effect, an unintended secondary reaction to medication; an effect that is aside from the desired effect of a treatment.

siderocyte, a red blood corpuscle that contains iron in a form other than hematin.

sideroderma, a disorder of iron metabolism that causes a bronze discoloration of the skin.

sideropenia, iron deficiency in the blood or the body.

sideropenic, pertaining to sideropenia.

sideroscope, a device used to find metal particles in the eye.

siderosis, a form of pneumoconiosis caused by dust or fumes containing iron particles being inhaled, as in occupations such as arc-welding.

siderous, pertaining to or containing iron.

sigh, deep inspiration preceded by an audible, slower expiration; suspirium.

sight, the act of seeing; having the faculty of vision.

sightless, blind.

sigmoid, shaped like the letter S; pertaining to the sigmoid colon.

sigmoidectomy, surgical excision of all or part of the sigmoid colon.

sigmoid flexure, the lower segment of the descending colon between the crest and the rectum, shaped like the letter S.

sigmoiditis, inflammation of the sigmoid colon.

sigmoidoscope, an endoscope with an illuminated end used for examination of the sigmoid flexure.

sgimoidoscopy, examination of the sigmoid colon with a sigmoidoscope.

sigmoidostomy, a surgical creation of an artificial opening from the sigmoid colon to the body surface.

sign, any existing evidence of an abnormal nature in the body or of an organ.

signa, meaning "mark", used in writing prescriptions; designated "S" or "sig".

signature, that part of a prescription which gives instructions for use of medication.

sign language, hand signs or gestures used as a substitute for speech by the deaf.

silicon, a nonmetallic element found in soil which occurs in traces in skeletal structures such as teeth and bone.

silicone, any organic compound in which all or part of the carbon has been replaced by silicon, used in preparations of oils, greases, synthetic rubber, and resins.

silicosis, a lung condition caused by inhalation of dust of stone, sand, or flint containing silica, resulting in nodular, fibrotic changes in the lungs.

silicotic, pertaining to silicosis.

silver nitrate, a chemical element which is used as a local anti- infective, or prophylaxis of opthalmia neonatorum, a purulent conjunctivitis in the newborn.

silver protein, silver made colloidal in combination with protein, used in solutions as an active germicide.

simple, not complex; something not mixed or compounded; being deficient in intellect; a medicinal herb, or plant.

simple fracture, fracture without torn ligaments or broken skin; bone fracture without complications.

simulate, to feign illness or disease.

simulation, feigning disease or symptoms of a disease.

simulator, one who simulates; malingerer; something that simulates.

sinapism, a mustard plaster.

sincipital, pertaining to the sinciput.

sinciput, upper and front portion of the head.

Sinequan, trademark for doxepin hydrochloride used in treatment of psychoneurosis to alleviate symptoms of anxiety, tension, depression, sleep disturbances, guilt, fear, apprehension, worry, and lack of energy.

sinew, a tendon of a muscle.

singuitus, hiccup.

sinister, on the left side; left.

sinistral, pertaining to the left side; left-handed.

sinistraural, hearing better with the left ear.

sinistrocardia, a displacement of the heart to the left side of the medial line of the body.

sinistrocerebral, pertaining to or situated in the left cerebral hemisphere.

sinistrocular, having stronger vision in the left eye.

sinistromanual, left-handed.

sinistropedal, using the left foot more than the right; left-footed.

sinistrotorsion, a turning or twisting to the left, as of the eye.

sinuitis, sinusitis; inflammation of a sinus.

sinuous, winding or bending in and out.

sinus, a cavity, recess, or passage, as in bone; dilated channel or vessel for venous blood; any cavity having a narrow opening leading to an abscess.

sinusal, pertaining to a sinus.

sinusitis, inflammation of a sinus, especially of a paranasal sinus.

sinusoid, resembling a sinus.

sinusotomy, surgical incision of a sinus.

sitiergia, hysterical refusal to take food, probably related to anorexia nervosa.

sitiology, the science of nutrition; dietetics.

sitomania, periodic bulimia; excessive hunger, or abnormal craving for food.

sitophobia, an abnormal repugnance to food, either generally or to certain selective dishes.

sitosterol, any of a group of sterols from closely related plants used in varying combinations as an anticholesterolemic substance in the synthetic production of steroid hormone drugs.

sitotherapy, treatment by diet.

situs, a position, or the site of a body part or organ.

sitz bath, a bath in which to sit with water covering the hips; hip bath.

skeletal, pertaining to the skeleton.

skeleton, the bones of the body collectively, forming the framework. The human body consists of 206 bones.

Skene's glands, glands which lie inside of the posterior floor of the urethra in the female.

skenitis, inflammation of the Skene's glands or paraurethral ducts.

skiagram, an X-ray picture; roentgenograph.

skiagraph, an object made visible by a shadowed outline; a radiograph.

skiagraphy, the process of taking pictures with roentgen rays; radiography.

skiameter, an apparatus that determines differences in density and penetration of roentgen rays.

skiascope, an apparatus that examines by fluoroscope errors of refraction in the eye by observing movement of shadow and light; retinoscope.

skiascopy, shadow test of the eye to determine the refractive error; fluoroscopic examination of the body.

skin, the external covering of the body consisting of two layers, the epidermis and the corium. In the skin of the palms of the hands and soles of the feet there are five layers of epidermis.

skin graft, a viable section of skin transplanted in skin grafting.

skin grafting, the grafting of skin from another part of the body, or from a donor, to repair a defect or to replace skin that has been destroyed, as by burns.

skleriasis, progressive patches of hardened skin; scleroderma.

skin test, injected substances beneath the skin or applied to the surface of the skin to determine allergic sensitivity; scratch test; Schick test.

skull, the cranium; bony framework of the head.

sleep, a periodic and normal loss of consciousness in which bodily functions are reduced since the body and mind are at rest.

sleeping sickness, an infectious disease, usually fatal, marked by fever, drowsiness, increased lethargy, muscular weakness, weight loss, and cerebral symptoms caused by a parasitic protozoan, Trypanosoma gambiense, introduced into the blood by the bite of a tsetse fly; encephalitis lethargica.

sleep walking, walking in one's sleep; somnambulism.

sling, a support, usually out of a triangular cotton cloth or material, for an injured upper extremity.

slipped disk, a displaced vertebral disk that causes pressure on the spinal nerve, creating extreme pain.

slough, to cast off or shed; necrotic (dead) matter separated from living tissue.

sloughing, formation of slough or dead matter; the separating of necrosed tissue from living tissue.

slow, mentally dull; having a retarded pulse; bradycardia.

smallpox, an acute viral disease marked by fever, macules and papules that leave small depressed scars on the skin; variola.

smear, a specimen prepared on a slide for microscopic study.

smegma, a cheesy secretion of sebaceous glands, consisting of desquamated epithelial cells found under the labia minora and the foreskin.

smegmatic, pertaining to the smegma.

smegmolith, a calcareous mass in the smegma.

smell, to perceive by stimulation of the olfactory nerves or olfactory sense; to render an offensive or pleasant odor.

smelling salts, ammonium carbonate used for resuscitation and stimulation.

snapping hip, a hip joint that slips with a snap due to displacement over the great trochanter of a tendinous band.

snare, a surgical device for excision of polyps, tumors, and other growths by encircling them at the base with a wire loop and closing the loop.

sneeze, to emit air forcibly through the mouth and nose by involuntary spasmodic contractions of muscles of expiration, due to irritation of nasal mucosa.

Snellen's chart, used to test visual acuity.

snore, noisy breathing during sleep through the mouth which causes a vibration of the uvula and soft palate.

snoring rale, a sonorous, low-pitched rale resembling a snore.

snow blindness, an irritation to the conjunctiva of the eye caused by reflection of the sun on the snow.

snuffles, catarrhal discharge from nasal mucous membranes while breathing, especially in infants with congenital syphilis.

soap, a chemical compound formed by an alkali acting on fatty acid, used for cleansing purposes.

SOAP, a process of recording progress notes in a problem-oriented assessment of data obtained subjectively from a patient.

sob, to weep with convulsive movements of the throat, involving a sudden inspiration accompanied by spasmodic closure of the glottis, resulting in a wail-like cry.

socialization, the process by which society integrates the individual and the way in which one learns to behave in a socially acceptable way.

sociobiology, the study that proposes that all human behavior has a biological basis and is controlled by the genes.

sociogenic, imposed by society.

sociologist, one who specializes in sociology.

sociology, the scientific study concerned with social relationships, social organization, and group behavior in contrast to individual behavior.

sociometry, the study of measurement of human social behavior.

sociopath, an individual with an antisocial personality; a psychopath.

socket, a hollow or cavity into which a correspondent part fits.

soda, usually applied to sodium bicarbonate, sodium hydroxide, or sodium carbonate.

soda lime, combined mixture of sodium hydroxide or caustic soda and calcium hydroxide or slaked lime, used in the production of ammonia and the absorption of moisture; combined mixture of calcium hydroxide with sodium or potassium, or both, used as an absorbent of carbon dioxide in equipment, such as in oxygen therapy.

sodium bicarbonate, used in the production of baking powder and as an antacid.

sodium chloride, common table salt.

sodium citrate, used as an anticoagulant in blood transfusions.

sodium iodide, used in preparation of a compound resembling potassium iodide.

sodium salicylate, a compound powder used as an analgesic and antipyretic.

sodium sulfate, used as a mild cathartic and diuretic; Glauber's salts.

sodomy, unnatural sexual intercourse; anal intercourse; bestiality; fellatio.

soft palate, soft part of the palate.

solar, pertaining to the sun.

solar plexus, a network of nerves behind the stomach and situated at the upper part of the abdomen in front of the aorta from which sympathetic fibers pass to the visceral organs.

sole, the undersurface or bottom part of the foot.

soleprint, a footprint used in hospitals to identify newborn infants.

solution, process of dissolving; a homogeneous mixture of one or more substances; a rupture or separation; termination of an illness.

solvent, any substance which has a dissolving effect upon another substance.

soma, the body as distinguished from the mind or psyche; body tissues distinguished from germinal tissues.

somatic, pertaining to the body, as somatic symptoms.

somatic cells, any of the body cells that compose various organs and tissue except reproductive cells or germ cells.

somatogenic, originating in the body.

somatology, the study of anatomy and physiology; the study of the structure, functions, and development of the human body.

somatopathy, bodily dysfunction as distinguished from mental dysfunction.

somatoplasm, the protoplasm of the body cells as distinguished from that of germ plasm.

somatopleure, the embryonic layer formed by ectoderm and somatic mesoderm.

somatopsychic, pertaining to both body and mind; relating to a physical disorder which manifests mental symptoms.

somatopsychosis, any mental dysfunction symptomatic of bodily disease.

somatotherapy, treatment focused at relieving or curing bodily ills.

somatotrophic, influencing body cells and stimulating growth.

somatotype, a particular body build based on a theory that certain types of body build are associated with personality types, such as endomorphy, mesomorphy, actomorphy.

somesthetic, sensibility to bodily sensations.

somite, any embryonic segment alongside the neural tube, forming the vertebral column and various organs.

somitic, pertaining to a somite.

somnambulate, walking while asleep.

somnambulism, the state of walking during sleep; a hypnotic state in which the individual has full possession of the senses but no subsequent memory.

somnambulist, one subject to somnambulism.

somniferous, producing or inducing sleep, as a narcotic or soporific.

somniloquism, habitual talking in one's sleep.

somnolence, unusual drowsiness; sleepiness.

somnolentia, inclined to sleep; drowsiness, or somnolence; a lack of natural sleep with disorientation and anxiety.

sonorous, a deep resonant sound.

sonovox, an electronic device used for transmitting sounds to be emitted through the mouth by a person whose larynx has been removed.

sopor, a very deep sleep; stupor.

soporiferous, producing sleep; soporific.

soporose, soporous, pertaining to profound sleep; coma.

sordes, undigested food in the stomach.

sore, any lesion of the skin or mucous membranes; tender or painful.

sore throat, inflammation of the pharynx; laryngitis; pharyngitis; tonsillitis.

souffle, a soft, blowing sound heard through a stethoscope in auscultation, as any cardiac or vascular murmur.

sound, the effect produced in the auditory organs by sound waves or certain vibrations; a noise, which is normal or abnormal, heard within the body; an instrument for exploring and detecting by sound any foreign body within a cavity.

space, an area, region, or cavity of the body; delimited area; the universe beyond earth.

Spanish fly, a blister beetle used in medicine as a counter-irritant or diuretic.

sparganosis, infestation with a variety of Sparganum.

Sparganum, the larva of tapeworms, especially of the genus Dibothriocephalus.

spargosis, distention of the female mammary glands with milk; swelling and thickening of the skin; elephantiasis.

spasm, a sudden, abnormal, involuntary muscular contraction; a transitory constriction of a passage or orifice; spasms may be clonic, described as alternating contraction and relaxation of involuntary muscles, or they may be tonic, described as sustained involuntary muscle contraction.

spasmodic, occurring in spasms; relating to the nature of a spasm.

spastic, characterized by spasms; a hypertonic state of muscles producing rigidity and awkward movements; an individual exhibiting spasticity, as occurs in cerebral palsy.

spasticity, hypertension of the muscles, or sustained increased muscular tension.

spay, to remove female sex glands, usually said of animals.

specialist, a medical practitioner who limits his practice to a particular branch of medicine or surgery.

specialty, the specific field of a specialist.

specific, pertaining to a species; restricted in application or effect to a particular function or structure; a drug indicated for a particular disease; pertaining to special affinity of an antigen for its corresponding antibody.

specimen, a small sample to determine the nature of the whole, as a small quantity of urine for diagnostic purposes or a segment of tissue for microscopic examination.

spectacles, a pair of lenses to aid defective vision or to protect the eyes from light rays or dust particles.

spectroscope, an instrument used for developing and analyzing spectra.

spectrum, a series of wavelengths of electromagnetic radiation obtained by refraction and diffraction of a ray of white light. The visible spectrum consists of the colors red, orange, yellow, green, blue, indigo and violet. The invisible spectrum includes rays such as X-ray, infrared, ultraviolet, cosmic, etc.; a measurable range of activity of bacteria which are affected by an antibiotic.

speculum, an instrument for examining canals or for opening a body orifice to permit visual inspection.

speech, the power to express thoughts and ideas by articulated vocal sounds and words.

sperm, semen; spermatozoon; reproductive seminal fluid in males.

spermacrasia, lack of spermatozoa in the semen.

spermatemphraxis, an obstruction that prevents the discharge of seminal fluid.

spermatic, pertaining to the semen; seminal.

spermatic cord, the cord suspending the testis within the scrotum, and which contains the blood vessels, lymphatics, nerves, and ductus deferens.

spermatid, a cell developed from a spermatocyte which becomes a mature reproductive cell or spermatozoon.

spermatism, the ejaculation of semen, voluntary or involuntary.

spermatocele, a cystic tumor of the epididymis which contains spermatozoa.

spermatocyte, a primary male germ cell that develops from the division of a spermatogonium and then itself divides into spermatids which give rise to spermatozoa.

spermatogenesis, the formation of mature spermatozoa.

spermatogenic, pertaining to the origin and development of spermatozoa.

spermatogonium, a primitive germ cell that gives rise to the spermatocyte.

spermatoid, resembling spermatozoa.

spermatology, the study of seminal fluid.

spermatolysis, the destruction of spermatozoa.

spermatopathy, any disease of sperm cells or their secreting glands or ducts.

spermatorrhea, involuntary discharge of semen without orgasm.

spermatozoic, pertaining to spermatozoa.

spermatozoon, the mature germ cell which is formed in the seminiferous tubules of the testes.

spermaturia, discharge of semen with urine.

spermiogenesis, the second stage in the formation of spermatozoa, in which the spermatids are transformed into functional spermatozoa.

sphenoid, wedge-shaped or cuneiform.

sphenoid bone, the large bone at the base of the skull which is wedge-shaped.

spherocyte, an erythrocyte which is spheroid in shape but more fragile, occurring in certain hemolytic anemias.

spheroid, having a body shaped like a sphere.

spheroidal, resembling a sphere.

sphincter, a ringlike, or circular muscle which closes a natural passage, as the anus.

sphincteral, pertaining to a sphincter.

sphincteralgia, pain in the anal sphincter muscles; pain in a sphincter muscle.

sphincterectomy, surgical excision of a sphincter.

sphincteritis, inflammation of a sphincter.

sphincterotomy, surgical incision of a sphincter.

sphygmogram, tracing of the pulse produced by a sphygmograph.

sphygmograph, an instrument which records differences of pulse in disease and health.

sphygmoid, resembling the pulse.

sphygmomanometer, an instrument for determining the blood pressure in an artery.

sphygmomanometric, pertaining to the blood pressure in an artery.

sphygmometer, an instrument that measures the pulse rate; sphymograph.

sphygmophone, an instrument which makes the pulse beat audible.

sphygmoscope, an instrument which makes the pulse beat visible.

sphygmotonometer, an instrument which measures the elasticity of arterial walls.

sphygmous, pertaining to the pulse.

sphygmus, a pulse.

spica, a reverse spiral bandage with turns crossing each other, resembling a spike of wheat.

spicule, a tiny, needle-shaped body.

spiculum, a sharp, small spike.

spiloma, a mole or skin discoloration; nevus.

spina bifida, the protrusion of the spinal membranes due to a defective closure of the bony encasement of the spinal cord which is a developmental anomaly.

spinal, pertaining to the backbone or spine.

spinal column, the vertebral column which encloses the spinal cord, consisting of thirty-two bones.

spinal cord, the ovoid column of nervous tissue extending through the spinal canal which serves as a center for spinal reflexes and a conducting pathway of impulses to and from the brain.

spine, the vertebral column.

spinobulbar, pertaining to the spinal cord and the medulla oblongata.

spinocerebellar, pertaining to the spinal cord and the cerebellum.

spinose, spinous, pertaining to the spine; spinelike.

spinous process, the prominence at the posterior part of each vertebra.

spireme, the continuous threadlike figure formed by the chromosome material during prophase of meiosis.

spirillemia, the condition caused by the presence of spirilla bacteria in the blood from the genus Spirillum.

Spirillum, a genus of gram-negative bacteria that causes fever in man resulting from a rat-bite.

spirit, any volatile liquor or a solution of volatile liquid in alcohol; alcohol.

spirochete, a slender threadlike bacteria which is spiral in shape that is from the genus Spirocheta causing diseases, as syphilis and yaws.

spirochetosis, infection caused by spirochetes.

spirograph, an instrument for recording respiratory movements.

spiroid, resembling a spiral.

spirometer, an instrument that determines the air capacity of the lungs; pneometer, pneumatometer.

spirometry, measurement of the air capacity of the lungs.

spirophore, a device used for artificial respiration; iron lung.

spit, saliva; to expectorate spittle; expectoration; sputum.

spittle, saliva; digestive fluid of the mouth.

splanchna, intestines or viscera.

splanchnemphraxis, obstruction of any internal organ, such as intestines.

splanchnic, pertaining to viscera or intestines.

splanchnicectomy, surgical excision of part of a splanchnic nerve.

splanchnic nerves, three nerves from the thoracic sympathetic ganglia that control the viscera.

splanchnicotomy, surgical procedure of incising a splanchnic nerve.

splanchnology, the branch of medicine concerned with the study of the viscera or intestines.

splanchnopathy, any diseased condition of the viscera.

splayfoot, flatfoot; talis valgus.

spleen, a spongy, glandlike organ situated in the upper part of the abdomen posterior and inferior to the stomach, important to blood formation, blood storage, blood filtration, and formation of antibodies.

splenadenoma, enlargement of the spleen due to hyperplasia of its pulp.

splenalgia, pain in the spleen.

splenectasis, enlargement of the spleen.

splenectomy, surgical removal of the spleen.

splenectopia, displacement of the spleen; floating spleen.

splenic, pertaining to the spleen.

splenitis, inflammation of the spleen.

splenius, a compress or bandage; a broad, flat, band-like muscle of the upper dorsal region and the back and side of the neck, which serves in rotating the head and neck.

splenocele, hernia of the spleen.

splenoma, a tumor of the spleen.

splenomegaly, an abnormal growth of the spleen; enlargement of the spleen.

splint, a rigid appliance made of bone, wood, metal, or plaster used to fixate a fractured or dislocated bone or to protect an injured part of the body.

splinting, application of a splint to fixate a fractured or dislocated bone; in dentistry, a fixed restoration of two or more teeth into a rigid unit; rigidity of muscles which occurs as a means of avoiding pain caused by movement.

spondylalgia, pain in the vertebrae.

spondylitis, inflammation of the vertebrae.

spondylopathy, any disorder of the vertebrae.

spondylosyndesis, a surgical formation of joining two vertebrae.

spondylotomy, surgical removal of part of the vertebral column.

sponge, a porous, absorbent mass of gauze or cotton surrounded by gauze used in surgery to mop up fluids; an elastic fibrous skeleton of certain marine animals.

spontaneity, the quality of being spontaneous; behavior or activity that is spontaneous.

spontaneous, occurring voluntarily, as arising from one's own impulses.

spontaneous fracture, fracture resulting from the state of the bone and causing little or no injury.

sporadic, intermittent; occurring singly and widely scattered.

spore, an oval, refractile body formed within bacteria, as in Bacillus and Clostridium, which is resistant to environmental changes and difficult to destroy.

spot, a small blemish or macula; scar; birthmark.

spotted fever, any various eruptive fevers: Typhus, Tick fever, Cerebrospinal meningitis, or Rocky Mountain spotted fever.

sprain, the wrenching of a joint without producing dislocation.

sprue, a chronic malabsorption syndrome applied to three closely related conditions: namely, tropical sprue, idiopathic steatorrhea (nontropical), and celiac. Tropical sprue and nontropical sprue affect adults. Celiac disease is limited to children, but all three conditions involve the mucosa of the small intestine resulting in impaired food absorption. Symptoms are diarrhea, bulky and foul stools which are usually greyish in color, weakness, loss of weight, and other conditions.

spud, a spadelike bladed surgical instrument used to dislodge foreign substances.

spur, a sharply pointed bony projection; calcar.

sputum, spittle; any mixed matter with saliva that is expectorated through the mouth.

squama, a thin, scaly platelike structure.

squint, strabismus; to partly close the eyes, as in excess light.

stabile, resistant to change; stable; fixed.

stability, the quality of being stable.

stable, fixed; resistant to change; steady.

staccato speech, jerky pronunciation of words and syllables; scanning speech.

stage, a time period in the course of disease.

stagnation, the cessation of motion; stasis.

stain, a dye or reagent used in staining specimen for microscopic examination.

stamina, endurance; having strength to endure conditions resulting from disease, fatigue, or privation.

stammer, speech disorder marked by involuntary pauses while speaking; stuttering.

standard, an established measurement or model of authority to which other similar things should conform.

stanch, to stop the flow of blood from a wound.

stapedectomy, surgical removal of the stapes in the ear.

stapedial, pertaining to the stapes.

stapes, the stirrup, one of the three small bones in the middle ear.

staphyle, the fleshy mass hanging from the soft palate; uvula.

staphylectomy, surgical excision of the uvula; staphylotomy.

staphylitis, inflammation of the uvula, or staphyle.

staphylococcus, any organism of the genus Staphylococcus causing body infection.

Staphylococcus aureus, a species commonly present on the skin and mucous membranes of the nose and mouth that causes inflammation and suppurative conditions such as boils, carbuncles, and internal abscesses.

staphylohemia, the presence of staphylococci in the blood.

staphylorrhaphy, suture of a cleft palate.

starch, any of a group of polysaccharides found in plants that are able to be hydrolized by water in the body into maltose and then into glucose which provide heat and energy for humans.

stasis, stoppage of the flow of blood, urine, or the contents of the intestines due to illness, or disease.

stasophobia, abnormal fear of standing up.

stat, at once.

state, condition of a patient; situation.

statistics, numerical facts pertaining to a certain subject, such as vital statistics which present human natality, morbidity, and mortality in a given population.

status, a condition or state.

statutory rape, sexual intercourse with a female under legal age of consent.

steapsin, a fat-splitting enzyme of the pancreatic juice; lipase.

stearate, salt or ester of stearic acid.

stearic acid, a fatty acid found in solid animal fats and in a few vegetable fats used in producing lubricants, cosmetics, and medicine preparations.

steariform, resembling fat.

stearodermia, a disease of the sebaceous glands of the skin.

stearrhea, an excessive secretion of sebum or fat.

steatitis, inflammation of adipose tissue.

steatoma, a lipoma; a fatty mass found within a sebaceous gland.

steatopathy, disease of the sebaceous glands of the skin.

steatopygia, abnormal fat accumulation of the buttocks.

steatorrhea, excessive secretion of sebaceous glands; fatty stools caused by pancreatic diseases.

stegnosis, checking an excess secretion or discharge; closing a passageway; constipation.

stellate, star-shaped; radiating from a center.

stenocephaly, an abnormal narrowness of the head.

stenosed, narrowed or constricted.

stenosis, narrowing of a body opening or passage.

stenotic, pertaining to stenosis.

stereoarthrolysis, surgical formation of a new movable joint in cases of bony ankylosis.

stereognosis, having the ability to recognize the form and nature of objects by touch.

sterile, barren; not fertile; aseptic; free from living microorganisms.

sterility, state of being sterile.

sterilization, complete destruction of all microorganisms; any procedure rendering an individual incapable of reproduction.

sterilizer, an appliance for sterilizing especially medical instruments, such as an autoclave or steam-pressure cooker.

sternal, pertaining to the sternum.

sternalgia, pain in the sternum.

sternocostal, pertaining to the sternum and ribs.

sternohyoid, pertaining to the sternum and hyoid bone.

sternoid, resembling the sternum.

sternum, the narrow, flat bone in the median line of the thorax; breastbone.

sternutatory, an agent that causes sneezing; inducing sneezing.

steroid, a group of fat-soluble organic compounds which includes many hormones, cardiac aglycones, bile acids, and sterols.

sterol, any of a group of substances which are related to fats and belong to the lipids found in animals or plants.

stertor, laborious breathing or snoring due to obstruction of the air passages.

stertorous, pertaining to laborious breathing or sonorous respiration; a snoring sound.

stethoscope, an instrument used in auscultation of sounds produced in the body, which consists of rubber tubing in a Y shape.

stethoscopic, pertaining to a stethoscope.

stethoscopy, examination by menas of the stethoscope.

sthenia, normal strength.

sthenic, active, vigorous, and strong.

stigma, a mark or pupuric lesion on the skin; any mental or physical peculiarity that helps to identify or diagnose a specific disease or condition.

stigmatic, pertaining to a stigma; marked with a stigma.

stigmatism, marked by the presence of stigmata; a condition of the eyes in which the rays of light are accurately focused on the retina.

stilbestrol, diethylstilbestrol, a synthetic estrogen.

stilet, stilette, a very small, sharp-pointed instrument used for probing; a wire used to pass through a flexible catheter.

stillbirth, the birth of a dead fetus.

stillborn, dead at birth.

stimulant, any agent that produces a transient surge of energy and strength of activity.

stimulate, to increase functional activity.

stimulation, the act of stimulating or that of being stimulated.

stimulus, any agent that produces functional or tropic reaction in a receptor, organ, or irritable tissue.

sting, a sharp sensation due to a prick, wound, astringent, or tiny pointed organ of bees, wasps, and certain other insects.

stirrup, stapes in the middle ear.

stitch, a sudden, temporary pain; a suture.

stoma, a mouthlike opening which is kept open to allow drainage.

stomach, the large musculomembranous pouch which is the principal organ of digestion extending from the esophagus to the duodenum, and consisting of a fundus, or cardiac part, a body, and a pyloric part.

stomachalgia, pain in the stomach.

stomachic, a medicine which aids functional activity of the stomach.

stomatitis, inflammation of the mouth.

stomatology, the branch of medicine concerned with diseases and treatments of the mouth.

stomatomycosis, any disease of the mouth caused by fungi.

stomatopathy, any disorder of the mouth.

stomatoplasty, plastic repair of the mouth.

stomodeum, the ectodermal depression in the embryo which becomes the front part of the mouth.

stone, a calculus.

stool, fecal discharge from the bowels.

strabismus, a squint; a disorder of vision due to the turning of one or both eyes so that both cannot be directed at the same point at the same time; cross-eyed.

strabometer, a device for measuring the degree of strabismus.

strabotomy, section of an ocular tendon, a surgical procedure used in treatment of strabismus.

strain, to overexercise; overexertion or overstretching of musculature; to filter.

strangulated, congestion by restriction, or hernial stricture.

strangulation, a choking or arrest of respiration by an obstruction of the air passages.

strangury, a condition in urination marked by slow and painful discharge of urine.

stratification, an arrangement in layers.

stratum, a layer.

Streptobacillus, a genus of gram-negative bacteria which are grouped together to form a chain, the causative agent of Haverhill fever.

streptococcus, spherical bacteria from the genus Streptococcus, usually resembling long chains which are nonmotile, some of which are dangerous pathogens of man causing infection.

streptokinase, a proteolytic enzyme present in hemolytic streptococci which break down blood clots and fibrinous material.

streptomycin, an antibiotic derived from soil fungus.

streptosepticemia, septicemia resulting from infection by streptococci.

stress, a forcibly exerted influence or pressure; any adverse stimulus that tends to disturb the homeostasis of an organism, such as a physical, mental, or emotional stressor.

stressor, an agent or condition capable of producing stress.

stria, a streak line, or ridge; a narrow band or stripe; in anatomy, the longitudinal collections of nerve fibers found in the brain.

stria atrohica, fine pinkish or purplish, scarlike lesions that later become white found on the skin of the abdomen, breasts, thighs, and buttocks, caused by weakening of elastic tissues associated with obesity, tumor, or pregnancy (striae gravidarum).

stricture, an abnormal contraction or narrowing of a passage, or duct; stenosis.

stridor, a harsh or high-pitched respiratory sound, caused by an obstruction of the air passages.

stroke, a sudden attack or affliction, such as apoplexy or paralysis.

stroma, supporting tissue or matrix around an organ.

Strongylus, a genus of nematode parasites which inhabit man and many animals producing serious pathological conditions.

strophanthin, a white, crystalline glucoside obtained from the dogbane plant family, used as a stimulant in certain heart diseases.

struma, an enlargement of the thyroid gland; goiter.

strychnine, a poisonous alkaloid derived from plants.

strychninism, chronic strychnine poisoning induced by overdosing.

stump, the distal part of a limb after amputation.

stupe, a hot, wet cloth for external application which may be medicated.

stupefactive, an agent that produces stupor.

stupor, partial or complete unconsciousness, or deadened sensibility, mental apathy, or reduced responsiveness.

stuporous, affected with stupor, or reduced responsiveness.

stuttering, a speech disorder marked by spasmodic repetition of sounds, especially consonants.

sty, stye, an inflammatory enlargement of a sebaceous gland on the eyelid near the edge.

stylet, a wire placed into a catheter or cannula to render it stiff, used as a probe to remove debris.

styloid, resembling a pillar; pertaining to the styloid process of the temporal bone.

stype, a tampon of cotton.

styptic, contracting a blood vessel; an astringent that checks a hemorrhage; hemostat; astringent.

subacute, somewhat acute; between acute and chronic, but having some acute features.

subarachnoid, between the arachnoid and the pia mater.

subcartilaginous, below the cartilage.

subclavian, below the clavicle.

subclavian artery, the main artery of the arm at the base of the neck beneath the clavicle.

subclavian vein, the main vein beneath the clavicle leading to the arm.

subclinical, pertaining to disorders without clinical manifestations.

subconscious, not clearly conscious; existing beyond consciousness.

subcortex, the substance of the brain underlying the cortex.

subculture, pertaining to a culture of bacteria derived from another culture; a culture derived from another culture.

subcutaneous, beneath the skin; an injection introduced beneath the skin.

subduct, to draw downward.

subfebrile, somewhat feverish, less than 101°F.

subglossal, below the tongue.

subiliac, below the ilium.

subject, an individual or animal subjected to treatment, observation, or experiment; a corpse for dissection.

subjective, perceived only by the subject or person, and not by the examiner.

sublatio retinae, detachment of the retina.

sublimation, a defense mechanism operating outside of conscious awareness in which unacceptable instinctual drives are exhibited in a personal and social acceptable way.

subliminal, below the threshold of sensation; subconscious.

sublingual, situated beneath the tongue.

submaxilla, mandible.

submaxillary, below the maxilla or lower jaw.

submaxillary gland, a salivary gland.

submicroscopic, a size too small to be seen with a microscope.

subnormal, less than normal intelligence.

subocular, situated beneath the eye.

suborbital, beneath the orbit of the eye.

subpharyngeal, beneath the pharynx.

subphrenic, below the diaphragm.

subscapular, below the scapula.

subscription, the directions for compounding ingredients in a prescription.

subsidence, gradual abatement of symptoms of a disease.

substantia alba, the white substance of the brain.

substantia cinerea, the gray matter of the brain and spinal cord.

succorrhea, an excessive flow of any body secretion or of a digestive fluid.

succus, fluid produced by a living tissue.

succussion, shaking of a patient to determine the presence of either fluid or gas in a body cavity.

suckle, to nurse from a breast.

sucrase, an enzyme in the intestinal juice.$ sucrose, a crystalline compound obtained from sugar cane, sugar beet and other sources which is hydrolyzed in the intestine to glucose and fructose.

sudation, sweating.

sudatorium, a hot-air bath to induce sweating.

sudor, perspiration, or sweating.

sudoriferous, conveying or producing sweat; secretion of perspiration.

sudorific, a drug that causes sweating.

suffocate, to asphyxiate; to smother; to choke by stopping respiration.

suffocation, the stoppage of respiration; asphyxiation.

sugar, a sweet carbohydrate belonging to one of two groups, either diasaccharides or monosaccharides; sucrose.

suggestibility, being susceptible to suggestion.

suggestion, an idea that is introduced to an individual from without.

suicidal, pertaining to or suggesting suicide.

suicide, taking one's own life; one who intentionally takes his own life.

sulcate, sulcated, furrowed or grooved.

sulcus, a slight depression or fissure, as of the brain.

sulfa drugs, any of the sulfonamide group which possesses bacteriostatic properties; sulfonamides.

sulfanilamide, a crystalline compound derived from sulfanilic acid, used for its potent antibacterial action.

sulfur, a colorless chemical element existing in several forms, used most commonly in pharmaceutical preparations and, in a dry form, as an insecticide and rodenticide.

sunburn, dermatitis caused by prolonged exposure to the sun's rays; to be affected with sunburn; actinodermatitis.

sunstroke, a condition due to excessive exposure to rays of the sun or extreme heat.

superciliary, pertaining to the eyebrow.

supercilium, the eyebrow.

superego, that part of the personality associated with morals, standards, ethics, and self-criticism; part of the psyche which is derived from the id and the ego that acts as a mediator of the ego; the conscience.

superfecundation, fertilization of two or more ova during the same menstrual cycle by two separate acts of coitus.

superfetation, the occurrence of a second conception after one already existing, resulting in two fetuses in the womb at the same time, but of different ages.

superficial, situated on or near the surface of the skin.

superficies, an outer surface.

superinduce, to bring on in addition to something that already exists.

supernormal, beyond what is normal; beyond average human intellect.

supernumerary, in excess of a normal number.

supersaturate, to saturate more of an ingredient than can be contained in a solution.

supinate, to turn the hand so that the palm faces upward; to rotate the foot and leg outward; to assume a position of supination.

supination, turning of the palm or foot upward; lying flat upon the back.

supinator, a muscle that produces the motion of turning the palm and hand upward.

supplemental, adding something to supply a need.

suppository, a semi-solid mass in the form of a cone for introduction into the rectum, vagina, or urethra where it dissolves; a vehicle for medicine to be absorbed.

suppress, to conceal; to restrain from course of action.

suppression, the act of suppressing; conscious effort to conceal unacceptable impulses, thoughts or feelings.

suppurant, the production of pus; any agent that causes the formation of pus.

suppuration, the formation of pus.

suppurative, producing the generation of pus; a drug that produces pus formation.

supraliminal, above the threshold of consciousness; conscious.

supramaxilla, the upper jawbone.

supraorbital, located above the orbit of the eye.

suprarenal, above the kidney; pertaining to an adrenal gland.

suprascapular, situated above the scapula or shoulder blade.

sura, the calf of the leg.

sural, pertaining to the calf of the leg.

surdity, deafness.

surdomute, a deaf-mute; one who is deaf and dumb.

surface, the exterior of the body.

surgeon, a specialist in surgery.

surgery, the branch of medicine concerned with operative procedures for correction of deformities, repair of injuries, diagnosis and cure of diseases, and the relief of suffering and prolongation of life in humans; a room where surgery is performed.

surrogate, a substitute; a thing or person who takes the place of something or someone.

susceptibility, the quality of being susceptible; capacity for feeling emotions; sensitiveness.

suspend, to cease temporarily.

suspension, a condition of cessation, as of animation or pain or of any vital process; a treatment of spinal disorders by suspending a patient by supporting the chin and shoulders.

suspensory ligament, any of a number of ligaments that support anatomical parts, such as the ring-shaped fibrous tissue which holds the lens of the eye.

suspiration, a sigh; the act of sighing.

sustentacular, supporting or sustaining.

sustentation, sustenance, or support of life.

susurrus, a soft murmuring sound; whisper; murmur.

suture, a stitch or stitches that unite the edges of a wound; the material used in stitching a wound; the line of union between the skull bones.

swab, a small bit of cotton or gauze applied to one end of a slender stick which is used for wiping or cleansing or as an applicator for medication.

sweat, perspiration; the substance secreted by the sweat glands.

sweat glands, tubular glands found on all surfaces of the body except the lips, glans penis, and inner surface of prepuce.

sweating, the process of excreting sweat.

swelling, a temporary enlargement of a body part; an abnormal protuberance; a tumor.

swoon, to faint.

sycoma, a large, soft wart.

sycosis, an inflammation of hair follicles of the beard and scalp.

syllepsis, impregnation; pregnancy or conception.

sylvian aqueduct, a narrow passage from the 3rd to 4th ventricle; aqueduct of Sylvius.

symbion, symbiont, an organism which lives with another in a state of symbiosis.

symbiosis, the living together of two different organisms in a close association with both benefiting from the relationship.

symbolia, having the ability to recognize the nature of objects through the sense of touch.

symbolism, a condition in which everything that occurs is interpreted as a symbol of the patient's own thoughts.

symmelus, a fetus with fused legs and one to three feet, or no feet.

symmetrical, pertaining to symmetry.

symmetry, correspondence in arrangement, form, and size of parts found on the opposite side of an axis.

sympathectomy, resection or interruption of some part of the sympathetic nervous system.

sympathetic nervous system, autonomic nervous system which stimulates the heartbeat, dilates the pupils, and contracts the blood vessels, and, in general, functions in opposition of the parasympathetic nervous system.

sympathin, a neurohormonal mediator of nerve impulses at the synapses of sympathetic nerves.

symphysion, most anterior point of the alveolar process of the lower jaw.

symphysis, line of fusion of two bones which are separate in early development, such as the mandible.

symptom, a condition that results or accompanies an illness or a disease from which a diagnosis may be made.

symptomatic, relating to a symptom or symptoms.

symptomatology, the branch of medicine concerned with symptoms; all of the symptoms of a given disease.

synapse, the junction where neural impulses are transmitted, either between two neurons or a neuron and an effector by the release of a chemical neurotransmitter, as acetylcholine or norepinephrine.

synapsis, a stage in meiosis in which homologous chromosomes from the male and female pronuclei pair off.

synaptic, pertaining to a synapse or synapsis.

synarthrosis, a fibrous joint in which two bones that unite cannot move freely; fixed articulation.

synchilia, congenital joining of the lips.

synclonus, a successive clonic contraction of various muscle groups; muscular tremors.

syncope, loss of consciousness; faint; generalized cerebral ischemia causing temporary unconsciousness.

syncytium, a multinucleated mass of protoplasm which is not divided into definite cell structures.

syndactyl, a fusion between adjacent digits of the hand or foot, so that they are more or less webbed together.

syndesis, synapsis; arthrodesis.

syndesmosis, connection of bones by ligaments formed by fibrous connective tissue other than a joint articulation.

syndesmotomy, surgical incision of a ligament.

syndesmus, a ligament.

syndrome, symptoms that occur together; complexus of symptoms.

syneresis, the contraction of a gel causing it to separate from the liquid, as a shrinkage of fibrin from a colloidal gel.

synergetic, cooperative action of muscles working together.

synergism, any cooperative action of two agents that produce more effective results which neither alone could produce, such as two drugs.

synergy, combined action of two or more organs or muscles; coordinated action.

synesthesia, a sensation in one area of the body from a stimulus applied to another area; a subjective sensation of another sense than the specific one being stimulated, as a sound which produces a visual sensation of color.

syngamy, sexual reproduction; the union of female and male gametes to form a zygote in fertilization.

synostosis, union between adjacent bones by the formation of osseous material.

synovia, the transparent lubricating fluid secreted by the synovial membranes present in joints, cavities, bursae, and tendon sheaths.

synovitis, inflammation of the synovial membrane.

synthesis, the process which involves the formation of a complex substance from a simpler compound, as in the synthesis of protein from an amino acid.

synthetic, artificially prepared; relating to synthesis.

syphilis, a venereal disease caused by Treponema pallidium, transmitted by direct sexual contact or in utero, marked by lesions which involve any body organ. The disease usually has three degenerative stages that occur over the course of many years; leus venera.

syphilogy, the study of syphilis and its treatment.

syringe, a small, tubular device for injecting fluids or withdrawing them from a blood vessel or cavity.

syringitis, inflammation of the eustachian tube.

syringomyelia, a disease of the spinal cord in which fluid accumulates in the cavities, replacing the nerve tissue and causing muscle atrophy and spasticity.

syringotome, a surgical instrument used in operating, as an incision of a fistula.

syssarcosis, muscular articulation of bones, as of the hyoid and patella.

systaltic, contracting and dilating of the heart alternately; pulsating.

system, organized grouping of related structures that act together for a common purpose; a method of practice based on specific principles; the human body as an anatomical whole.

systemic, pertaining to a specific system of parts; affecting the entire bodily system or the body as a whole.

systole, the period of contraction of the heart, especially of the ventricles; opposed to diastole.

systolic, pertaining to systole.

systremma, cramp in the calf muscles of the leg.

syzygium, a partial fusion of two structures.

syzygy, the fusion of two organs with each remaining distinct.

T

tabella, medicated material that is formed into a small disk; lozenge, tablet, or troche.

tabes, a gradual wasting or emaciation in any chronic disease.

tabes dorsalis, a late form of syphilis involving the degeneration of the spinal cord and sensory nerve trunks, causing muscular incoordination, intense pain, disturbances in sensation, and eventual paralysis.

tabetic, pertaining to or afflicted with tabes or tabes dorsalis.

tablature, separation or division of the cranial bones into inner and outer tables.

tablet, a small disk containing a solid dose of medicine.

taboparesis, general paralysis associated with tabes.

tache, a blemish, spot, or freckle on the skin.

tachistoscope, an apparatus used to test visual perception by exposing an object or group of objects to view for a selected brief period of time.

tachography, a recording of the movement and speed of the blood flow.

tachyarrhythmia, tachycardia associated with irregularity of normal heart rhythm.

tachycardia, an abnormal rapid heart rate, usually between 160-190 per minute.

tachylalia, speaking extremely rapidly.

tachyphagia, rapid eating.

tachyphrasia, extreme volubility of speech, often accompanying a mental disorder.

tachyphrenia, mental hyperactivity.

tachypnea, extremely rapid respiration.

tactile, pertaining to the sense of touch; touch.

tactile corpuscles, numerous elongated bodies that enclose the endings of afferent nerve fibers which serve as receptors for touch or for slight pressure beneath the epidermis of the finger tips, toes, soles, palms, lips, nipples, and tip of the tongue.

tactometer, a device that measures tactile sensibility.

tactus, touch.

taenia, a bandlike structure; a tapeworm.

taeniacide, an agent that is lethal to tapeworms.

taeniasis, infestation with tapeworms of the genus Taenia.

Tagement, trademark for cimetidine, used to decrease gastric acid secretion.

talalgia, pain in the heel or ankle.

talc, talcum powder, used as a dusting powder.

talipea, a congenital deformity of the foot; clubfoot.

talipomanus, clubhand.

talocalcaneal, pertaining to the talus and calcaneus.

talofibular, pertaining to the talus and fibula.

talpa, mole.

talus, the anklebone; the ankle.

Talwin, trademark for pentazocine used as an analgesic, anti-inflammatory, and antipyretic agent.

tampon, a pack, pad, or plug of cotton used in surgery to control hemorrhage or to absorb secretions, as produced in the nose or vagina; to plug with a tampon.

tannin, an acid substance found in the bark of certain plants and trees and in coffee and tea, used as an astringent, for burns, as an antidote for various poisons, and as a hemostatic; tannic acid.

tantalum, a noncorrosive chemical element used in replacement of cranial defects, for prosthetic appliances, and for fine sutures.

tantrum, a violent outburst of temper, anger, or rage.

tap, to drain of body accumulations of fluid by paracentesis.

tapeinocephaly, a flattening of the top of the skull or head.

tapetum, a layer of cells which cover a structure; a stratum in the human brain which is composed of fibers; a membranous layer, as in the retina.

tapeworm, a parasitic intestinal worm belonging to the class Cestoda, having a flat or bandlike form, characterized by having larval and adult stages in separate hosts.

taphophobia, a morbid fear of being buried alive.

tarantism, a nervous affection marked by manic or hysterical fits of dancing, melancholy, or stupor, believed to be attributed to the bite of a tarantula.

tarantula, a large, venomous spider feared by many, but relatively harmless.

tardive, late or tardy.

tardive dyskinesia, a serious side effect of antipsychotic drugs marked by grimacing, choreiform movements of the arms, fingers, ankles, and toes, and tonic contractions of the muscles of the neck and back, usually irreversible.

target, an area or an object toward which something is directed.

tarsal, pertaining to the tarsus of the foot.

tarsalgia, pain in the tarsus.

tarsalia, referring to the tarsal bones.

tarsectomy, surgical excision of the tarsus or tarsal bone.

tarsectopia, dislocation of the tarsus.

tarsitis, inflammation of the tarsus; inflammation of the upper eyelid.

tarsometatarsal, pertaining to the tarsus and metatarsus.

tarsoplasty, plastic surgery of an eyelid.

tarsotibial, pertaining to the tarsus and the tibia.

tarsotomy, surgical incision of the tarsal cartilage of an eyelid, or the tarsus of the foot.

tarsus, the proximal part of the foot; instep; the collection of bones between the tibia and metatarsus; the connective tissue plate along the edge of the eyelid.

tartar, the hard yallowish substance deposited on the teeth, mainly composed of calcium phosphate.

tastant, any salt capable of gustatory excitation that stimulates the sense of taste.

taste, the ability to distinguish flavor by the sense of taste; taste sensation occurs through stimulation of gustatory nerve endings in the tongue. Four distinguished qualities are: sweet, sour, salty, and bitter.

taste bud, a tiny end organ located on the surface of the tongue which mediates the sensation of taste.

taxis, the replacement of a displaced structure; reduction of a herniated tumor by manipulation, not by incision; the response of a mobile organism to a stimulus.

taxonomy, an orderly classification of organisms into categories according to correct or suitable names.

Tay-Sachs disease, an inherited disease that destroys the nervous system, caused by a lipid metabolism disorder which is always fatal. Tay-Sachs disease results from the absence of the enzyme hexosaminidase which is responsible for the breakdown of fat.

tears, a saline fluid secreted by the lacrimal glands that moistens the surface and cleanses the eyes of foreign particles.

tease, to pull apart or separate gently with very fine needles before microscopic examination.

teat, the nipple of a mammary gland.

technic, technique; expertness in performing the details of a procedure or operation.

technician, one skilled in specific technical procedures.

technologist, a technician who is highly trained and certified.

tectocephaly, having a roof-shaped cranium.

tectum, a roof-shaped structure.

teeth, hard, bony projections in the jaw. There are 32 permanent teeth, 16 in each jaw.

teething, the process of eruption of the teeth.

tegmen, a covering or integument.

tegmental, pertaining to the tegmentum.

tegmentum, a covering or roof; referring to the cerebral peduncle dorsal, a portion of the midbrain.

tegument, a natural covering of skin.

tegumental, pertaining to the skin.

teichopsia, attacks of temporary blindness, marked by zigzag lines appearing in the visual field, sometimes accompanying headache and mental or physical strain.

tela, a weblike structure.

telalgia, pain felt at a distance from its stimulus; pain referred.

telangiectasis, dilatation of the capillaries and other small blood vessels which cause an angioma of macular appearance, such as a birthmark in young children, or as caused by alcoholism, exposure to cold weather, diseases, and infections. May occur on the face, thighs, or nose.

telangitis, inflammation of the capillaries.

telencephalic, pertaining to the telencephalon.

telencephalon, endbrain; the anterior division of the forebrain.

teleneuron, a nerve ending.

teleopsia, a disturbance in vision in which objects appear to be farther away than they actually are.

telepathy, the communication of thought by means of extrasensory perception.

telesthesia, telepathy; the ability to respond to a stimulus beyond the usual range of perception.

telesystolic, pertaining to the termination of cardiac systole.

telolemma, the membrane covering the motor end plate in a striated muscle fiber.

telomere, pertaining to the ends of the chromosomes which have specific properties, such as having polarity that prevents reunion with any fragments after the chromosome has been broken.

telophase, the last of four stages of mitosis, and of two divisions of meiosis.

temperament, the combination of qualities, physical and mental, that determine personality.

temperature, heat or cold expressed in terms of a specific scale. Normal body temperature is 98.6° F or 37° C.

temple, the flattened area on either side of the forehead.

temporal, pertaining to the temple; pertaining to time; temporary.

temporal bone, one of the two bones on either side of the head.

temporalis, a muscle in the depression of the temporal bone which elevates the mandible.

temulence, intoxication; drunkenness.

tenaculum, a hooklike instrument used to grasp and hold parts in surgery or dissection.

tenalgia, pain in a tendon.

tenderness, sensitiveness to pain when pressure is applied to the skin.

tendinitis, inflammation of a tendon.

tendinous, resembling tendons; composed of tendons.

tendon, a fibrous cord of connective tissue by which a muscle is attached to a bone or cartilage.

tenesmus, painful straining in defecating or urinating.

tenia, taenia, a flat band of soft tissue; a tapeworm of the genus Taenia.

teniacide, an agent that is lethal to tapeworms.

teniafuge, an agent that expels tapeworms.

tennis elbow, radiohumeral bursitis; epicondylitis; pain caused by overexertion of the arm.

tenodesis, surgical fixation of the end of a tendon to a bone.

Tenon's capsule, a thin connective tissue that envelops the eyeball behind the conjunctiva.

tenontitis, inflammation of Tenon's capsule; tendinitis.

tenophyte, a growth in a tendon.

tenotomy, surgical section of a tendon.

tensile, pertaining to tension; capable of being stretched.

tension, the act of stretching or being stretched or strained.

tensor, any muscle that stretches or tightens a body part.

tent, a fabric covering placed over a patient's head for administering oxygen or vaporized medication.

tentative, a diagnosis which is subject to change because of insufficient data; experimental.

tenth nerve, vagus nerve.

tentum, the penis.

tenuity, the condition of being thin.

tenuous, slender or thin.

tephromyelitis, inflammation of the gray matter of the spinal cord.

teras, a deformed fetus; a monster.

teratology, the science dealing with monstrosities and malfomations of fetuses.

teratoma, congenital tumor that contains embryonic elements of the three primary germ layers, as teeth or hair; dermoid.

teratoid, resembling a monster.

terebration, the act of boring; boring pain; trephining.

teres, round and smooth; long and cylindrical.

term, parturition; a definite period; the normal nine months of pregnancy.

terminal, pertaining to an end; a termination, or ending.

terminology, the vocabulary of a science; nomenclature.

Terramycin, trademark for the oxy derivative of tetracycline, used as an antibiotic effective against rickettsias and some viruses.

tertiary syphilis, the third stage of syphilis and the most advanced stage.

test, an examination or trial; a chemical reaction; reagent.

testectomy, surgical removal of a testicle.

testicle, one of two oval-shaped glands of reproduction in the male; testis.

testicular, pertaining to the testis.

testitis, inflammation of the testicle or testicles.

testosterone, the principal male hormone responsible for secondary male sex characteristics.

tetanic, pertaining to tetanus.

tetanoid, resembling tetanus.

tetanus, an infectious disease, often fatal, caused by the neurotoxin of Clostridium tetani, marked by painful spasms of the voluntary muscles, especially those of the lower jaw and neck; lockjaw.

tetany, a condition characterized by painful muscle spasms, which are irregular and intermittent, usually occurring in the extremities due to an inability to utilize calcium salts.

tetracycline, a drug obtained naturally from certain soil bacilli of the genus Streptomyces or produced synthetically, used as an antibiotic.

tetrad, an arrangement of four chromosomes during meiosis by splitting off paired chromosomes.

tetralogy of Fallot, a congenital malformation of the heart involving pulmonic stenosis. As the infant grows, the pulmonary blood flow cannot increase causing right ventricular hypertrophy and shunting of blood from the right to the left ventricle, producing cyanosis. Growth of the child is poor, symptoms of fatigue, polycythemia and clubbing of the hands appear at the time cyanosis, a blue discoloration to the skin from lack of oxygen, becomes evident; a series of four congenital heart defects.

tetraparesis, muscular weakness present in all four extremities.

tetraplegia, quadriplegia.

tetraploidy, having four sets of chromosomes.

tetter, any of many cutaneous diseases, as impetigo, herpes, ringworm, and eczema.

textural, pertaining to the structure of tissues.

thalamencephalon, the part of the brain containing the optic thalami and the pineal gland.

thalamus, the region of the brain concerned with many bodily functions which lies between the hypothalamus and epithalamus, the center for sensory impulses to the cerebral cortex.

thalidomide, a sedative and hypnotic that causes serious congenital anomalies in the fetus when taken during early pregnancy.

thanatoid, resembling death.

thanatology, the science concerned with death and dying.

thanatophoric, lethal or deadly.

thanatos, in psychoanalysis, death instinct.

theca, a caselike structure or sheath.

thecal, pertaining to a sheath.

thecitis, inflammation of the sheath of a tendon.

thelalgia, pain in the nipples.

theleplasty, plastic surgery on a nipple.

thelitis, inflammation of a nipple.

thelium, a nipple or papilla.

thenar, the fleshy part of the hand below the thumb; palm.

theobromine, an alkaloid found in cacao seeds which have properties similar to caffeine, used as a smooth muscle relaxant, a diuretic, and as a myocardial stimulant and vasodilator.

theophobia, a morbid fear of God.

therapeutic, pertaining to therapeutics; curative.

therapeutics, the science of healing; scientific treatment of diseases and the application of remedies.

therapeutist, one skilled in therapeutics; a therapist.

therapy, the treatment of disease or a pathological condition.

therm, a unit of heat.

thermal, pertaining to heat.

thermoanesthesia, inability to distinguish between heat and cold.

thermocauterectomy, excision by thermocautery.

thermocautery, cautery by a heated wire or point.

thermogenesis, the production of heat within the body.

thermogram, a graphic record of variations of temperature.

thermograph, an instrument used for recording variations of temperature.

thermolabile, changed easily by heat; unstable.

thermolysis, a heat loss from the body due to evaporation; a chemical dissociation caused by heat.

thermomassage, the use of heat in massage.

thermometer, an instrument to measure heat.

thermophile, an organism that thrives in elevated temperatures.

thermophore, an apparatus for retaining heat.

thermoplegia, sunstroke; heatstroke.

thermostable, not destroyed by heat.

thermotaxis, the regulation and normal adjustment of the body to temperature; the movement of an organism toward or away from the stimulation of temperature or heat source.

thermotherapy, the therapeutic use of heat in treatment of disease.

thermotropism, the property within organisms to respond to heat stimulus.

thiamine, a B-complex vitamin compound found in animal and plant foods, dry yeast, and wheat germ which are the richest natural resources, essential to man for normal metabolism of both fats and carbohydrates; vitamin B$_1$.

thigh, that part of the leg between the knee and the hip.

thighbone, femur.

thigmesthesia, sense of touch; tactile sensibility.

thimerosal, used as a germicide and an antiseptic.

thinking, the process of forming concepts and images in one's mind.

thiopental, a short-acting barbiturate used in its salt form intravenously or rectally to induce general anesthesia.

thiouracil, an antithyroid drug used in treatment of hyperthyroidism, thyroiditis, and thyrotoxicosis which reduces the production of thyroid gland hormones.

third cranial nerve, regulates eye movements.

third-degree burn, implies a destruction of the full thickness of the skin, often of underlying fat, muscles and even bone, giving a pale white or charred appearance to the skin.

thirst, a craving for fluids, especially water.

thoracentesis, a puncture through the chest wall for tapping or removal of fluids; pleurocentesis.

thoracic, pertaining to the chest.

thoracic duct, the main lymphatic vessel of the body, which originates at the cisterna chyli on the abdomen.

thoracostomy, an opening of the chest wall for drainage or for an enlarged heart.

thoracotomy, surgical cutting into the chest wall.

thorax, the area between the base of the neck and the diaphragm.

Thorazine, trademark for chlorpromazine, a major tranquilizer used to treat severely excited psychiatric patients.

threadworm, term commonly applied to the pinworm which inhabits the intestines.

three-day fever, a viral disease which resembles dengue, transmitted by the sandfly.

threonine, one of the essential amino acids.

threshold, that point at which an effect is produced by a stimulus.

thrill, a vibration felt on palpation; to produce a sensation of tingling, as in excitement.

throat, the passage that extends from the nose and mouth to the lungs; pharynx; fauces.

throb, pulsating movement, as a heart beat,; palpitation.

throbbing, a pulsation, beating, or rhythmic movement.

throe, a severe pain, especially the sharp pain in childbirth.

thrombin, the enzyme that produces coagulation of the blood, resulting from the activation of prothrombin; a preparation used as a topical hemostatic that controls capillary bleeding.

thromboangitis, inflammation of a blood vessel.

thrombocyte, a blood platelet which aids in coagulation.

thromboembolism, an embolism carried by the blood from the site of origin to block another vessel.

thrombogenesis, clot formation.

thrombolysis, dissolution or breaking up of a thrombus.

thrombophlebitis, inflammation of a vein caused by a thrombus formation.

thromboplastic, acceleration of the formation of clots in the blood.

thromboplastin, a lipoprotein that promotes the conversion of prothrombin to thrombin.

thrombosis, formation of a thrombus.

thrombotic, pertaining to thrombosis.

thrombus, a blood clot that obstructs a blood vessel or a cavity of the heart.

thrush, a disease of the oral mucous membranes that forms whitish patches which become ulcerated, usually in infants and young children, caused by Candida albicans.

thumb, the first digit of the hand on the radial side.

thylacitis, inflammation of the sebaceous glands of the skin.

thymectomy, surgical removal of the thymus gland.

thymic, pertaining to the thymus gland.

thymion, a wart.

thymin, a hormone-like substance secreted by the thymus gland that impairs neuromuscular transmission.

thymine, a pyrimidine base found in DNA.

thymitis, inflammation of the thymus gland.

thymocyte, a lymphocyte produced by the thymus gland.

thymolysis, dissolution of thymus tissue.

thymolytic, thymus tissue destruction.

thymoma, a tumor arising from lymphoid or epithelial tissues of the thymus gland.

thymus, a ductless gland situated in the upper thoracic cavity, necessary in early life for the development of immunological functions, and which undergoes involution in adults.

thyroadenitis, inflammation of the thyroid gland.

thyrocele, a goiter.

thyrochondrotomy, surgical incision of the thyroid cartilage.

thyroid, a gland, in the neck, that partially surrounds the thyroid cartilage and upper rings of the trachea; thyroid secretions consist of two hormones, thyroxine and triiodothyronine, which help to regulate the metabolic rate, the growth process, and tissue differentiation. Thyroid extract is composed of dried thyroid glands of ox and sheep.

thyroid cartilage, the principal cartilage of the larynx which forms a v-shaped structure known as the Adam's apple.

thyroidectomy, surgical removal of part or all of the thyroid gland.

thyroiditis, inflammation of the thyroid gland.

thyroptosis, a displaced thyroid gland, partially or completely into the thorax.

thyrotome, a surgical instrument for excising the thyroid cartilage.

thyrotoxicosis, a disorder caused by an overactive thyroid gland; Graves' disease.

thyroxine, an iodine-containing hormone that is secreted by the thyroid gland responsible for increasing the rate of cell metabolism.

tibia, shinbone.

tibial, pertaining to the tibia.

tic, an involuntary, repetitive, compulsive movement of certain muscles of the face and shoulders.

tic douloureux, facial neuralgia accompanied by convulsive twitching.

tick, a parasitic mite or acarid of the genus Ixodes which buries its head into the skin of the host to suck blood, often transmitting diseases.

tick fever, an infectious disease transmitted by the bite of a woodtick; Rocky Mountain spotted fever.

tilmus, picking at bedsores in delirious patients.

tincture, diluted alcoholic solution used in preparation of a drug or a chemical substance, such as ginger, benzoin, guaiac, and others.

tinea, any of many different superficial fungal infections of the skin; ringworm.

tinnitus, a ringing or buzzing sound in the ear.

tissue, a grouping of similarly specialized cells that perform certain specific functions.

titillation, sensation produced by tickling, as in the throat; state of being tickled.

titubation, a staggering walk with shaking of the head and trunk, usually due to cerebellar diseases.

tocology, obstetrics.

toe, a digit of the foot.

Tofranil, trademark for imipramine preparations used to alleviate depression associated with specific mental conditions.

toilet, the cleansing and dressing of a wound.

tolbutamide, an oral hypoglycemic drug used to control uncomplicated, mild, stable diabetes mellitus in those who have some functioning islet cells; trademark name, Orinase.

tolerance, having the ability to endure without injury or effect.

tolerate, to resist the action of drugs or toxins.

tolmentum, a network of blood vessels found within the cortex of the brain and the cerebral surface of the pia mater.

tomography, a method of producing images of cross-sections of the body.

tonaphasia, the loss of recall of a tune due to cerebral lesions.

tone, having normal tension and vigor in muscles; tonus; a quality of sound or vocal production.

tone deafness, inability to distinguish musical pitch.

tongue, the freely moving muscular organ situated in the floor of the mouth which functions in mastication of food, taste, and in speech production.

tongue tie, a congenital shortening of the frenum which restricts tongue movement.

tonic, restoration of normal muscle tone; characterized by tension or contraction; an agent or remedy.

tonicity, the normal elastic tension of living muscles, arteries, etc.; in body fluid physiology, the effective osmotic pressure equivalent; tone.

tonography, recording the changes in intraocular pressure due to sustained pressure on the eyeball.

tonometer, a physiological instrument that measures the tension of the eyeball.

tonometric, pertaining to a tonometer or tonometry.

tonometry, measurement of tension of the eyeball.

tonsil, a rounded mass of lymphoid tissue, one on either side of the pharynx, which acts as a filter to protect the body from infection or invasion of bacteria.

tonsillar, pertaining to a tonsil.

tonsillectomy, surgical excision of a tonsil.

tonsillitis, inflammation of the tonsils.

tonus, the normal state of tension in muscles; a continuous contraction of a muscle.

tooth, one of the hard processes situated in the jaw which serves for biting and mastication of food.

toothache, pain in a tooth or area around the tooth.

tophus, a deposit of sodium biurate formed in the fibrous tissue near a joint, especially in gout.

topical, pertaining to a definite area; applied to a particular part of the body.

topography, a description of a specific part of the body.

tormen, a twisting or griping pain in the intestines.

torpor, sluggishness; abnormal inactivity; apathy.

torporific, causing torpor.

torque, rotary force; in dentistry, the rotation of a tooth on its axis by use of an orthodontic instrument.

torsion, the act of twisting, or state of being twisted.

torso, the trunk of the body, which excludes the head and limbs.

torticollis, wryneck; torsion of the neck caused by the contracted state of cervical muscles.

tortuous, full of many twists and turns.

torulus, a papilla or small elevation in the skin.

torus, a rounded swelling; a bulging or protuberant part.

touch, tactile sense; palpation by touching with the fingers.

tourniquet, a band that is placed tightly around a limb for the temporary arrest of circulation or hemorrhaging in the distal region.

toxalbumin, poisonous albumin or protein.

toxanemia, toxemia.

toxemia, the spread of bacterial toxins by the bloodstream, marked by fever, diarrhea, vomiting, quickened or depressed pulse and respirations, prostration.

toxemia of pregnancy, a specific hypertensive disease of pregnancy or of early puerperium (six week period after childbirth).

toxic, pertaining to a toxin or poison; poisonous.

toxicant, any toxic agent, or poison.

toxicity, having a toxic or poisonous quality; state of being toxic.

toxicoderma, a skin disease caused by poison.

toxicogenic, producing toxic or poisonous products.

toxicologist, one who specializes in the field of poisons and treatments.

toxicology, the science concerned with poisons, their effects, and antidotes.

toxicosis, any abnormal diseased condition due to poisoning or toxic action.

toxin, any organic poison of animal or plant origin; any poisonous substances produced by pathogenic organisms that cause disease in other living organisms.

toxin-antitoxin, a nearly neutral mixture of diphtheria toxin with an antitoxin, used for immunization against diphtheria.

toxinic, pertaining to a toxin.

toxipathy, any disease due to a poison.

toxiphobia, morbid fear of being poisoned.

toxoid, toxic properties of a toxin destroyed by a chemical agent, but still capable of inducing the formation of antibodies.

toxoplasmosis, a disease of the nervous system caused by Toxoplasma gondii, a parasitic protozoan, of which there is a congenital form and an acquired form.

trabecula, a supportive strand of connective tissue, which resembles a small beam extending from a structural part, as from a capsule into the enclosed organ.

trabecular, pertaining to a trabecula.

trachea, the windpipe; the membranous tube extending from the larynx to the bronchi.

tracheal, pertaining to the trachea.

tracheitis, inflammation of the trachea.

tracheobronchial, related to both the bronchi and the trachea.

tracheobronchoscopy, inspection of the trachea and bronchi with a bronchoscope.

tracheoscopy, inspection of the interior of the trachea with a laryngoscope.

tracheostomy, an incision of the trachea for the creation of an opening through the neck; used also for the insertion of a tube to relieve obstruction of the upper airway and to facilitate breathing or ventilation.

tracheotome, a surgical instrument for incising the trachea.

tracheotomy, surgical incision of the trachea.

trachitis, tracheitis, inflammation of the trachea.

trachoma, a contagious disease involving the conjunctiva and cornea of the eyes caused by Chlamydia trachomatis, marked by formation of granulations or tiny rounded growths.

trachomatous, pertaining to or affected with trachoma.

tract, a specific area of the body, especially of a system of related organs; a bundle of nerve fibers within the brain or spinal cord which compose a functional unit.

traction, the act of pulling or drawing.

tractus, a path or tract.

tragus, a cartilaginous projection in front of the external meatus of the ear.

trait, a distinguishing quality of an individual; a characteristic.

trance, an unconscious or hypnotic condition or state.

tranquilize, to render tranquil.

tranquilizer, drugs used in treatment of anxiety states, mental disorders, and neuroses.

transcription, synthesis of RNA using a DNA template.

transect, to cut across or divide.

transection, cross section.

transference, the unconscious transfer of attitudes and feelings to others that once were associated with parents, siblings, or significant others in forgotten childhood experiences; in psychiatry, the patient shifts any affect from one idea to another, or from one person to another by unconscious identification. Transference in the patient-physician relationship may be negative or positive.

transformation, the change of one tissue into another; degeneration.

transfuse, to transfer blood or blood components from one person into another directly into the blood stream.

transfusion, the process of transfusing.

transillumination, examination of a cavity or organ by the passage of a strong light through a body structure.

translocation, in genetics, the attachment of a fragment of one chromosome to another that is nonhomologous.

transmigration, the process of passing across or through, especially passage of white blood cells through the capillary membranes into the surrounding tissues; the passage of an ovum from the ovary to the uterus.

transmission, the transfer of disease from one individual to another; transfer of hereditary characteristics or traits.

transmutation, the process of evolution in which one species changes into another; change of properties of one substance into another.

transpiration, the discharge of moisture, air, or vapor through the skin or a membrane; perspiration.

transpire, to excrete perspiration through the pores in the skin.

transplant, a transfer of tissue in a graft to be transplanted from another person or from one body part to another site.

transplantation, the grafting of tissue or an organ from one person to another; grafting from one part of the body to another part.

transudation, a substance that has transuded; a fluid that has extruded from a tissue.

transude, to ooze through the pores of a membrane.

transverse, extending from side to side; lying crosswise.

transverse colon, that part of the colon that extends crosswise the abdominal cavity.

transversectomy, surgical removal of the transverse vertebral process.

transverse process, the right and left lateral projections from the posterior part of vertebra.

transvestism, the condition of finding sexual pleasure by wearing clothing appropriate to the opposite sex.

transvestite, one who has an uncontrollable compulsion to dress in clothing appropriate to the opposite sex.

trapezium, a bone in the wrist which is the first bone in the distal row of eight carpal bones.

trapezius, a large, flat triangular muscle that covers the posterior surface of the neck and shoulder serving to raise and lower the shoulder.

trauma, an injury or wound; an emotional shock causing injury to the subconscious which may have a lifelong effect.

traumatic, pertaining to trauma.

traumatism, an abnormal condition of the system produced by an injury or trauma.

treatment, the care and management of a patient; the application of medicinal remedies or surgery in combating disease or pathological conditions; therapy.

tremble, involuntary shaking or quivering.

tremor, involuntary quivering or shaking from fear, fever, or general weakness.

tremulous, marked by shaking, quivering, or trembling.

trench fever, recurrent fever caused by Rickettsia pediculi spread by body lice.

trench foot, a condition of the feet resembling frostbite, due to exposure to wet and cold for long periods, seen in trench warfare.

trench mouth, infection involving the tonsils and floor of the mouth caused by Vincent's bacillus, marked by inflammation, painful swelling, and ulceration; Vincent's angina.

trepan, to trephine.

trephine, a form of surgical trepan for removing a circular disk of skull bone; an instrument for removing a circular portion of cornea.

trepidation, trembling involuntary movements of the limbs due to fear or anxiety.

treponema, a spirochete of the genus Treponema, some of which are pathogenic and parasitic for man, as the organism that causes syphilis.

triceps, having three heads, as a triceps muscle that extends the lower arm.

trichiasis, an inversion of eyelashes that causes irritation by rubbing against the cornea of the eyeball.

trichina, a parasitic worm sometimes present in the muscular tissues of man as an encysted larva of the genus Trichinella.

trichinosis, a disease caused by Trichinella spiralis which is ingested into the system through eating pork insufficiently cooked. Symptoms include diarrhea, pain, nausea, fever, and later swelling of muscles, edema, stiffness, and many other conditions.

trichinous, infected with trichinae.

trichoid, resembling hair; hairlike.

trichologia, the pulling out of hair by some patients.

trichomadesis, abnormally premature loss of hair on the scalp.

trichome, a hairlike structure.

trichomegaly, a congenital condition marked by excessive hair growth of eyelashes and eyebrows associated with dwarfism, mental retardation, and degeneration of retina pigmentation.

trichomoniasis, an infection caused by Trichomonas vaginalis resulting in vaginitis and urethritis, marked by inflammation and persistent discharge with pruritus.

trichoptilosis, a splitting of the ends of hairs.

trichorrhea, an abnormally rapid falling of hair.

trichromatic, normal color vision in which one is able to see the three primary colors.

trichromic, able to distinguish only three colors of the spectrum of seven colors.

tricrotic, pertaining to three sphygmographic waves to one beat of the pulse.

tricuspid, having three cusps, as a tooth having three points or cusps; the tricuspid valve of the heart.

tricuspid valve, serving to prevent the back flow of blood from the right auricle into the right ventricle.

trifacial, pertaining to the 5th pair of cranial nerves; trigeminal.

trigeminal neuralgia, facial neuralgia; tic douloureux.

trigone, referring to the triangular space at the base of the bladder.

triorchidism, having three testes.

triplegia, paralysis involving three extremities.

triplet, one of three children produced at one birth.

trismus, a motor disturbance affecting the trigeminal nerve causing spasms of the masticatory muscles and difficulty in opening the mouth; an early symptom of tetanus.

trisomy, having an additional chromosome of one type in a diploid cell.

trituration, a reduction to a powdery substance by grinding or by friction, especially in a mixture of a medicinal preparation.

trocar, a surgical instrument with a sharp-tipped rod used to insert a cannula that serves to draw off body fluid from a cavity.

trochanter, a prominence on the upper part of the femur.

troche, a medicinal preparation that dissolves in the mouth.

trochlea, a pulley-shaped structure that provides a smooth surface over which tendons pass or with which other structures articulate.

trochlear, resembling a trochlea; pullylike.

trochoides, a pivot joint.

trombiculiasis, being infested with mites of the genus Trombicula.

trophic, pertaining to nutrition.

trophoblast, the outer edge of cells of the blastocyst that attaches the fertilized ovum to the uterine wall, and develops into the placenta and membranes serving to nourish and protect the developing embryo.

tropic, having to do with a turning or a change.

true ribs, the upper seven ribs on each side that articulate directly with the sternum attached by cartilages.

trunk, truncus, the main part of the body to which the head and limbs are attached.

truss, a device for retaining a reduced hernia which may be composed of elastic, canvas, or metallic material.

truth serum, a drug such as scopolamine, used to induce a state in which a patient or subject will talk unrestrainedly.

trypanosoma, a genus of parasitic flagellate protozoa present in the blood of man and other vertebrates, transmitted by insect vectors causing serious diseases, as sleeping sickness.

trypanosomiasis, any of the several diseases caused by a species of Trypanosoma; sleeping sickness.

trypsin, a proteolytic enzyme formed in the intestine from the action of enterokinase on trypsinogen which is secreted by the pancreas capable of converting proteins into proteoses, peptones, and polypeptides.

trypsinogen, a pancreatic juice converted into trypsin by enzyme action.

tryptic, relating to trypsin.

tryptophan, an amino acid in proteins necessary for tissue growth and repair; an essential amino acid necessary for human metabolism.

tsetse, a fly of Africa, genus Glossina, which transmits diseases, as sleeping sickness in man and domestic animals.

tubal, pertaining to a tube, especially the fallopian tube.

tubal pregnancy, a pregnancy occurring in one of the oviducts.

tube, any hollow, cylindrical organ or vessel.

tubercle, a minute rounded elevation on a bone; pertaining to a small rounded nodule of the skin; pertaining to tuberculosis.

tuberculation, the formation of many tubercles.

tuberculin, a sterile substance prepared from tubercle bacillus, used to determine the presence of a tuberculosis infection.

tuberculin test, a test to determine the presence of tuberculous infection based on a positive reaction to tuberculin.

tuberculosis, an infectious disease due to Mycobacterium, marked by the formation of tubercles and caseous necrosis in the tissues of an organ. The lung is the major site of the infection in man.

tuberculous, pertaining to or being affected with tuberculosis.

tuberosity, a protuberance or elevation of a bone.

tubule, tubular, a small tube.

tubulus, a tubule, or minute canal.

tularemia, a disease of rodents which is transmitted to man, by handling infected animals or by insects, causing intermittent fever and swelling of the lymph nodes.

tumescence, swelling; being swollen.

tumis, swollen; edematous.

tumor, an abnormal swelling, usually from inflammation; morbid enlargement; neoplasm; an uncontrolled new tissue growth in which the cells multiply or proliferate rapidly.

tunic, a coat or covering.

tunica, a tunic; a membrane covering or lining a body part or organ.

turbidity, a cloudiness or sedimentation in a solution.

turbinal, scroll-like structure; a turbinate bone.

turbinate, having a shape like a top; the spongy turbinate bone of the nasal concha.

turbinectomy, surgical excision of the turbinate bone.

turgescence, a swelling or distention of a part.

turgescent, growing turgid or swollen.

turgid, distended or swollen.

turgor, a condition of being turgid; normal fullness.

twelfth cranial nerve, one of a pair of cranial nerves extending to the base of the tongue; hypoglossal nerve.

twilight sleep, a state of partial anesthesia in which pain sensation is greatly reduced.

twin, one of two offspring born at the same birth.

twinge, afflicted with sudden, sharp pain or pains.

twitch, a spasmodic muscle contraction producing a jerking action; a brief contraction of muscles that is involuntary.

tyloma, a callosity.

tympanectomy, surgical excision of the tympanic membrane.

tympanic, pertaining to the tympanum; bell-like; resonant.

tympanic membrane, a membrane separating the tympanum or middle ear from the external ear; eardrum.

tympanites, distention or swelling of the abdomen resulting from a collection of air or gas in the peritoneal cavity.

tympanitis, pertaining to tympanites; bell-like quality.

tympanum, the middle ear cavity in the temporal bone.

tympany, a tympanic or bell-like percussion sound.

type, the general or prevailing character of a disease, a person, or a substance.

typhlology, the study of blindness, its causes and treatment.

typhoid, an infectious disease caused by the bacillus Salmonella typhosa, marked by intestinal inflammation and ulceration, usually acquired through ingestion of food or drink; typhoid fever; resembling typhus.

typhomania, delirium present with typhoid fever.

typhus, an acute infectious disease marked by high fever, severe nervous symptoms, macular eruptions of reddish spots, and severe headache, caused by Rickettsia prowazeki and transmitted to man by body lice; typhus fever.

tyrosinase, ferment that acts on tyrosine.

tyrosine, naturally occurring amino acid found in most proteins; a product of phenylalanine metabolism which is a precursor of thyroid hormones.

tyrosinuria, the presence of tyrosine in the urine.

tyrosis, the curdling of milk; the cheesy vomitus of infants; tyromatosis.

U

uaterium, a medicinal preparation for the ear.

uberous, fertile; prolific.

ulalgia, pain in the gums.

ulatropia, recession or shrinking of the gums.

ulcer, an open lesion of the skin or mucous membrane produced by the casting off of necrotic tissue, sometimes accompanied by pus formation.

ulcerate, to become ulcerous.

ulceration, the process of ulcerating.

ulcerous, pertaining to an ulcer; marked by ulcer formations.

ulcus, an ulcer.

ulectomy, surgical removal of scar tissue; gingivectomy.

ulitis, gingivitis; inflammation of the gums.

ulna, the long bone in the forearm between the wrist and the elbow, on the side opposite to the thumb.

ulnad, toward the ulna.

ulnar, relating to the ulna, to the ulna nerve, or the ulna artery.

ulocarcinoma, carcinoma or cancer of the gums.

ulorrhagia, bleeding gums.

ulosis, the formation of scar tissue.

ulotrichous, pertaining to short, wool-like hair.

ultramicroscope, a dark field microscope having powerful side illumination.

ultrasound, pertaining to frequencies greater than 20,000 vibrations per second.

ultrastructure, that structure visible only under the ultramicroscope and electron microscope.

ultraviolet, beyond the visible spectrum at its violet end.

ultraviolet rays, extremely hot invisible rays converted into heat by the ozone layer which protects life on earth. The therapeutic effects include heat production, pigmentation of the skin, aid in production of vitamin D, bactericidal effects, and various metabolism effects.

ultravirus, any filterable virus that can be demonstrated by inoculation test.

umbilectomy, surgical removal of the navel.

umbilical, pertaining to the navel or umbilicus; located centrally, like a navel.

umbilical cord, the cord that connects the placenta with the fetus.

umbilicate, pertaining to or shaped like a navel or umbilicus.

umbilicus, navel.

unciform, hook-shaped.

unciform bone, a hook-shaped bone of the wrist.

uncinariasis, hookworm disease; ancylostomiasis.

uncinate, hooked; hook-shaped.

uncinus, shaped like a hook.

unconscious, lacking awareness of the environment; insensible; that part of personality which contains complex feelings and drives of which we are unaware, and which are not accessible to our consciousness.

unconsciousness, state of being unconscious.

unction, application of a salve or ointment; an ointment.

unctuous, having a greasy or oily quality.

uncus, any structure that has a hook-shape; the anterior end of the hippocampal gyrus of the brain that is hook-shaped.

undersized, having a stature less than normal or average.

underweight, having a weight deficiency; the weight is at least 10 percent less than the average weight for persons of the same age, sex, height, and body build.

undifferentiated, primitive.

undine, a small flask for irrigating the eye, usually made of glass.

undulation, a wavelike motion; fluctuating; pulsating.

undulatory, pertaining to undulation.

ungual, pertaining to the nails.

unguent, an ointment.

unguiculate, having nails or claws; clawlike.

unguis, a finger nail or toe nail.

unhealthy, lacking health and not vigorous of body.

uniaxial, having one axis.

unicameral, having one cavity.

unicellular, composed of a single cell, as a protozoan.

unicornous, having a single cornu.

uniglandular, affecting only one gland.

unilateral, affecting one side.

unilocular, having only one chamber.

uninucleated, mononuclear.

union, a juncture, as of broken bone.

uniovular, developed from one germ cell or ovum; monozygotic.

unipara, primipara; having one pregnancy.

uniparous, producing one ovum or one child at a time.

unipolar, having a single pole; pertaining to a nerve cell having a single process.

unipotent, pertaining to a cell having the ability to develop into only kind of structure.

unisexual, pertaining to only one sex.

unit, one portion of a whole; one of anything.

unitary, referring to a single object or person.

unmyelinated, the absence of a myelin sheath around some nerve fibers.

unsaturated, having the ability to absorb more of a solute; referring to compounds in which two or more atoms are connected by double or triple bonds.

unsex, to castrate; deprive of gonads.

unstriated, pertaining to smooth muscles which have no striations.

urachus, an epitheloid cord surrounded by fibrous tissue connecting the apex of the urinary bladder with the umbilicus.

uracil, a component of pyrimidine found in nucleic acid.

uracrasia, a disordered condition of urine; enuresis.

uraniscus, palate.

uranoplasty, surgical repair of a cleft palate.

uranoschisis, cleft palate.

urarthritis, gouty arthritis.

urate, a salt of uric acid.

uratemia, urates in the blood.

uraturia, urates in the urine.

urea, the diamide of carbonic acid which is found in urine, blood, and lymph, and is the chief nitrogenous end-product of protein metabolism in the body.

ureapoiesis, the formation of urine.

ureameter, a device that determines the amount of urea in urine; ureometer.

urease, an enzyme which catalyzes the decomposition of urea into ammonium carbonate.

urelcosis, the ulceration of the urinary tract.

uremia, a toxic condition produced by excessive by-products of protein metabolism in the blood, causing symptoms of nausea, vomiting, vertigo, convulsions, dimness of vision, and coma.

uremic, pertaining to uremia.

uresis, the excretion of urine from the bladder; urination; voiding.

ureter, one of two tubes 10 to 12 inches long which extend from the kidneys to the posterior surface of the bladder.

ureteralgia, pain in the ureter.

ureterectasis, dilatation or stretching of the ureter.

ureterectomy, surgical excision of the ureter.

urethra, a passage which carries the urine from the bladder to the outside of the body.

urethralgia, pain in the urethra.

urethratresia, an occlusion of the urethra which prevents the passage of urine.

urethrectomy, surgical excision of the urethra.

urethremphraxis, a urethral obstruction; urethrophraxis.

urethritis, inflammation of the urethra.

urethrorrhagia, hemorrhaging from the urethra.

urethroscope, an instrument used to examine the interior of the urethra.

urethroscopy, visual inspection of the urethra by means of a urethroscope.

urgency, a sudden, involuntary need to urinate.

uric, pertaining to urine.

uric acid, a crystalline acid found in urine occurring as an end-product of purine metabolism.

urinal, a vessel used to collect urine, especially for bedridden patients.

urinalysis, a chemical analysis of urine.

urinary, pertaining to secreting or containing urine.

urinary bladder, the distensible receptacle for urine before it is voided.

urinary organs, pertaining to the structures of the urinary system, such as the kidneys, ureters, bladder, and urethra; urinary tract.

urinate, to discharge urine; void; to cast out waste material.

urination, the process of urinating.

urine, the fluid secreted from the blood by the kidneys, which is collected in the bladder and discharged by the urethra.

urinemia, uremia, the contamination of the blood with urinary constituents.

uriniferous, transporting or carrying urine.

uriniferous tubules, renal tubules extending from the Bowman's capsule of the kidney and serving to transport urine.

urinometer, an instrument that determines the specific gravity of urine.

urinous, resembling urine.

urobilin, brown-colored pigment formed by the oxidation of urobilinogen, found in stools or in urine after exposure to air.

urobilinogen, a colorless compound found in the intestines by reduction of bilirubin.

urochrome, the yellowish coloring matter in urine, closely related to urobilin.

urocyst, urinary bladder.

urocystitis, inflammation of the urinary bladder; cystitis.

urogenital, pertaining to the urinary and genital organs.

urography, X-ray of the urinary tract or part of it after the introduction of radiopaque substance.

urolith, a urinary calculus.

urologist, one who specializes in disorders of the urinary organs.

urology, the branch of science concerned with the study, diagnosis, and treatment of diseases of the urinary tract; urinology.

urometer, urinometer.

uroncus, a swelling due to retention of urine.

uropathy, any disease or condition of the urinary tract.

uropoiesis, formation of urine.

uropyoureter, an infected ureter with an accumulation of urine and pus.

urorrhagia, excessive secretion of urine; polyuria.

uroschesis, retention of urine.

urticant, producing itching or urticaria.

urticaria, hives or wheals which are either redder or paler than the surrounding area and are often attended by itching.

uteralgia, pain in the uterus.

uterine, pertaining to the uterus.

uteritis, inflammation of the uterus.

uteroplasty, plastic repair of the uterus.

uterotomy, surgical incision of the uterus.

uterus, the hollow muscular organ in females that serves the developing embryo after fertilization of the ovum; the womb.

utricle, one of two small sacs in the labyrinth of the inner ear.

utricular, pertaining to the nature of the utricle; having a utricle or utricles.

utriculitis, inflammation of the utricle.

uvea, the middle layer of the eye, composed of the ciliary muscle, the choroid, and the iris.

uveitis, inflammation of the uvea.

uvula, the small tissue projection extending from the middle of the soft palate in the throat.

uvulectomy, surgical excision of the uvula; cionectomy.

uvulitis, inflammation of the uvula.

uvulotomy, excising the uvula or part of it.

V

vaccigenous, to produce vaccine.

vaccin, pertaining to vaccine.

vaccinate, to inoculate with vaccine to provide immunity.

vaccination, the act of vaccinating with a vaccine by injection into the body.

vaccine, a suspension of killed microorganisms for prevention of infectious diseases.

vaccinia, a viral disease in cattle which is transmissible to man by inoculation of vaccinia virus used to induce antibody formation against smallpox.

vacciniform, having the nature of vaccinia or cowpox.

vacciniola, a secondary skin eruption sometimes following vaccinia.

vaccinogenous, producing vaccine.

vacuolar, possessing vacuoles.

vacuolation, the formation of vacuoles.

vacuole, a clear space within the cell protoplasm filled with air or fluid.

vacuous, empty.

vacuum, a space exhausted of its air or gaseous content.

vagal, pertaining to the vagus nerve.

vagina, a sheathlike structure; the canal within females between the vulva and the uterus.

vaginal, pertaining to the vagina, or any sheath.

vaginalitis, inflammation of the tunica of the testicles.

vaginate, to enclose in a sheath; enveloped by a sheath.

vaginectomy, surgical removal of the tunica of a testicle; excision of the vagina or part of it.

vaginismus, painful muscular spasms of the vagina.

vaginitis, inflammation of the vagina.

vaginodynia, pain in the vagina; colpopexy.

vaginoplasty, surgical repair of the vagina.

vaginoscope, an instrument used for inspecting the vagina.

vaginoscopy, visual examination of the vagina by a vaginoscope.

vaginotomy, incision of the vagina; colpotomy.

vagus, the 10th cranial nerve, a mixed nerve which has both motor and sensory functions.

valence, the degree of the combining power of an element or radical.

valeric acid, an acid extracted from the roots of the valerian plant, used in medicine.

valetudinarian, one seeking to recover health; invalid.

valgus, denoting a position, as being bent outward or twisted.

valine, an amino acid derived from the hydrolysis of proteins, essential for human metabolism.

Valium, trademark for diaezepam, used for management of anxiety disorders.

vallate, rim-shaped; a rim around a depression.

vallecular, a furrow or crevice, as on the back of the tongue.

valval, pertaining to a valve.

valvate, furnished with valves; resembling a valve.

valve, a membranous fold within a hollow organ that prevents a backward flow of fluid passing through it, as the entrance to the aorta from the left ventricle of the heart.

valvotomy, surgical incision into a valve.

valvular, pertaining to a valve.

valvulitis, inflammation of a valve.

vapor, a gaseous state of a substance; medicinal substance that is administered in the form of vapor which is inhaled.

vaporization, converting a liquid or solid into a vapor for inhalation as treatment for respiratory ailments.

varicella, chicken pox.

varices, dilated veins; plural of varix.

variciform, varicose.

varicocele, a varicose enlargement of the spermatic cord veins.

varicocelectomy, surgical removal of a portion of the scrotum to remove a varicocele.

varicose, distended or swollen veins; pertaining to varices.

varicose veins, veins that are enlarged and twisted, commonly found on the leg and thigh.

varicosity, a condition of being varicose; a varix; varicose vein.

varicotomy, a condition of being varicose; a varix; varicose vein.

varicotomy, surgical removal of a varix or varicose vein.

varicula, a varix of the conjunctiva of the eye.

variola, smallpox.

variolate, resembling a smallpox lesion; to vaccinate with smallpox virus.

varioloid, resembling smallpox; a mild form of smallpox.

varix, an abnormal, tortuous dilatation of a vein; varicose vein.

varus, denoting a deformity of the bone; bent inward; bowlegged.

vas, a duct or vessel.

vascular, pertaining to blood vessels.

vascularity, the condition of being vascular.

vasculitis, inflammation of a blood vessel; angiitis.

vasculum, a very small vessel.

vas deferens, the duct which transports sperm from the testis.

vasectomy, surgical removal of all or part of the vas deferens.

Vaseline, trademark for a translucent semisolid petroleum jelly used in medicinal preparations and for other purposes.

vasifactive, forming new vessels.

vasiform, resembling a tubular structure.

vasitis, inflammation of the vas deferens.

vasoconstrictor, causing a narrowing of blood vessels; an agent that causes constriction of blood vessels.

vasodepression, the lowering of blood pressure.

vasodepressor, an agent that produces vasodepression.

vasodilatation, dilatation of small arteries and arterioles.

vasodilator, causing relaxation or widening of blood vessels; an agent or nerve that dilates the blood vessels.

vasoinhibitor, a drug that depresses vasomotor nerves.

vasoligation, a surgical procedure involving the vas deferens which renders sterility.

vasomotor nerves, those nerves distributed over muscular coats of blood vessels which cause contraction or dilation of the inner diameter.

vasoparesis, partial paralysis or weakness of vasomotor nerves.

vasopressor, an agent which stimulates the contraction of the muscular tissue of blood vessels, such as adrenalin.

vasosection, surgical cutting of a vessel, especially the vas deferens.

vasospasm, spasm of any vessel.

vasostimulant, exciting vasomotor action.

vasotomy, surgical incision of the vas deferens.

vasotrophic, concerned with the nutrition of blood vessels.

vastus, great, referring to muscles.

vector, a carrier which transfers an infective microorganism from one host to another, usually an insect or tick.

vegetarian, one who eats no animal products, but lives on food of vegetable origin.

vegetation, an abnormal fungoid growth in the nasopharynx; a morbid outgrowth on any part, especially wartlike projections.

vehicle, an inactive substance used in a medicinal preparation for transporting the active ingredient; an excipient.

vein, a vessel carrying unaerated blood to the heart, excluding the pulmonary vein.

veinlet, small vein or venule.

velamen, a covering membrane, or skin covering.

velar, pertaining to velum, or veil.

vellication, spasms or twitching of muscular fibers.

velum, a veil-like structure.

vena, a vein.

vena cava, pertaining to either of two large veins that empties into the right atrium of the heart.

venenous, poisonous.

venereal disease, (VD); any disease contracted by sexual intercourse from an infected individual.

venereologist, one who specializes in venereology.

venereology, the branch of medicine concerned with the study and treatment of venereal diseases.

venesection, phlebotomy.

venipuncture, puncture of a vein for intravenous feeding, to administer medication, or for obtaining a blood specimen.

venom, poison or a toxic substance secreted by snakes, insects, or other animals.

venomous, poisonous.

venous, pertaining to the veins.

vent, an opening in any cavity.

venter, the abdomen or belly; a hollowed cavity.

ventilation, the process of supplying a room with a continuous flow of fresh air; oxygenation of the blood; the expression of feelings and thoughts in crisis intervention; abreaction.

ventricle, a small cavity, especially one of the two lower chambers of the heart; one of the connecting cavities of the brain.

ventricose, corpulent; big-bellied or a protruding abdomen; swelled out.

ventriculus, a ventricle; hollow organ, as the stomach.

venula, a small vein; venule.

venule, any of the small vessels from the capillary plexuses that join to form veins.

vergence, turning of one eye with reference to the other; convergence or divergence.

vermicide, an agent that is lethal to intestinal parasitic worms.

vermicular, resembling a worm in appearance or movement.

vermiform, having a wormlike shape.

vermiform appendix, a small tube opening into the cecum with its other end closed, varying from three to six inches long.

vermifuge, an agent that expels parasitic intestinal worms.

vermin, an external noxious parasitic animal or insect.

verminous, pertaining to, or infested with worms or vermin.

vermis, a worm.

vernix caseosa, a sebaceous covering consisting of exfoliations of outer skin layer, lanugo, and secretions from the sebaceous glands which envelops a fetus at birth, rendering a white, cheesy appearance to the skin of the newborn, believed to have beneficial protective properties.

verruca, a wart; a wartlike elevation.

verrucose, verrucous, having little warts on the surface.

version, the spontaneous or manual turning of the fetus in the uterus at childbirth.

vertebra, any of the 33 bones composing the vertebral or spinal column, of which there are: 7 cervical, 12 thoracic, 5 lumbar, 5 sacral, and 4 coccygeal vertebrae.

vertebral, pertaining to a vertebra or the vertebrae; spinal column.

vertebrate, having a backbone or spinal column; any member of the Vertebrata, animals having a vertebral column.

vertebrectomy, surgical excision of a vertebra.

vertex, the top of the head; the crown of the head.

vertical, pertaining to the top of the head; upright.

vertigo, a condition of dizziness.

vesica, the bladder.

vesical, pertaining to the urinary bladder.

vesicant, producing blisters; a substance that produces blisters.

vesication, the process of forming blisters.

vesicle, a sac containing fluid; a bladderlike cavity; a small blister; a small bladder.

vesicocele, a hernia of the bladder.

vesicular, pertaining to vesicles; composed of small saclike bodies or blisters.

vesiculation, the formation of vesicles.

vesiculectomy, surgical excision of the complete or part of a vesicle, usually the seminal vesicle.

vesiculitis, inflammation of a vesicle.

vessel, any tube, duct, or channel conveying fluid, such as blood.

vestibular, pertaining to a vestibule.

vestibule, any cavity or channel forming an entrance to another space.

vestibulogenic, arising from a vestibule of the ear.

vestibulotomy, surgical incision of the vestibule of the ear.

vestige, a small degenerate structure which functioned in the embryo or in a past generation.

vestigial, rudimentary.

viable, capable of sustaining an individual existence; having the ability to develop and grow after birth.

vial, a small bottle, usually containing medicine for administering as an injection.

vibration, rapidly moving to and fro; oscillation.

vibrator, a device used to produce a vibrating massage.

vibratory, causing or producing vibration.

vibrissae, long coarse hairs located in the vestibule of the nose in man.

vicarious, taking the place of another.

villi, minute vascular processes on the free surface of a membrane.

villiferous, having tufts of hair or villi.

villiform, resembling villi.

villose, covered with villi.

villus, a small hairlike vascular process on a free surface of a membrane.

Vincent's angina, a painful inflammatory disease of the tonsils, pharynx, and floor of the mouth; trench mouth.

viosterol, a preparation of vitamin D made from irradiated ergosterol in vegetable oil used as a substitute for cod-liver oil.

viral, relating to a virus, or caused by a virus.

viremia, viruses found in the blood.

virile, characteristic of a man; masculine or manly; having copulative power.

virilism, relating to male secondary characteristics in a female.

virility, the state of possessing normal sex characteristics in a male.

virologist, one who specializes in virology.

virology, the branch of science concerned with viruses and virus diseases.

virucide, an agent that destroys viruses.

virulence, the degree of pathogenicity possessed by microorganisms to produce disease.

virulent, infectious or highly poisonous; having a rapid and malignant course.

viruliferous, conveying or producing a virus.

virus, a minute infectious organism that causes disease in all life forms and which depends upon a living host for its metabolism and replication.

viscera, the interior organs within the cavities of the body, especially the abdomen and thorax.

visceral, pertaining to the viscera.

visceralgia, neuralgia of any of the viscera.

viscerogenic, originating in the viscera.

viscid, adhering and thick; having a glutinous or sticky quality.

viscosimeter, a device for measuring the viscosity of fluids.

viscosity, state of being sticky and resistant to flow.

viscous, thick, sticky, or gummy; having a glutinous quality.

viscus, any interior organ of the three large body cavities, especially the abdomen.

vision, sight; seeing; faculty of sensing light and color; an imaginary sight.

visual, pertaining to vision.

visual acuity, clarity of vision; sharpness.

visual field, the total area in which objects may be seen by the fixed eye.

visual purple, purple pigment in the rods of the retina; rhodopsin.

vital, pertaining to vital functions or processes; necessary to life.

vital signs, referring to temperature, pulse, respiration (TPR).

vital statistics, pertaining to a record of births, marriages, disease, and deaths in a population.

vitamin, an organic substance which occurs in natural foods and is necessary in trace amounts for normal metabolic functioning of the body.

vitamin A, fat-soluble vitamin occurring in two forms: retinol and dehydroretinol, found in egg yolk, fish-liver oils, liver, butter, cheese and many vegetables, necessary for night vision and for protecting epithelial tissue.

vitamin B_c, folic acid.

vitamin B complex, an important group of water-soluble vitamins isolated from liver, yeast, and other sources which include thiamine, riboflavin, niacin, niacinamide, the vitamin B_6 group, biotin, pantothenic acid, folic acid and others. The vitamin B complex group affects growth, appetite, lactation, and the gastrointestinal, nervous, and endocrine systems.

vitamin B_1, thiamine.

vitamin B_2, riboflavin.

vitamin B_6, pyridoxine.

vitamin B_{12}, cyanocobalmin, extracted from liver which is essential for red blood cell formation.

vitamin C, ascorbic acid which aids in growth, weight gain, appetite, blood-building, and prevents disease, such as scurvy.

vitamin D, fat-soluble vitamins found in fish-liver oils, milk products, eggs, and ultraviolet irradiation of ergosterol, necessary for absorption of calcium and phosphorus, valuable in normal bone formation of the skeleton and teeth.

vitamin E, a fat-soluble vitamin necessary in the body for reproduction, muscular development, and resistance of red blood cells to hemolysis, found in wheat germ, cereals, egg yolk, and beef liver.

vitamin G, riboflavin.

vitamin H, biotin.

vitamin K, found in green vegetables, important for normal clotting of the blood.

vitellin, a protein found in egg yolk.

vitiligo, destruction of melanocytes which form white patches on various sites of the body.

vitreous, pertaining to the vitreous humor of the eye; vitreous body; vitreous chamber.

vitreous body, a transparent jelly-like mass that fills the vitreous chamber; vitreous humor.

vitreous chamber, the cavity of the eyeball behind the lens.

vitreous humor, the transparent gelatinous substance that fills the chamber or cavity behind the lens of the eye; vitreous body.

vivisect, to dissect the body of an animal.

vivisection, the dissection of a living animal for purposes of demonstrating or studying physiological facts or for pathological investigation of diseases.

vocal cords, either of two tissue bands projecting into the cavity of the larynx which vibrate and produce vocal sounds of speech.

voice, the sounds uttered by living beings produced by vocal cord vibrations.

void, to urinate.

vola, a hollow surface, such as the sole of a foot or palm of a hand.

volar, the palm or foot surfaces.

volaris, palmar; concerning the palm of the hand.

volition, the act of choosing, or power of willing.

volume, a space occupied by a substance; the capacity of a container.

voluntary, pertaining to or under the control of the will.

voluntary muscles, voluntary musles are attached to the skeleton and are innervated by nerves coming from the brain or spinal cord; muscles subject to being controlled by the will.

volvulus, twisting of the bowel causing intestinal obstruction.

vomer, a bone of the skull which forms a large part of the nasal septum.

vomitory, an emetic; inducing vomiting.

vomitus, the ejected matter in vomiting.

vox, the voice.

vulnerability, susceptibility to injury, or disease.

vulnerable, easily injured.

vulnus, an injury or a wound.

vulsella, vulsellum, a special forceps with claw-like hooks.

vulva, external female genitalia, including the mons pubis, labia majora and minora, clitoris, and vestibule of the vagina.

vulvectomy, surgical excision of the vulva.

vulvitis, inflammation of the vulva.

vulvovaginal, pertaining to the vulva and vagina.

vulvovaginitis, inflammation of the vulva and vagina.

W

wad, a mass of fibrous material such as cotton, used for a surgical dressing or for packing.

waist, the section between the ribs and the hips in the human body.

Waldeyer's ring, the ring of tonsillar lymphatic tissue that surrounds the nasopharynx and oropharynx.

walleye, leukoma of the cornea; strabismus; exotropia.

ward, a large hospital room containing several or many patients.

wart, epidermal tumor originating from a virus; verruca.

Wassermann test, a test which detects syphilis.

wash, a solution for cleansing or for bathing a part; eyewash, or mouthwash.

waste, gradual decay, or reduction of bodily susbtance, health, or strength; to emaciate; excrement.

wasting, enfeebling, or causing loss of bodily strength.

water, a colorless, odorless, tasteless liquid, necessary to life of humans and animals; used in preparation of medicinal substances, as an aqueous solution.

water brash, gastric burning pain; heartburn.

waters, amniotic fluid; bag of water surrounding the fetus.

water-soluble, capable of dissolving in water, as many organic compounds.

wave, any wavelike pattern.

wax, a plastic substance obtained from plants or insects; cerumen, or ear wax.

waxy, pertaining to wax, or to the degeneration of body tissue resulting from accumulations of waxlike insoluble protein; characteristic of amyloid.

weak, lacking strength.

wean, the process of discontinuing breast feeding and substituting other nourishment.

wen, a sebaceous cyst; pillar cyst.

wet-nurse, a woman who suckles other infants.

wheal, a round, localized area of edema on the skin attended by severe itching which vanishes quickly; a lesion of urticaria.

wheeze, difficult breathing with a whistling sound resulting from narrowing of the lumen of a respiratory passageway.

whelk, a wheal; a pustule, nodule, tubercle, or pimple.

whiplash, an acute cervical sprain or injury caused by a sudden jerking of the head, as in an automobile accident.

whipworm, a parasitic nematode of the genus Trichuris.

white blood cell, leukocyte; white blood corpuscle.

white matter, nerve tissue of the brain and spinal cord.

whitlow, a felon; infected finger.

W.H.O., World Health Organization.

whooping cough, an infectious disease marked by catarrh of the respiratory tract with a peculiar cough, caused by Bordetella pertussis, especially in children.

will, having the power to control one's actions or emotions.

windpipe, the trachea.

wisdom tooth, the last molar tooth on each side of the jaw which usually erupts around the 25th year.

witch hazel, used as an astringent.

withdrawal, a pathological retreat from people and the world of reality; symptoms that occur when one abstains from drugs to which one is addicted; abstention from drugs.

withdrawal symptoms, a term used to describe effects of drug withdrawal in patients who have become addicted, which include nausea, vomiting, abdominal pain, tremors, and convulsions.

wolffian body, an embryonic body on each side of the spinal column; mesonephros.

womb, uterus.

woolsorter's disease, a pulmonary form of anthrax which develops in handlers of contaminated wool.

word blindness, inability to comprehend printed or written words, a form of aphasia; alexia.

word salad, the use of a mixture of words and phrases that lack meaning or logic, commonly seen in schizophrenia.

worm, a soft-bodied elongated invertebrate without limbs.

wound, an injury to the body caused by a physical means with rupture of normal skin and flesh.

wrinkle, a small crease or fold in the skin.

wrist, the joint between the forearm and hand; carpus.

wrist drop, a paralysis of the extensor muscles of the hand and fingers.

writer's cramp, an occupational disability caused by excessive writing.

wryneck, a contracted state of one or more neck muscles, resulting in an abnormal position of the head; torticollis.

Wunderlich's curve, a typical fever curve significant in typhoid fever.

X

xanthemia, yellowish pigment in the blood.

xanthine, a nitrogenous compound, related to uric acid, present in the blood and certain tissues of the body.

xanthinuria, an excretion of xanthine in large amounts with the urine.

xanthochromia, yellowish discoloration of patches of the skin or of the spinal fluid.

xanthocyanopia, a condition in which a person cannot distinguish between red and green, but can distinguish between yellow and blue; a form of color blindness.

xanthocyte, a cell that contains yellow pigment.

xanthoderma, yellow skin.

xanthodont, yellow teeth.

xanthoma, a condition marked by small, yellow nodules of the skin, especially of the eyelids.

xanthopsia, yellow vision.

xanthosis, jaundice.

X chromosome, one of the two sex chromosomes carrying female characteristics, which occur in pairs in the female cell and zygote, and with one Y chromosome in a male cell and zygote.

xenodiagnosis, a diagnosis or means of determining parasitic disease in humans by feeding an uninfected host on material believed to be infected and observing the results.

xenogenesis, reproduction of offspring unlike either parent.

xenogenous, a condition caused by a foreign body or toxin.

xenomenia, bleeding from other sites during menstruation.

xenophobia, abnormal fear of strangers.

xenophonia, an alteration in voice production, as in lack of bodily strength.

xenopthalmia, inflammation of the eye caused by a foreign body.

xeransis, a loss of moisture of the skin causing dryness.

xerocheilia, dryness of the lips.

xeroderma, excessive dryness of the skin; a form of ichthyosis.

xerophthalmia, an abnormal condition of the eye marked by dryness and thickening of the lining membrane of the lid and eyeball due to a deficiency of vitamin A.

xerostomia, dryness of the mouth.

xiphisternum, the lower portion of the sternum or xiphoid process.

xiphoid, relating to the sword-shaped xiphisternum.

xiphoiditis, inflammation of the cartilage xiphoid process.

X-linked, sex-linked, or transmitted by genes on the X-chromosome.

X-ray, to examine by roentgen rays.

X-ray therapy, used to treat certain diseases, as cancer.

Xylocaine, trademark for lidocaine, used in medicinal preparations.

xylometazoline, used as a topical nasal decongestant.

xylose, a pentose used in diagnostic tests of intestinal absorption.

xysma, membranous material in stools of diarrhea.

xyster, a surgical instrument used in surgery to scrape bone.

Y

yaw, a primary lesion of the skin due to yaws.

yawn, an involuntary opening of the mouth with a long inhalation, due to fatigue or drowsiness.

yawning, deep inspiration with the mouth wide open, resulting from fatigue or boredom.

yaws, an infectious tropical disease, marked by eruptions of tubercles on the skin, and rheumatism, caused by the spirochete Treponema pertenue.

Y bacillus, a bacillus that causes dysentery.

Y chromosome, one of a pair of sex chromosomes, an X and Y, that carry male characteristics.

yeast, a viscid substance composed of aggregated cells of small unicellular sac fungi, used to supplement B-complex vitamins.

yellow body, the corpus luteum formed in the cavity of the graafian follicle after the expulsion of the ovum, and which persists during pregnancy.

yellow fever, an acute infectious disease marked by jaundice, vomiting, epigastric tenderness, hemorrhages, and fever, transmitted by the bite of a female mosquito.

yoke, a connecting structure.

yolk, stored in the form of protein and fat granules in the ovum, as a nutrient.

Young's rule, a children's dose of medication is determined by adding 12 to the age and dividing the result by the age, making the quotient the denominator of a fraction, the numerator of which is 1. The proportion of adult medication to be given to a child is represented by the fraction.

youth, the period of adolescence.

Z

zein, protein derived from maize or corn.

Zeiss' gland, a sebaceous gland at the free edge of the eyelid.

zelotypia, a morbid interest in any project or cause.

zero, the point on a thermometer or other scale at which the graduation begins.

zestocausis, cauterization with steam.

zinc chloride, used as an astringent, antiseptic, and escharotic.

zinc oxide, used mostly in the form of ointment and as an antiseptic and astringent.

zoanthropy, a mental condition in which one has the delusion that he is an animal.

zoetic, pertaining to life; vital.

zona, a band or girdle; herpes zoster; zone.

zonesthesia, having the sensation of constriction, as by a girdle.

zoonosis, a disease transmissible to man by animals.

zoophagous, living on animal food.

zoophobia, pathological aversion toward animals.

zooplasty, transplantation of tissue from lower animals to the human body.

zootherapeutics, veterinary medicine.

zoster, herpes zoster; shingles.

zosteriform, resembling herpes zoster.

zygapophysis, one of the articular processes of the neural arch of a vertebra, usually occurring in pairs.

zygoma, the prominence of the cheekbone.

zygomatic, pertaining to the zygoma.

zygomatic arch, the formation on each side of the cheeks composed of each malar bone articulating with the zygomatic process.

zygomatic process, a thin projection that extends from the temporal bone; that part of the malar bone which forms the zygoma.

zygote, the union of male and female gametes to produce a new single-celled individual or zygote.

zymase, an enzyme found in yeast.

zyme, a fermenting substance.

zymogen, a substance that develops into an enzyme.

zymology, the science concerned with fermentation.

zymolysis, the change produced or the fermentative action of enzymes.

zymolytic, pertaining to zymolysis.

zymose, an enzyme responsible for the changes of a disaccharide into a monosaccharide.

zymosis, fermentation; an infectious disease.

zymosthenic, increasing the functional activity of an enzyme.

zymotic, pertaining to fermentation; relating to an infectious disease.

NUTRITIVE VALUES OF FOODS

Food	Measure	Weight	Water	Food energy	Protein	Fat	Carbohydrate	Calcium	Iron	Vitamin A Value	Thiamin	Riboflavin	Niacin	Ascorbic Acid
		Grams	Percent	Calories	Grams	Grams	Grams	Milligrams	Milligrams	Int'l. Units	Milligrams	Milligrams	Milligrams	Milligrams
Dairy and Related Products														
Cheese:														
Natural:														
Blue	1 oz	28	42	100	6	8	1	150	0.1	200	0.01	0.11	0.3	0
Camembert	1 wedge	38	52	115	8	9	Trace	147	.1	350	.01	.19	.2	0
Cheddar:														
Cut pieces	1 oz	28	37	115	7	9	Trace	204	.2	300	.01	.11	Trace	0
	1 cu in	17.2	37	70	4	6	Trace	124	.1	180	Trace	.06	Trace	0
Shredded	1 cup	113	37	455	28	37	1	815	.8	1,200	.03	.42	.1	0
Cottage														
Creamed (4% fat):														
Large curd	1 cup	225	79	235	28	10	6	135	.3	370	.05	.37	.3	Trace
Small curd	1 cup	210	79	220	26	9	6	126	.3	340	.04	.34	.3	Trace
Low fat (2%)	1 cup	226	79	205	31	4	8	155	.4	160	.05	.42	.3	Trace
Low fat (1%)	1 cup	226	82	165	28	2	6	138	.3	80	.05	.37	.3	Trace
Cream	1 oz	28	54	100	2	10	1	23	.3	400	Trace	.06	Trace	0
Mozzarella, made with—														
Whole milk	1 oz	28	48	90	6	7	1	163	.1	260	Trace	.08	Trace	0
Part skim milk	1 oz	28	49	80	8	5	1	207	.1	180	.01	.10	Trace	0
Parmesan, grated	1 oz	28	18	130	12	9	1	390	.3	200	.01	.11	.1	0
Provolone	1 oz	28	41	100	7	8	1	214	.1	230	.01	.09	Trace	0
Ricotta, made with—														
Whole milk	1 cup	246	72	428	28	32	7	509	.9	1,210	.03	.48	.3	0
Part skim milk	1 cup	246	74	340	28	19	13	669	1.1	1,060	.05	.46	.2	0
Romano	1 oz	28	31	110	9	8	1	302	—	160	—	.11	Trace	0
Swiss	1 oz	28	37	105	8	8	1	272	Trace	240	.01	.10	Trace	0
Pasteurized process cheese:														
American	1 oz	28	39	105	6	9	Trace	174	.1	340	.01	.10	Trace	0
Swiss	1 oz	28	42	95	7	7	1	219	.2	230	Trace	.08	Trace	0
Pasteurized process cheese food, American	1 oz	28	43	95	6	7	2	163	.2	260	.01	.13	Trace	0
Pasteurized process cheese spread, American	1 oz	28	48	82	5	6	2	159	.1	220	.01	.12	Trace	0
Cream, sweet:														
Half-and-half	1 cup	242	81	315	7	28	10	254	.2	260	.08	.36	.2	2
	1 tbsp	15	81	20	Trace	2	1	16	Trace	20	.01	.02	Trace	Trace
Light, coffee, or table	1 cup	240	74	470	6	46	9	231	.1	1,730	.08	.36	.1	2
	1 tbsp	15	74	30	Trace	3	1	14	Trace	110	Trace	.02	Trace	Trace
Whipping, unwhipped (volume about double when whipped):														
Light	1 tbsp	15	64	45	Trace	5	Trace	10	Trace	170	Trace	.02	Trace	Trace
Heavy	1 tbsp	15	58	80	Trace	6	Trace	10	Trace	220	Trace	.02	Trace	Trace
Whipped topping, (pressurized)	1 tbsp	3	61	10	Trace	1	Trace	3	Trace	30	Trace	Trace	Trace	0
Cream, sour	1 tbsp	12	71	25	Trace	3	1	14	Trace	90	Trace	.02	Trace	Trace
Cream products, imitation:														
Creamers, powdered	1 tsp	2	2	10	Trace	1	1	Trace	Trace	Trace	0	Trace	0	0
Whipped topping, pressurized	1 tbsp	4	60	10	Trace	1	1	Trace	Trace	20	0	0	0	0
Milk:														
Fluid:														
Whole (3.3% fat)	1 cup	244	88	150	8	8	11	291	.1	310	.09	.40	.2	2
Lowfat (2%)	1 cup	244	89	120	8	5	12	297	.1	500	.10	.40	.2	2
Lowfat (1%)	1 cup	244	90	100	8	3	12	300	.1	500	.10	.41	.2	2
Nonfat (skim)	1 cup	245	91	85	8	Trace	12	302	.1	500	.09	.37	.2	2
Buttermilk	1 cup	245	90	100	8	2	12	285	.1	80	.08	.38	.1	2
Canned:														
Evaporated, unsweetened	1 cup	252	74	340	17	19	25	657	.5	610	.12	.80	.5	5
Sweetened, condensed	1 cup	306	27	980	24	27	166	868	.6	1,000	.28	1.27	.6	8
Dried:														
Nonfat instant	1 cup	68	4	245	24	Trace	35	837	.2	1,610	.28	1.19	.6	4
Milk beverages:														
Chocolate milk (commercial):														
Regular	1 cup	250	82	210	8	8	26	280	.6	300	.09	.41	.3	2
Lowfat (2%)	1 cup	250	84	180	8	5	26	284	.6	500	.10	.42	.3	2
Lowfat (1%)	1 cup	250	85	160	8	3	26	287	.6	500	.10	.40	.2	2

(Dashes (—) denote lack of reliable data for a constituent believed to be present in measurable amount)

Food	Measure	Weight	Water	Food energy	Protein	Fat	Carbohydrate	Calcium	Iron	Vitamin A Value	Thiamin	Riboflavin	Niacin	Ascorbic Acid
		Grams	Percent	Calories	Grams	Grams	Grams	Milligrams	Milligrams	Int'l. Units	Milligrams	Milligrams	Milligrams	Milligrams
Milk beverages-Continued														
Eggnog (commercial)	1 cup	254	74	340	10	19	34	330	.5	890	.09	.48	.3	4
Milk desserts, frozen:														
Ice cream:														
Regular (about 11% fat):														
Hardened	1 cup	133	61	270	5	14	32	176	.1	540	.05	.33	.1	1
Soft serve (frozen custard)	1 cup	173	60	375	7	23	38	236	.4	790	.08	.45	.2	1
Rich (about 16% fat)	1 cup	148	59	350	4	24	32	151	.1	900	.04	.28	.1	1
Ice milk (about 4.3% fat)	1 cup	131	69	185	5	6	29	176	.1	210	.08	.35	.1	1
Soft serve (about 2.6% fat)	1 cup	175	70	225	8	5	38	274	.3	180	.12	.54	.2	1
Sherbet (about 2% fat)	1 cup	193	66	270	2	4	59	103	.3	190	.03	.09	.1	4
Milk desserts, other:														
Custard, baked	1 cup	265	77	305	14	15	29	297	1.1	930	.11	.50	.3	1
Puddings:														
Tapioca cream	1 cup	165	72	220	8	8	28	173	.7	480	.07	.30	.2	2
From mix (chocolate):														
Regular (cooked)	1 cup	260	70	320	9	8	59	265	.8	340	.05	.39	.3	2
Instant	1 cup	260	69	325	8	7	63	374	1.3	340	.08	.39	.3	2
Yogurt:														
Made with lowfat milk:														
Fruit-flavored	8 oz	227	75	230	10	3	42	343	.2	120	.08	.40	.2	1
Plain	8 oz	227	85	145	12	4	16	415	.2	150	.10	.49	.3	2
Made with nonfat milk	8 oz	227	85	125	13	Trace	17	452	.2	20	.11	.53	.3	2
Made with whole milk	8 oz	227	88	140	8	7	11	274	.1	280	.07	.32	.2	1
Eggs														
Eggs, large (24 oz per dozen):														
Fried in butter	1 egg	46	72	85	5	6	1	26	.9	290	.03	.13	Trace	0
Hard-cooked	1 egg	50	75	80	6	6	1	28	1.0	260	.04	.14	Trace	0
Poached	1 egg	50	74	80	6	6	1	28	1.0	260	.04	.13	Trace	0
Scrambled (milk added) in butter. Also omelet.	1 egg	64	76	95	6	7	1	47	.9	310	.04	.16	Trace	0
Fats, Oils; Related Products														
Butter:														
Regular	1 tbsp	14	16	100	Trace	12	Trace	3	Trace	430	Trace	Trace	Trace	0
Whipped	1 tbsp	9	16	65	Trace	8	Trace	2	Trace	290	Trace	Trace	Trace	0
Fats, cooking (vegetable shortenings)	1 tbsp	13	0	110	0	13	0	0	0	—	0	0	0	0
Margarine:														
Regular	1 tbsp	14	16	100	Trace	12	Trace	3	Trace	470	Trace	Trace	Trace	0
Soft	1 tbsp	14	16	100	Trace	12	Trace	3	Trace	470	Trace	Trace	Trace	0
Whipped	1 tbsp	9	16	70	Trace	8	Trace	2	Trace	310	Trace	Trace	Trace	0
Oils, salad or cooking:														
Corn	1 tbsp	14	0	120	0	14	0	0	0	—	0	0	0	0
Olive	1 tbsp	14	0	120	0	14	0	0	0	—	0	0	0	0
Peanut	1 tbsp	14	0	120	0	14	0	0	0	—	0	0	0	0
Safflower	1 tbsp	14	0	120	0	14	0	0	0	—	0	0	0	0
Soybean oil, hydrogenated	1 tbsp	14	0	120	0	14	0	0	0	—	0	0	0	0
Soybean-cottonseed oil blend, hydrogenated	1 tbsp	14	0	120	0	14	0	0	0	—	0	0	0	0
Salad dressings:														
Commercial:														
Blue cheese	1 tbsp	15	32	75	1	8	1	12	Trace	30	Trace	.02	Trace	Trace
French	1 tbsp	16	39	65	Trace	6	3	2	.1	—	—	—	—	—
Italian	1 tbsp	15	28	85	Trace	9	1	2	Trace	Trace	Trace	Trace	Trace	—
Mayonnaise	1 tbsp	14	15	100	Trace	11	Trace	3	.1	40	Trace	.01	Trace	—
Mayonnaise type	1 tbsp	15	41	65	Trace	6	2	2	Trace	30	Trace	Trace	Trace	—
Tartar sauce, regular	1 tbsp	14	34	75	Trace	8	1	3	.1	30	Trace	Trace	Trace	Trace
Thousand Island	1 tbsp	16	32	80	Trace	8	2	2	.1	50	Trace	Trace	Trace	Trace
Fish, Shellfish, Meat, Poultry; Related Products														
Fish and shellfish:														
Bluefish, baked with butter or margarine	3 oz	85	68	135	22	4	0	25	0.6	40	.09	.08	1.6	—
Clams:														
Raw, meat only	3 oz	85	82	65	11	1	2	59	5.2	90	.08	.15	1.1	8
Canned, solids and liquid	3 oz	85	86	45	7	1	2	47	3.5	—	.01	.09	.9	—
Crabmeat (white or king), canned	1 cup	135	77	135	24	3	1	61	1.1	—	.11	.11	2.6	—
Fish sticks, breaded, cooked, frozen	1 oz	28	66	50	5	3	2	3	.1	0	.01	.02	.5	—
Haddock, breaded, fried	3 oz	85	66	140	17	5	5	34	1.0	—	.03	.06	2.7	2
Oysters, raw, meat only	1 cup	240	85	160	20	4	8	226	13.2	740	.34	.43	6.0	—
Salmon, pink, canned, solids and liquid	3 oz	85	71	120	17	5	0	167	.7	60	.03	.16	6.8	—

Food	Measure	Weight	Water	Food energy	Pro-tein	Fat	Carbo-hydrate	Calcium	Iron	Vitamin A Value	Thiamin	Ribo-flavin	Niacin	Ascorbic Acid
		Grams	Per-cent	Cal-ories	Grams	Grams	Grams	Milli-grams	Milli-grams	Int'l. Units	Milli-grams	Milli-grams	Milli-grams	Milli-grams
Fish and shellfish—Continued														
Sardines, Atlantic, canned in oil, drained solids	3 oz	85	62	175	20	9	0	372	2.5	190	.02	.17	4.6	—
Scallops, frozen, breaded, fried, reheated	6 scallops	90	60	175	16	8	9	—	—	—	—	—	—	—
Shad, baked with butter or margarine, bacon	3 oz	85	64	170	20	10	0	20	.5	30	.11	.22	7.3	—
Shrimp:														
Canned meat	3 oz	85	70	100	21	1	1	98	2.6	50	.01	.03	1.5	—
French fried	3 oz	85	57	190	17	9	9	61	1.7	—	.03	.07	2.3	—
Tuna, canned in oil, drained solids	3 oz	85	61	170	24	7	0	7	1.6	70	.04	.10	10.1	—
Tuna salad	1 cup	205	70	350	30	22	7	41	2.7	590	.08	.23	10.3	2
Meat and meat products:														
Bacon, broiled or fried, crisp	2 slices	15	8	85	4	8	Trace	2	.5	0	.08	.05	.8	—
Beef, cooked:														
Cuts braised, simmered or pot roasted:														
Lean and fat	3 oz	85	53	245	23	16	0	10	2.9	30	.04	.18	3.6	—
Lean only	2.5 oz	72	62	140	22	5	0	10	2.7	10	.04	.17	3.3	
Ground beef, broiled:														
Lean with 10% fat	3 oz	85	60	185	23	10	0	10	3.0	20	.08	.20	5.1	—
Lean with 21% fat	2.9 oz	82	54	235	20	17	0	9	2.6	30	.07	.17	4.4	—
Roast, oven cooked, no liquid added:														
Relatively fat, such as rib:														
Lean and fat	3 oz	85	40	375	17	33	0	8	2.2	70	.05	.13	3.1	—
Lean only	1.8 oz	51	57	125	14	7	0	6	1.8	10	.04	.11	2.6	—
Relatively lean, such as heel of round:														
Lean and fat	3 oz	85	62	165	25	7	0	11	3.2	10	.06	.19	4.5	—
Lean only	2.8 oz	78	65	125	24	3	0	10	3.0	Trace	.06	.18	4.3	—
Steak:														
Relatively fat—sirloin, broiled:														
Lean and fat	3 oz	85	44	330	20	27	0	9	2.5	50	.05	.15	4.0	—
Lean only	2 oz	56	59	115	18	4	0	7	2.2	10	.05	.14	3.6	—
Relatively lean—round, braised:														
Lean and fat	3 oz	85	55	220	24	13	0	10	3.0	20	.07	.19	4.8	—
Lean only	2.4 oz	68	61	130	21	4	0	9	2.5	10	.05	.16	4.1	—
Beef, canned:														
Corned beef	3 oz	85	59	185	22	10	0	17	3.7	—	.01	.20	2.9	—
Corned beef hash	1 cup	220	67	400	19	25	24	29	4.4	—	.02	.20	4.6	—
Beef, dried, chipped	2½-oz jar	71	48	145	24	4	0	14	3.6	—	.05	.23	2.7	0
Beef and vegetable stew	1 cup	245	82	220	16	11	15	29	2.9	2,400	.15	.17	4.7	17
Chili con carne with beans, canned	1 cup	255	72	340	19	16	31	82	4.3	150	.08	.18	3.3	—
Heart, beef, lean, braised	3 oz	85	61	160	27	5	1	5	5.0	20	.21	1.04	6.5	1
Lamb, cooked:														
Chop, rib, broiled:														
Lean and fat	3.1 oz	89	43	360	18	32	0	8	1.0	—	.11	.19	4.1	—
Lean only	2 oz	57	60	120	16	6	0	6	1.1	—	.09	.15	3.4	—
Leg, roasted:														
Lean and fat	3 oz	85	54	235	22	16	0	9	1.4	—	.13	.23	4.7	—
Lean only	2.5 oz	71	62	130	20	5	0	9	1.4	—	.12	.21	4.4	—
Shoulder, roasted:														
Lean and fat	3 oz	85	50	285	18	23	0	9	1.0	—	.11	.20	4.0	—
Lean only	2.3 oz	64	61	130	17	6	0	8	1.0	—	.10	.18	3.7	—
Liver, beef, fried	3 oz	85	56	195	22	9	5	9	7.5	45,390	.22	3.56	14.0	23
Pork, cured, cooked:														
Ham, light cure, lean and fat, roasted	3 oz	85	54	245	18	19	0	8	2.2	0	.40	.15	3.1	—
Luncheon meat:														
Boiled ham, slice	1 oz	28	59	65	5	5	0	3	.8	0	.12	.04	.7	—
Canned, spiced or unspiced	1 slice	60	55	175	9	15	1	5	1.3	0	.19	.13	1.8	—
Pork, fresh, cooked:														
Chop, loin, broiled:														
Lean and fat	2.7 oz	78	42	305	19	25	0	9	2.7	0	.75	.22	4.5	—
Lean only	2 oz	56	53	150	17	9	0	7	2.2	0	.63	.18	3.8	—
Roast, oven cooked, no liquid added:														
Lean and fat	3 oz	85	46	310	21	24	0	9	2.7	0	.78	.22	4.8	—
Lean only	2.4 oz	68	55	175	20	10	0	9	2.6	0	.73	.21	4.4	—
Shoulder cut, simmered:														
Lean and fat	3 oz	85	46	320	20	26	0	9	2.6	0	.46	.21	4.1	—
Lean only	2.2 oz	63	60	135	18	6	0	8	2.3	0	.42	.19	3.7	—
Sausages:														
Bologna, slice	1 slice	28	56	85	3	8	Trace	2	.5	—	.05	.06	.7	—

Food	Measure	Weight	Water	Food energy	Protein	Fat	Carbohydrate	Calcium	Iron	Vitamin A Value	Thiamin	Riboflavin	Niacin	Ascorbic Acid
		Grams	Percent	Calories	Grams	Grams	Grams	Milligrams	Milligrams	Int'l. Units	Milligrams	Milligrams	Milligrams	Milligrams
Sausages—Continued														
Braunschweiger, slice	1 slice	28	53	90	4	8	1	3	1.7	1,850	.05	.41	2.3	—
Brown and serve, browned	1 link	17	40	70	3	6	Trace	—	—	—	.02	.01	.2	—
Deviled ham, canned	1 tbsp	13	51	45	2	4	0	1	.3	0	.02	.01	.2	—
Frankfurter	1 frankfurter	56	57	170	7	15	1	3	.8	—	.08	.11	1.4	—
Pork link	1 link	13	35	60	2	6	Trace	1	.3	0	.10	.04	.5	—
Salami:														
Dry type, slice	1 slice	10	30	45	2	4	Trace	1	.4	—	.04	.03	.5	—
Cooked type, slice	1 slice	28	51	90	5	7	Trace	3	.7	—	.07	.07	1.2	—
Vienna sausage, canned	1 sausage	16	63	40	2	3	Trace	1	.3	—	.01	.02	.4	—
Veal, medium fat, cooked, bone removed:														
Cutlet, braised or broiled	3 oz	85	60	185	23	9	0	9	2.7	—	.06	.21	4.6	—
Rib, roasted	3 oz	85	55	230	23	14	0	10	2.9	—	.11	.26	6.6	—
Poultry and poultry products:														
Chicken, cooked:														
Breast, fried, bones removed, ½ breast	2.8 oz	79	58	160	26	5	1	9	1.3	70	.04	.17	11.6	—
Drumstick, fried, bones removed	1.3 oz	38	55	90	12	4	Trace	6	.9	50	.03	.15	2.7	—
Half broiler, broiled, bones removed	6.2 oz	176	71	240	42	7	0	16	3.0	160	.09	.34	15.5	—
Chicken chow mein:														
Canned	1 cup	250	89	95	7	Trace	18	45	1.3	150	.05	.10	1.0	13
Turkey, roasted, flesh without skin:														
Dark meat	4 pieces	85	61	175	26	7	0	—	2.0	—	.03	.20	3.6	—
Light meat	2 pieces	85	62	150	28	3	0	—	1.0	—	.04	.12	9.4	—
Light and dark meat:														
Chopped or diced	1 cup	140	61	265	44	9	0	11	2.5	—	.07	.25	10.8	—

Fruits and Fruit Products

Food	Measure	Weight	Water	Food energy	Protein	Fat	Carbohydrate	Calcium	Iron	Vitamin A Value	Thiamin	Riboflavin	Niacin	Ascorbic Acid
Apples, raw, unpeeled:														
2¾-in diam	1 apple	138	84	80	Trace	1	20	10	.4	120	.04	.03	.1	6
3¼-in diam	1 apple	212	84	125	Trace	1	31	15	.6	190	.06	.04	.2	8
Apple juice, bottled or canned	1 cup	248	88	120	Trace	Trace	30	15	1.5	—	.02	.05	.2	2
Applesauce, canned:														
Sweetened	1 cup	255	76	230	1	Trace	61	10	1.3	100	.05	.03	.1	3
Unsweetened	1 cup	244	89	100	Trace	Trace	26	10	1.2	100	.05	.02	.1	2
Apricots:														
Raw, without pits	3 apricots	107	85	55	1	Trace	14	18	.5	2,890	.03	.04	.6	11
Canned in heavy sirup	1 cup	258	77	220	2	Trace	57	28	.8	4,490	.05	.05	1.0	10
Dried:														
Uncooked	1 cup	130	25	340	7	1	86	87	7.2	14,170	.01	.21	4.3	16
Cooked, unsweetened, fruit and liquid	1 cup	250	76	215	4	1	54	55	4.5	7,500	.01	.13	2.5	8
Apricot nectar, canned	1 cup	251	85	145	1	Trace	37	23	.5	2,380	.03	.03	.5	36
Avocados, raw, whole, without skins and seeds:														
California, mid- and late-winter	1 avocado	216	74	370	5	37	13	22	1.3	630	.24	.43	3.5	30
Florida, late summer and fall	1 avocado	304	78	390	4	33	27	30	1.8	880	.33	.61	4.9	43
Banana, without peel	1 banana	119	76	100	1	Trace	26	10	.8	230	.06	.07	.8	12
Blackberries, raw	1 cup	144	85	85	2	1	19	46	1.3	290	.04	.06	.6	30
Blueberries, raw	1 cup	145	83	90	1	1	22	22	1.5	150	.04	.09	.7	20
Cantaloup. See Muskmelons														
Cherries:														
Sour (tart), red, pitted, canned, water pack	1 cup	244	88	105	2	Trace	26	37	.7	1,660	.07	.05	.5	12
Sweet, raw, without pits and stems	10 cherries	68	80	45	1	Trace	12	15	.3	70	.03	.04	.3	7
Cranberry juice cocktail, bottled, sweetened	1 cup	253	83	165	Trace	Trace	42	13	.8	Trace	.03	.03	.1	81
Cranberry sauce, sweetened, canned, strained	1 cup	277	62	405	Trace	1	104	17	.6	60	.03	.03	.1	6
Dates:														
Whole, without pits	10 dates	80	23	220	2	Trace	58	47	2.4	40	.07	.08	1.8	0
Chopped	1 cup	178	23	490	4	1	130	105	5.3	90	.16	.18	3.9	0
Fruit cocktail, canned, in heavy sirup	1 cup	255	80	195	1	Trace	50	23	1.0	360	.05	.03	1.0	5
Grapefruit:														
Raw, medium, 3¾-in diam														
Pink or red	½ grapefruit	241	89	50	1	Trace	13	20	.5	540	.05	.02	.2	44
White	½ grapefruit	241	89	45	1	Trace	12	19	.5	10	.05	.02	.2	44
Canned, sections with sirup	1 cup	254	81	180	2	Trace	45	33	.8	30	.08	.05	.5	76
Grapefruit juice:														
Raw, pink, red, or white	1 cup	246	90	95	1	Trace	23	22	.5	1,080	.10	.05	.5	93
Canned, white:														
Unsweetened	1 cup	247	89	100	1	Trace	24	20	1.0	20	.07	.05	.5	84
Sweetened	1 cup	250	86	135	1	Trace	32	20	1.0	30	.08	.05	.5	78

Food	Measure	Weight	Water	Food energy	Pro-tein	Fat	Carbo-hydrate	Calcium	Iron	Vitamin A Value	Thiamin	Ribo-flavin	Niacin	Ascorbic Acid
		Grams	Per-cent	Cal-ories	Grams	Grams	Grams	Milli-grams	Milli-grams	Int'l. Units	Milli-grams	Milli-grams	Milli-grams	Milli-grams
Grapefruit juice (cont.)														
Frozen, concentrate, unsweetened:														
Diluted with 3 parts water	1 cup	247	89	100	1	Trace	24	25	.2	20	.10	.04	.5	96
Dehydrated crystals, prepared with water	1 cup	247	90	100	1	Trace	24	22	.2	20	.10	.05	.5	91
Grapes, raw:														
Seedless	10 grapes	50	81	35	Trace	Trace	9	6	.2	50	.03	.02	.2	2
Seeded	10 grapes	60	81	40	Trace	Trace	10	7	.2	60	.03	.02	.2	2
Grapejuice:														
Canned or bottled	1 cup	253	83	165	1	Trace	42	28	.8	—	.10	.05	.5	Trace
Frozen concentrate, sweetened:														
Undiluted, 6-fl oz can	1 can	216	53	395	1	Trace	100	22	.9	40	.13	.22	1.5	32
Diluted with 3 parts water	1 cup	250	86	135	1	Trace	33	8	.3	10	.05	.08	.5	10
Grape drink, canned	1 cup	250	86	135	Trace	Trace	35	8	.3	—	.03	.03	.3	—
Lemon	1 lemon	74	90	20	1	Trace	6	19	.4	10	.03	.01	.1	39
Lemon juice:														
Raw	1 cup	244	91	60	1	Trace	20	17	.5	50	.07	.02	.2	112
Canned or bottled, unsweetened	1 cup	244	92	55	1	Trace	19	17	.5	50	.07	.02	.2	102
Frozen, single strength, unsweetened, 6-fl oz can	1 can	183	92	40	1	Trace	13	13	.5	40	.05	.02	.2	81
Lemonade concentrate, frozen:														
Undiluted, 6-fl oz can	1 can	219	49	425	Trace	Trace	112	9	.4	40	.05	.06	.7	66
Diluted with 4⅓ parts water	1 cup	248	89	105	Trace	Trace	28	2	.1	10	.01	.02	.2	17
Limeade concentrate, frozen:														
Undiluted, 6-fl oz can	1 can	218	50	410	Trace	Trace	108	11	.2	Trace	.02	.02	.2	26
Diluted with 4⅓ parts water	1 cup	247	89	100	Trace	Trace	27	3	Trace	Trace	Trace	Trace	Trace	6
Lime juice:														
Raw	1 cup	246	90	65	1	Trace	22	22	.5	20	.05	.02	.2	79
Canned, unsweetened	1 cup	246	90	65	1	Trace	22	22	.5	20	.05	.02	.2	52
Muskmelons														
Cantaloup, orange-fleshed	½ melon	477	91	80	2	Trace	20	38	1.1	9,240	.11	.08	1.6	90
Honeydew	1/10 melon	226	91	50	1	Trace	11	21	.6	60	.06	.04	.9	34
Oranges, raw:														
Whole, 2⅝-in diam	1 orange	131	86	65	1	Trace	16	54	.5	260	.13	.05	.5	66
Sections without membranes	1 cup	180	86	90	2	Trace	22	74	.7	360	.18	.07	.7	90
Orange juice:														
Raw, all varieties	1 cup	248	88	110	2	Trace	26	27	.5	500	.22	.07	1.0	124
Canned, unsweetened	1 cup	249	87	120	2	Trace	28	25	1.0	500	.17	.05	.7	100
Frozen concentrate:														
Undiluted, 6-fl oz can	1 can	213	55	360	5	Trace	87	75	.9	1,620	.68	.11	2.8	360
Diluted with 3 parts water	1 cup	249	87	120	2	Trace	29	25	.2	540	.23	.03	.9	120
Dehydrated crystals, prepared with water (1 lb yields about 1 gal)	1 cup	248	88	115	1	Trace	27	25	.5	500	.20	.07	1.0	109
Orange and grapefruit juice:														
Frozen concentrate:														
Undiluted, 6-fl oz can	1 can	210	59	330	4	1	78	61	.8	800	.48	.06	2.3	302
Diluted with 3 parts water	1 cup	248	88	110	1	Trace	26	20	.2	270	.15	.02	.7	102
Papayas, raw, ½-in cubes	1 cup	140	89	55	1	Trace	14	28	.4	2,450	.06	.06	.4	78
Peaches:														
Raw:														
Whole, 2½-in diam	1 peach	100	89	40	1	Trace	10	9	.5	1,330	.02	.05	1.0	7
Sliced	1 cup	170	89	65	1	Trace	16	15	.9	2,260	.03	.09	1.7	12
Canned, yellow-fleshed, solids and liquid:														
Sirup pack	1 cup	256	79	200	1	Trace	51	10	.8	1,100	.03	.05	1.5	8
Water pack	1 cup	244	91	75	1	Trace	20	10	.7	1,100	.02	.07	1.5	7
Dried:														
Uncooked	1 cup	160	25	420	5	1	109	77	9.6	6,240	.02	.30	8.5	29
Cooked, unsweetened, halves and juice,	1 cup	250	77	205	3	1	54	38	4.8	3,050	.01	.15	3.8	5
Frozen, sliced, sweetened:														
10-oz container	1 container	284	77	250	1	Trace	64	11	1.4	1,850	.03	.11	2.0	116
Cup	1 cup	250	77	220	1	Trace	57	10	1.3	1,630	.03	.10	1.8	103
Pears:														
Raw, with skin, cored:														
Bartlett	1 pear	164	83	100	1	1	25	13	.5	30	.03	.07	.2	7
Bosc	1 pear	141	83	85	1	1	22	11	.4	30	.03	.06	.1	6
D'Anjou	1 pear	200	83	120	1	1	31	16	.6	40	.04	.08	.2	8
Canned, solids and liquid, sirup pack, heavy	1 cup	255	80	195	1	1	50	13	.5	10	.03	.05	.3	3
Pineapple:														
Raw, diced	1 cup	155	85	80	1	Trace	21	26	.8	110	.14	.05	.3	26
Canned, heavy sirup pack, solids and liquid:														
Crushed, chunks, tidbits	1 cup	255	80	190	1	Trace	49	28	.8	130	.20	.05	.5	18
Pineapple juice, unsweetened, canned	1 cup	250	86	140	1	Trace	34	38	.8	130	.13	.05	.5	80

Food	Measure	Weight	Water	Food energy	Pro-tein	Fat	Carbo-hydrate	Calcium	Iron	Vitamin A Value	Thiamin	Ribo-flavin	Niacin	Ascorbic Acid
		Grams	Per-cent	Cal-ories	Grams	Grams	Grams	Milli-grams	Milli-grams	Int'l. Units	Milli-grams	Milli-grams	Milli-grams	Milli-grams
Plums:														
Raw, without pits:														
Japanese and hybrid	1 plum	66	87	30	Trace	Trace	8	8	.3	160	.02	.02	.3	4
Prune-type	1 plum	28	79	20	Trace	Trace	6	3	.1	80	.01	.01	.1	1
Canned, heavy sirup pack														
Cup	1 cup	272	77	215	1	Trace	56	23	2.3	3,130	.05	.05	1.0	5
Prunes, dried														
Uncooked	5 large	49	28	110	1	Trace	29	22	1.7	690	.04	.07	.7	1
Cooked, unsweetened, fruit and liquid	1 cup	250	66	255	2	1	67	51	3.8	1,590	.07	.15	1.5	2
Prune juice, canned or bottled	1 cup	256	80	195	1	Trace	49	36	1.8	—	.03	.03	1.0	5
Raisins, seedless:														
Cup, not pressed down	1 cup	145	18	420	4	Trace	112	90	5.1	30	.16	.12	.7	1
Packet, ½ oz (1½ tbsp)	1 packet	14	18	40	Trace	Trace	11	9	.5	Trace	.02	.01	.1	Trace
Raspberries, red:														
Raw, capped, whole	1 cup	123	84	70	1	1	17	27	1.1	160	.04	.11	1.1	31
Frozen, sweetened, 10-oz container	1 container	284	74	280	2	1	70	37	1.7	200	.06	.17	1.7	60
Rhubarb, cooked, added sugar:														
From raw	1 cup	270	63	380	1	Trace	97	211	1.6	220	.05	.14	.8	16
From frozen, sweetened	1 cup	270	63	385	1	1	98	211	1.9	190	.05	.11	.5	16
Strawberries:														
Raw, whole berries, capped	1 cup	149	90	55	1	1	13	31	1.5	90	.04	.10	.9	88
Frozen, sweetened:														
Sliced, 10-oz container	1 container	284	71	310	1	1	79	40	2.0	90	.06	.17	1.4	151
Whole, 1-lb container	1 container	454	76	415	2	1	107	59	2.7	140	.09	.27	2.3	249
Tangerine, raw	1 tangerine	86	87	40	1	Trace	10	34	.3	360	.05	.02	.1	27
Tangerine juice, canned, sweetened	1 cup	249	87	125	1	Trace	30	44	.5	1,040	.15	.05	.2	54
Watermelon, raw, 4 by 8 in wedge	1 wedge	926	93	110	2	1	27	30	2.1	2,510	.13	.13	.9	30
Grain Products														
Bagel, 3-in diam:														
Egg	1 bagel	55	32	165	6	2	28	9	1.2	30	.14	.10	1.2	0
Water	1 bagel	55	29	165	6	1	30	8	1.2	0	.15	.11	1.4	0
Barley, pearled, uncooked	1 cup	200	11	700	16	2	158	32	4.0	0	.24	.10	6.2	0
Biscuits, from mix	1 biscuit	28	29	90	2	3	15	19	.6	Trace	.09	.08	.8	Trace
Breadcrumbs														
Dry, grated	1 cup	100	7	390	13	5	73	122	3.6	Trace	.35	.35	4.8	Trace
Soft. See White bread														
Breads:														
Cracked-wheat bread:														
Slice (18 per loaf)	1 slice	25	35	65	2	1	13	22	.5	Trace	.08	.06	.8	Trace
French or vienna bread, enriched:														
Slice:														
French	1 slice	35	31	100	3	1	19	15	.8	Trace	.14	.08	1.2	Trace
Vienna	1 slice	25	31	75	2	1	14	11	.6	Trace	.10	.06	.8	Trace
Italian bread, enriched:														
Slice	1 slice	30	32	85	3	Trace	17	5	.7	0	.12	.07	1.0	0
Raisin bread, enriched:														
Slice (18 per loaf)	1 slice	25	35	65	2	1	13	18	.6	Trace	.09	.06	.6	Trace
Rye bread:														
American, light, slice	1 slice	25	36	60	2	Trace	13	19	.5	0	.07	.05	.7	0
Pumpernickel, slice	1 slice	32	34	80	3	Trace	17	27	.8	0	.09	.07	.6	0
White bread,														
Soft-crumb type:														
Loaf, 1 lb														
Slice (22 per loaf)	1 slice	20	36	55	2	1	10	17	.5	Trace	.08	.05	.7	Trace
Slice, toasted	1 slice	17	25	55	2	1	10	17	.5	Trace	.06	.05	.7	Trace
Cubes	1 cup	30	36	80	3	1	15	25	.8	Trace	.12	.07	1.0	Trace
Crumbs	1 cup	45	36	120	4	1	23	38	1.1	Trace	.18	.11	1.5	Trace
Firm-crumb type:														
Loaf, 1 lb														
Slice (20 per loaf)	1 slice	23	35	65	2	1	12	22	.6	Trace	.09	.06	.8	Trace
Slice, toasted	1 slice	20	24	65	2	1	12	22	.6	Trace	.07	.06	.8	Trace
Whole-wheat bread:														
Soft-crumb type:														
Loaf, 1 lb														
Slice (16 per loaf)	1 slice	28	36	65	3	1	14	24	.8	Trace	.09	.03	.8	Trace
Slice, toasted	1 slice	24	24	65	3	1	14	24	.8	Trace	.07	.03	.8	Trace
Firm-crumb type:														
Loaf, 1 lb														
Slice (18 per loaf)	1 slice	25	36	60	3	1	12	25	.8	Trace	.06	.03	.7	Trace
Slice, toasted	1 slice	21	24	60	3	1	12	25	.8	Trace	.05	.03	.7	Trace
Breakfast cereals:														
Hot type, cooked:														
Corn (hominy) grits, enriched	1 cup	245	87	125	3	Trace	27	2	.7	Trace	.10	.07	1.0	0

Food	Measure	Weight	Water	Food energy	Pro-tein	Fat	Carbo-hydrate	Calcium	Iron	Vitamin A Value	Thiamin	Ribo-flavin	Niacin	Ascorbic Acid
		Grams	Per-cent	Cal-ories	Grams	Grams	Grams	Milli-grams	Milli-grams	Int'l. Units	Milli-grams	Milli-grams	Milli-grams	Milli-grams
Breakfast cereals—Continued														
Farina, quick-cooking, enriched	1 cup	245	89	105	3	Trace	22	147	.5	0	.12	.07	1.0	0
Oatmeal or rolled oats	1 cup	240	87	130	5	2	23	22	1.4	0	.19	.05	.2	0
Wheat, rolled	1 cup	240	80	180	5	1	41	19	1.7	0	.17	.07	2.2	0
Wheat, whole-meal	1 cup	245	88	110	4	1	23	17	1.2	0	.15	.05	1.5	0
Ready-to-eat:														
Bran flakes (40% bran), added sugar, salt, iron, vitamins	1 cup	35	3	105	4	1	28	19	12.4	1,650	.41	.49	4.1	12
Bran flakes with raisins, added sugar, salt, iron, vitamins	1 cup	50	7	145	4	1	40	28	17.7	2,350	.58	.71	5.8	18
Corn flakes:														
Plain, added sugar, salt, iron, vitamins	1 cup	25	4	95	2	Trace	21	1	.6	1,180	.29	.35	2.9	9
Sugar-coated, added salt, iron, vitamins	1 cup	40	2	155	2	Trace	37	1	1.0	1,880	.46	.56	4.6	14
Corn, puffed, plain, added sugar, salt, iron, vitamins	1 cup	20	4	80	2	1	16	4	2.3	940	.23	.28	2.3	7
Corn, shredded, added sugar, salt, iron, thiamin, niacin	1 cup	25	3	95	2	Trace	22	1	.6	0	.11	.05	.5	0
Oats, puffed, added sugar, salt, minerals, vitamins	1 cup	25	3	100	3	1	19	44	2.9	1,180	.29	.35	2.9	9
Rice, puffed:														
Plain, added iron, thiamin, niacin	1 cup	15	4	60	1	Trace	13	3	.3	0	.07	.01	.7	0
Presweetened, added salt, iron, vitamins	1 cup	28	3	115	1	0	26	3	1.1	1,250	.38	.43	5.0	15
Wheat flakes, added sugar, salt, iron, vitamins	1 cup	30	4	105	3	Trace	24	12	1.5	1,410	.35	.42	3.5	11
Wheat, puffed:														
Plain, added iron, thiamin, niacin	1 cup	15	3	55	2	Tra e	12	4	.6	0	.08	.03	1.2	0
Presweetened, added salt, iron, vitamins	1 cup	38	3	140	3	Trace	33	7	1.6	1,680	.50	.57	6.7	20
Wheat, shredded, plain	1 biscuit	25	7	90	2	1	20	11	.9	0	.06	.03	1.1	0
Wheat germ, without salt and sugar, toasted	1 tbsp	6	4	25	2	1	3	3	.5	10	.11	.05	.3	1
Buckwheat flour, light, sifted	1 cup	98	12	340	6	1	78	11	1.0	0	.08	.04	.4	0
Bulgur, canned, seasoned	1 cup	135	56	245	8	4	44	27	1.9	0	.08	.05	4.1	0
Cakes made from cake mixes with enriched flour:														
Angelfood:														
Piece, 1/12 of cake	1 piece	53	34	135	3	Trace	32	50	.2	0	.03	.08	.3	0
Coffeecake:														
Piece, 1/6 of cake	1 piece	72	30	230	5	7	38	44	1.2	120	.14	.15	1.3	Trace
Cupcakes, made with egg, milk, 2½-in diam:														
Without icing	1 cupcake	25	26	90	1	3	14	40	.3	40	.05	.05	.4	Trace
With chocolate icing	1 cupcake	36	22	130	2	5	21	47	.4	60	.05	.06	.4	Trace
Devil's food with chocolate icing:														
Piece, 1/16 of cake	1 piece	69	24	235	3	8	40	41	1.0	100	.07	.10	.6	Trace
Cupcake, 2½-in diam	1 cupcake	35	24	120	2	4	20	21	.5	50	.03	.05	.3	Trace
Gingerbread:														
Piece, 1/9 of cake	1 piece	63	37	175	2	4	32	57	.9	Trace	.09	.11	.8	Trace
White, 2 layer with chocolate icing:														
Piece, 1/16 of cake	1 piece	71	21	250	3	8	45	70	.7	40	.09	.11	.8	Trace
Yellow, 2 layer with chocolate icing:														
Piece, 1/16 of cake	1 piece	69	26	235	3	8	40	63	.8	100	.08	.10	.7	Trace
Cookies														
Brownies with nuts:														
From commercial recipe	1 brownie	20	11	85	1	4	13	9	.4	20	.03	.02	.2	Trace
Frozen, with chocolate icing	1 brownie	25	13	105	1	5	15	10	.4	50	.03	.03	.2	Trace
Chocolate chip:														
Commercial, 2¼-in diam, ⅜ in thick	4 cookies	42	3	200	2	9	29	16	1.0	50	.10	.17	.9	Trace
Fig bars	4 cookies	56	14	200	2	3	42	44	1.0	60	.04	.14	.9	Trace
Gingersnaps, 2-in diam, ¼ in thick	4 cookies	28	3	90	2	2	22	20	.7	20	.08	.06	.7	0
Macaroons, 2¾-in diam, ¼ in thick	2 cookies	38	4	180	2	9	25	10	.3	0	.02	.06	.2	0
Oatmeal with raisins, 2⅝-in diam, ¼ in thick	4 cookies	52	3	235	3	8	38	11	1.4	30	.15	.10	1.0	Trace

Food	Measure	Weight	Water	Food energy	Protein	Fat	Carbohydrate	Calcium	Iron	Vitamin A Value	Thiamin	Riboflavin	Niacin	Ascorbic Acid
		Grams	Percent	Calories	Grams	Grams	Grams	Milligrams	Milligrams	Int'l. Units	Milligrams	Milligrams	Milligrams	Milligrams
Cookies —Continued														
Plain, prepared from commercial chilled dough	4 cookies	48	5	240	2	12	31	17	.6	30	.10	.08	.9	0
Sandwich type (chocolate or vanilla)	4 cookies	40	2	200	2	9	28	10	.7	0	.06	.10	.7	0
Vanilla wafers	10 cookies	40	3	185	2	6	30	16	.6	50	.10	.09	.8	0
Crackers:														
Graham, plain, 2½-in square	2 crackers	14	6	55	1	1	10	6	.5	0	.02	.08	.5	0
Rye wafers, whole-grain	2 wafers	13	6	45	2	Trace	10	7	.5	0	.04	.03	.2	0
Saltines	4 crackers	11	4	50	1	1	8	2	.5	0	.05	.05	.4	0
Danish pastry, plain without fruit or nuts:														
Round piece	1 pastry	65	22	275	5	15	30	33	1.2	200	.18	.19	1.7	Trace
Ounce	1 oz	28	22	120	2	7	13	14	.5	90	.08	.08	.7	Trace
Doughnuts:														
Cake type, plain	1 doughnut	25	24	100	1	5	13	10	.4	20	.05	.05	.4	Trace
Yeast-leavened, glazed	1 doughnut	50	26	205	3	11	22	16	.6	25	.10	.10	.8	0
Macaroni, enriched, cooked (cut lengths, elbows, shells):														
Firm stage (hot)	1 cup	130	64	190	7	1	39	14	1.4	0	.23	.13	1.8	0
Tender stage:														
Cold macaroni	1 cup	105	73	115	4	Trace	24	8	.9	0	.15	.08	1.2	0
Hot macaroni	1 cup	140	73	155	5	1	32	11	1.3	0	.20	.11	1.5	0
Macaroni and cheese:														
Canned	1 cup	240	80	230	9	10	26	199	1.0	260	.12	.24	1.0	Trace
Muffins														
From mix, egg, milk:														
Corn	1 muffin	40	30	130	3	4	20	96	.6	100	.08	.09	.7	Trace
Noodles (egg noodles), enriched, cooked.	1 cup	160	71	200	7	2	37	16	1.4	110	.22	.13	1.9	0
Noodles, chow mein, canned	1 cup	45	1	220	6	11	26	—	—	—	—	—	—	—
Pancakes (4-in diam):														
Buckwheat, made from mix with egg and milk added	1 cake	27	58	55	2	2	6	59	.4	60	.04	.05	.2	Trace
Plain	1 cake	27	50	60	2	2	9	27	.4	30	.06	.07	.5	Trace
Made from mix with egg and milk added	1 cake	27	51	60	2	2	9	58	.3	70	.04	.06	.2	Trace
Pies, piecrust made with enriched flour, vegetable shortening (9-in diam):														
Apple:														
Sector, ⅐ of pie	1 sector	135	48	345	3	15	51	11	.9	40	.15	.11	1.3	2
Banana cream:														
Sector, ⅐ of pie	1 sector	130	54	285	6	12	40	86	1.0	330	.11	.22	1.0	1
Blueberry:														
Sector, ⅐ of pie	1 sector	135	51	325	3	15	47	15	1.4	40	.15	.11	1.4	4
Cherry:														
Sector, ⅐ of pie	1 sector	135	47	350	4	15	52	19	.9	590	.16	.12	1.4	Trace
Custard:														
Sector, ⅐ of pie	1 sector	130	58	285	8	14	30	125	1.2	300	.11	.27	.8	0
Lemon meringue:														
Sector, ⅐ of pie	1 sector	120	47	305	4	12	45	17	1.0	200	.09	.12	.7	4
Mince:														
Sector, ⅐ of pie	1 sector	135	43	365	3	16	56	38	1.9	Trace	.14	.12	1.4	1
Peach:														
Sector, ⅐ of pie	1 sector	135	48	345	3	14	52	14	1.2	990	.15	.14	2.0	4
Pecan:														
Sector, ⅐ of pie	1 sector	118	20	495	6	27	61	55	3.7	190	.26	.14	1.0	Trace
Pumpkin:														
Sector, ⅐ of pie	1 sector	130	59	275	5	15	32	66	1.0	3,210	.11	.18	1.0	Trace
Pizza (cheese) baked, ⅛ of 12-in diam pie	1 sector	60	45	145	6	4	22	86	1.1	230	.16	.18	1.6	4
Popcorn, popped:														
Plain	1 cup	6	4	25	1	Trace	5	1	.2	—	—	.01	.1	0
With oil and salt added	1 cup	9	3	40	1	2	5	1	.2	—	—	.01	.2	0
Sugar coated	1 cup	35	4	135	2	1	30	2	.5	—	—	.02	.4	0
Pretzels:														
Dutch, twisted	1 pretzel	16	5	60	2	1	12	4	.2	0	.05	.04	.7	0
Thin, twisted	10 pretzels	60	5	235	6	3	46	13	.9	0	.20	.15	2.5	0
Stick, 2¼ in long	10 pretzels	3	5	10	Trace	Trace	2	1	Trace	0	.01	.01	.1	0
Rice, white, enriched:														
Instant, ready-to-serve, hot	1 cup	165	73	180	4	Trace	40	5	1.3	0	.21	.15	1.7	0
Long grain:														
Cooked	1 cup	205	73	225	4	Trace	50	21	1.8	0	.23	.02	2.1	0
Rolls, commercial:														
Brown-and-serve	1 roll	26	27	85	2	2	14	20	.5	Trace	.10	.06	.9	Trace
Cloverleaf or pan	1 roll	28	31	85	2	2	15	21	.5	Trace	.11	.07	.9	Trace
Frankfurter and hamburger	1 roll	40	31	120	3	2	21	30	.8	Trace	.16	.10	1.3	Trace
Hard	1 roll	50	25	155	5	2	30	24	1.2	Trace	.20	.12	1.7	Trace
Hoagie or submarine, 11½ by 3 by 2½ in	1 roll	135	31	390	12	4	75	58	3.0	Trace	.54	.32	4.5	Trace

Food	Measure	Weight	Water	Food energy	Pro-tein	Fat	Carbo-hydrate	Calcium	Iron	Vitamin A Value	Thiamin	Ribo-flavin	Niacin	Ascorbic Acid
		Grams	Per-cent	Cal-ories	Grams	Grams	Grams	Milli-grams	Milli-grams	Int'l. Units	Milli-grams	Milli-grams	Milli-grams	Milli-grams
Spaghetti, enriched, cooked:														
Firm stage, "al dente," served hot	1 cup	130	64	190	7	1	39	14	1.4	0	.23	.13	1.8	0
Tender stage, served hot	1 cup	140	73	155	5	1	32	11	1.3	0	.20	.11	1.5	0
Spaghetti in tomato sauce with cheese:														
Canned	1 cup	250	80	190	6	2	39	40	2.8	930	.35	.28	4.5	10
Spaghetti with meat balls and tomato sauce:														
Canned	1 cup	250	78	260	12	10	29	53	3.3	1,000	.15	.18	2.3	5
Toaster pastries	1 pastry	50	12	200	3	6	36	54	1.9	500	.16	.17	2.1	Trace
Waffles, 7-in diam:														
From mix, egg and milk added	1 waffle	75	42	205	7	8	27	179	1.0	170	.14	.22	.9	Trace
Wheat flours:														
All-purpose enriched:														
Sifted, spooned	1 cup	115	12	420	12	1	88	18	3.3	0	.74	.46	6.1	0
Unsifted, spooned	1 cup	125	12	455	13	1	95	20	3.6	0	.80	.50	6.6	0
Cake flour, enriched, sifted, spooned	1 cup	96	12	350	7	1	76	16	2.8	0	.61	.38	5.1	0
Self-rising, unsifted, spooned	1 cup	125	12	440	12	1	93	331	3.6	0	.80	.50	6.6	0
Whole-wheat, from hard wheats, stirred	1 cup	120	12	400	16	2	85	49	4.0	0	.66	.14	5.2	0

Legumes (Dry), Nuts, Seeds; Related Products

Food	Measure	Weight	Water	Food energy	Pro-tein	Fat	Carbo-hydrate	Calcium	Iron	Vitamin A Value	Thiamin	Ribo-flavin	Niacin	Ascorbic Acid
Almonds, shelled:														
Chopped	1 cup	130	5	775	24	70	25	304	6.1	0	.31	1.20	4.6	Trace
Slivered, not pressed down	1 cup	115	5	690	21	62	22	269	5.4	0	.28	1.06	4.0	Trace
Beans, dry:														
Cooked, drained:														
Great Northern	1 cup	180	69	210	14	1	38	90	4.9	0	.25	.13	1.3	0
Pea (navy)	1 cup	190	69	225	15	1	40	95	5.1	0	.27	.13	1.3	0
Canned, solids and liquid:														
White with—														
Frankfurters (sliced)	1 cup	255	71	365	19	18	32	94	4.8	330	.18	.15	3.3	Trace
Pork and tomato sauce	1 cup	255	71	310	16	7	48	138	4.6	330	.20	.08	1.5	5
Pork and sweet sauce	1 cup	255	66	385	16	12	54	161	5.9	—	.15	.10	1.3	—
Red kidney	1 cup	255	76	230	15	1	42	74	4.6	10	.13	.10	1.5	—
Lima, cooked, drained	1 cup	190	64	260	16	1	49	55	5.9	—	.25	.11	1.3	—
Blackeye peas, cooked (with residual cooking liquid)	1 cup	250	80	190	13	1	35	43	3.3	30	.40	.10	1.0	—
Brazil nuts	1 oz	28	5	185	4	19	3	53	1.0	Trace	.27	.03	.5	—
Cashew nuts, roasted in oil	1 cup	140	5	785	24	64	41	53	5.3	140	.60	.35	2.5	—
Coconut meat, fresh:														
Piece, about 2 by 2 by ½ in	1 piece	45	51	155	2	16	4	6	.8	0	.02	.01	.2	1
Shredded or grated, not pressed down	1 cup	80	51	275	3	28	8	10	1.4	0	.04	.02	.4	2
Filberts (hazelnuts), chopped	1 cup	115	6	730	14	72	19	240	3.9	—	.53	—	1.0	Trace
Lentils, whole, cooked	1 cup	200	72	210	16	Trace	39	50	4.2	40	.14	.12	1.2	0
Peanuts, roasted in oil, salted	1 cup	144	2	840	37	72	27	107	3.0	—	.46	.19	24.8	0
Peanut butter	1 tbsp	16	2	95	4	8	3	9	.3	—	.02	.02	2.4	0
Peas, split, dry, cooked	1 cup	200	70	230	16	1	42	22	3.4	80	.30	.18	1.8	—
Pecans, chopped or pieces	1 cup	118	3	810	11	84	17	86	2.8	150	1.01	.15	1.1	2
Pumpkin and squash kernels, dry, hulled	1 cup	140	4	775	41	65	21	71	15.7	100	.34	.27	3.4	—
Sunflower seeds, dry, hulled	1 cup	145	5	810	35	69	29	174	10.3	70	2.84	.33	7.8	—
Walnuts:														
Black:														
Chopped or broken kernels	1 cup	125	3	785	26	74	19	Trace	7.5	380	.28	.14	.9	—
Ground (finely)	1 cup	80	3	500	16	47	12	Trace	4.8	240	.18	.09	.6	—
Persian or English, chopped (about 60 halves)	1 cup	120	4	780	18	77	19	119	3.7	40	.40	.16	1.1	2

Sugars and Sweets

Food	Measure	Weight	Water	Food energy	Pro-tein	Fat	Carbo-hydrate	Calcium	Iron	Vitamin A Value	Thiamin	Ribo-flavin	Niacin	Ascorbic Acid
Cake icings:														
Boiled, white:														
Plain	1 cup	94	18	295	1	0	75	2	Trace	0	Trace	.03	Trace	0
With coconut	1 cup	166	15	605	3	13	124	10	.8	0	.02	.07	0.3	0
Uncooked:														
Chocolate made with milk and butter	1 cup	275	14	1,035	9	38	185	165	3.3	580	.06	.28	.6	1
Creamy fudge from mix and water	1 cup	245	15	830	7	16	183	96	2.7	Trace	.05	.20	.7	Trace
White	1 cup	319	11	1,200	2	21	260	48	Trace	860	Trace	.06	Trace	Trace
Candy:														
Caramels, plain or chocolate	1 oz	28	8	115	1	3	22	42	.4	Trace	.01	.05	.1	Trace

Food	Measure	Weight	Water	Food energy	Pro-tein	Fat	Carbo-hydrate	Calcium	Iron	Vitamin A Value	Thiamin	Ribo-flavin	Niacin	Ascorbic Acid
		Grams	Per-cent	Cal-ories	Grams	Grams	Grams	Milli-grams	Milli-grams	Int'l. Units	Milli-grams	Milli-grams	Milli-grams	Milli-grams
Candy—Continued														
Chocolate:														
Milk, plain	1 oz	28	1	145	2	9	16	65	.3	80	.02	.10	.1	Trace
Semisweet, small pieces	6-oz	170	1	860	7	61	97	51	4.4	30	.02	.14	.9	0
Chocolate-coated peanuts	1 oz	28	1	160	5	12	11	33	.4	Trace	.10	.05	2.1	Trace
Fudge, chocolate, plain	1 oz	28	8	115	1	3	21	22	.3	Trace	.01	.03	.1	Trace
Gum drops	1 oz	28	12	100	Trace	Trace	25	2	.1	0	0	Trace	Trace	0
Hard	1 oz	28	1	110	0	Trace	28	6	.5	0	0	0	0	0
Marshmallows	1 oz	28	17	90	1	Trace	23	5	.5	0	0	Trace	Trace	0
Chocolate-flavored beverage powders (4 heaping tsp):														
With nonfat dry milk	1 oz	28	2	100	5	1	20	167	.5	10	.04	.21	.2	1
Without milk	1 oz	28	1	100	1	1	25	9	.6	—	.01	.03	.1	0
Honey, strained or extracted	1 tbsp	21	17	65	Trace	0	17	1	.1	0	Trace	.01	.1	Trace
Jams and preserves	1 tbsp	20	29	55	Trace	Trace	14	4	.2	Trace	Trace	.01	Trace	Trace
Jellies	1 tbsp	18	29	50	Trace	Trace	13	4	.3	Trace	Trace	.01	Trace	1
Sirups:														
Chocolate-flavored sirup:														
Thin type	1 fl oz	38	32	90	1	1	24	6	.6	Trace	.01	.03	.2	0
Fudge type	1 fl oz	38	25	125	2	5	20	48	.5	60	.02	.08	.2	Trace
Molasses, cane:														
Light (first extraction)	1 tbsp	20	24	50	—	—	13	33	.9	—	.01	.01	Trace	—
Blackstrap (third extraction)	1 tbsp	20	24	45	—	—	11	137	3.2	—	.02	.04	.4	—
Sorghum	1 tbsp	21	23	55	—	—	14	35	2.6	—	—	.02	Trace	—
Table blends, chiefly corn	1 tbsp	21	24	60	0	0	15	9	.8	0	0	0	0	0
Sugars:														
Brown, pressed down	1 cup	220	2	820	0	0	212	187	7.5	0	.02	.07	.4	0
White	1 tbsp	12	1	45	0	0	12	0	Trace	0	0	0	0	0
	1 packet	6	1	23	0	0	6	0	Trace	0	0	0	0	0
Vegetables and Vegetable Products														
Asparagus:														
Cooked:														
Cuts and tips:														
From raw	1 cup	145	94	30	3	Trace	5	30	.9	1,310	.23	.26	2.0	38
From frozen	1 cup	180	93	40	6	Trace	6	40	2.2	1,530	.25	.23	1.8	41
Spears:														
From raw	4 spears	60	94	10	1	Trace	2	13	.4	540	.10	.11	.8	16
From frozen	4 spears	60	92	15	2	Trace	2	13	.7	470	.10	.08	.7	16
Canned, spears	4 spears	80	93	15	2	Trace	3	15	1.5	640	.05	.08	.6	12
Beans:														
Lima, frozen, cooked, drained:														
Thick-seeded types (Fordhooks)	1 cup	170	74	170	10	Trace	32	34	2.9	390	.12	.09	1.7	29
Thin-seeded types (baby limas)	1 cup	180	69	210	13	Trace	40	63	4.7	400	.16	.09	2.2	22
Green:														
Cooked, drained:														
From raw	1 cup	125	92	30	2	Trace	7	63	.8	680	.09	.11	.6	15
From frozen:														
Cuts	1 cup	135	92	35	2	Trace	8	54	.9	780	.09	.12	.5	7
French style	1 cup	130	92	35	2	Trace	8	49	1.2	690	.08	.10	.4	9
Canned, drained solids	1 cup	135	92	30	2	Trace	7	61	2.0	630	.04	.07	.4	5
Yellow or wax:														
Cooked, drained:														
From raw	1 cup	125	93	30	2	Trace	6	63	.8	290	.09	.11	.6	16
From frozen	1 cup	135	92	35	2	Trace	8	47	.9	140	.09	.11	.5	8
Canned, drained solids	1 cup	135	92	30	2	Trace	7	61	2.0	140	.04	.07	.4	7
Bean sprouts														
Raw	1 cup	105	89	35	4	Trace	7	20	1.4	20	.14	.14	.8	20
Cooked, drained	1 cup	125	91	35	4	Trace	7	21	1.1	30	.11	.13	.9	8
Beets:														
Cooked, drained, peeled	1 cup	170	91	55	2	Trace	12	24	.9	30	.05	.07	.5	10
Canned, drained solids:														
Diced or sliced	1 cup	170	89	65	2	Trace	15	32	1.2	30	.02	.05	.2	5
Beet greens, leaves and stems, cooked, drained	1 cup	145	94	25	2	Trace	5	144	2.8	7,400	.10	.22	.4	22
Blackeye peas, cooked and drained:														
From raw	1 cup	165	72	180	13	1	30	40	3.5	580	.50	.18	2.3	28
From frozen	1 cup	170	66	220	15	1	40	43	4.8	290	.68	.19	2.4	15
Broccoli, cooked, drained:														
From raw:														
Stalk, medium size	1 stalk	180	91	45	6	1	8	158	1.4	4,500	.16	.36	1.4	162
Pieces	1 cup	155	91	40	5	Trace	7	136	1.2	3,880	.14	.31	1.2	140
From frozen:														
Stalk	1 stalk	30	91	10	1	Trace	1	12	.2	570	.02	.03	.2	22
Chopped	1 cup	185	92	50	5	1	9	100	1.3	4,810	.11	.22	.9	105

Food	Measure	Weight	Water	Food energy	Protein	Fat	Carbohydrate	Calcium	Iron	Vitamin A Value	Thiamin	Riboflavin	Niacin	Ascorbic Acid
		Grams	Percent	Calories	Grams	Grams	Grams	Milligrams	Milligrams	Int'l. Units	Milligrams	Milligrams	Milligrams	Milligrams
Brussels sprouts, cooked, drained:														
From raw, 7-8 sprouts	1 cup	155	88	55	7	1	10	50	1.7	810	.12	.22	1.2	135
From frozen	1 cup	155	89	50	5	Trace	10	33	1.2	880	.12	.16	.9	126
Cabbage:														
Raw:														
Coarsely shredded or sliced	1 cup	70	92	15	1	Trace	4	34	.3	90	.04	.04	.02	33
Cooked, drained	1 cup	145	94	30	2	Trace	6	64	.4	190	.06	.06	.4	48
Red, raw, coarsely shredded or sliced	1 cup	70	90	20	1	Trace	5	29	.6	30	.06	.04	.3	43
Savoy, raw, coarsely shredded or sliced	1 cup	70	92	15	2	Trace	3	47	.6	140	.04	.06	.2	39
Carrots:														
Raw, without crowns and tips, scraped:														
Whole, 7½ by 1⅛ in	1 carrot	72	88	30	1	Trace	7	27	.5	7,930	.04	.04	.4	6
Grated	1 cup	110	88	45	1	Trace	11	41	.8	12,100	.07	.06	.7	9
Cooked (crosswise cuts), drained	1 cup	155	91	50	1	Trace	11	51	.9	16,280	.08	.08	.8	9
Canned:														
Sliced, drained solids	1 cup	155	91	45	1	Trace	10	47	1.1	23,250	.03	.05	.6	3
Strained or junior (baby food)	1 oz (1¾ to 2 tbsp)	28	92	10	Trace	Trace	2	7	.1	3,690	.01	.01	.1	1
Cauliflower:														
Raw, chopped	1 cup	115	91	31	3	Trace	6	29	1.3	70	.13	.12	.8	90
Cooked, drained:														
From raw (flower buds)	1 cup	125	93	30	3	Trace	5	26	.9	80	.11	.10	.8	69
From frozen (flowerets)	1 cup	180	94	30	3	Trace	6	31	.9	50	.07	.09	.7	74
Celery, Pascal type, raw:														
Stalk, large outer	1 stalk	40	94	5	Trace	Trace	2	16	.1	110	.01	.01	.1	4
Pieces, diced	1 cup	120	94	20	1	Trace	5	47	.4	320	.04	.04	.4	11
Collards, cooked, drained:														
From raw (leaves without stems)	1 cup	190	90	65	7	1	10	357	1.5	14,820	.21	.38	2.3	144
From frozen (chopped)	1 cup	170	90	50	5	1	10	299	1.7	11,560	.10	.24	1.0	56
Corn, sweet:														
Cooked, drained:														
From raw, ear 5 by 1¾ in	1 ear	140	74	70	2	1	16	2	.5	310	.09	.08	1.1	7
From frozen:														
Ear, 5 in long	1 ear	229	73	120	4	1	27	4	1.0	440	.18	.10	2.1	9
Kernels	1 cup	165	77	130	5	1	31	5	1.3	580	.15	.10	2.5	8
Canned:														
Cream style	1 cup	256	76	210	5	2	51	8	1.5	840	.08	.13	2.6	13
Whole kernel:														
Vacuum pack	1 cup	210	76	175	5	1	43	6	1.1	740	.06	.13	2.3	11
Wet pack, drained solids	1 cup	165	76	140	4	1	33	8	.8	580	.05	.08	1.5	7
Cucumber slices:														
With peel	6 large	28	95	5	Trace	Trace	1	7	.3	70	.01	.01	.1	3
Without peel	6½ large	28	96	5	Trace	Trace	1	5	.1	Trace	.01	.01	.1	3
Dandelion greens, cooked, drained	1 cup	105	90	35	2	1	7	147	1.9	12,290	.14	.17	—	19
Endive, curly (including escarole), raw, small pieces	1 cup	50	93	10	1	Trace	2	41	.9	1,650	.04	.07	.3	5
Kale, cooked, drained:														
From raw leaves	1 cup	110	88	45	5	1	7	206	1.8	9,130	.11	.20	1.8	102
From frozen (leaf style)	1 cup	130	91	40	4	1	7	157	1.3	10,660	.08	.20	.9	49
Lettuce, raw:														
Boston types:														
Head, 5-in diam	1 head	220	95	25	2	Trace	4	57	3.3	1,580	.10	.10	.5	13
Leaves	1 outer or 2 inner or 3 heart leaves	15	95	Trace	Trace	Trace	Trace	5	.3	150	.01	.01	Trace	1
Crisphead, as Iceberg:														
Head, 6-in diam	1 head	567	96	70	5	1	16	108	2.7	1,780	.32	.32	1.6	32
Wedge, ¼ of head	1 wedge	135	96	20	1	Trace	4	27	.7	450	.08	.08	.4	8
Pieces, chopped or shredded	1 cup	55	96	5	Trace	Trace	2	11	.3	180	.03	.03	.2	3
Looseleaf, chopped or shredded pieces	1 cup	55	94	10	1	Trace	2	37	.8	1,050	.03	.04	.2	10
Mushrooms, raw, sliced or chopped	1 cup	70	90	20	2	Trace	3	4	.6	Trace	.07	.32	2.9	2
Mustard greens, cooked, drained	1 cup	140	93	30	3	1	6	193	2.5	8,120	.11	.20	.8	67
Okra pods, 3 by ⅝ in, cooked	10 pods	106	91	30	2	Trace	6	98	.5	520	.14	.19	1.0	21
Onions:														
Mature:														
Raw:														
Chopped	1 cup	170	89	65	3	Trace	15	46	.9	Trace	.05	.07	.3	17
Sliced	1 cup	115	89	45	2	Trace	10	31	.6	Trace	.03	.05	.2	12

Food	Measure	Weight	Water	Food energy	Pro-tein	Fat	Carbo-hydrate	Calcium	Iron	Vitamin A Value	Thiamin	Ribo-flavin	Niacin	Ascorbic Acid
		Grams	Per-cent	Cal-ories	Grams	Grams	Grams	Milli-grams	Milli-grams	Int'l. Units	Milli-grams	Milli-grams	Milli-grams	Milli-grams
Onions—Continued														
Cooked (whole or sliced)	1 cup	210	92	60	3	Trace	14	50	.8	Trace	.06	.06	.4	15
Young green, bulb (⅜ in diam) and white portion of top	6 onions	30	88	15	Trace	Trace	3	12	.2	Trace	.02	.01	.1	8
Parsley, raw, chopped	1 tbsp	4	85	Trace	Trace	Trace	Trace	7	.2	300	Trace	.01	Trace	6
Parsnips, cooked (diced or 2-in lengths)	1 cup	155	82	100	2	1	23	70	.9	50	.11	.12	.2	16
Peas, green:														
Canned:														
Whole, drained solids	1 cup	170	77	150	8	1	29	44	3.2	1,170	.15	.10	1.4	14
Strained (baby food)	1 oz	28	86	15	1	Trace	3	3	.3	140	.02	.03	.3	3
Frozen, cooked, drained	1 cup	160	82	110	8	Trace	19	30	3.0	960	.43	.14	2.7	21
Peppers, hot, red, dried	1 tsp	2	9	5	Trace	Trace	1	5	.3	1,300	Trace	.02	.2	Trace
Peppers, sweet, stem and seeds removed:														
Raw	1 pod	74	93	15	1	Trace	4	7	.5	310	.06	.06	.4	94
Cooked, boiled, drained	1 pod	73	95	15	1	Trace	3	7	.4	310	.05	.05	.4	70
Potatoes, cooked:														
Baked, peeled after baking	1 potato	156	75	145	4	Trace	33	14	1.1	Trace	.15	.07	2.7	31
Boiled:														
Peeled after boiling	1 potato	137	80	105	3	Trace	23	10	.8	Trace	.12	.05	2.0	22
Peeled before boiling	1 potato	135	83	90	3	Trace	20	8	.7	Trace	.12	.05	1.6	22
French-fried, strip, 2 to 3½ in long:														
Prepared from raw	10 strips	50	45	135	2	7	18	8	.7	Trace	.07	.04	1.6	11
Frozen, oven heated	10 strips	50	53	110	2	4	17	5	.9	Trace	.07	.01	1.3	11
Hashed brown, prepared from frozen	1 cup	155	56	345	3	18	45	28	1.9	Trace	.11	.03	1.6	12
Mashed, prepared from Raw:														
Milk added	1 cup	210	83	135	4	2	27	50	.8	40	.17	.11	2.1	21
Milk and butter added	1 cup	210	80	195	4	9	26	50	.8	360	.17	.11	2.1	19
Dehydrated flakes (without milk), water, milk, butter, and salt added	1 cup	210	79	195	4	7	30	65	.6	270	.08	.08	1.9	11
Potato chips, 1¾ by 2½ in oval cross section	10 chips	20	2	115	1	8	10	8	.4	Trace	.04	.01	1.0	3
Potato salad, made with cooked salad dressing	1 cup	250	76	250	7	7	41	80	1.5	350	.20	.18	2.8	28
Pumpkin, canned	1 cup	245	90	80	2	1	19	61	1.0	15,680	.07	.12	1.5	12
Radishes, raw	4 radishes	18	95	5	Trace	Trace	1	5	.2	Trace	.01	.01	.1	5
Sauerkraut, canned, solids and liquid	1 cup	235	93	40	2	Trace	9	85	1.2	120	.07	.09	.5	33
Spinach:														
Raw, chopped	1 cup	55	91	15	2	Trace	2	51	1.7	4,460	.06	.11	.3	28
Cooked, drained:														
From raw	1 cup	180	92	40	5	1	6	167	4.0	14,580	.13	.25	.9	50
From frozen:														
Chopped	1 cup	205	92	45	6	1	8	232	4.3	16,200	.14	.31	.8	39
Leaf	1 cup	190	92	45	6	1	7	200	4.8	15,390	.15	.27	1.0	53
Canned, drained solids	1 cup	205	91	50	6	1	7	242	5.3	16,400	.04	.25	.6	29
Squash, cooked:														
Summer, diced, drained	1 cup	210	96	30	2	Trace	7	53	.8	820	.11	.17	1.7	21
Winter, baked, mashed	1 cup	205	81	130	4	1	32	57	1.6	8,610	.10	.27	1.4	27
Sweet potatoes:														
Cooked:														
Baked in skin, peeled	1 potato	114	64	160	2	1	37	46	1.0	9,230	.10	.08	.8	25
Boiled in skin, peeled	1 potato	151	71	170	3	1	40	48	1.1	11,940	.14	.09	.9	26
Candied, 2½ by 2-in piece	1 piece	105	60	175	1	3	36	39	.9	6,620	.06	.04	.4	11
Canned:														
Solid pack (mashed)	1 cup	255	72	275	5	1	63	64	2.0	19,890	.13	.10	1.5	36
Vacuum pack, piece 2¾ by 1 in	1 piece	40	72	45	1	Trace	10	10	.3	3,120	.02	.02	.2	6
Tomatoes:														
Raw, 2⅗-in diam	1 tomato	135	94	25	1	Trace	6	16	.6	1,110	.07	.05	.9	28
Canned, solids and liquid	1 cup	241	94	50	2	Trace	10	14	1.2	2,170	.12	.07	1.7	41
Tomato catsup	1 tbsp	15	69	15	Trace	Trace	4	3	.1	210	.01	.01	.2	2
Tomato juice, canned:														
Glass (6 fl oz)	1 glass	182	94	35	2	Trace	8	13	1.6	1,460	.09	.05	1.5	29
Turnips, cooked, diced	1 cup	155	94	35	1	Trace	8	54	.6	Trace	.06	.08	.5	34
Turnip greens, cooked, drained:														
From raw (leaves and stems)	1 cup	145	94	30	3	Trace	5	252	1.5	8,270	.15	.33	.7	68
From frozen (chopped)	1 cup	165	93	40	4	Trace	6	195	2.6	11,390	.08	.15	.7	31
Vegetables, mixed, frozen	1 cup	182	83	115	6	1	24	46	2.4	9,010	.22	.13	2.0	15

The National Park System of the United States

The National Park System of the United States, now in the early years of its second century, comprises 337 areas covering some 79 million acres in 49 States, the District of Columbia, Guam, Puerto Rico, Saipan, and the Virgin Islands. These areas are of such national significance as to justify special recognition and protection in accordance with various acts of Congress.

By Act of March 1, 1872, Congress established Yellowstone National Park in the Territories of Montana and Wyoming "as a public park or pleasuring ground for the benefit and enjoyment of the people" and placed it "under exclusive control of the Secretary of the Interior." The founding of Yellowstone National Park began a worldwide national park movement. Today more than 100 nations contain some 1,200 national parks or equivalent preserves.

Additions to the National Park System are generally made through acts of Congress, and national parks can be created only through such acts. But the President has authority, under the Antiquities Act of 1906, to proclaim national monuments on lands already under federal jurisdiction. The Secretary of the Interior is usually asked by Congress for his recommendations on proposed additions to the System. Information about a specific site may be obtained by writing to the address that follows the name of the site on the list.

Nomenclature of Park System Areas

The diversity of the parks is reflected in the variety of titles given to them. These include such designations as national park, national preserve, national monument, national memorial, national historic site, national seashore, and national battlefield park.

Although some titles are self-explanatory, others have been used in many different ways. For example, the title "national monument" has been given to great natural reservations, historic military fortifications, prehistoric ruins, fossil sites, and to the Statue of Liberty. Brief definitions of the most common titles follow.

Areas added to the National Park System for their natural values are expanses or features of land or water of great scenic and scientific quality and are usually designated as national parks, monuments, preserves, seashores, lakeshores, or riverways. Such areas contain one or more distinctive attributes such as forest, grassland, tundra, desert, estuary, or river systems; they may contain "windows" on the past for a view of geological history, imposing landforms such as mountains, mesas, thermal areas, and caverns, and they may be habitats of abundant or rare wildlife and plantlife.

Generally, a **national park** covers a large area. It contains a variety of resources and encompasses sufficient land or water to ensure adequate protection of the resources.

A **national monument** is intended to preserve at least one nationally significant resource. It is usually smaller than a national park and lacks its diversity of attractions.

In 1974, Big Cypress and Big Thicket were authorized as the first **national preserves.** This category is established primarily for the protection of certain resources. Activities such as hunting and fishing or the extraction of minerals and fuels may be permitted if they do not jeopardize the natural values.

Preserving shoreline areas and off-shore islands, the **national lakeshores** and **national seashores** focus on the preservation of natural values while at the same time providing water-oriented recreation. Although national lakeshores can be established on any natural freshwater lake, the exiting four are all located on the Great Lakes. The national seashores are on the Atlantic, Gulf, and Pacific coasts.

National rivers and **wild and scenic riverways** preserve ribbons of land bordering on free-flowing streams which have not been dammed, channelized, or otherwise altered by man. Besides preserving rivers in their natural state, these areas provide opportunities for outdoor activities such as hiking and canoeing.

National scenic trails are generally long-distance footpaths winding through areas of natural beauty.

Although best known for its great scenic parks, more than half the areas of the National Park System preserve places and commemorate persons, events, and activities important in the Nation's history. These range from archaeological sites associated with prehistoric Indian civilizations to sites related to the lives of modern Americans. Historical areas are customarily preserved or restored to reflect their appearance during the period of their greatest historical significance.

In recent years, **national historic site** has been the title most commonly applied by Congress in authorizing the addition of such areas to the National Park System. A wide variety of titles— **national military park, national battlefield park, national battlefield site,** and **national battlefield**—has been used for areas associated with American military history. But other areas such as **national monuments** and **national historical parks** may include features associated with military history. **National historical parks** are commonly areas of greater physical extent and complexity than national historic sites. The lone **international historic site** refers to a site relevant to both U.S. and Canadian history.

The title **national memorial** is most often used for areas that are primarily commemorative. But they need not be sites or structures historically associated with their subjects. For example, the home of Abraham Lincoln in Springfield, Ill., is a national historic site, but the Lincoln Memorial in the District of Columbia is a national memorial.

Several areas administered by National Capital Region whose titles do not include the words national memorial are nevertheless classified as memorials. These are John F. Kennedy Center for the Performing Arts, Lincoln Memorial, Lyndon Baines Johnson Memorial Grove on the Potomac, Theodore Roosevelt Island, Thomas Jefferson Memorial, and the Washington Monument—all in the District of Columbia.

Originally, **national recreation areas** in the Park System were units surrounding reservoirs impounded by dams built by other federal agencies. The National Park Service manages many of these areas under cooperative agreements. The concept of recreational areas has grown to encompass other lands and waters set aside for recreational use by acts of Congress and now includes major areas in urban centers. There are also national recreation areas outside the National Park System that are administered by the Forest Service, U.S. Department of Agriculture.

National parkways encompass ribbons of land flanking roadways and offer an opportunity for leisurely driving through areas of scenic interest. They are not designed for high speed travel. Besides the areas set aside as parkways, other units of the National Park System include parkways within their boundaries.

Two areas of the National Park System have been set aside primarily as sites for the **performing arts.** These are Wolf Trap Farm Park for the Performing Arts, Virginia, America's first such national park, and the John F. Kennedy Center for the Performing Arts, D.C. Two historical areas, Ford's Theatre National Historic Site, D.C., and Chamizal National Memorial, Texas, also provide facilities for the performing arts.

Designation of Wilderness Areas

In the Wilderness Act of 1964, Congress directed three federal agencies, including the National Park Service, to study certain lands within their jurisdiction to determine the suitability of these lands for inclusion in the National Wilderness Preservation System.

By subsequent legislation, Congress has designated **wilderness areas** in many units of the National Park System. This designation (noted in this booklet in the listing by states) does not remove wilderness lands from the parks, but it does ensure that they will be managed to retain their "primeval character and influence, without permanent improvements or human habitation. . . ."

The Act provides, generally, that "there shall be no commercial enterprise and no permanent road within any wilderness area . . . and (except for emergency uses) no temporary road, no use of motor vehicles, motorized equipment or motorboats, no landing of aircraft, no other form of mechanical transport, and no structure or installation." Wilderness areas are open to hiking and, in some cases, horseback riding, primitive camping, and similar pursuits.

Parks in the Nation's Capital

As the Nation's Capital, Washington has a unique park system. Most of the public parks are administered by the Federal Government through National Capital Region of the National Park Service. These are listed under **District of Columbia.**

Alabama

Horseshoe Bend National Military Park (Route 1, Box 103, Daviston, AL 36256). On March 27, 1814, at the "horseshoe bend" in the Tallapoosa River, Gen. Andrew Jackson's forces broke the power of the Upper Creek Indian Confederacy and opened large parts of Alabama and Georgia for settlement. *Acreage—2,040.*

Natchez Trace National Scenic Trail (See Mississippi).

Natchez Trace Parkway (See Mississippi).

Russell Cave National Monument (Route 1, Box 175, Bridgeport, AL 35740). An almost continuous archaeological record of human habitation from at least 7000 BC to about AD 1650 is revealed in this cave. *Acreage—310.45.*

Tuskegee Institute National Historic Site (P.O. Drawer 10, Tuskegee Institute, AL 36088). Booker T. Washington founded this college for black Americans in 1881. Preserved here are the brick buildings the students constructed themselves, Washington's home, and the George Washington Carver Museum, which serves as park headquarters and visitor center. The college is still an active institution that owns most of the property within the national historic site. *Acreage—74.39.*

Alaska

Alagnak Wild River (c/o Katmai National Park and Preserve, P.O. Box 7, King Salmon, AK 99613). The Alagnak River flows from Kukaklek Lake in Katmai National Preserve and offers 69 miles of outstanding white-water floating. The river is also noted for abundant wildlife and sport fishing for five species of salmon. Portions of the main stem lie outside and westward of Katmai. *Acreage—24,038.*

Aniakchak National Monument and Preserve (P.O. Box 7, King Salmon, AK 99613). The Aniakchak Caldera, covering some 30 square miles, is one of the great dry calderas in the world. Located in the volcanically active Aleutian Mountains, the Aniakchak last erupted in 1931. The crater includes lava flows, cinder cones, and explosion pits, as well as Surprise Lake, source of the Aniakchak River, which cascades through a 1,500-foot gash in the crater wall. The site contains the Aniakchak Wild River. *Acreage—National monument: 139,500. National preserve: 475,500.*

Bering Land Bridge National Preserve (P.O. Box 220, Nome, AK 99762). Located on the Seward Peninsula in northwest Alaska, the preserve is a remnant of the land bridge that once connected Asia with North America more than 13,000 years ago. Paleontological and archaeological resources abound; large populations of migratory birds nest here. Ash explosion craters and lava flows, both of which are rare in the Arctic, are also present. *Acreage—2,770,000.*

Cape Krusenstern National Monument (P.O. Box 287, Kotzebue, AK 99752). Archaeological sites located along a succession of 114 lateral beach ridges illustrate Eskimo communities of every known cultural period in Alaska, dating back some 4,000 years. Older sites are located inland, along the foothills. The monument includes a representative example of the arctic coastline along the Chukchi Sea. *Acreage—660,000.*

Denali National Park and Preserve (P.O. Box 9, McKinley Park, AK 99755). The park contains North America's highest mountain, 20,320-foot Mount McKinley. Large glaciers of the Alaska Range, caribou, Dall sheep, moose, grizzly bears, and timber wolves are other highlights of this national park and preserve. *Acreage—National park: 4,700,000. National preserve: 1,330,000. Wilderness area: 1,900,000.*

Gates of the Arctic National Park and Preserve (P.O. Box 74680, Fairbanks, AK 99707). Lying entirely north of the Arctic Circle, the park and preserve includes a portion of the Central Brooks Range, the northernmost extension of the Rocky Mountains. Often referred to as the greatest remaining wilderness in North America, this second largest unit of the National Park System is characterized by jagged peaks, gentle arctic valleys, wild rivers, and numerous lakes. The forested southern slopes contrast to the barren northern reaches of the site at the edge of Alaska's "north slope." The park-preserve contains the Alatna, John, Kobuk, part of the Noatak, the North Fork of the Koyukuk, and the Tinayguk Wild Rivers. And with adjacent Kobuk Valley National Park and Noatak National Preserve, it is one of the largest park areas in the world. *Acreage—National park: 7,500,000. National preserve: 940,000. Wilderness area: 7,052,000.*

Glacier Bay National Park and Preserve (P.O. Box 1089, Juneau, AK 99802 or (in summer) Bartlett Cove, Gustavus, AK 99826). Great tidewater glaciers, a dramatic range of plant communities from rocky terrain recently covered by ice to lush temperate rain forest, and a large variety of animals, including brown and black bear, mountain goats, whales, seals, and eagles can be found within the park. Also included are Mount Fairweather, the highest peak in southeast Alaska, and the U.S. portion of the Alsek River. *Acreage—National park: 3,225,197.95. National preserve: 55,000. Wilderness area: 2,770,000.*

Katmai National Park and Preserve (P.O. Box 7, King Salmon, AK 99613). Variety marks this vast land: lakes, forests, mountains, and marshlands all abound in wildlife. The Alaska brown bear, the world's largest carnivore, thrives here, feeding upon red salmon that spawn in the many lakes and streams. Wild rivers and renowned sport fishing add to the attractions of this subarctic environment. Here, in 1912, Novarupta Volcano erupted violently, forming the ash-filled "Valley of Ten Thousand Smokes" where steam rose from countless fumaroles. Today only a few active vents remain. The park-preserve contains part of the Alagnak Wild River. *Acreage—National park: 3,716,000. National preserve: 374,000. Wilderness area: 3,473,000.*

Kenai Fjords National Park (P.O. Box 1727, Seward, AK 99664). The park, within 20 miles of Seward, includes one of the four major ice caps in the U.S., the 700-square-mile Harding Icefield and coastal fjords. Here a rich, varied rain forest is home to tens of thousands of breeding birds and adjoining marine waters support a multitude of sea lions, sea otters, and seals. *Acreage—670,000.*

Klondike Gold Rush National Historical Park (P.O. Box 517, Skagway, AK 99840) (See also Washington). Historic buildings in Skagway and portions of Chilkoot and White Pass Trails, all prominent in the 1898 gold rush, are included in the park. *Acreage—13,191.35.*

Kobuk Valley National Park (P.O. Box 287, Kotzebue, AK 99752). Embracing the central valley of the Kobuk River, the park, located entirely north of the Arctic Circle, includes a blend of biological, geological, and cultural resources. Here, in the northmost extent of the boreal forest, a rich array of arctic wildlife can be found, including caribou, grizzly and black bear, wolf, and fox. The 25-square-mile Great Kobuk Sand Dunes lie just south of the Kobuk River against the base of the Waring Mountains. Archaeological sites revealing more than 10,000 years of human occupation are among the most significant sites known in the Arctic. The park contains the Salmon Wild River. *Acreage— 1,750,000. Wilderness area: 190,000.*

Lake Clark National Park and Preserve (701 C Street, Box 61, Anchorage, AK 99513). Located in the heart of the Chigmit mountains along the western shore of Cook Inlet, the park-preserve contains great geologic diversity, including jagged peaks, granite spires, and two symmetrical active volcanoes. More than a score of glacial carved lakes rim the mountain mass. Lake Clark, more than 40 miles long, is not only the largest lake here, but it is also the headquarters for red salmon spawning. Merrill and Lake Clark Passes cut through the mountains and are lined by dozens of glaciers and hundreds of waterfalls that cascade over rocky ledges. The park-preserve contains the Chilikadrotna, Mulchatna, Tlikakila Wild Rivers. *Acreage—National park: 2,874,000. National preserve: 1,171,000. Wilderness area: 2,470,000.*

Noatak National Preserve (P.O. Box 287, Kotzebue, AK 99752). The Noatak River basin is the largest mountain-ringed river basin in the Nation still virtually unaffected by man. The preserve includes landforms of great scientific interest, including the 65-mile-long Grand Canyon of the Noatak, a transition zone and migration route for plants and animals between subarctic and arctic environments, and an array of flora among the most diverse anywhere in the earth's northern latitudes. Hundreds of archaeological sites and abundant wildlife populations add to the significance of the area. The preserve contains part of the Noatak Wild River. *Acreage—6,560,000. Wilderness area: 5,800,000.*

Sitka National Historical Park (P.O. Box 738, Sitka, AK 99835). The site of the 1804 fort and battle that marked the last major Tlingit Indian resistance to Russian colonization is preserved here. Tlingit totem poles and crafts are exhibited. The Russian Bishop's House, built in 1842, is the oldest intact piece of Russian American architecture. *Acreage—106.83.*

Wrangell-St. Elias National Park and Preserve (P.O. Box 29, Glenn Allen, AK 99588). The Chugach, Wrangell, and St. Elias mountain ranges converge here in what is often referred to as the "mountain kingdom of North America." The largest unit of the National Park System and a day's drive east of Anchorage, the park-preserve includes the continent's largest assemblage of glaciers and the greatest collection of peaks above 16,000 feet, including Mount St. Elias. At 18,008 feet it is the second highest peak in the U.S. Adjacent to Canada's Kluane National Park, the site is characterized by its remote mountains, valleys, and wild rivers, all rich in their concentrations of wildlife. *Acreage— National park: 8,945,000. National preserve: 4,255,000. Wilderness area: 8,700,000.*

Yukon-Charley Rivers National Preserve (P.O. Box 64, Eagle, AK 99738). Located along the Canadian border in central Alaska, the preserve protects 115 miles of the 1,800-mile Yukon River and the entire Charley River basin. Numerous old cabins and relics are reminders of the importance of the Yukon River during the 1898 gold rush. Paleontological and archaeological sites here add much to our knowledge of man and his environment thousands of years ago. Peregrine falcons nest in the high bluffs overlooking the river, while the rolling hills that make up the preserve are home to an abundant array of wildlife. The Charley, an 88-mile wild river, is considered by many to be the most spectacular river in Alaska. *Acreage—2,520,000.*

Arizona

Canyon de Chelly National Monument (P.O. Box 588, Chinle, AZ 86503). At the base of sheer red cliffs and in canyon wall caves are ruins of Indian villages built between AD 350 and 1300. Modern Navajo Indians live and farm here. Authorized Feb. 14, 1931. Boundary change: Mar. 1, 1933. *Acreage—83,840.*

Casa Grande National Monument (P.O. Box 518, Coolidge, AZ 85228). These perplexing ruins of a massive four-story build-ing, constructed of high-lime desert soil by Indians who farmed the Gila Valley 600 years ago, have raised many questions. *Acreage— 472.50.*

Chiricahua National Monument (Dos Cabezas Star Route, Box 6500, Willcox, AZ 85643). The varied rock formations here were created millions of years ago by volcanic activity, aided by erosion. *Acreage—11,134.80. Wilderness area: 9,440.*

Coronado National Memorial (Rural Route 1, Box 126, Hereford, AZ 85615). Our Hispanic heritage and the first European exploration of the Southwest, by Francisco Vasquez de Coronado in 1540–42, are commemorated here, near the point where Coronado's expedition entered what is now the United States. *Acreage—4,750.47.*

Fort Bowie National Historic Site (P.O. Box 158, Bowie, AZ 85605). Established in 1862, this fort was the focal point of military operations against Geronimo and his band of Apaches. The ruins can be reached only by trail. *Acreage—1,000.*

Glen Canyon National Recreation Area ((See Utah).

Grand Canyon National Park (P.O. Box 129, Grand Canyon, AZ 86023). The park, focusing on the world-famous Grand Canyon of the Colorado River, encompasses 177.7 miles of the river, with adjacent uplands, from the southern terminus of Glen Canyon National Recreation Area to the eastern boundary of Lake Mead National Recreation Area. The forces of erosion have exposed an immense variety of formations which illustrate vast periods of geological history. *Acreage—1,218,375.24.*

Hohokam Pima National Monument (c/o Casa Grande National Monument, P.O. Box 518, Coolidge, AZ 85228). Preserved here are the archeological remains of the Hohokam culture. Hohokam is a Pima Indian word meaning "those who have gone." NOT OPEN TO THE PUBLIC. *Acreage—1,690.*

Hubbell Trading Post National Historic Site (P.O. Box 150, Ganado, AZ 86505). This still-active trading post illustrates the influence of reservation traders on the Indians' way of life. *Acreage—160.09.*

Lake Mead National Recreation Area ((See Nevada).

Montezuma Castle National Monument (P.O. Box 219, Campe Verde, AZ 86322). One of the best-preserved cliff dwellings in the United States, this 5-story, 20-room castle is 90 percent intact. Montezuma Well is also of archeological and geological interest. *Acreage—857.69.*

Navajo National Monument (HC 63, Box 3, Tonalea, AZ 86044). Betatakin, Keet Seel, and Inscription House are three of the most elaborate cliff dwellings known. *Acreage—360.*

Organ Pipe Cactus National Monument (Route 1, Box 100, Ajo, AZ 85321). Sonoran Desert plants and animals found nowhere else in the United States are protected here as are traces of a historic trail, Camino del Diablo. *Acreage—330,688.86. Wilderness area: 312,600.*

Petrified Forest National Park (Petrified Forest National Park, AZ 86028). Trees that have petrified, or changed to multicolored stone, Indian ruins and petroglyphs, and portions of the colorful Painted Desert are features of the park. *Acreage— 93,492.57. Wilderness area: 50,260.*

Pipe Spring National Monument (Moccasin, AZ 86022). The historic fort and other structures, built here by Mormon pioneers, memorialize the struggle for exploration and settlement of the Southwest. *Acreage—40.*

Saguaro National Monument (Old Spanish Trail, Route 8, Box 695, Tucson, AZ 85730). Giant saguaro cacti, unique to the Sonoran Desert of southern Arizona and northwestern Mexico, sometimes reach a height of 50 feet in this cactus forest. *Acreage— 83,573.88. Wilderness area: 71,400.*

Sunset Crater National Monument (Route 3, Box 149, Flagstaff, AZ 86001). This volcanic cinder cone with summit crater was formed just before AD 1100. Its upper part is colored as if by sunset glow. *Acreage—3,040.*

Tonto National Monument (P.O. Box 707, Roosevelt, AZ 85545). These well-preserved cliff dwellings were occupied during the 13th and 14th centuries by Salado Indians who farmed in the Salt River Valley. *Acreage—1,120.*

Tumacacori National Monument (P.O. Box 67, Tumacacori, AZ 85640). This historic Spanish Catholic mission building stands near the site first visited by Jesuit Father Kino in 1691. *Acreage—16.52.*

Tuzigoot National Monument (P.O. Box 68, Clarkdale, AZ 86324). Ruins of a large Indian pueblo that flourished in the Verde Valley between AD 1100 and 1450 have been excavated here. *Acreage—809.30.*

Walnut Canyon National Monument (Walnut Canyon Road, Flagstaff, AZ 86001). These cliff dwellings were built in shallow caves under ledges of limestone by Pueblo Indians about 800 years ago. *Acreage—2,249.46.*

Wupatki National Monument (HC 33, Box 444A, Flagstaff, AZ 86001). Ruins of red sandstone pueblos built by farming Indians about AD 1065 are preserved here. The modern Hopi Indians are believed to be partly descended from these people. *Acreage—35,253.24.*

Arkansas

Arkansas Post National Memorial (Route 1, Box 16, Gillett, AR 72055). On this site the first permanent French settlement in the Lower Mississippi Valley was founded in 1686. *Acreage—389.18.*

Buffalo National River (P.O. Box 1173, Harrison, AR 72601). Offering both swift-running and placid stretches, the Buffalo is one of the few remaining unpolluted, free-flowing rivers in the lower 48 States. It courses through multicolored bluffs and past numerous springs along its 132-mile length. *Acreage—94,221.08. Wilderness area: 10,529.*

Fort Smith National Historic Site (P.O. Box 1406, Fort Smith, AR 72902). (Also in Oklahoma). This site was one of the first U.S. military posts in the Louisiana Territory and contains the remains of two frontier military forts and a federal court. Judge Isaac C. Parker, known as the "Hanging Judge," served here for 21 years and helped make the transition to civilized society. *Acreage—73.36.*

Hot Springs National Park (P.O. Box 1860, Hot Springs National Park, AR 71901). Although the 47 thermal springs fluctuate in flow from 750,000 to 950,000 gallons a day, the temperature remains near 143°F year round. Persons suffering from illness or injury often seek relief in the ancient tradition of thermal bathing. *Acreage—5,823.54.*

Pea Ridge National Military Park (Pea Ridge, AR 72751). The Union victory here on Mar. 7–8, 1862, in one of the major engagements of the Civil War west of the Mississippi, led to the Union's total control of Missouri. *Acreage—4,300.35.*

California

Cabrillo National Monument (P.O. Box 6670, San Diego, CA 92106). Juan Rodriquez Cabrillo, Portuguese explorer who claimed the West Coast of the United States for Spain in 1542, is memorialized here. Gray whales migrate offshore during the winter. Old Point Loma Lighthouse is restored to its most active period—the 1880s. Tidepools found on the west side of the park are excellent for studying southern California coastal ecology. *Acreage—143.94.*

Channel Islands National Park (1699 Anchors Way Drive, Ventura, CA 93003). The park consists of five islands off southern California: Anacapa, San Miguel, Santa Barbara, Santa Cruz, and Santa Rosa. On these islands you can find nesting sea birds, sea lion rookeries, and unique plants. Anacapa and Santa Barbara Islands are administered by the National Park Service; San Miguel, by the U.S. Navy and the National Park Service. A permit is needed to visit the latter. Santa Cruz and Santa Rosa are private property. *Acreage —249,353.77.*

Death Valley National Monument (Death Valley, CA 92328). (Also in Nevada). This large desert, nearly surrounded by high mountains, contains the lowest point in the Western Hemisphere. The area includes Scotty's Castle, the grandiose home of a famous prospector, and other remnants of gold and borax mining activity. *Acreage—2,067,627.68.*

Devils Postpile National Monument (c/o Sequoia and Kings Canyon National Parks, Three Rivers, CA 93271). Hot lava cooled and cracked some 900,000 years ago to form basalt columns 40 to 60 feet high resembling a giant pipe organ. The John Muir Trail between Yosemite and Kings Canyon National Parks crosses the monument. *Acreage—798.46.*

Eugene O'Neill National Historic Site (c/o John Muir NHS, 4202 Alhambra Avenue, Martinez, CA 94553). Tao House, near Danville, Calif., was built for Eugene O'Neill, who lived here from 1937 to 1944. Several of his best known plays, including "The Iceman Cometh" and "Long Day's Journey Into Night," were written here. The site is preserved as a memorial to the playwright. *Acreage—13.19.*

Fort Point National Historic Site (P.O. Box 29333, Presidio of San Francisco, CA 94129). This classic brick and granite mid-19th-century coastal fort is the only one of its style on the west coast of the United States. *Acreage—29.*

Golden Gate National Recreation Area (Fort Mason, San Francisco, CA 94123). The park encompasses shoreline areas of San Francisco, Marin, and San Mateo Counties, including ocean beaches, redwood forest, lagoons, marshes, ships of the National Maritime Museum, historic military properties, a cultural center at Fort Mason, and Alcatraz Island, site of the famous penitentiary. *Acreage—72,815.04.*

John Muir National Historic Site (4202 Alhambra Avenue, Martinez, CA 94553). The home of John Muir and adjacent Martinez Adobe commemorate Muir's contribution to conservation and literature. *Acreage—8.90.*

Joshua Tree National Monument (74485 National Monument Dr., Twentynine Palms, CA 92277). A representative stand of Joshua-trees and a great variety of plants and animals, including the desert bighorn, exist in this desert region. *Acreage—559,954.50. Wilderness area: 429,690.*

Kings Canyon National Park (Three Rivers, CA 93271). Two enormous canyons of the Kings River and the summit peaks of the High Sierra dominate this mountain wilderness. General Grant Grove, with its giant sequoias, is a detached section of the park. *Acreage—461,636.20. Wilderness area: 456,552.*

Lassen Volcanic National Park (Mineral, CA 96063). Lassen Peak erupted intermittently from 1914 to 1921. Evidence of current volcanic activity includes hot springs, steaming fumaroles, mud pots, and sulfurous vents. *Acreage—106,372.36. Wilderness area: 78,982.*

Lava Beds National Monument (P.O. Box 867, Tulelake, CA 96134). Volcanic activity spewed forth molten rock and lava here creating an incredibly rugged landscape—a natural fortress used by the Indians in the Modoc Indian War, 1872–73. *Acreage—46,559.87. Wilderness area: 28,460.*

Muir Woods National Monument (Mill Valley, CA 94941). This virgin stand of coastal redwoods was named for John Muir, writer and conservationist. *Acreage—553.55.*

Pinnacles National Monument (Paicines, CA 95043). Spire-like rock formations 500 to 1,200 feet high, with caves and a variety of volcanic features, rise above the smooth contours of the surrounding countryside. *Acreage—16,221.77. Wilderness area: 12,952.*

Point Reyes National Seashore (Point Reyes, CA 94956). This peninsula near San Francisco is noted for its long beaches backed by tall cliffs, lagoons and esteros, forested ridges, and off-shore bird and sea lion colonies. Part of the area remains a private pastoral zone. *Acreage—71,046.07. Land area: 53,883.98. Wilderness area: 25,370.*

Redwood National Park (1111 Second Street, Crescent City, CA 95531). Coastal redwood forests with virgin groves of ancient trees, including the world's tallest, thrive in the foggy climate here. The park includes 40 miles of scenic Pacific coastline. *Acreage—110,178.03. Land area: 106,000.*

Santa Monica Mountains National Recreation Area (22900 Ventura Boulevard, Suite 140, Woodland Hills, CA 91364). This park, a large, rugged landscape covered with chaparral, fronts on the sandy beaches north of Los Angeles. Established Nov. 10, 1978. *Acreage—150,000.*

Sequoia National Park (Three Rivers, CA 93271). Great groves of giant sequoias, the world's largest living things, Mineral King Valley, and Mount Whitney, the highest mountain in the U.S. outside of Alaska, are spectacular attractions here in the High Sierra. *Acreage—402,487.83. Wilderness area: 280,428.*

Whiskeytown-Shasta-Trinity National Recreation Area (P.O. Box 188, Whiskeytown, CA 96095). Whiskeytown Unit, with its mountainous backcountry and large reservoir, provides a multitude of outdoor recreation opportunities. Shasta and Trinity Units are administered by Forest Service, U.S. Dept. of Agriculture. *Acreage—42,503.43.*

Yosemite National Park (P.O. Box 577, Yosemite National Park, CA 95389). Granite peaks and domes rise high above broad meadows in the heart of the Sierra Nevada; groves of giant sequoias dwarf other trees and tiny wildflowers; and mountains, lakes and waterfalls. The park includes Yosemite Falls, the highest waterfalls in North America. *Acreage—761,170.18. Wilderness area: 677,600.*

Colorado

Bent's Old Fort National Historic Site (35110 Highway 194 East, La Junta, CO 81050). As a principal outpost of civilization on the Southern Plains in the early 1800s and a rendezvous for Indians, the post became the center of a vast fur-trading empire in the West. *Acreage—799.80.*

Black Canyon of the Gunnison National Monument (P.O. Box 1648, Montrose, CO 81402). Shadowed depths of this sheer-walled canyon accentuate the darkness of ancient rocks of obscure origin. *Acreage—20,762.70. Wilderness area: 11,180.*

Colorado National Monument (Fruita, CO 81521). Sheer-walled canyons, towering monoliths, weird formations, dinosaur fossils, and remains of prehistoric Indian cultures reflect the environment and history of this colorful sandstone country. *Acreage—20,453.93.*

Curecanti National Recreation Area (P.O.Box 1040, Gunnison, CO 81230). Three lakes—Blue Mesa, Morrow Point, and Crystal—extend for 40 miles along the Gunnison River. When full, Blue Mesa Lake, with a surface area of 14 square miles, is the largest lake in Colorado. *Acreage—42,114.47.*

Dinosaur National Monument (P.O. Box 210, Dinosaur, CO 81610). (Also in Utah). Spectacular canyons were cut by the Green and Yampa Rivers through upfolded mountains. A quarry contains fossil remains of dinosaurs and other ancient animals. *Acreage—211,141.69.*

Florissant Fossil Beds National Monument (P.O. Box 185, Florissant, CO 80816). A wealth of fossil insects, seeds, and leaves of the Oligocene Period are preserved here in remarkable detail. Here, too, is an unusual display of standing petrified sequoia stumps. *Acreage—5,998.09.*

Great Sand Dunes National Monument (Mosca, CO 81146). Among the largest and highest in the United States, these dunes were deposited over thousands of years by southwesterly winds blowing through the passes of the lofty Sangre de Cristo Mountains. *Acreage—38,662.18. Wilderness area: 33,450.*

Hovenweep National Monument (c/o Mesa Verde National Park, Mesa Verde National Park, CO 81330). (Also in Utah). Pre-Columbian Indians built these 6 groups of towers, pueblos, and cliff dwellings. *Acreage—784.93.*

Mesa Verde National Park (Mesa Verde National Park, CO 81330). These pre-Columbian cliff dwellings and other works of early man are the most notable and best preserved in the United States. *Acreage—52,085.14. Wilderness area: 8,100.*

Rocky Mountain National Park (Estes Park, CO 80517). The park's rich scenery, typifying the massive grandeur of the Rocky Mountains, is accessible by Trail Ridge Road, which crosses the Continental Divide. Peaks towering more than 14,000 feet shadow wildlife and wildflowers in these 412 square miles of the Rockies' Front Range. *Acreage—265,192.86. Wilderness area: 2,922.*

Yucca House National Monument (c/o Mesa Verde National Park, Mesa Verde National Park, CO 81330). Ruins of these large prehistoric Indian pueblos are as yet unexcavated. NOT OPEN TO THE PUBLIC. *Acreage—10.*

Connecticut

Appalachian National Scenic Trail (See Maine).

District of Columbia

Chesapeake and Ohio Canal National Historical Park (See Maryland).

Constitution Gardens (c/o National Capital Region, National Park Service, 1100 Ohio Drive, SW, Washington, DC 20242). Once the site of War Department office buildings, this 40-acre park was constructed during the American Revolution Bicentennial. On an island in a lake in the gardens is a memorial to the 56 Signers of the Declaration of Independence. *Acreage—40.*

Ford's Theatre National Historic Site (511 Tenth Street, NW, Washington, DC 20004). On Apr. 14, 1865, President Lincoln was shot while attending a show here. He was carried across the street to the Petersen house, where he died the next morning. The theater contains portions of the Olroyd Collection of Lincolniana. *Acreage—0.29.*

Frederick Douglass Home (1411 W Street, SE, Washington, DC 20020). From 1877 to 1895, this was the home of the Nation's leading 19th-century black spokesman. Among other achievements, he was U.S. minister to Haiti in 1889. *Acreage—8.08.*

John F. Kennedy Center for the Performing Arts (National Park Service, 2700 F Street, NW, Washington, DC 20566). Cultural events are presented in this structure designed by Edward Durell Stone. The building contains the Eisenhower Theater, a concert hall, an opera house, the American Film Institute Theater, the Terrace Theater, and restaurants. *Acreage—17.50.*

Lincoln Memorial (c/o National Capital Region, National Park Service, 1100 Ohio Drive, SW, Washington, DC 20242). This classical structure of great beauty contains a marble seated statue 19 feet high of the Great Emancipator by sculptor Daniel Chester French. Architect of the building was Henry Bacon. *Acreage—163.63.*

Lyndon Baines Johnson Memorial Grove on the Potomac (c/o George Washington Memorial Parkway, Turkey Run Park, McLean, VA 22101). A living memorial to the 36th President, the park overlooks the Potomac River vista of the Capital. The design features 500 white pines and inscriptions on Texas granite. *Acreage—17.*

National Capital Parks (1100 Ohio Drive, SW, Washington, DC 20242). (Also in Maryland)). The park system of the Nation's Capital comprises parks, parkways, and reservations in the Washington metropolitan area, including such properties as the Battleground National Cemetery, the President's Parks (Lafayette Park north of the White House and the Ellipse south of the White House), the parks flanking the Great Falls of the Potomac, a variety of military fortifications, and green areas. *Acreage—6,465.85.*

National Mall (c/o National Capital Region, National Park Service, 1100 Ohio Drive, SW, Washington, DC 20242). This landscaped park extending from the Capitol to the Washington Monument was envisioned as a formal park in the L'Enfant Plan for the city of Washington. *Acreage—146.35.*

Potomac Heritage National Scenic Trail (see Maryland)).

Rock Creek Park (5000 Glover Road, NW, Washington, DC 20015). One of the largest urban parks in the world, this wooded preserve contains natural, historical, and recreational features in the midst of Washington. *Acreage—1,754.37.*

Sewall-Belmont House National Historic Site (144 Constitution Avenue, NE, Washington, DC 20002). Rebuilt after fire damage from the War of 1812, this red brick house is one of the oldest on Capitol Hill. It has been the National Woman's Party headquarters since 1929 and commemorates the party's founder and women's suffrage leader, Alice Paul, and associates. *Acreage—0.35.*

Theodore Roosevelt Island (c/o George Washington Memorial Parkway, Turkey Run Park, McLean, VA 22101). On this wooded island sanctuary in the Potomac River, trails lead to an imposing statue of Roosevelt, the conservation-minded 26th President, by Paul Manship. His tenets on nature, manhood, youth, and the state are inscribed on tablets. *Acreage—88.50.*

Thomas Jefferson Memorial (c/o National Capital Region, National Park Service, 1100 Ohio Drive, SW, Washington, DC 20242). This circular, colonnaded structure in the classic style introduced in this country by Jefferson, memorializes the author of the Declaration of Independence and President from 1801 to 1809. The interior walls present inscriptions from his writings. The heroic statue was sculpted by Rudulph Evans; architects were John Russell Pope and associates, Otto Eggers and Daniel Higgins. *Acreage—18.36.*

Vietnam Veterans Memorial (c/o National Capital Region, National Park Service, 1100 Ohio Drive, SW, Washington, DC 20242). Located near the Lincoln Memorial at the west end of Constitution Gardens on the National Mall, the polished black granite wall is inscribed with the names of more than 58,000 persons who gave their lives or remain missing in the Vietnam war. The memorial was designed by Maya Ying Lin. A flagstaff and bronze statue of three Vietnam servicemen by Frederick Hart are included in an entrance plaza. *Acreage—2.*

Washington Monument (c/o National Capital Region, National Park Service, 1100 Ohio Drive, SW, Washington, DC 20242). A dominating feature of the Nation's Capital, this 555-foot obelisk honors the country's first President, George Washington. The architect-designer was Robert Mills. *Acreage—106.01.*

White House (c/o National Capital Region, National Park Service, 1100 Ohio Drive, SW, Washington, DC 20242). The White House has been the residence and office of the Presidents of the United States since November 1800. The cornerstone was laid Oct. 13, 1792, on the site selected by George Washington and included in the L'Enfant Plan. *Acreage—18.07.*

Florida

Big Cypress National Preserve (Star Route, Box 110, Ochopee, FL 33943). Adjoining the northwest section of Everglades National Park, this large area provides a freshwater supply crucial to the park's survival. Subtropical plant and animal life abounds in this ancestral home of the Seminole and Miccosukee Indians. *Acreage—570,000.*

Biscayne National Park (P.O. Box 1369, Homestead, FL 33090). Most of the park is reef and water, but within its boundaries about 33 keys, or islands, form a north-south chain, with Biscayne Bay on the west and the Atlantic Ocean on the east. *Acreage—173,274.37. Land area: 4,373.23.*

Canaveral National Seashore (P.O. Box 6447, Titusville, FL 32782). Twenty-five miles of undeveloped barrier island preserve the natural beach, dune, marsh, and lagoon habitats for a variety of wildlife, including many species of birds. The Kennedy Space Center occupies the southern end of the island. *Acreage—57,627.07. Land area: 29,545.07.*

Castillo de San Marcos National Monument (1 Castillo Drive, St. Augustine, FL 32084). Construction of this, the oldest masonry fort in the continental United States was started in 1672 by the Spanish to protect St. Augustine, first permanent settlement by Europeans in the United States, 1565. *Acreage—20.48.*

De Soto National Memorial (75th Street, NW, Bradenton, FL 33529). The landing of Spanish explorer Hernando de Soto in Florida in 1539 and the first extensive organized exploration of what is now the southern United States by Europeans are commemorated here. *Acreage—26.84.*

Everglades National Park (P.O. Box 279, Homestead, FL 33030). This largest remaining subtropical wilderness in the coterminous United States has extensive fresh- and saltwater areas, open Everglades prairies, and mangrove forests. Abundant wildlife includes rare and colorful birds. *Acreage—1,398,939.19. Wilderness area: 1,296,500. Water area: 625,000.*

Fort Caroline National Memorial (12713 Fort Caroline Road, Jacksonville, FL 32225). The fort overlooks the site of a French Huguenot colony of 1564–65, the second French attempt at settlement within the present United States. Here, the French and Spanish began two centuries of European colonial rivalry in North America. *Acreage—138.39*

Fort Jefferson National Monument (c/o Everglades National Park, P.O. Box 279, Homestead, FL 33030). Built in 1856 to help control the Florida Straits, this is the largest all-masonry fortification in the Western world; it served as a Federal military prison during and after the Civil War. The bird refuge and marine life here are features. *Acreage—64,700. Land area: 39.28*

Fort Matanzas National Monument (c/o Castillo de San Marcos National Monument, 1 Castillo Drive, St. Augustine, FL 32084). This Spanish fort was built, 1740–42, to protect St. Augustine from the British. *Acreage—227.76.*

Gulf Islands National Seashore (P.O. Box 100, Gulf Breeze, FL 32561). (See also Mississippi). Offshore islands and keys have both sparkling white sand beaches and historic forts and batteries. Mainland features of this unit, which is located near Pensacola, Fla., include the Naval Live Oaks Reservation, beaches, and military forts. All areas are accessible by car. *Acreage—65,816.64. Land area: 9,366.64.*

Georgia

Andersonville National Historic Site (Andersonville, GA 31711). This Civil War prisoner-of-war camp commemorates the sacrifices borne by American prisoners not only in the 1861–65 conflict but in all wars. Site includes Andersonville National Cemetery which has 16,000 interments, 1,004 unidentified. *Acreage—475.72.*

Appalachian National Scenic Trail (See Maine).

Chattahoochee River National Recreation Area (1900 Northridge Road, Dunwoody, GA 30338). A series of sites along a 48-mile stretch of the Chattahoochee River, extending into Atlanta, will be preserved so the public can look at the scenery, enjoy recreation, and visit historic spots. *Acreage—8,699.69.*

Chickamauga and Chattanooga National Military Park (P.O. Box 2128, Fort Oglethorpe, GA 30742). (Also in Tenn.). This park includes the Civil War battlefields of Chickamauga. Orchard Knob, Lookout Mountain, and Missionary Ridge. *Acreage—8,102.54.*

Cumberland Island National Seashore (P.O. Box 806, St. Marys, GA 31558). Magnificent and unspoiled beaches and dunes, marshes, and freshwater lakes make up the largest of Georgia's Golden Isles. Accessible by tour boat only. *Acreage—36,410.28. Land area: 26,153.10. Wilderness area: 8,840.*

Fort Frederica National Monument (Route 4, Box 286-C, St. Simons Island, GA 31522). Gen. James E. Oglethorpe built this British fort in 1736–48 during the Anglo-Spanish struggle for control of what is now the southeastern United States. *Acreage—216.35.*

Fort Pulaski National Monument (P.O. Box 98, Tybee Island, GA 31328). Bombardment of this early 19th-century fort by rifled cannon in 1862 first demonstrated the ineffectiveness of old-style masonry fortifications. *Acreage—5,623.10.*

Kennesaw Mountain National Battlefield Park (P.O. Box 1167, Marietta, GA 30061). Two engagements took place here between Union and Confederate forces during the Atlanta Campaign, June 20-July 2, 1864. *Acreage—2,884.38.*

Martin Luther King, Jr., National Historic Site (522 Auburn Avenue, NE, Atlanta, GA 30312). The birthplace, church, and grave of Dr. Martin Luther King, Jr., civil rights leader, are parts of this park. The neighborhood also includes the Martin Luther King, Jr., Center for Nonviolent Social Change, Inc. The surrounding 68.19-acre preservation district includes Sweet Auburn, the economic and cultural center of Atlanta's black community during most of the 20th century. *Acreage—23.16.*

Ocmulgee National Monument (1207 Emery Highway, Macon, GA 31201). Traces of 10,000 years of Southeastern Indian prehistory are preserved here, including the massive temple mounds of a Mississippian Indian ceremonial complex abandoned about AD 1100. *Acreage—683.48.*

Guam

War in the Pacific National Historical Park (P.O. Box FA, Agana, GU 96910). This park provides an opportunity to interpret events in the Pacific theater of World War II. It includes major historic sites associated with the 1944 battle for Guam, an example of the island-hopping military campaign against the Japanese. The park contains seven distinct units illustrating various aspects of the struggle. Aging gun emplacements and other military equipment that played a part in World War II also can be seen. *Acreage—1,957.89. Water area: 1,002.*

Hawaii

Haleakala National Park (P.O. Box 369, Makawao, HI 96768). The park preserves the outstanding features of Haleakala Crater on the island of Maui and protects the unique and fragile ecosystems of Kipahulu Valley, the scenic pools along 'Ohe'o Gulch, and many rare and endangered species. *Acreage—28,655.25. Wilderness area: 19,270.*

Hawaii Volcanoes National Park (Hawaii National Park, HI 96718). Active volcanism continues here, on the island of Hawaii, where at lower elevations luxuriant and often rare vegetation pro-

vides food and shelter for a variety of animals. *Acreage—229,177.03. Wilderness area: 123,100.*

Kalaupapa National Historical Park (c/o Pacific Area Office, National Park Service, 300 Ala Moana Boulevard, Honolulu, HI 96850). This park contains the site of the Molokai Island leprosy settlement (1886–1969), areas relating to early Hawaiian settlement, scenic and geologic resources, and habitats for rare and endangered species. Entry by pre-arranged tour only. *Acreage—10,902. Water area: 2,000.*

Kaloko-Honokohau National Historical Park (c/o Pacific Area Office National Park Service, 300 Ala Moana Boulevard, Honolulu, HI 96850). This was the site of Hawaiian settlements before arrival of European explorers. It includes 3 large fishponds, house sites, and other archeological remnants. The park is intended to preserve the native culture of Hawaii. *Acreage—1,160.91.*

Pu'uhonua o Honaunau National Historical Park (P.O. Box 128, Honaunau, Kona, HI 96726). Until 1819, vanquished Hawaiian warriors, noncombatants, and kapu breakers could escape death by reaching this sacred ground. Prehistoric house sites, royal fishponds, coconut groves, and spectacular shore scenery comprise the park. *Acreage—181.80.*

Puukohola Heiau National Historic Site (P.O. Box 4963, Kawaihae, HI 96743). Ruins of Puukohola Heiau ("Temple on the Hill of the Whale"), built by King Kamehameha the Great during his rise to power, are preserved. *Acreage—77.71.*

USS *Arizona* Memorial (c/o Pacific Area Office, National Park Service, Box 50165, Honolulu, HI 96850). This floating memorial marks the spot where the USS *Arizona* was sunk in Pearl Harbor Dec. 7, 1941, during the Japanese attack. *Acreage—None.*

Idaho

Craters of the Moon National Monument (P.O. Box 29, Arco, ID 83213). Volcanic cones, craters, lava flows, and caves make this an astonishing landscape. *Acreage—53,545.05. Wilderness area: 43,243.*

Nez Perce National Historical Park (P.O. Box 93, Spalding, ID 83551). The history and culture of the Nez Perce Indian country are preserved, commemorated, and interpreted here. Four federally-owned sites are administered by the National Park Service, and 20 sites through cooperative agreements. *Acreage—2,108.89.*

Yellowstone National Park (See Wyoming).

Illinois

Lincoln Home National Historic Site (426 S. Seventh Street, Springfield, IL 62701). Abraham Lincoln left his house here in 1861 to accept the Presidency. It was the only home he ever owned. *Acreage—12.24.*

Indiana

George Rogers Clark National Historical Park (401 S. Second Street, Vincennes, IN 47591). This classic memorial, near the site of old Fort Sackville, commemorates the seizure of the fort from the British by Lt. Col. George Rogers Clark, Feb. 25, 1779, and development of the region north of the Ohio River. The statue was sculpted by Hermon MacNeil. *Acreage—24.30.*

Indiana Dunes National Lakeshore (1100 N. Mineral Springs Rd., Porter, IN 46304). Magnificent dunes rise as high as 180 feet above Lake Michigan's southern shore. Other natural features include beaches, bogs, marshes, swamps, and prairie remnants; historic sites include an 1822 homestead and 1900 family farm, both partially restored. *Acreage—12,869.65.*

Lincoln Boyhood National Memorial (Lincoln City, IN 47552). On this southern Indiana farm, Abraham Lincoln grew from youth into manhood. His mother, Nancy Hanks Lincoln, is buried here. *Acreage—191.98.*

Iowa

Effigy Mounds National Monument (P.O. Box K, McGregor, IA 52157). The monument contains outstanding examples of prehistoric burial mounds, some in the shapes of birds and bears. *Acreage—1,475.53.*

Herbert Hoover National Historic Site (P.O. Box 607, West Branch, IA 52358). The birthplace, home, and boyhood neighborhood of the 31st President, 1929–33, the gravesite of President and Mrs. Hoover, and the Hoover Presidential Library and Museum are within the park. *Acreage—186.80.*

Kansas

Fort Larned National Historic Site (Route 3, Larned, KS 67550). From 1859 to 1878 this fort protected traffic along the Santa Fe Trail, was the key military base in the Indian war of 1868–69, and served as an Indian agency. Authorized Aug. 31, 1964. *Acreage—718.39.*

Fort Scott National Historic Site (Old Fort Boulevard, Fort Scott, KS 66701). Established in 1842 as a base for the U.S. Army's peacekeeping efforts along the "permanent Indian frontier," the fort was manned by U.S. Dragoons who served valiantly in the Mexican War. The post was abandoned in 1853 and reactivated during the Civil War as a supply and training center. The restored and reconstructed buildings of the fort today recreate the American frontier of the 1840s and 1850s. *Acreage—16.69.*

Kentucky

Abraham Lincoln Birthplace National Historic Site (R.F.D. 1, Hodgenville, KY 42748). An early 19th-century Kentucky cabin, believed to be the one in which Lincoln was born, is preserved in a memorial building at the site of his birth. *Acreage—116.50.*

Big South Fork National River and Recreation Area (See Tennessee).

Cumberland Gap National Historical Park (P.O. Box 840, Middlesboro, KY 40965). (Also in Virginia and Tennessee). This mountain pass on the Wilderness Road, explored by Daniel Boone, developed into a main artery of the great trans-Allegheny migration for settlement of "the Old West" and an important military objective in the Revolutionary and Civil Wars. *Acreage—20,274.42.*

Mammoth Cave National Park (Mammoth Cave, KY 42259). This series of underground passages—with beautiful limestone gypsum, travertine formations, deep pits and high domes, plus an underground river—has been explored and mapped for 300 miles, making this the longest recorded cave system in the world. *Acreage—52,394.94.*

Louisiana

Jean Lafitte National Historical Park and Preserve (U.S. Customs House, 423 Canal Street, Room 206, New Orleans, LA 70130). The park preserves significant examples of natural and historical resources of the Mississippi Delta and celebrates the cultural diversity of the region. The Chalmette Unit, located 7 miles east of New Orleans on St. Bernard Highway, marks the location where American forces were victorious in the Battle of New Orleans during the War of 1812 and contains the Chalmette National Cemetery. The French Quarter Unit provides an introduction to the culture of the Mississippi Delta Region and includes a visitor center on St. Ann Street adjacent to Jackson Square. The Barataria

Unit, located 15 miles south of New Orleans on La. 45, focuses on the ecology of the Mississippi River Delta and consists of bayous, freshwater swamps, and marshes. *Acreage—20,000.*

Maine

Acadia National Park (P.O. Box 177, Bar Harbor, ME 04609). The sea sets the mood here, uniting the rugged coastal area of Mount Desert Island (highest elevation on the eastern seaboard), picturesque Schoodic Peninsula on the mainland, and the spectacular cliffs of Isle au Haut. *Acreage—39,706.91.*

Appalachian National Scenic Trail (P.O. Box 236, Harpers Ferry, WV 25425). Approximately 2,000 miles of this scenic trail follow the Appalachian Mountains from Mount Katahdin, Maine, through New Hampshire, Vermont, Massachusetts, Connecticut, New York, New Jersey, Pennsylvania, Maryland, West Virginia, Virginia, Tennessee, and North Carolina, to Springer Mountain, Georgia. The trail is one of the two initial units of the National Trail System. *Acreage—115,863.04.*

Saint Croix Island International Historic Site (c/o Acadia National Park, P.O. Box 177, Bar Harbor, ME 04609). The attempted French settlement of 1604, which led to the founding of New France, is commemorated on Saint Croix Island in the Saint Croix River on the Canadian border. *Acreage—35.39.*

Maryland

Antietam National Battlefield (Box 158, Sharpsburg, MD 21782). Gen. Robert E. Lee's first invasion of the North was ended on this battlefield in 1862.
Antietam (Sharpsburg) National Cemetery—5,032 interments, 1,836 unidentified—adjoins the park; grave space is not available. *Park acreage—3,246.44. Cemetery acreage: 11.36.*

Appalachian National Scenic Trail (See Maine).

Assateague Island National Seashore (Route 2, Box 294, Berlin, MD 21811). (Also in Virginia). This 37-mile barrier island, with sandy beach, migratory waterfowl, and wild ponies, includes 9,021-acre Chincoteague National Wildlife Refuge. *Acreage—39,630.93. Land area: 15,977.67.*

Catoctin Mountain Park (Thurmont, MD 21788). Part of the forested ridge that forms the eastern rampart of the Appalachian Mountains in Maryland, this mountain park has sparkling streams and panoramic vistas of the Monocacy Valley. *Acreage—5,770.22.*

Chesapeake and Ohio Canal National Historical Park (Box 158, Sharpsburg, MD 21782). (Also in the District of Columbia and West Virginia). The park follows the route of the 184-mile canal along the Potomac River between Washington, D.C., and Cumberland, Md. The canal was built between 1828 and 1850. *Acreage—20,781.*

Clara Barton National Historic Site (5801 Oxford Road, Glen Echo, MD 20812). This 38-room home of the founder of the American Red Cross was for 7 years headquarters of that organization. *Acreage—8.59.*

Fort McHenry National Monument and Historic Shrine (Baltimore, MD 21230). Successful defense of this fort in the War of 1812, Sept. 13–14, 1814, inspired Francis Scott Key to write "The Star Spangled Banner." *Acreage—43.26.*

Fort Washington Park (National Capital Parks, East, 1900 Anacostia Drive, SE, Washington, DC 20019). This fort across the Potomac from Mt. Vernon was built to protect Washington, D.C. Construction was begun in 1814 to replace an 1809 fort destroyed by the British. The park has recreational facilities. *Acreage—341.*

George Washington Memorial Parkway (See Virginia).

Greenbelt Park (6501 Greenbelt Road, Greenbelt, MD 20770). Just 12 miles from Washington, D.C., this woodland park offers urban dwellers access to many forms of outdoor recreation, including camping all year. *Acreage—1,175.99.*

Hampton National Historic Site (535 Hampton Lane, Towson, MD 21204). This is a fine example of the lavish Georgian mansions built in America during the latter part of the 18th century. *Acreage—59.44.*

Harpers Ferry National Historical Park (See West Virginia).

Monocacy National Battlefield (c/o Antietam National Battlefield, Box 158, Sharpsburg, MD 21782). In a battle here July 9, 1864, Confederate Gen. Jubal T. Early defeated Union forces commanded by Brig. Gen. Lew Wallace. Wallace's troops delayed Early, however, enabling Union forces to marshal a successful defense of Washington, D.C. *Acreage—1,659.04.*

National Capital Parks (See District of Columbia).

Piscataway Park (National Capital Parks, East, 1900 Anacostia Drive, SE, Washington, DC 20019). The tranquil view from Mount Vernon of the Maryland shore of the Potomac is preserved as a pilot project in the use of easements to protect parklands from obtrusive urban expansion. *Acreage—4,262.52.*

Potomac Heritage National Scenic Trail (c/o National Capital Region, National Park Service, 1100 Ohio Drive, SW, Washington, DC 20242). (Also in D.C., Virginia, and Pennsylvania). The trail begins at the mouth of the Potomac River and follows both banks of the Potomac to the District of Columbia. For 175 miles it coincides with the Chesapeake and Ohio Canal Towpath. Then it turns north, ending at Conemaugh Gorge. NOT DEVELOPED FOR PUBLIC USE. *Acreage undetermined.*

Thomas Stone National Historic Site (c/o George Washington Birthplace National Monument, Washington's Birthplace, VA 22575). "Habre-de-Venture," a Georgian mansion built in 1771 near Port Tobacco, Md., was the home of Thomas Stone, 1771–87. A Signer of the Declaration of Independence, Stone was a delegate to the Continental Congress, 1775–78 and 1783–84. NOT OPEN TO THE PUBLIC. *Acreage—328.25.*

Massachusetts

Adams National Historic Site (135 Adams Street, Quincy, MA 02269). The home of Presidents John Adams and John Quincy Adams, of U.S. Minister to Great Britain Charles Francis Adams, and of the writers and historians Henry Adams and Brooks Adams, this house at 135 Adams Street reflects the influence of each of these distinguished men. The park also includes the birthplaces of the two presidents and the United First Parish Church, built by the Adams family. *Acreage—9.82.*

Appalachian National Scenic Trail (See Maine).

Boston National Historical Park (Charlestown Navy Yard, Boston, MA 02129). This park includes Faneuil Hall, Old North Church, Old State House, Bunker Hill, Old South Meeting House, Charlestown Navy Yard, berth for USS *Constitution*, Paul Revere House, and Dorchester Heights. *Acreage—41.03.*

Cape Cod National Seashore (South Wellfleet, MA 02663). Ocean beaches, dunes, woodlands, freshwater ponds, and marshes make up this park on outer Cape Cod. The area preserves notable examples of Cape Cod homes, an architectural style developed in the New England states during colonial times. *Acreage—43,526.06. Land area: 27,004.*

Frederick Law Olmsted National Historic Site (99 Warren Street, Brookline, MA 02146). The great conservationist, landscape architect, and founder of city planning lived and worked here at "Fairstead." An archival collection of more than 63,000 original photographs with 150,000 drawings and plans is housed at the site. *Acreage—1.75.*

John Fitzgerald Kennedy National Historic Site (83 Beals Street, Brookline, MA 02146). This house is the birthplace and early boyhood home of the 35th President. *Acreage—0.09.*

Longfellow National Historic Site (105 Brattle Street, Cambridge, MA 02138). Poet Henry Wadsworth Longfellow lived here from 1837 to 1882 while teaching at Harvard. The house had been General Washington's headquarters during the siege of Boston, 1775–76. *Acreage—1.98.*

Lowell National Historical Park (P.O. Box 1098, Lowell, MA 01853). America's first planned industrial community is commemorated by this park at the heart of the city. Elements of Lowell's factories, canal system, and the lifestyle of its people will be preserved and interpreted here. *Acreage—137.08.*

Minute Man National Historical Park (P.O. Box 160, Concord, MA 01742). Scene of the fighting on Apr. 19, 1775, that opened the American Revolution, the park includes North Bridge, the Minute Man statue by Daniel Chester French, and 4 miles of Battle Road between Lexington and Concord. The park also includes "The Wayside," home to a succession of remarkable people notable in the Nation's literary history: Bronson Alcott, Louisa May Alcott, Nathaniel Hawthorne, and Margaret Sidney. *Acreage—748.81.*

Salem Maritime National Historic Site (Custom House, 174 Derby Street, Salem, MA 01970). Structures preserved here date from the era when Salem ships opened trade with ports of the Far East. Structures of maritime significance include the Custom House, Derby Wharf, the Bonded Warehouse, and the West India Goods Store. *Acreage—8.95.*

Saugus Iron Works National Historic Site (244 Central Street, Saugus, MA 01906). This reconstruction of the first integrated ironworks in North America, begun in 1646, includes the ironworks, furnace, forge, and rolling and slitting mill. *Acreage—8.51.*

Springfield Armory National Historic Site (1 Armory Square, Springfield, MA 01105). From 1794 to 1968 Springfield Armory was a center for the manufacture of U.S. military small arms and the scene of many important technological advances. A large weapons museum is now housed in the original Main Arsenal Building. *Acreage—54.93.*

Michigan

Isle Royale National Park (87 North Ripley Street, Houghton, MI 49931). This forested island, the largest in Lake Superior, is distinguished by its wilderness character, timber wolves, moose herd, and pre-Columbian copper mines. *Acreage—571,790.11. Land area: 133,779.94. Wilderness area: 131,880.*

Pictured Rocks National Lakeshore (P.O. Box 40, Munising, MI 49862). Multicolored sandstone cliffs, broad beaches, sand bars, dunes, waterfalls, inland lakes, ponds, marshes, hardwood and coniferous forests, and numerous birds and animals comprise this scenic area on Lake Superior. This was the first national lakeshore. *Acreage—72,898.86. Land area: 63,122.08.*

Sleeping Bear Dunes National Lakeshore (400 Main Street, Frankfort, MI 49635). Beaches, massive sand dunes, forests, and lakes are outstanding characteristics of the Lake Michigan shoreline and two offshore islands. *Acreage—71,021.14. Land area: 58,473.*

Minnesota

Grand Portage National Monument (P.O. Box 666, Grand Marais, MN 55604). This 9-mile portage was a vital link on one of the principal routes for Indians, explorers, missionaries, and fur traders heading for the Northwest. The Grand Portage post of the North West Company has been reconstructed here. *Acreage—709.97.*

Lower Saint Croix National Scenic Riverway (See Wisconsin).

Pipestone National Monument (P.O. Box 727, Pipestone, MN 56164). From this quarry Indians obtained materials for making pipes used in ceremonies. Although George Catlin, the painter, was not the first white person to visit the quarries, he was the first person to describe them in print. Pipestone is known as Catlinite in his honor. The park includes the Upper Midwest Indian Cultural Center, which provides space for craftsmen to display their work and to demonstrate traditional crafts. *Acreage—281.78.*

Saint Croix National Scenic Riverway (See Wisconsin).

Voyageurs National Park (P.O. Box 50, International Falls, MN 56649). Interconnected northern lakes, once the route of the French-Canadian voyageurs, are surrounded by forest. Boaters ply the waters in summer. Snowmobilers and crosscountry skiers travel across the frozen lakes and wooded trails in winter. *Acreage—217,892.01. Land area: 138,828.*

Mississippi

Brices Cross Roads National Battlefield Site (c/o Natchez Trace Parkway, R.R. 1, NT-143, Tupelo, MS 38801). The Confederate cavalry was employed with extraordinary skill here during the battle of June 10, 1864. *Acreage—1.*

Gulf Islands National Seashore (3500 Park Road, Ocean Springs, MS 39564). (See also Florida). Sparkling beaches, historic ruins, and wildlife sanctuaries, accessible only by boat, can be found on the offshore islands of this unit, located near Pascagoula and Biloxi. On the mainland there's an urban park with a nature trail, picnic area, and a campground. *Acreage—73,958.82. Wilderness area: 1,800. Land area: 10,078.82.*

Natchez Trace National Scenic Trail (Southeast Region National Park Service, Richard B. Russell Building, 75 Spring Street, SW, Atlanta, GA 30303). (Also in Alabama and Tennessee). The trail extends from Nashville, Tenn., to Natchez, Miss., and parallels the existing parkway. NOT DEVELOPED FOR PUBLIC USE. *Acreage—10,995.*

Natchez Trace Parkway (R.R. 1, NT-143, Tupelo, MS 38801). (Also in Alabama and Tennessee). This historic route generally follows the old Indian trace, or trail, between Nashville, Tenn., and Natchez, Miss. (Of the estimated 449 miles, 358 are completed.) *Acreage—50,189.33.*

Tupelo National Battlefield (c/o Natchez Trace Parkway, R.R. 1, NT-143, Tupelo, MS 38801). Here, on July 13–14, 1864, Lt. Gen. Nathan Bedford Forrest's cavalry battled a Union force sent to keep Forrest from cutting the railroad supplying Maj. Gen. William T. Sherman's march on Atlanta. *Acreage—1.*

Vicksburg National Military Park (3201 Clay Street, Vicksburg, MS 39180). Fortifications of the 47-day siege of Vicksburg, which ended July 3, 1863, are remarkably well preserved here. Victory gave the North control of the Mississippi River and cut the Confederacy in two. Civil War gunboat USS *Cairo* and artifacts are on display.
Vicksburg National Cemetery—18,207 interments, 12,954 unidentified—adjoins the park; grave space is not available. *Park acreage—1,619.70. Cemetery acreage—116.28.*

Missouri

George Washington Carver National Monument (P.O. Box 38, Diamond, MO 64840). The birthplace and childhood home of George Washington Carver, the famous black agronomist, includes the Carver family cemetery and the site where Carver was born. *Acreage—210.*

Harry S Truman National Historic Site (P.O. Box 4139, Independence, MO 64075). Harry S Truman, the 33rd President, called this Victorian structure home from 1919 until his death in 1972. Constructed by Mrs. Truman's grandfather, it was known as the "Summer White House" from 1945 to 1953 and was the only home ever owned by the Trumans. *Acreage—0.78.*

Jefferson National Expansion Memorial National Historic Site (11 North 4th Street, St. Louis, MO 63102). This park on St. Louis' Mississippi riverfront memorializes Thomas Jefferson and others who directed territorial expansion of the United States. Eero Saarinen's prize-winning, stainless steel gateway arch commemorates westward pioneers. Visitors may ascend the 630-foot-high arch. In the nearby courthouse Dred Scott sued for freedom in the historic slavery case. *Acreage—90.96.*

Ozark National Scenic Riverways (P.O. Box 490, Van Buren, MO 63965). For about 134 miles the Current and Jacks Fork Rivers flow through the Ozark hills. Notable features include huge freshwater springs and numerous caves. *Acreage—80,788.34.*

Wilson's Creek National Battlefield (Postal Drawer C, Republic, MO 65738). The Confederate victory here on Aug. 10, 1861, was the first major engagement west of the Mississippi. It culminated in severe losses on both sides, yet Union troops were able to retreat and regroup. Major features include "Bloody Hill" and the recently restored 1852 Ray House. *Acreage—1,749.91.*

Montana

Big Hole National Battlefield (P.O. Box 237, Wisdom, MT 59761). Nez Perce Indians and U.S. Army troops fought here in 1877—a dramatic episode in the long struggle to confine the Nez Perce, and other Indians, to reservations. *Acreage—655.61.*

Bighorn Canyon National Recreation Area (P.O. Box 458, Fort Smith, MT 59035). (Also in Wyoming). Bighorn Lake, formed by Yellowtail Dam on the Bighorn River, extends 71 miles, including 47 miles through spectacular Bighorn Canyon. The Crow Indian Reservation borders a large part of the area. *Acreage—120,277.86.*

Custer Battlefield National Monument (P.O. Box 39, Crow Agency, MT 59022). The famous Battle of the Little Big Horn between twelve companies of the 7th U.S. Cavalry and the Sioux and Northern Cheyenne Indians was fought here on June 25–26, 1876. Lt. Col. George A. Custer and about 268 of his force were killed. Custer Battlefield National Cemetery with 4,487 interments, 277 unidentified, is included within the park. *Acreage—765.34.*

Fort Union Trading Post National Historic Site (See North Dakota).

Glacier National Park (West Glacier, MT 59936). With precipitous peaks ranging above 10,000 feet, this ruggedly beautiful land includes nearly 50 glaciers, many lakes and streams, a wide variety of wildflowers, and wildlife. *Acreage—1,013,594.67.*

Grant-Kohrs Ranch National Historic Site (P.O. Box 790, Deer Lodge, MT 59722). This was the home ranch area of one of the largest and best known 19th-century range ranches in the country. *Acreage—1,498.65.*

Yellowstone National Park (See Wyoming).

Nebraska

Agate Fossil Beds National Monument (P.O. Box 427, Gering, NE 69341). These renowned quarries contain numerous, well preserved Miocene mammal fossils and represent an important chapter in the evolution of mammals. *Acreage—3,055.22.*

Homestead National Monument of America (Route 3, Beatrice, NE 68310). One of the first claims under the Homestead Act of 1862 was filed for this land; includes Freeman School. *Acreage—194.57.*

Missouri National Recreational River (c/o Midwest Region, National Park Service, 1709 Jackson Street, Omaha, NE 68102). One of the last free-flowing stretches of the Missouri, this reach from Gavins Point Dam, near Yankton, S.D., to Ponca, Neb., still exhibits the river's dynamic character in its islands, bars, chutes, and snags. In all respects, the "Big Muddy" lives up to its name. *Acreage—14,941.*

Scotts Bluff National Monument (P.O. Box 427, Gering, NE 69341). Rising 800 feet above the valley floor, this massive promontory was a landmark on the Oregon Trail, associated with overland migration between 1843 and 1869 across the Great Plains. *Acreage—2,997.08.*

Nevada

Death Valley National Monument (See California).

Lake Mead National Recreation Area (601 Nevada Highway, Boulder City, NV 89005). (Also in Arizona). Lake Mead, formed by Hoover Dam, and Lake Mohave, by Davis Dam, on the Colorado River comprise this first national recreation area established by an act of Congress. *Acreage—1,496,600.52. Land area: 1,348,075.70.*

Lehman Caves National Monument (Baker, NV 89311). Tunnels and galleries decorated with stalactites and stalagmites honeycomb these caverns of light-gray and white marble. *Acreage—640.*

New Hampshire

Appalachian National Scenic Trail (See Maine).

Saint-Gaudens National Historic Site (R.R. #2, Cornish, NH 03745). Located in Cornish this memorial to sculptor Augustus Saint-Gaudens contains his home, "Aspet," and his studios and gardens. *Acreage—148.23.*

New Jersey

Appalachian National Scenic Trail (See Maine).

Delaware National Scenic River (See Pennsylvania).

Delaware Water Gap National Recreation Area (See Pennsylvania).

Edison National Historic Site (Main St. and Lakeside Ave., West Orange, NJ 07052). Laboratory and equipment used for 44 years by Thomas A. Edison for many of his experiments are here, as are his library, papers, and models of some of his inventions. The site also includes Glenmont, Edison's 23-room home, with original furnishings. *Acreage—21.25.*

Gateway National Recreation Area (See New York).

Morristown National Historical Park (Washington Place, Morristown, NJ 07960). During the Revolutionary War, Morristown was quarters for the Continental Army during two critical winters—Jan. 1777 and 1779–80. Ford Mansion, which served as George Washington's headquarters, is included in the park. *Acreage—1,675.94.*

Statue of Liberty National Monument (See New York).

New Mexico

Aztec Ruins National Monument (P.O. Box U, Aztec, NM 87410). Ruins of this large Pueblo Indian community of 12th-century masonry and timber buildings have been largely excavated and stabilized. The ruins, misnamed by settlers, are unrelated to the Aztecs of Mexico. *Acreage—27.14.*

Bandelier National Monument (Los Alamos, NM 87544). On the canyon-slashed slopes of the Pajarito Plateau are the ruins of many cliff houses of 15th-century Pueblo Indians. *Acreage—36,916.89. Wilderness area: 23,267.*

Capulin Mountain National Monument (Capulin, NM 88414). This symmetrical cinder cone is an interesting example of a geologically recent, extinct volcano. *Acreage—775.38.*

Carlsbad Caverns National Park (3225 National Parks Highway, Carlsbad, NM 88220). This series of connected caverns, with one of the world's largest underground chambers, has countless magnificent and curious formations. *Acreage—46,755.33. Wilderness area: 33,125.*

Chaco Culture National Historical Park (Star Route 4, Box 6500, Bloomfield, NM 87413). The canyon, with hundreds of smaller ruins, contains 13 major Indian ruins unsurpassed in the United States, representing the highest point of Pueblo pre-Columbian civilization. *Acreage—33,977.82.*

El Morro National Monument (Ramah, NM 87321). "Inscription Rock" is a soft sandstone monolith on which are carved hundreds of inscriptions, including those of 17th-century Spanish explorers and 19th-century American emigrants and settlers. The monument also includes pre-Columbian petroglyphs. *Acreage—1,278.72.*

Fort Union National Monument (Watrous, NM 87753). Three U.S. Army forts were built on this site—a key defensive point on the Santa Fe Trail—and were occupied from 1851 to 1891. Ruins of the last fort, which was the largest military post in the Southwest, have been stabilized. *Acreage—720.60.*

Gila Cliff Dwellings National Monument (Route 11, Box 100, Silver City, NM 88061). These well-preserved cliff dwellings in natural cavities on the face of an overhanging cliff were inhabited from about AD 1280 to the early 1300s. *Acreage—533.13.*

Pecos National Monument (P.O. Drawer 11, Pecos, NM 87552). The park contains the ruins of the ancient Pueblo of Pecos and the remains of two Spanish missions, one built in the 17th, and the other, in the 18th century. In later years, the ruins became a landmark on the Santa Fe Trail. *Acreage—364.80.*

Salinas National Monument (Box 496, Mountainair, NM 87036). Salinas takes its name from salt lakes that have been of great importance to this region. The park contains the ruins of three major pueblos, plus four large churches built by the Franciscan fathers. The area has been abandoned since 1670. *Acreage—1,076.94.*

White Sands National Monument (P.O. Box 458, Alamogordo, NM 88310). The park contains the world's largest gypsum dunefield covering nearly 230 square miles. The glistening white dunes rise 60 feet high. Small animals have adapted to this harsh environment by developing light, protective coloration. Plants also have adapted, extending root systems to remain atop the ever-shifting dunes. *Acreage—144,458.24.*

New York

Appalachian National Scenic Trail (See Maine).

Castle Clinton National Monument (Manhattan Sites, National Park Service, 26 Wall Street, New York, NY 10005). Built 1808–11, this structure served successively as a defense for New York harbor, a promenade and entertainment center, and an immigration depot through which more than 8 million people entered the United States from 1855 to 1890. It is located in Battery Park, Manhattan. *Acreage—1.*

Delaware National Scenic River (See Pennsylvania).

Eleanor Roosevelt National Historic Site (249 Albany Post Road, Bellfield Headquarters, Hyde Park, NY 12538). Mrs. Roosevelt used her ''Val-Kill'' estate as a personal retreat from her busy life. The pastoral setting of the cottage, built for her by FDR in 1925, includes fields, trees, swamps, and ponds. She also used the estate to entertain friends and dignitaries and to promote the many causes that interested her. *Acreage—180.50.*

Federal Hall National Memorial (Manhattan Sites, National Park Service, 26 Wall Street, New York, NY 10005). This graceful building is on the site of the original Federal Hall where the trial of John Peter Zenger, involving freedom of the press, was held in 1735; the Stamp Act Congress convened, 1765; the Second Continental Congress met, 1785; Washington took the oath as first U.S. President, and the Bill of Rights was adopted, 1789. Present building was completed in 1842 as a federal customs house. The statue of Washington on the steps of the building is by John Quincy Adams Ward. *Acreage—0.45.*

Fire Island National Seashore (120 Laurel Street, Patchogue, NY 11772). This barrier island off the south shore of Long Island offers the opportunity for beach-oriented recreation and ecological observations. The 32-mile-long island faces the Atlantic Ocean while protecting the waters of Great South Bay and the mainland of Long Island behind it. Much of the land in the seashore, which is almost within sight of New York City's skyscrapers, has a quality of wilderness amazing for its proximity to this great metropolis. *Acreage—19,578.55. Land area: 16,486.43. Wilderness area: 1,363.*

Fort Stanwix National Monument (112 E. Park Street, Rome, NY 13440). The American stand here in August 1777 was a major factor in repulsing the British invasion from Canada. The fort was also the site of the treaty of Fort Stanwix with the Iroquois Nov. 5, 1768. The current fort is a complete reconstruction. *Acreage—15.52.*

Gateway National Recreation Area (Floyd Bennett Field, Bldg. 69, Brooklyn, NY 11234). (Also in New Jersey). With beaches, marshes, islands, and adjacent waters in the New York harbor area, this park offers urban residents a wide range of recreational opportunities. The Sandy Hook Unit, in New Jersey, features beaches, plant and animal life, and historic structures, including Sandy Hook Lighthouse (1764), thought to be the oldest operational light in the United States. *Acreage—26,310.93.*

General Grant National Memorial (Manhattan Sites National Park Service, 26 Wall Street, New York, NY 10005). This memorial to Ulysses S. Grant, the Union commander who brought the Civil War to an end, includes the tombs of General and Mrs. Grant. As the President of the United States (1869–77), Grant signed the act establishing the first national park, Yellowstone, Mar. 1, 1872. The memorial is on Riverside Drive near West 122nd Street. *Acreage—0.76.*

Hamilton Grange National Memorial (287 Convent Avenue, New York, NY 10031). ''The Grange,'' named after his grandfather's estate in Scotland, was the home of Alexander Hamilton, statesman and first Secretary of the Treasury. *Acreage—0.71.*

Home of Franklin D. Roosevelt National Historic Site (249 Albany Post Road, Bellfield Headquarters, Hyde Park, NY 12538). This was the birthplace, lifetime residence, and ''Summer White House'' of the 32nd President. He entertained many distinguished visitors here. The gravesites of President and Mrs. Roosevelt are in the Rose Garden. *Acreage—290.34.*

Martin Van Buren National Historic Site (P.O. Box 545, Route 9H, Kinderhook, NY 12106). Lindenwald, south of Albany, was the home of the eighth President—a leader in the growth and emergence of Jacksonian Democracy—for 21 years until his death in 1862. *Acreage—39.58.*

Sagamore Hill National Historic Site (Cove Neck Road, Box 304, Oyster Bay, NY 11771). This estate was the home of Theodore Roosevelt from 1885 until his death in 1919. Used as the ''Summer White House'' 1901–08, it contains original furnishings. The Old Orchard Museum is on the grounds. *Acreage—78.*

Saratoga National Historical Park (R.D. 2, Box 33, Stillwater, NY 12170). The American victory here over the British in 1777 was the turning point of the Revolution and one of the decisive battles in world history. Maj. Gen. Philip Schuyler's country home and the 154-foot Saratoga monument are nearby. *Acreage—3,415.08.*

Statue of Liberty National Monument (Liberty Island, New York, NY 10004). (Also in New Jersey). The famous 152-foot copper statue bearing the torch of freedom was a gift of the French people in 1886 to commemorate the alliance of the two nations in the American Revolution. It was designed by Frederick Bartholdi. The monument includes the American Museum of Immigration, in the base of the statue, and Ellis Island, an immigration port from 1892 to 1954. *Acreage—58.38.*

Theodore Roosevelt Birthplace National Historic Site (28 E. 20th Street, New York, NY 10003). The 26th President was born in a brownstone house here on Oct. 27, 1858. Demolished in 1916, it was reconstructed in the 1920s to include museum and period rooms. *Acreage—0.11.*

Theodore Roosevelt Inaugural National Historic Site (641 Delaware Avenue, Buffalo, NY 14202). Theodore Roosevelt took the oath of office as President of the United States on Sept. 14, 1901, here in the Ansley Wilcox House after the assassination of President William McKinley. *Acreage—1.*

Upper Delaware Scenic and Recreational River (See Pennsylvania).

Vanderbilt Mansion National Historic Site (249 Albany Post Road, Bellfield Headquarters, Hyde Park, NY 12538). This palatial mansion is a fine example of homes built by 19th-century millionaires. This particular home was constructed by Frederick W. Vanderbilt, a grandson of Cornelius Vanderbilt. *Acreage—211.65.*

Women's Rights National Historical Park (P.O. Box 70, Seneca Falls, NY 13148). Located in Seneca Falls, this park commemorates the beginning of the women's struggle for equal rights and includes the Wesleyan Methodist Chapel, the site of the 1848 Women's Rights Convention, and the homes and offices of Elizabeth Cady Stanton, Amelia Jenks Bloomer, and other notable early women's rights activists. LIMITED PUBLIC FACILITIES. *Acreage—4.99.*

North Carolina

Appalachian National Scenic Trail (see Maine).

Blue Ridge Parkway (700 Northwestern Bank Bldg., Asheville, NC 28801). (Also in Virginia). Following the crest of the Blue Ridge Mountains, this scenic parkway averages 3,000 feet above sea level, embracing several large recreational areas and preserving mountain folk culture and scenic areas. First national parkway. *Acreage—82,117.37.*

Cape Hatteras National Seashore (Route 1, Box 675, Manteo, NC 27954). Beaches, migratory waterfowl, fishing, and points of historical interest, including the Cape Hatteras Lighthouse overlooking the ''graveyard of the Atlantic,'' are special features of the first national seashore. *Acreage—30,319.43. Land area: 26,326.24.*

Cape Lookout National Seashore (P.O. Box 690, Beaufort, NC 28516). This series of undeveloped barrier islands extends 55 miles along the lower Outer Banks embracing beaches, dunes, salt marshes, historic Portsmouth Village, and Cape Lookout Lighthouse. *Acreage—28,414.74. Land area: 8,741.*

Carl Sandburg Home National Historic Site (P.O. Box 395, Flat Rock, NC 28731). ''Connemara'' was the farm home of the noted poet-author for the last 22 years of his life. During his residence here, several of his books were published. *Acreage—263.52.*

Fort Raleigh National Historic Site (c/o Cape Hatteras National Seashore, Route 1, Box 675, Manteo, NC 27954). The first English settlement in North America was attempted here (1585–87). The fate of Sir Walter Raleigh's "Lost Colony" remains a mystery. *Acreage—157.27.*

Great Smoky Mountains National Park (See Tennessee).

Guilford Courthouse National Military Park (P.O. Box 9806, Greensboro, NC 27429). The battle fought here on Mar. 15, 1781, opened the campaign that led to Yorktown and the end of the Revolution. *Acreage—220.25.*

Moores Creek National Battlefield (P.O. Box 69, Currie, NC 28435). The battle on Feb. 27, 1776, between North Carolina Patriots and Loyalists, is commemorated here. The Patriot victory notably advanced the revolutionary cause in the South. *Acreage—86.52.*

Wright Brothers National Memorial (c/o Cape Hatteras National Seashore, Route 1, Box 675, Manteo, NC 27954). The first sustained flight in a heavier-than-air machine was made here by Wilbur and Orville Wright on Dec. 17, 1903. *Acreage—431.40.*

North Dakota

Fort Union Trading Post National Historic Site (Buford Route, Williston, ND 58801). (Also in Montana). The trading post that stood here was the principal fur-trading depot in the Upper Missouri River region from 1829 to 1867. Fort Union served the Dakotas, Montana, and the Prairie Provinces. *Acreage—434.04.*

Knife River Indian Villages National Historic Site (R.R. 1, Box 168, Stanton, ND 58571). Remnants of historic and prehistoric Indian villages, last occupied in 1845 by the Hidatsa, contain an array of artifacts of Plains Indian culture. NO FEDERAL FACILITIES. *Acreage—1,293.35.*

Theodore Roosevelt National Park (Medora, ND 58645). The park includes scenic badlands along the Little Missouri River and part of Theodore Roosevelt's Elkhorn Ranch. Established as Theodore Roosevelt National Memorial Park. *Acreage—70,416.39. Wilderness area: 29,920.*

Ohio

Cuyahoga Valley National Recreation Area (15610 Vaughn Road, Brecksville, OH 44141). This recreation area links the urban centers of Cleveland and Akron, preserving the rural character of the Cuyahoga River Valley and such historic resources as the Ohio and Erie Canal system that were built during the nineteenth century. *Acreage—32,460.19.*

James A. Garfield National Historic Site (Lawnfield, 1950 Mentor Avenue, Mentor, OH 44060). This site preserves property associated with the life of the 20th President. The site is currently managed by a private organization and is open to the public. *Acreage—7.82.*

Mound City Group National Monument (16062 State Route 104, Chillicothe, OH 45601). Twenty-three burial mounds of Hopewell Indians (200 BC-AD 500) yielded copper breastplates, tools, obsidian blades, shells, ornaments of grizzly bear teeth, and stone pipes carved as birds and animals. These provide insights into the ceremonial customs of these prehistoric people. *Acreage—217.50.*

Perry's Victory and International Peace Memorial (P.O. Box 549, Put-in-Bay, OH 43456). Commodore Oliver H. Perry won the greatest naval battle of the War of 1812 on Lake Erie. The memorial—the world's most massive Doric column—was constructed in 1912–15 "to inculcate the lessons of international peace by arbitration and disarmament." It was designed by Joseph Freedlander. *Acreage—25.38.*

William Howard Taft National Historic Site (2038 Auburn Ave., Cincinnati, OH 45219). This house was the birthplace and boyhood home of the only man to serve both as President and Chief Justice of the United States—27th President, 1909–13; U.S. Chief Justice, 1921–30. BEING RESTORED, LIMITED FEDERAL FACILITIES. *Acreage—3.07.*

Oklahoma

Chickasaw National Recreation Area (P.O. Box 201, Sulphur, OK 73086). The manmade Lake of the Arbuckles provides water recreation for an extensive Midwest area, and numerous cold mineral- and freshwater springs, including bromide waters, surface here. *Acreage—9,521.91. Water area: 2,409.*

Fort Smith National Historic Site (See Arkansas).

Oregon

Crater Lake National Park (P.O. Box 7, Crater Lake, OR 97604). This deep blue lake lies in the heart of Mount Mazama, an ancient volcanic peak that collapsed centuries ago. The lake is encircled by multicolored lava walls reaching 500 to 2,000 feet above the lake waters. *Acreage—183,227.05.*

Fort Clatsop National Memorial (Route 3, Box 604-FC, Astoria, OR 97103). The Lewis and Clark Expedition camped here in the winter of 1805–06. *Acreage—125.20.*

John Day Fossil Beds National Monument (420 W. Main Street, John Day, OR 97845). Plant and animal fossils show five epochs, from Eocene to end of Pleistocene. *Acreage—14,011.90.*

Oregon Caves National Monument (19000 Caves Highway, Cave Junction, OR 97523). Groundwater dissolving marble bedrock formed these cave passages and intricate flowstone formations. *Acreage—487.98.*

Pennsylvania

Allegheny Portage Railroad National Historic Site (P.O. Box 247, Cresson, PA 16630). Traces of the first railroad crossing of the Allegheny Mountains can still be seen here. An inclined plane railroad, it permitted transportation of passengers and freight over the mountains, providing a critical link in the Pennsylvania Mainline Canal system and with the West. Built between 1831 and 1834, it was abandoned by 1857. *Acreage—1,134.91.*

Appalachian National Scenic Trail (See Maine).

Delaware National Scenic River (c/o Delaware Water Gap National Recreation Area, Bushkill, PA 18324). (Also in New Jersey). This park contains the 41 miles of the Delaware River that lie within the boundaries of Delaware Water Gap National Recreation Area. The free-flowing stream offers swimming, boating, and fishing opportunities. *Acreage—1,973.33.*

Delaware Water Gap National Recreation Area (Bushkill, PA 18324). (Also in New Jersey). This scenic area preserves relatively unspoiled land on both the New Jersey and Pennsylvania sides of the middle Delaware River. The river segment flows through the famous gap in the Appalachian Mountains. The park sponsors a craft village and several environmental education centers. *Acreage—66,696.97.*

Edgar Allan Poe National Historic Site (c/o Independence National Historical Park, 313 Walnut Street, Philadelphia, PA 19106). The life and work of this gifted American author are portrayed in this three-building complex at 532 N. Seventh Street where Poe lived, 1843–44. *Acreage—0.52.*

Eisenhower National Historic Site (c/o Gettysburg National Military Park, Gettysburg, PA 17325). This was the only home ever owned by Gen. Dwight D. Eisenhower and his wife, Mamie. It served as a refuge when he was President and as a retirement home after he left office. *Acreage—690.46.*

Fort Necessity National Battlefield (R.D. 2, Box 528, Farmington, PA 15437). Colonial troops commanded by Col. George Washington, then 22 years old, were defeated here in the opening battle of the French and Indian War on July 3, 1754. The park includes the nearby monument to Maj. Gen. Edward Braddock and the early 19th-century Mount Washington Tavern and Jumonville Glen, site of the first skirmishing of the French and Indian War, May 28, 1754. *Acreage—902.80.*

Friendship Hill National Historic Site (R.D. 2, Box 528, Farmington, PA 15437). This stone and brick home on the Monongahela River near Point Marion, Pa., belonged to Albert Gallatin, Secretary of the Treasury, 1801–13, under Presidents Jefferson and Madison. UNDERGOING RESTORATION. *Acreage—674.56.*

Gettysburg National Military Park (Gettysburg, PA 17325). The great Civil War battle fought here July 1–3, 1863, repulsed the second Confederate invasion of the North. Gettysburg National Cemetery—7,036 interments, 1668 unidentified—adjoins the park. President Lincoln delivered his Gettysburg Address here in dedicating the cemetery Nov. 19, 1863. *Park acreage—3,865.11. Cemetery acreage—20.58.*

Hopewell Furnace National Historic Site (R.D. 1, Box 345, Elverson, PA 19520). This is one of the finest examples of a rural American 19th-century ironmaking village. The buildings include a blast furnace, the ironmaster's mansion, and auxiliary structures. Hopewell Village was founded in 1771 by Mark Bird, the first ironmaster. The furnace operated until 1883. *Acreage—848.06.*

Independence National Historical Park (313 Walnut Street, Philadelphia, PA 19106). The park includes structures and sites in central Philadelphia associated with the American Revolution and the founding and growth of the United States: Independence Hall, Congress Hall, Old City Hall, the First and Second Banks of the United States, Franklin Court, and others. *Acreage—44.85.*

Johnstown Flood National Memorial (c/o Allegheny Portage Railroad National Historic Site, P.O. Box 247, Cresson, PA 16630). A total of 2,209 people died in the Johnstown Flood of 1889, caused by a break in the South Fork Dam. Clara Barton successfully led the Red Cross in its first disaster relief effort. *Acreage—163.47.*

Potomac Heritage National Scenic Trail (See Maryland).

Thaddeus Kosciuszko National Memorial (c/o Independence National Historical Park, 313 Walnut Street, Philadelphia, PA 19106). The life and work of this Polish-born patriot and hero of the American Revolution are commemorated at 301 Pine Street, Philadelphia. *Acreage—0.02.*

Upper Delaware Scenic and Recreational River (Drawer C, Narrowsburg, NY 12764). (Also in New York). This is a 75-mile stretch of free-flowing river between Hancock and Sparrow Bush, N.Y., along the Pennsylvania border. LIMITED FEDERAL FACILITIES. *Acreage—75,000.*

Valley Forge National Historical Park (Valley Forge, PA 19481). Site of the Continental Army's winter encampment, 1777–78, the park contains General Washington's headquarters, original earthworks, a variety of monuments and markers, and re-creations of log buildings and cannon used by colonial troops. *Acreage—3,464.89.*

Puerto Rico

San Juan National Historic Site (P.O. Box 712, Old San Juan, PR 00902). These massive masonry fortifications, oldest in the territorial limits of the United States, were begun by the Spanish in the 16th century to protect a strategic harbor guarding the sea lanes to the New World. *Acreage—75.13.*

Rhode Island

Roger Williams National Memorial (P.O. Box 367, Annex Station, Providence, RI 02901). This memorial honors the founder of Rhode Island and a pioneer in religious freedom. *Acreage—4.56.*

South Carolina

Congaree Swamp National Monument (P.O. Box 11938, Columbia, SC 29211). Located on an alluvial floodplain 20 miles southeast of Columbia, the park contains the last significant tract of virgin southern bottomland hardwoods in the southeastern United States. NO FEDERAL FACILITIES. *Acreage—15,138.25.*

Cowpens National Battlefield (P.O. Box 308, Chesnee, SC 29323). Brig. Gen. Daniel Morgan won a decisive Revolutionary War victory here over British Lt. Col. Banastre Tarleton on Jan. 17, 1781. *Acreage—841.56.*

Fort Sumter National Monument (1214 Middle Street, Sullivans Island, SC 29482). The first engagement of the Civil War took place here on Apr. 12, 1861. The park also embraces Fort Moultrie, scene of the patriot victory of June 28, 1776—one of the early defeats of the British in the Revolutionary War. The fort has been restored to reflect 171 years of seacoast defense. *Acreage—189.32.*

Kings Mountain National Military Park (P.O. Box 31, Kings Mountain, NC 28086). American frontiersmen defeated the British here on Oct. 7, 1780, at a critical point during the Revolution. *Acreage—3,945.29.*

Ninety Six National Historic Site (P.O. Box 496, Ninety Six, SC 29666). This important colonial backcountry trading village and government seat after 1769 was held briefly by the British during the Revolutionary War and is the scene of Nathanael Greene's siege in 1781. The site contains earthwork embankments of a 1781 fortification, the remains of two historic villages, a colonial plantation complex, and numerous prehistoric sites. *Acreage—989.14.*

South Dakota

Badlands National Park (P.O. Box 6, Interior, SD 57750). Carved by erosion, this scenic landscape contains animal fossils of 40 million years ago. Prairie grasslands support bison, bighorn sheep, deer, and antelope. *Acreage—243,302.33. Wilderness area: 64,250.*

Jewel Cave National Monument (P.O. Box 351, Custer, SD 57730). Limestone caverns consist of a series of chambers connected by narrow passages, with many side galleries and fine calcite crystal encrustations. *Acreage—1,273.51.*

Missouri National Recreational River (See Nebraska).

Mount Rushmore National Memorial (Keystone, SD 57751). Colossal heads of Presidents George Washington, Thomas Jefferson, Abraham Lincoln, and Theodore Roosevelt were sculpted by Gutzon Borglum on the face of a granite mountain. *Acreage—1,278.45.*

Wind Cave National Park (Hot Springs, SD 57747). These limestone caverns in the scenic Black Hills are decorated by beautiful boxwork and calcite crystal formations. Elk, deer, pronghorn, prairie dogs, and bison live in the park. *Acreage—28,292.08.*

Tennessee

Andrew Johnson National Historic Site (Depot Street, Greenville, TN 37744). The site includes two homes and the tailor shop of the 17th President, who served from 1865 to 1869, and the Andrew Johnson National Cemetery, where the President, members of his family, and veterans of many wars are buried. *Acreage—16.68.*

Appalachian National Scenic Trail (See Maine).

Big South Fork National River and Recreation Area (P.O. Drawer 630, Oneida, TN 37841). (Also in Kentucky). The free-flowing Big South Fork of the Cumberland River and its tributaries pass through scenic gorges and valleys containing a wide range of natural and historical features. Ninety miles of streams are within the boundaries. The U.S. Army Corps of Engineers is coordinating planning and development of the area. *Acreage—122,960.*

Chickamauga and Chattanooga National Park (See Georgia).

Cumberland Gap National Historical Park (See Kentucky).

Fort Donelson National Military Park (P.O. Box F, Dover, TN 37058). The first major victory for the Union Army in the Civil War occurred here in February 1862 under the leadership of Ulysses S. Grant. Fort Donelson (Dover) National Cemetery—1,197 interments, 512 unidentified—adjoins the park. *Park acreage—536.66. Cemetery acreage—15.34.*

Great Smoky Mountains National Park (Gatlinburg, TN 37738). (Also in North Carolina). Loftiest range east of the Black Hills and one of the oldest uplands on Earth, the Smokies have a diversified and luxuriant plantlife, often of extraordinary size. *Acreage—520,269.44.*

Natchez Trace National Scenic Trail (See Mississippi).

Natchez Trace Parkway (See Mississippi).

Obed Wild and Scenic River (P.O. Drawer 630, Oneida, TN 37841). The Obed River and its two main tributaries, Clear Creek and Daddy's Creek, cut into the Cumberland Plateau of East Tennessee, providing some of the most rugged scenery in the southeast. Forty-five miles of streams are protected within the park. *Acreage—5,099.84.*

Shiloh National Military Park (Shiloh, TN 38376). The bitter battle fought here Apr. 6–7, 1862, prepared the way for Maj. Gen. U.S. Grant's successful siege of Vicksburg. Well-preserved prehistoric Indian mounds overlook the river. Shiloh (Pittsburg Landing) National Cemetery—3,761 interments, 2,370 unidentified—adjoins the park. *Park acreage—3,837.50. Cemetery acreage—10.05.*

Stones River National Battlefield (Route 10, Box 495, Old Nashville Highway, Murfreesboro, TN 37130). The fierce mid-winter battle, which began the federal offensive to trisect the Confederacy, took place here Dec. 31, 1862–Jan. 2, 1863. Stones River (Murfreesboro) National Cemetery—6,831 interments, 2,562 unidentified—adjoins the park; grave space not available. *Park acreage—330.86. Cemetery acreage—20.09.*

Texas

Alibates Flint Quarries National Monument (c/o Lake Meredith Recreation Area, P.O. Box 1438, Fritch, TX 79036). For more than 10,000 years, pre-Columbian Indians dug agatized dolomite from quarries here to make projectile points, knives, scrapers, and other tools. *Acreage—1,370.97.*

Amistad National Recreation Area (P.O. Box 420367, Del Rio, TX 78842). Boating and watersports highlight activities in the U.S. section of Amistad Reservoir on the Rio Grande. *Acreage—57,292.44.*

Big Bend National Park (Big Bend National Park, TX 79834). Mountains contrast with desert within the great bend of the Rio Grande, where a variety of unusual geological formations are found. *Acreage—741,118.40.*

Big Thicket National Preserve (P.O. Box 7408, Beaumont, TX 77706). A great number of plant and animal species coexist in this "biological crossroads of North America." Study and research opportunities are excellent. *Acreage—85,849.55.*

Chamizal National Memorial (P.O. Box 722, El Paso, TX 79944). The peaceful settlement of a 99-year boundary dispute between the United States and Mexico is memorialized here. The Chamizal Treaty, ending the dispute, was signed in 1963. An amphitheater and 500-seat auditorium are used by theatrical groups from both nations. *Acreage—54.90.*

Fort Davis National Historic Site (P.O. Box 1456, Fort Davis, TX 79734). A key post in the West Texas defensive system, the fort guarded emigrants on the San Antonio-El Paso road from 1854 to 1891. *Acreage—460.*

Guadalupe Mountains National Park (3225 National Park Highway, Carlsbad, NM 88220). Rising from the desert, this mountain mass contains portions of the world's most extensive and significant Permian limestone fossil reef. Also featured are a tremendous earth fault, lofty peaks, unusual flora and fauna, and a colorful record of the past. *Acreage—76,293.06. Wilderness area: 46,850.*

Lake Meredith Recreation Area (P.O. Box 1438, Fritch TX 79036). Manmade Lake Meredith on the Canadian River is a popular water-activity center in the Southwest. *Acreage—44,977.63. Land area: 7,768.*

Lyndon B. Johnson National Historical Park (P.O. Box 329, Johnson City, TX 78636). The park consists of the birthplace, boyhood home, and ranch of the 36th President, 1963–69, and his grandparents' old ranch. *Acreage—1,477.78.*

Padre Island National Seashore (9405 S. Padre Island Drive, Corpus Christi, TX 78418). Noted for its wide sand beaches, excellent fishing and abundant bird and marine life, this barrier island stretches along the Gulf Coast for 80.5 miles. *Acreage—130,696.83.*

Palo Alto Battlefield National Historic Site (P.O. Box 191, Brownsville, TX 78520). The park contains the site of the first of two important Mexican War battles fought on American soil. Gen. Zachary Taylor's victory here made invasion of Mexico possible. *Acreage—50.*

Rio Grande Wild and Scenic River (c/o Big Bend National Park, Big Bend National Park, TX 79834). A 191.2-mile strip on the American shore of the Rio Grande in the Chihuahuan Desert protects the river. It begins in Big Bend National Park and continues downstream to the Terrell-Val Verde County Line. *Acreage—Boundaries not established.*

San Antonio Missions National Historical Park (727 E. Durango Boulevard, San Antonio, TX 78206). Four Spanish frontier missions, part of a colonization system that stretched across the Spanish Southwest in the 17th, 18th, and 19th centuries, are commemorated here. Included in the park is an irrigation system with related historic dam and aqueduct system. *Acreage—477.43.*

Utah

Arches National Park (Moab, UT 84532). Extraordinary products of erosion in the form of giant arches, windows, pinnacles, and pedestals change color constantly as the sun moves overhead. *Acreage—73,378.98.*

Bryce Canyon National Park (Bryce Canyon, UT 84717). In horseshoe-shaped amphitheaters along the edge of the Paunsaugunt Plateau in southern Utah stand innumerable highly colored and bizarre pinnacles, walls, and spires, perhaps the most colorful and unusual eroded forms in the world. *Acreage—35,835.08.*

Canyonlands National Park (Moab, UT 84532). In this geological wonderland, rocks, spires, and mesas rise more than 7,800 feet. Here, too, are petroglyphs left by Indians about 1,000 years ago. *Acreage—337,570.43.*

Capitol Reef National Park (Torrey, UT 84775). Narrow high-walled gorges cut through a 60-mile uplift of sandstone cliffs with highly colored sedimentary formations. Dome-shaped white-cap rock along the Fremont River accounts for the name. *Acreage—241,904.26.*

Cedar Breaks National Monument (P.O. Box 749, Cedar City, UT 84720). A huge natural amphitheater has eroded into the variegated Pink Cliffs (Wasatch Formation), 2,000 feet thick at this point. *Acreage—6,154.60.*

Dinosaur National Monument (See Colorado).

Glen Canyon National Recreation Area (P.O. Box 1507, Page, AZ 86040). (Also in Arizona). Lake Powell, formed by the Colorado River, stretches for 186 miles behind one of the highest dams in the world. *Acreage—1,236,880.*

Golden Spike National Historic Site (P.O. Box W, Brigham City, UT 84302). Completion of the first transcontinental railroad in the United States was celebrated here where the Central Pacific Railroad and the Union Pacific Railroad met here in 1869. *Acreage—2,735.28.*

Hovenweep National Monument (See Colorado).

Natural Bridges National Monument (c/o Canyonlands National Park, Moab, UT 84532). Three natural bridges, carved out of sandstone, are protected here. The highest is 220 feet above the streambed, with a span of 268 feet. *Acreage—7,791.*

Rainbow Bridge National Monument (c/o Glen Canyon National Recreation Area, P.O. Box 1507, Page, AZ 86040). Greatest of the world's known natural bridges, this symmetrical, salmon-pink sandstone span rises 290 feet above the floor of Bridge Canyon. *Acreage—160.*

Timpanogos Cave National Monument (R.R. 3, Box 200, American Fork, Ut 84003). The colorful limestone cavern on the side of Mount Timpanogos is noted for helictites—water-created formations that grow in all directions and shapes, regardless of the pull of gravity. *Acreage—250.*

Zion National Park (Springdale, UT 84767). Colorful canyon and mesa scenery includes erosion and rock-fault patterns that create phenomenal shapes and landscapes. Evidence of former volcanic activity is here, too. *Acreage—146,551.10.*

Vermont

Appalachian National Scenic Trail (See Maine).

Virginia

Appalachian National Scenic Trail (See Maine).

Appomattox Court House National Historical Park (P.O. Box 218, Appomattox, VA 24522). Here on Apr. 9, 1865, Gen. Robert E. Lee surrendered the Confederacy's largest field army to Lt. Gen. Ulysses S. Grant. *Acreage—1,325.08.*

Arlington House, The Robert E. Lee Memorial (c/o George Washington Memorial Parkway, Turkey Run Park, McLean, VA 22101). This home of the Custis and Lee families overlooks the Potomac River and Washington, D.C. *Acreage—27.91.*

Assateague Island National Seashore (See Maryland).

Blue Ridge Parkway (See North Carolina).

Booker T. Washington National Monument (Route 1, Box 195, Hardy, VA 24101). This site was the birthplace and early

childhood home of the famous black leader and educator. *Acreage—223.92.*

Colonial National Historical Park (P.O. Box 210, Yorktown, VA 23690). This park encompasses most of Jamestown Island, site of the first permanent English settlement; Yorktown, scene of the culminating battle of the American Revolution in 1781; a 23-mile parkway connecting these and other colonial sites with Williamsburg; and Cape Henry Memorial, which marks the first landing of Jamestown's colonists in 1607. Yorktown National Cemetery, containing Civil War gravesites—2,183 interments, 1,434 unidentified—adjoins the park; grave space is not available. *Park acreage—9,316.37. Cemetery acreage—2.91.*

Cumberland Gap National Historical Park (See Kentucky).

Fredericksburg and Spotsylvania County Battlefields Memorial National Military Park (P.O. Box 679, Fredericksburg, VA 22404). Portions of four major Civil War Battlefields— Fredericksburg, Chancellorsville, the Wilderness, Spotsylvania Court House—Chatham Manor, and several smaller historic sites comprise the park. The battles occurred between 1862 and 1864. Fredericksburg National Cemetery—15,333 interments, 12,746 unidentified—is near the park; grave space is not available. *Park acreage—5,909.02. Cemetery acreage—12.*

George Washington Birthplace National Monument (Washington's Birthplace, VA 22575). Birthplace of the first U.S. President, the park includes a memorial mansion and gardens, and the tombs of his father, grandfather, and great-grandfather. *Acreage—538.23.*

George Washington Memorial Parkway (Turkey Run Park, McLean, VA 22101). (Also in Maryland). This landscaped riverfront parkway links many landmarks in the life of George Washington. It connects Mount Vernon and Great Falls on the Virginia side of the Potomac and Great Falls with Chain Bridge on the Maryland side. The parkway includes natural, historical, and recreational areas. *Acreage—7,141.63.*

Harpers Ferry National Historical Park (See West Virginia).

Maggie L. Walker National Historic Site (c/o Richmond National Battlefield Park, 3215 E. Broad St., Richmond, VA 23223). This rowhouse at 110½ E. Leigh Street, Richmond, was the home of the daughter of an ex-house slave who became the first woman president of an American financial institution. *Acreage—1.29.*

Manassas National Battlefield Park (P.O. Box 1830, Manassas, VA 22110). The Battles of First and Second Manassas were fought here July 21, 1861, and Aug. 28–30, 1862. The 1861 battle was the first test of Northern and Southern military prowess. Here, Confederate Brig. Gen. Thomas J. Jackson acquired his nickname "Stonewall." *Acreage—4,513.39.*

Petersburg National Battlefield (P.O. Box 549, Petersburg, VA 23803). The Union Army waged a 10-month campaign here 1864–65 to seize Petersburg, center of the railroads supplying Richmond and Gen. Robert E. Lee's army. Also includes City Point in Hopewell, Va., where Ulysses S. Grant made his headquarters at Appomattox Manor for the final ten months of the war. Poplar Grove (Petersburg) National Cemetery—6,315 interments, 4,110 unidentified—is near the park; grave space is not available. *Park acreage—2,735.38. Cemetery acreage—8.72.*

Potomac Heritage National Scenic Trail (See Maryland).

Prince William Forest Park (P.O. Box 209, Triangle, VA 22172). In this forested watershed of Quantico Creek, pines and hardwoods have replaced worn-out farmland. *Acreage—18,571.55.*

Richmond National Battlefield Park (3215 East Broad Street, Richmond, VA 23223). The park commemorates several battles to capture Richmond, the Confederate capital, during the Civil War. *Acreage—771.41.*

Shenandoah National Park (Route 4, Box 292, Luray, VA 22835). Skyline Drive winds through hardwood forests along the crest of this outstanding portion of the Blue Ridge Mountains, with spectacular vistas of historic Shenandoah Valley and the Piedmont. *Acreage—195,072. Wilderness area: 79,579.*

Wolf Trap Farm Park for the Performing Arts (1551 Trap Road, Vienna, VA 22180). At this first national park for the performing arts, Filene Center can accommodate an audience of 7,000, including 3,500 on the sloping lawn in a setting of rolling hills and woods. The stagehouse is 10 stories high and the stage 116 feet wide by 64 feet deep. *Acreage—130.28.*

Virgin Islands

Buck Island Reef National Monument (Box 160, Christiansted, St. Croix, VI 00820). Coral grottoes, sea fans, gorgonias, and tropical fishes—along an underwater trail—make this one of the finest marine gardens in the Caribbean. The island is a rookery for frigate birds and pelicans and the habitat of green turtles. *Acreage—880. Land area: 143.*

Christiansted National Historic Site (P.O. Box 160, Christiansted, St. Croix, VI 00820). Colonial development of the Virgin Islands is commemorated by 18th- and 19th-century structures in the capital of the former Danish West Indies on St. Croix Island. Discovered by Columbus in 1493, St. Croix was purchased by the United States in 1917 from Denmark. *Acreage—27.15.*

Virgin Islands National Park (P.O. Box 7789, Charlotte Amalie, St. Thomas, VI 00801). The park covers about three-fourths of St. John Island and Hassel Island in St. Thomas harbor and includes quiet coves, blue-green waters, and white sandy beaches fringed by lush green hills. Here, too, are early Carib Indian relics and the remains of Danish colonial sugar plantations. *Acreage—14,695.85. Water area: 5,650.*

Washington

Coulee Dam National Recreation Area (P.O. Box 37, Coulee Dam, WA 99116). Formed by Grand Coulee Dam (part of the Columbia River Basin project), 130-mile long Franklin D. Roosevelt Lake is the principal recreation feature here. *Acreage—100,390.31.*

Fort Vancouver National Historic Site (Vancouver, WA 98661-3897). From 1825 to 1849, Fort Vancouver was the western headquarters of the Hudson's Bay Company's fur trading operations. Under the leadership of John McLoughlin, the fort became the center of political, cultural, commercial, and manufacturing activities in the Pacific Northwest. When American pioneers arrived in the Oregon Country during the 1830s and 1840s, they came to Fort Vancouver for supplies to begin their farms. *Acreage—208.89.*

Klondike Gold Rush National Historical Park (117 South Main Street, Seattle, WA 98104). (See also Alaska). News of the Alaska gold strike spread from Seattle across the country, and from here most prospectors left for the gold fields. Today the park has a visitor center in the Pioneer Square Historic District, which was the center of Gold Rush activity.

Lake Chelan National Recreation Area (800 State Street, Sedro Woolley, WA 98284). Here the beautiful Stehekin Valley, with a portion of fjordlike Lake Chelan, adjoins the southern unit of North Cascades National Park. *Acreage—61,890.07.*

Mount Rainier National Park (Tahoma Woods, Star Route, Ashford, WA 98304). This greatest single-peak glacial system in the United States radiates from the summit and slopes of an ancient volcano, with dense forests and subalpine flowered meadows below. *Acreage—235,404.*

North Cascades National Park (800 State Street, Sedro Woolley, WA 98284). High jagged peaks intercept moisture-laden winds, producing glaciers, icefalls, waterfalls, and other water phenomena in this wild alpine region where lush forests and meadows, plant and animal communities thrive in the valleys. *Acreage—504,780.94.*

Olympic National Park (600 East Park Avenue, Port Angeles, WA 98362). This mountain wilderness contains the finest remnant of Pacific Northwest rain forest. The park features alpine meadows, lakes, and streams. The Olympic mountains tower more than 5,000 feet, and there are at least 60 glaciers in the mountains. In addition there are 50 miles of wild, scenic ocean shore. Rare Roosevelt elk are among the many kinds of animals found in the park. *Acreage—914,576.46.*

Ross Lake National Recreation Area (800 State Street, Sedro Woolley, WA 98284). Ringed by mountains, this National Recreation Area offers many outdoor recreation opportunities along the upper reaches of the Skagit River, between the north and south units of North Cascades National Park. *Acreage—117,574.09.*

San Juan Island National Historical Park (P.O. Box 429, Friday Harbor, WA 98250). This park marks the historic events on the island from 1853 to 1872 in connection with final settlement of the Oregon Territory's northern boundary, including the so-called Pig War of 1859. *Acreage—1,751.99.*

Whitman Mission National Historic Site (Route 2, Box 247, Walla Walla, WA 99362). Dr. and Mrs. Marcus Whitman ministered to spiritual and physical needs of the Indians here until they were slain by a few of them in 1847. The mission was a landmark on the Oregon Trail. *Acreage—98.15.*

West Virginia

Appalachian National Scenic Trail (See Maine).

Chesapeake and Ohio Canal National Historical Park (See Maryland).

Harpers Ferry National Historical Park (P.O. Box 65, Harpers Ferry, WV 25425) (Also in Maryland and Virginia). Because of its strategic location at the confluence of the Shenandoah and Potomac Rivers, this town changed hands many times during the Civil War. John Brown's raid took place here in 1859. *Acreage—2,238.37.*

New River Gorge National River (P.O. Drawer V, Oak Hill, WV 25901). A rugged, whitewater river, flowing northward through deep canyons, the New is among the oldest rivers on the continent. The free-flowing, 50-mile section from Hinton to Fayetteville is abundant in natural, scenic, historic, and recreational features. *Acreage—62,024.*

Wisconsin

Apostle Islands National Lakeshore (Route 1, Box 4, Bayfield, WI 54814). Twenty picturesque islands and an 11-mile strip of adjacent Bayfield Peninsula along the south shore of Lake Superior comprise this park. *Acreage—67,884.84. Land area: 16,321.90.*

Lower Saint Croix National Scenic Riverway (c/o Saint Croix National Scenic Riverway, P.O. Box 708, St. Croix Falls, WI 54024). (Also in Minnesota). Recreational opportunities for much of the upper Midwest are provided here along this 27-mile segment of the St. Croix River, a component of the Wild and Scenic Rivers System. *Acreage—9,465.14.*

Saint Croix National Scenic Riverway (P.O. Box 708, Saint Croix Falls, WI 54024). (Also in Minnesota). About 200 miles of the beautiful St. Croix River and its Namekagon tributary make up this area, an initial component of the National Wild and Scenic Rivers System. *Acreage—68,793.33.*

Wyoming

Bighorn Canyon National Recreation Area (See Montana).

Devils Tower National Monument (Devils Tower, WY 82714). This 865-foot tower of columnar rock, the remains of a volcanic intrusion, is the Nation's first national monument. *Acreage—1,346.91.*

Fort Laramie National Historic Site (Fort Laramie, WY 82212). A fur-trade post once stood here, but the surviving buildings are those of a major military post that guarded covered-wagon trails to the West, 1849–90. *Acreage—832.45.*

Fossil Butte National Monument (P.O. Box 527, Kemerer, WY 83101). An abundance of rare fish fossils, 40–65 million years old, is evidence of former habitation of this now semiarid region. *Acreage—8,198.*

Grand Teton National Park (F.O. Drawer 170, Moose, WY 83012). The most impressive part of the Teton Range, this series of blue-gray peaks rising more than a mile above the sagebrush flats was once a noted landmark for Indians and "mountain men." The park includes part of Jackson Hole, winter feeding ground of the largest American elk herd. *Acreage—310,520.94.*

John D. Rockefeller, Jr., Memorial Parkway (c/o Grand Teton National Park. P.O. Drawer 170, Moose, WY 83012). Linking West Thumb in Yellowstone with the South Entrance of Grand Teton National Park, this scenic 82-mile corridor commemorates Rockefeller's role in aiding establishment of many parks, including Grand Teton. *Acreage—23,777.22.*

Yellowstone National Park (P.O. Box 168, Yellowstone National Park, WY 82190). (Also in Montana and Idaho). Old Faithful and some 10,000 other geysers and hot springs make this the Earth's greatest geyser area. Here, too, are lakes, waterfalls, high mountain meadows, and the Grand Canyon of the Yellowstone—all set apart in 1872 as the world's first national park. *Acreage—2,219,822.70.*

DECLARATION OF INDEPENDENCE
In Congress, July 4, 1776

THE UNAMIMOUS DECLARATION OF THE
THIRTEEN UNITED STATES OF AMERICA,

When in the Course of human events, it becomes necessary for one people to dissolve the political bands which have connected them with another, and to assume among the Powers of the earth, the separate and equal station to which the Laws of Nature and of Nature's God entitle them, a decent respect to the opinions of mankind requires that they should declare the causes which impel them to the separation.

We hold these truths to be self-evident, that all men are created equal, that they are endowed by their Creator with certain unalienable Rights, that among these are Life, Liberty and the pursuit of Happiness. That to secure these rights, Governments are instituted among Men, deriving their just powers from the consent of the governed, That whenever any Form of Government becomes destructive of these ends, it is the Right of the People to alter or to abolish it, and to institute new Government, laying its foundation on such principles and organizing its powers in such form, as to them shall seem most likely to effect their Safety and Happiness. Prudence, indeed, will dictate that Governments long established should not be changed for light and transient causes; and accordingly all experience hath shown, that mankind are more disposed to suffer, while evils are sufferable, than to right themselves by abolishing the forms to which they are accustomed. But when a long train of abuses and usurpations, pursuing invariably the same Object evinces a design to reduce them under absolute Despotism, it is their right, it is their duty, to throw off such Government, and to provide new Guards for their future security.—Such has been the patient sufference of these Colonies; and such is now the necessity which constrains them to alter their former Systems of Government. The history of the present King of Great Britain is a history of repeated injuries and usurpations, all having in direct object the establishment of an absolute Tyranny over these States. To prove this, let Facts be submitted to a candid world.

He has refused his Assent to Laws, the most wholesome and necessity for the public good.

He has forbidden his Governors to pass Laws of immediate and pressing importance, unless suspended in their operation till his Assent should be obtained; and when so suspended, he has utterly neglected to attend to them.

He has refused to pass other Laws for the accommodation of large districts of people, unless those people would relinquish the right of Representation in the Legislature, a right inestimable to them and formidable to tyrants only.

He has called together legislative bodies at places unusual, uncomfortable, and distant from the depository of their Public Records, for the sole purpose of fatiguing them into compliance with his measures.

He has dissolved Representative Houses repeatedly, for opposing with manly firmness his invasions on the rights of the people.

He has refused for a long time, after such dissolutions, to cause others to be elected; whereby the Legislative Powers, incapable of Annihilation, have returned to the People at large for their exercise; the State remaining in the mean time exposed to all the dangers of invasion from without, and convulsions within.

He has endeavoured to prevent the populations of these States; for that purpose obstructing the Laws of Naturalization of Foreigners; refusing to pass others to encourage their migration hither, and raising the conditions of new Appropriations of Lands.

He has obstructed the Administration of Justice, by refusing his Assent to Laws for establishing Judiciary Powers.

He has made Judges dependent on his Will alone, for the tenure of their offices, and the amount and payment of their salaries.

He has erected a multitude of New Offices, and sent hither swarms of Officers to harass our People, and eat out their substance.

He has kept among us, in times of peace, Standing Armies without the Consent of our legislature.

He has affected to render the Military independent of and superior to the Civil Power.

He has combined with others to subject us to a jurisdiction foreign to our constitution, and unacknowledged by our laws; giving his Assent to their acts of pretended legislation:

For quartering large bodies of armed troops among us:

For protecting them, by a mock Trial, from Punishment for any Murders which they should commit on the Inhabitants of these States:

For cutting off our Trade with all parts of the world:

For imposing taxes on us without our Consent:

For depriving us in many cases, of the benefits of Trial by Jury:

For transporting us beyond Seas to be tried for pretended offences:

For abolishing the free System of English Laws in a neighbouring Province, establishing therein an Arbitrary government, and enlarging its Boundaries so as to render it at once an example and fit instrument for introducing the same absolute rule into these Colonies:

For taking away our Charters, abolishing our most valuable Laws, and altering fundamentally the Forms of our Governments:

For suspending our own Legislature, and declaring themselves invested with Power to legislate for us in all cases whatsoever.

He has abdicated Government here, by declaring us out of his Protection and waging War against us.

He has plundered our seas, ravaged our Coasts, burnt our towns, and destroyed the lives of our people.

He is at this time transporting large armies of foreign mercenaries to complete the works of death, desolation and tyranny, already begun with circumstances of Cruelty & perfidy scarcely paralleled in the most barbarous ages, and totally unworthy the Head of a civilized nation.

He has constrained our fellow Citizens taken Captive on the high Seas to bear Arms against their Country, to become the executioners of their friends and Brethren, or to fall themselves by their Hands.

He has excited domestic insurrections amongst us, and has endeavoured to bring on the inhabitants of our frontiers, the merciless Indian Savages, whose known rule of warfare, is an undistinguished destruction of all ages, sexes and conditions.

In every stage of these Oppressions We have Petitioned for Redress in the most humble terms: Our repeated Petitions have been answered only by repeated injury. A Prince, whose character is thus marked by every act which may define a Tyrant, is unfit to be the ruler of a free People.

Nor have We been wanting in attention to our British brethren. We have warned them from time to time of attempts by their legislature to extend an unwarrantable jurisdiction over us. We have reminded them of the circumstances of our emigration and settlement here. We have appealed to their native justice and magnanimity, and we have conjured them by the ties of our common kindred to disavow these usurpations, which, would inevitably interrupt our connections and correspondence. They too have been deaf to the voice of justice and of consanguinity. We must, therefore, acquiesce in the necessity, which denounces our Separation, and hold them, as we hold the rest of mankind, Enemies in War, in Peace Friends.

We, therefore, the Representatives of the United States of America, in General Congress, Assembled, appealing to the Supreme Judge of the world for the rectitude of our intentions, do, in the Name, and by Authority of the good People of these Colonies, solemnly publish and declare, That these United Colonies are, and of Right ought to be Free and Independent States; that they are Absolved from all Allegiance to the British Crown, and that all political connection between them and the State of Great Britain, is and ought to be totally dissolved; and that as Free and Independent States, they have full Power to levy War, conclude Peace, contract Alliances, establish Commerce, and to do all other Acts and Things which Independent States may of right do. And for the support of this Declaration, with a firm reliance on the Protection of Divine Providence, we mutually pledge to each other our Lives, our Fortunes and our sacred Honor.

New Hampshire
Josiah Bartlett
Wm. Whipple
Matthew Thornton

Massachusetts Bay
John Hancock
Saml. Adams
John Adams
Robt. Treat Paine
Elbridge Gerry

Rhode Island
Step. Hopkins
William Ellery

Connecticut
Roger Sherman
Sam. Huntington
Wm. Williams
Oliver Wolcott
Matthew Thornton

New York
Wm. Floyd
Phil. Livingston
Frans. Lewis
Lewis Morris

New Jersey
Richd. Stockton
Jno. Witherspoon
Fras. Hopkinson
John Hart
Abra. Clark

Pennsylvania
Robt. Morris
Benjamin Rush
Benj. Franklin
John Morton
Geo. Clymer
Jas. Smith
Geo. Taylor
James Wilson
Geo. Ross

Delaware
Caesar Rodney
Geo. Read
Tho. M'Kean

Maryland
Samuel Chase
Wm. Paca
Thos. Stone
Charles Carroll of Carrollton

Virginia
George Wythe
Richard Henry Lee
Th. Jefferson
Benj. Harrison
Ths. Nelson, j.
Francis Lightfoot Lee
Carter Braxton

North Carolina
Wm. Hooper
Joseph Hewes
John Penn

South Carolina
Edward Rutledge
Thos. Heyward, Junr.
Thomnas Lynch, Junr.
Arthur Middleton

Georgia
Button Gwinnett
Lyman Hall
Geo. Walton

THE CONSTITUTION OF THE UNITED STATES

WE THE PEOPLE of the United States, in Order to form a more perfect Union, establish Justice, insure domestic Tranquility, provide for the common defence, promote the general Welfare, and secure the Blessings of Liberty to ourselves and our Posterity, do ordain and establish this Constitution for the United States of America.

ARTICLE 1

SECTION 1. All legislative Powers herein granted shall be vested in a Congress of the United States, which shall consist of a Senate and House of Representatives.

SECTION 2. The House of Representatives shall be composed of Members chosen every second Year by the People of the several States, and the Electors in each State shall have the Qualifications requisite for Electors of the most numerous Branch of the State Legislature.

No Person shall be a Representative who shall not have attained to the Age of twenty five Years, and been seven Years a Citizen of the United States, and who shall not, when elected, be an Inhabitant of that State in which he shall be chosen.

[Representatives and direct Taxes shall be apportioned among the several States which may be included within the Union, according to their respective Numbers, which shall be determined by adding to the whole Number of free Persons, including those bound to Service for a Term of Years, and excluding Indians not taxed, three fifths of all other Persons.][1] The actual Enumeration shall be made within three Years after the first Meeting of the Congress of the United States, and within every subsequent Term of ten Years, in such Manner as they shall by Law direct. The Number of Representatives shall not exceed one for every thirty Thousand, but each State shall have at Least one Representative; and until such enumeration shall be made, the State of New Hampshire shall be entitled to chuse three, Massachusetts eight, Rhode-Island and Providence Plantations one, Connecticut five, New-York six, New Jersey four, Pennsylvania eight, Delaware one, Maryland six, Virginia ten, North Carolina five, South Carolina five, and Georgia three.

When vacancies happen in the Representation from any State, the Executive Authority thereof shall issue Writs of Election to fill such Vacancies.

The House of Representatives shall chuse their Speaker and other Officers; and shall have the sole Power of Impeachment.

SECTION 3. The Senate of the United States shall be composed of two Senators from each State, [chosen by the Legislature thereof,][2] for six Years; and each Senator shall have one Vote.

Immediately after they shall be assembled in Consequences of the first Election, they shall be divided as equally as may be into three Classes. The Seats of the Senators of the first Class shall be vacated at the Expiration of the second Year, of the second Class at the Expiration of the fourth Year, and of the third Class at the Expiration of the sixth Year, so that one third may be chosen every second Year; [and if Vacancies happen by Resignation, or otherwise, during the Recess of the Legislature of any State, the Executive thereof may make temporary Appointments until the next Meeting of the Legislature, which shall then fill such Vacancies.][3]

No person shall be a Senator who shall not have attained to the Age of thirty Years, and been nine Years a Citizens of the United States, and who shall not, when elected, be an Inhabitant of that State for which he shall be chosen.

The Vice President of the United States shall be President of the Senate, but shall have no Vote, unless they be equally divided.

The Senate shall chuse their other Officers, and also a President pro tempore, in

---

[1] The clause included in brackets is amended by the 14th Amendment, Section 2.
[2] The qualification in brackets is amended by the 17th Amendment.
[3] The clause in brackets is amended by the 17th Amendment.
[4] The part in brackets is amended by the 20th Amendment, Section 2.

the Absence of the Vice President, or when he shall exercise the Office of President of the United States.

The Senate shall have the sole Power to try all Impeachments. When sitting for that Purpose, they shall be on Oath or Affirmation. When the President of the United States is tried, the Chief Justice shall preside: And no Person shall be convicted without the Concurrence of two thirds of the Members present.

Judgment in Cases of Impeachment shall not extend further than to removal from Office, and disqualification to hold and enjoy any Office of honor, Trust or Profit under the United States: but the Party convicted shall nevertheless be liable and subject to Indictment, Trial, Judgment and Punishment, according to Law.

SECTION 4. The Times, Places and Manner of holding Elections for Senators and Representatives, shall be prescribed in each State by the Legislature thereof; but the Congress may at any time by Law make or alter such Regulations, except as to the Places of chusing Senators.

The Congress shall assemble at least once in every Year, and such Meeting shall [be on the first Monday in December,[4 unless they shall by Law appoint a different Day.

SECTION 5. Each House shall be the Judge of the Elections., Returns and Qualifications of its own Members, and a Majority of each shall constitute a Quorum to do Business; but a smaller Number may adjourn from day to day, and may be authorized to compel the Attendance of absent Members, in such Manner, and under such Penalties as each House may provide.

Each House may determine the Rules of its Proceedings, punish its Members for disorderly Behaviour, and, with the Concurrence of two thirds, expel a Member.

Each House shall keep a Journal of its Proceedings, and from time to time publish the same, excepting such Parts as may in their Judgment require Secrecy; and the Yeas and Nays of the Members of either House on any question shall, at the Desire of one fifth of those Present, be entered on the Journal.

Neither House, during the Session of Congress, shall, without the Consent of the other, adjourn for more than three days, nor to any other Place than that in which the two Houses shall be sitting.

SECTION 6. The Senators and Representatives shall receive a Compensation for their Services, to be ascertained by Law, and paid out of the Treasury of the United States. They shall in all Cases, except Treason, Felony and Breach of the Peace, be privileged from Arrest during their Attendance at the Session of their respective Houses, and in going to and returning from the same; and for any Speech or Debate in either House, they shall not be questioned in any other Place.

No Senator or Representative shall, during the Time for which he was elected, be appointed to any civil Office under the Authority of the United States, which shall have been created, or the Emoluments whereof shall have been encreased during such time; and no Person holding any Office under the United States, shall be a Member of either House during his Continuance in Office.

SECTION 7. All Bills for raising Revenue shall originate in the House of Representatives; but the Senate may propose or concur with Amendments as on other Bills.

Every Bill which shall have passed the House of Representatives and the Senate, shall, before it become a Law, be presented to the President of the United States; If he approve he shall sign it, but if not he shall return it, with his Objections to that House in which it shall have originated, who shall enter the Objections at large on their Journal, and proceed to reconsider it. If after such Reconsideration two thirds of that House shall agree to pass the Bill, it shall be sent, together with the Objections, to the other House, by which it shall likewise be reconsidered, and if approved by two thirds of that House, it shall become a Law. But in all such Cases the Votes of both Houses shall be determined by yeas and Nays, and the Names of the Persons voting for and against the Bill shall be entered on the Journal of each House respectively. If any Bill shall not be returned by the President within ten Days (Sundays excepted) after it shall have been presented to him, the Same shall be a Law, in like Manner as if he had signed it, unless the Congress by their Adjournment prevent its Return, in which Case it shall not be a Law.

Every Order, Resolution, or Vote to which the Concurrence of the Senate and House of Representatives may be necessary (except on a question of Adjournment) shall be presented to the President of the United States; and before the Same shall take Effect, shall be approved by him, or being disapproved by him, shall be repassed by two thirds of the Senate and House of Representatives, according to the Rules and Limitations prescribed in the Case of a Bill.

SECTION 8. The Congress shall have Power To lay and collect Taxes, Duties, Imposts and Excises, to pay the Debts and provide for the common Defence and general Welfare of the United States; but all Duties, Imposts and Excises shall be uniform throughout the United States;

To borrow Money on the credit of the United States;

To regulate Commerce with foreign Nations, and among the several States, and with the Indian Tribes;

To establish an uniform Rule of Naturalization, and uniform Laws on the subject of Bankruptcies throughout the United States;

To coin Money, regulate the Value thereof, and of foreign Coin, and fix the Standard of Weights and Measures;

To provide for the Punishment of counterfeiting the Securities and current Coin of the United States;

To establish Post Offices and post Roads;

To promote the Progress of Science and useful Arts, by securing for limited Times to Authors and Inventors the exclusive Right to their respective Writings and Discoveries;

To constitute Tribunals inferior to the supreme Court;

To define and punish Piracies and Felonies committed on the high Seas, and Offences against the Law of the Nations;

To declare War, grant Letters of Marque and Reprisal, and make Rules concerning Captures on Land and Water;

To raise and support Armies, but no Appropriation of Money to that Use shall be for a longer Term than two Years;

To provide and maintain a Navy;

To make Rules for the Government and Regulation of the land and naval Forces;

To provide for calling forth the Militia to execute the Laws of the Union, suppress Insurrections and repel Invasions;

To provide for organizing, arming, and disciplining, the Militia, and for governing such Part of them as may be employed in the Service of the United States, reserving to the State respectively, the Appointment of the Officers, and the Authority of training the Militia according to the discipline prescribed by Congress;

To exercise exclusive Legislation in all Cases whatsoever, over such District (not exceeding ten Miles square) as may, by Cession of particular States, and the Acceptance of Congress, become the Seat of the Government of the United States, and to exercise like Authority over all Places purchased by the Consent of the Legislature of the State in which the Same shall be, for the Erection of Forts, Magazines, Arsenals, dock-Yards, and other needful Buildings; —And

To make all Laws which shall be necessary and proper for carrying into Execution the foregoing Powers, and all other Powers vested by this Constitution in the Government of the United States, or in any Department or Officer thereof.

SECTION 9. The Migration or Importation of such Persons as any of the States now existing shall think proper to admit, shall not be prohibited by the Congress prior to the Year one thousand eight hundred and eight, but a Tax or duty may be imposed on such Importation, not exceeding ten dollars for each Person.

The Privilege of the Writ of Habeas Corpus shall not be suspended, unless when in Cases of Rebellion or Invasion the public Safety may require it.

No Bill of Attainder or ex post facto Law shall be passed.

No Capitation, or other direct, Tax shall be laid, unless in Proportion to the Census or Enumeration herein before directed to be taken.

No Tax or Duty shall be laid on Articles exported from any State.

No Preference shall be given by any Regulation or Commerce or Revenue to the Ports of one State over those of another: nor shall Vessels bound to, or from, one State, be obliged to enter, clear, or pay Duties in another.

No Money shall be drawn from the Treasury, but in Consequence of Appropriations made by Law; and a regular Statement and Account of the Receipts and Expenditures of all public Money shall be published from time to time.

No Title of Nobility shall be granted by the United States: And no Person holding any Office of Profit or Trust under them, shall, without the Consent of the Congress, accept of any present, Emolument, Office, or Title, of any kind whatever, from any King, Prince or foreign State.

SECTION 10. No State shall enter into any Treaty, Alliance, or Confederation; grant Letters of Marque and Reprisal; coin Money; emit Bills of Credit; make any Thing but gold and silver Coin a Tender in

Payment of Debts; pass any Bill of Attainder, ex post facto Law, or Law, impairing the Obligation of Contracts, or grant any Title of Nobility.

No State shall, without the Consent of the Congress, lay any Imposts or Duties on Imports or Exports, except what may be absolutely necessary for executing it's inspection Laws; and the net Produce of all Duties and Imposts, laid by any State on Imports or Exports, shall be for the Use of the Treasury of the United States; and all such Laws shall be subject to the Revision and Controul of the Congress.

No State shall, without the Consent of Congress, lay any Duty of Tonnage, keep Troops, or Ships of War in time of Peace, enter into any Agreement or Compact with another State, or with a foreign Power, or engage in War, unless actually invaded, or in such imminent Danger as will not admit of delay.

ARTICE II

SECTION 1. The executive Power shall be vested in a President of the United States of America. He shall hold his Office during the Term of four Years, and, together with the Vice President, chosen for the same Term, be elected, as follows

Each State shall appoint, in such Manner as the Legislature thereof may direct, a Number of Electors, equal to the whole Number of Senators and Representatives to which the State may be entitled in the Congress: but no Senator or Representative, or Person holding an Office of Trust or Profit under the United States, shall be appointed an Elector.

[The Electors shall meet in their respective States, and vote by Ballot for two Persons, of whom at least shall not be an Inhabitant of the same State with themselves. And they shall make a List of all the Persons voted for, and of the Number of Votes for each; which List they shall sign and certify, and transmit sealed to the Seat of the Government of the United States directed to the President of the Senate. The President of the Senate shall, in the Presence of the Senate and House of Representatives, open all the Certificates, and the Votes shall then be counted. The Person having the greatest Number of Votes shall be the President, if such Number be a Majority of the whole Number of Electors appointed; and if there be more than one who have such Majority, and have an equal Number of Votes, then the House of Representatives shall immediately chuse by Ballot one of them for President; and if no person have a Majority, then from the five highest on the List the said House shall in like Manner chuse the President. But in chusing the President, the Votes shall be taken by States, the Representation from each State having one Vote; A quorum for this Purpose shall consist of a Member or Members from two thirds of the States, and a Majority of all the States shall be necessary to a Choice. In every Case, after the Choice of the President, the Person having the greatest Number of Votes of the Electors shall be the Vice President. But if there should remain two or more who have equal Votes, the Senate shall chuse from them by Ballot the Vice President.][5]

The Congress may determine the Time of chusing the Electors, and the Day on which they shall give their Votes; which Day shall be the same throughout the United States.

No Person except a natural born Citizen, or a Citizen of the United States, at the time of the Adoption of this Constitution, shall be eligible to the Office of President; neither shall any Person be eligible to that Office who shall not have attained to the Age of thirty five Years, and been fourteen Years a Resident within the United States.

[In Case of the Removal of the President from Office, or of his Death, Resignation, or Inability to discharge the Powers and Duties of the said Office, the Same shall devolve on the Vice President, and the Congress may by Law provide for the Case of Removal, Death, Resignation or Inability, both of the President and Vice President, declaring what Officer shall then act as President, and such Officer shall act accordingly, until the Disability be removed, or a President shall be elected.][6]

The President shall, at stated Times, receive for his Services, a Compensation, which shall neither be encreased nor diminished during the Period for which he shall have been elected, and he shall not receive within that Period any other Emolument from the United States, or any of them.

Before he enter on the Execution of his Office, he shall take the following Oath or Affirmation:—"I do solemnly swear (or affirm) that I will faithfully execute the Office of President of the United States, and will to the best of my Ability, preserve, protect and defend the Constitution of the United States."

SECTION 2. The President shall be Commander in Chief of the Army and Navy of the United States, and of the Militia of the several States, when called into the actual Service of the United States; he may require the Opinion, in writing, of the principal Officer in each of the executive Departments, upon any Subject relating to the Duties of their respective Offices, and he shall have Power to grant Reprieves and Pardons for Offences against the United States, except in Cases of Impeachment.

He shall have Power, by and with the Advice and Consent of the Senate, to make Treaties, provided two thirds of the Senators present concur; and he shall nominate, and by and with the Advice and Consent of the Senate, shall appoint Ambassadors, other public Ministers and Consuls, Judges of the supreme Court, and all other Officers of the United States, whose Appointments are not herein otherwise provided for, and which shall be established by Law: but the Congress may by Law vest the Appointment of such inferior Officers, as they think proper, in the President alone, in the Courts of Law, or in the Heads of Departments.

The President shall have Power to fill up all Vacancies that may happen during the Recess of the Senate, by granting Commissions which shall expire at the End of their next Session.

SECTION 3. He shall from time to time give to the Congress Information of the State of the Union, and recommend to their Consideration such Measures as he shall judge necessary and expedient; he may, on extraordinary Occasions, convene both Houses, or either of them, and in Case of Disagreement between them, with Respect to the Time of Adjournment, he may adjourn them to such Time as he shall think proper; he shall receive Ambassadors and other public Ministers; he shall take Care that the Laws be faithfully executed, and shall Commission all the Officers of the United States.

SECTION— 4. The President, Vice President and all civil Officers of the United States, shall be removed from Office on Impeachment for, and Conviction of, Treason, Bribery, or other high Crimes and Misdemeanors.

ARTICLE III

SECTION 1. The judicial Power of the United States, shall be vested in one supreme Court, and in such inferior Courts as the Congress may time to time ordain and establish. The Judges, both of the supreme and inferior Courts, shall hold their Offices during good Behaviour, and shall, at stated Times, receive for their Services, a Compensation, which shall not be diminished during their Continuance in Office.

SECTION 2. The judicial Power shall extend to all Cases, in Law and Equity, arising under this Constitution, the Laws of the United States, and Treaties made, or which shall be made, under their Authority;—to all Cases affecting Ambassadors, other public Ministers and Consuls;—to all Cases of admiralty and maritime Jurisdiction;—to Controversies to which the United States shall be a Party;—to Controversies between two or more States;—[between a State and Citizens of another State;][7]—between Citizens of different States,—between Citizens of the same State claiming Lands under Grants of different States, and between a State, or the Citizens thereof, and foreign States, Citizens or Subjects.

In all Cases affecting Ambassadors, other public Ministers and Consuls, and those in which a State shall be Party, the Supreme Court shall have original Jurisdiction. In all the other Cases before mentioned, the Supreme Court shall have appellate Jurisdiction, both as to Law and Fact, with such Exceptions, and under such Regulations as the Congress shall make.

The Trial of all Crimes, except in Cases of Impeachment, shall be by Jury; and such Trial shall be held in the State where the said Crimes shall have been committed; but when not committed within any State, the Trial shall be at such Place or Places as the Congress may by Law have directed.

SECTION 3. Treason against the United States, shall consist only in levying War against them, or in adhering to their enemies, giving them Aid and Comfort. No Person shall be convicted of Treason unless on the Testimony of two Witnesses to the same overt Act, or on Confession in open Court.

---

[5] The clause in brackets has been superseded by the 12th Amendment.
[6] The clause in brackets is affected by the 25th Amendment.

[7] The part in brackets is limited by the 11th Amendment.

THE PRESIDENCY

In the course of some 200 years, the presidency of the United States has become the most powerful office in the world. The duties and responsibilities of the office are immense. Unlike many of the democratic governments of Europe and elsewhere that have both a chief of state and a head of government, the U.S. system of government has only one chief executive, the president. The holder of that office serves not only as head of government but also in the primarily ceremonial post of chief of state. As chief of state, the president performs many of the public and ceremonial duties undertaken by the king or queen of the United Kingdom, other monarchs, and the governor-general of Canada and other Commonwealth nations. Although some of the duties the president performs as chief of state may seem trivial, the role helps the occupant of the office maintain contact with the overall populace. As head of government, the president is the chief executive of the nation, the director of the government. In addition the president serves as commander in chief of the armed forces of the United States and the voice of the American people.

According to presidential scholar Clinton Rossiter, the presidency is a one-person job. The person "who holds it can never escape making the final decisions in each of many areas in which the American people and their constitution hold "him or her responsible." A sign on the presidential desk of Harry S. Truman, the nation's chief executive from April 1945 to January 1953, said it perfectly: "The buck stops here." According to Rossiter, "that, in the end, is the essence of the presidency. It is the one office in all of the land whose occupant is forbidden to pass the buck." Recognizing the value of President Truman's words, a White House successor of entirely different political persuasion adopted the motto for his administration 28 years later.

George Washington took the presidential oath in New York on April 30, 1789. The 20th amendment set the inauguration date as January 20.

The Role and Duties of the President

The role of the president has expanded considerably beyond that envisaged by the Founding Fathers in the Constitution. During such crises as the Civil War, world wars I and II, and the depression of the 1930s, Congress and the nation both turned to the executive for leadership and guidance. Crisis powers given to the president were to a great extent retained afterward, thereby adding new stature to the office. Likewise, as foreign affairs increased in importance during the 20th century, the president's role as the voice of the nation added new prestige and responsibilities to the office. Governmental efforts to provide for the social and economic welfare of its citizens, initiated in the depression of 1929-33 and subsequently expanded, have contributed to the president's duties and powers in the economic and social spheres. Likewise, the necessity for an expanded bureaucracy serving the president has heightened his prestige and influence at the expense of the legislative branch.

Such figures as Thomas Jefferson, Andrew Jackson, Abraham Lincoln, Theodore Roosevelt, Woodrow Wilson, Franklin D. Roosevelt, and Harry S. Truman have shaped the presidency. Normally regarded as "strong presidents," these individuals, exercising their prerogatives as leaders of the nation, utilized their influence to initiate major changes in American society. In so doing they added to the magnitude of the office. Although the Vietnam war and the Watergate scandal of Richard Nixon's administration strained the presidency during the 1960s and early 1970s, President Gerald Ford and his successors worked hard, and successfully, to restore the office to its former status.

The President as Leader of the Nation. The president as leader of the nation is confronted with a multiplicity of problems and tasks. As the only executive official elected by the people at large (the vice-president is assigned a legislative post as president of the Senate), he represents the nation to the world. His responsibilities do not stop there, for he is the chief policymaker for domestic and foreign affairs. In this capacity, although he is acknowledged as the leader of one of the political parties, he must represent all the people.

John Marshall, who was to become chief justice of the United States, recognized, as secretary of state, the inherent responsibilities of the president in the domain of foreign affairs. "The president," he noted in 1799, "is the sole organ of the nation in its external relations, and its sole representative with foreign nations." In receiving the credentials of foreign delegates the president exercises the prerogative of recognizing or rejecting the credentials of other governments. Likewise, he has the power to withdraw such recognition. He alone may address foreign governments or be addressed by them. Diplomatic communications are generally carried out through the numerous ministers and envoys who represent the president and the United States in other countries.

The president, with the advice and consent of the Senate, consummates treaties in his capacity as leader of the nation. (He signs treaties as chief of state.) Should he ignore the Senate's role in treaty making, especially by disregarding the Senate in the making of a pact, the president may endanger his own position. Thus President Wilson, by ignoring the senators in the negotiations on the Treaty of Versailles and the League of Nations, created acrimonious feelings that later led to the rejection by the United States of the treaty and the league. In addition to this, the president must recognize the need for congressional appropriations for his foreign policy measures. Consequently he must cultivate congressional support for his programs.

As leader of the nation, the president must determine the course of foreign and domestic policy. The Constitution stipulates that the executive "shall from time to time give to the Congress Information of the State of the Union, and recommend to their Consideration such Measures as he shall judge necessary and expedient." In his messages to Congress, including those on the annual budget, the state of the union, and the economic condition of the nation, the president suggests the programs and measures for legislative enactment that he considers vital to the nation's welfare and betterment.

Elected by the people, the president, unlike members of Congress, represents the entire nation rather than a district or state. Hence he must be a national leader. This he accomplishes by diverse means. In addition to his messages to Congress, he utilizes television and radio, including the live televised address and press conference, to inform the people of his position concerning the issues and problems confronting the nation.

Although elected specifically as a member of one political party, the president must work with both parties in determining public policy. Nevertheless, as the nominee of a specific party, he must also work toward the realization of that party's programs and goals. To prevent a complete cleavage in society, however, the president, along with the leaders of his party and the opposition, often works out programs on crucial matters like foreign affairs and national defense that are generally acceptable to both parties. If the president's party holds a majority in Congress that is in accord with his views, the president is more likely to see his program enacted. However, if his party is in a minority, or if the members of his own party disagree with his specific programs, the president's legislative measures may be ignored or defeated by Congress.

Early in 1986, President Ronald Reagan urged a major U.S. arms sale to Saudi Arabia. The Republican-controlled Senate and the Democratic-controlled House of Representatives passed a resolution blocking the sale. The president then vetoed the resolution and began a major campaign to have his veto sustained. On the morning that the Senate was to vote on the measure, all 100 senators were invited to breakfast at the White House; many senators also received presidential telephone calls on the issue. Although the merits of the sale were considered during Senate debate, some supporters of the president's position simply pointed out that the "prestige of the presidency" was "at stake" with the vote. The veto was sustained in the Senate by one vote. Eight senators, who originally voted against the sale, voted to sustain the veto. The incident is a classical example of the political clout and power of the presidency.

The President as Commander in Chief. Article II, Section 2, of the Constitution states that the president is "Commander in Chief of the Army and Navy . . . and of the Militia of the several States, when called into the actual Service of the United States."

This provision assures civilian control of the military. Although this stipulation grants the executive broad powers, the chief executive is limited somewhat by those powers left solely to Congress. These powers include the right of Congress to declare war, to appropriate funds for the armed forces, and to conscript men for military service.

Nevertheless, the executive's powers are extensive. He selects the key figures in the military establishment, including the secretary of defense, the secretaries of the Army, Navy, and Air Force, and the military chiefs of staff. He recommends the defense budget to Congress and administers laws pertaining to the defense of the nation. He directs strategy in times of war, and is held responsible for the success or failure of the entire defense program. As noted previously, the president has often been delegated extraordinary wartime powers. These include the right to make decisions pertaining to the fundamental military strategy of the nation and, on the domestic scene, to initiate measures, including the invoking of martial law if necessary, designed to win a war. In fact, in the 175 years between the late 1790s and the early 1970s, U.S. troops had been sent into military hostilities some 200 times without a declaration of war. In the age of the Cold War and possible nuclear conflict, the case for congressional involvement in decisions involving military force seemed to be weaker than at any time in U.S. history. In the event of a nuclear attack against the United States, there very likely would not be time for a president to consult Congress.

The Vietnam war of the 1960s and early 1970s, which took some 57,000 American lives and cost the nation billions of dollars, marked a turning point. In 1964 the Congress, responding to an alleged attack on U.S. vessels in the Gulf of Tonkin off Vietnam, passed a resolution authorizing the president to take the steps needed, "including the use of armed force," to assist South Vietnam preserve its freedom. As the U.S. involvement in the conflict mounted, so did congressional discontent with the implications of the Tonkin Gulf Resolution. By the early 1970s, Congress was debating legislation to limit the president's war-making power. Finally in October 1973, the Senate and House of Representatives passed the War Powers Resolution. Although President Richard M. Nixon vetoed the measure, there was sufficient support in Congress to override the veto.

The purpose of the War Powers Resolution is stated in Section 2(a):

> to fulfill the intent of the framers of the Constitution of the United States and insure that the collective judgment of both the Congress and the president will apply to the introduction of United States armed forces into hostilities, or into situations where imminent involvement in hostilities is clearly indicated by the circumstances, and to the continued use of such forces in hostilities or in such situations.

The resolution requires the president to keep Congress informed both before and during any involvement by U.S. forces in hostilities. Under Section 4(a), the president is required to report to Congress within 48 hours when U.S. troops are introduced:

> (1) into hostilities or into situations where imminent involvement in hostilities is clearly indicated by the circumstances;
> (2) into the territory, airspace or waters of a foreign nation, while equipped for combat, except for deployments which relate solely to supply, replacement, repair, or training of such forces; or
> (3) in numbers which substantially enlarge United States armed forces equipped for combat already located in a foreign nation.

A written report must be submitted to the speaker of the House of Representatives and the president pro tempore of the Senate setting forth:

> a—the circumstances necessitating the introduction of the United States armed forces;
> b—the constitutional and legislative authority under which such introduction took place; and
> c—the estimated scope and duration of the hostilities or involvement

Only in the first circumstance (U.S. forces likely to be engaged in combat) is the length of the commitment limited by the resolution. In that event, Section 5(b) of the resolution requires the president to withdraw U.S. troops within 60 to 90 days unless the Congress authorizes their continued presence. The resolution also contains a provision, 5(c), permitting Congress, by concurrent resolution without approval by the president, to order the withdrawal of U.S. troops from hostilities abroad.

Since passage of the act, Presidents Gerald Ford, Jimmy Carter, and Reagan sought ways to avoid the trigger mechanism in Section 5(b). The three presidents reported to the Congress under the act's provisions but often without citing which precise provision in the act applied to their deployment of forces. In this way they have been able to avoid the 60- to 90-day clock. As a result, the role of Congress in the deployment of U.S. troops abroad has not been any greater after enactment of the resolution than before.

The Presidency in History

Origins of the Office. The presidency, and what is often termed the "presidential system of government," is of distinctly American origin. Political philosophers such as John Locke (1632-1704) and Baron de Montesquieu (1689-1755) had written earlier on the separation of legislative and executive functions, but the transition from theory to practice was left to the framers of the Constitution. The term "president" was not new, however, for it had been applied to the presiding officer of legislative bodies in the colonies and in the Continental Congress. Likewise the New York constitution of 1777 and the Massachusetts constitution of 1780 suggested an independent executive, whose powers were somewhat comparable to those later granted to the president of the United States.

Delegates to the Constitutional Convention in Philadelphia in 1787 faced a dilemma when they considered establishing a "national executive." The majority of the framers of the constitution wanted an executive power capable of reaching the remotest parts of the Union, "not only for the purpose of enforcing national laws but also . . . for the purpose of bringing assistance to the states in grave emergencies of domestic disorder." The framers also wanted to avoid stirring up popular fear of the monarchy.

George P. A. Healy's "The Peacemakers" shows President Lincoln meeting with his military advisers toward the end of the Civil War. The U.S. Constitution clearly states that the president is commander in chief.

At the convention, Roger Sherman of Connecticut favored the notion of subordinating the chief executive to a legislature. According to James Madison's *Notes,* Sherman "considered the executive magistracy as nothing more than an institution for carrying the will of the legislature into effect," and he "wished that the number [of executives] might not be fixed, but that the legislature should be at liberty to appoint one or more as experience might dictate." Delegate James Wilson of Pennsylvania took an opposite view and argued in favor of a single executive with broad powers. Wilson, as James Madison recorded in his diary of the convention's proceedings, "preferred a single magistrate, as giving most energy, dispatch, and responsibility to the office." The executive, Wilson argued, should be independent of the legislature, and to preserve this status should be vested with an absolute veto over legislative enactments. Otherwise, the legislature would "at any moment sink it [the executive] into nonexistence." Furthermore the president should be elected directly by the people. Wilson had to compromise on a number of points, including the last one, for the convention decided that the president should be elected indirectly by the people through a college of electors. However, the core of Wilson's ideas, supported especially by Madison and Gouverneur Morris, was incorporated into the final document.

Section 1 of Article II of the Constitution clearly spells out and defines the basis of and qualifications for the office of president. It states:

Terry Arthur, The White House

The duties of the president are many. As "the sole organ of the nation in its foreign relations," Ronald Reagan met with Soviet General Secretary Gorbachev in 1985. In accordance with the Constitution, Jimmy Carter, *below left,*

> The executive Power shall be vested in a President of the United States of America. He shall hold his Office during the Term of four Years. . . .
>
> No Person except a natural born Citizen, or a Citizen of the United States, at the time of the Adoption of this Constitution, shall be eligible to the Office of President; neither shall any person be eligible to that Office who shall not have attained the Age of thirty five Years, and been fourteen Years a Resident within the United States.
>
> In Case of the Removal of the President from Office, or of his Death, Resignation, or Inability to discharge the Powers and Duties of the said Office, the Same shall devolve on the Vice-President, and the Congress may by Law provide for the Case of Removal, Death, Resignation or Inability, both of the President and Vice-President, declaring what Officer shall then act as President, and such Officer shall act accordingly, until the Disability be removed, or a President shall be elected.
>
> The President shall, at stated Times, receive for his Services, a Compensation, which shall neither be encreased nor diminished during the Period for which he shall have been elected, and he shall not receive within that period any other Emolument from the United States, or any of them.
>
> Before he enter on the Execution of his Office, he shall take the following Oath or Affirmation: —"I do solemnly swear (or affirm) that I will faithfully execute the Office of President of the United States, and will to the best of my Ability, preserve, protect and defend the Constitution of the United States."

© Arthur Grace, Sygma

Four constitutional amendments, relating directly to the presidency, were approved subsequently. The 12th amendment, proclaimed on Sept. 25, 1804, clarified the election procedure and defined the office of vice-president. A confused 1800 election result encouraged passage of the 12th amendment. The 20th, or Lame Duck amendment, was proclaimed on Feb. 6, 1933, and reduced the period between the election and inauguration of a president. The inauguration date now would be January 20, not March 4 as previously, and the session of Congress that had been held in the interim period was eliminated.

Franklin D. Roosevelt, an extremely active chief executive who took full advantage of his power, was the first and only president to be elected to four terms. As a result, sentiment in favor of limiting a president's time in office arose, and the 22nd amendment, limiting the president to two terms, was proclaimed on March 1, 1951.

The crises caused by the illness of President Dwight D. Eisenhower and the 1963 assassination of President John F. Kennedy focused attention on the issue of presidential succession and the

need to establish a procedure for filling the vice-presidency when that office becomes vacant. As a result, the 25th amendment was passed by Congress, ratified by the states and proclaimed on Feb. 24, 1967.

Section I of the 25th amendment states that in case of the removal of the president from office or of his death or resignation, the vice-president shall become president. Section II provides that "whenever there is a vacancy in the office of vice-president, the president shall nominate a vice-president who shall take the office upon confirmation by a majority vote of both houses of Congress." Prior to the 25th amendment, the vice-presidency had been vacant on 16 occasions. Gerald R. Ford and Nelson A. Rockefeller were appointed vice-president by Presidents Nixon and Ford, respectively, and took office in accordance with the terms of the 25th amendment.

The amendment also provides for a means of dealing with a much more difficult aspect of presidential power: namely, that of

The John Fitzgerald Kennedy Library

outlined the "State of the Union" to Congress. John Kennedy used the televised news conference to outline his program and objectives. Before a large audience, Lyndon Johnson signed the Civil Rights Bill on July 2, 1964. GOP leader Reagan campaigned for his reelection and the election of other Republicans in 1984.

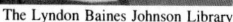

The Lyndon Baines Johnson Library

Jack Kightlinger, The White House

presidential disability or inability to perform the powers and duties of the office. It provides for the resolution of the presidential inability problem in three ways. First, the president may declare his own inability, whereupon his "powers and duties shall be discharged by the vice-president as acting president." In this instance, the president may reclaim the powers and duties of the office by stating his ability to perform. Second, in the event the president cannot declare his own inability, the vice-president and a majority of the Cabinet may declare that such an inability exists, whereupon the "vice-president shall immediately assume the powers and duties of the office as acting president." Third, in the event that the vice-president and a majority of the Cabinet conclude that the president is unable to perform the powers and duties of the office and the president disagrees with this conclusion, the matter will be decided by Congress. "If the Congress, within 21 days . . . determines by two-thirds vote of both Houses that the president is unable to discharge the powers and duties of his office, the vice-

president shall . . . discharge the same as acting president; otherwise, the president shall resume the powers and duties of his office."

At various times there have been calls for reform of the presidency. A single, six-year term as well as a parliamentary government system have been suggested. During the 1950s, Sen. John W. Bricker, a Republican from Ohio, proposed an amendment to limit the power of the president under executive agreements. Generally, such efforts to change the office have not met with much success.

As presidential scholar Thomas E. Cronin has noted, "the original job of presidency has grown and yet the Founding Fathers wrote a marvelously flexible job description that is almost as appropriate today as it was when the nation was a new republic. The flexibility plus the willingness of the American people to place confidence in effective presidents give a president an enormous opportunity to serve the nation."

PR-5

George Washington

1st president, 1789-97   Federalist

1732. Born on February 22 in Westmoreland county, VA.
1752. Inherited Mount Vernon, an estate on the Potomac.
1755-58. Was commander in chief of Virginian troops for the balance of the French and Indian War.
1759. On January 6, married Martha Dandridge Custis, a widow with two children.
1759-74. Served in the Virginia House of Burgesses.
1774. Was a delegate to the First Continental Congress.
1775. Elected a delegate to the Second Continental Congress; named commander in chief of the Continental Army.
1776. Forced British troops to evacuate Boston; after a series of defeats in New York, crossed the Delaware River on December 25-26 to take 1,000 British prisoners.
1781. Defeated British forces at Yorktown. Lord Cornwallis surrendered to end the Revolutionary War.
1787. Served as president of the Constitutional Convention.
1789. Unanimously elected president of the United States.
1797. Retired to Mount Vernon after two terms as president.
1798. Named commander in chief of new U.S. Army.
1799. Died on December 14 at Mount Vernon.

Highlights of Presidency

1789. Judiciary Act established federal court system; first tax laws were adopted.
1791. Bank Act established a nationwide banking system. □ The Bill of Rights became law on December 15.
1792. Unanimously reelected to a second term. □ Coinage Act gave the government power to mint coins.
1793. On April 22, proclaimed U.S. neutrality in war between Britain and France.
1794. Federal troops suppressed the Whiskey Rebellion, armed resistance to excise tax.
1795. The Jay Treaty, under which Britain gave up its frontier forts and ensured continued trade with the United States, was ratified.
1796. Delivered Farewell Address, announcing his retirement and advocating a strong central government and neutrality in foreign affairs.

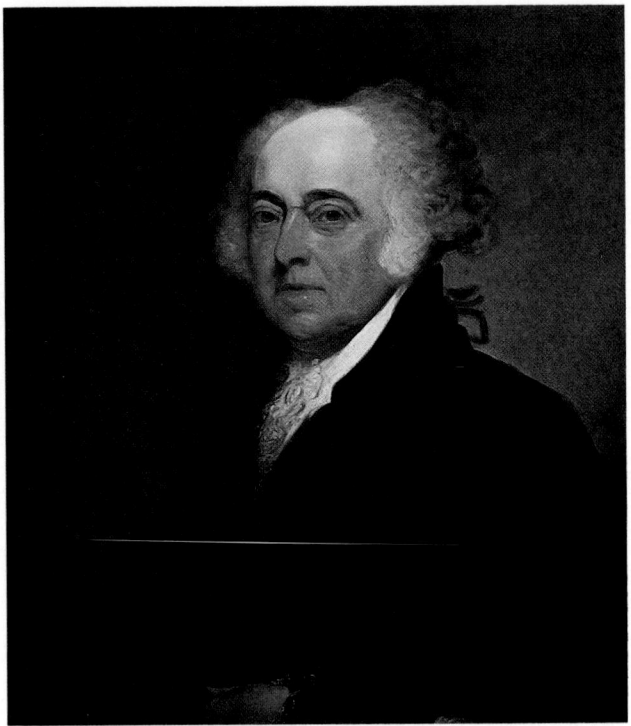

John Adams

2nd president, 1797-1801   Federalist

1735. Born on October 30 in Braintree (now Quincy), MA.
1755. Graduated from Harvard College.
1758. Began law practice in Braintree.
1764. Married Abigail Smith on October 25. Five children would be born to the couple.
1765. Wrote resolutions opposing the British Stamp Act.
1775. As a delegate to the Second Continental Congress, argued for independence and the formation of a Continental Army.
1776. Headed Continental Board of War and Ordnance; served on committee drafting Declaration of Independence.
1779. Drafted most of the Massachusetts state constitution.
1780. In France and the Netherlands, negotiated treaties and a $1,400,000 loan for the United States.
1782. Helped negotiate peace treaty with Britain (the Treaty of Paris, signed Sept. 3, 1783).
1785-1788. Was U.S. minister to Britain.
1789. Elected as the nation's first vice-president.
1792. Reelected vice-president.
1796. As the Federalist candidate, successfully opposed Thomas Jefferson, the Democratic-Republican candidate, in presidential election. Jefferson became vice-president.
1801. Retired to Braintree.
1826. Died on July 4 in Braintree.

Highlights of Presidency

1797. XYZ Affair, in which French agents demanded a bribe to conclude favorable treaty negotiations, brought the United States to the brink of war with France. (Peace was secured by the Convention of 1800.)
1798. Alien and Sedition Acts, giving the president power to imprison or banish foreigners and making criticism of the government a crime, were adopted. The laws, supported by the Federalists, were highly unpopular.
1800. U.S. capital moved from Philadelphia to Washington, D.C. □ In the presidential election, Adams and the Federalists were defeated by the Democratic-Republican candidates, Thomas Jefferson and Aaron Burr.

Thomas Jefferson

3rd president, 1801-09   Democratic-Republican

1743. Born on April 13 at Shadwell, VA.
1762. Graduated from the College of William and Mary.
1767. Admitted to the bar; began practicing law.
1769. Elected to the Virginia House of Burgesses.
1772. Married Martha Wayles Skelton on January 1. The couple would have a son and five daughters, but only two daughters would live to maturity.
1775. Elected a delegate to the First Continental Congress.
1776. As a delegate to the Second Continental Congress, chosen to write the Declaration of Independence.
1776-79. A member of the Virginia House of Delegates, supported proposals on land reform and religious freedom.
1779-81. Served as governor of Virginia.
1783-84. As delegate to Congress from Virginia, helped establish the nation's coinage system.
1785-89. Served as minister to France.
1790-93. Was secretary of state under George Washington.
1796. Accepted Democratic-Republican nomination for president but was narrowly defeated by John Adams and thus became vice-president.
1800. In the presidential election, defeated Adams but tied with his running mate, Aaron Burr. The election went to the House of Representatives, which chose Jefferson on Feb. 17, 1801.
1809. Retired to his Virginia estate, Monticello.
1819. Founded the University of Virginia.
1826. Died on July 4 at Monticello.

Highlights of Presidency

1803. Supreme Court ruling in *Marbury v. Madison* established the principle that the court could declare unconstitutional a law passed by Congress. □ The Louisiana Territory was purchased from France.
1804. Elected to a second term as president. □ Meriwether Lewis and William Clark began to explore the Northwest.
1805. A peace treaty was signed with Tripoli, ending a four-year war.
1808. The importation of African slaves into the United States became illegal.
1809. The 1807 Embargo Act, prohibiting exports and sailings to foreign ports, was replaced by a law banning trade with Britain and France.

James Madison

4th president, 1809-17   Democratic-Republican

1751. Born on March 16 at Port Conway, VA.
1771. Graduated from the College of New Jersey (now Princeton University).
1776. Served on the committee that drafted Virginia's constitution and declaration of rights.
1777. Elected to Virginia governor's council, where he served under Patrick Henry and Thomas Jefferson.
1780. Elected to Congress as a delegate from Virginia.
1784. Returned to Virginia, where he served in the legislature.
1787. As a delegate to the Constitutional Convention, argued for a strong central government and a system of checks and balances. Also contributed to *The Federalist* papers.
1788. Debated for and won Virginian ratification of the U.S. Constitution.
1789-97. Served in the House of Representatives.
1794. Married Dolley Payne Todd on September 15.
1798. Wrote the Virginia Resolutions, defending states' rights and opposing the Alien and Sedition Acts.
1801-09. Was secretary of state under Thomas Jefferson.
1808. Elected president over Federalist candidate C. C. Pinckney.
1817. Retired to his Virginia estate, Montpelier.
1826. Succeeded Jefferson as rector of the University of Virginia.
1836. Died on June 28 at Montpelier.

Highlights of Presidency

1810. Congress ended a ban on trade with Britain and France, who continued to be at war.
1811. Trade with Britain was ended again, after Britain continued to enforce its blockade of France by attacking U.S. ships. □ Indian forces allied under Chief Tecumseh were defeated in the Battle of Tippecanoe on November 7.
1812. Citing continued attacks on its ships, the United States declared war on Britain in June. □ Reelected to a second term.
1814. Treaty of Ghent, ending the War of 1812, was signed on December 24. British troops earlier had burned the White House.
1815. Began a wide-ranging domestic program that included reorganization of the National Bank and development of roads and canals.

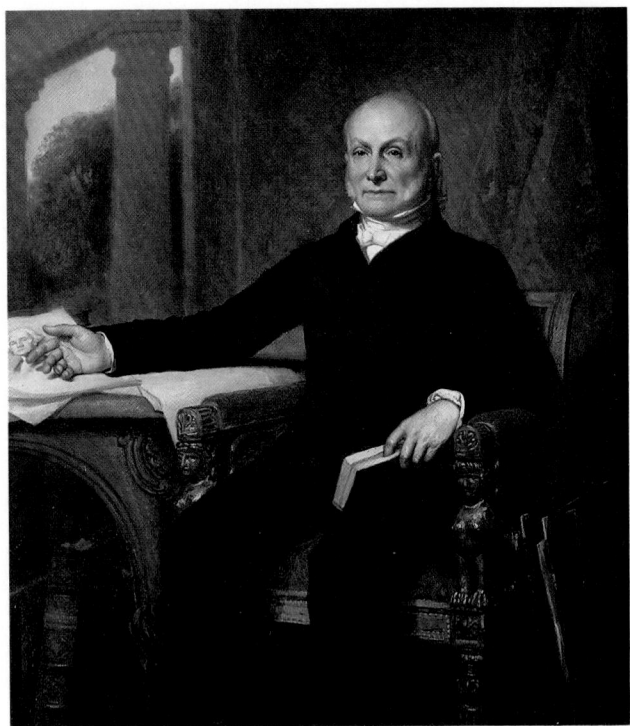

James Monroe

5th president, 1817-25   Democratic-Republican

1758. Born on April 28 in Westmoreland county, VA.
1774. Entered the College of William and Mary.
1776. Left school to join the Virginia Militia, enrolling as a lieutenant. Fought at White Plains and Trenton.
1782. Elected to the Virginia House of Delegates.
1783. Elected to Congress of the Confederation.
1786. Married Elizabeth Kortright of New York City on Febraury 16, and returned to Virginia to practice law. The couple would have two daughters, Eliza and Maria, and a son who died in infancy.
1790. Elected to the U.S. Senate, where he opposed greater centralization of government.
1794. Named minister to France by President Washington. His pro-France sympathies led to his recall in 1796.
1799. Elected governor of Virginia.
1803. Sent by President Jefferson to France, to negotiate the Louisiana Purchase. Subsequently named minister to Britain.
1808. Defeated by James Madison in bid for the Democratic-Republican presidential nomination.
1811. Appointed secretary of state by President Madison. His attempts to avert war with Britain were unsuccessful.
1814. Replaced John Armstrong as secretary of war following the British burning of Washington.
1816. Elected president by a wide margin.
1825. Retired to Oak Hill, near Leesburg, VA.
1829. Presided over the Virginia Constitutional Convention.
1830. Moved to New York to live with his daughter.
1831. Died on July 4 in New York City.

Highlights of Presidency

1818. The Convention of 1818 fixed the boundary between the United States and British North America.
1819. Spain agreed to give Florida to the United States in exchange for the cancellation of $5 million in debts.
1820. Congress adopted the Missouri Compromise, temporarily quieting sectional disputes over the expansion of slavery. □ Won election to a second term in a nearly unanimous vote.
1822. Vetoed a plan for the federal government to improve internal roads.
1823. On December 2, proclaimed the Monroe Doctrine, warning European powers not to interfere in U.S. affairs.

John Quincy Adams

6th president, 1825-29   Democratic-Republican

1767. Born on July 11 in Braintree (now Quincy), MA, the second child and eldest son of John and Abigail Adams.
1787. Graduated from Harvard College.
1790. Began law practice in Boston.
1791. Wrote the first of three series of articles supporting President Washington's policy of neutrality.
1797. On July 26, married Louisa Catherine Johnson. The couple would have four children.
1797-1801. Served as U.S. minister to Prussia.
1803. Elected to the U.S. Senate as a Federalist; however, his independent policies led the party to replace him before the end of his term.
1809-14. Was minister to Russia.
1814. Served on commission negotiating the Treaty of Ghent, ending the War of 1812.
1815-17. Was minister to Britain.
1817. Appointed secretary of state under James Monroe.
1824. Ran for president, opposed by Henry Clay, William Crawford, and Andrew Jackson (all Democratic-Republicans). Jackson received the most votes, but as none of the four had a majority, the election went to the House of Representatives. In the House, Clay, who had won the fewest electoral votes and was thus out of the running, threw his support to Adams and ensured his election in Febraury 1825.
1829. Returned to Quincy after four years as president.
1830. Elected to the House of Representatives, where he would serve for 17 years. As a Congressman, argued for government's right to free slaves and against the annexation of Texas.
1848. Died on February 23 in the Capitol.

Highlights of Presidency

1825. Divisions in the Democratic-Republican Party increased when Adams appointed Henry Clay secretary of state, leading to charges that the two men had made a bargain in the election of 1824. □ Opposition in Congress prevented Adams from enacting most of his domestic program. □ Erie Canal, linking New York City and the Great Lakes, was completed.
1828. Congress imposed stiff duties on imported manufactured goods. □ Soundly defeated by Andrew Jackson in bid for reelection.

Andrew Jackson

7th president, 1829-37   Democrat

1767. Born on March 15 in Waxhaw settlement, SC.
1780. Joined South Carolina militia; captured by the British in 1781.
1787. Admitted to the bar, after reading law in North Carolina.
1791. In August, married Rachel Donelson Robards. The couple remarried on Jan. 17, 1794, on learning that Mrs. Jackson's divorce from her first husband was not final until 1793. They had no children.
1796. After being a member of the Tennessee constitutional convention, was elected to the House of Representatives.
1797. Won a U.S. Senate seat; resigned a year later.
1798-1804. Served on the superior court of Tennessee.
1806. Killed Charles Dickinson, a Nashville lawyer, in a duel sparked by remarks he made about Mrs. Jackson.
1812. Mobilized a force of 2,500 for the War of 1812.
1815. Defeated the British in the Battle of New Orleans.
1817. Successfully led an expedition into Florida, to stop Seminole raids on U.S. territory.
1821. Named provisional governor of Florida.
1823-25. Served in the U.S. Senate.
1824. Opposed John Quincy Adams, Henry Clay, and William Crawford in the presidential election. Although Jackson won the most votes, no candidate had a majority, and the House chose Adams.
1828. Won a sweeping victory in the presidential race.
1837. Retired to the Hermitage, his estate near Nashville.
1845. Died on June 8 at the Hermitage.

Highlights of Presidency

1829. Among his first acts as president were to place some 2,000 of his supporters in government jobs and establish a "kitchen cabinet" of informal advisers.
1832. Won a second term. □ On December 10, federal troops were sent to South Carolina over the state's attempt to nullify federal tariff laws.
1833. Removed government funds from the Bank of the United States after vetoing a new charter for the bank in 1832.
1835. Final installment of national debt was paid, making Jackson the only president to clear the debt.
1836. On July 11, issued the Specie Circular, ordering that federal lands be purchased only in gold and silver.

Martin Van Buren

8th president, 1837-41   Democrat

1782. Born on December 5 in Kinderhook, NY.
1800. Named a delegate to the New York congressional caucus.
1803. Began law practice in Kinderhook.
1807. Married Hannah Hoes on February 21. The couple would have four sons.
1813-20. Was a member of the New York state Senate; also served as state attorney general (1816-19).
1821-28. As a U.S. senator, opposed international alliances and the extension of the slave trade.
1828. Elected governor of New York but resigned after two months to become secretary of state under Andrew Jackson.
1829-31. As secretary of state, settled a dispute with Britain over West Indies trade and obtained an agreement whereby France would pay claims for U.S. ships damaged in the Napoleonic wars.
1831. Resigned as secretary of state, bringing about the resignation of the rest of the cabinet and allowing Jackson to reorganize it.
1832. Elected vice-president as Jackson's running mate.
1836. Elected president with a wide electoral majority.
1841. Returned to his farm near Kinderhook, which he named Lindenwald.
1848. Nominated for president by the antislavery Free Soil Party, which had split from the Democrats. The party split opened the way for the election of the Whig candidate, Zachary Taylor.
1862. Died on July 24 at Kinderhook.

Highlights of Presidency

1837. On May 10, banks closed in Philadelphia and New York City, marking the start of the Panic of 1837. The panic, touched off by inflation and land speculation, was followed by an economic depression that lasted the rest of Van Buren's term.
1839. A boundary dispute between Maine and New Brunswick brought the United States to the brink of war with Britain.
1840. At Van Buren's urging, Congress established an independent treasury to hold federal funds. An attempt to safeguard funds from private bank failures, the treasury was abolished in 1841 but reinstated in 1846. □ Defeated by William Henry Harrison in the November presidential election.

William Henry Harrison

9th president, 1841   Whig

1773. Born on February 8 in Charles City county, VA.
1790. Left college to study medicine.
1791. Abandoned his studies to enlist in the army, serving in the Northwest Territory.
1795. Married Anna Symmes in November. The couple subsequently had ten children, only four of whom survived their father.
1798. After resigning from the army, appointed secretary of the Northwest Territory in June. Was elected the first delegate to Congress from the Northwest Territory in 1799.
1800. Following the division of the Northwest Territories into Ohio and Indiana, appointed governor of Indiana.
1809. As governor, negotiated the Treaty of Fort Wayne, which secured approximately 3 million acres (1.2 million ha) of land from four Indian tribes.
1811. In the Battle of Tippecanoe on November 7, defeated a federation of Indian tribes under the Shawnee chief Tecumseh, that was protesting the Treaty of Fort Wayne.
1812. Placed in command of the Army of the Northwest during the War of 1812.
1813. In October, won a major victory over combined British and Indian forces in the Battle of the Thames, in southern Ontario.
1814. Resigned from the army.
1816. Elected to the U.S. House of Representatives.
1819. Elected to the Ohio state Senate.
1825. Elected to the U.S. Senate.
1828. Resigned his Senate seat to become minister to Colombia. However, his outspoken views on democracy offended President Simón Bolívar, and he was recalled a month after his arrival there.
1836. Defeated for the presidency by Martin Van Buren.
1840. With John Tyler as his running mate, campaigned successfully for the presidency on the slogan "Tippecanoe and Tyler too."

Highlights of Presidency

1841. Inaugurated on March 4 as 9th president, delivering the longest inaugural address on record, in which he promised not to run for a second term. Having contracted pneumonia in late March, died at the White House on April 4.

John Tyler

10th president, 1841-45   Whig

1790. Born on March 29 in Charles City county, VA.
1807. Graduated from William and Mary College.
1809. Admitted to the bar.
1811. Elected to the Virginia House of Delegates.
1813. Married Letitia Christian on March 29. The couple would have eight children.
1816-21. Served in the U.S. House of Representatives.
1823. Elected again to the Virginia House of Delegates.
1825. Elected governor of Virginia.
1827. Elected to the U.S. Senate. His stand in favor of states rights eventually led him to break with the Democrats and ally himself with the Whigs.
1836. Resigned his Senate seat rather than follow the instructions of the Virginia legislature to expunge a vote of censure against Andrew Jackson. As a Whig, lost bid for the vice-presidency to Richard M. Johnson.
1840. Elected vice-president.
1841. Succeeded to the presidency following the death of William Henry Harrison.
1844. Two years after the death of his first wife, married Julia Gardiner on June 22. The couple subsequently had seven children.
1845. Retired to Sherwood Forest, his estate near Charles City, after one term as president.
1861. In February, chaired a peace convention attempting to avert the Civil War. □ At a Virginia convention, voted in favor of secession.
1862. Died on January 18 in Richmond, VA, before taking his seat in the Confederate House.

Highlights of Presidency

1841. Vetoed banking bills supported by the Whigs, prompting the resignation of his cabinet. Tyler quickly named a new cabinet, but the Whig Party disowned him.
1842. Seminole War in Florida ended; boundary dispute between Maine and New Brunswick settled.
1843. In January, the Whigs introduced impeachment resolutions in the House, but the measures were defeated.
1844. A treaty with China opened the Far East to U.S. traders.
1845. Among his last acts in office, signed bills permitting Texas and Florida to be admitted to the Union.

James Knox Polk

11th president, 1845-49   Democrat

1795. Born on November 2 in Mecklenburg county, NC, the eldest of ten children.

1806. Moved with his family to the Duck River valley in central Tennessee.

1818. Graduated from the University of North Carolina.

1820. Admitted to the bar and began practicing law in Columbia, TN.

1821. Became chief clerk of the Tennessee Senate.

1823. Elected to the Tennessee House of Representatives.

1824. Married Sarah Childress on January 1. There were no children from the marriage.

1825. Elected to the first of seven consecutive terms in the U.S. House of Representatives, where he quickly became known as a strong supporter of Andrew Jackson.

1832. As chairman of the House Ways and Means Committee, supported President Jackson's efforts to abolish the national bank.

1835. Became speaker of the House.

1839. Resigned his House seat to run for governor of Tennessee, winning by a slim margin.

1840. Sought the Democratic vice-presidential nomination but was turned down at the party's national convention.

1841. Defeated for a second term as governor.

1843. Again defeated in a bid for the governorship.

1844. At the Democratic presidential convention, the party split between opponents and supporters of Martin Van Buren. Polk took the nomination on the ninth ballot, the first "dark horse" candidate. He won the election by a slim margin, campaigning on a platform of territorial expansion.

1849. Died in Nashville, TN, on June 15, a few months after leaving the presidency.

Highlights of Presidency

1846. Two key pieces of Polk's domestic program, bills setting new tariffs and reestablishing a federal treasury, were adopted. □ A treaty with Britain settled a dispute over Oregon, giving both nations part of the territory.

1848. A treaty with Mexico ended two-year war and gave the United States control of most of present-day Arizona, California, Colorado, Nevada, New Mexico, Utah, and Wyoming. □ Gold was discovered in California in December.

Zachary Taylor

12th president, 1849-50   Whig

1784. Born on November 24 near Barboursville, VA.

1785. Moved with his family to a plantation near Louisville, KY, where he grew up and was educated by tutors.

1808. Entered the U.S. Army as a first lieutenant.

1810. Married Margaret Mackall Smith on June 21. The couple subsequently had six children, two of whom died in infancy.

1812. As commander of a company under William Henry Harrison, successfully defended Fort Harrison from Indian attack; subsequently brevetted a major.

1814. Led U.S. troops against British and Indian forces at Credit Island in Illinois Territory; outnumbered, he was forced to withdraw after some initial successes.

1829-32. Was Indian superintendent in the Northwest, at Fort Snelling, MN.

1832. Promoted to colonel; fought in the Black Hawk War.

1837-40. Earned the nickname "Old Rough and Ready" while fighting the Seminole Indians in Florida.

1841. Named commander of the second department of the army's western division, with headquarters at Fort Smith, AR.

1846. Advanced with a small army to the Rio Grande, in anticipation of conflict with Mexico. After war began, defeated Mexican forces at two battles, at Palo Alto and Resaca de la Palma, forcing their retreat across the Rio Grande. Later launched an attack against Monterrey, capturing the city after a prolonged fight.

1847. Leading a force mostly of volunteers, defeated a much larger Mexican force under Santa Anna at the Battle of Buena Vista, February 22-23; the battle secured U.S. victory in the war and made Taylor a national hero.

1848. Elected president as the Whig Party candidate, defeating Lewis Cass of the Democratic Party and Martin Van Buren, who ran on the Free Soil ticket.

1850. Died in the White House on July 9.

Highlights of Presidency

1849. Sectional debates over the extension of slavery occupied Congress, with Taylor supporting the admission of California without conditions.

1850. The United States and Britain signed the Clayton-Bulwer Treaty guaranteeing the neutrality of a future canal across Central America.

Millard Fillmore

13th president, 1850-53   Whig

1800. Born on January 7 in Cayuga county, NY.
1814. Apprenticed to a firm of clothmakers.
1823. Began to practice law in East Aurora, NY.
1826. Married Abigail Powers, a teacher, on February 5. The couple would have two children.
1828. Elected to the New York state House of Representatives on an Anti-Masonic platform. Was reelected twice.
1830. Moved to Buffalo, and began a law practice.
1832. Elected to the House of Representatives, again on the Anti-Masonic ticket.
1836. Reelected to the House as a Whig. Kept House seat until 1843.
1840. Became chairman of the Ways and Means Committee. He used that position to guide new protectionist tariff laws through Congress.
1844. Lost bid for the governorship of New York.
1846. Became the first chancellor of the University of Buffalo.
1847. Elected New York state comptroller.
1848. Elected vice-president, on the Whig ticket with Zachary Taylor.
1850. Zachary Taylor died in office on July 9. Took presidential oath the following day.
1853. Resumed his law practice in Buffalo.
1856. Nominated for president by the Whig Party and the American (Know-Nothing) Party. Ran third in the election, which James Buchanan won.
1858. Five years after the death of his first wife, married Caroline Carmichael McIntosh on February 10.
1874. Died on March 8 in Buffalo.

Highlights of Presidency

1850. In September, Congress passed the Compromise of 1850, which delayed conflict over slavery by admitting California as a free state, organizing the territories of Utah and New Mexico without reference to slavery, abolishing slavery in the District of Columbia, and establishing a stronger fugitive slave law.
1852. Authorized a mission to Japan by Commodore Matthew C. Perry. □ Rejected in his bid for nomination for a full term by Northern antislavery Whigs, who favored Gen. Winfield Scott.

Franklin Pierce

14th president, 1853-57   Democrat

1804. Born on November 23 in Hillsborough Lower Village, NH.
1824. Graduated from Bowdoin College.
1827. Admitted to the New Hampshire bar.
1829. Elected to the New Hampshire state legislature.
1833. Elected to the U.S. House of Representatives, where he became known as a supporter of Andrew Jackson.
1834. Married Jane Means Appleton in November. The couple later had three sons, all of whom died young.
1837. Elected to the U.S. Senate.
1842. Resigned his Senate seat under pressure from his wife, a temperance advocate. Returned to Concord to practice law and conduct a temperance drive.
1845. Appointed federal district attorney for New Hampshire.
1847. After enlisting to serve in the Mexican War, promoted to colonel and then brigadier general. Led an army to join Winfield Scott in attacking Mexico City and was wounded at Churubusco.
1852. After being nominated by the Democrats on the 49th ballot, defeated Whig candidate Winfield Scott for the presidency.
1853. En route to Washington, the Pierces' only surviving child, Benjamin, was killed in a train accident.
1857. After leaving office, traveled widely.
1860. Settled permanently in Concord.
1869. Died on October 8 in Concord.

Highlights of Presidency

1853. The Gadsden Purchase settled boundary disputes with Mexico and gave the United States a southern railway route to the Pacific.
1854. The Kansas Nebraska Act, endorsed by Pierce despite misgivings, was adopted. The law touched off rivalry between pro- and anti-slavery settlers that eventually led to fighting. □ The Ostend Manifesto, a document detailing a plan to buy Cuba from Spain, caused a furor when it was leaked to the press.
1856. Ordered federal troops into Kansas in an effort to end the fighting there. □ The Democrats, concerned about Pierce's connection with the Kansas issue, nominated James Buchanan for the presidency.

James Buchanan

15th president, 1857-61   Democrat

1791. Born on April 23 near Mercersburg, PA.
1809. Graduated from Dickinson College in Carlisle, PA.
1813. Admitted to the Pennsylvania bar and founded a law practice.
1814. After brief service in the War of 1812, elected as a Federalist to the Pennsylvania state assembly.
1819. Became engaged to Ann Caroline Coleman, but the engagement was broken when her parents disapproved. She died a week later, and Buchanan never married.
1820. Elected to Congress, where he served five terms.
1831. Appointed minister to Russia.
1834. Elected to the Senate from Pennsylvania. Served there until 1845, chairing the Foreign Relations Committee.
1845. Named secretary of state by President Polk.
1852. Supporters of Buchanan and Stephen A. Douglas split the Democratic Party, giving the presidential nomination and the election to Franklin Pierce.
1853. Appointed by Pierce to be minister to Britain.
1856. Running on a "Save the Union" platform as the Democratic presidential candidate, defeated Republican John C. Frémont and Whig Millard Fillmore.
1861. Returned to Wheatland, his estate near Lancaster, PA, where he remained a supporter of the Union.
1866. Published an account of his administration.
1868. Died on June 1 at Wheatland.

Highlights of Presidency

1857. Endorsing the concept of popular sovereignty, recommended that Congress approve a pro-slavery Kansas constitution. (Kansas antislavery forces had boycotted a vote on the measure.) The constitution was rejected, and the debate on it cost Buchanan Northern support.
1858. Northern candidates opposing Buchanan won a majority in both houses of Congress.
1859. John Brown was seized at Harpers Ferry and hanged for his attempt to start a slave revolt.
1860. Did not run for reelection but supported his vice-president, John C. Breckinridge, who was defeated in the November election by Abraham Lincoln.
1861. Seven Southern states formed the Confederacy on February 4.

Abraham Lincoln

16th president, 1861-65   Republican

1809. Born on February 12 in a log cabin in Hardin county, KY.
1832. Living in New Salem, IL, worked odd jobs. Served 80 days in Illinois militia during Black Hawk War. Lost election to Illinois House of Representatives.
1834. Elected to first of four consecutive two-year terms to Illinois House; aligned with Whigs.
1837. Became partner in Springfield, IL, law practice.
1842. Married Mary Todd Lincoln on November 4. The couple would have four sons.
1847-49. Served one two-year term in the U.S. House of Representatives, then resumed law practice in Springfield.
1858. Running as a Republican, lost election to U.S. Senate. Debates with opponent Stephen A. Douglas gained national attention.
1860. Elected president on the Republican ticket.
1865. Shot by actor John Wilkes Booth at Ford's Theater in Washington, DC, on April 14. Died early the next morning.

Highlights of Presidency

1861. On April 12, Confederate forces attacked Fort Sumter in Charleston, SC, setting off the Civil War. Lincoln moved quickly to mobilize the Union by executive order.
1862. Five days after the Battle of Antietam, Lincoln announced on September 22 that all slaves in states still in rebellion would be freed in 100 days.
1863. On January 1, formally issued Emancipation Proclamation. □ In the Battle of Gettysburg in southern Pennsylvania in July, Union forces led by Gen. George C. Meade turned back Gen. Robert E. Lee and the Confederate army. Lee retreated to Virginia, marking a major turning point in the war. □ At the dedication of the Soldiers' National Cemetery, Lincoln delivered the Gettysburg Address on November 19.
1864. The advancing Union army of Gen. William T. Sherman captured Atlanta on September 2. Sherman continued his "March to the Sea," taking Savannah in December. □ In November, Lincoln was elected to a second term, defeating Gen. George B. McClellan.
1865. On April 9, General Lee and Gen. Ulysses S. Grant signed terms of Confederate surrender at Appomattox, VA.

Andrew Johnson

17th president, 1865-69   Republican

1808. Born on December 29 in Raleigh, NC.
1827. Married Eliza McCardle on May 17. The Johnsons would have five children.
1835. Elected to the Tennessee state legislature for the first of three terms. Defeated in 1837 but elected in 1839 and 1841.
1843-53. Represented Tennessee's first district in the U.S. House of Representatives.
1853. Narrowly defeated the Whig candidate to become governor of Tennessee. Served two two-year terms.
1857-62. As a U.S. senator, he supported the Union.
1862-65. Was military governor of occupied Tennessee.
1864. Running with Abraham Lincoln on the National Union (Republican) ticket, the former Democrat was elected vice-president.
1865. Sworn in as president on April 15 following the assassination of President Lincoln.
1874. Five years after leaving the White House, and after several bids for office, elected again to U.S. Senate.
1875. Died on July 31 near Carter Station, TN.

Highlights of Presidency

1865. On March 29, issued Amnesty Proclamation, pardoning all Confederates except those with property in excess of $20,000 and certain Confederate leaders. □ The 13th amendment, abolishing slavery, was proclaimed.
1866. Was engaged in an ongoing dispute with Congress over Reconstruction and the power of the president in Southern states.
1867. Over Johnson's continual vetoes, Congress passed its own series of Reconstruction laws, enforcing Negro suffrage and making ratification of the 14th amendment (granting citizenship to all persons born or naturalized in the United States) a condition for readmission to the Union. □ On March 30, the United States signed a treaty with Russia for the purchase of Alaska for $7,200,000.
1868. Ignoring the 1867 Tenure of Office Act, Johnson ordered the removal of Edwin M. Stanton as secretary of war in March. He later became the only president ever to be impeached by the House, but was acquitted in the Senate on May 26 by a one-vote margin. □ The 14th amendment was proclaimed on July 28.

Ulysses Simpson Grant

18th president, 1869-77   Republican

1822. Born on April 27 in Point Pleasant, OH.
1843. Graduated from West Point.
1846-48. Fought in Mexican War under Generals Zachary Taylor and Winfield Scott. Distinguished himself for bravery and was promoted to 1st lieutenant.
1848. Married Julia Dent on August 22. The couple would become the parents of four children.
1854. Resigned army commission and took up farming in Missouri.
1861. After outbreak of Civil War, named colonel of 21st Illinois Volunteers, then brigadier general.
1862. Tooks Forts Henry and Donelson, the first major Union victories in the war. Defeated at Shiloh.
1863. Forced Confederate surrender at Vicksburg, another major Union victory. Also won Battle of Chattanooga.
1864. Appointed lieutenant general and given command of all U.S. armies.
1865. Accepted surrender of Gen. Robert E. Lee at Appomattox.
1868. Elected president on the Republican ticket.
1885. Shortly after completing his two-volume *Personal Memoirs,* died of cancer at Mount McGregor, NY, on July 23.

Highlights of Presidency

1869. The first transcontinental railroad was completed.
1870. Ratification of 15th amendment, granting citizens the right to vote regardless of race, was proclaimed on March 30.
1872. Amnesty Act, restoring civil rights to citizens of the South, was enacted. □ Despite charges of widespread corruption in his administration, Grant won reelection, defeating Horace Greeley.
1873. Widespread bank failures set off panic. Depression lasted five years.
1875. Signed Specie Resumption Act, a "hard money" measure designed to contract the amount of paper currency in circulation. □ Civil Rights Act, giving equal rights to blacks in public accommodations and jury duty, was passed.
1876. Hayes nominated for president by Republican Party, making Grant a "lame duck." □ Col. George Custer and his 7th Cavalry massacred at Little Big Horn, MT.

Rutherford Birchard Hayes

19th president, 1877-81   Republican

1822. Born on October 4 in Delaware, OH.
1842. Earned B.A. degree from Kenyon College in Gambier, OH.
1845. Graduated from Harvard Law School, admitted to the Ohio bar and began practice of law.
1852. Married Lucy Ware Webb on December 30. The couple would have seven sons and one daughter.
1856. Helped found Ohio Republican Party.
1858. Elected city solicitor of Cincinnati; served four years.
1861. At the outbreak of the Civil War, appointed major in 23rd Ohio Volunteer Infantry. Wounded several times in combat and eventually rose to major general.
1864. Still in service, nominated and elected to U.S. House of Representatives, representing Ohio's second district. Won reelection in 1866. Supported Radical Reconstruction and impeachment of President Andrew Johnson.
1867. Nominated for governor of Ohio, resigned from Congress, and won election. Reelected in 1869. As governor, worked for social reforms.
1872. Ran for Congress and lost. Returned to private life.
1875. At urging of Ohio Republicans, ran for governor on a "sound money" platform. Election victory made him a national figure.
1876. Won Republican presidential nomination on the seventh ballot. In the most controversial presidential election in U.S. history, appeared to lose to Samuel J. Tilden. The outcome was disputed, and a special electoral commission was appointed. On March 2, 1877, it declared Hayes the winner.
1893. Died at Spiegel Grove, the family estate in Fremont, OH, on January 17.

Highlights of Presidency

1877. Within two months of taking office, withdrew federal troops from the South—ending the era of Reconstruction—and appointed a former Confederate, David M. Key, to be postmaster general. □ Called out federal troops to quell violent, widespread railroad strikes.
1878. Favoring a "hard-money" policy (specie backing of paper currency), vetoed Bland-Allison Silver Purchase Bill; Congress overrode veto.
1880. Kept pledge to serve only one term.

James Abram Garfield

20th president, 1881   Republican

1831. Born on November 19 near Cleveland, OH.
1848. Struck out on own and worked on a canal boat. Six weeks later, returned home seriously ill. Decided to get an education.
1851. Entered Western Reserve Eclectic Institute (later Hiram College). Studied and taught for three years.
1856. Graduated from Williams College. Returned to Hiram College, where he taught ancient languages and literature for five years, served as principal, and became a lay preacher for the Disciples of Christ.
1858. Married Lucretia Rudolph on November 11. Seven children would be born to the Garfields.
1859. Admitted to the Ohio bar. □ Elected to the state Senate.
1861. Volunteered for Union army after outbreak of Civil War. Made colonel of 42nd Ohio Volunteer Infantry. Appointed major general for gallantry at Battle of Chickamauga.
1862. While still in the service, elected to U.S. House of Representatives as a radical Republican.
1863. Resigned military commission to take seat in Congress. A member of the House until 1880, he supported Lincoln policies and Radical Reconstruction. Favored specie payment as opposed to paper money. Served as Republican minority leader from 1876.
1876. Was a member of electoral commission for disputed Hayes-Tilden presidential election, voted consistently for Hayes on a strict party line.
1880. Elected to U.S. Senate in January. At the Republican National Convention in May, nominated for president as compromise choice on 36th ballot. Chester A. Arthur chosen as running mate to placate disgruntled "Stalwart" faction. Despite party split, won narrow victory over Democrat Winfield S. Hancock in November election.
1881. Died on September 19 at Elberon, NJ, eleven weeks after taking an assassin's bullet.

Highlights of Presidency

1881. Inaugurated on March 4 as 20th president of the United States, age 49. □ Shot on July 12 while entering a Washington railroad station by Charles J. Guiteau, a disappointed office-seeker in the new administration. Guiteau shouted: "I am a 'Stalwart' and Arthur is president now."

Chester Alan Arthur

21st president, 1881-85   Republican

1829. Born on October 5 in Fairfield, VT.
1848. Graduated from Union College in Schenectady, NY. Took up private law studies and teaching.
1854. Admitted to the bar after receiving training in a New York city law office.
1856. Formed law firm in New York City. Gradually became known as a leading New York attorney.
1859. Married Ellen Lewis Herndon on October 25. The Arthurs would become the parents of three children.
1861. After outbreak of Civil War, became inspector general and quartermaster of New York, responsible for furnishing supplies to large numbers of troops.
1863. Returned to private law practice.
1871. Appointed by President Ulysses Grant as collector for the Port of New York.
1878. After a year-long federal investigation of the New York Customs House for political patronage and mismanagement, Arthur was removed from the position of collector by President Rutherford B. Hayes. The action created a rift in the Republican Party.
1880. As a member of the party's "Stalwart" faction, supported Grant at Republican National Convention in May. When the convention settled on James Garfield as a compromise candidate, Arthur was nominated as vice-president to placate "Stalwarts." Garfield-Arthur ticket narrowly won November election.
1881. On September 20, took oath as 21st president, one day after the death of President Garfield.
1886. Died in New York City on November 18.

Highlights of Presidency

1882. Vetoed the Chinese Exclusion Bill as well as a "pork barrel" appropriation for river and harbor improvement. Was overridden by Congress on both measures.
1883. The Pendleton Civil Service Act, a major reform of federal civil service, was signed into law on January 16. Tariff reform legislation and the Edmunds Anti-Polygamy Bill, aimed at the Mormons in Utah, also passed.
1884. With major railroads reaching the Pacific Coast, westward settlement came into full swing. □ Defeated for Republican presidential nomination by James G. Blaine.

Grover Cleveland

22nd and 24th president, 1885-89, 1893-97   Democrat

1837. Born on March 18 in Caldwell, NJ.
1841. Family moved to Fayetteville, NY. Spent his boyhood there and in nearby Clinton.
1853. After father's death, moved to Buffalo, NY. Worked for an uncle and later as a law clerk.
1859. Admitted to the bar and entered law practice.
1863-65. Was assistant district attorney of Erie county, NY.
1871-73. Served as sheriff of Erie county.
1881. Elected mayor of Buffalo.
1882. Backed by reform Democrats, elected governor of New York.
1884. Nominated for president at Democratic National Convention. Narrowly defeated James G. Blaine in November.
1886. Married Frances Folsom in a White House ceremony on June 2. The couple would have five children.
1888. Lost election for second term to Benjamin Harrison, despite garnering a larger popular vote. After leaving office, practiced law in New York City.
1892. Elected a second time to the presidency, defeating Harrison.
1908. Died on July 24 in Princeton, NJ, where he had settled after leaving the White House.

Highlights of Presidency

1886. Dedicated the Statue of Liberty in New York Harbor on October 28.
1887. Interstate Commerce Act, the first major federal program to regulate railroads and private business, was adopted. □ Tenure of Office Act was repealed.
1893. Financial panic began, leading to a four-year depression. □ Sherman Silver Purchase Act of 1890 was repealed.
1894. Jacob S. Coxey led march on Washington of 500 unemployed Midwesterners. "Coxey's Army" demanded unemployment relief. □ In July, President Cleveland called out federal troops to quell Pullman strike rioting in Chicago. To keep U.S. mails moving, trains ran under military guard.
1895. In support of Monroe Doctrine, Cleveland received Congressional authorization to appoint commission to resolve border dispute between Venezuela and British Guiana.
1896. Lost Democratic presidential nomination to William Jennings Bryan.

Benjamin Harrison

23rd president, 1889-93   Republican

1833. Born on August 20 in North Bend, OH, the grandson of
William Henry Harrison, 9th president of the United States.
1852. Graduated from Miami University in Oxford, OH.
1853. Married Caroline Lavinia Scott on October 20. The
couple would have a son and a daughter.
1854. Admitted to the bar and established law practice in
Indianapolis.
1857. Ran successfully for city attorney of Indianapolis.
1860. Elected reporter of Indiana supreme court; reelected
twice.
1862. After the outbreak of the Civil War, raised the 70th
Indiana Volunteer Regiment. By 1865, had risen to rank of
brigadier general.
1876. Lost election for governorship of Indiana.
1877. Became Republican Party leader in Indiana.
1880. Elected to U.S. Senate.
1888. Defeated Grover Cleveland in November presidential race
despite having fewer popular votes.
1896. Married Mary Lord Dimmick on April 6. A daughter,
Elizabeth, was born in 1897. (The first Mrs. Harrison had
died in 1892.)
1897. Published *This Country of Ours,* a series of essays on
how the federal government works.
1899. Acted as senior counsel for Venezuela in dispute with
Great Britain over boundary with British Guiana.
1901. Died on March 13 in Indianapolis.

Highlights of Presidency

1889. The first Pan American Conference, encouraging
cooperation between the United States and Latin America, was
held in Washington.
1890. Four major bills were signed into law: Sherman Antitrust
Act, outlawing trusts and monopolies that hinder trade;
Sherman Silver Purchase Act, increasing amount of silver that
could be coined; McKinley Tariff Act, setting duties at record
high levels; and Dependent Pension Act, benefiting Civil War
veterans. □ Battle of Wounded Knee, last major conflict
between Indians and U.S. troops, was fought on December
29.
1892. Defeated for reelection by Grover Cleveland. Did not
campaign because of wife's illness.

William McKinley

25th president, 1897-1901   Republican

1843. Born on January 29 in Niles, OH.
1860. Studies at Allegheny College in Meadville, PA, cut short
by illness. Taught school briefly.
1861. At outset of Civil War, enlisted as private in 23rd Ohio
Regiment, under Rutherford B. Hayes. Saw considerable
action and left the Army a brevet major.
1865-67. Studied law in an Ohio law office and at Albany
(NY) Law School. Admitted to bar and opened practice in
Canton, OH.
1869. Elected prosecuting attorney of Stark county, OH.
1871. Married Ida Saxton on January 25. Two daughters would
be born to the couple; both died very young.
1877. Entered U.S. Congress as representative of Ohio's
seventeenth district. Served until 1891, except for 1884-85.
1891. Elected governor of Ohio. Served two terms.
1892. Had backing for Republican presidential nomination, but
supported incumbent Benjamin Harrison.
1896. Defeated William Jennings Bryan in November
presidential election.
1901. Died on September 14 in Buffalo, NY, eight days after
being shot at Pan-American Exposition.

Highlights of Presidency

1897. Dingley Tariff passed, raising average duty to a record
57%.
1898. On February 15, the U.S. battleship *Maine* was blown up
in Havana harbor. On April 25, the United States declared war
on Spain. In Battle of Manila Bay on May 1, Adm. George
Dewey led major U.S. victory over Spain.
1899. Treaty of Paris, ending the war, was approved by the
U.S. Senate on February 6. Spain ceded Philippines, Puerto
Rico, and Guam and agreed to independence for Cuba. □ In
May, U.S. troops captured Emilio Aguinaldo, ending revolt in
the Philippines. □ In September, U.S. Secretary of State John
Hay sent notes to major European nations calling for Open
Door trade policy toward China.
1900. U.S. troops joined international force in putting down
Boxer Rebellion in China. □ Gold Standard Act passed,
making the gold dollar the sole standard of currency.
1901. With Theodore Roosevelt as running-mate, reelected for
a second term.

Theodore Roosevelt

26th president, 1901-09   Republican

1858. Born on October 27 in New York City.
1880. Graduated from Harvard University. Married Alice Hathaway Lee on October 27.
1881-84. Served in New York state legislature.
1884. Wife died following birth of daughter, Alice. Mother died the same day. Dropped out of politics and became cattle rancher in Dakota Territory; also wrote history.
1886. Married Edith Kermit Carow on December 2. Four sons and a daughter would be born to the couple.
1887-89. Lived as sportsman and gentleman-scholar at Sagamore Hill, estate at Oyster Bay, NY. Continued career as historian. Most important work, *The Winning of the West,* was published in four volumes, 1889-96. He would write a total of some 40 books.
1889. Appointed to U.S. Civil Service Commission.
1895. Became police commissioner of New York City.
1897. Appointed assistant secretary of the Navy by President William McKinley.
1898. After outbreak of Spanish-American War, organized First U.S. Volunteer Cavalry (Rough Riders). As colonel, led charge up Kettle Hill in battle of San Juan. □ In November, elected governor of New York; as such, sponsored tax reform and fought spoils system.
1900. Elected vice-president.
1901. On September 14, sworn in as 26th president after the assassination of President McKinley.
1912. Left GOP and ran for the presidency on his new Progressive ("Bull Moose") ticket. Shot during campaign, but recovered. Lost election to Democrat Woodrow Wilson.
1919. Died on January 6 at Sagamore Hill.

Highlights of Presidency

1903. Panama signed treaty for a canal under U.S. sovereignty. □ Department of Commerce and Labor was created.
1904. Won election to full term.
1906. Awarded Nobel Peace Prize for arbitrating end of Russo-Japanese War. □ Hepburn Act, authorizing Interstate Commerce Commission to regulate railroad rates, and the Pure Food and Drug Act were enacted.
1907. Financial panic and depression started.
1908. Supported William Howard Taft for the presidency.

William Howard Taft

27th president, 1909-13   Republican

1857. Born on September 15 in Cincinnati, OH.
1878. Graduated from Yale University.
1880. Graduated from Cincinnati Law School and admitted to the Ohio bar.
1881. Became assistant prosecuting attorney of Hamilton county; served two years.
1886. Married Helen Herron on June 19. The Tafts would have three children.
1887. Appointed judge on the Ohio superior court. Elected to his own term the following year.
1890. Named U.S. solicitor-general.
1892. Chosen U.S. Circuit Court judge for the 6th district by President Benjamin Harrison.
1900. Named by President McKinley to head the commission charged with terminating U.S. military rule in Philippines.
1901. Became first civil governor of the Philippines.
1904. Appointed secretary of war by President Roosevelt.
1908. Won race for the presidency.
1913-21. Served as professor of law at Yale University. During World War I, was also joint chairman of the National War Labor Board.
1921. Appointed chief justice of the U.S. Supreme Court by President Warren Harding. Served until Feb. 3, 1930.
1930. Died on March 8 in Washington, DC.

Highlights of Presidency

1909. Payne-Aldrich Act passed, lowering tariffs.
1911. Standard Oil Co. dissolved by Supreme Court under Sherman Antitrust Act. Administration also effected dissolution of tobacco trusts and proceeded with scores of other antitrust suits.
1912. New Mexico and Arizona admitted to the union, the last of the 48 contiguous states. □ President Taft won renomination by Republican Party but lost election to Democrat Woodrow Wilson. "Bull Moose" candidacy of Theodore Roosevelt split the Republican vote.
1913. The 16th amendment, authorizing income taxes, was proclaimed on February 25. The 17th amendment, calling for direct popular election of U.S. senators, went into effect two months after Taft left office. □ Department of Commerce and Labor divided into separate departments.

(Thomas) Woodrow Wilson

28th president, 1913-21   Democrat

1856. Born on December 28 in Staunton, VA.
1879. Earned a A.B. from the College of New Jersey (now Princeton University).
1882. Admitted to the bar, but did not prosper as a lawyer.
1885. Married Ellen Louise Axson in Rome, GA on June 24. Three daughters would be born to the couple.
1886. Awarded a doctor's degree from Johns Hopkins University. His first book, *Congressional Government* (1885), analyzing the U.S. government, was his dissertation.
1890-1902. After teaching at Bryn Mawr College and Wesleyan University, served as a professor at Princeton University.
1902-10. Was president of Princeton University.
1911-13. Served as governor of New Jersey.
1912. Elected president.
1915. Married Edith Bolling Galt on December 18. (The first Mrs. Wilson died on Aug. 6, 1914.)
1919. Suffered a paralytic stroke in Washington, DC.
1924. Died on February 3 in Washington.

Highlights of Presidency

1913. The Federal Reserve Bill became law.
1914. The Clayton Antitrust Bill and the Federal Trade Bill were enacted. □ In April, Wilson ordered the U.S. Navy to occupy Veracruz, Mexico, during a dispute with President Victoriano Huerta. U.S.-Mexican relations remained troubled during Wilson era. □ In August, the president proclaimed neutrality as war broke out in Europe.
1915. More than 100 Americans were killed as a German submarine torpedoed the British liner *Lusitania* on May 7.
1916. Narrowly reelected.
1917. The United States purchased the Virgin Islands from Denmark. □ On April 6, Congress declared war on Germany.
1918. In a speech to Congress on January 8, outlined Fourteen Points as a basis for a peace settlement. □ On November 11, an armistice ending World War I was signed.
1920. For a second time, the U.S. Senate refused to ratify the 1919 Treaty of Versailles with Germany. □ Wilson was awarded the Nobel Peace Prize for 1919 for advocating the establishment of a League of Nations. □ The 19th amendment, giving woman the right to vote, was ratified. The 18th or Prohibition amendment had been proclaimed Jan. 29, 1919.

Warren Gamaliel Harding

29th president, 1921-23   Republican

1865. Born on November 2 in Blooming Grove, OH.
1882. Graduated from Ohio Central College in Iberin.
1884. Bought the Marion *Star*, a small, struggling weekly, and devoted himself to it wholly for some 15 years. The *Star* eventually became one of the most successful small-town newspapers in the state.
1891. Married Florence Kling DeWolfe on July 8.
1898. Elected to the Ohio state Senate; reelected in 1900. Served as floor leader during second term.
1902. Elected lieutenant governor of Ohio.
1910. Ran unsuccessfully for governor.
1912. Delivered nominating address for President Taft at GOP convention. Political fortunes began to rise.
1914. Elected to U.S. Senate.
1920. Won Republican nomination for president and campaigned on "Return to Normalcy" slogan. Easily defeated James M. Cox in November election.
1923. Returning from a trip to Alaska, died in San Francisco on August 2.

Highlights of Presidency

1921. In May, Congress set up a national quota system for immigration. □ In June, the Budget and Accounting Act was signed into law; the Bureau of the Budget was created. □ On July 2, the president signed joint congressional resolution of peace with Germany, Austria, and Hungary. Treaties were signed in August. □ On November 12, the International Conference on Limitation of Armaments opened in Washington. It lasted until Feb. 6, 1922. Major powers agreed to limit naval construction.
1921-22. Ordered federal troops into West Virginia during coal strike of 1921. Sweeping federal injunction issued against Railway Shopmen's Strike of 1922.
1922. Fordney-McCumber Act, raising tariffs on manufactured goods to highest level to date, signed into law.
1923. In June, the president set out on transcontinental "Voyage of Understanding" to promote U.S. participation in the World Court. Took ill on his way back. For months, evidence of corruption in his administration had been coming to light. After his death, several high officials were linked to Teapot Dome and other scandals.

Calvin Coolidge

30th president, 1923-29   Republican

1872. Born on July 4 in Plymouth Notch, VT.
1895. Graduated from Amherst College.
1897. Admitted to the Massachusetts bar.
1898. Elected city councilman of Northampton, MA.
1905. Married Grace Anna Goodhue on October 4. They would become the parents of two sons.
1906. Elected to the Massachusetts House of Representatives. Served two one-year terms.
1909. Elected mayor of Northampton. Reelected in 1910.
1911. Entered state Senate. Won reelection twice. In third term, elected president of Senate.
1915. Ran successfully for lieutenant governor of Massachusetts. Served three years.
1918. Elected governor of Massachusetts. Gained prominence in 1919 by calling out the National Guard in the Boston police strike, declaring, ''There is no right to strike against the public safety by anybody, anywhere, anytime.''
1920. Lost Republican presidential nomination to Warren G. Harding; selected as vice-presidential candidate.
1923. On August 3, sworn in as 30th president after the death of President Harding.
1929. Published *The Autobiography of Calvin Coolidge*.
1933. Died on January 5 in Northampton.

Highlights of Presidency

1924. Pressed for investigations and prosecutions relating to scandals involving members of the Harding administration. □ Was elected president in his own right.
1925. U.S. Marines sent to Nicaragua after outbreak of civil war. In 1927, the president sent Henry Stimson to work out compromise, but Gen. Augusto César Sandino launched guerrilla war that lasted until withdrawal of U.S. troops in 1933.
1926. Vetoed the McNary-Haugen farm bill, which called for dumping of agricultural surpluses. Vetoed the relief measure again in 1928.
1927. Despite strong party support, announced on August 2: ''I do not choose to run for president in 1928.''
1928. Kellogg-Briand Pact, an agreement ''to renounce war as an instrument of national policy,'' was signed in Paris by 15 nations on August 24.

Herbert Clark Hoover

31st president, 1929-33   Republican

1874. Born on August 10 in West Branch, IA.
1895. Graduated from Stanford University.
1897. Began his career as a mining engineer.
1899. Married Lou Henry on February 10. The couple would become the parents of two sons.
1912. Appointed a trustee of Stanford University.
1914-15. Directed the American Relief Committee, organized to aid Americans stranded in Europe as World War I began.
1915-19. Directed the Commission for Relief in Belgium.
1917-19. Served as U.S. food administrator.
1921-28. Was U.S. secretary of commerce.
1928. Defeated New York Gov. Alfred E. Smith in the presidential race.
1942. *The Problems of Lasting Peace,* written by Hoover with Hugh Gibson, was published.
1951-52. Published his memoirs in three volumes.
1955. On June 30, retired after serving as chairman of two Commissions on Organization of the Executive Branch of Government.
1959-61. *An American Epic,* a three-volume study of his experience in international relief work, appeared.
1964. Died on October 20 in New York City.

Highlights of Presidency

1929. After taking oath of office on March 4, the new president called Congress into special session in April. Two months later the Agricultural Marketing Act, designed to assist farmers suffering from low incomes during an era of prosperity, was enacted. □ The New York Stock Market crashed on October 29, beginning a severe economic depression that dominated the Hoover presidency.
1930. The London Naval Conference limited the number of small vessels, battleships, and cruisers various nations could construct. □ On February 3, the president named Charles Evans Hughes chief justice of the Supreme Court.
1932. On January 7, Secretary of State Henry L. Stimson announced the Stimson Doctrine, declaring that the United States would not recognize territorial conquest. □ Also in January, Congress established the Reconstruction Finance Corporation. □ In November, Hoover was defeated in bid for reelection by Franklin D. Roosevelt.

Franklin Delano Roosevelt

32nd president, 1933-45   Democrat

1882. Born on January 30 in Hyde Park, NY.
1904. Earned B.A. degree from Harvard University.
1905. On March 17, married Anna Eleanor Roosevelt, a fifth cousin and a niece of President Theodore Roosevelt. A daughter and five sons would be born to the Roosevelts.
1907. Passed New York State Bar examination, withdrew from Columbia Law School, hired by Wall Street law firm.
1911-13. Was a New York state senator.
1913-20. Served as assistant secretary of the Navy.
1920. Ran unsuccessfully for vice-president on Democratic ticket with James M. Cox. Returned to law practice.
1921. Stricken with polio while vacationing in Campobello, ME. He would never regain the use of his legs.
1928. Elected to first of two terms as governor of New York.
1932. Elected president over incumbent Republican Herbert Hoover.
1945. Died on April 12 at Warm Springs, GA.

Highlights of Presidency

1933. During first 100 days as president, launched New Deal relief measures. Revived the banking industry; delivered the first of 28 "Fireside Chats." □ In December, the 21st amendment, ending Prohibition, was ratified.
1934. Became the first president to visit Latin America.
1935. Social Security Act passed; Works Progress Administration (WPA) was established; Wagner Act, creating National Labor Relations Board (NLRB), was enacted.
1936. Amid economic improvement, reelected in a landslide over Alfred M. Landon. Also reelected in 1940 and 1944.
1937. President's plan to "reform" the Supreme Court was criticized as a "court-packing scheme" and rejected.
1939. Hitler overran Poland, and war was declared in Europe.
1941. Congress enacted Lend-Lease, giving the president power to supply military equipment to U.S. allies. □ On December 7, Japanese launched surprise attack on Pearl Harbor. Congress declared war the next day.
1944. June 6, D-Day: Allied forces landed on the Normandy coast of France.
1945. Yalta Conference held in the Crimea in February. Roosevelt, Britain's Winston Churchill, and USSR's Joseph Stalin discussed the terms of peace and the postwar world.

Harry S. Truman

33d president, 1945-53   Democrat

1884. Born on May 8 in Lamar, MO.
1901. Graduated from high school. Studied at the Kansas City Law School (1923-25).
1906-17. Worked on family farm in Grandview, MO.
1917-18. Served with the American Expeditional Force.
1919. On June 28, married Elizabeth (Bess) Wallace. A daughter, (Mary) Margaret would be born in 1924.
1922. Failed to succeed in clothing business. Elected judge of the Jackson county court. Lost reelection in 1924.
1926-34. Was presiding judge of the Jackson county court.
1934. Won first of two terms to the U.S. Senate.
1941-44. Served as chairman of a special Senate committee on defense.
1944. Running with F. D. Roosevelt, elected vice-president.
1945. On April 12, sworn in as president following the sudden death of President Roosevelt.
1953. Began retirement during which he traveled widely, wrote memoirs, and remained politically active.
1972. Died in Kansas City on December 26.

Highlights of Presidency

1945. On May 7, Germany surrendered ending World War II in Europe. □ On June 26, the UN Charter was signed. □ From July 17 to August 2, Truman attended the Potsdam Conference. □ After atomic bombs were dropped on Hiroshima and Nagasaki, Japan surrendered in September.
1946. Ordered the seizure of nation's railroads in face of a strike threat.
1947. On March 12, outlined the Truman Doctrine—U.S. aid to Greece, Turkey, and other nations "threatened by armed minorities and outside pressure." □ In June, the Marshall Plan (economic and technical assistance for Europe) was announced, and Congress overrode presidential veto of Taft Hartley labor bill.
1948. In a "political upset," won full term.
1949. In January, granted recognition to new state of Israel. □ The North Atlantic Treaty Organization was set up.
1950. U.S. forces entered combat in Korea.
1951. Relieved Gen. Douglas MacArthur of his command in the Far East.
1952. Declined to seek reelection.

Dwight David Eisenhower

34th president, 1953-61   Republican

1890. Born on October 14 in Denison, TX.
1915. Graduated from the U.S. Military Academy.
1916. Married Mary (Mamie) Geneva Doud on July 1. The couple would have two sons; one died in childhood.
1918. Took command of a tank training center in Gettysburg, PA.
1929-33. Served under the assistant secretary of war.
1935-39. Was a senior assistant to Gen. Douglas MacArthur in the Philippines.
1942. With United States fighting in World War II, became commander of the European Theater of Operations.
1943. Appointed supreme commander of the Allied Expeditionary Force.
1944. Directed the landing of allied forces in Normandy.
1945. Succeeded George Marshall as Army chief of staff.
1948. Installed as president of Columbia University.
1950. Became supreme commander of the forces of the North Atlantic Treaty Organization.
1952. Retired from the Army; elected president.
1955. Suffered a heart attack.
1961. Restored to the rank of general of the Army.
1965. The second and final volume of his memoirs was published.
1969. Died on March 28 in Washington.

Highlights of Presidency

1953. The Department of Health, Education, and Welfare was established. □ The Korean War ended. □ Eisenhower nominated Earl Warren as chief justice of the Supreme Court.
1956. After Egypt nationalized the Suez Canal, the president refused to join Britain, France, and Israel in an invasion of Egypt. □ Denounced the USSR for crushing Hungarian uprising. □ Reelected to a second term.
1957. Signed the Eisenhower Doctrine, promising that the United States would resist Communist aggression in the Middle East. □ Sent federal troops to Little Rock, AK, to ensure the integration of Central High School.
1959. The National Aeronautics and Space Administration was formed.
1960. After Soviets downed a U.S. reconnaissance flight, summit conference with Premier Nikita Khrushchev collapsed.

John Fitzgerald Kennedy

35th president, 1961-63   Democrat

1917. Born on May 29 in Brookline, MA.
1935. Studied at the London School of Economics.
1940. Graduated from Harvard University.
1941. Commissioned an ensign in the U.S. Navy.
1944. Received the Navy and Marine Corps Medal for his conduct while commander of a PT boat that was sunk by the Japanese in the Solomon Islands in 1943.
1945. Worked as a newspaper correspondent.
1947-53. Represented Massachusetts' 11th district in the U.S. House of Representatives.
1952. Elected to the U.S. Senate, defeating the Republican incumbent, Henry Cabot Lodge, by more than 70,000 votes.
1953. Married Jacqueline Bouvier on September 12 in Newport, RI. A daughter and a son would be born to the Kennedys. A second son died two days after birth in August 1963.
1956. Defeated in an open contest for the Democratic vice-presidential nomination.
1957. Won a Pulitzer Prize for *Profiles in Courage*.
1958. Reelected to the U.S. Senate.
1960. Defeated Richard M. Nixon for the presidency.
1963. Assassinated on November 22 in Dallas, TX.

Highlights of Presidency

1961. Established the Peace Corps. □ In April, a force of anti-Castro Cubans, trained by the Central Intelligence Agency, staged an unsuccessful attempt to establish a beachhead at the Bay of Pigs, Cuba. □ In August, East Germany constructed a wall separating East and West Berlin.
1962. On February 20, Lt. Col. John H. Glenn, Jr., became the first American to orbit the earth. □ After U.S. aerial reconnaissance revealed that Soviet offensive missiles were being installed in Cuba, the United States established a naval "quarantine" around Cuba in October. The Soviets then withdrew their missiles.
1963. On August 5, the United States, Britain, and the USSR signed a nuclear test-ban agreement, prohibiting atmospheric testing of nuclear weapons. □ On August 28, more than 200,000 persons staged a march in Washington, dramatizing the demands of blacks for equal rights. □ South Vietnam President Ngo Dinh Diem was overthrown on November 1.

Lyndon Baines Johnson

36th president, 1963-69   Democrat

1908. Born on August 27 near Johnson City, TX.
1930. After graduating from Southwest Texas State Teachers College in San Marcos, TX, taught school in Houston.
1931. Became secretary to U.S. Rep. Richard M. Kleberg.
1934. Married Claudia Alta ("Lady Bird") Taylor on November 17. The Johnsons would become the parents of two daughters.
1935-37. Headed the National Youth Administration in Texas.
1937-49. Served in the U.S. House of Representatives.
1941. Defeated in a special election for the U.S. Senate.
1942. After President Roosevelt ordered all congressmen on active military duty to return to Washington, concluded a brief tour of duty with the U.S. Navy.
1948. Elected to the U.S. Senate. Won reelection in 1954.
1955. In January, elected Senate majority leader. □ In July, suffered a major heart attack.
1960. After losing the Democratic presidential nomination to John F. Kennedy, ran successfully in the vice-presidential spot.
1963. Sworn in as 36th president following the assassination of President Kennedy.
1971. The president's memoirs, *The Vantage Point: Perspectives of the Presidency, 1963-1969,* were published.
1973. Died on January 22 near Johnson City, TX.

Highlights of Presidency

1964. Signed an $11.5 billion tax-reduction bill and a major civil-rights bill. □ Proclaimed a war on poverty. □ Elected to a full presidential term.
1965. On February 7, ordered the bombing of targets in North Vietnam and began escalating U.S. troop strength in Indochina. □ In April, ordered U.S. troops into the Dominican Republic to end a rebellion. □ Signed legislation setting up Medicare and the Department of Housing and Urban Development.
1966. The Department of Transportation was formed.
1967. Nominated Thurgood Marshall, a black, as an associate justice of the Supreme Court. □ Met with Soviet Premier Aleksei Kosygin in Glassboro, NJ.
1968. Withdrew from the 1968 presidential race and ordered a reduction in the bombing of North Vietnam.

Richard Milhous Nixon

37th president, 1969-74   Republican

1913. Born on January 9 in Yorba Linda, CA.
1934. Graduated from Whittier College.
1937. Received a law degree from Duke University Law School.
1940. Married Thelma Catherine ("Pat") Ryan on June 21. Two daughters would be born to the Nixons.
1942-45. Served in the U.S. Navy.
1947-51. Was a member of the U.S. House of Representatives.
1948. Participated in the House Committee of Un-American Activities investigation of Algier Hiss.
1950. Won election to the U.S. Senate.
1952. Nominated as Dwight D. Eisenhower's running mate on the Republican presidential ticket. Elected easily.
1955. Performed various presidential duties as President Eisenhower recuperated from a heart attack.
1956. The Eisenhower-Nixon ticket was reelected.
1960. Lost close presidential race to John F. Kennedy.
1962. His first book, *Six Crises,* was published. □ Lost California's gubernatorial contest to the Democratic incumbent, Edmund G. ("Pat") Brown.
1968. Elected president.

Highlights of Presidency

1969. On July 20, Neil A. Armstrong became the first man to walk on the moon.
1970. On April 30, announced that U.S. combat troops were being sent into Cambodia to destroy enemy sanctuaries.
1972. Visited China in February. □ Meeting in Moscow with Soviet General Secretary Leonid Brezhnev in May, signed agreements limiting antiballistic missile (ABM) systems and offensive missile launchers. □ In June, five men were arrested for breaking into the headquarters of the Democratic National Committee. The subsequent investigation of the "Watergate affair" led to the downfall of the Nixon presidency. □ Overwhelmingly reelected.
1973. The Vietnam cease-fire agreement was signed in January. □ On October 10, Spiro T. Agnew resigned as vice-president and pleaded no contest to one count of income tax evasion. The president named Gerald R. Ford as his successor.
1974. Toured Middle East in June. □ Resigned as president, effective at noon on August 9.

Gerald Rudolph Ford

38th president, 1974-77   Republican

1913. Born on July 14 in Omaha, NE.

1935. Graduated from the University of Michigan, where he starred on the football team.

1941. After graduating from Yale Law School, returned to Grand Rapids to practice law. While at Yale, served as assistant football coach and boxing coach.

1942-46. During 47 months in the U.S. Navy, was awarded ten battle stars for service in the South Pacific.

1948. Elected to the U.S. House of Representatives from Michigan's fifth district. Won reelection 12 times. □ Married Elizabeth Bloomer on October 15. Three sons and a daughter were born to the couple.

1963. Elected chairman of the House GOP Conference. □ Named by President Johnson to serve on the Warren Commission, the official investigation into the assassination of President Kennedy.

1965. Successfully challenged Charles A. Halleck for the post of House minority leader.

1973. Under the terms of the 25th amendment, took the oath as vice-president on December 6.

1974. Following the resignation of President Nixon, inaugurated as the 38th chief executive on August 9.

1980. An attempt by Ronald Reagan to persuade the former president to join him as the vice-presidential candidate on the GOP ticket failed.

Highlights of Presidency

1974. Nominated Nelson A. Rockefeller as vice-president. □ Granted Richard M. Nixon an "absolute" pardon for all federal crimes he may have "committed or taken part in" while president. □ In Vladivostok, USSR, joined Soviet General Secretary Brezhnev in signing a tentative agreement listing the number of offensive strategic nuclear weapons and delivery vehicles through 1985.

1975. In April, South Vietnam surrendered to the Communists, ending the war in Southeast Asia. U.S. evacuation airlift from the nation was completed. □ In May, U.S. forces rescued 39 crewmen of the U.S. merchant ship *Mayaguez*, seized by Cambodia.

1976. Led the nation in marking its 200th birthday. □ Defeated by Jimmy Carter in his bid to win a full term.

James Earl ("Jimmy") Carter, Jr.

39th president, 1977-81   Democrat

1924. Born on October 1 in Plains, GA.

1935. Baptized into the First Baptist Church of Plains.

1946. Graduated from the U.S. Naval Academy. Married Rosalynn Smith on July 7. The couple would become the parents of three sons and a daughter.

1946-53. Served in the U.S. Navy. Duty included work under Hyman Rickover.

1953. Following the death of his father, resigned from the Navy and returned to Plains to run the family farm.

1963-67. Served two terms in the Georgia Senate.

1966. Ran third in Georgia's Democratic primary for the gubernatorial nomination.

1971-75. Served as governor of Georgia.

1975. Published his first book, *Why Not the Best?*

1976. Defeated Gerald R. Ford for the presidency.

1982. Named a distinguished professor at Emory University. □ His memoirs, *Keeping Faith: Memoirs of a President*, were published.

Highlights of Presidency

1977. In September, signed treaties providing for U.S. operation of the Panama Canal to the end of 1999 and for the permanent neutralization of the canal.

1978. With Israeli Prime Minister Menahem Begin and Egypt's President Anwar el-Sadat, signed the "Framework of Peace in the Middle East" and the "Framework for the Conclusion of a Peace Treaty Between Egypt and Israel." The agreements followed 11 days of U.S.-sponsored talks at Camp David. □ In December, China and the United States agreed to establish diplomatic relations.

1979. Signed a bill creating the U.S. Department of Education; a Department of Energy was established in 1977. □ Reached Strategic Arms Limitation Agreement with Soviet President Brezhnev. □ Protesting U.S. support of the Shah, radical Iranian students seized a group of American diplomats and embassy officials in Teheran in November. The "hostage crisis" clouded the remaining months of the Carter presidency.

1980. After defeating Sen. Edward M. Kennedy for the Democratic presidential nomination, lost election to Ronald Reagan by a wide margin.

Ronald Wilson Reagan

40th president, 1981-   Republican

1911. Born on February 6 in Tampico, IL.

1932. After graduating from Eureka (IL) College, worked as a sports announcer for radio stations in Davenport and Des Moines, IA.

1937. Made film debut in *Love Is on the Air*. Appeared in more than 50 movies during a 27-year career as an actor.

1940. Married Jane Wyman on January 25. The couple would become the parents of a daughter and an adopted son, and be divorced in 1948.

1942-45. Served in the U.S. Army Air Forces.

1947-52; 1959. Was president of the Screen Actors Guild.

1952. Married actress Nancy Davis on March 4. The couple would have a daughter and a son.

1952-62. Served as a spokesperson for General Electric.

1962. Officially joined the Republican Party, after being a liberal Democrat during his younger years.

1967-75. Was governor of California.

1976. Failed to capture the GOP presidential nomination from the incumbent Gerald Ford.

1980. Elected president in a landslide win over Jimmy Carter and third party candidate John Anderson.

Highlights of Presidency

1981. On January 20, inaugurated as the 40th president. Moments later, 52 Americans, who had been held hostage in Iran since November 1979, were released. □ In July, nominated Sandra Day O'Connor as an associate justice of the U.S. Supreme Court. □ On August 13, signed into law the Economic Recovery Tax Bill and Omnibus Budget Reconciliation Bill.

1983. With U.S. forces participating in a multinational peacekeeping force in Lebanon, 241 U.S. servicemen are killed in terrorist attack in October. □ That same month, U.S.

troops invade the Caribbean island of Grenada in an "effort to restore order and democracy."

1984. Reelected in a landslide.

1985. In November, met with Soviet General Secretary Mikhail Gorbachev in Geneva.

1986. American warplanes bombed "terrorist-related targets" in Tripoli and Benghazi, Libya, in April.

Ronald Reagan, the 40th chief executive, welcomed his three predecessors to the White House in October 1981.

The White House

PRESIDENTIAL ELECTIONS 1789-1984

		PARTIES	POP-ULAR VOTE	ELEC-TORAL VOTE
1789[1]	George Washington			69
	John Adams			34
	John Jay			9
	R. H. Harrison			6
	John Rutledge			6
	John Hancock			4
	George Clinton			3
	Samuel Huntington			2
	John Milton			2
	James Armstrong			1
	Benjamin Lincoln			1
	Edward Telfair			1
	(Not voted)			12
1792[1]	George Washington	Federalist		132
	John Adams	Federalist		77
	George Clinton	Dem.-Rep.		50
	Thomas Jefferson			4
	Aaron Burr			1
1796[1]	John Adams	Federalist		71
	Thomas Jefferson	Dem.-Rep.		68
	Thomas Pinckney	Federalist		59
	Aaron Burr	Anti-Federalist		30
	Samuel Adams	Dem.-Rep.		15
	Oliver Ellsworth	Federalist		11
	George Clinton	Dem.-Rep.		7
	John Jay	Ind.-Fed.		5
	James Iredell	Federalist		3
	George Washington	Federalist		2
	John Henry	Independent		2
	S. Johnston	Ind.-Fed.		2
	C. C. Pinckney	Ind.-Fed.		1
1800[1]	Thomas Jefferson	Dem.-Rep.		73
	Aaron Burr	Dem.-Rep.		73
	John Adams	Federalist		65
	C. C. Pinckney	Federalist		64
	John Jay	Federalist		1
1804	Thomas Jefferson	Dem.-Rep.		162
	C. C. Pinckney	Federalist		14
1808	James Madison	Dem.-Rep.		122
	C. C. Pinckney	Federalist		47
	George Clinton	Ind.-Rep.		6
	(Not voted)			1
1812	James Madison	Dem.-Rep.		128
	DeWitt Clinton	Fusion		89
	(Not voted)			1
1816	James Monroe	Dem.-Rep.		183
	Rufus King	Federalist		34
	(Not voted)			4
1820	James Monroe	Dem.-Rep.		231
	John Q. Adams	Ind.-Rep.		1
	(Not voted)			3
1824	John Q. Adams	No distinct	108,740	84[2]
	Andrew Jackson	party	153,544	99[2]
	Henry Clay	designations	47,136	37
	W. H. Crawford		46,618	41
1828	Andrew Jackson	Democratic	647,286	178
	John Q. Adams	Nat.-Rep.	508,064	83
1832	Andrew Jackson	Democratic	687,502	219
	Henry Clay	Nat. Rep.	530,189	49
	William Wirt	Anti-Masonic	—	7
	John Floyd	Nullifiers	—	11
	(Not voted)			2
1836	Martin Van Buren	Democratic	765,483	170
	William H. Harrison	Whig		73
	Hugh L. White	Whig	739,795[3]	26
	Daniel Webster	Whig		14
	W. P. Mangum	Anti-Jackson		11

		PARTIES	POP-ULAR VOTE	ELEC-TORAL VOTE
1840	William H. Harrison	Whig	1,274,624	234
	Martin Van Buren	Democratic	1,127,781	60
1844	James K. Polk	Democratic	1,338,464	170
	Henry Clay	Whig	1,300,097	105
	James G. Birney	Liberty	62,300	—
1848	Zachary Taylor	Whig	1,360,967	163
	Lewis Cass	Democratic	1,222,342	127
	Martin Van Buren	Free Soil	291,263	—
1852	Franklin Pierce	Democratic	1,601,117	254
	Winfield Scott	Whig	1,385,453	42
	John P. Hale	Free Soil	155,825	—
1856	James Buchanan	Democratic	1,832,955	174
	John C. Fremont	Republican	1,339,932	114
	Millard Fillmore	American	871,731	8
1860	Abraham Lincoln	Republican	1,865,593	180
	J. C. Breckinridge	Democratic (S)	848,356	72
	Stephen A. Douglas	Democratic	1,382,713	12
	John Bell	Con. Union	592,906	39
1864	Abraham Lincoln	Republican	2,206,938	212
	George B. McClellan	Democratic	1,803,787	21
	(Not voted)		—	81
1868	Ulysses S. Grant	Republican	3,013,421	214
	Horatio Seymour	Democratic	2,706,829	80
	(Not voted)		—	23
1872	Ulysses S. Grant	Republican	3,596,745	286[4]
	Horace Greeley	Democratic	2,843,446	—
	Charles O'Connor	Straight Dem.	29,489	—
	Thomas A. Hendricks	Ind.-Dem.	—	42
	B. Gratz Brown	Democratic	—	18
	Charles J. Jenkins	Democratic	—	2
	David Davis	Democratic	—	1
	(Not voted)		—	17
1876	Rutherford B. Hayes	Republican	4,036,572	185
	Samuel J. Tilden	Democratic	4,284,020	184
	Peter Cooper	Greenback	81,737	—
1880	James A. Garfield	Republican	4,453,295	214
	Winfield S. Hancock	Democratic	4,414,082	155
	James B. Weaver	Green.-Labor	308,578	—
	Neal Dow	Prohibition	10,305	—
1884	Grover Cleveland	Democratic	4,879,507	219
	James G. Blaine	Republican	4,850,293	182
	Benjamin F. Butler	Green.-Labor	175,370	—
	John P. St. John	Prohibition	150,369	—
1888	Benjamin Harrison	Republican	5,447,129	233
	Grover Cleveland	Democratic	5,537,857	168
	Clinton B. Fisk	Prohibition	249,506	—
	Anson J. Streeter	Union Labor	146,935	—
1892	Grover Cleveland	Democratic	5,555,426	277
	Benjamin Harrison	Republican	5,182,690	145
	James B. Weaver	People's	1,029,846	22
	John Bidwell	Prohibition	264,133	—
	Simon Wing	Soc. Labor	21,164	—
1896	William McKinley	Republican	7,102,246	271
	William J. Bryan	Democratic[5]	6,492,559	176
	John M. Palmer	Nat. Dem.	133,148	—
	Joshua Levering	Prohibition	132,007	—
	Charles H. Matchett	Soc. Labor	36,274	—
	Charles E. Bentley	Nationalist	13,969	—
1900	William McKinley	Republican	7,218,491	292
	William J. Bryan	Democratic[5]	6,356,734	155
	John C. Wooley	Prohibition	208,914	—
	Eugene V. Debs	Socialist	87,814	—
	Wharton Barker	People's	50,373	—
	Jos. F. Malloney	Soc. Labor	39,739	—

Year	Candidate	Party	Popular	Electoral
1904	Theodore Roosevelt	Republican	7,628,461	336
	Alton B. Parker	Democratic	5,084,223	140
	Eugene V. Debs	Socialist	402,283	—
	Silas C. Swallow	Prohibition	258,536	—
	Thomas E. Watson	People's	117,183	—
	Charles H. Corregan	Soc. Labor	31,249	—
1908	William H. Taft	Republican	7,675,320	321
	William J. Bryan	Democratic	6,412,294	162
	Eugene V. Debs	Socialist	420,793	—
	Eugene W. Chafin	Prohibition	253,840	—
	Thomas L. Hisgen	Independence	82,872	—
	Thomas E. Watson	People's	29,100	—
	August Gillhaus	Soc. Labor	14,021	—
1912	Woodrow Wilson	Democratic	6,296,547	435
	Theodore Roosevelt	Progressive	4,118,571	88
	William H. Taft	Republican	3,486,720	8
	Eugene V. Debs	Socialist	900,672	—
	Eugene W. Chafin	Prohibition	206,275	—
	Arthur E. Reimer	Soc. Labor	28,750	—
1916	Woodrow Wilson	Democratic	9,127,695	277
	Charles E. Hughes	Republican	8,533,507	254
	A. L. Benson	Socialist	585,113	—
	J. Frank Hanly	Prohibition	220,506	—
	Arthur E. Reimer	Soc. Labor	13,403	—
1920	Warren G. Harding	Republican	16,143,407	404
	James M. Cox	Democratic	9,130,328	127
	Eugene V. Debs	Socialist	919,799	—
	P. P. Christensen	Farmer-Labor	265,411	—
	Aaron S. Watkins	Prohibition	189,408	—
	James E. Ferguson	American	48,000	—
	W. W. Cox	Soc. Labor	31,715	—
1924	Calvin Coolidge	Republican	15,718,211	382
	John W. Davis	Democratic	8,385,283	136
	Robert M. LaFollette	Progressive	4,831,289	13
	Herman P. Faris	Prohibition	57,520	—
	Frank T. Johns	Soc. Labor	36,428	—
	William Z. Foster	Workers	36,386	—
	GIlbert O. Nations	American	23,967	—
1928	Herbert C. Hoover	Republican	21,391,993	444
	Alfred E. Smith	Democratic	15,016,169	87
	Norman Thomas	Socialist	267,835	—
	Verne L. Reynolds	Soc. Labor	21,603	—
	William Z. Foster	Workers	21,181	—
	William F. Varney	Prohibition	20,106	—
1932	Franklin D. Roosevelt	Democratic	22,809,638	472
	Herbert C. Hoover	Republican	15,758,901	59
	Norman Thomas	Socialist	881,951	—
	William Z. Foster	Communist	102,785	—
	William D. Upshaw	Prohibition	81,869	—
	Verne L. Reynolds	Soc. Labor	33,276	—
	William H. Harvey	Liberty	53,425	—
1936	Franklin D. Roosevelt	Democratic	27,752,869	523
	Alfred M. Landon	Republican	16,674,665	8
	William Lemke	Union	882,479	—
	Norman Thomas	Socialist	187,720	—
	Earl Browder	Communist	80,159	—
	D. Leigh Colvin	Prohibition	37,847	—
	John W. Aiken	Soc. Labor	12,777	—
1940	Franklin D. Roosevelt	Democratic	27,307,819	449
	Wendell L. Willkie	Republican	22,321,018	82
	Norman Thomas	Socialist	99,557	—
	Roger Q. Babson	Prohibition	57,812	—
	Earl Browder	Communist	46,251	—
	John W. Aiken	Soc. Labor	14,892	—
1944	Franklin D. Roosevelt	Democratic	25,606,585	432
	Thomas E. Dewey	Republican	22,014,745	99
	Norman Thomas	Socialist	80,518	—
	Claude A. Watson	Prohibition	74,758	—
	Edward A. Teichert	Soc. Labor	45,336	—
1948	Harry S. Truman	Democratic	24,179,345	303
	Thomas E. Dewey	Republican	21,991,291	189
	Strom Thurmond	States' Rights	1,176,125	39
	Henry Wallace	Progressive	1,157,326	—
	Norman Thomas	Socialist	139,572	—
	Claude A. Watson	Prohibition	103,900	—
	Edward A. Teichert	Soc. Labor	29,241	—
	Farrell Dobbs	Soc. Workers	13,614	—
1952	Dwight D. Eisenhower	Republican	33,936,234	442
	Adlai E. Stevenson	Democratic	27,314,992	89
	Vincent Hallinan	Progressive	140,023	—
	Stuart Hamblen	Prohibition	72,949	—
	Eric Hass	Soc. Labor	30,267	—
	Darlington Hoopes	Socialist	20,203	—
	Douglas A. MacArthur	Constitution	17,205	—
	Farrell Dobbs	Soc. Workers	10,312	—
1956	Dwight D. Eisenhower	Republican	35,590,472	457
	Adlai E. Stevenson	Democratic	26,022,752	73[6]
	T. Coleman Andrews	States' Rights	111,178	—
	Eric Hass	Soc. Labor	44,450	—
	Enoch A. Holtwick	Prohibition	41,937	—
1960	John F. Kennedy	Democratic	34,226,731	303[7]
	Richard M. Nixon	Republican	34,108,157	219
	Eric Hass	Soc. Labor	47,522	—
	Rutherford L. Decker	Prohibition	46,203	—
	Orval E. Faubus	Nat. S. Rights	44,977	—
	Farrell Dobbs	Soc. Workers	40,165	—
	Charles L. Sullivan	Constitution	18,162	—
1964	Lyndon B. Johnson	Democratic	43,129,566	486
	Barry M. Goldwater	Republican	27,178,188	52
	Eric Hass	Soc. Labor	45,219	—
	Clifton DeBerry	Soc. Workers	32,720	—
	E. Harold Munn	Prohibition	23,267	—
1968	Richard M. Nixon	Republican	31,785,480	301
	Hubert H. Humphrey	Democratic	31,275,166	191
	George C. Wallace	Amer. Ind.	9,906,473	46
	Henning A. Blomen	Soc. Labor	52,588	—
	Dick Gregory		47,133[8]	—
	Fred Halstead	Soc. Workers	41,388	—
	Eldridge Cleaver	Peace-Freedom	36,563	—
	Eugene J. McCarthy		25,552[9]	—
	E. Harold Munn	Prohibition	15,123	—
1972	Richard M. Nixon	Republican	41,170,000	520[10]
	George McGovern	Democratic	29,170,000	17
	John Schmitz	American	1,099,482	—
	Benjamin Spock	People's	78,756	—
1976	Jimmy Carter	Democratic	40,831,000	297
	Gerald Ford	Republican	39,148,000	240[11]
	Eugene McCarthy	Independent	756,691	—
	Roger MacBride	Libertarian	173,011	—
1980	Ronald Reagan	Republican	43,904,000	489
	Jimmy Carter	Democratic	35,484,000	49
	John Anderson	Independent	5,720,060	—
	Ed Clark	Libertarian	921,299	—
1984	Ronald Reagan	Republican	54,455,000	525
	Walter Mondale	Democratic	37,577,000	13
	David Bergland	Libertarian	228,314	—
	Lyndon H. LaRouche	Independent	78,807	—

—Represents Zero

[1] Prior to the election of 1804, each elector voted for 2 candidates for president; the one receiving the highest number of votes, if a majority, was declared elected president, the next highest, vice-president. This provision was modified by adoption of the 12th amendment, which was declared ratified by the legislatures of three fourths of the states in a proclamation of the secretary of state, Sept. 25, 1804. [2] No candidate having a majority in the electoral college, the election was decided in the House of Representatives. [3] Whig tickets were pledged to various candidates in various states. [4] Greeley died shortly after the election and presidential electors supporting him cast their votes as indicated, including 3 for Greeley, which were not counted. [5] Includes a variety of joint tickets with People's Party electors committed to Bryan. [6] 1 Democratic elector in Alabama voted for Walter Jones. [7] 6 Democratic electors in Alabama, all 8 unpledged Democratic electors in Mississippi, and 1 Republican elector in Oklahoma voted for Sen. Harry F. Byrd. [8] Total vote for Gregory includes write-in votes as well as votes for the Freedom and Peace Party, the Peace Freedom Alternative, the Peace and Freedom Party, and the New Party. [9] Total vote for McCarthy includes write-in votes as well as votes for the Alternative in November Party, and the New Party. [10] John Hospers of California received one vote from an elector of Virginia. [11] An elector from the state of Washington voted for Ronald Reagan.

Party Abbreviations: Dem.-Rep. (Democratic-Republican); Ind.-Fed. (Independent-Federalist); Ind.-Rep. (Independent-Republican); Nat. Rep. (National Republican); Con. Union (Constitution Union); Ind.-Dem. (Independent-Democratic); Green.-Labor (Greenback-Labor); Soc. Labor (Socialist Labor); Nat. Dem. (National Democratic); Soc. Workers (Socialist Workers); Nat. S. Rights (National States Rights); Amer. Inc. (American Independent).

THE VICE-PRESIDENTS

1. JOHN ADAMS (1735-1826). Federalist. Served under George Washington, 1789-97; home state: MA; profession: lawyer.

2. THOMAS JEFFERSON (1743-1826). Democratic-Republican. Served under John Adams, 1797-1801; home state: VA; profession: lawyer, planter, public official.

3. AARON BURR (1756-1836). Democratic-Republican. Served under Thomas Jefferson, 1801-05; home state: NY; profession: public official.

4. GEORGE CLINTON (1739-1812). Democratic-Republican. Served under Thomas Jefferson, 1805-09, James Madison, 1809-12; home state: NY; profession: public official.

5. ELBRIDGE GERRY (1744-1814). Democratic-Republican. Served under James Madison, 1813-14; home state: MA; profession: public official.

6. DANIEL D. TOMPKINS (1774-1825). Democratic-Republican. Served under James Monroe, 1817-25; home state: NY; profession: lawyer and public official.

7. JOHN C. CALHOUN (1782-1850). Served as Democratic-Republican under John Quincy Adams, 1825-29; as Democrat under Andrew Jackson, 1829-32; home state: SC; profession: lawyer and public official.

8. MARTIN VAN BUREN (1782-1862). Democrat. Served under Andrew Jackson, 1833-37; home state: NY; profession: lawyer and public official.

9. RICHARD M. JOHNSON (1780-1850). Democrat. Served under Martin Van Buren, 1837-41; home state: KY; profession: public official.

10. JOHN TYLER (1790-1862). Whig. Served under William H. Harrison, March 4-April 4, 1841; home state: VA; profession: lawyer and public official.

11. GEORGE M. DALLAS (1792-1864). Democrat. Served under James K. Polk, 1845-49; home state: PA; profession: public official and diplomat.

12. MILLARD FILLMORE (1800-1874). Whig. Served under Zachary Taylor, 1849-50; home state: NY; profession: teacher, lawyer, public official.

13. WILLIAM R. D. KING (1786-1853). Democrat. Served under Franklin Pierce, March 4-April 18, 1853; home state: AL; profession: lawyer, public official, diplomat.

14. JOHN C. BRECKINRIDGE (1821-75). Democrat. Served under James Buchanan, 1857-61; home state: KY; profession: lawyer and public official.

15. HANNIBAL HAMLIN (1809-1891). Republican. Served under Abraham Lincoln, 1861-65; home state: ME; profession: lawyer and public official.

16. ANDREW JOHNSON (1808-1875). National Union (Republican). Served under Abraham Lincoln, March 4-April 15, 1865; home state: TN; profession: tailor and public official.

17. SCHUYLER COLFAX (1823-1885). Republican. Served under Ulysses S. Grant, 1869-73; home state: IN; profession: newspaperman and public official.

18. HENRY WILSON (1812-1875). Republican. Served under Ulysses S. Grant, 1873-75; home state: MA; profession: factory owner and public official.

19. WILLIAM A. WHEELER (1819-1887). Republican. Served under Rutherford B. Hayes, 1877-81; home state: NY; profession: businessman and public official.

20. CHESTER A. ARTHUR (1829-1886). Republican. Served under James A. Garfield, March 4-Sept. 20, 1881; home state: NY; profession: lawyer.

21. THOMAS A. HENDRICKS (1819-1885). Democrat. Served under Grover Cleveland, March 4-Nov. 25, 1885; home state: IN; profession: lawyer and public official.

22. LEVI P. MORTON (1824-1920). Republican. Served under Benjamin Harrison, 1889-93; home state: NY; profession: banker and public official.

23. ADLAI E. STEVENSON (1835-1914). Democrat. Served under G. Cleveland, 1893-97; home state: IL; profession: public official.

24. GARRET A. HOBART (1844-1899). Republican. Served under William McKinley, 1897-99; home state: NJ; profession: lawyer and public official.

25. THEODORE ROOSEVELT (1858-1919). Republican. Served under William McKinley, March 4-Sept. 14, 1901; home state: NY; profession: historian and public official.

26. CHARLES W. FAIRBANKS (1852-1918). Republican. Served under Theodore Roosevelt, 1905-09; home state: IN; profession: financier and public official.

27. JAMES S. SHERMAN (1855-1912). Republican. Served under William Howard Taft, 1909-12; home state: NY; profession: public official.

28. THOMAS R. MARSHALL (1854-1925). Democrat. Served under Woodrow Wilson, 1913-21; home state: IN; profession: lawyer and public official.

29. CALVIN COOLIDGE (1872-1933). Republican. Served under Warren G. Harding, 1921-23; home state: MA; profession: lawyer and public official.

30. CHARLES G. DAWES (1865-1951). Republican. Served under Calvin Coolidge, 1925-29; home state: IL; profession: financier and diplomat.

31. CHARLES CURTIS (1860-1936). Republican. Served under Herbert Hoover, 1929-33; home state: KS; profession: lawyer and public official.

32. JOHN N. GARNER (1868-1967). Democrat. Served under Franklin D. Roosevelt, 1933-41; home state: TX; profession: public official.

33. HENRY A. WALLACE (1888-1965). Democrat. Served under Franklin D. Roosevelt, 1941-45; home state: IA; profession: editor and agribusinessman.

34. HARRY S. TRUMAN (1884-1972). Democrat. Served under Franklin D. Roosevelt, Jan. 20-April 12, 1945; home state: MO; profession: public official.

35. ALBEN W. BARKLEY (1877-1956). Democrat. Served under Harry S. Truman, 1949-53; home state: KY; profession: public official.

36. RICHARD M. NIXON (1913-   ). Republican. Served under Dwight D. Eisenhower, 1953-61; home state: CA; profession: public official.

37. LYNDON B. JOHNSON (1908-1973). Democrat. Served under John F. Kennedy, Jan. 20, 1961-Nov. 22, 1963; home state: TX; profession: public official.

38. HUBERT H. HUMPHREY (1911-1978). Democrat. Served under L. B. Johnson, 1965-69; home state: MN; profession: public official.

39. SPIRO T. AGNEW (1918-   ). Republican. Served under R. M. Nixon, Jan. 20, 1969-Oct. 10, 1973; home state: MD; profession: public official.

40. GERALD R. FORD (1913-   ). Republican. Served under R. M. Nixon, Dec. 6, 1973-Aug. 9, 1974; home state: MI; profession: public official.

41. NELSON A. ROCKEFELLER (1908-1979). Republican. Served under Gerald R. Ford, Dec. 19, 1974-Jan. 20, 1977; home state: NY; profession: public official.

42. WALTER F. MONDALE (1928-   ). Democrat. Served under Jimmy Carter, 1977-81; home state: MN; profession: public official.

43. GEORGE BUSH (1924-   ). Republican. Served under Ronald Reagan, 1981-   ; home state: TX; profession: oilman and public official.

The White House

THE WHITE HOUSE

The White House, located at 1600 Pennsylvania Avenue, N.W., in Washington DC, has been the home of every U.S. president since John Adams. The presidential mansion is situated on some 18 acres (7.3 hectares) of land amid a parklike setting. The building's main section measures 170 feet (52 meters) long and 85 feet (26 meters) deep. Its 2½ stories are mounted on an English basement, which, because of the slope of the land, becomes a ground floor on the south side. Two wings flank the original structure. The West Wing was constructed in 1902, following a Congressional appropriation of $65,196. It contains the Oval (presidential) Office, the Roosevelt or staff meeting room, a reception room, and the Cabinet Room. French doors within the president's office open onto the Rose Garden, which continues to follow the plan of an 18th century flower garden. The president regularly receives official visitors in the Rose Garden. The East Wing was built in 1942 and contains offices for presidential aides. The Jacqueline Kennedy Garden, so named by Mrs. Lyndon B. Johnson in honor of her predecessor, is off the East Wing and is used by the First Lady as a reception area.

Prior to 1902, the ground floor served as the president's work area. This floor now features the Library, which was completely reorganized in 1962; the Vermeil or Gold Room, which serves as a display room as well as a ladies' sitting room; the China or "Presidential Collection Room," which includes a wide exhibit of White House China; the Diplomatic Reception Room, formerly a boiler room; and the Map Room, from which President Franklin D. Roosevelt monitored the events of World War II.

Although the rooms of the first (state) floor have been refurbished many times over the years, the floor has not changed architecturally since the White House was designed by John Hoban in 1792. The East Room, three reception rooms (the Green Room, Blue Room, and Red Room), the State Dining Room, and the Family Dining Room comprise the first floor. With the exception of the Family Dining Room, these rooms are open to the public. The East Room, called the "Public Audience Room" by Hoban, retains its classical style of the early 19th century. It has been the scene of many White House dances, concerts, weddings, funerals, and bill-signing ceremonies. Gerald R. Ford took the oath of office in the East Room when he succeeded Richard M. Nixon as chief executive. The State Dining Room was originally much smaller and functioned as a drawing room, office, and cabinet room. The dining hall now can seat as many as 140 guests. The second floor includes the Queen's Suite, formerly the Rose Guest Room and now a sitting room and bedroom; the Lincoln Bedroom, which was the office and the cabinet room of the 16th chief executive; the adjoining Lincoln Sitting Room; and a former Cabinet Room, which was designated the Treaty Room during the John Kennedy administration to reflect the many important decisions made in it. The private quarters of the president and his family are located on the west end of the second floor.

History. Construction of the White House was begun in 1792 after an architectural competition won by James Hoban, an Irish-born architect who had immigrated to America some years earlier. After many delays and financial problems the building was habitable (but not completed) in 1800, when President John Adams and his wife, Abigail, moved in. Hoban's original drawing of the north façade, which has survived, reflects the English-Palladian architecture of the mid-18th century.

Thomas Jefferson, the second president to occupy the White House, employed the gifted architect Benjamin H. Latrobe in 1806 to help design the east and west pavilions. The latter has survived in its nearly original state. Latrobe also made designs for the north and south porticoes which were executed in a modified form at a later date.

In 1814 during the War of 1812, British forces burned all of the public buildings in Washington. The White House was not spared. With the exception of a Gilbert Stuart portrait of George Washington, now in the East Room, all of the furnishings from the Adams, Jefferson, and Madison administrations were destroyed. Under James Hoban's supervision the White House was rebuilt and was

ready for occupancy in 1817, refurnished in the Empire Style with items imported from France by President James Monroe. However, in the architecture of the building, and particularly in the interior, Hoban returned to his earlier Palladian style and did not repeat the neoclassic innovations made by Latrobe. The scorched exterior walls were painted white. There is misconception that this is why the building was called the White House. Actually it had borne that name since it was first built.

Throughout the 19th century the interior of the White House went through each successive decorative style, but the exterior appearance of the building remained the same. Gas lighting was introduced in 1849 and central heating in 1853. The first bathroom was installed in 1877. In 1833 pipes bringing water from a nearby spring replaced the pump formerly used. After 1853 water was piped in from the city's water system. Electricity came to the White House during the residency of Benjamin Harrison.

In 1902, during the administration of President Theodore Roosevelt, the White House underwent its first major renovation, under the direction of the architectural firm of McKim, Mead, and White. The rooms of the first floor were stripped of their Victorian

The White House: The large North Entrance Hall, *top left,* was part of James Hoban's original architectural plan for the mansion. Prior to completion of the West Wing in the early 1900s, the hall was a reception area. The oval Blue Room, *bottom left,* includes French Empire style furnishings from the James Monroe administration. Although each president can alter the design and decor of the Oval Office, tradition dictates the correct positions of the U.S. and presidential flags. The Lincoln Bedroom, *right,* which was used by the 16th chief executive as an office and cabinet room, was decorated with bedroom furniture from the Lincoln era during the Truman years. George P.A. Healy's portrait of Lincoln hangs over the mantel in the State Dining Room. As many as 140 guests can dine in the gold- and white-dominated room. The Cabinet Room, overlooking the Rose Garden, was added to the West Wing in 1909.

overlay and returned to their early-19th-century appearance. The grand staircase was moved into the entrance hall to permit the creation of the State Dining Room at the southwest corner of the building.

In 1949, during the administration of President Harry S. Truman, the White House was found unsafe for occupancy. The exterior walls were retained while the interior fabric of the building was removed and rebuilt on a steel and concrete frame. Great care was taken to preserve the original woodwork, marble mantlepieces, and decorative plasterwork. The original floor plan was followed faithfully. A balcony, now known as the Truman Balcony, was built on the second-floor level of the South portico. It has become a favorite spot of presidential families.

Under the guidance of Mrs. John F. Kennedy, the restoration of the interior of the White House to its original late-18th and early-19th-century appearance was begun. A Fine Arts Committee, composed of museum specialists and others, was formed to direct the work of restoration. This committee was further strenghtened by a special Advisory Committee and a Paintings Committee. Prior to this there had been little attempt to preserve or to use historic White House furnishings, and the rooms of the first floor were largely furnished with reproductions. Many important objects were recovered from White House storage areas. Other outstanding examples of American cabinetmaking and the decorative arts were supplied by generous donors. Mrs. Kennedy felt strongly that "everything in the White House must have a reason for being there." Subsequently, the Committee for the Preservation of the White House and the permanent office of curator were established by President Johnson. Additional pieces of valuable furniture and American paintings were acquired for the White House during the Nixon administration, and the principal rooms of the first and ground floors were redecorated during the Nixon years. After moving to the executive mansion in January 1981, Mrs. Ronald Reagan oversaw the remodeling of the first and second floor rooms and several preservation projects.

For the American public, the executive mansion has become a national palace as well as a home for the chief executive. For, in the words of President Dwight D. Eisenhower, the "White House has been and should always remain a place to be venerated by its occupants as well as by all Americans."

On the University of Texas campus in Austin, the Lyndon Baines Johnson Library, *above,* houses the papers of the 36th president's career in public service. The "Kennedy rocker," his desk, and other memorabilia are displayed at the John Fitzgerald Kennedy Library in Boston.

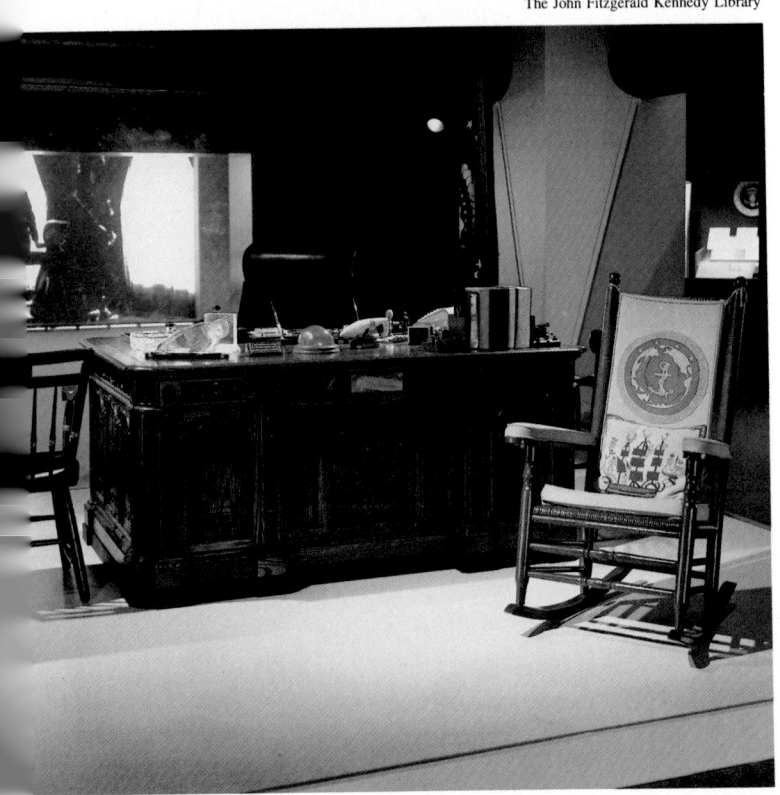

U. S. PRESIDENTIAL LIBRARIES

At various times in American history, Congress has appropriated funds to maintain the papers of former presidents. These collections, extending from the administration of George Washington to the era of Calvin Coolidge and including some 2 million manuscripts, are located in the Library of Congress. The first separate presidential library, the Franklin D. Roosevelt Library in Hyde Park, was established by a joint resolution of Congress in 1939 and was dedicated on July 4, 1940. The other presidential libraries are:

Herbert Hoover Presidential Library; located in West Branch, IA; dedicated on Aug. 10, 1962.

Harry S. Truman Presidential Library; located in Independence, MO; dedicated on July 6, 1957.

Dwight D. Eisenhower Presidential Library; located in Abilene, KS; dedicated on May 1, 1962.

John F. Kennedy Presidential Library; located in Boston, MA; dedicated on Oct. 20, 1979.

Lyndon B. Johnson Presidential Library; located in Austin, TX; dedicated on May 22, 1971.

Gerald R. Ford Presidential Library; located in Ann Arbor, MI; dedicated on April 27, 1981.

Jimmy Carter Presidential Library; located in Atlanta, GA; scheduled for dedication in late 1986.

They were built with private monies, donated to the federal government, and are administrated by the National Archives.

The Congress shall have Power to declare the Punishment of Treason, but no Attainder of Treason shall work Corruption of Blood, or Forfeiture except during the Life of the Person attainted.

ARTICLE IV

SECTION 1. Full Faith and Credit shall be given in each State to the Public Acts, Records, and judicial Proceedings of every other State. And the Congress may by general Laws prescribe the Manner in which such Acts, Records and Proceedings shall be proved, and the Effect thereof.

SECTION 2. The Citizens of each State shall be entitled to all Privileges and Immunities of Citizens in the several States.

A Person charged in any State with Treason, Felony, or other Crime, who shall flee from Justice, and be found in another State, shall on Demand of the executive Authority of the State from which he fled, be delivered up to be removed to the State having Jurisdiction of the Crime.

[No Person held to Service or Labour in one State, under the Laws thereof, escaping into another, shall, in Consequence of any Law or Regulation therein, be discharged from such Service or Labour, but shall be delivered up on Claim of the Party to whom such Service or Labour may be due.][8]

SECTION 3. New States may be admitted by the Congress into this Union; but no new States shall be formed or erected within the Jurisdiction of any other State; nor any State be formed by the Junction of two or more States, or Parts of States, without the Consent of the Legislatures of the States concerned as well as of the Congress.

The Congress shall have Power to dispose of and make all needful Rules and Regulations respecting the Territory or other Property belonging to the United States; and nothing in this Constitution shall be so construed as to Prejudice any Claims of the United States, or of any particular State.

SECTION 4. The United States shall guarantee to every State in this Union a Republican Form of Government, and shall protect each of them against Invasion; and on Application of the Legislature, or of the Executive (when the Legislature cannot be convened) against domestic Violence.

ARTICLE V

The Congress, whenever two thirds of both Houses shall deem it necessary, shall propose Amendments to this Constitution, or, on the Application of the Legislatures of two thirds of the several States, shall call a Convention for proposing Amendments, which, in either Case, shall be valid to all Intents and Purposes, as Part of this Constitution, when ratified by the Legislatures of three fourths of the several States, or by Conventions in three fourths thereof, as the one or the other Mode of Ratification may be proposed by the Congress; Provided that no Amendment which may be made prior to the Year One thousand eight hundred and eight shall in any Manner affect the first and fourth Clauses in the Ninth Section of the first Article; and that no State, without its Consent, shall be deprived of it's equal Suffrage in the Senate.

ARTICLE VI

All Debts contracted and Engagements entered into, before the Adoption of this Constitution, shall be as valid against the United States under this Constitution, as under the Confederation.

This Constitution, and the Laws of the United States which shall be made in Pursuance thereof; and all Treaties made, or which shall be made, under the Authority of the United States, shall be the supreme Law of the Land; and the Judges in every State shall be bound thereby, any Thing in the Constitution or Laws of any State to the Contrary notwithstanding.

The Senators and Representatives before mentioned, and the Members of the several State Legislatures, and all executive and judicial Officers, both of the United States and of the several States, shall be bound by Oath or Affirmation, to support this Constitution; but no religious Test shall ever be required as a Qualification to any Office or public Trust under the United States.

ARTICLE VII

The Ratification of the Conventions of nine States, shall be sufficient for the Establishment of this Constitution between the States so ratifying the Same.

Done in Convention by the Unanimous Consent of the States present the Seventeenth Day of September in the Year of our Lord one thousand seven hundred and Eighty seven and of the Independence of the United States of America the Twelfth. In witness whereof We have hereunto subscribed our Names,

New Hampshire
John Langdon
Nicholas Gilman

Massachusetts
Nathaniel Gorham
Rufus King

Connecticut
Wm. Saml. Johnson
Roger Sherman

New York
Alexander Hamilton

New Jersey
Wil. Livingston
David Brearley
Wm. Paterson
Jona. Dayton

Pennsylvania
B. Franklin
Thomas Mifflin
Robt. Morris
Geo. Clymer
Thos. FitzSimons
Jared Ingersoll
James Wilson
Gouv. Morris

Delaware
Geo. Read
Gunning Bedford, jun.
John Dickinson
Richard Bassett
Jaco. Broom

Maryland
James McHenry
Dan. of St. Thos. Jenifer
Danl. Carroll

Virginia
Go. Washington
John Blair
James Madison, Jr.

North Carolina
Wm. Blount,
Richd. Dobbs Spaight
Hu. Williamson

South Carolina
J. Rutledge
Charles Cotesworth Pinckney
Charles Pinckney
Pierce Butler

Georgia
William Few
Abr. Baldwin

---

[8] The clause in brackets is superseded by the 13th Amendment.

AMENDMENTS TO THE CONSTITUTION

Articles in addition to, and Amendment of the Constitution of the United States of America, proposed by Congress, and ratified by the Legislatures of the several States, pursuant to the fifth Article of the original Constitution. [The first ten amendments went into effect November 3, 1791.]

AMENDMENT I

Congress shall make no law respecting an establishment of religion, or prohibiting the free exercise thereof; or abridging the freedom of speech, or of the press; or the right of the people peaceably to assemble, and to petition the government for a redress of grievances.

AMENDMENT II

A well regulated Militia, being necessary to the security of a free State, the right of the people to keep and bear Arms, shall not be infringed.

AMENDMENT III

No Soldier shall, in time of peace be quartered in any house, without the consent of the Owner, nor in time of war, but in a manner to be prescribed by law.

AMENDMENT IV

The right of the people to be secure in their persons, houses, papers, and effects, against unreasonable searches and seizures, shall not be violated, and no Warrants shall issue, but upon probable cause, supported by Oath or affirmation, and particularly describing the place to be searched, and the persons or things to be seized.

AMENDMENT V

No person shall be held to answer for a capital, or otherwise infamous crime, unless on a presentment or indictment of a Grand Jury, except in cases arising in the land or naval forces, or in the Militia, when in actual service in time of War or public danger; nor shall any person be subject for the same offence to be twice put in jeopardy of life or limb; nor shall be compelled in any criminal case to be a witness against himself, nor be deprived of life, liberty, or property, without due process of law; nor shall private property be taken for public use, without just compensation.

AMENDMENT VI

In all criminal prosecutions, the accused shall enjoy the right to a speedy and public trial, by an impartial jury of the State and district wherein the crime shall have been committed, which district shall have been previously ascertained by law, and to be informed of the nature and cause of the accusation; to be confronted with the witnesses against him; to have compulsory process for obtaining witnesses in his favor, and to have the Assistance of Counsel for his defence.

AMENDMENT VII

In Suits at common law, where the value in controversy shall exceed twenty dollars, the right of trial by jury shall be preserved, and no fact tried by a jury, shall be otherwise re-examined in any Court of United States, than according to the rules of the common law.

AMENDMENT VIII

Excessive bail shall not be required, nor excessive fines imposed, nor cruel and unusual punishments inflicted.

AMENDMENT IX

The enumeration in the Constitution, of certain rights, shall not be construed to deny or disparage others retained by the people.

AMENDMENT X

The powers not delegated to the United States by the Constitution, nor prohibited by it to the States, are reserved to the States respectively, or to the people.

AMENDMENT XI[9]
January 8, 1798

The Judicial power of the United States shall not be construed to extend to any suit in law or equity, commenced or prosecuted against one of the United States by Citizens of another State, or by Citizens or Subjects of any Foreign State.

AMENDMENT XII[10]
September 25, 1804

The Electors shall meet in their respective states, and vote by ballot for President and Vice-President, one of whom, at least, shall not be an inhabitant of the same state with themselves; they shall name in their ballots the person voted for as President, and in distinct ballots the person voted for as Vice-President, and they shall make distinct lists of all persons voted for as President, and of all persons voted for as Vice-President, and of the number of votes for each, which lists they shall sign and certify, and transmit sealed to the seat of the government of the United States, directed to the President of the Senate;—The President of the Senate shall, in the presence of the Senate and House of Representatives, open all the certificates and the votes shall then be counted;—The person having the greatest number of votes for President, shall be the President, if such number be a majority of the whole number of Electors appointed; and if no person have such majority, then from the persons having the highest numbers not exceeding three on the list of those voted for as President, the House of Representatives shall choose immediately, by ballot, the President. But in choosing the President, the votes shall be taken by states, the representation from each state having one vote; a quorum for this purpose shall consist of a member or members from two-thirds of the states, and a majority of all the states shall be necessary to a choice. [And if the House of Representatives shall not choose a President whenever the right of choice shall devolve upon them, before the fourth day of March next following, then the Vice-President shall act as President, as in the case of the death or other constitutional disability of the President.][11]—The person having the greatest number of votes as Vice-President, shall be the Vice-President, if such number be a majority of the whole number of Electors appointed, and if no person have a majority, then from the two highest numbers on the list, the Senate shall choose the Vice-President; a quorum for the purpose shall consist of two-thirds of the whole number of Senators, and a majority of the whole number shall be necessary to a choice. But no person constitutionally ineligible to the office of President shall be eligible to that of Vice-President of the United States.

AMENDMENT XIII
December 18, 1865

SECTION 1. Neither slavery nor involuntary servitude, except as a punishment for crime whereof the party shall have been duly convicted, shall exist within the United States, or any place subject to their jurisdiction.

SECTION 2. Congress shall have power to enforce this article by appropriate legislation.

AMENDMENT XIV
July 28, 1868

SECTION 1. All persons born or naturalized in the United States, and subject to the jurisdiction thereof, are citizens of the United States and of the State wherein they reside. No State shall make or enforce any law which shall abridge the privileges or immunities of citizens of the United States; nor shall any State deprive any person of life, liberty, or property, without due process of law; nor deny to any person within its jurisdiction the equal protection of the laws.

SECTION 2. Representatives shall be apportioned among the several States according to their respective numbers, counting the whole number of persons in each State, excluding Indians not taxed. But when the right to vote at any election for the choice of electors for President and Vice President of the United States, Representatives in Congress, the Executive and Judicial officers of a State, or the members of the Legislature thereof, is denied to any of the male inhabitants of such State, being twenty-one years of age, and citizens of the United States, or in any way abridged, except for participation in rebellion, or other crime, the basis of representation therein shall be reduced in the proportion which the number of such

---

[9] Amendment XI qualifies Article III, Section 2.
[10] This amendment replaces Clause 3 in Article II, Section I, and annuls it.
[11] The clause in brackets is superseded by the 20th Amendment, Section 3.

male citizens shall bear to the whole number of male citizens twenty-one years of age in such State.

SECTION 3. No person shall be a Senator or Representative in Congress, or elector of President and Vice President, or hold any office, civil or military, under the United States, or under any State, who, having previously taken an oath, as a member of Congress, or as an officer of the United States, or as a member of any State legislature, or as an executive or judicial officer of any State, to support the Constitution of the United States, shall have engaged in insurrection or rebellion against the same, or given aid or comfort to the enemies thereof. But Congress may by a vote of two-thirds of each House, remove such disability.

SECTION 4. The validity of the public debt of the United States, authorized by law, including debts incurred for payment of pensions and bounties for services in suppressing insurrection or rebellion, shall not be questioned. But neither the United States nor any State shall assume or pay any debt or obligation incurred in aid of insurrection or rebellion against the United States, or any claim for the loss or emancipation of any slave; but all such debts, obligations and claims shall be held illegal and void.

SECTION 5. The Congress shall have power to enforce, by appropriate legislation, the provisions of this article.

AMENDMENT XV
March 30, 1870

SECTION 1. The right of citizens of the United States to vote shall not be denied or abridged by the United States or by any State on account of race, color, or previous condition of servitude—

SECTION 2. The Congress shall have power to enforce this article by appropriate legislation—

AMENDMENT XVI
February 25, 1913

The Congress shall have power to lay and collect taxes on incomes, from whatever source derived, without apportionment among the several States, and without regard to any census or enumeration.

AMENDMENT XVII
May 31, 1913

The Senate of the United States shall be composed of two senators from each State, elected by the people thereof, for six years; and each Senator shall have one vote. The electors in each State shall have the qualifications requisite for electors of the most numerous branch of the State legislature.

When vacancies happen in the representation of any State in the Senate, the executive authority of such State shall issue writs of election to fill such vacancies: *Provided,* That the legislature of any State may empower the executive thereof to make temporary appointments until the people fill the vacancies by election as the legislature may direct.

This amendment shall not be so construed as to affect the election or term of any senator chosen before it becomes valid as part of the Constitution.

AMENDMENT XVIII
January 29, 1919

After one year from the ratification of this article, the manufacture, sale, or transportation of intoxicating liquors within, the importation thereof into, or the exportation thereof from the United States and all territory subject to the jurisdiction thereof for beverage purposes is hereby prohibited.

The Congress and the several States shall have concurrent power to enforce this article by appropriate legislation.

This article shall be inoperative unless it shall have been ratified as an amendment to the Constitution by the legislatures of the several States, as provided in the Constitution, within seven years from the date of the submission hereof to the States by Congress.

AMENDMENT XIX
August 26, 1920

The right of citizens of the United States to vote shall not be denied or abridged by the United States or by any States on account of sex.

Congress shall have power by appropriate legislation to enforce the provisions of this article.

AMENDMENT XX
February 6, 1933

SECTION 1. The terms of the President and Vice-President shall end at noon on the twentieth day of January, and the terms of Senators and Representatives at noon on the third day of January, of the years in which such terms would have ended if this article had not been ratified; and the terms of their successors shall then begin.

SECTION 2. The Congress shall assemble at least once in every year, and such meeting shall begin at noon on the third day of January, unless they shall by law appoint a different day.

SECTION 3. If, at the time fixed for the beginning of the term of the President, the President-elect shall have died, the Vice-President-elect shall become President. If a President shall not have been chosen before the time fixed for the beginning of his term or if the President-elect shall have failed to qualify, then the Vice-President-elect shall act as President until a President shall have qualified; and the Congress may by law provide for the case wherein neither a President-elect nor a Vice-President-elect have qualified, declaring who shall then act as President, or the manner in which one who is to act shall be selected, and such person shall act accordingly until a President or Vice-President shall have qualified.

SECTION 4. The Congress may by law provide for the case of the death of any of the persons from whom the House of Representatives may choose a President whenever the right of choice shall have devolved upon them, and for the case of the death of any of the persons from whom the Senate may choose a Vice-President whenever the right of choice shall have devolved upon them.

SECTION 5. Sections 1 and 2 shall take ef-

fect on the 15th day of October following the ratification of this article.

SECTION 6. This article shall be inoperative unless it shall have been ratified as an amendment to the Constitution by the legislatures of three-fourths of the several States within seven years from the date of its submission.

AMENDMENT XXI
December 5, 1933

SECTION 1. The eighteenth article of amendment to the Constitution of the United States is hereby repealed.

SECTION 2. The transportation or importation into any State, Territory, or possession of the United States for delivery or use therein of intoxicating liquors, in violation of the laws thereof, is hereby prohibited.

SECTION 3. This article shall be inoperative unless it shall have been ratified as an amendment to the Constitution by conventions in the several States, as provided in the Constitution, within seven years from the date of the submission hereof to the States by the Congress.

AMENDMENT XXII
February 26, 1951

SECTION 1. No person shall be elected to the office of the President more than twice, and no person who has held the office of President, or acted as President, for more than two years of a term to which some other person was elected President shall be elected to the office of the President more than once. But this Article shall not apply to any person holding the office of President when this Article was proposed by the Congress, and shall not prevent any person who may be holding the office of President, or acting as President, during the term within which this Article becomes operative from holding the office of President or acting as President during the remainder of such term.

SECTION 2. This article shall be inoperative unless it shall have been ratified as an amendment to the Constitution by the legislatures of three-fourths of the several States within seven years from the date of its submission to the States by the Congress.

AMENDMENT XXIII
April 3, 1961

SECTION 1. The District constituting the seat of Government of the United States shall appoint in such manner as the Congress may direct:

A number of electors of President and Vice President equal to the whole number of Senators and Representatives in Congress to which the District would be entitled if it were a State, but in no event more than the least populous State; they shall be in addition to those appointed by the States, but they shall be considered, for the purposes of the election of President and Vice President, to be electors appointed by a State; and they shall meet in the District and perform such duties as provided by the twelfth article of amendment.

SECTION 2. The Congress shall have power to enforce this article by appropriate legislation.

AMENDMENT XXIV
February 4, 1964

SECTION 1. The right of citizens of the United States to vote in any primary or other election for President or Vice President, for electors for President or Vice President, or for Senator or Representative in Congress, shall not be denied or abridged by the United States or any State by reason of failure to pay any poll tax or other tax.

SECTION 2. The Congress shall have power to enforce this article by appropriate legislation.

AMENDMENT XXV
February 10, 1967

SECTION 1. In case of removal of the President from office or of his death or resignation, the Vice President shall become President.

SECTION 2. Whenever there is a vacancy in the office of the Vice President, the President shall nominate a Vice President who shall take the office upon confirmation by a majority vote of both Houses of Congress.

SECTION 3. Whenever the President transmits to the President pro tempore of the Senate and the Speaker of the House of Representatives his written declaration that he is unable to discharge the powers and duties of his office, and until he transmits to them a written declaration to the contrary, such powers and duties shall be discharged by the Vice President as Acting President.

SECTION 4. Whenever the Vice President and a majority of either the principal officers of the executive departments or of such other body as Congress may by law provide, transmit to the President pro tempore of the Senate and the Speaker of the House of Representatives their written declaration that the President is unable to discharge the powers and duties of his office, the Vice President shall immediately assume the powers and duties of the office as Acting President.

Thereafter, when the President transmits to the President pro tempore of the Senate and the Speaker of the House of Representatives his written declaration that no inability exists, he shall resume the powers and duties of his office unless the Vice President and a majority of either the principal officers of the executive department or of such other body as Congress may by law provide, transmit within four days to the President pro tempore of the Senate and the Speaker of the House of Representatives their written declaration that the President is unable to discharge the powers and duties of his office. Thereupon Congress shall decide the issue, assembling within forty-eight hours for that purpose if not in session. If the Congress, within twenty-one days after receipt of the latter written declaration, or, if Congress is not in session, within twenty-one days after Congress is required to assemble, determines by two-thirds vote of both Houses that the President is unable to discharge the powers and duties of his office, the Vice President shall continue to discharge the same as Acting President; otherwise, the President shall resume the powers and duties of his office.

AMENDMENT XXVI
June 30, 1971

SECTION 1. The right of citizens of the United States, who are eighteen years of age or older, to vote shall not be denied or abridged by the United States or by any State on account of age.

SECTION 2. The Congress shall have power to enforce this article by appropriate legislation.

QUOTATION DICTIONARY

ABILITY *Also see:* ACTION, CHARACTER, DISCRETION, FORCE, GENIUS, PERSEVERANCE, POWER, STRENGTH, SUCCESS.

There is something that is much more scarce, something finer far, something rarer than ability. It is the ability to recognize ability.

ELBERT HUBBARD

Consider the postage stamp: its usefulness consists in the ability to stick to one thing till it gets there.

JOSH BILLINGS

The question, "Who ought to be boss?" is like asking "Who ought to be the tenor in the quartet?" Obviously, the man who can sing tenor.

HENRY FORD

Executive ability is deciding quickly and getting somebody else to do the work.

JOHN G. POLLARD

They are able because they think they are able.

VERGIL

Ability is of little account without opportunity.

NAPOLEON BONAPARTE

Natural abilities are like natural plants; they need pruning by study.

FRANCIS BACON

The wind and the waves are always on the side of the ablest navigators.

EDWARD GIBBON

ABSENCE *Also see:* LONELINESS, MEMORY, WANT.

Is not absence death to those who love?

ALEXANDER POPE

Absence diminishes little passions and increases great ones, as wind extinguishes candles and fans a fire.

FRANÇOIS DE LA ROCHEFOUCALD

The absent are never without fault. Nor the present without excuse.

BENJAMIN FRANKLIN

When a man is out of sight, it is not too long before he is out of mind.

THOMAS À KEMPIS

The absent are like children, helpless to defend themselves.

CHARLES READE

The absent are always in the wrong.

ENGLISH PROVERB

Absence and death are the same—only that in death there is no suffering.

WALTER S. LANDOR

ABSTINENCE *Also see:* DRUNKENNESS, MODERATION, SACRIFICE.

Complete abstinence is easier than perfect moderation.

ST. AUGUSTINE

Always rise from the table with an appetite, and you will never sit down without one.

WILLIAM PENN

All philosophy lies in two words, sustain and abstain.

EPICTETUS

The only way for a rich man to be healthy is by exercise and abstinence, to live as if he were poor.

WILLIAM TEMPLE

Abstaining is favorable both to the head and the pocket.

HORACE GREELEY

ABSURDITY *Also see:* RIDICULE, SARCASM.

In politics, an absurdity is not a handicap.

NAPOLEON BONAPARTE

There is nothing so absurd or ridiculous that has not at some time been said by some philosopher.

OLIVER GOLDSMITH

It is the height of absurdity to sow little but weeds in the first half of one's lifetime and expect to harvest a valuable crop in the second half.

PERCY JOHNSTON

Almost all absurdity of conduct arises from the imitation of those whom we cannot resemble.

SAMUEL JOHNSON

ABUSE *Also see:* CRUELTY, INJURY, POLLUTION, SLANDER.

Abuse is the weapon of the vulgar.

SAMUEL GRISWOLD GOODRICH

The best security against revolution is in constant correction of abuses and the introduction of needed improvements.

RICHARD WHATELY

I never yet heard man or woman much abused that I was not inclined to think the better of them, and to transfer the suspicion or dislike to the one who found pleasure in pointing out the defects of another.

JANE PORTER

There is none more abusive to others than they that lie most open to it themselves.

SENECA

Anyone entrusted with power will abuse it if not also animated with the love of truth and virtue.

JEAN DE LA FONTAINE

ACCURACY *Also see:* FACTS, FIDELITY, PUNCTU-
ALITY, SCIENCE.

Accuracy is the twin brother of honesty; inaccuracy, of dishonesty.

CHARLES SIMMONS

Accuracy is to a newspaper what virtue is to a lady, but a
newspaper can always print a retraction.

ADLAI E. STEVENSON

Accuracy of statement is one of the first elements of truth;
inaccuracy is a near kin to falsehood.

TRYON EDWARDS

Even a stopped clock is right twice a day.

ANONYMOUS

From principles is derived probability, but truth or certainty is obtained only from facts.

NATHANIEL HAWTHORNE

ACHIEVEMENT *Also see:* ACTION, AIM, AMBITION,
DECISION, LABOR, PUR-
POSE, SUCCESS, WORK.

I feel that the greatest reward for doing is the opportunity
to do more.

JONAS SALK

Mere longevity is a good thing for those who watch Life
from the side lines. For those who play the game, an hour
may be a year, a single day's work an achievement for eternity.

GABRIEL HEATTER

Do not attempt to do a thing unless you are sure of yourself;
but do not relinquish it simply because someone else is not
sure of you.

STEWART E. WHITE

Every man who is high up loves to think that he has done it
all himself; and the wife smiles, and lets it go at that.

JAMES MATTHEW BARRIE

Life affords no higher pleasure than that of surmounting
difficulties, passing from one step of success to another,
forming new wishes and seeing them gratified.

SAMUEL JOHNSON

ACTION *Also see:* ACHIEVEMENT, DESIRE, LABOR,
PROGRESS, WORK.

Thought is the blossom; language the bud; action the fruit
behind it.

RALPH WALDO EMERSON

Positive anything is better than negative nothing.

ELBERT HUBBARD

Our grand business is not to see what lies dimly at a distance, but to do what lies clearly at hand.

THOMAS CARLYLE

The actions of men are the best interpreters of their
thoughts.

JOHN LOCKE

Think like a man of action and act like a man of thought.

HENRI BERGSON

What you do speaks so loud that I cannot hear what you
say.

RALPH WALDO EMERSON

Action may not always bring happiness; but there is no
happiness without action.

BENJAMIN DISRAELI

It is by acts and not by ideas that people live.

ANATOLE FRANCE

Thought and theory must precede all salutary action; yet
action is nobler in itself than either thought or theory.

WILLIAM WORDSWORTH

Action to be effective must be directed to clearly conceived
ends.

JAWAHARLAL NEHRU

Indolence is a delightful but distressing state; we must be
doing something to be happy. Action is no less necessary
than thought to the instinctive tendencies of the human
frame.

MAHATMA GANDHI

ADAPTABILITY *See also:* CONFORMITY.

Make yourself necessary to somebody.

RALPH WALDO EMERSON

Complete adaptation to environment means death. The essential point in all response is the desire to control environment.

JOHN DEWEY

One learns to itch where one can scratch.

ERNEST BRAMAH

Adaptability is not imitation. It means power of resistance
and assimilation.

MAHATMA GANDHI

ADMIRATION *Also see:* FAME, FOOL, LOVE,
PRAISE, RESPECT.

We always love those who admire us; we do not always love
those whom we admire.

FRANÇOIS DE LA ROCHEFOUCAULD

The only things one can admire at length are those one admires without knowing why.

JEAN ROSTAND

Fools admire, but men of sense approve.

ALEXANDER POPE

A fool always finds a greater fool to admire him.

NICOLAS BOLLEAU-DESPRÉAUX

Admiration is a very short-lived passion, that immediately
decays upon growing familiar with its object.

JOSEPH ADDISON

ADVANCEMENT . . . See PROGRESS

ADVENTURE *Also see:* DANGER, DISCOVERY, IN-
VENTION, SPACE, TRAVEL.

Without adventure civilization is in full decay.

ALFRED NORTH WHITEHEAD

Who dares nothing, need hope for nothing.

JOHANN VON SCHILLER

You can't cross the sea merely by standing and staring at the water. Don't let yourself indulge in vain wishes.

RABINDRANATH TAGORE

We live in a wonderful world that is full of beauty, charm and adventure. There is no end to the adventures that we can have if only we seek them with our eyes open.

JAWAHARLAL NEHRU

ADVERSITY Also see: AFFLICTION, CALAMITY, MISERY, PROSPERITY.

By trying we can easily learn to endure adversity—another man's I mean.

MARK TWAIN

Adversity makes men, and prosperity makes monsters.

VICTOR HUGO

Little minds are tamed and subdued by misfortune; but great minds rise above them.

WASHINGTON IRVING

Prosperity is not without many fears and distastes; adversity not without many comforts and hopes.

FRANCIS BACON

Adversity is the first path to truth.

LORD BYRON

The good things of prosperity are to be wished; but the good things that belong to adversity are to be admired.

SENECA

Prosperity is a great teacher; adversity is a greater. Possession pampers the mind; privation trains and strengthens it.

WILLIAM HAZLITT

ADVERTISING Also see: ART, BUSINESS, PUBLICITY.

The business that considers itself immune to the necessity for advertising sooner or later finds itself immune to business.

DERBY BROWN

Advertising is the foot on the accelerator, the hand on the throttle, the spur on the flank that keeps our economy surging forward.

ROBERT W. SARNOFF

Doing business without advertising is like winking at a girl in the dark. You know what you are doing, but nobody else does.

STEUART H. BRITT

The product that will not sell without advertising will not sell profitably with advertising.

ALBERT LASKER

Advertising promotes that divine discontent which makes people strive to improve their economic status.

RALPH S. BUTLER

ADVICE Also see: CAUTION, EXPERIENCE, HELP, WISDOM.

Advice is like snow; the softer it falls the longer it dwells upon, and the deeper it sinks into the mind.

SAMUEL TAYLOR COLERIDGE

Advice is seldom welcome, and those who need it the most, like it the least.

LORD CHESTERFIELD

It is easy when we are in prosperity to give advice to the afflicted.

AESCHYLUS

In those days he was wiser than he is now—he used frequently to take my advice.

WINSTON CHURCHILL

Men give away nothing so liberally as their advice.

FRANÇOIS DE LA ROCHEFOUCAULD

No man is so foolish but he may sometimes give another good counsel, and no man so wise that he may not easily err if he takes no other counsel than his own. He that is taught only by himself has a fool for a master.

BEN JONSON

It is only too easy to make suggestions and later try to escape the consequences of what we say.

JAWAHARLAL NEHRU

The only thing to do with good advice is to pass it on. It is never of any use to oneself.

OSCAR WILDE

He that won't be counselled can't be helped.

BENJAMIN FRANKLIN

There is as much difference between the counsel that a friend giveth, and that a man giveth himself, as there is between the counsel of a friend and a flatterer.

FRANCIS BACON

AFFECTION Also see: ADMIRATION, FRIENDSHIP, KISS, LOVE.

A slight touch of friendly malice and amusement towards those we love keeps our affections for them from turning flat.

LOGAN P. SMITH

Talk not of wasted affection; affection never was wasted.

HENRY WADSWORTH LONGFELLOW

Caresses, expressions of one sort or another, are necessary to the life of the affections as leaves are to the life of a tree.

NATHANIEL HAWTHORNE

The affections are like lightning: you cannot tell where they will strike till they have fallen.

JOHN BAPTISTE LACORDAIRE

A woman's life is a history of the affections.

WASHINGTON IRVING

I never met a man I didn't like.

WILL ROGERS

AFFLICTION See also: ADVERSITY, CALAMITY, DISEASE, PAIN, SORROW, SUFFERING.

The gem cannot be polished without friction, nor man perfected without trials.

CHINESE PROVERB

Strength is born in the deep silence of long-suffering hearts; not amid joy.

FELICIA HEMANS

Affliction, like the iron-smith, shapes as it smites.

CHRISTIAN NESTELL BOVEE

I thank God for my handicaps, for through them, I have found myself, my work and my God.

HELEN KELLER

As threshing separates the wheat from the chaff, so does affliction purify virtue.

RICHARD E. BURTON

Humanity either makes, or breeds, or tolerates all its afflictions.

H. G. WELLS

Affliction comes to us, not to make us sad but sober; not to make us sorry but wise.

HENRY WARD BEECHER

AGE Also see: AVARICE, YOUTH.

I refuse to admit I'm more than fifty-two, even if that does make my sons illegitimate.

LADY ASTOR

If wrinkles must be written upon our brows, let them not be written upon the heart. The spirit should never grow old.

JAMES A. GARFIELD

Age ... is a matter of feeling, not of years.

GEORGE WILLIAM CURTIS

Age does not depend upon years, but upon temperament and health. Some men are born old, and some never grow so.

TRYON EDWARDS

A man is not old as long as he is seeking something.

JEAN ROSTAND

The woman who tells her age is either too young to have anything to lose or too old to have anything to gain.

CHINESE PROVERB

The older I grow the more I distrust the familiar doctrine that age brings wisdom.

H. L. MENCKEN.

AGGRESSION Also see: ANGER, ENEMY, WAR.

The truth is often a terrible weapon of aggression. It is possible to lie, and even to murder, with the truth.

ALFRED ADLER

It is the habit of every aggressor nation to claim that it is acting on the defensive.

JAWAHARLAL NEHRU

Civilized society is perpetually menaced with disintegration through this primary hostility of men towards one another ...

SIGMUND FREUD

AGITATION Also see: ARGUMENT, DISSENT.

Agitation is that part of our intellectual life where vitality results; there ideas are born, breed and bring forth.

GEORGE EDWARD WOODBERRY

Those who profess to favor freedom, and yet depreciate agitation, are men who want rain without thunder and lightning. They want the ocean without the roar of its many waters.

FREDERICK DOUGLASS

Agitation is the marshalling of the conscience of a nation to mold its laws.

ROBERT PEEL

AGNOSTICISM Also see: ATHEISM, GOD, SKEPTICISM.

Agnosticism simply means that a man shall not say he knows or believes that for which he has no grounds for professing to believe.

THOMAS HUXLEY

Agnosticism is the philosophical, ethical and religious dry-rot of the modern world.

F. E. ABBOT

There is only one greater folly than that of the fool who says in his heart there is no God, and that is the folly of the people that says with its head that it does not know whether there is a God or not.

OTTO VON BISMARK

I am an agnostic; I do not pretend to know what many ignorant men are sure of.

CLARENCE DARROW

AGREEMENT Also see: COMPROMISE, CONFORMITY, UNDERSTANDING, UNITY.

We hardly find any persons of good sense save those who agree with us.

FRANCOIS DE LA ROCHEFOUCAULD

When two men in business always agree, one of them is unnecessary.

WILLIAM WRIGLEY, JR.

There is no conversation more boring than the one where everybody agrees.

MICHEL DE MONTAIGNE

I have never in my life learned anything from any man who agreed with me.

DUDLEY FIELD MALONE

The fellow that agrees with everything you say is either a fool or he is getting ready to skin you.

KIN HUBBARD

You may easily play a joke on a man who likes to argue—agree with him.

ED HOWE

AIM Also see: AMBITION, DESIRE, END, IDEAL, PURPOSE, PURSUIT.

Aim at the sun, and you may not reach it; but your arrow will fly far higher than if aimed at an object on a level with yourself.

JOEL HAWES

In great attempts it is glorious even to fall.

CASSIUS

Not failure, but low aim, is crime.

JAMES RUSSELL LOWELL

High aims form high characters, and great objects bring out great minds.

TRYON EDWARDS

AMBIGUITY *Also see:* DOUBT

Those who write clearly have readers, those who write obscurely have commentators.

ALBERT CAMUS

I fear explanations explanatory of things explained.

ABRAHAM LINCOLN

Clearly spoken, Mr. Fogg; you explain English by Greek.

BENJAMIN FRANKLIN

That must be wonderful; I have no idea of what it means.

MOLIÈRE

AMBITION *Also see:* AIM, CONSCIENCE, DESIRE, EFFORT, GLORY, IDEAL, PURPOSE, SUCCESS, WORTH, ZEAL.

You can't hold a man down without staying down with him.

BOOKER T. WASHINGTON

Ambition is the last refuge of failure.

OSCAR WILDE

We grow small trying to be great.

E. STANLEY JONES

Too low they build who build below the skies.

EDWARD YOUNG

Hitch your wagon to a star.

RALPH WALDO EMERSON

Most people would succeed in small things if they were not troubled with great ambitions.

HENRY WADSWORTH LONGFELLOW

He who surpasses or subdues mankind, must look down on the hate of those below.

LORD BYRON

Ambition is so powerful a passion in the human breast, that however high we reach we are never satisfied.

NICCOLÒ MACHIAVELLI

All ambitions are lawful except those which climb upward on the miseries or credulities of mankind.

JOSEPH CONRAD

If you wish to reach the highest, begin at the lowest.

PUBLILIUS SYRUS

When you are aspiring to the highest place, it is honorable to reach the second or even the third rank.

CICERO

Some folks can look so busy doing nothin' that they seem indispensable.

KIN HUBBARD

The men who succeed are the efficient few. They are the few who have the ambition and will power to develop themselves.

HERBERT N. CASSON

No bird soars too high if he soars with his own wings.

WILLIAM BLAKE

It seems to me we can never give up longing and wishing while we are thoroughly alive. There are certain things we feel to be beautiful and good, and we must hunger after them.

GEORGE ELIOT

The very substance of the ambitious is merely the shadow of a dream.

WILLIAM SHAKESPEARE

AMERICA *Also see:* DEMOCRACY, NATION, PARTY, PATRIOTISM, PRESIDENT.

America has believed that in differentiation, not in uniformity, lies the path of progress. It acted on this belief; it has advanced human happiness, and it has prospered.

LOUIS D. BRANDEIS

America is not a mere body of traders; it is a body of free men. Our greatness is built upon our freedom—is moral, not material. We have a great ardor for gain; but we have a deep passion for the rights of man.

WOODROW WILSON

A citizen of America will cross the ocean to fight for democracy, but won't cross the street to vote in a national election.

BILL VAUGHAN

If there is one word that describes our form of society in America, it may be the word—voluntary.

LYNDON BAINES JOHNSON

Intellectually I know that America is no better than any other country; emotionally I know she is better than every country.

SINCLAIR LEWIS

I am certain that, however great the hardships and the trials which loom ahead, our America will endure and the cause of human freedom will triumph.

CORDELL HULL

I would rather see the United States respected than loved by other nations.

HENRY CABOT LODGE

Wake up, America.

AUGUSTUS P. GARDNER

America lives in the heart of every man everywhere who wishes to find a region where he will be free to work out his destiny as he chooses.

WOODROW WILSON

Our country is still young and its potential is still enormous. We should remember, as we look toward the future, that the more fully we believe in and achieve freedom and equal opportunity—not simply for ourselves but for others—the greater our accomplishments as a nation will be.

HENRY FORD II

The interesting and inspiring thing about America is that she asks nothing for herself except what she has a right to ask for humanity itself.

WOODROW WILSON

If the American dream is for Americans only, it will remain our dream and never be our destiny.

RENÉ DE VISME WILLIAMSON

Our country, right or wrong. When right, to be kept right; when wrong, to be put right.

CARL SCHURZ

The country's honor must be upheld at home and abroad.

THEODORE ROOSEVELT

In the field of world policy, I would dedicate this nation to the policy of the good neighbor.

FRANKLIN DELANO ROOSEVELT

Let our object be our country, our whole country, and nothing but our country.

DANIEL WEBSTER

America . . . a great social and economic experiment, noble in motive and far-reaching in purpose.

HERBERT HOOVER

America is not merely a nation but a nation of nations.

LYNDON BAINES JOHNSON

AMIABILITY Also *see:* AGREEMENT, CHEERFUL-NESS, COURTESY, HAPPINESS.

Natural amiableness is too often seen in company with sloth, with uselessness, with the vanity of fashionable life.

WILLIAM ELLERY CHANNING

How easy to be amiable in the midst of happiness and success.

ANNE SOPHIE SWETCHINE

An inexhaustible good nature is one of the most precious gifts of heaven, spreading itself like oil over the troubled sea of thought, and keeping the mind smooth and equable in the roughest weather.

WASHINGTON IRVING

AMUSEMENT Also *see:* ENJOYMENT, JOY, PLEA-SURE, REVERIE.

. . . the happiness of those who cannot think.

ALEXANDER POPE

The only way to amuse some people is to slip and fall on an icy pavement.

ED HOWE

True enjoyment comes from activity of the mind and exercise of the body; the two are ever united.

HUMBOLDT

You can't live on amusement. It is the froth on water—an inch deep and then the mud.

GEORGE MACDONALD

I am a great friend to public amusements, for they keep people from vice.

SAMUEL JOHNSON

If those who are the enemies of innocent amusements had the direction of the world, they would take away the spring, and youth, the former from the year, the latter from human life.

HONORÉ DE BALZAC

The real character of a man is found out by his amusements.

JOSHUA REYNOLDS

Life is worth living, but only if we avoid the amusements of grown-up people.

ROBERT LYND

The mind ought sometimes to be diverted, that it may return the better to thinking.

PHAEDRUS

ANCESTRY Also *see:* ARISTOCRACY.

Everyone has ancestors and it is only a question of going back far enough to find a good one.

HOWARD KENNETH NIXON

Whoever serves his country well has no need of ancestors.

VOLTAIRE

Every man is his own ancestor, and every man his own heir. He devises his own future, and he inherits his own past.

H. F. HEDGE

Everyone has something ancestral, even if it is nothing more than a disease.

ED HOWE

Some men by ancestry are only the shadow of a mighty name.

LUCAN

The man who has nothing to boast of but his illustrious ancestry, is like the potato—the best part under ground.

THOMAS OVERBURY

It is of no consequence of what parents a man is born, so he be man of merit.

HORACE

We inherit nothing truly, but what our actions make us worthy of.

GEORGE CHAPMAN

It is indeed a desirable thing to be well descended, but the glory belongs to our ancestors.

PLUTARCH

We are all omnibuses in which our ancestors ride, and every now and then one of them sticks his head out and embarrasses us.

OLIVER WENDELL HOLMES

ANGER Also *see:* AGGRESSION, QUARREL, TEMPER.

When angry count four; when very angry, swear.

MARK TWAIN

Men often make up in wrath what they want in reason.

WILLIAM ROUNSEVILLE ALGER

Anger blows out the lamp of the mind.

ROBERT GREEN INGERSOLL

To rule one's anger is well; to prevent it is still better.

TRYON EDWARDS

Beware the fury of a patient man

JOHN DRYDEN

An angry man opens his mouth and shuts up his eyes.

CATO

Anger is seldom without argument but seldom with a good one.

HALIFAX

Anger and intolerance are the twin enemies of correct understanding.

MAHATMA GANDHI

An angry man is again angry with himself when he returns to reason.

PUBLILIUS SYRUS

Anger is a momentary madness, so control your passion or it will control you.

HORACE

Anger begins with folly, and ends with repentance.

H. G. BOHN

Keep cool; anger is not an argument.

DANIEL WEBSTER

The greatest remedy for anger is delay.

SENECA

When a man is wrong and won't admit it, he always gets angry.

HALIBURTON

ANTICIPATION *Also see:* ANXIETY, DISAPPOINT-
MENT, HOPE.

Nothing is so good as it seems beforehand.

GEORGE ELIOT

If pleasures are greatest in anticipation, just remember that this is also true of trouble.

ELBERT HUBBARD

What we anticipate seldom occurs, what we least expected generally happens.

BENJAMIN DISRAELI

Few enterprises of great labor or hazard would be undertaken if we had not the power of magnifying the advantages we expect from them.

SAMUEL JOHNSON

Our desires always disappoint us; for though we meet with something that gives us satisfaction, yet it never thoroughly answers our expectation.

FRANÇOIS DE LA ROCHEFOUCAULD

Nothing is so wretched or foolish as to anticipate misfortunes. What madness is it to be expecting evil before it comes.

SENECA

ANXIETY *Also see:* ANTICIPATION, FEAR, WORRY.

The natural role of twentieth-century man is anxiety.

NORMAN MAILER

The thinner the ice, the more anxious is everyone to see whether it will bear.

JOSH BILLINGS

We have a lot of anxieties, and one cancels out another very often.

WINSTON CHURCHILL

Do not anticipate trouble, or worry about what may never happen. Keep in the sunlight.

BENJAMIN FRANKLIN

God never built a Christian strong enough to carry today's duties and tomorrow's anxieties piled on the top of them.

THEODORE LEDYARD CUYLER

The misfortunes hardest to bear are those which never came.

JAMES RUSSELL LOWELL

Borrow trouble for yourself, if that's your nature, but don't lend it to your neighbors.

RUDYARD KIPLING

APATHY *Also see:* IDLENESS, NEGLECT, WORK.

Apathy is a sort of living oblivion.

HORACE GREELEY

There is no calamity which a great nation can invite which equals that which follows a supine submission to wrong and injustice.

GROVER CLEVELAND

The apathy of the people is enough to make every statue leap from its pedestal and hasten the resurrection of the dead.

WILLIAM LLOYD GARRISON

The tyranny of a prince in an oligarchy is not so dangerous to the public welfare as the apathy of a citizen in a democracy.

MONTESQUIEU

Most people are on the world, not in it—having no conscious sympathy or relationship to anything about them—undiffused, separate, and rigidly alone like marbles of polished stone, touching but separate.

JOHN MUIR

Nothing for preserving the body like having no heart.

JOHN PETIT-SENN

APPEARANCE *Also see:* DRESS, FASHION, ILLU-
SION, REALITY.

How little do they see what is, who frame their hasty judgments upon that which seems.

ROBERT SOUTHEY

The world is governed more by appearances than by realities, so that it is fully as necessary to seem to know something as to know it.

DANIEL WEBSTER

You are only what you are when no one is looking.

ROBERT C. EDWARDS

Half the work that is done in this world is to make things appear what they are not.

ELIAS ROOT BEADLE

You may turn into an archangel, a fool, or a criminal—no one will see it. But when a button is missing—everyone sees that.

ERICH M. REMARQUE

When I see a bird that walks like a duck and swims like a duck and quacks like a duck, I call that bird a duck.

RICHARD CARDINAL CUSHING

APPETITE *Also see:* DESIRE, EATING, GLUTTON, HUNGER.

Reason should direct and appetite obey.

CICERO

Let the stoics say what they please, we do not eat for the good of living, but because the meat is savory and the appetite is keen.

RALPH WALDO EMERSON

Animals feed; man eats. Only the man of intellect and judgment knows how to eat.

ANTHELME BRILLAT-SAVARIN

A well-governed appetite is a great part of liberty.

SENECA

ARGUMENT *Also see:* DIFFERENCE, DISSENT, QUARREL.

Debate is the death of conversation.

EMIL LUDWIG

People generally quarrel because they cannot argue.

GILBERT K. CHESTERTON

A long dispute means both parties are wrong.

VOLTAIRE

Behind every argument is someone's ignorance.

LOUIS D. BRANDEIS

The best way I know of to win an argument is to start by being in the right.

LORD HALLSHAM

He who establishes his argument by noise and command shows that his reason is weak.

MICHEL DE MONTAIGNE

Weak arguments are often thrust before my path; but although they are most unsubstantial, it is not easy to destroy them. There is not a more difficult feat known than to cut through a cushion with a sword.

RICHARD WHATELY

Any fact is better established by two or three good testimonies than by a thousand arguments.

NATHANIEL EMMONS

The sounder your argument, the more satisfaction you get out of it.

ED HOWE

Argument, as usually managed, is the worst sort of conversation.

JONATHAN SWIFT

ARISTOCRACY *Also see:* ANCESTRY, KING, RANK.

What is aristocracy? A corporation of the best, of the bravest.

THOMAS CARLYLE

I am an aristocrat. I love liberty; I hate equality.

JOHN RANDOLPH

Democracy means government by the uneducated, while aristocracy means government by the badly educated.

GILBERT K. CHESTERTON

There is a natural aristocracy among men. The grounds of this are virtue and talent.

THOMAS CARLYLE

Aristocracy is always cruel.

WENDELL PHILLIPS

Some will always be above others. Destroy the equality today, and it will appear again tomorrow.

RALPH WALDO EMERSON

The aristocrat is the democrat ripe and gone to seed.

RALPH WALDO EMERSON

ART *Also see:* ARTIST

If art is to nourish the roots of our culture, society must set the artist free to follow his vision wherever it takes him.

JOHN FITZGERALD KENNEDY

Art, like morality, consists in drawing the line somewhere.

GILBERT K. CHESTERTON

Art is an effort to create, beside the real world, a more human world.

ANDRÉ MAUROIS

Art is the most intense mode of individualism that the world has known.

OSCAR WILDE

The art of a people is a true mirror of their minds.

JAWAHARLAL NEHRU

The course of Nature is the art of God.

EDWARD YOUNG

Art is a form of catharsis.

DOROTHY PARKER

In art the hand can never execute anything higher than the heart can inspire.

RALPH WALDO EMERSON

Science and art belong to the whole world, and before them vanish the barriers of nationality.

JOHANN WOLFGANG VON GOETHE

Art is a collaboration between God and the artist, and the less the artist does the better.

ANDRÉ GIDE

Supreme art is a traditional statement of certain heroic and religious truth, passed on from age to age, modified by individual genius, but never abandoned.

WILLIAM BUTLER YEATS

The true work of art is but a shadow of the divine perfection.

MICHELANGEO

Nothing is so poor and melancholy as art that is interested in itself and not in its subject.

GEORGE SANTAYANA

Art is the desire of a man to express himself, to record the reactions of his personality to the world he lives in.

AMY LOWELL

We must never forget that art is not a form of propaganda, it is a form of truth.

JOHN FITZGERALD KENNEDY

ARTIST *Also see:* ART.

The artist does not illustrate science (but) he frequently responds to the same interests that a scientist does.

LEWIS MUMFORD

The work of art may have a moral effect, but to demand moral purpose from the artist is to make him ruin his work.

JOHANN WOLFGANG VON GOETHE

One puts into one's art what one has not been capable of putting into one's existence. It is because he was unhappy that God created the world.

HENRI DE MONTHERIANT

Every artist dips his brush in his own soul, and paints his own nature into his pictures.

HENRY WARD BEECHER

ASPIRATION . . . See AMBITION

ASSASSINATION *Also see:* MURDER, SLANDER.

Assassination: the extreme form of censorship.

GEORGE BERNARD SHAW

Assassination has never changed the history of the world.

BENJAMIN DISRAELI

Woe to the hand that shed this costly blood.

WILLIAM SHAKESPEARE

Yet each man kills the thing he loves,
By each let this be heard,
Some do it with a bitter look,
Some with a flattering word,
The coward does it with a kiss,
The brave man with a sword!

OSCAR WILDE

Some men are alive simply because it is against the law to kill them.

ED HOWE

I'm proud of the fact that I never invented weapons to kill.

THOMAS A. EDISON

ATHEISM *Also see:* AGNOSTICISM, DOUBT, GOD, SKEPTICISM, SOUL.

I am an atheist, thank God!

ANONYMOUS

I don't believe in God because I don't believe in Mother Goose.

CLARENCE DARROW

Nobody talks so constantly about God as those who insist that there is no God.

HEYWOOD BROUN

There are no atheists in the foxholes of Bataan.

DOUGLAS MACARTHUR

Atheism is rather in the life than in the heart of man.

FRANCIS BACON

The atheist has no hope.

J. F. CLARKE

An atheist is a man who has no invisible means of support.

FULTON J. SHEEN

AUTHORITY *Also see:* DEMOCRACY, GOVERNMENT, KING, POWER, PRESIDENT.

Nothing is more gratifying to the mind of man than power or dominion.

JOSEPH ADDISON

Every great advance in natural knowledge has involved the absolute rejection of authority.

THOMAS HUXLEY

The wisest have the most authority.

PLATO

All authority belongs to the people.

THOMAS JEFFERSON

If you wish to know what a man is, place him in authority.

YUGOSLAV PROVERB

Authority without wisdom is like a heavy ax without an edge, fitter to bruise than polish.

ANNE BRADSTREET

Authority is no stronger than the man who wields it.

DOLORES E. MCGUIRE

AUTOMATION *Also see:* MACHINE, SCIENCE, WORK.

The Christian notion of the possibility of redemption is incomprehensible to the computer.

VANCE PACKARD

If it keeps up, men will atrophy all his limbs but the push-button finger.

FRANK LLOYD WRIGHT

Jobs are physically easier, but the worker now takes home worries instead of an aching back.

HOMER BIGART

We live in a time when automation is ushering in a second industrial revolution.

ADLAI E. STEVENSON

AVARICE *Also see:* GREED, MISER, MONEY, SELFISHNESS, WEALTH.

If you would abolish avarice, you must abolish its mother, luxury.

CICERO

Avarice increases with the increasing pile of gold.

JUVENAL

Avarice in old age is foolish; for what can be more absurd than to increase our provisions for the road the nearer we approach to our journey's end.

CICERO

The avaricious man is like the barren sandy ground of the desert which sucks in all the rain and dew with greediness, but yields no fruitful herbs or plants for the benefit of others.

ZENO

Avarice is always poor.

SAMUEL JOHNSON

AVERAGE *Also see:* CONFORMITY, MAJORITY, MODERATION.

The average person puts only 25% of his energy and ability into his work. The world takes off its hat to those who put in more than 50% of their capacity, and stands on its head for those few and far between souls who devote 100%.

ANDREW CARNEGIE

I am only an average man but, by George, I work harder at it than the average man.

THEODORE ROOSEVELT

Not doing more than the average is what keeps the average down.

WILLIAM M. WINANS

A jury is a group of twelve people of average ignorance.

HERBERT SPENCER

BABY *Also see:* BIRTH, CHILDREN, FAMILY.

A baby is God's opinion that the world should go on.

CARL SANDBURG

The worst feature of a new baby is its mother's singing.

KIN HUBBARD

Babies are such a nice way to start people.

DON HEROLD

When the first baby laughed for the first time, the laugh broke into a thousand pieces and they all went skipping about, and that was the beginning of fairies.

JAMES MATTHEW BARRIE

BACHELOR

By persistently remaining single a man converts himself into a permanent public temptation.

OSCAR WILDE

Bachelors know more about women than married men; if they didn't, they'd be married too.

H. L. MENCKEN

A bachelor never quite gets over the idea that he is a thing of beauty and a boy forever.

HELEN ROWLAND

Bachelors have consciences, married men have wives.

H. L. MENCKEN

The only good husbands stay bachelors: They're too considerate to get married.

FINLEY PETER DUNNE

A single man has not nearly the value he would have in a state of union. He is an incomplete animal. He resembles the odd half of a pair of scissors.

BENJAMIN FRANKLIN

BARGAIN *Also see:* ADVERTISING, ECONOMY, GAIN, SALESMANSHIP.

. . . anything a customer thinks a store is losing money on.

KIN HUBBARD

Sometimes one pays most for the things one gets for nothing.

ALBERT EINSTEIN

Nothing is cheap which is superfluous, for what one does not need, is dear at a penny.

PLUTARCH

There are very honest people who do not think that they have had a bargain unless they have cheated a merchant.

ANATOLE FRANCE

BEAUTY *Also see:* APPEARANCE, ART, ARTIST, BLUSH, CHARM.

Beauty is not caused. It is.

EMILY DICKINSON

There is no cosmetic for beauty like happiness.

COUNTESS OF BLESSINGTON

Nothing's beautiful from every point of view.

HORACE

Beauty is power; a smile is its sword.

CHARLES READE

Truth exists for the wise, beauty for the feeling heart.

JOHANN VON SCHILLER

Beauty is the first present nature gives to women and the first it takes away.

GEORGE BROSSIN MÉRÉ

In every man's heart there is a secret nerve that answers to the vibrations of beauty.

CHRISTOPHER MORLEY

Beauty is only skin deep, but it's a valuable asset if you're poor or haven't any sense.

KIN HUBBARD

BEHAVIOR *Also see:* CHARM, COURTESY, MANNERS, MORALITY.

Behavior is a mirror in which every one displays his image.

JOHANN WOLFGANG VON GOETHE

Be nice to people on your way up because you'll meet them on your way down.

WILSON MIZNER

As a rule, there is no surer way to the dislike of men than to behave well where they have behaved badly.

LEW WALLACE

With a gentleman I am always a gentleman and a half, and with a fraud I try to be a fraud and a half.

OTTO VON BISMARCK

The reason the way of the transgressor is hard is because it's so crowded.

KIN HUBBARD

When man learns to understand and control his own behavior as well as he is learning to understand and control the behavior of crop plants and domestic animals, he may be justified in believing that he has become civilized.

E. C. STAKMAN

BELIEF *Also see:* ATHEISM, BUSINESS, CALAMITY, CONFIDENCE, CREDULITY, FAITH, HOPE, OPINION, PREJUDICE, RELIGION, THEORY, TRUST.

Nothing is so firmly believed as that which we least know.

MICHEL DE MONTAIGNE

It is always easier to believe than to deny. Our minds are naturally affirmative.

JOHN BURROUGHS

One person with a belief is equal to a force of ninety-nine who have only interests.

JOHN STUART MILL

Every time a child says "I don't believe in fairies" there is a little fairy somewhere that falls down dead.

JOHN MATTHEW BARRIE

Believe that life is worth living, and your belief will help create the fact.

WILLIAM JAMES

The practical effect of a belief is the real test of its soundness.

JAMES A. FROUDE

BENEVOLENCE ... See GENEROSITY

BIBLE *Also see:* GOD

The Bible is a window in this prison of hope, through which we look into eternity.

JOHN SULLIVAN DWIGHT

The total absence of humor from the Bible is one of the most singular things in all literature.

ALFRED NORTH WHITEHEAD

All human discoveries seem to be made only for the purpose of confirming more and more strongly the truths that come on high and are contained in the sacred writings.

JOHN F. HERSCHEL

To say nothing of its holiness or authority, the Bible contains more specimens of genius and taste than any other volume in existence.

WALTER S. LANDOR

Most people are bothered by those passages of Scripture they do not understand, but the passages that bother me are those I do understand.

MARK TWAIN

The Bible may be the truth, but it is not the whole truth and nothing but the truth.

SAMUEL BUTLER

BIGOTRY *Also see:* INTOLERANCE, OPINION, PERSECUTION, PREJUDICE, RACE, REASON, ZEAL.

Wisdom has never made a bigot, but learning has.

JOSH BILLINGS

A man must be both stupid and uncharitable who believes there is no virtue or truth but on his own side.

JOSEPH ADDISON

The mind of the bigot is like the pupil of the eye; the more light you pour upon it, the more it will contract.

OLIVER WENDELL HOLMES

Bigotry dwarfs the soul by shutting out the truth.

EDWIN HUBBEL CHAPIN

BIRTH *Also see:* ANCESTRY, BABY, BIRTH CONTROL, CHILDREN, DEATH, FAMILY.

About the only thing we have left that actually discriminates in favor of the plain people is the stork.

KIN HUBBARD

There is (sic) two things in life for which we are never fully prepared, and that is—twins.

JOSH BILLINGS

The fate of nations is intimately bound up with their powers of reproduction. All nations and all empires first felt decadence gnawing at them when their birth rate fell off.

BENITO MUSSOLINI

If nature had arranged that husbands and wives should have children alternatively, there would never be more than three in a family.

LAURENCE HOUSMAN

BIRTH CONTROL *Also see:* BIRTH, POPULATION, SEX.

Prevention of birth is a precipitation of murder.

TERTULLIAN

However we may pity the mother whose health and even life is imperiled by the performance of her natural duty, there yet remains no sufficient reason for condoning the direct murder of the innocent.

PIUS XI

No woman can call herself free who does not own and control her body. No woman can call herself free until she can choose consciously whether she will or will not be a mother.

MARGARET H. SANGER

BLINDNESS *Also see:* EYE.

In the country of the blind the one-eyed man is king.

ERASMUS

A blind man will not thank you for a looking-glass.

THOMAS FULLER

There's none so blind as they that won't see.

JONATHAN SWIFT

My darkness has been filled with the light of intelligence, and behold, the outer day-lit world was stumbling and groping in social blindness.

HELEN KELLER

Hatred is blind, as well as love.

THOMAS FULLER

What a blind person needs is not a teacher but another self.

HELEN KELLER.

BLOOD *Also see:* ANCESTRY, CHILDREN, REVOLU-
TION, WAR.

Blood will tell, but often it tells too much.

DON MARQUIS

No one need think that the world can be ruled without
blood. The civil sword shall and must be red and bloody.

MARTIN LUTHER

The future can be anything we want it to be, providing we
have the faith and that we realize that peace, no less than
war, required "blood and sweat and tears."

CHARLES F. KETTERING

The blood of the martyrs is the seed of the church.

TERTULLIAN

Peace, above all things, is to be desired, but blood must
sometimes be spilled to obtain it on equable and lasting
terms.

ANDREW JACKSON

Blood is a cleansing and sanctifying thing, and the nation
that regards it as the final horror has lost its manhood ...
there are many things more horrible than bloodshed, and
slavery is one of them!

PADRAIC PEARSE

BLUSH *Also see:* CRIME.

Man is the only animal that blushes. Or needs to.

MARK TWAIN

When a girl ceases to blush, she has lost the most powerful
charm of her beauty.

GREGORY I

The man that blushes is not quite a brute.

EDWARD YOUNG

BOASTING ... See VANITY

BODY *Also see:* HEALTH, MORALITY, SOUL.

A healthy body is a guest chamber for the soul: a sick body
is a prison.

FRANCIS BACON

A human being is an ingenious assembly of portable plumbing.

CHRISTOPHER MORLEY

We are bound to our bodies like an oyster is to its shell.

PLATO

All of us have mortal bodies, composed of perishable matter, but the soul lives forever: it is a portion of the Diety
housed in our bodies.

FLAVIUS JOSEPHUS

Our body is a well-set clock, which keeps good time, but if it
be too much or indiscreetly tampered with, the alarm runs
out before the hour.

JOSEPH HALL

BOLDNESS *Also see:* CONFIDENCE, COURAGE,
COWARDICE, GALLANTRY.

Fortune befriends the bold.

JOHN DRYDEN

Who bravely dares must sometimes risk a fall.

TOBIAS G. SMOLLETT

Fools rush in where angels fear to tread.

ALEXANDER POPE

When you cannot make up your mind which of two evenly
balanced courses of action you should take—choose the
bolder.

W. J. SLIM

Boldness is ever blind, for it sees not dangers and inconven-
iences; whence it is bad in council though good in execution.

FRANCIS BACON

It is wonderful what strength of purpose and boldness and
energy of will are roused by the assurance that we are doing
our duty.

WALTER SCOTT

In great straits and when hope is small, the boldest counsels
are the safest.

LIVY

BOOK *Also see:* BIBLE, CENSORSHIP, HISTORY,
LEARNING, LITERATURE, READ-
ING, WORD.

If I have not read a book before, it is, for all intents and
purposes, new to me whether it was printed yesterday or
three hundred years ago.

WILLIAM HAZLITT

That is a good book which is opened with expectation and
closed in profit.

AMOS BRONSON ALCOTT

Some books leave us free and some books make us free.

RALPH WALDO EMERSON

The books that help you the most are those which make
you think the most.

THEODORE PARKER

A book is a mirror: If an ass peers into it, you can't expect
an apostle to look out.

G. C. LICHTENBERG

Read the best books first, or you may not have a chance to
read them all.

HENRY DAVID THOREAU

This is the best book ever written by any man on the wrong
side of a question of which he is profoundly ignorant.

THOMAS B. MACAULAY

A house is not a home unless it contains food and fire for the
mind as well as the body.

MARGARET FULLER

Some books are to be tasted; others swallowed; and some to
be chewed and digested.

FRANCIS BACON

The man who does not read good books has no advantage
over the man who can't read them.

MARK TWAIN

Books, like friends, should be few and well chosen.

SAMUEL PATERSON

BORE and BOREDOM Also see: COMMUNICATION, CONVERSATION, LOQUACITY.

Bore, n. A person who talks when you wish him to listen.

AMBROSE BIERCE

There are few wild beasts more to be dreaded than a communicative man having nothing to communicate.

CHRISTIAN NESTELL BOVEE

The capacity of human beings to bore one another seems to be vastly greater than that of any other animal.

H. L. MENCKEN

Any subject can be made interesting, and therefore any subject can be made boring.

HILAIRE BELLOC

The man who lets himself be bored is even more contemptible than the bore.

SAMUEL BUTLER

A man who spends so much time talking about himself that you can't talk about yourself.

MELVILLE D. LANDON

A guy who wraps up a two-minute idea in a two-hour vocabulary.

WALTER WINCHELL

BORROWING Also see: CREDIT, DEBT.

The shoulders of a borrower are always a little straighter than those of a beggar.

MORRIS LEOPOLD ERNST

If you would know the value of money, go try to borrow some; for he that goes a-borrowing goes a-sorrowing.

BENJAMIN FRANKLIN

The human species, according to the best theory I can form of it, is composed of two distinct races: the men who borrow, and the men who lend.

CHARLES LAMB

Only an inventor knows how to borrow, and every man is or should be an inventor.

RALPH WALDO EMERSON

Live within your income, even if you have to borrow money to do so.

JOSH BILLINGS

Lots of fellows think a home is only good to borrow money on.

KIN HUBBARD

He who borrows sells his freedom.

GERMAN PROVERB

Creditors have better memories than debtors.

PROVERB

BOYS Also see: AGE, BACHELOR, CHILDREN, GIRLS, YOUTH.

I am convinced that every boy, in his heart, would rather steal second base than an automobile.

THOMAS CAMBELL CLARK

When you can't do anything else to a boy, you can make him wash his face.

ED HOWE

Boys will be boys, and so will a lot of middle-aged men.

KIN HUBBARD

Boys are beyond the range of anybody's sure understanding, at least when they are between the ages of 18 months and 90 years.

JAMES THURBER

A man can never quite understand a boy, even when he has been a boy.

GILBERT K. CHESTERTON

Of all wild beasts, the most difficult to manage.

PLATO

A boy is a magical creatue—you can lock him out of your workshop, but you can't lock him out of your heart.

ALLAN BECK

BREVITY Also see: CONVERSATION, LOQUACITY, SIMPLICITY, WORDS.

Never be so brief as to become obscure.

TRYON EDWARDS

The more you say, the less people remember. The fewer the words, the greater the profit.

FÉNELON

Brevity is the best recommendation of speech, whether in a senator or an orator.

CICERO

If you would be pungent, be brief; for it is with words as with sunbeams—the more they are condensed, the deeper they burn.

ROBERT SOUTHEY

The fewer the words, the better the prayer.

MARTIN LUTHER

Brevity is a great charm of eloquence.

CICERO

BROTHERHOOD Also see: CITIZENSHIP, EQUALITY, FAMILY, FRIENDSHIP, HUMANITY, MAN, SELFISHNESS.

On this shrunken globe, men can no longer live as strangers.

ADLAI E. STEVENSON

We must learn to live together as brothers or perish together as fools.

MARTIN LUTHER KING

We do not want the men of another color for our brothers-in-law, but we do want them for our brothers.

BOOKER T. WASHINGTON

Brotherhood is the very price and condition of man's survival.

CARLOS P. ROMULO

We live in a world that has narrowed into a neighborhood before it has broadened into a brotherhood.

LYNDON BAINES JOHNSON

It is easier to love humanity than to love one's neighbor.

ERIC HOFFER

BUSINESS Also see: ACTION, ADVERTISING, EMPLOYMENT, INDUSTRY, FINANCE, PURSUIT, SPECULATION, WORK.

There are two times in a man's life when he should not speculate: when he can't afford it, and when he can.

MARK TWAIN

All business proceeds on beliefs, or judgments of probabilities, and not on certainties.

CHARLES ELIOT

It is not the crook in modern business that we fear but the honest man who does not know what he is doing.

OWEN D. YOUNG

The successful business man sometimes makes his money by ability and experience; but he generally makes it by mistake.

GILBERT K. CHESTERTON

Business is a combination of war and sport.

ANDRÉ MAUROIS

A man to carry on a successful business must have imagination. He must see things as in a vision, a dream of the whole thing.

CHARLES M. SCHWAB

The best mental effort in the game of business is concentrated on the major problem of securing the consumer's dollar before the other fellow gets it.

STUART CHASE

A friendship founded on business is better than a business founded on friendship.

JOHN D. ROCKEFELLER

BUSY Also see: BUSINESS, INDUSTRY, PERSEVERANCE, WORK.

It is not enough to be busy; so are the ants. The question is: What are we busy about?

HENRY DAVID THOREAU

The busy have no time for tears.

LORD BYRON

Whoever admits that he is too busy to improve his methods has acknowledged himself to be at the end of his rope. And that is always the saddest predicament which anyone can get into.

J. OGDEN ARMOUR

What we hope ever to do with ease, we must learn first to do with diligence.

SAMUEL JOHNSON

The successful people are the ones who can think up things for the rest of the world to keep busy at.

DON MARQUIS

Who makes quick use of the moment, is a genius of prudence.

JOHANN KASPAR LAVATER

Occupation is the necessary basis of all enjoyment.

LEIGH HUNT

Busy souls have no time to be busybodies.

AUSTIN O'MALLEY

CALAMITY Also see: ADVERSITY, AFFLICTION, ANTICIPATION, CRISIS, DEBT, MISERY, WAR.

Calamities are of two kinds. Misfortune to ourselves, and good fortune to others.

AMBROSE BIERCE

He who forsees calamities, suffers them twice over.

BEILBY PORTEUS

Calamity is the perfect glass wherein we truly see and know ourselves.

WILLIAM DAVENANT

Calamity is the test of integrity.

SAMUEL RICHARDSON

It is only from the belief of the goodness and wisdom of a supreme being, that our calamities can be borne in the manner which becomes a man.

HENRY MACKENZIE

CANDOR Also see: HONESTY, SINCERITY, TRUTH.

Candor is the brightest gem of criticism.

BENJAMIN DISRAELI

Examine what is said, not him who speaks.

ARABIAN PROVERB

Friends, if we be honest with ourselves, we shall be honest with each other.

GEORGE MACDONALD

Frank and explicit—that is the right line to take when you wish to conceal your own mind and confuse the minds of others.

BENJAMIN DISRAELI

Nothing astonishes men so much as common sense and plain dealing.

RALPH WALDO EMERSON

There is no wisdom like frankness.

BENJAMIN DISRAELI

A "No" uttered from deepest conviction is better and greater than a "Yes" merely uttered to please, or what is worse, to avoid trouble.

MAHATMA GANDHI

CAPITALISM *Also see:* BUSINESS, FINANCE, MONEY.

The fundamental idea of modern capitalism is not the right of the individual to possess and enjoy what he has earned, but the thesis that the exercise of this right redounds to the general good.

RALPH BARTON PERRY

Capital is that part of wealth which is devoted to obtaining further wealth.

ALFRED MARSHALL

The dynamo of our economic system is self-interest which may range from mere petty greed to admirable types of self-expression.

FELIX FRANKFURTER

The inherent vice of capitalism is the unequal sharing of blessings; the inherent virtue of socialism is the equal sharing of miseries.

WINSTON CHURCHILL

Capitalism and communism stand at opposite poles. Their essential difference is this: The communist, seeing the rich man and his fine home, says: "No man should have so much." The capitalist, seeing the same thing, says: "All men should have as much."

PHELPS ADAMS

CATASTROPHE . . . See CALAMITY

CAUSE *Also see:* EFFICIENCY, MOTIVE, PURPOSE, RESULT.

That cause is strong, which has not a multitude, but a strong man behind it.

JAMES RUSSELL LOWELL

We are all ready to be savage in some cause. The difference between a good man and a bad one is the choice of the cause.

WILLIAM JAMES

No cause is helpless if it is just. Errors, no matter how popular, carry the seeds of their own destruction.

JOHN W. SCOVILLE

No man is worth his salt who is not ready at all times to risk his well-being, to risk his body, to risk his life, in a great cause.

THEODORE ROOSEVELT

The humblest citizen of all the land, when clad in the armor of a righteous cause, is stronger than all the hosts of Error.

WILLIAM JENNINGS BRYAN

The mark of the immature man is that he wants to die nobly for a cause, while the mark of a mature man is that he wants to live humbly for one.

WILHELM STEKEL

The probability that we may fail in the struggle ought not to deter us from the support of a cause we believe to be just.

ABRAHAM LINCOLN

Ours is an abiding faith in the cause of human freedom. We know it is God's cause.

THOMAS E. DEWEY

Men are blind in their own cause.

HEYWOOD BROUN

It is not a field of a few acres of ground, but a cause, that we are defending, and whether we defeat the enemy in one battle, or by degrees, the consequences will be the same.

THOMAS PAINE

Respectable men and women content with good and easy living are missing some of the most important things in life. Unless you give yourself to some great cause you haven't even begun to live.

WILLIAM P. MERRILL

CAUTION *Also see:* ADVICE, COWARDICE, DISCRETION, PRUDENCE, SAFETY, VIGILANCE.

I don't like these cold, precise, perfect people, who, in order not to speak wrong, never speak at all, and in order not to do wrong, never do anything.

HENRY WARD BEECHER

Among mortals second thoughts are wisest.

EURIPIDES

The chief danger in life is that you may take too many precautions.

ALFRED ADLER

Deliberate with caution, but act with decision; and yield with graciousness, or oppose with firmness.

CHARLES HOLE

Be slow of tongue and quick of eye.

MIGUEL DE CERVANTES

It is a good thing to learn caution from the misfortunes of others.

PUBLILIUS SYRUS

CENSORSHIP *Also see:* ASSASSINATION, FREEDOM, FREEDOM OF PRESS, FREEDOM OF SPEECH, NEWSPAPER.

Only the suppressed word is dangerous.

LUDWIG BÖRNE

I am opposed to censorship. Censors are pretty sure fools. I have no confidence in the suppression of everyday facts.

JAMES ROBINSON

Censorship reflects a society's lack of confidence in itself.

POTTER STEWART

He is always the severest censor of the merit of others who has the least worth of his own.

ELIAS LYMAN MAGGON

Every burned book enlightens the world.

RALPH WALDO EMERSON

Pontius Pilate was the first great censor, and Jesus Christ the first great victim of censorship.

BEN LINDSAY

If there had been a censorship of the press in Rome we should have had today neither Horace nor Juvenal, nor the philosophical writings of Cicero.

VOLTAIRE

CENSURE *Also see:* ABUSE, CRITICISM.

Censure is the tax a man pays to the public for being eminent.

JONATHAN SWIFT

The readiest and surest way to get rid of censure, is to correct ourselves.

DEMOSTHENES

He who would acquire fame must not show himself afraid of censure. The dread of censure is the death of genius.

WILLIAM GILMORE SIMMS

The censure of those who are opposed to us, is the highest commendation that can be given us.

SEIGNEUR DE SAINT-EVREMOND

It is folly for an eminent man to think of escaping censure, and a weakness to be affected with it. All the illustrious persons of antiquity, and indeed of every age in the world, have passed through this fiery persecution.

JOSEPH ADDISON

I find that the pain of a little censure, even when it is unfounded, is more acute than the pleasure of much praise.

THOMAS JEFFERSON

CERTAINTY *Also see:* CONFIDENCE, DOUBT, FACT, KNOWLEDGE, QUESTION, SUCCESS.

To be absolutely certain about something, one must know everything or nothing about it.

OLIN MILLER

Convictions are more dangerous foes of truth than lies.

NIETZSCHE

In these matters the only certainty is that there is nothing certain.

PLINY THE ELDER

If we begin with certainties, we shall end in doubts; but if we begin with doubts, and are patient in them, we shall end in certainties.

FRANCIS BACON

There is nothing certain in a man's life but that he must lose it.

OWEN MEREDITH

CHANGE *Also see:* IMPROVEMENT, PROGRESS, REFORM, REVOLUTION, VARIETY.

All change is not growth; all movement is not forward.

ELLEN GLASGOW

He that will not apply new remedies must expect new evils.

FRANCIS BACON

The world hates change, yet it is the only thing that has brought progress.

CHARLES F. KETTERING

Everyone thinks of changing the world, but no one thinks of changing himself.

LEO TOLSTOI

We are restless because of incessant change, but we would be frightened if change were stopped.

LYMAN LLOYD BRYSON

There is nothing permanent except change.

HERACLITUS

Things do not change, we do.

HENRY DAVID THOREAU

Christians are supposed not merely to endure change, nor even to profit by it, but to cause it.

HARRY EMERSON FOSDICK

I've never met a person, I don't care what his condition, in whom I could not see possibilities. I don't care how much a man may consider himself a failure, I believe in him, for he can change the thing that is wrong in his life any time he is ready and prepared to do it. Whenever he develops the desire, he can take away from his life the thing that is defeating it. The capacity for reformation and change lies within.

PRESTON BRADLEY

Life belongs to the living, and he who lives must be prepared for changes.

JOHANN WOLFGANG VON GOETHE

We emphasize that we believe in change because we were born of it, we have lived by it, we prospered and grew great by it. So the status quo has never been our god, and we ask no one else to bow down before it.

CARL T. ROWAN

CHARACTER *Also see:* FAME, INDIVIDUALITY, MORALITY, PERSONALITY, QUALITY, REPUTATION, TEMPER.

Let us not say, Every man is the architect of his own fortune; but let us say, Every man is the architect of his own character.

GEORGE DANA BOARDMAN

Weakness of character is the only defect which cannot be amended.

FRANÇOIS DE LA ROCHEFOUCAULD

Characters do not change. Opinions alter, but characters are only developed.

BENJAMIN DISRAELI

You must look into people, as well as at them.

LORD CHESTERFIELD

Make the most of yourself, for that is all there is of you.

RALPH WALDO EMERSON

Character is not made in a crisis—it is only exhibited.

ROBERT FREEMAN

A man never discloses his own character so clearly as when he describes another's.

JEAN PAUL RICHTER

The four cornerstones of character on which the structure of this nation was built are: Initiative, Imagination, Individuality and Independence.

EDWARD RICKENBACKER

There is no such thing as a "self-made" man. We are made up of thousands of others. Everyone who has ever done a kind deed for us, or spoken one word of encouragement to us, has entered into the make-up of our character and of our thoughts, as well as our success.

GEORGE MATTHEW ADAMS

Every man has three characters—that which he exhibits, that which he has, and that which he thinks he has.

ALPHONSE KARR

CHARITY Also see: GENEROSITY, HEART, HELP, HUMANITY, KINDNESS, LOVE, OSTENTATION, TOLERANCE.

Charity: a thing that begins at home, and usually stays there.

ELBERT HUBBARD

Not he who has much is rich, but he who gives much.

ERICH FROMM

As the purse is emptied, the heart is filled.

VICTOR HUGO

He who waits to do a great deal of good at once, will never do anything.

SAMUEL JOHNSON

The truly generous is the truly wise, and he who loves not others, lives unblest.

HENRY HOME

A bone to the dog is not charity. Charity is the bone shared with the dog, when you are just as hungry as the dog.

JACK LONDON

Though I speak with the tongues of men and angels and have not charity, I am become as sounding brass, or a tinkling cymbal.

I CORINTHIANS 13:1–3

Charity sees the need, not the cause.

GERMAN PROVERB

With malice toward none, with charity for all, with firmness in the right as God gives us to see the right, let us finish the work we are in.

ABRAHAM LINCOLN

Every charitable act is a stepping stone towards heaven.

HENRY WARD BEECHER

If you haven't got any charity in your heart, you have the worst kind of heart trouble.

BOB HOPE

What we frankly give, forever is our own.

GEORGE GRANVILLE

One must be poor to know the luxury of giving.

GEORGE ELIOT

It is more blessed to give than to receive.

ACTS. 20:35

CHARM Also see: BEAUTY, BLUSH, GRACE.

A really plain woman is one who, however beautiful, neglects to charm.

EDGAR SALTUS

There is no personal charm so great as the charm of a cheerful temperament.

HENRY VAN DYKE

Charm is more than beauty.

YIDDISH PROVERB

CHEERFULNESS Also see: CHARM, HAPPINESS, HUMOR, JOY, OPTIMISM, SMILE.

A good laugh is sunshine in a house.

WILLIAM MAKEPEACE THACKERAY

The best way to cheer yourself up is to try to cheer somebody else up.

MARK TWAIN

So of cheerfulness, or a good temper, the more it is spent, the more it remains.

RALPH WALDO EMERSON

The true source of cheerfulness is benevolence.

P. GODWIN

Wondrous is the strength of cheerfulness, and its power of endurance—the cheerful man will do more in the same time, will do it better, will preserve it longer, than the sad or sullen.

THOMAS CARLYLE

I feel an earnest and humble desire, and shall till I die, to increase the stock of harmless cheerfulness.

CHARLES DICKINS

Health is the condition of wisdom, and the sign is cheerfulness—an open and noble temper.

RALPH WALDO EMERSON

Cheer up! The worst is yet to come!

PHILANDER JOHNSON

The cheerful live longest in years, and afterwards in our regards. Cheerfulness is the off-shoot of goodness.

CHRISTIAN NESTELL BOVEE

CHILDREN Also see: BIRTH, BOYS, FAMILY, FATHER, GIRLS, YOUTH.

It is dangerous to confuse children with angels.

DAVID FYFE

Childhood sometimes does pay a second visit to man; youth never.

ANNA JAMESON

The best way to make children good is to make them happy.

OSCAR WILDE

The child is father of the man.

WILLIAM WORDSWORTH

The potential possibilities of any child are the most intriguing and stimulating in all creation.

RAY L. WILBUR

Pretty much all the honest truth telling there is in the world is done by children.

OLIVER WENDELL HOLMES

Don't take up a man's time talking about the smartness of your children; he wants to talk to you about the smartness of his children.

ED HOWE

Children are our most valuable natural resource.

HERBERT HOOVER

Better to be driven out from among men than to be disliked of children.

RICHARD HENRY DANA

A child is a curly, dimpled lunatic.

RALPH WALDO EMERSON

Children in a family are like flowers in a bouquet: there's always one determined to face in an opposite direction from the way the arranger desires.

MARCELENE COX

We've had bad luck with our kids—they've all grown up.

CHRISTOPHER MORELY

Children are poor men's riches.

ENGLISH PROVERB

If a child annoys you, quiet him by brushing his hair. If this doesn't work, use the other side of the brush on the other end of the child.

ANONYMOUS

CHOICE Also see: DECISION, DESIRE, DESTINY, FREEDOM, LIBERTY.

Between two evils, choose neither; between two goods, choose both.

TRYON EDWARDS

Life often presents us with a choice of evils rather than of goods.

CHARLES CALEB COLTON

When you have to make a choice and don't make it, that in itself is a choice.

WILLIAM JAMES

He who chooses the beginning of a road chooses the place it leads to. It is the means that determine the end.

HARRY EMERSON FOSDICK

A man is too apt to forget that in this world he cannot have everything. A choice is all that is left him.

H. MATHEWS

CHRISTIANITY Also see: BROTHERHOOD, CHURCH, FAITH, RELIGION.

Christianity is a battle, not a dream.

WENDELL PHILLIPS

Christian: one who believes that the New Testament is a divinely inspired book admirably suited to the spiritual needs of his neighbors.

AMBROSE BIERCE

Christianity has not been tried and found wanting; it has been found difficult and not tried.

GILBERT K. CHESTERTON

No man ever repented of being a Christian on his death bed.

HANNAH MORE

Christianity does not remove you from the world and its problems; it makes you fit to live in it, triumphantly and usefully.

CHARLES TEMPLETON

If a man cannot be a Christian in the place where he is, he cannot be a Christian anywhere.

HENRY WARD BEECHER

Christianity is a missionary religion, converting, advancing, aggressive, encompassing the world; a non-missionary church is in the band of death.

FRIEDRICH MAX MÜLLER

CHURCH and STATE Also see: CHRISTIANITY, RELIGION

The church is actually patronized by the social order as a means of stabilizing and perpetuating the existing system.

C. C. MORRISON

In the relationship between man and religion, the state is firmly committed to a position of neutrality.

THOMAS CAMPBELL CLARK

The church is the only place where someone speaks to me and I do not have to answer back.

CHARLES DEGAULLE

No religion can long continue to maintain its purity when the church becomes the subservient vassal of the state.

FELIX ADLER

CITIZENSHIP Also see: AMERICA, COUNTRY, DUTY, HEROISM, PATRIOTISM, RIGHTS.

Citizenship consists in the service of the country.

JAWAHARLAL NEHRU

Voting is the least arduous of a citizen's duties. He has the prior and harder duty of making up his mind.

RALPH BARTON PERRY

The first requisite of a good citizen in this republic of ours is that he should be able and willing to pull his weight.

THEODORE ROOSEVELT

Citizenship comes first today in our crowded world. . . . No man can enjoy the privileges of education and thereafter with a clear conscience break his contract with society.

ISAIAH BOWMAN

Every good citizen makes his country's honor his own, and cherishes it not only as precious but as sacred. He is willing to risk his life in its defense and is conscious that he gains protection while he gives it.

ANDREW JACKSON

Let us at all times remember that all American citizens are brothers of a common country, and should dwell together in bonds of fraternal feeling.

ABRAHAM LINCOLN

Now the trumpet summons us again—not as a call to bear arms, though arms we need—not as a call to battle, though embattled we are—but a call to bear the burden of a long twilight struggle year in and year out, "rejoicing in hope, patient in tribulation"—a struggle against the common enemies of man: tyranny, poverty, disease and war itself.

JOHN FITZGERALD KENNEDY

If you will help run our government in the American way, then there will never be danger of our government running America in the wrong way.

OMAR N. BRADLEY

CIVILIZATION Also see: ADVENTURE, BEHAVIOR, CULTURE, DOUBT, IMPROVEMENT, PROGRESS.

Anyone can be a barbarian; it requires a terrible effort to remain a civilized man.

LEONARD SIDNEY WOOLF

The true test of civilization is, not the census, nor the size of the cities, nor the crops, but the kind of man that the country turns out.

RALPH WALDO EMERSON

Civilization begins with order, grows with liberty, and dies with chaos.

WILL DURANT

You can't say civilization isn't advancing: in every war, they kill you in a new way.

WILL ROGERS

The three great elements of modern civilization, Gunpowder, Printing, and the Protestant Religion.

THOMAS CARLYLE

Civilization is the order and freedom promoting cultural activity.

WILL DURANT

In the advance of civilization, it is new knowledge which paves the way, and the pavement is eternal.

W. R. WHITNEY

Civilization ceases when we no longer respect and no longer put into their correct places the fundamental values, such as work, family and country; such as the individual, honor and religion.

R. P. LEBRET

Every advance in civilization has been denounced as unnatural while it was recent.

BETRAND RUSSELL

The true civilization is where evey man gives to every other every right that he claims for himself.

ROBERT GREEN INGERSOLL

All the things now enjoyed by civilization have been created by some man and sold by another man before anybody really enjoyed the benefits of them.

JAMES G. DALY

CLASS *Also see:* ARISTOCRACY, ORDER, SOCIETY.

All mankind is divided into three classes: those that are immovable, those that are movable, and those that move.

ARABIAN PROVERB

There is nothing to which men cling more tenaciously than the privileges of class.

LEONARD SIDNEY WOOLF

Let him who expects one class of society to prosper in the highest degree, while the other is in distress, try whether one side of the face can smile while the other is pinched.

THOMAS FULLER

The distinctions separating the social classes are false; in the last analysis they rest on force.

ALBERT EINSTEIN

The ignorant classes are the dangerous classes.

HENRY WARD BEECHER

I never would believe that Providence had sent a few men into the world, ready booted and spurred to ride, and millions ready saddled and bridled to be ridden.

RICHARD RUMBOLD

Other lands have their vitality in a few, a class, but we have it in the bulk of our people.

WALT WHITMAN

CLEVERNESS *Also see:* CYNIC, INTELLIGENCE, WIT.

Clever men are good, but they are not the best.

THOMAS CARLYLE

Cleverness is serviceable for everything, sufficient for nothing.

AMIEL

The doctrine of human equality reposes on this: that there is no man really clever who has not found that he is stupid.

GILBERT K. CHESTERTON

Cleverness is not wisdom.

EURIPIDES

The desire to seem clever often keeps us from being so.

FRANÇOIS DE LA ROCHEFOUCAULD

It is great cleverness to know how to conceal our cleverness.

FRANÇOIS DE LA ROCHEFOUCAULD

COMMITTEE

If you want to kill any idea in the world today, get a committee working on it.

CHARLES F. KETTERING

When it comes to facing up to serious problems, each candidate will pledge to appoint a committee. And what is a committee? A group of the unwilling, picked from the unfit, to do the unnecessary. But it all sounds great in a campaign speech.

RICHARD LONG HARKNESS

To get something done a committee should consist of three men, two of whom are absent.

ANONYMOUS

A committee is a group that keeps minutes and loses hours.

MILTON BERLE

A cul-de-sac to which ideas are lured and then quietly strangled.

JOHN A. LINCOLN

COMMON SENSE *Also see:* CANDOR, INTELLIGENCE, PRUDENCE, REASON, UNDERSTANDING.

Common sense is very uncommon.

HORACE GREELEY

Common sense is in spite of, not as the result of education.

VICTOR HUGO

He was one of those men who possess almost every gift, except the gift of the power to use them.

CHARLES KINGSLEY

Common sense is instinct, and enough of it is genius.

JOSH BILLINGS

Common sense and nature will do a lot to make the pilgrimage of life not too difficult.

W. SOMERSET MAUGHAM

Nothing is more fairly distributed than common sense: no one thinks he needs more of it than he already has.

DESCARTES

Common sense is the knack of seeing things as they are, and doing things as they ought to be done.

JOSH BILLINGS

COMMUNICATION *Also see:* CONVERSATION, NEWSPAPER, TELEVISION.

A world community can exist only with world communication, which means something more than extensive short-wave facilities scattered about the globe. It means common understanding, a common tradition, common ideas, and common ideals.

ROBERT M. HUTCHINS

News is that which comes from the North, East, West and South, and if it comes from only one point on the compass, then it is a class publication and not news.

BENJAMIN DISRAELI

The fantastic advances in the field of electronic communication constitute a greater danger to the privacy of the individual.

EARL WARREN

We shall never be able to remove suspicion and fear as potential causes of war until communication is permitted to flow, free and open, across international boundaries.

HARRY S. TRUMAN

COMMUNISM *Also see:* ARISTOCRACY, CAPITALISM, DEMOCRACY.

Communism is a society where each one works according to his abilities and gets according to his needs.

PIERRE JOSEPH PROUDHON

The theory of Communism may be summed up in one sentence: abolish all private property.

KARL MARX

Communism possesses a language which every people can understand—its elements are hunger, envy, and death.

HEINRICH HEINE

A communist is like a crocodile: when it opens its mouth you cannot tell whether it is trying to smile or preparing to eat you up.

WINSTON CHURCHILL

Communism is the death of the soul. It is the organization of total conformity—in short, of tyranny—and it is committed to making tyranny universal.

ADLAI E. STEVENSON

Communism has nothing to do with love. Communism is an excellent hammer which we use to destroy our enemy.

MAO TSE-TUNG

I never agree with Communists or any other kind of kept men.

H. L. MENCKEN

Communism means barbarism.

JAMES RUSSELL LOWELL

COMPASSION *Also see:* KINDNESS, MERCY, PITY, SYMPATHY.

The dew of compassion is a tear.

LORD BYRON

The mind is no match with the heart in persuasion; constitutionality is no match with compassion.

EVERETT M. DIRKSEN

The value of compassion cannot be over-emphasized. Anyone can criticize. It takes a true believer to be compassionate. No greater burden can be borne by an individual than to know no one cares or understands.

ARTHUR H. STAINBACK

Man may dismiss compassion from his heart, but God never will.

WILLIAM COWPER

COMPETITION . . . *See* RIVALRY

COMPLAINT *Also see:* DISCONTENT.

Had we not faults of our own, we should take less pleasure in complaining of others.

FÉNELON

Constant complaint is the poorest sort of pay for all the comforts we enjoy.

BENJAMIN FRANKLIN

I will not be as those who spend the day in complaining of headache, and the night in drinking the wine that gives it.

JOHANN WOLFGANG VON GOETHE

The usual fortune of complaint is to excite contempt more than pity.

SAMUEL JOHNSON

We have no more right to put our discordant states of mind into the lives of those around us and rob them of their sunshine and brightness than we have to enter their houses and steal their silverware.

JULIA MOSS SETON

The wheel that squeaks the loudest is the one that gets the grease.

JOSH BILLINGS

The wheel that squeaks the loudest is the first to be replaced.

ANONYMOUS

COMPLIMENT *Also see:* FLATTERY, PRAISE.

If you can't get a compliment any other way, pay yourself one.

MARK TWAIN

When a man makes a woman his wife, it's the highest compliment he can pay her, and it's usually the last.

HELEN ROWLAND

I have been complimented many times and they always embarrass me; I always feel that they have not said enough.

MARK TWAIN

Don't tell a woman she's pretty; tell her there's no other woman like her, and all roads will open to you.

JULES RENARD

COMPROMISE *Also see:* AGREEMENT, EXPEDIENCY.

Better bend than break.

SCOTTISH PROVERB

Compromise is never anything but an ignoble truce between the duty of a man and the terror of a coward.

REGINALD WRIGHT KAUFFMAN

Compromise makes a good umbrella, but a poor roof; it is temporary expedient, often wise in party politics, almost sure to be unwise in statesmanship.

JAMES RUSSELL LOWELL

It is the weak man who urges compromise—never the strong man.

ELBERT HUBBARD

People talk about the middle of the road as though it were unacceptable. Actually, all human problems, excepting morals, come into the gray areas. Things are not all black and white. There have to be compromises. The middle of the road is all of the usable surface. The extremes, right and left, are in the gutters.

DWIGHT D. EISENHOWER

Life cannot subsist in society but by reciprocal concessions.

SAMUEL JOHNSON

Real life is, to most men, a long second-best, a perpetual compromise between the ideal and the possible; but the world of pure reason knows no compromise, no practical limitations, no barrier to the creative activity.

BERTRAND RUSSELL

From the beginning of our history the country has been afflicted with compromise. It is by compromise that human rights have been abandoned.

CHARLES SUMNER

All government, indeed every human benefit and enjoyment, every virtue, and every prudent act, is founded on compromise and barter.

EDMUND BURKE

CONCEIT . . . See VANITY.

CONDUCT . . . See BEHAVIOR.

CONFESSION *Also see:* CONSCIENCE, GUILT, SIN.

To confess a fault freely is the next thing to being innocent of it.

PUBLILIUS SYRUS

Nothing spoils a confession like repentance.

ANATOLE FRANCE

It is the confession, not the priest, that gives us absolution.

OSCAR WILDE

Open confession is good for the soul.

SCOTTISH PROVERB

The confession of evil works is the first beginning of good works.

ST. AUGUSTINE

CONFIDENCE *Also see:* BELIEF, BOLDNESS, CENSORSHIP, DOUBT, FAITH, SECURITY, SELF-CONFIDENCE, TRUST.

I have great faith in fools—self-confidence my friends call it.

EDGAR ALLAN POE

For they conquer who believe they can.

JOHN DRYDEN

Have confidence that if you have done a little thing well, you can do a bigger thing well too.

STOREY

If once you forfeit the confidence of your fellow-citizens, you can never regain their respect and esteem.

ABRAHAM LINCOLN

Only trust thyself, and another shall not betray thee.

WILLIAM PENN

True prosperity is the result of well-placed confidence in ourselves and our fellow man.

BURT

CONFORMITY *Also see:* ADAPTABILITY, AGREEMENT, CUSTOM, TRADITION.

Conform and be dull.

J. FRANK DOBIE

Our wretched species is so made that those who walk on the well-trodden path always throw stones at those who are showing a new road.

VOLTAIRE

The surest way to corrupt a youth is to instruct him to hold in higher esteem those who think alike than those who think differently.

NIETZSCHE

If a man does not keep pace with his companions, perhaps it is because he hears a different drummer. Let him step to the music which he hears, however measured or far away.

HENRY DAVID THOREAU

Singularity in the right hath ruined many; happy those who are convinced of the general opinion.

BENJAMIN FRANKLIN

We are discreet sheep; we wait to see how the drove is going, and then go with the drove.

MARK TWAIN

CONSCIENCE *Also see:* HONOR, MORALITY, VIRTUE.

Conscience—the only incorruptible thing about us.

HENRY FIELDING

The only tyrant I accept in this world is the still voice within.

MAHATMA GANDHI

No ear can hear nor tongue can tell the tortures of the inward hell!

LORD BYRON

Conscience is a mother-in-law whose visit never ends.

H. L. MENCKEN

Conscience is the mirror of our souls, which represents the errors of our lives in their full shape.

GEORGE BANCROFT

He who sacrifices his conscience to ambition burns a picture to obtain the ashes.

CHINESE PROVERB

'Tis the business of little minds to shrink; but he whose heart is firm, and whose conscience approves his conduct, will pursue his principles unto death.

THOMAS PAINE

CONSCIENTIOUS OBJECTION ... See DRAFT.

CONSERVATION Also see: NATURE, POLLUTION.

Conservaton is ethically sound. It is rooted in our love of the land, our respect for the rights of others, our devotion to the rule of law.

LYNDON BAINES JOHNSON

As soils are depleted, human health, vitality and intelligence go with them.

LOUIS BROMFIELD

Conservation means the wise use of the earth and its resources for the lasting good of men.

GIFFORD PINCHOT

World-wide practice of Conservation and the fair and continued access by all nations to the resources they need are the two indispensable foundations of continuous plenty and of permanent peace.

GIFFORD PINCHOT

CONTEMPT ... See HATE.

CONTENTMENT Also see: AMUSEMENT, ENJOY-MENT, HAPPINESS, JOY, PEACE.

The secret of contentment is knowing how to enjoy what you have, and to be able to lose all desire for things beyond your reach.

LIN YUTANG

Nothing contributes more to a person's peace of mind than having no opinions at all.

G. C. LICHTENBERG

It is right to be contented with what we have, never with what we are.

JAMES MACKINTOSH

One who is contented with what he has done will never become famous for what he will do.

CHRISTIAN NESTELL BOVEE

Since we cannot get what we like, let us like what we can get.

SPANISH PROVERB

My motto is: Contented with little, yet wishing for more.

CHARLES LAMB

If you are content, you have enough to live comfortably.

PLAUTUS

CONTRAST Also see: DIFFERENCE.

The superiority of some men is merely local. They are great because their associates are little.

SAMUEL JOHNSON

Where there is much light, the shadow is deep.

JOHANN WOLFGANG VON GOETHE

Joy and grief are never far apart.

ROBERT ELDRIDGE WILLMOTT

The rose and the thorn, and sorrow and gladness are linked together.

SAADI

The lustre of diamonds is invigorated by the interposition of darker bodies; the lights of a picture are created by the shades; the highest pleasure which nature has indulged to sensitive perception is that of rest after fatigue.

SAMUEL JOHNSON

CONVERSATION Also see: ARGUMENT, GOSSIP, LOQUACITY.

Conversation is an art in which man has all mankind for competitors.

RALPH WALDO EMERSON

Silence is one great art of conversation.

WILLIAM HAZLITT

Not only to say the right thing in the right place, but far more difficult, to leave unsaid the wrong thing at the tempting moment.

GEORGE SALA

Conceit causes more conversation than wit.

FRANÇOIS DE LA ROCHEFOUCAULD

Conversation would be vastly improved by the constant use of four simple words: I do not know.

ANDRÉ MAUROIS

Never hold anyone by the button or the hand in order to be heard out; for if people are unwilling to hear you, you had better hold your tongue than them.

LORD CHESTERFIELD

Conversation should be pleasant without scurrility, witty without affectation, free without indecency, learned without conceitedness, novel without falsehood.

WILLIAM SHAKESPEARE

COUNTRY Also see: AMERICA, CITIZENSHIP, DE-MOCRACY, NATION, PATRIOTISM.

So long as you are ready to die for humanity, the life of your country is immortal.

GUISEPPE MAZZINI

I have no country to fight for: my country is the earth, and I am a citizen of the world.

EUGENE V. DEBS

Our country. In her intercourse with foreign nations may she always be in the right; but our country right or wrong!

STEPHEN DECATUR

The world is my country, all mankind are my brethren, and to do good is my religion.

THOMAS PAINE

There is no such thing as a little country. The greatness of a people is no more determined by their number than the greatness of a man is determined by his height.

VICTOR HUGO

The most certain test by which we judge whether a country is really free is the amount of security enjoyed by minorities.

LORD ACTON

Let it be borne on the flag under which we rally in every exigency, that we have one country, one constitution, one destiny.

DANIEL WEBSTER

Our country is the world—our countrymen are mankind.

WILLIAM LLOYD GARRISON

There is no greater sign of a general decay of virtue in a nation, than a want of zeal in its inhabitants for the good of their country.

JOSEPH ADDISON

My kind of loyalty was loyalty to one's country, not to its institutions or its officeholders. The country is the real thing, the substantial thing, the eternal thing; it is the thing to watch over, and care for, and be loyal to.

MARK TWAIN

COURAGE *Also see:* BOLDNESS, COWARDICE, DANGER, DEFEAT, FIRMNESS, HEROISM, SPIRIT.

Courage is almost a contradiction in terms: it means a strong desire to live taking the form of readiness to die.

GILBERT K. CHESTERTON

The greatest test of courage on earth is to bear defeat without losing heart.

ROBERT GREEN INGERSOLL

It takes vision and courage to create—it takes faith and courage to prove.

OWEN D. YOUNG

I'd rather give my life than be afraid to give it.

LYNDON BAINES JOHNSON

Courage is resistance to fear, mastery of fear—not absence of fear.

MARK TWAIN

This is no time for ease and comfort. It is the time to dare and endure.

WINSTON CHURCHILL

Far better it is to dare mighty things, to win glorious triumphs, even though checkered by failure, than to take rank with those poor spirits who neither enjoy much nor suffer much, because they live in the grey twilight that knows not victory nor defeat.

THEODORE ROOSEVELT

Last, but by no means least, courage—moral courage, the courage of one's convictions, the courage to see things through. The world is in a constant conspiracy against the brave. It's the age-old struggle—the roar of the crowd on one side and the voice of your conscience on the other.

DOUGLAS MACARTHUR

Give us the fortitude to endure the things which cannot be changed, and the courage to change the things which should be changed, and the wisdom to know one from the other.

OLIVER J. HART

No man in the world has more courage than the man who can stop after eating one peanut.

CHANNING POLLOCK

COURT *Also see:* JUSTICE, LAW.

A court is a place where what was confused before becomes more unsettled than ever.

HENRY WALDORF FRANCIS

Dictum is what a court thinks but is afraid to decide.

HENRY WALDORF FRANCIS

The place of justice is a hallowed place.

FRANCIS BACON

The penalty for laughing in a courtroom is six months in jail; if it were not for this penalty, the jury would never hear the evidence.

H. L. MENCKEN

COURTESY *Also see:* CHARM, CULTURE, GALLANTRY, MANNERS.

Life is not so short but that there is always time for courtesy.

RALPH WALDO EMERSON

It is better to have too much courtesy than too little, provided you are not equally courteous to all, for that would be injustice.

BALTASAR GRACIÁN

Courtesies of a small and trivial character are the ones which strike deepest in the grateful and appreciating heart.

HENRY CLAY

Nothing is ever lost by courtesy. It is the cheapest of the pleasures; costs nothing and conveys much. It pleases him who gives and him who receives, and thus, like mercy, it is twice blessed.

ERASTUS WIMAN

If a man be gracious and courteous to strangers, it shows he is a citizen of the world.

FRANCIS BACON

Politeness is the art of choosing among one's real thoughts.

ABEL STEVENS

True politeness consists in being easy one's self, and in making every one about one as easy as one can.

ALEXANDER POPE

COWARDICE *Also see:* FEAR, SILENCE.

The cowards never started—and the weak died along the way.

ANONYMOUS

Great occasions do not make heroes or cowards; they simply unveil them to the eyes of men.

BISHOP WESTCOTT

A coward is much more exposed to quarrels than a man of spirit.

THOMAS JEFFERSON

At the bottom of a good deal of the bravery that appears in the world there lurks a miserable cowardice. Men will face powder and steel because they cannot face public opinion.

EDWIN HUBBEL CHAPIN

It is better to be the widow of a hero than the wife of a coward.

DOLORES IBARRURI

Fear has its use but cowardice has none.

MAHATMA GANDHI

To know what is right and not to do it is the worst cowardice.

CONFUCIUS

The people to fear are not those who disagree with you, but those who disagree with you and are too cowardly to let you know.

NAPOLEON BONAPARTE

Faint heart ne'er won fair lady.

MIGUEL DE CERVANTES

It is the coward who fawns upon those above him. It is the coward who is insolent whenever he dares be so.

JUNIUS

How many feasible projects have miscarried through despondency, and been strangled in their birth by a cowardly imagination.

JEREMY COLLIER

Dishonesty, cowardice and duplicity are never impulsive.

GEORGE A. KNIGHT

A cowardly cur barks more fiercely than it bites.

QUINTUS CURTIUS RUFUS

CREATIVITY *Also see:* ACTION, ART, GOD, INVENTION, LITERATURE.

Ideas are the root of creation.

ERNEST DIMNET

Man was made at the end of the week's work when God was tired.

MARK TWAIN

It is wise to learn; it is God-like to create.

JOHN SAXE

Had I been present at the creation of the world I would have proposed some improvements.

ALFONSO X

Creation is a drug I can't do without.

CECIL B. DEMILLE

The merit of originality is not novelty; it is sincerity.

THOMAS CARLYLE

CREDIT *Also see:* BORROWING, DEBT, REPUTATION.

The surest way to establish your credit is to work yourself into the position of not needing any.

MAURICE SWITZER

The private control of credit is the modern form of slavery.

UPTON SINCLAIR

No man's credit is as good as his money

ED HOWE

Remember that credit is money.

BENJAMIN FRANKLIN

Nothing so cements and holds together all the parts of a society as faith or credit, which can never be kept up unless men are under some force or necessity of honestly paying what they owe to one another.

CICERO

Men ... are sent into the world with bills of credit, and seldom draw to their full extent.

HORACE WALPOLE

Credit is like a looking-glass, which when once sullied by a breath, may be wiped clear again; but if once cracked can never be repaired.

WALTER SCOTT

Buying on trust is the way to pay double.

ANONYMOUS

Acquaintance: a person whom we know well enough to borrow from, but not well enough to lend to.

AMBROSE BIERCE

CREDULITY *Also see:* BELIEF, DOUBT, FAITH, INNOCENCE, LYING.

Credulity is belief in slight evidence, with no evidence, or against evidence.

TRYON EDWARDS

The only disadvantage of an honest heart is credulity.

PHILIP SIDNEY

The great masses of the people ... will more easily fall victims to a great lie than to a small one.

ADOLF HITLER

I prefer credulity to skepticism and cynicism for there is more promise in almost anything than in nothing at all.

RALPH BARTON PERRY

I cannot spare the luxury of believing that all things beautiful are what they seem.

FITZ-GREENE HALLECK

Let us believe neither half of the good people tell us of ourselves, nor half the evil they say of others.

JOHN PETIT-SENN

The more gross the fraud, the more glibly will it go down and the more greedily will it be swallowed, since folly will always find faith wherever imposters will find impudence.

CHRISTIAN NESTELL BOVEE

CRIME *Also see:* DISHONESTY, FRAUD, GUILT, MURDER, RIOT, SIN, VICE, WICKEDNESS, WRONG.

All crime is a kind of disease and should be treated as such.

MAHATMA GANDHI

Society prepares the crime; the criminal commits it.

HENRY THOMAS BUCKLE

We enact many laws that manufacture criminals, and then a few that punish them.

ALLEN TUCKER

And who are the greater criminals—those who sell the instruments of death, or those who buy them and use them?

ROBERT EMMET SHERWOOD

Providence sees to it that no man gets happiness out of crime.

VITTORIO ALTIERI

The real significance of crime is in its being a breach of faith with the community of mankind.

JOSEPH CONRAD

Purposelessness is the fruitful mother of crime.

CHARLES H. PARKHURST

Whoever profits by the crime is guilty of it.

ANONYMOUS

What is crime amongst the multitude, is only vice among the few.

BENJAMIN DISRAELI

Capital punishment is as fundamentally wrong as a cure for crime as charity is wrong as a cure for poverty.

HENRY FORD

Crime is a product of social excess.

LENIN

If poverty is the mother of crimes, want of sense is the father.

JEAN DE LA BRUYÈRE

Few men have virtue to withstand the highest bidder.

GEORGE WASHINGTON

Small crimes always precede great ones. Never have we seen timid innocence pass suddenly to extreme licentiousness.

JEAN BAPTISTE RACINE

Organized crime constitutes nothing less than a guerilla war against society.

LYNDON BAINES JOHNSON

Fear follows crime, and is its punishment.

VOLTAIRE

We easily forget crimes that are known only to ourselves.

FRANÇOIS DE LA ROCHEFOUCAULD

CRISIS *Also see:* CALAMITY, CHARACTER.

Every little thing counts in a crisis.

JAWAHARLAL NEHRU

These are the times that try men's souls.

THOMAS PAINE

Crises and deadlocks when they occur have at least this advantage, that they force us to think.

JAWAHARLAL NEHRU

Crises refine life. In them you discover what you are.

ALLAN K. CHALMERS

The wise man does not expose himself needlessly to danger, since there are few things for which he cares sufficiently; but he is willing, in great crises, to give even his life—knowing that under certain conditions it is not worth-while to live.

ARISTOTLE

. . . as we wake or sleep, we grow strong or we grow weak, and at last some crisis shows us what we have become.

BISHOP WESTCOTT

CRITICISM *Also see:* ADVICE, CENSURE, JUDGMENT, PRAISE.

I never give them hell; I just tell them the truth and they think it is hell.

HARRY S. TRUMAN

Blame is safer than praise.

RALPH WALDO EMERSON

To avoid criticism do nothing, say nothing, be nothing.

ELBERT HUBBARD

Remember that nobody will ever get ahead of you as long as he is kicking you in the seat of the pants.

WALTER WINCHELL

Each generation produces its squad of "moderns" with pea-shooters to attack Gibralter.

CHANNING POLLOCK

Criticism, as it was first instituted by Aristotle, was meant as a standard of judging well.

SAMUEL JOHNSON

It is much easier to be critical than to be correct.

BENJAMIN DISRAELI

The public is the only critic whose opinion is worth anything at all.

MARK TWAIN

CRUELTY *Also see:* ABUSE, EVIL, INJURY, PUNISHMENT, VIOLENCE, WAR.

If it were absolutely necessary to choose, I would rather be guilty of an immoral act than of a cruel one.

ANATOLE FRANCE

One of the ill effects of cruelty is that it makes the bystanders cruel.

THOMAS FOWELL BUXTON

All cruelty springs from hard-heartedness and weakness.

SENECA

Cruelty and fear shake hands together.

HONORÉ DE BALZAC

Cruelty, like every other vice, requires no motive outside of itself; it only requires opportunity.

GEORGE ELIOT

Cruelty is a part of nature, at least of human nature, but it is the one thing that seems unnatural to us.

ROBINSON JEFFERS

CULTURE *Also see:* ART, CIVILIZATION, COURTESY, LITERATURE, MANNERS.

Culture is the habit of being pleased with the best and knowing why.

HENRY VAN DYKE

Every man's ability may be strengthened or increased by culture.

JOHN ABBOTT

The acquiring of culture is the development of an avid hunger for knowledge and beauty.

JESSE BENNETT

No culture can live, if it attempts to be exclusive.

MAHATMA GANDHI

Culture is the widening of the mind and of the spirit.

JAWAHARLAL NEHRU

That is true culture which helps us to work for the social betterment of all.

HENRY WARD BEECHER

The end of culture is right living.

W. SOMERSET MAUGHAM

CUNNING ... See DECEIT

CURIOSITY Also see: INTEREST, QUESTION, SCIENCE, SPECULATION, WONDER.

The first and simplest emotion which we discover in the human mind, is curiosity.

EDMUND BURKE

One of the secrets of life is to keep our intellectual curiosity acute.

WILLIAM LYON PHELPS

Creatures whose mainspring is curiosity enjoy the accumulating of facts far more than the pausing at times to reflect on those facts.

CLARENCE DAY

It is a shameful thing to be weary of inquiry when what we search for is excellent.

CICERO

The important thing is not to stop questioning. Curiosity has its own reason for existing. One cannot help but be in awe when he contemplates the mysteries of eternity, of life, of the marvelous structure of reality. It is enough if one tries merely to comprehend a little of this mystery every day. Never lose a holy curiosity.

ALBERT EINSTEIN

Curiosity is as much the parent of attention, as attention is of memory.

RICHARD WHATELY

CUSTOM Also see: CONFORMITY, FASHION, HABIT, TRADITION.

Custom meets us at the cradle and leaves us only at the tomb.

ROBERT GREEN INGERSOLL

The old ways are the safest and surest ways.

CHARLES CALEB COLTON

The custom and fashion of today will be the awkwardness and outrage of tomorrow—so arbitrary are these transient laws.

ALEXANDRE DUMAS

Take the course opposite to custom and you will almost always do well.

JEAN-JACQUES ROUSSEAU

Men will sooner surrender their rights than their customs.

MORITZ GUEDMANN

Custom governs the world; it is the tyrant of our feelings and our manners and rules the world with the hand of a despot.

J. BARTLETT

There is nothing that strengthens a nation like reading of a nation's own history, whether that history is recorded in books or embodied in customs, institutions and monuments.

JOSEPH ANDERSON

Men commonly think according to their inclinations, speak according to their learning and imbibed opinions, but generally act according to custom.

FRANCIS BACON

There is no tyrant like custom, and no freedom where its edicts are not resisted.

CHRISTIAN NESTELL BOVEE

Ancient custom has the force of law.

LEGAL MAXIM

CYNIC Also see: CREDULITY, DOUBT, PESSIMISM, PREJUDICE, SARCASM, SKEPTICISM.

It takes a clever man to turn cynic and a wise man to be clever enough not to.

FANNIE HURST

A cynic is a man who knows the price of everything, and the value of nothing.

OSCAR WILDE

A cynic is just a man who found out when he was ten that there wasn't any Santa Claus, and he's still upset.

J. G. COZZENS

A cynic is a man who, when he smells flowers, looks around for a coffin.

H. L. MENCKEN

A cynic can chill and dishearten with a single word.

RALPH WALDO EMERSON

The only deadly sin I know is cynicism.

HENRY L. STIMSON

The cynic is one who never sees a good quality in a man, and never fails to see a bad one.

HENRY WARD BEECHER

DANGER Also see: ADVENTURE, BOLDNESS, CALAMITY, CAUTION, CENSORSHIP, COURAGE, FEAR.

As soon as there is life there is danger.

RALPH WALDO EMERSON

In this world there is always danger for those who are afraid of it.

GEORGE BERNARD SHAW

The most dangerous thing in the world is to try to leap a chasm in two jumps.

WILLIAM LLOYD GEORGE

If we survive danger it steels our courage more than anything else.

REINHOLD NIEBUHR

A timid person is frightened before a danger, a coward during the time, and a courageous person afterwards.

JEAN PAUL RICHTER

This country has come to feel the same when Congress is in session as when the baby gets hold of a hammer.

WILL ROGERS

We cannot banish dangers, but we can banish fears. We must not demean life by standing in awe of death.

DAVID SARNOFF

The mere apprehension of a coming evil has put many into a situation of the utmost danger.

LUCAN

There is danger when a man throws his tongue into high gear before he gets his brain a-going.

C. C. PHELPS

The person who runs away exposes himself to that very danger more than a person who sits quietly.

JAWAHARLAL NEHRU

We are confronted by a first danger, the destructiveness of applied atomic energy. And then we are confronted by a second danger, that we do not enough appreciate the first danger.

RAYMOND G. SWING

DEATH *Also see:* ABSENCE, BIRTH, CIVILIZATION, COMMUNISM, COWARDICE, DANGER, DEFEAT, DESPAIR, DESTINY, DISEASE, LIFE, IMMORTALITY.

Nothing in this life became him like leaving it.

WILLIAM SHAKESPEARE

I never think he is quite ready for another world who is altogether weary of this.

HUGH HAMILTON

All say, "How hard it is that we have to die"—a strange complaint to come from the mouths of people who have had to live.

MARK TWAIN

Some people are so afraid to die that they never begin to live.

HENRY VAN DYKE

Most people would rather die than think: many do.

BERTRAND RUSSELL

God's finger touched him, and he slept.

ALFRED, LORD TENNYSON

The gods conceal from men the happiness of death, that they may endure life.

LUCAN

Men fear death, as if unquestionably the greatest evil, and yet no man knows that it may not be the greatest good.

WILLIAM MITFORD

Death—the last sleep? No, it is the final awakening.

WALTER SCOTT

I look upon life as a gift from God. I did nothing to earn it. Now that the time is coming to give it back, I have no right to complain.

JOYCE CARY

Good men must die, but death cannot kill their names.

PROVERB

I am ready to meet my maker, but whether my maker is prepared for the great ordeal of meeting me is another matter.

WINSTON CHURCHILL

Death is a very dull, dreary affair, and my advice to you is to have nothing whatever to do with it.

W. SOMERSET MAUGHAM

DEBT *Also see:* BORROWING, CREDIT, MONEY.

Some debts are fun when you are acquiring them, but none are fun when you set about retiring them.

OGDEN NASH

Debt is a prolific mother of folly and of crime.

BENJAMIN DISRAELI

A small debt produces a debtor; a large one, an enemy.

PUBLILIUS SYRUS

A habit of debt is very injurious to the memory.

AUSTIN O'MALLEY

Some people use one half their ingenuity to get into debt, and the other half to avoid paying it.

GEORGE D. PRENTICE

We often pay our debts not because it is only fair that we should, but to make future loans easier.

FRANÇOIS DE LA ROCHEFOUCAULD

Debt is the fatal disease of republics, the first thing and the mightiest to undermine governments and corrupt the people.

WENDELL PHILLIPS

Debt is the worst poverty.

THOMAS FULLER

Our national debt, after all, is an internal debt, owed not only by the nation but to the nation. If our children have to pay the interest they will pay that interest to themselves.

FRANKLIN DELANO ROOSEVELT

Do not accustom yourself to consider debt only as an inconvenience; you will find it a calamity.

SAMUEL JOHNSON

A man in debt is so far a slave.

RALPH WALDO EMERSON

Never spend your money before you have it.

THOMAS JEFFERSON

Debt is the slavery of the free.

PUBLILIUS SYRUS

DECEIT *Also see:* FRAUD, SKEPTICISM.

You can fool some of the people all the time, and all of the people some of the time, but you cannot fool all of the people all the time.

ABRAHAM LINCOLN

The sure way to be cheated is to think one's self more cunning than others.

FRANÇOIS DE LA ROCHEFOUCAULD

It is double the pleasure to deceive the deceiver.

JEAN DE LA FONTAINE

All deception in the course of life is indeed nothing else but a lie reduced to practice, and falsehood passing from words into things.

ROBERT SOUTH

Hateful to me as the gates of Hades is that man who hides one thing in his heart and speaks another.

HOMER

DECENCY Also see: CENSORSHIP, MODESTY, MORALITY, VIRTUE.

Decency is the least of all laws, but yet it is the law which is most strictly observed.

FRANÇOIS DE LA ROCHEFOUCAULD

Don't overestimate the decency of the human race.

H. L. MENCKEN

We are decent 99 percent of the time, when we could easily be vile.

R. W. RILS

No law reaches it, but all right-minded people observe it.

CHAMFORT

DECISION Also see: CHOICE.

It does not take much strength to do things, but it requires great strength to decide on what to do.

ELBERT HUBBARD

I hate to see things done by halves. If it be right, do it boldly,—if it be wrong leave it undone.

BERNARD GILPIN

When possible make the decisions now, even if action is in the future. A reviewed decision usually is better than one reached at the last moment.

WILLIAM B. GIVEN, JR.

All our final decisions are made in a state of mind that is not going to last.

MARCEL PROUST

DEFEAT Also see: COURAGE, FAILURE, VICTORY.

What is defeat? Nothing but education, nothing but the first step to something better.

WENDELL PHILLIPS

There are some defeats more triumphant than victories.

MICHEL DE MONTAIGNE

It is defeat that turns bone to flint; it is defeat that turns gristle to muscle; it is defeat that makes men invincible.

HENRY WARD BEECHER

Politics has become so expensive that it takes a lot of money even to be defeated.

WILL ROGERS

Defeat is not the worst of failures. Not to have tried is the true failure.

GEORGE EDWARD WOODBERRY

Believe you are defeated, believe it long enough, and it is likely to become a fact.

NORMAN VINCENT PEALE

I would rather lose in a cause that I know some day will triumph than to triumph in a cause that I know some day will fail.

WENDELL L. WILLKIE

Defeat never comes to any man until he admits it.

JOSEPHUS DANIELS

Those who are prepared to die for any cause are seldom defeated.

JAWAHARLAL NEHRU

The problems of victory are more agreeable than those of defeat, but they are no less difficult.

WINSTON CHURCHILL

Defeat should never be a source of courage, but rather a fresh stimulant.

ROBERT SOUTH

DELIGHT ... See JOY

DELUSION Also see: REALITY, SELF-KNOWLEDGE.

No man is happy without a delusion of some kind. Delusions are as necessary to our happiness as realities.

CHRISTIAN NESTELL BOVEE

The worst deluded are the self-deluded.

CHRISTIAN NESTELL BOVEE

Love is the delusion that one woman differs from another.

H. L. MENCKEN

DEMOCRACY Also see: AMERICA, EQUALITY, FREEDOM, LIBERTY.

Democracy is good. I say this because other systems are worse.

JAWAHARLAL NEHRU

Democracy is based upon the conviction that there are extraordinary possibilities in ordinary people.

HARRY EMERSON FOSDICK

In a democracy, the individual enjoys not only the ultimate power but carries the ultimate responsibility.

NORMAN COUSINS

Democracy ... is a system of self-determination. It's the right to make the wrong choice.

JOHN PATRICK

Too many people expect wonders from democracy, when the most wonderful thing of all is just having it.

WALTER WINCHELL

Democracy is the government of the people, by the people, for the people.

ABRAHAM LINCOLN

As I would not be a slave, so I would not be a master. This expresses my idea of democracy.

ABRAHAM LINCOLN

Man's capacity for justice makes democracy possible, but man's inclination to injustice makes democracy necessary.

REINHOLD NIEBUHR

In free countries, every man is entitled to express his opinions—and every other man is entitled not to listen.

G. NORMAN COLLIE

DEPENDENCE *Also see:* FREEDOM, INDEPENDENCE.

There is no dependence that can be sure but a dependence upon one's self.

JOHN GAY

He who imagines he can do without the world deceives himself much; but he who fancies the world cannot do without him is still more mistaken.

FRANÇOIS DE LA ROCHEFOUCAULD

No degree of knowledge attainable by man is able to set him above the want of hourly assistance.

SAMUEL JOHNSON

Depend on no man, on no friend but him who can depend on himself. He only who acts conscientiously toward himself, will act so toward others.

JOHANN KASPAR LAVATER

There is no one subsists by himself alone.

OWEN FELLTHAM

DESIRE *Also see:* AMBITION, LOVE, PASSION, WANT.

Desire is the essence of a man.

BENEDICT SPINOZA

It is much easier to suppress a first desire than to satisfy those that follow.

FRANÇOIS DE LA ROCHEFOUCAULD

There are two tragedies in life. One is not get your heart's desire. The other is to get it.

GEORGE BERNARD SHAW

By annihilating the desires, you annihilate the mind. Every man without passions has within him no principle of action, nor motive to act.

CLAUDE ADRIEN HELVÉTIUS

All human activity is prompted by desire.

BERTRAND RUSSELL

We trifle when we assign limits to our desires, since nature hath set none.

CHRISTIAN NESTELL BOVEE

Every human mind is a great slumbering power until awakened by a keen desire and by definite resolution to do.

EDGAR F. ROBERTS

You will become as small as your controlling desire; as great as your dominant aspiration.

JAMES ALLEN

DESPAIR *Also see:* DISAPPOINTMENT, HOPE, PAIN, POVERTY, SORROW.

The man who lives only by hope will die with despair.

ITALIAN PROVERB

When we are flat on our backs there is no way to look but up.

ROGER W. BABSON

Despair is like forward children, who, when you take away one of their playthings, throw the rest into the fire for madness. It grows angry with itself, turns its own executioner, and revenges its misfortunes on its own head.

PIERRE CHARRON

It becomes no man to nurse despair, but, in the teeth of clenched antagonisms, to follow up the worthiest till he die.

ALFRED, LORD TENNYSON

It is a miserable state of mind to have few things to desire, and many things to fear.

FRANCIS BACON

The fact that God has prohibited despair gives misfortune the right to hope all things, and leaves hope free to dare all things.

ANNE SOPHIE SWETCHINE

DESTINY *Also see:* FATE, FORTUNE, FUTURE, GOD.

Destiny is no matter of chance. It is a matter of choice: It is not a thing to be waited for, it is a thing to be achieved.

WILLIAM JENNINGS BRYAN

Lots of folks confuse bad management with destiny.

KIN HUBBARD

Destiny: A tyrant's authority for crime and a fool's excuse for failure.

AMBROSE BIERCE

Men heap together the mistakes of their lives, and create a monster they call Destiny.

JOHN OLIVER HOBBES

Our destiny changes with our thought; we shall become what we wish to become, do what we wish to do, when our habitual thought corresponds with our desire.

ORISON S. MARDEN

DIFFERENCE *Also see:* ARGUMENT, CONTRAST, QUARREL, VARIETY.

The difference is no less real because it is of degree.

BENJAMIN NATHAN CARDOZO

The difference between the right word and the almost right word is the difference between lightning and the lightning bug.

MARK TWAIN

If men would consider not so much wherein they differ, as wherein they agree, there would be far less of uncharitableness and angry feeling in the world.

JOSEPH ADDISON

Honest differences are often a healthy sign of progress.

MAHATMA GANDHI

If by saying that all men are born equal, you mean that they are equally born, it is true, but true in no other sense; birth, talent, labor, virtue, and providence, are forever making differences.

EUGENE EDWARDS

Where there is no difference, there is only indifference.

LOUIS NIZER

DIFFICULTY *Also see:* ADVERSITY, ANXIETY, LABOR.

Difficulties are meant to rouse, not discourage. The human spirit is to grow strong by conflict.

WILLIAM ELLERY CHANNING

No man who is occupied in doing a very difficult thing, and doing it very well, ever loses his self-respect.

GEORGE BERNARD SHAW

There are two ways of meeting difficulties: you alter the difficulties or you alter yourself meeting them.

PHYLLIS BOTTOME

Difficulties strengthen the mind, as labor does the body.

SENECA

Undertake something that is difficult; it will do you good. Unless you try to do something beyond what you have already mastered, you will never grow.

RONALD E. OSBORN

DIGNITY Also see: HONOR, PRIDE, RIGHTS, WORK.

True dignity is never gained by place, and never lost when honors are withdrawn.

PHILIP MASSINGER

There is a healthful hardiness about real dignity that never dreads contact and communion with others however humble.

WASHINGTON IRVING

No race can prosper till it learns that there is as much dignity in tilling a field as in writing a poem.

BOOKER T. WASHINGTON

When boasting ends, there dignity begins.

OWEN D. YOUNG

Our dignity is not in what we do, but what we understand.

GEORGE SANTAYANA

Human rights rest on human dignity. The dignity of man is an ideal worth fighting for and worth dying for.

ROBERT MAYNARD

The ultimate end of all revolutionary social change is to establish the sanctity of human life, the dignity of man, the right of every human being to liberty and well-being.

EMMA GOLDMAN

DILIGENCE Also see: BUSY, EFFORT, INDUSTRY, LABOR, PERSEVERANCE, WORK.

The expectations of life depend upon diligence; the mechanic that would perfect his work must first sharpen his tools.

CONFUCIUS

Diligence is the mother of good luck.

BENJAMIN FRANKLIN

He who labors diligently need never despair; for all things are accomplished by diligence and labor.

MENANDER OF ATHENS

What we hope ever to do with ease, we must learn first to do with diligence.

SAMUEL JOHNSON

Few things are impossible to diligence and skill ... Great works are performed, not by strength, but perseverance.

SAMUEL JOHNSON

DIPLOMACY Also see: DISCRETION, JUDGMENT, POLITICS, TACT.

I have discovered the art of deceiving diplomats. I speak the truth, and they never believe me.

CAMILLO DI CAVOUR

Diplomacy is to do and say the nastiest things in the nicest way.

ISAAC GOLDBERG

To say nothing, especially when speaking, is half the art of diplomacy.

WILL DURANT

A diplomat is a person who can tell you to go to Hell in such a way that you actually look forward to the trip.

ANONYMOUS

The principle of give and take is the principle of diplomacy—give one and take ten.

MARK TWAIN

Diplomacy is the art of letting someone have your way.

DANIELE VARE

Diplomacy is a disguised war, in which states seek to gain by barter and intrigue, by the cleverness of arts, the objectives which they would have to gain more clumsily by means of war.

RANDOLPH BOURNE

Let us never negotiate out of fear. But let us never fear to negotiate.

JOHN FITZGERALD KENNEDY

This is the devilish thing about foreign affairs: they are foreign and will not always conform to our whims.

JAMES RESTON

DISAPPOINTMENT Also see: DEFEAT, FAILURE, HOPE.

Man must be disappointed with the lesser things of life before he can comprehend the full value of the greater.

EDWARD G. BULWER-LYTTON

Disappointment is the nurse of wisdom.

BOYLE ROCHE

Too many people miss the silver lining because they're expecting gold.

MAURICE SEITTER

Disappointment to a noble soul is what cold water is to burning metal; it strengthens, tempers, intensifies, but never destroys it.

ELIZA TABOR

The disappointment of manhood succeeds the delusion of youth.

BENJAMIN DISRAELI

If you expect perfection from people your whole life is a series of disappointments, grumblings and complaints. If, on the contrary, you pitch your expectations low, taking folks as the inefficient creatures which they are, you are frequently surprised by having them perform better than you had hoped.

BRUCE BARTON

DISARMAMENT *Also see:* NUCLEAR WARFARE, WAR.

The notion that disarmament can put a stop to war is contradicted by the nearest dogfight.

GEORGE BERNARD SHAW

Today, every inhabitant of this planet must contemplate the day when it may no longer be habitable. Every man, woman and child lives under a nuclear sword of Damocles, hanging by the slenderest of threads, capable of being cut at any moment by accident, miscalculation or madness. The weapons of war must be abolished before they abolish us.

JOHN FITZGERALD KENNEDY

The best way to begin disarming is to begin—and the United States is ready to conclude firm agreements in these areas and to consider any other reasonable proposal.

LYNDON BAINES JOHNSON

There is no more dangerous misconception than this which misconstrues the arms race as the cause rather than a symptom of the tensions and divisions which threaten nuclear war. If the history of the past fifty years teaches us anything, it is that peace does not follow disarmament—disarmament follows peace.

BERNARD M. BARUCH

DISCIPLINE *Also see:* CHEERFULNESS, ORDER, PARENTS.

To be in good moral condition requires at least as much training as to be in good physical condition.

JAWAHARLAL NEHRU

A stern discipline pervades all nature, which is a little cruel that it may be very kind.

EDMUND SPENSER

You never will be the person you can be if pressure, tension, and discipline are taken out of your life.

JAMES G. BILKEY

What we do on some great occasion will probably depend on what we already are; and what we are will be the result of previous years of self-discipline.

H. P. LIDDON

Man is still responsible. He must turn the alloy of modern experience into the steel of mastery and character. His success lies not with the stars but with himself. He must carry on the fight of self-correction and discipline.

FRANK CURTIS WILLIAMS

He that has learned to obey will know how to command.

SOLON

If the self-discipline of the free cannot match the iron discipline of the mailed fist, in economic, scientific, and all other kinds of struggles as well as the military, then the peril of freedom will continue to rise.

JOHN FITZGERALD KENNEDY.

DISCONTENT *Also see:* ANXIETY, COMPLAINT, CONTENTMENT, DISSENT, REBELLION.

One thing only has been lent to youth and age in common—discontent.

MATTHEW ARNOLD

Restlessness and discontent are the necessities of progress.

THOMAS EDISON

Discontent is the first step in the progress of a man or a nation.

OSCAR WILDE

Discontent is something that follows ambition like a shadow.

HENRY H. HASKINS

Who is not satisfied with himself will grow; who is not sure of his own correctness will learn many things.

CHINESE PROVERB

The discontented man finds no easy chair.

BENJAMIN FRANKLIN

Who with a little cannot be content, endures an everlasting punishment.

ROBERT HERRICK

DISCOVERY *Also see:* INVENTION, ORIGINALITY.

What is wanted is not the will to believe but the wish to find out, which is the exact opposite.

BERTRAND RUSSELL

If I have ever made any valuable discoveries, it has been owing more to patient attention, than to any other talent.

ISAAC NEWTON

Great discoveries and improvements invariably involve the cooperation of many minds. I may be given credit for having blazed the trail but when I look at the subsequent developments I feel the credit is due to others rather than to myself.

ALEXANDER GRAHAM BELL

Through every rift of discovery some seeming anomaly drops out of the darkness, and falls, as a golden link, into the great chain of order.

EDWIN HUBBEL CHAPIN

DISCRETION *Also see:* CAUTION, COMMON SENSE, JUDGMENT, PRUDENCE.

Be discreet in all things, and so render it unnecessary to be mysterious about any.

FIRST DUKE OF WELLINGTON

I have never been hurt by anything I didn't say.

CALVIN COOLIDGE

If thou art a master, be sometimes blind; if a servant, sometimes deaf.

THOMAS FULLER

Discretion in speech is more than eloquence.

FRANCIS BACON

Great ability without discretion comes almost invariably to a tragic end.

GAMBETTA

An ounce of discretion is worth a pound of learning.

PROVERB

Philosophy is nothing but discretion.

JOHN SELDEN

DISCUSSION ... See CONVERSATION

DISEASE *Also see:* AFFLICTION, CRIME, DEATH, DEBT, HEALTH, MEDICINE, PAIN.

Some remedies are worse than the diseases.

PUBILIUS SYRUS

Disease is a physical process that generally begins that equality which death completes.

SAMUEL JOHNSON

We classify disease as error, which nothing but Truth or Mind can heal.

MARY BAKER EDDY

Disease is the retribution of outraged Nature.

HOSEA BALLOU

A bodily disease may be but a symptom of some ailment in the spiritual past.

NATHANIEL HAWTHORNE

We are the carriers of health and disease—either the divine health of courage and nobility or the demonic diseases of hate and anxiety.

JOSHUA LOTH LIEBMAN

There are no such things as incurables; there are only things for which man has not found a cure.

BERNARD M. BARUCH

Sickness and disease are in weak minds the sources of melancholy; but that which is painful to the body, may be profitable to the soul. Sickness puts us in mind of our mortality, and, while we drive on heedlessly in the full career of worldly pomp and jollity, kindly pulls us by the ear, and brings us to a proper sense of our duty.

RICHARD E. BURTON

It is with disease of the mind, as with those of the body; we are half dead before we understand our disorder, and half cured when we do.

CHARLES CALEB COLTON

DISHONESTY *Also see:* CRIME, DECEIT, FRAUD, HYPOCRISY, INJUSTICE, LYING.

If all mankind were suddenly to practice honesty, many thousands of people would be sure to starve.

G. C. LICHTENBERG

Honesty pays, but it doesn't seem to pay enough to suit some people.

KIN HUBBARD

Don't place too much confidence in the man who boasts of being as honest as the day is long. Wait until you meet him at night.

ROBERT C. EDWARDS

False words are not only evil in themselves, but they infect the soul with evil.

SOCRATES

Hope of ill gain is the beginning of loss.

DEMOCRITUS

Dishonesty, cowardice and duplicity are never impulsive.

GEORGE A. KNIGHT

DISSENT *Also see:* ARGUMENT, DIFFERENCE, DIFFICULTY, QUARREL.

Dissent does not include the freedom to destroy the system of law which guarantees freedom to speak, assemble and march in protest. Dissent is not anarchy.

SEYMOUR F. SIMON

The United States can ... be proud that it has institutions and a structure that permit its citizens to express honest dissent, even though those who do so may be maligned by the highest official in the land.

NEW YORK TIMES

In a number of cases dissenting opinions have in time become the law.

CHARLES EVANS HUGHES

Those who begin coercive elimination of dissent soon find themselves exterminating dissenters. Compulsory unification of opinion achieves only the unanimity of the graveyard.

FELIX FRANKFURTER

Mere unorthodoxy or dissent from the prevailing mores is not to be condemned. The absence of such voices would be a symptom of grave illness in our society.

EARL WARREN

Thought that is silenced is always rebellious. ... Majorities, of course, are often mistaken. This is why the silencing of minorities is always dangerous. Criticism and dissent are the indispensable antidote to major delusions.

ALAN BARTH

DISTRUST *Also see:* DOUBT, FAITH, FEAR, SUSPICION.

The disease of mutual distrust among nations is the bane of modern civilization.

FRANZ BOAS

However much we may distrust men's sincerity, we always believe they speak to us more sincerely than to others.

FRANÇOIS DE LA ROCHEFOUCAULD

What loneliness is more lonely than distrust?

GEORGE ELIOT

The man who trusts men will make fewer mistakes than he who distrusts them.

CAMILLO DI CAVOUR

DOUBT *Also see:* AGNOSTICISM, DISTRUST, FAITH, INCREDULITY, SKEPTICISM, SUSPICION, WISDOM.

We know accurately only when we know little; with knowledge doubt enters.

JOHANN WOLFGANG VON GOETHE

I respect faith, but doubt is what gets you an education.

WILSON MIZNER

Men become civilized, not in proportion to their willingness to believe, but in proportion to their readiness to doubt.

H. L. MENCKEN

Doubt is the beginning, not the end, of wisdom.

GEORGE ILES

Just think of the tragedy of teaching children not to doubt.

CLARENCE DARROW

Faith keeps many doubts in her pay. If I could not doubt, I should not believe.

HENRY DAVID THOREAU

In all affairs it's a healthy thing now and then to hang a question mark on the things you have long taken for granted.

BERTRAND RUSSELL

DRAFT *Also see:* SOLDIER, WAR.

Peacetime conscription is the greatest step toward regimentation and militarism ever undertaken by the Congress of the United States.

BURTON KENDALL WHEELER

A young man who does not have what it takes to perform military service is not likely to have what it takes to make a living.

JOHN FITZGERALD KENNEDY

Pressed into service means pressed out of shape.

ROBERT FROST

People have not been horrified by war to a sufficient extent . . . War will exist until that distant day when the conscientious objector enjoys the same reputation and prestige as the warrior does today.

JOHN FITZGERALD KENNEDY

DREAM *Also see:* AMERICA, DEMOCRACY, ILLUSION, IMAGINATION, REVERIE.

Keep true to the dreams of thy youth.

JOHANN VON SCHILLER

Dreaming permits each and every one of us to be quietly and safely insane every night of our lives.

CHARLES WILLIAM DEMENT

The smaller the head, the bigger the dream.

AUSTIN O'MALLEY

Dreaming is an act of pure imagination, attesting in all men a creative power, which, if it were available in waking, would make every man a Dante or Shakespeare.

H. F. HEDGE

If one advances confidently in the directions of his dreams, and endeavors to live the life which he has imagined, he will meet with a success unexpected in common hours.

HENRY DAVID THOREAU

Dreams are nothing but incoherent ideas, occasioned by partial or imperfect sleep.

BENJAMIN RUSH

All men of action are dreamers.

JAMES G. HUNEKER

The more a man dreams, the less he believes.

H. L. MENCKEN

People who insist on telling their dreams are among the terrors of the breakfast table.

MAX BEERBOHM

The end of wisdom is to dream high enough to lose the dream in the seeking of it.

WILLIAM FAULKNER

Toil, feel, think, hope; you will be sure to dream enough before you die, without arranging it.

JOHN STERLING

It is difficult to say what is impossible, for the dream of yesterday is the hope of today and the reality of tomorrow.

ROBERT H. GODDARD

A lost but happy dream may shed its light upon our waking hours, and the whole day may be infected with the gloom of a dreary or sorrowful one; yet of neither may we be able to recover a trace.

WALTER DE LA MARE

DRESS *Also see:* APPEARANCE, FASHION, TASTE.

Be careless in your dress if you must, but keep a tidy soul.

MARK TWAIN

The body is the shell of the soul, and dress the husk of that shell; but the husk often tells what the kernel is.

ANONYMOUS

Eat to please thyself, but dress to please others.

BENJAMIN FRANKLIN

Clothes don't make the man, but clothes have got many a man a good job.

HERBERT HAROLD VREELAND

There is new strength, repose of mind, and imspiration in fresh apparel.

ELLA WHEELER WILCOX

The well-dressed man is he whose clothes you never notice.

W. SOMERSET MAUGHAM

No man is esteemed for gay garments but by fools and women.

SIR WALTER RALEIGH

If a woman rebels against high-heeled shoes, she should take care to do it in a very smart hat.

GEORGE BERNARD SHAW

Good clothes open all doors.

THOMAS FULLER

Clothes make the man.

LATIN PROVERB

Do not conceive that fine clothes make fine men, any more than fine feathers make fine birds. A plain, genteel dress is more admired, obtains more credit in the eyes of the judicious and sensible.

GEORGE WASHINGTON

Keeping your clothes well pressed will keep you from looking hard pressed.

COLEMAN COX

DRUGS *Also see:* CRIME.

The time has come to stop the sale of slavery to the young.

LYNDON BAINES JOHNSON

We have drugs to make women speak, but none to keep them silent.

ANATOLE FRANCE

The young physician starts life with 20 drugs for each disease, and the old physician ends life with one drug for 20 diseases.

WILLIAM OSLER

DRUNKENNESS *Also see:* ABSTINENCE, VICE.

The sight of a drunkard is a better sermon against that vice than the best that was ever preached on the subject.

JOHN FAUCIT SAVILLE

Drunkenness is the ruin of a person. It is premature old age. It is temporary death.

ST. BASIL

Alcoholism is tragically high on the list of our nation's health problems. Five million Americans are alcoholics. They bring incalculable grief to millions of families. They cost their families, their employers and society billions of dollars.

LYNDON BAINES JOHNSON

Extensive interviews show that not one alcoholic has ever actually seen a pink elephant.

YALE UNIVERSITY, CENTER OF ALCOHOL STUDIES

Always remember, that I have taken more out of alcohol than alcohol has taken out of me.

WINSTON CHURCHILL

Drunkenness is temporary suicide: the happiness that it brings is merely negative, a momentary cessation of unhappiness.

BERTRAND RUSSELL

Drunkenness is not a mere matter of intoxicating liquors; it goes deeper—far deeper. Drunkenness is the failure of a man to control his thoughts.

DAVID GRAYSON

Drunkenness is nothing else but a voluntary madness.

SENECA

DUTY *Also see:* AFFECTION, AUTHORITY, BOLDNESS, BUSY, RESPONSIBILITY, RIGHTS.

Only aim to do your duty, and mankind will give you credit where you fail.

THOMAS JEFFERSON

Men do less than they ought, unless they do all that they can.

THOMAS CARLYLE

The reward of one duty is the power to fulfill another.

GEORGE ELIOT

. . . it is just as hard to do your duty when men are sneering at you as when they are shooting at you.

WOODROW WILSON

A duty dodged is like a debt unpaid; it is only deferred, and we must come back and settle the account at last.

JOSEPH F. NEWTON

Let us do our duty in our shop or our kitchen, in the market, the street, the office, the school, the home, just as faithfully as if we stood in the front rank of some great battle, and knew that victory for mankind depended on our bravery, strength and skill. When we do that, the humblest of us will be serving in that great army which achieves the welfare of the world.

THEODORE PARKER

Never mind your happiness; do your duty.

WILL DURANT

It is the duty of the government to make it difficult for people to do wrong, easy to do right.

WILLIAM E. GLADSTONE

A man who neglects his duty as a citizen is not entitled to his rights as a citizen.

TIORIO

Knowledge of our duties is the most essential part of the philosophy of life. If you escape duty you avoid action. The world demands results.

GEORGE W. GOETHALS

Who escapes a duty, avoids a gain.

THEODORE PARKER

EARTH *Also see:* NATURE, WORLD, UNIVERSE.

The earth is given as a common for men to labor and live in.

THOMAS JEFFERSON

How far must suffering and misery go before we see that even in the day of vast cities and powerful machines, the good earth is our mother and that if we destroy her, we destroy ourselves?

PAUL BIGELOW SEARS

The earth and its resources belong of right to its people.

GIFFORD PINCHOT

There is enough for all. The earth is a generous mother; she will provide in plentiful abundance food for all her children if they will but cultivate her soil in justice and in peace.

BOURKE COCKRAN

Our earth is but a small star in a great universe. Yet of it we can make, if we choose, a planet unvexed by war, untroubled by hunger or fear, undivided by senseless distinctions of race, color or theory.

STEPHEN VINCENT BENÉT

Earth, thou great footstool of our God, who reigns on high; thou fruitful source of all our raiment, life, and food; our house, our parent, and our nurse.

ISAAC WATTS

The pagans do not know God, and love only the earth. The Jews know the true God, and love only the earth. The Christians know the true God, and do not love the earth.

BLAISE PASCAL

"The earth is the Lord's fullness thereof": this is no longer a hollow dictum of religion, but a directive for economic action toward human brotherhood.

LEWIS MUMFORD

EATING *Also see:* GLUTTON.

Eat, drink, and be merry, for tomorrow ye diet.

WILLIAM GILMORE BEYMER

To eat is human; to digest, divine.

C. T. COPELAND

The way to a man's heart is through his stomach.

FANNY FERN

He who does not mind his belly will hardly mind anything else.

SAMUEL JOHNSON

There is no love sincerer than the love of food.

GEORGE BERNARD SHAW

When it comes to eating, you can sometimes help yourself more by helping yourself less.

RICHARD ARMOUR

Tell me what you eat, and I will tell you what you are.

ANTHELME BRILLAT-SAVARIN

A saw few die of hunger; of eating, a hundred thousand.

BENJAMIN FRANKLIN

The proof of the pudding is in the eating.

MIGUEL DE CERVANTES

Part of the secret of success in life is to eat what you like and let the food fight it out inside.

MARK TWAIN

The difference between a rich man and a poor man is this— the former eats when he pleases, and the latter when he can get it.

SIR WALTER RALEIGH

ECONOMY Also see: BARGAIN, MONEY, PRUDENCE.

There can be no economy where there is no efficiency.

BEACONSFIELD

Without economy none can be rich, and with it few will be poor.

SAMUEL JOHNSON

Nothing is cheap which is superfluous, for what one does not need, is dear at a penny.

PLUTARCH

Beware of little expenses; a small leak will sink a great ship.

BENJAMIN FRANKLIN

Ere you consult your fancy, consult your purse.

BENJAMIN FRANKLIN

He who will not economize will have to agonize.

CONFUCIUS

The world abhors closeness, and all but admires extravagance; yet a slack hand shows weakness, and a tight hand strength.

THOMAS FOWELL BUXTON

I place economy among the first and most important virtues, and public debt as the greatest of dangers. . . . We must make our choice between economy and liberty, or profusion and servitude. If we can prevent the government from wasting the labors of the people under the pretense of caring for them, they will be happy.

THOMAS JEFFERSON

Economy is a way of spending money without getting any pleasure out of it.

ARMAND SALACROU

Economy is for the poor; the rich may dispense with it.

CHRISTIAN NESTELL BOVEE

Let honesty and industry be thy constant companions, and spend one penny less than thy clear gains; then shall thy pocket begin to thrive; creditors will not insult, nor want oppress, nor hungerness bite, nor nakedness freeze thee.

BENJAMIN FRANKLIN

EDUCATION Also see: CULTURE, DEFEAT, DOUBT, READING, STUDY.

Only the educated are free.

EPICTETUS

Education is a better safeguard of liberty than a standing army.

EDWARD EVERETT

Education is a progressive discovery of our ignorance.

WILL DURANT

I have never let my schooling interfere with my education.

MARK TWAIN

Education makes people easy to lead, but difficult to drive; easy to govern, but impossible to enslave.

HENRY PETER BROUGHAM

If a man empties his purse into his head, no man can take it away from him. An investment in knowledge always pays the best interest.

BENJAMIN FRANKLIN

Education is a social process . . . Education is growth. . . . Education is, not a preparation for life; education is life itself.

JOHN DEWEY

Education is that which discloses to the wise and disguises from the foolish their lack of understanding.

AMBROSE BIERCE

Education is too important to be left solely to the educators.

FRANCIS KEPPEL

He who opens a school door, closes a prison.

VICTOR HUGO

The best education in the world is that by struggling to get a living.

WENDELL PHILLIPS

My father must have had some elementary education for he could read and write and keep accounts inaccurately.

GEORGE BERNARD SHAW

Our progress as a nation can be no swifter than our progress in education.

JOHN FITZGERALD KENNEDY

EFFICIENCY Also see: ABILITY, DILIGENCE, GENIUS, INDUSTRY, ORDER, TECHNOLOGY.

It is more than probable that the average man could, with no injury to his health, incease his efficiency fifty percent.

WALTER SCOTT

A sense of the value of time—that is, of the best way to divide one's time into one's various activities—is an essential preliminary to efficient work; it is the only method of avoiding hurry.

ARNOLD BENNETT

In the old world that is passing, in the new world that is coming, national efficiency has been and will be a controlling factor in national safety and welfare.

GIFFORD PINCHOT

Loyal and efficient work in a great cause, even though it may not be immediately recognized, ultimately bears fruit.

JAWAHARLAL NEHRU

We want the spirit of America to be efficient; we want American character to be efficient; we want American character to display itself in what I may, perhaps, be allowed to call spiritual efficiency—clear disinterested thinking and fearless action along the right lines of thought.

WOODROW WILSON

Obviously, the highest type of efficiency is that which can utilize existing material to the best advantage.

JAWAHARLAL NEHRU

EFFORT *Also see:* ACHIEVEMENT, ACTION, DILIGENCE, ENERGY, INDUSTRY, LABOR, PERSEVERANCE, WORK.

It is hard to fail, but it is worse never to have tried to succeed. In this life we get nothing save by effort.

THEODORE ROOSEVELT

The only method by which people can be supported is out of the effort of those who are earning their own way. We must not create a deterrent to hard work.

ROBERT A. TAFT

A law of nature rules that energy cannot be destroyed. You change its form from coal to steam, from steam to power in the turbine, but you do not destroy energy. In the same way, another law governs human activity and rules that honest effort cannot be lost, but that some day the proper benefits will be forthcoming.

PAUL SPEICHER

Things don't turn up in this world until somebody turns them up.

JAMES A. GARFIELD

Many a man never fails because he never tries.

NORMAN MACEWAN

EGOTISM . . . See VANITY

ELOQUENCE *Also see:* LOQUACITY.

True eloquence consists in saying all that is proper, and nothing more.

FRANÇOIS DE LA ROCHEFOUCAULD

Eloquence is logic on fire.

LYMAN BEECHER

Eloquence is the child of knowledge.

BENJAMIN DISRAELI

Noise proves nothing. Often a hen who has merely laid an egg cackles as if she had laid an asteroid.

MARK TWAIN

There is no eloquence without a man behind it.

RALPH WALDO EMERSON

True eloquence does not consist in speech. Words and phrases may be marshalled in every way, but they cannot compass it. It must consist in the man, in the subject, and in the occasion. It comes, if at all, like the outbreaking of a fountain from the earth, or the bursting forth of volcanic fires, with spontaneous, original native force.

DANIEL WEBSTER

EMINENCE . . . *See* ESTEEM

EMOTION *Also see:* CURIOSITY, PASSION, REASON, SENTIMENT.

When dealing with people remember you are not dealing with creatures of logic, but with creatures of emotion, creatures bristling with prejudice, and motivated by pride and vanity.

DALE CARNEGIE

Emotion is not something shameful, subordinate, second-rate; it is a supremely valid phase of humanity at its noblest and most mature.

JOSHUA LOTH LIEBMAN

The young man who has not wept is a savage, and the old man who will not laugh is a fool.

GEORGE SANTAYANA

By starving emotions we become humorless, rigid and stereotyped; by repressing them we become literal, reformatory and holier-than-thou; encouraged, they perfume life; discouraged, they poison it.

JOSEPH COLLINS

EMPLOYMENT *Also see:* BUSINESS, BUSY, EFFORT, WORK.

Not to enjoy life, but to employ life, ought to be our aim and inspiration.

JOHN ROSS MACDUFF

Each man's task is his life preserver.

GEORGE B. EMERSON

When you hire people that are smarter than you are, you prove you are smarter than they are.

R. H. GRANT

Early to bed and early to rise probably indicates unskilled labor.

JOHN CIARDI

Employment, which Galen calls "nature's physician," is so essential to human happiness that indolence is justly considered as the mother of misery.

RICHARD E. BURTON

The employer generally gets the employees he deserves.

WALTER GILBEY

END and MEANS *Also see:* AIM, DEATH, PURPOSE, RESULT.

The end must justify the means.

MATTHEW PRIOR

Knowledge of means without knowledge of ends is animal training.

EVERETT DEAN MARTIN

If well thou hast begun, go on; it is the end that crowns us, not the fight.

ROBERT HERRICK

Freedom is only good as a means; it is no end in itself.

HERMAN MELVILLE

The end justifies the means only when the means used are such as actually bring about the desired and desirable end.

JOHN DEWEY

In everything we ought to look to the end.

JEAN DE LA FONTAINE

ENDURANCE *Also see:* PATIENCE, STRENGTH, TOLERANCE, WILL.

To endure is the first thing that a child ought to learn, and that which he will have the most need to know.

JEAN JACQUES ROUSSEAU

Whatever necessity lays upon thee, endure; whatever she commands, do.

JOHANN WOLFGANG VON GOETHE

Endurance is patience concentrated.

THOMAS CARLYLE

Still achieving, still pursuing, learn to labor and to wait.

HENRY WADSWORTH LONGFELLOW

There is a strength of quiet endurance as significant of courage as the most daring feats of prowess.

HENRY THEODORE TUCKERMAN

ENEMY *Also see:* CITIZENSHIP, DEBT, FORGIVE-NESS, FRIENDSHIP, QUARREL.

There is no little enemy.

BENJAMIN FRANKLIN

A man's greatness can be measured by his enemies.

DON PLATT

Observe your enemies, for they first find out your faults.

ANTISTHENES

If you have no enemies, you are apt to be in the same predicament in regard to friends.

ELBERT HUBBARD

Our real enemies are the people who make us feel so good that we are slowly, but inexorably, pulled down into the quicksand of smugness and self-satisfaction.

SYDNEY HARRIS

Man is his own worst enemy.

CICERO

In order to have an enemy, one must be somebody. One must be a force before he can be resisted by another force. A malicious enemy is better than a clumsy friend.

ANNE SOPHIE SWETCHINE

Nothing would more contribute to make a man wise than to have always an enemy in his view.

LORD HALIFAX

An enemy is anyone who tells the truth about you.

ELBERT HUBBARD

ENERGY *Also see:* AVERAGE, EFFICIENCY, EF-FORT, FORCE, INDUSTRY, POWER, SPIRIT, STRENGTH, ZEAL.

The world belongs to the energetic.

RALPH WALDO EMERSON

Energy and persistence conquer all things.

BENJAMIN FRANKLIN

There is no genius in life like the genius of energy and industry.

DONALD GRANT MITCHELL

Energy will do anything that can be done in the world; and no talents, no circumstances, no opportunities will make a two-legged animal a man without it.

JOHANN WOLFGANG VON GOETHE

The real difference between men is energy. A strong will, a settled purpose, an invincible determination, can accomplish almost anything; and in this lies the distinction between great men and little men.

THOMAS FULLER

ENJOYMENT *Also see:* AMUSEMENT, CHEERFUL-NESS, CONTENTMENT, JOY, LEISURE, PLEASURE.

The first half of life consists of the capacity to enjoy without the chance; the last half consists of the chance without the capacity.

MARK TWAIN

True enjoyment comes from activity of the mind and exercise of the body; the two are ever united.

HUMBOLDT

If your capacity to acquire has outstripped your capacity to enjoy, you are on the way to the scrap-heap.

GLEN BUCK

May we never let the things we can't have, or don't have, or shouldn't have, spoil our enjoyment of the things we do have and can have. As we value our happiness let us not forget it, for one of the greatest lessons in life is learning to be happy without the things we cannot or should not have.

RICHARD L. EVANS

ENTHUSIASM *Also see:* OPTIMISM, PASSION, ZEAL.

The enthusiasm of old men is singularly like that of infancy.

GÉRARD DE NERVAL

The worst bankrupt in the world is the man who has lost his enthusiasm.

H. W. ARNOLD

Every great and commanding movement in the annals of the world is the triumph of enthusiasm. Nothing great was ever achieved without it.

RALPH WALDO EMERSON

No person who is enthusiastic about his work has anything to fear from life.

SAMUEL GOLDWYN

EQUALITY *Also see:* ARISTOCRACY, CLEVERNESS, DEMOCRACY, DIFFERENCE, RACE, RIGHTS.

All human beings are born free and equal in dignity and rights.

U.N., DECLARATION OF HUMAN RIGHTS, ART. 1.

Men are equal; it is not birth but virtue that makes the difference.

VOLTAIRE

There are many humorous things in the world: among them the white man's notion that he is less savage than the other savages.

MARK TWAIN

We hold these truths to be self-evident, that all men are created equal.

THOMAS JEFFERSON

Complete equality means universal irresponsibility.

T. S. ELIOT

If there be a human being who is freer than I, then I shall necessarily become his slave. If I am freer than any other, then he will become my slave. Therefore equality is an absolutely necessary condition of freedom.

MIKHAIL A. BAKUNIN

ERROR Also see: CAUSE, TRUTH, WRONG.

It takes less time to do a thing right than it does to explain why you did it wrong.

HENRY WADSWORTH LONGFELLOW

The man who makes no mistakes does not usually make anything.

EDWARD PHELPS

An error doesn't become a mistake until you refuse to correct it.

ORLANDO A. BATTISTA

If I have erred, I err in company with Abraham Lincoln.

THEODORE ROOSEVELT

Error is discipline through which we advance.

WILLIAM ELLERY CHANNING

Sometimes we may learn more from a man's errors, than from his virtues.

HENRY WADSWORTH LONGFELLOW

A man whose errors take ten years to correct is quite a man.

J. ROBERT OPPENHEIMER

ESTEEM Also see: ADMIRATION, HONOR.

The chief ingredients in the composition of those qualities that gain esteem and praise, are good nature, truth, good sense, and good breeding.

JOSEPH ADDISON

Oftentimes nothing profits more than self-esteem, grounded on what is just and right.

JOHN MILTON

Esteem has more engaging charms than friendship and even love. It captivates hearts better, and never makes ingrates.

FRANÇOIS DE LA ROCHEFOUCAULD

ETERNITY Also see: BIBLE, FUTURE, GOD, HEAVEN, HELL, IMMORTAL- ITY, TIME.

Eternity is not an everlasting flux of time, but time is a short parenthesis in a long period.

JOHN DONNE

Eternity is in love with the productions of time.

WILLIAM BLAKE

All great natures delight in stability; all great men find eternity affirmed in the very promise of their faculties.

RALPH WALDO EMERSON

Eternity has no gray hairs! The flowers fade, the heart withers, man grows old and dies, the world lies down in the sepulchre of ages, but time writes no wrinkles on the brow of eternity.

REGINALD HEBER

The sum of all sums is eternity.

LUCRETIUS

The thought of eternity consoles for the shortness of life.

LUC DE CLAPIERS

I leave eternity to Thee; for what is man that he could live the lifetime of his God?

HERMAN MELVILLE

EVIL Also see: CREDULITY, DANGER, VICE.

It is a sin to believe evil of others, but it is seldom a mistake.

H. L. MENCKEN

There is nothing evil save that which perverts the mind and shackles the conscience.

ST. AMBROSE

I never wonder to see men wicked, but I often wonder to see them not ashamed.

JONATHAN SWIFT

Evil often triumphs, but never conquers.

JOSEPH ROUX

A person may cause evil to others not only by his actions but by his inaction, and in either case he is justly accountable to them for the injury.

JOHN STUART MILL

There are a thousand hacking at the branches of evil to one who is striking at the root.

HENRY DAVID THOREAU

Evil events from evil causes spring.

ARISTOPHANES

It is privilege that causes evil in the world, not wickedness, and not men.

LINCOLN STEFFENS

It is the law of our humanity that man must know good through evil. No great principle ever triumphed but through much evil. No man ever progressed to greatness and goodness but through great mistakes.

FREDERICK W. ROBERTSON

All that is necessary for the triumph of evil is that good men do nothing.

EDMUND BURKE

Evil unchecked grows, evil tolerated poisons the whole system.

JAWAHARLAL NEHRU

EVOLUTION *Also see:* CHANGE.

All modern men are descended from a worm-like creature, but it shows more on some people.

WILL CUPPY

Some call it evolution and others call it God.

W. H. CARRUTH

The question is this: is man an ape or an angel? I am on the side of the angels. I repudiate with indignation and adhorrence these new-fangled theories

BENJAMIN DISRAELI

One touch of Darwin makes the whole world kin.

GEORGE BERNARD SHAW

We must remember that there are no shortcuts in evolution

LOUIS D. BRANDEIS

Concerning what ultimately becomes of the individual it (evolution) has added nothing and subtracted nothing.

ROBERT A. MILLIKAN

We are descended not only from monkeys, but also from monks.

ELBERT HUBBARD

EXAGGERATION *Also see:* ELOQUENCE, LOQUACITY.

We always weaken whatever we exaggerate.

JEAN FRANÇOIS DE LAHARPE

Exaggeration is a blood relation to falsehood and nearly as blameable.

HOSEA BALLOU

There are people so addicted to exaggeration they can't tell the truth without lying.

JOSH BILLINGS

Some so speak in exaggerations and superlatives that we need to make a large discount from their statements before we can come at their real meaning.

TRYON EDWARDS

Exaggeration is a department of lying.

BALTASAR GRACIÁN

EXAMPLE *Also see:* CONFORMITY, INFLUENCE

Example is not the main thing in life—it is the only thing.

ALBERT SCHWEITZER

Other men are lenses through which we read our own minds.

FRANCOIS DE LA ROCHEFOUCAULD

Old men are fond of giving good advice to console themselves for their inability to give bad examples.

FRANÇOIS DE LA ROCEFOUCAULD

The first great gift we can bestow on others is a good example.

MORELL

Few things are harder to put up with than the annoyance of a good example.

MARK TWAIN

The rotten apple spoils his companion.

BENJAMIN FRANKLIN

I have ever deemed it more honorable and more profitable, too, to set a good example than to follow a bad one.

THOMAS JEFFERSON

First find the man in yourself if you will inspire manliness in others.

AMOS BRONSON ALCOTT

EXCELLENCE . . . See PERFECTION

EXCUSES *Also see:* FAILURE, REGRET.

Don't make excuses, make good.

ELBERT HUBBARD

An excuse is worse and more terrible than a lie; for an excuse is a lie guarded.

ALEXANDER POPE

He that is good for making excuses is seldom good for anything else

BENJAMIN FRANKLIN

We have forty million reasons for failure, but not a single excuse.

RUDYARD KIPLING

Uncalled-for excuses are practical confessions.

CHARLES SIMMONS

EXPECTATION . . . See ANTICIPATION.

EXPEDIENCY *Also see:* COMPROMISE, OPPORTUNITY

I believe the moral losses of expediency always far outweigh the temporary gains.

WENDELL L. WILKIE

When private virtue is hazarded on the perilous cast of expediency, the pillars of the republic, however apparent their stability, are infected with decay at the very center.

EDWIN HUBBEL CHAPIN

No man is justified in doing evil on the ground of expedience.

THEODORE ROOSEVELT

Expedients are for the hour; principles for the ages.

HENRY WARD BEECHER

EXPERIENCE *Also see:* AGE, THEORY.

Men are wise in proportion, not to their experience, but to their capacity for experience.

GEORGE BERNARD SHAW

Experience is a school where a man learns what a big fool he has been.

JOSH BILLINGS

Experience is a hard teacher because she gives the test first, the lesson afterwards.

VERNON SANDERS LAW

Nothing is a waste of time if you use the experience wisely.

RODIN

Experience is something you get too late to do anything about the mistakes you made while getting it.

ANONYMOUS

When I was a boy of fourteen, my father was so ignorant I could hardly stand to have the old man around. But when I got to be twenty-one, I was astonished at how much the old man had learned in seven years.

MARK TWAIN

Experience is one thing you can't get for nothing.

OSCAR WILDE

QD-39

Experience increases our wisdom but doesn't reduce our follies.

JOSH BILLINGS

EXTRAVAGANCE *Also see:* DESIRE, ECONOMY.

Extravagance is the luxury of the poor; penury is the luxury of the rich.

OSCAR WILDE

An extravagance is anything you buy that is of no earthly use to your wife.

FRANKLIN P. JONES

He who buys what he needs not, sells what he needs.

JAPANESE PROVERB

All decent people live beyond their incomes; those who aren't respectable live beyond other people's; a few gifted individuals manage to do both.

SAKI

EXTREMES *Also see:* EXTRAVAGANCE, RADICAL, REVERIE.

Mistrust the man who finds everything good; the man who finds everything evil; and still more the man who is indifferent to everything.

JOHANN KASPAR LAVATER

I would remind you that extremism in the defense of liberty is no vice. And let me also remind you that moderation in the pursuit of justice is no virtue.

BARRY M. GOLDWATER

In everything the middle course is best; all things in excess bring trouble.

PLAUTUS

Too austere a philosophy makes few wise men; too rigorous politics, few good subjects; too hard a religion, few persons whose devotion is of long continuance.

SEIGNEUR DE SAINT-EVREMOND

EYE *Also see:* ADVENTURE, BIGOTRY, ORIGINALITY, VISION.

Men are born with two eyes, but only one tongue, in order that they should see twice as much as they say.

CHARLES CALEB COLTON

One of the most wonderful things in nature is a glance of the eye; it transcends speech; it is the bodily symbol of identity.

RALPH WALDO EMERSON

The eye of the master will do more work than both his hands.

BENJAMIN FRANKLIN

An eye can threaten like a loaded and levelled gun, or it can insult like hissing or kicking; or, in its altered mood, by beams of kindness, it can make the heart dance for joy.

RALPH WALDO EMERSON

FACTS *Also see:* ACCURACY, COMPROMISE, CURIOSITY, EMOTION, THEORY.

Facts are facts and will not disappear on account of your likes.

JAWAHARLAL NEHRU

Get your facts first, and then you can distort them as much as you please.

MARK TWAIN

We should keep so close to facts that we never have to remember the second time what we said the first time.

F. MARION SMITH

A fact in itself is nothing. It is valuable only for the idea attached to it, or for the proof which it furnishes.

CLAUDE BERNARD

If you get all the facts, your judgment can be right; if you don't get all the facts, it can't be right.

BERNARD M. BARUCH

Comment is free but facts are sacred.

CHARLES P. SCOTT

FAILURE *Also see:* AMBITION, BOLDNESS, DEFEAT, DESPAIR, EFFORT, FATE, SUCCESS, WAR.

Show me a thoroughly satisfied man and I will show you a failure.

THOMAS A. EDISON

The only people who never fail are those who never try.

ILKA CHASE

Failures are divided into two classes—those who thought and never did, and those who did and never thought.

JOHN CHARLES SALAK

A failure is a man who has blundered but is not able to cash in the experience.

ELBERT HUBBARD

A man can fail many times, but he isn't a failure until he begins to blame somebody else.

JOHN BURROUGHS

FAITH *Also see:* ATHEISM, BELIEF, CONFIDENCE, COURAGE, CREDIT, CRIME, DOUBT, EFFORT, FEAR, RELIGION.

The smallest seed of faith is better than the largest fruit of happiness.

HENRY DAVID THOREAU

When faith is lost, when honor dies, the man is dead.

JOHN GREENLEAF WHITTIER

We have not lost faith, but we have transferred it from God to the medical profession.

GEORGE BERNARD SHAW

I can believe anything provided it is incredible.

OSCAR WILDE

Faith is love taking the form of aspiration.

WILLIAM ELLERY CHANNING

I always prefer to believe the best of everybody—it saves so much trouble.

RUDYARD KIPLING

FAME *Also see:* ADMIRATION, ESTEEM, GLORY, HONOR, NAME, REPUTATION, VANITY.

Fame is proof that people are gullible.

RALPH WALDO EMERSON

Fame usually comes to those who are thinking about something else.

HORACE GREELEY

The fame of great men ought to be judged always by the means they used to acquire it.

FRANÇOIS DE LA ROCHEFOUCAULD

The lust of fame is the last that a wise man shakes off.

TACITUS

Even the best things are not equal to their fame.

HENRY DAVID THOREAU

The highest form of vanity is love of fame.

GEORGE SANTAYANA

FAMILIARITY *Also see:* FRIENDSHIP.

Familiarity is a magician that is cruel to beauty but kind to ugliness.

OUIDA

All objects lose by too familiar a view.

JOHN DRYDEN

Familiarity breeds contempt—and children.

MARK TWAIN

Though familiarity may not breed contempt, it takes off the edge of admiration.

WILLIAM HAZLITT

Nothing is wonderful when you get used to it.

ED HOWE

Familiarity is the root of the closest friendships, as well as the intensest hatreds.

ANTOINE RIVAROL

FAMILY *Also see:* ANCESTRY, BIRTH, CHILDREN.

If you cannot get rid of the family skeleton, you may as well make it dance.

GEORGE BERNARD SHAW

A happy family is but an earlier heaven.

JOHN BOWRING

The family is one of nature's masterpieces.

GEORGE SANTAYANA

None but a mule denies his family.

ANONYMOUS

The family you come from isn't as important as the family you're going to have.

RING LARDNER

I would rather start a family than finish one.

DON MARQUIS

Family life is too intimate to be preserved by the spirit of justice. It can be sustained by a spirit of love which goes beyond justice.

REINHOLD NIEBUHR

FANATICISM *Also see:* ENTHUSIASM, TYRANNY, ZEAL.

Fanaticism consists in redoubling your efforts when you have forgotten your aim.

GEORGE SANTAYANA

A fanatic is one who can't change his mind and won't change the subject.

WINSTON CHURCHILL

The worst vice of the fanatic is his sincerity.

OSCAR WILDE

Fanaticism, the false fire of an overheated mind.

WILLIAM COWPER

A fanatic is a man who does what he thinks the Lord would do if only He knew the facts of the case.

FINLEY PETER DUNNE

FASHION *Also see:* APPEARANCE, DRESS.

Fashion is a form of ugliness so intolerable that we have to alter it every six months.

OSCAR WILDE

Fashion is what one wears oneself. What is unfashionable is what other people wear.

OSCAR WILDE

Every generation laughs at the old fashions, but follows religiously the new.

HENRY DAVID THOREAU

Fashion is the science of appearances, and it inspires one with the desire to seem rather than to be.

EDWIN HUBBEL CHAPIN

Ten years before its time, a fashion is indecent; ten years after, it is hideous; but a century after, it is romantic.

JAMES LAVER

Be not too early in the fashion, nor too long out of it; nor at any time in the extremes of it.

JOHANN KASPAR LAVATER

FATE *Also see:* CHARACTER, DESTINY, FORTUNE.

I do not believe in the word Fate. It is the refuge of every self-confessed failure.

ANDREW SOUTAR

What a man thinks of himself, that it is which determines, or rather indicates, his fate.

HENRY DAVID THOREAU

We make our own fortunes and we call them fate.

BENJAMIN DISRAELI

There is no good arguing with the inevitable.

JAMES RUSSELL LOWELL

Fate is the friend of the good, the guide of the wise, the tyrant of the foolish, the enemy of the bad.

WILLIAM ROUNSEVILLE ALGER

Fate often puts all the material for happiness and prosperity into a man's hands just to see how miserable he can make himself.

DON MARQUIS

FATHER *Also see:* CHILDREN, FAMILY, PARENT.

Paternity is a career imposed on you without any inquiry into your fitness.

ADLAI E. STEVENSON

The fundamental defect of fathers is that they want their children to be a credit to them.

BERTRAND RUSSELL

No man is responsible for his father. That is entirely his mother's affair.

MARGARET TURNBULL

The worst misfortune that can happen to an ordinary man is to have an extraordinary father.

AUSTIN O'MALLEY

I don't want to be a pal, I want to be a father.

CLIFTON FADIMAN

Every father expects his boy to do the things he wouldn't do when he was young.

KIN HUBBARD

FAULT *Also see:* COMPLAINT, CONFESSION, ENEMY, WEAKNESS.

People who have no faults are terrible; there is no way of taking advantage of them.

ANATOLE FRANCE

His only fault is that he has none.

PLINY THE ELDER

A benevolent man should allow a few faults in himself, to keep his friends in countenance.

BENJAMIN FRANKLIN

If you are pleased at finding faults, you are displeased at finding perfections.

JOHANN KASPAR LAVATER

We confess small faults, in order to insinuate that we have no great ones.

FRANÇOIS DE LA ROCHEFOUCAULD

I like a friend better for having faults that one can talk about.

WILLIAM HAZLITT

The greatest of faults, I should say, is to be conscious of none.

THOMAS CARLYLE

FEAR *Also see:* BOLDNESS, COURAGE, COWARD-ICE, CRIME, CRUELTY, DANGER, DISEASE, SUPERSTITION.

The man who fears suffering is already suffering from what he fears.

MICHEL DE MONTAIGNE

He who fears being conquered is sure of defeat.

NAPOLEON BONAPARTE

The only thing we have to fear is fear itself.

FRANKLIN DELANO ROOSEVELT

Logic and cold reason are poor weapons to fight fear and distrust. Only faith and generosity can overcome them.

JAWAHARLAL NEHRU

If a man harbors any sort of fear, it percolates through all his thinking, damages his personality, makes him landlord to a ghost.

LLOYD DOUGLAS

FEELINGS . . . See EMOTION

FIDELITY *Also see:* LOYALTY.

Another of our highly prized virtues is fidelity. We are immensely pleased with ourselves when we are faithful.

IDA ROSS WYLIE

An ideal wife is one who remains faithful to you but tries to be just as charming as if she weren't.

SACHA GUITRY

It is better to be faithful than famous.

THEODORE ROOSEVELT

Constancy is the complement of all other human virtues.

GIUSEPPE MAZZINI

Nothing is more noble, nothing more venerable than fidelity. Faithfulness and truth are the most sacred excellences and endowments of the human mind.

CICERO

FINANCE *Also see:* BUSINESS, GAIN, MONEY, SPECULATION.

High finance isn't burglary or obtaining money by false pretenses, but rather a judicious selection from the best features of those fine arts.

FINLEY PETER DUNNE

A financier is a pawn-broker with imagination.

ARTHUR WING PINERO

Alexander Hamilton originated the put and take system in our national treasury: the taxpayers put it in, and the politicians take it out.

WILL ROGERS

One-third of the people in the United States promote, while the other two-thirds provide.

WILL ROGERS

Financial sense is knowing that certain men will promise to do certain things, and fail.

ED HOWE

FIRMNESS *Also see:* DECISION, RESOLUTION.

The greatest firmness is the greatest mercy.

HENRY WADSWORTH LONGFELLOW

Firmness of purpose is one of the most necessary sinews of character, and one of the best instruments of success. Without it genius wastes its efforts in a maze of inconsistencies.

LORD CHESTERFIELD

The superior man is firm in the right way, and not merely firm.

CONFUCIUS

That which is called firmness in a king is called obstinacy in a donkey.

LORD ERSKINE

It is only persons of firmness that can have real gentleness. Those who appear gentle are, in general, only a weak character, which easily changes into asperity.

FRANÇOIS DE LA ROCHEFOUCAULD

FLATTERY *Also see:* COMPLIMENT, PRAISE.

Flattery is from the teeth out. Sincere appreciation is from the heart out.

DALE CARNEGIE

None are more taken in with flattery than the proud, who wish to be the first and are not.

BENEDICT SPINOZA

It is easy to flatter: it is harder to praise.

JEAN PAUL RICHTER

Flattery is like cologne water, to be smelt of, not swallowed.

JOSH BILLINGS

FOOL *Also see:* ADMIRATION, BROTHERHOOD, DESPAIR, QUESTION.

The best way to convince a fool that he is wrong is to let him have his own way.

JOSH BILLINGS

Let us be thankful for the fools; but for them the rest of us could not succeed.

MARK TWAIN

What the fool does in the end, the wise man does in the beginning.

PROVERB

A fool can no more see his own folly than he can see his ears.

WILLIAM MAKEPEACE THACKERAY

FORCE *Also see:* CUSTOM, POWER, REVOLUTION, VIOLENCE, WAR.

When force is necessary, it must be applied boldly, decisively and completely. But one must know the limitations of force; one must know when to blend force with a maneuver, the blow with an agreement.

LEON TROTSKY

Force is not a remedy.

JOHN BRIGHT

Right reason is stronger than force.

JAMES A. GARFIELD

Force is all-conquering, but its victories are short-lived.

ABRAHAM LINCOLN

The power that is supported by force alone will have cause often to tremble.

LAJOS KOSSUTH

FORGIVENESS *Also see:* MERCY.

To err is human; to forgive, divine.

ALEXANDER POPE

The weak can never forgive. Forgiveness is the attribute of the strong.

MAHATMA GANDHI

Forgive many things in others; nothing in yourself.

AUSONIUS

It is easier to forgive an enemy than a friend.

MADAME DOROTHÉE DELUZY

"I can forgive, but I cannot forget," is only another way of saying, "I will not forgive." Forgiveness ought to be like a cancelled note—torn in two, and burned up, so that it never can be shown against one.

HENRY WARD BEECHER

Humanity is never so beautiful as when praying for forgiveness, or else forgiving another.

JEAN PAUL RICHTER

FORTUNE *Also see:* FATE, MERIT, PURSUIT, WEALTH.

Fortune is ever seen accompanying industry.

OLIVER GOLDSMITH

Fortune is the rod of the weak, and the staff of the brave.

JAMES RUSSELL LOWELL

Every man is the architect of his own fortune.

SALLUST

Fortune is a great deceiver. She sells very dear the things she seems to give us.

VINCENT VOITURE

Nature magically suits a man to his fortunes, by making them the fruit of his character.

RALPH WALDO EMERSON

FRAUD *Also see:* DECEIT, DISHONESTY.

It is fraud to accept what you cannot repay.

PUBLILIUS SYRUS

The first and worst of all frauds is to cheat oneself.

GAMALIEL BAILEY

For the most part fraud in the end secures for its companions repentance and shame.

CHARLES SIMMONS

The more gross the fraud the more glibly will it go down, and the more greedily be swallowed, since folly will always find faith where impostors will find imprudence.

CHARLES CALEB COLTON

FREEDOM *Also see:* BOOK, BORROWING, COUNTRY, DISCIPLINE, EDUCATION, END AND MEANS, EQUALITY, FREEDOM OF PRESS, FREEDOM OF SPEECH, INDEPENDENCE, LIBERTY, SECURITY.

I know but one freedom and that is the freedom of mind.

ANTOINE DE SAINT-EXUPÉRY

No man is free who is not a master of himself.

EPICTETUS

Freedom is not worth having if it does not connote freedom to err.

MAHATMA GANDHI

The unity of freedom has never relied on uniformity of opinion.

JOHN FITZGERALD KENNEDY

A hungry man is not a free man.

ADLAI E. STEVENSON

Only our individual faith in freedom can keep us free.

DWIGHT D. EISENHOWER

The cost of freedom is always high, but Americans have always paid it. And one path we shall never choose, and that is the path of surrender, or submission.

JOHN FITZGERALD KENNEDY

Freedom rings where opinions clash.

ADLAI E. STEVENSON

FREEDOM of the PRESS *Also see:* CENSORSHIP, LIBERTY.

Our liberty depends on the freedom of the press, and that cannot be limited without being lost.

THOMAS JEFFERSON

The liberty of the press is a blessing when we are inclined to write against others, and a calamity when we find ourselves overborne by the multitude of our assailants.

SAMUEL JOHNSON

The free press is the mother of all our liberties and of our progress under liberty.

ADLAI E. STEVENSON

The press is not only free, it is powerful. That power is ours. It is the proudest that man can enjoy.

BENJAMIN DISRAELI

Let it be impressed upon your minds, let it be instilled into your children, that the liberty of the press is the palladium of all the civil, political, and religious rights.

JUNIUS

FREEDOM of SPEECH *Also see:* CENSORSHIP, DISSENT, LIBERTY, FREEDOM OF THE PRESS.

I disapprove of what you say, but will defend to the death your right to say it.

VOLTAIRE

I have always been among those who believed that the greatest freedom of speech was the greatest safety, because if a man is a fool the best thing to do is to encourage him to advertise the fact by speaking.

WOODROW WILSON

I realize that there are certain limitations placed upon the right of free speech. I may not be able to say all I think, but I am not going to say anything I do not think.

EUGENE V. DEBS

Free speech is to a great people what winds are to oceans and malarial regions, which waft away the elements of disease and bring new elements of health; and where free speech is stopped, miasma is bred, and death comes fast.

HENRY WARD BEECHER

Better a thousandfold abuse of free speech than denial of free speech. The abuse dies in a day, but the denial stays the life of the people, and entombs the hope of the race.

CHARLES BRADLAUGH

FRIENDSHIP *Also see:* AFFECTION, BROTHERHOOD, ENEMY, FAMILIARITY, LOVE, PRAISE.

The only way to have a friend is to be one.

RALPH WALDO EMERSON

Friendship is always a sweet responsibility, never an opportunity.

KAHLIL GIBRAN

If a man does not make new acquaintances as he advances through life, he will soon find himself left alone; one should keep his friendships in constant repair.

SAMUEL JOHNSON

Friendship is one mind in two bodies.

MENCIUS

Acquaintance: a degree of friendship called slight when its object is poor or obscure, and intimate when he is rich or famous.

AMBROSE BIERCE

The best way to keep your friends is not to give them away.

WILSON MIZNER

Friendship without self-interest is one of the rare and beautiful things of life.

JAMES FRANCIS BYRNES

Friendship is almost always the union of a part of one mind with a part of another: people are friends in spots.

GEORGE SANTAYANA

FRUGALITY ... See ECONOMY

FUTURE *Also see:* PAST, PRESENT.

When all else is lost, the future still remains.

CHRISTIAN NESTELL BOVEE

I never think of the future. It comes soon enough.

ALBERT EINSTEIN

I like the dreams of the future better than the history of the past.

PATRICK HENRY

My interest is in the future because I am going to spend the rest of my life there.

CHARLES F. KETTERING

The trouble with our times is that the future is not what it used to be.

PAUL VALERY

GAIN *Also see:* DUTY.

Sometimes the best gain is to lose.

GEORGE HERBERT

For everything you have missed you have gained something.

RALPH WALDO EMERSON

Gain cannot be made without some other person's loss.

PUBLILIUS SYRUS

The true way to gain much, is never to desire to gain too much.

FRANCIS BEAUMONT

No gain is so certain as that which proceeds from the economical use of what you already have.

LATIN PROVERB

GALLANTRY *Also see:* COURTESY, FLATTERY.

Gallantry of the mind is saying the most empty things in an agreeable manner.

FRANÇOIS DE LA ROCHEFOUCAULD

To give up your seat in a car to a woman, and tread on your neighbor's foot to get even.

ELBERT HUBBARD

To do a perfectly unselfish act for selfish motives.

ELBERT HUBBARD

GENEROSITY *Also see:* ARISTOCRACY, CHARITY, FEAR, KINDNESS.

Generosity during life is a very different thing from generosity in the hour of death; one proceeds from genuine liberality and benevolence, the other from pride or fear.

HORACE MANN

Generosity is giving more than you can, and pride is taking less than you need.

KAHLIL GIBRAN

What seems to be generosity is often no more than disguised ambition, which overlooks a small interest in order to secure a great one.

FRANÇOIS DE LA ROCHEFOUCAULD

If there be any truer measure of a man than by what he does, it must be by what he gives.

ROBERT SOUTH

GENIUS *Also see:* ABILITY, ART, COMMON SENSE.

Genius does what it must, and talent does what it can.

EDWARD G. BULWER-LYTTON

When human power becomes so great and original that we can account for it only as a kind of divine imagination, we call it genius.

WILLIAM CRASHAW

Genius is entitled to respect only when it promotes the peace and improves the happiness of mankind.

LORD ESSEX

Genius begins great works; labor alone finishes them.

JOSEPH JOUBERT

Genius is one per cent inspiration and ninety-nine per cent perspiration.

THOMAS A. EDISON

To believe your own thought, to believe that what is true for you in your private heart is true for all men—that is genius.

RALPH WALDO EMERSON

Genius without education is like silver in the mine.

BENJAMIN FRANKLIN

Genius is the ability to act rightly without precedent—the power to do the right thing the first time.

ELBERT HUBBARD

When Nature has work to be done, she creates a genius to do it.

RALPH WALDO EMERSON

No great genius is without an admixture of madness.

ARISTOTLE

GENTLEMAN *Also see:* COURTESY.

. . . one who never hurts anyone's feelings unintentionally.

OLIVER HERFORD

This is the final test of a gentleman: his respect for those who can be of no possible service to him.

WILLIAM LYON PHELPS

A true man of honor feels humbled himself when he cannot help humbling others.

ROBERT E. LEE

The man who is always talking about being a gentleman, never is one.

ROBERT S. SURTEES

GIRLS *Also see:* WOMAN.

A homely girl hates mirrors.

PROVERB

I am fond of children—except boys.

LEWIS CARROLL

Some girls never know what they are going to do from one husband to another.

TOM MASSON

I never expected to see the day when girls would get sunburned in the places they do now.

WILL ROGERS

GLORY *Also see:* FAME, HONOR.

For glory gives herself only to those who have always dreamed of her.

CHARLES DE GAULLE

Glory built on selfish principles, is shame and guilt.

WILLIAM COWPER

Our greatest glory consists not in never falling, but in rising every time we fall.

OLIVER GOLDSMITH

Real glory springs from the silent conquest of ourselves.

JOSEPH P. THOMPSON

Glory paid to our ashes comes too late.

MARTIAL

GLUTTON *Also see:* ABSTINENCE, APPETITE, EATING.

Their kitchen is their shrine, the cook their priest, the table their altar, and their belly their god.

CHARLES BUCK

Glutton: one who digs his grave with his teeth.

FRENCH PROVERB

The fool that eats till he is sick must fast till he is well.

GEORGE W. THORNBURY

One meal a day is enough for a lion, and it ought to be for a man.

GEORGE FORDYCE

In general, mankind, since the improvement of cookery, eats twice as much as nature requires.

BENJAMIN FRANKLIN

One should eat to live, not live to eat.

BENJAMIN FRANKLIN

GOD *Also see:* AGNOSTICISM, ARTIST, ATHEISM, BABY, CREATIVITY, DEMOCRACY, DISHONESTY, EARTH, FAITH, FREEDOM OF THE PRESS, HEAVEN, RELIGION.

I fear God, and next to God I chiefly fear him who fears Him not.

SAADI

God enters by a private door into every individual.

RALPH WALDO EMERSON

God is not a cosmic bell-boy for whom we can press a button to get things.

HARRY EMERSON FOSDICK

God never made His work for man to mend.

JOHN DRYDEN

God is more truly imagined than expressed, and He exists more truly than He is imagined.

ST. AUGUSTINE

God is the brave man's hope, and not the coward's excuse.

PLUTARCH

When we know what God is, we shall be gods ourselves.

GEORGE BERNARD SHAW

We love the Lord, of course, but we often wonder what He finds in us.

ED HOWE

You can believe in God without believing in immortality, but it is hard to see how anyone can believe in immortality and not believe in God.

ERNEST DIMNET

The best way to know God is to love many things.

VINCENT VAN GOGH

Two men please God—who serves Him with all his heart because he knows Him; who seeks Him with all his heart because he knows Him not.

NIKITA IVANOVICH PANIN

Men talk of "finding God," but no wonder it is difficult; He is hidden in that darkest hiding-place, your heart. You yourself are a part of Him.

CHRISTOPHER MORLEY

In the faces of men and women I see God.

WALT WHITMAN

GOLD *Also see:* AVARICE, MISER.

The man who works for the gold in the job rather than for the money in the pay envelope, is the fellow who gets on.

JOSEPH FRENCH JOHNSON

Gold will be slave or master.

HORACE

A mask of gold hides all deformities.

THOMAS DEKKER

It is much better to have your gold in the hand than in the heart.

THOMAS FULLER

Curst greed of gold, what crimes thy tyrant power has caused.

VERGIL

Gold has worked down from Alexander's time ... When something holds good for two thousand years I do not believe it can be so because of prejudice or mistaken theory.

BERNARD M. BARUCH

GOSSIP *Also see:* CONVERSATION, SLANDER.

Of every ten persons who talk about you, nine will say something bad, and the tenth will say something good in a bad way.

ANTOINE RIVAROL

Gossip is always a personal confession either of malice or imbecility.

JOSIAH GILBERT HOLLAND

The only time people dislike gossip is when you gossip about them.

WILL ROGERS

Truth is not exciting enough to those who depend on the characters and lives of their neighbors for all their amusement.

GEORGE BANCROFT

There isn't much to be seen in a little town, but what you hear makes up for it.

KIN HUBBARD

That which is everybody's business is nobody's business.

IZAAK WALTON

GOVERNMENT *Also see:* AUTHORITY, CITIZEN-SHIP, COMPROMISE, DE-MOCRACY, PARTY, POLITICS.

The best of all governments is that which teaches us to govern ourselves.

JOHANN WOLFGANG VON GOETHE

Good government is no substitute for self-government.

MAHATMA GANDHI

The government is us; we are the government, you and I.

THEODORE ROOSEVELT

You can't run a government solely on a business basis . . . Government should be human. It should have a heart.

HERBERT HENRY LEHMAN

All free governments are managed by the combined wisdom and folly of the people.

JAMES A. GARFIELD

No man is good enough to govern another man without that other's consent.

ABRAHAM LINCOLN

My experience in government is that when things are non-controversial and beautifully coordinated, there is not much going on.

JOHN FITZGERALD KENNEDY

He mocks the people who proposes that the government shall protect the rich that they in turn may care for the laboring poor.

GROVER CLEVELAND

GRACE

Beauty and grace command the world.

PARK BENJAMIN

A graceful and pleasing figure is a perpetual letter of recommendation.

FRANCIS BACON

Gracefulness has been defined to be the outward expression of the inward harmony of the soul.

WILLIAM HAZLITT

He does it with a better grace, but I do it more natural.

WILLIAM SHAKESPEARE

Grace is to the body, what good sense is to the mind.

FRANÇOIS DE LA ROCHEFOUCAULD

God appoints our graces to be nurses to other men's weaknesses.

HENRY WARD BEECHER

GRATITUDE

Gratitude is one of the least articulate of the emotions, especially when it is deep.

FELIX FRANKFURTER

Gratitude is the heart's memory.

FRENCH PROVERB

Gratitude is a duty which ought to be paid, but which none have a right to expect.

JEAN JACQUES ROUSSEAU

If you pick up a starving dog and make him prosperous, he will not bite you. This is the principal difference between a dog and a man.

MARK TWAIN

Gratitude is not only the greatest of virtues, but the parent of all the others.

CICERO

There is as much greatness of mind in acknowledging a good turn, as in doing it.

SENECA

GRAVE *Also see:* DEATH, MONUMENT.

The only difference between a rut and a grave is their dimensions.

ELLEN GLASGOW

A grave, wherever found, preaches a short and pithy sermon to the soul.

NATHANIEL HAWTHORNE

The grave is still the best shelter against the storms of destiny.

G. C. LICHTENBERG

There is but one easy place in this world, and that is the grave.

HENRY WARD BEECHER

We weep over the graves of infants and the little ones taken from us by death; but an early grave may be the shortest way to heaven.

TRYON EDWARDS

GRAVITY *Also see:* SORROW.

There is gravity in wisdom, but no particular wisdom in gravity.

JOSH BILLINGS

Too much gravity argues a shallow mind.

JOHANN KASPAR LAVATER

Those wanting wit affect gravity, and go by the name of solid men.

JOHN DRYDEN

GREED *Also see:* AVARICE, DESIRE, MISER, SELFISHNESS.

The greed of gain has no time or limit to its capaciousness. Its one object is to produce and consume. It has pity neither for beautiful nature nor for living human beings. It is ruthlessly ready without a moment's hesitation to crush beauty and life out of them, molding them into money.

RABINDRANATH TAGORE

The covetous man pines in plenty, like Tantalus up to the chin in water, and yet thirsty.

THOMAS ADAMS

It is economic slavery, the savage struggle for a crumb, that has converted mankind into wolves and sheep . . .

ALEXANDER BERKMAN

There is no fire like passion, there is no shark like hatred, there is no snare like folly, there is no torrent like greed.

BUDDHA

GRIEF *Also see:* AFFLICTION, MISERY, SORROW.

The only cure for grief is action.

GEORGE HENRY LEWES

Excess of grief for the dead is madness; for it is an injury to the living, and the dead know it not.

XENOPHON

Grief is the agony of an instant; the indulgence of grief the blunder of a life.

BENJAMIN DISRAELI

While grief is fresh, every attempt to divert only irritates. You must wait till it be digested, and then amusement will dissipate the remains of it.

SAMUEL JOHNSON

GUEST

Nobody can be as agreeable as an uninvited guest.

KIN HUBBARD

No one can be so welcome a guest that he will not annoy his host after three days.

PLAUTUS

Every guest hates the others, and the host hates them all.

ALBANIAN PROVERB

The first day, a guest; the second, a burden; the third, a pest.

EDOUARD R. LABOULAYE

GUILT *Also see:* CONSCIENCE, CRIME, REPENTENCE.

Every man is guilty of all the good he didn't do.

VOLTAIRE

The guilty is he who meditates a crime; the punishment is his who lays the plot.

CONTE VITTORIO ALFIERI

The greatest incitement to guilt is the hope of sinning with impunity.

CICERO

From the body of one guilty deed a thousand ghostly fears and haunting thoughts proceed.

WILLIAM WORDSWORTH

He who flees from trial confesses his guilt.

PUBLILIUS SYRUS

It is base to filch a purse, daring to embezzle a million, but it is great beyond measure to steal a crown. The sin lessens as the guilt increases.

JOHANN VON SCHILLER

Suspicion always haunts the guilty mind.

WILLIAM SHAKESPEARE

Men's minds are too ready to excuse guilt in themselves.

LIVY

Every guilty person is his own hangman.

SENECA

HABIT *Also see:* DEBT, DUTY, TRADITION.

Each year, one vicious habit rooted out, in time ought to make the worst man good.

BENJAMIN FRANKLIN

Habit, if not resisted, soon becomes necessity.

ST. AUGUSTINE

A single bad habit will mar an otherwise faultless character, as an ink-drop soileth the pure white page.

HOSEA BALLOU

The unfortunate thing about this world is that the good habits are much easier to give up than the bad ones.

W. SOMERSET MAUGHAM

The chains of habit are too weak to be felt until they are too strong to be broken.

SAMUEL JOHNSON

Habit converts luxurious enjoyments into dull and daily necessities.

ALDOUS HUXLEY

Good habits result from resisting temptation.

ANCIENT PROVERB

HAIR

By common consent gray hairs are a crown of glory; the only object of respect that can never excite envy.

GEORGE BANCROFT

Gray hair is a sign of age, not of wisdom.

GREEK PROVERB

The hair is the richest ornament of women.

MARTIN LUTHER

HAPPINESS *Also see:* APPEARANCE, BEAUTY, CHEERFULNESS, DUTY, ENJOYMENT, FAITH, FATE, PLEASURE, SECURITY, ZEST.

It is pretty hard to tell what does bring happiness; poverty and wealth have both failed.

KIN HUBBARD

Happiness is not a reward—it is a consequence. Suffering is not a punishment—it is a result.

ROBERT GREEN INGERSOLL

Be happy while you're living, for you're a long time dead.

SCOTTISH PROVERB

To fill the hour—that is happiness.

RALPH WALDO EMERSON

The grand essentials of happiness are: something to do, something to love, and something to hope for.

ALLAN K. CHALMERS

Happiness is like a sunbeam, which the least shadow intercepts, while adversity is often as the rain of spring.

CHINESE PROVERB

Happiness isn't something you experience; it's something you remember.

OSCAR LEVANT

HARDSHIP ... See ADVERSITY

HASTE

No man who is in a hurry is quite civilized.

WILL DURANT

Manners require time, and nothing is more vulgar than haste.

RALPH WALDO EMERSON

Though I am always in haste, I am never in a hurry.

JOHN WESLEY

Take time for all things: great haste makes great waste.

BENJAMIN FRANKLIN

Make haste slowly.

LATIN PROVERB

Rapidity does not always mean progress, and hurry is akin to waste.

CHARLES A. STODDARD

HATE Also see: BLINDNESS, ENEMY.

Hatred does not cease by hatred, but only by love; this is the eternal rule.

BUDDHA

Hatred is the madness of the heart.

LORD BYRON

Heaven has no rage like love to hatred turned.

WILLIAM CONGREVE

A man who lives, not by what he loves but what he hates, is a sick man.

ARCHIBALD MACLEISH

When our hatred is violent, it sinks us even beneath those we hate.

FRANÇOIS DE LA ROCHEFOUCAULD

It is better to be hated for what you are than to be loved for what you are not.

ANDRÉ GIDE

Hatred is self-punishment.

HOSEA BALLOU

I shall never permit myself to stoop so low as to hate any man.

BOOKER T. WASHINGTON

National hatred is something peculiar. You will always find it strongest and most violent where there is the lowest degree of culture.

JOHANN WOLFGANG VON GOETHE

HEALTH Also see: BODY, CHEERFULNESS, DISEASE.

He who has health, has hope; and he who has hope, has everything.

ARABIAN PROVERB

To become a thoroughly good man is the best prescription for keeping a sound mind and a sound body.

FRANCIS BOWEN

It is a weariness disease to preserve health by too strict a regimen.

FRANÇOIS DE LA ROCHEFOUCAULD

The only way to keep your health is to eat what you don't want, drink what you don't like, and do what you'd rather not.

MARK TWAIN

There's a lot of people in this world who spend so much time watching their health that they haven't the time to enjoy it.

JOSH BILLINGS

HEART Also see: CHARITY, COMPASSION, CONFIDENCE, COURAGE, GREED, GOVERNMENT, LOVE.

The head learns new things, but the heart forever more practices old experiences.

HENRY WARD BEECHER

The heart has reasons that reason does not understand.

JACQUES BÈNIGNE BOSSUET

There is no instinct like that of the heart.

LORD BYRON

The heart of a fool is in his mouth, but the mouth of the wise man is in his heart.

BENJAMIN FRANKLIN

Nothing is less in our power than the heart, and far from commanding we are forced to obey it.

JEAN JACQUES ROUSSEAU

Two things are bad for the heart—running up stairs and running down people.

BERNARD M. BARUCH

HEAVEN Also see: AMBITION, DEMOCRACY, FAMILY, HELL, HOME.

Heaven will be inherited by every man who has heaven in his soul.

HENRY WARD BEECHER

The few men who have managed to reach heaven must be terribly spoiled by this time.

ED HOWE

On earth there is no heaven, but there are pieces of it.

JULES RENARD

I don't like to commit myself about heaven and hell—you see, I have friends in both places.

MARK TWAIN

To get to heaven, turn right and keep straight.

ANONYMOUS

The main object of religion is not to get a man into heaven, but to get heaven into him.

THOMAS HARDY

HELL Also see: CHRISTIANITY, DECEIT, DIPLOMACY, HEAVEN.

Hell is truth seen too late.

TRYON EDWARDS

There may be some doubt about hell beyond the grave but there is no doubt about there being one on this side of it.

ED HOWE

I never give them hell; I just tell the truth and they think it's hell.

HARRY S. TRUMAN

If there is no hell, a good many preachers are obtaining money under false pretenses.

WILLIAM A. SUNDAY

The wicked work harder to reach hell than the righteous to reach heaven.

JOSH BILLINGS

To be in hell is to drift; to be in heaven is to steer.

GEORGE BERNARD SHAW

The road to Hell is paved with good intentions.

KARL MARX

HELP *Also see:* CHARITY, GENEROSITY.

God helps them that help themselves.

PROVERB

Nothing makes one feel so strong as a call for help.

GEORGE MACDONALD

Every great man is always being helped by everybody; for his gift is to get good out of all things and all persons.

JOHN RUSKIN

When a person is down in the world, an ounce of help is better than a pound of preaching.

EDWARD G. BULWAR-LYTTON

The race of mankind would perish did they cease to aid each other. We cannot exist without mutual help. All therefore that need aid have a right to ask it from their fellowmen; and no one who has the power of granting can refuse it without guilt.

WALTER SCOTT

HEROISM *Also see:* COURAGE.

Self-trust is the essence of heroism.

RALPH WALDO EMERSON

The world's battlefields have been in the heart chiefly; more heroism has been displayed in the household and the closet, than on the most memorable battlefields in history.

HENRY WARD BEECHER

Heroes are not known by the loftiness of their carriage; the greatest braggarts are generally the merest cowards.

JEAN JACQUES ROUSSEAU

A hero is no braver than an ordinary man, but he is braver five minutes longer.

RALPH WALDO EMERSON

Hero worship is strongest where there is least regard for human freedom.

HERBERT SPENCER

Hero-worship is mostly idol gossip.

ANONYMOUS

HISTORY *Also see:* CUSTOM, SPIRIT, TRADITION.

History is little more than the register of the crimes, follies and misfortunes of mankind.

EDWARD GIBBON

The men who make history have not time to write it.

METTERNICH

The main thing is to make history, not to write it.

OTTO VON BISMARCK

No historian can take part with—or against—the forces he has to study. To him even the extinction of the human race should merely be a fact to be grouped with other vital statistics.

HENRY BROOKS ADAMS

History repeats itself, and that's one of the things that's wrong with history.

CLARENCE DARROW

History is nothing but a pack of tricks that we play upon the dead.

VOLTAIRE

HOME *Also see:* FAMILY, FATHER.

A hundred men may make an encampment, but it takes a woman to make a home.

CHINESE PROVERB

Home is where the heart is.

PLINY THE ELDER

Home is the place where, when you have to go there, they have to take you in.

ROBERT FROST

Home is the most popular, and will be the most enduring of all earthly establishments.

CHANNING POLLOCK

Home interprets heaven. Home is heaven for beginners.

CHARLES H. PARKHURST

He is the happiest, be he king or peasant, who finds peace in his home.

JOHANN WOLFGANG VON GOETHE

Home life is no more natural to us than a cage is to a cockatoo.

GEORGE BERNARD SHAW

HONESTY *Also see:* ACCURACY, CANDOR, DISHONESTY, DISTRUST, TRUTH.

I would give no thought of what the world might say of me, if I could only transmit to posterity the reputation of an honest man.

SAM HOUSTON

Honesty is the rarest wealth anyone can possess, and yet all the honesty in the world ain't lawful tender for a loaf of bread.

JOSH BILLINGS

Honesty pays, but it don't seem to pay enough to suit some people.

KIN HUBBARD

We must make the world honest before we can honestly say to our children that honesty is the best policy.

GEORGE BERNARD SHAW

Make yourself an honest man, and then you may be sure there is one less rascal in the world.

THOMAS CARLYLE

Honesty is the best policy—when there is money in it.

MARK TWAIN

HONOR *Also see:* DIGNITY, DRESS, ESTEEM, GLORY, RESPECT.

It is better to deserve honors and not have them than to have them and not deserve them.

MARK TWAIN

The difference between a moral man and a man of honor is that the latter regrets a discreditable act even when it has worked.

H. L. MENCKEN

Honor lies in honest toil.

GROVER CLEVELAND

Better to die ten thousand deaths than wound my honor.

JOSEPH ADDISON

The louder he talked of his honor, the faster we counted our spoons.

RALPH WALDO EMERSON

When faith is lost, when honor dies, the man is dead!

JOHN GREENLEAF WHITTIER

HOPE *Also see:* ANTICIPATION, ATHEISM, BELIEF, BIBLE, CREDULITY, DESPAIR, DISAPPOINTMENT, FAITH, TRUST.

To the sick, while there is life there is hope.

CICERO

Hope for the best, but prepare for the worst.

ENGLISH PROVERB

A woman's hopes are woven of sunbeams; a shadow annihilates them.

GEORGE ELIOT

We should not expect something for nothing but we all do, and we call it hope.

ED HOWE

He that lives upon hope will die fasting.

BENJAMIN FRANKLIN

In all things it is better to hope than to despair.

JOHANN WOLFGANG VON GOETHE

Hope is the parent of faith.

CYRUS A. BARTOL

HUMANITY *Also see:* AMERICA, BROTHERHOOD, EMOTION, FORGIVENESS, HUMILITY.

We cannot despair of humanity, since we ourselves are human beings.

ALBERT EINSTEIN

There are times when one would like to hang the whole human race, and finish the farce.

MARK TWAIN

There is nothing on earth divine except humanity.

WALTER SAVAGE LANDOR

The true grandeur of humanity is in moral elevation, sustained, enlightened and decorated by the intellect of man.

CHARLES SUMNER

Humanity to me is not a mob. A mob is a degeneration of humanity. A mob is humanity going the wrong way.

FRANK LLOYD WRIGHT

HUMAN NATURE *Also see:* BROTHERHOOD, LIFE, MAN, SOCIETY.

We have provided for the survival of man against all enemies except his fellow man.

LYMAN LLOYD BRYSON

It is human nature to think wisely and act foolishly.

ANATOLE FRANCE

It is easier to love humanity as a whole than to love one's neighbor.

ERIC HOFFER

HUMILITY *Also see:* MODESTY.

I feel coming on a strange disease—humility.

FRANK LLOYD WRIGHT

The first of all other virtues—for other people.

OLIVER WENDELL HOLMES

Without humility there can be no humanity.

JOHN BUCHAN

HUMOR *Also see:* BIBLE, JESTING, WIT.

If I had no sense of humor, I would long ago have committed suicide.

MAHATMA GANDHI

A man isn't poor if he can still laugh.

RAYMOND HITCHCOCK

Good humor is one of the best articles of dress one can wear in society.

WILLIAM MAKEPEACE THACKERAY

If I studied all my life, I couldn't think up half the number of funny things passed in one session of congress.

WILL ROGERS

Everything is funny as long as it is happening to somebody else.

WILL ROGERS

Whenever you find humor, you find pathos close by his side.

EDWIN PERCY WHIPPLE

HUNGER *Also see:* APPETITE, CULTURE, FREEDOM, GLUTTON, POPULATION.

An empty stomach is not a good political advisor.

ALBERT EINSTEIN

Hunger does not breed reform; it breeds madness, and all the ugly distempers that make an ordered life impossible.

WOODROW WILSON

A hungry man is not a free man.

ADLAI E. STEVENSON

A hungry people listens not to reason, nor cares for justice, nor is bent by any prayers.

SENECA

No one can worship God or love his neighbor on an empty stomach.

WOODROW WILSON

HUSBAND *Also see:* GIRLS, MARRIAGE.

All husbands are alike, but they have different faces so you can tell them apart.

ANONYMOUS

An archaeologist is the best husband any woman can have: the older she gets, the more interested he is in her.

AGATHA CHRISTIE

The husband who wants a happy marriage should learn to keep his mouth shut and his checkbook open.

GROUCHO MARX

Husbands never become good; they merely become proficient.

H. L. MENCKEN

A good husband should be deaf and a good wife should be blind.

FRENCH PROVERB

HYPOCRISY *Also see:* DECEIT, LYING, OSTENTATION.

A hypocrite is the kind of politician who would cut down a redwood tree, then mount the stump and make a speech for conservation.

ADLAI E. STEVENSON

A bad man is worse when he pretends to be a saint.

FRANCIS BACON

It is with pious fraud as with a bad action; it begets a calamitous necessity of going on.

THOMAS PAINE

Hypocrite: the man who murdered both his parents ... pleaded for mercy on the grounds that he was an orphan.

ABRAHAM LINCOLN

Every man alone is sincere; at the entrance of a second person hypocrisy begins.

RALPH WALDO EMERSON

IDEA *Also see:* ACTION, COMMITTEE, COMMUNI-CATION, CREATIVITY, FACTS, THOUGHT.

Ideas are the root of creation.

ERNEST DIMNET

Ideas are the factors that lift civilization. They create revolutions. There is more dynamite in an idea than in many bombs.

JOHN H. VINCENT

There is one thing stronger than all the armies in the world, and that is an idea whose time has come.

VICTOR HUGO

The vitality of thought is in adventure. *Ideas won't keep.* Something must be done about them. When the idea is new, its custodians have fervor, live for it, and if need be, die for it.

ALFRED NORTH WHITEHEAD

IDEAL *Also see:* AMERICA, COMMUNICATION.

The attainment of an ideal is often the beginning of a disillusion.

STANLEY BALDWIN

Words without actions are the assassins of idealism.

HERBERT HOOVER

Some men see things as they are and say why. I dream things that never were and say, why not?

ROBERT F. KENNEDY

What we need most, is not so much to realize the ideal as to idealize the real.

H. F. HEDGE

Ideals are like the stars: we never reach them, but like the mariners of the sea, we chart our course by them.

CARL SCHURZ

IDLENESS *Also see:* ACTION, LEISURE.

Prolonged ideas paralyzes initiative.

ANONYMOUS

The way to be nothing is to do nothing.

NATHANIEL HOWE

It is impossible to enjoy idling thoroughly unless one has plenty of work to do.

JEROME K. JEROME

Idleness is the stupidity of the body, and stupidity is the idleness of the mind.

JOHANN G. SEUME

Idleness is an inlet to disorder, and makes way for licentiousness. People who have nothing to do are quickly tired of their own company.

JEREMY COLLIER

An idle brain is the devil's workshop.

ENGLISH PROVERB

Purity of mind and idleness are incompatible.

MAHATMA GANDHI

IDOLATRY *Also see:* GOD.

We boast our emancipation from many superstitions; but if we have broken any idols, it is through a transfer of idolatry.

RALPH WALDO EMERSON

The idol is the measure of the worshipper.

JAMES RUSSELL LOWELL

Belief in a cruel God makes a cruel man.

THOMAS PAINE

Whatever a man seeks, honors, or exalts more than God, this is the god of his idolatry.

WILLIAM B. ULLATHORNE

When men have gone so far as to talk as though their idols have come to life, it is time that someone broke them.

RICHARD H. TAWNEY

IGNORANCE Also see: DIGNITY, FOOL, HAPPINESS, KNOWLEDGE, MYSTERY, PREJUDICE.

He knows so little and knows it so fluently.

ELLEN GLASGOW

Ignorance is a voluntary misfortune.

NICHOLAS LING

Have the courage to be ignorant of a great number of things, in order to avoid the calamity of being ignorant of everything.

SYDNEY SMITH

Everybody is ignorant, only on different subjects.

WILL ROGERS

There is nothing more frightful than ignorance in action.

JOHANN WOLFGANG VON GOETHE

Most ignorance is vincible ignorance. We don't know because we don't want to know.

ALDOUS HUXLEY

Ignorance breeds monsters to fill up the vacancies of the soul that are unoccupied by the verities of knowledge.

HORACE MANN

ILLNESS ... See DISEASE

ILLUSION Also see: IMAGINATION, REVERIE.

Nothing is more sad than the death of an illusion.

ARTHUR KOESTLER

Better a dish of illusion and a hearty appetite for life, than a feast of reality and indigestion therewith.

HARRY A. OVERSTREET

It is respectable to have no illusions, and safe, and profitable—and dull.

JOSEPH CONRAD

The one person who has more illusions than the dreamer is the man of action.

OSCAR WILDE

IMAGINATION Also see: BUSINESS, COWARDICE, CREATIVITY, DREAM, GENIUS, MOB.

He who has imagination without learning has wings and no feet.

JOSEPH JOUBERT

Imagination rules the world.

NAPOLEON BONAPARTE

Imagination disposes of everything; it creates beauty, justice, and happiness, which are everything in this world.

BLAISE PASCAL

Imagination is a quality given a man to compensate him for what he is not, and a sense of humor was provided to console him for what he is.

OSCAR WILDE

Science does not know its debt to imagination.

RALPH WALDO EMERSON

IMITATION Also see: ADAPTABILITY, CONFORMITY, ORIGINALITY.

Imitation belittles.

CHRISTIAN NESTELL BOVEE

There is much difference between imitating a good man and counterfeiting him.

BENJAMIN FRANKLIN

To copy others is necessary, but to copy oneself is pathetic.

PABLO PICASSO

Men are so constituted that every one undertakes what he sees another successful in, whether he has aptitude for it or not.

JOHANN WOLFGANG VON GOETHE

IMMORTALITY Also see: CONVERSATION, ETERNITY, GOD, LIFE.

The average man does not know what to do with this life, yet wants another one which will last forever.

ANATOLE FRANCE

The first requisite for immortality is death.

STANISLAW J. LEC

The best argument I know for an immortal life is the existence of a man who deserves one.

WILLIAM JAMES

Immortality is the genius to move others long after you yourself have stopped moving.

FRANK ROONEY

If your contribution has been vital there will always be somebody to pick up where you left off, and that will be your claim to immortality.

WALTER GROPIUS

IMPOSSIBILITY Also see: PERFECTION.

The Difficult is that which can be done immediately; the Impossible that which takes a little longer.

GEORGE SANTAYANA

Most of the things worth doing in the world had been declared impossible before they were done.

LOUIS D. BRANDEIS

Nothing is impossible; there are ways that lead to everything, and if we had sufficient will we should always have sufficient means. It is often merely for an excuse that we say things are impossible.

FRANÇOIS DE LA ROCHEFOUCAULD

It is difficult to say what is impossible, for the dream of yesterday is the hope of today and the reality of tomorrow.

ROBERT H. GODDARD

IMPROVEMENT *Also see:* PROGRESS, SELF-IMPROVEMENT.

People seldom improve when they have no other model but themselves to copy after.

OLIVER GOLDSMITH

Where we cannot invent, we may at least improve.

CHARLES CALEB COLTON

As long as I can conceive something better than myself I cannot be easy unless I am striving to bring it into existence or clearing the way for it.

GEORGE BERNARD SHAW

Much of the wisdom of one age, is the folly of the next.

CHARLES SIMMONS

INACTIVITY . . . See CHANGE.

INCREDULITY *Also see:* AGNOSTICISM, DISTRUST, DOUBT, SKEPTICISM.

Incredulity robs us of many pleasures, and gives us nothing in return.

JAMES RUSSELL LOWELL

The amplest knowledge has the largest faith. Ignorance is always incredulous.

ROBERT ELDRIDGE WILLMOTT

The curse of man, and the cause of nearly all his woe, is his stupendous capacity for believing the incredible.

H. L. MENCKEN

INDECISION

There is no more miserable human being than one in whom nothing is habitual but indecision.

WILLIAM JAMES

While the mind is in doubt it is driven this way and that by a slight impulse.

TERENCE

He is no wise man who will quit a certainty for an uncertainty.

SAMUEL JOHNSON

Indecision is debilitating; it feeds upon itself; it is, one might almost say, habit-forming. Not only that, but it is contagious; it transmits itself to others.

H. A. HOPF

Indecision has often given an advantage to the other fellow because he did his thinking beforehand.

MAURICE SWITZER

INDEPENDENCE *Also see:* DEPENDENCE, FREEDOM, INDIVIDUALITY, LIBERTY.

Without moral and intellectual independence, there is no anchor for national independence.

DAVID BEN-GURION

I would rather sit on a pumpkin and have it all to myself than be on a crowded velvet cushion.

HENRY DAVID THOREAU

So live that you can look any man in the eye and tell him to go to hell.

ANONYMOUS

There is no more independence in politics than there is in jail.

WILL ROGERS

Can anything be so elegant as to have few wants, and to serve them one's self?

RALPH WALDO EMERSON

(I am) lord of myself, accountable to none.

BENJAMIN FRANKLIN

INDIVIDUALITY *Also see:* CHARACTER, ORIGINALITY, PERSONALITY, PROPERTY.

The worth of the state, in the long run, is the worth of the individuals composing it.

JOHN STUART MILL

The whole theory of the universe is directed unerringly to one single individual.

WALT WHITMAN

An institution is the lengthened shadow of one man.

RALPH WALDO EMERSON

That so few now dare to be eccentric marks the chief danger of the time.

JOHN STUART MILL

Individuality is the aim of political liberty.

JAMES FENIMORE COOPER

INDOLENCE . . . See Idleness

INDUSTRY *Also see:* BUSINESS, BUSY, DILIGENCE, FORTUNE, LABOR.

No thoroughly occupied man was ever yet very miserable.

LETITIA LANDON

It is better to wear out than to rust out.

RICHARD CUMBERLAND

The more we do, the more we can do.

WILLIAM HAZLITT

A man who gives his children habits of industry provides for them better than by giving them a fortune.

RICHARD WHATELY

If you have great talents, industry will improve them; if moderate abilities, industry will supply their deficiencies. Nothing is denied to well-directed labor; nothing is ever to be attained without it.

JOSHUA REYNOLDS

In the ordinary business of life, industry can do anything which genius can do, and very many things which it cannot.

HENRY WARD BEECHER

INEQUALITY *Also see:* DIFFERENCE, EQUALITY.

One half of the world must sweat and groan that the other half may dream.

HENRY WADSWORTH LONGFELLOW

No amount of artificial reinforcement can offset the natural inequalities of human individuals.

HENRY P. FAIRCHILD

Can one preach at home inequality of races and nations and advocate abroad good-will towards all men?

DOROTHY THOMPSON

People differ in capacity, skill, health, strength; and unequal fortune is a necessary result of unequal condition. Such inequality is far from being disadvantageous either to individuals or to the community.

LEO XIII

INFERIORITY Also see: IGNORANCE, INEQUALITY, RACE.

The surrender of life is nothing to sinking down into acknowledgement of inferiority.

JOHN C. CALHOUN

No man likes to have his intelligence or good faith questioned, especially if he has doubts about it himself.

HENRY BROOKS ADAMS

We must interpret a bad temper as a sign of inferiority.

ALFRED ADLER

No one can make you feel inferior without your consent.

ELEANOR ROOSEVELT

Exaggerated sensitiveness is an expression of the feeling of inferiority.

ALFRED ADLER

No two men can be half an hour together but one shall acquire an evident superiority over the other.

SAMUEL JOHNSON

INFLUENCE Also see: AUTHORITY, POWER.

The humblest individual exerts some influence, either for good or evil, upon others.

HENRY WARD BEECHER

No man should think himself a zero, and think he can do nothing about the state of the world.

BERNARD M. BARUCH

Blessed is the influence of one true, loving human soul on another.

GEORGE ELIOT

The least movement is of importance to all nature. The entire ocean is affected by a pebble.

BLAISE PASCAL

We perceive and are affected by changes too subtle to be described.

HENRY DAVID THOREAU

I am a part of all that I have met.

ALFRED, LORD TENNYSON

INGRATITUDE Also see: GRATITUDE, SELFISHNESS.

Next to ingratitude the most painful thing to bear is gratitude.

HENRY WARD BEECHER

Nothing more detestable does the earth produce than an ungrateful man.

AUSONIUS

A proud man is seldom a grateful man, for he never thinks he gets as much as he deserves.

HENRY WARD BEECHER

Too great haste to repay an obligation is a kind of ingratitude.

FRANÇOIS DE LA ROCHEFOUCAULD

One ungrateful man does an injury to all who stand in need of aid.

PUBLILIUS SYRUS

INHERITANCE

We pay for the mistakes of our ancestors, and it seems only fair that they should leave us the money to pay with.

DON MARQUIS

Who comes for the inheritance is often made to pay for the funeral.

YIDDISH PROVERB

What madness it is for a man to starve himself to enrich his heir, and so turn a friend into an enemy! For his joy at your death will be proportioned to what you leave him.

SENECA

Enjoy what thou has inherited from thy sires if thou wouldst really possess it. What we employ and use is never an oppressive burden; what the moment brings forth, that only can it profit by.

JOHANN WOLFGANG VON GOETHE

INJURY Also see: ABUSE, JUSTICE, SLANDER, VENGEANCE

No man ever did a designed injury to another, but at the same time he did a greater to himself.

LORD KAMES

If the other person injures you, you may forget the injury; but if you injure him you will always remember.

KAHLIL GIBRAN

The natural principle of war is to do the most harm to our enemy with the least harm to ourselves; and this of course is to be effected by strategem.

WASHINGTON IRVING

Never does the human soul appear so strong as when it foregoes revenge and dares to forgive an injury.

EDWIN HUBBEL CHAPIN

The injury we do and the one we suffer are not weighed in the same scale.

AESOP

INJUSTICE Also see: JUSTICE.

If thou suffer injustice, console thyself; the true unhappiness is in doing it.

DEMOCRITUS

Those who commit injustice bear the greatest burden.

HOSEA BALLOU

A book might be written on the injustice of the just

ANTHONY HOPE

He who commits injustice is ever made more wretched than he who suffers it.

PLATO

Whatever the human law may be, neither an individual nor a nation can commit the least act of injustice against the obscurest individual without having to pay the penalty for it.

HENRY DAVID THOREAU

INNOCENCE *Also see:* GUILT, IGNORANCE, JUSTICE.

Innocence most often is a good fortune and not a virtue.

ANATOLE FRANCE

They that know no evil will suspect none.

BEN JONSON

To be innocent is to be not guilty; but to be virtuous is to overcome our evil inclinations.

WILLIAM PENN

It is better that ten guilty persons escape than that one innocent suffer.

WILLIAM BLACKSTONE

INSANITY *Also see:* ACCURACY.

Insanity is often the logic of an accurate mind overtaxed.

OLIVER WENDELL HOLMES

I teach that all men are mad.

HORACE

We do not have to visit a madhouse to find disordered minds; our planet is the mental institution of the universe.

JOHANN WOLFGANG VON GOETHE

When we remember we are all mad, the mysteries disappear and life stands explained.

MARK TWAIN

INSTINCT *Also see:* COMMON SENSE.

Instinct is the nose of the mind.

MADAME DE GIRARDIN

Instinct is action taken in pursuance of a purpose, but without conscious perception of what the purpose is.

VAN HARTMANN

Instinct is untaught ability.

ALEXANDER BALN

The active part of man consists of powerful instincts, some of which are gentle and continuous; others violent and short; some baser, some nobler, and all necessary.

FRANCIS W. NEWMAN

It is the rooted instinct in men to admire what is better and more beautiful than themselves.

JAMES RUSSELL LOWELL

INSULT *Also see:* ABUSE, INJURY, IRONY.

A gentleman will not insult me, and no man not a gentleman can insult me.

FREDERICK DOUGLASS

He who puts up with insult invites injury.

PROVERB

The best way to procure insults is to submit to them.

WILLIAM HAZLITT

If you can't ignore an insult, top it; if you can't top it, laugh it off; and if you can't laugh it off, it's probably deserved.

RUSSELL LYNES

A graceful taunt is worth a thousand insults.

LOUIS NIZER

INTEGRITY ... See HONESTY

INTELLIGENCE *Also see:* COMMON SENSE, JUDGMENT, KNOWLEDGE, PERCEPTION, PRUDENCE.

It is impossible to underrate human intelligence—beginning with one's own.

HENRY BROOKS ADAMS

When you don't have an education, you've got to use your brains.

ANONYMOUS

There is nobody so irritating as somebody with less intelligence and more sense than we have.

DON HEROLD

A weak mind is like a microscope, which magnifies trifling things but cannot receive great ones.

LORD CHESTERFIELD

There is no such thing as an underestimate of average intelligence.

HENRY BROOKS ADAMS

INTEREST *Also see:* GAIN.

There are no uninteresting things, there are only uninterested people.

GILBERT K. CHESTERTON

A man's interest in the world is only an overflow from his interest in himself.

GEORGE BERNARD SHAW

Only free peoples can hold their purpose and their honor steady to a common end and prefer the interest of mankind to any narrow interest of their own.

WOODROW WILSON

It is a cursed evil to any man to become as absorbed in any subject as I am in mine.

CHARLES DARWIN

INTOLERANCE *Also see:* ANGER, BIGOTRY, PREJUDICE.

Nothing dies so hard, or rallies so often as intolerance.

HENRY WARD BEECHER

Intolerance has been the curse of every age and state.

SAMUEL DAVIES

Whoever kindles the flames of intolerance in America is lighting a fire underneath his own home.

HAROLD E. STASSEN

Bigotry and intolerance, silenced by argument, endeavors to silence by persecution, in old days by fire and sword, in modern days by the tongue.

CHARLES SIMMONS

INVENTION *Also see:* DISCOVERY.

Invention is the talent of youth, as judgment is of age.

JONATHAN SWIFT

Only an inventor knows how to borrow, and every man is or should be an inventor.

RALPH WALDO EMERSON

The march of invention has clothed mankind with powers of which a century ago the boldest imagination could not have dreamt.

HENRY GEORGE

A tool is but the extension of a man's hand, and a machine is but a complex tool. And he that invents a machine augments the power of a man and the well-being of mankind.

HENRY WARD BEECHER

JAZZ *Also see:* MUSIC.

Jazz will endure as long as people hear it through their feet instead of their brains.

JOHN PHILIP SOUSA

The chief trouble with jazz is that there is not enough of it; some of it we have to listen to twice.

DON HEROLD

Jazz may be a thrilling communion with the primitive soul; or it may be an ear-splitting bore.

WINTHROP SARGEANT

Jazz tickles your muscles, symphonies stretch your soul.

PAUL WHITEMAN

JEALOUSY *Also see:* RIVALRY, SARCASM.

There is never jealousy where there is not strong regard.

WASHINGTON IRVING

Jealousy lives upon doubts. It becomes madness or ceases entirely as soon as we pass from doubt to certainty.

FRANÇOIS DE LA ROCHEFOUCAULD

Jealousy is the injured lover's hell.

JOHN MILTON

The way to hold a husband is to keep him a little jealous; the way to lose him is to keep him a little more jealous.

H. L. MENCKEN

In jealousy there is more of self-love than of love to another.

FRANÇOIS DE LA ROCHEFOUCAULD

Lots of people know a good thing the minute the other fellow sees it first.

JOB E. HEDGES

JESTING *Also see:* HUMOR, WIT.

Many a true word is spoken in jest.

ENGLISH PROVERB

Jesting is often only indigence of intellect.

JEAN DE LA BRUYÈRE

Judge of a jest when you have done laughing.

WILLIAM LLOYD

The jest loses its point when he who makes it is the first to laugh.

JOHANN VON SCHILLER

JOURNALISM *Also see:* NEWSPAPER.

Journalists do not live by words alone, although sometimes they have to eat them.

ADLAI E. STEVENSON

Get your facts first, and then you can distort 'em as you please.

MARK TWAIN

A news sense is really a sense of what is important, what is vital, what has color and life—what people are interested in. That's journalism.

BURTON RASCOE

A journalist is a grumbler, a censurer, a giver of advice, a regent of sovereigns, a tutor of nations. Four hostile newspapers are more to be feared than a thousand bayonets.

NAPOLEON BONAPARTE

Half my lifetime I have earned my living by selling words, and I hope thoughts.

WINSTON CHURCHILL

JOY *Also see:* ENJOYMENT, HAPPINESS, PLEASURE, SMILE.

Tranquil pleasures last the longest; we are not fitted to bear the burden of great joys.

CHRISTIAN NESTELL BOVEE

One can endure sorrow alone, but it takes two to be glad.

ELBERT HUBBARD

In this world, full often, our joys are only the tender shadows which our sorrows cast.

HENRY WARD BEECHER

Great joy, especially after a sudden change of circumstances, is apt to be silent, and dwells rather in the heart than on the tongue.

HENRY FIELDING

JUDAISM *Also see:* RELIGION.

The builders of Judaism utilized emotion in order to sublimate the passions, the angers, the dreams, of the people.

JOSHUA LOTH LIEBMAN

To be a Jew is a destiny.

VICKI BAUM

Judaism lives not in an abstract creed, but in its institutions.

AUERBACH

Historically the profoundest meaning of Passover is something which sets Judaism apart from other religions. It marks the birth of a nation. Out of a mass of slaves, Moses fashioned a nation and gave them a faith. From that day to this, Jews have never ceased to be a people.

PHILIP S. BERNSTEIN

JUDGMENT *Also see:* DECISION, PRUDENCE, WISDOM.

You shall judge of a man by his foes as well as by his friends.

JOSEPH CONRAD

We judge ourselves by what we feel capable of doing; others judge us by what we have done.

HENRY WADSWORTH LONGFELLOW

Everyone complains of the badness of his memory, but nobody of his judgment.

FRANÇOIS DE LA ROCHEFOUCAULD

One cool judgment is worth a thousand hasty councils. The thing to do is to supply light and not heat.

WOODROW WILSON

Hesitancy in judgment is the only true mark of the thinker.

DAGOBERT D. RUNES

The average man's judgment is so poor, he runs a risk every time he uses it.

ED HOWE

JUSTICE *Also see:* CAUSE, COURT, EQUALITY, LAW, RIGHTS.

Justice is the great interest of man on earth.

DANIEL WEBSTER

Justice is the ligament which holds civilized beings and civilized nations together.

DANIEL WEBSTER

Justice is the insurance which we have on our lives and property. Obedience is the premium which we pay for it.

WILLIAM PENN

There is no such thing as justice—in or out of court.

CLARENCE DARROW

Whenever a separation is made between liberty and justice, neither, in my opinion, is safe.

EDMUND BURKE

Though force can protect in emergency, only justice, fairness, consideration and cooperation can finally lead men to the dawn of eternal peace.

DWIGHT D. EISENHOWER

Justice is the firm and continuous desire to render to everyone that which is his due.

JUSTINIAN

Rather suffer an injustice than commit one.

ANONYMOUS

An honest man nearly always thinks justly.

JEAN JACQUES ROUSSEAU

Justice and power must be brought together, so that whatever is just may be powerful, and whatever is powerful may be just.

BLAISE PASCAL

One man's word is no man's word; we should quietly hear both sides.

JOHANN WOLFGANG VON GOETHE

KILLING . . . See ASSASSINATION.

KINDNESS *Also see:* CHARITY, HELP.

Human kindness has never weakened the stamina or softened the fiber of a free people. A nation does not have to be cruel in order to be tough.

FRANKLIN DELANO ROOSEVELT

The best portion of a good man's life is his little, nameless, unremembered acts of kindness and of love.

WILLIAM WORDSWORTH

We hate the kindness which we understand.

HENRY DAVID THOREAU

A kind heart is a fountain of gladness, making everything in its vicinity freshen into smiles.

WASHINGTON IRVING

Kindness is a language the dumb can speak and the deaf can hear and understand.

CHRISTIAN NESTELL BOVEE

You cannot do a kindness too soon, for you never know how soon it will be too late.

RALPH WALDO EMERSON

KING *Also see:* ARISTOCRACY, BLINDNESS.

A king is one who has "few things to desire and many things to fear."

FRANCIS BACON

Wise kings generally have wise counsellors; and he must be a wise man himself who is capable of distinguishing one.

DIOGENES

Royalty consists not in vain pomp, but in great virtues.

AGESILAUS II

Every king springs from a race of slaves, and every slave had kings among his ancestors.

PLATO

The right kind of monarchy is one where everybody goes about with the permanent conviction that the king can do no wrong.

GILBERT K. CHESTERTON

KISS *Also see:* AFFECTION, PAIN.

A kiss is a lovely trick designed by nature to stop speech when words become superfluous.

INGRID BERGMAN

It is the passion that is in a kiss that gives to it its sweetness; it is the affection in a kiss that sanctifies it.

CHRISTIAN NESTELL BOVEE

A man snatches the first kiss, pleads for the second, demands the third, takes the fourth, accepts the fifth—and endures all the rest.

HELEN ROWLAND

A peculiar proposition. Of no use to one, yet absolute bliss to two. The small boy gets it for nothing, the young man has to lie for it, and the old man has to buy it. The baby's right, the lover's privilege, and the hypocrite's mask. To a young girl, faith; to a married woman, hope; and to an old maid, charity.

V.P.I SKIPPER

KNOWLEDGE Also see: CIVILIZATION, DANGER, DOUBT, DUTY, EDUCATION, POWER.

I am not young enough to know everything.

JAMES MATTHEW BARRIE

Knowledge is like money: the more he gets, the more he craves.

JOSH BILLINGS

Knowledge is knowing that we cannot know.

RALPH WALDO EMERSON

What a man knows is everywhere at war with what he wants.

JOSEPH WOOD KRUTCH

Knowledge is the small part of ignorance that we arrange and classify.

AMBROSE BIERCE

All wish to possess knowledge, but few, comparatively speaking, are willing to pay the price.

JUVENAL

LABOR Also see: AUTOMATION, EFFORT, EMPLOYMENT, INDUSTRY, LEISURE, MACHINE, WAGE, WORK.

Labor is man's greatest function. He is nothing, he can do nothing, he can achieve nothing, he can fulfill nothing, without working.

ORVILLE DEWEY

The fruit derived from labor is the sweetest of all pleasures.

LUC DE CLAPIERS

Excellence in any department can be attained only by the labor of a lifetime; it is not to be purchased at a lesser price.

SAMUEL JOHNSON

There is no real wealth but the labor of man.

PERCY BYSSHE SHELLEY

It is only through labor and painful effort, by grim energy and resolute courage, that we move on to better things.

THEODORE ROOSEVELT

I pity the man who wants a coat so cheap that the man or woman who produces the cloth will starve in the process.

BENJAMIN HARRISON

LANGUAGE Also see: CONVERSATION, LITERATURE, MUSIC, SPEECH, WORD.

Language is the blood of the soul into which thoughts run and out of which they grow.

OLIVER WENDELL HOLMES

Language is the dress of thought.

SAMUEL JOHNSON

Language is only the instrument of science, and words are but the signs of ideas.

SAMUEL JOHNSON

Think like a wise man but communicate in the language of the people.

WILLIAM BUTLER YEATS

LAUGHTER Also see: BABY, CHEERFULNESS, HUMOR, SMILE.

Those who bring sunshine to the lives of others cannot keep it from themselves.

JAMES MATTHEW BARRIE

Men show their character in nothing more clearly than by what they think laughable.

JOHANN WOLFGANG VON GOETHE

The young man who has not wept is a savage, and the old man who will not laugh is a fool.

GEORGE SANTAYANA

If you don't learn to laugh at trouble, you won't have anything to laugh at when you're old.

ED HOWE

Laughter is the sun that drives winter from the human face.

VICTOR HUGO

He laughs best who laughs last.

ENGLISH PROVERB

I can usually judge a fellow by what he laughs at.

WILSON MIZNER

LAW Also see: DISSENT, EQUALITY, GOVERNMENT.

Petty laws breed great crimes.

OUIDA

A law is valuable not because it is law, but because there is right in it.

HENRY WARD BEECHER

If we desire respect for the law, we must first make the law respectable.

LOUIS D. BRANDEIS

The best way to get a bad law repealed is to enforce it strictly.

ABRAHAM LINCOLN

It is the spirit and not the form of law that keeps justice alive.

EARL WARREN

Laws that do not embody public opinion can never be enforced.

ELBERT HUBBARD

We can not expect to breed respect for law and order among people who do not share the fruits of our freedom.

HUBERT H. HUMPHREY

LEADERSHIP Also see: AUTHORITY, COURAGE, HEROISM.

And when we think we lead, we are most led.

LORD BYRON

Leadership is the other side of the coin of loneliness, and he who is a leader must always act alone. And acting alone, accept everything alone.

FERDINAND EDRALIN MARCOS

Leadership: The art of getting someone else to do something you want done because he wants to do it.

DWIGHT D. EISENHOWER

If the blind lead the blind, both shall fall into the ditch.

MATTHEW 15:14

The final test of a leader is that he leaves behind him in other men the conviction and the will to carry on.

WALTER LIPPMANN

LEARNING Also see: DISCRETION, EDUCATION, KNOWLEDGE, STUDY, TEACHING.

The brighter you are the more you have to learn.

DON HEROLD

I've known countless people who were reservoirs of learning yet never had a thought.

WILSON MIZNER

The wisest mind has something yet to learn.

GEORGE SANTAYANA

To be proud of learning is the greatest ignorance.

JEREMY TAYLOR

I am always ready to learn, but I do not always like being taught.

WINSTON CHURCHILL

He who adds not to his learning diminishes it.

THE TALMUD

Wear your learning like your watch, in a private pocket, and do not pull it out and strike it merely to show that you have one.

LORD CHESTERFIELD

LEISURE Also see: IDLENESS, OPPORTUNITY, REST.

Leisure is a beautiful garment, but it will not do for constant wear.

ANONYMOUS

The end of labor is to gain leisure.

ARISTOTLE

We give up leisure in order that we may have leisure, just as we go to war in order that we may have peace.

ARISTOTLE

He does not seem to me to be a free man who does not sometimes do nothing.

CICERO

Employ thy time well, if thou meanest to gain leisure.

BENJAMIN FRANKLIN

In this theater of man's life, it is reserved only for God and angels to be lookers-on.

PYTHAGORAS

LIBERTY Also see: DEMOCRACY, FREEDOM of PRESS, JUSTICE, RIGHTS.

Absolute liberty is absence of restraint; responsibility is restraint; therefore, the ideally free individual is responsible to himself.

HENRY BROOKS ADAMS

Liberty, not communism, is the most contagious force in the world.

EARL WARREN

Liberty is the only thing you can't have unless you give it to others.

WILLIAM ALLEN WHITE

Liberty means responsibility. That is why most men dread it.

GEORGE BERNARD SHAW

What light is to the eyes—what air is to the lungs—what love is to the heart, liberty is to the soul of man.

ROBERT GREEN INGERSOLL

Liberty is always dangerous, but it is the safest thing we have.

HARRY EMERSON FOSDICK

LIFE Also see: AMUSEMENT, CERTAINTY, CHANGE, CHOICE, EMPLOYMENT, ENJOYMENT, IMMORTALITY, MAN, SOUL.

We are here to add what we can to life, not to get what we can from it.

WILLIAM OSLER

Life is not lost by dying; life is lost minute by minute, day by dragging day, in all the thousand small uncaring ways.

STEPHEN VINCENT BENÉT

The best use of life is to spend it for something that outlasts life.

WILLIAM JAMES

Life is a series of little deaths out of which life always returns.

CHARLES FEIDELSON, JR.

Life is a tragedy for those who feel, and a comedy for those who think.

JEAN DE LA BRUYÈRE

Let us so live that when we come to die even the undertaker will be sorry.

MARK TWAIN

Do not take life too seriously; you will never get out of it alive.

ELBERT HUBBARD

Life is like a cash register, in that every account, every thought, every deed, like every sale, is registered and recorded.

FULTON J. SHEEN

LIGHT

There are two kinds of light—the glow that illuminates, and the glare that obscures.

JAMES THURBER

The thing to do is supply light and not heat.

WOODROW WILSON

Light is the symbol of truth.

JAMES RUSSELL LOWELL

The pursuit of perfection, then, is the pursuit of sweetness and light.

MATTHEW ARNOLD

LITERATURE Also see: BOOK, LANGUAGE, PLAGIARISM, READING.

Literature is the immortality of speech.

AUGUST WILHELM VON SCHLEGEL

Great literature is simply language charged with meaning to the utmost possible degree.

EZRA POUND

Writing is the only profession where no one considers you ridiculous if you earn no money.

JULES RENARD

Literature is the art of writing something that will be read twice.

CYRIL CONNOLLY

The decline of literature indicates the decline of a nation.

JOHANN WOLFGANG VON GOETHE

Our high respect for a well-read man is praise enough of literature.

RALPH WALDO EMERSON

LOGIC Also see: ARGUMENT, REASON, PHILOSOPHY, SCIENCE.

Logic is the art of going wrong with confidence.

JOSEPH WOOD KRUTCH

Logic: an instrument used for bolstering a prejudice.

ELBERT HUBBARD

Logic is the anatomy of thought.

JOHN LOCKE

Man is not logical and his intellectual history is a record of mental reserves and compromises. He hangs on to what he can in his old beliefs even when he is compelled to surrender their logical basis.

JOHN DEWEY

Men are apt to mistake the strength of their feeling for the strength of their argument. The heated mind resents the chill touch and relentless scrutiny of logic.

WILLIAM E. GLADSTONE

LONELINESS Also see: ABSENCE, DISTRUST, LEADERSHIP, SOLITUDE.

In cities no one is quiet but many are lonely; in the country, people are quiet but few are lonely.

GEOFFREY FRANCIS FISHER

People are lonely because they build walls instead of bridges.

JOSEPH F. NEWTON

Language has created the word *loneliness* to express the pain of being alone, and the word *solitude* to express the glory of being alone.

PAUL TILLICH

LOQUACITY Also see: BORE, DIPLOMACY, ELOQUENCE

He who talks much cannot talk well.

CARLO GOLDONI

Every absurdity has a champion to defend it, for error is always talkative.

OLIVER GOLDSMITH

They always talk who never think, and who have the least to say.

MATTHEW PRIOR

Speaking much is a sign of vanity, for he that is lavish with words is a niggard in deed.

SIR WALTER RALEIGH

LOSS Also see: ADVERSITY, DEFEAT, GAIN, WASTE.

When wealth is lost, nothing is lost; when health is lost, something is lost; when character is lost, all is lost.

GERMAN MOTTO

It's the good loser who finally loses out.

KIN HUBBARD

The cheerful loser is the winner.

ELBERT HUBBARD

Lose an hour in the morning, and you will spend all day looking for it.

RICHARD WHATELY

LOVE Also see: AFFECTION, DEATH, DELUSION, FAITH, MARRIAGE, PASSION.

If there is anything better than to be loved it is loving.

ANONYMOUS

The way to love anything is to realize that it might be lost.

GILBERT K. CHESTERTON

Love built on beauty, soon as beauty, dies.

JOHN DONNE

To love is to place our happiness in the happiness of another.

GOTTFRIED WILHELM VON LEIBNITZ

Love gives itself; it is not bought.

HENRY WADSWORTH LONGFELLOW

It is better to have loved and lost, than not to have loved at all.

ALFRED, LORD TENNYSON

He that falls in love with himself will have no rivals.

BENJAMIN FRANKLIN

Love: the delusion that one woman differs from another.

H. L. MENCKEN

There is only one sort of love, but there are a thousand copies.

FRANÇOIS DE LA ROCHEFOUCAULD

I never knew how to worship until I knew how to love.
HENRY WARD BEECHER

There is a Law that man should love his neighbor as himself. In a few years it should be as natural to mankind as breathing or the upright gait; but if he does not learn it he must perish.
ALFRED ADLER

We are shaped and fashioned by what we love.
JOHANN WOLFGANG VON GOETHE

LOYALTY Also see: COUNTRY, DIPLOMACY, FIDELITY.

Loyalty means nothing unless it has at its heart the absolute principle of self-sacrifice.
WOODROW WILSON

Fidelity purchased with money, money can destroy.
SENECA

We join ourselves to no party that does not carry the American flag, and keep step to the music of the Union.
RUFUS CHOATE

My country right or wrong; when right, to keep her right; when wrong, to put her right.
CARL SCHURZ

Loyalty . . . is a realization that America was born of revolt, flourished in dissent, became great through experimentation.
HENRY S. COMMANGER

LUCK Also see: CHANCE, DESTINY, DIGNITY, FORTUNE.

The only sure thing about luck is that it will change.
WILSON MIZNER

Shallow men believe in luck. Strong men believe in cause and effect.
RALPH WALDO EMERSON

Chance favors the prepared mind.
LOUIS PASTEUR

Good luck is a lazy man's estimate of a worker's success.
ANONYMOUS

I believe in luck: how else can you explain the success of those you dislike?
JEAN COCTEAU

It is the mark of an inexperienced man not to believe in luck.
JOSEPH CONRAD

A pound of pluck is worth a ton of luck.
JAMES A. GARFIELD

LUXURY Also see: AVARICE, EXTRAVAGANCE, WEALTH.

War destroys men, but luxury destroys mankind; at once corrupts the body and the mind.
JOHN CROWNE

Give us the luxuries of life and we'll dispense with the necessaries.
OLIVER WENDELL HOLMES

On the soft bed of luxury most kingdoms have expired.
EDWARD YOUNG

Possessions, outward success, publicity, luxury—to me these have always been contemptible. I believe that a simple and unassuming manner of life is best for everyone, best for both the body and the mind.
ALBERT EINSTEIN

Luxury is the first, second and third cause of the ruin of republics.
EDWARD PAYSON

LYING Also see: CREDULITY, DECEIT, DISHONESTY, EXCUSES, HYPOCRISY, LOQUACITY.

You can best reward a liar by believing nothing of what he says.
ARISTIPPUS

I do not mind lying, but I hate inaccuracy.
SAMUEL BUTLER

One ought to have a good memory when he has told a lie.
CORNEILLE

The liar's punishment is not in the least that he is not believed, but that he cannot believe anyone else.
GEORGE BERNARD SHAW

Any fool can tell the truth, but it requires a man of some sense to know how to lie well.
SAMUEL BUTLER

MACHINE Also see: AUTOMATION, TECHNOLOGY.

One machine can do the work of fifty ordinary men. No machine can do the work of one extraordinary man.
ELBERT HUBBARD

A tool is but the extension of a man's hand, and a machine is but a complex tool. He that invents a machine augments the power of man and the well-being of mankind.
HENRY WARD BEECHER

On mechanical slavery, on the slaver of the machine, the future of the world depends.
OSCAR WILDE

To me, there is something superbly symbolic in the fact that an astronaut, sent up as assistant to a series of computers, found that he worked more accurately and more intelligently than they. Inside the capsule, man is still in charge.
ADLAI E. STEVENSON

MAJORITY Also see: DEMOCRACY, MINORITY.

There is one body that knows more than anybody, and that is everybody.
ALEXANDRE DE TALLEYRAND-PÉRIGORD

Any man more right than his neighbors, constitutes a majority of one.
HENRY DAVID THOREAU

The voice of the majority is no proof of justice.

JOHANN VON SCHILLER

When you get too big a majority, you're immediately in trouble.

SAM RAYBURN

It is my principle that the will of the majority should always prevail.

THOMAS JEFFERSON

MAN *Also see:* AVERAGE, BELIEF, BOOK, BOYS, CAUSE, CITIZENSHIP, CLASS, FAILURE, FATHER, FOOL, GOD, HUMAN NATURE, MACHINE, WOMAN.

Man is a reasoning rather than a reasonable animal.

ALEXANDER HAMILTON

Man is a piece of the universe made alive.

RALPH WALDO EMERSON

The ablest man I ever met is the man you think you are.

FRANKLIN DELANO ROOSEVELT

Man is a special being, and if left to himself, in an isolated condition, would be one of the weakest creatures; but associated with his kind, he works wonders.

DANIEL WEBSTER

I am the inferior of any man whose rights I trample under foot. Men are not superior by reason of the accidents of race or color. They are superior who have the best heart—the best brain. The superior man ... stands erect by bending above the fallen. He rises by lifting others.

ROBERT GREEN INGERSOLL

MANNERS *Also see:* BEHAVIOR, COURTESY, GENTLEMAN, HASTE.

To succeed in the world it is not enough to be stupid, you must also be well-mannered.

VOLTAIRE

Nothing so much prevents our being natural as the desire of appearing so.

FRANÇOIS DE LA ROUCHEFOUCAULD

A man's own good breeding is the best security against other people's ill manners.

LORD CHESTERFIELD

Savages we call them because their manners differ from ours.

BENJAMIN FRANKLIN

Manners easily and rapidly mature into morals.

HORACE MANN

MARRIAGE *Also see:* ANCESTRY, BACHELOR, HUSBAND, SEX, WIFE.

The difficulty with marriage is that we fall in love with a personality, but must live with a character.

PETER DEVRIES

Marriage is that relation between man and woman in which the independence is equal, the dependence mutual, and the obligation reciprocal.

LOUIS K. ANSPACHER

Men marry to make an end; women to make a beginning.

ALEXIS DUPUY

It takes two to make a marriage a success and only one to make it a failure.

HERBERT SAMUEL

I guess the only way to stop divorce is to stop marriage.

WILL ROGERS

Well-married, a man is winged: ill-matched, he is shackled.

HENRY WARD BEECHER

A successful marriage is an edifice that must be rebuilt every day.

ANDRÉ MAUROIS

God help the man who won't marry until he finds a perfect woman, and God help him still more if he finds her.

BENJAMIN TILLETT

Marriage resembles a pair of shears, so joined that they cannot be separated; often moving in opposite directions, yet always punishing any one who comes between them.

SYDNEY SMITH

MARTYR *Also see:* HEROISM, SACRIFICE.

The way of the world is, to praise dead saints, and persecute living ones.

NATHANIEL HOWE

It is more difficult, and it calls for higher energies of soul, to live a martyr than to die one.

HORACE MANN

It is the cause and not merely the death that makes the martyr.

NAPOLEON BONAPARTE

MATURITY *Also see:* AGE.

Maturity is often more absurd than youth and very frequently is most unjust to youth.

THOMAS A. EDISON

The immature man wants to die nobly for a cause, while the mature man wants to live humanely for one.

WILHELM STEKEL

Maturity is the time of life when, if you had the time, you'd have the time of your life.

ANONYMOUS

Only the middle-aged have all their five senses in the keeping of their wits.

HERVEY ALLEN

MAXIM

Pithy sentences are like sharp nails which force truth upon our memory.

DENIS DIDEROT

Maxims are the condensed good sense of nations.

JAMES MACKINTOSH

Maxims are like lawyers who must need to see but one side of the case.

FRANK GELETT BURGESS

All maxims have their antagonist maxims; proverbs should be sold in pairs, a single one being but a half truth.

WILLIAM MATHEWS

MEANS ... See END and MEANS

MEDICINE *Also see:* DISEASE, DRUGS, HEALTH, PROFESSION.

The only profession that labors incessantly to destroy the reason for its own existence.

JAMES BRYCE

God heals and the doctor takes the fee.

BENJAMIN FRANKLIN

He is the best physician who is the most ingenious inspirer of hope.

SAMUEL TAYLOR COLERIDGE

MEDITATION ... See THOUGHT

MEMORY *Also see:* LYING, MONUMENT.

Memory is the cabinet of imagination, the treasury of reason, the registry of conscience, and the council chamber of thought.

ST. BASIL

Unless we remember we cannot understand.

EDWARD M. FORSTER

Those who cannot remember the past are condemned to repeat it.

GEORGE SANTAYANA

Recollection is the only paradise from which we cannot be turned out.

JEAN PAUL RICHTER

A retentive memory is a good thing, but the ability to forget is the true token of greatness.

ELBERT HUBBARD

Every man's memory is his private literature.

ALDOUS HUXLEY

MERCY *Also see:* COMPASSION, FIRMNESS, FORGIVENESS, PITY.

Sweet mercy is nobility's true badge.

WILLIAM SHAKESPEARE

Mercy among the virtues is like the moon among the stars ... It is the light that hovers above the judgment seat.

EDWIN HUBBEL CHAPIN

Hate shuts her soul when dove-eyed mercy pleads.

CHARLES SPRAGUE

MERIT *Also see:* CREDIT, WORTH.

If you wish your merit to be known, acknowledge that of other people.

ORIENTAL PROVERB

Contemporaries appreciate the man rather than his merit; posterity will regard the merit rather than the man.

CHARLES CALEB COLTON

The world rewards the appearance of merit oftener than merit itself.

FRANÇOIS DE LA ROCHEFOUCAULD

It never occurs to fools that merit and good fortune are closely united.

JOHANN WOLFGANG VON GOETHE

MIND *Also see:* DISEASE, INTELLIGENCE, NATION, REASON, SELF-KNOWLEDGE, UNDERSTANDING.

Few minds wear out; more rust out.

CHRISTIAN NESTELL BOVEE

Commonplace minds usually condemn what is beyond the reach of their understanding.

FRANÇOIS DE LA ROCHEFOUCAULD

The mind is like the stomach. It is not how much you put into it that counts, but how much it digests.

ALBERT JAY NOCK

I not only use all the brains I have, but all that I can borrow.

WOODROW WILSON

The defects of the mind, like those of the face, grow worse as we grow old.

FRANÇOIS DE LA ROCHEFOUCAULD

Life is not a static thing. The only people who do not change their minds are incompetents in asylums, who can't, and those in cemeteries.

EVERETT M. DIRKSEN

MINORITY *Also see:* MAJORITY.

Every new opinion, at its starting, is precisely in a minority of one.

THOMAS CARLYLE

That cause is strong which has not a multitude, but one strong man behind it.

JAMES RUSSELL LOWELL

The only tyrannies from which men, women and children are suffering in real life are the tyrannies of minorities.

THEODORE ROOSEVELT

The minority of a country is never known to agree, except in its efforts to reduce and oppress the majority.

JAMES FENIMORE COOPER

The political machine works because it is a united minority acting against a divided majority.

WILL DURANT

MIRTH ... See JOY

MISER *Also see:* AVARICE, GOLD, GREED, MONEY, SELFISHNESS.

The miser, poor fool, not only starves his body, but also his own soul.

THEODORE PARKER

The happiest miser on earth is the man who saves up every friend he can make.

ROBERT EMMET SHERWOOD

The devil lies brooding in the miser's chest.

THOMAS FULLER

Misers mistake gold for good, whereas it is only a means of obtaining it.

FRANÇOIS DE LA ROCHEFOUCAULD

The miser, starving his brother's body, starves also his own soul, and at death shall creep out of his great estate of injustice, poor and naked and miserable.

THEODORE PARKER

MISERY *Also see:* ADVERSITY, GRIEF, PAIN, SORROW.

He that is down need fear no fall.

JOHN BUNYAN

There is no greater grief than to remember days of joy when misery is at hand.

DANTE

Man is only miserable so far as he thinks himself so.

JACOPO SANNAZARO

There are a good many real miseries in life that we cannot help smiling at, but they are the smiles that make wrinkles and not dimples.

OLIVER WENDELL HOLMES

A misery is not to be measured from the nature of the evil, but from the temper of the sufferer.

JOSEPH ADDISON

MOB *Also see:* RIOT, VIOLENCE.

A mob is a group of persons with heads but no brains.

THOMAS FULLER

The nose of a mob is its imagination. By this, at any time, it can be quietly led.

EDGAR ALLAN POE

The mob is man voluntarily descending to the nature of the beast.

RALPH WALDO EMERSON

Get together a hundred or two men, however sensible they may be, and you are very likely to have a mob.

SAMUEL JOHNSON

The mob is the mother of tyrants.

DIOGENES

It is proof of a bad cause when it is applauded by the mob.

SENECA

MODERATION *Also see:* ABSTINENCE, BARGAIN, SELF-CONTROL.

In everything the middle road is the best; all things in excess bring trouble to men.

PLAUTUS

Moderation in temper is always a virtue; but moderation in principle is always a vice.

THOMAS PAINE

Moderation is a fatal thing: nothing succeeds like excess.

OSCAR WILDE

To go beyond the bounds of moderation is to outrage humanity.

BLAISE PASCAL

The pursuit, even of the best things, ought to be calm and tranquil.

CICERO

He will always be a slave who does not know how to live upon a little.

HORACE

MODESTY *Also see:* BLUSH, HUMILITY, MERIT.

Modesty is not only an ornament, but also a guard to virtue.

JOSEPH ADDISON

There's a lot to be said for the fellow who doesn't say it himself.

MAURICE SWITZER

Modesty may make a fool seem a man of sense.

JONATHAN SWIFT

It is easy for a somebody to be modest, but it is difficult to be modest when one is a nobody.

JULES RENARD

Modesty is the only sure bait when you angle for praise.

LORD CHESTERFIELD

With people of only moderate ability modesty is mere honesty; but with those who possess great talent it is hypocrisy.

ARTHUR SCHOPENHAUER

MONEY *Also see:* BORROWING, CREDIT, DEBT, DIPLOMACY, ECONOMY, FINANCE, GOLD, KNOWLEDGE, WEALTH.

He that is of the opinion money will do everything may well be suspected of doing everything for money.

BENJAMIN FRANKLIN

The safest way to double your money is to fold it over once and put it in your pocket.

KIM HUBBARD

The use of money is all the advantage there is in having it.

BENJAMIN FRANKLIN

Money often costs too much.

RALPH WALDO EMERSON

Money is not required to buy one necessity of the soul.

HENRY DAVID THOREAU

Money does all things for reward. Some are pious and honest as long as they thrive upon it, but if the devil himself gives better wages, they soon change their party.

SENECA

Put not your trust in money, but put your money in trust.

OLIVER WENDELL HOLMES

MONUMENT *Also see:* ACHIEVEMENT, GRAVE.

Deeds, not stones, are the true monuments of the great.

JOHN L. MOTLEY

The marble keeps merely a cold and sad memory of a man who would else be forgotten. No man who needs a monument ever ought to have one.

NATHANIEL HAWTHORNE

Monuments are the grappling-irons that bind one generation to another.

JOSEPH JOUBERT

If I have done any deed worthy of remembrance, that deed will be my monument. If not, no monument can preserve my memory.

AGESILAUS II

MORALITY *Also see:* ART, BOREDOM, MANNERS, VIRTUE.

Moralizing and morals are two entirely different things and are always found in entirely different people.

DON HEROLD

So far, about morals, I know only that what is moral is what you feel good after and what is immoral is what you feel bad after.

ERNEST HEMINGWAY

To denounce moralizing out of hand is to pronounce a moral judgment.

H. L. MENCKEN

All sects are different, because they come from men; morality is everywhere the same, because it comes from God.

VOLTAIRE

MORTALITY . . . See DEATH

MOTHER *Also see:* BIRTH, BIRTH CONTROL, CHILDREN, CLEVERNESS, DESTINY, EARTH, FATHER, PARENT, WIFE, WOMAN.

Men are what their mothers made them.

RALPH WALDO EMERSON

A mother is not a person to lean on but a person to make leaning unnecessary.

DOROTHY CANFIELD FISHER

The hand that rocks the cradle is the hand that rules the world.

W. S. ROSS

God could be not everywhere, and therefore he made mothers.

JEWISH PROVERB

All that I am, or hope to be, I owe to my angel mother.

ABRAHAM LINCOLN

MURDER *Also see:* ASSASSINATION, BIRTH CONTROL.

Every unpunished murder takes away something from the security of every man's life.

DANIEL WEBSTER

Criminals do not die by the hands of the law; they die by the hands of other men.

GEORGE BERNARD SHAW

It is forbidden to kill; therefore all murderers are punished unless they kill in large numbers and to the sound of trumpets.

VOLTAIRE

The very emphasis of the commandment: Thou shalt not kill, makes it certain that we are descended from an endlessly long chain of generations of murderers, whose love of murder was in their blood as it is perhaps also in ours.

SIGMUND FREUD

MUSIC *Also see:* JAZZ

Music is well said to be the speech of angels.

THOMAS CARLYLE

After silence that which comes nearest to expressing the inexpressible is music.

ALDOUS HUXLEY

Music is the only language in which you cannot say a mean or sarcastic thing.

LORD ERSKINE

Music is the universal language of mankind.

HENRY WADSWORTH LONGFELLOW

Music is harmony, harmony is perfection, perfection is our dream, and our dream is heaven.

AMIEL

Composers should write tunes that chauffeurs and errand boys can whistle.

THOMAS BEECHAM

MYSTERY *Also see:* SECRECY.

All is mystery; but he is a slave who will not struggle to penetrate the dark veil.

BENJAMIN DISRAELI

It is hard to say whether the doctors of law or divinity have made the greater advances in the lucrative business of mystery.

EDMUND BURKE

The most beautiful experience we can have is the mysterious. It is the fundamental emotion which stands at the cradle of true art and true science.

ALBERT EINSTEIN

It is the dim haze of mystery that adds enchantment to pursuit.

ANTOINE RIVAROL

Mystery is another name for our ignorance; if we were omniscient, all would be perfectly plain.

TRYON EDWARDS

NAME *Also see:* REPUTATION.

A person with a bad name is already half-hanged.

PROVERB

To live in mankind is far more than to live in a name

VACHEL LINDSAY

A good name, like good will, is got by many actions and lost by one.

LORD JEFFERY

The invisible thing called a Good Name is made up of the breath of numbers that speak well of you.

LORD HALIFAX

What's in a name? That which we call a rose by any other name would smell as sweet.

WILLIAM SHAKESPEARE

Nicknames stick to people, and the most ridiculous are the most adhesive.

THOMAS C. HALIBURTON

NATION Also see: AMERICA, UNITED NATIONS, UNITY.

A nation is a totality of men united through community of fate into a community of character.

OTTO BAUER

The nation's honor is dearer than the nation's comfort; yes, than the nation's life itself.

WOODROW WILSON

A nation, like a person, has a mind—a mind that must be kept informed and alert, that must know itself, that understands the hopes and needs of its neighbors—all the other nations that live within the narrowing circle of the world.

FRANKLIN DELANO ROOSEVELT

No nation is fit to sit in judgment upon any other nation.

WOODROW WILSON

NATIONALISM Also see: CITIZENSHIP, PATRIOTISM.

We are in the midst of a great transition from narrow nationalism to international partnership.

LYNDON BAINES JOHNSON

There is a higher form of patriotism than nationalism, and that higher form is not limited by the boundaries of one's country; but by a duty to mankind to safeguard the trust of civilization.

OSCAR S. STRAUSS

Born in iniquity and conceived in sin, the spirit of nationalism has never ceased to bend human institutions to the service of dissension and distress.

THORSTEIN VEBLEN

The root of the problem is very simply stated: if there were no sovereign independent states, if the states of the civilized world were organized in some sort of federalism, as the states of the American Union, for instance, are organized, there would be no international war as we know it ... The main obstacle is nationalism.

NORMAN ANGELL

NATURE Also see: ART, BEAUTY, CRUELTY, EARTH, FAMILY, FORTUNE, KISS.

The ignorant man marvels at the exceptional; the wise man marvels at the common; the greatest wonder of all is the regularity of nature.

GEORGE DANA BOARDMAN

Nature encourages no looseness, pardons no errors.

RALPH WALDO EMERSON

Nature creates ability; luck provides it with opportunity.

FRANÇOIS DE LA ROCHEFOUCAULD

Whether man is disposed to yield to nature or to oppose her, he cannot do without a correct understanding of her language.

JEAN ROSTAND

I love to think of nature as an unlimited broadcasting station, through which God speaks to us every hour, if we only will tune in.

GEORGE WASHINGTON CARVER

Man must go back to nature for information.

THOMAS PAINE

NECESSITY Also see: CIVILIZATION, ENDURANCE, HABIT, LUXURY, WANT.

Make yourself necessary to somebody.

RALPH WALDO EMERSON

Necessity is the mother of invention.

JONATHAN SWIFT

Our necessities are few but our wants are endless.

JOSH BILLINGS

Necessity is the plea for every infringement of human freedom. It is the argument of tyrants; it is the creed of slaves.

WILLIAM PITT

It is surprising what a man can do when he has to, and how little most men will do when they don't have to.

WALTER LINN

Whatever necessity lays upon thee, endure; whatever she commands, do.

JOHANN WOLFGANG VON GOETHE

Necessity is blind until it becomes conscious. Freedom is the consciousness of necessity.

KARL MARX

NEGLECT Also see: IDLENESS, PROCRASTINATION.

He that thinks he can afford to be negligent is not far from being poor.

SAMUEL JOHNSON

It is the neglect of timely repair that makes rebuilding necessary.

RICHARD WHATELY

It will generally be found that men who are constantly lamenting their ill luck are only reaping the consequences of their own neglect, mismanagement, and improvidence, or want of application.

SAMUEL SMILES

NEUTRALITY Also see: TOLERANCE.

Neutral men are the devil's allies.

EDWIN HUBBEL CHAPLIN

Neutrality, as a lasting principle, is an evidence of weakness.

LAJOS KOSSUTH

People who demand neutrality in any situation are usually not neutral but in favor of the status quo.

MAX EASTMAN

NEWSPAPER *Also see:* FREEDOM OF THE PRESS, JOURNALISM.

Newspapers are the schoolmasters of the common people.

HENRY WARD BEECHER

A newspaper should be the maximum of information, and the minimum of comment.

RICHARD COBDEN

Newspapers are the world's mirrors.

JAMES ELLIS

We live under a government of men and morning newspapers.

WENDELL PHILLIPS

The man who reads nothing at all is better educated than the man who reads nothing but newspapers.

THOMAS JEFFERSON

Were it left to me to decide whether we should have a government without newspapers or newspapers without government, I should not hesitate a moment to prefer the latter.

THOMAS JEFFERSON

NOVELTY *Also see:* ORIGINALITY, VARIETY.

It is not only old and early impressions that deceive us; the charms of novelty have the same power.

BLAISE PASCAL

Novelty is the great parent of pleasure.

ROBERT SOUTH

Some degree of novelty must be one of the materials in almost every instrument which works upon the mind; and curiosity blends itself, more or less, with all our pleasures.

EDMUND BURKE

In science, as in common life, we frequently see that a novelty in system, or in practice, cannot be duly appreciated till time has sobered the enthusiasm of its advocates.

MAUD

NUCLEAR WARFARE *Also see:* TECHNOLOGY, WAR.

We've opened a door—maybe a treasure house, maybe only the realization of a maniac's dream of destruction.

JOHN ANDERSON

People who talk of outlawing the atomic bomb are mistaken—what needs to be outlawed is war.

LESLIE RICHARD GROVES

Idealists maintain that all nations should share the atomic bomb. Pessimists maintain that they will.

PUNCH

The hydrogen bomb is history's exclamation point. It ends an age-long sentence of manifest violence.

MARSHALL MCLUHAN

We develop weapons, not to wage war, but to prevent war. Only in the clear light of this greater truth can we properly examine the lesser matter of the testing of our nuclear weapons.

DWIGHT D. EISENHOWER

OBEDIENCE *Also see:* CHILDREN, DUTY, JUSTICE

Wicked men obey from fear; good men, from love.

ARISTOTLE

The only safe ruler is he who has learned to obey willingly.

THOMAS À KEMPIS

There are two kinds of men who never amount to much: those who cannot do what they are told, and those who can do nothing else.

CYRUS H. CURTIS

OBLIGATION ... See DUTY

OBSCURITY ... See AMBIGUITY

OBSERVATION *Also see:* PERCEPTION, SCIENCE.

Observation—activity of both eyes and ears.

HORACE MANN

If I were to prescribe one process in the training of men which is fundamental to success in any direction, it would be thoroughgoing training in the habit of observation. It is a habit which every one of us should be seeking ever more to perfect.

EUGENE G. GRACE

Every man who observes vigilantly and resolves steadfastly grows unconsciously into genius.

EDWARD G. BULWER-LYTTON

OPINION *Also see:* BELIEF, FORCE, FREEDOM, IDEA, JUDGMENT, MINORITY, OPPRESSION, PREJUDICE.

The foolish and the dead alone never change their opinions.

JAMES RUSSELL LOWELL

People do not seem to realize that their opinion of the world is also a confession of character.

RALPH WALDO EMERSON

He that never changes his opinions, never corrects his mistakes, and will never be wiser on the morrow than he is today.

TRYON EDWARDS

Opinions cannot survive if one has no chance to fight for them.

THOMAS MANN

Public opinion is a weak tyrant, compared with our private opinion—what a man thinks of himself, that is which determines, or rather indicates his fate.

HENRY DAVID THOREAU

OPPORTUNITY *Also see:* ABILITY, ACHIEVEMENT, CHANCE, CIVILIZATION, FORTUNE, LUCK.

A wise man will make more opportunities than he finds.

FRANCIS BACON

You will never "find" time for anything. If you want time you must make it.

CHARLES BUXTON

Do not wait for extraordinary circumstances to do good; try to use ordinary situations.

JEAN PAUL RICHTER

The commonest form, one of the most often neglected, and the safest opportunity for the average man to seize, is hard work.

ARTHUR BRISBANE

OPPRESSION Also see: ABUSE, CRUELTY, TYRANNY.

You can't hold a man down without staying down with him.

BOOKER T. WASHINGTON

A desire to resist oppression is implanted in the nature of man.

TACITUS

He that would make his own liberty secure must guard even his enemy from oppression; for if he violates this duty, he establishes a precedent that will reach to himself.

THOMAS PAINE

OPTIMISM Also see: CHEERFULNESS, PESSIMISSM, TRADITION.

In these times you have to be an optimist to open your eyes in the morning.

CARL SANDBURG

The only limit to our realization of tomorrow will be our doubts of today.

FRANKLIN DELANO ROOSEVELT

There is no sadder sight than a young pessimist, except an old optimist.

MARK TWAIN

Optimist: a proponent of the doctrine that black is white.

AMBROSE BIERCE

The optimist proclaims that we live in the best of all possible worlds; and the pessimist fears this is true.

JAMES BRANCH CABELL

The habit of looking on the bright side of every event is worth more than a thousand pounds a year.

SAMUEL JOHNSON

ORDER Also see: CIVILIZATION, DISCOVERY, EFFICIENCY.

A place for everything, everything in its place.

BENJAMIN FRANKLIN

The art of progress is to preserve order amid change, and to preserve change amid order.

ALFRED NORTH WHITEHEAD

He who has no taste for order, will be often wrong in his judgment, and seldom considerate or conscientious in his actions.

JOHANN KASPAR LAVATER

ORIGINALITY Also see: CREATIVITY, FASHION, INVENTION, PLAGIARISM.

Originality is simply a pair of fresh eyes.

THOMAS WENTWORTH HIGGINSON

It is better to create than to be learned; creating is the true essence of life.

BARTHOLD GEORG NIEBUHR

The merit of originality is not novelty, it is sincerity. The believing man is the original man; he believes for himself, not for another.

THOMAS CARLYLE

Originality is nothing but judicious imitation.

VOLTAIRE

OSTENTATION Also see: PRETENSION, PRIDE.

Ostentation is the signal flag of hypocrisy.

EDWIN HUBBLE CHAPIN

Whatever is done without ostentation, and without the people being witnesses of it, is in my opinion, most praiseworthy: not that the public eye should be entirely avoided, for good actions desire to be placed in the light; but notwithstanding this, the greatest theater for virtue is conscience.

CICERO

Pride is the master sin of the devil, and the devil is the father of lies.

EDWIN HUBBEL CHAPIN

That which is given with pride and ostentation is rather an ambition than a bounty.

SENECA

The charity that hastens to proclaim its good deeds, ceases to be charity, and is only pride and ostentation.

WILLIAM HUTTON

PAIN Also see: SUFFERING.

Pain adds rest unto pleasure, and teaches the luxury of health.

MARTIN F. TUPPER

The pain of the mind is worse than the pain of the body.

PUBLILIUS SYRUS

Pain dies quickly, and lets her weary prisoners go; the fiercest agonies have shortest reign.

WILLIAM CULLEN BRYANT

Pain and pleasure, like light and darkness, succeed each other.

LAURENCE STERNE

Pain is life—the sharper, the more evidence of life.

CHARLES LAMB

Man endures pain as an undeserved punishment; woman accepts it as a natural heritage.

ANONYMOUS

PARDON ... See FORGIVENESS

PARENTS

The joys of parents are secret, and so are their griefs and fears.

FRANCIS BACON

The first half of our lives is ruined by our parents and the second half by our children.

CLARENCE DARROW

We never know the love of the parent till we become parents ourselves.

HENRY WARD BEECHER

The most important thing a father can do for his children is to love their mother.

THEODORE M. HESBURGH

How many hopes and fears, how many ardent wishes and anxious apprehensions are twisted together in the threads that connect the parent with the child!

SAMUEL GRISWOLD GOODRICH

PARTY *Also see:* GOVERNMENT, POLITICS.

He serves his party best who serves the country best.

RUTHERFORD B. HAYES

Any party which takes credit for the rain must not be surprised if its opponents blame it for the drought.

DWIGHT W. MORROW

I know my Republican friends were glad to see my wife feeding an elephant in India. She gave him sugar and nuts. But of course the elephant wasn't satisfied.

JOHN FITZGERALD KENNEDY

The best system is to have one party govern and the other party watch.

THOMAS B. REED

Party honesty is party expediency.

GROVER CLEVELAND

PASSION *Also see:* ANGER, DESIRE, EMOTION, ENTHUSIASM, PATIENCE, POETRY.

Act nothing in furious passion. It's putting to sea in a storm.

THOMAS FULLER

Passion is universal humanity. Without it religion, history, romance and art would be useless.

HONORÉ DE BALZAC

The passions are like fire, useful in a thousand ways and dangerous only in one, through their excess.

CHRISTIAN NESTELL BOVEE

He only employs his passion who can make no use of his reason.

CICERO

Our passions are like convulsion fits, which, though they make us stronger for the time, leave us the weaker ever after.

JONATHAN SWIFT

He submits to be seen through a microscope, who suffers himself to be caught in a fit of passion.

JOHANN KASPAR LAVATER

PAST *Also see:* FUTURE, HISTORY, PRESENT.

I tell you the past is a bucket of ashes.

CARL SANDBURG

Those who cannot remember the past are condemned to repeat it.

GEORGE SANTAYANA

The free world must now prove itself worthy of its own past.

DWIGHT D. EISENHOWER

Study the past if you would divine the future.

CONFUCIUS

The present contains nothing more than the past, and what is found in the effect was already in the cause.

HENRI BERGSON

PATIENCE *Also see:* ANGER, ENDURANCE.

Adopt the pace of nature: her secret is patience.

RALPH WALDO EMERSON

He that can have patience can have what he will.

BENJAMIN FRANKLIN

They also serve who only stand and wait.

JOHN MILTON

Our patience will achieve more than our force.

EDMUND BURKE

Everything comes to him who hustles while he waits.

THOMAS A. EDISON

Patience is bitter, but its fruit is sweet.

JEAN JACQUES ROUSSEAU

Patience and time do more than strength or passion.

JEAN DE LA FONTAINE

PATRIOTISM *Also see:* CITIZENSHIP, COUNTRY, NATIONALISM.

Patriotism is easy to understand in America; it means looking out for yourself by looking out for your country.

CALVIN COOLIDGE

I only regret that I have but one life to give for my country.

NATHAN HALE

Ask not what your country can do for you: Ask what you can do for your country.

JOHN FITZGERALD KENNEDY

Love of country is like love of woman—he loves her best who seeks to bestow on her the highest good.

FELIX ADLER

A man's country is not a certain area of land, of mountains, rivers, and woods, but it is a principle; and patriotism is loyalty to that principle.

GEORGE WILLIAM CURTIS

You'll never have a quiet world till you knock the patriotism out of the human race.

GEORGE BERNARD SHAW

A man's feet must be planted in his country, but his eyes should survey the world.

GEORGE SANTAYANA

PEACE *Also see:* BLOOD, DISARMAMENT, HOME, LEISURE, LOYALTY, WAR.

Peace, in international affairs, is a period of cheating between two periods of fighting.

AMBROSE BIERCE

If they want peace, nations should avoid the pin-pricks that precede cannonshots.

NAPOLEON BONAPARTE

Peace is rarely denied to the peaceful.

JOHANN VON SCHILLER

Peace is the one condition of survival in this nuclear age.

ADLAI E. STEVENSON

We seek peace, knowing that peace is the climate of freedom.

DWIGHT D. EISENHOWER

If we are to live together in peace, we must come to know each other better.

LYNDON BAINES JOHNSON

PERCEPTION *Also see:* SCIENCE, UNDERSTANDING.

Only in quiet waters things mirror themselves undistorted. Only in a quiet mind is adequate perception of the world.

HANS MARGOLIUS

The heart has eyes which the brain knows nothing of.

CHARLES H. PARKHURST

To see what is right, and not do it, is want of courage, or of principle.

CONFUCIUS

The clearsighted do not rule the world, but they sustain and console it.

AGNES REPPLIER

PERFECTION

Trifles make perfection, and perfection is no trifle.

MICHELANGELO

Aim at perfection in everything, though in most things it is unattainable. However, they who aim at it, and persevere, will come much nearer to it than those whose laziness and despondency make them give it up as unattainable.

LORD CHESTERFIELD

Perfection is attained by slow degrees; it requires the hand of time.

VOLTAIRE

No good work whatever can be perfect, and the demand for perfection is always a sign of a misunderstanding of the ends of art.

JOHN RUSKIN

This is the very perfection of a man, to find out his own imperfections.

ST. AUGUSTINE

The artist who aims at perfection in everything achieves it in nothing.

DELACROIX

It is reasonable to have perfection in our eye that we may always advance toward it, though we know it can never be reached.

SAMUEL JOHNSON

PERSEVERANCE *Also see:* DIGNITY, DILIGENCE, ENDURANCE, PATIENCE, PURPOSE.

The difference between perseverance and obstinacy is, that one often comes from a strong will, and the other from a strong won't.

HENRY WARD BEECHER

Consider the postage stamp, my son. It secures success through its ability to stick to one thing till it gets there.

JOSH BILLINGS

We make way for the man who boldly pushes past us.

CHRISTIAN NESTELL BOVEE

There is no failure except in no longer trying. There is no defeat except from within, no really insurmountable barrier save our own inherent weakness of purpose.

KIN HUBBARD

Perseverance is more prevailing than violence; and many things which cannot be overcome when they are together yield themselves up when taken little by little.

PLUTARCH

PERSONALITY *Also see:* CHARACTER, INDIVIDUALITY, MATURITY.

Everyone is a moon, and has a dark side which he never shows to anybody.

MARK TWAIN

Some persons are likeable in spite of their unswerving integrity.

DON MARQUIS

If you have anything really valuable to contribute to the world it will come through the expression of your own personality, that single spark of divinity that sets you off and makes you different from every other living creature.

BRUCE BARTON

Personality is to a man what perfume is to a flower.

CHARLES M. SCHWAB

PESSIMISM *Also see:* CYNIC, OPTIMISM, SKEPTICISM, TRADITION.

A pessimist is one who feels bad when he feels good for fear he'll feel worse when he feels better.

ANONYMOUS

Cheer up, the worst is yet to come.

PHILANDER JOHNSON

PHILOSOPHY *Also see:* DISCRETION, GOD, REASON, RELIGION, SCIENCE, THEORY.

Philosophy: unintelligible answers to insoluble problems.

HENRY BROOKS ADAMS

The philosophy of one century is the common sense of the next.

HENRY WARD BEECHER

All philosophy lies in two words, sustain and abstain.

EPICTETUS

Philosophy is an unusually ingenious attempt to think fallaciously.

BERTRAND RUSSELL

Philosphy is the science which considers truth.

ARISTOTLE

Philosophy, when superficially studied, excites doubt; when thoroughly explored, it dispels it.

FRANCIS BACON

PITY Also see: COMPASSION, SYMPATHY.

Pity is best taught by fellowship in woe.

SAMUEL TAYLOR COLERIDGE

Compassion is the only one of the human emotions the Lord permitted Himself and it has carried the divine flavor ever since.

DAGOBERT D. RUNES

We pity in others only those evils which we have ourselves experienced.

JEAN JACQUES ROUSSEAU

Pity is not natural to man. Children and savages are always cruel. Pity is acquired and improved by the cultivation of reason. We may have uneasy sensations from seeing a creature in distress, without pity; but we have not pity unless we wish to relieve him.

SAMUEL JOHNSON

PLAGIARISM Also see: ORIGINALITY, WRITER.

When you take stuff from one writer, it's plagiarism; but when you take it from many writers, it's research.

WILSON MIZNER

About the most originality that any writer can hope to achieve honestly is to steal with good judgment.

JOSH BILLINGS

Literature is full of coincidences, which some love to believe are plagiarisms. There are thoughts always abroad in the air which it takes more wit to avoid than to hit upon.

OLIVER WENDELL HOLMES

A certain awkwardness marks the use of borrowed thoughts; but as soon as we have learned what to do with them, they become our own.

RALPH WALDO EMERSON

Every man is a borrower and a mimic, life is theatrical and literature a quotation.

RALPH WALDO EMERSON

PLEASURE Also see: ANXIETY, CHEERFULNESS, COURTESY, JOY.

That man is the richest whose pleasures are the cheapest.

HENRY DAVID THOREAU

In diving to the bottom of pleasure we bring up more gravel than pearls.

HONORÉ DE BALZAC

We tire of those pleasures we take, but never of those we give.

JOHN PETIT-SENN

The average man does not get pleasure out of an idea because he thinks it is true; he thinks it is true because he gets pleasure out of it.

H. L. MENCKEN

Whenever you are sincerely pleased you are nourished.

RALPH WALDO EMERSON

To make pleasures pleasant shorten them.

CHARLES BUXTON

POETRY Also see: ARTIST.

With me poetry has not been a purpose, but a passion.

EDGAR ALLAN POE

Writing free verse is like playing tennis with the net down.

ROBERT FROST

When power leads man toward arrogance, poetry reminds him of his limitations. When power narrows the areas of man's concern, poetry reminds him of the richness and diversity of his existence. When power corrupts, poetry cleanses.

JOHN FITZGERALD KENNEDY

Poetry comes nearer to vital truth than history.

PLATO

You will not find poetry anywhere unless you bring some of it with you.

JOSEPH JOUBERT

Poetry is the utterance of deep and heart-felt truth—the true poet is very near the oracle.

EDWIN HUBBEL CHAPIN

POLITICS Also see: DEFEAT, GOVERNMENT, INDEPENDENCE, PARTY, POWER, PROFESSION, PROSPERITY, REVOLUTION.

Politics is a profession; a serious, complicated and, in its true sense, a noble one.

DWIGHT D. EISENHOWER

Politics is too serious a matter to be left to the politicians.

CHARLES DE GAULLE

Politics is the conduct of public affairs for private advantage.

AMBROSE BIERCE

A politician thinks of the next election; a statesman, of the next generation.

J. F. CLARKE

Politicans are the same all over. They promise to build a bridge even where there is no river.

NIKITA KHRUSHCHEV

The political world is stimulating. It's the most interesting thing you can do. It beats following the dollar.

JOHN FITZGERALD KENNEDY

POLLUTION *Also see:* CONSERVATION.

Among these treasures of our land is water—fast becoming our most valuable, most prized, most critical resource. A blessing where properly used—but it can bring devastation and ruin when left uncontrolled.

DWIGHT D. EISENHOWER

We in Government have begun to recognize the critical work which must be done at all levels—local, State and Federal—in ending the pollution of our waters.

ROBERT F. KENNEDY

The American people have a right to air that they and their children can breathe without fear.

LYNDON BAINES JOHNSON

As soils are depleted, human health, vitality and intelligence go with them.

LOUIS BROMFIELD

POPULARITY *Also see:* FAME, REPUTATION.

Avoid popularity if you would have peace.

ABRAHAM LINCOLN

Popular opinion is the greatest lie in the world.

THOMAS CARLYLE

Popularity is exhausting. The life of the party almost always winds up in a corner with an overcoat over him.

WILSON MIZNER

True popularity is not the popularity which is followed after, but the popularity which follows after.

LORD MANSFIELD

To his dog, every man is Napoleon; hence the constant popularity of dogs.

ALDOUS HUXLEY

Whatever is popular deserves attention.

JAMES MACKINTOSH

Avoid popularity; it has many snares, and no real benefit.

WILLIAM PENN

POPULATION *Also see:* BIRTH, BIRTH CONTROL.

We have been God-like in our planned breeding of our domesticated plants and animals, but we have been rabbit-like in our unplanned breeding of ourselves.

ARNOLD JOSEPH TOYNBEE

The hungry world cannot be fed until and unless the growth of its resources and the growth of its population come into balance. Each man and woman—and each nation—must make decisions of conscience and policy in the face of this great problem.

LYNDON BAINES JOHNSON

POVERTY *Also see:* AVARICE, LUXURY, PRIDE, TAX, WANT.

Poverty is the step-mother of genius.

JOSH BILLINGS

Poverty often deprives a man of all spirit and virtue; it is hard for an empty bag to stand upright.

BENJAMIN FRANKLIN

I thank fate for having made me born poor. Poverty taught me the true value of the gifts useful to life.

ANATOLE FRANCE

For every talent that poverty has stimulated it has blighted a hundred.

JOHN W. GARDNER

In a country well governed poverty is something to be ashamed of. In a country badly governed wealth is something to be ashamed of.

CONFUCIUS

Hard as it may appear in individual cases, dependent poverty ought to be held disraceful.

THOMAS ROBERT MALTHUS

The child was diseased at birth, stricken with a hereditary ill that only the most vital men are able to shake off. I mean poverty—the most deadly and prevalent of all diseases.

EUGENE O'NEILL

POWER *Also see:* ABUSE, AUTHORITY, BEAUTY, DESIRE, FORCE, PARTY, PATIENCE, POETRY, VIOLENCE.

Most powerful is he who has himself in his own power.

SENECA

We cannot live by power, and a culture that seeks to live by it becomes brutal and sterile. But we can die without it.

MAX LERNER

Man is born to seek power, yet his actual condition makes him a slave to the power of others.

HANS J. MORGENTHAU

I know of nothing sublime which is not some modification of power.

EDMUND BURKE

There is no knowledge that is not power.

RALPH WALDO EMERSON

We often say how impressive power is. But I do not find it impressive at all. The guns and the bombs, the rockets and the warships, are all symbols of human failure. They are necessary symbols. They protect what we cherish. But they are witness to human folly.

LYNDON BAINES JOHNSON

Power will intoxicate the best hearts, as wine the strongest heads. No man is wise enough, nor good enough to be trusted with unlimited power.

CHARLES CALEB COLTON

PRAISE *Also see:* FLATTERY, MODESTY.

When we disclaim praise, it is only showing our desire to be praised a second time.

FRANÇOIS DE LA ROCHEFOUCAULD

Get someone else to blow your horn and the sound will carry twice as far.

WILL ROGERS

He who praises everybody, praises nobody.

SAMUEL JOHNSON

I can live for two months on a good compliment.

MARK TWAIN

PRAYER

Practical prayer is harder on the soles of your shoes than on the knees of your trousers.

AUSTIN O'MALLEY

Certain thoughts are prayers. There are moments when, whatever be the attitude of the body, the soul is on its knees.

VICTOR HUGO

No man ever prayed heartily without learning something.

RALPH WALDO EMERSON

God hears no more than the heart speaks; and if the heart be dumb, God will certainly be deaf.

THOMAS BROOKS

Pray as if everything depended on God, and work as if everything depended upon man.

FRANCIS CARDINAL SPELLMAN

Prayer is a confession of one's own unworthiness and weakness.

MAHATMA GANDHI

PREACHING Also see: SIN.

Only the sinner has a right to preach.

CHRISTOPHER MORLEY

The world is dying for want, not of good preaching, but of good hearing.

GEORGE DANA BOARDMAN

One of the proofs of the divinity of our gospel is the preaching it has survived.

WOODROW WILSON

The minister's brain is often the "poor-box" of the church.

EDWIN PERCY WHIPPLE

The test of a preacher is that his congregation goes away saying, not "What a lovely sermon" but, "I will do something!"

ST. FRANCIS DE SALES

The best of all the preachers are the men who live their creeds.

EDGAR A. GUEST

PREJUDICE Also see: BIGOTRY, INTOLERANCE, QUESTION, RACE.

To lay aside all prejudices, is to lay aside all principles. He who is destitute of principles is governed by whims.

FRIEDRICH H. JACOBI

Prejudice, which sees what it pleases, cannot see what is plain.

AUBREY T. DE VERA

A prejudice is a vagrant opinion without visible means of support.

AMBROSE BIERCE

When dealing with people, remember you are not dealing with creatures of logic, but with creatures of emotion, creatures bristling with prejudice and motivated by pride and vanity.

DALE CARNEGIE

The time is past when Christians in America can take a long spoon and hand the gospel to the black man out the back door.

MORDECAI W. JOHNSON

He that is possessed with a prejudice is possessed with a devil, and one of the worst kinds of devils, for it shuts out the truth, and often leads to ruinous error.

TRYON EDWARDS

PRESENT Also see: PAST, TIME.

He to whom the present is the only thing that is present, knows nothing of the age in which he lives.

OSCAR WILDE

The future is purchased by the present.

SAMUEL JOHNSON

Those who live to the future must always appear selfish to those who live to the present.

RALPH WALDO EMERSON

PRESIDENT

No man will ever bring out of the Presidency the reputation which carries him into it.

THOMAS JEFFERSON

I seek the Presidency not because it offers me a chance to be somebody but because it offers a chance to do something.

RICHARD M. NIXON

The American presidency will demand more than ringing manifestos issued from the rear of the battle. It will demand that the President place himself in the very thick of the fight; that he care passionately about the fate of the people he leads . . .

JOHN FITZGERALD KENNEDY

President means chief servant.

MAHATMA GANDHI

My most fervent prayer is to be a President who can make it possible for every boy in this land to grow to manhood by loving his country—instead of dying for it.

LYNDON BAINES JOHNSON

When I was a boy I was told that anybody could become President; I'm beginning to believe.

CLARENCE DARROW

PRETENSION Also see: OSTENTATION, PRIDE, SCANDAL, SELF-CONFIDENCE.

The only good in pretending is the fun we get out of fooling ourselves that we fool somebody.

BOOTH TARKINGTON

The hardest tumble a man can make is to fall over his own bluff.

AMBROSE BIERCE

When there is much pretension, much has been borrowed; nature never pretends.

JOHANN KASPAR LAVATER

Pretension almost always overdoes the original, and hence exposes itself.

HOSEA BALLOU

We had better appear what we are, than affect to appear what we are not.

FRANÇOIS DE LA ROCHEFOUCAULD

PRIDE *Also see:* OSTENTATION, PRETENSION, RIVALRY, TAX, VANITY.

There is this paradox in pride—it makes some men ridiculous, but prevents others from becoming so.

CHARLES CALEB COLTON

Pride is an admission of weakness; it secretly fears all competition and dreads all rivals.

FULTON J. SHEEN

The infinitely little have a pride infinitely great.

VOLTAIRE

To be proud and inaccessible is to be timid and weak.

JEAN BAPTISTE MASILLON

Pride is seldom delicate; it will please itself with very mean advantages.

SAMUEL JOHNSON

PRIVACY *Also see:* COMMUNICATION, LONELINESS, SOLITUDE.

Privacy is the right to be alone—the most comprehensive of rights, and the right most valued by civilized man.

LOUIS D. BRANDEIS

Modern Americans are so exposed, peered at, inquired about, and spied upon as to be increasingly without privacy—members of a naked society and denizens of a goldfish bowl.

EDWARD V. LONG

Far from the madding crowd's ignoble strife.

THOMAS GRAY

PROCRASTINATION *Also see:* ACTION, IDLENESS, NEGLECT.

Procrastination is the art of keeping up with yesterday.

DON MARQUIS

Even if you're on the right track—you'll get run over if you just sit there.

ARTHUR GODFREY

Never leave that till tomorrow which you can do today.

BENJAMIN FRANKLIN

Putting off an easy thing makes it hard, and putting off a hard one makes it impossible.

GEORGE H. LORIMER

PRODUCTION *Also see:* ECONOMY, EFFICIENCY, INDUSTRY, LABOR.

Production is the only answer to inflation.

CHESTER BOWLES

The goose lays the golden egg. Payrolls make consumers.

GEORGE HUMPHEY

It is one of the greatest errors to put any limitation upon production. ... We have not the power to produce more than there is a potential to consume.

LOUIS D. BRANDEIS

Unless each man produces more than he receives, increases his output, there will be less for him than all the others.

BERNARD M. BARUCH

PROFANITY *Also see:* WICKEDNESS.

Nothing is greater, or more fearful sacrilege than to prostitute the great name of God to the petulancy of an idle tongue.

JEREMY TAYLOR

The foolish and wicked practice of profane cursing and swearing is a vice so mean and low that every person of sense and character detests and despises it.

GEORGE WASHINGTON

Profaneness is a brutal vice. He who indulges in it is no gentleman.

EDWIN HUBBEL CHAPIN

PROFESSION *Also see:* MEDICINE, POLITICS.

I hold every man a debtor to his profession.

FRANCIS BACON

Medicine is my lawful wife and literature my mistress; when I get tired of one, I spend the night with the other.

ANTON CHEKHOV

In all professions each affects a look and an exterior to appear what he wishes the world to believe that he is. Thus we may say that the whole world is made up of appearances.

FRANÇOIS DE LA ROCHEFOUCAULD

We forget that the most successful statesmen have been professionals. Lincoln was a professional politician.

FELIX FRANKFURTER

PROFIT ... See GAIN

PROGRESS *Also see:* AMERICA, BEHAVIOR, DIFFERENCE, DIFFICULTY, DISCONTENT, EDUCATION, IMPROVEMENT, ORDER, SELF-IMPROVEMENT.

He that is good, will infallibly become better, and he that is bad, will as certainly become worse; for vice, virtue and time are three things that never stand still.

CHARLES CALEB COLTON

All that is human must retrograde if it does not advance.

EDWARD GIBBON

The reasonable man adapts himself to the world, but the unreasonable man tries to adapt the world to him—therefore, all progress depends upon the unreasonable man.

SAMUEL BUTLER

Social advance depends as much upon the process through which it is secured as upon the result itself.

JANE ADDAMS

Speak softly, and carry a big stick; you will go far.

THEODORE ROOSEVELT

Those who work most for the world's advancement are the ones who demand least.

HENRY DOHERTY

PROMISE ... See VOW

PROPAGANDA Also see: ART, DECEIT, RELIGION, TRUTH, WORD.

Propaganda must not serve the truth, especially insofar as it might bring out something favorable for the opponent.

ADOLF HITLER

Some of mankind's most terrible misdeeds have been committed under the spell of certain magic words or phrases.

JAMES BRYANT CONANT

A propagandist is a specialist in selling attitudes and opinions.

HANS SPEIER

We have made the Reich by propaganda.

JOSEPH PAUL GOEBBELS

Today the world is the victim of propaganda because people are not intellectually competent. More than anything the United States needs effective citizens competent to do their own thinking.

WILLIAM MATHER LEWIS

PROPERTY Also see: WEALTH.

Mine is better than ours.

BENJAMIN FRANKLIN

Private property began the instant somebody had a mind of his own.

E. E. CUMMINGS

Property is the fruit of labor; property is desirable; it is a positive good in the world.

ABRAHAM LINCOLN

Ultimately property rights and personal rights are the same thing.

CALVIN COOLIDGE

What we call real estate—the solid ground to build a house on—is the broad foundation on which nearly all the guilt of this world rests.

NATHANIAL HAWTHORNE

It is preoccupation with possession, more than anything else, that prevents men from living freely and nobly.

BERTRAND RUSSELL

PROSPERITY Also see: ADVERSITY, ADVICE, WEALTH.

Prosperity makes friends, adversity tries them.

PUBLILIUS SYRUS

Prosperity is something the businessmen created for politicians to take credit for.

BRUNSWICK (GA.) PILOT

The prosperous man is never sure that he is loved for himself.

LUCAN

Prosperity is the surest breeder of insolence I know.

MARK TWAIN

When prosperity comes, do not use all of it.

CONFUCIUS

PROVIDENCE Also see: GOD, FATE.

There are many scapegoats for our sins, but the most popular is providence.

MARK TWAIN

Friends, I agree with you in Providence; but I believe in the Providence of the most men, the largest purse, and the longest cannon.

ABRAHAM LINCOLN

God's providence is on the side of clear heads.

HENRY WARD BEECHER

The longer I live, the more convincing proofs I see of this truth, that God governs in the affairs of man; and if a sparrow cannot fall to the ground without his notice, is it probable that an empire can rise without his aid?

BENJAMIN FRANKLIN

PRUDENCE Also see: MODERATION, QUESTION, WISDOM.

The prudence of the best heads is often defeated by the tenderness of the best of hearts.

HENRY FIELDING

It is by the goodness of God that in our country we have those three unspeakably precious things: freedom of speech, freedom of conscience, and the prudence never to practice either.

MARK TWAIN

Prudence is an attitude that keeps life safe, but does not often make it happy.

SAMUEL JOHNSON

There is nothing more imprudent than excessive prudence.

CHARLES CALEB COLTON

PSYCHOLOGY Also see: MIND

Anybody who is 25 or 30 years old has physical scars from all sorts of things, from tuberculosis to polio. It's the same with the mind.

MOSES R. KAUFMAN

Psychoanalysis has changed American psychology from a diagnostic to a therapeutic science, not because so many patients are cured by the psychoanalytic technique, but because of the new understanding of psychiatric patients it has given us, and the new and different concept of illness and health.

KARL A. MENNINGER

PUBLIC *Also see:* PUBLICITY, TASTE.

If there's anything a public servant hates to do it's something for the public.

KIN HUBBARD

The public is wiser than the wisest critic.

GEORGE BANCROFT

In a free and republican government, you cannot restrain the voice of the multitude.

GEORGE WASHINGTON

That miscellaneous collection of a few wise and many foolish individuals, called the public.

JOHN STUART MILL

The public have neither shame nor gratitude.

WILLIAM HAZLITT

The public is a ferocious beast: one must either chain it up or flee from it.

VOLTAIRE

PUBLICITY *Also see:* ADVERTISING, NEWSPAPER.

Without publicity there can be no public support, and without public support every nation must decay.

BENJAMIN DISRAELI

Publicity, publicity, PUBLICITY is the greatest moral factor and force in our public life.

JOSEPH PULITZER

Modern business and persons and organizations that seek publicity must recognize their obligations to the public and to the press.

HENRY F. WOODS, JR.

PUNCTUALITY

I could never think well of a man's intellectual or moral character, if he was habitually unfaithful to his appointments.

NATHANIEL EMMONS

Unfaithfulness in the keeping of an appointment is an act of clear dishonesty. You may as well borrow a person's money as his time.

HORACE MANN

Punctuality is one of the cardinal business virtues: always insist on it in your subordinates.

DON MARQUIS

PUNISHMENT *Also see:* CRIME, DISCONTENT, LYING, PAIN, SIN.

Punishment is justice for the unjust.

ST. AUGUSTINE

We are not punished for our sins, but by them.

ELBERT HUBBARD

If punishment makes not the will supple it hardens the offender.

JOHN LOCKE

It is as expedient that a wicked man be punished as that a sick man be cured by a physician; for all chastisement is a kind of medicine.

PLATO

Crime and punishment grow out of one stem.

RALPH WALDO EMERSON

PURPOSE *Also see:* AIM, FIRMNESS, IDEAL, INSTINCT, SUCCESS.

The secret of success is constancy to purpose.

BENJAMIN DISRALLI

Great minds have purposes, others have wishes.

WASHINGTON IRVING

Only the consciousness of a purpose that is mightier than any man and worthy of all men can fortify and inspirit and compose the souls of men.

WALTER LIPPMANN

The good man is the man who, no matter how morally unworthy he has been, is moving to become better.

JOHN DEWEY

PURSUIT *Also see:* ADVENTURE, ENTHUSIASM, MYSTERY.

The rapture of pursuing is the prize the vanquished gain.

HENRY WADSWORTH LONGFELLOW

The crowning fortune of a man is to be born to some pursuit which finds him employment and happiness, whether it be to make baskets, or broadswords, or canals, or statues, or songs.

RALPH WALDO EMERSON

Men tire themselves in pursuit of rest.

LAURENCE STERNE

QUALITY *Also see:* PUBLIC, VALUE, WORTH.

We are never so ridiculous by the qualities we have, as by those we affect to have.

FRANÇOIS DE LA ROCHEFOUCAULD

It is the quality of our work which will please God and not the quantity.

MAHATMA GANDHI

Nothing endures but personal qualities.

WALT WHITMAN

I think there is only one quality worse than hardness of heart, and that is softness of head.

THEODORE ROOSEVELT

Many individuals have, like uncut diamonds, shining qualities beneath a rough exterior.

JUVENAL

QUARREL *Also see:* ANGER, ARGUMENT, CHEERFULNESS, COWARDICE.

When chickens quit quarreling over their food they often find that there is enough for all of them. I wonder if it might not be the same with the human race.

DON MARQUIS

People generally quarrel because they cannot argue.

GILBERT K. CHESTERTON

He that blows the coals in quarrels he has nothing to do with has no right to complain if the sparks fly in his face.

BENJAMIN FRANKLIN

Two cannot fall out if one does not choose.

SPANISH PROVERB

A long dispute means that both parties are wrong.

VOLTAIRE

I never take my own side in a quarrel.

ROBERT FROST

In quarreling the truth is always lost.

PUBLILIUS SYRUS

QUESTION *Also see:* CONVERSATION, CURIOSITY, DOUBT.

No man really becomes a fool until he stops asking questions.

CHARLES STEINMETZ

A fool may ask more questions in an hour than a wise man can answer in seven years.

ENGLISH PROVERB

No question is so difficult to answer as that to which the answer is obvious.

GEORGE BERNARD SHAW

Man will not live without answers to his questions.

HANS MORGENTHAU

Judge a man by his questions rather than his answers.

VOLTAIRE

He must be very ignorant for he answers every question he is asked.

VOLTAIRE

A prudent question is one-half of wisdom.

FRANCIS BACON

QUIET *Also see:* REST, SILENCE.

The good and the wise lead quiet lives.

EURIPIDES

To have a quiet mind is to possess one's mind wholly; to have a calm spirit is to possess one's self.

HAMILTON MABIE

An inability to stay quiet is one of the conspicuous failings of mankind.

WALTER BAGEHOT

God gives quietness at last.

JOHN GREENLEAF WHITTIER

Quiet is what home would be without children.

ANONYMOUS

Stillness of person and steadiness of features are signal marks of good breeding.

OLIVER WENDELL HOLMES

QUOTATION *Also see:* MAXIM, PLAGIARISM, WRITER.

The profoundest thought or passion sleeps as in a mine, until an equal mind and heart finds and publishes it.

RALPH WALDO EMERSON

He presents me with what is always an acceptable gift who brings me news of a great thought before unknown. He enriches me without impoverishing himself.

RALPH WALDO EMERSON

Certain brief sentences are peerless in their ability to give one the feeling that nothing remains to be said.

JEAN ROSTAND

Next to the originator of a good sentence is the first quoter of it.

RALPH WALDO EMERSON

RACE *Also see:* DIGNITY, PREJUDICE.

Mere connection with what is known as a superior race will not permanently carry an individual forward unless the individual has worth.

BOOKER T. WASHINGTON

The difference of race is one of the reasons why I fear war may always exist; because race implies difference, difference implies superiority, and superiority leads to predominance.

BENJAMIN DISRAELI

The existence of any pure race with special endowments is a myth, as is the belief that there are races all of whose members are foredoomed to eternal inferiority.

FRANZ BOAS

A heavy guilt rests upon us for what the whites of all nations have done to the colored peoples. When we do good to them, it is not benevolence—it is atonement.

ALBERT SCHWEITZER

At the heart of racism is the religious assertion that God made a creative mistake when He brought some people into being.

FRIEDRICH OTTO HERTZ

When white and black and brown and every other color decide they're going to live together as Christians, then and only then are we going to see an end to these troubles.

BARRY M. GOLDWATER

RADICAL *Also see:* EXTREMES, REBELLION, REVOLUTION, VIOLENCE.

A radical is one who speaks the truth.

CHARLES A. LINDBERGH

If a man is right, he can't be too radical; if he is wrong, he can't be too conservative.

JOSH BILLINGS

A radical man is a man with both feet firmly planted in the air.

FRANKLIN DELANO ROOSEVELT

I am trying to do two things: dare to be a radical and not a fool, which is a matter of no small difficulty.

JAMES A. GARFIELD

RANK *Also see:* ANCESTRY, CLASS.

It is an interesting question how far men would retain their relative rank if they were divested of their clothes.

HENRY DAVID THOREAU

Rank and riches are chains of gold, but still chains.

GIOVANNI RUFFINI

To be vain of one's rank or place, is to show that one is below it.

STANISLAS I

What men prize most is a privilege, even if it be that of chief mourner at a funeral.

JAMES RUSSELL LOWELL

READING *Also see:* BOOK, LITERATURE, NEWSPAPER.

I divide all readers into two classes: those who read to remember and those who read to forget.

WILLIAM LYON PHELPS

Reading is to the mind what exercise is to the body.

JOSEPH ADDISON

We should be as careful of the books we read, as of the company we keep. The dead very often have more power than the living.

TRYON EDWARDS

No entertainment is so cheap as reading, nor any pleasure so lasting.

MARY WORTLEY MONTAGU

Reading is a basic tool in the living of a good life.

MORTIMER J. ADLER

Read the best books first, or you may not have a chance to read them all.

HENRY DAVID THOREAU

REALITY *Also see:* APPEARANCE, DREAM, ILLUSION, TRUTH.

Facts are facts and will not disappear on account of your likes.

JAWAHARLAL NEHRU

A theory must be tempered with reality.

JAWAHARLAL NEHRU

I accept reality and dare not question it.

WALT WHITMAN

The realist is the man, who having weighed all the visible factors in a given situation and having found that the odds are against him, decides that fighting is useless.

RAOUL DE SALES

REASON *Also see:* ANGER, ARGUMENT, COMMON SENSE, FORCE, HEART, LOGIC, MIND, TEMPER, UNDERSTANDING.

Most of our so-called reasoning consists in finding arguments for going on believing as we already do.

JAMES ROBINSON

Reason has never failed men. Only force and repression have made the wrecks in the world.

WILLIAM ALLEN WHITE

Man has received direct from God only one instrument wherewith to know himself and to know his relation to the universe—he has no other—and that instrument is reason.

LEO TOLSTOI

Man is a reasoning rather than a reasonable animal.

ALEXANDER HAMILTON

An appeal to the reason of the people has never been known to fail in the long run.

JAMES RUSSELL LOWELL

Error of opinion may be tolerated where reason is left free to admit it.

THOMAS JEFFERSON

Reason can in general do more than blind force.

GALLUS

Many are destined to reason wrongly; others, not to reason at all; and others, to persecute those who do reason.

VOLTAIRE

REBELLION *Also see:* DISSENT, OPPRESSION, REVOLUTION, RIOT, TREASON.

Rebellion against tyrants is obedience to God.

BENJAMIN FRANKLIN

As long as the world shall last there will be wrongs, and if no man objected and no man rebelled, those wrongs would last forever.

CLARENCE DARROW

An oppressed people are authorized whenever they can to rise and break their fetters.

HENRY CLAY

Men seldom, or rather never for a length of time and deliberately, rebel against anything that does not deserve rebelling against.

THOMAS CARLYLE

It doesn't take a majority to make a rebellion; it takes only a few determined leaders and a sound cause.

H. L. MENCKEN

REFLECTION . . . See THOUGHT

REFORM *Also see:* IMPROVEMENT, PROGRESS.

Nothing so needs reforming as other people's habits.

MARK TWAIN

Reform must come from within, not from without. You cannot legislate for virtue.

JAMES CARDINAL GIBBONS

What is a man born for but to be a reformer, a remaker of what has been made, a denouncer of lies, a restorer of truth and good?

RALPH WALDO EMERSON

The church is always trying to get other people to reform; it might not be a bad idea to reform itself.

MARK TWAIN

I think I am better than the people who are trying to reform me.

ED HOWE

REGRET *Also see:* REMORSE.

Regret is an appalling waste of energy; you can't build on it; it's only good for wallowing in.

KATHERINE MANSFIELD

I only regret that I have but one life to give for my country.

NATHAN HALE

For of all sad words of tongue or pen, the saddest are these: "It might have been!"

JOHN GREENLEAF WHITTIER

RELIGION *Also see:* CHRISTIANITY, CHURCH and
STATE, CONSCIENCE,
HEAVEN, HYPROCRISY,
JUDAISM, PREACHING.

All religions must be tolerated, for every man must get to heaven in his own way.

FREDERICK THE GREAT

Many have quarreled about religion that never practiced it.

BENJAMIN FRANKLIN

Religion is the sum of the expansive impulses of a being.

HENRY H. ELLIS

Every man, either to his terror or consolation, has some sense of religion.

JAMES HARRINGTON

Science without religion is lame; religion without science is blind.

ALBERT EINSTEIN

Measure not men by Sundays, without regarding what they do all the week after.

THOMAS FULLER

To swallow and follow, whether old doctrine or new propaganda, is a weakness still dominating the human mind.

CHARLOTTE P. GILBERT

Our hope of immortality does not come from any religions, but nearly all religions come from that hope.

ROBERT GREEN INGERSOLL

You can change your faith without changing gods, and vice versa.

STANISLAW J. LEC

REMORSE *Also see:* GRIEF, GUILT, REGRET.

Remorse is the pain of sin.

THEODORE PARKER

To be left alone, and face to face with my own crime, had been just retribution.

HENRY WADSWORTH LONGFELLOW

Remorse is the echo of a lost virtue.

EDWARD G. BULWER-LYTTON

Remorse: beholding heaven and feeling hell.

GEORGE MOORE

REPENTANCE *Also see:* CONFESSION, GUILT, SIN.

It is much easier to repent of sins that we have committed than to repent of those that we intend to commit.

JOSH BILLINGS

Of all acts of man repentance is the most divine. The greatest of all faults is to be conscious of none.

THOMAS CARLYLE

True repentance is to cease from sinning.

AMBROSE OF MILAN

Bad men are full of repentance.

ARISTOTLE

Great is the difference betwixt a man's being frightened at, and humbled for his sins.

THOMAS FULLER

REPETITION *Also see:* LOQUACITY.

Iteration, like friction, is likely to generate heat instead of progress.

GEORGE ELIOT

There is no absurdity so palpable but that it may be firmly planted in the human head if you only begin to inculcate it before the age of five, by constantly repeating it with an air of great solemnity.

ARTHUR SCHOPENHAUER

REPUTATION *Also see:* CHARACTER, FAME, NAME,
PERSONALITY, SLANDER.

A reputation once broken may possibly be repaired, but the world will always keep their eyes on the spot where the crack was.

JOSEPH HALL

Good will, like a good name, is got by many actions, and lost by one.

LORD JEFFREY

Associate with men of good quality if you esteem your own reputation; for it is better to be alone than in bad company.

GEORGE WASHINGTON

A doctor's reputation is made by the number of eminent men who die under his care.

GEORGE BERNARD SHAW

The two most precious things this side of the grave are our reputation and our life. But it is to be lamented that the most contemptible whisper may deprive us of the one, and the weakest weapon of the other.

CHARLES CALEB COLTON

What people say behind your back is your standing in the community.

ED HOWE

RESENTMENT . . . See DISCONTENT

RESIGNATION *Also see:* ENDURANCE,
RETIREMENT.

Resignation is the courage of Christian sorrow.

ALEXANDER VINET

A wise man cares not for what he cannot have.

JACK HERBERT

For after all, the best thing one can do when it's raining is to let it rain.

HENRY WADSWORTH LONGFELLOW

What is called resignation is confirmed desperation.

HENRY DAVID THOREAU

We cannot conquer fate and necessity, yet we can yield to them in such a manner as to be greater than if we could.

WALTER S. LANDOR

RESOLUTION Also see: AIM, FIRMNESS, PURPOSE, SECURITY, VOW.

The block of granite which is an obstacle in the pathway of the weak, becomes a stepping-stone in the pathway of the strong.

THOMAS CARLYLE

Either I will find a way, or I will make one.

PHILIP SIDNEY

It is always during a passing state of mind that we make lasting resolutions.

MARCEL PROUST

Resolve to perform what you ought; perform without fail what you resolve.

BENJAMIN FRANKLIN

Resolve and thou art free.

HENRY WADSWORTH LONGFELLOW

RESPECT Also see: ADMIRATION, TYRANNY.

I must respect the opinions of others even if I disagree with them.

HERBERT HENRY LEHMAN

I don't know what a scoundrel is like, but I know what a respectable man is like, and it's enough to make one's flesh creep.

J. M. MAISTRE

Men are respectable only as they respect.

RALPH WALDO EMERSON

RESPONSIBILITY Also see: DISCIPLINE, DUTY, RIGHTS.

Responsibility is the thing people dread most of all. Yet it is the one thing in the world that develops us, give us manhood or womanhood fibre.

FRANK CRANE

Responsibility educates.

WENDELL PHILLIPS

Every human being has a work to carry on within, duties to perform abroad, influence to exert, which are peculiarly his, and which no conscience but his own can teach.

WILLIAM ELLERY CHANNING

The only way to get rid of responsibilities is to discharge them.

WALTER S. ROBERTSON

Responsibility is the price of greatness.

WINSTON CHURCHILL

REST Also see: SLEEP.

Eternal rest sounds comforting in the pulpit; well, you try it once, and see how heavy time will hang on your hands.

MARK TWAIN

Rest is a good thing, but boredom is its brother.

VOLTAIRE

Rest: the sweet sauce of labor.

PLUTARCH

Put off thy cares with thy clothes; so shall thy rest strengthen thy labor, and so thy labor sweeten thy rest.

FRANCIS QUARLES

RESULT Also see: ABILITY, CAUSE, END and MEANS

Results! Why, man, I have gotten a lot of results. I know several thousand things that won't work.

THOMAS A. EDISON

It has been my observation and experience, and that of my family, that nothing human works out well.

DON MARQUIS

The man who gets the most satisfactory results is not always the man with the most brilliant single mind, but rather the man who can best coordinate the brains and talents of his associates.

W. ALTON JONES

RETIREMENT Also see: LABOR, RESIGNATION, REST, WORK.

The worst of work nowadays is what happens to people when they cease to work.

GILBERT K. CHESTERTON

Don't think of retiring from the world until the world will be sorry that you retire.

SAMUEL JOHNSON

The best time to start thinking about your retirement is before the boss does.

ANONYMOUS

A man is known by the company that keeps him on after retirement age.

ANONYMOUS

REVENGE ... See VENGEANCE

REVERIE Also see: DREAM, ILLUSION.

Sit in reverie and watch the changing color of the waves that break upon the idle seashore of the mind.

HENRY WADSWORTH LONGFELLOW

To lose one's self in reverie, one must be either very happy, or very unhappy. Reverie is the child of extremes.

ANTOINE RIVAROL

Reverie is when ideas float in our mind without reflection or regard of the understanding.

JOHN LOCKE

Do anything rather than give yourself to reverie.

WILLIAM ELLERY CHANNING

REVOLUTION *Also see:* CHANGE, GOVERNMENT, TYRANNY, VIOLENCE.

Revolution: in politics, an abrupt change in the form of mis-government.

AMBROSE BIERCE

Revolutions are not trifles, but spring from trifles.

ARISTOTLE

Make revolution a parent of settlement, and not a nursery of future revolutions.

EDMUND BURKE

Those who make peaceful revolution impossible will make violent revolution inevitable.

JOHN FITZGERALD KENNEDY

Any people anywhere being inclined and having the power have the right to rise up and shake off the existing government, and force a new one that suits them better.

ABRAHAM LINCOLN

Revolutions have never lightened the burden of tyranny: they have only shifted it to another shoulder.

GEORGE BERNARD SHAW

It is impossible to predict the time and progress of revolution. It is governed by its own more or less mysterious laws.

LENIN

REWARD *Also see:* ACHIEVEMENT, AMBITION, SUCCESS.

The reward of a thing well done is to have done it.

RALPH WALDO EMERSON

No man, who continues to add something to the material, intellectual and moral well-being of the place in which he lives, is left long without proper reward.

BOOKER T. WASHINGTON

He that does good for good's sake seeks neither paradise nor reward, but he is sure of both in the end.

WILLIAM PENN

Not in rewards, but in the strength to strive, the blessing lies.

J. T. TOWBRIDGE

The effects of our actions may be postponed but they are never lost. There is an inevitable reward for good deeds and an inescapable punishment for bad. Meditate upon this truth, and seek always to earn good wages from Destiny.

WU MING FU

No person was ever honored for what he received. Honor has been the reward for what he gave.

CALVIN COOLIDGE

Let the motive be in the deed and not in the event. Be not one whose motive for action is the hope of reward.

KREESHNA

RIDICULE *Also see:* ABSURDITY, IRONY, JESTING, SARCASM.

Mockery is the weapon of those who have no other.

HUBERT PIERIOT

Ridicule is the first and last argument of fools.

CHARLES SIMMONS

Resort is had to ridicule only when reason is against us.

THOMAS JEFFERSON

Ridicule is the language of the devil.

THOMAS CARLYLE

Man learns more readily and remembers more willingly what excites his ridicule than what deserves esteem and respect.

HORACE

RIGHTS *Also see:* CUSTOM, DIGNITY, EQUALITY, FREEDOM OF THE PRESS, PRIVACY, PROPERTY, WAGE.

Many a person seems to think it isn't enough for the government to guarantee him the pursuit of happiness. He insists it also run interference for him.

ANONYMOUS

No man was ever endowed with a right without being at the same time saddled with a responsibility.

GERALD W. JOHNSON

We hold these truths to be self-evident, that all men are created equal, that they are endowed by their Creator with certain unalienable rights, that among these are life, liberty, and the pursuit of happiness.

THOMAS JEFFERSON

No man has a right to do what he pleases, except when he pleases to do right.

CHARLES SIMMONS

In giving rights to others which belong to them, we give rights to ourselves and to our country.

JOHN FITZGERALD KENNEDY

From the equality of rights springs identity of our highest interests; you cannot subvert your neighbor's rights without striking a dangerous blow at your own.

CARL SCHURZ

RIOT *Also see:* MOB, REBELLION, REVOLUTION, VIOLENCE.

No nation, no matter how enlightened, can endure criminal violence. If we cannot control it, we are admitting to the world and to ourselves that our laws are no more than a facade that crumbles when the winds of crisis rise.

ALAN BIBLE

The poor suffer twice at the rioter's hands. First, his destructive fury scars their neighborhood; second, the atmosphere of accomodation and consent is changed to one of hostility and resentment.

LYNDON BAINES JOHNSON

If we resort to lawlessness, the only thing we can hope for is civil war, untold bloodshed, and the end of our dreams.

ARCHIE LEE MOORE

RISK *Also see:* DANGER.

The policy of being too cautious is the greatest risk of all.

JAWAHARLAL NEHRU

The willingness to take risks is our grasp of faith.

GEORGE E. WOODBERRY

Don't be afraid to take a big step if one is indicated; you can't cross a chasm in two small jumps.

WILLIAM LLOYD GEORGE

Every noble acquisition is attended with its risks; he who fears to encounter the one must not expect to obtain the other.

METASTASIO

Risk is a part of God's game, alike for men and nations.

GEORGE E. WOODBERRY

Who bravely dares must sometimes risk a fall.

TOBIAS G. SMOLLETT

RIVALRY *Also see:* AMBITION, JEALOUSY, SUCCESS.

In ambition, as in love, the successful can afford to be indulgent toward their rivals.

CHRISTIAN NESTELL BOVEE

If we devote our time disparaging the products of our business rivals, we hurt business generally, reduce confidence, and increase discontent.

EDWARD N. HURLEY

It is the privilege of posterity to set matters right between those antagonists who, by their rivalry for greatness, divided a whole age.

JOSEPH ADDISON

Competition is the keen cutting edge of business, always shaving away at costs.

HENRY FORD II

Anybody can win unless there happens to be a second entry.

GEORGE ADE

RUMOR . . . See GOSSIP

SACRIFICE *Also see:* COMPROMISE, HEROISM, MARTYR.

Good manners are made up of petty sacrifices.

RALPH WALDO EMERSON

In this world it is not what we take up, but what we give up, that makes us rich.

HENRY WARD BEECHER

One-half of knowing what you want is knowing what you must give up before you get it.

SIDNEY HOWARD

They never fail who die in a great cause.

LORD BYRON

No sacrifice short of individual liberty, individual self-respect, and individual enterprise is too great a price to pay for permanent peace.

CLARK H. MINOR

SADNESS . . . See SORROW

SAFETY *Also see:* SECURITY, SELF-RESPECT, VIGILANCE.

It is better to be safe than sorry.

AMERICAN PROVERB

A ship in harbor is safe, but that is not what ships are built for.

JOHN A. SHEDD

He that's secure is not safe.

BENJAMIN FRANKLIN

Let the people know the truth and the country is safe.

ABRAHAM LINCOLN

SARCASM *Also see:* CRITICISM, HUMOR, IRONY, RIDICULE.

Sarcasm is the language of the devil, for which reason I have long since as good as renounced it.

THOMAS CARLYLE

Blows are sarcasms turned stupid.

GEORGE ELIOT

A sneer is the weapon of the weak.

JAMES RUSSELL LOWELL

To "leave a sting within a brother's heart."

EDWARD YOUNG

SCANDAL *Also see:* GOSSIP, REPUTATION, SLANDER.

There is so much good in the worst of us, and so much bad in the best of us, that it hardly becomes any one of us to talk about the rest of us.

ANONYMOUS

Everybody says it, and what everybody says must be true.

JAMES FENIMORE COOPER

How awful to reflect that what people say of us is true.

LOGAN P. SMITH

The objection of the scandalmonger is not that she tells of racy doings, but that she pretends to be indignant about them.

H. L. MENCKEN

Scandal: gossip made tedious by morality.

OSCAR WILDE

Scandal dies sooner of itself, than we could kill it.

BENJAMIN RUSH

SCHOOL . . . See EDUCATION

SCIENCE *Also see:* ART, ARTIST, FASHION, IMAGINATION, NOVELTY, RELIGiON.

Science is nothing but perception.

PLATO

Every great advance in science has issued from a new audacity of imagination.

JOHN DEWEY

It stands to the everlasting credit of science that by acting on the human mind it has overcome man's insecurity before himself and before nature.

ALBERT EINSTEIN

Science is simply common sense at its best—that is, rigidly accurate in observation, and merciless to fallacy in logic.

THOMAS HUXLEY

It will free man from his remaining chains, the chains of gravity which still tie him to this planet. It will open to him the gates of heaven.

WERNHER VON BRAUN

SECRECY Also see: TRUST.

To keep your secret is wisdom; but to expect others to keep it is folly.

SAMUEL JOHNSON

I usually get my stuff from people who promised somebody else that they would keep it a secret.

WALTER WINCHELL

Secrets are things we give to others to keep for us.

ELBERT HUBBARD

Where secrecy or mystery begins, vice or roguery is not far off.

SAMUEL JOHNSON

Trust him not with your secrets, who, when left alone in your room, turns over your papers.

JOHANN KASPAR LAVATER

SECURITY Also see: COUNTRY, MURDER, REWARD, WAGE.

Too many people are thinking of security instead of opportunity.

JAMES F. BYRNES

Each one of us requires the spur of insecurity to force us to do our best.

HAROLD W. DODDS

Happiness has many roots, but none more important than security.

E. R. STETTINIUS, JR.

Security is the priceless product of freedom. Only the strong can be secure, and only in freedom can men produce those material resources which can secure them from want at home and against aggression from abroad.

B. E. HUTCHINSON

Security is mostly a superstition. It does not exist in nature, nor do the children of men as a whole experience it. Avoiding danger is no safer in the long run than outright exposure. Life is either a daring adventure, or nothing.

HELEN KELLER

In no direction that we turn do we find ease or comfort. If we are honest and if we have the will to win we find only danger, hard work and iron resolution.

WENDELL K. WILLKIE

SELF-CONFIDENCE Also see: BEHAVIOR, CONFIDENCE, RESOLUTION.

Do not attempt to do a thing unless you are sure of yourself; but do not relinquish it simply because someone else is not sure of you.

STEWART E. WHITE

Calm self-confidence is as far from conceit as the desire to earn a decent living is remote from greed.

CHANNING POLLOCK

The history of the world is full of men who rose to leadership, by sheer force of self-confidence, bravery and tenacity.

MAHATMA GANDHI

They can conquer who believe they can.

VERGIL

SELF-CONTROL Also see: BEHAVIOR, CHARACTER, QUIET.

It is by presence of mind in untried emergencies that the native metal of man is tested.

JAMES RUSSELL LOWELL

The best time for you to hold your tongue is the time you feel you must say something or bust.

JOSH BILLINGS

Such power there is in clear-eyed self-restraint.

JAMES RUSSELL LOWELL

SELF-IMPROVEMENT Also see: CHANGE, HABIT, PURPOSE, REFORM.

There is no use whatever trying to help people who do not help themselves. You cannot push anyone up a ladder unless he be willing to climb himself.

ANDREW CARNEGIE

I tell you that as long as I can conceive something better than myself I cannot be easy unless I am striving to bring it in to existence or clearing the way for it.

GEORGE BERNARD SHAW

People seldom improve when they have no other model but themselves to copy after.

OLIVER GOLDSMITH

All of us, who are worth anything, spend our manhood in unlearning the follies, or expiating the mistakes of our youth.

PERCY BYSSHE SHELLEY

SELFISHNESS Also see: AVARICE, GALLANTRY.

The man who lives by himself and for himself is likely to be corrupted by the company he keeps.

CHARLES H. PARKHURST

He who lives only to benefit himself confers on the world a benefit when he dies.

TERTULLIAN

Selfishness is the greatest curse of the human race.

WILLIAM E. GLADSTONE

Next to the very young, the very old are the most selfish.

WILLIAM MAKEPEACE THACKERAY

SELF-KNOWLEDGE *Also see:* HEROISM, QUIET, REASON, REVERIE.

It's not only the most difficult thing to know one's self, but the most inconvenient.

JOSH BILLINGS

We know what we are, but know not what we may be.

WILLIAM SHAKESPEARE

He that knows himself, knows others; and he that is ignorant of himself, could not write a very profound lecture on other men's heads.

CHARLES CALEB COLTON

Other men's sins are before our eyes; our own are behind our backs.

SENECA

SELF-RESPECT *Also see:* LOYALTY, PRIDE, SACRIFICE.

It is necessary to the happiness of a man that he be mentally faithful to himself.

THOMAS PAINE

Never violate the sacredness of your individual self-respect.

THEODORE PARKER

He that respects himself is safe from others; He wears a coat of mail that none can pierce.

HENRY WADSWORTH LONGFELLOW

No more duty can be urged upon those who are entering the great theater of life than simple loyalty to their best convictions.

EDWIN HUBBEL CHAPIN

SELF-SACRIFICE *Also see:* GENEROSITY, HEROISM, LOYALTY, REWARD, SACRIFICE.

Self-sacrifice is the real miracle out of which all the reported miracles grow.

RALPH WALDO EMERSON

Many men have been capable of doing a wise thing, more a cunning thing, but very few a generous thing.

ALEXANDER POPE

Self-sacrifice is never entirely unselfish, for the giver never fails to receive.

DOLORES E. MCGUIRE

For anything worth having one must pay the price; and the price is always work, patience, love, self-sacrifice—no paper currency, no promises to pay, but the gold of real service.

JOHN BURROUGHS

The men and women who have the right ideals . . . are those who have the courage to strive for the happiness which comes only with labor and effort and self-sacrifice, and those whose joy in life springs in part from power of work and sense of duty.

THEODORE ROOSEVELT

SENSUALITY *Also see:* GLUTTON, REVERIE, SEX, SOUL, VICE.

The body of a sensualist is the coffin of a dead soul.

CHRISTIAN NESTELL BOVEE

Sensual pleasures are like soap bubbles, sparkling, effervescent. The pleasures of intellect are calm, beautiful, sublime, ever enduring.

JOHN H. AUGHEY

If sensuality were happiness, beasts were happier than men; but human felicity is lodged in the soul, not in the flesh.

SENECA

All sensuality is one, though it takes many forms, as all purity is one. It is the same whether a man eat, or drink, or cohabit, or sleep sensually. They are but one appetite, and we only need to see a person do any one of these things to know how great a sensualist he is.

HENRY DAVID THOREAU

Human brutes, like other beasts, find snares and poison in the provision of life, and are allured by their appetites to their destruction.

JONATHAN SWIFT

SENTIMENT *Also see:* EMOTION, PASSION, REVERIE.

A sentimentalist is simply one who desires to have the luxury of an emotion without paying for it.

OSCAR WILDE

Sentimentality is the only sentiment that rubs you the wrong way.

W. SOMERSET MAUGHAM

He who molds the public sentiment . . . makes statues and decisions possible or impossible to make.

ABRAHAM LINCOLN

Society is infested by persons who, seeing that the sentiments please, counterfeit the expression of them. These we call sentimentalists—talkers who mistake the description for the thing, saying for having.

RALPH WALDO EMERSON

Sentimentality—that's what we call the sentiment we don't share.

GRAHAM GREENE

Sentiment is the poetry of the imagination.

ALPHONSE DE LAMARTINE

SEX *Also see:* BIRTH, SENSUALITY.

Sex has become one of the most discussed subjects of modern times. The Victorians pretended it did not exist; the moderns pretend that nothing else exists.

FULTON J. SHEEN

Sex is a flame which uncontrolled may scorch; properly guided, it will light the torch of eternity.

JOSEPH FETTERMAN

Some things are better than sex, and some are worse, but there's nothing exactly like it.

W. C. FIELDS

Sex lies at the roof of life, and we can never learn to reverence life until we know how to understand sex.

HAVELOCK ELLIS

The sexes were made for each other, and only in the wise and loving union of the two is the fullness of health and duty and happiness to be expected.

WILLIAM HALL

SILENCE *Also see:* CONVERSATION, LOQUACITY, UNDERSTANDING.

Silence is the ultimate weapon of power.

CHARLES DE GAULLE

Silence is one of the hardest arguments to refute.

JOSH BILLINGS

Silence is foolish if we are wise, but wise if we are foolish.

CHARLES CALEB COLTON

Still waters run deep.

ENGLISH PROVERB

Blessed is the man who, having nothing to say, abstains from giving wordy evidence of the fact.

GEORGE ELIOT

If you keep your mouth shut you will never put your foot in it.

AUSTIN O'MALLEY

If you don't say anything, you won't be called on to repeat it.

CALVIN COOLIDGE

SIMPLICITY *Also see:* BREVITY, TASTE, TRUTH.

When thought is too weak to be simply expressed, it's clear proof that it should be rejected.

LUC DE CLAPIERS

Nothing is more simple than greatness; indeed, to be simple is to be great.

RALPH WALDO EMERSON

Everything should be made as simple as possible, but not simpler.

ALBERT EINSTEIN

The whole is simpler than the sum of its parts.

WILLARD GIBBS

Simplicity is the glory of expression.

WALT WHITMAN

SIN *Also see:* DEATH, EVIL, GUILT, HUMANITY, PREACHING, PROVIDENCE, PUNISHMENT, REMORSE, REPENTANCE, WICKEDNESS.

He that falls into sin is a man; that grieves at it, is a saint; that boasteth of it, is a devil.

THOMAS FULLER

He that is without sin among you, let him cast the first stone.

JOHN 8:7

Men are not punished for their sins, but by them.

ELBERT HUBBARD

Sin is not harmful because it is forbidden, but it is forbidden because it is hurtful.

BENJAMIN FRANKLIN

Man-like it is to fall into sin; fiendlike it is to dwell therein.

HENRY WADSWORTH LONGFELLOW

Only the sinner has a right to preach.

CHRISTOPHER MORLEY

There is no sin except stupidity.

OSCAR WILDE

SINCERITY . . . See HONESTY

SKEPTICISM *Also see:* CREDULITY, CYNIC, DOUBT, PESSIMISM.

Skeptics are never deceived.

FRENCH PROVERB

Skepticism, riddling the faith of yesterday, prepared the way for the faith of tomorrow.

ROMAIN ROLLAND

The path of sound credence is through the thick forest of skepticism.

GEORGE JEAN NATHAN

Skepticism is the chastity of the intellect.

GEORGE SANTAYANA

Skepticism: the mark and even the pose of the educated mind.

JOHN DEWEY

Great intellects are skeptical.

NIETZSCHE

SLANDER *Also see:* GOSSIP, INJURY, REPUTATION, SCANDAL.

To murder character is as truly a crime as to murder the body: the tongue of the slanderer is brother to the dagger of the assassin.

TRYON EDWARDS

I hate the man who builds his name on the ruins of another's fame.

JOHN GAY

Never throw mud. You may miss your mark, but you will have dirty hands.

JOSEPH PARKER

Slander is the revenge of a coward, and dissimulation of his defense.

SAMUEL JOHNSON

Character assassination is at once easier and surer than physical assault; and it involves far less risk for the assassin. It leaves him free to commit the same deed over and over again, and may, indeed, win him the honors of a hero even in the country of his victims.

ALAN BARTH

The worthiest people are the most injured by slander, as is the best fruit which the birds have been pecking at.

JONATHON SWIFT

SLEEP *Also see:* REST, SUCCESS.

Sleep she as sound as careless infancy.

WILLIAM SHAKESPEARE

It is a delicious moment, certainly, that of being well-nestled in bed and feeling that you shall drop gently to sleep. The good is to come, not past; the limbs are tired enough to render the remaining in one posture delightful; the labor of the day is gone.

LEIGH HUNT

Living is a disease from which sleep gives us relief eight hours a day.

CHAMFORT

Sleep is the twin of death.

HOMER

SMILE *Also see:* BEAUTY, CHEERFULNESS, KINDNESS.

Smiles form the channels of a future tear.

LORD BYRON

Wrinkles should merely indicate where smiles have been.

MARK TWAIN

Wear a smile and have friends; wear a scowl and have wrinkles. What do we live for if not to make the world less difficult for each other?

GEORGE ELIOT

There are many kinds of smiles, each having a distinct character. Some announce goodness and sweetness, others betray sarcasm, bitterness and pride; some soften the countenance by their languishing tenderness, others brighten by their spiritual vivacity.

JOHANN KASPAR LAVATER

SMOKING *Also see:* HABIT.

To cease smoking is the easiest thing I ever did; I ought to know because I've done it a thousand times.

MARK TWAIN

Much smoking kills live men and cures dead swine.

GEORGE D. PRENTICE

I tried to stop smoking cigarettes by telling myself I just didn't want to smoke, but I didn't believe myself.

BARBARA KELLY

The best way to stop smoking is to carry wet matches.

ANONYMOUS

SOCIETY *Also see:* CLASS, HUMANITY, HUMOR, MAN, POVERTY, SENTIMENT.

Society is like a lawn where every roughness is smoothed, every bramble eradicated, and where the eye is delighted by the smiling verdure of a velvet surface.

WASHINGTON IRVING

To get into the best society nowadays, one has either to feed people, amuse people, or shock people.

OSCAR WILDE

One great society alone on earth: the noble living and the noble dead.

WILLIAM WORDSWORTH

The pillars of truth and the pillars of freedom—they are the pillars of society.

HENRIK IBSEN

SOLDIER *Also see:* CITIZENSHIP, COURAGE, DRAFT, DUTY, WAR.

A good soldier, like a good horse, cannot be of a bad color.

OLIVER WENDELL HOLMES

I want to see you shoot the way you shout.

THEODORE ROOSEVELT

Every citizen should be a soldier. This was the case with the Greeks and Romans, and must be that of every free state.

THOMAS JEFFERSON

Theirs is not to make reply,
    Theirs is not to reason why,
Theirs is but to do and die.

ALFRED, LORD TENNYSON

But in a larger sense we cannot dedicate, we cannot consecrate, we cannot hallow this ground. The brave men, living and dead, who struggled here, have consecrated it far above our poor power to add or detract.

ABRAHAM LINCOLN

SOLITUDE *Also see:* LONELINESS.

I live in that solitude which is painful in youth, but delicious in the years of maturity.

ALBERT EINSTEIN

Solitude, though it may be silent as light, is like light, the mightiest of agencies; for solitude is essential to man.

THOMAS DE QUINCEY

I never found a companion that was so companionable as solitude.

HENRY DAVID THOREAU

It is easy in the world to live after the world's opinions; it is easy in solitude to live after your own; but the great man is he who in the midst of the crowd keeps with perfect sweetness the independence of solitude.

RALPH WALDO EMERSON

The right to be alone—the most comprehensive of rights, and the right most valued by civilized man.

LOUIS D. BRANDEIS

SORROW *Also see:* AFFLICTION, GRIEF, GUILT, HUMOR, RESIGNATION.

Into each life some rain must fall.

HENRY WADSWORTH LONGFELLOW

There can be no rainbow without a cloud and a storm.

J. H. VINCENT

Sorrow makes men sincere.

HENRY WARD BEECHER

The world is so full of care and sorrow that it is a gracious debt we owe to one another to discover the bright crystals of delight hidden in somber circumstances and irksome tasks.

HELEN KELLER

Out of suffering have emerged the strongest souls.

EDWIN HUBBEL CHAPIN

Earth has no sorrow that heaven cannot heal.

THOMAS MOORE

Where there is sorrow, there is holy ground.

OSCAR WILDE

SOUL *Also see:* BODY, CONFESSION, CONSCIENCE, CRIME, DRESS, HEAVEN, INFLUENCE, MISER, NEGLECT, PRAYER, PURPOSE, SENSUALITY.

The one thing in the world, of value, is the active soul.

RALPH WALDO EMERSON

The soul, like the body, lives by what it feeds on.

JOSIAH GILBERT HOLLAND

Most people sell their souls and live with a good conscience on the proceeds.

LOGAN P. SMITH

My mind is inescapable of conceiving such a thing as a soul. I may be in error, and man may have a soul; but I simply do not believe it.

THOMAS A. EDISON

The wealth of a soul is measured by how much it can feel; its poverty by how little.

WILLIAM ROUNSEVILLE ALGER

SPACE *Also see:* SCIENCE, TECHNOLOGY.

Here's one small step for a man . . . one giant leap for mankind.

NEIL ARMSTRONG

There is beauty in space, and it is orderly. There is no weather, and there is regularity. It is predictable . . . Everything in space obeys the laws of physics. If you know these laws and obey them, space will treat you kindly. And don't tell me man doesn't belong out there. Man belongs wherever he wants to go.

WERNHER VON BRAUN

The moon and other celestial bodies should be free for exploration and use by all countries. No country should be permitted to advance a claim of sovereignty.

LYNDON BAINES JOHNSON

The sky is no longer the limit.

RICHARD M. NIXON

God has no intention of setting a limit to the efforts of man to conquer space.

PLUS XII

SPECULATION *Also see:* BUSINESS, FINANCE.

Speculation is only a word covering the making of money out of the manipulation of prices, instead of supplying goods and services.

HENRY FORD

A speculator is a man who observes the future, and acts before it occurs.

BERNARD M. BARUCH

If there were no bad speculations there could be no good investments; if there were no wild ventures there would be no brilliantly successful enterprises.

F. W. HIRST

There will always be speculation of some kind. If you throw it out of an organized exchange, you throw it out into the street.

H. C. EMERY

SPEECH *Also see:* ELOQUENCE, LANGUAGE, LOQUACITY, MUSIC.

Speak softly, and carry a big stick.

THEODORE ROOSEVELT

It usually takes more than three weeks to prepare a good impromptu speech.

MARK TWAIN

Speak clearly, if you speak at all; carve every word before you let it fall.

OLIVER WENDELL HOLMES

Half the world is composed of people who have something to say and can't, and the other half who have nothing to say and keep on saying it.

ROBERT FROST

Speech is power: speech is to persuade, to convert, to compel.

RALPH WALDO EMERSON

We speak little if not egged on by vanity.

FRANÇOIS DE LA ROCHEFOUCAULD

Speech is human nature itself, with none of the artificiality of written language.

ALFRED NORTH WHITEHEAD

SPIRIT *Also see:* COWARDICE, CULTURE, ENERGY, ENTHUSIASM, ZEAL.

One truth stands firm. All that happens in world history rests on something spiritual. If the spiritual is strong, it creates world history. If it is weak, it suffers world history.

ALBERT SCHWEITZER

It must be of the spirit if we are to save the flesh.

DOUGLAS MACARTHUR

Great men are they who see that the spiritual is stronger than any material force.

RALPH WALDO EMERSON

There are only two forces in the world, the sword and the spirit. In the long run the sword will always be conquered by the spirit.

NAPOLEON BONAPARTE

He that loseth wealth, loseth much; he that loseth friends, loseth more; but he that loseth his spirit loseth all.

SPANISH MAXIM

STRENGTH *Also see:* CHEERFULNESS, RESOLU-
TION, REWARD, WILL.

O, it is excellent to have a giant's strength, but it is tyrannous to use it like a giant.

WILLIAM SHAKESPEARE

Don't hit at all if it is honorably possible to avoid hitting,
but never hit soft.

THEODORE ROOSEVELT

We acquire the strength we have overcome.

RALPH WALDO EMERSON

Concentration is the secret of strength.

RALPH WALDO EMERSON

I wish to preach not the doctrine of ignoble ease, but the
doctrine of strenuous life.

THEODORE ROOSEVELT

Don't expect to build up the weak by pulling down the
strong.

CALVIN COLLIDGE

STRESS . . . See ANXIETY

STUDY *Also see:* LEARNING, SELF-IMPROVEMENT,
THOUGHT.

No student knows his subject: the most he knows is where
and how to find out the things he does not know.

WOODROW WILSON

The world's great men have not commonly been great
scholars, nor its great scholars great men.

OLIVER WENDELL HOLMES

The mind of the scholar, if he would leave it large and liberal, should come in contact with other minds.

HENRY WADSWORTH LONGFELLOW

There are more men ennobled by study than by nature.

CICERO

I would live to study, and not study to live.

FRANCIS BACON

The more we study the more we discover our ignorance.

PERCY BYSSHE SHELLEY

SUCCESS *Also see:* ACHIEVEMENT, AMBITION,
CONFIDENCE, DEFEAT,
ENEMY, LUCK, POPULARITY,
REWARD, VICTORY.

If A equals success, then the formula is A equals X plus Y
and Z, with X being work, Y play, and Z keeping your
mouth shut.

ALBERT EINSTEIN

If man has good corn, or wood, or boards, or pigs to sell,
or can make better chairs or knives, crucibles, or church
organs, than anybody else, you will find a broad, hard-
beaten road to his house, tho it be in the woods.

RALPH WALDO EMERSON

There is only one success—to spend your life in your own
way.

CHRISTOPHER MORLEY

Try not to become a man of success but rather try to become a man of value.

ALBERT EINSTEIN

The gent who wakes up and finds himself a success hasn't
been asleep.

WILSON MIZNER

SUFFERING *Also see:* ABSENCE, AFFLICTION,
FEAR, PAIN, REWARD,
SORROW.

I have suffered too much in this world not to hope for another.

JEAN JACQUES ROUSSEAU

It requires more courage to suffer than to die.

NAPOLEON BONAPARTE

It is a glorious thing to be indifferent to suffering, but only
to one's own suffering.

ROBERT LYND

The salvation of the world is in man's suffering.

WILLIAM FAULKNER

Suffering becomes beautiful when anyone bears great calamities with cheerfulness, not through insensibility but
through greatness of mind.

ARISTOTLE

We are healed of a suffering only by experiencing it in full.

MARCEL PROUST

SUPERSTITION *Also see:* BELIEF, CREDULITY,
IDOLATRY, IGNORANCE,
SECURITY.

Superstition is a senseless fear of God.

CICERO

Superstition is . . . religion which is incongruous with intelligence.

JOHN TYNDALL

Superstition is the poison of the mind.

JOSEPH LEWIS

Superstition, idolatry, and hypocrisy have ample wages, but
truth goes begging.

MARTIN LUTHER

Superstition is the religion of feeble minds.

EDMUND BURKE

Superstitions are, for the most part, but the shadows of
great truths.

TRYON EDWARDS

SUSPICION *Also see:* DISTRUST, DOUBT, GUILT.

Suspicions which may be unjust need not be stated.

ABRAHAM LINCOLN

The less we know the more we suspect.

JOSH BILLINGS

The louder he talked of his honor, the faster we counted our
spoons.

RALPH WALDO EMERSON

A woman of honor should not expect of others things she would not do herself.

MARQUERITE DE VALOIS

SYMPATHY *Also see:* COMPASSION, KINDNESS, MERCY, PITY.

Sympathy is a virtue unknown in nature.

PAUL EIPPER

Harmony of aim, not identity of conclusion, is the secret of sympathetic life.

RALPH WALDO EMERSON

A sympathetic heart is like a spring of pure water bursting forth from the mountain side.

ANONYMOUS

TACT *Also see:* COURTESY, DIPLOMACY, DISCRETION, GALLANTRY.

Tact: the ability to describe others as they see themselves.

ABRAHAM LINCOLN

Be kind and considerate to others, depending somewhat upon who they are.

DON HEROLD

Tact is one of the first mental virtues, the absence of which is often fatal to the best of talents; it supplies the place of many talents.

WILLIAM GILMORE SIMMS

Don't flatter yourself that friendship authorizes you to say disagreeable things to your intimates. The nearer you come into relation with a person, the more necessary do tact and courtesy become.

OLIVER WENDELL HOLMES

TALENT . . . See ABILITY

TALKING . . . See LOQUACITY

TASTE *Also see:* DESIRE, TEMPER, VARIETY, VULGARITY.

Taste is the feminine of genius.

EDWARD FITZGERALD

I would rather be able to appreciate things I cannot have than to have things I am not able to appreciate.

ELBERT HUBBARD

Partial culture runs to the ornate; extreme culture to simplicity.

CHRISTIAN NESTELL BOVEE

Taste is, so to speak, the microscope of the judgment.

JEAN JACQUES ROUSSEAU

Bad taste is a species of bad morals.

CHRISTIAN NESTELL BOVEE

TAX *Also see:* CENSURE, GOVERNMENT.

Death and taxes are inevitable.

THOMAS C. HALIBURTON

The income tax has made more liars out of the American people than gold has.

WILL ROGERS

The power to tax involves the power to destroy.

JOHN MARSHALL

For every benefit you receive a tax is levied.

RALPH WALDO EMERSON

The tax collector must love poor people—he's creating so many of them.

BILL VAUGHAN

To tax and to please, no more than to love and to be wise, is not given to men.

EDMUND BURKE

Taxes are the sinews of the state.

CICERO

TEACHING *Also see:* EDUCATION, KNOWLEDGE, LEARNING.

You cannot teach a man anything; you can only help him find it within himself.

GALILEO

One good schoolmaster is worth a thousand priests.

ROBERT GREEN INGERSOLL

Knowledge exists to be imparted.

RALPH WALDO EMERSON

The teacher is one who makes two ideas grow where only one grew before.

ELBERT HUBBARD

The man who can make hard things easy is the educator.

RALPH WALDO EMERSON

A teacher affects eternity; he can never tell where his influence stops.

HENRY BROOKS ADAMS

TECHNOLOGY *Also see:* SCIENCE, SPACE.

The economic and technological triumphs of the past few years have not solved as many problems as we thought they would, and, in fact, have brought us new problems we did not foresee.

HENRY FORD II

What is more difficult, to think of an encampment on the moon or of Harlem rebuilt? Both are now within the reach of our resources. Both now depend upon human decision and human will.

ADLAI E. STEVENSON

As nuclear and other technological achievements continue to mount, the normal life span will continue to climb. The hourly productivity of the worker will increase.

DWIGHT D. EISENHOWER

TELEVISION *Also see:* COMMUNICATIoN.

Television is now so desparately hungry for material that they're scraping the top of the barrel.

GORE VIDAL

Time has convinced me of one thing: Television is for appearing on—not for looking at.

NOEL COWARD

I hate television. I hate it as much as peanuts. But I can't stop eating peanuts.

ORSON WELLES

TEMPER *Also see:* ANGER, MISERY, MODERATION, SELF-CONTROL.

The worst-tempered people I've ever met were people who knew they were wrong.

WILSON MIZNER

A tart temper never mellows with age; and a sharp tongue is the only edged tool that grows keener with constant use.

WASHINGTON IRVING

Man is a rational animal who always loses his temper when called upon to act in accordance with the dictates of reason.

OSCAR WILDE

Men lose their tempers in defending their taste.

RALPH WALDO EMERSON

TEMPTATION *Also see:* COWARDICE, DESIRE, PASSION, SELF-CONTROL.

Few men have virtue to withstand the highest bidder.

GEORGE WASHINGTON

I can resist anything except temptation.

OSCAR WILDE

There are several good protections against temptations, but the surest is cowardice.

MARK TWAIN

He who cannot resist temptation is not a man.

HORACE MANN

The only way to get rid of a temptation is to yield to it.

OSCAR WILDE

As the Sandwich-Islander believes that the strength and valor of the enemy he kills passes into himself, so we gain the strength of the temptations we resist.

RALPH WALDO EMERSON

THEOLOGY *Also see:* ATHEISM, CHRISTIANITY, HELL, JUDAISM, RELIGION.

My theology, briefly, is that the universe was dictated but not signed.

CHRISTOPHER MORLEY

Theology is a science of mind applied to God.

HENRY WARD BEECHER

The best theology is rather a divine life than a divine knowledge.

JEREMY TAYLOR

Theology is but our ideas of truth classified and arranged.

HENRY WARD BEECHER

As the grave grows nearer my theology is growing strangely simple, and it begins and ends with Christ as the only Savior of the lost.

HENRY BENJAMIN WHIPPLE

Let us put theology out of religion. Theology has always sent the worst to heaven, the best to hell.

ROBERT GREEN INGERSOLL

THEORY *Also see:* FACTS, PHILOSOPHY, REALITY.

Science is organized common sense where many a beautiful theory was killed by an ugly fact.

THOMAS HUXLEY

A little experience often upsets a lot of theory.

CADMAN

There can be no theory of any account unless it corroborate with the theory of the earth.

WALT WHITMAN

I never once made a discovery . . . I speak without exaggeration that I have constructed *three thousand* different theories in connection with the electric light . . . Yet in only two cases did my experiments prove the truth of my theory.

THOMAS A. EDISON

A theory is no more like a fact than a photograph is like a person.

ED HOWE

In scientific work, those who refuse to go beyond fact rarely get as far as fact.

THOMAS HUXLEY

THOUGHT *Also see:* ACTION, DISSENT, LANGUAGE, LOGIC, PLAGIARISM, POLITICS, PROPAGANDA, QUOTATION, REVERIE, SELF-KNOWLEDGE, STUDY.

Great thoughts reduced to practice become great acts.

WILLIAM HAZLITT

You are today where your thoughts have brought you; you will be tomorrow where your thoughts take you.

JAMES ALLEN

The soul of God is poured into the world through the thoughts of men.

RALPH WALDO EMERSON

I've known countless people who were reservoirs of learning, yet never had a thought.

WILSON MIZNER

Learning without thought is labor lost.

CONFUCIUS

THRIFT . . . See ECONOMY

TIME *Also see:* BUSY, EFFICIENCY, ETERNITY, HASTE, OPPORTUNITY, PRESENT, PUNCTUALITY, REST, WASTE.

Lost time is never found again.

JOHN H. AUGHEY

Dost thou love life? Then do not squander time, for that is the stuff life is made of.

BENJAMIN FRANKLIN

As if you could kill time without injuring eternity.

HENRY DAVID THOREAU

Time is like money; the less we have of it to spare the further we make it go.

JOSH BILLINGS

Lost, yesterday, somewhere between sunrise and sunset, two golden hours, each set with sixty diamond minutes. No reward is offered for they are gone forever.

HORACE MANN

TOLERANCE Also see: INTOLERANCE, LIBERTY, RIGHTS.

Tolerance is another word for difference.

W. SOMERSET MAUGHAM

No man has a right in America to treat any other man "tolerantly" for tolerance is the assumption of superiority. Our liberties are equal rights of every citizen.

WENDELL K. WILLKIE

It is easy to be tolerant of the principles of other people if you have none of your own.

HERBERT SAMUEL

Tolerance is the oil which takes the friction out of life.

WILBERT E. SCHEER

Tolerance comes with age. I see no fault committed that I myself could not have committed at some time or other.

JOHANN WOLFGANG VON GOETHE

I have seen gross intolerance shown in support of tolerance.

SAMUEL TAYLOR COLERIDGE

TRADITION Also see: CUSTOM.

Traditionalists are pessimists about the future and optimists about the past.

LEWIS MUMFORD

It takes an endless amount of history to make even a little tradition.

HENRY JAMES

Tradition does not mean that the living are dead, but that the dead are living.

GILBERT K. CHESTERTON

Tradition is an important help to history, but its statements should be carefully scrutinized before we rely on them.

JOSEPH ADDISON

TRAGEDY Also see: ADVERSITY, DESIRE, LIFE, SORROW.

The tragedy of life is not so much what men suffer, but rather what they miss.

THOMAS CARLYLE

There are two tragedies in life: one is to lose your heart's desire, the other is to gain it.

GEORGE BERNARD SHAW

The world is a comedy to those who think, a tragedy to those who feel.

HORACE WALPOLE

TRANQUILITY ... See PEACE

TRAVEL Also see: ADVENTURE, SPACE, WORLD.

The world is a book, and those who do not travel, read only a page.

ST. AUGUSTINE

A man travels the world over in search of what he needs, and returns home to find it.

GEORGE MOORE

The man who gets out alone can start today; but he who travels with another must wait till that other is ready.

HENRY DAVID THOREAU

The traveler sees what he sees, the tourist sees what he has come to see.

GILBERT K. CHESTERTON

TREASON Also see: INGRATITUDE, REBELLION.

We are a rebellious nation. Our whole history is treason; our blood was attained before we were born; our creeds were infidelity to the mother church; our constitution treason to our fatherland.

THEODORE PARKER

Is there not some chosen curse, some hidden thunder in the stores of heaven, red with uncommon wrath, to blast the man who owes his greatness to his country's ruin!

JOSEPH ADDISON

There is something peculiarly sinister and insidious in even a charge of disloyalty. Such a charge all too frequently places a strain on the reputation of an individual which is indelible and lasting, regardless of the complete innocence later proved.

JOHN LORD O'BRIAN

Write on my gravestone: "Infidel, Traitor."—infidel to every church that compromises with wrong; traitor to every government that oppresses the people.

WENDELL PHILLIPS

TRIFLES Also see: AFFECTION, SIMPLICITY.

Little things affect little minds.

BENJAMIN DISRAELI

It is the little bits of things that fret and worry us; we can dodge an elephant, but we can't dodge a fly.

JOSH BILLINGS

Little strokes fell great oaks.

BENJAMIN FRANKLIN

The creation of a thousand forests is in one acorn.

RALPH WALDO EMERSON

A small leak will sink a great ship.

BENJAMIN FRANKLIN

There is nothing too little for so little a creature as man. It is by studying little things that we attain the great art of having as little misery and as much happiness as possible.

SAMUEL JOHNSON

Trifles make perfection—and perfection is no trifle.

MICHELANGELO

TROUBLE . . . See ANXIETY

TRUST *Also see:* CONFIDENCE, CREDIT, DISHON-
ESTY, ILLUSION, MONEY, SE-
CRECY, SYMPATHY, WEALTH.

When a man has no reason to trust himself, he tusts in luck.

ED HOWE

Put your trust in God, but keep your powder dry.

OLIVER CROMWELL

Trust men and they will be true to you; treat them greatly
and they will show themselves great.

RALPH WALDO EMERSON

Woe to the man whose heart has not learned while young to
hope, to love—and to put its trust in life.

JOSEPH CONRAD

You may be deceived if you trust too much, but you will live
in torment if you don't trust enough.

FRANK CRANE

TRUTH *Also see:* BIBLE, BIGOTRY, CHILDREN, DI-
PLOMACY, ENEMY, ERROR, GOS-
SIP, LYING, MAXIM, PHILOSOPHY,
PREJUDICE, PROPAGANDA, RADI-
CAL, REFORM, SAFETY, SCAN-
DAL, SUPERSTITION, TIME.

Rather than love, than money, than fame, give me truth.

HENRY DAVID THOREAU

Men occasionally stumble over the truth, but most of them
pick themselves up and hurry off as if nothing happened.

WINSTON CHURCHILL

Never tell the truth to people who are not worthy of it.

MARK TWAIN

Truth is always served by great minds, even if they fight it.

JEAN ROSTAND

Everyone wishes to have truth on his side, but not everyone
wishes to be on the side of truth.

RICHARD WHATELY

When you want to fool the world, tell the truth.

OTTO VON BISMARCK

The pure and simple truth is rarely pure and never simple.

OSCAR WILDE

The truth is more important than the facts.

FRANK LLOYD WRIGHT

The greatest homage we can pay to truth, is to use it.

JAMES RUSSELL LOWELL

It is easier to perceive error than to find truth, for the former lies on the surface and is easiy seen, while the latter lies
in the depth, where few are willing to search for it.

JOHANN WOLFGANG VON GOETHE

Truth is the property of no individual but is the treasure of
all men.

RALPH WALDO EMERSON

The greatest friend of truth is Time, her greatest enemy is
Prejudice, and her constant companion is Humility.

CHARLES CALEB COLTON

It is man that makes truth great, not truth that makes man
great.

CONFUCIUS

As scarce as truth is, the supply has always been in excess of
the demand.

JOSH BILLINGS

TYRANNY *Also see:* COMMUNISM, CONSCIENCE,
DESTINY, MOB, REBELLION,
REVOLUTION, UNITY.

Every tyrant who has lived has believed in freedom—for
himself.

ELBERT HUBBARD

Tyranny and anarchy are never far asunder.

JEREMY BENTHAM

Hateful is the power, and pitiable is the life, of those who
wish to be feared rather than loved.

CORNELIUS NEPOS

Resistance to tyrants is obedience to God.

THOMAS JEFFERSON

Tyrants are seldom free; the cares and the instruments of
their tyranny enslave them.

GEORGE SANTAYANA

There is a secret pride in every human heart that revolts at
tyranny. You may order and drive an individual, but you
cannot make him respect you.

WILLIAM HAZLITT

UGLINESS *Also see:* BEAUTY.

Better an ugly face than an ugly mind.

JAMES ELLIS

There is a sort of charm in ugliness, if the person has some
redeeming qualities and is only ugly enough.

JOSH BILLINGS

Heaven sometimes hedges a rare character about with un-
gainliness and odium, as the burr that protects the fruit.

RALPH WALDO EMERSON

UNDERSTANDING *Also see:* ANGER, COMMUNICA-
TION, MIND, PERCEP-
TION, PITY, REVERIE,
WORD.

Understanding is a two-way street.

ELEANOR ROOSEVELT

Whatever you cannot understand, you cannot possess.

JOHANN WOLFGANG VON GOETHE

There is a great difference between knowing and understanding: you can know a lot about something and not
really understand it.

CHARLES F. KETTERING

The improvement of understanding is for two ends: first, our own increase of knowledge; secondly, to enable us to deliver that knowledge to others.

JOHN LOCKE

UNHAPPINESS ... See SORROW

UNION *Also see:* ECONOMICS, LABOR, WORK.

The labor movement's basic purpose is to achieve a better life for its members. A union that fails in this purpose has failed utterly.

NEW YORK TIMES

We must hang together or assuredly we shall hang separately.

BENJAMIN FRANKLIN

The trade union movement represents the organized economic power of the workers ... It is in reality the most potent and the most direct social insurance the workers can establish.

SAMUEL GOMPERS

All for one; one for all.

ALEXANDER DUMAS

UNITED NATIONS

The United Nations is our one great hope for a peaceful and free world.

RALPH BUNCHE

This organization is created to prevent you from going to hell. It isn't created to take you to heaven.

HENRY CABOT LODGE

The whole basis of the United Nations is the right of all nations—great or small—to have weight, to have a vote, to be attended to, to be a part of the twentieth century.

ADLAI E. STEVENSON

We have actively sought and are actively seeking to make the United Nations an effective instrument of international cooperation.

DEAN ACHESON

The United Nations is designed to make possible lasting freedom and independence for all its members.

HARRY S. TRUMAN

UNITY *Also see:* LOYALTY, MARRIAGE, STRENGTH.

Men's hearts ought not to be set against one another, but set with one another, and all against evil only.

THOMAS CARLYLE

There are no problems we cannot solve together, and very few that we can solve by ourselves.

LYNDON BAINES JOHNSON

We cannot be separated in interest or divided in purpose. We stand together until the end.

WOODROW WILSON

One country, one constitution, one destiny.

DANIEL WEBSTER

We come to reason, not to dominate. We do not seek to have our way, but to find a common way.

LYNDON BAINES JOHNSON

A house divided against itself cannot stand.

ABRAHAM LINCOLN

United we stand, divided we fall.

G. P. MORRIS

UNIVERSE *Also see:* EARTH, MAN, SCIENCE, SPACE, TECHNOLOGY.

The Universe is but one vast symbol of God.

THOMAS CARLYLE

The universe is one of God's thoughts.

JOHANN VON SCHILLER

The universe is duly in order, everything in its place.

WALT WHITMAN

An infinite universe is at each moment opened to our view. And this universe is the sign and symbol of infinite Power, Intelligence, Purity, Bliss, and Love.

WILLIAM ELLERY CHANNING

We are all fellow passengers on a dot of earth. And each of us, in the span of time, has really only a moment among our companions.

LYNDON BAINES JOHNSON

UNIVERSITY *Also see:* EDUCATION, TEACHING.

The university most worthy of rational admiration is that one in which your lonely thinker can feel himself lonely, most positively furthered, and most richly fed.

WILLIAM JAMES

The task of a university is the creation of the future, so far as rational thought and civilized modes of appreciation can affect the issue.

ALFRED NORTH WHITEHEAD

This institution will be based on the illimitable freedom of the human mind. For here we are not afraid to follow truth wherever it may lead, not tolerate error as long as reason is left free to combat it.

THOMAS JEFFERSON

A university should be a place of light, of liberty, and of learning.

BENJAMIN DISRAELI

VACATION *Also see:* REST, VARIETY.

No man needs a vacation so much as the man who has just had one.

ELBERT HUBBARD

A vacation is over when you begin to yearn for your work.

MORRIS FISHBEIN

If some people didn't tell you, you'd never know they'd been away on a vacation.

KIN HUBBARD

A period of travel and relaxation when you take twice the clothes and half the money you need.

ANONYMOUS

VALOR ... See COURAGE

VALUE *Also see:* CIVILIZATION, MERIT, SUCCESS, WORTH.

Some values are ... like sugar on the doughnut, legitimate, desirable, but insufficient, apart from the doughnut itself. We need substance as well as frosting.

RALPH T. FLEWELLING

I conceive that the great part of the miseries of mankind are brought upon them by false estimates they have made of the value of things.

BENJAMIN FRANKLIN

What we obtain too cheap, we esteem too lightly; it is dearness only that gives everything its value.

THOMAS PAINE

The value of a principle is the number of things it will explain; and there is no good theory of disease which does not at once suggest a cure.

RALPH WALDO EMERSON

Nothing can have value without being an object of utility.

KARL MARX

All that is valuable in human society depends upon the opportunity for development accorded the individual.

ALBERT EINSTEIN

VANITY *Also see:* CURIOSITY, FAME, FAULT, LONELINESS, LOQUACITY, RANK, SPEECH.

A vain man finds it wise to speak good or ill of himself; a modest man does not talk of himself.

JEAN DE LA BRUYÈRE

It is our own vanity that makes the vanity of others intolerable to us.

FRANÇOIS DE LA ROCHEFOUCAULD

Vanity as an impulse has without doubt been of far more benefit to civilization than modesty has ever been.

WILLIAM E. WOODWARD

To be a man's own fool is bad enough; but the vain man is everybody's.

WILLIAM PENN

The highest form of vanity is love of fame.

GEORGE SANTAYANA

A man who is not a fool can rid himself of every folly except vanity.

JEAN JACQUES ROUSSEAU

The only cure for vanity is laughter, and the only fault that's laughable is vanity.

HENRI BERGSON

VARIETY *Also see:* CHANGE, ORIGINALITY.

Variety's the very spice of life, that gives it all its flavor.

WILLIAM COWPER

Variety of mere nothings gives more pleasure than uniformity of something.

JEAN PAUL RICHTER

It takes all sorts to make a world.

ENGLISH PROVERB

The most delightful pleasures cloy without variety.

PUBLILIUS SYRUS

Sameness is the mother of disgust, variety the cure.

PETRARCH

VENGEANCE *Also see:* ANGER, HATE, INJURY, SLANDER.

Vengeance has no foresight.

NAPOLEON BONAPARTE

Revenge is the abject pleasure of an abject mind.

JUVENAL

Avenge not yourselves, but rather give place unto wrath: for it is written, Vengeance is mine; I will repay, saith the Lord.

ROMANS 12:19

Revenge is an act of passion; vengeance of justice. Injuries are revenged; crimes are avenged.

JOSEPH JOUBERT

VICE *Also see:* CRIME, CRUELTY, EVIL, FANATICISM, PROFANITY, SELFISHNESS, SIN, WICKEDNESS.

This is the essential evil of vice, that it debases man.

EDWIN HUBBEL CHAPIN

One big vice in a man is apt to keep out a great many smaller ones.

BRET HARTE

Vices are often habits rather than passions.

ANTOINE RIVAROL

It has been my experience that folks who have no vices have very few virtues.

ABRAHAM LINCOLN

Men wish to be saved from the mischiefs of their vices, but not from their vices.

RALPH WALDO EMERSON

It is but a step from companionship to slavery when one associates with vice.

HOSEA BALLOU

Our faith comes in moments; our vice is habitual.

WILLIAM ELLERY CHANNING

There will be vice as long as there are men.

TACITUS

VICTORY *Also see:* CHARACTER, DEFEAT, SUCCESS, WAR.

One may know how to gain a victory, and know not how to use it.

BARCA

The greatest conquerer is he who overcomes the enemy without a blow.

CHINESE PROVERB

We should wage war not to win war, but to win peace.

PAUL HOFFMAN

Victories that are easy are cheap. Those only are worth having which come as the result of hard fighting.

HENRY WARD BEECHER

The god of victory is said to be one-handed, but peace gives victory on both sides.

RALPH WALDO EMERSON

It is fatal to enter any war without the will to win it.

DOUGLAS MACARTHUR

VIGILANCE *Also see:* CAUTION, PRUDENCE, WISDOM.

Eternal vigilance is the price of liberty.

THOMAS JEFFERSON

He is most free from danger, who, even when safe, is on his guard.

PUBLILIUS SYRUS

There is a significant Latin proverb; to wit: Who will guard the guards?

JOSH BILLINGS

They that are on their guard and appear ready to receive their adversaries, are in much less danger of being attacked than the supine, secure and negligent.

BENJAMIN FRANKLIN

Experience should teach us to be most on our guard to protect liberty when the government's purposes are beneficent.

LOUIS D. BRANDEIS

VIOLENCE *Also see:* HATE, PERSEVERANCE, REVOLUTION, RIOT, TELEVISION, WAR.

Nothing good ever comes of violence.

MARTIN LUTHER

Degeneracy follows every autocratic system of violence, for violence inevitably attracts moral inferiors. Time has proven that illustrious tyrants are succeeded by scoundrels.

ALBERT EINSTEIN

There is a violence that liberates, and a violence that enslaves; there is a violence that is moral and a violence that is immoral.

BENITO MUSSOLINI

It is organized violence on top which creates individual violence at the bottom. It is the accumulated indignation against organized wrong, organized crime, organized injustice, which drives the political offender to act.

EMMA GOLDMAN

Violence cannot build a better society. Disruption and disorder nourish repression, not justice. They strike at the freedom of every citizen. The community cannot—it will not—tolerate coercion and mob rule.

COMMISSION ON CIVIL DISORDER, 1968

VIRTUE *Also see:* ARISTOCRACY, INNOCENCE, MERCY, MODESTY, WORTH.

Virtue is like a rich stone, best plain set.

FRANCIS BACON

If you can be well without health, you may be happy without virtue.

EDMUND BURKE

Perfect virtue is to do unwitnessed that which we should be capable of doing before all the world.

FRANÇOIS DE LA ROCHEFOUCAULD

The person who talks most of his own virtue is often the least virtuous.

JAWAHARLAL NEHRU

Virtue consists, not in abstaining from vice, but in not desiring it.

GEORGE BERNARD SHAW

The only reward of virtue is virtue.

RALPH WALDO EMERSON

VISION *Also see:* BLINDNESS, COURAGE, CYNIC, EYE, IDEAL, IMAGINATION, TOLERANCE, WONDER.

It is never safe to look into the future with eyes of fear.

EDWARD H. HARRIMAN

No man that does not see visions will ever realize any high hope or undertake any high enterprise.

WOODROW WILSON

The farther back you can look, the farther forward you are likely to see.

WINSTON CHURCHILL

Where there is no vision a people perish.

RALPH WALDO EMERSON

You see things and you say "Why?"; but I dream things that never were and I say "Why not?"

GEORGE BERNARD SHAW

VOICE *Also see:* DISSENT, PUBLIC, SPEECH, VIOLENCE, WORD.

The sweetest of all sounds is that of the voice of the woman we love.

JEAN DE LA BRUYÈRE

There is no index so sure as the voice.

TANCRED

A man's style is his mind's voice. Wooden minds, wooden voices.

RALPH WALDO EMERSON

It is the still small voice that the soul heeds; not the deafening blasts of doom.

WILLIAM D. HOWELLS

The human voice is the organ of the soul.

HENRY WADSWORTH LONGFELLOW

VOTE *Also see:* AMERICA, CITIZENSHIP, DEMOC-
RACY, POLITICS.

Where annual elections end, there slavery begins.
JOHN QUINCY ADAMS

Vote for the man who promises least—he'll be the least disappointing.
BERNARD BARUCH

Always vote for principle, though you may vote alone, and
you may cherish the sweetest reflection that your vote is
never lost.
JOHN QUINCY ADAMS

The future of this republic is in the hands of the American
voter.
DWIGHT D. EISENHOWER

Giving every man a vote has no more made men wise and
free than Christianity has made them good.
H. L. MENCKEN

When a fellow tells me he's bipartisan, I know he's going to
vote against me.
HARRY S. TRUMAN

There can no longer be anyone too poor to vote.
LYNDON BAINES JOHNSON

VOID . . . See ABSENCE

VOW *Also see:* MARRIAGE, POLITICS, RESOLUTION

Your capacity to keep your vow will depend on the purity of
your life.
MAHATMA GANDHI

Hasty resolutions are of the nature of vows, and to be
equally avoided.
WILLIAM PENN

A vow is fixed and unalterable determination to do a thing,
when such a determination is related to something noble
which can only uplift the man who makes the resolve.
MAHATMA GANDHI

Vows made in storms are forgotten in calm.
THOMAS FULLER

Personally, I hold that a man, who deliberately and intelligently takes a pledge and then breaks it, forfeits his manhood.
MAHATMA GANDHI

VULGARITY *Also see:* ABUSE, AMBITION, HASTE,
PROFANITY, TELEVISION,
TASTE.

Vulgarity is more obvious in satin than in homespun.
NATHANIEL P. WILLIS

Vulgarity is the conduct of other people, just as falsehoods
are the truths of other people.
OSCAR WILDE

By vulgarity I mean that vice of civilization which makes
man ashamed of himself and his next of kin, and pretend to
be somebody else.
SOLOMON SCHECHTER

A thing is not vulgar merely because it is common.
WILLIAM HAZLITT

WAGE *Also see:* CAPITALISM, EMPLOYMENT,
LABOR, REWARD, UNION.

Low wages are not cheap wages.
LOUIS D. BRANDEIS

It is but a truism that labor is most productive where its
wages are largest. Poorly paid labor is inefficient labor, the
world over.
HENRY GEORGE

No business which depends for existence on paying less
than living wages to its workers has any right to continue in
this country.
FRANKLIN DELANO ROOSEVELT

The high wage begins down in the shop. If it is not created
there it cannot get into pay envelopes. There will never be a
system invented which will do away with the necessity for
work.
HENRY FORD

"A fair day's wage for a fair day's work": it is as just a demand as governed men ever made of governing. It is the
everlasting right of man.
THOMAS CARLYLE

Men who do things without being told draw the most wages.
EDWIN H. STUART

WANT *Also see:* DESIRE, INDEPENDENCE, NECES-
SITY, POVERTY, SECURITY,
SPEECH, WASTE.

Our necessities never equal our wants.
BENJAMIN FRANKLIN

The keener the want the lustier the growth.
WENDELL PHILLIPS

It is not from nature, but from education and habits, that
our wants are chiefly derived.
HENRY FIELDING

He can feel no little wants who is in pursuit of grandeur.
JOHANN KASPAR LAVATER

The fewer our wants, the nearer we resemble the gods.
SOCRATES

WAR *Also see:* BLOOD, CAUSE, CIVILIZATION, DI-
PLOMACY, DISARMAMENT, HERO-
ISM, NUCLEAR WARFARE, PEACE,
POWER, RACE, SOLDIER, UNITED
NATIONS, YOUTH.

Soldiers usually win the battles and generals get the credit
for them.
NAPOLEON BONAPARTE

The tragedy of war is that it uses man's best to do man's
worst.
HARRY EMERSON FOSDICK

I don't know whether war is an interlude during peace, or
peace is an interlude during war.
GEORGES CLEMENCEAU

War is the science of destruction.
JOHN ABBOTT

No one can guarantee success in war, but only deserve it.
WINSTON CHURCHILL

When people speak to you about a preventive war, you tell them to go and fight it. After my experience, I have come to hate war. War settles nothing.
DWIGHT D. EISENHOWER

The essence of war is violence. Moderation in war is imbecility.
JOHN A. FISHER

There was never a good war, or a bad peace.
BENJAMIN FRANKLIN

Only two great groups of animals, men and ants, indulge in highly organized mass warfare.
CHARLES H. MASKINS

There is no such thing as an inevitable war. If war comes it will be from failure of human wisdom.
ANDREW B. LAW

War is hell.
WILLIAM TECUMSEH SHERMAN

The next World War will be fought with stones.
ALBERT EINSTEIN

Diplomats are just as essential in starting a war as soldiers are in finishing it.
WILL ROGERS

I have never advocated war except as a means of peace.
ULYSSES S. GRANT

WASTE *Also see:* LOSS, PURSUIT, REFORM, RE-
GRET, WAGE.

Waste neither time nor money, but make the best use of both. Without industry and frugality, nothing will do, and with them everything.
BENJAMIN FRANKLIN

The waste of life occasioned by trying to do too many things at once is appalling.
ORISON S. MARDEN

Short as life is, we make it still shorter by the careless waste of time.
VICTOR HUGO

A man who dares to waste one hour of life has not discovered the value of life.
CHARLES DARWIN

Waste is worse than loss. The time is coming when every person who lays claim to ability will keep the question of waste before him constantly. The scope of thrift is limitless.
THOMAS A. EDISON

WEAKNESS *Also see:* COWARDICE, CRUELTY,
NEUTRALITY, PRIDE.

There are two kinds of weakness, that which breaks and that which bends.
JAMES RUSSELL LOWELL

Better make a weak man your enemy than your friend.
JOSH BILLINGS

Our strength grows out of our weakness.
RALPH WALDO EMERSON

A weak mind is like a microscope, which magnifies trifling things but cannot receive great ones.
LORD CHESTERFIELD

You cannot run away from weakness; you must some time fight it out or perish; and if that be so, why not now, and where you stand?
ROBERT LOUIS STEVENSON

What is bad? All that proceeds from weakness.
NIETZSCHE

WEALTH *Also see:* CAPITALISM, LOSS, MONEY, OP-
PORTUNITY, PROSPERITY,
VALUE.

Surplus wealth is a sacred trust which its possessor is bound to adminster in his lifetime for the good of the community.
ANDREW CARNEGIE

It is sheer madness to live in want in order to be wealthy when you die.
JUVENAL

The gratification of wealth is not found in mere possession or in lavish expenditure, but in its wise application.
MIGUEL DE CERVANTES

There's nothing so comfortable as a small bankroll. A big one is always in danger.
WILSON MIZNER

He is richest who is content with the least, for content is the wealth of nature.
SOCRATES

Without a rich heart wealth is an ugly beggar.
RALPH WALDO EMERSON

WEATHER

Sunshine is delicious, rain is refreshing, wind braces up, snow is exhilarating; there is no such thing as bad weather, only different kinds of good weather.
JOHN RUSKIN

Don't knock the weather; nine-tenths of the people couldn't start a conversation if it didn't change once in a while.
KIN HUBBARD

Everybody talks about the weather but nobody does anything about it.
CHARLES DUDLEY WARNER

Change of weather is the discourse of fools.
THOMAS FULLER

WICKEDNESS *Also see:* EVIL, PROFANITY, PUN-
ISHMENT, REPENTANCE,
SIN.

To see and listen to the wicked is already the beginning of wickedness.
CONFUCIUS

It is a satistical fact that the wicked work harder to reach hell than the righteous do to enter heaven.
JOSH BILLINGS

The sun also shines on the wicked.
SENECA

The world loves a spice of wickedness.
HENRY WADSWORTH LONGFELLOW

No wickedness proceeds on any grounds of reason.

LIVY

God bears with the wicked, but not forever.

MIGUEL DE CERVANTES

There is wickedness in the intention of wickedness, even though it be not perpetrated in the act.

CICERO

WIFE *Also see:* ACHIEVEMENT, COMPLIMENT, FIDELITY, HUSBAND, MARRIAGE, MOTHER.

I chose my wife, as she did her wedding gown, for qualities that would wear well.

OLIVER GOLDSMITH

Wives are young men's mistresses, companions for middle age, and old men's nurses.

FRANCIS BACON

Of all the home remedies, a good wife is best.

KIN HUBBARD

Heaven will be no heaven to me if I do not meet my wife there.

ANDREW JACKSON

All married women are not wives.

JAPANESE PROVERB

A wife is a gift bestowed upon man to reconcile him to the loss of paradise.

JOHANN WOLFGANG VON GOETHE

A wife is essential to great longevity; she is the receptacle of half a man's cares, and two-thirds of his ill-humor.

CHARLES READE

WILL *Also see:* AIM, DESIRE, PURPOSE, RESOLUTION, TECHNOLOGY, VICTORY.

People do not lack strength; they lack will.

VICTOR HUGO

Great souls have wills; feeble ones have only wishes.

CHINESE PROVERB

To deny the freedom of the will is to make morality impossible.

JAMES A. FROUDE

Will is character in action.

WILLIAM MCDOUGALL

Strength does not come from physical capacity. It comes from an indomitable will.

MAHATMA GANDHI

No action will be considered blameless, unless the will was so, for by the will the act was dictated.

SENECA

WISDOM *Also see:* COMMON SENSE, JUDGMENT, KNOWLEDGE, LEARNING, QUESTION.

The wisest man is generally he who thinks himself the least so.

NICOLAS BOILEAU-DESPRÉAUX

One of the greatest pieces of economic wisdom is to know what you do not know.

JOHN KENNETH GALBRAITH

It is unwise to be too sure of one's own wisdom. It is healthy to be reminded that the strongest might weaken and the wisest might err.

MAHATMA GANDHI

It is more easy to be wise for others than for ourselves.

FRANÇOIS DE LA ROCHEFOUCAULD

Nine-tenths of wisdom consists in being wise in time.

THEODORE ROOSEVELT

The older I grow the more I distrust the familiar doctrine that age brings wisdom.

H. L. MENCKEN

WIT *Also see:* FOOL, HUMOR, INSANITY, JESTING, MATURITY.

If it were not for the company of fools, a witty man would often be greatly at a loss.

FRANÇOIS DE LA ROCHEFOUCAULD

Wit is the salt of conversation, not the food.

WILLIAM HAZLITT

The next best thing to being witty one's self, is to be able to quote another's wit.

CHRISTIAN NESTELL BOVEE

A wise man will live as much within his wit as within his income.

LORD CHESTERFIELD

Wit makes its own welcome, and levels all distinctions. No dignity, no learning, no force of character, can make any stand against good wit.

RALPH WALDO EMERSON

WOMAN *Also see:* DRESS, SEX, WIFE.

There is nothing enduring in life for a woman except what she builds in a man's heart.

JUDITH ANDERSON

The way to fight a woman is with your hat. Grab it and run.

JOHN BARRYMORE

She is not made to be the admiration of all, but the happiness of one.

EDMUND BURKE

Being a woman is a terribly difficult task since it consists principally in dealing with men.

JOSEPH CONRAD

A woman's guess is much more accurate than a man's certainty.

RUDYARD KIPLING

Of all the rights of women, the greatest is to be a mother.

LIN YUTANG

A beautiful lady is an accident of nature. A beautiful old lady is a work of art.

LOUIS NIZER

WONDER *Also see:* CURIOSITY, DOUBT, PHILOSO-
PHY, VISION.

The world will never starve for want of wonders, but for
want of wonder.

GILBERT K. CHESTERTON

It was through the feeling of wonder that men now and at
first began to philosophize.

ARISTOTLE

He who can no longer pause to wonder and stand rapt in
awe, is as good as dead; his eyes are closed.

ALBERT EINSTEIN

As knowledge increases, wonder deepens.

CHARLES MORGAN

Men love to wonder and that is the seed of our science.

RALPH WALDO EMERSON

WORDS *Also see:* BREVITY, DIFFERENCE, JOUR-
NALISM, LANGUAGE, LOQUAC-
ITY, POETRY, PROPAGANDA,
SPEECH.

One great use of words is to hide our thoughts.

VOLTAIRE

Eating words has never given me indigestion.

WINSTON CHURCHILL

The finest words in the world are only vain sounds, if you
cannot comprehend them.

ANATOLE FRANCE

A thousand words will not leave so deep an impression as
one deed.

HENRIK IBSEN

The safest words are always those which bring us most
directly to facts.

CHARLES H. PARKHURST

Without knowing the force of words, it is impossible to
know men.

CONFUCIUS

Suit the action to the word, the word to the action.

WILLIAM SHAKESPEARE

WORK *Also see:* AUTOMATION, DILIGENCE, EF-
FORT, INDUSTRY, LABOR, RE-
TIREMENT, WAGE, ZEAL.

Nothing is really work unless you would rather be doing
something else.

JAMES MATTHEW BARRIE

A man is a worker. If he is not that he is nothing.

JOSEPH CONRAD

Work is the meat of life, pleasure the dessert.

BERTIE CHARLES FORBES

I like work; it fascinates me. I can sit and look at it for
hours.

JEROME K. JEROME

Work is the greatest thing in the world, so we should always
save some of it for tomorrow.

DON HEROLD

The world is filled with willing people; some willing to work,
the rest willing to let them.

ROBERT FROST

Labor disgraces no man, but occasionally men disgrace
labor.

ULYSSES S. GRANT

WORLD *Also see:* CITIZENSHIP, COUNTRY, EARTH,
RETIREMENT, UNIVERSE.

The world gets better every day—then worse again in the
evening.

KIN HUBBARD

The world always had the same bankrupt look, to foregoing
ages as to us.

RALPH WALDO EMERSON

He who imagines he can do without the world deceives
himself much; but he who fancies the world cannot do
without him is still more mistaken.

FRANÇOIS DE LA ROCHEFOUCAULD

The only fence against the world is a thorough knowledge
of it.

JOHN LOCKE

We can only change the world by changing men.

CHARLES WELLS

The world is not growing worse and it is not growing better—it is just turning around as usual.

FINLEY PETER DUNNE

WORRY *Also see:* ANXIETY, AUTOMATION, FEAR,
TRIFLES.

The freedom now desired by many is not freedom to do and
dare but freedom from care and worry.

JAMES TRUSLOW ADAMS

Worry is interest paid on trouble before it is due.

WILLIAM RALPH INGE

I have lost everything, and I am so poor now that I really
cannot afford to let anything worry me.

JOSEPH JEFFERSON

As a cure for worrying, work is better than whiskey.

RALPH WALDO EMERSON

Worry is the interest paid by those who borrow trouble.

GEORGE LYON

Don't tell me that worry doesn't do any good. I know better.
The things I worry about don't happen.

ANONYMOUS

There is nothing that wastes the body like worry, and one
who has any faith in God should be ashamed to worry about
anything whatsoever.

MAHATMA GANDHI

The reason why worry kills more people than work is that
more people worry than work.

ROBERT FROST

WORTH *Also see:* MERIT, QUALITY, RACE, RESPECT.

I believe in the supreme worth of the individual and in his right to life, liberty, and the pursuit of happiness.

JOHN D. ROCKEFELLER

It's not what you pay a man, but what he costs you that counts.

WILL ROGERS

For anything worth having one must pay the price; and the price is always work, patience, love, self-sacrifice.

JOHN BURROUGHS

He is rich or poor according to what he *is*, not according to what he *has*.

HENRY WARD BEECHER

Where quality is the thing sought after, the thing of supreme quality is cheap, whatever the price one has to pay for it.

WILLIAM JAMES

WRITER *Also see:* AMBIGUITY, BOOK, HISTORY, JOURNALISM, LITERATURE, POETRY, QUOTATION, TRUTH, WORD.

Talent alone cannot make a writer. There must be a man behind the book.

RALPH WALDO EMERSON

Nothing gives an author so much pleasure as to find his works respectfully quoted by other learned authors.

BENJAMIN FRANKLIN

Your manuscript is both good and original, but the part that is good is not original, and the part that is original is not good.

SAMUEL JOHNSON

The most original authors are not so because they advance what is new, but because they put what they have to say as if it had never been said before.

JOHANN WOLFGANG VON GOETHE

Every compulsion is put upon writers to become safe, polite, obedient, and sterile.

SINCLAIR LEWIS

You become a good writer just as you become a good joiner: by planing down your sentences.

ANATOLE FRANCE

WRITING . . . See JOURNALISM

WRONG *Also see:* APATHY, CRUELTY, ERROR, EVIL, FOOL, FRAUD, SIN, VICE, WICKEDNESS.

It is better to suffer wrong than to do it, and happier to be sometimes cheated than not to trust.

SAMUEL JOHNSON

Wrong is but falsehood put in practice.

WALTER S. LANDOR

There are few people who are more often in the wrong than those who cannot endure to be so.

FRANÇOIS DE LA ROCHEFOUCAULD

The man who says "I may be wrong, but—" does not believe there can be any such possibility.

KIN HUBBARD

YEARS . . . See AGE

YOUTH *Also see:* AGE, AMERICA, BOYS, CHILDREN, DEBT, DISAPPOINTMENT, GIRLS, MATURITY, SELF-IMPROVEMENT, SENSUALITY.

It is not possible for civilization to flow backwards while there is youth in the world.

HELEN KELLER

Youth is the first victim of war; the first fruit of peace. It takes 20 years or more of peace to make a man; it takes only 20 seconds of war to destroy him.

BAUDOUIN I

Older men declare war. But it is the youth that must fight and die.

HERBERT HOOVER

For God's sake, give me the young man who has brains enough to make a fool of himself.

ROBERT LOUIS STEVENSON

It is better to be a young June-bug than an old bird of paradise.

MARK TWAIN

Youth is that period when a young boy knows everything but how to make a living.

CAREY WILLIAMS

The Youth of a Nation are the trustees of posterity.

BENJAMIN DISRAELI

Youth is a wonderful thing: what a crime to waste it on children.

GEORGE BERNARD SHAW

In youth we run into difficulties, in old age difficulties run into us.

JOSH BILLINGS

Youth comes but once in a lifetime.

HENRY WADSWORTH LONGFELLOW

ZEAL *Also see:* AMBITION, ENTHUSIASM, FANATICISM, PURPOSE, SPIRIT, WILL.

Zeal without humanity is like a ship without a rudder, liable to be stranded at any moment.

OWEN FELLTHAM

The greatest dangers to liberty lurk in insidious encroachment by men of zeal, well-meaning, but without understanding.

LOUIS D. BRANDEIS

Experience shows that success is due less to ability than to zeal. The winner is he who gives himself to his work, body and soul.

CHARLES BUXTON

Zeal is very blind, or badly regulated, when it encroaches upon the rights of others.

QUESNEL

There is no greater sign of a general decay of virtue in a nation, than a want of zeal in its inhabitants for the good of their country.

JOSEPH ADDISON

Zeal is fit only for wise men but is found mostly in fools.

ANCIENT PROBERB

BUSINESS DICTIONARY

ABANDONMENT 1) The elimination from use of a fixed asset.
2) The relinquishing of salvage to the insurers with a view to claiming the full amount of insurance.
3) The relinquishment of a property right by voluntary surrender or neglect.

ABILITY-TO-PAY CONCEPT Idea that those with more wealth or income should proportionally pay more than those with less wealth or income. The progressive tax on income is one example of this idea. A surgeon charging a rich patient much more for an identical operation than he charges a poor patient is another example.

ABSOLUTE ADVANTAGE A condition in which an individual, country, district, or company can make or sell a product below the cost of another. See "comparative advantage."

ABSTRACT OF TITLE A brief statement of the legal evidences of real estate ownership. An abstract of title gives the history of a parcel of land, starting with the original grant and following through each transfer of title to the present titleholder. It also recites all mortgages outstanding on the property and any defects that would cause a cloud on the title. See "cloud on title."

ACCELERATED AMORTIZATION 1) A writing off of the cost of a machine or facility in a shorter period of time than has been customary for the item. This technique reduces income taxes during the period and has been permitted by the federal government as an incentive to production of needed items.
2) Where payment date of the principal of a debt (such as a mortgage) is accelerated by special agreement.

ACCELERATION CLAUSE A clause in a note, bond, or mortgage which provides that in the event of a default by the debtor the entire balance outstanding shall become due and payable.

ACCELERATION PREMIUM Wage plan in which increased production by workers results in an increased rate of pay.

ACCEPTANCE 1) Agreeing to an offer made.
2) A time draft (bill of exchange) on the face of which the drawee has written the word "accepted," the date it is payable, usually the place where it is payable, and his signature. Thus an acceptance is an obligation which the drawee has agreed to pay at maturity. After accepting the draft, the drawee is known as the acceptor. See "bank acceptance" and "trade acceptance."

ACCEPTANCE CREDIT That type of credit which is the result of the substitution of the credit of a more widely known organization such as that of a bank for the credit of a lesser known firm or individual such as a bank's customer or a trade customer. The substitution comes when the bank or other firm "accepts" the commercial paper of its customer.

ACCEPTANCE LIABILITY The total liability which the bank assumes when accepting negotiable instruments drawn upon it by its customers. A record of the instruments so accepted is usually maintained in account form for each customer in a separate ledger, termed the acceptance liability ledger.

ACCESSION 1) The process whereby property which belongs to one person becomes the property of another by reason of its being added to or incorporated with the property of the latter.
2) Attainment to an office; elevation.

ACCESSORIAL SERVICE A service rendered by a carrier in addition to a transportation service, such as assorting, packing, precooling, heating, storage, substitution of tonnage, etc.

ACCESSORY EQUIPMENT Those industrial goods that do not become part of the physical product and which are exhausted only after repeated use, such as major installations, or installation equipment, and auxiliary accessories, or auxiliary equipment.

ACCIDENTAL DEATH BENEFIT Provision for payment of an additional amount in the event death results from an accidental cause or means. See "double indemnity, health and accident" and "double indemnity, life."

ACCIDENTAL MEANS The unexpected or undesigned cause of an accident. The "means" which caused the mishap must be accidental in order to claim policy benefits.

ACCOMMODATION ENDORSEMENT When a person signs or endorses a note or draft solely for the purpose of inducing a bank to lend money to a borrower whose credit is not substantial enough to warrant a loan, such an endorsement is called an accommodation endorsement. The endorser, while being liable to repay the amount in full, ordinarily does not expect to do so. He derives no benefit from the transaction, but acts as a guarantor or surety for the borrower. Another form of accommodation endorsement is the practice among banks of endorsing the acceptances of other banks for a fee, in order to make them acceptable for purchase in the acceptance market.

ACCOMMODATION LINE An insurance company at times will accept from an agent or broker whose entire account is satisfactory, business which would ordinarily be rejected on a strict underwriting basis. Such business is known as an "accommodation line." Insurance that, by itself, would not be acceptable to an insurer, written as an accommodation where the possibility of securing other desirable business seems to justify it.

ACCORD AND SATISFACTION The settlement of a dispute by an executed agreement between the parties whereby the aggrieved party accepts something different from his original right or claim.

ACCOUNT A contract arrangement, written or unwritten, to purchase and take delivery, payment to be made later as arranged; also a record of a transaction.

ACCOUNTABILITIES Those items for which a person, firm, or corporation must render an account, although he or it may not be personally liable for them. For example, an official is responsible for the cash and other assets under his control and must account for them. Moreover, even if a trustee has disbursed all funds confided to his care and has relieved himself of liability, he is still obligated to account for them and the items are, therefore, accountabilities.

ACCOUNT ANALYSIS The process of analyzing an account to determine activity, the size of the balance at given times, the cost of handling transactions on the account, the profit and loss on the account, etc.

ACCOUNTANT An individual who is competent in accounting, systems, audits, balance sheets, profit and loss statements, and bookkeeping. Some accountants are Certified or Registered Public Accountants.

ACCOUNT BALANCE The difference between the debit and the credit sides of an account.

ACCOUNTING The art of recording, classifying, and summarizing in a significant manner and in terms of money, transactions and events which are, in part at least, of a financial character, and interpreting the results thereof.

ACCOUNTING CLASSIFICATIONS Uniform system of accounts prescribed by some authority such as a governmental agency or recommended by a trade association or other authoritative group.

ACCOUNTING PERIOD A time interval at the end of which an analysis is made of the information contained in the bookkeeping records. It is also the period of time covered by the profit and loss statement. It may be any length of time desired, but it is usually a month, three months, six months, or a year.

ACCOUNT IN TRUST An account opened by an individual to be held in trust and maintained for the benefit of another. In the absence of a legally constituted trust fund, withdrawals from the account are subject to the approval of the party establishing the account. An example is an educational fund established by an individual for the benefit of a minor.

ACCOUNTS PAYABLE A current liability representing the amount owed by an individual or a business to a creditor for merchandise or services purchased on open account or short-term credit.

ACCOUNTS RECEIVABLE 1) Money owed by customers for merchandise sold to them on open account—that is, without the giving of a note or other evidence of debt.
2) Any amount owed to a business by a customer, any other individual, or another business on a current account.

ACCRETION The increase or extension of the boundaries, or the acquisition of land by the gradual or imperceptible action of natural forces as by the washing up of sand or soil from the sea or a river, or by a gradual recession of the water from the usual watermark.

ACCRUAL BASIS A method of keeping accounts that shows expenses incurred and income earned for a given fiscal period, even though such expenses and income have not been actually paid or received in cash.

ACCRUE 1) To be gained or obtained; to proceed, arise, or come from; such as, a profit or loss accrues from a commercial transaction.

2) As applied to a right, to come into existence as an enforceable claim; as, a cause of action has accrued when the right to sue has become vested and exercisable.

ACCRUED EXPENSE Expense incurred but not yet paid.

ACCRUED INCOME Income earned but not yet collected. See "asset, accrued."

ACCRUED INTEREST Interest earned but not collected.

ACCUMULATED DIVIDEND The amount of money due the equity holder which has not been paid.

ACCUMULATION 1) Percentage addition to policy benefits as a reward to the insured for continuous renewal. The opposite of the term "amortization."
2) The purchase of a security or securities in such a way that securities are obtained without causing the price to materially increase. The purchase orders are frequently executed when the market is soft and on the down side. If the orders to purchase are expertly executed the price is not "run up" and additional accumulation may be made at relatively favorable prices.
3) The spread between the face amount of a bond and the discount price.

ACKNOWLEDGEMENT 1) A formal declaration made by a person before a competent officer, a notary public, or a court to the effect that he has executed an instrument.
2) The certificate of such a declaration.

ACROSS-THE-BOARD A uniform action such as granting all employees a wage increase of the same amount per hour or the same percent of their wage per hour.

ACT OF GOD An accident or event that is the result of natural causes, without any human intervention or agency, that could not have been prevented by reasonable foresight or care, such as floods, lightning, earthquake, or storms.

ACTS OF BANKRUPTCY Any act enumerated under Section 3 of the National Bankruptcy Act, the most common being the inability to pay debts as they mature of not less than $1,000 and voluntarily appearing in a bankruptcy court or by involuntary bankruptcy in which creditors who are unpaid petition the bankruptcy court.

ACTUARIAL ASSUMPTIONS Estimates of future experience with respect to the rates of mortality, disability, turnover, ages at retirement, rate of investment, income, and salary trends. Such estimates are generally determined from past experience, modified for possible changes in conditions which may affect the future experience.

ACTUARIAL VALUATION A mathematical determination of the financial condition of a retirement plan. It includes the computation of the present monetary value of benefits payable to present members, and the present monetary value of future employer and employee contributions, giving effect to mortality among active and retired members and also to the rates of disability, retirement, withdrawal from service, salary, and interest.

ACTUARY A professional expert in pension and life insurance matters, particularly trained in mathematical, statistical, and accounting methods and procedures, and in insurance probabilities.

ADDITION An addition to a fixed asset already recorded in the property ledger (as distinguished from a newly acquired asset). Examples are additional floor space added to an existing building, and new attachments to a piece of equipment.

ADDITIONAL EXTENDED COVERAGE An endorsement for policies covering dwellings and similar property, extending the coverage to include insurance against direct loss caused by water damage from plumbing and heating systems, rupture or bursting of steam of hot water heating systems, vandalism and malicious mischief, vehicles owned or operated by the insured or by a tenant, glass breakage, ice, snow, and freezing, as well as fall of trees, and collapse.

ADJUSTED TRIAL BALANCE A merger of the trial balance columns of the work sheet with the adjustment columns. The adjusted trial balance represents the trial balance that would be obtained if it were prepared immediately after the adjusting entries were posted.

ADJUSTER An individual who acts for the company or the insured in the settlement of claims. He leads to agreement about the amount of a loss and the company's liability. Adjusters may be salaried employees of adjusting organizations operated by insurance companies, individuals operating independently and engaged by the companies to adjust a particular loss, and special agents or staff adjusters employed by the company. The term "claim representative" is used interchangeably. Not to be confused with public adjusters who represent claimants only.

ADJUSTING ENTRIES Those entries made in a journal at the end of an accounting period to correct errors that have been found and to assign expenses and income to the correct time period by such devices as use of deferred charges and prepaid expenses.

ADMINISTERED PRICE A price which is not the result of the full play of supply and demand but rather has been arrived at by some restraints such as monopoly, duopoly, oligopoly, or government action.

ADMINISTRATION 1) Direction and evaluation by supervisory personnel including both administrative duties and administrative functions.
2) The care and management of an estate by an executor, an administrator, a trustee, or a guardian.

ADMINISTRATIVE EXPENSE Expenses chargeable to the managerial, general administrative and policy phases of a business in contrast to sales, manufacturing, or cost of goods expense.

ADMINISTRATIVE LAW As distinguished from common law or statute law, administrative law results from the regulations of a governmental body, either state or federal, which is responsible for carrying out statute law.

ADMINISTRATOR A person or an institution appointed by a court to settle an estate when the decedent has left no will, when no executor has been named in the will if the decedent has left one, or when the named executor has died or is unwilling to serve.

ADMIRALTY COURT A court having jurisdiction on maritime questions and offenses, including suits involving marine insurance contracts and general average adjustments.

ADMISSION BY INVESTMENT Term meaning that a new partner is admitted into a partnership by contributing additional cash to the business, thereby increasing the assets and the proprietorship of the business.

ADMITTED COMPANY A company is termed "admitted" within a given state when licensed to do business in that state. An insurer of another state or country licensed under the insurance law of a state to do business in that state.

ADMITTED TO DEALINGS Official approval by an exchange and the SEC to a security whereby it is "admitted to the list"; *i.e.,* The security has the privilege of being traded on the particular exchange to which it is admitted.

AD VALOREM Designates an assessment of taxes or duties against property or goods. Literally, "according to the value." Ad valorem duties are those estimated at a percentage of the value of the goods.

ADVANCE 1) A loan.
2) An increase in price.
3) A payment on account.

ADVANCE BILL A bill of exchange drawn in advance of the shipment of goods.

ADVERSE POSSESSION A possession inconsistent with the right of the true owner.

ADVERTISING The practice of bringing to the public's notice the good qualities of something in order to induce the public to buy or invest in it.

ADVERTISING AGENCY A business which prepares advertising for its customers and performs other related services such as market research.

ADVERTISING MEDIA The means through which advertisements are conveyed to the consumers or users whom they are designed to influence. Magazines, newpapers, radio, television, and direct mail are all media.

AFFIDAVIT A statement in writing sworn to before a person authorized by law to take oaths; it is made without cross-examination and in this respect differs from a deposition.

AFFILIATED COMPANY Under the Investment Company Act, a company in which there is any direct or indirect ownership of 5 percent or more of the outstanding voting securities.

AFTER-ACQUIRED CLAUSE That portion of a mortgage which states that any additional property which the mortgagor acquires after the mortgage is drawn will also be security for the loan.

AGE CHANGE In insurance, the date halfway between natural birth dates when the age of an individual, for the purpose of life insurance rating, changes to the next higher age, insurance age being the nearer birthday. Annuity age is commonly the last previous birthday.

AGENCY 1) The status or the relation between an agent and his principal.
2) A term used to describe certain types of accounts in trust institutions. The main distinguishing characteristic of an agency is that the title to the property does not pass to the

trust institution but remains in the name of the owner of the property, who is known as the principal. See "agent."

AGENCY SHOP A form of union security under which all employees, nonmembers as well as members of a union, pay union dues as a condition of employment.

AGENT A person who is authorized to act for or represent another person (usually called the principal) in dealing with a third party.

AGENTS' QUALIFICATION LAWS Laws which each state passes, setting up standards of specific knowledge and qualification that an agent must meet in order to be legally permitted to practice certain professions and occupations in that state. *i.e.,* brokers, agents, factors.

AGGREGATE CORPORATION An incorporated venture having more than one stockholder.

AGGREGATE-OF-INTERMEDIATES CLAUSE A provision in Section 4 of the Interstate Commerce Act which prohibits a through rate higher than the sum of intermediate rates except as authorized by the Commission after investigation.

AGING ACCOUNTS RECEIVABLE The process of analyzing each customer's account to determine how old each unpaid charge is. It is one basis for determining the estimate of bad debts expense. See "accounts receivable."

AGREED-AMOUNT CLAUSE Policy provision in which the holder agrees to carry a stated or determinable amount of insurance. An amount of insurance specified in the contract as being sufficient to nullify the effect of a coinsurance, average, or contribution clause of the contract.

AGRICULTURAL PAPER Those acceptances, notes, and similar documents which have arisen out of agricultural, farming, or ranching transactions rather than trade, commerce, or industry.

AIR RIGHTS The rights vested by grant (fee simple, lease agreement, or other conveyance) of an estate in real property to build upon, occupy, or use, in the manner and degree permitted, all or any portion of space above the ground or any other stated elevation without vertical planes, the basis of which corresponds with the boundaries of the real estate described in the grant.

ALEATORY CONTRACT The parties to a contract realize that the values given up by each party will not be equal. When such is the fact, it is an "aleatory contract."

ALL-COMMODITY RATE A freight rate, usually a carload rate, applying to a shipment regardless of the nature of the commodities included, subject to stated exceptions and conditions; also called all-freight rate.

ALLOCATION The crediting of a receipt in its entirety or the charging of a disbursement in its entirety to one account, as to the principal account or to the income account; to be distinguished from apportionment.

ALLOTMENT A share, part, or portion granted or distributed.

ALLOWANCE FOR BAD DEBTS Same as "Reserve for Bad Debts"; an account for showing the estimated loss on uncollectible debts as an offset against the value shown for accounts receivable.

ALLOWANCE FOR DEPRECIATION An account recording the accumulation of periodical credits made to reduce the value of fixed assets as a result of depreciation. See "depreciation."

ALLOWED TIME That amount of time that employers permit their employees to have for such purposes as adjusting their machines, taking care of personal needs, etc., when the employees are on a piecework basis.

ALLOY That combination of base metal such as copper, zinc, or tin which is added to precious metals such as silver or gold to provide against abrasion.

ALTERATION 1) A change or rearrangement in the structural parts of something.
2) Applied to a building or structure, alteration is a change or rearrangement in the structural parts or in the exit facilities; or an enlargement, whether by extending on a side or by increasing in height; including work, other than repairs, that would affect safety or a vital element of an elevator, plumbing, gas piping, wiring, ventilating or heating installation; the term "alter" in its various moods and tenses and its participial forms, refers to the making of an alteration.
3) Any change involving an erasure or rewriting in the date, amount, or payee of a check or other negotiable instrument. In accounting records, necessary alterations are best made by crossing out the "old" figure, leaving it legible, and writing the correct one above or below the original.

AMALGAMATION The uniting or combining of two or more businesses.

AMERICAN EXPERIENCE TABLE OF MORTALITY A listing by age of the probable death rates among insurance risks.

AMERICAN FEDERATION OF LABOR AND CONGRESS OF INDUSTRIAL ORGANIZATIONS The national labor organization in the United States made up of national, international, and local unions.

AMERICAN STOCK EXCHANGE A leading securities exchange located in New York City. Formerly known as the Outdoor Market or New York Curb Exchange because it initially conducted operations outdoors at Wall and Hanover Streets. Moved indoors at 86 Trinity Place in 1921. Present name was adopted in 1953. It is the largest market for foreign securities in the United States.

AMORTIZATION The gradual reduction of a debt by means of periodic payments sufficient to meet current interest and extinguish the debt at maturity. When the debt involves real property, often the periodic payments include a sum sufficient to pay taxes and insurance on the property. In connection with bond investment, the gradual extinguishment of a premium or a discount until the book value of the bond is equal to par value at maturity or at the earliest call date, as the case may be.

AMORTIZED MORTGAGE A mortgage payable in installments, usually monthly, both as to principal and interest.

AMORTIZED VALUE The investment value of a security is determined by the process of amortization. This value is appropriate for use in connection with bonds which are fully secured and are not in default as to either principal or interest.

ANARCHISM The abolishment of ownership of private property and of coercive government.

ANCILLARY Subordinate or auxiliary; used in such terms as ancillary administration, ancillary administrator, and ancillary guardian.

ANNUAL REPORT 1) The yearly report made by a company at the close of the fiscal year, stating the company's receipts and disbursements, assets and liabilities. Such a statement usually includes an account of the progress made by the company during the year.
2) The annual report, as of December 31, of an insurer to the state insurance department, showing assets and liabilities, receipts and disbursements, and other information.

ANNUAL WAGE The rate of pay for one year's work including such agreed upon time off for vacation and/or sick leave.

ANNUITY A series of periodic payments for a fixed future period or for life, payable monthly, semiannually, annually, or at other specified intervals. It is frequently used to describe a part of the retirement allowance derived from the accumulated contributions made by the member, as distinguished from that part of the retirement allowance financed by employer's contributions which is called a "pension."

ANNUITY BOND An investment, usually one not providing a maturity date.

ANNUITY, CASH REFUND A life annuity with an agreement that the insurer, on the death of the annuitant, will pay in a lump sum to a beneficiary any amount by which the consideration paid to the insurer exceeds the payments made to the annuitant.

ANNUITY CERTAIN An annuity payable for a specified period of time, regardless of the time of death of the annuitant.

ANNUITY, DEFERRED An annuity under which payments will begin at some specified future date provided the specified beneficiary is alive at such date.

ANNUITY, GROUP A pension plan providing annuities at retirement to a group of persons under a master contract. It is usually issued to an employer for the benefit of employees. The individual members of the group hold certificates as evidence of their coverage. The most common type of group annuity provides for the purchase each year of a paid-up deferred annuity for each member, the total amount received by the member at retirement being the sum of these deferred annuities. Another type is the deposit administration plan.

ANNUITY, VARIABLE An annuity in which the insurance company agrees to pay an amount of money to the beneficiary. The amount will vary with the value of equities purchased as investments by the insurance companies. Most annuities are fixed as to the annual amount of payment but the variable annuity is not. Proponents of variable annuities believe that they provide a better hedge against inflation than the fixed annuities; however, variable annuities are not permitted to be sold in many states.

ANTICIPATION RATE A discount or rebate for payment prior to the stated terms of payment.

ANTICIPATION, RIGHT OF The privilege given the mortgagor, by a provision in the mortgage instruments, to pay all or any portion of the outstanding balance of the obligation prior to its due date without penalty.

ANTI-INJUNCTION LAW (NORRIS-LAGUARDIA ACT) A federal statute restricting the use of injunctions by federal courts in labor disputes. Many state statutes have used this act as a model.

ANTI-RACKETEERING ACT Federal statute forbidding robbery or extortion that affects interstate commerce.

ANTI-STRIKEBREAKING ACT (BYRNES ACT) Federal law which prohibits interstate transportation of strikebreakers.

ANTITRUST Opposed to trusts or large combinations of capital.

APPORTIONED TAX The distribution of a tax by the collecting unit among other governmental units.

APPORTIONMENT CLAUSE A clause found in an insurance policy which distributes the insurance in proportion to the total coverage. Thus, you may have two $1,000 fire insurance policies on a building and one of them provides extended coverage against windstorm and the other does not. In the event of a $100 loss from a windstorm, you would only receive $50 or 50% of the loss. If both policies had provided this extended coverage, you would receive full payment, however, of the loss.

APPRAISAL 1) Evaluation of a specific piece of personal or real property, or the property of another as a whole.
2) The value placed on the property evaluated.

APPRAISAL CLAUSE A clause in an insurance policy which provides that the insured or the insurance company shall have the right to demand an appraisal to fix or determine the amount of damage in terms of money. This would also refer to loss as well as damage.

APPRAISAL SURPLUS The excess of appraised values over book values.

APPRAISE Estimate the value.

APPRAISED VALUE The values arrived at in an appraisal of property.

APPRECIATION The increase in the value of an asset in excess of its depreciable cost due to economic and other conditions, as distinguished from increases in value due to improvements or additions made to it.

APPRENTICE A worker serving a special training period in preparation to admission to full status as a skilled tradesman.

APPROPRIATION An authorized sum of money set aside, frequently in a separate fund, to pay certain known or anticipated costs of a given item or service.

APPURTENANCE Something belonging or attached to something else and passing as incident to the principal thing; as, a right-of-way (the appurtenance) over land (the principal thing).

ARBITRAGE The buying of stocks, bonds, or other securities in one market and selling in another.

ARBITRATION The hearing and determination of a controversy between parties by a person or persons chosen by the parties, or appointed under statutory authority, instead of hearing and determination by a judicial tribunal.

ARBITRATION CLAUSE A provision in a contract requiring that disputes arising out of or relating to the collective bargaining agreement be finally determined by arbitration.

ARBITRATION OF EXCHANGE The prices of bills of exchange payable in foreign currency vary in different financial centers in the world. Therefore, a person in country A may find it profitable to purchase a bill of exchange in country B for payment in country C. This is arbitration of exchange.

AREA AGREEMENT A collective-bargaining agreement covering a given physical or geographical region, its terms and conditions governing all companies which participate.

AREA-WIDE BARGAINING Negotiating between a single union and the management of different companies in that skill or trade within a geographic area such as a state or section.

ARREARS Amounts past due and unpaid. A bond or preferred stock is "in arrears" when interest or dividends have fallen due but have not been paid.

ARSON The willful and malicious burning of property; if someone deliberately sets fire to a property, that is arson. If an individual carries fire insurance the damage will be paid for under the terms of the policy just as though the fire had started accidentally; however, if it can be proved that the insured himself was the arsonist, that is, he started the fire himself or had some one do it for him for the purposes of collecting damages, the insurance is automatically voided.

ARTICLES OF ASSOCIATION A certificate similar to one of incorporation which is used by non-stock companies such as charitable, eleemosynary and mutual corporations. It sets forth the pertinent data on the organization and is filed with the appropriate governmental agencies upon approval and becomes part of the public record.

ARTICLES OF COPARTNERSHIP The written agreement by which a partnership is formed.

ARTICLES OF INCORPORATION A certificate of incorporation which sets forth the pertinent data on a corporation. The certificate is filed with the appropriate governmental agencies upon approval and becomes part of the public record.

AS IS Goods which are sold "as is" have not the usual implied warranties and may be damaged or shopworn; for these reasons the prices are usually lowered from the regular prices.

ASKED PRICE 1) That price at which a commodity or security is offered for sale either over the counter or on an exchange.
2) In the case of open-end shares, the price (including the selling charge or load) at which the buyer may purchase stock from the investment company. In the case of closed-end shares, the lowest price at which the stock is then offered for sale in the public market.

ASSESSED VALUATION A valuation set upon real estate or other property by a government as a basis for levying taxes or for condemnation purposes.

ASSESSMENT 1) A share of expenses.
2) The attempt to raise additional capital by making a levy on a security, the assumption being that without assessment for additional capital the corporation will experience difficulties but with additional capital the projected success of the corporation will more than compensate for the levy.
3) An appraisal or estimate.

ASSESSMENT ROLL In the case of real property, the official list containing the legal description of each parcel of property and its assessed valuation. In the case of other property, the official list containing the name and address of each owner of such property and its assessed value.

ASSESSOR The designated public official who makes the official estimate of value.

ASSET Anything owned by a business or by an individual which has commercial or exchange value. Assets may consist of specific property or of claims against others, in contrast to obligations due to others (liabilities).

ASSET, ACCRUED Assets arising from revenues earned but not yet due, such as unbilled utility sales accrued since bills were last rendered to customers and accrued interest on investments. See "accrue."

ASSET, CAPITAL Those assets which are not readily convertible into cash and in the ordinary course of business are not so converted, more often termed fixed assets.

ASSET, CURRENT Those assets which are readily convertible into cash without substantial loss; included are cash, investments, notes and accounts receivable, and inventories.

ASSET, DEAD Those assets which are not productive of income under normal operations. A standby machine tool or a high-cost facility that is not used except in emergencies is a dead asset during those periods it is not in use.

ASSET, DEFERRED Assets which are not readily convertible into cash, or subject to current settlement.

ASSET, FIXED Assets of a long-term character which are intended to continue to be held or used, such as land, buildings, machinery, furniture, and other equipment. The term does not indicate the immobility of an asset which is the distinctive characteristic of "fixture." See "asset, capital."

ASSET, FLOATING A quick asset such as cash, government bonds or prime listed securities.

ASSET, FROZEN Any asset which cannot be used by its owner because of legal action. The owner cannot use it, nor can he dispose of the asset until the process of law has been completed and a decision passed down from the courts.

ASSET, HYPOTHECATED Things pledged without transferring possession or title.

ASSET, INTANGIBLE Something to which a business enterprise attaches an arbitrary dollar value, not because it has real value in itself but because it helps to produce real values in a going business. Patents, trademarks, service marks, franchises, and goodwill are examples of intangible assets.

ASSET, LIQUID Those assets, generally current assets, which may be quickly turned into cash.

ASSET, NOMINAL An asset whose value is inconsiderable, doubtful or difficult to evaluate such as judgments or claims in reorganization. Accounting conventions generally recommend that nominal assets be written down and carried at some token value. The customary amount is one dollar. This calls attention to the asset but also conservatively values it. Goodwill, copyrights and such assets may be considered at times to be nominal assets.

ASSET, TANGIBLE Those assets which are of a physical and material nature (perceptible to touch) as distinguished from intangible assets which are imperceptible to touch. Examples of tangible assets are: Cash, land, buildings, etc.

ASSET VALUE PER SHARE, NET With regard to investment companies, this is the ratio of the current asset value of securities held in the portfolio minus all liabilities divided by the number of shares outstanding. This figure is computed at least once daily by investment companies and indicates investment progress. A load charge, or commission, is added to this net asset value per share to get the selling price of most mutual fund shares.

ASSET, WASTING Assets which are exhausted through use or lose their value through the passage of time, such as oil wells, mining claims, and patents.

ASSIGNED ACCOUNT An account, such as an accounts receivable account, which has been assigned to a bank as security for a loan by the borrower. In theory, the bank actually takes possession of the account pledged, and when this account is paid by the borrower's customer, it should be paid directly to the bank to reduce the borrower's loan. In actual practice, and in order not to jeopardize the relationship between the borrower and his customer (whose account has been pledged), the bank will allow the account to be paid by the borrower in the normal manner, and rely upon the integrity of the borrower to apply this payment against the loan balance.

ASSIGNED RISK A risk which insurance underwriters do not care to insure but which, because of state law or otherwise, must be insured. The insurance is, therefore, handled through a pool of insurers and assigned to companies in turn.

ASSIGNEE One to whom property, or a limited interest, is transferred.

ASSIGNMENT The transfer of title to certain property, usually securities. The assignment form usually contains the wording, "sell, assign, and transfer unto."

ASSIGNOR One who transfers property he possesses.

ASSOCIATION AGREEMENT A collective-bargaining agreement applicable to all members of the employer association which has negotiated it.

ASSUMPTION OF RISK The common-law doctrine, since superseded by various states' Workmen's Compensation Laws, which held that employees seeking employment in an occupation assumed the risk of injury in that activity.

ASSURANCE Same as insurance. Term widely used in England and Canada.

ASSURED An interchangeable word that is the same in meaning as insured.

AT SIGHT A term used in the body of negotiable instruments indicating that payment is due upon presentation or demand.

ATTACHED ACCOUNT An account against which a court order has been issued, permitting disbursement of the attached balance only with the consent of the court.

ATTACHMENT 1) A legal process by which property is taken into custody or possession.
2) The instrument which issues from such a process.

ATTESTATION CLAUSE The clause of a document containing the formal declaration of the act of witnessing; in the case of a will, the clause immediately following the signature of the testator and usually beginning, "signed, sealed, published, and declared by the said . . ."

AT THE MARKET An order "at the market" is executed at the current price.

ATTORNEY-AT-LAW A person who is legally qualified and authorized to represent and act for clients in legal proceedings; to be distinguished from an attorney-in-fact.

ATTORNEY-IN-FACT A person who, as agent, is given written authorization by another person to transact business for his principal out of court; to be distinguished from an attorney-at-law. See "power of attorney."

ATTRACTIVE NUISANCE A dangerous place, condition, or object which is particularly attractive to people, particularly children. In these cases the courts have frequently held that where "attractiveness" exists, the owner is under a duty to take steps to prevent injury to those that may be attracted, and the owner may be held liable for failure to do so.

AUDIT In general, an examination of accounting documents and of supporting evidence for the purpose of reaching an informed opinion concerning their propriety. An examination intended to serve as a basis for an expression of opinion regarding the fairness, consistency, and conformity with accepted accounting principles of statements prepared by a corporation or other entity for submission to the public or to other interested parties.

AUDIT FUNCTION Periodic or continuous verification of a firm's assets and liabilities. This function is performed by an auditor. The auditor is responsible for the carrying out of this verification.

AUDITOR An officer of a firm who is in charge of all audit functions. In some firms he is directly responsible to the board of directors.

AUDITOR'S CERTIFICATE A statement signed by an auditor in which he states that he has examined the financial statements, the system of internal control, the accounting records, and supporting evidence in accordance with generally accepted auditing standards and in which he expresses his opinion, based on such examination, regarding the financial condition of a business firm or any of its enterprises, the results from operations, and any facts which he has investigated in his professional capacity. See "unqualified certificate."

AUDIT TRAIL An auditing concept that provides, in a step-by-step fashion, the history of an account by carrying in the account master file the date and serial number of the last previous transaction. This allows the auditor to trace back all transactions affecting the account.

AUTHENTICATION 1) The legal verification of a document, proving it genuine or true.
2) The signing, by the trustee, of a certificate on a bond for the purpose of identifying it being issued under a certain indenture, thus validating the bond.

AUTHORITY TO PURCHASE (LETTER OF CREDIT) This term is generally used in connection with Far Eastern trade. It is a substitute for a commercial letter of credit and permits the bank to which it is directed to purchase drafts drawn on an importer rather than on a bank. Drafts drawn under authority to purchase have to be marked with the "A/P" number and must conform to the conditions of the letter of authority to purchase. Drafts drawn under "A/P's" are usually confined to United States dollar transactions and branch or correspondent banks in the cities where such drafts originate.

AUTHORIZED CAPITAL STOCK The total amount of stock that a corporation is permitted by its charter to issue.

AUTHORIZED INVESTMENT An investment that is authorized by a trust instrument; to be distinguished from a legal investment.

AUTHORIZED ISSUE The amount of a security issue stipulated in a corporation's charter which can be changed only by amendment.

AUTHORIZED POWER The power assigned to a radio station by the Federal Communications Commission and specified in the instrument of authorization. The authorized power does not necessarily correspond to the power used by the Commission for purposes of its Master Frequency Record (MFR) and notification to the Bureau of the International Telecommunications Union.

AUTHORIZER The individual in charge of the credit department designated to approve or disapprove requests for purchases to be charged to credit accounts.

AUTOMATIC CHECK-OFF A deduction made by an employer from an employee's paycheck that goes into effect without any authorization by the employee, such as union dues sent directly to the union.

AUTOMATIC COVER Coverage provided in many forms of insurance usually for a specified period and limited amount, to cover increasing values, newly acquired and changing interests.

AUTOMATIC PREMIUM LOAN A contractual agreement by an insurance company to utilize the cash value of the insurance policy to pay a past-due premium. This prevents a lapse in coverage. A feature in a life insurance policy providing that any premium not paid by the end of the grace period (usually 31 days) be automatically paid by a policy loan if there is sufficient cash value.

AUTOMATIC REINSTATEMENT CLAUSE A clause in an insurance policy which provides for the automatic reinstatement of the full face value of the policy after payment for a loss. See "reinstatement."

AUTOMATION Advanced mechanization or technical developments, including continuous-flow production processes controlled by electronics, electronic computing machines, and self-regulating machines which perform precise operations in sequence.

AUTONOMOUS INVESTMENT The formation of new capital without regard for the cost of the investment in terms of interest rate or of national income. Most investments by public agencies are autonomous while most investments by private profit-seeking individuals or agencies would be induced.

AUTONOMOUS TARIFF Import duties resulting from action by the legislative body and not from commercial treaties.

AUXILIARY EQUIPMENT Accessory equipment necessary for the operation of something, such as a facility or plant. Example: Pumps, stokers, fans, etc.

AVAILABILITY DATE In banking, the date on which a check drawn on an out-of-town bank will be considered as having been converted into cash.

AVERAGE See "general average" and "particular average."

AVERAGE CLAUSE 1) In insurance, a term loosely used to mean pro rata distribution or a coinsurance clause.
2) A clause providing that the insurer shall be liable in the event of loss for not more than that proportion of the loss which the amount of the insurance under the policy bears to a specified percentage of the acutal cash value of the property insured. See "coinsurance clause" and "pro rata distribution clause."

AVERAGE DAILY BALANCE In finance, the average amount of money that a depositor keeps on deposit, determined by adding the daily balances of his account for a given length of time and dividing the total by the number of days covered.

AVERAGE OUT To conclude a trade or commitment in the market without loss, or at a profit, by the process of averaging; i.e., buying securities at different prices, but selling at a time when price is equal to or better than the average price of purchases.

AVERAGING UP OR DOWN The practice of making purchases of the same security at different price levels, thereby arriving at a higher or a lower average cost than the first commitment.

AWARD A decision of an arbitrator; to be distinguished from a decree and a judgment.

BACKHAUL To haul a shipment back over a part of a route which it has traveled.

BACKLOG An accumulation of work or orders not completed.

BACK PAY 1) Wages due for past services, often the difference between money already received and a higher amount resulting from a change in wage rates.

2) Under the National Labor Relations Act "back pay" is the amount a discriminatorily discharged employee would have earned if no discrimination had occurred, minus his earnings during the discrimination period.

BACKTRACKING Exercise of seniority rights to displace junior employees by longer-service workers when business conditions require temporary layoffs or the discontinuance of departments.

BAILEE The person to whom goods are committed in trust.

BAILMENT The delivery of personal property by one person to another for some specific purpose, such as for use, repairs, or safekeeping, but without passing title to the property. The person delivering the property is known as the bailor; the person receiving it, the bailee.

BAILOR One who delivers goods to another in trust for some particular purpose.

BALANCED FUND An investment company which at all times holds bonds and/or preferred stocks and cash in varying ratios to its holdings of common stocks, in order to maintain relatively greater stability of both capital and income.

BALANCE OF PAYMENTS In international finance, the difference between all visible and invisible trade payments made by a nation to foreign creditors and the visible and invisible items paid by foreign debtors during a stated period of time. Invisible items would include such payments of foreign exchange for insurance, shipping and immigrant remittances.

BALANCE OF TRADE In international finance, the relationship, expressed in monetary units between a nation's exports and imports. If the exports exceed the imports the term "favorable balance of trade" is used. If imports exceed the exports it is termed "unfavorable balance of trade." Annual figures are generally used.

BALANCE SHEET A detailed listing of assets, liabilities, and capital accounts (net worth) showing the financial condition of a company on a given date. The balance sheet of a bank is generally referred to as a statement of condition.

BALANCE-SHEET ACCOUNTS Accounts designated to show the assets, liabilities, and corporate surplus or deficit of the corporation.

BALLOON LOAN A loan in which small periodic payments are made during the term of the loan. These sums are not sufficient to pay the full loan so that at the end of the period there is a need to refinance the loan since the last payment is a balloon or large amount that was not expected to be paid in full. Credit insurance of level term or decreasing term life may be written to cover the loan.

BANK An organization, normally a corporation, chartered by the state or federal government, the principal functions of which are: To receive demand deposits and pay customers' checks drawn against them; to receive time deposits and pay interest thereon; to discount notes, make loans, and invest in government or other securities; to collect checks, drafts, notes, etc.; to issue drafts and cashier's checks; to certify depositors' checks; when authorized by a chartering government, it may act in a fiduciary or trustee capacity.

BANK ACCEPTANCE A draft drawn on a bank and accepted by the bank.

BANK CALL The demand made upon a bank by a supervisory authority for a sworn statement of the bank's condition as of a certain date.

BANK CHARGE PLAN Usually a copyrighted plan brought to a community by a bank or private organization under charter or franchise for providing a complete credit service including credit authorization, issuance of credit cards, and billing and collection of 30-day accounts for member stores. Most banks charge 5% or less of total credit sales for their service.

BANK CHECK A check drawn by a bank on itself and signed by an authorized officer. Savings banks do not usually draw such checks. Also called treasurer's check, officer's check, or cashier's check.

BANK CREDIT The credit created by commercial banks through the media of loans and discounts—granted with or without collateral. The amount of credit so extended is controlled in part by the rediscount rates established by the Federal Reserve Board.

BANK DEBITS The sum total of all debits (made up of sight drafts honored and checks and other instruments) drawn against deposited funds of individuals, partnerships, corporations, and other legal entities during a given period of time—usually reported by banks daily.

BANK DISCOUNT The charge, generally expressed as a percent of the face amount of the commercial paper or personal note which is made by a bank, for payment of the paper or note before its maturity.

BANK DRAFT A check drawn by a bank against funds deposited to its account in another bank.

BANK-ELIGIBLE ISSUES Issues of United States Treasury obligations eligible for immediate purchase by commercial banks—mainly those due or callable within ten years.

BANK EXAMINER A person who as the representative of a federal or state bank supervisory authority examines the banks under its jurisdction with respect to their financial condition, management, and policies.

BANK EXCHANGES Those items such as checks, notes, drafts, etc., which are collected through a clearinghouse system.

BANK NOTE A noninterest-bearing promissory note of a bank issued for general circulation as money and payable to the bearer on demand. In the United States only the Federal Reserve Banks now issue bank notes.

BANK OF DISCOUNT Those banks, generally commercial banks, which will extend credit on acceptances, bills of exchange and notes.

BANK-POST REMITTANCE Any bill of exchange of foreign origin which a bank has honored and pays through the use of the mail either by money order or by cash.

BANK RATE The interest rate charged by the bank on typical loans. Also the discount rate established by a central bank. This is the rate that the commercial bank must pay to discount or borrow from the central bank.

BANK RUN A situation in which abnormally large withdrawals are made on a bank out of fear that the bank may close.

BANKRUPTCY A state of conditions in which the financial position of an individual, corporation or other legal entity is such as to cause them to be actually or legally bankrupt. Such condition is commonly referred to as a condition of insolvency.

BANK STATEMENT A monthly statement of account which a bank renders to each of its depositors. It shows in detail the amounts deposited, the checks paid by the bank, and the balance on hand at the end of the month.

BARGAINING AGENT Union recognized or designated as the exclusive representative of employees in a bargaining unit.

BARGAINING RIGHTS 1) Rights of workers to negotiate through chosen representatives concerning terms and conditions of employment.
2) The right of the union designated by a majority of the workers in an appropriate bargaining unit to represent the group in collective bargaining.

BARGAINING UNIT The employee group that, in the light of all factors of related skill and interest, is the appropriate unit for collective bargaining.

BAROMETERS Those business indexes which are used to evaluate the condition of a market or economy. Industrial production, total employment, freight car loadings, etc., are among some of the statistical series which are considered to be barometers.

BARTER The exchange, without the use of money, of one item or service for another.

BASE PAY Wages paid, exclusive of overtime, premiums and bonuses.

BASE PERIOD Many statistical series choose a "base period" or normal period which is given the weight or value of 100. As the time series are computed the current data are related to the base. If the measurement in the base period, for example, was 200 units and current measurement is 300 units, one could express the base as 100 and current as 150. By reducing the data to a percentage of the base period, complex data may be more easily evaluated.

BASE RATE The straight-time rate of pay, excluding premiums, incentive bonuses, etc.

BASIC CROPS Those agricultural commodities designated by the Congress as such. Currently corn, cotton, peanuts, rice, tobacco and wheat are considered as being basic crops. As such, they are under price support programs.

BASIC YIELD A concept similar to pure interest; that is, the annual rate of return in percent on a risk-free investment such as a long-term United States Government bond. Even in this illustration there is some risk including the effect of inflation on purchasing power of the future income from the bond.

BASING POINT A technique for quoting prices of products. The buyer figures his delivered cost from the geographic point used as the base even though the product is not necessarily shipped from there.

BASIS POINT A measure for small differences in yields; 100 basis points equaling 1%. For example, there is a 20 basis point spread (difference) between bonds quoted at yields of 1.30% and 1.10%.

BATCH PROOF A system for proving deposits, usually performed in the following sequence: Deposits are assembled in groups of various sizes; deposit tickets are sorted into one group; checks are sorted into several classifications, as clearings, transit, bookkeeping, etc.; cash release tickets are sorted according to tellers; deposit tickets, checks, and cash release tickets are listed on a "batch" or "block" sheet in their respective columns; the total of the deposits and other credits should equal the recapitulation of the checks and other debits.

BEAR Someone who believes the stock market will decline. See "bull."

BEARER The individual who has physical possession of a negotiable instrument which is payable to the bearer.

BEARER FORM In a form payable to bearer, the security having no registered owner.

BEAR MARKET A period of generally declining market prices.

BEAR POSITION Means a "short position" or the prevailing market position of a pessimist; *i.e.,* one who has sold securities short in hopes that the market will turn downward, at which point securities will be bought at a lower price to give a net profit.

BENCH MARKS Identification symbols on stone, metal, or other durable matter permanently fixed in the ground from which differences of elevation are measured as in tidal observation or topographical surveys.

BENEFICIARY One who receives benefits, profits, or advantages.

BENEFITS-RECEIVED TAX PRINCIPLE Concept that a person or company should be taxed in the same proportion to the benefits he receives from the tax agency. The use of a gasoline tax to build better roads for the motorists is an illustration of this principle.

BEQUEATH To give personal property by will; to be distinguished from devise.

BEQUEST A gift of personal property by will; a legacy.

BEST BID The highest price anyone is willing to pay for something offered for sale. This bid is the relevant one in establishing the market for a stock.

BETTERMENT An improvement in a property which is considered to add to the investment or capital cost as distinguished from repairs or replacements where the original character or cost is unchanged.

BID A price offered subject, unless otherwise stated, to immediate acceptance for a specific amount of a commodity or a stock.

BID-AND-ASKED PRICE   The price at which an owner offers to sell (asked) and the price at which someone has agreed to buy (bid). Usually used in reference to stocks and bonds but may apply to any property in which there is an active trade.

BIDDING UP   The act of successively raising the price bid for a security or commodity to higher levels for fear of failing to have an order executed before an advance is under way.

BID PRICE   In the case of open-end shares, the price at which the holder may redeem his shares; in most cases it is the current net asset value per share. In the case of closed-end shares, the highest price then offered for stock in the public market.

BILL   1) A note or bill of exchange.
2) A document showing the amount that is due a creditor which is given or sent to a debtor.
3) A bill of sale, a way bill, a due bill, or paper money such as a ten dollar bill.

BILL DISCOUNTED   A promissory note or bill of exchange from which the bank deducts, in advance, its fee or interest for lending the money (usually to the holder or endorser).

BILL OF CREDIT   A written instrument in which the drawer requests the firm or individual addressed to advance credit to the bearer or named firm or individual at the risk of the drawer.

BILL OF EXCHANGE   An unconditional order in writing, addressed by one person to another, signed by the person issuing it, which requires the person to whom it is addressed to pay a specified sum of money to the order of a third person. Used interchangeably with "draft."

BILL OF LADING   A document issued by a railroad or other carrier. It acknowledges the receipt of specified goods for transportation to a certain place, it sets forth the contract between the shipper and the carrier, and it provides for proper delivery of the goods.

BILL OF MATERIAL   A prescheduled list of materials and component assemblies required for a given work assignment or job.

BILL OF SALE   A formal legal document which conveys title to, or right or interest in, specific personal property from the seller to the buyer.

BILLS PAYABLE   1) A comprehensive term that includes the sum total of notes and trade acceptances which a business owes to trade creditors and which the business must pay at their maturity.
2) The sum of money which a member bank has borrowed, on its own collateral note, from the Federal Reserve Bank.

BILLS RECEIVABLE   A comprehensive term that includes the total of all notes and trade acceptances given by customers, usually in payment of merchandise, which the debtors must pay at maturity.

BIMETALLISM   The "free" or unlimited coinage of two metals, generally of gold and silver. The coins have full legal tender value and an established relationship or ratio of value such as sixteen ounces of silver of a standard fineness

or purity to one ounce of gold of a standard fineness or purity.

BINDER   1) A temporary agreement which obligates the several parties of the contract. In insurance, the insurance company is obligated to pay if the loss insured against occurs before the policy is written.
2) A preliminary agreement to provide immediate insurance until a policy can be written, either by an agent or by a company. It should contain a definite time limit, should be in writing, and clearly designate the company in which the risk is bound, the amount and the perils insured against, as well as the type of insurance.
3) A temporary insurance contract pending execution of the policy contract. Except for specified differences, the terms of the binder are by implication those of the contract which is intended to replace it.

BLACKLIST   1) A list of persons considered to be undesirable and to be avoided such as bad credit risks.
2) List of union members circulated among employers to advise them of the union activities of job applicants.
3) List of contractors who have violated Federal Government Walsh-Healey Act specifications.

BLACK MARKET   A place where illegal transactions take place. Generally those violations involve rationing, price, or exchange controls.

BLANK BILL   A bill of exchange with no payee designated.

BLANK ENDORSEMENT   The endorsement or signature of an individual or company on an instrument such as a check or note making it payable to the bearer and thus negotiable without restrictions.

BLANKET INJUNCTIONS   Injunctions prohibiting, in the future, acts or violations that have not actually been committed in the case presently before the court.

BLANKET MORTGAGE   A mortgage that takes in or "covers" all the assets or property of the debtor.

BLANKET POLICY   A broad type of insurance coverage, commonly used in fire and burglary insurance.

BLANKET RATE   An insurance rate applied to more than one property or subject of insurance.

BLOCKAGE   1) Placing an account subject to United States Treasury control because of enemy or suspected enemy interest.
2) A discount from the established market for which a large block of stock of a single corporation would have to be sold if the entire holding were placed on the market at a given date (a term used in connection with federal estate tax).

BLOCKED ACCOUNT   Any account in a bank the handling of which is closely circumscribed by government regulations. The term in this country is used to designate any account whose administration is subject to United States Treasury license because of enemy or suspected enemy interest.

BLOCKED CURRENCY   A device used by some nations to discriminate against certain types of holders of the claims against a nation. It is generally used to try to control foreign exchange rates and the balance of payments as well as trade movement. Blocked currencies are quoted at discounts from the unblocked or regular currency of a nation. At times the blocked currency may be used only in certain regulated ways and may involve the need for special permits from the monetary authorities.

BLOCK POLICY A policy covering all the property of the insured (usually a merchant) against most perils, including transportation. It may also cover property of others held by the insured on consignment, goods sold but not delivered, goods left for repairs, or goods otherwise held. It usually covers both on and off the insured's premises.

BLUE CHIP 1) Something of exceptionally high quality or value.
2) Common stock in a company known nationally for quality and wide acceptance of its products or services and for its ability to make money and pay dividends in good times and bad. Usually such stocks are relatively high-priced and offer relatively low yields.

BLUE-COLLAR WORKERS Workers employed in a plant or in production, as distinguished from white-collar workers employed in an office.

BLUE-SKY LAWS A popular name for laws various states have enacted to protect the public against securities frauds. These laws pertain to the punishment of persons who sell illegal stocks, and they provide jurisdiction over investment companies. The term is believed to have originated when a judge ruled that a particular stock had about the same value as a patch of blue sky.

BOARD LOT A round lot. The regular unit of trade for the designated exchange. The board or round lot on the New York Stock Exchange is generally 100 shares of stock or $1,000 par value for a bond unless an exception is made.

BOARD OF DIRECTORS Those individuals elected by the stockholders of a corporation to manage the business. An inside board has directors who are also active in the day-to-day operation of the firm while an outside board is made up of individuals who do not make active day-to-day decisions in the business but are rather concerned with policy and broad general direction.

BOARD OF GOVERNORS OF THE FEDERAL RESERVE SYSTEM A board of seven members (located at Washington) which supervises, coordinates, and controls the operations of the twelve Federal Reserve Banks and branches. The Board has regulatory powers with respect to member banks.

BOARD OF TRADE A chamber of commerce or a produce exchange.

BOARD OF TRUSTEES The body in an institution which manages and administrates the organization, establishes the policies under which it is to be operated, appoints the officers, etc.

BODILY INJURY Injury to the body of a person. The term is usually specifically defined in an insurance policy, and these individual definitions have variations.

BOILER-ROOM OPERATION A dubious operation involving the sale of very speculative and frequently valueless securities through the use of high-pressure phone techniques and misleading literature. The appeal of quick profit and rapid price change is used to stimulate the unsophisti-

cated to purchase the security without making a proper investigation as to the merits of the security.

BOND 1) An interest-bearing certificate of debt, usually issued in series by which the issuer (a government or corporation) obligates itself to pay the principal amount and interest at a specified time, usually five years or more after date of issue. Bonds may be distinguished from promissory notes or other evidences of debt because of their formal execution under seal and certification by a bank or trust company that they are authorized by the board of directors of a corporation or other governing body. Corporate bonds are usually secured by a lien against certain specified property. Bonds may be issued in "bearer" form or "registered."
2) An obligation of an insurance company to protect the insured against financial loss caused by the acts or omissions of another person or persons known as the principal. A fidelity bond on employees would reimburse the insured up to the limits of the policy for the loss caused by dishonesty of the covered employee. Originally it meant any obligation under seal.
3) In a noninsurance sense, a bond is a debt instrument consisting of a promise to pay and usually issued on the security of a mortgage or a deed of trust or on the credit of the issuer.

BOND, ADJUSTMENT The term used for income bonds that have been issued out of a reorganization. See "bond, income."

BOND, ASSUMED Bonds which originally were the obligation of one corporation but which for some reason such as a subsidiary relationship have been assumed as obligations as well by another corporation. Most assumed bonds are found in the area of railway divisional bonds in which the parent company has assumed the interests and principal obligation of the original debtor, which is a division of a system.

BOND, BEARER Bonds whose proceeds (principal and interest) are payable to the bearer, that is, to whoever has physical possession. Since there is no identification, such bonds always have attached coupons, which are cut and presented to collect the interest.

BOND, BID A guarantee that a contractor will enter into a contract on which he has bid if it is awarded to him and furnish a contract bond as required by the terms of the contract.

BOND, BLANKET A broad fidelity bond covering all employees of a firm and in the case of financial institutions including insurance against enumerated hazards.

BOND, CALLABLE Bonds which the issuing corporation or body may redeem before their maturity. Generally some premium is paid by the issuing corporation to the holder of the bond should it be called. Interest stops when a bond is called.

BOND, COLLATERAL TRUST An issue of bonds for which collateral has been pledged to guarantee repayment of the principal. This type of bond usually arises out of intercompany transactions where the parent company will issue bonds with securities of a subsidiary as the underlying collateral.

BOND, CONSOLIDATED A debt instrument issued to take the place of two or more previously issued bonds. This may be done to simplify a debt structure or to take advantage of a lower prevailing interest rate.

BOND, CONTINUED A debt instrument that does not have to be redeemed at maturity but can continue to earn interest. The Series E bonds have been "continued." Extended bonds.

BOND, CONTRACT A guarantee of the faithful performance of a construction contract and the payment of all labor and material bills incident thereto. In those situations where two bonds are required, one to cover performance and the other to cover payment of labor and material, the former is known as a performance bond and the latter as a payment bond.

BOND, CONVERTIBLE Bonds having the special provision for being converted into stock at a certain time and at a specified price.

BOND, COUPON Bonds to which are attached coupons representing the interest payments. As the interest becomes due, the coupons are clipped and presented for payment.

BOND, DEBENTURE Bonds which represent a company's funded debt backed only by its credit and not secured by a pledge or mortgage of property.

BOND, DEFERRED A debt instrument in which a due payment has been postponed until some future time.

BONDED WAREHOUSE A warehouse owned by persons approved by the United States Treasury Department and under bond or guarantee for the strict observance of the revenue laws; utilized for storing goods until duties are paid or goods are otherwise properly released.

BOND, EXTENDED Continued bonds; bonds which have matured without the debtor paying the principal but which the debtor agrees to extend or continue to pay at some future date.

BOND, FIDELITY A bond covering the risk of loss due to larceny, embezzlement, or culpable negligence and the faithful discharge of an employee's duties.

BOND, FOREIGN Foreign bonds may take even more forms than domestic bonds. Some domestic issues of a nation become foreign bonds by being moved from their country of origin. Foreign bonds which are deliberately sold abroad are external bonds; those that are payable in dollars are called foreign dollar bonds. Some foreign bonds are payable in more than one currency at the option of the holder and some are tied to price indexes as to value of principal. Foreign bonds that have defaulted may be assented or stamped. Those still in default are sold flat. They may be obligations of nations, states, municipalities or of foreign corporations.

BOND, GOVERNMENT Obligations of the United States Government regarded as the highest grade issues in existence. Obligations of governments other than the United States are generally designated as foreign government bonds.

BOND, GUARANTEED Bond on which the principal or income or both are guaranteed by another corporation or parent company in case of default by the issuing corporation.

BOND, INCOME An obligation upon which interest is payable to the extent earned in each year except that interest not earned and unpaid may be either fully or partially cumulative according to the terms of the contract. The income bond may be or may not be secured by the pledge of either real or personal property.

BOND, INDEMNITY A written instrument under seal by which the signer, usually together with his surety or bondsman, guarantees to protect another against loss. An indemnity bond in which the obligation assumed by the surety is not a fixed amount is known as an open penalty form of indemnity bond.

BOND, INTERCHANGEABLE A bond in either coupon or registered form which may be converted to the other form or back to its original form at the option of the holder. There may be some service charge for such conversion.

BOND, JOINT AND SEVERAL A debt instrument in which the holder may look to payment from more than one party up to the full face amount of the security. These securities are mostly associated with railroad financing for such facilities as terminals used by more than one railroad. The users of the terminal agree to be responsible for the payment in the event the others default. The holder may only collect the face amount once, but he may collect from all or only one of the obligors.

BOND, JUNIOR Bonds which are not senior; that is, are secondary or subordinate to another issue which in the event of liquidation would have a prior claim to the junior bonds. See "bond, senior," "senior interest," or "senior securities."

BOND, LEGAL Bonds that state or federal law prescribe as suitable and legal investments for fiduciary institutions. In a number of states a "legal list" states by name and issue those investments that a fiduciary or trustee may purchase and hold for the beneficiary.

BOND, MORTGAGE A bond secured by a mortgage on a property. The value of the property may or may not equal the value of the so-called mortgage bonds issued against it. See "bond, debenture."

BOND, OPEN-END A mortgage bond of an issue which does not have a limitation on the number or amounts of bonds which may be issued under the mortgage though some relationship may be required to the number and amount of bonds to the value of the property mortgaged.

BOND, REGISTERED A bond which is registered on the books of the issuing company in the name of the owner. It can be transferred only when endorsed by the registered owner. See "bond, bearer" and "bond, coupon."

BOND, REVENUE Bonds the principal of and interest on which are to be paid solely from earnings; usually those of a municipally owned utility or other public service enterprise the revenues and possibly the properties of which are pledged for this purpose.

BOND, SENIOR Bonds which have first or prior claim to the assets of the debtor in the event of liquidation.

BOND, SERIAL An issue of bonds in which a certain proportion of the bonds are retired at regular intervals. Serial bonds are issued where the security depreciates through use of obsolescence, and they usually provide that the bonds outstanding shall not exceed the value of the security.

BOND, SINKING FUND   A bond which has as one of its features the requirement that the debtor provides and maintains a sinking fund to provide for the ultimate repayment and retirement of the bond.

BOND, SURETY   A bond or guarantee usually given by a bonding company to answer for the debt, default, or miscarriage of another. The surety (company) binds itself to pay if the obligor shall default in his obligation.

BOND, UNITED STATES SAVINGS   A nonnegotiable bond issued in different series such as E, F, and G, the most commonly issued being the series E. Such bonds are issued in small, odd units such as $18.75 with a maturity value of $25 or $37.50 with a maturity value of $50. The typical period such bonds were originally issued for was 10 years, but, because of changed interest rates, the maturity has been altered rather than the redemption amount.

BONUS   Anything, although generally money, which is given without legal obligation by an individual or firm in addition to that which is required for some action.

BONUS STOCK   A sweetening device used to encourage the sale of another class of securities. For example, the issuing of a share or shares of a common stock for each unit of purchase of a preferred stock. The bonus stock may be given to the ultimate purchaser, the salesman, or the underwriter of the issue.

BOOK CREDIT   Those items shown on the ledger accounts which represent obligations of firms and individuals which are not secured by notes or other security. Also described as book accounts or open book accounts.

BOOK OF FINAL ENTRY   A book to which information is transferred from a book of original entry. The ledger is a book of final entry.

BOOK OF ORIGINAL ENTRY   A book in which transactions are recorded completely, one after another, in the order in which they occur. The journal is a book of original entry.

BOOKS (CLOSE)   The date the transfer agent closes the transfer books of a corporation and checks the stockholder list to determine those eligible to vote or receive dividends.

BOOKS (OPEN)   The date the transfer agent opens a corporation's transfer books to resume the normal business of transferring stocks after they had been closed to check the stockholder list.

BOOK VALUE   1) The price at which assets are carried on a financial statement.
2) The value of each share of common or capital stock based on the values at which the assets of a corporation are carried on the balance sheet. It is obtained by deducting from total assets all liabilities of the corporation and dividing the remainder by the number of shares outstanding.

BOOM   A period of rapidly rising prices, characterized by substantial excess of demand for goods and services, full employment, sharply increasing demand for and supply of luxury items, inflation, rising interest rates, abnormal commercial and industrial plant expansion, and profitable use of marginal (and even submarginal) agents of production, and a carefree attitude by a substantial part of the public.

BORROWED RESERVES   Discounts and advances from Federal Reserve Banks; mainly advances secured by United States Government securities or eligible paper.

BORROWED STOCKS   Stocks that brokers borrow for the purpose of providing delivery on short sales made for their clients.

BOTTOM OUT   A condition in which something with a variable value such as the national economy, a security, or a business condition, after reaching a low point or phase, has started to rise or improve.

BOYCOTT   Refusal to buy from or sell to a certain company. To stop buying or using certain products.

BRANCH BANKING   Any bank which maintains complete banking facilities in offices away from its main office, or head office, may be considered as carrying on branch banking business. The separated units are called branches or offices and are permitted among the various classes of banks in the several states under certain conditions. Generally speaking, national banks are allowed to have branches in a state under the same conditions granted to a state-chartered bank. That is, if a state bank is permitted to have statewide branches, then the same privilege is afforded national banks. At present, few states permit statewide banking. The majority do, however, permit branches within city limits.

BRAND   A design, mark, symbol or other device which distinguishes one line or type of goods from those of a competitor.

BRAND NAME   1) Special name registered to prevent copying.
2) An expression that has come into use to refer to a well-established, quality product.

BREACH OF CONTRACT   Breaking an agreement; refusing to do one's part in the agreement.

BREACH OF PROMISE   Violation of one's plighted word, especially of a promise to marry.

BREACH OF TRUST   Violation of a duty which a trustee owes to a beneficiary.

BREAK EVEN   To have neither a profit nor a loss at the termination of a transaction but to have just covered the costs incurred.

BREAK-EVEN POINT   Where the income from the business just equals the cost of doing business leaving neither a profit nor a loss.

BROKEN LOT   An odd lot. Generally, less than one hundred shares of a stock or less than the usual unit of measurement or unit of sale of any item.

BROKER   A middleman who brings together buyers and sellers of the same product, service, commodity, or security and executes the orders, charging a commission for this service. In contrast to a principal or dealer, the broker does not own or take a position in the item being sold.

BROKERAGE 1) The business of a broker.
2) The fee or commission paid by a client to a broker for the execution of his order.

BROKERAGE ACCOUNT A client's account which is managed by the broker on behalf of and subject to the client's order.

BROKER-AGENT One who is licensed to act both as broker and as agent. While generally one is either a broker or an agent, some individuals maintain two offices, one as a broker and the other as an agent.

BROKER'S LOAN Loans made to stock brokers and secured by stock exchange collateral. Statistics on this type of loan are tabulated by the Federal Reserve Banks and others as a guide to the investing public.

BUDGET 1) An estimate of the income and expenditures for a future period of time, usually one year.
2) A systematic estimate or plan for a future fiscal period of a business.
3) A limited allotment or appropriation for a specific purpose, such as an advertising budget.

BUDGETARY ACCOUNTS Those accounts necessary to reflect budget operations and conditions, such as estimated revenues, appropriations, and encumbrances, as distinguished from proprietary accounts. See "proprietary accounts."

BUDGETARY CONTROL A plan to control all operations in order to secure maximum profit from a minimum capital investment. This is accomplished by setting standards against which actual performance can be measured. An efficient budgetary control program not only detects inefficiencies but also definitely fixes responsibility upon the proper person or persons.

BUDGET, CASH A summary of anticipated receipts and disbursements for a forthcoming period. It is generally used in forecasting cash requirements to meet future bond redemptions, dividends, plant expansions, etc.

BUFFER-STOCK PLAN As a stabilizing device to help reduce cyclical fluctuations, a federal agency buys certain commodities at a minimum price and sells them at a higher price. The prices would be determined by normal costs of production and normal price fluctuations.

BUILDING AND LOAN ASSOCIATION See "savings and loan association."

BUILDING LOAN A mortgage loan which is made to finance the construction of a building. It is advanced in stages as the construction work progresses. See "construction loan."

BUILT-IN STABILIZERS Those business and government practices, policies, customs and laws which tend to automatically moderate fluctuations in business or economy. Unemployment insurance, social security, and progressive income taxes illustrate such stabilizers.

BULK-LINE COSTS Those costs in any industry at which over 80% of the goods are produced. On the basis of such bulk-line costs, price fixing or stablization programs can be established.

BULL One who believes the market will rise. See "bear."

BULLION Precious metals such as platinum, gold, or silver which are cast in ingots or bars and considered merely as metal.

BULL MARKET A period of generally increasing market prices.

BULL POSITION Refers to the prevailing status of market optimists, or bulls. If most of the market is on the buying side, *i.e.,* leading securities are being acquired by institutions and individual investors, this is said to be a strong bull position.

BUMPING Exercise of seniority rights to displace junior employees by longer-service workers when business conditions require temporary layoffs or the discontinuance of departments.

BUSINESS AGENT Person employed by an individual or a group to represent them and to protect their interests. An example would be a business agent appointed by a local union or several locals to conduct union activities and negotiate with employers.

BUSINESS BAROMETER 1) A composite of weighted index numbers used to estimate the level of business.
2) A single index of a business activity which is considered to be reflective of business activity such as total employment.

BUSINESS CYCLES Broad swings up and down in the state of business.

BUSINESS INSURANCE TRUST A trust of life insurance policy contracts created in connection with a business enterprise. The term is applied both to a trust created for the liquidation of business interests and to a trust created for credit purposes or otherwise for the benefit of a business enterprise.

BUSINESSMAN'S RISK The justifiable risk taken in a business or securities venture based on the assumption that a businessman is situated to handle the risk emotionally and financially.

BUSINESS RISK There are a number of different risks which are involved in granting credit. These include insurable risks, moral risks, and the risk from acts of God such as floods and earthquakes. One major risk, the business risk, involves the ability of a businessman to operate his business in an efficient and profitable manner.

BUYERS' MARKET A period of a lessening demand; prices are on a downward trend thus giving the buyer an advantage over the seller.

BUYERS' STRIKE A situation in which the buyers of a product stop their purchases. This may be because the price is simply too high, or it may be caused by a concerted attempt by organizers to exert pressure on the sellers to force price reductions.

BUYER'S SURPLUS An economic concept to recognize that many buyers would pay more for a product than the seller has asked. The difference between what the buyer pays and what he would pay if he had to is known as the buyer's surplus.

BUYING ON MARGIN Many items are bought without the purchaser paying immediately the whole price. Examples of buying on margin include purchase of a home with a mortgage or of a security with a partial payment and borrowing the difference from his broker or bank. Margin refers to the proportion of down payment that is made by the purchaser. The Board of Governors of the Federal Reserve Board has the right to establish margin requirements for the purchase of listed securities. This is a selective credit control.

BUYING ON SCALE A method used in purchasing securities in which the broker is instructed to buy a given number of shares at given intervals of a price decline. Since the buyer does not know how low the price will drop, by buying on scale as the price drops his average cost per share also drops.

BUY-SELL AGREEMENT An agreement wherein owners of a business arrange to transfer their respective ownership interests upon the death of one, or upon some other event, so as to provide continued control of the business or some other desired end.

BYLAWS Regulations, ordinances, or rules enacted by an organization for its own government and in accordance with which its affairs are to be conducted.

BY-PRODUCT A substance that is produced as an incident of a major product. In meat packing certain glands are used to make medicine. The major product is meat; the by-product, in this illustration, is medicine.

BYRNES ACT Federal law which prohibits interstate transportation of strikebreakers.

CABLE RATE A term used in foreign exchange to refer to the rates quoted for a cable transfer of foreign exchange. The cable rate is higher than the check, demand, 30-, 60-, or 90-day bill of exchange rate.

CALL To demand payment immediately or at a specified date.

CALLABLE Redeemable at option of issuer. Applied to a bond or preferred stock that is subject to redemption, usually on or after a specified date or dates, under designated terms and at a stated price or scale of prices.

CALL-BACK PAY Wages for a minimum number of hours sometimes guaranteed workers called back to work outside of their scheduled working hours.

CALL-IN PAY Wages to which an employee is entitled under a union contract or by custom when required to report and there is not a full day's work available.

CALL LOAN A loan made on a day-to-day basis, callable on twenty-four hours' notice. Typically, loans made to members of the New York Stock Exchange to facilitate the exchange of securities.

CALL MONEY Money loaned by banks to brokers which is subject to call (demand payment) at the discretion of the lender.

CALL-MONEY MARKET Those financial institutions which are active in providing call money. Today brokers individually arrange with the big banks for their day-to-day needs to finance margin purchases.

CALL PAY The reimbursement paid to an employee who upon reporting for work as scheduled is not assigned to a job or work.

CALL PRICE The price at which a corporation or other obligor is permitted to redeem securities containing call provisions. To compensate for this privilege, a price above par is usually paid.

CALL PURCHASE A technique for purchasing commodities in which the seller has some option of pricing in the future within a stated range of the present price.

CALL REPORT Banking authorities such as the Comptroller of the Currency, Federal Reserve Banks, Federal Deposit Insurance Corporation and State Superintendent of Banking call a minimum of three times and sometimes four times a year for the banks under their supervision to provide statements of condition as of the call date. The actual date is not released prior to the "call" so that banks may not engage in "window dressing" activities.

CANCELLATION Rendering null and void. This may be done by use of rubber stamps which are used to print the word canceled or a perforation device to cut similar words on a document. In some cases the instrument is burned or cremated.

CANNIBALIZATION To completely dismantle a vehicle or unit, salvaging usable parts and discarding worn-out items as unserviceable material.

CAPACITY FACTOR The ratio of the average load on a machine, plant or system for a given period of time (commonly one year) to the capacity of the machine or equipment. This factor is based on nameplate capacity except when otherwise qualified.

CAPITAL 1) Savings or accumulated wealth put to economic use such as invested in business, banking, production, etc.
2) In an accounting sense, the excess of assets over liabilities.
3) In a corporation, it is the sum of the various capital stock accounts, surplus, and undivided profits; hence capital is synonymous with net worth.
4) The ownership interest in a business.
5) In finance, the total tangible assets of a firm.

CAPITAL ACCOUNT 1) An account maintained in the name of the owner, or owners, of a business and which indicates his or their equity in that business—usually at the close of the last accounting period.
2) Accounts which show what has been invested in an enterprise.

CAPITAL BUDGET The formal estimate of anticipated sales and purchases of capital items as compared with ordinary income receipts and expenditures.

CAPITAL CHARGES Sums required to satisfy interest upon and amortization of monies invested in an enterprise.

CAPITAL CONSUMPTION ALLOWANCES A measure of the plant and equipment worn-out, damaged or rendered obsolete during a given period of time.

CAPITAL COSTS Cost of improvements which extend the useful life of property and/or add to value. Not deductible for tax purposes in the year incurred but depreciable over their useful lives.

CAPITAL EXPENDITURES Expenditures for the original cost of fixed assets and expenditures that increase the value for fixed assets.

CAPITAL GAINS (AND LOSSES) The difference between purchase price and selling price in the sale of assets. The computation is used primarily in tax computations.

CAPITAL GAINS TAX RATES The tax charged against any gains or profits earned in the transactions of assets. Net profits resulting from sale or exchange of securities held for more than six months are subject to federal taxation at one-half the taxpayer's regular rate with a maximum effective rate of 25 percent. Net profits resulting from sale or exchange of securities held six months or less are taxable at the taxpayer's regular rate.

CAPITAL GOODS Commodities such as raw materials, which are used to produce other goods, either consumer goods or other capital goods.

CAPITAL INVESTMENTS A collective term representing the amounts invested in capital, fixed assets, or in long-term securities as contrasted with those funds invested in current assets or short-term securities. Generally speaking, capital investments include all funds invested in assets which, during the normal course of business, are not expected to be realized upon during the ensuing fiscal period.

CAPITALISM The free-enterprise system founded upon private property right, freedom of choice of occupation, limited governmental regulation for the preservation of order, and conviction that the price system permits the best incentive through profit, thus economic growth.

CAPITALIZATION Total amount of the various securities issued by a corporation. Capitalization may include bonds, debentures, preferred and common stock. Bonds and debentures are usually carried on the books of the issuing company in terms of their par or face value. Preferred and common shares may be carried in terms of par or stated value. Stated value may be an abitrary figure decided upon by the directors or may represent the amount received by the company from the sale of the securities at the time of issuance. See "par."

CAPITALIZATION RATE 1) The relationship of income to capital investment or value, expressed as a percentage.
2) The (percentage) rate at which an anticipated future income stream is discounted to present worth, *i.e.*, market value.

CAPITALIZE 1) To convert money which may be used in production.
2) To apply something to the purposes of business.
3) To include in the investment account expenditures for purchase or construction of property, or for organization.
4) To issue securities to represent such investment.
5) To divide income by a rate of interest to obtain principal.

CAPITALIZED VALUE The asset value (principal) of a given number of income dollars determined on the basis of an assumed rate of return. For example, the capitalized value of a $500 perpetual income at a rate of 5% is $10,000 (obtained by dividing $500 by .05).

CAPITALIZED-VALUE STANDARD See "earning-capacity standard."

CAPITAL LEVY A tax on capital as contrasted to income. The tax is on the total appraised or reported valuation as contrasted with a capital gains tax which is only on the appreciated value of the capital.

CAPITAL LOAN A loan which cannot be repaid without disposing of capital assets, in contrast to a loan, for example, to purchase merchandise, the sale of which will provide funds to repay the loan.

CAPITAL RATING Many mercantile agencies divide their evaluation of a credit risk into two phases, one being an estimation of the net worth of a business which is called the capital rating and the second phase which refers to the payment record of the subject as to his practice of discounting, paying on time or of being slow.

CAPITAL REQUIREMENTS 1) The total monetary investment essential to the establishment and operation of an enterprise.
2) The appraised investment in plant facilities and normal working capital. It may or may not include appraised cost of business rights such as patents, contracts and charters.

CAPITAL STOCK That evidence of ownership in a corporation, in the form of stock certificates, issued in exchange for money or property or out of accumulated earnings. Stock which takes precedence in the distribution of earnings and assets is known as preferred stock. Stock which enjoys no such precedence is generally called common stock, or sometimes capital stock.

CAPITAL STRUCTURE The distribution of a corporation's capital among its several component parts, such as stock, bonds, and surplus.

CAPITAL SURPLUS Paid-in surplus, donated surplus and revaluation surplus; that is, surplus other than earned surplus. Surplus not arising from profits of operation but from such sources as sale of capital stock at premium, profit on dealings in a corporation's own stock, donated stock, appraisal valuations, and surplus shown by the accounts at the time of organization.

CAPITAL TURNOVER A term commonly used by the credit department of a lending institution which represents the number of times the outstanding capital has "turned over" in relation to the net sales for a given period of time, frequently a year.

CARLOADINGS The number of railroad freight cars loaded during a stated time period. Formerly this was regarded as a good index of business activity, but inroads of trucking and air freight have caused the figures to have a downward bias.

CARRIER'S LIEN Right of carrier to retain property which it has transported, as security for the collection of charges.

CARRYING CHARGES 1) Generally, expenses incident to the continued ownership or use of property, as taxes on real property.
2) Specifically, charges made for carrying a debtor, as interest charged on a margin account with a broker.

CARRYING VALUE The value of a fixed asset remaining after its accumulated depreciation reserve has been deducted from its original depreciable cost.

CARRY-OVERS AND CARRY-BACKS There are two kinds of carry-overs and carry-backs available to corporations for federal income tax purposes: Net operating loss, and unused excess profits credit. The net operating loss carry-over or carry-back is the excess of the deductions allowed under the income tax law over the statutory gross income, with certain exceptions, additions and limitations. The excess profits credit carry-over or carry-back is the excess of the excess profits credit over the excess profits net income. It is to be understood that an operating deficit will not necessarily produce a carry-over or a carry-back for income tax purposes.

CARTEL Syndicate, combine, or trust generally formed to regulate prices and output in some field.

CASH 1) A term associated with any business transaction involving the handling of currency (paper money) and specie (metal coins).
2) In the broader sense, the term "cash" as used in banks includes any item which the bank will immediately credit for deposit or make payment in currency or specie.

CASH AUDIT An audit of cash transactions for a stated period, for the purpose of determining that all cash received has been recorded, that all disbursements have been properly authorized and vouched, and that the balance of cash is either on hand or on deposit. A cash audit can be limited from a complete inquiry into all cash transactions (a complete cash audit) to one involving only some of them (a limited cash audit). Such an audit establishes the accountability of the persons responsible for cash.

CASH BASIS The system of accounting under which revenues are accounted for only when received in cash, and expenditures are accounted for only when paid.

CASH BOOK A book of original entry in which the cash receipts journal and the cash payments journal are brought together to form one book.

CASH DISCOUNT A deduction that the seller offers to allow on the amount of an invoice to encourage prompt payment by the purchaser by a certain date.

CASH DIVIDEND Declared dividends that are payable in cash. In this case, cash would include checks as distinguished from a stock or commodity dividend.

CASH FLOW 1) The sources and uses of a company's cash funds over a designated period. In the preparation of a cash-flow statement, both income and balance sheet items are traced in order to highlight the financial progress of a company.
2) Disposition of funds received by a revenue bond project.

CASHIER'S CHECK A check signed by a cashier or other authorized officer of a bank drawn by the bank on itself.

CASH ITEMS Items (commonly checks and coupons) which a bank accepts for immediate credit to depositors' accounts.

CASH MARKET The spot market as contrasted with the futures market.

CASH ON DELIVERY Abbreviated COD. That transaction which requires the buyer to pay cash upon receipt of the goods.

CASH POSITION The percentage of cash to total net assets indicates relative cash positions. It includes cash and United States Government securities, and is the net amount after deducting current liabilities.

CASH RESERVE 1) An amount of cash, or very liquid securities quickly convertible to cash, kept in reserve for special purposes or to protect against sudden emergency need.
2) Those legal requirements for banks to maintain legal reserves. Banks that are members of the Federal Reserve System keep their cash reserves on deposit with their district Federal Reserve Bank and are permitted to count some of their till cash also as part of their legal reserves. The cash reserves of state nonmember banks are determined by the individual state law.

CASH SURRENDER SALE The amount which an insurance company will pay the insured on the cancellation of a policy.

CASUAL WORKER A temporary employee who does not acquire any seniority rights or fringe benefits. He is typically hired because of an unanticipated increase in activity or unforeseen development which is not expected to continue for a long period of time.

CATASTROPHE HAZARD The hazard of loss by reason of a simultaneous peril to which all insured in a group or a large number of insureds are subject.

CAVEAT EMPTOR A Latin phrase for: Let the buyer beware.

CAVEATOR An interested party who gives notice to some officer not to do a certain act until the party is heard in opposition, as the caveator of a will offered for probate.

CAVEAT VENDITOR A Latin phrase for: Let the seller beware.

CEASE-AND-DESIST ORDER Order issued by a court or government agency directing a business, employer, or union to end an unfair or illegal practice or policy.

CEILING PRICES Maximum prices under some system of price controls.

CENTRAL BANK A bank which deals chiefly with other banks in holding the banking reserves of its county or district and normally government agencies or government-related agencies and operates in the broad public interest. In the United States, central banking functions are carried on by the twelve regional Federal Reserve Banks under the supervision of the Board of Governors of the Federal Reserve System. In many other countries there is but a single institution that functions as a central bank, *e.g.,* Bank of England.

CERTIFICATE A written or printed statement or declaration of truth that can be used to prove a fact (birth certificate, school certificate, ownership, etc.).

CERTIFICATE OF ACCOUNTS That document and statement which is issued by a certified public accountant which states the accountant's evaluation of the books of accounts of a firm which he has audited or from which he has prepared statements.

CERTIFICATE OF BENEFICIAL INTEREST A legal instrument which is issued to owners of a business. The document describes the owner's equity and is commonly used in voting trusts.

CERTIFICATE OF CLAIM A contingent promise of the Federal Housing Administration to reimburse an insured mortgagee for certain costs incurred during foreclosure of an insured mortgage provided the proceeds from the sale of the property acquired are sufficient to cover those costs.

CERTIFICATE OF DEPOSIT Evidence of an investment with an association or bank. Has no stockholders' liability and carries no voting rights. Resembles an investment certificate.

CERTIFICATE OF INCORPORATION The franchise or charter issued by the state to the original petitioners of an approved corporation. Such franchise or charter consitutes the authority granted by the state for the organization to transact business as a corporation.

CERTIFICATE OF INDEBETEDNESS A short-term negotiable promissory note issued by a government or a corporation to show and evidence a floating indebtedness.

CERTIFICATE OF INSURANCE 1) A statement of insurance coverage taking the place of the policy as evidence of insurance and often transferring the right to collect claims to the holder of the certificate.
2) A document evidencing the fact that an insurance policy has been written and includes a statement of the coverage of the policy in general terms. It is frequently found where there are group plans. Thus a master policy is issued to the company, and certificates of insurance are given to the individuals covered by the terms of the policy.
3) In group insurance, a statement issued to a member of the group certifying that an insurance contract has been written and containing a summary of the terms applicable to that member.
4) In insurance other than marine or group, a statement that a specified insured and risk are covered to a specified extent, but ordinarily without responsibility on the part of the insurer to notify the certificate holder of termination of the insurance.

CERTIFICATE OF NECESSITY A certificate issued by a federal authority certifying that certain emergency facilities are necessary in the interest of national welfare, which permits the accelerated amortization of all or a part of the cost of the facilities for income tax purposes.

CERTIFICATE OF ORIGIN A certificate issued by the proper authorities which accompanies the documents attached to a draft covering the shipment of goods. The certificate usually specifies the origin of material or labor used in the production of such merchandise.

CERTIFICATE OF PROTEST That document which a notary public prepares when a dishonored negotiable instrument is again presented but not paid. The certificate is legal evidence that presentation has been made and refused.

CERTIFICATE OF PUBLIC CONVENIENCE AND NECESSITY A license granted to a private enterprise such as a public utility by the state. This allows government to protect existing franchises from injurious competition.

CERTIFICATION 1) The act of testifying to the truth or validity of something through a written statement.
2) Formal finding by the National Labor Relations Board that a union has been duly selected by a majority of the employees in a bargaining unit and is therefore the exclusive bargaining agent for all employees in the unit.
3) The processing of checks in which the bank guarantees the signature of the drawer and that the drawer has that amount in his account. The amount of the certification is deducted from the drawer's account and held until the certified check is presented for payment.

CERTIFIED CHECK A depositor's check across the face of which an authorized official of the bank has stamped the word "certified," the bank's name, and signed his own name. By its certification, the bank guarantees that sufficient funds have been set aside from the depositor's account to pay the check when payment is demanded.

CERTIFIED PUBLIC ACCOUNTANT An accountant to whom a state has given a certificate showing that he has met prescribed requirements designed to insure competence on the part of the public practitioner in accounting and that he is permitted to use the designation Certified Public Accountant, commonly abbreviated as C.P.A.

CERTIORARI A proceeding to review in a competent court the action of an inferior tribunal, board, or officer exercising judicial functions, when such action is alleged to be without jurisdiction or otherwise illegal.

CERTIORARI, WRIT OF The method used to direct inferior courts, officers, boards or tribunals to certify to the superior court the record of their proceedings for inspection and review.

CESSION 1) A yielding of property or a right to another.
2) Reinsurance, or the amount ceded as reinsurance.

CHAIN BANKING A term used to refer to an arrangement by which control of a number of banks is exercised through entire or majority ownership of stock by a group of individuals who take an active part in formulating the policies of the banks in the group. See "group banking."

CHAIN OF TITLE The succession of conveyances from some accepted starting point whereby the present holder of real property derives his title.

CHAMBER OF COMMERCE An organization of businessmen designed to advance the interests of its members. Three levels are noted: The Chamber of Commerce of the United States is at the national level, the state level, and the city or town level.

CHANNEL OF DISTRIBUTION The path by which goods move from the producer to the consumer.

CHARGE 1) The setting or stating of a price for a good or service.
2) To set down the amount that is due from someone.
3) A price.

CHARGE-OFF The act of writing off an account to its present value. This may be to zero or some amount lower than the amount the account is being carried at prior to the writing down or off. It is the result of the recognition of the change in value of an asset. Thus, an account receivable which has proven not to be collectible may be charged off.

CHARITABLE TRUST A trust created for the benefit of a community, ordinarily without a definite beneficiary; as, a trust for educational purposes. The same as a public trust; opposed to a private trust.

CHARITY An agency, institution, or organization in existence and operation for the benefit of an indefinite number of persons and conducted for educational, religious, scientific, medical, or other beneficent purposes.

CHARTER 1) The grant of rights from a state to a business corporation such as the right to incorporate and transact business.
2) It also means the renting or leasing of a ship, aircraft, bus, etc.

CHARTERED ACCOUNTANT A member of an Institute of Chartered Accountants in the British Empire. Admission to such institutes is dependent upon serving a period of apprenticeship and passing an entrance examination.

CHARTS 1) Any tabular lists of instructions or facts, oftentimes plotted on graph paper.
2) Records of price changes in a stock or market average kept on graph paper with the associated volume of transactions. Analysts utilize these in trying to determine future market action and the resulting actions they should take.

CHATTEL Every species of property, movable or immovable, which is less than a life estate in land.

CHATTEL MORTGAGE A legal document in which personal property (chattels) is made security for payment of a debt but is left in the hands of the debtor so long as payments are kept up as contracted.

CHATTEL, PERSONAL An article of personal property, as distinguished from an interest in real property.

CHATTEL, REAL Any item of property which is connected or concerned or annexed with or to real estate.

CHEAP MONEY The economic condition characterized by low interest rates and high price level. Inflationary.

CHECK 1) A restraint or hindrance.
2) A mark used to note that an item has been attended to.
3) A written order on a bank for the payment of money to a stated person or to bearer on demand out of funds which the drawer of the check has in his account in the bank.

CHECK CURRENCY Demand deposits created by a bank loan and subject to withdrawal by check as contrasted with paper money or coin.

CHECKOFF A system by which union dues and other assessments are deducted from the employees' pay checks by the employer, either automatically or on specific authorization from the workers.

CHEQUE The designation of a check in Canada and other foreign countries. See "check."

CHICAGO BOARD OF TRADE The largest grain exchange in the world where spot or futures contracts are made in a large range of agricultural products.

CHILD LABOR Under the 1938 Fair Labor Standards Act it is the gainful employment of individuals under sixteen years of age in nonexcepted activities such as on a farm during vacation from school. In some hazardous activities the age is raised to eighteen.

CHOSE IN ACTION A right to personal property which has not been reduced to possession or enjoyment but which is recoverable in an action at law; for example, a patent right, a copyright, a royalty right, a right growing out of a contract or out of damage to person or to property, or a right under a life insurance policy. While the right itself is the chose in action, the evidence of the right, such as the life insurance policy, sometimes is referred to as if it were the chose in action. To be distinguished from a chose in possession.

CHOSE IN POSSESSION Any article of tangible personal property in actual, rightful possession, such as a watch, an automobile or a piece of furniture; to be distinguished from a chose in action.

CHURNING 1) Continuous buying and selling of securities which does not move the market very much in either direction.
2) An illegal practice referring to a broker's frequent attempts to buy and sell securities for his clients in order to generate commissions.

CIRCULAR LETTER OF CREDIT A document, usually issued by a bank, that is not addressed to any specific bank or agency. The bank agrees to accept drafts upon it if they are within the terms of the letter.

CIRCULATING CAPITAL As contrasted with fixed capital which is relatively permanent, circulating capital is used synonymously with working capital.

CIRCULATING MEDIUM 1) Money.
2) An item of exchange which is generally accepted without endorsement.

CIRCULATION STATEMENT The monthly report of the Treasury of the United States which gives the amount of money outstanding, and the amount of currency which is held by the Federal Reserve Banks and the United States Treasury.

CIVIL AUTHORITY CLAUSE Provision in a fire policy which provides that the insured is protected against damages which may be caused by firemen, policemen, or other civil authorities in their efforts to check fire.

CIVIL CORPORATION An artificial being, created by law for the purpose of engaging in the business purposes stated in its charter which is granted by the state.

CIVIL LAW The legal system prevailing in the European, Asiatic, Central American, and South American countries which inherited their legal systems from Rome; in other words, in practically all except the English-speaking countries. Compare common law.

CLAIM 1) A right to demand as due a title to any debt.
2) To demand, assert as true.

CLAIM AGAINST ESTATE 1) A demand made upon the estate to do or to forbear some act as a matter of duty. A common example would be the claim submitted by a creditor for a debt owed him by the decedent at the time of his death.
2) A title.

CLASSIFICATION 1) A systematic method of arranging or designating.
2) An individual class or group, as insurance underwriting classifications, or stock classifications.

CLASSIFIED STOCK Equity security divided into groups such as Class A and Class B. The difference between the two classes will be determined by the provisions of the charter and bylaws. Typically the difference between A and B classes of stock is the right of voting.

CLASSIFIED TAX A tax in which different tax rates are assigned to each class of property. Thus a luxurious property may be taxed at a higher rate than a simple property.

CLASS RATE In insurance, the premium rate applicable to a specified class of risk. See "minimum rate."

CLASS SYSTEM A stagger system for the election of members of a board of directors. Each group or "class" has a term of more than one year. Only one class would be voted upon for election in any one year. This permits a perpetuation of control and makes it difficult to unseat the existing management or administration of a corporation.

CLAYTON ACT Federal statute passed in 1914 as an amendment to the Sherman Antitrust Act. Notable for its declaration that human labor is not "a commodity or article of commerce" and for its privileging of certain labor activities.

CLEAN BILL OF EXCHANGE A bill of exchange which has no other documents attached to it such as a bill of lading.

CLEAN BILL OF LADING A bill of lading which has not been changed or modified by such limitation clauses as may be added by a carrier such as "shipper's load and count."

CLEAN DRAFT A sight or time draft which has no other documents attached to it. This is to be distinguished from "documentary draft." See "draft" and "documentary draft."

CLEAN LETTER OF CREDIT A letter of credit which does not require such documents as bills of lading as a condition of acceptance by a bank. Such letters are issued only to prime risks.

CLEAR This term has three meanings in banking circles: The clearing of a check is the collection and final payment of it through a clearinghouse; the clearing of active securities through a stock exchange clearinghouse; a legal term meaning "free from encumbrances," such as "clear title" referring to title of property or goods. In transportation, the term refers to the certification given by customs that a vessel may depart since it has complied with the customs requirements.

CLEARING Domestic clearing (clearing within a country) is the offsetting of bank counterclaims and the settlement of balances; it may be either local or nationwide. This is carried on at a clearinghouse. International clearing is the settlement of balances between countries through the medium of foreign exchange.

CLEARING AGREEMENT Accord between participating nations whereby buyers of foreign goods or services pay for them with their own domestic currency. Periodically the central banks of the agreeing nations will balance at the previously agreed upon rates of exchange.

CLEARINGHOUSE A place where representatives of banks meet each day at an agreed time to exchange checks, drafts, and similar items drawn on each other and to settle the resulting balances.

CLEARINGS The incoming cash letters of items which must be proved, sorted, returned if necessary, and for which settlement must be made.

CLOCK OVERTIME Overtime paid because more than the contract-specified "regular rate" hours are worked in the day or week even though the statutory maximum regular rate hours are not exceeded.

CLOSED CONTRACT OF INSURANCE An insurance contract under which rates and policy provisions cannot be changed. Fraternal insurance companies are not permitted to write this type of insurance.

CLOSED CORPORATION A corporation whose shares are not held by the general public but rather by a small group such as members of a family or the management of a company. The term "close corporation" means the same but is used less frequently.

CLOSED-END INVESTMENT COMPANY A management investment company which has raised its capital by means of a public offering, over a limited period of time, of a fixed amount of common stock (and which may also have raised capital by the issuance of senior securities). The stock of a closed-end investment company is bought and sold on securities exchanges or over-the-counter markets, as are the securities of business corporations.

CLOSED-END INVESTMENT TRUST An investment fund which allows only the original prescribed number of shares to be distributed.

CLOSED MORTGAGE A corporate trust indenture under which bonds have been authenticated and delivered (as an original issue) to the extent authorized under the indenture. Compare open-end mortgage.

CLOSED SHOP A form of union security in which the employer obligates himself to hire and retain in employ only union members.

CLOSED UNION A union which unreasonably withholds union membership.

CLOSING CHARGES The expenses or costs incurred in the sale, transfer, or pledging of property, such as recording fees and title-examination fees, which must be provided for and distributed among the parties upon the consummation of the transaction.

CLOSING ENTRIES In accounting, those journal entries which are used to balance and close the nominal accounts into summary accounts which in turn are transferred into the income statement or profit and loss statement and balance sheet.

CLOUD ON TITLE A defect in the owner's title to property arising from a written instrument or judgment or from an order of court purporting to create an interest in or lien upon the property, and therefore impairing the marketability of the owner's title though the interest or lien may be shown by evidence to be invalid.

CODICIL An amendment or supplement to a will. It must be executed with all the formalities of the will itself.

COGNOVIT NOTE A form of note (legal evidence of indebtedness) which is both a promissory note and chattel mortgage. The borrower, within the wording of the instrument, waives his right of action to the chattel property in case of his default in any payments agreed to in the transaction. The holder is entitled to enter judgment without a trial.

COINSURANCE 1) Insurance held jointly with another or others.
2) A system of insurance in which the insured is obligated to maintain coverage on a risk at a stipulated percentage of the property's full value, or in the event of loss suffer a penalty in proportion to the deficiency.

COLLATERAL Security pledged to insure an agreement or pledge, such as for the payment of a loan.

COLLATERAL HEIR An individual who is not a brother, sister, aunt, uncle, niece or nephew of a deceased person and thus not in a direct line of descent.

COLLATERAL LOAN A loan which is secured by the pledge of specific property, the borrower depositing with the lender either the property itself or a document bearing evidence of title to the property.

COLLATERAL NOTE A promissory note which is secured by the pledge of specific property.

COLLATERAL SECURITY Real or personal property which is put up or pledged for a loan as to be distinguished from a coendorsement.

COLLATERAL SURETY Commercial paper, such as stocks or bonds, which is placed with the lender as security for the payment of a loan.

COLLATERAL VALUE That estimate of value of the thing put up as security for a loan which is made by the lender. In the case of securities and traded commodities, the lender may be further restricted in his valuation by regulations of an appropriate body such as the exchange or Federal Reserve Board.

COLLECTION CHARGES Those fees charged for collecting drafts, notes, coupons and accounts receivable. Since most banks are on a "par" collection system for checks there is no direct charge from such banks. However, in some rural areas there still are "non-par banks"; these banks do charge a fee for paying checks that are not directly presented to them.

COLLECTION ITEM (As distinguished from a cash item.) In banking, an item which is received for collection and credit to a depositor's account after final payment. Collection items are usually subject to special instructions regarding delivery of documents when attached, protested, etc., and in most banks are subject to a special fee for handling which is called a collection charge.

COLLECTION RATIO The ratio of receivables (accounts, notes, and interest) to net sales and it indicates the efficiency of a business in collecting its accounts with customers.

COLLECTIVE BARGAINING The process of negotiating a union contract or settling grievances in line with the grievance procedure provided in an existing contract, with union representatives on one side, and management representatives on the other.

COLLECTIVE OWNERSHIP Possession of a good in common with no particular part or proportion assigned to anyone. A public building or road is owned by the taxpayers of the district or subdivision; however, no one taxpayer can identify or claim any particular part.

COLLECTIVISM A governmental system that operates with most decisions being reached by the centralized government. Communism is an example of a government using the collectivism system.

COLLUSION A secret agreement between two or more persons to defraud a third party of his rights, to injure him, to deceive a court, or to obtain an unlawful object.

COMAKER A person who signs the note of another as an additional maker for the purpose of strengthening the credit of the principal maker.

COMBINATION IN RESTRAINT OF TRADE Any agreement or understanding between individuals or companies with the objective of restricting competition in the sale, production, or the distribution of a good or service.

COMBINATION PLAN In insurance, a retirement plan which combines two or more of the established methods of funding, such as a combination of group annuities for current service benefits and individual annuities for prior service benefits, or a life insurance program with a self-administered retirement plan.

COMBINED ENTRY (compound entry) One that contains more than two bookkeeping elements. Such an entry may consist of two or more debits and one credit, or one debit and two or more credits. It may also consist of several debits and several credits.

COMMERCE Trade, communication, etc., between the states and between nations; the basis for Congressional labor legislation through exercise of its "commerce power."

COMMERCIAL BANK A banking corporation which accepts demand deposits subject to check and makes short-term loans to business enterprises, regardless of the scope of its other services.

COMMERCIAL BILL Those bills of exchange which have resulted from a commercial business transaction as compared to the noncommercial bills such as a banker's bill. In theory, a commercial bill, if discounted, would provide a desirable expansion of the money supply while a bill arising out of, say, a financial speculation, would generally be undesirable and inflationary, if rediscounted.

COMMERCIAL CREDIT That credit used by manufacturers, retailers, wholesalers, jobbers, and commission agents for the production and distribution of goods. It is distinguished from investment, agricultural, bank, and personal credit.

COMMERCIAL CREDIT COMPANY A finance or credit company. One which buys and sells installment contracts and open book accounts which are obtained from retailers and wholesalers. At times they also engage in factoring.

COMMERCIAL DISCOUNTS That discount which is given to encourage prompt payment of a commercial account.

COMMERCIAL DRAFT A written order signed by one person or firm requesting another person or firm to pay a stated sum of money to a third party.

COMMERCIAL LETTER OF CREDIT An instrument by which a bank lends its credit to a customer to enable him to finance the purchase of goods. Addressed to the seller, it authorizes him to draw drafts on the bank under the terms stated in the letter.

COMMERCIAL LOAN A short-term loan made by a bank to a business enterprise for use in the production, manufacture, or distribution of goods or in the financing of related services.

COMMERCIAL PAPER This term applies to notes, drafts, bills of exchange, and other negotiable paper originating from commercial transactions (the transfer and movement of goods). These are usually notes or acceptances with a definite maturity date which are received by a business enterprise in payment for goods sold or services rendered.

COMMERCIAL POLICY 1) An administrative plan of action on the part of government, business, or some other organization to stimulate or retard sale, production or distribution of a good or service.
2) An accident or health insurance policy sold to persons in less hazardous occupations such as sales, teaching, clerical, business administration, etc.

COMMERCIAL TREATY The agreement between two or more nations which enumerates the rights and responsibilities of individuals and companies doing business between the two nations.

COMMISSION 1) A percentage of the principal or of the income (or of both) which a fiduciary receives as compensation for its services; to be distinguished from allowance, charge, and fee.
2) Formal, written authority granting certain privileges or powers, or commanding the performance of certain duties or acts.

COMMISSION BROKER An agent who executes the public's orders for the purchase or sale of securities or commodities, for which he receives a percentage of the transaction as his compensation. See "dealer."

COMMISSION HOUSE A brokerage firm, in securities or commodities or both, that buys and sells for its customers for a commission of the transaction.

COMMISSION MERCHANT A business that is established for the purpose of selling goods as the consignee for producers, merchants, and manufacturers.

COMMODITY Economic goods such as raw or semi-processed materials which may be quoted either on a cash or immediate delivery basis or on a futures basis. Such commodities are frequently quoted in the financial or business sections of newspapers and have agreed upon standards of quality or type.

COMMODITY AGREEMENT Contract between producers to control marketing or production of the covered commodity for the purpose of preventing price decline.

COMMODITY CREDIT CORPORATION A corporation formed by the government of the United States for the purpose of providing the facility for the United States Department of Agriculture's programs of agricultural price support and related activities such as storage, transportation, sale, loans and purchase.

COMMODITY EXCHANGE An association of member traders in agricultural products which have standards of quality. The typical exchange deals primarily in futures which provide the opportunity of hedging. Spot or actual commodity transactions may also take place on some exchanges but the proportionate volume is much smaller than the futures contracts.

COMMODITY EXCHANGE ACT The 1936 Act which created the Commodity Exchange Commission which regulates trading in the contract markets and has other broad powers to prevent fraud and manipulation in covered commodities and to establish limits in trading for the purpose of preventing excessive speculation.

COMMODITY EXCHANGE AUTHORITY The unit within the United States Department of Agriculture which enforces the Commodity Exchange Act of 1936.

COMMODITY EXCHANGE COMMISSION The Secretary of Agriculture, the Secretary of Commerce, and the Attorney General are designated by the Commodity Exchange Act of 1936 as the Commodity Exchange Commission.

COMMODITY PAPER Any note, draft or other document with accompanying warehouse receipts or bills of lading for commodities. In the event of default, the lender may sell the commodities up to the value of the loan and the expense of collection.

COMMON CAPITAL STOCK Represents the funds invested by the residual owners whose claims to income and assets are subordinated to all other claims. See "common stock."

COMMON CARRIER A business engaged in transportation on a hire basis. It is required by the terms of its charter to charge uniform rates and within the limits of its facilities to serve all comers.

COMMON DISASTER Sudden and extraordinary misfortune which brings about the simultaneous or near-simultaneous death of two or more associated persons.

COMMON-DISASTER CLAUSE In insurance, a clause that provides for an alternative beneficiary in event both the insured and the original beneficiary die at the same time in an accident.

COMMON LAW An unwritten system of laws which has grown out of custom and traditional usage. It originated in England and its form of development was different from that of Roman (civil) law. Compare civil law.

COMMON-LAW DEFENSES 1) Defense pleas which are based on common law, rather than civil law.
2) Pleas which would defeat an insured workman's suit against his employer (and which are still effective in the absence of Workmen's Compensation or Employer's Liability legislation). They are: Contributory negligence on employee's part, injury caused by fellow servant, assumption of risk by the employee in the course of his work.

COMMON MARKET A group of West European countries who have negotiated to build a common tariff wall against outside interests while gradually disintegrating tariffs among themselves.

COMMON STOCK A security representing ownership of a corporation's assets. The right of common stock to dividends and assets ranks after the requirements of bonds, debentures and preferred stocks. Normally, increases in asset values and earnings beyond the fixed claims of bonds and preferred stocks rebound to the benefit of the common stock. Similarly, common stocks are affected first by decreases in asset values and earnings. Generally, shares of common stock have voting rights.

COMMON-STOCK DIVIDENDS Dividends declared on common stock during the year whether or not they were paid during the year. Unless otherwise qualified, it is the amount of such dividends charged to retained income (earned surplus) and includes those payable in cash or stock.

COMMUNISM A political and economic theory calling for the complete abolition of all private property and complete control by the community of all matters including labor, religion, politics and social relations. As an emotionally charged word, communism must be interpreted within the context of its use.

COMMUNITY PROPERTY Property in which a husband and wife have each an undivided one-half interest by reason of their marital status; recognized in all civil-law countries and in certain states of the United States.

COMMUTED VALUE Present value of future payments due or receivable, computed on the basis of a given rate of interest.

COMPANY An association of persons, whether incorporated or not, for the purpose of carrying on some business.

COMPARATIVE ADVANTAGE Situation in which an individual, firm, locality or nation can produce a good or service cheaper than another.

COMPARATIVE STATEMENT The income, expense, profit and loss, balance sheet or other financial statements of the same concern for two or more consecutive years that are analyzed to determine the increase or decrease in their component items, frequently for credit purposes.

COMPENSATING BALANCE The amount of a commercial loan which the banker requires his borrower to keep with the bank.

COMPENSATION Something given or received as an equivalent for services, debt, loss, suffering; idemnity.

COMPENSATORY DUTY An import duty of an amount sufficient to balance a domestic excise tax, or a foreign producer's governmental subsidy.

COMPETENCY A fitness or sufficiency to undertake something, such as to enter into a contract. For example, in insurance, the company must have the charter and permission of the state to write business. The other party to the insurance contract must have the mental faculties to be able to contract.

COMPLAINT The allegation of damages or accusation of crime, with an offer to prove the truth and fact of same.

COMPLETE AUDIT An audit in which an examination is made of the system of internal control and of the details of all of the books of account, including subsidiary records and supporting documents, as to legality, mathematical ac-

curacy, complete accountability, and application of accepted accounting principles. One of the main features of a complete audit is that the auditor is not expected to make any qualifications in his report except such as are imposed by lack of information, that is, physical inability to get the facts. See "limited audit."

COMPOSITE DEMAND The complete schedule of demand for a good or service.

COMPOSITE SUPPLY The complete supply schedule for a good or service, or function.

COMPOSITION SETTLEMENT The acceptance by a creditor of an amount smaller than that which he is legally entitled to from a debtor. In doing this he waives his right to the full amount.

COMPOUND DUTY A specific tariff duty in addition to an ad valorem duty.

COMPOUND INTEREST Interest upon principal plus accrued interest.

COMPTROLLER In large firms this office is often held by a vice president with the title "Vice President and Comptroller." The duties of a comptroller generally embrace the audit functions of the firm and the establishment of control over all systems in use in operations. The comptroller also is one of the key officers in the future planning of the firm's operations.

COMPTROLLER OF THE CURRENCY An appointed official who is responsible for the chartering, supervision, and liquidation of national banks. His office is located in the Treasury Department.

COMPTROLLER'S CALL The Comptroller of the Currency may "call" upon all national banks to submit a complete financial report of their activities at any given date. Reports must, according to law, be submitted at his call at least three times a year. These "called reports" must also be published in all local newspapers in the town nearest to the bank.

CONCESSION 1) A deviation from higher regular terms or previous conditions.
2) The right to use property for a stated purpose or purposes.

CONCILIATION Attempt by third party, a conciliator, to aid the settling of a labor dispute by hearing both sides and offering advice and nonbinding suggestions.

CONDEMNATION The legal taking of private property for the public use and interest. The taking of such property must be through the exercise of due process of law.

CONDITIONAL ENDORSEMENT An endorsement of a negotiable instrument which states and imposes conditions upon the transferee. The instrument may still be negotiated within the terms of the condition but the individual who has made the conditional endorsement has the right to the proceeds of the instrument should the conditions not be fulfilled.

CONDITIONAL GIFT A gift of property by will which is subject to some condition specified in the will or in the trust instrument; opposed to an absolute gift.

CONDITIONAL SALE A sale in which the transfer of title to property (real or personal) is dependent upon the performance of a stipulated condition.

CONDITIONAL SALES CONTRACT An installment contract which stipulates that title to the property referred to in the contract shall not pass to the purchaser until the price is fully paid in cash.

CONDITION PRECEDENT A qualification or restriction which must happen or be performed before the contract or estate dependent upon it can arise or vest.

CONDITION SUBSEQUENT A condition, by the failure or nonperformance of which an estate already vested is defeated.

CONDOMINIUM The common ownership of a piece of property by one or more individuals, each of whom owns an absolute undivided interest in the property, or a portion of it. It is an interest which has all of the characteristics associated with free ownership, such as alienability, mortgageability, divisability and inheritability.

CONFESSION OF JUDGMENT An admission by a party to whom an act or liability is imputed.

CONFIRMED LETTER OF CREDIT A foreign bank wishing to issue a letter of credit to a local concern may request a local bank in the city in which the beneficiary is located to confirm this credit to the beneficiary. The purpose of this confirmation is to lend the prestige and responsibility of the local bank to the transaction because the status of the foreign bank may be unknown to the beneficiary. The confirming bank assumes responsibility for the payment of all drafts drawn under the credit and usually charges a fee for doing so.

CONFISCATION The governmental seizure of private property without compensation for the action.

CONFLICT OF LAWS That branch of the law which is concerned with the legal principles applicable in a situation wherein the law of two or more jurisdictions is claimed to be applicable by the parties to the controversy and the laws of the two or more jurisdictions are in conflict with one another.

CONGLOMERATE The term used to describe a corporate consolidation in which one company acquires another in a different industry.

CONSENT DECREE The settlement of equity cases whereby the defendant agrees to stop certain actions that caused the case to be brought. This agreement is expressed as a judicial decree and the legal suit is dropped.

CONSERVATOR The appointed official charged with the protection of the interests in an estate. He may protect the creditors of a bank or a declared incompetent as well as see that certain laws that are in the public interest are enforced.

CONSIDERATION Something of value given by one party to another in exchange for the promise or act of such other party.

CONSIGNEE The person to whom articles are shipped.

CONSIGNMENT The act of an individual or company of delivery or transfer of goods to an agent to be cared for or sold.

CONSIGNOR The owner of goods sent to a consignee.

CONSOLIDATED The results obtained when the accounts of a parent company and its subsidiary companies are combined to reflect the financial position and results of operations of the group as if it operated as a single entity. Such a consolidation involves proper intercompany eliminations and minority interest adjustments.

CONSOLIDATED BALANCE SHEET A balance sheet showing the financial condition of a corporation and its subsidiaries. See "balance sheet."

CONSOLIDATED MORTGAGE A mortgage on several separate units of property which are covered by the consolidated mortgage.

CONSTANT COST Costs of production may be fixed or variable. The fixed or constant costs are those that do not change with changes in production. The variable costs of production do change with the volume of production. If reference is made to unit costs of production then many of the fixed costs of total production will become variable unit costs.

CONSTRUCTION LOAN Funds extended on the security of real estate for the purpose of constructing improvements on the property and usually advanced during the period of construction.

CONSTRUCTIVE DISCHARGE A form of discrimination that forces a worker to "quit."

CONSTRUCTIVE EVICTION The act whereby the owner does not provide the tenant with such comfort or peace as the tenant desires so that the tenant will, therefore, voluntarily break the lease.

CONSTRUCTIVE MILEAGE An arbitrary mileage allowed to a transportation line in dividing joint rates, etc., on a mileage pro-rate (not the actual mileage). Also arbitrary mileage allowed train and engine employees for mileage paid for and not run.

CONSTRUCTIVE TRUST A trust imposed by a court of equity as a means of doing justice, without regard to the intention of the parties, in a situation in which a person who holds title to property is under a duty to convey it to another person; to be distinguished from an express trust and a resulting trust.

CONSUL A nation's foreign service officer located in a foreign country who represents his nation's tourists, businessmen and other traveling nationals.

CONSUMER CREDIT Credit extended by a bank to borrowers (usually individuals) for personal use and for the purchase of consumer goods and services. Repayable in regular equal installments. Loans may be secured or unsecured, depending upon pertinent factors.

CONSUMER GOODS Commodities whose ultimate use is to contribute directly to the satisfaction of human wants or desires—such as shoes and food—as distinguished from producers' or capital goods.

CONSUMER PRICE INDEX A measure of the average change in prices of goods and services purchased by city wage earner and clerical worker families. The index represents the total cost of a selected "market basket" of goods and services expressed as a percentage of the average cost of the same "market basket" in a selected period.

CONSUMERS' COOPERATIVE An association of ultimate consumers organized to purchase goods and services primarily for use by or resale to the membership.

CONSUMPTION The use of a good or service to satisfy a desire.

CONTEMPLATION OF DEATH Act of considering and acting upon the possibility of death. In estate taxes, transfers near the date of death are commonly considered transfers in contemplation of death and as such taxable in the estate even though they would be excludable had the decedent lived a greater number of years.

CONTINGENCY RESERVE A reserve created to cover the deficiency that might arise in departments where an original appropriation proves to be inadequate to cover the necessary expenditures. In some instances, the law prohibits the creation of such a reserve.

CONTINGENT BENEFICIARY The beneficiary whose interest is conditioned upon a future occurrence which may or may not take place. Unless or until the condition takes place, the interest is only contingent.

CONTINGENT DUTY In international trade, a countervailing duty levied on an importation to offset a subsidy or similar export aid granted by the exporting nation.

CONTINGENT FUND An amount of money set aside to take care of the expenses of emergencies. These emergencies may not be predictable, but the fund should be able to permit the company to continue to operate in the event the contingencies develop.

CONTINGENT INTEREST A future interest in real or personal property that is dependent upon the fulfillment of a stated condition. Thus, the interest may never come into existence. To be distinguished from vested interest.

CONTINGENT REMAINDER A future interest in property that is dependent upon the fulfillment of a stated condition before the termination of a prior estate; to be distinguished from a vested remainder.

CONTINUING AGREEMENT That phase of a regular borrower's loan agreement with his bank which simplifies his borrowing since the borrower does not have to make a loan application and sign a note every time he borrows. Once the continuing agreement is signed the borrower may borrow within the terms of the contract on a continuing basis.

CONTINUING GUARANTY A form given to a bank by a person to guarantee repayment of a loan to another party. This guaranty promises payment by the guarantor in the event of default by the borrower and is so worded that it may apply to a current loan or to one made at a later date. The guaranty may or may not pledge collateral as security for the loan.

CONTINUITY OF COVERAGE In insurance, a clause attached or contained in a fidelity bond which takes the place of another bond and agrees to pay the losses that would be recoverable under the first bond except that the discovery period has expired. This would be in a case where losses have been caused by a dishonest employee and have not been discovered, though they have occurred at various times stretching over a period of time, that time being a period under which several bonds had been insured. This may involve a chain of several bonds, each one superseding a prior obligation. Those losses will be covered if the chain of bonds is unbroken and each has included continuity of coverage clause.

CONTINUOUS AUDIT An audit in which the detailed work is performed either continuously or at short, regular intervals throughout the fiscal period, usually at the shortest intervals (*e.g.,* weekly or monthly) at which subsidiary records are closed and made available for audit in controllable form. Such "continuous" work leads up to the completion of the audit upon the closing of the accounting records at the end of the fiscal year.

CONTINUOUS MARKET The market for a security or commodity which is so broad that normal amounts may usually be sold with little difficulty and small price variation.

CONTRACT An agreement between two or more parties to do or not to do some lawful thing for a lawful consideration.

CONTRACT CARRIER A motor carrier transporting goods for one or more concerns under contract specifically designed to cover type of service, special equipment, etc.

CONTRACT CLAUSE That portion of the United States Constitution which prohibits any state from impairing the rights and obligations of legal contracts.

CONTRACT FOR DEED An agreement by a seller to deliver the deed to the property when certain conditions have been fulfilled, such as the completion of certain payments and provisions of insurance. It has similar features to a mortgage.

CONTRACT MARKET Any commodity exchange which may engage in the business of futures contracts and is approved by the Secretary of Agriculture subject to the Commodity Exchange Administration supervision.

CONTRACT OF SALE A written document whereby an owner agrees to convey title to a property when the purchaser has completed paying for the property under the terms of the contract.

CONTRACTOR A person who contracts to perform work or to supply materials under specified conditions.

CONTRACT RENT That amount agreed upon between a tenant and owner for the use of real estate for a stated period of time. This contract rent may be higher or lower than the theoretical economic rent which is the difference between the productivity of the land and marginal land.

CONTRACTUAL PLAN By common usage, an investment-accumulation plan with a stated paying-in period and provision for regular investments at monthly or quarterly dates. Substantially synonymous with prepaid charge plan.

CONTRIBUTION Something given such as money, time, personal or real property, etc.

CONTRIBUTORY PENSION A retirement system in which the employer and the employee both make payments for the benefit of the employee. The system may in addition be vested, that is, subject to tenure; the employee, upon termination of employment, may take his and his employer's contribution with him. A nonvested pension would not have the employer's contribution go with the employee until actual retirement.

CONTROL 1) Power or authority to manage or administrate.
2) Maintaining records and preparing reports to meet corporate legal and tax requirements and measure the results of the company operations; providing accounting services structured for use by managers in planning and controlling the business.

CONTROLLED ACCOUNT 1) A discretionary account.
2) A trading account in securities or commodities in which the principal does not necessarily instruct his broker to buy or sell but rather gives a power of attorney for his broker to exercise his own discretion.
3) An account which a salesman is able to take with him in the event he changes firms.

CONTROLLED ECONOMY The administration of the means of production and consumption by a large amount of government planning and controls with only nominal use of the price system, the objective being to direct and guide the economy.

CONTROLLED INFLATION That economic situation in which the monetary and fiscal authorities of a nation deliberately create inflationary conditions, generally through increasing the supply of money. The objective is to pull the economy out of a recession or period of deflation into prosperity. By such controls as the authorities have over the money supply they are able to reduce the increase in inflation as they approach their goal.

CONTROLLING ACCOUNT In bookkeeping, an account, usually kept in the general ledger, which receives the aggregate of the debit and of the credit postings to a number of identical, similar, or related accounts called subsidiary accounts so that its balance equals the aggregate of the balance in these accounts. See "general ledger" and "subsidiary account."

CONTROLLING COMPANY A parent company that controls other companies through several devices. Some of them are: Through stock ownership, through interlocking boards of directors, by use of a holding company, through leases, patents, copyrights and common management.

CONTROLLING INTEREST In a legal sense slightly over fifty percent of the voting stock will control any corporation, and thus constitute a controlling interest. However, in a de facto sense, many corporations may be controlled by a much smaller percentage of voting stock if the rest of the stock is widely dispersed and not active in voting.

CONVENIENCE GOODS Those consumer goods which are of low price which consumers wish to purchase with little effort and for which they generally do not "shop."

CONVENTIONAL LOAN A non-Federal Housing Administration or Veterans Administration loan on property whose principal usually is not extinguished by periodic payments if it is a nonamortized conventional loan.

CONVENTIONAL MORTGAGE LOAN A mortgage loan made directly to the borrower without government insurance or guaranty.

CONVENTION VALUES Values at which the Commissioner of Insurance permits certain securities to be carried on insurance companies' books. Also known as "commissioner's values." The values are used during very abnormal business conditions, such as in periods of panic and severe depression.

CONVERSION 1) The exchange of personal or real property of one nature for that of another nature.
2) The exchange of one type of security for another, as for example—the exchange of bonds for stock.
3) The exchanging of a charter granted by the state for a federal charter, etc.
4) The appropriation of, dealing with, or using the property of another without right or consent as though it were one's own.

CONVERSION PRICE That amount or rate at which a holder of a convertible bond may exchange it for the stock of the same corporation. This price may be fixed or determinable.

CONVERTIBLE Subject to exchanging for something else; as, stock convertible to bonds, or bonds to stock, or an asset convertible to cash.

CONVEYANCE 1) The transfer of ownership of property.
2) The instrument by which title to property is transferred.

COOLING-OFF-PERIOD A period of time (usually 30 to 90 days) during which a union is barred from striking, or an employer from locking out his employees. The period may be required by law or be a part of a labor agreement.

COOPERATIVE A type of business enterprise that is owned by its customers.

COOPERATIVE MARKETING The process by which groups composed of producers, middlemen, consumers, or combinations of them act collectively in buying or selling or both.

COPARTNERSHIP (or PARTNERSHIP) A company of partners, as distinguished from a proprietorship or a corporation.

COPYRIGHT The exclusive legal right of writers, composers, playwrights and artists to publish and dispose of their works for a period of time.

CORNER Buying of a stock or commodity on a scale large enough to give the buyer, or buying group, control over the price. A person who must buy that stock or commodity, for example one who is short, is forced to do business at an arbitrarily high price with those who engineered the corner. See "short."

CORN-HOG RATIO That relationship between the selling price of corn and the selling price of hogs. The farmer knowing how many pounds a hog will gain from eating one bushel of corn is able to decide whether it is more profitable to sell the corn or to feed it to his hogs and sell the hogs.

CORPORATE AGENT Trust companies act as agents for corporations, governments, and municipalities for various transactions. In each case, a fee is charged for the particular service rendered.

CORPORATE FIDUCIARY A trust institution serving in fiduciary capacity, such as executor, administrator, trustee, or guardian.

CORPORATE RESOLUTION A document given to a bank by a corporation defining the authority vested in each of its officers who may sign and otherwise conduct the business of the corporation with the bank. Corporate resolutions usually are given with or without borrowing powers. These powers are granted by the board of directors of the firm.

CORPORATE STOCK The equity shares of a corporation. These shares may be common, preferred or classified. The term corporate stock is also used occasionally to refer to bonds of some municipalities.

CORPORATE SURETY 1) Insurance provided by a surety company as compared to surety provided by an individual.
2) The writing of bonds by a corporation as obligor.

CORPORATE TRUST A trust created by a corporation, typical of which is a trust to secure a bond issue.

CORPORATION A form of business organization that may have many owners with each owner liable only for the amount of his investment in the business. It is an artificial person created by state or federal law. As defined by the Supreme Court of the United States, a corporation is "an artificial being, invisible, intangible, and existing only in contemplation of law."

CORPORATION FINANCE That area of business which is concerned with providing the funds needed by a business. This would include the technique of organizing and raising the initial capital of the corporation, the provision of working capital through proper cash-flow practices, the emergency steps needed in the event of insolvency or bankruptcy, as well as those techniques such as dividend policies which will permit a corporation to obtain needed capital for expansion.

CORPORATION INCOME TAX A progressive tax levied on earnings of corporations and Massachusetts trusts by either the federal or state government.

CORPORATION SOLE A one-man corporation, the authority, duties and powers of which are attached to and go with the office and not the natural person who for the time being holds the office.

CORRESPONDENT BANK One which carries a deposit balance for a bank located in another city or engages in an exchange of services with that bank.

CORRESPONDENT FIRM A brokerage firm that maintains a mutually advantageous business and financial association with another brokerage firm. This quite often occurs between one firm located in a city where there is an exchange and another out-of-town firm which has business executed and cleared by the member firm.

COST The amount, measured in money, of cash expended or other property transferred, capital stock issued, services performed, or a liability incurred, in consideration of goods or services received or to be received.

COST ACCOUNTING That method of accounting which provides for the assembling and recording of all the elements of cost incurred to accomplish a purpose, to carry on an activity, or operation, or to complete a unit of work or a specific job.

COST, BOOK The cost of acquisition shown in the general ledger of an individual partnership or corporation which generally includes direct and indirect costs, financing costs, and all development costs, except preliminary operating losses.

COST, CENTER A purely arbitrary division or unit of a plant set up for costing purposes only. It may be a man at a bench, a machine or group of machines, a department, a floor, or an entire building.

COST, DIRECT Costs computed and identified directly with a specific product, job or function. It usually refers to identifiable costs of raw materials, labor, overhead, etc.

COST, EXPIRED Costs which are not applicable to the production of future revenues and, for that reason, are treated as deductions from current revenues or are charged against retained earnings. Examples are costs of products or other assets sold or disposed of and current expenses.

COST, INDIRECT A cost not particularly identifiable with a specific product, job or function.

COST-OF-GOODS SOLD A firm's production cost or inventory value of the products the company sells, which appear in the profit and loss statement.

COST OF LIVING A misnomer frequently applied to an index developed by the Bureau of Labor Statistics, Department of Labor. The proper designation is consumer price index. It shows the relationship of wages to the cost of commodities. See "consumer price index."

COST-OF-LIVING ADJUSTMENT The device found in some union contracts which provides that the employer shall adjust his hourly rate up or down in sympathetic relationship to some index such as the consumer price index so that the covered employees will maintain the same purchasing power.

COST-OF-MERCHANDISE SOLD In accounting, the result obtained by subtracting the ending merchandise inventory from the sum of the beginning merchandise inventory and the net purchases for the month.

COST PLUS CONTRACTS An agreement by which the buyer pays the seller or producer his costs of the product and also a percentage of the costs in addition for his profits. Contracts for production of devices of unknown costs such as a space vehicle may take this form. Where costs are better known, it is probable that a fixed price contract will be used.

COST UNIT A term used in cost accounting to designate the unit of product or service whose cost is computed. These units are selected for the purpose of comparing the actual cost with a standard cost or with actual costs of units produced under different circumstances or at different places and times. See "unit cost" and "work unit."

COUNSEL Legal advice; also a lawyer or lawyers engaged to give such advice or to conduct a case in court.

COUNTER CHECK   A form of check provided by a bank for the convenience of the depositor. A counter check can be cashed only by the drawer personally.

COUNTERPART FUND   The amount of domestic currency a nation sets aside as an offset adjustment for loans or gifts from abroad.

COUNTERSIGN   To sign what has already been signed in order to verify the authenticity of an instrument.

COUNTY AGENT   The man or woman jointly employed by the Department of Agriculture of the United States, county government and state agricultural school (land grant college) to bring to farm families improved farm practices and agricultural research.

COUPON   One of a series of promissory notes of consecutive maturities attached to a bond or other debt certificate and intended to be detached and presented on their respective due dates for payment of interest.

COUPON POLICY   An insurance policy also called guaranteed investment policy. A type of policy sold by some nonparticipating companies as a competitive offering. Typically it is a 20-payment life policy with attached coupons. Each coupon is redeemable in cash at the end of each policy year. Since the coupon is guaranteed, it has a selling feature over dividends.

COURT OF CLAIMS   That federal court which handles all claims against the United States which arise out of any contract with the Government, regulation of the President or act of Congress as well as claims directed to it by the Senate or House of Representatives.

COURT OF EQUITY   Courts applying a system of jurisprudence more flexible than that of the common law in order to work justice where the common law, by reason of its rigidity, fails to recognize a right or is unable to enforce it.

COURT TRUST   A trust coming under the immediate supervision of the court, such as a trust by order of court or, in some states, a trust under will.

COVENANT   A promise, incorporated in a trust indenture or other formal instrument, to perform certain acts or to refrain from the performance of certain acts.

COVER   1) In securities transactions, shorts are said to cover when they buy back the contracts they had previously sold, thereby liquidating their position.
2) An insurance contract.
3) The backing for some instrument; such as, the bond has a cover of gold or securities.

COVERAGE   1) Frequently used interchangeably with the word "protection" or "insurance." The extent of the insurance afforded under an insurance contract.
2) The extent of membership under a retirement plan. The term is frequently applied to the types of employees included under a plan. The guarantee against specific losses provided under the terms of a policy of insurance.
3) As used in credit analysis, coverage is the amount of one item in a financial statement in relationship to another item. Thus, if accounts payable is shown as $1,000 and cash as $2,000, the coverage of cash is two times.

CRAFT UNION   A labor organization, the membership in which is restricted to individuals possessing or working a specific skill or trade.

CREDIT   1) Used in general sense means act of allowing person or persons immediate use of goods or services with payment deferred until an agreed future date.
2) Used in bookkeeping sense means an entry on ledger signifying cash payment, merchandise returned, or an allowance. Opposite of "debit."

CREDIT AGENCY   Those companies which make a business of providing credit and collection information. See "mercantile agency."

CREDIT BUREAU   Place where information about payment records of individuals and firms and all other relevant data are assembled. Information released to members and nonmembers on request. Credit bureaus can be merchant-owned, that is, ownership held by local merchants and others, or can be privately owned.

CREDIT CONTROLS   Those restraints which are imposed by authoritative bodies. The Federal Reserve Board controls credit in several ways: Reserve requirements for member banks; open-market operations; rediscount rates; margin requirements. In addition, in periods of national emergency, other regulating devices are used to regulate credit such as the fiscal operation of the United States Treasury, gold sterilization and action by the American Bankers' Association.

CREDIT INSTRUMENTS   Any document, contract or paper which may be used to obtain credit. This would include paper money not redeemable in standard money, checks, notes, drafts, bills of exchange, traveler's checks, letters of credit, coupons, money orders, and cashier's checks. The above are debt credit instruments. In addition, such things as preferred and common stock certificates may be classified as equity credit instruments.

CREDIT INTERCHANGE   Information on credit may be interchanged in two ways: Direct—in which two creditors exchange their credit experience for mutual benefit; by use of a central clearing bureau in which accounts of certain categories, such as 30-day past-due accounts are listed and sent to the bureau which in turn collates the data for its members.

CREDIT LINE   The maximum amount of credit a financial institution or trade firm will extend to a customer. The customer may in many cases be unaware of the trade credit line.

CREDIT MEMORANDUM   A special business form that is issued by the seller to the buyer and that contains a record of the credit which the seller has granted for returns, allowances, overcharges, and similar items.

CREDITOR   One to whom money or its equivalent is owed.

CREDITOR NATION   A country which on a net basis is owed more by foreigners than it owes to them. Such a nation would tend to have a "favorable" balance of trade.

CREDIT RATING   The appraisal of one's credit standing, ability and willingness to pay obligations.

CREDIT UNION   A cooperative financial society organized within and limited to a specific group of people. Any group of people with common interests are eligible to form a credit union. Each union is self-managed and is intended to provide a convenient system of saving money and of lending funds to members in need at lawful rates of interest. It functions under either state or federal law and supervision.

CRITICAL MATERIALS Those commodities determined by the agency enforcing the Strategic and Critical Materials Stockpiling Act of 1946 to be essential to national defense and which are in short supply below anticipated national emergency needs.

CROP YEAR The commodity term referring to the period from the harvest of a crop to the next year. Harvest dates vary for different crops.

CROSSING The function performed by a broker in handling both sides of a transaction, *i.e.*, buying a security from one customer and simultaneously selling the same to another customer. This is legal, but a broker-member of a stock exchange must first publicly offer the security for sale at a price higher than his bid; then if no buyer appears, he may consummate the transaction with himself.

CROSS-PICKETING When two rival unions picket the same business each contending they are representatives of the striking employees.

CROSS-PURCHASE AGREEMENT Plan of partnership insurance that has each partner individually buying and maintaining enough insurance on the life or lives of other partners to fund the purchase of the others' equity.

CUM DIVIDENDS With dividends; corporate stock may be termed ex-dividend which means that the buyer is not entitled to a declared dividend or cum-dividend which means that the buyer is entitled to the declared dividend.

CUM RIGHTS With rights; corporate stock which still has the privilege of buying a stated amount of stock to be newly issued. Generally, the new stock is of a different class.

CUMULATIVE An arrangement whereby a dividend or interest which, if not paid when due or received when due, is added to that which is to be paid in the future.

CUMULATIVE DIVIDEND See "accumulated dividend."

CUMULATIVE VOTING A method of voting for corporate directors which enables the shareholder to multiply the number of his shares by the number of directorships being voted on and cast the total for one director or a selected group of directors.

CURATOR An individual or a trust institution appointed by a court to care for the property or person (or both) or a minor or an incompetent. In some cases a curator is essentially the same as a temporary administrator or a temporary guardian.

CURRENCY Technically, any form of money which serves as circulating medium and includes both paper money and metallic money (coins). In banking terminology, however, the term generally refers to paper money only.

CURRENT DEBT See "liabilities, current."

CURRENT RATIO The ratio of current assets to current liabilities, indicating the ability of a business to pay its current liabilities in cash as they fall due.

CURRENT YIELD The expression as a percentage of the annual income to the investment, *e.g.*, annual income is five dollars and investment is one hundred dollars then current yield is five percent. See "return."

CURTAIL SCHEDULE A list of the amounts by which the principal of an obligation is to be reduced by partial payments and of the dates when these payments are to become due.

CUSTODIAN One whose duty it is to hold, safeguard, and account for property committed to his care.

CUSTODY ACCOUNT An agency account concerning which the main duties of the custodian (agent) are to safekeep and preserve the property and perform ministerial acts with respect to the property as directed by the principal. The agent has no investment or management responsibilities. To be distinguished from a managing agency account and a safekeeping account.

CUSTOMS BROKER The licensed individual who for a fee handles the necessary papers and steps in obtaining clearance of goods through the customs.

CUSTOMS DUTY A tax levied on goods imported into the United States. In some nations it may also refer to the tax on goods exported from that country.

CUSTOMS UNION Tariff Union—The treaty between two or more nations to reduce or do away with customs duties between themselves and to adopt a similar policy of tariff regulations with nations not a party to the customs union.

CUTBACK The reduction in the volume of work or workers because of a decline in orders or sales or source of supply.

CUTTHROAT COMPETITION Severe but independent endeavoring by two or more firms for the business patronage by the offer of very advantageous terms to the buyer. These terms may actually cause the failure of one or more of the competitors because of low-profit margin.

CYBERNETICS The field of technology involved in the comparative study of the control and intracommunication of information, handling machines and nervous systems of animals and man in order to understand and improve communication.

CYCLICAL STOCKS Stocks which move directly with the general business cycle, *i.e.*, advancing when business improves and declining when business slackens.

CYCLICAL THEORY A theory reflected in the stock market which claims that there are identifiable, regular cycles in which the volume of trade rises or falls. The Major Cycle in which business and commodity prices move up or down, alternatingly, spans about 30 years. The Minor Cycle, and best known one, spans about 8–11 years within the trend of the Major Cycle. The Short-Term Cycle of approximately 2 years is a sharper fluctuation within the Minor Cycle.

CYCLICAL UNEMPLOYMENT Unemployment which has been caused by the drop in business-activity level.

DAMAGES The estimated compensation paid for a specified injury, loss, or wrong sustained.

DAYLIGHT TRADING Effecting a purchase and sale of a commodity or a security during the same day so that one does not hold a "position" in the item traded overnight or longer. Scalpers generally engage in "daylight trading" and probably more is done in commodities than in securities.

DAY LOAN This is a loan made for one day only for the convenience of stock brokers. The loan is granted for the purchase of securities. When the securities are delivered, they are pledged as collateral to secure a regular call loan.

DAY ORDER An order to buy or sell stock at a specified price which expires on the day the order is given unless executed. An investor may also specify a longer time or good until canceled. See "limit order" and "good until canceled."

DAYS OF GRACE The reasonable length of time allowed, without suffering a loss or penalty, for postponed payment or for the presentment for payment of certain financial documents.

DEAD TIME Time during which production employees wait for materials or for machinery adjustments and for which pay is sometimes provided.

DEALER A person or firm that transacts business as a principal rather than as an agent. See "principal."

DEATH BENEFIT A benefit payable to the survivors or a beneficiary of a member upon his death while a member of a retirement plan.

DEATH TAXES Taxes imposed on property or on the transfer of property at the owner's death; a general term covering estate taxes, inheritance taxes and other succession or transfer taxes.

DEBASEMENT Reducing the quality, purity, or content, or otherwise altering the accepted intrinsic value of the coinage of a realm.

DEBENTURE An obligation not secured by a specific lien on property; usually an unsecured note or bond of a corporation.

DEBENTURE STOCK Stock issued under a contract to pay a specified return at specified intervals. In this sense, it may be considered a special type of preferred stock. It is to be distinguished from debentures which represent a bond in form as compared with a share of stock.

DEBIT In an accounting sense, an entry which will increase an asset or expense account and will decrease a liability or income account. In insurance, accounts receivable. Compare "credit."

DEBT A contract evidencing an amount owed by one party to another for money, goods, or services.

DEBT FINANCING The long-term borrowing of money by a business, usually in exchange for debt securities or a note, for the purpose of obtaining working capital or other funds necessary to operational needs or for the purpose of retiring current or other indebtedness.

DEBT LIMIT The maximum amount of gross or net debt legally permitted.

DEBTOR A person or company who owes money.

DEBTOR NATION A country which on a net basis owes more to foreigners than it is owed by them. Such a nation would tend to have an "unfavorable" balance of trade.

DEBT SERVICE The amount of principal and interest that falls due within a stated period such as a year which must be paid by a debtor.

DECEASED ACCOUNT An account carried on deposit in a bank in the name and title of a deceased person. As soon as the death of a depositor is ascertained, the bank segregates the account, and withholds payment until authorized by a court of law to make such payment to the legal heirs. Tax waivers and authorized claims to the deposited account are known to the bank before payment may be made.

DECEDENT A deceased person.

DECENTRALIZATION 1) The distribution of power and administration from a central authority to regional and local governing bodies.
2) Dispersion from a center, as the outward growth or movement of a retail center.
3) The redistribution of population and industry from the urban areas to outlying, suburban districts.

DECLARATION OF TRUST An acknowledgment, usually but not necessarily in writing, by one holding or taking title to property that he holds the property in trust for the benefit of someone else.

DECLARATORY JUDGMENT The judgment or decision of a court interpreting an instrument or declaring what the law on the given matter is under a statutory proceeding that authorizes the court to enter such a judgment in a case that is not being litigated.

DECREASING COSTS The situation in which the per unit cost of production declines. This is generally associated with increased production when a business is operating below normal capacity.

DECREE The decision of a court of equity, admiralty, probate, or divorce; to be distinguished from the judgment of a court of law.

DEDICATE To put aside one's private property for some public purpose, such as to make a private road public.

DEDUCTIBLE COVERAGE CLAUSE Provision that in return for a reduced rate the insured will assume losses below a specified amount.

DEED A written transfer of title to property, usually real estate.

DEED, ADMINISTRATOR'S A deed by a person lawfully appointed to manage and settle the estate of a deceased person who has left no executor.

DEED, EXECUTOR'S A deed by a person named by the decedent in his will to manage and settle his estate.

DEED, MORTGAGED A deed by way of mortgage which has the effect of a mortgage on the property conveyed and imposes a lien on the granted estate.

DEED OF ASSIGNMENT The document which is used to appoint an assignee such as an individual or a fiduciary institution to take over an insolvent firm. The assignment states the powers and functions of the appointed firm or individual.

DEED OF TRUST An instrument that conveys or transfers to a trustee the title to property as security for the payment of a debt, giving the trustee the power to sell the property in order to satisfy the debt in the event of default on the part of the debtor. The instrument becomes void on the payment of the debt when due.

DEFALCATION The misappropriation or embezzlement of money or property by one to whom it has been entrusted, usually, by reason of his employment.

DEFAULT Failure to meet a legal obligation.

DEFENDANT A person required to make answer in an action or suit in law or equity or in a criminal action.

DEFERRED AVAILABILITY This term is used in Federal Reserve Bank statements. At all times there are checks traveling throughout the United States in the process of collection for member banks of the Federal Reserve System. These are contingent assets and are designated "deferred availability items."

DEFERRED CHARGES Expenditures which are not chargeable to the fiscal period in which made but are carried on the asset side of the balance sheet pending amortization or other disposition; for example, discount on bonds issued.

DEFERRED CREDITS Credit balances or items which will be spread over following accounting periods either as additions to revenue or as reductions of expenses. Examples are taxes collected in advance and premiums on bonds issued.

DEFERRED DEMAND Demand for goods or services which cannot be met because the goods or services are not available. It is expected that if they do become available, the deferred demand will be met.

DEFERRED INCOME The income account which is used to record income which has been paid in advance but not as yet earned. The prepayment of rent or insurance are illustrations of items that become deferred income for the recipient.

DEFICIENCY JUDGMENT A court order authorizing collection from a debtor of any part of a debt that remains unsatisfied after foreclosure and sale of collateral.

DEFICIT 1) The excess of liabilities over assets (negative net worth); a term used indicating obligations or expenditures for items which are in excess of the amount allotted for those items in a financial budget.
2) The excess of obligations and expenditures as a whole affecting a given budget period which is in excess of the budget established for the period.

DEFICIT FINANCING The process or methods used to meet a deficit. The term has most frequently been used during recent years in connection with the government's procedure in meeting its operating deficits through the sale of large quantities of bonds.

DEFLATION An economic condition generally characterized by declining prices and depressed business. For contrast see "inflation."

DEGRESSIVE TAX A progressive tax in which each progressive step is at a lower rate than the previous step.

DELAYED OPENING A situation caused by an accumulation of buy or sell orders before the opening of a stock exchange. Efforts are made to find counterbalancing offers, usually with institutions, firms, or individuals who have a large interest in the security, to prevent the opening price from varying sharply from the previous day's close. The specialist in the stock will often sell some of his inventory in the security, or "short" it, to help arrange a reasonable opening price.

DELINQUENCY Failure to pay an obligation when due; sometimes this term is extended to cover the amount of the delinquency.

DELINQUENT TAX A tax still unpaid after its due date. The taxpayer or his property may be assessed a penalty or lien or be foreclosed for nonpayment of taxes.

DELIVERY 1) The transfer of the possession of a thing from one person to another.
2) The certificate representing shares bought "regular way" on the New York Stock Exchange normally is delivered to the purchaser's broker on the fourth business day after the transaction. If a seller wants to delay delivery of the certificates, he may have his broker offer the stock "seller's option," instead of "regular way," and he may specify the number of days, from five up to sixty, for delivery. A stock offered "seller's option" may command a lesser price than if offered "regular way." See "bid," "cash sale," "offer," and "transfer."

DELIVERY NOTICE 1) A formal notice certifying that delivery of something will occur on a certain date, or has already occurred.
2) The notification of delivery of the actual commodity on the contract, issued by the seller of the futures to the buyer.

DELIVERY POINTS In commodities dealing, those locations designated by futures exchanges at which the commodity covered by a futures contract may be delivered in fulfillment of the contract.

DEMAND The amount of a good or service that will be purchased at various prices at a given time in a market. In another sense, it may be the amount of a good or services that will be purchased at the current price in a market. The first concept is one of a schedule of demand while the latter is one of a point of demand.

DEMAND BILL A sight bill of exchange.

DEMAND DEPOSIT Deposits that are payable on demand at any time the depositor elects. The Federal Reserve Board and the various state laws define these deposits as being payable within 30 days after deposit. They are drawn against by check, and no notice of withdrawal is necessary.

DEMAND DRAFT A draft that is payable on demand. Also called sight draft.

DEMAND LOAN A loan with no fixed maturity date, payable upon demand of the bank. Borrower is billed at specified intervals for the interest due the bank.

DEMAND NOTE A promissory note payable on demand of the holder of the note as payee or transferee.

DEPARTMENT STORE A retail store which handles a wide variety of lines of goods, such as, women's ready-to-wear and accessories, men's and boys' wear, piece goods, smallwares, and house furnishings, and which is organized into separate departments for purposes of promotion, service, and control.

DEPENDENCY ALLOWANCE A payment or tax reduction for individuals who have dependents as defined by the government or other determining body.

DEPENDENT A person who is dependent for support upon another; to be distinguished from one who merely derives a benefit from the earnings of another.

DEPLETION Reduction, through removal or use of an asset; an exhaustion of natural resources such as mineral deposits, timber, and water.

DEPLETION ALLOWANCE The provision of the Internal Revenue Code that wasting assets such as oil wells, mines, quarries, shell banks, etc., may deduct from taxable income a percentage of the income from the asset.

DEPOSIT Money placed with a banking or other institution, or with a person either as a general deposit subject to check, or as a special deposit made for some specified purpose; securities lodged with a banking or other institution or with a person for some particular purpose; sums deposited by customers for electric meters, water meters, etc., and by contractors and others to accompany and guarantee their bids. Money put down to insure and guarantee the fulfillment of an agreement, such as a deposit offered to hold an apartment for a specific length of time.

DEPOSIT ADMINISTRATION PLAN 1) A type of pension plan, usually under a master group annuity contract, providing for the accumulation of contributions in an undivided fund out of which annuities are purchased as the individual members of the group retire.
2) An insured pension arrangement. Periodic contributions of the employer are not allocated to the purchase of annuities for a particular employee until he is ready to retire. A feature of the plan is that the employer may hire his own independent actuarial consultants.

DEPOSITARY One who receives a deposit of money, securities, instruments, or other property.

DEPOSIT CURRENCY The effect of a typical loan from a bank. The bank credits the borrower's account with the amount of the loan. This, in turn, may be withdrawn by check or cash.

DEPOSIT FUNCTION The business of receiving money on deposit for safekeeping and convenience. This function includes the receiving of demand deposits subject to check and the receiving of savings (time) deposits at interest.

DEPOSIT FUNDS Those funds which are established to account for collections that are either (a) held in suspense temporarily and later refunded or paid into some other fund of the government, or (b) held by the government as banker or agent for others. Such funds are not available for paying salaries, expenses, grants, or other expenditures of the government and, therefore, are excluded from total budget receipts or expenditures.

DEPOSIT INSURANCE See "Federal Deposit Insurance Corporation."

DEPOSITION The written testimony of a witness, under oath, before a qualified officer, to be used in place of the oral testimony of the witness at a trial.

DEPOSIT LINE That approximate-average amount which a depositor tends to keep in his bank account. With a knowledge of the deposit line, a lending officer can judge not only the probable profitability of an account but also can relate it to a loan application.

DEPOSIT LOAN Most loans are made by the banker crediting the borrower's account with a "loan deposit" in the amount of the loan as distinguished from presenting the borrower with currency when granting a loan.

DEPOSITORY A bank in which funds or securities are deposited by others, usually under the terms of a specific depository agreement. Also, a bank in which government funds are deposited or in which other banks are permitted by law to maintain required reserves. The term "depository" and "depositary" have come to be used interchangeably in banking.

DEPRECIABLE COST The value of a fixed asset that is subject to depreciation. Sometimes this is the original cost, and sometimes it is the original cost less an estimated salvage value.

DEPRECIATION 1) Expiration in service life of fixed assets, other than wasting assets, attributable to wear and tear through use and lapse of time, obsolescence, inadequacy, or other physical or functional cause.
2) The proportion of the cost of a fixed asset other than a wasting asset charged as an expense during a particular period.

DEPRECIATION, ACCELERATED Higher than normal rate of depreciation either for tax purposes or because of greater than normal use.

DEPRESSION A sustained period of falling prices, characterized by excess of supply over demand, accumulating inventories, falling employment and rising welfare costs, deflation, abnormal commercial and industrial plant contraction, uneven drop in personal incomes, and fear and caution on the part of the public.

DERIVATIVE DEPOSIT The typical result of a commercial loan is the action of the bank in crediting the account of the borrower with the amount of the loan. This deposit is derived from the loan.

DERIVED DEMAND That need for a good or service which has come about as a result of the demand for another good or service.

DESCRIPTIVE LABELING To state the attributes of a good without the use of objective standards such as grades.

DE SON TORT "Of his own wrongdoing." An expression found in such phrases as executor de son tort and guardian de son tort.

DETERIORATION Physical wear-out; decay, impairment, wasting away, and wear and tear through action of the elements, age, and use.

DEVALUATION The reduction in the value of the precious or semiprecious metal content of a monetary unit or the reduction in the exchange value of a nation's currency as a result of action by some agency such a a central bank, an exchange stabilization fund or the International Money Fund.

DEVELOPMENT 1) The gradual unfolding by which something such as a plan or a method comes to be.
2) Applying scientific and technologic knowledge to create new or modify existing products and processes so they will best achieve stated performance and economic requirements.
3) A photographic image.
4) A real-estate investment enterprise, usually on a large-scale basis.

DEVISE 1) To contrive, invent, or bequeath something.
2) A gift of real property by will; to be distinguished from bequest.
3) A will, or a clause in a will.

DIAGONAL EXPANSION The increase in a firm's activity by such devices as the utilization of by-products or addition of a closely related line.

DIFFERENCE ACCOUNT In bookkeeping, an account carried in the general ledger where all differences from the true balances, such as averages and shortages, of the firm are recorded.

DIFFERENTIAL 1) Relation to a distinction or difference.
2) A difference in a wage rate for similar work done of comparable quality, which reflects a variable such as the race or sex of the worker, location, etc.
3) In investment trading, refers to the odd-lot differential, or compensation, received by an odd-lot broker for his services. A differential is added to the price of buy orders and subtracted from the price of sell orders.

DIFFUSION THEORY OF TAXATION The concept that a tax is transferred on to other than the original taxpayer by such techniques as price changes, increases in rents and even lower wages to employees of the taxpayer. While it is true that some taxes may be transferred by the taxpayer, not all fall in this class.

DILUTION 1) The watering down or weakening of something.
2) The reduction in the value of an asset such as a stock. See "watered stock."

DIRECT ADVERTISING Advertising that is sent or given right to the customer, rather than being generally given or exposed to the public. A letter is direct, a newspaper ad is not.

DIRECT COST An expense that is free from any intervening conditions. An immediate cost as compared with an indirect cost.

DIRECT EARNINGS In cases where a firm has subsidiary companies, the direct earnings of the parent company are the amounts earned by it without the upstream dividends of the subsidiaries.

DIRECT FINANCING The obtaining of equity or debt capital without the use of a middleman or underwriter. See "direct placement."

DIRECT HEIR A person in the direct line of the decedent; as father, mother, son, daughter. See "collateral heir" and "heir."

DIRECT LABOR The amount of the wages paid to employees whose time may be charged to specific finished products.

DIRECT MAIL Marketing goods directly to the consumer through the mail.

DIRECT MARKETING Technique of distribution in which goods go from producer to consumer without going through a middleman.

DIRECT OBLIGATION An obligation of the drawer or maker of the instrument as distinguished from the indirect obligation of an endorser of the instrument.

DIRECTOR 1) One who is charged with administering, leading, or supervising something.
2) Person elected by shareholders at the annual meeting to direct company policies. The directors appoint the president, vice presidents and all other operating officers. Directors decide, among other matters, if and when dividends shall be paid.

DIRECT REDUCTION MORTGAGE (D.R.M.) A direct reduction mortgage is liquidated over the life of the mortgage in equal monthly payments. Each monthly payment consists of an amount to cover interest, reduction in principal, taxes and insurance. The interest is computed on an outstanding principal balance monthly. As the principal balance is reduced the amount of interest becomes less, thereby providing a larger portion of the monthly payment to be applied to the reduction of principal. As taxes and insurance are paid by the mortgagee (lending association), these disbursements are added to the principal balance. This procedure follows throughout the life of the mortgage.

DIRECT SELLING The process whereby the producer sells to the user, ultimate consumer, or retailer without intervening middlemen.

DIRECT TAX A levy which the taxed individual or firm may not transfer to someone else in the form of higher prices, rent or interest charge.

DIRECT VERIFICATION A method of bank audit whereby the auditor of a bank sends a request for the verification of the balances of deposits or loans as of a stated date to the depositors or borrowers. Verifications are returned directly to the auditor confirming the correctness of balances or listing discrepancies.

DISABILITY BENEFIT A feature added to a life insurance policy providing for waiver of premium and sometimes payment of monthly income upon the furnishing of proof that the injured has become totally and permanently disabled.

DISABLING INJURY An injury which causes loss of working time beyond the day or shift on which the injury occurs.

DISBURSEMENT Money paid out in discharge of a debt or an expense; to be distinguished from distribution.

DISBURSEMENT SCHEDULE A list or tabular statement of the amounts to be disbursed on specific dates in accordance with agreements entered into in a mortgage-loan type of transaction.

DISCHARGE 1) To unload, free, dismiss.
2) Ending of the employment relationship by act of the employer. See "constructive discharge."

DISCHARGE OF BANKRUPTCY An order which terminates bankruptcy proceedings, usually relieving the debtor of all legal responsibility for certain specified obligations.

DISCLAIMER A document, or a clause within a document, which renounces or repudiates the liability of an otherwise responsible party, in the event of a noncompliance on the part of another party to other certain conditions within the instrument, or in the event of other named external conditions, or losses incurred due to the delivery of goods being in disagreement with the weight or count made by the shipper of the goods.

DISCOUNT 1) A deduction from the stated or list price of something.
2) A deduction given for prompt payment.
3) Interest deducted from the face value of a note at the time a loan is made. On other loans interest is collected at the time a note is paid.
4) The amount by which a security is priced below par; that is, the opposite of premium. A $1,000 bond with a market price of $950 has a discount of $50.

DISCOUNTED VALUE Present value of future payments due or receivable, computed on the basis of a given rate of interest.

DISCOUNT HOUSE 1) A retail establishment which sells brand-name merchandise at a lower price than the general retailer. To accomplish this, some of the customary services such as credit and delivery may not be available.
2) One of the functions of a commercial credit company.

DISCOUNT MARKET That part of the money market in which commercial paper is traded. Institutions in the discount market include commercial banks, note dealers, commercial paper houses and discount houses. In addition, the Federal Reserve Banks by their rediscounting function are important factors in the market.

DISCOUNT ON SECURITIES The amount or percentage by which a security (a bond or a share of stock) is bought or sold for less than its face, or par, value; opposed to premium on securities.

DISCOUNT RATE That interest rate which a lender charges when it discounts an obligation such as a note or bill of exchange. The discount rate will vary by type of borrower, security, maturity, the supply and demand for funds in the market and the policy of the lender.

DISCRETIONARY TRUST 1) A trust which entitles the beneficiary only to so much of the income or principal as the trustee in its uncontrolled discretion shall see fit to give him or to apply to his use.
2) An investment company which is not limited in its policy to any one class, or type, of stock or security but may invest in any or all of a broad range of securities.

DISCRIMINATION An unfair distinction such as unequal treatment of workers, whether by the disparate application of hiring or employment rules or the conditions of employment, because of race, creed, sex, or union membership or activity. In many cases, discrimination is an "unfair labor practice" under federal or state laws.

DISCRIMINATORY TAXES Contributions exacted by the government for the purpose of helping special interests. The tax is imposed on those the special interests oppose.

DISHONOR 1) The refusal of the drawee to accept or to pay a check, draft, or bill of exchange when it is presented to him for acceptance or for payment, as the case may be.
2) The refusal of the maker to pay a note when it is presented to him for payment.

DISMISSAL WAGE Generally a lump-sum payment made to a worker whose employment is permanently ended for causes beyond the worker's control by an emloyer and which is in addition to any back wages or salary due the worker.

DISPOSABLE PERSONAL INCOME Personal income less personal taxes and non-tax payments to government.

DISTANT DELIVERY Delivery scheduled to be made during one of the more distant months ahead, and at least two months away.

DISTRESSED SALE A forced liquidation of a thing. The assumption is that the seller does not receive as high a price for his good as he would under normal selling conditions.

DISTRIBUTION 1) The dividing up of something among several or many parties, such as profits to stockholders or owners, or money to creditors.
2) In law, the apportionment by a court of the personal property (or its proceeds) of one who died intestate among those entitled to receive the property according to the applicable statute of distribution; to be distinguished from disbursement.
3) The division of the aggregate income of any society among its members, or among the factors of production. Dispersal of goods throughout the community.
4) Selling, over a period of time, of a large block of stock without unduly depressing the market price.

DISTRIBUTORS Middlemen; wholesalers.

DIVERSIFICATION 1) To be going in many different ways or directions, rather than being limited to just a few or one area.
2) Spreading investments among different companies in different fields. Diversification is also offered by the securities of many individual companies because of the wide range of their activities.

DIVEST To annul; to take away a vested right.

DIVIDED COVERAGE Division of insurance that would normally be covered by one insurance policy between two or more companies.

DIVIDENDS The proportion of the net earnings of a corporation paid to the stockholders as their share of the profits. Dividends become payable only when declared by the board of directors. They are commonly distributed at regular intervals (quarterly, semiannually, or annually).

DIVISION OF LABOR The employment of workers in such a way that each does a relatively simple and limited number of operations. The product frequently is on an assembly line or conveyor belt. Each worker, after completing his phase of the total job, passes it to the next until its final completion.

DOCUMENTARY DRAFT A draft accompanied by a shipping document, bill of lading, insurance certificate, etc., these documents having intrinsic value. Instructions for disposition of the document usually accompany the draft.

DOLE Welfare payments.

DOLLAR Monetary unit of Canada, Ethiopia, Liberia and the United States.

DOLLAR ACCEPTANCE A bill of exchange or acceptance which may be drawn in a foreign or domestic country but is payable in dollars. While Canada, Ethiopia, Liberia and the United States all have the dollar as their monetary unit, it is generally assumed that the dollar is a United States dollar.

DOLLAR BILL OF EXCHANGE See "dollar acceptance."

DOLLAR-COST AVERAGING The systematic investment in investment company shares of the same amount of money at regular intervals over a period of years regardless of the prices of such shares at the time of purchase.

DOLLAR GAP (DOLLAR DEFICIT) The difference in dollars for a nation which has not earned as many dollars as it has spent in a given period of time.

DOLLAR STABILIZATION 1) Those acts by monetary authorities such as the International Monetary Fund, the Exchange Stabilization Fund, the Federal Reserve Board, and the United States Treasury which have as their purpose the reduction in the fluctuation of the international exchange value of the dollar.
2) It also has been used to designate an idea of economist Irving Fisher which would result in a compensated dollar which would be tied to the commodities rather than gold.

DOMESTIC ACCEPTANCE In a strict sense, any acceptance which has the drawer, the drawee and the place of payment within the same state. However, the term is generally loosely used to refer to any acceptance which has the drawer, drawee and the place of payment in the United States.

DOMESTIC BILL Any of numerous documents such as sight or time drafts which are drawn and payable within the same state. In a looser sense, any of numerous documents which are drawn and payable in the United States.

DOMESTIC EXCHANGE As distinguished from foreign exchange, any acceptance, check, draft or similar document which is drawn and payable in the United States. In a foreign nation, any acceptance, check, draft or similar document which is drawn and payable in that nation would be considered as domestic exchange.

DOMICILE The place where one has his true, fixed, and permanent home, and to which, whenever he is absent, he has the intention of returning.

DONATED SURPLUS In accounting, a capital surplus account that contains a record of the par value of donated stock that is in the treasury of the corporation and of the proceeds from donated stock that has been sold.

DOUBLE BUDGET A system of segregating capital expenditures from recurring expense items so that an annual income statement will not be distorted during those years of heavy capital investment.

DOUBLE-ENTRY BOOKKEEPING That system of bookkeeping under which both the debit and the credit elements of each transaction are recorded.

DOUBLE INDEMNITY Feature of some insurance policies that provides for twice the face amount of the policy to be paid if death results from stated but generally accidental causes.

DOUBLE TAXATION 1) The taxing body imposing two taxes on what is essentially the same thing.
2) Double taxation of dividends—the federal government taxes corporate profits once as corporate income; any part of the remaining profits distributed as dividends to stockholders is taxed again as income to the recipient stockholer.

DOWER The right which a widow has in some states to share in the real property of her deceased husband.

DOW-JONES AVERAGES Those averages of industrials, rails and utilities which are published by The Wall Street Journal and publications using their service. The figures refer to stock market quotations of the securities which make up the averages.

DOWN PAYMENT The cash payment that the purchaser of merchandise sold on an installment-payment plan is required to make at the time of the sale.

DOWN PERIOD The period of time during which a plant is closed for maintenance or repairs.

DOW THEORY A theory of market analysis based upon the performance of the Dow-Jones industrial and rail stock price averages.

DRAFT Bill of exchange—a signed written order addressed by one person (the drawer) to another person (the drawee) directing the latter to pay a specified sum of money to the order of a third person (the payee).

DRAWEE The party who is directed to pay the sum specified in a check, draft, or bill of exchange.

DRAWER Any party or company who draws a draft or check upon another party for the payment of funds.

DRAWING ACCOUNT Money available to owners or salesmen to be used for expenses which will be deducted from future earnings.

DRAYAGE The cost of moving articles in a for-hire vehicle.

DROP SHIPPER A wholesaler who does not store goods though he does take title. Also called desk jobber.

DUAL-PAY SYSTEM Wage plan with two systems of computing pay in which the employee is allowed to choose the one which will give him the most compensation.

DUAL UNIONISM Situation existing when the jurisdictional claims of one union infringe of the jurisdiction of another union.

DUE BILL A statement of an amount that is owed.

DUE DATE The date upon which a note, draft, bond, coupon, etc., becomes payable; the maturity date.

DUMP 1) To discard, get rid of, scrap.
2) The sale of a large amount of goods or securities in a disorganizing way, frequently with little regard to price or impact on the market.

DUN AND BRADSTREET Largest and oldest existing agency supplying information and credit ratings on and for all types of business concerns.

DURABLE GOODS Products into which are built long series of continuing services; products that last and continue to serve; usually applied to "hard goods"—metal, wood, etc.

DURESS Compulsion or constraint by force or fear of personal violence, prosecution, or imprisonment which induces a person to do what he does not want to do or to refrain from doing something he has a legal right to do. Sometimes the word is used with reference to the making of a will, as that it was made under duress.

DUTY A customs duty or tax on imports.

DYNAMIC ECONOMY Situation in which an economy is characterized by growth and change.

EARMARKED GOLD Gold in the fiduciary possession of one nation's central bank for another nation's central bank, treasury or stabilization fund.

EARNED INCOME The amount received for goods or services delivered and for which no future liability is anticipated.

EARNED PREMIUM Premium for that portion of an insurance policy period which has expired and for which protection was provided.

EARNED SURPLUS The undistributed corporation profits resulting from the regular operations of the business.

EARNEST MONEY Money which is paid as an evidence of good faith or intent to complete a transaction and may be forfeited by the willful failure to complete the transaction.

EARNING-CAPACITY STANDARD The capitalized value standard. The annual earnings of a business divided by an appropriate interest rate. The rate is estimated by the risk involved in the business. A very risky business would be capitalized at a higher percentage than a more stable business.

EARNINGS Synonym for "net income," particularly over a period of years. In the singular, the term is often combined with another word in the expression "earning power," referring to the demonstrated ability of an enterprise to earn net income.

EARNINGS REPORT A statement, also called an income statement, issued by a company showing its earnings or losses over a given period. The earnings report lists the income earned, expenses, and the net result. See "balance sheet."

EASEMENT The acquired, or reserved, privilege or right of use of property the ownership of which is held by another, such as the right of passage.

ECCLESIASTICAL CORPORATION A nonprofit corporation established by churchmen for a religious, educational or charitable purpose.

ECONOMIC 1) Pertaining to the production, distribution and consumption of wealth to the material means of satisfying human needs and desires.
2) Concerning the administration of the income and expenditure of a household, business, community, government, or other organization.

ECONOMIC DEMAND The desire to buy backed by the necessary money to make active purchasing possible—an actual "offer to buy at price" market situation.

ECONOMIC DETERMINISM The concept that economic factors cause social change.

ECONOMIC FRICTION Any human characteristic which distorts and reduces the operation of economic principles. Religion, taboos and customs may serve as examples of economic friction.

ECONOMIC GOOD Any service or thing that has utility and is not free.

ECONOMIC HARMONY Concept that the profit system as determined for the individual actually works out for the best interest of society as a whole.

ECONOMIC IMPERIALISM The use of large-scale power on the part of an organization to buy or sell to dominate a subject and to force the subject, individual, firm, or nation to take additional steps of cooperation or submission.

ECONOMIC LAW Not a law in the legal sense but rather a generalization about economic relationships and probabilities.

ECONOMIC MOBILIZATION The concentration of the people and business firms of an area upon some activity such as a war or depression so that production is directed to meet the goal such as winning the war or improving business conditions.

ECONOMIC PLANNING A relative term to indicate a scheme or method of obtaining some economic goal. Such planning may be done by an individual, firm or nation. The degree of planning may vary from the modest establishment of some goal such as a rate of growth for gross national product to the almost complete regimentation of all the productive forces in a nation.

ECONOMIC RENT A philosophic concept of the true value of a property as compared with the contract rent which would be expressed in monetary units and might not be necessarily indicative of the true value, being possibly either over or under the economic rent.

ECONOMICS The study of the factors which affect the production, distribution and consumption of wealth and of the use of the earth's resources to satisfy the needs and desires of man.

ECONOMIC SANCTIONS The provision for securing conformity to a position, decree or law by economic steps such as boycott, embargo, credit controls or trade restrictions.

ECONOMIC STRIKES   Strikes called to force changes in wages, hours, or other working conditions, rather than in protest against unfair labor practices.

ECONOMIC SYSTEM   The orderly collection of economic principles, laws, and attitudes into a plan for the operation of a society. The system may be established by governmental legislation or developed by evolutionary steps. The three major economic systems today are capitalism, socialism, and communism with many nations modifying a system to their own particular level of economic need or development.

ECONOMIC UNION   The treaty between signing nations to adopt and follow similar economic steps such as customs, taxation and other economic policies.

ECONOMIC WARFARE   The use of such economic devices as control of credit, raw material, transportation, copyrights, patents, foreign exchange, blacklists, and economic pressure on neutral nations to stop trading with an enemy for the purpose of weakening and thus conquering the enemy.

ECONOMIC WEALTH   Those scarce material things that man finds of use. While businessmen consider money, securities and mortgages as being wealth, the economist considers that these are instruments that represent wealth and not wealth itself.

ECONOMIES OF SCALE   Efficiencies which result from the producer having the proper proportions of land, labor and machinery to meet a given market.

ECONOMY OF ABUNDANCE   That state of economic activity characterized by full employment and the satisfaction of material wants at a level of plenty.

ECONOMY OF SCARCITY   That state of economic activity at less than full employment and where consumers are unable to satisfy reasonable material wants.

EFFECTIVE DATE   The date on which something goes into effect such as a contract or agreement, insurance policy, etc.

EFFECTIVE INTEREST RATE OR YIELD   The rate or earnings on a bond investment based on the actual price paid for the bond, the coupon rate, the maturity date, and the length of time between interest dates; in contrast with the nominal interest rate.

EJECTMENT   An action brought to regain possession of real property from a party wrongfully in possession of it.

ELASTIC DEMAND   Demand which fluctuates at a greater proportionate rate than the rate of change of price for a product.

ELASTIC SUPPLY   Supply which fluctuates at a greater proportionate rate than the rate of change of price for a product.

ELECTION   The choice of an alternative right or course. Thus, the right of a widow to take the share of her deceased husband's estate to which she is entitled under the law, despite a contrary provision in the will, is known as the widow's election.

ELEEMOSYNARY   Pertaining or devoted to nonprofit purposes or charity; as, an eleemosynary institution.

ELEEMOSYNARY CORPORATION   A corporation devoted to giving relief to the poor, or to some other charitable purpose.

ELIGIBLE PAPER   Those documents, securities, notes and bills which are acceptable by a financial institution such as the Federal Reserve Bank for rediscounting purposes.

ELKINS ACT   "An act to further regulate commerce with foreign nations and among the states." One of the important provisions of this act makes it a misdemeanor, punishable by heavy penalties, to accept or receive rebates, concessions, or discriminations as there defined.

EMBARGO   Any prohibition imposed by law upon commerce either in general or in one or more of its branches.

EMBEZZLEMENT   The fraudulent appropriation to one's own use of the money or property entrusted to his care.

EMERSON EFFICIENCY SYSTEM   An incentive plan whereby a direct laborer is paid a minimum guarantee until his production reaches two-thirds of standard. Beyond that point, he is paid a rapidly increasing bonus. In addition, when his production exceeds 100% of standard, he is paid an additional bonus (usually 20%) on the total time. Generally, this bonus is calculated monthly, rather than on individual jobs. This is done to discourage alternate spurts and lags in the workers' output.

EMINENT DOMAIN   The inherent right of certain legally constituted governing bodies to take title to a possession of real property, with just compensation to its owner, for the public good.

EMPLOYEE BENEFITS   Advantages besides salary or wage that an employee may have through his employment. Sometimes called fringe benefits.

EMPLOYEE SERVICES   Maintaining the general welfare of employees on the job and assisting them with problems related to their security and personal well-being.

EMPLOYEES' TRUST   A trust established by an employer (usually a corporation) for the benefit of employees.

ENCROACHMENT   1) The act of trespassing upon the domain of another. Partial or gradual invasion or intrusion. 2) Encroachment of low-value district upon high-class residential section.

ENCUMBRANCE   1) Something which holds back or weighs down.
2) A lien or claim against title to property which, unless removed, prevents the passing of full and complete title. See "unencumbered property."

ENDORSEMENT   1) A show of support, a verification. Backing up.
2) A signature on the back of a negotiable instrument, made primarily for the purpose of transferring the rights of the holder to some other person. For variations see "indorsee," "indorser."

ENDOWMENT   Gift to an institution for a specific purpose such as money or property given to hospitals for research purposes.

ENDOWMENT FUND A fund whose principal must be maintained inviolate but whose income may be expended.

ENFORCED LIQUIDATION In investment trading, condition caused by the failure of a security owner to maintain sufficient equity in his margin account.

ENGEL'S LAW The economic concept that the proportion of a family's budget that goes for food goes up as the income goes down.

ENTAIL The system of land ownership and succession which may restrict the inheritance of land to a particular class of heirs such as the eldest son.

ENTITY That which exists as separate and complete in itself. A corporation is an entity, separate and distinct from its stockholders.

ENTREPRENEUR One who assumes the financial risk of the initiation, operation and management of a given business or undertaking.

ENVIRONMENT 1) The total surrounding conditions of influence and atmosphere.
2) The sum total of economic, physical, and social influencing factors which affect the desirability of property, and hence its value.

EQUALIZATION OF ASSESSMENTS The periodic review of real property values in a political division such as a county. As a result of the review by trained land appraisers, new values are given the various plots of land and the tax burden is equitably apportioned.

EQUATION PRICE The price reached by the adjusting action of competition in any market at any time, or in a unit of time, such that the demand and supply become equal at that price.

EQUILIBRIUM Economic or physical condition which tends to maintain itself in the same situation.

EQUIPMENT Physical property of a more of less permanent nature ordinarily useful in carrying on operations, other than land, buildings, or improvements to either of them. Examples are machinery, tools, trucks, cars, ships, furniture, and furnishings.

EQUIPMENT TRUST A corporate trust established for the purpose of financing the purchase of equipment; commonly resorted to by railroads for the purpose of rolling stock.

EQUIPMENT TRUST CERTIFICATE A type of security, generally issued by a railroad, to pay for new equipment. Title to the equipment, such as a locomotive, is held by a trustee until the notes are paid off. An equipment trust certificate is usually secured by a first lien on the equipment.

EQUITABLE CHARGE A charge on property imposed by and enforceable in a court of equity, as distinguished from a charge enforceable in a court of law.

EQUITABLE OWNERSHIP The estate or interest of a person who has a beneficial right in property the legal ownership of which is in another person. A beneficiary of trust has an equitable estate or interest in the trust property.

EQUITABLE TITLE A right to the benefits of property which is recognized by and enforceable only in a court of equity; to be distinguished from legal title.

EQUITIES A term used synonymously with common stocks or capital stocks to designate securities that are owned capital rather than owed capital. The stockholders' equity in a company may be stated inclusive or exclusive of preferred stock.

EQUITY 1) An interest of an ownership nature, as distinguished from an interest of a creditor nature. The value of collateral over and above the amount of the obligation it secures.
2) A system of legal principles and rules developed to supplement and correct a system of law that had become too narrow and rigid in scope and application. Its characteristic is flexibility and its aim is the administration of justice.

EQUITY CAPITAL Money furnished by owners of the business.

EQUITY FINANCING The acquisition of money for capital or operating purposes in exchange for a share or shares in the business being financed.

EQUITY RATE Rate applied to very large insurance risks that have had outstandingly good or bad records of claims so that the ordinary rates would not truly represent the risk.

ESCALATOR CLAUSE Union-contract provision for the raising and lowering of wages according to changes in the cost-of-living index or similar standard.

ESCAPE CLAUSE A provision in maintenance-of-membership union contracts giving union members an "escape period" during which they can resign membership. Members who do not resign must remain members for the duration of the contract.

ESCHEAT The reversion of land to the state by the failure of persons legally entitled to hold the same. Also, the reversion to the state of certain funds after a stated period of inactivity pertaining to them, or of other property the ownership of which is unknown or in doubt.

ESCROW A written agreement among three or more persons, under which documents or property is deposited with one of the persons as custodian to be delivered to the grantee only upon the fulfillment of certain specified conditions.

ESCROW FUNDS As applied to mortgage loans, represents reserves established for the payment of taxes and insurance when due. Reserves are collected monthly by the mortgagee as part of the regular payment.

ESTATE 1) The right, title, or interest which a person has in any property; to be distinguished from the property itself which is the subject matter of the interest.
2) A large palatial private residence usually consisting of extensive grounds and several buildings.
3) The property of a decedent.

ESTATE TAX A tax imposed on a decedent's estate as such and not on the distributive shares of the estate or on the right to receive the shares; to be distinguished from an inheritance tax.

ESTIMATE 1) In appraising, an opinion developed from analysis of an adequate data program by one qualified to develop such an opinion; hence, the opinion of an informed person.
2) A preliminary opinion of the approximate cost of doing certain work.

ESTOPPEL The legal principle which precludes a person from alleging in an action what is contrary to his previous action or admission or which bars him from denying a misrepresentation of a fact when another person has acted upon that misrepresentation to his detriment. The person so precluded or barred is said to be estopped.

EVICTION The depriving by due process of law of a person or persons from the possession of land in keeping with the judgment of the court.

EXCESS-PROFITS TAX A levy designed to take away from a business "abnormal" profits which have resulted from some emergency situation such as war.

EXCESS RESERVES A term used to designate the amount of funds held in reserve by banks in excess of the legal minimum requirements, whether the funds are on deposit in the Federal Reserve Bank, in a bank approved as a depository, or in the cash reserve carried within its own vaults.

EXCHANGE 1) An organization or place for transacting business or settling accounts between parties at some distance from each other.
2) An organization for trading in securities or commodities.
3) The volume of funds available for use in another city or country.
4) An amount charged for the collection of a check or other financial instrument.

EXCHANGE ACQUISITION A method of filling an order to buy a large block of stock on the floor of the exchange. Under certain circumstances, a member-broker can facilitate the purchase of a block by soliciting orders to sell. All orders to sell the security are lumped together and offset with the buy order in the regular auction market. The price to the buyer may be on a net basis or on a commission basis.

EXCHANGE CHARGE A fee or service charge made by the drawee bank on the presenting bank for its services in paying negotiable instruments. The Federal Reserve Act forbids drawee banks to make such charges against Federal Reserve Banks on checks in process of collection. The reason is to assure that check money will be payable throughout the country at its face value.

EXCHANGE RATE The price of one nation's currency expressed in terms of another nation's currency.

EXCHANGE STABILIZATION (or) **EQUALIZATION FUND** The sum of money, or the organization handling the money, used to purchase or sell gold, foreign exchange, and domestic currency for the purposes of keeping the exchange rate within a very limited range. See "exchange rate."

EXCISE TAX A tax levied by the federal and state governments upon the manufacture, sale, or consumption of certain commodities, or a tax levied on the right, privilege, or permission to engage in a certain business, trade, occupation, or sport.

EXCLUSION 1) A restriction or limitation.
2) Provision of part of the insurance contract limiting the scope of the coverage. Certain causes and conditions, listed in the policy, which are not covered.

EXCLUSIVE LISTING An agreement providing that a specific broker shall be the sole agent of the owner of a property, giving the broker the sole right to sell or rent the property within a specified time.

EX DIVIDEND When a dividend is declared by a corporation, it is payable on a designated date to stockholders of record as of a stated date. When stock is sold prior to the stated date, the dividend belongs to the buyer and not to the seller. When the stock is sold subsequent to the stated date and prior to the date of payment, the dividend belongs to the seller and not to the buyer. It is then said to sell ex dividend. (The New York Stock Exchange, however, has a special rule to the effect that the stock becomes ex dividend three business days prior to the stated date. Most other exchanges follow the New York rule.)

EXECUTION A formal judicial order which directs a public officer, usually a sheriff, to execute or carry into effect a final judgment or decree of a court.

EXECUTIVE The individual engaged in the administrative function, be it private or public, who plans and controls the execution of the activity.

EXECUTOR A person or an institution named by an individual in his will to settle his estate in accordance with the terms of his will.

EX GRATIA PAYMENT Settlement of a claim which an insurance company does not think it is legally obligated to pay to prevent an even larger expense of defending itself in the courts. Strike suits or threats of suit may result in an ex gratia payment.

EXHAUST PRICE That price at which a broker is forced to sell a security which was margined and subsequently has dropped in price. Prior to reaching the exhaust price, the broker will request his customer to provide additional margin or cover. In the event that the customer does not provide the needed margin, the security will be sold by the broker when the stock drops to the exhaust price so that the broker himself will not suffer any loss.

EX OFFICIO By virtue of his office.

EXONERATION 1) The act of clearing, freeing from blame, acquitting.
2) The act of relieving one of what otherwise would be or might be a liability or a duty.

EXPANSION 1) That phase of a business cycle or fluctuation in which there is an increase in industrial activity. Periods of expansion are associated with recovery and prosperity.
2) A broadening or extending of the operation or territory of a business or organization.

EXPEDITING CHARGES Funds expended to replace or repair damage to prevent even larger claims.

EXPENDABLE 1) That which is capable of being consumed or used up in production or service.
2) That which can be sacrificed or given up.

EXPENDITURE An actual payment or the creation of an obligation to make a future payment for some benefit, item, or service rendered.

EXPENSE In its broadest sense it includes all expired costs which are deductible from revenues. Narrower use of the term refers to such items as operating, selling or administrative expenses, interest, and taxes.

EXPENSE RATIO The ratio of expenses to income.

EXPORT Goods shipped outside a country. To ship goods outside a country.

EXPORT BOUNTY That premium or subsidy paid to an exporter of covered goods. The subsidy is generally paid by the government for the purpose of stimulating an industry.

EXPORT-IMPORT BANK That governmental agency formed in 1934, and expanded in 1945, to engage in the general banking business but not to compete with private banking activities in helping exports and imports of the United States. Most of such help is tied to price-supported agricultural products.

EXPORT LICENSE The document issued by a government which will permit a stated amount of the described commodity to be exported. Items such as gold, arms, munitions and drugs may require such a license.

EXPRESS TRUST A trust stated orally or in writing with the terms of the trust definitely prescribed; to be distinguished from a resulting trust or a constructive trust.

EXPROPRIATION The act or process whereby private property is taken for public purpose or use, or the rights therein modified by a sovereignty or any entity vested with the necessary legal authority, *e.g.,* where property is acquired under eminent domain.

EX RIGHTS Without the rights. Corporations raising additional money may do so by offering their stockholders the right to subscribe to new or additional stock, usually at a discount from the prevailing market price. The buyer of a stock selling ex rights is not entitled to the rights. See "ex dividend" and "rights."

EXTENDED COVERAGE A clause in an insurance policy or of an endorsement of a policy which provides extra or additional coverage for other hazards or risks than those provided for under the basic provisions of the policy.

EXTERNAL ECONOMICS Reduction in costs of a firm which have resulted from outside factors over which the firm has no control.

EXTRA DIVIDEND A supplementary dividend in cash or stock. A dividend in addition to the one which a firm has regularly been paying.

EX WARRANTS Without warrants. A security trading ex warrants indicates that the warrants have been retained or exercised by the seller.

FABRICATED MATERIALS Those industrial goods which become a part of the finished product and which have undergone processing beyond that required for raw materials but not so much as finished parts.

FACE OF THE NOTE The amount stated on the note. It is also known as the principal.

FACE VALUE The principal value of a note, bond, or other instrument. The value upon which interest is computed, if an interest-bearing instrument.

FACT-FINDING BOARD A group of persons appointed by an organization such as a business or a government to investigate, collect and make known the facts regarding a specific situation or problem.

FACTOR 1) A type of commission merchant who often advances funds to the consignor, identified chiefly with the raw cotton and naval stores trades.
2) A specialized commercial banker, performing the function of financing for producers of, and dealers in, many varieties of products and occasionally combining this function with that of selling. The term "factor" was formerly synonymous with "commission merchant."

FACTOR COST The market price of a product from which is deducted all costs that are not factors of production such as transfer payments and depreciation.

FACTORING A means of advancing credit whereby the factor purchases at a discount and without recourse the accounts receivable of a firm. The factor assumes complete responsibility for the credit investigation and collection.

FACTORS OF PRODUCTION Land, capital, labor, and management when used to produce wealth.

FAIR-EMPLOYMENT PRACTICES Policy of firing, promoting, etc., without regard for race, sex, or religious background.

FAIR LABOR STANDARDS ACT The federal Wage-Hour Law which establishes minimum-wage and overtime-pay requirements and child-labor restrictions.

FAIR-MARKET VALUE A legal term variously interpreted by the courts but in general connoting a price obtainable in the market which is fair and reasonable in view of the conditions currently existing.

FAIR RETURN An income on invested capital used in the activity that will permit the business to raise additional capital for normal growth.

FAIR TRADE LAWS Federal and state legislation on resale price agreements generally designed to restrict price cutting by establishing minimum retail prices for products whose manufacturers comply with the provisions of the fair trade laws.

FAIR VALUE 1) Value that is reasonable and consistent with all the known facts.
2) Under the Investment Company Act, value determined in good faith by the board of directors for those securities and assets for which there is no market quotation readily available.

FALSE PRETENSES Refers to any untrue statements or representations made with the intention of obtaining something of value such as property or money.

FANNIE MAE Nickname. See "Federal National Mortgage Association."

FARM BLOC The senators and representatives of states with extensive agricultural interests who tend to vote on agricultural legislation as a group or bloc.

FARM COOPERATIVE An association of farmers for the purpose of markets and/or purchasing goods for its members.

FARM CREDIT ADMINISTRATION Established in 1933, it comprises twelve Federal Land Banks, twelve Federal Intermediate Credit Banks, twelve Production Credit Corporations, twelve District Banks for Cooperatives, the Federal Farm Mortgage Corporation and related agencies.

FARMERS HOME ADMINISTRATION Created in 1946 to aid in the financing of farm homes and improvements; it also helps finance purchase of seed, equipment, fertilizer, and livestock.

FARMERS' MARKET A privately owned retail center with central management that rents booth space usually on a short-term basis to a large number of merchants. Generally located in a suburban or rural area, it has simple facilities, ample parking, and large assortments of low-priced nonfood merchandise as well as food lines. It enjoys a low overhead and heavy traffic. A carnival atmosphere prevails, and an auction is frequently featured. The name is misleading because farmers today play an insignificant part, either as owners or tenants of these markets.

FARM SURPLUSES Those agricultural products which have been acquired under loan or support programs by the government.

FASCISM While usually regarded as a political system, fascism, in the business sense, worked through a mercantilistic guild system of "sindacati" or controlled unions organized along occupational lines and "corporazioni" which were similar to producers' guilds. The deaths of Hitler and Mussolini in 1945 and the defeat of the Axis powers brought about the end of this system.

FAVORABLE BALANCE OF TRADE A situation in which the value of the merchandise and service exports exceed the merchandise and service imports for a nation for a period of time. The difference is made up by shipment of gold, obtaining holdings of foreign exchange or making of foreign investments.

FEATHERBEDDING Labor practices that are not productive or which result in the employee being paid for work which he did not do.

FEDERAL ADVISORY COUNCIL Twelve men, one from each Federal Reserve District, who have no power except to give advice to the Board of Governors of the Federal Reserve System regarding business conditions and related economic factors.

FEDERAL CREDIT UNION A cooperative association organized under the Federal Credit Union Act for the purpose of accepting savings from its members, making loans to them at low interest rates, and rendering other financial services to its members. Cooperatives offering similar services also operate under state charters.

FEDERAL CROP INSURANCE CORPORATION Facility for insurance of growing crops by an instrumentality of the United States Government. No element of compulsion is involved.

FEDERAL DEBT LIMIT A limit imposed by law (Second Liberty Bond Act, as amended) on the aggregate face amount of outstanding obligations issued, or guaranteed as to principal and interest, by the United States except such guaranteed obligations as may be held by the Secretary of the Treasury.

FEDERAL DEPOSIT INSURANCE CORPORATION A corporation established by federal authority to provide insurance of demand and time deposits in participating banks up to a maximum of a specified amount.

FEDERAL FUNDS 1) Funds owned or set aside for use by a federal government such as the United States or Switzerland.
2) Bank deposits at the Federal Reserve Banks or at correspondent banks. Banks, which find themselves with temporary excess reserves not needed for transactions purposes, can lend these balances, overnight or for a few days, to banks which have temporary reserve deficiencies.

FEDERAL HOME LOAN BANK SYSTEM A system established in 1932 to serve as a mortgage credit reserve system for home mortgage lending institutions. Members may obtain advances on home mortgage collateral and may borrow from Federal Home Loan Banks under certain conditions.

FEDERAL HOUSING ADMINISTRATION An instrumentality of the United States Government that provides an insurance protection to mortgage holders of mortgages issued under its supervision.

FEDERAL INTERMEDIATE CREDIT BANKS Twelve regional banks established by Congress for the purpose of providing intermediate credit for ranchers and farmers by rediscounting the agricultural paper of financial institutions.

FEDERAL LABOR UNION A union which was affiliated directly with the American Federation of Labor prior to its merger with the Congress of Industrial Organizations and which had no national officers except those of the American Federation of Labor's executive council.

FEDERAL LAND BANKS Twelve regional banks established by Congress for such purposes as providing long-term mortgage loans to farmers through National Farm Loan Associations.

FEDERAL MEDIATION AND CONCILIATION SERVICE Independent agency created by the Taft-Hartley Act in 1947 to attempt to settle labor disputes which substantially affect interstate commerce.

FEDERAL NATIONAL MORTGAGE ASSOCIATION A corporation organized in 1938 under the provisions of the National Housing Act of 1934, as amended. It provides a secondary mortgage market for the purchase and sale of Federal Housing Administration insured and Veterans Administration guaranteed loans.

FEDERAL OPEN MARKET COMMITTEE The Board of Governors of the Federal Reserve System plus the president of the New York Federal Reserve Bank and four of the remaining Federal Reserve Bank presidents from the other eleven Federal Reserve Banks. The four are chosen on a rotating basis. The committee determines the broad policy of open market operations which are conducted through the Federal Reserve Bank of New York as agent for the system.

FEDERAL POWER COMMISSION The governmental agency established in 1920 to regulate interstate operations of private utilities in such things as issuance of securities, rates and site location.

FEDERAL RESERVE ACT   As amended, this act establishes and provides for the operation of the Federal Reserve System. See "Federal Reserve Banks" and "Federal Reserve System."

FEDERAL RESERVE AGENT   The Class "C" director and chairman of the board of directors of a Federal Reserve District Bank whose major function is safeguarding the collateral for Federal Reserve notes in his possession.

FEDERAL RESERVE BANKS   (Twelve in number plus branches.) Federal banking corporations that deal principally with their member banks and with the government. They deal with the general public only to a limited extent. They act as agents in maintaining reserves, issuing money in the form of bank notes, and lending money to other banks.

FEDERAL RESERVE BOARD   The seven-member Board of Governors of the Federal Reserve System located in Washington, D.C. Members are appointed for fourteen-year terms by the President with Senate approval and devote their full time to board business. No two members come from the same district. One term expires every two years.

FEDERAL RESERVE CITIES   The head office and number of each of the twelve Federal Reserve Banks follows: 1. Boston, 2. New York, 3. Philadelphia, 4. Cleveland, 5. Richmond, 6. Atlanta, 7. Chicago, 8. St. Louis, 9. Minneapolis, 10. Kansas City, 11. Dallas, 12. San Francisco. These are known as the twelve Federal Reserve cities.

FEDERAL RESERVE NOTE   A noninterest-bearing promissory note of a Federal Reserve Bank issued for general circulation as money and payable to the bearer on demand.

FEDERAL RESERVE SYSTEM   The central banking system of the United States, created by an act of Congress (Federal Reserve Act) in 1913. It consists of regional bankers' banks (twelve Federal Reserve Banks and their branches), which are controlled and supervised by the Board of Governors in Washington, and national and state member banks. It has wide powers in controlling credit and the flow of money, as well as regulating its member banks.

FEDERAL SAVINGS AND LOAN ASSOCIATION The title given to one of the associations established by the Home Owners Loan Act of 1933 and amended in the Home Owners Loan Act of 1934, approved on April 27, 1934. This act permitted existing and newly formed mutual savings banks and building and loan associations to come under a federal charter. Under the federal charter, these institutions are governed and regulated by the Federal Home Loan Bank Board.

FEDERAL SAVINGS AND LOAN INSURANCE CORPORATION   An organization created in 1934 for the purpose of insuring the shares and accounts of all federal savings and loan associations and of such state-chartered savings and loan associations as apply for insurance and meet the requirements of the corporation.

FEDERAL TORT CLAIMS ACT   Permits the United States to be sued for damage to property or personal injuries under circumstances such that if the federal government were an individual it would be liable. Previous to this the concept of sovereignty that a government cannot be sued without its permission was in effect.

FEDERAL TRADE COMMISSION   The United States agency formed in 1914 to prevent restraint of trade and unfair pricing and advertising in interstate commerce.

FEDERAL UNEMPLOYMENT INSURANCE TAX Dual state and federal tax based on merit rating to provide insurance benefits for unemployment of covered individuals.

FEE SIMPLE   An absolute fee, that is, an estate of inheritance without limitation to any particular class of heirs and with no restrictions upon alienation; sometimes known as fee simple absolute; the largest estate a person may own.

FEE TAIL   An estate limited to a particular class of heirs of the person to whom the property or estate is granted.

FIDUCIARY   An individual, corporation, or association, such as a bank or trust company, to whom certain property is given to hold in trust, according to the trust agreement under which this property is held. The property may be utilized, or invested, for the benefit of the property owner to the best ability of the fiduciary. Administrators and executors of estates, and trustees of organizations are common examples of fiduciaries. Investments of trust funds, unless specified in the trust indenture, are usually restricted by law.

FIDUCIARY SERVICE   A service performed by an individual or a corporation acting in a trust capacity. A banking institution authorized to do a trust business may perform fiduciary services, for example, by acting as executor or administrator of estates, guardian of minors, and trustee under wills.

FIELD WAREHOUSE RECEIPT   A receipt issued by a field warehouseman for inventory or for other property stored on the owner's premises. The part of the owner's premises on which the property is stored must be leased to the warehouseman to comply with the Federal Warehouse Receipts Act. Banks accepting field warehouse receipts as collateral for loans are, therefore, protected by having legal possession of the property pledged.

FIFO   See "first in, first out."

FINANCE   As a noun, the system by which the income of a company is raised and administered. As a verb, to conduct financial operations or to furnish money. Deals with methods for supplying capital needed to acquire, develop, and operate real property.

FINANCE COMPANY   A discount house or commercial credit company. At times it is also used to refer to a personal loan company.

FINANCIAL INSOLVENCY   That situation in which a firm, individual, government, or other organization is not able to pay its debts as they mature even though the assets may exceed the liabilities.

FINANCIAL INVESTMENT   The purchase of sound stocks or bonds as compared to real investment in a capital asset such as real estate or plant and machinery.

FINANCIAL SERVICES   1) All related services provided by banks and financial institutions to their customers.

2) Those financial organizations established to rate securities, publish investor services, etc., such as Moody's Investor's Service and Standard and Poor's Corporation.

FINANCIAL SOLVENCY That situation in which a business is able to meet its current debts with its current assets.

FINANCIAL STATEMENT A summary of figure facts showing the financial condition of a business. It is an itemized listing of assets (what the business owns), liabilities (what the business owes), and net worth of capital account (the owners' equity in the business). A balance sheet of a bank is called a statement of condition.

FINDER'S FEE The amount an intermediary between a lender and a borrower obtains for bringing the two together, provided that financing is consummated.

FINE The penalty charged the violator by a government or authority such as a union for breaking a law or rule.

FINISHED GOODS Goods that have gone through the manufacturing process and that have been made ready for sale.

FIRM-COMMITMENT OFFERING A securities issue whereby the risk of selling the entire issue is assumed by the underwriting brokers. Some agreements specify only a "best efforts" approach without the assumption of risk by the underwriters.

FIRST IN, FIRST OUT Accounting method of valuing inventory on the basis of first in, first out. That is, an entire inventory may have been acquired at slightly different prices and time intervals. The accountant upon receiving the notice of a sale of part of that inventory will compute his cost and profit on the oldest or first price for his markup. This method is referred to as "fifo." For contrast see "lifo," or "last in, first out."

FIRST LIEN The best and highest priority claim against an asset.

FIRST MORTGAGE The senior mortgage, thus having precedent and priority over all other mortgages taken out on a property.

FISCAL 1) Financial matters, in general.
2) Of or pertaining to the public treasury or revenue.

FISCAL AGENT 1) In general, a person or organization serving as another's financial agent.
2) An agent for a corporation or organization to handle certain matters relating specifically to taxes in connection with an issue of bonds.
3) An agent for a national, state or municipal government or governmental body to pay its bonds and coupons or to perform certain other duties related to financial matters.

FISCAL PERIOD Any period at the end of which a unit determines its financial condition, the results of its operations, and closes its books.

FISCAL POLICY In a general sense, a government's activities concerned with taxes, receipts, debt expenditures, currency and trust funds.

FISCAL YEAR The accounting year of a firm, government, or other organization.

FIXED CAPITAL Capital invested in fixed assets, such as land, buildings, machinery, etc.

FIXED CHARGES Expenses the amount of which is more or less fixed.

FIXED COSTS Those indirect or overhead expenses of a business activity which do not vary with the volume of activity.

FIXED DEBT A permanent debt extending over a length of time, such as that represented by bonds.

FIXED INCOME Any constant income which does not fluctuate over time, such as that from bonds, annuities and preferred stocks.

FIXED INVESTMENT TRUST An investment company established as a nondiscretionary trust and which is limited to a stated and agreed upon list of securities.

FIXED-PRICE CONTRACT An agreement by which the buyer pays the seller or producer a stipulated amount.

FIXED SHIFT Established working period; same hours of work over an extensive period.

FIXING THE PRICE 1) Setting a price for something in advance (as through an agreement between producers or by government edict) rather than through the free enterprise system.
2) The computation of the price at which a spot commodity will be billed. The price is determined after a call sale permits a differential to be established with a specific futures contract.

FIXTURES Appurtenances which are affixed to the building or land and generally in such a way that they cannot be moved without causing damage to either the property or themselves.

FLEXIBLE SCHEDULE Situation in which work period and working hours are not fixed but vary in accordance with production requirements.

FLEXIBLE TARIFF A schedule of duties which the Tariff Commission may adjust within certain maximum ranges as their discretion would indicate.

FLOAT Checks, in the process of being collected and converted into cash, which represent funds not available to the bank for investment purposes, although immediate credit is usually given to the depositor. Float is an important factor in analyzing customer accounts in order to compute service charges.

FLOATING CAPITAL Capital which is identified as being in the form of current assets rather than fixed assets.

FLOATING DEBT Liabilities (except bonds) payable on demand or at any early date; for example, accounts payable, bank loans, notes or warrants.

FLOATING SUPPLY The amount of a security or commodity which is in the hands of speculators and traders as distinguished from investors or users of the commodity.

FLOOR BROKER Any person who, in or surrounding any pit, ring, post, or other place provided by a contract market for the meeting of persons similarly engaged, engages in executing for others any order for the purchase or sale of commodity or security on or subject to the rules of any contract market, and who for such services receives or accepts a prescribed fee or brokerage.

FLOOR-PLAN FINANCING A type of financing which supplies the capital to permit a dealer in a certain product or products to acquire samples of the product or products to display for sale, and which is liquidated when the sale is consummated.

FLOOR TRADER Any member of a stock or commodity exchange who trades on the floor for his own account.

FLOW CHART 1) A visual device which shows the movement of some product, item, authority or other economic factor from one point or place to another.
2) In electronic data processing, a symbolic representation of program logic or computer processing.

FLUID SAVINGS Savings in a liquid form such as cash or demand deposits which may be used at the discretion of the holder.

FORCED SALE The act of selling property under compulsion as to time and place. Usually a sale made by virtue of a court order, ordinarily at public auction.

FORECASTING Predicting reasonable probabilities about the future of something, such as sales of a product, economic conditions, etc.

FORECLOSURE The process by which a mortgagor of real or personal property, or other owner of property subject to a lien, is deprived of his interest therein. The usual modern method is sale of the property by court procedings or outside of court.

FOREIGN AGENCY An agency of a domestically domiciled firm which is located outside the country. The major consideration is that the legal relationship is one of agency as compared to branch or subsidiary operation.

FOREIGN BILL A bill drawn in one state and payable in another state or country.

FOREIGN BILL OF EXCHANGE The system by which the balances arising out of transactions between countries are settled. The currency used in making the settlement.

FOREIGN CORPORATION A corporation organized under the laws of a state other than the state in which it is doing business.

FOREIGN CORRESPONDENT 1) The firm or individual in a foreign nation which acts for a principal as an agent.
2) A reporter of news from a foreign source.

FOREIGN DEPOSITS Those deposits which are payable at a financial institution outside the jurisdiction of the United States Government and payable in the currency of the country in which the depository is located.

FOREIGN EXCHANGE The conversion of money of one country into its equal of another country.

FOREIGN EXCHANGE RATE The price relationship between the currencies of two countries.

FOREIGN TRADE ZONE A free port or area where foreign merchandise may be imported without being required

to pay duties on the condition that it is not used domestically and is shipped to some other country.

FORFEITURE The automatic loss of cash, property, or rights, as a punishment for not complying with legal provisions and as compensation for the resulting damages or losses. The term should not be confused with "confiscation." The latter term designates the actual taking over of the forfeited property by the government. Even after property has been forfeited, it cannot be said to be confiscated until the governmental unit claims it.

FORGERY The alteration of any document, instrument, or signature, with the intent to defraud or prejudice any individual constitutes forgery, which is a statutory crime, punishable by imprisonment.

FORMULA INVESTING An investment technique. One formula calls for the shifting of funds from common shares to preferred shares or bonds as the market, on average, rises above a common predetermined point—and the return of funds to common share investments as the market average declines.

FORWARD EXCHANGE A means of hedging against the fluctuation of a foreign exchange rate by purchasing a bill of foreign exchange that is payable at some future or forward period of time.

FORWARDING AGENT That individual or company which handles the function of collecting and shipping merchandise for others.

FOUNDATION 1) The base or lowest part of a structure upon which everything else rests or is founded upon.
2) Basic principles or policies.
3) A permanent fund established by contributions from one source (as the Carnegie Foundation) or from many sources (as the Cleveland Foundation) for charitable, educational, religious or other benevolent uses or purposes.

FOUNDERS' STOCK Stock which is issued to the promoters or founders for their services in forming a new corporation.

FRACTION 1) A portion of a whole.
2) In investments, a term generally applied to holdings of less than one share, resulting from rights and stock dividends. Since they are not entitled to dividends, they are usually disposed of by sale or rounded out, by the purchase of additional fractions, to full shares.

FRACTIONAL RESERVE The present system of commercial banking in the United States in which any bank is legally required to maintain only a part of any deposit in the form of reserves such as till cash or deposits with a central bank. The difference between the required reserves and the actual reserves may then be lent to borrowers.

FRANCHISE 1) Liberty, freedom, right, privilege.
2) A special privilege granted by a government permitting the continuing use of public property, such as city streets, and usually involving the elements of monopoly and regulation.
3) A right given by a corporation or business firm to another to sell or distribute a certain product or service in a given area or section, in return for some compensation or a share of the profits.

FRANCHISE CLAUSE In marine insurance, a policy feature providing that no claims below a stated amount are to be paid by the insurance company, but, if the claims are above that amount, the entire amount will be paid. This clause discourages the submission of small claims that cost more to process than the actual settlement amount.

FRANCHISE TAX   The charge made by a governmental unit for the right to exercise a private monopoly such as a public utility or bus line.

FRANKING   The exemption from having to pay for the postage on United States mail which is granted to members of Congress and certain other departments and executives of the nation for certain uses of the mails.

FREE AND OPEN MARKET   A market in which supply and demand are expressed without restraint in terms of price. Contrast with a controlled market in which supply, demand and price may all be regulated.

FREEHOLD ESTATE   A legal estate in land commonly referred to as an estate of inheritance. The two most important freehold estates are the fee simple estate and the life estate. See "chattel."

FREE PORT   See "foreign trade zone."

FREE RIDE   The situation where an individual is in a position to take advantage of circumstances to obtain a profit without exposing himself to risk.

FREE TRADE   A situation in which customs duties and restrictions on exports or imports are absent and no governmental actions are permitted to interfere with foreign commerce.

FRICTIONAL UNEMPLOYMENT   That situation where people are not working because of technical factors. A migratory farm laborer experiences frictional unemployment for the period in transit from one job to another even though he is assured of the job upon arrival.

FRINGE BENEFITS   See "employee benefits."

FRINGE ISSUE   Provisions in a labor agreement that involve compensation to the employee other than hourly wages or incentive earnings, such as vacations, overtime, sick leave, holidays, etc.

FROZEN ACCOUNT   An account that has been suspended in payment until a court order or legal process again makes the account available for withdrawal.

FROZEN CREDITS   Loans which would normally have been called and matured, but, due to economic conditions, it is recognized by the creditor that such a step would precipitate the bankruptcy of the debtor and thus preclude any substantial payment. As a result, such credits may be carried or extended, with the hope of liquidation when the debtor has recovered. Also described as frozen loans.

FULL COVERAGE   Any form of insurance which provides for payment, without deduction, of all losses up to the amount of the insurance occasioned by hazards covered. See "all risks insurance."

FULL EMPLOYMENT   The situation when all able people who are in the labor market and wishing employment may find gainful work. During full employment people may, however, not be working for such technical reasons as frictional unemployment and vacations.

FULL FAITH AND CREDIT DEBT   Usually state debt for which the credit of the government, implying the power of taxation, is unconditionally pledged.

FULL LOT   A "round" or "board" lot. Generally, 100 shares of stock traded on the New York Stock Exchange.

FULLY PAID STOCK   Legally issued stock for which the corporation has received at least the amount of the par value in goods, services or money.

FULLY REGISTERED   A term generally applied to bonds which are registered as to principal and income. In this form, a bond is not negotiable and interest is remitted by the disbursing agent to the registered owner.

FUNCTION   A more or less arbitrary subdivision of the total activity area, which, when the size or nature of the business justifies it, can best be performed by a specialist.

FUNCTIONAL OBSOLESCENCE   The reduction in the value of a real estate property because that property does not possess the technological features of more efficient or newer property.

FUND   Stock; capital; cash or currency; to be distinguished from other kinds of property. As distinguished from a reserve, an asset or group of assets segregated for some specified purpose.

FUNDED DEBT   Usually interest-bearing bonds of a company. Could include long-term bank loans. Does not include short-term loans, preferred or common stock.

FUNDED PENSION PLAN   A systematic method used by the insurer of a pension insurance plan to accumulate the amount or fund which will be needed to meet the claims of the plan.

FUNDING   The act of converting a shorter maturity debt into a longer maturity. Some authorities use the term to refer to the conversion of debt into equity but they appear to be in the minority.

FUTURE-EXCHANGE CONTRACT   A contract for the purchase or sale of foreign exchange to be delivered at a future date and at a rate determined in the present.

FUTURES   Agreements to buy and receive or to sell and deliver a commodity at a future date, with these distinguishing features: All trades in the same contract, such as the grain contract, have the same unit of trading, 5,000 bushels; the terms of all trades are standardized; a trade, therefore, may be offset later by an opposite trade through the same clearing member; all trades must be made by open outcry in the pit within the hours prescribed; the contract has a basic grade but more than one grade is deliverable; delivery is made during a single calendar month; the trades are cleared through a clearinghouse daily.

GAIN   Profits; winnings; advantage. To obtain, earn, or increase.

GAIN SHARING   A wage plan in which a bonus is paid for production in excess of standard.

GARNISHEE   The party upon whom a garnishment is served.

GARNISHMENT   A notice summoning a third party, in whose hands the effects of the defendant are attached, not to pay the money or deliver the goods to the defendant but to appear in court and answer to the suit of the plaintiff to the extent of his liability to the defendant.

GENERAL AUDIT An audit which embraces all financial transactions and records and which is made regularly at the close of an accounting period.

GENERAL DEPOSITORY A bank which is a member of the Federal Reserve System and which is permitted to handle deposits of the United States Treasury.

GENERAL FUND The fund that is available for any legally authorized purpose and which is therefore used to account for all revenues and all activities not provided for in other funds. The general fund is used to finance the ordinary operations of a unit.

GENERAL LEDGER A company's general book of accounts in which all financial transactions are recorded or summarized.

GENERAL LEGACY A gift of personal property by will which is not a particular thing as distinguished from all others of the same kind; to be distinguished from specific legacy.

GENERAL LOAN AND COLLATERAL AGREEMENT A continuing agreement under which an investment broker borrows on the security of stocks and bonds which are listed on an exchange. A broker's loan.

GENERAL PARTNERSHIP A firm formed by two or more people, each having the power to bind the firm and all partners by his actions and in which all partners are fully liable for the debts of the partnership.

GENERAL STRIKE A situation in which many industries and business firms are struck by their workers with the attempt at paralysis of the business in the area.

GENERAL TARIFF A single-schedule tariff, that is, one single rate of duty on a product no matter what country exported it. It is also called a unilinear tariff.

GENTLEMEN'S AGREEMENT An unsigned, unsecured contract based upon the faith of both parties that each will perform.

GEOGRAPHIC WAGE DIFFERENTIALS Differences in wage rates based upon locations of plants or industries.

GIFT The value of a donated asset acquired without cost to the recipient or regard to its donor. The use of the gift may or may not be restricted.

GIFT TAX An excise tax levied by the federal government and many states on the gift or transfer of property. Most taxes of gifts are progressive and have minimum exemptions.

GIVE AN ORDER 1) To issue a command or instruction expected to be followed.
2) An instruction to an investment broker to buy or sell a security in a certain amount which may, or may not, include specifications of a price or time limit.

GOING CONCERN A successful business with the prospects of continuing.

GOING-CONCERN VALUE An intangible value said to inhere in an operating plant or common carrier or utility with business established because it is an actual operation, as distinguished from one newly constituted and not yet in operation which has yet to establish its business and reputation.

GOLD BULLION STANDARD Sometimes called the rich man's standard because the paper currency of the nation which is on the gold bullion standard may be exchanged into gold freely but only in sizeable amounts such as a gold bar which might be worth over $5,000.

GOLD CERTIFICATE ACCOUNT Gold certificates on hand and due from the Treasury. The certificates, on hand and due from the Treasury, are backed 100 percent by gold owned by the United States Government. They count as legal reserve, the minimum the Reserve Banks are required to maintain being 25 percent of their combined Federal Reserve note and deposit liabilities.

GOLD EXCHANGE STANDARD The monetary system in which a nation ties its currency to another nation's gold standard by providing that the first nation's currency may be exchanged for the currency of the nation that is on the gold standard. The exchange is pegged at a fixed rate which is maintained by the monetary authorities. This makes the one nation's gold do double-duty but will also permit the gold exchange nation to earn interest on funds which are not tied up in gold bullion or coin by purchasing bonds of the nation which is on the gold standard.

GOLD POINTS The upper and lower limits in the rates of foreign exchange between two nations which are on the gold standard. When these limits or points are reached, it then becomes profitable to ship gold rather than purchase foreign exchange.

GOLD SETTLEMENT FUND The Interdistrict Settlement Fund. See "gold wire" for illustration of operation of the fund.

GOLD STANDARD A monetary system with gold or specific weight as the unit of value.

GOLD STOCK Value of gold owned by a government.

GOLD WIRE A term used principally in Federal Reserve Banks to describe the telegraphic transfer of gold between Federal Reserve Banks through the medium of the Federal Reserve Board in Washington. These transfers arise from the settlement of inter-bank balances in the Federal Reserve System and occur daily. The gold involved is on deposit with the Treasurer of the United States.

GOOD DELIVERY Certain basic qualifications must be met before a security sold on the exchange may be delivered. The security must be in proper form to comply with the contract of sale and to transfer title by delivery to the purchaser. If these qualifications are met, then the security is ready for "good delivery."

GOODS AND CHATTELS The term commonly used to describe and identify all of the tangible (touchable) personal property in an estate, such as jewelry, furniture, tools, equipment.

GOODS IN PROCESS Goods in a factory on which some operations have been performed but that have not been completed.

GOOD UNTIL CANCELED (G.T.C.) An order or instruction given by the customer to his investment broker to be effective until the customer rescinds the order.

GOODWILL An intangible asset that represents the difference between the book value of a business and its purchase (or sale) price when the latter is greater than the book value. It is based on reputation, established business, location, etc.

GOVERNMENTAL DEPOSITORY Any bank which has been selected and approved to receive deposits of a government or agency of a government. Generally, the term is used to distinguish a bank which is designated as a depository for the United States Government.

GOVERNMENTS 1) Those administrative bodies which rule, control and direct the actions of their members, citizens, etc.
2) As used in the United States, all types of securities issued by the Federal Government (United States Treasury obligations), including in its broad concept, securities issued by agencies of the Federal Government.

GRACE PERIOD A formally specified extension of time beyond the due date for payment of insurance premiums, taxes or other obligations, or for performing a specific duty, such as renewing a driver's license.

GRADED TAX A local tax structure designed to stimulate construction and land utilization by taxing unimproved land at a higher rate or base than improved land.

GRADE LABELING The inclusion on a label or container of an objective designation which may be compared with a recognized standard. Meat labeled Prime or Choice and milk labeled Grade A or B are examples of this type.

GRADING Grading is the process of sorting individual units of a product according to predetermined standards or classes.

GRAIN EXCHANGES Those commodity exchanges upon which trading in spot and futures of grain takes place.

GRAIN PIT That portion of the trading area of a commodity or grain exchange in which the pit traders or commodity brokers transact their business. The physical appearance is of a series of concentric rings with each ring representing a different contract period.

GRANT To admit as true; to allow; to give.

GRANTEE 1) One who receives a grant.
2) A person to whom property is transferred by deed or to whom property rights are granted by means of a trust instrument or some other document.

GRANTOR A person who executes and delivers a deed or other instrument by which property rights are conveyed or otherwise transferred to another.

GRANTS-IN-AID Sums of money given by the federal government to a state or local government for specified purposes. They represent federal support for a state or locally administered program.

GRAVEYARD SHIFT The shift employed from midnight until 8 a.m.

GRAY MARKET A legal market in which goods in short supply can be purchased at premiums over normal trade prices.

GREENBACKS Technically, only the inconvertible notes issued during the Civil War period which were legal tender for all public and private debts except interest on national debt or import duties. Today, the term is used to refer to any of the paper money issues of the Federal Reserve Banks or the United States Treasury.

GRESHAM'S LAW The general theory is that if two kinds of money of equal nominal value are in circulation, the general public may prefer one over the other, because of metal content or because one is more easily mutilated or debased, and will tend to hoard the "good money" and spend the "bad money." This drives the "good money" out of circulation, while keeping the "bad money" or inferior money in circulation. The term also applies to available balances in depositors' accounts.

GRIEVANCE An employee's or employer's dissatisfaction with some aspect of the employment relationship. May or may not be limited to dissatisfaction due to interpretation of the contract.

GRIEVANCE PROCEDURE Grievance procedure of a union contract is an orderly way to resolve disputes by successive steps, usually beginning with negotiations between union stewards and foremen and ending with meetings between top union and company officials.

GROSS DEBT The total amount of debt without any reduction for such deductions as sinking funds.

GROSS INCOME The whole, entire or total amount of income without having been subject to deduction.

GROSS INTEREST The total price paid for the use of a thing which includes the cost of the capital and the cost of the administration of the transaction.

GROSS LEASE A lease of property under which the lessor agrees to meet all charges which would normally be incurred by the owner of the property.

GROSS MARGIN (For purposes of marketing.) Sales revenue less the cost of goods sold (adjusted for inventory depreciation and merchandise shortages).

GROSS NATIONAL DEBT The total outstanding debt of a national government including duplications and overlapping entries.

GROSS NATIONAL PRODUCT (GNP) The market value of the output of goods and services produced by the nation's economy in a year.

GROSS PROFIT The result of net sales revenue minus the cost of goods sold.

GROSS PROFIT ON SALES The amount by which the net sales exceeds the cost of the merchandise sold.

GROSS SALES The total sales of all merchandise sold to customers before deducting the returned sales.

GROSS YIELD The return obtained from an investment before deduction of costs and losses involved in procuring and managing the investment. See "net yield."

GROUND RENT A price paid each year or for a term of years for the right to occupy and improve a piece of land.

GROUP BANKING A form of banking enterprise whereby a group of people form a holding company for purpose of acquiring a majority of the capital stock of several banks in order to control their operations.

GROUP-BONUS WAGE PLAN An incentive plan used where the efforts of more than one man are required to perform basically related direct labor operations. The incentive for the group as a whole is first computed and then distributed to the individuals on some equitable basis.

GROUP MEDICINE A plan of medical insurance to provide such services as medical examinations and treatment of illness for a group such as employees of a company.

GROWTH STOCK Stock that is characterized by the prospect of its increase in market value rather than by the amount of cash dividends it earns for the stockholder.

GUARANTEE To make oneself liable or responsible for the performance of something; a surety; a promise or pledge.

GUARANTEED ANNUAL WAGE A contractual obligation for an employer to provide an employee a minimum amount of income during a year. This amount may be less than a fully employed worker might earn but does provide at least an assured minimum.

GUARANTEED LETTER OF CREDIT A term used to describe those traveler's letters of credit or commercial letters of credit where the party requesting the credit issuance does not pay the bank in cash for the equivalent amount of the credit upon its issuance. Reimbursement to the bank is guaranteed by the applicant for this accommodation and is often backed by collateral security or the merchandise itself.

GUARANTEED MORTGAGE A mortgage on which there is a guarantee of payment of principal or interest or both. In years prior to 1930 this was frequently done by a mortgage guarantee corporation. Today most such mortgages are of the Federal Housing Administration or Veterans Administration variety.

GUARANTEED MORTGAGE CERTIFICATE A document indicating a stated partial interest in a bond and mortgage which is held by a trustee. A mortgage loan company, in turn, guarantees such certificates for a typical fee of about one half of one percent of the principal per year.

GUARANTEED WAGE PLANS Systems under which the employer states, in advance, that for a specific period he will pay a predetermined amount to, or retain in service at some employment or in any event with pay, a previously specified number of his workers, whether or not they have work to do.

GUARANTY A written promise by one person (the guarantor) to be liable for the debt of another person (the principal debtor) in the event that the principal debtor fails to perform his obligation and provided the guarantor is notified of that fact by the creditor. A guaranty must be in writing to be enforceable by law.

GUARANTY FUND A fund which a mutual savings bank in certain states must create through subscriptions or out of earnings, in order to meet possible losses resulting from decline in value of investments or from other unforeseen contingencies. In other states such a fund is known as the surplus fund.

GUARDIAN An individual appointed by a court to manage the affairs or person (or both) of a minor or a mentally incompetent individual. A corporation appointed by a court to manage the affairs of a minor or a mentally incompetent person.

HABEAS CORPUS A writ directing one who has custody of another to bring him before the court to determine the right to hold such person in custody.

HALLMARK The indented mark made on gold and silver which shows the degree of purity and fineness of the metal.

HAND-TO-MOUTH OPERATION The technique of operating a business with the smallest amount of goods, labor, machinery, capital and other facilities adequate to take care of current and immediate requirements.

HARD COPY A visible record which may be read by the human eye.

HARD MONEY Has three different meanings. The context will indicate which one to use: 1) A situation in which interest rates are high and loans are hard to arrange. 2) Metallic currency. 3) A nation's currency which is desired by foreigners in lieu of a "soft" currency which may be the domestic or other foreign currency.

HARDWARE 1) The mechanical equipment necessary for conducting an activity, to be distinguished from the planning and theory that went into the activity. 2) The physical equipment or devices forming a computer and peripheral equipment.

HATCH ACT Federal statute which, as amended by the Taft-Hartley Act, forbids corporations or unions to make contributions or expenditures in connection with elections for certain federal offices.

HAZARD A dangerous condition which may create or increase the probability of loss or injury.

HEAD TAX A poll tax or charge made upon any immigrant entering the United States.

HEALTH AND WELFARE PLAN Plan providing insurance payments to employees in case of sickness or accident.

HEALTH CERTIFICATE State of health completed by an insured, usually as a request for reinstatement of a policy.

HEALTH HAZARD Health reasons, personal and family, or occupational, indicative of an added insurance risk incurred above that considered standard.

HEAVY INDUSTRY One involved in manufacturing basic products such as metals or which manufactures equipment such as machines.

HEAVY MARKET A declining market caused by an inadequate supply of bids to buy securities to offset the supply of offerings.

HEDGING A type of economic insurance used by dealers in commodities and securities, manufacturers and other producers to prevent loss due to price fluctuations. This is obtained by counterbalancing a present sale or purchase by a purchase or sale of a similar commodity, or of a different commodity, usually for delivery at some future date, the desired result being that the profit or loss on a current sale or purchase will be offset by the loss or profit on the future purchase or sale.

HEIR A person who inherits real property; to be distinguished from next of kin and from distributee. An heir of the body is an heir in the direct line of the decedent. A son, for example, is the heir of the body of his father or mother. See "collateral heir," "direct heir" and "next of kin."

HEIRS-AT-LAW The persons who inherit the real property of a person who dies without a valid will disposing of his property.

HIDDEN ASSETS Those assets publicly reported at different value than their true worth. May involve the risk of tax penalty as well as being merely misleading.

HIDDEN INFLATION That phase of inflation which is not revealed by economic indicators. Generally, hidden inflation takes the form of a reduction in quality.

HIDDEN TAX A governmental levy of which the ultimate user is unaware. Generally, an indirect tax.

HIERARCHY A specified rank or order of persons or things; thus, a series of persons or things classified by rank or order.

HIGH CREDIT Highest amount of credit extended to a particular customer at one time.

HIGHEST AND BEST USE The utilization of a property which will produce the highest or maximum net return over the life of the property. The term does not necessarily refer to an intensive development of the site but considers the site in terms of the maximum net return.

HIGH FINANCE 1) Very complicated financial transactions such as associated with recapitalization of a complicated corporate structure as distinguished from low or simple financial transactions such as a small bank loan.
2) Borrowing to the maximum of one's credit.
3) The use of others' funds in a speculative way which may result in a loss to the owner of the funds.

HI-LO INDEX A moving average of individual stocks that reach new highs and new lows each day. Often indicates a change in the market that some of the other market indicators will not show. Variations in the average of the new highs and lows may indicate a deteriorating or rebounding market in general while an average such as the Dow-Jones Industrials might show a neutral or even opposite action in the blue chip issues.

HIRING HALL Headquarters from which a union fills requests for workers.

HOLDER IN DUE COURSE A person who has taken a negotiable instrument (check, note or bill of exchange) under the following conditions: That it is complete; that it is not overdue or to his knowledge previously dishonored; that he took it in good faith for value; and that at the time it was negotiated to him he had no notice of any infirmity in the instrument or defect in the title of the person negotiating it.

HOLDER OF RECORD The owners of a corporation's securities as they appear in the records of the firm's transfer agent on a certain date. These individuals or organizations are then entitled to any benefits or dividends declared.

HOLD-HARMLESS AGREEMENT Liability of one party is assumed by a second party; frequently the second party is an insurance company.

HOLDING COMPANY A corporation which exercises control over other companies through title to their securities, primarily voting issues.

HOLDOVER TENANT A tenant who remains in possession of leased property after the expiration of the lease term.

HOME LOAN A real estate loan for which the security is residential property.

HOMESTEAD The land and buildings thereon occupied by the owner as a home for himself and family, if any, and in most states protected to some extent by statute against the claims of creditors.

HOMESTEAD ASSOCIATION A term given in some states to an institution that operates as a savings and loan association. See "savings and loan association."

HOMEWORK A piecework production system in which the entrepreneuer provides material to be processed in a person's home.

HONOR The payment of a demand negotiable instrument, or the acceptance for future payment of a time negotiable instrument, upon presentation. See "acceptance."

HORIZONTAL EXPANSION The establishment of facilities to permit a firm to expand its business in the same product it is producing or selling.

HORIZONTAL UNION Union which covers workers or groups of similar status though of different crafts or classes.

HOT MONEY Funds which move from investment situation or institution to investment situation or institution in a short period of time generally to obtain a higher rate of return or greater safety and at times to avoid taxes or regulation. It may also be a designation for currency which was illegally acquired and subject to being traced.

HOURLY-RATE WAGE PLAN A plan whereby the worker is paid a fixed amount per hour regardless of what he produces.

HOUSING AUTHORITY An agency set up by either the federal state or local government to construct or manage public housing generally for lower income group tenants.

HYPOTHECATION Originally, a pledge to secure an obligation without delivery of title or possession; now, generally any pledge to secure an obligation, such as the hypothecation of securities for a loan.

HYPOTHESIS The tentative explanation of a situation based upon the logical development of subject data.

IDLE MONEY Uninvested, available funds.

ILLEGAL-PURPOSE DOCTRINE Test applied by some courts in determining whether union activities, lawful in themselves, were invalid because of their objectives.

ILLEGAL STRIKE A strike that is called in violation of law, such as a strike that ignores "cooling-off" period restrictions or some absolute statutory ban, or a strike that disregards the "no strike" order or agreement of the parent or local union.

IMMEDIATE BENEFICIARY (Also called present beneficiary and primary beneficiary). A beneficiary of a trust who is entitled to receive immediate benefits from the trust property, whether or not limited to income, opposed to ultimate beneficiary.

IMMEDIATE ORDER Also called a "fill, or kill" order, or one that must be executed at a stipulated price as soon as it reaches the exchange floor, or be canceled.

IMPAIRED CAPITAL A condition in which the capital of a business is worth less than its stated capital.

IMPARTIAL CHAIRMAN Term often applied to a permanent arbitrator, named for the life of the union contract, and usually selected by mutual agreement. The term indicates his function of presiding over the union contract and its observance by both parties.

IMPERSONAL ACCOUNT An account in a set of books of record which is other than that of an individual or firm.

IMPLIED TRUST A trust created by operation of law or by judicial construction to be distinguished from an express trust.

IMPLIED WARRANTY Representation, not in writing, that insurable conditions exist.

IMPORT To bring goods from another country into one's own country.

IMPORT CREDIT A commercial letter of credit issued for the purpose of financing the importation of goods.

IMPORT LICENSE Permission obtained from a government to import stated quantities of enumerated goods.

IMPORT QUOTA The amount of a product which a nation will permit to be imported during a stated period.

IMPORT RATE A railroad transport rate established specifically for application on import traffic and generally less, when so published, than domestic rate.

IMPOST To classify so as to establish a customs duty.

IMPREST FUND (PETTY CASH FUND) A system commonly employed in business which provides a fund of a designated amount (by debiting petty cash and crediting cash) out of which payments for expenses of small amounts are made.

IMPROPER IMPROVEMENT Improvements which do not conform to the best utilization of the site.

IMPROVEMENTS Buildings, other structures and other attachments or annexations to land which are intended to remain so attached or annexed, such as sidewalks, trees, drives, tunnels, drains and sewers.

IMPUTED An estimate of value in the event that a cash payment is not made for a good or service.

IMPUTED INTEREST An estimate of value, charge of interest due for the use of capital even though a cash payment is not made. Implicit interest.

INACTIVE CORPORATION One which neither operates property nor administers its financial affairs. If it maintains an organization, it does so only for the purpose of complying with legal requirements and maintaining title to property or franchises.

INACTIVE STOCK An issue traded on an exchange or in the over-the-counter market in which there is a relatively low volume of transactions. Volume may be no more than a few hundred shares a week or even less. On the New York Stock Exchange most inactive stocks are traded in 10-share units rather than the customary 100. See "round lot."

INACTIVE TRUST A trust in which the trustee has no duty except to hold title to the property.

INCENTIVE WAGES Method of wage payment by which workers receive extra pay for extra production.

INCHOATE Not yet completed. Contracts are inchoate until executed by all the parties who should join in their execution, and a widow's right to dower is inchoate so long as her husband lives.

INCIDENCE OF TAXATION The individual or firm that actually has the burden of a tax even though not formally paying it.

IN-CLEARING ITEMS Items received by a bank as a result of a clearinghouse exchange are commonly called incoming clearings, or shorted to "in-clearings."

INCOME A stream of benefits generally measured in terms of money as of a certain time; a flow of services. It is the source of value. Loosely, the money a person or company has coming in from any source. Exactly, income is made up of the amount received from both earnings and investments.

INCOME FUND Investment company whose primary objective is generous current income. May be balanced fund, common stock fund, bond fund or preferred stock fund.

INCOME RETURN The amount of annual income paid on an investment. The percent obtained by dividing the amount of annual income paid on an investment by the cost or purchase price.

INCOME STATEMENT A record of income and expense relating to the operations of a business; a summary of transactions from the sale of goods or services. Operating statement and profit and loss statement are other terms that are sometimes applied to this accounting record.

INCOME TAX That tax, federal, state or local, which is levied on the income of individuals or firms.

INCOMPETENT One who is legally incapable of managing his affairs because of mental (not physical) deficiency.

INCONTESTABLE CLAUSE Standard policy provision. A policy cannot be contested by the insurer after a given length of time. See "contestable clause."

INCONVERTIBLE MONEY Irredeemable money. Money which may not be converted into the standard. United States money is inconvertible since it is not redeemable in gold.

INCORPORATE To form into a corporation; become a corporation.

INCREASING COSTS A production situation in which the cost per production unit goes up as production volume goes up.

INCREASING RETURNS A situation in which production is increased even though there has been no increase in the various factors of production such as land, labor, capital or management. This may be due to a more efficient utilization of one or more of the factors. The term is also used to describe a situation in which an additional unit of any of the factors of production results in an increase in production more than was caused by a prior unit of the same factor.

INCREMENT That which is gained or added.

INCREMENTAL COST The cost of one more unit; marginal cost.

INCUMBRANCE A lien or liability attached to real property. See "encumbrance."

INDEFEASIBLE Incapable of being annulled or rendered void; as, an indefeasible title to property.

INDEMNITY That which is given as compensation or security for loss.

INDENTURE A written agreement under which bonds or debentures are issued, setting forth maturity date, interest rate, security and other terms.

INDEPENDENT CONTRACTOR One who agrees to perform certain actions for another and is responsible only for the results but not subject to direction of the party hiring him.

INDEPENDENT UNION A labor organization, not company-dominated, which is not affiliated with the AFL-CIO and remains independent of any federation.

INDETERMINATE APPROPRIATION An appropriation which is not limited either to any definite period of time or to any definite amount, or to both time and amount.

INDIRECT COST Also called overhead, fixed cost or supplementary cost. A cost which does not vary with the volume of activity. A real estate tax is an example of an indirect cost.

INDIRECT EXCHANGE The technique used in arbitrage of foreign exchange in buying foreign exchange in one market and promptly selling it in another market at a rate that will yield a profit over the purchase price plus the expenses of transaction.

INDIRECT LABOR The amount of the wages paid to employees who work in the factory but whose time may not be charged to specific finished products.

INDIRECT PRODUCTION The modern system of production which involves the use of capital and tools. Thus, to make most products one first makes a machine to make the product. Only in a very primitive society does one find direct production.

INDIRECT STANDARD The monetary system which does not directly convert its currency into a standard metal such as gold or silver but permits, as a right of ownership, the exchange of the domestic currency into the currency of a nation that is on a metal standard. The ratio of exchange is established and maintained with only infrequent changes.

INDIRECT TAX A levy by a governmental unit which can easily be passed on to some other individual or firm. To the individual or firm that bears the final burden of the tax it is an indirect tax.

INDIVIDUAL INCOME TAX Income taxes may be on the income of people or companies such as corporations. That portion of the total collection of taxes paid by people. It is either a state or federal tax and also has progressive features after a minimum deduction.

INDIVIDUALISM The economic social structure which is characterized by free enterprise and the right of private property as well as profit system.

INDIVIDUAL PROPRIETORSHIP A business owned by one person. The individual owner has all the rights to profits from the business as well as all the liabilities and losses.

INDORSEE The holder of a negotiable instrument to whom it has been transferred by indorsement.

INDORSER A person who signs his name on the back of a negotiable instrument, such as a check, draft, or promissory note, for the purpose of transferring his title to the instrument or of guaranteeing payment.

INDUCED CONSUMPTION The increased purchases which are derived from consumers as a result of capital investment. To build a plant, direct and indirect employees must be hired; these, upon being paid, buy consumer goods. These goods, in turn, provide income and thus consumption for the related activities.

INDUCED INVESTMENT The capital investment in such forms as plant and machinery produced as a result of increases in spending by consumers.

INDUSTRIAL BANK A financial institution that derives its funds through a form of savings known as "investment shares" and invests these funds by specializing in the financing of businesses through the assignment of pledged accounts receivable.

INDUSTRIAL GOODS Goods which are destined for use in producing other goods or rendering services as contrasted with goods destined to be sold to the ultimate consumer.

INDUSTRIAL PLANT RESERVE Any productive facility for manufacturing defense material subject to administration by a government agency for that purpose.

INDUSTRIAL RELATIONS Insuring that the working relationships between management and employees and the job satisfaction of and work opportunities for the company's personnel are developed and maintained in the best interests of the company and its employees.

INDUSTRIAL RESEARCH The systematic investigation of opportunities for improvement of products or production in a commercial or business sense. Applied research as compared with pure research which does not require a materialistic goal.

INDUSTRIAL REVOLUTION That period starting in the late 18th century in which rapid advancements were made in production largely due to the use of steam and machinery.

INDUSTRIAL UNION A union whose membership includes any worker in a particular industry, regardless of the particular skills the members are exercising. Membership is secured largely from semiskilled and unskilled workers.

INDUSTRY A particular branch of trade or manufacture.

INDUSTRY-WIDE BARGAINING The labor relations activity designed to set a pattern of policy for an entire industry and the employees in that industry.

INELASTIC DEMAND Demand which does not change at a proportionate rate with the rate of change in price.

INELASTIC SUPPLY Supply which does not change at a proportionate rate with the rate of change in price.

INFERIOR GOODS Products and services which, as income increases, tend to be consumed in smaller amounts.

INFIRMITY Any known act, or visible omission in detail, in the creation or transfer of title that would invalidate an instrument is known as an infirmity.

INFLATION A rapid and sharp increase in the general price level generally associated with an increase in the supply or velocity of money.

INFLATIONARY GAP The amount by which government and private spending exceeds the amount needed to maintain a stable price level and full employment.

INFLATIONARY SPIRAL That condition in the rapidly increasing price level which leads workers to demand higher wages, which increases costs, which in turn leads sellers and producers to ask even higher prices.

INFRINGEMENT The act of violating; breach nonfulfillment.

INHERENT VICE A condition in property which causes deterioration or damage; for example, the painting of damp wood.

INHERITANCE That estate in property, technically real property but in general usage any property, which has come about through a bequest by will or devise or through intestate descent.

INHERITANCE TAX A tax on the right to receive property by inheritance; to be distinguished from an estate tax.

INJUNCTION An order of a court of equity directing a person to do or refrain from doing some act.

IN KIND Generally refers to payment of a loss through replacing the damage to a destroyed property with the same type of property, the option generally being with the insuring company.

INPUT 1) That which is put in or inserted into.
2) Information or data transferred or to be transferred from an external storage medium into the internal storage of the computer.
3) Describing the routines which direct input as defined in (2) or the devices from which such information is available to the computer.
4) The device or collective set of devices necessary for input as defined in (2).

INSANITY A mental condition, or impairment, which results in a person's being declared legally incompetent.

INSIDER REPORTS The monthly reports required by the Securities and Exchange Commission that must be filed by the officers, directors and stockholders who own more than 10% of any corporation whose securities are listed on a national securities exchange. Included are records of all purchases and sales made during the previous month and the total number of shares held at the end of the month. These reports, along with the information on what action investment funds are taking, make it possible to know which securities have gained or lost favor with people who are close to the market.

INSOLVENCY The inability to pay one's debts in the ordinary course of business.

INSTALLATION EQUIPMENT Those industrial goods that do not become part of the physical product and which are exhausted only after repeated use, such as boilers, power lathes, and bank vaults.

INSTALLMENT A part payment.

INSTALLMENT SALES Sales that are made on terms by which the customer pays part of the selling price at the time of sale and signs a written contract covering the settlement of the balance in periodic payments.

INSTITUTIONALISM The increase of governmental activities affecting the social existence of a people.

INSTITUTION ECONOMICS That school of economics which stresses the importance of the social environment or institutions on the economic behavior of individuals.

INSTRUMENT A written document that gives formal expression to a legal act or agreement.

INSTRUMENTAL CAPITAL Goods which may be used to produce capital such as machine tools.

INSTRUMENTALITIES A term often applied to agencies of the federal government and whose obligations are not the direct obligation of the federal government. However, there is an implied support; for example, Federal Land Bank bonds.

INSURABLE INTEREST Such an interest in the subject matter of life or property insurance as will entitle the person possessing the interest to obtain insurance on it.

INSURANCE The contractual relationship which exists when one party, for a consideration, agrees to reimburse another for loss caused by designated contingencies.

INSURANCE, ACCIDENT Insurance against the loss of earning power sustained through disabling accident, only.

INSURANCE, ACCOUNTS RECEIVABLE Insurance against loss due to inability to collect outstanding accounts receivable because of damage to or destruction of records by a peril insured against.

INSURANCE, ALL-RISK A name given to a policy which covers against the loss caused by all perils except those which are specifically excluded by the terms of the policy. Ordinary policies, contrarywise, name the peril or perils which are specifically covered in that policy.

INSURANCE, ASSESSMENT Plan of insurance for which either the amount of insurance, or the number and amount of assessments or premiums, are variable.

INSURANCE, AUTOMOBILE LIABILITY Indemnity policy for legal liability for bodily injury or damage to others arising from accidents of ownership or operation of an automobile.

INSURANCE, BUSINESS Accident and sickness coverage issued primarily to indemnify a business against loss of time because of the disability of a key employee.

INSURANCE, BUSINESS INTERRUPTION Protection for the owner of a business from losses which would be sustained during a period when the business is not operating due to such occurrences as fire or other hazards.

INSURANCE CARRIER The insurance company, since it assumes the financial responsibility for the risks of the policyholders.

INSURANCE, CASUALTY Insurance protection for accident or injury to persons or property.

INSURANCE, COMBINATION POLICY An insurance policy, or more often, two policies printed on one joined sheet, which provides coverage against several hazards under the one document.

INSURANCE, COMMERCIAL Accident and sickness insurance intended primarily to be sold to workers in commerce and business as contrasted to industrial workers.

INSURANCE, COOPERATIVE Refers to mutual associations such as fraternal, employee, industrial or trade union groups. The profit motive is not the factor in this type of insurance but rather the accomplishment of some social end or goal.

INSURANCE COVERAGE The total amount of insurance carried.

INSURANCE, CREDIT Two different types of insurance. 1) Issued by insurance companies on accounts receivables. Claim payment is made if the account receivable proves uncollectable.
2) A type of insurance more properly called credit life insurance.

INSURANCE, CREDIT LIFE Life insurance issued by a life insurance company on the lives of borrowers to cover payment of loans (usually small loans repayable in installments) in case of death.

INSURANCE, EMPLOYER'S LIABILITY Protects an employer against the claims for damages which arise out of the injuries to employees in the course of their work. A workmen's compensation policy insures the employer against liability under state compensation laws. Employer's liability insurance provides protection in cases not covered by the compensation laws.

INSURANCE, ENDOWMENT Provides for payment of the face amount to the insured on maturity, or to the beneficiary on prior death of the insured. Combination of pure endowment and term insurance.

INSURANCE, EXCESS A policy or bond covering the insured against certain hazards, which applies only to loss or damage in excess of a stated amount.

INSURANCE, EXTENDED TERM A form of insurance available as a nonforfeiture option. It provides the original amount of insurance for a limited period of time.

INSURANCE, FAMILY INCOME Insurance that provides an income to the beneficiary to the end of a specified period from the inception of the insurance if the insured dies within that period. The face amount of the insurance is paid at the end of the income period or when the insured dies after the end of the period.

INSURANCE, FIRE Contract prescribed by each state subject to modification by endorsements insuring against direct loss by fire, lightning and other defined causes.

INSURANCE, FLEET POLICY An insurance contract covering a number of automobiles, usually owned by companies who provide them for certain employees.

INSURANCE, FLOATER POLICY A policy under the terms of which protection follows movable property, covering it wherever it may be; *e.g.,* a policy on tourists' baggage.

INSURANCE, FRATERNAL A system of cooperative protection furnished by a fraternal order to its members on a nonprofit basis.

INSURANCE, GOVERNMENT Protection issued by the United States Government in amounts up to $10,000, to those who have served or are serving in the armed forces, intended to cover the added hazards of war. The insurance is usually issued on a term basis with the option of converting to a permanent plan.

INSURANCE, GRADED PREMIUM LIFE A type of modified life insurance in which the premiums increase each year for the first several years and then level off.

INSURANCE, GROUP Any insurance plan by which a number of employees (and their dependents) or other homogeneous groups, are insured under a single policy, issued to their employer or leader with individual certificates given to each insured individual or family unit.

INSURANCE, GROUP CREDITOR Contract issued to the creditor on the lives of his debtors to pay the amount of the indebtedness in the event of death.

INSURANCE, GROUP DISABILITY Provides benefits for a group of individuals, usually employees of the covered company, to compensate for losses such as time lost because of accident, or sickness, hospitalization cost, medical or surgical expense.

INSURANCE, GUARANTEED PREMIUM REDUCTION (GPR) Policies for which an annual reduction in premiums is available as specified in the contract.

INSURANCE, HEALTH Insurance for loss due to disability sustained because of disease.

INSURANCE, HOMEOWNER'S POLICY A form of package policy including fire and allied lines, theft insurance and comprehensive personal liability.

INSURANCE, INDUSTRIAL Insurance designed primarily for hourly wage workers exposed to some degree of occupational hazard and having difficulty in accumulating an amount of money to pay an annual or semiannual premium.

INSURANCE, JOINT LIFE Insurance on two or more persons, the benefits of which are payable on the first death.

INSURANCE, KEYMAN Protection of a business firm against the financial loss caused by the death of or disablement of a vital member of the firm.

INSURANCE, LEVEL PREMIUM Insurance for which the cost is distributed evenly over the period during which premiums are paid.

INSURANCE, LIABILITY Insurance provided by casualty and surety companies as a protection against the loss of property or of the earning power of an individual or company.

INSURANCE, LIFE Insurance providing for payment of a specified amount on the insured's death either to his estate or to a designated beneficiary.

INSURANCE, LIMITED PAYMENT LIFE Whole of life insurance for which number of premiums payable is limited, and after which the policy becomes fully paid.

INSURANCE, LIMITED POLICY A policy providing insurance against specified types of accidents or restricted in indemnity payments as contrasted with full coverage policies.

INSURANCE, MAJOR MEDICAL EXPENSE Contractual protection for large surgical, hospital, or medical expenses.

INSURANCE, MARINE That form of coverage which is primarily concerned with the protection of goods in transit and the means of transportation. This term is applied in common usage to risks involving ocean transit.

INSURANCE, MORTGAGE Title II of the 1934 National Housing Act provided a system of insurance on mortgage loans popularly known as FHA or Federal Housing Administration insurance. Insurance companies have declining term policies on the life of the mortgagor which are popularly called mortgage insurance.

INSURANCE, NONASSESSABLE Insurance under which the premium rate is guaranteed and no additional assessments may be required.

INSURANCE, NONCANCELLABLE A policy which the insurer is obligated to continue in force during the period for which the policy was written, and so long as payment of premiums is made when due.

INSURANCE, OLD AGE AND SURVIVORS See "Social Security Act."

INSURANCE, ORDINARY Life insurance on an annual premium basis as distinguished from industrial or group insurance. Term loosely used for whole life insurance.

INSURANCE, PAID-UP Policy for which all required premiums have been paid, and under which the company is liable for benefits as provided by the terms of the policy.

INSURANCE, PARTICIPATING Insurance issued by a mutual or mixed company providing for participation in dividend distribution.

INSURANCE, PARTNERSHIP Insurance coverage on the lives of business partners, the purpose being to enable the remaining partner, on death of the other, to purchase the business and to cushion the loss of executive ability.

INSURANCE, PRODUCTS LIABILITY Protection provided against claims arising from the utilization of the covered product manufactured, sold, handled or distributed by the insured or others trading under his name if the accident occurs after possession has been relinquished to others and away from premises owned, rented or controlled by the insured.

INSURANCE, PROTECTION AND INDEMNITY Insurance against loss due to claims for damages against vessel owners or operators not covered by the basic marine insurance contract, often written by mutual associations called clubs.

INSURANCE, RENEWABLE TERM Term insurance providing the right to renew at the end of the term for another term or terms, without evidence of insurability.

INSURANCE, REPLACEMENT Insurance under which the loss payable is the replacement cost of the property new. The excess over the depreciated replacement cost is payable only if the property is actually replaced.

INSURANCE, RETIREMENT INCOME Insurance payable on death before a specified age, with provision of a life annuity certain if the insured attains that age.

INSURANCE, SCHEDULE OF The list of individual items covered under one policy as the various buildings, animals and other property in farm insurance or the list of the rings, bracelets, etc., insured under a jewelry floater.

INSURANCE, SELF- The systematic provision of a fund to provide for the loss which the individual or firm may have. The endeavor of one who is subject to a risk to lay aside sums periodically which in time will provide a fund to cover any loss which occurs.

INSURANCE, SINGLE PREMIUM A life insurance contract that provides that for the consideration of a premium paid only once, the insurance company will assume the liability on the contract.

INSURANCE, SOCIAL Old age benefit insurance, federal unemployment insurance, state unemployment insurance, and disability insurance are examples of social insurance. The insurance is generally established by state or federal government with progressive benefits for the less favorably situated social groups.

INSURANCE, SPECIFIC A policy coverage that goes into detail as to the description of the property covered as compared to a blanket coverage, applying separately to specifically named objects or locations.

INSURANCE, STRAIGHT LIFE A plan of insurance for the whole of life with premium payable until death. See "insurance, ordinary."

INSURANCE, SUBSTANDARD Coverage issued to those who do not qualify for insurance at regular rates, usually due to being high risks.

INSURANCE, TERM A plan of insurance payable at death providing death occurs within a specified period. In fire and accident insurance it is a policy contract for a period of more than one year.

INSURANCE, TITLE Insurance against financial loss resulting from claims arising out of defects in the title to real property, which are existent but undisclosed at the time the policy is issued by the title company.

INSURANCE TRUST A trust composed partly or wholly of life insurance policy contracts.

INSURANCE, UNDER- A condition in which not enough insurance is carried to cover the insurable value, and especially to satisfy a coinsurance clause. Insurance less in amount than the possible loss to which it applies.

INSURANCE, UNEMPLOYMENT A form of social security that pays a weekly income to workers while they are unemployed.

INSURANCE, WHOLE LIFE A plan of insurance for the whole of life, payable at death.

INSURANCE, WORKMEN'S COMPENSATION Social insurance that provides that employees may collect from their employer for injuries sustained in the course of their employment.

INSURED An individual or business organization protected in case of some loss or damage, under the terms of the insurance policy.

INSURED PENSION PLANS Retirement and other employee benefit plans, the source of the benefits of which is life insurance paid for wholly or partially by the employer.

INSURER The party to the insurance contract who promises to pay losses or render service.

INTANGIBLE PROPERTY Property which cannot be touched or realized with the senses, such as a legally enforceable right. The right possessed by the holder of a promissory note or bond is intangible property, the paper and writing being only the evidence of that right.

INTENSIVE CULTIVATION Use of large proportions of fertilizer, machinery, labor and other capital on relatively limited agricultural acreage.

INTERCHANGEABLE PARTS Those segments of a whole product, which being duplicated could be reassembled at random and fit together and operate efficiently.

INTERDISTRICT SETTLEMENT FUND That part of the Federal Reserve System, located in Washington, D.C., which serves as a clearinghouse for the twelve Federal Reserve Banks in settling the difference between the debits and credits each of the banks has with the other eleven, thus minimizing the need to transfer funds. The fund is settled daily.

INTEREST The sum paid for the use of borrowed money or credit.

INTEREST RATE A percentage that expresses the relationship between the interest for one year and the principal.

INTERLOCKING DIRECTORS Directors of two or more similar corporations who simultaneously hold office in the corporations. The inference generally is that this device will tie the policies of the two companies together and reduce the competition between them.

INTERNAL AUDIT A routine and continuous check on the accuracy of all accounting records.

INTERNAL CONTROL 1) To have control come from within the organization or firm.
2) A plan of organization under which employees' duties are so arranged and records and procedures so designed as to make it possible to exercise effective accounting control over assets, liabilities, revenues and expenditures.

INTERNAL IMPROVEMENT Any governmental capital expenditure such as a dam, bridge, or road within the boundaries of the government.

INTERNAL NATIONAL DEBT The sum total of all the private and public indebtedness of a domestic nature of a nation as distinguished from the external debt or foreign debt.

INTERNAL REVENUE For the United States Government: All receipts from federal taxes excluding the amounts collected as customs. For a business: All receipts from the operation of the business. This would not include such amounts as earnings on outside investments.

INTERNAL REVENUE SERVICE That agency of the government which collects and administers the collection of the internal revenue taxes.

INTERNATIONAL BALANCE OF PAYMENTS The sum total of all the receipts of a nation from the other nations of the world and all the payments made by that nation to all the other nations of the world. If the nation has received more than it has paid it is described as having a favorable balance of payments.

INTERNATIONAL BANK FOR RECONSTRUCTION AND DEVELOPMENT See "World Bank."

INTERNATIONAL DOUBLE TAXATION The situation in which two sovereign powers tax a property or income. To prevent this inequity most modern nations have tax treaties which result in the reduction of the tax burden of the individual or company who would otherwise be subject to full double taxation.

INTERNATIONAL ECONOMICS The section of the broad field of economics which concerns itself with balances of payments, foreign exchange, international capital movements and related subject areas.

INTERNATIONAL GOLD BULLION STANDARD A gold bullion standard with the limitation that gold may be freely obtained in the form of bullion only for purposes of export. This prevents it from being hoarded for domestic purposes and gives a central bank greater control over the limited amount of gold.

INTERNATIONAL MONETARY FUND A companion institution to the nations with foreign exchange to meet temporary needs in their balance of international payments and thus avoid nationalistic trade barriers and currency depreciation.

INTERNATIONAL TRADE ORGANIZATION Affiliate of the United Nations whose purpose is to help trade between the various nations by encouragement of tariff reduction and other such steps which will help international trade.

INTERNATIONAL UNION Union whose membership includes employees in at least one other country in addition to the United States, usually Canada.

INTERNATIONAL UNIT A statistical device used to put data from various nations on a uniform base so that the different economies may be compared.

INTERSTATE CARRIER A common carrier doing business across state boundaries.

INTERSTATE COMMERCE A very broad term used to refer not only to shipments of goods between states but also to the methods of transportation and manufacture of goods which move over state borders.

INTERSTATE COMMERCE ACT Comprises the original act to regulate commerce, approved February 4, 1887, and many amendments.

INTERSTATE COMMERCE COMMISSION The agency created by the Congress in 1887 to obtain reports, establish rate structures and prevent discrimination and other abuses from railroads. Amendments since then have increased the powers of the commission to include pipe lines, motor lines, and interstate barge and boat lines under their control provided they fall within the broad definition of interstate commerce.

INTESTATE A person who dies without making a will; not disposed of by will.

INTESTATE SUCCESSION The descent and distribution of property of a person who dies without a valid will.

INTRASTATE COMMERCE Business in one state only; never crossing state lines.

INTRASTATE TRAFFIC Traffic moving wholly within one state, that is, originating and terminating in the same state and not passing en route outside the state.

INTRINSIC VALUE The value possessed by a particular thing considered in itself.

INVENTORY A detailed list showing quantities, descriptions and values of property and goods, and frequently also units of measure and unit prices.

INVENTORY CONTROL 1) An internal system for keeping adequate inventory at hand.

2) A governmental device used in emergencies to regulate inventories for the purpose of better utilization of the goods and to prevent hoarding.

INVENTORY VALUATION ADJUSTMENT 1) A method of removing the influence of price inflation from inventories stated in monetary units. This may be done by the use of various price indexes.
2) Corporate profits and income of an unincorporated enterprise include inventory profit or loss in customary business accounting. Current output in the national income accounts, however, includes only the value of the change in volume in inventories. The adjustment is that which is necessary to take account of this departure from business accounting. No valuation adjustment is necessary for farm inventories because farm income is measured exclusive of inventory profits.

INVESTMENT The use of money for the purpose of making more money, to gain income or increase capital, or both. Safety of principal is an important consideration.

INVESTMENT BANKING The business of underwriting and distributing corporate and government securities.

INVESTMENT BILL A discounted bill of exchange held to maturity as an investment.

INVESTMENT CERTIFICATE Certificate issued by associations which shows the amount of money an individual has invested with them. They do not carry any stockholders' liability and have no voting rights. Not to be confused with investment accounts.

INVESTMENT COMPANY A financial institution through which investors pool their money to obtain supervision and diversification of their investments.

INVESTMENT COMPANY ACT Federal statute enacted in 1940 for the registration and regulation of investment companies.

INVESTMENT COUNSELOR One who is professionally engaged in rendering investment advisory and supervisory services.

INVESTMENT CREDIT The long term extension of funds for purchase of such fixed assets as machinery, buildings or land as compared with the furnishing of working capital credit for inventory or accounts receivable and wages.

INVESTMENT PORTFOLIO The list of the various securities owned by a bank, an individual, a business enterprise, or other organization.

INVESTMENT RATINGS A number of investment services such as Moody's, Fitch's, Standard & Poor's, Value Line, etc., rate securities by various devices such as letters, numbers, or similar devices. In addition, bank examiners and "legal list" states assign investment classifications to securities. These ratings attempt to assign securities to certain general classes of quality or investment attributes.

INVESTMENT TRUST A company which uses its capital to invest in other companies.

INVISIBLE ITEMS OF TRADE Those nontangible items that are part of a balance of payments. Such expenditures as purchase of foreign insurance, foreign shipping, tourist expenditures and remittances by immigrants to their former countries are the major invisible items of trade.

INVOICE An itemized statement of merchandise or services bought or sold with the date, terms, methods of shipment if any, cost, and any other pertinent details.

INVOLUNTARY BANKRUPTCY An individual or firm judicially declared insolvent as a result of a petition filed with a competent court by the required number of unpaid and past-due creditors.

IRREVOCABLE LETTER OF CREDIT A contract by the issuer to accept drafts as conditioned by the contract and to charge them against their account. The letter is good (irrevocable) for a stated period of time.

IRREVOCABLE TRUST A trust that cannot be altered by the person who created the trust.

ISSUE 1) Any of a company's securities, or the act of distributing such securities.
2) All persons who have descended from a common ancestor; a broader term than children.

ISSUED STOCK That portion of the authorized stock which is treasury stock or outstanding in the possession of the stockholders as distinguished from unissued stock.

ITEMIZED APPROPRIATION A restriction of an appropriation to be made only for and in the amounts itemized.

JOB ACCOUNT An account pertaining either to an operation which occurs regularly (a "standing order") or to a specific piece of work (a "job order"), showing all charges for material and labor used and other expenses incurred, together with any allowances or other credit.

JOBBER 1) A middleman who buys from wholesale dealers and sells to retailers.
2) A merchant dealing in special, odd, or job lots.

JOB CLASSIFICATION Job ratings based on analysis of the requirements of the work.

JOB DESCRIPTION Written summary of the important features and requirements of a job. Usually based on a job analysis.

JOB EVALUATION System for fixing the relative value of jobs as they exist in a plant or office.

JOB LOT 1) An odd assortment of various merchandise.
2) A form of contract having a smaller unit of trading than the regular contract.

JOINT ACCOUNT An account owned by two or more people, subject to check or withdrawal by all signatures of all joint owners.

JOINT AGREEMENT The contract between union and management where more than one union or employer is involved.

JOINT COSTS The manufacturing costs of two or more products which, by the nature of production, are processed together.

JOINT DEMAND The type of demand in which two or more products or services must be brought together if utility is to be produced.

JOINT STOCK COMPANY A form of business organization in which the capital contribution of the partners is represented by transferable shares. It differs from the corporate form of organization in that each of the partners has unlimited liability, and is similar from the standpoint that death or transfer of membership does not terminate operations.

JOINT TENANCY An estate held by two or more persons in which the interest of anyone dying passes to the surviving tenant.

JOINT VENTURE Something undertaken by two or more parties.

JOURNAL A book in which any of the records of a business are first written.

JOURNEYMAN Worker in a traditional craft who has gone through an apprenticeship and mastered the type of work involved in the craft; qualified craftsman.

JUDGMENT 1) An opinion or discretion.
2) The decision or sentence of a court of law; to be distinguished from a decree. The obligation created by such a decision or sentence.

JUDGMENT CREDITOR The creditor who has been granted a judgment against a debtor by an appropriate court of jurisdiction.

JUDGMENT DEBTOR The debtor against whom a judgment has been obtained, which has been recorded.

JUDGMENT LIEN A charge rendered in a state or federal court on a piece of land or personal property against one who owes a debt. When applied to personal property it is generally termed an attachment.

JUDGMENT NOTE A note given by a debtor to a creditor acknowledging the debt and one which, if remaining unpaid at maturity, authorizes the creditor to appear in a court at law and confess judgment without process to the maker.

JUDICIAL SETTLEMENT The settlement of an account in accordance with the order, judgment or decree of a proper court, the effect of which in many states is determined by statute.

JUNIOR INTEREST 1) A legal right that is subordinate to another interest.
2) A mortgage participation junior to another participation.

JUNIOR LIEN A lien placed upon a property that has a senior lien already made and recorded. The rights are enforceable only after the previous liens have been satisfied.

JURISDICTION Legal right, power, or authority to hear and determine a cause; as, the jurisdiction of a court.

JURISDICTIONAL DISPUTE 1) A conflict over who or what body has the legal authority to preside or govern in a specific area.
2) A conflict that may involve either a dispute between two unions, as to which shall represent a group of employees in

collective bargaining, or as to which union's members shall perform a certain type of work.

JURISDICTIONAL STRIKE Work stoppage as a result of a jurisdictional dispute.

KEY INDUSTRY A dominant industry in its field or in the general economy.

KEYNESIAN An economic concept similar in logic or reasoning to the theories of John Meynard Keynes, British economist of major importance during the 1930's and 1940's. One of his ideas calls for large governmental spending and deficits during business recessions as a counter-cyclical device. Another states that wages not only are a cost of business but also are a major factor in demand; thus increased wages lead to increased production to meet the demand.

KICKBACK 1) An illegal or dishonest rebate secretly given a buyer by a seller for granting the order or contract, such as a payoff given to a crooked politician for a defense contract.
2) An illegal payment made by a worker to someone in a position of firing him so that he will not be laid off or given unpleasant duties.

KIND In the phrase "distribution in kind," distribution of the property itself and not the cash value of the property.

KITING Technique of drawing checks against deposits that have to clear through the banking system. Kiting takes advantage of the time needed for checks to clear and permits the kiter to use funds that are not his.

LABOR Manual workers; manual exertion; a factor of production.

LABOR AGREEMENT A trade agreement. The contractual relationship between the employer and the union representing his employees which covers the conditions of employment which will prevail for the period of the contract.

LABOR FORCE All persons 14 years of age or over in the United States who are employed or able, willing, and seeking work. Civilian labor force excludes all who are members of the armed forces and in institutions.

LABOR GRADE A technique of job evaluation in which levels of skill required for the various jobs are established.

LABOR MANAGEMENT RELATIONS ACT (Taft-Hartley Act) Federal statute which amends the National Labor Relations Act to regulate some union activities, authorizes damage suits for collective bargaining violations and certain strikes and boycotts, and sets up procedures for trying to settle "national emergency strikes."

LABOR RELATIONS Term ordinarily used to denote all matters arising out of the employer-employee relationship which involve collective action on the part of the employees; most intimately associated with collective bargaining and concerted activities.

LABOR-SAVING MACHINERY Mechanical devices that reduce the need for workers and create problems of technological unemployment.

LABOR THEORY OF VALUE The theory that the value of anything is closely related to the amount of labor required to make it.

LABOR TURNOVER The ratio or percentage which is computed by dividing the average number of employees for the covered period by the number of newly hired employees. This indicates the ratio of new employees to the average number of workers usually employed. This figure may also be adjusted for an annual rate.

LABOR UNION Any organization of employees which has as its purpose the improvement of the condition of its members. The union may act as the representative of its members in negotiating with employers.

LAISSEZ FAIRE Economic system in which very little government control is exercised over business.

LAME DUCK 1) A speculator whose venture has not succeeded.
2) An elected official who is still in office but whose position has been filled by another who will take over at a later date. The term refers to the official's inability to speak from a position of meaningful authority or influence as he might have during his actual term of office.

LAND In a legal sense, the solid part of the surface of the earth as distinguished from water; any ground, soil, or earth whatsoever, regarded as the subject of ownership, and everything annexed to it, whether by nature; e.g., trees, and everything in or on the earth, such as minerals and running water, or annexed to it by man, as buildings, fences, etc. In an economic sense, land consists of all those elements in the wealth of a nation which are supposed to be furnished by nature, as distinguished from those improvements which owe their value to the labor and organizing power of man.

LAND BANK 1) An agricultural program which has as its purpose the retirement of land from active agricultural purposes by a government subsidy to encourage the transfer of use into such activities as tree cultivation. Also called "Soil Bank."
2) A Federal Land Bank
3) A state cooperative to assist savings and loan associations.
4) A bank which instead of having capital uses land as the basis for issuing currency and extending credit such as the Land Bank founded in New England in 1740.

LAND CONTRACT A legal instrument to deliver a deed to the property given to the purchaser of the real estate, who customarily pays a small portion of the purchase price when the contract is signed and agrees to pay additional sums at specified intervals and in specified amounts until the total purchase price is paid. Since the possession of the land, that is, the ownership, does not become final until the whole payments have been made, this serves as a means of financing some properties in certain states.

LAND GRANT The land given to an individual or organization by the federal government for the purpose of stimulating or accomplishing certain goals.

LAND IMPROVEMENTS Physical changes in, or construction of, a more or less permanent nature attached to or appurtenant to land, of such character as to increase its utility and/or value.

LAND PATENT The document used by the United States Government to transfer title of a land grant to the new owner.

LAND TAX A property tax on real estate.

LAND TRUST An unincorporated association for holding real property by putting the title in one or more trustees for the benefit of the members whose interests are evidenced by land trust certificates.

LAND TRUST CERTIFICATE An instrument which grants participation in benefits of the ownership of real estate, while the title remains in a trustee.

LAND-VALUE TAX The levy by a government unit on the value of the land alone. The land value is an appraised value rather than one sales value.

LAPSE (noun) The falling of a gift into the residuary estate by reason of the death of the legatee or devisee during the testator's lifetime. Such a gift is known as a lapsed legacy or lapsed devise.

LARCENY Theft; taking and carrying away the goods of another.

LAST IN, FIRST OUT An accounting technique which assigns the value of an inventory from the cost of the most recent purchases. The balance sheet valuation of inventory is computed on the purchase price of earlier purchases and thus minimizes income taxes in periods of inflation. For contrast see "first in, first out." (fifo).

LAST WIL The will last executed by a person. Since all former wills ordinarily are revoked by the last one, the term is used to emphasize the fact that it is the latest and, therefore, the effective will of the maker.

LATE CHARGE A special fee demanded in connection with any payment on a mortgage loan or other obligation that is not made when due.

LAWFUL MONEY All forms of money which, by federal law, is endowed with legal tender for the payment of all debts, both public and private. See "legal tender."

LAYOFF Temporary, prolonged or final separation as a result of lack of work or business.

LAYOFF LOAN Generally considered to be one within the legal limit of the country bank but taken by the city bank to assist a country bank that is highly loaned up.

LEASE A contract by which the possession and use of real estate or other property is conveyed for a certain specified term and at a specified rent.

LEASEBACK A technique of financing and handling real estate. The original owner sells the property and simultaneously leases it back. There are a number of advantages and disadvantages to such a practice. Advantages include frequent tax savings; disadvantages include loss of a hedge in a period of inflation.

LEASED DEPARTMENT Part or subdivision of a store which is rented to an independent operator as a concession.

LEASEHOLDS Rights to the use of real estate by virtue of the lease, usually for a specified term of years, for which a

consideration is paid, as distinguished from the ownership of the real estate.

LEDGER A record of final entry in bookkeeping.

LEGACY A gift of personal property by will; the same as a bequest. A person receiving such a gift is called a legatee.

LEGAL ENTITY A thing, other than a person, that exists, can sue, be sued, and otherwise dealt with as if it were a natural person; in this sense, a corporation, a state, or a city is a legal entity.

LEGAL INTEREST That maximum interest rate established by state law which is used in contracts which have omitted mention of a rate.

LEGAL INVESTMENT An investment that conforms to the requirements of the statutes. A term used principally with reference to investments by trustees and other fiduciaries and by savings banks; often abbreviated to legals. To be distinguished from an authorized investment.

LEGAL LIST A list of investments selected by various states in which certain institutions and fiduciaries, such as insurance companies and banks, may invest. Legal lists are restricted to high-quality securities meeting certain specifications. See "prudent man law."

LEGAL PERSON Description of a corporation's condition of being subject to laws just as if it were a person.

LEGAL RATE OF INTEREST The maximum rate of interest that is permitted by the laws of the state having jurisdiction over the legality of a transaction. Interest in excess of this legal rate is termed usury. See "usury."

LEGAL RESERVE 1) The minimum reserve which an insurance company must keep to meet future claims and obligations as they are calculated under the state insurance code.
2) A bank's legal reserve is the portion of its deposits (demand and time) which it is required by law to maintain in the form of cash or readily available balances to meet the demands of the depositors.

LEGAL SECURITY That stock or bond which a fiduciary such as a trust company or trustee may purchase and hold for beneficiaries. In some states these are published in a legal list.

LEGAL TENDER Coin or currency required by law to be accepted in payment of obligations.

LENDER One who makes a trade of putting money to interest; a money lender.

LESSEE One who possesses the right to use or occupy a property under a lease; the tenant.

LESSOR The person, corporation, or other legal entity that leases property to a lessee.

LETTER OF ATTORNEY A written document which evidences a power of attorney.

LETTER OF CREDIT An instrument issued by a bank to an individual or corporation by which the bank substitutes its own credit for that of the individual or corporation.

LETTER OF TRUST A letter of lien. A letter which states that the signer-agent is holding merchandise or property for a seller until such times as the seller is paid for the goods.

LETTER PATENT A sealed and signed document from a government which grants a special right, privilege, property, or title such as the exclusive right to make or sell an invention.

LEVEL CHARGE PLAN An investment accumulation plan under which the selling charges are spread over the entire life of the investment program.

LEVERAGE 1) In securities investment, the effect on the per share earnings of the common stock of a company when large sums must be paid for bond interest or preferred stock dividends, or both, before the common stock is entitled to share in earnings. Leverage may be advantageous for the common stock when earnings are good but may work against the common stock when earnings decline.
2) Financial leverage refers to the controlling of a certain amount of investment worth with a smaller amount of money, such as controlling a land investment with a down payment, receiving the benefits of appreciation while making payments.

LEVY (verb) To impose taxes or special assessments. (noun) The total of taxes or special assessments imposed on a governmental unit.

LIABILITY A debt or responsibility that is owed or assumed.

LIABILITY, CAPITAL A comprehensive term which includes all long-term indebtedness of a corporation which is represented by the outstanding capital stock (liability to owners) and mortgages and bonded indebtedness (liability to outside creditors).

LIABILITY, CENTRAL The grouping together on one record of all liabilities of a borrower, such as loans both direct and indirect, consumer credit, letters of credit, guarantees, and other accommodations. The purpose of this record is to prevent over-extensions of credit to the borrower.

LIABILITY, COMMON LAW A party's responsibility for injuries or damage imposed upon a second party because of the first party's actions, by that part of the law based upon custom and usage as established by the courts, as distinguished from liability under statutes passed by a legislative body.

LIABILITY, CONTINGENT A liability which is dependent upon certain events occurring before it becomes an active liability.

LIABILITY, CONTRACTUAL Liability over and above that which would be imposed by law which a person assumes under the terms of a contract.

LIABILITY, CORPORATE PROFITS TAX Federal and state taxes levied on corporate earnings of a given year. This measures taxes for the year in which they are incurred, not necessarily for the year in which they are paid.

LIABILITY, CUMULATIVE When one bond is canceled and another issued to take its place and the first bond has a discovery period, the surety company is exposed to the possibility of a loss equal to the aggregate sum of the two bonds.

LIABILITY, CURRENT Those pecuniary obligations ordinarily intended to be paid in the usual course of business within a relatively short time, normally within a year, out of earnings.

LIABILITY, DEPOSIT The total of time, demand and certificate of deposits as well as other special deposits such as Christmas Club, Vacation Club and escrow accounts which a bank owes its customers.

LIABILITY, DIRECT A known primary obligation requiring the payment of a certain sum of money either now or at some determinable future date. See "prime maker."

LIABILITY, FIXED A long-term debt; recurring expenses.

LIABILITY, INDIRECT BUSINESS TAX AND NON-TAX All tax liabilities incurred by business, except for corporate income and social insurance taxes, plus general government nontax revenues for business. Nontax liabilities consist mainly of certain charges for government products and services, of fines and penalties, of donations, and of special assessments by state and local governments. Note that tax and nontax liability consists of payments incurred, not payments made.

LIABILITY, JOINT Liability for which more than one person or company share responsibility.

LIABILITY, LEGAL An obligation enforceable by law most often considered in a monetary sense.

LIABILITY, LIMITED Responsibility in event of bankruptcy limited to the amount invested in the business.

LIABILITY LIMITS The sum or sums beyond which a liability insurance company does not protect the insured on a particular policy.

LIABILITY, PRIMARY A direct liability as differentiated from an indirect or contingent liability.

LIABILITY, SECONDARY A contingent liability.

LIAISON The contact maintained between units, in order to ensure concerted action.

LICENSE The document embodying the formal permission from a legally constituted governing authority to carry on a certain activity, the conduct of which would otherwise be illegal. Usually used for revenue and/or regulatory purposes.

LIEN A charge or claim against the property of another until some claim against that person is paid or satisfied.

LIFE ESTATE A freehold interest in land, the duration of which is confined to the life of one or more persons or contingent upon certain happenings.

LIFE EXPECTANCY The length of time a person of a given age may be expected to live according to the statistical tables that have been worked out.

LIFE TENANT One who owns an estate in real property for his own lifetime or for another person's lifetime or for an indefinite period bounded by a lifetime.

LIFO See "last in, first out."

LIMITED (LTD.) A corporation. While mostly associated with British or Canadian business firms using the corporate form and thus having limited liability, the term is sometimes used in the United States and has the same meaning.

LIMITED AUDIT An audit in which the effectiveness of the system of internal control and the mathematical accuracy, legality, propriety, and completeness of all transactions are determined by examining only selected items.

LIMITED DEPOSITARY A Federal Reserve System member bank which under stated restrictions may receive governmental deposits.

LIMITED PARTNER A member of a partnership who as a result of giving up an active voice in management and publicly announcing in the legally required way that he is a limited partner acquires limited liability.

LIMITED PARTNERSHIP A partnership consisting of both general and special partners, with at least one member, the manager, being fully responsible for all debts.

LINE OF CREDIT A term applied to a maximum amount of credit which a bank will extend to a particular borrower (usually a business concern) over a stated period, subject to certain conditions which must be met by the borrower, such as maintaining a specified balance in his checking account.

LIQUIDATION The process of paying the liabilities of a business, selling the assets, and distributing the remaining cash to the owner or owners of the business.

LIQUIDITY 1) A term used to describe the solvency of a business, and which has special reference to the degree of readiness in which assets can be converted into cash without loss.
2) The ability of the market in a particular security to absorb a reasonable amount of buying or selling at reasonable price changes.

LIQUIDITY PREFERENCE The tendency for people to keep their assets in a form that is cash or easily converted into cash rather than in a frozen form.

LISTED SECURITIES Securities that have been accepted for trading on a recognized securities exchange.

LISTING The record of property for sale or lease and services being booked or sold by a broker or agent who has been authorized in writing by the owners and/or managers to act as their agent or representative.

LIST PRICE The posted, published price which may at times be reduced by such devices as volume discounts, commissions, discounts for prompt payment, or other rebate.

LITIGATION The act of carrying on a lawsuit.

LIVING TRUST A trust that becomes operative during the lifetime of the settlor; opposed to a trust under will.

LLOYD'S ASSOCIATION A group of individual insurance underwriters who make contributions to a common fund. The individual contributors are liable for the amount of the risk placed after their respective names in the policy in proportion to their contribution. Any individual underwriter is not liable for the others' assumed risk or loss.

LLOYD'S OF LONDON An insurance carrier in the nature of a board of trade or insurance mart, where individual underwriters gather for the purpose of quoting rates and accepting insurance on all manner of risks. Lloyd's is bound by few restrictive regulations and is free to develop special coverages to meet nearly all manner of insurance situations.

LOAN Money advanced to a borrower usually to be repaid with interest, and evidenced by notes, bonds, etc.

LOAN INTEREST Explicit interest. The amount paid for the use of capital or money.

LOAN RATE The charge at which loan funds can be had at a given time and at a given lending source.

LOAN VALUE The largest amount that can be borrowed on an item, such as the wholesale price of a car or the security of the cash value of a live insurance policy. The idea is for the lender not to be overcommitted in the event of default on the part of the borrower.

LOCAL UNION The basic unit in union organization. The local has its own constitution and bylaws, and elects its own officers, but it is chartered by the international with which it is affiliated.

LOCKED-IN An investor is said to be locked-in when he has a profit on a security he owns but does not sell because his profit would immediately become subject to the capital gains tax. See "capital gain."

LOCKOUT Shutdown of a plant by the employer to discourage union membership or activity.

LOCKUP Refers to securities that have been withdrawn from circulation and placed in a safe-deposit box for purposes of long-term investment.

LONG 1) Signifies ownership of securities. "I am long 100 United States Steel" means the speaker owns 100 shares. See "short."
2) One is said to be net "long" of the futures market if he has bought more contracts than he has sold—the opposite of "short."

LONG AND SHORT HAUL CLAUSE The Fourth Section of the Interstate Commerce Act, Part I, which prohibits a transportation line from charging more for a shorter than for a longer haul over the same route, except by special permission of the Interstate Commerce Commission, hence the term "Long and Short Haul Clauses."

LONG POSITION A market attitude of one who actually owns securities, that is, one who is expecting a rise in prices or holding for income as opposed to one who has a short position.

LONG TERM A period of six months or more as opposed to the short or near-term period of less than six months. Long-term securities profits are accorded a more favorable tax treatment than short-term gains.

LONG-TERM TREND 1) A pattern to be studied or analyzed for a period of six months or more.

2) The basic direction in which market prices seem likely to move over a period of time in the future.

LOSS LEADERS (price leaders) Items which a dealer sells at very low prices, sometimes below cost, in order to increase store traffic. The dealer hopes the people who come to buy the low-priced items will buy enough other goods at profitable prices to more than make up for the loss he suffers on the leaders.

LOSS-PAYABLE CLAUSE A clause in an insurance contract providing for payment of a loss, for which the insurer is liable to the insured, to someone other than the insured, such as a bank holding a lien on an auto which it has financed.

LOSS RESERVE That portion of the assets of an insurance company kept in a readily available form to meet probable claims. A fund provided for the payment of losses which have been incurred but are not yet due.

LUMP-SUM Full payment made in one sum, and at one time.

LUMP-SUM APPROPRIATION An appropriation made for a stated purpose, or for a named department, without specifying further the amounts that may be spent for specific activities or for particular objects of expenditure.

LUXURY TAX A levy upon products which are not deemed to be necessities, such as liquor, jewelry, tobacco, etc.

MAINTENANCE OF MEMBERSHIP A union security system under which an employee is not required to join the union, but if he does, or, if already a member, he fails to resign during the "escape period," he binds himself to remain a member for the duration of the union contract.

MAJOR TREND The basic direction in which stock prices are moving over a period of time regardless of temporary movements contrary to trend. Also called the primary movement.

MAKER Any individual, proprietorship, corporation, or other legal entity who signs a check, draft, note, or other type of negotiable instrument as a primary responsible party is known as the maker.

MAKE-WORK PRACTICES Labor policies that compel, through hiring of extra help, the spreading of available work.

MANAGED CURRENCY A manipulated money. The currency is not permitted to respond to "natural laws" of such factors as gold points or supply and demand.

MANAGEMENT The administration and policy makers of a business or other organization. In a corporation it is the board of directors, elected by the stockholders, and the officers of the corporation, appointed by the board of directors.

MANAGEMENT FEE The amount paid to the investment adviser for its services.

MANAGEMENT STOCK 1) The stock owned by the management of a corporation.
2) Stock which having extra voting privileges can control a corporation.

MANIFEST A document listing the contents, value, origin, destination, carrier and time a cargo is shipped.

MANIPULATION 1) Operating or managing skillfully with the hands.
2) An illegal or false operation. Buying or selling a security for the purpose of creating false or misleading appearance of active trading or for the purpose of raising or depressing the price to induce purchase or sale by others.

MAN-LAND RATIO The number of people per unit of land as a method of measuring the density of population.

MANUFACTURER'S AGENT An agent who generally operates on an extended contractual basis; sells with an exclusive territory; handles noncompeting but related lines of goods; and possesses limited authority with regard to prices and terms of sale.

MANUFACTURER'S BRAND A manufacturer's or producer's brand usually enjoying wide territorial distribution.

MARGIN 1) A reserve amount or quantity. An excess of time or money over what is actually needed or required.
2) The amount deposited by a client with his broker to protect the broker against loss on contracts being carried or to be carried by the broker.

MARGINAL COST That amount of money one extra unit of production will add to the total cost of production.

MARGINAL EFFICIENCY OF CAPITAL The relationship between the return and the cost of an additional unit of capital.

MARGINAL LAND That which barely pays the cost of working or using. Land whereon the costs of operating approximately equal the gross income.

MARGINAL PRODUCER The manufacturer who is just meeting his production costs at the price he is receiving for his product.

MARGINAL REVENUE The gross income, or sale price of an additional unit of production.

MARGINAL SELLER The individual or firm which will drop out, or refuse to sell, in the event that the price of the product or service is reduced.

MARGINAL TRADING The purchasing of a security or commodity in which the buyer does not pay for the transaction entirely with his own funds but rather borrows part of the purchase price.

MARGINAL UTILITY The amount of satisfaction gained by consuming an additional unit of good.

MARGIN CALL A demand upon a customer to put up money or securities with the broker. The call is made when a purchase is made; also if a customer's equity in a margin account declines below a minimum standard set by the Exchange or by the firm. See "margin."

MARGIN OF CULTIVATION That state of utilization of agricultural land in which the income produced by the last unit of labor, capital, or management will just meet the cost of the unit.

MARGIN OF SAFETY The balance of income remaining after payment of fixed charges (or after payment of preferred dividends), expressed as a percentage of gross revenues (net sales); hence the approximate percentage by which gross revenues can decline or operating expenses can increase before the continued payment of bond interest (or of bond interest plus preferred dividends) is endangered.

MARITAL DEDUCTION The portion of a decedent's estate that may be given to the surviving wife or husband without its becoming subject to the federal estate tax levied against the decedent's estate.

MARITIME LAW Rules of conduct or action set forth by specific court (Admiralty) having jurisdiction on maritime questions and offenses.

MARKDOWN The reduction of an originally established selling price.

MARKET 1) An aggregate composed of a prospective buyer (or buyers), and a seller (or sellers), that brings to focus the conditions and forces which determine prices.
2) The aggregate demand of the potential buyers of a commodity or service.
3) The place or area in which buyers and sellers function.
4) To perform business activities which direct the flow of goods and services from producer to consumer or user.

MARKETABILITY The relative ease and quickness with which a good, property, commodity, or service can be sold; salability.

MARKET ANALYSIS A subdivision of marketing research which involves the measurement of the extent of a market and the determination of its characteristics.

MARKET DEMAND The total quantity of a good which is demanded at any one time at a given price.

MARKETING Directing and encouraging the flow of goods from producer to consumer or user.

MARKETING AGREEMENT 1) A price-fixing or similar arrangement between producers of like products. Usually illegal.
2) That system of agricultural products distribution and price-fixing permitted by law involving the approval of two-thirds of the producers and products covered by the agreement. Upon submission and acceptance by the United States Department of Agriculture the restrictions become binding not only on the agreeing majority but also on the disagreeing minority.

MARKETING COOPERATIVE One of over 7,000 organizations having over 2,000,000 members devoted to aiding their members market their products which are primarily agricultural in nature. Present tax provisions give them a distinct advantage over commercial corporations in the same field.

MARKETING RESEARCH Gathering, recording and analyzing facts relating to the transfer and sale of products.

MARKET ORDER An order to a stock broker from a client to buy or sell stocks or bonds at the price prevailing when the order reaches the market.

MARKET PENETRATION Extent to which a given establishment, firm or plant shares or dominates the sales in a given market area.

MARKET PRICE 1) That price which prevails in a market at a given period of time.
2) The point of intersection of a supply and a demand schedule of a market.
3) In the case of a security, market price is usually considered the last reported price at which the stock or bond sold.

MARKET VALUE The price of a good, property, service, security, or commodity, as determined by current market transactions.

MARKUP The amount added to the cost of merchandise or services when they are first priced to cover expenses and provide a profit; also called initial markup.

MARXIAN Any economic or political concept believed to have been proposed by, or which follows the philosophy of Karl Marx—communism.

MASSACHUSETTS TRUST An unincorporated organization created for profit under a written instrument or declaration of trust, by the terms of which the property held in trust is managed by compensated trustees for the benefit of a person whose legal interests are represented by transferable certificates of participation or shares; also called business trust.

MASS PICKETING Patrolling by large numbers of closely ranked persons, often strikers, preventing access to company premises and often conveying threats of violence.

MASS PRODUCTION Production by machinery; assembly line; in great quantity.

MATERIAL COST That cost of a product which is due only to the cost of raw material and would not include such indirect expenses as wages, rent, interest and management costs.

MATURE ECONOMY That stage of development of a nation's economy where a decline in the rate of growth has occurred on a relatively permanent basis. During the 1930's a number of economists described the United States as a mature economy. However, the growth periods following 1950 indicate that they mistook a cyclical reversal for a long-term trend.

MATURITY The time when a note, draft, acceptance, bond, insurance policy or other instrument becomes due for payments.

MATURITY DATE The date upon which a financial obligation or other contract becomes due for payments or expires.

MATURITY VALUE The amount that must be paid on the date a financial obligation becomes due.

MAXIMUM-HOUR LEGISLATION Part of the Fair Labor Standards Act of 1938 as amended, which covers employees in interstate commerce and restricts regular hourly minimum rates to a forty-hour week. Hours in excess of 40 are reimbursed at a rate of 150% of the regular rate.

MEASURED DAY RATE A technique for piecework compensation based upon the employees' production for the preceding day.

MECHANIC'S LIEN A claim against title to property placed by or for the benefit of one who has performed labor or has furnished material in improving the property.

MEDIATOR Serves as a referee to help people decide for themselves, but does not impose a binding decision. Advises with worker and employer in labor disputes.

MEDIUM OF EXCHANGE Any commodity (commonly money) which is widely accepted in payment for goods and services and in settlement of debts, and is accepted without reference to the standing of the person who offers it in payment.

MEMBER BANK The term applied to any bank, either national or state, that is a member of the Federal Reserve System. A state bank that is not a member of the system is termed a nonmember bank.

MEMBER CORPORATION A securities brokerage firm, organized as a corporation, with at least one member of the New York Stock Exchange who is a director and a holder of voting stock in the corporation.

MEMBER FIRM A securities brokerage firm organized as a partnership and having at least one general partner who is a member of the New York Stock Exchange.

MEMORANDUM ACCOUNT The record of an account maintained by a bank which is not included in its assets or liabilities. An example is the record of a bad debt written off, on which subsequent recoveries are anticipated.

MEMORANDUM BUYING A marketing and selling technique in which the producer is not paid for his goods until the retailer has sold the merchandise to the consumer.

MERCANTILE AGENCY That organization such as Dun and Bradstreet or local credit bureau which supplies credit information on applicants for credit to its members. In addition, the agency may also perform other functions, such as collection of past-due accounts and trade-collection statistics.

MERCANTILISM The system of business from about 1550 to 1850 in England in which great emphasis was put on retention of a favorable balance of trade.

MERCHANDISE Goods bought for the purpose of resale.

MERCHANDISE TURNOVER The number of times that a business buys and sells a stock of goods during a year.

MERCHANDISING The process of distributing a product or a service by systematic and carefully planned promotion and directed sales effort.

MERCHANTABLE Salable in the ordinary way; fit for ordinary uses to which it is put.

MERCHANT MARINE A nation's facilities and equipment for carrying on trade and international commerce on the ocean.

MERCHANT MIDDLEMAN A middleman who takes title to the goods he stocks and sells.

MERGER When two or more businesses join together and form a single company.

MERIT RATING 1) In insurance, a system used in measuring the differences of a specific risk from some moral, or other standard, in order to correct the manual rate for that risk.
2) In personnel administration, the regular review of an employee's performance. Merit rating may be for purposes of promotion, layoff, firing or training.

METES AND BOUNDS A method of describing land through the use of boundaries and measurements of a parcel of real estate.

MIDDLEMAN A business concern that specializes in performing functions or rendering services immediately involved in the purchase and/or sale of goods in the process of their flow from producer to consumer.

MINERAL RIGHTS The right or title to all or to certain, specified minerals in a given tract of land.

MINIMUM RATE 1) In insurance rating, a general class for risks of low hazard, with many units in the class. Opposed to "schedule rate" and "specific rate." See "class rate."
2) In public utility rates, it is the rate established by the regulatory body below which a utility may not charge for a service.

MINIMUM WAGE Lowest amount of money that may be paid to workers, as prescribed by law.

MINOR A person under legal age, that is, under the age at which he or she is accorded full civil rights; the same as an infant.

MINT The establishment or place where coins are made from metal under the supervision of an authorized governmental official.

MINUTE BOOK A book in which is kept an official record of the proceedings of various meetings such as stockholders' meetings and board of directors' meetings.

MISSIONARY SALESMAN A salesman employed by a manufacturer to make contact with and work with the customers of his distributors, usually for the purpose of developing goodwill and stimulating demand, helping or inducing them to promote the sale of his employer's goods, helping them train their salesmen to do so, and often taking orders for delivery by such distributors.

MIXED ACCOUNTS In accounting and bookkeeping, accounts whose balances are part asset and part expense or part liability and part income.

MIXED ECONOMY Most western economies today are mixed economies in that they have characteristics of both capitalism and socialism in varying degrees.

MIXED PROPERTY Property which has some of the attributes of both real property and personal property, such as fixtures and keys to a house.

MODEL A representation of a thing in miniature or, in the case of economics, in mathematical terms.

MODIFIED UNION SHOP Provision in a contract that requires all new employees to join the union within a stated period after employment, but does not require present employees to join the union. However, all employees who are or who become union members must retain membership in good standing as a condition of employment.

MONETARY RESERVES The amount of gold and silver held by the Treasury or monetary authorities to secure the issue of credit money in circulation.

MONETARY STANDARD The standard upon which a country's money is issued.

MONETARY SYSTEM Description of the legal standard money of a nation and the related legislation on reserves, coinage, and methods of redemption and conversion.

MONETARY UNIT A country's unit of money.

MONEY Those things which are generally acceptable in any society, and which pass freely from hand to hand as mediums of exchange.

MONEY BROKER An individual or firm, sometimes called a "finder" who brings those needing money to those who lend money and for this expects a fee. See "finder's fee."

MONEY IN CIRCULATION Total amount of currency and coin outside the Treasury and the Federal Reserve Banks.

MONEY MARKET Market for short-term, high-grade, open-market assets.

MONEY RATES Those rates of interest which lenders are charging various classes of borrowers.

MONEY WAGE That amount paid to an employee in money.

MONOMETALLISM A single-standard monetary system in which one metal, generally gold, is given free and unlimited coinage.

MONOPOLISTIC COMPETITION That situation in which one or two buyers or sellers can influence the price of a product in a market.

MONOPOLY Exclusive control of a commodity or service in a particular market.

MONTHLY INVESTMENT PLAN A methodical investment technique introduced by members of the New York Stock Exchange in 1954 to allow a public investor to acquire stock on a regular, convenient basis, with payments ranging from $40 every three months to $1000 every month.

MORAL HAZARD Refers to the risk resulting from the personal habits of the insured which may increase the possibility of loss due to carelessness or dishonesty.

MORATORIUM That period of time, generally some emergency such as war, depression, or bank holiday, during which the normal activities and transactions of everyday life, either personal or business, are temporarily postponed.

MORE-FAVORABLE-TERMS CLAUSE That part of a union contract in which the union agrees not to negotiate any more favorable terms with the employer's competitors than the employer has agreed to. In this case, the term refers to favoring an employer and not the union.

MORNING LOAN Loans made by banks to stockbrokers on an unsecured basis for the purpose of the broker handling his stock deliveries until reimbursed by his customer.

MORTALITY TABLE A table showing the probable death rate per year, and expectation of life at any given age.

MORTGAGE An instrument by which the borrower (mortgagor) gives the lender (mortgagee) a lien on real estate as security for a loan. The borrower continues to use the property, and when the loan is repaid, the lien is removed.

MORTGAGE BANKER A banker who specializes in mortgage financing; an operator of a mortgage financing company. They also disburse funds for taxes, insurance, etc., as escrow agents.

MORTGAGE CERTIFICATE An interest in a mortgage evidenced by the instrument, generally a fractional portion of the mortgage, which certifies as to the agreement between the mortgagees who hold the certificates and the mortgagor as to such terms as principal, amount, date of payment, and place of payment.

MORTGAGE CLAUSE Clause in an insurance policy which makes the proceeds payable to the holder of a mortgage on the insured property to the extent of his interest in that property.

MORTGAGE COMPANY Mortgage financing companies are mortgagees themselves, as well as being mortgage agents for other large mortgagees. Serving as mortgage agents, these mortgage bankers collect payments, maintain complete mortgage records, and make remittances to the mortgagees for a set fee or service charge.

MORTGAGEE The institution, group or person which lends the money in a mortgage transaction.

MORTGAGE LOAN A loan secured by a mortgage on real estate. Also called a real estate loan.

MORTGAGE, OPEN-END A mortgage which permits the mortgagee to make additional advances, to be added to the principal balance to be secured by the mortgage, without prejudice to the position of the mortgagee as a senior lienor or encumbrancer.

MORTGAGOR An owner of property who executes a mortgage pledging that property as security for a debt.

MOST-FAVORED-NATION CLAUSE That part of an international commercial treaty in which the signatory nations agree to grant to no other nation trade concessions or duties more favorable than granted to the signatory nations.

MOTOR CARRIER ACT Federal statute under which the Interstate Commerce Commission may regulate hours of service of interstate passenger and freight motor vehicle operators.

MULTICRAFT UNION A union which members of several different crafts, trades, or occupations may join.

MULTILATERAL AGREEMENT The accord of more than two individuals, firms, governments, or parties.

MULTILINEAR TARIFF A tariff which has a separate schedule of duties for each nation or group of nations. Also called multiple tariff.

MULTIPLE CURRENCY SYSTEM A method of control for foreign exchange. The domestic currency may only be exchanged into foreign currency through a government agency or controlled bank. The rate of exchange will vary according to the product or use being made of the exchange. Generally, essentials such as farm machinery and tools are given a more favorable rate than luxuries.

MULTIPLE EXPANSION OF DEPOSITS (OR CREDIT) The nature of operation of a fractional reserve commercial banking system such as is found in the United States. A bank with excess reserves makes a loan and thus creates a deposit; when the deposit is withdrawn and spent it tends to be deposited in a bank creating excess reserves which, in turn, may be lent and cause a multiple expansion of credit or deposits. The rate of expansion is determined by the reserve requirement. A 10% reserve requirement in theory could have an expansion of ten times, while a 20% would have a five times expansion potential.

MULTIPLIER PRINCIPLE The ratio between the increase in income and the increase in the formation of new capital used by followers of Keynes to recommend large-scale government spending during depressions as a means of increasing national income.

MUNICIPAL Pertaining to the local government of a town or city.

MUNICIPAL CORPORATION An incorporated political subdivision such as a town, county or city.

MUNICIPAL IMPROVEMENT CERTIFICATES Certificates issued in lieu of bonds for the financing of special improvements.

MUNICIPALS A word which in its broad sense designates the securities of any state, or of any political subdivision of a state, including cities, counties, towns, villages, districts and authorities.

MUNICIPAL SOCIALISM The situation in which a municipality owns and operates one or more utilities such as transit lines, waterworks, power generators, or gas producers.

MUTUAL BENEFIT ASSOCIATION Fraternal societies, social groups, other organizations, or corporations for the relief of members of the group operating on a corporate or assessment insurance plan. The features of this plan provide that the payment of losses is not met by fixed premiums payable in advance, but by assessments intended to liquidate specific losses.

MUTUAL COMPANY A company with a corporate form but no stock; profits being dispersed on the basis of the amount of business a member did with the company.

MUTUAL FUND The shorter and more popular term for an open-end investment company.

MUTUAL INSURANCE COMPANIES Companies with no capital stock, owned by policyholders. Trustees of the company are chosen by the policyholders. The earnings of the company, over and above the payments of the losses and operating expenses and reserves, are the property of the policyholders.

MUTUAL MORTGAGE INSURANCE FUND A fund (established under the provisions of the National Housing Act) into which mortgage insurance premiums and other specified revenue of the Federal Housing Administration are paid and from which losses are met.

MUTUAL SAVINGS BANK A bank that is owned by the depositors and managed for them by a self-perpetuating board of trustees. It has no capital stock and therefore no stockholders.

NARROW MARKET A thin market. A condition in the securities' market characterized by low volume of trading and slight variation in quotations.

NATIONAL ADVISORY COUNCIL ON INTERNATIONAL MONETARY AND FINANCIAL PROBLEMS Comprised of the Secretary of State, the Secretary of the Treasury, the Secretary of Commerce, Chairman of the Board of Governors of the Federal Reserve System and the Export-Import Bank. Its function is to coordinate the policies of the United States in the World Bank and the International Monetary Fund.

NATIONAL ASSOCIATION OF SECURITIES DEALERS A voluntary association of brokers and dealers handling over-the-counter securities, formed after the Maloney Act of 1938. This special legislation was passed to regulate the over-the-counter market. The association has importance to members because they receive reduced commission from each other.

NATIONAL BANK A corporation organized under a federal banking law (National Bank Act), and authorized to do a general or commercial banking business—that is, receive deposits subject to check, and make loans. It usually performs a variety of other functions as well. A national bank must have the word "national" in its corporate title.

NATIONAL BANK ACT The legislation under which national banks were formed and operate. See "national bank."

NATIONAL BANK NOTE A type of currency issued in the United States. National bank notes are backed by two types of United States Government bonds—2% consols of 1930, and the 2% Panama Canal bonds of 1916-36 and 1918-38. These bonds were called for redemption by the Bank Act of 1935, and so no further issuance of national bank notes was authorized. They are being retired from circulation. National bank notes are in denominations of 5, 10, 20, 50, and 100 dollars, and each has a brown seal and the issuing bank's charter number on its face.

NATIONAL BANKRUPTCY ACT This act, as frequently amended, has established uniform laws on bankruptcy in all the states. In its present state it contains numerous chapters covering the procedures for handling the various bankrupt organizations ranging from individual through corporate, municipal, and railroad reorganization.

NATIONAL BRAND A manufacturer's or producer's brand usually enjoying wide territorial distribution.

NATIONAL BUREAU OF STANDARDS Part of the United States Department of Commerce. Works in areas of testing, standardization, measurement, and values.

NATIONAL CAPITALISM Economic and political system in which the national government exercises great control over the use of capital and may engage in competition with private enterprise in such sectors as power and utilities.

NATIONAL DEBT The total amount owed by a national government.

NATIONAL ECONOMY The entire economic life of a country.

NATIONAL INCOME A measure of the aggregate earnings of a nation's labor and property which result in the production of new goods and services in a given period of time.

NATIONAL INDUSTRIAL RECOVERY ACT Legislation enacted in 1933 which established the Public Works Administration and the National Recovery Administration. Parts of the act were declared unconstitutional by the Supreme Court of the United States in 1935.

NATIONALIZATION The conversion from private ownership and operation of a business activity to control and operation and, at times, ownership by a national government.

NATIONAL LABOR RELATIONS ACT Federal statute, originally known as the Wagner Act and now a part of the Taft-Hartley Act, which guarantees to employees in industries affecting interstate commerce the right to self-organization, to bargain collectively and to engage in concerted activities.

NATIONAL LABOR RELATIONS BOARD (NLRB) Agency established to determine collective-bargaining representatives and prevent unfair labor practices.

NATIONAL MINIMUM A federal social welfare policy which establishes a standard of living below which people should not experience because of public charitable assistance and welfare, or social security.

NATIONAL PRODUCT See "gross national product."

NATIONAL SECURITY EXCHANGE A stock and securities exchange classified as such by the Securities Exchange Commission. Included are most of the larger exchanges in the United States. Only a few small exchanges are not designated as national security exchanges. Not to be confused with National Stock Exchange.

NATIONAL STOCK EXCHANGE Newest stock exchange, founded in 1960 in New York City. The third stock exchange in that city, the other two being the New York Stock Exchange and the American Stock Exchange. Not to be confused with national security exchange.

NATIONAL UNION A union with local unions and members throughout the United States but without foreign local unions or members.

NATIONAL WEALTH The monetary sum of all the material assets owned by citizens and institutions of a country as of a stated time and which are within the borders of the nation, plus the material assets owned outside the nation. A number of nations assume a balance between assets owned abroad and assets within a nation owned by foreigners, and thus count all material assets, irrespective of ownership within their borders. Material assets are used to prevent duplication of counting assets such as currency or securities.

NATURAL CAPITAL Land when used as a factor of production.

NATURAL MONOPOLY A situation characterized by the obviousness of having only one producer of a service rather than many competitors. Electrical production and other utilities are typical natural monopolies. A natural monopoly may also come about because of unique mineral deposits, water flow, or soil characteristics. The owner of land upon which may be found minerals that are not to be found on other lands may be considered to have a natural monopoly.

NATURAL RIGHTS The rights to life, liberty, and the pursuit of happiness provided the pursuit does not infringe upon the rights of others. Governments do not have the legal sanction to deny natural rights under the Declaration of Independence of the United States.

NEAR-MONEY Time deposits in commercial banks, savings and loan shares, Treasury bills, and other very liquid assets are considered near-money since they may be converted into money very easily.

NEGATIVE-PLEDGE CLAUSE A covenant in an indenture to the effect that the corporation will not pledge any of its assets unless the notes or debentures outstanding under the particular indenture are at least equally secured by such pledge; also called the covenant of equal coverage.

NEGLIGENCE Failure to do what a reasonably prudent individual would ordinarily do under the circumstances of a particular case, or doing what a prudent person would not have done.

NEGOTIABLE Something which can be sold or transferred to another for money or in payment of a debt.

NEPOTISM Practice by those in positions of power and influence such as corporate management or public office, of giving promotions, higher earnings, better jobs, and other benefits to employees who are their relatives or friends.

NET COST 1) The actual cost of something, after all income or other financial gain is subtracted from the gross cost.
2) In insurance, the total premiums paid on a policy, minus any dividends, and the surrender value as of the date of the determination of the so-called net cost.

NET DEBT The total of all debt after deducting such items as sinking funds.

NET EARNINGS The amount of the gross income less the operating expenses and any other expenses and before payment of any dividends.

NET FREE OR NET BORROWED RESERVES Excess reserves less member bank borrowings from Federal Reserve Banks. The resulting difference is called net free when positive, and net borrowed when negative.

NET INCOME In general, synonymous with net earnings, but considered a broader and better term; the balance remaining, after deducting from the gross income all operating expense, maintenance, taxes and losses pertaining to operating properties, excepting interest or other financial charges on borrowed or other capital.

NET LEASE A lease where, in addition to the rental stipulated, the lessee assumes payment of all property charges such as taxes, insurance and maintenance.

NET NATIONAL DEBT National debt less such amounts held in United States trust accounts.

NET NATIONAL PRODUCT A measure of the aggregate market value of all goods and services which do not replace wornout, damaged or obsolete capital goods, and which are produced by the economy within a given period of time. Thus, it equals gross national product less capital consumption allowances.

NET OPTION A written instrument which grants the right to purchase property at a specified price to the owner.

NET PRICE The price paid after all deductions such as discounts, rebates, allowances and kickbacks.

NET PROFIT The actual profit realized by a business over a specified period of time, or for an individual transaction or sale, after deducting all costs from gross receipts.

NET SALES Sales minus discounts, allowances, and returns.

NET WORTH The excess of the assets of an individual or an enterprise over all his or its liabilities.

NET YIELD The return obtained from an investment after deduction of costs and losses involved in procuring and managing the investment.

NEW DEAL The popular designation for the political policies and administration of the late President of the United States, Franklin D. Roosevelt.

NEW ISSUE A stock or bond sold by a corporation for the first time. Proceeds may be used to retire outstanding securities of the company, for new plants or equipment, or for additional working capital.

NEW YORK STOCK EXCHANGE The major security exchange in the world. It is an unincorporated association in which membership is limited in number and may be obtained only upon acceptance by a membership committee. Such membership is called "a seat." See "stock exchanges."

NEXT OF KIN The person or persons in the nearest degree of blood relationship to a person.

NO-LIMIT ORDER Means the opposite of a limit order; in other words, it is a market order because it has no stipulation as to prices. May be either a buy or sell order.

NO-LOAD FUND A mutual fund which has no sales organization but whose sponsor sells shares directly to the public for little or no commission (load charge).

NOMINAL ACCOUNT In bookkeeping, a ledger account which is closed out when the books are balanced.

NOMINAL INTEREST RATE The contractual interest rate shown on the face and in the body of a bond, and representing the amount of interest to be paid, in contrast with the effective interest rate.

NOMINAL QUOTE The probable price of a security, based upon an evaluation of previous prices of the security or of similar securities.

NOMINAL YIELD The amount of interest stated on an instrument's face. The amount of dividend stated on the face of the stock (if preferred).

NONASSESSABLE STOCK A type of security which cannot be assessed in the event of insolvency or failure, *i.e.,*

it is fully paid for. Most stocks are of this nature, thus the holder cannot be assessed.

NONCONFORMING USE Any building or land lawfully occupied by a use at the time of the passage of a zoning resolution or subsequent amendments thereto, which does not conform after the passage of the resolution or amendments thereto, with all the regulations of the district in which said building or land is situated.

NONFORFEITURE OPTIONS Options available to an insured after policy values have been established.

NON-INTEREST-BEARING NOTE A note on which the maker is not required to pay interest.

NONOPERATING INCOME An increase in the income of a business that is derived from gains through the financial control of the business rather than through sales or other operations of the business. It is also known as financial income, nonrecurring income, or other income.

NONPAR ITEM Item for which the drawee bank will not remit to a collecting bank without deducting an exchange charge.

NONPROFIT INSTITUTIONS Enterprises set up to do some useful service and seek no profit; colleges, schools, churches, also such foundations established to better business relationships and understanding with and by the public, etc.

NONRECOURSE A situation in which the holder of an instrument does not have the legal right to compel a prior endorser or drawer to pay the amount of the negotiable instrument if it is dishonored. This may be because of a prior endorsement having the term "nonrecourse" as part of the endorsement. Or it may be because the holder is not "in due course."

NONWAIVER AGREEMENT Assent by the insured that investigation and determination of the value of the claim by the insurance company does not constitute an admission that the insurance company has assumed liability.

NO-PAR VALUE Having no face value.

NORMAL PRICE That price which will balance the supply and demand for a product for an extended period of time and to which the price will tend to return upon fluctuation up or down. Sometimes called the equilibrium price.

NOTARY PUBLIC A quasi-public official appointed by a state governor or other appointing authority to perform designated duties, such as attesting signatures on documents and administering oaths.

NOTE A written promise to pay a definite sum of money on demand or at a specified tie.

NOTES PAYABLE An account in the ledger showing the liability for notes given by the business.

NOTES RECEIVABLE Promissory notes received by the business from its customers.

NUISANCE TAX A levy or duty which provides less revenue than the value of the time needed to compute and pay the tax.

OBJECTIVE VALUE The price which an economic good can command in terms of other goods in the market.

OBLIGATION An amount of money or contracted performance one is morally or legally bound to pay or carry out.

OBLIGEE One to whom an obligation is owed, such as a bondholder.

OBLIGOR One who has an obligation to discharge, such as a corporation which issues bonds.

OBSOLESCENCE The decrease in value caused by changes in models and new inventions that render previous versions or models out of date.

OCCUPATIONAL LEVEL The degree of vocational skill, such as laborer, foreman, semiprofessional, professional, or other intermediate classifications.

OCCUPATION TAX A privilege tax for engaging in a covered line of business activity. Plumbers, barbers, and most professions have to pay such a tax as a license to engage in the designated activity.

OCCUPIED 1) Presently in possession or use.
2) Applied to a building, shall be construed as though followed by the words "or intended, arranged or designed to be occupied."

OCCURRENCE A continuance or repeated exposure to conditions which result in injury. A clause frequently found under a personal liability policy; *e.g.*, all damages which arise out of the same general conditions are considered as arising from one occurrence. A leaky gas heater in a home might cause illness over a period of days without the person exposed to it being completely overcome at any one time. Such illness would be described as due to one occurrence under terms of a personal liability policy.

ODD LOT An amount of stock less than the established 100-share unit of 10-share unit of trading: From 1 to 99 shares for the great majority of issues, 1 to 9 for so-called inactive stocks. See "round lot" and "inactive stock."

ODD-LOT DEALER A broker or a dealer who assembles orders to buy or sell smaller quantities of a security than the normal trading unit and who consolidates such orders into a round-lot transaction.

OFF-BOARD This term may refer to transactions over-the-counter in unlisted securities, or, in a special situation, to a transaction involving a block of listed shares which was not executed on a national securities exchange. See "over-the-counter" and "secondary distribution."

OFFER 1) To present for acceptance or refusal.
2) The price at which a seller will sell.

OFFERING PRICE See "asked price."

OFFICIAL EXCHANGE RATE The rate at which the monetary authority of a nation will exchange its currency for the currency of another nation.

OFFICER'S CHECK Same as cashier's check.

ONE-THOUSAND-HOUR CLAUSE A provision of the Fair Labor Standards Act which limits a worker covered under the Act to no more than one thousand hours of work during a single 26-week period.

ON MARGIN Securities which have been purchased by a customer who borrowed part of the purchase price from the broker, *i.e.*, they are not fully paid for.

OPEN ACCOUNT Credit (usually unsecured) extended to an individual, firm, corporation, or other legal entity based on an estimate of the general ability to pay, as distinguished from credit extended that is supported by a note, mortgage, or other formal written evidence of indebtedness.

OPEN CERTIFICATE An insurance policy under which the rates and policy provisions may be changed. Fraternal insurance companies are required by law to issue this type of certificate.

OPEN COMPETITION A trade designation for the practice of firms in an industry of exchanging trade data such as prices, backlog of orders, past-due accounts, orders, production rate, etc.

OPEN-DOOR POLICY A policy whereby citizens and goods of foreign nations receive the same treatment as domestic citizens and goods.

OPEN-END CONTRACT The contract of a supplier to furnish all the required designated material to a purchaser for a stated period of time, even though the total volume is not known at the time the contract is signed.

OPEN-END INVESTMENT COMPANY A company, popularly known as a "mutual fund," which stands ready to redeem its shares at any time, usually at the prevailing net asset value per share. With rare exceptions, such companies also continuously offer new shares to investors.

OPEN-END INVESTMENT TRUST An investment trust in which the trustee, by the terms of the trust, is authorized to invest in shares of stock other than those in the trust at the time of the inception of the trust or of the participation in the trust.

OPENING The time or price at which trading begins in a commodity or security. Some orders to buy or sell are to be executed at the "opening."

OPENING ENTRY 1) In accounting and bookkeeping, an entry that is made in the general journal to record the assets, liabilities, and proprietorship of a new business at the time the business is organized, or of a going concern at the time a new set of books is opened.
2) The first entry that is made in opening a new set of books. It is recorded in the general journal and presents a complete record of the assets, the liabilities, and the proprietorship as of the date of the entry.

OPENING PRICE The price of the first transaction in the security during the day is termed the opening price and constitutes one of the important quotations carried in financial publications. See "opening" and "opening range."

OPENING RANGE Commodities, unlike securities, are often traded at several prices at the opening or close of the market. Buying or selling orders at the opening might be filled at any point in such a price range for the commodity.

OPEN INTEREST In a contract market, it is the total position on one side of the market shown by all clearing brokers at any given time. In any one delivery month the short interest equals the long interest; in other words, the total number of contracts sold equals the total number bought.

OPEN LETTER OF CREDIT   An open letter has no restrictions on the presenting of documents such as bills of lading against drafts, and is paid simply on a valid draft. See "letter of credit."

OPEN MARKET   A highly competitive and broad market without limitations as to the qualifications of either the purchaser or seller.

OPEN-MARKET OPERATIONS   The actions of the Federal Reserve Bank of New York in carrying out the instructions of the Federal Open Market Committee to buy and sell government securities as one of the major tools of monetary policy. In most cases, bills are bought or sold for the accounts of the twelve Federal Reserve Banks. Buying creates excess reserves and eases the interst-rate structure. Selling government securities reduces reserves and firms interest rates.

OPEN MORTGAGE   A past-due mortgage which is being held by the mortgagee without requiring refinancing or the execution of an extension agreement.

OPEN ORDER   An order to buy or sell a security at a specified price. An open order remains in effect until executed or canceled by the customer.

OPEN SHOP   A shop in which union membership is neither required as a condition of securing, nor of retaining employment.

OPEN TRADE   A transaction which has not yet been closed.

OPEN UNION   A labor union which does not restrict membership by any discriminatory devices such as by establishing bloodline relationship to existing members, high initiation fees, or race.

OPERATING COST   Cost of maintenance, utilities, office supplies, salaries, and such, required to keep a business or organization running.

OPERATING EXPENSE   All expenses incurred in the normal operation of a business or other organization.

OPERATING PROFIT   For purposes of marketing, gross margin (gross profit), less operating expenses (including salaries of managers, whether proprietors or employees), fixed plant and equipment cost, and sometimes interest on invested capital.

OPERATING RATIO   The ratio of the operating expenses to the operating revenues.

OPERATING STATEMENT   A tabulation of data, generally of a financial nature, such as income and outgo for a stated period such as week, month, or year.

OPTIMUM POPULATION   The population which can produce the greatest per capita output with a given amount of land, capital, and technology.

OPTION   The right to buy something at a certain price within a certain time.

OPTIONAL DIVIDEND   A dividend in which the shareholder has the right of choice of a cash dividend or a stock dividend.

ORDER   Has several meanings. 1) A written instruction or commission to do something such as buy, sell, negotiate, or supply.
2) A direction from a proper court of jurisdiction.
3) Regulation.

ORDER BILL OF LADING   A special form of bill of lading that is used in C.O.D. freight shipments. It is negotiable, and is good only to the person in whose favor it is drawn or the person to whom it is endorsed.

ORDINARY INTEREST   Interest computed on the basis of 360 days to the year—12 months of 30 days each.

ORDINARY RENT   The periodic payment for the use of such capital goods as machinery or land.

ORIGINAL COST   All costs associated with the acquisition of a fixed asset necessary to place it in effective use.

ORIGINAL-ISSUE STOCK   Those shares which were initially issued at the time the corporation was formed and are part of the starting capitalization.

OTHER EXPENSE   An expense not considered to be one of the regular operating expenses of a business or other organization.

OTHER INCOME   A financial gain derived from unusual sources, not regular routine operation transactions of a business, or not from an individual's usual source of income.

OUTLAW STRIKES   Work stoppages which lack the approval of the national or international union and usually violate either a collective agreement or the union constitution.

OUTLAY   That which is laid out or expended; cost.

OUT-OF-POCKET COSTS   Costs which are paid out or owed in cash.

OUTSIDE BROKER   An investment broker who does not belong to the local board or exchange.

OUTSIDE MARKET   Means over-the-counter, or a market where unlisted securities are traded.

OVER-AND-SHORT ACCOUNT   An account carried in the general ledger. Overages and shortages from all sources, and their nature, are posted to this account, which is also termed a "suspense" or "differences" account in banks. At the end of the fiscal period, this account is closed out to profit and loss, and becomes either an increase or a decrease to the undivided profits account in the general ledger.

OVERBOUGHT   An opinion as to price levels. May refer to a security which has had a sharp rise, or to the market as a whole after a period of vigorous buying, which, it may be argued, has left prices "too high." See "technical position."

OVERCAPITALIZED   1) A corporation whose capital is valued at less than the property which secures it.
2) A corporation whose assets exceed the need of the business. The business has too much capacity for the market for its production. Since these two meanings of the same term

vary so much, care must be taken to be sure of the context. See "watered stock."

OVERDRAFT 1) The amount by which checks, drafts, or other demands for payment on the treasury or on a bank exceed the amount of the credit against which they are drawn.
2) The amount by which requisitions, purchase orders, or audited vouchers exceed the appropriation or other credit to which they are chargeable.

OVEREXTENSION 1) Credit received or extended beyond the debtor's ability to pay.
2) The condition where a dealer in securities obligates himself for an amount beyond his borrowing power or ability to pay.
3) The expansion of buildings, equipment, etc., by a business concern which is in excess of its present or prospective future needs.

OVERHEAD Expenses, such as rent or insurance, which are not included in the actual running and operating of a business, organization, or other enterprise.

OVERLAPPING DEBT The proportionate share of the debts of local government units located wholly or in part within the limits of the reporting government which must be borne by property within such government.

OVERPRODUCTION A supply of goods greater than can be sold within a reasonable time at a price sufficient to keep a business or industry producing the product.

OVERRIDE A commission paid to managerial personnel in addition to their basic compensation.

OVERSOLD An opinion—the reverse of overbought. A single security or a market which, it is believed, has declined to an unreasonable level. See "technical position."

OVERSUBSCRIPTION The situation in which, for a given issue of securities, more orders have been received than can be filled.

OVER-THE-COUNTER A term for the method of trading when securities are not listed on a recognized securities exchange and when transactions are made either by a broker acting directly on behalf of the buyer and seller or directly by a dealer.

OVERTIME Hours worked in excess of the maximum regular number of hours fixed by statute or collective agreement.

OWNERSHIP CERTIFICATE A form furnished by the Collector of Internal Revenue for the filing of information as to the ownership of bonds containing a tax-free covenant. An ownership certificate must accompany the deposit of coupons from such bonds.

OWNERSHIP UTILITY The feeling of satisfaction in possessing things. Since most things are acquired by work, exchange, or purchase, one would not acquire something unless it provided greater satisfaction or ownership utility than that which was used to acquire it.

PACKAGED MORTGAGE PLAN A mortgage plan that permits the borrower to include as part of the mortgaged real estate such household equipment as refrigerators, ranges, and home laundries, thus bringing these articles under the lien of the mortgage.

PAID-IN CAPITAL Capital contributed by stockholders and credited to accounts other than capital stock.

PAID-IN SURPLUS That amount of surplus which was not earned but contributed to the corporation.

PAID-UP STOCK Capital stock upon which the initial purchaser from the issuing corporation has paid in goods, services, or money an amount at least as much as the par value.

PAPER PROFIT An unrealized profit on a security still held which would become realized profit if sold immediately. Paper profits become realized profits only when the security is sold.

PAR Technically, 100 percent; full value.

PARALLEL STANDARDS A monetary system in which two or more metals are coined but in which there is no exchange ratio between the metals.

PAR EXCHANGE RATE The rate or price in gold, designated by the International Monetary Fund, in cooperation with a nation's monetary authorities, at which that currency may be exchanged for the currency of another member nation of the IMF whose currency is computed on the same basis. The nations need not be on a gold standard for in this case only gold is used as the common denominator for all the IMF members' currency.

PAR ITEMS Items for which a drawee bank will remit to another bank without charge.

PARITY 1) The relationship of one foreign currency to another as indicated by their exchange value in gold or silver.
2) The relationship of agricultural prices in covered commodities, such as wheat and corn, to a base period of prices which farmers had to pay. The base period is used to measure the increase in prices for the commodities which the farmer purchases.

PAR LIST A list (issued by the Federal Reserve System) of banks which will remit in full for items payable to them.

PARTIAL LIMITATION CLAUSE A provision in an insurance policy for the payment of the total loss when a loss is more than a specified amount.

PARTIAL MONOPOLY A condition of partial monopoly in which there are so few sellers of a product or service that each may affect the price and market and, in view of this, can judge the probable impact of his actions on the other sellers.

PARTICIPATION CERTIFICATE An instrument that evidences a proportionate interest in a security or group of securites held by a trustee for the benefit of a group of investors.

PARTICIPATION LOAN Limitations have been set up by the banking laws whereby banks are not permitted to lend more than a fixed percent of their capital and surplus to any one borrower. (In most states, this fixed percent is approximately 10%.) This limitation causes banks to invite other banks to participate in making a large loan. If the financial background and credit position of the borrower warrants the large loan, several banks may each lend a portion of the amount to the borrower. The participating banks work together in handling the loan, and work out a joint agreement as to the liquidation program of the loan, since some of the banks may wish to be paid off ahead of other banks.

PARTITION A division of property held jointly or in common. It may be effected by consent of parties or by compulsion of law.

PARTNERSHIP An association of two or more persons for the conduct of an enterprise other than in corporate form. The rights, duties, and responsibilities of the people so associated may be covered by a partnership agreement or, if not, they are determined by law.

PARTNERSHIP CERTIFICATE A certificate filed with a bank showing the interest of each partner in a business enterprise operating as a partnership.

PARTY WALL A dividing wall erected upon and over a line separating two adjoining properties and in which the owners of the respective parcels have common rights to its use.

PAR VALUE The principal or nominal value appearing on a bond, note, coupon, or other instrument calling for the payment of money.

PAR-VALUE STOCK Stock that has been assigned a definite value and the value is printed on the stock certificates.

PASSED DIVIDEND Omission of a regular or scheduled dividend.

PASSIVE TRADE BALANCE A trade deficit; an unfavorable balance of trade.

PASSIVE TRUST A trust in which the trustee has no active duties to perform being merely a titleholder; the same as bare, dry, or naked trust; opposed to an active trust.

PATENT 1) A special license issued by the federal government that insures to an inventor the exclusive right to manufacture his invention for a period of seventeen years. 2) The title deed by which the United States or a state conveys its lands.

PATENT OFFICE That agency of the government which is in charge of records, granting of patents, and determining who is correct where conflicts regarding priority arise.

PATERNALISM The actions of a company or a government in providing social-welfare benefits for workers or citizens.

PATTERN BARGAINING Collective bargaining in which the union tries to apply identical terms, conditions, or demands to a number of employers in an industry although the employers act individually rather than as a group.

PAY 1) To remit; to give money or some other medium of exchange for goods delivered or services rendered. 2) To pay a check in cash, as when a check is paid by the paying teller. 3) To charge a check against a customer's account, as in the case of a check coming through the clearings.

PAYEE The person or firm to whom a promissory note or a check is payable.

PAYER The party primarily responsible for the payment of the amount owed as evidenced by a given negotiable instrument.

PAYMENT BILL A bill which is presented for payment rather than acceptance.

PAYROLL TAXES Taxes based on the wages and salaries of employees. They are also known as employment taxes.

PEGGED PRICE 1) The agreed, customary, or legal price at which any commodity has been fixed. 2) A price level for a particular security at which buying support nearly always develops and prevents a decline—thus "pegging" the price.

PENNSYLVANIA RULE A rule that requires credit of extraordinary dividends received in trust on the basis of the source of such dividends; to income if declared from earnings of the corporation during the life of the trust, and to principal if from earnings accumulated before commencement of the trust.

PENNY STOCKS Low-priced issues, often highly speculative, selling at less than $1 a share. Frequently used as a term of disparagement, although a few penny stocks have developed into investment-caliber issues.

PENSION A regular allowance made to someone who has worked a certain number of years, attained a certain age, suffered some injury, retired, etc.

PENSION PLAN An arrangement evidenced by a written agreement providing for the accumulation of funds from a corporation, or its employees, or both, to be used for monthly or other periodic payments to employees of the corporation after their retirement.

PENSION POOL A system for the payment of pension to workers in a limited geographic area in which subscribing employers all contribute according to some formula to a common fund or pool for their employees' pensions. In the event that any employee transfers from one of the subscribing employer's firm to another subscribing employer's firm, he has not lost any of the pension rights.

PER CAPITA A term expressing the result of dividing stated sums by the applicable number of people (population figures), thereby relating the sums to an amount per person, such as the proportion of a community's total debt per person.

PERCENTAGE LEASE A lease providing for payment of rent based on a percentage of the gross sales or the sales over a fixed amount.

PER-CONTRA ITEM In bookkeeping, a ledger account which exactly offsets some other ledger account.

PER DIEM Per day.

PERFECT COMPETITION The market situation where no one trader can materially affect the market for a product.

PERIL Cause of a possible loss. Perils include such things as fires, windstorms, explosions, damage suits, robbery, and accidents.

PERMISSIVE-WAGE ADJUSTMENT System authorizing the opening of negotiations for new wage rates at stated intervals during the life of a union contract, or when either party can demonstrate a significant change in factors such as prevailing wages, price of product, etc.

PERMIT A document giving the right to perform some action.

PERPETUAL INVENTORY (Book inventories) Records maintained for a manufacturing business so that they show a continuous inventory of such items as raw materials, goods in process, and finished goods.

PERPETUITY Duration without limitation as to time. See "rule against perpetuities."

PER PROCURATION The signature of a principal made by his agent. The agent instead of having power of attorney is given limited authority by the principal. The words "per procuration" call attention to the limitation, and the holder of the instrument is within his rights in requesting a statement in which the authority for the signature is given.

PERQUISITE Any incidental gain or profit from work beyond monetary wages. Meals or clothing furnished an employee are examples of such benefits.

PERSON An individual, partnership, association, joint stock company, trust, or corporation.

PERSONAL DISTRIBUTION The division of the total income of individuals among themselves.

PERSONAL FINANCE COMPANY A personal loan company which lends individuals relatively modest amounts of money at rates of interest which are generally higher than bank rates.

PERSONAL HOLDING COMPANY A device used by individuals for tax minimization. The Internal Revenue Code defines the conditions under which a corporation is considered to be a personal holding company and thus subject to special surtaxes.

PERSONAL INCOME 1) Income earned or received by an individual.
2) National income, less various kinds of income not actually received by individuals (*i.e.,* undistributed corporate profits, corporate taxes, contributions for social insurance), plus certain receipts which do not arise from production (*i.e.,* transfer payments and government interest).

PERSONAL PROPERTY The rights, powers, and privileges a person has in movable things both corporeal (as furniture and jewelry) and incorporeal (as stocks and bonds).

PERSONAL PROPERTY FLOATER An insurance policy with broad coverage for personal property either at home or away. Contractual coverage of insured's personal effects against loss or theft.

PERSONAL PROPERTY TAX A tax on personal property such as home furnishings, jewelry, securities, and bank balances but not real estate.

PERSONAL SAVING The difference between disposable personal income and personal consumption expenditures. Personal saving includes the changes in cash and deposits, security holdings, indebtedness, reserves of life insurance companies and mutual savings institutions, the net investment of unincorporated enterprises and the acquisition of real property net of depreciation. Personal saving includes saving by individuals, nonprofit institutions, and private pension, health, welfare and trust funds.

PERSONAL SURETY A person who agrees to be financially responsible for the debt of another person.

PERSONALTY Personal property.

PERSONNEL People employed in a business or other occupation.

PER STIRPES (by the branch) A term used in the distribution of property; distribution to persons as members of a family (per stirpes), and not as individuals (per capita). Two or more children of the same parent take per stirpes when together they take what the parent, if living, would take. For example, "I give my estate to my son A and to my grandsons C, D and E (the sons of my deceased son B). My grandsons are to take per stirpes." C, D and E take, as the sons of B (not as individuals), each receiving one-sixth of the estate (one-third of the one-half to which B would be entitled if living), while A receives one-half of the estate. Taking per stirpes is also known as taking by right of representation.

PETTY CASH A sum of money, either in the form of currency or a special bank deposit, set aside for the purpose of making change or immediate payments of comparatively small amounts. See "imprest fund."

PHYSICAL DISTRIBUTION Moving and handling products from the point of storage to the point of consumption or use.

PHYSICAL INVENTORY To take account of stock by actually hand-counting and listing all merchandise on hand.

PHYSICAL VALUE A term erroneously used to designate an estimate of reproduction or replacement cost, or the estimated value of physical assets as distinct from nonphysical assets.

PICKETING Union's patrolling alongside the premises of a business to organize the workers, to gain recognition as a bargaining agent, or to publicize a labor dispute with the owner or with some other firm with which the owner deals.

PIECE-RATE PLAN A form of incentive plan whereby direct labor is paid a standard amount for each piece produced. See "direct labor."

PIECEWORK A means of paying workers by the number of items the worker processes during a period of time such as hour, day, or week.

PIGGYBACK TRUCKING Transporting loaded truck trailers to distant points on railroad flatcars, rather than by pulling them over the highways by tractors.

PILFERAGE Any petty thievery or the theft of a portion of property such as theft of a tire from an automobile.

PLACE UTILITY That added value gained by having a product where it is used or consumed.

PLAGIARISM Literary or artistic theft; representing someone else's work as one's own.

PLAINTIFF Individual who brings a lawsuit against a defendant.

PLANT The building and equipment used by a business, usually a manufacturing concern.

PLAT A map or plan of an identified area of land.

PLEDGE 1) To place something as security; guarantee. 2) The transference of property, such as the cash value of a life insurance policy, to a creditor as security for a debt.

PLOTTAGE INCREMENT The increase or appreciation of the unit value resulting from the joining together of smaller lots, parcels, or land units into one large single ownership, the resulting total value being larger than the individual unit values.

POINT In the case of shares of stock, a point means $1. If General Motors shares rise 3 points, each share has risen $3. In the case of bonds, a point means $10, since a bond is quoted as a percentage of $1,000. A bond which rises 3 points gains 3 percent of $1,000, or $30 in value. An advance from 87 to 90 would mean an advance in dollar value from $870 to $900 for each $1,000 bond. In the case of market averages, the word point means merely that and no more. If, for example, the Dow-Jones industrial average rises from 1750.50 to 1751.50, it has risen a point. A point in the averages, however, is not equivalent to $1. See "average."

POINT OF IDEAL PROPORTIONS That theoretical balance of the capital, land, labor, and entrepreneurial ability in a business which would provide the greatest profit.

POINT OF INDIFFERENCE That theoretical balance of capital, land, and entrepreneurial ability in a business where one additional unit of any of the productive factors would just equal the probable return from such factor. At this point the business manager is indifferent in increasing his volume because his profit will not increase.

POLICY 1) A plan of action; a way of doing things. 2) A written agreement about insurance.

POLICYHOLDER The person insured or the one having control of the policy. Usually, but not necessarily, the insured.

POLICY LOAN A loan made by an insurance company to a policyholder on the security of the cash value of his policy.

POLICY RESERVES The funds that an insurance company holds specifically for the fulfillment of its policy obligations. Reserves are so calculated that, together with the future premiums and interest earnings, they will enable the company to pay all future claims.

POLICY VALUE Amount of cash available to the insured on surrender of the policy.

POLITICAL ECONOMY A term, still used extensively in Europe for the subject-matter area; known as economics in the United States.

POLL TAX A head tax or capitation tax formerly associated with the payment required in some states before one could vote. It might, however, be tied to some other privilege.

POOL A combination of resources, or funds for some common purpose or benefit.

PORTAL-TO-PORTAL ACT Federal statute limiting employees' Wage-Hour Law suits based on "portal" claims.

PORTAL-TO-PORTAL PAY Payment for time spent in traveling to and from the entrance to the employer's premises and the work area.

PORT AUTHORITY The agency authorized by a state, states, or federal government which is empowered to regulate, plan, and finance traffic through a port.

PORT DIFFERENTIAL In commerce, the difference between through rates on the same class or commodity to or from competing ports, from or to the same point.

PORTFOLIO Holdings of securities by an individual or institution. A portfolio may contain bonds, preferred stocks, and common stocks of various types of enterprises.

PORT OF ENTRY Any seaport, airport, or place where customs duties are collected.

POSSESSION The right to exclusive occupancy and use of real property.

POSTAUDIT An audit made after the transactions to be audited have taken place and have been recorded or have been approved for recording by designated officials, if such approval is required. See "preaudit."

POSTDATE To date an instrument a time after that on which it is made.

POSTING The process of transferring journal entries to the ledger.

POTENTIAL DEMAND A loose term signifying an estimation of how much demand would or will exist for something at some time in the future. It is generally based on projection of economic trends and relationships.

POTENTIAL STOCK The difference between the total authorized capital stock and the actually issued stock.

POVERTY The level of living at which an individual has so little of the necessities of life that his ability to retain physical efficiency has declined.

POWER IN TRUST A power which the donee (the trustee) is under a duty to exercise in favor of the beneficiary of the trust.

POWER OF ALIENATION The power to assign, transfer, or otherwise dispose of property.

POWER OF ATTORNEY A written document authorizing a named person to perform certain acts in place of the signer. It is usually acknowledged before a public officer or witness and is void on the death of the signer.

PREAUDIT An examination for the purpose of determining the propriety of proposed financial transactions and of financial transactions which have already taken place but have not yet been recorded, or, if such approval is required, before the approval of the financial transactions by designated officials for recording. There is frequently confusion between the audit as a whole and the auditing of individual transactions. For example, if we speak of an audit as a whole, then an independent auditor may be said to be performing a postaudit, since most of the transactions whose propriety he examines have already been approved for recording. The independent auditor may, however, also have to deal with transactions which have not been approved for recording (for example, accrued salaries and wages) but in speaking of an audit as a whole we may ignore these and say that the audit under consideration is a postaudit. On the other hand, if the audit of individual transactions is involved, the independent auditor, in the case illustrated, would be performing a postaudit with respect to most of the transactions, but a preaudit with respect to some of them. Sometimes the term "preaudit" is used as a synonym for "internal audit" (*q.v.*) but such usage is not recommended. See "postaudit."

PRECATORY WORDS Expressions in a will praying or requesting (but not directing) that a thing be done or not done.

PRECLUSIVE BUYING The purchase of goods and services, not for the purpose of one's own normal use, but rather for the purpose of preventing someone else from buying them.

PREEMPTIVE RIGHTS A prior right or privilege, such as the right of a stockholder to be offered the privilege of buying additional shares before the stock is offered to others.

PREFABRICATED 1) A wall or other unit fabricated prior to erection or installation on a building or structure foundation.
2) The manufacturing of a modular unit or standard item which permits the manufactured part to be assembled at some other site, rather than fully manufactured there.

PREFERENTIAL DUTY A customs duty that varies when levied on similar items because of the country of origin, type of labor used to make the product, or some other reason.

PREFERENTIAL SHOP A business which has a labor-relations policy of favoring union members over nonunion employees.

PREFERRED CREDITOR A creditor whose claim takes legal preference over the claim of another (such as government taxes over the amount owed to an individual).

PREFERRED STOCK A class of stock with a claim on the company's earnings before payment may be made on the common stock and usually entitled to priority over the common stock and usually entitled to dividends at a specified rate—when declared by the board of directors and before payment of a dividend on the common stock—depending upon the terms of the issue. See "preferred stock, cumulative" and "preferred stock, participating."

PREFERRED STOCK, CALLABLE Can be called in for payment at a stated price.

PREFERRED STOCK, CUMULATIVE A stock having a provision that if one or more dividends are omitted, the omitted dividends must be paid up before dividends may be paid on the company's common stock.

PREFERRED STOCK, PARTICIPATING A preferred stock which is entitled to its stated dividend and, also, to additional dividends on a specified basis upon payment of dividends on the common stock.

PREMIUM 1) A consideration (price) paid for a contract of insurance.
2) A fee charged for the granting of a loan.
3) The amount by which a security is priced over par. A $1,000 bond with a market price of $1,050 has a premium of $50.

PREMIUM DISCOUNT PLAN A plan available in some rating jurisdictions providing for a percentage reduction on premium dependent upon the size of the premium. In workmen's compensation insurance it is recognized that the proportionate cost of issuing and servicing a policy is less as the premium increases. The premium discount plan gives the policyholder the benefit of this reduction.

PREMIUM LOAN A policy loan made for the purpose of paying premiums.

PREMIUM ON SECURITIES The amount by which a security (a bond or a share of stock) is bought or sold for more than its face or par value; opposed to discount on securities.

PREMIUM PAY A rate of pay, higher than that paid for normal working hours, that is given as compensation for work performed during inconvenient hours or uncomfortable conditions.

PREMIUM RATE 1) The price per unit of insurance.
2) In security trading, it is the premium which must be paid to borrow stocks for a short sale when the stocks are not selling flat.

PREMIUM STOCK A stock which lends at a premium, *i.e.*, an amount has been charged for loaning it to someone who borrowed it to make delivery on a short sale. Also may denote an above-average, superior stock; an established leader.

PREPAID CHARGE PLAN An accumulation plan under which the major deductions for selling charges are made during the first year or two of the program. Investor must complete program in order to minimize purchasing expenses.

PREPAID EXPENSE An expenditure, often recurrent, for benefits as yet not received. Unexpired insurance is a prepaid expense from the policyholder's point of view.

PREPAID TRANSPORTATION CHARGES Transportation charges paid at the shipping point by the person who is sending the shipment.

PREPAYMENT PENALTY A special charge, provided for in a mortgage contract, which may be collected from the mortgagor if he repays all or a part of the loan in advance of the due date.

PRESENTATION A legal term used in connection with negotiable instruments. The act of presentation technically means the actual delivery of a negotiable instrument by a holder in due course to the drawee for acceptance, or to the maker for payment. Upon presentation, the holder in due course requests acceptance of a draft, or requests payment of the instrument from the maker of a note, check, etc. See "negotiable."

PRESENT VALUE 1) The current value of something, taking into account depreciation, appreciation, wear and tear, etc.
2) The discounted value of a certain sum due and payable at a certain specified future date.

PRICE The amount, in the current medium of exchange, which is asked or received in exchange for an economic good.

PRICE CONTROLS The restrictions on price increases by some agency such as the Office of Price Stabilization or Office of Price Administration. Both of these agencies were emergency activities caused by war.

PRICE DISCRIMINATION The charging of different prices for a good or service to similar customers.

PRICED OUT OF THE MARKET A market situation in which the price asked for a product has eliminated many potential buyers and thus the volume of sales and profits has declined.

PRICE-EARNINGS RATIO The price of a stock divided by its earnings per share.

PRICE-FIXING or **STABILIZATION** Holding prices at a certain level. Often attempted by governments, but generally illegal if attempted by private firms.

PRICE INDEX A statistical device for showing the percentage change in the price of a thing or a group of things from the base period which is assigned the value of one hundred.

PRICE LEADERSHIP A situation in which a major producer of a product establishes a price and other producers in the same field adopt that price as their own.

PRICE LEVEL A relative position in the scale of prices as determined by a comparison of prices (of labor, materials, capital, etc.), as of one time with prices as of other times.

PRICE SUPPORTS Any of many ways to keep prices from falling below some preconceived level. Agricultural prices in the United States are in many cases supported by such devices as subsidies, loans, government purchases, soil banks, and school lunch programs.

PRICE SYSTEM An economy in which goods and services are produced for profit and the amounts produced and consumed are determined by price.

PRIMA FACIE At first view. Prima facie evidence is such as in law sufficient to establish a fact, unless rebutted.

PRIMARY BOYCOTT The action by a union to prevent the handling, purchase, or use of a product of an employer with whom the union has a dispute.

PRIMARY DEPOSIT A deposit in a bank which is created by an inflow of cash or checks as compared with a deposit created by the commercial bank making a loan and crediting the account of the borrower with a deposit for the amount of the loan. The latter is a derivative deposit. However, a derivative deposit, when withdrawn by check may become a primary deposit in the receiving bank.

PRIMARY DISTRIBUTION Also called primary offering. The original sale of a company's securities. See "investment banking" and "secondary distribution."

PRIMARY INDUSTRIES Those which take their materials directly from natural resources; mining, agriculture, trapping, or fishing.

PRIMARY RESERVES Those assets of a bank, consisting of cash and balances on deposit with other banks, which are immediately available for the payment of liabilities.

PRIME BILL OF EXCHANGE A draft or trade acceptance which states on the face of the instrument that it was created through a business transaction involving the movement of goods.

PRIME COST A direct cost; an operating cost; a running cost; a cost which fluctuates directly with the volume of production, such as the cost of the raw material.

PRIME RATE The minimum interest rate on bank loans as set by commercial banks and granted to only top business borrowers. The rate is influenced by the size of the loan, larger loans receiving better rates; and by general business conditions, geographical area, availability of reserves, etc.

PRIMOGENITURE The right of the eldest son to inherit such things as real estate or title to the exclusion of other children in the family.

PRINCIPAL 1) The sum of money stated in a contract, an account, or a financial instrument as distinguished from the sum actually to be paid; in other words, the amount of a loan or debt exclusive of interest.
2) A person who is primarily liable on an obligation.
3) A person who appoints another person to act for him as agent.

PRIORITY Legal preference.

PRIORITY SYSTEM A technique for distributing a limited supply of goods among the members of the society on some basis other than complete reliance on price sovereignty. In periods of emergency, where supplies are abnormally limited, it may be deemed more socially desirable to have a distribution of scarce products based on allocation. Ration books, ration stamps, and similar devices are used in the consumer area. Certificates of necessity and quotas may be used in the production area.

PRIVATE BANK An unincorporated institution which is owned and operated by an individual or a partnership. It may or may not be subject to supervision by the banking authorities, depending on the laws of the particular state in which it is located.

PRIVATE BRANDS Brands sponsored by merchants or agents as distinguished from those sponsored by manufacturers or producers.

PRIVATE CARRIER An individual contract carrier as compared to a common or public carrier.

PRIVATE CORPORATION A corporation founded and operated for purposes of making money for the stockholders of the company.

PRIVATE DEBT The monetary amount owed by the people and businesses of a nation and not including the amount owed by the governmental units, federal, state, or local.

PRIVATE ENTERPRISE Those profit-seeking activities carried out by private individuals in any business form. Activities of government agencies, even if producing profits, do not come under the heading of private enterprise.

PRIVATE PROPERTY That which is individually owned. The right of an individual or firm to use and dispose of goods or things within the normal police powers of a government.

PRIVATE TRUST 1) A trust created for the benefit of a designated beneficiary or designated beneficiaries; as a trust for the benefit of the settlor's or the testator's wife and children; opposed to a charitable (or public) trust.
2) A trust created under a declaration of trust or under a trust agreement; as a living trust or an insurance trust; opposed to a trust coming under the immediate supervision of a court. See "court trust."

PRIVILEGE Synonymous to a stock-option contract, such as a call or put, which permits one of the parties to exercise some right or privilege stated in the contract during the specified time period.

PROBATE COURT A court having jurisdiction of the proof of wills, the settlement of estates and, usually, of guardianships. In some states it is the district court.

PROBATE OF WILL Formal proof before the proper officer or court that the instrument offered is the last will of the decedent, as it purports and is alleged to be.

PROBATIONARY EMPLOYEE A worker hired with the understanding that he may be discharged with or without cause during an initial trial period.

PROCEEDS A very general term used to designate the total amount realized or received in any transaction, whether it be a sale, an issue of stock, the collection of receivables, a donation, or the borrowing of money.

PRODUCE EXCHANGE 1) A spot market for such items as perishable agricultural products.
2) A contract market in which futures contracts are bought and sold for products of agriculture.

PRODUCERS' CAPITAL See "instrumental capital."

PRODUCERS' COOPERATIVE MARKETING That type of cooperative marketing which involves primarily the sale of goods or services of the associated producing membership.

PRODUCTION The creation of something capable of satisfying a need.

PRODUCTION FACTORS Measurements such as time series and economic indexes which provide data on productivity.

PRODUCTION FUNCTION A curve or schedule which shows how total quantity of a product will vary with changing proportions of factors of production such as labor and machinery.

PRODUCTIVITY That which a man or machine produces within a stated period of time. It may also be expressed as an increase in the rate of production from one period to another.

PRODUCTIVITY THEORY That attempt to explain wage rates in terms of the value or productivity of work performed.

PROFIT The excess of the selling price over all costs and expenses incurred in making the sale. The reward to the entrepreneur for the risks assumed by him in the establishment, operation, and management of a given enterprise or undertaking. See "entrepreneur."

PROFIT AND LOSS ACCOUNT 1) Account transferred from accounts receivable to separate ledger.
2) Amount deducted from accounts receivable balance.
3) An account deemed to be uncollectible, or an account which is a certain number of months past-due, becomes eligible for transfer to the "profit and loss account" ledger.

PROFIT AND LOSS STATEMENT See "income statement."

PROFIT-SHARING PLAN An arrangement between an employer and his employees by which employees are to receive a fixed share of all or part of the profits.

PROGRESSIVE TAXATION Any tax which has the rate increase as the item that is subject to tax increases in size or amount. The income tax, federal or state, is an example of a progressive tax.

PROLETARIAT Workers, unskilled and semiskilled. Wage earners.

PROMISSORY NOTE An unconditional written promise to pay a fixed amount of money at a definite time. It is signed by the person or persons agreeing to make the payment.

PROMOTER An individual, who acting as a middleman, brings together the various needed factors of a venture in business, especially as they are associated with a new firm.

PROOF OF LOSS In insurance, a written statement complying with certain conditions made by the insured and given to the insurance company. Its purpose is to place before the company sufficient information concerning the loss to enable it to determine its liability under the policy or bond.

PROPERTY That which one owns; the possession or possessions of a particular owner.

PROPERTY ACCOUNT In bookkeeping, a real account. An account that is not closed out when a balance is taken but is continued to the next accounting period.

PROPERTY TAX A general property tax. A levy by a governmental unit on any asset. The asset may be real, such as land and buildings, or it may be personal such as deposits, or securities.

PROPORTIONALITY, LAW OF An economic concept which states that in any act of production there is an optimum point of production by using the correct proportions of land, labor, capital, and management. Also known as law of variable proportions.

PROPORTIONAL TAXATION A tax levy designed to apply the same rate of taxation to the property subject to the tax. Thus, a property valued at twice the amount of another property would pay the same rate which would result in a monetary amount of twice the tax on the second property.

PROPRIETARY CORPORATION A nonoperating parent company of a nonoperating controlling company.

PROPRIETORSHIP The owner of the business; ownership.

PROPRIETORY ACCOUNTS Those accounts which show actual financial condition and operations such as actual assets, liabilities, reserves, surplus, revenues and expenditures, as distinguished from budgetary accounts.

PRO RATA In proportion to the total amount.

PRO RATA DISTRIBUTION CLAUSE In a fire insurance policy, it provides that the amount of insurance written shall apply to each building or location in that proportion which the value of each building or location bears to the total value of the described property.

PRO RATA LIABILITY CLAUSE Provides that the insurance company is liable for not more than the proportion of loss which the amount insured under the policy bears to all insurance policies covering the loss.

PRO RATA RATE A premium rate charged for a short term, at the same proportion of the rate for a longer term as the short term bears to the longer term.

PROSPECTUS 1) An outline or plan of a proposed enterprise or undertaking.
2) A brief description of a property for sale or lease, usually including basic specifications.
3) A detailed statement issued by a company prior to the sale of new or additional securities, giving a full description of facts and information as required by the Securities and Exchange Commission.

PROTECTIONISM The practice of protecting a nation's industries from foreign competition.

PROTECTIVE TARIFF A customs duty schedule which permits domestic producers of the scheduled items to be able to profitably sell and continue to produce without fear of the competition of imported similar products.

PROTEST A written statement by a notary public, or other authorized person, under seal for the purpose of giving formal notice to parties secondarily liable that an instrument has been dishonored, either by refusal to accept or by refusal to make payment.

PROXY A person authorized to act for another.

PRUDENT INVESTMENT COST The amount arrived at in valuation of a business or property which considers original cost of the property but deducts from that amount those expenses or frills which a prudent man would not accept.

PRUDENT MAN RULE An investment standard. In some states, the law requires that a fiduciary, such as a trustee, may invest the fund's money only in a list of securities designated by the state—the so-called legal list. In other states, the trustee may invest in a security if it is one which a prudent man of discretion and intelligence, who is seeking a reasonable income and preservation of capital, would buy.

PSYCHIC INCOME The nonmonetary return from activity. While all people may obtain a feeling of satisfaction from their work, certain activities such as teaching, preaching, the creative arts, and social work are considered to provide psychic income to those engaged in such fields. In part, this is used to explain why people will do such things when they could earn more in other activities.

PUBLIC ADMINISTRATOR A county officer whose main official duty is to settle the estates of persons who die intestate.

PUBLIC CARRIER Individual or company offering to transport people or merchandise for a fee. Such public or common carriers are required by law to accept shipments from all who request and pay for their services.

PUBLIC CORPORATION Any corporation formed by and for a governmental agency to help in the conducting of public activities.

PUBLIC CREDIT The credit of a government or subdivision of a government as distinguished from the private credit of private firms or individuals.

PUBLIC DEBT That total or subtotal of the debt of any or all governments, federal, state, or local.

PUBLIC DOMAIN 1) The portion of the land owned by the government.
2) That situation in which the period of copyright or patent has passed and anyone may freely use or reproduce the thing patented or copyrighted.

PUBLIC FINANCE Those financial activities which are associated with any phase of government. Taxes, customs, public debt, public expenditures, and related fields all comprise public finance.

PUBLIC GOOD Those economic goods or services which the government, federal, state, or local, makes available without direct costs to its citizens. It would include such things as public roads, public health programs, public libraries, public parks, and education.

PUBLIC HOUSING ADMINISTRATION That part of the United States Housing and Home Finance Agency which is concerned with the provision of financing and legislation on the national level for local public housing.

PUBLIC OWNERSHIP The control and ownership of some productive facility for providing some good or service to the citizens of a community or nation by an agency of government. Public ownership is not uncommon in the public utility fields.

PUBLIC PROPERTY That property which is owned by other than the individual or individuals or private corporations; that is, property whose ownership is vested in the community.

PUBLIC REVENUE Any income received by the government such as from taxes, customs, franchises, or services.

PUBLIC SERVICE COMMISSION That state agency which establishes rates and supervises public-utility corporations.

PUBLIC SPACE Any area where the public may freely enter in the normal course of business and during business hours. A private establishment such as a store or bank has a space for the public and customers to transact their business. Such an area is called public space.

PUBLIC TRUST The same as a charitable trust; opposed to a private trust.

PUBLIC UTILITY In the generally accepted sense, privately owned (as opposed to publicly owned) corporations engaged in public-service enterprises supplying electricity, gas, telephone, water, and other services.

PUBLIC WAREHOUSE Those storage facilities which are available to the general public as distinguished from private warehouses which are for the exclusive use of one firm.

PUBLIC WORKS The activities of governmental agencies in providing public improvements such as roads, parks, sewers, and other physical structures as compared with services.

PUMP PRIMING The expenditure of governmental funds, generally during periods of depression, for the purpose of creating jobs and demand for material which in turn will cause recovery.

PURCHASE A term applicable to every method of acquiring property except by descent—that is, by right of blood, or by charitable gift.

PURCHASE MONEY MORTGAGE A mortgage given by the purchaser to the seller as security for the payment of a part of the purchase price of property.

PURCHASE ORDER A document which authorizes the delivery of specified merchandise or the rendering of certain services and the making of a charge for them.

PURCHASING POWER The capacity to purchase possessed by an individual buyer, a group of buyers, or the aggregate of the buyers in an area or a market.

PURCHASING POWER OF THE DOLLAR A measurement of the quantity (not quality) of goods and services that a dollar will buy compared with the amount that it could buy in some base period. It is obtained by taking the reciprocal of a price index, usually the consumers' price index.

PURE COMPETITION The market situation where no one trader can materially affect the market price of a product.

PURE INTEREST A theoretical concept that excludes all costs for risk and overhead from the cost paid for capital. See "consols."

PUT A contract to have the option to sell a security within a stated time and amount to the drawer of the option. It is the opposite of a call. See "call."

PYRAMIDING Has two major meanings: 1) A situation where a series of holding companies own stock in related holding or operating companies. Generally, the holding is for control and speculative profit and does not serve as an improvement in the operating efficiency of the individual companies.
2) The use of the increased value of a purchased security above the margin requirement is used as the collateral to purchase additional securities, also on margin. In turn, if these increase in price over the margin required, additional purchases are made. It tends to magnify profits in a bull market and magnify losses in a bear market.

QUALIFIED ACCEPTANCE In reality, a counteroffer to another's original offer. To be binding, original acceptance must be unqualified. Since a condition or qualification is made by one party the other must accept the qualification completely before the contract has both offer and acceptance. If changes are made, then an entirely new offer is being presented for approval or rejection.

QUALIFIED ENDORSEMENT Use of such words or terms as "without recourse" preceding the endorsement which serves as a limitation of the warranties of the one making the endorsement.

QUALIFIED REPORT A report with exceptions or inadequate facts so that full credence should not be given to the finding. A credit report on an applicant for insurance may qualify some of the findings.

QUANTITY THEORY OF MONEY The belief that prices are related directly to the quantity of money in circulation. As the quantity of money increases, prices increase; as the money in circulation decreases prices also decrease. Modern economists add additional factors to the equation of exchange and various formulas express the idea.

QUASI CONTRACT 1) An obligation similar in character to that of a contract, but which arises not from an agreement between the parties but from some relationship between them, or from a voluntary act by one or more of them. For example, the management of the affairs of another without authority, or the management of a common property without authority.
2) Situation imposed by law to prevent unjust enrichment or injustice and not dependent on agreement of the parties to the contract.

QUASI CORPORATION A political subdivision such as an unincorporated town that operates in the manner of an incorporated municipality.

QUASI-PUBLIC CORPORATION An incorporated organization that is privately operated but in which some general interest of the public is evident.

QUICKIE STRIKES Work stoppages called without advance notice, usually because of some employer practice resented by the employees or the local union, and usually not authorized by the national or international union.

QUICK RATIO The ratio between the quick assets and the current liabilities; an indication of the ability of a business to pay all of its current liabilities quickly in cash.

QUITCLAIM DEED A deed by which the owner of real estate conveys to another whatever title or interest he has to the property, but which makes no representation that the property is free from encumbrances, except those created by the owner himself.

QUORUM The minimum number of persons necessary to transact business of a corporation, legislative body, assembly, etc.

QUOTA SAMPLE The division of a statistical universe into groups and then taking a sample of these groups in the same proportion these groups have to the total.

RACK JOBBER A wholesaler serving retail stores, especially supermarkets; offers a complete service in the merchandising of certain items of nonfood departments—housewares, toiletries, toys, and soft goods—thus relieving the store of inventory as well as merchandising activities; selects, assembles, prices, and delivers merchandise, and arranges and maintains the display on the shelves or racks on the dealer's floors; sells principally on a consignment basis but frequently on other terms.

RAILWAY LABOR ACT Federal statute recognizing the right of collective bargaining in the railroad and airline industries.

RANGE 1) The discrepancy between the highest and lowest values in a sample.
2) In the land laws of the United States, a strip of land six miles wide, running north and south, marked off by government survey.

RATE That fixed relationship between two series of data. Such as a 10% rate of interest on a loan, or a wage rate of 6 dollars per hour, or a tax rate of one dollar of tax for every hundred dollars of valuation.

RATE BASE Those factors such as cost of plant, equipment, labor, rent, capital charges and other costs which are included in a consideration for establishing a rate. The rate base permits the businessman to obtain a fair and reasonable return.

RATE OF EXCHANGE The ratio at which foreign currency exchanges for a domestic currency. See "foreign exchange."

RATE OF RETURN 1) The yield obtainable on a security based on its purchase price or its current market price. This may be the amortized yield to maturity on a bond or the current income return.
2) The income earned by a public utility company on its property or capital investment, expressed as a percentage.

RATE REGULATION The establishment of a rate or a maximum or minimum range of rate fluctuation by some authoritative body such as a Public Utility Commission.

RATE WAR A destructive type of competition in which the various sellers of a good or service progressively decrease their prices even below their costs for the purposes of driving their competitors out of business.

RATIFICATION Confirmation of a contract or act done by oneself or by his agent.

RATING 1) The evaluation of the moral or other risk of an individual or organization.
2) The making of insurance, freight, or other rates or charges.

RATING, EXPERIENCE Determination of the insurance premium rate for an individual risk partially or wholly on the basis of that risk's own experience.

RATIONING OF EXCHANGE A system which requires exporters to sell all foreign exchange to the government for domestic currency. The government then sells foreign exchange to those importers engaged in approved activities.

RAW MATERIALS Articles that are either changed in form or united with other articles in a manufacturing business to become a part of the finished products of the factory.

REAL ESTATE The right, title or interest that a person has in real property, as distinguished from the property itself, which is the subject matter of the interest.

REAL ESTATE TAX That tax or amount of money levied by taxing authority against the ownership of real estate for purposes of financing the functioning of the government.

REALIZATION The act or process of converting an asset or the total assets of an individual or business into cash.

REALIZED PROFIT OR LOSS A profit or loss resulting from the sale or other disposal of a security, as distinguished from a paper profit or loss.

REAL MONEY Money, the composition of which contains one or more metals having intrinsic value, as distinguished from representative money such as currency issued by a realm, and checks, drafts, etc., issued by legal entities in society.

REAL PROPERTY Land, buildings, and other improvements to property that may legally be classifed as real, in contrast to personal.

REAL WAGES Wages in terms of goods and services that money wages will buy.

RECAPITALIZATION Any change in the existing capital structure of a corporation. This may involve changing the value of stock, issuing new stocks or bonds, or calling in bonds or callable preferred.

RECAPTURE CLAUSE A clause in an agreement providing for retaking or recovering possession. As used in percentage leases, to take a portion of earnings or profits above a fixed amount of rent.

RECEIVABLE An asset in the form of an account which is due from a borrower.

RECEIVER A person appointed, ordinarily by a court of equity jurisdiction, to receive and hold in trust, money or other property which is the subject of litigation, pending the suit, as in case of a person incompetent to manage his property, or of the dissolution and winding up of a partnership or a corporation.

RECEIVER'S CERTIFICATE A note issued by a receiver for the purpose of obtaining working capital to keep a distressed corporation in operation. The note is generally for a short term and given a priority over other open-book accounts. The exact priority is determined by authority of the court.

RECEIVERSHIP The status of a carrier's property while in charge of a receiver appointed by a court of equity. See "trusteeship."

RECESSION   That phase of a business cycle characterized by a reduction in the level of production and employment from the previous phase.

RECIPROCAL BUSINESS   An order to buy or sell securities given by one person or firm to another in return for a more or less equivalent order, or business favor, previously granted. Quite often, brokerage firms will have a correspondent relationship with another firm which may be a member of a particular stock exchange, and orders brought in may be repaid by another type of business in return.

RECIPROCAL EXCHANGE   An unincorporated association organized to write insurance for its members. Members are both insurers and policyholders. Each member is liable for his proportionate share of total liabilities but may be assessed for additional funds if they are needed.

RECIPROCAL LAW   State laws providing for equal privileges to all alien insurers as accorded domestic insurers in alien states. See "retaliatory law."

RECIPROCITY   Equality between citizens and businesses of two countries with respect to commercial privileges in trade, tariffs, taxation, and related governmental restrictions.

RECLAMATION   1) A negotiable instrument such as a check or note which has incorrectly been posted through a clearinghouse and is now to be corrected or reclaimed.
2) The process of making a heretofore unproductive asset such as eroded land productive by restoring through terracing and good land management.

RECONCILIATION   1) Bringing into agreement or harmony.
2) Adjusting amounts which should be equal.

RECONVERSION   The administrative and tool changes necessary to permit a business, industry, or economy to produce a different style or type of product or service.

RECORDATION   In connection with a mortgage, the recording of the fact that a lien has been created against certain property, described in the mortgage, such entry usually being made in the appropriate public record of the county or other jurisdiction in which the particular property is located.

RECORD DATE   The day designated by a corporation for the determination of holders entitled to a dividend, previously declared.

RECOURSE   The right to require performance of an obligation by an indorser, assignor, or other prior holder of an instrument.

RECOVERY   1) That phase of a business cycle characterized by improvement in the level of business. Recovery is generally preceded by recession or depression but precedes prosperity.
2) Money or other valuables that an insurance company obtains from subrogation, salvage, or reinsurance.

REDEEMABLE STOCK   A preferred stock which is callable.

REDEMPTION   The liquidation of an indebtedness whether on maturity or prior to maturity, such as the retirement of a bond issue prior to its maturity date.

REDEMPTION FUND   A fund created for the purpose of retiring an obligation maturing serially, or purchasing them as they become available.

REDEMPTION PRICE   The price at which a bond may be redeemed before maturity, at the option of the issuing company. Redemption value also applies to the price the company must pay to call in certain types of preferred stock. See "preferred stock, callable."

REDISCOUNT   The process by which a Federal Reserve or other bank discounts for a member or customer bank the notes, drafts, or acceptances which the member or customer bank has already discounted for its customers. The rediscounted paper itself.

REDISCOUNT RATE   The interest rate charged by one of the twelve Federal Reserve Banks to a member bank on eligible commercial paper which the member bank has used as collateral for a loan.

REDRAFT   A cross bill. When a check or other bill of exchange which has been presented for payment and is dishonored, and as a result is protested, the holder of the instrument may draw a bill of exchange for the original amount of the obligation plus the cost of the notary and other protest expenses. This new instrument is known as a redraft or cross bill.

REEXPORT   A product which has been imported into a foreign trade zone of a country and then is exported in relatively the same basic form.

REFEREE   1) A person appointed in court proceedings for the judicial settlement of a trustee's accounts to conduct hearings with the interested parties and report his findings to the court.
2) A medical examiner who, in addition to the regular duties, also secures special underwriting reports.

REFINANCING   The payment of indebtedness with funds obtained through the creation of a new obligation or obligations.

REFORMATION OF CONTRACT   Proof in a court of equity that a contract does not state the true intentions of both parties will permit reformation of the contract to correct the contract.

REFUNDING   The refinancing of an indebtedness on or before its maturity in order to reduce the fixed interest charge or to reduce the amount of fixed payment, due to the inability to conveniently liquidate an indebtedness when it matures.

REGISTER   A record for the consecutive entry of a certain class of events, documents, or transactions, with a proper notation of all the required particulars.

REGISTER CHECK   The title given to a check used in parts of the United States in lieu of cashier's checks or bank drafts.

REGISTERED REPRESENTATIVE   Present name for the older term "customer's man." The registered representative is an employee of a stock exchange member firm, registered with the exchange as having passed certain tests and met certain requirements, authorized to serve the public customers of his firm. Also known as "customer's broker."

REGISTRAR In connection with stock, the agent which affixes its signature to each stock certificate issued, the object being the prevention of overissuance. In connection with bonds, the agent which maintains the record of ownership of registered bonds.

REGISTRATION STATEMENT A statement which sets forth certain facts as prescribed by statute and by rules and regulations issued thereunder, and which (subject to certain exceptions) must be filed with the Securities and Exchange Commission prior to a public offering of new securities.

REGRESSIVE TAX A tax designed so that the rate goes down as the value of the thing taxed goes up. A tax which will fall proportionately more on the poor than on the rich. A tax on food would be regressive because poor people spend a larger proportion of their income on food than the wealthy.

REGULATION Q A requirement of the Federal Reserve Board which limits the amount of interest that may be paid by covered commercial banks to their depositors on time deposits.

REHYPOTHECATE To transfer to another a note which is secured by the hypothecation of property.

REINSTATEMENT Restoration of an insurance policy to full force and effect upon presentation of evidence of insurability satisfactory to the company, together with payment of premiums due. For life policies, an additional charge for interest may be made. See "automatic reinstatement clause."

REINSURANCE Insurance for the insurer. A portion or all of a risk is transferred from the issuing company to a reinsurer to prevent undue fluctuations in death claims. The insured, being covered under the standard terms of the issuing company, deals directly with the original insurer and is in no way affected by a reinsuring agreement.

RELEASE 1) A written statement that an obligation has been satisfied.
2) The giving up of a claim by the person entitled to it, to the person against whom the claim exists.

RELEASE OF MORTGAGE The act of releasing or relinquishing the claim against property established by a mortgage. The instrument by which such a release is effected.

REMAINDER The estate in property created simultaneously with other estates, such as a life estate, by a single grant and consisting of the rights and interests contingent upon and remaining after the termination of the other estate.

REMAINDERMAN The person who is entitled to an estate after the prior estate has expired. Originally the term applied, and in many states still does apply, to real property only.

REMARGINING The act of putting up additional margin against a loan. When securities have dropped in price, brokers may require their customers who have margin accounts to provide additional collateral either in the form of other securities or of cash.

RENT The return in money, labor, or chattel provisions which are given by the renter to the owner of the land in compensation for the use or right of use of the real estate.

RENT CONTROL Control by a government agency of the amount to be charged as rent.

REOPENING CLAUSE Clause in a collective bargaining agreement providing for reopening negotiations as to wage rates, etc., during the term of the agreement.

REORGANIZATION The changing of the capital structure of a corporation which is in distress financially under the appropriate legislation such as the National Bankruptcy Act. The objective is to remove the cause of the failure, make a fair settlement with the creditors, and permit the corporation to stay in business.

REPATRIATION The liquidation of foreign investments and return of the proceeds to the nation of the investor. In a broader sense, it means the return to one's own country of either persons or things.

REPLACEMENT COST The cost as of a certain date of a property which can render similar service (but need not necessarily be of the same structural form) as the property to be replaced. See "reproduction cost."

REPLACEMENT DEMAND The demand for goods which is attributable to similar goods being consumed, worn-out, or obsolete.

REPLEVIN The writ by which, or the action in which, personal property wrongfully taken is returned to the rightful owner.

REPORTING PAY Guaranteed payment to employees who report for work at their usual time and find no work to do.

REPOSSESSION Legal procedure where seller or financer of goods on installment basis repossesses goods because of failure of purchaser to fulfill agreement.

REPRESENTATIVE GOODS Those evidences of ownership of wealth such as notes, bonds, stocks, and money are considered to be representative goods.

REPRESENTATIVE MONEYS Those paper moneys which have full standard money backing or are freely redeemable in the standard such as gold or silver.

REPRODUCTION COST Normal cost of the exact duplication of a property as of a certain date.

REPUDIATION The intentional and willful refusal to pay a debt in whole or in part. The term usually refers to the willful act of a government or a subdivision thereof.

REPURCHASE AGREEMENT An agreement by one individual or firm to buy back, under certain terms, the thing which it originally sold to the second party of the transaction.

REQUIRED RESERVES Those liquid assets state-chartered banks are required to maintain by the state Superintendent of Banking and which member banks are required to maintain by the Federal Reserve authorities.

REQUISITION A written demand or request, usually from one department in a firm or organization to the purchasing officer or to another department, for specified articles or services.

RESALE PRICE AGREEMENT A contract between a producer and a seller whereby the seller agrees to not price the subject product below a certain minimum level.

RESCIND To cancel a contract or order so that both parties may be put, as far as possible, in the same position as before making the contract.

RESEARCH AND DEVELOPMENT Applying the processes, operations, and techniques of science and technology to create products, processes, and services which may benefit an enterprise.

RESERVE 1) A portion of the earnings which has been set aside to take care of any possible losses in the conduct of the business or organization.
2) Funds which are set aside by an insurance company for the purpose of meeting obligations as they fall due. A liability set up by an insurer for a particular purpose.
3) A portion of a bank's funds which has been set aside for the purpose of assuring its ability to meet its liabilities to depositors in cash. Minimum reserves to be maintained against demand and time deposits are usually specified by banking law. See "legal reserve."

RESERVE CITY BANK A member bank of the Federal Reserve System which is located in cities designated by the Federal Reserve Act, as amended, as reserve cities. Banks are divided for reserve requirements by the Act into two classes, reserve city banks and country banks.

RESERVE FOR BAD DEBTS Same as allowance for bad debts; the amount recorded on the books that represents the estimated reduction in the value of the accounts receivable because of estimated and anticipated losses on bad debts from uncollectible accounts.

RESERVE FOR DEPRECIATION Same as allowance for depreciation; the accumulated estimated decrease in the value of a fixed asset because of depreciation; the total depreciation that has been recorded for a fixed asset since the time the asset was put into service.

RESERVE RATIO The proportion of deposit liability which a bank keeps as reserves. The ratio required by member banks of the Federal Reserve System varies by type of deposit, time, or demand, and by location of bank in country or reserve city. It is in the form of deposits with the regional Federal Reserve Bank and a minor amount may be vault cash.

RESIDENCE EMPLOYEE An employee whose duties are incidental to the ownership, maintenance, or use of personal residential premises and to the personal, rather than the business activities of his employer.

RESIDUARY LEGATEE A person to whom is given the remainder of testator's personal property after all other legacies have been satisfied.

RESISTANCE POINTS Those points or areas of price fluctuation at which a security or security average comes to a resistance or stop prior to moving in a direction.

RESTRAINT OF TRADE Activities which interfere with the regular marketing process. Generally, the illegal restraint of trade is prohibited by the Sherman Antitrust Act.

RESTRICTIVE ENDORSEMENT An endorsement on a negotiable instrument which limits its negotiability.

RESULTING TRUST A trust which results in law from the acts of the parties, regardless of whether they intend to create a trust, as when a person disposes of property under circumstances which raise an inference that he does not intend that the person taking or holding the property shall have the beneficial interest in it; to be distinguished from an express trust and a constructive trust.

RETAIL Dealing with the final consumer of goods or service involved; handling sales in small quantities and amounts.

RETAILER A person or firm engaged in selling merchandise for personal, household, or farm consumption, and rendering services incidental to the sale of the merchandise.

RETAINED EARNINGS That part of the net profits of a corporation which has not been paid out as dividends.

RETALIATORY CUSTOMS DUTY A duty that discriminates against imports from a specific nation on the basis or reason that that nation discriminates against the first nation in some way.

RETALIATORY LAW State law imposing requirements on all alien companies equal to those imposed on domestic companies operating in alien states. See "reciprocal law."

RETENTION POLICY An insurance contract in which the insured agrees to pay all losses up to a specified amount in consideration of a lower premium. This policy is legal only in certain states. Certain states permit a retention class insurance policy to be sold. Under such a policy the insured pays 50% of the usual premium. When the total loss reaches this figure, the insured then has full coverage for all losses above that figure.

RETROACTIVE RESTORATION 1) Reinstatement of a bond or policy to its original face value after a loss has been paid, for the purposes of providing payment should prior losses be discovered at a future date.
2) Automatic restoration of the original amount of an insurance contract or bond, after payment of loss, to cover prior undiscovered as well as future losses not connected with the one previously paid.

RETURN See "yield."

RETURNS TO SCALE Refers to the rate of change of output when increasing amounts of the factors of production are used.

REVALUATION The revaluation or restoration of purchasing power to an inflated currency.

REVENUE Revenue results from the sale of goods and the rendering of services, and is measured by the charge made to customers, clients, or tenants for goods and services furnished to them. It also includes gains from the sale or exchange of assets (other than stock in trade), interest and dividends earned on investments, and other increases in the owner's equity except those arising from capital contributions and capital adjustments.

REVENUE EXPENDITURES Those expenditures that do not increase the value of the fixed assets but that are necessary to maintain the assets in an efficient operating condition.

REVENUE STAMPS (documentary stamps) Adhesive stamps issued by the federal or a state government, which must be purchased and affixed, in amounts provided by law, to documents or instruments representing original issues, sales, and transfers of stocks and bonds, deeds of conveyances, and certain types of foreign insurance policies.

REVERSE SPLIT Also called a split down; the opposite of a stock split. The number of outstanding shares of a corporation is reduced, and the market price of these remaining shares is increased.

REVERSING ENTRIES General journal entries made at the beginning of a new fiscal period to reverse the adjusting entries that were recorded at the end of the preceding period.

REVERSION The interest in an estate remaining in the grantor after a particular interest, less than the whole estate, has been granted by the owner to another person; to be distinguished from remainder. The reversion remains in the grantor; the remainder goes to some grantee.

REVOCABLE LETTER OF CREDIT A letter of credit which may be canceled.

REVOLVING FUND A fund provided to carry out a cycle of operations. The amounts expended from the fund are restored thereto either from earnings from operations, or from transfers by other funds, so that the original capital of the fund is kept intact. See "imprest fund" and "working capital fund."

REVOLVING LETTER OF CREDIT A letter of credit issued for a specific amount which renews itself for the same amount over a given period. Usually the unused renewable portion of the credit is cumulative, so long as drafts are drawn before the expiration of the credit.

RIDER A document or form containing special provisions that are not contained in the policy contract. Such forms are to be added or attached to the policy.

RIGHT-OF-WAY The term has two significances: 1) As a privilege to pass or cross, it is an easement over another's land.
2) It is also used to describe that strip of land which railroad companies use for a roadbed, or as dedicated to public use for roadway, walk or other way.

RIGHTS 1) The legal privileges, protections, and options available to all people by a government and its laws.
2) The privilege extended by an issuer to existing security holders to subscribe to new or additional securities, usually at a price below the current market and in a fixed relationship to the amount of securities owned by each holder.

RIGHT-TO-WORK LAW State law prohibiting union shop, closed shop, or any other union-security arrangement which requires employees to join a union as a condition of retaining employment.

RIPARIAN Pertaining to, or living on, the bank of a river, a lake, or of a tidewater; specifically, the use of lands lying between the high-water mark and the low-water mark. Local legal regulations determine the extent of the riparian right of the upland owner.

RISK CAPITAL 1) Venture capital.
2) That proportion of a total capitalization which is not secured by a lien or mortgage.
3) Common stock in a new enterprise.

ROBINSON-PATMAN ACT Passed in 1936. Prohibits firms engaged in interstate commerce from charging different buyers different prices for the same good unless there is a difference in cost.

ROLLBACK A governmental attempt to reduce a price to some previous level either through verbal request to manufacturers or distributors to lower their profit margins, or by a subsidy or tax rebate.

ROLLING STOCK That property of a railroad that is on wheels, such as freight cars, locomotives, and other rolling equipment.

ROLL OVER The procedure of repeated investment of the proceeds of short-term securites upon maturity.

ROTATING SHIFT An assignment of a worker in a plant that is operating on more than one shift, in such a way that he does not continually work in one shift, but spends a relatively short amount of time in a week or month on all the shifts.

ROUND LOT A unit of trading or a multiple thereof. On the New York Stock Exchange, the unit of trading is generally 100 shares in stocks, and $1,000 par value in the case of bonds.

ROUND TURN The offsetting sale or purchase to a previous purchase or sale, thus completing the transaction and resulting in a profit or loss.

ROYALTY 1) Agreements by which an author, musician, or inventor receives a certain payment on each copy of his work which is sold.
2) A payment reserved by the grantor of a patent, lease of a mine, oil property, or similar right and payable proportionately to the use made of the right or output by the grantee.

RULE AGAINST PERPETUITIES A rule of common law that makes void any estate or interest in property so limited that it will not take effect or vest within a period measured by a life or lives in being at the time of the creation of the estate plus twenty-one years. In many states, the rule has been modified by statute. In some states, it is known as the rule against remoteness of vesting.

RULE OF REASON Interpretation of a rule or law in which consideration of the reasonableness of a situation or act is taken into the basis of judgment.

RUN The action by a large number of people doing the same thing. A run on a bank is caused by an abnormally large number of withdrawals. A run on a product or commodity may be caused by some scare, such as war or strike.

RUNAWAY INFLATION A very sharp increase in the general price level. The severe inflation becomes part of an inflationary spiral in which higher prices lead to demands for higher wages, which in turn leads to higher prices.

RUNNING COSTS See "direct cost," "operating cost," "prime cost," and "variable cost."

SABOTAGE Malicious destruction, waste, or damage of an employer's property or equipment, or the obstruction and interference with normal operations, typically during an industrial dispute or strike.

SAFEKEEPING A service rendered by banks, especially banks in large metropolitan areas, where securities and valuables of all types and descriptions are protected in the vaults of the bank for the customer for a service fee.

SALARY A fixed compensation periodically paid to a person by an employer for regular work or services.

SALES The amount of goods and services sold.

SALES BUDGET An estimate of the probable dollar sales and probable selling costs for a specified period.

SALES CHARGE The amount charged in connection with the issuance of shares of a mutual fund and their distribution to the public. It is added to the net asset value per share in the determination of the offering price.

SALES FORECAST An estimate of dollar or unit sales for a specified future period under a proposed marketing plan or program. The forecast may be for a specified item or the entire line; it may be for a market as a whole or for any portion thereof.

SALES MANAGEMENT The planning, direction, and control of personal selling, including recruiting, selecting, training, equipping, assigning, routing, supervising, paying, and motivating as these tasks apply to the personal sales force.

SALES POTENTIAL The share of a market potential which a company expects to achieve.

SALES QUOTA A statement of the amount of sales that each salesman, supervisor, and branch manager is expected to complete during a future fiscal period.

SALES TAX A tax on sales that the seller collects from customers and pays to the state or federal government.

SALVAGE 1) The recovery reducing the amount of loss. As a verb, meaning to save endangered property and to enhance the value of damaged property.
2) In marine insurance it means the cost of saving property exposed to a peril.
3) In suretyship it is that which is recovered from the principal or an indemnitor to offset in whole, or in part, the loss and expense paid by a surety in satisfying its obligation under a bond.

SALVAGE VALUE The value attached to a fixed asset at the time it is retired from service.

SATISFACTION OF JUDGMENT Legal procedure followed when debtor pays amount of judgment, together with interest and costs. "Satisfaction of judgment" is then entered on records of Court of Record.

SATURATION POINT That point in the securities market when the supply of stocks begins to exceed the demand. This coincides with the peak of a market cycle.

SAVINGS Money, or goods and other valuable property set aside from earnings, investments, etc.,—left over after the costs of living have been met.

SAVINGS AND LOAN ASSOCIATION A financial corporation organized under state or federal statute for the primary purpose of selling shares to individuals, the proceeds of which are largely invested in home mortgages. The return to the investor is in the form of a dividend on shares, and not as interest on deposits.

SAVINGS BANK A corporation chartered by the state to receive savings deposits, primarily from people of moderate means. It invests these deposits for the most part in securities (bonds) and real estate mortgages.

SCAB A union term generally applied to a worker who refuses to join co-workers in a strike. Sometimes applied to members of a nonstriking union who pass through a striking union's picket line.

SCALING A technique of trading in commodities or securities by placing orders for purchase or sale at intervals of price, rather than placing the order in full at the market or at a price.

SCALPING A speculative attempt to obtain a quick profit by purchase of a security at an initial offering price with the expectation that the issue, being oversubscribed, will then advance in price at which time the security may then be sold. In some cases, the sale will be consummated by the scalper before he is required to pay for his purchase. Thus, no capital was tied up or little capital in terms of the total transactions. Scalping is also found on commodity exchanges where the scalper buys and sells during the trading day in equal amounts, so that at the end of the trading period he has no position—either long or short.

SCARCITY VALUE The rate of worth of a thing which is fixed in supply.

SCHEDULE 1) In business, a schedule refers to some systematic plan for future production or action tied to stated periods of time.
2) In economics, a schedule refers to a systematic recording of the amount, supply, rate, or other measurement of one factor which will be utilized, supplied, demanded, or otherwise developed in terms of some other factor.
3) An enumeration of various properties covered by an insurance policy. A system for computing rates.

SCHEDULED PROPERTY In insurance, the listing of a specific dollar amount against each item covered by one insurance policy.

SCRAP The material residue left from certain manufacturing operations. The term scrap is frequently erroneously applied to spoilage. See "spoilage."

SCRIP Any temporary document which entitles the holder or bearer to receive stock or a fractional share of stock in a corporation, cash, or some other article of value upon demand, or at some specified future date.

SEAL In law, any impression, device, sign, or mark which is recognized by judicial decision or by statute law making the instrument on which it is placed enforceable at law.

SEALED BID A technique for submitting an offer to buy or perform something. All interested parties are invited to submit (in a sealed envelope) their bid to buy or perform something, such as a construction of a building or other type of work. The bids are all opened at one time and the most attractive bid is accepted.

SEASONAL ADJUSTMENT Allowance made in monthly or other periodical data for seasonal fluctuations.

SEASONAL FLUCTUATION The tendency for certain economic factors to increase or diminish each year in a relatively predictable way tied to seasons of the year.

SEASONAL RISK An insured property that is only used for part of the year. A summer cottage at the shore, or a vegetable-packing plant are examples of seasonal risks.

SEASONAL UNEMPLOYMENT That unemployment which results from the operations of the seasons.

SEAT A traditional figure of speech for a membership on a securities or commodity exchange. Price and admission requirements vary.

SECONDARY BOYCOTT Refusal to deal with a neutral party in a labor dispute, usually accompanied by a demand that he bring pressure upon the employer involved in the dispute to accede to the boycotter's terms.

SECONDARY DISTRIBUTION Also known as a secondary offering. The redistribution of a block of stock sometime after it has been sold by the issuing company.

SECONDARY PICKETING The picketing by union members of an employer with whom the union has no direct relations in an effort to force that employer to stop dealing with another employer with whom the union does have a dispute.

SECONDARY RESERVES Those assets of a bank that are convertible into cash on short notice by sale in the open market or by rediscount.

SECONDARY STRIKE A strike called against one employer with a view to influencing another. See "strike."

SECTION OF LAND One of the portions of one square mile each, or 640 acres, into which the public lands of the United States are divided; one thirty-sixth part of a township. Much of this public land has been sold to individuals, or homesteaded.

SECULAR TREND A long-term irregular trend, as compared with a seasonal variation or business cycle movement.

SECURED CREDITOR An individual or firm that has a claim on the debtor's assets in the form of definite collateral such as a real estate mortgage on the debtor's land.

SECURED LOAN Loans that are made certain of payment by the pledging of valuable property to be forfeited in case of default.

SECURITIES Literally, things given, deposited, or pledged to assure the fulfillment of an obligation. In this narrow sense a mortgage is security; but the term is now generally used in a broader sense to include stocks as well as bonds, notes, and other evidences of indebtedness.

SECURITIES AND EXCHANGE COMMISSION Established by Congress to help protect investors. The Securities and Exchange Commission (SEC) administers the Securities Act of 1933, the Securities Exchange Act of 1934, the Trust Indenture Act, the Investment Company Act, the Investment Adviser's Act, and the Public Utility Holding Company Act.

SECURITY CAPITAL That proportion of a total capitalization which is relatively secured by a lien or mortgage. The rest of the capitalization consists of risk capital.

SELECTIVE SELLING The policy of selling only to dealers and distributors who meet the seller's requirements, such as size of orders, volume of purchases, profitability, or area, or type of operations.

SELF-INTEREST Greater consideration for one's own interest than for the interest of others.

SELF-LIQUIDATING LOAN A short-term commercial loan, usually supported by a lien on a given product or commodities, which is liquidated from the proceeds of the sale of the product or commodities. See "floor-plan financing."

SELLER'S MARKET A market in which goods are scarce so that buyers compete among themselves to obtain supplies.

SELLING AGAINST THE BOX A method of protecting a paper profit. Let's say you own 100 shares of XYZ which has advanced in price, and you think the price may decline. So you sell 100 shares short, borrowing 100 shares to make delivery. You retain in your security box the 100 shares which you own. If XYZ declines, the profit on your short sale is exactly offset by the loss in the market value of the stock you own. If XYZ advances, the loss on your short sale is exactly offset by the profit in the market value of stock you have retained. You can close out your short sale by buying 100 shares to return to the person from whom you borrowed, or you can send him the 100 shares which you own. See "hedge" and "short sale."

SELLING GROUP A combination of securities dealers operating under the leadership of a syndicate department of an underwriting firm, and participating in the public sale of an issue of securities.

SELLING SHORT See "short sale."

SEMISKILLED LABOR Persons whose work requires manipulative ability of a high order, but is limited to a well-defined work routine.

SENIORITY System granting preference in security, promotions, authority, and rewards to employees in accordance with their length of service.

SENIOR LIEN The lien which has prior claim before other liens.

SENIOR SECURITIES Securities having a prior claim on assets and earnings; usually bonds and preferred stocks as contrasted with common stocks.

SEQUESTERED ACCOUNT In bookkeeping and accounting, a term used to describe an account that has been impounded under due process of law. Since disbursement of such an account is subject to court action, the account is usually set up in a separate control. See "attached account."

SERVICE BUSINESS Business that does things for you, rather than sells you goods. Examples of services include the public utilities, such as telephone, transportation, etc., as well as such trades as laundry, dry cleaning, maintenance and repair work, etc.

SERVICE WHOLESALER A merchant middleman who sells to retailers and other merchants and/or to industrial, institutional, and commercial users but who does not sell in significant amounts to ultimate consumers.

SERVICING 1) The extra obligations or related functions performed by the seller of a good or service, regarding his product.
2) In connection with bonded indebtedness, the payment by the obligor of the interest and principal as they become due. In mortgage financing, the performance by the mortgagee or his agent of the many services which must be taken care of while the mortgage is held by the institution, such as searching of title, billing, collection of interest and principal payments, reinspections and reappraisals of the real property, readjustment of the terms of the mortgage contract when necessary, tax follow-up work, etc.

SETTLEMENT 1) An agreement between two or more parties regarding a matter of mutual interest.
2) The winding up and distribution of an estate by an executor or an administrator; to be distinguished from the administration of an estate by a trustee or a guardian.
3) A property arrangement, as between a husband and wife, or a parent and child, frequently involving a trust.

SEVERANCE PAY Generally a lump-sum payment made to a worker whose employment is permanently ended for causes beyond the worker's control by an employer, and which is in addition to any back wages or salary due the worker.

SEVERANCE TAX That levy made for removing natural resources such as oil, wood, shell, coal, or minerals.

SHAREHOLDER Coowners of specific percentages of the whole.

SHARES The equal interests into which the capital stock of a corporation is divided, the ownership usually being evidenced by certificates called stock certificates.

SHARE TENANT (SHARECROPPER) One who tills the soil owned by another and who receives payment for his labor, services, and effort, in form of a given stipulated share of the crop or crops he produces.

SHERIFF'S DEED An instrument drawn under order of court to convey title to property sold to satisfy a judgment at law.

SHERIFF'S SALE A sale of real or personal property made by a sheriff or other like ministerial officer, in obedience to an execution or other similar mandate of the court.

SHERMAN ANTITRUST ACT Federal legislation which declares illegal every contract, combination, or conspiracy, in restraint of normal trade.

SHIFT DIFFERENTIAL A premium wage, sometimes based on a percentage, sometimes a flat sum, paid workers on other than the day shift to compensate them for their inconvenient working hours.

SHIFTING TAXATION The ability of an individual or firm which is taxed to transfer the incidence of the tax to some other person or body.

SHOP CHAIRMAN Union steward usually chosen by the department stewards to serve as chairman over all the stewards in the plant and to deal with higher management representatives in adjusting grievances.

SHOP STEWARD Union man ordinarily elected to represent workers in a particular shop or department. He collects dues, solicits for new members, announces meetings, and receives, investigates, and attempts the adjustment of grievances.

SHORT In finance, one who has sold commodities or securities that he does not own at the time of the sale. He sells in expectation of buying them back at a lower price.

SHORT COVERING Buying stock to return stock previously borrowed to make a delivery on a short sale.

SHORT HUNDREDWEIGHT (SH CWT) 100 avoirdupois pounds.

SHORT INTEREST The total of the short sales in a security or a commodity or on an exchange which are outstanding. Typically, short-interest figures are released by exchanges on a weekly basis.

SHORT POSITION Stocks sold short and not covered as of a particular date.

SHORT RUN 1) In manufacturing, a short, one-time job.
2) A period which will vary from situation to situation. In a business it is the time within which a company can change price or production with a given fixed plant, but not change the size of its plant or terminate operations.

SHORT SALE In investment trading, a short sale is made by instructing one's broker to sell a stock which one does not own. In order to do this, the broker borrows the shares to be sold, and the seller hopes to be able to buy them back at a lower price in order to profit. Eventually, the short seller must purchase the shares sold short in order to replace the stock borrowed.

SHORT-TERM DEBT Notes, drafts, acceptances, or other similar evidences of indebtedness payable on demand or which, by their terms, are payable within one year or less from the date of issuance.

SHRINKAGE 1) Contraction in size, volume, weight, or texture of a product caused by exposure to the elements or handling.
2) The tendency for the dollar to buy less and less all the time. This is commonly referred to as the "shrinking dollar."

SIGHT BILL OF EXCHANGE Any bill of exchange that becomes due and payable when presented by the holder to the party upon whom it is drawn. See "draft."

SIGHT DRAFT A commercial draft payable upon presentation.

SILENT PARTNER One who is known to the public as a member of the firm but who does not take an active part in the management of the business.

SIMPLE INTEREST The interest arising from the principal sum only.

SINGLE ENTRY An accounting system which does not use double-entry bookkeeping techniques.

SINGLE-NAME PAPER A note for which only one legal entity—the maker—is obligated to make payment at maturity. A legal distinction exists in single-name paper, in that if the obligation is incurred for one purpose, or one common interest, the paper may have more than one maker or endorser, and still be termed single-name paper.

SINKING FUND   An accumulation of amounts set aside periodically by municipalities or corporations, which will be sufficient to satisfy a debt, such as a bond issue, at maturity. See "amortization.

SINKING-FUND DEPRECIATION METHOD   A plan for depreciating fixed assets through the medium of establishing an actual cash fund in the hands of a trustee to be used for subsequent replacement of the assets.

SIT-DOWN STRIKE   A strike in which the workers refuse to work but stay inside the employer's factory.

SITE   1) The area on which anything is, has been, or is to be located.
2) A location or plot of ground delineated for a specific purpose or function.
3) Lands made suitable for building purposes by dividing into lots, laying out streets, and the like.

SIXTY-DAY NOTICE   1) The notice that, under the Taft-Hartley Act, must be given by either party to a collective bargaining agreement when desiring to reopen or terminate it. No strike or lockout may be begun during this sixty days.
2) Notice required to be given to the Internal Revenue Department in those cases where the decedent's gross taxable estate exceeds or may exceed the exemption under the federal estate tax law.

SIZE OF THE MARKET   In the securities business, this term describes the number of round lots bid for at the highest price showing on the specialist's book, and the total number being offered for sale simultaneously at the lowest price quoted, at any specific moment. An answer to a request for the size of the market might be "4 and 2," which means that four hundred shares have been bid for at the highest price, and two hundred shares are offered at the lowest price on the book.

SKILLED LABOR   Persons working at a craft who possess thorough and comprehensive knowledge of the process and can exercise independent judgment, usually having a high degree of manual dexterity.

SLANDER   Malicious speaking of false and defamatory words concerning another, whereby he is injured. Liability for slander is a risk of newspapers, magazines, radio, and television.

SLIDING SCALE   Wage rates automatically adjusted to changes of the selling price of the commodity.

SLIDING-SCALE TARIFF   A customs duty tied to a formula so that the duties fluctuate in some relationship to the prevailing price of the import.

SLOWDOWN   A concerted and sustained refusal by working men to produce at the normal production rate.

SMALL BUSINESS   There are many different definitions depending upon the source of the term. The Small Business Administration, the Census Bureau, the National Industrial Conference Board, the Investment Bankers' Association and others have defined the term with somewhat different characteristics. Some definitions permit as many as 500 employees to work for a small business. Others use sales of less than 200,000 dollars a year. Others use relative size in an industry. Still others consider public financing and corporations that are not closed to indicate a business that is not small. For exact meaning, one must know the source using the term and even the time since the Small Business Administration has modified its original definition.

SMUGGLE   Taking goods or persons into or out of a nation without obtaining permission to do so, or without payment of duties, or purchasing travel tickets from the carrier.

SOCIALISM   The political and economic system in which the government owns and operates production facilities.

SOCIAL SECURITY ACT   Federal legislation providing social insurance on a national scale.

SOCIAL SECURITY TAX   A general term used to refer to any tax imposed under the terms of the Social Security Act; a tax assessed against certain workers and their employers under the terms of the Social Security Act.

SOFT MONEY   Has three different meanings—the context will indicate which one to use. A situation in which interest rates are low and loans are easy to arrange. A paper rather than metallic currency. A nation's currency which is not desired by foreigners in lieu of a "hard" currency which may be domestic or other foreign currency.

SOIL BANK   A governmental attempt to help solve the problem of oversupply of agricultural commodities by paying the farmer-owner to plant trees or grasses in place of crops.

SOLDIERING   A slowdown and deliberate attempt to not produce or work at a normal level or rate.

SOLE PROPRIETORSHIP   Ownership by one person of an entire business.

SOLVENT   Condition in which assets exceed liabilities. Condition in which debtor is able to pay his debts as they mature.

SPECIAL AGENT   Individual representing his company in an exclusive territory. He supervises certain agents of the company and the operations of his company.

SPECIAL ASSESSMENT   A tax levied against certain real estate owners to pay for public improvements that are assumed to specifically benefit their property.

SPECIAL-ASSESSMENT BOND   Bonds payable from the proceeds of special assessments.

SPECIAL DEPOSIT   A fund esetablished for the payment of interest, dividends, or other debts, or to insure the performance of contracts, and other deposits of a special nature as distinguished from sinking funds.

SPECIAL DEPOSITARY   A bank authorized by the United States Treasury to receive as deposits the proceeds of sales of government bonds.

SPECIAL ENDORSEMENT   A negotiable instrument made out to the order of John Jones, for example, would have a special endorsement if he endorsed it with the words "Pay to the order of Frank Brown" and then signed it "John Jones." This is an unqualified endorsement which limits the negotiability to Frank Brown or his order.

SPECIALIST   A member of a stock exchange who assumes two responsibilities: First, to maintain an orderly market, insofar as reasonably practicable, in the stocks in which he is registered as a specialist. In order to maintain an orderly market, the specialist must be prepared to buy or sell for his own account, to a reasonable degree, when there is a temporary disparity between supply and demand. Second, the specialist acts as a broker's broker. When a commission broker on the exchange floor receives a limit order, say, to buy at $50 a stock then selling at $60—he cannot wait at the particular post where the stock is traded until the price reaches the specified level. So he leaves the order with the specialist, who will try to execute it in the market if and when the stock declines to the specified price. At all times the specialist must put his customers' interests above his own.

SPECIALIST'S BOOK Also called simply, the book. It is composed of orders that have come to the specialist in a security on the stock-exchange floor at prices limited to other than the prevailing market price. The orders are kept in a book, to be executed at such time as the market price reaches their limitations. A specialist will have a book on each security in which he specializes, standing ready to accept orders from brokers who are unable to execute them.

SPECIALIZATION OF LABOR See "division of labor."

SPECIALIZED CAPITAL GOODS Those capital goods which have use in limited roles of production. The term is one of degree. Some tools are more specialized than others. Some buildings are more specialized in their use than others.

SPECIALIZED MANAGEMENT TRUST An investment company whose investment policy is confined to securities of businesses found in one industry such as oils, electronics, or aircraft.

SPECIALTY GOODS Those consumers' goods on which a significant group of buyers characteristically insist and for which they are willing to make a special purchasing effort. These goods do not have a general consumer-appeal.

SPECIALTY SHOP A retail store that makes its appeal on the basis of a restricted class of shopping goods.

SPECIFICATION A detailed description of a thing, specifically about any work to be done, building, etc.

SPEED-UP A system designed to increase worker productivity.

SPENDING UNIT A family, a group of individuals, or, in some cases, an individual that spends as a unit. Income generally is pooled, meals eaten together, and the property is considered for their joint use, and is possessed by the unit.

SPENDTHRIFT TRUST A trust in which the interest of a beneficiary cannot be assigned or disposed of by him, or attached, or otherwise reached by his creditors.

SPIN-OFF Division of a corporate business into two or more companies by the original corporation transferring certain of the properties to another corporation formed for that purpose, and then distributing the new corporation's stock to the original corporation's stockholders in proportion to their holdings. See "split-off" and "split-up."

SPLIT The division of the outstanding shares of a corporation into a larger number of shares.

SPLIT-OFF Division of a corporate business into two or more companies by the original corporation transferring certain of the corporate properties to another corporation formed for that purpose. The original stockholders turn in part of their old stock in exchange for the new stock. See "spin-off" and "split-up."

SPLIT OPENING That situation on a commodity or security exchange in which a security or a commodity has simultaneous opening prices which are spread, or different. This can occur when a number of traders at a trading post break up into groups and the sales take place in two groups at the same time but at different prices.

SPLIT ORDER An order to buy or to sell a given commodity or security which, because of the large size of the transaction, might cause a material price fluctuation, is "split" or executed in smaller units over a period of time.

SPLIT SHIFT A term for a regular daily work period which is divided into two or more parts, rather than being continuous.

SPLIT-UP 1) Division of a corporate business into two or more companies by the original corporation transferring all of the property to two or more new corporations formed for that purpose, and then exchanging the old stock of the original corporation for the stock of the new corporations. In most cases the original corporation would then go out of business.
2) Split-up also may be used to refer to the division of the number of existing shares into a larger number, such as a two-for-one stock split. See "spin-off" and "split-off."

SPOILAGE Production which does not meet dimensional or quality standards. Rejects. See "scrap."

SPOT In commodity trading and foreign exchange, this term indicates ready delivery as compared with some future time.

SPOT PRICE The selling price of the physical commodity.

SPREAD 1) The difference between the bid and asked price.
2) The use of both a put and a call on a specific security.
3) The purchase of one futures contract and the simultaneous sale of the same commodity, but in a different month, with both the sale and purchase remaining open until one of the contracts matures.

STABILIZATION Action by government, labor, or business to reduce fluctuations.

STABILIZATION FUND Fund established in 1934, as a result of the devaluation of the dollar, with two billion dollars to stabilize exchange values of the United States dollar, to deal in such things as foreign exchange and gold, and to invest in direct obligations of the United States Government. Under the Bretton Woods Agreement much of the assets of the fund were used to contribute to the International Bank for Reconstruction and Development and the International Monetary Fund. See "World Bank."

STABLE MONEY Money which does not fluctuate much in purchasing power. One of the goals of the Federal Reserve authorities is to maintain a stable level of prices.

STAGNATION Condition of an economy, business, industry, security, or commodity in which activity and volume has dropped substantially from previous levels.

STAGNATION THESIS Keynesian economic concept that mature economies tend to drop in their rate of growth of production for several reasons such as oversaving, decline in population rate of growth, or loss of geographic frontiers.

STAMP TAX A tax on legal documents, certificates, and papers which requires that revenue stamps be affixed to the documents to indicate that payment of the tax has been made.

STANDARD AND POOR'S CORPORATION A leading organization in the field of financial service which provides corporate information such as dividend, stock and bond reports as well as other pertinent records.

STANDARD AND POOR'S 500-STOCK PRICE INDEX A popular gauge of stock market movements as computed by Standard & Poor's Corporation from the price action of 425 leading industrial issues, 25 railroads, and 50 utilities. The average market prices of these stocks during 1941–43 are used as the base period, and the Index shows the relationship with today's average prices.

STANDARD COST A predetermined cost of product expected to be attained during the period to which it applies, based upon average efficiency in use of materials, average of expected prices for the period, and normal hours of operation over the period. Used as the basis for judging efficiency and for determining net profit.

STANDARD-COST SYSTEM A method of operating cost accounts whereby quantity variations and price variations from standard costs of production are recorded for each element by periods.

STANDARDIZATION The determination of basic limits or grades in the form of specifications to which manufactured goods must conform, and classes into which the products of agriculture and the extractive industries may be sorted.

STANDARD MONEY Primary money. A monetary unit which is made of the standard such as gold. A coin which is worth as much as its face value—if used as a commodity or medium of exchange.

STANDARD OF LIVING Those luxuries and necessities which an individual or class of people generally possess or use.

STATE BANK A corporation organized under the general banking law of a state and authorized to do a commercial banking business—that is, receive deposits subject to check, and make loans. It usually performs a variety of other functions as well. In a broader sense, a state bank is any bank chartered by the state.

STATED VALUE The value given to a corporation's stock and carried on the books if there is no assigned par value.

STATEMENT 1) An account; a list of bills due, sent periodically to customers.
2) A report sent, usually monthly, to a depositor in a bank or a debtor of a business firm.

STATEMENT OF CONDITION A financial picture of an association or business which shows the amount and character of its assets, liabilities, and reserves as of a certain date; also known as the balance sheet.

STATIC ECONOMY An economy which is at equilibrium. That is, the forces of supply and demand which are equated by price are such that little change in production or demand is created.

STATUTE A law established by the act of the legislature.

STATUTE OF FRAUDS A statute, first enacted in England in 1677, designed to prevent many fraudulent practices by requiring proof of a specific kind, usually in writing, of the important transactions of business, declaring that no action shall be brought or that no contract shall be allowed to be good when the transaction is not so evidenced.

STATUTE OF LIMITATIONS The periods fixed by statute within which suits must be brought if legal redress is to be obtained. At the expiration of these periods, suits are forever barred. Periods vary in the several states and within a state according to the rights to be enforced.

STATUTES OF WILLS Statutes (the first one passed in 1541) providing that no will shall be valid, and no devise or bequest shall be valid, unless the will is in writing, signed and attested in the manner provided by the statute.

STERLING That which has a standard of fineness or value such as established by the government of Great Britain for silver or gold or bank notes.

STERLING AREA Those nations since 1939 which have been closely tied to the British pound and the monetary policies of the British Empire.

STEWARD Union employee in plant or department who represents other employees in handling grievances, and who sees that terms specified in the contract are complied with. Also called committeeman.

STOCK Supply of goods and merchandise in store for sale. Shares of ownership in a corporation which pay dividends, or share in the profits.

STOCK-BONUS TRUST A trust established by a corporation to enable its employees to receive benefits in the form of the corporation's stock as a reward for meritorious service, seniority, or as a means of sharing in the profits of the enterprise.

STOCKBROKER An individual or firm engaged in the business of buying and selling securities for others.

STOCK CERTIFICATE The printed evidence of a stockholder's ownership in a corporation.

STOCK DIVIDEND This is a dividend which consists of additional shares, rather than a money dividend.

STOCK EXCHANGE An association of brokers and dealers engaged in the business of buying and selling securities. The place where such brokers and dealers meet to do their trading.

STOCK INSURANCE COMPANY Association of persons formed for the purpose of issuing insurance coverage on the lives of others.

STOCK-OPTION CONTRACT A negotiable instrument, also called a "paper" or "privilege," which gives the purchaser the right to buy (call) or sell (put) the number of shares of stock designated in the contract at a fixed price within a stated period of time.

STOCKPILE A quantity of essential products originally obtained to meet inventory requirements.

STOCK SPLIT The division of shares of stock of a corporation among its present stockholders which goes to increase the number of outstanding shares, but does not increase the capitalization of the company.

STOCK-TRANSFER TAX The federal and/or state tax on sale or transfer and, in some cases, loan of stock.

STOCK WARRANTS See "rights" and "warrant."

STOP-LIMIT ORDER In investment trading, a form of a stop order from a client to his stockbroker, by which a specific price limit is set. Any price below this will not be accepted if it is a sell order, or any price above this will not be accepted if this is a buy order.

STOP-LOSS ORDER or **STOP ORDER** An order issued by a client to his stockbroker entered to buy or sell specific securities when the market reaches a specific point.

STOP PAYMENT ORDER An order issued by a depositor to his bank instructing it to refuse payment of the check or checks specified in the order.

STOP PRICE In investment trading, that price where a client's stop order to his broker becomes a market order.

STRADDLE 1) The simultaneous purchase of options to buy and sell a specific security.
2) The exercising of both a put and a call in the same security.
3) In commodities, the simultaneous sale of one futures month with the purchase of the same commodity in a different month.

STRAIGHT BILL OF LADING A bill of lading which states a specific person to whom the goods should be delivered and which is not negotiable.

STRAIGHT LETTER OF CREDIT An irrevocable letter of credit which has been confirmed. See "letter of credit."

STRAIGHT-LINE METHOD A method of accounting for depreciation which spreads the depreciation charges uniformly over the estimated service life of the property.

STRAIGHT-TERM MORTGAGE LOAN A mortgage loan granted for a fixed term of years, the entire loan becoming due at the end of that time.

STRATEGIC MATERIALS See "critical materials."

STREET BROKER An over-the-counter broker as distinguished from a broker who is a member of an exchange.

STREET CERTIFICATE A security or stock certificate which has been made out to a broker, and which the broker has endorsed, so that it is negotiable and thus may be transferred to others.

STRETCH-OUT 1) Actions by workers to try to extend the period of their employment by taking longer than is customary to do a job.
2) An increase in the work load of an employee by an employer without any added payment.

STRIKE A concerted and sustained refusal by workingmen to perform some or all of the services for which they were hired.

STRIKEBREAKERS Workers hired during a strike primarily for the purpose of defeating the strike.

STRIKE VOTE A vote conducted among employees in the bargaining unit on the question of whether they should go out on strike.

STRIKING PRICE In investment trading, the fixed price at which a stock may be bought in a call contract, or sold in a put contract.

STRUCK-WORK CLAUSE Collective bargaining agreement clause which permits employees to work on materials coming from a strike-bound plant.

SUBJECTIVE VALUE The value which an individual may place upon goods for his own purposes, which may differ from their general or usual value.

SUBPOENA A writ or order commanding by law the person named in it to appear and testify in a legal proceeding.

SUBROGATION The substitution of one person in the place of another with reference to a lawful claim or right.

SUBSCRIBER One who agrees in writing to purchase certain securities offerings such as a certain number of shares of designated stock of a given corporation, or a certain number of bonds of a given stipulated (par) value.

SUBSCRIPTION The offer to purchase a certain offering, as a certain number of shares of stipulated stock or bonds, for a stipulated amount of money. Such offer is not binding unless accepted by the proper authorized representatives of the issuing firm or corporation. See "subscriber."

SUBSCRIPTION PRICE The offering price at which new or additional security issues of a corporation may be purchased.

SUBSCRIPTION RIGHTS A privilege to the stockholders of a corporation to purchase proportionate amounts of a new issue of securities, at an established price, usually below the current market price; also, the negotiable certificate evidencing such privilege.

SUBSIDIARY ACCOUNT One of a group of related accounts which support in detail the debit and credit summaries recorded in a controlling account.

SUBSIDIARY COMPANY A company which is under the control of another company. Generally this is accomplished by the ownership of sufficient shares of the subsidiary to direct policy.

SUBSIDIARY LEDGER A separate ledger containing detailed information that is summarized in a controlling account in the general ledger.

SUBSIDY A grant of money from a government or other organization to a person or industrial plan considered beneficial to the public.

SUBSISTENCE That amount of the necessities of life just adequate to keep one alive.

SUBSTITUTION, LAW OF Economic concept that if one product or service may be readily exchanged or substituted for another the prices of the two must be relatively close.

SUCCESSION The act or fact of a person's becoming entitled to property of a deceased person, whether by operation of law upon his dying intestate, or by taking under his will.

SUCCESSION TAX 1) A tax upon the transmission of property by a deceased person, in which case it will be charged upon the whole estate, regardless of the manner in which it is to be distributed, in which case it is called a probate or estate tax.
2) The more common form of a tax on the privilege of taking property by will or by inheritance or by succession in any other form upon the death of the owner, and in such case it is imposed upon each legacy or distributive share of the estate as it is received.

SUMMARIZING ENTRY An entry in journal form that is written below the footings in a columnar journal to show that the debits and the credits are equal.

SUMMONS A written order commanding a defendant to appear in court and answer to the charge of the plaintiff.

SUNK COSTS A fixed expense that probably cannot be recovered without total liquidation. A building, well, road, foundation, special jigs or dies all represent sunk costs.

SUPERMARKET Large retail store typically having at least such departments as meat, produce, dairy, and grocery, operating on a cash-and-carry technique.

SUPERSENIORITY Seniority superior to, and not based upon, length of service; often granted to union officers.

SUPPLEMENTARY COSTS Those fixed, indirect, or overhead expenses of a business activity which do not vary with the volume of activity.

SUPPLY AND DEMAND, LAW OF The theory that the price of a product fluctuates in the same direction as demand and in the opposite direction of the supply.

SUPPORT THE MARKET In investment trading, the entering of buy orders at or slightly below the prevailing market level to support and stabilize the existing prices and promote a rise in prices if possible.

SURETY One who promises to answer for a debt or obligation to a third person on behalf of a second person.

SURPLUS 1) Supply of a commodity above requirements.
2) The accumulated profits of past periods left invested in a business. In a bank it represents the amount paid in by the stockholders in addition to their capital stock subscriptions when the bank is organized and amounts (not available for dividends) added to capital from earnings.

SURPLUS RESERVE A reserve representing the segregation of surplus for specified purposes. An example is a reserve for inventories.

SURRENDER CHARGE Small fee charged upon discontinuance of an insurance policy within the first years. Net values are shown in policies and rate manual.

SURRENDER VALUE (CASH SURRENDER VALUE) A term used in insurance designating the progressive increase in the percentage of, or the amount of the total life insurance in force that will be paid to the policyholder when he elects to surrender his policy and receive such proportionate part. The cash surrender value of a policy is the amount frequently used to determine the amount of money that will be loaned against the policy.

SURROGATE A probate judge.

SURTAX An extra tax on something already taxed.

SUSPEND TRADING In investment trading, an action which can be taken if there is evidence that an orderly market may be threatened because of some unusual event. Might be invoked if there is a sudden influx of buy or sell orders, and continued so long as necessary.

SUSPENSE ACCOUNT A bookkeeping account which carries charges or credits temporarily, pending the determination of the proper account or accounts to which they are to be posted.

SWEATSHOP A factory which has poor physical working conditions such as inadequate lighting, lack of sanitation, unsafe machinery, and bad ventilation.

SWEETHEART CONTRACT Term of derision for an agreement negotiated by an employer and a union granting concessions to the employer or the union, the usual purpose being to keep a rival union out.

SWING TIME Time employee lunches, or is unemployed, during his tour of duty.

SYMMETALLISM 1) A monetary system in which the paper currency is redeemable in two or more metals which are paid in a fixed and proportionate combination.
2) A standard coin which is a combination of two or more precious metals.

SYMPATHETIC STRIKE Concerted work stoppage by employees of Employer A to express sympathy for striking employees of Employer B, and to exert indirect pressure on B.

SYNDICATE A combination of people or firms formed to carry out some project requiring large resources of capital.

TACIT COLLUSION Conspiracy without evidence except from the results. In cases of oligopoly when one buyer or seller takes an action such as changing a bid or asked price and the same action is promptly taken by another in a consistent pattern, courts of law may hold that tacit collusion exists.

TAFT-HARTLEY ACT Federal statute which amends the National Labor Relations Act to regulate some union activities, authorizes damage suits for collective bargaining violations and certain strikes and boycotts, and sets up procedures for trying to settle "national emergency strikes."

TAKE-HOME PAY The amount of wages or salary left to the worker after taxes, any insurance, and other deductions have been taken out.

TANGIBLE PROPERTY Property which can be touched or realized with the senses, such as a chair; opposed to intangible property, such as an insurance policy.

TARE WEIGHT As applied to a carload, weight of the car exclusive of its contents.

TARIFF 1) Duties imposed on exports and imports.
2) A published schedule showing the rates, fares, charges, classification of freight, rules and regulations applying to the various kinds of transportation and incidental services.

TARIFF FOR REVENUE A tariff not designed for protection of domestic manufacturers but to obtain taxes for the government.

TARIFF UNION See "customs union."

TAX 1) To assess or determine judicially the amount of levy for the support of certain government functions for public purposes.
2) A charge or burden, usually pecuniary, laid upon persons or property for public purposes.
3) A forced contribution of wealth to meet the public needs of a government.

TAX ABATEMENT Amount of tax abated; deduction; decrease rebate, especially of a tax or burden improperly laid. The act of abating such tax or burden.

TAXABLE ESTATE The gross estate of a citizen or resident less allowable administrative expenses, indebtedness, taxes, losses, transfers for public, charitable, and religious uses, transfers to a surviving spouse, and the specific exemption of $60,000.

TAX ANTICIPATION NOTES Notes (sometimes called "warrants") issued in anticipation of collection of taxes, usually retirable only from tax collections, and frequently only from the proceeds of the tax levy whose collection they anticipate.

TAX ASSESSMENT The placing of a value on real or personal property for tax purposes.

TAX AVOIDANCE The use of legal means to minimize one's taxes.

TAX BASE The thing or right upon which the computation of a tax is determined.

TAX COLLECTOR That elected or appointed government official who is responsible for the collection of those taxes within his area of responsibility. In addition, certain administrative functions are also performed.

TAX COMMISSION That elected or appointed group on a local, state, or national level charged with administration of specific types of taxes.

TAX COURT OF THE UNITED STATES Special federal court which deals only with internal revenue cases.

TAX DODGE Any legal or illegal attempt to avoid taxes.

TAX EVASION The use of illegal means to reduce one's taxes.

TAX EXEMPTION The excuse or freedom and immunity from tax, or a portion of a tax.

TAX FORECLOSURE Seizure of property, because of unpaid taxes, by the duly authorized officials of the public authority empowered to tax.

TAX LIMIT The maximum rate or amount of general property tax which a local government may levy.

TAXPAYER 1) One who pays taxes.
2) A building erected for the primary purpose of producing revenues to meet the taxes on the land. When the land has ripened, the taxpayer is demolished and a more substantial structure put up in its place. Thus the building and property with the "taxpayer" is producing some return, generally enough to pay the taxes.

TAX RATE The amount of tax stated in terms of a unit of the tax base; for example, 25 mills per dollar of assessed valuation.

TAX ROLL The official list showing the amount of taxes levied against each taxpayer or property.

TAX SALE The sale of property, sometimes at auction, for nonpayment of taxes.

TAX SELLING The practice of effecting securities that will realize a capital gain or loss which is desired as an offset to the losses or gains realized in the same tax period. The purpose of this practice is to minimize the tax impact of the seller's capital transactions during a tax period.

TAX SHARING That condition in which more than one governmental level or division divide tax receipts among themselves.

TAYLOR DIFFERENTIAL PIECE-RATE SYSTEM An incentive plan for paying direct labor based on a modified piece-rate plan. The worker is paid at one rate for each piece produced up to a standard production per hour, and at a higher rate on each piece, if he exceeds his standard. Due to wage-and-hour legislation, a minimum guarantee is generally associated with this plan. See "direct labor" and "piece-rate plan."

TECHNICAL POSITION A term applied to the various internal factors affecting the market, opposed to external forces such as earnings, dividends, political considerations and general economic conditions. Some internal factors considered in appraising the market's technical position include the size of the short interest, whether the market has had a sustained advance or decline without interruption, a sharp advance or decline on small volume, and the amount of credit in use in the market. See "overbought" and "oversold."

TECHNICIAN Also called a chartist because his analysis of a particular security or market is based primarily upon the technical, or chart-formation, aspect of the changes taking place.

TECHNOLOGICAL UNEMPLOYMENT Job loss caused by changes in production methods or the installation of labor-saving devices.

TECHNOLOGY The application of sciences, especially to engineering, administration, and production, in the use of machines to increase productivity.

TENANCY The holding of real property by any form of title.

TENANCY AT WILL A tenancy in which the tenant holds the property at the will or pleasure of the grantor.

TENANCY BY THE ENTIRETY Tenancy by a husband and wife in such a manner that, except in concert with the other, neither husband nor wife has a disposable interest in the property during the lifetime of the other. Upon the death of either, the property goes to the survivor. To be distinguished from joint tenancy and tenancy in common.

TENANCY FOR YEARS A tenancy for a definite period of time—for example, a year or ninety-nine years. It cannot be terminated by either party alone, except at the expiration of the time agreed upon.

TENANCY IN COMMON The holding of property by two or more persons in such a manner that each has an undivided interest which, upon his death, passes as such to his heirs or devisees and not to the survivor or survivors; the same as an estate in common; to be distinguished from joint tenancy and tenancy by the entirety.

TENANT One who holds or possesses real estate by any kind of title, either in fee, for life, for years, or at will. In a more limited and popular sense, a tenant is one who has the temporary use of real estate which belongs to another.

TENDER The unconditional offer of payment by a debtor to the creditor of the amount owed.

TERMINAL WAGE That amount paid to an employee upon his dismissal.

TERM LOAN A loan scheduled to run for more than one year and usually repayable in annual or more frequent payments. Term loan should be differentiated from term issue and serial issue.

TERMS OF TRADE Those discounts from the list price which may be taken if payment is made within a stated period, such as ten days from the date of delivery.

TESTAMENTARY DISPOSITION The disposition of property by deed, will, or otherwise in such a manner that it shall not take effect unless or until the grantor dies.

TESTATE Having made and left a valid will; opposed to intestate.

TESTATOR A deceased person who left a will setting forth the disposition of his wealth (total assets).

THIN MARKET A market in which there are comparatively few bids to buy, or offers to sell, or both. The phrase may apply to a single security or to the entire stock market.

THIRD MARKET Trading in the over-the-counter market of securities listed on an exchange.

THROUGH BILL OF LADING That type of bill of lading which is used in the event that more than one carrier will be handling a shipment so that processing of documents is minimized at the intermediate connecting stations. See "bill of lading."

TICKLER Any record or file established to serve as a reminder of action to be taken on a fixed future date. It is always arranged in the order of dates on which such action is to be taken.

TIED LOAN A loan in which the granting of the loan is conditioned (tied) to the borrower using the proceeds for a very specific purchase from a named supplier.

TIGHT CREDIT That condition in an economy in which credit accommodations are difficult to obtain and in which interest rates tend to increase.

TILL MONEY Money set aside for use by a teller at his window as distinguished from money in the vault, on deposit in other banks, etc.

TIME-AND-MOTION STUDY Analysis of the motions and measurements of the time an average workers needs to perform a given job.

TIME BILL A bill of exchange that has a fixed or determinable date of payment as contrasted with a sight or demand bill.

TIME DEPOSIT A deposit from which the customer has the right to withdraw funds at a specified date thirty or more days after the date of deposit, or from which, if the bank so requires, the customer may withdraw funds only by giving the bank written notice thirty days or more in advance of the contemplated withdrawal.

TIME DRAFT A draft that is payable at a fixed or determinable future time.

TIME-OFF PLAN System under which an employee who works overtime in some week of the pay period is given a sufficient number of hours off during some other week in the same pay period to offset the overtime week so that the usual wage for the pay period covers the total pay, including overtime, due the worker for each separate work week.

TIME UTILITY That value added to a good or service by time. Many products, especially agricultural products, by being stored, gain time utility.

TIMEWORK Work where wages are based on the time it takes to do the job rather than by the piece.

TITLE The right to ownership of property. Evidence or proof of ownership.

TOLERANCE That fractional allowance of variation from a given standard.

TOLL As used today, it is a charge for the use of some facility of a fairly public nature such as a toll bridge, a toll road, or a toll tunnel. Many years ago the term was applied to a rent paid at a market or fair.

TONNAGE The contents of a vessel or ship in which 100 cubic feet is computed as one registered ton. The tax on a vessel, computed on its cubic contents, is also called tonnage.

TOP OUT The gradual leveling off of market prices after an extended upward climb. Also may refer to a temporary peak in the market or in a particular stock which is unlikely to be surpassed in the near future.

TORRENS CERTIFICATE A certificate issued by a public official, known as a registrar of titles, establishing an indefeasible title in an indicated owner.

TORRENS REGISTRATION System of registration of land title as opposed to registration or recording of evidence of such title. The originator of the system was Sir Richard Torrens, 1814–1884, reformer of Australian Land Laws.

TORT A wrong arising independently of a contract; a private wrong as distinguished from a crime.

TOTAL AND PERMANENT DISABILITY Complete inability to work with little prospect of improvement or recovery.

TOTAL LOSS The complete destroying or ruining of a property. A claim of sufficient size to require settlement of the maximum amount of insurance on the covered property.

TOTAL RESERVES Member bank deposits with Federal Reserve Banks plus member bank vault cash. The sum required and excess reserves.

TOTAL UTILITY A theoretical total of the sum of all the utility, time, place, quantity, possession, etc., which a quantity of a good would have considering the diminishing utility of a quantity of goods.

TOTTEN TRUST Trust created by deposit of one's own money in his own name as trustee for another. Title is vested in the record owner (trustee), who during his life holds it on a revocable trust for the named beneficiary. At the death of the depositor a presumption arises that an absolute trust was created as to the balance on hand at the death of the depositor.

TRADE The buying, selling, or exchanging of commodities either by wholesale or by retail, within a country or between countries.

TRADE ACCEPTANCE A written promise drawn by the seller of merchandise at the time of sale and signed by the purchaser.

TRADE AGREEMENT See "labor agreement."

TRADE ASSOCIATION Businesses in the same line of work promoting their common interest.

TRADE BARRIERS Those restrictions or regulations which tend to reduce the freedom of movement of products and services from one area to another.

TRADE CHANNEL The path of distribution of goods from producer to consumer.

TRADE DEFICIT An adverse balance of trade. A passive trade balance.

TRADE DISCOUNT The deduction from the list price.

TRADE GAP The difference between the larger amount of imports of merchandise and the lesser amount of exports of merchandise in a given period.

TRADE-IN The part of a sale represented by trading an old product for a new product, as contrasted to the part of the sale completed by payment of money.

TRADEMARK Symbol identifying a business or product.

TRADE NAME The name by which a product is known in commercial circles.

TRADER One who buys and sells. In investment trading, one who transacts for his own account for short-term profit.

TRADE UNION Generally the members of such a union are limited to a specific occupation or trade. See "labor union."

TRADING AREA 1) A district whose boundaries are usually determined by the economical buying or selling range for a commodity or group of related commodities from a center of distribution.
2) The "pit" or "floor" of a stock or commodity exchange.

TRADING LIMIT In most North American commodity contract markets there is a maximum price change permitted for a single session. These limits vary in the different commodity markets. After prices have advanced or declined to the permissible daily limits, trading automatically ceases unless, of course, offers appear at the permissible upper-trading limit, or, on the other hand, bids appear at the permissible lower limit.

TRANSACTIONS TAX A turnover or sales tax.

TRANSFER The passage of property or rights, with title, from one person to another.

TRANSFER AGENT A bank, a trust company, or an individual appointed by a corporation to see that all the requirements are met in connection with the transfer of its stock.

TRANSFER BOOKS Ledgers required to be kept by the county auditor, showing all transfers of real estate within the county.

TRANSFER IN CONTEMPLATION OF DEATH A transfer of property by gift made in apprehension of death arising from some existing bodily condition or impending peril, and not the general expectation of eventual decease commonly entertained by all persons.

TRANSFER PAYMENTS Payments to individuals by government and business for which no goods or services are currently rendered.

TRANSFER TAX A tax imposed upon the transfer of ownership of stocks and bonds, usually paid by affixing, and canceling, stamps to the certificates or other documents evidencing the transfer of ownership.

TRANSIT ITEMS Cash items which are payable outside the town or city of the bank receiving them for credit to customers' accounts.

TRANSIT RATE A transportation rate restricted in its application to traffic which has been or will be milled, stored, or otherwise specially treated in transit.

TRANSPLACEMENT (or SLIDE) An error caused by moving all the digits of an amount to the right or the left without changing the order of the digits.

TRAVELER'S LETTER OF CREDIT A letter addressed by a bank to its correspondent banks either in the same country or in foreign countries, authorizing the person named in the letter to draw drafts on the correspondent banks to the extent of the credit specified. The person in whose favor the letter of credit is issued deposits with the issuing bank a sum of money equal to the total amount of the credit plus the bank's charges for this service.

TREASURER'S CHECK See "cashier's check."

TREASURY BILLS Noncoupon obligations; sold at discount through competitive bidding; generally having original maturities of three months, and one year.

TREASURY CERTIFICATES OF INDEBTEDNESS Obligations which usually mature in 9 to 12 months from date of issue.

TREASURY NOTES Coupon obligations having original maturities of from one to five years.

TREASURY STOCK Stock that has been issued and that is later reacquired by the corporation.

TREND 1) The general course or prevailing tendency of something.
2) In economics, the direction prices or other indicators are taking.

TRIAL BALANCE The proof of the equality of the debits and the credits in the ledger.

TRIANGULAR TRADE Trade between three nations in which a rough balance exists. However, balance does not exist between any two in a direct sense, without the trade between them and the third nation.

TRUE INTEREST See "pure interest" and "net interest."

TRUNK LINE A transportation line operating over an extensive territory.

TRUST An arrangement by which an individual or a corporation as trustee holds the title to property for the benefit of one or more persons, usually under the terms of a will or a written agreement.

TRUST ADMINISTRATOR A person in the employment of a trust institution who handles trust accounts in the sense of having direct contacts and dealings with trust customers and beneficiaries.

TRUST COMPANY A corporation, one of whose stated objectives is to engage in trust business.

TRUST DEED A written agreement, under seal, conveying property (usually real but sometimes personal property) from the owner to a trustee for the accomplishment of the objectives set forth in the agreement.

TRUSTEE One to whom property is legally committed in trust.

TRUSTEE IN BANKRUPTCY A qualified person elected by the creditors to take charge of the property of the bankrupt.

TRUST FUND Technically, only money held in trust; but frequently applied to all the property held in trust in a given account.

TRUST INDENTURE An instrument in writing which contains a description of all property originally placed in

the trust, the agreement as to the rights of the trustee in administering the property, the rights of all beneficiaries named, along with their proportionate share in the trust, the duration of the trusteeship, the distribution of income from the trust principal to the life-tenants, and the distribution of the trust property of the remaindermen at the termination of the trust.

TRUST RECEIPT A formal receipt issued by a trustee for property held in trust; used in certain commercial transactions.

TRUST UNDER WILL A trust created by a valid will, to become operative only on the death of the testator; the same as a testamentary trust and opposed to a living trust.

TURN The completed transaction of a purchase and sale of a commodity or a security. It may be a long purchase followed by a sale, or a short sale followed by a long purchase. The last transaction completes the "turn."

TURNOVER 1) The volume of business in a security or the entire market.
2) Number of employees who are separated from the payroll.
3) The ratio obtained by dividing sales for a period such as a month or year by some related figure such as accounts receivables, capital, or inventory. To be clearly understood the term "turnover" should in addition have reference to the time and item which has turned over.

TWO-YEAR RULE National Labor Relations Board rule holding the first two years of a collective bargaining agreement to be a reasonable period during which rival claims to representation will not be considered.

TYING CONTRACT Any contract which forbids the buyer or the lessee to transact business with competitors of the supplier.

ULTIMATE CONSUMER One who buys and/or uses goods or services to satisfy personal or household wants rather than for resale or use in business, institutional, or industrial operations.

ULTRA VIRES An act beyond the powers legally granted a corporation.

UNCOLLECTED CASH ITEMS Checks in the process of collection for which payment has not yet been received from the banks on which the checks are drawn.

UNCONFIRMED LETTER OF CREDIT A letter of credit in which the issuing bank has processed all the necessary documents and advised the financial institution upon which the letter is drawn, but the institution has not confirmed, acknowledged, and accepted the advice of the letter. See "letter of credit."

UNDERDEVELOPED COUNTRY A state or nation which has the potential for greater productivity but which has a real per capita income below the average of Western nations.

UNDERLYING MORTGAGE A mortgage which has priority over some other mortgage.

UNDER THE RULE When a member of an exchange does not complete delivery of a security in terms of the rules of the exchange, the security is purchased by an official of the exchange who makes the delivery under the rule.

UNDERWRITER 1) In insurance, the individual whose duty it is to determine the acceptability of insurance risks. A person whose duty it is to select risks for insurance and to determine in what amounts, and on what terms, the insurance company will accept the risks.
2) One who arranges for the distribution and sale of a large block of securities and who assumes responsibility for paying the net purchase price to the seller at a predetermined price. In most instances, the underwriter deals in a new issue and with the issuing company.

UNDERWRITING PROFIT That portion of the earnings of an insurance company that comes from the function of underwriting. It is found by deducting incurred losses and expenses from earned premiums. It excludes the earnings from investments either in the form of income from securities or sale of securities at a profit.

UNDISTRIBUTED PROFITS See "earned surplus."

UNDISTRIBUTED-PROFITS TAX A federal tax levied on companies with large amounts of undistributed profits for which there is no valid business reason.

UNDUE INFLUENCE The influence which one person exerts over another person to the point where the latter is prevented from exercising his own free will.

UNEARNED DISCOUNT Interest collected but not yet earned.

UNEARNED INCOME See "deferred credits."

UNEARNED INCREMENT The increase in the value of property that can be attributed to changing social or economic conditions beyond the control of the titleholder as distinguished from that increase in value that can be attributed to the improvements made or additions added by the efforts of the titleholder.

UNEARNED PREMIUM In insurance, that part of the original insurance premium paid in advance and not yet earned by the insurance company, and therefore due the policyholder if the policy should be canceled.

UNEARNED PREMIUM RESERVE The fund set aside by an insurance company to provide for the payment of unearned premiums on canceled policies.

UNECONOMIC Any production or service which has higher costs than the values produced.

UNENCUMBERED An asset owned which is free from all claims made by, or granted to, another.

UNENCUMBERED PROPERTY Property that is free and clear of assessments, liens, easements, claims, and exceptions of all kinds. See "encumbrance."

UNFAIR LABOR PRACTICES Those employer or union activities that are classed as unfair by federal or state labor relations acts.

UNFAIR TRADE PRACTICES Those actions by a business or industry designed to increase the profits which violate a high code of ethics. These would include such actions as bribing a competitor's employees, short weight, false product description, misleading advertising, etc.

UNFAVORABLE BALANCE OF PAYMENTS A condition in which the monetary value of exports of goods and services is less than the monetary value of imports of goods and services for a stated period of time. These services would include such things as earnings on foreign investments, insurance, and shipping fees. The portion or difference in the balance is generally made up by export of gold or the acquisition of claims against the country by foreigners.

UNFAVORABLE BALANCE OF TRADE A condition in which the monetary value of exports of merchandise is less than the monetary value of imports of merchandise for a stated period of time.

UNFUNDED DEBT Debt which is short-term and not represented by formal securities such as bonds. See "floating debt."

UNILATERAL AGREEMENT An obligation which is binding on only one party to the agreement.

UNION Formal organization of workers formed primarily for the purpose of dealing collectively with their employer on matters pertaining to their employment.

UNION CERTIFICATION The recognition by an authorized governmental agency that a particular union has complied with the legal provisions to be considered as the rightful bargaining agent for employees of a firm.

UNION LABEL Recognized imprint on a product indicating the item was made under union conditions.

UNION REGISTRATION Filing by unions with the Secretary of Labor of the descriptions of their internal organization and procedures, the copies of their constitutions and bylaws, and the annual financial reports required by the Taft-Hartley Act as a first step before unions may pursue their rights under that statute.

UNION SECURITY CLAUSE Provision in union contract that fixes the position of the union in the plant and its relation to the workers and their jobs.

UNION SHOP Form of union security under which an employer may hire nonunion workers who must, however, become members after they are employed as a condition of retaining their employee status.

UNISSUED STOCK That portion of the authorized capital stock of a corporation which is not outstanding or issued.

UNIT COST A term used in cost accounting to denote the cost of producing a unit of product or rendering a unit of service.

UNIVERSE The total from which a sample is taken.

UNLIMITED MORTGAGE A mortgage with an open-end. This permits the borrower to finance under a single mortgage rather than being forced to issue several. While the mortgage has an open-end, it generally has certain restrictions such as the ratio of debt instruments to the total value of the assets securing the debt.

UNLISTED SECURITIES The opposite of listed securities. See "listed securities" and "over-the-counter."

UNPRODUCTIVE CONSUMPTION The process of consumption by individuals who are not productive. The ill, the institutionalized, and those in prisons, in most cases, are examples of unproductive consumption.

UNQUALIFIED CERTIFICATE An auditor's certificate which contains no qualifications or exceptions.

UNREALIZED PROFITS The existence of paper profits which have not yet been made actual.

UNSATISFIED JUDGMENT FUNDS A fund created by state law in several states. Reimbursement is made to persons having claims arising out of automobile accidents who have been unable to collect from the party responsible for the accident because the party is not insured or is financially not in a position to pay.

UNSECURED CREDITOR A general creditor such as the tradesman who sold the merchandise to the debtor on open-book account. His claim is subordinate to the claim of a creditor who has priority because of such features as a mortgage or other security.

UNSECURED LOAN A loan made by a bank, based upon credit information on the borrower and his integrity, to repay his obligations. The loan is not secured by collateral, but is made on the signature of the borrower.

UNVALUED STOCK Stock which has no par or stated value. The term is a misnomer since it must have value to be bought and sold, but the unvalued reference is to the value which the issuer of the stock carries it on the books. The trend in recent years is away from unvalued or no-par stock because it is generally taxed as if it had a value of $100 par.

USE TAX That tax, imposed in several states for the purpose of putting on the same tax basis products which are bought in another state to avoid the first state's sales tax.

USE VALUE That value determined on the basis of the amount paid for the actual use of a property as compared with the holding of a property out of use.

USURY Lending money over the legal rate of interest.

UTILITY For business usage see "public utility." In an economic sense, it is that quality of anything which will satisfy a human want.

UTILITY OR OTHER-ENTERPRISE FUND A fund established to finance the construction, operation, and maintenance of municipally owned utilities, such as gas, water, and light plants, transportation facilities, and other self-supporting enterprises such as airports and housing projects.

UTILITY THEORY OF VALUE The oversimplified explanation of value which directly relates value to the utility of goods and services.

UTILIZATION FACTOR The ratio of an average electric-power load (kilowatts) over a designated period of time to the net capability in the same period of time. This ratio represents the average use made of the net capability of equipment over a specific period of time.

VALORIZATION The action of some influential body such as a governmental agency which arbitrarily sets a price on a good or service. The price may be, but probably is not, a price which the free workings of the market would determine.

VALUATION Appraised or estimated worth.

VALUE 1) Value in use ... The worth of any economic wealth, product, service, etc., to one possessing it. Many things not for sale have great value in use, which may at times be described roughly in dollar terms.
2) Value in exchange ... The worth of anything in the marketplace—"Price" represents value as agreed to in an actual sale.

VALUE ADDED The selling price of produced goods less the cost of the raw material used in production.

VALUE DATE In accounting and bookkeeping for banks, the date on which an entry made on an account is considered effective. The value date has no relation to the entry date, since it is based on the collection or payment of items which may be received from a depositor, or sent to a depository bank. Its use is generally associated with foreign accounts maintained with, or by, a bank.

VALUED POLICY An insurance policy which provides that a special amount shall be paid in event of a total loss of the property.

VARIABLE COST That prime cost which fluctuates with the level of production. See "direct cost."

VARIABLE PROPORTIONS, LAW OF See "proportionality, law of."

VELOCITY OF CIRCULATION The rate at which money and those substitutes such as checks are transferred from one holder to the next.

VENDEE The person who purchases, or agrees to purchase, an item of property or service.

VENDOR (vender) The person who sells, or agrees to sell, an item of property or service.

VENDOR'S LIEN An equitable lien which a vendor of property or services has thereon for the unpaid purchase money.

VENTURE CAPITAL See "risk capital."

VENUE The place or county where a suit is brought.

VERTICAL EXPANSION 1) The establishment of facilities to permit a firm to expand its business from the basic raw material, through processing and manufacturing and distribution to the sale to ultimate consumer. Vertical expansion may start at any level of activity, be it production or distribution. The main feature is that control is maintained by one firm at all levels. Naturally, there are degrees of less than full vertical expansion.
2) The consolidation of companies involved in similar product areas.

VERTICAL INTEGRATION Ownership or control of the various levels of production and distribution for a class of merchandise generally from raw material to the ultimate consumer.

VERTICAL UNION A union which represents workers of different skills and occupations but with a common industry.

VESTED Placed firmly in the possession of a person or persons; fixed.

VESTED INTEREST An immediate, fixed interest in real or personal property although the right of possession and enjoyment may be postponed until some future date, or until the happening of some event; to be distinguished from a contingent interest.

VESTED REMAINDER A fixed interest in real property, with the right of possession and enjoyment postponed until the termination of the prior estate; to be distinguished from a contingent remainder.

VISIBLE ITEMS OF TRADE Those exports and imports of recorded goods, but not including the invisible items of insurance and shipping, paid by or to foreigners.

VITAL STATISTICS Generally, those statistics pertaining to deaths, births, population, and similar areas.

VOIDABLE CONTRACT A valid contract that may be rescinded by one of the parties due to such grounds as fraud, duress, insanity, incompetency, or minority.

VOLUNTARY BANKRUPTCY That state of insolvency of an individual, corporation, or other legal entity in which the debtor has petitioned a competent court and been judged insolvent and has had his property assigned for the benefit of his creditors.

VOLUNTARY PLAN A type of accumulation plan for investment on a regular basis but without any total-time period or ultimate investment amount specified. The sales charge is applicable individually to each purchase made.

VOLUNTARY TRUST A trust created by the voluntary act of the settlor and not conditioned upon his death; the same as a living trust; to be distinguished from a trust under will or testamentary trust.

VOTING STOCK Stock in a corporation in which the holders are entitled to vote for the directors.

VOTING TRUST A device whereby the owner of shares turns over the control of the stock to a trustee who exchanges a voting trust certificate for the stock. The certificate gives the holder all the rights he previously had as to dividends and equity, but transfers the right to vote to the trustee for a stated period of time. At the end of that time the trust may be dissolved and the shares reexchanged for the trust certificates or the trust may be renewed.

VOUCHER A document which evidences the propriety of transactions and usually indicates the accounts in which they are to be recorded.

VOUCHER CHECK A check that contains on its face a brief summary of the voucher to show the purpose for which the check is issued.

VOUCHER REGISTER A special book of original entry in which all the vouchers of a business using the voucher system are recorded.

VOUCHER SYSTEM A system which calls for the preparation of vouchers for all transactions involving payments, and for the recording of such vouchers in a special book of original entry known as a voucher register in the order in which payment is approved.

WAGE Payment for services rendered, especially the pay for workers by hour, day, week, or month.

WAGE AND SALARY STABILIZATION Statutorily backed program for holding wages and salaries as closely as possible to existing levels as an anti-inflation measure. Also referred to as wage and price control.

WAGE DIFFERENTIALS Different rates of pay for the same general type of work, the variations resulting from differences in conditions under which the work is done, differences in performance standards, and differences in the types of workers.

WAGE DIVIDEND That additional payment to employees beyond their regular wages which represents a sharing with the stockholders of a corporation of the earnings of the business.

WAGE PLAN Any system by which a worker's compensation is determined.

WAGE-PRICE SPIRAL A situation in a period of inflation in which the granting of higher wages is followed by the manufacturer increasing his prices, which in turn leads to increases in the cost of living, followed by escalator-clause increases in wages and demands from nonescalator-clause workers for higher wages. The spiral lasts as long as a sellers' market lasts but tapers off when a buyers' market returns.

WAGES AND HOURS ACT See "Fair Labor Standards Act."

WAGNER ACT Federal statute, originally known as the Wagner Act and now a part of the Taft-Hartley Act, which guarantees to employees in industries affecting interstate commerce the right to self-organization, to bargain collectively, and to engage in concerted activities.

WAIVER The voluntary relinquishment of a right, privilege, or advantage. The document by which the relinquishment is evidenced.

WAIVER OF PREMIUM A provision that under certain conditions an insurance policy will be kept in full force by the insurance company without the payment of premiums. It is used most often as a total and permanent disability benefit and may be available in certain other cases.

WALKOUT A workers' strike against an employer or employers.

WALSH-HEALEY PUBLIC CONTRACTS ACT Federal statute fixing wage, hour, and working conditions for most federal supply contracts in excess of $10,000.

WAR CLAUSE A clause in an insurance contract relieving the insurer of liability, or reducing its liability, for loss caused by war.

WARD A person who by reason of minority, mental incompetence, or other incapacity is under the protection of the court either directly or through a guardian, committee, curator, conservator, or tutor.

WAR ECONOMY The changes in an economy from peacetime practices to a sharp increase in governmental intervention in the form of controls, rationing, and production for the war effort rather than the peacetime production of consumer goods.

WAREHOUSE LOANS Loans, generally made by a bank on the collateral of warehouse receipts, which are evidence of material which is stored in a public warehouse.

WAREHOUSE RECEIPT A receipt for goods stored in a warehouse and an agreement between the warehouseman and the person storing the goods. By its terms the warehouseman promises to keep the goods safely and to redeliver them upon the surrender of the receipt, properly indorsed, and payment of the storage charges. The receipt is also evidence that the owner or holder has title to the stored goods.

WARRANT 1) Warrants are evidences of indebtedness incurred by legal entities, and which will be duly redeemed for cash or check when presented to the drawee of the warrant.
2) An option to buy a specified number of shares of the issuing company's stock at a specified price. The warrant may be valid for a limited period of time only, or it may be valid permanently.
3) An official paper, ordered by the proper government official, giving authority to arrest.
4) To guarantee; authorize; justify.

WARRANTY A pledge that a certain matter is true; statements of a seller that goods sold are of a certain quality; a legal guarantee.
In insurance assertions or undertakings on the part of the insured to the strict and literal truth of all statements made.

WARRANTY DEED A deed conveying real property containing the usual covenants of warranty of title.

WASH SALE An illegal security manipulation where a security is bought and sold by the same interest to give the impression of market activity and price rise. This may be done by using different brokers and instructing one to buy and the other to sell at the same time.

WASTE 1) Material which is lost in a manufacturing process or which has no appreciable recovery value.
2) Spoil or destruction of real property done or permitted by the tenant in possession to the prejudice of the heir or owner of the remainder or reversion.

WATER RIGHTS A property consisting of the rights to a water supply.

WAYBILL A record prepared at the point of shipment showing the origin, destination, consignee and consignor for a shipment.

WEIGHTED AVERAGE INVENTORY PLAN A method of inventory valuation whereby the unit cost is arrived at by dividing the total cost of the inventory by the number of units. This "weights" the unit cost toward the cost of those units which make up a larger portion of the inventory.

WELFARE ECONOMICS Those economic policies and actions taken by any governmental agency which have as their primary goal improvement of social conditions.

WELFARE STATE A condition in which welfare economics has become dominant and, as a result, many areas of free enterprise have disappeared.

WHEELER-LEA ACT Amendment to the Federal Trade Commission Act. Passed in 1938, it makes unfair trade practices and deceptive advertising illegal.

WHEN ISSUED In investment trading, a short form of "when, as and if issued." The term indicates a conditional transaction in a security authorized for issuance but not as yet actually issued. All "when issued" transactions are on an "if" basis, to be settled if and when the actual security is issued and the exchange or National Association of Securities Dealers rules the transactions are to be settled.

WHITE-COLLAR WORKERS Workers in office and clerical jobs as distinguished from production workers and maintenance workers.

WHOLE COVERAGE Any form of insurance which provides for payment of all losses without any deductions.

WHOLESALE PRICE INDEX A measure of the average change in the prices of 2,000 commodities at the primary market level (usually the level at which the commodity is first sold commercially in substantial volume).

WHOLESALER A merchant middleman who sells to retailers and other merchants and/or to industrial, institutional, and commercial users but who does not sell in significant amounts to ultimate consumers.

WILDCAT STRIKE A strike called without the consent of the organized union, or in violation of a bargaining agreement "no strike" clause.

WINDFALL PROFIT An unexpected and unusually high profit.

WIRE HOUSE A member firm of the Stock Exchange with branch offices linked together by a communications network.

WITH EXCHANGE A designation on a check or draft of "payable with exchange" or "with exchange" indicates that any collection or exchange charges will be against the payer in the event it is a check, or the drawee in the event it is a draft.

WITHHOLDING TAX Making a deduction at the source of income for part of the wage earner's income-tax liability.

WITHOUT PREJUDICE Part of an insurance policy nonwaiver agreement that holds that the insured who signs the agreement cannot legally construe certain actions, such as the determination of the value of a claim by the insurance company to an admission of liability on their part.

WITHOUT RECOURSE Words used in endorsing a note or bill to denote that the future holder is not to look to the endorser in case of nonpayment.

WORKING CAPITAL That portion of the capital of a business enterprise which is not invested in fixed assets but is kept liquid to care for day-to-day working needs. In an accounting sense, the excess of current assets over current liabilities.

WORKING-CAPITAL FUND A fund established to finance activities, usually of a manufacturing or service nature, such as shops and garages, asphalt plants, and central purchases and stores departments. Sometimes called a revolving fund.

WORKING CONTROL Theoretically, ownership of 51 percent of a company's voting stock is necessary to exercise control. In practice—and this is particularly true in case of a large corporation—effective control sometimes can be exerted through ownership, individually or by a group acting in concert, of less than 50 percent.

WORK-IN-PROCESS INVENTORY   The asset value of the incompleted products which are in various stages of manufacture.

WORKMEN'S COMPENSATION   State laws under which workers or their relatives receive compensation for work-incurred illness, injury, or fatality.

WORK RELIEF   That type of employment which has as its immediate goal the provision of income to the workers, and the economic stimulation which such payments will have on a depressed economy. While projects may be completed such as roads, reforestation, and other public work projects, these are less directly of importance than the income-spending generated.

WORK-SHARING   Plan by which available work is distributed as evenly as possible among all workers when production slackens, or by which working time is generally reduced to prevent layoffs.

WORK SHEET   In accounting, a working trial balance that includes columns for adjustments and for an adjusted trial balance.

WORK UNIT   The parts into which a job or operation is subdivided for cost accounting and other purposes. See "cost unit."

WORLD BANK   Formerly the International Bank for Reconstruction and Development. Formed in 1945 for the purposes of helping finance the reconstruction of productive facilities destroyed during World War II and the development of member nations. It does not compete with regular commercial banks since the loans it makes are to governments, or to business firms which have the backing of their government, by the endorsement of their loan contract. The World Bank also will participate with commercial banks in making loans.

WORLD-WIDE COVERAGE   An insurance policy clause in some policies that provides coverage in any place in the world. Jewelry, fur, personal effects, and personal property floaters may have this clause.

WRIT   An order of a court commanding that the will of the court be obeyed.

WRITE-DOWN   The reduction in the quotation of a thing or a ledger account to bring the present quotation in line with current values.

WRITE-OFF   An instrument or receivable account which has been determined to be uncollectable, since there are no known visible assets available with which the obligor can liquidate the obligation. Write-offs are charged as losses to either the surplus or the undivided profits account.

WRITE-UP   The increase in the quotation of a thing or of a ledger account to bring the present quotation in line with current values.

YIELD   The annual rate of return from a security, expressed as a percentage of the amount invested.

YIELD TEST   Measurement applied to bond investments. It is the relationship of the yield of bonds the holder has in his portfolio individually to the yield of fully taxable United States Government bonds of the same maturity. Yields of such corporate bonds of over $1\frac{1}{2}$ percent higher than the United States Government bonds require that they be valued at market price rather than amortized value.

YIELD TO MATURITY   That rate of return expressed in a percentage that will be obtained on an investment if the investment is held to maturity. It takes into consideration that few investments are bought exactly at par, and thus have a capital gain or loss in addition to the rate of return stated on the face of the instrument.

ZONE PRICING   Technique of charging all purchasers of material who are located within a stated geographical district the same delivered price for equal quantities of the material.

ZONING   The process of establishing by legislation certain restrictions upon the use to which property may be put.

Dictionary Usage Guide

PRONUNCIATION
KEY USED
IN THIS
DICTIONARY

ə	*adjust, bacillus, colony*
æ	*cat, apple, laugh*
ɑ	*father, guitar, art*
ɛə	*bear, aerial*
ei	*snake, alien, parade*
b	*banana, rebel, ebb*
tʃ	*charm, fetch, ratchet*
d	*dog, elder, feed*
e	*egg, exit, request*
i:	*even, relief, sneeze*
iə	*fear, career, earring*
f	*fee, effort, rough*
g	*goat, hog, bigger*
h	*house, behind*
i	*fish, kitten, corrosive*
ai	*tiger, bright*
dʒ	*general, legend, dodge*
ʒ	*leisure, corsage*
k	*kill, luck, vacation*
l	*life, lily, dull*
ʼl	*rabble, trouble*
m	*moon, lemon, dam*
n	*night, train, canal*
ʼn	*redden*
ŋ	*bring, wearing*
ɒ	*lock, rotten*
ɔ	*fawn, court*
ou	*vote, elope, low*
au	*cow, round*
ɔi	*void, royal*
p	*pack, slipper, wrap*
r	*rise, errand, paper*
s	*silly, whisper, juice*

Guide words showing the alphabetical range of entries on the page

Syllabicated main entry
See Part 1A.

Usage labels
See Part 4B.

Derivative forms
See Part 1D.

Encyclopedic entry
See Part 3.

Plural form
See Part 1C.

Pronounced derivative
See Part 1D.

Multiple definitions in single part of speech
See Part 3A.

---

ab·ne·gate (æbnigeit) *pres. part.* **ab·ne·gat·ing** *past* and *past part.* **ab·ne·gat·ed** *v.t.* to renounce, give up (a right etc.) [fr. L. *abnegare* (*abnegatus*), to deny]

ab·ne·ga·tion (æbnigéiʃən) *n.* renunciation, denial [fr. L. *abnegatio* (*abnegationis*)]

ab·nor·mal (æbnɔ́rməl) *adj.* different from the norm or average, unusual ‖ pertaining to that which is not normal, *abnormal psychology* **ab·nor·mal·i·ty** (æbnɔrmǽliti:) *pl.* **ab·nor·mal·i·ties** *n.* [fr. F. *anormal* and L. *abnormis*]

ABO a classification of blood groups (A, B, AB or O) with regard to their use in transfusion

a·board (əbɔ́rd, əbóurd) **1.** *adj.* and *adv.* on or into a ship, plane, train etc. **2.** *prep.* on board, *aboard the last ship*

a·bode (əbóud) *n.* (*old-fash., rhet.*) the place someone lives in (*old-fash., rhet.*) residence, *he took up his abode at the east gate of the city* [fr. ABIDE]

abode alt. *past* and *past part.* of ABIDE

ab·ohm (æbóum) *n.* the cgs electromagnetic unit of resistance equal to 10^{-9} ohm

a·bol·ish (əbɒ́liʃ) *v.t.* to do away with completely, put an end to (laws, customs, taxes, privileges etc.) [F. *abolir* (*aboliss-*)]

ab·o·li·tion (æbəliʃən) *n.* the act of abolishing ‖ (esp. *hist.*) the movement against slavery **ab·o·li·tion·ism, ab·o·li·tion·ist** *ns* [F. or fr. L. *abolitio* (*abolitionis*)] —The movement to abolish the international slave trade and the institution of chattel slavery was largely religious. It centered in Great Britain, the U.S.A. and western Europe, between c. 1783 and 1888. Following the pioneer work of Granville Sharp, the struggle was led by the Quakers, who had outlawed slavery in Pennsylvania as early as 1675. Under the leadership of William Wilberforce they obtained, almost singlehandedly, the abolition of the slave trade in the British Empire and the U.S.A. by acts of Parliament and Congress in 1808. In England the struggle then became one for emancipation, while in the U.S.A. the act of Congress was blatantly defied. The U.S. movement, led chiefly by William Llyod Garrison, Theodore Dwight Weld, and Frederick Douglass, was obstructed by the U.S. Constitution's toleration of slavery and by the South's economic defense of it. Only after the Civil War could the 13th amendment outlawing slavery be enacted. In 1862 the U.S.A. adhered to an international agreement reached in 1842 affording the reciprocal right of search, which thereafter put an end to the slave trade

ab·o·ma·sum (æbəméisəm) *pl.* **ab·o·ma·sa** (æbəméisə) *n.* the fourth chamber of the stomach of a ruminant [Mod. L. fr. *ab*, from + *omasum*, bullock's tripe]

A-bomb (éibɒm) *n.* atomic bomb

a·bom·i·na·ble (əbɒ́minəbʼl) *adj.* causing intense disgust, *an abominable crime* [F.]

abominable snowman a bearlike creature said to inhabit the high Himalayas

a·bom·i·na·bly (əbɒ́minəbli:) *adv.* in an abominable way

a·bom·i·nate (əbɒ́mineit) *pres. part.* **a·bom·i·nat·ing** *past* and *past part.* **a·bom·i·nat·ed** *v.t.* (*rhet.*) to detest [fr. L. *abominari* (*abominatus*)]

a·bom·i·na·tion (əbɒminéiʃən) *n.* disgust ‖ a loathsome act or thing [F.]

ab·o·rig·i·nal (æbərídʒinəl) **1.** *adj.* existing from the earliest times ‖ pertaining to aborigines **2.** *n.* an aborigine **ab·o·rig·i·nal·i·ty** (æbərídʒinǽliti:) *n.* [fr. L. *ab origine*, from the beginning]

ab·o·rig·i·ne (æbərídʒini:) *n.* a native inhabitant of a country, esp. before colonization. *an Australian aborigine* ‖ (*pl.*) the native plants and animals of a region [fr. L. *aborigines* pl. n., inhabitants from the beginning]

a·bort (əbɔ́rt) *v.i.* (*med.*) to give birth to a fetus before it is viable ‖ (*biol.*) to become arrested in development ‖ to come to nothing, *their plans aborted* ‖ (*space*, of a missile) to stop before completion of the scheduled flight ‖ *v.t.* (*space*) to bring (a missile flight) to an end before completion of schedule [fr. L. *aboriri* (*abortus*), to die, to abort]

a·bor·ti·fa·cient (əbɔrtiféiʃənt) **1.** *n.* something which produces an abortion **2.** *adj.* producing an abortion [fr. L. *aboriri* (*abortus*), to abort + *faciens* (*facientis*), causing]

a·bor·tion (əbɔ́rʃən) *n.* the spontaneous or induced expulsion from the womb of a nonviable human fetus ‖ a monstrous person or thing ‖ the failure of a project or attempt **a·bór·tion·ist** *n.* a